BUTTERWORTHS
AND CONSUMER
DBOOK

BUTTERWORTHS
COMMERCIAL AND CONSUMER LAW
HANDBOOK

Eighth edition

Consultant Editors

RICHARD B MAWREY QC
Barrister, Henderson Chambers

TOBIAS RILEY-SMITH
Barrister, Henderson Chambers

Members of the LexisNexis Group worldwide

United Kingdom	Reed Elsevier (UK) Limited trading as LexisNexis, 1–3 Strand, London WC2N 5JR
Australia	Reed International Books Australia Pty Ltd trading as LexisNexis, Chatswood, New South Wales
Austria	LexisNexis Verlag ARD Orac GmbH & Co KG, Vienna
Benelux	LexisNexis Benelux, Amsterdam
Canada	LexisNexis Canada, Markham, Ontario
China	LexisNexis China, Beijing and Shanghai
France	LexisNexis SA, Paris
Germany	LexisNexis GmbH, Dusseldorf
Hong Kong	LexisNexis Hong Kong, Hong Kong
India	LexisNexis India, New Delhi
Italy	Giuffrè Editore, Milan
Japan	LexisNexis Japan, Tokyo
Malaysia	Malayan Law Journal Sdn Bhd, Kuala Lumpur
New Zealand	LexisNexis New Zealand Ltd, Wellington
Singapore	LexisNexis Singapore, Singapore
South Africa	LexisNexis, Durban
USA	LexisNexis, Dayton, Ohio

© Reed Elsevier (UK) Ltd 2015

Published by LexisNexis
This is a Butterworths title

A CIP Catalogue record for this book is available from the British Library.

ISBN for this volume: 978 1 4057 9614 9

Printed and bound by CPI Group (UK) Ltd, Croydon, CR0 4YY

Visit LexisNexis at www.lexisnexis.co.uk

PREFACE

In each of the recent Editions of this work we have commented on the fact that the interval between Editions had dropped dramatically in recent years. No sooner had one Edition emerged when a new raft of legislation was produced by both the UK government and by the European Union. The zeal for innovation, particularly in the field of consumer law, seemed inexhaustible.

The reason why the interval between this Edition and the last (7th) Edition is slightly longer than that between the 6th and 7th Editions is not due to a slackening of that zeal. *Au contraire.* As will be seen, the period since 2012 has been one of major change. The sole reason why this Edition did not appear in the summer of 2014 was the elephantine gestation of the Consumer Rights Act 2015. The Bill took two Parliamentary years to complete and, even then, barely made it over the line before the general election.

The major change since the 7th Edition has been the complete reorganisation of the regulatory system for financial services and the subsuming of consumer credit into that system. New bodies have been created such as the Financial Conduct Authority and the Prudential Regulation Authority, and old bodies such as the Financial Services Authority and the Office of Fair Trading have either transformed into the new bodies or, in the case of the OFT, been abolished.

Regulation of consumer credit is now, therefore, part of the overall regulation of financial services by the FCA. This has meant that large areas of the Consumer Credit Act 1974 have been repealed and those areas are now covered by provisions of the Financial Services and Markets Act 2000 and its subordinate legislation. At the same time, however, the parts of the 1974 Act and its subordinate legislation that govern the making, administration and enforcement of regulated agreements have been kept in force. The practitioner thus has two principal Acts to master instead of one.

The Consumer Rights Act 2015 is a major piece of legislation which replaces much of the existing law of sale of goods, hire and hire-purchase, contracts for services and unfair contract terms, in addition to providing a proper statutory basis for the law relating to supply of software. It derives from EU Directive 2011/83/EU which we pre-figured in the last Edition. This Act has been augmented by the Consumer Protection (Amendment) Regulations 2014, SI 2014/870, which create a wide range of civil claims for misleading or aggressive practices.

Although this book is principally devoted to reproducing the relevant legislation at all levels, we have felt it necessary to include the principal codes of practice issued by the FCA in relation to consumer credit law. Though not, strictly speaking, legislation, their force is tantamount to that of a statutory instrument and (through the medium of FSMA 2000) they give rise to a number of important civil law rights for the consumer. These handbooks and sourcebooks, in particular CONC, are vital to the administration of consumer credit law, but the reader should bear in mind that, unlike legislation, they can be altered at very short notice. Thus while the main provisions of CONC will differ little from edition to edition, if exactitude is required, the practitioner will have to consult the appropriate version of CONC at the relevant time by means of the FCA website.

Clearly since 1 April 2014, which was the date of the transfer of consumer credit regulation from the OFT (under CCA 1974) to the FCA (under FSMA 2000), the law covered by a Handbook of this kind must necessarily overlap with the law relating to financial services, although this overlap has been kept to a minimum, and readers are directed to its companion volume Butterworths Securities and Financial Services Law Handbook. Nonetheless, the editorial team will be very grateful for any reader's comments as to material which might usefully have been included in this Edition but was not.

As always, the real credit for this Edition must go to the in-house team at LexisNexis who do virtually all the work of sourcing the material and putting it into attractive and manageable form. In particular they are masters of incorporating obscure amending statutory instruments into the parent legislation so that the nature and date of the amendment are clear to see. The fact that this tribute is repeated in each Edition does not make it any the less heartfelt.

This Handbook follows the standard Butterworths Handbooks style, with amendments made by new legislation incorporated into the text of existing legislation. Details of the provenance of changes are given in the NOTES which include, where appropriate, details of any savings and transitional provisions in the implementing legislation. Commencement information is given at provision level for Acts and statutory instruments in cases where the provision came into force within the last 5 years (ie, on or after 1 August 2010) or where it is not yet in force for all or some purposes. If no commencement information is given at provision level then the provision in question was brought into force for all purposes before 1 August 2010. In the text:

- an ellipsis (. . .) indicates that text has been repealed or revoked (or is outside the scope of this Handbook);
- square brackets denote text that has been inserted or substituted;
- italicised text is prospectively repealed or substituted, or repealed subject to savings (in the case of prospective substitutions the 'new' text is set out in the notes).

The contents of this Edition of the Handbook take into account materials available as at 1 August 2015.

Richard B. Mawrey QC

Tobias Riley-Smith

August 2015

CONTENTS

PART 2   STATUTORY INSTRUMENTS

PART 3   FCA HANDBOOK MATERIALS

PART 4   OTHER MATERIALS

APPENDIX: CONSUMER CREDIT ACT 1974 (PRE CCA 2006) ....**[A.1]**

ALPHABETICAL LIST OF CONTENTS

PART 1
STATUTES

STATUTE OF FRAUDS (1677)

(29 Car 2 c 3)

An Act for prevention of Frauds and Perjuryes

NOTES

The short title was given to this Act by the Short Titles Act 1896.

1–3   (*Repealed by the Law of Property Act 1925, s 207, Sch 7.*)

[1.1]
4   No action against executors, etc, upon a special promise, or upon any agreement, or contract for sale of lands, etc, unless agreement, etc, be in writing, and signed
. . .   noe action shall be brought   . . .   whereby to charge the defendant upon any speciall promise to answere for the debt default or miscarriages of another person   . . .   unlesse the agreement upon which such action shall be brought or some memorandum or note thereof shall be in writeing and signed by the partie to be charged therewith or some other person thereunto by him lawfully authorized.

NOTES

First words omitted repealed by the Statute Law Revision Act 1883 and the Statute Law Revision Act 1948; second words omitted repealed by the Law Reform (Enforcement of Contracts) Act 1954, s 1; final words omitted repealed by the Law of Property Act 1925, s 207, Sch 7, and the Law Reform (Enforcement of Contracts) Act 1954, s 1.

5–24   (*Ss 5, 6, 12, 18–21, 22 repealed by the Wills Act 1837, s 2; ss 7–9 repealed by the Law of Property Act 1925, s 207, Sch 7; ss 10, 11, 23 repealed by the Administration of Estates Act 1925, s 56, Sch 2; ss 13, 14 repealed by the Civil Procedure Acts Repeal Act 1879, s 2, Schedule, Pt I; ss 15, 16 repealed by the Sale of Goods Act 1893, s 60, Schedule, s 17 repealed by the Statute Law Revision and Civil Procedure Act 1881; s 24 repealed by the Law of Property Act 1925, s 207, Sch 7 and by the Administration of Estates Act 1925, s 56, Sch 2.*)

LIFE ASSURANCE ACT 1774

(14 Geo 3 c 48)

ARRANGEMENT OF SECTIONS

An Act for regulating Insurances upon Lives, and for prohibiting all such Insurances except in cases where the Persons insuring shall have an Interest in the Life or Death of the Persons insured

NOTES

The short title was given to this Act by the Short Titles Act 1896. It is also known as the Gambling Act 1774.

Exemptions: this Act is excluded in relation to insurance by local authorities against accidents to their members and voluntary assistants by the Local Government Act 1972, ss 140(3), 140C(3), and in relation to insurance by internal drainage boards against accidents to their members by the Land Drainage Act 1991, s 1, Sch 2, para 1(3).

[1.2]
Whereas it hath been found by experience that the making insurances on lives or other events wherein the assured shall have no interest hath introduced a mischievous kind of gaming:

[1.3]
1   No insurance to be made on lives, etc, by persons having no interest etc
From and after the passing of this Act no insurance shall be made by any person or persons, bodies politick or corporate, on the life or lives of any person or persons, or on any other event or events whatsoever, wherein the person or persons for whose use, benefit, or on whose account such policy or policies shall be made, shall have no interest, or by way of gaming or wagering; and that every assurance made contrary to the true intent and meaning hereof shall be null and void to all intents and purposes whatsoever.

[1.4]
2 No policies on lives without inserting the names of persons interested, etc
And . . . it shall not be lawful to make any policy or policies on the life or lives of any person or persons, or other event or events, without inserting in such policy or policies the person or persons name or names interested therein, or for whose use, benefit, or on whose account such policy is so made or underwrote.

NOTES
Words omitted repealed by the Statute Law Revision Act 1888.
Validation of certain group policies: certain group policies are excluded from the effect of this section with retrospective effect, by the Insurance Companies Amendment Act 1973, s 50.

[1.5]
3 How much may be recovered where the insured hath interest in lives
And . . . in all cases where the insured hath interest in such life or lives, event or events, no greater sum shall be recovered or received from the insurer or insurers than the amount of value of the interest of the insured in such life or lives, or other event or events.

NOTES
Words omitted repealed by the Statute Law Revision Act 1888.

[1.6]
4 Not to extend to insurances on ships, goods, etc
Provided, always, that nothing herein contained shall extend or be construed to extend to insurances bona fide made by any person or persons on ships, goods, or merchandises, but every such insurance shall be as valid and effectual in the law as if this Act had not been made.

FIRES PREVENTION (METROPOLIS) ACT 1774

(14 Geo 3 c 78)

ARRANGEMENT OF SECTIONS

An Act . . . for the more effectually preventing Mischiefs by Fire within the Cities of London and Westminster and the Liberties thereof, and other the Parishes, Precincts, and Places within the Weekly Bills of Mortality, the Parishes of Saint Mary-le-bon, Paddington, Saint Pancras and Saint Luke at Chelsea, in the County of Middlesex . . .

NOTES
Short title: given to this Act by the Short Titles Act 1896.
Long title: words omitted repealed by the Statute Law Revision Act 1887. This Act applies to the whole of England.

(Whole Act, except ss 83, 86, repealed by the Metropolitan Fire Brigade Act 1865, s 34.)

[1.7]
83 Money insured on houses burnt how to be applied
And in order to deter and hinder ill-minded persons from wilfully setting their house or houses or other buildings on fire with a view of gaining to themselves the insurance money, whereby the lives and fortunes of many families may be lost or endangered: Be it further enacted by the authority aforesaid, that it shall and may be lawful to and for the respective governors or directors of the several insurance offices for insuring houses or other buildings against loss by fire, and they are hereby authorised and required, upon the request of any person or persons interested in or intitled unto any house or houses or other buildings which may hereafter be burnt down, demolished or damaged by fire, or upon any grounds of suspicion that the owner or owners, occupier or occupiers, or other person or persons who shall have insured such house or houses or other buildings have been guilty of fraud, or of wilfully setting their house or houses or other buildings on fire, to cause the insurance money to be laid out and expended, as far as the same will go, towards rebuilding, reinstating or repairing such house or houses or other buildings so burnt down, demolished or damaged by fire, unless the party or parties claiming such insurance money shall, within sixty days next after his, her or their claim is adjusted, give a sufficient security to the governors or directors of the insurance office where such house or houses or other buildings are insured, that the same insurance money shall be laid out and expended as aforesaid, or unless the said insurance money shall be in that time settled and disposed of to and amongst all the contending parties, to the satisfaction and approbation of such governors or directors of such insurance office respectively.

[1.8]
86 No action to lie against a person where the fire accidentally begins
And . . . no action, suit or process whatever shall be had, maintained or prosecuted against any person in whose house, chamber, stable, barn or other building, or on whose estate any fire shall . . . accidentally begin, nor shall any recompence be made by such person for any damage suffered thereby, any law, usage or custom to the contrary notwithstanding: . . . provided that no contract or agreement made between landlord and tenant shall be hereby defeated or made void.

NOTES
First words omitted repealed by the Statute Law Revision Act 1888; second words omitted repealed by the Statute Law Revision Act 1948; final words omitted repealed by the Statute Law Revision Act 1958 and by virtue of the Statute Law Revision Act 1861.

STATUTE OF FRAUDS AMENDMENT ACT 1828

(9 Geo 4 c 14)

ARRANGEMENT OF SECTIONS

An Act for rendering a written Memorandum necessary to the Validity of certain Promises and Engagements

[9 May 1828]

NOTES
The short title was given to this Act by the Short Titles Act 1896. It is also known as Lord Tenterden's Act.

1–5   *(Ss 1, 3, 4 repealed by the Limitation Act 1939, s 34, Schedule, and the Statute of Limitations Act (Northern Ireland) 1958, s 75, Schedule; s 2 repealed by the Statute Law Revision Act 1890; s 5 repealed by the Statute Law Revision Act 1875.)*

[1.9]
6 Action not maintainable on representations of character, etc, unless they be in writing signed by the party chargeable
No action shall be brought whereby to charge any person upon or by reason of any representation or assurance made or given concerning or relating to the character, conduct, credit, ability, trade, or dealings of any other person, to the intent or purpose that such other person may obtain credit, money, or goods upon, unless such representation or assurance be made in writing, signed by the party to be charged therewith.

7, 8   *(S 7 repealed by the Sale of Goods Act 1893, s 60, Schedule; s 8 repealed by the Limitation Act 1939, s 34, Schedule, and the Statute of Limitations Act (Northern Ireland) 1958, s 75, Schedule.)*

[1.10]
9 Act not to extend to Scotland
Nothing in this Act contained shall extend to Scotland.

10   *(Repealed by the Statute Law Revision Act 1873.)*

AUCTIONEERS ACT 1845

(8 & 9 Vict c 15)

An Act . . . to impose a new Duty on the Licence to be taken out by all Auctioneers in the United Kingdom

[8 May 1845]

NOTES
The short title was given to this Act by the Short Titles Act 1896. Words omitted repealed by the Statute Law Revision Act 1891.

1–6   *(S 1 repealed by the Statute Law Revision Act 1875; ss 2–6 repealed retrospectively by the Finance Act 1949, ss 14, 52(9), (10), Sch 11, Pt I.)*

[1.11]
7 Auctioneer, before commencing any sale, shall affix or suspend a ticket or board containing his full christian and surname and place of residence

. . . Every auctioneer, before beginning any auction, shall affix or suspend, or cause to be affixed or suspended, a ticket or board, containing his true and full christian and surname and residence painted, printed, or written in large letters publicly visible and legible, in some conspicuous part of the room or place where the auction is held, so that all persons may easily read the same, and shall also keep such ticket or board so affixed or suspended during the whole time of such auction being held; and if any auctioneer begins any auction, or acts as auctioneer at any auction, in any room or place where his name and residence is not so painted or written on a ticket or board so affixed or suspended, and kept affixed or suspended as aforesaid, he shall forfeit for every such offence the sum of twenty pounds.

NOTES
Words omitted repealed by the Statute Law Revision Act 1891.
The sum of twenty pounds: this Act does not state whether this offence is to be tried summarily or on indictment. In the case of an offence that is triable on indictment only, there is now no limit to the fine that may be imposed; see the Criminal Law Act 1977, s 32.
The particulars which under this section must be displayed in some conspicuous part of the room, etc, where the auction is held include a copy of the Auctions (Bidding Agreements) Act 1927 and the Auctions (Bidding Agreements) Act 1969; see s 3 of the 1927 Act at **[1.363]** and s 4 of the 1969 Act at **[1.461]**.

8, 9 *(S 8 repealed retrospectively by the Finance Act 1949, ss 14, 52(9), (10), Sch 11, Pt I; s 9 repealed by the Statute Law Revision Act 1875.)*

COMMON LAW PROCEDURE ACT 1854

(17 & 18 Vict c 125)

ARRANGEMENT OF SECTIONS

An Act for the further Amendment of the Process, Practice, and Mode of Pleading in and enlarging the Jurisdiction of the Superior Courts of Common Law at Westminster, and of the Superior Courts of Common Law of the Counties Palatine of Lancaster and Durham . . .

[12 August 1854]

NOTES
Long title: words omitted repealed by the Statute Law Revision and Civil Procedure Act 1883, s 3, Schedule, and the Statute Law Revision Act 1892. Repeals by those Acts were, however, subject to savings of jurisdiction established by the repealed enactments and savings of the application of the repealed enactments to local courts.

1–86 *(Ss 1, 2, 18, 19, 31–58, 60–86 repealed by the Statute Law Revision and Civil Procedure Act 1883, s 3, Schedule and ss 21–27, 30 repealed by the Statute Law Revision Act 1892, all subject to the savings mentioned in the Introductory Note to this Act; ss 3–17 repealed by the Arbitration Act 1889, s 26, Sch 2; s 20 repealed by the Oaths Act 1888, s 6, Schedule; ss 28, 29 repealed by the Inland Revenue Repeal Act 1870, s 2, Schedule; s 59 repealed by the Courts Act 1971, s 56, Sch 11, Pt I.)*

[1.12]
87 Actions on lost negotiable instruments
In case of any action founded upon a . . . negotiable instrument, it shall be lawful for the court or a judge to order that the loss of such instrument shall not be set up, provided an indemnity is given, to the satisfaction of the court or judge, or a master, against the claims of any other person upon such negotiable instrument.

NOTES
Words omitted, which related to bills of exchange, repealed by the Statute Law Revision Act 1892.

88–98 *(S 88 repealed by the Common Law Procedure Act 1860, s 35; s 89 repealed by the Statute Law Revision Act 1892 and ss 90–96 repealed by the Statute Law Revision and Civil Procedure Act 1883, s 3, Schedule, subject to the savings mentioned in the Introductory Note to this Act; ss 97, 98 repealed by the Supreme Court of Judicature (Officers) Act 1879, s 29, Sch 2.)*

[1.13]
99   Interpretation of terms
In the construction of this Act the word "court" shall be understood to mean any one of the Superior Courts of Common Law at Westminster: and the word "judge" shall be understood to mean a judge or baron of any of the said courts; and the word "master" shall be understood to mean a master of any of the said courts; and the word "action" shall be understood to mean any personal action in any of the said courts.

NOTES
Repealed by the Statute Law Revision and Civil Procedure Act 1883, s 3, Schedule, subject to the savings mentioned in the Introductory Note to this Act.

Superior Courts of Common Law: the jurisdiction of the former Courts of Common Law was vested in the High Court by the Supreme Court of Judicature (Consolidation) Act 1925, ss 18, 224 (repealed), see now the Senior Courts Act 1981, s 19, Sch 4, para 1.

100–105   *(Ss 100–102, 104, 105 repealed by the Statute Law Revision and Civil Procedure Act 1883, s 3, Schedule, and s 103 repealed by the Statute Law Revision Act 1892, subject to the savings mentioned in the Introductory Note to this Act.)*

[1.14]
106   Short title of Act
In citing this Act in any instrument, document, or proceeding, it shall be sufficient to use the expression, "The Common Law Procedure Act 1854."

[1.15]
107   Act not to extend to Ireland or Scotland
Nothing in this Act shall extend to Ireland or Scotland   . . .

NOTES
Words omitted repealed by the Statute Law Revision Act 1875.

MERCANTILE LAW AMENDMENT ACT 1856

(19 & 20 Vict c 97)

ARRANGEMENT OF SECTIONS

An Act to amend the Laws of England and Ireland affecting Trade and Commerce

[29 July 1856]

1, 2   *(Repealed by the Sale of Goods Act 1893, s 60, Schedule.)*

[1.16]
3   Written guarantee not to be invalid by reason that the consideration does not appear in writing
No special promise to be made by any person   . . .   to answer for the debt default, or miscarriage of another person, being in writing, and signed by the party to be charged therewith, or some other person by him thereunto lawfully authorised, shall be deemed invalid to support an action, suit, or other proceeding to charge the person by whom such promise shall have been made, by reason only that the consideration for such promise does not appear in writing or by necessary inference from a written document.

NOTES
Words omitted repealed by the Statute Law Revision Act 1892.

4   *(Repealed by the Partnership Act 1890, s 48, Schedule.)*

[1.17]
5   Surety who discharges the liability to be entitled to assignment of all securities held by the creditor, and to stand in the place of the creditor
Every person who, being surety for the debt or duty of another, or being liable with another for any debt or duty, shall pay such debt or perform such duty, shall be entitled to have assigned to him, or to a trustee for him, every judgment specialty, or other security which shall be held by the creditor

in respect of such debt or duty, whether such judgment, specialty, or other security shall or shall not be deemed at law to have been satisfied by the payment of the debt or performance of the duty, and such person shall be entitled to stand in the place of the creditor, and to use all the remedies, and, if need be, and upon a proper indemnity, to use the name of the creditor, in any action or other proceeding, at law or in equity, in order to obtain from the principal debtor, or any co-surety, co-contractor, or co-debtor, as the case may be, indemnification for the advances made and loss sustained by the person who shall have so paid such debt or performed such duty, and such payment or performance so made by such surety shall not be pleadable in bar of any such action or other proceeding by him: Provided always, that no co-surety, cocontractor, or codebtor shall be entitled to recover from any other co-surety, cocontractor, or codebtor, by the means aforesaid, more than the just proportion to which, as between those parties themselves, such last-mentioned person shall be justly liable.

6, 7 *(Repealed by the Bills of Exchange Act 1882, s 96, Sch 2.)*

[1.18]
8 Definition of home port
In relation to the rights and remedies of persons having claims for repairs done to or supplies furnished to or for, ships, every port within the United Kingdom of Great Britain and Ireland, the Islands of Man, Guernsey, Jersey, Alderney, and Sark, and the islands adjacent to any of them, being part of the dominions of Her Majesty, shall be deemed a home port.

9–15 *(Ss 9–14 repealed by the Limitation Act 1939, s 34, Schedule, and the Statute of Limitations Act (Northern Ireland) 1958, s 75, Schedule; s 15 repealed by the Statute Law Revision Act 1894.)*

[1.19]
16 Short title
In citing this Act, it shall be sufficient to use the expression "The Mercantile Law Amendment Act 1856."

[1.20]
17 Extent
Nothing in this Act shall extend to Scotland.

POLICIES OF ASSURANCE ACT 1867

(30 & 31 Vict c 144)

ARRANGEMENT OF SECTIONS

An Act to enable Assignees of Policies of Life Assurance to sue thereon in their own names

[20 August 1867]

(Preamble repealed by the Statute Law Revision Act 1893.)

[1.21]
1 Assignees of life policies, empowered to sue
Any person or corporation now being or hereafter becoming entitled, by assignment or other derivative title, to a policy of life assurance, and possessing at the time of action brought the right in equity to receive and the right to give an effectual discharge to the assurance company liable under such policy for monies thereby assured or secured, shall be at liberty to sue at law in the name of such person or corporation to recover such monies.

[1.22]
2 Defence or reply on equitable grounds
In any action on a policy of life assurance, a defence on equitable grounds, or a reply to such defence on similar grounds, may be respectively pleaded and relied upon in the same manner and to the same extent as in any other personal action.

[1.23]
3 Notice of assignment
No assignment made after the passing of this Act of a policy of life assurance shall confer on the assignee therein named, his executors, administrators, or assigns, any right to sue for the amount of such policy, or the monies assured or secured thereby, until a written notice of the date and purport of such assignment shall have been given to the assurance company liable under such policy at their principal place of business for the time being, or in case they have two or more principal places of business, then at some one of such principal places of business, either in England or Scotland or Ireland; and the date on which such notice shall be received shall regulate the priority of all claims under any assignment; and a payment bona fide made in respect of any policy by any assurance company before the date on which such notice shall have been received shall be as valid against the assignee giving such notice as if this Act had not been passed.

[1.24]
4 Principal place of business to be specified on policies
Every assurance company shall, on every policy issued by them after the thirtieth day of September one thousand eight hundred and sixty-seven, specify their principal place or principal places of business at which notices of assignment may be given in pursuance of this Act.

[1.25]
5 Mode of assignment
Any such assignment may be made either by endorsement on the policy or by a separate instrument in the words or to the effect set forth in the schedule hereto, such endorsement or separate instrument being duly stamped.

[1.26]
6 Receipt of notice of assignment
Every assurance company to whom notice shall have been duly given of the assignment of any policy under which they are liable shall, upon the request in writing of any person by whom any such notice was given or signed, or of his executors or administrators, and upon payment in each case of a fee not exceeding [25p] deliver an acknowledgment in writing, under the hand of the manager, secretary, treasurer, or other principal officer of the assurance company, of their receipt of such notice; and every such written acknowledgment, if signed by a person being de jure or de facto the manager, secretary, treasurer, or other principal officer of the assurance company whose acknowledgment the same purports to be, shall be conclusive evidence as against such assurance company of their having duly received the notice to which such acknowledgment relates.

NOTES
Sum in square brackets substituted by virtue of the Decimal Currency Act 1969, s 10(1).

[1.27]
7 Interpretation
In the construction and for the purposes of this Act the expression "policy of life assurance" or "policy" shall mean any instrument by which the payment of monies by or out of the funds of an assurance company, on the happening of any contingency depending on the duration of human life, is assured or secured; and the expression "assurance company" shall mean and include every corporation, association, society, or company now or hereafter carrying on the business of assuring lives, or survivorships, either alone or in conjunction with any other object or objects.

[1.28]
8 Saving of contracts under 16 & 17 Vict c 45, or 27 & 28 Vict c 43, and of engagements by friendly societies
Provided always, that this Act shall not apply to any policy of assurance granted or to be granted or to any contract for a payment on death entered into or to be entered into in pursuance of the provisions of the Government Annuities Act 1853, and the Government Annuities Act 1864, or either of those Acts, or to any engagement for payment on death by any friendly society.

NOTES
Government Annuities Act 1853 and Government Annuities Act 1864: repealed with savings by the Government Annuities Act 1929, s 66, Sch 2, Pt II, see now Pt II of that Act.

[1.29]
9 Short title
For all purposes this Act may be cited as "The Policies of Assurance Act 1867."

SCHEDULE

Section 5

[1.30]

I *A.B.*, of, &c, in consideration of, &c, do hereby assign unto *C.D.*, of, &c, his executors, administrators, and assigns, the [within] policy of assurance granted, &c [*here describe the policy*].

In witness, &c

BILLS OF SALE ACT 1878

(41 & 42 Vict c 31)

ARRANGEMENT OF SECTIONS

SCHEDULES

An Act to consolidate and amend the Law for preventing Frauds upon Creditors by secret Bills of Sale of Personal Chattels

[22 July 1878]

NOTES

Bills of Sale Acts 1878 and 1882: by the Bills of Sale Act (1878) Amendment Act 1882, s 1, that Act and this Act may be cited together as the Bills of Sale Acts 1878 and 1882; see **[1.56]**.

Application: this Act shall not apply to a security agreement which creates or provides for an international interest; see the International Interests in Aircraft Equipment (Cape Town Convention) Regulations 2015, SI 2015/912, reg 50, Sch 5, Pt 2, para 6.

[1.31]
1　Short title
This Act may be cited for all purposes as the Bills of Sale Act 1878.

[1.32]
2　Commencement
. . . the first day of January one thousand eight hundred and seventy-nine, . . . is in this Act referred to as the commencement of this Act.

NOTES

Words omitted repealed by the Statute Law Revision Act 1894.

[1.33]

3 Application

This Act shall apply to every bill of sale executed on or after the first day of January one thousand eight hundred and seventy-nine (whether the same be absolute, or subject or not subject to any trust) whereby the holder or grantee has power, either with or without notice, and either immediately or at any future time, to seize or take possession of any personal chattels comprised in or made subject to such bill of sale.

NOTES

Application, construction and partial repeal of this Act: this Act remains in force so far as it relates to absolute bills of sale executed after its commencement; as to bills of sale given as security for the payment of money it is to be construed as one with the Bills of Sale Act (1878) Amendment Act 1882 (by virtue of s 3 of the 1882 Act at **[1.58]**), but as to such bills of sale only, this Act is repealed as far as it is inconsistent with the 1882 Act (by virtue of s 15 of the 1882 Act at **[1.71]**).

[1.34]

4 Interpretation of terms

In this Act the following words and expressions shall have the meanings in this section assigned to them respectively, unless there be something in the subject or context repugnant to such construction; (that is to say),

The expression "bill of sale" shall include bills of sale, assignments, transfers, declarations of trust without transfer, inventories of goods with receipt thereto attached, or receipts for purchase moneys of goods, and other assurances of personal chattels, and also powers of attorney, authorities, or licenses to take possession of personal chattels as security for any debt, and also any agreement, whether intended or not to be followed by the execution of any other instrument, by which a right in equity to any personal chattels, or to any charge or security thereon, shall be conferred, but shall not include the following documents; that is to say, assignments for the benefit of the creditors of the person making or giving the same, marriage settlements, transfers or assignments of any ship or vessel or any share thereof, transfers of goods in the ordinary course of business of any trade or calling, bills of sale of goods in foreign parts or at sea, bills of lading, India warrants, warehouse-keepers' certificates, warrants or orders for the delivery of goods, or any other documents used in the ordinary course of business as proof of the possession or control of goods, or authorising or purporting to authorise, either by indorsement or by delivery, the possessor of such document to transfer or receive goods thereby represented:

The expression "personal chattels" shall mean goods, furniture, and other articles capable of complete transfer by delivery, and (when separately assigned or charged) fixtures and growing crops, but shall not include chattel interests in real estate, nor fixtures (except trade machinery as herein-after defined), when assigned together with a freehold or leasehold interest in any land or building to which they are affixed, nor growing crops when assigned together with any interest in the land on which they grow, nor shares or interests in the stock, funds, or securities of any government, or in the capital or property of incorporated or joint stock companies, nor choses in action, nor any stock or produce upon any farm or lands which by virtue of any covenant or agreement or of the custom of the country ought not to be removed from any farm where the same are at the time of making or giving of such bill of sale:

Personal chattels shall be deemed to be in the "apparent possession" of the person making or giving a bill of sale, so long as they remain or are in or upon any house, mill, warehouse, building, works, yard, land, or other premises occupied by him, or are used and enjoyed by him in any place whatsoever, notwithstanding that formal possession thereof may have been taken by or given to any other person:

"Prescribed" means prescribed by rules made under the provisions of this Act.

[1.35]

5 Application of Act to trade machinery

From and after the commencement of this Act trade machinery shall, for the purposes of this Act, be deemed to be personal chattels, and any mode of disposition of trade machinery by the owner thereof which would be a bill of sale as to any other personal chattels shall be deemed to be a bill of sale within the meaning of this Act.

For the purposes of this Act—

"Trade machinery" means the machinery used in or attached to any factory or workshop;

     1st   Exclusive of the fixed motive-powers, such as the water-wheels and steam-engines, and the steam-boilers, donkey-engines, and other fixed appurtenances of the said motive-powers; and,

     2nd   Exclusive of the fixed power machinery, such as the shafts, wheels, drums, and their fixed appurtenances, which transmit the action of the motive-powers to the other machinery, fixed and loose, and

     3rd   Exclusive of the pipes for steam gas and water in the factory or workshop.

The machinery or effects excluded by this section from the definition of trade machinery shall not be deemed to be personal chattels within the meaning of this Act.

"Factory or workshop" means any premises on which any manual labour is exercised by way of trade, or for purposes of gain, in or incidental to the following purposes or any of them; that is to say,

(a) In or incidental to the making any article or part of an article; or

(b) In or incidental to the altering, repairing, ornamenting, finishing, of any article; or

(c) In or incidental to the adapting for sale any article.

[1.36]
6 Certain instruments giving powers of distress to be subject to this Act

Every attornment instrument or agreement, not being a mining lease, whereby a power of distress is given or agreed to be given by any person to any other person by way of security for any present future or contingent debt or advance, and whereby any rent is reserved or made payable as a mode of providing for the payment of interest on such debt or advance, or otherwise for the purpose of such security only, shall be deemed to be a bill of sale, within the meaning of this Act, of any personal chattels which may be seized or taken under such power of distress.

Provided, that nothing in this section shall extend to any mortgage of any estate or interest in any land tenement or hereditament which the mortgagee, being in possession, shall have demised to the mortgagor as his tenant at a fair and reasonable rent.

[1.37]
7 Fixtures or growing crops not to be deemed separately assigned when the land passes by the same instrument

No fixtures or growing crops shall be deemed, under this Act, to be separately assigned or charged by reason only that they are assigned by separate words, or that power is given to sever them from the land or building to which they are affixed, or from the land on which they grow, without otherwise taking possession of or dealing with such land or building, or land, if by the same instrument any freehold or leasehold interest in the land or building to which such fixtures are affixed, or in the land on which such crops grow, is also conveyed or assigned to the same persons or person.

The same rule of construction shall be applied to all deeds or instruments, including fixtures or growing crops, executed before the commencement of this Act, and then subsisting and in force, in all questions arising under any bankruptcy liquidation assignment for the benefit of creditors, or execution of any process of any court, which shall take place or be issued after the commencement of this Act.

[1.38]
8 Avoidance of unregistered bill of sale in certain cases

Every bill of sale to which this Act applies shall be duly attested and shall be registered under this Act, within seven days after the making or giving thereof, and shall set forth the consideration for which such bill of sale was given, otherwise such bill of sale, as against all trustees or assignees of the estate of the person whose chattels, or any of them, are comprised in such bill of sale under the law relating to bankruptcy or liquidation, or under any assignment for the benefit of the creditors of such person, and also as against all sheriffs officers and other persons seizing any chattels comprised in such bill of sale, in the execution of any process of any court authorising the seizure of the chattels of the person by whom or of whose chattels such bill has been made, and also as against every person on whose behalf such process shall have been issued, shall be deemed fraudulent and void so far as regards the property in or right to the possession of any chattels comprised in such bill of sale which, at or after the time of filing the petition for bankruptcy or liquidation, or of the execution of such assignment, or of executing such process (as the case may be), and after the expiration of such seven days are in the possession or apparent possession of the person making such bill of sale (or of any person against whom the process has issued under or in the execution of which such bill has been made or given, as the case may be).

NOTES

This section is in terms repealed by the Bills of Sale Act (1878) Amendment Act 1882, s 15 at **[1.71]**, but notwithstanding that, the effect of the Bills of Sale Act (1878) Amendment Act 1882, s 3 at **[1.58]**, is that the repeal applies only to bills of sale to which the later Act applies, so that this section remains in force so far as regards bills of sale not given as a security for money (ie, absolute bills of sale).

[1.39]
9 Avoidance of certain duplicate bills of sale

Where a subsequent bill of sale is executed within or on the expiration of seven days after the execution of a prior unregistered bill of sale, and comprises all or any part of the personal chattels comprised in such prior bill of sale, then, if such subsequent bill of sale is given as a security for the same debt as is secured by the prior bill of sale, or for any part of such debt, it shall, to the extent to which it is a security for the same debt or part thereof, and so far as respects the personal chattels or part thereof comprised in the prior bill, be absolutely void, unless it is proved to the satisfaction of the court having cognizance of the case that the subsequent bill of sale was bona fide given for the purpose of correcting some material error in the prior bill of sale, and not for the purpose of evading this Act.

[1.40]

10   Mode of registering bills of sale

A bill of sale shall be attested and registered under this Act in the following manner—

(1)   The execution of every bill of sale shall be attested by a solicitor of the [Senior Courts], and the attestation shall state that before the execution of the bill of sale the effect thereof has been explained to the grantor by the attesting solicitor.

(2)   Such bill, with every schedule or inventory thereto annexed or therein referred to, and also a true copy of such bill and of every such schedule or inventory, and of every attestation of the execution of such bill of sale, together with an affidavit of the time of such bill of sale being made or given, and of its due execution and attestation, and a description of the residence and occupation of the person making or giving the same (or in case the same is made or given by any person under or in the execution of any process, then a description of the residence and occupation of the person against whom such process issued), and of every attesting witness to such bill of sale, shall be presented to and the said copy and affidavit shall be filed with the registrar within seven clear days after the making or giving of such bill of sale, in like manner as a warrant of attorney in any personal action given by a trader is now by law required to be filed:

(3)   If the bill of sale is made or given subject to any defeasance or condition, or declaration of trust not contained in the body thereof such defeasance, condition, or declaration shall be deemed to be part of the bill, and shall be written on the same paper or parchment therewith before the registration, and shall be truly set forth in the copy filed under this Act therewith and as part thereof, otherwise the registration shall be void.

In case two or more bills of sale are given, comprising in whole or in part any of the same chattels, they shall have priority in the order of the date of their registration respectively as regards such chattels.

A transfer or assignment of a registered bill of sale need not be registered.

NOTES

Sub-s (1): as regards absolute bills of sale the requirements of sub-s (1) must still be observed, for, although repealed by the Bills of Sale Act (1878) Amendment Act 1882, s 10, it remains in force so far as absolute bills are concerned by virtue of s 3 of that Act at **[1.58]**; words in square brackets substituted by the Constitutional Reform Act 2005, s 59(5), Sch 11, Pt 2, para 4(1), (3).

Local registration: see the Bills of Sale Act (1878) Amendment Act 1882, s 11 at **[1.67]**, and the Bills of Sale (Local Registration) Rules 1960, SI 1960/2326.

[1.41]

11   Renewal of registration

The registration of a bill of sale, whether executed before or after the commencement of this Act, must be renewed once at least every five years, and if a period of five years elapses from the registration or renewed registration of a bill of sale without a renewal or further renewal (as the case may be), the registration shall become void.

The renewal of a registration shall be effected by filing with the registrar an affidavit stating the date of the bill of sale and of the last registration thereof, and the names, residences, and occupations of the parties thereto as stated therein, and that the bill of sale is still a subsisting security.

Every such affidavit may be in the form set forth in the schedule (A.) to this Act annexed.

A renewal of registration shall not become necessary by reason only of a transfer or assignment of a bill of sale.

[1.42]

12   Form of register

The registrar shall keep a book (in this Act called "the register") for the purposes of this Act, and shall, upon the filing of any bill of sale or copy under this Act, enter therein in the form set forth in the second schedule (B) to this Act annexed, or in any other prescribed form, the name, residence and occupation of the person by whom the bill was made or given (or in case the same was made or given by any person under or in the execution of process, then the name residence and occupation of the person against whom such process was issued, and also the name of the person or persons to whom or in whose favour the bill was given), and the other particulars shown in the said schedule or to be prescribed under this Act, and shall number all such bills registered in each year consecutively, according to the respective dates of their registration.

Upon the registration of any affidavit of renewal the like entry shall be made, with the addition of the date and number of the last previous entry relating to the same bill, and the bill of sale or copy originally filed shall be thereupon marked with the number affixed to such affidavit of renewal.

The registrar shall also keep an index of the names of the grantors of registered bills of sale with reference to entries in the register of the bills of sale given by each such grantor.

Such index shall be arranged in divisions corresponding with the letters of the alphabet, so that all grantors whose surnames begin with the same letter (and no others) shall be comprised in one division, but the arrangement within each such division need not be strictly alphabetical.

[1.43]
13   The registrar
The masters of the [Senior Courts] attached to the Queen's Bench Division of the High Court of Justice, or such other officers as may for the time being be assigned for this purpose under the provisions of the Supreme Court of Judicature Acts, 1873 and 1875, shall be the registrar for the purposes of this Act, and any one of the said masters may perform all or any of the duties of the registrar.

NOTES
Words in square brackets substituted by the Constitutional Reform Act 2005, s 59(5), Sch 11, Pt 2, para 4(1), (3).
Supreme Court of Judicature Acts 1873 and 1875: repealed by the Supreme Court of Judicature (Consolidation) Act 1925, s 226, Sch 6 (repealed).

[1.44]
14   Rectification of register
Any judge of the High Court of Justice on being satisfied that the omission to register a bill of sale or an affidavit or renewal thereof within the time prescribed by this Act, or the omission or mis-statement of the name residence or occupation of any person, was accidental or due to inadvertence, may in his discretion order such omission or mis-statement to be rectified by the insertion in the register of the true name residence or occupation, or by extending the time for such registration on such terms and conditions (if any) as to security, notice by advertisement or otherwise, or as to any other matter, as he thinks fit to direct.

[1.45]
15   Entry of satisfaction
Subject to and in accordance with any rules to be made under and for the purposes of this Act, the registrar may order a memorandum of satisfaction to be written upon any registered copy of a bill of sale, upon the prescribed evidence being given that the debt (if any) for which such bill of sale was made or given has been satisfied or discharged.

[1.46]
16   Copies may be taken, etc
Any person shall be entitled to have an office copy or extract of any registered bill of sale, and affidavit of execution filed therewith, or copy thereof, and of any affidavit filed therewith, if any, or registered affidavit of renewal, upon paying for the same at the like rate as for office copies of judgments of the High Court of Justice, and any copy of a registered bill of sale, and affidavit purporting to be an office copy thereof, shall in all courts and before all arbitrators or other persons, be admitted as prima facie evidence thereof, and of the fact and date of registration as shown thereon . . .

NOTES
Words omitted repealed by the Bills of Sale Act (1878) Amendment Act 1882, s 16.

[1.47]
17   Affidavits
Every affidavit required by or for the purposes of this Act may be sworn before a master of any division of the High Court of Justice, or before any commissioner empowered to take affidavits in the [Senior Courts] . . .

NOTES
Words in square brackets substituted by the Constitutional Reform Act 2005, s 59(5), Sch 11, Pt 2, para 4(1), (3); words omitted repealed by the Perjury Act 1911, s 17 (repealed), see now s 2(2) of that Act.

18   (*Repealed by the Statute Law Revision Act 1950.*)

[1.48]
19   Collection of fees under 38 & 39 Vict c 77 s 26
Section twenty-six of the Supreme Court of Judicature Act 1875, and any enactments for the time being in force amending or substituted for that section shall apply to fees under this Act, and an order under that section may, if need be, be made in relation to such fees accordingly.

NOTES
Supreme Court of Judicature 1875, s 26: repealed by the Supreme Court of Judicature (Consolidation) Act 1925, s 226, Sch 6 (repealed).

[1.49]
20   Order and disposition
Chattels comprised in a bill of sale which has been and continues to be duly registered under this Act shall not be deemed to be in the possession, order, or disposition of the grantor of the bill of sale within the meaning of the Bankruptcy Act 1869.

NOTES

The provisions of this section are not affected, so far as regards absolute bills of sale, by the repeal of the section by the Bills of Sale Act (1878) Amendment Act 1882, s 15 at **[1.71]**, the effect of s 3 of the 1882 Act at **[1.58]** being that the repeal only applies to bills which are within the latter Act (ie, bills given as security for the payment of money).

Bankruptcy Act 1869: repealed by the Bankruptcy Act 1883, s 169, Sch 5 (repealed). See now the Insolvency Act 1986, s 283 and cf ss 307–309, 338 of that Act.

[1.50]
21   Rules

Rules for the purposes of this Act may be made and altered from time to time by the like persons and in the like manner in which rules and regulations may be made under and for the purposes of the Supreme Court of Judicature Acts 1873 and 1875.

NOTES

Supreme Court of Judicature Acts 1873 and 1875: repealed as to the relevant provisions for the purposes of this section by the Supreme Court of Judicature (Consolidation) Act 1925, s 226, Sch 6 (repealed).

Rules: the Bills of Sale (Local Registration) Rules 1960, SI 1960/2326.

[1.51]
22   Time for registration

When the time for registering a bill of sale expires on a Sunday, or other day on which the registrar's office is closed, the registration shall be valid if made on the next following day on which the office is open.

[1.52]
23   As to bills of sale and under repealed Acts

. . . Except as is herein expressly mentioned with respect to construction and with respect to renewal of registration, nothing in this Act shall affect any bill of sale executed before the commencement of this Act, and as regards bills of sale so executed the Acts hereby repealed shall continue in force.

Any renewal after the commencement of this Act of the registration of a bill of sale executed before the commencement of this Act, and registered under the Acts hereby repealed, shall be made under this Act in the same manner as the renewal of a registration made under this Act.

NOTES

Words omitted repealed the Bills of Sale Act 1854 and the Bills of Sale Act 1866 and were themselves repealed by the Statute Law Revision Act 1894.

[1.53]
24   Extent of Act

This Act shall not extend to Scotland or to Ireland.

SCHEDULES

SCHEDULE A

Section 11

[1.54]

I [*AB*] of do swear that a bill of sale, bearing date the day of 18 [*insert the date of the bill,*] and made between [*insert the names and descriptions of the parties in the original bill of sale*] and which said bill of sale [*or, and a copy of which said bill of sale, as the case may be*] was registered on the day of 18 [*insert date of registration*], is still a subsisting security.

Sworn, & *c.*

SCHEDULE B

Section 12

[1.55]

Satis-faction entered	No	By whom given (or against whom process issued)			To whom given	Nature of In-stru-ment	Date	Date of Registra-tion	Date of Registra-tion of affidavit of re-newal
		Name	Resi-dence	Occupa-tion					

BILLS OF SALE ACT (1878) AMENDMENT ACT 1882

(45 & 46 Vict c 43)

ARRANGEMENT OF SECTIONS

An Act to amend the Bills of Sale Act 1878

[18 August 1882]

NOTES

Application: this Act shall not apply to a security agreement which creates or provides for an international interest; see the International Interests in Aircraft Equipment (Cape Town Convention) Regulations 2015, SI 2015/912, reg 50, Sch 5, Pt 2, para 7.

[1.56]
1   Short title
This Act may be cited for all purposes as the Bills of Sale Act (1878) Amendment Act 1882; and this Act and the Bills of Sale Act 1878 may be cited together as the Bills of Sale Acts 1878 and 1882.

[1.57]
2   Commencement of Act
This Act shall come into operation on the first day of November one thousand eight hundred and eighty-two, which date is herein-after referred to as the commencement of this Act.

[1.58]
3   Construction of Act
The Bills of Sale Act 1878 is herein-after referred to as "the principal Act," and this Act shall, so far as is consistent with the tenor thereof, be construed as one with the principal Act; but unless the context otherwise requires shall not apply to any bill of sale duly registered before the commencement of this Act so long as the registration thereof is not avoided by non-renewal or otherwise.

The expression "bill of sale," and other expressions in this Act, have the same meaning as in the principal Act, except as to bills of sale or other documents mentioned in section four of the principal Act, which may be given otherwise than by way of security for the payment of money, to which last-mentioned bills of sale and other documents this Act shall not apply.

[1.59]
4   Bill of sale to have schedule of property attached thereto
Every bill of sale shall have annexed thereto or written thereon a schedule containing an inventory of the personal chattels comprised in the bill of sale; and such bill of sale, save as herein-after mentioned, shall have effect only in respect of the personal chattels specifically described in the said schedule; and shall be void, except as against the grantor, in respect of any personal chattels not so specifically described.

[1.60]
5   Bill of sale not to affect after acquired property
Save as herein-after mentioned, a bill of sale shall be void, except as against the grantor, in respect of any personal chattels specifically described in the schedule thereto of which the grantor was not the true owner at the time of the execution of the bill of sale.

[1.61]
6   Exception as to certain things
Nothing contained in the foregoing sections of this Act shall render a bill of sale void in respect of any of the following things; (that is to say,)
(1)   Any growing crops separately assigned or charged where such crops were actually growing at the time when the bill of sale was executed.
(2)   Any fixtures separately assigned or charged, and any plant, or trade machinery where such fixtures, plant, or trade machinery are used in, attached to, or brought upon any land, farm, factory, workshop, shop, house, warehouse, or other place in substitution for any of the like fixtures, plant, or trade machinery specifically described in the schedule to such bill of sale.

[1.62]
7   Bill of sale with power to seize except in certain events to be void
Personal chattels assigned under a bill of sale shall not be liable to be seized or taken possession of by the grantee for any other than the following causes—
(1)   If the grantor shall make default in payment of the sum or sums of money thereby secured at the time therein provided for payment, or in the performance of any covenant or agreement contained in the bill of sale and necessary for maintaining the security;
(2)   If the grantor shall become a bankrupt, or suffer the said goods or any of them to be distrained[, or taken control of using the power in Schedule 12 to the Tribunals, Courts and Enforcement Act 2007,] for rent, rates, or taxes;
(3)   If the grantor shall fraudulently either remove or suffer the said goods, or any of them, to be removed from the premises;
(4)   If the grantor shall not, without reasonable excuse, upon demand in writing by the grantee, produce to him his last receipts for rent, rates, and taxes;
(5)   If execution shall have been levied against the goods of the grantor under any judgment at law:
Provided that the grantor may within five days from the seizure or taking possession of any chattels on account of any of the above-mentioned causes, apply to the High Court, or to a judge thereof in chambers, and such court or judge, if satisfied that by payment of money or otherwise the said cause of seizure no longer exists, may restrain the grantee from removing or selling the said chattels, or may make such other order as may seem just.

NOTES

Sub-s (2): words in square brackets inserted by the Tribunals, Courts and Enforcement Act 2007, s 62(3), Sch 13, paras 17, 18.

[1.63]
[7A   Defaults under consumer credit agreements
(1)   Paragraph (1) of section 7 of this Act does not apply to a default relating to a bill of sale given by way of security for the payment of money under a regulated agreement to which section 87(1) of the Consumer Credit Act 1974 applies—
(a)   unless the restriction imposed by section 88(2) of that Act has ceased to apply to the bill of sale; or
(b)   if, by virtue of section 89 of that Act, the default is to be treated as not having occurred.
(2)   Where paragraph (1) of section 7 of this Act does apply in relation to a bill of sale such as is mentioned in subsection (1) of this section, the proviso to that section shall have effect with the substitution of "county court" for "High Court".]

NOTES

Inserted by the Consumer Credit Act 1974, s 192(3)(a), Sch 4, para 1.

[1.64]
8   Bill of sale to be void unless attested and registered
Every bill of sale shall be duly attested, and shall be registered under the principal Act within seven clear days after the execution thereof, or if it is executed in any place out of England then within seven clear days after the time at which it would in the ordinary course of post arrive in England if posted immediately after the execution thereof; and shall truly set forth the consideration for which it was given; otherwise such bill of sale shall be void in respect of the personal chattels comprised therein.

NOTES

Principal Act: ie, the Bills of Sale Act 1878.

[1.65]
9   Form of bill of sale
A bill of sale made or given by way of security for the payment of money by the grantor thereof shall be void unless made in accordance with the form in the schedule to this Act annexed.

[1.66]
10   Attestation
The execution of every bill of sale by the grantor shall be attested by one or more credible witness or witnesses, not being a party or parties thereto . . .

NOTES
Words omitted repealed by the Statute Law Revision Act 1898.

[1.67]
11   Local registration of contents of bills of sale
Where the affidavit (which under section ten of the principal Act is required to accompany a bill of sale when presented for registration) describes the residence of the person making or giving the same or of the person against whom the process is issued to be in some place outside [the London insolvency district] or where the bill of sale describes the chattels enumerated therein as being in some place outside [the London insolvency district], the registrar under the principal Act shall forthwith and within three clear days after registration in the principal registry, and in accordance with the prescribed directions, transmit an abstract in the prescribed form of the contents of such bill of sale to the [county court].

Every abstract so transmitted shall be filed, kept, and indexed by the . . . county court in the prescribed manner, and any person may search, inspect, make extracts from, and obtain copies of the abstract so registered in the like manner, and upon the like terms as to payment or otherwise as near as may be as in the case of bills of sale registered by the registrar under the principal Act.

NOTES
Words in first and second pairs of square brackets substituted by the Insolvency Act 1985, s 235(1), Sch 8, para 1, for savings, see the Insolvency Act 1986, s 437, Sch 11, Pt II, para 10; words in final pair of square brackets substituted, and words omitted repealed, by the Crime and Courts Act 2013, s 17(5), Sch 9, Pt 2, para 15, for transitional provision see the Crime and Courts Act 2013 (Commencement No 10 and Transitional Provision) Order 2014, SI 2014/954, art 3.
Registration: the Bills of Sale (Local Registration) Rules 1960, SI 1960/2326, regulate the local registration of bills of sale.
Principal Act: ie, the Bills of Sale Act 1878.

[1.68]
12   Bill of sale under £30 to be void
Every bill of sale made or given in consideration of any sum under thirty pounds shall be void.

[1.69]
13   Chattels not to be removed or sold
All personal chattels seized or of which possession is taken . . . under or by virtue of any bill of sale (whether registered before or after the commencement of this Act), shall remain on the premises where they were so seized or so taken possession of, and shall not be removed or sold until after the expiration of five clear days from the day they were so seized or so taken possession of.

NOTES
Words omitted repealed by the Statute Law Revision Act 1898.

[1.70]
14   Bill of sale not to protect chattels against poor and parochial rates
A bill of sale to which this Act applies shall be no protection in respect of personal chattels included in such bill of sale which but for such bill of sale would have been liable to distress under a warrant[, or subject to a warrant of control,] for the recovery of taxes and poor and other parochial rates.

NOTES
Words in square brackets inserted by the Tribunals, Courts and Enforcement Act 2007, s 62(3), Sch 13, paras 17, 19.

[1.71]
15   Repeal of part of Bills of Sale Act 1878
. . . . all . . . . enactments contained in the principal Act which are inconsistent with this Act are repealed . . . .

NOTES
Words omitted repealed by the Statute Law Revision Act 1898.
Principal Act: ie, the Bills of Sale Act 1878.

[1.72]
16   Inspection of registered bills of sale

. . . any person shall be entitled at all reasonable times to search the register on payment of a fee of [five pence], or such other fee as may be prescribed, and subject to such regulations as may be prescribed, and shall be entitled at all reasonable times to inspect, examine, and make extracts from any and every registered bill of sale without being required to make a written application, or to specify any particulars in reference thereto, upon payment of [five pence] for each bill of sale inspected, and such payment shall be made by a judicature stamp: Provided that the said extracts shall be limited to the dates of execution registration, renewal of registration, and satisfaction, to the names, addresses, and occupations of the parties, to the amount of the consideration, and to any further prescribed particulars.

NOTES

Words omitted repealed by the Statute Law Revision Act 1898; words in square brackets substituted by virtue of the Decimal Currency Act 1969, s 10(1).

[1.73]
17   Debentures to which Act not to apply

Nothing in this Act shall apply to any debentures issued by any mortgage, loan or other incorporated company [or by any limited liability partnership], and secured upon the capital stock or goods, chattels, and effects of such company [or a limited liability partnership].

NOTES

Words in square brackets inserted and added by the Limited Liability Partnerships Regulations 2001, SI 2001/1090, reg 9, Sch 5, para 1.

[1.74]
18   Extent of Act

This Act shall not extend to Scotland or Ireland.

SCHEDULE
FORM OF BILL OF SALE

Section 9

[1.75]

This Indenture made the day of, between *AB* of the one part, and *CD* of the other part, witnesseth that in consideration of the sum of £ now paid to *AB* by *CD* the receipt of which the said *AB* hereby acknowledges [*or whatever else the consideration may be*], he the said *AB* doth hereby assign unto *CD*, his executors, administrators, and assigns, all and singular the several chattels and things specifically described in the schedule hereto annexed by way of security for the payment of the sum of £   , and interest thereon at the rate of per cent per annum [*or whatever else may be the rate*]. And the said *AB* doth further agree and declare that he will duly pay to the said *CD* the principal sum aforesaid, together with the interest then due, by equal payments of £   on the day of [*or whatever else may be the stipulated times or time of payment*]. And the said *AB* doth also agree with the said *CD* that he will [*here insert terms as to insurance, payment of rent or otherwise, which the parties may agree to for the maintenance or defeasance of the security*].

Provided always, that the chattels hereby assigned shall not be liable to seizure or to be taken possession of by the said *CD* for any cause other than those specified in section seven of the Bills of Sale Act (1878) Amendment Act 1882.

In Witness, &c.

Signed and sealed by the said *AB* in the presence of me *EF* [*add witness' name, address, and description*].

BILLS OF EXCHANGE ACT 1882

(45 & 46 Vict c 61)

ARRANGEMENT OF SECTIONS

PART I
PRELIMINARY

PART II
BILLS OF EXCHANGE

An Act to codify the law relating to Bills of Exchange, Cheques, and Promissory Notes

[18 August 1882]

NOTES

By the Bills of Exchange (Time of Noting) Act 1917, s 2, the Bills of Exchange Act 1882 and the 1917 Act may be cited by the collective title of the Bills of Exchange Acts 1882 to 1917.

PART I
PRELIMINARY

[1.76]
1　Short title
This Act may be cited as the Bills of Exchange Act, 1882.

[1.77]
2　Interpretation of terms
In this Act, unless the context otherwise requires,—
　　"Acceptance" means an acceptance completed by delivery or notification.
　　"Action" includes counter claim and set off.
　　"Banker" includes a body of persons whether incorporated or not who carry on the business of
　　　　banking.
　　"Bankrupt" includes any person whose estate is vested in a trustee or assignee under the law for
　　　　the time being in force relating to bankruptcy.
　　"Bearer" means the person in possession of a bill or note which is payable to bearer.
　　"Bill" means bill of exchange, and "note" means promissory note.
　　"Delivery" means transfer of possession, actual or constructive, from one person to another.
　　"Holder" means the payee or indorsee of a bill or note who is in possession of it, or the bearer
　　　　thereof.
　　"Indorsement" means an indorsement completed by delivery.
　　"Issue" means the first delivery of a bill or note, complete in form to a person who takes it as a
　　　　holder.
　　"Person" includes a body of persons whether incorporated or not.
　　["Postal operator" has the meaning given by [section 27 of the Postal Services Act 2011].]
　　"Value" means valuable consideration.
　　"Written" includes printed, and "writing" includes print.

NOTES

Definition "Postal operator" inserted by the Postal Services Act 2000 (Consequential Modifications No 1) Order 2001, SI 2001/1149, art 3(1), Sch 1, para 4(1), (2); words in square brackets therein substituted by the Postal Services Act 2011, s 91(1), (2), Sch 12, Pt 3, para 73.

PART II
BILLS OF EXCHANGE

Form and interpretation

[1.78]
3　Bill of exchange defined
(1)　A bill of exchange is an unconditional order in writing, addressed by one person to another, signed by the person giving it, requiring the person to whom it is addressed to pay on demand or at a fixed or determinable future time a sum certain in money to or to the order of a specified person, or to bearer.
(2)　An instrument which does not comply with these conditions, or which orders any act to be done in addition to the payment of money, is not a bill of exchange.
(3)　An order to pay out of a particular fund is not unconditional within the meaning of this section; but an unqualified order to pay, coupled with (a) an indication of a particular fund out of which the drawee is to re-imburse himself or a particular account to be debited with the amount, or (b) a statement of the transaction which gives rise to the bill, is unconditional.
(4)　A bill is not invalid by reason—
　　(a)　That it is not dated;
　　(b)　That it does not specify the value given, or that any value has been given therefor;
　　(c)　That it does not specify the place where it is drawn or the place where it is payable.

NOTES

Bill of exchange: a bill of exchange drawn on or after 15 February 1971 is invalid if the sum payable is an amount of money wholly or partly in shillings or pence, see the Decimal Currency Act 1969, s 2(1).

[1.79]

4   Inland and foreign bills

(1)   An inland bill is a bill which is or on the face of it purports to be (a) both drawn and payable within the British Islands, or (b) drawn within the British Islands upon some person resident therein. Any other bill is a foreign bill.

For the purposes of this Act "British Islands" mean any part of the United Kingdom of Great Britain and Ireland the islands of Man, Guernsey, Jersey Alderney, and Sark, and the islands adjacent to any of them being part of the dominions of Her Majesty.

(2)   Unless the contrary appear on the face of the bill the holder may treat it as an inland bill.

[1.80]

5   Effect where different parties to bill are the same person

(1)   A bill may be drawn payable to, or to the order of, the drawer; or it may be drawn payable to, or to the order of, the drawee.

(2)   Where in a bill drawer and drawee are the same person, or where the drawee is a fictitious person or a person not having capacity to contract, the holder may treat the instrument, at his option, either as a bill of exchange or as a promissory note.

[1.81]

6   Address to drawee

(1)   The drawee must be named or otherwise indicated in a bill with reasonable certainty.

(2)   A bill may be addressed to two or more drawees whether they are partners or not, but an order addressed to two drawees in the alternative or to two or more drawees in succession is not a bill of exchange.

[1.82]

7   Certainty required as to payee

(1)   Where a bill is not payable to bearer, the payee must be named or otherwise indicated therein with reasonable certainty.

(2)   A bill may be made payable to two or more payees jointly, or it may be made payable in the alternative to one of two, or one or some of several payees. A bill may also be made payable to the holder of an office for the time being.

(3)   Where the payee is a fictitious or non-existing person the bill may be treated as payable to bearer.

[1.83]

8   What bills are negotiable

(1)   When a bill contains words prohibiting transfer, or indicating an intention that it should not be transferable, it is valid as between the parties thereto, but is not negotiable.

(2)   A negotiable bill may be payable either to order or to bearer.

(3)   A bill is payable to bearer which is expressed to be so payable, or on which the only or last indorsement is an indorsement in blank.

(4)   A bill is payable to order which is expressed to be so payable, or which is expressed to be payable to a particular person, and does not contain words prohibiting transfer or indicating an intention that it should not be transferable.

(5)   Where a bill, either originally or by indorsement, is expressed to be payable to the order of a specified person, and not to him or his order, it is nevertheless payable to him or his order at his option.

[1.84]

9   Sum payable

(1)   The sum payable by a bill is a sum certain within the meaning of this Act, although it was required to be paid—

(a)   With interest.

(b)   By stated instalments.

(c)   By stated instalments, with a provision that upon default in payment of any instalment the whole shall become due.

(d)   According to an indicated rate of exchange or according to a rate of exchange to be ascertained as directed by the bill.

(2)   Where the sum payable is expressed in words and also in figures, and there is a discrepancy between the two, the sum denoted by the words is the amount payable.

(3)   Where a bill is expressed to be payable with interest, unless the instrument otherwise provides, interest runs from the date of the bill, and if the bill is undated from the issue thereof.

[1.85]
10 Bill payable on demand
(1)   A bill is payable on demand—
  (a)   Which is expressed to be payable on demand, or at sight, or on presentation; or
  (b)   In which no time for payment was expressed.
(2)   Where a bill is accepted or indorsed when it is overdue, it shall, as regards the acceptor who so accepts, or any indorser who so indorses it, be deemed a bill payable on demand.

[1.86]
11 Bill payable at a future time
A bill is payable at a determinable future time within the meaning of this Act which is expressed to be payable—
  (1)   At a fixed period after date or sight.
  (2)   On or at a fixed period after the occurrence of a specified event which is certain to happen, though the time of happening may be uncertain.
    An instrument expressed to be payable on a contingency is not a bill, and the happening of the event does not cure the defect.

[1.87]
12 Omission of date in bill payable after date
Where a bill expressed to be payable at a fixed period after date is issued undated, or where the acceptance of a bill payable at a fixed period after sight is undated, any holder may insert therein the true date of issue or acceptance, and the bill shall be payable accordingly.
    Provided that (1) where the holder in good faith and by mistake inserts a wrong date, and (2) in every case where a wrong date is inserted, if the bill subsequently comes into the hands of a holder in due course the bill shall not be avoided thereby, but shall operate and be payable as if the date so inserted had been the true date.

[1.88]
13 Ante-dating and post-dating
(1)   Where a bill or an acceptance or any indorsement on a bill is dated, the date shall, unless the contrary be proved, be deemed to be the true date of the drawing, acceptance, or indorsement, as the case may be.
(2)   A bill is not invalid by reason only that it is ante-dated or post-dated, or that it bears date on a Sunday.

[1.89]
14 Computation of time of payment
Where a bill is not payable on demand the day on which it falls due is determined as follows—
  [(1)   The bill is due and payable in all cases on the last day of the time of payment as fixed by the bill or, if that is a non-business day, on the succeeding business day.]
  (2)   Where a bill is payable at a fixed period after date, after sight, or after the happening of a specified event, the time of payment is determined by excluding the day from which the time is to begin to run and by including the day of payment.
  (3)   Where a bill is payable at a fixed period after sight, the time begins to run from the date of the acceptance if the bill be accepted, and from the date of noting or protest if the bill be noted or protested for non-acceptance, or for non-delivery.
  (4)   The term "month" in a bill means calendar month.

NOTES
  Sub-s (1): substituted by the Banking and Financial Dealings Act 1971, s 3(2).

[1.90]
15 Case of need
The drawer of a bill and any indorser may insert therein the name of a person to whom the holder may resort in case of need, that is to say, in case the bill is dishonoured by non-acceptance or non-payment. Such person is called the referee in case of need. It is in the option of the holder to resort to the referee in case of need or not as he may think fit.

[1.91]
16 Optional stipulations by drawer or indorser
The drawer of a bill, and any indorser, may insert therein an express stipulation—
  (1)   Negativing or limiting his own liability to the holder.
  (2)   Waiving as regards himself some or all of the holder's duties.

[1.92]
17 Definition and requisites of acceptance
(1)   The acceptance of a bill is the signification by the drawee of his assent to the order of the drawer.
(2)   An acceptance is invalid unless it complies with the following conditions, namely—

(a) It must be written on the bill and be signed by the drawee. The mere signature of the drawee without additional words is sufficient.

(b) It must not express that the drawee will perform his promise by any other means than the payment of money.

[1.93]

18 Time for acceptance

A bill may be accepted—

(1) Before it has been signed by the drawer, or while otherwise incomplete:

(2) When it is overdue, or after it has been dishonoured by a previous refusal to accept, or by non-payment:

(3) When a bill payable after sight is dishonoured by non-acceptance, and the drawee subsequently accepts it, the holder, in the absence of any different agreement, is entitled to have the bill accepted as of the date of first presentment to the drawee for acceptance.

[1.94]

19 General and qualified acceptances

(1) An acceptance is either (a) general or (b) qualified.

(2) A general acceptance assents without qualification to the order of the drawer. A qualified acceptance in expressed terms varies the effect of the bill as drawn.

In particular an acceptance is qualified which is—

(a) conditional, that is to say, which makes payment by the acceptor dependent on the fulfilment of a condition therein stated:

(b) partial, that is to say, an acceptance to pay part only of the amount for which the bill is drawn:

(c) local, that is to say, an acceptance to pay only at a particular specified place:

An acceptance to pay at a particular place is a general acceptance, unless it expressly states that the bill is to be paid there only and not elsewhere:

(d) qualified as to time:

(e) the acceptance of some one or more of the drawees, but not of all.

[1.95]

20 Inchoate instruments

(1) Where a simple signature on a blank . . . paper is delivered by the signer in order that it may be converted into a bill, it operates as a prima facie authority to fill it up as a complete bill for any amount . . . , using the signature for that of the drawer, or the acceptor, or an indorser; and, in like manner, when a bill is wanting in any material particular, the person in possession of it has a prima facie authority to fill up the omission in any way he thinks fit.

(2) In order that any such instrument when completed may be enforceable against any person who became a party thereto prior to its completion, it must be filled up within a reasonable time, and strictly in accordance with the authority given. Reasonable time for this purpose is a question of fact.

Provided that if any such instrument after completion is negotiated to a holder in due course it shall be valid and effectual for all purposes in his hands, and he may enforce it as if it had been filled up within a reasonable time and strictly in accordance with the authority given.

NOTES

Sub-s (1): words omitted repealed by the Finance Act 1970, s 36(8), Sch 8, Pt V and the Finance Act (Northern Ireland) 1970, s 19, Sch 3, Pt III.

[1.96]

21 Delivery

(1) Every contract on a bill, whether it be the drawer's, the acceptor's, or an indorser's, is incomplete and revocable, until delivery of the instrument in order to give effect thereto.

Provided that where an acceptance is written on a bill, and the drawee gives notice to or according to the directions of the person entitled to the bill that he has accepted it, the acceptance then becomes complete and irrevocable.

(2) As between immediate parties, and as regards a remote party other than a holder in due course, the delivery—

(a) in order to be effectual must be made either by or under the authority of the party drawing, accepting, or indorsing, as the case may be:

(b) may be shown to have been conditional or for a special purpose only, and not for the purpose of transferring the property in the bill.

But if the bill be in the hands of a holder in due course a valid delivery of the bill by all parties prior to him so as to make them liable to him is conclusively presumed.

(3) Where a bill is no longer in the possession of a party who has signed it as drawer, acceptor, or indorser, a valid and unconditional delivery by him is presumed until the contrary is proved.

Capacity and authority of parties

[1.97]
22 Capacity of parties

(1) Capacity to incur liability as a party to a bill is co-extensive with capacity to contract.

Provided that nothing in this section shall enable a corporation to make itself liable as drawer, acceptor, or indorser of a bill unless it is competent to it so to do under the law for the time being in force relating to corporations.

(2) Where a bill is drawn or indorsed by an infant, minor, or corporation having no capacity or power to incur liability on a bill, the drawing or indorsement entitles the holder to receive payment of the bill, and to enforce it against any other party thereto.

[1.98]
23 Signature essential to liability

No person is liable as drawer, indorser, or acceptor of a bill who has not signed it as such: Provided that

    (1)   Where a person signs a bill in a trade or assumed name, he is liable thereon as if he had signed it in his own name:

    (2)   The signature of the name of a firm is equivalent to the signature by the person so signing of the names of all persons liable as partners in that firm.

[1.99]
24 Forged or unauthorised signature

Subject to the provisions of this Act, where a signature on a bill is forged or placed thereon without the authority of the person whose signature it purports to be, the forged or unauthorised signature is wholly inoperative, and no right to retain the bill or to give a discharge therefor or to enforce payment thereof against any party thereto can be acquired through or under that signature, unless the party against whom it is sought to retain or enforce payment of the bill is precluded from setting up the forgery or want of authority.

Provided that nothing in this section shall affect the ratification of an unauthorised signature not amounting to a forgery.

[1.100]
25 Procuration signatures

A signature by procuration operates as notice that the agent has but a limited authority to sign, and the principal is only bound by such signature if the agent in so signing was acting within the actual limits of his authority.

[1.101]
26 Person signing as agent or in representative capacity

(1) Where a person signs a bill as drawer, indorser, or acceptor, and adds words to his signature, indicating that he signs for or on behalf of a principal, or in a representative character, he is not personally liable thereon; but the mere addition to his signature of words describing him as an agent, or as filling a representative character, does not exempt him from personal liability.

(2) In determining whether a signature on a bill is that of the principal or that of the agent by whose hand it is written, the construction most favourable to the validity of the instrument shall be adopted.

The consideration for a bill

[1.102]
27 Value and holder for value

(1) Valuable consideration for a bill may be constituted by,—

    (a)   Any consideration sufficient to support a simple contract;

    (b)   An antecedent debt or liability. Such a debt or liability is deemed valuable consideration whether the bill is payable on demand or at a future time.

(2) Where value has at any time been given for a bill the holder is deemed to be a holder for value as regards the acceptor and all parties to the bill who became parties prior to such time.

(3) Where the holder of a bill has a lien on it arising either from contract or by implication of law, he is deemed to be a holder for value to the extent of the sum for which he has a lien.

[1.103]
28 Accommodation bill or party

(1) An accommodation party to a bill is a person who has signed a bill as drawer, acceptor, or indorser, without receiving value therefor, and for the purpose of lending his name to some other person.

(2) An accommodation party is liable on the bill to a holder for value; and it is immaterial whether, when such holder took the bill, he knew such party to be an accommodation party or not.

[1.104]
29   Holder in due course
(1)   A holder in due course is a holder who has taken a bill, complete and regular on the face of it, under the following conditions; namely,
-   (a)   That he became the holder of it before it was overdue, and without notice that it had been previously dishonoured, if such was the fact:
-   (b)   That he took the bill in good faith and for value, and that at the time the bill was negotiated to him he had no notice of any defect in the title of the person who negotiated it.

(2)   In particular the title of a person who negotiates a bill is defective within the meaning of this Act when he obtained the bill, or the acceptance thereof, by fraud, duress, or force and fear, or other unlawful means, or an illegal consideration, or when he negotiates it in breach of faith, or under such circumstances as amount to a fraud.

(3)   A holder (whether for value or not), who derives his title to a bill through a holder in due course, and who is not himself a party to any fraud or illegality affecting it, has all the rights of that holder in due course as regards the acceptor and all parties to the bill prior to that holder.

[1.105]
30   Presumption of value and good faith
(1)   Every party whose signature appears on a bill is prima facie deemed to have become a party thereto for value.

(2)   Every holder of a bill is prima facie deemed to be a holder in due course; but if in an action on a bill it is admitted or proved that the acceptance, issue, or subsequent negotiation of the bill is affected with fraud, duress, or force and fear, or illegality, the burden of proof is shifted, unless and until the holder proves that, subsequent to the alleged fraud or illegality, value has in good faith been given for the bill.

Negotiation of bills

[1.106]
31   Negotiation of bill
(1)   A bill is negotiated when it is transferred from one person to another in such a manner as to constitute the transferee the holder of the bill.

(2)   A bill payable to bearer is negotiated by delivery.

(3)   A bill payable to order is negotiated by the indorsement of the holder completed by delivery.

(4)   Where the holder of a bill payable to his order transfers it for value without indorsing it, the transfer gives the transferee such title as the transferor had in the bill, and the transferee in addition acquires the right to have the indorsement of the transferor.

(5)   Where any person is under obligation to indorse a bill in a representative capacity, he may indorse the bill in such terms as to negative personal liability.

[1.107]
32   Requisites of a valid indorsement
An indorsement in order to operate as a negotiation must comply with the following conditions, namely,—
-   (1)   It must be written on the bill itself and be signed by the indorser. The simple signature of the indorser on the bill, without additional words, is sufficient.
        An indorsement written on an allonge, or on a "copy" of a bill issued or negotiated in a country where "copies" are recognised, is deemed to be written on the bill itself.
-   (2)   It must be an indorsement of the entire bill. A partial indorsement, that is to say, an indorsement which purports to transfer to the indorsee a part only of the amount payable, or which purports to transfer the bill to two or more indorsees severally, does not operate as a negotiation of the bill.
-   (3)   Where a bill is payable to the order of two or more payees or indorsees who are not partners all must indorse, unless the one indorsing has authority to indorse for the others.
-   (4)   Where, in a bill payable to order, the payee or indorsee is wrongly designated, or his name is mis-spelt, he may indorse the bill as therein described, adding, if he think fit, his proper signature.
-   (5)   Where there are two or more indorsements on a bill, each indorsement is deemed to have been made in the order in which it appears on the bill, until the contrary is proved.
-   (6)   An indorsement may be made in blank or special. It may also contain terms making it restrictive.

[1.108]
33   Conditional indorsement
Where a bill purports to be indorsed conditionally the condition may be disregarded by the payer, and payment to the indorsee is valid whether the condition has been fulfilled or not.

[1.109]
34   Indorsement in blank and special indorsement
(1)   An indorsement in blank specifies no indorsee, and a bill so indorsed becomes payable to bearer.

(2) A special indorsement specifies the person to whom, or to whose order, the bill is to be payable.

(3) The provisions of this Act relating to a payee apply with the necessary modifications to an indorsee under a special indorsement.

(4) When a bill has been indorsed in blank, any holder may convert the blank indorsement into a special indorsement by writing above the indorser's signature a direction to pay the bill to or to the order of himself or some other person.

[1.110]
35 Restrictive indorsement
(1) An indorsement is restrictive which prohibits the further negotiation of the bill or which expresses that it is a mere authority to deal with the bill as thereby directed and not a transfer of the ownership thereof, as, for example, if a bill be indorsed "Pay D only," or "Pay D for the account of X," or "Pay D or order for collection."

(2) A restrictive indorsement gives the indorsee the right to receive payment of the bill and to sue any party thereto that his indorser could have sued, but gives him no power to transfer his rights as indorsee unless it expressly authorise him to do so.

(3) Where a restrictive indorsement authorises further transfer, all subsequent indorsees take the bill with the same rights and subject to the same liabilities as the first indorsee under the restrictive indorsement.

[1.111]
36 Negotiation of overdue or dishonoured bill
(1) Where a bill is negotiable in its origin it continues to be negotiable until it has been (a) restrictively indorsed or (b) discharged by payment or otherwise.

(2) Where an overdue bill is negotiated, it can only be negotiated subject to any defect of title affecting it at its maturity, and thenceforward no person who takes it can acquire or give a better title than that which the person from whom he took it had.

(3) A bill payable on demand is deemed to be overdue within the meaning and for the purposes of this section, when it appears on the face of it to have been in circulation for an unreasonable length of time. What is an unreasonable length of time for this purpose is a question of fact.

(4) Except where an indorsement bears date after the maturity of the bill, every negotiation is prima facie deemed to have been effected before the bill was overdue.

(5) Where a bill which is not overdue has been dishonoured any person who takes it with notice of the dishonour takes it subject to any defect of title attaching thereto at the time of dishonour, but nothing in this sub-section shall affect the rights of a holder in due course.

[1.112]
37 Negotiation of bill to party already liable thereon
Where a bill is negotiated back to the drawer, or to a prior indorser or to the acceptor, such party may, subject to the provisions of this Act, re-issue and further negotiate the bill, but he is not entitled to enforce payment of the bill against any intervening party to whom he was previously liable.

[1.113]
38 Rights of the holder
The rights and powers of the holder of a bill are as follows—
    (1) He may sue on the bill in his own name:
    (2) Where he is a holder in due course, he holds the bill free from any defect of title of prior parties, as well as from mere personal defences available to prior parties among themselves, and may enforce payment against all parties liable on the bill:
    (3) Where his title is defective (a) if he negotiates the bill to a holder in due course, that holder obtains a good and complete title to the bill, and (b) if he obtains payment of the bill the person who pays him in due course gets a valid discharge for the bill.

General duties of the holder

[1.114]
39 When presentment for acceptance is necessary
(1) Where a bill is payable after sight, presentment for acceptance is necessary in order to fix the maturity of the instrument.

(2) Where a bill expressly stipulates that it shall be presented for acceptance, or where a bill is drawn payable elsewhere than at the residence or place of business of the drawee, it must be presented for acceptance before it can be presented for payment.

(3) In no other case is presentment for acceptance necessary in order to render liable any party to the bill.

(4) Where the holder of a bill, drawn payable elsewhere than at the place of business or residence of the drawee, has not time, with the exercise of reasonable diligence, to present the bill for acceptance before presenting it for payment on the day that it falls due, the delay caused by presenting the bill for acceptance before presenting it for payment is excused, and does not discharge the drawer and indorsers.

[1.115]
40   Time for presenting bill payable after sight
(1)   Subject to the provisions of this Act, when a bill payable after sight is negotiated, the holder must either present it for acceptance or negotiate it within a reasonable time.
(2)   If he do not do so, the drawer and all indorsers prior to that holder are discharged.
(3)   In determining what is a reasonable time within the meaning of this section, regard shall be had to the nature of the bill, the usage of trade with respect to similar bills, and the facts of the particular case.

[1.116]
41   Rules as to presentment for acceptance, and excuses for non-presentment
(1)   A bill is duly presented for acceptance which is presented in accordance with the following rules—
    (a)   The presentment must be made by or on behalf of the holder to the drawee or to some person authorised to accept or refuse acceptance on his behalf at a reasonable hour on a business day and before the bill is overdue:
    (b)   Where a bill is addressed to two or more drawees, who are not partners, presentment must be made to them all, unless one has authority to accept for all, then presentment may be made to him only:
    (c)   Where the drawee is dead presentment may be made to his personal representative:
    (d)   Where the drawee is bankrupt, presentment may be made to him or to his trustee:
    (e)   Where authorised by agreement or usage, a presentment through [a postal operator] is sufficient.
(2)   Presentment in accordance with these rules is excused, and a bill may be treated as dishonoured by non-acceptance—
    (a)   Where the drawee is dead or bankrupt, or is a fictitious person or a person not having capacity to contract by bill:
    (b)   Where, after the exercise of reasonable diligence, such presentment cannot be effected:
    (c)   Where, although the presentment has been irregular, acceptance has been refused on some other ground.
(3)   The fact that the holder has reason to believe that the bill, on presentment, will be dishonoured does not excuse presentment.

NOTES
  Sub-s (1): words in square brackets in para (e) substituted by the Postal Services Act 2000 (Consequential Modifications No 1) Order 2001, SI 2001/1149, art 3(1), Sch 1, para 4(1), (3).

[1.117]
42   Non-acceptance
When a bill is duly presented for acceptance and is not accepted within the customary time, the person presenting it must treat it as dishonoured by non-acceptance. If he do not, the holder shall lose his right of recourse against the drawer and indorsers.

[1.118]
43   Dishonour by non-acceptance and its consequences
(1)   A bill is dishonoured by non-acceptance—
    (a)   when it is duly presented for acceptance, and such an acceptance as is prescribed by this Act is refused or cannot be obtained; or
    (b)   when presentment for acceptance is excused and the bill is not accepted.
(2)   Subject to the provisions of this Act when a bill is dishonoured by nonacceptance, an immediate right of recourse against the drawer and indorsers accrues to the holder, and no presentment for payment is necessary.

[1.119]
44   Duties as to qualified acceptances
(1)   The holder of a bill may refuse to take a qualified acceptance, and if he does not obtain an unqualified acceptance may treat the bill as dishonoured by non-acceptance.
(2)   Where a qualified acceptance is taken, and the drawer or an indorser has not expressly or impliedly authorised the holder to take a qualified acceptance, or does not subsequently assent thereto, such drawer or indorser is discharged from his liability on the bill.
  The provisions of this subsection do not apply to a partial acceptance, whereof due notice has been given. Where a foreign bill has been accepted as to part, it must be protested as to the balance.
(3)   When the drawer or indorser of a bill receives notice of a qualified acceptance, and does not within a reasonable time express his dissent to the holder he shall be deemed to have assented thereto.

[1.120]
45   Rules as to presentment for payment
Subject to the provisions of this Act a bill must be duly presented for payment. If it be not so presented the drawer and indorsers shall be discharged.

A bill is duly presented for payment which is presented in accordance with the following rules—

(1) Where the bill is not payable on demand, presentment must be made on the day it falls due.

(2) Where the bill is payable on demand, then, subject to the provisions of this Act, presentment must be made within a reasonable time after its issue in order to render the drawer liable, and within a reasonable time after its indorsement, in order to render the indorser liable.

In determining what is a reasonable time, regard shall be had to the nature of the bill, the usage of trade with regard to similar bills, and the facts of the particular case.

(3) Presentment must be made by the holder or by some person authorised to receive payment on his behalf at a reasonable hour on a business day, at the proper place as herein-after defined, either to the person designated by the bill as payer, or to some person authorised to pay or refuse payment on his behalf if with the exercise of reasonable diligence such person can there be found.

(4) A bill is presented at the proper place—

(a) Where a place of payment is specified in the bill and the bill is there presented.

(b) Where no place of payment is specified, but the address of the drawee or acceptor is given in the bill, and the bill is there presented.

(c) Where no place of payment is specified and no address given, and the bill is presented at the drawee's or acceptor's place of business if known, and if not, at his ordinary residence if known.

(d) In any other case if presented to the drawee or acceptor wherever he can be found, or if presented at his last known place of business or residence.

(5) Where a bill is presented at the proper place, and after the exercise of reasonable diligence no person authorised to pay or refuse payment can be found there, no further presentment to the drawee or acceptor is required.

(6) Where a bill is drawn upon, or accepted by two or more persons who are not partners, and no place of payment is specified, presentment must be made to them all.

(7) Where the drawee or acceptor of a bill is dead, and no place of payment is specified, presentment must be made to a personal representative, if such there be, and with the exercise of reasonable diligence he can be found.

(8) Where authorised by agreement or usage a presentment through [a postal operator] is sufficient.

NOTES

Rule (8): words in square brackets substituted by the Postal Services Act 2000 (Consequential Modifications No 1) Order 2001, SI 2001/1149, art 3(1), Sch 1, para 4(1), (4).

[1.121]
46   Excuses for delay or non-presentment for payment
(1) Delay in making presentment for payment is excused when the delay is caused by circumstances beyond the control of the holder, and not imputable to his default, misconduct, or negligence. When the cause of delay ceases to operate presentment must be made with reasonable diligence.

(2) Presentment for payment is dispensed with,—

(a) Where, after the exercise of reasonable diligence presentment, as required by this Act, cannot be effected.
The fact that the holder has reason to believe that the bill will, on presentment, be dishonoured, does not dispense with the necessity for presentment.

(b) Where the drawee is a fictitious person.

(c) As regards the drawer where the drawee or acceptor is not bound as between himself and the drawer, to accept or pay the bill, and the drawer has no reason to believe that the bill would be paid if presented.

(d) As regards an indorser, where the bill was accepted or made for the accommodation of that indorser, and he has no reason to expect that the bill would be paid if presented.

(e) By waiver of presentment, express or implied.

[1.122]
47   Dishonour by non-payment
(1) A bill is dishonoured by non-payment (a) when it is duly presented for payment and payment is refused or cannot be obtained, or (b) when presentment is excused and the bill is overdue and unpaid.

(2) Subject to the provisions of this Act, when a bill is dishonoured by non-payment, an immediate right of recourse against the drawer and indorsers accrues to the holder.

[1.123]
48   Notice of dishonour and effect of non-notice
Subject to the provisions of this Act, when a bill has been dishonoured by nonacceptance or by non-payment, notice of dishonour must be given to the drawer and each indorser, and any drawer or indorser to whom such notice is not given is discharged: Provided that—

(1)   Where a bill is dishonoured by non-acceptance, and notice of dishonour is not given, the rights of a holder in due course, subsequent to the omission, shall not be prejudiced by the omission.

(2)   Where a bill is dishonoured by non-acceptance, and due notice of dishonour is given, it shall not be necessary to give notice of a subsequent dishonour by non-payment unless the bill shall in the meantime have been accepted.

[1.124]
49   Rules as to notice of dishonour

Notice of dishonour in order to be valid and effectual must be given in accordance with the following rules—

(1)   The notice must be given by or on behalf of the holder, or by or on behalf of an indorser who, at the time of giving it, is himself liable on the bill.

(2)   Notice of dishonour may be given by an agent either in his own name, or in the name of any party entitled to give notice whether that party be his principal or not.

(3)   Where the notice is given by or on behalf of the holder, it enures for the benefit of all subsequent holders and all prior indorsers who have a right of recourse against the party to whom it is given.

(4)   Where notice is given by or on behalf of an indorser entitled to give notice as herein-before provided, it enures for the benefit of the holder and all indorsers subsequent to the party to whom notice is given.

(5)   The notice may be given in writing or by personal communication, and may be given in any terms which sufficiently identify the bill, and intimate that the bill has been dishonoured by non-acceptance or non-payment.

(6)   The return of a dishonoured bill to the drawer or an indorser is, in point of form, deemed a sufficient notice of dishonour.

(7)   A written notice need not be signed, and an insufficient written notice may be supplemented and validated by verbal communication. A misdescription of the bill shall not vitiate the notice unless the party to whom the notice is given is in fact misled thereby.

(8)   Where notice of dishonour is required to be given to any person, it may be given either to the party himself, or to his agent in that behalf.

(9)   Where the drawer or indorser is dead, and the party giving notice knows it, the notice must be given to a personal representative if such there be, and with the exercise of reasonable diligence he can be found.

(10)   Where the drawer or indorser is bankrupt, notice may be given either to the party himself or to the trustee.

(11)   Where there are two or more drawers or indorsers who are not partners, notice must be given to each of them, unless one of them has authority to receive such notice for the others.

(12)   The notice may be given as soon as the bill is dishonoured and must be given within a reasonable time thereafter.

     In the absence of special circumstances notice is not deemed to have been given within a reasonable time, unless—

     (a)   where the person giving and the person to receive notice reside in the same place, the notice is given or sent off in time to reach the latter on the day after the dishonour of the bill;

     (b)   where the person giving and the person to receive notice reside in different places, the notice is sent off on the day after the dishonour of the bill, if there be a post at a convenient hour on that day, and if there be no post on that day then by the next post thereafter.

(13)   Where a bill when dishonoured is in the hands of an agent, he may either himself give notice to the parties liable on the bill, or he may give notice to his principal. If he give notice to his principal, he must do so within the same time as if he were the holder, and the principal upon receipt of such notice has himself the same time for giving notice as if the agent had been an independent holder.

(14)   Where a party to a bill receives due notice of dishonour, he has after the receipt of such notice the same period of time for giving notice to antecedent parties that the holder has after the dishonour.

(15)   Where a notice of dishonour is duly addressed and posted, the sender is deemed to have given due notice of dishonour, notwithstanding any miscarriage by [a postal operator].

NOTES

Rule (15): words in square brackets substituted by the Postal Services Act 2000 (Consequential Modifications No 1) Order 2001, SI 2001/1149, art 3(1), Sch 1, para 4(1), (5).

[1.125]
50 Excuses for non-notice and delay
(1) Delay in giving notice of dishonour is excused where the delay is caused by circumstances beyond the control of the party giving notice, and not imputable to his default, misconduct, or negligence. When the cause of delay ceases to operate the notice must be given with reasonable diligence.
(2) Notice of dishonour is dispensed with—
(a) When, after the exercise of reasonable diligence, notice as required by this Act cannot be given to or does not reach the drawer or indorser sought to be charged:
(b) By waiver express or implied. Notice of dishonour may be waived before the time of giving notice has arrived, or after the omission to give due notice:
(c) As regards the drawer in the following cases, namely, (1) where drawer and drawee are the same person, (2) where the drawee is a fictitious person or a person not having capacity to contract, (3) where the drawer is the person to whom the bill is presented for payment, (4) where the drawee or acceptor is as between himself and the drawer under no obligation to accept or pay the bill, (5) where the drawer has countermanded payment:
(d) As regards the indorser in the following cases, namely, (1) where the drawee is a fictitious person or a person not having capacity to contract, and the indorser was aware of the fact at the time he indorsed the bill, (2) where the indorser is the person to whom the bill is presented for payment, (3) where the bill was accepted or made for his accommodation.

[1.126]
51 Noting or protest of bill
(1) Where an inland bill has been dishonoured it may, if the holder think fit, be noted for non-acceptance or non-payment, as the case may be; but it shall not be necessary to note or protest any such bill in order to preserve the recourse against the drawer or indorser.
(2) Where a foreign bill, appearing on the face of it to be such, has been dishonoured by non-acceptance it must be duly protested for non-acceptance, and where such a bill, which has not been previously dishonoured by non-acceptance, is dishonoured by non-payment it must be duly protested for non-payment. If it be not so protested the drawer and indorsers are discharged. Where a bill does not appear on the face of it to be a foreign bill, protest thereof in case of dishonour is unnecessary.
(3) A bill which has been protested for non-acceptance may be subsequently protested for non-payment.
(4) Subject to the provisions of this Act, when a bill is noted or protested, [it may be noted on the day of its dishonour and must be noted not later than the next succeeding business day]. When a bill has been duly noted, the protest may be subsequently extended as of the date of the noting.
(5) Where the acceptor of a bill becomes bankrupt or insolvent or suspends payment before it matures, the holder may cause the bill to be protested for better security against the drawer and indorsers.
(6) A bill must be protested at the place where it is dishonoured: Provided that—
(a) When a bill is presented through [a postal operator], and returned by post dishonoured, it may be protested at the place to which it is returned and on the day of its return if received during business hours, and if not received during business hours, then not later than the next business day:
(b) When a bill drawn payable at the place of business or residence of some person other than the drawee has been dishonoured by non-acceptance, it must be protested for non-payment at the place where it is expressed to be payable, and no further presentment for payment to, or demand on, the drawee is necessary.
(7) A protest must contain a copy of the bill, and must be signed by the notary making it, and must specify—
(a) The person at whose request the bill is protested:
(b) The place and date of protest, the cause or reason for protesting the bill, the demand made, and the answer given, if any, or the fact that the drawee or acceptor could not be found.
[(7A) In subsection (7) "notary" includes a person who, for the purposes of the Legal Services Act 2007, is an authorised person in relation to any activity which constitutes a notarial activity (within the meaning of that Act).]
(8) Where a bill is lost or destroyed, or is wrongly detained from the person entitled to hold it, protest may be made on a copy or written particulars thereof.
(9) Protest is dispensed with by any circumstance which would dispense with notice of dishonour. Delay in noting or protesting is excused when the delay is caused by circumstances beyond the control of the holder, and not imputable to his default, misconduct, or negligence. When the cause of delay ceases to operate the bill must be noted or protested with reasonable diligence.

NOTES

Sub-s (4): words in square brackets substituted by the Bills of Exchange (Time of Noting) Act 1917, s 1.

Sub-s (6): words in square brackets in para (a) substituted by the Postal Services Act 2000 (Consequential Modifications No 1) Order 2001, SI 2001/1149, art 3(1), Sch 1, para 4(1), (6).

Sub-s (7A): inserted by the Legal Services Act 2007, s 208(1), Sch 21, paras 8, 9.

[1.127]
52   Duties of holder as regards drawee or acceptor
(1)   When a bill is accepted generally presentment for payment is not necessary in order to render the acceptor liable.
(2)   When by the terms of a qualified acceptance presentment for payment is required, the acceptor, in the absence of an express stipulation to that effect, is not discharged by the omission to present the bill for payment on the day that it matures.
(3)   In order to render the acceptor of a bill liable it is not necessary to protest it, or that notice of dishonour should be given to him.
(4)   [Subject to Part 4A (presentment by electronic means),] where the holder of a bill presents it for payment, he shall exhibit the bill to the person from whom he demands payment, and when a bill is paid the holder shall forthwith deliver it up to the party paying it.

NOTES

Sub-s (4): words in square brackets added by the Small Business, Enterprise and Employment Act 2015, s 13(1), (3), (6), as from 31 July 2016. Note that this amendment has effect in relation to presentment of instruments after 31 July 2016, including instruments created before that time.

Liabilities of parties

[1.128]
53   Funds in hands of drawee
(1)   A bill, of itself, does not operate as an assignment of funds in the hands of the drawee available for the payment thereof, and the drawee of a bill who does not accept as required by this Act is not liable on the instrument. This sub-section shall not extend to Scotland.
(2)   (*Applies to Scotland only.*)

[1.129]
54   Liability of acceptor
The acceptor of a bill, by accepting it—
   (1)   Engages that he will pay it according to the tenor of his acceptance:
   (2)   Is precluded from denying to a holder in due course:
      (a)   The existence of the drawer, the genuineness of his signature, and his capacity and authority to draw the bill;
      (b)   In the case of a bill payable to drawer's order, the then capacity of the drawer to indorse, but not the genuineness or validity of his indorsement;
      (c)   In the case of a bill payable to the order of a third person, the existence of the payee and his then capacity to indorse, but not the genuineness or validity of his indorsement.

[1.130]
55   Liability of drawer or indorser
(1)   The drawer of a bill by drawing it—
   (a)   Engages that on due presentment it shall be accepted and paid according to its tenor, and that if it be dishonoured he will compensate the holder or any indorser who is compelled to pay it, provided that the requisite proceedings on dishonour be duly taken;
   (b)   Is precluded from denying to a holder in due course the existence of the payee and his then capacity to indorse.
(2)   The indorser of a bill by indorsing it—
   (a)   Engages that on due presentment it shall be accepted and paid according to its tenor, and that if it be dishonoured he will compensate the holder or a subsequent indorser who is compelled to pay it, provided that the requisite proceedings on dishonour be duly taken;
   (b)   Is precluded from denying to a holder in due course the genuineness and regularity in all respects of the drawer's signature and all previous indorsements;
   (c)   Is precluded from denying to his immediate or a subsequent indorsee that the bill was at the time of his indorsement a valid and subsisting bill, and that he had then a good title thereto.

[1.131]
56   Stranger signing bill liable as indorser
Where a person signs a bill otherwise than as drawer or acceptor, he thereby incurs the liabilities of an indorser to a holder in due course.

[1.132]
57   Measure of damages against parties to dishonoured bill
Where a bill is dishonoured, the measure of damages, which shall be deemed to be liquidated damages, shall be as follows—
   (1)   The holder may recover from any party liable on the bill, and the drawer who has been compelled to pay the bill may recover from the acceptor, and an indorser who has been compelled to pay the bill may recover from the acceptor or from the drawer, or from a prior indorser—
      (a)   The amount of the bill:

(b) Interest thereon from the time of presentment for payment if the bill is payable on demand, and from the maturity of the bill in any other case:

(c) The expenses of noting, or, when protest is necessary, and the protest has been extended, the expenses of protest.

(2) . . .

(3) Where by this Act interest may be recovered as damages, such interest may, if justice require it, be withheld wholly or in part, and where a bill is expressed to be payable with interest at a given rate, interest as damages may or may not be given at the same rate as interest proper.

NOTES

Sub-s (2): repealed by the Administration of Justice Act 1977, ss 4, 32(4), Sch 5, Pt I.

[1.133]
58 Transferor by delivery and transferee
(1) Where the holder of a bill payable to bearer negotiates it by delivery without indorsing it he is called a "transferor by delivery."
(2) A transferor by delivery is not liable on the instrument.
(3) A transferor by delivery who negotiates a bill thereby warrants to his immediate transferee being a holder for value that the bill is what it purports to be, that he has a right to transfer it, and that at the time of transfer he is not aware of any fact which renders it valueless.

Discharge of bill

[1.134]
59 Payment in due course
(1) A bill is discharged by payment in due course by or on behalf of the drawee or acceptor.
"Payment in due course" means payment made at or after the maturity of the bill to the holder thereof in good faith and without notice that his title to the bill is defective.
(2) Subject to the provisions herein-after contained, when a bill is paid by the drawer or an indorser it is not discharged; but
(a) Where a bill payable to, or to the order of, a third party is paid by the drawer, the drawer may enforce payment thereof against the acceptor, but may not re-issue the bill.
(b) Where a bill is paid by an indorser, or where a bill payable to drawer's order is paid by the drawer, the party paying it is remitted to his former rights as regards the acceptor or antecedent parties and he may, if he thinks fit, strike out his own subsequent indorsements, and again negotiate the bill.
(3) Where an accommodation bill is paid in due course by the party accommodated the bill is discharged.

NOTES

Sub-s (2): the word "and" appears to be needed between "own" and "subsequent", but does not appear in the Queen's Printer's copy of the Act.

[1.135]
60 Banker paying demand draft whereon indorsement is forged
When a bill payable to order on demand is drawn on a banker, and the banker on whom it is drawn pays the bill in good faith and in the ordinary course of business, it is not incumbent on the banker to show that the indorsement of the payee or any subsequent indorsement was made by or under the authority of the person whose indorsement it purports to be, and the banker is deemed to have paid the bill in due course, although such indorsement has been forged or made without authority.

[1.136]
61 Acceptor the holder at maturity
When the acceptor of a bill is or becomes the holder of it at or after its maturity, in his own right, the bill is discharged.

[1.137]
62 Express waiver
(1) When the holder of a bill at or after its maturity absolutely and unconditionally renounces his rights against the acceptor the bill is discharged.
The renunciation must be in writing, unless the bill is delivered up to the acceptor.
(2) The liabilities of any party to a bill may in like manner be renounced by the holder before, at, or after its maturity; but nothing in this section shall affect the rights of a holder in due course without notice of the renunciation.

[1.138]
63 Cancellation
(1) Where a bill is intentionally cancelled by the holder or his agent, and the cancellation is apparent thereon, the bill is discharged.

(2)   In like manner any party liable on a bill may be discharged by the intentional cancellation of his signature by the holder or his agent. In such case any indorser who would have had a right of recourse against the party whose signature is cancelled is also discharged.

(3)   A cancellation made unintentionally, or under a mistake, or without the authority of the holder is inoperative; but where a bill or any signature thereon appears to have been cancelled the burden of proof lies on the party who alleges that the cancellation was made unintentionally, or under a mistake, or without authority.

[1.139]

64   Alteration of bill

(1)   Where a bill or acceptance is materially altered without the assent of all parties liable on the bill, the bill is avoided except as against a party who has himself made, authorised, or assented to the alteration, and subsequent indorsers.

Provided that,

> Where a bill has been materially altered, but the alteration is not apparent, and the bill is in the hands of a holder in due course, such holder may avail himself of the bill as if it had not been altered, and may enforce payment of it according to its original tenour.

(2)   In particular the following alterations are material, namely, any alteration of the date, the sum payable, the time of payment, the place of payment and, where a bill has been accepted generally, the addition of a place of payment without the acceptor's assent.

Acceptance and payment for honour

[1.140]

65   Acceptance for honour *suprà protest*

(1)   Where a bill of exchange has been protested for dishonour by non-acceptance, or protested for better security, and is not overdue, any person, not being a party already liable thereon, may, with the consent of the holder, intervene and accept the bill *suprà protest*, for the honour of any party liable thereon, or for the honour of the person for whose account the bill is drawn.

(2)   A bill may be accepted for honour for part only of the sum for which it is drawn.

(3)   An acceptance for honour *suprà protest* in order to be valid must—

  (a)   be written on the bill, and indicate that it is an acceptance for honour:

  (b)   be signed by the acceptor for honour.

(4)   Where an acceptance for honour does not expressly state for whose honour it is made, it is deemed to be an acceptance for the honour of the drawer.

(5)   Where a bill payable after sight is accepted for honour, its maturity is calculated from the date of the noting for non-acceptance, and not from the date of the acceptance for honour.

[1.141]

66   Liability of acceptor for honour

(1)   The acceptor for honour of a bill by accepting it engages that he will, on due presentment, pay the bill according to the tenor of his acceptance, if it is not paid by the drawee, provided it has been duly presented for payment, and protested for non-payment, and that he receives notice of these facts.

(2)   The acceptor for honour is liable to the holder and to all parties to the bill subsequent to the party for whose honour he has accepted.

[1.142]

67   Presentment to acceptor for honour

(1)   Where a dishonoured bill has been accepted for honour *suprà protest*, or contains a reference in case of need, it must be protested for non-payment before it is presented for payment to the acceptor for honour, or referee in case of need.

(2)   Where the address of the acceptor for honour is in the same place where the bill is protested for non-payment, the bill must be presented to him not later than the day following its maturity; and where the address of the acceptor for honour is in some place other than the place where it was protested for non-payment, the bill must be forwarded not later than the day following its maturity for presentment to him.

(3)   Delay in presentment or non-presentment is excused by any circumstance which would excuse delay in presentment for payment or non-presentment for payment.

(4)   When a bill of exchange is dishonoured by the acceptor for honour it must be protested for non-payment by him.

[1.143]

68   Payment for honour *suprà protest*

(1)   Where a bill has been protested for non-payment, any person may intervene and pay it *suprà protest* for the honour of any party liable thereon, or for the honour of the person for whose account the bill is drawn.

(2)   Where two or more persons offer to pay a bill for the honour of different parties, the person whose payment will discharge most parties to the bill shall have the preference.

(3) Payment for honour *suprà protest*, in order to operate as such and not as a mere voluntary payment, must be attested by a notarial act of honour which may be appended to the protest or form an extension of it.

(4) The notarial act of honour must be founded on a declaration made by the payer for honour, or his agent in that behalf, declaring his intention to pay the bill for honour, and for whose honour he pays.

(5) Where a bill has been paid for honour, all parties subsequent to the party for whose honour it is paid are discharged, but the payer for honour is subrogated for, and succeeds to both the rights and duties of, the holder as regards the party for whose honour he pays, and all parties liable to that party.

(6) The payer for honour on paying to the holder the amount of the bill and the notarial expenses incidental to its dishonour is entitled to receive both the bill itself and the protest. If the holder do not on demand deliver them up he shall be liable to the payer for honour in damages.

(7) Where the holder of a bill refuses to receive payment *suprà protest* he shall lose his right of recourse against any party who would have been discharged by such payment.

Lost instruments

[1.144]
69 Holder's right to duplicate of lost bill
Where a bill has been lost before it is overdue the person who was the holder of it may apply to the drawer to give him another bill of the same tenor, giving security to the drawer if required to indemnify him against all persons whatever in case the bill alleged to have been lost shall be found again.

If the drawer on request as aforesaid refuses to give such duplicate bill he may be compelled to do so.

[1.145]
70 Action on lost bill
In any action or proceeding upon a bill, the court or a judge may order that the loss of the instrument shall not be set up, provided an indemnity be given to the satisfaction of the court or judge against the claims of any other person upon the instrument in question.

NOTES
Repealed in relation to Northern Ireland by the Judicature (Northern Ireland) Act 1978, s 122, Sch 7, Pt I.

Bill in a set

[1.146]
71 Rules as to sets
(1) Where a bill is drawn in a set, each part of the set being numbered, and containing a reference to the other parts the whole of the parts constitute one bill.

(2) Where the holder of a set indorses two or more parts to different persons, he is liable on every such part, and every indorser subsequent to him is liable on the part he has himself indorsed as if the said parts were separate bills.

(3) Where two or more parts of a set are negotiated to different holders in due course, the holder whose title first accrues is as between such holders deemed the true owner of the bill; but nothing in this sub-section shall affect the rights of a person who in due course accepts or pays the part first presented to him.

(4) The acceptance may be written on any part, and it must be written on one part only.

If the drawee accepts more than one part, and such accepted parts get into the hands of different holders in due course, he is liable on every such part as if it were a separate bill.

(5) When the acceptor of a bill drawn in a set pays it without requiring the part bearing his acceptance to be delivered up to him, and that part at maturity is outstanding in the hands of a holder in due course, he is liable to the holder thereof.

(6) Subject to the preceding rules, where any one part of a bill drawn in a set is discharged by payment or otherwise, the whole bill is discharged.

Conflict of laws

[1.147]
72 Rules where laws conflict
Where a bill drawn in one country is negotiated, accepted, or payable in another, the rights, duties, and liabilities of the parties thereto are determined as follows—

(1) The validity of a bill as regards requisites in form is determined by the law of the place of issue, and the validity as regards requisites in form of the supervening contracts, such as acceptance, or indorsement, or acceptance *suprà protest*, is determined by the law of the place where such contract was made.

Provided that—

(a) Where a bill is issued out of the United Kingdom it is not invalid by reason only that it is not stamped in accordance with the law of the place of issue:

(b) Where a bill, issued out of the United Kingdom, conforms, as regards requisites in form, to the law of the United Kingdom, it may, for the purpose of enforcing payment thereof, be treated as valid as between all persons who negotiate, hold, or become parties to it in the United Kingdom.

(2) Subject to the provisions of this Act, the interpretation of the drawing, indorsement, acceptance, or acceptance *suprà protest* of a bill, is determined by the law of the place where such contract is made.

Provided that where an inland bill is indorsed in a foreign country the indorsement shall as regards the payer be interpreted according to the law of the United Kingdom.

(3) The duties of the holder with respect to presentment for acceptance or payment and the necessity for or sufficiency of a protest or notice of dishonour, or otherwise, are determined by the law of the place where the act is done or the bill is dishonoured.

(4) . . .

(5) Where a bill is drawn in one country and is payable in another, the due date thereof is determined according to the law of the place where it is payable.

NOTES

Sub-s (4): repealed by the Administration of Justice Act 1977, ss 4, 32(4), Sch 5, Pt I.

PART III
CHEQUES ON A BANKER

[1.148]
73 Cheque defined

A cheque is a bill of exchange drawn on a banker payable on demand.

Except as otherwise provided in this Part, the provisions of this Act applicable to a bill of exchange payable on demand apply to a cheque.

NOTES

Cheque: certain warrants are deemed cheques by virtue of the National Loans Act 1968, s 14(7).

[1.149]
74 Presentment of cheque for payment

Subject to the provisions of this Act—

(1) Where a cheque is not presented for payment within a reasonable time of its issue, and the drawer or the person on whose account it is drawn had the right at the time of such presentment as between him and the banker to have the cheque paid and suffers actual damage through the delay, he is discharged to the extent of such damage, that is to say, to the extent to which such drawer or person is a creditor of such banker to a larger amount than he would have been had such cheque been paid.

(2) In determining what is a reasonable time regard shall be had to the nature of the instrument, the usage of trade and of bankers, and the facts of the particular case.

(3) The holder of such cheque as to which such drawer or person is discharged shall be a creditor, in lieu of such drawer or person, of such banker to the extent of such discharge, and entitled to recover the amount from him.

[1.150]
[74A Presentment of cheque for payment: alternative place of presentment

Where the banker on whom a cheque is drawn—

(a) has by notice published in the London, Edinburgh and Belfast Gazettes specified an address at which cheques drawn on him may be presented, and

(b) has not by notice so published cancelled the specification of that address, the cheque is also presented at the proper place if it is presented there.]

NOTES

Inserted by the Deregulation (Bills of Exchange) Order 1996, SI 1996/2993, art 3.

[1.151]
[74B Presentment of cheque for payment: alternative means of presentment by banker

(1) A banker may present a cheque for payment to the banker on whom it is drawn by notifying him of its essential features by electronic means or otherwise, instead of by presenting the cheque itself.

(2) If a cheque is presented for payment under this section, presentment need not be made at the proper place or at a reasonable hour on a business day.

(3) If, before the close of business on the next business day following presentment of a cheque under this section, the banker on whom the cheque is drawn requests the banker by whom the cheque was presented to present the cheque itself—

(a) the presentment under this section shall be disregarded, and

(b) this section shall not apply in relation to the subsequent presentment of the cheque.

(4)   A request under subsection (3) above for the presentment of a cheque shall not constitute dishonour of the cheque by non-payment.

(5)   Where presentment of a cheque is made under this section, the banker who presented the cheque and the banker on whom it is drawn shall be subject to the same duties in relation to the collection and payment of the cheque as if the cheque itself had been presented for payment.

(6)   For the purposes of this section, the essential features of a cheque are—

    (a)   *the serial number of the cheque,*

    (b)   *the code which identifies the banker on whom the cheque is drawn,*

    (c)   *the account number of the drawer of the cheque, and*

    (d)   *the amount of the cheque is entered by the drawer of the cheque.]*

NOTES

Inserted, together with s 74C, by the Deregulation (Bills of Exchange) Order 1996, SI 1996/2993, art 4(1), in relation to cheques drawn on or after 28 November 1996.

Repealed, together with s 74C, by the Small Business, Enterprise and Employment Act 2015, s 13(1), (4), (6), as from 31 July 2016. Note that this repeal has effect in relation to presentment of instruments after 31 July 2016, including instruments created before that time.

[1.152]
[74C   Cheques presented for payment under section 74B: disapplication of section 52(4)
Section 52(4) above—

    (a)   so far as relating to presenting a bill for payment, shall not apply to presenting a cheque for payment under section 74B above, and

    (b)   so far as relating to a bill which is paid, shall not apply to a cheque which is paid following presentment under that section.]

NOTES

Inserted as noted to s 74B at **[1.151]**.
Repealed as noted to s 74B at **[1.151]**.

[1.153]
75   Revocation of banker's authority
The duty and authority of a banker to pay a cheque drawn on him by his customer are determined by—

    (1)   Countermand of payment:

    (2)   Notice of the customer's death.

[75A]   *(Inserted, in relation to Scotland only, by the Law Reform (Miscellaneous Provisions) (Scotland) Act 1985, s 11(b) and repealed by the Banking Act 2009, s 254(4)(b).)*

Crossed cheques

[1.154]
76   General and special crossings defined
(1)   Where a cheque bears across its face an addition of—

    (a)   The words "and company" or any abbreviation thereof between two parallel transverse lines, either with or without the words "not negotiable"; or

    (b)   Two parallel transverse lines simply, either with or without the words "not negotiable";

that addition constitutes a crossing, and the cheque is crossed generally.

(2)   Where a cheque bears across its face an addition of the name of a banker, either with or without the words "not negotiable," that addition constitutes a crossing, and the cheque is crossed specially and to that banker.

NOTES

Application: the provisions of this Act relating to crossed cheques are applied to dividend warrants by s 95 of this Act at **[1.179]**, and to instruments (other than cheques) to which the Cheques Act 1957, s 4 applies (see s 5 of the 1957 Act at **[1.386]**).

[1.155]
77   Crossing by drawer or after issue
(1)   A cheque may be crossed generally or specially by the drawer.

(2)   Where a cheque is uncrossed, the holder may cross it generally or specially.

(3)   Where a cheque is crossed generally the holder may cross it specially.

(4)   Where a cheque is crossed generally or specially, the holder may add the words "not negotiable."

(5)   Where a cheque is crossed specially, the banker to whom it is crossed may again cross it specially to another banker for collection.

(6)   Where an uncrossed cheque, or a cheque crossed generally, is sent to a banker for collection, he may cross it specially to himself.

NOTES

Application: see the note to s 76 at **[1.154]**.

[1.156]
78   Crossing a material part of cheque
A crossing authorised by this Act is a material part of the cheque; it shall not be lawful for any person to obliterate or, except as authorised by this Act, to add to or alter the crossing.

NOTES
  Application: see the note to s 76 at **[1.154]**.

[1.157]
79   Duties of banker as to crossed cheques
(1)   Where a cheque is crossed specially to more than one banker except when crossed to an agent for collection being a banker, the banker on whom it is drawn shall refuse payment thereof.

(2)   Where the banker on whom a cheque is drawn which is so crossed nevertheless pays the same, or pays a cheque crossed generally otherwise than to a banker, or if crossed specially otherwise than to the banker to whom it is crossed, or his agent for collection being a banker, he is liable to the true owner of the cheque for any loss he may sustain owing to the cheque having been so paid.

Provided that where a cheque is presented for payment which does not at the time of presentment appear to be crossed, or to have had a crossing which has been obliterated, or to have been added to or altered otherwise than as authorised by this Act, the banker paying the cheque in good faith and without negligence shall not be responsible or incur any liability, nor shall the payment be questioned by reason of the cheque having been crossed, or of the crossing having been obliterated or having been added to or altered otherwise than as authorised by this Act, and of payment having been made otherwise than to a banker or to the banker to whom the cheque is or was crossed, or to his agent for collection being a banker, as the case may be.

NOTES
  Application: see the note to s 76 at **[1.154]**.

[1.158]
80   Protection to banker and drawer where cheque is crossed
Where the banker, on whom a crossed cheque [(including a cheque which under section 81A below or otherwise is not transferable)] is drawn, in good faith and without negligence pays it, if crossed generally, to a banker, and if crossed specially, to the banker to whom it is crossed, or his agent for collection being a banker, the banker paying the cheque, and, if the cheque has come into the hands of the payee, the drawer, shall respectively be entitled to the same rights and be placed in the same position as if payment of the cheque had been made to the true owner thereof.

NOTES
  Words in square brackets inserted by the Cheques Act 1992, s 2.
  Application: see the note to s 76 at **[1.154]**.

[1.159]
81   Effect of crossing on holder
Where a person takes a crossed cheque which bears on it the words "not negotiable," he shall not have and shall not be capable of giving a better title to the cheque than that which the person from whom he took it had.

NOTES
  Application: see the note to s 76 at **[1.154]**.

[1.160]
[81A   Non-transferable cheques
(1)   Where a cheque is crossed and bears across its face the words "account payee" or "a/c payee", either with or without the word "only", the cheque shall not be transferable, but shall only be valid as between the parties thereto.

(2)   A banker is not to be treated for the purposes of section 80 above as having been negligent by reason only of his failure to concern himself with any purported indorsement of a cheque which under subsection (1) above or otherwise is not transferable.]

NOTES
  Inserted by the Cheques Act 1992, s 1.
  Application: see the note to s 76 at **[1.154]**.

82   (*Repealed by the Cheques Act 1957, s 6(3), Schedule; see now s 4 of that Act at* **[1.385]**.)

PART IV
PROMISSORY NOTES

[1.161]
83 Promissory note defined

(1) A promissory note is an unconditional promise in writing made by one person to another signed by the maker, engaging to pay, on demand or at a fixed or determinable future time, a sum certain in money, to, or to the order of, a specified person or to bearer.

(2) An instrument in the form of a note payable to maker's order is not a note within the meaning of this section unless and until it is indorsed by the maker.

(3) A note is not invalid by reason only that it contains also a pledge of collateral security with authority to sell or dispose thereof.

(4) A note which is, or on the face of it purports to be, both made and payable within the British Islands is an inland note. Any other note is a foreign note.

[1.162]
84 Delivery necessary

A promissory note is inchoate and incomplete until delivery thereof to the payee or bearer.

[1.163]
85 Joint and several notes

(1) A promissory note may be made by two or more makers, and they may be liable thereon jointly, or jointly and severally according to its tenour.

(2) Where a note runs "I promise to pay" and is signed by two or more persons it is deemed to be their joint and several note.

[1.164]
86 Note payable on demand

(1) Where a note payable on demand has been indorsed, it must be presented for payment within a reasonable time of the indorsement. If it be not so presented the indorser is discharged.

(2) In determining what is reasonable time, regard shall be had to the nature of the instrument, the usage of trade, and the facts of the particular case.

(3) Where a note payable on demand is negotiated, it is not deemed to be overdue, for the purpose of affecting the holder with defects of title of which he had no notice, by reason that it appears that a reasonable time for presenting it for payment has elapsed since its issue.

[1.165]
87 Presentment of note for payment

(1) Where a promissory note is in the body of it made payable at a particular place, it must be presented for payment at that place in order to render the maker liable. In any other case, presentment for payment is not necessary in order to render the maker liable.

(2) Presentment for payment is necessary in order to render the indorser of a note liable.

(3) Where a note is in the body of it made payable at a particular place, presentment at that place is necessary in order to render an indorser liable; but when a place of payment is indicated by way of memorandum only, presentment at that place is sufficient to render the indorser liable, but a presentment to the maker elsewhere, if sufficient in other respects, shall also suffice.

[(4) This section is subject to Part 4A (presentment by electronic means).]

NOTES

Sub-s (4): added by the Small Business, Enterprise and Employment Act 2015, s 13(5), (6), as from 31 July 2016. Note that this repeal has effect in relation to presentment of instruments after 31 July 2016, including instruments created before that time.

[1.166]
88 Liability of maker

The maker of a promissory note by making it—
  (1) Engages that he will pay it according to its tenour;
  (2) Is precluded from denying to a holder in due course the existence of the payee and his then capacity to indorse.

[1.167]
89 Application of Part II to notes

(1) Subject to the provisions in this part, and except as by this section provided, the provisions of this Act relating to bills of exchange apply, with the necessary modifications, to promissory notes.

(2) In applying those provisions the maker of a note shall be deemed to correspond with the acceptor of a bill, and the first indorser of a note shall be deemed to correspond with the drawer of an accepted bill payable to drawer's order.

(3) The following provisions as to bills do not apply to notes; namely, provisions relating to—
  (a) Presentment for acceptance;
  (b) Acceptance;
  (c) Acceptance *suprà protest*;
  (d) Bills in a set.

(4)   Where a foreign note is dishonoured, protest thereof is unnecessary.

[PART 4A
PRESENTMENT OF CHEQUES AND OTHER INSTRUMENTS BY
ELECTRONIC MEANS

[1.168]
89A   Presentment of instruments by electronic means
(1)   Presentment for payment of an instrument to which this section applies may be effected by provision of an electronic image of both faces of the instrument, instead of by presenting the physical instrument, if the person to whom presentment is made accepts the presentment as effective.

This is subject to regulations under subsection (2) and to section 89C.

(2)   The Treasury may by regulations prescribe circumstances in which subsection (1) does not apply.

(3)   Regulations under subsection (2) may in particular prescribe circumstances by reference to—
   (a)   descriptions of instrument;
   (b)   arrangements under which presentment is made;
   (c)   descriptions of persons by or to whom presentment is made;
   (d)   descriptions of persons receiving payment or on whose behalf payment is received.

(4)   Where presentment for payment is made under subsection (1)—
   (a)   any requirement—
      (i)   that the physical instrument must be exhibited, presented or delivered on or in connection with presentment or payment (including after presentment or payment or in connection with dishonour for non-payment), or
      (ii)   as to the day, time or place on or at which presentment of the physical instrument may be or is to be made, and
   (b)   any other requirement which is inconsistent with subsection (1),
does not apply.

(5)   Subsection (4) does not affect any requirement as to the latest time for presentment.

(6)   References in subsections (4) and (5) to a requirement are to a requirement or prohibition, whether imposed by or under any enactment, by a rule of law or by the instrument in question.

(7)   Where an instrument is presented for payment under this section—
   (a)   any banker providing the electronic image,
   (b)   any banker to whom it is provided, and
   (c)   any banker making payment of the instrument as a result of provision of the electronic image,
are subject to the same duties in relation to collection and payment of the instrument as if the physical instrument had been presented.

This is subject to any provision made by or under this Part.]

NOTES
   Commencement: 26 March 2015 (certain purposes); 31 July 2016 (otherwise). See further the note below.
   Pt 4A (ss 89A–89F) inserted by the Small Business, Enterprise and Employment Act 2015, s 13(1), (2), (6), as from 26 March 2015 (for the purpose of enabling the making of Regulations), and as from 31 July 2016 (otherwise). Note that this amendment has effect in relation to presentment of instruments after 31 July 2016, including instruments created before that time.

[1.169]
[89B   Instruments to which section 89A applies
(1)   Subject to subsection (2), section 89A applies to—
   (a)   a cheque, or
   (b)   any other bill of exchange or any promissory note or other instrument—
      (i)   which appears to be intended by the person creating it to enable a person to obtain payment from a banker indicated in it of the sum so mentioned,
      (ii)   payment of which requires the instrument to be presented, and
      (iii)   which, but for section 89A, could not be presented otherwise than by presenting the physical instrument.

(2)   Section 89A does not apply to any banknote (within the meaning given in section 208 of the Banking Act 2009).

(3)   The reference in subsection (1) to the person creating an instrument is—
   (a)   in the case of a bill of exchange, a reference to the drawer;
   (b)   in the case of a promissory note, a reference to the maker.

(4)   For the purposes of subsection (1)(b)(i) an indication may be by code or number and need not indicate that payment is intended to be obtained from the banker.]

NOTES
   Commencement: 26 March 2015 (certain purposes); 31 July 2016 (otherwise). See further the note to s 89A at **[1.168]**.
   Inserted as noted to s 89A at **[1.168]**.

[1.170]
[89C   Banker's obligation in relation to accepting physical instrument for presentment
Provision of an electronic image of an instrument does not constitute presentment of the instrument under section 89A if the arrangements between—
    (a)   the banker authorised to collect payment of the instrument on behalf of a customer, and
    (b)   that customer,
do not permit the customer to pay in the physical instrument but instead require an electronic image to be provided (whether to that banker or to any other person).]

NOTES
Commencement: 26 March 2015 (certain purposes); 31 July 2016 (otherwise). See further the note to s 89A at **[1.168]**. Inserted as noted to s 89A at **[1.168]**.

[1.171]
[89D   Copies of instruments and evidence of payment
(1)   The Treasury may by regulations make provision for—
    (a)   requiring a copy of an instrument paid as a result of presentment under section 89A to be provided, on request, to the creator of the instrument by the banker who paid the instrument;
    (b)   a copy of an instrument provided in accordance with the regulations to be evidence of receipt by a person identified in accordance with the regulations of the sum payable by the instrument.
(2)   Regulations under subsection (1)(a) may in particular—
    (a)   prescribe the manner and form in which a copy is to be provided;
    (b)   require the copy to be certified to be a true copy of the electronic image provided to the banker making the payment on presentment under section 89A;
    (c)   provide for the copy to be accompanied by prescribed information;
    (d)   require any copy to be provided free of charge or permit charges to be made for the provision of copies in prescribed circumstances.
(3)   The reference in subsection (1)(a) to the creator of the instrument is—
    (a)   in the case of a bill of exchange, a reference to the drawer;
    (b)   in the case of a promissory note, a reference to the maker.]

NOTES
Commencement: 26 March 2015 (certain purposes); 31 July 2016 (otherwise). See further the note to s 89A at **[1.168]**. Inserted as noted to s 89A at **[1.168]**.

[1.172]
[89E   Compensation in cases of presentment by electronic means
(1)   The Treasury may by regulations make provision for the responsible banker to compensate any person for any loss of a kind specified by the regulations which that person incurs in connection with electronic presentment or purported electronic presentment of an instrument.
(2)   In this section "electronic presentment or purported electronic presentment of an instrument" includes—
    (a)   presentment of an instrument to which section 89A applies under that section;
    (b)   presentment of any other instrument by any means involving provision of an electronic image by which it may be presented for payment;
    (c)   purported presentment for payment by any means involving provision of an electronic image of an instrument that may not be presented for payment in that way;
    (d)   provision, in purported presentment for payment, of—
        (i)   an electronic image that purports to be, but is not, an image of a physical instrument (including an image that has been altered electronically), or
        (ii)   an electronic image of an instrument which has no legal effect; or
    (e)   provision, in presentment or purported presentment for payment, of an electronic image which has been stolen.
(3)   In this section, the "responsible banker", in relation to electronic presentment or purported electronic presentment of an instrument, means—
    (a)   the banker who is authorised to collect payment of the instrument on a customer's behalf, or
    (b)   if the holder of the instrument is a banker, that banker.
(4)   In this section—
    (a)   references to an instrument include references to an instrument which has no legal effect (whether because it has been fraudulently altered or created, or because it has been discharged, or otherwise);
    (b)   in relation to an electronic image which is not an image of a physical instrument, references to the instrument are to a purported instrument (of which it purports to be an image); and

(c)   in relation to an instrument which is not a bill of exchange or promissory note, references to the holder are to the payee or indorsee of the instrument who is in possession of it or, if it is payable to bearer, the person in possession of it.

(5)   Regulations under this section may in particular make provision for—

(a)   the responsible banker to be required to pay compensation irrespective of fault;

(b)   the amount of compensation to be reduced by virtue of anything done, or any failure to act, by the person to whom compensation is payable.

(6)   Nothing in this section or regulations under it is to be taken to—

(a)   prevent the responsible banker claiming a contribution from any other person, or

(b)   affect any remedy available to the responsible banker in contract or otherwise.

(7)   Except so far as regulations under this section provide expressly, nothing in this section or regulations under it is to be taken to affect any liability of the responsible banker which exists apart from this section or any such regulations.]

NOTES

Commencement: 26 March 2015 (certain purposes); 31 July 2016 (otherwise). See further the note to s 89A at **[1.168]**. Inserted as noted to s 89A at **[1.168]**.

[1.173]
[89F   Supplementary

(1)   Regulations under this Part may—

(a)   include incidental, supplementary and consequential provision;

(b)   make transitory or transitional provision or savings;

(c)   make different provision for different cases or circumstances or for different purposes;

(d)   make provision subject to exceptions.

(2)   The power to make regulations under this Part is exercisable by statutory instrument.

(3)   An instrument containing—

(a)   regulations under section 89A or 89D, or

(b)   the first regulations to be made under section 89E,

may not be made unless a draft of the instrument has been laid before, and approved by resolution of, each House of Parliament.

(4)   An instrument containing any other regulations under section 89E is subject to annulment in pursuance of a resolution of either House of Parliament.

(5)   For the purposes of this Part, a banker collects payment of an instrument on behalf of a customer by—

(a)   receiving payment of the instrument for the customer, or

(b)   receiving payment of the instrument for the banker (but not as holder), having—

(i)   credited the customer's account with the amount of the instrument, or

(ii)   otherwise given value to the customer in respect of the instrument.

(6)   Section 89E(4) applies for the purposes of subsection (5) in its application to section 89E.]

NOTES

Commencement: 26 March 2015 (certain purposes); 31 July 2016 (otherwise). See further the note to s 89A at **[1.168]**. Inserted as noted to s 89A at **[1.168]**.

PART V
SUPPLEMENTARY

[1.174]
90   Good faith

A thing is deemed to be done in good faith, within the meaning of this Act where it is in fact done honestly, whether it is done negligently or not.

[1.175]
91   Signature

(1)   Where, by this Act, any instrument or writing is required to be signed by any person it is not necessary that he should sign it with his own hand, but it is sufficient if his signature is written thereon by some other person by or under his authority.

(2)   In the case of a corporation, where, by this Act, any instrument or writing is required to be signed, it is sufficient if the instrument or writing be sealed with the corporate seal.

But nothing in this section shall be construed as requiring the bill or note of a corporation to be under seal.

[1.176]
92   Computation of time

Where, by this Act, the time limited for doing any act or thing is less than three days, in reckoning time, non-business days are excluded.

"Non-business days" for the purposes of this Act mean—

(a)   [Saturday] Sunday, Good Friday, Christmas Day:

(b)   A bank holiday under [the Banking and Financial Dealings Act 1971]:

(c)   A day appointed by Royal proclamation as a public fast or thanksgiving day:

[(d)   a day declared by an order under section 2 of the Banking and Financial Dealings Act 1971 to be a non-business day].

Any other day is a business day.

NOTES

Words in square brackets in para (a) and the whole of para (d) inserted, and words in square brackets in para (b) substituted, by the Banking and Financial Dealings Act 1971, ss 3(1), (3), 4(4).

[1.177]
93   When noting equivalent to protest
For the purposes of this Act, where a bill or note is required to be protested within a specified time or before some further proceeding is taken, it is sufficient that the bill has been noted for protest before the expiration of the specified time or the taking of the proceeding; and the formal protest may be extended at any time thereafter as of the date of the noting.

[1.178]
94   Protest when notary not accessible
[(1)]   Where a dishonoured bill or note is authorised or required to be protested, and the services of a notary cannot be obtained at the place where the bill is dishonoured, any householder or substantial resident of the place may, in the presence of two witnesses, give a certificate, signed by them, attesting the dishonour of the bill, and the certificate shall in all respects operate as if it were a formal protest of the bill.

The form given in Schedule 1 to this Act may be used with necessary modifications, and if used shall be sufficient.

[(2)   In subsection (1), "notary" includes a person who, for the purposes of the Legal Services Act 2007, is an authorised person in relation to any activity which constitutes a notarial activity (within the meaning of that Act).]

NOTES

Sub-s (1): numbered as such by the Legal Services Act 2007, s 208(1), Sch 21, paras 8, 10(a).

Sub-s (2): added by the Legal Services Act 2007, s 208(1), Sch 21, paras 8, 10(b).

[1.179]
95   Dividend warrants may be crossed
The provisions of this Act as to crossed cheques shall apply to a warrant for payment of dividend.

96   (*Repealed by the Statute Law Revision Act 1898.*)

[1.180]
97   Savings
(1)   The rules in bankruptcy relating to bills of exchange, promissory notes, and cheques, shall continue to apply thereto notwithstanding anything in this Act contained.

(2)   The rules of common law including the law merchant, save in so far as they are inconsistent with the express provisions of this Act, shall continue to apply to bills of exchange, promissory notes, and cheques.

(3)   Nothing in this Act or in any repeal effected thereby shall affect—

(a)   . . . any law or enactment for the time being in force relating to the revenue:

(b)   The provisions of the Companies Act, 1862, or Acts amending it, or any Act relating to joint stock banks or companies:

(c)   The provisions of any Act relating to or confirming the privileges of the Bank of England or the Bank of Ireland respectively:

(d)   The validity of any usage relating to dividend warrants, or the indorsements thereof.

NOTES

Sub-s (3): words omitted from para (a) repealed by the Statute Law Revision Act 1898.

Companies Act 1862: repealed by the Companies Consolidation Act 1908 (itself repealed by the Companies Act 1929, s 381, Sch 12, Pt I (itself repealed by the Companies Act 1948, s 459, Sch 17)), the Companies Act (Northern Ireland) 1932, s 336(1), Sch 10, Pt I and the Company Law Amendment Act (Northern Ireland) 1950, s 2).

98   (*Applies to Scotland only.*)

[1.181]
99   Construction with other Acts, etc
Where any Act or document refers to any enactment repealed by this Act, the Act or document shall be construed, and shall operate, as if it referred to the corresponding provisions of this Act.

100   (*Applies to Scotland only.*)

SCHEDULES

FIRST SCHEDULE

Section 94

[1.182]
Form of protest which may be used when the services of a notary cannot be obtained.

Know all men that I, *AB* [householder], of   in the county of   in the United Kingdom, at the request of *CD*, there being no notary public available, did on the   day of   188
at   demand payment [*or* acceptance] of the bill of exchange hereunder written, from *EF*, to which demand he made answer [state answer, if any] wherefore I now, in the presence of *GH* and *JK* do protest the said bill of exchange.

(Signed) *AB*

GH Witnesses.

JK

NB—The bill itself should be annexed, or a copy of the bill and all that is written thereon should be underwritten.

SECOND SCHEDULE

(*Second Schedule repealed by the Statute Law Revision Act 1898.*)

FACTORS ACT 1889

(52 & 53 Vict c 45)

ARRANGEMENT OF SECTIONS

Preliminary

An Act to amend and consolidate the Factors Acts

[26 August 1889]

Preliminary

[1.183]
1 Definitions
For the purposes of this Act—
   (1)   The expression "mercantile agent" shall mean a mercantile agent having in the customary course of his business as such agent authority either to sell goods, or to consign goods for the purpose of sale, or to buy goods, or to raise money on the security of goods:

(2)   A person shall be deemed to be in possession of goods or of the documents of title to goods, where the goods or documents are in his actual custody or are held by any other person subject to his control or for him or on his behalf:

(3)   The expression "goods" shall include wares and merchandise:

(4)   The expression "document of title" shall include any bill of lading, dock warrant, warehouse-keeper's certificate, and warrant or order for the delivery of goods, and any other document used in the ordinary course of business as proof of the possession or control of goods, or authorising or purporting to authorise, either by endorsement or by delivery, the possessor of the document to transfer or receive goods thereby represented:

(5)   The expression "pledge" shall include any contract pledging, or giving a lien or security on, goods, whether in consideration of an original advance or of any further or continuing advance or of any pecuniary liability:

(6)   The expression "person" shall include any body of persons corporate or unincorporate.

Dispositions by mercantile agents

[1.184]
2   Powers of mercantile agent with respect to disposition of goods
(1)   Where a mercantile agent is, with the consent of the owner, in possession of goods or of the documents of title to goods, any sale, pledge, or other disposition of the goods, made by him when acting in the ordinary course of business of a mercantile agent, shall, subject to the provisions of this Act, be as valid as if he were expressly authorised by the owner of the goods to make the same, provided that the person taking under the disposition acts in good faith, and has not at the time of the disposition notice that the person making the disposition has not authority to make the same.

(2)   Where a mercantile agent has, with the consent of the owner, been in possession of goods or of the documents of title to goods, any sale, pledge, or other disposition, which would have been valid if the consent had continued shall be valid notwithstanding the determination of the consent: provided that the person taking under the disposition has not at the time thereof notice that the consent has been determined.

(3)   Where a mercantile agent has obtained possession of any documents of title to goods by reason of his being or having been, with the consent of the owner, in possession of the goods represented thereby, or of any other documents of title to the goods, his possession of the first-mentioned documents shall, for the purposes of this Act, be deemed to be with the consent of the owner.

(4)   For the purposes of this Act the consent of the owner shall be presumed in the absence of evidence to the contrary.

[1.185]
3   Effect of pledges of documents of title
A pledge of the documents of title to goods shall be deemed to be a pledge of the goods.

[1.186]
4   Pledge for antecedent debt
Where a mercantile agent pledges goods as security for a debt or liability due from the pledgor to the pledgee before the time of the pledge, the pledgee shall acquire no further right to the goods than could have been enforced by the pledgor at the time of the pledge.

[1.187]
5   Rights acquired by exchange of goods or documents
The consideration necessary for the validity of a sale, pledge, or other disposition, of goods, in pursuance of this Act, may be either a payment in cash, or the delivery or transfer of other goods, or of a document of title to goods, or of a negotiable security, or any other valuable consideration; but where goods are pledged by a mercantile agent in consideration of the delivery or transfer of other goods, or of a document of title to goods, or of a negotiable security, the pledgee shall acquire no right or interest in the goods so pledged in excess of the value of the goods, documents, or security when so delivered or transferred in exchange.

[1.188]
6   Agreements through clerks, etc
For the purposes of this Act an agreement made with a mercantile agent through a clerk or other person authorised in the ordinary course of business to make contracts of sale or pledge on his behalf shall be deemed to be an agreement with the agent.

[1.189]
7   Provisions as to consignors and consignees
(1)   Where the owner of goods has given possession of the goods to another person for the purpose of consignment or sale, or has shipped the goods in the name of another person, and the consignee of the goods has not had notice that such person is not the owner of the goods, the consignee shall, in respect of advances made to or for the use of such person, have the same lien on the goods as if such person were the owner of the goods, and may transfer any such lien to another person.

(2)   Nothing in this section shall limit or effect the validity of any sale, pledge, or disposition, by a mercantile agent.

Dispositions by sellers and buyers of goods

[1.190]
8   Disposition by seller remaining in possession
Where a person, having sold goods, continues, or is, in possession of the goods or of the documents of title to the goods, the delivery or transfer by that person, or by a mercantile agent acting for him, of the goods or documents of title under any sale, pledge, or other disposition thereof, or under any agreement for sale pledge, or other disposition thereof, to any person receiving the same in good faith and without notice of the previous sale, shall have the same effect as if the person making the delivery or transfer were expressly authorised by the owner of the goods to make the same.

[1.191]
9   Disposition by buyer obtaining possession
Where a person, having bought or agreed to buy goods, obtains with the consent of the seller possession of the goods or the documents of title to the goods, the delivery or transfer, by that person or by a mercantile agent acting for him, of the goods or documents of title, under any sale, pledge, or other disposition thereof, or under any agreement for sale, pledge, or other disposition thereof, to any person receiving the same in good faith and without notice of any lien or other right of the original seller in respect of the goods, shall have the same effect as if the person making the delivery or transfer were a mercantile agent in possession of the goods or documents of title with the consent of the owner.
   [For the purposes of this section—
   (i)   the buyer under a conditional sale agreement shall be deemed not to be a person who has bought or agreed to buy goods, and
   (ii)   "conditional sale agreement" means an agreement for the sale of goods which is a consumer credit agreement within the meaning of the Consumer Credit Act 1974 under which the purchase price or part of it is payable by instalments, and the property in the goods is to remain in the seller (notwithstanding that the buyer is to be in possession of the goods) until such conditions as to the payment of instalments or otherwise as may be specified in the agreement are fulfilled.]

NOTES
   Words in square brackets added by the Consumer Credit Act 1974, s 192(3)(a), Sch 4, Pt I, para 2.

[1.192]
10   Effect of transfer of documents on vendor's lien or right of stoppage in transitu
Where a document of title to goods has been lawfully transferred to a person as a buyer or owner of the goods, and that person transfers the document to a person who takes the document in good faith and for valuable consideration, the last-mentioned transfer shall have the same effect for defeating any vendor's lien or right of stoppage in transitu as the transfer of a bill of lading has for defeating the right of stoppage in transitu.

Supplemental

[1.193]
11   Mode of transferring documents
For the purposes of this Act, the transfer of a document may be by endorsement, or, where the document is by custom or by its express terms transferable by delivery, or makes the goods deliverable to the bearer, then by delivery.

[1.194]
12   Saving for rights of true owner
(1)   Nothing in this Act shall authorise an agent to exceed or depart from his authority as between himself and his principal, or exempt him from any liability, civil or criminal, for so doing.
(2)   Nothing in this Act shall prevent the owner of goods from recovering the goods from an agent or his trustee in bankruptcy at any time before the sale or pledge thereof, or shall prevent the owner of goods pledged by an agent from having the right to redeem the goods at any time before the sale thereof, on satisfying the claim for which the goods were pledged, and paying to the agent, if by him required, any money in respect of which the agent would by law be entitled to retain the goods or the documents of title thereto, or any of them, by way of lien as against the owner, or from recovering from any person with whom the goods have been pledged any balance of money remaining in his hands as the produce of the sale of the goods after deducting the amount of his lien.
(3)   Nothing in this Act shall prevent the owner of goods sold by an agent from recovering from the buyer the price agreed to be paid for the same, or any part of that price, subject to any right of set off on the part of the buyer against the agent.

[1.195]
13 Saving for common law powers of agent
The provisions of this Act shall be construed in amplification and not in derogation of the powers exercisable by an agent independently of this Act.

14, 15 *(Repealed by the Statute Law Revision Act 1908.)*

[1.196]
16 Extent of Act
This Act shall not extend to Scotland.

NOTES
The Factors (Scotland) Act 1890 extended this Act to Scotland, subject to certain provisions. This section should, therefore, be regarded as spent.

[1.197]
17 Short title
This Act may be cited as the Factors Act 1889.

(Schedule repealed by virtue of the Statute Law Revision Act 1908.)

BILLS OF SALE ACT 1890

(53 & 54 Vict c 53)

ARRANGEMENT OF SECTIONS

An Act to exempt certain letters of hypothecation from the operation of the Bills of Sale Act 1882
[10 August 1890]

[1.198]
[1 Exemption of letters of hypothecation of imported goods from 41 & 42 Vict c 31, and 45 & 46 Vict c 43, s 9
An instrument charging or creating any security on or declaring trusts of imported goods given or executed at any time prior to their deposit in a warehouse, factory, or store, or to their being reshipped for export, or delivered to a purchaser not being the person giving or executing such instrument shall not be deemed a bill of sale within the meaning of the Bills of Sale Acts 1878 and 1882.]

NOTES
Substituted by the Bills of Sale Act 1891, s 1.

[1.199]
2 Savings of 46 & 47 Vict c 52, s 44
Nothing in this Act shall affect the operation of section forty-four of the Bankruptcy Act 1883 in respect of any goods comprised in any such instrument as is hereinbefore described, if such goods would but for this Act be goods within the meaning of sub-section three of that section.

NOTES
Bankruptcy Act 1883, s 44: repealed by the Bankruptcy Act 1914, s 168, Sch 6 (repealed). See now the Insolvency Act 1986, s 283, and cf ss 307–309, 338 of that Act.

[1.200]
3 Short title
This Act may be cited as the Bills of Sale Act 1890.

PARTNERSHIP ACT 1890

(53 & 54 Vict c 39)

ARRANGEMENT OF SECTIONS

An Act to declare and amend the Law of Partnership

[14 August 1890]

Nature of Partnership

[1.201]
1 Definition of Partnership
(1) Partnership is the relation which subsists between persons carrying on a business in common with a view of profit.
(2) But the relation between members of any company or association which is—
[(a) registered under the Companies Act 2006, or]
(b) Formed or incorporated by or in pursuance of any other Act of Parliament or letters patent, or Royal Charter; . . .
(c) . . .
is not a partnership within the meaning of this Act.

NOTES
Sub-s (2): para (a) substituted by the Companies Act 2006 (Consequential Amendments, Transitional Provisions and Savings) Order 2009, SI 2009/1941, art 2(1), Sch 1, para 2; para (c) and word immediately preceding it repealed by the Statute Law (Repeals) Act 1998.

[1.202]
2 Rules for determining existence of partnership
In determining whether a partnership does or does not exist, regard shall be had to the following rules:
(1) Joint tenancy, tenancy in common, joint property, common property, or part ownership does not of itself create a partnership as to anything so held or owned, whether the tenants or owners do or do not share any profits made by the use thereof.
(2) The sharing of gross returns does not of itself create a partnership, whether the persons sharing such returns have or have not a joint or common right or interest in any property from which or from the use of which the returns are derived.
(3) The receipt by a person of a share of the profits of a business is prima facie evidence that he is a partner in the business, but receipt of such a share, or of a payment contingent on or varying with the profits of a business, does not of itself make him a partner in the business; and in particular—
(a) The receipt by a person of a debt or other liquidated amount by instalments or otherwise out of the accruing profits of a business does not of itself make him a partner in the business or liable as such:
(b) A contract for the remuneration of a servant or agent of a person engaged in a business by a share of the profits of the business does not of itself make the servant or agent a partner in the business or liable as such:
(c) A person being the widow[, widower, surviving civil partner] or child of a deceased partner, and receiving by way of annuity a portion of the profits made in the business in which the deceased person was a partner, is not by reason only of such receipt a partner in the business or liable as such:
(d) The advance of money by way of loan to a person engaged or about to engage in any business on a contract with that person that the lender shall receive a rate of interest varying with the profits, or shall receive a share of the profits arising from carrying on the business, does not of itself make the lender a partner with the person or persons carrying on the business or liable as such. Provided that the contract is in writing, and signed by or on behalf of all the parties thereto:
(e) A person receiving by way of annuity or otherwise a portion of the profits of a business in consideration of the sale by him of the goodwill of the business is not by reason only of such receipt a partner in the business or liable as such.

NOTES
Sub-s (3): words in square brackets in para (c) inserted by the Civil Partnership Act 2004, s 261(1), Sch 27, para 2.

[1.203]
3 Postponement of rights of person lending or selling in consideration of share of profits in case of insolvency
In the event of any person to whom money has been advanced by way of loan upon such a contract as is mentioned in the last foregoing section, or of any buyer of a goodwill in consideration of a share of the profits of the business, being adjudged a bankrupt, entering into an arrangement to pay his creditors less than [100p] in the pound, or dying in insolvent circumstances, the lender of the loan shall not be entitled to recover anything in respect of his loan, and the seller of the goodwill shall not be entitled to recover anything in respect of the share of profits contracted for, until the claims of the other creditors of the borrower or buyer for valuable consideration in money or money's worth have been satisfied.

NOTES

Sum in square brackets substituted by virtue of the Decimal Currency Act 1969, s 10(1).

[1.204]
4   Meaning of firm

(1) Persons who have entered into partnership with one another are for the purposes of this Act called collectively a firm, and the name under which their business is carried on is called the firm-name.

(2) (*Applies to Scotland only.*)

Relations of Partners to persons dealing with them

[1.205]
5   Power of partner to bind the firm

Every partner is an agent of the firm and his other partners for the purpose of the business of the partnership; and the acts of every partner who does any act for carrying on in the usual way business of the kind carried on by the firm of which he is a member bind the firm and his partners, unless the partner so acting has in fact no authority to act for the firm in the particular matter, and the person with whom he is dealing either knows that he has no authority, or does not know or believe him to be a partner.

[1.206]
6   Partners bound by acts on behalf of firm

An act or instrument relating to the business of the firm done or executed in the firm-name, or in any other manner showing an intention to bind the firm, by any person thereto authorised, whether a partner or not, is binding on the firm and all the partners.

Provided that this section shall not affect any general rule of law relating to the execution of deeds or negotiable instruments.

[1.207]
7   Partner using credit of firm for private purposes

Where one partner pledges the credit of the firm for a purpose apparently not connected with the firm's ordinary course of business, the firm is not bound, unless he is in fact specially authorised by the other partners; but this section does not affect any personal liability incurred by an individual partner.

[1.208]
8   Effect of notice that firm will not be bound by acts of partner

If it has been agreed between the partners that any restriction shall be placed on the power of any one or more of them to bind the firm, no act done in contravention of the agreement is binding on the firm with respect to persons having notice of the agreement.

[1.209]
9   Liability of partners

Every partner in a firm is liable jointly with the other partners, and in Scotland severally also, for all debts and obligations of the firm incurred while he is a partner; and after his death his estate is also severally liable in a due course of administration for such debts and obligations, so far as they remain unsatisfied, but subject in England or Ireland to the prior payment of his separate debts.

[1.210]
10   Liability of the firm for wrongs

Where, by any wrongful act or omission of any partner acting in the ordinary course of the business of the firm, or with the authority of his co-partners, loss or injury is caused to any person not being a partner in the firm, or any penalty is incurred, the firm is liable therefor to the same extent as the partner so acting or omitting to act.

[1.211]
11   Misapplication of money or property received for or in custody of the firm

In the following cases; namely—

    (a) Where one partner acting within the scope of his apparent authority receives the money or property of a third person and misapplies it; and

    (b) Where a firm in the course of its business receives money or property of a third person, and the money or property so received is misapplied by one or more of the partners while it is in the custody of the firm;

the firm is liable to make good the loss.

[1.212]
12   Liability for wrongs joint and several

Every partner is liable jointly with his co-partners and also severally for everything for which the firm while he is a partner therein becomes liable under either of the two last preceding sections.

[1.213]
13 Improper employment of trust-property for partnership purposes
If a partner, being a trustee, improperly employs trust-property in the business or on the account of the partnership, no other partner is liable for the trust property to the persons beneficially interested therein:

Provided as follows—
(1) This section shall not affect any liability incurred by any partner by reason of his having notice of a breach of trust; and
(2) Nothing in this section shall prevent trust money from being followed and recovered from the firm if still in its possession or under its control.

[1.214]
14 Persons liable by "holding out"
(1) Every one who by words spoken or written or by conduct represents himself, or who knowingly suffers himself to be represented, as a partner in a particular firm, is liable as a partner to any one who has on the faith of any such representation given credit to the firm, whether the representation has or has not been made or communicated to the person so giving credit by or with the knowledge of the apparent partner making the representation or suffering it to be made.
(2) Provided that where after a partner's death the partnership business is continued in the old firm's name, the continued use of that name or of the deceased partner's name as part thereof shall not of itself make his executors or administrators estate or effects liable for any partnership debts contracted after his death.

[1.215]
15 Admissions and representations of partners
An admission or representation made by any partner concerning the partnership affairs, and in the ordinary course of its business, is evidence against the firm.

[1.216]
16 Notice to acting partner to be notice to the firm
Notice to any partner who habitually acts in the partnership business of any matter relating to partnership affairs operates as notice to the firm, except in the case of a fraud on the firm committed by or with the consent of that partner.

[1.217]
17 Liabilities of incoming and outgoing partners
(1) A person who is admitted as a partner into an existing firm does not thereby become liable to the creditors of the firm for anything done before he became a partner.
(2) A partner who retires from a firm does not thereby cease to be liable for partnership debts or obligations incurred before his retirement.
(3) A retiring partner may be discharged from any existing liabilities, by an agreement to that effect between himself and the members of the firm as newly constituted and the creditors, and this agreement may be either expressed or inferred as a fact from the course of dealing between the creditors and the firm as newly constituted.

[1.218]
18 Revocation of continuing guaranty by change in firm
A continuing guaranty or cautionary obligation given either to a firm or to a third person in respect of the transactions of a firm is, in the absence of agreement to the contrary, revoked as to future transactions by any change in the constitution of the firm to which, or of the firm in respect of the transactions of which, the guaranty or obligation was given.

Relations of Partners to one another

[1.219]
19 Variation by consent of terms of partnership
The mutual rights and duties of partners, whether ascertained by agreement or defined by this Act, may be varied by the consent of all the partners, and such consent may be either express or inferred from a course of dealing.

[1.220]
20 Partnership property
(1) All property and rights and interests in property originally brought into the partnership stock or acquired, whether by purchase or otherwise, on account of the firm, or for the purposes and in the course of the partnership business, are called in this Act partnership property, and must be held and applied by the partners exclusively for the purposes of the partnership and in accordance with the partnership agreement.
(2) Provided that the legal estate or interest in any land, or in Scotland the title to and interest in any heritable estate, which belongs to the partnership shall devolve according to the nature and tenure thereof, and the general rules of law thereto applicable, but in trust, so far as necessary, for the persons beneficially interested in the land under this section.

(3) Where co-owners of an estate or interest in any land, or in Scotland of any heritable estate, not being itself partnership property, are partners as to profits made by the use of that land or estate, and purchase other land or estate out of the profits to be used in like manner, the land or estate so purchased belongs to them, in the absence of an agreement to the contrary, not as partners, but as co-owners for the same respective estates and interests as are held by them in the land or estate first mentioned at the date of the purchase.

[1.221]
21   Property bought with partnership money
Unless the contrary intention appears, property bought with money belonging to the firm is deemed to have been bought on account of the firm.

22   (*Repealed by the Trusts of Land and Appointment of Trustees Act 1996, s 25(2), Sch 4, subject to savings contained in s 25(4), (5) thereof.*)

[1.222]
23   Procedure against partnership property for a partner's separate judgment debt
(1) . . . A writ of execution shall not issue against any partnership property except on a judgment against the firm.
(2) The High Court, or a judge thereof, . . . , [or the county court in England and Wales or a county court in Northern Ireland,] may, on the application by summons of any judgment creditor of a partner, make an order charging that partner's interest in the partnership property and profits with payment of the amount of the judgment debt and interest thereon, and may by the same or a subsequent order appoint a receiver of that partner's share of profits (whether already declared or accruing), and of any other money which may be coming to him in respect of the partnership, and direct all accounts and inquiries, and give all other orders and directions which might have been directed or given if the charge had been made in favour of the judgment creditor by the partner, or which the circumstances of the case may require.
(3) The other partner or partners shall be at liberty at any time to redeem the interest charged, or in case of a sale being directed, to purchase the same.
(4) . . .
(5) This section shall not apply to Scotland.

NOTES
    Sub-s (1): words omitted repealed by the Statute Law Revision Act 1908.
    Sub-s (2): words omitted repealed by the Courts Act 1971, s 56(4), Sch 11, Pt II; words in square brackets substituted by the Crime and Courts Act 2013, s 17(5), Sch 9, Pt 3, para 118, for transitional provision see the Crime and Courts Act 2013 (Commencement No 10 and Transitional Provision) Order 2014, SI 2014/954, art 3.
    Sub-s (4): repealed by the Statute Law (Repeals) Act 1998.

[1.223]
24   Rules as to interests and duties of partners subject to special agreement
The interests of partners in the partnership property and their rights and duties in relation to the partnership shall be determined, subject to any agreement express or implied between the partners, by the following rules—
    (1) All the partners are entitled to share equally in the capital and profits of the business, and must contribute equally towards the losses whether of capital or otherwise sustained by the firm.
    (2) The firm must indemnify every partner in respect of payments made and personal liabilities incurred by him—
       (a) In the ordinary and proper conduct of the business of the firm; or,
       (b) In or about anything necessarily done for the preservation of the business or property of the firm.
    (3) A partner making, for the purpose of the partnership, any actual payment or advance beyond the amount of capital which he has agreed to subscribe, is entitled to interest at the rate of five per cent per annum from the date of the payment or advance.
    (4) A partner is not entitled, before the ascertainment of profits, to interest on the capital subscribed by him.
    (5) Every partner may take part in the management of the partnership business.
    (6) No partner shall be entitled to remuneration for acting in the partnership business.
    (7) No person may be introduced as a partner without the consent of all existing partners.
    (8) Any difference arising as to ordinary matters connected with the partnership business may be decided by a majority of the partners, but no change may be made in the nature of the partnership business without the consent of all existing partners.
    (9) The partnership books are to be kept at the place of business of the partnership (or the principal place, if there is more than one), and every partner may, when he thinks fit, have access to and inspect and copy any of them.

[1.224]
25 Expulsion of partner
No majority of the partners can expel any partner unless a power to do so has been conferred by express agreement between the partners.

[1.225]
26 Retirement from partnership at will
(1) Where no fixed term has been agreed upon for the duration of the partnership, any partner may determine the partnership at any time on giving notice of his intention so to do to all the other partners.
(2) Where the partnership has originally been constituted by deed, a notice in writing, signed by the partner giving it, shall be sufficient for this purpose.

[1.226]
27 Where partnership for term is continued over, continuance on old terms presumed
(1) Where a partnership entered into for a fixed term is continued after the term has expired, and without any express new agreement, the rights and duties of the partners remain the same as they were at the expiration of the term, so far as is consistent with the incidents of a partnership at will.
(2) A continuance of the business by the partners or such of them as habitually acted therein during the term, without any settlement or liquidation of the partnership affairs, is presumed to be a continuance of the partnership.

[1.227]
28 Duty of partners to render accounts, etc
Partners are bound to render true accounts and full information of all things affecting the partnership to any partner or his legal representatives.

[1.228]
29 Accountability of partners for private profits
(1) Every partner must account to the firm for any benefit derived by him without the consent of the other partners from any transaction concerning the partnership, or from any use by him of the partnership property name or business connexion.
(2) This section applies also to transactions undertaken after a partnership has been dissolved by the death of a partner, and before the affairs thereof have been completely wound up, either by any surviving partner or by the representatives of the deceased partner.

[1.229]
30 Duty of partner not to compete with firm
If a partner, without the consent of the other partners, carries on any business of the same nature as and competing with that of the firm, he must account for and pay over to the firm all profits made by him in that business.

[1.230]
31 Rights of assignee of share in partnership
(1) An assignment by any partner of his share in the partnership, either absolute or by way of mortgage or redeemable charge, does not, as against the other partners, entitle the assignee, during the continuance of the partnership, to interfere in the management or administration of the partnership business or affairs, or to require any accounts of the partnership transactions, or to inspect the partnership books, but entitles the assignee only to receive the share of profits to which the assigning partner would otherwise be entitled, and the assignee must accept the account of profits agreed to by the partners.
(2) In case of a dissolution of the partnership, whether as respects all the partners or as respects the assigning partner, the assignee is entitled to receive the share of the partnership assets to which the assigning partner is entitled as between himself and the other partners, and, for the purpose of ascertaining that share, to an account as from the date of the dissolution.

Dissolution of Partnership, and its consequences

[1.231]
32 Dissolution by expiration or notice
Subject to any agreement between the partners, a partnership is dissolved—
  (a) If entered into for a fixed term, by the expiration of that term:
  (b) If entered into for a single adventure or undertaking, by the termination of that adventure or undertaking:
  (c) If entered into for an undefined time, by any partner giving notice to the other or others of his intention to dissolve the partnership.
  In the last-mentioned case the partnership is dissolved as from the date mentioned in the notice as the date of dissolution, or, if no date is so mentioned, as from the date of the communication of the notice.

[1.232]
33   Dissolution by bankruptcy, death or charge
(1)   Subject to any agreement between the partners, every partnership is dissolved as regards all the partners by the death or bankruptcy of any partner.

(2)   A partnership may, at the option of the other partners, be dissolved if any partner suffers his share of the partnership property to be charged under this Act for his separate debt.

[1.233]
34   Dissolution by illegality of partnership
A partnership is in every case dissolved by the happening of any event which makes it unlawful for the business of the firm to be carried on or for the members of the firm to carry it on in partnership.

[1.234]
35   Dissolution by the Court
On application by a partner the Court may decree a dissolution of the partnership in any of the following cases:

(a)   . . .

(b)   When a partner, other than the partner suing, becomes in any other way permanently incapable of performing his part of the partnership contract:

(c)   When a partner, other than the partner suing, has been guilty of such conduct as, in the opinion of the Court, regard being had to the nature of the business, is calculated to prejudicially affect the carrying on of the business:

(d)   When a partner, other than the partner suing, wilfully or persistently commits a breach of the partnership agreement, or otherwise so conducts himself in matters relating to the partnership business that it is not reasonably practicable for the other partner or partners to carry on the business in partnership with him:

(e)   When the business of the partnership can only be carried on at a loss:

(f)   Whenever in any case circumstances have arisen which, in the opinion of the Court, render it just and equitable that the partnership be dissolved.

NOTES

Para (a) repealed by the Mental Health Act 1959, s 149(2), Sch 8.

[1.235]
36   Rights of persons dealing with firm against apparent members of firm
(1)   Where a person deals with a firm after a change in its constitution he is entitled to treat all apparent members of the old firm as still being members of the firm until he has notice of the change.

(2)   An advertisement in the London Gazette as to a firm whose principal place of business is in England or Wales, in the Edinburgh Gazette as to a firm whose principal place of business is in Scotland, and in the [Belfast] Gazette as to a firm whose principal place of business is in Ireland, shall be notice as to persons who had not dealings with the firm before the date of the dissolution or change so advertised.

(3)   The estate of a partner who dies, or who becomes bankrupt, or of a partner who, not having been known to the person dealing with the firm to be a partner, retires from the firm, is not liable for partnership debts contracted after the date of the death, bankruptcy, or retirement respectively.

NOTES

Sub-s (2): word in square brackets substituted by virtue of the General Adaptation of Enactments (Northern Ireland) Order 1921, SR & O 1921/1804, art 7.

[1.236]
37   Right of partners to notify dissolution
On the dissolution of a partnership or retirement of a partner any partner may publicly notify the same, and may require the other partner or partners to concur for that purpose in all necessary or proper acts, if any, which cannot be done without his or their concurrence.

[1.237]
38   Continuing authority of partners for purposes of winding up
After the dissolution of a partnership the authority of each partner to bind the firm, and the other rights and obligations of the partners, continue notwithstanding the dissolution so far as may be necessary to wind up the affairs of the partnership, and to complete transactions begun but unfinished at the time of the dissolution[, and in relation to any prosecution of the partnership by virtue of section 1 of the Partnerships (Prosecution) (Scotland) Act 2013], but not otherwise.

     Provided that the firm is in no case bound by the acts of a partner who has become bankrupt; but this proviso does not affect the liability of any person who has after the bankruptcy represented himself or knowingly suffered himself to be represented as a partner of the bankrupt.

NOTES

Sub-s (1): words in square brackets inserted by the Partnerships (Prosecution) (Scotland) Act 2013, s 6(1), (2).

[1.238]
39   Rights of partners as to application of partnership property
On the dissolution of a partnership every partner is entitled, as against the other partners in the firm, and all persons claiming through them in respect of their interests as partners, to have the property of the partnership applied in payment of the debts and liabilities of the firm, and to have the surplus assets after such payment applied in payment of what may be due to the partners respectively after deducting what may be due from them as partners to the firm; and for that purpose any partner or his representatives may on the termination of the partnership apply to the Court to wind up the business and affairs of the firm.

[1.239]
40   Apportionment of premium where partnership prematurely dissolved
Where one partner has paid a premium to another on entering into a partnership for a fixed term, and the partnership is dissolved before the expiration of that term otherwise than by the death of a partner, the Court may order the repayment of the premium, or of such part thereof as it thinks just, having regard to the terms of the partnership contract and to the length of time during which the partnership has continued; unless

   (a)   the dissolution is, in the judgment of the Court, wholly or chiefly due to the misconduct of the partner who paid the premium; or

   (b)   the partnership has been dissolved by an agreement containing no provision for a return of any part of the premium.

[1.240]
41   Rights where partnership dissolved for fraud or misrepresentation
Where a partnership contract is rescinded on the ground of the fraud or misrepresentation of one of the parties thereto, the party entitled to rescind is, without prejudice to any other right, entitled—

   (a)   to a lien on, or right of retention of, the surplus of the partnership assets, after satisfying the partnership liabilities, for any sum of money paid by him for the purchase of a share in the partnership and for any capital contributed by him, and is

   (b)   to stand in the place of the creditors of the firm for any payments made by him in respect of the partnership liabilities, and

   (c)   to be indemnified by the person guilty of the fraud or making the representation against all the debts and liabilities of the firm.

[1.241]
42   Right of outgoing partner in certain cases to share profits made after dissolution
(1)   Where any member of a firm has died or otherwise ceased to be a partner, and the surviving or continuing partners carry on the business of the firm with its capital or assets without any final settlement of accounts as between the firm and the outgoing partner or his estate, then, in the absence of any agreement to the contrary, the outgoing partner or his estate is entitled at the option of himself or his representatives to such share of the profits made since the dissolution as the Court may find to be attributable to the use of his share of the partnership assets, or to interest at the rate of five per cent per annum on the amount of his share of the partnership assets.
(2)   Provided that where by the partnership contract an option is given to surviving or continuing partners to purchase the interest of a deceased or outgoing partner, and that option is duly exercised, the estate of the deceased partner, or the outgoing partner or his estate, as the case may be, is not entitled to any further or other share of profits; but if any partner assuming to act in exercise of the option does not in all material respects comply with the terms thereof, he is liable to account under the foregoing provisions of this section.

[1.242]
43   Retiring or deceased partner's share to be a debt
Subject to any agreement between the partners, the amount due from surviving or continuing partners to an outgoing partner or the representatives of a deceased partner in respect of the outgoing or deceased partner's share is a debt accruing at the date of the dissolution or death.

[1.243]
44   Rule for distribution of assets on final settlement of accounts
In settling accounts between the partners after a dissolution of partnership, the following rules shall, subject to any agreement, be observed:

   (a)   Losses, including losses and deficiencies of capital, shall be paid first out of profits, next out of capital, and lastly, if necessary, by the partners individually in the proportion in which they were entitled to share profits:

   (b)   The assets of the firm including the sums, if any, contributed by the partners to make up losses or deficiencies of capital, shall be applied in the following manner and order:

      1.   In paying the debts and liabilities of the firm to persons who are not partners therein:

      2.   In paying to each partner rateably what is due from the firm to him for advances as distinguished from capital:

      3.   In paying to each partner rateably what is due from the firm to him in respect of capital:

4. The ultimate residue, if any, shall be divided among the partners in the proportion in which profits are divisible.

Supplemental

[1.244]
45 Definitions of "court" and "business"
In this Act, unless the contrary intention appears,—
The expression "court" includes every court and judge having jurisdiction in the case:
The expression "business" includes every trade, occupation, or profession.

[1.245]
46 Saving for rules of equity and common law
The rules of equity and of common law applicable to partnership shall continue in force except so far as they are inconsistent with the express provisions of this Act.

47–49 (*S 47 applies to Scotland only; ss 48, 49 repealed by the Statute Law Revision Act 1908.*)

[1.246]
50 Short title
This Act may be cited as the Partnership Act 1890.

SCHEDULE

(*Schedule repealed by the Statute Law Revision Act 1908.*)

MARINE INSURANCE ACT 1906

(6 Edw 7 c 41)

ARRANGEMENT OF SECTIONS

An Act to codify the Law relating to Marine Insurance

[21 December 1906]

NOTES

    Marine Insurance Acts 1906 and 1909. By the Marine Insurance (Gambling Policies) Act 1909, s 2, at **[1.358]**, that Act and this Act may be cited together by this collective title.

Marine Insurance

[1.247]
1   Marine insurance defined
A contract of marine insurance is a contract whereby the insurer undertakes to indemnify the assured, in manner and to the extent thereby agreed, against marine losses, that is to say, the losses incident to marine adventure.

[1.248]
2   Mixed sea and land risks
(1)   A contract of marine insurance may, by its express terms, or by usage of trade, be extended so as to protect the assured against losses on inland waters or on any land risk which may be incidental to any sea voyage.

(2)   Where a ship in course of building, or the launch of a ship, or any adventure analogous to a marine adventure, is covered by a policy in the form of a marine policy, the provisions of this Act, in so far as applicable, shall apply thereto; but, except as by this section provided, nothing in this Act shall alter or affect any rule of law applicable to any contract of insurance other than a contract of marine insurance as by this Act defined.

[1.249]
3   Marine adventure and maritime perils defined
(1)   Subject to the provisions of this Act, every lawful marine adventure may be the subject of a contract of marine insurance.

(2)   In particular there is a marine adventure where—

   (a)   Any ship goods or other moveables are exposed to maritime perils. Such property is in this Act referred to as "insurable property";

   (b)   The earning or acquisition of any freight, passage money, commission, profit, or other pecuniary benefit, or the security for any advances, loan, or disbursements, is endangered by the exposure of insurable property to maritime perils;

   (c)   Any liability to a third party may be incurred by the owner of, or other person interested in or responsible for, insurable property, by reason of maritime perils.

"Maritime perils" means the perils consequent on, or incidental to, the navigation of the sea, that is to say, perils of the seas, fire, war perils, pirates, rovers, thieves, captures, seisures, restraints, and detainments of princes and peoples, jettisons, barratry, and any other perils, either of the like kind or which may be designated by the policy.

Insurable Interest

[1.250]
4 Avoidance of wagering or gaming contracts
(1) Every contract of marine insurance by way of gaming or wagering is void.
(2) A contract of marine insurance is deemed to be a gaming or wagering contract—
   (a) Where the assured has not an insurable interest as defined by this Act, and the contract is entered into with no expectation of acquiring such an interest; or
   (b) Where the policy is made "interest or no interest," or "without further proof of interest than the policy itself," or "without benefit of salvage to the insurer," or subject to any other like term:
   Provided that, where there is no possibility of salvage, a policy may be effected without benefit of salvage to the insurer.

[1.251]
5 Insurable interest defined
(1) Subject to the provisions of this Act, every person has an insurable interest who is interested in a marine adventure.
(2) In particular a person is interested in a marine adventure where he stands in any legal or equitable relation to the adventure or to any insurable property at risk therein, in consequence of which he may benefit by the safety or due arrival of insurable property, or may be prejudiced by its loss, or damage thereto, or by the detention thereof, or may incur liability in respect thereof.

[1.252]
6 When interest must attach
(1) The assured must be interested in the subject-matter insured at the time of the loss though he need not be interested when the insurance is effected:
   Provided that where the subject-matter is insured "lost or not lost," the assured may recover although he may not have acquired his interest until after the loss, unless at the time of effecting the contract of insurance the assured was aware of the loss, and the insurer was not.
(2) Where the assured has no interest at the time of the loss, he cannot acquire interest by any act or election after he is aware of the loss.

[1.253]
7 Defeasible or contingent interest
(1) A defeasible interest is insurable, as also is a contingent interest.
(2) In particular, where the buyer of goods has insured them, he has an insurable interest, notwithstanding that he might, at his election, have rejected the goods, or have treated them as at the seller's risk, by reason of the latter's delay in making delivery or otherwise.

[1.254]
8 Partial interest
A partial interest of any nature is insurable.

[1.255]
9 Re-insurance
(1) The insurer under a contract of marine insurance has an insurable interest in his risk, and may re-insure in respect of it.
(2) Unless the policy otherwise provides, the original assured has no right or interest in respect of such re-insurance.

[1.256]
10 Bottomry
The lender of money on bottomry or respondentia has an insurable interest in respect of the loan.

[1.257]
11 Master's and seamen's wages
The master or any member of the crew of a ship has an insurable interest in respect of his wages.

[1.258]
12 Advance freight
In the case of advance freight, the person advancing the freight has an insurable interest, in so far as such freight is not repayable in case of loss.

[1.259]
13 Charges of insurance
The assured has an insurable interest in the charges of any insurance which he may effect.

[1.260]
14   Quantum of interest
(1)   Where the subject-matter insured is mortgaged, the mortgagor has an insurable interest in the full value thereof, and the mortgagee has an insurable interest in respect of any sum due or to become due under the mortgage.

(2)   A mortgagee, consignee, or other person having an interest in the subject matter insured may insure on behalf and for the benefit of other persons interested as well as for his own benefit.

(3)   The owner of insurable property has an insurable interest in respect of the full value thereof, notwithstanding that some third person may have agreed, or be liable, to indemnify him in case of loss.

[1.261]
15   Assignment of interest
Where the assured assigns or otherwise parts with his interest in the subject-matter insured, he does not thereby transfer to the assignee his rights under the contract of insurance, unless there be an express or implied agreement with the assignee to that effect.

But the provisions of this section do not affect a transmission of interest by operation of law.

Insurable Value
[1.262]
16   Measure of insurable value
Subject to any express provision or valuation in the policy, the insurable value of the subject-matter insured must be ascertained as follows—

(1)   In insurance on ship, the insurable value is the value, at the commencement of the risk, of the ship, including her outfit, provisions and stores for the officers and crew, money advanced for seamen's wages, and other disbursements (if any) incurred to make the ship fit for the voyage or adventure contemplated by the policy, plus the charges of insurance upon the whole:

     The insurable value, in the case of a steamship, includes also the machinery, boilers, and coals and engine stores if owned by the assured, and, in the case of a ship engaged in a special trade, the ordinary fittings requisite for that trade:

(2)   In insurance on freight, whether paid in advance or otherwise, the insurable value is the gross amount of the freight at the risk of the assured, plus the charges of insurance:

(3)   In insurance on goods or merchandise, the insurable value is the prime cost of the property insured, plus the expenses of and incidental to shipping and the charges of insurance upon the whole:

(4)   In insurance on any other subject-matter, the insurable value is the amount at the risk of the assured when the policy attaches, plus the charges of insurance.

Disclosure and Representations
[1.263]
17   Insurance is uberrimae fidei
A contract of marine insurance is a contract based upon the utmost good faith, *and, if the utmost good faith be not observed by either party, the contract may be avoided by the other party.*

NOTES

Words in italics repealed by the Insurance Act 2015, s 14(3)(a), as from 12 August 2016. Note that s 14(3)(b) of the 2015 Act provides that the application of this section (as so amended) is subject to the provisions of the 2015 Act and the Consumer Insurance (Disclosure and Representations) Act 2012. Note also that this amendment applies only in relation to (a) contracts of insurance entered into after the end of the period of 18 months beginning with the day on which the 2015 Act was passed (12 February 2015), and (b) variations, agreed after the end of that period, to contracts of insurance entered into at any time (see s 22(1) of the 2015 Act at **[1.2219]**.

See further, in relation to a contract of marine insurance which is a consumer insurance contract, the Consumer Insurance (Disclosure and Representations) Act 2012, s 2(5)(b) at **[1.2144]**.

[1.264]
18   *Disclosure by assured*
(1)   *Subject to the provisions of this section, the assured must disclose to the insurer, before the contract is concluded, every material circumstance which is known to the assured, and the assured is deemed to know every circumstance which, in the ordinary course of business, ought to be known by him. If the assured fails to make such disclosure, the insurer may avoid the contract.*

(2)   *Every circumstance is material which would influence the judgment of a prudent insurer in fixing the premium, or determining whether he will take the risk.*

(3)   *In the absence of inquiry the following circumstances need not be disclosed, namely—*

     (a)   *Any circumstance which diminishes the risk;*

     (b)   *Any circumstance which is known or presumed to be known to the insurer. The insurer is presumed to know matters of common notoriety or knowledge, and matters which an insurer in the ordinary course of his business, as such, ought to know;*

     (c)   *Any circumstance as to which information is waived by the insurer;*

    (d)   Any circumstance which it is superfluous to disclose by reason of any express or implied warranty.

(4)   Whether any particular circumstance, which is not disclosed, be material or not is, in each case, a question of fact.

(5)   The term "circumstance" includes any communication made to, or information received by, the assured.

[(6)   This section does not apply in relation to a contract of marine insurance if it is a consumer insurance contract within the meaning of the Consumer Insurance (Disclosure and Representations) Act 2012.]

NOTES

Repealed, together with ss 19, 20, by the Insurance Act 2015, s 21(2), as from 12 August 2016. Note that this amendment applies only in relation to (a) contracts of insurance entered into after the end of the period of 18 months beginning with the day on which the 2015 Act was passed (12 February 2015), and (b) variations, agreed after the end of that period, to contracts of insurance entered into at any time (see s 22(1) of the 2015 Act at **[1.2218]**.

Sub-s (6): added by the Consumer Insurance (Disclosure and Representations) Act 2012, s 11(2)(a).

[1.265]
19 *Disclosure by agent effecting insurance*
[(1)] Subject to the provisions of the preceding section as to circumstances which need not be disclosed, where an insurance is effected for the assured by an agent, the agent must disclose to the insurer—

    (a)   Every material circumstance which is known to himself, and an agent to insure is deemed to know every circumstance which in the ordinary course of business ought to be known by, or to have been communicated to, him; and

    (b)   Every material circumstance which the assured is bound to disclose, unless it come to his knowledge too late to communicate it to the agent.

[(2)   This section does not apply in relation to a contract of marine insurance if it is a consumer insurance contract within the meaning of the Consumer Insurance (Disclosure and Representations) Act 2012.]

NOTES

Repealed as noted to s 18 at **[1.265]**.

Sub-s (1) numbered as such and sub-s (2) added by the Consumer Insurance (Disclosure and Representations) Act 2012, s 11(2)(b).

[1.266]
20 *Representations pending negotiation of contract*
(1)   Every material representation made by the assured or his agent to the insurer during the negotiations for the contract, and before the contract is concluded, must be true. If it be untrue the insurer may avoid the contract.

(2)   A representation is material which would influence the judgment of a prudent insurer in fixing the premium, or determining whether he will take the risk.

(3)   A representation may be either a representation as to a matter of fact, or as to a matter of expectation or belief.

(4)   A representation as to matter of fact is true, if it be substantially correct, that is to say, if the difference between what is represented and what is actually correct would not be considered material by a prudent insurer.

(5)   A representation as to a matter of expectation or belief is true if it be made in good faith.

(6)   A representation may be withdrawn or corrected before the contract is concluded.

(7)   Whether a particular representation be material or not is, in each case, a question of fact.

[(8)   This section does not apply in relation to a contract of marine insurance if it is a consumer insurance contract within the meaning of the Consumer Insurance (Disclosure and Representations) Act 2012.]

NOTES

Repealed as noted to s 18 at **[1.265]**.

Sub-s (8): added by the Consumer Insurance (Disclosure and Representations) Act 2012, s 11(2)(c).

[1.267]
21 When contract is deemed to be concluded
A contract of marine insurance is deemed to be concluded when the proposal of the assured is accepted by the insurer, whether the policy be then issued or not; and, for the purpose of showing when the proposal was accepted, reference may be made to the slip or covering note or other customary memorandum of the contract, . . .

NOTES

Words omitted repealed by the Finance Act 1959, s 37(5), Sch 8, Pt II, and the Finance Act (Northern Ireland) 1959, s 17(2), Sch 3, Pt II.

The Policy

[1.268]
22 Contract must be embodied in policy
Subject to the provisions of any statute, a contract of marine insurance is inadmissible in evidence unless it is embodied in a marine policy in accordance with this Act. The policy may be executed and issued either at the time when the contract is concluded, or afterwards.

[1.269]
23 What policy must specify
A marine policy must specify—
    (1)   The name of the assured, or of some person who effects the insurance on his behalf:
    (2)–(5). . .

NOTES

Sub-ss (2)–(5): repealed by the Finance Act 1959, ss 30(5), (7), 37(5), Sch 8, Pt II, and the Finance Act (Northern Ireland) 1959, ss 5(5), (7), 17(2), Sch 3, Pt II.

[1.270]
24 Signature of insurer
(1)   A marine policy must be signed by or on behalf of the insurer, provided that in the case of a corporation the corporate seal may be sufficient, but nothing in this section shall be construed as requiring the subscription of a corporation to be under seal.
(2)   Where a policy is subscribed by or on behalf of two or more insurers, each subscription, unless the contrary be expressed, constitutes a distinct contract with the assured.

[1.271]
25 Voyage and time policies
(1)   Where the contract is to insure the subject-matter "at and from", or from one place to another or others, the policy is called a "voyage policy", and where the contract is to insure the subject-matter for a definite period of time the policy is called a "time policy". A contract for both voyage and time may be included in the same policy.
(2)   . . .

NOTES

Sub-s (2): repealed by the Finance Act 1959, ss 30(5), (7), 37(5), Sch 8, Pt II, and the Finance Act (Northern Ireland) 1959, ss 5(5), (7), 17(2), Sch 3, Pt II.

[1.272]
26 Designation of subject-matter
(1)   The subject-matter insured must be designated in a marine policy with reasonable certainty.
(2)   The nature and extent of the interest of the assured in the subject-matter insured need not be specified in the policy.
(3)   Where the policy designates the subject-matter insured in general terms, it shall be construed to apply to the interest intended by the assured to be covered.
(4)   In the application of this section regard shall be had to any usage regulating the designation of the subject-matter insured.

[1.273]
27 Valued policy
(1)   A policy may be either valued or unvalued.
(2)   A valued policy is a policy which specifies the agreed value of the subject matter insured.
(3)   Subject to the provisions of this Act, and in the absence of fraud, the value fixed by the policy is, as between the insurer and assured, conclusive of the insurable value of the subject intended to be insured, whether the loss be total or partial.
(4)   Unless the policy otherwise provides, the value fixed by the policy is not conclusive for the purpose of determining whether there has been a constructive total loss.

[1.274]
28 Unvalued policy
An unvalued policy is a policy which does not specify the value of the subject-matter insured, but, subject to the limit of the sum insured, leaves the insurable value to be subsequently ascertained, in the manner herein-before specified.

[1.275]
29 Floating policy by ship or ships
(1)   A floating policy is a policy which describes the insurance in general terms, and leaves the name of the ship or ships and other particulars to be defined by subsequent declaration.
(2)   The subsequent declaration or declarations may be made by indorsement on the policy, or in other customary manner.

(3) Unless the policy otherwise provides, the declarations must be made in the order of dispatch or shipment. They must, in the case of goods, comprise all consignments within the terms of the policy, and the value of the goods or other property must be honestly stated, but an omission or erroneous declaration may be rectified even after loss or arrival, provided the omission or declaration was made in good faith.

(4) Unless the policy otherwise provides, where a declaration of value is not made until after notice of loss or arrival, the policy must be treated as an unvalued policy as regards the subject-matter of that declaration.

[1.276]
30 Construction of terms in policy
(1) A policy may be in the form in the First Schedule to this Act.
(2) Subject to the provisions of this Act, and unless the context of the policy otherwise requires, the terms and expressions mentioned in the First Schedule to this Act shall be construed as having the scope and meaning in that schedule assigned to them.

[1.277]
31 Premium to be arranged
(1) Where an insurance is effected at a premium to be arranged, and no arrangement is made, a reasonable premium is payable.
(2) Where an insurance is effected on the terms that an additional premium is to be arranged in a given event, and that event happens but no arrangement is made, then a reasonable additional premium is payable.

Double Insurance

[1.278]
32 Double insurance
(1) Where two or more policies are effected by or on behalf of the assured on the same adventure and interest or any part thereof, and the sums insured exceed the indemnity allowed by this Act, the assured is said to be over-insured by double insurance.
(2) Where the assured is over-insured by double insurance—
  (a) The assured, unless the policy otherwise provides, may claim payment from the insurers in such order as he may think fit, provided that he is not entitled to receive any sum in excess of the indemnity allowed by this Act;
  (b) Where the policy under which the assured claims is a valued policy, the assured must give credit as against the valuation for any sum received by him under any other policy without regard to the actual value of the subject-matter insured;
  (c) Where the policy under which the assured claims is an unvalued policy he must give credit, as against the full insurable value, for any sum received by him under any other policy;
  (d) Where the assured receives any sum in excess of the indemnity allowed by this Act, he is deemed to hold such sum in trust for the insurers, according to their right of contribution among themselves.

Warranties, etc

[1.279]
33 Nature of warranty
(1) A warranty, in the following sections relating to warranties, means a promissory warranty, that is to say, a warranty by which the assured undertakes that some particular thing shall or shall not be done, or that some condition shall be fulfilled, or whereby he affirms or negatives the existence of a particular state of facts.
(2) A warranty may be express or implied.
(3) A warranty, as above defined, is a condition which must be exactly complied with, whether it be material to the risk or not. *If it be not so complied with, then, subject to any express provision in the policy, the insurer is discharged from liability as from the date of the breach of warranty, but without prejudice to any liability incurred by him before that date.*

NOTES
   Sub-s (3): words in italics repealed by the Insurance Act 2015, s 10(7)(a), as from 12 August 2016.

[1.280]
34 When breach of warranty excused
(1) Non-compliance with a warranty is excused when, by reason of a change of circumstances, the warranty ceases to be applicable to the circumstances of the contract, or when compliance with the warranty is rendered unlawful by any subsequent law.
(2) Where a warranty is broken, the assured cannot avail himself of the defence that the breach has been remedied, and the warranty complied with, before loss.
(3) A breach of warranty may be waived by the insurer.

NOTES
   Repealed by the Insurance Act 2015, s 10(7)(b), as from 12 August 2016.

[1.281]
35　Express warranties
(1)　An express warranty may be in any form of words from which the intention to warrant is to be inferred.
(2)　An express warranty must be included in, or written upon, the policy, or must be contained in some document incorporated by reference into the policy.
(3)　An express warranty does not exclude an implied warranty, unless it be inconsistent therewith.

[1.282]
36　Warranty of neutrality
(1)　Where insurable property, whether ship or goods, is expressly warranted neutral, there is an implied condition that the property shall have a neutral character at the commencement of the risk, and that, so far as the assured can control the matter, its neutral character shall be preserved during the risk.
(2)　Where a ship is expressly warranted "neutral" there is also an implied condition that, so far as the assured can control the matter, she shall be properly documented, that is to say, that she shall carry the necessary papers to establish her neutrality, and that she shall not falsify or suppress her papers, or use simulated papers. If any loss occurs through breach of this condition, the insurer may avoid the contract.

[1.283]
37　No implied warranty of nationality
There is no implied warranty as to the nationality of a ship, or that her nationality shall not be changed during the risk.

[1.284]
38　Warranty of good safety
Where the subject-matter insured is warranted "well" or "in good safety" on a particular day, it is sufficient if it be safe at any time during that day.

[1.285]
39　Warranty of seaworthiness of ship
(1)　In a voyage policy there is an implied warranty that at the commencement of the voyage the ship shall be seaworthy for the purpose of the particular adventure insured.
(2)　Where the policy attaches while the ship is in port, there is also an implied warranty that she shall, at the commencement of the risk, be reasonably fit to encounter the ordinary perils of the port.
(3)　Where the policy relates to a voyage which is performed in different stages, during which the ship requires different kinds of or further preparation or equipment, there is an implied warranty that at the commencement of each stage the ship is seaworthy in respect of such preparation or equipment for the purposes of that stage.
(4)　A ship is deemed to be seaworthy when she is reasonably fit in all respects to encounter the ordinary perils of the seas of the adventure insured.
(5)　In a time policy there is no implied warranty that the ship shall be seaworthy at any stage of the adventure, but where, with the privity of the assured, the ship is sent to sea in an unseaworthy state, the insurer is not liable for any loss attributable to unseaworthiness.

[1.286]
40　No implied warranty that goods are seaworthy
(1)　In a policy on goods or other moveables there is no implied warranty that the goods or moveables are seaworthy.
(2)　In a voyage policy on goods or other moveables there is an implied warranty that at the commencement of the voyage the ship is not only seaworthy as a ship, but also that she is reasonably fit to carry the goods or other moveables to the destination contemplated by the policy.

[1.287]
41　Warranty of legality
There is an implied warranty that the adventure insured is a lawful one, and that, so far as the assured can control the matter, the adventure shall be carried out in a lawful manner.

The Voyage

[1.288]
42　Implied condition as to commencement of risk
(1)　Where the subject-matter is insured by a voyage policy "at and from" or "from" a particular place, it is not necessary that the ship should be at that place when the contract is concluded, but there is an implied condition that the adventure shall be commenced within a reasonable time, and that if the adventure be not so commenced the insurer may avoid the contract.
(2)　The implied condition may be negatived by showing that the delay was caused by circumstances known to the insurer before the contract was concluded, or by showing that he waived the condition.

[1.289]
43 Alteration of port of departure
Where the place of departure is specified by the policy, and the ship instead of sailing from that place sails from any other place, the risk does not attach.

NOTES
Repealed by the Insurance Act 2015, s 21(2), as from 12 August 2016. Note that this amendment applies only in relation to (a) contracts of insurance entered into after the end of the period of 18 months beginning with the day on which the 2015 Act was passed (12 February 2015), and (b) variations, agreed after the end of that period, to contracts of insurance entered into at any time (see s 22(1) of the 2015 Act at **[1.2218]**.

[1.290]
44 Sailing for different destination
Where the destination is specified in the policy, and the ship, instead of sailing for that destination, sails for any other destination, the risk does not attach.

[1.291]
45 Change of voyage
(1) Where, after the commencement of the risk, the destination of the ship is voluntarily changed from the destination contemplated by the policy, there is said to be a change of voyage.
(2) Unless the policy otherwise provides, where there is a change of voyage, the insurer is discharged from liability as from the time of change, that is to say, as from the time when the determination to change it is manifested; and it is immaterial that the ship may not in fact have left the course of voyage contemplated by the policy when the loss occurs.

[1.292]
46 Deviation
(1) Where a ship, without lawful excuse, deviates from the voyage contemplated by the policy, the insurer is discharged from liability as from the time of deviation, and it is immaterial that the ship may have regained her route before any loss occurs.
(2) There is a deviation from the voyage contemplated by the policy—
    (a) Where the course of the voyage is specifically designated by the policy, and that course is departed from; or
    (b) Where the course of the voyage is not specifically designated by the policy, but the usual and customary course is departed from.
(3) The intention to deviate is immaterial; there must be a deviation in fact to discharge the insurer from his liability under the contract.

[1.293]
47 Several ports of discharge
(1) Where several ports of discharge are specified by the policy, the ship may proceed to all or any of them, but, in the absence of any usage or sufficient cause to the contrary, she must proceed to them, or such of them as she goes to, in the order designated by the policy. If she does not there is a deviation.
(2) Where the policy is to "ports of discharge", within a given area, which are not named, the ship must, in the absence of any usage or sufficient cause to the contrary, proceed to them, or such of them as she goes to, in their geographical order. If she does not there is a deviation.

[1.294]
48 Delay in voyage
In the case of a voyage policy, the adventure insured must be prosecuted throughout its course with reasonable dispatch, and, if without lawful excuse it is not so prosecuted, the insurer is discharged from liability as from the time when the delay became unreasonable.

[1.295]
49 Excuses for deviation or delay
(1) Deviation or delay in prosecuting the voyage contemplated by the policy is excused—
    (a) Where authorised by any special term in the policy; or
    (b) Where caused by circumstances beyond the control of the master and his employer; or
    (c) Where reasonably necessary in order to comply with an express or implied warranty; or
    (d) Where reasonably necessary for the safety of the ship or subject-matter insured; or
    (e) For the purpose of saving human life, or aiding a ship in distress where human life may be in danger; or
    (f) Where reasonably necessary for the purpose of obtaining medical or surgical aid for any person on board the ship; or
    (g) Where caused by the barratrous conduct of the master or crew, if barratry be one of the perils insured against.
(2) When the cause excusing the deviation or delay ceases to operate, the ship must resume her course, and prosecute her voyage, with reasonable dispatch.

Assignment of Policy

[1.296]
50   When and how policy is assignable
(1)   A marine policy is assignable unless it contains terms expressly prohibiting assignment. It may be assigned either before or after loss.
(2)   Where a marine policy has been assigned so as to pass the beneficial interest in such policy, the assignee of the policy is entitled to sue thereon in his own name; and the defendant is entitled to make any defence arising out of the contract which he would have been entitled to make if the action had been brought in the name of the person by or on behalf of whom the policy was effected.
(3)   A marine policy may be assigned by indorsement thereon or in other customary manner.

[1.297]
51   Assured who has no interest cannot assign
Where the assured has parted with or lost his interest in the subject-matter insured, and has not, before or at the time of so doing, expressly or impliedly agreed to assign the policy, any subsequent assignment of the policy is inoperative:
    Provided that nothing in this section affects the assignment of a policy after loss.

The Premium

[1.298]
52   When premium payable
Unless otherwise agreed, the duty of the assured or his agent to pay the premium, and the duty of the insurer to issue the policy to the assured or his agent, are concurrent conditions, and the insurer is not bound to issue the policy until payment or tender of the premium.

[1.299]
53   Policy effected through broker
(1)   Unless otherwise agreed, where a marine policy is effected on behalf of the assured by a broker, the broker is directly responsible to the insurer for the premium, and the insurer is directly responsible to the assured for the amount which may be payable in respect of losses, or in respect of returnable premium.
(2)   Unless otherwise agreed, the broker has, as against the assured, a lien upon the policy for the amount of the premium and his charges in respect of effecting the policy; and, where he has dealt with the person who employs him as a principal, he has also a lien on the policy in respect of any balance on any insurance account which may be due to him from such person, unless when the debt was incurred he had reason to believe that such person was only an agent.

[1.300]
54   Effect of receipt on policy
Where a marine policy effected on behalf of the assured by a broker acknowledges the receipt of the premium, such acknowledgment is, in the absence of fraud, conclusive as between the insurer and the assured, but not as between the insurer and broker.

Loss and Abandonment

[1.301]
55   Included and excluded losses
(1)   Subject to the provisions of this Act, and unless the policy otherwise provides, the insurer is liable for any loss proximately caused by a peril insured against, but, subject as aforesaid, he is not liable for any loss which is not proximately caused by a peril insured against.
(2)   In particular,—
    (a)   The insurer is not liable for any loss attributable to the wilful misconduct of the assured, but, unless the policy otherwise provides, he is liable for any loss proximately caused by a peril insured against, even though the loss would not have happened but for the misconduct or negligence of the master or crew;
    (b)   Unless the policy otherwise provides, the insurer on ship or goods is not liable for any loss proximately caused by delay, although the delay be caused by a peril insured against;
    (c)   Unless the policy otherwise provides, the insurer is not liable for ordinary wear and tear, ordinary leakage and breakage, inherent vice or nature of the subject-matter insured, or for any loss proximately caused by rats or vermin, or for any injury to machinery not proximately caused by maritime perils.

[1.302]
56   Partial and total loss
(1)   A loss may be either total or partial. Any loss other than a total loss, as herein-after defined, is a partial loss.
(2)   A total loss may be either an actual total loss, or a constructive total loss.
(3)   Unless a different intention appears from the terms of the policy, an insurance against total loss includes a constructive, as well as an actual, total loss.
(4)   Where the assured brings an action for a total loss and the evidence proves only a partial loss, he may, unless the policy otherwise provides, recover for a partial loss.

(5)   Where goods reach their destination in specie, but by reason of obliteration of marks, or otherwise, they are incapable of identification, the loss, if any, is partial, and not total.

[1.303]
57   Actual total loss
(1)   Where the subject-matter insured is destroyed, or so damaged as to cease to be a thing of the kind insured, or where the assured is irretrievably deprived thereof, there is an actual total loss.
(2)   In the case of an actual total loss no notice of abandonment need be given.

[1.304]
58   Missing ship
Where the ship concerned in the adventure is missing, and after the lapse of a reasonable time no news of her has been received, an actual total loss may be presumed.

[1.305]
59   Effect of transhipment, etc
Where, by a peril insured against, the voyage is interrupted at an intermediate port or place, under such circumstances as, apart from any special stipulation in the contract of affreightment, to justify the master in landing and re-shipping the goods or other moveables, or in transhipping them, and sending them on to their destination, the liability of the insurer continues, notwithstanding the landing or transhipment.

[1.306]
60   Constructive total loss defined
(1)   Subject to any express provision in the policy, there is a constructive total loss where the subject-matter insured is reasonably abandoned on account of its actual total loss appearing to be unavoidable, or because it could not be preserved from actual total loss without an expenditure which would exceed its value when the expenditure had been incurred.
(2)   In particular, there is a constructive total loss—
  (i)   Where the assured is deprived of the possession of his ship or goods by a peril insured against, and (a) it is unlikely that he can recover the ship or goods, as the case may be, or (b) the cost of recovering the ship or goods, as the case may be, would exceed their value when recovered; or
  (ii)   In the case of damage to a ship, where she is so damaged by a peril insured against that the cost of repairing the damage would exceed the value of the ship when repaired.
     In estimating the cost of repairs, no deduction is to be made in respect of general average contributions to those repairs payable by other interests, but account is to be taken of the expense of future salvage operations and of any future general average contributions to which the ship would be liable if repaired; or
  (iii)   In the case of damage to goods, where the cost of repairing the damage and forwarding the goods to their destination would exceed their value on arrival.

[1.307]
61   Effect of constructive total loss
Where there is a constructive total loss the assured may either treat the loss as a partial loss, or abandon the subject-matter insured to the insurer and treat the loss as if it were an actual total loss.

[1.308]
62   Notice of abandonment
(1)   Subject to the provisions of this section, where the assured elects to abandon the subject-matter insured to the insurer, he must give notice of abandonment. If he fails to do so the loss can only be treated as a partial loss.
(2)   Notice of abandonment may be given in writing, or by word of mouth, or partly in writing and partly by word of mouth, and may be given in terms which indicate the intention of the assured to abandon his insured interest in the subject matter insured unconditionally to the insurer.
(3)   Notice of abandonment must be given with reasonable diligence after the receipt of reliable information of the loss, but where the information is of a doubtful character the assured is entitled to a reasonable time to make inquiry.
(4)   Where notice of abandonment is properly given, the rights of the assured are not prejudiced by the fact that the insurer refuses to accept the abandonment.
(5)   The acceptance of an abandonment may be either express or implied from the conduct of the insurer. The mere silence of the insurer after notice is not an acceptance.
(6)   Where a notice of abandonment is accepted the abandonment is irrevocable. The acceptance of the notice conclusively admits liability for the loss and the sufficiency of the notice.
(7)   Notice of abandonment is unnecessary where, at the time when the assured receives information of the loss, there would be no possibility of benefit to the insurer if notice were given to him.
(8)   Notice of abandonment may be waived by the insurer.
(9)   Where an insurer has re-insured his risk, no notice of abandonment need be given by him.

[1.309]
63 Effect of abandonment
(1) Where there is a valid abandonment the insurer is entitled to take over the interest of the assured in whatever may remain of the subject-matter insured, and all proprietary rights incidental thereto.
(2) Upon the abandonment of a ship, the insurer thereof is entitled to any freight in course of being earned, and which is earned by her subsequent to the casualty causing the loss, less the expenses of earning it incurred after the casualty; and, where the ship is carrying the owner's goods, the insurer is entitled to a reasonable remuneration for the carriage of them subsequent to the casualty causing the loss.

Partial Losses (including Salvage and General Average and Particular Charges)

[1.310]
64 Particular average loss
(1) A particular average loss is a partial loss of the subject-matter insured, caused by a peril insured against, and which is not a general average loss.
(2) Expenses incurred by or on behalf of the assured for the safety or preservation of the subject-matter insured, other than general average and salvage charges, are called particular charges. Particular charges are not included in particular average.

[1.311]
65 Salvage charges
(1) Subject to any express provision in the policy, salvage charges incurred in preventing a loss by perils insured against may be recovered as a loss by those perils.
(2) "Salvage charges" means the charges recoverable under maritime law by a salvor independently of contract. They do not include the expenses of services in the nature of salvage rendered by the assured or his agents, or any person employed for hire by them, for the purpose of averting a peril insured against. Such expenses, where properly incurred, may be recovered as particular charges or as a general average loss, according to the circumstances under which they were incurred.

[1.312]
66 General average loss
(1) A general average loss is a loss caused by or directly consequential on a general average act. It includes a general average expenditure as well as a general average sacrifice.
(2) There is a general average act where any extraordinary sacrifice or expenditure is voluntarily and reasonably made or incurred in time of peril for the purpose of preserving the property imperilled in the common adventure.
(3) Where there is a general average loss, the party on whom it falls is entitled, subject to the conditions imposed by maritime law, to a rateable contribution from the other parties interested, and such contribution is called a general average contribution.
(4) Subject to any express provision in the policy, where the assured has incurred a general average expenditure, he may recover from the insurer in respect of the proportion of the loss which falls upon him; and, in the case of a general average sacrifice, he may recover from the insurer in respect of the whole loss without having enforced his right of contribution from the other parties liable to contribute.
(5) Subject to any express provision in the policy, where the assured has paid, or is liable to pay, a general average contribution in respect of the subject insured, he may recover therefor from the insurer.
(6) In the absence of express stipulation, the insurer is not liable for any general average loss or contribution where the loss was not incurred for the purpose of avoiding, or in connexion with the avoidance of, a peril insured against.
(7) Where ship, freight, and cargo, or any two of those interests, are owned by the same assured, the liability of the insurer in respect of general average losses or contributions is to be determined as if those subjects were owned by different persons.

Measure of Indemnity

[1.313]
67 Extent of liability of insurer for loss
(1) The sum which the assured can recover in respect of a loss on a policy by which he is insured, in the case of an unvalued policy to the full extent of the insurable value, or, in the case of a valued policy to the full extent of the value fixed by the policy, is called the measure of indemnity.
(2) Where there is a loss recoverable under the policy, the insurer, or each insurer if there be more than one, is liable for such proportion of the measure of indemnity as the amount of his subscription bears to the value fixed by the policy in the case of a valued policy, or to the insurable value in the case of an unvalued policy.

[1.314]
68 Total loss
Subject to the provisions of this Act and to any express provision in the policy, where there is a total loss of the subject-matter insured,—
(1)   If the policy be a valued policy, the measure of indemnity is the sum fixed by the policy:
(2)   If the policy be an unvalued policy, the measure of indemnity is the insurable value of the subject-matter insured.

[1.315]
69 Partial loss of ship
Where a ship is damaged, but is not totally lost, the measure of indemnity, subject to any express provision in the policy, is as follows—
(1)   Where the ship has been repaired, the assured is entitled to the reasonable cost of the repairs, less the customary deductions, but not exceeding the sum insured in respect of any one casualty:
(2)   Where the ship has been only partially repaired, the assured is entitled to the reasonable cost of such repairs, computed as above, and also to be indemnified for the reasonable depreciation, if any, arising from the unrepaired damage, provided that the aggregate amount shall not exceed the cost of repairing the whole damage, computed as above:
(3)   Where the ship has not been repaired, and has not been sold in her damaged state during the risk, the assured is entitled to be indemnified for the reasonable depreciation arising from the unrepaired damage, but not exceeding the reasonable cost of repairing such damage, computed as above.

[1.316]
70 Partial loss of freight
Subject to any express provision in the policy, where there is a partial loss of freight, the measure of indemnity is such proportion of the sum fixed by the policy in the case of a valued policy, or of the insurable value in the case of an unvalued policy, as the proportion of freight lost by the assured bears to the whole freight at the risk of the assured under the policy.

[1.317]
71 Partial loss of goods, merchandise, etc
Where there is a partial loss of goods, merchandise, or other moveables, the measure of indemnity, subject to any express provision in the policy, is as follows—
(1)   Where part of the goods, merchandise or other moveables insured by a valued policy is totally lost, the measure of indemnity is such proportion of the sum fixed by the policy as the insurable value of the part lost bears to the insurable value of the whole, ascertained as in the case of an unvalued policy:
(2)   Where part of the goods, merchandise, or other moveables insured by an unvalued policy is totally lost, the measure of indemnity is the insurable value of the part lost, ascertained as in case of total loss:
(3)   Where the whole or any part of the goods or merchandise insured has been delivered damaged at its destination, the measure of indemnity is such proportion of the sum fixed by the policy in the case of a valued policy, or of the insurable value in the case of an unvalued policy, as the difference between the gross sound and damaged values at the place of arrival bears to the gross sound value:
(4)   "Gross value" means the wholesale price or, if there be no such price, the estimated value, with, in either case, freight, landing charges, and duty paid beforehand; provided that, in the case of goods or merchandise customarily sold in bond, the bonded price is deemed to be the gross value. "Gross proceeds" means the actual price obtained at a sale where all charges on sale are paid by the sellers.

[1.318]
72 Apportionment of valuation
(1)   Where different species of property are insured under a single valuation, the valuation must be apportioned over the different species in proportion to their respective insurable values, as in the case of an unvalued policy. The insured value of any part of a species is such proportion of the total insured value of the same as the insurable value of the part bears to the insurable value of the whole, ascertained in both cases as provided by this Act.
(2)   Where a valuation has to be apportioned, and particulars of the prime cost of each separate species, quality, or description of goods cannot be ascertained, the division of the valuation may be made over the net arrived sound values of the different species, qualities, or descriptions of goods.

[1.319]
73 General average contributions and salvage charges
(1)   Subject to any express provision in the policy, where the assured has paid, or is liable for, any general average contribution, the measure of indemnity is the full amount of such contribution, if the subject-matter liable to contribution is insured for its full contributory value; but, if such subject-matter be not insured for its full contributory value, or if only part of it be insured, the

indemnity payable by the insurer must be reduced in proportion to the under insurance, and where there has been a particular average loss which constitutes a deduction from the contributory value, and for which the insurer is liable, that amount must be deducted from the insured value in order to ascertain what the insurer is liable to contribute.

(2)   Where the insurer is liable for salvage charges the extent of his liability must be determined on the like principle.

[1.320]
74   Liabilities to third parties

Where the assured has effected an insurance in express terms against any liability to a third party, the measure of indemnity, subject to any express provision in the policy, is the amount paid or payable by him to such third party in respect of such liability.

[1.321]
75   General provisions as to measure of indemnity

(1)   Where there has been a loss in respect of any subject-matter not expressly provided for in the foregoing provisions of this Act, the measure of indemnity shall be ascertained, as nearly as may be, in accordance with those provisions, in so far as applicable to the particular case.

(2)   Nothing in the provisions of this Act relating to the measure of indemnity shall affect the rules relating to double insurance, or prohibit the insurer from disproving interest wholly or in part, or from showing that at the time of the loss the whole or any part of the subject-matter insured was not at risk under the policy.

[1.322]
76   Particular average warranties

(1)   Where the subject-matter insured is warranted free from particular average, the assured cannot recover for a loss of part, other than a loss incurred by a general average sacrifice unless the contract contained in the policy be apportionable; but, if the contract be apportionable, the assured may recover for a total loss of any apportionable part.

(2)   Where the subject-matter insured is warranted free from particular average, either wholly or under a certain percentage, the insurer is nevertheless liable for salvage charges, and for particular charges and other expenses properly incurred pursuant to the provisions of the suing and labouring clause in order to avert a loss insured against.

(3)   Unless the policy otherwise provides, where the subject-matter insured is warranted free from particular average under a specified percentage, a general average loss cannot be added to a particular average loss to make up the specified percentage.

(4)   For the purpose of ascertaining whether the specified percentage has been reached, regard shall be had only to the actual loss suffered by the subject-matter insured. Particular charges and the expenses of and incidental to ascertaining and proving the loss must be excluded.

[1.323]
77   Successive losses

(1)   Unless the policy otherwise provides, and subject to the provisions of this Act, the insurer is liable for successive losses, even though the total amount of such losses may exceed the sum insured.

(2)   Where, under the same policy, a partial loss, which has not been repaired or otherwise made good, is followed by a total loss, the assured can only recover in respect of the total loss:

     Provided that nothing in this section shall affect the liability of the insurer under the suing and labouring clause.

[1.324]
78   Suing and labouring clause

(1)   Where the policy contains a suing and labouring clause, the engagement thereby entered into is deemed to be supplementary to the contract of insurance, and the assured may recover from the insurer any expenses properly incurred pursuant to the clause, notwithstanding that the insurer may have paid for a total loss, or that the subject-matter may have been warranted free from particular average, either wholly or under a certain percentage.

(2)   General average losses and contributions and salvage charges, as defined by this Act, are not recoverable under the suing and labouring clause.

(3)   Expenses incurred for the purpose of averting or diminishing any loss not covered by the policy are not recoverable under the suing and labouring clause.

(4)   It is the duty of the assured and his agents, in all cases, to take such measures as may be reasonable for the purpose of averting or minimising a loss.

Rights of Insurer on Payment

[1.325]
79 Right of subrogation
(1)   Where the insurer pays for a total loss, either of the whole, or in the case of goods of any apportionable part, of the subject-matter insured, he thereupon becomes entitled to take over the interest of the assured in whatever may remain of the subject-matter so paid for, and he is thereby subrogated to all the rights and remedies of the assured in and in respect of that subject-matter as from the time of the casualty causing the loss.
(2)   Subject to the foregoing provisions, where the insurer pays for a partial loss, he acquires no title to the subject-matter insured, or such part of it as may remain, but he is thereupon subrogated to all rights and remedies of the assured in and in respect of the subject-matter insured as from the time of the casualty causing the loss, in so far as the assured has been indemnified, according to this Act, by such payment for the loss.

[1.326]
80 Right of contribution
(1)   Where the assured is over-insured by double insurance, each insurer is bound, as between himself and the other insurers, to contribute rateably to the loss in proportion to the amount for which he is liable under his contract.
(2)   If any insurer pays more than his proportion of the loss, he is entitled to maintain an action for contribution against the other insurers, and is entitled to the like remedies as a surety who has paid more than his proportion of the debt.

[1.327]
81 Effect of under insurance
Where the assured is insured for an amount less than the insurable value or, in the case of a valued policy, for an amount less than the policy valuation, he is deemed to be his own insurer in respect of the uninsured balance.

Return of Premium

[1.328]
82 Enforcement of return
Where the premium or a proportionate part thereof is, by this Act, declared to be returnable,—
    (a)   If already paid, it may be recovered by the assured from the insurer; and
    (b)   If unpaid, it may be retained by the assured or his agent.

[1.329]
83 Return by agreement
Where the policy contains a stipulation for the return of the premium, or a proportionate part thereof, on the happening of a certain event, and that event happens, the premium, or, as the case may be, the proportionate part thereof, is thereupon returnable to the assured.

[1.330]
84 Return for failure of consideration
(1)   Where the consideration for the payment of the premium totally fails, and there has been no fraud or illegality on the part of the assured or his agents, the premium is thereupon returnable to the assured.
(2)   Where the consideration for the payment of the premium is apportionable and there is a total failure of any apportionable part of the consideration, a proportionate part of the premium is, under the like conditions, thereupon returnable to the assured.
(3)   In particular—
    (a)   Where the policy is void, or is avoided by the insurer as from the commencement of the risk, the premium is returnable, provided that there has been no fraud or illegality on the part of the assured; but if the risk is not apportionable, and has once attached, the premium is not returnable;
    (b)   Where the subject-matter insured, or part thereof, has never been imperilled, the premium, or, as the case may be, a proportionate part thereof, is returnable:
        Provided that where the subject-matter has been insured "lost or not lost" and has arrived in safety at the time when the contract is concluded, the premium is not returnable unless, at such time, the insurer knew of the safe arrival.
    (c)   Where the assured has no insurable interest throughout the currency of the risk, the premium is returnable, provided that this rule does not apply to a policy effected by way of gaming or wagering;
    (d)   Where the assured has a defeasible interest which is terminated during the currency of the risk, the premium is not returnable;
    (e)   Where the assured has over-insured under an unvalued policy, a proportionate part of the premium is returnable;
    (f)   Subject to the foregoing provisions, where the assured has over-insured by double insurance, a proportionate part of the several premiums is returnable:

Provided that, if the policies are effected at different times, and any earlier policy has at any time borne the entire risk, or if a claim has been paid on the policy in respect of the full sum insured thereby, no premium is returnable in respect of that policy, and when the double insurance is effected knowingly by the assured no premium is returnable.

NOTES

Note: this section is to be read subject to the provisions of the Insurance Act 2015, Sch 1 (Insurers' remedies for qualifying breaches) in relation to contracts of marine insurance which are non-consumer insurance contracts; see Sch 1, para 12 to that Act at **[1.2222]**.

See further, in relation to contracts of marine insurance which are consumer insurance contracts, the Consumer Insurance (Disclosure and Representations) Act 2012, s 4(3), Sch 1, Pt 4 at **[1.2146]**, **[1.2158]**.

See further, the Insurance Act 2015, Sch 1, Pt 3, para 12, which provides that this section is to be read subject to the provisions of that Schedule in relation to contracts of marine insurance which are non-consumer insurance.

Mutual Insurance

[1.331]
85 Modification of Act in case of mutual insurance
(1)   Where two or more persons mutually agree to insure each other against marine losses there is said to be a mutual insurance.
(2)   The provisions of this Act relating to the premium do not apply to mutual insurance, but a guarantee, or such other arrangement as may be agreed upon, may be substituted for the premium.
(3)   The provisions of this Act, in so far as they may be modified by the agreement of the parties, may in the case of mutual insurance be modified by the terms of the policies issued by the association, or by the rules and regulations of the association.
(4)   Subject to the exceptions mentioned in this section, the provisions of this Act apply to a mutual insurance.

Supplemental

[1.332]
86 Ratification by assured
Where a contract of marine insurance is in good faith effected by one person on behalf of another, the person on whose behalf it is effected may ratify the contract even after he is aware of a loss.

[1.333]
87 Implied obligations varied by agreement or usage
(1)   Where any right, duty, or liability would arise under a contract of marine insurance by implication of law, it may be negatived or varied by express agreement, or by usage, if the usage be such as to bind both parties to the contract.
(2)   The provisions of this section extend to any right, duty, or liability declared by this Act which may be lawfully modified by agreement.

[1.334]
88 Reasonable time, etc, a question of fact
Where by this Act any reference is made to reasonable time, reasonable premium, or reasonable diligence, the question what is reasonable is a question of fact.

[1.335]
89 Slip as evidence
Where there is a duly stamped policy, reference may be made, as heretofore, to the slip or covering note, in any legal proceeding.

[1.336]
90 Interpretation of terms
In this Act, unless the context or subject-matter otherwise requires,—
   "Action" includes counter-claim and set off:
   "Freight" includes the profit derivable by a shipowner from the employment of his ship to carry
      his own goods or moveables, as well as freight payable by a third party, but does not
      include passage money:
   "Moveables" means any moveable tangible property, other than the ship, and includes money,
      valuable securities, and other documents:
   "Policy" means a marine policy.

[1.337]
91 Savings
(1)   Nothing in this Act, or in any repeal effected thereby, shall affect—
   (a)   The provisions of the Stamp Act 1891, or any enactment for the time being in force relating
      to the revenue;
   (b)   The provisions of the Companies Act 1862, or any enactment amending or substituted for
      the same;
   (c)   The provisions of any statute not expressly repealed by this Act.

(2) The rules of the common law including the law merchant, save in so far as they are inconsistent with the express provisions of this Act, shall continue to apply to contracts of marine insurance.

NOTES

Companies Act 1862: repealed by the Companies (Consolidation) Act 1908.

92, 93 (*Repealed by the Statute Law Revision Act 1927.*)

[1.338]
94 Short title
This Act may be cited as the Marine Insurance Act 1906.

SCHEDULES

FIRST SCHEDULE
FORM OF POLICY

Section 30

[1.339]
Be it known that   as well in   own name as for and in the name and names of all and every other person or persons to whom the same doth, may, or shall appertain, in part or in all doth make assurance and cause   and them, and every of them, to be insured lost or not lost, at and from

Upon any kind of goods and merchandise, and also upon the body, tackle, apparel, ordnance, munition, artillery, boat, and other furniture, of and in the good ship or vessel called the whereof is master under God, for this present voyage,   or whosoever else shall go for master in the said ship, or by whatsoever other name or names the said ship, or the master thereof, is or shall be named or called; beginning the adventure upon the said goods and merchandises from the loading thereof aboard the said ship.

upon the said ship, etc

and so shall continue and endure, during her abode there, upon the said ship, etc

And further, until the said ship, with all her ordnance, tackle, apparel, etc, and goods and merchandises whatsoever shall be arrived at

upon the said ship, etc, until she hath moored at anchor twenty-four hours in good safety; and upon the goods and merchandises, until the same be there discharged and safely landed. And it shall be lawful for the said ship, etc, in this voyage to proceed and sail to and touch and stay at any ports or places whatsoever

without prejudice to this insurance. The said ship, etc, goods and merchandises, etc, for so much as concerns the assured by agreement between the assured and assurers in this policy, are and shall be valued at

Touching the adventures and perils which we the assurers are contented to bear and do take upon us in this voyage: they are of the seas, men of war, fire, enemies, pirates, rovers, thieves, jettisons, letters of mart and countermart, surprisals, takings at sea, arrests, restraints, and detainments of all kings, princes, and people, of what nation, condition, or quality soever, barratry of the master and mariners, and of all other perils, losses, and misfortunes, that have or shall come to the hurt, detriment, or damage of the said goods and merchandises, and ship, etc, or any part thereof. And in case of any loss or misfortune it shall be lawful to the assured, their factors, servants and assigns, to sue, labour, and travel for, in and about the defence, safeguards, and recovery of the said goods and merchandises, and ship, etc, or any part thereof, without prejudice to this insurance; to the charges whereof we, the assurers, will contribute each one according to the rate and quantity of his sum herein assured. And it is especially declared and agreed that no acts of the insurer or insured in recovering, saving, or preserving the property insured shall be considered as a waiver, or acceptance of abandonment. And it is agreed by us, the insurers, that this writing or policy of assurance shall be of as much force and effect as the surest writing or policy of assurance heretofore made in Lombard Street, or in the Royal Exchange, or elsewhere in London. And so we, the assurers, are contented, and do hereby promise and bind ourselves, each one for his own part, our heirs, executors, and goods to the assured, their executors, administrators, and assigns, for the true performance of the premises, confessing ourselves paid the consideration due unto us for this assurance by the assured, at and after the rate of

IN WITNESS whereof we, the assurers, have subscribed our names and sums assured in London.

N.B.—Corn, fish, salt, fruit, flour, and seed are warranted free from average, unless general, or the ship be stranded—sugar, tobacco, hemp, flax, hides and skins are warranted free from average, under five pounds per cent., and all other goods, also the ship and freight, are warranted free from average, under three pounds per cent. unless general, or the ship be stranded.

RULES FOR CONSTRUCTION OF POLICY

The following are the rules referred to by this Act for the construction of a policy in the above or other like form, where the context does not otherwise require—

1. Where the subject-matter is insured "lost or not lost," and the loss has occurred before the contract is concluded, the risk attaches, unless at such time the assured was aware of the loss, and the insurer was not.

2. Where the subject-matter is insured "from" a particular place, the risk does not attach until the ship starts on the voyage insured.

3.—
    (a)   Where a ship is insured "at and from" a particular place, and she is at that place in good safety when the contract is concluded, the risk attaches immediately.
    (b)   If she be not at that place when the contract is concluded, the risk attaches as soon as she arrives there in good safety, and, unless the policy otherwise provides, it is immaterial that she is covered by another policy for a specified time after arrival.
    (c)   Where chartered freight is insured "at and from" a particular place, and the ship is at that place in good safety when the contract is concluded the risk attaches immediately. If she be not there when the contract is concluded, the risk attaches as soon as she arrives there in good safety.
    (d)   Where freight, other than chartered freight, is payable without special conditions and is insured "at and from" a particular place, the risk attaches pro rata as the goods or merchandise are shipped; provided that if there be cargo in readiness which belongs to the shipowner, or which some other person has contracted with him to ship, the risk attaches as soon as the ship is ready to receive such cargo.

4. Where goods or other moveables are insured "from the loading thereof," the risk does not attach until such goods or moveables are actually on board, and the insurer is not liable for them while in transit from the shore to ship.

5. Where the risk on goods or other moveables continues until they are "safely landed," they must be landed in the customary manner and within a reasonable time after arrival at the port of discharge, and if they are not so landed the risk ceases.

6. In the absence of any further license or usage, the liberty to touch and stay "at any port or place whatsoever" does not authorise the ship to depart from the course of her voyage from the port of departure to the port of destination.

7. The term "perils of the seas" refers only to fortuitous accidents or casualties of the seas. It does not include the ordinary action of the winds and waves.

8. The term "pirates" includes passengers who mutiny and rioters who attack the ship from the shore.

9. The term "thieves" does not cover clandestine theft or a theft committed by any one of the ship's company, whether crew or passengers.

10. The term "arrests, etc, of kings, princes, and people" refers to political or executive acts, and does not include a loss caused by riot or by ordinary judicial process.

11. The term "barratry" includes every wrongful act wilfully committed by the master or crew to the prejudice of the owner, or, as the case may be, the charterer.

12. The term "all other perils" includes only perils similar in kind to the perils specifically mentioned in the policy.

13. The term "average unless general" means a partial loss of the subject-matter insured other than a general average loss, and does not include "particular charges."

14. Where the ship has stranded, the insurer is liable for the excepted losses, although the loss is not attributable to the stranding, provided that when the stranding takes place the risk has attached and, if the policy be on goods, that the damaged goods are on board.

15. The term "ship" includes the hull, materials and outfit, stores and provisions for the officers and crew, and, in the case of vessels engaged in a special trade, the ordinary fittings requisite for the trade, and also, in the case of a steamship, the machinery, boilers, and coals and engine stores, if owned by the assured.

16. The term "freight" includes the profit derivable by a shipowner from the employment of his ship to carry his own goods or moveables, as well as freight payable by a third party, but does not include passage money.

17. The term "goods" means goods in the nature of merchandise, and does not include personal effects or provisions and stores for use on board.

In the absence of any usage to the contrary, deck cargo and living animals must be insured specifically, and not under the general denomination of goods.

NOTES

The form of policy contained in this Schedule is the same as the model policy called "the Lloyd's policy" which was in common use for marine insurances in the UK for about 200 years. This has largely been superseded by a modern standard form of marine policy issued by Lloyd's.

SECOND SCHEDULE

(*Second Schedule repealed by the Statute Law Revision Act 1927.*)

LIMITED PARTNERSHIPS ACT 1907

(1907 c 24)

ARRANGEMENT OF SECTIONS

An Act to establish Limited Partnership

[28 August 1907]

[1.340]
1   Short title
This Act may be cited for all purposes as the Limited Partnerships Act 1907.

NOTES

Whole Act repealed, in relation to Northern Ireland, by the Companies Act 2006, s 1286(2)(b). See also the Companies Act 2006, s 1286(1)(b), which extends the enactments in force in Great Britain relating to limited partnerships to Northern Ireland.

2 (*Repealed by the Statute Law Revision Act 1927.*)

[1.341]
3   Interpretation of terms
In the construction of this Act the following words and expressions shall have the meanings respectively assigned to them in this section, unless there be something in the subject or context repugnant to such construction—

"Firm," "firm name," and "business" have the same meanings as in the Partnership Act 1890;

"General partner" shall mean any partner who is not a limited partner as defined by this Act.

NOTES

Repealed (in relation to Northern Ireland) as noted to s 1 at **[1.340]**.

[1.342]
4   Definition and constitution of limited partnership

(1)   . . . Limited partnerships may be formed in the manner and subject to the conditions by this Act provided.

(2)   A limited partnership . . . must consist of one or more persons called general partners, who shall be liable for all debts and obligations of the firm, and one or more persons to be called limited partners, who shall at the time of entering into such partnership contribute thereto a sum or sums as capital or property valued at a stated amount, and who shall not be liable for the debts or obligations of the firm beyond the amount so contributed.

(3)   A limited partner shall not during the continuance of the partnership, either directly or indirectly, draw out or receive back any part of his contribution, and if he does so draw out or receive back any such part shall be liable for the debts and obligations of the firm up to the amount so drawn out or received back.

(4)   A body corporate may be a limited partner.

NOTES

Repealed (in relation to Northern Ireland) as noted to s 1 at **[1.340]**.

Sub-s (1): words omitted repealed by the Statute Law Revision Act 1927.

Sub-s (2): words omitted repealed by the Banking Act 1979, ss 46(b), 51(2), Sch 7, and by the Regulatory Reform (Removal of 20 Member Limit in Partnerships etc) Order 2002, SI 2002/3203, art 3, and in relation to Northern Ireland, by the Partnerships etc (Removal of Twenty Member Limit) (Northern Ireland) Order 2003, SI 2003/2904, arts 3(1), 4, Schedule.

Modified, in relation to a partnership scheme in respect of which an authorisation order is made under the Financial Services and Markets Act 2000, s 261D(1), by the Collective Investment in Transferable Securities (Contractual Scheme) Regulations 2013, SI 2013/1388, reg 16(1), (3).

[1.343]
5   Registration of limited partnership required

Every limited partnership must be registered as such in accordance with the provisions of this Act
. . .

NOTES

Repealed (in relation to Northern Ireland) as noted to s 1 at **[1.340]**; words omitted repealed by the Legislative Reform (Limited Partnerships) Order 2009, SI 2009/1940, art 8, in relation to limited partnerships for which registration applications are received on or after 1 October 2009.

[1.344]
6   Modifications of general law in case of limited partnerships

(1)   A limited partner shall not take part in the management of the partnership business, and shall not have power to bind the firm—

Provided that a limited partner may by himself or his agent at any time inspect the books of the firm and examine into the state and prospects of the partnership business, and may advise with the partners thereon.

If a limited partner takes part in the management of the partnership business he shall be liable for all debts and obligations of the firm incurred while he so takes part in the management as though he were a general partner.

(2)   A limited partnership shall not be dissolved by the death or bankruptcy of a limited partner, and the lunacy of a limited partner shall not be a ground for dissolution of the partnership by the court unless the lunatic's share cannot be otherwise ascertained and realised.

(3)   In the event of the dissolution of a limited partnership its affairs shall be wound up by the general partners unless the court otherwise orders.

(4)   . . .

(5)   Subject to any agreement expressed or implied between the partners—

   (a)   Any difference arising as to ordinary matters connected with the partnership business may be decided by a majority of the general partners;

   (b)   A limited partner may, with the consent of the general partners, assign his share in the partnership, and upon such an assignment the assignee shall become a limited partner with all the rights of the assignor;

   (c)   The other partners shall not be entitled to dissolve the partnership by reason of any limited partner suffering his share to be charged for his separate debt;

   (d)   A person may be introduced as a partner without the consent of the existing limited partners;

   (e)   A limited partner shall not be entitled to dissolve the partnership by notice.

NOTES

Repealed (in relation to Northern Ireland) as noted to s 1 at **[1.340]**.

Sub-s (4): repealed by the Companies (Consolidation) Act 1908, s 286, Sch 6, Pt I.

Modified, in relation to a partnership scheme in respect of which an authorisation order is made under the Financial Services and Markets Act 2000, s 261D(1), by the Collective Investment in Transferable Securities (Contractual Scheme) Regulations 2013, SI 2013/1388, reg 16(1), (4).

[1.345]
7 Law as to private partnerships to apply where not excluded by this Act
Subject to the provisions of this Act, the Partnership Act 1890 and the rules of equity and of common law applicable to partnerships, except so far as they are inconsistent with the express provisions of the last-mentioned Act, shall apply to limited partnerships.

NOTES
Repealed (in relation to Northern Ireland) as noted to s 1 at **[1.340]**.
Modified, in relation to a partnership scheme in respect of which an authorisation order is made under the Financial Services and Markets Act 2000, s 261D(1), by the Collective Investment in Transferable Securities (Contractual Scheme) Regulations 2013, SI 2013/1388, reg 16(1), (5).

[1.346]
[8 Duty to register
The registrar shall register a limited partnership if an application is made to the registrar in accordance with section 8A.]

NOTES
Substituted by the Legislative Reform (Limited Partnerships) Order 2009, SI 2009/1940, arts 3(2), 4, in relation to limited partnerships for which registration applications are received on or after 1 October 2009.
Repealed (in relation to Northern Ireland) as noted to s 1 at **[1.340]**.

[1.347]
[8A Application for registration
(1) An application for registration must—
  (a) specify the firm name, complying with section 8B, under which the limited partnership is to be registered,
  (b) contain the details listed in subsection (2),
  (c) be signed or otherwise authenticated by or on behalf of each partner, and
  (d) be made to the registrar for the part of the United Kingdom in which the principal place of business of the limited partnership is to be situated.
(2) The required details are—
  (a) the general nature of the partnership business,
  (b) the name of each general partner,
  (c) the name of each limited partner,
  (d) the amount of the capital contribution of each limited partner (and whether the contribution is paid in cash or in another specified form),
  (e) the address of the proposed principal place of business of the limited partnership, and
  (f) the term (if any) for which the limited partnership is to be entered into (beginning with the date of registration).]

NOTES
Inserted by the Legislative Reform (Limited Partnerships) Order 2009, SI 2009/1940, arts 3(2), 5, in relation to limited partnerships for which registration applications are received on or after 1 October 2009.
Repealed (in relation to Northern Ireland) as noted to s 1 at **[1.340]**.

[1.348]
[8B Name of limited partnership
(1) This section sets out conditions which must be satisfied by the firm name of a limited partnership as specified in the application for registration.
(2) The name must end with—
  (a) the words "limited partnership" (upper or lower case, or any combination), or
  (b) the abbreviation "LP" (upper or lower case, or any combination, with or without punctuation).
(3) But if the principal place of business of a limited partnership is to be in Wales, its firm name may end with—
  (a) the words "partneriaeth cyfyngedig" (upper or lower case, or any combination), or
  (b) the abbreviation "PC" (upper or lower case, or any combination, with or without punctuation).]

NOTES
Inserted by the Legislative Reform (Limited Partnerships) Order 2009, SI 2009/1940, arts 3(2), 6, in relation to limited partnerships for which registration applications are received on or after 1 October 2009.
Repealed (in relation to Northern Ireland) as noted to s 1 at **[1.340]**.

[1.349]
[8C Certificate of registration
(1) On registering a limited partnership the registrar shall issue a certificate of registration.
(2) The certificate must be—
  (a) signed by the registrar, or
  (b) authenticated with the registrar's seal.

(3) The certificate must state—
    (a) the firm name of the limited partnership given in the application for registration,
    (b) the limited partnership's registration number,
    (c) the date of registration, and
    (d) that the limited partnership is registered as a limited partnership under this Act.
(4) The certificate is conclusive evidence that a limited partnership came into existence on the date of registration.]

NOTES

Inserted by the Legislative Reform (Limited Partnerships) Order 2009, SI 2009/1940, arts 3(2), 7, in relation to limited partnerships for which registration applications are received on or after 1 October 2009.

Repealed (in relation to Northern Ireland) as noted to s 1 at **[1.340]**.

[1.350]

9 Registration of changes in partnerships

(1) If during the continuance of a limited partnership any change is made or occurs in—
    (a) the firm name,
    (b) the general nature of the business,
    (c) the principal place of business,
    (d) the partners or the name of any partner,
    (e) the term or character of the partnership,
    (f) the sum contributed by any limited partner,
    (g) the liability of any partner by reason of his becoming a limited instead of a general partner or a general instead of a limited partner,
a statement, signed by the firm, specifying the nature of the change shall within seven days be sent by post or delivered to the registrar . . .
(2) If default is made in compliance with the requirements of this section each of the general partners shall, on conviction under the Summary Jurisdiction Acts, be liable to a fine not exceeding one pound for each day during which the default continues.

NOTES

Repealed (in relation to Northern Ireland) as noted to s 1 at **[1.340]**.

Sub-s (1): words omitted repealed by the Companies Act 2006 (Consequential Amendments, Transitional Provisions and Savings) Order 2009, SI 2009/1941, art 2(1), Sch 1, para 3(1), (2).

Modified, in relation to a partnership scheme in respect of which an authorisation order is made under the Financial Services and Markets Act 2000, s 261D(1), by the Collective Investment in Transferable Securities (Contractual Scheme) Regulations 2013, SI 2013/1388, reg 16(1), (6).

[1.351]

10 Advertisement in Gazette of statement of general partner becoming a limited partner and of assignment of share of limited partner

(1) Notice of any arrangement or transaction under which any person will cease to be a general partner in any firm, and will become a limited partner in that firm, or under which the share of a limited partner in a firm will be assigned to any person, shall be forthwith advertised in the Gazette, and until notice of the arrangement or transaction is so advertised the arrangement or transaction shall, for the purposes of this Act, be deemed to be of no effect.
(2) For the purposes of this section, the expression "the Gazette" means—
In the case of a limited partnership registered in England, the London Gazette.
In the case of a limited partnership registered in Scotland, the Edinburgh Gazette.
In the case of a limited partnership registered in [Northern Ireland], the [Belfast] Gazette.

NOTES

Repealed (in relation to Northern Ireland) as noted to s 1 at **[1.340]**.

Sub-s (2): words in square brackets substituted by the Companies Act 2006 (Consequential Amendments, Transitional Provisions and Savings) Order 2009, SI 2009/1941, art 2(1), Sch 1, para 3(1), (3).

Modified, in relation to a partnership scheme in respect of which an authorisation order is made under the Financial Services and Markets Act 2000, s 261D(1), by the Collective Investment in Transferable Securities (Contractual Scheme) Regulations 2013, SI 2013/1388, reg 16(1), (7).

11, 12 *(S 11 repealed by the Finance Act 1973, s 59(7), Sch 22, Pt V and the Finance (Miscellaneous Provisions) (Northern Ireland) Order 1973, SI 1973/1323, art 10(1), Sch 4; s 12 repealed by the Perjury Act 1911, s 17, Schedule and the Perjury Act (Northern Ireland) 1946, s 16(3), Schedule.)*

[1.352]

13 Registrar to file statement and issue certificate of registration

On receiving any statement made in pursuance of this Act the registrar shall cause the same to be filed, and he shall send by post to the firm from whom such statement shall have been received a certificate of the registration thereof.

NOTES

Repealed (in relation to Northern Ireland) as noted to s 1 at **[1.340]**.

[1.353]
14 Register and index to be kept
. . . The registrar shall keep . . . a register and an index of all the limited partnerships registered as aforesaid, and of all the statements registered in relation to such partnerships.

NOTES

Repealed (in relation to Northern Ireland) as noted to s 1 at **[1.340]**.

Words omitted repealed by the Companies Act 2006 (Consequential Amendments, Transitional Provisions and Savings) Order 2009, SI 2009/1941, art 2(1), Sch 1, para 3(1), (4).

[1.354]
[15 The registrar
[(1) The registrar of companies is the registrar of limited partnerships.
(2) In this Act—
  (a) references to the registrar in relation to the registration of a limited partnership are to the registrar to whom the application for registration is to be made (see section 8A(1)(d));
  (b) references to registration in a particular part of the United Kingdom are to registration by the registrar for that part of the United Kingdom;
  (c) references to the registrar in relation to any other matter relating to a limited partnership are to the registrar for the part of the United Kingdom in which the partnership is registered.]

NOTES

Substituted by the Companies Act 2006 (Consequential Amendments, Transitional Provisions and Savings) Order 2009, SI 2009/1941, art 2(1), Sch 1, para 3(1), (5).

Repealed (in relation to Northern Ireland) as noted to s 1 at **[1.340]**.

[1.355]
16 Inspection of statements registered
(1) Any person may inspect the statements filed by the registrar . . . ; and any person may require a certificate of the registration of any limited partnership, or a copy of or extract from any registered statement, to be certified by the registrar, . . .
(2) A certificate of registration or a copy of or extract from any statement registered under this Act, if duly certified to be a true copy under the hand of the registrar . . . (whom it shall not be necessary to prove to be the registrar . . .) shall, in all legal proceedings, civil or criminal, and in all cases whatsoever be received in evidence.

NOTES

Repealed (in relation to Northern Ireland) as noted to s 1 at **[1.340]**.

Sub-s (1): words omitted repealed by the Companies Act 2006, ss 1063(7)(a), 1295, Sch 16 and the Companies Act 2006 (Consequential Amendments, Transitional Provisions and Savings) Order 2009, SI 2009/1941, art 2(1), Sch 1, para 3(1), (6)(a).

Sub-s (2): words omitted repealed by SI 2009/1941, art 2(1), Sch 1, para 3(1), (6)(b).

[1.356]
17 Power to Board of Trade to make rules
The Board of Trade may make rules . . . concerning any of the following matters—
  (a) . . .
  (b) The duties or additional duties to be performed by the registrar for the purposes of this Act;
  (c) The performance by assistant registrars and other officers of acts by this Act required to be done by the registrar;
  (d) The forms to be used for the purposes of this Act;
  (e) Generally, the conduct and regulation of registration under this Act and any matters incidental thereto.

NOTES

Repealed (in relation to Northern Ireland) as noted to s 1 at **[1.340]**.

Words omitted repealed by the Companies Act 2006, ss 1063(7)(b), 1295, Sch 16.

Rules: the Limited Partnerships (Forms) Rules 2009, SI 2009/2160.

MARINE INSURANCE (GAMBLING POLICIES) ACT 1909

(9 Edw 7 c 12)

ARRANGEMENT OF SECTIONS

An Act to prohibit Gambling on Loss by Maritime Perils

[20 October 1909]

[1.357]
1   Prohibition of gambling on loss by maritime perils

(1)   If—

  (a)   any person effects a contract of marine insurance without having any bona fide interest, direct or indirect, either in the safe arrival of the ship in relation to which the contract is made or in the safety or preservation of the subject-matter insured, or a bona fide expectation of acquiring such an interest; or

  (b)   any person in the employment of the owner of a ship, not being a part owner of the ship, effects a contract of marine insurance in relation to the ship, and the contract is made "interest or no interest," or "without further proof of interest than the policy itself," or "without benefit of salvage to the insurer," or subject to any other like term,

the contract shall be deemed to be a contract by way of gambling on loss by maritime perils, and the person effecting it shall be guilty of an offence, and shall be liable, on summary conviction, to imprisonment . . . for a term not exceeding six months or to a fine not exceeding [level 3 on the standard scale], and in either case to forfeit to the Crown any money he may receive under the contract.

(2)   Any broker or other person through whom, and any insurer with whom, any such contract is effected shall be guilty of an offence and liable on summary conviction to the like penalties if he acted knowing that the contract was by way of gambling on loss by maritime perils within the meaning of this Act.

(3)   Proceedings under this Act shall not be instituted without the consent in England of the Attorney-General, in Scotland of the Lord Advocate, and in Ireland of the Attorney-General for Ireland.

(4)   Proceedings shall not be instituted under this Act against a person (other than a person in the employment of the owner of the ship in relation to which the contract was made) alleged to have effected a contract by way of gambling on loss by maritime perils until an opportunity has been afforded him of showing that the contract was not such a contract as aforesaid, and any information given by that person for that purpose shall not be admissible in evidence against him in any prosecution under this Act.

(5)   If proceedings under this Act are taken against any person (other than a person in the employment of the owner of the ship in relation to which the contract was made) for effecting such a contract, and the contract was made "interest or no interest," or "without further proof of interest than the policy itself," or "without benefit of salvage to the insurer," or subject to any other like term, the contract shall be deemed to be a contract by way of gambling on loss by maritime perils unless the contrary is proved.

(6)   For the purpose of giving jurisdiction under this Act, every offence shall be deemed to have been committed either in the place in which the same actually was committed or in any place in which the offender may be.

(7)   Any person aggrieved by an order or decision of a court of summary jurisdiction under this Act, may appeal to [the Crown Court].

(8)   For the purposes of this Act the expression "owner" includes charterer.

(9)   Subsection (7) of this section shall not apply to Scotland.

NOTES

Sub-s (1): words omitted repealed by virtue of the Criminal Justice Act 1948, s 1(2); reference to a level on the standard scale substituted by virtue of the Criminal Justice Act 1982, ss 38, 46.

Sub-s (7): words in square brackets substituted by the Courts Act 1971, s 56, Sch 9, Pt I.

[1.358]
2   Short title

This Act may be cited as the Marine Insurance (Gambling Policies) Act 1909, and the Marine Insurance Act 1906 and this Act may be cited together as the Marine Insurance Acts 1906 and 1909.

Part 1   Statutes

ADMINISTRATION OF JUSTICE ACT 1925

(15 & 16 Geo 5 c 28)

ARRANGEMENT OF SECTIONS

Miscellaneous

An Act to amend the law with respect to the jurisdiction and business of the Supreme Court in England and with respect to the judges, officers and offices thereof and otherwise with respect to the administration of justice

[7 May 1925]

1–21 *(Ss 1–18, 21 repealed by the Supreme Court of Judicature (Consolidation) Act 1925, s 226(1), Sch 6; s 19 repealed by the Courts Act 1971, s 56(4), Sch 11, Pt IV; s 20 repealed by the County Courts Act 1934, s 193, Sch 5.)*

Miscellaneous

[1.359]
22 Registration of deeds of arrangement
(1)   The office for the registration of deeds of arrangement under the Deeds of Arrangement Act 1914 (in this section referred to as "the Act of 1914"), shall be transferred to the Board of Trade, and the registrar for the purposes of the Act of 1914 shall be appointed by the Board of Trade, and references in that Act to the registrar of bills of sale or to the registrar for the purposes of that Act shall be construed as references to the registrar so appointed.
(2)   Subsection (1) of section five of the Act of 1914 (which provides that a copy of every deed to be registered shall be presented to the registrar) shall have effect as if it provided that there shall be presented to the registrar such number of copies of the deed and of every schedule or inventory annexed thereto or referred to therein as he may deem to be necessary for the purpose of carrying out the requirements of the Act of 1914 as amended by this section.
(3)   . . .
(4)   . . . all . . . fees whatsoever to be taken under the Act of 1914 shall be prescribed by order made by the Lord Chancellor with the concurrence of the Treasury and not otherwise, and all such . . . fees shall be paid into such account as the Treasury may direct.
(5)   Subject to the provisions of subsection (4) of this section, rules for carrying into effect the provisions of the Act of 1914, as amended by this section, other than the provisions of section seven thereof, may be made [by the Lord Chief Justice with the concurrence of the Lord Chancellor and] of the President of the Board of Trade, and, subject as aforesaid, the expression "prescribed" in the Act of 1914 shall mean prescribed by rules made under this subsection.
[(5A)   The Lord Chief Justice may nominate a judicial office holder (as defined in section 109(4) of the Constitutional Reform Act 2005) to exercise his functions under subsection (5).]
(6)   This section shall be construed as one with the Act of 1914.

NOTES
Repealed by the Deregulation Act 2015, s 19, Sch 6, Pt 1, para 1(2), as from 1 October 2015, except in relation to a deed of arrangement registered under the Deeds of Arrangement Act 1914, s 5, before the date on which the repeal comes into force if, immediately before that date, the estate of the debtor who executed the deed of arrangement has not been finally wound up.
Sub-s (3): repealed by the Statute Law (Repeals) Act 1989.
Sub-s (4): words omitted repealed by the Statute Law (Repeals) Act 1989.
Sub-s (5): words in square brackets substituted by the Constitutional Reform Act 2005, s 15(1), Sch 4, Pt 1, para 19(1), (2).
Sub-s (5A): inserted by the Constitutional Reform Act 2005, s 15(1), Sch 4, Pt 1, para 19(1), (3).
Rules: the Deeds of Arrangement Rules 1925, SR & O 1925/795; the Deeds of Arrangement Rules 1941, SI 1941/1253; the Deeds of Arrangement (Amendment) Rules 1962, SI 1962/297.
Orders: the Deeds of Arrangement Fees Order 1984, SI 1984/887.

[1.360]
23 Local registration of bills of sale under Bills of Sale Acts 1878 and 1882
(1)   Section eleven of the Bills of Sale Act (1878) Amendment Act 1882 (which makes provision for the local registration of the contents of bills of sale), shall have effect as if it required the registrar of bills of sale to transmit to county court registrars copies of the bills instead of abstracts of the contents of the bills, and references in that section to the abstract transmitted and the abstract registered shall be construed accordingly.

(2)   Section ten of the Bills of Sale Act 1878 shall have effect as though it required the presentation to the registrar on the registration of a bill of sale, in addition to the copy of the bill of sale mentioned in paragraph (2) of that section, of such number of copies of the bill and every schedule and inventory annexed thereto as the registrar may deem to be necessary for the purpose of carrying out the requirements of the said section eleven as amended by this section.

24–28   (*Ss 24–26 repealed by the Supreme Court of Judicature (Consolidation) Act 1925, s 226(1), Sch 6; s 27 repealed by the Statute Law Revision Act 1950; s 28 spent.*)

[1.361]
29   Short title, interpretation and extent
(1)   This Act may be cited as the Administration of Justice Act 1925.
(2)   . . .
(3)   This Act shall not extend to Scotland or Northern Ireland.
(4), (5)   . . .

NOTES
   Sub-s (2): repealed by the Statute Law (Repeals) Act 1973.
   Sub-ss (4), (5): repealed by the Statute Law Revision Act 1950.

SCHEDULES

SCHEDULES 1–5

(*Schs 1–3 repealed by the Supreme Court of Judicature (Consolidation) Act 1925, s 226(1), Sch 6; Schs 4, 5 repealed by the Statute Law Revision Act 1950.*)

AUCTIONS (BIDDING AGREEMENTS) ACT 1927

(17 & 18 Geo 5 c 12)

ARRANGEMENT OF SECTIONS

An Act to render illegal certain agreements and transactions affecting bidding at auctions
[29 July 1927]

[1.362]
1   Certain bidding agreements to be illegal
(1)   If any dealer agrees to give, or gives, or offers any gift or consideration to any other person as an inducement or reward for abstaining, or for having abstained, from bidding at a sale by auction either generally or for any particular lot, or if any person agrees to accept, or accepts, or attempts to obtain from any dealer any such gift or consideration as aforesaid, he shall be guilty of an offence under this Act, and shall be liable on summary conviction to a fine not exceeding one hundred pounds, or to a term of imprisonment for any period not exceeding six months, or to both such fine and such imprisonment:
   Provided that, where it is proved that a dealer has previously to an auction entered into an agreement in writing with one or more persons to purchase goods at the auction bona fide on a joint account and has before the goods were purchased at the auction deposited a copy of the agreement with the auctioneer, such an agreement shall not be treated as an agreement made in contravention of this section.
(2)   For the purposes of this section the expression "dealer" means a person who in the normal course of his business attends sales by auction for the purpose of purchasing goods with a view to reselling them.
(3)   In England and Wales a prosecution for an offence under this section shall not be instituted without the consent of the Attorney-General   . . .

NOTES
   Sub-s (3): words omitted repealed by the Law Officers Act 1997, s 3(2), Schedule.
   Shall be liable on summary conviction: by virtue of the Auctions (Bidding Agreements) Act 1969, s 1(1) at **[1.459]**, this offence is now triable either way, and the penalty that may be imposed upon conviction on indictment is a fine or imprisonment for a short term not exceeding two years, or both. By virtue of the Magistrates' Courts Act 1980, s 32(2), the penalty that may be imposed on summary conviction for an offence triable either way is imprisonment for a term not exceeding six months or a fine not exceeding the "prescribed sum", or both. By s 32(9) of the 1980 Act, the prescribed sum is currently £5,000.

2   (*Repealed by the Statute Law (Repeals) Act 2004.*)

[1.363]
3 Copy of Act to be exhibited at sale
The particulars which under section seven of the Auctioneers Act 1845, are required to be affixed or suspended in some conspicuous part of the room or place where the auction is held shall include a copy of this Act, and that section shall have effect accordingly.

[1.364]
4 Short title, commencement and extent
(1) This Act may be cited as the Auctions (Bidding Agreements) Act 1927 . . .
(2) This Act shall not extend to Northern Ireland.

NOTES
Sub-s (1): words omitted repealed by the Statute Law Revision Act 1950.

THIRD PARTIES (RIGHTS AGAINST INSURERS) ACT 1930

(20 & 21 Geo 5 c 25)

ARRANGEMENT OF SECTIONS

An Act to confer on third parties rights against insurers of third-party risks in the event of the insured becoming insolvent, and in certain other events

[10 July 1930]

NOTES
This Act does not apply in relation to any contract of insurance to which such a certificate as is mentioned in the Merchant Shipping Act 1995, s 163 relates, by s 165(5) of that Act.
Whole Act repealed by the Third Parties (Rights against Insurers) Act 2010, s 20(3), Sch 4, as from a day to be appointed and subject to transitional provisions and savings in s 20(2) of, and Sch 3, para 3 to, the 2010 Act at **[1.2080]**, **[1.2083]**.

[1.365]
1 Rights of third parties against insurers on bankruptcy, etc, of the insured
(1) Where under any contract of insurance a person (hereinafter referred to as the insured) is insured against liabilities to third parties which he may incur, then—
  (a)   in the event of the insured becoming bankrupt or making a composition or arrangement with his creditors; or
  (b)   in the case of the insured being a company, in the event of a winding-up order [. . .] being made, or a resolution for a voluntary winding-up being passed, with respect to the company, [or of the company entering administration,] or of a receiver or manager of the company's business or undertaking being duly appointed, or of possession being taken, by or on behalf of the holders of any debentures secured by a floating charge, of any property comprised in or subject to the charge [or of [a voluntary arrangement proposed for the purposes of Part I of the Insolvency Act 1986 being approved under that Part]];
if, either before or after that event, any such liability as aforesaid is incurred by the insured, his rights against the insurer under the contract in respect of the liability shall, notwithstanding anything in any Act or rule of law to the contrary, be transferred to and vest in the third party to whom the liability was so incurred.
(2) Where [the estate of any person falls to be administered in accordance with an order under section [421 of the Insolvency Act 1986]], then, if any debt provable in bankruptcy [in Scotland, any claim accepted in the sequestration] is owing by the deceased in respect of a liability against which he was insured under a contract of insurance as being a liability to a third party, the deceased debtor's rights against the insurer under the contract in respect of that liability shall, notwithstanding anything in [any such order], be transferred to and vest in the person to whom the debt is owing.
(3) In so far as any contract of insurance made after the commencement of this Act in respect of any liability of the insured to third parties purports, whether directly or indirectly, to avoid the contract or to alter the rights of the parties thereunder upon the happening to the insured of any of the events specified in paragraph (a) or paragraph (b) of subsection (1) of this section or upon the [estate of any person falling to be administered in accordance with an order under section [421 of the Insolvency Act 1986]], the contract shall be of no effect.

(4)   Upon a transfer under subsection (1) or subsection (2) of this section, the insurer shall, subject to the provisions of section three of this Act, be under the same liability to the third party as he would have been under to the insured, but—

  (a)   if the liability of the insurer to the insured exceeds the liability of the insured to the third party, nothing in this Act shall affect the rights of the insured against the insurer in respect of the excess; and

  (b)   if the liability of the insurer to the insured is less than the liability of the insured to the third party, nothing in this Act shall affect the rights of the third party against the insured in respect of the balance.

(5)   For the purposes of this Act, the expression "liabilities to third parties", in relation to a person insured under any contract of insurance, shall not include any liability of that person in the capacity of insurer under some other contract of insurance.

(6)   This Act shall not apply—

  (a)   where a company is wound up voluntarily merely for the purposes of reconstruction or of amalgamation with another company; or

  (b)   to any case to which subsections (1) and (2) of section seven of the Workmen's Compensation Act 1925 applies.

NOTES

Repealed as noted at the beginning of this Act.

Sub-s (1): words omitted repealed (originally inserted by the Insolvency Act 1985, s 235(1), Sch 8, para 7(2)(a)), and words in second pair of square brackets inserted, by the Enterprise Act 2002 (Insolvency) Order 2003, SI 2003/2096, arts 4, 6, Schedule, paras 1, 2, except in any case where a petition for an administration order was presented before 15 September 2003; words in third (outer) pair of square brackets inserted by the Insolvency Act 1985, s 235(1), Sch 8, para 7(2)(a); words in fourth (inner) pair of square brackets substituted by the Insolvency Act 1986, s 439(2), Sch 14.

Sub-s (2): words in first (outer) and fourth pairs of square brackets substituted by the Insolvency Act 1985, s 235(1), Sch 8, para 7(2)(b); words in second (inner) pair of square brackets substituted by the Insolvency Act 1986, s 439(2), Sch 14; words in third pair of square brackets inserted by the Bankruptcy (Scotland) Act 1985, s 75(1), Sch 7, Pt I, para 6(1).

Sub-s (3): words in first (outer) pair of square brackets inserted by the Insolvency Act 1985, s 235(1), Sch 8, para 7(2)(c); words in second (inner) pair of square brackets substituted by the Insolvency Act 1986, s 439(2), Sch 14.

Workman's Compensation Act 1925: repealed, subject to savings, by the National Insurance (Industrial Injuries) Act 1946, now itself repealed by the Social Security Act 1973, ss 100, 101, Schs 26, 28, Pt I and the Social Security (Consequential Provisions) Act 1975, s 1(2), (5), Sch 1, Pt I.

[1.366]
2   Duty to give necessary information to third parties

(1)   In the event of any person becoming bankrupt or making a composition or arrangement with his creditors, or in the event of [the estate of any person falling to be administered in accordance with an order under section [421 of the Insolvency Act 1986]], or in the event of a winding-up order [. . .] being made, or a resolution for a voluntary winding-up being passed, with respect to any company [or of the company entering administration] or of a receiver or manager of the company's business or undertaking being duly appointed or of possession being taken by or on behalf of the holders of any debentures secured by a floating charge of any property comprised in or subject to the charge it shall be the duty of the bankrupt, debtor, personal representative of the deceased debtor or company, and, as the case may be, of the trustee in bankruptcy, trustee, liquidator, [administrator,] receiver, or manager, or person in possession of the property to give at the request of any person claiming that the bankrupt, debtor, deceased debtor, or company is under a liability to him such information as may reasonably be required by him for the purpose of ascertaining whether any rights have been transferred to and vested in him by this Act and for the purpose of enforcing such rights, if any, and any contract of insurance, in so far as it purports, whether directly or indirectly, to avoid the contract or to alter the rights of the parties thereunder upon the giving of any such information in the events aforesaid or otherwise to prohibit or prevent the giving thereof in the said events shall be of no effect.

[(1A)   The reference in subsection (1) of this section to a trustee includes a reference to the supervisor of a [voluntary arrangement proposed for the purposes of, and approved under, Part I or Part VIII of the Insolvency Act 1986].]

(2)   If the information given to any person in pursuance of subsection (1) of this section discloses reasonable ground for supposing that there have or may have been transferred to him under this Act rights against any particular insurer, that insurer shall be subject to the same duty as is imposed by the said subsection on the persons therein mentioned.

(3)   The duty to give information imposed by this section shall include a duty to allow all contracts of insurance, receipts for premiums, and other relevant documents in the possession or power of the person on whom the duty is so imposed to be inspected and copies thereof to be taken.

NOTES

Repealed as noted at the beginning of this Act.

Sub-s (1): words in first (outer) pair of square brackets substituted and words in fifth pair of square brackets inserted by the Insolvency Act 1985, s 235(1), Sch 8, para 7(3)(a); words in second (inner) pair of square brackets substituted by the Insolvency Act 1986, s 439(2), Sch 14; words omitted repealed (originally inserted by the Insolvency Act 1985, s 235(1), Sch 8, para 7(3)(a)), and words in fourth pair of square brackets inserted, by the Enterprise Act 2002 (Insolvency) Order 2003, SI 2003/2096, arts 4, 6, Schedule, paras 1, 2, except in any case where a petition for an administration order was presented before 15 September 2003.

Sub-s (1A): inserted by the Insolvency Act 1985, s 235(1), Sch 8, para 7(3)(b); words in square brackets substituted by the Insolvency Act 1986, s 439(2), Sch 14.

[1.367]
3   Settlement between insurers and insured persons
Where the insured has become bankrupt or where in the case of the insured being a company, a winding-up order [or an administration order] has been made or a resolution for a voluntary winding-up has been passed, with respect to the company, no agreement made between the insurer and the insured after liability has been incurred to a third party and after the commencement of the bankruptcy or winding-up [or the day of the making of the administration order], as the case may be, nor any waiver, assignment, or other disposition made by, or payment made to the insured after the commencement [or day] aforesaid shall be effective to defeat or affect the rights transferred to the third party under this Act, but those rights shall be the same as if no such agreement, waiver, assignment, disposition or payment had been made.

NOTES
Repealed as noted at the beginning of this Act.
Words in square brackets inserted by the Insolvency Act 1985, s 235(1), Sch 8, para 7(4).

[1.368]
[3A   Application to limited liability partnerships
(1)   This Act applies to limited liability partnerships as it applies to companies.
(2)   In its application to limited liability partnerships, references to a resolution for a voluntary winding-up being passed are references to a determination for a voluntary winding-up being made.]

NOTES
Repealed as noted at the beginning of this Act.
Inserted by the Limited Liability Partnerships Regulations 2001, SI 2001/1090, reg 9(1), Sch 5, para 2.

4   *(Applies to Scotland only; repealed as noted at the beginning of this Act.)*

[1.369]
5   Short title
This Act may be cited as the Third Parties (Rights Against Insurers) Act 1930.

NOTES
Repealed as noted at the beginning of this Act.

LAW REFORM (FRUSTRATED CONTRACTS) ACT 1943

(6 & 7 Geo 6 c 40)

ARRANGEMENT OF SECTIONS

An Act to amend the law relating to the frustration of contracts

[5 August 1943]

[1.370]
1   Adjustment of rights and liabilities of parties to frustrated contracts
(1)   Where a contract governed by English law has become impossible of performance or been otherwise frustrated, and the parties thereto have for that reason been discharged from the further performance of the contract, the following provisions of this section shall, subject to the provisions of section two of this Act, have effect in relation thereto.
(2)   All sums paid or payable to any party in pursuance of the contract before the time when the parties were so discharged (in this Act referred to as "the time of discharge") shall, in the case of sums so paid, be recoverable from him as money received by him for the use of the party by whom the sums were paid, and, in the case of sums so payable, cease to be so payable:
Provided that, if the party to whom the sums were so paid or payable incurred expenses before the time of discharge in, or for the purpose of, the performance of the contract, the court may, if it

considers it just to do so having regard to all the circumstances of the case, allow him to retain or, as the case may be, recover the whole or any part of the sums so paid or payable, not being an amount in excess of the expenses so incurred.

(3)   Where any party to the contract has, by reason of anything done by any other party thereto in, or for the purpose of, the performance of the contract, obtained a valuable benefit (other than a payment of money to which the last foregoing subsection applies) before the time of discharge, there shall be recoverable from him by the said other party such sum (if any), not exceeding the value of the said benefit to the party obtaining it, as the court considers just, having regard to all the circumstances of the case and, in particular,—

(a)   the amount of any expenses incurred before the time of discharge by the benefited party in, or for the purpose of, the performance of the contract, including any sums paid or payable by him to any other party in pursuance of the contract and retained or recoverable by that party under the last foregoing subsection, and

(b)   the effect, in relation to the said benefit, of the circumstances giving rise to the frustration of the contract.

(4)   In estimating, for the purposes of the foregoing provisions of this section, the amount of any expenses incurred by any party to the contract, the court may, without prejudice to the generality of the said provisions, include such sum as appears to be reasonable in respect of overhead expenses and in respect of any work or services performed personally by the said party.

(5)   In considering whether any sum ought to be recovered or retained under the foregoing provisions of this section by any party to the contract, the court shall not take into account any sums which have, by reason of the circumstances giving rise to the frustration of the contract, become payable to that party under any contract of insurance unless there was an obligation to insure imposed by an express term of the frustrated contract or by or under any enactment.

(6)   Where any person has assumed obligations under the contract in consideration of the conferring of a benefit by any other party to the contract upon any other person, whether a party to the contract or not, the court may, if in all the circumstances of the case it considers it just to do so, treat for the purposes of subsection (3) of this section any benefit so conferred as a benefit obtained by the person who has assumed the obligations as aforesaid.

[1.371]
2   Provision as to application of this Act

(1)   This Act shall apply to contracts, whether made before or after the commencement of this Act, as respects which the time of discharge is on or after the first day of July, nineteen hundred and forty-three, but not to contracts as respects which the time of discharge is before the said date.

(2)   This Act shall apply to contracts to which the Crown is a party in like manner as to contracts between subjects.

(3)   Where any contract to which this Act applies contains any provision which, upon the true construction of the contract, is intended to have effect in the event of circumstances arising which operate, or would but for the said provision operate, to frustrate the contract, or is intended to have effect whether such circumstances arise or not, the court shall give effect to the said provision and shall only give effect to the foregoing section of this Act to such extent, if any, as appears to the court to be consistent with the said provision.

(4)   Where it appears to the court that a part of any contract to which this Act applies can properly be severed from the remainder of the contract, being a part wholly performed before the time of discharge, or so performed except for the payment in respect of that part of the contract of sums which are or can be ascertained under the contract, the court shall treat that part of the contract as if it were a separate contract and had not been frustrated and shall treat the foregoing section of this Act as only applicable to the remainder of that contract.

(5)   This Act shall not apply—

(a)   to any charterparty, except a time charterparty or a charterparty by way of demise, or to any contract (other than a charterparty) for the carriage of goods by sea; or

(b)   to any contract of insurance, save as is provided by subsection (5) of the foregoing section; or

(c)   to any contract to which [section 7 of the Sale of Goods Act 1979] (which avoids contracts for the sale of specific goods which perish before the risk has passed to the buyer) applies, or to any other contract for the sale, or for the sale and delivery, of specific goods, where the contract is frustrated by reason of the fact that the goods have perished.

NOTES

Sub-s (5): words in square brackets in para (c) substituted by the Sale of Goods Act 1979, s 63, Sch 2, para 2.

[1.372]
3   Short title and interpretation

(1)   This Act may be cited as the Law Reform (Frustrated Contracts) Act 1943.

(2)   In this Act the expression "court" means, in relation to any matter, the court or arbitrator by or before whom the matter falls to be determined.

ARBITRATION ACT 1950

(14 Geo 6 c 27)

ARRANGEMENT OF SECTIONS

PART II
ENFORCEMENT OF CERTAIN FOREIGN AWARDS

PART III
GENERAL

An Act to consolidate the Arbitration Acts 1889 to 1934

[28 July 1950]

1–34   *(Ss 1–20, 22–34 repealed by the Arbitration Act 1996, s 107(2), Sch 4; s 21 repealed by the Arbitration Act 1979, ss 1(1), 8(3).)*

PART II
ENFORCEMENT OF CERTAIN FOREIGN AWARDS

[1.373]
35   Awards to which Part II applies
(1)   This Part of this Act applies to any award made after the twenty-eighth day of July, nineteen hundred and twenty-four—
  (a)   in pursuance of an agreement for arbitration to which the protocol set out in the First Schedule to this Act applies; and
  (b)   between persons of whom one is subject to the jurisdiction of some one of such Powers as His Majesty, being satisfied that reciprocal provisions have been made, may by Order in Council declare to be parties to the convention set out in the Second Schedule to this Act, and of whom the other is subject to the jurisdiction of some other of the Powers aforesaid; and
  (c)   in one of such territories as His Majesty, being satisfied that reciprocal provisions have been made, may by Order in Council declare to be territories to which the said convention applies;
and an award to which this Part of this Act applies is in this Part of this Act referred to as "a foreign award".
(2)   His Majesty may by a subsequent Order in Council vary or revoke any Order previously made under this section.
(3)   Any Order in Council under section one of the Arbitration (Foreign Awards) Act 1930, which is in force at the commencement of this Act shall have effect as if it had been made under this section.

NOTES
  Orders in Council: the Arbitration (Foreign Awards) Order 1984, SI 1984/1168. In addition, the following orders also have effect by virtue of sub-s (3) above, as if made under this section: the Arbitration (Foreign Awards) No 1 Order 1930, SR & O 1930/674; the Arbitration (Foreign Awards) No 2 Order 1930, SR & O 1930/1096; the Arbitration (Foreign Awards) No 1 Order 1931, SR & O 1931/166; the Arbitration (Foreign Awards) No 2 Order 1931, SR & O 1931/669; the Arbitration (Foreign Awards) No 3 Order 1931, SR & O 1931/898; the Arbitration (Foreign Awards) No 1 Order 1933, SR & O 1933/42; the Arbitration (Foreign Awards) No 1 Order 1935, SR & O 1935/133; the Arbitration (Foreign Awards) No 2 Order 1938, SR & O 1938/1360; the Arbitration (Foreign Awards) No 1 Order 1939, SR & O 1939/152. Note, although none of these Orders have been revoked, they have been largely superseded by SI 1984/1168 or have become obsolete following political and other changes in the countries concerned.

[1.374]
36   Effect of foreign awards
(1)   A foreign award shall, subject to the provisions of this Part of this Act, be enforceable in England either by action or in the same manner as the award of an arbitrator is enforceable by virtue of [section 66 of the Arbitration Act 1996].

(2)   Any foreign award which would be enforceable under this Part of this Act shall be treated as binding for all purposes on the persons as between whom it was made, and may accordingly be relied on by any of those persons by way of defence, set off or otherwise in any legal proceedings in England, and any references in this Part of this Act to enforcing a foreign award shall be construed as including references to relying on an award.

NOTES

Sub-s (1): words in square brackets substituted by the Arbitration Act 1996, s 107(1), Sch 3, para 10.

[1.375]
37   Conditions for enforcement of foreign awards
(1)   In order that a foreign award may be enforceable under this Part of this Act it must have—
   (a)   been made in pursuance of an agreement for arbitration which was valid under the law by which it is governed;
   (b)   been made by the tribunal provided for in the agreement or constituted in manner agreed upon by the parties;
   (c)   been made in conformity with the law governing the arbitration procedure;
   (d)   become final in the country in which it was made;
   (e)   been in respect of a matter which may lawfully be referred to arbitration under the law of England;
and the enforcement thereof must not be contrary to the public policy or the law of England.
(2)   Subject to the provisions of this subsection, a foreign award shall not be enforceable under this Part of this Act if the court dealing with the case is satisfied that—
   (a)   the award has been annulled in the country in which it was made; or
   (b)   the party against whom it is sought to enforce the award was not given notice of the arbitration proceedings in sufficient time to enable him to present his case, or was under some legal incapacity and was not properly represented; or
   (c)   the award does not deal with all the questions referred or contains decisions on matters beyond the scope of the agreement for arbitration:
Provided that, if the award does not deal with all the questions referred, the court may, if it thinks fit, either postpone the enforcement of the award or order its enforcement subject to the giving of such security by the person seeking to enforce it as the court may think fit.
(3)   If a party seeking to resist the enforcement of a foreign award proves that there is any ground other than the non-existence of the conditions specified in paragraphs (a), (b) and (c) of subsection (1) of this section, or the existence of the conditions specified in paragraphs (b) and (c) of subsection (2) of this section, entitling him to contest the validity of the award, the court may, if it thinks fit, either refuse to enforce the award or adjourn the hearing until after the expiration of such period as appears to the court to be reasonably sufficient to enable that party to take the necessary steps to have the award annulled by the competent tribunal.

[1.376]
38   Evidence
(1)   The party seeking to enforce a foreign award must produce—
   (a)   the original award or a copy thereof duly authenticated in manner required by the law of the country in which it was made; and
   (b)   evidence proving that the award has become final; and
   (c)   such evidence as may be necessary to prove that the award is a foreign award and that the conditions mentioned in paragraphs (a), (b) and (c) of subsection (1) of the last foregoing section are satisfied.
(2)   In any case where any document required to be produced under subsection (1) of this section is in a foreign language, it shall be the duty of the party seeking to enforce the award to produce a translation certified as correct by a diplomatic or consular agent of the country to which that party belongs, or certified as correct in such other manner as may be sufficient according to the law of England.
(3)   Subject to the provisions of this section, rules of court may be made under section [84 of the [Senior Courts Act 1981]], with respect to the evidence which must be furnished by a party seeking to enforce an award under this Part of this Act.

NOTES

Sub-s (3): words in first (outer) pair of square brackets substituted by the Senior Courts Act 1981, s 152(1), Sch 5; words in second (inner) pair of square brackets substituted by the Constitutional Reform Act 2005, s 59(5), Sch 11, Pt 1, para 1(2).

[1.377]
39   Meaning of "final award"
For the purposes of this Part of this Act, an award shall not be deemed final if any proceedings for the purpose of contesting the validity of the award are pending in the country in which it was made.

[1.378]
40   Saving for other rights, etc
Nothing in this Part of this Act shall—

(a) prejudice any rights which any person would have had of enforcing in England any award or of availing himself in England of any award if neither this Part of this Act nor Part I of the Arbitration (Foreign Awards) Act 1930, had been enacted; or

(b) apply to any award made on an arbitration agreement governed by the law of England.

41–43 (*S 41 applies to Scotland only and repealed with transitional provisions by the Arbitration (Scotland) Act 2010, s 29, Sch 2; s 42(1), (2) apply to Northern Ireland only; s 42(3) repealed with savings by the Arbitration Act 1996, s 107(2), Sch 4; s 42(4) repealed by the Judicature (Northern Ireland) Act 1978, s 122(2), Sch 7, Pt I; s 43 repealed by the Statute Law (Repeals) Act 1978.*)

PART III
GENERAL

[1.379]
44 Short title, commencement and repeal
(1) This Act may be cited as the Arbitration Act 1950.
(2) This Act shall come into operation on the first day of September, nineteen hundred and fifty.
(3) The Arbitration Act 1889, the Arbitration Clauses (Protocol) Act 1924, and the Arbitration Act 1934 are hereby repealed except in relation to arbitrations commenced (within the meaning of subsection (2) of section twenty-nine of this Act) before the commencement of this Act, and the Arbitration (Foreign Awards) Act 1930 is hereby repealed; and any reference in any Act or other document to any enactment hereby repealed shall be construed as including a reference to the corresponding provision of this Act.

SCHEDULES

SCHEDULES 1, 2

(*Sch 1 (Protocol on Arbitration Clauses signed on behalf of His Majesty at a meeting of the Assembly of the League of Nations held on 24 September 1923) and Sch 2 (Convention on the Exclusion of Foreign Arbitral Awards signed at Geneva on behalf of His Majesty on 26 September 1927) outside the scope of this work.*)

ACCOMMODATION AGENCIES ACT 1953

(1 & 2 Eliz 2 c 23)

ARRANGEMENT OF SECTIONS

An Act to prohibit the taking of certain commissions in dealings with persons seeking houses or flats to let and the unauthorised advertisement for letting of houses and flats

[14 July 1953]

[1.380]
1 Illegal commissions and advertisements
(1) Subject to the provisions of this section, any person who, . . .
(a) demands or accepts payment of any sum of money in consideration of registering, or undertaking to register, the name or requirements of any person seeking the tenancy of a house;
(b) demands or accepts payment of any sum of money in consideration of supplying, or undertaking to supply, to any person addresses or other particulars of houses to let; or
(c) issues any advertisement, list or other document describing any house as being to let without the authority of the owner of the house or his agent,
shall be guilty of an offence.
(2) A person shall not be guilty of an offence under this section by reason of his demanding or accepting payment from the owner of a house of any remuneration payable to him as agent for the said owner.
(3) A person being a solicitor [or an authorised person] shall not be guilty of an offence under this section by reason of his demanding or accepting payment of any remuneration in respect of business done by him as such.
(4) A person shall not be guilty of an offence under this section by reason of his demanding or accepting any payment in consideration of the display in a shop, or of the publication in a newspaper, of any advertisement or notice, or by reason of the display or publication as aforesaid of an advertisement or notice received for the purpose in the ordinary course of business.

(5)   Any person guilty of an offence under this section shall be liable on summary conviction to a fine not exceeding [level 3 on the standard scale] *or to imprisonment for a term not exceeding three months, or to both such fine and imprisonment.*

(6)   In this section the following expressions have the meanings hereby assigned to them that is to say—

> ["authorised person" means a person (other than a solicitor) who, for the purposes of the Legal Services Act 2007, is an authorised person in relation to an activity which is a reserved legal activity (within the meaning of that Act);]

> "house" includes any part of a building which is occupied or intended to be occupied as a dwelling;

> "newspaper" includes any periodical or magazine;

> "owner", in relation to a house, means the person having power to grant a lease of the house.

NOTES

Sub-s (1): words omitted repealed by the Expiring Laws Act 1969.

Sub-s (3): words in square brackets inserted by the Legal Services Act 2007, s 208(1), Sch 21, para 22(a).

Sub-s (5): reference to a level on the standard scale substituted by virtue of the Criminal Justice Act 1982, ss 38, 46; words in italics repealed by the Criminal Justice Act 2003, s 332, Sch 37, Pt 9, as from a day to be appointed.

Sub-s (6): definition "authorised person" inserted by the Legal Services Act 2007, s 208(1), Sch 21, para 22(b).

Solicitors: references to solicitors are modified so as to include references to recognised bodies within the meaning of the Administration of Justice Act 1985, s 9, by the Solicitors' Recognised Bodies Order 1991, SI 1991/2684, arts 3–5, Sch 1.

[1.381]

2   Short title, extent, commencement and duration

(1)   This Act may be cited as the Accommodation Agencies Act 1953.

(2)   This Act shall not extend to Northern Ireland.

(3)   This Act shall come into operation one month after the date on which it is passed.

(4)   . . .

NOTES

Sub-s (4): repealed by the Expiring Laws Act 1969, s 1.

CHEQUES ACT 1957

(5 & 6 Eliz 2 c 36)

ARRANGEMENT OF SECTIONS

An Act to amend the law relating to cheques and certain other instruments

[17 July 1957]

[1.382]

1   Protection of bankers paying unindorsed or irregularly indorsed cheques, etc

(1)   Where a banker in good faith and in the ordinary course of business pays a cheque drawn on him which is not indorsed or is irregularly indorsed, he does not, in doing so, incur any liability by reason only of the absence of, or irregularity in, indorsement, and he is deemed to have paid it in due course.

(2)   Where a banker in good faith and in the ordinary course of business pays any such instrument as the following, namely,—

> (a)   a document issued by a customer of his which, though not a bill of exchange, is intended to enable a person to obtain payment from him of the sum mentioned in the document;

> (b)   a draft payable on demand drawn by him upon himself, whether payable at the head office or some other office of his bank;

he does not, in doing so, incur any liability by reason only of the absence of, or irregularity in, indorsement, and the payment discharges the instrument.

[1.383]
2 Rights of bankers collecting cheques not indorsed by holders
A banker who gives value for, or has a lien on, a cheque payable to order which the holder delivers to him for collection without indorsing it, has such (if any) rights as he would have had if, upon delivery, the holder had indorsed it in blank.

[1.384]
3 Unindorsed cheques as evidence of payment
[(1)] An unindorsed cheque which appears to have been paid by the banker on whom it is drawn is evidence of the receipt by the payee of the sum payable by the cheque.
[(2) For the purposes of subsection (1) above, a copy of a cheque to which that subsection applies is evidence of the cheque if—
   (a)   the copy is made by the banker in whose possession the cheque is after presentment and,
   (b)   it is certified by him to be a true copy of the original.]

NOTES
Sub-s (1): numbered as such by the Deregulation (Bills of Exchange) Order 1996, SI 1996/2993, art 5.
Sub-s (2): added by SI 1996/2993, art 5.

[1.385]
4 Protection of bankers collecting payment of cheques, etc
(1) Where a banker, in good faith and without negligence,—
   (a)   receives payment for a customer of an instrument to which this section applies; or
   (b)   having credited a customer's account with the amount of such an instrument, receives payment thereof for himself;
and the customer has no title, or a defective title, to the instrument, the banker does not incur any liability to the true owner of the instrument by reason only of having received payment thereof,—
(2) This section applies to the following instruments, namely,—
   (a)   cheques [(including cheques which under section 81A(1) of the Bills of Exchange Act 1882 or otherwise are not transferable)];
   (b)   any document issued by a customer of a banker which, though not a bill of exchange, is intended to enable a person to obtain payment from that banker of the sum mentioned in the document;
   (c)   any document issued by a public officer which is intended to enable a person to obtain payment from the Paymaster General or the Queen's and Lord Treasurer's Remembrancer of the sum mentioned in the document but is not a bill of exchange;
   (d)   any draft payable on demand drawn by a banker upon himself, whether payable at the head office or some other office of his bank.
(3) A banker is not to be treated for the purposes of this section as having been negligent by reason only of his failure to concern himself with absence of, or irregularity in, indorsement of an instrument.

NOTES
Sub-s (2): words in square brackets in para (a) inserted by the Cheques Act 1992, s 3.

[1.386]
5 Application of certain provisions of Bills of Exchange Act, 1882, to instruments not being bills of exchange
The provisions of the Bills of Exchange Act, 1882, relating to crossed cheques shall, so far as applicable, have effect in relation to instruments (other than cheques) to which the last foregoing section applies as they have effect in relation to cheques.

[1.387]
6 Construction, saving and repeal
(1) This Act shall be construed as one with the Bills of Exchange Act, 1882.
(2) The foregoing provisions of this Act do not make negotiable any instrument which, apart from them, is not negotiable.
(3) . . .

NOTES
Sub-s (3): repealed by the Statute Law (Repeals) Act 1974.

[1.388]
7 Provisions as to Northern Ireland
This Act extends to Northern Ireland, . . .

NOTES
Words omitted repealed by the Northern Ireland Constitution Act 1973, s 41(1), Sch 6, Pt I.

[1.389]

8   Short title and commencement

(1)   This Act may be cited as the Cheques Act 1957.

(2)   This Act shall come into operation at the expiration of a period of three months beginning with the day on which it is passed.

SCHEDULE

(*Schedule repealed by the Statutes Law (Repeals) Act 1974.*)

CORPORATE BODIES' CONTRACTS ACT 1960

(8 & 9 Eliz 2 c 46)

ARRANGEMENT OF SECTIONS

An Act to amend the law governing the making of contracts by or on behalf of bodies corporate; and for connected purposes

[29 July 1960]

[1.390]

1   Cases where contracts need not be under seal

(1)   Contracts may be made on behalf of any body corporate, wherever incorporated, as follows—

   (a)   a contract which if made between private persons would be by law required to be in writing, signed by the parties to be charged there-with, may be made on behalf of the body corporate in writing signed by any person acting under its authority, express or implied, and

   (b)   a contract which if made between private persons would by law be valid although made by parol only, and not reduced into writing, may be made by parol on behalf of the body corporate by any person acting under its authority, express or implied.

(2)   A contract made according to this section shall be effectual in law, and shall bind the body corporate and its successors and all other parties thereto.

(3)   A contract made according to this section may be varied or discharged in the same manner in which it is authorised by this section to be made.

(4)   Nothing in this section shall be taken as preventing a contract under seal from being made by or on behalf of a body corporate.

(5)   This section shall not apply to the making, variation or discharge of a contract before the commencement of this Act but shall apply whether the body corporate gave its authority before or after the commencement of this Act.

[1.391]

[2   Exclusion of companies etc

This Act does not apply to—

   (a)   a company registered under the Companies Act 2006,

   (b)   a company incorporated outside the United Kingdom, or

   (c)   a limited liability partnership.]

NOTES

Substituted by the Companies Act 2006 (Consequential Amendments, Transitional Provisions and Savings) Order 2009, SI 2009/1941, art 2(1), Sch 1, para 8.

3   (*Repealed by the Northern Ireland Constitution Act 1973, s 41, Sch 6, Pt I.*)

[1.392]

4   Short title, repeal and extent

(1)   This Act may be cited as the Corporate Bodies' Contracts Act 1960.

(2)   . . .

(3)   This Act shall not affect the law of Scotland or   . . .   of Northern Ireland.

NOTES

Sub-s (2): repealed by the Statute Law (Repeals) Act 1974.

Sub-s (3): words omitted repealed by the Northern Ireland Constitution Act 1973, s 41(1), Sch 6, Pt I.

SCHEDULE

(Schedule repealed by the Statute Law (Repeals) Act 1974.)

HIRE-PURCHASE ACT 1964

(1964 c 53)

ARRANGEMENT OF SECTIONS

An Act to amend the law relating to hire-purchase and credit-sale, and, in relation thereto, to amend the enactments relating to the sale of goods; to make provision with respect to dispositions of motor vehicles which have been let or agreed to be sold by way of hire-purchase or conditional sale; to amend the Advertisements (Hire-Purchase) Act 1957; and for purposes connected with the matters aforesaid

[16 July 1964]

1–26 *(Ss 1–24 (Pt I) repealed by the Hire-Purchase Act 1965, s 59, Sch 6; ss 25, 26 (Pt II) repealed by the Hire-Purchase (Scotland) Act 1965, s 55, Sch 6.)*

[PART III
TITLE TO MOTOR VEHICLES ON HIRE-PURCHASE OR CONDITIONAL SALE

[1.393]
27 Protection of purchasers of motor vehicles
(1)   This section applies where a motor vehicle has been bailed or (in Scotland) hired under a hire-purchase agreement, or has been agreed to be sold under a conditional sale agreement, and, before the property in the vehicle has become vested in the debtor, he disposes of the vehicle to another person.
(2)   Where the disposition referred to in subsection (1) above is to a private purchaser, and he is a purchaser of the motor vehicle in good faith, without notice of the hire-purchase or conditional sale agreement (the "relevant agreement") that disposition shall have effect as if the creditor's title to the vehicle has been vested in the debtor immediately before that disposition.
(3)   Where the person to whom the disposition referred to in subsection (1) above is made (the "original purchaser") is a trade or finance purchaser, then if the person who is the first private purchaser of the motor vehicle after that disposition (the "first private purchaser") is a purchaser of the vehicle in good faith without notice of the relevant agreement, the disposition of the vehicle to the first private purchaser shall have effect as if the title of the creditor to the vehicle had been vested in the debtor immediately before he disposed of it to the original purchaser.
(4)   Where, in a case within subsection (3) above—
  (a)   the disposition by which the first private purchaser becomes a purchaser of the motor vehicle in good faith without notice of the relevant agreement is itself a bailment or hiring under a hire-purchase agreement, and
  (b)   the person who is the creditor in relation to that agreement disposes of the vehicle to the first private purchaser, or a person claiming under him, by transferring to him the property in the vehicle in pursuance of a provision in the agreement in that behalf,
the disposition referred to in paragraph (b) above (whether or not the person to whom it is made is a purchaser in good faith without notice of the relevant agreement) shall as well as the disposition referred to in paragraph (a) above, have effect as mentioned in subsection (3) above.
(5)   The preceding provisions of this section apply—
  (a)   notwithstanding anything in [section 21 of the Sale of Goods Act 1979] (sale of goods by a person not the owner), but
  (b)   without prejudice to the provisions of the Factors Act (as defined by [section 61(1) of the said Act of 1979]) or of any other enactment enabling the apparent owner of goods to dispose of them as if he were the true owner.
(6)   Nothing in this section shall exonerate the debtor from any liability (whether criminal or civil) to which he would be subject apart from this section; and, in a case where the debtor disposes of the motor vehicle to a trade or finance purchaser, nothing in this section shall exonerate—

(a)   that trade or finance purchaser; or

(b)   any other trade or finance purchaser who becomes a purchaser of the vehicle and is not a person claiming under the first private purchaser,

from any liability (whether criminal or civil) to which he would be subject apart from this section.]

NOTES

Part III (ss 27–29) substituted by the Consumer Credit Act 1974, s 192(3)(a), Sch 4, para 22.

Sub-s (5): words in square brackets substituted by the Sale of Goods Act 1979, s 63, Sch 2, para 4.

[1.394]

[28   Presumptions relating to dealings with motor vehicles

(1)   Where in any proceedings (whether criminal or civil) relating to a motor vehicle it is proved—

(a)   that the vehicle was bailed or (in Scotland) hired under a hire-purchase agreement, or was agreed to be sold under a conditional sale agreement and

(b)   that a person (whether a party to the proceedings or not) became a private purchaser of the vehicle in good faith without notice of the hire-purchase or conditional sale agreement (the "relevant agreement"),

this section shall have effect for the purposes of the operation of section 27 of this Act in relation to those proceedings.

(2)   It shall be presumed for those purposes, unless the contrary is proved, that the disposition of the vehicle to the person referred to in subsection (1)(b) above (the "relevant purchaser") was made by the debtor.

(3)   If it is proved that that disposition was not made by the debtor, then it shall be presumed for those purposes, unless the contrary is proved—

(a)   that the debtor disposed of the vehicle to a private purchaser purchasing in good faith without notice of the relevant agreement, and

(b)   that the relevant purchaser is or was a person claiming under the person to whom the debtor so disposed of the vehicle.

(4)   If it is proved that the disposition of the vehicle to the relevant purchaser was not made by the debtor, and that the person to whom the debtor disposed of the vehicle (the "original purchaser") was a trade or finance purchaser, then it shall be presumed for those purposes, unless the contrary is proved,—

(a)   that the person who, after the disposition of the vehicle to the original purchaser, first became a private purchaser of the vehicle was a purchaser in good faith without notice of the relevant agreement, and

(b)   that the relevant purchaser is or was a person claiming under the original purchaser.

(5)   Without prejudice to any other method of proof, where in any proceedings a party thereto admits a fact, that fact shall, for the purposes of this section, be taken as against him to be proved in relation to those proceedings.]

NOTES

Substituted as noted to s 27 at **[1.393]**.

[1.395]

[29   Interpretation of Part III

(1)   In this Part of this Act—

"conditional sale agreement" means an agreement for the sale of goods under which the purchase price or part of it is payable by instalments, and the property in the goods is to remain in the seller (notwithstanding that the buyer is to be in possession of the goods) until such conditions as to the payment of instalments or otherwise as may be specified in the agreement are fulfilled;

"creditor" means the person by whom goods are bailed or (in Scotland) hired under a hire-purchase agreement or as the case may be, the seller under a conditional sale agreement, or the person to whom his rights and duties have passed by assignment or operation of law;

"disposition" means any sale or contract of sale (including a conditional sale agreement), any bailment or (in Scotland) hiring under a hire-purchase agreement and any transfer of the property in goods in pursuance of a provision in that behalf contained in a hire-purchase agreement, and includes, any transaction purporting to be a disposition (as so defined), and "dispose of" shall be construed accordingly;

"hire-purchase agreement" means an agreement, other than a conditional sale agreement, under which—

(a)   goods are bailed or (in Scotland) hired in return for periodical payments by the person to whom they are bailed or hired, and

(b)   the property in the goods will pass to that person if the terms of the agreement are complied with and one or more of the following occurs—

(i)   the exercise of an option to purchase by that person,

(ii)   the doing of any other specified act by any party to the agreement,

(iii)   the happening of any other specified events; and

"motor vehicle" means a mechanically propelled vehicle intended or adapted for use on roads to which the public has access.

(2)   In this Part of this Act, "trade or finance purchaser" means a purchaser who, at the time of the disposition made to him, carries on a business which consists, wholly or partly,—

(a)   of purchasing motor vehicles for the purpose of offering or exposing them for sale, or

(b)   of providing finance by purchasing motor vehicles for the purpose of bailing or (in Scotland) hiring them under hire-purchase agreements or agreeing to sell them under conditional sale agreements,

and "private purchaser" means a purchaser who, at the time of the disposition made to him, does not carry on any such business.

(3)   For the purposes of this Part of this Act a person becomes a purchaser of a motor vehicle if, and at the time when, a disposition of the vehicle is made to him; and a person shall be taken to be a purchaser of a motor vehicle without notice of a hire-purchase agreement or conditional sale agreement if, at the time of the disposition made to him, he has no actual notice that the vehicle is or was the subject of any such agreement.

(4)   In this Part of this Act the "debtor" in relation to a motor vehicle which has been bailed or hired under a hire-purchase agreement, or, as the case may be, agreed to be sold under a conditional sale agreement, means the person who at the material time (whether the agreement has before that time been terminated or not) is either—

(a)   the person to whom the vehicle is bailed or hired under that agreement, or

(b)   is, in relation to the agreement, the buyer, including a person who at the time is, by virtue of section 130(4) of the Consumer Credit Act 1974 treated as a bailee or (in Scotland) a custodier of the vehicle.

(5)   In this Part of this Act any reference to the title of the creditor to a motor vehicle which has been bailed or (in Scotland) hired under a hire-purchase agreement, or agreed to be sold under a conditional sale agreement, and is disposed of by the debtor, is a reference to such title (if any) to the vehicle as, immediately before that disposition, was vested in the person who then was the creditor in relation to the agreement.]

NOTES

Substituted as noted to s 27 at **[1.393]**.

30–32   ((*Pt IV*) *repealed by the Advertisements (Hire-Purchase) Act 1967, s 8(2), Sch 2.*)

PART V
SUPPLEMENTARY PROVISIONS

33–36   (*S 33 repealed by the Hire-Purchase Act 1965, s 59, Sch 6; ss 34–36 repealed by the Consumer Credit Act 1974, s 192(3)(b), Sch 5.*)

[1.396]
37   Short title, citation and extent
(1)   This Act may be cited as the Hire-Purchase Act 1964.
(2)–(4)   . . .
(5)   This Act shall not extend to Northern Ireland.

NOTES

Sub-s (2): repealed by the Hire-Purchase Act 1965, s 59, Sch 6.
Sub-s (3): repealed by the Hire-Purchase (Scotland) Act 1965, s 55, Sch 6.
Sub-s (4): repealed by the Hire-Purchase Act 1965, s 55, Sch 6, and the Hire-Purchase (Scotland) Act 1965, s 55, Sch 6.

SCHEDULES

SCHEDULES 1–7

(*Schs 1, 4 (in part), 5, 6, repealed by the Hire-Purchase Act 1965, s 55, Sch 6; Schs 2, 3, 7 repealed by the Hire-Purchase (Scotland) Act 1965, s 55, Sch 6; Schs 3, 4 (remainder) repealed by the Advertisements (Hire-Purchase) Act 1967, s 8(2), Sch 2.*)

CARRIAGE OF GOODS BY ROAD ACT 1965

(1965 c 37)

ARRANGEMENT OF SECTIONS

An Act to give effect to the Convention on the Contract for the International Carriage of Goods by Road signed at Geneva on 19th May 1956; and for purposes connected therewith

[5 August 1965]

[1.397]
1   Convention to have force of law
Subject to the following provisions of this Act, the provisions of the Convention on the Contract for the International Carriage of Goods by Road (in this Act referred to as "the Convention"), as set out in the Schedule to this Act, shall have the force of law in the United Kingdom so far as they relate to the rights and liabilities of persons concerned in the carriage of goods by road under a contract to which the Convention applies.

NOTES
   Convention on the Contract for the International Carriage of Goods by Road: signed at Geneva on 19 May 1956; see Cmnd 2260.

[1.398]
2   Designation of High Contracting Parties
(1)   Her Majesty may by Order in Council from time to time certify who are the High Contracting Parties to the Convention and in respect of what territories they are respectively parties.
(2)   An Order in Council under this section shall, except so far as it has been superseded by a subsequent Order, be conclusive evidence of the matters so certified.

NOTES
   Orders in Council: the Carriage of Goods by Road (Parties to Convention) Order 1967, SI 1967/1683; the Carriage of Goods by Road (Parties to Convention) (Amendment) Order 1980, SI 1980/697.

[1.399]
3   Power of court to take account of other proceedings
(1)   A court before which proceedings are brought to enforce a liability which is limited by article 23 in the Schedule to this Act may at any stage of the proceedings make any such order as appears to the court to be just and equitable in view of the provisions of the said article 23 and of any other proceedings which have been, or are likely to be, commenced in the United Kingdom or elsewhere to enforce the liability in whole or in part.
(2)   Without prejudice to the preceding subsection, a court before which proceedings are brought to enforce a liability which is limited by the said article 23 shall, where the liability is, or may be, partly enforceable in other proceedings in the United Kingdom or elsewhere, have jurisdiction to award an amount less than the court would have awarded if the limitation applied solely to the proceedings before the court, or to make any part of its award conditional on the result of any other proceedings.

[1.400]
4   Registration of foreign judgments
(1)   Subject to the next following subsection, Part I of the Foreign Judgments (Reciprocal Enforcement) Act 1933 (in this section referred to as "the Act of 1933") shall apply, whether or not it would otherwise have so applied, to any judgment which—
   (a)   has been given in any such action as is referred to in paragraph 1 of article 31 in the Schedule to this Act, and
   (b)   has been so given by any court or tribunal of a territory in respect of which one of the High Contracting Parties, other than the United Kingdom, is a party to the Convention, and
   (c)   has become enforceable in that territory.
(2)   In the application of Part I of the Act of 1933 in relation to any such judgment as is referred to in the preceding subsection, section 4 of that Act shall have effect with the omission of subsections (2) and (3).

(3) The registration, in accordance with Part I of the Act of 1933, of any such judgment as is referred to in subsection (1) of this section shall constitute, in relation to that judgment, compliance with the formalities for the purposes of paragraph 3 of article 31 in the Schedule to this Act.

[1.401]
5 Contribution between carriers
(1) Where a carrier under a contract to which the Convention applies is liable in respect of any loss or damage for which compensation is payable under the Convention, nothing in [section 1 of the Civil Liability (Contribution) Act 1978], or section 3(2) of the Law Reform (Miscellaneous Provisions) (Scotland) Act 1940 shall confer on him any right to recover contribution in respect of that loss or damage from any other carrier who, in accordance with article 34 in the Schedule to this Act, is a party to the contract of carriage.
(2) The preceding subsection shall be without prejudice to the operation of article 37 in the Schedule to this Act.

NOTES
Sub-s (1): words in square brackets substituted by the Civil Liability (Contribution) Act 1978, s 9(1), Sch 1, para 7.

[1.402]
6 Actions against High Contracting Parties
Every High Contracting Party to the Convention shall, for the purposes of any proceedings brought in a court in the United Kingdom in accordance with the provisions of article 31 in the Schedule to this Act to enforce a claim in respect of carriage undertaken by that Party, be deemed to have submitted to the jurisdiction of that court, and accordingly rules of court may provide for the manner in which any such action is to be commenced and carried on; but nothing in this section shall authorise the issue of execution, or in Scotland the execution of diligence, against the property of any High Contracting Party.

[1.403]
7 Arbitrations
(1) Any reference in the preceding provisions of this Act to a court includes a reference to an arbitration tribunal acting by virtue of article 33 in the Schedule to this Act.
(2) For the purposes of article 32 in the Schedule to this Act, as it has effect (by virtue of the said article 33) in relation to arbitrations,—
    [(a) as respects England and Wales and Northern Ireland, the provisions of section 14(3) to (5) of the Arbitration Act 1996 (which determine the time at which an arbitration is commenced) apply;]
    (c) *(applies to Scotland only.)*

NOTES
Sub-s (2): para (a) substituted, for original paras (a), (b), by the Arbitration Act 1996, s 107, Sch 3, para 21, Sch 4.

[1.404]
8 Resolution of conflicts between Conventions on carriage of goods
(1) If it appears to Her Majesty in Council that there is any conflict between the provisions of this Act (including the provisions of the Convention as set out in the Schedule to this Act) and any provisions relating to the carriage of goods for reward by land, sea or air contained in—
    (a) any other Convention which has been signed or ratified by or on behalf of Her Majesty's Government in the United Kingdom before the passing of this Act, or
    (b) any enactment of the Parliament of the United Kingdom giving effect to such a Convention,
Her Majesty may by Order in Council make such provision as may seem to Her to be appropriate for resolving that conflict by amending or modifying this Act or any such enactment.
(2) Any statutory instrument made by virtue of this section shall be subject to annulment in pursuance of a resolution of either House of Parliament.

[1.405]
[8A Amendments consequential on revision of Convention
(1) If at any time it appears to Her Majesty in Council that Her Majesty's Government in the United Kingdom have agreed to any revision of the Convention, Her Majesty may by Order in Council make such amendment of—
    [(a) this Act; and]
    (c) section 5(1) of the Carriage by Air and Road Act 1979,
as appear to Her to be appropriate in consequence of the revision.
(2) In the preceding subsection "revision" means an omission from, addition to or alteration of the Convention and includes replacement of the Convention or part of it by another convention.
(3) An Order in Council under this section shall not be made unless a draft of the Order has been laid before Parliament and approved by a resolution of each House of Parliament.]

NOTES

Inserted by the Carriage by Air and Road Act 1979, s 3(3).

Sub-s (1): para (a) substituted, for original paras (a), (b), by the International Transport Conventions Act 1983, s 9, Sch 2, para 2.

[1.406]
9   Application to British possessions, etc

Her Majesty may by Order in Council direct that this Act shall extend, subject to such exceptions, adaptations and modifications as may be specified in the Order, to—

(a)   the Isle of Man;

(b)   any of the Channel Islands;

(c)   any colony;

(d)   . . .

NOTES

Para (d) repealed by the Statute Law (Repeals) Act 1993.

Orders in Council: the Carriage of Goods by Road (Gibraltar) Order 1967, SI 1967/820; the Carriage of Goods by Road (Gibraltar) (Amendment) Order 1981, SI 1981/604; the Carriage of Goods by Road (Isle of Man) Order 1981, SI 1981/1543; the Carriage of Goods by Road (Guernsey) Order 1986, SI 1986/1882.

10, 11   (*S 10 applies to Scotland only; s 11 applies to Northern Ireland only.*)

[1.407]
12   Orders in Council

An Order in Council made under any of the preceding provisions of this Act may contain such transitional and supplementary provisions as appear to Her Majesty to be expedient and may be varied or revoked by a subsequent Order in Council made under that provision.

[1.408]
13   Application to Crown

This Act shall bind the Crown.

[1.409]
14   Short title, interpretation and commencement

(1)   This Act may be cited as the Carriage of Goods by Road Act 1965.

(2)   The persons who, for the purposes of this Act, are persons concerned in the carriage of goods by road under a contract to which the Convention applies are—

(a)   the sender,

(b)   the consignee,

(c)   any carrier who, in accordance with article 34 in the Schedule to this Act or otherwise, is a party to the contract of carriage,

(d)   any person for whom such a carrier is responsible by virtue of article 3 in the Schedule to this Act,

(e)   any person to whom the rights and liabilities of any of the persons referred to in paragraphs (a) to (d) to this subsection have passed (whether by assignment or assignation or by operation of law).

(3)   Except in so far as the context otherwise requires, any reference in this Act to an enactment shall be construed as a reference to that enactment as amended or extended by or under any other enactment.

(4)   This Act shall come into operation on such day as Her Majesty may by Order in Council appoint; but nothing in this Act shall apply in relation to any contract or the carriage of goods by road made before the day so appointed.

NOTES

Orders in Council: the Carriage of Goods by Road Act 1965 (Commencement) Order 1967, SI 1967/819.

SCHEDULE
CONVENTION ON THE CONTRACT FOR THE INTERNATIONAL CARRIAGE OF GOODS BY ROAD

Section 1

CHAPTER I
SCOPE OF APPLICATION

Article 1

[1.410]
1. This Convention shall apply to every contract for the carriage of goods by road in vehicles for reward, when the place of taking over of the goods and the place designated for delivery, as specified in the contract, are situated in two different countries, of which at least one is a Contracting country, irrespective of the place of residence and the nationality of the parties.

2. For the purposes of this Convention, "vehicles" means motor vehicles, articulated vehicles, trailers and semi-trailers as defined in article 4 of the Convention on Road Traffic dated 19th September 1949.

3. This Convention shall apply also where carriage coming within its scope is carried out by States or by governmental institutions or organizations.

4. This Convention shall not apply:
   (a)   to carriage performed under the terms of any international postal convention;
   (b)   to funeral consignments;
   (c)   to furniture removal.

5. The Contracting Parties agree not to vary any of the provisions of this Convention by special agreements between two or more of them, except to make it inapplicable to their frontier traffic or to authorise the use in transport operations entirely confined to their territory of consignment notes representing a title to the goods.

Article 2

1. Where the vehicle containing the goods is carried over part of the journey by sea, rail, inland waterways or air, and, except where the provisions of article 14 are applicable, the goods are not unloaded from the vehicle, this Convention shall nevertheless apply to the whole of the carriage. Provided that to the extent that it is proved that any loss, damage or delay in delivery of the goods which occurs during the carriage by the other means of transport was not caused by an act or omission of the carrier by road, but by some event which could only have occurred in the course of and by reason of the carriage by that other means of transport, the liability of the carrier by road shall be determined not by this Convention but in the manner in which the liability of the carrier by the other means of transport would have been determined if a contract for the carriage of the goods alone had been made by the sender with the carrier by the other means of transport in accordance with the conditions prescribed by law for the carriage of goods by that means of transport. If, however, there are no such prescribed conditions, the liability of the carrier by road shall be determined by this Convention.

2. If the carrier by road is also himself the carrier by the other means of transport, his liability shall also be determined in accordance with the provisions of paragraph 1 of this article, but as if, in his capacities as carrier by road and as carrier by the other means of transport, he were two separate persons.

CHAPTER II
PERSONS FOR WHOM THE CARRIER IS RESPONSIBLE

Article 3

For the purposes of this Convention the carrier shall be responsible for the acts and omissions of his agents and servants and of any other persons of whose services he makes use for the performance of the carriage, when such agents, servants or other persons are acting within the scope of their employment, as if such acts or omissions were his own.

CHAPTER III
CONCLUSION AND PERFORMANCE OF THE CONTRACT OF CARRIAGE

Article 4

The contract of carriage shall be confirmed by the making out of a consignment note. The absence, irregularity or loss of the consignment note shall not affect the existence or the validity of the contract of carriage which shall remain subject to the provisions of this Convention.

Article 5

1. The consignment note shall be made out in three original copies signed by the sender and by the carrier. These signatures may be printed or replaced by the stamps of the sender and the carrier if the law of the country in which the consignment note has been made out so permits. The first copy shall be handed to the sender, the second shall accompany the goods and the third shall be retained by the carrier.

2. When the goods which are to be carried have to be loaded in different vehicles, or are of different kinds or are divided into different lots, the sender or the carrier shall have the right to require a separate consignment note to be made out for each vehicle used, or for each kind or lot of goods.

Article 6

1. The consignment note shall contain the following particulars:
- (a) the date of the consignment note and the place at which it is made out;
- (b) the name and address of the sender;
- (c) the name and address of the carrier;
- (d) the place and the date of taking over of the goods and the place designated for delivery;
- (e) the name and address of the consignee;
- (f) the description in common use of the nature of the goods and the method of packing, and, in the case of dangerous goods, their generally recognised description;
- (g) the number of packages and their special marks and numbers;
- (h) the gross weight of the goods or their quantity otherwise expressed;
- (i) charges relating to the carriage (carriage charges, supplementary charges, customs duties and other charges incurred from the making of the contract to the time of delivery);
- (j) the requisite instructions for Customs and other formalities;
- (k) a statement that the carriage is subject, notwithstanding any clause to the contrary, to the provisions of this Convention.

2. Where applicable, the consignment note shall also contain the following particulars:
- (a) a statement that transhipment is not allowed;
- (b) the charges which the sender undertakes to pay;
- (c) the amount of "cash on delivery" charges;
- (d) a declaration of the value of the goods and the amount representing special interest in delivery;
- (e) the sender's instructions to the carrier regarding insurance of the goods;
- (f) the agreed time-limit within which the carriage is to be carried out;
- (g) a list of the documents handed to the carrier.

3. The parties may enter in the consignment note any other particulars which they may deem useful.

Article 7

1. The sender shall be responsible for all expenses, loss and damage sustained by the carrier by reason of the inaccuracy or inadequacy of:
- (a) the particulars specified in article 6, paragraph 1(b), (d), (e), (f), (g), (h) and (j);
- (b) the particulars specified in article 6, paragraph 2;
- (c) any other particulars or instructions given by him to enable the consignment note to be made out or for the purpose of their being entered therein.

2. If, at the request of the sender, the carrier enters in the consignment note the particulars referred to in paragraph 1 of this article, he shall be deemed, unless the contrary is proved, to have done so on behalf of the sender.

3. If the consignment note does not contain the statement specified in article 6, paragraph 1(k), the carrier shall be liable for all expenses, loss and damage sustained through such omission by the person entitled to dispose of the goods.

Article 8

1. On taking over the goods, the carrier shall check:
  (a) the accuracy of the statements in the consignment note as to the number of packages and their marks and numbers, and
  (b) the apparent condition of the goods and their packaging.

2. Where the carrier has no reasonable means of checking the accuracy of the statements referred to in paragraph 1(a) of this article, he shall enter his reservations in the consignment note together with the grounds on which they are based. He shall likewise specify the grounds for any reservations which he makes with regard to the apparent condition of the goods and their packaging. Such reservations shall not bind the sender unless he has expressly agreed to be bound by them in the consignment note.

3. The sender shall be entitled to require the carrier to check the gross weight of the goods or their quantity otherwise expressed. He may also require the contents of the packages to be checked. The carrier shall be entitled to claim the cost of such checking. The result of the checks shall be entered in the consignment note.

Article 9

1. The consignment note shall be *prima facie* evidence of the making of the contract of carriage, the conditions of the contract and the receipt of the goods by the carrier.

2. If the consignment note contains no specific reservations by the carrier, it shall be presumed, unless the contrary is proved, that the goods and their packaging appeared to be in good condition when the carrier took them over and that the number of packages, their marks and numbers corresponded with the statements in the consignment note.

Article 10

The sender shall be liable to the carrier for damage to persons, equipment or other goods, and for any expenses due to defective packing of the goods, unless the defect was apparent or known to the carrier at the time when he took over the goods and he made no reservations concerning it.

Article 11

1. For the purposes of the Customs or other formalities which have to be completed before delivery of the goods, the sender shall attach the necessary documents to the consignment note or place them at the disposal of the carrier and shall furnish him with all the information which he requires.

2. The carrier shall not be under any duty to enquire into either the accuracy or the adequacy of such documents and information. The sender shall be liable to the carrier for any damage caused by the absence, inadequacy or irregularity of such documents and information, except in the case of some wrongful act or neglect on the part of the carrier.

3. The liability of the carrier for the consequences arising from the loss or incorrect use of the documents specified in and accompanying the consignment note or deposited with the carrier shall be that of an agent, provided that the compensation payable by the carrier shall not exceed that payable in the event of loss of the goods.

Article 12

1. The sender has the right to dispose of the goods, in particular by asking the carrier to stop the goods in transit, to change the place at which delivery is to take place or to deliver the goods to a consignee other than the consignee indicated in the consignment note.

2. This right shall cease to exist when the second copy of the consignment note is handed to the consignee or when the consignee exercises his right under article 13, paragraph 1; from that time onwards the carrier shall obey the orders of the consignee.

3. The consignee shall, however, have the right of disposal from the time when the consignment note is drawn up, if the sender makes an entry to that effect in the consignment note.

4. If in exercising his right of disposal the consignee has ordered the delivery of the goods to another person, that other person shall not be entitled to name other consignees.

5. The exercise of the right of disposal shall be subject to the following conditions:
  (a) that the sender or, in the case referred to in paragraph 3 of this article, the consignee who wishes to exercise the right produces the first copy of the consignment note on which the new instructions to the carrier have been entered and indemnifies the carrier against all expenses, loss and damage involved in carrying out such instructions;

(b)   that the carrying out of such instructions is possible at the time when the instructions reach the person who is to carry them out and does not either interfere with the normal working of the carrier's undertaking or prejudice the senders or consignees of other consignments;

(c)   that the instructions do not result in a division of the consignment.

6. When, by reason of the provisions of paragraph 5(b) of this article, the carrier cannot carry out the instructions which he receives, he shall immediately notify the person who gave him such instructions.

7. A carrier who has not carried out the instructions given under the conditions provided for in this article, or who has carried them out without requiring the first copy of the consignment note to be produced, shall be liable to the person entitled to make a claim for any loss or damage caused thereby.

Article 13

1. After arrival of the goods at the place designated for delivery, the consignee shall be entitled to require the carrier to deliver to him, against a receipt, the second copy of the consignment note and the goods. If the loss of the goods is established or if the goods have not arrived after the expiry of the period provided for in article 19, the consignee shall be entitled to enforce in his own name against the carrier any rights arising from the contract of carriage.

2. The consignee who avails himself of the rights granted to him under paragraph 1 of this article shall pay the charges shown to be due on the consignment note, but in the event of dispute on this matter the carrier shall not be required to deliver the goods unless security has been furnished by the consignee.

Article 14

1. If for any reason it is or becomes impossible to carry out the contract in accordance with the terms laid down in the consignment note before the goods reach the place designated for delivery, the carrier shall ask for instructions from the person entitled to dispose of the goods in accordance with the provisions of article 12.

2. Nevertheless, if circumstances are such as to allow the carriage to be carried out under conditions differing from those laid down in the consignment note and if the carrier has been unable to obtain instructions in reasonable time from the person entitled to dispose of the goods in accordance with the provisions of article 12, he shall take such steps as seem to him to be in the best interests of the person entitled to dispose of the goods.

Article 15

1. Where circumstances prevent delivery of the goods after their arrival at the place designated for delivery, the carrier shall ask the sender for his instructions. If the consignee refuses the goods the sender shall be entitled to dispose of them without being obliged to produce the first copy of the consignment note.

2. Even if he has refused the goods, the consignee may nevertheless require delivery so long as the carrier has not received instructions to the contrary from the sender.

3. When circumstances preventing delivery of the goods arise after the consignee, in exercise of his rights under article 12, paragraph 3, has given an order for the goods to be delivered to another person, paragraphs 1 and 2 of this article shall apply as if the consignee were the sender and that other person were the consignee.

Article 16

1. The carrier shall be entitled to recover the cost of his request for instructions, and any expenses entailed in carrying out such instructions, unless such expenses were caused by the wrongful act or neglect of the carrier.

2. In the cases referred to in article 14, paragraph 1, and in article 15, the carrier may immediately unload the goods for account of the person entitled to dispose of them and thereupon the carriage shall be deemed to be at an end. The carrier shall then hold the goods on behalf of the person so entitled. He may however entrust them to a third party, and in that case he shall not be under any liability except for the exercise of reasonable care in the choice of such third party. The charges due under the consignment note and all other expenses shall remain chargeable against the goods.

3. The carrier may sell the goods, without awaiting instructions from the person entitled to dispose of them, if the goods are perishable or their condition warrants such a course, or when the storage expenses would be out of proportion to the value of the goods. He may also proceed to the sale of the goods in other cases if after the expiry of a reasonable period he has not received from the person entitled to dispose of the goods instructions to the contrary which he may reasonably be required to carry out.

4. If the goods have been sold pursuant to this article, the proceeds of sale, after deduction of the expenses chargeable against the goods, shall be placed at the disposal of the person entitled to dispose of the goods. If these charges exceed the proceeds of sale, the carrier shall be entitled to the difference.

5. The procedure in the case of sale shall be determined by the law or custom of the place where the goods are situated.

CHAPTER IV
LIABILITY OF THE CARRIER

Article 17

1. The carrier shall be liable for the total or partial loss of the goods and for damage thereto occurring between the time when he takes over the goods and the time of delivery, as well as for any delay in delivery.

2. The carrier shall however be relieved of liability if the loss, damage or delay was caused by the wrongful act or neglect of the claimant, by the instructions of the claimant given otherwise than as the result of a wrongful act or neglect on the part of the carrier, by inherent vice of the goods or through circumstances which the carrier could not avoid and the consequences of which he was unable to prevent.

3. The carrier shall not be relieved of liability by reason of the defective condition of the vehicle used by him in order to perform the carriage, or by reason of the wrongful act or neglect of the person from whom he may have hired the vehicle or of the agents or servants of the latter.

4. Subject to article 18, paragraphs 2 to 5, the carrier shall be relieved of liability when the loss or damage arises from the special risks inherent in one or more of the following circumstances:

- (a) use of open unsheeted vehicles, when their use has been expressly agreed and specified in the consignment note;
- (b) the lack of, or defective condition of packing in the case of goods which, by their nature, are liable to wastage or to be damaged when not packed or when not properly packed;
- (c) handling, loading, stowage or unloading of the goods by the sender, the consignee or persons acting on behalf of the sender or the consignee;
- (d) the nature of certain kinds of goods which particularly exposes them to total or partial loss or to damage, especially through breakage, rust, decay, desiccation, leakage, normal wastage, or the action of moth or vermin;
- (e) insufficiency or inadequacy of marks or numbers on the packages;
- (f) the carriage of livestock.

5. Where under this article the carrier is not under any liability in respect of some of the factors causing the loss, damage or delay, he shall only be liable to the extent that those factors for which he is liable under this article have contributed to the loss, damage or delay.

Article 18

1. The burden of proving that loss, damage or delay was due to one of the causes specified in article 17, paragraph 2, shall rest upon the carrier.

2. When the carrier establishes that in the circumstances of the case, the loss or damage could be attributed to one or more of the special risks referred to in article 17, paragraph 4, it shall be presumed that it was so caused. The claimant shall however be entitled to prove that the loss or damage was not, in fact, attributable either wholly or partly to one of these risks.

3. This presumption shall not apply in the circumstances set out in article 17, paragraph 4(a), if there has been an abnormal shortage, or a loss of any package.

4. If the carriage is performed in vehicles specially equipped to protect the goods from the effects of heat, cold, variations in temperature or the humidity of the air, the carrier shall not be entitled to claim the benefit of article 17, paragraph 4(d), unless he proves that all steps incumbent on him in the circumstances with respect to the choice, maintenance and use of such equipment were taken and that he complied with any special instructions issued to him.

5. The carrier shall not be entitled to claim the benefit of article 17, paragraph 4(f), unless he proves that all steps normally incumbent on him in the circumstances were taken and that he complied with any special instructions issued to him.

Article 19

Delay in delivery shall be said to occur when the goods have not been delivered within the agreed time-limit or when, failing an agreed time-limit, the actual duration of the carriage having regard to the circumstances of the case, and in particular, in the case of partial loads, the time required for making up a complete load in the normal way, exceeds the time it would be reasonable to allow a diligent carrier.

Article 20

1. The fact that goods have not been delivered within thirty days following the expiry of the agreed time-limit, or, if there is no agreed time-limit, within sixty days from the time when the carrier took over the goods, shall be conclusive evidence of the loss of the goods, and the person entitled to make a claim may thereupon treat them as lost.

2. The person so entitled may, on receipt of compensation for the missing goods, request in writing that he shall be notified immediately should the goods be recovered in the course of the year following the payment of compensation. He shall be given a written acknowledgment of such request.

3. Within the thirty days following receipt of such notification, the person entitled as aforesaid may require the goods to be delivered to him against payment of the charges shown to be due on the consignment note and also against refund of the compensation he received less any charges included therein but without prejudice to any claims to compensation for delay in delivery under article 23 and, where applicable, article 26.

4. In the absence of the request mentioned in paragraph 2 or of any instructions given within the period of thirty days specified in paragraph 3, or if the goods are not recovered until more than one year after the payment of compensation, the carrier shall be entitled to deal with them in accordance with the law of the place where the goods are situated.

Article 21

Should the goods have been delivered to the consignee without collection of the "cash on delivery" charge which should have been collected by the carrier under the terms of the contract of carriage, the carrier shall be liable to the sender for compensation not exceeding the amount of such charge without prejudice to his right of action against the consignee.

Article 22

1. When the sender hands goods of a dangerous nature to the carrier, he shall inform the carrier of the exact nature of the danger and indicate, if necessary, the precautions to be taken. If this information has not been entered in the consignment note, the burden of proving, by some other means, that the carrier knew the exact nature of the danger constituted by the carriage of the said goods shall rest upon the sender or the consignee.

2. Goods of a dangerous nature which, in the circumstances referred to in paragraph 1 of this article, the carrier did not know were dangerous, may, at any time or place, be unloaded, destroyed or rendered harmless by the carrier without compensation; further, the sender shall be liable for all expenses, loss or damage arising out of their handing over for carriage or of their carriage.

Article 23

1. When, under the provisions of this Convention, a carrier is liable for compensation in respect of total or partial loss of goods, such compensation shall be calculated by reference to the value of the goods at the place and time at which they were accepted for carriage.

2. The value of the goods shall be fixed according to the commodity exchange price or, if there is no such price, according to the current market price or, if there is no commodity exchange price or current market price, by reference to the normal value of goods of the same kind and quality.

[3. Compensation shall not, however, exceed 8.33 units of account per kilogram of gross weight short.]

4. In addition, the carriage charges, Customs duties and other charges incurred in respect of the carriage of the goods shall be refunded in full in case of total loss and in proportion to the loss sustained in case of partial loss, but no further damages shall be payable.

5. In the case of delay, if the claimant proves that damage has resulted therefrom the carrier shall pay compensation for such damage not exceeding the carriage charges.

6. Higher compensation may only be claimed where the value of the goods or a special interest in delivery has been declared in accordance with articles 24 and 26.

[**7.** The unit of account mentioned in this Convention is the Special Drawing Right as defined by the International Monetary Fund. The amount mentioned in paragraph 3 of this article shall be converted into the national currency of the State of the Court seised of the case on the basis of the value of that currency on the date of the judgment or the date agreed upon by the Parties.]

Article 24

The sender may, against payment of a surcharge to be agreed upon, declare in the consignment note a value for the goods exceeding the limit laid down in article 23, paragraph 3, and in that case the amount of the declared value shall be substituted for that limit.

Article 25

1. In case of damage, the carrier shall be liable for the amount by which the goods have diminished in value, calculated by reference to the value of the goods fixed in accordance with article 23, paragraphs 1, 2 and 4.

2. The compensation may not, however, exceed:
  (a)   if the whole consignment has been damaged, the amount payable in the case of total loss;
  (b)   if part only of the consignment has been damaged, the amount payable in the case of loss of the part affected.

Article 26

1. The sender may, against payment of a surcharge to be agreed upon, fix the amount of a special interest in delivery in the case of loss or damage or of the agreed time-limit being exceeded, by entering such amount in the consignment note.

2. If a declaration of a special interest in delivery has been made, compensation for the additional loss or damage proved may be claimed, up to the total amount of the interest declared, independently of the compensation provided for in articles 23, 24 and 25.

Article 27

1. The claimant shall be entitled to claim interest on compensation payable. Such interest, calculated at five per centum per annum, shall accrue from the date on which the claim was sent in writing to the carrier or, if no such claim has been made, from the date on which legal proceedings were instituted.

2. When the amounts on which the calculation of the compensation is based are not expressed in the currency of the country in which payment is claimed, conversion shall be at the rate of exchange applicable on the day and at the place of payment of compensation.

Article 28

1. In cases where, under the law applicable, loss, damage or delay arising out of carriage under this Convention gives rise to an extra-contractual claim, the carrier may avail himself of the provisions of this Convention which exclude his liability or which fix or limit the compensation due.

2. In cases where the extra-contractual liability for loss, damage or delay of one of the persons for whom the carrier is responsible under the terms of article 3 is in issue, such person may also avail himself of the provisions of this Convention which exclude the liability of the carrier or which fix or limit the compensation due.

Article 29

1. The carrier shall not be entitled to avail himself of the provisions of this chapter which exclude or limit his liability or which shift the burden of proof if the damage was caused by his wilful misconduct or by such default on his part as, in accordance with the law of the court or tribunal seised of the case, is considered as equivalent to wilful misconduct.

2. The same provision shall apply if the wilful misconduct or default is committed by the agents or servants of the carrier or by any other persons of whose services he makes use for the performance of the carriage, when such agents, servants or other persons are acting within the scope of their employment. Furthermore, in such a case such agents, servants or other persons shall not be entitled to avail themselves, with regard to their personal liability, of the provisions of this chapter referred to in paragraph 1.

CHAPTER V
CLAIMS AND ACTIONS

Article 30

1. If the consignee takes delivery of the goods without duly checking their condition with the carrier or without sending him reservations giving a general indication of the loss or damage, not later than the time of delivery in the case of apparent loss or damage and within seven days of delivery, Sundays and public holidays excepted, in the case of loss or damage which is not apparent, the fact of his taking delivery shall be *prima facie* evidence that he has received the goods in the condition described in the consignment note. In the case of loss or damage which is not apparent the reservations referred to shall be made in writing.

2. When the condition of the goods has been duly checked by the consignee and the carrier, evidence contradicting the result of this checking shall only be admissible in the case of loss or damage which is not apparent and provided that the consignee has duly sent reservations in writing to the carrier within seven days, Sundays and public holidays excepted, from the date of checking.

3. No compensation shall be payable for delay in delivery unless a reservation has been sent in writing to the carrier, within twenty-one days from the time that the goods were placed at the disposal of the consignee.

4. In calculating the time-limits provided for in this Article the date of delivery, or the date of checking, or the date when the goods were placed at the disposal of the consignee, as the case may be, shall not be included.

5. The carrier and the consignee shall give each other every reasonable facility for making the requisite investigations and checks.

Article 31

1. In legal proceedings arising out of carriage under this Convention, the plaintiff may bring an action in any court or tribunal of a contracting country designated by agreement between the parties and, in addition, in the courts or tribunals of a country within whose territory
  (a)   the defendant is ordinarily resident, or has his principal place of business, or the branch or agency through which the contract of carriage was made, or
  (b)   the place where the goods were taken over by the carrier or the place designated for delivery is situated,
and in no other courts or tribunals.

2. Where in respect of a claim referred to in paragraph 1 of this article an action is pending before a court or tribunal competent under that paragraph, or where in respect of such a claim a judgment has been entered by such a court or tribunal no new action shall be started between the same parties on the same grounds unless the judgment of the court or tribunal before which the first action was brought is not enforceable in the country in which the fresh proceedings are brought.

3. When a judgment entered by a court or tribunal of a contracting country in any such action as is referred to in paragraph 1 of this article has become enforceable in that country, it shall also become enforceable in each of the other contracting States, as soon as the formalities required in the country concerned have been complied with. The formalities shall not permit the merits of the case to be re-opened.

4. The provisions of paragraph 3 of this article shall apply to judgments after trial, judgments by default and settlements confirmed by an order of the court, but shall not apply to interim judgments or to awards of damages, in addition to costs against a plaintiff who wholly or partly fails in his action.

5. Security for costs shall not be required in proceedings arising out of carriage under this Convention from nationals of contracting countries resident or having their place of business in one of those countries.

Article 32

1. The period of limitation for an action arising out of carriage under this Convention shall be one year. Nevertheless, in the case of wilful misconduct, or such default as in accordance with the law of the court or tribunal seised of the case, is considered as equivalent to wilful misconduct, the period of limitation shall be three years. The period of limitation shall begin to run:
   (a)   in the case of partial loss, damage or delay in delivery, from the date of delivery;
   (b)   in the case of total loss, from the thirtieth day after the expiry of the agreed time-limit or where there is no agreed time-limit from the sixtieth day from the date on which the goods were taken over by the carrier;
   (c)   in all other cases, on the expiry of a period of three months after the making of the contract of carriage.
   The day on which the period of limitation begins to run shall not be included in the period.

2. A written claim shall suspend the period of limitation until such date as the carrier rejects the claim by notification in writing and returns the documents attached thereto. If a part of the claim is admitted the period of limitation shall start to run again only in respect of that part of the claim still in dispute. The burden of proof of the receipt of the claim, or of the reply and of the return of the documents, shall rest with the party relying upon these facts. The running of the period of limitation shall not be suspended by further claims having the same object.

3. Subject to the provisions of paragraph 2 above, the extension of the period of limitation shall be governed by the law of the court or tribunal seised of the case. That law shall also govern the fresh accrual of rights of action.

4. A right of action which has become barred by lapse of time may not be exercised by way of counter-claim or set-off.

Article 33

The contract of carriage may contain a clause conferring competence on an arbitration tribunal if the clause conferring competence on the tribunal provides that the tribunal shall apply this Convention.

CHAPTER VI
PROVISIONS RELATING TO CARRIAGE PERFORMED BY SUCCESSIVE CARRIERS

Article 34

If carriage governed by a single contract is performed by successive road carriers, each of them shall be responsible for the performance of the whole operation, the second carrier and each succeeding carrier becoming a party to the contract of carriage, under the terms of the consignment note, by reason of his acceptance of the goods and the consignment note.

Article 35

1. A carrier accepting the goods from a previous carrier shall give the latter a dated and signed receipt. He shall enter his name and address on the second copy of the consignment note. Where applicable, he shall enter on the second copy of the consignment note and on the receipt reservations of the kind provided for in article 8, paragraph 2.

2. The provisions of article 9 shall apply to the relations between successive carriers.

Article 36

Except in the case of a counter-claim or a set-off raised in an action concerning a claim based on the same contract of carriage, legal proceedings in respect of liability for loss, damage or delay may only be brought against the first carrier, the last carrier or the carrier who was performing that portion of the carriage during which the event causing the loss, damage or delay occurred; an action may be brought at the same time against several of these carriers.

Article 37

A carrier who has paid compensation in compliance with the provisions of this Convention, shall be entitled to recover such compensation, together with interest thereon and all costs and expenses incurred by reason of the claim, from the other carriers who have taken part in the carriage, subject to the following provisions:
   (a)   the carrier responsible for the loss or damage shall be solely liable for the compensation whether paid by himself or by another carrier;

(b)   when the loss or damage has been caused by the action of two or more carriers, each of them shall pay an amount proportionate to his share of liability; should it be impossible to apportion the liability, each carrier shall be liable in proportion to the share of the payment for the carriage which is due to him;

(c)   if it cannot be ascertained to which carriers liability is attributable for the loss or damage, the amount of the compensation shall be apportioned between all the carriers as laid down in (b) above.

Article 38

If one of the carriers is insolvent, the share of the compensation due from him and unpaid by him shall be divided among the other carriers in proportion to the share of the payment for the carriage due to them.

Article 39

1. No carrier against whom a claim is made under articles 37 and 38 shall be entitled to dispute the validity of the payment made by the carrier making the claim if the amount of the compensation was determined by judicial authority after the first mentioned carrier had been given due notice of the proceedings and afforded an opportunity of entering an appearance.

2. A carrier wishing to take proceedings to enforce his right of recovery may make his claim before the competent court or tribunal of the country in which one of the carriers concerned is ordinarily resident, or has his principal place of business or the branch or agency through which the contract of carriage was made. All the carriers concerned may be made defendants in the same action.

3. The provisions of article 31, paragraphs 3 and 4, shall apply to judgments entered in the proceedings referred to in articles 37 and 38.

4. The provisions of article 32 shall apply to claims between carriers. The period of limitation shall, however, begin to run either on the date of the final judicial decision fixing the amount of compensation payable under the provisions of this Convention, or, if there is no such judicial decision, from the actual date of payment.

Article 40

Carriers shall be free to agree among themselves on provisions other than those laid down in articles 37 and 38.

CHAPTER VII
NULLITY OF STIPULATIONS CONTRARY TO THE CONVENTION

Article 41

1. Subject to the provisions of Article 40, any stipulation which would directly or indirectly derogate from the provisions of this Convention shall be null and void. The nullity of such a stipulation shall not involve the nullity of the other provisions of the contract.

2. In particular, a benefit of insurance in favour of the carrier or any other similar clause, or any clause shifting the burden of proof shall be null and void.

[Chapter VIII of the Convention is not reproduced. This deals with the coming into force of the Convention, the settlement of disputes between the High Contracting Parties and related matters.]

PROTOCOL OF SIGNATURE

1. This Convention shall not apply to traffic between the United Kingdom of Great Britain and Northern Ireland and the Republic of Ireland.

NOTES

Article 23: para 3 substituted and para 7 added by the Carriage by Air and Road Act 1979, s 4(2).

ARBITRATION (INTERNATIONAL INVESTMENT DISPUTES) ACT 1966

(1966 c 41)

ARRANGEMENT OF SECTIONS

Enforcement of Convention Awards

An Act to implement an international Convention on the settlement of investment disputes between States and nationals of other States

[13 December 1966]

NOTES

Transfer of functions: functions under this Act, so far as exercisable in relation to Northern Ireland, are transferred to the Department of Justice, by the Northern Ireland Act 1998 (Devolution of Policing and Justice Functions) Order 2010, SI 2010/976, arts 15(1), 28–31, Sch 17, para 2.

Enforcement of Convention Awards

[1.411]
1 Registration of Convention awards
(1) This section has effect as respects awards rendered pursuant to the Convention on the settlement of investment disputes between States and nationals of other States which was opened for signature in Washington on 18th March 1965.

That Convention is in this Act called "the Convention", and its text is set out in the Schedule to this Act.
(2) A person seeking recognition or enforcement of such an award shall be entitled to have the award registered in the High Court subject to proof of the prescribed matters and to the other provisions of this Act.
(3) . . .
(4) In addition to the pecuniary obligations imposed by the award, the award shall be registered for the reasonable costs of and incidental to registration.
(5) If at the date of the application for registration the pecuniary obligations imposed by the award have been partly satisfied, the award shall be registered only in respect of the balance, and accordingly if those obligations have then been wholly satisfied, the award shall not be registered.
(6) The power to make rules of court under section [84 of the [Senior Courts Act 1981]] shall include power—
    (a) to prescribe the procedure for applying for registration under this section, and to require an applicant to give prior notice of his intention to other parties,
    (b) to prescribe the matters to be proved on the application and the manner of proof, and in particular to require the applicant to furnish a copy of the award certified pursuant to the Convention,
    (c) to provide for the service of notice of registration of the award by the applicant on other parties,
and in this and the next following section "prescribed" means prescribed by rules of court.
(7) For the purposes of this and the next following section—
    (a) "award" shall include any decision interpreting, revising or annulling an award, being a decision pursuant to the Convention, and any decision as to costs which under the Convention is to form part of the award,
    (b) an award shall be deemed to have been rendered pursuant to the Convention on the date on which certified copies of the award were pursuant to the Convention dispatched to the parties.

(8) This and the next following section shall bind the Crown (but not so as to make an award enforceable against the Crown in a manner in which a judgment would not be enforceable against the Crown).

NOTES

Sub-s (3): repealed by the Administration of Justice Act 1977, ss 4(1), (2), (4), 32(4), Sch 5, Pt I, except in relation to awards registered before 29 August 1977.

Sub-s (6): words in first (outer) pair of square brackets substituted by the Senior Courts Act 1981, s 152(1), Sch 5; words in second (inner) pair of square brackets substituted by the Constitutional Reform Act 2005, s 59(5), Sch 11, Pt 1, para 1(2).

[1.412]
2 Effect of registration
(1) Subject to the provisions of this Act, an award registered under section 1 above shall, as respects the pecuniary obligations which it imposes, be of the same force and effect for the purposes of execution as if it had been a judgment of the High Court given when the award was rendered pursuant to the Convention and entered on the date of registration under this Act, and, so far as relates to such pecuniary obligations—
   (a) proceedings may be taken on the award,
   (b) the sum for which the award is registered shall carry interest,
   (c) the High Court shall have the same control over the execution of the award,
as if the award had been such a judgment of the High Court.
(2) Rules of court under section [84 of the [Senior Courts Act 1981]] may contain provisions requiring the court on proof of the prescribed matters to stay execution of any award registered under this Act so as to take account of cases where enforcement of the award has been stayed (whether provisionally or otherwise) pursuant to the Convention, and may provide for the provisional stay of execution of the award where an application is made pursuant to the Convention which, if granted, might result in a stay of enforcement of the award.

NOTES

Sub-s (2): words in first (outer) pair of square brackets substituted by the Senior Courts Act 1981, s 152(1), Sch 5; words in second (inner) pair of square brackets substituted by the Constitutional Reform Act 2005, s 59(5), Sch 11, Pt 1, para 1(2).

Procedural Provisions

[1.413]
[3 Application of provisions of Arbitration Act 1996
(1) The Lord Chancellor may by order direct that any of the provisions contained in sections 36 and 38 to 44 of the Arbitration Act 1996 (provisions concerning the conduct of arbitral proceedings, &c) shall apply to such proceedings pursuant to the Convention as are specified in the order with or without any modifications or exceptions specified in the order.
(2) Subject to subsection (1), the Arbitration Act 1996 shall not apply to proceedings pursuant to the Convention, but this subsection shall not be taken as affecting section 9 of that Act (stay of legal proceedings in respect of matter subject to arbitration).
(3) An order made under this section—
   (a) may be varied or revoked by a subsequent order so made, and
   (b) shall be contained in a statutory instrument.]

NOTES

Substituted by the Arbitration Act 1996, s 107(1), Sch 3, para 24.

Immunities and Privileges

[1.414]
4 Status, immunities and privileges conferred by the Convention
(1) In Section 6 of Chapter I of the Convention (which governs the status, immunities and privileges of the International Centre for Settlements of Investment Disputes established by the Convention, of members of its Council and Secretariat and of persons concerned with conciliation or arbitration under the Convention) Articles 18 to 20, Article 21 (a) (with Article 22 as it applies Article 21 (a)), Article 23 (1) and Article 24 shall have the force of law.
(2) Nothing in Article 24 (1) of the Convention as given the force of law by this section shall be construed as—
   (a) entitling the said Centre to import goods free of customs duty without any restriction on their subsequent sale in the country to which they were imported, or
   (b) conferring on that Centre any exemption from duties or taxes which form part of the price of goods sold, or
   (c) conferring on that Centre any exemption from duties or taxes which are no more than charges for services rendered.
(3) For the purposes of Article 20 and Article 21 (a) of the Convention as given the force of law by this section, a statement to the effect that the said Centre has waived an immunity in the circumstances specified in the statement, being a statement certified by the Secretary-General of the said Centre (or by the person acting as Secretary-General), shall be conclusive evidence.

Supplemental

[1.415]
5 Government contribution to expenses under the Convention

The Treasury may discharge any obligations of Her Majesty's Government in the United Kingdom arising under Article 17 of the Convention (which obliges the Contracting States to meet any deficit of the International Centre for Settlement of Investment Disputes established under the Convention), and any sums required for that purpose shall be met out of money provided by Parliament.

[1.416]
6 Application to British possessions, etc

(1) Her Majesty may by Order in Council direct that the provisions of this Act shall extend, with such exceptions, adaptations and modifications as may be specified in the Order, to—
   (a) the Isle of Man,
   (b) any of the Channel Islands,
   (c) any colony, or any country or place outside Her Majesty's dominions in which for the time being Her Majesty has jurisdiction, or any territory consisting partly of one or more colonies and partly of one or more such countries or places.

(2) An Order in Council under this section—
   (a) may contain such transitional and other supplemental provisions as appear to Her Majesty to be expedient;
   (b) may be varied or revoked by a subsequent Order in Council under this section.

NOTES

Orders in Council: the Arbitration (International Investment Disputes) Act 1966 (Application to Colonies etc) Order 1967, SI 1967/159; the Arbitration (International Investment Disputes) Act 1966 (Application to Tonga) Order 1967, SI 1967/585; the Arbitration (International Investment Disputes) (Guernsey) Order 1968, SI 1968/1199; the Arbitration (International Investment Disputes) (Jersey) Order 1979, SI 1979/572.

7, 8 *(S 7 applies to Scotland only; s 8 applies to Northern Ireland only.)*

[1.417]
9 Short title and commencement

(1) This Act may be cited as the Arbitration (International Investment Disputes) Act 1966.
(2) This Act shall come into force on such day as Her Majesty may by Order in Council certify to be the day on which the Convention comes into force as regards the United Kingdom.

NOTES

Orders in Council: the Arbitration (International Investment Disputes) Act 1966 (Commencement) Order 1966, SI 1966/1597.

SCHEDULE
TEXT OF CONVENTION

Section 1

CONVENTION ON THE SETTLEMENT OF INVESTMENT DISPUTES BETWEEN STATES AND NATIONALS OF OTHER STATES

PREAMBLE

[1.418]
The Contracting States

Considering the need for international co-operation for economic development, and the role of private international investment therein;

Bearing in mind the possibility that from time to time disputes may arise in connection with such investment between Contracting States and nationals of other Contracting States;

Recognizing that while such disputes would usually be subject to national legal processes, international methods of settlement may be appropriate in certain cases;

Attaching particular importance to the availability of facilities for international conciliation or arbitration to which Contracting States and nationals of other Contracting States may submit such disputes if they so desire;

Desiring to establish such facilities under the auspices of the International Bank for Reconstruction and Development;

Recognizing that mutual consent by the parties to submit such disputes to conciliation or to arbitration through such facilities constitutes a binding agreement which requires in particular that due consideration be given to any recommendation of conciliators, and that any arbitral award be complied with; and

Declaring that no Contracting State shall by the mere fact of its ratification acceptance or approval of this Convention and without its consent be deemed to be under any obligation to submit any particular dispute to conciliation or arbitration.

Have agreed as follows:

CHAPTER I
INTERNATIONAL CENTRE FOR SETTLEMENT OF INVESTMENT DISPUTES

SECTION 1
ESTABLISHMENT AND ORGANIZATION

Article 1

(1)   There is hereby established the International Centre for Settlement of Investment Disputes (hereinafter called the Centre).

(2)   The purpose of the Centre shall be to provide facilities for conciliation and arbitration of investment disputes between Contracting States and nationals of other Contracting States in accordance with the provisions of this Convention.

Article 2

The seat of the Centre shall be at the principal office of the International Bank for Reconstruction and Development (hereinafter called the Bank).

The seat may be moved to another place by decision of the Administrative Council adopted by a majority of two-thirds of its members.

Article 3

The Centre shall have an Administrative Council and a Secretariat and shall maintain a Panel of Conciliators and a Panel of Arbitrators.

SECTION 2
THE ADMINISTRATIVE COUNCIL

Article 4

(1)   The Administrative Council shall be composed of one representative of each Contracting State. An alternate may act as representative in case of his principal's absence from a meeting or inability to act.

(2)   In the absence of a contrary designation, each governor and alternate governor of the Bank appointed by a Contracting State shall be *ex officio* its representative and its alternate respectively.

Article 5

The President of the Bank shall be ex officio Chairman of the Administrative Council (hereinafter called the Chairman) but shall have no vote. During his absence or inability to act and during any vacancy in the office of President of the Bank, the person for the time being acting as President shall act as Chairman of the Administrative Council.

Article 6

(1)   Without prejudice to the powers and functions vested in it by other provisions of this Convention, the Administrative Council shall
    (a)   adopt the administrative and financial regulations of the Centre;
    (b)   adopt the rules of procedure for the institution of conciliation and arbitration proceedings;
    (c)   adopt the rules of procedure for conciliation and arbitration proceedings (hereinafter called the Conciliation Rules and the Arbitration Rules);
    (d)   approve arrangements with the Bank for the use of the Bank's administrative facilities and services;
    (e)   determine the conditions of service of the Secretary-General and of any Deputy Secretary-General;
    (f)   adopt the annual budget of revenues and expenditures of the Centre;
    (g)   approve the annual report on the operation of the Centre.
The decisions referred to in sub-paragraphs (a), (b), (c) and (f) above shall be adopted by a majority of two-thirds of the members of the Administrative Council.

(2)   The Administrative Council may appoint such committees as it considers necessary.

(3)   The Administrative Council shall also exercise such other powers and perform such other functions as it shall determine to be necessary for the implementation of the provisions of this Convention.

Article 7

(1)   The Administrative Council shall hold an annual meeting and such other meetings as may be determined by the Council, or convened by the Chairman, or convened by the Secretary-General at the request of not less than five members of the Council.

(2)   Each member of the Administrative Council shall have one vote and, except as otherwise herein provided, all matters before the Council shall be decided by a majority of the votes cast.

(3)   A quorum for any meeting of the Administrative Council shall be a majority of its members.

(4)   The Administrative Council may establish, by a majority of two-thirds of its members, a procedure whereby the Chairman may seek a vote of the Council without convening a meeting of the Council. The vote shall be considered valid only if the majority of the members of the Council cast their votes within the time limit by the said procedure.

Article 8

Members of the Administrative Council and the Chairman shall serve without remuneration from the Centre.

SECTION 3
THE SECRETARIAT

Article 9

The Secretariat shall consist of a Secretary-General, one or more Deputy Secretaries-General and staff.

Article 10

(1)   The Secretary-General and any Deputy Secretary-General shall be elected by the Administrative Council by a majority of two-thirds of its members upon the nomination of the Chairman for a term of service not exceeding six years and shall be eligible for re-election. After consulting the members of the Administrative Council, the Chairman shall propose one or more candidates for each such office.

(2)   The offices of Secretary-General and Deputy Secretary-General shall be incompatible with the exercise of any political function. Neither the Secretary-General nor any Deputy Secretary-General may hold any other employment or engage in any other occupation except with the approval of the Administrative Council.

(3)   During the Secretary-General's absence or inability to act, and during any vacancy of the office of Secretary-General, the Deputy Secretary-General shall act as Secretary-General. If there shall be more than one Deputy Secretary-General, the Administrative Council shall determine in advance the order in which they shall act as Secretary-General.

Article 11

The Secretary-General shall be the legal representative and the principal officer of the Centre and shall be responsible for its administration, including the appointment of staff, in accordance with the provisions of this Convention and the rules adopted by the Administrative Council. He shall perform the function of registrar and shall have the power to authenticate arbitral awards rendered pursuant to this Convention, and to certify copies thereof.

SECTION 4
THE PANELS

Article 12

The Panel of Conciliators and the Panel of Arbitrators shall each consist of qualified persons, designated as hereinafter provided, who are willing to serve thereon.

Article 13

(1) Each Contracting State may designate to each Panel four persons who may but need not be its nationals.

(2) The Chairman may designate ten persons to each Panel. The persons so designated to a Panel shall each have a different nationality.

Article 14

(1) Persons designated to serve on the Panels shall be persons of high moral character and recognized competence in the fields of law, commerce, industry or finance, who may be relied upon to exercise independent judgment. Competence in the field of law shall be of particular importance in the case of persons on the Panel of Arbitrators.

(2) The Chairman, in designating persons to serve on the Panels, shall in addition pay due regard to the importance of assuring representation on the Panels of the principal legal systems of the world and of the main forms of economic activity.

Article 15

(1) Panel members shall serve for renewable periods of six years.

(2) In case of death or resignation of a member of a Panel, the authority which designated the member shall have the right to designate another person to serve for the remainder of that member's term.

(3) Panel members shall continue in office until their successors have been designated.

Article 16

(1) A person may serve on both Panels.

(2) If a person shall have been designated to serve on the same Panel by more than one Contracting State, or by one or more Contracting States and the Chairman, he shall be deemed to have been designated by the authority which first designated him or, if one such authority is the State of which he is a national, by that State.

(3) All designations shall be notified to the Secretary-General and shall take effect from the date on which the notification is received.

SECTION 5
FINANCING THE CENTRE

Article 17

If the expenditure of the Centre cannot be met out of charges for the use of its facilities, or out of other receipts, the excess shall be borne by Contracting States which are members of the Bank in proportion to their respective subscriptions to the capital stock of the Bank, and by Contracting States which are not members of the Bank in accordance with rules adopted by the Administrative Council.

SECTION 6
STATUS, IMMUNITIES AND PRIVILEGES

Article 18

The Centre shall have full international legal personality. The legal capacity of the Centre shall include the capacity
  (a) to contract;
  (b) to acquire and dispose of movable and immovable property;
  (c) to institute legal proceedings.

Article 19

To enable the Centre to fulfil its functions, it shall enjoy in the territories of each Contracting State the immunities and privileges set forth in this Section.

Article 20

The Centre, its property and assets shall enjoy immunity from all legal process, except when the Centre waives this immunity.

Article 21

The Chairman, the members of the Administrative Council, persons acting as conciliators or arbitrators or members of a Committee appointed pursuant to paragraph (3) of Article 52, and the officers and employees of the Secretariat

(a) shall enjoy immunity from legal process with respect to acts performed by them in the exercise of their functions, except when the Centre waives this immunity;

(b) not being local nationals, shall enjoy the same immunities from immigration restrictions, alien registration requirements and national service obligations, the same facilities as regards exchange restrictions and the same treatment in respect of travelling facilities as are accorded by Contracting States to the representatives, officials and employees of comparable rank of other Contracting States.

Article 22

The provisions of Article 21 shall apply to persons appearing in proceedings under this Convention as parties, agents, counsel, advocates, witnesses or experts; provided, however, that sub-paragraph (b) thereof shall apply only in connection with their travel to and from, and their stay at, the place where the proceedings are held.

Article 23

(1) The archives of the Centre shall be inviolable, wherever they may be.

(2) With regard to its official communications, the Centre shall be accorded by each Contracting State treatment not less favourable than that accorded to other international organizations.

Article 24

(1) The Centre, its assets, property and income, and its operations and transactions authorized by this Convention shall be exempt from all taxation and customs duties. The Centre shall also be exempt from liability for the collection or payment of any taxes or customs duties.

(2) Except in the case of local nationals, no tax shall be levied on or in respect of expense allowances paid by the Centre to the Chairman or members of the Administrative Council, or on or in respect of salaries, expense allowances or other emoluments paid by the Centre to officials or employees of the Secretariat.

(3) No tax shall be levied on or in respect of fees or expense allowances received by persons acting as conciliators, or arbitrators, or members of a Committee appointed pursuant to paragraph (3) of Article 52, in proceedings under this Convention, if the sole jurisdictional basis for such tax is the location of the Centre or the place where such proceedings are conducted or the place where such fees or allowances are paid.

CHAPTER II
JURISDICTION OF THE CENTRE

Article 25

(1) The jurisdiction of the Centre shall extend to any legal dispute arising directly out of an investment, between a Contracting State (or any constituent subdivision or agency of a Contracting State designated to the Centre by that State) and a national of another Contracting State, which the parties to the dispute consent in writing to submit to the Centre. When the parties have given their consent, no party may withdraw its consent unilaterally.

(2) "National of another Contracting State" means:

(a) any natural person who had the nationality of a Contracting State other than the State party to the dispute on the date on which the parties consented to submit such dispute to conciliation or arbitration as well as on the date on which the request was registered pursuant to paragraph (3) of Article 28 or paragraph (3) of Article 36, but does not include any person who on either date also had the nationality of the Contracting State party to the dispute; and

(b)   any juridical person which had the nationality of a Contracting State other than the State party to the dispute on the date on which the parties consented to submit such dispute to conciliation or arbitration and any juridical person which had the nationality of the Contracting State party to the dispute on that date and which, because of foreign control, the parties have agreed should be treated as a national of another Contracting State for the purposes of this Convention.

(3)   Consent by a constituent subdivision or agency of a Contracting State shall require the approval of that State unless that State notifies the Centre that no such approval is required.

(4)   Any Contracting State may, at the time of ratification, acceptance or approval of this Convention or at any time thereafter, notify the Centre of the class or classes of disputes which it would or would not consider submitting to the jurisdiction of the Centre. The Secretary-General shall forthwith transmit such notification to all Contracting States. Such notification shall not constitute the consent required by paragraph (1).

Article 26

Consent of the parties to arbitration under this Convention shall, unless otherwise stated, be deemed consent to such arbitration to the exclusion of any other remedy. A Contracting State may require the exhaustion of local administrative or judicial remedies as a condition of its consent to arbitration under this Convention.

Article 27

(1)   No Contracting State shall give diplomatic protection, or bring an international claim, in respect of a dispute which one of its nationals and another Contracting State shall have consented to submit or shall have submitted to arbitration under this Convention, unless such other Contracting State shall have failed to abide by and comply with the award rendered in such dispute.

(2)   Diplomatic protection, for the purposes of paragraph (1), shall not include informal diplomatic exchanges for the sole purpose of facilitating a settlement of the dispute.

CHAPTER III
CONCILIATION

SECTION 1
REQUEST FOR CONCILIATION

Article 28

(1)   Any Contracting State or any national of a Contracting State wishing to institute conciliation proceedings shall address a request to that effect in writing to the Secretary-General who shall send a copy of the request to the other party.

(2)   The request shall contain information concerning the issues in dispute, the identity of the parties and their consent to conciliation in accordance with the rules of procedure for the institution of conciliation and arbitration proceedings.

(3)   The Secretary-General shall register the request unless he finds, on the basis of the information contained in the request, that the dispute is manifestly outside the jurisdiction of the Centre. He shall forthwith notify the parties of registration or refusal to register.

SECTION 2
CONSTITUTION OF THE CONCILIATION COMMISSION

Article 29

(1)   The Conciliation Commission (hereinafter called the Commission) shall be constituted as soon as possible after registration of a request pursuant to Article 28.

(2)
(a)   The Commission shall consist of a sole conciliator or any uneven number of conciliators appointed as the parties shall agree.
(b)   Where the parties do not agree upon the number of conciliators and the method of their appointment, the Commission shall consist of three conciliators, one conciliator appointed by each party and the third, who shall be the president of the Commission, appointed by agreement of the parties.

Article 30

If the Commission shall not have been constituted within 90 days after notice of registration of the request has been dispatched by the Secretary-General in accordance with paragraph (3) of Article 28, or such other period as the parties may agree, the Chairman shall, at the request of either party and after consulting both parties as far as possible, appoint the conciliator or conciliators not yet appointed.

Article 31

(1)   Conciliators may be appointed from outside the Panel of Conciliators, except in the case of appointments by the Chairman pursuant to Article 30.

(2)   Conciliators appointed from outside the Panel of Conciliators shall possess the qualities stated in paragraph (1) of Article 14.

SECTION 3
CONCILIATION PROCEEDINGS

Article 32

(1)   The Commission shall be the judge of its own competence.

(2)   Any objection by a party to the dispute that that dispute is not within the jurisdiction of the Centre, or for other reasons is not within the competence of the Commission, shall be considered by the Commission which shall determine whether to deal with it as a preliminary question or to join it to the merits of the dispute.

Article 33

Any conciliation proceeding shall be conducted in accordance with the provisions of this Section and, except as the parties otherwise agree, in accordance with the Conciliation Rules in effect on the date on which the parties consented to conciliation. If any question of procedure arises which is not covered by this Section or the Conciliation Rules or any rules agreed by the parties, the Commission shall decide the question.

Article 34

(1)   It shall be the duty of the Commission to clarify the issues in dispute between the parties and to endeavour to bring about agreement between them upon mutually acceptable terms. To that end, the Commission may at any stage of the proceedings and from time to time recommend terms of settlement to the parties. The parties shall cooperate in good faith with the Commission in order to enable the Commission to carry out its functions, and shall give their most serious consideration to its recommendations.

(2)   If the parties reach agreement, the Commission shall draw up a report noting the issues in dispute and recording that the parties have reached agreement. If, at any stage of the proceedings, it appears to the Commission that there is no likelihood of agreement between the parties, it shall close the proceedings and shall draw up a report noting the submission of the dispute and recording the failure of the parties to reach agreement. If one party fails to appear or participate in the proceedings, the Commission shall close the proceedings and shall draw up a report noting that party's failure to appear or participate.

Article 35

Except as the parties to the dispute shall otherwise agree, neither party to a conciliation proceeding shall be entitled in any other proceeding, whether before arbitrators or in a court of law or otherwise, to invoke or rely on any views expressed or statements or admissions or offers of settlement made by the other party in the conciliation proceedings, or the report or any recommendations made by the Commission.

CHAPTER IV
ARBITRATION

SECTION 1
REQUEST FOR ARBITRATION

Article 36

(1) Any Contracting State or any national of a Contracting State wishing to institute arbitration proceedings shall address a request to that effect in writing to the Secretary-General who shall send a copy of the request to the other party.

(2) The request shall contain information concerning the issues in dispute, the identity of the parties and their consent to arbitration in accordance with the rules of procedure for the institution of conciliation and arbitration proceedings.

(3) The Secretary-General shall register the request unless he finds, on the basis of the information contained in the request, that the dispute is manifestly outside the jurisdiction of the Centre. He shall forthwith notify the parties of registration or refusal to register.

SECTION 2
CONSTITUTION OF THE TRIBUNAL

Article 37

(1) The Arbitral Tribunal (hereinafter called the Tribunal) shall be constituted as soon as possible after registration of a request pursuant to Article 36.

(2)
   (a)   The Tribunal shall consist of a sole arbitrator or any uneven number of arbitrators appointed as the parties shall agree.
   (b)   Where the parties do not agree upon the number of arbitrators and the method of their appointment, the Tribunal shall consist of three arbitrators, one arbitrator appointed by each party and the third, who shall be the president of the Tribunal, appointed by agreement of the parties.

Article 38

If the Tribunal shall not have been constituted within 90 days after notice of registration of the request has been dispatched by the Secretary-General in accordance with paragraph (3) of Article 36, or such other period as the parties may agree, the Chairman shall, at the request of either party and after consulting both parties as far as possible, appoint the arbitrator or arbitrators not yet appointed. Arbitrators appointed by the Chairman pursuant to this Article shall not be nationals of the Contracting State party to the dispute or of the Contracting State whose national is a party to the dispute.

Article 39

The majority of the arbitrators shall be nationals of States other than the Contracting State party to the dispute and the Contracting State whose national is a party to the dispute; provided, however, that the foregoing provisions of this Article shall not apply if the sole arbitrator or each individual member of the Tribunal has been appointed by agreement of the parties.

Article 40

(1) Arbitrators may be appointed from outside the Panel of Arbitrators, except in the case of appointments by the Chairman pursuant to Article 38.

(2) Arbitrators appointed from outside the Panel of Arbitrators shall possess the qualities stated in paragraph (1) of Article 14.

SECTION 3
POWERS AND FUNCTIONS OF THE TRIBUNAL

Article 41

(1) The Tribunal shall be the judge of its own competence.

(2)   Any objection by a party to the dispute that that dispute is not within the jurisdiction of the Centre, or for other reasons is not within the competence of the Tribunal, shall be considered by the Tribunal which shall determine whether to deal with it as a preliminary question or to join it to the merits of the dispute.

Article 42

(1)   The Tribunal shall decide a dispute in accordance with such rules of law as may be agreed by the parties. In the absence of such agreement, the Tribunal shall apply the law of the Contracting State party to the dispute (including its rules on the conflict of laws) and such rules of international law as may be applicable.

(2)   The Tribunal may not bring in a finding of *non liquet* on the ground of silence or obscurity of the law.

(3)   The provisions of paragraphs (1) and (2) shall not prejudice the power of the Tribunal to decide a dispute *ex aequo et bono* if the parties so agree.

Article 43

Except as the parties otherwise agree, the Tribunal may, if it deems it necessary at any stage of the proceedings,
  (a)   call upon the parties to produce documents or other evidence, and
  (b)   visit the scene connected with the dispute, and conduct such enquiries there as it may deem appropriate.

Article 44

Any arbitration proceeding shall be conducted in accordance with the provisions of this Section and, except as the parties otherwise agree, in accordance with the Arbitration Rules in effect on the date on which the parties consented to arbitration. If any question of procedure arises which is not covered by this Section or the Arbitration Rules or any rules agreed by the parties, the Tribunal shall decide the question.

Article 45

(1)   Failure of a party to appear or to present his case shall not be deemed an admission of the other party's assertions.

(2)   If a party fails to appear or to present his case at any stage of the proceedings the other party may request the Tribunal to deal with the questions submitted to it and to render an award. Before rendering an award, the Tribunal shall notify, and grant a period of grace to, the party failing to appear or to present its case, unless it is satisfied that that party does not intend to do so.

Article 46

Except as the parties otherwise agree, the Tribunal shall, if requested by a party, determine any incidental or additional claims or counter-claims arising directly out of the subject-matter of the dispute provided that they are within the scope of the consent of the parties and are otherwise within the jurisdiction of the Centre.

Article 47

Except as the parties otherwise agree, the Tribunal may, if it considers that the circumstances so require, recommend any provisional measures which should be taken to preserve the respective rights of either party.

SECTION 4
THE AWARD

Article 48

(1)   The Tribunal shall decide questions by a majority of the votes of all its members.

(2)   The award of the Tribunal shall be in writing and shall be signed by the members of the Tribunal who voted for it.

(3)   The award shall deal with every question submitted to the Tribunal, and shall state the reasons upon which it is based.

(4) Any member of the Tribunal may attach his individual opinion to the award, whether he dissents from the majority or not, or a statement of his dissent.

(5) The Centre shall not publish the award without the consent of the parties.

Article 49

(1) The Secretary-General shall promptly dispatch certified copies of the award to the parties. The award shall be deemed to have been rendered on the date on which the certified copies were dispatched.

(2) The Tribunal upon the request of a party made within 45 days after the date on which the award was rendered may after notice to the other party decide any question which it had omitted to decide in the award, and shall rectify any clerical, arithmetical or similar error in the award. Its decision shall become part of the award and shall be notified to the parties in the same manner as the award. The periods of time provided for under paragraph (2) of Article 51 and paragraph (2) of Article 52 shall run from the date on which the decision was rendered.

SECTION 5
INTERPRETATION, REVISION AND ANNULMENT OF THE AWARD

Article 50

(1) If any dispute shall arise between the parties as to the meaning or scope of an award, either party may request interpretation of the award by an application in writing addressed to the Secretary-General.

(2) The request shall, if possible, be submitted to the Tribunal which rendered the award. If this shall not be possible, a new Tribunal shall be constituted in accordance with Section 2 of this Chapter. The Tribunal may, if it considers that the circumstances so require, stay enforcement of the award pending its decision.

Article 51

(1) Either party may request revision of the award by an application in writing addressed to the Secretary-General on the ground of discovery of some fact of such a nature as decisively to affect the award, provided that when the award was rendered that fact was unknown to the Tribunal and to the applicant and that the applicant's ignorance of that fact was not due to negligence.

(2) The application shall be made within 90 days after the discovery of such fact and in any event within three years after the date on which the award was rendered.

(3) The request shall, if possible, be submitted to the Tribunal which rendered the award. If this shall not be possible, a new Tribunal shall be constituted in accordance with Section 2 of this Chapter.

(4) The Tribunal may, if it considers that the circumstances so require, stay enforcement of the award pending its decision. If the applicant requests stay of enforcement of the award in his application, enforcement shall be stayed provisionally until the Tribunal rules on such request.

Article 52

(1) Either party may request annulment of the award by an application in writing addressed to the Secretary-General on one or more of the following grounds:
   (a)   that the Tribunal was not properly constituted;
   (b)   that the Tribunal has manifestly exceeded its powers;
   (c)   that there was corruption on the part of a member of the Tribunal;
   (d)   that there has been a serious departure from a fundamental rule of procedure; or
   (e)   that the award has failed to state the reasons on which it is based.

(2) The application shall be made within 120 days after the date on which the award was rendered except that when annulment is requested on the ground of corruption such application shall be made within 120 days after discovery of the corruption and in any event within three years after the date on which the award was rendered.

(3) On receipt of the request the Chairman shall forthwith appoint from the Panel of Arbitrators an *ad hoc* Committee of three persons. None of the members of the Committee shall have been a member of the Tribunal which rendered the award, shall be of the same nationality as any such member, shall be a national of the State party to the dispute or of the State whose national is a party

to the dispute, shall have been designated to the Panel of Arbitrators by either of those States, or shall have acted as a conciliator in the same dispute. The Committee shall have the authority to annul the award or any part thereof on any of the grounds set forth in paragraph (1).

(4) The provisions of Articles 41–45, 48, 49, 53 and 54, and of Chapters VI and VII shall apply *mutatis mutandis* to proceedings before the Committee.

(5) The Committee may, if it considers that circumstances so require, stay enforcement of the award pending its decision. If the applicant requests a stay of enforcement of the award in his application, enforcement shall be stayed provisionally until the Committee rules on such request.

(6) If the award is annulled the dispute shall, at the request of either party, be submitted to a new Tribunal constituted in accordance with Section 2 of this Chapter.

SECTION 6
RECOGNITION AND ENFORCEMENT OF THE AWARD

Article 53

(1) The award shall be binding on the parties and shall not be subject to any appeal or to any other remedy except those provided for in this Convention. Each party shall abide by and comply with the terms of the award except to the extent that enforcement shall have been stayed pursuant to the relevant provisions of this Convention.

(2) For the purposes of this Section, "award" shall include any decision interpreting, revising or annulling such award pursuant to Articles 50, 51 or 52.

Article 54

(1) Each Contracting State shall recognize an award rendered pursuant to this Convention as binding and enforce the pecuniary obligations imposed by that award within its territories as if it were a final judgment of a court in that State. A Contracting State with a federal constitution may enforce such an award in or through its federal courts and may provide that such courts shall treat the award as if it were a final judgment of the courts of a constituent state.

(2) A party seeking recognition or enforcement in the territories of a Contracting State shall furnish to a competent court or other authority which such State shall have designated for this purpose a copy of the award certified by the Secretary-General. Each Contracting State shall notify the Secretary-General of the designation of the competent court or other authority for this purpose and of any subsequent change in such designation.

(3) Execution of the award shall be governed by the laws concerning the execution of judgments in force in the State in whose territories such execution is sought.

Article 55

Nothing in Article 54 shall be construed as derogating from the law in force in any Contracting State relating to immunity of that State or of any foreign State from execution.

CHAPTER V
REPLACEMENT AND DISQUALIFICATION OF CONCILIATORS AND ARBITRATORS

Article 56

(1) After a Commission or a Tribunal has been constituted and proceedings have begun, its composition shall remain unchanged; provided, however, that if a conciliator or an arbitrator should die, become incapacitated, or resign, the resulting vacancy shall be filled in accordance with the provisions of Section 2 of Chapter III or Section 2 of Chapter IV.

(2) A member of the Commission or Tribunal shall continue to serve in that capacity notwithstanding that he shall have ceased to be a member of the Panel.

(3) If a conciliator or arbitrator appointed by a party shall have resigned without the consent of the Commission or Tribunal of which he was a member, the Chairman shall appoint a person from the appropriate Panel to fill the resulting vacancy.

Article 57

A party may propose to a Commission or Tribunal the disqualification of any of its members on account of any fact indicating a manifest lack of the qualities required by paragraph (1) of Article 14. A party to arbitration proceedings may, in addition, propose the disqualification of an arbitrator on the ground that he was ineligible for appointment to the Tribunal under Section 2 of Chapter IV.

Article 58

The decision on any proposal to disqualify a conciliator or arbitrator shall be taken by the other members of the Commission or Tribunal as the case may be, provided that where those members are equally divided, or in the case of a proposal to disqualify a sole conciliator or arbitrator, or a majority of the conciliators or arbitrators, the Chairman shall take that decision. If it is decided that the proposal is well-founded the conciliator or arbitrator to whom the decision relates shall be replaced in accordance with the provisions of Section 2 of Chapter III or Section 2 of Chapter IV.

CHAPTER VI
COST OF PROCEEDINGS

Article 59

The charges payable by the parties for the use of the facilities of the Centre shall be determined by the Secretary-General in accordance with the regulations adopted by the Administrative Council.

Article 60

(1)   Each Commission and each Tribunal shall determine the fees and expenses of its members within limits established from time to time by the Administrative Council and after consultation with the Secretary-General.

(2)   Nothing in paragraph (1) of this Article shall preclude the parties from agreeing in advance with the Commission or Tribunal concerned upon the fees and expenses of its members.

Article 61

(1)   In the case of conciliation proceedings the fees and expenses of members of the Commission as well as the charges for the use of the facilities of the Centre, shall be borne equally by the parties. Each party shall bear any other expenses it incurs in connection with the proceedings.

(2)   In the case of arbitration proceedings the Tribunal shall, except as the parties otherwise agree, assess the expenses incurred by the parties in connection with the proceedings, and shall decide how and by whom those expenses, the fees and expenses of the members of the Tribunal and the charges for the use of the facilities of the Centre shall be paid. Such decision shall form part of the award.

CHAPTER VII
PLACE OF PROCEEDINGS

Article 62

Conciliation and arbitration proceedings shall be held at the seat of the Centre except as hereinafter provided.

Article 63

Conciliation and arbitration proceedings may be held, if the parties so agree,
  (a)   at the seat of the Permanent Court of Arbitration or of any other appropriate institution, whether private or public, with which the Centre may make arrangements for that purpose; or
  (b)   at any other place approved by the Commission or Tribunal after consultation with the Secretary-General.

CHAPTER VIII
DISPUTES BETWEEN CONTRACTING STATES

Article 64

Any dispute arising between Contracting States concerning the interpretation or application of this Convention which is not settled by negotiation shall be referred to the International Court of Justice by the application of any party to such dispute, unless the States concerned agree to another method of settlement.

CHAPTER IX
AMENDMENT

Article 65

Any Contracting State may propose amendment of this Convention. The text of a proposed amendment shall be communicated to the Secretary-General not less than 90 days prior to the meeting of the Administrative Council at which such amendment is to be considered and shall forthwith be transmitted by him to all the members of the Administrative Council.

Article 66

(1) If the Administrative Council shall so decide by a majority of two-thirds of its members, the proposed amendment shall be circulated to all Contracting States for ratification, acceptance or approval. Each amendment shall enter into force 30 days after dispatch by the depositary of this Convention of a notification to Contracting States that all Contracting States have ratified, accepted or approved the amendment.

(2) No amendment shall affect the rights and obligations under this Convention of any Contracting State or of any of its constituent subdivisions or agencies, or of any national of such State arising out of consent to the jurisdiction of the Centre given before the date of entry into force of the amendment.

CHAPTER X
FINAL PROVISIONS

Article 67

This Convention shall be open for signature on behalf of States members of the Bank. It shall also be open for signature on behalf of any other State which is a party to the Statute of the International Court of Justice and which the Administrative Council, by a vote of two-thirds of its members, shall have invited to sign the Convention.

Article 68

(1) This Convention shall be subject to ratification, acceptance or approval by the signatory States in accordance with their respective constitutional procedures.

(2) This Convention shall enter into force 30 days after the date of deposit of the twentieth instrument of ratification, acceptance or approval. It shall enter into force for each State which subsequently deposits its instrument of ratification, acceptance or approval 30 days after the date of such deposit.

Article 69

Each Contracting State shall take legislative or other measures as may be necessary for making the provisions of this Convention effective in its territories.

Article 70

This Convention shall apply to all territories for whose international relations a Contracting State is responsible, except those which are excluded by such State by written notice to the depositary of this Convention either at the time of ratification, acceptance or approval or subsequently.

Article 71

Any Contracting State may denounce this Convention by written notice to the depositary of this Convention. The denunciation shall take effect six months after receipt of such notice.

Article 72

Notice by a Contracting State pursuant to Article 70 or 71 shall not affect the rights or obligations under this Convention of that State or of any of its constituent subdivisions or agencies or of any national of that State arising out of consent to the jurisdiction of the Centre given by one of them before such notice was received by the depositary.

Article 73

Instruments of ratification, acceptance or approval of this Convention and of amendments thereto shall be deposited with the Bank which shall act as the depositary of this Convention. The depositary shall transmit certified copies of this Convention to States members of the Bank and to any other State invited to sign the Convention.

Article 74

The depositary shall register this Convention with the Secretariat of the United Nations in accordance with Article 102 of the Charter of the United Nations and the Regulations thereunder adopted by the General Assembly.

Article 75

The depositary shall notify all signatory States of the following:
  (a)   signatures in accordance with Article 67;
  (b)   deposits of instruments of ratification, acceptance and approval in accordance with Article 73;
  (c)   the date on which this Convention enters into force in accordance with Article 68;
  (d)   exclusions from territorial application pursuant to Article 70;
  (e)   the date on which any amendment of this Convention enters into force in accordance with Article 66; and
  (f)   denunciations in accordance with Article 71.

DONE at Washington in the English, French and Spanish languages, all three texts being equally authentic, in a single copy which shall remain deposited in the archives of the International Bank for Reconstruction and Development, which has indicated by its signature below its agreement to fulfil the functions with which it is charged under this Convention.

(Here follow the signatures)

MISREPRESENTATION ACT 1967

(1967 c 7)

ARRANGEMENT OF SECTIONS

An Act to amend the law relating to innocent misrepresentations and to amend sections 11 and 35 of the Sale of Goods Act 1893

[22 March 1967]

[1.419]
1   Removal of certain bars to rescission for innocent misrepresentation
Where a person has entered into a contract after a misrepresentation has been made to him, and—
  (a)   the misrepresentation has become a term of the contract; or
  (b)   the contract has been performed;
or both, then, if otherwise he would be entitled to rescind the contract with-out alleging fraud, he shall be so entitled, subject to the provisions of this Act, notwithstanding the matters mentioned in paragraphs (a) and (b) of this section.

[1.420]

2 Damages for misrepresentation

(1) Where a person has entered into a contract after a misrepresentation has been made to him by another party thereto and as a result thereof he has suffered loss, then, if the person making the misrepresentation would be liable to damages in respect thereof had the misrepresentation been made fraudulently, that person shall be so liable notwithstanding that the misrepresentation was not made fraudulently, unless he proves that he had reasonable ground to believe and did believe up to the time the contract was made that the facts represented were true.

(2) Where a person has entered into a contract after a misrepresentation has been made to him otherwise than fraudulently, and he would be entitled, by reason of the misrepresentation, to rescind the contract, then, if it is claimed, in any proceedings arising out of the contract, that the contract ought to be or has been rescinded, the court or arbitrator may declare the contract subsisting and award damages in lieu of rescission, if of opinion that it would be equitable to do so, having regard to the nature of the misrepresentation and the loss that would be caused by it if the contract were upheld, as well as to the loss that rescission would cause to the other party.

(3) Damages may be awarded against a person under subsection (2) of this section whether or not he is liable to damages under subsection (1) thereof, but where he is so liable any award under the said subsection (2) shall be taken into account in assessing his liability under the said subsection (1).

[(4) This section does not entitle a person to be paid damages in respect of a misrepresentation if the person has a right to redress under Part 4A of the Consumer Protection from Unfair Trading Regulations 2008 (SI 2008/1277) in respect of the conduct constituting the misrepresentation.

(5) Subsection (4) does not prevent a debtor from bringing a claim under section 75(1) of the Consumer Credit Act 1974 against a creditor under a debtor-creditor-supplier agreement in a case where, but for subsection (4), the debtor would have a claim against the supplier in respect of a misrepresentation (and, where section 75 of that Act would otherwise apply, it accordingly applies as if the debtor had a claim against the supplier).]

NOTES

Sub-ss (4), (5): added by the Consumer Protection (Amendment) Regulations 2014, SI 2014/870, reg 5.

[1.421]

[3 Avoidance of provision excluding liability for misrepresentation

[(1)] If a contract contains a term which would exclude or restrict—

    (a) any liability to which a party to a contract may be subject by reason of any misrepresentation made by him before the contract was made; or

    (b) any remedy available to another party to the contract by reason of such a misrepresentation,

that term shall be of no effect except in so far as it satisfies the requirement of reasonableness as stated in section 11(1) of the Unfair Contract Terms Act 1977; and it is for those claiming that the term satisfies that requirement to show that it does.]

[(2) This section does not apply to a term in a consumer contract within the meaning of Part 2 of the Consumer Rights Act 2015 (but see the provision made about such contracts in section 62 of that Act).]

NOTES

Substituted by the Unfair Contract Terms Act 1977, s 8(1).

Sub-s (1) numbered as such and sub-s (2) added by the Consumer Rights Act 2015, s 75, Sch 4, para 1, as from 1 October 2015 (for transitional provisions see the Consumer Rights Act 2015 (Commencement No 3, Transitional Provisions, Savings and Consequential Amendments) Order 2015, SI 2015/1630, arts 6–8 at **[2.1220]** et seq).

4 (*Repealed by the Sale of Goods Act 1979, s 63(2), Sch 3.*)

[1.422]

5 Saving for past transactions

Nothing in this Act shall apply in relation to any misrepresentation or contract of sale which is made before the commencement of this Act.

[1.423]

6 Short title, commencement and extent

(1) This Act may be cited as the Misrepresentation Act 1967.

(2) This Act shall come into operation at the expiration of the period of one month beginning with the date on which it is passed.

(3) This Act . . . does not extend to Scotland.

(4) This Act does not extend to Northern Ireland.

NOTES

Sub-s (3): words omitted repealed by the Sale of Goods Act 1979, ss 62, 63, Sch 3.

UNIFORM LAWS ON INTERNATIONAL SALES ACT 1967

(1967 c 45)

ARRANGEMENT OF SECTIONS

An Act to give effect to two Conventions with respect to the international sale of goods; and for purposes connected therewith

[14 July 1967]

[1.424]
1   Application of Uniform Law on the International Sale of Goods
(1)   In this Act "the Uniform Law on Sales" means the Uniform Law on the International Sale of Goods forming the Annex to the First Convention and set out, with the modification provided for by Article III of that Convention, in Schedule 1 to this Act; and "the First Convention" means the Convention relating to a Uniform Law on the International Sale of Goods done at The Hague on 1st July 1964.
(2)   The Uniform Law on Sales shall, subject to the following provisions of this section, have the force of law in the United Kingdom.
(3)   While an Order of Her Majesty in Council is in force declaring that a declaration by the United Kingdom under Article V of the First Convention (application only by choice of parties) has been made and not withdrawn the Uniform Law on Sales shall apply to a contract of sale only if it has been chosen by the parties to the contract as the law of the contract.
[(4)   In determining the extent of the application of the Uniform Law on Sales by virtue of Article 4 thereof (choice of parties)—
   (a)   in relation to a contract made before 18th May 1973, no provision of the law of any part of the United Kingdom shall be regarded as a mandatory provision within the meaning of that Article;
   (b)   in relation to a contract made on or after 18th May 1973 and before 1st February 1978, no provision of that law shall be so regarded except sections 12 to 15, 55 and 56 of the Sale of Goods Act 1979;
   (c)   in relation to a contract made on or after 1st February 1978, no provision of that law shall be so regarded except sections [12 to 15B] of the Sale of Goods Act 1979 [and sections 9 to 17, 19 to 24 and 28 to 32 of the Consumer Rights Act 2015].]
(5)   If Her Majesty by Order in Council declares what States are Contracting States and in respect of what territories or what declarations under Article II of the First Convention are for the time being in force, the Order shall, while in force, be conclusive for the purposes of paragraph 1 or, as the case may be, paragraph 5 of Article 1 of the Uniform Law on Sales; but any Order in Council under this subsection may be varied or revoked by a subsequent Order in Council.
(6)   The Uniform Law on Sales shall not apply to contracts concluded before such date as Her Majesty may by Order in Council declare to be the date on which the First Convention comes into force in respect of the United Kingdom.
(7)   Any Order in Council under the preceding provisions of this section shall be laid before Parliament after being made.
(8)   An Order in Council made under subsection (3) of this section may be revoked by a subsequent Order in Council; but no recommendation shall be made to Her Majesty in Council to make an Order under this subsection unless a draft thereof has been laid before and approved by each House of Parliament.

NOTES
   Sub-s (4): substituted by the Sale of Goods Act 1979, s 63, Sch 2, para 15; words in first pair of square brackets substituted by the Sale and Supply of Goods Act 1994, s 7(1), Sch 2 para 3; words in second pair of square brackets inserted by the Consumer Rights Act 2015 (Consequential Amendments) Order 2015, SI 2015/1726, art 2, Schedule, Pt 1, para 1, in relation to contracts entered into on or after 1 October 2015.
   Orders in Council: the Uniform Laws on International Sales Order 1972, SI 1972/973; the Uniform Laws on International Sales Order 1987, SI 1987/2061.

Part 1   Statutes

[1.425]
2 Application of Uniform Law on the Formation of Contracts for the International Sale of Goods

(1) In this Act "the Uniform Law on Formation" means the Law forming Annex I to the Second Convention as set out, with the modifications provided for by paragraph 3 of Article I of that Convention, in Schedule 2 to this Act; and "the Second Convention" means the Convention relating to a Uniform Law on the Formation of Contracts for the International Sale of Goods done at the Hague on 1st July 1964.

(2) Subject to subsection (3) of this section the Uniform Law on Formation shall have the force of law in the United Kingdom.

(3) The Uniform Law on Formation shall not apply to offers, replies and acceptances made before such date as Her Majesty may by Order in Council declare to be the date on which the Second Convention comes into force in respect of the United Kingdom.

(4) An Order in Council under this section shall be laid before Parliament after being made.

NOTES
Orders in Council: the Uniform Laws on International Sales Order 1972, SI 1972/973.

[1.426]
3 Revision of Uniform Laws

(1) If by any international Convention the Uniform Law on Sales or the Uniform Law on Formation is amended Her Majesty may by Order in Council modify the Schedules to this Act in such manner as appears to Her necessary for the purpose of giving effect to the Convention.

(2) No recommendation shall be made to Her Majesty in Council to make an Order under this section unless a draft thereof has been laid before and approved by each House of Parliament.

[1.427]
4 Application to Isle of Man and Channel Islands

Her Majesty may by Order in Council direct that the provisions of this Act shall extend, with such exceptions, adaptations and modifications as may be specified in the Order, to the Isle of Man or any of the Channel Islands; and an Order in Council under this section may be varied or revoked by a subsequent Order in Council.

[1.428]
5 Short title

This Act may be cited as the Uniform Laws on International Sales Act 1967.

SCHEDULES

SCHEDULE 1

THE UNIFORM LAW ON THE INTERNATIONAL SALE OF GOODS

Section 1

CHAPTER I—SPHERE OF APPLICATION OF THE LAW

Article 1

[1.429]
1. The present Law shall apply to contracts of sale of goods entered into by parties whose places of business are in the territories of different Contracting States, in each of the following cases:

(a) where the contract involves the sale of goods which are at the time of the conclusion of the contract in the course of carriage or will be carried from the territory of one State to the territory of another;

(b) where the acts constituting the offer and the acceptance have been effected in the territories of different States;

(c) where delivery of the goods is to be made in the territory of a State other than that within whose territory the acts constituting the offer and the acceptance have been effected.

2. Where a party to the contract does not have a place of business, reference shall be made to his habitual residence.

3. The application of the present Law shall not depend on the nationality of the parties.

4. In the case of contracts by correspondence, offer and acceptance shall be considered to have been effected in the territory of the same State only if the letters, telegrams or other documentary communications which contain them have been sent and received in the territory of that State.

5. For the purpose of determining whether the parties have their places of business or habitual residences in "different States", any two or more States shall not be considered to be "different States" if a valid declaration to that effect made under Article II of the Convention dated the 1st day of July 1964 relating to a Uniform Law on the International Sale of Goods is in force in respect of them.

Article 2

Rules of private international law shall be excluded for the purposes of the application of the present Law, subject to any provision to the contrary in the said Law.

Article 3

The parties to a contract of sale shall be free to exclude the application thereto of the present Law either entirely or partially. Such exclusion may be express or implied.

Article 4

The present Law shall also apply where it has been chosen as the law of the contract by the parties, whether or not their places of business or their habitual residences are in different States and whether or not such States are Parties to the Convention dated the 1st day of July 1964 relating to the Uniform Law on the International Sale of Goods, to the extent that it does not affect the application of any mandatory provisions of law which would have been applicable if the parties had not chosen the Uniform Law.

Article 5

1. The present Law shall not apply to sales:
(a) of stocks, shares, investment securities, negotiable instruments or money;
(b) of any ship, vessel or aircraft, which is or will be subject to registration;
(c) of electricity;
(d) by authority of law or on execution or distress.

2. The present Law shall not affect the application of any mandatory provision of national law for the protection of a party to a contract which contemplates the purchase of goods by that party by payment of the price by instalments.

Article 6

Contracts for the supply of goods to be manufactured or produced shall be considered to be sales within the meaning of the present Law, unless the party who orders the goods undertakes to supply an essential and substantial part of the materials necessary for such manufacture or production.

Article 7

The present Law shall apply to sales regardless of the commercial or civil character of the parties or of the contracts.

Article 8

The present Law shall govern only the obligations of the seller and the buyer arising from a contract of sale. In particular, the present Law shall not, except as otherwise expressly provided therein, be concerned with the formation of the contract, nor with the effect which the contract may have on the property in the goods sold, nor with the validity of the contract or of any of its provisions or of any usage.

CHAPTER II—GENERAL PROVISIONS

Article 9

1. The parties shall be bound by any usage which they have expressly or impliedly made applicable to their contract and by any practices which they have established between themselves.

2. They shall also be bound by usages which reasonable persons in the same situation as the parties usually consider to be applicable to their contract. In the event of conflict with the present Law, the usages shall prevail unless otherwise agreed by the parties.

3. Where expressions, provisions or forms of contract commonly used in commercial practice are employed, they shall be interpreted according to the meaning usually given to them in the trade concerned.

Article 10

For the purposes of the present Law, a breach of contract shall be regarded as fundamental wherever the party in breach knew, or ought to have known, at the time of the conclusion of the contract, that a reasonable person in the same situation as the other party would not have entered into the contract if he had foreseen the breach and its effects.

Article 11

Where under the present Law an act is required to be performed "promptly", it shall be performed within as short a period as possible, in the circumstances, from the moment when the act could reasonably be performed.

Article 12

For the purposes of the present Law, the expression "current price" means a price based upon an official market quotation, or, in the absence of such a quotation, upon those factors which, according to the usage of the market, serve to determine the price.

Article 13

For the purposes of the present Law, the expression "a party knew or ought to have known", or any similar expression, refers to what should have been known to a reasonable person in the same situation.

Article 14

Communications provided for by the present Law shall be made by the means usual in the circumstances.

Article 15

A contract of sale need not be evidenced by writing and shall not be subject to any other requirements as to form. In particular, it may be proved by means of witnesses.

Article 16

Where under the provisions of the present Law one party to a contract of sale is entitled to require performance of any obligation by the other party, a court shall not be bound to enter or enforce a judgment providing for specific performance except in accordance with the provisions of Article VII of the Convention dated the 1st day of July 1964 relating to a Uniform Law on the International Sale of Goods.

Article 17

Questions concerning matters governed by the present Law which are not expressly settled therein shall be settled in conformity with the general principles on which the present Law is based.

CHAPTER III—OBLIGATIONS OF THE SELLER

Article 18

The seller shall effect delivery of the goods, hand over any documents relating thereto and transfer the property in the goods, as required by the contract and the present Law.

SECTION I.—DELIVERY OF THE GOODS

Article 19

1. Delivery consists in the handing over of goods which conform with the contract.

2. Where the contract of sale involves carriage of the goods and no other place for delivery has been agreed upon, delivery shall be effected by handing over the goods to the carrier for transmission to the buyer.

3. Where the goods handed over to the carrier are not clearly appropriated to performance of the contract by being marked with an address or by some other means, the seller shall, in addition to handing over the goods, send to the buyer notice of the consignment and, if necessary, some document specifying the goods.

Sub-Section 1.—Obligations of the Seller as Regards the Date and Place of Delivery
A.—Date of Delivery

Article 20

Where the parties have agreed upon a date for delivery or where such date is fixed by usage, the seller shall, without the need for any other formality, be bound to deliver the goods at that date, provided that the date thus fixed is determined or determinable by the calendar or is fixed in relation to a definite event, the date of which can be ascertained by the parties.

Article 21

Where by agreement of the parties or by usage delivery shall be effected within a certain period (such as a particular month or season), the seller may fix the precise date of delivery, unless the circumstances indicate that the fixing of the date was reserved to the buyer.

Article 22

Where the date of delivery has not been determined in accordance with the provisions of Articles 20 or 21, the seller shall be bound to deliver the goods within a reasonable time after the conclusion of the contract, regard being had to the nature of the goods and to the circumstances.
B.—Place of Delivery

Article 23

1. Where the contract of sale does not involve carriage of the goods, the seller shall deliver the goods at the place where he carried on business at the time of the conclusion of the contract, or, in the absence of a place of business, at his habitual residence.

2. If the sale relates to specific goods and the parties knew that the goods were at a certain place at the time of the conclusion of the contract, the seller shall deliver the goods at that place. The same rule shall apply if the goods sold are unascertained goods to be taken from a specified stock or if they are to be manufactured or produced at a place known to the parties at the time of the conclusion of the contract.
C.—Remedies for the seller's failure to perform his obligations as regards the date and place of delivery

Article 24

1. Where the seller fails to perform his obligations as regards the date or the place of delivery, the buyer may, as provided in Articles 25 to 32:
    (a)   require performance of the contract by the seller;
    (b)   declare the contract avoided.

2. The buyer may also claim damages as provided in Article 82 or in Articles 84 to 87.

3. In no case shall the seller be entitled to apply to a court or arbitral tribunal to grant him a period of grace.

Article 25

The buyer shall not be entitled to require performance of the contract by the seller, if it is in conformity with usage and reasonably possible for the buyer to purchase goods to replace those to which the contract relates. In this case the contract shall be ipso facto avoided as from the time when such purchase should be effected.

(a) Remedies as regards the date of delivery

Article 26

1. Where the failure to deliver the goods at the date fixed amounts to a fundamental breach of the contract, the buyer may either require performance by the seller or declare the contract avoided. He shall inform the seller of his decision within a reasonable time; otherwise the contract shall be ipso facto avoided.

2. If the seller requests the buyer to make known his decision under paragraph 1 of this Article and the buyer does not comply promptly, the contract shall be ipso facto avoided.

3. If the seller has effected delivery before the buyer has made known his decision under paragraph 1 of this Article and the buyer does not exercise promptly his right to declare the contract avoided, the contract cannot be avoided.

4. Where the buyer has chosen performance of the contract and does not obtain it within a reasonable time, he may declare the contract avoided.

Article 27

1. Where failure to deliver the goods at the date fixed does not amount to a fundamental breach of the contract, the seller shall retain the right to effect delivery and the buyer shall retain the right to require performance of the contract by the seller.

2. The buyer may however grant the seller an additional period of time of reasonable length. Failure to deliver within this period shall amount to a fundamental breach of the contract.

Article 28

Failure to deliver the goods at the date fixed shall amount to a fundamental breach of the contract whenever a price for such goods is quoted on a market where the buyer can obtain them.

Article 29

Where the seller tenders delivery of the goods before the date fixed, the buyer may accept or reject delivery; if he accepts, he may reserve the right to claim damages in accordance with Article 82.

(b) Remedies as regards the place of delivery

Article 30

1. Where failure to deliver the goods at the place fixed amounts to a fundamental breach of the contract, and failure to deliver the goods at the date fixed would also amount to a fundamental breach, the buyer may either require performance of the contract by the seller or declare the contract avoided. The buyer shall inform the seller of his decision within a reasonable time; otherwise the contract shall be ipso facto avoided.

2. If the seller requests the buyer to make known his decision under paragraph 1 of this Article and the buyer does not comply promptly, the contract shall be ipso facto avoided.

3. If the seller has transported the goods to the place fixed before the buyer has made known his decision under paragraph 1 of this Article and the buyer does not exercise promptly his right to declare the contract avoided, the contract cannot be avoided.

Article 31

1. In cases not provided for in Article 30, the seller shall retain the right to effect delivery at the place fixed and the buyer shall retain the right to require performance of the contract by the seller.

2. The buyer may however grant the seller an additional period of time of reasonable length. Failure to deliver within this period at the place fixed shall amount to a fundamental breach of the contract.

Article 32

1. If delivery is to be effected by handing over the goods to a carrier and the goods have been handed over at a place other than that fixed, the buyer may declare the contract avoided, whenever the failure to deliver the goods at the place fixed amounts to a fundamental breach of the contract. He shall lose this right if he has not promptly declared the contract avoided.

2. The buyer shall have the same right, in the circumstances and on the conditions provided in paragraph 1 of this Article, if the goods have been despatched to some place other than that fixed.

3. If despatch from a place or to a place other than that fixed does not amount to a fundamental breach of the contract, the buyer may only claim damages in accordance with Article 82.

Sub-Section 2.—Obligations of the Seller as Regards the Conformity of the Goods
A.—Lack of conformity

Article 33

1. The seller shall not have fulfilled his obligation to deliver the goods, where he has handed over:
- (a) part only of the goods sold or a larger or a smaller quantity of the goods than he contracted to sell;
- (b) goods which are not those to which the contract relates or goods of a different kind;
- (c) goods which lack the qualities of a sample or model which the seller has handed over or sent to the buyer, unless the seller has submitted it without any express or implied undertaking that the goods would conform therewith;
- (d) goods which do not possess the qualities necessary for their ordinary or commercial use;
- (e) goods which do not possess the qualities for some particular purpose expressly or impliedly contemplated by the contract;
- (f) in general, goods which do not possess the qualities and characteristics expressly or impliedly contemplated by the contract.

2. No difference in quantity, lack of part of the goods or absence of any quality or characteristic shall be taken into consideration where it is not material.

Article 34

In the cases to which Article 33 relates, the rights conferred on the buyer by the present Law exclude all other remedies based on lack of conformity of the goods.

Article 35

1. Whether the goods are in conformity with the contract shall be determined by their conditions at the time when risk passes. However, if risk does not pass because of a declaration of avoidance of the contract or of a demand for other goods in replacement, the conformity of the goods with the contract shall be determined by their condition at the time when risk would have passed had they been in conformity with the contract.

2. The seller shall be liable for the consequences of any lack of conformity occurring after the time fixed in paragraph 1 of this Article if it was due to an act of the seller or of a person for whose conduct he is responsible.

Article 36

The seller shall not be liable for the consequences of any lack of conformity of the kind referred to in sub-paragraphs (d), (e) or (f) of paragraph 1 of Article 33, if at the time of the conclusion of the contract the buyer knew, or could not have been unaware of, such lack of conformity.

Article 37

If the seller has handed over goods before the date fixed for delivery he may, up to that date, deliver any missing part or quantity of the goods or deliver other goods which are in conformity with the contract or remedy any defects in the goods handed over, provided that the exercise of this right does not cause the buyer either unreasonable inconvenience or unreasonable expense.

B.—Ascertainment and notification of lack of conformity

Article 38

1. The buyer shall examine the goods, or cause them to be examined, promptly.

2. In case of carriage of the goods the buyer shall examine them at the place of destination.

3. If the goods are redespatched by the buyer without transhipment and the seller knew or ought to have known, at the time when the contract was concluded, of the possibility of such redespatch, examination of the goods may be deferred until they arrive at the new destination.

4. The methods of examination shall be governed by the agreement of the parties or, in the absence of such agreement, by the law or usage of the place where the examination is to be effected.

Article 39

1. The buyer shall lose the right to rely on a lack of conformity of the goods if he has not given the seller notice thereof promptly after he has discovered the lack of conformity or ought to have discovered it. If a defect which could not have been revealed by the examination of the goods provided for in Article 38 is found later, the buyer may nonetheless rely on that defect, provided that he gives the seller notice thereof promptly after its discovery. In any event, the buyer shall lose the right to rely on a lack of conformity of the goods if he has not given notice thereof to the seller within a period of two years from the date on which the goods were handed over, unless the lack of conformity constituted a breach of a guarantee covering a longer period.

2. In giving notice to the seller of any lack of conformity, the buyer shall specify its nature and invite the seller to examine the goods or to cause them to be examined by his agent.

3. Where any notice referred to in paragraph 1 of this Article has been sent by letter, telegram or other appropriate means, the fact that such notice is delayed or fails to arrive at its destination shall not deprive the buyer of the right to rely thereon.

Article 40

The seller shall not be entitled to rely on the provisions of Articles 38 and 39 if the lack of conformity relates to facts of which he knew, or of which he could not have been unaware, and which he did not disclose.

C.—Remedies for lack of conformity

Article 41

1. Where the buyer has given due notice to the seller of the failure of the goods to conform with the contract, the buyer may, as provided in Articles 42 to 46:
  (a) require performance of the contract by the seller;
  (b) declare the contract avoided;
  (c) reduce the price.

2. The buyer may also claim damages as provided in Article 82 or in Articles 84 to 87.

Article 42

1. The buyer may require the seller to perform the contract:
  (a) if the sale relates to goods to be produced or manufactured by the seller, by remedying defects in the goods, provided the seller is in a position to remedy the defects;
  (b) if the sale relates to specific goods, by delivering the goods to which the contract refers or the missing part thereof;
  (c) if the sale relates to unascertained goods, by delivering other goods which are in conformity with the contract or by delivering the missing part or quantity, except where the purchase of goods in replacement is in conformity with usage and reasonably possible.

2. If the buyer does not obtain performance of the contract by the seller within a reasonable time, he shall retain the rights provided in Articles 43 to 46.

Article 43

The buyer may declare the contract avoided if the failure of the goods to conform to the contract and also the failure to deliver on the date fixed amount to fundamental breaches of the contract. The buyer shall lose his right to declare the contract avoided if he does not exercise it promptly after giving the seller notice of the lack of conformity or, in the case to which paragraph 2 of Article 42 applies, after the expiration of the period referred to in that paragraph.

Article 44

1. In cases not provided for in Article 43, the seller shall retain, after the date fixed for the delivery of the goods, the right to deliver any missing part or quantity of the goods or to deliver other goods which are in conformity with the contract or to remedy any defect in the goods handed over, provided that the exercise of this right does not cause the buyer either unreasonable inconvenience or unreasonable expense.

2. The buyer may however fix an additional period of time of reasonable length for the further delivery or for the remedying of the defect. If at the expiration of the additional period the seller has not delivered the goods or remedied the defect, the buyer may choose between requiring the performance of the contract or reducing the price in accordance with Article 46 or, provided that he does so promptly, declare the contract avoided.

Article 45

1. Where the seller has handed over part only of the goods or an insufficient quantity or where part only of the goods handed over is in conformity with the contract, the provisions of Articles 43 and 44 shall apply in respect of the part or quantity which is missing or which does not conform with the contract.

2. The buyer may declare the contract avoided in its entirety only if the failure to effect delivery completely and in conformity with the contract amounts to a fundamental breach of the contract.

Article 46

Where the buyer has neither obtained performance of the contract by the seller nor declared the contract avoided, the buyer may reduce the price in the same proportion as the value of the goods at the time of the conclusion of the contract has been diminished because of their lack of conformity with the contract.

Article 47

Where the seller has proffered to the buyer a quantity of unascertained goods greater than that provided for in the contract, the buyer may reject or accept the excess quantity. If the buyer rejects the excess quantity, the seller shall be liable only for damages in accordance with Article 82. If the buyer accepts the whole or part of the excess quantity, he shall pay for it at the contract rate.

Article 48

The buyer may exercise the rights provided in Articles 43 to 46, even before the time fixed for delivery, if it is clear that goods which would be handed over would not be in conformity with the contract.

Article 49

1. The buyer shall lose his right to rely on lack of conformity with the contract at the expiration of a period of one year after he has given notice as provided in Article 39, unless he has been prevented from exercising his right because of fraud on the part of the seller.

2. After the expiration of this period, the buyer shall not be entitled to rely on the lack of conformity, even by way of defence to an action. Nevertheless, if the buyer has not paid for the goods and provided that he has given due notice of the lack of conformity promptly, as provided in Article 39, he may advance as a defence to a claim for payment of the price a claim for a reduction in the price or for damages.

SECTION II.—HANDING OVER OF DOCUMENTS

Article 50

Where the seller is bound to hand over to the buyer any documents relating to the goods, he shall do so at the time and place fixed by the contract or by usage.

Article 51

If the seller fails to hand over documents as provided in Article 50 at the time and place fixed or if he hands over documents which are not in conformity with those which he was bound to hand over, the buyer shall have the same rights as those provided under Articles 24 to 32 or under Articles 41 to 49, as the case may be.

SECTION III.—TRANSFER OF PROPERTY

Article 52

1. Where the goods are subject to a right or claim of a third person, the buyer, unless he agreed to take the goods subject to such right or claim, shall notify the seller of such right or claim, unless the seller already knows thereof, and request that the goods should be freed therefrom within reasonable time or that other goods free from all rights and claims of third persons be delivered to him by the seller.

2. If the seller complies with a request made under paragraph 1 of this Article and the buyer nevertheless suffers a loss, the buyer may claim damages in accordance with Article 82.

3. If the seller fails to comply with a request made under paragraph 1 of this Article and a fundamental breach of the contract results thereby, the buyer may declare the contract avoided and claim damages in accordance with Articles 84 to 87. If the buyer does not declare the contract avoided or if there is no fundamental breach of the contract, the buyer shall have the right to claim damages in accordance with Article 82.

4. The buyer shall lose his right to declare the contract avoided if he fails to act in accordance with paragraph 1 of this Article within a reasonable time from the moment when he became aware or ought to have become aware of the right or claim of the third person in respect of the goods.

Article 53

The rights conferred on the buyer by Article 52 exclude all other remedies based on the fact that the seller has failed to perform his obligation to transfer the property in the goods or that the goods are subject to a right or claim of a third person.

SECTION IV.—OTHER OBLIGATIONS OF THE SELLER

Article 54

1. If the seller is bound to despatch the goods to the buyer, he shall make, in the usual way and on the usual terms, such contracts as are necessary for the carriage of the goods to the place fixed.

2. If the seller is not bound by the contract to effect insurance in respect of the carriage of the goods, he shall provide the buyer, at his request, with all information necessary to enable him to effect such insurance.

Article 55

1. If the seller fails to perform any obligation other than those referred to in Articles 20 to 53, the buyer may:
- (a) where such failure amounts to a fundamental breach of the contract, declare the contract avoided, provided that he does so promptly, and claim damages in accordance with Articles 84 to 87, or
- (b) in any other case, claim damages in accordance with Article 82.

2. The buyer may also require performance by the seller of his obligation, unless the contract is avoided.

CHAPTER IV—OBLIGATIONS OF THE BUYER

Article 56

The buyer shall pay the price for the goods and take delivery of them, as required by the contract and the present law.

SECTION I.—PAYMENT OF THE PRICE
A.—*Fixing the price*

Article 57

Where a contract has been concluded but does not state a price or make provision for the determination of the price, the buyer shall be bound to pay the price generally charged by the seller at the time of the conclusion of the contract.

Article 58

Where the price is fixed according to the weight of the goods, it shall, in case of doubt, be determined by the net weight.

B.—Place and date of payment

Article 59

1. The buyer shall pay the price to the seller at the seller's place of business or, if he does not have a place of business, at his habitual residence, or, where the payment is to be made against the handing over of the goods or of documents, at the place where such handing over takes place.

2. Where, in consequence of a change in the place of business or habitual residence of the seller subsequent to the conclusion of the contract, the expenses incidental to payment are increased, such increase shall be borne by the seller.

Article 60

Where the parties have agreed upon a date for the payment of the price or where such date is fixed by usage, the buyer shall, without the need for any other formality, pay the price at that date.

C.—Remedies for non-payment

Article 61

1. If the buyer fails to pay the price in accordance with the contract and with the present law, the seller may require the buyer to perform his obligation.

2. The seller shall not be entitled to require payment of the price by the buyer if it is in conformity with usage and reasonably possible for the seller to resell the goods. In that case the contract shall be ipso facto avoided as from the time when such resale should be effected.

Article 62

1. Where the failure to pay the price at the date fixed amounts to a fundamental breach of the contract, the seller may either require the buyer to pay the price or declare the contract avoided. He shall inform the buyer of his decision within a reasonable time; otherwise the contract shall be ipso facto avoided.

2. Where the failure to pay the price at the date fixed does not amount to a fundamental breach of the contract, the seller may grant to the buyer an additional period of time of reasonable length. If the buyer has not paid the price at the expiration of the additional period, the seller may either require the payment of the price by the buyer or, provided that he does so promptly, declare the contract avoided.

Article 63

1. Where the contract is avoided because of failure to pay the price, the seller shall have the right to claim damages in accordance with Articles 84 to 87.

2. Where the contract is not avoided, the seller shall have the right to claim damages in accordance with Articles 82 and 83.

Article 64

In no case shall the buyer be entitled to apply to a court or arbitral tribunal to grant him a period of grace for the payment of the price.

SECTION II.—TAKING DELIVERY

Article 65

Taking delivery consists in the buyer's doing all such acts as are necessary in order to enable the seller to hand over the goods and actually taking them over.

Article 66

1. Where the buyer's failure to take delivery of the goods in accordance with the contract amounts to a fundamental breach of the contract or gives the seller good grounds for fearing that the buyer will not pay the price, the seller may declare the contract avoided.

2. Where the failure to take delivery of the goods does not amount to a fundamental breach of the contract, the seller may grant to the buyer an additional period of time of reasonable length. If the buyer has not taken delivery of the goods at the expiration of the additional period, the seller may declare the contract avoided, provided that he does so promptly.

Article 67

1. If the contract reserves to the buyer the right subsequently to determine the form, measurement or other features of the goods (sale by specification) and he fails to make such specification either on the date expressly or impliedly agreed upon or within a reasonable time after receipt of a request from the seller, the seller may declare the contract avoided, provided that he does so promptly, or make the specification himself in accordance with the requirements of the buyer in so far as these are known to him.

2. If the seller makes the specification himself, he shall inform the buyer of the details thereof and shall fix a reasonable period of time within which the buyer may submit a different specification. If the buyer fails to do so the specification made by the seller shall be binding.

Article 68

1. Where the contract is avoided because of the failure of the buyer to accept delivery of the goods or to make a specification, the seller shall have the right to claim damages in accordance with Articles 84 to 87.

2. Where the contract is not avoided, the seller shall have the right to claim damages in accordance with Article 82.

SECTION III.—OTHER OBLIGATIONS OF THE BUYER

Article 69

The buyer shall take the steps provided for in the contract, by usage or by laws and regulations in force, for the purpose of making provision for or guaranteeing payment of the price, such as the acceptance of a bill of exchange, the opening of a documentary credit or the giving of a banker's guarantee.

Article 70

1. If the buyer fails to perform any obligation other than those referred to in Sections I and II of this Chapter, the seller may:
  (a) where such failure amounts to a fundamental breach of the contract, declare the contract avoided, provided that he does so promptly, and claim damages in accordance with Articles 84 to 87; or
  (b) in any other case, claim damages in accordance with Article 82.

2. The seller may also require performance by the buyer of his obligation, unless the contract is avoided.

CHAPTER V
PROVISIONS COMMON TO THE OBLIGATIONS OF THE SELLER AND OF THE BUYER

SECTION I.—CONCURRENCE BETWEEN DELIVERY OF THE GOODS AND PAYMENT OF THE PRICE

Article 71

Except as otherwise provided in Article 72, delivery of the goods and payment of the price shall be concurrent conditions. Nevertheless, the buyer shall not be obliged to pay the price until he has had an opportunity to examine the goods.

Article 72

1. Where the contract involves carriage of the goods and where delivery is, by virtue of paragraph 2 of Article 19, effected by handing over the goods to the carrier, the seller may either postpone despatch of the goods until he receives payment or proceed to despatch them on terms that reserve to himself the right of disposal of the goods during transit. In the latter case, he may require that the goods shall not be handed over to the buyer at the place of destination except against payment of the price and the buyer shall not be bound to pay the price until he has had an opportunity to examine the goods.

2. Nevertheless, when the contract requires payment against documents, the buyer shall not be entitled to refuse payment of the price on the ground that he has not had the opportunity to examine the goods.

Article 73

1. Each party may suspend the performance of his obligations whenever, after the conclusion of the contract, the economic situation of the other party appears to have become so difficult that there is good reason to fear that he will not perform a material part of his obligations.

2. If the seller has already despatched the goods before the economic situation of the buyer described in paragraph 1 of this Article becomes evident, he may prevent the handing over of the goods to the buyer even if the latter holds a document which entitles him to obtain them.

3. Nevertheless, the seller shall not be entitled to prevent the handing over of the goods if they are claimed by a third person who is a lawful holder of a document which entitles him to obtain the goods, unless the document contains a reservation concerning the effects of its transfer or unless the seller can prove that the holder of the document, when he acquired it, knowingly acted to the detriment of the seller.

Section II.—Exemptions

Article 74

1. Where one of the parties has not performed one of his obligations, he shall not be liable for such non-performance if he can prove that it was due to circumstances which, according to the intention of the parties at the time of the conclusion of the contract, he was not bound to take into account or to avoid or to overcome; in the absence of any expression of the intention of the parties, regard shall be had to what reasonable persons in the same situation would have intended.

2. Where the circumstances which gave rise to the non-performance of the obligation constituted only a temporary impediment to performance, the party in default shall nevertheless be permanently relieved of his obligation if, by reason of the delay, performance would be so radically changed as to amount to the performance of an obligation quite different from that contemplated by the contract.

3. The relief provided by this Article for one of the parties shall not include the avoidance of the contract under some other provision of the present Law or deprive the other party of any right which he has under the present Law to reduce the price, unless the circumstances which entitled the first party to relief were caused by the act of the other party or of some person for whose conduct he was responsible.

Section III.—Supplementary Rules Concerning the Avoidance of the Contract
A.—Supplementary grounds for avoidance

Article 75

1. Where, in the case of contracts for delivery of goods by instalments, by reason of any failure by one party to perform any of his obligations under the contract in respect of any instalment, the other party has good reason to fear failure of performance in respect of future instalments, he may declare the contract avoided for the future, provided that he does so promptly.

2. The buyer may also, provided that he does so promptly, declare the contract avoided in respect of future deliveries or in respect of deliveries already made or both, if by reason of their interdependence such deliveries would be worthless to him.

Article 76

Where prior to the date fixed for performance of the contract it is clear that one of the parties will commit a fundamental breach of the contract, the other party shall have the right to declare the contract avoided.

Article 77

Where the contract has been avoided under Article 75 or Article 76, the party declaring the contract avoided may claim damages in accordance with Articles 84 to 87.

B.—Effects of avoidance

Article 78

1. Avoidance of the contract releases both parties from their obligations thereunder, subject to any damages which may be due.

2. If one party has performed the contract either wholly or in part, he may claim the return of whatever he has supplied or paid under the contract. If both parties are required to make restitution, they shall do so concurrently.

Article 79

1. The buyer shall lose his right to declare the contract avoided where it is impossible for him to return the goods in the condition in which he received them.

2. Nevertheless, the buyer may declare the contract avoided:
- (a) if the goods or part of the goods have perished or deteriorated as a result of the defect which justifies the avoidance;
- (b) if the goods or part of the goods have perished or deteriorated as a result of the examination prescribed in Article 38;
- (c) if part of the goods have been consumed or transformed by the buyer in the course of normal use before the lack of conformity with the contract was discovered;
- (d) if the impossibility of returning the goods or of returning them in the condition in which they were received is not due to the act of the buyer or of some other person for whose conduct he is responsible;
- (e) if the deterioration or transformation of the goods is unimportant.

Article 80

The buyer who has lost the right to declare the contract avoided by virtue of Article 79 shall retain all the other rights conferred on him by the present Law.

Article 81

1. Where the seller is under an obligation to refund the price, he shall also be liable for the interest thereon at the rate fixed by Article 83, as from the date of payment.

2. The buyer shall be liable to account to the seller for all benefits which he has derived from the goods or part of them, as the case may be:
- (a) where he is under an obligation to return the goods or part of them,
- (b) where it is impossible for him to return the goods or part of them, but the contract is nevertheless avoided.

SECTION IV.—SUPPLEMENTARY RULES CONCERNING DAMAGES
A.—Damages where the contract is not avoided

Article 82

Where the contract is not avoided, damages for a breach of contract by one party shall consist of a sum equal to the loss, including loss of profit, suffered by the other party. Such damages shall not exceed the loss which the party in breach ought to have foreseen at the time of the conclusion of the contract, in the light of the facts and matters which then were known or ought to have been known to him, as a possible consequence of the breach of the contract.

Article 83

Where the breach of contract consists of delay in the payment of the price, the seller shall in any event be entitled to interest on such sum as is in arrear at a rate equal to the official discount rate in the country where he has his place of business or, if he has no place of business, his habitual residence, plus 1 per cent.

B.—Damages where the contract is avoided

Article 84

1. In case of avoidance of the contract, where there is a current price for the goods, damages shall be equal to the difference between the price fixed by the contract and the current price on the date on which the contract is avoided.

2. In calculating the amount of damages under paragraph 1 of this Article, the current price to be taken into account shall be that prevailing in the market in which the transaction took place or, if there is no such current price or if its application is inappropriate, the price in a market which serves as a reasonable substitute, making due allowance for differences in the cost of transporting the goods.

Article 85

If the buyer has bought goods in replacement or the seller has resold goods in a reasonable manner, he may recover the difference between the contract price and the price paid for the goods bought in replacement or that obtained by the resale.

Article 86

The damages referred to in Articles 84 and 85 may be increased by the amount of any reasonable expenses incurred as a result of the breach or up to the amount of any loss, including loss of profit, which should have been foreseen by the party in breach, at the time of the conclusion of the contract, in the light of the facts and matters which were known or ought to have been known to him, as a possible consequence of the breach of the contract.

Article 87

If there is no current price for the goods, damages shall be calculated on the same basis as that provided in Article 82.

C.—General provisions concerning damages

Article 88

The party who relies on a breach of the contract shall adopt all reasonable measures to mitigate the loss resulting from the breach. If he fails to adopt such measures, the party in breach may claim a reduction in the damages.

Article 89

In case of fraud, damages shall be determined by the rules applicable in respect of contracts of sale not governed by the present law.

Section V.—Expenses

Article 90

The expenses of delivery shall be borne by the seller; all expenses after delivery shall be borne by the buyer.

Section VI.—Preservation of the Goods

Article 91

Where the buyer is in delay in taking delivery of the goods or in paying the price, the seller shall take reasonable steps to preserve the goods; he shall have the right to retain them until he has been reimbursed his reasonable expenses by the buyer.

Article 92

1. Where the goods have been received by the buyer, he shall take reasonable steps to preserve them if he intends to reject them; he shall have the right to retain them until he has been reimbursed his reasonable expenses by the seller.

2. Where goods despatched to the buyer have been put at his disposal at their place of destination and he exercises the right to reject them, he shall be bound to take possession of them on behalf of the seller, provided that this may be done without payment of the price and without unreasonable inconvenience or unreasonable expense. This provision shall not apply where the seller or a person authorised to take charge of the goods on his behalf is present at such destination.

Article 93

The party who is under an obligation to take steps to preserve the goods may deposit them in the warehouse of a third person at the expense of the other party provided that the expense incurred is not unreasonable.

Article 94

1. The party who, in the cases to which Articles 91 and 92 apply, is under an obligation to take steps to preserve the goods may sell them by any appropriate means, provided that there has been unreasonable delay by the other party in accepting them or taking them back or in paying the costs of preservation and provided that due notice has been given to the other party of the intention to sell.

2. The party selling the goods shall have the right to retain out of the proceeds of sale an amount equal to the reasonable costs of preserving the goods and of selling them and shall transmit the balance to the other party.

Article 95

Where, in the cases to which Articles 91 and 92 apply, the goods are subject to loss or rapid deterioration or their preservation would involve unreasonable expense, the party under the duty to preserve them is bound to sell them in accordance with Article 94.

CHAPTER VI—PASSING OF THE RISK

Article 96

Where the risk has passed to the buyer, he shall pay the price notwithstanding the loss or deterioration of the goods, unless this is due to the act of the seller or of some other person for whose conduct the seller is responsible.

Article 97

1. The risk shall pass to the buyer when delivery of the goods is effected in accordance with the provisions of the contract and the present Law.

2. In the case of the handing over of goods which are not in conformity with the contract, the risk shall pass to the buyer from the moment when the handing over has, apart from the lack of conformity, been effected in accordance with the provisions of the contract and of the present Law, where the buyer has neither declared the contract avoided nor required goods in replacement.

Article 98

1. Where the handing over of the goods is delayed owing to the breach of an obligation of the buyer, the risk shall pass to the buyer as from the last date when, apart from such breach, the handing over could have been made in accordance with the contract.

2. Where the contract relates to a sale of unascertained goods, delay on the part of the buyer shall cause the risk to pass only when the seller has set aside goods manifestly appropriated to the contract and has notified the buyer that this has been done.

3. Where unascertained goods are of such a kind that the seller cannot set aside a part of them until the buyer takes delivery, it shall be sufficient for the seller to do all acts necessary to enable the buyer to take delivery.

Article 99

1. Where the sale is of goods in transit by sea, the risk shall be borne by the buyer as from the time at which the goods were handed over to the carrier.

2. Where the seller, at the time of the conclusion of the contract, knew or ought to have known that the goods had been lost or had deteriorated, the risk shall remain with him until the time of the conclusion of the contract.

Article 100

If, in a case to which paragraph 3 of Article 19 applies, the seller, at the time of sending the notice or other document referred to in that paragraph knew or ought to have known that the goods had been lost or had deteriorated after they were handed over to the carrier, the risk shall remain with the seller until the time of sending such notice or document.

Article 101

The passing of the risk shall not necessarily be determined by the provisions of the contract concerning expenses.

SCHEDULE 2
THE UNIFORM LAW ON THE FORMATION OF CONTRACTS FOR THE INTERNATIONAL SALE OF GOODS

Section 2

Article 1

[1.430]
The present Law shall apply to the formation of contracts of sale of goods which, if they were concluded, would be governed by the Uniform Law on the International Sale of Goods.

Article 2

1. The provisions of the following Articles shall apply except to the extent that it appears from the preliminary negotiations, the offer, the reply, the practices which the parties have established between themselves or usage, that other rules apply.

2. However, a term of the offer stipulating that silence shall amount to acceptance is invalid.

Article 3

An offer or an acceptance need not be evidenced by writing and shall not be subject to any other requirement as to form. In particular, they may be proved by means of witnesses.

Article 4

1. The communication which one person addresses to one or more specific persons with the object of, concluding a contract of sale shall not constitute an offer unless it is sufficiently definite to permit the conclusion of the contract by acceptance and indicates the intention of the offeror to be bound.

2. This communication may be interpreted by reference to and supplemented by the preliminary negotiations, any practices which the parties have established between themselves, usage and the provisions of the Uniform Law on the International Sale of Goods.

Article 5

1. The offer shall not bind the offeror until it has been communicated to the offeree; it shall lapse if its withdrawal is communicated to the offeree before or at the same time as the offer.

2. After an offer has been communicated to the offeree it can be revoked unless the revocation is not made in good faith or in conformity with fair dealing or unless the offer states a fixed time for acceptance or otherwise indicates that it is firm or irrevocable.

3. An indication that the offer is firm or irrevocable may be express or implied from the circumstances, the preliminary negotiations, any practices which the parties have established between themselves or usage.

4. A revocation of an offer shall only have effect if it has been communicated to the offeree before he has despatched his acceptance or has done any act treated as acceptance under paragraph 2 of Article 6.

Article 6

1. Acceptance of an offer consists of a declaration by any means whatsoever to the offeror.

2. Acceptance may also consist of the despatch of the goods or of the price or of any other act which may be considered to be equivalent to the declaration referred to in paragraph 1 of this Article either by virtue of the offer or as a result of practices which the parties have established between themselves or usage.

Article 7

1. An acceptance containing additions, limitations or other modifications shall be a rejection of the offer and shall constitute a counter-offer.

2. However, a reply to an offer which purports to be an acceptance but which contains additional or different terms which do not materially alter the terms of the offer shall constitute an acceptance unless the offeror promptly objects to the discrepancy; if he does not so object, the terms of the contract shall be the terms of the offer with the modifications contained in the acceptance.

Article 8

1. A declaration of acceptance of an offer shall have effect only if it is communicated to the offeror within the time he has fixed or, if no such time is fixed, within a reasonable time, due account being taken of the circumstances of the transaction, including the rapidity of the means of communication employed by the offeror, and usage. In the case of an oral offer, the acceptance shall be immediate, if the circumstances do not show that the offeree shall have time for reflection.

2. If a time for acceptance is fixed by an offeror in a letter or in a telegram, it shall be presumed to begin to run from the day the letter was dated or the hour of the day the telegram was handed in for despatch.

3. If an acceptance consists of an act referred to in paragraph 2 of Article 6, the act shall have effect only if it is done within the period laid down in paragraph 1 of the present Article.

Article 9

1. If the acceptance is late, the offeror may nevertheless consider it to have arrived in due time on condition that he promptly so informs the acceptor orally or by despatch of a notice.

2. If however the acceptance is communicated late, it shall be considered to have been communicated in due time, if the letter or document which contains the acceptance shows that it has been sent in such circumstances that if its transmission had been normal it would have been communicated in due time; this provision shall not however apply if the offeror has promptly informed the acceptor orally or by despatch of a notice that he considers his offer as having lapsed.

Article 10

An acceptance cannot be revoked except by a revocation which is communicated to the offeror before or at the same time as the acceptance.

Article 11

The formation of the contract is not affected by the death of one of the parties or by his becoming incapable of contracting before acceptance unless the contrary results from the intention of the parties, usage or the nature of the transaction.

Article 12

1. For the purposes of the present Law, the expression "to be communicated" means to be delivered at the address of the person to whom the communication is directed.

2. Communications provided for by the present Law shall be made by the means usual in the circumstances.

Article 13

1. "Usage" means any practice or method of dealing which reasonable persons in the same situation as the parties usually consider to be applicable to the formation of their contract.

2. Where expressions, provisions or forms of contract commonly used in commercial practice are employed, they shall be interpreted according to the meaning usually given to them in the trade concerned.

TRADE DESCRIPTIONS ACT 1968

(1968 c 29)

ARRANGEMENT OF SECTIONS

Prohibition of false trade descriptions

Misstatements other than false trade descriptions

Prohibition of importation of certain goods

Provisions as to offences

Defences

Enforcement

Miscellaneous and supplemental

An Act to replace the Merchandise Marks Acts 1887 to 1953 by fresh provisions prohibiting misdescriptions of goods, services, accommodation and facilities provided in the course of trade; to prohibit false or misleading indications as to the price of goods; to confer power to require information or instructions relating to goods to be marked on or to accompany the goods or to be included in advertisements; to prohibit the unauthorised use of devices or emblems signifying royal awards; to enable the Parliament of Northern Ireland to make laws relating to merchandise marks; and for purposes connected with those matters

[30 May 1968]

Prohibition of false trade descriptions

[1.431]
1 Prohibition of false trade descriptions
(1)   . . .
[(2)   Sections 2 to 4 shall have effect for the interpretation of expressions used in this Act.]

NOTES
Sub-s (1): repealed by the Consumer Protection from Unfair Trading Regulations 2008, SI 2008/1277, reg 30(1), (3), Sch 2, Pt 1, paras 7, 8(a), Sch 4.
Sub-s (2): substituted by SI 2008/1277, reg 30(1), Sch 2, Pt 1, paras 7, 9.

[1.432]
2 Trade description
(1)   A trade description is an indication, direct or indirect, and by whatever means given of any of the following matters with respect to any goods or parts of goods, that is to say—
  (a)   quantity, size or gauge;
  (b)   method of manufacture, production, processing or reconditioning;
  (c)   composition;
  (d)   fitness for purpose, strength, performance, behaviour or accuracy;
  (e)   any physical characteristics not included in the preceding paragraphs;
  (f)   testing by any person and results thereof;
  (g)   approval by any person or conformity with a type approved by any person;
  (h)   place or date of manufacture, production, processing or reconditioning;
  (i)   person by whom manufactured, produced, processed or reconditioned;
  (j)   other history, including previous ownership or use.
(2)   The matters specified in subsection (1) of this section shall be taken—
  (a)   in relation to any animal, to include sex, breed or cross, fertility and soundness;
  (b)   in relation to any semen, to include the identity and characteristics of the animal from which it was taken and measure of dilution.
(3)   In this section "quantity" includes length, width, height, area, volume, capacity, weight and number.
(4)   Notwithstanding anything in the preceding provisions of this section, the following shall be deemed not to be trade descriptions, that is to say, any description or mark applied in pursuance of—
  (a), (b) . . .
  (c)   the Plant Varieties and Seeds Act 1964;
  (d)   the Agriculture and Horticulture Act 1964 [or any Community grading rules within the meaning of Part III of that Act];
  (e)   the Seeds Act (Northern Ireland) 1965;
  (f)   the Horticulture Act (Northern Ireland) 1966;
  [(g)   the Consumer Protection Act 1987;]
  [(h)   the Plant Varieties Act 1997;]
[any statement made in respect of, or mark applied to, any material in pursuance of Part IV of the Agriculture Act 1970, any name or expression to which a meaning has been assigned under section 70 of that Act when applied to any material in the circumstances specified in that section]
   . . .   any mark prescribed by a system of classification compiled under section 5 of the Agriculture Act 1967 [and any designation, mark or description applied in pursuance of a scheme brought into force under section 6(1) or an order made under section 25(1) of the Agriculture Act 1970].
(5)   Notwithstanding anything in the preceding provisions of this section,
  [(a)] where provision is made under [the Food Safety Act 1990] or the [Food Safety (Northern Ireland) Order 1991] [or the Consumer Protection Act 1987] prohibiting the application of a description except to goods in the case of which the requirements specified in that provision are complied with, that description, when applied to such goods, shall be deemed not to be a trade description;
  [(b)] where by virtue of any provision [of Chapter 1 of Part 13 of the Human Medicines Regulations 2012] anything which, in accordance with this Act, constitutes the application of a trade description to goods is subject to any requirements or restrictions imposed by that provision, any particular description specified in that provision, when applied to goods in circumstances to which those requirements or restrictions are applicable, shall be deemed not to be a trade description]
  [(c)   where any description of a veterinary medicinal product is required to be applied to the product by an authorisation for the product granted under the Veterinary Medicines Regulations 2006, that description, when applied to the product, shall be deemed not to be a trade description.]

NOTES

Sub-s (4): para (a) repealed, and words in square brackets in para (d) added, by the European Communities Act 1972, s 4, Sch 3, Pt II, Sch 4, para 4(2); para (b) repealed by the Deregulation Act 2015, s 107, Sch 23, Pt 6, para 34(1), (5)(a); para (g) inserted by the Consumer Safety Act 1978, s 7(8), substituted by the Consumer Protection Act 1987, s 48(1), Sch 4, para 2(1); para (h) inserted by the Plant Varieties Act 1997, s 51(4); other words in square brackets substituted or added and second words omitted repealed by the Agriculture Act 1970, ss 6(4), 87(3), 113(3), Sch 5, Pt V.

Sub-s (5): para (a) numbered as such and para (b) added by the Medicines Act 1968, s 135(1), Sch 5, para 16; in para (a), words in first pair of square brackets substituted by the Food Safety Act 1990, s 59(1), Sch 3, para 6, words in second pair of square brackets substituted by the Food Safety (Northern Ireland) Order 1991, SI 1991/762, art 51(1), Sch 2, para 8, and words in third pair of square brackets substituted by the Consumer Protection Act 1987, s 48(1), Sch 4, para 2(1); words in square brackets in para (b) substituted by the Human Medicines Regulations 2012, SI 2012/1916, reg 348, Sch 34, Pt 2, para 37; para (c) added by the Veterinary Medicines Regulations 2006, SI 2006/2407, reg 44(3), Sch 9, Pt 1, para 2.

[1.433]

3   False trade description

(1)   A false trade description is a trade description which is false to a material degree.

(2)   A trade description which, though not false, is misleading, that is to say, likely to be taken for such an indication of any of the matters specified in section 2 of this Act as would be false to a material degree, shall be deemed to be a false trade description.

(3)   Anything which, though not a trade description, is likely to be taken for an indication of any of those matters and, as such an indication, would be false to a material degree, shall be deemed to be a false trade description.

(4)   A false indication, or anything likely to be taken as an indication which would be false, that any goods comply with a standard specified or recognised by any person or implied by the approval of any person shall be deemed to be a false trade description, if there is no such person or no standard so specified, recognised or implied.

[1.434]

4   Applying a trade description to goods

(1)   A person applies a trade description to goods if he—

    (a)   affixes or annexes it to or in any manner marks it on or incorporates it with—

       (i)   the goods themselves, or

       (ii)   anything in, on or with which the goods are supplied; or

    (b)   places the goods in, on or with anything which the trade description has been affixed or annexed to, marked on or incorporated with, or places any such thing with the goods; or

    (c)   uses the trade description in any manner likely to be taken as referring to the goods.

(2)   An oral statement may amount to the use of a trade description.

(3)   Where goods are supplied in pursuance of a request in which a trade description is used and circumstances are such as to make it reasonable to infer that the goods are supplied as goods corresponding to that trade description, the person supplying the goods shall be deemed to have applied that trade description to the goods.

[1.435]

5   *Trade descriptions used in advertisements*

(1)   The following provisions of this section shall have effect where in an advertisement a trade description is used in relation to any class of goods.

(2)   The trade description shall be taken as referring to all goods of the class, whether or not in existence at the time the advertisement is published—

    (a)   for the purpose of determining whether an offence has been committed under paragraph (a) of section 1(1) of this Act; and

    (b)   where goods of the class are supplied or offered to be supplied by a person publishing or displaying the advertisement, also for the purpose of determining whether an offence has been committed under paragraph (b) of the said section 1(1).

(3)   In determining for the purposes of this section whether any goods are of a class to which a trade description used in an advertisement relates regard shall be had not only to the form and content of the advertisement but also to the time, place, manner and frequency of its publication and all other matters making it likely or unlikely that a person to whom the goods are supplied would think of the goods as belonging to the class in relation to which the trade description is used in the advertisement.

NOTES

Repealed by the Consumer Protection from Unfair Trading Regulations 2008, SI 2008/1277, reg 30(1), (3), Sch 2, Pt 1, paras 7, 8(b), Sch 4, subject to transitional provisions and savings in reg 30(2) of, and Sch 3, para 1 to, those Regulations at **[2.595]**, **[2.597]**.

6–10   *(Repealed by the Consumer Protection from Unfair Trading Regulations 2008, SI 2008/1277, reg 30(1), (3), Sch 2, Pt 1, paras 7, 8(c), (d), Sch 4.)*

Misstatements other than false trade descriptions

11 (*Repealed by the Consumer Protection Act 1987, s 48(3), Sch 5.*)

[1.436]
12 False representations as to royal approval or award, etc
(1) If any person, in the course of any trade or business, gives, by whatever means, any false indication, direct or indirect, that any goods or services supplied by him or any methods adopted by him are or are of a kind supplied to or approved by Her Majesty or any member of the Royal Family, he shall, subject to the provisions of this Act, be guilty of an offence.
(2) If any person, in the course of any trade or business, uses, without the authority of Her Majesty, any device or emblem signifying the Queen's Award to Industry or anything so nearly resembling such a device or emblem as to be likely to deceive, he shall, subject to the provisions of this Act, be guilty of an offence.
[(3) A person shall not be guilty of an offence under subsection (1) or (2) by reason of doing anything that is a commercial practice unless the commercial practice is unfair.
    In this subsection "commercial practice" and "unfair" have the same meaning as in the Consumer Protection from Unfair Trading Regulations 2008.]

NOTES
Sub-s (3): added by the Consumer Protection from Unfair Trading Regulations 2008, SI 2008/1277, reg 30(1), Sch 2, Pt 1, paras 7, 10.

13–15 (*Repealed by the Consumer Protection from Unfair Trading Regulations 2008, SI 2008/1277, reg 30(1), (3), Sch 2, Pt 1, paras 7, 8(e), Sch 4.*)

Prohibition of importation of certain goods

[1.437]
16 Prohibition of importation of goods bearing false indication of origin
Where a false trade description is applied to any goods outside the United Kingdom and the false indication, or one of the false indications, given, or likely to be taken as given, thereby is an indication of the place of manufacture, production, processing or reconditioning of the goods or any part thereof, the goods shall not be imported into the United Kingdom.

17 (*Inserted the Trade Marks Act 1938, s 64A (repealed).*)

Provisions as to offences

[1.438]
18 Penalty for offences
A person guilty of an offence under this Act for which no other penalty is specified shall be liable—
    (a)   on summary conviction, to a fine not exceeding [the prescribed sum] and
    (b)   on conviction on indictment, to a fine or imprisonment for a term not exceeding two years or both.

NOTES
Reference to the prescribed sum in para (a) substituted by virtue of the Magistrates' Courts Act 1980, s 32(2).

[1.439]
19 Time limit for prosecutions
(1) No prosecution for an offence under this Act shall be commenced after the expiration of three years from the commission of the offence or one year from its discovery by the prosecutor, whichever is the earlier.
(2) Notwithstanding anything in [section 127(1) of the Magistrates' Courts Act 1980], a magistrates' court may try an information for an offence under this Act if the information was laid at any time within twelve months from the commission of the offence.
(3) (*Applies to Scotland only.*)
(4) Subsections (2) and (3) of this section do not apply where—
    (a)   the offence was committed by the making of an oral statement; or
    (b)   *the offence was one of supplying goods to which a false trade description is applied, and the trade description was applied by an oral statement; or*
    (c)   *the offence was one where a false trade description is deemed to have been applied to goods by virtue of section 4(3) of this Act and the goods were supplied in pursuance of an oral request.*

NOTES
Sub-s (2): words in square brackets substituted by the Magistrates' Courts Act 1980, s 154, Sch 7, para 75.
Sub-s (4): paras (b), (c) repealed by the Consumer Protection from Unfair Trading Regulations 2008, SI 2008/1277, reg 30(3), Sch 4, subject to transitional provisions and savings in reg 30(2) of, and Sch 3, para 2 to, those Regulations at **[2.595]**, **[2.597]**.

[1.440]
20 Offences by corporations
(1) Where an offence under this Act which has been committed by a body corporate is proved to have been committed with the consent and connivance of, or to be attributable to any neglect on the part of, any director, manager, secretary or other similar officer of the body corporate, or any person who was purporting to act in any such capacity, he as well as the body corporate shall be guilty of that offence and shall be liable to be proceeded against and punished accordingly.
(2) In this section "director", in relation to any body corporate established by or under any enactment for the purpose of carrying on under national ownership any industry or part of an industry or undertaking, being a body corporate whose affairs are managed by the members thereof, means a member of that body corporate.

[1.441]
21 Accessories to offences committed abroad
(1), (2) . . .
(3) Any person who, in the United Kingdom, assists in or induces the commission outside the United Kingdom of an act which, if committed in the United Kingdom, would be an offence under section 12 of this Act shall be guilty of an offence.

NOTES

Sub-ss (1), (2): repealed by the Consumer Protection from Unfair Trading Regulations 2008, SI 2008/1277, reg 30(1), (3), Sch 2, Pt 1, paras 7, 8(f), Sch 4.

22 *(Repealed by the Consumer Protection from Unfair Trading Regulations 2008, SI 2008/1277, reg 30(1), (3), Sch 2, Pt 1, paras 7, 8(g), Sch 4.)*

[1.442]
23 Offences due to fault of other person
Where the commission by any person of an offence under this Act is due to the act or default of some other person that other person shall be guilty of the offence, and a person may be charged with and convicted of the offence by virtue of this section whether or not proceedings are taken against the first-mentioned person.

Defences

[1.443]
24 Defence of mistake, accident, etc
(1) In any proceedings for an offence under this Act it shall, subject to subsection (2) of this section, be a defence for the person charged to prove—
   (a)   that the commission of the offence was due to a mistake or to reliance on information supplied to him or to the act or default of another person, an accident or some other cause beyond his control; and
   (b)   that he took all reasonable precautions and exercised all due diligence to avoid the commission of such an offence by himself or any person under his control.
(2) If in any case the defence provided by the last foregoing subsection involves the allegation that the commission of the offence was due to the act or default of another person or to reliance on information supplied by another person, the person charged shall not, without leave of the court, be entitled to rely on that defence unless, within a period ending seven clear days before the hearing, he has served on the prosecutor a notice in writing giving such information identifying or assisting in the identification of that other person as was then in his possession.
(3) In any proceedings for an offence under this Act of supplying or offering to supply goods to which a false trade description is applied it shall be a defence for the person charged to prove that he did not know, and could not with reasonable diligence have ascertained, that the goods did not conform to the description or that the description had been applied to the goods.

NOTES

Sub-s (3): repealed by the Consumer Protection from Unfair Trading Regulations 2008, SI 2008/1277, reg 30(3), Sch 4, subject to transitional provisions and savings in reg 30(2) of, and Sch 3, para 3 to, those Regulations at **[2.595]**, **[2.597]**.

[1.444]
25 Innocent publication of advertisement
In proceedings for an offence under this Act committed by the publication of an advertisement it shall be a defence for the person charged to prove that he is a person whose business it is to publish or arrange for the publication of advertisements and that he received the advertisement for publication in the ordinary course of business and did not know and had no reason to suspect that its publication would amount to an offence under this Act.

Enforcement

[1.445]
26 Enforcing authorities
(1) It shall be the duty of every local weights and measures authority to enforce within their area the provisions of this Act and of any order made under this Act; . . .
[(1A) For the investigatory powers available to a local weights and measures authority for the purposes of the duty in subsection (1), see Schedule 5 to the Consumer Rights Act 2015.]
(2) Every local weights and measures authority shall, whenever the Board of Trade so direct, make to the Board a report on the exercise of their functions under this Act in such form and containing such particulars as the Board may direct.
(3), (4) . . .
(5) (*Applies to Scotland only.*)

NOTES
Sub-s (1): words omitted repealed by the Weights and Measures Act 1985, ss 96(1), 98(1), Sch 11, para 18(2), Sch 13, Pt I.
Sub-s (1A): inserted by the Consumer Rights Act 2015, s 77(2), Sch 6, paras 2, 3, as from 1 October 2015 (for transitional provisions see the Consumer Rights Act 2015 (Commencement No 3, Transitional Provisions, Savings and Consequential Amendments) Order 2015, SI 2015/1630, arts 6–8 at **[2.1220]** et seq).
Sub-ss (3), (4): repealed by the Local Government, Planning and Land Act 1980, ss 1(4), 194, Sch 4, para 10(a), Sch 34, Pt IV.

[1.446]
27 *Power to make test purchases*
A local weights and measures authority shall have power to make, or to authorise any of their officers to make on their behalf, such purchases of goods, and to authorise any of their officers to secure the provision of such services, accommodation or facilities, as may appear expedient for the purpose of determining whether or not the provisions of this Act and any order made thereunder are being complied with.

NOTES
Repealed by the Consumer Rights Act 2015, s 77(2), Sch 6, paras 2, 4, as from 1 October 2015 (for transitional provisions see the Consumer Rights Act 2015 (Commencement No 3, Transitional Provisions, Savings and Consequential Amendments) Order 2015, SI 2015/1630, arts 6–8 at **[2.1220]** et seq).

[1.447]
28 *Power to enter premises and inspect and seize goods and documents*
(1) A duly authorised officer of a local weights and measures authority or of a Government department may, at all reasonable hours and on production, if required, of his credentials, exercise the following powers, that is to say,—
  (a) he may, for the purpose of ascertaining whether any offence under this Act has been committed, inspect any goods and enter any premises other than premises used only as a dwelling;
  (b) if he has reasonable cause to suspect that an offence under this Act has been committed, he may, for the purpose of ascertaining whether it has been committed, require any person carrying on a trade or business or employed in connection with a trade or business to produce any books or documents relating to the trade or business and may take copies of, or of any entry in, any such book or document;
  (c) if he has reasonable cause to believe that an offence under this Act has been committed, he may seize and detain any goods for the purpose of ascertaining, by testing or otherwise, whether the offence has been committed;
  (d) he may seize and detain any goods or documents which he has reason to believe may be required as evidence in proceedings for an offence under this Act;
  (e) he may, for the purpose of exercising his powers under this subsection to seize goods, but only if and to the extent that it is reasonably necessary in order to secure that the provisions of this Act and of any order made thereunder are duly observed, require any person having authority to do so to break open any container or open any vending machine and, if that person does not comply with the requirement, he may do so himself.
(2) An officer seizing any goods or documents in the exercise of his powers under this section shall inform the person from whom they are seized and, in the case of goods seized from a vending machine, the person whose name and address are stated on the machine as being the proprietor's or, if no name and address are so stated, the occupier of the premises on which the machine stands or to which it is affixed.
(3) If a justice of the peace, on sworn information in writing—
  (a) is satisfied that there is reasonable ground to believe either—
    (i) that any goods, books or documents which a duly authorised officer has power under this section to inspect are on any premises and that their inspection is likely to disclose evidence of the commission of an offence under this Act; or
    (ii) that any offence under this Act has been, is being or is about to be committed on any premises; and
  (b) is also satisfied either—

   (i)   *that admission to the premises has been or is likely to be refused and that notice of intention to apply for a warrant under this subsection has been given to the occupier; or*

  (ii)   *that an application for admission, or the giving of such a notice, would defeat the object of the entry or that the premises are unoccupied or that the occupier is temporarily absent and it might defeat the object of the entry to await his return,*

the justice may by warrant under his hand, which shall continue in force for a period of one month, authorise an officer of a local weights and measures authority or of a Government department to enter the premises, if need be by force.

   . . .

(4) An officer entering any premises by virtue of this section may take with him such other persons and such equipment as may appear to him necessary; and on leaving any premises which he has entered by virtue of a warrant under the preceding subsection he shall, if the premises are unoccupied or the occupier is temporarily absent, leave them as effectively secured against trespassers as he found them.

(5)   . . .

[(5A)   . . .]

(6) If any person who is not a duly authorised officer of a local weights and measures authority or of a Government department purports to act as such under this section he shall be guilty of an offence.

(7) Nothing in this section shall be taken to compel the production by a solicitor of a document containing a privileged communication made by or to him in that capacity or to authorise the taking of possession of any such document which is in his possession.

NOTES

Repealed by the Consumer Rights Act 2015, s 77(2), Sch 6, paras 2, 5, as from 1 October 2015 (for transitional provisions see the Consumer Rights Act 2015 (Commencement No 3, Transitional Provisions, Savings and Consequential Amendments) Order 2015, SI 2015/1630, arts 6–8 at **[2.1220]** et seq).

Sub-s (3): words omitted apply to Scotland only.

Sub-s (5): repealed by the Enterprise Act 2002, ss 247(a), 278(2), Sch 26.

Sub-s (5A): inserted by the Consumer Credit Act 1974, s 192(3)(a), Sch 4, Pt I, para 28; repealed by the Enterprise Act 2002, ss 247(a), 278(2), Sch 26.

Seize and detain goods: the powers of seizure conferred by sub-s (1)(c), (d) are powers of seizure to which the Criminal Justice and Police Act 2001, s 50 apply (additional powers of seizure from premises); see s 50 of, and Sch 1, Pt 1, para 9 to, that Act.

[1.448]

29 *Obstruction of authorised officers*

(1) Any person who—

   (a)   *wilfully obstructs an officer of a local weights and measures authority or of a Government department acting in pursuance of this Act; or*

  (b)   *wilfully fails to comply with any requirement properly made to him by such an officer under section 28 of this Act; or*

  (c)   *without reasonable cause fails to give such an officer so acting any other assistance or information which he may reasonably require of him for the purpose of the performance of his functions under this Act,*

shall be guilty of an offence and liable, on summary conviction, to a fine not exceeding [level 3 on the standard scale].

(2) If any person, in giving any such information as is mentioned in the preceding subsection, makes any statement which he knows to be false, he shall be guilty of an offence.

(3) Nothing in this section shall be construed as requiring a person to answer any question or give any information if to do so might incriminate him.

NOTES

Repealed by the Consumer Rights Act 2015, s 77(2), Sch 6, paras 2, 6, as from 1 October 2015 (for transitional provisions see the Consumer Rights Act 2015 (Commencement No 3, Transitional Provisions, Savings and Consequential Amendments) Order 2015, SI 2015/1630, arts 6–8 at **[2.1220]** et seq).

Sub-s (1): reference to a level on the standard scale substituted by virtue of the Criminal Justice Act 1982, ss 38, 46.

[1.449]

30 *Notice of test and intended prosecution*

(1) Where any goods seized or purchased by an officer in pursuance of this Act are submitted to a test, then—

   (a)   *if the goods were seized, the officer shall inform the person mentioned in section 28(2) of this Act of the result of the test;*

  (b)   *if the goods were purchased and the test leads to the institution of proceedings for an offence under this Act, the officer shall inform the person from whom the goods were purchased, or, in the case of goods sold through a vending machine, the person mentioned in section 28(2) of this Act, of the result of the test;*

and shall, where as a result of the test proceedings for an offence under this Act are instituted against any person, allow him to have the goods tested on his behalf if it is reasonably practicable to do so.

(2)–(4) . . .

NOTES

Repealed by the Consumer Rights Act 2015, s 77(2), Sch 6, paras 2, 7, as from 1 October 2015 (for transitional provisions see the Consumer Rights Act 2015 (Commencement No 3, Transitional Provisions, Savings and Consequential Amendments) Order 2015, SI 2015/1630, arts 6–8 at **[2.1220]** et seq).

Sub-ss (2)–(4): repealed by the Fair Trading Act 1973, s 139, Sch 13.

[1.450]
31 Evidence by certificate
(1)   The Board of Trade may by regulations provide that certificates issued by such persons as may be specified by the regulations in relation to such matters as may be so specified shall, subject to the provisions of this section, be received in evidence of those matters in any proceedings under this Act.
(2)   Such a certificate shall not be received in evidence—
  (a)   unless the party against whom it is to be given in evidence has been served with a copy thereof not less than seven days before the hearing; or
  (b)   if that party has, not less than three days before the hearing, served on the other party a notice requiring the attendance of the person issuing the certificate.
(3)   *(Applies to Scotland only.)*
(4)   For the purposes of this section any document purporting to be such a certificate as is mentioned in this section shall be deemed to be such a certificate unless the contrary is shown.
(5)   Regulations under this section shall be made by statutory instrument which shall be subject to annulment in pursuance of a resolution of either House of Parliament.

Miscellaneous and supplemental

32   *(Repealed by the Consumer Protection from Unfair Trading Regulations 2008, SI 2008/1277, reg 30(1), (3), Sch 2, Pt 1, paras 7, 8(h), Sch 4.)*

[1.451]
33   *Compensation for loss, etc of goods seized under s 28*
(1)   Where, in the exercise of his powers under section 28 of this Act, an officer of a local weights and measures authority or of a Government department seizes and detains any goods and their owner suffers loss by reason thereof or by reason that the goods, during the detention, are lost or damaged or deteriorate, then, unless the owner is convicted of an offence under this Act committed in relation to the goods, the authority or department shall be liable to compensate him for the loss so suffered.
(2)   Any disputed question as to the right to or the amount of any compensation payable under this section shall be determined by arbitration and, in Scotland, by a single arbiter appointed, failing agreement between the parties, by the sheriff.

NOTES

Repealed by the Consumer Rights Act 2015, s 77(2), Sch 6, paras 2, 8, as from 1 October 2015 (for transitional provisions see the Consumer Rights Act 2015 (Commencement No 3, Transitional Provisions, Savings and Consequential Amendments) Order 2015, SI 2015/1630, arts 6–8 at **[2.1220]** et seq).

[1.452]
34   Trade marks containing trade descriptions
The fact that a trade description is a trade mark, or part of a trade mark, ... does not prevent it from being a false trade description when applied to any goods, except where the following conditions are satisfied, that is to say—
  (a)   that it could have been lawfully applied to the goods if this Act had not been passed; and
  (b)   that on the day this Act is passed the trade mark either is registered under the Trade Marks Act 1938 or is in use to indicate a connection in the course of trade between such goods and the proprietor of the trade mark; and
  (c)   that the trade mark as applied is used to indicate such a connection between the goods and the proprietor of the trade mark or[, in the case of a registered trade mark, a person licensed to use it]; and
  (d)   that the person who is the proprietor of the trade mark is the same person as, or a successor in title of, the proprietor on the day this Act is passed.

NOTES

Words omitted repealed, and words in square brackets substituted, by the Trade Marks Act 1994, s 106(1), Sch 4, para 4.

Modification: references to trade marks or registered trade marks within the meaning of the Trade Marks Act 1938 shall, unless the context otherwise requires, be construed as references to trade marks or registered trade marks within the meaning of the Trade Marks Act 1994; see the Trade Marks Act 1994, Sch 4, para 1.

Trade Marks Act 1938: repealed and replaced by the Trade Marks Act 1994.

[1.453]

35 Saving for civil rights

A contract for the supply of any goods shall not be void or unenforceable by reason only of a contravention of any provision of this Act.

[1.454]

36 Country of origin

(1) For the purposes of this Act goods shall be deemed to have been manufactured or produced in the country in which they last underwent a treatment or process resulting in a substantial change.

(2) The Board of Trade may by order specify—

(a) in relation to any description of goods, what treatment or process is to be regarded for the purposes of this section as resulting or not resulting in a substantial change;

(b) in relation to any description of goods different parts of which were manufactured or produced in different countries, or of goods assembled in a country different from that in which their parts were manufactured or produced, in which of those countries the goods are to be regarded for the purposes of this Act as having been manufactured or produced.

NOTES

Orders: the Trade Descriptions (Country of Origin) (Cutlery) Order 1981, SI 1981/122.

37 (*Repealed by the Consumer Protection from Unfair Trading Regulations 2008, SI 2008/1277, reg 30(1), (3), Sch 2, Pt 1, paras 7, 8(i), Sch 4.*)

[1.455]

38 Orders

(1) Any power to make an order under the preceding provisions of this Act shall be exercisable by statutory instrument, which shall be subject to annulment in pursuance of a resolution of either House of Parliament, and includes power to vary or revoke such an order by a subsequent order.

(2) Any order under the preceding provisions of this Act which relates to any . . . fertilisers or any goods used as pesticides or for similar purposes shall be made by the Board of Trade acting jointly with the following Ministers, that is to say, if the order extends to England and Wales, the Minister of Agriculture, Fisheries and Food, and if it extends to Scotland or Northern Ireland, the Secretary of State concerned.

[(2A) Any order under the preceding provisions of this Act which relates to any agricultural, horticultural or fishery produce, whether processed or not, food, feeding stuffs or the ingredients of food or feeding stuffs shall be made by the Board of Trade acting jointly with the following Ministers, that is to say, if the order extends to England and Wales, the Secretary of State concerned with health and if it extends to Scotland or Northern Ireland, the Secretary of State concerned.

(2B) Before making an order to which subsection (2) or (2A) of this section applies the Board of Trade shall consult the Food Standards Agency.]

(3) The following provisions shall apply to the making of an order under [section 36 of this Act], that is to say—

(a) before making the order the Board of Trade shall consult with such organisations as appear to them to be representative of interests substantially affected by it and shall publish, in such manner as the Board think appropriate, notice of their intention to make the order and of the place where copies of the proposed order may be obtained; and

(b) the order shall not be made until the expiration of a period of twenty-eight days from the publication of the notice and may then be made with such modifications (if any) as the Board of Trade think appropriate having regard to any representations received by them.

NOTES

Sub-s (2): words omitted repealed by the Food Standards Act 1999, s 40(1), (4), Sch 5, para 4(1), (2), Sch 6.

Sub-ss (2A), (2B): inserted by the Food Standards Act 1999, s 40(1), Sch 5, para 4(1), (3).

Sub-s (3): words in square brackets substituted by the Consumer Protection from Unfair Trading Regulations 2008, SI 2008/1277, reg 30(1), Sch 2, Pt 1, paras 7, 11.

Minister of Agriculture, Fisheries and Food: now the Secretary of State for Environment, Food and Rural Affairs; see the Secretaries of State for Transport, Local Government and the Regions and for Environment, Food and Rural Affairs Order 2001, SI 2001/2568.

Transfer of functions in relation to Wales: as to the transfer of functions under this section to the National Assembly for Wales, see the National Assembly for Wales (Transfer of Functions) Order 1999, SI 1999/672.

[1.456]

39 Interpretation

(1) The following provisions shall have effect, in addition to sections [2 to 4] of this Act, for the interpretation in this Act of expressions used therein, that is to say,—

"advertisement" includes a catalogue, a circular and a price list;

"goods" includes ships and aircraft, things attached to land and growing crops;

"premises" includes any place and any stall, vehicle, ship or aircraft; and

"ship" includes any boat and any other description of vessel used in navigation.

(2) For the purposes of this Act, a trade description or statement published in any newspaper, book or periodical or in any film or sound or television broadcast [or in any programme included in any programme service (within the meaning of the Broadcasting Act 1990) other than a sound or television broadcasting service] shall not be deemed to be a trade description applied or statement made in the course of a trade or business unless it is or forms part of an advertisement.

NOTES

Sub-s (1): words in square brackets substituted by the Consumer Protection from Unfair Trading Regulations 2008, SI 2008/1277, reg 30(1), Sch 2, Pt 1, paras 7, 12.

Sub-s (2): repealed by SI 2008/1277, reg 30(1), (3), Sch 2, Pt 1, paras 7, 8(j), Sch 4, subject to transitional provisions and savings in reg 30(2) of, and Sch 3, para 4 to, those Regulations at **[2.595]**, **[2.597]**; words in square brackets originally inserted by the Cable and Broadcasting Act 1984, s 57(1), Sch 5, para 19, substituted by the Broadcasting Act 1990, s 203(1), Sch 20, para 11.

[1.457]
40   Provisions as to Northern Ireland
(1)   This Act shall apply to Northern Ireland subject to the following modifications, that is to say—
   (a)   section 19(2) shall apply as if for the references to [section 127(1) of the Magistrates' Courts Act 1980] and the trial and laying of an information there were substituted respectively references to [Article 19(1) of the Magistrates' Courts (Northern Ireland) Order 1981] and the hearing and determination and making of a complaint [and as if for the word "under" there were substituted the words "under section 29(1) of"];
   (b)   section 26 and subsections (2) to (4) of section 30 shall not apply but it shall be the duty of the Ministry of Commerce for Northern Ireland to enforce the provisions of this Act and of any order made under it (other than the provisions of section 42 of this Act);
   (c)   *sections 27 to 29 and 33 shall apply as if for references to a local weights and measures authority and any officer of such an authority there were substituted respectively references to the said Ministry and any of its officers.*
[(1A)   For the investigatory powers available to the Department of Enterprise, Trade and Investment in Northern Ireland for the purposes of the duty in subsection (1)(b), see Schedule 5 to the Consumer Rights Act 2015.]
(2)–(5)   . . .
(6)   Nothing in this Act shall authorise any department of the Government of Northern Ireland to incur any expenses attributable to the provisions of this Act until provision has been made by the Parliament of Northern Ireland for those expenses to be defrayed out of moneys provided by that Parliament.
(7)   . . .

NOTES

Sub-s (1): in para (a) words in first pair of square brackets substituted by the Magistrates' Courts Act 1980, s 154, Sch 7, para 74, words in second pair of square brackets substituted by the Magistrates' Courts (Northern Ireland) Order 1981, SI 1981/1675, art 170(2), Sch 6, Pt 1, para 13, words in third pair of square brackets inserted by the Criminal Justice (Northern Ireland) Order 1980, SI 1980/704, art 12, Sch 1, Pt II, para 43; para (c) repealed by the Consumer Rights Act 2015, s 77(2), Sch 6, paras 2, 9(1), (2), as from 1 October 2015 (for transitional provisions see the Consumer Rights Act 2015 (Commencement No 3, Transitional Provisions, Savings and Consequential Amendments) Order 2015, SI 2015/1630, arts 6–8 at **[2.1220]** et seq).

Sub-s (1A): inserted by the Consumer Rights Act 2015, s 77(2), Sch 6, paras 2, 9(1), (3), as from 1 October 2015 (for transitional provisions see SI 2015/1630, arts 6–8 at **[2.1220]** et seq).

Sub-ss (2)–(4), (7): repealed by the Northern Ireland Constitution Act 1973, s 41(1), Sch 6, Pt I.

Sub-s (5): repealed by the Northern Ireland (Modification of Enactments—No 1) Order 1973, SI 1973/2163, art 14(2), Sch 6.

41, 42   *(S 41 outside the scope of this work; s 42 repealed by the Statute Law (Repeals) Act 1975.)*

[1.458]
43   Short title and commencement
(1)   This Act may be cited as the Trade Descriptions Act 1968.
(2)   This Act shall come into force on the expiration of the period of six months beginning with the day on which it is passed.

SCHEDULES

SCHEDULES 1, 2

(Sch 1 in so far as unrepealed outside the scope of this work; Sch 2 repealed by the Statute Law (Repeals) Act 1975.)

AUCTIONS (BIDDING AGREEMENTS) ACT 1969

(1969 c 56)

ARRANGEMENT OF SECTIONS

An Act to amend the law with respect to proceedings for offences under the Auctions (Bidding Agreements) Act 1927; to make fresh provision as to the rights of a seller of goods by auction where an agreement subsists that a person or persons shall abstain from bidding for the goods; and for connected purposes

[22 October 1969]

[1.459]
1   Offences under Auctions (Bidding Agreements) Act 1927 to be indictable as well as triable summarily, and extension of time for bringing summary proceedings
(1)   Offences under section 1 of the Auctions (Bidding Agreements) Act 1927 (which, as amended by the Criminal Justice Act 1967, renders a dealer who agrees to give, or gives, or offers a gift or consideration to another as an inducement or reward for abstaining, or for having abstained, from bidding at a sale by auction punishable on summary conviction with a fine not exceeding £400 or imprisonment for a term not exceeding six months, or both, and renders similarly punishable a person who agrees to accept, or accepts, or attempts to obtain from a dealer any such gift or consideration as aforesaid) shall be triable on indictment as well as summarily; and the penalty that may be imposed on a person on conviction on indictment of an offence under that section shall be imprisonment for a term not exceeding two years or a fine or both.
(2)   . . .
(3)   *(Applies to Scotland only.)*
(4)   . . .
(5)   This section applies only to offences committed after the commencement of this Act.

NOTES
   Sub-ss (2), (4): repealed, in relation to England and Wales, by the Criminal Law Act 1977, s 65(5), Sch 13.

[1.460]
2   Persons convicted not to attend or participate in auctions
(1)   On any such summary conviction or conviction on indictment as is mentioned in section 1 above, the court may order that the person so convicted or that person and any representative of him shall not (without leave of the court) for a period from the date of such conviction—
    (a)   in the case of a summary conviction, of not more than one year, or
    (b)   in the case of a conviction on indictment, of not more than three years,
enter upon any premises where goods intended for sale by auction are on display or to attend or participate in any way in any sale by auction.
(2)   In the event of a contravention of an order under this section, the person who contravenes it (and, if he is the representative of another, that other also) shall be guilty of an offence and liable—
    (a)   on summary conviction, to a fine not exceeding [the prescribed sum];
    (b)   on conviction on indictment, to imprisonment for a term not exceeding two years or to a fine or to both.
(3)   In any proceedings against a person in respect of a contravention of an order under this section consisting in the entry upon premises where goods intended for sale by auction were on display, it shall be a defence for him to prove that he did not know, and had no reason to suspect, that goods so intended were on display on the premises, and in any proceedings against a person in respect of a contravention of such an order consisting in his having done something as the representative of another, it shall be a defence for him to prove that he did not know, and had no reason to suspect, that that other was the subject of such an order.
(4)   A person shall not be guilty of an offence under this section by reason only of his selling property by auction or causing it to be so sold.

NOTES
   Sub-s (2): reference to the prescribed sum substituted by virtue of the Magistrates' Courts Act 1980, s 32(7).

[1.461]
3 Rights of seller of goods by auction where agreement subsists that some person shall abstain from bidding for the goods
(1) Where goods are purchased at an auction by a person who has entered into an agreement with another or others that the other or the others (or some of them) shall abstain from bidding for the goods (not being an agreement to purchase the goods bona fide on a joint account) and he or the other party, or one of the other parties, to the agreement is a dealer, the seller may avoid the contract under which the goods are purchased.
(2) Where a contract is avoided by virtue of the foregoing subsection, then, if the purchaser has obtained possession of the goods and restitution thereof is not made, the persons who were parties to the agreement that one or some of them should abstain from bidding for the goods the subject of the contract shall be jointly and severally liable to make good to the seller the loss (if any) he sustained by reason of the operation of the agreement.
(3), (4) . . .
(5) In this section, "dealer" has the meaning assigned to it by section 1(2) of the Auctions (Bidding Agreements) Act 1927.

NOTES
Sub-ss (3), (4): repealed by the Statute Law (Repeals) Act 2004.

[1.462]
4 Copy of Act to be exhibited at sale
Section 3 of the Auctions (Bidding Agreements) Act 1927 (copy of Act to be exhibited at sale) shall have effect as if the reference to that Act included a reference to this Act.

[1.463]
5 Short title, commencement and extent
(1) This Act may be cited as the Auctions (Bidding Agreements) Act 1969.
(2) . . .
(3) This Act shall not extend to Northern Ireland.

NOTES
Sub-s (2): repealed by the Statute Law (Repeals) Act 2004.

ADMINISTRATION OF JUSTICE ACT 1970

(1970 c 31)

ARRANGEMENT OF SECTIONS

An Act to make further provision about the courts (including assizes), their business, jurisdiction and procedure; to enable a High Court judge to accept appointment as arbitrator or umpire under an arbitration agreement; to amend the law respecting the enforcement of debt and other liabilities; to amend section 106 of the Rent Act 1968; and for miscellaneous purposes connected with the administration of justice

[29 May 1970]

1–39 ((*Pts I–IV) outside the scope of this work.*)

PART V
MISCELLANEOUS PROVISIONS

[1.464]
40 Punishment for unlawful harassment of debtors
(1) A person commits an offence if, with the object of coercing another person to pay money claimed from the other as a debt due under a contract, he—
(a) harasses the other with demands for payment which, in respect of their frequency or the manner or occasion of making any such demand, or of any threat or publicity by which any demand is accompanied, are calculated to subject him or members of his family or household to alarm, distress or humiliation;

(b)   falsely represents, in relation to the money claimed, that criminal proceedings lie for failure to pay it;

(c)   falsely represents himself to be authorised in some official capacity to claim or enforce payment; or

(d)   utters a document falsely represented by him to have some official character or purporting to have some official character which he knows it has not.

(2)   A person may be guilty of an offence by virtue of subsection (1)(a) above if he concerts with others in the taking of such action as is described in that paragraph, notwithstanding that his own course of conduct does not by itself amount to harassment.

(3)   Subsection (1)(a) above does not apply to anything done by a person which is reasonable (and otherwise permissible in law) for the purpose—

(a)   of securing the discharge of an obligation due, or believed by him to be due, to himself or to persons for whom he acts, or protecting himself or them from future loss; or

(b)   of the enforcement of any liability by legal process.

[(3A)   Subsection (1) above does not apply to anything done by a person to another in circumstances where what is done is a commercial practice within the meaning of the Consumer Protection from Unfair Trading Regulations 2008 and the other is a consumer in relation to that practice.]

(4)   A person guilty of an offence under this section shall be liable on summary conviction to a fine of not more than [level 5 on the standard scale].

NOTES

Sub-s (3A): inserted by the Consumer Protection from Unfair Trading Regulations 2008, SI 2008/1277, reg 30(1), Sch 2, Pt 1, para 13.

Sub-s (4): reference to a level on the standard scale substituted by virtue of the Criminal Justice Act 1982, ss 35, 38, 46.

41–51   (*In so far as unrepealed, outside the scope of this work.*)

PART VI
GENERAL

52, 53   (*S 52 outside the scope of this work; s 53 repealed by the Northern Ireland Constitution Act 1973, s 41(1), Sch 6, Pt I.*)

[1.465]
54   Citation, interpretation, repeals, commencement and extent
(1)   This Act may be cited as the Administration of Justice Act 1970.
(2)   References in this Act to any enactment include references to that enactment as amended or extended by or under any other enactment, including this Act.
(3)–(6)   . . .

NOTES

Sub-ss (3), (5), (6): outside the scope of this work.

Sub-s (4): repealed by the Statute Law (Repeals) Act 2004.

Orders: the Administration of Justice Act 1970 (Commencement No 1) Order 1970, SI 1970/886; the Administration of Justice Act 1970 (Commencement No 2) Order 1970, SI 1970/1207; the Administration of Justice Act 1970 (Commencement No 3) Order 1970, SI 1970/1962; the Administration of Justice Act 1970 (Commencement No 4) Order 1970, SI 1971/834; the Administration of Justice Act 1970 (Commencement No 5) Order 1970, SI 1971/1244.

SCHEDULES

SCHEDULES 1–11

(*Schs 1–11 outside the scope of this work.*)

CARRIAGE OF GOODS BY SEA ACT 1971

(1971 c 19)

ARRANGEMENT OF SECTIONS

Schedule—The Hague Rules as amended by the Brussels Protocol. . . . .[1.473]

An Act to amend the law with respect to the carriage of goods by sea

[8 April 1971]

NOTES

Hovercraft: by the Hovercraft (Civil Liability) Order 1986, SI 1986/1305, arts 4, 5, 10, Sch 2, Sch 4, this Act applies, with modifications, in relation to the carriage of goods by hovercraft (other than passengers' baggage) as it applies in relation to goods on board or carried by ship.

[1.466]
1 Application of Hague Rules as amended
(1) In this Act, "the Rules" means the International Convention for the unification of certain rules of law relating to bills of lading signed at Brussels on 25th August 1924, as amended by the Protocol signed at Brussels on 23rd February 1968 [and by the Protocol signed at Brussels on 21st December 1979].
(2) The provisions of the Rules, as set out in the Schedule to this Act, shall have the force of law.
(3) Without prejudice to subsection (2) above, the said provisions shall have effect (and have the force of law) in relation to and in connection with the carriage of goods by sea in ships where the port of shipment is a port in the United Kingdom, whether or not the carriage is between ports in two different States within the meaning of Article X of the Rules.
(4) Subject to subsection (6) below, nothing in this section shall be taken as applying anything in the Rules to any contract for the carriage of goods by sea, unless the contract expressly or by implication provides for the issue of a bill of lading or any similar document of title.
(5) . . .
(6) Without prejudice to Article X(c) of the Rules, the Rules shall have the force of law in relation to—
    (a)   any bill of lading if the contract contained in or evidenced by it expressly provides that the Rules shall govern the contract, and
    (b)   any receipt which is a non-negotiable document marked as such if the contract contained in or evidenced by it is a contract for the carriage of goods by sea which expressly provides that the Rules are to govern the contract as if the receipt were a bill of lading,
but subject, where paragraph (b) applies, to any necessary modifications and in particular with the omission in Article III of the Rules of the second sentence of paragraph 4 and of paragraph 7.
(7) If and so far as the contract contained in or evidenced by a bill of lading or receipt within paragraph (a) or (b) of subsection (6) above applies to deck cargo or live animals, the Rules as given the force of law by that subsection shall have effect as if Article I(c) did not exclude deck cargo and live animals.
In this subsection "deck cargo" means cargo which by the contract of carriage is stated as being carried on deck and is so carried.

NOTES

Sub-s (1): words in square brackets inserted by the Merchant Shipping Act 1981, s 2(1); this amendment continues to have effect by virtue of the Merchant Shipping Act 1995, s 314(2), Sch 13, para 45(1), (2).
Sub-s (5): repealed by the Merchant Shipping Act 1981, s 5(3), Schedule.

[1.467]
[1A Conversion of special drawing rights into sterling
(1) For the purposes of Article IV of the Rules the value on a particular day of one special drawing right shall be treated as equal to such a sum in sterling as the International Monetary Fund have fixed as being the equivalent of one special drawing right—
    (a)   for that day; or
    (b)   if no sum has been so fixed for that day, for the last day before that day for which a sum has been so fixed.
(2) A certificate given by or on behalf of the Treasury stating—
    (a)   that a particular sum in sterling has been fixed as aforesaid for a particular day; or
    (b)   that no sum has been so fixed for a particular day and that a particular sum in sterling has been so fixed for a day which is the last day for which a sum has been so fixed before the particular day,
shall be conclusive evidence of those matters for the purposes of subsection (1) above; and a document purporting to be such a certificate shall in any proceedings be received in evidence and, unless the contrary is proved, be deemed to be such a certificate.
(3) The Treasury may charge a reasonable fee for any certificate given in pursuance of subsection (2) above, and any fee received by the Treasury by virtue of this subsection shall be paid into the Consolidated Fund.]

NOTES

Inserted by the Merchant Shipping Act 1995, s 314(2), Sch 13, para 45(1), (3).

[1.468]

2   Contracting States, etc

(1)   If Her Majesty by Order in Council certifies to the following effect, that is to say, that for the purposes of the Rules—

(a)   a State specified in the Order is a contracting State, or is a contracting State in respect of any place or territory so specified; or

(b)   any place or territory specified in the Order forms part of a State so specified (whether a contracting State or not),

the Order shall, except so far as it has been superseded by a subsequent Order, be conclusive evidence of the matters so certified.

(2)   An Order in Council under this section may be varied or revoked by a subsequent Order in Council.

NOTES

Orders in Council: the Carriage of Goods by Sea (Parties to Convention) Order 1985, SI 1985/443; the Carriage of Goods by Sea (Parties to Convention) (Amendment) Order 2000, SI 2000/1103.

[1.469]

3   Absolute warranty of seaworthiness not to be implied in contracts to which Rules apply

There shall not be implied in any contract for the carriage of goods by sea to which the Rules apply by virtue of this Act any absolute undertaking by the carrier of the goods to provide a seaworthy ship.

[1.470]

4   Application of Act to British possessions, etc

(1)   Her Majesty may by Order in Council direct that this Act shall extend, subject to such exceptions, adaptations and modifications as may be specified in the Order, to all or any of the following territories, that is—

(a)   any colony (not being a colony for whose external relations a country other than the United Kingdom is responsible),

(b)   any country outside Her Majesty's dominions in which Her Majesty has jurisdiction in right of Her Majesty's Government of the United Kingdom.

(2)   An Order in Council under this section may contain such transitional and other consequential and incidental provisions as appear to Her Majesty to be expedient, including provisions amending or repealing any legislation about the carriage of goods by sea forming part of the law of any of the territories mentioned in paragraphs (a) and (b) above.

(3)   An Order in Council under this section may be varied or revoked by a subsequent Order in Council.

NOTES

Orders in Council: the Carriage of Goods by Sea (Bermuda) Order 1980, SI 1980/1507; the Carriage of Goods by Sea (Overseas Territories) Order 1982, SI 1982/1664; the Merchant Shipping (Revocation) (Bermuda) Order 2002, SI 2002/3147.

[1.471]

5   Extension of application of Rules to carriage from ports in British possessions, etc

(1)   Her Majesty may by Order in Council provide that section 1(3) of this Act shall have effect as if the reference therein to the United Kingdom included a reference to all or any of the following territories, that is—

(a)   the Isle of Man;

(b)   any of the Channel Islands specified in the Order;

(c)   any colony specified in the Order (not being a colony for whose external relations a country other than the United Kingdom is responsible);

(d)   . . .

(e)   any country specified in the Order, being a country outside Her Majesty's dominions in which Her Majesty has jurisdiction in right of Her Majesty's Government of the United Kingdom.

(2)   An Order in Council under this section may be varied or revoked by a subsequent Order in Council.

NOTES

Sub-s (1): para (d) repealed by the Statute Law (Repeals) Act 1989.

[1.472]

6   Supplemental

(1)   This Act may be cited as the Carriage of Goods by Sea Act 1971.

(2)   It is hereby declared that this Act extends to Northern Ireland.

(3)   The following enactments shall be repealed, that is—

(a)   the Carriage of Goods by Sea Act 1924,

(b)   section 12(4)(a) of the Nuclear Installations Act 1965, and without prejudice to section 38(1) of the Interpretation Act 1889, the reference to the said Act of 1924 in section 1(1)(i)(ii) of the Hovercraft Act 1968 shall include a reference to this Act.

[(4)   It is hereby declared that for the purposes of Article VIII of the Rules section 186 of the Merchant Shipping Act 1995 (which entirely exempts shipowners and others in certain circumstances or loss of, or damage to, goods) is a provision relating to limitation of liability.]

(5)   This Act shall come into force on such day as Her Majesty may by Order in Council appoint, and, for the purposes of the transition from the law in force immediately before the day appointed under this subsection to the provisions of this Act, the Order appointing the day may provide that those provisions shall have effect subject to such transitional provisions as may be contained in the Order.

NOTES

Sub-s (4): substituted by the Merchant Shipping Act 1995, s 314(3), Sch 13, para 45(1), (4).

Interpretation Act 1889, s 38(1): repealed by the Interpretation Act 1978, s 25, Sch 3; see now s 17(2)(a) of, and Sch 2, para 3 to, the 1978 Act.

Orders in Council: the Carriage of Goods by Sea Act 1971 (Commencement) Order 1977, SI 1977/981.

SCHEDULE
THE HAGUE RULES AS AMENDED BY THE BRUSSELS PROTOCOL 1968

Section 3

Article I

[1.473]

In these Rules the following words are employed, with the meanings set out below—

  (a) "Carrier" includes the owner or the charterer who enters into a contract of carriage with a shipper.

  (b) "Contract of carriage" applies only to contracts of carriage covered by a bill of lading or any similar document of title, in so far as such document relates to the carriage of goods by sea, including any bill of lading or any similar document as aforesaid issued under or pursuant to a charter party from the moment at which such bill of lading or similar document of title regulates the relations between a carrier and a holder of the same.

  (c) "Goods" includes goods, wares, merchandise, and articles of every kind whatsoever except live animals and cargo which by the contract of carriage is stated as being carried on deck and is so carried.

  (d) "Ship" means any vessel used for the carriage of goods by sea.

  (e) "Carriage of goods" covers the period from the time when the goods are loaded on to the time they are discharged from the ship.

Article II

Subject to the provisions of Article VI, under every contract of carriage of goods by sea the carrier, in relation to the loading, handling, stowage, carriage, custody, care and discharge of such goods, shall be subject to the responsibilities and liabilities, and entitled to the rights and immunities hereinafter set forth.

Article III

1. The carrier shall be bound before and at the beginning of the voyage to exercise due diligence to—

  (a) Make the ship seaworthy.

  (b) Properly man, equip and supply the ship.

  (c) Make the holds, refrigerating and cool chambers, and all other parts of the ship in which goods are carried, fit and safe for their reception, carriage and preservation.

2. Subject to the provisions of Article IV, the carrier shall properly and carefully load, handle, stow, carry, keep, care for, and discharge the goods carried.

3. After receiving the goods into his charge the carrier or the master or agent of the carrier shall, on demand of the shipper, issue to the shipper a bill of lading showing among other things—

  (a) The leading marks necessary for identification of the goods as the same are furnished in writing by the shipper before the loading of such goods starts, provided such marks are stamped or otherwise shown clearly upon the goods if uncovered, or on the cases or coverings in which such goods are contained, in such a manner as should ordinarily remain legible until the end of the voyage.

  (b) Either the number of packages or pieces, or the quantity, or weight, as the case may be, as furnished in writing by the shipper.

  (c) The apparent order and condition of the goods.

Provided that no carrier, master or agent of the carrier shall be bound to state or show in the bill of lading any marks, number, quantity, or weight which he has reasonable ground for suspecting not accurately to represent the goods actually received, or which he has had no reasonable means of checking.

4. Such a bill of lading shall be prima facie evidence of the receipt by the carrier of the goods as therein described in accordance with paragraph 3 (a), (b) and (c). However, proof to the contrary shall not be admissible when the bill of lading has been transferred to a third party acting in good faith.

5. The shipper shall be deemed to have guaranteed to the carrier the accuracy at the time of shipment of the marks, number, quantity and weight, as furnished by him, and the shipper shall indemnify the carrier against all loss, damages and expenses arising or resulting from inaccuracies in such particulars. The right of the carrier to such indemnity shall in no way limit his responsibility and liability under the contract of carriage to any person other than the shipper.

6. Unless notice of loss or damage and the general nature of such loss or damage be given in writing to the carrier or his agent at the port of discharge before or at the time of the removal of the goods into the custody of the person entitled to delivery thereof under the contract of carriage, or, if the loss or damage be not apparent, within three days, such removal shall be prima facie evidence of the delivery by the carrier of the goods as described in the bill of lading.

The notice in writing need not be given if the state of the goods has, at the time of their receipt, been the subject of joint survey or inspection.

Subject to paragraph 6*bis* the carrier and the ship shall in any event be discharged from all liability whatsoever in respect of the goods, unless suit is brought within one year of their delivery or of the date when they should have been delivered. This period may, however, be extended if the parties so agree after the cause of action has arisen.

In the case of any actual or apprehended loss or damage the carrier and the receiver shall give all reasonable facilities to each other for inspecting and tallying the goods.

6bis. An action for indemnity against a third person may be brought even after the expiration of the year provided for in the preceding paragraph if brought within the time allowed by the law of the Court seized of the case. However, the time allowed shall be not less than three months, commencing from the day when the person bringing such action for indemnity has settled the claim or has been served with process in the action against himself.

7. After the goods are loaded the bill of lading to be issued by the carrier, master, or agent of the carrier, to the shipper shall, if the shipper so demands, be a "shipped" bill of lading, provided that if the shipper shall have previously taken up any document of title to such goods, he shall surrender the same as against the issue of the "shipped" bill of lading, but at the option of the carrier such document of title may be noted at the port of shipment by the carrier, master, or agent with the name or names of the ship or ships upon which the goods have been shipped and the date or dates of shipment, and when so noted, if it shows the particulars mentioned in paragraph 3 of Article III, shall for the purpose of this article be deemed to constitute a "shipped" bill of lading.

8. Any clause, covenant, or agreement in a contract of carriage relieving the carrier or the ship from liability for loss or damage to, or in connection with, goods arising from negligence, fault, or failure in the duties and obligations provided in this article or lessening such liability otherwise than as provided in these Rules, shall be null and void and of no effect. A benefit of insurance in favour of the carrier or similar clause shall be deemed to be a clause relieving the carrier from liability.

Article IV

1. Neither the carrier nor the ship shall be liable for loss or damage arising or resulting from unseaworthiness unless caused by want of due diligence on the part of the carrier to make the ship seaworthy, and to secure that the ship is properly manned, equipped and supplied, and to make the holds, refrigerating and cool chambers and all other parts of the ship in which goods are carried fit and safe for their reception, carriage and preservation in accordance with the provisions of paragraph 1 of Article III. Whenever loss or damage has resulted from unseaworthiness the burden of proving the exercise of due diligence shall be on the carrier or other person claiming exemption under this article.

2. Neither the carrier nor the ship shall be responsible for loss or damage arising or resulting from—

   (a)   Act, neglect, or default of the master, mariner, pilot, or the servants of the carrier in the navigation or in the management of the ship.

   (b)   Fire, unless caused by the actual fault or privity of the carrier.

   (c)   Perils, dangers and accidents of the sea or other navigable waters.

   (d)   Act of God.

   (e)   Act of war.

   (f)   Act of public enemies.

   (g)   Arrest or restraint of princes, rulers or people, or seizure under legal process.

   (h)   Quarantine restrictions.

   (i)   Act or omission of the shipper or owner of the goods, his agent or representative.

   (j)   Strikes or lockouts or stoppage or restraint of labour from whatever cause, whether partial or general.

   (k)   Riots and civil commotions.

   (l)   Saving or attempting to save life or property at sea.

   (m)   Wastage in bulk or weight or any other loss or damage arising from inherent defect, quality or vice of the goods.

   (n)   Insufficiency of packing.

   (o)   Insufficiency or inadequacy of marks.

   (p)   Latent defects not discoverable by due diligence.

   (q)   Any other cause arising without the actual fault or privity of the carrier, or without the fault or neglect of the agents or servants of the carrier, but the burden of proof shall be on the person claiming the benefit of this exception to show that neither the actual fault or privity of the carrier nor the fault or neglect of the agents or servants of the carrier contributed to the loss or damage.

3. The shipper shall not be responsible for loss or damage sustained by the carrier or the ship arising or resulting from any cause without the act, fault or neglect of the shipper, his agents or his servants.

4. Any deviation in saving or attempting to save life or property at sea or any reasonable deviation shall not be deemed to be an infringement or breach of these Rules or of the contract of carriage, and the carrier shall not be liable for any loss or damage resulting therefrom.

5.

   (a)   Unless the nature and value of such goods have been declared by the shipper before shipment and inserted in the bill of lading, neither the carrier nor the ship shall in any event be or become liable for any loss or damage to or in connection with the goods in an amount exceeding [666.67 units of account] per package or unit or [2 units of account per kilogramme] of gross weight of the goods lost or damaged, whichever is the higher.

   (b)   The total amount recoverable shall be calculated by reference to the value of such goods at the place and time at which the goods are discharged from the ship in accordance with the contract or should have been so discharged.
   The value of the goods shall be fixed according to the commodity exchange price, or, if there be no such price, according to the current market price, or, if there be no commodity exchange price or current market price, by reference to the normal value of goods of the same kind and quality.

   (c)   Where a container, pallet or similar article of transport is used to consolidate goods, the number of packages or units enumerated in the bill of lading as packed in such article of transport shall be deemed the number of packages or units for the purpose of this paragraph as far as these packages or units are concerned. Except as aforesaid such article of transport shall be considered the package or unit.

   [(d)   The unit of account mentioned in this Article is the special drawing right as defined by the International Monetary Fund. The amounts mentioned in sub-paragraph (a) of this paragraph shall be converted into national currency on the basis of the value of that currency on a date to be determined by the law of the Court seized of the case.]

   (e)   Neither the carrier nor the ship shall be entitled to the benefit of the limitation of liability provided for in this paragraph if it is proved that the damage resulted from an act or omission of the carrier done with intent to cause damage, or recklessly and with knowledge that damage would probably result.

   (f)   The declaration mentioned in sub-paragraph (a) of this paragraph, if embodied in the bill of lading, shall be prima facie evidence, but shall not be binding or conclusive on the carrier.

   (g)   By agreement between the carrier, master or agent of the carrier and the shipper other maximum amounts than those mentioned in sub-paragraph (a) of this paragraph may be fixed, provided that no maximum amount so fixed shall be less than the appropriate maximum mentioned in that sub-paragraph.

   (h)   Neither the carrier nor the ship shall be responsible in any event for loss or damage to, or in connection with, goods if the nature or value thereof has been knowingly mis-stated by the shipper in the bill of lading.

6. Goods of an inflammable, explosive or dangerous nature to the shipment whereof the carrier, master or agent of the carrier has not consented with knowledge of their nature and character, may at any time before discharge be landed at any place, or destroyed or rendered innocuous by the carrier without compensation and the shipper of such goods shall be liable for all damages and expenses directly or indirectly arising out of or resulting from such shipment. If any such goods shipped with such knowledge and consent shall become a danger to the ship or cargo, they may in like manner be landed at any place, or destroyed or rendered innocuous by the carrier without liability on the part of the carrier except to general average, if any.

Article IV bis

1. The defences and limits of liability provided for in these Rules shall apply in any action against the carrier in respect of loss or damage to goods covered by a contract of carriage whether the action be founded in contract or in tort.

2. If such an action is brought against a servant or agent of the carrier (such servant or agent not being an independent contractor), such servant or agent shall be entitled to avail himself of the defences and limits of liability which the carrier is entitled to invoke under these Rules.

3. The aggregate of the amounts recoverable from the carrier, and such servants and agents, shall in no case exceed the limit provided for in these Rules.

4. Nevertheless, a servant or agent of the carrier shall not be entitled to avail himself of the provisions of this article, if it is proved that the damage resulted from an act or omission of the servant or agent done with intent to cause damage or recklessly and with knowledge that damage would probably result.

Article V

A carrier shall be at liberty to surrender in whole or in part all or any of his rights and immunities or to increase any of his responsibilities and obligations under these Rules, provided such surrender or increase shall be embodied in the bill of lading issued to the shipper. The provisions of these Rules shall not be applicable to charter parties, but if bills of lading are issued in the case of a ship under a charter party they shall comply with the terms of these Rules.

Nothing in these Rules shall be held to prevent the insertion in a bill of lading of any lawful provision regarding general average.

Article VI

Notwithstanding the provisions of the preceding articles, a carrier, master or agent of the carrier and a shipper shall in regard to any particular goods be at liberty to enter into any agreement in any terms as to the responsibility and liability of the carrier for such goods, and as to the rights and immunities of the carrier in respect of such goods, or his obligation as to seaworthiness, so far as this stipulation is not contrary to public policy, or the care or diligence of his servants or agents in regard to the loading, handling, stowage, carriage, custody, care and discharge of the goods carried by sea, provided that in this case no bill of lading has been or shall be issued and that the terms agreed shall be embodied in a receipt which shall be a non-negotiable document and shall be marked as such.

Any agreement so entered into shall have full legal effect.

Provided that this article shall not apply to ordinary commercial shipments made in the ordinary course of trade, but only to other shipments where the character or condition of the property to be carried or the circumstances, terms and conditions under which the carriage is to be performed are such as reasonably to justify a special agreement.

Article VII

Nothing herein contained shall prevent a carrier or a shipper from entering into any agreement, stipulation, condition, reservation or exemption as to the responsibility and liability of the carrier or the ship for the loss or damage to, or in connection with, the custody and care and handling of goods prior to the loading on, and subsequent to the discharge from, the ship on which the goods are carried by sea.

Article VIII

The provisions of these Rules shall not affect the rights and obligations of the carrier under any statute for the time being in force relating to the limitation of the liability of owners of sea-going vessels.

Article IX

These Rules shall not affect the provisions of any international Convention or national law governing liability for nuclear damage.

Article X

The provisions of these Rules shall apply to every bill of lading relating to the carriage of goods between ports in two different States if:

(a)   the bill of lading is issued in a contracting State, or

(b)   the carriage is from a port in a contracting State, or

(c)   the contract contained in or evidenced by the bill of lading provides that these Rules or legislation of any State giving effect to them are to govern the contract,

whatever may be the nationality of the ship, the carrier, the shipper, the consignee, or any other interested person.

[The last two paragraphs of this article are not reproduced. They require contracting States to apply the Rules to bills of lading mentioned in the article and authorise them to apply the Rules to other bills of lading.]

[Articles 11 to 16 of the International Convention for the unification of certain rules of law relating to bills of lading signed at Brussels on 25th August 1924 are not reproduced. They deal with the coming into force of the Convention, procedure for ratification, accession and denunciation, and the right to call for a fresh conference to consider amendments to the Rules contained in the Convention.]

NOTES

Article IV: words in square brackets in para 5 substituted by the Merchant Shipping Act 1981, s 2(3), (4); this amendment continues to have effect by virtue of the Merchant Shipping Act 1995, s 314(2), Sch 13, para 45(2).

Words in italics in square brackets at the end of the Schedule are as set out in the Queen's Printer's version of the Act.

POWERS OF ATTORNEY ACT 1971

(1971 c 27)

ARRANGEMENT OF SECTIONS

An Act to make new provision in relation to powers of attorney and the delegation by trustees of their trusts, powers and discretions

[12 May 1971]

[1.474]
1   Execution of powers of attorney
(1)   An instrument creating a power of attorney shall be [executed as a deed by] the donor of the power.
(2)   . . .
(3)   This section is without prejudice to any requirement in, or having effect under, any other Act as to the witnessing of instruments creating powers of attorney and does not affect the rules relating to the execution of instruments by bodies corporate.

NOTES

Sub-s (1): words in square brackets substituted by the Law of Property (Miscellaneous Provisions) Act 1989, ss 1(8), Sch 1, para 6(a).

Sub-s (2): repealed by the Law of Property (Miscellaneous Provisions) Act 1989, ss 1, 4, Sch 1, para 6(b), Sch 2.

2   *(Repealed by the Senior Courts Act 1981, s 152(4), Sch 7.)*

[1.475]
3   Proof of instruments creating powers of attorney
(1)   The contents of an instrument creating a power of attorney may be proved by means of a copy which—
(a)   is a reproduction of the original made with a photographic or other device for reproducing documents in facsimile; and
(b)   contains the following certificate or certificates signed by the donor of the power or by a solicitor[, authorised person] or stockbroker, that is to say—
(i)   a certificate at the end to the effect that the copy is a true and complete copy of the original; and

(ii)   if the original consists of two or more pages, a certificate at the end of each page of the copy to the effect that it is a true and complete copy of the corresponding page of the original.

(2)   Where a copy of an instrument creating a power of attorney has been made which complies with subsection (t) of this section, the contents of the instrument may also be proved by means of a copy of that copy if the further copy itself complies with that subsection, taking references in it to the original as references to the copy from which the further copy is made.

(3)   In this section ["authorised person" means a person (other than a solicitor) who, for the purposes of the Legal Services Act 2007, is an authorised person in relation to any activity which constitutes a notarial activity (within the meaning of that Act) and] "stockbroker" means a member of any stock exchange within the meaning of the Stock Transfer Act 1963 or the Stock Transfer Act (Northern Ireland) 1963.

(4)   This section is without prejudice to section 4 of the Evidence and Powers of Attorney Act 1940 (proof of deposited instruments by office copy) and to any other method of proof authorised by law.

(5)   For the avoidance of doubt, in relation to an instrument made in Scotland the references to a power of attorney in this section and in section 4 of the Evidence and Powers of Attorney Act 1940 include references to a factory and commission.

NOTES

Sub-ss (1), (3): words in square brackets substituted by the Legal Services Act 2007, s 208(1), Sch 21, para 26.

Solicitors' incorporated practices: the provisions of sub-s (1)(b) of this section are applied, with modifications, in relation to a "recognised body" under the Administration of Justice Act 1985, s 9, by the Solicitors' Recognised Bodies Order 1991, SI 1991/2684, arts 2–5, Sch 1.

[1.476]
4   Powers of attorney given as security

(1)   Where a power of attorney is expressed to be irrevocable and is given to secure—

(a)   a proprietary interest of the donee of the power; or

(b)   the performance of an obligation owed to the donee,

then, so long as the donee has that interest or the obligation remains undischarged, the power shall not be revoked—

(i)   by the donor without the consent of the donee; or

(ii)   by the death, incapacity or bankruptcy of the donor or, if the donor is a body corporate, by its winding up or dissolution.

(2)   A power of attorney given to secure a proprietary interest may be given to the person entitled to the interest and persons deriving title under him to that interest, and those persons shall be duly constituted donees of the power for all purposes of the power but without prejudice to any right to appoint substitutes given by the power.

(3)   This section applies to powers of attorney whenever created.

[1.477]
5   Protection of donee and third persons where power of attorney is revoked

(1)   A donee of a power of attorney who acts in pursuance of the power at a time when it has been revoked shall not, by reason of the revocation, incur any liability (either to the donor or to any other person) if at that time he did not know that the power had been revoked.

(2)   Where a power of attorney has been revoked and a person, without knowledge of the revocation, deals with the donee of the power, the transaction between them shall, in favour of that person, be as valid as if the power had then been in existence.

(3)   Where the power is expressed in the instrument creating it to be irrevocable and to be given by way of security then, unless the person dealing with the donee knows that it was not in fact given by way of security, he shall be entitled to assume that the power is incapable of revocation except by the donor acting with the consent of the donee and shall accordingly be treated for the purposes of subsection (2) of this section as having knowledge of the revocation only if he knows that it has been revoked in that manner.

(4)   Where the interest of a purchaser depends on whether a transaction between the donee of a power of attorney and another person was valid by virtue of subsection (2) of this section, it shall be conclusively presumed in favour of the purchaser that that person did not at the material time know of the revocation of the power if—

(a)   the transaction between that person and the donee was completed within twelve months of the date on which the power came into operation; or

(b)   that person makes a statutory declaration, before or within three months after the completion of the purchase, that he did not at the material time know of the revocation of the power.

(5)   Without prejudice to subsection (3) of this section, for the purposes of this section knowledge of the revocation of a power of attorney includes knowledge of the occurrence of any event (such as the death of the donor) which has the effect of revoking the power.

(6)   In this section "purchaser" and "purchase" have the meanings specified in section 205(1) of the Law of Property Act 1925.

(7) This section applies whenever the power of attorney was created but only to acts and transactions after the commencement of this Act.

[1.478]
6 Additional protection for transferees under stock exchange transactions
(1) Without prejudice to section 5 of this Act, where—
   (a)   the donee of a power of attorney executes, as transferor, an instrument transferring registered securities; and
   (b)   the instrument is executed for the purposes of a stock exchange transaction,
it shall be conclusively presumed in favour of the transferee that the power had not been revoked at the date of the instrument if a statutory declaration to that effect is made by the donee of the power on or within three months after that date.
(2) In this section "registered securities" and "stock exchange transaction" have the same meanings as in the Stock Transfer Act 1963.

[1.479]
7 Execution of instruments etc by donee of power of attorney
[(1) If the donee of a power of attorney is an individual, he may, if he thinks fit—
   (a)   execute any instrument with his own signature, and]
   (b)   do any other thing in his own name,
by the authority of the donor of the power; and any [instrument executed or thing done in that manner shall, subject to subsection (1A) of this section, be as effective as if executed by the donee in any manner which would constitute due execution of that instrument by the donor or, as the case may be, as if done by the donee in the name of the donor].
[(1A) Where an instrument is executed by the donee as a deed, it shall be as effective as if executed by the donee in a manner which would constitute due execution of it as a deed by the donor only if it is executed in accordance with section 1(3)(a) of the Law of Property (Miscellaneous Provisions) Act 1989.]
(2) For the avoidance of doubt it is hereby declared that an instrument to which subsection (3) . . . of section 74 of the Law of Property Act 1925 applies may be executed either as provided in [that subsection] or as provided in this section.
(3) . . .
(4) This section applies whenever the power of attorney was created.

NOTES
Sub-s (1): words in first pair of square brackets substituted by the Law of Property (Miscellaneous Provisions) Act 1989, s 1(8), Sch 1, para 7; words in second pair of square brackets substituted by the Regulatory Reform (Execution of Deeds and Documents) Order 2005, SI 2005/1906, art 10(1), Sch 1, paras 5, 6, except in relation to any instrument executed before 15 September 2005.
Sub-s (1A): inserted by SI 2005/1906, art 10(1), Sch 1, paras 5, 7, except in relation to any instrument executed before 15 September 2005.
Sub-s (2): words in square brackets substituted, and words omitted repealed, by the Law of Property (Miscellaneous Provisions) Act 1989, ss 1(8), 4, Sch 1, para 7, Sch 2.
Sub-s (3): repealed by SI 2005/1906, art 10, Sch 1, paras 5, 8, Sch 2, except in relation to any instrument executed before 15 September 2005.

8, 9 (*S 8 repealed by the Statute Law (Repeals) Act 2004; s 9 repealed by the Trustee Delegation Act 1999, s 12, Schedule.*)

[1.480]
10 Effect of general power of attorney in specified form
(1) Subject to subsection (2) of this section, a general power of attorney in the form set out in Schedule 1 to this Act, or in a form to the like effect but expressed to be made under this Act, shall operate to confer—
   (a)   on the donee of the power; or
   (b)   if there is more than one donee, on the donees acting jointly or acting jointly or severally, as the case may be,
authority to do on behalf of the donor anything which he can lawfully do by an attorney.
(2) [Subject to section 1 of the Trustee Delegation Act 1999, this section] does not apply to functions which the donor has as a trustee or personal representative or as a tenant for life or statutory owner within the meaning of the Settled Land Act 1925.

NOTES
Sub-s (2): words in square brackets substituted by the Trustee Delegation Act 1999, s 3.

[1.481]
11 Short title, repeals, consequential amendments, commencement and extent
(1) This Act may be cited as the Powers of Attorney Act 1971.
(2) The enactments specified in Schedule 2 to this Act are hereby repealed to the extent specified in the third column of that Schedule.
(3), (4) . . .

(5)   Section 3 of this Act extends to Scotland and Northern Ireland but, save as aforesaid, this Act extends to England and Wales only.

NOTES

Sub-s (3): in part amends the Law of Property Act 1925, s 125(2); remainder repealed by the Senior Courts Act 1981, s 152(4), Sch 7.

Sub-s (4): repealed by the Statute Law (Repeals) Act 2004.

SCHEDULES

SCHEDULE 1
FORM OF GENERAL POWER OF ATTORNEY FOR PURPOSES OF SECTION 10

Section 10

[1.482]

THIS GENERAL POWER OF ATTORNEY is made this   day of
19   by AB of

I appoint CD of [*or* CD of   and EF

of   jointly *or* jointly and severally] to be my attorney[s]

in accordance with section 10 of the Powers of Attorney Act 1971.

IN WITNESS etc,

NOTES

Prescribed form: for a Welsh language form, see the Powers of Attorney (Welsh Language Forms) Order 2000, SI 2000/215.

SCHEDULE 2

(*Sch 2 (Repeals) outside the scope of this work.*)

UNSOLICITED GOODS AND SERVICES ACT 1971

(1971 c 30)

ARRANGEMENT OF SECTIONS

An Act to make provision for the greater protection of persons receiving unsolicited goods, and to amend the law with respect to charges for entries in directories

[12 May 1971]

NOTES

Unsolicited Goods and Services Acts 1971 and 1975: by the Unsolicited Goods and Services (Amendment) Act 1975, s 4(1), see **[1.694]**, that Act and this Act may be cited together by this collective title.

1   (*Repealed by the Consumer Protection (Distance Selling) Regulations 2000, SI 2000/2334, reg 22(4)*).

[1.483]
2   Demands and threats regarding payment

(1)   A person who, not having reasonable cause to believe there is a right to payment, in the course of any trade or business makes a demand for payment, or asserts a present or prospective right to payment, for what he knows are unsolicited goods sent (after the commencement of this Act) to another person with a view to his acquiring them [for the purposes of his trade or business], shall be guilty of an offence and on summary conviction shall be liable to a fine not exceeding [level 4 on the standard scale].

(2)   A person who, not having reasonable cause to believe there is a right to payment, in the course of any trade or business and with a view to obtaining any payment for what he knows are unsolicited goods sent as aforesaid—

    (a)   threatens to bring any legal proceedings; or

    (b)   places or causes to be placed the name of any person on a list of defaulters or debtors or threatens to do so; or

    (c)   invokes or causes to be invoked any other collection procedure or threatens to do so,

shall be guilty of an offence and shall be liable on summary conviction to a fine not exceeding [level 5 on the standard scale].

NOTES

Sub-s (1): words in first pair of square brackets inserted by the Consumer Protection (Distance Selling) Regulations 2000, SI 2000/2334, reg 22(1), (3), in relation to goods sent after 31 October 2000; reference to a level on the standard scale substituted by virtue of the Criminal Justice Act 1982, ss 38, 46.

Sub-s (2): references to a level on the standard scale substituted by virtue of the Criminal Justice Act 1982, ss 38, 46.

[1.484]
3   Directory entries

[(1)   A person ("the purchaser") shall not be liable to make any payment, and shall be entitled to recover any payment made by him, by way of charge for including or arranging for the inclusion in a directory of an entry relating to that person or his trade or business, unless—

    (a)   there has been signed by the purchaser or on his behalf an order complying with this section,

    (b)   there has been signed by the purchaser or on his behalf a note complying with this section of his agreement to the charge and before the note was signed, a copy of it was supplied, for retention by him, to him or a person acting on his behalf, . . .

    (c)   there has been transmitted by the purchaser or a person acting on his behalf an electronic communication which includes a statement that the purchaser agrees to the charge and the relevant condition is satisfied in relation to that communication[, or

    (d)   the charge arises under a contract in relation to which the conditions in section 3B(1) (renewed and extended contracts) are met.]

(2)   A person shall be guilty of an offence punishable on summary conviction with a fine not exceeding [the prescribed sum] if, in a case where a payment in respect of a charge would . . . be recoverable from him in accordance with the terms of subsection (1) above, he demands payment, or asserts a present or prospective right to payment, of the charge or any part of it, without knowing or having reasonable cause to believe [that—

    (a)   the entry to which the charge relates was ordered in accordance with this section,

    (b)   a proper note of the agreement has been duly signed, or

    (c)   the requirements set out in subsection (1)(c) [or (d)] above have been met].

(3)   For the purposes of [this section—

    (a)]   an order for an entry in a directory must be made by means of an order form or other stationery belonging to the [purchaser[,which may be sent electronically but which must bear] his name and address (or one or more of his addresses);] and

    [(b)]   the note [of a person's agreement to a charge must—

        (i)   specify the particulars set out in Part 1 of the Schedule to the Regulatory Reform (Unsolicited Goods and Services Act 1971) (Directory Entries and Demands for Payment) Order 2005, and

        (ii)   give reasonable particulars of the entry in respect of which the charge would be payable.]

[(3A)   In relation to an electronic communication which includes a statement that the purchaser agrees to a charge for including or arranging the inclusion in a directory of any entry, the relevant condition is that—

    (a)   before the electronic communication was transmitted the information referred to in subsection (3B) below was communicated to the purchaser, and

    (b)   the electronic communication can readily be produced and retained in a visible and legible form.

(3B)   That information is—

    (a)   the following particulars—

        (i)   the amount of the charge;

        (ii)   the name of the directory or proposed directory;

        (iii)   the name of the person producing the directory;

        (iv)   the geographic address at which that person is established;

        (v)   if the directory is or is to be available in printed form, the proposed date of publication of the directory or of the issue in which the entry is to be included;

        (vi)   if the directory or the issue in which the entry is to be included is to be put on sale, the price at which it is to be offered for sale and the minimum number of copies which are to be available for sale;

       (vii)   if the directory or the issue in which the entry is to be included is to be distributed free of charge (whether or not it is also to be put on sale), the minimum number of copies which are to be so distributed;

       (viii)   if the directory is or is to be available in a form other than in printed form, adequate details of how it may be accessed; and

   (b)   reasonable particulars of the entry in respect of which the charge would be payable.

(3C)   In this section "electronic communication" has the same meaning as in the Electronic Communications Act 2000.]

(4)   Nothing in this section shall apply to a payment due under a contract entered into before the commencement of this Act, or entered into by the acceptance of an offer made before that commencement.

NOTES

Sub-s (1): substituted by the Unsolicited Goods and Services Act 1971 (Electronic Communications) Order 2001, SI 2001/2778, arts 2, 3; word omitted repealed and words in square brackets added by the Regulatory Reform (Unsolicited Goods and Services Act 1971) (Directory Entries and Demands for Payment) Order 2005, SI 2005/55, art 2(1)–(3).

Sub-s (2): reference to the prescribed sum substituted by virtue of the Magistrates' Courts Act 1980, s 32(2); words omitted repealed and words in third (inner) pair of square brackets inserted by SI 2005/55, art 2(1), (4); words in second (outer) pair of square brackets substituted, by SI 2001/2778, arts 2, 4(b).

Sub-s (3): words in first pair of square brackets substituted, para (b) numbered as such, and words in final pair of square brackets substituted by SI 2005/55, art 2(1), (5); words in second (outer) pair of square brackets substituted by SI 2001/2778, art 5; words in third (inner) pair of square brackets substituted by the Unsolicited Goods and Services Act 1971 (Electronic Commerce) (Amendment) Regulations 2005, SI 2005/148, reg 2.

Sub-ss (3A)–(3C): inserted by SI 2001/2778, art 6.

Summary conviction: see the Unsolicited Goods and Services (Amendment) Act 1975, s 3 at **[1.693]**, which provides that the offence under sub-s (2) may be prosecuted on indictment.

3A   *(Inserted by the Unsolicited Goods and Services (Amendment) Act 1975, s 1; repealed by the Regulatory Reform (Unsolicited Goods and Services Act 1971) (Directory Entries and Demands for Payment) Order 2005, SI 2005/55, art 2(1), (6).)*

[1.485]
[3B   Renewed and extended contracts

(1)   The conditions referred to in section 3(1)(d) above are met in relation to a contract ("the new contract") if—

   (a)   a person ("the purchaser") has entered into an earlier contract ("the earlier contract") for including or arranging for the inclusion in a particular issue or version of a directory ("the earlier directory") of an entry ("the earlier entry") relating to him or his trade or business;

   (b)   the purchaser was liable to make a payment by way of a charge arising under the earlier contract for including or arranging for the inclusion of the earlier entry in the earlier directory;

   (c)   the new contract is a contract for including or arranging for the inclusion in a later issue or version of a directory ("the later directory") of an entry ("the later entry") relating to the purchaser or his trade or business;

   (d)   the form, content and distribution of the later directory is materially the same as the form, content and distribution of the earlier directory;

   (e)   the form and content of the later entry is materially the same as the form and content of the earlier entry;

   (f)   if the later directory is published other than in electronic form—

       (i)   the earlier directory was the last, or the last but one, issue or version of the directory to be published before the later directory, and

       (ii)   the date of publication of the later directory is not more than 13 months after the date of publication of the earlier directory;

   (g)   if the later directory is published in electronic form, the first date on which the new contract requires the later entry to be published is not more than the relevant period after the last date on which the earlier contract required the earlier entry to be published;

   (h)   if it was a term of the earlier contract that the purchaser renew or extend the contract—

       (i)   before the start of the new contract the relevant publisher has given notice in writing to the purchaser containing the information set out in Part 3 of the Schedule to the Regulatory Reform (Unsolicited Goods and Services Act 1971) (Directory Entries and Demands for Payment) Order 2005; and

       (ii)   the purchaser has not written to the relevant publisher withdrawing his agreement to the renewal or extension of the earlier contract within the period of 21 days starting when he receives the notice referred to in sub-paragraph (i); and

   (i)   if the parties to the earlier contract and the new contract are different—

       (i)   the parties to both contracts have entered into a novation agreement in respect of the earlier contract; or

       (ii)   the relevant publisher has given the purchaser the information set out in Part 4 of the Schedule to the Regulatory Reform (Unsolicited Goods and Services Act 1971) (Directory Entries and Demands for Payment) Order 2005.

(2)   For the purposes of subsection (1)(d) and (e), the form, content or distribution of the later directory, or the form or content of the later entry, shall be taken to be materially the same as that of the earlier directory or the earlier entry (as the case may be), if a reasonable person in the position of the purchaser would—

(a)   view the two as being materially the same; or

(b)   view that of the later directory or the later entry as being an improvement on that of the earlier directory or the earlier entry.

(3)   For the purposes of subsection (1)(g) "the relevant period" means the period of 13 months or (if shorter) the period of time between the first and last dates on which the earlier contract required the earlier entry to be published.

(4)   For the purposes of subsection (1)(h) and (i) "the relevant publisher" is the person with whom the purchaser has entered into the new contract.

(5)   The information referred to in subsection (1)(i)(ii) must be given to the purchaser prior to the conclusion of the new contract.]

NOTES

Inserted by the Regulatory Reform (Unsolicited Goods and Services Act 1971) (Directory Entries and Demands for Payment) Order 2005, SI 2005/55, art 2(1), (7).

[1.486]
4   Unsolicited publications

(1)   A person shall be guilty of an offence if he sends or causes to be sent to another person any book, magazine or leaflet (or advertising material for any such publication) which he knows or ought reasonably to know is unsolicited and which describes or illustrates human sexual techniques.

(2)   A person found guilty of an offence under this section shall be liable on summary conviction to a fine not exceeding [level 5 on the standard scale].

(3)   A prosecution for an offence under this section shall not in England and Wales be instituted except by, or with the consent of, the Director of Public Prosecutions.

NOTES

Sub-s (2): reference to a level on the standard scale substituted by virtue of the Criminal Justice Act 1982, ss 38, 46.

[1.487]
5   Offences by corporations

(1)   Where an offence under this Act which has been committed by a body corporate is proved to have been committed with the consent or connivance of, or to be attributable to any neglect on the part of, any director, manager, secretary, or other similar officer of the body corporate, or of any person who was purporting to act in any such capacity, he as well as the body corporate shall be guilty of that offence and shall be liable to be proceeded against and punished accordingly.

(2)   Where the affairs of a body corporate are managed by its members, this section shall apply in relation to the acts or defaults of a member in connection with his functions of management as if he were a director of the body corporate.

[1.488]
6   Interpretation

(1)   In this Act, unless the context or subject matter otherwise requires,—

"acquire" includes hire;

"send" includes deliver, and "sender" shall be construed accordingly;

"unsolicited" means, in relation to goods sent to any person, that they are sent without any prior request made by him or on his behalf.

[(2)   For the purposes of this Act, any invoice or similar document stating the amount of any payment shall be regarded as asserting a right to the payment unless it complies with the conditions set out in Part 2 of the Schedule to the Regulatory Reform (Unsolicited Goods and Services Act 1971) (Directory Entries and Demands for Payment) Order 2005.]

[(3)   Nothing in section 3 or 3B affects the rights of any consumer under the Consumer Contracts (Information, Cancellation and Additional Charges) Regulations 2013.]

NOTES

Sub-s (2): substituted by the Regulatory Reform (Unsolicited Goods and Services Act 1971) (Directory Entries and Demands for Payment) Order 2005, SI 2005/55, art 2(1), (8)(a).

Sub-s (3): added by SI 2005/55, art 2(1), (8)(b); substituted by the Consumer Contracts (Information, Cancellation and Additional Charges) Regulations 2013, SI 2013/3134, reg 47, Sch 4, para 1, with effect in relation to contracts entered into on or after 13 June 2014.

[1.489]
7   Citation, commencement and extent

(1)   This Act may be cited as the Unsolicited Goods and Services Act 1971.

(2)   This Act shall come into force at the expiration of three months beginning with the day on which it is passed.

(3)   This Act does not extend to Northern Ireland.

SUPPLY OF GOODS (IMPLIED TERMS) ACT 1973

(1973 c 13)

ARRANGEMENT OF SECTIONS

Hire-purchase agreements

An Act to amend the law with respect to the terms to be implied in contracts of sale of goods and hire-purchase agreements and on the exchange of goods for trading stamps, and with respect to the terms of conditional sale agreements: and for connected purposes

[18 April 1973]

1–7 (*Repealed by the Sale of Goods Act 1979, s 63(2), Sch 3.*)

Hire-purchase agreements

[1.490]

[8   Implied terms as to title

(1)   In every *hire-purchase agreement*, other than one to which subsection (2) below applies, there is—

   (a)   an implied [term] on the part of the creditor that he will have a right to sell the goods at the time when the property is to pass; and

   (b)   an implied [term] that—

     (i)   the goods are free, and will remain free until the time when the property is to pass, from any charge or encumbrance not disclosed or known to the person to whom the goods are bailed or (in Scotland) hired before the agreement is made, and

     (ii)   that person will enjoy quiet possession of the goods except so far as it may be disturbed by any person entitled to the benefit of any charge or encumbrance so disclosed or known.

(2)   In a *hire-purchase agreement*, in the case of which there appears from the agreement or is to be inferred from the circumstances of the agreement an intention that the creditor should transfer only such title as he or a third person may have, there is—

   (a)   an implied [term] that all charges or encumbrances known to the creditor and not known to the person to whom the goods are bailed or hired have been disclosed to that person before the agreement is made; and

   (b)   an implied [term] that neither—

     (i)   the creditor; nor

     (ii)   in a case where the parties to the agreement intend that any title which may be transferred shall be only such title as a third person may have, that person; nor

     (iii)   anyone claiming through or under the creditor or that third person otherwise than under a charge or encumbrance disclosed or known to the person to whom the goods are bailed or hired, before the agreement is made;

will disturb the quiet possession of the person to whom the goods are bailed or hired.

[(3)   As regards England and Wales and Northern Ireland, the term implied by subsection (1)(a) above is a condition and the terms implied by subsections (1)(b), (2)(a) and (2)(b) above are warranties.]]

NOTES

Substituted, together with ss 9–11, 12, by the Consumer Credit Act 1974, s 192(3)(a), Sch 4, para 35.

Sub-ss (1), (2): for the words in italics there are substituted the words "relevant hire-purchase agreement" by the Consumer Rights Act 2015, s 60, Sch 1, paras 1, 2, as from 1 October 2015 (for transitional provisions see the Consumer Rights Act 2015 (Commencement No 3, Transitional Provisions, Savings and Consequential Amendments) Order 2015, SI 2015/1630, arts 6–8 at **[2.1220]** et seq); words in square brackets substituted by the Sale and Supply of Goods Act 1994, s 7(1), Sch 2 para 4(1), (2)(a).

Sub-s (3): added by the Sale and Supply of Goods Act 1994, s 7(1), Sch 2 para 4(1), (2)(b).

[1.491]
[9   Bailing or hiring by description
(1)   Where under a *hire-purchase agreement* goods are bailed or (in Scotland) hired by description, there is an implied [term] that the goods will correspond with the description, and if under the agreement the goods are bailed or hired by reference to a sample as well as a description, it is not sufficient that the bulk of the goods corresponds with the sample if the goods do not also correspond with the description.
[(1A)   As regards England and Wales and Northern Ireland, the term implied by subsection (1) above is a condition.]
(2)   Goods shall not be prevented from being bailed or hired by description by reason only that, being exposed for sale, bailment or hire, they are selected by the person to whom they are bailed or hired.]

NOTES
Substituted as noted to s 8 at **[1.490]**.
Sub-s (1): for the words in italics there are substituted the words "relevant hire-purchase agreement" by the Consumer Rights Act 2015, s 60, Sch 1, paras 1, 2, as from 1 October 2015 (for transitional provisions see the Consumer Rights Act 2015 (Commencement No 3, Transitional Provisions, Savings and Consequential Amendments) Order 2015, SI 2015/1630, arts 6–8 at **[2.1220]** et seq); word in square brackets substituted by the Sale and Supply of Goods Act 1994, s 7(1), Sch 2, para 4(1), (3)(a).
Sub-s (1A): inserted by the Sale and Supply of Goods Act 1994, s 7(1), Sch 2, para 4(1), (3)(b).

[1.492]
[10   Implied undertakings as to quality or fitness
(1)   Except as provided by this section and section 11 below and subject to the provisions of any other enactment, including any enactment of the Parliament of Northern Ireland, or the Northern Ireland Assembly, there is no implied [term] as to the quality or fitness for any particular purpose of goods bailed or (in Scotland) hired under a *hire-purchase agreement*.
[(2)   Where the creditor bails or hires goods under a *hire purchase agreement* in the course of a business, there is an implied term that the goods supplied under the agreement are of satisfactory quality.
(2A)   For the purposes of this Act, goods are of satisfactory quality if they meet the standard that a reasonable person would regard as satisfactory, taking account of any description of the goods, the price (if relevant) and all the other relevant circumstances.
(2B)   For the purposes of this Act, the quality of goods includes their state and condition and the following (among others) are in appropriate cases aspects of the quality of goods—
    (a)   fitness for all the purposes for which goods of the kind in question are commonly supplied,
    (b)   appearance and finish,
    (c)   freedom from minor defects,
    (d)   safety, and
    (e)   durability.
(2C)   The term implied by subsection (2) above does not extend to any matter making the quality of goods unsatisfactory—
    (a)   which is specifically drawn to the attention of the person to whom the goods are bailed or hired before the agreement is made,
    (b)   where that person examines the goods before the agreement is made, which that examination ought to reveal, or
    (c)   where the goods are bailed or hired by reference to a sample, which would have been apparent on a reasonable examination of the sample.]
[(2D)   If the person to whom the goods are bailed or hired deals as consumer or, in Scotland, if the goods are hired to a person under a consumer contract, the relevant circumstances mentioned in subsection (2A) above include any public statements on the specific characteristics of the goods made about them by the creditor, the producer or his representative, particularly in advertising or on labelling.
(2E)   A public statement is not by virtue of subsection (2D) above a relevant circumstance for the purposes of subsection (2A) above in the case of a contract of hire-purchase, if the creditor shows that—
    (a)   at the time the contract was made, he was not, and could not reasonably have been, aware of the statement,
    (b)   before the contract was made, the statement had been withdrawn in public or, to the extent that it contained anything which was incorrect or misleading, it had been corrected in public, or
    (c)   the decision to acquire the goods could not have been influenced by the statement.
(2F)   Subsections (2D) and (2E) above do not prevent any public statement from being a relevant circumstance for the purposes of subsection (2A) above (whether or not the person to whom the goods are bailed or hired deals as consumer or, in Scotland, whether or not the goods are hired to a person under a consumer contract) if the statement would have been such a circumstance apart from those subsections.]

(3) Where the creditor bails or hires goods under a *hire-purchase agreement* in the course of a business and the person to whom the goods are bailed or hired, expressly or by implication, makes known—

    (a)   to the creditor in the course of negotiations conducted by the creditor in relation to the making of the *hire-purchase agreement*, or

    (b)   to a credit-broker in the course of negotiations conducted by that broker in relation to goods sold by him to the creditor before forming the subject matter of the *hire-purchase agreement*,

any particular purpose for which the goods are being bailed or hired, there is an implied [term] that the goods supplied under the agreement are reasonably fit for that purpose, whether or not that is a purpose for which such goods are commonly supplied, except where the circumstances show that the person to whom the goods are bailed or hired does not rely, or that it is unreasonable for him to rely, on the skill or judgment of the creditor or credit-broker.

(4) An implied [term] as to quality or fitness for a particular purpose may be annexed to a *hire-purchase agreement* by usage.

(5) The preceding provisions of this section apply to a *hire-purchase agreement* made by a person who in the course of a business is acting as agent for the creditor as they apply to an agreement made by the creditor in the course of a business, except where the creditor is not bailing or hiring in the course of a business and either the person to whom the goods are bailed or hired knows that fact or reasonable steps are taken to bring it to the notice of that person before the agreement is made.

(6) In subsection (3) above and this subsection—

    (a)   "credit-broker" means a person acting in the course of a business of credit brokerage.

    (b)   "credit brokerage" means the effecting of introductions of individuals desiring to obtain credit—

        (i)   to persons carrying on any business so far as it relates to the provision of credit, or

        (ii)   to other persons engaged in credit brokerage.]

[(7) As regards England and Wales and Northern Ireland, the terms implied by subsections (2) and (3) above are conditions.]

[(8) . . .]

NOTES

Substituted as noted to s 8 at **[1.490]**.

Sub-ss (1), (3), (4): words in square brackets substituted by the Sale and Supply of Goods Act 1994, s 7(1), Sch 2, para 4(1), (4)(b); for the words in italics in each place there are substituted the words "relevant hire-purchase agreement" by the Consumer Rights Act 2015, s 60, Sch 1, paras 1, 2, as from 1 October 2015 (for transitional provisions see the Consumer Rights Act 2015 (Commencement No 3, Transitional Provisions, Savings and Consequential Amendments) Order 2015, SI 2015/1630, arts 6–8 at **[2.1220]** et seq).

Sub-ss (2), (2A), (2B), (2C): substituted, for original sub-s (2), by the Sale and Supply of Goods Act 1994, s 7(1), Sch 2, para 4(1), (4)(a); in sub-s (2) for the words in italics there are substituted the words "relevant hire-purchase agreement" by the Consumer Rights Act 2015, s 60, Sch 1, paras 1, 2, as from 1 October 2015 (for transitional provisions see note above).

Sub-ss (2D)–(2F): inserted by the Sale and Supply of Goods to Consumers Regulations 2002, SI 2002/3045, reg 13(1), (2); repealed by the Consumer Rights Act 2015, s 60, Sch 1, paras 1, 3(1), (2), as from 1 October 2015 (for transitional provisions see note above).

Sub-s (5): for the words in italics there are substituted the words "relevant hire-purchase agreement" by the Consumer Rights Act 2015, s 60, Sch 1, paras 1, 2, as from 1 October 2015 (for transitional provisions see note above).

Sub-s (7): added by the Sale and Supply of Goods Act 1994, s 7(1), Sch 2, para 4(1), (4)(c).

Sub-s (8): added by SI 2002/3045, art 13(1), (3), and repealed by the Consumer Rights Act 2015, s 60, Sch 1, paras 1, 3(1), (3), as from 1 October 2015 (for transitional provisions see note above); applies to Scotland only.

[1.493]
[11 Samples

[(1)] Where under a *hire-purchase agreement* goods are bailed or (in Scotland) hired by reference to a sample, there is an implied [term]—

    (a)   that the bulk will correspond with the sample in quality; and

    (b)   that the person to whom the goods are bailed or hired will have a reasonable opportunity of comparing the bulk with the sample; and

    (c)   that the goods will be free from any defect, [making their quality unsatisfactory], which would not be apparent on reasonable examination of the sample.

[(2) As regards England and Wales and Northern Ireland, the term implied by subsection (1) above is a condition.]]

NOTES

Substituted as noted to s 8 at **[1.490]**.

Sub-s (1): numbered as such, and words in square brackets substituted, by the Sale and Supply of Goods Act 1994, s 7(1), Sch 2, para 4(1), (5)(a)–(c); for the words in italics there are substituted the words "relevant hire-purchase agreement" by the Consumer Rights Act 2015, s 60, Sch 1, paras 1, 2, as from 1 October 2015 (for transitional provisions see the Consumer Rights Act 2015 (Commencement No 3, Transitional Provisions, Savings and Consequential Amendments) Order 2015, SI 2015/1630, arts 6–8 at **[2.1220]** et seq).

Sub-s (2): added by the Sale and Supply of Goods Act 1994, s 7(1), Sch 2, para 4(1), (5)(d).

[1.494]
[11A   Modification of remedies for breach of statutory condition in non-consumer cases
(1)   Where in the case of a *hire purchase agreement*—
  (a)   the person to whom goods are bailed would, apart from this subsection, have the right to reject them by reason of a breach on the part of the creditor of a term implied by section 9, 10 or 11(1)(a) or (c) above, but
  (b)   the breach is so slight that it would be unreasonable for him to reject them,
then, if the person to whom the goods are bailed does not deal as consumer, the breach is not to be treated as a breach of condition but may be treated as a breach of warranty.
(2)   This section applies unless a contrary intention appears in, or is to be implied from, the agreement.
(3)   It is for the creditor to show—
  (a)   that a breach fell within subsection (1)(b) above, and
  (b)   *that the person to whom the goods were bailed did not deal as consumer.*
(4)   The references in this section to dealing as consumer are to be construed in accordance with Part I of the Unfair Contract Terms Act 1977.
(5)   This section does not apply to Scotland.]

NOTES
Inserted by the Sale and Supply of Goods Act 1994, s 7(1), Sch 2, para 4(1), (6).
Sub-s (1): for the first words in italics there are substituted the words "relevant hire-purchase agreement", and second words in italics repealed by the Consumer Rights Act 2015, s 60, Sch 1, paras 1, 2, 4(1), (2), as from 1 October 2015 (for transitional provisions see the Consumer Rights Act 2015 (Commencement No 3, Transitional Provisions, Savings and Consequential Amendments) Order 2015, SI 2015/1630, arts 6–8 at **[2.1220]** et seq).
Sub-s (3): para (b) substituted by the Consumer Rights Act 2015, s 60, Sch 1, paras 1, 4(1), (3), as from 1 October 2015 (for transitional provisions see note above), as follows:

"(b)   that the agreement was a relevant hire-purchase agreement".

Sub-s (4): repealed by the Consumer Rights Act 2015, s 60, Sch 1, paras 1, 4(1), (4), as from 1 October 2015 (for transitional provisions see note above).

[1.495]
[12   Exclusion of implied terms
An express term does not negative a term implied by this Act unless inconsistent with it.]

NOTES
Substituted as noted to s 8 at **[1.490]**; further substituted by the Sale and Supply of Goods Act 1994, s 7(1), Sch 2 para 4(1), (7).

12A, 13   *(S 12A inserted in relation to Scotland only, by the Sale and Supply of Goods Act 1994, s 7(1), Sch 2 para 4(1), (8); s 13 repealed by the Unfair Contract Terms Act 1977, s 31(4), Sch 4.)*

[1.496]
[14   Special provisions as to conditional sale agreements
(1)   [Section 11(4) of the Sale of Goods Act 1979] (whereby in certain circumstances a breach of a condition in a contract of sale is treated only as a breach of warranty) shall not apply to [a conditional sale agreement where the buyer deals as consumer within Part I of the Unfair Contract Terms Act 1977 . . .].
(2)   In England and Wales and Northern Ireland a breach of a condition (whether express or implied) to be fulfilled by the seller under any such agreement shall be treated as a breach of warranty, and not as grounds for rejecting the goods and treating the agreement as repudiated, if (but only if) it would have fallen to be so treated had the condition been contained or implied in a corresponding hire-purchase agreement as a condition to be fulfilled by the creditor.]

NOTES
Substituted, together with s 15, by the Consumer Credit Act 1974, s 192(3)(a), Sch 4, para 36.
Repealed by the Consumer Rights Act 2015, s 60, Sch 1, paras 1, 6, as from 1 October 2015 (for transitional provisions see the Consumer Rights Act 2015 (Commencement No 3, Transitional Provisions, Savings and Consequential Amendments) Order 2015, SI 2015/1630, arts 6–8 at **[2.1220]** et seq). Note also that Sch 1, para 2 to the 2015 Act provides for the substitution of all occurrences of "hire-purchase agreement" (or "hire purchase agreement") in this Act (with the exception of s 15(1)) with the words "relevant hire-purchase agreement". Given the repeal of this section, it is assumed that this general substitution is not applicable here.
Sub-s (1): words in first pair of square brackets substituted by the Sale of Goods Act 1979, s 63, Sch 2, para 16; words in second pair of square brackets substituted by the Unfair Contract Terms Act 1977, s 31(3), Sch 3; words omitted repealed by the Statute Law (Repeals) Act 1981.

[1.497]
[15   Supplementary
(1)   In sections 8 to 14 above and this section—
  "business" includes a profession and the activities of any government department (including a Northern Ireland department), [or local or public authority];

"buyer" and "seller" includes a person to whom rights and duties under a conditional sale agreement have passed by assignment or operation of law;

. . .

"conditional sale agreement" means an agreement for the sale of goods under which the purchase price or part of it is payable by instalments, and the property in the goods is to remain in the seller (notwithstanding that the buyer is to be in possession of the goods) until such conditions as to the payment of instalments or otherwise as may be specified in the agreement are fulfilled;

. . .

"creditor" means the person by whom the goods are bailed or (in Scotland) hired under a hire-purchase agreement or the person to whom his rights and duties under the agreement have passed by assignment or operation of law; and

"hire-purchase agreement" means an agreement, other than a conditional sale agreement, under which—

(a)   goods are bailed or (in Scotland) hired in return for periodical payments by the person to whom they are bailed or hired, and

(b)   the property in the goods will pass to that person if the terms of the agreements are complied with and one or more of the following occurs—

    (i)   the exercise of an option to purchase by that person,

    (ii)   the doing of any other specified act by any party to the agreement,

    (iii)   the happening of any other specified event.

[and a hire-purchase agreement is relevant if it is not a contract to which Chapter 2 of Part 1 of the Consumer Rights Act 2015 applies;]

[*"producer" means the manufacturer of goods, the importer of goods into the European Economic Area or any person purporting to be a producer by placing his name, trade mark or other distinctive sign on the goods;*]

(2)   . . .

(3)   In section 14(2) above "corresponding hire-purchase agreement" means, in relation to a conditional sale agreement, a hire-purchase agreement relating to the same goods as the conditional sale agreement and made between the same parties and at the same time and in the same circumstances and, as nearly as may be, in the same terms as the conditional sale agreement.

(4)   Nothing in sections 8 to 13 above shall prejudice the operation of any other enactment including any enactment of the Parliament of Northern Ireland or the Northern Ireland Assembly or any rule of law whereby any [term], other than one relating to quality or fitness, is to be implied in any *hire-purchase agreement.*]

NOTES

Substituted as noted to s 14 at **[1.496]**.

Sub-s (1): in definition "business" words in square brackets substituted, and second definition omitted repealed, by the Unfair Contract Terms Act 1977, s 31(3), (4), Schs 3, 4; first definition omitted repealed by the Sale and Supply of Goods Act 1994, s 7(1), Sch 2 para 4(1), (9)(a), Sch 3; in definition "hire-purchase agreement" words in square brackets added by the Consumer Rights Act 2015, s 60, Sch 1, paras 1, 7(1), (2)(a), as from 1 October 2015 (for transitional provisions see the Consumer Rights Act 2015 (Commencement No 3, Transitional Provisions, Savings and Consequential Amendments) Order 2015, SI 2015/1630, arts 6–8 at **[2.1220]** et seq); definition "producer" inserted by the Sale and Supply of Goods to Consumers Regulations 2002, SI 2002/3045, art 13(1), (4) and repealed by the Consumer Rights Act 2015, s 60, Sch 1, paras 1, 7(1), (2)(b), as from 1 October 2015 (for transitional provisions see note above).

Sub-s (2): repealed by the Sale and Supply of Goods Act 1994, s 7(1), Sch 2 para 4(1), (9)(b), Sch 3.

Sub-s (3): repealed by the Consumer Rights Act 2015, s 60, Sch 1, paras 1, 7(1), (3), as from 1 October 2015 (for transitional provisions see note above). Note also that Sch 1, para 2 to the 2015 Act provides for the substitution of all occurrences of "hire-purchase agreement" (or "hire purchase agreement") in this Act (with the exception of sub-s (1) above) with the words "relevant hire-purchase agreement". Given the repeal of this subsection, it is assumed that this general substitution is not applicable here.

Sub-s (4): word in square brackets substituted by the Sale and Supply of Goods Act 1994, s 7(1), Sch 2 para 4(1), (9)(c); for the words in italics there are substituted the words "relevant hire-purchase agreement" by the Consumer Rights Act 2015, s 60, Sch 1, paras 1, 2, as from 1 October 2015 (for transitional provisions see note above).

16   (*Repealed in relation to England, Wales and Scotland by the Regulatory Reform (Trading Stamps) Order 2005, SI 2005/871, art 6, Schedule and in relation to Northern Ireland by the Law Reform (Miscellaneous Provisions) (Northern Ireland) Order 2005, SI 2005/1452, art 24, Sch 2.*)

Miscellaneous

[1.498]

17 **Northern Ireland**

(1)   It is hereby declared that this Act extends to Northern Ireland.

(2)   . . .

NOTES

Sub-s (2): repealed by the Northern Ireland Constitution Act 1973, s 41(1), Sch 6, Part I.

[1.499]
18 Short title, citation, interpretation, commencement, repeal and saving
(1) This Act may be cited as the Supply of Goods (Implied Terms) Act 1973.
(2) . . .
(3) This Act shall come into operation at the expiration of a period of one month beginning with the date on which it is passed.
(4) . . .
(5) This Act does not apply to contracts of sale or *hire-purchase agreements* made before its commencement.

NOTES
Sub-s (2): repealed by the Sale of Goods Act 1979, s 63(2), Sch 3.
Sub-s (4): repeals the Hire-Purchase Act 1965, ss 17–20, 29(3)(c), the Hire-Purchase (Scotland) Act 1965, ss 17–20, 29(3)(c), and the Hire-Purchase Act (Northern Ireland) 1966, ss 17–20, 29(3)(c).
Sub-s (5): for the words in italics there are substituted the words "relevant hire-purchase agreements" by virtue of the Consumer Rights Act 2015, s 60, Sch 1, paras 1, 2, as from 1 October 2015 (for transitional provisions see the Consumer Rights Act 2015 (Commencement No 3, Transitional Provisions, Savings and Consequential Amendments) Order 2015, SI 2015/1630, arts 6–8 at **[2.1220]** et seq).

FAIR TRADING ACT 1973

(1973 c 41)

ARRANGEMENT OF SECTIONS

PART IX
AMENDMENTS OF RESTRICTIVE TRADE PRACTICES ACTS

PART XI
PYRAMID SELLING AND SIMILAR TRADING SCHEMES

PART XII
MISCELLANEOUS AND SUPPLEMENTARY PROVISIONS

An Act to provide for the appointment of a Director General of Fair Trading and of a Consumer Protection Advisory Committee, and to confer on the Director General and the Committee so appointed, on the Secretary of State, on the Restrictive Practices Court and on certain other courts new functions for the protection of consumers; to make provisions, in substitution for the Monopolies and Restrictive Practices (Inquiry and Control) Act 1948 and the Monopolies and Mergers Act 1965, for the matters dealt with in those Acts and related matters, including restrictive labour practices; to amend the Restrictive Trade Practices Act 1956 and the Restrictive Trade Practices Act 1968, to make provision for extending the said Act of 1956 to agreements relating to services, and to transfer to the Director General of Fair Trading the functions of the Registrar of Restrictive Trading Agreements; to make provision with respect to pyramid selling and similar trading schemes; to make new provision in place of section 30(2) to (4) of the Trade Descriptions Act 1968; and for purposes connected with those matters

[25 July 1973]

NOTES
Director General of Fair Trading: the Enterprise Act 2002, s 2(1), provided that, as from the coming into force of that section (on 1 April 2003), the functions of the Director General of Fair Trading, his property, rights and liabilities were transferred to the Office of Fair Trading. Accordingly, (by virtue of s 2(2), (3) of the 2002 Act) the office of the Director was abolished, and any reference to the Director in any enactment, instrument or other document passed or made before the commencement of s 2(1) had, in so far as is necessary, effect as if it were a reference to the Office of Fair Trading (for

transitional provisions in connection with the transfer, see Sch 24, para 6 to the 2002 Act). Section 2 of the 2002 Act was repealed by the Enterprise and Regulatory Reform Act 2013, s 26(3), Sch 5, Pt 4, para 229, as from 1 April 2014. Part 3 of the 2013 Act (ss 25–28) abolished the Office of Fair Trading (and the Competition Commission) and provided for the transfer of its functions to the newly created Competition and Markets Authority.

Note also that certain functions of the Director under this Act were transferred, partly transferred, or were to be exercised concurrently, or after consultation with, specific industry regulators; ie, the Director General of Telecommunications, the Director General of Water Services, the Gas and Electricity Markets Authority, the Rail Regulator, and the Civil Aviation Authority. See the Telecommunications Act 1984, the Water Industry Act 1991, the Gas Act 1986, the Electricity Act 1989, the Railways Act 1993, and the Transport Act 2000.

1–93B (*Pt I: ss 1, 2, 6–11 repealed by the Enterprise Act 2002, s 278(2), Sch 26; s 3 repealed by ss 10(1)(a), 278(2) of, and Sch 26 to, the 2002 Act; s 4 repealed by the Competition Act 1998, s 74(1), (3), Sch 12, para 1(1), (2), Sch 14, Pt I; s 5 repealed by the Enterprise Act 2002 and Media Mergers (Consequential Amendments) Order 2003, SI 2003/3180, art 2, Schedule, para 1(1), (2); s 12 repealed by ss 9, 278(2) of, and Sch 26 to, the 2002 Act; Pt II: ss 13–22 repealed by the Enterprise Act 2002, ss 10(1)(b), 278(2), Sch 26, subject to savings in relation to any Orders made under that section and its continued operation in so far as applying to the revocation of any such Order (see s 10(2)–(4) of the 2002 Act at* **[1.1704]**; *ss 24–33 repealed by the Consumer Protection from Unfair Trading Regulations 2008, SI 2008/1277, reg 30(1), (3), Sch 2, Pt 1, para 15, Sch 4, subject to savings in reg 30(2) of and Sch 3, para 15 to, those Regulations at* **[2.595]**, **[2.597]**; *ss 34–93B (Pts III–VIII) insofar as unrepealed outside the scope of this work; Pt VIII: ss 84, 86, 88–93 repealed by the Enterprise Act 2002, s 278(2), Sch 26; ss 85, 87 repealed by the Enterprise Act 2002 and Media Mergers (Consequential Amendments) Order 2003, SI 2003/3180, art 2, Schedule, para 1(1), (6), (7); s 93A inserted by the Companies Act 1989, s 148 and repealed by the Enterprise Act 2002, s 278(2), Sch 26; s 93B inserted by the Companies Act 1989, s 151 and repealed by the Civil Aviation Act 2012, s 76(4), Sch 9, para 1.*)

PART IX
AMENDMENTS OF RESTRICTIVE TRADE PRACTICES ACTS

[1.500]
94 Transfer of functions of Registrar to Director
(1) Subject to the transitional provisions having effect by virtue of section 139 of this Act, the functions of the Registrar of Restrictive Trading Agreements are hereby transferred to the Director,
. . .
(2)   . . .

NOTES
Sub-s (1): words omitted repealed by the Statute Law (Repeals) Act 2004.
Sub-s (2): repealed by the Resale Prices Act 1976, s 29, Sch 3, Pt I.
The Director: see the note "Director General of Fair Trading" at the beginning of this Act.

95–117 (*Ss 95–106, ss 107–117 (Pt X) repealed by the Restrictive Trade Practices Act 1976.*)

PART XI
PYRAMID SELLING AND SIMILAR TRADING SCHEMES

[1.501]
[118 Trading schemes to which Part XI applies
(1)   This Part of this Act applies to any trading scheme if—
  (a)   the prospect is held out to participants of receiving payments or other benefits in respect of any of the matters specified in subsection (2) of this section; and
  (b)   (subject to subsection (7) of this section) either or both of the conditions in subsections (3) and (4) of this section are fulfilled in relation to the scheme.
(2)   The matters referred to in paragraph (a) of subsection (1) of this section are—
  (a)   the introduction by any person of other persons who become participants in a trading scheme;
  (b)   the continued participation of participants in a trading scheme;
  (c)   the promotion, transfer or other change of status of participants within a trading scheme;
  (d)   the supply of goods or services by any person to or for other persons;
  (e)   the acquisition of goods or services by any person.
(3)   The condition in this subsection is that—
  (a)   goods or services, or both, are to be provided by the person promoting the scheme (in this Part of this Act referred to as "the promoter") or, in the case of a scheme promoted by two or more persons acting in concert (in this Part of this Act referred to as "the promoters"), by one or more of those persons; and
  (b)   the goods or services so provided—
     (i)   are to be supplied to or for other persons under transactions effected by participants (whether in the capacity of agents of the promoter or of one of the promoters or in any other capacity), or

(ii) are to be used for the purposes of the supply of goods or services to or for other persons under such transactions.

(4) The condition in this subsection is that goods or services, or both, are to be supplied by the promoter or any of the promoters to or for persons introduced to him or any of the other promoters (or an employee or agent of his or theirs) by participants.

(5) For the purposes of this Part of this Act a prospect of a kind mentioned in paragraph (a) of subsection (1) of this section shall be treated as being held out to a participant whether it is held out so as to confer on him a legally enforceable right or not.

(6) This Part of this Act does not apply to any trading scheme—

[(a) under which the promoter or any of the promoters or participants is to carry on, or to purport to carry on, a relevant regulated activity;] or

(b) which otherwise falls within a description prescribed by regulations made by the Secretary of State by statutory instrument.

[(6A) For the purposes of subsection (6)(a), "relevant regulated activity" means—

(a) dealing in investments as principal or agent;

(b) arranging deals in investments;

[(ba) operating a multilateral trading facility;]

(c) managing investments;

(d) safeguarding and administering investments;

(e) sending dematerialised instructions;

[(ea) managing a UCITS;

(eb) acting as trustee or depositary of a UCITS;

(ec) managing an AIF;

(ed) acting as trustee or depositary of an AIF;]

(f) establishing etc a collective investment scheme;

(g) advising on investments,

and paragraphs (a) to (g) must be read with section 22 of the Financial Services and Markets Act 2000, any relevant order under that section, and Schedule 2 to that Act.]

(7) The Secretary of State may by order made by statutory instrument—

(a) disapply paragraph (b) of Subsection (1) of this section in relation to a trading scheme of a kind specified in the order; or

(b) amend or repeal paragraph (a) of subsection (6) of this section;

and no such order, and no order varying or revoking any such order, shall be made under this subsection unless a draft of the order has been laid before Parliament and approved by a resolution of each House of Parliament.

(8) In this Part of this Act—

"goods" includes property of any description and a right to, or interest in, property;

"participant" means, in relation to a trading scheme, a person (other than the promoter or any of the promoters) participating in the scheme;

"trading scheme" includes any arrangements made in connection with the carrying on of a business, whether those arrangements are made or recorded wholly or partly in writing or not;

and any reference to the provision or supply of goods shall be construed as including a reference to the grant or transfer of a right or interest.

(9) In this section any reference to the provision or supply of goods or services by a person shall be construed as including a reference to the provision or supply of goods or services under arrangements to which that person is a party.]

NOTES

Substituted by the Trading Schemes Act 1996, s 1.

Sub-s (6): para (a) substituted by the Financial Services and Markets Act 2000 (Consequential Amendments and Repeals) Order 2001, SI 2001/3649, art 284(1), (2).

Sub-s (6A): inserted by SI 2001/3649, art 284(1), (3); para (ba) inserted by the Financial Services and Markets Act 2000 (Regulated Activities) (Amendment No 3) Order 2006, SI 2006/3384, art 31; paras (ea)–(ed) inserted by the Alternative Investment Fund Managers Regulations 2013, SI 2013/1773, reg 80, Sch 1, Pt 2, para 38.

Regulations: the Trading Schemes (Exclusion) Regulations 1997, SI 1997/31 at **[2.118]**; the Trading Schemes (Exclusion) (Amendment) Regulations 1997, SI 1997/1887.

[1.502]

119 Regulations relating to such trading schemes

(1) Regulations made by the Secretary of State by statutory instrument may make provision with respect to the issue, circulation or distribution of [any form of advertisement, prospectus, circular or notice which contains any information] calculated to lead directly or indirectly to persons becoming participants in such a trading scheme, and may prohibit any such [advertisement, prospectus, circular or notice] from being issued, circulated or distributed unless it complies with such requirements as to the matters to be included or not included in it as may be prescribed by the regulations.

(2) Regulations made by the Secretary of State by statutory instrument may prohibit the promoter or any of the promoters of, or any participant in, a trading scheme to which this Part of this Act applies from—

(a)   supplying any goods to a participant in the trading scheme, or
(b)   supplying any training facilities or other services for such a participant, or
(c)   providing any goods or services under a transaction effected by such a participant, or
(d)   being a party to any arrangements under which goods or services are supplied or provided as mentioned in any of the preceding paragraphs, or
(e)   accepting from any such participant any payment, or any undertaking to make a payment, in respect of any goods or services supplied or provided as mentioned in any of paragraphs (a) to (d) of this subsection or in respect of any goods or services to be so supplied or provided,

unless (in any such case) such requirements as are prescribed by the regulations are complied with.

(3)   Any requirements prescribed by regulations under subsection (2) of this section shall be such as the Secretary of State considers necessary or expedient for the purpose of preventing participants in trading schemes to which this Part of this Act applies from being unfairly treated; and, without prejudice to the generality of this subsection, any such requirements may include provisions—

(a)   requiring the rights and obligations of every participant under such a trading scheme to be set out in full in an agreement in writing made between the participant and the promoter or (if more than one) each of the promoters;
(b)   specifying rights required to be conferred on every such participant, and obligations required to be assumed by the promoter or promoters, under any such trading scheme; or
(c)   imposing restrictions on the liabilities to be incurred by such a participant in respect of any of the matters mentioned in paragraphs (a) to (e) of subsection (2) of this section.

(4)   Regulations made under subsection (2) of this section—

(a)   may include provision for enabling a person who has made a payment as a participant in a trading scheme to which this Part of this Act applies, in circumstances where any of the requirements prescribed by the regulations were not complied with, to recover the whole or part of that payment from any person to whom or for whose benefit it was paid, and
(b)   subject to any provision made in accordance with the preceding paragraph, may prescribe the degree to which anything done in contravention of the regulations is to be treated as valid or invalid for the purposes of any civil proceedings.

(5)   The power to make regulations under this section may be exercised so as to make different provision—

(a)   in relation to different descriptions of trading schemes to which this Part of this Act applies, or
(b)   in relation to trading schemes which are or were in operation on a date specified in the regulations and trading schemes which are or were not in operation on that date,

or in relation to different descriptions of participants in such trading schemes.

NOTES

Sub-s (1): words in square brackets substituted by the Trading Schemes Act 1996, s 2(1).
Regulations: the Trading Schemes Regulations 1997, SI 1997/30 at **[2.105]**.

[1.503]
120   Offences under Part XI

(1)   Subject to the next following section, any person who issues, circulates or distributes, or causes another person to issue, circulate or distribute, a [advertisement, prospectus, circular or notice] in contravention of any regulations made under subsection (1) of section 119 of this Act shall be guilty of an offence.

(2)   Any person who contravenes any regulations made under subsection (2) of that section shall be guilty of an offence.

(3)   If any person who is a participant in a trading scheme to which this Part of this Act applies, or has applied or been invited to become a participant in such a trading scheme,—

(a)   makes any payment to or for the benefit of the promoter or (if there is more than one) any of the promoters, or to or for the benefit of a participant in the trading scheme, and
(b)   is induced to make that payment by reason that the prospect is held out to him of receiving payments or other benefits in respect of the introduction of other persons who become participants in the trading scheme,

any person to whom or for whose benefit that payment is made shall be guilty of an offence.

(4)   If the promoter or any of the promoters of a trading scheme to which this Part of this Act applies, or any other person acting in accordance with such a trading scheme, by holding out to any person such a prospect as is mentioned in subsection (3)(b) of this section, attempts to induce him—

(a)   if he is already a participant in the trading scheme, to make any payment to or for the benefit of the promoter or any of the promoters or to or for the benefit of a participant in the trading scheme, or
(b)   if he is not already a participant in the trading scheme, to become such a participant and to make any such payment as is mentioned in the preceding paragraph,

the person attempting to induce him to make that payment shall be guilty of an offence.

(5)   In determining, for the purposes of subsection (3) or subsection (4) of this section, whether an inducement or attempt to induce is made by holding out such a prospect as is therein mentioned, it shall be sufficient if such a prospect constitutes or would constitute a substantial part of the inducement.

(6)   Where the person by whom an offence is committed under subsection (3) or subsection (4) of this section is not the sole promoter of the trading scheme in question, any other person who is the promoter or (as the case may be) one of the promoters of the trading scheme shall, subject to the next following section, also be guilty of that offence.

(7)   Nothing in subsections (3) to (6) of this section shall be construed as limiting the circumstances in which the commission of any act may constitute an offence under subsection (1) or subsection (2) of this section.

(8)   In this section any reference to the making of a payment to or for the benefit of a person shall be construed as including the making of a payment partly to or for the benefit of that person and partly to or for the benefit of one or more other persons.

NOTES

Sub-s (1): words in square brackets substituted by the Trading Schemes Act 1996, s 2(2).

[1.504]
121   Defences in certain proceedings under Part XI
(1)   Where a person is charged with an offence under subsection (1) of section 120 of this Act in respect of an advertisement, it shall be a defence for him to prove that he is a person whose business it is to publish or arrange for the publication of advertisements, and that he received the advertisement for publication in the ordinary course of business and did not know, and had no reason to suspect, that its publication would amount to an offence under that subsection.

(2)   Where a person is charged with an offence by virtue of subsection (6) of section 120 of this Act, it shall be a defence for him to prove—
  (a)   that the trading scheme to which the charge relates was in operation before the commencement of this Act, and
  (b)   that the act constituting the offence was committed without his consent or connivance.

[1.505]
122   Penalties for offences under Part XI
A person guilty of an offence under this Part of this Act shall be liable—
  (a)   on summary conviction, to a fine not exceeding [the prescribed sum] or to imprisonment for a term not exceeding three months or to both;
  (b)   on conviction on indictment, to a fine or to imprisonment for a term not exceeding two years or to both.

NOTES

Reference to the prescribed sum substituted by virtue of the Magistrates' Courts Act 1980, s 32(2).

[1.506]
123   Enforcement provisions
(1)   The provisions of sections 29 to 32 of this Act shall have effect for the purposes of this Part of this Act as if in those provisions—
  (a)   references to a weights and measures authority or a duly authorised officer of such an authority were omitted, and
  (b)   any reference to an offence under section 23 of this Act were a reference to an offence under this Part of this Act.

(2)   For the purposes of the application to Northern Ireland of those provisions as applied by the preceding subsection—
  (a)   any reference to the Secretary of State shall be construed as a reference to the Ministry of Commerce for Northern Ireland, and
  (b)   paragraphs (c) and (d) of section 33(2) of this Act shall have effect for the purposes of the application of Part II of this Act to Northern Ireland.

PART XII
MISCELLANEOUS AND SUPPLEMENTARY PROVISIONS

124–128   (*Ss 124, 125 repealed by the Enterprise Act 2002, s 278(2), Sch 26; s 126 repealed by the Patents Act 1977, s 132(7), Sch 6; s 127 outside the scope of this work; s 128 repealed by the Restrictive Trade Practices Act 1976, s 44, Sch 6.*)

[1.507]
129   Time-limit for prosecutions
(1)   No prosecution for an offence under this Act shall be commenced after the expiration of three years from the commission of the offence or one year from its discovery by the prosecutor, whichever is the earlier.

(2)   Notwithstanding anything in [section 127(1) of the Magistrates' Courts Act 1980], a magistrates' court may try an information for an offence under this Act if the information was laid within twelve months from the commission of the offence.

(3)   (*Applies to Scotland only.*)

(4)   In the application of this section to Northern Ireland, for the references in subsection (2) to [section 127(1) of the Magistrates' Courts Act 1980], and to the trial and laying of an information there shall be substituted respectively references to [Article 19(1) of the Magistrates' Courts (Northern Ireland) Order 1981] and to the hearing and determination and making of a complaint [and as if in that subsection for the words "an offence under this Act" there were substituted the words "an offence under section 30(1) . . . of this Act"].

130, 131   (*Repealed by the Enterprise Act 2002, s 278(2), Sch 26.*)

[1.508]
132   Offences by bodies corporate
(1)   Where an offence under . . . , . . . , . . . [section 93B] or Part XI of this Act, which has been committed by a body corporate, is proved to have been committed with the consent or connivance of, or to be attributable to any neglect on the part of, any director, manager, secretary or other similar officer of the body corporate, or any person who was purporting to act in any such capacity, he as well as the body corporate shall be guilty of that offence and be liable to be proceeded against and punished accordingly.

(2)   Where the affairs of a body corporate are managed by its members, subsection (1) of this section shall apply in relation to the acts and defaults of a member in connection with his functions of management as if he were a director of the body corporate.

133   (*Repealed by the Enterprise Act 2002, ss 247(b), 278(2), Sch 26.*)

[1.509]
134   Provisions as to orders
(1)   Any statutory instrument whereby any order is made under any of the preceding provisions of this Act, other than a provision which requires a draft of the order to be laid before Parliament before making the order, or whereby any regulations are made under this Act, shall be subject to annulment in pursuance of a resolution of either House of Parliament.

(2)   Any power conferred by any provision of this Act to make an order by statutory instrument shall include power to revoke or vary the order by a subsequent order made under that provision.

[1.510]
135   Financial provisions
(1)   The Secretary of State shall pay all remuneration, allowances or other sums payable under this Act to or in respect of persons who are or have been members of the Advisory Committee . . . and shall defray—

(a)   . . .
(b)   to such amount as the Secretary of State with the approval of the Minister for the Civil Service may determine, all other expenses duly incurred by the Advisory Committee   . . .

(2)   There shall be defrayed out of moneys provided by Parliament—
(a)   all expenses incurred by the Secretary of State in consequence of the provisions of this Act;
(b)   any expenses incurred in consequence of those provisions by any other Minister of the Crown or government department, not being a Minister or department of the Government of Northern Ireland;
(c)   the remuneration of, and any travelling or other allowances payable under this Act to, the Director and any staff of the Director, any other sums payable under this Act to or in respect of the Director, and any expenses duly incurred by the Director or by any of his staff in consequence of the provisions [of this or any other Act];
(d)   any increase attributable to this Act in the sums payable out of moneys so provided under the Superannuation Act 1972.

(3)   . . .

NOTES

Sub-s (1): words omitted repealed by the Competition Act 1998, s 74(1), (3), Sch 12, para 1(1), (15), Sch 14, Pt I.

Sub-s (2): words in square brackets in para (c) inserted by the Competition Act 1980, s 32(2).

Sub-s (3): repealed by the Northern Ireland (Modification of Enactments—No 1) Order 1973, SI 1973/2163, art 14(2), Sch 6.

Minister for the Civil Service: now the Treasury, by virtue of the Transfer of Functions (Civil Service and Treasury) Order 1981, SI 1981/1670.

The Director: see the note "Director General of Fair Trading" at the beginning of this Act.

136 (*Repealed by the Statute Law (Repeals) Act 1977.*)

[1.511]
137 General interpretation provisions

(1)   In this Act—

"the Act of 1948" means the Monopolies and Restrictive Practices (Inquiry and Control) Act 1948;

. . .

"the Act of 1965" means the Monopolies and Mergers Act 1965;

. . .

"contract of employment" means a contract of service or of apprenticeship, whether it is express or implied, and (if it is express) whether it is oral or in writing;

"scale" (where the reference is to the scale on which any services are, or are to be, made available, supplied or obtained) means scale measured in terms of money or money's worth or in any other manner.

(2)   Except in so far as the context otherwise requires, in this Act, . . . , the following expressions have the meanings hereby assigned to them respectively, that is to say—

. . .

"agreement" means any agreement or arrangement, in whatever way and in whatever form it is made, and whether it is, or is intended to be, legally enforceable or not;

"business" includes a professional practice and includes any other undertaking which is carried on for gain or reward or which is an undertaking in the course of which goods or services are supplied otherwise than free of charge;

. . .

"consumer" (subject to subsection (6) of this section) means any person who is either—

(a)   a person to whom goods are or are sought to be supplied (whether by way of sale or otherwise) in the course of a business carried on by the person supplying or seeking to supply them, or

(b)   a person for whom services are or are sought to be supplied in the course of a business carried on by the person supplying or seeking to supply them,

and who does not receive or seek to receive the goods or services in the course of a business carried on by him;

"enactment" includes an enactment of the Parliament of Northern Ireland;

"goods" includes buildings and other structures, and also includes ships, aircraft and hovercraft,

. . . ;

"merger situation qualifying for investigation" has the meaning assigned to it by section 64(8) of this Act;

"Minister" includes a government department but shall not by virtue of this provision be taken to include the establishment consisting of the Director and his staff, and, except where the contrary is expressly provided, does not include any Minister or department of the Government of Northern Ireland;

. . .

"practice" means any practice, whether adopted in pursuance of an agreement or otherwise;

. . .

"supply", in relation to the supply of goods, includes supply by way of sale, lease, hire or hire-purchase, and, in relation to buildings or other structures, includes the construction of them by a person for another person;

. . .

(3)   In the provisions of this Act . . . "the supply of services" does not include the rendering of any services under a contract of employment but, . . .

(a)   includes the undertaking and performance for gain or reward of engagements (whether professional or other) for any matter other than the supply of goods, and

(b)   includes both the rendering of services to order and the provision of services by making them available to potential users; [and

(c)   includes the making of arrangements for a person to put or keep on land a caravan (within the meaning of Part I of the Caravan Sites and Control of Development Act 1960) other than arrangements by virtue of which the person may occupy the caravan as his only or main residence] [and

(d)   includes the making of arrangements for the use by public service vehicles (within the meaning of the Public Passenger Vehicles Act 1981) of a parking place which is used as a point at which passengers on services provided by means of such vehicles may be taken up or set down] [and

(e)   includes the making of arrangements permitting use of the tunnel system (within the meaning of the Channel Tunnel Act 1987) by a person operating services for the carriage of passengers or goods by rail] [and

[(f)   includes the making of arrangements, by means of such an agreement as is mentioned in paragraph 29 of Schedule 2 to the Telecommunications Act 1984, for the sharing of the use of any electronic communications apparatus, and]]

[(g)   includes the supply of network services and station services, within the meaning of Part I of the Railways Act 1993;]

and any reference in those provisions to services supplied or to be supplied, or to services provided or to be provided, shall be construed accordingly.

[(3A)   The Secretary of State may by order made by statutory instrument—

(a)   provide that "the supply of services" in the provisions of this Act is to include, or to cease to include, any activity specified in the order which consists in, or in making arrangements in connection with, permitting the use of land; and

(b)   for that purpose, amend or repeal any of paragraphs (c), (d), (e) or (g) of subsection (3) above.

(3B)   No order under subsection (3A) above is to be made unless a draft of the order has been laid before Parliament and approved by a resolution of each House of Parliament.

(3C)   The provisions of Schedule 9 to this Act apply in the case of a draft of any such order as they apply in the case of a draft of an order to which section 91(1) above applies.]

(4)   . . .

(5)   For the purposes of the provisions of this Act . . . , any two bodies corporate are to be treated as interconnected if one of them is a body corporate of which the other is a subsidiary (within the meaning of [section 1159 of the Companies Act 2006]) or if both of them are subsidiaries (within the meaning of that section) of one and the same body corporate; and in those provisions "interconnected bodies corporate" shall be construed accordingly, and "group of interconnected bodies corporate" means a group consisting of two or more bodies corporate all of whom are interconnected with each other.

(6)   For the purposes of the application of any provision of this Act in relation to goods or services of a particular description or to which a particular practice applies, "consumers" means persons who are consumers (as defined by subsection (2) of this section) in relation to goods or services of that description or in relation to goods or services to which that practice applies.

(7)   . . .

(8)   Except in so far as the context otherwise requires, any reference in this Act to an enactment shall be construed as a reference to that enactment as amended or extended by or under any other enactment, including this Act.

NOTES

Sub-s (1): definition "the Act of 1976" (omitted) repealed by the Resale Prices Act 1976, s 29, Sch 3, Pt I; definition "the Act of 1964" (omitted) repealed by the Competition Act 1998 (Transitional, Consequential and Supplemental Provisions) Order 2000, SI 2000/311, art 9(1), (6); definition "the Act of 1968" (omitted) repealed by the Restrictive Trade Practices Act 1976, s 44, Sch 6; definition "assignment" (omitted) repealed by the Enterprise Act 2002 and Media Mergers (Consequential Amendments) Order 2003, SI 2003/3180, art 2, Schedule, para 1(1), (10)(a).

Sub-s (2): first words omitted repealed by the Restrictive Trade Practices Act 1976, s 44, Sch 6; definitions "the Advisory Committee" and "the Director" (both omitted) repealed by the Enterprise Act 2002, s 278(2), Sch 26; definitions "commercial activities in the United Kingdom", "complex monopoly situation", "group", "merger reference", "monopoly reference", "newspaper merger reference", "price", "produce", "uncompetitive practices", "worker" (all omitted) repealed by SI 2003/3180, art 2, Schedule, para 1(1), (10)(b); definition "the Commission" (omitted) repealed by the Enterprise and Regulatory Reform Act 2013 (Competition) (Consequential, Transitional and Saving Provisions) Order 2014, SI 2014/892, art 2, Sch 1, Pt 2, para 28(a); words omitted from definition "goods" repealed by the Electricity Act 1989, s 112(4), Sch 18.

Sub-s (3): words omitted repealed by the Restrictive Trade Practices Act 1976, s 44, Sch 6; para (c) and word immediately preceding it inserted by the Competition Act 1980, s 23; para (d) and word immediately preceding it inserted by the Transport Act 1985, s 116(1); para (e) and word immediately preceding it inserted by the Channel Tunnel Act 1987, s 33(10); para (f) and word immediately preceding it inserted by the Broadcasting Act 1990, s 192(1), para (f) and word immediately following it substituted by the Communications Act 2003, s 406(1), Sch 17, para 44; para (g) and word immediately preceding it inserted by the Railways Act 1993, s 66(4).

Sub-ss (3A)–(3C): inserted by the Competition Act 1998, s 68.

Sub-s (4): repealed by the Electricity Act 1989, s 112(4), Sch 18.

Sub-s (5): words omitted repealed by the Restrictive Trade Practices Act 1976, s 44, Sch 6; words in square brackets substituted by the Companies Act 2006 (Consequential Amendments, Transitional Provisions and Savings) Order 2009, SI 2009/1941, art 2(1), Sch 1, para 26.

Sub-s (7): repealed by SI 2003/3180, art 2, Schedule, para 1(1), (10)(c).

[1.512]
138   Supplementary interpretation provisions

(1)   This section applies to the following provisions of this Act, that is to say, section 2(4), . . . section 137(6), and the definition of "consumer" contained in section 137(2).

(2)   For the purposes of any provisions to which this section applies it is immaterial whether any person supplying goods or services has a place of business in the United Kingdom or not.

(3)   For the purposes of any provisions to which this section applies any goods or services supplied wholly or partly outside the United Kingdom, if they are supplied in accordance with arrangements made in the United Kingdom, whether made orally or by one or more documents delivered in the United Kingdom or by correspondence posted from and to addresses in the United Kingdom, shall be treated as goods supplied to, or services supplied for, persons in the United Kingdom.

(4)   In relation to the supply of goods under a hire-purchase agreement, a credit-sale agreement or a conditional sale agreement, the person conducting any antecedent negotiations, as well as the owner or seller, shall for the purposes of any provisions to which this section applies be treated as a person supplying or seeking to supply the goods.

[(5)   In subsection (4) of this section, the following expressions have the meanings given by, or referred to in, section 189 of the Consumer Credit Act 1974—

"antecedent negotiations",

"conditional sale agreement",

"credit-sale agreement",

"hire-purchase agreement".]

(6)   In any provisions to which this section applies—
  (a)   any reference to a person to or for whom goods or services are supplied shall be construed as including a reference to any guarantor of such a person, and
  (b)   any reference to the terms or conditions on or subject to which goods or services are supplied shall be construed as including a reference to the terms or conditions on or subject to which any person undertakes to act as such a guarantor;

and in this subsection "guarantor", in relation to a person to or for whom goods or services are supplied, includes a person who undertakes to indemnify the supplier of the goods or services against any loss which he may incur in respect of the supply of the goods or services to or for that person.

(7)   For the purposes of any provisions to which this section applies goods or services supplied by a person carrying on a business shall be taken to be supplied in the course of that business if payment for the supply of the goods or services is made or (whether under a contract or by virtue of an enactment or otherwise) is required to be made.

NOTES

Sub-s (1): words omitted repealed by the Enterprise Act 2002, s 278(2), Sch 26.

Sub-s (5): substituted by the Consumer Credit Act 1974, s 192(3)(a), Sch 4, Pt I, para 37.

[1.513]
139   Amendments, repeals and transitional provisions
(1)   Subject to the transitional provisions and savings contained in Schedule 11 to this Act—
  (a)   the enactments specified in Schedule 12 to this Act shall have effect subject to the amendments specified in that Schedule (being minor amendments or amendments consequential upon the preceding provisions of this Act), and
  (b)   the enactments specified in Schedule 13 to this Act are hereby repealed to the extent specified in the third column of that Schedule.
(2)   The provisions of Schedule 11 to this Act shall have effect for the purposes of this Act.

[1.514]
140   Short title, citation, commencement and extent
(1)   This Act may be cited as the Fair Trading Act 1973.
(2), (3)   . . .
(4)   Where any provision of this Act, other than a provision contained in Schedule 11, refers to the commencement of this Act, it shall be construed as referring to the day appointed under this section for the coming into operation of that provision.
(5)   This Act extends to Northern Ireland.

NOTES

Sub-s (2): repealed by the Restrictive Trade Practices Act 1976, s 44, Sch 6.

Sub-s (3): repealed by the Statute Law (Repeals) Act 2004.

Orders: the Fair Trading Act 1973 (Commencement No 1) Order 1973, SI 1973/1545; the Fair Trading Act 1973 (Commencement No 2) Order 1973, SI 1973/1652.

SCHEDULES

SCHEDULES 1–13

(Schs 1, 2 repealed by the Enterprise Act 2002, ss 10(1)(a), 278(2), Sch 26; Sch 3 repealed by the Competition Act 1998, s 74(1), (3), Sch 12, para 1(1), (2), Sch 14, Pt I; Schs 4–9 repealed by

the Enterprise Act 2002, s 278, Sch 26; Sch 10 repealed by the Restrictive Trade Practices Act 1976, s 44, Sch 6; Sch 11 (Transitional Provisions and Savings) outside the scope of this work; Sch 12, in so far as unrepealed, contains miscellaneous amendments; Sch 13 contains repeals.)

PRICES ACT 1974

(1974 c 24)

ARRANGEMENT OF SECTIONS

An Act to authorise the payment of food subsidies; to confer on the Secretary of State power to regulate the price of food and certain other goods and on the Price Commission additional powers for preventing or restricting increases in prices and charges; to make provision for requiring prices to be indicated on or in relation to goods offered or exposed for sale by retail and for requiring information as to the range within which food and certain other goods are commonly being sold by retail within the United Kingdom to be displayed by retailers dealing in those goods; to confer power to abolish the Pay Board; and for purposes connected with those matters

[9 July 1974]

1–3 *(S 1 repealed by the Statute Law (Repeals) Act 1989; s 2 repealed by the Statute Law (Repeals) Act 2004; s 3 repealed by the Price Commission Act 1977, ss 16(4), 22(7), Sch 3.)*

[1.515]
4 Price marking
[(1) The Secretary of State may by order make provision for securing—
  (a) that prices are indicated on or in relation to goods which a person indicates are or may be for sale by retail, whether or not the goods are in existence when he does so;
  (b) that charges are indicated for services which a person indicates are or may be provided, except services which he indicates are or may be provided only for the purposes of business carried on by other persons;
  (c) that prices of such goods or charges for such services are not indicated in a manner which the Secretary of State considers inappropriate and that no part of a penny except one half-penny is specified in the amount of an indicated price or charge.]
(2) Without prejudice to the generality of subsection (1) above, an order under this section [may specify the kinds of goods or services to which and the circumstances in which the order applies and]—
  (a) may make provision as to the manner in which any price [or charge] is to be indicated;
  (b) may require that the price [or charge] to be indicated on or in relation to any goods [or services] shall be, or shall include, a price [or charge] expressed by reference to such unit or units of measurement as may be specified in the order;
  (c) may, in relation to goods [or services] subject to value added tax, make provision as to the circumstances in which the price [or charge] to be indicated may or may not be exclusive of the tax and as to the indication to be given of the tax included in, or payable in addition to, the price [or charge];
  (d) may make different provision in relation to different circumstances and may contain such supplementary provisions as the Secretary of State thinks necessary or expedient.
[(3) Before making an order under this section the Secretary of State shall consult, in such manner as appears to him to be appropriate having regard to the subject-matter and urgency of the order, with such organisations representative of interests substantially affected by the order as appear to him, having regard to those matters, to be appropriate.]
(4) The power to make an order under this section shall be exercisable by statutory instrument and includes power to vary or revoke a previous order; and a statutory instrument containing an order under this section shall be subject to annulment in pursuance of a resolution of either House of Parliament.
(5) In the application of this section to Northern Ireland for any reference to the Secretary of State there shall be substituted a reference to the Department of Commerce for Northern Ireland and any order made by the Department under this section shall be [a statutory rule for the purposes of the Statutory Rules Act (Northern Ireland) 1958 and be] subject to negative resolution within the

meaning of section 41(6) of the Interpretation Act (Northern Ireland) 1954 as if it were a statutory instrument within the meaning of that Act; and subsection (4) above shall not apply to any such order except in so far as that subsection confers a power to vary or revoke a previous order.

NOTES

Sub-s (1): substituted by the Price Commission Act 1977, s 16(1).

Sub-ss (2), (5): words in square brackets inserted by the Price Commission Act 1977, s 16(2)(a), (3).

Sub-s (3): substituted by the Statute Law (Repeals) Act 2004, s 1(2), Sch 2, para 11.

Orders: the Price Marking Order 2004, SI 2004/102 at **[2.299]**; the Price Marking (Amendment) Order 2009, SI 2009/3231; the Indication of Prices (Beds) (Revocation) Order 2012, SI 2012/1816.

5, 6 (*S 5 repealed by the Statute Law (Repeals) Act 2004; s 6 repealed by the Statute Law (Repeals) Act 1989.*)

[1.516]

7 Enforcement

The Schedule to this Act shall have effect . . . for the enforcement of orders under section . . . 4 . . . above.

NOTES

Words omitted repealed by the Statute Law (Repeals) Act 2004.

[1.517]

8 Financial provisions

(1) There shall be paid out of moneys provided by Parliament—

    (a) the expenses of any government department in respect of the administration of this Act;

    (b) any increase attributable to this Act in the sums so payable under any other Act.

(2) . . .

NOTES

Sub-s (2): repealed by the Statute Law (Repeals) Act 1989.

[1.518]

9 Short title and interpretation

(1) This Act may be cited as the Prices Act 1974.

(2) In this Act "food" means food and drink for human consumption.

(3) In this Act any reference to any enactment is a reference to that enactment as amended by or under any subsequent enactment.

(4) . . .

NOTES

Sub-s (4): repealed by the Statute Law (Repeals) Act 2004.

SCHEDULE
ENFORCEMENT

Section 7

Food subsidies

[1.519]

1, 2. . . .

3. *(1) A duly authorised officer of the Secretary of State or the Minister of Agriculture, Fisheries and Food may, at all reasonable hours and on production, if required, of his credentials, exercise the powers specified in sub-paragraph (2) below for the purpose of determining—*

    (a) whether any payment is to be, or has been, properly made under any scheme under section 1 of this Act or falls to be repaid in accordance with any conditions subject to which it was made or falls to be made to the Secretary of State by virtue of any order under subsection (7) of that section; or

    (b) whether any condition required to be observed under paragraph 2 above has been contravened.

(2) The said powers are—

    (a) a power to inspect and take samples of any goods and to enter any land or any premises other than premises used only as a dwelling; and

    (b) a power to require any person carrying on business, or employed in connection with a business, to produce any documents relating to the business, and a power of making extracts from, or making copies of, the documents.

(3) Any person who—

    (a) wilfully obstructs an officer acting under this paragraph; or

    (b) wilfully fails to comply with a requirement imposed under this paragraph,

shall be guilty of an offence and liable on summary conviction to a fine not exceeding [level 5 on the standard scale].

(4) Any person who, with intent to deceive, produces, in compliance with a requirement under this paragraph, a document which to his knowledge is or may be misleading, false or deceptive in a material particular shall be guilty of an offence and liable on summary conviction to a fine not exceeding [level 5 on the standard scale].

(5) Nothing in this paragraph shall be construed as compelling the production by a barrister, advocate or solicitor of a document containing a privileged communication made by or to him in that capacity.

(6) In this paragraph "premises" include any stall, vehicle or vessel.

4. . . .

Price regulation, price marking and price range notices

5. (1) Any person who contravenes an order under section . . . 4 . . . of this Act shall be guilty of an offence and liable—
    (a) on conviction on indictment, to a fine;
    (b) on summary conviction, to a fine not exceeding [the prescribed sum].

(2) . . .

(3) Section 23 of the Trade Descriptions Act 1968 (offences due to fault of other person) and section 24(1) and (2) of that Act (defence of mistake, accident etc.) shall have effect in relation to an offence in respect of an order under section 4 of this Act as they have effect in relation to an offence under that Act.

6. It shall be the duty of every local weights and measures authority to enforce within their area any such order as is mentioned in paragraph 5(1) above.

7. A local weights and measures authority may make, or may authorise any of their officers to make, any purchases of goods [and any contracts for services] for the purpose of determining whether any such order is being complied with.

8. (1) Proceedings for an offence under paragraph 5 above shall not be instituted except by or on behalf of a local weights and measures authority.

(2) Proceedings for any such offence shall not be instituted—
    (a) unless there has been served on the person charged a notice in writing of the date and nature of the offence alleged, being (except where he is a street trader) a notice served before the expiration of the period of thirty days beginning with that date; or
    (b) after the expiration of the period of three months beginning with that date.

(3) Such a notice as is mentioned in sub-paragraph (2)(a) above may be served on any person either by serving it on him personally or by sending it to him by post at his usual or last known residence or place of business in the United Kingdom or, in the case of a company, at the company's registered office.

(4) Sub-paragraph (1) above does not apply to Scotland.

9. (1) A duly authorised officer of a local weights and measures authority may, at all reasonable hours and on production, if required, of his credentials, exercise any of the powers specified in paragraph 3(2) above and any of the powers specified in sub-paragraph (2) below for the purpose of determining whether an offence under paragraph 5 above has been committed.

(2) The said powers are—
    (a) a power to seize and detain any document or goods which the officer has reason to believe may be required as evidence in proceedings for such an offence; and
    (b) a power to seize and detain any goods if the officer has reason to believe that their examination is likely to produce evidence of the commission of any such offence.

(3) Any person who—
    (a) wilfully obstructs an officer acting under this paragraph; or
    (b) wilfully fails to comply with a requirement imposed under this paragraph; or
    (c) without reasonable cause fails to give to any officer acting under this paragraph any other assistance or information which the officer may reasonably require for the performance by the officer of his functions under this Schedule,
shall be guilty of an offence and liable on summary conviction to a fine not exceeding [level 5 on the standard scale].

(4) Any person who, with intent to deceive, produces or gives, in compliance with a requirement under this paragraph, a document or information which to his knowledge is or may be misleading, false or deceptive in a material particular shall be guilty of an offence and liable on summary conviction to a fine not exceeding [level 5 on the standard scale].

(5) Nothing in this paragraph shall be construed as requiring a person to answer any question or give any information if to do so might incriminate him or as authorising the taking of possession of any such document as is mentioned in paragraph 3(5) above which is in the possession of a barrister, advocate or solicitor.

10. Where a local weights and measures authority have made arrangements for the discharge of any of their functions as such by another local authority, the powers conferred by paragraph 9 above shall also be exercisable by a duly authorised officer of that other local authority.

11, 12.   . . .

Offences by bodies corporate

13. Where an offence under this Schedule committed by a body corporate is proved to have been committed with the consent or connivance of, or to be attributable to any neglect on the part of, any director, manager, secretary or other similar officer of the body corporate or any person who was purporting to act in any such capacity, he as well as the body corporate shall be guilty of the offence and shall be liable to be proceeded against and punished accordingly.

14. (*Outside the scope of this work.*)

NOTES

Paras 1, 2, 4: repealed by the Statute Law (Repeals) Act 1989.

Para 3: repealed, except as it has effect for the purposes of para 9 by the Statute Law (Repeals) Act 1989; references to a level on the standard scale in sub-paras (3), (4) substituted by virtue of the Criminal Justice Act 1982, ss 38, 46.

Para 5: words omitted repealed by the Statute Law (Repeals) Act 2004; reference to the prescribed sum substituted by virtue of the Magistrates' Courts Act 1980, s 32(2).

Para 7: words in square brackets inserted by the Price Commission Act 1977, s 16(2)(b).

Para 9: references to a level on the standard scale in sub-paras (3), (4) substituted by virtue of the Criminal Justice Act 1982, ss 38, 46.

Para 11: repealed by the Statute Law (Repeals) Act 2004.

Para 12: repealed by the Enterprise Act 2002, ss 247(c), 278(2), Sch 26.

Minister of Agriculture, Fisheries and Food: now the Secretary of State for Environment, Food and Rural Affairs; see the Secretaries of State for Transport, Local Government and the Regions and for Environment, Food and Rural Affairs Order 2001, SI 2001/2568.

Seize and detain documents, etc: the powers of seizure conferred by para 9(2) are powers to which the Criminal Justice and Police Act 2001, s 50 apply (additional powers of seizure from premises); see s 50 of, and Sch 1, Pt 1, para 18 to, that Act.

CONSUMER CREDIT ACT 1974

(1974 c 39)

ARRANGEMENT OF SECTIONS

PART II
CREDIT AGREEMENTS, HIRE AGREEMENTS AND LINKED TRANSACTIONS

PART IV
SEEKING BUSINESS

Canvassing etc

PART V
ENTRY INTO CREDIT OR HIRE AGREEMENTS

Preliminary matters

Making the agreement

Withdrawal from certain agreements

Cancellation of certain agreements within cooling-off period

Exclusion of certain agreements from Part V

PART VA
CURRENT ACCOUNT OVERDRAFTS

PART VI
MATTERS ARISING DURING CURRENCY OF CREDIT OR HIRE AGREEMENTS

PART VII
DEFAULT AND TERMINATION

Information sheets

PART IX
JUDICIAL CONTROL

PART X
ANCILLARY CREDIT BUSINESS

PART XI
ENFORCEMENT OF ACT

PART XII
SUPPLEMENTAL

An Act to establish for the protection of consumers a new system, administered by the Director General of Fair Trading, of licensing and other control of traders concerned with the provision of credit, or the supply of goods on hire or hire-purchase, and their transactions, in place of the present enactments regulating moneylenders, pawnbrokers and hire-purchase traders and their transactions, and for related matters

31 July 1974

NOTES

   The text of the Consumer Credit Act 1974 reproduced here includes all amendments to the Act, including prospective amendments, as at 1 August 2015. Commencement dates for amendments are shown in the notes to each provision.

   For the text of the 1974 Act as it had effect on 15 June 2006, prior to amendments made by the Consumer Credit Act 2006, and subsequent amendments, see the Appendix at [A.1].

   Director General of Fair Trading: the Enterprise Act 2002, s 2(1), provided that, as from the coming into force of that section (on 1 April 2003), the functions of the Director General of Fair Trading, his property, rights and liabilities were transferred to the Office of Fair Trading. Accordingly, (by virtue of s 2(2), (3) of the 2002 Act) the office of the Director was abolished, and any reference to the Director in any enactment, instrument or other document passed or made before the commencement of s 2(1) had, in so far as is necessary, effect as if it were a reference to the Office of Fair Trading (for transitional provisions in connection with the transfer, see Sch 24, para 6 to the 2002 Act). Section 2 of the 2002 Act was repealed by the Enterprise and Regulatory Reform Act 2013, s 26(3), Sch 5, Pt 4, para 229, as from 1 April 2014. Part 3 of the 2013 Act (ss 25–28) abolished the Office of Fair Trading (and the Competition Commission) and provided for the transfer of its functions to the newly created Competition and Markets Authority.

1–7   (*Ss 1–7 (Pt I) repealed by the Financial Services and Markets Act 2000 (Regulated Activities) (Amendment) (No 2) Order 2013, SI 2013/1881, art 20(1), (2), as from 26 July 2013 (certain purposes), and as from 1 April 2014 (remaining purposes), for transitional provisions see Pt 8 thereof at* **[2.1007]** *et seq.*)

PART II
CREDIT AGREEMENTS, HIRE AGREEMENTS AND LINKED TRANSACTIONS

[1.520]
8 Consumer credit agreements

(1) A [consumer] credit agreement is an agreement between an individual ("the debtor") and any other person ("the creditor") by which the creditor provides the debtor with credit of any amount.

(2) . . .

[(3) A consumer credit agreement is a regulated agreement within the meaning of this Act if it is a regulated credit agreement for the purposes of Chapter 14A of Part 2 of the Regulated Activities Order.]

[(4) Subsection (1) does not apply in relation to an agreement that is a green deal plan (see instead section 189B).]

NOTES

Sub-s (1): word in square brackets substituted by the Consumer Credit Act 2006, s 2(1)(a), as from 31 October 2008: for effect and transitional provisions, see the Consumer Credit Act 2006 (Commencement No 4 and Transitional Provisions) Order 2008, SI 2008/831, arts 2(1), 4, Sch 1.

Sub-s (2): repealed by the Consumer Credit Act 2006, ss 2(1)(b), 70, Sch 4, as from 31 October 2008; for effect and transitional provisions, see SI 2008/831, arts 2(1), 4, Sch 1.

Sub-s (3): substituted by the Financial Services and Markets Act 2000 (Regulated Activities) (Amendment) (No 2) Order 2013, SI 2013/1881, art 20(1), (3), as from 26 July 2013 (certain purposes), and as from 1 April 2014 (remaining purposes), for transitional provisions see Pt 8 thereof at **[2.1007]** et seq; further substituted by the Mortgage Credit Directive Order 2015, SI 2015/910, art 3, Sch 1, Pt 1, paras 2(1), (2), as from 21 March 2016 (note that the 2015 Order also comes into force on 20 April 2015 and 21 December 2015 for limited other purposes, and for transitional provisions, see Part 4 of that Order at **[2.1194]** et seq), as follows:

"(3) A consumer credit agreement is a regulated credit agreement within the meaning of this Act if it—
    (a)   is a regulated credit agreement for the purposes of Chapter 14A of Part 2 of the Regulated Activities Order; and
    (b)   is not an agreement of the type described in Article 3(1)(b) of Directive 2014/17/EU of the European Parliament and of the Council of 4th February 2014 on credit agreements for consumers relating to residential immovable property.".

Sub-s (4): added by the Consumer Credit Act 1974 (Green Deal) (Amendment) Order 2014, SI 2014/436, art 3, as from 28 February 2014, except in relation to a green deal plan (within the meaning of the Energy Act 2011, s 1) made before that date; see art 1(3) thereof.

[1.521]
9 Meaning of credit

(1) In this Act "credit" includes a cash loan, and any other form of financial accommodation.

(2) Where credit is provided otherwise than in sterling, it shall be treated for the purposes of this Act as provided in sterling of an equivalent amount.

(3) Without prejudice to the generality of subsection (1), the person by whom goods are bailed or (in Scotland) hired to an individual under a hire-purchase agreement shall be taken to provide him with fixed-sum credit to finance the transaction of an amount equal to the total price of the goods less the aggregate of the deposit (if any) and the total charge for credit.

(4) For the purposes of this Act, an item entering into the total charge for credit shall not be treated as credit even though time is allowed for its payment.

[1.522]
10 Running-account credit and fixed-sum credit

(1) For the purposes of this Act—
    (a)   running-account credit is a facility under a [consumer] credit agreement whereby the debtor is enabled to receive from time to time (whether in his own person, or by another person) from the creditor or a third party cash, goods and services (or any of them) to an amount or value such that, taking into account payments made by or to the credit of the debtor, the credit limit (if any) is not at any time exceeded; and
    (b)   fixed-sum credit is any other facility under a [consumer] credit agreement whereby the debtor is enabled to receive credit (whether in one amount or by instalments).

(2) In relation to running-account credit, "credit limit" means, as respects any period, the maximum debit balance which, under the credit agreement, is allowed to stand on the account during that period, disregarding any term of the agreement allowing that maximum to be exceeded merely temporarily.

(3) For the purposes of [any provision of this Act that specifies an amount of credit (except section 17(1)(a))] running-account credit shall be taken not to exceed the amount specified in [that provision] ("the specified amount") if—
    (a)   the credit limit does not exceed the specified amount; or
    (b)   whether or not there is a credit limit, and if there is, notwithstanding that it exceeds the specified amount,—
        (i)   the debtor is not enabled to draw at any one time an amount which, so far as (having regard to section 9(4)) it represents credit, exceeds the specified amount, or

(ii) the agreement provides that, if the debit balance rises above a given amount (not exceeding the specified amount), the rate of the total charge for credit increases or any other condition favouring the creditor or his associate comes into operation, or

(iii) at the time the agreement is made it is probable, having regard to the terms of the agreement and any other relevant considerations, that the debit balance will not at any time rise above the specified amount.

NOTES

Sub-s (1): words in square brackets substituted by the Consumer Credit Act 2006, s 5(2)(a), as from 6 April 2008.

Sub-s (3): words in square brackets substituted by the Consumer Credit (EU Directive) Regulations 2010, SI 2010/1010, regs 2, 44, as from 1 February 2011, with effect in relation to certain agreements before that date, as provided for in regs 101, 101A of the 2010 Regulations at [**2.804**], [**2.805**].

[1.523]
11   Restricted-use credit and unrestricted-use credit
(1)   A restricted-use credit agreement is a regulated consumer credit agreement—
  (a) to finance a transaction between the debtor and the creditor, whether forming part of that agreement or not, or
  (b) to finance a transaction between the debtor and a person (the "supplier") other than the creditor, or
  (c) to refinance any existing indebtedness of the debtor's, whether to the creditor or another person,
and "restricted-use credit" shall be construed accordingly.
(2)   An unrestricted-use credit agreement is a regulated consumer credit agreement not falling within subsection (1), and "unrestricted-use credit" shall be construed accordingly.
(3)   An agreement does not fall within subsection (1) if the credit is in fact provided in such a way as to leave the debtor free to use it as he chooses, even though certain uses would contravene that or any other agreement.
(4)   An agreement may fall within subsection (1)(b) although the identity of the supplier is unknown at the time the agreement is made.

[1.524]
12   Debtor-creditor-supplier agreements
A debtor-creditor-supplier agreement is a regulated consumer credit agreement being—
  (a) a restricted-use credit agreement which falls within section 11(1)(a), or
  (b) a restricted-use credit agreement which falls within section 11(1)(b) and is made by the creditor under pre-existing arrangements, or in contemplation of future arrangements, between himself and the supplier, or
  (c) an unrestricted-use credit agreement which is made by the creditor under pre-existing arrangements between himself and a person (the "supplier") other than the debtor in the knowledge that the credit is to be used to finance a transaction between the debtor and the supplier.

[1.525]
13   Debtor-creditor agreements
A debtor-creditor agreement is a regulated consumer credit agreement being—
  (a) a restricted-use credit agreement which falls within section 11(1)(b) but is not made by the creditor under pre-existing arrangements, or in contemplation of future arrangements, between himself and the supplier, or
  (b) a restricted-use credit agreement which falls within section 11(1)(c), or
  (c) an unrestricted-use credit agreement which is not made by the creditor under pre-existing arrangements between himself and a person (the "supplier") other than the debtor in the knowledge that the credit is to be used to finance a transaction between the debtor and the supplier.

[1.526]
14   Credit-token agreements
(1)   A credit-token is a card, check, voucher, coupon, stamp, form, booklet or other document or thing given to an individual by a person carrying on a consumer credit business, who undertakes—
  (a) that on the production of it (whether or not some other action is also required) he will supply cash, goods and services (or any of them) on credit, or
  (b) that where, on the production of it to a third party (whether or not any other action is also required), the third party supplies cash, goods and services (or any of them), he will pay the third party for them (whether or not deducting any discount or commission), in return for payment to him by the individual.
(2)   A credit-token agreement is a regulated agreement for the provision of credit in connection with the use of a credit-token.
(3)   Without prejudice to the generality of section 9(1), the person who gives to an individual an undertaking falling within subsection (1)(b) shall be taken to provide him with credit drawn on whenever a third party supplies him with cash, goods or services.

(4)   For the purposes of subsection (1), use of an object to operate a machine provided by the person giving the object or a third party shall be treated as the production of the object to him.

[1.527]
15   Consumer hire agreements
(1)   A consumer hire agreement is an agreement made by a person with an individual (the "hirer") for the bailment or (in Scotland) the hiring of goods to the hirer, being an agreement which—
    (a)   is not a hire-purchase agreement, and
    (b)   is capable of subsisting for more than three months, . . .
    (c)   . . .
[(2)   A consumer hire agreement is a regulated agreement with the meaning of this Act if it is a regulated consumer hire agreement for the purposes of Chapter 14B of Part 2 of the Regulated Activities Order.]

NOTES
  Sub-s (1): para (c) and word "and" immediately preceding it repealed by the Consumer Credit Act 2006, ss 2(2), 70, Sch 4, as from 6 April 2008.
  Sub-s (2): substituted by the Financial Services and Markets Act 2000 (Regulated Activities) (Amendment) (No 2) Order 2013, SI 2013/1881, art 20(1), (4), as from 26 July 2013 (certain purposes), and as from 1 April 2014 (remaining purposes), for transitional provisions see Pt 8 thereof at **[2.1007]** et seq.

16, 16A–16C   (*Repealed by the Financial Services and Markets Act 2000 (Regulated Activities) (Amendment) (No 2) Order 2013, SI 2013/1881, art 20(1), (5)–(8), as from 26 July 2013 (certain purposes), and as from 1 April 2014 (remaining purposes), for transitional provisions see Pt 8 thereof at* **[2.1007]** *et seq (ss 16A–16B as inserted by the Consumer Credit Act 2006, ss 3, 4, as from 31 October 2008: s 16C as inserted by the Legislative Reform (Consumer Credit) Order 2008, SI 2008/2826, art 3(1)), as from 31 October 2008.*)

[1.528]
17   Small agreements
(1)   A small agreement is—
    (a)   a regulated consumer credit agreement for credit not exceeding [£50], other than a hire-purchase or conditional sale agreement; or
    (b)   a regulated consumer hire agreement which does not require the hirer to make payments exceeding [£50],
being an agreement which is either unsecured or secured by a guarantee or indemnity only (whether or not the guarantee or indemnity is itself secured).
[(2)   For the purposes of paragraph (a) of subsection (1), running-account credit shall be taken not to exceed the amount specified in that paragraph if the credit limit does not exceed that amount.]
(3)   Where—
    (a)   two or more small agreements are made at or about the same time between the same parties, and
    (b)   it appears probable that they would instead have been made as a single agreement but for the desire to avoid the operation of provisions of this Act which would have applied to that single agreement but, apart from this subsection, are not applicable to the small agreements,
this Act applies to the small agreements as if they were regulated agreements other than small agreements.
(4)   If, apart from this subsection, subsection (3) does not apply to any agreements but would apply if, for any party or parties to any of the agreements, there were substituted an associate of that party, or associates of each of those parties, as the case may be, then subsection (3) shall apply to the agreements.

NOTES
  Sub-s (1): sums in square brackets substituted by the Consumer Credit (Increase of Monetary Limits) Order 1983, SI 1983/1878, art 3, Schedule, Pt I, as from 1 January 1984.
  Sub-s (2): substituted by the Consumer Credit (EU Directive) Regulations 2010, SI 2010/1010, regs 2, 45, as from 1 February 2011, with effect in relation to certain agreements before that date, as provided for in regs 101, 101A of the 2010 Regulations at **[2.804]**, **[2.805]**.

[1.529]
18   Multiple agreements
(1)   This section applies to an agreement (a "multiple agreement") if its terms are such as—
    (a)   to place a part of it within one category of agreement mentioned in this Act, and another part of it within a different category of agreements so mentioned, or within a category of agreement not so mentioned, or
    (b)   to place it, or a part of it, within two or more categories of agreement so mentioned.
(2)   Where a part of an agreement falls within subsection (1), that part shall be treated for the purposes of this Act as a separate agreement.
(3)   Where an agreement falls within subsection (1)(b), it shall be treated as an agreement in each of the categories in question, and this Act shall apply to it accordingly.

(4) Where under subsection (2) a part of a multiple agreement is to be treated as a separate agreement, the multiple agreement shall (with any necessary modifications) be construed accordingly; and any sum payable under the multiple agreement, if not apportioned by the parties, shall for the purposes of proceedings in any court relating to the multiple agreement be apportioned by the court as may be requisite.

(5) In the case of an agreement for running-account credit, a term of the agreement allowing the credit limit to be exceeded merely temporarily shall not be treated as a separate agreement or as providing fixed-sum credit in respect of the excess.

(6) This Act does not apply to a multiple agreement so far as the agreement relates to goods if under the agreement payments are to be made in respect of the goods in the form of rent (other than a rent-charge) issuing out of land.

[1.530]
19 Linked transactions
(1) A transaction entered into by the debtor or hirer, or a relative of his, with any other person ("the other party"), except one for the provision of security, is a linked transaction in relation to an actual or prospective regulated agreement (the "principal agreement") of which it does not form part if—

    (a)   the transaction is entered into in compliance with a term of the principal agreement; or

    (b)   the principal agreement is a debtor-creditor-supplier agreement and the transaction is financed, or to be financed, by the principal agreement; or

    (c)   the other party is a person mentioned in subsection (2), and a person so mentioned initiated the transaction by suggesting it to the debtor or hirer, or his relative, who enters into it—

        (i)   to induce the creditor or owner to enter into the principal agreement, or

        (ii)   for another purpose related to the principal agreement, or

        (iii)   where the principal agreement is a restricted-use credit agreement, for a purpose related to a transaction financed, or to be financed, by the principal agreement.

(2) The persons referred to in subsection (1)(c) are—

    (a)   the creditor or owner, or his associate;

    (b)   a person who, in the negotiation of the transaction, is represented by a credit-broker who is also a negotiator in antecedent negotiations for the principal agreement;

    (c)   a person who, at the time the transaction is initiated, knows that the principal agreement has been made or contemplates that it might be made.

(3) A linked transaction entered into before the making of the principal agreement has no effect until such time (if any) as that agreement is made.

(4) Regulations may exclude linked transactions of the prescribed description from the operation of subsection (3).

NOTES

    Regulations: the Consumer Credit (Linked Transactions) (Exemptions) Regulations 1983, SI 1983/1560 (revoked) at **[2.43]**.

[1.531]
[20 Total charge for credit
In this Act, "the total charge for credit" has the meaning given by the Regulated Activities Order for the purposes of Chapter 14A of Part 2 of that Order.]

NOTES

    Commencement: 26 July 2013 (for certain purposes); 1 April 2014 (remaining purposes).

    Substituted by the Financial Services and Markets Act 2000 (Regulated Activities) (Amendment) (No 2) Order 2013, SI 2013/1881, art 20(1), (9), as from 26 July 2013 (certain purposes), and as from 1 April 2014 (remaining purposes), for transitional provisions see Pt 8 thereof at **[2.1007]** et seq.

21–41ZB (*Ss 21–41ZB (Pt III) repealed by the Financial Services and Markets Act 2000 (Regulated Activities) (Amendment) (No 2) Order 2013, SI 2013/1881, art 20(1), (10), as from 26 July 2013 (certain purposes), and as from 1 April 2014 (remaining purposes), for transitional provisions see Pt 8 thereof at* **[2.1007]** *et seq.*)

PART IV
SEEKING BUSINESS

43–47 (*Ss 43–45, 47 repealed by the Financial Services and Markets Act 2000 (Regulated Activities) (Amendment) (No 2) Order 2013, SI 2013/1881, art 20(1), (11)–(14), as from 26 July 2013 (certain purposes), and as from 1 April 2014 (remaining purposes), for transitional provisions see Pt 8 thereof at* **[2.1007]** *et seq; s 46 repealed by the Consumer Protection from Unfair Trading Regulations 2008, SI 2008/1277, reg 30(1), (3), Sch 2, Pt 1, paras 17, 18, Sch 4, as from 26 May 2008.*)

Canvassing etc

[1.532]
48 Definition of canvassing off trade premises (regulated agreements)

(1) An individual (the "canvasser") canvasses a regulated agreement off trade premises if he solicits the entry (as debtor or hirer) of another individual (the "consumer") into the agreement by making oral representations to the consumer, or any other individual, during a visit by the canvasser to any place (not excluded by subsection (2)) where the consumer, or that other individual, as the case may be, is, being a visit—

    (a)   carried out for the purpose of making such oral representations to individuals who are at that place, but

    (b)   not carried out in response to a request made on a previous occasion.

(2) A place is excluded from subsection (1) if it is a place where a business is carried on (whether on a permanent or temporary basis) by—

    (a)   the creditor or owner, or

    (b)   a supplier, or

    (c)   the canvasser, or the person whose employee or agent the canvasser is, or

    (d)   the consumer.

[1.533]
49 Prohibition of canvassing debtor-creditor agreements off trade premises

(1) It is an offence to canvass debtor-creditor agreements off trade premises.

(2) It is also an offence to solicit the entry of an individual (as debtor) into a debtor-creditor agreement during a visit carried out in response to a request made on a previous occasion, where—

    (a)   the request was not in writing signed by or on behalf of the person making it, and

    (b)   if no request for the visit had been made, the soliciting would have constituted the canvassing of a debtor-creditor agreement off trade premises.

(3) Subsections (1) and (2) do not apply to any soliciting for an agreement enabling the debtor to overdraw on a current account of any description kept with the creditor, where—

    (a)   the [FCA] has determined that current accounts of that description kept with the creditor are excluded from subsections (1) and (2), and

    (b)   the debtor already keeps an account with the creditor (whether a current account or not).

(4) A determination under subsection (3)(a)—

    (a)   may be made subject to such conditions as the [FCA] thinks fit, and

    (b)   shall be made only where the [FCA] is of opinion that it is not against the interests of debtors.

(5) If soliciting is done in breach of a condition imposed under subsection (4)(a), the determination under subsection (3)(a) does not apply to it.

NOTES

Sub-ss (3), (4): words in square brackets substituted by the Financial Services Act 2012 (Consumer Credit) Order 2013, SI 2013/1882, art 7(1), (2), as from 26 July 2013 (certain purposes), and as from 1 April 2014 (remaining purposes).

References to the FCA, etc: as to the abolition of the office of the Director General of Fair Trading and the substitution of the original references to the Director (and related expressions), see the note preceding s 8 at **[1.520]**.

[1.534]
50 Circulars to minors

(1) A person commits an offence who, with a view to financial gain, sends to a minor any document inviting him to—

    (a)   borrow money, or

    (b)   obtain goods on credit or hire, or

    (c)   obtain services on credit, or

    (d)   apply for information or advice on borrowing money or otherwise obtaining credit, or hiring goods.

(2) In proceedings under subsection (1) in respect of the sending of a document to a minor, it is a defence for the person charged to prove that he did not know, and had no reasonable cause to suspect, that he was a minor.

(3) Where a document is received by a minor at any school or educational establishment for minors, a person sending it to him at that establishment knowing or suspecting it to be such an establishment shall be taken to have reasonable cause to suspect that he is a minor.

[1.535]
51 Prohibition of unsolicited credit-tokens

(1) It is an offence to give a person a credit-token if he has not asked for it.

(2) To comply with subsection (1) a request must be contained in a document signed by the person making the request, unless the credit-token agreement is a small debtor-creditor-supplier agreement.

(3) Subsection (1) does not apply to the giving of a credit-token to a person—

    (a)   for use under a credit-token agreement already made, or

(b)　in renewal or replacement of a credit-token previously accepted by him under a credit-token agreement which continues in force, whether or not varied.

NOTES

Repealed by the Financial Services and Markets Act 2000 (Regulated Activities) (Amendment) (No 2) Order 2013, SI 2013/1881, art 20(1), (15), as from 26 July 2013 (certain purposes), and as from 1 April 2014 (remaining purposes), for transitional provisions see Pt 8 thereof at **[2.1007]** et seq (kept for reference only).

51A, 51B, 52–54　*(Ss 51A–54 repealed by the Financial Services and Markets Act 2000 (Regulated Activities) (Amendment) (No 2) Order 2013, SI 2013/1881, art 20(1), (16)–(20), as from 26 July 2013 (certain purposes), and as from 1 April 2014 (remaining purposes), for transitional provisions see Pt 8 thereof at* **[2.1007]** *et seq (ss 51A, 51B as inserted by the Financial Services Act 2010, s 15(1), (2)).)*

PART V
ENTRY INTO CREDIT OR HIRE AGREEMENTS
Preliminary matters

[1.536]
55　Disclosure of information
(1)　Regulations may require specified information to be disclosed in the prescribed manner to the debtor or hirer before a regulated agreement is made.
[(2)　If regulations under subsection (1) are not complied with, the agreement is enforceable against the debtor or hirer on an order of the court only (and for these purposes a retaking of goods or land to which the agreement relates is an enforcement of the agreement).]

NOTES

Sub-s (2): substituted by the Consumer Credit (EU Directive) Regulations 2010, SI 2010/1010, regs 2, 16, as from 1 February 2011, with effect in relation to certain agreements before that date, as provided for in regs 101, 101A of the 2010 Regulations at **[2.804]**, **[2.805]**.

Regulations: the Consumer Credit (Disclosure of Information) Regulations 2004, SI 2004/1481 at **[2.315]**; the Consumer Credit (Disclosure of Information) Regulations 2010, SI 2010/1013 at **[2.814]**; the Consumer Credit (Amendment) Regulations 2010, SI 2010/1969; the Consumer Credit (Green Deal) Regulations 2012, SI 2012/2798 at **[2.967]**.

[1.537]
[55A　*Pre-contractual explanations etc*
(1)　Before a regulated consumer credit agreement, other than an excluded agreement, is made, the creditor must—
　(a)　*provide the debtor with an adequate explanation of the matters referred to in subsection (2) in order to place him in a position enabling him to assess whether the agreement is adapted to his needs and his financial situation,*
　(b)　*advise the debtor—*
　　(i)　*to consider the information which is required to be disclosed under section 55(1), and*
　　(ii)　*where this information is disclosed in person to the debtor, that the debtor is able to take it away,*
　(c)　*provide the debtor with an opportunity to ask questions about the agreement, and*
　(d)　*advise the debtor how to ask the creditor for further information and explanation.*
(2)　The matters referred to in subsection (1)(a) are—
　(a)　*the features of the agreement which may make the credit to be provided under the agreement unsuitable for particular types of use,*
　(b)　*how much the debtor will have to pay periodically and, where the amount can be determined, in total under the agreement,*
　(c)　*the features of the agreement which may operate in a manner which would have a significant adverse effect on the debtor in a way which the debtor is unlikely to foresee,*
　(d)　*the principal consequences for the debtor arising from a failure to make payments under the agreement at the times required by the agreement including legal proceedings and, where this is a possibility, repossession of the debtor's home, and*
　(e)　*the effect of the exercise of any right to withdraw from the agreement and how and when this right may be exercised.*
(3)　The advice and explanation may be given orally or in writing except as provided in subsection (4).
(4)　Where the explanation of the matters specified in paragraphs (a), (b) or (e) of subsection (2) is given orally or in person to a debtor, the explanation of the matters specified in paragraphs (c) and (d) of that subsection, and the advice required to be given by subsection (1)(b), must be given orally to him.
(5)　Subsections (1) to (4) do not apply to a creditor if a credit intermediary (see section 160A) has complied with those subsections in respect of the agreement.
(6)　For the purposes of this section an agreement is an excluded agreement if it is—

(a)   *an agreement under which the creditor provides the debtor with credit which exceeds £60, 260, or*

(b)   *an agreement secured on land.*

(7)   Where the regulated consumer credit agreement is an agreement under which a person takes an article in pawn—

    (a)   *the obligation in subsection (1)(a) only relates to the matters listed in paragraphs (d) and (e) of subsection (2), and*

    (b)   *the obligations in subsection (1)(b) and (d) do not apply.]*

NOTES

Inserted by the Consumer Credit (EU Directive) Regulations 2010, SI 2010/1010, regs 2, 3 (as amended by the Consumer Credit (Amendment) Regulations 2010, SI 2010/1969, regs 4, 6), with effect in relation to certain agreements before 1 February 2011, as provided for in regs 101, 101A of the 2010 Regulations at **[2.804]**, **[2.805]**; repealed by the Financial Services and Markets Act 2000 (Regulated Activities) (Amendment) (No 2) Order 2013, SI 2013/1881, art 20(1), (21), as from 26 July 2013 (certain purposes), and as from 1 April 2014 (remaining purposes), for transitional provisions see Pt 8 thereof at **[2.1007]** et seq (kept for reference only).

[1.538]

[55B   Assessment of creditworthiness

(1)   Before making a regulated consumer credit agreement, other than an excluded agreement, the creditor must undertake an assessment of the creditworthiness of the debtor.

(2)   Before significantly increasing—

    (a)   *the amount of credit to be provided under a regulated consumer credit agreement, other than an excluded agreement, or*

    (b)   *a credit limit for running-account credit under a regulated consumer credit agreement, other than an excluded agreement,*

the creditor must undertake an assessment of the debtor's creditworthiness.

(3)   A creditworthiness assessment must be based on sufficient information obtained from—

    (a)   *the debtor, where appropriate, and*

    (b)   *a credit reference agency, where necessary.*

(4)   For the purposes of this section an agreement is an excluded agreement if it is—

    (a)   *an agreement secured on land, or*

    (b)   *an agreement under which a person takes an article in pawn.]*

NOTES

Inserted by the Consumer Credit (EU Directive) Regulations 2010, SI 2010/1010, regs 2, 5, with effect in relation to certain agreements before 1 February 2011, as provided for in regs 101, 101A of the 2010 Regulations at **[2.804]**, **[2.805]**; repealed by the Financial Services and Markets Act 2000 (Regulated Activities) (Amendment) (No 2) Order 2013, SI 2013/1881, art 20(1), (22), as from 26 July 2013 (certain purposes), and as from 1 April 2014 (remaining purposes), for transitional provisions see Pt 8 thereof at **[2.1007]** et seq (kept for reference only).

[1.539]

[55C   Copy of draft consumer credit agreement

(1)   Before a regulated consumer credit agreement, other than an excluded agreement, is made, the creditor must, if requested, give to the debtor without delay a copy of the prospective agreement (or such of its terms as have at that time been reduced to writing).

(2)   Subsection (1) does not apply if at the time the request is made, the creditor is unwilling to proceed with the agreement.

(3)   A breach of the duty imposed by subsection (1) is actionable as a breach of statutory duty.

(4)   For the purposes of this section an agreement is an excluded agreement if it is—

    (a)   an agreement secured on land,

    (b)   an agreement under which a person takes an article in pawn,

    (c)   an agreement under which the creditor provides the debtor with credit which exceeds £60,260 [and which is not a residential renovation agreement], or

    (d)   an agreement entered into by the debtor wholly or predominantly for the purposes of a business carried on, or intended to be carried on, by him.

[(5)   Article 60C(5) and (6) of the Regulated Activities Order applies for the purposes of subsection (4)(d).]]

NOTES

Inserted by the Consumer Credit (EU Directive) Regulations 2010, SI 2010/1010, regs 2, 6, with effect in relation to certain agreements before 1 February 2011, as provided for in regs 101, 101A of the 2010 Regulations at **[2.804]**, **[2.805]**.

Sub-s (4): in sub-para (c) words in square brackets inserted by the Mortgage Credit Directive Order 2015, SI 2015/910, art 3, Sch 1, Pt 1, para 2(1), (3), as from 21 March 2016 (note that the 2015 Order also comes into force on 20 April 2015 and 21 December 2015 for limited other purposes, and for transitional provisions, see Part 4 of that Order at **[2.1194]** et seq).

Sub-s (5): substituted by the Financial Services and Markets Act 2000 (Regulated Activities) (Amendment) (No 2) Order 2013, SI 2013/1881, art 20(1), (23), as from 26 July 2013 (certain purposes), and as from 1 April 2014 (remaining purposes), for transitional provisions see Pt 8 thereof at **[2.1007]** et seq.

[1.540]

56 Antecedent negotiations

(1) In this Act "antecedent negotiations" means any negotiations with the debtor or hirer—

(a) conducted by the creditor or owner in relation to the making of any regulated agreement, or

(b) conducted by a credit-broker in relation to goods sold or proposed to be sold by the credit-broker to the creditor before forming the subject-matter of a debtor-creditor-supplier agreement within section 12(a), or

(c) conducted by the supplier in relation to a transaction financed or proposed to be financed by a debtor-creditor-supplier agreement within section 12(b) or (c),

and "negotiator" means the person by whom negotiations are so conducted with the debtor or hirer.

(2) Negotiations with the debtor in a case falling within subsection (1)(b) or (c) shall be deemed to be conducted by the negotiator in the capacity of agent of the creditor as well as in his actual capacity.

(3) An agreement is void if, and to the extent that, it purports in relation to an actual or prospective regulated agreement—

(a) to provide that a person acting as, or on behalf of, a negotiator is to be treated as the agent of the debtor or hirer, or

(b) to relieve a person from liability for acts or omissions of any person acting as, or on behalf of, a negotiator.

(4) For the purposes of this Act, antecedent negotiations shall be taken to begin when the negotiator and the debtor or hirer first enter into communication (including communication by advertisement), and to include any representations made by the negotiator to the debtor or hirer and any other dealings between them.

[1.541]

57 Withdrawal from prospective agreement

(1) The withdrawal of a party from a prospective regulated agreement shall operate to apply this Part to the agreement, any linked transaction and any other thing done in anticipation of the making of the agreement as it would apply if the agreement were made and then cancelled under section 69.

(2) The giving to a party of a written or oral notice which, however expressed, indicates the intention of the other party to withdraw from a prospective regulated agreement operates as a withdrawal from it.

(3) Each of the following shall be deemed to be the agent of the creditor or owner for the purpose of receiving a notice under subsection (2)—

(a) a credit-broker or supplier who is the negotiator in antecedent negotiations, and

(b) any person who, in the course of a business carried on by him, acts on behalf of the debtor or hirer in any negotiations for the agreement.

(4) Where the agreement, if made, would not be a cancellable agreement, subsection (1) shall nevertheless apply as if the contrary were the case.

NOTES

Regulations: the Consumer Credit (Repayment of Credit on Cancellation) Regulations 1983, SI 1983/1559.

[1.542]

58 Opportunity for withdrawal from prospective land mortgage

(1) Before sending to the debtor or hirer, for his signature, an unexecuted agreement in a case where the prospective regulated agreement is to be secured on land (the "mortgaged land"), the creditor or owner shall give the debtor or hirer a copy of the unexecuted agreement which contains a notice in the prescribed form indicating the right of the debtor or hirer to withdraw from the prospective agreement, and how and when the right is exercisable, together with a copy of any other document referred to in the unexecuted agreement.

(2) Subsection (1) does not apply to—

(a) a restricted-use credit agreement to finance the purchase of the mortgaged land, or

(b) an agreement for a bridging loan in connection with the purchase of the mortgaged land or other land.

NOTES

Regulations: the Consumer Credit (Cancellation Notices and Copies of Documents) Regulations 1983, SI 1983/1557; the Consumer Credit (Amendment) Regulations 2010, SI 2010/1969.

[1.543]

59 Agreement to enter future agreement void

(1) An agreement is void if, and to the extent that, it purports to bind a person to enter as debtor or hirer into a prospective regulated agreement.

(2) Regulations may exclude from the operation of subsection (1) agreements such as are described in the regulations.

NOTES
Regulations: the Consumer Credit (Agreements to Enter Prospective Agreements) (Exemptions) Regulations 1983, SI 1983/1552.

Making the agreement

[1.544]
60 Form and content of agreements

(1) The [Treasury] shall make regulations as to the form and content of documents embodying regulated agreements, and the regulations shall contain such provisions as appear to [them] appropriate with a view to ensuring that the debtor or hirer is made aware of—

- (a) the rights and duties conferred or imposed on him by the agreement,
- (b) the amount and rate of the total charge for credit (in the case of a consumer credit agreement),
- (c) the protection and remedies available to him under this Act, and
- (d) any other matters which, in the opinion of the [Treasury], it is desirable for him to know about in connection with the agreement.

(2) Regulations under subsection (1) may in particular—

- (a) require specified information to be included in the prescribed manner in documents, and other specified material to be excluded;
- (b) contain requirements to ensure that specified information is clearly brought to the attention of the debtor or hirer, and that one part of a document is not given insufficient or excessive prominence compared with another.

(3) If, on an application made to the [FCA] by a person carrying on a consumer credit business or a consumer hire business, it appears to the [FCA] impracticable for the applicant to comply with any requirement of regulations under subsection (1) in a particular case, [it] may, by notice to the applicant, direct that the requirement be waived or varied in relation to such agreements, and subject to such conditions (if any), as [it] may specify, and this Act and the regulations shall have effect accordingly.

(4) The [FCA] shall give a notice under subsection (3) only if [it] is satisfied that to do so would not prejudice the interests of debtors or hirers.

[(5) An application may be made under subsection (3) only if it relates to—

- (a) a consumer credit agreement secured on land,
- (b) a consumer credit agreement under which a person takes an article in pawn,
- (c) a consumer credit agreement under which the creditor provides the debtor with credit which exceeds £60,260 [and which is not a residential renovation agreement],
- (d) a consumer credit agreement entered into by the debtor wholly or predominantly for the purposes of a business carried on, or intended to be carried on, by him, or
- (e) a consumer hire agreement.

[(6) Article 60C(5) and (6) of the Regulated Activities Order applies for the purposes of subsection (5)(d).]]

NOTES
Sub-s (1): words in square brackets substituted by the Financial Services Act 2012 (Consumer Credit) Order 2013, SI 2013/1882, art 7(1), (3)(a), as from 26 July 2013 (certain purposes), and as from 1 April 2014 (remaining purposes).

Sub-s (3): words in first and second pairs of square brackets substituted by SI 2013/1882, art 7(1), (3)(b), as from 26 July 2013 (certain purposes), and as from 1 April 2014 (remaining purposes); words in third and final pairs of square brackets substituted by the Enterprise Act 2002, s 278(1), Sch 25, para 6(1), (23).

Sub-s (4): word in first pair of square brackets substituted by SI 2013/1882, art 7(1), (3)(c), as from 26 July 2013 (certain purposes), and as from 1 April 2014 (remaining purposes); word in second pair of square brackets substituted by the Enterprise Act 2002, s 278(1), Sch 25, para 6(1), (23).

Sub-s (5): inserted, together with sub-s (6), by the Consumer Credit (EU Directive) Regulations 2010, SI 2010/1010, regs 2, 7, as from 1 February 2011, with effect in relation to certain agreements before that date, as provided for in regs 101, 101A of the 2010 Regulations at **[2.804]**, **[2.805]**.; in sub-para (c) words in square brackets inserted by the Mortgage Credit Directive Order 2015, SI 2015/910, art 3, Sch 1, Pt 1, para 2(1), (4), as from 21 March 2016 (note that the 2015 Order also comes into force on 20 April 2015 and 21 December 2015 for limited other purposes, and for transitional provisions, see Part 4 of that Order at **[2.1194]** et seq).

Sub-s (6): inserted as noted to sub-s (5); substituted by the Financial Services and Markets Act 2000 (Regulated Activities) (Amendment) (No 2) Order 2013, SI 2013/1881, art 20(1), (24), as from 26 July 2013 (certain purposes), and as from 1 April 2014 (remaining purposes), for transitional provisions see Pt 8 thereof at **[2.1007]** et seq.

References to the FCA, etc: as to the abolition of the office of the Director General of Fair Trading and the substitution of the original references to the Director (and related expressions), see the note preceding s 8 at **[1.520]**.

Regulations: the Consumer Credit (Agreements) Regulations 1983, SI 1983/1553; the Consumer Credit (Agreements) Regulations 2010, SI 2010/1014 at **[2.829]**.

[1.545]
61 Signing of agreement

(1) A regulated agreement is not properly executed unless—

- (a) a document in the prescribed form itself containing all the prescribed terms and conforming to regulations under section 60(1) is signed in the prescribed manner both by the debtor or hirer and by or on behalf of the creditor or owner, and

(b)   the document embodies all the terms of the agreement, other than implied terms, and

(c)   the document is, when presented or sent to the debtor or hirer for signature, in such a state that all its terms are readily legible.

(2)   In addition, where the agreement is one to which section 58(1) applies, it is not properly executed unless—

(a)   the requirements of section 58(1) were complied with, and

(b)   the unexecuted agreement was sent, for his signature, to the debtor or hirer [by an appropriate method] not less than seven days after a copy of it was given to him under section 58(1), and

(c)   during the consideration period, the creditor or owner refrained from approaching the debtor or hirer (whether in person, by telephone or letter, or in any other way) except in response to a specific request made by the debtor or hirer after the beginning of the consideration period, and

(d)   no notice of withdrawal by the debtor or hirer was received by the creditor or owner before the sending of the unexecuted agreement.

(3)   In subsection (2)(c), "the consideration period" means the period beginning with the giving of the copy under section 58(1) and ending—

(a)   at the expiry of seven days after the day on which the unexecuted agreement is sent, for his signature, to the debtor or hirer, or

(b)   on its return by the debtor or hirer after signature by him,

whichever first occurs.

(4)   Where the debtor or hirer is a partnership or an unincorporated body of persons, subsection (1)(a) shall apply with the substitution for "by the debtor or hirer" of "by or on behalf of the debtor or hirer".

NOTES

Sub-s (2): in para (b) words in square brackets substituted by the Consumer Credit Act 1974 (Electronic Communications) Order 2004, SI 2004/3236, art 2(1), (2), as from 31 December 2004.

Regulations: the Consumer Credit (Agreements) Regulations 1983, SI 1983/1553; the Consumer Credit (Agreements) (Amendment) Regulations 2004, SI 2004/1482; the Consumer Credit (Miscellaneous Amendments) Regulations 2004, SI 2004/2619; the Consumer Credit (Agreements) Regulations 2010, SI 2010/1014 at **[2.829]**; the Consumer Credit (Amendment) Regulations 2010, SI 2010/1969.

[1.546]
[61A   Duty to supply copy of executed consumer credit agreement

(1)   Where a regulated consumer credit agreement, other than an excluded agreement, has been made, the creditor must give a copy of the executed agreement, and any other document referred to in it, to the debtor.

(2)   Subsection (1) does not apply if—

(a)   a copy of the unexecuted agreement (and of any other document referred to in it) has already been given to the debtor, and

(b)   the unexecuted agreement is in identical terms to the executed agreement.

(3)   In a case referred to in subsection (2), the creditor must inform the debtor in writing—

(a)   that the agreement has been executed,

(b)   that the executed agreement is in identical terms to the unexecuted agreement a copy of which has already been given to the debtor, and

(c)   that the debtor has the right to receive a copy of the executed agreement if the debtor makes a request for it at any time before the end of the period referred to in section 66A(2).

(4)   Where a request is made under subsection (3)(c) the creditor must give a copy of the executed agreement to the debtor without delay.

(5)   If the requirements of this section are not observed, the agreement is not properly executed.

(6)   For the purposes of this section, an agreement is an excluded agreement if it is—

(a)   a cancellable agreement, or

(b)   an agreement—

(i)   secured on land,

(ii)   under which the creditor provides the debtor with credit which exceeds £60,260, or

(iii) entered into by the debtor wholly or predominantly for the purposes of a business carried on, or intended to be carried on, by him,

unless the creditor or a credit intermediary has complied with or purported to comply with regulation 3(2) of the Consumer Credit (Disclosure of Information) Regulations 2010.

[(6A)   An agreement is not an excluded agreement by virtue of subsection (6)(b)(ii) if it is a residential renovation agreement.]

[(7)   Article 60C(5) and (6) of the Regulated Activities Order applies for the purposes of subsection (6)(b)(iii).

(8)   In this section, "credit intermediary" means a person who in the course of business—

(a)   carries on any of the activities specified in article 36A(1)(d) to (f) of the Regulated Activities Order for a consideration that is or includes a financial consideration, and

(b)   does not do so as a creditor.]]

Part 1 Statutes

NOTES

Inserted by the Consumer Credit (EU Directive) Regulations 2010, SI 2010/1010, regs 2, 8, as from 1 February 2011, with effect in relation to certain agreements before that date, as provided for in regs 101, 101A of the 2010 Regulations at **[2.804]**, **[2.805]**.

Sub-s (6A): inserted by the Mortgage Credit Directive Order 2015, SI 2015/910, art 3, Sch 1, Pt 1, para 2(1), (5), as from 21 March 2016 (note that the 2015 Order also comes into force on 20 April 2015 and 21 December 2015 for limited other purposes, and for transitional provisions, see Part 4 of that Order at **[2.1194]** et seq).

Sub-ss (7), (8): substituted, for original sub-s (7), by the Financial Services and Markets Act 2000 (Regulated Activities) (Amendment) (No 2) Order 2013, SI 2013/1881, art 20(1), (25), as from 26 July 2013 (certain purposes), and as from 1 April 2014 (remaining purposes), for transitional provisions see Pt 8 thereof at **[2.1007]** et seq.

[1.547]
[61B   Duty to supply copy of overdraft agreement
(1)   Where an authorised business overdraft agreement or an authorised non-business overdraft agreement has been made, a document containing the terms of the agreement must be given to the debtor.
(2)   The creditor must provide the document referred to in subsection (1) to the debtor before or at the time the agreement is made unless—
   (a)   the creditor has provided the debtor with the information referred to in regulation 10(3) of the Consumer Credit (Disclosure of Information) Regulations 2010, in which case it may be provided after the agreement is made,
   (b)   the creditor has provided the debtor with the information referred to in regulation 10(3)(c), (e), (f), (h) and (k) of those Regulations, in which case it must be provided immediately after the agreement is made, or
   (c)   the agreement is an agreement of a description referred to in regulation 10(4)(b) of those Regulations, in which case it must be provided immediately after the agreement is made.
(3)   If the requirements of this section are not observed, the agreement is enforceable against the debtor on an order of the court only (and for these purposes a retaking of goods or land to which the agreement relates is an enforcement of the agreement).]

NOTES

Inserted by the Consumer Credit (EU Directive) Regulations 2010, SI 2010/1010, regs 2, 9 (as amended by the Consumer Credit (Amendment) Regulations 2010, SI 2010/1969, regs 4, 7), as from 1 February 2011, with effect in relation to certain agreements before that date, as provided for in regs 101, 101A of the 2010 Regulations at **[2.804]**, **[2.805]**.

[1.548]
62   Duty to supply copy of unexecuted agreement[: excluded agreements]
(1)   If [in the case of a regulated agreement which is an excluded agreement] the unexecuted agreement is presented personally to the debtor or hirer for his signature, but on the occasion when he signs it the document does not become an executed agreement, a copy of it, and of any other document referred to in it, must be there and then delivered to him.
(2)   If the unexecuted agreement is sent to the debtor or hirer for his signature, a copy of it, and of any other document referred to in it, must be sent to him at the same time.
(3)   A regulated agreement [which is an excluded agreement] is not properly executed if the requirements of this section are not observed.
[(4)   In this section, "excluded agreement" has the same meaning as in section 61A.]

NOTES

Section heading: words in square brackets inserted by the Consumer Credit (EU Directive) Regulations 2010, SI 2010/1010, regs 2, 10(a), as from 1 February 2011, with effect in relation to certain agreements before that date, as provided for in regs 101, 101A of the 2010 Regulations at **[2.804]**, **[2.805]**.

Sub-ss (1), (3): words in square brackets inserted by SI 2010/1010, regs 2, 10(b), (c), as from 1 February 2011, with effect in relation to certain agreements before that date, as provided for in regs 101, 101A of the 2010 Regulations at **[2.804]**, **[2.805]**.

Sub-s (4): added by SI 2010/1010, regs 2, 10(d), as from 1 February 2011, with effect in relation to certain agreements before that date, as provided for in regs 101, 101A of the 2010 Regulations at **[2.804]**, **[2.805]**.

[1.549]
63   Duty to supply copy of executed agreement[: excluded agreements]
(1)   If [in the case of a regulated agreement which is an excluded agreement] the unexecuted agreement is presented personally to the debtor or hirer for his signature, and on the occasion when he signs it the document becomes an executed agreement, a copy of the executed agreement, and of any other document referred to in it, must be there and then delivered to him.
(2)   A copy of the executed agreement, and of any other document referred to in it, must be given to the debtor or hirer within the seven days following the making of the agreement unless—
   (a)   subsection (1) applies, or
   (b)   the unexecuted agreement was sent to the debtor or hirer for his signature and, on the occasion of his signing it, the document became an executed agreement.
(3)   In the case of a cancellable agreement, a copy under subsection (2) must be sent [by an appropriate method].

(4) In the case of a credit-token agreement, a copy under subsection (2) need not be given within the seven days following the making of the agreement if it is given before or at the time when the credit-token is given to the debtor.

(5) A regulated agreement [which is an excluded agreement] is not properly executed if the requirements of this section are not observed.

[(6) In this section, "excluded agreement" has the same meaning as in section 61A.]

NOTES

Section heading: words in square brackets inserted by the Consumer Credit (EU Directive) Regulations 2010, SI 2010/1010, regs 2, 11(a), as from 1 February 2011, with effect in relation to certain agreements before that date, as provided for in regs 101, 101A of the 2010 Regulations at **[2.804]**, **[2.805]**.

Sub-s (1): words in square brackets inserted by SI 2010/1010, regs 2, 11(b), as from 1 February 2011, with effect in relation to certain agreements before that date, as provided for in regs 101, 101A of the 2010 Regulations at **[2.804]**, **[2.805]**.

Sub-s (3): words in square brackets substituted by the Consumer Credit Act 1974 (Electronic Communications) Order 2004, SI 2004/3236, art 2(1), (3), as from 31 December 2004.

Sub-s (5): words in square brackets inserted by SI 2010/1010, regs 2, 11(c), as from 1 February 2011, with effect in relation to certain agreements before that date, as provided for in regs 101, 101A of the 2010 Regulations at **[2.804]**, **[2.805]**.

Sub-s (6): added by SI 2010/1010, regs 2, 11(d), as from 1 February 2011, with effect in relation to certain agreements before that date, as provided for in regs 101, 101A of the 2010 Regulations at **[2.804]**, **[2.805]**.

[1.550]
64 Duty to give notice of cancellation rights

(1) In the case of a cancellable agreement, a notice in the prescribed form indicating the right of the debtor or hirer to cancel the agreement, how and when that right is exercisable, and the name and address of a person to whom notice of cancellation may be given,—

   (a) must be included in every copy given to the debtor or hirer under section 62 or 63, and

   (b) except where section 63(2) applied, must also be sent [by an appropriate method] to the debtor or hirer within the seven days following the making of the agreement.

(2) In the case of a credit-token agreement, a notice under subsection (1)(b) need not be sent [by an appropriate method] within the seven days following the making of the agreement if either—

   (a) it is sent [by an appropriate method] to the debtor or hirer before the credit-token is given to him, or

   (b) it is sent [by an appropriate method] to him together with the credit-token.

(3) Regulations may provide that except where section 63(2) applied a notice sent under subsection (1)(b) shall be accompanied by a further copy of the executed agreement, and of any other document referred to in it.

(4) Regulations may provide that subsection (1)(b) is not to apply in the case of agreements such as are described in the regulations, being agreements made by a particular person, if—

   (a) on an application by that person to the [FCA], the [FCA] has determined that, having regard to—

      (i) the manner in which antecedent negotiations for agreements with the applicant of that description are conducted, and

      (ii) the information provided to debtors or hirers before such agreements are made,

      the requirement imposed by subsection (1)(b) can be dispensed with without prejudicing the interests of debtors or hirers; and

   (b) any conditions imposed by the [FCA] in making the determination are complied with.

(5) A cancellable agreement is not properly executed if the requirements of this section are not observed.

NOTES

Sub-ss (1), (2): words in square brackets substituted by the Consumer Credit Act 1974 (Electronic Communications) Order 2004, SI 2004/3236, art 2(1), (4), as from 31 December 2004.

Sub-s (4): words in square brackets substituted by the Financial Services Act 2012 (Consumer Credit) Order 2013, SI 2013/1882, art 7(1), (4), as from 26 July 2013 (certain purposes), and as from 1 April 2014 (remaining purposes).

References to the FCA, etc: as to the abolition of the office of the Director General of Fair Trading and the substitution of the original references to the Director (and related expressions), see the note preceding s 8 at **[1.520]**.

Regulations: the Consumer Credit (Cancellation Notices and Copies of Documents) Regulations 1983, SI 1983/1557; the Consumer Credit (Notice of Cancellation Rights) (Exemptions) Regulations 1983, SI 1983/1558; the Consumer Credit (Cancellation Notices and Copies of Documents) (Amendment) Regulations 1984, SI 1984/1108; the Consumer Credit (Miscellaneous Amendments) Regulations 2004, SI 2004/2619.

[1.551]
65 Consequences of improper execution

(1) An improperly-executed regulated agreement is enforceable against the debtor or hirer on an order of the court only.

(2) A retaking of goods or land to which a regulated agreement relates is an enforcement of the agreement.

[1.552]
66   Acceptance of credit-tokens

(1)   The debtor shall not be liable under a credit-token agreement for use made of the credit-token by any person unless the debtor had previously accepted the credit-token, or the use constituted an acceptance of it by him.

(2)   The debtor accepts a credit-token when—

    (a)   it is signed, or

    (b)   a receipt for it is signed, or

    (c)   it is first used,

either by the debtor himself or by a person who, pursuant to the agreement, is authorised by him to use it.

[Withdrawal from certain agreements

[1.553]
66A   Withdrawal from consumer credit agreement

(1)   The debtor under a regulated consumer credit agreement, other than an excluded agreement, may withdraw from the agreement, without giving any reason, in accordance with this section.

(2)   To withdraw from an agreement under this section the debtor must give oral or written notice of the withdrawal to the creditor before the end of the period of 14 days beginning with the day after the relevant day.

(3)   For the purposes of subsection (2) the relevant day is whichever is the latest of the following—

    (a)   the day on which the agreement is made;

    (b)   where the creditor is required to inform the debtor of the credit limit under the agreement, the day on which the creditor first does so;

    (c)   in the case of an agreement to which section 61A (duty to supply copy of executed consumer credit agreement) applies, the day on which the debtor receives a copy of the agreement under that section or on which the debtor is informed as specified in subsection (3) of that section;

    (d)   in the case of an agreement to which section 63 (duty to supply copy of executed agreement: excluded agreements) applies, the day on which the debtor receives a copy of the agreement under that section.

(4)   Where oral notice under this section is given to the creditor it must be given in a manner specified in the agreement.

(5)   Where written notice under this section is given by facsimile transmission or electronically—

    (a)   it must be sent to the number or electronic address specified for the purpose in the agreement, and

    (b)   where it is so sent, it is to be regarded as having been received by the creditor at the time it is sent (and section 176A does not apply).

(6)   Where written notice under this section is given in any other form—

    (a)   it must be sent by post to, or left at, the postal address specified for the purpose in the agreement, and

    (b)   where it is sent by post to that address, it is to be regarded as having been received by the creditor at the time of posting (and section 176 does not apply).

(7)   Subject as follows, where the debtor withdraws from a regulated consumer credit agreement under this section—

    (a)   the agreement shall be treated as if it had never been entered into, and

    (b)   where an ancillary service relating to the agreement is or is to be provided by the creditor, or by a third party on the basis of an agreement between the third party and the creditor, the ancillary service contract shall be treated as if it had never been entered into.

(8)   In the case referred to in subsection (7)(b) the creditor must without delay notify any third party of the fact that the debtor has withdrawn from the agreement.

(9)   Where the debtor withdraws from an agreement under this section—

    (a)   the debtor must repay to the creditor any credit provided and the interest accrued on it (at the rate provided for under the agreement), but

    (b)   the debtor is not liable to pay to the creditor any compensation, fees or charges except any non-returnable charges paid by the creditor to a public administrative body.

(10)   An amount payable under subsection (9) must be paid without undue delay and no later than the end of the period of 30 days beginning with the day after the day on which the notice of withdrawal was given (and if not paid by the end of that period may be recovered by the creditor as a debt).

(11)   Where a regulated consumer credit agreement is a conditional sale, hire-purchase or credit-sale agreement and—

    (a)   the debtor withdraws from the agreement under this section after the credit has been provided, and

    (b)   the sum payable under subsection (9)(a) is paid in full by the debtor,

title to the goods purchased or supplied under the agreement is to pass to the debtor on the same terms as would have applied had the debtor not withdrawn from the agreement.

(12)   In subsections (2), (4), (5), (6) and (9)(a) references to the creditor include a person specified by the creditor in the agreement.

(13)   In subsection (7)(b) the reference to an ancillary service means a service that relates to the provision of credit under the agreement and includes in particular an insurance or payment protection policy.

(14)   For the purposes of this section, an agreement is an excluded agreement if it is—

   (a)   an agreement for credit exceeding £60,260[, other than a residential renovation agreement],

   (b)   an agreement secured on land,

   (c)   a restricted-use credit agreement to finance the purchase of land, or

   (d)   an agreement for a bridging loan in connection with the purchase of land.]

NOTES

Inserted, together with preceding cross-heading, by the Consumer Credit (EU Directive) Regulations 2010, SI 2010/1010, regs 2, 13 (as amended by the Consumer Credit (Amendment) Regulations 2010, SI 2010/1969, regs 4, 8), as from 1 February 2011, with effect in relation to certain agreements before that date, as provided for in regs 101, 101A of the 2010 Regulations at [**2.804**], [**2.805**].

Sub-s (14): in para (a) words in square brackets inserted by the Mortgage Credit Directive Order 2015, SI 2015/910, art 3, Sch 1, Pt 1, para 2(1), (6), as from 21 March 2016 (note that the 2015 Order also comes into force on 20 April 2015 and 21 December 2015 for limited other purposes, and for transitional provisions, see Part 4 of that Order at [**2.1194**] et seq).

Transitional provision: SI 2010/1969, regs 4, 8 amended SI 2010/1010, reg 13 so as to include the words "the day after" in the text of sub-s (2) reproduced above. SI 2010/1969, reg 46 provides that the insertion of these words does not apply to an agreement to which the Consumer Credit Act 1974, s 66A applies if the relevant day in relation to the agreement falls on or before 26 August 2010.

Cancellation of certain agreements within cooling-off period

[1.554]
67   Cancellable agreements
[(1)]   [Subject to subsection (2)] A regulated agreement may be cancelled by the debtor or hirer in accordance with this Part if the antecedent negotiations included oral representations made when in the presence of the debtor or hirer by an individual acting as, or on behalf of, the negotiator, unless—

   (a)   the agreement is secured on land, or is a restricted-use credit agreement to finance the purchase of land or is an agreement for a bridging loan in connection with the purchase of land, or

   (b)   the unexecuted agreement is signed by the debtor or hirer at premises at which any of the following is carrying on any business (whether on a permanent or temporary basis)—

      (i)   the creditor or owner;

      (ii)   any party to a linked transaction (other than the debtor or hirer or a relative of his);

      (iii)   the negotiator in any antecedent negotiations.

[(2)   This section does not apply where section 66A applies.]

NOTES

Sub-s (1): original provision renumbered as such and words in square brackets inserted by the Consumer Credit (EU Directive) Regulations 2010, SI 2010/1010, regs 2, 14(a), as from 1 February 2011, with effect in relation to certain agreements before that date, as provided for in regs 101, 101A of the 2010 Regulations at [**2.804**], [**2.805**].

Sub-s (2): added by SI 2010/1010, regs 2, 14(b), as from 1 February 2011, with effect in relation to certain agreements before that date, as provided for in regs 101, 101A of the 2010 Regulations at [**2.804**], [**2.805**].

[1.555]
68   Cooling-off period
The debtor or hirer may serve notice of cancellation of a cancellable agreement between his signing of the unexecuted agreement and—

   (a)   the end of the fifth day following the day on which he received a copy under section 63(2) or a notice under section 64(1)(b), or

   (b)   if (by virtue of regulations made under section 64(4)) section 64(1)(b) does not apply, the end of the fourteenth day following the day on which he signed the unexecuted agreement.

[1.556]
69   Notice of cancellation
(1)   If within the period specified in section 68 the debtor or hirer under a cancellable agreement serves on—

   (a)   the creditor or owner, or

   (b)   the person specified in the notice under section 64(1), or

   (c)   a person who (whether by virtue of subsection (6) or otherwise) is the agent of the creditor or owner,

a notice (a "notice of cancellation") which, however expressed and whether or not conforming to the notice given under section 64(1), indicates the intention of the debtor or hirer to withdraw from the agreement, the notice shall operate—

   (i)   to cancel the agreement, and any linked transaction, and

   (ii)   to withdraw any offer by the debtor or hirer, or his relative, to enter into a linked transaction.

(2) In the case of a debtor-creditor-supplier agreement for restricted-use credit financing—

    (a) the doing of work or supply of goods to meet an emergency, or

    (b) the supply of goods which, before service of the notice of cancellation, had by the act of the debtor or his relative become incorporated in any land or thing not comprised in the agreement or any linked transaction,

subsection (1) shall apply with the substitution of the following for paragraph (i)—

        "(i) to cancel only such provisions of the agreement and any linked transaction as—

            (aa) relate to the provision of credit, or

            (bb) require the debtor to pay an item in the total charge for credit, or

            (cc) subject the debtor to any obligation other than to pay for the doing of the said work, or the supply of the said goods".

(3) Except so far as is otherwise provided, references in this Act to the cancellation of an agreement or transaction do not include a case within subsection (2).

(4) Except as otherwise provided by or under this Act, an agreement or transaction cancelled under subsection (1) shall be treated as if it had never been entered into.

(5) Regulations may exclude linked transactions of the prescribed description from subsection (1)(i) or (ii).

(6) Each of the following shall be deemed to be the agent of the creditor or owner for the purpose of receiving a notice of cancellation—

    (a) a credit-broker or supplier who is the negotiator in antecedent negotiations, and

    (b) any person who, in the course of a business carried on by him, acts on behalf of the debtor or hirer in any negotiations for the agreement.

[(7) Whether or not it is actually received by him, a notice of cancellation sent to a person shall be deemed to be served on him—.

    (a) in the case of a notice sent by post, at the time of posting, and

    (b) in the case of a notice transmitted in the form of an electronic communication in accordance with section 176A(1), at the time of the transmission.]

NOTES

Sub-s (7): substituted by the Consumer Credit Act 1974 (Electronic Communications) Order 2004, SI 2004/3236, art 2(1), (5), as from 31 December 2004.

Regulations: the Consumer Credit (Linked Transactions) (Exemptions) Regulations 1983, SI 1983/1560 (revoked) at **[2.43]**.

[1.557]
70 Cancellation: recovery of money paid by debtor or hirer

(1) On the cancellation of a regulated agreement, and of any linked transaction,—

    (a) any sum paid by the debtor or hirer, or his relative, under or in contemplation of the agreement or transaction, including any item in the total charge for credit, shall become repayable, and

    (b) any sum, including any item in the total charge for credit, which but for the cancellation is, or would or might become, payable by the debtor or hirer, or his relative, under the agreement or transaction shall cease to be, or shall not become, so payable, and

    (c) in the case of a debtor-creditor-supplier agreement falling within section 12(b) any sum paid on the debtor's behalf by the creditor to the supplier shall become repayable to the creditor.

(2) If, under the terms of a cancelled agreement or transaction, the debtor or hirer, or his relative, is in possession of any goods, he shall have a lien on them for any sum repayable to him under subsection (1) in respect of that agreement or transaction, or any other linked transaction.

(3) A sum repayable under subsection (1) is repayable by the person to whom it was originally paid, but in the case of a debtor-creditor-supplier agreement falling within section 12(b) the creditor and the supplier shall be under a joint and several liability to repay sums paid by the debtor, or his relative, under the agreement or under a linked transaction falling within section 19(1)(b) and accordingly, in such a case, the creditor shall be entitled, in accordance with rules of court, to have the supplier made a party to any proceedings brought against the creditor to recover any such sums.

(4) Subject to any agreement between them, the creditor shall be entitled to be indemnified by the supplier for loss suffered by the creditor in satisfying his liability under subsection (3), including costs reasonably incurred by him in defending proceedings instituted by the debtor.

(5) Subsection (1) does not apply to any sum which, if not paid by a debtor, would be payable by virtue of section 71, and applies to a sum paid or payable by a debtor for the issue of a credit-token only where the credit-token has been returned to the creditor or surrendered to a supplier.

(6) If the total charge for credit includes an item in respect of a fee or commission charged by a credit-broker, the amount repayable under subsection (1) in respect of that item shall be the excess over [£5] of the fee or commission.

(7) If the total charge for credit includes any sum payable or paid by the debtor to a credit-broker otherwise than in respect of a fee or commission charged by him, that sum shall for the purposes of subsection (6) be treated as if it were such a fee or commission.

(8) So far only as is necessary to give effect to section 69(2), this section applies to an agreement or transaction within that subsection as it applies to a cancelled agreement or transaction.

NOTES

  Sub-s (6): sum in square brackets substituted by the Consumer Credit (Further Increase of Monetary Amounts) Order 1998, SI 1998/997, art 3, Schedule, as from 1 May 1998.

[1.558]
71 Cancellation: repayment of credit

(1) Notwithstanding the cancellation of a regulated consumer credit agreement, other than a debtor-creditor-supplier agreement for restricted-use credit, the agreement shall continue in force so far as it relates to repayment of credit and payment of interest.

(2) If, following the cancellation of a regulated consumer credit agreement, the debtor repays the whole or a portion of a credit—

  (a)   before the expiry of one month following service of the notice of cancellation, or

  (b)   in the case of a credit repayable by instalments, before the date on which the first instalment is due,

no interest shall be payable on the amount repaid.

(3) If the whole of a credit repayable by instalments is not repaid on or before the date specified in subsection (2) (b), the debtor shall not be liable to repay any of the credit except on receipt of a request in writing in the prescribed form, signed by or on behalf of the creditor, stating the amounts of the remaining instalments (recalculated by the creditor as nearly as may be in accordance with the agreement and without extending the repayment period), but excluding any sum other than principal and interest.

(4) Repayment of a credit, or payment of interest, under a cancelled agreement shall be treated as duly made if it is made to any person on whom, under section 69, a notice of cancellation could have been served, other than a person referred to in section 69(6)(b).

NOTES

  Regulations: the Consumer Credit (Repayment of Credit on Cancellation) Regulations 1983, SI 1983/1559.

[1.559]
72 Cancellation: return of goods

(1) This section applies where any agreement or transaction relating to goods, being—

  (a)   a restricted-use debtor-creditor-supplier agreement, a consumer hire agreement, or a linked transaction to which the debtor or hirer under any regulated agreement is a party, or

  (b)   a linked transaction to which a relative of the debtor or hirer under any regulated agreement is a party,

is cancelled after the debtor or hirer (in a case within paragraph (a)) or the relative (in a case within paragraph (b)) has acquired possession of the goods by virtue of the agreement or transaction.

(2) In this section—

  (a)   "the possessor" means the person who has acquired possession of the goods as mentioned in subsection (1),

  (b)   "the other party" means the person from whom the possessor acquired possession, and

  (c)   "the pre-cancellation period" means the period beginning when the possessor acquired possession and ending with the cancellation.

(3) The possessor shall be treated as having been under a duty throughout the pre-cancellation period—

  (a)   to retain possession of the goods, and

  (b)   to take reasonable care of them.

(4) On the cancellation, the possessor shall be under a duty, subject to any lien, to restore the goods to the other party in accordance with this section, and meanwhile to retain possession of the goods and take reasonable care of them.

(5) The possessor shall not be under any duty to deliver the goods except at his own premises and in pursuance of a request in writing signed by or on behalf of the other party and served on the possessor either before, or at the time when, the goods are collected from those premises.

(6) If the possessor—

  (a)   delivers the goods (whether at his own premises or elsewhere) to any person on whom, under section 69, a notice of cancellation could have been served (other than a person referred to in section 69(6)(b)), or

  (b)   sends the goods at his own expense to such a person,

he shall be discharged from any duty to retain the goods or deliver them to any person.

(7) Where the possessor delivers the goods as mentioned in subsection (6)(a) his obligation to take care of the goods shall cease; and if he sends the goods as mentioned in subsection (6)(b), he shall be under a duty to take reasonable care to see that they are received by the other party and not damaged in transit, but in other respects his duty to take care of the goods shall cease.

(8) Where, at any time during the period of 21 days following the cancellation, the possessor receives such a request as is mentioned in subsection (5), and unreasonably refuses or unreasonably fails to comply with it, his duty to take reasonable care of the goods shall continue until he delivers or sends the goods as mentioned in subsection (6), but if within that period he does not receive such a request his duty to take reasonable care of the goods shall cease at the end of that period.

(9)   The preceding provisions of this section do not apply to—
  (a)   perishable goods, or
  (b)   goods which by their nature are consumed by use and which, before the cancellation, were so consumed, or
  (c)   goods supplied to meet an emergency, or
  (d)   goods which, before the cancellation, had become incorporated in any land or thing not comprised in the cancelled agreement or a linked transaction.
(10)   Where the address of the possessor is specified in the executed agreement, references in this section to his own premises are to that address and no other.
(11)   Breach of a duty imposed by this section is actionable as a breach of statutory duty.

[1.560]
73   Cancellation: goods given in part-exchange
(1)   This section applies on the cancellation of a regulated agreement where, in antecedent negotiations, the negotiator agreed to take goods in part-exchange (the "part-exchange goods") and those goods have been delivered to him.
(2)   Unless, before the end of the period of ten days beginning with the date of cancellation, the part-exchange goods are returned to the debtor or hirer in a condition substantially as good as when they were delivered to the negotiator, the debtor or hirer shall be entitled to recover from the negotiator a sum equal to the part-exchange allowance (as defined in subsection (7)(b)).
(3)   In the case of a debtor-creditor-supplier agreement within section 12(b), the negotiator and the creditor shall be under a joint and several liability to pay to the debtor a sum recoverable under subsection (2).
(4)   Subject to any agreement between them, the creditor shall be entitled to be indemnified by the negotiator for loss suffered by the creditor in satisfying his liability under subsection (3), including costs reasonably incurred by him in defending proceedings instituted by the debtor.
(5)   During the period of ten days beginning with the date of cancellation, the debtor or hirer, if he is in possession of goods to which the cancelled agreement relates, shall have a lien on them for—
  (a)   delivery of the part-exchange goods, in a condition substantially as good as when they were delivered to the negotiator, or
  (b)   a sum equal to the part-exchange allowance;
and if the lien continues to the end of that period it shall thereafter subsist only as a lien for a sum equal to the part-exchange allowance.
(6)   Where the debtor or hirer recovers from the negotiator or creditor, or both of them jointly, a sum equal to the part-exchange allowance, then, if the title of the debtor or hirer to the part-exchange goods has not vested in the negotiator, it shall so vest on the recovery of that sum.
(7)   For the purposes of this section—
  (a)   the negotiator shall be treated as having agreed to take goods in part-exchange if, in pursuance of the antecedent negotiations, he either purchased or agreed to purchase those goods or accepted or agreed to accept them as part of the consideration for the cancelled agreement, and
  (b)   the part-exchange allowance shall be the sum agreed as such in the antecedent negotiations or, if no such agreement was arrived at, such sum as it would have been reasonable to allow in respect of the part-exchange goods if no notice of cancellation had been served.
(8)   In an action brought against the creditor for a sum recoverable under subsection (2), he shall be entitled, in accordance with rules of court, to have the negotiator made a party to the proceedings.

Exclusion of certain agreements from Part V

[1.561]
74   Exclusion of certain agreements from Part V
[(1)   Except as provided in subsections (1A) to (2), this Part does not apply to—
  (a)   a non-commercial agreement,
  (b)   a debtor-creditor agreement enabling the debtor to overdraw on a current account,
  (c)   a debtor-creditor agreement to finance the making of such payments arising on, or connected with, the death of a person as may be prescribed, or
  (d)   a small debtor-creditor-supplier agreement for restricted-use credit.
(1A)   Section 56 (antecedent negotiations) applies to a non-commercial agreement.
(1B)   Where an agreement that falls within subsection (1)(b) is an authorised business overdraft agreement the following provisions apply—
  (a)   . . .
  (b)   section 56 (antecedent negotiations);
  (c)   section 60 (regulations on form and content of agreements);
  (d)   section 61B (duty to supply copy of overdraft agreement).
(1C)   Where an agreement that falls within subsection (1)(b) is an authorised non-business overdraft agreement the following provisions apply—
  (a)   section 55 (regulations on disclosure of information);
  (b)   . . .
  (c)   section 55C (copy of draft consumer credit agreement);

    (d)   section 56 (antecedent negotiations);

    (e)   section 60 (regulations on form and content of agreements);

    (f)   section 61B (duty to supply copy of overdraft agreement).

(1D)   Where an agreement that falls within subsection (1)(b) would be an authorised non-business overdraft agreement but for the fact that the credit is not repayable on demand or within three months the following provisions apply—

    (a)   section 55 (regulations on disclosure of information);

    (b), (c). . .

    (d)   section 55C (copy of draft consumer credit agreement);

    (e)   section 56 (antecedent negotiations);

    (f)   section 60 (regulations on form and content of agreements);

    (g)   section 61 (signing of agreement);

    (h)   section 61A (duty to supply copy of executed agreement);

    (i)   section 66A (withdrawal from consumer credit agreement).

(1E)   In the case of an agreement that falls within subsection (1)(b) but does not fall within subsection (1B), (1C) or (1D), section 56 (antecedent negotiations) applies.

(1F)   The following provisions apply to a debtor-creditor agreement to finance the making of such payments arising on, or connected with, the death of a person as may be prescribed—

    (a)   section 55 (regulations on disclosure of information);

    (b), (c). . .

    (d)   section 55C (copy of draft consumer credit agreement);

    (e)   section 56 (antecedent negotiations);

    (f)   section 60 (regulations on form and content of agreements);

    (g)   section 61 (signing of agreement);

    (h)   section 61A (duty to supply copy of executed agreement);

    (i)   section 66A (withdrawal from consumer credit agreement).

(2)   The following provisions apply to a small debtor-creditor-supplier agreement for restricted-use credit—

    (a)   section 55 (regulations on disclosure of information);

    (b)   section 56 (antecedent negotiations);

    (c)   section 66A (withdrawal from consumer credit agreement).]

[(2A)   In the case of an agreement to which Part 2 or 3 of the Consumer Contracts (Information, Cancellation and Additional Charges) Regulations 2013 applies, the reference in subsection (2) to a small agreement is to be read as if in section 17(1)(a) and (b) "£42" were substituted for "£50".]

(3)   [Subsection (1)(c) applies] only where the [FCA] so determines, and such a determination—

    (a)   may be made subject to such conditions as the [FCA] thinks fit, and

    (b)   shall be made only if the [FCA] is of opinion that it is not against the interests of debtors.

[(3A)   . . .]

(4)   If any term of an agreement falling within subsection [(1)(d)] is expressed in writing, regulations under section 60(1) shall apply to that term (subject to section 60(3)) as if the agreement was a regulated agreement not falling within subsection [(1)(d)].

NOTES

Sub-ss (1), (1A)–(1F), (2): substituted for original sub-ss (1), (2), by the Consumer Credit (EU Directive) Regulations 2010, SI 2010/1010, regs 2, 17(1), (2), as from 1 February 2011, with effect in relation to certain agreements before that date, as provided for in regs 101, 101A of the 2010 Regulations at **[2.804]**, **[2.805]**.

Sub-ss (1B)–(1D), (1F): paras omitted repealed by Financial Services and Markets Act 2000 (Regulated Activities) (Amendment) (No 2) Order 2013, SI 2013/1881, art 20(1), (26), as from 26 July 2013 (certain purposes), and as from 1 April 2014 (remaining purposes), for transitional provisions see Pt 8 thereof at **[2.1007]** et seq.

Sub-s (2A): inserted by the Consumer Protection (Cancellation of Contracts Concluded away from Business Premises) Regulations 1987, SI 1987/2117, reg 9, as from 1 July 1988; substituted by the Consumer Contracts (Information, Cancellation and Additional Charges) Regulations 2013, SI 2013/3134, reg 47, Sch 4, para 2, in relation to contracts entered into on or after 13 June 2014.

Sub-s (3): words in square brackets substituted by the Financial Services Act 2012 (Consumer Credit) Order 2013, SI 2013/1882, art 7(1), (5), as from 26 July 2013 (certain purposes), and as from 1 April 2014 (remaining purposes).

Sub-s (3A): added by the Banking Act 1979, s 38(1), as from 1 October 1979, and repealed by SI 2010/1010, regs 2, 17(1), (4), as from 1 February 2011, with effect in relation to certain agreements before that date, as provided for in regs 101, 101A of the 2010 Regulations at **[2.804]**, **[2.805]**.

Sub-s (4): references in square brackets in both places substituted by SI 2010/1010, regs 2, 17(1), (5), as from 1 February 2011, with effect in relation to certain agreements before that date, as provided for in regs 101, 101A of the 2010 Regulations at **[2.804]**, **[2.805]**.

References to the FCA, etc: as to the abolition of the office of the Director General of Fair Trading and the substitution of the original references to the Director (and related expressions), see the note preceding s 8 at **[1.520]**.

Regulations: the Consumer Credit (Payments Arising on Death) Regulations 1983, SI 1983/1554.

[PART VA
CURRENT ACCOUNT OVERDRAFTS

[1.562]

74A *Information to be provided on a current account agreement*

(1)   This section applies to a current account agreement where—

(a)   there is the possibility that the account-holder may be allowed to overdraw on the current account without a pre-arranged overdraft or exceed a pre-arranged overdraft limit, and

(b)   if the account-holder did so, this would be a regulated consumer credit agreement.

(2)   The current account agreement must include the following information at the time it is made—

(a)   the rate of interest charged on the amount by which an account-holder overdraws on the current account or exceeds the pre-arranged overdraft limit,

(b)   any conditions applicable to that rate,

(c)   any reference rate on which that rate is based,

(d)   information on any changes to the rate of interest (including the periods that the rate applies and any conditions or procedure applicable to changing that rate), and

(e)   any other charges payable by the debtor under the agreement (and the conditions under which those charges may be varied).

(3)   The account-holder must be informed in writing at least annually of the information in subsection (2).

(4)   For the purposes of subsections (2) and (3) where different rates of interest are charged in different circumstances, the creditor must provide the information in subsection (2)(a) to (d) in respect of each rate.

(5)   Subsection (3) does not apply where the overdraft or excess would be secured on land.]

NOTES

Inserted, together with preceding Part heading, by the Consumer Credit (EU Directive) Regulations 2010, SI 2010/1010, regs 2, 21 (as amended by the Consumer Credit (Amendment) Regulations 2010, SI 2010/1969, regs 4, 9), as from 1 February 2011, with effect in relation to certain agreements before that date, as provided for in regs 101, 101A of the 2010 Regulations at **[2.804]**, **[2.805]**; repealed, together with s 74B, by the Financial Services and Markets Act 2000 (Regulated Activities) (Amendment) (No 2) Order 2013, SI 2013/1881, art 20(1), (27), as from 26 July 2013 (certain purposes), and as from 1 April 2014 (remaining purposes), for transitional provisions see Pt 8 thereof at **[2.1007]** et seq (kept for reference only).

[1.563]

[74B   Information to be provided on significant overdrawing without prior arrangement

(1)   Where—

(a)   the holder of a current account overdraws on the account without a pre-arranged overdraft, or exceeds a pre-arranged overdraft limit, for a period exceeding one month,

(b)   the amount of that overdraft or excess is significant throughout that period,

(c)   that overdraft or excess is a regulated consumer credit agreement, and

(d)   the account-holder has not been informed in writing of the matters mentioned in subsection (2) within that period,

the account-holder must be informed in writing of those matters without delay.

(2)   The matters referred to in subsection (1) are—

(a)   the fact that the current account is overdrawn or the overdraft limit has been exceeded,

(b)   the amount of that overdraft or excess,

(c)   the rate of interest charged on it, and

(d)   any other charges payable by the debtor in relation to it (including any penalties and any interest on those charges).

(3)   For the purposes of subsection (1)(b) the amount of the overdraft or excess is to be treated as significant if—

(a)   the account-holder is liable to pay a charge for which he would not otherwise be liable,

(b)   the overdraft or excess is likely to have an adverse effect on the debtor's ability to receive further credit (including any effect on the information about the debtor held by a credit reference agency), or

(c)   it otherwise appears significant, having regard to all the circumstances.

(4)   Where the overdraft or excess is secured on land, subsection (1)(a) is to be read as if the reference to one month were a reference to three months.]

NOTES

Inserted by the Consumer Credit (EU Directive) Regulations 2010, SI 2010/1010, regs 2, 22 (as amended by the Consumer Credit (Amendment) Regulations 2010, SI 2010/1969, regs 4, 10(1), (3)), as from 1 February 2011, with effect in relation to certain agreements before that date, as provided for in regs 100–101A of the 2010 Regulations at **[2.803]–[2.805]**; repealed as noted to s 74A at **[1.562]** (kept for reference only).

PART VI

MATTERS ARISING DURING CURRENCY OF CREDIT OR HIRE AGREEMENTS

[1.564]

75   Liability of creditor for breaches by supplier

(1)   If the debtor under a debtor-creditor-supplier agreement falling within section 12(b) or (c) has, in relation to a transaction financed by the agreement, any claim against the supplier in respect of a misrepresentation or breach of contract, he shall have a like claim against the creditor, who, with the supplier, shall accordingly be jointly and severally liable to the debtor.

(2)   Subject to any agreement between them, the creditor shall be entitled to be indemnified by the supplier for loss suffered by the creditor in satisfying his liability under subsection (1), including costs reasonably incurred by him in defending proceedings instituted by the debtor.

(3)   Subsection (1) does not apply to a claim—

(a)   under a non-commercial agreement, ...

(b)   so far as the claim relates to any single item to which the supplier has attached a cash price not exceeding [£100] or more than [£30,000][, or

(c)   under a debtor-creditor-supplier agreement for running-account credit—

(i)   which provides for the making of payments by the debtor in relation to specified periods which, in the case of an agreement which is not secured on land, do not exceed three months, and

(ii)   which requires that the number of payments to be made by the debtor in repayments of the whole amount of the credit provided in each such period shall not exceed one.]

(4)   This section applies notwithstanding that the debtor, in entering into the transaction, exceeded the credit limit or otherwise contravened any term of the agreement.

(5)   In an action brought against the creditor under subsection (1) he shall be entitled, in accordance with rules of court, to have the supplier made a party to the proceedings.

NOTES

Sub-s (3): word omitted from para (a) repealed and para (c) and word preceding it inserted by the Consumer Credit (EU Directive) Regulations 2010, SI 2010/1010, regs 2, 24, as from 1 February 2011, with effect in relation to certain agreements before that date, as provided for in regs 101, 101A of the 2010 Regulations at **[2.804]**, **[2.805]**; sums in square brackets in para (b) substituted by the Consumer Credit (Increase of Monetary Limits) Order 1983, SI 1983/1878, arts 3, 4, Schedule, Pts I, II, as from 1 May 1998.

[1.565]
[75A   Further provision for liability of creditor for breaches by supplier

(1)   If the debtor under a linked credit agreement has a claim against the supplier in respect of a breach of contract the debtor may pursue that claim against the creditor where any of the conditions in subsection (2) are met.

(2)   The conditions in subsection (1) are—

(a)   that the supplier cannot be traced,

(b)   that the debtor has contacted the supplier but the supplier has not responded,

(c)   that the supplier is insolvent, or

(d)   that the debtor has taken reasonable steps to pursue his claim against the supplier but has not obtained satisfaction for his claim.

(3)   The steps referred to in subsection (2)(d) need not include litigation.

(4)   For the purposes of subsection (2)(d) a debtor is to be deemed to have obtained satisfaction where he has accepted a replacement product or service or other compensation from the supplier in settlement of his claim.

(5)   In this section "linked credit agreement" means a regulated consumer credit agreement which serves exclusively to finance an agreement for the supply of specific goods or the provision of a specific service and where—

(a)   the creditor uses the services of the supplier in connection with the preparation or making of the credit agreement, or

(b)   the specific goods or provision of a specific service are explicitly specified in the credit agreement.

(6)   This section does not apply where—

(a)   the cash value of the goods or service is £30,000 or less,

(b)   the linked credit agreement is for credit which exceeds £60,260 [and is not a residential renovation agreement], or

(c)   the linked credit agreement is entered into by the debtor wholly or predominantly for the purposes of a business carried on, or intended to be carried on, by him.

[(7)   Article 60C(5) and (6) of the Regulated Activities Order applies for the purposes of subsection (6)(c).]

(8)   This section does not apply to an agreement secured on land.]

NOTES

Inserted by the Consumer Credit (EU Directive) Regulations 2010, SI 2010/1010, regs 2, 25 (as amended by the Consumer Credit (Amendment) Regulations 2010, SI 2010/1969, regs 4, 11), as from 1 February 2011, with effect in relation to certain agreements before that date, as provided for in regs 100–101A of the 2010 Regulations at **[2.803]**–**[2.805]**.

Sub-s (6): in para (b) words in square brackets inserted by the Mortgage Credit Directive Order 2015, SI 2015/910, art 3, Sch 1, Pt 1, para 2(1), (7), as from 21 March 2016 (note that the 2015 Order also comes into force on 20 April 2015 and 21 December 2015 for limited other purposes, and for transitional provisions, see Part 4 of that Order at **[2.1194]** et seq).

Sub-s (7): substituted by the Financial Services and Markets Act 2000 (Regulated Activities) (Amendment) (No 2) Order 2013, SI 2013/1881, art 20(1), (28), as from 26 July 2013 (certain purposes), and as from 1 April 2014 (remaining purposes), for transitional provisions see Pt 8 thereof at **[2.1007]** et seq.

[1.566]
76 Duty to give notice before taking certain action

(1) The creditor or owner is not entitled to enforce a term of a regulated agreement by—
  (a) demanding earlier payment of any sum, or
  (b) recovering possession of any goods or land, or
  (c) treating any right conferred on the debtor or hirer by the agreement as terminated, restricted or deferred,

except by or after giving the debtor or hirer not less than seven days' notice of intention to do so.
(2) Subsection (1) applies only where—
  (a) a period for the duration of the agreement is specified in the agreement, and
  (b) that period has not ended when the creditor or owner does an act mentioned in subsection (1),

but so applies notwithstanding that, under the agreement, any party is entitled to terminate it before the end of the period so specified.
(3) A notice under subsection (1) is ineffective if not in the prescribed form.
(4) Subsection (1) does not prevent a creditor from treating the right to draw on any credit as restricted or deferred and taking such steps as may be necessary to make the restriction or deferment effective.
(5) Regulations may provide that subsection (1) is not to apply to agreements described by the regulations.
(6) Subsection (1) does not apply to a right of enforcement arising by reason of any breach by the debtor or hirer of the regulated agreement.

NOTES

Regulations: the Consumer Credit (Enforcement, Default and Termination Notices) Regulations 1983, SI 1983/1561; the Consumer Credit (Enforcement, Default and Termination Notices) (Amendment) Regulations 2004, SI 2004/3237.

[1.567]
77 Duty to give information to debtor under fixed-sum credit agreement

(1) The creditor under a regulated agreement for fixed-sum credit, within the prescribed period after receiving a request in writing to that effect from the debtor and payment of a fee of [£1], shall give the debtor a copy of the executed agreement (if any) and of any other document referred to in it, together with a statement signed by or on behalf of the creditor showing, according to the information to which it is practicable for him to refer,—
  (a) the total sum paid under the agreement by the debtor;
  (b) the total sum which has become payable under the agreement by the debtor but remains unpaid, and the various amounts comprised in that total sum, with the date when each became due; and
  (c) the total sum which is to become payable under the agreement by the debtor, and the various amounts comprised in that total sum, with the date, or mode of determining the date, when each becomes due.
(2) If the creditor possesses insufficient information to enable him to ascertain the amounts and dates mentioned in subsection (1)(c), he shall be taken to comply with that paragraph if his statement under subsection (1) gives the basis on which, under the regulated agreement, they would fall to be ascertained.
[(2A) Subsection (2B) applies if the regulated agreement is a green deal plan . . .
(2B) The duty imposed on the creditor by subsection (1) may be discharged by another person acting on the creditor's behalf.]
(3) Subsection (1) does not apply to—
  (a) an agreement under which no sum is, or will or may become, payable by the debtor, or
  (b) a request made less than one month after a previous request under that subsection relating to the same agreement was complied with.
(4) If the creditor under an agreement fails to comply with subsection (1)—
  (a) he is not entitled, while the default continues, to enforce the agreement; . . .
  (b) . . .
(5) This section does not apply to a non-commercial agreement.

NOTES

Sub-s (1): sum in square brackets substituted by the Consumer Credit (Further Increase in Monetary Amounts) Order 1998, SI 1998/997, art 3, Schedule, as from 1 May 1998.

Sub-ss (2A), (2B): inserted by the Energy Act 2011, s 27(1), (2), as from 28 January 2013; words omitted from sub-para (2A) repealed by the Consumer Credit Act 1974 (Green Deal) (Amendment) Order 2014, SI 2014/436, art 8(2), as from 28 February 2014, except in relation to a green deal plan (within the meaning of the Energy Act 2011, s 1) made before that date; see art 1(3) thereof.

Sub-s (4): words omitted repealed by the Consumer Protection from Unfair Trading Regulations 2008, SI 2008/1277, reg 30(1), (3), Sch 2, Pt 1, paras 17, 19, Sch 4, as from 26 May 2008.

Regulations: the Consumer Credit (Prescribed Periods for Giving Information) Regulations 1983, SI 1983/1569.

[1.568]

[77A   Statements to be provided in relation to fixed-sum credit agreements

[(1)   The creditor under a regulated agreement for fixed-sum credit must give the debtor statements under this section.

(1A)   The statements must relate to consecutive periods.

(1B)   The first such period must begin with either—

(a)   the day on which the agreement is made, or

(b)   the day the first movement occurs on the debtor's account with the creditor relating to the agreement.

(1C)   No such period may exceed a year.

(1D)   For the purposes of subsection (1C), a period of a year which expires on a non-working day may be regarded as expiring on the next working day.

(1E)   Each statement under this section must be given to the debtor before the end of the period of thirty days beginning with the day after the end of the period to which the statement relates.]

(2)   Regulations may make provision about the form and content of statements under this section.

[(2A)   Subsection (2B) applies if the regulated agreement is a green deal plan . . .

(2B)   Any duty imposed on the creditor by this section may be discharged by another person acting on the creditor's behalf.]

(3)   The debtor shall have no liability to pay any sum in connection with the preparation or the giving to him of a statement under this section.

(4)   The creditor is not required to give the debtor any statement under this section once the following conditions are satisfied—

(a)   that there is no sum payable under the agreement by the debtor; and

(b)   that there is no sum which will or may become so payable.

(5)   Subsection (6) applies if at a time before the conditions mentioned in subsection (4) are satisfied the creditor fails to give the debtor—

(a)   a statement under this section within the period mentioned in subsection [(1E)]; . . .

(b)   . . .

(6)   Where this subsection applies in relation to a failure to give a statement under this section to the debtor—

(a)   the creditor shall not be entitled to enforce the agreement during the period of non-compliance;

(b)   the debtor shall have no liability to pay any sum of interest to the extent calculated by reference to the period of non-compliance or to any part of it; and

(c)   the debtor shall have no liability to pay any default sum which (apart from this paragraph)—

(i)   would have become payable during the period of non-compliance; or

(ii)   would have become payable after the end of that period in connection with a breach of the agreement which occurs during that period (whether or not the breach continues after the end of that period).

(7)   In this section "the period of non-compliance" means, in relation to a failure to give a statement under this section to the debtor, the period which—

(a)   begins immediately after the end of the period mentioned in . . . subsection (5); and

(b)   ends at the end of the day on which the statement is given to the debtor or on which the conditions mentioned in subsection (4) are satisfied, whichever is earlier.

(8)   This section does not apply in relation to a non-commercial agreement or to a small agreement.]

[(9)   This section does not apply where the holder of a current account overdraws on the account without a pre-arranged overdraft or exceeds a pre-arranged overdraft limit.]

NOTES

Inserted by the Consumer Credit Act 2006, s 6, as from 16 June 2006 (sub-s (2)) and as from 1 October 2008 (remainder), subject to transitional provisions in s 69(1) of, and Sch 3, paras 1, 2 to, that Act at **[1.1945]**, **[1.1947]**.

Sub-ss (1), (1A)–(1E): substituted for original sub-s (1) by the Legislative Reform (Consumer Credit) Order 2008, SI 2008/2826, art 4(a), as from 31 October 2008; for transitional provisions see the note below.

Sub-ss (2A), (2B): inserted by the Energy Act 2011, s 27(1), (3), as from 28 January 2013; words omitted from sub-para (2A) repealed by the Consumer Credit Act 1974 (Green Deal) (Amendment) Order 2014, SI 2014/436, art 8(2), as from 28 February 2014, except in relation to a green deal plan (within the meaning of the Energy Act 2011, s 1) made before that date; see art 1(3) thereof.

Sub-s (5): reference in square brackets substituted and words omitted repealed by SI 2008/2826, art 4(b), as from 31 October 2008; for transitional provisions see the note below.

Sub-s (7): words omitted repealed by SI 2008/2826, art 4(c), as from 31 October 2008; for transitional provisions see the note below.

Sub-s (9): added by the Consumer Credit (EU Directive) Regulations 2010, SI 2010/1010, regs 2, 23, as from 1 February 2011, with effect in relation to certain agreements before that date, as provided for in regs 101, 101A of the 2010 Regulations at **[2.804]**, **[2.805]**.

Transitional provisions: the Legislative Reform (Consumer Credit) Order 2008, SI 2008/2826, art 5, provides that this section as amended by SI 2008/2826, art 4 (as noted above), applies to agreements whenever made and that it has effect in relation to agreements made before 1 October 2008, as if the period mentioned in sub-s (1B) were a period beginning no later than 1 October 2008 and ending no later than 30 September 2009; and sub-s (1C) did not apply. Accordingly, s 77A prior to the amendments made by SI 2008/2826, art 4, read as follows:

"[77A Statements to be provided in relation to fixed-sum credit agreements

(1) The creditor under a regulated agreement for fixed-sum credit—

  (a) shall, within the period of one year beginning with the day after the day on which the agreement is made, give the debtor a statement under this section; and

  (b) after the giving of that statement, shall give the debtor further statements under this section at intervals of not more than one year.

(2) Regulations may make provision about the form and content of statements under this section.

(3) The debtor shall have no liability to pay any sum in connection with the preparation or the giving to him of a statement under this section.

(4) The creditor is not required to give the debtor any statement under this section once the following conditions are satisfied—

  (a) that there is no sum payable under the agreement by the debtor; and

  (b) that there is no sum which will or may become so payable.

(5) Subsection (6) applies if at a time before the conditions mentioned in subsection (4) are satisfied the creditor fails to give the debtor—

  (a) a statement under this section within the period mentioned in subsection (1)(a); or

  (b) such a statement within the period of one year beginning with the day after the day on which such a statement was last given to him.

(6) Where this subsection applies in relation to a failure to give a statement under this section to the debtor—

  (a) the creditor shall not be entitled to enforce the agreement during the period of non-compliance;

  (b) the debtor shall have no liability to pay any sum of interest to the extent calculated by reference to the period of non-compliance or to any part of it; and

  (c) the debtor shall have no liability to pay any default sum which (apart from this paragraph)—

    (i) would have become payable during the period of non-compliance; or

    (ii) would have become payable after the end of that period in connection with a breach of the agreement which occurs during that period (whether or not the breach continues after the end of that period).

(7) In this section "the period of non-compliance" means, in relation to a failure to give a statement under this section to the debtor, the period which—

  (a) begins immediately after the end of the period mentioned in paragraph (a) or (as the case may be) paragraph (b) of subsection (5); and

  (b) ends at the end of the day on which the statement is given to the debtor or on which the conditions mentioned in subsection (4) are satisfied, whichever is earlier.

(8) This section does not apply in relation to a non-commercial agreement or to a small agreement.]".

Regulations: the Consumer Credit (Information Requirements and Duration of Licences and Charges) Regulations 2007, SI 2007/1167 at **[2.399]**; the Consumer Credit (Information Requirements and Duration of Licences and Charges) (Amendment) Regulations 2008, SI 2008/1751; the Consumer Credit (Green Deal) Regulations 2012, SI 2012/2798 at **[2.967]**; the Consumer Credit (Information Requirements and Duration of Licences and Charges) (Amendment) Regulations 2014, SI 2014/2369.

[1.569]
[77B Fixed-sum credit agreement: statement of account to be provided on request

(1) This section applies to a regulated consumer credit agreement—

  (a) which is for fixed-sum credit,

  (b) which is of fixed duration,

  (c) where the credit is repayable in instalments by the debtor, and

  (d) which is not an excluded agreement.

(2) Upon a request from the debtor, the creditor must as soon as reasonably practicable give to the debtor a statement in writing which complies with subsections (3) to (5).

(3) The statement must include a table showing the details of each instalment owing under the agreement as at the date of the request.

(4) Details to be provided under subsection (3) must include—

  (a) the date on which the instalment is due,

  (b) the amount of the instalment,

  (c) any conditions relating to payment of the instalment, and

  (d) a breakdown of the instalment showing how much of it is made up of capital repayment, interest payment and other charges.

(5) Where the rate of interest is variable or the charges under the agreement may be varied, the statement must also indicate clearly and concisely that the information in the table is valid only until the rate of interest or charges are varied.

(6) The debtor may make a request under subsection (2) at any time that the agreement is in force unless a previous request has been made less than a month before and has been complied with.

(7) The debtor shall have no liability to pay any sum in connection with the preparation or the giving of a statement under this section.

[(7A) Subsection (7B) applies if the regulated agreement is a green deal plan . . .

(7B) The duty imposed on the creditor by this section may be discharged by another person acting on the creditor's behalf.]

(8) A breach of the duty imposed by this section is actionable as a breach of statutory duty.

(9) For the purposes of this section, an agreement is an excluded agreement if it is—

  (a) an agreement secured on land,

  (b) an agreement under which a person takes an article in pawn,

(c) an agreement under which the creditor provides the debtor with credit which exceeds £60,260 [and which is not a residential renovation agreement], or

(d) an agreement entered into by the debtor wholly or predominantly for the purpose of a business carried on, or intended to be carried on, by him.

[(10) Article 60C(5) and (6) of the Regulated Activities Order applies for the purposes of subsection (9)(d).]]

NOTES

Inserted by the Consumer Credit (EU Directive) Regulations 2010, SI 2010/1010, regs 2, 26, as from 1 February 2011, with effect in relation to certain agreements before that date, as provided for in regs 100–101A of the 2010 Regulations at **[2.803]–[2.805]**.

Sub-ss (7A), (7B): inserted by the Energy Act 2011, s 27(1), (4), as from 28 January 2013; words omitted from sub-para (7A) repealed by the Consumer Credit Act 1974 (Green Deal) (Amendment) Order 2014, SI 2014/436, art 8(2), as from 28 February 2014, except in relation to a green deal plan (within the meaning of the Energy Act 2011, s 1) made before that date; see art 1(3) thereof.

Sub-s (9): in sub-para (c) words in square brackets inserted by the Mortgage Credit Directive Order 2015, SI 2015/910, art 3, Sch 1, Pt 1, para 2(1), (8), as from 21 March 2016 (note that the 2015 Order also comes into force on 20 April 2015 and 21 December 2015 for limited other purposes, and for transitional provisions, see Part 4 of that Order at **[2.1194]** et seq).

Sub-s (10): substituted by the Financial Services and Markets Act 2000 (Regulated Activities) (Amendment) (No 2) Order 2013, SI 2013/1881, art 20(1), (29), as from 26 July 2013 (certain purposes), and as from 1 April 2014 (remaining purposes), for transitional provisions see Pt 8 thereof at **[2.1007]** et seq.

[1.570]
78 Duty to give information to debtor under running-account credit agreement
(1) The creditor under a regulated agreement for running-account credit, within the prescribed period after receiving a request in writing to that effect from the debtor and payment of a fee of [£1], shall give the debtor a copy of the executed agreement (if any) and of any other document referred to in it, together with a statement signed by or on behalf of the creditor showing, according to the information to which it is practicable for him to refer,—

(a) the state of the account, and

(b) the amount, if any, currently payable under the agreement by the debtor to the creditor, and

(c) the amounts and due dates of any payments which, if the debtor does not draw further on the account, will later become payable under the agreement by the debtor to the creditor.

(2) If the creditor possesses insufficient information to enable him to ascertain the amounts and dates mentioned in subsection (1)(c), he shall be taken to comply with that paragraph if his statement under subsection (1) gives the basis on which, under the regulated agreement, they would fall to be ascertained.

(3) Subsection (1) does not apply to—

(a) an agreement under which no sum is, or will or may become, payable by the debtor, or

(b) a request made less than one month after a previous request under that subsection relating to the same agreement was complied with.

(4) Where running-account credit is provided under a regulated agreement, the creditor shall give the debtor statements in the prescribed form, and with the prescribed contents—

(a) showing according to the information to which it is practicable for him to refer, the state of the account at regular intervals of not more than twelve months, and

(b) where the agreement provides, in relation to specified periods, for the making of payments by the debtor, or the charging against him of interest or any other sum, showing according to the information to which it is practicable for him to refer the state of the account at the end of each of those periods during which there is any movement in the account.

[(4A) Regulations may require a statement under subsection (4) to contain also information in the prescribed terms about the consequences of the debtor—

(a) failing to make payments as required by the agreement; or

(b) only making payments of a prescribed description in prescribed circumstances.]

(5) A statement under subsection (4) shall be given within the prescribed period after the end of the period to which the statement relates.

(6) If the creditor under an agreement fails to comply with subsection (1)—

(a) he is not entitled, while the default continues, to enforce the agreement; . . .

(b) . . .

(7) This section does not apply to a non-commercial agreement, and subsections [(4) to (5)] do not apply to a small agreement.

NOTES

Sub-s (1): sum in square brackets substituted by the Consumer Credit (Further Increase in Monetary Amounts) Order 1998, SI 1998/997, art 3, Schedule, as from 1 May 1998.

Sub-s (4A): inserted by the Consumer Credit Act 2006, s 7(1), as from 16 June 2006, subject to transitional provisions in s 69(1) of, and Sch 3, paras 1, 3 to, that Act at **[1.1945]**, **[1.1947]**.

Sub-s (6): words omitted repealed by the Consumer Protection from Unfair Trading Regulations 2008, SI 2008/1277, reg 30(1), (3), Sch 2, Pt 1, paras 17, 20, Sch 4, as from 26 May 2008.

Sub-s (7): words in square brackets substituted by the Consumer Credit Act 2006, s 7(2), as from 16 June 2006.

Regulations: the Consumer Credit (Prescribed Periods for Giving Information) Regulations 1983, SI 1983/1569; the Consumer Credit (Running-Account Credit) Information Regulations 1983, SI 1983/1570; the Consumer Credit

(Information Requirements and Duration of Licences and Charges) Regulations 2007, SI 2007/1167 at **[2.399]**; the Consumer Credit (Information Requirements and Duration of Licences and Charges) (Amendment) Regulations 2008, SI 2008/1751.

[1.571]
[78A Duty to give information to debtor on change of rate of interest
(1)   Where the rate of interest charged under a regulated consumer credit agreement, other than an excluded agreement, is to be varied, the creditor must inform the debtor in writing of the matters mentioned in subsection (3) before the variation can take effect.
(2)   But subsection (1) does not apply where—
  (a)   the agreement provides that the creditor is to inform the debtor in writing periodically of the matters mentioned in subsection (3) in relation to any variation, at such times as may be provided for in the agreement,
  (b)   the agreement provides that the rate of interest is to vary according to a reference rate,
  (c)   the reference rate is publicly available,
  (d)   information about the reference rate is available on the premises of the creditor, and
  (e)   the variation of the rate of interest results from a change to the reference rate.
(3)   The matters referred to in subsections (1) and (2)(a) are—
  (a)   the variation in the rate of interest,
  (b)   the amount of any payments that are to be made after the variation has effect, if different, expressed as a sum of money where practicable, and
  (c)   if the number or frequency of payments changes as a result of the variation, the new number or frequency.
(4)   In the case of an agreement mentioned in subsection (5) this section applies as follows—
  (a)   the obligation in subsection (1) only applies if the rate of interest increases, and
  (b)   subsection (3) is to be read as if paragraphs (b) and (c) were omitted.
(5)   The agreements referred to in subsection (4) are—
  (a)   an authorised business overdraft agreement,
  (b)   an authorised non-business overdraft agreement, or
  (c)   an agreement which would be an authorised non-business overdraft agreement but for the fact that the credit is not repayable on demand or within three months.
(6)   For the purposes of this section an agreement is an excluded agreement if it is—
  (a)   a debtor-creditor agreement arising where the holder of a current account overdraws on the account without a pre-arranged overdraft or exceeds a pre-arranged overdraft limit, or
  (b)   an agreement secured on land.]

NOTES
Inserted by the Consumer Credit (EU Directive) Regulations 2010, SI 2010/1010, regs 2, 27, as from 1 February 2011, with effect in relation to certain agreements before that date, as provided for in regs 100–101A of the 2010 Regulations at **[2.803]–[2.805]**.

[1.572]
79   Duty to give hirer information
(1)   The owner under a regulated consumer hire agreement, within the prescribed period after receiving a request in writing to that effect from the hirer and payment of a fee of [£1], shall give to the hirer a copy of the executed agreement and of any other document referred to in it, together with a statement signed by or on behalf of the owner showing, according to the information to which it is practicable for him to refer, the total sum which has become payable under the agreement by the hirer but remains unpaid and the various amounts comprised in that total sum, with the date when each became due.
(2)   Subsection (1) does not apply to—
  (a)   an agreement under which no sum is, or will or may become, payable by the hirer, or
  (b)   a request made less than one month after a previous request under that subsection relating to the same agreement was complied with.
(3)   If the owner under an agreement fails to comply with subsection (1)—
  (a)   he is not entitled, while the default continues, to enforce the agreement; . . .
  (b)   . . .
(4)   This section does not apply to a non-commercial agreement.

NOTES
Sub-s (1): sum in square brackets substituted by the Consumer Credit (Further Increase in Monetary Amounts) Order 1998, SI 1998/997, art 3, Schedule, as from 1 May 1998.
Sub-s (3): words omitted repealed by the Consumer Protection from Unfair Trading Regulations 2008, SI 2008/1277, reg 30(1), (3), Sch 2, Pt 1, paras 17, 21, Sch 4, as from 26 May 2008.
Regulations: the Consumer Credit (Prescribed Periods for Giving Information) Regulations 1983, SI 1983/1569.

[1.573]
80 Debtor or hirer to give information about goods
(1) Where a regulated agreement, other than a non-commercial agreement, requires the debtor or hirer to keep goods to which the agreement relates in his possession or control, he shall, within seven working days after he has received a request in writing to that effect from the creditor or owner, tell the creditor or owner where the goods are.
(2) If the debtor or hirer fails to comply with subsection (1), and the default continues for 14 days, he commits an offence.

[1.574]
81 Appropriation of payments
(1) Where a debtor or hirer is liable to make to the same person payments in respect of two or more regulated agreements, he shall be entitled, on making any payment in respect of the agreements which is not sufficient to discharge the total amount then due under all the agreements, to appropriate the sum so paid by him—
   (a)   in or towards the satisfaction of the sum due under any one of the agreements, or
   (b)   in or towards the satisfaction of the sums due under any two or more of the agreements in such proportions as he thinks fit.
(2)   If the debtor or hirer fails to make any such appropriation where one or more of the agreements is—
   (a)   a hire-purchase agreement or conditional sale agreement, or
   (b)   a consumer hire agreement, or
   (c)   an agreement in relation to which any security is provided,
the payment shall be appropriated towards the satisfaction of the sums due under the several agreements respectively in the proportions which those sums bear to one another.

NOTES
   Repealed by the Financial Services and Markets Act 2000 (Regulated Activities) (Amendment) (No 2) Order 2013, SI 2013/1881, art 20(1), (30), as from 26 July 2013 (certain purposes), and as from 1 April 2014 (remaining purposes), for transitional provisions see Pt 8 thereof at **[2.1007]** et seq (kept for reference only).

[1.575]
82 Variation of agreements
(1) Where, under a power contained in a regulated agreement, the creditor or owner varies the agreement, the variation shall not take effect before notice of it is given to the debtor or hirer in the prescribed manner.
[(1A) Subsection (1) does not apply to a variation in the rate of interest charged under an agreement not secured on land (see section 78A).
(1B) Subsection (1) does not apply to a variation in the rate of interest charged under an agreement secured on land if—
   (a)   the agreement falls within subsection (1D), and
   (b)   the variation is a reduction in the rate.
(1C) Subsection (1) does not apply to a variation in any other charge under an agreement if—
   (a)   the agreement falls within subsection (1D), and
   (b)   the variation is a reduction in the charge.
(1D) The agreements referred to in subsections (1B) and (1C) are—
   (a)   an authorised business overdraft agreement,
   (b)   an authorised non-business overdraft agreement, or
   (c)   an agreement which would be an authorised non-business overdraft agreement but for the fact that the credit is not repayable on demand or within three months.
(1E) Subsection (1) does not apply to a debtor-creditor agreement arising where the holder of a current account overdraws on the account without a pre-arranged overdraft or exceeds a pre-arranged overdraft limit.]
(2) Where an agreement (a "modifying agreement") varies or supplements an earlier agreement, the modifying agreement shall for the purposes of this Act be treated as—
   (a)   revoking the earlier agreement, and
   (b)   containing provisions reproducing the combined effect of the two agreements,
and obligations outstanding in relation to the earlier agreement shall accordingly be treated as outstanding instead in relation to the modifying agreement.
[(2A) Subsection (2) does not apply if [the earlier agreement or] the modifying agreement is an exempt agreement . . .]
[(2B) Subsection (2) does not apply if the modifying agreement varies—
   (a)   the amount of the repayment to be made under the earlier agreement, or
   (b)   the duration of the agreement,
as a result of the discharge of part of the debtor's indebtedness under the earlier agreement by virtue of section 94(3).]
(3) If the earlier agreement is a regulated agreement but (apart from this subsection) the modifying agreement is not then, [unless the modifying agreement is—
   (a)   for running account credit; or

(b)   an exempt agreement . . . ,

it shall be treated as a regulated agreement.]

(4)   If the earlier agreement is a regulated agreement for running-account credit, and by the modifying agreement the creditor allows the credit limit to be exceeded but intends the excess to be merely temporary, Part V (except section 56) shall not apply to the modifying agreement.

(5)   If—

     (a)   the earlier agreement is a cancellable agreement, and

     (b)   the modifying agreement is made within the period applicable under section 68 to the earlier agreement,

then, whether or not the modifying agreement would, apart from this subsection, be a cancellable agreement, it shall be treated as a cancellable agreement in respect of which a notice may be served under section 68 not later than the end of the period applicable under that section to the earlier agreement.

[(5A)   Subsection (5) does not apply where the modifying agreement is an exempt agreement . . .]

(6)   Except under subsection (5), a modifying agreement shall not be treated as a cancellable agreement.

[(6A)   If—

     (a)   the earlier agreement is an agreement to which section 66A (right of withdrawal) applies, and

     (b)   the modifying agreement is made within the period during which the debtor may give notice of withdrawal from the earlier agreement (see section 66A(2)),

then, whether or not the modifying agreement would, apart from this subsection, be an agreement to which section 66A applies, it shall be treated as such an agreement in respect of which notice may be given under subsection (2) of that section within the period referred to in paragraph (b) above.

(6B)   Except as provided for under subsection (6A) section 66A does not apply to a modifying agreement.]

(7)   This section does not apply to a non-commercial agreement.

[(8)   In this section, an "exempt agreement" means an agreement which is an exempt agreement for the purposes of Chapter 14A of Part 2 of the Regulated Activities Order by virtue of article 60C(2) (regulated mortgage contracts and regulated home purchase plans) or article 60D (exemption relating to the purchase of land for non-residential purposes) of that Order.]

NOTES

Sub-ss (1A)–(1E): inserted by the Consumer Credit (EU Directive) Regulations 2010, SI 2010/1010, regs 2, 28, as from 1 February 2011, with effect in relation to certain agreements before that date, as provided for in regs 100–101A of the 2010 Regulations at **[2.803]–[2.805]**.

Sub-s (2A): inserted by the Financial Services and Markets Act 2000 (Consequential Amendments) Order 2005, SI 2005/2967, art 2(1), (2), as from 16 November 2005; words in first pair of square brackets inserted by the Financial Services and Markets Act 2000 (Consequential Amendments) Order 2008, SI 2008/733, art 2, as from 6 April 2008; words omitted repealed by Financial Services and Markets Act 2000 (Regulated Activities) (Amendment) (No 2) Order 2013, SI 2013/1881, art 20(1), (31)(a), as from 26 July 2013 (certain purposes), and as from 1 April 2014 (remaining purposes), for transitional provisions see Pt 8 thereof at **[2.1007]** et seq.

Sub-s (2B): inserted by SI 2010/1010, regs 2, 29, as from 1 February 2011, with effect in relation to certain agreements before that date as provided for in regs 100–101A of the 2010 Regulations at **[2.803]–[2.805]**.

Sub-s (3): words in square brackets substituted by SI 2005/2967, art 2(1), (3), as from 16 November 2005; words omitted therein repealed by SI 2013/1881, art 20(1), (31)(b), as from 26 July 2013 (certain purposes), and as from 1 April 2014 (remaining purposes), for transitional provisions see Pt 8 thereof at **[2.1007]** et seq.

Sub-s (5A): inserted by SI 2005/2967, art 2(1), (4), as from 16 November 2005; words omitted repealed by SI 2013/1881, art 20(1), (31)(c), as from 26 July 2013 (certain purposes), and as from 1 April 2014 (remaining purposes), for transitional provisions see Pt 8 thereof at **[2.1007]** et seq.

Sub-ss (6A), (6B): inserted by SI 2010/1010, regs 2, 15, as from 1 February 2011, with effect in relation to certain agreements before that date, as provided for in regs 101, 101A of the 2010 Regulations at **[2.804]**, **[2.805]**.

Sub-s (8): added by SI 2013/1881, art 20(1), (31)(d), as from 26 July 2013 (certain purposes), and as from 1 April 2014 (remaining purposes), for transitional provisions see Pt 8 thereof at **[2.1007]** et seq.

Regulations: the Consumer Credit (Notice of Variation of Agreements) Regulations 1977, SI 1977/328; the Consumer Credit (Notice of Variation of Agreements) (Amendment) Regulations 1979, SI 1979/661; the Consumer Credit (Notice of Variation of Agreements) (Amendment No 2) Regulations 1979, SI 1979/667.

[1.576]

[82A   Assignment of rights

(1)   Where rights of a creditor under a regulated consumer credit agreement are assigned to a third party, the assignee must arrange for notice of the assignment to be given to the debtor—

     (a)   as soon as reasonably possible, or

     (b)   if, after the assignment, the arrangements for servicing the credit under the agreement do not change as far as the debtor is concerned, on or before the first occasion that they do.

(2)   This section does not apply to an agreement secured on land.]

NOTES

Inserted by the Consumer Credit (EU Directive) Regulations 2010, SI 2010/1010, regs 2, 36, as from 1 February 2011, with effect in relation to certain agreements before that date, as provided for in regs 100–101A of the 2010 Regulations at

[2.803]–[2.805]; repealed by the Financial Services and Markets Act 2000 (Regulated Activities) (Amendment) (No 2) Order 2013, SI 2013/1881, art 20(1), (32), as from 26 July 2013 (certain purposes), and as from 1 April 2014 (remaining purposes), for transitional provisions see Pt 8 thereof at **[2.1007]** et seq (kept for reference only).

[1.577]

83 Liability for misuse of credit facilities

(1) The debtor under a regulated consumer credit agreement shall not be liable to the creditor for any loss arising from use of the credit facility by another person not acting, or to be treated as acting, as the debtor's agent.

(2) This section does not apply to a non-commercial agreement, or to any loss in so far as it arises from misuse of an instrument to which section 4 of the Cheques Act 1957 applies.

[1.578]

84 Misuse of credit-tokens

(1) Section 83 does not prevent the debtor under a credit-token agreement from being made liable to the extent of [£50] (or the credit limit if lower) for loss to the creditor arising from use of the credit-token by other persons during a period beginning when the credit-token ceases to be in the possession of any authorised person and ending when the credit-token is once more in the possession of an authorised person.

(2) Section 83 does not prevent the debtor under a credit-token agreement from being made liable to any extent for loss to the creditor from use of the credit-token by a person who acquired possession of it with the debtor's consent.

(3) Subsections (1) and (2) shall not apply to any use of the credit-token after the creditor has been given oral or written notice that it is lost or stolen, or is for any other reason liable to misuse.

[(3A), (3B) . . .]

[(3C) . . .]

(4) Subsections (1) and (2) shall not apply unless there are contained in the credit-token agreement in the prescribed manner particulars of the name, address and telephone number of a person stated to be the person to whom notice is to be given under subsection (3).

(5) Notice under subsection (3) takes effect when received, but where it is given orally, and the agreement so requires, it shall be treated as not taking effect if not confirmed in writing within seven days.

(6) Any sum paid by the debtor for the issue of the credit-token, to the extent (if any) that it has not been previously offset by use made of the credit token, shall be treated as paid towards satisfaction of any liability under subsection (1) or (2).

(7) The debtor, the creditor, and any person authorised by the debtor to use the credit-token, shall be authorised persons for the purposes of subsection (1).

(8) Where two or more credit-tokens are given under one credit-token agreement, the preceding provisions of this section apply to each credit-token separately.

NOTES

Sub-s (1): sum in square brackets substituted by the Consumer Credit (Further Increase in Monetary Amounts) Order 1998, SI 1998/997, art 3, Schedule, as from 1 May 1998.

Sub-ss (3A), (3B): inserted by the Consumer Protection (Distance Selling) Regulations 2000, SI 2000/2334, reg 21(5), as from 31 October 2000 and repealed by virtue of the Payment Services Regulations 2009, SI 2009/209, reg 126, Sch 6, Pt 2, para 3, as from 1 November 2009.

Sub-s (3C): inserted by the Financial Services (Distance Marketing) Regulations 2004, SI 2004/2095, reg 14(4), as from 31 October 2004 (in relation to distance contracts made on or after that date) and repealed by virtue of the Payment Services Regulations 2009, SI 2009/209, reg 126, Sch 6, Pt 2, para 5(c), as from 1 November 2009.

Regulations: the Consumer Credit (Credit-Token Agreements) Regulations 1983, SI 1983/1555.

[1.579]

85 Duty on issue of new credit-tokens

(1) Whenever, in connection with a credit-token agreement, a credit-token (other than the first) is given by the creditor to the debtor, the creditor shall give the debtor a copy of the executed agreement (if any) and of any other document referred to in it.

(2) If the creditor fails to comply with this section—

    (a) he is not entitled, while the default continues, to enforce the agreement; . . .

    (b) . . .

(3) This section does not apply to a small agreement.

NOTES

Sub-s (2): words omitted repealed by the Consumer Protection from Unfair Trading Regulations 2008, SI 2008/1277, reg 30(1), (3), Sch 2, Pt 1, paras 17, 22, Sch 4, as from 26 May 2008.

[1.580]

86 Death of debtor or hirer

(1) The creditor or owner under a regulated agreement is not entitled, by reason of the death of the debtor or hirer, to do an act specified in paragraphs (a) to (e) of section 87(1) if at the death the agreement is fully secured.

(2) If at the death of the debtor or hirer a regulated agreement is only partly secured or is unsecured, the creditor or owner is entitled, by reason of the death of the debtor or hirer, to do an act specified in paragraphs (a) to (e) of section 87(1) on an order of the court only.

(3) This section applies in relation to the termination of an agreement only where—

   (a) a period for its duration is specified in the agreement, and

   (b) that period has not ended when the creditor or owner purports to terminate the agreement,

but so applies notwithstanding that, under the agreement, any party is entitled to terminate it before the end of the period so specified.

(4) This section does not prevent the creditor from treating the right to draw on any credit as restricted or deferred, and taking such steps as may be necessary to make the restriction or deferment effective.

(5) This section does not affect the operation of any agreement providing for payment of sums—

   (a) due under the regulated agreement, or

   (b) becoming due under it on the death of the debtor or hirer,

out of the proceeds of a policy of assurance on his life.

(6) For the purposes of this section an act is done by reason of the death of the debtor or hirer if it is done under a power conferred by the agreement which is—

   (a) exercisable on his death, or

   (b) exercisable at will and exercised at any time after his death.

PART VII
DEFAULT AND TERMINATION

[Information sheets

[1.581]
86A [FCA] to prepare information sheets on arrears and default

(1) The [FCA shall prepare and issue] an arrears information sheet and a default information sheet.

(2) The arrears information sheet shall include information to help debtors and hirers who receive notices under section 86B or 86C

(3) The default information sheet shall include information to help debtors and hirers who receive default notices.

(4) Regulations may make provision about the information to be included in an information sheet.

(5) An information sheet takes effect for the purposes of this Part at the end of the period of three months beginning with the day on which [it is issued] [or on such later date as the FCA may specify in relation to the information sheet].

[(6) If the FCA revises an information sheet after it has been issued, it shall issue the revised information sheet.]

(7) A revised information sheet takes effect for the purposes of this Part at the end of the period of three months beginning with the day on which [it is issued] [or on such later date as the FCA may specify in relation to the information sheet].]

NOTES

Inserted, together with preceding cross-heading, by the Consumer Credit Act 2006, s 8, as from 31 January 2006, subject to transitional provisions in s 69(1) of, and Sch 3, paras 1, 5 to, that Act at **[1.1945]**, **[1.1947]**.

Section heading, sub-s (1): words in square brackets substituted by the Financial Services Act 2012 (Consumer Credit) Order 2013, SI 2013/1882, art 7(1), (6), (7)(a), as from 26 July 2013 (certain purposes), and as from 1 April 2014 (remaining purposes).

Sub-s (5): words in first pair of square brackets substituted by SI 2013/1882, art 7(1), (7)(b), as from 26 July 2013 (certain purposes), and as from 1 April 2014 (remaining purposes); words in second pair of square brackets inserted by the Financial Services and Markets Act 2000 (Regulated Activities) (Amendment) Order 2014, SI 2014/366, art 3(1), (2), as from 14 February 2014 (for certain purposes), and as from 1 April 2014 (remaining purposes).

Sub-s (6): substituted by SI 2013/1882, art 7(1), (7)(c), as from 26 July 2013 (certain purposes), and as from 1 April 2014 (remaining purposes).

Sub-s (7): words in first pair of square brackets substituted by SI 2013/1882, art 7(1), (7)(d), as from 26 July 2013 (certain purposes), and as from 1 April 2014 (remaining purposes); words in second pair of square brackets inserted by SI 2014/366, art 3(1), (2).

[Sums in arrears and default sums

[1.582]
86B Notice of sums in arrears under fixed-sum credit agreements etc

(1) This section applies where at any time the following conditions are satisfied—

   (a) that the debtor or hirer under an applicable agreement is required to have made at least two payments under the agreement before that time;

   (b) that the total sum paid under the agreement by him is less than the total sum which he is required to have paid before that time;

   (c) that the amount of the shortfall is no less than the sum of the last two payments which he is required to have made before that time;

   (d) that the creditor or owner is not already under a duty to give him notices under this section in relation to the agreement; and

(e) if a judgment has been given in relation to the agreement before that time, that there is no sum still to be paid under the judgment by the debtor or hirer.

(2) The creditor or owner—

    (a) shall, within the period of 14 days beginning with the day on which the conditions mentioned in subsection (1) are satisfied, give the debtor or hirer a notice under this section; and

    (b) after the giving of that notice, shall give him further notices under this section at intervals of not more than six months.

(3) The duty of the creditor or owner to give the debtor or hirer notices under this section shall cease when either of the conditions mentioned in subsection (4) is satisfied; but if either of those conditions is satisfied before the notice required by subsection (2)(a) is given, the duty shall not cease until that notice is given.

(4) The conditions referred to in subsection (3) are—

    (a) that the debtor or hirer ceases to be in arrears;

    (b) that a judgment is given in relation to the agreement under which a sum is required to be paid by the debtor or hirer.

(5) For the purposes of subsection (4)(a) the debtor or hirer ceases to be in arrears when—

    (a) no [payments], which he has ever failed to [make] under the agreement when required, [are] still owing;

    (b) no default sum, which has ever become payable under the agreement in connection with his failure to pay any sum under the agreement when required, is still owing;

    (c) no sum of interest, which has ever become payable under the agreement in connection with such a default sum, is still owing; and

    (d) no other sum of interest, which has ever become payable under the agreement in connection with his failure to pay any sum under the agreement when required, is still owing.

(6) A notice under this section shall include a copy of the current arrears information sheet under section 86A.

(7) The debtor or hirer shall have no liability to pay any sum in connection with the preparation or the giving to him of a notice under this section.

(8) Regulations may make provision about the form and content of notices under this section.

(9) In the case of an applicable agreement under which the debtor or hirer must make all payments he is required to make at intervals of one week or less, this section shall have effect as if in subsection (1)(a) and (c) for "two" there were substituted "four".

(10) If an agreement mentioned in subsection (9) was made before the beginning of the relevant period, only amounts resulting from failures by the debtor or hirer to make payments he is required to have made during that period shall be taken into account in determining any shortfall for the purposes of subsection (1)(c).

(11) In subsection (10) "relevant period" means the period of 20 weeks ending with the day on which the debtor or hirer is required to have made the most recent payment under the agreement.

[(12) In this section "applicable agreement" means an agreement which falls within subsection (12A) or (12B).

(12A) An agreement falls within this subsection if—

    (a) it is a regulated agreement for fixed-sum credit; and

    (b) it is not—

        (i) a non-commercial agreement;

        (ii) a small agreement; or

        (iii) a green deal plan . . .

(12B) An agreement falls within this subsection if—

    (a) it is a regulated consumer hire agreement; and

    (b) it is neither a non-commercial agreement nor a small agreement.]

[(13) In this section—

    (a) "payments" in relation to an applicable agreement which is a regulated agreement for fixed-sum credit means payments to be made at predetermined intervals provided for under the terms of the agreement; and

    (b) "payments" in relation to an applicable agreement which is a regulated consumer hire agreement means any payments to be made by the hirer in relation to any period in consideration of the bailment or hiring to him of goods under the agreement.]]

NOTES

Inserted, together with preceding cross-heading, by the Consumer Credit Act 2006, s 9, as from 16 June 2006 (sub-s (8)) and as from 1 October 2008 (remainder), subject to transitional provisions in s 69(1) of, and Sch 3, paras 1, 6 to, that Act at **[1.1945]**, **[1.1947]**.

Sub-s (5): words in square brackets substituted by the Legislative Reform (Consumer Credit) Order 2008, SI 2008/2826, art 8(a), as from 31 October 2008.

Sub-ss (12), (12A), (12B): substituted for original sub-s (12) by the Energy Act 2011, s 28, as from 28 January 2013; in sub-s (12A) words omitted from para (b)(iii) repealed by the Consumer Credit Act 1974 (Green Deal) (Amendment) Order 2014, SI 2014/436, art 8(2), as from 28 February 2014, except in relation to a green deal plan (within the meaning of the Energy Act 2011, s 1) made before that date; see art 1(3) thereof.

Sub-s (13): added by SI 2008/2826, art 8(b), as from 31 October 2008.

Regulations: the Consumer Credit (Information Requirements and Duration of Licences and Charges) Regulations 2007, SI 2007/1167 at **[2.399]**; the Consumer Credit (Information Requirements and Duration of Licences and Charges) (Amendment) Regulations 2008, SI 2008/1751.

[1.583]
[86C Notice of sums in arrears under running-account credit agreements
(1) This section applies where at any time the following conditions are satisfied—
  (a) that the debtor under an applicable agreement is required to have made at least two payments under the agreement before that time;
  (b) that the last two payments which he is required to have made before that time have not been made;
  (c) that the creditor has not already been required to give a notice under this section in relation to either of those payments; and
  (d) if a judgment has been given in relation to the agreement before that time, that there is no sum still to be paid under the judgment by the debtor.
(2) The creditor shall, no later than the end of the period within which he is next required to give a statement under section 78(4) in relation to the agreement, give the debtor a notice under this section.
(3) The notice shall include a copy of the current arrears information sheet under section 86A.
(4) The notice may be incorporated in a statement or other notice which the creditor gives the debtor in relation to the agreement by virtue of another provision of this Act.
(5) The debtor shall have no liability to pay any sum in connection with the preparation or the giving to him of the notice.
(6) Regulations may make provision about the form and content of notices under this section.
(7) In this section "applicable agreement" means an agreement which—
  (a) is a regulated agreement for running-account credit; and
  (b) is neither a non-commercial agreement nor a small agreement.
[(8) In this section "payments" means payments to be made at predetermined intervals provided for under the terms of the agreement.]]

NOTES
Inserted by the Consumer Credit Act 2006, s 10, as from 16 June 2006 (sub-s (6)) and as from 1 October 2008 (remainder), subject to transitional provisions in s 69(1) of, and Sch 3, paras 1, 7 to, that Act at **[1.1945]**, **[1.1947]**.
Sub-s (8): added by the Legislative Reform (Consumer Credit) Order 2008, SI 2008/2826, art 9, as from 31 October 2008.
Regulations: the Consumer Credit (Information Requirements and Duration of Licences and Charges) Regulations 2007, SI 2007/1167 at **[2.399]**.

[1.584]
[86D Failure to give notice of sums in arrears
(1) This section applies where the creditor or owner under an agreement is under a duty to give the debtor or hirer notices under section 86B but fails to give him such a notice—
  (a) within the period mentioned in subsection (2)(a) of that section; or
  (b) within the period of six months beginning with the day after the day on which such a notice was last given to him.
(2) This section also applies where the creditor under an agreement is under a duty to give the debtor a notice under section 86C but fails to do so before the end of the period mentioned in subsection (2) of that section.
(3) The creditor or owner shall not be entitled to enforce the agreement during the period of non-compliance.
(4) The debtor or hirer shall have no liability to pay—
  (a) any sum of interest to the extent calculated by reference to the period of non-compliance or to any part of it; or
  (b) any default sum which (apart from this paragraph)—
    (i) would have become payable during the period of non-compliance; or
    (ii) would have become payable after the end of that period in connection with a breach of the agreement which occurs during that period (whether or not the breach continues after the end of that period).
(5) In this section "the period of non-compliance" means, in relation to a failure to give a notice under section 86B or 86C to the debtor or hirer, the period which—
  (a) begins immediately after the end of the period mentioned in (as the case may be) subsection (1)(a) or (b) or (2); and
  (b) ends at the end of the day mentioned in subsection (6).
(6) That day is—
  (a) in the case of a failure to give a notice under section 86B as mentioned in subsection (1)(a) of this section, the day on which the notice is given to the debtor or hirer;
  (b) in the case of a failure to give a notice under that section as mentioned in subsection (1)(b) of this section, the earlier of the following—
    (i) the day on which the notice is given to the debtor or hirer;

(ii)   the day on which the condition mentioned in subsection (4)(a) of that section is satisfied;

(c)   in the case of a failure to give a notice under section 86C, the day on which the notice is given to the debtor.]

NOTES
Inserted by the Consumer Credit Act 2006, s 11, as from 1 October 2008.

[1.585]
[86E   Notice of default sums

(1)   This section applies where a default sum becomes payable under a regulated agreement by the debtor or hirer.

(2)   The creditor or owner shall, within the prescribed period after the default sum becomes payable, give the debtor or hirer a notice under this section.

(3)   The notice under this section may be incorporated in a statement or other notice which the creditor or owner gives the debtor or hirer in relation to the agreement by virtue of another provision of this Act.

(4)   The debtor or hirer shall have no liability to pay interest in connection with the default sum to the extent that the interest is calculated by reference to a period occurring before the 29th day after the day on which the debtor or hirer is given the notice under this section.

(5)   If the creditor or owner fails to give the debtor or hirer the notice under this section within the period mentioned in subsection (2), he shall not be entitled to enforce the agreement until the notice is given to the debtor or hirer.

(6)   The debtor or hirer shall have no liability to pay any sum in connection with the preparation or the giving to him of the notice under this section.

(7)   Regulations may—
(a)   provide that this section does not apply in relation to a default sum which is less than a prescribed amount;
(b)   make provision about the form and content of notices under this section.

(8)   This section does not apply in relation to a non-commercial agreement or to a small agreement.]

NOTES
Inserted by the Consumer Credit Act 2006, s 12, as from 16 June 2006 (sub-s (2), for the purpose of prescribing the period referred to therein) and as from 1 October 2008 (remainder), subject to transitional provisions in s 69(1) of, and Sch 3, paras 1, 8 to, that Act at **[1.1945]**, **[1.1947]**.
Regulations: the Consumer Credit (Information Requirements and Duration of Licences and Charges) Regulations 2007, SI 2007/1167 at **[2.399]**.

[1.586]
[86F   Interest on default sums

(1)   This section applies where a default sum becomes payable under a regulated agreement by the debtor or hirer.

(2)   The debtor or hirer shall only be liable to pay interest in connection with the default sum if the interest is simple interest.]

NOTES
Inserted by the Consumer Credit Act 2006, s 13, as from 1 October 2008, subject to transitional provisions in s 69(1) of, and Sch 3, paras 1, 9 to, that Act at **[1.1945]**, **[1.1947]**.

Default notices

[1.587]
87   Need for default notice

(1)   Service of a notice on the debtor or hirer in accordance with section 88 (a "default notice") is necessary before the creditor or owner can become entitled, by reason of any breach by the debtor or hirer of a regulated agreement,—
(a)   to terminate the agreement, or
(b)   to demand earlier payment of any sum, or
(c)   to recover possession of any goods or land, or
(d)   to treat any right conferred on the debtor or hirer by the agreement as terminated, restricted or deferred, or
(e)   to enforce any security.

(2)   Subsection (1) does not prevent the creditor from treating the right to draw upon any credit as restricted or deferred, and taking such steps as may be necessary to make the restriction or deferment effective.

(3)   The doing of an act by which a floating charge becomes fixed is not enforcement of a security.

(4)   Regulations may provide that subsection (1) is not to apply to agreements described by the regulations.

[(5)   Subsection (1)(d) does not apply in a case referred to in section 98A(4) (termination or suspension of debtor's right to draw on credit under open-end agreement).]

NOTES

Sub-s (5): added by the Consumer Credit (EU Directive) Regulations 2010, SI 2010/1010, regs 2, 37, as from 1 February 2011, with effect in relation to certain agreements before that date, as provided for in regs 100–101A of the 2010 Regulations at **[2.803]–[2.805]**.

[1.588]
88 Contents and effect of default notice

(1)   The default notice must be in the prescribed form and specify—
   (a) the nature of the alleged breach;
   (b) if the breach is capable of remedy, what action is required to remedy it and the date before which that action is to be taken;
   (c) if the breach is not capable of remedy, the sum (if any) required to be paid as compensation for the breach, and the date before which it is to be paid.

(2)   A date specified under subsection (1) must not be less than [14] days after the date of service of the default notice, and the creditor or owner shall not take action such as is mentioned in section 87(1) before the date so specified or (if no requirement is made under subsection (1)) before those [14] days have elapsed.

(3)   The default notice must not treat as a breach failure to comply with a provision of the agreement which becomes operative only on breach of some other provision, but if the breach of that other provision is not duly remedied or compensation demanded under subsection (1) is not duly paid, or (where no requirement is made under subsection (1)) if the [14] days mentioned in subsection (2) have elapsed, the creditor or owner may treat the failure as a breach and section 87(1) shall not apply to it.

(4)   The default notice must contain information in the prescribed terms about the consequences of failure to comply with it [and any other prescribed matters relating to the agreement].

[(4A)   The default notice must also include a copy of the current default information sheet under section 86A.]

(5)   A default notice making a requirement under subsection (1) may include a provision for the taking of action such as is mentioned in section 87(1) at any time after the restriction imposed by subsection (2) will cease, together with a statement that the provision will be ineffective if the breach is duly remedied or the compensation duly paid.

NOTES

Sub-ss (2), (3): number in square brackets in each place it appears substituted by the Consumer Credit Act 2006, s 14(1), as from 1 October 2006, subject to transitional provisions in s 69(1) of, and Sch 3, paras 1, 10 to, that Act at **[1.1945]**, **[1.1947]**.

Sub-s (4): words in square brackets added by the Consumer Credit Act 2006, s 14(2), as from 16 June 2006, subject to transitional provisions in s 69(1) of, and Sch 3, paras 1, 2 to, that Act at **[1.1945]**, **[1.1947]**.

Sub-s (4A): inserted by the Consumer Credit Act 2006, s 14(3), as from 1 October 2008, subject to transitional provisions in s 69(1) of, and Sch 3, paras 1, 10 to, that Act at **[1.1945]**, **[1.1947]**.

Regulations: the Consumer Credit (Enforcement, Default and Termination Notices) Regulations 1983, SI 1983/1561; the Consumer Credit (Enforcement, Default and Termination Notices) (Amendment) Regulations 1984, SI 1984/1109; the Consumer Credit (Enforcement, Default and Termination Notices) (Amendment) Regulations 2004, SI 2004/3237; the Consumer Credit (Enforcement, Default and Termination Notices) (Amendment) Regulations 2006, SI 2006/3094; the Consumer Credit (Information Requirements and Duration of Licences and Charges) Regulations 2007, SI 2007/1167 at **[2.399]**.

[1.589]
89 Compliance with default notice

If before the date specified for that purpose in the default notice the debtor or hirer takes the action specified under section 88(1)(b) or (c) the breach shall be treated as not having occurred.

Further restriction of remedies for default

[1.590]
90 Retaking of protected hire-purchase etc goods

(1)   At any time when—
   (a) the debtor is in breach of a regulated hire-purchase or a regulated conditional sale agreement relating to goods, and
   (b) the debtor has paid to the creditor one-third or more of the total price of the goods, and
   (c) the property in the goods remains in the creditor,
the creditor is not entitled to recover possession of the goods from the debtor except on an order of the court.

(2)   Where under a hire-purchase or conditional sale agreement the creditor is required to carry out any installation and the agreement specifies, as part of the total price, the amount to be paid in respect of the installation (the "installation charge") the reference in subsection (1)(b) to one third of the total price shall be construed as a reference to the aggregate of the installation charge and one third of the remainder of the total price.

(3)   In a case where—
   (a) subsection (1)(a) is satisfied, but not subsection (1)(b), and

(b)   subsection (1)(b) was satisfied on a previous occasion in relation to an earlier agreement, being a regulated hire-purchase or regulated conditional sale agreement, between the same parties, and relating to any of the goods comprised in the later agreement (whether or not other goods were also included),

subsection (1) shall apply to the later agreement with the omission of paragraph (b).

(4)   If the later agreement is a modifying agreement, subsection (3) shall apply with the substitution, for the second reference to the later agreement, of a reference to the modifying agreement.

(5)   Subsection (1) shall not apply, or shall cease to apply, to an agreement if the debtor has terminated, or terminates, the agreement.

(6)   Where subsection (1) applies to an agreement at the death of the debtor, it shall continue to apply (in relation to the possessor of the goods) until the grant of probate or administration, or (in Scotland) confirmation (on which the personal representative would fall to be treated as the debtor).

(7)   Goods falling within this section are in this Act referred to as "protected goods".

[1.591]
91   Consequences of breach of s 90
If goods are recovered by the creditor in contravention of section 90—
   (a)   the regulated agreement, if not previously terminated, shall terminate, and
   (b)   the debtor shall be released from all liability under the agreement, and shall be entitled to recover from the creditor all sums paid by the debtor under the agreement.

[1.592]
92   Recovery of possession of goods or land
(1)   Except under an order of the court, the creditor or owner shall not be entitled to enter any premises to take possession of goods subject to a regulated hire-purchase agreement, regulated conditional sale agreement or regulated consumer hire agreement.

(2)   At any time when the debtor is in breach of a regulated conditional sale agreement relating to land, the creditor is entitled to recover possession of the land from the debtor, or any person claiming under him, on an order of the court only.

(3)   An entry in contravention of subsection (1) or (2) is actionable as a breach of statutory duty.

[1.593]
93   Interest not to be increased on default
The debtor under a regulated consumer credit agreement shall not be obliged to pay interest on sums which, in breach of the agreement, are unpaid by him at a rate—
   (a)   where the total charge for credit includes an item in respect of interest, exceeding the rate of that interest, or
   (b)   in any other case, exceeding what would be the rate of the total charge for credit if any items included in the total charge for credit by virtue of [rules made by the FCA under paragraph (2)(d) of article 60M of the Regulated Activities Order] were disregarded.

NOTES
   In para (b) words in square brackets substituted by the Financial Services and Markets Act 2000 (Regulated Activities) (Amendment) (No 2) Order 2013, SI 2013/1881, art 20(1), (33), as from 26 July 2013 (certain purposes), and as from 1 April 2014 (remaining purposes), for transitional provisions see Pt 8 thereof at **[2.1007]** et seq.

93A   *(Applies to Scotland only.)*

Early payment by debtor

[1.594]
94   Right to complete payments ahead of time
(1)   The debtor under a regulated consumer credit agreement is entitled at any time, by notice to the creditor and the payment to the creditor of all amounts payable by the debtor to him under the agreement [and any amount which the creditor claims under section 95A(2)] [or section 95B(2)] (less any rebate allowable under section 95), to discharge the debtor's indebtedness under the agreement.

(2)   A notice under subsection (1) may embody the exercise by the debtor of any option to purchase goods conferred on him by the agreement, and deal with any other matter arising on, or in relation to, the termination of the agreement.

[(3)   The debtor under a regulated consumer credit agreement, other than an agreement secured on land, is entitled at any time to discharge part of his indebtedness by taking the steps in subsection (4).

(4)   The steps referred to in subsection (3) are as follows—
   (a)   he provides notice to the creditor,
   (b)   he pays to the creditor some of the amount payable by him to the creditor under the agreement before the time fixed by the agreement, and
   (c)   he makes the payment—
        (i)   before the end of the period of 28 days beginning with the day following that on which notice under paragraph (a) was received by the creditor, or

      (ii)   on or before any later date specified in the notice.

(5)   Where a debtor takes the steps in subsection (4) his indebtedness shall be discharged by an amount equal to the sum of the amount paid and any rebate allowable under section 95 less any amount which the creditor claims under section 95A(2) [or section 95B(2)].

(6)   A notice—

    (a)   under subsection (1), other than a notice relating to a regulated consumer credit agreement secured on land, or

    (b)   under subsection (4)(a),

need not be in writing.]

NOTES

Sub-s (1): words in first pair of square brackets inserted by the Consumer Credit (EU Directive) Regulations 2010, SI 2010/1010, regs 2, 30(a), as from 1 February 2011, with effect in relation to certain agreements before that date, as provided for in regs 100–101A of the 2010 Regulations at **[2.803]–[2.805]**; words in second pair of square brackets inserted by the Energy Act 2011, s 29(1), (3)(a), as from 21 March 2012 (for certain purposes), and as from 28 January 2013 (for remaining purposes).

Sub-s (3): added, together with sub-ss (4)–(6), by SI 2010/1010, regs 2, 30(b), as from 1 February 2011, with effect in relation to certain agreements before that date, as provided for in regs 100–101A of the 2010 Regulations at **[2.803]–[2.805]**.

Sub-ss (4), (6): added as noted to sub-s (3) above.

Sub-s (5): added as noted to sub-s (3) above; words in square brackets inserted by the Energy Act 2011, s 29(1), (3)(b), as from 21 March 2012 (for certain purposes), and as from 28 January 2013 (for remaining purposes).

[1.595]

95   Rebate on early settlement

(1)   Regulations may provide for the allowance of a rebate of charges for credit to the debtor under a regulated consumer credit agreement where, under section 94, on refinancing, on breach of the agreement, or for any other reason, his indebtedness is discharged [or is discharged in part] or becomes payable before the time fixed by the agreement, or any sum becomes payable by him before the time so fixed.

(2)   Regulations under subsection (1) may provide for calculation of the rebate by reference to any sums paid or payable by the debtor or his relative under or in connection with the agreement (whether to the creditor or some other person), including sums under linked transactions and other items in the total charge for credit.

NOTES

Sub-s (1): words in square brackets inserted by the Consumer Credit (EU Directive) Regulations 2010, SI 2010/1010, regs 2, 31, as from 1 February 2011, with effect in relation to certain agreements before that date, as provided for in regs 100–101A of the 2010 Regulations at **[2.803]–[2.805]**.

Regulations: the Consumer Credit (Early Settlement) Regulations 2004, SI 2004/1483 at **[2.319]**; the Consumer Credit (Miscellaneous Amendments) Regulations 2004, SI 2004/2619; the Consumer Credit (Green Deal) Regulations 2012, SI 2012/2798 at **[2.967]**.

[1.596]

[95A   Compensatory amount

(1)   This section applies where—

    (a)   a regulated consumer credit agreement, other than an agreement secured on land, provides for the rate of interest on the credit to be fixed for a period of time, and

    (b)   under section 94 the debtor discharges all or part of his indebtedness during that period.

(2)   The creditor may claim an amount equal to the cost which the creditor has incurred as a result only of the debtor's indebtedness being discharged during that period if—

    (a)   the amount of the payment under section 94 exceeds £8,000 or, where more than one such payment is made in any 12 month period, the total of those payments exceeds £8,000,

    (b)   the agreement is not a debtor-creditor agreement enabling the debtor to overdraw on a current account, and

    (c)   the amount of the payment under section 94 is not paid from the proceeds of a contract of payment protection insurance.

(3)   The amount in subsection (2)—

    (a)   must be fair,

    (b)   must be objectively justified, and

    (c)   must not exceed whichever is the lower of—

        (i)   the relevant percentage of the amount of the payment under section 94, and

        (ii)   the total amount of interest that would have been paid by the debtor under the agreement in the period from the date on which the debtor makes the payment under section 94 to the date fixed by the agreement for the discharge of the indebtedness of the debtor.

(4)   In subsection (3)(c)(i) "relevant percentage" means—

    (a)   1%, where the period from the date on which the debtor makes the payment under section 94 to the date fixed by the agreement for the discharge of the indebtedness of the debtor is more than one year, or

    (b)   0.5%, where that period is equal to or less than one year.]

NOTES

Inserted by the Consumer Credit (EU Directive) Regulations 2010, SI 2010/1010, regs 2, 32 (as amended by the Consumer Credit (Amendment) Regulations 2011, SI 2011/11, regs 2, 3), as from 1 February 2011, with effect in relation to certain agreements before that date, as provided for in regs 100–101A of the 2010 Regulations at **[2.803]–[2.805]**.

[1.597]
[95B Compensatory amount: green deal finance
(1) This section applies where—
  (a) a regulated consumer credit agreement provides for the rate of interest on the credit to be fixed for a period of time ("the fixed rate period"),
  (b) the agreement is a green deal plan . . . which is of a duration specified for the purposes of this section in regulations, and
  (c) under section 94 the debtor discharges all or part of his indebtedness during the fixed rate period.
(2) The creditor may claim an amount equal to the cost which the creditor has incurred as a result only of the debtor's indebtedness being discharged during the fixed rate period if—
  (a) the amount of the payment under section 94 is not paid from the proceeds of a contract of payment protection insurance, and
  (b) such other conditions as may be specified for the purposes of this section in regulations are satisfied.
(3) The amount in subsection (2)—
  (a) must be fair,
  (b) must be objectively justified,
  (c) must be calculated by the creditor in accordance with provision made for the purposes of this section in regulations, and
  (d) must not exceed the total amount of interest that would have been paid by the debtor under the agreement in the period from the date on which the debtor makes the payment under section 94 to the date fixed by the agreement for the discharge of the indebtedness of the debtor.
(4) If a creditor could claim under either section 95A or this section, the creditor may choose under which section to claim.]

NOTES

Inserted by the Energy Act 2011, s 29(1), (2), as from 21 March 2012 (in so far as necessary for the purposes of interpreting the Energy Act 2011, ss 1–41 and enabling the exercise of any power under those sections to make an order or regulations or to issue a code of practice), and as from 28 January 2013 (otherwise).

Sub-s (1): words omitted from para (b) repealed by the Consumer Credit Act 1974 (Green Deal) (Amendment) Order 2014, SI 2014/436, art 8(2), as from 28 February 2014, except in relation to a green deal plan (within the meaning of the Energy Act 2011, s 1) made before that date; see art 1(3) thereof.

[1.598]
96 Effect on linked transactions
(1) Where for any reason the indebtedness of the debtor under a regulated consumer credit agreement is discharged before the time fixed by the agreement, he, and any relative of his, shall at the same time be discharged from any liability under a linked transaction, other than a debt which has already become payable.
(2) Subsection (1) does not apply to a linked transaction which is itself an agreement providing the debtor or his relative with credit.
(3) Regulations may exclude linked transactions of the prescribed description from the operation of subsection (1).

[1.599]
97 Duty to give information
(1) The creditor under a regulated consumer credit agreement, within the prescribed period after he has received a request . . . to that effect from the debtor, shall give the debtor a statement in the prescribed form indicating, according to the information to which it is practicable for him to refer, the amount of the payment required to discharge the debtor's indebtedness under the agreement, together with the prescribed particulars showing how the amount is arrived at.
(2) Subsection (1) does not apply to a request made less than one month after a previous request under that subsection relating to the same agreement was complied with.
[(2A) A request under subsection (1) need not be in writing unless the agreement is secured on land.]
(3) If the creditor fails to comply with subsection (1)—
  (a) he is not entitled, while the default continues, to enforce the agreement; . . .
  (b) . . .

Part 1 Statutes

NOTES

Sub-s (1): words omitted repealed by the Consumer Credit (EU Directive) Regulations 2010, SI 2010/1010, regs 2, 33(a), as from 1 February 2011, with effect in relation to certain agreements before that date, as provided for in regs 100–101A of the 2010 Regulations at **[2.803]–[2.805]**.

Sub-s (2A): inserted by SI 2010/1010, regs 2, 33(b), as from 1 February 2011, with effect in relation to certain agreements before that date, as provided for in regs 100–101A of the 2010 Regulations at **[2.803]–[2.805]**.

Sub-s (3): words omitted repealed by the Consumer Protection from Unfair Trading Regulations 2008, SI 2008/1277, reg 30(1), (3), Sch 2, Pt 1, paras 17, 23, Sch 4, as from 28 May 2008.

Regulations: the Consumer Credit (Settlement Information) Regulations 1983, SI 1983/1564; the Consumer Credit (Early Settlement) Regulations 2004, SI 2004/1483 at **[2.319]**; the Consumer Credit (Green Deal) Regulations 2012, SI 2012/2798 at **[2.967]**.

[1.600]

[97A   Duty to give information on partial repayment

(1)   Where a debtor under a regulated consumer credit agreement—

(a)   makes a payment by virtue of which part of his indebtedness is discharged under section 94, and

(b)   at the same time or subsequently requests the creditor to give him a statement concerning the effect of the payment on the debtor's indebtedness,

the creditor must give the statement to the debtor before the end of the period of seven working days beginning with the day following that on which the creditor receives the request.

(2)   The statement shall be in writing and shall contain the following particulars—

(a)   a description of the agreement sufficient to identify it,

(b)   the name, postal address and, where appropriate, any other address of the creditor and the debtor,

(c)   where the creditor is claiming an amount under section 95A(2) [or section 95B(2)], that amount and the method used to determine it,

(d)   the amount of any rebate to which the debtor is entitled—

(i)   under the agreement, or

(ii)   by virtue of section 95 where that is higher,

(e)   where the amount of the rebate mentioned in paragraph (d)(ii) is given, a statement indicating that this amount has been calculated having regard to the Consumer Credit (Early Settlement) Regulations 2004,

(f)   where the debtor is not entitled to any rebate, a statement to this effect,

(g)   any change to—

(i)   the number, timing or amount of repayments to be made under the agreement, or

(ii)   the duration of the agreement,

which results from the partial discharge of the indebtedness of the debtor, and

(h)   the amount of the debtor's indebtedness remaining under the agreement at the date the creditor gives the statement.]

NOTES

Inserted by the Consumer Credit (EU Directive) Regulations 2010, SI 2010/1010, regs 2, 34, as from 1 February 2011, with effect in relation to certain agreements before that date, as provided for in regs 100–101A of the 2010 Regulations at **[2.803]–[2.805]**.

Sub-s (2): words in square brackets in para (c) inserted by the Energy Act 2011, s 29(1), (4), as from 21 March 2012 (for certain purposes), and as from 28 January 2013 (for remaining purposes).

Termination of agreements

[1.601]

98   Duty to give notice of termination (non-default cases)

(1)   The creditor or owner is not entitled to terminate a regulated agreement except by or after giving the debtor or hirer not less than seven days' notice of the termination.

(2)   Subsection (1) applies only where—

(a)   a period for the duration of the agreement is specified in the agreement, and

(b)   that period has not ended when the creditor or owner does an act mentioned in subsection (1),

but so applies notwithstanding that, under the agreement, any party is entitled to terminate it before the end of the period so specified.

(3)   A notice under subsection (1) is ineffective if not in the prescribed form.

(4)   Subsection (1) does not prevent a creditor from treating the right to draw on any credit as restricted or deferred and taking such steps as may be necessary to make the restriction or deferment effective.

(5)   Regulations may provide that subsection (1) is not to apply to agreements described by the regulations.

(6)   Subsection (1) does not apply to the termination of a regulated agreement by reason of any breach by the debtor or hirer of the agreement.

NOTES

Regulations: the Consumer Credit (Enforcement, Default and Termination Notices) Regulations 1983, SI 1983/1561; Consumer Credit (Enforcement, Default and Termination Notices) (Amendment) Regulations 2004, SI 2004/3237.

[1.602]

[98A Termination etc of open-end consumer credit agreements

(1) The debtor under a regulated open-end consumer credit agreement, other than an excluded agreement, may by notice terminate the agreement, free of charge, at any time, subject to any period of notice not exceeding one month provided for by the agreement.

(2) Notice under subsection (1) need not be in writing unless the creditor so requires.

(3) Where a regulated open-end consumer credit agreement, other than an excluded agreement, provides for termination of the agreement by the creditor—

(a) the termination must be by notice served on the debtor, and

(b) the termination may not take effect until after the end of the period of two months, or such longer period as the agreement may provide, beginning with the day after the day on which notice is served.

(4) Where a regulated open-end consumer credit agreement, other than an excluded agreement, provides for termination or suspension by the creditor of the debtor's right to draw on credit—

(a) to terminate or suspend the right to draw on credit the creditor must serve a notice on the debtor before the termination or suspension or, if that is not practicable, immediately afterwards,

(b) the notice must give reasons for the termination or suspension, and

(c) the reasons must be objectively justified.

(5) Subsection (4)(a) and (b) does not apply where giving the notice—

(a) is prohibited by an EU obligation, or

(b) would, or would be likely to, prejudice—

(i) the prevention or detection of crime,

(ii) the apprehension or prosecution of offenders, or

(iii) the administration of justice.

(6) An objectively justified reason under subsection (4)(c) may, for example, relate to—

(a) the unauthorised or fraudulent use of credit, or

(b) a significantly increased risk of the debtor being unable to fulfil his obligation to repay the credit.

(7) Subsections (1) and (3) do not affect any right to terminate an agreement for breach of contract.

(8) For the purposes of this section an agreement is an excluded agreement if it is—

(a) an authorised non-business overdraft agreement,

(b) an authorised business overdraft agreement,

(c) a debtor-creditor agreement arising where the holder of a current account overdraws on the account without a pre-arranged overdraft or exceeds a pre-arranged overdraft limit, or

(d) an agreement secured on land.]

NOTES

Inserted by the Consumer Credit (EU Directive) Regulations 2010, SI 2010/1010, regs 2, 38, as from 1 February 2011, with effect in relation to certain agreements before that date, as provided for in regs 100–101A of the 2010 Regulations at [2.803]–[2.805].

[1.603]

99 Right to terminate hire-purchase etc agreements

(1) At any time before the final payment by the debtor under a regulated hire-purchase or regulated conditional sale agreement falls due, the debtor shall be entitled to terminate the agreement by giving notice to any person entitled or authorised to receive the sums payable under the agreement.

(2) Termination of an agreement under subsection (1) does not affect any liability under the agreement which has accrued before the termination.

(3) Subsection (1) does not apply to a conditional sale agreement relating to land after the title to the land has passed to the debtor.

(4) In the case of a conditional sale agreement relating to goods, where the property in the goods, having become vested in the debtor, is transferred to a person who does not become the debtor under the agreement, the debtor shall not thereafter be entitled to terminate the agreement under subsection (1).

(5) Subject to subsection (4), where a debtor under a conditional sale agreement relating to goods, terminates the agreement under this section after the property in the goods has become vested in him, the property in the goods shall thereupon vest in the person (the "previous owner") in whom it was vested immediately before it became vested in the debtor:

Provided that if the previous owner has died, or any other event has occurred whereby that property, if vested in him immediately before that event, would thereupon have vested in some other person, the property shall be treated as having devolved as if it had been vested in the previous owner immediately before his death or immediately before that event, as the case may be.

[1.604]
100   Liability of debtor on termination of hire-purchase etc agreement
(1)   Where a regulated hire-purchase or regulated conditional sale agreement is terminated under section 99 the debtor shall be liable, unless the agreement provides for a smaller payment, or does not provide for any payment, to pay to the creditor the amount (if any) by which one-half of the total price exceeds the aggregate of the sums paid and the sums due in respect of the total price immediately before the termination.
(2)   Where under a hire-purchase or conditional sale agreement the creditor is required to carry out any installation and the agreement specifies, as part of the total price, the amount to be paid in respect of the installation (the "installation charge") the reference in subsection (1) to one-half of the total price shall be construed as a reference to the aggregate of the installation charge and one-half of the remainder of the total price.
(3)   If in any action the court is satisfied that a sum less than the amount specified in subsection (1) would be equal to the loss sustained by the creditor in consequence of the termination of the agreement by the debtor, the court may make an order for the payment of that sum in lieu of the amount specified in subsection (1).
(4)   If the debtor has contravened an obligation to take reasonable care of the goods or land, the amount arrived at under subsection (1) shall be increased by the sum required to recompense the creditor for that contravention, and subsection (2) shall have effect accordingly.
(5)   Where the debtor, on the termination of the agreement, wrongfully retains possession of goods to which the agreement relates, then, in any action brought by the creditor to recover possession of the goods from the debtor, the court, unless it is satisfied that having regard to the circumstances it would not be just to do so, shall order the goods to be delivered to the creditor without giving the debtor an option to pay the value of the goods.

[1.605]
101   Right to terminate hire agreement
(1)   The hirer under a regulated consumer hire agreement is entitled to terminate the agreement by giving notice to any person entitled or authorised to receive the sums payable under the agreement.
(2)   Termination of an agreement under subsection (1) does not affect any liability under the agreement which has accrued before the termination.
(3)   A notice under subsection (1) shall not expire earlier than eighteen months after the making of the agreement, but apart from that the minimum period of notice to be given under subsection (1), unless the agreement provides for a shorter period, is as follows.
(4)   If the agreement provides for the making of payments by the hirer to the owner at equal intervals, the minimum period of notice is the length of one interval or three months, whichever is less.
(5)   If the agreement provides for the making of such payments at differing intervals, the minimum period of notice is the length of the shortest interval or three months, whichever is less.
(6)   In any other case, the minimum period of notice is three months.
(7)   This section does not apply to—
  (a)   any agreement which provides for the making by the hirer of payments which in total (and without breach of the agreement) exceed [£1,500] in any year, or
  (b)   any agreement where—
    (i)   goods are bailed or (in Scotland) hired to the hirer for the purposes of a business carried on by him, or the hirer holds himself out as requiring the goods for those purposes, and
    (ii)   the goods are selected by the hirer, and acquired by the owner for the purposes of the agreement at the request of the hirer from any person other than the owner's associate, or
  (c)   any agreement where the hirer requires, or holds himself out as requiring, the goods for the purpose of bailing or hiring them to other persons in the course of a business carried on by him.
(8)   If, on an application made to the [FCA] by a person carrying on a consumer hire business, it appears to the [FCA] that it would be in the interest of hirers to do so, [it] may . . . direct that[, subject to such conditions (if any) as it may specify, this section shall not apply to consumer hire agreements made by the applicant; and this Act shall have effect accordingly].
[(8A)   If it appears to the [FCA] that it would be in the interests of hirers to do so, it may . . . direct that, subject to such conditions (if any) as it may specify, this section shall not apply to a consumer hire agreement if the agreement falls within a specified description; and this Act shall have effect accordingly.]
(9)   In the case of a modifying agreement subsection (3) shall apply with the substitution, for "the making of the agreement" of "the making of the original agreement".

NOTES
   References to the FCA, etc: as to the abolition of the office of the Director General of Fair Trading and the substitution of the original references to the Director (and related expressions), see the note preceding s 8 at **[1.520]**.

Sub-s (7): sum in square brackets substituted by the Consumer Credit (Further Increase in Monetary Amounts) Order 1998, SI 1998/997, art 3, Schedule, as from 1 May 1998.

Sub-s (8): words in first and second pairs of square brackets substituted, and words omitted repealed, by the Financial Services Act 2012 (Consumer Credit) Order 2013, SI 2013/1882, art 7(1), (8)(a), as from 26 July 2013 (certain purposes), and as from 1 April 2014 (remaining purposes); word in third pair of square brackets substituted by the Enterprise Act 2002, s 278(1), Sch 25, para 6(1), (26); words in final pair of square brackets substituted by the Consumer Credit Act 2006, s 63(2), as from 16 June 2006.

Sub-s (8A): inserted by the Consumer Credit Act 2006, s 63(1); word in square brackets substituted, and words omitted repealed, by SI 2013/1882, art 7(1), (8)(b), as from 26 July 2013 (certain purposes), and as from 1 April 2014 (remaining purposes).

[1.606]
102 Agency for receiving notice of rescission
(1) Where the debtor or hirer under a regulated agreement claims to have a right to rescind the agreement, each of the following shall be deemed to be the agent of the creditor or owner for the purpose of receiving any notice rescinding the agreement which is served by the debtor or hirer—
  (a) a credit-broker or supplier who was the negotiator in antecedent negotiations, and
  (b) any person who, in the course of a business carried on by him, acted on behalf of the debtor or hirer in any negotiations for the agreement.
(2) In subsection (1) "rescind" does not include—
  (a) service of a notice of cancellation, or
  (b) termination of an agreement under section 99 or 101, or by the exercise of a right or power in that behalf expressly conferred by the agreement.

[1.607]
103 Termination statements
(1) If an individual (the "customer") serves on any person (the "trader") a notice—
  (a) stating that—
    (i) the customer was the debtor or hirer under a regulated agreement described in the notice, and the trader was the creditor or owner under the agreement, and
    (ii) the customer has discharged his indebtedness to the trader under the agreement, and
    (iii) the agreement has ceased to have any operation; and
  (b) requiring the trader to give the customer a notice, signed by or on behalf of the trader, confirming that those statements are correct,
the trader shall, within the prescribed period after receiving the notice, either comply with it or serve on the customer a counter-notice stating that, as the case may be, he disputes the correctness of the notice or asserts that the customer is not indebted to him under the agreement.
(2) Where the trader disputes the correctness of the notice he shall give particulars of the way in which he alleges it to be wrong.
(3) Subsection (1) does not apply in relation to any agreement if the trader has previously complied with that subsection on the service of a notice under it with respect to that agreement.
(4) Subsection (1) does not apply to a non-commercial agreement.
(5) . . .
[(6) A breach of the duty imposed by subsection (1) is actionable as a breach of statutory duty.]

NOTES
Sub-s (5): repealed by the Consumer Protection from Unfair Trading Regulations 2008, SI 2008/1277, reg 30(1), (3), Sch 2, Pt 1, paras 17, 24(a), Sch 4, as from 26 May 2008.
Sub-s (6): added by SI 2008/1277, reg 30(1), Sch 2, Pt 1, paras 17, 24(b), as from 26 May 2008.
Regulations: the Consumer Credit (Prescribed Periods for Giving Information) Regulations 1983, SI 1983/1569.

104 (*Applies to Scotland only.*)

PART VIII
SECURITY

General

[1.608]
105 Form and content of securities
(1) Any security provided in relation to a regulated agreement shall be expressed in writing.
(2) Regulations may prescribe the form and content of documents ("security instruments") to be made in compliance with subsection (1).
(3) Regulations under subsection (2) may in particular—
  (a) require specified information to be included in the prescribed manner in documents, and other specified material to be excluded;
  (b) contain requirements to ensure that specified information is clearly brought to the attention of the surety, and that one part of a document is not given insufficient or excessive prominence compared with another.
(4) A security instrument is not properly executed unless—

   (a)   a document in the prescribed form, itself containing all the prescribed terms and conforming to regulations under subsection (2), is signed in the prescribed manner by or on behalf of the surety, and

   (b)   the document embodies all the terms of the security, other than implied terms, and

   (c)   the document, when presented or sent for the purpose of being signed by or on behalf of the surety, is in such a state that its terms are readily legible, and

   (d)   when the document is presented or sent for the purpose of being signed by or on behalf of the surety there is also presented or sent a copy of the document.

(5)   A security instrument is not properly executed unless—

   (a)   where the security is provided after, or at the time when, the regulated agreement is made, a copy of the executed agreement, together with a copy of any other document referred to in it, is given to the surety at the time the security is provided, or

   (b)   where the security is provided before the regulated agreement is made, a copy of the executed agreement, together with a copy of any other document referred to in it, is given to the surety within seven days after the regulated agreement is made.

(6)   Subsection (1) does not apply to a security provided by the debtor or hirer.

(7)   If—

   (a)   in contravention of subsection (1) a security is not expressed in writing, or

   (b)   a security instrument is improperly executed,

the security (so far as provided in relation to a regulated agreement) is enforceable against the surety on an order of the court only.

(8)   If an application for an order under subsection (7) is dismissed (except on technical grounds only) section 106 (ineffective securities) shall apply to the security.

(9)   Regulations under section 60(1) shall include provision requiring documents embodying regulated agreements also to embody any security provided in relation to a regulated agreement by the debtor or hirer.

NOTES

Regulations: the Consumer Credit (Agreements) Regulations 1983, SI 1983/1553; the Consumer Credit (Guarantees and Indemnities) Regulations 1983, SI 1983/1556; the Consumer Credit (Agreements) (Amendment) Regulations 2004, SI 2004/1482; the Consumer Credit (Miscellaneous Amendments) Regulations 2004, SI 2004/2619; the Consumer Credit (Agreements) Regulations 2010, SI 2010/1014 at **[2.829]**; the Consumer Credit (Amendment) Regulations 2010, SI 2010/1969.

[1.609]
106   Ineffective securities

Where, under any provision of this Act, this section is applied to any security provided in relation to a regulated agreement, then, subject to section 177 (saving for registered charges),—

   (a)   the security, so far as it is so provided, shall be treated as never having effect;

   (b)   any property lodged with the creditor or owner solely for the purposes of the security as so provided shall be returned by him forthwith;

   (c)   the creditor or owner shall take any necessary action to remove or cancel an entry in any register, so far as the entry relates to the security as so provided; and

   (d)   any amount received by the creditor or owner on realisation of the security shall, so far as it is referable to the agreement, be repaid to the surety.

[1.610]
107   Duty to give information to surety under fixed-sum credit agreement

(1)   The creditor under a regulated agreement for fixed-sum credit in relation to which security is provided, within the prescribed period after receiving a request in writing to that effect from the surety and payment of a fee of [£1], shall give to the surety (if a different person from the debtor)—

   (a)   a copy of the executed agreement (if any) and of any other document referred to in it;

   (b)   a copy of the security instrument (if any); and

   (c)   a statement signed by or on behalf of the creditor showing, according to the information to which it is practicable for him to refer,—

       (i)   the total sum paid under the agreement by the debtor,

       (ii)   the total sum which has become payable under the agreement by the debtor but remains unpaid, and the various amounts comprised in that total sum, with the date when each became due, and

       (iii)   the total sum which is to become payable under the agreement by the debtor, and the various amounts comprised in that total sum, with the date, or mode of determining the date, when each becomes due.

(2)   If the creditor possesses insufficient information to enable him to ascertain the amount and dates mentioned in subsection (1)(c) (iii), he shall be taken to comply with that sub-paragraph if his statement under subsection (1)(c) gives the basis on which, under the regulated agreement, they would fall to be ascertained.

(3)   Subsection (1) does not apply to—

   (a)   an agreement under which no sum is, or will or may become, payable by the debtor, or

   (b)   a request made less than one month after a previous request under that subsection relating to the same agreement was complied with.

(4)   If the creditor under an agreement fails to comply with subsection (1)—

   (a) he is not entitled, while the default continues, to enforce the security, so far as provided in relation to the agreement;   . . .

   (b) . . .

(5)   This section does not apply to a non-commercial agreement.

NOTES

Sub-s (1): sum in square brackets substituted by the Consumer Credit (Further Increase in Monetary Amounts) Order 1998, SI 1998/997, art 3, Schedule, as from 1 May 1998.

Sub-s (4): words omitted repealed by the Consumer Protection from Unfair Trading Regulations 2008, SI 2008/1277, reg 30(1), (3), Sch 2, Pt 1, paras 17, 25, Sch 4.

Regulations: the Consumer Credit (Prescribed Periods for Giving Information) Regulations 1983, SI 1983/1569.

[1.611]

108   Duty to give information to surety under running-account credit agreement

(1)   The creditor under a regulated agreement for running-account credit in relation to which security is provided, within the prescribed period after receiving a request in writing to that effect from the surety and payment of a fee of [£1], shall give to the surety (if a different person from the debtor)—

   (a) a copy of the executed agreement (if any) and of any other document referred to in it;

   (b) a copy of the security instrument (if any); and

   (c) a statement signed by or on behalf of the creditor showing, according to the information to which it is practicable for him to refer,—

      (i) the state of the account, and

      (ii) the amount, if any, currently payable under the agreement by the debtor to the creditor, and

      (iii) the amounts and due dates of any payments which, if the debtor does not draw further on the account, will later become payable under the agreement by the debtor to the creditor.

(2)   If the creditor possesses insufficient information to enable him to ascertain the amounts and dates mentioned in subsection (1)(c)(iii), he shall be taken to comply with that sub-paragraph if his statement under subsection (1)(c) gives basis on which, under the regulated agreement, they would fall to be ascertained.

(3)   Subsection (1) does not apply to—

   (a) an agreement under which no sum is, or will or may become, payable by the debtor, or

   (b) a request made less than one month after a previous request under that subsection relating to the same agreement was complied with.

(4)   If the creditor under an agreement fails to comply with subsection (1)—

   (a) he is not entitled, while the default continues, to enforce the security, so far as provided in relation to the agreement;   . . .

   (b) . . .

(5)   This section does not apply to a non-commercial agreement.

NOTES

Sub-s (1): sum in square brackets substituted by the Consumer Credit (Further Increase in Monetary Amounts) Order 1998, SI 1998/997, art 3, Schedule, as from 1 May 1998.

Sub-s (4): words omitted repealed by the Consumer Protection from Unfair Trading Regulations 2008, SI 2008/1277, reg 30(1), (3), Sch 2, Pt 1, paras 17, 26, Sch 4, as from 26 May 2008.

Regulations: the Consumer Credit (Prescribed Periods for Giving Information) Regulations 1983, SI 1983/1569.

[1.612]

109   Duty to give information to surety under consumer hire agreement

(1)   The owner under a regulated consumer hire agreement in relation to which security is provided, within the prescribed period after receiving a request in writing to that effect from the surety and payment of a fee of [£1], shall give to the surety (if a different person from the hirer)—

   (a) a copy of the executed agreement and of any other document referred to in it;

   (b) a copy of the security instrument (if any); and

   (c) a statement signed by or on behalf of the owner showing, according to the information to which it is practicable for him to refer, the total sum which has become payable under the agreement by the hirer but remains unpaid and the various amounts comprised in that total sum, with the date when each became due.

(2)   Subsection (1) does not apply to—

   (a) an agreement under which no sum is, or will or may become, payable by the hirer, or

   (b) a request made less than one month after a previous request under that subsection relating to the same agreement was complied with.

(3)   If the owner under an agreement fails to comply with subsection (1)—

   (a) he is not entitled, while the default continues, to enforce the security, so far as provided in relation to the agreement;   . . .

   (b) . . .

(4)   This section does not apply to a non-commercial agreement.

NOTES

Sub-s (1): sum in square brackets substituted by the Consumer Credit (Further Increase in Monetary Amounts) Order 1998, SI 1998/997, art 3, Schedule, as from 1 May 1998.

Sub-s (3): words omitted repealed by the Consumer Protection from Unfair Trading Regulations 2008, SI 2008/1277, reg 30(1), (3), Sch 2, Pt 1, paras 17, 27, Sch 4, as from 26 May 2008.

Regulations: the Consumer Credit (Prescribed Periods for Giving Information) Regulations 1983, SI 1983/1569.

[1.613]
110   Duty to give information to debtor or hirer
(1)   The creditor or owner under a regulated agreement, within the prescribed period after receiving a request in writing to that effect from the debtor or hirer and payment of a fee of [£1], shall give the debtor or hirer a copy of any security instrument executed in relation to the agreement after the making of the agreement.
(2)   Subsection (1) does not apply to—
  (a)   a non-commercial agreement, or
  (b)   an agreement under which no sum is, or will or may become, payable by the debtor or hirer, or
  (c)   a request made less than one month after a previous request under subsection (1) relating to the same agreement was complied with.
(3)   If the creditor or owner under an agreement fails to comply with subsection (1)—
  (a)   he is not entitled, while the default continues, to enforce the security (so far as provided in relation to the agreement);   . . .
  (b)   . . .

NOTES

Sub-s (1): sum in square brackets substituted by the Consumer Credit (Further Increase in Monetary Amounts) Order 1998, SI 1998/997, art 3, Schedule, as from 1 May 1998.

Sub-s (3): words omitted repealed by the Consumer Protection from Unfair Trading Regulations 2008, SI 2008/1277, reg 30(1), (3), Sch 2, Pt 1, paras 17, 28, Sch 4, as from 26 May 2008.

Regulations: the Consumer Credit (Prescribed Periods for Giving Information) Regulations 1983, SI 1983/1569.

[1.614]
111   Duty to give surety copy of default etc notice
(1)   When a default notice or a notice under section 76(1) or 98(1) is served on a debtor or hirer, a copy of the notice shall be served by the creditor or owner on any surety (if a different person from the debtor or hirer).
(2)   If the creditor or owner fails to comply with subsection (1) in the case of any surety, the security is enforceable against the surety (in respect of the breach or other matter to which the notice relates) on an order of the court only.

112   (*Repealed by the Financial Services and Markets Act 2000 (Regulated Activities) (Amendment) (No 2) Order 2013, SI 2013/1881, art 20(1), (34), as from 26 July 2013 (certain purposes), and as from 1 April 2014 (remaining purposes), for transitional provisions see Pt 8 thereof at* **[2.1007]** *et seq.*)

[1.615]
113   Act not to be evaded by use of security
(1)   Where a security is provided in relation to an actual or prospective regulated agreement, the security shall not be enforced so as to benefit the creditor or owner, directly or indirectly, to an extent greater (whether as respects the amount of any payment or the time or manner of its being made) than would be the case if the security were not provided and any obligations of the debtor or hirer, or his relative, under or in relation to the agreement were carried out to the extent (if any) to which they would be enforced under this Act.
(2)   In accordance with subsection (1), where a regulated agreement is enforceable on an order of the court or the [FCA] only, any security provided in relation to the agreement is enforceable (so far as provided in relation to the agreement) where such an order has been made in relation to the agreement, but not otherwise.
(3)   Where—
  (a)   a regulated agreement is cancelled under section 69(1) or becomes subject to section 69(2), or
  (b)   a regulated agreement is terminated under section 91, or
  (c)   in relation to any agreement an application for an order under section [65(1) or 124(1) or a notice under section 28A of the Financial Services and Markets Act 2000] is dismissed (except on technical grounds only), or
  (d)   a declaration is made by the court under section 142(1) (refusal of enforcement order) as respects any regulated agreement,
section 106 shall apply to any security provided in relation to the agreement.
(4)   Where subsection (3)(d) applies and the declaration relates to a part only of the regulated agreement, section 106 shall apply to the security only so far as it concerns that part.

(5)   In the case of a cancelled agreement, the duty imposed on the debtor or hirer by section 71 or 72 shall not be enforceable before the creditor or owner has discharged any duty imposed on him by section 106 (as applied by subsection (3)(a)).

(6)   If the security is provided in relation to a prospective agreement or transaction, the security shall be enforceable in relation to the agreement or transaction only after the time (if any) when the agreement is made; and until that time the person providing the security shall be entitled, by notice to the creditor or owner, to require that section 106 shall thereupon apply to the security.

(7)   Where an indemnity [or guarantee] is given in a case where the debtor or hirer is a minor, or [an indemnity is given in a case where he] is otherwise not of full capacity, the reference in subsection (1) to the extent to which his obligations would be enforced shall be read in relation to the indemnity [or guarantee] as a reference to the extent to which [those obligations] would be enforced if he were of full capacity.

(8)   Subsections (1) to (3) also apply where a security is provided in relation to an actual or prospective linked transaction, and in that case—

(a)   references to the agreement shall be read as references to the linked transaction, and

(b)   references to the creditor or owner shall be read as references to any person (other than the debtor or hirer, or his relative) who is a party, or prospective party, to the linked transaction.

NOTES

Sub-s (2): word in square brackets substituted by the Financial Services Act 2012 (Consumer Credit) Order 2013, SI 2013/1882, art 7(1), (9), as from 26 July 2013 (certain purposes), and as from 1 April 2014 (remaining purposes).

Sub-s (3): in para (c) words in square brackets substituted by the Financial Services and Markets Act 2000 (Regulated Activities) (Amendment) (No 2) Order 2013, SI 2013/1881, art 20(1), (35), as from 26 July 2013 (certain purposes), and as from 1 April 2014 (remaining purposes), for transitional provisions see Pt 8 thereof at **[2.1007]** et seq.

Sub-s (7): words in square brackets inserted or substituted by the Minors' Contracts Act 1987, s 4(1), as from 9 June 1987.

References to the FCA, etc: as to the abolition of the office of the Director General of Fair Trading and the substitution of the original references to the Director (and related expressions), see the note preceding s 8 at **[1.520]**.

Pledges

[1.616]
114   Pawn-receipts
(1)   At the time he receives the article, a person who takes any article in pawn under a regulated agreement shall give to the person from whom he receives it a receipt in the prescribed form (a "pawn-receipt").

(2)   A person who takes any article in pawn from an individual whom he knows to be, or who appears to be and is, a minor commits an offence.

(3)   This section and sections [117] to 122 do not apply to—

(a)   a pledge of documents of title [or of bearer bonds], or

(b)   a non-commercial agreement.

NOTES

Sub-s (3): reference in first pair of square brackets substituted by the Financial Services and Markets Act 2000 (Regulated Activities) (Amendment) (No 2) Order 2013, SI 2013/1881, art 20(1), (36), as from 26 July 2013 (certain purposes), and as from 1 April 2014 (remaining purposes), for transitional provisions see Pt 8 thereof at **[2.1007]** et seq; words in second pair of square brackets inserted by the Banking Act 1979, s 38(2).

Regulations: the Consumer Credit (Agreements) Regulations 1983, SI 1983/1553; the Consumer Credit (Pawn Receipts) Regulations 1983, SI 1983/1566; the Consumer Credit (Agreements) (Amendment) Regulations 2004, SI 2004/1482; the Consumer Credit (Miscellaneous Amendments) Regulations 2004, SI 2004/2619; the Consumer Credit (Agreements) Regulations 2010, SI 2010/1014 at **[2.829]**.

115   (*Repealed by the Financial Services and Markets Act 2000 (Regulated Activities) (Amendment) (No 2) Order 2013, SI 2013/1881, art 20(1), (37), as from 26 July 2013 (certain purposes), and as from 1 April 2014 (remaining purposes), for transitional provisions see Pt 8 thereof at* **[2.1007]** *et seq.*)

[1.617]
116   Redemption period
(1)   A pawn is redeemable at any time within six months after it was taken.

(2)   Subject to subsection (1), the period within which a pawn is redeemable shall be the same as the period fixed by the parties for the duration of the credit secured by the pledge, or such longer period as they may agree.

(3)   If the pawn is not redeemed by the end of the period laid down by subsections (1) and (2) (the "redemption period"), it nevertheless remains redeemable until it is realised by the pawnee under section 121, except where under section 120(1)(a) the property in it passes to the pawnee.

(4)   No special charge shall be made for redemption of a pawn after the end of the redemption period, and charges in respect of the safe keeping of the pawn shall not be at a higher rate after the end of the redemption period than before.

[1.618]
117 Redemption procedure
(1) On surrender of the pawn-receipt, and payment of the amount owing, at any time when the pawn is redeemable, the pawnee shall deliver the pawn to the bearer of the pawn-receipt.
(2) Subsection (1) does not apply if the pawnee knows or has reasonable cause to suspect that the bearer of the pawn-receipt is neither the owner of the pawn nor authorised by the owner to redeem it.
(3) The pawnee is not liable to any person in tort or delict for delivering the pawn where subsection (1) applies, or refusing to deliver it where the person demanding delivery does not comply with subsection (1) or, by reason of subsection (2), subsection (1) does not apply.

[1.619]
118 Loss etc of pawn-receipt
(1) A person (the "claimant") who is not in possession of the pawn-receipt but claims to be the owner of the pawn, or to be otherwise entitled or authorised to redeem it, may do so at any time when it is redeemable by tendering to the pawnee in place of the pawn-receipt—
  (a) a statutory declaration made by the claimant in the prescribed form, and with the prescribed contents, or
  (b) where the pawn is security for fixed-sum credit not exceeding [£75] or running-account credit on which the credit limit does not exceed [£75], and the pawnee agrees, a statement in writing in the prescribed form, and with the prescribed contents, signed by the claimant.
(2) On compliance by the claimant with subsection (1), section 117 shall apply as if the declaration or statement were the pawn-receipt, and the pawn-receipt itself shall become inoperative for the purposes of section 117.

NOTES
Sub-s (1): sums in square brackets substituted by the Consumer Credit (Further Increase in Monetary Amounts) Order 1998, SI 1998/997, art 3, Schedule, as from 1 May 1998.
Regulations: the Consumer Credit (Loss of Pawn Receipts) Regulations 1983, SI 1983/1567.

[1.620]
119 Unreasonable refusal to deliver pawn
(1) If a person who has taken a pawn under a regulated agreement refuses without reasonable cause to allow the pawn to be redeemed, he commits an offence.
(2) On the conviction in England or Wales of a pawnee under subsection (1) where the offence does not amount to theft, [section 148 of the Powers of Criminal Courts (Sentencing) Act 2000 (restitution orders)] shall apply as if the pawnee had been convicted of stealing the pawn.
(3) On the conviction in Northern Ireland of a pawnee under subsection (1) where the offence does not amount to theft, section 27 (orders for restitution) of the Theft Act (Northern Ireland) 1969, and any provision of the Theft Act (Northern Ireland) 1969 relating to that section, shall apply as if the pawnee had been convicted of stealing the pawn.

NOTES
Sub-s (2): words in square brackets substituted by the Powers of Criminal Courts (Sentencing) Act 2000, s 165(1), Sch 9, para 45, as from 25 August 2000.

[1.621]
120 Consequence of failure to redeem
(1) If at the end of the redemption period the pawn has not been redeemed—
  (a) notwithstanding anything in section 113, the property in the pawn passes to the pawnee where[—
    (i) the redemption period is six months,
    (ii) the pawn is security for fixed-sum credit not exceeding £75 or running-account credit on which the credit limit does not exceed £75, and
    (iii) the pawn was not immediately before the making of the regulated consumer credit agreement a pawn under another regulated consumer credit agreement in respect of which the debtor has discharged his indebtedness in part under section 94(3); or]
  (b) in any other case the pawn becomes realisable by the pawnee.
(2) Where the debtor or hirer is entitled to apply to the court for a time order under section 129, subsection (1) shall apply with the substitution, for "at the end of the redemption period" of "after the expiry of five days following the end of the redemption period".

NOTES
Sub-s (1): words in square brackets substituted by the Consumer Credit (EU Directive) Regulations 2010, SI 2010/1010, regs 2, 35, as from 1 February 2011, with effect in relation to certain agreements before that date, as provided for in regs 100–101A of the 2010 Regulations at **[2.803]–[2.805]**.

[1.622]
121   Realisation of pawn
(1)   When a pawn has become realisable by him, the pawnee may sell it, after giving to the pawnor (except in such cases as may be prescribed) not less than the prescribed period of notice of the intention to sell, indicating in the notice the asking price and such other particulars as may be prescribed.
(2)   Within the prescribed period after the sale takes place, the pawnee shall give the pawnor the prescribed information in writing as to the sale, its proceeds and expenses.
(3)   Where the net proceeds of sale are not less than the sum which, if the pawn had been redeemed on the date of the sale, would have been payable for its redemption, the debt secured by the pawn is discharged and any surplus shall be paid by the pawnee to the pawnor.
(4)   Where subsection (3) does not apply, the debt shall be treated as from the date of sale as equal to the amount by which the net proceeds of sale fall short of the sum which would have been payable for the redemption of the pawn on that date.
(5)   In this section the "net proceeds of sale" is the amount realised (the "gross amount") less the expenses (if any) of the sale.
(6)   If the pawnor alleges that the gross amount is less than the true market value of the pawn on the date of sale, it is for the pawnee to prove that he and any agents employed by him in the sale used reasonable care to ensure that the true market value was obtained, and if he fails to do so subsections (3) and (4) shall have effect as if the reference in subsection (5) to the gross amount were a reference to the true market value.
(7)   If the pawnor alleges that the expenses of the sale were unreasonably high, it is for the pawnee to prove that they were reasonable, and if he fails to do so subsections (3) and (4) shall have effect as if the reference in subsection (5) to expenses were a reference to reasonable expenses.

NOTES
   Regulations: the Consumer Credit (Realisation of Pawn) Regulations 1983, SI 1983/1568; the Consumer Credit (Realisation of Pawn) (Amendment) Regulations 1998, SI 1998/998.

122   (*Applies to Scotland only.*)

Negotiable instruments

[1.623]
123   Restrictions on taking and negotiating instruments
(1)   A creditor or owner shall not take a negotiable instrument, other than a bank note or cheque, in discharge of any sum payable—
   (a)   by the debtor or hirer under a regulated agreement, or
   (b)   by any person as surety in relation to the agreement.
(2)   The creditor or owner shall not negotiate a cheque taken by him in discharge of a sum payable as mentioned in subsection (1), except to a banker (within the meaning of the Bills of Exchange Act 1882).
(3)   The creditor or owner shall not take a negotiable instrument as security for the discharge of any sum payable as mentioned in subsection (1).
(4)   A person takes a negotiable instrument as security for the discharge of a sum if the sum is intended to be paid in some other way, and the negotiable instrument is to be presented for payment only if the sum is not paid in that way.
(5)   This section does not apply where the regulated agreement is a non-commercial agreement.
(6)   The [Treasury] may by order provide that this section shall not apply where the regulated agreement has a connection with a country outside the United Kingdom.

NOTES
   Sub-s (6): word in square brackets substituted by the Financial Services Act 2012 (Consumer Credit) Order 2013, SI 2013/1882, art 7(1), (10), as from 26 July 2013 (certain purposes), and as from 1 April 2014 (remaining purposes).
   Orders: the Consumer Credit (Negotiable Instruments) (Exemption) Order 1984, SI 1984/435.

[1.624]
124   Consequences of breach of s 123
(1)   After any contravention of section 123 has occurred in relation to a sum payable as mentioned in section 123(1)(a), the agreement under which the sum is payable is enforceable against the debtor or hirer on an order of the court only.
(2)   After any contravention of section 123 has occurred in relation to a sum payable by any surety, the security is enforceable on an order of the court only.
(3)   Where an application for an order under subsection (2) is dismissed (except on technical grounds only) section 106 shall apply to the security.

[1.625]
125   Holders in due course
(1)   A person who takes a negotiable instrument in contravention of section 123(1) or (3) is not a holder in due course, and is not entitled to enforce the instrument.

(2)   Where a person negotiates a cheque in contravention of section 123(2), his doing so constitutes a defect in his title within the meaning of the Bills of Exchange Act 1882.

(3)   If a person mentioned in section 123(1)(a) or (b) ("the protected person") becomes liable to a holder in due course of an instrument taken from the protected person in contravention of section 123(1) or (3), or taken from the protected person and negotiated in contravention of section 123(2), the creditor or owner shall indemnify the protected person in respect of that liability.

(4)   Nothing in this Act affects the rights of the holder in due course of any negotiable instrument.

Land mortgages

[1.626]

[126   Enforcement of land mortgages

(1)   A land mortgage securing an agreement of one the following types is enforceable (so far as is provided in relation to the agreement) on an order of the court only—

    (a)   a regulated agreement;

    (b)   a regulated mortgage contract;

    (c)   a consumer credit agreement which would, but for article 60D of the Regulated Activities Order (exempt agreements: exemption relating to the purchase of land for non-residential purposes), be a regulated agreement.

(2)   Subject to section 140A(5) (unfair relationships between creditors and debtors), a regulated mortgage contract which would, but for article 60C(2) of the Regulated Activities Order (exempt agreements: exemption relating to the nature of the agreement), be a regulated agreement is to be treated for the purposes of Part 9 (judicial control) as if it were a regulated agreement.

(3)   In this section, "regulated mortgage contract" has the meaning given by article 61(3) of the Regulated Activities Order (regulated mortgage contracts)).]

NOTES

Commencement: 30 March 2014.

Substituted by the Financial Services and Markets Act 2000 (Regulated Activities) (Amendment) (No 2) Order 2013, SI 2013/1881, art 20(1), (38) (as substituted by SI 2014/506, art 5(1), (4)), as from 30 March 2014, for transitional provisions see Pt 8 thereof at **[2.1007]** et seq.

PART IX
JUDICIAL CONTROL

Enforcement of certain regulated agreements and securities

[1.627]

127   Enforcement orders in cases of infringement

(1)   In the case of an application for an enforcement order under—

    [(za)   section 55(2) (disclosure of information), or]

    [(zb)   section 61B(3) (duty to supply copy of overdraft agreement), or]

    (a)   section 65(1) (improperly executed agreements), or

    (b)   section 105(7)(a) or (b) (improperly executed security instruments), or

    (c)   section 111(2) (failure to serve copy of notice on surety), or

    (d)   section 124(1) or (2) (taking of negotiable instrument in contravention of section 123),

the court shall dismiss the application if, but   . . .   only if, it considers it just to do so having regard to—

    (i)   prejudice caused to any person by the contravention in question, and the degree of culpability for it; and

    (ii)   the powers conferred on the court by subsection (2) and sections 135 and 136.

(2)   If it appears to the court just to do so, it may in an enforcement order reduce or discharge any sum payable by the debtor or hirer, or any surety, so as to compensate him for prejudice suffered as a result of the contravention in question.

(3)–(5)   . . .

NOTES

Sub-s (1): paras (za), (zb) inserted by the Consumer Credit (EU Directive) Regulations 2010, SI 2010/1010, regs 2, 12, 18, as from 1 February 2011, with effect in relation to certain agreements before that date, as provided for in regs 101, 101A of the 2010 Regulations at **[2.804]**, **[2.805]**; words omitted repealed by the Consumer Credit Act 2006, s 70, Sch 4, as from 6 April 2007, subject to transitional provisions in s 69(1) of, and Sch 3, paras 1, 11(a) to, that Act at **[1.1945]**, **[1.1947]**.

Sub-ss (3)–(5): repealed by the Consumer Credit Act 2006, ss 15, 70, Sch 4, as from 6 April 2007, subject to transitional provisions in s 69(1) of, and Sch 3, paras 1, 11(b) to, that Act at **[1.1945]**, **[1.1947]**.

Regulations: the Consumer Credit (Agreements) Regulations 1983, SI 1983/1553.

[1.628]

128   Enforcement orders on death of debtor or hirer

The court shall make an order under section 86(2) if, but only if, the creditor or owner proves that he has been unable to satisfy himself that the present and future obligations of the debtor or hirer under the agreement are likely to be discharged.

Extension of time

[1.629]
129 Time orders
(1) [Subject to subsection (3) below,] if it appears to the court just to do so—
  (a) on an application for an enforcement order; or
  (b) on an application made by a debtor or hirer under this paragraph after service on him of—
      (i) a default notice, or
      (ii) a notice under section 76(1) or 98(1); or
  [(ba) on an application made by a debtor or hirer under this paragraph after he has been given a notice under section 86B or 86C; or]
  (c) in an action brought by a creditor or owner to enforce a regulated agreement or any security, or recover possession of any goods or land to which a regulated agreement relates,
the court may make an order under this section (a "time order").
(2) A time order shall provide for one or both of the following, as the court considers just—
  (a) the payment by the debtor or hirer or any surety of any sum owed under a regulated agreement or a security by such instalments, payable at such times, as the court, having regard to the means of the debtor or hirer and any surety, considers reasonable;
  (b) the remedying by the debtor or hirer of any breach of a regulated agreement (other than the non-payment of money) within such period as the court may specify.
(3) *(Applies to Scotland only.)*

NOTES
Sub-s (1): words in first pair of square brackets inserted by Debtors (Scotland) Act 1987, s 108(1), Sch 6, para 17, in relation to Scotland only; para (ba) inserted by the Consumer Credit Act 2006, s 16(1), as from 1 October 2008, subject to transitional provisions in s 69(1) of, and Sch 3, paras 1, 12 to, that Act at **[1.1945]**, **[1.1947]**.

[1.630]
[129A Debtor or hirer to give notice of intent etc to creditor or owner
(1) A debtor or hirer may make an application under section 129(1)(ba) in relation to a regulated agreement only if—
  (a) following his being given the notice under section 86B or 86C, he gave a notice within subsection (2) to the creditor or owner; and
  (b) a period of at least 14 days has elapsed after the day on which he gave that notice to the creditor or owner.
(2) A notice is within this subsection if it—
  (a) indicates that the debtor or hirer intends to make the application;
  (b) indicates that he wants to make a proposal to the creditor or owner in relation to his making of payments under the agreement; and
  (c) gives details of that proposal.]

NOTES
Inserted by the Consumer Credit Act 2006, s 16(2), as from 1 October 2008, subject to transitional provisions in s 69(1) of, and Sch 3, paras 1, 12 to, that Act at **[1.1945]**, **[1.1947]**.

[1.631]
130 Supplemental provisions about time orders
(1) Where in accordance with rules of court an offer to pay any sum by instalments is made by the debtor or hirer and accepted by the creditor or owner, the court may in accordance with rules of court make a time order under section 129(2)(a) giving effect to the offer without hearing evidence of means.
(2) In the case of a hire-purchase or conditional sale agreement only, a time order under section 129(2)(a) may deal with sums which, although not payable by the debtor at the time the order is made, would if the agreement continued in force become payable under it subsequently.
(3) A time order under section 129(2)(a) shall not be made where the regulated agreement is secured by a pledge if, by virtue of regulations made under section 76(5), 87(4) or 98(5), service of a notice is not necessary for enforcement of the pledge.
(4) Where, following the making of a time order in relation to a regulated hire-purchase or conditional sale agreement or a regulated consumer hire agreement, the debtor or hirer is in possession of the goods, he shall be treated (except in the case of a debtor to whom the creditor's title has passed) as a bailee or (in Scotland) a custodier of the goods under the terms of the agreement, notwithstanding that the agreement has been terminated.
(5) Without prejudice to anything done by the creditor or owner before the commencement of the period specified in a time order made under section 129(2)(b) ("the relevant period"),—
  (a) he shall not while the relevant period subsists take in relation to the agreement any action such as is mentioned in section 87(1);
  (b) where—
      (i) a provision of the agreement ("the secondary provision") becomes operative only on breach of another provision of the agreement ("the primary provision"), and

(ii)   the time order provides for the remedying of such a breach of the primary provision within the relevant period,

he shall not treat the secondary provision as operative before the end of that period;

(c)   if while the relevant period subsists the breach to which the order relates is remedied it shall be treated as not having occurred.

(6)   On the application of any person affected by a time order, the court may vary or revoke the order.

[Interest

[1.632]
130A   Interest payable on judgment debts etc

(1)   If the creditor or owner under a regulated agreement wants to be able to recover from the debtor or hirer post-judgment interest in connection with a sum that is required to be paid under a judgment given in relation to the agreement (the "judgment sum"), he—

(a)   after the giving of that judgment, shall give the debtor or hirer a notice under this section (the "first required notice"); and

(b)   after the giving of the first required notice, shall give the debtor or hirer further notices under this section at intervals of not more than six months.

(2)   The debtor or hirer shall have no liability to pay post-judgment interest in connection with the judgment sum to the extent that the interest is calculated by reference to a period occurring before the day on which he is given the first required notice.

(3)   If the creditor or owner fails to give the debtor or hirer a notice under this section within the period of six months beginning with the day after the day on which such a notice was last given to the debtor or hirer, the debtor or hirer shall have no liability to pay post-judgment interest in connection with the judgment sum to the extent that the interest is calculated by reference to the whole or to a part of the period which—

(a)   begins immediately after the end of that period of six months; and

(b)   ends at the end of the day on which the notice is given to the debtor or hirer.

(4)   The debtor or hirer shall have no liability to pay any sum in connection with the preparation or the giving to him of a notice under this section.

(5)   A notice under this section may be incorporated in a statement or other notice which the creditor or owner gives the debtor or hirer in relation to the agreement by virtue of another provision of this Act.

(6)   Regulations may make provision about the form and content of notices under this section.

(7)   This section does not apply in relation to post-judgment interest which is required to be paid by virtue of any of the following—

(a)   section 4 of the Administration of Justice (Scotland) Act 1972;

(b)   Article 127 of the Judgments Enforcement (Northern Ireland) Order 1981;

(c)   section 74 of the County Courts Act 1984.

(8)   This section does not apply in relation to a non-commercial agreement or to a small agreement.

(9)   In this section "post-judgment interest" means interest to the extent calculated by reference to a period occurring after the giving of the judgment under which the judgment sum is required to be paid.]

NOTES

Inserted, together with preceding cross-heading, by the Consumer Credit Act 2006, s 17, as from 16 June 2006 (sub-ss (6), (9)), and as from 1 October 2008 (remainder), subject to transitional provisions in s 69(1) of, and Sch 3, paras 1, 13 to, that Act at **[1.1945]**, **[1.1947]**.

Regulations: the Consumer Credit (Information Requirements and Duration of Licences and Charges) Regulations 2007, SI 2007/1167 at **[2.399]**; the Consumer Credit (Information Requirements and Duration of Licences and Charges) (Amendment) Regulations 2008, SI 2008/1751.

Protection of property pending proceedings

[1.633]
131   Protection orders

The court, on the application of the creditor or owner under a regulated agreement, may make such orders as it thinks just for protecting any property of the creditor or owner, or property subject to any security, from damage or depreciation pending the determination of any proceedings under this Act, including orders restricting or prohibiting use of the property or giving directions as to its custody.

Hire and hire-purchase etc agreements

[1.634]
132   Financial relief for hirer

(1)   Where the owner under a regulated consumer hire agreement recovers possession of goods to which the agreement relates otherwise than by action, the hirer may apply to the court for an order that—

(a) the whole or part of any sum paid by the hirer to the owner in respect of the goods shall be repaid, and

(b) the obligation to pay the whole or part of any sum owed by the hirer to the owner in respect of the goods shall cease,

and if it appears to the court just to do so, having regard to the extent of the enjoyment of the goods by the hirer, the court shall grant the application in full or in part.

(2) Where in proceedings relating to a regulated consumer hire agreement the court makes an order for the delivery to the owner of goods to which the agreement relates the court may include in the order the like provision as may be made in an order under subsection (1).

[1.635]
133 Hire-purchase etc agreements: special powers of court

(1) If, in relation to a regulated hire-purchase or conditional sale agreement, it appears to the court just to do so—

(a) on an application for an enforcement order or time order; or

(b) in an action brought by the creditor to recover possession of goods to which the agreement relates,

the court may—

(i) make an order (a "return order") for the return to the creditor of goods to which the agreement relates,

(ii) make an order (a "transfer order") for the transfer to the debtor of the creditor's title to certain goods to which the agreement relates ("the transferred goods"), and the return to the creditor of the remainder of the goods.

(2) In determining for the purposes of this section how much of the total price has been paid ("the paid-up sum"), the court may—

(a) treat any sum paid by the debtor, or owed by the creditor, in relation to the goods as part of the paid-up sum;

(b) deduct any sum owed by the debtor in relation to the goods (otherwise than as part of the total price) from the paid-up sum,

and make corresponding reductions in amounts so owed.

(3) Where a transfer order is made, the transferred goods shall be such of the goods to which the agreement relates as the court thinks just; but a transfer order shall be made only where the paid-up sum exceeds the part of the total price referable to the transferred goods by an amount equal to at least one-third of the unpaid balance of the total price.

(4) Notwithstanding the making of a return order or transfer order, the debtor may at any time before the goods enter the possession of the creditor, on payment of the balance of the total price and the fulfilment of any other necessary conditions, claim the goods ordered to be returned to the creditor.

(5) When, in pursuance of a time order or under this section, the total price of goods under a regulated hire-purchase agreement or regulated conditional sale agreement is paid and any other necessary conditions are fulfilled, the creditor's title to the goods vests in the debtor.

(6) If, in contravention of a return order or transfer order, any goods to which the order relates are not returned to the creditor, the court, on the application of the creditor, may—

(a) revoke so much of the order as relates to those goods, and

(b) order the debtor to pay the creditor the unpaid portion of so much of the total price as is referable to those goods.

(7) For the purposes of this section, the part of the total price referable to any goods is the part assigned to those goods by the agreement or (if no such assignment is made) the part determined by the court to be reasonable.

[1.636]
134 Evidence of adverse detention in hire-purchase etc cases

(1) Where goods are comprised in a regulated hire-purchase agreement, regulated conditional sale agreement or regulated consumer hire agreement, and the creditor or owner—

(a) brings an action or makes an application to enforce a right to recover possession of the goods from the debtor or hirer, and

(b) proves that a demand for the delivery of the goods was included in the default notice under section 88(5), or that, after the right to recover possession of the goods accrued but before the action was begun or the application was made, he made a request in writing to the debtor or hirer to surrender the goods,

then, for the purposes of the claim of the creditor or owner to recover possession of the goods, the possession of them by the debtor or hirer shall be deemed to be adverse to the creditor or owner.

(2) In subsection (1) "the debtor or hirer" includes a person in possession of the goods at any time between the debtor's or hirer's death and the grant of probate or administration, or (in Scotland) confirmation.

(3) Nothing in this section affects a claim for damages for conversion or (in Scotland) for delict.

Supplemental provisions as to orders

[1.637]
135 Power to impose conditions, or suspend operation of order
(1) If it considers it just to do so, the court may in an order made by it in relation to a regulated agreement include provisions—
    (a)   making the operation of any term of the order conditional on the doing of specified acts by any party to the proceedings;
    (b)   suspending the operation of any term of the order either—
        (i)   until such time as the court subsequently directs, or
        (ii)   until the occurrence of a specified act or omission.
(2) The court shall not suspend the operation of a term requiring the delivery up of goods by any person unless satisfied that the goods are in his possession or control.
(3) In the case of a consumer hire agreement, the court shall not so use its powers under subsection (1)(b) as to extend the period for which, under the terms of the agreement, the hirer is entitled to possession of the goods to which the agreement relates.
(4) On the application of any person affected by a provision included under subsection (1), the court may vary the provision.

[1.638]
136 Power to vary agreements and securities
The court may in an order made by it under this Act include such provision as it considers just for amending any agreement or security in consequence of a term of the order.

137–140 (*Repealed by the Consumer Credit Act 2006, ss 22(3), 70, Sch 4, as from 6 April 2007, subject to transitional provisions in s 69(1) of, and Sch 3, paras 1, 15 to, that Act at* **[1.1945]**, **[1.1947]**.)

[Unfair relationships

[1.639]
140A Unfair relationships between creditors and debtors
(1) The court may make an order under section 140B in connection with a credit agreement if it determines that the relationship between the creditor and the debtor arising out of the agreement (or the agreement taken with any related agreement) is unfair to the debtor because of one or more of the following—
    (a)   any of the terms of the agreement or of any related agreement;
    (b)   the way in which the creditor has exercised or enforced any of his rights under the agreement or any related agreement;
    (c)   any other thing done (or not done) by, or on behalf of, the creditor (either before or after the making of the agreement or any related agreement).
(2) In deciding whether to make a determination under this section the court shall have regard to all matters it thinks relevant (including matters relating to the creditor and matters relating to the debtor).
(3) For the purposes of this section the court shall (except to the extent that it is not appropriate to do so) treat anything done (or not done) by, or on behalf of, or in relation to, an associate or a former associate of the creditor as if done (or not done) by, or on behalf of, or in relation to, the creditor.
(4) A determination may be made under this section in relation to a relationship notwithstanding that the relationship may have ended.
(5) An order under section 140B shall not be made in connection with a credit agreement which is an exempt agreement [for the purposes of Chapter 14A of Part 2 of the Regulated Activities Order by virtue of article 60C(2) of that Order (regulated mortgage contracts and regulated home purchase plans)].]

NOTES
   Inserted, together with preceding cross-heading, by the Consumer Credit Act 2006, s 19, as from 6 April 2007, subject to transitional provisions in s 69(1) of, and Sch 3, paras 1, 14 to, that Act at **[1.1945]**, **[1.1947]**.
   Sub-s (5): words in square brackets substituted by the Financial Services and Markets Act 2000 (Regulated Activities) (Amendment) (No 2) Order 2013, SI 2013/1881, art 20(1), (39), as from 26 July 2013 (certain purposes), and as from 1 April 2014 (remaining purposes), for transitional provisions see Pt 8 thereof at **[2.1007]** et seq.

[1.640]
[140B Powers of court in relation to unfair relationships
(1) An order under this section in connection with a credit agreement may do one or more of the following—
    (a)   require the creditor, or any associate or former associate of his, to repay (in whole or in part) any sum paid by the debtor or by a surety by virtue of the agreement or any related agreement (whether paid to the creditor, the associate or the former associate or to any other person);

(b)   require the creditor, or any associate or former associate of his, to do or not to do (or to cease doing) anything specified in the order in connection with the agreement or any related agreement;

(c)   reduce or discharge any sum payable by the debtor or by a surety by virtue of the agreement or any related agreement;

(d)   direct the return to a surety of any property provided by him for the purposes of a security;

(e)   otherwise set aside (in whole or in part) any duty imposed on the debtor or on a surety by virtue of the agreement or any related agreement;

(f)   alter the terms of the agreement or of any related agreement;

(g)   direct accounts to be taken, or (in Scotland) an accounting to be made, between any persons.

(2) An order under this section may be made in connection with a credit agreement only—

    (a)   on an application made by the debtor or by a surety;

    (b)   at the instance of the debtor or a surety in any proceedings in any court to which the debtor and the creditor are parties, being proceedings to enforce the agreement or any related agreement; or

    (c)   at the instance of the debtor or a surety in any other proceedings in any court where the amount paid or payable under the agreement or any related agreement is relevant.

(3) An order under this section may be made notwithstanding that its effect is to place on the creditor, or any associate or former associate of his, a burden in respect of an advantage enjoyed by another person.

(4) An application under subsection (2)(a) may only be made—

    (a)   in England and Wales, to the county court;

    (b)   in Scotland, to the sheriff court;

    (c)   in Northern Ireland, to the High Court (subject to subsection (6)).

(5) In Scotland such an application may be made in the sheriff court for the district in which the debtor or surety resides or carries on business.

(6) In Northern Ireland such an application may be made to the county court if the credit agreement is an agreement under which the creditor provides the debtor with—

    (a)   fixed-sum credit not exceeding £15,000; or

    (b)   running-account credit on which the credit limit does not exceed £15,000.

(7) Without prejudice to any provision which may be made by rules of court made in relation to county courts in Northern Ireland, such rules may provide that an application made by virtue of subsection (6) may be made in the county court for the division in which the debtor or surety resides or carries on business.

(8) A party to any proceedings mentioned in subsection (2) shall be entitled, in accordance with rules of court, to have any person who might be the subject of an order under this section made a party to the proceedings.

(9) If, in any such proceedings, the debtor or a surety alleges that the relationship between the creditor and the debtor is unfair to the debtor, it is for the creditor to prove to the contrary.]

NOTES

Inserted by the Consumer Credit Act 2006, s 20, as from 6 April 2007, subject to transitional provisions in s 69(1) of, and Sch 3, paras 1, 14, 16 to, that Act at **[1.1945]**, **[1.1947]**.

[1.641]
[140C Interpretation of ss 140A and 140B

(1) In this section and in sections 140A and 140B "credit agreement" means any agreement between an individual (the "debtor") and any other person (the "creditor") by which the creditor provides the debtor with credit of any amount.

(2) References in this section and in sections 140A and 140B to the creditor or to the debtor under a credit agreement include—

    (a)   references to the person to whom his rights and duties under the agreement have passed by assignment or operation of law;

    (b)   where two or more persons are the creditor or the debtor, references to any one or more of those persons.

(3) The definition of "court" in section 189(1) does not apply for the purposes of sections 140A and 140B.

(4) References in sections 140A and 140B to an agreement related to a credit agreement (the "main agreement") are references to—

    (a)   a credit agreement consolidated by the main agreement;

    (b)   a linked transaction in relation to the main agreement or to a credit agreement within paragraph (a);

    (c)   a security provided in relation to the main agreement, to a credit agreement within paragraph (a) or to a linked transaction within paragraph (b).

(5) In the case of a credit agreement which is not a regulated consumer credit agreement, for the purposes of subsection (4) a transaction shall be treated as being a linked transaction in relation to that agreement if it would have been such a transaction had that agreement been a regulated consumer credit agreement.

(6)   For the purposes of this section and section 140B the definitions of "security" and "surety" in section 189(1) apply (with any appropriate changes) in relation to—

   (a)   a credit agreement which is not a consumer credit agreement as if it were a consumer credit agreement; and

   (b)   a transaction which is a linked transaction by virtue of subsection (5).

(7)   For the purposes of this section a credit agreement (the "earlier agreement") is consolidated by another credit agreement (the "later agreement") if—

   (a)   the later agreement is entered into by the debtor (in whole or in part) for purposes connected with debts owed by virtue of the earlier agreement; and

   (b)   at any time prior to the later agreement being entered into the parties to the earlier agreement included—

      (i)   the debtor under the later agreement; and

      (ii)   the creditor under the later agreement or an associate or a former associate of his.

(8)   Further, if the later agreement is itself consolidated by another credit agreement (whether by virtue of this subsection or subsection (7)), then the earlier agreement is consolidated by that other agreement as well.]

NOTES

Inserted by the Consumer Credit Act 2006, s 21, as from 6 April 2007, subject to transitional provisions in s 69(1) of, and Sch 3, paras 1, 16, 17 to, that Act at **[1.1945]**, **[1.1947]**.

140D   (*Inserted by the Consumer Credit Act 2006, s 22(1); repealed by the Financial Services and Markets Act 2000 (Regulated Activities) (Amendment) (No 2) Order 2013, SI 2013/1881, art 20(1), (40), as from 26 July 2013 (certain purposes), and as from 1 April 2014 (remaining purposes), for transitional provisions see Pt 8 thereof at* **[2.1007]** *et seq.)*

Miscellaneous

[1.642]

141   Jurisdiction and parties

(1)   In England and Wales, the county court shall have jurisdiction to hear and determine—

   (a)   any action by the creditor or owner to enforce a regulated agreement or any security relating to it;

   (b)   any action to enforce any linked transaction against the debtor or hirer or his relative;

and such an action shall not be brought in any other court.

(2)   Where an action or application is brought in the High Court which, by virtue of this Act, ought to have been brought in the county court it shall not be treated as improperly brought, but shall be transferred to the county court.

(3)–(3B)   (*Apply to Scotland only.*)

(4)   In Northern Ireland the county court shall have jurisdiction to hear and determine any action or application falling within subsection (1).

(5)   Except as may be provided by rules of court, all the parties to a regulated agreement, and any surety, shall be made parties to any proceedings relating to the agreement.

[1.643]

142   Power to declare rights of parties

(1)   Where under any provision of this Act a thing can be done by a creditor or owner on an enforcement order only, and either—

   (a)   the court dismisses (except on technical grounds only) an application for an enforcement order, or

   (b)   where no such application has been made or such an application has been dismissed on technical grounds only, an interested party applies to the court for a declaration under this subsection,

the court may if it thinks just make a declaration that the creditor or owner is not entitled to do that thing, and thereafter no application for an enforcement order in respect of it shall be entertained.

(2)   Where—

   (a)   a regulated agreement or linked transaction is cancelled under section 69(1), or becomes subject to section 69(2), or

   (b)   a regulated agreement is terminated under section 91, and an interested party applies to the court for a declaration under this subsection, the court may make a declaration to that effect.

143, 144   (*Apply to Northern Ireland only.*)

PART X
ANCILLARY CREDIT BUSINESS

Definitions

[1.644]

145   Types of ancillary credit business

(1)   An ancillary credit business is any business so far as it comprises or relates to—

(a)   credit brokerage,
(b)   debt-adjusting,
(c)   debt-counselling,
(d)   debt-collecting,
[(da) debt administration,]
[(db) the provision of credit information services, or]
(e)   the operation of a credit reference agency.
[(2) "Credit brokerage" means the carrying on of an activity of the kind specified by article 36A(1)(a) to (c) of the Regulated Activities Order (credit broking), disregarding the effect of paragraph (2) of that article.]
[(5) "Debt adjusting" means the carrying on of an activity of the kind specified by article 39D of that Order (debt adjusting).]
[(6) "Debt-counselling" means the carrying on of an activity of the kind specified by article 39E of that Order (debt-counselling).]
[(7) "Debt-collecting" means the carrying on of an activity of the kind specified by article 39F of that Order (debt-collecting).]
[(7A) "Debt administration" means the carrying on of an activity of the kind specified by article 39G of that Order (debt administration), disregarding the effect of paragraph (3) of that article.]
[(7B) A person ("P") provides credit information services if P carries on, by way of business, an activity of the kind specified by article 89A(1) or (2) of that Order (providing credit information services).]
[(8) A person ("P") operates a credit reference agency if P carries on, by way of business, an activity of the kind specified by article 89B of that Order (providing credit references).]

NOTES
Sub-s (1): para (da) substituted (for original word "or" in para (d)) and para (db) inserted, by the Consumer Credit Act 2006, ss 24(1), 25(1), as from 1 October 2008.
Sub-s (2): substituted, for original sub-ss (2)–(4), by the Financial Services and Markets Act 2000 (Regulated Activities) (Amendment) (No 2) Order 2013, SI 2013/1881, art 20(1), (41)(a), as from 26 July 2013 (certain purposes), and as from 1 April 2014 (remaining purposes), for transitional provisions see Pt 8 thereof at **[2.1007]** et seq.
Sub-ss (5)–(7), (8): substituted by SI 2013/1881, art 20(1), (41)(b)–(d), (g), as from 26 July 2013 (certain purposes), and as from 1 April 2014 (remaining purposes), for transitional provisions see Pt 8 thereof at **[2.1007]** et seq.
Sub-ss (7A), (7B): substituted, for original sub-s-ss (7A)–(7D) (as inserted by the Consumer Credit Act 2006, s 24(2), 25(2)), by SI 2013/1881, art 20(1), (41)(e), (f), as from 26 July 2013 (certain purposes), and as from 1 April 2014 (remaining purposes), for transitional provisions see Pt 8 thereof at **[2.1007]** et seq.

146–150 *(Repealed by the Financial Services and Markets Act 2000 (Regulated Activities) (Amendment) (No 2) Order 2013, SI 2013/1881, art 20(1), (42), as from 26 July 2013 (certain purposes), and as from 1 April 2014 (remaining purposes), for transitional provisions see Pt 8 thereof at* **[2.1007]** *et seq.)*

Seeking business

151–152 *(Repealed by the Financial Services and Markets Act 2000 (Regulated Activities) (Amendment) (No 2) Order 2013, SI 2013/1881, art 20(1), (42), as from 26 July 2013 (certain purposes), and as from 1 April 2014 (remaining purposes), for transitional provisions see Pt 8 thereof at* **[2.1007]** *et seq.)*

[1.645]
153 Definition of canvassing off trade premises (agreements for ancillary credit services)
(1) An individual (the "canvasser") canvasses off trade premises the services of a person carrying on an ancillary credit business if he solicits the entry of another individual (the "consumer") into an agreement for the provision to the consumer of those services by making oral representations to the consumer, or any other individual, during a visit by the canvasser to any place (not excluded by subsection (2)) where the consumer, or that other individual, as the case may be, is, being a visit—
(a)   carried out for the purpose of making such oral representations to individuals who are at that place, but
(b)   not carried out in response to a request made on a previous occasion.
(2) A place is excluded from subsection (1) if it is a place where (whether on a permanent or temporary basis)—
(a)   the ancillary credit business is carried on, or
(b)   any business is carried on by the canvasser or the person whose employee or agent the canvasser is, or by the consumer.

[1.646]
154 Prohibition of canvassing certain ancillary credit services off trade premises
It is an offence to canvass off trade premises the services of a person carrying on a business of credit brokerage, debt-adjusting[, debt-counselling or the provision of credit information services].

NOTES
Words in square brackets substituted by the Consumer Credit Act 2006, s 25(4)(b).

[1.647]

155 Right to recover brokerage fees

(1) [Subject to subsection (2A),] the excess over [£5] of a fee or commission for his services charged by a credit-broker to an individual to whom this subsection applies shall cease to be payable or, as the case may be, shall be recoverable by the individual if the introduction does not result in his entering into a relevant agreement within the six months following the introduction (disregarding any agreement which is cancelled under section 69(1) or becomes subject to section 69(2)).

(2) Subsection (1) applies to an individual who sought an introduction for a purpose which would have been fulfilled by his entry into—

    (a)   a regulated agreement, or

    (b)   in the case of an individual [desiring to obtain credit to finance the acquisition or provision of a dwelling occupied or to be occupied by that individual or a relative of that individual], an agreement for credit secured on land,[

    (c)   a credit agreement which is an exempt agreement for the purposes of Chapter 14A of Part 2 of the Regulated Activities Order, or

    (d)   an agreement which is not a regulated credit agreement or a regulated consumer hire agreement but which would be such an agreement if the law applicable to the agreement were the law of a part of the United Kingdom.]

[(2A) But subsection (1) does not apply where—

    (a)   the fee or commission relates to the effecting of an introduction of a kind mentioned in [article 36E of the Regulated Activities Order (activities in relation to certain agreements relating to land)]; and

    (b)   the person charging that fee or commission is an authorised person or an appointed representative, within the meaning of the Financial Services and Markets Act 2000.]

(3) An agreement is a relevant agreement for the purposes of subsection (1) in relation to an individual if it is an agreement such as is referred to in subsection (2) in relation to that individual.

(4) In the case of an individual desiring to obtain credit under a consumer credit agreement, any sum payable or paid by him to a credit-broker otherwise than as a fee or commission for the credit-broker's services shall for the purposes of subsection (1) be treated as such a fee or commission if it enters, or would enter, into the total charge for credit.

NOTES

Sub-s (1): words in first pair of square brackets inserted by the Financial Services and Markets Act 2000 (Regulated Activities) (Amendment) (No 1) Order 2003, SI 2003/1475, art 22(1), (2), as from 31 October 2004; sum in second pair of square brackets substituted by the Consumer Credit (Further Increase in Monetary Amounts) Order 1998, SI 1998/997, art 3, Schedule, as from 1 May 1998.

Sub-s (2): in para (b) words in square brackets substituted, and paras (c), (d) substituted, for original para (c), by the Financial Services and Markets Act 2000 (Regulated Activities) (Amendment) (No 2) Order 2013, SI 2013/1881, art 20(1), (43)(a), as from 26 July 2013 (certain purposes), and as from 1 April 2014 (remaining purposes), for transitional provisions see Pt 8 thereof at **[2.1007]** et seq.

Sub-s (2A): inserted by SI 2003/1475, art 22(1), (3), as from 31 October 2004; in para (a) words in square brackets substituted by SI 2013/1881, art 20(1), (43)(b), as from 26 July 2013 (certain purposes), and as from 1 April 2014 (remaining purposes), for transitional provisions see Pt 8 thereof at **[2.1007]** et seq.

156 (*Repealed by the Financial Services and Markets Act 2000 (Regulated Activities) (Amendment) (No 2) Order 2013, SI 2013/1881, art 20(1), (44), as from 26 July 2013 (certain purposes), and as from 1 April 2014 (remaining purposes), for transitional provisions see Pt 8 thereof at* **[2.1007]** *et seq.*)

Credit reference agencies

[1.648]

157 Duty to disclose name etc of agency

[(A1) Where a creditor under a prospective regulated agreement, other than an excluded agreement, decides not to proceed with it on the basis of information obtained by the creditor from a credit reference agency, the creditor must, when informing the debtor of the decision—

    (a)   inform the debtor that this decision has been reached on the basis of information from a credit reference agency, and

    (b)   provide the debtor with the particulars of the agency including its name, address and telephone number.]

(1) [In any other case,] a creditor, owner or negotiator, within the prescribed period after receiving a request in writing to that effect from the debtor or hirer, shall give him notice of the name and address of any credit reference agency from which the creditor, owner or negotiator has, during the antecedent negotiations, applied for information about his financial standing.

(2) Subsection (1) does not apply to a request received more than 28 days after the termination of the antecedent negotiations, whether on the making of the regulated agreement or otherwise.

[(2A) A creditor is not required to disclose information under this section if such disclosure—

    (a)   contravenes the Data Protection Act 1998,

    (b)   is prohibited by any EU obligation,

(c)   would create or be likely to create a serious risk that any person would be subject to violence or intimidation, or

(d)   would, or would be likely to, prejudice—
   (i)   the prevention or detection of crime,
   (ii)   the apprehension or prosecution of offenders, or
   (iii)   the administration of justice.]

(3)   If the creditor, owner or negotiator fails to comply with subsection [(A1) or] (1) he commits an offence.

[(4)   For the purposes of subsection (A1) an agreement is an excluded agreement if it is—
   (a)   a consumer hire agreement, or
   (b)   an agreement secured on land.]

NOTES

Sub-ss (A1), (2A): inserted by the Consumer Credit (EU Directive) Regulations 2010, SI 2010/1010, regs 2, 40(1), (2), (4), as from 1 February 2011, with effect in relation to certain agreements before that date, as provided for in regs 101, 101A of the 2010 Regulations at [**2.804**], [**2.805**].

Sub-ss (1), (3): words in square brackets inserted by SI 2010/1010, regs 2, 40(1), (3), (5), as from 1 February 2011, with effect in relation to certain agreements before that date, as provided for in regs 101, 101A of the 2010 Regulations at [**2.804**], [**2.805**].

Sub-s (4): added by SI 2010/1010, regs 2, 40(1), (6), as from 1 February 2011, with effect in relation to certain agreements before that date, as provided for in regs 101, 101A of the 2010 Regulations at [**2.804**], [**2.805**].

Regulations: the Consumer Credit (Credit Reference Agency) Regulations 2000, SI 2000/290.

[1.649]

158   Duty of agency to disclose filed information

(1)   A credit reference agency, within the prescribed period after receiving,
   [(a)   a request in writing to that effect from a consumer,] and
   (b)   such particulars as the agency may reasonably require to enable them to identify the file, and
   (c)   a fee of [£2],
shall give the consumer a copy of the file relating to [it] kept by the agency.

(2)   When giving a copy of the file under subsection (1), the agency shall also give the consumer a statement in the prescribed form of [the consumer's] rights under section 159.

(3)   If the agency does not keep a file relating to the consumer it shall give [the consumer] notice of that fact, but need not return any money paid.

(4)   If the agency contravenes any provision of this section it commits an offence.

[(4A)   In this section "consumer" means—
   (a)   a partnership consisting of two or three persons not all of whom are bodies corporate; or
   (b)   an unincorporated body of persons which does not consist entirely of bodies corporate and is not a partnership.]

(5)   In this Act "file", in relation to an individual, means all the information about him kept by a credit reference agency, regardless of how the information is stored and "copy of the file", as respects information not in plain English, means a transcript reduced into plain English.

NOTES

Sub-s (1): para (a) substituted by the Consumer Credit Act 2006, s 5(5), as from 6 April 2007; sum in square brackets in para (c) substituted by the Consumer Credit (Further Increase of Monetary Amounts) Order 1998, SI 1998/997, Schedule, para 3, as from 1 May 1998.

Sub-ss (2), (3): words in square brackets substituted by the Data Protection Act 1998, s 62(1)(b), (c), as from 1 March 2000, subject to savings in Sch 14, para 20 to that Act.

Sub-s (4A): inserted by the Consumer Credit Act 2006, s 5(6), as from 6 April 2007.

Regulations: the Consumer Credit (Credit Reference Agency) Regulations 2000, SI 2000/290.

[1.650]

159   Correction of wrong information

[(1)   Any individual (the "objector") given—
   (a)   information under section 7 of the Data Protection Act 1998 by a credit reference agency, or
   (b)   information under section 158,
who considers that an entry in his file is incorrect, and that if it is not corrected he is likely to be prejudiced, may give notice to the agency requiring it either to remove the entry from the file or amend it.]

(2)   Within 28 days after receiving a notice under subsection (1), the agency shall by notice inform the [objector] that it has—
   (a)   removed the entry from the file, or
   (b)   amended the entry, or
   (c)   taken no action,
and if the notice states that the agency has amended the entry it shall include a copy of the file so far as it comprises the amended entry.

(3) Within 28 days after receiving a notice under subsection (2) or, where no such notice was given, within 28 days after the expiry of the period mentioned in subsection (2), the [objector] may, unless he has been informed by the agency that it has removed the entry from his file, serve a further notice on the agency requiring it to add to the file an accompanying notice of correction (not exceeding 200 words) drawn up by the [objector] and include a copy of it when furnishing information included in or based on that entry.

(4) Within 28 days after receiving a notice under subsection (3), the agency, unless it intends to apply to the [the relevant authority] under subsection (5), shall by notice inform the [objector] that it has received the notice under subsection (3) and intends to comply with it.

(5) If—

(a)   the [objector] has not received a notice under subsection (4) within the time required, or

(b)   it appears to the agency that it would be improper for it to publish a notice of correction because it is incorrect, or unjustly defames any person, or is frivolous or scandalous, or is for any other reason unsuitable,

the [objector] or, as the case may be, the agency may, in the prescribed manner and on payment of [the prescribed fee], apply to the [the relevant authority], who may make such order on the application as he thinks fit.

(6) If a person to whom an order under this section is directed fails to comply with it within the period specified in the order he commits an offence.

[(7) The [Information Commissioner] may vary or revoke any order made by him under this section.

(8) In this section "the relevant authority" means—

(a)   where the objector is a partnership or other unincorporated body of persons, the [FCA], and

(b)   in any other case, the [Information Commissioner].]

NOTES

Sub-s (1): substituted by the Data Protection Act 1998, s 62(1), (2), as from 1 March 2000, for savings see Sch 14, para 20 thereto and the Data Protection Act 1998 (Commencement) Order 2000, SI 2000/183, art 2(2).

Sub-ss (2)–(4): words in square brackets substituted by the Data Protection Act 1998, s 62(3), as from 1 March 2000, for savings see Sch 14, para 20 thereto and SI 2000/183, art 2(2).

Sub-s (5): words in first, second and final pairs of square brackets substituted by the Data Protection Act 1998, s 62(3), as from 1 March 2000, for savings see Sch 14, para 20 thereto and SI 2000/183, art 2(2); words in third pair of square brackets substituted by the Financial Services and Markets Act 2000 (Regulated Activities) (Amendment) (No 2) Order 2013, SI 2013/1881, art 20(1), (45), as from 26 July 2013 (certain purposes), and as from 1 April 2014 (remaining purposes), for transitional provisions see Pt 8 thereof at **[2.1007]** et seq.

Sub-s (7): added, together with sub-s (8), by the Data Protection Act 1998, s 62(4), as from 1 March 2000, for savings see Sch 14, para 20 thereto and SI 2000/183, art 2(2)); words in square brackets substituted by the Freedom of Information Act 2000, s 18(4), Sch 2, Pt I, para 7.

Sub-s (8): added as noted to sub-s (7); in para (a) word in square brackets substituted by the Financial Services Act 2012 (Consumer Credit) Order 2013, SI 2013/1882, art 7(1), (11), as from 26 July 2013 (certain purposes), and as from 1 April 2014 (remaining purposes); in para (b) words in square brackets substituted by the Freedom of Information Act 2000, s 18(4), Sch 2, Pt I, para 7, as from 30 January 2001.

References to the FCA, etc: as to the abolition of the office of the Director General of Fair Trading and the substitution of the original references to the Director (and related expressions), see the note preceding s 8 at **[1.520]**.

Regulations: the Consumer Credit (Credit Reference Agency) Regulations 2000, SI 2000/290.

[1.651]
160 Alternative procedure for business consumers

(1) The [FCA], on an application made by a credit reference agency, may direct that this section shall apply to the agency if [it] is satisfied—

(a)   that compliance with section 158 in the case of consumers who carry on a business would adversely affect the service provided to its customers by the agency, and

(b)   that, having regard to the methods employed by the agency and to any other relevant factors, it is probable that consumers carrying on a business would not be prejudiced by the making of the direction.

(2) Where an agency to which this section applies receives a request, particulars and a fee under section 158(1) from a consumer who carries on a business, and section 158(3) does not apply, the agency, instead of complying with section 158, may elect to deal with the matter under the following subsections.

(3) Instead of giving the consumer a copy of the file, the agency shall within the prescribed period give notice to the consumer that it is proceeding under this section, and by notice give the consumer such information included in or based on entries in the file as the [FCA] may direct, together with a statement in the prescribed form of the consumer's rights under subsections (4) and (5).

(4) If within 28 days after receiving the information given [to the consumer] under subsection (3), or such longer period as the [FCA] may allow, the consumer—

(a)   gives notice to the [FCA] that [the consumer] is dissatisfied with the information, and

(b)   satisfies the [FCA] that [the consumer] has taken such steps in relation to the agency as may be reasonable with a view to removing the cause of [the consumer's] dissatisfaction, and

(c)   pays the [FCA] [the prescribed fee],

the [FCA] may direct the agency to give the [FCA] a copy of the file, and the [FCA] may disclose to the consumer such of the information on the file as the [FCA] thinks fit.

(5)   Section 159 applies with any necessary modifications to information given to the consumer under this section as it applies to information given under section 158.

(6)   If an agency making an election under subsection (2) fails to comply with subsection (3) or (4) it commits an offence.

[(7)   In this section "consumer" has the same meaning as in section 158.]

NOTES

Sub-s (1): word in first pair of square brackets substituted by the Financial Services Act 2012 (Consumer Credit) Order 2013, SI 2013/1882, art 7(1), (12), as from 26 July 2013 (certain purposes), and as from 1 April 2014 (remaining purposes); word in second pair of square brackets substituted by the Enterprise Act 2002, s 278(1), Sch 25, para 6(1), (31)(b).

Sub-s (3): word in square brackets substituted by SI 2013/1882, art 7(1), (12), as from 26 July 2013 (certain purposes), and as from 1 April 2014 (remaining purposes).

Sub-s (4): words in first, fourth, sixth and seventh pairs of square brackets substituted by the Data Protection Act 1998, s 62(5)(a), as from 1 March 2000, for savings see Sch 14, para 20 thereto and the Data Protection Act 1998 (Commencement) Order 2000, SI 2000/183, art 2(2); all references to "FCA" in square brackets substituted by SI 2013/1882, art 7(1), (12), as from 26 July 2013 (certain purposes), and as from 1 April 2014 (remaining purposes); in sub-s (c) words in second pair of square brackets substituted by the Financial Services and Markets Act 2000 (Regulated Activities) (Amendment) (No 2) Order 2013, SI 2013/1881, art 20(1), (46), as from 26 July 2013 (certain purposes), and as from 1 April 2014 (remaining purposes), for transitional provisions see Pt 8 thereof at **[2.1007]** et seq.

Sub-s (7): added by the Data Protection Act 1998, s 62(5)(b), as from 1 March 2000; for savings see Sch 14, para 20 thereto and SI 2000/183, art 2(2).

References to the FCA, etc: as to the abolition of the office of the Director General of Fair Trading and the substitution of the original references to the Director (and related expressions), see the note preceding s 8 at **[1.520]**.

Regulations: the Consumer Credit (Credit Reference Agency) Regulations 2000, SI 2000/290.

160A   (*Inserted by the Consumer Credit (EU Directive) Regulations 2010, SI 2010/1010, regs 2, 41, as from 1 February 2011, with effect in relation to certain agreements before that date; repealed by the Financial Services and Markets Act 2000 (Regulated Activities) (Amendment) (No 2) Order 2013, SI 2013/1881, art 20(1), (44), as from 26 July 2013 (certain purposes), and as from 1 April 2014 (remaining purposes), for transitional provisions see Pt 8 thereof at* **[2.1007]** *et seq.*)

PART XI
ENFORCEMENT OF ACT

[1.652]
161   Enforcement authorities
(1)   The following authorities ("enforcement authorities") have a duty to enforce this Act and regulations made under it—
   (a)   . . .
   (b)   in Great Britain, the local weights and measures authority,
   (c)   in Northern Ireland, the Department of Commerce for Northern Ireland.
[(1A)   Subsection (1) does not limit any function of the FCA in relation to the enforcement of this Act or regulations made under it.]
[(1B)   For the investigatory powers available to a local weights and measures authority or the Department of Enterprise, Trade and Investment in Northern Ireland for the purposes of the duty in subsection (1), see Schedule 5 to the Consumer Rights Act 2015.]
(2)   . . .
(3)   Every local weights and measures authority shall, whenever the [FCA] requires, report to [it] in such form and with such particulars as [it] requires on the exercise of their functions under this Act.
(4)–(6)   . . .

NOTES

Sub-s (1): para (a) repealed by the Financial Services and Markets Act 2000 (Regulated Activities) (Amendment) (No 2) Order 2013, SI 2013/1881, art 20(1), (48)(a), as from 26 July 2013 (certain purposes), and as from 1 April 2014 (remaining purposes), for transitional provisions see Pt 8 thereof at **[2.1007]** et seq.

Sub-s (1A): inserted by SI 2013/1881, art 20(1), (48)(b), as from 26 July 2013 (certain purposes), and as from 1 April 2014 (remaining purposes), for transitional provisions see Pt 8 thereof at **[2.1007]** et seq.

Sub-s (1B): inserted by the Consumer Rights Act 2015, s 77, Sch 6, paras 12, 13, as from 1 October 2015 (for transitional provisions see the Consumer Rights Act 2015 (Commencement No 3, Transitional Provisions, Savings and Consequential Amendments) Order 2015, SI 2015/1630, arts 6–8 at **[2.1220]** et seq).

Sub-s (2): repealed by the Enterprise Act 2002, s 278, Sch 25, para 6(1), (32)(b), Sch 26, as from 1 April 2003.

Sub-s (3): word in first pair of square brackets substituted by the Financial Services Act 2012 (Consumer Credit) Order 2013, SI 2013/1882, art 7(1), (13), as from 26 July 2013 (certain purposes), and as from 1 April 2014 (remaining purposes); words in second and final pairs of square brackets substituted by the Enterprise Act 2002, s 278(1), Sch 25, para 6(1), (32)(c).

Sub-ss (4)–(6): repealed by the Local Government, Planning and Land Act 1980, ss 1(4), 194, Sch 4, para 10, Sch 34, Pt IV, as from 13 November 1980.

References to the FCA, etc: as to the abolition of the office of the Director General of Fair Trading and the substitution of the original references to the Director (and related expressions), see the note preceding s 8 at **[1.520]**.

[1.653]

162 *Powers of entry and inspection*

(1) *A duly authorised officer of an enforcement authority, at all reasonable hours and on production, if required, of his credentials, may—*

(a) *in order to ascertain whether a breach of any provision of or under this Act has been committed, inspect any goods and enter any premises (other than premises used only as a dwelling);*

(b) *if he has reasonable cause to suspect that a breach of any provision of or under this Act has been committed, in order to ascertain whether it has been committed, require any person—*

    (i) *carrying on, or employed in connection with, a business to produce any . . . documents relating to it; or*

    (ii) *having control of any information relating to a business [to provide him with that information];*

(c) *if he has reasonable cause to believe that a breach of any provision of or under this Act has been committed, seize and detain any goods in order to ascertain (by testing or otherwise) whether such a breach has been committed;*

(d) *seize and detain any goods . . . or documents which he has reason to believe may be required as evidence in proceedings for an offence under this Act;*

(e) *for the purpose of exercising his powers under this subsection to seize goods . . . or documents, but only if and to the extent that it is reasonably necessary for securing that the provisions of this Act and of any regulations made under it are duly observed, require any person having authority to do so to break open any container and, if that person does not comply, break it open himself.*

(2) *An officer seizing goods . . . or documents in exercise of his powers under this section shall not do so without informing the person he seizes them from.*

(3) *If a justice of the peace, on sworn information in writing, or, in Scotland, a sheriff or a magistrate or justice of the peace, on evidence on oath,—*

(a) *is satisfied that there is reasonable ground to believe either—*

    (i) *that any goods . . . or documents which a duly authorised officer has power to inspect under this section are on any premises and their inspection is likely to disclose evidence of a breach of any provision of or under this Act; or*

    (ii) *that a breach of any provision of or under this Act has been, is being or is about to be committed on any premises; and*

(b) *is also satisfied either—*

    (i) *that admission to the premises has been or is likely to be refused and that notice of intention to apply for a warrant under this subsection has been given to the occupier; or*

    (ii) *that an application for admission, or the giving of such a notice, would defeat the object of the entry or that the premises are unoccupied or that the occupier is temporarily absent and it might defeat the object of the entry to wait for his return,*

the justice or, as the case may be, the sheriff or magistrate may by warrant under his hand, which shall continue in force for a period of one month, authorise an officer of an enforcement authority to enter the premises (by force if need be).

(4) *An officer entering premises by virtue of this section may take such other persons and equipment with him as he thinks necessary; and on leaving premises entered by virtue of a warrant under subsection (3) shall, if they are unoccupied or the occupier is temporarily absent, leave them as effectively secured against trespassers as he found them.*

(5) *. . .*

(6) *A person who is not a duly authorised officer of an enforcement authority, but purports to act as such under this section, commits an offence.*

(7) *. . .*

[(8) *. . .]*

NOTES

Repealed by the Consumer Rights Act 2015, s 77, Sch 6, paras 12, 14, as from 1 October 2015 (for transitional provisions see the Consumer Rights Act 2015 (Commencement No 3, Transitional Provisions, Savings and Consequential Amendments) Order 2015, SI 2015/1630, arts 6–8 at **[2.1220]** et seq).

Sub-s (1): words omitted repealed and words in square brackets substituted by the Consumer Credit Act 2006, ss 51(2), 70, Sch 4, as from 6 April 2008.

Sub-ss (2), (3): words omitted repealed by the Consumer Credit Act 2006, s 70, Sch 4, as from 6 April 2008.

Sub-s (5): repealed by the Financial Services and Markets Act 2000 (Regulated Activities) (Amendment) (No 2) Order 2013, SI 2013/1881, art 20(1), (49), as from 26 July 2013 (certain purposes), and as from 1 April 2014 (remaining purposes), for transitional provisions see Pt 8 thereof at **[2.1007]** et seq.

Sub-s (7): repealed by the Consumer Credit Act 2006, s 70, Sch 4, as from 6 April 2008.

Sub-s (8): added by the Consumer Credit Act 2006, s 51(2), as from 6 April 2008; repealed by SI 2013/1881, art 20(1), (49), as from 26 July 2013 (certain purposes), and as from 1 April 2014 (remaining purposes), for transitional provisions see Pt 8 thereof at **[2.1007]** et seq.

References to the FCA, etc: as to the abolition of the office of the Director General of Fair Trading and the substitution of the original references to the Director (and related expressions), see the note preceding s 8 at **[1.520]**.

Seize and detain goods, etc: the powers of seizure conferred by sub-s (1)(c), (d) are powers to which the Criminal Justice and Police Act 2001, s 50 apply (additional powers of seizure from premises); see s 50 of, and Sch 1, Pt 1, para 19 to, that Act.

See further, in relation to the application of this section, with modifications, in respect of contraventions of certain provisions of the Financial Services and Markets Act 2000: the Financial Services Act 2012 (Consumer Credit) Order 2013, SI 2013/1882, art 8(1), (2).

Regulations: the Consumer Credit (Entry and Inspection) Regulations 1977, SI 1977/331.

[1.654]
163 Compensation for loss
(1) Where, in exercising his powers under section 162, an officer of an enforcement authority seizes and detains goods and their owner suffers loss by reason of—
 (a) that seizure, or
 (b) the loss, damage or deterioration of the goods during detention,
then, unless the owner is convicted of an offence under this Act committed in relation to the goods, the authority shall compensate him for the loss so suffered.
(2) Any dispute as to the right to or amount of any compensation under subsection (1) shall be determined by arbitration.

NOTES
Repealed by the Consumer Rights Act 2015, s 77, Sch 6, paras 12, 15, as from 1 October 2015 (for transitional provisions see the Consumer Rights Act 2015 (Commencement No 3, Transitional Provisions, Savings and Consequential Amendments) Order 2015, SI 2015/1630, arts 6–8 at **[2.1220]** et seq).

See further, in relation to the application of this section, with modifications, in respect of contraventions of certain provisions of the Financial Services and Markets Act 2000: the Financial Services Act 2012 (Consumer Credit) Order 2013, SI 2013/1882, art 8(1), (3).

[1.655]
164 Power to make test purchases etc
(1) An enforcement authority may—
 (a) make, or authorise any of their officers to make on their behalf, such purchases of goods; and
 (b) authorise any of their officers to procure the provision of such services or facilities or to enter into such agreements or other transactions,
as may appear to them expedient for determining whether any provisions made by or under this Act are being complied with.
(2) Any act done by an officer authorised to do it under subsection (1) shall be treated for the purposes of this Act as done by him as an individual on his own behalf.
(3) Any goods seized by an officer under this Act may be tested, and in the event of such a test he shall inform the person mentioned in section 162(2) of the test results.
(4) Where any test leads to proceedings under this Act, the enforcement authority shall—
 (a) if the goods were purchased, inform the person they were purchased from of the test results, and
 (b) allow any person against whom the proceedings are taken to have the goods tested on his behalf if it is reasonably practicable to do so.

NOTES
Repealed by the Consumer Rights Act 2015, s 77, Sch 6, paras 12, 16, as from 1 October 2015 (for transitional provisions see the Consumer Rights Act 2015 (Commencement No 3, Transitional Provisions, Savings and Consequential Amendments) Order 2015, SI 2015/1630, arts 6–8 at **[2.1220]** et seq).

See further, in relation to the application of this section, with modifications, in respect of contraventions of certain provisions of the Financial Services and Markets Act 2000: the Financial Services Act 2012 (Consumer Credit) Order 2013, SI 2013/1882, art 8(1), (4).

[1.656]
165 Obstruction of authorised officers
(1) Any person who—
 (a) wilfully obstructs an officer of an enforcement authority acting in pursuance of this Act; or
 (b) wilfully fails to comply with any requirement properly made to him by such an officer under section 162; or
 (c) without reasonable cause fails to give such an officer (so acting) other assistance or information he may reasonably require in performing his functions under this Act,
commits an offence.
[(1A) . . .]
(2) If any person, in giving such information as is mentioned in subsection (1)(c), makes any statement which he knows to be false, he commits an offence.
(3) Nothing in this section requires a person to answer any question or give any information if to do so might incriminate that person or (where that person is [married or a civil partner) the spouse or civil partner] of that person.

NOTES

Repealed by the Consumer Rights Act 2015, s 77, Sch 6, paras 12, 17, as from 1 October 2015 (for transitional provisions see the Consumer Rights Act 2015 (Commencement No 3, Transitional Provisions, Savings and Consequential Amendments) Order 2015, SI 2015/1630, arts 6–8 at **[2.1220]** et seq).

Sub-s (1A): inserted by the Consumer Credit Act 2006, s 51(4), as from 6 April 2008; repealed by the Financial Services and Markets Act 2000 (Regulated Activities) (Amendment) (No 2) Order 2013, SI 2013/1881, art 20(1), (50), as from 26 July 2013 (certain purposes), and as from 1 April 2014 (remaining purposes), for transitional provisions see Pt 8 thereof at **[2.1007]** et seq.

Sub-s (3): words in square brackets substituted by the Civil Partnership Act 2004, s 261(1), Sch 27, para 50, as from 5 December 2005.

See further, in relation to the application of this section, with modifications, in respect of contraventions of certain provisions of the Financial Services and Markets Act 2000: the Financial Services Act 2012 (Consumer Credit) Order 2013, SI 2013/1882, art 8(1), (5).

[1.657]
166   Notification of convictions and judgments to [FCA]

Where a person is convicted of an offence or has a judgment given against him by or before any court in the United Kingdom and it appears to the court—

    (a)   having regard to the functions of the [FCA under the Financial Services and Markets Act 2000 or] this Act, that the conviction or judgment should be brought to the [FCA's] attention, and

    (b)   that it may not be brought to [its] attention unless arrangements for that purpose are made by the court,

the court may make such arrangements notwithstanding that the proceedings have been finally disposed of.

NOTES

Section heading, words in first and second pairs of square brackets substituted by the Financial Services Act 2012 (Consumer Credit) Order 2013, SI 2013/1882, art 7(1), (14), (15), as from 26 July 2013 (certain purposes), and as from 1 April 2014 (remaining purposes); word in final pair of square brackets substituted by the Enterprise Act 2002, s 278(1), Sch 25, para 6(1), (34), as from 1 April 2003, for transitional and transitory provisions and savings see the 2002 Act, s 276, Sch 24, paras 2–6.

References to the FCA, etc: as to the abolition of the office of the Director General of Fair Trading and the substitution of the original references to the Director (and related expressions), see the note preceding s 8 at **[1.520]**.

[1.658]
167   Penalties

(1)   An offence under a provision of this Act specified in column 1 of Schedule 1 is triable in the mode or modes indicated in column 3, and on conviction is punishable as indicated in column 4 (where a period of time indicates the maximum term of imprisonment, and a monetary amount indicates the maximum fine, for the offence in question).

(2)   . . .

NOTES

Sub-s (2): repealed by the Financial Services and Markets Act 2000 (Regulated Activities) (Amendment) (No 2) Order 2013, SI 2013/1881, art 20(1), (51), as from 26 July 2013 (certain purposes), and as from 1 April 2014 (remaining purposes), for transitional provisions see Pt 8 thereof at **[2.1007]** et seq.

[1.659]
168   Defences

(1)   In any proceedings for an offence under this Act it is a defence for the person charged to prove—

    (a)   that his act or omission was due to a mistake, or to reliance on information supplied to him, or to an act or omission by another person, or to an accident or some other cause beyond his control, and

    (b)   that he took all reasonable precautions and exercised all due diligence to avoid such an act or omission by himself or any person under his control.

(2)   If in any case the defence provided by subsection (1) involves the allegation that the act or omission was due to an act or omission by another person or to reliance on information supplied by another person, the person charged shall not, without leave of the court, be entitled to rely on that defence unless, within a period ending seven clear days before the hearing, he has served on the prosecutor a notice giving such information identifying or assisting in the identification of that other person as was then in his possession.

[1.660]
169   Offences by bodies corporate

Where at any time a body corporate commits an offence under this Act with the consent or connivance of, or because of neglect by, any individual, the individual commits the like offence if at that time—

    (a)   he is a director, manager, secretary or similar officer of the body corporate, or

    (b)   he is purporting to act as such an officer, or

(c)   the body corporate is managed by its members, of whom he is one.

[1.661]
170   No further sanctions for breach of Act
(1)   A breach of any requirement made (otherwise than by any court) by or under this Act shall incur no civil or criminal sanction as being such a breach, except to the extent (if any) expressly provided by or under this Act [or by or under the Financial Services and Markets Act 2000 by virtue of an order made under section 107 of the Financial Services Act 2012].
(2)   In exercising [its] functions under this Act the [FCA] may take account of any matter appearing to [it] to constitute a breach of a requirement made by or under this Act, whether or not any sanction for that breach is provided by or under this Act and, if it is so provided, whether or not proceedings have been brought in respect of the breach.
(3)   Subsection (1) does not prevent the grant of an injunction, or the making of an order of certiorari, mandamus or prohibition or as respects Scotland the grant of an interdict or of an order under section 91 of the Court of Session Act 1868 (order for specific performance of statutory duty).

NOTES
   Sub-s (1): words in square brackets added by the Financial Services Act 2012 (Consumer Credit) Order 2013, SI 2013/1882, art 7(1), (16)(a), as from 26 July 2013 (certain purposes), and as from 1 April 2014 (remaining purposes).
   Sub-s (2): words in first and third pairs of square brackets substituted by the Enterprise Act 2002, s 278(1), Sch 25, para 6(1), (35), as from 1 April 2003, for transitional and transitory provisions and savings see the 2002 Act, s 276, Sch 24, paras 2–6; word in second pair of square brackets substituted by SI 2013/1882, art 7(1), (16)(b), as from 26 July 2013 (certain purposes), and as from 1 April 2014 (remaining purposes).
   References to the FCA, etc: as to the abolition of the office of the Director General of Fair Trading and the substitution of the original references to the Director (and related expressions), see the note preceding s 8 at **[1.520]**.
   Court of Session Act 1868, s 91: repealed by the Court of Session Act 1988.

[1.662]
171   Onus of proof in various proceedings
(1)   If an agreement contains a term signifying that in the opinion of the parties section 10(3)(b)(iii) does not apply to the agreement, it shall be taken not to apply unless the contrary is proved.
(2)   It shall be assumed in any proceedings, unless the contrary is proved, that when a person initiated a transaction as mentioned in section 19(1)(c) he knew the principal agreement had been made, or contemplated that it might be made.
(3)   . . .
(4)   In proceedings brought by the creditor under a credit-token agreement—
   (a)   it is for the creditor to prove that the credit-token was lawfully supplied to the debtor, and was accepted by him, and
   (b)   if the debtor alleges that any use made of the credit-token was not authorised by him, it is for the creditor to prove either—
      (i)   that the use was so authorised, or
      (ii)   that the use occurred before the creditor had been given notice under section 84(3).
(5)   In proceedings under section 50(1) in respect of a document received by a minor at any school or other educational establishment for minors, it is for the person sending it to him at that establishment to prove that he did not know or suspect it to be such an establishment.
(6)   In proceedings under section 119(1) it is for the pawnee to prove that he had reasonable cause to refuse to allow the pawn to be redeemed.
(7)   . . .

NOTES
   Sub-s (3): repealed by the Financial Services and Markets Act 2000 (Regulated Activities) (Amendment) (No 2) Order 2013, SI 2013/1881, art 20(1), (52), as from 26 July 2013 (certain purposes), and as from 1 April 2014 (remaining purposes), for transitional provisions see Pt 8 thereof at **[2.1007]** et seq.
   Sub-s (7): repealed by the Consumer Credit Act 2006, s 70, Sch 4, as from 6 April 2007, subject to transitional provisions in s 69(1) of, and Sch 3, paras 1, 15(5)(c) to, that Act at **[1.1945]**, **[1.1947]**.

[1.663]
172   Statements by creditor or owner to be binding
(1)   A statement by a creditor or owner is binding on him if given under—
   section 77(1),
   section 78(1),
   section 79(1),
   section 97(1),
   section 107(1)(c),
   section 108(1)(c), or
   section 109(1)(c).
(2)   Where a trader—
   (a)   gives a customer a notice in compliance with section 103(1)(b), or

(b)   gives a customer a notice under section 103(1) asserting that the customer is not indebted to him under an agreement,

the notice is binding on the trader.

(3)   Where in proceedings before any court—

(a)   it is sought to rely on a statement or notice given as mentioned in subsection (1) or (2), and

(b)   the statement or notice is shown to be incorrect,

the court may direct such relief (if any) to be given to the creditor or owner from the operation of subsection (1) or (2) as appears to the court to be just.

[1.664]

173   Contracting-out forbidden

(1)   A term contained in a regulated agreement or linked transaction, or in any other agreement relating to an actual or prospective regulated agreement or linked transaction, is void if, and to the extent that, it is inconsistent with a provision for the protection of the debtor or hirer or his relative or any surety contained in this Act or in any regulation made under this Act.

(2)   Where a provision specifies the duty or liability of the debtor or hirer or his relative or any surety in certain circumstances, a term is inconsistent with that provision if it purports to impose, directly or indirectly, an additional duty or liability on him in those circumstances.

(3)   Notwithstanding subsection (1), a provision of this Act under which a thing may be done in relation to any person on an order of the court or the [FCA] only shall not be taken to prevent its being done at any time with that person's consent given at that time, but the refusal of such consent shall not give rise to any liability.

NOTES

Sub-s (3): word in square brackets substituted by the Financial Services and Markets Act 2000 (Regulated Activities) (Amendment) (No 2) Order 2013, SI 2013/1881, art 20(1), (53), as from 26 July 2013 (certain purposes), and as from 1 April 2014 (remaining purposes), for transitional provisions see Pt 8 thereof at **[2.1007]** et seq.

References to the FCA, etc: as to the abolition of the office of the Director General of Fair Trading and the substitution of the original references to the Director (and related expressions), see the note preceding s 8 at **[1.520]**.

PART XII
SUPPLEMENTAL

General

174   (*Repealed by the Enterprise Act 2002, ss 247(d), 278(2), Sch 26, as from 20 June 2003.*)

[1.665]

[174A   Powers to require provision of information or documents etc

(1)   Every power conferred on a relevant authority by or under this Act (however expressed) to require the provision or production of information or documents includes the power—

(a)   to require information to be provided or produced in such form as the authority may specify, including, in relation to information recorded otherwise than in a legible form, in a legible form;

(b)   to take copies of, or extracts from, any documents provided or produced by virtue of the exercise of the power;

(c)   to require the person who is required to provide or produce any information or document by virtue of the exercise of the power—

(i)   to state, to the best of his knowledge and belief, where the information or document is;

(ii)   to give an explanation of the information or document;

(iii)   to secure that any information provided or produced, whether in a document or otherwise, is verified in such manner as may be specified by the authority;

(iv)   to secure that any document provided or produced is authenticated in such manner as may be so specified;

(d)   to specify a time at or by which a requirement imposed by virtue of paragraph (c) must be complied with.

(2)   Every power conferred on a relevant authority by or under this Act (however expressed) to inspect or to seize documents at any premises includes the power to take copies of, or extracts from, any documents inspected or seized by virtue of the exercise of the power.

(3)   But a relevant authority has no power under this Act—

(a)   to require another person to provide or to produce,

(b)   to seize from another person, or

(c)   to require another person to give access to premises for the purposes of the inspection of, any information or document which the other person would be entitled to refuse to provide or produce in proceedings in the High Court on the grounds of legal professional privilege or (in Scotland) in proceedings in the Court of Session on the grounds of confidentiality of communications.

(4)   In subsection (3) "communications" means—

(a)   communications between a professional legal adviser and his client;

    (b)   communications made in connection with or in contemplation of legal proceedings and for the purposes of those proceedings.

[(5)   In this section, "relevant authority" means an enforcement authority or an officer of an enforcement authority.]

NOTES

  Inserted by the Consumer Credit Act 2006, s 51(5).

  Sub-s (5): substituted by the Financial Services and Markets Act 2000 (Regulated Activities) (Amendment) (No 2) Order 2013, SI 2013/1881, art 20(1), (54), as from 26 July 2013 (certain purposes), and as from 1 April 2014 (remaining purposes), for transitional provisions see Pt 8 thereof at **[2.1007]** et seq.

  See further, in relation to the application of this section, with modifications, in respect of contraventions of certain provisions of the Financial Services and Markets Act 2000: the Financial Services Act 2012 (Consumer Credit) Order 2013, SI 2013/1882, art 8(1), (6).

[1.666]
175 Duty of persons deemed to be agents

Where under this Act a person is deemed to receive a notice or payment as agent of the creditor or owner under a regulated agreement, he shall be deemed to be under a contractual duty to the creditor or owner to transmit the notice, or remit the payment, to him forthwith.

[1.667]
176 Service of documents

(1) A document to be served under this Act by one person ("the server") on another person ("the subject") is to be treated as properly served on the subject if dealt with as mentioned in the following subsections.

(2) The document may be delivered or sent [by an appropriate method] to the subject, or addressed to him by name and left at his proper address.

(3) For the purposes of this Act, a document sent by post to, or left at, the address last known to the server as the address of a person shall be treated as sent by post to, or left at, his proper address.

(4) Where the document is to be served on the subject as being the person having any interest in land, and it is not practicable after reasonable inquiry to ascertain the subject's name or address, the document may be served by—

    (a)   addressing it to the subject by the description of the person having that interest in the land (naming it), and

    (b)   delivering the document to some responsible person on the land or affixing it, or a copy of it, in a conspicuous position on the land.

(5) Where a document to be served on the subject as being a debtor, hirer or surety, or as having any other capacity relevant for the purposes of this Act, is served at any time on another person who—

    (a)   is the person last known to the server as having that capacity, but

    (b)   before that time had ceased to have it,

the document shall be treated as having been served at that time on the subject.

(6) Anything done to a document in relation to a person who (whether to the knowledge of the server or not) has died shall be treated for the purposes of subsection (5) as service of the document on that person if it would have been so treated had he not died.

[(7) The following enactments shall not be construed as authorising service on the Public Trustee (in England and Wales) or the Probate Judge (in Northern Ireland) of any document which is to be served under this Act—

    section 9 of the Administration of Estates Act 1925;

    section 3 of the Administration of Estates Act (Northern Ireland) 1955.]

(8) References in the preceding subsections to the serving of a document on a person include the giving of the document to that person.

NOTES

  Sub-s (2): words in square brackets substituted by the Consumer Credit Act 1974 (Electronic Communications) Order 2004, SI 2004/3236, art 2(1), (6), as from 31 December 2004.

  Sub-s (7): substituted by the Law of Property (Miscellaneous Provisions) Act 1994, s 21(1), Sch 1, para 6, as from 1 July 1995.

[1.668]
[176A Electronic transmission of documents

(1) A document is transmitted in accordance with this subsection if—

    (a)   the person to whom it is transmitted agrees that it may be delivered to him by being transmitted to a particular electronic address in a particular electronic form,

    (b)   it is transmitted to that address in that form, and

    (c)   the form in which the document is transmitted is such that any information in the document which is addressed to the person to whom the document is transmitted is capable of being stored for future reference for an appropriate period in a way which allows the information to be reproduced without change.

(2)   A document transmitted in accordance with subsection (1) shall, unless the contrary is proved, be treated for the purposes of this Act, except section 69, as having been delivered on the working day immediately following the day on which it is transmitted.

(3)   In this section, "electronic address" includes any number or address used for the purposes of receiving electronic communications.]

NOTES

Inserted by the Consumer Credit Act 1974 (Electronic Communications) Order 2004, SI 2004/3236, art 2(1), (7), as from 31 December 2004.

[1.669]
177   Saving for registered charges
(1)   Nothing in this Act affects the rights of a proprietor of a registered charge (within the meaning of the [Land Registration Act 2002]), who—
- (a)   became the proprietor under a transfer for valuable consideration without notice of any defect in the title arising (apart from this section) by virtue of this Act, or
- (b)   derives title from such a proprietor.

(2)   Nothing in this Act affects the operation of section 104 of the Law of Property Act 1925 (protection of purchaser where mortgagee exercises power of sale).

(3)   Subsection (1) does not apply to a proprietor carrying on [a consumer credit business, a consumer hire business or a business of debt-collecting or debt administration].

(4)   Where, by virtue of subsection (1), a land mortgage is enforced which apart from this section would be treated as never having effect, the original creditor or owner shall be liable to indemnify the debtor or hirer against any loss thereby suffered by him.

(5)   (*Applies to Scotland only.*)

(6)   In the application of this section to Northern Ireland—
- (a)   any reference to the proprietor of a registered charge (within the meaning of the [Land Registration Act 2002]) shall be construed as a reference to the registered owner of a charge under the Local Registration of Title (Ireland) Act 1891 or Part IV of the Land Registration Act (Northern Ireland) 1970, and
- (b)   for the reference to section 104 of the Law of Property Act 1925 there shall be substituted a reference to section 21 of the Conveyancing and Law of Property Act 1881 and section 5 of the Conveyancing Act 1911.

NOTES

Sub-ss (1), (6): words in square brackets substituted by the Land Registration Act 2002, s 133, Sch 11, para 11, as from 13 October 2003.
Sub-s (3): words in square brackets substituted by the Consumer Credit Act 2006, s 24(5), as from 1 October 2008.
Conveyancing and Law of Property Act 1881, s 21: repealed by the Law of Property Act 1925, s 207, Sch 7.
Conveyancing Act 1911: repealed by the Settled Land Act 1925, the Trustee Act 1925 and the Law of Property Act 1925.

[1.670]
178   Local Acts
The [Treasury] or the Department of Commerce for Northern Ireland may by order make such amendments or repeals of any provision of any local Act as appears to the [Treasury] or, as the case may be, the Department, necessary or expedient in consequence of the replacement by this Act of the enactments relating to pawnbrokers and moneylenders.

NOTES

Words in square brackets substituted by the Financial Services Act 2012 (Consumer Credit) Order 2013, SI 2013/1882, art 7(1), (17), as from 26 July 2013 (certain purposes), and as from 1 April 2014 (remaining purposes).
Orders: the Consumer Credit (Local Acts) Order 1984, SI 1984/1107.

Regulations, orders, etc

[1.671]
179   Power to prescribe form etc of secondary documents
(1)   Regulations may be made as to the form and content of credit-cards, trading-checks, receipts, vouchers and other documents or things issued by creditors, owners or suppliers under or in connection with regulated agreements or by other persons in connection with linked transactions, and may in particular—
- (a)   require specified information to be included in the prescribed manner in documents, and other specified material to be excluded;
- (b)   contain requirements to ensure that specified information is clearly brought to the attention of the debtor or hirer, or his relative, and that one part of a document is not given insufficient or excessive prominence compared with another.

(2)   If a person issues any document or thing in contravention of regulations under subsection (1) then, as from the time of the contravention but without prejudice to anything done before it, this Act shall apply as if the regulated agreement had been improperly executed by reason of a contravention of regulations under section 60(1).

[1.672]
180 Power to prescribe form etc of copies
(1) Regulations may be made as to the form and content of documents to be issued as copies of any executed agreement, security instrument or other document referred to in this Act, and may in particular—
(a) require specified information to be included in the prescribed manner in any copy, and contain requirements to ensure that such information is clearly brought to the attention of a reader of the copy;
(b) authorise the omission from a copy of certain material contained in the original, or the inclusion of such material in condensed form.
(2) A duty imposed by any provision of this Act . . . to supply a copy of any document—
(a) is not satisfied unless the copy supplied is in the prescribed form and conforms to the prescribed requirements;
(b) is not infringed by the omission of any material, or its inclusion in condensed form, if that is authorised by regulations;
and references in this Act to copies shall be construed accordingly.
(3) Regulations may provide that a duty imposed by this Act to supply a copy of a document referred to in an unexecuted agreement or an executed agreement shall not apply to documents of a kind specified in the regulations.

NOTES
Sub-s (2): words omitted repealed by the Financial Services and Markets Act 2000 (Regulated Activities) (Amendment) (No 2) Order 2013, SI 2013/1881, art 20(1), (55), as from 26 July 2013 (certain purposes), and as from 1 April 2014 (remaining purposes), for transitional provisions see Pt 8 thereof at **[2.1007]** et seq.
Regulations: the Consumer Credit (Cancellation Notices and Copies of Documents) Regulations 1983, SI 1983/1557; the Consumer Credit (Cancellation Notices and Copies of Documents) (Amendment) Regulations 1984, SI 1984/1108; the Consumer Credit (Agreements and Cancellation Notices and Copies of Documents) (Amendment) Regulations 1985, SI 1985/666; the Consumer Credit (Cancellation Notices and Copies of Documents) (Amendment) Regulations 1989, SI 1989/591; the Consumer Credit (Miscellaneous Amendments) Regulations 2004, SI 2004/2619; the Consumer Credit (Amendment) Regulations 2010, SI 2010/1969.

[1.673]
181 Power to alter monetary limits etc
(1) The [Treasury] may by order made by statutory instrument amend, or further amend, any of the following provisions of this Act so as to reduce or increase a sum mentioned in that provision, namely, sections . . . 17(1), . . . [. . .] 70(6), 75(3)(b), 77(1), 78(1), 79(1), 84(1), 101(7)(a), 107(1), 108(1), 109(1), 110(1), . . . , . . . [140B(6),] 155(1) and 158(1).
(2) An order under subsection (1) amending section . . . , 17(1), . . . [. . .] 75(3)(b) . . . [or 140B(6)] shall be of no effect unless a draft of the order has been laid before and approved by each House of Parliament.

NOTES
Sub-s (1): word in first pair of square brackets substituted by the Financial Services Act 2012 (Consumer Credit) Order 2013, SI 2013/1882, art 7(1), (18), as from 26 July 2013 (certain purposes), and as from 1 April 2014 (remaining purposes); first, third (in square brackets) and fourth numbers omitted repealed by the Financial Services and Markets Act 2000 (Regulated Activities) (Amendment) (No 2) Order 2013, SI 2013/1881, art 20(1), (56)(a), as from 26 July 2013 (certain purposes), and as from 1 April 2014 (remaining purposes), for transitional provisions see Pt 8 thereof at **[2.1007]** et seq; second number omitted repealed, and third number in square brackets (omitted) inserted (as from 6 April 2008), fifth number omitted repealed and second number in square brackets inserted (as from 6 April 2007) by the Consumer Credit Act 2006, ss 5(7), 22(4)(a), 53(3)(a), 70, Sch 4, subject to transitional provisions in s 69(1) of, and Sch 3, paras 1, 15(5)(d) to, that Act at **[1.1945], [1.1947]**;
Sub-s (2): first and third (in square brackets) numbers omitted repealed by SI 2013/1881, art 20(1), (56)(b), as from 26 July 2013 (certain purposes), and as from 1 April 2014 (remaining purposes), for transitional provisions see Pt 8 thereof at **[2.1007]** et seq; second number omitted repealed and third number in square brackets (omitted) inserted (as from 6 April 2008), fourth number omitted repealed and second number in square brackets inserted (as from 6 April 2007) by the Consumer Credit Act 2006, ss 5(7), 22(4)(b), 53(3)(b), 70, Sch 4, subject to transitional provisions in s 69(1) of, and Sch 3, paras 1, 15(5)(e) to, that Act at **[1.1945], [1.1947]**.
Orders: the Consumer Credit (Increase of Monetary Limits) Order 1983, SI 1983/1878; the Consumer Credit (Increase of Monetary Limits) (Amendment) Order 1998, SI 1998/996; the Consumer Credit (Further Increase of Monetary Amounts) Order 1998, SI 1998/997.

[1.674]
182 Regulations and orders
(1) Any power of the [Treasury] to make regulations or orders under this Act, except the power conferred by sections . . . 181 and 192, shall be exercisable by statutory instrument subject to annulment in pursuance of a resolution of either House of Parliament.
[(1A) . . .]
(2) Where a power to make regulations or orders [. . .] is exercisable by the [Treasury] [. . .] by virtue of this Act, regulations or orders [. . .] made in the exercise of that power may—
(a) make different provision in relation to different cases or classes of case, and
(b) exclude certain cases or classes of case, and
(c) contain such transitional provisions as the [Treasury] thinks fit.

(3) Regulations may provide that specified expressions, when used as described by the regulations, are to be given the prescribed meaning, notwithstanding that another meaning is intended by the person using them.

(4) Any power conferred on the [Treasury] by this Act to make orders includes power to vary or revoke an order so made.

NOTES

Sub-s (1): word in square brackets substituted by the Financial Services Act 2012 (Consumer Credit) Order 2013, SI 2013/1882, art 7(1), (19), as from 26 July 2013 (certain purposes), and as from 1 April 2014 (remaining purposes); reference omitted repealed by the Financial Services and Markets Act 2000 (Regulated Activities) (Amendment) (No 2) Order 2013, SI 2013/1881, art 20(1), (57), as from 26 July 2013 (certain purposes), and as from 1 April 2014 (remaining purposes), for transitional provisions see Pt 8 thereof at **[2.1007]** et seq.

Sub-s (1A): inserted by the Consumer Credit Act 2006, s 58(2), as from 1 December 2007, and repealed by the Transfer of Functions of the Consumer Credit Appeals Tribunal Order 2009, SI 2009/1835, art 4(1), Sch 1, paras 1, 7(a), as from 1 September 2009, subject to transitional provisions and savings in Sch 4 thereto at **[2.791]**.

Sub-s (2): words in first, third and fourth pairs of square brackets (omitted) inserted by the Consumer Credit Act 2006, s 58(3), and repealed by SI 2009/1835, art 4(1), Sch 1, paras 1, 7(b)(i), (ii), as from 1 September 2009, subject to transitional provisions and savings in Sch 4 thereto at **[2.791]**; word in second pair of square brackets substituted by SI 2013/1882, art 7(1), (19), as from 26 July 2013 (certain purposes), and as from 1 April 2014 (remaining purposes).

Sub-s (4): word in square brackets substituted by SI 2013/1882, art 7(1), (19), as from 26 July 2013 (certain purposes), and as from 1 April 2014 (remaining purposes).

[1.675]
[183 Determinations etc by [FCA]
(1) The [FCA] may vary or revoke any determination made, or direction given, by it under this Act.
(2) . . .]

NOTES

Substituted by the Consumer Credit Act 2006, s 64.

Section heading, sub-s (1): words in square brackets substituted by the Financial Services Act 2012 (Consumer Credit) Order 2013, SI 2013/1882, art 7(1), (20), as from 26 July 2013 (certain purposes), and as from 1 April 2014 (remaining purposes).

Sub-s (2): repealed by the Financial Services and Markets Act 2000 (Regulated Activities) (Amendment) (No 2) Order 2013, SI 2013/1881, art 20(1), (58), as from 26 July 2013 (certain purposes), and as from 1 April 2014 (remaining purposes), for transitional provisions see Pt 8 thereof at **[2.1007]** et seq.

Interpretation

[1.676]
184 Associates
[(1) A person is an associate of an individual if that person is—
  (a) the individual's husband or wife or civil partner,
  (b) a relative of—
    (i) the individual, or
    (ii) the individual's husband or wife or civil partner, or
  (c) the husband or wife or civil partner of a relative of—
    (i) the individual, or
    (ii) the individual's husband or wife or civil partner.]

(2) A person is an associate of any person with whom he is in partnership, and of the husband or wife [or civil partner] or a relative of any individual with whom he is in partnership.

(3) A body corporate is an associate of another body corporate—
  (a) if the same person is a controller of both, or a person is a controller of one and persons who are his associates, or he and persons who are his associates, are the controllers of the other; or
  (b) if a group of two or more persons is a controller of each company, and the groups either consist of the same persons or could be regarded as consisting of the same persons by treating (in one or more cases) a member of either group as replaced by a person of whom he is an associate.

(4) A body corporate is an associate of another person if that person is a controller of it or if that person and persons who are his associates together are controllers of it.

(5) In this section "relative" means brother, sister, uncle, aunt, nephew, niece, lineal ancestor or lineal descendant, . . . references to a husband or wife include a former husband or wife and a reputed husband [or wife, and references to a civil partner include a former civil partner] [and a reputed civil partner]; and for the purposes of this subsection a relationship shall be established as if any illegitimate child, step-child or adopted child of a person [were the legitimate child of the relationship in question].

NOTES

Sub-s (1): substituted by the Civil Partnership Act 2004, s 261(1), Sch 27, para 51(1), (2), as from 5 December 2005.

Sub-s (2): words in square brackets inserted by the Civil Partnership Act 2004, s 261(1), Sch 27, para 51(1), (3), as from 5 December 2005.

Sub-s (5): word omitted repealed and words in first and third pairs of square brackets substituted by the Civil Partnership Act 2004, s 261(1), (4), Sch 27, para 51(1), (4), Sch 30, as from 5 December 2005; words in second pair of square brackets inserted by the Civil Partnership Act 2004 (Overseas Relationships and Consequential, etc Amendments) Order 2005, SI 2005/3129, art 4(4), Sch 4, para 2, as from 5 December 2005.

[1.677]
185 Agreement with more than one debtor or hirer
(1) Where an actual or prospective regulated agreement has two or more debtors or hirers (not being a partnership or an unincorporated body of persons)—
  (a) anything required by or under this Act to be done to or in relation to the debtor or hirer shall be done to or in relation to each of them; and
  (b) anything done under this Act by or on behalf of one of them shall have effect as if done by or on behalf of all of them.
[(1A) . . .]
[(2) Notwithstanding subsection (1)(a), where credit is provided under an agreement to two or more debtors jointly, in performing his duties—
  (a) in the case of fixed-sum credit, under section 77A, or
  (b) in the case of running-account credit, under section 78(4), the creditor need not give statements to any debtor who has signed and given to him a notice (a "dispensing notice") authorising him not to comply in the debtor's case with section 77A or (as the case may be) 78(4).
(2A) A dispensing notice given by a debtor is operative from when it is given to the creditor until it is revoked by a further notice given to the creditor by the debtor.
(2B) But subsection (2) does not apply if (apart from this subsection) dispensing notices would be operative in relation to all of the debtors to whom the credit is provided.
(2C) Any dispensing notices operative in relation to an agreement shall cease to have effect if any of the debtors dies.
(2D) A dispensing notice which is operative in relation to an agreement shall be operative also in relation to any subsequent agreement which, in relation to the earlier agreement, is a modifying agreement.]
(3) Subsection (1)(b) does not apply for the purposes of section 61(1)(a) . . .
(4) Where a regulated agreement has two or more debtors or hirers (not being a partnership or an unincorporated body of persons), section 86 applies to the death of any of them.
(5) An agreement for the provision of credit, or the bailment or (in Scotland) the hiring of goods, to two or more persons jointly where—
  (a) one or more of those persons is an individual, and
  (b) one or more of them is a [not an individual],
is a consumer credit agreement or consumer hire agreement if it would have been one had they all been individuals; and [each person within paragraph (b)] shall accordingly be included among the debtors or hirers under the agreement.
(6) Where subsection (5) applies, references in this Act to the signing of any document by the debtor or hirer shall be construed in relation to a body corporate as referring to a signing on behalf of the body corporate [within paragraph (b) of that subsection].

NOTES
  Sub-s (1A): inserted by the Consumer Credit (EU Directive) Regulations 2010, SI 2010/1010, regs 2, 4, as from 1 February 2011; repealed by the Financial Services and Markets Act 2000 (Regulated Activities) (Amendment) (No 2) Order 2013, SI 2013/1881, art 20(1), (59), as from 26 July 2013 (certain purposes), and as from 1 April 2014 (remaining purposes), for transitional provisions see Pt 8 thereof at [**2.1007**] et seq.
  Sub-ss (2), (2A)–(2D): substituted for original sub-s (2) by the Consumer Credit Act 2006, s 7(3), as from 1 October 2008, subject to transitional provisions in s 69(1) of, and Sch 3, paras 1, 4 to, that Act at [**1.1945**], [**1.1947**].
  Sub-s (3): words omitted repealed by the Consumer Credit Act 2006, s 70, Sch 42, as from 6 April 2007, subject to transitional provisions and savings in s 69(1) of, and Sch 3, paras 1, 11(c) to, that Act at [**1.1945**], [**1.1947**].
  Sub-s (5): words in square brackets substituted by the Consumer Credit Act 2006, s 5(8), as from 6 April 2007.
  Sub-s (6): words in square brackets added by the Consumer Credit Act 2006, s 5(9), as from 6 April 2007.

[1.678]
186 Agreement with more than one creditor or owner
Where an actual or prospective regulated agreement has two or more creditors or owners, anything required by or under this Act to be done to, or in relation to, or by, the creditor or owner shall be effective if done to, or in relation to, or by, any one of them.

[1.679]
187 Arrangements between creditor and supplier
(1) A consumer credit agreement shall be treated as entered into under pre-existing arrangements between a creditor and a supplier if it is entered into in accordance with, or in furtherance of, arrangements previously made between persons mentioned in subsection (4)(a), (b) or (c).
(2) A consumer credit agreement shall be treated as entered into in contemplation of future arrangements between a creditor and a supplier if it is entered into in the expectation that arrangements will subsequently be made between persons mentioned in subsection (4)(a), (b) or (c) for the supply of cash, goods and services (or any of them) to be financed by the consumer credit agreement.

(3)　Arrangements shall be disregarded for the purposes of subsection (1) or (2) if—
(a)　they are arrangements for the making, in specified circumstances, of payments to the supplier by the creditor, and
(b)　the creditor holds himself out as willing to make, in such circumstances, payments of the kind to suppliers generally.
[(3A)　Arrangements shall also be disregarded for the purposes of subsections (1) and (2) if they are arrangements for the electronic transfer of funds from a current account at a bank within the meaning of the Bankers' Books Evidence Act 1879.]
(4)　The persons referred to in subsections (1) and (2) are—
(a)　the creditor and the supplier;
(b)　one of them and an associate of the other's;
(c)　an associate of one and an associate of the other's.
(5)　Where the creditor is an associate of the supplier's, the consumer credit agreement shall be treated, unless the contrary is proved, as entered into under pre-existing arrangements between the creditor and the supplier.

NOTES

Sub-s (3A): inserted by the Banking Act 1987, s 89, as from 1 October 1987.

[1.680]
[187A　Definition of "default sum"
(1)　In this Act "default sum" means, in relation to the debtor or hirer under a regulated agreement, a sum (other than a sum of interest) which is payable by him under the agreement in connection with a breach of the agreement by him.
(2)　But a sum is not a default sum in relation to the debtor or hirer simply because, as a consequence of his breach of the agreement, he is required to pay it earlier than he would otherwise have had to.]

NOTES

Inserted by the Consumer Credit Act 2006, s 18(1), as from 16 June 2006.

[1.681]
188　Examples of use of new terminology
(1)　Schedule 2 shall have effect for illustrating the use of terminology employed in this Act.
(2)　The examples given in Schedule 2 are not exhaustive.
(3)　In the case of conflict between Schedule 2 and any other provision of this Act, that other provision shall prevail.
(4)　The [Treasury] may by order amend Schedule 2 by adding further examples or in any other way.

NOTES

Sub-s (4): word in square brackets substituted by the Financial Services Act 2012 (Consumer Credit) Order 2013, SI 2013/1882, art 7(1), (21), as from 26 July 2013 (certain purposes), and as from 1 April 2014 (remaining purposes).

[1.682]
189　Definitions
(1)　In this Act, unless the context otherwise requires—
"advertisement" includes every form of advertising, whether in a publication, by television or radio, by display of notices, signs, labels, showcards or goods, by distribution of samples, circulars, catalogues, price lists or other material, by exhibition of pictures, models or films, or in any other way, and references to the publishing of advertisements shall be construed accordingly;
. . .
"ancillary credit business" has the meaning given by section 145(1);
"antecedent negotiations" has the meaning given by section 56;
. . .
["appropriate method" means–
(a)　post, or
(b)　transmission in the form of an electronic communication in accordance with section 176A(1);]
"assignment", in relation to Scotland, means assignation;
"associate" shall be construed in accordance with section 184;
["authorised business overdraft agreement" means a debtor-creditor agreement which provides authorisation in advance for the debtor to overdraw on a current account, where the agreement is entered into by the debtor wholly or predominantly for the purposes of the debtor's business (see subsection (2A));
"authorised non-business overdraft agreement" means a debtor-creditor agreement which provides authorisation in advance for the debtor to overdraw on a current account where—
(a)　the credit must be repaid on demand or within three months, and

(b)   the agreement is not entered into by the debtor wholly or predominantly for the purposes of the debtor's business (see subsection (2A));]

[. . .]

"bill of sale" has the meaning given by section 4 of the Bills of Sale Act 1878 or, for Northern Ireland, by section 4 of the Bills of Sale (Ireland) Act 1879;

["building society" means a building society within the meaning of the Building Societies Act 1986;]

"business" includes profession or trade, and references to a business apply subject to subsection (2);

"cancellable agreement" means a regulated agreement which, by virtue of section 67, may be cancelled by the debtor or hirer;

"canvass" shall be construed in accordance with sections 48 and 153;

"cash" includes money in any form;

"charity" means as respects England and Wales a charity registered under [the Charities Act 2011] or an exempt charity (within the meaning of that Act), [as respects] Northern Ireland an institution or other organisation established for charitable purposes only ("organisation" including any persons administering a trust and "charitable" being construed in the same way as if it were contained in the Income Tax Acts) [and as respects Scotland a body entered in the Scottish Charity Register];

"conditional sale agreement" means an agreement for the sale of goods or land under which the purchase price or part of it is payable by instalments, and the property in the goods or land is to remain in the seller (notwithstanding that the buyer is to be in possession of the goods or land) until such conditions as to the payment of instalments or otherwise as may be specified in the agreement are fulfilled;

"consumer credit agreement" has the meaning given by section 8, and includes a consumer credit agreement which is cancelled under section 69(1), or becomes subject to section 69(2), so far as the agreement remains in force;

["consumer credit business" means any business being carried on by a person so far as it comprises or relates to—

(a)   the provision of credit by him, or

(b)   otherwise his being a creditor,

under regulated consumer credit agreements;]

"consumer hire agreement" has the meaning given by section 15;

["consumer hire business" means any business being carried on by a person so far as it comprises or relates to—

(a)   the bailment or (in Scotland) the hiring of goods by him, or

(b)   otherwise his being an owner,

under regulated consumer hire agreements;]

"controller", in relation to a body corporate, means a person—

(a)   in accordance with whose directions or instructions the directors of the body corporate or of another body corporate which is its controller (or any of them) are accustomed to act, or

(b)   who, either alone or with any associate or associates, is entitled to exercise or control the exercise of, one third or more of the voting power at any general meeting of the body corporate or of another body corporate which is its controller;

"copy" shall be construed in accordance with section 180;

. . .

"court" means in relation to England and Wales the county court, in relation to Scotland the sheriff court and in relation to Northern Ireland the High Court or the county court;

"credit" shall be construed in accordance with section 9;

"credit-broker" means a person carrying on a business of credit brokerage;

"credit brokerage" has the meaning given by section 145(2);

["credit information services" [is to be read in accordance with] section 145(7B);]

["credit intermediary" has the meaning given by section 160A;]

"credit limit" has the meaning given by section 10(2);

"creditor" means [(except in relation to green deal plans: see instead section 189B(2))] the person providing credit under a consumer credit agreement or the person to whom his rights and duties under the agreement have passed by assignment or operation of law, and in relation to a prospective consumer credit agreement, includes the prospective creditor;

"credit reference agency" [is to be read in accordance with] section 145(8);

"credit-sale agreement" means an agreement for the sale of goods, under which the purchase price or part of it is payable by instalments, but which is not a conditional sale agreement;

"credit-token" has the meaning given by section 14(1);

"credit-token agreement" means a regulated agreement for the provision of credit in connection with the use of a credit-token;

"debt-adjusting" has the meaning given by section 145(5);

["debt administration" has the meaning given by section 145(7A);]

"debt-collecting" has the meaning given by section 145(7);

"debt-counselling" has the meaning given by section 145(6);

"debtor" means [(except in relation to green deal plans: see instead section 189B(3))] the individual receiving credit under a consumer credit agreement or the person to whom his rights and duties under the agreement have passed by assignment or operation of law, and in relation to a prospective consumer credit agreement includes the prospective debtor;

"debtor-creditor agreement" has the meaning given by section 13;

"debtor-creditor-supplier agreement" has the meaning given by section 12;

"default notice" has the meaning given by section 87(1);

["default sum" has the meaning given by section 187A;]

"deposit" means [. . .] any sum payable by a debtor or hirer by way of deposit or down-payment, or credited or to be credited to him on account of any deposit or down-payment, whether the sum is to be or has been paid to the creditor or owner or any other person, or is to be or has been discharged by a payment of money or a transfer or delivery of goods or by any other means;

. . .

["documents" includes information recorded in any form;]

"electric line" has the meaning given by [the Electricity Act 1989] or, for Northern Ireland, [the Electricity (Northern Ireland) Order 1992];

["electronic communication" means an electronic communication within the meaning of the Electronic Communications Act 2000 (c 7);]

"embodies" and related words shall be construed in accordance with subsection (4);

"enforcement authority" has the meaning given by section 161(1);

"enforcement order" means an order under section 65(1), 105(7)(a) or (b), 111(2) or 124(1) or (2);

"executed agreement" means a document, signed by or on behalf of the parties, embodying the terms of a regulated agreement, or such of them as have been reduced to writing;

. . .

["FCA" means the Financial Conduct Authority;]

"finance" means to finance wholly or partly and "financed" and "refinanced" shall be construed accordingly;

"file" and "copy of the file" have the meanings given by section 158(5);

"fixed-sum credit" has the meaning given by section 10(1)(b);

"friendly society" means a society registered [or treated as registered under the Friendly Societies Act 1974 or the Friendly Societies Act 1992] . . . ;

"future arrangements" shall be construed in accordance with section 187;

. . .

"give", means, deliver or send [by an appropriate method] to;

"goods" has the meaning given by [section 61(1) of the Sale of Goods Act 1979];

["green deal plan" has the meaning given by section 1 of the Energy Act 2011;]

. . .

"High Court" means Her Majesty's High Court of Justice, or the Court of Session in Scotland or the High Court of Justice in Northern Ireland;

"hire-purchase agreement" means an agreement, other than a conditional sale agreement, under which—

    (a)   goods are bailed or (in Scotland) hired in return for periodical payments by the person to whom they are bailed or hired, and

    (b)   the property in the goods will pass to that person if the terms of the agreement are complied with and one or more of the following occurs—

        (i)   the exercise of an option to purchase by that person,

        (ii)   the doing of any other specified act by any party to the agreement,

        (iii)   the happening of any other specified event;

"hirer" means the individual to whom goods are bailed or (in Scotland) hired under a consumer hire agreement, or the person to whom his rights and duties under the agreement have passed by assignment or operation of law, and in relation to a prospective consumer hire agreement includes the prospective hirer;

["individual" includes—

    (a)   a partnership consisting of two or three persons not all of whom are bodies corporate; and

    (b)   an unincorporated body of persons which does not consist entirely of bodies corporate and is not a partnership;]

"installation" means—

    (a)   the installing of any electric line or any gas or water pipe,

    (b)   the fixing of goods to the premises where they are to be used, and the alteration of premises to enable goods to be used on them,

    (c)   where it is reasonably necessary that goods should be constructed or erected on the premises where they are to be used, any work carried out for the purpose of constructing or erecting them on those premises;

. . .

"judgment" includes an order or decree made by any court;

"land", includes an interest in land, and in relation to Scotland includes heritable subjects of whatever description;

"land improvement company" means an improvement company as defined by section 7 of the Improvement of Land Act 1899;

"land mortgage" includes any security charged on land;

. . .

. . .

"linked transaction" has the meaning given by section 19(1);

"local authority", in relation to England . . . , means . . . a county council, a London borough council, a district council, the Common Council of the City of London, or the Council of Isles of Scilly, [in relation to Wales means a county council or a county borough council,] and in relation to Scotland, means a [council constituted under section 2 of the Local Government etc (Scotland) Act 1994], and, in relation to Northern Ireland, means a district council;

. . .

"modifying agreement" has the meaning given by section 82(2);

"mortgage", in relation to Scotland, includes any heritable security;

"multiple agreement" has the meaning given by section 18(1);

"negotiator" has the meaning given by section 56(1);

"non-commercial agreement" means a consumer credit agreement or a consumer hire agreement not made by the creditor or owner in the course of a business carried on by him;

"notice" means notice in writing;

"notice of cancellation" has the meaning given by section 69(1);

[. . .]

["open-end" in relation to a consumer credit agreement, means of no fixed duration;]

"owner" means a person who bails or (in Scotland) hires out goods under a consumer hire agreement or the person to whom his rights and duties under the agreement have passed by assignment or operation of law, and in relation to a prospective consumer hire agreement, includes the prospective bailor or persons from whom the goods are to be hired;

"pawn" means any article subject to a pledge;

"pawn-receipt" has the meaning given by section 114;

"pawnee" and "pawnor" include any person to whom the rights and duties of the original pawnee or the original pawnor, as the case may be, have passed by assignment or operation of law;

"payment" includes tender;

. . .

"pledge" means the pawnee's rights over an article taken in pawn;

"prescribed" means prescribed by regulations made by the Secretary of State;

"pre-existing arrangements" shall be construed in accordance with section 187;

"principal agreement" has the meaning given by section 19(1);

"protected goods" has the meaning given by section 90(7);

. . .

"redemption period" has the meaning given by section 116(3);

["Regulated Activities Order" means the Financial Services and Markets Act 2000 (Regulated Activities) Order 2001;]

["regulated agreement" means a consumer credit agreement which is a regulated agreement (within the meaning of section 8(3)) or a consumer hire agreement which is a regulated agreement (within the meaning of section 15(2));]

"regulations" means regulations made by the [Treasury];

"relative", except in section 184, means a person who is an associate by virtue of section 184(1);

"representation" includes any condition or warranty, and any other statement or undertaking, whether oral or in writing;

["residential renovation agreement" means a consumer credit agreement—

    (a)   which is unsecured; and

    (b)   the purpose of which is the renovation of residential property, as described in Article 2(2a) of Directive 2008/48/EC of the European Parliament and of the Council of 23rd April 2008 on credit agreements for consumers.]

"restricted-use credit agreement" and "restricted-use credit" have the meanings given by section 11(1);

"rules of court", in relation to Northern Ireland means, in relation to the High Court, rules made under section 7 of the Northern Ireland Act 1962, and, in relation to any other court, rules made by the authority having for the time being power to make rules regulating the practice and procedure in that court;

"running-account credit" shall be construed in accordance with section 10;

"security", in relation to an actual or prospective consumer credit agreement or consumer hire agreement, or any linked transaction, means a mortgage, charge, pledge, bond, debenture, indemnity, guarantee, bill, note or other right provided by the debtor or hirer, or at his request (express or implied), to secure the carrying out of the obligations of the debtor or hirer under the agreement;

"security instrument" has the meaning given by section 105(2);

"serve on" means deliver or send [by an appropriate method] to;

"signed" shall be construed in accordance with subsection (3);

"small agreement" has the meaning given by section 17(1), and "small" in relation to an agreement within any category shall be construed accordingly;

. . .

"supplier" has the meaning given by section 11(1)(b) or 12(c) or 13(c) or, in relation to an agreement falling within section 11(1)(a), means the creditor, and includes a person to whom the rights and duties of a supplier (as so defined) have passed by assignment or operation of law, or (in relation to a prospective agreement) the prospective supplier;

"surety" means the person by whom any security is provided, or the person to whom his rights and duties in relation to the security have passed by assignment or operation of law;

"technical grounds" shall be construed in accordance with subsection (5);

"time order" has the meaning given by section 129(1);

["total charge for credit" has the meaning given by section 20;]

"total price" means the total sum payable by the debtor under a hire-purchase agreement or a conditional sale agreement, including any sum payable on the exercise of an option to purchase, but excluding any sum payable as a penalty or as compensation or damages for a breach of the agreement;

[. . .]

"unexecuted agreement" means a document embodying the terms of a prospective regulated agreement, or such of them as it is intended to reduce to writing;

. . .

"unrestricted-use credit agreement" and "unrestricted-use credit" have the meanings given by section 11(2);

"working day" means any day other than—

(a) Saturday or Sunday,
(b) Christmas Day or Good Friday,
(c) a bank holiday within the meaning given by section 1 of the Banking and Financial Dealings Act 1971.

[(1A) In sections . . . 70(4), 73(4) and 75(2) . . . "costs", in relation to proceedings in Scotland, means expenses.]

(2) A person is not to be treated as carrying on a particular type of business merely because occasionally he enters into transactions belonging to a business of that type.

[(2A) For the purpose of the definitions of "authorised business overdraft agreement" and "authorised non-business overdraft agreement" [article 60C(5) and (6) of the Regulated Activities Order applies].]

(3) Any provision of this Act requiring a document to be signed is complied with by a body corporate if the document is sealed by that body.

This subsection does not apply to Scotland.

(4) A document embodies a provision if the provision is set out either in the document itself or in another document referred to in it.

(5) An application dismissed by the court . . . shall, if the court . . . so certifies, be taken to be dismissed on technical grounds only.

(6) Except in so far as the context otherwise requires, any reference in this Act to an enactment shall be construed as a reference to that enactment as amended by or under any other enactment, including this Act.

(7) In this Act, except where otherwise indicated—

(a) a reference to a numbered Part, section or Schedule is a reference to the Part or section of, or the Schedule to, this Act so numbered, and
(b) a reference in a section to a numbered subsection is a reference to the subsection of that section so numbered, and
(c) a reference in a section, subsection or Schedule to a numbered paragraph is a reference to the paragraph of that section, subsection or Schedule so numbered.

NOTES

Sub-s (1) is amended as follows:

definitions "advertiser", "appeal period", "exempt agreement", "group licence", "licence", "licensed", "licensee", "quotation", "register", "specified fee", "standard licence" and "unlicensed" (omitted) repealed, in definitions "credit information services" and "credit reference agency" words in square brackets substituted, words omitted from definition "deposit" (inserted by SI 2001/3649, art 176(b)) repealed, definition "Regulated Activities Order" inserted and definitions "regulated agreement" and "total charge for credit" substituted by the Financial Services and Markets Act 2000 (Regulated Activities) (Amendment) (No 2) Order 2013, SI 2013/1881, art 20(1), (60)(a), as from 26 July 2013 (certain purposes), and as from 1 April 2014 (remaining purposes), for transitional provisions see Pt 8 thereof at **[2.1007]** et seq.

definitions "appropriate method", "electronic communication" inserted and in definitions "give" and "serve on", words in square brackets substituted by the Consumer Credit Act 1974 (Electronic Communications) Order 2004, SI 2004/3236, art 2(1), (8), (9), as from 31 December 2004;

definitions "authorised business overdraft agreement", "authorised non-business overdraft agreement", "credit intermediary" and "open-end" inserted by the Consumer Credit (EU Directive) Regulations 2010, SI 2010/1010, regs 2, 19(1), (2), 39, 42, as from 30 April 2010;

definition "authorised institution" inserted by the Banking Act 1987, s 88, as from 1 October 1987, and repealed by the Financial Services and Markets Act 2000 (Consequential Amendments and Repeals) Order 2001, SI 2001/3649, art 176(a), as from 1 December 2001;

definition "building society" substituted by the Building Societies Act 1986, s 120, Sch 18, Pt I, para 10(4), as from 1 January 1987;

in definition "charity" words in first pair of square brackets substituted by the Charities Act 2011, s 354(1), Sch 7, Pt 2, para 29, as from 14 March 2012, words in second pair of square brackets substituted and words in third pair of square brackets added by the Charities and Trustee Investment (Scotland) Act 2005 (Consequential Provisions and Modifications) Order 2006, SI 2006/242, art 5, Schedule, Pt 1, para 1, as from 1 April 2006;

definitions "consumer credit business", "consumer hire business" substituted, definition "costs" (omitted) repealed, and definition "documents" inserted, by the Consumer Credit Act 2006, ss 23(a), (b), 51(6), 70, Sch 4, as from 6 April 2008;

definitions "credit information services", "debt administration", "default sum" inserted, by the Consumer Credit Act 2006, ss 18(2), 24(6), 25(5), as from 16 June 2006;

in definitions "creditor" and "debtor" words in square brackets inserted, and definition "green deal plan" inserted, by the Consumer Credit Act 1974 (Green Deal) (Amendment) Order 2014, SI 2014/436, art 5, as from 28 February 2014, except in relation to a green deal plan (within the meaning of the Energy Act 2011, s 1) made before that date; see art 1(3) thereof.

definition "Director" (omitted) repealed by the Enterprise Act 2002, s 278, Sch 25, para 6(1), (38)(a)(i), Sch 26, as from 1 April 2003;

in definition "electric line" words in first pair of square brackets substituted by the Electricity Act 1989, s 112(1), Sch 16, para 17(1), (3), as from 31 March 1990, words in second pair of square brackets substituted by the Electricity (Northern Ireland) Order 1992, SI 1992/231, art 95(1), Sch 12, para 15;

definition "FCA" inserted, definitions "general notice" and "OFT" omitted (definition "OFT" as inserted by the Enterprise Act 2002, s 278(1), Sch 25, para 6(1), (38)(a)(iii), as from 1 April 2003) repealed, in definition "regulations" words in square brackets substituted, by the Financial Services Act 2012 (Consumer Credit) Order 2013, SI 2013/1882, art 7(1), (22), as from 26 July 2013 (certain purposes), and as from 1 April 2014 (remaining purposes).

in definition "friendly society" words in square brackets substituted by SI 2001/3649, art 176(c), as from 1 December 2001, words omitted repealed by the Friendly Societies Act 1992, s 120, Sch 22, Pt I, as from 1 January 1994;

in definition "goods" words in square brackets substituted by the Sale of Goods Act 1979, s 63, Sch 2, para 18, as from 1 January 1980;

definition "individual" substituted by the Consumer Credit Act 2006, s 1, as from 6 April 2007, subject to transitional provisions and savings in the Consumer Credit Act 2006 (Commencement No 2 and Transitional Provisions and Savings) Order 2007, SI 2007/123, arts 4, 5 and s 69(1) of, and Sch 3, paras 1, 17, 29 to, the 2006 Act at **[1.1945]**, **[1.1947]**;

definition "insurance company" (omitted) repealed by SI 2001/3649, art 176(a), as from 1 December 2001;

in definition "local authority" words omitted in the first place repealed, and words in first pair of square brackets inserted, by the Local Government (Wales) Act 1994, s 66(6), (8), Sch 16, para 45, Sch 18, as from 1 April 1996, words omitted in the second place repealed by the Local Government Act 1985, s 102, Sch 17, as from 16 July 1985, and words in second pair of square brackets substituted by the Local Government etc (Scotland) Act 1994, s 180(1), Sch 13, para 94, as from 1 April 1996;

definition "minor" (omitted) repealed by the Age of Legal Capacity (Scotland) Act 1991, s 10, Sch 2;

definition "personal credit agreement" (omitted) repealed by the Consumer Credit Act 2006, s 70, Sch 4, as from 31 October 2008: for effect and transitional provisions, see the Consumer Credit Act 2006 (Commencement No 4 and Transitional Provisions) Order 2008, SI 2008/831, arts 2(1), 4, Sch 1;

definition "residential renovation agreement" inserted by the Mortgage Credit Directive Order 2015, SI 2015/910, art 3, Sch 1, Pt 1, para 2(1), (9), as from 21 March 2016 (note that the 2015 Order also comes into force on 20 April 2015 and 21 December 2015 for limited other purposes, and for transitional provisions, see Part 4 of that Order at **[2.1194]** et seq).

Sub-s (1A): inserted by the Consumer Credit Act 2006, s 27(3), as from 6 April 2008; first words omitted repealed by SI 2013/1881, art 20(1), (60)(b), as from 26 July 2013 (certain purposes), and as from 1 April 2014 (remaining purposes), for transitional provisions see Pt 8 thereof at **[2.1007]** et seq; second words omitted repealed by SI 2009/1835, art 4(1), Sch 1, paras 1, 8(b), as from 1 September 2009, subject to transitional provisions and savings in Sch 4 thereto at **[2.791]**.

Sub-s (2A): inserted by the Consumer Credit (EU Directive) Regulations 2010, SI 2010/1010, regs 2, 19(1), (3), as from 30 April 2010; words in square brackets substituted by SI 2013/1881, art 20(1), (60)(c), as from 26 July 2013 (certain purposes), and as from 1 April 2014 (remaining purposes), for transitional provisions see Pt 8 thereof at **[2.1007]** et seq.

Sub-s (5): words omitted repealed by SI 2013/1881, art 20(1), (60)(d), as from 26 July 2013 (certain purposes), and as from 1 April 2014 (remaining purposes), for transitional provisions see Pt 8 thereof at **[2.1007]** et seq.

References to the FCA, etc: as to the abolition of the office of the Director General of Fair Trading and the substitution of the original references to the Director (and related expressions), see the note preceding s 8 at **[1.520]**.

189A (*Inserted by the Financial Services and Markets Act 2000 (Consequential Amendments and Repeals) Order 2001, SI 2001/3649, art 177; repealed by the Financial Services and Markets Act 2000 (Regulated Activities) (Amendment) (No 2) Order 2013, SI 2013/1881, art 20(1), (61), as from 26 July 2013 (certain purposes), and as from 1 April 2014 (remaining purposes), for transitional provisions see Pt 8 thereof at* **[2.1007]** *et seq.*)

[1.683]
[189B   Green deal plans
(1)   A green deal plan is to be treated as a consumer credit agreement for the purposes of this Act if (and only if)—
   (a)   the property in relation to the plan is a domestic property at the time when the plan is commenced, or

(b) if paragraph (a) does not apply, the occupier or owner of the property who makes the arrangement for the plan is an individual.

(2) In the application of this Act to a green deal consumer credit agreement—
  (a) the creditor is to be treated as being—
    (i) the green deal provider (within the meaning of Chapter 1 of Part 1 of the Energy Act 2011) for the plan, or
    (ii) the person to whom the provider's rights and duties under the plan have passed by assignment or operation of law,
  (b) credit is to be treated as advanced under the agreement of an amount equal to the amount of the improvement costs, and
  (c) the advance of credit is to be treated as made on the completion of the installation of the energy efficiency improvements to the property (but this paragraph is subject to any term of the green deal plan providing that part of the advance is to be treated as made on completion of any part of the installation).

(3) A reference in a provision of this Act listed in the first column of the table in Schedule 2A to the debtor is, in the application of the provision in relation to a green deal consumer credit agreement, to be read as a reference to—
  (a) a person who at the relevant time falls (or fell) within the description or descriptions specified in the corresponding entry in the second column of the table, or
  (b) if more than one description is specified and at the relevant time different persons fall (or fell) within the descriptions, each of those persons,
and except as provided by this subsection, a person is not and is not to be treated as the debtor in relation to the agreement.

(4) Where by virtue of subsection (3) a reference to the debtor in a listed provision is to be read as a reference to the improver, it is to be assumed in applying the provision in relation to the green deal consumer credit agreement that the improver is provided with credit on the terms of the green deal plan.

(5) Where by virtue of subsection (3) a reference to the debtor in a listed provision is to be read as a reference to a person who is not the improver, it is to be assumed in applying the provision in relation to the green deal consumer credit agreement—
  (a) if the provision in question is any of sections 94 to 97A (which together make provision about early payment by the debtor), that the person is provided with credit on terms that the person is liable to pay all the instalments under the green deal plan;
  (b) in any other case, that the person is provided with credit on those terms of the green deal plan that bind or benefit the person for any period by virtue of regulations under section 6(2)(b) of the Energy Act 2011.

(6) References in this section and in Schedule 2A to the "improver", "first bill payer", "current bill payer" and "previous bill payer" are to be read as follows—
  (a) a person is the "improver" if the person—
    (i) is the owner or occupier of the property, and
    (ii) is the person who makes (or has made or proposes to make) the arrangement for the green deal plan,
    but this is subject to section 189C(4) in cases where the person is not an individual;
  (b) a person is the "first bill payer" if the person is liable to pay the energy bills for the property at the time when the green deal plan is commenced;
  (c) a person is the "current bill payer" if the person is liable by virtue of section 1(6)(a) of the Energy Act 2011 to pay instalments under the plan as a result of being for the time being liable to pay the energy bills for the property;
  (d) a person is a "previous bill payer" if, as a result of previously falling within paragraph (c) for an earlier period, the person has an outstanding payment liability under the plan in respect of that period.

(7) References in this Act to a prospective consumer credit agreement, and references to the creditor and debtor in relation to such an agreement, are to be read in accordance with this section in the case of prospective green deal consumer credit agreements.

(8) In this section and in section 189C—
  "domestic property" means a building or part of a building that is occupied as a dwelling or (if not occupied) is intended to be occupied as a dwelling;
  "energy bill" has the same meaning as in section 1 of the Energy Act 2011;
  "energy efficiency improvements" has the meaning given by section 2(4) of the Energy Act 2011;
  "green deal consumer credit agreement" means a green deal plan that is to be treated as a consumer credit agreement for the purposes of this Act by virtue of subsection (1);
  "improvement costs", in relation to a green deal plan, are the costs of the energy efficiency improvements to the property which are to be paid by instalments under the plan after the time when credit is to be treated as being advanced by virtue of subsection (2) (but ignoring any interest or other charges for credit in determining those costs);
  "listed provision" means a provision of this Act listed in the first column of Schedule 2A;
  "occupier" and "owner" have the same meanings as in Chapter 1 of Part 1 of the Energy Act 2011;

"property", in relation to a green deal plan, means the property to which the energy efficiency improvements under the plan are or are intended to be made.]

NOTES

Commencement: 28 February 2014.

Inserted, together with ss 189C, 189D, by the Consumer Credit Act 1974 (Green Deal) (Amendment) Order 2014, SI 2014/436, art 6, as from 28 February 2014, except in relation to a green deal plan (within the meaning of the Energy Act 2011, s 1) made before that date; see art 1(3) thereof.

[1.684]
[189C   Section 189B: supplementary provision
(1)   A green deal consumer credit agreement is to be treated—
   (a)   as an agreement for fixed-sum credit within the meaning of section 10(1)(b);
   (b)   as a credit agreement for the purposes of sections 140A and 140B (and section 140C(1) is to be read accordingly).
(2)   Where a green deal consumer credit agreement is a regulated agreement within the meaning of this Act (see section 8(3)), it is to be treated as a restricted-use agreement that falls within section 11(1)(a).
(3)   Sections 81, 140C(2) and 176(5) do not apply in the case of a green deal consumer credit agreement.
(4)   A person who is not an individual is to be treated as the improver in relation to any listed provision in the first column of the table in Schedule 2A only if the corresponding entry in the second column of the table so specifies.
(5)   For the purposes of section 189B—
   (a)   a green deal plan is commenced when—
      (i)   the occupier or owner of the property signs in the prescribed manner a document in relation to the plan in accordance with section 61(1) (requirements as to form and content of regulated agreements), or
      (ii)   if the occupier or owner of the property does not sign such a document, the green deal plan is made;
   (b)   a person is liable to pay the energy bills for a property at any time if the person would be treated as the bill payer for the property at that time for the purposes of Chapter 1 of Part 1 of the Energy Act 2011 (see section 2(3) and (10)).]

NOTES

Commencement: 28 February 2014.

Inserted as noted to s 189B at **[1.683]**.

[1.685]
[189D   Section 189B: temporary provision
(1)   For the period beginning on the date when this section comes into force and ending on 31st March 2014, the table in Schedule 2A is to be read as if it included the following entries—

Section of this Act	*References to "debtor" are to be read as references to the . . .*
Sections 16, 16A, 16B, 16C	—improver
Section 20	—improver —first bill payer
Section 40	—improver (including an improver who is not an individual) —current bill payer —previous bill payer
Section 55A	—improver —first bill payer, except for the purposes of subsection (1)(b)
Section 55B	—improver —first bill payer
Section 82A	—improver —current bill payer —previous bill payer
Section 145	—current bill payer —previous bill payer
Section 149	—improver (including an improver who is not an individual) —current bill payer —previous bill payer
Section 160A	—improver

(2)   This section ceases to have effect on 1st April 2014.]

NOTES
Commencement: 28 February 2014.
Inserted as noted to s 189B at **[1.683]**.

Miscellaneous

[1.686]
190   Financial provisions
(1)   There shall be defrayed out of money provided by Parliament—
  (a)   all expenses incurred by the Secretary of State in consequence of the provisions of this Act;
  (b)   any expenses incurred in consequence of those provisions by any other Minister of the Crown or Government department;
  (c)   any increase attributable to this Act in the sums payable out of money so provided under the Superannuation Act 1972 or the Fair Trading Act 1973.
(2)   . . .

NOTES
Sub-s (2): repealed by the Financial Services and Markets Act 2000 (Regulated Activities) (Amendment) (No 2) Order 2013, SI 2013/1881, art 20(1), (62), as from 26 July 2013 (certain purposes), and as from 1 April 2014 (remaining purposes), for transitional provisions see Pt 8 thereof at **[2.1007]** *et seq*.
References to the FCA, etc: as to the abolition of the office of the Director General of Fair Trading and the substitution of the original references to the Director (and related expressions), see the note preceding s 8 at **[1.520]**.

191   (*Applies to Northern Ireland only.*)

[1.687]
192   Transitional and commencement provisions, amendments and repeals
(1)   The provisions of Schedule 3 shall have effect for the purposes of this Act.
(2)   The appointment of a day for the purposes of any provision of Schedule 3 shall be effected by an order of the Secretary of State made by statutory instrument; and any such order shall include a provision amending Schedule 3 so as to insert an express reference to the day appointed.
(3)   Subject to subsection (4)—
  (a)   the enactments specified in Schedule 4 shall have effect subject to the amendments specified in that Schedule (being minor amendments or amendments consequential on the preceding provisions of this Act), and
  (b)   the enactments specified in Schedule 5 are hereby repealed to the extent shown in column 3 of that Schedule.
(4)   The Secretary of State shall by order made by statutory instrument provide for the coming into operation of the amendments contained in Schedule 4 and the repeals contained in Schedule 5, and those amendments and repeals shall have effect only as provided by an order so made.

NOTES
Orders: the Consumer Credit Act 1974 (Commencement No 1) Order 1975, SI 1975/2123; the Consumer Credit Act 1974 (Commencement No 2) Order 1977, SI 1977/325; the Consumer Credit Act 1974 (Commencement No 3) Order 1977, SI 1977/802; the Consumer Credit Act 1974 (Commencement No 4) Order 1977, SI 1977/2163; the Consumer Credit Act 1974 (Commencement No 5) Order 1979, SI 1979/1685; the Consumer Credit Act 1974 (Commencement No 6) Order 1980, SI 1980/50; the Consumer Credit Act 1974 (Commencement No 7) Order 1981, SI 1981/280; the Consumer Credit Act 1974 (Commencement No 8) Order 1983, SI 1983/1551; the Consumer Credit Act 1974 (Commencement No 9) Order 1984, SI 1984/436; the Consumer Credit Act 1974 (Commencement No 10) Order 1989, SI 1989/1128.

[1.688]
193   Short title and extent
(1)   This Act may be cited as the Consumer Credit Act 1974.
(2)   This Act extends to Northern Ireland.

SCHEDULES

SCHEDULE A1

(*Inserted by the Consumer Credit Act 2006, s 55(2), Sch 1, as from 6 April 2008; repealed by the Transfer of Functions of the Consumer Credit Appeals Tribunal Order 2009, SI 2009/1835, art 4(1), Sch 1, paras 1, 9, as from 1 September 2009, subject to transitional provisions and savings in Sch 4 thereto at* **[2.791]**.)

SCHEDULE 1
PROSECUTION AND PUNISHMENT OF OFFENCES

Section 167

[1.689]

1 Section	2 Offence	3 Mode of prosecution	4 Imprisonment or fine
. . .	. . .	. . .	. . .
. . .	. . .	. . .	. . .
. . .	. . .	. . .	. . .
. . .	. . .	. . .	. . .
. . .	. . .	. . .	. . .
49(1)	Canvassing debtor-creditor agreements off trade premises.	(a) Summarily. (b) On indictment.	[The prescribed sum]. 1 year or a fine or both.
49(2)	Soliciting debtor-creditor agreements during visits made in response to previous oral requests.	(a) Summarily. (b) On indictment.	[The prescribed sum]. 1 year or a fine or both.
50(1)	Sending circulars to minors.	(a) Summarily. (b) On indictment.	[The prescribed sum]. 1 year or a fine or both.
[. . .	. . .	. . .	. . .]
80(2)	Failure to tell creditor or owner whereabouts of goods.	Summarily.	[Level 3 on the standard scale.]
114(2)	Taking pledges from minors.	(a) Summarily. (b) On indictment.	[The prescribed sum]. 1 year or a fine or both.
119(1)	Unreasonable refusal to allow pawn to be redeemed.	Summarily.	[Level 4 on the standard scale.]
154	Canvassing ancillary credit services off trade premises.	(a) Summarily. (b) On indictment.	[The prescribed sum]. 1 year or a fine or both.
157(3)	Refusal to give name etc of credit reference agency.	Summarily.	[Level 4 on the standard scale.]
158(4)	Failure of credit reference agency to disclose filed information.	Summarily.	[Level 4 on the standard scale.]
159(6)	Failure of credit reference agency to correct information.	Summarily.	[Level 4 on the standard scale.]
160(6)	Failure of credit reference agency to comply with section 160(3) or (4).	Summarily.	[Level 4 on the standard scale.]
[. . .	. . .	. . .	. . .]
162(6)	*Impersonation of enforcement authority officers.*	*(a) Summarily.* *(b) On indictment.*	*[The prescribed sum].* *2 years or a fine or both.*
165(1)	*Obstruction of enforcement authority officers.*	*Summarily.*	*[Level 4 on the standard scale.]*

1 **Section**	2 **Offence**	3 **Mode of prosecution**	4 **Imprisonment or fine**
165(2)	Giving false information to enforcement authority officers.	(a) Summarily. (b) On indictment.	[The prescribed sum]. 2 years or a fine or both.
. . .	. . .	. . .	. . .
. . .	. . .	. . .	. . .

NOTES

Entries relating to ss 7, 39(1), 39(2), 39(3), 45, 47(1), 51(1), 51A(1) (as inserted by the Financial Services Act 2010, s 15(1), (3)), 115, 160A, 167(2) and 174(5) (omitted) repealed by the Financial Services and Markets Act 2000 (Regulated Activities) (Amendment) (No 2) Order 2013, SI 2013/1881, art 20(1), (64), as from 26 July 2013 (certain purposes), and as from 1 April 2014 (remaining purposes), for transitional provisions see Pt 8 thereof at **[2.1007]** et seq.

Entries relating to ss 46(1), 77(4), 78(6), 79(3), 85(2), 97(3), 103(5), 107(4), 108(4), 109(3) and 110(3) (omitted) repealed by the Consumer Protection from Unfair Trading Regulations 2008, SI 2008/1277, reg 30(3), Sch 4, as from 26 May 2008.

Entry relating to s 160A inserted by the Consumer Credit (EU Directive) Regulations 2010, SI 2010/1010, regs 2, 43, as from 1 February 2011, with effect in relation to certain agreements before that date, as provided for in regs 101, 101A of the 2010 Regulations at **[2.804]**, **[2.805]**.

Entries relating to ss 162(6), 165(1) and 165(2) repealed by the Consumer Rights Act 2015, s 77, Sch 6, para 12, 18, as from 1 October 2015 (for transitional provisions see the Consumer Rights Act 2015 (Commencement No 3, Transitional Provisions, Savings and Consequential Amendments) Order 2015, SI 2015/1630, arts 6–8 at **[2.1220]** et seq).

References to the prescribed sum substituted by virtue of the Magistrates' Courts Act 1980, s 32(2).

References to a level on the standard scale substituted by virtue of the Criminal Justice Act 1982, ss 38, 46.

References to the FCA, etc: as to the abolition of the office of the Director General of Fair Trading and the substitution of the original references to the Director (and related expressions), see the note preceding s 8 at **[1.520]**.

SCHEDULE 2
EXAMPLES OF USE OF NEW TERMINOLOGY

Section 188(1)

PART I
LIST OF TERMS

[1.690]

Term	Defined in section	Illustrated by example(s)
Advertisement	189(1)	2
. . .	. . .	. . .
Antecedent negotiations	56	1, 2, 3, 4
Cancellable agreement	67	4
Consumer credit agreement	8	5, 6, 7, 15, 19, 21
Consumer hire agreement	15	20, 24
Credit	9	16, 19, 21
Credit-broker	189(1)	2
Credit limit	10(2)	6, 7, 19, 22, 23
Creditor	189(1)	1, 2, 3, 4
Credit-sale agreement	189(1)	5
Credit-token	14	3, 14, 16
Credit-token agreement	14	3, 14, 16, 22
Debtor-creditor agreement	13	8, 16, 17, 18
Debtor-creditor-supplier agreement	12	8, 16
Fixed-sum credit	10	9, 10, 17, 23
Hire-purchase agreement	189(1)	10
Individual	189(1)	19, 24
Linked transaction	19	11
Modifying agreement	82(2)	24
Multiple agreement	18	16, 18
Negotiator	56(1)	1, 2, 3, 4
. . .	. . .	. . .
Pre-existing arrangements	187	8, 21
Restricted-use credit	11	10, 12, 13, 14, 16

Term	Defined in section	Illustrated by example(s)
Running-account credit	10	15, 16, 18, 23
Small agreement	17	16, 17, 22
Supplier	189(1)	3, 14
Total charge for credit	20	5, 10
Total price	189(1)	10
Unrestricted-use credit	11	8, 12, 16, 17, 18

NOTES

Entry relating to "advertiser" (omitted) repealed by the Financial Services and Markets Act 2000 (Regulated Activities) (Amendment) (No 2) Order 2013, SI 2013/1881, art 20(1), (65)(a), as from 26 July 2013 (certain purposes), and as from 1 April 2014 (remaining purposes), for transitional provisions see Pt 8 thereof at **[2.1007]** et seq.

Entry relating to "personal credit agreement" (omitted) repealed by the Consumer Credit Act 2006, s 70, Sch 4, as from 31 October 2008.

PART II
EXAMPLES

Example 1

[1.691]

Facts. Correspondence passes between an employee of a moneylending company (writing on behalf of the company) and an individual about the terms on which the company would grant him a loan under a regulated agreement.

Analysis. The correspondence constitutes antecedent negotiations falling within section 56(1)(a), the moneylending company being both creditor and negotiator.

Example 2

Facts. Representations are made about goods in a poster displayed by a shopkeeper near the goods, the goods being selected by a customer who has read the poster and then sold by the shopkeeper to a finance company introduced by him (with whom he has a business relationship). The goods are disposed of by the finance company to the customer under a regulated hire-purchase agreement.

Analysis. The representations in the poster constitute antecedent negotiations falling within section 56(1)(b), the shopkeeper being the credit-broker and negotiator and the finance company being the creditor. The poster is an advertisement and the shopkeeper is the advertiser.

Example 3

Facts. Discussions take place between a shopkeeper and a customer about goods the customer wishes to buy using a credit-card issued by the D Bank under a regulated agreement.

Analysis. The discussions constitute antecedent negotiations falling within section 56(1)(c), the shopkeeper being the supplier and negotiator and the D Bank the creditor. The credit-card is a credit-token as defined in section 14(1), and the regulated agreement under which it was issued is a credit-token agreement as defined in section 14(2).

Example 4

Facts. Discussions take place and correspondence passes between a secondhand car dealer and a customer about a car, which is then sold by the dealer to the customer under a regulated conditional sale agreement. Subsequently, on a revocation of that agreement by consent, the car is resold by the dealer to a finance company introduced by him (with whom he has a business relationship), who in turn dispose of it to the same customer under a regulated hire-purchase agreement.

Analysis. The discussions and correspondence constitute antecedent negotiations in relation both to the conditional sale agreement and the hire-purchase agreement. They fall under section 56(1)(a) in relation to the conditional sale agreement, the dealer being the creditor and the negotiator. In relation to the hire-purchase agreement they fall within section 56(1)(b), the dealer continuing to be treated as the negotiator but the finance company now being the creditor. Both agreements are cancellable if the discussions took place when the individual conducting the negotiations (whether the "negotiator" or his employee or agent) was in the presence of the debtor, unless the unexecuted agreement was signed by the debtor at trade premises (as defined in section 67(b)). If the discussions all took place by telephone however, or the unexecuted agreement was signed by the debtor on trade premises (as so defined) the agreements are not cancellable.

Example 5

Facts. E agrees to sell to F (an individual) an item of furniture in return for 24 monthly instalments of £10 payable in arrears. The property in the goods passes to F immediately.

Analysis. This is a credit-sale agreement (see definition of "credit-sale agreement" in section 189(1)). The credit provided amounts to £240 less the amount which [constitutes the total charge for credit (within the meaning given by section 20)]. (This amount is required to be deducted by section 9(4)). Accordingly the agreement falls within section 8(2) and is a consumer credit agreement.

Example 6

Facts. The G Bank grants H (an individual) an unlimited overdraft, with an increased rate of interest on so much of any debit balance as exceeds £2,000.

Analysis. Although the overdraft purports to be unlimited, the stipulation for increased interest above £2,000 brings the agreement within section 10(3)(b)(ii) and it is a consumer credit agreement.

Example 7

Facts. J is an individual who owns a small shop which usually carries a stock worth about £1,000. K makes a stocking agreement under which he undertakes to provide on short-term credit the stock needed from time to time by J without any specified limit.

Analysis. Although the agreement appears to provide unlimited credit, it is probable, having regard to the stock usually carried by J, that his indebtedness to K will not at any time rise above £5,000. Accordingly the agreement falls within section 10(3)(b)(iii) and is a consumer credit agreement.

Example 8

Facts. U, a moneylender, lends £500 to V (an individual) knowing he intends to use it to buy office equipment from W. W introduced V to U, it being his practice to introduce customers needing finance to him. Sometimes U gives W a commission for this and sometimes not. U pays the £500 direct to V.

Analysis. Although this appears to fall under section 11(1)(b), it is excluded by section 11(3) and is therefore (by section 11(2)) an unrestricted-use credit agreement. Whether it is a debtor-creditor agreement (by section 13(c)) or a debtor-creditor-supplier agreement (by section 12(c)) depends on whether the previous dealings between U and W amount to "pre-existing arrangements", that is whether the agreement can be taken to have been entered into "in accordance with, or in furtherance of" arrangements previously made between U and W, as laid down in section 187(1).

Example 9

Facts. A agrees to lend B (an individual) £4,500 in nine monthly instalments of £500.

Analysis. This is a cash loan and is a form of credit (see section 9 and definition of "cash" in section 189(1)). Accordingly it falls within section 10(1)(b) and is fixed-sum credit amounting to £4,500.

Example 10

Facts. C (in England) agrees to bail goods to D (an individual) in return for periodical payments. The agreement provides for the property in the goods to pass to D on payment of a total of £7,500 and the exercise by D of an option to purchase. The sum of £7,500 includes a down-payment of £1,000. It also includes an amount which, according to regulations made under section 20(1), constitutes a total charge for credit of £1,500.

Analysis. This is a hire-purchase agreement with a deposit of £1,000 and a total price of £7,500 (see definitions of "hire-purchase agreement", "deposit" and "total price" in section 189(1)). By section 9(3), it is taken to provide credit amounting to £7,500 – (£1,500 + £1,000), which equals £5,000. Under section 8(2), the agreement is therefore a consumer credit agreement, and under sections 9(3) and 11(1) it is a restricted-use credit agreement for fixed-sum credit. A similar result would follow if the agreement by C had been a hiring agreement in Scotland.

Example 11

Facts. X (an individual) borrows £500 from Y (Finance). As a condition of the granting of the loan X is required—

   (a)   to execute a second mortgage on his house in favour of Y (Finance), and

   (b)   to take out a policy of insurance on his life with Y (Insurances).

In accordance with the loan agreement, the policy is charged to Y (Finance) as collateral security for the loan. The two companies are associates within the meaning of section 184(3).

Analysis. The second mortgage is a transaction for the provision of security and accordingly does not fall within section 19(1), but the taking out of the insurance policy is a linked transaction falling within section 19(1)(a). The charging of the policy is a separate transaction (made between different parties) for the provision of security and again is excluded from section 19(1). The only linked transaction is therefore the taking out of the insurance policy. If X had not been required by the loan agreement to take out the policy, but it had been done at the suggestion of Y (Finance) to induce them to enter into the loan agreement, it would have been a linked transaction under section 19(1)(c)(i) by virtue of section 19(2)(a).

Example 12

Facts. The N Bank agrees to lend O (an individual) £2,000 to buy a car from P. To make sure the loan is used as intended, the N Bank stipulates that the money must be paid by it direct to P.

Analysis. The agreement is a consumer credit agreement by virtue of section 8(2). Since it falls within section 11(1)(b), it is a restricted-use credit agreement, P being the supplier. If the N Bank had not stipulated for direct payment to the supplier, section 11(3) would have operated and made the agreement into one for unrestricted-use credit.

Example 13

Facts. Q, a debt-adjuster, agrees to pay off debts owed by R (an individual) to various moneylenders. For this purpose the agreement provides for the making of a loan by Q to R in return for R's agreeing to repay the loan by instalments with interest. The loan money is not paid over to R but retained by Q and used to pay off the moneylenders.

Analysis. This is an agreement to refinance existing indebtedness of the debtor's, and if the loan by Q does not exceed £5,000 is a restricted-use credit agreement falling within section 11(1)(c).

Example 14

Facts. On payment of £1, S issues to T (an individual) a trading check under which T can spend up to £20 at any shop which has agreed, or in future agrees, to accept S's trading checks.

Analysis. The trading check is a credit-token falling within section 14(1)(b). The credit-token agreement is a restricted-use credit agreement within section 11(1)(b), any shop in which the credit-token is used being the "supplier". The fact that further shops may be added after the issue of the credit-token is irrelevant in view of section 11(4).

Example 15

Facts. A retailer, L, agrees with M (an individual) to open an account in M's name and, in return for M's promise to pay a specified minimum sum into the account each month and to pay a monthly charge for credit, agrees to allow to be debited to the account, in respect of purchases made by M from L, such sums as will not increase the debit balance at any time beyond the credit limit, defined in the agreement as a given multiple of the specified minimum sum.

Analysis. This arrangement provides credit falling within the definition of running-account credit in section 10(1)(a). Provided the credit limit is not over £5,000, the agreement falls within section 8(2) and is a consumer credit agreement for running-account credit.

Example 16

Facts. Under an unsecured agreement, A (Credit), an associate of the A Bank, issues to B (an individual) a credit-card for use in obtaining cash on credit from A (Credit), to be paid by branches of the A Bank (acting as agent of A (Credit)), or goods or cash from suppliers or banks who have agreed to honour credit-cards issued by A (Credit). The credit limit is £30.

Analysis. This is a credit-token agreement falling within section 14(1)(a) and (b). It is a regulated consumer credit agreement for running-account credit. Since the credit limit does not exceed £30, the agreement is a small agreement. So far as the agreement relates to goods it is a debtor-creditor-supplier agreement within section 12(b), since it provides restricted-use credit under section 11(1)(b). So far as it relates to cash it is a debtor-creditor agreement within section 13(c) and the credit it provides is unrestricted-use credit. This is therefore a multiple agreement. In that the whole agreement falls within several of the categories of agreement mentioned in this Act, it is, by section 18(3), to be treated as an agreement in each of those categories. So far as it is a debtor-creditor-supplier agreement providing restricted-use credit it is, by section 18(2), to be treated as a separate agreement; and similarly so far as it is a debtor-creditor agreement providing unrestricted-used credit. (See also Example 22.)

Example 17

Facts. The manager of the C Bank agrees orally with D (an individual) to open a current account in D's name. Nothing is said about overdraft facilities. After maintaining the account in credit for some weeks, D draws a cheque in favour of E for an amount exceeding D's credit balance by £20. E presents the cheque and the Bank pay it.

Analysis. In drawing the cheque D, by implication, requests the Bank to grant him an overdraft of £20 on its usual terms as to interest and other charges. In deciding to honour the cheque, the Bank by implication accepts the offer. This constitutes a regulated small consumer credit agreement for unrestricted-use, fixed-sum credit. It is a debtor-creditor agreement, and falls within section 74(1)(b) . . . (Compare Example 18.)

Example 18

Facts. F (an individual) has had a current account with the G Bank for many years. Although usually in credit, the account has been allowed by the Bank to become overdrawn from time to time. The maximum such overdraft has been is about £1,000. No explicit agreement has ever been made about overdraft facilities. Now, with a credit balance of £500, F draws a cheque for £1,300.

Analysis. It might well be held that the agreement with F (express or implied) under which the Bank operate his account includes an implied term giving him the right to overdraft facilities up to say £1,000. If so, the agreement is a regulated consumer credit agreement for unrestricted-use, running-account credit. It is a debtor-creditor agreement, and falls within section 74(1)(b) . . . It is also a multiple agreement, part of which (i.e. the part not dealing with the overdraft), as referred to in section 18(1)(a), falls within a category of agreement not mentioned in this Act. (Compare Example 17.)

Example 19

Facts. H (a finance house) agrees with J (a partnership of individuals) to open an unsecured loan account in J's name on which the debit balance is not to exceed £7,000 (having regard to payments into the account made from time to time by J). Interest is to be payable in advance on this sum, with provision for yearly adjustments. H is entitled to debit the account with interest, a "setting-up" charge, and other charges. Before J has an opportunity to draw on the account it is initially debited with £2,250 for advance interest and other charges.

Analysis. This is a personal running-account credit agreement (see sections 8(1) and 10(1)(a), and definition of "individual" in section 189(1)). By section 10(2) the credit limit is £7,000. By section 9(4) however the initial debit of £2,250, and any other charges later debited to the account by H, are not to be treated as credit even though time is allowed for their payment. Effect is given to this by section 10(3). Although the credit limit of £7,000 exceeds the amount (£5,000) specified in section 8(2) as the maximum for a consumer credit agreement, so that the agreement is not within section 10(3)(a), it is caught by section 10(3)(b)(i). At the beginning J can effectively draw (as credit) no more than £4,750, so the agreement is a consumer credit agreement.

Example 20

Facts. K (in England) agrees with L (an individual) to bail goods to L for a period of three years certain at £2,000 a year, payable quarterly. The agreement contains no provision for the passing of the property in the goods to L.

Analysis. This is not a hire-purchase agreement (see paragraph (b) of the definition of that term in section 189(1)) and is capable of subsisting for more than three months. Paragraphs (a) and (b) of section 15(1) are therefore satisfied, but paragraph (c) is not. The payments by L must exceed £5,000 if he conforms to the agreement. It is true that under section 101 L has a right to terminate the agreement on giving K three months' notice expiring not earlier than eighteen months after the making of the agreement, but that section applies only where the agreement is a regulated consumer hire agreement apart from the section (see subsection (1)). So the agreement is not a consumer hire agreement, though it would be if the hire charge were say £1,500 a year, or there were a "break" clause in it operable by either party before the hire charges exceeded £5,000. A similar result would follow if the agreement by K had been a hiring agreement in Scotland.

Example 21

Facts. The P Bank decides to issue cheque cards to its customers under a scheme whereby the Bank undertakes to honour cheques of up to £30 in every case where the payee has taken the cheque in reliance on the cheque card, whether the customer has funds in his account or not. The P Bank writes to the major retailers advising them of this scheme and also publicises it by advertising. The Bank issues a cheque card to Q (an individual), who uses it to pay by cheque for goods costing £20 bought by Q from R, a major retailer. At the time, Q has £500 in his account at the P Bank.

Analysis. The agreement under which the cheque card is issued to Q is a consumer credit agreement even though at all relevant times Q has more than £30 in his account. This is because Q is free to draw out his whole balance and then use the cheque card, in which case the Bank has bound itself to honour the cheque. In other words the cheque card agreement provides Q with credit, whether he avails himself of it or not. Since the amount of the credit is not subject to any express limit, the cheque card can be used any number of times. It may be presumed however that section 10(3)(b)(iii) will apply. The agreement is an unrestricted-use debtor-creditor agreement (by section 13(c)). Although the P Bank wrote to R informing R of the P Bank's willingness to honour any cheque taken by R in reliance on a cheque card, this does not constitute pre-existing arrangements as mentioned in section 13(c) because section 187(3) operates to prevent it. The agreement is not a credit-token agreement within section 14(1)(b) because payment by the P Bank to R, would be a payment of the cheque and not a payment for the goods.

Example 22

Facts. The facts are as in Example 16. On one occasion B uses the credit-card in a way which increases his debit balance with A (Credit) to £40. A (Credit) writes to B agreeing to allow the excess on that occasion only, but stating that it must be paid off within one month.

Analysis. In exceeding his credit limit B, by implication, requests A (Credit) to allow him a temporary excess (compare Example 17). A (Credit) is thus faced by B's action with the choice of treating it as a breach of contract or granting his implied request. He does the latter. If he had done the former, B would be treated as taking credit to which he was not entitled (section 14(3)) and, subject to the terms of his contract with A (Credit), would be liable to damages for breach of contract. As it is, the agreement to allow the excess varies the original credit-token agreement by adding a new term. Under section 10(2), the new term is to be disregarded in arriving at the credit limit, so that the credit-token agreement at no time ceases to be a small agreement. By section 82(2) the later agreement is deemed to revoke the original agreement and contain provisions reproducing the combined effect of the two agreements. By section 82(4), this later agreement is exempted from Part V (except section 56).

Example 23

Facts. Under an oral agreement made on 10th January, X (an individual) has an overdraft on his current account at the Y Bank with a credit limit of £100. On 15th February, when his overdraft standards at £90, X draws a cheque for £25. It is the first time that X has exceeded his credit limit, and on 16th February the bank honours the cheque.

Analysis. The agreement of 10th January is a consumer credit agreement for running-account credit. The agreement of 15th–16th February varies the earlier agreement by adding a term allowing the credit limit to be exceeded merely temporarily. By section 82(2) the later agreement is deemed to revoke the earlier agreement and reproduce the combined effect of the two agreements. By section 82(4), Part V of this Act (except section 56) does not apply to the later agreement. By section 18(5), a term allowing a merely temporary excess over the credit limit is not to be treated as a separate agreement, or as providing fixed-sum credit. The whole of the £115 owed to the Bank by X on 16th February is therefore running-account credit.

Example 24

Facts. On 1st March 1975 Z (in England) enters into an agreement with A (an unincorporated body of persons) to bail to A equipment consisting of two components (component P and component Q). The agreement is not a hire-purchase agreement and is for a fixed term of 3 years, so paragraphs (a) and (b) of section 15(1) are both satisfied. The rental is payable monthly at a rate of £2,400 a year, but the agreement provides that this is to be reduced to £1,200 a year for the remainder of the agreement if at any time during its currency A returns component Q to the owner Z. On 5th May 1976 A is incorporated as A Ltd., taking over A's assets and liabilities. On 1st March 1977, A Ltd. returns component Q. On 1st January 1978, Z and A Ltd. agree to extend the earlier agreement by one year, increasing the rental for the final year by £250 to £1,450.

Analysis. When entered into on 1st March 1975, the agreement is a consumer hire agreement. A falls within the definition of "individual" in section 189(1) and if A returns component Q before 1st May 1976 the total rental will not exceed £5,000 (see section 15(1)(c)). When this date is passed without component Q having been returned it is obvious that the total rental must now exceed £5,000. Does this mean that the agreement then ceases to be a consumer hire agreement? The answer is no, because there has been no change in the terms of the agreement, and without such a change the agreement cannot move from one category to the other. Similarly, the fact that A's rights and duties under the agreement pass to a body corporate on 5th May 1976 does not cause the agreement to cease to be a consumer hire agreement (see the definition of "hirer" in section 189(1)).

The effect of the modifying agreement of 1st January 1978 is governed by section 82(2), which requires it to be treated as containing provisions reproducing the combined effect of the two actual agreements, that is to say as providing that—

(a) obligations outstanding on 1st January 1978 are to be treated as outstanding under the modifying agreement;

(b) the modifying agreement applies at the old rate of hire for the months of January and February 1978, and

(c) for the year beginning 1st March 1978 A Ltd. will be the bailee of component P at a rental of £1,450.

The total rental under the modifying agreement is £1,850. Accordingly the modifying agreement is a regulated agreement. Even if the total rental under the modifying agreement exceeded £5,000 it would still be regulated because of the provisions of section 82(3).

NOTES

Example 5: words in square brackets substituted by the Financial Services and Markets Act 2000 (Regulated Activities) (Amendment) (No 2) Order 2013, SI 2013/1881, art 20(1), (65)(b), as from 26 July 2013 (certain purposes), and as from 1 April 2014 (remaining purposes), for transitional provisions see Pt 8 thereof at **[2.1007]** et seq.

Examples 17, 18: words omitted repealed by the Consumer Credit (EU Directive) Regulations 2010, SI 2010/1010, regs 2, 20, as from 1 February 2011, with effect in relation to certain agreements before that date, as provided for in regs 101, 101A of the 2010 Regulations at **[2.804]**, **[2.805]**.

[SCHEDULE 2A]
MEANING OF "DEBTOR" IN RELATION TO GREEN DEAL AGREEMENTS
[1.692]

Section of this Act	*References to "debtor" are to be read as references to the . . .*
Section 19	—improver
Section 55	—improver
Section 55C	—improver —first bill payer
Section 56	—improver —first bill payer
Section 57	—improver
Section 59	—improver
Sections 60 and 61	—improver (including an improver who is not an individual)
Section 61A	—improver

Section of this Act	References to "debtor" are to be read as references to the . . .
Sections 62, 63, 64	—improver
Section 65	—improver —current bill payer —previous bill payer
Section 66A	—improver
Sections 67, 68, 69, 70, 71, 72, 73	—improver
Section 75A	—improver
Sections 76 and 77	—current bill payer —previous bill payer
Section 77A	—current bill payer
Section 77B	—improver —current bill payer
Section 78A	—improver —current bill payer
Section 80	—improver
Section 82	—improver —current bill payer —previous bill payer
Section 86	—current bill payer —previous bill payer
Section 86E	—current bill payer —previous bill payer
Section 86F	—current bill payer —previous bill payer
Section 87	—current bill payer —previous bill payer
Section 89	—current bill payer —previous bill payer
Section 93	—current bill payer —previous bill payer
Sections 94, 95, 95A, 95B, 96, 97, 97A	—improver —current bill payer
Section 98	—current bill payer —previous bill payer
Sections 102, 103, 105, 107, 110, 113	—improver
Sections 123, 124	—current bill payer —previous bill payer
Section 127	—improver —current bill payer —previous bill payer
Sections 128, 129, 130, 130A	—current bill payer —previous bill payer
Sections 140A, 140B, 140C	—improver —current bill payer —previous bill payer
Section 141(1), (2), (3A), (3B)	—improver —current bill payer —previous bill payer
Section 157	—improver —first bill payer
Section 173	—improver —current bill payer —previous bill payer
Section 179	—improver —first bill payer —current bill payer —previous bill payer

Section of this Act	References to "debtor" are to be read as references to the . . .
Section 185(1), (2), (2A), (2B), (2C), (2D), (4)	—current bill payer
Section 187A	—current bill payer —previous bill payer
Section 189(1), so far as relating to definition of "security"	—improver]

NOTES

Commencement: 28 February 2014.

Inserted by the Consumer Credit Act 1974 (Green Deal) (Amendment) Order 2014, SI 2014/436, art 7, as from 28 February 2014, except in relation to a green deal plan (within the meaning of the Energy Act 2011, s 1) made before that date; see art 1(3) thereof.

SCHEDULES 3 AND 4

(Sch 3 (Transitional and Commencement Provisions), Sch 4 (Minor and Consequential Amendments) outside the scope of this work.)

UNSOLICITED GOODS AND SERVICES (AMENDMENT) ACT 1975

(1975 c 13)

ARRANGEMENT OF SECTIONS

An Act to amend the Unsolicited Goods and Services Act 1971, to enable the Secretary of State to make regulations with respect to the contents and form of notes of agreement, invoices and similar documents and to provide for conviction on indictment in relation to an offence under s 3(2) of the said Act; and for connected matters

[20 March 1975]

NOTES

Unsolicited Goods and Services Acts 1971 and 1975: by s 4(1) of this Act, see **[1.694]**, that Act and this Act may be cited together by this collective title.

1, 2 *(S 1 inserts the Unsolicited Goods and Services Act 1971, s 3A (repealed); s 2 repealed in part, remainder spent.)*

[1.693]

3 Provision for offence under section 3(2) of the Act of 1971 to be prosecuted on indictment

(1) An offence under section 3(2) of the Act of 1971 may be prosecuted on indictment; and a person convicted on indictment of an offence under that section shall be liable to a fine.

(2) . . .

NOTES

Sub-s (2): repealed by the Statute Law (Repeals) Act 2004.

[1.694]

4 Short title, citation, commencement, transitional provisions and extent

(1) This Act may be cited as the Unsolicited Goods and Services (Amendment) Act 1975 and the Unsolicited Goods and Services Act 1971 and this Act may be cited together as the Unsolicited Goods and Services Acts 1971 and 1975.

(2)–(4) . . .

(5) This Act shall not extend to Northern Ireland.

NOTES

Sub-ss (2)–(4): repealed by the Statute Law (Repeals) Act 2004.

Orders: the Unsolicited Goods and Services (Amendment) Act 1975 (Commencement No 1) Order 1975, SI 1975/731.

INDUSTRY ACT 1975

(1975 c 68)

ARRANGEMENT OF SECTIONS

An Act to establish a National Enterprise Board; to confer on the Secretary of State power to prohibit the passing to persons not resident in the United Kingdom of control of undertakings engaged in manufacturing industry, and power to acquire compulsorily the capital or assets of such undertakings where control has passed to such persons or there is a probability that it will pass; to amend the Industry Act 1972 and the Development of Inventions Act 1967; to make provision for the disclosure of information relating to manufacturing undertakings to the Secretary of State or the Minister of Agriculture, Fisheries and Food, and to trade unions; and for connected purposes

[12 November 1975]

1–10 ((*Pt I*) *ss 1–3, 5–10 repealed by the British Technology Group Act 1991, s 17(2), Sch 2, Pts II, III; s 4 repealed by the Industry Act 1980, ss 9, 21, Sch 2.*)

PART II
POWERS IN RELATION TO TRANSFERS OF CONTROL OF IMPORTANT
MANUFACTURING UNDERTAKINGS TO NON-RESIDENTS

[1.695]
11   General extent of powers in relation to control of important manufacturing undertakings
(1)   The powers conferred by this Part of this Act shall have effect in relation to changes of control of important manufacturing undertakings.
(2)   In this Part of this Act—
    "important manufacturing undertaking" means an undertaking which, in so far as it is carried on in the United Kingdom, is wholly or mainly engaged in manufacturing industry and appears to the Secretary of State to be of special importance to the United Kingdom or to any substantial part of the United Kingdom.

[1.696]
12   Meaning of "change of control"
(1)   There is a change of control of an important manufacturing undertaking for the purposes of this Part of this Act only upon the happening of a relevant event.
(2)   In subsection (1) above "relevant event" means any event as a result of which—
   (a)   the person carrying on the whole or part of the undertaking ceases to be resident in the United Kingdom;
   (b)   a person not resident in the United Kingdom acquires the whole or part of the undertaking;

(c)   a body corporate resident in the United Kingdom but controlled by a person not so resident acquires the whole or part of the undertaking;

(d)   a person not resident in the United Kingdom becomes able to exercise or control the exercise of the first, second or third qualifying percentage of votes in a body corporate carrying on the whole or part of the undertaking or in any other body corporate which is in control of such a body; or

(e)   a person resident in the United Kingdom and able to exercise or control the exercise of the first, second or third qualifying percentage of votes in a body corporate carrying on the whole or part of the undertaking or in any other body corporate which is in control of such a body ceases to be resident in the United Kingdom.

(3)   For the purposes of subsection (2) above—

(a)   a body corporate or individual entitled to cast 30 per cent or more of the votes that may be cast at any general meeting of a body corporate, is in control of that body; and

(b)   control of a body corporate which has control of another body corporate gives control of the latter body.

(4)   Any power to direct the holder of shares or stock in a body corporate as to the exercise of his votes at a general meeting of that body corporate is to be treated as entitlement to cast the votes in respect of the shares or stock in question.

(5)   Two or more persons acting together in concert may be treated as a single person for the purposes of any provision of this Part of this Act relating to change of control.

(6)   For the purposes of this Part of this Act—

(a)   the first qualifying percentage of votes is 30 per cent;

(b)   the second qualifying percentage is 40 per cent; and

(c)   the third qualifying percentage is 50 per cent;

and the references to votes in this subsection are references to votes that may be cast at a general meeting.

[1.697]
13   Power to make orders

(1)   If it appears to the Secretary of State—

(a)   that there is a serious and immediate probability of a change of control of an important manufacturing undertaking; and

(b)   that that change of control would be contrary to the interests of the United Kingdom, or contrary to the interests of any substantial part of the United Kingdom,

he may by order (in this Part of this Act referred to as a "prohibition order") specify the undertaking and

(i)   prohibit that change of control; and

(ii)   prohibit or restrict the doing of things which in his opinion would constitute or lead to it;

and may make such incidental or supplementary provision in the order as appears to him to be necessary or expedient.

(2)   Subject to subsection (3) below, if—

(a)   the conditions specified in paragraphs (a) and (b) of subsection (1) above are satisfied, or

(b)   a prohibition order has been made in relation to an important manufacturing undertaking, or

(c)   the Secretary of State has learnt of circumstances which appear to him to constitute a change of control of an important manufacturing undertaking, occurring on or after 1st February 1975, and is satisfied that that change is contrary to the interests of the United Kingdom, or contrary to the interests of any substantial part of the United Kingdom,

the Secretary of State may by order made with the approval of the Treasury (in this Part of this Act referred to as a "vesting order") direct that on a day specified in the order—

(i)   share capital and loan capital to which this subsection applies, or

(ii)   any assets which are employed in the undertaking,

shall vest in . . . in himself or in nominees for . . . himself and may make such incidental or supplementary provision in the order as appears to him to be necessary or expedient.

(3)   A vesting order may only be made if the Secretary of State is satisfied that the order is necessary in the national interest and that, having regard to all the circumstances, that interest cannot, or cannot appropriately, be protected in any other way.

(4)   The share capital and loan capital to which subsection (2) above applies are—

(a)   in any case where the Secretary of State considers that the interests mentioned in subsection (2)(c) above cannot, or cannot appropriately, be protected unless all the share capital of any relevant body corporate vests by virtue of the order, the share capital of that body corporate, together with so much (if any) of the loan capital of that body as may be specified in the order,

(b)   in any other case, that part of the share capital of any relevant body corporate which, at the time that the draft of the order is laid before Parliament under section 15 (3) below, appears to the Secretary of State to be involved in the change of control.

(5)   In this section "relevant body corporate" means—

(a)   a body corporate incorporated in the United Kingdom carrying on in the United Kingdom as the whole or the major part of its business there the whole or part of an important manufacturing undertaking, or

(b)   a body corporate incorporated in the United Kingdom—

    (i)   which is the holding company of a group of companies carrying on in the United Kingdom as the whole or the major part of their business there the whole or part of an important manufacturing undertaking, and

    (ii)   as to which one of the conditions specified in subsection (6) below is satisfied.

(6)   The conditions mentioned in subsection (5) above are—

(a)   that it appears to the Secretary of State that there is a serious and immediate probability of the happening of an event in relation to the company which would constitute a change of control of the undertaking, or

(b)   that the Secretary of State has learnt of circumstances relating to the company which appear to him to constitute a change of control of the undertaking on or after 1st February 1975.

[(7)   In sections (1)(b) and (2)(c) "interests" means interests which relate to public policy, public security or public health.

(8)   In subsection (3) "the national interest" means the national interest in relation to public policy, public security or public health.]

NOTES

Sub-s (2): words omitted repealed by the British Technology Group Act 1991, s 17(2), Sch 2, Pt I.

Sub-ss (7), (8): added by the Industry Act 1975 (Prohibition and Vesting Order) Regulations 1998, SI 1998/3035, reg 2.

[1.698]
14   Notices to extend vesting orders to other holdings

(1)   Where 30 per cent or more of the share capital of the body corporate vests in the Secretary of State . . . by virtue of a vesting order, the Secretary of State shall serve on the holders of all the share capital that does not so vest, and on any other persons who to his knowledge have a present or prospective right to subscribe for share capital of the body corporate, within 28 days of the making of the order, a notice informing them of the making of the order and of the right of each of them to require the order to extend to the share capital or rights held by him.

(2)   The recipient of a notice under subsection (1) above may, within three months of the date of the notice, serve on the Secretary of State a counter-notice requiring the order to extend to the share capital or rights held by the recipient in the body corporate.

(3)   A vesting order shall have effect, from the date of a counter-notice, as if the share capital or rights specified in the notice had been specified in the vesting order.

(4)   Subsections (1) to (3) above shall have the same effect in relation to share capital vesting in nominees for the Secretary of State . . . as in relation to share capital vesting as mentioned in those subsections.

NOTES

Sub-ss (1), (4): words omitted repealed by the British Technology Group Act 1991, s 17(2), Sch 2, Pt I.

[1.699]
15   Parliamentary control of orders

(1)   A prohibition order shall be laid before Parliament after being made, and the order shall cease to have effect at the end of the period of 28 days beginning on the day on which it was made (but without prejudice to anything previously done by virtue of the order or to the making of a new order) unless during that period it is approved by resolution of each House of Parliament.

(2)   In reckoning the period mentioned in subsection (1) above no account shall be taken of any time during which Parliament is dissolved or prorogued or during which both Houses are adjourned for more than four days.

(3)   A vesting order shall not be made unless a draft of the order has been laid before and approved by resolution of each House of Parliament.

(4)   A draft of a vesting order shall not be laid before Parliament—

(a)   in a case such as is mentioned in paragraph (a) of section 13(2) above, after the end of a period of three months from the service of a notice under section 16(7) below of the Secretary of State's intention to lay the draft before Parliament;

(b)   in a case such as is mentioned in paragraph (b) of that subsection (2), after the end of a period of three months from the making of the prohibition order unless such circumstances as are mentioned in paragraph (a) or (c) of that subsection exist at the time when the draft of the order is laid before Parliament under subsection (3) above; and

(c)   in a case such as is mentioned in paragraph (c) of that subsection, after the end of a period of three months from the date on which the Secretary of State learnt of circumstances such as are mentioned in that paragraph.

(5) On the expiry of 28 days from the laying of the draft of a vesting order in a House of Parliament the order shall proceed in that House, whether or not it has been referred to a Committee under Standing Orders of that House relating to Private Bills, as if its provisions would require to be enacted by a Public Bill which cannot be referred to such a Committee.

(6) In reckoning, for purposes of proceedings in either House of Parliament, the period mentioned in subsection (5) above, no account shall be taken of any time during which Parliament is dissolved or prorogued or during which that House is adjourned for more than four days.

[1.700]
16 Contents of vesting order
(1) Without prejudice to the generality of section 13(2) above, a vesting order may contain provisions by virtue of which rights, liabilities or incumbrances to which assets or capital which will vest by virtue of the order are subject—
  (a) will be extinguished in consideration of the payment of compensation as provided under section 19 below, or
  (b) will be transferred to the Secretary of State . . . . , or
  (c) will be charged on the compensation under section 19 below.

(2) A vesting order which provides for the vesting of assets employed in an undertaking may prohibit or set aside any transfer of assets so employed or of any right in respect of such assets.

(3) A vesting order may include such provisions as the Secretary of State considers necessary or expedient to safeguard—
  (a) any capital which will vest by virtue of the order; and
  (b) any assets—
    (i) of a body corporate whose capital will so vest, or
    (ii) of any subsidiary of such a body corporate;
and may in particular, but without prejudice to the generality of this subsection, prohibit or set aside the transfer of any such capital or assets or any right in respect of such capital or assets.

(4) A vesting order setting aside a transfer of capital or a transfer of assets such as are mentioned in subsection (2) above shall entitle the Secretary of State . . . to recover the capital or assets transferred.

(5) A vesting order setting aside a transfer of assets such as are mentioned in subsection (3)(b) above shall entitle the body corporate or subsidiary to recover the assets transferred.

(6) Any vesting order setting aside a transfer shall give the person entitled to recover the capital or assets a right to be compensated in respect of the transfer.

(7) The transfers to which this section applies include transfers made before the draft of the order is laid before Parliament but after the Secretary of State has served notice on the person concerned of his intention to lay a draft order.

(8) In subsection (7) above "the person concerned" means—
  (a) in the case of an order such as is mentioned in paragraph (i) of section 13(2) above, the relevant body corporate, and
  (b) in the case of an order such as is mentioned in paragraph (ii) of that subsection, the person carrying on the undertaking.

(9) The Secretary of State shall publish a copy of any such notice in the London Gazette, the Edinburgh Gazette and the Belfast Gazette as soon as practicable after he has served it.

NOTES
Sub-ss (1), (4): words omitted repealed by the British Technology Group Act 1991, s 17(2), Sch 2, Pt I.

[1.701]
17 Remedies for contravention of prohibition orders
(1) No criminal proceedings shall lie against any person on the ground that he has committed, or aided, abetted, counselled or procured the commission of, or conspired or attempted to commit, or incited others to commit, any contravention of a prohibition order.

(2) Nothing in subsection (1) above shall limit any right of any person to bring civil proceedings in respect of any contravention or apprehended contravention of a prohibition order, and (without prejudice to the generality of the preceding words) compliance with any such order shall be enforceable by civil proceedings by the Crown for an injunction or interdict or for any other appropriate relief.

NOTES
See further, in relation to England, Wales and Northern Ireland, the Serious Crime Act 2007, s 63(1), Sch 6, Pt 1, para 3, which provides that the reference in sub-s (1) above to (or to conduct amounting to) the common law offence of inciting the commission of another offence, has effect (as from the day that offence is abolished) as a reference to (or to conduct amounting to) offences under the Serious Crime Act 2007, Pt 2.

[1.702]
18 Territorial scope of orders
(1) Nothing in a prohibition order shall have effect so as to apply to any person in relation to his conduct outside the United Kingdom unless he is—
  (a) a citizen of the United Kingdom and Colonies or,

(b)   a body corporate incorporated in the United Kingdom or,

(c)   a person carrying on business in the United Kingdom either alone or in partnership with one or more other persons,

but in a case falling within paragraph (a), (b) or (c) above, any such order may extend to acts or omissions outside the United Kingdom.

(2)   For the purposes of this Part of this Act a body corporate shall be deemed not to be resident in the United Kingdom if it is not incorporated in the United Kingdom.

[1.703]
19 Compensation orders

(1)   No vesting order shall be made until there has also been laid before both Houses of Parliament an order (in this Part of this Act referred to as a "compensation order") providing for the payment of compensation for the acquisition of the capital or assets and for any extinguishment or transfer of rights, liabilities or encumbrances in question.

(2)   A compensation order shall be subject to special parliamentary procedure.

(3)   A compensation order—

(a)   shall identify the persons or descriptions of persons to be paid compensation and determine their rights and duties in relation to any compensation paid to them;

(b)   shall specify the manner in which compensation is to be paid;

(c)   shall provide for the payment of interest on compensation in respect of the relevant period;

(d)   may make different provision in relation to different descriptions of capital or assets and different rights, liabilities or incumbrances; and

(e)   may contain incidental and supplementary provisions;

and in paragraph (c) above "the relevant period" means—

(i)   in relation to capital or assets, the period commencing with the date on which the capital or assets vest in . . . the Secretary of State or their or his nominees and ending with the date of payment of compensation; and

(ii)   in relation to rights, liabilities and incumbrances, the period commencing with the date on which they are extinguished and ending on the date of payment.

(4)   Compensation may be paid out—

(a)   out of moneys provided by Parliament, or

(b)   by the issue of government stock (that is to say, stock the principal whereof and the interest whereon is charged on the National Loans Fund with recourse to the Consolidated Fund),

and the power conferred by subsection (3)(b) above is a power to provide for compensation by one or both of the means specified in this subsection.

(5)   The proviso to section 6(2) of the Statutory Orders (Special Procedure) Act 1945 (power to withdraw an order or submit it to Parliament for further consideration by means of a Bill for its confirmation) shall have effect in relation to compensation orders as if for the words "may by notice given in the prescribed manner, withdraw the order or may" there were substituted the word "shall".

NOTES

Sub-s (3): words omitted repealed by the British Technology Group Act 1991, s 17(2), Sch 2, Pt I.

[1.704]
20 Arbitration of disputes relating to vesting and compensation orders

(1)   Any dispute to which this section applies shall be determined under Schedule 3 to this Act.

(2)   Where any such dispute has been submitted to a tribunal constituted under that Schedule, any other dispute to which this section applies shall be determined by the same tribunal.

(3)   This section applies to a dispute which arises out of a vesting order or a compensation order and to which one of the parties is the Secretary of State . . . or a body corporate the whole or part of whose share capital has vested by virtue of the order in either of them or in nominees for either of them—

(a)   if the provisions of the order require it to be submitted to arbitration; or

(b)   if one of the parties wishes it to be so submitted;

and where this section applies to a dispute which arises out of an order, it also applies to any dispute which arises out of a related order.

(4)   A vesting order and a compensation order are related for the purposes of this section if they relate to the same capital or assets.

NOTES

Sub-s (3): words omitted repealed by the British Technology Group Act 1991, s 17(2), Sch 2, Pt I.

21–34 *((Pts III, IV) s 21 repealed by the Industry Act 1980, ss 19, 21, Sch 2; s 22 repealed by the Industrial Development Act 1982, s 19, Sch 3; ss 23–25 amend the Industry Act 1972, s 10, and insert s 10A of that Act; s 26 repealed by the British Technology Group Act 1991, s 17(2), Sch 2, Pt I; s 27 repealed by the Budget Responsibility and National Audit Act 2011, s 10(a); ss 28–34 repealed by the Industry Act 1980, ss 19, 21, Sch 2.)*

PART V
GENERAL AND SUPPLEMENTARY

[1.705]
35 Expenses

Any expenses of the Secretary of State or the Minister of Agriculture, Fisheries and Food incurred in consequence of the provisions of this Act, including any increase attributable to those provisions in sums payable under any other Act, shall be defrayed out of money provided by Parliament.

NOTES

Minister of Agriculture, Fisheries and Food: now the Secretary of State for Environment, Food and Rural Affairs; see the Secretaries of State for Transport, Local Government and the Regions and for Environment, Food and Rural Affairs Order 2001, SI 2001/2568.

[1.706]
36 Service of documents

(1) Any notice or other document required or authorised by or by virtue of this Act to be served on any person may be served on him either by delivering it to him or by leaving it at his proper address or by sending it by post.

(2) Any notice or other document so required or authorised to be served on a body corporate or a firm shall be duly served if it is served on the secretary or clerk of that body or a partner of that firm.

(3) For the purposes of this section, and of section 26 of the Interpretation Act 1889 in its application to this section, the proper address of a person, in the case of a secretary or clerk of a body corporate, shall be that of the registered or principal office of that body, in the case of a partner of a firm shall be that of the principal office of the firm, and in any other case shall be the last known address of the person to be served.

NOTES

Interpretation Act 1889, s 26: repealed by the Interpretation Act 1978, s 25, Sch 3, and replaced by s 7 of, and Sch 2, para 3 to, that Act.

[1.707]
37 Interpretation

(1) In this Act, unless the context otherwise requires—

. . .

"enactment" includes an enactment of the Parliament of Northern Ireland or the Northern Ireland Assembly;

"holding company" means a holding company as defined by [section 1159 of the Companies Act 2006];

"industry" includes any description of commercial activity, and any section of an industry, and "industrial" has a corresponding meaning;

"manufacturing industry" means, subject to subsection (3) below, activities which are described in any of the minimum list headings in Orders III to XIX (inclusive) of the Standard Industrial Classification;

. . .

["Standard Industrial Classification" means the revised edition published by Her Majesty's Stationery Office in 1968 of the publication of that name prepared by the Central Statistical Office [of the Chancellor of the Exchequer];]

"subsidiary" means a subsidiary as defined by [section 1159 of the Companies Act 2006];

. . .

(2) . . .

(3) In determining the extent to which an undertaking is engaged in manufacturing industry, the following activities shall be treated as manufacturing industry so far as they relate to products manufactured or to be manufactured by the undertaking—

research,
transport,
distribution,
repair and maintenance of machinery,
sales and marketing,
storage,
mining and quarrying,
production and distribution of energy and heating,
administration,
training of staff,
packaging.

(4) . . .

(5) Except in so far as the context otherwise requires, any reference in this Act to an enactment shall be construed as a reference to that enactment as amended, applied or extended by or under any other enactment, including this Act.

NOTES

Sub-s (1): definitions "accounting year" and "wholly owned subsidiary" (omitted) repealed by the British Technology Group Act 1991, s 17(2), Sch 2, Pt I; words in square brackets in definitions "holding company" and "subsidiary" substituted by the Companies Act 2006 (Consequential Amendments, Transitional Provisions and Savings) Order 2009, SI 2009/1941, art 2(1), Sch 1, para 33; definitions "the Ministers" and "planning agreement" (omitted) repealed by the Industry Act 1980, s 21, Sch 2; definition "Standard Industrial Classification" substituted by the Co-operative Development Agency and Industrial Development Act 1984, s 5(2), Sch 1, Pt II, para 1, words in square brackets inserted by the Transfer of Functions (Economic Statistics) Order 1989, SI 1989/992, art 6(4), Sch 2, para 2(a).

Sub-ss (2), (4): repealed by the British Technology Group Act 1991, s 17(2), Sch 2, Pt I.

[1.708]
38 Orders
(1)   Any power to make an order conferred by this Act shall be exercisable by statutory instrument.
(2)   Any power to make an order conferred by any provision of this Act shall include power to make an order varying or revoking any order previously made under that provision.
(3)   It is hereby declared that any power of giving directions or making determinations conferred on the Secretary of State by any provision of this Act includes power to vary or revoke directions or determinations given or made under that provision.

[1.709]
39 Citation etc
(1)   This Act may be cited as the Industry Act 1975.
(2)   . . .
(3)   The enactments specified in Schedule 8 to this Act are repealed to the extent mentioned in column 3 of that Schedule.
(4)   It is hereby declared that this Act extends to Northern Ireland.
(5)   Notwithstanding the provisions—
  (a)   of section 12(3) of the Statutory Orders (Special Procedure) Act 1945, . . .
  (b)   . . .
the former Act shall apply to any compensation order which extends to Northern Ireland, . . .
(6)   This Act shall come into force on such day as the Secretary of State may by order made by statutory instrument appoint.
(7)   An order under subsection (6) above may appoint different days for different provisions and for different purposes.

NOTES

Sub-s (2): repealed by the Industrial Development Act 1982, s 19, Sch 3.
Sub-s (5): words omitted repealed by the Industry Act 1980, s 21, Sch 2.
Orders: the Industry Act 1975 (Commencement) Order 1975, SI 1975/1881.

SCHEDULES
SCHEDULES 1 AND 2

(Sch 1, paras 1–6, 11–17 repealed by the British Technology Group Act 1991, s 17(2), Sch 2, Pt III; Sch 1, paras 7–10, 18, 20, Sch 2, paras 1–7, 8(1), (2), (4) repealed by the British Technology Group Act 1991, s 17(2), Sch 2, Pt I; Sch 1, para 19 repealed by the Financial Services Act 1986, s 212(3), Sch 17, Pt I and again by the British Technology Group Act 1991, s 17(2), Sch 2, Pt I; Sch 2, para 8(3) repealed by the Industry Act 1980, s 21, Sch 2 and again by the British Technology Group Act 1991, s 17(2), Sch 2, Pt I.)

SCHEDULE 3
ARBITRATION

Section 20

PART I
GENERAL

Establishment of Tribunal
[1.710]
1. If a party to a dispute such as is mentioned in subsection (1) of section 20 above serves on the other party or parties to the dispute, at a time when no proceedings relating to it have been commenced in any court, a notice that he wishes the dispute to be determined by arbitration, the Secretary of State shall by order establish a tribunal to determine the dispute and any other dispute such as is mentioned in subsection (2) of that section.

2. An order under paragraph 1 above shall be laid before each House of Parliament.

3. A tribunal shall be a court of record and shall have an official seal which shall be judicially noticed.

4. [(1)] A tribunal shall, as the Lord Chancellor may[, after consulting the Lord Chief Justice of England and Wales, the Lord President of the Court of Session and the Lord Chief Justice of Northern Ireland,] direct, either sit as a single tribunal or sit in two or more divisions and, subject to paragraph 5 below, shall, for the hearing of any proceedings, consist of—

  (a) a president who shall be—
     [[(i) a person who satisfies the judicial-appointment eligibility condition on a 5-year basis; or]
      (ii) a member of the Bar of Northern Ireland or [solicitor of the Court of Judicature of Northern Ireland] of at least [5] years' standing,]
      appointed by the Lord Chancellor, and
  (b) two other members appointed by the Secretary of State, one being a person of experience in business and the other being a person of experience in finance.

[(2) The Lord Chief Justice of England and Wales may nominate a judicial office holder (as defined in section 109(4) of the Constitutional Reform Act 2005) to exercise his functions under this paragraph.

(3) The Lord President of the Court of Session may nominate a judge of the Court of Session who is a member of the First or Second Division of the Inner House of that Court to exercise his functions under this paragraph.

(4) The Lord Chief Justice of Northern Ireland may nominate any of the following to exercise his functions under this paragraph—

  (a) the holder of one of the offices listed in Schedule 1 to the Justice (Northern Ireland) Act 2002;
  (b) a Lord Justice of Appeal (as defined in section 88 of that Act).]

5. *(Applies to Scotland only.)*

6. [(1)] [Subject, in the case of the president of a tribunal, to sub-paragraph (2) below] the members of a tribunal shall hold office for such period as may be determined at the time of their respective appointments and shall be eligible for reappointment but, notwithstanding that the period for which a member was appointed has not expired—

  (a) a member may, at any time by not less than one month's notice in writing to his appointor, resign his office;
  (b) the appointor of a member may declare the office of that member vacant on the ground that he is unfit to continue in his office; and
  (c) if any member [is the subject of a bankruptcy restrictions order [or an interim bankruptcy restrictions order, or a debt relief restrictions order or interim debt relief restrictions order under Schedule 4ZB of the Insolvency Act 1986]] or, in Scotland, if sequestration of a member's estate is awarded . . . ., his office shall thereupon become vacant.

[(2) No appointment of a person to be the president of a tribunal shall be such as to extend beyond the day on which he attains the age of 70 years; but this paragraph is subject to section 26(4) to (6) of the Judicial Pensions and Retirement Act 1993 (power to authorise continuance in office up to the age of 75 years).]

7. If any member of a tribunal becomes, by reason of illness or other infirmity, temporarily incapable of performing the duties of his office, his appointor shall appoint some other fit person to discharge his duties for any period not exceeding 6 months at any one time, and the person so appointed shall during that period have the same powers as the person in whose place he was appointed.

8. In this Part of this Schedule, "appointor", in relation to a member of a tribunal means—

  (a) in the case of a member appointed under sub-paragraph (a) of [paragraph 4(1)] above, the Lord Chancellor or, if paragraph 5 above applies, the Lord President of the Court of Session; and
  (b) in the case of any other member, the Secretary of State.

[**8A.** Where the appointor is, by virtue of paragraph 8(a), the Lord Chancellor, the power conferred by paragraph 6(1)(b) may be exercised only with the concurrence of the appropriate senior judge.

8B. The appropriate senior judge is the Lord Chief Justice of England and Wales, unless the member to be removed exercises functions wholly or mainly in Northern Ireland, in which case it is the Lord Chief Justice of Northern Ireland.]

9, 10. . . .

Staff and expenses

11. A tribunal may appoint such officers as they consider necessary for assisting them in the proper execution of their duties.

12. (1)   There shall be paid to members of a tribunal such remuneration (whether by way of salaries or fees) and such allowances as the Secretary of State may, with the approval of the Minister for the Civil Service, determine.

(2)   There shall be paid to any officer appointed under paragraph 11 above and any person to whom proceedings are referred by the tribunal under paragraph 27 below for inquiry and report such remuneration (whether by way of salary or fees) and such allowances as the tribunal may, with the approval of the Secretary of State given with the consent of the Minister for the Civil Service, determine.

(3)   The Secretary of State shall pay any such remuneration and allowances and any other expenses of a tribunal shall be defrayed by the Secretary of State out of money provided by Parliament.

NOTES

Para 4: sub-para (1) numbered as such, words in first pair of square brackets inserted, and sub-paras (2)–(4) added, by the Constitutional Reform Act 2005, s 15(1), Sch 4, Part 1, paras 81(1), (2); sub-para (1)(a)(i), (ii) substituted by the Courts and Legal Services Act 1990, s 71(2), Sch 10, para 39; sub-para (1)(a)(i) further substituted and number in sub-para (1)(a)(ii) substituted by the Tribunals, Courts and Enforcement Act 2007, s 50, Sch 10, Pt 1, para 12; words in square brackets in sub-para (1)(a)(ii) substituted by the Constitutional Reform Act 2005, s 59, Sch 11, Pt 3, para 5.

Para 6: sub-para (1) numbered as such, the words in square brackets in that paragraph inserted, and sub-para (2) added, by the Judicial Pensions and Retirement Act 1993, s 26(10), Sch 6, para 52; in sub-para (1)(c) words in first (outer) pair of square brackets substituted and words omitted repealed by the Enterprise Act 2002 (Disqualification from Office: General) Order 2006, SI 2006/1722, art 2(2), Sch 2, Pt 1, para 1; words in second (inner) pair of square brackets substituted by the Tribunals, Courts and Enforcement Act 2007 (Consequential Amendments) Order 2012, SI 2012/2404, art 3(2), Sch 2, para 9, for transitional provisions see art 6 thereof.

Para 8: words in square brackets substituted by the Constitutional Reform Act 2005, s 15(1), Sch 4, Part 1, paras 81(1), (4).

Paras 8A, 8B: inserted by the Constitutional Reform Act 2005, s 15(1), Sch 4, Part 1, paras 81(1), (5).

Para 9: amends the House of Commons Disqualification Act 1975, Sch 1, Pt II, and the Northern Ireland Assembly Disqualification Act 1975, Sch 1, Pt II.

Para 10: repealed by the Tribunals and Inquiries Act 1992, s 18(2), Sch 4, Pt I.

Minister for the Civil Service: now the Treasury, see the Transfer of Functions (Minister for the Civil Service and Treasury) Order 1981, SI 1981/1670.

PART II
PROCEEDINGS

Proceedings other than Scottish proceedings

[1.711]
13. Paragraphs 14 to 17 below shall have effect with respect to proceedings of a tribunal other than those which, by virtue of paragraph 18 below, are to be treated as Scottish proceedings.

14. The provisions of [Part I of the Arbitration Act 1996] with respect to—
  (a)   the administration of oaths and the taking of affirmations,
  (b)   the correction in awards of mistakes and errors,
  (c)   the summoning, attendance and examination of witnesses and the production of documents, and
  (d)   the costs of the reference and award,
shall, with any necessary modifications, apply in respect of such proceedings but, except as provided by this paragraph, the provisions of [that Part] shall not apply to any such proceedings.

15. A tribunal may, and if so ordered by the Court of Appeal shall, state in the form of a special case for determination by the Court of Appeal any question of law which may arise in such proceedings.

16. An appeal shall lie to the Court of Appeal on any question of law or fact from any determination or order of the tribunal with respect to compensation under section 16(6) above.

17. (1)   Subject to the provisions of this Schedule, the procedure in or in connection with any such proceedings shall be such as may be determined by rules made by the Lord Chancellor by statutory instrument.

(2)   A statutory instrument containing rules made under this paragraph shall be subject to annulment in pursuance of a resolution of either House of Parliament.

18–25. (*Apply to Scotland only.*)

All proceedings

26. Every order of a tribunal—

(a)   shall be enforceable in England and Wales and Northern Ireland as if it were an order of the High Court; and

(b)   may be recorded for execution in the books of Council and Session and may be enforced accordingly.

27. A tribunal may, at any stage in any proceedings before them, refer to a person or persons appointed by them for the purpose any question arising in the proceedings, other than a question which in their opinion is primarily one of law, for inquiry and report, and the report of any such person or persons may be adopted wholly or partly by the tribunal and, if so adopted, may be incorporated in an order of the tribunal.

NOTES

Para 14: words in square brackets substituted by the Arbitration Act 1996, s 107(1), Sch 3, para 30.

SCHEDULES 4–8

(Sch 4 repealed by the Industry Act 1980, s 21, Sch 2 and the Industrial Development Act 1982, s 19, Sch 3; Sch 5 repealed by the Budget Responsibility and National Audit Act 2011, s 10(a); Sch 6 repealed by the Industry Act 1980, s 21, Sch 2; Sch 7 repealed by the Industrial Development Act 1982, s 19, Sch 3; Sch 8 (Repeals) outside the scope of this work.)

TORTS (INTERFERENCE WITH GOODS) ACT 1977

(1977 c 32)

ARRANGEMENT OF SECTIONS

Preliminary

An Act to amend the law concerning conversion and other torts affecting goods

[22 July 1977]

Preliminary

[1.712]
1 Definition of "wrongful interference with goods"
In this Act "wrongful interference", or "wrongful interference with goods", means—
(a) conversion of goods (also called trover),
(b) trespass to goods,
(c) negligence so far as it results in damage to goods or to an interest in goods,
(d) subject to section 2, any other tort so far as it results in damage to goods or to an interest in goods

[and references in this Act (however worded) to proceedings for wrongful interference or to a claim or right to claim for wrongful interference shall include references to proceedings by virtue of Part I of the Consumer Protection Act 1987 [or Part II of the Consumer Protection (Northern Ireland) Order 1987] (product liability) in respect of any damage to goods or to an interest in goods or, as the case may be, to a claim or right to claim by virtue of that Part in respect of any such damage].

NOTES
   Words in first (outer) pair of square brackets added by the Consumer Protection Act 1987, s 48, Sch 4; words in second (inner) pair of square brackets inserted by the Consumer Protection (Northern Ireland) Order 1987, SI 1987/2049, art 35(1), Sch 3, para 3.

Detention of goods

[1.713]
2 Abolition of detinue
(1) Detinue is abolished.
(2) An action lies in conversion for loss or destruction of goods which a bailee has allowed to happen in breach of his duty to his bailor (that is to say it lies in a case which is not otherwise conversion, but would have been detinue before detinue was abolished).

[1.714]
3 Form of judgment where goods are detained
(1) In proceedings for wrongful interference against a person who is in possession or in control of the goods relief may be given in accordance with this section, so far as appropriate.
(2) The relief is—
(a) an order for delivery of the goods, and for payment of any consequential damages, or
(b) an order for delivery of the goods, but giving the defendant the alternative of paying damages by reference to the value of the goods, together in either alternative with payment of any consequential damages, or
(c) damages.
(3) Subject to rules of court—
(a) relief shall be given under only one of paragraphs (a), (b) and (c) of subsection (2),
(b) relief under paragraph (a) of subjection (2) is at the discretion of the court, and the claimant may choose between the others.
(4) If it is shown to the satisfaction of the court that an order under subsection (2)(a) has not been complied with, the court may—
(a) revoke the order, or the relevant part of it, and
(b) make an order for payment of damages by reference to the value of the goods.
(5) Where an order is made under subsection (2)(b) the defendant may satisfy the order by returning the goods at any time before execution of judgment, but without prejudice to liability to pay any consequential damages.
(6) An order for delivery of the goods under subsection (2)(a) or (b) may impose such conditions as may be determined by the court, or pursuant to rules of court, and in particular, where damages by reference to the value of the goods would not be the whole of the value of the goods, may require an allowance to be made by the claimant to reflect the difference.
  For example, a bailor's action against the bailee may be one in which the measure of damages is not the full value of the goods, and then the court may order delivery of the goods, but require the bailor to pay the bailee a sum reflecting the difference.
(7) Where under subjection (1) or subsection (2) of section 6 an allowance is to be made in respect of an improvement of the goods, and an order is made under subsection (2)(a) or (b), the court may assess the allowance to be made in respect of the improvement, and by the order require, as a condition for delivery of the goods, that allowance to be made by the claimant.
(8) This section is without prejudice—
(a) to the remedies afforded by section 133 of the Consumer Credit Act 1974, or
(b) to the remedies afforded by sections 35, 42 and 44 of the Hire-Purchase Act 1965, or to those sections of the Hire-Purchase Act (Northern Ireland) 1966 (so long as those sections respectively remain in force), or
(c) to any jurisdiction to afford ancillary or incidental relief.

NOTES
Hire-Purchase Act 1965, ss 35, 42, 44: repealed by the Consumer Credit Act 1974, s 192(3), (4), Sch 5, Pt I.
Hire-Purchase Act (Northern Ireland) 1966: repealed by the Consumer Credit Act 1974, s 192(3), (4), Sch 5, Pt II.

[1.715]
4 Interlocutory relief where goods are detained
(1)   In this section "proceedings" means proceedings for wrongful interference.
(2)   On the application of any person in accordance with rules of court, the High Court shall, in such circumstances as may be specified in the rules, have power to make an order providing for the delivery up of any goods which are or may become the subject matter of subsequent proceedings in the court, or as to which any question may arise in proceedings.
(3)   Delivery shall be, as the order may provide, to the claimant or to a person appointed by the court for the purpose, and shall be on such terms and conditions as may be specified in the order.
(4)   The power to make rules of court [for the High Court in England and Wales] . . . or under section 7 of the Northern Ireland Act 1962 shall include power to make rules of court as to the manner in which an application for such an order can be made, and as to the circumstances in which such an order can be made; and any such rules may include such incidental, supplementary and consequential provisions as the authority making the rules may consider necessary or expedient.
(5)   The preceding provisions of this section shall have effect in relation to county courts [in Northern Ireland] as they have effect in relation to the High Court [in Northern Ireland], and as if in those provisions references to rules of court and to section . . . or section 7 of the Northern Ireland Act 1962 included references to county court rules and to . . . [Article 47 of the County Courts (Northern Ireland) Order 1980].
[(6)   Subsections (1) to (4) have effect in relation to the county court in England and Wales as they have effect in relation to the High Court in England and Wales.]
[(6)   Subsections (1) to (4) apply in relation to the family court in England and Wales as they apply in relation to the High Court in England and Wales, but as if references in those subsections to rules of court (including references to rules of court under any particular enactment) were references to Family Procedure Rules.]

NOTES
Sub-s (4): words in square brackets substituted and words omitted repealed by the Crime and Courts Act 2013, s 17(5), Sch 9, Pt 3, para 133(a)(i), (ii), for transitional provision see SI 2014/954, art 3.
Sub-s (5): words in first and second pair of square brackets inserted, and words omitted repealed, by the Crime and Courts Act 2013, s 17(5), Sch 9, Pt 3, para 133(b), for transitional provision see SI 2014/954, art 3; words in final pair of square brackets substituted by the County Courts (Northern Ireland) Order 1980, SI 1980/397, art 68(2), Sch 1, Pt II.
First sub-s (6): inserted by the Crime and Courts Act 2013, s 17(5), Sch 9, Pt 3, para 133(c), for transitional provision see SI 2014/954, art 3.
Second sub-s (6): inserted by the Crime and Courts Act 2013, s 17(6), Sch 10, Pt 2, para 37, for transitional provision see SI 2014/954, art 3.
Northern Ireland Act 1962, s 7: repealed by the Judicature (Northern Ireland) Act 1978, s 122, Sch 7, Pt I. By virtue of s 122(1) of, and Sch 5, Pt I, para 3 to, the 1978 Act, the reference in this section to rules made under s 7 of the 1962 Act is to be construed as a reference to rules of court made under s 55 of the 1978 Act.
County Courts Act 1984, s 75: repealed by the Civil Procedure Act 1997, s 10, Sch 2, para 2(1), (6).

Damages

[1.716]
5 Extinction of title on satisfaction of claim for damages
(1)   Where damages for wrongful interference are, or would fall to be, assessed on the footing that the claimant is being compensated—
   (a)   for the whole of his interest in the goods, or
   (b)   for the whole of his interest in the goods subject to a reduction for contributory negligence,
payment of the assessed damages (under all heads), or as the case may be settlement of a claim for damages for the wrong (under all heads), extinguishes the claimant's title to that interest.
(2)   In subsection (1) the reference to the settlement of the claim includes—
   (a)   where the claim is made in court proceedings, and the defendant has paid a sum into court to meet the whole claim, the taking of that sum by the claimant, and
   (b)   where the claim is made in court proceedings, and the proceedings are settled or compromised, the payment of what is due in accordance with the settlement or compromise, and
   (c)   where the claim is made out of court and is settled or compromised, the payment of what is due in accordance with the settlement or compromise.
(3)   It is hereby declared that subsection (1) does not apply where damages are assessed on the footing that the claimant is being compensated for the whole of his interest in the goods, but the damages paid are limited to some lesser amount by virtue of any enactment or rule of law.
(4)   Where under section 7(3) the claimant accounts over to another person (the "third party") so as to compensate (under all heads) the third party for the whole of his interest in the goods, the third party's title to that interest is extinguished.

(5)   This section has effect subject to any agreement varying the respective rights of the parties to the agreement, and where the claim is made in court proceedings has effect subject to any order of the court.

[1.717]
6   Allowance for improvement of the goods
(1)   If in proceedings for wrongful interference against a person (the "improver") who has improved the goods, it is shown that the improver acted in the mistaken but honest belief that he had a good title to them, an allowance shall be made for the extent to which, at the time as at which the goods fall to be valued in assessing damages, the value of the goods is attributable to the improvement.
(2)   If, in proceedings for wrongful interference against a person ("the purchaser") who has purported to purchase the goods—
    (a)   from the improver, or
    (b)   where after such a purported sale the goods passed by a further purported sale on one or more occasions, on any such occasion,
it is shown that the purchaser acted in good faith, an allowance shall be made on the principle set out in subsection (1).
    For example, where a person in good faith buys a stolen car from the improver and is sued in conversion by the true owner the damages may be reduced to reflect the improvement, but if the person who bought the stolen car from the improver sues the improver for failure of consideration, and the improver acted in good faith, subsection (3) below will ordinarily make a comparable reduction in the damages he recovers from the improver.
(3)   If in a case within subsection (2) the person purporting to sell the goods acted in good faith, then in proceedings by the purchaser for recovery of the purchase price because of failure of consideration, or in any other proceedings founded on that failure of consideration, an allowance shall, where appropriate, be made on the principle set out in subsection (1).
(4)   This section applies, with the necessary modifications, to a purported bailment or other disposition of goods as it applies to a purported sale of goods.

Liability to two or more claimants

[1.718]
7   Double liability
(1)   In this section "double liability" means the double liability of the wrongdoer which can arise—
    (a)   where one of two or more rights of action for wrongful interference is founded on a possessory title, or
    (b)   where the measure of damages in an action for wrongful interference founded on a proprietary title is or includes the entire value of the goods, although the interest is one of two or more interests in the goods.
(2)   In proceedings to which any two or more claimants are parties, the relief shall be such as to avoid double liability of the wrongdoer as between those claimants.
(3)   On satisfaction, in whole or in part, of any claim for an amount exceeding that recoverable if subsection (2) applied, the claimant is liable to account over to the other person having a right to claim to such extent as will avoid double liability.
(4)   Where, as the result of enforcement of a double liability, any claimant is unjustly enriched to any extent, he shall be liable to reimburse the wrongdoer to that extent.
    For example, if a converter of goods pays damages first to a finder of the goods, and then to the true owner, the finder is unjustly enriched unless he accounts over to the true owner under subsection (3); and then the true owner is unjustly enriched and becomes liable to reimburse the converter of the goods.

[1.719]
8   Competing rights to the goods
(1)   The defendant in an action for wrongful interference shall be entitled to show, in accordance with rules of court, that a third party has a better right than the plaintiff as respects all or any part of the interest claimed by the plaintiff, or in right of which he sues, and any rule of law (sometimes called jus tertii) to the contrary is abolished.
(2)   Rules of court relating to proceedings for wrongful interference may—
    (a)   require the plaintiff to give particulars of his title,
    (b)   require the plaintiff to identify any person who, to his knowledge, has or claims any interest in the goods,
    (c)   authorise the defendant to apply for directions as to whether any person should be joined with a view to establishing whether he has a better right than the plaintiff, or has a claim as a result of which the defendant might be doubly liable,
    (d)   where a party fails to appear on an application within paragraph (c), or to comply with any direction given by the court on such an application, authorise the court to deprive him of any right of action against the defendant for the wrong either unconditionally, or subject to such terms or conditions as may be specified.

(3)   Subsection (2) is without prejudice to any other power of making rules of court.

[1.720]
9   Concurrent actions
(1)   This section applies where goods are the subject of two or more claims for wrongful interference (whether or not the claims are founded on the same wrongful act, and whether or not any of the claims relates also to other goods).
(2)   Where goods are the subject of two or more claims under section 6 this section shall apply as if any claim under section 6(3) were a claim for wrongful interference.
(3)   If proceedings have been brought [in England and Wales in the county court or in Northern Ireland] in a county court on one of those claims, [rules of court or] county court rules may waive, or allow a court to waive, any limit (financial or territorial) on the jurisdiction of county courts in [the County Courts Act 1984] or the County Courts [(Northern Ireland) Order 1980] so as to allow another of those claims to be brought in the [same] court.
(4)   If proceedings are brought [in England and Wales in the county court or in Northern Ireland] on one of the claims in the High Court, and proceedings on any other are brought in a county court, whether prior to the High Court proceedings or not, the High Court may, on the application of the defendant, after notice has been given to the claimant in the county court proceedings—
   (a)   order that the county court proceedings be transferred to the High Court, and
   (b)   order security for costs or impose such other terms as the court thinks fit.

NOTES
Sub-s (3): words in first and second pairs of square brackets inserted, and word in final pair of square brackets substituted, by the Crime and Courts Act 2013, s 17(5), Sch 9, Pt 3, para 133(d), (e), for transitional provision see SI 2014/954, art 3; words in third pair of square brackets substituted by the County Courts Act 1984, s 148(1), Sch 2, Pt V, para 65; words in fourth pair of square brackets substituted by the County Courts (Northern Ireland) Order 1980, SI 1980/397, art 68(2), Sch 1, Pt II.
Sub-s (4): words in first pair of square brackets inserted by the Crime and Courts Act 2013, s 17(5), Sch 9, Pt 3, para 133(d), for transitional provision see SI 2014/954, art 3.

Conversion and trespass to goods

[1.721]
10   Co-owners
(1)   Co-ownership is no defence to an action founded on conversion or trespass to goods where the defendant without the authority of the other co-owner—
   (a)   destroys the goods, or disposes of the goods in a way giving a good title to the entire property in the goods, or otherwise does anything equivalent to the destruction of the other's interest in the goods, or
   (b)   purports to dispose of the goods in a way which would give a good title to the entire property in the goods if he was acting with the authority of all co-owners of the goods.
(2)   Subsection (1) shall not effect the law concerning execution or enforcement of judgments, or concerning any form of distress.
(3)   Subsection (1)(a) is by way of restatement of existing law so far as it relates to conversion.

[1.722]
11   Minor amendments
(1)   Contributory negligence is no good defence in proceedings founded on conversion, or on intentional trespass to goods.
(2)   Receipt of goods by way of pledge is conversion if the delivery of the goods is conversion.
(3)   Denial of title is not of itself conversion.

Uncollected goods

[1.723]
12   Bailee's power of sale
(1)   This section applies to goods in the possession or under the control of a bailee where—
   (a)   the bailor is in breach of an obligation to take delivery of the goods or, if the terms of the bailment so provide, to give directions as to their delivery, or
   (b)   the bailee could impose such an obligation by giving notice to the bailor, but is unable to trace or communicate with the bailor, or
   (c)   the bailee can reasonably expect to be relieved of any duty to safeguard the goods on giving notice to the bailor, but is unable to trace or communicate with the bailor.
(2)   In the cases in Part I of Schedule 1 to this Act a bailee may, for the purposes of subsection (1), impose an obligation on the bailor to take delivery of the goods, or as the case may be to give directions as to their delivery, and in those cases the said Part I sets out the methods of notification.
(3)   If the bailee—
   (a)   has in accordance with Part II of Schedule 1 to this Act given notice to the bailor of his intention to sell the goods under this subsection, or
   (b)   has failed to trace or communicate with the bailor with a view to giving him such a notice, after having taken reasonable steps for the purpose,
and is reasonably satisfied that the bailor owns the goods, he shall be entitled, as against the bailor, to sell the goods.

(4)   Where subsection (3) applies but the bailor did not in fact own the goods, a sale under this section, or under section 13, shall not give a good title as against the owner, or as against a person claiming under the owner.

(5)   A bailee exercising his powers under subsection (3) shall be liable to account to the bailor for the proceeds of sale, less any costs of sale, and—

  (a)   the account shall be taken on the footing that the bailee should have adopted the best method of sale reasonably available in the circumstances, and

  (b)   where subsection (3)(a) applies, any sum payable in respect of the goods by the bailor to the bailee which accrued due before the bailee gave notice of intention to sell the goods shall be deductible from the proceeds of sale.

(6)   A sale duly made under this section gives a good title to the purchaser as against the bailor.

(7)   In this section, section 13, and Schedule 1 to this Act,

  (a)   "bailor" and "bailee" include their respective successors in title, and

  (b)   references to what is payable, paid or due to the bailee in respect of the goods include references to what would be payable by the bailor to the bailee as a condition of delivery of the goods at the relevant time.

(8)   This section, and Schedule 1 to this Act, have effect subject to the terms of the bailment.

(9)   This section shall not apply where the goods were bailed before the commencement of this Act.

[1.724]
13   Sale authorised by the court

(1)   If a bailee of the goods to which section 12 applies satisfies the court that he is entitled to sell the goods under section 12, or that he would be so entitled if he had given any notice required in accordance with Schedule 1 to this Act, the court—

  (a)   may authorise the sale of the goods subject to such terms and conditions, if any, as may be specified in the order, and

  (b)   may authorise the bailee to deduct from the proceeds of sale any costs of sale and any amount due from the bailor to the bailee in respect of the goods, and

  (c)   may direct the payment into court of the net proceeds of sale, less any amount deducted under paragraph (b), to be held to the credit of the bailor.

(2)   A decision of the court authorising a sale under this section shall, subject to any right of appeal, be conclusive, as against the bailor, of the bailee's entitlement to sell the goods, and gives a good title to the purchaser as against the bailor.

(3)   [In this section "the court", in relation to England and Wales, means the High Court or the county court and, in relation to Northern Ireland, means the High Court or a county court, save that a county court in Northern Ireland has jurisdiction in the proceedings only if] the value of the goods does not exceed the county court limit mentioned in Article 10(1) of the County Courts (Northern Ireland) Order 1980].

NOTES

Sub-s (3): words in square brackets substituted by the Crime and Courts Act 2013, s 17(5), Sch 9, Pt 3, para 133(f), for transitional provision see SI 2014/954, art 3.

Supplemental

[1.725]
14   Interpretation

(1)   In this Act, unless the context otherwise requires—

  . . .

  "enactment" includes an enactment contained in an Act of the Parliament of Northern Ireland or an Order in Council made under the Northern Ireland (Temporary Provisions) Act 1972, or in a Measure of the Northern Ireland Assembly,

  "goods" includes all chattels personal other than things in action and money,

  "High Court" includes the High Court of Justice in Northern Ireland.

(2)   References in this Act to any enactment include references to that enactment as amended, extended or applied by or under that or any other enactment.

NOTES

Sub-s (1): definition omitted repealed by the High Court and County Courts Jurisdiction Order 1991, SI 1991/724, art 2(8), Schedule, Pt I.

[1.726]
15   Repeal

(1)   The Disposal of Uncollected Goods Act 1952 is hereby repealed.

(2)   In England and Wales that repeal shall not affect goods bailed before the commencement of this Act.

(3)   *(Applies to Scotland only.)*

NOTES
Disposal of Uncollected Goods Act 1952: replaced by ss 12, 13 at **[1.723]**, **[1.724]**, and Sch 1 at **[1.729]**, et seq.

[1.727]
16   Extent and application to the Crown
(1)   Section 15 shall extend to Scotland, but otherwise this Act shall not extend to Scotland.

(2)   This Act, except section 15, extends to Northern Ireland.

(3)   This Act shall bind the Crown, but as regards the Crown's liability in tort shall not bind the Crown further than the Crown is made liable in tort by the Crown Proceedings Act 1947.

[1.728]
17   Short title, etc
(1)   This Act may be cited as the Torts (Interference with Goods) Act 1977.

(2)   This Act shall come into force on such day as the Lord Chancellor may by order contained in a statutory instrument appoint, and such an order may appoint different dates for different provisions or for different purposes.

(3)   Schedule 2 to this Act contains transitional provisions.

NOTES
Orders: the Torts (Interference with Goods) Act 1977 (Commencement No 1) Order 1977, SI 1977/1910; the Torts (Interference with Goods) Act 1977 (Commencement No 2) Order 1978, SI 1978/627; the Torts (Interference with Goods) Act 1977 (Commencement No 3) Order 1980, SI 1980/2024.

SCHEDULES

SCHEDULE 1
UNCOLLECTED GOODS

Section 12

PART I
POWER TO IMPOSE OBLIGATION TO COLLECT GOODS

[1.729]

1. (1)   For the purposes of section 12(1) a bailee may, in the circumstances specified in this Part of this Schedule, by notice given to the bailor impose on him an obligation to take delivery of the goods.

(2)   The notice shall be in writing, and may be given either—
   (a)   by delivering it to the bailor, or
   (b)   by leaving it at his proper address, or
   (c)   by post.

(3)   The notice shall—
   (a)   specify the name and address of the bailee, and give sufficient particulars of the goods and the address or place where they are held, and
   (b)   state that the goods are ready for delivery to the bailor, or where combined with a notice terminating the contract of bailment, will be ready for delivery when the contract is terminated, and
   (c)   specify the amount, if any, which is payable by the bailor to the bailee in respect of the goods and which became due before the giving of the notice.

(4)   Where the notice is sent by post it may be combined with a notice under Part II of this Schedule if the notice is sent by post in a way complying with paragraph 6(4).

(5)   References in this Part of this Schedule to taking delivery of the goods include, where the terms of the bailment admit, references to giving directions as to their delivery.

(6)   This Part of this Schedule is without prejudice to the provisions of any contract requiring the bailor to take delivery of the goods.

Goods accepted for repair or other treatment

2. If a bailee has accepted goods for repair or other treatment on the terms (expressed or implied) that they will be re-delivered to the bailor when the repair or other treatment has been carried out, the notice may be given at any time after the repair or other treatment has been carried out.

Goods accepted for valuation or appraisal

3. If a bailee has accepted goods in order to value or appraise them, the notice may be given at any time after the bailee has carried out the valuation or appraisal.

Storage, warehousing, etc

4. (1) If a bailee is in possession of goods which he has held as custodian, and his obligation as custodian has come to an end, the notice may be given at any time after the ending of the obligation, or may be combined with any notice terminating his obligation as custodian.

(2) This paragraph shall not apply to goods held by a person as mercantile agent, that is to say by a person having in the customary course of his business as a mercantile agent authority either to sell goods or to consign goods for the purpose of sale, or to buy goods, or to raise money on the security of goods.

Supplemental

5. Paragraphs 2, 3 and 4 apply whether or not the bailor has paid any amount due to the bailee in respect of the goods, and whether or not the bailment is for reward, or in the course of business, or gratuitous.

PART II
NOTICE OF INTENTION TO SELL GOODS

[1.730]
6. (1) A notice under section 12(3) shall
   (a) specify the name and address of the bailee, and give sufficient particulars of the goods and the address or place where they are held, and
   (b) specify the date on or after which the bailee proposes to sell the goods, and
   (c) specify the amount, if any, which is payable by the bailor to the bailee in respect of the goods, and which became due before the giving of the notice.

(2) The period between giving of the notice and the date specified in the notice as that on or after which the bailee proposes to exercise the power of sale shall be such as will afford the bailor a reasonable opportunity of taking delivery of the goods.

(3) If any amount is payable in respect of the goods by the bailor to the bailee, and became due before giving of the notice, the said period shall be not less than three months.

(4) The notice shall be in writing and shall be sent by post in a registered letter, or by the recorded delivery service.

7. (1) The bailee shall not give a notice under section 12(3), or exercise his right to sell the goods pursuant to such a notice, at a time when he has notice that, because of a dispute concerning the goods, the bailor is questioning or refusing to pay all or any part of what the bailee claims to be due to him in respect of the goods.

(2) This paragraph shall be left out of account in determining under section 13(1) whether a bailee of goods is entitled to sell the goods under section 12, or would be so entitled if he had given any notice required in accordance with this Schedule.

Supplemental

8. For the purposes of this Schedule, and of section 26 of the Interpretation Act 1889 in its application to this Schedule, the proper address of the person to whom a notice is to be given shall be—
   (a) in the case of a body corporate, a registered or principal office of the body corporate, and
   (b) in any other case, the last known address of the person.

NOTES
   Interpretation Act 1889, s 26: repealed by the Interpretation Act 1978, s 25, Sch 3, and replaced by s 7 of, and Sch 2, para 3 to, that Act.

SCHEDULE 2

(Sch 2 (Transitional) outside the scope of this work.)

UNFAIR CONTRACT TERMS ACT 1977

(1977 c 50)

ARRANGEMENT OF SECTIONS

PART I
AMENDMENT OF LAW FOR ENGLAND AND WALES
AND NORTHERN IRELAND

Introductory

PART III
PROVISIONS APPLYING TO WHOLE OF UNITED KINGDOM

An Act to impose further limits on the extent to which under the law of England and Wales and Northern Ireland civil liability for breach of contract, or for negligence or other breach of duty, can be avoided by means of contract terms and otherwise, and under the law of Scotland civil liability can be avoided by means of contract terms

[26 October 1977]

PART I
AMENDMENT OF LAW FOR ENGLAND AND WALES AND NORTHERN IRELAND

Introductory

[1.731]
1   Scope of Part I

(1)   For the purposes of this Part of this Act, "negligence" means the breach—

   (a)   of any obligation, arising from the express or implied terms of a contract, to take reasonable care or exercise reasonable skill in the performance of the contract;

   (b)   of any common law duty to take reasonable care or exercise reasonable skill (but not any stricter duty);

   (c)   of the common duty of care imposed by the Occupiers' Liability Act 1957 or the Occupiers' Liability Act (Northern Ireland) 1957.

(2)   This Part of this Act is subject to Part III; and in relation to contracts, the operation of sections 2 *to* 4 and 7 is subject to the exceptions made by Schedule 1.

(3)   In the case of both contract and tort, sections 2 to 7 apply (except where the contrary is stated in section 6(4)) only to business liability, that is liability for breach of obligations or duties arising—

   (a)   from things done or to be done by a person in the course of a business (whether his own business or another's); or

   (b)   from the occupation of premises used for business purposes of the occupier;

and references to liability are to be read accordingly [but liability of an occupier of premises for breach of an obligation or duty towards a person obtaining access to the premises for recreational or educational purposes, being liability for loss or damage suffered by reason of the dangerous state of the premises, is not a business liability of the occupier unless granting that person such access for the purposes concerned falls within the business purposes of the occupier].

(4)   In relation to any breach of duty or obligation, it is immaterial for any purpose of this Part of this Act whether the breach was inadvertent or intentional, or whether liability for it arises directly or vicariously.

NOTES

Sub-s (2): for the words in italics there is substituted the figure ", 3" by the Consumer Rights Act 2015, s 75, Sch 4, paras 2, 3, as from 1 October 2015 (except for the purpose of a contract to supply a consumer transport service), and as from 6 April 2016 (otherwise) (for transitional provisions see the Consumer Rights Act 2015 (Commencement No 3, Transitional Provisions, Savings and Consequential Amendments) Order 2015, SI 2015/1630, arts 6–8 at **[2.1220]** et seq).

Sub-s (3): words in square brackets added by the Occupiers' Liability Act 1984, s 2.

Avoidance of liability for negligence, breach of contract, etc

[1.732]

2   Negligence liability

(1)   A person cannot by reference to any contract term or to a notice given to persons generally or to particular persons exclude or restrict his liability for death or personal injury resulting from negligence.

(2)   In the case of other loss or damage, a person cannot so exclude or restrict his liability for negligence except in so far as the term or notice satisfies the requirement of reasonableness.

(3)   Where a contract term or notice purports to exclude or restrict liability for negligence a person's agreement to or awareness of it is not of itself to be taken as indicating his voluntary acceptance of any risk.

[(4)   This section does not apply to—

   (a)   a term in a consumer contract, or

   (b)   a notice to the extent that it is a consumer notice,

(but see the provision made about such contracts and notices in sections 62 and 65 of the Consumer Rights Act 2015).]

NOTES

Sub-s (4): added by the Consumer Rights Act 2015, s 75, Sch 4, paras 2, 4, as from 1 October 2015 (except for the purpose of a contract to supply a consumer transport service), and as from 6 April 2016 (otherwise) (for transitional provisions see the Consumer Rights Act 2015 (Commencement No 3, Transitional Provisions, Savings and Consequential Amendments) Order 2015, SI 2015/1630, arts 6–8 at **[2.1220]** et seq).

[1.733]

3   Liability arising in contract

(1)   This section applies as between contracting parties where one of them deals *as consumer or* on the other's written standard terms of business.

(2)   As against that party, the other cannot by reference to any contract term—

   (a)   when himself in breach of contract, exclude or restrict any liability of his in respect of the breach; or

   (b)   claim to be entitled—

      (i)   to render a contractual performance substantially different from that which was reasonably expected of him, or

      (ii)   in respect of the whole or any part of his contractual obligation, to render no performance at all,

except in so far as (in any of the cases mentioned above in this subsection) the contract term satisfies the requirement of reasonableness.

[(3)   This section does not apply to a term in a consumer contract (but see the provision made about such contracts in section 62 of the Consumer Rights Act 2015).]

NOTES

Sub-s (1): words in italics repealed by the Consumer Rights Act 2015, s 75, Sch 4, paras 2, 5(1), (2), as from 1 October 2015 (except for the purpose of a contract to supply a consumer transport service), and as from 6 April 2016 (otherwise) (for transitional provisions see the Consumer Rights Act 2015 (Commencement No 3, Transitional Provisions, Savings and Consequential Amendments) Order 2015, SI 2015/1630, arts 6–8 at **[2.1220]** et seq).

Sub-s (3): added by the Consumer Rights Act 2015, s 75, Sch 4, paras 2, 5(1), (3), as from 1 October 2015 (except for the purpose of a contract to supply a consumer transport service), and as from 6 April 2016 (otherwise) (for transitional provisions see note above).

[1.734]

4   Unreasonable indemnity clauses

(1)   A person dealing as consumer cannot by reference to any contract term be made to indemnify another person (whether a party to the contract or not) in respect of liability that may be incurred by the other for negligence or breach of contract, except in so far as the contract term satisfies the requirement of reasonableness.

(2)   This section applies whether the liability in question—

   (a)   is directly that of the person to be indemnified or is incurred by him vicariously;

   (b)   is to the person dealing as consumer or to someone else.

NOTES

Repealed by the Consumer Rights Act 2015, s 75, Sch 4, paras 2, 6, as from 1 October 2015 (except for the purpose of a contract to supply a consumer transport service), and as from 6 April 2016 (otherwise) (for transitional provisions see the Consumer Rights Act 2015 (Commencement No 3, Transitional Provisions, Savings and Consequential Amendments) Order 2015, SI 2015/1630, arts 6–8 at **[2.1220]** et seq).

Liability arising from sale or supply of goods

[1.735]

5   "Guarantee" of consumer goods

(1)   In the case of goods of a type ordinarily supplied for private use or consumption, where loss or damage—

(a)   *arises from the goods proving defective while in consumer use; and*

(b)   *results from the negligence of a person concerned in the manufacture or distribution of the goods,*

liability for the loss or damage cannot be excluded or restricted by reference to any contract term or notice contained in or operating by reference to a guarantee of the goods.

(2)   For these purposes—

(a)   *goods are to be regarded as "in consumer use" when a person is using them, or has them in his possession for use, otherwise than exclusively for the purposes of a business; and*

(b)   *anything in writing is a guarantee if it contains or purports to contain some promise or assurance (however worded or presented) that defects will be made good by complete or partial replacement, or by repair, monetary compensation or otherwise.*

(3)   This section does not apply as between the parties to a contract under or in pursuance of which possession or ownership of the goods passed.

NOTES

Repealed by the Consumer Rights Act 2015, s 75, Sch 4, paras 2, 7, as from 1 October 2015 (for transitional provisions see the Consumer Rights Act 2015 (Commencement No 3, Transitional Provisions, Savings and Consequential Amendments) Order 2015, SI 2015/1630, arts 6–8 at **[2.1220]** et seq).

[1.736]

6   Sale and hire-purchase

(1)   Liability for breach of the obligations arising from—

(a)   [section 12 of the Sale of Goods Act 1979] (seller's implied undertakings as to title, etc);

(b)   section 8 of the Supply of Goods (Implied Terms) Act 1973 (the corresponding thing in relation to hire-purchase),

cannot be excluded or restricted by reference to any contract term.

[(1A)   Liability for breach of the obligations arising from—

(a)   section 13, 14 or 15 of the 1979 Act (seller's implied undertakings as to conformity of goods with description or sample, or as to their quality or fitness for a particular purpose);

(b)   section 9, 10 or 11 of the 1973 Act (the corresponding things in relation to hire purchase),

cannot be excluded or restricted by reference to a contract term except in so far as the term satisfies the requirement of reasonableness.]

(2)   As against a person dealing as consumer, liability for breach of the obligations arising from—

(a)   *[section 13, 14 or 15 of the 1979 Act] (seller's implied undertakings as to conformity of goods with description or sample, or as to their quality or fitness for a particular purpose);*

(b)   *section 9, 10 or 11 of the 1973 Act (the corresponding things in relation to hire-purchase),*

cannot be excluded or restricted by reference to any contract term.

(3)   As against a person dealing otherwise than as consumer, the liability specified in subsection (2) above can be excluded or restricted by reference to a contract term, but only in so far as the term satisfies the requirement of reasonableness.

(4)   The liabilities referred to in this section are not only the business liabilities defined by section 1(3), but include those arising under any contract of sale of goods or hire-purchase agreement.

[(5)   This section does not apply to a consumer contract (but see the provision made about such contracts in section 31 of the Consumer Rights Act 2015).]

NOTES

Sub-ss (1), (2): words in square brackets substituted by the Sale of Goods Act 1979, s 63, Sch 2, para 19.

Sub-ss (1A), (5): inserted and added respectively by the Consumer Rights Act 2015, s 75, Sch 4, paras 2, 8(1), (2), (4), as from 1 October 2015 (for transitional provisions see the Consumer Rights Act 2015 (Commencement No 3, Transitional Provisions, Savings and Consequential Amendments) Order 2015, SI 2015/1630, arts 6–8 at **[2.1220]** et seq).

Sub-ss (2), (3): repealed by the Consumer Rights Act 2015, s 75, Sch 4, paras 2, 8(1), (3), as from 1 October 2015 (for transitional provisions see note above).

[1.737]

7 Miscellaneous contracts under which goods pass

(1)   Where the possession or ownership of goods passes under or in pursuance of a contract not governed by the law of sale of goods or hire-purchase, subsections (2) to (4) below apply as regards the effect (if any) to be given to contract terms excluding or restricting liability for breach of obligation arising by implication of law from the nature of the contract.

[(1A)   Liability in respect of the goods' correspondence with description or sample, or their quality or fitness for any particular purpose, cannot be excluded or restricted by reference to such a term except in so far as the term satisfies the requirement of reasonableness.]

(2)   As against a person dealing as consumer, liability in respect of the goods' correspondence with description or sample, or their quality or fitness for any particular purpose, cannot be excluded or restricted by reference to any such term.

(3)   As against a person dealing otherwise than as consumer, that liability can be excluded or restricted by reference to such a term, but only in so far as the term satisfies the requirement of reasonableness.

[(3A)   Liability for breach of the obligations arising under section 2 of the Supply of Goods and Services Act 1982 (implied terms about title etc in certain contracts for the transfer of the property in goods) cannot be excluded or restricted by references to any such term.]

(4)   Liability in respect of—

   (a)   the right to transfer ownership of the goods, or give possession; or

   (b)   the assurance of quiet possession to a person taking goods in pursuance of the contract,

cannot [(in a case to which subsection (3A) above does not apply)] be excluded or restricted by reference to any such term except in so far as the term satisfies the requirement of reasonableness.

[(4A)   This section does not apply to a consumer contract (but see the provision made about such contracts in section 31 of the Consumer Rights Act 2015).]

(5)   . . .

NOTES

Sub-ss (1A), (4A): inserted by the Consumer Rights Act 2015, s 75, Sch 4, paras 2, 9(1), (2), (4), as from 1 October 2015 (for transitional provisions see the Consumer Rights Act 2015 (Commencement No 3, Transitional Provisions, Savings and Consequential Amendments) Order 2015, SI 2015/1630, arts 6–8 at **[2.1220]** et seq).

Sub-ss (2), (3): repealed by the Consumer Rights Act 2015, s 75, Sch 4, paras 2, 9(1), (3), as from 1 October 2015 (for transitional provisions see note above).

Sub-s (3A): inserted by the Supply of Goods and Services Act 1982, s 17(2).

Sub-s (4): words in square brackets inserted by the Supply of Goods and Services Act 1982, s 17(3).

Sub-s (5): repealed in relation to England and Wales by the Regulatory Reform (Trading Stamps) Order 2005, SI 2005/871, art 6, Schedule, and in relation to Northern Ireland by the Law Reform (Miscellaneous Provisions) (Northern Ireland) Order 2005, SI 2005/1452, art 24, Sch 2.

Other provisions about contracts

8   *(Substitutes the Misrepresentation Act 1967, s 3 at* **[1.421]***, and the Misrepresentation Act (Northern Ireland) 1967, s 3.)*

[1.738]

9 Effect of breach

(1)   Where for reliance upon it a contract term has to satisfy the requirement of reasonableness, it may be found to do so and be given effect accordingly notwithstanding that the contract has been terminated either by breach or by a party electing to treat it as repudiated.

(2)   Where on a breach the contract is nevertheless affirmed by a party entitled to treat it as repudiated, this does not of itself exclude the requirement of reasonableness in relation to any contract term.

NOTES

Repealed by the Consumer Rights Act 2015, s 75, Sch 4, paras 2, 10, as from 1 October 2015 (except for the purpose of a contract to supply a consumer transport service), and as from 6 April 2016 (otherwise) (for transitional provisions see the Consumer Rights Act 2015 (Commencement No 3, Transitional Provisions, Savings and Consequential Amendments) Order 2015, SI 2015/1630, arts 6–8 at **[2.1220]** et seq).

[1.739]

10 Evasion by means of secondary contract

A person is not bound by any contract term prejudicing or taking away rights of his which arise under, or in connection with the performance of, another contract, so far as those rights extend to the enforcement of another's liability which this Part of this Act prevents that other from excluding or restricting.

Explanatory provisions

[1.740]

11   The "reasonableness" test

(1)   In relation to a contract term, the requirement of reasonableness for the purposes of this Part of this Act, section 3 of the Misrepresentation Act 1967 and section 3 of the Misrepresentation Act (Northern Ireland) 1967 is that the term shall have been a fair and reasonable one to be included having regard to the circumstances which were, or ought reasonably to have been, known to or in the contemplation of the parties when the contract was made.

(2)   In determining for the purposes of section 6 or 7 above whether a contract term satisfies the requirement of reasonableness, regard shall be had in particular to the matters specified in Schedule 2 to this Act; but this subsection does not prevent the court or arbitrator from holding, in accordance with any rule of law, that a term which purports to exclude or restrict any relevant liability is not a term of the contract.

(3)   In relation to a notice (not being a notice having contractual effect), the requirement of reasonableness under this Act is that it should be fair and reasonable to allow reliance on it, having regard to all the circumstances obtaining when the liability arose or (but for the notice) would have arisen.

(4)   Where by reference to a contract term or notice a person seeks to restrict liability to a specified sum of money, and the question arises (under this or any other Act) whether the term or notice satisfies the requirement of reasonableness, regard shall be had in particular (but without prejudice to subsection (2) above in the case of contract terms) to—

    (a)   the resources which he could expect to be available to him for the purpose of meeting the liability should it arise; and

    (b)   how far it was open to him to cover himself by insurance.

(5)   It is for those claiming that a contract term or notice satisfies the requirement of reasonableness to show that it does.

[1.741]

12   *"Dealing as consumer"*

(1)   A party to a contract "deals as consumer" in relation to another party if—

    (a)   he neither makes the contract in the course of a business nor holds himself out as doing so; and

    (b)   the other party does make the contract in the course of a business; and

    (c)   in the case of a contract governed by the law of sale of goods or hire-purchase, or by section 7 of this Act, the goods passing under or in pursuance of the contract are of a type ordinarily supplied for private use or consumption.

[(1A)   But if the first party mentioned in subsection (1) is an individual paragraph (c) of that subsection must be ignored.]

[(2)   But the buyer is not in any circumstances to be regarded as dealing as consumer—

    (a)   if he is an individual and the goods are second hand goods sold at public auction at which individuals have the opportunity of attending the sale in person;

    (b)   if he is not an individual and the goods are sold by auction or by competitive tender.]

(3)   Subject to this, it is for those claiming that a party does not deal as consumer to show that he does not.

NOTES

Repealed by the Consumer Rights Act 2015, s 75, Sch 4, paras 2, 11, as from 1 October 2015 (except for the purpose of a contract to supply a consumer transport service), and as from 6 April 2016 (otherwise) (for transitional provisions see the Consumer Rights Act 2015 (Commencement No 3, Transitional Provisions, Savings and Consequential Amendments) Order 2015, SI 2015/1630, arts 6–8 at **[2.1220]** et seq).

Sub-s (1A): inserted by the Sale and Supply of Goods to Consumers Regulations 2002, SI 2002/3045, reg 14(1), (2).

Sub-s (2): substituted by SI 2002/3045, reg 14(1), (3).

[1.742]

13   Varieties of exemption clause

(1)   To the extent that this Part of this Act prevents the exclusion or restriction of any liability it also prevents—

    (a)   making the liability or its enforcement subject to restrictive or onerous conditions;

    (b)   excluding or restricting any right or remedy in respect of the liability, or subjecting a person to any prejudice in consequence of his pursuing any such right or remedy;

    (c)   excluding or restricting rules of evidence or procedure;

and (to that extent) sections 2 *and 5 to* 7 also prevent excluding or restricting liability by reference to terms and notices which exclude or restrict the relevant obligation or duty.

(2)   But an agreement in writing to submit present or future differences to arbitration is not to be treated under this Part of this Act as excluding or restricting any liability.

NOTES

Sub-s (1): for the words in italics there are substituted the words ", 6 and" by the Consumer Rights Act 2015, s 75, Sch 4, paras 2, 12, as from 1 October 2015 (except for the purpose of a contract to supply a consumer transport service), and as from

6 April 2016 (otherwise) (for transitional provisions see the Consumer Rights Act 2015 (Commencement No 3, Transitional Provisions, Savings and Consequential Amendments) Order 2015, SI 2015/1630, arts 6–8 at **[2.1220]** et seq).

[1.743]
14   Interpretation of Part I
In this Part of this Act—
   "business" includes a profession and the activities of any government department or local or public authority;
   ["consumer contract" has the same meaning as in the Consumer Rights Act 2015 (see section 61);
   "consumer notice" has the same meaning as in the Consumer Rights Act 2015 (see section 61);]
   "goods" has the same meaning as in [the Sale of Goods Act 1979];
   "hire-purchase agreement" has the same meaning as in the Consumer Credit Act 1974;
   "negligence" has the meaning given by section 1(1);
   "notice" includes an announcement, whether or not in writing, and any other communication or pretended communication; and
   "personal injury" includes any disease and any impairment of physical or mental condition.

NOTES
   Definitions "consumer contract" and "consumer notice" inserted by the Consumer Rights Act 2015, s 75, Sch 4, paras 2, 13, as from 1 October 2015 (except for the purpose of a contract to supply a consumer transport service), and as from 6 April 2016 (otherwise) (for transitional provisions see the Consumer Rights Act 2015 (Commencement No 3, Transitional Provisions, Savings and Consequential Amendments) Order 2015, SI 2015/1630, arts 6–8 at **[2.1220]** et seq).
   Words in square brackets in definition "goods" substituted by the Sale of Goods Act 1979, s 63, Sch 2, para 20.

15–25   (*(Pt II) applies to Scotland only.*)

PART III
PROVISIONS APPLYING TO WHOLE OF UNITED KINGDOM

Miscellaneous

[1.744]
26   International supply contracts
(1)   The limits imposed by this Act on the extent to which a person may exclude or restrict liability by reference to a contract term do not apply to liability arising under such a contract as is described in subsection (3) below.
(2)   The terms of such a contract are not subject to any requirement of reasonableness under section 3 *or 4*: and nothing in Part II of this Act shall require the incorporation of the terms of such a contract to be fair and reasonable for them to have effect.
(3)   Subject to subsection (4), that description of contract is one whose characteristics are the following—
   (a)   either it is a contract of sale of goods or it is one under or in pursuance of which the possession or ownership of goods passes; and
   (b)   it is made by parties whose places of business (or, if they have none, habitual residences) are in the territories of different States (the Channel Islands and the Isle of Man being treated for this purpose as different States from the United Kingdom).
(4)   A contract falls within subsection (3) above only if either—
   (a)   the goods in question are, at the time of the conclusion of the contract, in the course of carriage, or will be carried, from the territory of one State to the territory of another; or
   (b)   the acts constituting the offer and acceptance have been done in the territories of different States; or
   (c)   the contract provides for the goods to be delivered to the territory of a State other than that within whose territory those acts were done.

NOTES
   Sub-s (2): words in italics repealed by the Consumer Rights Act 2015, s 75, Sch 4, paras 2, 23, as from 1 October 2015 (except for the purpose of a contract to supply a consumer transport service), and as from 6 April 2016 (otherwise) (for transitional provisions see the Consumer Rights Act 2015 (Commencement No 3, Transitional Provisions, Savings and Consequential Amendments) Order 2015, SI 2015/1630, arts 6–8 at **[2.1220]** et seq).

[1.745]
27   Choice of law clauses
(1)   Where the [law applicable to] a contract is the law of any part of the United Kingdom only by choice of the parties (and apart from that choice would be the law of some country outside the United Kingdom) sections 2 to 7 and 16 to 21 of this Act do not operate as part [of the law applicable to the contract].
(2)   This Act has effect notwithstanding any contract term which applies or purports to apply the law of some country outside the United Kingdom, where *(either or both)*—

(a) the term appears to the court, or arbitrator or arbiter to have been imposed wholly or mainly for the purpose of enabling the party imposing it to evade the operation of this Act; *or*

(b) *in the making of the contract one of the parties dealt as consumer, and he was then habitually resident in the United Kingdom, and the essential steps necessary for the making of the contract were taken there, whether by him or by others on his behalf.*

(3) *(Applies to Scotland only.)*

NOTES

Sub-s (1): words in square brackets substituted by the Contracts (Applicable Law) Act 1990, s 5, Sch 4, para 4.

Sub-s (2): words in italics repealed by the Consumer Rights Act 2015, s 75, Sch 4, paras 2, 24(1), (2), as from 1 October 2015 (except for the purpose of a contract to supply a consumer transport service), and as from 6 April 2016 (otherwise) (for transitional provisions see the Consumer Rights Act 2015 (Commencement No 3, Transitional Provisions, Savings and Consequential Amendments) Order 2015, SI 2015/1630, arts 6–8 at **[2.1220]** et seq).

Sub-s (3): repealed by the Consumer Rights Act 2015, s 75, Sch 4, paras 2, 24(1), (3), as from 1 October 2015 (except for the purpose of a contract to supply a consumer transport service), and as from 6 April 2016 (otherwise) (for transitional provisions see note above).

[1.746]

28 Temporary provision for sea carriage of passengers

(1) This section applies to a contract for carriage by sea of a passenger or of a passenger and his luggage where the provisions of the Athens Convention (with or without modification) do not have, in relation to the contract, the force of law in the United Kingdom.

(2) In a case where—

(a) *the contract is not made in the United Kingdom, and*

(b) *neither the place of departure nor the place of destination under it is in the United Kingdom,*

a person is not precluded by this Act from excluding or restricting liability for loss or damage, being loss or damage for which the provisions of the Convention would, if they had the force of law in relation to the contract, impose liability on him.

(3) In any other case, a person is not precluded by this Act from excluding or restricting liability for that loss or damage—

(a) *in so far as the exclusion or restriction would have been effective in that case had the provisions of the Convention had the force of law in relation to the contract; or*

(b) *in such circumstances and to such extent as may be prescribed, by reference to a prescribed term of the contract.*

(4) For the purposes of subsection (3)(a), the values which shall be taken to be the official values in the United Kingdom of the amounts (expressed in gold francs) by reference to which liability under the provisions of the Convention is limited shall be such amounts in sterling as the Secretary of State may from time to time by order made by statutory instrument specify.

(5) In this section,—

(a) *the references to excluding or restricting liability include doing any of those things in relation to the liability which are mentioned in section 13 or section 25(3) and (5); and*

(b) *"the Athens Convention" means the Athens Convention relating to the Carriage of Passengers and their Luggage by Sea, 1974; and*

(c) *"prescribed" means prescribed by the Secretary of State by regulations made by statutory instrument;*

and a statutory instrument containing the regulations shall be subject to annulment in pursuance of a resolution of either House of Parliament.

NOTES

Repealed by the Consumer Rights Act 2015, s 75, Sch 4, paras 2, 25, as from 1 October 2015 (except for the purpose of a contract to supply a consumer transport service), and as from 6 April 2016 (otherwise) (for transitional provisions see the Consumer Rights Act 2015 (Commencement No 3, Transitional Provisions, Savings and Consequential Amendments) Order 2015, SI 2015/1630, arts 6–8 at **[2.1220]** et seq).

The Athens Convention: Cmnd 6326; set out in the Merchant Shipping Act 1979, Sch 3 and given the force of law by s 14 of that Act (as from 1 January 1996, replaced by the Merchant Shipping Act 1995, Sch 6 and s 183 respectively); brought fully into force on 30 April 1987 by the Merchant Shipping Act 1979 (Commencement No 11) Order 1987, SI 1987/635.

Modifications: the Merchant Shipping Act 1995, s 184(2), provides that Orders in Council made under s 184(1) of the Act may modify this section as the Secretary of State considers appropriate. By the Carriage of Passengers and their Luggage by Sea (Interim Provisions) Order 1980, SI 1980/1092 (made under s 16(1), (2) of the 1979 Act and now having effect under s 184 of the 1995 Act), this section ceased to apply to any contract to which that Order applies on 1 January 1981, but continues to apply to any contract made before that date. Contracts made after 30 April 1987 are governed by the Athens convention, subject, in the case of contracts for domestic carriage, to modifications contained in the Carriage of Passengers and their Luggage by Sea (Domestic Carriage) Order 1987, SI 1987/670.

Orders: as a result of the coming into force of the 1976 Protocol to the Athens Convention which replaced the references to gold francs in the Convention with references to special drawing rights, no equivalents for gold francs are now provided for by order under this section.

[1.747]
29 Saving for other relevant legislation
(1) Nothing in this Act removes or restricts the effect of, or prevents reliance upon, any contractual provision which—
  (a) is authorised or required by the express terms or necessary implication of an enactment; or
  (b) being made with a view to compliance with an international agreement to which the United Kingdom is a party, does not operate more restrictively than is contemplated by the agreement.
(2) A contract term is to be taken—
  (a) for the purposes of Part I of this Act, as satisfying the requirement of reasonableness; and
  (b) (*applies to Scotland only*),
if it is incorporated or approved by, or incorporated pursuant to a decision or ruling of, a competent authority acting in the exercise of any statutory jurisdiction or function and is not a term in a contract to which the competent authority is itself a party.
(3) In this section—
  "competent authority" means any court, arbitrator or arbiter, government department or public authority;
  "enactment" means any legislation (including subordinate legislation) of the United Kingdom or Northern Ireland and any instrument having effect by virtue of such legislation; and
  "statutory" means conferred by an enactment.

30 (*Repealed by the Consumer Safety Act 1978, s 10(1), Sch 3.*)

General

[1.748]
31 Commencement; amendments; repeals
(1) This Act comes into force on 1st February 1978.
(2) Nothing in this Act applies to contracts made before the date on which it comes into force, but subject to this, it applies to liability for any loss or damage which is suffered on or after that date.
(3) The enactments specified in Schedule 3 to this Act are amended as there shown.
(4) The enactments specified in Schedule 4 to this Act are repealed to the extent specified in column 3 of that Schedule.

[1.749]
32 Citation and extent
(1) This Act may be cited as the Unfair Contract Terms Act 1977.
(2) Part I of this Act extends to England and Wales and to Northern Ireland; but it does not extend to Scotland.
(3) Part II of this Act extends to Scotland only.
(4) This Part of this Act extends to the whole of the United Kingdom.

SCHEDULES
SCHEDULE 1
SCOPE OF SECTIONS 2 *TO* 4 AND 7

Section 1(2)

[1.750]
1. Sections 2 *to* 4 of this Act do not extend to—
  (a) any contract of insurance (including a contract to pay an annuity on human life);
  (b) any contract so far as it relates to the creation or transfer of an interest in land, or to the termination of such an interest, whether by extinction, merger, surrender, forfeiture or otherwise;
  (c) any contract so far as it relates to the creation or transfer of a right or interest in any patent, trade mark, copyright [or design right], registered design, technical or commercial information or other intellectual property, or relates to the termination of any such right or interest;
  (d) any contract so far as it relates—
    (i) to the formation or dissolution of a company (which means any body corporate or unincorporated association and includes a partnership), or
    (ii) to its constitution or the rights or obligations of its corporators or members;
  (e) any contract so far as it relates to the creation or transfer of securities or of any right or interest in securities.
  [(f) anything that is governed by Article 6 of Regulation (EU) No 181/2011 of the European Parliament and of the Council of 16 February 2011 concerning the rights of passengers in bus and coach transport and amending Regulation (EC) No 2006/2004.]

2. Section 2(1) extends to—
  (a) any contract of marine salvage or towage;
  (b) any charterparty of a ship or hovercraft; and

(c)   any contract for the carriage of goods by ship or hovercraft;

but subject to this sections 2 *to 4* and 7 do not extend to any such contract *except in favour of a person dealing as consumer.*

3. Where goods are carried by ship or hovercraft in pursuance of a contract which either—

(a)   specifies that as the means of carriage over part of the journey to be covered, or

(b)   makes no provision as to the means of carriage and does not exclude that means,

then sections 2(2), *3 and 4* do not, *except in favour of a person dealing as consumer,* extend to the contract as it operates for and in relation to the carriage of the goods by that means.

4. Section 2(1) and (2) do not extend to a contract of employment, except in favour of the employee.

5. Section 2(1) does not affect the validity of any discharge and indemnity given by a person, on or in connection with an award to him of compensation for pneumoconiosis attributable to employment in the coal industry, in respect of any further claim arising from his contracting that disease.

NOTES

Schedule heading: for the words in italics there is substituted the figure ", 3" by the Consumer Rights Act 2015, s 75, Sch 4, paras 2, 26(1), (2), as from 1 October 2015 (except for the purpose of a contract to supply a consumer transport service), and as from 6 April 2016 (otherwise) (for transitional provisions see the Consumer Rights Act 2015 (Commencement No 3, Transitional Provisions, Savings and Consequential Amendments) Order 2015, SI 2015/1630, arts 6–8 at **[2.1220]** et seq).

Para 1: for the first words in italics there are substituted the words "and 3", and second words in italics repealed, by the Consumer Rights Act 2015, s 75, Sch 4, paras 2, 26(1), (3), as from 1 October 2015 (except for the purpose of a contract to supply a consumer transport service), and as from 6 April 2016 (otherwise) (for transitional provisions see note above); words in square brackets in sub-para (c) inserted by the Copyright, Designs and Patents Act 1988, s 303(1), Sch 7, para 24; sub-para (f) added by the Rights of Passengers in Bus and Coach Transport (Exemptions and Enforcement) Regulations 2013, SI 2013/1865, reg 13(5).

Para 2: for the first words in italics there is substituted the figure ", 3", and second words in italics repealed, by the Consumer Rights Act 2015, s 75, Sch 4, paras 2, 26(1), (4), as from 1 October 2015 (except for the purpose of a contract to supply a consumer transport service), and as from 6 April 2016 (otherwise) (for transitional provisions see note above).

Para 3: for the words in italics there are substituted the words "and 3", and second words in italics repealed, by the Consumer Rights Act 2015, s 75, Sch 4, paras 2, 26(1), (5), as from 1 October 2015 (except for the purpose of a contract to supply a consumer transport service), and as from 6 April 2016 (otherwise) (for transitional provisions see note above).

Modification: References to trade marks or registered trade marks within the meaning of the Trade Marks Act 1938 shall, unless the context otherwise requires, be construed as references to trade marks or registered trade marks within the meaning of the Trade Marks Act 1994; see the Trade Marks Act 1994, Sch 4, para 1.

SCHEDULE 2
"GUIDELINES" FOR APPLICATION OF REASONABLENESS TEST

Sections 11(2), 24(2)

[1.751]
The matters to which regard is to be had in particular for the purposes of sections *6(3), 7(3) and (4),* 20 and 21 are any of the following which appear to be relevant—

(a)   the strength of the bargaining positions of the parties relative to each other, taking into account (among other things) alternative means by which the customer's requirements could have been met;

(b)   whether the customer received an inducement to agree to the term, or in accepting it had an opportunity of entering into a similar contract with other persons, but without having to accept a similar term;

(c)   whether the customer knew or ought reasonably to have known of the existence and extent of the term (having regard, among other things, to any custom of the trade and any previous course of dealing between the parties);

(d)   where the term excludes or restricts any relevant liability if some condition is not complied with, whether it was reasonable at the time of the contract to expect that compliance with that condition would be practicable;

(e)   whether the goods were manufactured, processed or adapted to the special order of the customer.

NOTES

For the words in italics there are substituted the words "6(1A), 7(1A) and (4)," by the Consumer Rights Act 2015, s 75, Sch 4, paras 2, 27, as from 1 October 2015 (except for the purpose of a contract to supply a consumer transport service), and as from 6 April 2016 (otherwise) (for transitional provisions see the Consumer Rights Act 2015 (Commencement No 3, Transitional Provisions, Savings and Consequential Amendments) Order 2015, SI 2015/1630, arts 6–8 at **[2.1220]** et seq).

SCHEDULES 3 AND 4

(Sch 3, in so far as unrepealed, specifies amendments of the Supply of Goods (Implied Terms) Act 1973, ss 14, 15 (as originally enacted and as substituted by the Consumer Credit Act 1974); Sch 4 specifies certain enactments repealed by s 31(4).)

STATE IMMUNITY ACT 1978

(1978 c 33)

ARRANGEMENT OF SECTIONS

PART I
PROCEEDINGS IN UNITED KINGDOM BY OR AGAINST OTHER STATES

Immunity from jurisdiction

An Act to make new provision with respect to proceedings in the United Kingdom by or against other States; to provide for the effect of judgments given against the United Kingdom in the courts of States parties to the European Convention on State Immunity; to make new provision with respect to the immunities and privileges of heads of State; and for connected purposes

[20 July 1978]

PART I
PROCEEDINGS IN UNITED KINGDOM BY OR AGAINST OTHER STATES

Immunity from jurisdiction

[1.752]
1   General immunity from jurisdiction
(1)   A State is immune from the jurisdiction of the courts of the United Kingdom except as provided in the following provisions of this Part of this Act.
(2)   A court shall give effect to the immunity conferred by this section even though the State does not appear in the proceedings in question.

Exceptions from immunity

[1.753]
2   Submission to jurisdiction
(1)   A State is not immune as respects proceedings in respect of which it has submitted to the jurisdiction of the courts of the United Kingdom.

(2)   A State may submit after the dispute giving rise to the proceedings has arisen or by a prior written agreement; but a provision in any agreement that it is to governed by the law of the United Kingdom is not to be regarded as a submission.

(3)   A State is deemed to have submitted—

    (a)   if it has instituted the proceedings; or

    (b)   subject to subsections (4) and (5) below, if it has intervened or taken any step in the proceedings.

(4)   Subsection (3)(b) above does not apply to intervention or any step taken for the purpose only of—

    (a)   claiming immunity; or

    (b)   asserting an interest in property in circumstances such that the State would have been entitled to immunity if the proceedings had been brought against it.

(5)   Subsection (3)(b) above does not apply to any step taken by the State in ignorance of facts entitling it to immunity if those facts could not reasonably have been ascertained and immunity is claimed as soon as reasonably practicable.

(6)   A submission in respect of any proceedings extends to any appeal but not to any counter-claim unless it arises out of the same legal relationship or facts as the claim.

(7)   The head of a State's diplomatic mission in the United Kingdom, or the person for the time being performing his functions, shall be deemed to have authority to submit on behalf of the State in respect of any proceedings; and any person who has entered into a contract on behalf of and with the authority of a State shall be deemed to have authority to submit on its behalf in respect of proceedings arising out of the contract.

[1.754]
3   Commercial transactions and contracts to be performed in United Kingdom

(1)   A State is not immune as respects proceedings relating to—

    (a)   a commercial transaction, entered into by the State; or

    (b)   an obligation of the State which by virtue of a contract (whether a commercial transaction or not) falls to be performed wholly or partly in the United Kingdom.

(2)   This section does not apply if the parties to the dispute are States or have otherwise agreed in writing; and subsection (1)(b) above does not apply if the contract (not being a commercial transaction) was made in the territory of the State concerned and the obligation in question is governed by its administrative law.

(3)   In this section "commercial transaction" means—

    (a)   any contract for the supply of goods or services;

    (b)   any loan or other transaction for the provision of finance and any guarantee or indemnity in respect of any such transaction or of any other financial obligation; and

    (c)   any other transaction or activity (whether of a commercial, industrial, financial, professional or other similar character) into which a State enters or in which it engages otherwise than in the exercise of sovereign authority;

but neither paragraph of subsection (1) above applies to a contract of employment between a State and an individual.

[1.755]
4   Contracts of employment

(1)   A State is not immune as respects proceedings relating to a contract of employment between the State and an individual where the contract was made in the United Kingdom or the work is to be wholly or partly performed there.

(2)   Subject to subsections (3) and (4) below, this section does not apply if—

    (a)   at the time when the proceedings are brought the individual is a national of the State concerned; or

    (b)   at the time when the contract was made the individual was neither a national of the United Kingdom nor habitually resident there; or

    (c)   the parties to the contract have otherwise agreed in writing.

(3)   Where the work is for an office, agency or establishment maintained by the State in the United Kingdom for commercial purposes, subsection (2) (a) and (b) above do not exclude the application of this section unless the individual was, at the time when the contract was made, habitually resident in that State.

(4)   Subsection (2)(c) above does not exclude the application of this section where the law of the United Kingdom requires the proceedings to be brought before a court of the United Kingdom.

(5)   In subsection (2)(b) above "national of the United Kingdom" [means—

    (a)   a British citizen, a [British overseas territories citizen][, a British National (Overseas)] or a British Overseas citizen; or

    (b)   a person who under the British Nationality Act 1981 is a British subject; or

    (c)   a British protected person (within the meaning of that Act)].

(6)   In this section "proceedings relating to a contract of employment" includes proceedings between the parties to such a contract in respect of any statutory rights or duties to which they are entitled or subject as employer or employee.

NOTES

Sub-s (5): words in first (outer) pair of square brackets substituted by the British Nationality Act 1981, s 52(6), Sch 7; in para (a), words in first pair of square brackets substituted by virtue of the British Overseas Territories Act 2002, s 2(3); words in second pair of square brackets inserted by the Hong Kong (British Nationality) Order 1986, SI 1986/948, art 8, Schedule.

[1.756]
5   Personal injuries and damage to property
A State is not immune as respects proceedings in respect of—
    (a)   death or personal injury; or
    (b)   damage or loss of tangible property,
caused by an act or omission in the United Kingdom.

[1.757]
6   Ownership, possession and use of property
(1)   A State is not immune as respects proceedings relating to—
    (a)   any interest of the State in, or its possession or use of, immovable property in the United Kingdom; or
    (b)   any obligation of the State arising out of its interest in, or its possession or use of, any such property.
(2)   A State is not immune as respects proceedings relating to any interest of the State in movable or immovable property, being an interest arising by way of succession, gift or bona vacantia.
(3)   The fact that a State has or claims an interest in any property shall not preclude any court from exercising in respect of it any jurisdiction relating to the estates of deceased persons or persons of unsound mind or to insolvency, the winding up of companies or the administration of trusts.
(4)   A court may entertain proceedings against a person other than a State notwithstanding that the proceedings relate to property—
    (a)   which is in the possession or control of a State; or
    (b)   in which a State claims an interest,
if the State would not have been immune had the proceedings been brought against it or, in a case within paragraph (b) above, if the claim is neither admitted nor supported by prima facie evidence.

[1.758]
7   Patents, trade-marks etc
A State is not immune as respects proceedings relating to—
    (a)   any patent, trade-mark design or plant breeders' rights belonging to the State and registered or protected in the United Kingdom or for which the State has applied in the United Kingdom;
    (b)   an alleged infringement by the State in the United Kingdom of any patent, trade-mark, design, plant breeders' rights or copyright; or
    (c)   the right to use a trade or business name in the United Kingdom.

NOTES

References to trade marks or registered trade marks within the meaning of the Trade Marks Act 1938 shall, unless the context otherwise requires, be construed as references to trade marks or registered trade marks within the meaning of the Trade Marks Act 1994; see the Trade Marks Act 1994, Sch 4, para 1.

[1.759]
8   Membership of bodies corporate etc
(1)   A State is not immune as respects proceedings relating to its membership of a body corporate, an unincorporated body or a partnership which—
    (a)   has members other than States; and
    (b)   is incorporated or constituted under the law of the United Kingdom or is controlled from or has its principal place of business in the United Kingdom,
being proceedings arising between the State and the body or its other members or, as the case may be, between the State and the other partners.
(2)   This section does not apply if provision to the contrary has been made by an agreement in writing between the parties to the dispute or by the constitution or other instrument establishing or regulating the body or partnership in question.

[1.760]
9   Arbitrations
(1)   Where a State has agreed in writing to submit a dispute which has arisen, or may arise, to arbitration, the State is not immune as respects proceedings in the courts of the United Kingdom which relate to the arbitration.
(2)   This section has effect subject to any contrary provision in the arbitration agreement and does not apply to any arbitration agreement between States.

[1.761]
10 Ships used for commercial purposes
(1) This section applies to—
(a) Admiralty proceedings; and
(b) proceedings on any claim which could be made the subject of Admiralty proceedings.
(2) A State is not immune as respects—
(a) an action in rem against a ship belonging to that State; or
(b) an action in personam for enforcing a claim in connection with such a ship,
if, at the time when the cause of action arose, the ship was in use or intended for use for commercial purposes.
(3) Where an action in rem is brought against a ship belonging to a State for enforcing a claim in connection with another ship belonging to that State, subsection (2)(a) above does not apply as respects the first-mentioned ship unless, at the time when the cause of action relating to the other ship arose, both ships were in use or intended for use for commercial purposes.
(4) A State is not immune as respects—
(a) an action in rem against a cargo belonging to that State if both the cargo and the ship carrying it were, at the time when the cause of action arose, in use or intended for use for commercial purposes; or
(b) an action in personam for enforcing a claim in connection with such a cargo if the ship carrying it was in use or intended for use as aforesaid.
(5) In the foregoing provisions references to a ship or cargo belonging to a State include references to a ship or cargo in its possession or control or in which it claims an interest; and, subject to subsection (4) above, subsection (2) above applies to property other than a ship as it applies to a ship.
(6) Sections 3 to 5 above do not apply to proceedings of the kind described in subsection (1) above if the State in question is a party to the Brussels Convention and the claim relates to the operation of a ship owned or operated by that State, the carriage of cargo or passengers on any such ship or the carriage of cargo owned by that State on any other ship.

[1.762]
11 Value added tax, customs duties etc
A State is not immune as respects proceedings relating to its liability for—
(a) value added tax, and duty of customs or excise or any agricultural levy; or
(b) rates in respect of premises occupied by it for commercial purposes.

Procedure

[1.763]
12 Service of process and judgements in default of appearance
(1) Any writ or other document required to be served for instituting proceedings against a State shall be served by being transmitted through the Foreign and Commonwealth Office to the Ministry of Foreign Affairs of the State and service shall be deemed to have been effected when the writ or document is received at the Ministry.
(2) Any time for entering an appearance (whether prescribed by rules of court or otherwise) shall begin to run two months after the date on which the writ or document is received as aforesaid.
(3) A State which appears in proceedings cannot thereafter object that subsection (1) above has not been complied with in the case of those proceedings.
(4) No judgment in default of appearance shall be given against a State except on proof that subsection (1) above has been complied with and that the time for entering an appearance as extended by subsection (2) above has expired.
(5) A copy of any judgment given against a State in default of appearance shall be transmitted through the Foreign and Commonwealth Office to the Ministry of Foreign Affairs of that State and any time for applying to have the judgment set aside (whether prescribed by rules of court or otherwise) shall begin to run two months after the date on which the copy of the judgment is received at the Ministry.
(6) Subsection (1) above does not prevent the service of a writ or other document in any manner to which the State has agreed and subsections (2) and (4) above do not apply where service is effected in any such manner.
(7) This section shall not be construed as applying to proceedings against a State by way of counter-claim or to an action in rem; and subsection (1) above shall not be construed as affecting any rules of court whereby leave is required for the service of process outside the jurisdiction.

[1.764]
13 Other procedural privileges
(1) No penalty by way of committal or fine shall be imposed in respect of any failure or refusal by or on behalf of a State to disclose or produce any document or other information for the purposes of proceedings to which it is a party.
(2) Subject to subsections (3) and (4) below—
(a) relief shall not be given against a State by way of injunction or order for specific performance or for the recovery of land or other property; and

(b)   the property of a State shall not be subject to any process for the enforcement of a judgment or arbitration award or, in an action in rem, for its arrest, detention or sale.

(3)   Subsection (2) above does not prevent the giving of any relief or the issue of any process with the written consent of the State concerned; and any such consent (which may be contained in a prior agreement) may be expressed so as to apply to a limited extent or generally; but a provision merely submitting to the jurisdiction of the courts is not to be regarded as a consent for the purposes of this subsection.

(4)   Subsection (2)(b) above does not prevent the issue of any process in respect of property which is for the time being in use or intended for use for commercial purposes; but, in a case not falling within section 10 above, this subsection applies to property of a State party to the European Convention on State Immunity only if—

(a)   the process is for enforcing a judgment which is final within the meaning of section 18(1)(b) below and the State has made a declaration under Article 24 of the Convention; or

(b)   the process is for enforcing an arbitration award.

(5)   The head of a State's diplomatic mission in the United Kingdom, or the person for the time being performing his functions, shall be deemed to have authority to give on behalf of the State any such consent as is mentioned in subsection (3) above and, for the purposes of subsection (4) above, his certificate to the effect that any property is not in use or intended for use by or on behalf of the State for commercial purposes shall be accepted as sufficient evidence of that fact unless the contrary is proved.

(6)   (*Applies to Scotland only.*)

Supplementary provisions

[1.765]
14   States entitled to immunities and privileges
(1)   The immunities and privileges conferred by this Part of this Act apply to any foreign or commonwealth State other than the United Kingdom; and references to a State include references to—

(a)   the sovereign or other head of that State in his public capacity;

(b)   the government of that State; and

(c)   any department of that government,

but not to any entity (hereafter referred to as a "separate entity") which is distinct from the executive organs of the government of the State and capable of suing or being sued.

(2)   A separate entity is immune from the jurisdiction of the courts of the United Kingdom if, and only if—

(a)   the proceedings relate to anything done by it in the exercise of sovereign authority; and

(b)   the circumstances are such that a State (or, in the case of proceedings to which section 10 above applies, a State which is not a party to the Brussels Convention) would have been so immune.

(3)   If a separate entity (not being a State's central bank or other monetary authority) submits to the jurisdiction in respect of proceedings in the case of which it is entitled to immunity by virtue of subsection (2) above, subsections (1) to (4) of section 13 above shall apply to it in respect of those proceedings as if references to a State were references to that entity.

(4)   Property of a State's central bank or other monetary authority shall not be regarded for the purposes of subsection (4) of section 13 above as in use or intended for use for commercial purposes; and where any such bank or authority is a separate entity subsections (1) to (3) of that section shall apply to it as if references to a State were references to the bank or authority.

(5)   Section 12 above applies to proceedings against the constituent territories of a federal State; and Her Majesty may by Order in Council provide for the other provisions of this Part of this Act to apply to any such constituent territory specified in the Order as they apply to a State.

(6)   Where the provisions of this Part of this Act do not apply to a constituent territory by virtue of any such Order subsections (2) and (3) above shall apply to it as if it were a separate entity.

NOTES

Orders: the State Immunity (Federal States) Order 1979, SI 1979/457; the State Immunity (Federal States) Order 1993, SI 1993/2809.

[1.766]
15   Restriction and extension of immunities and privileges
(1)   If it appears to Her Majesty that the immunities and privileges conferred by this Part of this Act in relation to any State—

(a)   exceed those accorded by the law of that State in relation to the United Kingdom; or

(b)   are less than those required by any treaty, convention or other international agreement to which that State and the United Kingdom are parties,

Her Majesty may by Order in Council provide for restricting or, as the case may be, extending those immunities and privileges to such extent as appears to Her Majesty to be appropriate.

(2)   Any statutory instrument containing an Order under this section shall be subject to annulment in pursuance of a resolution of either House of Parliament.

NOTES

Orders: the State Immunity (Merchant Shipping) (Revocation) Order 1999, SI 1999/668.

[1.767]
16 Excluded matters

(1) This Part of this Act does not affect any immunity or privilege conferred by the Diplomatic Privileges Act 1964 or the Consular Relations Act 1968; and—

  (a) section 4 above does not apply to proceedings concerning the employment of the members of a mission within the meaning of the Convention scheduled to the said Act of 1964 or of the members of a consular post within the meaning of the Convention scheduled to the said Act of 1968;

  (b) section 6(1) above does not apply to proceedings concerning a State's title to or its possession of property used for the purposes of a diplomatic mission.

(2) This Part of this Act does not apply to proceedings relating to anything done by or in relation to the armed forces of a State while present in the United Kingdom and, in particular, has effect subject to the Visiting Forces Act 1952.

(3) This Part of this Act does not apply to proceedings to which section 17(6) of the Nuclear Installations Act 1965 applies.

(4) This Part of this Act does not apply to criminal proceedings.

(5) This Part of this Act does not apply to any proceedings relating to taxation other than those mentioned in section 11 above.

[1.768]
17 Interpretation of Part I

(1) In this Part of this Act—

  "the Brussels Convention" means the International Convention for the Unification of Certain Rules Concerning the Immunity of State-owned Ships signed in Brussels on 10th April 1926;

  "commercial purposes" means purposes of such transactions or activities as are mentioned in section 3(3) above;

  "ship" includes hovercraft.

(2) In sections 2(2) and 13(3) above references to an agreement include references to a treaty, convention or other international agreement.

(3) For the purposes of sections 3 to 8 above the territory of the United Kingdom shall be deemed to include any [British overseas territory] in respect of which the United Kingdom is a party to the European Convention on State Immunity.

(4) In sections 3(1), 4(1), 5 and 16(2) above references to the United Kingdom includes references to its territorial waters and any area designated under section 1(7) of the Continental Shelf Act 1964.

(5) (*Applies to Scotland only.*)

NOTES

Sub-s (3): words in square brackets substituted by virtue of the British Overseas Territories Act 2002, s 1(2).

PART II
JUDGMENTS AGAINST UNITED KINGDOM IN CONVENTION STATES

[1.769]
18 Recognition of judgments against United Kingdom

(1) This section applies to any judgment given against the United Kingdom by a court in another State party to the European Convention on State Immunity, being a judgment—

  (a) given in proceedings in which the United Kingdom was not entitled to immunity by virtue of provisions corresponding to those of sections 2 to 11 above; and

  (b) which is final, that is to say, which is not or is no longer subject to appeal or, if given in default of appearance, liable to be set aside.

(2) Subject to section 19 below, a judgment to which this section applies shall be recognised in any court in the United Kingdom as conclusive between the parties thereto in all proceedings founded on the same cause of action and may be relied on by way of defence or counter-claim in such proceedings.

(3) Subsection (2) above (but not section 19 below) shall have effect also in relation to any settlement entered into by the United Kingdom before a court in another State party to the Convention which under the law of that State is treated as equivalent to a judgment.

(4) In this section references to a court in a State party to the Convention include references to a court in any territory in respect of which it is a party.

[1.770]
19 Exceptions to recognition

(1) A court need not give effect to section 18 above in the case of a judgment—

(a) if to do so would be manifestly contrary to public policy or if any party to the proceedings in which the judgment was given had no adequate opportunity to present his case; or

(b) if the judgment was given without provisions corresponding to those of section 12 above having been complied with and the United Kingdom has not entered an appearance or applied to have the judgment set aside.

(2) A court need not give effect to section 18 above in the case of a judgment—

(a) if proceedings between the same parties, based on the same facts and having the same purpose—

    (i) are pending before a court in the United Kingdom and were the first to be instituted; or

    (ii) are pending before a court in another State party to the Convention, were the first to be instituted and may result in a judgment to which that section will apply; or

(b) if the result of the judgment is inconsistent with the result of another judgment given in proceedings between the same parties and—

    (i) the other judgment is by a court in the United Kingdom and either those proceedings were the first to be instituted or the judgment of that court was given before the first-mentioned judgment became final within the meaning of subsection (1)(b) of section 18 above; or

    (ii) the other judgment is by a court in another State party to the Convention and that section has already become applicable to it.

(3) Where the judgment was given against the United Kingdom in proceedings in respect of which the United Kingdom was not entitled to immunity by virtue of a provision corresponding to section 6(2) above, a court need not give effect to section 18 above in respect of the judgment if the court that gave the judgment—

(a) would not have had jurisdiction in the matter if it had applied rules of jurisdiction corresponding to those applicable to such matters in the United Kingdom; or

(b) applied a law other than that indicated by the United Kingdom rules of private international law and would have reached a different conclusion if it had applied the law so indicated.

(4) In subsection (2) above references to a court in the United Kingdom include references to a court in any [British overseas territory] in respect of which the United Kingdom is a party to the Convention, and references to a court in another State party to the Convention include references to a court in any territory in respect of which it is a party.

NOTES

Sub-s (4): words in square brackets substituted by virtue of the British Overseas Territories Act 2002, s 1(2).

PART III
MISCELLANEOUS AND SUPPLEMENTARY

[1.771]
20   Heads of State

(1) Subject to the provisions of this section and to any necessary modifications, the Diplomatic Privileges Act 1964 shall apply to—

(a) a sovereign or other head of State;

(b) members of his family forming part of his household; and

(c) his private servants,

as it applies to the head of a diplomatic mission, to members of his family forming part of his household and to his private servants.

(2) The immunities and privileges conferred by virtue of subsection (1) (a) and (b) above shall not be subject to the restrictions by reference to nationality or residence mentioned in Article 37(1) or 38 in Schedule 1 to the said Act of 1964.

(3) Subject to any direction to the contrary by the Secretary of State, a person on whom immunities and privileges are conferred by virtue of subsection (1) above shall be entitled to the exemption conferred by section 8 (3) of the Immigration Act 1971.

(4) Except as respects value added tax and duties of customs or excise, this section does not affect any question whether a person is exempt from, or immune as respects proceedings relating to, taxation.

(5) This section applies to the sovereign or other head of any State on which immunities and privileges are conferred by Part I of this Act and is without prejudice to the application of that Part to any such sovereign or head of State in his public capacity.

[1.772]
21   Evidence by certificate

A certificate by or on behalf of the Secretary of State shall be conclusive evidence on any question—

(a) whether any country is a State for the purposes of Part I of this Act, whether any territory is a constituent territory of a federal State for those purposes or as to the person or persons to be regarded for those purposes as the head or government of a State;

(b) whether a State is a party to the Brussels Convention mentioned in Part I of this Act.

(c) whether a State is a party to the European Convention on State Immunity, whether it has made a declaration under Article 24 of that Convention or as to the territories in respect of which the United Kingdom or any other State is a party;

(d) whether, and if so when, a document has been served or received as mentioned in section 12(1) or (5) above.

[1.773]
22 General interpretation

(1) In this Act "court" includes any tribunal or body exercising judicial functions; and references to the courts or law of the United Kingdom include references to the courts or law of any part of the United Kingdom.

(2) In this Act references to entry of appearance and judgments in default of appearance include references to any corresponding procedures.

(3) In this Act "the European Convention on State Immunity" means the Convention of that name signed in Basle in 16th May 1972.

(4) In this Act "[British overseas territory]" means—

(a) any of the Channel Islands;

(b) the Isle of Man;

(c) any colony other than one for whose external relations a country other than the United Kingdom is responsible; or

(d) any country or territory outside Her Majesty's dominions in which Her Majesty has jurisdiction in right of the government of the United Kingdom.

(5) Any power conferred by this Act to make an Order in Council includes power to vary or revoke a previous Order.

NOTES
Sub-s (4): words in square brackets substituted by virtue of the British Overseas Territories Act 2002, s 1(2).

[1.774]
23 Short title, repeals commencement and extent

(1) This Act may be cited as the State Immunity Act 1978.

(2) . . .

(3) Subject to subsection (4) below, Parts I and II of this Act do not apply to proceedings in respect of matters that occurred before the date of the coming into force of this Act and, in particular—

(a) sections 2(2) and 13(3) do not apply to any prior agreement, and

(b) sections 3, 4 and 9 do not apply to any transaction, contract or arbitration agreement, entered into before that date.

(4) Section 12 above applies to any proceedings instituted after the coming into force of this Act.

(5) This Act shall come into force on such date as may be specified by an order made by the Lord Chancellor by statutory instrument.

(6) This Act extends to Northern Ireland.

(7) Her Majesty may by Order in Council extend any of the provisions of this Act, with or without modification, to any [British overseas territory].

NOTES
Sub-s (2): repeals the Administration of Justice (Miscellaneous Provisions) Act 1938, s 13, and the Law Reform (Miscellaneous Provisions) (Scotland) Act 1940, s 7.

Sub-s (7): words in square brackets substituted by virtue of the British Overseas Territories Act 2002, s 1(2).

Orders: the State Immunity Act 1978 (Commencement) Order 1978, SI 1978/1572; the State Immunity (Overseas Territories) Order 1979, SI 1979/458, the State Immunity (Guernsey) Order 1980, SI 1980/871, the State Immunity (Isle of Man) Order 1981, SI 1981/1112, the State Immunity (Jersey) Order 1985, SI 1985/1642.

CIVIL LIABILITY (CONTRIBUTION) ACT 1978

(1978 c 47)

ARRANGEMENT OF SECTIONS

Proceedings for contribution

An Act to make new provision for contribution between persons who are jointly or severally, or both jointly and severally, liable for the same damage and in certain other similar cases where two or more persons have paid or may be required to pay compensation for the same damage; and to amend the law relating to proceedings against persons jointly liable for the same debt or jointly or severally, or both jointly and severally, liable for the same damage

[31 July 1978]

Proceedings for contribution

[1.775]
1   Entitlement to contribution

(1)   Subject to the following provisions of this section, any person liable in respect of any damage suffered by another person may recover contribution from any other person liable in respect of the same damage (whether jointly with him or otherwise).

(2)   A person shall be entitled to recover contribution by virtue of subsection (1) above notwithstanding that he has ceased to be liable in respect of the damage in question since the time when the damage occurred, provided that he was so liable immediately before he made or was ordered or agreed to make the payment in respect of which the contribution is sought.

(3)   A person shall be liable to make contribution by virtue of subsection (1) above notwithstanding that he has ceased to be liable in respect of the damage in question since the time when the damage occurred, unless he ceased to be liable by virtue of the expiry of a period of limitation or prescription which extinguished the right on which the claim against him in respect of the damage was based.

(4)   A person who has made or agreed to make any payment in bona fide settlement or compromise of any claim made against him in respect of any damage (including a payment into court which has been accepted) shall be entitled to recover contribution in accordance with this section without regard to whether or not he himself is or ever was liable in respect of the damage, provided, however, that he would have been liable assuming that the factual basis of the claim against him could be established.

(5)   A judgment given in any action brought in any part of the United Kingdom by or on behalf of the person who suffered the damage in question against any person from whom contribution is sought under this section shall be conclusive in the proceedings for contribution as to any issue determined by that judgment in favour of the person from whom the contribution is sought.

(6)   References in this section to a person's liability in respect of any damage are references to any such liability which has been or could be established in an action brought against him in England and Wales by or on behalf of the person who suffered the damage; but it is immaterial whether any issue arising in any such action was or would be determined (in accordance with the rules of private international law) by reference to the law of a country outside England and Wales.

NOTES

Disapplication: this section and s 2 do not apply where liability for contribution between persons liable in respect of the same damage is governed by European Parliament and Council Regulation 1371/2007/EC on rail passengers' rights and obligations; see the Rail Passengers' Rights and Obligations Regulations 2010, SI 2010/1504, reg 5(1), (2).

[1.776]
2 Assessment of contribution

(1)   Subject to subsection (3) below, in any proceedings for contribution under section 1 above the amount of the contribution recoverable from any person shall be such as may be found by the court to be just and equitable having regard to the extent of that person's responsibility for the damage in question.

(2)   Subject to subsection (3) below, the court shall have power in any such proceedings to exempt any person from liability to make contribution, or to direct that the contribution to be recovered from any person shall amount to a complete indemnity.

(3)   Where the amount of the damages which have or might have been awarded in respect of the damage in question in any action brought in England and Wales by or on behalf of the person who suffered it against the person from whom the contribution is sought was or would have been subject to—

   (a)   any limit imposed by or under any enactment or by any agreement made before the damage occurred;

   (b)   any reduction by virtue of section 1 of the Law Reform (Contributory Negligence) Act 1945 or section 5 of the Fatal Accidents Act 1976; or

   (c)   any corresponding limit or reduction under the law of a country outside England and Wales;

the person from whom the contribution is sought shall not by virtue of any contribution awarded under section 1 above be required to pay in respect of the damage a greater amount than the amount of those damages as so limited or reduced.

NOTES
   Disapplication: see the note to s 1 at **[1.775]**.

Proceedings for the same debt or damage

[1.777]
3   Proceedings against persons jointly liable for the same debt or damage

Judgment recovered against any person liable in respect of any debt or damage shall not be a bar to an action, or to the continuance of an action, against any other person who is (apart from any such bar) jointly liable with him in respect of the same debt or damage.

[1.778]
4   Successive actions against persons liable (jointly or otherwise) for the same damage

If more than one action is brought in respect of any damage by or on behalf of the person by whom it was suffered against persons liable in respect of the damage (whether jointly or otherwise) the plaintiff shall not be entitled to costs in any of those actions, other than that in which judgment is first given, unless the court is of the opinion that there was reasonable ground for bringing the action.

Supplemental

[1.779]
5   Application to the Crown

Without prejudice to section 4(1) of the Crown Proceedings Act 1947 (indemnity and contribution), this Act shall bind the Crown, but nothing in this Act shall be construed as in any way affecting Her Majesty in Her private capacity (including in right of Her Duchy of Lancaster) or the Duchy of Cornwall.

[1.780]
6   Interpretation

(1)   A person is liable in respect of any damage for the purposes of this Act if the person who suffered it (or anyone representing his estate or dependants) is entitled to recover compensation from him in respect of that damage (whatever the legal basis of his liability, whether tort, breach of contract, breach of trust or otherwise).

(2)   References in this Act to an action brought by or on behalf of the person who suffered any damage include references to an action brought for the benefit of his estate or dependants.

(3)   In this Act "dependants" has the same meaning as in the Fatal Accidents Act 1976.

(4)   In this Act, except in section 1(5) above, "action" means an action brought in England and Wales.

[1.781]
7   Savings

(1)   Nothing in this Act shall affect any case where the debt in question became due or (as the case may be) the damage in question occurred before the date on which it comes into force.

(2)   A person shall not be entitled to recover contribution or liable to make contribution in accordance with section 1 above by reference to any liability based on breach of any obligation assumed by him before the date on which this Act comes into force.

(3)   The right to recover contribution in accordance with section 1 above supersedes any right, other than an express contractual right, to recover contribution (as distinct from indemnity) otherwise than under this Act in corresponding circumstances; but nothing in this Act shall affect—
- (a)   any express or implied contractual or other right to indemnity; or
- (b)   any express contractual provision regulating or excluding contribution;

which would be enforceable apart from this Act (or render enforceable any agreement for indemnity or contribution which would not be enforceable apart from this Act).

8   *(Applies to Northern Ireland only.)*

[1.782]
9   Consequential amendments and repeals
(1)   The enactments specified in Schedule 1 to this Act shall have effect subject to the amendments set out in that Schedule, being amendments consequential on the preceding provisions of this Act.
(2)   The enactments specified in Schedule 2 to this Act are hereby repealed to the extent specified in column 3 of that Schedule.

[1.783]
10   Short title, commencement and extent
(1)   This Act may be cited as the Civil Liability (Contribution) Act 1978.
(2)   This Act shall come into force on 1st January next following the date on which it is passed.
(3)   This Act, with the exception of paragraph 1 of Schedule 1 thereto, does not extend to Scotland.

SCHEDULES

SCHEDULES 1, 2

(Sch 1 (Consequential Amendments) and Sch 2 (Repeals) outside the scope of this work.)

BANKING ACT 1979

(1979 c 37)

ARRANGEMENT OF SECTIONS

PART IV
MISCELLANEOUS AND GENERAL

An Act to regulate the acceptance of deposits in the course of a business; to confer functions on the Bank of England with respect to the control of institutions carrying on deposit-taking businesses; to give further protection to persons who are depositors with such institutions; to make provision with respect to advertisements inviting the making of deposits; to restrict the use of names and descriptions associated with banks and banking; to prohibit fraudulent inducement to make a deposit; to amend the Consumer Credit Act 1974 and the law with respect to instruments to which section 4 of the Cheques Act 1957 applies; to repeal certain enactments relating to banks and banking; and for purposes connected therewith

[4 April 1979]

1–37   *((Pts I–III) repealed by the Banking Act 1987, s 108(2), Sch 7, Pt I.)*

PART IV
MISCELLANEOUS AND GENERAL

38–46   *(S 38 amends the Consumer Credit Act 1974, ss 74, 114, 185(2) at* **[1.561]**, **[1.616]**, **[1.677]***; ss 39–46 repealed by the Banking Act 1987, s 108(2), Sch 7, Pt I.)*

[1.784]
47   Defence of contributory negligence
In any circumstances in which proof of absence of negligence on the part of a banker would be a defence in proceedings by reason of section 4 of the Cheques Act 1957, a defence of contributory negligence shall also be available to the banker notwithstanding the provisions of section 11(1) of the Torts (Interference with Goods) Act 1977.

48–51   *(Ss 48–50 repealed by the Banking Act 1987, s 108(2), Sch 7, Pt I; s 51(1) introduces Sch 6 to this Act (consequential amendments); s 51(2) repealed by the Statute Law (Repeals) Act 2004.)*

[1.785]
52 Short title, commencement and extent
(1) This Act may be cited as the Banking Act 1979.

(2) This Act extends to Northern Ireland.

(3) . . .

(4) Any reference in any provision of this Act to "the appointed day" shall be construed as a reference to the day appointed for the purposes of that provision; and any reference in this Act to the day appointed for the purposes of any provision of this Act—

    (a) shall be construed as a reference to the day appointed under this section for the coming into operation of that provision; and

    (b) where different days are appointed for different purposes of that provision, shall be construed, unless an order under this section otherwise provides, as a reference to the first day so appointed.

NOTES

Sub-s (3): repealed by the Statute Law (Repeals) Act 2004.

Orders: the Banking Act 1979 (Commencement No 1) Order 1979, SI 1979/938; the Banking Act 1979 (Commencement No 2) Order 1982, SI 1982/188; the Banking Act 1979 (Commencement No 3) Order 1985, SI 1985/797.

SCHEDULES

SCHEDULES 1–7

(Schs 1–5, 7 repealed by the Banking Act 1987, s 108(2), Sch 7, Pt I; Sch 6, in so far as unrepealed, specifies consequential amendments made by s 51(1).)

ESTATE AGENTS ACT 1979

(1979 c 38)

ARRANGEMENT OF SECTIONS

Application of Act

An Act to make provision with respect to the carrying on of and to persons who carry on, certain activities in connection with the disposal and acquisition of interests in land; and for purposes connected therewith

[4 April 1979]

Application of Act

[1.786]
1 Estate agency work
(1) This Act applies, subject to subsections (2) to (4) below to things done by any person in the course of a business (including a business in which he is employed) pursuant to instructions received from another person (in this section referred to as "the client") who wishes to dispose of or acquire an interest in land—
   (a)   for the purpose of, or with a view to, effecting the introduction to the client of a third person who wishes to acquire or, as the case may be, dispose of such an interest; and
   (b)   after such an introduction has been effected in the course of that business, for the purpose of securing the disposal or, as the case may be, the acquisition of that interest;
and in this Act the expression "estate agency work" refers to things done as mentioned above to which this Act applies.
(2) This Act does not apply to things done—
   (a)   in the course of his profession by a practising solicitor or a person employed by him [or by an incorporated practice (within the meaning of the Solicitors (Scotland) Act 1980) or a person employed by it]; or
   (b)   in the course of credit brokerage, within the meaning of the Consumer Credit Act 1974; or
   (c)   . . .
   (d)   in the course of carrying out any survey or valuation pursuant to a contract which is distinct from that under which other things falling within subsection (1) above are done; or
   (e)   in connection with applications and other matters arising under [the Town and Country Planning Act 1990, the Planning (Listed Buildings and Conservation Areas) Act 1990, the Planning (Hazardous Substances) Act 1990] or [the Town and Country Planning (Scotland) Act 1997, the Planning (Listed Buildings and Conservation Areas) (Scotland) Act 1997, the Planning (Hazardous Substances) (Scotland) Act 1997] or the Planning (Northern Ireland) [Order 1991].
(3) This Act does not apply to things done by any person—
   (a)   pursuant to instructions received by him in the course of his employment in relation to an interest in land if his employer is the person who, on his own behalf, wishes to dispose of or acquire that interest; or
   (b)   in relation to any interest in any property if the property is subject to a mortgage and he is the receiver of the income of it; or

    (c)   in relation to a present, prospective or former employee of his or of any person by whom he also is employed if the things are done by reason of the employment (whether past, present or future).

[(4) This Act does not apply to the following things when done by a person who does no other things which fall within subsection (1) above—

    (a)   publishing advertisements or disseminating information;

    (b)   providing a means by which—

        (i)   a person who wishes to acquire or dispose of an interest in land can, in response to such an advertisement or dissemination of information, make direct contact with a person who wishes to dispose of or, as the case may be, acquire an interest in land;

        (ii)   the persons mentioned in sub-paragraph (i) can continue to communicate directly with each other.]

(5) In this section—

    (a)   "practising solicitor" means, except in Scotland, a solicitor who is qualified to act as such under section 1 of the Solicitors Act 1974 or Article 4 of the Solicitors (Northern Ireland) Order 1976, and in Scotland includes a firm of practising solicitors;

    (b)   "mortgage" includes a debenture and any other charge on property for securing money or money's worth; and

    (c)   any reference to employment is a reference to employment under a contract of employment.

NOTES

Sub-s (2): words in square brackets in para (a) inserted by the Law Reform (Miscellaneous Provisions) (Scotland) Act 1985, s 56, Sch 1, Pt I, para 40; para (c) repealed by the Financial Services and Markets Act 2000 (Dissolution of the Insurance Brokers Registration Council) (Consequential Provisions) Order 2001, SI 2001/1283, art 3(1); in para (e) words in first pair of square brackets substituted by the Planning (Consequential Provisions) Act 1990, s 4, Sch 2, para 42, words in second pair of square brackets substituted by the Planning (Consequential Provisions) (Scotland) Act 1997, s 4, Sch 2, para 28, words in third pair of square brackets substituted by the Planning (Northern Ireland) Order 1991, SI 1991/1220, art 133(1), Sch 5.

Sub-s (4): substituted by the Enterprise and Regulatory Reform Act 2013, s 70.

Solicitors: references to solicitors in sub-ss (2)(a), (5)(a) are modified so as to include references to recognised bodies within the meaning of the Administration of Justice Act 1985, s 9, by the Solicitors' Recognised Bodies Order 1991, SI 1991/2684, arts 3–5, Sch 1.

Disapplication: this Act does not apply to things done in the course of the provision of conveyancing services by a licensed body which has been granted a licence by the Council for Licensed Conveyancers: see the Legal Services Act 2007 (Designation as a Licensing Authority) Order 2011, SI 2011/2038, art 3, Schedule, para 4.

[1.787]
2 Interests in land

(1) Subject to subsection (3) below, any reference in this Act to disposing of an interest in land is a reference to—

    (a)   transferring a legal estate in fee simple absolute in possession; or

    (b)   transferring or creating, elsewhere than in Scotland, a lease which, by reason of the level of the rent, the length of the term or both, has a capital value which may be lawfully realised on the open market; or

    (c)   *(applies to Scotland only)*;

and any reference to acquiring an interest in land shall be construed accordingly.

(2) In subsection (1)(b) above the expression "lease" includes the rights and obligations arising under an agreement to grant a lease.

(3) Notwithstanding anything in subsections (1) and (2) above, references in this Act to disposing of an interest in land do not extend to disposing of—

    (a)   the interest of a creditor whose debt is secured by way of a mortgage or charge of any kind over land or an agreement for any such mortgage or charge; or

    (b)   *(applies to Scotland only)*.

Orders by [the lead enforcement authority]

[1.788]
3 Orders prohibiting unfit persons from doing estate agency work

(1) The power of [the [lead enforcement authority]] to make an order under this section with respect to any person shall not be exercisable unless the [lead enforcement authority] is satisfied that that person—

    (a)   [has committed]—

        (i)   an offence involving fraud or other dishonesty or violence, or

        (ii)   an offence under any provision of this Act, other than section 10(6), section 22(3) or section 23(4), or

        (iii)   any other offence which, at the time it was committed, was specified for the purposes of this section by an order made by the Secretary of State; or

    (b)   has committed discrimination in the course of estate agency work; or

    [(ba) has failed to comply with an undertaking accepted from him under section 217, 218 or 219 of the Enterprise Act 2002 and given in relation to estate agency work; or (bb) has failed to comply with an enforcement order under section 217 of the Enterprise Act 2002 which was made against him in relation to estate agency work; or]

(c) has failed to comply with any obligation imposed on him under any of sections 15 and 18 to *21* below; or

[(ca) has engaged in estate agency work in relation to residential property in breach of the duty imposed by an order under section 23A(1) below; or]

[(cb) has failed to comply with any requirement imposed on him under *section 9(1) or 11(1A)(b) below*; or]

(d) has engaged in a practice which, in relation to estate agency work, has been declared undesirable by an order made by the Secretary of State;

and the provisions of Schedule 1 to the Act shall have effect for supplementing paragraphs (a) and (b) above.

(2) Subject to subsection (1) above, if the [lead enforcement authority] is satisfied that any person is unfit to carry on estate agency work generally or of a particular description [it] may make an order prohibiting that person—

(a) from doing any estate agency work at all; or

(b) from doing estate agency work of a description specified in the order;

and in determining whether a person is so unfit the [lead enforcement authority] may, in addition to taking account of any matters falling within subsection (1) above, also take account of whether, in the course of estate agency work or any other business activity, that person has engaged in any practice which involves breaches of a duty owed by virtue of any enactment, contract or rule of law and which is material to his fitness to carry on estate agency work.

(3) For the purposes of [paragraphs (ba) to (d)] of subsection (1) above,—

(a) anything done by a person in the course of his employment shall be treated as done by his employer as well as by him, whether or not it was done with the employer's knowledge or approval, unless the employer shows that he took such steps as were reasonably practicable to prevent the employee from doing that act, or from doing in the course of his employment acts of that description; and

(b) anything done by a person as agent for another person with the authority (whether express or implied, and whether precedent or subsequent) of that person shall be treated as done by that other person as well as by him; and

(c) anything done by a business associate of a person shall be treated as done by that person as well, unless he can show that the act was done without his connivance or consent.

(4) In an order under this section the [lead enforcement authority] shall specify as the grounds for the order those matters falling within paragraphs (a) to (d) of subsection (1) above to which [it] is satisfied and on which, accordingly, [it] relies to give [it] power to make the order.

(5) If the [lead enforcement authority] considers it appropriate, [it] may in an order under this section limit the scope of the prohibition imposed by the order to a particular part of or area within the United Kingdom.

(6) An order under paragraph (a)(iii) or paragraph (d) of subsection (1) above—

(a) shall be made by statutory instrument;

(b) shall be laid before Parliament after being made; and

(c) shall cease to have effect (without prejudice to anything previously done in reliance on the order) after the expiry of the period of twenty-eight days beginning with the date on which it was made unless within that period it has been approved by a resolution of each House of Parliament.

(7) In reckoning for the purposes of subsection (6)(c) above any period of twenty-eight days, no account shall be taken of any period during which Parliament is dissolved or prorogued or during which both Houses are adjourned for more than four days.

(8) A person who fails without reasonable excuse to comply with an order of the [lead enforcement authority] under this section shall be liable on conviction on indictment or on summary conviction to a fine which on summary conviction shall not exceed the statutory maximum.

NOTES

Cross-heading: words in square brackets substituted by the Public Bodies (Abolition of the National Consumer Council and Transfer of the Office of Fair Trading's Functions in relation to Estate Agents etc) Order 2014, SI 2014/631, art 5(3)(a), Sch 2, Pt 1, para 1(1), (2), for transitional provisions and savings see art 5(3)(a), Sch 2, Pt 4 thereof at **[2.1133]**, **[2.1134A]**.

Sub-s (1): words in first (outer) pair of square brackets substituted by the Enterprise Act 2002, s 278(1), Sch 25, para 9(1), (2)(a); and words in second (inner) and third pairs of square brackets substituted by SI 2014/631, art 5(3)(a), Sch 2, Pt 1, para 1(1), (3)(a), for transitional provisions and savings see note above; words in square brackets in para (a) substituted, and paras (ba), (bb), (ca), (cb) inserted, by the Consumers, Estate Agents and Redress Act 2007, ss 53(2), 55(1)–(3), 58(2), and for the number in italics in para (c) there is substituted the number "21A" by the Consumers, Estate Agents and Redress Act 2007, s 54(2), as from a day to be appointed; in para (cb) for the words in italics there are substituted the words "paragraph 14 or 27 of Schedule 5 to the Consumer Rights Act 2015" by the Consumer Rights Act 2015, s 77(2), Sch 6, paras 19, 20, as from 1 October 2015 (for transitional provisions see the Consumer Rights Act 2015 (Commencement No 3, Transitional Provisions, Savings and Consequential Amendments) Order 2015, SI 2015/1630, arts 6–8 at **[2.1220]** et seq).

Sub-s (2): words in first and final pairs of square brackets substituted by SI 2014/631, art 5(3)(a), Sch 2, Pt 1, para 1(1), (3)(b), for transitional provisions and savings see note above; word in second pair of square brackets substituted by the Enterprise Act 2002, s 278(1), Sch 25, para 9(1), (2)(c).

Sub-s (3): words in square brackets substituted by the Consumers, Estate Agents and Redress Act 2007, s 63(1), Sch 7, para 1.

Sub-s (4): words in first pair of square brackets substituted by SI 2014/631, art 5(3)(a), Sch 2, Pt 1, para 1(1), (3)(b), for transitional provisions and savings see note above; words in second, third and final pairs of square brackets substituted by the Enterprise Act 2002, s 278(1), Sch 25, para 9(1), (2)(d).

Sub-s (5): words in first pair of square brackets substituted by SI 2014/631, art 5(3)(a), Sch 2, Pt 1, para 1(1), (3)(b), for transitional provisions and savings see note above; word in second pair of square brackets substituted by the Enterprise Act 2002, s 278(1), Sch 25, para 9(1), (2)(d).

Sub-s (8): words in square brackets substituted by SI 2014/631, art 5(3)(a), Sch 2, Pt 1, para 1(1), (3)(b), for transitional provisions and savings see note above.

Orders: the Estate Agents (Undesirable Practices) (No 2) Order 1991, SI 1991/1032; the Estate Agents (Specified Offences) (No 2) Order 1991, SI 1991/1091; the Estate Agents (Specified Offences) (No 2) (Amendment) Order 1992, SI 1992/2833.

[1.789]
4 Warning orders
[(1) If the [lead enforcement authority] is satisfied that any of subsections (1A), (1B) or (1C) apply in relation to a person it may by order notify that person that it is satisfied of the matters mentioned in that subsection.

(1A) This subsection applies in relation to a person if—
- (a) in the course of estate agency work, he has engaged in conduct falling within paragraph (a), (b), (c), (ca) or (cb) of section 3(1); and
- (b) were he to engage again in any conduct falling within that paragraph, the [lead enforcement authority] would consider him unfit and proceed to make a prohibition order.

(1B) This subsection applies in relation to a person if—
- (a) in the course of estate agency work, he has engaged in conduct constituting a failure to comply with—
  - (i) an undertaking mentioned in section 3(1)(ba); or
  - (ii) an enforcement order mentioned in section 3(1)(bb); and
- (b) were he to fail again to comply with that undertaking or order by engaging in the same or similar conduct, the [lead enforcement authority] would consider him unfit and proceed to make a prohibition order.

(1C) This subsection applies in relation to a person if—
- (a) in the course of estate agency work, he has engaged in a practice mentioned in section 3(1)(d); and
- (b) were he to engage again in that practice, the [lead enforcement authority] would consider him unfit and proceed to make a prohibition order.]

(2) An order under this section shall state whether, in the opinion of the [lead enforcement authority], [further conduct as mentioned in subsection (1A)(b) or (1B)(b) or engaging again in the practice specified in the order, as the case may be,] would render the person to whom the order is addressed unfit to carry on estate agency work generally or estate agency work of a description specified in the order.

(3) If, after an order has been made under this section, the person to whom it is addressed [engages in further conduct as mentioned in subsection (1A)(b) or (1B)(b) or engages again in the practice specified in the order, as the case may be,] then, for the purposes of this Act, that fact shall be treated as conclusive evidence that he is unfit to carry on estate agency work as stated in the order in accordance with subsection (2) above; and the [lead enforcement authority] may proceed to make an order under section 3 above accordingly.

[(4) In this section "unfit" means unfit as mentioned in subsection (2) of section 3 and "prohibition order" means an order under that section.]

NOTES
Sub-ss (1), (1A)–(1C): substituted, for original sub-s (1), by the Consumers, Estate Agents and Redress Act 2007, s 56(1), (2); words in square brackets substituted by the Public Bodies (Abolition of the National Consumer Council and Transfer of the Office of Fair Trading's Functions in relation to Estate Agents etc) Order 2014, SI 2014/631, art 5(3)(a), Sch 2, Pt 1, para 1(1), (4)(a), for transitional provisions and savings see art 5(3)(a), Sch 2, Pt 4 thereof at **[2.1133]**, **[2.1134A]**.

Sub-s (2): words in first pair of square brackets substituted by SI 2014/631, art 5(3)(a), Sch 2, Pt 1, para 1(1), (4)(a), for transitional provisions and savings see note above; words in second pair of square brackets substituted by the Consumers, Estate Agents and Redress Act 2007, s 56(1), (3).

Sub-s (3): words in first pair of square brackets substituted by the Consumers, Estate Agents and Redress Act 2007, s 56(1), (4); words in second pair of square brackets substituted by SI 2014/631, art 5(3)(a), Sch 2, Pt 1, para 1(1), (4)(a), for transitional provisions and savings see note above.

Sub-s (4): added by the Consumers, Estate Agents and Redress Act 2007, s 56(1), (5).

[1.790]
5 Supplementary provisions as to orders under sections 3 and 4
(1) The provisions of Part I of Schedule 2 to this Act shall have effect—
- (a) with respect to the procedure to be followed before an order is made by the [lead enforcement authority] under section 3 or section 4 above; and
- (b) in connection with the making and coming into operation of any such order.

(2)   Where an order is made by the [lead enforcement authority] under section 3 or section 4 above, against a partnership, it may, if the [lead enforcement authority] thinks it appropriate, have effect also as an order against some or all of the partners individually, and in such a case the order shall so provide and shall specify the names of the partners affected by the order.

(3)   Nothing in [section 113 of the Equality Act 2010 (proceedings)] or Article 62 of the Sex Discrimination (Northern Ireland) Order 1976 [or Article 51 of the Race Relations (Northern Ireland) Order 1997] (restriction of sanctions for breaches of   . . .   [those Orders]) shall be construed as applying to the making of an order by the [lead enforcement authority] under section 3 above.

(4)   . . .

(5)   In any case where—

(a)   an order of the [lead enforcement authority] under section 3 above specifies as grounds for the order the fact that the person concerned committed discrimination by reason of the existence of any such finding or notice as is referred to in paragraph 2 of Schedule 1 to this Act, and

(b)   the period expires at the end of which, by virtue of paragraph 3 of that Schedule, the person concerned would no longer be treated for the purposes of section 3(1)(b) above as having committed discrimination by reason only of that finding or notice,

then, unless the order also specifies other grounds which remain valid, the order shall cease to have effect at the end of that period.

NOTES

Sub-ss (1), (2): words in square brackets substituted by the Public Bodies (Abolition of the National Consumer Council and Transfer of the Office of Fair Trading's Functions in relation to Estate Agents etc) Order 2014, SI 2014/631, art 5(3)(a), Sch 2, Pt 1, para 1(1), (4)(b), for transitional provisions and savings see art 5(3)(a), Sch 2, Pt 4 thereof at **[2.1133]**, **[2.1134A]**.

Sub-s (3): words in first pair of square brackets substituted and words omitted repealed by the Equality Act 2010, s 211, Sch 26, Pt 1, paras 4, 5, Sch 27, Pt 1 (as amended by the Equality Act 2010 (Consequential Amendments, Saving and Supplementary Provisions) Order 2010, SI 2010/2279, arts 2, 12, 13, Sch 1, para 2, Sch 2); words in second pair of square brackets inserted, and words in third pair of square brackets substituted, by the Race Relations (Northern Ireland) Order 1997, SI 1997/869, art 73, Sch 2, para 2(1); words in final pair of square brackets substituted by SI 2014/631, art 5(3)(a), Sch 2, Pt 1, para 1(1), (4)(b), for transitional provisions and savings see note above.

Sub-s (4): repealed by the Consumers, Estate Agents and Redress Act 2007, ss 55(1), (4), 64, Sch 8.

Sub-s (5): words in square brackets substituted by SI 2014/631, art 5(3)(a), Sch 2, Pt 1, para 1(1), (4)(b), for transitional provisions and savings see note above.

[1.791]
6   Revocation and variation of orders under sections 3 and 4

(1)   On an application made to [it] by the person in respect of whom the [lead enforcement authority] has made an order under section 3 or section 4 above, the [lead enforcement authority] may revoke or vary the order.

(2)   An application under subsection (1) above—

(a)   shall state the reasons why the applicant considers that the order should be revoked or varied;

(b)   in the case of an application for a variation, shall indicate the variation which the applicant seeks; and

(c)   shall be accompanied by the prescribed fee.

(3)   If the [lead enforcement authority] decides to accede to an application under subsection (1) above, [it] shall give notice in writing of [its] decision to the applicant and, upon the giving of that notice, the revocation or, as the case may be, the variation specified in the application shall take effect.

(4)   The [lead enforcement authority] may decide to refuse an application under subsection (1) above—

(a)   where it relates to an order under section 3 above, if [it] considers that the applicant remains unfit to carry on any estate agency work at all or, as the case may be, estate agency work of the description which is prohibited by the order; and

(b)   where it relates to an order under section 4 above, if [it] considers that the applicant may [engage in further conduct as mentioned in subsection (1A)(b) or (1B)(b) of that section or engage again in the practice specified in the order, as the case may be].

(5)   If, on an application under subsection (1) above, the [lead enforcement authority] decides that—

(a)   [it] cannot accede to the application because [it] considers that the applicant remains unfit to carry on any estate agency work at all in a particular part of or area within the United Kingdom or remains unfit to carry on estate agency work of a particular description (either throughout the United Kingdom or in a particular part of or area within it), or, as the case may be, remains likely to fail to comply with a relevant statutory obligation or to engage in a particular practice, but

(b)   the order to which the application relates could, without detriment to the public, be varied in favour of the applicant,

the [lead enforcement authority] may make such a variation accordingly.

(6) The provisions of Part II of Schedule 2 to this Act shall have effect in relation to any application to the [lead enforcement authority] under subsection (1) above and the provisions of Part I of that Schedule shall have effect—

    (a)   with respect to the procedure to be followed before the [lead enforcement authority] comes to a decision under subsection (4) or subsection (5) above; and

    (b)   in connection with the making and coming into operation of such a decision.

(7)   . . .

NOTES

Sub-s (1): word in first pair of square brackets substituted by the Enterprise Act 2002, s 278(1), Sch 25, para 9(1), (5); words in second and final pairs of square brackets substituted by the Public Bodies (Abolition of the National Consumer Council and Transfer of the Office of Fair Trading's Functions in relation to Estate Agents etc) Order 2014, SI 2014/631, art 5(3)(a), Sch 2, Pt 1, para 1(1), (4)(c), for transitional provisions and savings see art 5(3)(a), Sch 2, Pt 4 thereof at **[2.1133]**, **[2.1134A]**.

Sub-ss (3), (5): words in first pair of square brackets substituted by SI 2014/631, art 5(3)(a), Sch 2, Pt 1, para 1(1), (4)(c), for transitional provisions and savings see note above; words in second and final pairs of square brackets substituted by the Enterprise Act 2002, s 278(1), Sch 25, para 9(1), (5).

Sub-s (4): words in first pair of square brackets substituted by SI 2014/631, art 5(3)(a), Sch 2, Pt 1, para 1(1), (4)(c), for transitional provisions and savings see note above; words in second and third pairs of square brackets substituted by the Enterprise Act 2002, s 278(1), Sch 25, para 9(1), (5); words in final pair of square brackets substituted by the Consumers, Estate Agents and Redress Act 2007, s 63(1), Sch 7, para 2(a).

Sub-s (6): words in square brackets substituted by SI 2014/631, art 5(3)(a), Sch 2, Pt 1, para 1(1), (4)(c), for transitional provisions and savings see note above.

Sub-s (7): repealed by the Consumers, Estate Agents and Redress Act 2007, ss 63(1), 64, Sch 7, para 2(b), Sch 8.

Regulations: the Estate Agents (Fees) Regulations 1982, SI 1982/637.

[1.792]
7 Appeals

(1)   A person who receives notice under paragraph 9 of Schedule 2 to this Act of—

    (a)   a decision of the [lead enforcement authority] to make an order in respect of him under section 3 or section 4 above, or

    (b)   a decision of the [lead enforcement authority] under subsection (4) or subsection (5) of section 6 above on an application made by him,

may appeal against the decision to the [First-tier Tribunal].

(2)   On an appeal under subsection (1) above the [First-tier Tribunal] may give such directions for disposing of the appeal as [it] thinks just . . .

(3)–(6)   . . .

NOTES

Sub-s (1): words in first and second pairs of square brackets substituted by the Public Bodies (Abolition of the National Consumer Council and Transfer of the Office of Fair Trading's Functions in relation to Estate Agents etc) Order 2014, SI 2014/631, art 5(3)(a), Sch 2, Pt 1, para 1(1), (4)(d), for transitional provisions and savings see art 5(3)(a), Sch 2, Pt 4 thereof at **[2.1133]**, **[2.1134A]**; words in final pair of square brackets substituted by the Transfer of Functions (Estate Agents Appeals and Additional Scheduled Tribunal) Order 2009, SI 2009/1836, art 5(1), Sch 1, paras 2, 3(a).

Sub-s (2): words in square brackets substituted and words omitted repealed by SI 2009/1836, art 5(1), Sch 1, paras 2, 3(b).

Sub-ss (3)–(6): repealed by SI 2009/1836, art 5(1), Sch 1, paras 2, 3(c).

[1.793]
8 Register of orders etc

(1)   The [lead enforcement authority] shall establish and maintain a register on which there shall be entered particulars of every order made by [it] under section 3 or section 4 above and of [its] decision on any application for revocation or variation of such an order.

(2)   The particulars referred to in subsection (1) above shall include—

    (a)   the terms of the order and of any variation of it; and

    (b)   the date on which the order or variation came into operation or is expected to come into operation or if an appeal against the decision is pending and the order or variation has in consequence not come into operation, a statement to that effect.

(3)   The [lead enforcement authority] may, of [its] own motion or on the application of any person aggrieved, rectify the register by the addition, variation or removal of any particulars; and the provisions of Part II of Schedule 2 to this Act shall have effect in relation to an application under this subsection.

(4)   If it comes to the attention of the [lead enforcement authority] that any order of which particulars appear in the register is no longer in operation, [it] shall remove those particulars from the register.

(5)   Any person shall be entitled on payment of the prescribed fee—

    (a)   to inspect the register during such office hours as may be specified by a general notice made by the [lead enforcement authority] and to take copies of any entry, or

    (b)   to obtain from the [lead enforcement authority] a copy, certified by [it] to be correct, of any entry in the register.

(6)   A certificate given by the [lead enforcement authority] under subsection (5)(b) above shall be conclusive evidence of the fact that, on the date on which the certificate was given, the particulars contained in the copy to which the certificate relates were entered on the register; and particulars of any matters required to be entered on the register which are so entered shall be evidence and, in Scotland, sufficient evidence of those matters and shall be presumed, unless the contrary is proved, to be correct.

NOTES

Sub-s (1): words in first pair of square brackets substituted by the Public Bodies (Abolition of the National Consumer Council and Transfer of the Office of Fair Trading's Functions in relation to Estate Agents etc) Order 2014, SI 2014/631, art 5(3)(a), Sch 2, Pt 1, para 1(1), (4)(e), for transitional provisions and savings see art 5(3)(a), Sch 2, Pt 4 thereof at **[2.1133]**, **[2.1134A]**; words in second and final pairs of square brackets substituted by the Enterprise Act 2002, s 278(1), Sch 25, para 9(1), (7).

Sub-ss (3), (4): words in first pair of square brackets substituted by SI 2014/631, art 5(3)(a), Sch 2, Pt 1, para 1(1), (4)(e), for transitional provisions and savings see note above; words in second pair of square brackets substituted by the Enterprise Act 2002, s 278(1), Sch 25, para 9(1), (7).

Sub-s (5): words in first and second pairs of square brackets substituted by SI 2014/631, art 5(3)(a), Sch 2, Pt 1, para 1(1), (4)(e), for transitional provisions and savings see note above; word in final pair of square brackets substituted by the Enterprise Act 2002, s 278(1), Sch 25, para 9(1), (7).

Sub-s (6): words in square brackets substituted by SI 2014/631, art 5(3)(a), Sch 2, Pt 1, para 1(1), (4)(e), for transitional provisions and savings see note above.

Regulations: the Estate Agents (Fees) Regulations 1982, SI 1982/637.

Information, entry and inspection

[1.794]
9   Information for the [lead enforcement authority]
(1)   The [lead enforcement authority] may, for the purpose of assisting [it]—
    (a)   to determine whether to make an order under section 3 or section 4 above, and
    (b)   in the exercise of any of [its] functions under sections 5, 6 and 8 above and 13 and 17 below,
by notice require any person to furnish to [it] such information as may be specified or described in the notice or to produce to [it] any documents so specified or described.
(2)   A notice under this section—
    (a)   may specify the way in which and the time within which it is to be complied with and, in the case of a notice requiring the production of documents, the facilities to be afforded for making extracts, or taking copies of, the documents; and
    (b)   may be varied or revoked by a subsequent notice.
(3)   Nothing in this section shall be taken to require a person who has acted as counsel or solicitor for any person to disclose any privileged communication made by or to him in that capacity.
(4)   A person who—
    (a)   . . .
    (b)   in furnishing any information in compliance with [a notice under this section], makes any statement which he knows to be false in a material particular or recklessly makes any statement which is false in a material particular, or
    (c)   with intent to deceive, produces in compliance with such a notice a document which is false in a material particular,
shall be liable on conviction on indictment or on summary conviction to a fine which, on summary conviction, shall not exceed the statutory maximum.
(5)   . . .
(6)   It shall be the duty of—
    [(a)   the Commission for Equality and Human Rights, and]
    (b)   the Equal Opportunities Commission for Northern Ireland   . . .
    (c)   . . .
to furnish to the [lead enforcement authority] such information relating to any finding, notice, injunction or order falling within paragraph 2 of Schedule 1 to this Act as is in their possession and appears to them to be relevant to the functions of the [lead enforcement authority] under this Act.

NOTES

Section heading: words in square brackets substituted by the Public Bodies (Abolition of the National Consumer Council and Transfer of the Office of Fair Trading's Functions in relation to Estate Agents etc) Order 2014, SI 2014/631, art 5(3)(a), Sch 2, Pt 1, para 1(1), (4)(f), for transitional provisions and savings see art 5(3)(a), Sch 2, Pt 4 thereof at **[2.1133]**, **[2.1134A]**.

Sub-ss (1)–(4): repealed by the Consumer Rights Act 2015, s 77(2), Sch 6, paras 19, 21, as from 1 October 2015 (for transitional provisions see the Consumer Rights Act 2015 (Commencement No 3, Transitional Provisions, Savings and Consequential Amendments) Order 2015, SI 2015/1630, arts 6–8 at **[2.1220]** et seq).

Sub-s (1): words in first pair of square brackets substituted by SI 2014/631, art 5(3)(a), Sch 2, Pt 1, para 1(1), (4)(g), for transitional provisions and savings see note above; words in second, third, fourth and final pairs of square brackets substituted by the Enterprise Act 2002, s 278(1), Sch 25, para 9(1), (8).

Sub-s (4): para (a) repealed and words in square brackets in para (b) substituted by the Consumers, Estate Agents and Redress Act 2007, ss 58(1), (3), 64, Sch 8.

Sub-s (5): repealed by the Enterprise Act 2002, s 278(2), Sch 26.

Sub-s (6): para (a) substituted, and para (c) and word omitted immediately preceding it repealed, by the Equality Act 2006, ss 40, 91, Sch 3, paras 36, 37, Sch 4; words in second and final pairs of square brackets substituted by SI 2014/631, art 5(3)(a), Sch 2, Pt 1, para 1(1), (4)(g), for transitional provisions and savings see note above.

[1.795]

[9A   Notice of convictions and judgments
(1)   This section applies if—
   (a)   a person is convicted of an offence by or before a court in the United Kingdom, or
   (b)   a judgment is given against a person by a court in civil proceedings in the United Kingdom.
(2)   The court may make arrangements to bring the conviction or judgment to the attention of the lead enforcement authority if it appears to the court that—
   (a)   having regard to the functions of the lead enforcement authority under this Act it is expedient for the conviction or judgment to be brought to the attention of the lead enforcement authority, and
   (b)   without such arrangements the conviction or judgment may not be brought to the attention of the lead enforcement authority.]

NOTES
Commencement: 31 March 2014.
Inserted by the Public Bodies (Abolition of the National Consumer Council and Transfer of the Office of Fair Trading's Functions in relation to Estate Agents etc) Order 2014, SI 2014/631, art 5(3)(a), Sch 2, Pt 1, para 1(1), (5), for transitional provisions and savings see art 5(3)(a), Sch 2, Pt 4 thereof at **[2.1133]**, **[2.1134A]**.

10   (*Repealed by the Enterprise Act 2002, ss 247(e), 278(2), Sch 26; see further, in so far as this section remains in force, the Railways and Transport Safety Act 2003, s 16(5), Sch 2, Pt 2, para 19(e).*)

[1.796]

11   Powers of entry and inspection
[(1)   If a duly authorised officer of an enforcement authority ("an officer") has reasonable cause to suspect—
   (a)   that an offence has been committed under this Act;
   (b)   that a person has failed to comply with an obligation imposed on him under any of sections 15 and 18 to 21A; or
   (c)   that a person has engaged in a practice mentioned in section 3(1)(d);
he may, in order to ascertain whether the offence has been committed, whether the person has failed to comply with the obligation or whether the person has engaged in the practice (as the case may be), exercise any power specified in subsection (1A).
(1A)   The powers are—
   (a)   to enter any premises (other than premises used only as a dwelling);
   (b)   to require—
      (i)   any person carrying on, or employed in connection with, a business to produce any books or document relating to it, or
      (ii)   any person having control of any information relating to a business which is stored in any electronic form to produce the information in a form in which it can be taken away and in which it is visible and legible (or from which it can readily be produced in a visible and legible form);
   (c)   to take copies of, or of any entry in, any books or documents produced or provided in pursuance of a requirement imposed under paragraph (b).
(1B)   An officer may seize and detain any books or documents which he has reason to believe may be required as evidence—
   (a)   in proceedings for an offence under this Act; or
   (b)   in proceedings under any of sections 3, 4, 6 or 7 relating to an allegation—
      (i)   that an offence has been committed under this Act;
      (ii)   that a person has failed to comply with an obligation imposed on him under any of sections 15 and 18 to 21A; or
      (iii)   that a person has engaged in a practice mentioned in section 3(1)(d).
(1C)   If it is not reasonably practicable to exercise any power under subsection (1A)(c) to take a copy of, or of any entry in, a book or document, an officer may seize and detain the book or document for the purpose of inspecting it (or any entry in it).
(1D)   A book or document which is seized in exercise of the power under subsection (1C) must be returned to the person from whom it was seized unless an officer has reason to believe that the book or document may be required as evidence in any proceedings mentioned in subsection (1B).
(1E)   Any power conferred by subsection (1) to (1C) may be exercised at all reasonable hours.
(1F)   An officer exercising any such power must, if required, produce his credentials.]
(2)   An officer seizing books or documents in exercise of his powers under this section shall not do so without informing the person from whom he seizes them.

(3)   If and so long as any books or documents which have been seized under this section are not required as evidence in connection with proceedings which have been begun for an offence under this Act, the enforcement authority by whose officer they were seized shall afford to the person to whom the books or documents belong and to any person authorised by him in writing reasonable facilities to inspect them and to take copies of or make extracts from them.

[(4)   An appropriate judicial officer may, by warrant under his hand, authorise an officer of an enforcement authority to enter any premises, by force if need be, if on sworn information in writing or, in Scotland, on evidence on oath the appropriate judicial officer—

    (a)   is satisfied that there is reasonable ground to believe that either of the conditions in subsection (4A) applies; and

    (b)   is also satisfied that at least one of the conditions in subsection (4B) applies.

(4A)   The conditions in this subsection are—

    (a)   that any books or documents which a duly authorised officer has power to inspect under this section are on the premises and their inspection is likely to disclose evidence—

        (i)   that an offence has been committed under this Act;

        (ii)   that a person has failed to comply with an obligation imposed on him under any of sections 15 and 18 to 21A; or

        (iii)   that a person has engaged in a practice mentioned in section 3(1)(d);

    (b)   that an offence under this Act has been, is being or is about to be committed on the premises.

(4B)   The conditions in this subsection are—

    (a)   that admission to the premises has been or is likely to be refused and that notice of intention to apply for a warrant under subsection (4) has been given to the occupier;

    (b)   that an application for admission, or the giving of such a notice of intention, would defeat the object of the entry;

    (c)   that the premises are unoccupied;

    (d)   that the occupier is temporarily absent and it might defeat the object of the entry to wait for his return.

(4C)   A warrant issued under subsection (4) shall continue in force for a period of one month.

(4D)   In subsection (4) "appropriate judicial officer" means—

    (a)   in England and Wales, a justice of the peace;

    (b)   in Scotland, the sheriff or a justice of the peace;

    (c)   in Northern Ireland, a lay magistrate.]

(5)   An officer entering premises by virtue of this section may take such other persons and equipment with him as he thinks necessary, and on leaving premises entered by virtue of a warrant under subsection (4) above shall, if the premises are unoccupied or the occupier is temporarily absent, leave them as effectively secured against trespassers as he found them.

(6), (7)   . . .

(8)   Nothing in this section shall be taken to require a person who has acted as [a relevant lawyer] for any person to produce a document containing a privileged communication made by or to him in that capacity or authorises the seizing of any such document in his possession.

[(9)   For the purposes of subsection (8) "relevant lawyer" means counsel, a solicitor or other legal representative communications with whom may be the subject of a claim to privilege.]

NOTES

Repealed by the Consumer Rights Act 2015, s 77(2), Sch 6, paras 19, 22, as from 1 October 2015 (for transitional provisions see the Consumer Rights Act 2015 (Commencement No 3, Transitional Provisions, Savings and Consequential Amendments) Order 2015, SI 2015/1630, arts 6–8 at **[2.1220]** et seq).

Sub-ss (1), (1A)–(1F): substituted for original sub-s (1) by the Consumers, Estate Agents and Redress Act 2007, s 57(1), (2).

Sub-ss (4), (4A)–(4D): substituted for original sub-s (4) by the Consumers, Estate Agents and Redress Act 2007, s 57(1), (3).

Sub-ss (6), (7): repealed by the Public Bodies (Abolition of the National Consumer Council and Transfer of the Office of Fair Trading's Functions in relation to Estate Agents etc) Order 2014, SI 2014/631, art 5(3)(a), Sch 2, Pt 1, para 1(1), (6), for transitional provisions and savings see art 5(3)(a), Sch 2, Pt 4 thereof at **[2.1133]**, **[2.1134A]**.

Sub-s (8): words in square brackets substituted by the Legal Services Act 2007, s 208(1), Sch 21, para 41(a).

Sub-s (9): added by the Legal Services Act 2007, s 208(1), Sch 21, para 41(b).

Seize and detain books or documents, etc: the powers of seizure conferred by sub-s (1B) are powers to which the Criminal Justice and Police Act 2001, s 50 apply (additional powers of seizure from premises); see s 50 of, and Sch 1, Pt 1, para 24 to, that Act.

Regulations: the Estate Agents (Entry and Inspection) Regulations 1981, SI 1981/1519.

[1.797]

[11A   Failure to produce information

(1)   If on an application made by a duly authorised officer of an enforcement authority it appears to the court that a person ("the defaulter") has failed to do something that he is required to do by virtue of section 9(1) or 11(1A)(b) the court may make an order under this section.

(2)   An order under this section may require the defaulter—

    (a)   to do the thing that it appears he failed to do within such period as may be specified in the order;

    (b)   otherwise to take such steps to remedy the consequences of the failure as may be so specified.

(3)   If the defaulter is a body corporate, a partnership or an unincorporated association, the order may require any officer who is (wholly or partly) responsible for the failure to meet such costs of the application as are specified in the order.

(4)   In this section—

"court" means—

[(za)   in England and Wales, the High Court or the county court;]

(a)   in . . . Northern Ireland, the High Court or a county court;

(b)   in Scotland, the Court of Session or the sheriff;

"officer" means—

(a)   in relation to a body corporate, a person holding a position of director, manager or secretary of the body or any similar position;

(b)   in relation to a partnership or an unincorporated association, a member of the partnership or association.

(5)   In subsection (4) "director" means, in relation to a body corporate whose affairs are managed by its members, a member of the body.]

NOTES

Inserted by the Consumers, Estate Agents and Redress Act 2007, s 58(1).

Repealed by the Consumer Rights Act 2015, s 77(2), Sch 6, paras 19, 23, as from 1 October 2015 (for transitional provisions see the Consumer Rights Act 2015 (Commencement No 3, Transitional Provisions, Savings and Consequential Amendments) Order 2015, SI 2015/1630, arts 6–8 at **[2.1220]** et seq).

Sub-s (4): in definition "court" para (za) inserted, and words omitted from para (a) repealed, by the Crime and Courts Act 2013, s 17(5), Sch 9, Pt 3, para 82(a), for transitional provision see the Crime and Courts Act 2013 (Commencement No 10 and Transitional Provision) Order 2014, SI 2014/954, art 3.

Clients' money and accounts

[1.798]
12   Meaning of "clients' money" etc

(1)   In this Act "clients' money", in relation to a person engaged in estate agency work, means any money received by him in the course of that work which is a contract or pre-contract deposit—

(a)   in respect of the acquisition of an interest in land in the United Kingdom, or

(b)   in respect of a connected contract,

whether that money is held or received by him as agent, bailee, stakeholder or in any other capacity.

(2)   In this Act "contract deposit" means any sum paid by a purchaser—

(a)   which in whole or in part is, or is intended to form part of, the consideration for acquiring such an interest as is referred to in subsection (1)(a) above or for a connected contract; and

(b)   which is paid by him at or after the time at which he acquires the interest or enters into an enforceable contract to acquire it.

(3)   In this Act "pre-contract deposit" means any sum paid by any person—

(a)   in whole or in part as an earnest of his intention to acquire such an interest as is referred to in subsection (1)(a) above, or

(b)   in whole or in part towards meeting any liability of his in respect of the consideration for the acquisition of such an interest which will arise if he acquires or enters into an enforceable contract to acquire the interest, or

(c)   in respect of a connected contract,

and which is paid by him at a time before he either acquires the interest or enters into an enforceable contract to acquire it.

(4)   In this Act "connected contract", in relation to the acquisition of an interest in land, means a contract which is conditional upon such an acquisition or upon entering into an enforceable contract for such an acquisition (whether or not it is also conditional on other matters).

[1.799]
13   Clients' money held on trust or as agent

(1)   It is hereby declared that clients' money received by any person in the course of estate agency work in England, Wales or Northern Ireland—

(a)   is held by him on trust for the person who is entitled to call for it to be paid over to him or to be paid on his direction or to have it otherwise credited to him, or

(b)   if it is received by him as stakeholder, is held by him on trust for the person who may become so entitled on the occurrence of the event against which the money is held.

(2)   (Applies to Scotland only.)

(3)   The provisions of sections 14 and 15 below as to the investment of clients' money, the keeping of accounts and records and accounting for interest shall have effect in place of the corresponding duties which would be owed by a person holding clients' money as trustee, or in Scotland as agent, under the general law.

(4)   Where an order of the [lead enforcement authority] under section 3 above has the effect of prohibiting a person from holding clients' money the order may contain provision—

(a)   appointing another person as trustee, or in Scotland as agent, in place of the person to whom the order relates to hold and deal with clients' money held by that person when the order comes into effect; and

(b)   requiring the expenses and such reasonable remuneration of the new trustee or agent as may be specified in the order to be paid by the person to whom the order relates or, if the order so provides, out of the clients' money;

but nothing in this subsection shall affect the power conferred by section 41 of the Trustee Act 1925 or section 40 of the Trustee Act (Northern Ireland) 1958 to appoint a new trustee to hold clients' money.

(5)   For the avoidance of doubt it is hereby declared that the fact that any person has or may have a lien on clients' money held by him does not affect the operation of this section and also that nothing in this section shall prevent such a lien from being given effect.

NOTES

Sub-s (4): words in square brackets substituted by the Public Bodies (Abolition of the National Consumer Council and Transfer of the Office of Fair Trading's Functions in relation to Estate Agents etc) Order 2014, SI 2014/631, art 5(3)(a), Sch 2, Pt 1, para 1(1), (7)(a), for transitional provisions and savings see art 5(3)(a), Sch 2, Pt 4 thereof at **[2.1133]**, **[2.1134A]**.

[1.800]
14   Keeping of client accounts

(1)   Subject to such provision as may be made by accounts regulations, every person who receives clients' money in the course of estate agency work shall, without delay, pay the money into a client account maintained by him or by a person in whose employment he is.

(2)   In this Act a "client account" means a current or deposit account which—

  (a)   is with an institution authorised for the purposes of this section, and

  (b)   is in the name of a person who is or has been engaged in estate agency work; and

  (c)   contains in its title the word "client".

(3)   The Secretary of State may make provision by regulations (in this section referred to as "accounts regulations") as to the opening and keeping of client accounts, the keeping of accounts and records relating to clients' money and the auditing of those accounts; and such regulations shall be made by statutory instrument which shall be subject to annulment in pursuance of a resolution of either House of Parliament.

(4)   As to the opening and keeping of client accounts, accounts regulations may in particular specify—

  (a)   the institutions which are authorised for the purposes of this section;

  (b)   any persons or classes of persons to whom, or any circumstances in which, the obligation imposed by subsection (1) above does not apply;

  (c)   any circumstances in which money other than clients' money may be paid into a client account; and

  (d)   the occasions on which, and the persons to whom, money held in a client account may be paid out.

(5)   As to the auditing of accounts relating to clients' money, accounts regulations may in particular make provision—

  (a)   requiring such accounts to be drawn up in respect of specified accounting periods and to be audited by a qualified auditor within a specified time after the end of each such period;

  (b)   requiring the auditor to report whether in his opinion the requirements of this Act and of the accounts regulations have been complied with or have been substantially complied with;

  (c)   as to the matters to which such a report is to relate and the circumstances in which a report of substantial compliance may be given; and

  (d)   requiring a person who maintains a client account to produce on demand to a duly authorised officer of an enforcement authority the latest auditor's report.

[(6)   Subject to subsection (7) below, "qualified auditor" in subsection (5)(a) above means a person who is [eligible for appointment as a statutory auditor under Part 42 of the Companies Act 2006].

(7)   A person is not a qualified auditor for the purposes of subsection (5)(a) above if, in the case of a client account maintained by a company, he is [prohibited from acting as statutory auditor of the company by virtue of section 1214 of the Companies Act 2006 (independence requirement)].]

(8)   A person who—

  (a)   contravenes any provision of this Act or of accounts regulations as to the manner in which clients' money is to be dealt with or accounts and records relating to such money are to be kept, or

  (b)   fails to produce an auditor's report when required to do so by accounts regulations,

shall be liable on summary conviction to a fine not exceeding [level 4 on the standard scale].

NOTES

Sub-s (6): substituted, together with sub-s (7), by the Companies Act 1989 (Eligibility for Appointment as Company Auditor) (Consequential Amendments) Regulations 1991, SI 1991/1997, reg 2, Schedule, para 33; words in square brackets substituted by the Companies Act 2006 (Consequential Amendments etc) Order 2008, SI 2008/948, art 3(1)(a), 6, Sch 1, Pt 1, para 8(1), (2).

Sub-s (7): substituted as noted to sub-s (6); words in square brackets substituted by SI 2008/948, art 3(1)(a), 6, Sch 1, Pt 1, para 8(1), (3).

Sub-s (8): reference to a level on the standard scale substituted by virtue of the Criminal Justice Act 1982, ss 38, 46.

[1.801]
15 Interest on clients' money

(1)   Accounts regulations may make provision for requiring a person who has received any clients' money to account, in such cases as may be prescribed by the regulations, to the person who is or becomes entitled to the money for the interest which was, or could have been, earned by putting the money in a separate deposit account at an institution authorised for the purposes of section 14 above.

(2)   The cases in which a person may be required by accounts regulations to account for interest as mentioned in subsection (1) above may be defined, amongst other things, by reference to the amount of the sum held or received by him or the period for which it is likely to be retained, or both.

(3)   Except as provided by accounts regulations and subject to subsection (4) below, a person who maintains a client account in which he keeps clients' money generally shall not be liable to account to any person for interest received by him on money in that account.

(4)   Nothing in this section or in accounts regulations shall affect any arrangement in writing, whenever made, between a person engaged in estate agency work and any other person as to the application of, or of any interest on, money in which that other person has or may have an interest.

(5)   Failure of any person to comply with any provision of accounts regulations made by virtue of this section may be taken into account by the [lead enforcement authority] in accordance with section 3(1)(c) above and may form the basis of a civil claim for interest which was or should have been earned on clients' money but shall not render that person liable to any criminal penalty.

(6)   In this section "accounts regulations" has the same meaning as in section 14 above.

NOTES

Sub-s (5): words in square brackets substituted by the Public Bodies (Abolition of the National Consumer Council and Transfer of the Office of Fair Trading's Functions in relation to Estate Agents etc) Order 2014, SI 2014/631, art 5(3)(a), Sch 2, Pt 1, para 1(1), (7)(b), for transitional provisions and savings see art 5(3)(a), Sch 2, Pt 4 thereof at **[2.1133]**, **[2.1134A]**.

[1.802]
16 Insurance cover for clients' money

(1)   Subject to the provisions of this section, a person may not accept clients' money in the course of estate agency work unless there are in force authorised arrangements under which, in the event of his failing to account for such money to the person entitled to it, his liability will be made good by another.

(2)   The Secretary of State may by regulations made by statutory instrument, which shall be subject to annulment in pursuance of a resolution of either House of Parliament—

    (a)   specify any persons or classes of persons to whom subsection (1) above does not apply;

    (b)   specify arrangements which are authorised for the purposes of this section including arrangements to which an enforcement authority nominated for the purpose by the Secretary of State or any other person so nominated is a party;

    (c)   specify the terms and conditions upon which any payment is to be made under such arrangements and any circumstances in which the right to any such payment may be excluded or modified;

    (d)   provide that any limit on the amount of any such payment is to be not less than a specified amount;

    (e)   require a person providing authorised arrangements covering any person carrying on estate agency work to issue a certificate in a form specified in the regulations certifying that arrangements complying with the regulations have been made with respect to that person; and

    (f)   prescribe any matter required to be prescribed for the purposes of subsection (4) below.

(3)   Every guarantee entered into by a person (in this subsection referred to as "the insurer") who provides authorised arrangements covering another person (in this subsection referred to as "the agent") carrying on estate agency work shall enure for the benefit of every person from whom the agent has received clients' money as if—

    (a)   the guarantee were contained in a contract made by the insurer with every such person; and

    (b)   except in Scotland, that contract were under seal; and

    (c)   where the guarantee is given by two or more insurers, they had bound themselves jointly and severally.

(4)   No person who carries on estate agency work may describe himself as an "estate agent" or so use any name or in any way hold himself out as to indicate or reasonably be understood to indicate that he is carrying on a business in the course of which he is prepared to act as a broker in the acquisition or disposal of interests in land unless, in such manner as may be prescribed,—

    (a)   there is displayed at his place of business, and

    (b)   there is included in any relevant document issued or displayed in connection with his business,

any prescribed information relating to arrangements authorised for the purposes of this section.

(5)   For the purposes of subsection (4) above—

    (a)   any business premises at which a person carries on estate agency work and to which the public has access is a place of business of his; and

(b)   "relevant document" means any advertisement, notice or other written material which might reasonably induce any person to use the services of another in connection with the acquisition or disposal of an interest in land.

(6)   A person who fails to comply with any provision of subsection (1) or subsection (4) above or of regulations under subsection (2) above which is binding on him shall be liable on conviction on indictment or on summary conviction to a fine which, on summary conviction, shall not exceed the statutory maximum.

NOTES

Commencement: to be appointed.

[1.803]

17   Exemptions from section 16

(1)   If, on an application made to [it] in that behalf, the [lead enforcement authority] considers that a person engaged in estate agency work may, without loss of adequate protection to consumers, be exempted from all or any of the provisions of subsection (1) of section 16 above or of regulations under subsection (2) of that section, [it] may issue to that person a certificate of exemption under this section.

(2)   An application under subsection (1) above—

   (a)   shall state the reasons why the applicant considers that he should be granted a certificate of exemption; and

   (b)   shall be accompanied by the prescribed fee.

(3)   A certificate of exemption under this section—

   (a)   may impose conditions of exemption on the person to whom it is issued;

   (b)   may be issued to have effect for a period specified in the certificate or without limit of time.

(4)   If and so long as—

   (a)   a certificate of exemption has effect, and

   (b)   the person to whom it is issued complies with any conditions of exemption specified in the certificate,

that person shall be exempt, to the extent so specified, from the provisions of subsection (1) of section 16 above and of any regulations made under subsection (2) of that section.

(5)   If the [lead enforcement authority] decides to refuse an application under subsection (1) above [it] shall give the applicant notice of [its] decision and of the reasons for it, including any facts which in [its] opinion justify the decision.

(6)   If a person who made an application under subsection (1) above is aggrieved by a decision of the [lead enforcement authority]—

   (a)   to refuse his application, or

   (b)   to grant him a certificate of exemption subject to conditions,

he may appeal against the decision to the Secretary of State; and subsections (2) to (6) of section 7 above shall apply to such an appeal as they apply to an appeal under that section.

(7)   A person who fails to comply with any condition of exemption specified in a current certificate of exemption issued to him shall be liable on conviction on indictment or on summary conviction to a fine which, on summary conviction, shall not exceed the statutory maximum.

NOTES

Commencement: to be appointed.

Sub-s (1): words in first and final pairs of square brackets substituted by the Enterprise Act 2002, s 278(1), Sch 25, para 9(1), (10); words in second pair of square brackets substituted by the Public Bodies (Abolition of the National Consumer Council and Transfer of the Office of Fair Trading's Functions in relation to Estate Agents etc) Order 2014, SI 2014/631, art 5(3)(a), Sch 2, Pt 1, para 1(1), (7)(c), for transitional provisions and savings see art 5(3)(a), Sch 2, Pt 4 thereof at **[2.1133]**, **[2.1134A]**.

Sub-s (5): words in first pair of square brackets substituted by SI 2014/631, art 5(3)(a), Sch 2, Pt 1, para 1(1), (7)(c), for transitional provisions and savings see note above; words in second, third and final pairs of square brackets substituted by the Enterprise Act 2002, s 278(1), Sch 25, para 9(1), (10).

Sub-s (6): words in square brackets substituted by SI 2014/631, art 5(3)(a), Sch 2, Pt 1, para 1(1), (7)(c), for transitional provisions and savings see note above.

Regulation of other aspects of estate agency work

[1.804]

18   Information to clients of prospective liabilities

(1)   Subject to subsection (2) below, before any person (in this section referred to as "the client") enters into a contract with another (in this section referred to as "the agent") under which the agent will engage in estate agency work on behalf of the client, the agent shall give the client—

   (a)   the information specified in subsection (2) below; and

   (b)   any additional information which may be prescribed under subsection (4) below.

(2)   The following is the information to be given under subsection (1)(a) above—

   (a)   particulars of the circumstances in which the client will become liable to pay remuneration to the agent for carrying out estate agency work;

   (b)   particulars of the amount of the agent's remuneration for carrying out estate agency work or, if that amount is not ascertainable at the time the information is given, particulars of the manner in which the remuneration will be calculated;

(c)   particulars of any payments which do not form part of the agent's remuneration for carrying out estate agency work or a contract or pre-contract deposit but which, under the contract referred to in subsection (1) above, will or may in certain circumstances be payable by the client to the agent or any other person and particulars of the circumstances in which any such payments will become payable; and

(d)   particulars of the amount of any payment falling within paragraph (c) above or, if that amount is not ascertainable at the time the information is given, an estimate of that amount together with particulars of the manner in which it will be calculated.

(3)   If, at any time after the client and the agent have entered into such a contract as is referred to in subsection (1) above, the parties are agreed that the terms of the contract should be varied so far as they relate to the carrying out of estate agency work or any payment falling within subsection (2)(c) above, the agent shall give the client details of any changes which, at the time the statement is given, fall to be made in the information which was given to the client under subsection (1) above before the contract was entered into.

(4)   The Secretary of State may by regulations—

(a)   prescribe for the purposes of subsection (1)(b) above additional information relating to any estate agency work to be performed under the contract; and

(b)   make provision with respect to the time and the manner in which the obligation of the agent under subsection (1) or subsection (3) above is to be performed;

and the power to make regulations under this subsection shall be exercisable by statutory instrument which shall be subject to annulment in pursuance of a resolution of either House of Parliament.

(5)   If any person—

(a)   fails to comply with the obligation under subsection (1) above with respect to a contract or with any provision of regulations under subsection (4) above relating to that obligation, or

(b)   fails to comply with the obligation under subsection (3) above with respect to any variation of a contract or with any provision of regulations under subsection (4) above relating to that obligation,

the contract or, as the case may be, the variation of it shall not be enforceable by him except pursuant to an order of the court under subsection (6) below.

(6)   If, in a case where subsection (5) above applies in relation to a contract or a variation of a contract, the agent concerned makes an application to the court for the enforcement of the contract or, as the case may be, of a contract as varied by the variation—

(a)   the court shall dismiss the application if, but only if, it considers it just to do so having regard to prejudice caused to the client by the agent's failure to comply with his obligation and the degree of culpability for the failure; and

(b)   where the court does not dismiss the application, it may nevertheless order that any sum payable by the client under the contract or, as the case may be, under the contract as varied shall be reduced or discharged so as to compensate the client for prejudice suffered as a result of the agent's failure to comply with his obligation.

(7)   In this section—

(a)   references to the enforcement of a contract or variation include the withholding of money in pursuance of a lien for money alleged to be due under the contract or as a result of the variation; and

(b)   "the court" means any court having jurisdiction to hear and determine matters arising out of the contract.

NOTES

Regulations: the Estate Agents (Provision of Information) Regulations 1991, SI 1991/859.

[1.805]
19 Regulation of pre-contract deposits outside Scotland

(1)   No person may, in the course of estate agency work in England, Wales or Northern Ireland, seek from any other person (in this section referred to as a "prospective purchaser") who wishes to acquire an interest in land in the United Kingdom, a payment which, if made, would constitute a pre-contract deposit in excess of the prescribed limit.

(2)   If, in the course of estate agency work, any person receives from a prospective purchaser a pre-contract deposit which exceeds the prescribed limit, so much of that deposit as exceeds the prescribed limit shall forthwith be either repaid to the prospective purchaser or paid to such other person as the prospective purchaser may direct.

(3)   In relation to a prospective purchaser, references in subsections (1) and (2) above to a pre-contract deposit shall be treated as references to the aggregate of all the payments which constitute pre-contract deposits in relation to his proposed acquisition of a particular interest in land in the United Kingdom.

(4)   In this section "the prescribed limit" means such limit as the Secretary of State may by regulations prescribe; and such limit may be so prescribed either as a specific amount or as a percentage or fraction of a price or other amount determined in any particular case in accordance with the regulations.

(5)   The power to make regulations under this section shall be exercisable by statutory instrument which shall be subject to annulment in pursuance of a resolution of either House of Parliament.

Statutes

Part 1

(6) Failure by any person to comply with subsection (1) or subsection (2) above may be taken into account by the [lead enforcement authority] in accordance with section 3(1)(c) above but shall not render that person liable to any criminal penalty nor constitute a ground for any civil claim, other than a claim for the recovery of such an excess as is referred to in subsection (2) above.

(7) This section does not form part of the law of Scotland.

NOTES

Commencement: to be appointed.

Sub-s (6): words in square brackets substituted by the Public Bodies (Abolition of the National Consumer Council and Transfer of the Office of Fair Trading's Functions in relation to Estate Agents etc) Order 2014, SI 2014/631, art 5(3)(a), Sch 2, Pt 1, para 1(1), (7)(d), for transitional provisions and savings see art 5(3)(a), Sch 2, Pt 4 thereof at **[2.1133]**, **[2.1134A]**.

20 (*Applies to Scotland only.*)

[1.806]
21 Transactions in which an estate agent has a personal interest
(1) A person who is engaged in estate agency work (in this section referred to as an "estate agent") and has a personal interest in any land shall not enter into negotiations with any person with respect to the acquisition or disposal by that person of any interest in that land until the estate agent has disclosed to that person the nature and extent of his personal interest in it.

(2) In any case where the result of a proposed disposal of an interest in land or of such a proposed disposal and other transactions would be that an estate agent would have a personal interest in that land, the estate agent shall not enter into negotiations with any person with respect to the proposed disposal until he has disclosed to that person the nature and extent of that personal interest.

(3) Subsections (1) and (2) above apply where an estate agent is negotiating on his own behalf as well as where he is negotiating in the course of estate agency work.

(4) An estate agent may not seek or receive a contract or pre-contract deposit in respect of the acquisition or proposed acquisition of—
   (a) a personal interest of his in land in the United Kingdom; or
   (b) any other interest in any such land in which he has a personal interest.

(5) For the purposes of this section, an estate agent has a personal interest in land if—
   (a) he has a beneficial interest in the land or in the proceeds of sale of any interest in it; or
   (b) he knows or might reasonably be expected to know that any of the following persons has such a beneficial interest, namely,—
      (i) his employer or principal, or
      (ii) any employee or agent of his, or
      (iii) any associate of his or of any person mentioned in sub-paragraphs (i) and (ii) above.

(6) Failure by an estate agent to comply with any of the preceding provisions of this section may be taken into account by the [lead enforcement authority] in accordance with section 3(1)(c) above but shall not render the estate agent liable to any criminal penalty nor constitute a ground for any civil claim.

NOTES

Sub-s (6): words in square brackets substituted by the Public Bodies (Abolition of the National Consumer Council and Transfer of the Office of Fair Trading's Functions in relation to Estate Agents etc) Order 2014, SI 2014/631, art 5(3)(a), Sch 2, Pt 1, para 1(1), (7)(f), for transitional provisions and savings see art 5(3)(a), Sch 2, Pt 4 thereof at **[2.1133]**, **[2.1134A]**.

[1.807]
[21A Duty to keep permanent records
(1) A person engaged in estate agency work shall—
   (a) keep records for the purposes of this section ("the permanent records"); and
   (b) ensure that anything required by subsection (3) to be included in the permanent records is kept for a period of at least six years beginning with the day on which it is included.

(2) In the case of a person engaged in estate agency work in the course of employment the duties under subsection (1) are duties of the employer (and not the employee).

(3) A person engaged in estate agency work shall ensure that a record of any information or event to which this subsection applies is included in the permanent records kept by that person or his employer (as the case may be).

(4) Subsection (3) applies to—
   (a) information the person concerned is required to give by section 18(1) or (3) and any prescribed information relating to the giving of that information;
   (b) information the person concerned is required to disclose by section 21(1) or (2) and any prescribed information relating to the disclosure of that information;
   (c) any offer of a prescribed description received by the person concerned and any prescribed information relating to the making of the offer;
   (d) any action of a prescribed description taken by the person concerned in relation to such an offer and any prescribed information relating to that action; and
   (e) any other information or event of a prescribed description.

(5) If the person concerned is acting in the course of employment, it is also the duty of the employer to ensure that the record of the information or event is included in the permanent records; but the employer is not to be regarded as having breached his duty if he shows that he took such steps as were reasonably practicable to ensure that the duty under subsection (3) was complied with by his employees.

(6) The Secretary of State may by regulations make provision as to—

    (a)   the manner in which the permanent records are to be kept;

    (b)   the place or places at which they are to be kept.

(7) In this section "prescribed" means prescribed by regulations made by the Secretary of State.

(8) Any power to make regulations under this section shall be exercisable by statutory instrument which shall be subject to annulment in pursuance of a resolution of either House of Parliament.]

NOTES

Commencement: to be appointed.

Inserted by the Consumers, Estate Agents and Redress Act 2007, s 54(1), as from a day to be appointed.

[1.808]

22 Standards of competence

(1) The Secretary of State may by regulations made by statutory instrument make provision for ensuring that persons engaged in estate agency work satisfy minimum standards of competence.

(2) If the Secretary of State exercises his power to make regulations under subsection (1) above, he shall in the regulations prescribe a degree of practical experience which is to be taken as evidence of competence and, without prejudice to the generality of subsection (1) above, the regulations may, in addition,—

    (a)   prescribe professional or academic qualifications which shall also be taken to be evidence of competence;

    (b)   designate any body of persons as a body which may itself specify professional qualifications the holding of which is to be taken as evidence of competence;

    (c)   make provision for and in connection with the establishment of a body having power to examine and inquire into the competence of persons engaged or professing to engage in estate agency work; and

    (d)   delegate to a body established as mentioned in paragraph (c) above powers of the Secretary of State with respect of the matters referred to in paragraph (a) above;

and any reference in the following provisions of this section to a person who has attained the required standard of competence is a reference to a person who has that degree of practical experience which, in accordance with the regulations, is to be taken as evidence of competence or, where the regulations so provide, holds such qualifications or otherwise fulfils such conditions as, in accordance with the regulations, are to be taken to be evidence of competence.

(3) After the day appointed for the coming into force of this subsection—

    (a)   no individual may engage in estate agency work on his own account unless he has attained the required standard of competence;

    (b)   no member of a partnership may engage in estate agency work on the partnership's behalf unless such number of the partners as may be prescribed have attained the required standard of competence; and

    (c)   no body corporate or unincorporated association may engage in estate agency work unless such numbers and descriptions of the officers, members or employees as may be prescribed have attained the required standard of competence;

and any person who contravenes this subsection shall be liable on conviction on indictment or on summary conviction to a fine which, on summary conviction, shall not exceed the statutory maximum.

(4) In subsection (3) above "prescribed" means prescribed by the Secretary of State by order made by statutory instrument, which shall be subject to annulment in pursuance of a resolution of either House of Parliament.

(5) No regulations shall be made under this section unless a draft of them has been laid before Parliament and approved by a resolution of each House.

NOTES

Commencement: to be appointed.

[1.809]

23 Bankrupts not to engage in estate agency work

(1) An individual who is adjudged bankrupt after the day appointed for the coming into force of this section or, in Scotland, whose estate is sequestrated after that day shall not engage in estate agency work of any description except as an employee of another person.

[(1A) An individual in respect of whom a debt relief order (under Part 7A of the Insolvency Act 1986) is made shall not engage in estate agency work of any description except as an employee of another person.]

(2) The prohibition imposed on an individual by subsection (1) above shall cease to have effect if and when—

(a)   the adjudication of bankruptcy against him is annulled, or, in Scotland, the sequestration of his estate is recalled [or reduced]; or

[(b)   he is discharged from bankruptcy.]

[(2A)   The prohibition imposed on an individual by subsection (1A) shall cease to have effect if and when—

(a)   the debt relief order is revoked for reasons falling within section 251(L)(2)(a) or (c) of the Insolvency Act 1986;

(b)   the individual is discharged from all the qualifying debts specified under the debt relief order at the end of the moratorium period applicable to the order; or

(c)   the debt relief order is revoked and a period of one year has elapsed beginning with the effective date for the order.]

(3)   [The references in this section] to employment of an individual by another person does not include employment of him by a body corporate of which he is a director or controller.

(4)   If a person engages in estate agency work in contravention [of this section] he shall be liable on conviction on indictment or on summary conviction to a fine which on summary conviction shall not exceed the statutory maximum.

NOTES

Sub-ss (1A), (2A): inserted by the Tribunals, Courts and Enforcement Act 2007 (Consequential Amendments) Order 2012, SI 2012/2404, art 3(2), Sch 2, para 10(1)–(3).

Sub-s (2): words in square brackets in para (a) inserted by the Bankruptcy (Scotland) Act 1985, s 75, Sch 7, para 17; para (b) substituted by the Insolvency Act 1985, s 235, Sch 8, para 33.

Sub-ss (3), (4): words in square brackets substituted by SI 2012/2404, art 3(2), Sch 2, para 10(1), (4), (5).

[Redress schemes

[1.810]
23A   Redress schemes

(1)   The Secretary of State may by order require persons who engage in estate agency work in relation to residential property ("relevant estate agency work") to be members of an approved redress scheme for dealing with complaints in connection with that work.

(2)   An order may provide for the duty to apply—

(a)   only to specified descriptions of persons who engage in estate agency work; and

(b)   in relation to any relevant estate agency work carried out by a person to whom the duty applies or only in relation to specified descriptions of work (which may be framed by reference to descriptions of residential property).

(3)   An order may also provide for the duty not to apply in relation to complaints of any specified description (which may be framed by reference to a description of person making a complaint).

(4)   In subsections (1) and (2)(a), the reference to persons who engage in estate agency work does not include a reference to persons who engage in that work in the course of their employment.

(5)   The power to make an order shall be exercisable by statutory instrument which shall be subject to annulment in pursuance of a resolution of either House of Parliament.

(6)   Before making an order the Secretary of State must be satisfied that all persons who are to be subject to the duty will be eligible to join a suitable approved redress scheme before the duty applies to them.

For this purpose the Secretary of State may disregard persons who cannot lawfully engage in the relevant estate agency work to which the duty applies.

(7)   Nothing in this section prevents an approved redress scheme from providing—

(a)   for membership to be open to persons who are not subject to the duty;

(b)   for the investigation and determination of any complaints in relation to which the duty does not apply, where the members concerned have voluntarily accepted the jurisdiction of the scheme over those complaints;

(c)   for the exclusion from investigation and determination under the scheme of any complaint in such cases or circumstances as may be specified in or determined under the scheme.

(8)   For the purposes of this section—

(a)   a "redress scheme" is a scheme which provides for complaints against members of the scheme to be investigated and determined by an independent person ("the ombudsman");

(b)   a redress scheme is "approved" if—

(i)   it is for the time being approved by the [lead enforcement authority] under Schedule 3; or

(ii)   it is administered by or on behalf of the Secretary of State and designated by him as an approved redress scheme for the purposes of this section;

(c)   a "complaint" is a complaint made by a person by virtue of his being or having been a seller or buyer of residential property;

(d)   "seller", in relation to residential property, means a person who claims that he is or may become interested in disposing of an interest in land in respect of that property (and includes a person who disposes of such an interest);

(e)   "buyer", in relation to residential property, means a person who claims that he is or may become interested in acquiring an interest in land in respect of that property (and includes a person who acquires such an interest).

(9)   The Secretary of State may not designate a scheme as an approved redress scheme for the purposes of this section unless the Secretary of State is satisfied that the scheme is one which could be approved by the [lead enforcement authority] in accordance with paragraphs 2 to 5 of Schedule 3.

(10)   Schedule 3 (which makes further provision in connection with the approval of redress schemes etc.) shall have effect.

(11)   In this section—

"order" means an order under subsection (1);

"the duty" means the requirement under an order to be a member of an approved redress scheme.]

NOTES

Inserted, together with preceding cross-heading and ss 23B, 23C, by the Consumers, Estate Agents and Redress Act 2007, s 53(1), Sch 6, paras 1, 2.

Sub-ss (8), (9): words in square brackets substituted by the Public Bodies (Abolition of the National Consumer Council and Transfer of the Office of Fair Trading's Functions in relation to Estate Agents etc) Order 2014, SI 2014/631, art 5(3)(a), Sch 2, Pt 1, para 1(1), (7)(g), for transitional provisions and savings see art 5(3)(a), Sch 2, Pt 4 thereof at **[2.1133]**, **[2.1134A]**.

Orders: the Estate Agents (Redress Scheme) Order 2008, SI 2008/1712 at **[2.598]**.

[1.811]
[23B   Enforcement

(1)   If a duly authorised officer of an enforcement authority   . . .   believes that a person has engaged (or is engaging) in estate agency work in relation to residential property in breach of the duty imposed by an order under section 23A(1) he may give a penalty charge notice to that person.

(2)   A penalty charge notice may not be given after the end of the period of six months beginning with the day (or in the case of a continuing breach the last day) on which the breach of duty was committed.

(3)   Schedule 4 (which makes further provision in connection with penalty charge notices) shall have effect.

(4)   An enforcement authority other than the [lead enforcement authority] must notify the [lead enforcement authority] if it believes that a person has engaged (or is engaging) in estate agency work in relation to residential property in breach of the duty imposed by an order under section 23A(1).]

NOTES

Inserted as noted to s 23A at **[1.810]**.

Sub-s (1): words omitted repealed by the Public Bodies (Abolition of the National Consumer Council and Transfer of the Office of Fair Trading's Functions in relation to Estate Agents etc) Order 2014, SI 2014/631, art 5(3)(a), Sch 2, Pt 1, para 1(1), (8)(a), for transitional provisions and savings see art 5(3)(a), Sch 2, Pt 4 thereof at **[2.1133]**, **[2.1134A]**.

Sub-s (4): words in square brackets substituted by SI 2014/631, art 5(3)(a), Sch 2, Pt 1, para 1(1), (8)(b), for transitional provisions and savings see note above.

See further: the Estate Agents (Redress Scheme) (Penalty Charge) Regulations 2008, SI 2008/1713 at **[2.600]** specify the amount of the penalty charge in a notice given to a person under sub-s (1) as £1000.

[1.812]
[23C   Meaning of residential property

(1)   For the purposes of sections 23A and 23B "residential property"—

(a)   has the meaning given by subsection (2); but

(b)   does not include land of a description specified in an order made by the Secretary of State for the purposes of this section.

(2)   "Residential property" means any land that consists of or includes a building or part of a building—

(a)   the whole or part of which is used as a dwelling or as more than one dwelling; or

(b)   that is (or is to be) offered for sale on the basis that the whole or part of it is suitable for such use or is intended to be so suitable by the time the seller disposes of his interest in it.

(3)   In subsection (2), the reference to a building or part of a building (so far as relating to paragraph (b) of that subsection) includes a reference to a building or part that is being or is to be constructed.

(4)   A description of land specified by order under subsection (1)(b) may be framed by reference to the purpose or purposes for which the land (or part of it) is or is intended to be used.

(5)   The power to make an order under subsection (1)(b) shall be exercisable by statutory instrument which shall be subject to annulment in pursuance of a resolution of either House of Parliament.]

NOTES

Inserted as noted to s 23A at **[1.810]**.

Supervision, enforcement, publicity etc

24   (*Sub-s (1) repealed by the Tribunals and Inquiries Act 1992, s 18(2), Sch 4, Pt I; sub-s (2) repealed by the Tribunals, Courts and Enforcement Act 2007, ss 48(1), 146, Sch 8, para 8, Sch 23, Pt 1.*)

[1.813]
25   General duties of [lead enforcement authority]
(1)   Subject to section 26(3) below, it is the duty of the [lead enforcement authority]—
   (a)   generally to superintend the working and enforcement of this Act, and
   (b)   where necessary or expedient, [itself] to take steps to enforce this Act.
(2)   It is the duty of the [lead enforcement authority], so far as appears to [it] to be practicable and having regard both to the national interest and the interests of persons engaged in estate agency work and of consumers to keep under review and from time to time advise the Secretary of State about—
   (a)   social and commercial developments in the United Kingdom and elsewhere relating to the carrying on of estate agency work and related activities; and
   (b)   the working and enforcement of this Act.
(3)   The [lead enforcement authority] shall arrange for the dissemination, in such form and manner as [it] considers appropriate, of such information and advice as it may appear to [it] expedient to give the public in the United Kingdom about the operation of this Act.

NOTES
Section heading: words in square brackets substituted by the Public Bodies (Abolition of the National Consumer Council and Transfer of the Office of Fair Trading's Functions in relation to Estate Agents etc) Order 2014, SI 2014/631, art 5(3)(a), Sch 2, Pt 1, para 1(1), (9)(a), for transitional provisions and savings see art 5(3)(a), Sch 2, Pt 4 thereof at **[2.1133]**, **[2.1134A]**.
Sub-ss (1)–(3): words in first pair of square brackets substituted by SI 2014/631, art 5(3)(a), Sch 2, Pt 1, para 1(1), (9)(b), for transitional provisions and savings see note above; all other words in square brackets substituted by the Enterprise Act 2002, s 278(1), Sch 25, para 9(1), (12).

[1.814]
26   Enforcement authorities
(1)   Without prejudice to section 25(1) above, the following authorities (in this Act referred to as "enforcement authorities") have a duty to enforce this Act—
   (a)   the [lead enforcement authority],
   (b)   in Great Britain, a local weights and measures authority, and
   (c)   in Northern Ireland, the Department of Commerce for Northern Ireland.
[(1A)   For the investigatory powers available to an authority for the purposes of the duty in subsection (1), see Schedule 5 to the Consumer Rights Act 2015.]
(2)   . . .
(3)   (*Applies to Scotland only.*)
(4)   Every local weights and measures authority shall, whenever the [lead enforcement authority] requires, report to [it] in such form and with such particulars as [it] requires on the exercise of their functions under this Act.
(5)–(8)   . . .

NOTES
Sub-s (1): words in square brackets substituted by the Public Bodies (Abolition of the National Consumer Council and Transfer of the Office of Fair Trading's Functions in relation to Estate Agents etc) Order 2014, SI 2014/631, art 5(3)(a), Sch 2, Pt 1, para 1(1), (10)(a), for transitional provisions and savings see art 5(3)(a), Sch 2, Pt 4 thereof at **[2.1133]**, **[2.1134A]**.
Sub-s (1A): inserted by the Consumer Rights Act 2015, s 77(2), Sch 6, paras 19, 24, as from 1 October 2015 (for transitional provisions see the Consumer Rights Act 2015 (Commencement No 3, Transitional Provisions, Savings and Consequential Amendments) Order 2015, SI 2015/1630, arts 6–8 at **[2.1220]** et seq).
Sub-s (4): words in first pair of square brackets substituted by SI 2014/631, art 5(3)(a), Sch 2, Pt 1, para 1(1), (10)(a), for transitional provisions and savings see note above; words in second and final pairs of square brackets substituted by the Enterprise Act 2002, s 278(1), Sch 25, para 9(1), (13)(a), (c).
Sub-s (2): repealed by the Enterprise Act 2002, s 278, Sch 25, para 9(1), (13)(b), Sch 26.
Sub-ss (5)–(8): repealed by the Local Government, Planning and Land Act 1980, ss 1(4), 194, Sch 4, para 10, Sch 34, Pt IV.

[1.815]
27   *Obstruction and personation of authorised officers*
(*1*)   *Any person who*—
   (a)   *wilfully obstructs an authorised officer, or*
   (b)   . . .
   (c)   *without reasonable cause fails to give an authorised officer [any] assistance or information he may reasonably require in performing his functions under this Act, or*
   (d)   *in giving information to an authorised officer, makes any statement which he knows to be false,*
shall be liable on summary conviction to a fine not exceeding [level 4 on the standard scale].
[(1A)   A failure to give assistance or information shall not constitute an offence under subsection (1)(c) if it is also a failure in relation to which an authorised officer may apply for an order under section 11A above.]

(2)   A person who is not an authorised officer but purports to act as such shall be liable on summary conviction to a fine not exceeding [level 5 on the standard scale].

(3)   In this section "authorised officer" means a duly authorised officer of an enforcement authority who is acting in pursuance of this Act.

(4)   Nothing in subsection (1) above requires a person to answer any question or give any information if to do so might incriminate that person or that person's [spouse or civil partner].

NOTES

Repealed by the Consumer Rights Act 2015, s 77(2), Sch 6, paras 19, 25, as from 1 October 2015 (for transitional provisions see the Consumer Rights Act 2015 (Commencement No 3, Transitional Provisions, Savings and Consequential Amendments) Order 2015, SI 2015/1630, arts 6–8 at [2.1220] et seq).

Sub-s (1): para (b) repealed and word in square brackets in para (c) substituted by the Consumers, Estate Agents and Redress Act 2007, ss 58(4)(a), 64, Sch 8; reference to a level on the standard scale substituted by virtue of the Criminal Justice Act 1982, ss 38, 46.

Sub-s (1A): inserted by the Consumers, Estate Agents and Redress Act 2007, s 58(4)(b).

Sub-s (2): reference to a level on the standard scale substituted by virtue of the Criminal Justice Act 1982, ss 38, 46.

Sub-s (4): words in square brackets substituted by the Civil Partnership Act 2004, s 261(1), Sch 27, para 62.

Supplementary

[1.816]
28   General provisions as to offences

(1)   In any proceedings for an offence under this Act it shall be a defence for the person charged to prove that he took all reasonable precautions and exercised all due diligence to avoid the commission of an offence by himself or any person under his control.

(2)   Where an offence under this Act committed by a body corporate is proved to have been committed with the consent or connivance of, or to be attributable to any neglect on the part of, any director, manager, secretary or other similar officer of the body corporate, or any person who was purporting to act in any such capacity, he as well as the body corporate shall be guilty of that offence and shall be liable to be proceeded against and punished accordingly.

[1.817]
29   Service of notices etc

(1)   Any notice which under this Act is to be given to any person by the [lead enforcement authority] shall be so given—
   (a)   by delivering it to him, or
   (b)   by leaving it at his proper address, or
   (c)   by sending it by post to him at that address.

(2)   Any such notice may—
   (a)   in the case of a body corporate or unincorporated association, be given to the secretary or clerk of that body or association; and
   (b)   in the case of a partnership, be given to a partner or a person having the control or management of the partnership business.

(3)   Any application or other document which under this Act may be made or given to the [lead enforcement authority] may be so made or given by sending it by post to the [lead enforcement authority] at such address as may be specified for the purposes of this Act by a general notice.

(4)   For the purposes of subsections (1) and (2) above and section 7 of the Interpretation Act 1978 (service of documents by post) in its application to those subsections, the proper address of any person to whom a notice is to be given shall be his last-known address, except that—
   (a)   in the case of a body corporate or their secretary or clerk, it shall be the address of the registered or principal office of that body;
   (b)   in the case of an unincorporated association or their secretary or clerk, it shall be that of the principal office of that association;
   (c)   in the case of a partnership or a person having the control or management of the partnership business, it shall be that of the principal office of the partnership;
and for the purposes of this subsection the principal office of a company registered outside the United Kingdom or of an unincorporated association or partnership carrying on business outside the United Kingdom shall be their principal office within the United Kingdom.

(5)   If the person to be given any notice mentioned in subsection (1) above has specified an address within the United Kingdom other than his proper address, within the meaning of subsection (4) above, as the one at which he or someone on his behalf will accept notices under this Act, that address shall also be treated for the purposes mentioned in subsection (4) above as his proper address.

NOTES

Sub-ss (1), (3): words in square brackets substituted by the Public Bodies (Abolition of the National Consumer Council and Transfer of the Office of Fair Trading's Functions in relation to Estate Agents etc) Order 2014, SI 2014/631, art 5(3)(a), Sch 2, Pt 1, para 1(1), (10)(b), for transitional provisions and savings see art 5(3)(a), Sch 2, Pt 4 thereof at [2.1133], [2.1134A].

[1.818]

30 Orders and regulations

(1) Before making any order or regulations under any provision of this Act to which this subsection applies, the Secretary of State shall consult the [lead enforcement authority], such bodies representative of persons carrying on estate agency work, such bodies representative of consumers and such other persons as he thinks fit.

(2) Subsection (1) above applies to paragraphs (a)(iii) and (d) of section 3(1) above and to sections 14, 15, 16, 18, 19[, 21A] and 22 above.

(3) Any power of the Secretary of State to make orders or regulations under this Act—

    (a) may be so exercised as to make different provision in relation to different cases or classes of cases and to exclude certain cases or classes of case; and

    (b) includes power to make such supplemental, incidental and transitional provisions as he thinks fit.

NOTES

Sub-s (1): words in square brackets substituted by the Public Bodies (Abolition of the National Consumer Council and Transfer of the Office of Fair Trading's Functions in relation to Estate Agents etc) Order 2014, SI 2014/631, art 5(3)(a), Sch 2, Pt 1, para 1(1), (10)(c), for transitional provisions and savings see art 5(3)(a), Sch 2, Pt 4 thereof at **[2.1133]**, **[2.1134A]**.

Sub-s (2): number in square brackets inserted by the Consumers, Estate Agents and Redress Act 2007, s 63(1), Sch 7, para 3, as from a day to be appointed.

Regulations: the Estate Agents (Accounts) Regulations 1981, SI 1981/1520.

[1.819]

31 Meaning of "business associate" and "controller"

(1) The provisions of this section shall have effect for determining the meaning of "business associate" and "controller" for the purposes of this Act.

(2) As respects acts done in the course of a business carried on by a body corporate, every director and controller of that body is a business associate of it.

(3) As respects acts done in the course of a business carried on by a partnership, each partner is a business associate of every other member of the partnership and also of the partnership itself and, in the case of a partner which is a body corporate, every person who, by virtue of subsection (2) above, is a business associate of that body is also a business associate of every other member of the partnership.

(4) As respects acts done in the course of a business carried on by an unincorporated association, every officer of the association and any other person who has the management or control of its activities is a business associate of that association.

(5) In relation to a body corporate "controller" means a person—

    (a) in accordance with whose directions or instructions the directors of the body corporate or of any other body corporate which is its controller (or any of them) are accustomed to act; or

    (b) who, either alone or with any associate or associates, is entitled to exercise, or control the exercise of, one third or more of the voting power at any general meeting of the body corporate or of another body corporate which is its controller.

[1.820]

32 Meaning of "associate"

(1) In this Act "associate" includes a business associate and otherwise has the meaning given by the following provisions of this section.

(2) A person is an associate of another if he is the spouse [or civil partner] or a relative of that other or of a business associate of that other.

(3) In subsection (2) above "relative" means brother, sister, uncle, aunt, nephew, niece, lineal ancestor or linear descendant, ... references to a spouse include a former spouse and a [reputed spouse, and references to a civil partner include a former civil partner] [and a reputed civil partner]; and for the purposes of this subsection a relationship shall be established as if an illegitimate child or stepchild of a person [were the legitimate child of the relationship in question].

(4) A body corporate is an associate of another body corporate—

    (a) if the same person is a controller of both, or a person is a controller of one and persons who are his associates, or he and persons who are his associates, are controllers of the other; or

    (b) if a group of two or more persons is a controller of each company, and the groups either consist of the same persons or could be regarded as consisting of the same persons by treating (in one or more cases) a member of either group as replaced by a person of whom he is an associate.

(5) An unincorporated association is an associate of another unincorporated association if any person—

    (a) is an officer of both associations;

    (b) has the management or control of the activities of both associations; or

    (c) is an officer of one association and has the management or control of the activities of the other association.

(6) A partnership is an associate of another partnership if—

    (a) any person is a member of both partnerships; or

(b) a person who is a member of one partnership is an associate of a member of the other partnership; or

(c) a member of one partnership has an associate who is also an associate of a member of the other partnership.

NOTES

Sub-s (1): words in square brackets substituted by the Public Bodies (Abolition of the National Consumer Council and Transfer of the Office of Fair Trading's Functions in relation to Estate Agents etc) Order 2014, SI 2014/631, art 5(3)(a), Sch 2, Pt 1, para 1(1), (10)(c), for transitional provisions and savings see art 5(3)(a), Sch 2, Pt 4 thereof at **[2.1133]**, **[2.1134A]**.

Sub-s (2): words in square brackets inserted by the Civil Partnership Act 2004, s 261(1), Sch 27, para 63(1), (2).

Sub-s (3): word omitted repealed and words in first and third pairs of square brackets substituted by the Civil Partnership Act 2004, s 261(1), (4), Sch 27, para 63(1), (3), Sch 30; words in second pair of square brackets inserted by the Civil Partnership Act 2004 (Overseas Relationships and Consequential, etc Amendments) Order 2005, SI 2005/3129, art 4(4), Sch 4, para 5.

[1.821]
33 General interpretation provisions

(1) In this Act, unless the context otherwise requires—

"associate" has the meaning assigned to it by section 32 above and "business associate" has the meaning assigned to it by section 31 above;

"client account" has the meaning assigned to it by section 14(2) above;

"clients' money" has the meaning assigned to it by section 12(1) above;

"connected contract", in relation to the acquisition of an interest in land, has the meaning assigned to it by section 12(4) above;

"contract deposit" has the meaning assigned to it by section 12(2) above;

"controller", in relation to a body corporate, has the meaning assigned to it by section 31(5) above;

. . .

"enforcement authority" has the meaning assigned to it by section 26(1) above;

"estate agency work" has the meaning assigned to it by section 1(1) above;

"general notice" means a notice published by the [lead enforcement authority] at a time and in a manner appearing to [it] suitable for securing that the notice is seen within a reasonable time by persons likely to be affected by it;

["the lead enforcement authority" means Powys County Council;]

[. . .]

"pre-contract deposit" has the meaning assigned to it by section 12(3) above;

"prescribed fee" means such fee as may be prescribed by regulations made by the Secretary of State;

. . .

"unincorporated association" does not include a partnership.

(2) The power to make regulations under subsection (1) above prescribing fees shall be exercisable by statutory instrument which shall be subject to annulment in pursuance of a resolution of either House of Parliament.

NOTES

Sub-s (1): definition "Director" (omitted) repealed, in definition "general notice" second word in square brackets substituted, and definition "OFT" (omitted) inserted, by the Enterprise Act 2002, s 278, Sch 25, para 9(1), (15), Sch 26; in definition "general notice" words in first pair of square brackets substituted, definition "OFT" (omitted) repealed, and definition "the lead enforcement authority" inserted, by the Public Bodies (Abolition of the National Consumer Council and Transfer of the Office of Fair Trading's Functions in relation to Estate Agents etc) Order 2014, SI 2014/631, art 5(3)(a), Sch 2, Pt 1, para 1(1), (11), for transitional provisions and savings see art 5(3)(a), Sch 2, Pt 4 thereof at **[2.1133]**, **[2.1134A]**; definition "the statutory maximum" (omitted) repealed by the Statute Law (Repeals) Act 1993.

[1.822]
34 Financial provisions

(1) There shall be defrayed out of moneys provided by Parliament—

(a) any expenses incurred by the Secretary of State in consequence of the provisions of this Act; and

(b) any increase attributable to this Act in the sums payable out of moneys so provided under any other Act.

(2) Any fees [paid to the lead enforcement authority under this Act] shall be paid into the Consolidated Fund.

NOTES

Sub-s (2): words in square brackets substituted by the Public Bodies (Abolition of the National Consumer Council and Transfer of the Office of Fair Trading's Functions in relation to Estate Agents etc) Order 2014, SI 2014/631, art 5(3)(a), Sch 2, Pt 1, para 1(1), (12), for transitional provisions and savings see art 5(3)(a), Sch 2, Pt 4 thereof at **[2.1133]**, **[2.1134A]**.

35 *(Repealed by the Statute Law (Repeals) Act 1981.)*

[1.823]
36 Short title, commencement and extent
(1) This Act may be cited as the Estate Agents Act 1979.

(2) This Act shall come into force on such day as the Secretary of State may by order made by statutory instrument appoint and different days may be so appointed for different provisions and for different purposes.

(3) This Act extends to Northern Ireland.

NOTES

Orders: the Estate Agents Act 1979 (Commencement No 1) Order 1981, SI 1981/1517.

SCHEDULES

SCHEDULE 1
PROVISIONS SUPPLEMENTARY TO SECTION 3(1)

Section 3(1)

[Spent convictions

[1.824]
1. A person is not to be treated for the purposes of section 3(1)(a) of this Act as having committed an offence if he has been convicted of that offence and that conviction is to be treated as spent for the purposes of the Rehabilitation of Offenders Act 1974 or any corresponding enactment for the time being in force in Northern Ireland.]

Discrimination

[2. (1) A person commits discrimination for the purposes of section 3(1)(b) in the following cases only.

(2) The first case is where—
   (a) the person has been found to have contravened a relevant equality provision, and
   (b) no appeal against the finding is pending or can be brought.

(3) The second case is where—
   (a) the person has been given an unlawful act notice under section 21 of the Equality Act 2006,
   (b) the notice specifies a relevant equality provision as the provision by virtue of which the act in question is unlawful, and
   (c) no appeal against the giving of the notice is pending or can be brought.

(4) The third case is where—
   (a) the person is the subject of an injunction, interdict or order under section 24 of the Equality Act 2006 (unlawful acts), and
   (b) the unlawful act in question is a contravention of a relevant equality provision.

(5) The relevant equality provisions are—
   (a) Parts 3 and 4 of the Equality Act 2010 (services and premises) so far as relating to discrimination and victimisation, and
   (b) section 112 of that Act (aiding contraventions) in relation to either of those Parts of that Act so far as relating to discrimination and victimisation.]

3. After the expiry of the period of five years beginning on the day on which any such finding or notice as is referred to in paragraph 2 above became final, no person shall be treated for the purposes of section 3(1)(b) of this Act as having committed [a contravention of a relevant equality provision] by reason only of that finding or notice.

[4. For the purposes of paragraphs 2 and 3 "discrimination" and "victimisation" have the same meaning as in the Equality Act 2010.]

5. In the application of paragraphs 2 to 4 above to Northern Ireland references to the 1975 Act shall be construed as references to the Sex Discrimination (Northern Ireland) Order 1976, and in particular—
   (a) the references to sections 38, 39 and 40 of the 1975 Act shall be construed as references to Articles 39, 40 and 41 of that Order;
   (b) the reference to subsections (1) and (4) of section 82 of the 1975 Act shall be construed as a reference to paragraphs (1), (2) and (5) of Article 2 of that Order; and
   (c) other references to numbered sections of the 1975 Act shall be construed as references to the Articles of that Order bearing the same number.

[6. In the application of paragraphs 2 to 4 above to Northern Ireland references to the 1976 Act shall be construed as references to the Race Relations (Northern Ireland) Order 1997, and in particular the references to sections 29, 30, 31, 57, 62, 63(2)(a) and (4) and 78(1) and (4) of the 1976 Act shall be construed as references to Articles 29, 30, 31, 54, 59, 60(2)(a) and (4) and 2(2) and (3) respectively of that Order.]

NOTES

Para 1: substituted by the Consumers, Estate Agents and Redress Act 2007, s 55(1), (5).

Para 2: substituted by the Equality Act 2010, s 211(1), Sch 26, Pt 1, paras 4, 6(1), (2) (as inserted by the Equality Act 2010 (Consequential Amendments, Saving and Supplementary Provisions) Order 2010, SI 2010/2279, arts 2, 12, Sch 1, para 2).

Para 3: words in square brackets substituted by the Equality Act 2010, s 211(1), Sch 26, Pt 1, paras 4, 6(1), (3) (as inserted by SI 2010/2279, arts 2, 12, Sch 1, para 2).

Para 4: substituted by the Equality Act 2010, s 211(1), Sch 26, Pt 1, paras 4, 6(1), (4) (as inserted by SI 2010/2279, arts 2, 12, Sch 1, para 2).

Para 6: substituted for part of original para 5 by the Race Relations (Northern Ireland) Order 1997, SI 1997/869, art 73, Sch 2, para 2(2).

SCHEDULE 2
PROCEDURE ETC

Sections 5, 6, 8 (3)

PART I
ORDERS AND DECISIONS UNDER SECTIONS 3, 4 AND 6

Introductory

[1.825]

1. (1) In this Schedule—

(a) subject to sub-paragraph (2) below, references to "the person affected" are to the person in respect of whom the [lead enforcement authority] proposes to make, or has made, an order under section 3 or section 4 of this Act, or who has made an application under section 6 of this Act for the variation or revocation of such an order; and

(b) references to the [lead enforcement authority's] "proposal" are to any proposal of [its] to make such an order or to make a decision under subsection (4) or subsection (5) of section 6 of this Act on such an application.

(2) In the case of a proposal of the [lead enforcement authority] to make an order under section 3 or section 4 of this Act against a partnership where, by virtue of section 5(2) of this Act, [it] intends that the order shall have effect as an order against some or all of the partners individually, references in the following provisions of this Schedule to the person affected shall be construed, except where the contrary is provided, as references to each of the partners affected by the order, as well as to the partnership itself.

Notice of proposal

2. (1) The [lead enforcement authority] shall give to the person affected a notice informing him of the proposal and of the [lead enforcement authority's] reason for it; but paragraph 1(2) above shall not apply for the purposes of this sub-paragraph.

(2) In the case of a proposal to make an order, the notice under sub-paragraph (1) above shall inform the person affected of the substance of the proposed order and, in the case of a proposal to make an order under section 3 of this Act, shall—

(a) set out those matters falling within subsection (1) of that section which the [lead enforcement authority] intends should be specified as the grounds for the order, and

(b) specify any other matters of which the [lead enforcement authority] has taken account under subsection (2) of that section, and

(c) if the [lead enforcement authority] proposes to rely on section 4(3) of this Act to establish the unfitness of the person affected, state that fact.

(3) The notice given under sub-paragraph (1) above shall invite the person affected, within such period of not less than twenty-one days as may be specified in the notice—

(a) to submit to the [lead enforcement authority] his representations in writing as to why the order should not be made or, as the case may be, should be varied or revoked in accordance with the application, and

(b) to give notice to the [lead enforcement authority], if he thinks fit, that he wishes to make such representations orally,

and where notice is given under paragraph (b) above the [lead enforcement authority] shall arrange for the oral representations to be heard.

Hearing of representations

3. Where the [lead enforcement authority] receives notice under paragraph 2(3)(b) above [it] shall give the person affected not less than twenty-one days notice, or such shorter notice as the person affected may consent to accept, of the date, time and place at which representations are to be heard.

4. (1) In the course of hearing oral representations the [lead enforcement authority] shall, at the request of the person affected, permit any other person (in addition to the person affected) to make representations on his behalf or to give evidence or to introduce documents for him.

(2) The [lead enforcement authority] shall not refuse to admit evidence solely on the grounds that it would not be admissible in a court of law.

5. If the [lead enforcement authority] adjourns the hearing [it] shall give the person affected reasonable notice of the date, time and place at which the hearing is to be resumed.

Decision

6. (1)   The [lead enforcement authority] shall take into account in deciding whether to proceed with [its] proposal any written or oral representations made in accordance with the preceding provisions of this Schedule.

(2)   If the [lead enforcement authority] considers that [it] should proceed with [its] proposal but for a reason which differs, or on grounds which differ, from those set out in the notice of the proposal under paragraph 2 above, [it] shall give a further notice under that paragraph.

(3)   In any case where—

(a)   a notice under paragraph 2 above gives more than one reason for the proposal or (in the case of a proposal to make an order under section 3 of this Act) sets out more than one matter which the [lead enforcement authority] intends should be specified as the grounds for the order, and

(b)   it appears to the [lead enforcement authority] that one or more of those reasons should be abandoned or, as the case may be, that one or more of those matters should not be so specified,

the [lead enforcement authority] may nevertheless decide to proceed with [its] proposal on the basis of any other reason given in the notice or, as the case may be, on any other grounds set out in the notice.

7. If the [lead enforcement authority] decides not to proceed with [its] proposal [it] shall give notice of that decision to the person affected and, in the case of a notice of a decision on an application under section 6 of this Act, such a notice shall be combined with a notice under subsection (3) of that section.

8. If the [lead enforcement authority] decides to proceed with [its] proposal [it] may, if [it] thinks fit having regard to any representations made to [it]—

(a)   where the proposal is for the making of an order, make the order in a form which varies from that of the proposed order mentioned in the notice under paragraph 2 above, or

(b)   where the proposal is to vary an order, make a variation other than that mentioned in the notice under paragraph 2 above, or

(c)   where the proposal is to refuse to revoke an order, vary the order.

Notification of decision

9. (1)   Notice of the decision to make the order, and of the terms of the order or, as the case may be, notice of the decision on the application for variation or revocation of the order, shall be given to the person affected, together with the [lead enforcement authority's] reasons for [its] decision, including the facts which in [its] opinion justify the decision.

(2)   The notice referred to in sub-paragraph (1) above shall also inform the person affected of his right to appeal against the decision and of the period within which an appeal may be brought and of how notice of appeal may be given.

10. (1)   Subject to sub-paragraph (2) below, the order to which the decision relates or, as the case may be, any variation of an order for which the decision provides shall not come into operation until any appeal under section 7(1) of this Act and any further appeal has been finally determined or the period within which such an appeal may be brought has expired.

(2)   Where the [lead enforcement authority] states in the notice referred to in paragraph 9(1) above that [it] is satisfied that there are special circumstances which require it, an order shall come into operation immediately upon the giving of notice of the decision to make it.

NOTES

References to "lead enforcement authority" or "lead enforcement authority's" in square brackets substituted by the Public Bodies (Abolition of the National Consumer Council and Transfer of the Office of Fair Trading's Functions in relation to Estate Agents etc) Order 2014, SI 2014/631, art 5(3)(a), Sch 2, Pt 1, para 1(1), (13)(a), for transitional provisions and savings see art 5(3)(a), Sch 2, Pt 4 thereof at **[2.1133]**, **[2.1134A]**; all other words in square brackets substituted by the Enterprise Act 2002, s 278(1), Sch 25, para 9(1), (16).

PART II
APPLICATIONS UNDER SECTIONS 6(1) AND 8(3)

[1.826]

11. Any reference in this Part of this Schedule to an application is a reference to an application to the [lead enforcement authority] under section 6(1) or section 8(3) of this Act, and any reference to the applicant shall be construed accordingly.

12. An application shall be in writing and be in such form and accompanied by such particulars as the [lead enforcement authority] may specify by general notice.

13. The [lead enforcement authority] may by notice require the applicant to publish details of his application at a time and times and in a manner specified in the notice.

14. If an application does not comply with paragraph 12 above or if an applicant fails to comply with a notice under *section 9 of this Act* requiring the furnishing of information *or the production of documents* in connection with the application, the [lead enforcement authority] may decline to proceed with the application.

NOTES

Paras 11–13: words in square brackets substituted by the Public Bodies (Abolition of the National Consumer Council and Transfer of the Office of Fair Trading's Functions in relation to Estate Agents etc) Order 2014, SI 2014/631, art 5(3)(a), Sch 2, Pt 1, para 1(1), (13)(b), for transitional provisions and savings see art 5(3)(a), Sch 2, Pt 4 thereof at **[2.1133]**, **[2.1134A]**.

Para 14: for the first words in italics there are substituted the words "paragraph 14 of Schedule 5 to the Consumer Rights Act 2015", and second words in italics repealed by the Consumer Rights Act 2015, s 77(2), Sch 6, paras 19, 26, as from 1 October 2015 (for transitional provisions see the Consumer Rights Act 2015 (Commencement No 3, Transitional Provisions, Savings and Consequential Amendments) Order 2015, SI 2015/1630, arts 6–8 at **[2.1220]** et seq); words in square brackets substituted by the Public Bodies (Abolition of the National Consumer Council and Transfer of the Office of Fair Trading's Functions in relation to Estate Agents etc) Order 2014, SI 2014/631, art 5(3)(a), Sch 2, Pt 1, para 1(1), (13)(b), for transitional provisions and savings see note above.

[SCHEDULE 3
REDRESS SCHEMES

Section 23A(10)

Approval of redress schemes

[1.827]
1. A redress scheme may be approved for the purposes of section 23A by the [lead enforcement authority] acting in accordance with paragraphs 2 to 8.

2. (1) A scheme may not be approved unless the [lead enforcement authority] considers that—
  (a) the provisions of the scheme; and
  (b) the manner in which it will be operated (so far as can be judged from facts known to the authority);
are satisfactory for the purposes of section 23A.

(2) Without prejudice to the generality of sub-paragraph (1), a scheme must not be approved unless the [lead enforcement authority] considers that it makes satisfactory provision about—
  (a) the complaints which may be made under the scheme (which may include complaints about non-compliance with the provisions of a code of practice or other document);
  (b) the ombudsman's duties and powers in relation to the investigation and determination of complaints (which may include power to decide not to investigate or determine a particular complaint);
  (c) the redress which the ombudsman may require members to provide to complainants, which must include the types of redress specified in sub-paragraph (3);
  (d) the enforcement of any requirement to provide redress imposed on a member in accordance with the scheme.

(3) The types of redress mentioned in sub-paragraph (2)(c) are—
  (a) providing an apology or explanation;
  (b) paying compensation; and
  (c) taking such other actions in the interests of the complainant as the ombudsman may specify.

3. (1) In determining whether a scheme, or any provisions mentioned in paragraph 2(2), are satisfactory the [lead enforcement authority] must have regard to—
  (a) the interests of members of the scheme and of sellers and buyers of residential properties; and
  (b) such principles as—
    (i) in the opinion of the [lead enforcement authority] constitute generally accepted principles of best practice in relation to consumer redress schemes, and
    (ii) it is reasonable to regard as applicable to the scheme.

(2) In considering the interests mentioned in sub-paragraph (1)(a), the [lead enforcement authority] may have regard to the number of other redress schemes which are (or are likely to become) approved redress schemes.

4. The [lead enforcement authority] must not approve a scheme unless it considers that the scheme makes satisfactory provision about the provision of information by the ombudsman or the scheme administrator to—
  (a) persons exercising functions under other approved schemes;
  (b) persons exercising functions under other consumer redress schemes; and
  (c) the [lead enforcement authority] or any other person exercising regulatory functions in relation to the activities of persons engaging in estate agency work.

5. The [lead enforcement authority] must not approve a scheme if it considers that the scheme provides for membership to be revoked on any unfair grounds.

Applications for approval to the [lead enforcement authority]

6. An application for approval by the [lead enforcement authority] of a redress scheme must—
  (a) be made in such manner as the [lead enforcement authority] may determine; and
  (b) be accompanied by such information as the [lead enforcement authority] may require.

7. Where the [lead enforcement authority] is proposing to refuse an application for approval it must give the applicant a notice stating—
  (a) that it is proposing to refuse the application;
  (b) the grounds for the proposed refusal; and
  (c) that representations about the proposed refusal may be made within such period of not less than 30 days as is specified in the notice.

8. If the [lead enforcement authority] decides to refuse an application for approval, it must give the applicant a notice stating—
  (a) the [lead enforcement authority]'s decision to refuse the application; and
  (b) the reasons for the decision.

Notification of changes to an approved scheme

9. The scheme administrator of a redress scheme which is approved by the [lead enforcement authority] must notify the [lead enforcement authority] of any change to the scheme before the end of the period of 14 days beginning with the day on which the change is made.

Withdrawal of approval by the [lead enforcement authority]

10. The [lead enforcement authority] may withdraw approval of a redress scheme which is for the time being approved by it.

11. Before withdrawing approval of a scheme, the [lead enforcement authority] must give the scheme administrator a notice stating—
  (a) that it proposes to withdraw its approval;
  (b) the grounds for the proposed withdrawal of approval; and
  (c) that representations about the proposed withdrawal may be made within such period of not less than 30 days as is specified in the notice.

12. The [lead enforcement authority] must give the scheme administrator a notice stating—
  (a) its decision on a proposal to withdraw approval; and
  (b) the reasons for its decision.

13. If the [lead enforcement authority] decides to withdraw approval of a scheme—
  (a) the withdrawal has effect from such date as may be specified in the notice under paragraph 12;
  (b) the scheme administrator must give a copy of the notice under paragraph 12 to every member of the scheme.

Revocation of designation by the Secretary of State

14. If the Secretary of State decides to revoke his designation of a scheme for the purposes of section 23A, he must give every member of the scheme a notice stating—
  (a) that he has decided to revoke the designation;
  (b) the reasons for his decision; and
  (c) the date from which the revocation has effect.

Defamation proceedings

15. For the purposes of the law relating to defamation, proceedings under an approved redress scheme in relation to the investigation and determination of a complaint are to be treated in the same way as proceedings before a court.

Interpretation

16. In this Schedule—
  "redress scheme" has the meaning given in section 23A(8)(a);
  "approved redress scheme" has the meaning given in section 23A(8)(b);
  "buyer", in relation to residential property, has the meaning given in section 23A(8)(e);
  "complaint" has the meaning given in section 23A(8)(c);
  "ombudsman" means the independent person mentioned in section 23A(8)(a);
  "residential property" has the meaning given in section 23C;
  "scheme administrator", in relation to a redress scheme, means the person who administers the scheme;
  "seller", in relation to residential property, has the meaning given by section 23A(8)(d).]

NOTES

Schedule inserted by the Consumers, Estate Agents and Redress Act 2007, s 53(1), Sch 6, paras 1, 3.

Words in square brackets substituted by the Public Bodies (Abolition of the National Consumer Council and Transfer of the Office of Fair Trading's Functions in relation to Estate Agents etc) Order 2014, SI 2014/631, art 5(3)(a), Sch 2, Pt 1, para 1(1), (14), for transitional provisions and savings see art 5(3)(a), Sch 2, Pt 4 thereof at **[2.1133]**, **[2.1134A]**.

[SCHEDULE 4
PENALTY NOTICES UNDER SECTION 23B(1)

Section 23B(3)

[1.828]

1. A penalty charge notice given to a person under section 23B(1) by a duly authorised officer of an enforcement authority . . . must—

   (a)   state the officer's belief that that person has committed a breach of the duty imposed by an order under section 23A(1);

   (b)   give such other particulars of the circumstances as may be necessary to give reasonable notice of the breach of duty;

   (c)   require that person, within a period specified in the notice—

      (i)   to pay a penalty charge specified in the notice; or

      (ii)   to give notice to the enforcement authority that he wishes to review the notice;

   (d)   state the effect of paragraph 8;

   (e)   specify the person to whom and the address at which the penalty charge may be paid and the method or methods by which payment may be made; and

   (f)   specify the person to whom and the address at which a notice requesting a review may be sent (and to which any representations relating to the review may be addressed).

2. The penalty charge specified in the notice shall be of such amount (not exceeding £1,000) as may be prescribed for the time being by regulations made by the Secretary of State.

3. (1) The period specified under paragraph 1(c) must not be less than 28 days beginning with the day after that on which the penalty charge notice was given.

(2) The enforcement authority may extend the period for complying with the requirement mentioned in paragraph 1(c) in any particular case if they consider it appropriate to do so.

4. The enforcement authority may, if they consider that the penalty charge notice ought not to have been given, give the recipient a notice withdrawing the penalty charge notice.

5. (1) If, within the period specified under paragraph 1(c) (or that period as extended under paragraph 3(2)), the recipient of the penalty charge notice gives notice to the enforcement authority requesting a review, the authority shall—

   (a)   consider any representations made by the recipient and all other circumstances of the case;

   (b)   decide whether to confirm or withdraw the notice; and

   (c)   give notice of their decision to the recipient.

(2) A notice under sub-paragraph (1)(c) confirming the penalty charge notice must also state the effect of paragraphs 6(1) to (3) and 8(1) and (3).

(3) If the authority are not satisfied—

   (a)   that the recipient committed the breach of duty specified in the notice;

   (b)   that the notice was given within the time allowed by section 23B(2) and complies with the other requirements imposed by or under this Schedule; and

   (c)   that in the circumstances of the case it was appropriate for a penalty charge notice to be given to the recipient;

they shall withdraw the penalty charge notice.

6. (1) If after a review the penalty charge notice is confirmed by the enforcement authority, the recipient may, within the period of 28 days beginning with the day after that on which the notice under paragraph 5(1)(c) is given, appeal [in England and Wales to the county court or, in Northern Ireland,] to a county court or, in Scotland, to the sheriff against the penalty charge notice.

(2) The county court or the sheriff may extend the period for appealing against the notice.

(3) Such an appeal must be on one (or more) of the following grounds—

   (a)   that the recipient did not commit the breach of duty specified in the penalty charge notice;

   (b)   that the notice was not given within the time allowed by section 23B(2) or does not comply with any other requirement imposed by or under this Schedule; or

   (c)   that in the circumstances of the case it was inappropriate for the notice to be given to the recipient.

(4) An appeal against a penalty charge notice shall be by way of a rehearing; and the county court or sheriff shall either uphold the notice or quash it.

7. If the penalty charge notice is withdrawn or quashed, the authority shall repay any amount previously paid as a penalty charge in pursuance of the notice.

8. (1) The amount of the penalty charge is recoverable from the recipient of the penalty charge notice as a debt owed to the authority unless—

    (a)   the notice has been withdrawn or quashed; or

    (b)   the charge has been paid.

(2) Proceedings for the recovery of the penalty charge may not be commenced before the end of the period mentioned in paragraph 5(1).

(3) And if within that period the recipient of the penalty charge notice gives notice to the authority that he wishes the authority to review the penalty charge notice, such proceedings may not be commenced—

    (a)   before the end of the period mentioned in paragraph 6(1); and

    (b)   where the recipient appeals against the penalty charge notice, before the end of the period of 28 days beginning with the day on which the appeal is withdrawn or determined.

9. In proceedings for the recovery of the penalty charge, a certificate which—

    (a)   purports to be signed by or on behalf of the person having responsibility for the financial affairs of the enforcement authority; and

    (b)   states that payment of the penalty charge was or was not received by a date specified in the certificate;

is evidence of the facts stated.

10. Section 29 (service of notices etc) applies in relation to—

    (a)   any penalty charge notice which is to be given under section 23B(1) by a duly authorised officer of an enforcement authority . . . ; and

    (b)   any notice which is to be given under paragraph 5(1)(c) of this Schedule by such an enforcement authority;

as it applies in relation to any notice which under this Act is to be given to any person [by the lead enforcement authority].

11. The Secretary of State may by regulations make provision supplementary or incidental to the provisions of this Schedule, including in particular provision prescribing—

    (a)   the form of penalty charge notices or of any other notice mentioned in this Schedule;

    (b)   circumstances in which penalty charge notices may not be given;

    (c)   the method or methods by which penalty charges may be paid.

12. Any power to make regulations under this Schedule shall be exercisable by statutory instrument which shall be subject to annulment in pursuance of a resolution of either House of Parliament.]

NOTES

Schedule inserted by the Consumers, Estate Agents and Redress Act 2007, s 53(1), Sch 6, paras 1, 4.

Paras 1, 10: words omitted repealed, and words in square brackets substituted, by the Public Bodies (Abolition of the National Consumer Council and Transfer of the Office of Fair Trading's Functions in relation to Estate Agents etc) Order 2014, SI 2014/631, art 5(3)(a), Sch 2, Pt 1, para 1(1), (15), for transitional provisions and savings see art 5(3)(a), Sch 2, Pt 4 thereof at **[2.1133]**, **[2.1134A]**.

Para 6: in sub-para (1) words in square brackets inserted by the Crime and Courts Act 2013, s 17(5), Sch 9, Pt 3, para 82(b).

Regulations: the Estate Agents (Redress Scheme) (Penalty Charge) Regulations 2008, SI 2008/1713 at **[2.600]**.

SALE OF GOODS ACT 1979

(1979 c 54)

ARRANGEMENT OF SECTIONS

An Act to consolidate the law relating to the sale of goods

[6 December 1979]

PART I
CONTRACTS TO WHICH ACT APPLIES

[1.829]
1 Contracts to which Act applies
(1)   This Act applies to contracts of sale of goods made on or after (but not to those made before) 1 January 1894.
(2)   In relation to contracts made on certain dates, this Act applies subject to the modification of certain of its sections as mentioned in Schedule 1 below.
(3)   Any such modification is indicated in the section concerned by a reference to Schedule 1 below.
(4)   Accordingly, where a section does not contain such a reference, this Act applies in relation to the contract concerned without such modification of the section.
[(5)   Certain sections or subsections of this Act do not apply to a contract to which Chapter 2 of Part 1 of the Consumer Rights Act 2015 applies.
(6)   Where that is the case it is indicated in the section concerned.]

NOTES
Sub-ss (5), (6): added by the Consumer Rights Act 2015, s 60, Sch 1, paras 8, 9, as from 1 October 2015 (for transitional provisions see the Consumer Rights Act 2015 (Commencement No 3, Transitional Provisions, Savings and Consequential Amendments) Order 2015, SI 2015/1630, arts 6–8 at **[2.1220]** et seq).

PART II
FORMATION OF THE CONTRACT

Contract of sale

[1.830]
2   Contract of sale

(1)   A contract of sale of goods is a contract by which the seller transfers or agrees to transfer the property in goods to the buyer for a money consideration, called the price.

(2)   There may be a contract of sale between one part owner and another.

(3)   A contract of sale may be absolute or conditional.

(4)   Where under a contract of sale the property in the goods is transferred from the seller to the buyer the contract is called a sale.

(5)   Where under a contract of sale the transfer of the property in the goods is to take place at a future time or subject to some condition later to be fulfilled the contract is called an agreement to sell.

(6)   An agreement to sell becomes a sale when the time elapses or the conditions are fulfilled subject to which the property in the goods is to be transferred.

[1.831]
3   Capacity to buy and sell

(1)   Capacity to buy and sell is regulated by the general law concerning capacity to contract and to transfer and acquire property.

(2)   Where necessaries are sold and delivered to a minor or to a person who by reason of . . . drunkenness is incompetent to contract, he must pay a reasonable price for them.

(3)   In subsection (2) above "necessaries" means goods suitable to the condition in life of the minor or other person concerned and to his actual requirements at the time of the sale and delivery.

NOTES

Sub-s (2): words "mental incapacity or" (omitted) repealed, in relation to England and Wales, by the Mental Capacity Act 2005, s 67(1), Sch 6, para 24.

Formalities of contract

[1.832]
4   How contract of sale is made

(1)   Subject to this and any other Act, a contract of sale may be made in writing (either with or without seal), or by word of mouth, or partly in writing and partly by word of mouth, or may be implied from the conduct of the parties.

(2)   Nothing in this section affects the law relating to corporations.

Subject matter of contract

[1.833]
5   Existing or future goods

(1)   The goods which form the subject of a contract of sale may be either existing goods, owned or possessed by the seller, or goods to be manufactured or acquired by him after the making of the contract of sale, in this Act called future goods.

(2)   There may be a contract for the sale of goods the acquisition of which by the seller depends on a contingency which may or may not happen.

(3)   Where by a contract of sale the seller purports to effect a present sale of future goods, the contract operates as an agreement to sell the goods.

[1.834]
6   Goods which have perished

Where there is a contract for the sale of specific goods, and the goods without the knowledge of the seller have perished at the time when the contract is made, the contract is void.

[1.835]
7   Goods perishing before sale but after agreement to sell

Where there is an agreement to sell specific goods and subsequently the goods, without any fault on the part of the seller or buyer, perish before the risk passes to the buyer, the agreement is avoided.

The price

[1.836]
8   Ascertainment of price

(1)   The price in a contract of sale may be fixed by the contract, or may be left to be fixed in a manner agreed by the contract, or may be determined by the course of dealing between the parties.

(2)   Where the price is not determined as mentioned in subsection (1) above the buyer must pay a reasonable price.

(3)   What is a reasonable price is a question of fact dependent on the circumstances of each particular case.

[1.837]
9   Agreement to sell at valuation
(1)   Where there is an agreement to sell goods on the terms that the price is to be fixed by the valuation of a third party, and he cannot or does not make the valuation, the agreement is avoided; but if the goods or any part of them have been delivered to and appropriated by the buyer he must pay a reasonable price for them.

(2)   Where the third party is prevented from making the valuation by the fault of the seller or buyer, the party not at fault may maintain an action for damages against the party at fault.

[Implied terms etc]

[1.838]
10   Stipulations about time
(1)   Unless a different intention appears from the terms of the contract, stipulations as to time of payment are not of the essence of a contract of sale.

(2)   Whether any other stipulation as to time is or is not of the essence of the contract depends on the terms of the contract.

(3)   In a contract of sale "month" prima facie means calendar month.

NOTES
Cross-heading preceding this section substituted by the Sale and Supply of Goods Act 1994, s 7(1), Sch 2, para 5(1), (10).

[1.839]
11   When condition to be treated as warranty
[(1)   This section does not apply to Scotland.]

(2)   Where a contract of sale is subject to a condition to be fulfilled by the seller, the buyer may waive the condition, or may elect to treat the breach of the condition as a breach of warranty and not as a ground for treating the contract as repudiated.

(3)   Whether a stipulation in a contract of sale is a condition, the breach of which may give rise to a right to treat the contract as repudiated, or a warranty, the breach of which may give rise to a claim for damages but not to a right to reject the goods and treat the contract as repudiated, depends in each case on the construction of the contract; and a stipulation may be a condition, though called a warranty in the contract.

(4)   [Subject to section 35A below] where a contract of sale is not severable and the buyer has accepted the goods or part of them, the breach of a condition to be fulfilled by the seller can only be treated as a breach of warranty, and not as a ground for rejecting the goods and treating the contract as repudiated, unless there is an express or implied term of the contract to that effect.

[(4A)   Subsection (4) does not apply to a contract to which Chapter 2 of Part 1 of the Consumer Rights Act 2015 applies (but see the provision made about such contracts in sections 19 to 22 of that Act).]

(5)   . . .

(6)   Nothing in this section affects a condition or warranty whose fulfilment is excused by law by reason of impossibility or otherwise.

(7)   Paragraph 2 of Schedule 1 below applies in relation to a contract made before 22 April 1967 or (in the application of this Act to Northern Ireland) 28 July 1967.

NOTES
Sub-s (1): substituted by the Sale and Supply of Goods Act 1994, s 7(1), Sch 2, para 5(1), (2).

Sub-s (4): words in square brackets inserted by the Sale and Supply of Goods Act 1994, s 3(2).

Sub-s (4A): inserted by the Consumer Rights Act 2015, s 60, Sch 1, paras 8, 10, as from 1 October 2015 (for transitional provisions see the Consumer Rights Act 2015 (Commencement No 3, Transitional Provisions, Savings and Consequential Amendments) Order 2015, SI 2015/1630, arts 6–8 at **[2.1220]** et seq).

Sub-s (5): repealed by the Sale and Supply of Goods Act 1994, s 7, Sch 2, para 5(1), (2), Sch 3.

[1.840]
12   Implied terms about title, etc
(1)   In a contract of sale, other than one to which subsection (3) below applies, there is an implied [term] on the part of the seller that in the case of a sale he has a right to sell the goods, and in the case of an agreement to sell he will have such a right at the time when the property is to pass.

(2)   In a contract of sale, other than one to which subsection (3) below applies, there is also an implied [term] that—
    (a)   the goods are free, and will remain free until the time when the property is to pass, from any charge or encumbrance not disclosed or known to the buyer before the contract is made, and

    (b)   the buyer will enjoy quiet possession of the goods except so far as it may be disturbed by the owner or other person entitled to the benefit of any charge or encumbrance so disclosed or known.

(3)   This subsection applies to a contract of sale in the case of which there appears from the contract or is to be inferred from its circumstances an intention that the seller should transfer only such title as he or a third person may have.

(4) In a contract to which subsection (3) above applies there is an implied [term] that all charges or encumbrances known to the seller and not known to the buyer have been disclosed to the buyer before the contract is made.

(5) In a contract to which subsection (3) above applies there is also an implied [term] that none of the following will disturb the buyer's quiet possession of the goods, namely—

    (a)   the seller;

    (b)   in a case where the parties to the contract intend that the seller should transfer only such title as a third person may have, that person;

    (c)   anyone claiming through or under the seller or that third person otherwise than under a charge or encumbrance disclosed or known to the buyer before the contract is made.

[(5A) As regards England and Wales and Northern Ireland, the term implied by subsection (1) above is a condition and the terms implied by subsections (2), (4) and (5) above are warranties.]

(6) Paragraph 3 of Schedule 1 below applies in relation to a contract made before 18 May 1973.

[(7) This section does not apply to a contract to which Chapter 2 of Part 1 of the Consumer Rights Act 2015 applies (but see the provision made about such contracts in section 17 of that Act).]

NOTES

Sub-ss (1), (2), (4), (5): words in square brackets substituted by the Sale and Supply of Goods Act 1994, s 7(1), Sch 2, para 5(1), (3)(a).

Sub-s (5A): inserted by the Sale and Supply of Goods Act 1994, s 7(1), Sch 2, para 5(1), (3)(b).

Sub-s (7): added by the Consumer Rights Act 2015, s 60, Sch 1, paras 8, 11, as from 1 October 2015 (for transitional provisions see the Consumer Rights Act 2015 (Commencement No 3, Transitional Provisions, Savings and Consequential Amendments) Order 2015, SI 2015/1630, arts 6–8 at **[2.1220]** et seq).

[1.841]
13 Sale by description

(1) Where there is a contract for the sale of goods by description, there is an implied [term] that the goods will correspond with the description.

[(1A) As regards England and Wales and Northern Ireland, the term implied by subsection (1) above is a condition.]

(2) If the sale is by sample as well as by description it is not sufficient that the bulk of the goods corresponds with the sample if the goods do not also correspond with the description.

(3) A sale of goods is not prevented from being a sale by description by reason only that, being exposed for sale or hire, they are selected by the buyer.

(4) Paragraph 4 of Schedule 1 below applies in relation to a contract made before 18th May 1973.

[(5) This section does not apply to a contract to which Chapter 2 of Part 1 of the Consumer Rights Act 2015 applies (but see the provision made about such contracts in section 11 of that Act).]

NOTES

Sub-s (1): word in square brackets substituted by the Sale and Supply of Goods Act 1994, s 7(1), Sch 2, para 5(1), (4)(a).

Sub-s (1A): inserted by the Sale and Supply of Goods Act 1994, s 7(1), Sch 2, para 5(1), (4)(b).

Sub-s (5): added by the Consumer Rights Act 2015, s 60, Sch 1, paras 8, 12, as from 1 October 2015 (for transitional provisions see the Consumer Rights Act 2015 (Commencement No 3, Transitional Provisions, Savings and Consequential Amendments) Order 2015, SI 2015/1630, arts 6–8 at **[2.1220]** et seq).

[1.842]
14 Implied terms about quality or fitness

(1) Except as provided by this section and section 15 below and subject to any other enactment, there is no implied [term] about the quality or fitness for any particular purpose of goods supplied under a contract of sale.

[(2) Where the seller sells goods in the course of a business, there is an implied term that the goods supplied under the contract are of satisfactory quality.

(2A) For the purposes of this Act, goods are of satisfactory quality if they meet the standard that a reasonable person would regard as satisfactory, taking account of any description of the goods, the price (if relevant) and all the other relevant circumstances.

(2B) For the purposes of this Act, the quality of goods includes their state and condition and the following (among others) are in appropriate cases aspects of the quality of goods—

    (a)   fitness for all the purposes for which goods of the kind in question are commonly supplied,

    (b)   appearance and finish,

    (c)   freedom from minor defects,

    (d)   safety, and

    (e)   durability.

(2C) The term implied by subsection (2) above does not extend to any matter making the quality of goods unsatisfactory—

    (a)   which is specifically drawn to the buyer's attention before the contract is made,

    (b)   where the buyer examines the goods before the contract is made, which that examination ought to reveal, or

    (c)   in the case of a contract for sale by sample, which would have been apparent on a reasonable examination of the sample.]

[(2D)   If the buyer deals as consumer or, in Scotland, if a contract of sale is a consumer contract, the relevant circumstances mentioned in subsection (2A) above include any public statements on the specific characteristics of the goods made about them by the seller, the producer or his representative, particularly in advertising or on labelling.

(2E)   A public statement is not by virtue of subsection (2D) above a relevant circumstance for the purposes of subsection (2A) above in the case of a contract of sale, if the seller shows that—

   (a)   at the time the contract was made, he was not, and could not reasonably have been, aware of the statement,

   (b)   before the contract was made, the statement had been withdrawn in public or, to the extent that it contained anything which was incorrect or misleading, it had been corrected in public, or

   (c)   the decision to buy the goods could not have been influenced by the statement.

(2F)   Subsections (2D) and (2E) above do not prevent any public statement from being a relevant circumstance for the purposes of subsection (2A) above (whether or not the buyer deals as consumer or, in Scotland, whether or not the contract of sale is a consumer contract) if the statement would have been such a circumstance apart from those subsections.]

(3)   Where the seller sells goods in the course of a business and the buyer, expressly or by implication, makes known—

   (a)   to the seller, or

   (b)   where the purchase price or part of it is payable by instalments and the goods were previously sold by a credit-broker to the seller, to that credit-broker,

any particular purpose for which the goods are being bought, there is an implied [term] that the goods supplied under the contract are reasonably fit for that purpose, whether or not that is a purpose for which such goods are commonly supplied, except where the circumstances show that the buyer does not rely, or that it is unreasonable for him to rely, on the skill or judgment of the seller or credit-broker.

(4)   An implied [term] about quality or fitness for a particular purpose may be annexed to a contract of sale by usage.

(5)   The preceding provisions of this section apply to a sale by a person who in the course of a business is acting as agent for another as they apply to a sale by a principal in the course of a business, except where that other is not selling in the course of a business and either the buyer knows that fact or reasonable steps are taken to bring it to the notice of the buyer before the contract is made.

[(6)   As regard England and Wales and Northern Ireland, the terms implied by subsections (2) and (3) above are conditions.]

(7)   Paragraph 5 of Schedule 1 below applies in relation to a contract made on or after 18 May 1973 and before the appointed day, and paragraph 6 in relation to one made before 18th May 1973.

(8)   In subsection (7) above and paragraph 5 of Schedule 1 below references to the appointed day are to the day appointed for the purposes of those provisions by an order of the Secretary of State made by statutory instrument.

[(9)   This section does not apply to a contract to which Chapter 2 of Part 1 of the Consumer Rights Act 2015 applies (but see the provision made about such contracts in sections 9, 10 and 18 of that Act).]

NOTES

Sub-ss (1), (3), (4): words in square brackets substituted by the Sale and Supply of Goods Act 1994, s 7(1), Sch 2, para 5(1). (5)(a).

Sub-ss (2)–(2C): substituted, for original sub-s (2), by the Sale and Supply of Goods Act 1994, s 1(1).

Sub-ss (2D)–(2F): inserted by the Sale and Supply of Goods to Consumers Regulations 2002, SI 2002/3045, reg 3; repealed by the Consumer Rights Act 2015, s 60, Sch 1, paras 8, 13(1), (2), as from 1 October 2015 (for transitional provisions see the Consumer Rights Act 2015 (Commencement No 3, Transitional Provisions, Savings and Consequential Amendments) Order 2015, SI 2015/1630, arts 6–8 at **[2.1220]** et seq).

Sub-s (6): substituted by the Sale and Supply of Goods Act 1994, s 7(1), Sch 2, para (1), 5(5)(b).

Sub-s (9): added by the Consumer Rights Act 2015, s 60, Sch 1, paras 8, 13(1), (3), as from 1 October 2015 (for transitional provisions see note above).

Orders: the Sale of Goods Act 1979 (Appointed Day) Order 1983, SI 1983/1572 (appointing 19 May 1985 for the purposes of sub-s (7)).

Sale by sample

[1.843]
15   Sale by sample

(1)   A contract of sale is a contract for sale by sample where there is an express or implied term to that effect in the contract.

(2)   In the case of a contract for sale by sample there is an implied [term]—

   (a)   that the bulk will correspond with the sample in quality;

   (b)   . . .

   (c)   that the goods will be free from any defect, [making their quality unsatisfactory], which would not be apparent on reasonable examination of the sample.

[(3)   As regards England and Wales and Northern Ireland, the term implied by subsection (2) above is a condition.]

(4)   Paragraph 7 of Schedule 1 below applies in relation to a contract made before 18 May 1973.

[(5)   This section does not apply to a contract to which Chapter 2 of Part 1 of the Consumer Rights Act 2015 applies (but see the provision made about such contracts in sections 13 and 18 of that Act).]

NOTES

Sub-s (2): words in square brackets substituted, and para (b) repealed, by the Sale and Supply of Goods Act 1994, ss 1(2), 7, Sch 2, para 5(1), (6)(a), Sch 3.

Sub-s (3): substituted by the Sale and Supply of Goods Act 1994, s 7, Sch 2, para 5(1), (6)(b).

Sub-s (5): added by the Consumer Rights Act 2015, s 60, Sch 1, paras 8, 14, as from 1 October 2015 (for transitional provisions see the Consumer Rights Act 2015 (Commencement No 3, Transitional Provisions, Savings and Consequential Amendments) Order 2015, SI 2015/1630, arts 6–8 at **[2.1220]** et seq).

[Miscellaneous

[1.844]
15A   Modifications of remedies for breach of condition in non-consumer cases
(1)   Where in the case of a contract of sale—
  (a)   the buyer would, apart from this subsection, have the right to reject goods by reason of a breach on the part of the seller of a term implied by section 13, 14 or 15 above, but
  (b)   the breach is so slight that it would be unreasonable for him to reject them,
then, if the buyer does not deal as consumer, the breach is not to be treated as a breach of condition but may be treated as a breach of warranty.
(2)   This section applies unless a contrary intention appears in, or is to be implied from, the contract.
(3)   It is for the seller to show that a breach fell within subsection (1)(b) above.
(4)   This section does not apply to Scotland.]

NOTES

Inserted, together with preceding cross-heading, by the Sale and Supply of Goods Act 1994, s 4(1).

Sub-s (1): words in italics repealed by the Consumer Rights Act 2015, s 60, Sch 1, paras 8, 15, as from 1 October 2015 (for transitional provisions see the Consumer Rights Act 2015 (Commencement No 3, Transitional Provisions, Savings and Consequential Amendments) Order 2015, SI 2015/1630, arts 6–8 at **[2.1220]** et seq).

15B   (*Inserted by the Sale and Supply of Goods Act 1994, s 5(1) and applies to Scotland only.*)

PART III
EFFECTS OF THE CONTRACT

Transfer of property as between seller and buyer

[1.845]
16   Goods must be ascertained
[Subject to section 20A below] where there is a contract for the sale of unascertained goods no property in the goods is transferred to the buyer unless and until the goods are ascertained.

NOTES

Words in square brackets inserted by the Sale of Goods (Amendment) Act 1995, s 1(1).

[1.846]
17   Property passes when intended to pass
(1)   Where there is a contract for the sale of specific or ascertained goods the property in them is transferred to the buyer at such time as the parties to the contract intend it to be transferred.
(2)   For the purpose of ascertaining the intention of the parties regard shall be had to the terms of the contract, the conduct of the parties and the circumstances of the case.

[1.847]
18   Rules for ascertaining intention
Unless a different intention appears, the following are rules for ascertaining the intention of the parties as to the time at which the property in the goods is to pass to the buyer.
  Rule 1.—Where there is an unconditional contract for the sale of specific goods in a deliverable state the property in the goods passes to the buyer when the contract is made, and it is immaterial whether the time of payment or the time of delivery, or both, be postponed.
  Rule 2.—Where there is a contract for the sale of specific goods and the seller is bound to do something to the goods for the purpose of putting them into a deliverable state, the property does not pass until the thing is done and the buyer has notice that it has been done.
  Rule 3.—Where there is a contract for the sale of specific goods in a deliverable state but the seller is bound to weigh, measure, test, or do some other act or thing with reference to the goods for the purpose of ascertaining the price, the property does not pass until the act or thing is done and the buyer has notice that it has been done.

Rule 4.—When goods are delivered to the buyer on approval or on sale or return or other similar terms the property in the goods passes to the buyer:—

(a)   when he signifies his approval or acceptance to the seller or does any other act adopting the transaction;

(b)   if he does not signify his approval or acceptance to the seller but retains the goods without giving notice of rejection, then, if a time has been fixed for the return of the goods, on the expiration of that time, and, if no time has been fixed, on the expiration of a reasonable time.

Rule 5.—

(1)   Where there is a contract for the sale of unascertained or future goods by description, and goods of that description and in a deliverable state are unconditionally appropriated to the contract, either by the seller with the assent of the buyer or by the buyer with the assent of the seller, the property in the goods then passes to the buyer; and the assent may be express or implied, and may be given either before or after the appropriation is made.

(2)   Where, in pursuance of the contract, the seller delivers the goods to the buyer or to a carrier or other bailee or custodier (whether named by the buyer or not) for the purpose of transmission to the buyer, and does not reserve the right of disposal, he is to be taken to have unconditionally appropriated the goods to the contract.

[(3)   Where there is a contract for the sale of a specified quantity of unascertained goods in a deliverable state forming part of a bulk which is identified either in the contract or by subsequent agreement between the parties and the bulk is reduced to (or to less than) that quantity, then, if the buyer under that contract is the only buyer to whom goods are then due out of the bulk—

(a)   the remaining goods are to be taken as appropriated to that contract at the time when the bulk is so reduced; and

(b)   the property in those goods then passes to that buyer.

(4)   Paragraph (3) above applies also (with the necessary modifications) where a bulk is reduced to (or to less than) the aggregate of the quantities due to a single buyer under separate contracts relating to that bulk and he is the only buyer to whom goods are then due out of that bulk.]

NOTES

Paras (3), (4) of Rule 5 added by the Sale of Goods (Amendment) Act 1995, s 1(2).

[1.848]
19   Reservation of right of disposal

(1)   Where there is a contract for the sale of specific goods or where goods are subsequently appropriated to the contract, the seller may, by the terms of the contract or appropriation, reserve the right of disposal of the goods until certain conditions are fulfilled; and in such a case, notwithstanding the delivery of the goods to the buyer, or to a carrier or other bailee or custodier for the purpose of transmission to the buyer, the property in the goods does not pass to the buyer until the conditions imposed by the seller are fulfilled.

(2)   Where goods are shipped, and by the bill of lading the goods are deliverable to the order of the seller or his agent, the seller is prima facie to be taken to reserve the right of disposal.

(3)   Where the seller of goods draws on the buyer for the price, and transmits the bill of exchange and bill of lading to the buyer together to secure acceptance or payment of the bill of exchange, the buyer is bound to return the bill of lading if he does not honour the bill of exchange, and if he wrongfully retains the bill of lading the property in the goods does not pass to him.

[1.849]
[20   Passing of risk]

(1)   Unless otherwise agreed, the goods remain at the seller's risk until the property in them is transferred to the buyer, but when the property in them is transferred to the buyer the goods are at the buyer's risk whether delivery has been made or not.

(2)   But where delivery has been delayed through the fault of either buyer or seller the goods are at the risk of the party at fault as regards any loss which might not have occurred but for such fault.

(3)   Nothing in this section affects the duties or liabilities of either seller or buyer as a bailee or custodier of the goods of the other party.

[(4)   *In a case where the buyer deals as consumer or, in Scotland, where there is a consumer contract in which the buyer is a consumer, subsections (1) to (3) above must be ignored and the goods remain at the seller's risk until they are delivered to the consumer.*]

NOTES

Section heading: substituted by the Sale and Supply of Goods to Consumers Regulations 2002, SI 2002/3045, reg 4(1).

Sub-s (4): added by SI 2002/3045, reg 4(1), (2); substituted by the Consumer Rights Act 2015, s 60, Sch 1, paras 8, 17(1), as from 1 October 2015 (for transitional provisions see the Consumer Rights Act 2015 (Commencement No 3, Transitional Provisions, Savings and Consequential Amendments) Order 2015, SI 2015/1630, arts 6–8 at **[2.1220]** et seq), as follows:

"(4) This section does not apply to a contract to which Chapter 2 of Part 1 of the Consumer Rights Act 2015 applies (but see the provision made about such contracts in section 29 of that Act).".

[1.850]
[20A Undivided shares in goods forming part of a bulk
(1) This section applies to a contract for the sale of a specified quantity of unascertained goods if the following conditions are met—
    (a) the goods or some of them form part of a bulk which is identified either in the contract or by subsequent agreement between the parties; and
    (b) the buyer has paid the price for some or all of the goods which are the subject of the contract and which form part of the bulk.
(2) Where this section applies, then (unless the parties agree otherwise), as soon as the conditions specified in paragraphs (a) and (b) of subsection (1) above are met or at such later time as the parties may agree—
    (a) property in an undivided share in the bulk is transferred to the buyer, and
    (b) the buyer becomes an owner in common of the bulk.
(3) Subject to subsection (4) below, for the purposes of this section, the undivided share of a buyer in a bulk at any time shall be such share as the quantity of goods paid for and due to the buyer out of the bulk bears to the quantity of goods in the bulk at that time.
(4) Where the aggregate of the undivided shares of buyers in a bulk determined under subsection (3) above would at any time exceed the whole of the bulk at that time, the undivided share in the bulk of each buyer shall be reduced proportionately so that the aggregate of the undivided shares is equal to the whole bulk.
(5) Where a buyer has paid the price for only some of the goods due to him out of a bulk, any delivery to the buyer out of the bulk shall, for the purposes of this section, be ascribed in the first place to the goods in respect of which payment has been made.
(6) For the purposes of this section payment of part of the price for any goods shall be treated as payment for a corresponding part of the goods.]

NOTES
Inserted, together with s 20B, by the Sale of Goods (Amendment) Act 1995, s 1(3).

[1.851]
[20B Deemed consent by co-owner to dealings in bulk goods
(1) A person who has become an owner in common of a bulk by virtue of section 20A above shall be deemed to have consented to—
    (a) any delivery of goods out of the bulk to any other owner in common of the bulk, being goods which are due to him under his contract;
    (b) any dealing with or removal, delivery or disposal of goods in the bulk by any other person who is an owner in common of the bulk in so far as the goods fall within that co-owner's undivided share in the bulk at the time of the dealing, removal, delivery or disposal.
(2) No cause of action shall accrue to anyone against a person by reason of that person having acted in accordance with paragraph (a) or (b) of subsection (1) above in reliance on any consent deemed to have been given under that subsection.
(3) Nothing in this section or section 20A above shall—
    (a) impose an obligation on a buyer of goods out of a bulk to compensate any other buyer of goods out of that bulk for any shortfall in the goods received by that other buyer;
    (b) affect any contractual arrangement between buyers of goods out of a bulk for adjustments between themselves; or
    (c) affect the rights of any buyer under his contract.]

NOTES
Inserted as noted to s 20A at **[1.850]**.

Transfer of title

[1.852]
21 Sale by person not the owner
(1) Subject to this Act, where goods are sold by a person who is not their owner, and who does not sell them under the authority or with the consent of the owner, the buyer acquires no better title to the goods than the seller had, unless the owner of the goods is by his conduct precluded from denying the seller's authority to sell.
(2) Nothing in this Act affects—
    (a) the provisions of the Factors Acts or any enactment enabling the apparent owner of goods to dispose of them as if he were their true owner;
    (b) the validity of any contract of sale under any special common law or statutory power of sale or under the order of a court of competent jurisdiction.

[1.853]

22   Market overt

(1)   . . .

(2)   This section does not apply to Scotland.

(3)   Paragraph 8 of Schedule 1 below applies in relation to a contract under which goods were sold before 1st January 1968 or (in the application of this Act to Northern Ireland) 29th August 1967.

NOTES

     Sub-s (1): repealed by the Sale of Goods (Amendment) Act 1994, ss 1, 3(2), in relation to any contract for sale of goods made after 3 January 1995.

[1.854]

23   Sale under voidable title

When the seller of goods has a voidable title to them, but his title has not been avoided at the time of the sale, the buyer acquires a good title to the goods, provided he buys them in good faith and without notice of the seller's defect of title.

[1.855]

24   Seller in possession after sale

Where a person having sold goods continues or is in possession of the goods, or of the documents of title to the goods, the delivery or transfer by that person, or by a mercantile agent acting for him, of the goods or documents of title under any sale, pledge, or other disposition thereof, to any person receiving the same in good faith and without notice of the previous sale, has the same effect as if the person making the delivery or transfer were expressly authorised by the owner of the goods to make the same.

[1.856]

25   Buyer in possession after sale

(1)   Where a person having bought or agreed to buy goods obtains, with the consent of the seller, possession of the goods or the documents of title to the goods, the delivery or transfer by that person, or by a mercantile agent acting for him, of the goods or documents of title, under any sale, pledge, or other disposition thereof, to any person receiving the same in good faith and without notice of any lien or other right of the original seller in respect of the goods, has the same effect as if the person making the delivery or transfer were a mercantile agent in possession of the goods or documents of title with the consent of the owner.

(2)   For the purposes of subsection (1) above—

    (a)   the buyer under a conditional sale agreement is to be taken not to be a person who has bought or agreed to buy goods, and

    (b)   "conditional sale agreement" means an agreement for the sale of goods which is a consumer credit agreement within the meaning of the Consumer Credit Act 1974 under which the purchase price or part of it is payable by instalments, and the property in the goods is to remain in the seller (notwithstanding that the buyer is to be in possession of the goods) until such conditions as to the payment of instalments or otherwise as may be specified in the agreement are fulfilled.

(3)   Paragraph 9 of Schedule 1 below applies in relation to a contract under which a person buys or agrees to buy goods and which is made before the appointed day.

(4)   In subsection (3) above and paragraph 9 of Schedule 1 below references to the appointed day are to the day appointed for the purposes of those provisions by an order of the Secretary of State made by statutory instrument.

NOTES

     Orders: the Sale of Goods Act 1979 (Appointed Day) Order 1983, SI 1983/1572 (appointing 19 May 1985 for the purposes of sub-s (3)).

[1.857]

26   Supplementary to sections 24 and 25

In sections 24 and 25 above "mercantile agent" means a mercantile agent having in the customary course of his business as such agent authority either—

    (a)   to sell goods, or

    (b)   to consign goods for the purpose of sale, or

    (c)   to buy goods, or

    (d)   to raise money on the security of goods.

PART IV
PERFORMANCE OF THE CONTRACT

[1.858]

27   Duties of seller and buyer

It is the duty of the seller to deliver the goods, and of the buyer to accept and pay for them, in accordance with the terms of the contract of sale.

[1.859]
28 Payment and delivery are concurrent conditions
Unless otherwise agreed, delivery of the goods and payment of the price are concurrent conditions, that is to say, the seller must be ready and willing to give possession of the goods to the buyer in exchange for the price and the buyer must be ready and willing to pay the price in exchange for possession of the goods.

[1.860]
29 Rules about delivery
(1) Whether it is for the buyer to take possession of the goods or for the seller to send them to the buyer is a question depending in each case on the contract, express or implied, between the parties.
(2) Apart from any such contract, express or implied, the place of delivery is the seller's place of business if he has one, and if not, his residence; except that, if the contract is for the sale of specific goods, which to the knowledge of the parties when the contract is made are in some other place, then that place is the place of delivery.
(3) Where under the contract of sale the seller is bound to send the goods to the buyer, but no time for sending them is fixed, the seller is bound to send them within a reasonable time.
[(3A) Subsection (3) does not apply to a contract to which Chapter 2 of Part 1 of the Consumer Rights Act 2015 applies (but see the provision made about such contracts in section 28 of that Act).]
(4) Where the goods at the time of sale are in the possession of a third person, there is no delivery by seller to buyer unless and until the third person acknowledges to the buyer that he holds the goods on his behalf; but nothing in this section affects the operation of the issue or transfer of any document of title to goods.
(5) Demand or tender of delivery may be treated as ineffectual unless made at a reasonable hour; and what is a reasonable hour is a question of fact.
(6) Unless otherwise agreed, the expenses of and incidental to putting the goods into a deliverable state must be borne by the seller.

NOTES

Sub-s (3A): inserted by the Consumer Rights Act 2015, s 60, Sch 1, paras 8, 18, as from 1 October 2015 (for transitional provisions see the Consumer Rights Act 2015 (Commencement No 3, Transitional Provisions, Savings and Consequential Amendments) Order 2015, SI 2015/1630, arts 6–8 at **[2.1220]** et seq).

[1.861]
30 Delivery of wrong quantity
(1) Where the seller delivers to the buyer a quantity of goods less than he contracted to sell, the buyer may reject them, but if the buyer accepts the goods so delivered he must pay for them at the contract rate.
(2) Where the seller delivers to the buyer a quantity of goods larger than he contracted to sell, the buyer may accept the goods included in the contract and reject the rest, or he may reject the whole.
[(2A) A buyer *who does not deal as consumer* may not—
   (a) where the seller delivers a quantity of goods less than he contracted to sell, reject the goods under subsection (1) above, or
   (b) where the seller delivers a quantity of goods larger than he contracted to sell, reject the whole under subsection (2) above,
if the shortfall or, as the case may be, excess is so slight that it would be unreasonable for him to do so.
(2B) It is for the seller to show that a shortfall or excess fell within subsection (2A) above.
(2C) Subsections (2A) and (2B) above do not apply to Scotland.
(2D), (2E) *(Apply to Scotland only.)*]
(3) Where the seller delivers to the buyer a quantity of goods larger than he contracted to sell and the buyer accepts the whole of the goods so delivered he must pay for them at the contract rate.
(4) . . .
(5) This section is subject to any usage of trade, special agreement, or course of dealing between the parties.
[(6) This section does not apply to a contract to which Chapter 2 of Part 1 of the Consumer Rights Act 2015 applies (but see the provision made about such contracts in section 25 of that Act).]

NOTES

Sub-ss (2A)–(2E): inserted by the Sale and Supply of Goods Act 1994, ss 4(2), 5(2); in sub-s (2A) words in italics repealed by the Consumer Rights Act 2015, s 60, Sch 1, paras 8, 19(1), (2), as from 1 October 2015 (for transitional provisions see the Consumer Rights Act 2015 (Commencement No 3, Transitional Provisions, Savings and Consequential Amendments) Order 2015, SI 2015/1630, arts 6–8 at **[2.1220]** et seq).

Sub-s (4): repealed by the Sale and Supply of Goods Act 1994, ss 3(3), 7(2), Sch 3.

Sub-s (6): added by the Consumer Rights Act 2015, s 60, Sch 1, paras 8, 19(1), (3), as from 1 October 2015 (for transitional provisions see note above).

[1.862]

31   Instalment deliveries

(1)   Unless otherwise agreed, the buyer of goods is not bound to accept delivery of them by instalments.

(2)   Where there is a contract for the sale of goods to be delivered by stated instalments, which are to be separately paid for, and the seller makes defective deliveries in respect of one or more instalments, or the buyer neglects or refuses to take delivery of or pay for one or more instalments, it is a question in each case depending on the terms of the contract and the circumstances of the case whether the breach of contract is a repudiation of the whole contract or whether it is a severable breach giving rise to a claim for compensation but not to a right to treat the whole contract as repudiated.

[(3)   This section does not apply to a contract to which Chapter 2 of Part 1 of the Consumer Rights Act 2015 applies (but see the provision made about such contracts in section 26 of that Act).]

NOTES

Sub-s (3): added by the Consumer Rights Act 2015, s 60, Sch 1, paras 8, 20, as from 1 October 2015 (for transitional provisions see the Consumer Rights Act 2015 (Commencement No 3, Transitional Provisions, Savings and Consequential Amendments) Order 2015, SI 2015/1630, arts 6–8 at **[2.1220]** et seq).

[1.863]

32   Delivery to carrier

(1)   Where, in pursuance of a contract of sale, the seller is authorised or required to send the goods to the buyer, delivery of the goods to a carrier (whether named by the buyer or not) for the purpose of transmission to the buyer is prima facie deemed to be a delivery of the goods to the buyer.

(2)   Unless otherwise authorised by the buyer, the seller must make such contract with the carrier on behalf of the buyer as may be reasonable having regard to the nature of the goods and the other circumstances of the case; and if the seller omits to do so, and the goods are lost or damaged in course of transit, the buyer may decline to treat the delivery to the carrier as a delivery to himself or may hold the seller responsible in damages.

(3)   Unless otherwise agreed, where goods are sent by the seller to the buyer by a route involving sea transit, under circumstances in which it is usual to insure, the seller must give such notice to the buyer as may enable him to insure them during their sea transit; and if the seller fails to do so, the goods are at his risk during such sea transit.

[(4)   *In a case where the buyer deals as consumer or, in Scotland, where there is a consumer contract in which the buyer is a consumer, subsections (1) to (3) above must be ignored, but if in pursuance of a contract of sale the seller is authorised or required to send the goods to the buyer, delivery of the goods to the carrier is not delivery of the goods to the buyer.*]

NOTES

Sub-s (4): added by the Sale and Supply of Goods to Consumers Regulations 2002, SI 2002/3045, reg 4(3); substituted by the Consumer Rights Act 2015, s 60, Sch 1, paras 8, 21, as from 1 October 2015 (for transitional provisions see the Consumer Rights Act 2015 (Commencement No 3, Transitional Provisions, Savings and Consequential Amendments) Order 2015, SI 2015/1630, arts 6–8 at **[2.1220]** et seq), as follows:

"(4)   This section does not apply to a contract to which Chapter 2 of Part 1 of the Consumer Rights Act 2015 applies (but see the provision made about such contracts in section 29 of that Act).".

[1.864]

33   Risk where goods are delivered at distant place

[(1)]   Where the seller of goods agrees to deliver them at his own risk at a place other than that where they are when sold, the buyer must nevertheless (unless otherwise agreed) take any risk of deterioration in the goods necessarily incident to the course of transit.

[(2)   This section does not apply to a contract to which Chapter 2 of Part 1 of the Consumer Rights Act 2015 applies (but see the provision made about such contracts in section 29 of that Act).]

NOTES

Sub-s (1): numbered as such and sub-s (2) added by the Consumer Rights Act 2015, s 60, Sch 1, paras 8, 22, as from 1 October 2015 (for transitional provisions see the Consumer Rights Act 2015 (Commencement No 3, Transitional Provisions, Savings and Consequential Amendments) Order 2015, SI 2015/1630, arts 6–8 at **[2.1220]** et seq).

[1.865]

34   Buyer's right of examining the goods

[(1)]   . . .   Unless otherwise agreed, when the seller tenders delivery of goods to the buyer, he is bound on request to afford the buyer a reasonable opportunity of examining the goods for the purpose of ascertaining whether they are in conformity with the contract [and, in the case of a contract for sale by sample, of comparing the bulk with the sample.]

[(2)   Nothing in this section affects the operation of section 22 (time limit for short-term right to reject) of the Consumer Rights Act 2015.]

NOTES

Sub-s (1): numbered as such by the Consumer Rights Act 2015, s 60, Sch 1, paras 8, 23(1), (2), as from 1 October 2015 (for transitional provisions see the Consumer Rights Act 2015 (Commencement No 3, Transitional Provisions, Savings and Consequential Amendments) Order 2015, SI 2015/1630, arts 6–8 at **[2.1220]** et seq); words omitted repealed, and words in square brackets added, by the Sale and Supply of Goods Act 1994, ss 2(2), 7(2), Sch 3.

Sub-s (2): added by the Consumer Rights Act 2015, s 60, Sch 1, paras 8, 23(1), (3), as from 1 October 2015 (for transitional provisions see note above).

[1.866]

35 Acceptance

(1) The buyer is deemed to have accepted the goods [subject to subsection (2) below—
  (a) when he intimates to the seller that he has accepted them, or
  (b) when the goods have been delivered to him and he does any act in relation to them which is inconsistent with the ownership of the seller.

(2) Where goods are delivered to the buyer, and he has not previously examined them, he is not deemed to have accepted them under subsection (1) above until he has had a reasonable opportunity of examining them for the purpose—
  (a) of ascertaining whether they are in conformity with the contract, and
  (b) in the case of a contract for sale by sample, of comparing the bulk with the sample.

(3) Where the buyer deals as consumer or (in Scotland) the contract of sale is a consumer contract, the buyer cannot lose his right to rely on subsection (2) above by agreement, waiver or otherwise.

(4) The buyer is also deemed to have accepted the goods when after the lapse of a reasonable time he retains the goods without intimating to the seller that he has rejected them.

(5) The questions that are material in determining for the purposes of subsection (4) above whether a reasonable time has elapsed include whether the buyer has had a reasonable opportunity of examining the goods for the purpose mentioned in subsection (2) above.

(6) The buyer is not by virtue of this section deemed to have accepted the goods merely because—
  (a) he asks for, or agrees to, their repair by or under an arrangement with the seller, or
  (b) the goods are delivered to another under a sub-sale or other disposition.

(7) Where the contract is for the sale of goods making one or more commercial units, a buyer accepting any goods included in a unit is deemed to have accepted all the goods making the unit; and in this subsection "commercial unit" means a unit division of which would materially impair the value of the goods or the character of the unit.

(8)] Paragraph 10 of Schedule 1 below applies in relation to a contract made before 22nd April 1967 or (in the application of this Act of Northern Ireland) 28th July 1967.

[(9) This section does not apply to a contract to which Chapter 2 of Part 1 of the Consumer Rights Act 2015 applies (but see the provision made about such contracts in section 21 of that Act).]

NOTES

In sub-s (1) words in square brackets substituted, together with sub-ss (2)–(7), and sub-s (8) numbered as such, by the Sale and Supply of Goods Act 1994, s 2(1).

Sub-s (3): repealed by the Consumer Rights Act 2015, s 60, Sch 1, paras 8, 24(1), (2), as from 1 October 2015 (for transitional provisions see the Consumer Rights Act 2015 (Commencement No 3, Transitional Provisions, Savings and Consequential Amendments) Order 2015, SI 2015/1630, arts 6–8 at **[2.1220]** et seq).

Sub-s (9): added by the Consumer Rights Act 2015, s 60, Sch 1, paras 8, 24(1), (3), as from 1 October 2015 (for transitional provisions see note above).

[1.867]

[35A Right of partial rejection

(1) If the buyer—
  (a) has the right to reject the goods by reason of a breach on the part of the seller that affects some or all of them, but
  (b) accepts some of the goods, including, where there are any goods unaffected by the breach, all such goods,

he does not by accepting them lose his right to reject the rest.

(2) In the case of a buyer having the right to reject an instalment of goods, subsection (1) above applies as if references to the goods were references to the goods comprised in the instalment.

(3) For the purposes of subsection (1) above, goods are affected by a breach if by reason of the breach they are not in conformity with the contract.

(4) This section applies unless a contrary intention appears in, or is to be implied from, the contract.

[(5) This section does not apply to a contract to which Chapter 2 of Part 1 of the Consumer Rights Act 2015 applies (but see the provision made about such contracts in section 21 of that Act).]]

NOTES

Inserted by the Sale and Supply of Goods Act 1994, s 3(1).

Sub-s (5): added by the Consumer Rights Act 2015, s 60, Sch 1, paras 8, 25, as from 1 October 2015 (for transitional provisions see the Consumer Rights Act 2015 (Commencement No 3, Transitional Provisions, Savings and Consequential Amendments) Order 2015, SI 2015/1630, arts 6–8 at **[2.1220]** et seq).

[1.868]
36   Buyer not bound to return rejected goods

[(1)]   Unless otherwise agreed, where goods are delivered to the buyer, and he refuses to accept them, having the right to do so, he is not bound to return them to the seller, but it is sufficient if he intimates to the seller that he refuses to accept them.

[(2)   This section does not apply to a contract to which Chapter 2 of Part 1 of the Consumer Rights Act 2015 applies (but see the provision made about such contracts in section 20 of that Act).]

NOTES

Sub-s (1): numbered as such and sub-s (2) added by the Consumer Rights Act 2015, s 60, Sch 1, paras 8, 26, as from 1 October 2015 (for transitional provisions see the Consumer Rights Act 2015 (Commencement No 3, Transitional Provisions, Savings and Consequential Amendments) Order 2015, SI 2015/1630, arts 6–8 at **[2.1220]** et seq).

[1.869]
37   Buyer's liability for not taking delivery of goods

(1)   When the seller is ready and willing to deliver the goods, and requests the buyer to take delivery, and the buyer does not within a reasonable time after such request take delivery of the goods, he is liable to the seller for any loss occasioned by his neglect or refusal to take delivery, and also for a reasonable charge for the care and custody of the goods.

(2)   Nothing in this section affects the rights of the seller where the neglect or refusal of the buyer to take delivery amounts to a repudiation of the contract.

PART V
RIGHTS OF UNPAID SELLER AGAINST THE GOODS

Preliminary

[1.870]
38   Unpaid seller defined

(1)   The seller of goods is an unpaid seller within the meaning of this Act—

    (a)   when the whole of the price has not been paid or tendered;

    (b)   when a bill of exchange or other negotiable instrument has been received as conditional payment, and the condition on which it was received has not been fulfilled by reason of the dishonour of the instrument or otherwise.

(2)   In this Part of this Act "seller" includes any person who is in the position of a seller, as, for instance, an agent of the seller to whom the bill of lading has been indorsed, or a consignor or agent who has himself paid (or is directly responsible for) the price.

[1.871]
39   Unpaid seller's rights

(1)   Subject to this and any other Act, notwithstanding that the property in the goods may have passed to the buyer, the unpaid seller of goods, as such, has by implication of law—

    (a)   a lien on the goods or right to retain them for the price while he is in possession of them;

    (b)   in case of the insolvency of the buyer, a right of stopping the goods in transit after he has parted with the possession of them;

    (c)   a right of re-sale as limited by this Act.

(2)   Where the property in goods has not passed to the buyer, the unpaid seller has (in addition to his other remedies) a right of withholding delivery similar to and co-extensive with his rights of lien or retention and stoppage in transit where the property has passed to the buyer.

40   (*Repealed by the Debtors (Scotland) Act 1987, s 108(3), Sch 8.*)

Unpaid seller's lien

[1.872]
41   Seller's lien

(1)   Subject to this Act, the unpaid seller of goods who is in possession of them is entitled to retain possession of them until payment or tender of the price in the following cases:—

    (a)   where the goods have been sold without any stipulation as to credit;

    (b)   where the goods have been sold on credit but the term of credit has expired;

    (c)   where the buyer becomes insolvent.

(2)   The seller may exercise his lien or right of retention notwithstanding that he is in possession of the goods as agent or bailee or custodier for the buyer.

[1.873]
42 Part delivery
Where an unpaid seller has made part delivery of the goods, he may exercise his lien or right of retention on the remainder, unless such part delivery has been made under such circumstances as to show an agreement to waive the lien or right of retention.

[1.874]
43 Termination of lien
(1) The unpaid seller of goods loses his lien or right of retention in respect of them—
  (a) when he delivers the goods to a carrier or other bailee or custodier for the purpose of transmission to the buyer without reserving the right of disposal of the goods;
  (b) when the buyer or his agent lawfully obtains possession of the goods;
  (c) by waiver of the lien or right of retention.
(2) An unpaid seller of goods who has a lien or right of retention in respect of them does not lose his lien or right of retention by reason only that he has obtained judgment or decree for the price of the goods.

Stoppage in transit

[1.875]
44 Right of stoppage in transit
Subject to this Act, when the buyer of goods becomes insolvent the unpaid seller who has parted with the possession of the goods has the right of stopping them in transit, that is to say, he may resume possession of the goods as long as they are in course of transit, and may retain them until payment or tender of the price.

[1.876]
45 Duration of transit
(1) Goods are deemed to be in course of transit from the time when they are delivered to a carrier or other bailee or custodier for the purpose of transmission to the buyer, until the buyer or his agent in that behalf takes delivery of them from the carrier or other bailee or custodier.
(2) If the buyer or his agent in that behalf obtains delivery of the goods before their arrival at the appointed destination, the transit is at an end.
(3) If, after the arrival of the goods at the appointed destination, the carrier or other bailee or custodier acknowledges to the buyer or his agent that he holds the goods on his behalf and continues in possession of them as bailee or custodier for the buyer or his agent, the transit is at an end, and it is immaterial that a further destination for the goods may have been indicated by the buyer.
(4) If the goods are rejected by the buyer, and the carrier or other bailee or custodier continues in possession of them, the transit is not deemed to be at an end, even if the seller has refused to receive them back.
(5) When goods are delivered to a ship chartered by the buyer it is a question depending on the circumstances of the particular case whether they are in the possession of the master as a carrier or as agent to the buyer.
(6) Where the carrier or other bailee or custodier wrongfully refuses to deliver the goods to the buyer or his agent in that behalf, the transit is deemed to be at an end.
(7) Where part delivery of the goods has been made to the buyer or his agent in that behalf, the remainder of the goods may be stopped in transit, unless such part delivery has been made under such circumstances as to show an agreement to give up possession of the whole of the goods.

[1.877]
46 How stoppage in transit is effected
(1) The unpaid seller may exercise his right of stoppage in transit either by taking actual possession of the goods or by giving notice of his claim to the carrier or other bailee or custodier in whose possession the goods are.
(2) The notice may be given either to the person in actual possession of the goods or to his principal.
(3) If given to the principal, the notice is ineffective unless given at such time and under such circumstances that the principal, by the exercise of reasonable diligence, may communicate it to his servant or agent in time to prevent a delivery to the buyer.
(4) When notice of stoppage in transit is given by the seller to the carrier or other bailee or custodier in possession of the goods, he must re-deliver the goods to, or according to the directions of, the seller; and the expenses of the re-delivery must be borne by the seller.

Re-sale etc by buyer

[1.878]
47 Effect of sub-sale etc by buyer
(1) Subject to this Act, the unpaid seller's right of lien or retention or stoppage in transit is not affected by any sale or other disposition of the goods which the buyer may have made, unless the seller has assented to it.

(2)   Where a document of title to goods has been lawfully transferred to any person as buyer or owner of the goods, and that person transfers the document to a person who takes it in good faith and for valuable consideration, then—

   (a)   if the last-mentioned transfer was by way of sale the unpaid seller's right of lien or retention or stoppage in transit is defeated; and

   (b)   if the last-mentioned transfer was made by way of pledge or other disposition for value, the unpaid seller's right of lien or retention or stoppage in transit can only be exercised subject to the rights of the transferee.

Rescission: and re-sale by seller

[1.879]
48   Rescission: and re-sale by seller
(1)   Subject to this section, a contract of sale is not rescinded by the mere exercise by an unpaid seller of his right of lien or retention or stoppage in transit.

(2)   Where an unpaid seller who has exercised his right of lien or retention or stoppage in transit re-sells the goods, the buyer acquires a good title to them as against the original buyer.

(3)   Where the goods are of a perishable nature, or where the unpaid seller gives notice to the buyer of his intention to re-sell, and the buyer does not within a reasonable time pay or tender the price, the unpaid seller may re-sell the goods and recover from the original buyer damages for any loss occasioned by his breach of contract.

(4)   Where the seller expressly reserves the right of re-sale in case the buyer should make default, and on the buyer making default re-sells the goods, the original contract of sale is rescinded but without prejudice to any claim the seller may have for damages.

[PART VA
ADDITIONAL RIGHTS OF BUYER IN CONSUMER CASES

[1.880]
48A   Introductory
(1)   This section applies if—

   (a)   the buyer deals as consumer or, in Scotland, there is a consumer contract in which the buyer is a consumer, and

   (b)   the goods do not conform to the contract of sale at the time of delivery.

(2)   If this section applies, the buyer has the right—

   (a)   under and in accordance with section 48B below, to require the seller to repair or replace the goods, or

   (b)   under and in accordance with section 48C below—

      (i)   to require the seller to reduce the purchase price of the goods to the buyer by an appropriate amount, or

      (ii)   to rescind the contract with regard to the goods in question.

(3)   For the purposes of subsection (1)(b) above goods which do not conform to the contract of sale at any time within the period of six months starting with the date on which the goods were delivered to the buyer must be taken not to have so conformed at that date.

(4)   Subsection (3) above does not apply if—

   (a)   it is established that the goods did so conform at that date;

   (b)   its application is incompatible with the nature of the goods or the nature of the lack of conformity.]

NOTES
Part VA (ss 48A–48F) inserted by the Sale and Supply of Goods to Consumers Regulations 2002, SI 2002/3045, reg 5; repealed by the Consumer Rights Act 2015, s 60, Sch 1, paras 8, 27, as from 1 October 2015 (for transitional provisions see the Consumer Rights Act 2015 (Commencement No 3, Transitional Provisions, Savings and Consequential Amendments) Order 2015, SI 2015/1630, arts 6–8 at **[2.1220]** et seq).

[1.881]
[48B   Repair or replacement of the goods
(1)   If section 48A above applies, the buyer may require the seller—

   (a)   to repair the goods, or

   (b)   to replace the goods.

(2)   If the buyer requires the seller to repair or replace the goods, the seller must—

   (a)   repair or, as the case may be, replace the goods within a reasonable time but without causing significant inconvenience to the buyer;

   (b)   bear any necessary costs incurred in doing so (including in particular the cost of any labour, materials or postage).

(3)   The buyer must not require the seller to repair or, as the case may be, replace the goods if that remedy is—

   (a)   impossible, or

   (b)   disproportionate in comparison to the other of those remedies, or

   (c)   disproportionate in comparison to an appropriate reduction in the purchase price under paragraph (a), or rescission under paragraph (b), of section 48C(1) below.

(4) One remedy is disproportionate in comparison to the other if the one imposes costs on the seller which, in comparison to those imposed on him by the other, are unreasonable, taking into account—

(a) the value which the goods would have if they conformed to the contract of sale,

(b) the significance of the lack of conformity, and

(c) whether the other remedy could be effected without significant inconvenience to the buyer.

(5) Any question as to what is a reasonable time or significant inconvenience is to be determined by reference to—

(a) the nature of the goods, and

(b) the purpose for which the goods were acquired.]

NOTES

Inserted and repealed as noted to s 48A at **[1.880]**.

[1.882]

[48C Reduction of purchase price or rescission of contract

(1) If section 48A above applies, the buyer may—

(a) require the seller to reduce the purchase price of the goods in question to the buyer by an appropriate amount, or

(b) rescind the contract with regard to those goods,

if the condition in subsection (2) below is satisfied.

(2) The condition is that—

(a) by virtue of section 48B(3) above the buyer may require neither repair nor replacement of the goods; or

(b) the buyer has required the seller to repair or replace the goods, but the seller is in breach of the requirement of section 48B(2)(a) above to do so within a reasonable time and without significant inconvenience to the buyer.

(3) For the purposes of this Part, if the buyer rescinds the contract, any reimbursement to the buyer may be reduced to take account of the use he has had of the goods since they were delivered to him.]

NOTES

Inserted and repealed as noted to s 48A at **[1.880]**.

[1.883]

[48D Relation to other remedies etc

(1) If the buyer requires the seller to repair or replace the goods the buyer must not act under subsection (2) until he has given the seller a reasonable time in which to repair or replace (as the case may be) the goods.

(2) The buyer acts under this subsection if—

(a) in England and Wales or Northern Ireland he rejects the goods and terminates the contract for breach of condition;

(b) in Scotland he rejects any goods delivered under the contract and treats it as repudiated;

(c) he requires the goods to be replaced or repaired (as the case may be).]

NOTES

Inserted and repealed as noted to s 48A at **[1.880]**.

[1.884]

[48E Powers of the court

(1) In any proceedings in which a remedy is sought by virtue of this Part the court, in addition to any other power it has, may act under this section.

(2) On the application of the buyer the court may make an order requiring specific performance or, in Scotland, specific implement by the seller of any obligation imposed on him by virtue of section 48B above.

(3) Subsection (4) applies if—

(a) the buyer requires the seller to give effect to a remedy under section 48B or 48C above or has claims to rescind under section 48C, but

(b) the court decides that another remedy under section 48B or 48C is appropriate.

(4) The court may proceed—

(a) as if the buyer had required the seller to give effect to the other remedy, or if the other remedy is rescission under section 48C

(b) as if the buyer had claimed to rescind the contract under that section.

(5) If the buyer has claimed to rescind the contract the court may order that any reimbursement to the buyer is reduced to take account of the use he has had of the goods since they were delivered to him.

(6) The court may make an order under this section unconditionally or on such terms and conditions as to damages, payment of the price and otherwise as it thinks just.]

NOTES
Inserted and repealed as noted to s 48A at **[1.880]**.

[1.885]
[48F   Conformity with the contract
For the purposes of this Part, goods do not conform to a contract of sale if there is, in relation to the goods, a breach of an express term of the contract or a term implied by section 13, 14 or 15 above.]

NOTES
Inserted and repealed as noted to s 48A at **[1.880]**.

PART VI
ACTIONS FOR BREACH OF THE CONTRACT
Seller's remedies

[1.886]
49   Action for price
(1)   Where, under a contract of sale, the property in the goods has passed to the buyer and he wrongfully neglects or refuses to pay for the goods according to the terms of the contract, the seller may maintain an action against him for the price of the goods.
(2)   Where, under a contract of sale, the price is payable on a day certain irrespective of delivery and the buyer wrongfully neglects or refuses to pay such price, the seller may maintain an action for the price, although the property in the goods has not passed and the goods have not been appropriated to the contract.
(3)   (*Applies to Scotland only.*)

[1.887]
50   Damages for non-acceptance
(1)   Where the buyer wrongfully neglects or refuses to accept and pay for the goods, the seller may maintain an action against him for damages for non-acceptance.
(2)   The measure of damages is the estimated loss directly and naturally resulting, in the ordinary course of events, from the buyer's breach of contract.
(3)   Where there is an available market for the goods in question the measure of damages is prima facie to be ascertained by the difference between the contract price and the market or current price at the time or times when the goods ought to have been accepted or (if no time was fixed for acceptance) at the time of the refusal to accept.

Buyer's remedies

[1.888]
51   Damages for non-delivery
(1)   Where the seller wrongfully neglects or refuses to deliver the goods to the buyer, the buyer may maintain an action against the seller for damages for non-delivery.
(2)   The measure of damages is the estimated loss directly and naturally resulting, in the ordinary course of events, from the seller's breach of contract.
(3)   Where there is an available market for the goods in question the measure of damages is prima facie to be ascertained by the difference between the contract price and the market or current price of the goods at the time or times when they ought to have been delivered or (if no time was fixed) at the time of the refusal to deliver.
[(4)   This section does not apply to a contract to which Chapter 2 of Part 1 of the Consumer Rights Act 2015 applies (but see the provision made about such contracts in section 19 of that Act).]

NOTES
Sub-s (4): added by the Consumer Rights Act 2015, s 60, Sch 1, paras 8, 28, as from 1 October 2015 (for transitional provisions see the Consumer Rights Act 2015 (Commencement No 3, Transitional Provisions, Savings and Consequential Amendments) Order 2015, SI 2015/1630, arts 6–8 at **[2.1220]** et seq).

[1.889]
52   Specific performance
(1)   In any action for breach of contract to deliver specific or ascertained goods the court may, if it thinks fit, on the plaintiff's application, by its judgment or decree direct that the contract shall be performed specifically, without giving the defendant the option of retaining the goods on payment of damages.
(2)   The plaintiff's application may be made at any time before judgment or decree.
(3)   The judgment or decree may be unconditional, or on such terms and conditions as to damages, payment of the price and otherwise as seem just to the court.
(4)   (*Applies to Scotland only.*)
[(5)   This section does not apply to a contract to which Chapter 2 of Part 1 of the Consumer Rights Act 2015 applies (but see the provision made about such contracts in section 19 of that Act).]

NOTES

Sub-s (5): added by the Consumer Rights Act 2015, s 60, Sch 1, paras 8, 29, as from 1 October 2015 (for transitional provisions see the Consumer Rights Act 2015 (Commencement No 3, Transitional Provisions, Savings and Consequential Amendments) Order 2015, SI 2015/1630, arts 6–8 at **[2.1220]** et seq).

[1.890]
53 Remedy for breach of warranty
(1)   Where there is a breach of warranty by the seller, or where the buyer elects (or is compelled) to treat any breach of a condition on the part of the seller as a breach of warranty, the buyer is not by reason only of such breach of warranty entitled to reject the goods; but he may—
  (a)   set up against the seller the breach of warranty in diminution or extinction of the price, or
  (b)   maintain an action against the seller for damages for the breach of warranty.
(2)   The measure of damages for breach of warranty is the estimated loss directly and naturally resulting, in the ordinary course of events, from the breach of warranty.
(3)   In the case of breach of warranty of quality such loss is prima facie the difference between the value of the goods at the time of delivery to the buyer and the value they would have had if they had fulfilled the warranty.
(4)   The fact that the buyer has set up the breach of warranty in diminution or extinction of the price does not prevent him from maintaining an action for the same breach of warranty if he has suffered further damage.
[(4A)   This section does not apply to a contract to which Chapter 2 of Part 1 of the Consumer Rights Act 2015 applies (but see the provision made about such contracts in section 19 of that Act).]
[(5)   This section does not apply to Scotland.]

NOTES

Sub-s (4A): inserted by the Consumer Rights Act 2015, s 60, Sch 1, paras 8, 30, as from 1 October 2015 (for transitional provisions see the Consumer Rights Act 2015 (Commencement No 3, Transitional Provisions, Savings and Consequential Amendments) Order 2015, SI 2015/1630, arts 6–8 at **[2.1220]** et seq).

Sub-s (5): substituted by the Sale and Supply of Goods Act 1994, s 7(1), Sch 2, para 5(1), (7).

53A   *(Inserted by the Sale and Supply of Goods Act 1994, s 5(3) and applies to Scotland only.)*

Interest, etc

[1.891]
54 Interest
[(1)]   Nothing in this Act affects the right of the buyer or the seller to recover interest or special damages in any case where by law interest or special damages may be recoverable, or to recover money paid where the consideration for the payment of it has failed.
[(2)   This section does not apply to a contract to which Chapter 2 of Part 1 of the Consumer Rights Act 2015 applies (but see the provision made about such contracts in section 19 of that Act).]

NOTES

Sub-s (1): numbered as such and sub-s (2) added by the Consumer Rights Act 2015, s 60, Sch 1, paras 8, 32, as from 1 October 2015 (for transitional provisions see the Consumer Rights Act 2015 (Commencement No 3, Transitional Provisions, Savings and Consequential Amendments) Order 2015, SI 2015/1630, arts 6–8 at **[2.1220]** et seq).

PART VII
SUPPLEMENTARY

[1.892]
55 Exclusion of implied terms
(1)   Where a right, duty or liability would arise under a contract of sale of goods by implication of law, it may (subject to the Unfair Contract Terms Act 1977) be negatived or varied by express agreement, or by the course of dealing between the parties, or by such usage as binds both parties to the contract.
[(1A)   Subsection (1) does not apply to a contract to which Chapter 2 of Part 1 of the Consumer Rights Act 2015 applies (but see the provision made about such contracts in section 31 of that Act).]
(2)   An express [term] does not negative a [term] implied by this Act unless inconsistent with it.
(3)   Paragraph 11 of Schedule 1 below applies in relation to a contract made on or after 18th May 1973 and before 1st February 1978, and paragraph 12 in relation to one made before 18th May 1973.

NOTES

Sub-s (1A): inserted by the Consumer Rights Act 2015, s 60, Sch 1, paras 8, 33, as from 1 October 2015 (for transitional provisions see the Consumer Rights Act 2015 (Commencement No 3, Transitional Provisions, Savings and Consequential Amendments) Order 2015, SI 2015/1630, arts 6–8 at **[2.1220]** et seq).

Sub-s (2): words in square brackets substituted by the Sale and Supply of Goods Act 1994, s 7(1), Sch 2, para 5(1), (8).

[1.893]
56   Conflict of laws
Paragraph 13 of Schedule 1 below applies in relation to a contract made on or after 18th May 1973 and before 1st February 1978, so as to make provision about conflict of laws in relation to such a contract.

[1.894]
57   Auction sales
(1)   Where goods are put up for sale by auction in lots, each lot is prima facie deemed to be the subject of a separate contract of sale.

(2)   A sale by auction is complete when the auctioneer announces its completion by the fall of the hammer, or in other customary manner; and until the announcement is made any bidder may retract his bid.

(3)   A sale by auction may be notified to be subject to a reserve or upset price, and a right to bid may also be reserved expressly by or on behalf of the seller.

(4)   Where a sale by auction is not notified to be subject to a right to bid by or on behalf of the seller, it is not lawful for the seller to bid himself or to employ any person to bid at the sale, or for the auctioneer knowingly to take any bid from the seller or any such person.

(5)   A sale contravening subsection (4) above may be treated as fraudulent by the buyer.

(6)   Where, in respect of a sale by auction, a right to bid is expressly reserved (but not otherwise) the seller or any one person on his behalf may bid at the auction.

58   (*Applies to Scotland only.*)

[1.895]
59   Reasonable time a question of fact
Where a reference is made in this Act to a reasonable time the question what is a reasonable time is a question of fact.

[1.896]
60   Rights etc enforceable by action
Where a right, duty or liability is declared by this Act, it may (unless otherwise provided by this Act) be enforced by action.

[1.897]
61   Interpretation
(1)   In this Act, unless the context or subject matter otherwise requires—

"action" includes counterclaim and set-off, and in Scotland condescendence and claim and
        compensation;

["bulk" means a mass or collection of goods of the same kind which—
        (a)   is contained in a defined space or area; and
        (b)   is such that any goods in the bulk are interchangeable with any other goods therein
             of the same number or quantity;]

"business" includes a profession and the activities of any government department (including a
        Northern Ireland department) or local or public authority;

"buyer" means a person who buys or agrees to buy goods;

[*"consumer contract" has the same meaning as in section 25(1) of the Unfair Contract Terms
        Act 1977; and for the purposes of this Act the onus of proving that a contract is not to be
        regarded as a consumer contract shall lie on the seller*]

"contract of sale" includes an agreement to sell as well as a sale;

"credit-broker" means a person acting in the course of a business of credit brokerage carried on
        by him, that is a business of effecting introductions of individuals desiring to obtain
        credit—
        (a)   to persons carrying on any business so far as it relates to the provision of credit, or
        (b)   to other persons engaged in credit brokerage;

"delivery" means voluntary transfer of possession from one person to another [except that in
        relation to sections 20A and 20B above it includes such appropriation of goods to the
        contract as results in property in the goods being transferred to the buyer;]

"document of title to goods" has the same meaning as it has in the Factors Acts;

"Factors Acts" means the Factors Act 1889, the Factors (Scotland) Act 1890, and any enactment
        amending or substituted for the same;

"fault" means wrongful act or default;

"future goods" means goods to be manufactured or acquired by the seller after the making of the
        contract of sale;

"goods" includes all personal chattels other than things in action and money, and in Scotland all
        corporeal moveables except money; and in particular "goods" includes emblements,
        industrial growing crops, and things attached to or forming part of the land which are
        agreed to be severed before sale or under the contract of sale [and includes an undivided
        share in goods;]

"plaintiff" includes pursuer, complainer, claimant in a multiplepoinding and defendant or defender counter-claiming;

[*"producer" means the manufacturer of goods, the importer of goods into the European Economic Area or any person purporting to be a producer by placing his name, trade mark or other distinctive sign on the goods;*]

"property" means the general property in goods, and not merely a special property;

. . .

[*"repair" means, in cases where there is a lack of conformity in goods for the purposes of section 48F of this Act, to bring the goods into conformity with the contract;*]

"sale" includes a bargain and sale as well as a sale and delivery;

"seller" means a person who sells or agrees to sell goods;

"specific goods" means goods identified and agreed on at the time a contract of sale is made [and includes an undivided share, specified as a fraction or percentage, of goods identified and agreed on as aforesaid];

"warranty" (as regards England and Wales and Northern Ireland) means an agreement with reference to goods which are the subject of a contract of sale, but collateral to the main purpose of such contract, the breach of which gives rise to a claim for damages, but not to a right to reject the goods and treat the contract as repudiated.

(2)   . . .

(3)   A thing is deemed to be done in good faith within the meaning of this Act when it is in fact done honestly, whether it is done negligently or not.

(4)   A person is deemed to be insolvent within the meaning of this Act if has either ceased to pay his debts in the ordinary course of business or he cannot pay his debts as they become due, . . .

(5)   Goods are in a deliverable state within the meaning of this Act when they are in such a state that the buyer would under the contract be bound to take delivery of them.

[*(5A)   References in this Act to dealing as consumer are to be construed in accordance with Part I of the Unfair Contract Terms Act 1977; and, for the purposes of this Act, it is for a seller claiming that the buyer does not deal as consumer to show that he does not.*]

(6)   As regards the definition of "business" in subsection (1) above, paragraph 14 of Schedule 1 below applies in relation to a contract made on or after 18th May 1973 and before 1st February 1978, and paragraph 15 in relation to one made before 18th May 1973.

NOTES

Sub-s (1): definition "bulk" inserted, and words in square brackets in definitions "delivery", "goods" and "specific goods" added, by the Sale of Goods (Amendment) Act 1995, s 2; definition "consumer contract" inserted, and definition "quality" (omitted) repealed, by the Sale and Supply of Goods Act 1994, s 7, Sch 2, para 5(1), (9)(a), Sch 3; definition "consumer contract" repealed by the Consumer Rights Act 2015, s 60, Sch 1, paras 8, 35(1), (2)(a), as from 1 October 2015 (for transitional provisions see the Consumer Rights Act 2015 (Commencement No 3, Transitional Provisions, Savings and Consequential Amendments) Order 2015, SI 2015/1630, arts 6–8 at [**2.1220**] et seq); first definition omitted applies to Scotland only; definitions "producer" and "repair" inserted by the Sale and Supply of Goods to Consumers Regulations 2002, SI 2002/3045, reg 6 and repealed by the Consumer Rights Act 2015, s 60, Sch 1, paras 8, 35(1), (2)(b), (c), as from 1 October 2015 (for transitional provisions see note above).

Sub-s (2): repealed by the Sale and Supply of Goods Act 1994, s 7, Sch 2, para 5(1), (9)(b), Sch 3.

Sub-s (4): words omitted repealed by the Insolvency Act 1985, s 235, Sch 10, Pt III, the Bankruptcy (Scotland) Act 1985, s 75(2), Sch 8, and the Insolvency Act 1986, s 437, Sch 11, Pt II.

Sub-s (5A): inserted by the Sale and Supply of Goods Act 1994, s 7, Sch 2, para 5(9)(c); repealed by the Consumer Rights Act 2015, s 60, Sch 1, paras 8, 35(1), (3), as from 1 October 2015 (for transitional provisions see note above).

[1.898]
62   Savings: rules of law etc

(1)   The rules in bankruptcy relating to contracts of sale apply to those contracts, notwithstanding anything in this Act.

(2)   The rules of the common law, including the law merchant, except in so far as they are inconsistent with the provisions of *this Act*, and in particular the rules relating to the law of principal and agent and the effect of fraud, misrepresentation, duress or coercion, mistake, or other invalidating cause, apply to contracts for the sale of goods.

(3)   Nothing in this Act or the Sale of Goods Act 1893 affects the enactments relating to bills of sale, or any enactment relating to the sale of goods which is not expressly repealed or amended by this Act or that.

(4)   The provisions of this Act about contracts of sale do not apply to a transaction in the form of a contract of sale which is intended to operate by way of mortgage, pledge, charge, or other security.

(5)   (*Applies to Scotland only.*)

NOTES

Sub-s (2): for the words in italics there are substituted the words substitute "legislation including this Act and the Consumer Rights Act 2015" by the Consumer Rights Act 2015, s 60, Sch 1, paras 8, 36, as from 1 October 2015 (for transitional provisions see the Consumer Rights Act 2015 (Commencement No 3, Transitional Provisions, Savings and Consequential Amendments) Order 2015, SI 2015/1630, arts 6–8 at [**2.1220**] et seq).

Sale of Goods Act 1893: mostly repealed by s 63(2) of, Sch 3 to, this Act; remainder repealed by the Supreme Court Act 1981, s 152(4), Sch 7.

[1.899]
63 Consequential amendments, repeals and savings
(1) Without prejudice to section 17 of the Interpretation Act 1978 (repeal and re-enactment), the enactments mentioned in Schedule 2 below have effect subject to the amendments there specified (being amendments consequential on this Act).

(2) The enactments mentioned in Schedule 3 below are repealed to the extent specified in column 3, but subject to the savings in Schedule 4 below.

(3) The savings in Schedule 4 below have effect.

[1.900]
64 Short title and commencement
(1) This Act may be cited as the Sale of Goods Act 1979.

(2) This Act comes into force on 1 January 1980.

SCHEDULES

SCHEDULES 1–4

(Sch 1 (Modification of this Act for certain contracts), Sch 2 (Consequential amendments), Sch 3 (Repeals), Sch 4 (Savings) outside the scope of this work.)

PROTECTION OF TRADING INTERESTS ACT 1980

(1980 c 11)

ARRANGEMENT OF SECTIONS

An Act to provide protection from requirements, prohibitions and judgments imposed or given under the laws of countries outside the United Kingdom and affecting the trading or other interests of persons in the United Kingdom

[20 March 1980]

[1.901]
1 Overseas measures affecting United Kingdom trading interests
(1) If it appears to the Secretary of State—
- (a) that measures have been or are proposed to be taken by or under the law of any overseas country for regulating or controlling international trade; and
- (b) that those measures, in so far as they apply or would apply to things done or to be done outside the territorial jurisdiction of that country by persons carrying on business in the United Kingdom, are damaging or threaten to damage the trading interests of the United Kingdom,

the Secretary of State may by order direct that this section shall apply to those measures either generally or in their application to such cases as may be specified in the order.

(2) The Secretary of State may by order make provision for requiring, or enabling the Secretary of State to require, a person in the United Kingdom who carries on business there to give notice to the Secretary of State of any requirement or prohibition imposed or threatened to be imposed on that person pursuant to any measures in so far as this section applies to them by virtue of an order under subsection (1) above.

(3) The Secretary of State may give to any person in the United Kingdom who carries on business there such directions for prohibiting compliance with any such requirement or prohibition as aforesaid as he considers appropriate for avoiding damage to the trading interests of the United Kingdom.

(4) The power of the Secretary of State to make orders under subsection (1) or (2) above shall be exercisable by statutory instrument subject to annulment in pursuance of a resolution of either House of Parliament.

(5) Directions under subsection (3) above may be either general or special and may prohibit compliance with any requirement or prohibition either absolutely or in such cases or subject to such conditions as to consent or otherwise as may be specified in the directions; and general directions under that subsection shall be published in such manner as appears to the Secretary of State to be appropriate.

(6) In this section "trade" includes any activity carried on in the course of a business of any description and "trading interests" shall be construed accordingly.

NOTES

Orders: the Protection of Trading Interests (US Re-export Control) Order 1982, SI 1982/885; the Protection of Trading Interests (US Antitrust Measures) Order 1983, SI 1983/900; the Protection of Trading Interests (US Cuban Assets Control Regulations) Order 1992, SI 1992/2449.

[1.902]
2 Documents and information required by overseas courts and authorities

(1) If it appears to the Secretary of State—

    (a)   that a requirement has been or may be imposed on a person or persons in the United Kingdom to produce to any court, tribunal or authority of an overseas country any commercial document which is not within the territorial jurisdiction of that country or to furnish any commercial information to any such court, tribunal or authority; or

    (b)   that any such authority has imposed or may impose a requirement on a person or persons in the United Kingdom to publish any such document or information,

the Secretary of State may, if it appears to him that the requirement is inadmissible by virtue of subsection (2) or (3) below, give directions for prohibiting compliance with the requirement.

(2) A requirement such as is mentioned in subsection (1)(a) or (b) above is inadmissible—

    (a)   if it infringes the jurisdiction of the United Kingdom or is otherwise prejudicial to the sovereignty of the United Kingdom; or

    (b)   if compliance with the requirement would be prejudicial to the security of the United Kingdom or to the relations of the government of the United Kingdom with the government of any other country.

(3) A requirement such as is mentioned in subsection (1)(a) above is also inadmissible—

    (a)   if it is made otherwise than for the purposes of civil or criminal proceedings which have been instituted in the overseas country; or

    (b)   if it requires a person to state what documents relevant to any such proceedings are or have been in his possession, custody or power or to produce for the purposes of any such proceedings any documents other than particular documents specified in the requirement.

(4) Directions under subsection (1) above may be either general or special and may prohibit compliance with any requirement either absolutely or in such cases or subject to such conditions as to consent or otherwise as may be specified in the directions; and general directions under that subsection shall be published in such manner as appears to the Secretary of State to be appropriate.

(5) For the purposes of this section the making of a request or demand shall be treated as the imposition of a requirement if it is made in circumstances in which a requirement to the same effect could be or could have been imposed; and

    (a)   any request or demand for the supply of a document or information which, pursuant to the requirement of any court, tribunal or authority of an overseas country, is addressed to a person in the United Kingdom; or

    (b)   any requirement imposed by such a court, tribunal or authority to produce or furnish any document or information to a person specified in the requirement,

shall be treated as a requirement to produce or furnish that document or information to that court, tribunal or authority.

(6) In this section "commercial document" and "commercial information" mean respectively a document or information relating to a business of any description and "document" includes any record or device by means of which material is recorded or stored.

[1.903]
3 Offences under ss 1 and 2

(1) Subject to subsection (2) below, any person who without reasonable excuse fails to comply with any requirement imposed under subsection (2) of section 1 above or knowingly contravenes any directions given under subsection (3) of that section or section 2(1) above shall be guilty of an offence and liable—

    (a)   on conviction on indictment, to a fine;

    (b)   on summary conviction, to a fine not exceeding the statutory maximum.

(2) A person who is neither a citizen of the United Kingdom and Colonies nor a body corporate incorporated in the United Kingdom shall not be guilty of an offence under subsection (1) above by reason of anything done or omitted outside the United Kingdom in contravention of directions under section 1(3) or 2(1) above.

(3) No proceedings for an offence under subsection (1) above shall be instituted in England, Wales or Northern Ireland except by the Secretary of State or with the consent of the Attorney General or, as the case may be, the Attorney General for Northern Ireland.

(4)   Proceedings against any person for an offence under this section may be taken before the appropriate court in the United Kingdom having jurisdiction in the place where that person is for the time being.

(5)   . . .

NOTES

Sub-s (5): repealed by the Statute Law (Repeals) Act 1993.

[1.904]

4   Restriction of Evidence (Proceedings in Other Jurisdictions) Act 1975

A court in the United Kingdom shall not make an order under section 2 of the Evidence (Proceedings in Other Jurisdictions) Act 1975 for giving effect to a request issued by or on behalf of a court or tribunal of an overseas country if it is shown that the request infringes the jurisdiction of the United Kingdom or is otherwise prejudicial to the sovereignty of the United Kingdom; and a certificate signed by or on behalf of the Secretary of State to the effect that it infringes that jurisdiction or is so prejudicial shall be conclusive evidence of that fact.

[1.905]

5   Restriction on enforcement of certain overseas judgments

(1)   A judgment to which this section applies shall not be registered under Part II of the Administration of Justice Act 1920 or Part I of the Foreign Judgments (Reciprocal Enforcement) Act 1933 and no court in the United Kingdom shall entertain proceedings at common law for the recovery of any sum payable under such a judgment.

(2)   This section applies to any judgment given by a court of an overseas country, being—

(a)   a judgment for multiple damages within the meaning of subsection (3) below;

(b)   a judgment based on a provision or rule of law specified or described in an order under subsection (4) below and given after the coming into force of the order; or

(c)   a judgment on a claim for contribution in respect of damages awarded by a judgment falling within paragraph (a) or (b) above.

(3)   In subsection (2)(a) above a judgment for multiple damages means a judgment for an amount arrived at by doubling, trebling or otherwise multiplying a sum assessed as compensation for the loss or damage sustained by the person in whose favour the judgment is given.

(4)   The Secretary of State may for the purposes of subsection (2)(b) above make an order in respect of any provision or rule of law which appears to him to be concerned with the prohibition or regulation of agreements, arrangements or practices designed to restrain, distort or restrict competition in the carrying on of business of any description or to be otherwise concerned with the promotion of such competition as aforesaid.

(5)   The power of the Secretary of State to make orders under subsection (4) above shall be exercisable by statutory instrument subject to annulment in pursuance of a resolution of either House of Parliament.

(6)   Subsection (2)(a) above applies to a judgement given before the date of the passing of this Act as well as to a judgment given on or after that date but this section does not affect any judgment which has been registered before that date under the provisions mentioned in subsection (1) above or in respect of which such proceedings as are there mentioned have been finally determined before that date.

NOTES

Orders: the Protection of Trading Interests (Australian Trade Practices) Order 1988, SI 1988/569.

[1.906]

6   Recovery of awards of multiple damages

(1)   This section applies where a court of an overseas country has given a judgment for multiple damages with the meaning of section 5(3) above against—

(a)   a citizen of the United Kingdom and Colonies; or

(b)   a body corporate incorporated in the United Kingdom or in a territory outside the United Kingdom for whose international relations Her Majesty's Government in the United Kingdom are responsible; or

(c)   a person carrying on business in the United Kingdom,

(in this section referred to as a "qualifying defendant") and an amount on account of the damages has been paid by the qualifying defendant either to the party in whose favour the judgment was given or to another party who is entitled as against the qualifying defendant to contribution in respect of the damages.

(2)   Subject to subsections (3) and (4) below, the qualifying defendant shall be entitled to recover from the party in whose favour the judgment was given so much of the amount referred to in subsection (1) above as exceeds the part attributable to compensation; and that part shall be taken to be such part of the amount as bears to the whole of it the same proportion as the sum assessed by the court that gave the judgment as compensation for the loss or damage sustained by that party bears to the whole of the damages awarded to that party.

(3)   Subsection (2) above does not apply where the qualifying defendant is an individual who was ordinarily resident in the overseas country at the time when the proceedings in which the judgment was given were instituted or a body corporate which had its principal place of business there at that time.

(4)   Subsection (2) above does not apply where the qualifying defendant carried on business in the overseas country and the proceedings in which the judgment was given were concerned with activities exclusively carried on in that country.

(5)   A court in the United Kingdom may entertain proceedings on a claim under this section notwithstanding that the person against whom the proceedings are brought is not within the jurisdiction of the court.

(6)   The reference in subsection (1) above to an amount paid by the qualifying defendant includes a reference to an amount obtained by execution against his property or against the property of a company which (directly or indirectly) is wholly owned by him; and references in that subsection and subsection (2) above to the party in whose favour the judgment was given or to a party entitled to contribution include references to any person in whom the rights of any such party have become vested by succession or assignment or otherwise.

(7)   This section shall, with the necessary modifications, apply also in relation to any order which is made by a tribunal or authority of an overseas country and would, if that tribunal or authority were a court, be a judgment for multiple damages within the meaning of section 5(3) above.

(8)   This section does not apply to any judgment given or order made before the passing of this Act.

[1.907]
7   Enforcement of overseas judgment under provision corresponding to s 6

(1)   If it appears to Her Majesty that the law of an overseas country provides or will provide for the enforcement in that country of judgments given under section 6 above, Her Majesty may by Order in Council provide for the enforcement in the United Kingdom of [judgments of any description specified in the Order which are given under any provision of the law of that country relating to the recovery of sums paid or obtained pursuant to a judgment for multiple damages within the meaning of section 5(3) above, whether or not that provision corresponds to section 6 above].

[(1A)   Such an Order in Council may, as respects judgments to which it relates—
   (a)   make different provisions for different descriptions of judgment; and
   (b)   impose conditions or restrictions on the enforcement of judgments of any description.]

(2)   An Order under this section may apply, with or without modification, any of the provisions of the Foreign Judgments (Reciprocal Enforcement) Act 1933.

NOTES
Sub-s (1): words in square brackets substituted by the Civil Jurisdiction and Judgments Act 1982, s 38.
Sub-s (1A): inserted by the Civil Jurisdiction and Judgments Act 1982, s 38.
Orders: the Reciprocal Enforcement of Foreign Judgments (Australia) Order 1994, SI 1994/1901.

[1.908]
8   Short title, interpretation, repeals and extent

(1)   This Act may be cited as the Protection of Trading Interests Act 1980.

(2)   In this Act "overseas country" means any country or territory outside the United Kingdom other than one for whose international relations Her Majesty's Government in the United Kingdom are responsible.

(3)   References in this Act to the law or a court, tribunal or authority of an overseas country include, in the case of a federal state, references to the law or a court, tribunal or authority of any constituent part of that country.

(4)   References in this Act to a claim for, or to entitlement to, contribution are references to a claim or entitlement based on an enactment or rule of law.

(5), (6)   . . .

(7)   This Act extends to Northern Ireland.

(8)   Her Majesty may by Order in Council direct that this Act shall extend with such exceptions, adaptations and modifications, if any, as may be specified in the Order to any territory outside the United Kingdom, being a territory for the international relations of which Her Majesty's Government in the United Kingdom are responsible.

NOTES
Sub-ss (5), (6): outside the scope of this work.
Orders in Council: the Protection of Trading Interests Act 1980 (Jersey) Order 1983, SI 1983/607; the Evidence (Proceedings in Other Jurisdictions) (Jersey) Order 1983, SI 1983/1700; the Protection of Trading Interests Act 1980 (Guernsey) Order 1983, SI 1983/1703; the Protection of Trading Interests Act 1980 (Isle of Man) Order 1983, SI 1983/1704.

COMPETITION ACT 1980

(1980 c 21)

ARRANGEMENT OF SECTIONS

Further references and investigations

Patents and agricultural schemes

General provisions about references and investigations

Supplementary

An Act to abolish the Price Commission; to make provision for the control of anticompetitive practices in the supply and acquisition of goods and the supply and securing of services; to provide for references of certain public bodies and other persons to the Monopolies and Mergers Commission; to provide for the investigation of prices and charges by the Director General of Fair Trading; to provide for the making of grants to certain bodies; to amend and provide for the amendment of the Fair Trading Act 1973; to make amendments with respect to the Restrictive Trade Practices Act 1976; to repeal the remaining provisions of the Counter-Inflation Act 1973; and for purposes connected therewith

[3 April 1980]

NOTES

Monopolies and Mergers Commission: the Monopolies and Mergers Commission was dissolved by the Competition Act 1998, s 45(3) at **[1.1307]**, which also transferred the functions of the Monopolies and Mergers Commission to the Competition Commission.

Director General of Fair Trading: the Enterprise Act 2002, s 2(1) provided that, as from the coming into force of that section (on 1 April 2003), the functions of the Director General of Fair Trading, his property, rights and liabilities were transferred to the Office of Fair Trading. Accordingly, (by virtue of s 2(2), (3) of the 2002 Act) the office of the Director was abolished, and any reference to the Director in any enactment, instrument or other document passed or made before the commencement of s 2(1) had, in so far as is necessary, effect as if it were a reference to the Office of Fair Trading (for transitional provisions in connection with the transfer, see Sch 24, para 6 to the 2002 Act). Section 2 of the 2002 Act was repealed by the Enterprise and Regulatory Reform Act 2013, s 26(3), Sch 5, Pt 4, para 229, as from 1 April 2014. Part 3 the 2013 Act (ss 25–28) abolished the Office of fair Trading (and the Competition Commission) and provided for the transfer of its functions to the newly created Competition and Markets Authority.

1–10   *(S 1 repealed by the Statute Law (Repeals) Act 1989; ss 2–10 repealed by the Competition Act 1998, ss 17, 74(3), Sch 14, Pt I.)*

Further references and investigations

[1.909]
11   References of public bodies and certain other persons to the [CMA]

(1)   The Secretary of State may at any time refer to the [CMA] any question relating to—

   (a)   the efficiency and costs of, [or]

   (b)   the service provided by,   . . .

   (c)   . . .

a person falling within subsection (3) below and specified in the reference, including any question whether, in relation to a matter falling within [paragraph (a) or (b)] above, the person is pursuing a course of conduct which operates against the public interest.

(2)   . . .

(3)   The persons referred to in subsection (1) above are—

   (a)   any body corporate—

      (i)   which supplies goods or services by way of business,

      (ii)   the affairs of which are managed by its members, and

      (iii)   the members of which hold office as such by virtue of their appointment to that or another office by a Minister under any enactment; or [(aa) any publicly owned railway company, within the meaning of the Railways Act 1993, which supplies network services or station services, within the meaning of Part I of that Act; or]

[(b) any person (not falling within paragraph (a) above) who provides in Northern Ireland a bus service within the meaning of section 14 of the Finance Act (Northern Ireland) 1966; or]

[(bb) any person who provides a railway passenger service in pursuance of an agreement entered into by Transport for London or any of its subsidiaries (within the meaning of the Greater London Authority Act 1999) by virtue of section 156(2) or (3) of the Greater London Authority Act 1999; or]

[(c) the [Environment Agency];] or

[(cc) . . .]

[(ca) Scottish water;]

(d) any board administering a scheme under the Agricultural Marketing Act 1958 [or the Agricultural Marketing (Northern Ireland) Order 1982]; or

(e) any body corporate with a statutory duty to promote and assist the maintenance and development of the efficient supply of any goods or services by a body falling within paragraphs (a) to (d) above; or

(f) any subsidiary, within the meaning of [section 1159 of the Companies Act 2006], of a body falling within paragraphs (a) to (e) above.

(4) The Secretary of State may by order exclude from subsection (3)(b) [or (bb)] above persons of such descriptions as may be specified in the order.

(5) No question concerning a person falling within subsection (3)(b) [or (bb)] above or a subsidiary of a body falling within [either of those paragraphs] may be referred to the [CMA] under this section unless it relates to the carriage of passengers by the person or, as the case may be, the subsidiary.

(6) The Secretary of State may at any time by notice given to the [CMA] vary a reference under this section.

(7) On making a reference under this section or on varying such a reference under subsection (6) above the Secretary of State shall arrange for the reference or, as the case may be, the variation to be published in such manner as he considers most suitable for bringing it to the attention of persons who in his opinion would be affected by it or be likely to have an interest in it.

(8) On a reference under this section the [CMA] shall investigate and report on any question referred to them but shall exclude from their investigation and report consideration of—

(a) any question relating to the appropriateness of any financial obligations or guidance as to financial objectives (however expressed) imposed on or given to the person in question by or under any enactment, or otherwise by a Minister; . . .

(b) . . .

[(9), (9A)] . . .

(10) A report of the [CMA] on a reference under this section shall be made to the Secretary of State and shall state, with reasons, the conclusions of the [CMA] with respect to any question referred to them and, where the [CMA] conclude that the person specified in the reference is pursuing a course of conduct which operates against the public interest, the report may include recommendations as to what action (if any) should be taken by the person for the purpose of remedying or preventing what the [CMA] consider are the adverse effects of that course of conduct.

[(10A) The functions of the CMA with respect to a reference under this section (including functions under sections 109 to 115 of the Enterprise Act 2002, as applied by section 11B) are to be carried out on behalf of the CMA by a group constituted for the purpose by the chair of the CMA under Schedule 4 to the Enterprise and Regulatory Reform Act 2013.]

(11) In this section "Minister" includes a Northern Ireland department and the head of such a department.

NOTES

In the section heading and sub-ss (1), (5), (6), (8), (10), references to the "CMA" substituted (for original references to the "Commission") by the Enterprise and Regulatory Reform Act 2013, s 26(4), Sch 6, Pt 1, paras 1, 2(1), (2), (4). For various transitional provisions (including those relating to the abolition of the OFT and the Competition Commission, existing references to those bodies and provisions relating to continuity), see the Enterprise and Regulatory Reform Act 2013 (Commencement No 6, Transitional Provisions and Savings) Order 2014, SI 2014/416, Schedule at [**2.1126**]. This section is also amended as follows:

Sub-s (1): word in square brackets in para (a) inserted, para (c) and the word immediately preceding it repealed, and words in final pair of square brackets substituted, by the Enterprise Act 2002, s 278, Sch 25, para 10(1), (2)(a), Sch 26.

Sub-s (2): repealed by the Enterprise Act 2002, s 278, Sch 25, para 10(1), (2)(b).

Sub-s (3): para (aa) inserted by the Railways Act 1993, s 152(1), Sch 12, para 12(1); para (b) substituted by the Transport Act 1985, s 114(1); para (bb) inserted by the London Regional Transport Act 1984, s 71(3)(a), Sch 6, para 15, and substituted by the Transport for London (Consequential Provisions) Order 2003, SI 2003/1615, art 2, Sch 1, Pt 1, para 6; para (c) substituted by the Water Act 1989, s 190(1), Sch 25, para 59(1), and words in square brackets in that paragraph substituted by the Environment Act 1995 (Consequential Amendments) Regulations 1996, SI 1996/593, reg 2, Sch 1; para (ca) inserted by the Water Industry (Scotland) Act 2002 (Consequential Modifications) Order 2004, SI 2004/1822, art 2, Schedule, Pt 1, para 10; para (cc) inserted, in relation to Scotland only, by the Local Government etc (Scotland) Act 1994, s 72, and repealed by the Water Industry (Scotland) Act 2002, s 71, Sch 7, para 10; words in square brackets in para (d) substituted by the Agricultural Marketing (Northern Ireland) Order 1982, SI 1982/1080, art 46, Schs 8, 9; words in square brackets in para (f) substituted by the Companies Act 2006 (Consequential Amendments, Transitional Provisions and Savings) Order 2009, SI 2009/1941, art 2(1), Sch 1, para 42(a).

Sub-s (4): words in square brackets inserted by the London Regional Transport Act 1984, s 71(3)(a), Sch 6, para 15.

Sub-s (5): words in first pair of square brackets inserted, and words in second pair of square brackets substituted, by the London Regional Transport Act 1984, s 71(3)(a), Sch 6, para 15.

Sub-s (8): words omitted repealed by the Competition Act 1998, s 74(1), (3), Sch 12, para 4(1), (2), Sch 14, Pt I, subject to transitional provisions and savings in Sch 13, Pt V, para 40 of the 1998 Act at **[1.1374]**.

Sub-ss (9), (9A): substituted, for original sub-s (9), by the Competition Act 1998, s 74(1), Sch 12, para 4(1), (3), and repealed by the Enterprise Act 2002, s 278, Sch 25, para 10(1), (2)(b), Sch 26.

Sub-s (10A): inserted by the Enterprise and Regulatory Reform Act 2013, s 26(4), Sch 6, Pt 1, paras 1, 2(1), (3), subject to transitional provisions in SI 2014/416 as noted above.

Ministers of the Crown, etc: the Enterprise Act 2002, Sch 25, para 10(10) provides that for the purposes of the Scotland Act 1998, the amendments made by Sch 25, para 10(1)–(9) to that Act (including the amendments made to this section) shall be taken to be pre-commencement enactments within the meaning of the 1998 Act; references to a Minister of the Crown should be construed accordingly.

[1.910]
[11A References under section 11: time-limits
(1) Every reference under section 11 above shall specify a period (not longer than six months beginning with the date of the reference) within which a report on the reference is to be made.
(2) A report of the [CMA] on a reference under section 11 above shall not have effect (and no action shall be taken in relation to it under section 12 below) unless the report is made before the end of the period specified in the reference or such further period (if any) as may be allowed by the Secretary of State under subsection (3) below.
(3) The Secretary of State may, if he has received representations on the subject from the [CMA] and is satisfied that there are special reasons why the report cannot be made within the period specified in the reference, extend that period by no more than three months.
(4) No more than one extension is possible under subsection (3) above in relation to the same reference.
(5) The Secretary of State shall publish any extension made by him under subsection (3) above in such manner as he considers most suitable for bringing it to the attention of persons who in his opinion would be affected by it or be likely to have an interest in it.]

NOTES
Inserted, together with ss 11B–11D, by the Enterprise Act 2002, s 278(1), Sch 25, para 10(1), (3).
Sub-ss (2), (3): references to the "CMA" substituted (for original references to the "Commission") by the Enterprise and Regulatory Reform Act 2013, s 26(4), Sch 6, Pt 1, paras 1, 3. For various transitional provisions (including those relating to the abolition of the OFT and the Competition Commission, existing references to those bodies and provisions relating to continuity), see the Enterprise and Regulatory Reform Act 2013 (Commencement No 6, Transitional Provisions and Savings) Order 2014, SI 2014/416, Schedule at **[2.1126]**.
Ministers of the Crown, etc: see the note to s 11 at **[1.909]**.

[1.911]
[11B References under section 11: powers of investigation and penalties
(1) The following sections of Part 3 of the Enterprise Act 2002 shall apply, with the modifications mentioned in subsections (2) and (3) below, for the purposes of references under section 11 above as they apply for the purposes of references under that Part—
(a) section 109 (attendance of witnesses and production of documents etc);
(b) section 110 (enforcement of powers under section 109: general);
(c) section 111 (penalties);
(d) section 112 (penalties: main procedural requirements);
(e) section 113 (payments and interest by instalments);
(f) section 114 (appeals in relation to penalties);
(g) section 115 (recovery of penalties); and
(h) section 116 (statement of policy).
(2) Section 110 shall, in its application by virtue of subsection (1) above, have effect as if—
(a) subsection (2) were omitted;
(b) in subsection (4), for the word "publication" there were substituted "laying before both Houses of Parliament"; and
(c) in subsection (9) the words from "or section" to "section 65(3))" were omitted.
(3) Section 111(5)(b)(ii) shall, in its application by virtue of subsection (1) above, have effect as if—
(a) for the words "published (or, in the case of a report under section 50 or 65, given)" there were substituted "made";
(b) for the words "published (or given)", in both places where they appear, there were substituted "made"; and
(c) the words "by this Part" were omitted.]

NOTES
Inserted as noted to s 11A at **[1.910]**.
Ministers of the Crown, etc: see the note to s 11 at **[1.909]**.

[1.912]
[11C References under section 11: further supplementary provisions
(1) Section 117 of the Enterprise Act 2002 (false or misleading information) shall apply in relation to functions under this Act as it applies in relation to functions under Part 3 of that Act but as if, in subsections (1)(a) and (2)[—
  (a) the words ", OFCOM or the Secretary of State" were omitted, and
  (b) for the words "their functions" there were substituted "its functions".]
(2) Section 125 of the Enterprise Act 2002 (offences by bodies corporate) shall apply for the purposes of this Act as it applies for the purposes of Part 3 of that Act.
(3) For the purposes of section 12 below, a conclusion contained in a report of the [CMA] is to be disregarded if the conclusion is not that of at least two-thirds of the members of the group constituted [by the chair of the CMA for the purpose of carrying out the functions of the CMA with respect to the reference].]

NOTES
Inserted as noted to s 11A at **[1.910]**.
Sub-s (1): words in square brackets substituted (for words "the words ["the OFT, OFCOM,"] were omitted" (as amended by the Communications Act 2003, s 389(1), Sch 16, para 1)), by the Enterprise and Regulatory Reform Act 2013, s 26(4), Sch 6, Pt 1, paras 1, 4(1), (2). For various transitional provisions (including those relating to the abolition of the OFT and the Competition Commission, existing references to those bodies and provisions relating to continuity), see the Enterprise and Regulatory Reform Act 2013 (Commencement No 6, Transitional Provisions and Savings) Order 2014, SI 2014/416, Schedule at **[2.1126]**.
Sub-s (3): words in first and second pairs of square brackets substituted (for original words "Commission" and "in connection with the reference concerned in pursuance of paragraph 15 of Schedule 7 to the Competition Act 1998" respectively) by the Enterprise and Regulatory Reform Act 2013, s 26(4), Sch 6, Pt 1, paras 1, 4(1), (3), subject to transitional provisions in SI 2014/416 as noted above.
Ministers of the Crown, etc: see the note to s 11 at **[1.909]**.

[1.913]
[11D Interim orders
(1) Subsection (2) below applies where, in the circumstances specified in subsection (1) of section 12 below, the Secretary of State has under consideration the making of an order under subsection (5) of that section.
(2) The Secretary of State may by order, for the purpose of preventing pre-emptive action—
  (a) prohibit or restrict the doing of things which the Secretary of State considers would constitute pre-emptive action;
  (b) impose on any person concerned obligations as to the carrying on of any activities or the safeguarding of any assets;
  (c) provide for the carrying on of any activities or the safeguarding of any assets either by the appointment of a person to conduct or supervise the conduct of any activities (on such terms and with such powers as may be specified or described in the order) or in any other manner;
  (d) do anything which may be done by virtue of paragraph 19 of Schedule 8 to the Enterprise Act 2002 (information powers).
(3) An order under this section shall come into force at such time as is determined by or under the order.
(4) An order under this section shall, if it has not previously ceased to be in force, cease to be in force on the making of the order under section 12(5) below or (as the case may be) on the making of the decision not to make such an order.
(5) The Secretary of State shall publish any decision made by him not to make an order under section 12(5) below in such manner as he considers most suitable for bringing it to the attention of persons who in his opinion would be affected by it or would be likely to have an interest in it.
(6) The Secretary of State shall, as soon as reasonably practicable, consider any representations received by him in relation to varying or revoking an order under this section.
(7) The following provisions of Part 3 of the Enterprise Act 2002 shall apply in relation to orders under this section as they apply in relation to orders under paragraph 2 of Schedule 7 to that Act—
  (a) section 86(2) and (3) (enforcement orders: general provisions);
  (b) section 87 (delegated power of directions); and
  (c) section 94(1) to (5), (8) and (9) (rights to enforce orders).
(8) In this section "pre-emptive action" means action which might impede the making of an order under section 12(5) below.]

NOTES
Inserted as noted to s 11A at **[1.910]**.
Ministers of the Crown, etc: see the note to s 11 at **[1.909]**.

[1.914]
12 Orders following report under section 11

(1) This section applies where a report of the [CMA] on a reference under section 11 above concludes that the person specified in the reference is pursuing a course of conduct which operates against the public interest.

(2) If it appears to the Secretary of State that any other Minister has functions directly relating to the person specified in the reference or, in the case of a reference only concerning the activities of the person in a part of the United Kingdom, functions directly relating to the person in respect of his activities in that part, he shall send a copy of the report of the [CMA] on the reference to that Minister; and in subsection (3) below "the relevant Minister" means—

    (a)   in a case where it appears to the Secretary of State that any Minister (including himself) has such functions, that Minister, and

    (b)   in a case where it appears to the Secretary of State that no Minister has such functions, the Secretary of State.

(3) If—

    (a)   the relevant Minister considers it appropriate for the purpose of remedying or preventing what he considers are the adverse effects of the course of conduct specified in the report of the [CMA] as operating against the public interest, and

    (b)   the person specified in the reference does not fall within paragraph (d) of section 11(3) above and is not a subsidiary of a body falling within that paragraph,

he may by order direct the person to prepare within such time, if any, as may be specified in the order a plan for remedying or preventing such of those effects as are so specified; but where there is more than one relevant Minister no such order shall be made except by all the relevant Ministers acting jointly and where none of the relevant Ministers is the Secretary of State no such order shall be made except after consultation with him.

(4) It shall be the duty of a person to whom a direction is given under subsection (3) above to prepare such a plan as is mentioned in that subsection and to send a copy of that plan to the Minister or Ministers by whom the order containing the direction was made who shall lay it before Parliament; and, in a case where the plan involves the use by a body of its powers in relation to any subsidiary within the meaning of [section 1159 of the Companies Act 2006], the plan shall specify the manner in which the body proposes using those powers.

(5) Whether or not an order has been or may be made under subsection (3) above, the Secretary of State may, if he considers it appropriate for the purpose of remedying or preventing what he considers are the adverse effects of the course of conduct specified in the report of the [CMA] as operating against the public interest, [make an order under this subsection].

[(5A) An order under subsection (5) above may contain anything permitted by Schedule 8 to the Enterprise Act 2002, except paragraphs 8, 13 and 14 of that Schedule.

(5B) An order under subsection (5) above shall come into force at such time as is determined by or under the order.]

[(6) The following provisions of Part 3 of the Enterprise Act 2002 shall apply in relation to orders under subsection (5) above as they apply in relation to orders under paragraph 11 of Schedule 7 to that Act—

    (a)   section 86(2) and (3) (enforcement orders: general provisions);

    (b)   section 87 (delegated power of directions);

    (c)   section 88 (contents of certain enforcement orders);

    (d)   section 94(1) to (5), (8) and (9) (rights to enforce orders); and

    (e)   Schedule 10 (procedural requirements for orders).

(7) The Secretary of State shall publish any decision made by him to dispense with the requirements of Schedule 10 to the Enterprise Act 2002 as applied by subsection (6) above; and shall do so in such manner as he considers most suitable for bringing the decision to the attention of persons who in his opinion would be affected by it or be likely to have an interest in it.]

NOTES

Sub-ss (1)–(3): references to the "CMA" substituted (for original references to the "Commission") by the Enterprise and Regulatory Reform Act 2013, s 26(4), Sch 6, Pt 1, paras 1, 5. For various transitional provisions (including those relating to the abolition of the OFT and the Competition Commission, existing references to those bodies and provisions relating to continuity), see the Enterprise and Regulatory Reform Act 2013 (Commencement No 6, Transitional Provisions and Savings) Order 2014, SI 2014/416, Schedule at **[2.1126]**.

Sub-s (4): words in square brackets substituted by the Companies Act 2006 (Consequential Amendments, Transitional Provisions and Savings) Order 2009, SI 2009/1941, art 2(1), Sch 1, para 42(b).

Sub-s (5): word in first pair of square brackets substituted for original word "Commission" by the Enterprise and Regulatory Reform Act 2013, s 26(4), Sch 6, Pt 1, paras 1, 5, subject to transitional provisions in SI 2014/416 as noted above; words in second pair of square brackets substituted by the Enterprise Act 2002, s 278(1), Sch 25, para 10(4)(a).

Sub-ss (5A), (5B): inserted by the Enterprise Act 2002, s 278(1), Sch 25, para 10(4)(b).

Sub-ss (6), (7): substituted, for original sub-s (6), by the Enterprise Act 2002, s 278(1), Sch 25, para 10(4)(c).

Ministers of the Crown, etc: see the note to s 11 at **[1.909]**.

---

13   (*Repealed by the Enterprise Act 2002, ss 9, 278(2), Sch 26.*)

Patents and agricultural schemes

14 (*Repealed by the Copyright, Designs and Patents Act 1988, s 303(2), Sch 8.*)

[1.915]
15 Agricultural schemes: special provisions

(1)   . . .

(2)   The Secretary of State shall not—

(a), (b). . .

(c)   make or vary a reference under section 11 above,

in a case where the person to whom or to whose conduct or activities the investigation or reference relates falls within section 11(3)(d) above unless he has first consulted the relevant Minister.

(3), (4)   . . .

(5)   In this section "the relevant Minister" means—

(a)   in the case of a board administering a scheme under the said Act of 1958, the Minister who would have power to make an order under section 19 of that Act in relation to that board or the board administering that scheme, and

(b)   in the case of a board administering a scheme under [the said Order of 1982], the Department of Agriculture for Northern Ireland.

NOTES

Sub-s (1): repealed by the Enterprise Act 2002 and Media Mergers (Consequential Amendments) Order 2003, SI 2003/3180, art 2, Schedule, para 3.

Sub-s (2): para (a) repealed by the Deregulation and Contracting Out Act 1994, s 81(1), Sch 17; para (b) repealed by the Competition Act 1998, s 74(1), (3), Sch 12, para 4(1), (5), Sch 14, Pt I.

Sub-ss (3), (4): repealed by the Competition Act 1998, s 74(1), (3), Sch 12, para 4(1), (5), Sch 14, Pt I.

Sub-s (5): words in square brackets substituted by the Agricultural Marketing (Northern Ireland) Order 1982, SI 1982/1080, art 46(1), Schs 8, 9.

Act of 1958: ie, the Agricultural Marketing Act 1958.

Order of 1982: ie, the Agricultural Marketing (Northern Ireland) Order 1982, SI 1982/1080.

General provisions about references and investigations

[1.916]
16 General provisions as to reports

(1)   . . .

(2)   For the purposes of the law relating to defamation, absolute privilege shall attach to any report of the [CMA]   . . .   under this Act.

[(3)   . . .   ]

NOTES

Sub-s (1): repealed by the Enterprise Act 2002, s 278, Sch 25, para 10(5)(a), Sch 26.

Sub-s (2): reference to the "CMA" substituted (for original reference to the "Commission") by the Enterprise and Regulatory Reform Act 2013, s 26(4), Sch 6, Pt 1, paras 1, 6. For various transitional provisions (including those relating to the abolition of the OFT and the Competition Commission, existing references to those bodies and provisions relating to continuity), see the Enterprise and Regulatory Reform Act 2013 (Commencement No 6, Transitional Provisions and Savings) Order 2014, SI 2014/416, Schedule at [2.1126]; words omitted repealed by the Enterprise Act 2002, s 278, Sch 25, para 10(5)(b), Sch 26.

Sub-s (3): added by the Deregulation and Contracting Out Act 1994, s 39, Sch 11, para 4(1), (5); repealed by the Competition Act 1998, s 74(1), (3), Sch 12, para 4(1), (6), Sch 14, Pt I.

Ministers of the Crown, etc: see the note to s 11 at [1.909].

[1.917]
17 Laying before Parliament and publication of reports

(1)   Subject to subsection (2) below, the Secretary of State shall lay a copy of any report made to him under section   . . .   11(10)   . . .   above before each House of Parliament and shall arrange for the report to be published in such manner as appears to him appropriate.

(2)   The Secretary of State shall not lay a copy of a report made to him under section   . . .   11(10) above before either House of Parliament unless at least twenty-four hours before doing so he has transmitted to every person specified in the reference a copy of the report in the form in which it is laid (or by virtue of subsection (3) below is treated as being laid) before each House of Parliament.

(3)   If a report made to him under section   . . .   11(10)   . . .   above is presented by command of Her Majesty to either House of Parliament otherwise than at or during the time of a sitting of that House, the presentation of the report shall for the purposes of this section be treated as the laying of a copy of it before that House by the Secretary of State.

(4)   If it appears to the Secretary of State that the publication of any matter in a report made to him under section   . . .   11(10)   . . .   above would be [inappropriate], he shall exclude that matter from the copies of the report as laid before Parliament and from the report as published under this section.

[(5)   In deciding what is inappropriate for the purposes of subsection (4) the Secretary of State shall have regard to the considerations mentioned in section 244 of the Enterprise Act 2002.]

(6)　Any reference in [section] 12 above to a report of the [CMA] shall be construed as a reference to the report in the form in which copies of it are laid (or by virtue of subsection (3) of this section are treated as having been laid) before each House of Parliament under this section.

NOTES

Sub-ss (1), (3): first words omitted repealed by the Competition Act 1998, s 74(1), (3), Sch 12, para 4(1), (7)(a), (b), Sch 14, Pt I; second words omitted repealed by the Enterprise Act 2002, s 278, Sch 25, para 10(6)(a), Sch 26.

Sub-s (2): word omitted repealed by the Competition Act 1998, s 74(1), (3), Sch 12, para 4(1), (7)(b), Sch 14, Pt I.

Sub-s (4): first word omitted repealed by the Competition Act 1998, s 74(1), (3), Sch 12, para 4(1), (7)(a), (b), Sch 14, Pt I; second words omitted repealed, and word in square brackets substituted, by the Enterprise Act 2002, s 278, Sch 25, para 10(6)(a), (b), Sch 26.

Sub-s (5): substituted by the Enterprise Act 2002, s 278(1), Sch 25, para 10(6)(c).

Sub-s (6): word in first pair of square brackets substituted by the Competition Act 1998, s 74(1), Sch 12, para 4(1), (7)(c); reference to "CMA" substituted (for original reference to the "Commission") by the Enterprise and Regulatory Reform Act 2013, s 26(4), Sch 6, Pt 1, paras 1, 7. For various transitional provisions (including those relating to the abolition of the OFT and the Competition Commission, existing references to those bodies and provisions relating to continuity), see the Enterprise and Regulatory Reform Act 2013 (Commencement No 6, Transitional Provisions and Savings) Order 2014, SI 2014/416, Schedule at **[2.1126]**.

Ministers of the Crown, etc: see the note to s 11 at **[1.909]**.

18–30　*(Ss 18, 19(1)–(3), (5), (6), 20, 21, 24 repealed by the Enterprise Act 2002, s 278, Sch 25, para 10(1), (7), (1), Sch 26; s 19(4) repealed in part by the Agricultural Marketing (Northern Ireland) Order 1982, SI 1982/1080, art 46(2), Sch 9, remainder repealed by ss 247(f), 278(2) of, and Sch 26 to, the 2002 Act; s 19(7) repealed by the Statute Law (Repeals) Act 1993; ss 22, 25–30 repealed by the Competition Act 1998, s 74(1), (3), Sch 12, para 4(1), (11), (13), Sch 14, Pt I.)*

Supplementary

[1.918]
31　Orders and regulations
(1)　Any power of the Secretary of State to make orders　. . .　under this Act shall be exercisable by statutory instrument.

(2)　. . .

(3)　Any statutory instrument containing　. . .　an order under section　. . . , 11(4)[, 11D] or 12(3) or (5) above[, or section 111(4) or (6) or 114(3)(b) or (4)(b) of the Enterprise Act 2002 as applied by section 11B(1)(c) or (f) above,] shall be subject to annulment in pursuance of a resolution of either House of Parliament.

(4)　. . .

[(5)　Any power of the Secretary of State to make an order under this Act—
  (a)　may be exercised so as to make different provision for different cases or different purposes; and
  (b)　includes power to make such incidental, supplementary, consequential, transitory, transitional or saving provision as the Secretary of State considers appropriate.]

NOTES

Sub-s (1): words omitted repealed by the Enterprise Act 2002, s 278, Sch 25, para 10(8)(a), Sch 26.

Sub-s (2): repealed by the Competition Act 1998, s 74(1), (3), Sch 12, para 4(1), (14)(a), Sch 14, Pt I.

Sub-s (3): first words omitted repealed, words in first pair of square brackets inserted, and words in second pair of square brackets substituted, by the Enterprise Act 2002, s 278, Sch 25, para 10(8)(b), Sch 26; second words omitted repealed by the Competition Act 1998, s 74(1), (3), Sch 12, para 4(1), (14)(b), Sch 14, Pt I.

Sub-s (4): repealed by the Enterprise Act 2002, s 278, Sch 25, para 10(8)(c), Sch 26.

Sub-s (5): added by the Enterprise Act 2002, s 278(1), Sch 25, para 10(8)(d).

Ministers of the Crown, etc: see the note to s 11 at **[1.909]**.

[1.919]
32　Financial provisions
(1)　There shall be defrayed out of moneys provided by Parliament—
  (a)　any expenses incurred by the Secretary of State in consequence of the provisions of this Act; and
  (b)　any increase attributable to this Act in the sums payable out of moneys so provided under any other Act.

(2)　. . .

NOTES

Sub-s (2): amends the Fair Trading Act 1973, s 135(2)(c) at **[1.909]**.

[1.920]
33　Short title, interpretation, repeals, commencement and extent
(1)　This Act may be cited as the Competition Act 1980.

[(2)　Unless the context otherwise requires, in this Act "Minister" includes a government department and the following expressions shall have the same meanings as they have in Part 3 of the Enterprise Act 2002—
  "business"

["the CMA"]
"enactment"
"goods"
"services"
"supply (in relation to the supply of goods)"
"the supply of services".]

(3), (4)   . . .

(5)   This Act shall come into operation on such day as the Secretary of State may by order appoint, and different days may be so appointed for different provisions and for different purposes.

(6)   An order under this section appointing a day for the coming into operation of any provision of Schedule 2 to this Act may contain such savings with respect to the operation of that provision and such incidental and transitional provisions as appear to the Secretary of State to be appropriate.

(7)   Any reference in any provision of this Act to the appointed day shall be construed as a reference to the day appointed or, as the case may require, first appointed under this section for the coming into operation of that provision.

(8)   This Act extends to Northern Ireland.

NOTES

Sub-s (2): substituted by the Enterprise Act 2002, s 278(1), Sch 25, para 10(9); words in square brackets substituted (for original words "the Commission") by the Enterprise and Regulatory Reform Act 2013, s 26(4), Sch 6, Pt 1, paras 1, 8. For various transitional provisions (including those relating to the abolition of the OFT and the Competition Commission, existing references to those bodies and provisions relating to continuity), see the Enterprise and Regulatory Reform Act 2013 (Commencement No 6, Transitional Provisions and Savings) Order 2014, SI 2014/416, Schedule at [**2.1126**].

Sub-ss (3), (4): repealed by the Competition Act 1998, s 74(1), (3), Sch 12, para 4(1), (15)(b), Sch 14, Pt I.

Ministers of the Crown, etc: see the note to s 11 at [**1.909**].

Orders: the Competition Act 1980 (Commencement No 1) Order 1980, SI 1980/497; the Competition Act 1980 (Commencement No 2) Order 1980, SI 1980/978.

SCHEDULES

SCHEDULES 1 AND 2

(Sch 1 repealed by the Statute Law (Repeals) Act 1989; Sch 2 (Repeals) outside the scope of this work.)

SUPPLY OF GOODS AND SERVICES ACT 1982

(1982 c 29)

ARRANGEMENT OF SECTIONS

PART I
SUPPLY OF GOODS

PART 1B
ADDITIONAL RIGHTS OF TRANSFEREE IN CONSUMER CASES

PART II
SUPPLY OF SERVICES

PART III
SUPPLEMENTARY

An Act to amend the law with respect to the terms to be implied in certain contracts for the transfer of the property in goods, in certain contracts for the hire of goods and in certain contracts for the supply of a service; and for connected purposes

[13 July 1982]

PART I
SUPPLY OF GOODS

1–5A   (*Outside the scope of this work.*)

Contracts for the hire of goods

[1.921]
6   The contracts concerned
(1)   In this Act [in its application to England and Wales and Northern Ireland] a "*contract for the hire of goods*" means a contract under which one person bails or agrees to bail goods to another by way of hire, other than [a hire-purchase agreement][, and other than a contract to which Chapter 2 of Part 1 of the Consumer Rights Act 2015 applies].
(2)   . . .
(3)   For the purposes of this Act [in its application to England and Wales and Northern Ireland] a contract is a *contract for the hire of goods* whether or not services are also provided or to be provided under the contract, and   . . .   whatever is the nature of the consideration for the bailment or agreement to bail by way of hire.

NOTES
Sub-s (1): words in first pair of square brackets substituted by the Sale and Supply of Goods Act 1994, s 7(1), Sch 2, para 6(1), (6); for the words in italics there are substituted the words "relevant contract for the hire of goods", and words in final pair of square brackets added, by the Consumer Rights Act 2015, s 60, Sch 1, paras 37, 38(b), 42, as from 1 October 2015 (for transitional provisions see the Consumer Rights Act 2015 (Commencement No 3, Transitional Provisions, Savings and Consequential Amendments) Order 2015, SI 2015/1630, arts 6–8 at **[2.1220]** et seq); words in second pair of square brackets substituted in relation to England and Wales by the Regulatory Reform (Trading Stamps) Order 2005, SI 2005/871, art 5(b)(i) and in relation to Northern Ireland by the Law Reform (Miscellaneous Provisions) (Northern Ireland) Order 2005, SI 2005/1452, art 21(2)(b)(i).
Sub-s (2): repealed in relation to England and Wales by SI 2005/871, art 5(b)(ii) and in relation to Northern Ireland by SI 2005/1452, arts 21(2)(b)(ii), 24, Sch 2.
Sub-s (3): words in square brackets substituted by the Sale and Supply of Goods Act 1994, s 7(1), Sch 2, para 6(1), (6); for the words in italics there are substituted the words "relevant contract for the hire of goods" by the Consumer Rights Act 2015, s 60, Sch 1, paras 37, 38(b), as from 1 October 2015 (for transitional provisions see note above); words omitted repealed in relation to England and Wales by SI 2005/871, art 5(b)(iii) and in relation to Northern Ireland by SI 2005/1452, arts 21(2)(b)(iii), 24, Sch 2.

[1.922]
7   Implied terms about right to transfer possession, etc
(1)   In a *contract for the hire of goods* there is an implied condition on the part of the bailor that in the case of a bailment he has a right to transfer possession of the goods by way of hire for the period of the bailment and in the case of an agreement to bail he will have such a right at the time of the bailment.
(2)   In a *contract for the hire of goods* there is also an implied warranty that the bailee will enjoy quiet possession of the goods for the period of the bailment except so far as the possession may be disturbed by the owner or other person entitled to the benefit of any charge or encumbrance disclosed or known to the bailee before the contract is made.
(3)   The preceding provisions of this section do not affect the right of the bailor to repossess the goods under an express or implied term of the contract.

NOTES
Sub-ss (1), (2): for the words in italics there are substituted the words "relevant contract for the hire of goods" by the Consumer Rights Act 2015, s 60, Sch 1, paras 37, 38(b), as from 1 October 2015 (for transitional provisions see the Consumer Rights Act 2015 (Commencement No 3, Transitional Provisions, Savings and Consequential Amendments) Order 2015, SI 2015/1630, arts 6–8 at **[2.1220]** et seq).

[1.923]
8   Implied terms where hire is by description
(1)   This section applies where, under a *contract for the hire of goods*, the bailor bails or agrees to bail the goods by description.

(2) In such a case there is an implied condition that the goods will correspond with the description.

(3) If under the contract the bailor bails or agrees to bail the goods by reference to a sample as well as a description it is not sufficient that the bulk of the goods corresponds with the sample if the goods do not also correspond with the description.

(4) A contract is not prevented from falling within subsection (1) above by reason only that, being exposed for supply, the goods are selected by the bailee.

NOTES

Sub-s (1): for the words in italics there are substituted the words "relevant contract for the hire of goods" by the Consumer Rights Act 2015, s 60, Sch 1, paras 37, 38(b), as from 1 October 2015 (for transitional provisions see the Consumer Rights Act 2015 (Commencement No 3, Transitional Provisions, Savings and Consequential Amendments) Order 2015, SI 2015/1630, arts 6–8 at **[2.1220]** et seq).

[1.924]
9 Implied terms about quality or fitness

(1) Except as provided by this section and section 10 below and subject to the provisions of any other enactment, there is no implied condition or warranty about the quality or fitness for any particular purpose of goods bailed under a *contract for the hire of goods.*

[(2) Where, under such a contract, the bailor bails goods in the course of a business, there is an implied condition that the goods supplied under the contract are of satisfactory quality.

(2A) For the purposes of this section and section 10 below, goods are of satisfactory quality if they meet the standard that a reasonable person would regard as satisfactory, taking account of any description of the goods, the consideration for the bailment (if relevant) and all the other relevant circumstances.

[(2B) *If the bailee deals as consumer, the relevant circumstances mentioned in subsection (2A) above include any public statements on the specific characteristics of the goods made about them by the bailor, the producer or his representative, particularly in advertising or on labelling.*

(2C) *A public statement is not by virtue of subsection (2B) above a relevant circumstance for the purposes of subsection (2A) above in the case of a contract for the hire of goods, if the bailor shows that—*

  (a) *at the time the contract was made, he was not, and could not reasonably have been, aware of the statement,*

  (b) *before the contract was made, the statement had been withdrawn in public or, to the extent that it contained anything which was incorrect or misleading, it had been corrected in public, or*

  (c) *the decision to acquire the goods could not have been influenced by the statement.*

(2D) *Subsections (2B) and (2C) above do not prevent any public statement from being a relevant circumstance for the purposes of subsection (2A) above (whether or not the bailee deals as consumer) if the statement would have been such a circumstance apart from those subsections.]*

(3) The condition implied by subsection (2) above does not extend to any matter making the quality of goods unsatisfactory—

  (a) which is specifically drawn to the bailee's attention before the contract is made,

  (b) where the bailee examines the goods before the contract is made, which that examination ought to reveal, or

  (c) where the goods are bailed by reference to a sample, which would have been apparent on a reasonable examination of the sample.]

(4) Subsection (5) below applies where, under a *contract for the hire of goods*, the bailor bails goods in the course of a business and the bailee, expressly or by implication, makes known—

  (a) to the bailor in the course of negotiations conducted by him in relation to the making of the contract, or

  (b) to a credit-broker in the course of negotiations conducted by that broker in relation to goods sold by him to the bailor before forming the subject matter of the contract,

any particular purpose for which the goods are being bailed.

(5) In that case there is (subject to subsection (6) below) an implied condition that the goods supplied under the contract are reasonably fit for that purpose, whether or not that is a purpose for which such goods are commonly supplied.

(6) Subsection (5) above does not apply where the circumstances show that the bailee does not rely, or that it is unreasonable for him to rely, on the skill or judgment of the bailor or credit-broker.

(7) An implied condition or warranty about quality or fitness for a particular purpose may be annexed by usage to a *contract for the hire of goods.*

(8) The preceding provisions of this section apply to a bailment by a person who in the course of a business is acting as agent for another as they apply to a bailment by a principal in the course of a business, except where that other is not bailing in the course of a business and either the bailee knows that fact or reasonable steps are taken to bring it to the bailee's notice before the contract concerned is made.

(9) . . .

Part 1 Statutes

NOTES

Sub-ss (1), (4), (7): for the words in italics there are substituted the words "relevant contract for the hire of goods" by the Consumer Rights Act 2015, s 60, Sch 1, paras 37, 38(b), as from 1 October 2015 (for transitional provisions see the Consumer Rights Act 2015 (Commencement No 3, Transitional Provisions, Savings and Consequential Amendments) Order 2015, SI 2015/1630, arts 6–8 at **[2.1220]** et seq).

Sub-ss (2), (2A), (3): substituted, for original sub-ss (2), (3), by the Sale and Supply of Goods Act 1994, s 7(1), Sch 2, para 6(1), (7).

Sub-ss (2B)–(2D): inserted by the Sale and Supply of Goods to Consumers Regulations 2002, SI 2002/3045, reg 10(1), (2); repealed by the Consumer Rights Act 2015, s 60, Sch 1, paras 37, 43, as from 1 October 2015 (for transitional provisions see note above). Note also that Sch 1, paras 37, 38(b) to the 2015 Act provides for the substitution of all occurrences of "contract for the hire of goods" in this Act with the words "relevant contract for the hire of goods". Given the repeal of these subsections, it is assumed that this general substitution is not applicable in sub-s (2C).

Sub-s (9): repealed by the Sale and Supply of Goods Act 1994, s 7, Sch 2, para 6(1), (7), Sch 3.

[1.925]
10 Implied terms where hire is by sample

(1)   This section applies where, under a *contract for the hire of goods*, the bailor bails or agrees to bail the goods by reference to a sample.

(2)   In such a case there is an implied condition—

   (a)   that the bulk will correspond with the sample in quality; and

   (b)   that the bailee will have a reasonable opportunity of comparing the bulk with the sample; and

   (c)   that the goods will be free from any defect, [making their quality unsatisfactory], which would not be apparent on reasonable examination of the sample.

(3)   . . .

(4)   For the purposes of this section a bailor bails or agrees to bail goods by reference to a sample where there is an express or implied term to that effect in the contract concerned.

NOTES

Sub-s (1): for the words in italics there are substituted the words "relevant contract for the hire of goods" by the Consumer Rights Act 2015, s 60, Sch 1, paras 37, 38(b), as from 1 October 2015 (for transitional provisions see the Consumer Rights Act 2015 (Commencement No 3, Transitional Provisions, Savings and Consequential Amendments) Order 2015, SI 2015/1630, arts 6–8 at **[2.1220]** et seq).

Sub-s (2): words in square brackets in para (c) substituted by the Sale and Supply of Goods Act 1994, s 7(1), Sch 2, para 6(1), (8).

Sub-s (3): repealed by the Sale and Supply of Goods Act 1994, s 7, Sch 2, para 6(1), (8), Sch 3.

[1.926]
[10A Modification of remedies for breach of statutory condition in non-consumer cases

(1)   Where in the case of a *contract for the hire of goods*—

   (a)   the bailee would, apart from this subsection, have the right to treat the contract as repudiated by reason of a breach on the part of the bailor of a term implied by section 8, 9 or 10(2)(a) or (c) above, but

   (b)   the breach is so slight that it would be unreasonable for him to do so,

then, if the bailee does not deal as consumer, the breach is not to be treated as a breach of condition but may be treated as a breach of warranty.

(2)   This section applies unless a contrary intention appears in, or is to be implied from, the contract.

(3)   It is for the bailor to show that a breach fell within subsection (1)(b) above.]

NOTES

Inserted by the Sale and Supply of Goods Act 1994, s 7(1), Sch 2, para 6(1), (9).

Sub-s (1): for the first words in italics there are substituted the words "relevant contract for the hire of goods", and second words in italics repealed, by the Consumer Rights Act 2015, s 60, Sch 1, paras 37, 38(b), 44, as from 1 October 2015 (for transitional provisions see the Consumer Rights Act 2015 (Commencement No 3, Transitional Provisions, Savings and Consequential Amendments) Order 2015, SI 2015/1630, arts 6–8 at **[2.1220]** et seq).

Exclusion of implied terms, etc

[1.927]
11 Exclusion of implied terms, etc

(1)   Where a right, duty or liability would arise under a *contract for the transfer of goods* or a *contract for the hire of goods* by implication of law, it may (subject to subsection (2) below and the 1977 Act) be negatived or varied by express agreement, or by the course of dealing between the parties, or by such usage as binds both parties to the contract[, and other than a contract to which Chapter 2 of Part 1 of the Consumer Rights Act 2015 applies].

(2)   An express condition or warranty does not negative a condition or warranty implied by the preceding provisions of this Act unless inconsistent with it.

(3)   Nothing in the preceding provisions of this Act prejudices the operation of any other enactment or any rule of law whereby any condition or warranty (other than one relating to quality or fitness) is to be implied in a *contract for the transfer of goods* or a *contract for the hire of goods*.

NOTES

Sub-s (1): for the words in italics there are substituted the words "relevant contract for the transfer of goods" and "relevant contract for the hire of goods" respectively, and words in square brackets added, by the Consumer Rights Act 2015, s 60, Sch 1, paras 37, 38(a), (b), 45, as from 1 October 2015 (for transitional provisions see the Consumer Rights Act 2015 (Commencement No 3, Transitional Provisions, Savings and Consequential Amendments) Order 2015, SI 2015/1630, arts 6–8 at **[2.1220]** et seq).

Sub-s (3): for the words in italics there are substituted the words "relevant contract for the transfer of goods" and "relevant contract for the hire of goods" respectively by the Consumer Rights Act 2015, s 60, Sch 1, paras 37, 38(a), (b), as from 1 October 2015 (for transitional provisions see note above).

11A–11L *(Pt IA (ss 11A–11L) inserted by the Sale and Supply of Goods Act 1994, s 6, Sch 1, para 1 and applies to Scotland only.)*

[PART 1B
ADDITIONAL RIGHTS OF TRANSFEREE IN CONSUMER CASES

[1.928]
11M   Introductory
(1)   This section applies if—
(a)   the transferee deals as consumer or, in Scotland, there is a consumer contract in which the transferee is a consumer, and
(b)   the goods do not conform to the contract for the transfer of goods at the time of delivery.
(2)   If this section applies, the transferee has the right—
(a)   under and in accordance with section 11N below, to require the transferor to repair or replace the goods, or
(b)   under and in accordance with section 11P below—
(i)   to require the transferor to reduce the amount to be paid for the transfer by the transferee by an appropriate amount, or
(ii)   to rescind the contract with regard to the goods in question.
(3)   For the purposes of subsection (1)(b) above, goods which do not conform to the contract for the transfer of goods at any time within the period of six months starting with the date on which the goods were delivered to the transferee must be taken not to have so conformed at that date.
(4)   Subsection (3) above does not apply if—
(a)   it is established that the goods did so conform at that date;
(b)   its application is incompatible with the nature of the goods or the nature of the lack of conformity.
(5)   For the purposes of this section, "consumer contract" has the same meaning as in section 11F(3) above.]

NOTES

Part 1B (ss 11M–11S) inserted by the Sale and Supply of Goods to Consumers Regulations 2002, SI 2002/3045, reg 9; repealed by the Consumer Rights Act 2015, s 60, Sch 1, paras 37, 50, as from 1 October 2015 (for transitional provisions see the Consumer Rights Act 2015 (Commencement No 3, Transitional Provisions, Savings and Consequential Amendments) Order 2015, SI 2015/1630, arts 6–8 at **[2.1220]** et seq). Note also that Sch 1, paras 37, 38(a) to the 2015 Act provides for the substitution of all occurrences of "contract for the transfer of goods" in this Act with the words "relevant contract for the transfer of goods". Given the repeal of this Part, it is assumed that this general substitution is not applicable.

[1.929]
[11N   Repair or replacement of the goods
(1)   If section 11M above applies, the transferee may require the transferor—
(a)   to repair the goods, or
(b)   to replace the goods.
(2)   If the transferee requires the transferor to repair or replace the goods, the transferor must—
(a)   repair or, as the case may be, replace the goods within a reasonable time but without causing significant inconvenience to the transferee;
(b)   bear any necessary costs incurred in doing so (including in particular the cost of any labour, materials or postage).
(3)   The transferee must not require the transferor to repair or, as the case may be, replace the goods if that remedy is—
(a)   impossible,
(b)   disproportionate in comparison to the other of those remedies, or
(c)   disproportionate in comparison to an appropriate reduction in the purchase price under paragraph (a), or rescission under paragraph (b), of section 11P(1) below.
(4)   One remedy is disproportionate in comparison to the other if the one imposes costs on the transferor which, in comparison to those imposed on him by the other, are unreasonable, taking into account—
(a)   the value which the goods would have if they conformed to the contract for the transfer of goods,
(b)   the significance of the lack of conformity to the contract for the transfer of goods, and

(c)   whether the other remedy could be effected without significant inconvenience to the transferee.

(5)   Any question as to what is a reasonable time or significant inconvenience is to be determined by reference to—

(a)   the nature of the goods, and

(b)   the purpose for which the goods were acquired.]

NOTES

Inserted and repealed as noted to s 11M at **[1.928]**. Note also that Sch 1, paras 37, 38(a) to the 2015 Act provides for the substitution of all occurrences of "contract for the transfer of goods" in this Act with the words "relevant contract for the transfer of goods". Given the repeal of this Part, it is assumed that this general substitution is not applicable.

[1.930]

[11P   Reduction of purchase price or rescission of contract

(1)   If section 11M above applies, the transferee may—

(a)   require the transferor to reduce the purchase price of the goods in question to the transferee by an appropriate amount, or

(b)   rescind the contract with regard to those goods,

if the condition in subsection (2) below is satisfied.

(2)   The condition is that—

(a)   by virtue of section 11N(3) above the transferee may require neither repair nor replacement of the goods, or

(b)   the transferee has required the transferor to repair or replace the goods, but the transferor is in breach of the requirement of section 11N(2)(a) above to do so within a reasonable time and without significant inconvenience to the transferee.

(3)   If the transferee rescinds the contract, any reimbursement to the transferee may be reduced to take account of the use he has had of the goods since they were delivered to him.]

NOTES

Inserted and repealed as noted to s 11M at **[1.928]**.

[1.931]

[11Q   Relation to other remedies etc

(1)   If the transferee requires the transferor to repair or replace the goods the transferee must not act under subsection (2) until he has given the transferor a reasonable time in which to repair or replace (as the case may be) the goods.

(2)   The transferee acts under this subsection if—

(a)   in England and Wales or Northern Ireland he rejects the goods and terminates the contract for breach of condition;

(b)   in Scotland he rejects any goods delivered under the contract and treats it as repudiated; or

(c)   he requires the goods to be replaced or repaired (as the case may be).]

NOTES

Inserted and repealed as noted to s 11M at **[1.928]**.

[1.932]

[11R   Powers of the court

(1)   In any proceedings in which a remedy is sought by virtue of this Part the court, in addition to any other power it has, may act under this section.

(2)   On the application of the transferee the court may make an order requiring specific performance or, in Scotland, specific implement by the transferor of any obligation imposed on him by virtue of section 11N above.

(3)   Subsection (4) applies if—

(a)   the transferee requires the transferor to give effect to a remedy under section 11N or 11P above or has claims to rescind under section 11P, but

(b)   the court decides that another remedy under section 11N or 11P is appropriate.

(4)   The court may proceed—

(a)   as if the transferee had required the transferor to give effect to the other remedy, or if the other remedy is rescission under section 11P,

(b)   as if the transferee had claimed to rescind the contract under that section.

(5)   If the transferee has claimed to rescind the contract the court may order that any reimbursement to the transferee is reduced to take account of the use he has had of the goods since they were delivered to him.

(6)   The court may make an order under this section unconditionally or on such terms and conditions as to damages, payment of the price and otherwise as it thinks just.]

NOTES

Inserted and repealed as noted to s 11M at **[1.928]**.

[1.933]

[11S Conformity with the contract

(1) Goods do not conform to a contract for the supply or transfer of goods if—

 (a) there is, in relation to the goods, a breach of an express term of the contract or a term implied by section 3, 4 or 5 above or, in Scotland, by section 11C, 11D or 11E above, or

 (b) installation of the goods forms part of the contract for the transfer of goods, and the goods were installed by the transferor, or under his responsibility, in breach of the term implied by section 13 below or (in Scotland) in breach of any term implied by any rule of law as to the manner in which the installation is carried out.]

NOTES

Inserted as noted to s 11M at **[1.928]**. Note also that Sch 1, paras 37, 38(a) to the 2015 Act provides for the substitution of all occurrences of "contract for the transfer of goods" in this Act with the words "relevant contract for the transfer of goods". Given the repeal of this Part, it is assumed that this general substitution is not applicable.

PART II
SUPPLY OF SERVICES

[1.934]

12 The contracts concerned

(1) In this Act a *"contract for the supply of a service"* means, subject to subsection (2) below, a contract under which a person ("the supplier") agrees to carry out a service[, other than a contract to which Chapter 4 of Part 1 of the Consumer Rights Act 2015 applies].

(2) For the purposes of this Act, a contract of service or apprenticeship is not a *contract for the supply of a service*.

(3) Subject to subsection (2) above, a contract is a *contract for the supply of a service* for the purposes of this Act whether or not goods are also—

 (a) transferred or to be transferred, or

 (b) bailed or to be bailed by way of hire,

under the contract, and whatever is the nature of the consideration for which the service is to be carried out.

(4) The Secretary of State may by order provide that one or more of sections 13 to 15 below shall not apply to services of a description specified in the order, and such an order may make different provision for different circumstances.

(5) The power to make an order under subsection (4) above shall be exercisable by statutory instrument subject to annulment in pursuance of a resolution of either House of Parliament.

NOTES

Sub-s (1): for the words in italics there are substituted the words "relevant contract for the supply of a service", and words in square brackets added, by the Consumer Rights Act 2015, s 60, Sch 1, paras 37, 38(c), 51, as from 1 October 2015 (for transitional provisions see the Consumer Rights Act 2015 (Commencement No 3, Transitional Provisions, Savings and Consequential Amendments) Order 2015, SI 2015/1630, arts 6–8 at **[2.1220]** et seq).

Sub-ss (2), (3): for the words in italics there are substituted the words "relevant contract for the supply of a service" by the Consumer Rights Act 2015, s 60, Sch 1, paras 37, 38(c), as from 1 October 2015 (for transitional provisions see note above).

Orders: the Supply of Services (Exclusion of Implied Terms) Order 1982, SI 1982/1771 at **[2.19]**; the Supply of Services (Exclusion of Implied Terms) Order 1983, SI 1983/902 at **[2.21]**; the Supply of Services (Exclusion of Implied Terms) Order 1985, SI 1985/1 at **[2.45]**.

[1.935]

13 Implied term about care and skill

In a *contract for the supply of a service* where the supplier is acting in the course of a business, there is an implied term that the supplier will carry out the service with reasonable care and skill.

NOTES

For the words in italics there are substituted the words "relevant contract for the supply of a service" by the Consumer Rights Act 2015, s 60, Sch 1, paras 37, 38(c), as from 1 October 2015 (for transitional provisions see the Consumer Rights Act 2015 (Commencement No 3, Transitional Provisions, Savings and Consequential Amendments) Order 2015, SI 2015/1630, arts 6–8 at **[2.1220]** et seq).

[1.936]

14 Implied term about time for performance

(1) Where, under a *contract for the supply of a service* by a supplier acting in the course of a business, the time for the service to be carried out is not fixed by the contract, left to be fixed in a manner agreed by the contract or determined by the course of dealing between the parties, there is an implied term that the supplier will carry out the service within a reasonable time.

(2) What is a reasonable time is a question of fact.

NOTES

Sub-s (1): for the words in italics there are substituted the words "relevant contract for the supply of a service" by the Consumer Rights Act 2015, s 60, Sch 1, paras 37, 38(c), as from 1 October 2015 (for transitional provisions see the Consumer Rights Act 2015 (Commencement No 3, Transitional Provisions, Savings and Consequential Amendments) Order 2015, SI 2015/1630, arts 6–8 at **[2.1220]** et seq).

[1.937]
15   Implied term about consideration

(1)   Where, under a *contract for the supply of a service*, the consideration for the service is not determined by the contract, left to be determined in a manner agreed by the contract or determined by the course of dealing between the parties, there is an implied term that the party contracting with the supplier will pay a reasonable charge.

(2)   What is a reasonable charge is a question of fact.

NOTES

Sub-s (1): for the words in italics there are substituted the words "relevant contract for the supply of a service" by the Consumer Rights Act 2015, s 60, Sch 1, paras 37, 38(c), as from 1 October 2015 (for transitional provisions see the Consumer Rights Act 2015 (Commencement No 3, Transitional Provisions, Savings and Consequential Amendments) Order 2015, SI 2015/1630, arts 6–8 at **[2.1220]** et seq).

[1.938]
16   Exclusion of implied terms, etc

(1)   Where a right, duty or liability would arise under a *contract for the supply of a service* by virtue of this Part of this Act, it may (subject to subsection (2) below and the 1977 Act) be negatived or varied by express agreement, or by the course of dealing between the parties, or by such usage as binds both parties to the contract.

(2)   An express term does not negative a term implied by this Part of this Act unless inconsistent with it.

(3)   Nothing in this Part of this Act prejudices—

   (a)   any rule of law which imposes on the supplier a duty stricter than that imposed by section 13 or 14 above; or

   (b)   subject to paragraph (a) above, any rule of law whereby any term not inconsistent with this Part of this Act is to be implied in a *contract for the supply of a service*.

(4)   This Part of this Act has effect subject to any other enactment which defines or restricts the rights, duties or liabilities arising in connection with a service of any description.

NOTES

Sub-ss (1), (3): for the words in italics there are substituted the words "relevant contract for the supply of a service" by the Consumer Rights Act 2015, s 60, Sch 1, paras 37, 38(c), as from 1 October 2015 (for transitional provisions see the Consumer Rights Act 2015 (Commencement No 3, Transitional Provisions, Savings and Consequential Amendments) Order 2015, SI 2015/1630, arts 6–8 at **[2.1220]** et seq).

PART III
SUPPLEMENTARY

17   (*Sub-s (1) repealed by the Sale and Supply of Goods Act 1994, s 7(2), Sch 3; sub-ss (2), (3) amend the Unfair Contract Terms Act 1977, s 7 at* **[1.737]**.)

[1.939]
18   Interpretation: general

(1)   In the preceding provisions of this Act and this section—

   "bailee", in relation to a *contract for the hire of goods* means (depending on the context) a person to whom the goods are bailed under the contract, or a person to whom they are to be so bailed, or a person to whom the rights under the contract of either of those persons have passed;

   "bailor", in relation to a *contract for the hire of goods*, means (depending on the context) a person who bails the goods under the contract, or a person who agrees to do so, or a person to whom the duties under the contract of either of those persons have passed;

   "business" includes a profession and the activities of any government department or local or public authority;

   "credit-broker" means a person acting in the course of a business of credit brokerage carried on by him;

   "credit brokerage" means the effecting of introductions—

   (a)   of individuals desiring to obtain credit to persons carrying on any business so far as it relates to the provision of credit; or

   (b)   of individuals desiring to obtain goods on hire to persons carrying on a business which comprises or relates to the bailment [or as regards Scotland the hire] of goods under a *contract for the hire of goods*; or

   (c)   of individuals desiring to obtain credit, or to obtain goods on hire, to other credit-brokers;

   "enactment" means any legislation (including subordinate legislation) of the United Kingdom or Northern Ireland;

"goods" [includes all personal chattels, other than things in action and money, and as regards Scotland all corporeal moveables; and in particular "goods" includes] emblements, industrial growing crops, and things attached to or forming part of the land which are agreed to be severed before the transfer [bailment or hire] concerned or under the contract concerned . . . ;

"hire-purchase agreement" has the same meaning as in the 1974 Act;

[*"producer" means the manufacturer of goods, the importer of goods into the European Economic Area or any person purporting to be a producer by placing his name, trade mark or other distinctive sign on the goods;*]

"property", in relation to goods, means the general property in them and not merely a special property;

. . .

[*"repair" means, in cases where there is a lack of conformity in goods for the purposes of this Act, to bring the goods into conformity with the contract;*]

. . .

"transferee", in relation to a *contract for the transfer of goods*, means (depending on the context) a person to whom the property in the goods is transferred under the contract, or a person to whom the property is to be so transferred, or a person to whom the rights under the contract of either of those persons have passed;

"transferor", in relation to a *contract for the transfer of goods*, means (depending on the context) a person who transfers the property in the goods under the contract, or a person who agrees to do so, or a person to whom the duties under the contract of either of those persons have passed.

(2) In subsection (1) above, in the definitions of bailee, bailor, transferee and transferor, a reference to rights or duties passing is to their passing by assignment [assignation], operation of law or otherwise.

[(3) For the purposes of this Act, the quality of goods includes their state and condition and the following (among others) are in appropriate cases aspects of the quality of goods—

(a) fitness for all the purposes for which goods of the kind in question are commonly supplied,
(b) appearance and finish,
(c) freedom from minor defects,
(d) safety, and
(e) durability.

(4) *References in this Act to dealing as consumer are to be construed in accordance with Part I of the Unfair Contract Terms Act 1977; and, for the purposes of this Act, it is for the transferor or bailor claiming that the transferee or bailee does not deal as consumer to show that he does not.*]

NOTES

Sub-s (1): for the words in italics in definitions "bailee", "bailor" and "credit brokerage" there are substituted the words "relevant contract for the hire of goods", and for the words in italics in definitions "transferee" and "transferor" there are substituted the words "relevant contract for the transfer of goods", by the Consumer Rights Act 2015, s 60, Sch 1, paras 37, 38(a), (b), as from 1 October 2015 (for transitional provisions see the Consumer Rights Act 2015 (Commencement No 3, Transitional Provisions, Savings and Consequential Amendments) Order 2015, SI 2015/1630, arts 6–8 at **[2.1220]** et seq); words in square brackets in definitions "credit brokerage" and "goods" substituted, words omitted from definition "goods" and definition "quality" (omitted) repealed, by the Sale and Supply of Goods Act 1994, ss 6, 7, Sch 1, para 2, Sch 2, para 6(1), (10); definitions "producer" and "repair" inserted by the Sale and Supply of Goods to Consumers Regulations 2002, SI 2002/3045, reg 12 and repealed by the Consumer Rights Act 2015, s 60, Sch 1, paras 37, 52(1), as from 1 October 2015 (for transitional provisions see note above); definitions "redemption" and "trading stamps" (omitted) repealed in relation to England and Wales by the Regulatory Reform (Trading Stamps) Order 2005, SI 2005/871, art 5(e) and in relation to Northern Ireland by the Law Reform (Miscellaneous Provisions) (Northern Ireland) Order 2005, SI 2005/1452, art 21(2)(c).

Sub-s (2): word in square brackets inserted by the Sale and Supply of Goods Act 1994, s 6, Sch 1, para 3.

Sub-ss (3), (4): added by the Sale and Supply of Goods Act 1994, s 7(1), Sch 2, para 6(1), (10), and sub-s (4) repealed by the Consumer Rights Act 2015, s 60, Sch 1, paras 37, 52(2), as from 1 October 2015 (for transitional provisions see note above).

[1.940]
19 Interpretation: references to Acts
In this Act—

"the 1973 Act" means the Supply of Goods (Implied Terms) Act 1973;
"the 1974 Act" means the Consumer Credit Act 1974;
"the 1977 Act" means the Unfair Contract Terms Act 1977; and
"the 1979 Act" means the Sale of Goods Act 1979.

[1.941]
20 Citation, transitional provisions, commencement and extent
(1) This Act may be cited as the Supply of Goods and Services Act 1982.
(2) The transitional provisions in the Schedule to this Act shall have effect.
(3) Part I of this Act together with section 17 and so much of sections 18 and 19 above as relates to that Part shall not come into operation until 4th January 1983; and Part II of this Act together with so much of sections 18 and 19 above as relates to that Part shall not come into operation until such day as may be appointed by an order made by the Secretary of State.

(4) The power to make an order under subsection (3) above shall be exercisable by statutory instrument.

(5) No provision of this Act applies to a contract made before the provision comes into operation.

(6) This Act [except Part IA, which extends only to Scotland] extends to Northern Ireland [and Parts I and II do not extend] to Scotland.

NOTES

Sub-s (6): words in first pair of square brackets inserted, and words in second pair of square brackets substituted, by the Sale and Supply of Goods Act 1994, s 6, Sch 1, para 4.

Orders: the Supply of Goods and Services Act 1982 (Commencement) Order 1982, SI 1982/1770.

SCHEDULE

(Schedule spent.)

WEIGHTS AND MEASURES ACT 1985

(1985 c 72)

ARRANGEMENT OF SECTIONS

PART IV
REGULATION OF TRANSACTIONS IN GOODS

Part 1 Statutes

SCHEDULES

An Act to consolidate certain enactments relating to weights and measures

[30 October 1985]

1–20 *((Pts I–III) outside the scope of this work.)*

PART IV
REGULATION OF TRANSACTIONS IN GOODS

Transactions in particular goods

[1.942]
21 Transactions in goods mentioned in Schedules 4 to 7
Schedules 4, 5, 6 and 7 to this Act (which relate to transactions in the goods mentioned in those Schedules) shall have effect.

[1.943]
22 Orders relating to transactions in particular goods
(1)   The Secretary of State may by order make provision with respect to any goods specified in the order for all or any of the following purposes, that is to say, to ensure that, except in such cases or in such circumstances as may be so specified, the goods in question—
   (a)   are sold only by quantity expressed in such manner as may be so specified,
   (b)   are pre-packed, or are otherwise made up in or on a container for sale or for delivery after sale, only if the container is marked with such information as to the quantity of the goods as may be so specified,
   (c)   are pre-packed, or are otherwise made up for sale or for delivery after sale, only in or on a container of a size or capacity so specified,
   (d)   are sold, or are pre-packed, or are otherwise made up in or on a container for sale or for delivery after sale, or are made for sale, only in such quantities as may be so specified,
   (e)   are not sold without the quantity sold expressed in such manner as may be so specified being made known to the buyer at or before such time as may be so specified,
   (f)   are sold by means of, or are offered or exposed for sale in, a vending machine only if there is displayed on or in the machine—
      (i)   such information as to the quantity of the goods in question comprised in each item for sale by means of that machine as may be so specified, and
      (ii)   a statement of the name and address of the seller,
   (g)   are carried for reward only in pursuance of an agreement made by reference to the quantity of the goods in question expressed in such manner as may be so specified,
   (h)   in such circumstances as may be so specified, have associated with them in such manner as may be so specified a document containing a statement of the quantity of the goods in question expressed in such manner, and a statement of such other particulars, if any, as may be so specified, or
   (i)   when carried on a road vehicle along a highway are accompanied by a document containing such particulars determined in such manner as may be so specified as to the weight of the vehicle and its load apart from the goods in question.
(2)   An order under subsection (1) above may be made with respect to any goods, including goods to which any of the provisions of Schedule 4, 5, 6, or 7 to this Act applies, and may—
   (a)   make provision for any of the purposes mentioned in subsection (1) above in such manner, whether by means of amending, or of applying with or without modifications, or of excluding the application in whole or in part of, any of the provisions of this Act . . . or of any previous order under subsection (1) or otherwise,
   (b)   make such, if any, different provision for retail and other sales respectively, and
   (c)   contain such consequential, incidental or supplementary provision, whether by such means as mentioned in paragraph (a) above or otherwise,

as may appear to the Secretary of State to be expedient, and may in particular make provision in respect of contraventions of the order for which no penalty is provided by this Act for the imposition of penalties not exceeding those provided by section 84(6) below for an offence under this Act.

(3) Without prejudice to the generality of the powers conferred by paragraph (c) of subsection (1) above, an order made by virtue of that paragraph—

(a) may require a container to be marked with such information concerning it or its contents as is specified in the order, and

(b) in order to prevent size or capacity from giving a false impression of the quantity of the goods in a container, may prescribe a minimum quantity for the goods in a container of a given capacity.

(4) The minimum quantity referred to in subsection (3)(b) above may be expressed in the order by weight or volume, by percentage of the capacity of the container or in any other manner.

NOTES

Sub-s (2): words omitted from para (a) repealed by the Weights and Measures (Packaged Goods) Regulations 2006, SI 2006/659, reg 1(2), Sch 1, Pt 2, paras (1), (2), subject to transitional provisions in reg 21 thereof.

Orders: the Weights and Measures (Liquid Fuel carried by Road Tanker) Order 1985, SI 1985/778; the Weights and Measures Act 1963 (Various Foods) (Amendment) Order 1985, SI 1985/988; the Weights and Measures Act 1963 (Various Foods) (Amendment No 2) Order 1985, SI 1985/1980; the Weights and Measures (Carriage of Solid Fuel by Rail) Order 1987, SI 1987/216; the Weights and Measures (Knitting Yarns) Order 1988, SI 1988/895; the Weights and Measures (Intoxicating Liquor) Order, SI 1988/2039; the Weights and Measures (Miscellaneous Foods) Order 1988, SI 1988/2040; the Weights and Measures (Various Foods) (Amendment) Order 1990, SI 1990/1550; the Weights and Measures Act 1985 (Metrication) (Amendment) Order 1994, SI 1994/2866; the Weights and Measures (Metrication) (Miscellaneous Goods) (Amendment) Order 1994, SI 1994/2868; the Weights and Measures (Miscellaneous Foods) (Amendment) Order 2005, SI 2005/3057; the Weights and Measures (Cosmetic Products) Order 1994, SI 1994/1884; the Weights and Measures (Specified Quantities) (Unwrapped Bread and Intoxicating Liquor) Order 2011, SI 2011/2331. In addition, by virtue of the Interpretation Act 1978, s 17(2)(b), the following order has effect as if made under this section: the Weights and Measures Act 1963 (Cheese, Fish, Fresh Fruits and Vegetables, Meat and Poultry) Order 1984, SI 1984/1315.

[1.944]
23 Regulations as to information

(1) The Secretary of State may make regulations—

(a) as to the manner in which any container required by any of the provisions of Schedules 4, 5, 6 or 7 to this Act or of any other under section 22(1) above to be marked with information (including in particular information as to quantity or capacity) is to be so marked,

(b) as to the manner in which any information required by any such provision to be displayed on or in a vending machine is to be so displayed,

(c) as to the conditions which must be satisfied in marking with information as to the quantity of goods made up in it the container in or on which any goods are made up for sale (whether by way of pre-packing or otherwise) where those goods are goods on a sale of which (whether any sale or a sale of any particular description) the quantity of the goods sold is required by any such provision to be made known to the buyer at or before a particular time,

(d) as to the units of measurement to be used in marking any such container or machine with any information,

(e) for securing, in the case of pre-packed goods, that the container is so marked as to enable the packer to be identified,

(f) as to the method by which and conditions under which quantity is to be determined in connection with any information relating to quantity required by or under section 21 or 22 above, and

(g) permitting, in the case of such goods and in such circumstances as may be specified in the regulations, the weight of such articles used in making up the goods for sale as may be so specified to be included in the net weight of the goods for the purposes of this Part of this Act.

(2) Any person who contravenes any regulation made under subsection (1) above otherwise than by virtue of paragraph (f) or (g) of that subsection shall be guilty of an offence.

NOTES

Regulations: the Weights and Measures (Quantity Marking and Abbreviations of Units) Regulations 1987, SI 1987/1538; the Weights and Measures (Quantity Marking and Abbreviations of Units) (Amendment) Regulations 1988, SI 1988/627. In addition, by virtue of the Interpretation Act 1978, s 17(2)(b), the following regulations have effect as if made under this section: the Weights and Measures (Solid Fuel) Regulations 1978, SI 1978/238; the Weights and Measures (Milk and Solid Fuel Vending Machines) Regulations 1980, SI 1980/246.

[1.945]
24 Exemption from requirements imposed under sections 21 to 23

(1) The Secretary of State may by order grant, with respect to goods or sales of such descriptions as may be specified in the order, exemption, either generally or in such circumstances as may be so specified, from all or any of the requirements imposed by or under sections 21 to 23 above.

(2) Until otherwise provided by an order under subsection (1) above, the following shall be exempted from all requirements imposed by or under sections 21 to 23 above, that is to say—

- (a) goods made up in or on a container for sale only for use by Her Majesty's forces or by a visiting force within the meaning of any of the provisions of Part I of the Visiting Forces Act 1952 and not sold or offered, exposed or in any person's possession for sale for any other use,
- (b) any sale of goods in the case of which the buyer gives notice in writing to the seller before the sale is completed that the goods are being bought—
  - (i) for despatch to a destination outside Great Britain and any designated country, or
  - (ii) for use as stores within the meaning of the Customs and Excise Management Act 1979 in a ship or aircraft on a voyage or flight to an eventual destination outside the United Kingdom and the Isle of Man,
- (c) any goods sold for, or offered, exposed or in any person's possession for sale only for, use or consumption at the premises of the seller, not being intoxicating liquor, and
- (d) any assortment of articles of food pre-packed together for consumption together as a meal and ready for such consumption without being cooked, heated or otherwise prepared.

NOTES

Orders: the Weights and Measures (Liquid Fuel Carried by Road Tanker) Order 1985, SI 1985/778; the Weights and Measures Act 1963 (Various Foods) (Amendment) Order 1985, SI 1985/988; the Weights and Measures Act 1963 (Various Foods) (Amendment No 2) Order 1985, SI 1985/1980; the Weights and Measures (Carriage of Solid Fuel by Rail) Order 1987, SI 1987/216; the Weights and Measures (Intoxicating Liquor) Order, SI 1988/2039; the Weights and Measures (Miscellaneous Foods) Order 1988, SI 1988/2040; the Weights and Measures (Various Foods) (Amendment) Order 1990, SI 1990/1550; the Weights and Measures (Metrication) (Miscellaneous Goods) (Amendment) Order 1994, SI 1994/2868; the Weights and Measures (Cosmetic Products) Order 1994, SI 1994/1884; the Weights and Measures (Specified Quantities) (Unwrapped Bread and Intoxicating Liquor) Order 2011, SI 2011/2331. In addition, by virtue of the Interpretation Act 1978, s 17(2)(b), the following orders have effect as if made under this section: the Weights and Measures Act 1963 (Cheese, Fish, Fresh Fruits and Vegetables, Meat and Poultry) Order 1984, SI 1984/1315.

[1.946]
25 Offences relating to transactions in particular goods
(1) Subject to section 44 below, where any goods are required, when not pre-packed, to be sold only by quantity expressed in a particular manner or only in a particular quantity, any person shall be guilty of an offence who—

- (a) whether on his own behalf or on behalf of another person, offers or exposes for sale, sells or agrees to sell, or
- (b) causes or suffers any other person to offer or expose for sale, sell or agree to sell on his behalf,

those goods otherwise than by quantity expressed in that manner or, as the case may be, otherwise than in that quantity.
(2) Any person shall be guilty of an offence who—

- (a) whether on his own behalf or on behalf of another person, has in his possession for sale, sells or agrees to sell,
- (b) except in the course of carriage of the goods for reward, has in his possession for delivery after sale, or
- (c) causes or suffers any other person to have in his possession for sale or for delivery after sale, sell or agree to sell on behalf of the first-mentioned person,

any goods to which subsection (3) below applies, whether the sale is or is to be, by retail or otherwise.
(3) This subsection applies to any goods—

- (a) which are required to be pre-packed only in particular quantities but are not so pre-packed,
- (b) which are required to be otherwise made up in or on a container for sale or for delivery after sale only in particular quantities but are not so made up,
- (c) which are required to be made for sale only in particular quantities but are not so made,
- (d) which are required to be pre-packed only if the container is marked with particular information but are pre-packed otherwise than in or on a container so marked,
- (e) which are required to be otherwise made up in or on a container for sale or for delivery after sale only if the container is marked with particular information but are so made up otherwise than in or on a container so marked,
- (f) which are required to be pre-packed only in or on a container of a particular description but are not pre-packed in or on a container of that description, or
- (g) which are required to be otherwise made up in or on a container for sale or for delivery after sale only in or on a container of a particular description but are not so made up in or on a container of that description.

(4) In the case of any sale where the quantity of the goods sold expressed in a particular manner is required to be made known to the buyer at or before a particular time and that quantity is not so made known, the person by whom, and any other person on whose behalf, the goods were sold shall be guilty of an offence.

(5) Where any goods required to be sold by means of, or to be offered or exposed for sale in, a vending machine only if certain requirements are complied with are so sold, offered or exposed without those requirements being complied with, the seller or person causing the goods to be offered or exposed shall be guilty of an offence.

(6) The preceding provisions of this section have effect subject to sections 33 to 37 below.

[(7) For the purposes of this section the quantity of goods in a package, or of a loaf of bread, to which the packaged goods regulations apply shall be deemed to be the nominal quantity (within the meaning of those regulations) of the package or the loaf of bread.]

(8) In this section "required" means required by or under this Part of this Act.

NOTES

Sub-s (7): substituted by the Weights and Measures (Packaged Goods) Regulations 2006, SI 2006/659, reg 1(2), Sch 1, Pt 2, paras (1), (3), subject to transitional provisions in reg 21 thereof.

Quantity to be stated in writing

[1.947]

26 Quantity to be stated in writing in certain cases

(1) Subject to section 27 below, the provisions of this section shall have effect on any sale of goods—

   (a) which is required by or under this Part of this Act to be a sale by quantity expressed in a particular manner,

   (b) in the case of which the quantity of the goods sold expressed in a particular manner is so required to be made known to the buyer at or before a particular time, or

   (c) which, being a sale by retail not falling within paragraph (a) or (b) above, is, or purports to be, a sale by quantity expressed in a particular manner other than by number.

(2) Subject to subsections (4) to (6) below, unless the quantity of the goods sold expressed in the manner in question is made known to the buyer at the premises of the seller and the goods are delivered to the buyer at those premises on the same occasion as, and at or after the time when, that quantity is so made known to him, a statement in writing of that quantity shall be delivered to the consignee at or before delivery of the goods to him.

(3) If subsection (2) above is contravened then, subject to sections 33 to 37 below, the person by whom, and any other person on whose behalf, the goods were sold shall be guilty of an offence.

(4) If at the time when the goods are delivered the consignee is absent, it shall be sufficient compliance with subsection (2) above if the statement is left at some suitable place at the premises at which the goods are delivered.

(5) Subsection (2) above shall not apply to any sale otherwise than by retail where, by agreement with the buyer, the quantity of the goods sold is to be determined after their delivery to the consignee.

(6) Where any liquid goods are sold by capacity measurement and the quantity sold is measured at the time of delivery and elsewhere than at the premises of the seller, subsection (2) above shall not apply but, unless the quantity by capacity measurement of the goods sold is measured in the presence of the buyer, the person by whom the goods are delivered shall immediately after the delivery hand to the buyer, or if the buyer is not present leave at some suitable place at the premises at which the goods are delivered, a statement in writing of the quantity by capacity measurement delivered, and if without reasonable cause he fails so to do he shall be guilty of an offence.

[1.948]

27 Exemption from requirements of section 26

(1) The Secretary of State may by order grant, with respect to goods or sales of such descriptions as may be specified in the order, exemption, either generally or in such circumstances as may be so specified, from all or any of the requirements of section 26 above.

(2) Until otherwise provided by an order under subsection (1) above, nothing in section 26 above shall apply to—

   (a) a sale by retail from a vehicle of—

      (i) any of the following in a quantity not exceeding [110 kilograms], that is to say, any solid fuel within the meaning of Schedule 5 to this Act, and wood fuel, or

      (ii) any of the following in a quantity not exceeding [25 litres], that is to say, liquid fuel, lubricating oil, and any mixture of such fuel and oil,

   (b) a sale by retail of bread within the meaning of the Weights and Measures Act 1963 (Miscellaneous Foods) Order 1984,

   (c) goods made up for sale (whether by way of pre-packing or otherwise) in or on a container marked with a statement in writing with respect to the quantity of the goods expressed in the manner in question, being a container which is delivered with the goods,

   (d) a sale of goods in the case of which a document stating the quantity of the goods expressed in the manner in question is required to be delivered to the buyer or consignee of the goods by or under any other provision of this Part of this Act,

   (e) any such goods or sales as are mentioned in section 24(2)(a) to (d) above,

   (f) a sale of intoxicating liquor for consumption at the premises of the seller,

   (g) a sale by means of a vending machine, or

(h)   goods delivered at premises of the buyer by means of an installation providing a connection of a permanent nature between those premises and premises of the seller.

[(3)   Nothing in section 26 above shall apply to goods that are subject to the FIC Regulation.]

NOTES

Sub-s (2): words in square brackets in para (a) substituted by the Units of Measurement Regulations 1994, SI 1994/2867, reg 6(1), (4).

Sub-s (3): added by the Weights and Measures (Food) (Amendment) Regulations 2014, SI 2014/2975, regs 2, 3.

Weights and Measures 1963 (Miscellaneous Foods) Order 1984, SI 1984/1316: revoked and replaced by the Weights and Measures (Miscellaneous Foods) Order 1988, SI 1988/2040.

General offences

[1.949]

28   Short weight, etc

(1)   Subject to sections 33 to 37 below, any person who, in selling or purporting to sell any goods by weight or other measurement or by number, delivers or causes to be delivered to the buyer—

(a)   a lesser quantity than that purported to be sold, or

(b)   a lesser quantity than corresponds with the price charged,

shall be guilty of an offence.

(2)   For the purposes of this section—

[(a)   the quantity of goods in a package, or of a loaf of bread, to which the packaged goods regulations apply shall be deemed to be the nominal quantity (within the meaning of those regulations) of the package or the loaf of bread; and]

(b)   any statement, whether oral or in writing, as to the weight of any goods shall be taken, unless otherwise expressed, to be a statement as to the net weight of the goods.

(3)   Nothing in this section shall apply in relation to any such goods or sales as are mentioned in section 24(2)(a) or (b) above.

NOTES

Sub-s (2): para (a) substituted by the Weights and Measures (Packaged Goods) Regulations 2006, SI 2006/659, reg 1(2), Sch 1, Pt 2, paras (1), (4), subject to transitional provisions in reg 21 thereof.

29   (*Repealed by the Consumer Protection from Unfair Trading Regulations 2008, SI 2008/1277, reg 30(1), (3), Sch 2, Pt 1, para 31, Sch 4, subject to savings in reg 30(2) of, and Sch 3, paras 9, 11 to, those Regulations at* **[2.595]**, **[2.597]**.)

[1.950]

30   Quantity less than stated

(1)   If, in the case of any [goods that are pre-packed within the meaning of this Act or are prepacked food within the meaning of the FIC Regulation and (in either case) are] in or on a container marked with a statement in writing with respect to the quantity of the goods, the quantity of the goods is at any time found to be less than that stated, then, subject to sections 33 to 37 below—

(a)   any person who has those goods in his possession for sale shall be guilty of an offence, and

(b)   if it is shown that the deficiency cannot be accounted for by anything occurring after the goods had been sold by retail and delivered to, or to a person nominated in that behalf by, the buyer, any person by whom or on whose behalf those goods have been sold or agreed to be sold at any time while they were pre-packed [within the meaning of this Act or were prepacked food within the meaning of the FIC Regulation and (in either case) were] in or on the container in question, shall be guilty of an offence.

(2)   If—

(a)   in the case of a sale of or agreement to sell any goods which, not being pre-packed [within the meaning of this Act or prepacked food within the meaning of the FIC Regulation], are made up for sale or for delivery after sale in or on a container marked with a statement in writing with respect to the quantity of the goods, or

(b)   in the case of any goods which, in connection with their sale or an agreement for their sale, have associated with them a document containing such a statement,

the quantity of the goods is at any time found to be less than that stated, then, if it is shown that the deficiency cannot be accounted for by anything occurring after the goods had been delivered to, or to a person nominated in that behalf by, the buyer, and subject to sections 33 to 37 below and paragraph 10 of Schedule 4 to this Act, the person by whom, and any other person on whose behalf, the goods were sold or agreed to be sold shall be guilty of an offence.

(3)   Subsections (1) and (2) above shall have effect notwithstanding that the quantity stated is expressed to be the quantity of the goods at a specified time falling before the time in question, or is expressed with some other qualification of whatever description, except where—

(a)   that quantity is so expressed in pursuance of an express requirement of this Part of this Act or any instrument made under this Part, or

(b)   the goods, although falling within subsection (1) or subsection (2)(a) above—

(i)   are not required by or under this Part of this Act to be pre-packed as mentioned in subsection (1) [or required by the FIC Regulation to be prepacked food as mentioned in that subsection] or, as the case may be, to be made up for sale or for delivery after sale in or on a container only if the container is marked as mentioned in subsection (2)(a), and

(ii) are not goods on a sale of which (whether any sale or a sale of any particular description) the quantity sold is required by or under any provision of this Part of this Act other than section 26 [or required by the FIC Regulation], to be made known to the buyer at or before a particular time, or

(c) the goods, although falling within subsection (2)(b) above, are not required by or under this Part of this Act to have associated with them such a document as is mentioned in that provision.

(4) In any case to which, by virtue of paragraph (a), (b) or (c) of subsection (3) above, the provisions of subsection (1) or (2) above do not apply, if it is found at any time that the quantity of the goods in question is less than that stated and it is shown that the deficiency is greater than can be reasonably justified on the ground justifying the qualification in question, then, subject to sections 33 to 37 below—

(a) in the case of goods such as are mentioned in subsection (1) above, if it is further shown as mentioned in that subsection, then—

(i) where the container in question was marked in Great Britain, the person by whom, and any other person on whose behalf, the container was marked, or

(ii) where the container in question was marked outside Great Britain, the person by whom, and any other person on whose behalf, the goods were first sold in Great Britain,

shall be guilty of an offence;

(b) in the case of goods such as are mentioned in subsection (2) above, the person by whom, and any other person on whose behalf, the goods were sold or agreed to be sold shall be guilty of an offence if, but only if, he would, but for paragraph (a), (b) or (c) of subsection (3) above have been guilty of an offence under subsection (2).

(5) Subsection (2) of section 28 above shall have effect for the purposes of this section as it has effect for the purposes of that section.

(6) Nothing in this section shall apply in relation to any such goods or sales as are mentioned in section 24(2)(a) or (b) above.

NOTES

Sub-s (1): words in first pair of square brackets substituted, and words in second pair of square brackets inserted, by the Weights and Measures (Food) (Amendment) Regulations 2014, SI 2014/2975, regs 2, 4(a), (b).

Sub-ss (2), (3): words in square brackets inserted by SI 2014/2975, regs 2, 4(c)–(e).

[1.951]
31 Incorrect statements

(1) Without prejudice to section 30(2) to (4) above, if in the case of any goods required by or under this Part of this Act to have associated with them a document containing particular statements, that document is found to contain any such statement which is materially incorrect, any person who, knowing or having reasonable cause to suspect that statement to be materially incorrect, inserted it or caused it to be inserted in the document, or used the document for the purposes of this Part of this Act while that statement was contained in the document, shall be guilty of an offence.

(2) Subsection (2) of section 28 above shall have effect for the purposes of this section as it has effect for the purposes of that section.

(3) Nothing in this section shall apply in relation to any such goods or sales as are mentioned in section 24(2)(a) or (b) above.

[1.952]
[31A Non-compliance with certain requirements of the FIC Regulation

(1) Subject to subsection (2) below, a food business operator to which Article 1(3) of the FIC Regulation applies is guilty of an offence if that food business operator fails to comply with—

(a) any of the provisions of Article 8 of the FIC Regulation (responsibilities of food business operators) applicable to the food business operator, to the extent that the provisions relate to net quantity;

(b) Article 9(1)(e) of the FIC Regulation (mandatory indication of net quantity of food), except to the extent that it relates to a failure to comply with Article 13(5) of the FIC Regulation; or

(c) Chapter V of the FIC Regulation (voluntary food information), to the extent that it imposes requirements in respect of net quantity.

(2) A food business operator is not guilty of an offence under subsection (1) if the food business operator acts in accordance with any of the following—

(a) an exception contained in Chapter IV of the FIC Regulation;

(b) national measures adopted under Article 40 of the FIC Regulation (milk and milk products);

(c) national measures maintained under Article 42 of the FIC Regulation (measures adopted before 12 December 2011);

(d) transitional measures under Article 54(1) of the FIC Regulation.

(3) In this section "food business operator" and "net quantity" have the same meanings as in the FIC Regulation.]

NOTES

Commencement: 13 December 2014.

Inserted by the Weights and Measures (Food) (Amendment) Regulations 2014, SI 2014/2975, regs 2, 5.

[1.953]

32 Offences due to default of third person

Where the commission by any person of an offence under this Part of this Act [(other than section 31A)] or an instrument made under this Part is due to the act or default of some other person, the other person shall be guilty of an offence and may be charged with and convicted of the offence whether or not proceedings are taken against the first-mentioned person.

NOTES

Words in square brackets inserted by the Weights and Measures (Food) (Amendment) Regulations 2014, SI 2014/2975, regs 2, 6.

Defences

[1.954]

33 Warranty

(1) Subject to the following provisions of this section, in any proceedings for an offence under this Part of this Act or any instrument made under this Part, being an offence relating to the quantity or pre-packing of any goods, it shall be a defence for the person charged to prove—

(a) that he bought the goods from some other person—

    (i) as being of the quantity which the person charged purported to sell or represented, or which was marked on any container or stated in any document to which the proceedings relate, or

    (ii) as conforming with the statement marked on any container to which the proceedings relate, or with the requirements with respect to the pre-packing of goods of this Part of this Act or any instrument made under this Part,

as the case may require, and

(b) that he so bought the goods with a written warranty from that other person that they were of that quantity or, as the case may be, did so conform, and

(c) that at the time of the commission of the offence he did in fact believe the statement contained in the warranty to be accurate and had no reason to believe it to be inaccurate, and

(d) if the warranty was given by a person who at the time he gave it was resident outside Great Britain and any designated country, that the person charged had taken reasonable steps to check the accuracy of the statement contained in the warranty, and

(e) in the case of proceedings relating to the quantity of any goods, that he took all reasonable steps to ensure that, while in his possession, the quantity of the goods remained unchanged and, in the case of such or any other proceedings, that apart from any change in their quantity the goods were at the time of the commission of the offence in the same state as when he bought them.

(2) A warranty shall not be a defence in any such proceedings as are mentioned in subsection (1) above unless, not later than three days before the date of the hearing, the person charged has sent to the prosecutor a copy of the warranty with a notice stating that he intends to rely on it and specifying the name and address of the person from whom the warranty was received, and has also sent a like notice to that person.

(3) Where the person charged is the employee of a person who, if he had been charged, would have been entitled to plead a warranty as a defence under this section, subsection (1) above shall have effect—

(a) with the substitution, for any reference (however expressed) in paragraphs (a), (b), (d) and (e) to the person charged, of a reference to his employer, and

(b) with the substitution for paragraph (c) of the following—

    "(c) that at the time of the commission of the offence his employer did in fact believe the statement contained in the warranty to be accurate and the person charged had no reason to believe it to be inaccurate,".

(4) The person by whom the warranty is alleged to have been given shall be entitled to appear at the hearing and to give evidence.

(5) If the person charged in any such proceedings as are mentioned in subsection (1) above wilfully attributes to any goods a warranty given in relation to any other goods, he shall be guilty of an offence.

(6) A person who, in respect of any goods sold by him in respect of which a warranty might be pleaded under this section, gives to the buyer a false warranty in writing shall be guilty of an offence unless he proves that when he gave the warranty he took all reasonable steps to ensure that the statements contained in it were, and would continue at all relevant times to be, accurate.

(7) Where in any such proceedings as are mentioned in subsection (1) above ("the original proceedings") the person charged relies successfully on a warranty given to him or to his employer, any proceedings under subsection (6) above in respect of the warranty may, at the option of the prosecutor, be taken either before a court having jurisdiction in the place where the original proceedings were taken or before a court having jurisdiction in the place where the warranty was given.

(8) For the purposes of this section, any statement with respect to any goods which is contained in any document required by or under this Part of this Act to be associated with the goods or in any invoice, and, in the case of goods made up in or on a container for sale or for delivery after sale, any statement with respect to those goods with which that container is marked, shall be taken to be a written warranty of the accuracy of that statement.

[1.955]
34 Reasonable precautions and due diligence
(1) In any proceedings for an offence under this Part of this Act or any instrument made under this Part, it shall be a defence for the person charged to prove that he took all reasonable precautions and exercised all due diligence to avoid the commission of the offence.

(2) If in any case the defence provided by subsection (1) above involves an allegation that the commission of the offence in question was due to the act or default of another person or due to reliance on information supplied by another person, the person charged shall not, without the leave of the court, be entitled to rely on the defence unless, before the beginning of the period of seven days ending with the date when the hearing of the charge began, he served on the prosecutor a notice giving such information identifying or assisting in the identification of the other person as was then in his possession.

[1.956]
35 Subsequent deficiency
(1) This subsection applies to any proceedings for an offence under this Part of this Act, or any instrument made under this Part, by reason of the quantity—
  (a) of any goods made up for sale or for delivery after sale (whether by way of pre-packing or otherwise) in or on a container marked with an indication of quantity,
  (b) of any goods which, in connection with their sale or an agreement for their sale, have associated with them a document purporting to state the quantity of the goods, or
  (c) of any goods required by or under this Part of this Act to be pre-packed, or to be otherwise made up in or on a container for sale or for delivery after sale, or to be made for sale, only in particular quantities,

being less than that marked on the container or stated in the document in question or than the relevant particular quantity, as the case may be.

(2) In any proceedings to which subsection (1) above applies, it shall be a defence for the person charged to prove that the deficiency arose—
  (a) in a case falling within paragraph (a) of subsection (1) above, after the making up of the goods and the marking of the container,
  (b) in a case falling within paragraph (b) of that subsection, after the preparation of the goods for delivery in pursuance of the sale or agreement and after the completion of the document,
  (c) in a case falling within paragraph (c) of that subsection, after the making up or making, as the case may be, of the goods for sale,

and was attributable wholly to factors for which reasonable allowance was made in stating the quantity of the goods in the marking or document or in making up or making the goods for sale, as the case may be.

(3) In the case of a sale by retail of food, other than food pre-packed in a container which is, or is required by or under this Part of this Act [or the FIC Regulation] to be, marked with an indication of quantity, in any proceedings for an offence under this Part of this Act or any instrument made under this Part, by reason of the quantity delivered to the buyer being less than that purported to be sold, it shall be a defence for the person charged to prove that the deficiency was due wholly to unavoidable evaporation or drainage since the sale and that due care and precaution were taken to minimise any such evaporation or drainage.

(4) If in any proceedings for an offence under this Part of this Act or any instrument made under this Part, being an offence in respect of any deficiency in the quantity of any goods sold, it is shown that between the sale and the discovery of the deficiency the goods were with the consent of the buyer subjected to treatment which could result in a reduction in the quantity of those goods for delivery to, or to any person nominated in that behalf by, the buyer, the person charged shall not be found guilty of that offence unless it is shown that the deficiency cannot be accounted for by the subjecting of the goods to that treatment.

NOTES

Sub-s (3): words in square brackets inserted by the Weights and Measures (Food) (Amendment) Regulations 2014, SI 2014/2975, regs 2, 7.

[1.957]
36 Excess due to precautions

In any proceedings for an offence under this Part of this Act or any instrument made under this Part, being an offence in respect of any excess in the quantity of any goods, it shall be a defence for the person charged to prove that the excess was attributable to the taking of measures reasonably necessary in order to avoid the commission of an offence in respect of a deficiency in those or other goods.

[1.958]
37 Provisions as to testing

(1) If proceedings for an offence under this Part of this Act, or any instrument made under this Part, in respect of any deficiency or excess in the quantity—

    (a)   of any goods made up for sale (whether by way of pre-packing or otherwise) in or on a container marked with an indication of quantity, or

    (b)   of any goods which have been pre-packed or otherwise made up in or on a container for sale or for delivery after sale, or which have been made for sale, and which are required by or under this Part of this Act [or the FIC Regulation] to be pre-packed, or to be otherwise so made up, or to be so made, as the case may be, only in particular quantities,

are brought with respect to any article, and it is proved that, at the time and place at which that article was tested, other articles of the same kind, being articles which, or articles containing goods which, had been sold by the person charged or were in that person's possession for sale or for delivery after sale, were available for testing, the person charged shall not be convicted of such an offence with respect to that article unless a reasonable number of those other articles was also tested.

(2) In any proceedings for such an offence as is mentioned in subsection (1) above, the court—

    (a)   if the proceedings are with respect to one or more of a number of articles tested on the same occasion, shall have regard to the average quantity in all the articles tested,

    (b)   if the proceedings are with respect to a single article, shall disregard any inconsiderable deficiency or excess, and

    (c)   shall have regard generally to all the circumstances of the case.

(3) Subsections (1) and (2) above shall apply with the necessary modifications to proceedings for an offence in respect of the size, capacity or contents of a container as they apply to proceedings for an offence in respect of the excess or deficiency in the quantity of certain goods.

(4) Where by virtue of section 32 above a person is charged with an offence with which some other person might have been charged, the reference in subsection (1) above to articles or goods sold by or in the possession of the person charged shall be construed as a reference to articles or goods sold by or in the possession of that other person.

NOTES

Sub-s (1): words in square brackets inserted by the Weights and Measures (Food) (Amendment) Regulations 2014, SI 2014/2975, regs 2, 8.

Powers of inspectors

[1.959]
38 Special powers of inspectors with respect to certain goods

(1) Subsection (2) below applies where any person—

    (a)   makes in any manner any representation as to the quantity of any goods offered or exposed for sale by him, or

    (b)   has in his possession or charge awaiting or in the course of delivery to the buyer any goods which have been sold or agreed to be sold, and the sale is, or purports to be, or is required by or under this Part of this Act [or the FIC Regulation] to be, by quantity expressed in a particular manner, or is such that the quantity of the goods sold is required by or under any provision of this Part other than section 26 to be made known to the buyer at or before a particular time, or

    (c)   has in his possession or charge for sale, or awaiting or in the course of delivery to a buyer after they have been sold or agreed to be sold—

        (i)   any goods pre-packed or otherwise made up in or on a container for sale or for delivery after sale which are required by or under this Part of this Act [or the FIC Regulation] to be pre-packed, or to be otherwise so made up, as the case may be, only in particular quantities or only if the container is marked with particular information, or

        (ii)   any goods pre-packed in or on a container marked with an indication of quantity, or

        (iii)   any goods required by or under this Part of this Act [or the FIC Regulation] to be made for sale only in particular quantities, or

Part 1   Statutes

    (d)   has in his possession or charge for sale, or awaiting or in the course of delivery to a buyer after they have been sold or agreed to be sold, any goods subject to a requirement imposed by virtue of section 22(1)(c) above.

(2)   Where this subsection applies, the powers of an inspector under *section 79 below* shall, subject to subsection (4) below, include power to require the person referred to in subsection (1) above either to do in the presence of the inspector, or to permit the inspector to do, all or any of the following things, that is to say—

    (a)   weigh or otherwise measure or count the goods,

    (b)   weigh or otherwise measure any container in or on which the goods are made up,

    (c)   in the case of goods within subsection (1)(d) above, do anything else as respects the goods or container which is reasonably necessary to ascertain whether the requirement there mentioned is complied with, and which does not damage or depreciate the goods or container,

    (d)   if necessary for any of the purposes of paragraphs (a) to (c) above, break open any container of goods, or open any vending machine in which goods are offered or exposed for sale,

and, in the case of any of the goods which are not already sold, power to require that person to sell any of them to the inspector.

(3)   Where any container of goods is broken open under subsection (2) above and all requirements of, and of any instrument made under, this Part of this Act [or the FIC Regulation] which are applicable to those goods are found to have been complied with, then—

    (a)   if the container can be resealed without injury to the contents, the inspector may reseal it with a label certifying that all such requirements have been complied with, and

    (b)   if he does not reseal it or it cannot be so resealed without injury to the contents, the inspector shall at the request of the person referred to in subsection (1) above buy the goods on behalf of the local weights and measures authority.

(4)   . . .

NOTES

Sub-ss (1), (3): words in square brackets inserted by the Weights and Measures (Food) (Amendment) Regulations 2014, SI 2014/2975, regs 2, 9.

Sub-s (2): for the words in italics there are substituted the words "Schedule 5 to the Consumer Rights Act 2015" by the Consumer Rights Act 2015, s 77(2), Sch 6, paras 28, 29, as from 1 October 2015 (for transitional provisions see the Consumer Rights Act 2015 (Commencement No 3, Transitional Provisions, Savings and Consequential Amendments) Order 2015, SI 2015/1630, arts 6–8 at **[2.1220]** et seq).

Sub-s (4): repealed by the Food Safety Act 1990, s 59(1), (4), Sch 3, para 32, Sch 5.

[1.960]

39   Powers of inspectors with respect to certain documents

(1)   An inspector, subject to the production if so requested of his credentials, may require the person in charge of any document required by or under this Part of this Act to be associated with any goods to produce that document for inspection.

(2)   If the inspector has reasonable cause to believe that any document produced to him under subsection (1) above contains any inaccurate statement, he may either—

    (a)   seize and detain the document, giving in exchange a copy with an endorsement signed by him certifying that the original has been seized and giving particulars of any inaccuracy alleged, or

    (b)   without prejudice to any proceedings which may be taken by reason of any inaccuracy alleged, make on the document an endorsement signed by him giving particulars of any such inaccuracy;

and, except where the context otherwise requires, any reference in this Part of this Act to any such document includes a reference to a copy given in pursuance of paragraph (a) above.

[1.961]

40   Powers of inspectors with respect to goods carried on road vehicles

(1)   Subsection (2) below applies where, in the case of any goods being carried on a road vehicle,—

    (a)   the whole of the vehicle's load is being carried for sale to, or for delivery after sale to, the same person, and

    (b)   any document produced in pursuance of section 39(1) above by the person in charge of the vehicle purports, or is required by or under this Part of this Act, to state the quantity of the goods.

(2)   Where this subsection applies, the inspector may, for the purpose of the exercise of his powers under section 38(2) above do all or any of the following things, that is to say—

    (a)   require the goods to which the document relates to be unloaded from the vehicle;

    (b)   require the vehicle to be taken to the nearest suitable and available weighing or measuring equipment;

    (c)   require the person in charge of the vehicle to have it check-weighed.

(3)   The powers conferred by subsection (2) above shall be exercised only to such extent as may appear to the inspector reasonably necessary in order to secure that the provisions of this Act . . . and of any instrument made under those provisions are duly observed.

NOTES
   Sub-s (3): words omitted repealed by the Weights and Measures (Packaged Goods) Regulations 2006, SI 2006/659, reg 1(2), Sch 1, Pt 2, paras (1), (5), subject to transitional provisions in reg 21 thereof.

Miscellaneous and supplementary

[1.962]
41   Check-weighing of certain road vehicles
Where any road vehicle is loaded with goods for sale by weight to a single buyer of the whole of the vehicle's load, or for delivery to the buyer after they have been so sold, the buyer or seller of the goods, or any inspector who shows that he is authorised so to do by the buyer or seller of the goods, may require the person in charge of the vehicle to have it check-weighed, and if that person fails without reasonable cause to comply with any such requirement he shall be guilty of an offence.

[1.963]
42   *Power to make test purchases*
A local weights and measures authority shall have power to make, or to authorise an inspector to make on their behalf, such purchases of goods as may appear expedient for the purpose of determining whether or not the provisions of this Part of this Act and any instrument made under this Part, and the provisions of Parts II and III of this Act and any instrument made under either of those Parts [and the provisions of the FIC Regulation], are being complied with.

NOTES
   Repealed by the Consumer Rights Act 2015, s 77(2), Sch 6, paras 28, 30, as from 1 October 2015 (for transitional provisions see the Consumer Rights Act 2015 (Commencement No 3, Transitional Provisions, Savings and Consequential Amendments) Order 2015, SI 2015/1630, arts 6–8 at **[2.1220]** et seq).
   Words in square brackets inserted by the Weights and Measures (Food) (Amendment) Regulations 2014, SI 2014/2975, regs 2, 10.

43   *(Repealed by the Deregulation and Contracting Out Act 1994, ss 14, 81(1), Sch 17.)*

[1.964]
44   Selling by quantity
Where any goods are required by or under this Part of this Act to be sold only by quantity expressed in a particular manner—
   (a)   it shall be a sufficient compliance with that requirement in the case of any sale of, or agreement to sell, any such goods if the quantity of the goods expressed in the manner in question is made known to the buyer before the purchase price is agreed; and
   (b)   no person shall be guilty of an offence under section 25(1) above by reason of the exposing or offering for sale of such goods at any time if both the quantity of the goods expressed in the manner in question and the price at which they are exposed or offered for sale are made known at that time to any prospective buyer.

[1.965]
45   Making quantity known to a person
(1)   For the purposes of this Part of this Act, without prejudice to any other method of making known to a person the quantity of any goods expressed in a particular manner, that quantity shall be taken to be made known to that person—
   (a)   if the goods are weighed or otherwise measured or counted, as the case may require, in the presence of that person,
   (b)   if the goods are made up in or on a container marked with a statement in writing of the quantity of the goods expressed in the manner in question and the container is readily available for inspection by that person, or
   (c)   upon such a statement in writing being delivered to that person.
(2)   The Secretary of State may by order provide that subsection (3) below shall apply, in the case of such goods in such circumstances as are specified in the order, to any requirement so specified of, or of any instrument made under, this Part of this Act with respect to the making known to the buyer of the quantity by weight of such goods sold by retail.
(3)   In any case to which this subsection applies, the requirement specified in the order shall be taken to be satisfied if the goods are bought at premises at which weighing equipment of such description as may be prescribed—
   (a)   is kept available by the occupier of those premises for use without charge by any prospective buyer of such goods for the purpose of weighing for himself any such goods offered or exposed for sale by retail on those premises, and
   (b)   is so kept available in a position on those premises which is suitable and convenient for such use of the equipment, and

(c)   is reserved for use for that purpose at all times while those premises are open for retail transactions,

and a notice of the availability of the equipment for such use is displayed in a position on the premises where it may be readily seen by any such prospective buyer.

[1.966]
46   Weighing in presence of a person
For the purposes of this Part of this Act, a person shall not be taken to weigh or otherwise measure or count any goods in the presence of any other person unless he causes any equipment used for the purpose to be so placed, and so conducts the operation of weighing or otherwise measuring or counting the goods, as to permit that other person a clear and unobstructed view of the equipment, if any, and of the operation, and of any indication of quantity given by any such equipment as the result of that operation.

47–78   (*Ss 47–68 (Pt V) repealed by the Weights and Measures (Packaged Goods) Regulations 2006, SI 2006/659, reg 1(2), Sch 1, Pt 2, paras (1), (2), subject to transitional provisions in reg 21 thereof; ss 69–78 (Pt VI) outside the scope of this work.*)

PART VII
GENERAL

79–85   (*Outside the scope of this work.*)

Miscellaneous and supplementary

86–98   (*Outside the scope of this work.*)

[1.967]
99   Short title and commencement
(1)   This Act may be cited as the Weights and Measures Act 1985.
(2)   . . . this Act shall come into force at the end of the period of three months beginning with the day on which it is passed.

NOTES

Sub-s (2): words omitted repealed by the Deregulation and Contracting Out Act 1994, s 81, Sch 17.

SCHEDULES

SCHEDULES 1–5

(*Schs 1–5 outside the scope of this work.*)

SCHEDULE 6
MISCELLANEOUS GOODS OTHER THAN FOODS

Section 21

PART I
LIQUID FUEL AND LUBRICANTS

[1.968]
1. This Part of this Schedule applies to—
   (a)   liquid fuel, lubricating oil and any mixture of such fuel and oil, and
   (b)   lubricating grease.

2. Subject to paragraph 3 below, goods to which this Part of this Schedule applies—
   (a)   unless pre-packed, shall be sold only by net weight or by capacity measurement,
   (b)   shall be pre-packed only if the container is marked with an indication of quantity either by net weight or by capacity measurement, and
   (c)   in the case of lubricating oil in a quantity of [one litre] or less, shall be made up in a container for sale otherwise than by way of pre-packing only if the container is marked with an indication of quantity by capacity measurement.

3. Notwithstanding anything in paragraph 2 above, liquid fuel—
   (a)   when not pre-packed may be sold by volume, and
   (b)   may be pre-packed in a container marked with an indication of quantity by volume,
being in either case the volume of the gas which would be produced from the fuel in question at such temperature and such atmospheric pressure as are specified in regulations made by the Secretary of State with respect to fuel of the type in question or, if no such regulations are in force, as may be made known by the seller to the buyer before he pays for or takes possession of the fuel; and there shall be exempted from all requirements of paragraph 2 above goods of any description in a quantity of less than [250 grams] or of less than [250 millilitres]

NOTES

Paras 2, 3: words in square brackets substituted by the Weights and Measures Act 1985 (Metrication) (Amendment) Order 1994, SI 1994/2866, art 3(1), (6)(a), (b).

PART II
READY-MIXED CEMENT MORTAR AND READY-MIXED CONCRETE

[1.969]
4. This Part of this Schedule applies to ready-mixed cement mortar and ready-mixed concrete.

5. [(1)   Subject to the following provisions of this Part of this Schedule, any goods to which this Part of this Schedule applies—
   (a)   if made up in advance ready for retail sale or wholesale in a securely closed container, shall be sold only by volume, and
   (b)   if not so made up, shall be sold only by volume in a multiple of 0.1 cubic metre.]

(2)   There shall be exempted from the requirements of this paragraph any goods in a quantity of less than one cubic metre.

6. Part II of Schedule 4 to this Act, except sub-paragraph (3) of paragraph 7, shall apply for the purposes of this Part of this Schedule as if—
   (a)   any reference in the said Part II to ballast included a reference to goods to which this Part of this Schedule applies; and
   (b)   the reference in sub-paragraph (1) of paragraph 7 to paragraph 2 of Schedule 4 were a reference to paragraph 5 of this Schedule.

7. (*Applies to Scotland only.*)

NOTES

Para 5: sub-para (1) substituted by the Weights and Measures (Specified Quantities) (Pre-packed Products) Regulations 2009, SI 2009/663, reg 2(1), (4).

PART III
AGRICULTURAL LIMING MATERIALS, AGRICULTURAL SALT AND INORGANIC FERTILISERS

[1.970]
8. This Part of this Schedule applies—
   (a)   to agricultural liming materials, other than calcareous sand,
   (b)   to agricultural salt,
   (c)   to, and to any mixture consisting mainly of, inorganic fertilisers, other than such fertilisers or such a mixture made up into pellets or other articles for use as individual items, and
   (d)   to any mixture of any of the foregoing.

9. (1)   Goods to which this Part of this Schedule applies which are not pre-packed, other than liquid fertilisers, shall be sold only by quantity, being—
   (a)   quantity by net weight; or
   (b)   if the goods are sold in a container which does not exceed the permitted weight and the gross weight of the goods is not less than [25 kilograms], quantity either by net weight or by gross weight; or
   (c)   quantity by volume.

(2)   Goods to which this Part of this Schedule applies shall be pre-packed only if the container is marked with an indication of quantity, being—
   (a)   in the case of liquid fertilisers, quantity by capacity measurement;
   (b)   in any other case, quantity by net weight or, if the container does not exceed the permitted weight and the gross weight of the goods is not less than [25 kilograms], quantity either by net weight or by gross weight.

(3)   In this paragraph, "the permitted weight" means a weight or the rate of [650 grams per 50 kilograms] of the gross weight.

(4)   There shall be exempted from all requirements of this paragraph any sale of goods with a view to their industrial use.

10. Paragraphs 4 and 5 of Schedule 4 to this Act shall have effect as if any reference in those paragraphs to ballast included a reference to any goods to which this Part of this Schedule applies.

NOTES

Para 9: words in square brackets substituted by the Weights and Measures Act 1985 (Metrication) (Amendment) Order 1994, SI 1994/2866, art 3(1), (6)(c).

PART IV
WOOD FUEL

[1.971]

11. Subject to paragraphs 12 and 13 below—

    (a)   wood fuel which is not made up in a container for sale shall be sold by retail only by net weight;

    (b)   in the case of a sale by retail of wood fuel made up in a container for sale, the quantity by net weight of the fuel sold shall be made known to the buyer before he pays for or takes possession of it.

12. (1) Paragraph 11 above shall not have effect in any area unless the local weights and measures authority for that area so direct by byelaw.

(2) Not less than one month before making any byelaw by virtue of this paragraph, the local weights and measures authority shall give public notice of their intention to make it by advertisement in one or more newspapers circulating in the area to which the byelaw is to apply.

(3) The local weights and measures authority by whom any byelaw is made by virtue of this paragraph shall give notice of the making of the byelaw to the Secretary of State.

13. There shall be exempted from the requirements of paragraph 11 above any sale of wood fuel in a quantity which does not exceed [7.5 kilograms] or which exceeds [500 kilograms].

14. Paragraphs 9 and 10 of Schedule 5 to this Act shall have effect as if any reference in those paragraphs to solid fuel included a reference to wood fuel.

NOTES

    Para 13: words in square brackets substituted by the Weights and Measures Act 1985 (Metrication) (Amendment) Order 1994, SI 1994/2866, art 3(1), (6)(d).

(Pt V repealed by the Weights and Measures (Food) (Amendment) Regulations 2014, SI 2013/1478, reg 25, Sch 5, para 3.)

PART VI
SOAP

[1.972]

[16A. [(1)]   In this Part of this Schedule "soap" does not include any soap which is a cosmetic product . . .]

[(2)   "Cosmetic product" has the same meaning as in Regulation (EC) 1223/2009 of the European Parliament and of the Council on cosmetic products (recast), as amended from time to time.]

17. Subject to paragraph 18 below—

    (a)   soap in the form of a cake, tablet or bar shall be pre-packed only if the container is marked with an indication of quantity by net weight,

    (b)   liquid soap shall be pre-packed only if the container is marked with an indication of quantity by capacity measurement, and

    (c)   soap in any other form—

        (i)   unless pre-packed, shall be sold by retail only by net weight, and

        (ii)   shall be pre-packed only if the container is marked with an indication of quantity by net weight.

18. There shall be exempted from the requirements of this Part of this Schedule—

    (a)   liquid soap in a quantity of less than [125 millilitres], and

    (b)   soap in any other form in a quantity of less than [25 grams].

NOTES

    Para 16A: inserted by the Weights and Measures (Cosmetic Products) Order 1994, SI 1994/1884, art 3; sub-para (1) numbered as such, word omitted repealed, and sub-para (2) added, by the Cosmetic Products Enforcement Regulations 2013, SI 2013/1478, reg 25, Sch 5, para 4.

    Para 18: words in square brackets substituted by the Weights and Measures Act 1985 (Metrication) (Amendment) Order 1994, SI 1994/2866, art 3(1), (6)(e).

PART VII
MISCELLANEOUS GOODS TO BE SOLD BY OR MARKED WITH LENGTH

[1.973]

19. This Part of this Schedule applies to goods of any of the following descriptions, that is to say, bias binding, elastic, ribbon, tape and sewing thread.

20. Subject to paragraph 21 below, goods to which this Part of this Schedule applies—

    (a)   unless pre-packed, shall be sold by retail only by length, and

(b)   shall be pre-packed only if the container is marked with an indication of quantity by length.

21.   There shall be exempted from all requirements of paragraph 20 above goods of any description in a quantity of less than [one metre].

NOTES

Para 21: words in square brackets substituted by the Weights and Measures Act 1985 (Metrication) (Amendment) Order 1994, SI 1994/2866, art 3(1), (6)(f).

PART VIII
MISCELLANEOUS GOODS TO BE SOLD BY OR MARKED WITH NET WEIGHT

[1.974]
22.   This Part of this Schedule applies to—
   (a)   distemper,
   (b)   articles offered as feed for household pets, being manufactured feed or bird feed, other than animal feed in biscuit or cake form pre-packed in a quantity by number not exceeding sixteen,
   (c)   nails,
   (d)   paste paint,
   (e)   seeds, other than pea or bean seeds, and
   (f)   rolled oats.

23.   Subject to paragraphs 24 and 25 below, goods to which this Part of this Schedule applies—
   (a)   unless pre-packed, shall be sold by retail only by net weight, and
   (b)   shall be pre-packed only if the container is marked with an indication of quantity by net weight.

[24. The following shall be exempted from the requirements of this Part of this Schedule—
   (a)   distemper or paste paint in a quantity of less than 250 grams,
   (b)   bird seed in a quantity of less than 125 grams, and
   (c)   any other goods in a quantity of less than 25 grams.]

25.   Notwithstanding anything in paragraph 24 above, nails—
   (a)   when not pre-packed may be so sold by retail by number, and
   (b)   may be pre-packed in or on a container marked with an indication of quantity by number.

NOTES

Para 24: substituted by the Weights and Measures Act 1985 (Metrication) (Amendment) Order 1994, SI 1994/2866, art 3(1), (6)(g).

PART IX
MISCELLANEOUS GOODS TO BE MARKED WHEN PRE-PACKED WITH NET WEIGHT

[1.975]
26.   This Part of this Schedule applies to—
   (a)   Portland cement,
   (b)   cleansing powders and scouring powders,
   (c)   detergents, other than liquid detergents, and
   (d)   paint remover, other than liquid paint remover.

27.   Subject to paragraph 28 below, goods to which this Part of this Schedule applies shall be pre-packed only if the container is marked with an indication of quantity by net weight.

28.   There shall be exempted from the requirements of this Part of this Schedule goods of any description in a quantity of less than [25 grams].

NOTES

Para 28: words in square brackets substituted by the Weights and Measures Act 1985 (Metrication) (Amendment) Order 1994, SI 1994/2866, art 3(1), (6)(h).

PART X
MISCELLANEOUS GOODS TO BE SOLD BY OR MARKED WITH CAPACITY MEASUREMENT

[1.976]
29.   This Part of this Schedule applies to antifreeze fluid for internal combustion engines, linseed oil, paint (other than paste paint), paint thinner, turpentine, turpentine substitute, varnish, and wood preservative fluid (including fungicides and insecticides).

30.   Subject to paragraph 31 below, goods to which this Part of this Schedule applies—

(a)   unless pre-packed, shall be sold by retail only by capacity measurement, and
(b)   shall be pre-packed only if the container is marked with an indication of quantity by capacity measurement.

31. There shall be exempted from all requirements of this Part of this Schedule goods of any description in a quantity of less than [150 millilitres].

NOTES

Para 31: words in square brackets substituted by the Weights and Measures Act 1985 (Metrication) (Amendment) Order 1994, SI 1994/2866, art 3(1), (6)(i).

PART XI
MISCELLANEOUS GOODS TO BE MARKED WHEN PRE-PACKED WITH CAPACITY MEASUREMENT

[1.977]
32. This Part of this Schedule applies to enamel, lacquer, liquid detergents, liquid paint remover, petrifying fluid and rust remover.

33. Subject to paragraph 34 below, goods to which this Part of this Schedule applies shall be pre-packed only if the container is marked with an indication of quantity by capacity measurement.

[34. The following shall be exempted from the requirements of paragraph 33 above—
(a)   liquid detergents in a quantity of less than 125 millilitres, and
(b)   goods of any other description in a quantity of less than 150 millilitres.]

NOTES

Para 34: substituted by the Weights and Measures Act 1985 (Metrication) (Amendment) Order 1994, SI 1994/2866, art 3(1), (6)(j).

PART XII
MISCELLANEOUS GOODS TO BE SOLD BY OR MARKED WITH NET WEIGHT OR CAPACITY MEASUREMENT

[1.978]
35. This Part of this Schedule applies to—
(a)   polishes,
(b)   dressings, analogous to polishes, and
(c)   pea seeds and bean seeds.

36. Subject to paragraph 37 below, goods to which this Part of this Schedule applies—
(a)   unless pre-packed, shall be sold by retail only by net weight or by capacity measurement, and
(b)   shall be pre-packed only if the container is marked with an indication of quantity either by net weight or by capacity measurement.

37. The following shall be exempted from all the requirements of this Part of this Schedule, that is to say—
(a)   pea or bean seeds in a quantity of less than [250 grams] or of less than [250 millilitres], and
(b)   any other goods in a quantity of less than [30 grams] or of less than [30 millilitres].

NOTES

Para 37: words in square brackets substituted by the Weights and Measures Act 1985 (Metrication) (Amendment) Order 1994, SI 1994/2866, art 3(1), (6)(k).

PART XIII
MISCELLANEOUS GOODS TO BE MARKED WHEN PRE-PACKED WITH QUANTITY BY NUMBER

[1.979]
38. This Part of this Schedule applies—
(a)   to cheroots, cigarettes and cigars,
(b)   to postal stationery, that is to say, paper or cards for use in correspondence, and envelopes,
(b)   to, and to any mixture consisting mainly of, inorganic fertilisers, being such fertilisers or such a mixture made up into pellets or other articles for use as individual items, and
(d)   to manufactured animal feed in biscuit or cake form pre-packed in a quantity by number of sixteen or less.

39. Subject to paragraphs 40 and 41 below, goods to which this Part of this Schedule applies shall be pre-packed only if the container is marked with an indication of quantity by number.

40. In relation to postal stationery, the reference to number in paragraph 39 above shall be construed as a reference to number of sheets of paper, cards or envelopes, as the case may be, in the pad, confining band or other form of container; and postal stationery shall be exempted from the requirements of that paragraph if pre-packed as part of a collection of articles made up for sale together and including any article other than postal stationery and blotting or other paper.

41. There shall be exempted from the requirements of this Part of this Schedule any goods in a quantity by number of one.

SCHEDULE 7
COMPOSITE GOODS AND COLLECTIONS OF ARTICLES

Section 21

[1.980]
1. (1) This paragraph applies to any goods which, not being pre-packed, and not themselves being goods—
   (a) required by or under Part IV of this Act, except this paragraph, to be sold (whether on any sale or on a sale of any particular description) only by quantity expressed in a particular manner, or
   (b) on a sale of which (whether any sale or a sale of any particular description) the quantity of the goods sold expressed in a particular manner is required by or under Part IV of this Act, except this paragraph, to be made known to the buyer at or before a particular time, or
   (c) expressly exempted by or under Part IV of this Act, except this paragraph, from all such requirements as mentioned in paragraph (a) or (b) above which would otherwise apply to them,
consist of a mixture constituted wholly or mainly of goods of one or more descriptions to which there applies any such requirement made by reference to any of the following (whether exclusively or otherwise), that is to say, weight, capacity measurement or volume.

(2) Subject to paragraph 5 below, goods to which this paragraph applies shall be sold only by net weight or by capacity measurement or by volume.

2. (1) This paragraph applies to any goods which, not being aerosol products and not themselves being goods—
   (a) required by or under Part IV of this Act, except this paragraph, to be pre-packed only if the container is marked with an indication of quantity, or
   [(aa) that are subject to the FIC Regulation, or]
   (b) in the case of which when sold pre-packed (whether on any sale or on a sale of any particular description) the quantity of the goods sold expressed in a particular manner is required by or under Part IV of this Act, except this paragraph, to be made known to the buyer at or before a particular time, or
   (c) expressly exempted by or under Part IV of this Act, except this paragraph, from all such requirements as mentioned in paragraph (a) or (b) above which would otherwise apply to them,
consist of a mixture constituted wholly or mainly of goods of one or more descriptions to which there applies any such requirement made by reference to any of the following (whether exclusively or otherwise), that is to say, capacity measurement or volume.

(2) Subject to paragraph 5 below, goods to which this paragraph applies shall be pre-packed only if the container is marked with an indication of quantity either by net weight or by capacity measurement or by volume.

3. (1) This paragraph applies to aerosol products containing any goods required by or under Part IV of this Act, except this paragraph, to be pre-packed only if the container is marked with an indication of quantity expressed in a particular manner.

[(1A) This paragraph does not apply to aerosol products containing goods that are subject to the FIC Regulation.]

(2) Subject to paragraph 5 below, any aerosol product to which this paragraph applies shall be pre-packed only if the container is marked with—
   [(a) an indication of the total capacity of the container (indicated in such a way as to avoid giving a false impression of the quantity of goods in the container), and
   (b)] an indication of the quantity by [net volume] of the entire contents of the container.

4. (1) This paragraph applies to any collection of two or more items which, not itself being—
   (a) required by or under Part IV of this Act, except this paragraph, to be pre-packed only if the container is marked with particular information, or
   (b) expressly exempted by or under Part IV of this Act, except this paragraph, from any such requirement which would otherwise apply to it,
contains one or more articles to which any such requirement applies.

[(1A) This paragraph does not apply to a collection containing any goods that are subject to the FIC Regulation.]

(2)   Any collection to which this paragraph applies shall be pre-packed only if—

(a)   the container in which the collection is pre-packed is marked with an indication of the quantity of each of any such articles as mentioned in sub-paragraph (1) above contained in it, or

(b)   each of any such articles contained in the container is made up in an individual container marked with an indication of quantity,

being in either case the like indication of the quantity of each respectively of those articles as would have been required if that article had itself been pre-packed.

5. There shall be exempted from any requirement of paragraph 1, 2 or [3(2)(b)] above food of any description in a quantity of less than five grams or of less than five millilitres and goods of any other description in a quantity of less than [25 grams] or of less than [25 millilitres].

NOTES

Paras 2(1)(aa), 3(1A), 4(1A): inserted by the Weights and Measures (Food) (Amendment) Regulations 2014, SI 2014/2975, regs 2, 12.

Para 3: words in first pair of square brackets inserted and words in second pair of square brackets substituted by the Weights and Measures (Specified Quantities) (Pre-packed Products) Regulations 2009, SI 2009/663, reg 2(1), (5)(a).

Para 5: first reference in square brackets substituted by SI 2009/663, reg 2(1), (5)(b); words in second and third pairs of square brackets substituted by the Weights and Measures Act 1985 (Metrication) (Amendment) Order 1994, SI 1994/2866, art 3(1), (7).

SCHEDULES 8–13

(Schs 8–13 outside the scope of this work.)

MINORS' CONTRACTS ACT 1987

(1987 c 13)

ARRANGEMENT OF SECTIONS

An Act to amend the law relating to minors' contracts

[9 April 1987]

[1.981]
1   Disapplication of Infants Relief Act 1874 etc
The following enactments shall not apply to any contract made by a minor after the commencement of this Act—

(a)   the Infants Relief Act 1874 (which invalidates certain contracts made by minors and prohibits actions to enforce contracts ratified after majority), and

(b)   section 5 of the Betting and Loans (Infants) Act 1892 (which invalidates contracts to repay loans advanced during minority).

NOTES

Infants Relief Act 1874, Betting and Loans (Infants) Act 1892, s 5: repealed by s 4(2) of this Act.

[1.982]
2   Guarantees
Where—

(a)   a guarantee is given in respect of an obligation of a party to a contract made after the commencement of this Act, and

(b)   the obligation is unenforceable against him (or he repudiates the contract) because he was a minor when the contract was made

the guarantee shall not for that reason alone be unenforceable against the guarantor.

[1.983]
3   Restitution
(1)   Where—

(a)   a person ("the plaintiff") has after the commencement of this Act entered into a contract with another ("the defendant"), and

(b)   the contract is unenforceable against the defendant (or he repudiates it) because he was a minor when the contract was made,

the court may, if it is just and equitable to do so, require the defendant to transfer to the plaintiff any property acquired by the defendant under the contract, or any property representing it.
(2) Nothing in this section shall be taken to prejudice any other remedy available to the plaintiff.

4 (*Sub-s (1) amends the Consumer Credit Act 1974, s 113(7) at* **[1.615]**; *sub-s (2) repeals the Infants Relief Act 1874 and the Betting and Loans (Infants) Act 1892 (in accordance with s 1).*)

[1.984]
5 Short title, commencement and extent
(1) This Act may be cited as the Minors' Contracts Act 1987.
(2) This Act shall come into force at the end of the period of two months beginning with the date on which it is passed.
(3) This Act extends to England and Wales only.

CONSUMER PROTECTION ACT 1987

(1987 c 43)

ARRANGEMENT OF SECTIONS

PART I
PRODUCT LIABILITY

PART II
CONSUMER SAFETY

PART IV
ENFORCEMENT OF PARTS II AND III

PART V
MISCELLANEOUS AND SUPPLEMENTAL

An Act to make provision with respect to the liability of persons for damage caused by defective products; to consolidate with amendments the Consumer Safety Act 1978 and the Consumer Safety (Amendment) Act 1986; to make provision with respect to the giving of price indications; to amend Part I of the Health and Safety at Work etc Act 1974 and sections 31 and 80 of the Explosives Act 1875; to repeal the Trade Descriptions Act 1972 and the Fabrics (Misdescription) Act 1913; and for connected purposes

[15 May 1987]

PART I
PRODUCT LIABILITY

[1.985]
1 Purpose and construction of Part I
(1)   This Part shall have effect for the purpose of making such provision as is necessary in order to comply with the product liability Directive and shall be construed accordingly.
(2)   In this Part, except in so far as the context otherwise requires—

   . . .
     "dependant" and "relative" have the same meaning as they have in, respectively, the Fatal Accidents Act 1976 and the [Damages (Scotland) Act 2011];
     "producer", in relation to a product, means—
       (a)   the person who manufactured it;
       (b)   in the case of a substance which has not been manufactured but has been won or abstracted, the person who won or abstracted it;
       (c)   in the case of a product which has not been manufactured, won or abstracted but essential characteristics of which are attributable to an industrial or other process having been carried out (for example, in relation to agricultural produce), the person who carried out that process;
     "product" means any goods or electricity and (subject to subsection (3) below) includes a product which is comprised in another product, whether by virtue of being a component part or raw material or otherwise; and
     "the product liability Directive" means the Directive of the Council of the European Communities, dated 25th July 1985, (No 85/374/EEC) on the approximation of the laws, regulations and administrative provisions of the member States concerning liability for defective products.
(3)   For the purposes of this Part a person who supplies any product in which products are comprised, whether by virtue of being component parts or raw materials or otherwise, shall not be treated by reason only of his supply of that product as supplying any of the products so comprised.

NOTES
     Sub-s (1): definition "agricultural produce" (omitted) repealed in relation to England and Wales by the Consumer Protection Act 1987 (Product Liability) (Modification) Order 2000, SI 2000/2771, art 2(1), (2), and in relation to Scotland by the Consumer Protection Act 1987 (Product Liability) (Modification) (Scotland) Order 2001, SSI 2001/265, art 2(1), (2); in definition "dependant", words in square brackets substituted, in relation to Scotland, by the Damages (Scotland) Act 2011, s 15, Sch 1, para 4(1).

[1.986]
2 Liability for defective products
(1)   Subject to the following provisions of this Part, where any damage is caused wholly or partly by a defect in a product, every person to whom subsection (2) below applies shall be liable for the damage.
(2)   This subsection applies to—
     (a)   the producer of the product;
     (b)   any person who, by putting his name on the product or using a trade mark or other distinguishing mark in relation to the product, has held himself out to be the producer of the product;
     (c)   any person who has imported the product into a member State from a place outside the member States in order, in the course of any business of his, to supply it to another.

(3) Subject as aforesaid, where any damage is caused wholly or partly by a defect in a product, any person who supplied the product (whether to the person who suffered the damage, to the producer of any product in which the product in question is comprised or to any other person) shall be liable for the damage if—

    (a)   the person who suffered the damage requests the supplier to identify one or more of the persons (whether still in existence or not) to whom subsection (2) above applies in relation to the product;

    (b)   that request is made within a reasonable period after the damage occurs and at a time when it is not reasonably practicable for the person making the request to identify all those persons; and

    (c)   the supplier fails, within a reasonable period after receiving the request, either to comply with the request or to identify the person who supplied the product to him.

(4) . . .

(5) Where two or more persons are liable by virtue of this Part for the same damage, their liability shall be joint and several.

(6) This section shall be without prejudice to any liability arising otherwise than by virtue of this Part.

NOTES

    Sub-s (4): repealed in relation to England and Wales by the Consumer Protection Act 1987 (Product Liability) (Modification) Order 2000, SI 2000/2771, art 2(1), (3) and in relation to Scotland by the Consumer Protection Act 1987 (Product Liability) (Modification) (Scotland) Order 2001, SSI 2001/265, art 2(1), (3).

[1.987]
3 Meaning of "defect"

(1) Subject to the following provisions of this section, there is a defect in a product for the purposes of this Part if the safety of the product is not such as persons generally are entitled to expect; and for those purposes "safety", in relation to a product, shall include safety with respect to products comprised in that product and safety in the context of risks of damage to property, as well as in the context of risks of death or personal injury.

(2) In determining for the purposes of subsection (1) above what persons generally are entitled to expect in relation to a product all the circumstances shall be taken into account, including—

    (a)   the manner in which, and purposes for which, the product has been marketed, its get-up, the use of any mark in relation to the product and any instructions for, or warnings with respect to, doing or refraining from doing anything with or in relation to the product;

    (b)   what might reasonably be expected to be done with or in relation to the product; and

    (c)   the time when the product was supplied by its producer to another;

and nothing in this section shall require a defect to be inferred from the fact alone that the safety of a product which is supplied after that time is greater than the safety of the product in question.

[1.988]
4 Defences

(1) In any civil proceedings by virtue of this Part against any person ("the person proceeded against") in respect of a defect in a product it shall be a defence for him to show—

    (a)   that the defect is attributable to compliance with any requirement imposed by or under any [EU] obligation; or

    (b)   that the person proceeded against did not at any time supply the product to another; or

    (c)   that the following conditions are satisfied, that is to say—

        (i)   that the only supply of the product to another by the person proceeded against was otherwise than in the course of a business of that person's; and

        (ii)   that section 2(2) above does not apply to that person or applies to him by virtue only of things done otherwise than with a view to profit; or

    (d)   that the defect did not exist in the product at the relevant time; or

    (e)   that the state of scientific and technical knowledge at the relevant time was not such that a producer of products of the same description as the product in question might be expected to have discovered the defect if it had existed in his products while they were under his control; or

    (f)   that the defect—

        (i)   constituted a defect in a product ("the subsequent product") in which the product in question had been comprised; and

        (ii)   was wholly attributable to the design of the subsequent product or to compliance by the producer of the product in question with instructions given by the producer of the subsequent product.

(2) In this section "the relevant time", in relation to electricity, means the time at which it was generated, being a time before it was transmitted or distributed, and in relation to any other product, means—

    (a)   if the person proceeded against is a person to whom subsection (2) of section 2 above applies in relation to the product, the time when he supplied the product to another;

(b) if that subsection does not apply to that person in relation to the product, the time when the product was last supplied by a person to whom that subsection does apply in relation to the product.

NOTES

Sub-s (1): reference in square brackets in para (a) substituted by the Treaty of Lisbon (Changes in Terminology) Order 2011, SI 2011/1043, art 6(1)(e).

[1.989]

5 Damage giving rise to liability

(1) Subject to the following provisions of this section, in this Part "damage" means death or personal injury or any loss of or damage to any property (including land).

(2) A person shall not be liable under section 2 above in respect of any defect in a product for the loss of or any damage to the product itself or for the loss of or any damage to the whole or any part of any product which has been supplied with the product in question comprised in it.

(3) A person shall not be liable under section 2 above for any loss of or damage to any property which, at the time it is lost or damaged, is not—

(a) of a description of property ordinarily intended for private use, occupation or consumption; and

(b) intended by the person suffering the loss or damage mainly for his own private use, occupation or consumption.

(4) No damages shall be awarded to any person by virtue of this Part in respect of any loss of or damage to any property if the amount which would fall to be so awarded to that person, apart from this subsection and any liability for interest, does not exceed £275.

(5) In determining for the purposes of this Part who has suffered any loss of or damage to property and when any such loss or damage occurred, the loss or damage shall be regarded as having occurred at the earliest time at which a person with an interest in the property had knowledge of the material facts about the loss or damage.

(6) For the purposes of subsection (5) above the material facts about any loss of or damage to any property are such facts about the loss or damage as would lead a reasonable person with an interest in the property to consider the loss or damage sufficiently serious to justify his instituting proceedings for damages against a defendant who did not dispute liability and was able to satisfy a judgment.

(7) For the purposes of subsection (5) above a person's knowledge includes knowledge which he might reasonably have been expected to acquire—

(a) from facts observable or ascertainable by him; or

(b) from facts ascertainable by him with the help of appropriate expert advice which it is reasonable for him to seek;

but a person shall not be taken by virtue of this subsection to have knowledge of a fact ascertainable by him only with the help of expert advice unless he has failed to take all reasonable steps to obtain (and, where appropriate, to act on) that advice.

(8) Subsections (5) to (7) above shall not extend to Scotland.

[1.990]

6 Application of certain enactments

(1) Any damage for which a person is liable under section 2 above shall be deemed to have been caused—

(a) for the purposes of the Fatal Accidents Act 1976, by that person's wrongful act, neglect or default;

(b)–(d) *(apply to Scotland only.)*

(2) Where—

(a) a person's death is caused wholly or partly by a defect in a product, or a person dies after suffering damage which has been so caused;

(b) a request such as mentioned in paragraph (a) of subsection (3) of section 2 above is made to a supplier of the product by that person's personal representatives or, in the case of a person whose death is caused wholly or partly by the defect, by any dependant or relative of that person; and

(c) the conditions specified in paragraphs (b) and (c) of that subsection are satisfied in relation to that request,

this Part shall have effect for the purposes of the Law Reform (Miscellaneous Provisions) Act 1934, the Fatal Accidents Act 1976 and the [Damages (Scotland) Act 2011] as if liability of the supplier to that person under that subsection did not depend on that person having requested the supplier to identify certain persons or on the said conditions having been satisfied in relation to a request made by that person.

(3) Section 1 of the Congenital Disabilities (Civil Liability) Act 1976 shall have effect for the purposes of this Part as if—

(a) a person were answerable to a child in respect of an occurrence caused wholly or partly by a defect in a product if he is or has been liable under section 2 above in respect of any effect of the occurrence on a parent of the child, or would be so liable if the occurrence caused a parent of the child to suffer damage;

(b) the provisions of this Part relating to liability under section 2 above applied in relation to liability by virtue of paragraph (a) above under the said section 1; and

(c) subsection (6) of the said section 1 (exclusion of liability) were omitted.

(4) Where any damage is caused partly by a defect in a product and partly by the fault of the person suffering the damage, the Law Reform (Contributory Negligence) Act 1945 and section 5 of the Fatal Accidents Act 1976 (contributory negligence) shall have effect as if the defect were the fault of every person liable by virtue of this Part for the damage caused by the defect.

(5) In subsection (4) above "fault" has the same meaning as in the said Act of 1945.

(6) Schedule 1 to this Act shall have effect for the purpose of amending the Limitation Act 1980 and the Prescription and Limitation (Scotland) Act 1973 in their application in relation to the bringing of actions by virtue of this Part.

(7) It is hereby declared that liability by virtue of this Part is to be treated as liability in tort for the purposes of any enactment conferring jurisdiction on any court with respect to any matter.

(8) Nothing in this Part shall prejudice the operation of section 12 of the Nuclear Installations Act 1965 (rights to compensation for certain breaches of duties confined to rights under that Act).

NOTES

Sub-s (2): words in square brackets substituted, in relation to Scotland, by the Damages (Scotland) Act 2011, s 15, Sch 1, para 4(2)(b).

[1.991]
7 Prohibition on exclusions from liability

The liability of a person by virtue of this Part to a person who has suffered damage caused wholly or partly by a defect in a product, or to a dependant or relative of such a person, shall not be limited or excluded by any contract term, by any notice or by any other provision.

[1.992]
8 Power to modify Part I

(1) Her Majesty may by Order in Council make such modifications of this Part and of any other enactment (including an enactment contained in the following Parts of this Act, or in an Act passed after this Act) as appear to Her Majesty in Council to be necessary or expedient in consequence of any modification of the product liability Directive which is made at any time after the passing of this Act.

(2) An Order in Council under subsection (1) above shall not be submitted to Her Majesty in Council unless a draft of the Order has been laid before, and approved by a resolution of, each House of Parliament.

NOTES

Orders: the Consumer Protection Act 1987 (Product Liability) (Modification) Order 2000, SI 2000/2771.

[1.993]
9 Application of Part I to Crown

(1) Subject to subsection (2) below, this Part shall bind the Crown.

(2) The Crown shall not, as regards the Crown's liability by virtue of this Part, be bound by this Part further than the Crown is made liable in tort or in reparation under the Crown Proceedings Act 1947, as that Act has effect from time to time.

PART II
CONSUMER SAFETY

10 (*Repealed by the General Product Safety Regulations 2005, SI 2005/1803, reg 46(1), (2).*)

[1.994]
11 Safety regulations

(1) The Secretary of State may by regulations under this section ("safety regulations") make such provision as he considers appropriate . . . and for the purpose of securing—

(a) that goods to which this section applies are safe;

(b) that goods to which this section applies which are unsafe, or would be unsafe in the hands of persons of a particular description, are not made available to persons generally or, as the case may be, to persons of that description; and

(c) that appropriate information is, and inappropriate information is not, provided in relation to goods to which this section applies.

(2) Without prejudice to the generality of subsection (1) above, safety regulations may contain provision—

(a)   with respect to the composition or contents, design, construction, finish or packing of goods to which this section applies, with respect to standards for such goods and with respect to other matters relating to such goods;

(b)   with respect to the giving, refusal, alteration or cancellation of approvals of such goods, of descriptions of such goods or of standards for such goods;

(c)   with respect to the conditions that may be attached to any approval given under the regulations;

(d)   for requiring such fees as may be determined by or under the regulations to be paid on the giving or alteration of any approval under the regulations and on the making of an application for such an approval or alteration;

(e)   with respect to appeals against refusals, alterations and cancellations of approvals given under the regulations and against the conditions contained in such approvals;

(f)   for requiring goods to which this section applies to be approved under the regulations or to conform to the requirements of the regulations or to descriptions or standards specified in or approved by or under the regulations;

(g)   with respect to the testing or inspection of goods to which this section applies (including provision for determining the standards to be applied in carrying out any test or inspection);

(h)   with respect to the ways of dealing with goods of which some or all do not satisfy a test required by or under the regulations or a standard connected with a procedure so required;

(i)   for requiring a mark, warning or instruction or any other information relating to goods to be put on or to accompany the goods or to be used or provided in some other manner in relation to the goods, and for securing that inappropriate information is not given in relation to goods either by means of misleading marks or otherwise;

(j)   for prohibiting persons from supplying, or from offering to supply, agreeing to supply, exposing for supply or possessing for supply, goods to which this section applies and component parts and raw materials for such goods;

(k)   for requiring information to be given to any such person as may be determined by or under the regulations for the purpose of enabling that person to exercise any function conferred on him by the regulations.

(3)   Without prejudice as aforesaid, safety regulations may contain provision—

(a)   for requiring persons on whom functions are conferred by or under section 27 below to have regard, in exercising their functions so far as relating to any provision of safety regulations, to matters specified in a direction issued by the Secretary of State with respect to that provision;

(b)   for securing that a person shall not be guilty of an offence under section 12 below unless it is shown that the goods in question do not conform to a particular standard;

(c)   for securing that proceedings for such an offence are not brought in England and Wales except by or with the consent of the Secretary of State or the Director of Public Prosecutions;

(d)   for securing that proceedings for such an offence are not brought in Northern Ireland except by or with the consent of the Secretary of State or the Director of Public Prosecutions for Northern Ireland;

(e)   for enabling a magistrates' court in England and Wales or Northern Ireland to try an information or, in Northern Ireland, a complaint in respect of such an offence if the information was laid or the complaint made within twelve months from the time when the offence was committed;

(f)   (*applies to Scotland only*);

(g)   for determining the persons by whom, and the manner in which, anything required to be done by or under the regulations is to be done.

(4)   Safety regulations shall not provide for any contravention of the regulations to be an offence.

(5)   Where the Secretary of State proposes to make safety regulations it shall be his duty before he makes them—

(a)   to consult such organisations as appear to him to be representative of interests substantially affected by the proposal;

(b)   to consult such other persons as he considers appropriate; and

(c)   in the case of proposed regulations relating to goods suitable for use at work, to consult [the Health and Safety Executive] in relation to the application of the proposed regulations to Great Britain;

but the preceding provisions of this subsection shall not apply in the case of regulations which provide for the regulations to cease to have effect at the end of a period of not more than twelve months beginning with the day on which they come into force and which contain a statement that it appears to the Secretary of State that the need to protect the public requires that the regulations should be made without delay.

(6)   The power to make safety regulations shall be exercisable by statutory instrument subject to annulment in pursuance of a resolution of either House of Parliament and shall include power—

(a)   to make different provision for different cases; and

(b)   to make such supplemental, consequential and transitional provision as the Secretary of State considers appropriate.

(7)   This section applies to any goods other than—
    (a)   growing crops and things comprised in land by virtue of being attached to it;
    (b)   water, food, feeding stuff and fertiliser;
    (c)   gas which is, is to be or has been supplied by a person authorised to supply it by or under [section 7A of the Gas Act 1986 (licensing of gas suppliers and gas shippers) *or paragraph 5 of Schedule 2A to that Act (supply to very large customers an exception to prohibition on unlicensed activities)*] [or under Article 8(1)(c) of the Gas (Northern Ireland) Order 1996];
    (d)   controlled drugs and licensed medicinal products.

NOTES

Sub-s (1): words omitted repealed by the General Product Safety Regulations 2005, SI 2005/1803, reg 46(1), (3).

Sub-s (5): words in square brackets substituted by the Legislative Reform (Health and Safety Executive) Order 2008, SI 2008/960, art 22, Sch 3, subject to transitional provisions in art 21 of, and Sch 2 to, that Order.

Sub-s (7): words in first pair of square brackets in para (c) substituted by the Gas Act 1995, s 16(1), Sch 4, para 15(2); words in italics in para (c) repealed by the Utilities Act 2000, s 108, Sch 8, as from a day to be appointed; words in second pair of square brackets in para (c) inserted by the Gas (Northern Ireland) Order 1996, SI 1996/275, art 71(1), Sch 6.

Regulations: the Furniture and Furnishings (Fire) (Safety) Regulations 1988, SI 1988/1324; the Babies' Dummies (Safety) (Revocation) Regulations 1989, SI 1989/141; the Food Imitations (Safety) Regulations 1989, SI 1989/1291; the Furniture and Furnishings (Fire) (Safety) (Amendment) Regulations 1989, SI 1989/2358; the Tobacco Products Labelling (Safety) Regulations 1991, SI 1991/1530; the Oil Lamps (Safety) (Revocation) Regulations 1992, SI 1992/23; the Cigarettes (Maximum Tar Yield) (Safety) Regulations 1992, SI 1992/2783; the Tobacco for Oral Use (Safety) Regulations 1992, SI 1992/3134; the Furniture and Furnishings (Fire) (Safety) (Amendment) Regulations 1993, SI 1993/207; the Tobacco Products Labelling (Safety) Amendment Regulations 1993, SI 1993/1947; the Plugs and Sockets etc (Safety) Regulations 1994, SI 1994/1768; the Motor Vehicle Tyres (Safety) Regulations 1994, SI 1994/3117; the Electrical Equipment (Safety) Regulations 1994, SI 1994/3260; the Fireworks (Safety) (Revocation) Regulations 1995, SI 1995/415; the N-nitrosamines and N-nitrosatable Substances in Elastomer or Rubber Teats and Dummies (Safety) Regulations 1995, SI 1995/1012; the Gas Appliances (Safety) Regulations 1995, SI 1995/1629; the Dangerous Substances and Preparations (Safety) (Consolidation) (Amendment) Regulations 1996, SI 1996/2635; the Motor Vehicle Tyres (Safety) (Amendment) Regulations 1996, SI 1996/3227; the Motor Vehicle Tyres (Safety) (Amendment) Regulations 1997, SI 1997/815; the Cigarette Lighter Refill (Safety) Regulations 1999, SI 1999/1844; the Road Vehicles (Brake Linings Safety) Regulations 1999, SI 1999/2978; the Dangerous Substances and Preparations (Safety) (Consolidation) and Chemicals (Hazard Information and Packaging for Supply) (Amendment) Regulations 2000, SI 2000/2897; the Medical Devices Regulations 2002, SI 2002/618; the Tobacco Products (Manufacture, Presentation and Sale) (Safety) Regulations 2002 SI 2002/3041; the Motor Vehicle Tyres (Safety) (Amendment) Regulations 2003, SI 2003/1316; the Unlicensed Medicinal Products for Human Use (Transmissible Spongiform Encephalopathies) (Safety) Regulations 2003, SI 2003/1680; the Medical Devices (Amendment) Regulations 2003, SI 2003/1697; the Motor Vehicle Tyres (Safety) (Amendment) (No 2) Regulations 2003, SI 2003/2762; the Road Vehicles (Brake Linings Safety) (Amendment) Regulations 2003, SI 2003/3314; the Fireworks Regulations 2004, SI 2004/1836; the Medical Devices (Amendment) Regulations 2007, SI 2007/400; the Tobacco Products (Manufacture, Presentation and Sale) (Safety) (Amendment) Regulations 2007, SI 2007/2473; the Medical Devices (Amendment) Regulations 2008, SI 2008/2936; the Aerosol Dispensers Regulations 2009, SI 2009/2824; the Pedal Bicycles (Safety) Regulations 2010, SI 2010/198; the Pyrotechnic Articles (Safety) Regulations 2010, SI 2010/1554; the Furniture and Furnishings (Fire) (Safety) (Amendment) Regulations 2010, SI 2010/2205; the Toys (Safety) Regulations 2011, SI 2011/1881; the Medical Devices (Amendment) Regulations 2012, SI 2012/1426; the Product Safety (Revocation) Regulations 2012, SI 2012/1815; the Product Safety Amendment and Revocation Regulations 2012, SI 2012/2963; the Medical Devices (Amendment) Regulations 2013, SI 2013/2327; the Aerosol Dispensers (Amendment) Regulations 2014, SI 2014/1130.

By virtue of the Consumer Protection Act 1987 (Commencement No 1) Order 1987, SI 1987/1680, arts 6–9, the following regulations (which were made under the Consumer Protection Act 1961) have effect as if made under this section: the Cooking Utensils (Safety) Regulations 1972, SI 1972/1957; the Children's Clothing (Hood Cords) Regulations 1976, SI 1976/2; the Oil Heaters (Safety) Regulations 1977, SI 1977/167; the Nightwear (Safety) Regulations 1985, SI 1985/2043. Also, by virtue of the Interpretation Act 1978, s 17(2)(b), the following regulations (which were made under the Consumer Safety Act 1978, s 1) take effect under this section: the Filament Lamps for Vehicles (Safety) Regulations 1982, SI 1982/444; the Nightwear (Safety) Regulations 1985, SI 1985/2043.

[1.995]
12   Offences against the safety regulations

(1)   Where safety regulations prohibit a person from supplying or offering or agreeing to supply any goods or from exposing or possessing any goods for supply, that person shall be guilty of an offence if he contravenes the prohibition.

(2)   Where safety regulations require a person who makes or processes any goods in the course of carrying on a business—
    (a)   to carry out a particular test or use a particular procedure in connection with the making or processing of the goods with a view to ascertaining whether the goods satisfy any requirements of such regulations; or
    (b)   to deal or not to deal in a particular way with a quantity of the goods of which the whole or part does not satisfy such a test or does not satisfy standards connected with such a procedure,

that person shall be guilty of an offence if he does not comply with the requirement.

(3)   If a person contravenes a provision of safety regulations which prohibits or requires the provision, by means of a mark or otherwise, of information of a particular kind in relation to goods, he shall be guilty of an offence.

(4)   Where safety regulations require any person to give information to another for the purpose of enabling that other to exercise any function, that person shall be guilty of an offence if—
    (a)   he fails without reasonable cause to comply with the requirement; or

   (b)   in giving the information which is required of him—
       (i)   he makes any statement which he knows is false in a material particular; or
       (ii)   he recklessly makes any statement which is false in a material particular.

(5)   A person guilty of an offence under this section shall be liable on summary conviction to imprisonment for a term not exceeding six months or to a fine not exceeding level 5 on the standard scale or to both.

[1.996]
13   Prohibition notices and notices to warn

(1)   The Secretary of State may—

   (a)   serve on any person a notice ("a prohibition notice") prohibiting that person, except with the consent of the Secretary of State, from supplying, or from offering to supply, agreeing to supply, exposing for supply or possessing for supply, any relevant goods which the Secretary of State considers are unsafe and which are described in the notice;

   (b)   serve on any person a notice ("a notice to warn") requiring that person at his own expense to publish, in a form and manner and on occasions specified in the notice, a warning about any relevant goods which the Secretary of State considers are unsafe, which that person supplies or has supplied and which are described in the notice.

(2)   Schedule 2 to this Act shall have effect with respect to prohibition notices and notices to warn; and the Secretary of State may by regulations make provision specifying the manner in which information is to be given to any person under that Schedule.

(3)   A consent given by the Secretary of State for the purposes of a prohibition notice may impose such conditions on the doing of anything for which the consent is required as the Secretary of State considers appropriate.

(4)   A person who contravenes a prohibition notice or a notice to warn shall be guilty of an offence and liable on summary conviction to imprisonment for a term not exceeding six months or to a fine not exceeding level 5 on the standard scale or to both.

(5)   The power to make regulations under subsection (2) above shall be exercisable by statutory instrument subject to annulment in pursuance of a resolution of either House of Parliament and shall include power—

   (a)   to make different provision for different cases; and

   (b)   to make such supplemental, consequential and transitional provision as the Secretary of State considers appropriate.

(6)   In this section "relevant goods" means—

   (a)   in relation to a prohibition notice, any goods to which section 11 above applies; and

   (b)   in relation to a notice to warn, any goods to which that section applies or any growing crops or things comprised in land by virtue of being attached to it.

[(7)   A notice may not be given under this section in respect of any aspect of the safety of goods, or any risk or category of risk associated with goods, concerning which provision is contained in the General Product Safety Regulations 2005.]

NOTES

Sub-s (7): added by the General Product Safety Regulations 2005, SI 2005/1803, reg 46(1), (4).

[1.997]
14   Suspension notices

(1)   Where an enforcement authority has reasonable grounds for suspecting that any safety provision has been contravened in relation to any goods, the authority may serve a notice ("a suspension notice") prohibiting the person on whom it is served, for such period ending not more than six months after the date of the notice as is specified therein, from doing any of the following things without the consent of the authority, that is to say, supplying the goods, offering to supply them, agreeing to supply them or exposing them for supply.

(2)   A suspension notice served by an enforcement authority in respect of any goods shall—

   (a)   describe the goods in a manner sufficient to identify them;

   (b)   set out the grounds on which the authority suspects that a safety provision has been contravened in relation to the goods; and

   (c)   state that, and the manner in which, the person on whom the notice is served may appeal against the notice under section 15 below.

(3)   A suspension notice served by an enforcement authority for the purpose of prohibiting a person for any period from doing the things mentioned in subsection (1) above in relation to any goods may also require that person to keep the authority informed of the whereabouts throughout that period of any of those goods in which he has an interest.

(4)   Where a suspension notice has been served on any person in respect of any goods, no further such notice shall be served on that person in respect of the same goods unless—

   (a)   proceedings against that person for an offence in respect of a contravention in relation to the goods of a safety provision (not being an offence under this section); or

   (b)   proceedings for the forfeiture of the goods under section 16 or 17 below,

are pending at the end of the period specified in the first-mentioned notice.

(5)   A consent given by an enforcement authority for the purposes of subsection (1) above may impose such conditions on the doing of anything for which the consent is required as the authority considers appropriate.

(6)   Any person who contravenes a suspension notice shall be guilty of an offence and liable on summary conviction to imprisonment for a term not exceeding six months or to a fine not exceeding level 5 on the standard scale or to both.

(7)   Where an enforcement authority serves a suspension notice in respect of any goods, the authority shall be liable to pay compensation to any person having an interest in the goods in respect of any loss or damage caused by reason of the service of the notice if—

(a)   there has been no contravention in relation to the goods of any safety provision; and

(b)   the exercise of the power is not attributable to any neglect or default by that person.

(8)   Any disputed question as to the right to or the amount of any compensation payable under this section shall be determined by arbitration or, in Scotland, by a single arbiter appointed, failing agreement between the parties, by the sheriff.

NOTES

Modification: this section is applied, with modifications, for the purposes of the enforcement of the Supply of Machinery (Safety) Regulations 2008, SI 2008/1597, by SI 2008/1597, reg 20, Sch 5, paras 11, 12, 17, 18.

[1.998]
15   Appeals against suspension notices

(1)   Any person having an interest in any goods in respect of which a suspension notice is for the time being in force may apply for an order setting aside the notice.

(2)   An application under this section may be made—

(a)   to any magistrates' court in which proceedings have been brought in England and Wales or Northern Ireland—

(i)   for an offence in respect of a contravention in relation to the goods of any safety provision; or

(ii)   for the forfeiture of the goods under section 16 below;

(b)   where no such proceedings have been so brought, by way of complaint to a magistrates' court; or

(c)   (*applies to Scotland only.*)

(3)   On an application under this section to a magistrates' court in England and Wales or Northern Ireland the court shall make an order setting aside the suspension notice only if the court is satisfied that there has been no contravention in relation to the goods of any safety provision.

(4)   On an application under this section to the sheriff he shall make an order setting aside the suspension notice only if he is satisfied that at the date of making the order—

(a)   proceedings for an offence in respect of a contravention in relation to the goods of any safety provision; or

(b)   proceedings for the forfeiture of the goods under section 17 below,

have not been brought or, having been brought, have been concluded.

(5)   Any person aggrieved by an order made under this section by a magistrates' court in England and Wales or Northern Ireland, or by a decision of such a court not to make such an order, may appeal against that order or decision—

(a)   in England and Wales, to the Crown Court;

(b)   in Northern Ireland, to the county court;

and an order so made may contain such provision as appears to the court to be appropriate for delaying the coming into force of the order pending the making and determination of any appeal (including any application under section 111 of the Magistrates' Courts Act 1980 or Article 146 of the Magistrates' Courts (Northern Ireland) Order 1981 (statement of case)).

NOTES

Modification: this section is applied, with modifications, for the purposes of the enforcement of the Supply of Machinery (Safety) Regulations 2008, SI 2008/1597, by SI 2008/1597, reg 20, Sch 5, paras 11, 12, 17, 18.

[1.999]
16   Forfeiture: England and Wales and Northern Ireland

(1)   An enforcement authority in England and Wales or Northern Ireland may apply under this section for an order for the forfeiture of any goods on the grounds that there has been a contravention in relation to the goods of a safety provision.

(2)   An application under this section may be made—

(a)   where proceedings have been brought in a magistrates' court for an offence in respect of a contravention in relation to some or all of the goods of any safety provision, to that court;

(b)   where an application with respect to some or all of the goods has been made to a magistrates' court under section 15 above or section 33 below, to that court; and

(c)   where no application for the forfeiture of the goods has been made under paragraph (a) or (b) above, by way of complaint to a magistrates' court.

(3) On an application under this section the court shall make an order for the forfeiture of any goods only if it is satisfied that there has been a contravention in relation to the goods of a safety provision.

(4) For the avoidance of doubt it is declared that a court may infer for the purposes of this section that there has been a contravention in relation to any goods of a safety provision if it is satisfied that any such provision has been contravened in relation to goods which are representative of those goods (whether by reason of being of the same design or part of the same consignment or batch or otherwise).

(5) Any person aggrieved by an order made under this section by a magistrates' court, or by a decision of such a court not to make such an order, may appeal against that order or decision—

(a) in England and Wales, to the Crown Court;

(b) in Northern Ireland, to the county court;

and an order so made may contain such provision as appears to the court to be appropriate for delaying the coming into force of the order pending the making and determination of any appeal (including any application under section 111 of the Magistrates' Courts Act 1980 or Article 146 of the Magistrates' Courts (Northern Ireland) Order 1981 (statement of case)).

(6) Subject to subsection (7) below, where any goods are forfeited under this section they shall be destroyed in accordance with such directions as the court may give.

(7) On making an order under this section a magistrates' court may, if it considers it appropriate to do so, direct that the goods to which the order relates shall (instead of being destroyed) be released, to such person as the court may specify, on condition that that person—

(a) does not supply those goods to any person otherwise than as mentioned in section 46(7)(a) or (b) below; and

(b) complies with any order to pay costs or expenses (including any order under section 35 below) which has been made against that person in the proceedings for the order for forfeiture.

17 (*Applies to Scotland only.*)

[1.1000]
18 Power to obtain information

(1) If the Secretary of State considers that, for the purpose of deciding whether—

(a) to make, vary or revoke any safety regulations; or

(b) to serve, vary or revoke a prohibition notice; or

(c) to serve or revoke a notice to warn,

he requires information which another person is likely to be able to furnish, the Secretary of State may serve on the other person a notice under this section.

(2) A notice served on any person under this section may require that person—

(a) to furnish to the Secretary of State, within a period specified in the notice, such information as is so specified;

(b) to produce such records as are specified in the notice at a time and place so specified and to permit a person appointed by the Secretary of State for the purpose to take copies of the records at that time and place.

(3) A person shall be guilty of an offence if he—

(a) fails, without reasonable cause, to comply with a notice served on him under this section; or

(b) in purporting to comply with a requirement which by virtue of paragraph (a) of subsection (2) above is contained in such a notice—

   (i) furnishes information which he knows is false in a material particular; or

   (ii) recklessly furnishes information which is false in a material particular.

(4) A person guilty of an offence under subsection (3) above shall—

(a) in the case of an offence under paragraph (a) of that subsection, be liable on summary conviction to a fine not exceeding level 5 on the standard scale; and

(b) in the case of an offence under paragraph (b) of that subsection be liable—

   (i) on conviction on indictment, to a fine;

   (ii) on summary conviction, to a fine not exceeding the statutory maximum.

[1.1001]
19 Interpretation of Part II

(1) In this Part—

"controlled drug" means a controlled drug within the meaning of the Misuse of Drugs Act 1971;

"feeding stuff" and "fertiliser" have the same meanings as in Part IV of the Agriculture Act 1970;

"food" does not include anything containing tobacco but, subject to that, has the same meaning as in the [Food Safety Act 1990] or, in relation to Northern Ireland, the same meaning as in the [Food Safety (Northern Ireland) Order 1991];

"licensed medicinal product" means—

(a) any medicinal product within the meaning of the Medicines Act 1968 in respect of which a product licence within the meaning of that Act is for the time being in force;

. . .

     (b)   any other article or substance in respect of which any such licence is for the time being in force in pursuance of an order under section 104 or 105 of that Act (application of Act to other articles and substances); [or

     (c)   a veterinary medicinal product that has a marketing authorisation under the Veterinary Medicines Regulations 2006.]

"safe", in relation to any goods, means such that there is no risk, or no risk apart from one reduced to a minimum, that any of the following will (whether immediately or after a definite or indefinite period) cause the death of, or any personal injury to, any person whatsoever, that is to say—

     (a)   the goods;

     (b)   the keeping, use or consumption of the goods;

     (c)   the assembly of any of the goods which are, or are to be, supplied unassembled;

     (d)   any emission or leakage from the goods or, as a result of the keeping, use or consumption of the goods, from anything else; or

     (e)   reliance on the accuracy of any measurement, calculation or other reading made by or by means of the goods,

     and . . . "unsafe" shall be construed accordingly;

"tobacco" includes any tobacco product within the meaning of the Tobacco Products Duty Act 1979 and any article or substance containing tobacco and intended for oral or nasal use.

(2) In the definition of "safe" in subsection (1) above, references to the keeping, use or consumption of any goods are references to—

     (a)   the keeping, use or consumption of the goods by the persons by whom, and in all or any of the ways or circumstances in which, they might reasonably be expected to be kept, used or consumed; and

     (b)   the keeping, use or consumption of the goods either alone or in conjunction with other goods in conjunction with which they might reasonably be expected to be kept, used or consumed.

NOTES

Sub-s (1): in definition "food" words in first pair of square brackets substituted by the Food Safety Act 1990, s 59(1), Sch 3, para 37, words in second pair of square brackets substituted by the Food Safety (Northern Ireland) Order 1991, SI 1991/762, art 51(1), Sch 2, para 17; in definition "licensed medicinal product" word omitted repealed and words in square brackets added by the Veterinary Medicines Regulations 2006, SI 2006/2407, reg 44(3), Sch 9, Pt 1, para 7; in definition "safe" words omitted repealed by the General Product Safety Regulations 2005, SI 2005/1803, reg 46(1), (5).

20–26 (*Pt III repealed by the Consumer Protection from Unfair Trading Regulations 2008, SI 2008/1277, reg 30(1), (3), Sch 2, Pt 1, paras 33, 34, Sch 4, subject to savings in reg 30(2) of, and Sch 3, paras 5, 9, 11 to, those Regulations at* **[2.595]**, **[2.597]**.)

PART IV
ENFORCEMENT OF PARTS II AND III

[1.1002]
27   Enforcement

(1) Subject to the following provisions of this section—

     (a)   it shall be the duty of every weights and measures authority in Great Britain to enforce within their area the safety provisions . . . ; and

     (b)   it shall be the duty of every district council in Northern Ireland to enforce within their area the safety provisions.

(2) The Secretary of State may by regulations—

     (a)   wholly or partly transfer any duty imposed by subsection (1) above on a weights and measures authority or a district council in Northern Ireland to such other person who has agreed to the transfer as is specified in the regulations;

     (b)   relieve such an authority or council of any such duty so far as it is exercisable in relation to such goods as may be described in the regulations.

(3) The power to make regulations under subsection (2) above shall be exercisable by statutory instrument subject to annulment in pursuance of a resolution of either House of Parliament and shall include power—

     (a)   to make different provision for different cases; and

     (b)   to make such supplemental, consequential and transitional provision as the Secretary of State considers appropriate.

[(3A) For the investigatory powers available to a person for the purposes of the duty imposed by subsection (1), see Schedule 5 to the Consumer Rights Act 2015 (as well as section 29).]

(4) Nothing in this section shall authorise any weights and measures authority, or any person on whom functions are conferred by regulations under subsection (2) above, to bring proceedings in Scotland for an offence.

NOTES

Sub-s (1): words omitted repealed by the Consumer Protection from Unfair Trading Regulations 2008, SI 2008/1277, reg 30(3), Sch 4.

Sub-s (3A): inserted by the Consumer Rights Act 2015, s 77(2), Sch 6, paras 37, 38, as from 1 October 2015 (for transitional provisions see the Consumer Rights Act 2015 (Commencement No 3, Transitional Provisions, Savings and Consequential Amendments) Order 2015, SI 2015/1630, arts 6–8 at **[2.1220]** et seq).

Regulations: the Medical Devices Regulations 2002, SI 2002/618; the Unlicensed Medicinal Products for Human Use (Transmissible Spongiform Encephalopathies) (Safety) Regulations 2003, SI 2003/1680; the Fireworks Regulations 2004, SI 2004/1836.

[1.1003]
28 Test purchases

(1)   An enforcement authority shall have power, for the purpose of ascertaining whether any safety provision . . . has been contravened in relation to any goods, services, accommodation or facilities—

(a)   to make, or to authorise an officer of the authority to make, any purchase of any goods; or

(b)   to secure, or to authorise an officer of the authority to secure, the provision of any services, accommodation or facilities.

(2)   Where—

(a)   any goods purchased under this section by or on behalf of an enforcement authority are submitted to a test; and

(b)   the test leads to—

   (i)   the bringing of proceedings for an offence in respect of a contravention in relation to the goods of any safety provision . . . or for the forfeiture of the goods under section 16 or 17 above; or

   (ii)   the serving of a suspension notice in respect of any goods; and

(c)   the authority is requested to do so and it is practicable for the authority to comply with the request,

the authority shall allow the person from whom the goods were purchased or any person who is a party to the proceedings or has an interest in any goods to which the notice relates to have the goods tested.

(3)   The Secretary of State may by regulations provide that any test of goods purchased under this section by or on behalf of an enforcement authority shall—

(a)   be carried out at the expense of the authority in a manner and by a person prescribed by or determined under the regulations; or

(b)   be carried out either as mentioned in paragraph (a) above or by the authority in a manner prescribed by the regulations.

(4)   The power to make regulations under subsection (3) above shall be exercisable by statutory instrument subject to annulment in pursuance of a resolution of either House of Parliament and shall include power—

(a)   to make different provision for different cases; and

(b)   to make such supplemental, consequential and transitional provision as the Secretary of State considers appropriate.

(5)   Nothing in this section shall authorise the acquisition by or on behalf of an enforcement authority of any interest in land.

NOTES

Repealed by the Consumer Rights Act 2015, s 77(2), Sch 6, paras 37, 39, as from 1 October 2015 (for transitional provisions see the Consumer Rights Act 2015 (Commencement No 3, Transitional Provisions, Savings and Consequential Amendments) Order 2015, SI 2015/1630, arts 6–8 at **[2.1220]** et seq).

Sub-ss (1), (2): words omitted repealed by the Consumer Protection from Unfair Trading Regulations 2008, SI 2008/1277, reg 30(3), Sch 4.

Modification: this section is applied, with modifications, for the purposes of the enforcement of the Supply of Machinery (Safety) Regulations 2008, SI 2008/1597, by SI 2008/1597, reg 20, Sch 5, paras 11, 12, 17, 18.

[1.1004]
29 Powers of search etc

(1)   Subject to the following provisions of this Part, a duly authorised officer of an enforcement authority may at any reasonable hour and on production, if required, of his credentials exercise *any of the powers conferred by the following provisions of this section.*

(2)   The officer may, for the purposes of ascertaining whether there has been any contravention of any safety provision . . . , inspect any goods and enter any premises other than premises occupied only as a person's residence.

(3)   The officer may, for the purpose of ascertaining whether there has been any contravention of any safety provision, examine any procedure (including any arrangements for carrying out a test) connected with the production of any goods.

(4)   If the officer has reasonable grounds for suspecting that any goods are manufactured or imported goods which have not been supplied in the United Kingdom since they were manufactured or imported he may—

(a)   for the purpose of ascertaining whether there has been any contravention of any safety provision in relation to the goods, require any person carrying on a business, or employed in connection with a business, to produce any records relating to the business;

(b)   for the purpose of ascertaining (by testing or otherwise) whether there has been any such contravention, seize and detain the goods;

(c)   take copies of, or of any entry in, any records produced by virtue of paragraph (a) above.

(5)   If the officer has reasonable grounds for suspecting that there has been a contravention in relation to any goods of any safety provision . . . , he may—

(a)   for the purpose of ascertaining whether there has been any such contravention, require any person carrying on a business, or employed in connection with a business, to produce any records relating to the business;

(b)   for the purpose of ascertaining (by testing or otherwise) whether there has been any such contravention, seize and detain the goods;

(c)   take copies of, or of any entry in, any records produced by virtue of paragraph (a) above.

(6)   The officer may seize and detain—

(a)   any goods or records which he has reasonable grounds for believing may be required as evidence in proceedings for an offence in respect of a contravention of any safety provision . . . ;

(b)   any goods which he has reasonable grounds for suspecting may be liable to be forfeited under section 16 or 17 above.

(7)   If and to the extent that it is reasonably necessary to do so to prevent a contravention of any safety provision . . . , the officer may, for the purpose of exercising his power under subsection (4), *(5) or (6)* above to seize any goods *or records*—

(a)   require any person having authority to do so to open any container or to open any vending machine; and

(b)   himself open or break open any such container or machine where a requirement made under paragraph (a) above in relation to the container or machine has not been complied with.

NOTES

Sub-s (1): for the words in italics there are substituted the words "the power conferred by subsection (4)" by the Consumer Rights Act 2015, s 77(2), Sch 6, paras 37, 40(1), (2), as from 1 October 2015 (for transitional provisions see the Consumer Rights Act 2015 (Commencement No 3, Transitional Provisions, Savings and Consequential Amendments) Order 2015, SI 2015/1630, arts 6–8 at **[2.1220]** et seq).

Sub-ss (2), (5), (6): repealed by the Consumer Rights Act 2015, s 77(2), Sch 6, paras 37, 40(1), (3), as from 1 October 2015 (for transitional provisions see note above); words omitted repealed by the Consumer Protection from Unfair Trading Regulations 2008, SI 2008/1277, reg 30(3), Sch 4.

Sub-s (3): repealed by the Consumer Rights Act 2015, s 77(2), Sch 6, paras 37, 40(1), (3), as from 1 October 2015 (for transitional provisions see note above).

Sub-s (7): words omitted repealed by the Consumer Protection from Unfair Trading Regulations 2008, SI 2008/1277, reg 30(3), Sch 4; words in italics repealed by the Consumer Rights Act 2015, s 77(2), Sch 6, paras 37, 40(1), (4), as from 1 October 2015 (for transitional provisions see note above).

Seize and detain: the powers of seizure conferred by sub-ss (4)–(6) are powers to which the Criminal Justice and Police Act 2001, s 50 apply (additional powers of seizure from premises); see s 50 of, and Sch 1, Pt 1, para 45 to, that Act.

Modification: this section is applied, with modifications, for the purposes of the enforcement of the Supply of Machinery (Safety) Regulations 2008, SI 2008/1597, by SI 2008/1597, reg 20, Sch 5, paras 11, 12, 17, 18.

[1.1005]
30   Provisions supplemental to s 29

(1)   An officer seizing any goods *or records* under section 29 above shall inform the following persons that the goods *or records* have been so seized, that is to say—

(a)   the person from whom they are seized; and

(b)   in the case of imported goods seized on any premises under the control of the Commissioners of Customs and Excise, the importer of those goods (within the meaning of the Customs and Excise Management Act 1979).

(2)   If a justice of the peace—

(a)   is satisfied by any written information on oath that there are reasonable grounds for believing either—

(i)   that any *goods or* records which any officer has power to inspect under section 29 above are on any premises and that their inspection is likely to disclose evidence that there has been a contravention of any safety provision . . . ; or

(ii)   that such a contravention has taken place, is taking place or is about to take place on any premises; and

(b)   is also satisfied by any such information either—

(i)   that admission to the premises has been or is likely to be refused and that notice of intention to apply for a warrant under this subsection has been given to the occupier; or

(ii)   that an application for admission, or the giving of such a notice, would defeat the object of the entry or that the premises are unoccupied or that the occupier is temporarily absent and it might defeat the object of the entry to await his return, the justice may by warrant under this hand, which shall continue in force for a period of one month, authorise any officer of an enforcement authority to enter the premises, if need be by force.

(3) An officer entering any premises by virtue of *section 29 above or* a warrant under subsection (2) above may take with him such other persons and such equipment as may appear to him necessary.

(4) On leaving any premises which a person is authorised to enter by a warrant under subsection (2) above, that person shall, if the premises are unoccupied or the occupier is temporarily absent, leave the premises as effectively secured against trespassers as he found them.

(5) If any person who is not an officer of an enforcement authority purports to act as such under section 29 above or this section he shall be guilty of an offence and liable on summary conviction to a fine not exceeding level 5 on the standard scale.

(6) Where any goods seized by an officer under section 29 above are submitted to a test, the officer shall inform the persons mentioned in subsection (1) above of the result of the test and, if—

    (a)   proceedings are brought for an offence in respect of a contravention in relation to the goods of any safety provision . . . or for the forfeiture of the goods under section 16 or 17 above, or a suspension notice is served in respect of any goods; and

    (b)   the officer is requested to do so and it is practicable to comply with the request,

the officer shall allow any person who is a party to the proceedings or, as the case may be, has an interest in the goods to which the notice relates to have the goods tested.

(7) The Secretary of State may by regulations provide that any test of goods seized under section 29 above by an officer of an enforcement authority shall—

    (a)   be carried out at the expense of the authority in a manner and by a person prescribed by or determined under the regulations; or

    (b)   be carried out either as mentioned in paragraph (a) above or by the authority in a manner prescribed by the regulations.

(8) The power to make regulations under subsection (7) above shall be exercisable by statutory instrument subject to annulment in pursuance of a resolution of either House of Parliament and shall include power—

    (a)   to make different provision for different cases; and

    (b)   to make such supplemental, consequential and transitional provision as the Secretary of State considers appropriate.

(9) *(Applies to Scotland only.)*

(10) In the application of this section to Northern Ireland, the references in subsection (2) above to any information on oath shall be construed as references to any complaint on oath.

NOTES

Sub-s (1): words in italics in each place repealed, and for the figure in italics there is substituted the figure "29(4)" by the Consumer Rights Act 2015, s 77(2), Sch 6, paras 37, 41(1), (2), as from 1 October 2015 (for transitional provisions see the Consumer Rights Act 2015 (Commencement No 3, Transitional Provisions, Savings and Consequential Amendments) Order 2015, SI 2015/1630, arts 6–8 at **[2.1220]** et seq).

Sub-s (2): words in italics repealed, and for the figure in italics there is substituted the figure "29(4)" by the Consumer Rights Act 2015, s 77(2), Sch 6, paras 37, 41(1), (3), as from 1 October 2015 (for transitional provisions see note above); words omitted repealed by the Consumer Protection from Unfair Trading Regulations 2008, SI 2008/1277, reg 30(3), Sch 4.

Sub-s (3): words in italics repealed by the Consumer Rights Act 2015, s 77(2), Sch 6, paras 37, 41(1), (4), as from 1 October 2015 (for transitional provisions see note above).

Sub-ss (5), (7): for the figure in italics there is substituted the figure "29(4)" by the Consumer Rights Act 2015, s 77(2), Sch 6, paras 37, 41(1), (5), as from 1 October 2015 (for transitional provisions see note above).

Sub-s (6): for the figure in italics there is substituted the figure "29(4)" by the Consumer Rights Act 2015, s 77(2), Sch 6, paras 37, 41(1), (5), as from 1 October 2015 (for transitional provisions see note above); words omitted repealed by the Consumer Protection from Unfair Trading Regulations 2008, SI 2008/1277, reg 30(3), Sch 4.

Modification: this section is applied, with modifications, for the purposes of the enforcement of the Supply of Machinery (Safety) Regulations 2008, SI 2008/1597, by SI 2008/1597, reg 20, Sch 5, paras 11, 12, 17, 18.

[1.1006]

31 Power of customs officer to detain goods

(1) A customs officer may, for the purpose of facilitating the exercise by an enforcement authority or officer of such an authority of any functions conferred on the authority or officer by or under Part II of this Act, or by *or under this Part* in its application for the purposes of the safety provisions, seize any imported goods and detain them for not more than two working days.

(2) Anything seized and detained under this section shall be dealt with during the period of its detention in such manner as the Commissioners of Customs and Excise may direct.

(3) In subsection (1) above the reference to two working days is a reference to a period of forty-eight hours calculated from the time when the goods in question are seized but disregarding so much of any period as falls on a Saturday or Sunday or on Christmas Day, Good Friday or a day which is a bank holiday under the Banking and Financial Dealings Act 1971 in the part of the United Kingdom where the goods are seized.

(4) In this section and section 32 below "customs officer" means any officer within the meaning of the Customs and Excise Management Act 1979.

NOTES

Sub-s (1): for the words in italics there are substituted the words "section 29(4) of this Act or Schedule 5 to the Consumer Rights Act 2015" by the Consumer Rights Act 2015, s 77(2), Sch 6, paras 37, 42, as from 1 October 2015 (for transitional provisions see the Consumer Rights Act 2015 (Commencement No 3, Transitional Provisions, Savings and Consequential Amendments) Order 2015, SI 2015/1630, arts 6–8 at **[2.1220]** et seq).

Modification: this section is applied, with modifications, for the purposes of the enforcement of the Supply of Machinery (Safety) Regulations 2008, SI 2008/1597, by SI 2008/1597, reg 20, Sch 5, paras 11, 12, 17, 18.

[1.1007]
32 Obstruction of authorised officer

(1) Any person who—
   (a) intentionally obstructs any officer of an enforcement authority who is acting in pursuance of *any provision of this Part* or any customs officer who is *so acting*; or
   (b) intentionally fails to comply with any requirement made of him by any officer of an enforcement authority under *any provision of this Part*; or
   (c) without reasonable cause fails to give any officer of an enforcement authority who is so acting any other assistance or information which the officer may reasonably require of him for the purposes of the exercise of the officer's functions under *any provision of this Part*,

shall be guilty of an offence and liable on summary conviction to a fine not exceeding level 5 on the standard scale.

(2) A person shall be guilty of an offence if, in giving any information which is required of him by virtue of subsection (1)(c) above—
   (a) he makes any statement which he knows is false in a material particular; or
   (b) he recklessly makes a statement which is false in a material particular.

(3) A person guilty of an offence under subsection (2) above shall be liable—
   (a) on conviction on indictment, to a fine;
   (b) on summary conviction, to a fine not exceeding the statutory maximum.

NOTES

Sub-s (1): for the words in italics there are substituted the words "section 29(4)", "acting in pursuance of section 31", "section 29(4)", and "section 29(4)" respectively, by the Consumer Rights Act 2015, s 77(2), Sch 6, paras 37, 43, as from 1 October 2015 (for transitional provisions see the Consumer Rights Act 2015 (Commencement No 3, Transitional Provisions, Savings and Consequential Amendments) Order 2015, SI 2015/1630, arts 6–8 at **[2.1220]** et seq).

Modification: this section is applied, with modifications, for the purposes of the enforcement of the Supply of Machinery (Safety) Regulations 2008, SI 2008/1597, by SI 2008/1597, reg 20, Sch 5, paras 11, 12, 17, 18.

[1.1008]
33 Appeals against detention of goods

(1) Any person having an interest in any goods which are for the time being detained under *any provision of this Part* by an enforcement authority or by an officer of such an authority may apply for an order requiring the goods to be released to him or to another person.

(2) An application under this section may be made—
   (a) to any magistrates' court in which proceedings have been brought in England and Wales or Northern Ireland—
      (i) for an offence in respect of a contravention in relation to the goods of any safety provision . . . ; or
      (ii) for the forfeiture of the goods under section 16 above;
   (b) where no such proceedings have been so brought, by way of complaint to a magistrates' court; or
   (c) *(applies to Scotland only.)*

(3) On an application under this section to a magistrates' court or to the sheriff, an order requiring goods to be released shall be made only if the court or sheriff is satisfied—
   (a) that proceedings—
      (i) for an offence in respect of a contravention in relation to the goods of any safety provision . . . ; or
      (ii) for the forfeiture of the goods under section 16 or 17 above,
      have not been brought or, having been brought, have been concluded without the goods being forfeited; and
   (b) where no such proceedings have been brought, that more than six months have elapsed since the goods were seized.

(4) Any person aggrieved by an order made under this section by a magistrates' court in England and Wales or Northern Ireland, or by a decision of such a court not to make such an order, may appeal against that order or decision—
   (a) in England and Wales, to the Crown Court;
   (b) in Northern Ireland, to the county court;

and an order so made may contain such provision as appears to the court to be appropriate for delaying the coming into force of the order pending the making and determination of any appeal (including any application under section 111 of the Magistrates' Courts Act 1980 or Article 146 of the Magistrates' Courts (Northern Ireland) Order 1981 (statement of case)).

NOTES

　　Sub-s (1): for the words in italics there are substituted the words "section 29(4)" by the Consumer Rights Act 2015, s 77(2), Sch 6, paras 37, 44, as from 1 October 2015 (for transitional provisions see the Consumer Rights Act 2015 (Commencement No 3, Transitional Provisions, Savings and Consequential Amendments) Order 2015, SI 2015/1630, arts 6–8 at **[2.1220]** et seq).

　　Sub-ss (2), (3): words omitted repealed by the Consumer Protection from Unfair Trading Regulations 2008, SI 2008/1277, reg 30(3), Sch 4.

　　Modification: this section is applied, with modifications, for the purposes of the enforcement of the Supply of Machinery (Safety) Regulations 2008, SI 2008/1597, by SI 2008/1597, reg 20, Sch 5, paras 11, 12, 17, 18.

[1.1009]
34　Compensation for seizure and detention

(1)　Where an officer of an enforcement authority exercises any power under section *29* above to seize and detain goods, the enforcement authority shall be liable to pay compensation to any person having an interest in the goods in respect of any loss or damage caused by reason of the exercise of the power if—

　(a)　there has been no contravention in relation to the goods of any safety provision　. . . ; and

　(b)　the exercise of the power is not attributable to any neglect or default by that person.

(2)　Any disputed question as to the right to or the amount of any compensation payable under this section shall be determined by arbitration or, in Scotland, by a single arbiter appointed, failing agreement between the parties, by the sheriff.

NOTES

　　Sub-s (1): for the figure in italics there is substituted the figure "29(4)" by the Consumer Rights Act 2015, s 77(2), Sch 6, paras 37, 45, as from 1 October 2015 (for transitional provisions see the Consumer Rights Act 2015 (Commencement No 3, Transitional Provisions, Savings and Consequential Amendments) Order 2015, SI 2015/1630, arts 6–8 at **[2.1220]** et seq); words omitted repealed by the Consumer Protection from Unfair Trading Regulations 2008, SI 2008/1277, reg 30(3), Sch 4.

　　Modification: this section is applied, with modifications, for the purposes of the enforcement of the Supply of Machinery (Safety) Regulations 2008, SI 2008/1597, by SI 2008/1597, reg 20, Sch 5, paras 11, 12, 17, 18.

[1.1010]
35　Recovery of expenses of enforcement

(1)　This section shall apply where a court—

　(a)　convicts a person of an offence in respect of a contravention in relation to any goods of any safety provision　. . . ; or

　(b)　makes an order under section 16 or 17 above for the forfeiture of any goods.

(2)　The court may (in addition to any other order it may make as to costs or expenses) order the person convicted or, as the case may be, any person having an interest in the goods to reimburse an enforcement authority for any expenditure which has been or may be incurred by that authority—

　(a)　in connection with any seizure or detention of the goods by or on behalf of the authority; or

　(b)　in connection with any compliance by the authority with directions given by the court for the purposes of any order for the forfeiture of the goods.

NOTES

　　Sub-s (1): words omitted repealed by the Consumer Protection from Unfair Trading Regulations 2008, SI 2008/1277, reg 30(3), Sch 4.

　　Modification: this section is applied, with modifications, for the purposes of the enforcement of the Supply of Machinery (Safety) Regulations 2008, SI 2008/1597, by SI 2008/1597, reg 20, Sch 5, paras 11, 12, 17, 18.

PART V
MISCELLANEOUS AND SUPPLEMENTAL

36　(*Introduces Sch 3, containing amendments to legislation outside the scope of this work.*)

[1.1011]
37　[Power of Commissioners for Revenue and Customs to disclose information]

(1)　If they think it appropriate to do so for the purpose of facilitating the exercise by any person to whom subsection (2) below applies of any functions conferred on that person by or under Part II of this Act, or by or under Part IV of this Act in its application for the purposes of the safety provisions, [the Commissioners for Her Majesty's Revenue and Customs] may authorise the disclosure to that person of any information obtained [or held] for the purposes of the exercise [by Her Majesty's Revenue and Customs] of their functions in relation to imported goods.

(2)　This subsection applies to an enforcement authority and to any officer of an enforcement authority.

(3)　A disclosure of information made to any person under subsection (1) above shall be made in such manner as may be directed by [the Commissioners for Her Majesty's Revenue and Customs] and may be made through such persons acting on behalf of that person as may be so directed.

(4)　Information may be disclosed to a person under subsection (1) above whether or not the disclosure of the information has been requested by or on behalf of that person.

38   *(Repealed by the Enterprise Act 2002, ss 247(g), 278(2), Sch 26; see further, in so far as this section remains in force, the Railways and Transport Safety Act 2003, s 16(5), Sch 2, Pt 2, para 19(k).)*

[1.1012]
39   Defence of due diligence

(1)   Subject to the following provisions of this section, in proceedings against any person for an offence to which this section applies it shall be a defence for that person to show that he took all reasonable steps and exercised all due diligence to avoid committing the offence.

(2)   Where in any proceedings against any person for such an offence the defence provided by subsection (1) above involves an allegation that the commission of the offence was due—

    (a)   to the act or default of another; or

    (b)   to reliance on information given by another,

that person shall not, without the leave of the court, be entitled to rely on the defence unless, not less than seven clear days before the hearing of the proceedings, he has served a notice under subsection (3) below on the person bringing the proceedings.

(3)   A notice under this subsection shall give such information identifying or assisting in the identification of the person who committed the act or default or gave the information as is in the possession of the person serving the notice at the time he serves it.

(4)   It is hereby declared that a person shall not be entitled to rely on the defence provided by subsection (1) above by reason of his reliance on information supplied by another, unless he shows that it was reasonable in all the circumstances for him to have relied on the information, having regard in particular—

    (a)   to the steps which he took, and those which might reasonably have been taken, for the purpose of verifying the information; and

    (b)   to whether he had any reason to disbelieve the information.

(5)   This section shall apply to an offence under section . . . 12(1), (2) or (3), 13(4) [or 14(6)] above.

[1.1013]
40   Liability of persons other than principal offender

(1)   Where the commission by any person of an offence to which section 39 above applies is due to an act or default committed by some other person in the course of any business of his, the other person shall be guilty of the offence and may be proceeded against and punished by virtue of this subsection whether or not proceedings are taken against the first-mentioned person.

(2)   Where a body corporate is guilty of an offence under this Act (including where it is so guilty by virtue of subsection (1) above) in respect of any act or default which is shown to have been committed with the consent or connivance of, or to be attributable to any neglect on the part of, any director, manager, secretary or other similar officer of the body corporate or any person who was purporting to act in any such capacity he, as well as the body corporate, shall be guilty of that offence and shall be liable to be proceeded against and punished accordingly.

(3)   Where the affairs of a body corporate are managed by its members, subsection (2) above shall apply in relation to the acts and defaults of a member in connection with his functions of management as if he were a director of the body corporate.

[1.1014]
41 Civil proceedings

(1) An obligation imposed by safety regulations shall be a duty owed to any person who may be affected by a contravention of the obligation and, subject to any provision to the contrary in the regulations and to the defences and other incidents applying to actions for breach of statutory duty, a contravention of any such obligation shall be actionable accordingly.

(2) This Act shall not be construed as conferring any other right of action in civil proceedings, apart from the right conferred by virtue of Part I of this Act, in respect of any loss or damage suffered in consequence of a contravention of a safety provision . . .

(3) Subject to any provision to the contrary in the agreement itself, an agreement shall not be void or unenforceable by reason only of a contravention of a safety provision . . .

(4) Liability by virtue of subsection (1) above shall not be limited or excluded by any contract term, by any notice or (subject to the power contained in subsection (1) above to limit or exclude it in safety regulations) by any other provision.

(5) Nothing in subsection (1) above shall prejudice the operation of section 12 of the Nuclear Installations Act 1965 (rights to compensation for certain breaches of duties confined to rights under that Act).

(6) In this section "damage" includes personal injury and death.

NOTES

Sub-ss (2), (3): words omitted repealed by the Consumer Protection from Unfair Trading Regulations 2008, SI 2008/1277, reg 30(3), Sch 4.

[1.1015]
42 Reports etc

(1) It shall be the duty of the Secretary of State at least once in every five years to lay before each House of Parliament a report on the exercise during the period to which the report relates of the functions which under Part II of this Act, or under Part IV of this Act in its application for the purposes of the safety provisions, are exercisable by the Secretary of State, weights and measures authorities, district councils in Northern Ireland and persons on whom functions are conferred by regulations made under section 27(2) above.

(2) The Secretary of State may from time to time prepare and lay before each House of Parliament such other reports on the exercise of those functions as he considers appropriate.

(3) Every weights and measures authority, every district council in Northern Ireland and every person on whom functions are conferred by regulations under subsection (2) of section 27 above shall, whenever the Secretary of State so directs, make a report to the Secretary of State on the exercise of the functions exercisable by that authority or council under that section or by that person by virtue of any such regulations.

(4) A report under subsection (3) above shall be in such form and shall contain such particulars as are specified in the direction of the Secretary of State.

(5) The first report under subsection (1) above shall be laid before each House of Parliament not more than five years after the laying of the last report under section 8(2) of the Consumer Safety Act 1978.

[1.1016]
43 Financial provisions

(1) There shall be paid out of money provided by Parliament—

 (a) any expenses incurred or compensation payable by a Minister of the Crown or Government department in consequence of any provision of this Act; and

 (b) any increase attributable to this Act in the sums payable out of money so provided under any other Act.

(2) Any sums received by a Minister of the Crown or Government department by virtue of this Act shall be paid into the Consolidated Fund.

[1.1017]
44 Service of documents etc

(1) Any document required or authorised by virtue of this Act to be served on a person may be so served—

 (a) by delivering it to him or by leaving it at his proper address or by sending it by post to him at that address; or

 (b) if the person is a body corporate, by serving it in accordance with paragraph (a) above on the secretary or clerk of that body; or

 (c) if the person is a partnership, by serving it in accordance with that paragraph on a partner or on a person having control or management of the partnership business.

(2) For the purposes of subsection (1) above, and for the purposes of section 7 of the Interpretation Act 1978 (which relates to the service of documents by post) in its application to that subsection, the proper address of any person on whom a document is to be served by virtue of this Act shall be his last known address except that—

(a) in the case of service on a body corporate or its secretary or clerk, it shall be the address of the registered or principal office of the body corporate;

(b) in the case of service on a partnership or a partner or a person having the control or management of a partnership business, it shall be the principal office of the partnership;

and for the purposes of this subsection the principal officer of a company registered outside the United Kingdom or of a partnership carrying on business outside the United Kingdom is its principal office within the United Kingdom.

(3) The Secretary of State may by regulations make provision for the manner in which any information is to be given to any person under any provision of Part IV of this Act.

(4) Without prejudice to the generality of subsection (3) above regulations made by the Secretary of State may prescribe the person, or manner of determining the person, who is to be treated for the purposes of section *28(2) or* 30 above as the person from whom any goods were *purchased or* seized where the goods were *purchased or* seized from a vending machine.

(5) The power to make regulations under subsection (3) or (4) above shall be exercisable by statutory instrument subject to annulment in pursuance of a resolution of either House of Parliament and shall include power—

(a) to make different provision for different cases; and

(b) to make such supplemental, consequential and transitional provision as the Secretary of State considers appropriate.

NOTES

Sub-s (4): words in italics repealed by the Consumer Rights Act 2015, s 77(2), Sch 6, paras 37, 46, as from 1 October 2015 (for transitional provisions see the Consumer Rights Act 2015 (Commencement No 3, Transitional Provisions, Savings and Consequential Amendments) Order 2015, SI 2015/1630, arts 6–8 at **[2.1220]** et seq).

Modification: this section is applied, with modifications, for the purposes of the enforcement of the Supply of Machinery (Safety) Regulations 2008, SI 2008/1597, by SI 2008/1597, reg 20, Sch 5, paras 11, 12, 17, 18.

[1.1018]
45 Interpretation
(1) In this Act, except in so far as the context otherwise requires—

"aircraft" includes gliders, balloons and hovercraft;

"business" includes a trade or profession and the activities of a professional or trade association or of a local authority or other public authority;

"conditional sale agreement", "credit-sale agreement" and "hire-purchase agreement" have the same meanings as in the Consumer Credit Act 1974 but as if in the definitions in that Act "goods" had the same meaning as in this Act;

"contravention" includes a failure to comply and cognate expressions shall be construed accordingly;

"enforcement authority" means the Secretary of State, any other Minister of the Crown in charge of a Government department, any such department and any authority, council or other person on whom functions under this Act are conferred by or under section 27 above;

"gas" has the same meaning as in Part I of the Gas Act 1986;

"goods" includes substances, growing crops and things comprised in land by virtue of being attached to it and any ship, aircraft or vehicle;

"information" includes accounts, estimates and returns;

"magistrates' court", in relation to Northern Ireland, means a court of summary jurisdiction;

. . .

"modifications" includes additions, alterations and omissions, and cognate expressions shall be construed accordingly;

"motor vehicle" has the same meaning as in [the Road Traffic Act 1988];

"notice" means a notice in writing;

"notice to warn" means a notice under section 13(1)(b) above;

"officer", in relation to an enforcement authority, means a person authorised in writing to assist the authority in carrying out its functions under or for the purposes of the enforcement of any of the safety provisions or of any of the provisions made by or under Part III of this Act;

"personal injury" includes any disease and any other impairment of a person's physical or mental condition;

"premises" includes any place and any ship, aircraft or vehicle;

"prohibition notice" means a notice under section 13(1)(a) above;

"records" includes any books or documents and any records in non-documentary form;

"safety provision" means . . . any provision of safety regulations, a prohibition notice or a suspension notice;

"safety regulations" means regulations under section 11 above;

"ship" includes any boat and any other description of vessel used in navigation;

"subordinate legislation" has the same meaning as in the Interpretation Act 1978;

"substance" means any natural or artificial substance, whether in solid, liquid or gaseous form or in the form of a vapour, and includes substances that are comprised in or mixed with other goods;

"supply" and cognate expressions shall be construed in accordance with section 46 below;
"suspension notice" means a notice under section 14 above.

(2)   Except in so far as the context otherwise requires, references in this Act to a contravention of a safety provision shall, in relation to any goods, include references to anything which would constitute such a contravention if the goods were supplied to any person.

(3)   References in this Act to any goods in relation to which any safety provision has been or may have been contravened shall include references to any goods which it is not reasonably practicable to separate from any such goods.

(4)   . . .

(5)   (*Applies to Scotland only.*)

NOTES

Sub-s (1): definitions "mark" and "trade mark" (omitted) repealed by the Trade Marks Act 1994, s 106(2), Sch 5; words in square brackets in definition "motor vehicle" substituted by the Road Traffic (Consequential Provisions) Act 1988, s 4, Sch 3, para 35; in definition "safety provision" words omitted repealed by the General Product Safety Regulations 2005, SI 2005/1803, reg 46(1), (7).

Sub-s (4): repealed by the Trade Marks Act 1994, s 106(2), Sch 5.

[1.1019]
46   Meaning of "supply"

(1)   Subject to the following provisions of this section, references in this Act to supplying goods shall be construed as references to doing any of the following, whether as principal or agent, that is to say—

    (a)   selling, hiring out or lending the goods;

    (b)   entering into a hire-purchase agreement to furnish the goods;

    (c)   the performance of any contract for work and materials to furnish the goods;

    (d)   providing the goods in exchange for any consideration   . . .   other than money;

    (e)   providing the goods in or in connection with the performance of any statutory function; or

    (f)   giving the goods as a prize or otherwise making a gift of the goods;

and, in relation to gas or water, those references shall be construed as including references to providing the service by which the gas or water is made available for use.

(2)   For the purposes of any reference in this Act to supplying goods, where a person ("the ostensible supplier") supplies goods to another person ("the customer") under a hire-purchase agreement, conditional sale agreement or credit-sale agreement or under an agreement for the hiring of goods (other than a hire-purchase agreement) and the ostensible supplier—

    (a)   carries on the business of financing the provision of goods for others by means of such agreements; and

    (b)   in the course of that business acquired his interest in the goods supplied to the customer as a means of financing the provision of them for the customer by a further person ("the effective supplier"),

the effective supplier and not the ostensible supplier shall be treated as supplying the goods to the customer.

(3)   Subject to subsection (4) below, the performance of any contract by the erection of any building or structure on any land or by the carrying out of any other building works shall be treated for the purposes of this Act as a supply of goods in so far as, but only in so far as, it involves the provision of any goods to any person by means of their incorporation into the building, structure or works.

(4)   Except for the purposes of, and in relation to, notices to warn   . . . , references in this Act to supplying goods shall not include references to supplying goods comprised in land where the supply is effected by the creation or disposal of an interest in the land.

(5)   Except in Part I of this Act references in this Act to a person's supplying goods shall be confined to references to that person's supplying goods in the course of a business of his, but for the purposes of this subsection it shall be immaterial whether the business is a business of dealing in the goods.

(6)   For the purposes of subsection (5) above goods shall not be treated as supplied in the course of a business if they are supplied, in pursuance of an obligation arising under or in connection with the insurance of the goods, to the person with whom they were insured.

(7)   Except for the purposes of, and in relation to, prohibition notices or suspension notices, references in [Part 2 or Part 4] of this Act to supplying goods shall not include—

    (a)   references to supplying goods where the person supplied carries on a business of buying goods of the same description as those goods and repairing or reconditioning them;

    (b)   references to supplying goods by a sale of articles as scrap (that is to say, for the value of materials included in the articles rather than for the value of the articles themselves).

(8)   Where any goods have at any time been supplied by being hired out or lent to any person, neither a continuation or renewal of the hire or loan (whether on the same or different terms) nor any transaction for the transfer after that time of any interest in the goods to the person to whom they were hired or lent shall be treated for the purposes of this Act as a further supply of the goods to that person.

(9)   A ship, aircraft or motor vehicle shall not be treated for the purposes of this Act as supplied to any person by reason only that services consisting in the carriage of goods or passengers in that ship, aircraft or vehicle, or in its use for any other purpose, are provided to that person in pursuance of an agreement relating to the use of the ship, aircraft or vehicle for a particular period or for particular voyages, flights or journeys.

NOTES

Sub-s (1): words omitted from para (d) repealed in relation to England, Wales and Scotland by the Regulatory Reform (Trading Stamps) Order 2005, SI 2005/871, art 6, Schedule, and in relation to Northern Ireland by the Law Reform (Miscellaneous Provisions) (Northern Ireland) Order 2005, SI 2005/1452, art 24, Sch 2.

Sub-s (4): words omitted repealed by the Consumer Protection from Unfair Trading Regulations 2008, SI 2008/1277, reg 30(3), Sch 4.

Sub-s (7): words in square brackets substituted by SI 2008/1277, reg 30(1), Sch 2, Pt 1, paras 33, 37.

[1.1020]
47   Savings for certain privileges
(1)   Nothing in this Act shall be taken as requiring any person to produce any records if he would be entitled to refuse to produce those records in any proceedings in any court on the grounds that they are the subject of legal professional privilege or, in Scotland, that they contain a confidential communication made by or to an advocate or solicitor in that capacity, or as authorising any person to take possession of any records which are in the possession of a person who would be so entitled.
(2)   Nothing in this Act shall be construed as requiring a person to answer any question or give any information if to do so would incriminate that person or that person's spouse [or civil partner].

NOTES

Sub-s (2): words in square brackets inserted by the Civil Partnership Act 2004, s 261(1), Sch 27, para 126.

Modification: this section is applied, with modifications, for the purposes of the enforcement of the Supply of Machinery (Safety) Regulations 2008, SI 2008/1597, by SI 2008/1597, reg 20, Sch 5, paras 11, 12, 17, 18.

[1.1021]
48   Minor and consequential amendments and repeals
(1)   The enactments mentioned in Schedule 4 to this Act shall have effect subject to the amendments specified in that Schedule (being minor amendments and amendments consequential on the provisions of this Act).
(2)   The following Acts shall cease to have effect, that is to say—
   (a)   the Trade Descriptions Act 1972; and
   (b)   the Fabrics (Misdescription) Act 1913.
(3)   The enactments mentioned in Schedule 5 to this Act are hereby repealed to the extent specified in the third column of that Schedule.

[1.1022]
49   Northern Ireland
(1)   This Act shall extend to Northern Ireland with the exception of—
   (a)   the provisions of [Part 1];
   (b)   any provision amending or repealing an enactment which does not so extend; and
   (c)   any other provision so far as it has effect for the purposes of, or in relation to, a provision falling within paragraph (a) or (b) above.
(2)   . . .
(3)   An Order in Council under paragraph 1(1)(b) of Schedule 1 to the Northern Ireland Act 1974 (exercise of legislative functions for Northern Ireland) which states that it is made only for purposes corresponding to any of the provisions of this Act mentioned in subsection (1)(a) to (c) above—
   (a)   shall not be subject to paragraph 1(4) and (5) of that Schedule (affirmative resolution procedure and procedure in cases of urgency); but
   (b)   shall be subject to annulment in pursuance of a resolution of either House of Parliament.

NOTES

Sub-s (1): words in square brackets in para (a) substituted by the Consumer Protection from Unfair Trading Regulations 2008, SI 2008/1277, reg 30(1), Sch 2, Pt 1, paras 33, 37.

Sub-s (2): repealed by the Northern Ireland Act 1998, s 100(2), Sch 15.

[1.1023]
50   Short title, commencement and transitional provision
(1)   This Act may be cited as the Consumer Protection Act 1987.
(2)   This Act shall come into force on such day as the Secretary of State may by order made by statutory instrument appoint, and different days may be so appointed for different provisions or for different purposes.
(3)   The Secretary of State shall not make an order under subsection (2) above bringing into force the repeal of the Trade Descriptions Act 1972, a repeal of any provision of that Act or a repeal of that Act or of any provision of it for any purposes, unless a draft of the order has been laid before, and approved by a resolution of, each House of Parliament.

(4)   An order under subsection (2) above bringing a provision into force may contain such transitional provision in connection with the coming into force of that provision as the Secretary of State considers appropriate.

(5)   Without prejudice to the generality of the power conferred by subsection (4) above, the Secretary of State may by order provide for any regulations made under the Consumer Protection Act 1961 or the Consumer Protection Act (Northern Ireland) 1965 to have effect as if made under section 11 above and for any such regulations to have effect with such modifications as he considers appropriate for that purpose.

(6)   The power of the Secretary of State by order to make such provision as is mentioned in subsection (5) above, shall, in so far as it is not exercised by an order under subsection (2) above, be exercisable by statutory instrument subject to annulment in pursuance of a resolution of either House of Parliament.

(7)   Nothing in this Act or in any order under subsection (2) above shall make any person liable by virtue of Part I of this Act for any damage caused wholly or partly by a defect in a product which was supplied to any person by its producer before the coming into force of Part I of this Act.

(8)   Expressions used in subsection (7) above and in Part I of this Act have the same meanings in that subsection as in that Part.

NOTES

Trade Descriptions Act 1972: repealed by s 48(2), (3) of, and Sch 5 to, this Act.

Orders: the Consumer Protection Act 1987 (Commencement No 1) Order 1987, SI 1987/1680; the Consumer Protection Act 1987 (Commencement No 2) Order 1988, SI 1988/2041; the Consumer Protection Act 1987 (Commencement No 3) Order 1988, SI 1988/2076.

SCHEDULES

SCHEDULE 1

(Sch 1: Pt I amends the Limitation Act 1980; Pt II applies to Scotland only.)

SCHEDULE 2
PROHIBITION NOTICES AND NOTICES TO WARN

Section 13

PART I
PROHIBITION NOTICES

[1.1024]

1.   A prohibition notice in respect of any goods shall—

  (a)   state that the Secretary of State considers that the goods are unsafe;

  (b)   set out the reasons why the Secretary of State considers that the goods are unsafe;

  (c)   specify the day on which the notice is to come into force; and

  (d)   state that the trader may at any time make representations in writing to the Secretary of State for the purpose of establishing that the goods are safe.

2.   (1)   If representations in writing about a prohibition notice are made by the trader to the Secretary of State, it shall be the duty of the Secretary of State to consider whether to revoke the notice and—

  (a)   if he decides to revoke it, to do so;

  (b)   in any other case, to appoint a person to consider those representations, any further representations made (whether in writing or orally) by the trader about the notice and the statements of any witnesses examined under this Part of this Schedule.

(2)   Where the Secretary of State has appointed a person to consider representations about a prohibition notice, he shall serve a notification on the trader which—

  (a)   states that the trader may make oral representations to the appointed person for the purpose of establishing that the goods to which the notice relates are safe; and

  (b)   specifies the place and time at which the oral representations may be made.

(3)   The time specified in a notification served under sub-paragraph (2) above shall not be before the end of the period of twenty-one days beginning with the day on which the notification is served, unless the trader otherwise agrees.

(4)   A person on whom a notification has been served under sub-paragraph (2) above or his representative may, at the place and time specified in the notification—

  (a)   make oral representations to the appointed person for the purpose of establishing that the goods in question are safe; and

  (b)   call and examine witnesses in connection with the representations.

3. (1)   Where representations in writing about a prohibition notice are made by the trader to the Secretary of State at any time after a person has been appointed to consider representations about that notice, then, whether or not the appointed person has made a report to the Secretary of State, the following provisions of this paragraph shall apply instead of paragraph 2 above.

(2)   The Secretary of State shall, before the end of the period of one month beginning with the day on which he receives the representations, serve a notification on the trader which states—

(a)   that the Secretary of State has decided to revoke the notice, has decided to vary it or, as the case may be, has decided neither to revoke nor to vary it; or

(b)   that, a person having been appointed to consider representations about the notice, the trader may, at a place and time specified in the notification, make oral representations to the appointed person for the purpose of establishing that the goods to which the notice relates are safe.

(3)   The time specified in a notification served for the purposes of sub-paragraph (2)(b) above shall not be before the end of the period of twenty-one days beginning with the day on which the notification is served, unless the trader otherwise agrees or the time is the time already specified for the purposes of paragraph 2(2)(b) above.

(4)   A person on whom a notification has been served for the purposes of sub-paragraph (2)(b) above or his representative may, at the place and time specified in the notification—

(a)   make oral representations to the appointed person for the purpose of establishing that the goods in question are safe; and

(b)   call and examine witnesses in connection with the representations.

4. (1)   Where a person is appointed to consider representations about a prohibition notice, it shall be his duty to consider—

(a)   any written representations made by the trader about the notice, other than those in respect of which a notification is served under paragraph 3(2)(a) above;

(b)   any oral representations made under paragraph 2(4) or 3(4) above; and

(c)   any statements made by witnesses in connection with the oral representations,

and, after considering any matters under this paragraph, to make a report (including recommendations) to the Secretary of State about the matters considered by him and the notice.

(2)   It shall be the duty of the Secretary of State to consider any report made to him under sub-paragraph (1) above and, after considering the report, to inform the trader of his decision with respect to the prohibition notice to which the report relates.

5. (1)   The Secretary of State may revoke or vary a prohibition notice by serving on the trader a notification stating that the notice is revoked or, as the case may be, is varied as specified in the notification.

(2)   The Secretary of State shall not vary a prohibition notice so as to make the effect of the notice more restrictive for the trader.

(3)   Without prejudice to the power conferred by section 13(2) of this Act, the service of a notification under sub-paragraph (1) above shall be sufficient to satisfy the requirement of paragraph 4(2) above that the trader shall be informed of the Secretary of State's decision.

PART II
NOTICES TO WARN

[1.1025]
6. (1)   If the Secretary of State proposes to serve a notice to warn on any person in respect of any goods, the Secretary of State, before he serves the notice, shall serve on that person a notification which—

(a)   contains a draft of the proposed notice;

(b)   states that the Secretary of State proposes to serve a notice in the form of the draft on that person;

(c)   states that the Secretary of State considers that the goods described in the draft are unsafe;

(d)   sets out the reasons why the Secretary of State considers that those goods are unsafe; and

(e)   states that that person may make representations to the Secretary of State for the purpose of establishing that the goods are safe if, before the end of the period of fourteen days beginning with the day on which the notification is served, he informs the Secretary of State—

(i)   of his intention to make representations; and

(ii)   whether the representations will be made only in writing or both in writing and orally.

(2)   Where the Secretary of State has served a notification containing a draft of a proposed notice to warn on any person, he shall not serve a notice to warn on that person in respect of the goods to which the proposed notice relates unless—

(a)   the period of fourteen days beginning with the day on which the notification was served expires without the Secretary of State being informed as mentioned in sub-paragraph (1)(e) above;

(b) the period of twenty-eight days beginning with that day expires without any written representations being made by that person to the Secretary of State about the proposed notice; or

(c) the Secretary of State has considered a report about the proposed notice by a person appointed under paragraph 7(1) below.

7. (1) Where a person on whom a notification containing a draft of a proposed notice to warn has been served—

(a) informs the Secretary of State as mentioned in paragraph 6(1)(e) above before the end of the period of fourteen days beginning with the day on which the notification was served; and

(b) makes written representations to the Secretary of State about the proposed notice before the end of the period of twenty-eight days beginning with that day,

the Secretary of State shall appoint a person to consider those representations, any further representations made by that person about the draft notice and the statements of any witnesses examined under this Part of this Schedule.

(2) Where—

(a) the Secretary of State has appointed a person to consider representations about a proposed notice to warn; and

(b) the person whose representations are to be considered has informed the Secretary of State for the purposes of paragraph 6(1)(e) above that the representations he intends to make will include oral representations,

the Secretary of State shall inform the person intending to make the representations of the place and time at which oral representations may be made to the appointed person.

(3) Where a person on whom a notification containing a draft of a proposed notice to warn has been served is informed of a time for the purposes of sub-paragraph (2) above, that time shall not be—

(a) before the end of the period of twenty-eight days beginning with the day on which the notification was served; or

(b) before the end of the period of seven days beginning with the day on which that person is informed of the time.

(4) A person who has been informed of a place and time for the purposes of sub-paragraph (2) above or his representative may, at that place and time—

(a) make oral representations to the appointed person for the purpose of establishing that the goods to which the proposed notice relates are safe; and

(b) call and examine witnesses in connection with the representations.

8. (1) Where a person is appointed to consider representations about a proposed notice to warn, it shall be his duty to consider—

(a) any written representations made by the person on whom it is proposed to serve the notice; and

(b) in a case where a place and time has been appointed under paragraph 7(2) above for oral representations to be made by that person or his representative, any representations so made and any statements made by witnesses in connection with those representations,

and, after considering those matters, to make a report (including recommendations) to the Secretary of State about the matters considered by him and the proposal to serve the notice.

(2) It shall be the duty of the Secretary of State to consider any report made to him under sub-paragraph (1) above and, after considering the report, to inform the person on whom it was proposed that a notice to warn should be served of his decision with respect to the proposal.

(3) If at any time after serving a notification on a person under paragraph 6 above the Secretary of State decides not to serve on that person either the proposed notice to warn or that notice with modifications, the Secretary of State shall inform that person of the decision; and nothing done for the purposes of any of the preceding provisions of this Part of this Schedule before that person was so informed shall—

(a) entitle the Secretary of State subsequently to serve the proposed notice or that notice with modifications; or

(b) require the Secretary of State, or any person appointed to consider representations about the proposed notice, subsequently to do anything in respect of, or in consequence of, any such representations.

(4) Where a notification containing a draft of a proposed notice to warn is served on a person in respect of any goods, a notice to warn served on him in consequence of a decision made under sub-paragraph (2) above shall either be in the form of the draft or shall be less onerous than the draft.

9. The Secretary of State may revoke a notice to warn by serving on the person on whom the notice was served a notification stating that the notice is revoked.

PART III
GENERAL

[1.1026]

10. (1) Where in a notification served on any person under this Schedule the Secretary of State has appointed a time for the making of oral representations or the examination of witnesses, he may, by giving that person such notification as the Secretary of State considers appropriate, change that time to a later time or appoint further times at which further representations may be made or the examination of witnesses may be continued; and paragraphs 2(4), 3(4) and 7(4) above shall have effect accordingly.

(2) For the purposes of this Schedule the Secretary of State may appoint a person (instead of the appointed person) to consider any representations or statements, if the person originally appointed, or last appointed under this sub-paragraph, to consider those representations or statements has died or appears to the Secretary of State to be otherwise unable to act.

11. In this Schedule—
　　"the appointed person" in relation to a prohibition notice or a proposal to serve a notice to warn, means the person for the time being appointed under this Schedule to consider representations about the notice or, as the case may be, about the proposed notice;
　　"notification" means a notification in writing;
　　"trader", in relation to a prohibition notice, means the person on whom the notice is or was served.

SCHEDULES 3–5

(Schs 3–5 outside the scope of this work.)

LAW OF PROPERTY (MISCELLANEOUS PROVISIONS) ACT 1989

(1989 c 34)

ARRANGEMENT OF SECTIONS

An Act to make new provisions with respect to deeds and their execution and contracts for the sale or other disposition of interests in land; and to abolish the rule of law known as the rule in Bain v Fothergill

[27 July 1989]

[1.1027]
1 Deeds and their execution
(1) Any rule of law which—
　　(a)　restricts the substances on which a deed may be written;
　　(b)　requires a seal for the valid execution of an instrument as a deed by an individual; or
　　(c)　requires authority by one person to another to deliver an instrument as a deed on his behalf to be given by deed,
is abolished.
(2) An instrument shall not be a deed unless—
　　(a)　it makes it clear on its face that it is intended to be a deed by the person making it or, as the case may be, by the parties to it (whether by describing itself as a deed or expressing itself to be executed or signed as a deed or otherwise); and
　　(b)　it is validly executed as a deed[—
　　　　(i)　by that person or a person authorised to execute it in the name or on behalf of that person, or
　　　　(ii)　by one or more of those parties or a person authorised to execute it in the name or on behalf of one or more of those parties.]
[(2A) For the purposes of subsection (2)(a) above, an instrument shall not be taken to make it clear on its face that it is intended to be a deed merely because it is executed under seal.]
(3) An instrument is validly executed as a deed by an individual if, and only if—
　　(a)　it is signed—
　　　　(i)　by him in the presence of a witness who attests the signature; or
　　　　(ii)　at his direction and in his presence and the presence of two witnesses who each attest the signature; and

(b)   it is delivered as a deed . . .

(4)   In subsections (2) and (3) above "sign", in relation to an instrument, includes—

[(a)   an individual signing the name of the person or party on whose behalf he executes the instrument; and

(b)   making one's mark on the instrument,

and "signature" is to be construed accordingly.]

[(4A)   Subsection (3) above applies in the case of an instrument executed by an individual in the name or on behalf of another person whether or not that person is also an individual.]

(5)   Where [a relevant lawyer, or an agent or employee of a relevant lawyer], in the course of or in connection with a transaction . . . , purports to deliver an instrument as a deed on behalf of a party to the instrument, it shall be conclusively presumed in favour of a purchaser that he is authorised so to deliver the instrument.

(6)   In subsection (5) above—

["purchaser" has the same meaning] as in the Law of Property Act 1925;

["relevant lawyer" means a person who, for the purposes of the Legal Services Act 2007, is an authorised person in relation to an activity which constitutes a reserved instrument activity (within the meaning of that Act).]

. . .

(7)   Where an instrument under seal that constitutes a deed is required for the purposes of an Act passed before this section comes into force, this section shall have effect as to signing, sealing or delivery of an instrument by an individual in place of any provision of that Act as to signing, sealing or delivery.

(8)   The enactments mentioned in Schedule 1 to this Act (which in consequence of this section require amendments other than those provided by subsection (7) above) shall have effect with the amendments specified in that Schedule.

(9)   Nothing in subsection (1)(b), (2), (3), (7) or (8) above applies in relation to deeds required or authorised to be made under—

(a)   the seal of the county palatine of Lancaster;

(b)   the seal of the Duchy of Lancaster; or

(c)   the seal of the Duchy of Cornwall.

(10)   The references in this section to the execution of a deed by an individual do not include execution by a corporation sole and the reference in subsection (7) above to signing, sealing or delivery by an individual does not include signing, sealing or delivery by such a corporation.

(11)   Nothing in this section applies in relation to instruments delivered as deeds before this section comes into force.

NOTES

Sub-s (2): in sub-para (b) words in square brackets substituted, except in relation to any instrument executed before 15 September 2005, by the Regulatory Reform (Execution of Deeds and Documents) Order 2005, SI 2005/1906, art 7(3).

Sub-ss (2A), (4A): inserted, except in relation to any instrument executed before 15 September 2005, by SI 2005/1906, arts 7(4), 8.

Sub-s (3): words omitted repealed, except in relation to any instrument executed before 15 September 2005, by SI 2005/1906, art 10(2), Sch 2.

Sub-s (4): words in square brackets substituted, except in relation to any instrument executed before 15 September 2005, by SI 2005/1906, art 10(1), Sch 1, paras 13, 14.

Sub-s (5): words in square brackets substituted by the Legal Services Act 2007, s 208(1), Sch 21, para 81(a); words omitted repealed, except in relation to any instrument executed before 15 September 2005, by SI 2005/1906, arts 9, 10(2), Sch 2.

Sub-s (6): in definition "purchaser" words in square brackets substituted, and definition "interest in land" (omitted) repealed, except in relation to any instrument executed before 15 September 2005, by SI 2005/1906, art 10, Sch 1, paras 13, 15, Sch 2; definition "relevant lawyer" substituted (for definition "duly certificated notary public" as inserted by the Courts and Legal Services Act 1990, s 125(2), Sch 17, para 20) by the Legal Services Act 2007, s 208(1), Sch 21, para 81(b).

[1.1028]
2   Contracts for sale etc of land to be made by signed writing

(1)   A contract for the sale or other disposition of an interest in land can only be made in writing and only by incorporating all the terms which the parties have expressly agreed in one document or, where contracts are exchanged, in each.

(2)   The terms may be incorporated in a document either by being set out in it or by reference to some other document.

(3)   The document incorporating the terms or, where contracts are exchanged, one of the documents incorporating them (but not necessarily the same one) must be signed by or on behalf of each party to the contract.

(4)   Where a contract for the sale or other disposition of an interest in land satisfies the conditions of this section by reason only of the rectification of one or more documents in pursuance of an order of a court, the contract shall come into being, or be deemed to have come into being, at such time as may be specified in the order.

(5)   This section does not apply in relation to—

(a)   a contract to grant such a lease as is mentioned in section 54(2) of the Law of Property Act 1925 (short leases);

(b)   a contract made in the course of a public auction; or

[(c) a contract regulated under the Financial Services and Markets Act 2000, other than a regulated mortgage contract[, a regulated home reversion plan, a regulated home purchase plan or a regulated sale and rent back agreement];]

and nothing in this section affects the creation or operation of resulting, implied or constructive trusts.

(6) In this section—

"disposition" has the same meaning as in the Law of Property Act 1925;

"interest in land" means any estate, interest or charge in or over land . . .

["regulated mortgage contract"[, "regulated home reversion plan"[, "regulated home purchase plan" and "regulated sale and rent back agreement"]] must be read with—

(a) section 22 of the Financial Services and Markets Act 2000,

(b) any relevant order under that section, and

(c) Schedule 22 to that Act.]

(7) Nothing in this section shall apply in relation to contracts made before this section comes into force.

(8) Section 40 of the Law of Property Act 1925 (which is superseded by this section) shall cease to have effect.

NOTES

Sub-s (5): para (c) substituted by the Financial Services and Markets Act 2000 (Consequential Amendments and Repeals) Order 2001, SI 2001/3649, art 317(1), (2); words in square brackets in para (c) substituted by the Financial Services and Markets Act 2000 (Regulated Activities) (Amendment) Order 2009, SI 2009/1342, art 24(a).

Sub-s (6): words omitted from definition "interest in land" repealed by the Trusts of Land and Appointment of Trustees Act 1996, s 25(2), Sch 4, for savings in connection with the abolition of the doctrine of conversion, see ss 3, 18(3), 25(5) of the 1996 Act; definition "regulated mortgage contract" inserted by SI 2001/3649, art 317(1), (3), first (outer) words in square brackets inserted by the Financial Services and Markets Act 2000 (Regulated Activities) (Amendment) (No 2) Order 2006, SI 2006/2383, art 27(b), subject to transitional provisions in arts 37–39 of that Order, words in second (inner) pair of square brackets substituted by SI 2009/1342, art 24(b).

[1.1029]

3 Abolition of rule in Bain v Fothergill

The rule of law known as the rule in Bain v Fothergill is abolished in relation to contracts made after this section comes into force.

4 (*Introduces Sch 2 (repeals) outside the scope of this work.*)

[1.1030]

5 Commencement

(1) The provisions of this Act to which this subsection applies shall come into force on such day as the Lord Chancellor may by order made by statutory instrument appoint.

(2) The provisions to which subsection (1) above applies are—

(a) section 1 above; and

(b) section 4 above, except so far as it relates to section 40 of the Law of Property Act 1925.

(3) The provisions of this Act to which this subsection applies shall come into force at the end of the period of two months beginning with the day on which this Act is passed.

(4) The provisions of this Act to which subsection (3) above applies are—

(a) sections 2 and 3 above; and

(b) section 4 above, so far as it relates to section 40 of the Law of Property Act 1925.

NOTES

Orders: the Law of Property (Miscellaneous Provisions) Act 1989 (Commencement) Order 1990, SI 1990/1175.

[1.1031]

6 Citation

(1) This Act may be cited as the Law of Property (Miscellaneous Provisions) Act 1989.

(2) This Act extends to England and Wales only.

SCHEDULES

SCHEDULES 1, 2

(*Sch 1 repealed in part; remainder amends the Law of Property Act 1925, ss 52(2)(e), 74(2), 80(1), 81, and the Powers of Attorney Act 1971, ss 1, 7 at* **[1.474]**, **[1.479]***; Sch 2 (repeals) outside the scope of this work.*)

FOOD SAFETY ACT 1990

(1990 c 16)

ARRANGEMENT OF SECTIONS

An Act to make new provision in place of the Food Act 1984 (except Parts III and V), the Food and Drugs (Scotland) Act 1956 and certain other enactments relating to food; to amend Parts III and

V of the said Act of 1984 and Part I of the Food and Environment Protection Act 1985; and for connected purposes

[29 June 1990]

NOTES

The Act confers extensive powers to make subordinate legislation. Considerations of space preclude reference to all orders and regulations made under the Act. For details of orders and regulations made under the Act, and for modifications to the Act made by specific orders and regulations, specialist works on food and food safety should be consulted.

Transfer of functions in relation to Wales: as to the transfer of functions under this Act from Ministers of the Crown to the National Assembly for Wales, see the National Assembly for Wales (Transfer of Functions) Order 1999, SI 1999/672.

By the Transfer of Functions (Agriculture and Food) Order 1999, SI 1999/3141, arts 2(6), (7), 3, any function under this Act which is exercisable by the Minister of Agriculture, Fisheries and Food jointly with the Secretaries of State respectively concerned with health in England and food and health in Wales is hereby transferred to the Minister of Agriculture, Fisheries and Food and the Secretary of State acting jointly. The Minister for Agriculture, Fisheries and Food is now the Secretary of State for Environment, Food and Rural Affairs; see in general, the Secretaries of State for Transport, Local Government and the Regions and for Environment, Food and Rural Affairs Order 2001, SI 2001/2568. Note however, that by the Food Standards Act 1999, s 26(1), the functions of the Minister of Agriculture, Fisheries and Food under this Act ceased to be exercisable by that Minister on 1 April 2000. By s 26(3) of the 1999 Act, enforcement functions under directions or subordinate legislation made under this Act (or any power under this Act to confer such functions in directions or subordinate legislation) are unaffected.

PART I
PRELIMINARY

[1.1032]
1   Meaning of "food" and other basic expressions
[(1)   In this Act "food" has the same meaning as it has in Regulation (EC) No 178/2002.
(2)   In this Act "Regulation (EC) No 178/2002" means Regulation (EC) No 178/2002 of the European Parliament and of the Council laying down the general principles and requirements of food law, establishing the European Food Safety Authority and laying down procedures in matters of food safety.]
(3)   In this Act, unless the context otherwise requires—
"business" includes the undertaking of a canteen, club, school, hospital or institution, whether carried on for profit or not, and any undertaking or activity carried on by a public or local authority;
"commercial operation", in relation to any food or contact material, means any of the following, namely—
(a)   selling, possessing for sale and offering, exposing or advertising for sale;
(b)   consigning, delivering or serving by way of sale;
(c)   preparing for sale or presenting, labelling or wrapping for the purpose of sale;
(d)   storing or transporting for the purpose of sale;
(e)   importing and exporting;
and, in relation to any food source, means deriving food from it for the purpose of sale or for purposes connected with sale;
"contact material" means any article or substance which is intended to come into contact with food;
"food business" means any business in the course of which commercial operations with respect to food or food sources are carried out;
"food premises" means any premises used for the purposes of a food business;
"food source" means any growing crop or live animal, bird or fish from which food is intended to be derived (whether by harvesting, slaughtering, milking, collecting eggs or otherwise);
"premises" includes any place, any vehicle, stall or moveable structure and, for such purposes as may be specified in an order made by [the Secretary of State], any ship or aircraft of a description so specified.
(4)   The reference in subsection (3) above to preparing for sale shall be construed, in relation to any contact material, as a reference to manufacturing or producing for the purpose of sale.

NOTES

Sub-s (1), (2): substituted by the Food Safety Act 1990 (Amendment) Regulations 2004, SI 2004/2990, regs 2, 3.

Sub-s (3): in definition "premises" words in square brackets substituted by the Food Standards Act 1999, s 40(1), Sch 5, paras 7, 8.

Orders: see note at the beginning of this Act.

[1.1033]
2   Extended meaning of "sale" etc
(1)   For the purposes of this Act—
(a)   the supply of food, otherwise than on sale, in the course of a business; and
(b)   any other thing which is done with respect to food and is specified in an order made by [the Secretary of State],
shall be deemed to be a sale of the food, and references to purchasers and purchasing shall be construed accordingly.

(2)　This Act shall apply—
- (a)　in relation to any food which is offered as a prize or reward or given away in connection with any entertainment to which the public are admitted, whether on payment of money or not, as if the food were, or had been, exposed for sale by each person concerned in the organisation of the entertainment;
- (b)　in relation to any food which, for the purpose of advertisement or in furtherance of any trade or business, is offered as a prize or reward or given away, as if the food were, or had been, exposed for sale by the person offering or giving away the food; and
- (c)　in relation to any food which is exposed or deposited in any premises for the purpose of being so offered or given away as mentioned in paragraph (a) or (b) above, as if the food were, or had been, exposed for sale by the occupier of the premises;

and in this subsection "entertainment" includes any social gathering, amusement, exhibition, performance, game, sport or trial of skill.

NOTES

Sub-s (1): words in square brackets in para (b) substituted by the Food Standards Act 1999, s 40(1), Sch 5, paras 7, 8.

[1.1034]
3　Presumptions that food intended for human consumption
(1)　The following provisions shall apply for the purposes of this Act.

(2)　Any food commonly used for human consumption shall, if sold or offered, exposed or kept for sale, be presumed, until the contrary is proved, to have been sold or, as the case may be, to have been or to be intended for sale for human consumption.

(3)　The following, namely—
- (a)　any food commonly used for human consumption which is found on premises used for the preparation, storage, or sale of that food; and
- (b)　any article or substance commonly used in the manufacture of food for human consumption which is found on premises used for the preparation, storage or sale of that food,

shall be presumed, until the contrary is proved, to be intended for sale, or for manufacturing food for sale, for human consumption.

(4)　Any article or substance capable of being used in the composition or preparation of any food commonly used for human consumption which is found on premises on which that food is prepared shall, until the contrary is proved, be presumed to be intended for such use.

4–6　(*S 4 repealed by the Food Standards Act 1999, s 40(4), Sch 6; ss 5, 6 outside the scope of this work.*)

PART II
MAIN PROVISIONS

Food safety

[1.1035]
7　Rendering food injurious to health
(1)　Any person who renders any food injurious to health by means of any of the following operations, namely—
- (a)　adding any article or substance to the food;
- (b)　using any article or substance as an ingredient in the preparation of the food;
- (c)　abstracting any constituent from the food; and
- (d)　subjecting the food to any other process or treatment,

with intent that it shall be sold for human consumption, shall be guilty of an offence.

[(2)　In determining for the purposes of this section whether any food is injurious to health, regard shall be had to the matters specified in sub-paragraphs (a) to (c) of Article 14(4) of Regulation (EC) No 178/2002.]

(3)　. . .

NOTES

Sub-s (2): substituted by the General Food Regulations 2004, SI 2004/3279, regs 8, 9(a).
Sub-s (3): repealed by SI 2004/3279, regs 8, 9(b).

[1.1036]
8　Selling food not complying with food safety requirements
(1)　. . .

[(2)　For the purposes of this Part food fails to comply with food safety requirements if it is unsafe within the meaning of Article 14 of Regulation (EC) No. 178/2002 and references to food safety requirements or to food complying with such requirements shall be construed accordingly.]

(4)　For the purposes of this Part, any part of, or product derived wholly or partly from, an animal—
- (a)　which has been slaughtered in a knacker's yard, or of which the carcase has been brought into a knacker's yard; or

(b)   *(applies to Scotland only)*

shall be deemed to be unfit for human consumption.

(5)   *(Applies to Scotland only.)*

NOTES

Sub-s (1): repealed by the General Food Regulations 2004, SI 2004/3279, regs 8, 10(a).

Sub-s (2): substituted for original sub-ss (2), (3) by SI 2004/3279, regs 8, 10(b).

[1.1037]
9   Inspection and seizure of suspected food
(1)   An authorised officer of a food authority may at all reasonable times inspect any food intended for human consumption which—
 (a)   has been sold or is offered or exposed for sale; . . .
 (b)   is in the possession of, or has been deposited with or consigned to, any person for the purpose of sale or of preparation for sale; [or
 (c)   is otherwise placed on the market within the meaning of Regulation (EC) No 178/2002;]
and subsections (3) to (9) below shall apply where, on such an inspection, it appears to the authorised officer that any food fails to comply with food safety requirements.
(2)   The following provisions shall also apply where, otherwise than on such an inspection, it appears to an authorised officer of a food authority that any food is likely to cause food poisoning or any disease communicable to human beings.
(3)   The authorised officer may either—
 (a)   give notice to the person in charge of the food that, until the notice is withdrawn, the food or any specified portion of it—
   (i)   is not to be used for human consumption; and
   (ii)   either is not to be removed or is not to be removed except to some place specified in the notice; or
 (b)   seize the food and remove it in order to have it dealt with by a justice of the peace;
and any person who knowingly contravenes the requirements of a notice under paragraph (a) above shall be guilty of an offence.
(4)   Where the authorised officer exercises the powers conferred by subsection (3)(a) above, he shall, as soon as is reasonably practicable and in any event within 21 days, determine whether or not he is satisfied that the food complies with food safety requirements and—
 (a)   if he is so satisfied, shall forthwith withdraw the notice;
 (b)   if he is not so satisfied, shall seize the food and remove it in order to have it dealt with by a justice of the peace.
(5)   Where an authorised officer exercises the powers conferred by subsection (3)(b) or (4)(b) above, he shall inform the person in charge of the food of his intention to have it dealt with by a justice of the peace and—
 (a)   any person who under section 7[, regulation 19(1) of the Food Safety and Hygiene (England) Regulations 2013, so far as relating to the second entry in the list of specified EU provisions set out in column 1 of Schedule 2 to those Regulations] [or regulation [4(b)] of the General Food Regulations 2004] might be liable to a prosecution in respect of the food shall, if he attends before the justice of the peace by whom the food falls to be dealt with, be entitled to be heard and to call witnesses; and
 (b)   that justice of the peace may, but need not, be a member of the court before which any person is charged with an offence under that section in relation to that food.
(6)   If it appears to a justice of the peace, on the basis of such evidence as he considers appropriate in the circumstances, that any food falling to be dealt with by him under this section fails to comply with food safety requirements, he shall condemn the food and order—
 (a)   the food to be destroyed or to be so disposed of as to prevent it from being used for human consumption; and
 (b)   any expenses reasonably incurred in connection with the destruction or disposal to be defrayed by the owner of the food.
(7)   If a notice under subsection (3)(a) above is withdrawn, or the justice of the peace by whom any food falls to be dealt with under this section refuses to condemn it, the food authority shall compensate the owner of the food for any depreciation in its value resulting from the action taken by the authorised officer.
(8)   Any disputed question as to the right to or the amount of any compensation payable under subsection (7) above shall be determined by arbitration.
(9)   *(Applies to Scotland only.)*

NOTES

Sub-s (1): word omitted from para (a) repealed and para (c) and word immediately preceding it inserted by the General Food Regulations 2004, SI 2004/3279, regs 8, 11(a).

Sub-s (5): in para (a) words in first pair of square brackets inserted, in relation to England, by the Food Safety and Hygiene (England) Regulations 2013, SI 2013/2996, reg 36; words in second (outer) pair of square brackets substituted by SI 2004/3279, regs 8, 11(b) (this amendment no longer applies to England by virtue of SI 2013/2996, reg 40, Sch 9); reference in third (inner) square brackets substituted, in relation to Wales, by the Food (Miscellaneous Amendments) (Scotland) Regulations 2013, SI 2013/3049, reg 5.

[1.1038]

10 Improvement notices

(1) If an authorised officer of an enforcement authority has reasonable grounds for believing that the proprietor of a food business is failing to comply with any regulations to which this section applies, he may, by a notice served on that proprietor (in this Act referred to as an "improvement notice")—

(a) state the officer's grounds for believing that the proprietor is failing to comply with the regulations;

(b) specify the matters which constitute the proprietor's failure so to comply;

(c) specify the measures which, in the officer's opinion, the proprietor must take in order to secure compliance; and

(d) require the proprietor to take those measures, or measures which are at least equivalent to them, within such period (not being less than 14 days) as may be specified in the notice.

(2) Any person who fails to comply with an improvement notice shall be guilty of an offence.

(3) This section and section 11 below apply to any regulations under this Part which make provision—

(a) for requiring, prohibiting or regulating the use of any process or treatment in the preparation of food; or

(b) for securing the observance of hygienic conditions and practices in connection with the carrying out of commercial operations with respect to food or food sources.

[1.1039]

11 Prohibition orders

(1) If—

(a) the proprietor of a food business is convicted of an offence under any regulations to which this section applies; and

(b) the court by or before which he is so convicted is satisfied that the health risk condition is fulfilled with respect to that business,

the court shall by an order impose the appropriate prohibition.

(2) The health risk condition is fulfilled with respect to any food business if any of the following involves risk of injury to health, namely—

(a) the use for the purposes of the business of any process or treatment;

(b) the construction of any premises used for the purposes of the business, or the use for those purposes of any equipment; and

(c) the state or condition of any premises or equipment used for the purposes of the business.

[(2A) In subsection (2) above and in sections 12(4) and 13(1) "injury" includes any impairment, whether permanent or temporary.]

(3) The appropriate prohibition is—

(a) in a case falling within paragraph (a) of subsection (2) above, a prohibition on the use of the process or treatment for the purposes of the business;

(b) in a case falling within paragraph (b) of that subsection, a prohibition on the use of the premises or equipment for the purposes of the business or any other food business of the same class or description;

(c) in a case falling within paragraph (c) of that subsection, a prohibition on the use of the premises or equipment for the purposes of any food business.

(4) If—

(a) the proprietor of a food business is convicted of an offence under any regulations to which this section applies by virtue of section 10(3)(b) above; and

(b) the court by or before which he is so convicted thinks it proper to do so in all the circumstances of the case,

the court may, by an order, impose a prohibition on the proprietor participating in the management of any food business, or any food business of a class or description specified in the order.

(5) As soon as practicable after the making of an order under subsection (1) or (4) above (in this Act referred to as a "prohibition order"), the enforcement authority shall—

(a) serve a copy of the order on the proprietor of the business; and

(b) in the case of an order under subsection (1) above, affix a copy of the order in a conspicuous position on such premises used for the purposes of the business as they consider appropriate;

and any person who knowingly contravenes such an order shall be guilty of an offence.

(6) A prohibition order shall cease to have effect—

(a) in the case of an order under subsection (1) above, on the issue by the enforcement authority of a certificate to the effect that they are satisfied that the proprietor has taken sufficient measures to secure that the health risk condition is no longer fulfilled with respect to the business;

(b) in the case of an order under subsection (4) above, on the giving by the court of a direction to that effect.

(7) The enforcement authority shall issue a certificate under paragraph (a) of subsection (6) above within three days of their being satisfied as mentioned in that paragraph; and on an application by the proprietor for such a certificate, the authority shall—

(a) determine, as soon as is reasonably practicable and in any event within 14 days, whether or not they are so satisfied; and

(b) if they determine that they are not so satisfied, give notice to the proprietor of the reasons for that determination.

(8) The court shall give a direction under subsection (6)(b) above if, on an application by the proprietor, the court thinks it proper to do so having regard to all the circumstances of the case, including in particular the conduct of the proprietor since the making of the order; but no such application shall be entertained if it is made—

(a) within six months after the making of the prohibition order; or

(b) within three months after the making by the proprietor of a previous application for such a direction.

(9) Where a magistrates' court or, in Scotland, the sheriff makes an order under section 12(2) below with respect to any food business, subsection (1) above shall apply as if the proprietor of the business had been convicted by the court or sheriff of an offence under regulations to which this section applies.

(10) Subsection (4) above shall apply in relation to a manager of a food business as it applies in relation to the proprietor of such a business; and any reference in subsection (5) or (8) above to the proprietor of the business, or to the proprietor, shall be construed accordingly.

(11) In subsection (10) above "manager", in relation to a food business, means any person who is entrusted by the proprietor with the day to day running of the business, or any part of the business.

NOTES

Sub-s (2A): inserted by the General Food Regulations 2004, SI 2004/3279, regs 8, 12.

[1.1040]
12 Emergency prohibition notices and orders

(1) If an authorised officer of an enforcement authority is satisfied that the health risk condition is fulfilled with respect to any food business, he may, by a notice served on the proprietor of the business (in this Act referred to as an "emergency prohibition notice"), impose the appropriate prohibition.

(2) If a magistrates' court or, in Scotland, the sheriff is satisfied, on the application of such an officer, that the health risk condition is fulfilled with respect to any food business, the court or sheriff shall, by an order (in this Act referred to as an "emergency prohibition order"), impose the appropriate prohibition.

(3) Such an officer shall not apply for an emergency prohibition order unless, at least one day before the date of the application, he has served notice on the proprietor of the business of his intention to apply for the order.

(4) Subsections (2) and (3) of section 11 above shall apply for the purposes of this section as they apply for the purposes of that section, but as if the reference in subsection (2) to risk of injury to health were a reference to imminent risk of such injury.

(5) As soon as practicable after the service of an emergency prohibition notice, the enforcement authority shall affix a copy of the notice in a conspicuous position on such premises used for the purposes of the business as they consider appropriate; and any person who knowingly contravenes such a notice shall be guilty of an offence.

(6) As soon as practicable after the making of an emergency prohibition order, the enforcement authority shall—

(a) serve a copy of the order on the proprietor of the business; and

(b) affix a copy of the order in a conspicuous position on such premises used for the purposes of that business as they consider appropriate;

and any person who knowingly contravenes such an order shall be guilty of an offence.

(7) An emergency prohibition notice shall cease to have effect—

(a) if no application for an emergency prohibition order is made within the period of three days beginning with the service of the notice, at the end of that period;

(b) if such an application is so made, on the determination or abandonment of the application.

(8) An emergency prohibition notice or emergency prohibition order shall cease to have effect on the issue by the enforcement authority of a certificate to the effect that they are satisfied that the proprietor has taken sufficient measures to secure that the health risk condition is no longer fulfilled with respect to the business.

(9) The enforcement authority shall issue a certificate under subsection (8) above within three days of their being satisfied as mentioned in that subsection; and on an application by the proprietor for such a certificate, the authority shall—

(a) determine, as soon as is reasonably practicable and in any event within 14 days, whether or not they are so satisfied; and

(b) if they determine that they are not so satisfied, give notice to the proprietor of the reasons for that determination.

(10) Where an emergency prohibition notice is served on the proprietor of a business, the enforcement authority shall compensate him in respect of any loss suffered by reason of his complying with the notice unless—

(a)   an application for an emergency prohibition order is made within the period of three days beginning with the service of the notice; and

(b)   the court declares itself satisfied, on the hearing of the application, that the health risk condition was fulfilled with respect to the business at the time when the notice was served;

and any disputed question as to the right to or the amount of any compensation payable under this subsection shall be determined by arbitration or, in Scotland, by a single arbiter appointed, failing agreement between the parties, by the sheriff.

[1.1041]

13   Emergency control orders

(1)   If it appears to [the Secretary of State] that the carrying out of commercial operations with respect to food, food sources or contact materials of any class or description involves or may involve imminent risk of injury to health, he may, by an order (in this Act referred to as an "emergency control order"), prohibit the carrying out of such operations with respect to food, food sources or contact materials of that class or description.

(2)   Any person who knowingly contravenes an emergency control order shall be guilty of an offence.

(3)   [The Secretary of State] [or the Food Standards Agency] may consent, either unconditionally or subject to any condition that [the authority giving the consent] considers appropriate, to the doing in a particular case of anything prohibited by an emergency control order.

(4)   It shall be a defence for a person charged with an offence under subsection (2) above to show—

(a)   that consent had been given under subsection (3) above to the contravention of the emergency control order; and

(b)   that any condition subject to which that consent was given was complied with.

(5)   [The Secretary of State] [or the Food Standards Agency]—

(a)   may give such directions as appear to [the authority giving the directions] to be necessary or expedient for the purpose of preventing the carrying out of commercial operations with respect to any food, food sources or contact materials which [the authority giving the directions] believes, on reasonable grounds, to be food, food sources or contact materials to which an emergency control order applies; and

(b)   may do anything which appears to [the authority giving the directions] to be necessary or expedient for that purpose.

(6)   Any person who fails to comply with a direction under this section shall be guilty of an offence.

(7)   If the [the Secretary of State] [or the Food Standards Agency] does anything by virtue of this section in consequence of any person failing to comply with an emergency control order or a direction under this section, [that authority] may recover from that person any expenses reasonably incurred by [that authority] under this section.

[(8)   *(Applies to Scotland only.)*]

NOTES

Sub-s (1): words in square brackets substituted by the Food Standards Act 1999, s 40(1), Sch 5, paras 7, 8.

Sub-s (3): words in first and third pairs of square brackets substituted, and words in second pair of square brackets inserted, by the Food Standards Act 1999, s 40(1), Sch 5, paras 7, 11(1), (2).

Sub-s (5): words in first, third, fourth and fifth pairs of square brackets substituted, and words in second pair of square brackets inserted, by the Food Standards Act 1999, s 40(1), Sch 5, paras 7, 11(1), (3).

Sub-s (7): words in first, third and fourth pairs of square brackets substituted, and words in second pair of square brackets inserted, by the Food Standards Act 1999, s 40(1), Sch 5, paras 7, 11(1), (4).

Sub-s (8): added by the Food (Scotland) Act 2015, s 59, Schedule, para 3(1), (3).

Orders: see note at the beginning of this Act.

Consumer protection

[1.1042]

14   Selling food not of the nature or substance or quality demanded

(1)   Any person who sells to the purchaser's prejudice any food which is not of the nature or substance or quality demanded by the purchaser shall be guilty of an offence.

(2)   In subsection (1) above the reference to sale shall be construed as a reference to sale for human consumption; and in proceedings under that subsection it shall not be a defence that the purchaser was not prejudiced because he bought for analysis or examination.

[1.1043]

15   Falsely describing or presenting food

(1)   Any person who gives with any food sold by him, or displays with any food offered or exposed by him for sale or in his possession for the purpose of sale, a label, whether or not attached to or printed on the wrapper or container, which—

(a)   falsely describes the food; or

(b)   is likely to mislead as to the nature or substance or quality of the food,

shall be guilty of an offence.

(2)   Any person who publishes, or is a party to the publication of, an advertisement (not being such a label given or displayed by him as mentioned in subsection (1) above) which—

(a)   falsely describes any food; or

(b)   is likely to mislead as to the nature or substance or quality of any food,

shall be guilty of an offence.

(3)   Any person who sells, or offers or exposes for sale, or has in his possession for the purpose of sale, any food the presentation of which is likely to mislead as to the nature or substance or quality of the food shall be guilty of an offence.

(4)   In proceedings for an offence under subsection (1) or (2) above, the fact that a label or advertisement in respect of which the offence is alleged to have been committed contained an accurate statement of the composition of the food shall not preclude the court from finding that the offence was committed.

(5)   In this section references to sale shall be construed as references to sale for human consumption.

[15A–15D   (*Ss 15A–15D inserted by the Food (Scotland) Act 2015, s 33, and apply to Scotland only*).]

Regulations

[1.1044]
16   Food safety and consumer protection

(1)   [The Secretary of State] may by regulations make—

(a)   provision for requiring, prohibiting or regulating the presence in food or food sources of any specified substance, or any substance of any specified class, and generally for regulating the composition of food;

(b)   provision for securing that food is fit for human consumption and meets such microbiological standards (whether going to the fitness of the food or otherwise) as may be specified by or under the regulations;

(c)   provision for requiring, prohibiting or regulating the use of any process or treatment in the preparation of food;

(d)   provision for securing the observance of hygienic conditions and practices in connection with the carrying out of commercial operations with respect to food or food sources;

(e)   provision for imposing requirements or prohibitions as to, or otherwise regulating, the labelling, marking, presenting or advertising of food, and the descriptions which may be applied to food; and

(f)   such other provision with respect to food or food sources, including in particular provision for prohibiting or regulating the carrying out of commercial operations with respect to food or food sources, as appears to them to be necessary or expedient—

(i)   for the purpose of securing that food complies with food safety requirements or in the interests of the public health; or

(ii)   for the purpose of protecting or promoting the interests of consumers.

(2)   [The Secretary of State] may also by regulations make provision—

(a)   for securing the observance of hygienic conditions and practices in connection with the carrying out of commercial operations with respect to contact materials which are intended to come into contact with food intended for human consumption;

(b)   for imposing requirements or prohibitions as to, or otherwise regulating, the labelling, marking or advertising of such materials, and the descriptions which may be applied to them; and

(c)   otherwise for prohibiting or regulating the carrying out of commercial operations with respect to such materials.

(3)   Without prejudice to the generality of subsection (1) above, regulations under that subsection may make any such provision as is mentioned in Schedule 1 to this Act.

(4)   In making regulations under subsection (1) above, [the Secretary of State] shall have regard to the desirability of restricting, so far as practicable, the use of substances of no nutritional value as foods or as ingredients of foods.

(5)   In subsection (1) above and Schedule 1 to this Act, unless the context otherwise requires—

(a)   references to food shall be construed as references to food intended for sale for human consumption; and

(b)   references to food sources shall be construed as references to food sources from which such food is intended to be derived.

NOTES

Sub-ss (1), (2), (4): words in square brackets substituted by the Food Standards Act 1999, s 40(1), Sch 5, paras 7, 8.
Regulations: see note at the beginning of this Act.

[1.1045]

17 Enforcement of [EU] provisions

(1) [The Secretary of State] may by regulations make such provision with respect to food, food sources or contact materials, including in particular provision for prohibiting or regulating the carrying out of commercial operations with respect to food, food sources or contact materials, as appears to [him] to be called for by any [EU] obligation.

(2) As respects any directly applicable [EU] provision which relates to food, food sources or contact materials and for which, in [his] opinion, it is appropriate to provide under this Act, [the Secretary of State] may by regulations—

> (a)   make such provision as [he considers] necessary or expedient for the purpose of securing that the [EU] provision is administered, executed and enforced under this Act; and
>
> (b)   apply such of the provisions of this Act as may be specified in the regulations in relation to the [EU] provision with such modifications, if any, as may be so specified.

(3) In subsections (1) and (2) above references to food or food sources shall be construed in accordance with section 16(5) above.

NOTES

Section heading: reference in square brackets substituted by the Treaty of Lisbon (Changes in Terminology) Order 2011, SI 2011/1043, art 6(2)(c).

Sub-ss (1), (2): references to "EU" in square brackets in each place they appear substituted by SI 2011/1043, art 6(1)(e), (2)(c); other words in square brackets substituted by the Food Standards Act 1999, s 40(1), Sch 5, paras 7, 8, 12.

Regulations: see note at the beginning of this Act.

[1.1046]

18 Special provisions for particular foods etc

(1) [The Secretary of State] may by regulations make provision—

> (a)   for prohibiting the carrying out of commercial operations with respect to novel foods, or food sources from which such foods are intended to be derived, of any class specified in the regulations;
>
> (b)   for prohibiting the carrying out of such operations with respect to genetically modified food sources, or foods derived from such food sources, of any class so specified; or
>
> (c)   for prohibiting the importation of any food of a class so specified,

and (in each case) for excluding from the prohibition any food or food source which is of a description specified by or under the regulations and, in the case of a prohibition on importation, is imported at an authorised place of entry.

(2) [The Secretary of State] may also by regulations—

> (a)   prescribe, in relation to milk of any description, such a designation (in this subsection referred to as a "special designation") as [the Secretary of State considers] appropriate;
>
> (b)   provide for the issue by enforcement authorities of licences to producers and sellers of milk authorising the use of a special designation; and
>
> (c)   prohibit, without the use of a special designation, all sales of milk for human consumption, other than sales made with [the Secretary of State's] consent.

(3) In this section—

"authorised place of entry" means any port, aerodrome or other place of entry authorised by or under the regulations and, in relation to food in a particular consignment, includes any place of entry so authorised for the importation of that consignment;

"description", in relation to food, includes any description of its origin or of the manner in which it is packed;

"novel food" means any food which has not previously been used for human consumption in Great Britain, or has been so used only to a very limited extent.

(4) For the purposes of this section a food source is genetically modified if any of the genes or other genetic material in the food source—

> (a)   has been modified by means of an artificial technique; or
>
> (b)   is inherited or otherwise derived, through any number of replications, from genetic material which was so modified;

and in this subsection "artificial technique" does not include any technique which involves no more than, or no more than the assistance of, naturally occurring processes of reproduction (including selective breeding techniques or *in vitro* fertilisation).

NOTES

Sub-ss (1), (2): words in square brackets substituted by the Food Standards Act 1999, s 40(1), Sch 5, paras 7, 8, 13.

Regulations: see note at the beginning of this Act.

[1.1047]

19 Registration and licensing of food premises

(1) [The Secretary of State] may by regulations make provision—

> (a)   for the registration by enforcement authorities of premises used or proposed to be used for the purposes of a food business, and for prohibiting the use for those purposes of any premises which are not registered in accordance with the regulations; or

(b)   subject to subsection (2) below, for the issue by such authorities of licences in respect of the use of premises for the purposes of a food business, and for prohibiting the use for those purposes of any premises except in accordance with a licence issued under the regulations.

(2) [The Secretary of State] shall exercise the power conferred by subsection (1)(b) above only where it appears to [him] to be necessary or expedient to do so—

(a)   for the purpose of securing that food complies with food safety requirements or in the interests of the public health; or

(b)   for the purpose of protecting or promoting the interests of consumers.

NOTES

Sub-ss (1), (2): words in square brackets substituted by the Food Standards Act 1999, s 40(1), Sch 5, paras 7, 8, 14.

Regulations: see note at the beginning of this Act.

Defences etc

[1.1048]
20 Offences due to fault of another person

Where the commission by any person of an offence under any of the preceding provisions of this Part is due to an act or default of some other person, that other person shall be guilty of the offence; and a person may be charged with and convicted of the offence by virtue of this section whether or not proceedings are taken against the first-mentioned person.

[1.1049]
21 Defence of due diligence

(1) In any proceedings for an offence under any of the preceding provisions of this Part (in this section referred to as "the relevant provision"), it shall, subject to subsection (5) below, be a defence for the person charged to prove that he took all reasonable precautions and exercised all due diligence to avoid the commission of the offence by himself or by a person under his control.

(2) Without prejudice to the generality of subsection (1) above, a person charged with an offence under [section 14 or 15] above who neither—

(a)   prepared the food in respect of which the offence is alleged to have been committed; nor

(b)   imported it into Great Britain,

shall be taken to have established the defence provided by that subsection if he satisfies the requirements of subsection (3) or (4) below.

(3) A person satisfies the requirements of this subsection if he proves—

(a)   that the commission of the offence was due to an act or default of another person who was not under his control, or to reliance on information supplied by such a person;

(b)   that he carried out all such checks of the food in question as were reasonable in all the circumstances, or that it was reasonable in all the circumstances for him to rely on checks carried out by the person who supplied the food to him; and

(c)   that he did not know and had no reason to suspect at the time of the commission of the alleged offence that his act or omission would amount to an offence under the relevant provision.

(4) A person satisfies the requirements of this subsection if he proves—

(a)   that the commission of the offence was due to an act or default of another person who was not under his control, or to reliance on information supplied by such a person;

(b)   that the sale or intended sale of which the alleged offence consisted was not a sale or intended sale under his name or mark; and

(c)   that he did not know, and could not reasonably have been expected to know, at the time of the commission of the alleged offence that his act or omission would amount to an offence under the relevant provision.

(5) If in any case the defence provided by subsection (1) above involves the allegation that the commission of the offence was due to an act or default of another person, or to reliance on information supplied by another person, the person charged shall not, without leave of the court, be entitled to rely on that defence unless—

(a)   at least seven clear days before the hearing; and

(b)   where he has previously appeared before a court in connection with the alleged offence, within one month of his first such appearance,

he has served on the prosecutor a notice in writing giving such information identifying or assisting in the identification of that other person as was then in his possession.

(6) In subsection (5) above any reference to appearing before a court shall be construed as including a reference to being brought before a court.

NOTES

Sub-s (2): words in square brackets substituted by the General Food Regulations 2004, SI 2004/3279, regs 8, 13.

[1.1050]

22 Defence of publication in the course of business

In proceedings for an offence under any of the preceding provisions of this Part consisting of the advertisement for sale of any food, it shall be a defence for the person charged to prove—

    (a)   that he is a person whose business it is to publish or arrange for the publication of advertisements; and

    (b)   that he received the advertisement in the ordinary course of business and did not know and had no reason to suspect that its publication would amount to an offence under that provision.

23–26   *(Ss 23, 24, 26 outside the scope of this work; s 25 repealed by the Food Standards Act 1999, s 40(1), (4), Sch 5, para 15, Sch 6.)*

PART III
ADMINISTRATION AND ENFORCEMENT

Administration

[1.1051]

27 Appointment of public analysts

(1)   Every authority to whom this section applies, that is to say, every food authority in England and Wales and every [council constituted under section 2 of the Local Government etc (Scotland) Act 1994] in Scotland, shall appoint in accordance with this section one or more persons (in this Act referred to as "public analysts") to act as analysts for the purposes of this Act within the authority's area.

(2)   No person shall be appointed as a public analyst unless he possesses—

    (a)   such qualifications as may be prescribed by regulations made by [the Secretary of State]; or

    (b)   such other qualifications as [the Secretary of State] may approve,

and no person shall act as a public analyst for any area who is engaged directly or indirectly in any food business which is carried on in that area.

(3)   An authority to whom this section applies shall pay to a public analyst such remuneration as may be agreed, which may be expressed to be payable either—

    (a)   in addition to any fees received by him under this Part; or

    (b)   on condition that any fees so received by him are paid over by him to the authority.

(4)   An authority to whom this section applies who appoint only one public analyst may appoint also a deputy to act during any vacancy in the office of public analyst, or during the absence or incapacity of the holder of the office, and—

    (a)   the provisions of this section with respect to the qualifications, appointment, removal and remuneration of a public analyst shall apply also in relation to a deputy public analyst; and

    (b)   any reference in the following provisions of this Act to a public analyst shall be construed as including a reference to a deputy public analyst appointed under this subsection.

(5)   In subsection (1) above "food authority" does not include the council of a non-metropolitan district [in England] [(except where the county functions have been transferred to that council . . .)], the Sub-Treasurer of the Inner Temple or the Under Treasurer of the Middle Temple; and in subsection (2) above the reference to being engaged directly or indirectly in a food business includes a reference to having made such arrangements with a food business as may be prescribed by regulations made by [the Secretary of State].

NOTES

    Sub-s (1): words in square brackets substituted by the Local Government etc (Scotland) Act 1994, s 180(1), Sch 13, para 163(3).

    Sub-s (2): words in square brackets substituted by the Food Standards Act 1999, s 40(1), Sch 5, paras 7, 8.

    Sub-s (5): words in first pair of square brackets inserted by the Local Government (Wales) Act 1994, s 22(3), Sch 9, para 16(2); words in second pair of square brackets inserted by the Local Government Changes for England Regulations 1994, SI 1994/867, reg 24; words omitted repealed by the Local Government and Public Involvement in Health Act 2007, ss 22, 241, Sch 1, Pt 2, para 17, Sch 18, Pt 1; words in third pair of square brackets substituted by the Food Standards Act 1999, s 40(1), Sch 5, paras 7, 8.

    Regulations: see note at the beginning of this Act.

[1.1052]

28 Provision of facilities for examinations

(1)   A food authority, or a [council constituted under section 2 of the Local Government etc (Scotland) Act 1994] in Scotland, may provide facilities for examinations for the purposes of this Act.

(2)   In this Act "examination" means a microbiological examination and "examine" shall be construed accordingly.

NOTES

    Sub-s (1): words in square brackets substituted by the Local Government etc (Scotland) Act 1994, s 180(1), Sch 13, para 163(4).

Sampling and analysis etc

[1.1053]
29 Procurement of samples

An authorised officer of an enforcement authority may—

(a) purchase a sample of any food, or any substance capable of being used in the preparation of food;

(b) take a sample of any food, or any such substance, which—

   (i) appears to him to be intended for sale, or to have been sold, for human consumption; or

   (ii) is found by him on or in any premises which he is authorised to enter by or under section 32 below;

(c) take a sample from any food source, or a sample of any contact material, which is found by him on or in any such premises;

(d) take a sample of any article or substance which is found by him on or in any such premises and which he has reason to believe may be required as evidence in proceedings under any of the provisions of this Act or of regulations or orders made under it.

[1.1054]
30 Analysis etc of samples

(1) An authorised officer of an enforcement authority who has procured a sample under section 29 above shall—

(a) if he considers that the sample should be analysed, submit it to be analysed either—

   (i) by the public analyst for the area in which the sample was procured; or

   (ii) by the public analyst for the area which consists of or includes the area of the authority;

(b) if he considers that the sample should be examined, submit it to be examined by a food examiner.

(2) A person, other than such an officer, who has purchased any food, or any substance capable of being used in the preparation of food, may submit a sample of it—

(a) to be analysed by the public analyst for the area in which the purchase was made; or

(b) to be examined by a food examiner.

(3) If, in any case where a sample is proposed to be submitted for analysis under this section, the office of public analyst for the area in question is vacant, the sample shall be submitted to the public analyst for some other area.

(4) If, in any case where a sample is proposed to be or is submitted for analysis or examination under this section, the food analyst or examiner determines that he is for any reason unable to perform the analysis or examination, the sample shall be submitted or, as the case may be, sent by him to such other food analyst or examiner as he may determine.

(5) A food analyst or examiner shall analyse or examine as soon as practicable any sample submitted or sent to him under this section, but may, except where—

(a) he is the public analyst for the area in question; and

(b) the sample is submitted to him for analysis by an authorised officer of an enforcement authority,

demand in advance the payment of such reasonable fee as he may require.

(6) A food analyst or examiner who has analysed or examined a sample shall give to the person by whom it was submitted a certificate specifying the result of the analysis or examination.

(7) Any certificate given by a food analyst or examiner under subsection (6) above shall be signed by him, but the analysis or examination may be made by any person acting under his direction.

(8) In any proceedings under this Act, the production by one of the parties—

(a) of a document purporting to be a certificate given by a food analyst or examiner under subsection (6) above; or

(b) of a document supplied to him by the other party as being a copy of such a certificate,

shall be sufficient evidence of the facts stated in it unless, in a case falling within paragraph (a) above, the other party requires that the food analyst or examiner shall be called as a witness.

(9) In this section—

"food analyst" means a public analyst or any other person who possesses the requisite qualifications to carry out analyses for the purposes of this Act;

"food examiner" means any person who possesses the requisite qualifications to carry out examinations for the purposes of this Act;

"the requisite qualifications" means such qualifications as may be prescribed by regulations made by [the Secretary of State], or such other qualifications as [the Secretary of State] may approve;

"sample", in relation to an authorised officer of an enforcement authority, includes any part of a sample retained by him in pursuance of regulations under section 31 below;

and where two or more public analysts are appointed for any area, any reference in this section to the public analyst for that area shall be construed as a reference to either or any of them.

NOTES

Sub-s (9): in definition "the requisite qualifications" words in square brackets substituted by the Food Standards Act 1999, s 40(1), Sch 5, paras 7, 8.

Regulations: see note at the beginning of this Act.

[1.1055]
31 Regulation of sampling and analysis etc

(1) [The Secretary of State] may by regulations make provision for supplementing or modifying the provisions of sections 29 and 30 above.

(2) Without prejudice to the generality of subsection (1) above, regulations under that subsection may make provision with respect to—

(a) the matters to be taken into account in determining whether, and at what times, samples should be procured;

(b) the manner of procuring samples, including the steps to be taken in order to ensure that any samples procured are fair samples;

(c) the method of dealing with samples, including (where appropriate) their division into parts;

(d) the persons to whom parts of samples are to be given and the persons by whom such parts are to be retained;

(e) the notices which are to be given to, and the information which is to be furnished by, the persons in charge of any food, substance, contact material or food source of or from which samples are procured;

(f) the methods which are to be used in analysing or examining samples, or parts of samples, or in classifying the results of analyses or examinations;

(g) the circumstances in which a food analyst or examiner is to be precluded, by reason of a conflict of interest, from analysing or examining a particular sample or part of a sample; and

(h) the circumstances in which samples, or parts of samples, are to be or may be submitted for analysis or examination—

(i) to the Government Chemist, or to such other food analyst or examiner as he may direct; or

(ii) to a person determined by or under the regulations.

(3) In this section "food analyst" and "food examiner" have the same meanings as in section 30 above.

NOTES

Sub-s (1): words in square brackets substituted by the Food Standards Act 1999, s 40(1), Sch 5, paras 7, 8.

Regulations: see note at the beginning of this Act.

Powers of entry and obstruction etc

[1.1056]
32 Powers of entry

(1) An authorised officer of an enforcement authority shall, on producing, if so required, some duly authenticated document showing his authority, have a right at all reasonable hours—

(a) to enter any premises within the authority's area for the purpose of ascertaining whether there is or has been on the premises any contravention of the provisions of this Act, or of regulations or orders made under it; and

(b) to enter any business premises, whether within or outside the authority's area, for the purpose of ascertaining whether there is on the premises any evidence of any contravention within that area of any of such provisions; and

(c) in the case of an authorised officer of a food authority, to enter any premises for the purpose of the performance by the authority of their functions under this Act;

but admission to any premises used only as a private dwelling-house shall not be demanded as of right unless 24 hours' notice of the intended entry has been given to the occupier.

(2) If a justice of the peace, on sworn information in writing, is satisfied that there is reasonable ground for entry into any premises for any such purpose as is mentioned in subsection (1) above and either—

(a) that admission to the premises has been refused, or a refusal is apprehended, and that notice of the intention to apply for a warrant has been given to the occupier; or

(b) that an application for admission, or the giving of such a notice, would defeat the object of the entry, or that the case is one of urgency, or that the premises are unoccupied or the occupier temporarily absent,

the justice may by warrant signed by him authorise the authorised officer to enter the premises, if need be by reasonable force.

(3) Every warrant granted under this section shall continue in force for a period of one month.

(4) An authorised officer entering any premises by virtue of this section, or of a warrant issued under it, may take with him such other persons as he considers necessary, and on leaving any unoccupied premises which he has entered by virtue of such a warrant shall leave them as effectively secured against unauthorised entry as he found them.

(5)   An authorised officer entering premises by virtue of this section, or of a warrant issued under it, may inspect any records (in whatever form they are held) relating to a food business and, where any such records are [stored in any electronic form]—

    (a)   may have access to, and inspect and check the operation of, any computer and any associated apparatus or material which is or has been in use in connection with the records; and

    (b)   may require any person having charge of, or otherwise concerned with the operation of, the computer, apparatus or material to afford him such assistance as he may reasonably require.

(6)   Any officer exercising any power conferred by subsection (5) above may—

    (a)   seize and detain any records which he has reason to believe may be required as evidence in proceedings under any of the provisions of this Act or of regulations or orders made under it; and

    (b)   where the records are [stored in any electronic form], may require the records to be produced in a form in which they may be taken away.

(7)   If any person who enters any premises by virtue of this section, or of a warrant issued under it, discloses to any person any information obtained by him in the premises with regard to any trade secret, he shall, unless the disclosure was made in the performance of his duty, be guilty of an offence.

(8)   Nothing in this section authorises any person, except with the permission of the local authority under the Animal Health Act 1981, to enter any premises—

    (a)   in which an animal or bird affected with any disease to which that Act applies is kept; and

    (b)   which is situated in a place declared under that Act to be infected with such a disease.

(9)   *(Applies to Scotland only.)*

NOTES
> Sub-ss (5), (6): words in square brackets substituted by the Criminal Justice and Police Act 2001, s 70, Sch 2, Pt 2, para 18.
> Seize and detain: the powers of seizure conferred by sub-s (6) are powers to which the Criminal Justice and Police Act 2001, s 50 apply (additional powers of seizure from premises); see s 50 of, and Sch 1, Pt 1, para 50 to, that Act.

[1.1057]
33   Obstruction etc of officers
(1)   Any person who—

    (a)   intentionally obstructs any person acting in the execution of this Act; or

    (b)   without reasonable cause, fails to give to any person acting in the execution of this Act any assistance or information which that person may reasonably require of him for the performance of his functions under this Act,

shall be guilty of an offence.

(2)   Any person who, in purported compliance with [section 15C(1) above or] any such requirement as is mentioned in subsection (1)(b) above—

    (a)   furnishes information which he knows to be false or misleading in a material particular; or

    (b)   recklessly furnishes information which is false or misleading in a material particular,

shall be guilty of an offence.

(3)   Nothing in subsection (1)(b)[, section 15C(1) or section 15D(2)] above shall be construed as requiring any person to answer any question or give any information if to do so might incriminate him.

NOTES
> Sub-ss (2), (3): words in square brackets inserted by the Food (Scotland) Act 2015, s 59, Schedule, para 3(1), (4), in relation to Scotland only.

Offences

[1.1058]
34   Time limit for prosecutions
No prosecution for an offence under this Act which is punishable under [section 35(A1), (A2) or (2)] below shall be begun after the expiry of—

    (a)   three years from the commission of the offence; or

    (b)   one year from its discovery by the prosecutor,

whichever is the earlier.

NOTES
> Words in square brackets substituted by the Food (Scotland) Act 2015, s 59, Schedule, para 3(1), (5), in relation to Scotland only.

[1.1059]
35   Punishment of offences
[(A1), (A2)   *(Apply to Scotland only).*]

(1)   A person guilty of an offence under section 33(1) above shall be liable on summary conviction to a fine not exceeding level 5 on the standard scale or to imprisonment for a term not exceeding *three months* or to both.

[(1A)   *(Apply to Scotland only).*]

(2)   A person guilty of any other offence under this Act shall be liable—

  (a)   on conviction on indictment, to a fine or to imprisonment for a term not exceeding two years or to both;

  (b)   on summary conviction, to a fine not exceeding the relevant amount or to imprisonment for a term not exceeding six months or to both.

(3)   In subsection (2) above "the relevant amount" means—

  (a)   in the case of an offence under [section 7 or 14] above, £20,000;

  (b)   in any other case, the statutory maximum.

(4)   If a person who is—

  (a)   licensed under section 1 of the Slaughterhouses Act 1974 to keep a . . . knacker's yard;

  (b)   . . . ; or

  (c)   *(applies to Scotland only)*,

is convicted of an offence under Part II of this Act, the court may, in addition to any other punishment, cancel his licence or registration.

NOTES

   Sub-s (1): for the words in italics there are substituted the words "51 weeks" by the Criminal Justice Act 2003, s 280(2), Sch 26, para 42, as from a day to be appointed.

   Sub-s (3): words in square brackets substituted by the General Food Regulations 2004, SI 2004/3279, regs 8, 14.

   Sub-s (4): words omitted repealed by the Deregulation (Slaughterhouses Act 1974 and Slaughter of Animals (Scotland) Act 1980) Order 1996, SI 1996/2235, art 11, Schedule.

[1.1060]
36   Offences by bodies corporate

(1)   Where an offence under this Act which has been committed by a body corporate is proved to have been committed with the consent or connivance of, or to be attributable to any neglect on the part of—

  (a)   any director, manager, secretary or other similar officer of the body corporate; or

  (b)   any person who was purporting to act in any such capacity,

he as well as the body corporate shall be deemed to be guilty of that offence and shall be liable to be proceeded against and punished accordingly.

(2)   In subsection (1) above "director", in relation to any body corporate established by or under any enactment for the purpose of carrying on under national ownership any industry or part of an industry or undertaking, being a body corporate whose affairs are managed by its members, means a member of that body corporate.

36A–39   *(Outside the scope of this work.)*

PART IV
MISCELLANEOUS AND SUPPLEMENTAL

40–52   *(Outside the scope of this work.)*

Supplemental

53–59   *(Outside the scope of this work.)*

[1.1061]
60   Short title, commencement and extent

(1)   This Act may be cited as the Food Safety Act 1990.

(2)   The following provisions shall come into force on the day on which this Act is passed, namely—

   section 13;

   section 51; and

   paragraphs 12 to 15 of Schedule 2 and, so far as relating to those paragraphs, section 52.

(3)   Subject to subsection (2) above, this Act shall come into force on such day as the Ministers may by order appoint, and different days may be appointed for different provisions or for different purposes.

(4)   An order under subsection (3) above may make such transitional adaptations of any of the following, namely—

  (a)   the provisions of this Act then in force or brought into force by the order; and

  (b)   the provisions repealed by this Act whose repeal is not then in force or so brought into force,

as appear to the Ministers to be necessary or expedient in consequence of the partial operation of this Act.

(5)   This Act, except—

   this section;

   section 51

   section 58(2) to (4); and

   paragraphs 7, 29 and 30 of Schedule 3 and, so far as relating to those paragraphs, section 59(1),

does not extend to Northern Ireland.

NOTES

Orders: the Food Safety Act 1990 (Commencement No 1) Order 1990, SI 1990/1383; the Food Safety Act 1990 (Commencement No 2) Order 1990, SI 1990/2372; the Food Safety Act 1990 (Commencement No 3) Order 1992, SI 1992/57.

SCHEDULES

SCHEDULES 1–5

(Schs 1–5 outside the scope of this work.)

CONTRACTS (APPLICABLE LAW) ACT 1990

(1990 c 36)

ARRANGEMENT OF SECTIONS

An Act to make provision as to the law applicable to contractual obligations in the case of conflict of laws

[26 July 1990]

[1.1062]
1   Meaning of "the Conventions"
In this Act—
  (a)   "the Rome Convention" means the Convention on the law applicable to contractual obligations opened for signature in Rome on 19th June 1980 and signed by the United Kingdom on 7th December 1981;
  (b)   "the Luxembourg Convention" means the Convention on the accession of the Hellenic Republic to the Rome Convention signed by the United Kingdom in Luxembourg on 10th April 1984; and
  (c)   "the Brussels Protocol" means the first Protocol on the interpretation of the Rome Convention by the European Court signed by the United Kingdom in Brussels on 19th December 1988;
 [(d)   "the Funchal Convention" means the Convention on the accession of the Kingdom of Spain and the Portuguese Republic to the Rome Convention and the Brussels Protocol, with adjustments made to the Rome Convention by the Luxembourg Convention, signed by the United Kingdom in Funchal on 18th May 1992;]
 [(e)   "the 1996 Accession Convention" means the Convention on the accession of the Republic of Austria, the Republic of Finland and the Kingdom of Sweden to the Rome Convention and the Brussels Protocol, with the adjustments made to the Rome Convention by the Luxembourg Convention and the Funchal Convention, signed by the United Kingdom in Brussels on 29th November 1996;]
and [these Conventions and this Protocol] ate together referred to as "the Conventions".

NOTES

Para (d) added, and words in final pair of square brackets substituted, by the Contracts (Applicable Law) Act 1990 (Amendment) Order 1994, SI 1994/1900, arts 3, 4; para (e) added by the Contracts (Applicable Law) Act 1990 (Amendment) Order 2000, SI 2000/1825, art 3.

[1.1063]
2   Conventions to have force of law
(1)   Subject to subsections (2) and (3) below, the Conventions shall have the force of law in the United Kingdom.

[(1A)   The internal law for the purposes of Article 1(3) of the Rome Convention is whichever of the following are applicable, namely—
- (a)   the provisions of Schedule 3A to the Insurance Companies Act 1982 (law applicable to certain contracts of insurance with insurance companies), and
- (b)   the provisions of Schedule 20 to the Friendly Societies Act 1992 as applied by subsections (1)(a) and (2)(a) of section 101 of that Act (law applicable to certain contracts of insurance with friendly societies).]

(2)   Articles 7(1) and 10(1)(e) of the Rome Convention shall not have the force of law in the United Kingdom.

(3)   Notwithstanding Article 19(2) of the Rome Convention, the Conventions shall apply in the case of conflicts between the laws of different parts of the United Kingdom.

(4)   For ease of reference there are set out in [Schedules 1, 2, 3[, 3A and 3B]] to this Act respectively the English texts of—
- (a)   the Rome Convention;
- (b)   the Luxembourg Convention; . . .
- (c)   the Brussels Protocol[, and
- (d)   the Funchal Convention; and
- (e)   the 1996 Accession Convention.]]

NOTES

Sub-s (1A): inserted by the Insurance Companies (Amendment) Regulations 1993, SI 1993/174, reg 9; substituted by the Friendly Societies (Amendment) Regulations 1993, SI 1993/2519, reg 6(5).

Sub-s (4): words in first (outer) pair of square brackets substituted, word omitted repealed and original para (d) and the word immediately preceding it added, by the Contracts (Applicable Law) Act 1990 (Amendment) Order 1994, SI 1994/1900, arts 5, 6; words in second (inner) pair of square brackets substituted, and paras (d), (e) substituted for original para (d) by the Contracts (Applicable Law) Act 1990 (Amendment) Order 2000, SI 2000/1825, art 4.

[1.1064]
3   Interpretation of Conventions
(1)   Any question as to the meaning or effect of any provision of the Conventions shall, if not referred to the European Court in accordance with the Brussels Protocol, be determined in accordance with the principles laid down by, and any relevant decision of, the European Court.

(2)   Judicial notice shall be taken of any decision of, or expression of opinion by, the European Court on any such question.

(3)   Without prejudice to any practice of the courts as to the matters which may be considered apart from this subsection—
- (a)   the report on the Rome Convention by Professor Mario Giuliano and Professor Paul Lagarde which is reproduced in the Official Journal of the Communities of 31st October 1980 may be considered in ascertaining the meaning or effect of any provision of that Convention; and
- (b)   any report on the Brussels Protocol which is reproduced in the Official Journal of the [European Union] may be considered in ascertaining the meaning or effect of any provision of that Protocol.

NOTES

Sub-s (3): words in square brackets substituted by the Treaty of Lisbon (Changes in Terminology) Order 2011, SI 2011/1043, art 4(1).

[1.1065]
4   Revision of Conventions etc
(1)   If at any time it appears to Her Majesty in Council that Her Majesty's Government in the United Kingdom—
- (a)   have agreed to a revision of any of the Conventions (including, in particular, any revision connected with the accession to the Rome Convention of any state); or
- (b)   have given notification in accordance with Article 22(3) of the Rome Convention that either or both of the provisions mentioned in section 2(2) above shall have the force of law in the United Kingdom,

Her Majesty may by Order in Council make such consequential modifications of this Act or any other statutory provision, whenever passed or made, as Her Majesty considers appropriate.

(2)   An Order in Council under subsection (1) above shall not be made unless a draft of the Order has been laid before Parliament and approved by a resolution of each House.

(3)   In subsection (1) above—

"modifications" includes additions, omissions and alterations;

"revision" means an omission from, addition to or alteration of any of the Conventions and includes replacement of any of the Conventions to any extent by another convention, protocol or other description of international agreement; and "statutory provision" means any provision contained in an Act, or in any Northern Ireland legislation, or in—

(a) subordinate legislation (as defined in section 21(1) of the Interpretation Act 1978); or

(b) any instrument of a legislative character made under any Northern Ireland legislation.

[1.1066]
[4A Disapplication where the rules in the Rome I Regulations apply: England and Wales and Northern Ireland

(1) Nothing in this Act applies to affect the determination of issues relating to contractual obligations which fall to be determined under the Rome I Regulation.

(2) In this section the "Rome I Regulation" means Regulation (EC) No 593/2008 of the European Parliament and of the Council on the law applicable to contractual obligations, including that Regulation as applied by regulation 3 of the Law Applicable to Contractual Obligations (England and Wales and Northern Ireland) Regulations 2009 (conflicts falling within Article 22(2) of Regulation (EC) No 593/2008).

(3) This section extends to England and Wales and Northern Ireland only.]

NOTES
Inserted by the Law Applicable to Contractual Obligations (England and Wales and Northern Ireland) Regulations 2009, SI 2009/3064, reg 2.

4B, 5 (*S 4B inserted by the Law Applicable to Contractual Obligations (Scotland) Regulations 2009, SSI 2009/410, reg 2(a) and applies to Scotland only; s 5 introduces Sch 4 (consequential amendments) outside the scope of this work.*)

[1.1067]
6 Application to Crown
This Act binds the Crown.

[1.1068]
7 Commencement
This Act shall come into force on such day as the Lord Chancellor and the Lord Advocate may by order made by statutory instrument appoint; and different days may be appointed for different provisions or different purposes.

NOTES
Orders: the Contracts (Applicable Law) Act 1990 (Commencement No 1) Order 1991, SI 1991/707; the Contracts (Applicable Law) Act 1990 (Commencement No 2) Order 2004, SI 2004/3448.

[1.1069]
8 Extent

(1) [Except as provided by virtue of section 4B(3), this] Act extends to Northern Ireland.

(2) Her Majesty may by Order in Council direct that all or any of the provisions of this Act shall extend to any of the following territories, namely—

(a) the Isle of Man;

(b) any of the Channel Islands;

(c) Gibraltar;

(d) the Sovereign Base Areas of Akrotiri and Dhekelia (that is to say, the areas mentioned in section 2(1) of the Cyprus Act 1960).

(3) An Order in Council under subsection (2) above may modify this Act in its application to any of the territories mentioned in that subsection and may contain such supplementary provisions as Her Majesty considers appropriate; and in this subsection "modify" shall be construed in accordance with section 4 above.

NOTES
Sub-s (1): words in square brackets substituted for original word "This" in relation to Scotland only by the Law Applicable to Contractual Obligations (Scotland) Regulations 2009, SSI 2009/410, reg 2(b).

[1.1070]
9 Short title
This Act may be cited as the Contracts (Applicable Law) Act 1990.

SCHEDULES

SCHEDULE 1
THE ROME CONVENTION

Section 2

[1.1071]
The High Contracting Parties to the Treaty establishing the European Economic Community,

Anxious to continue in the field of private international law the work of unification of law which has already been done within the Community, in particular in the field of jurisdiction and enforcement of judgments,

Wishing to establish uniform rules concerning the law applicable to contractual obligations,

HAVE AGREED AS FOLLOWS—

TITLE I
SCOPE OF THE CONVENTION

Article 1
Scope of the Convention

1. The rules of this Convention shall apply to contractual obligations in any situation involving a choice between the laws of different countries.

2. They shall not apply to—
  (a) questions involving the status or legal capacity of natural persons, without prejudice to Article 11;
  (b) contractual obligations relating to—
    — wills and succession,
    — rights in property arising out of a matrimonial relationship,
    — rights and duties arising out of a family relationship, parentage, marriage or affinity, including maintenance obligations in respect of children who are not legitimate;
  (c) obligations arising under bills of exchange, cheques and promissory notes and other negotiable instruments to the extent that the obligations under such other negotiable instruments arise out of their negotiable character;
  (d) arbitration agreements and agreements on the choice of court;
  (e) questions governed by the law of companies and other bodies corporate or unincorporate such as the creation, by registration or otherwise, legal capacity, internal organisation or winding up of companies and other bodies corporate or unincorporate and the personal liability of officers and members as such for the obligations of the company or body;
  (f) the question whether an agent is able to bind a principal, or an organ to bind a company or body corporate or unincorporate, to a third party;
  (g) the constitution of trusts and the relationship between settlors, trustees and beneficiaries;
  (h) evidence and procedure, without prejudice to Article 14.

3. The rules of this Convention do not apply to contracts of insurance which cover risks situated in the territories of the Member States of the European Economic Community. In order to determine whether a risk is situated in these territories the court shall apply its internal law.

4. The preceding paragraph does not apply to contracts of re-insurance.

Article 2
Application of law of non-contracting States

Any law specified by this Convention shall be applied whether or not it is the law of a Contracting State.

TITLE II
UNIFORM RULES

Article 3
Freedom of choice

1. A contract shall be governed by the law chosen by the parties. The choice must be express or demonstrated with reasonable certainty by the terms of the contract or the circumstances of the case. By their choice the parties can select the law applicable to the whole or a part only of the contract.

2. The parties may at any time agree to subject the contract to a law other than that which previously governed it, whether as a result of an earlier choice under this Article or of other provisions of this Convention. Any variation by the parties of the law to be applied made after the conclusion of the contract shall not prejudice its formal validity under Article 9 or adversely affect the rights of third parties.

3. The fact that the parties have chosen a foreign law, whether or not accompanied by the choice of a foreign tribunal, shall not, where all the other elements relevant to the situation at the time of the choice are connected with one country only, prejudice the application of rules of the law of that country which cannot be derogated from by contract, hereinafter called "mandatory rules".

4. The existence and validity of the consent of the parties as to the choice of the applicable law shall be determined in accordance with the provisions of Articles 8, 9 and 11.

Article 4
Applicable law in the absence of choice

1. To the extent that the law applicable to the contract has not been chosen in accordance with Article 3, the contract shall be governed by the law of the country with which it is most closely connected. Nevertheless, a severable part of the contract which has a closer connection with another country may by way of exception be governed by the law of that other country.

2. Subject to the provisions of paragraph 5 of this Article, it shall be presumed that the contract is most closely connected with the country where the party who is to effect the performance which is characteristic of the contract has, at the time of conclusion of the contract, his habitual residence or, in the case of a body corporate or unincorporate, its central administration. However, if the contract is entered into in the course of that party's trade or profession, that country shall be the country in which the principal place of business is situated or, where under the terms of the contract the performance is to be effected through a place of business other than the principal place of business, the country in which that other place of business is situated.

3. Notwithstanding the provisions of paragraph 2 of this Article, to the extent that the subject matter of the contract is a right in immovable property or a right to use immovable property it shall be presumed that the contract is most closely connected with the country where the immovable property is situated.

4. A contract for the carriage of goods shall not be subject to the presumption in paragraph 2. In such a contract if the country in which, at the time the contract is concluded, the carrier has his principal place of business is also the country in which the place of loading or the place of discharge or the principal place of business of the consignor is situated, it shall be presumed that the contract is most closely connected with that country. In applying this paragraph single voyage charter-parties and other contracts the main purpose of which is the carriage of goods shall be treated as contracts for the carriage of goods.

5. Paragraph 2 shall not apply if the characteristic performance cannot be determined, and the presumptions in paragraphs 2, 3 and 4 shall be disregarded if it appears from the circumstances as a whole that the contract is more closely connected with another country.

Article 5
Certain consumer contracts

1. This Article applies to a contract the object of which is the supply of goods or services to a person ("the consumer") for a purpose which can be regarded as being outside his trade or profession, or a contract for the provision of credit for that object.

2. Notwithstanding the provisions of Article 3, a choice of law made by the parties shall not have the result of depriving the consumer of the protection afforded to him by the mandatory rules of the law of the country in which he has his habitual residence—
— if in that country the conclusion of the contract was preceded by a specific invitation addressed to him or by advertising, and he had taken in that country all the steps necessary on his part for the conclusion of the contract, or
— if the other party or his agent received the consumer's order in that country, or
— if the contract is for the sale of goods and the consumer travelled from that country to another country and there gave his order, provided that the consumer's journey was arranged by the seller for the purpose of inducing the consumer to buy.

3. Notwithstanding the provisions of Article 4, a contract to which this Article applies shall, in the absence of choice in accordance with Article 3, be governed by the law of the country in which the consumer has his habitual residence if it is entered into in the circumstances described in paragraph 2 of this Article.

4. This Article shall not apply to—
(a)   a contract of carriage;
(b)   a contract for the supply of services where the services are to be supplied to the consumer exclusively in a country other than that in which he has his habitual residence.

5. Notwithstanding the provisions of paragraph 4, this Article shall apply to a contract which, for an inclusive price, provides for a combination of travel and accommodation.

Article 6
Individual employment contracts

1. Notwithstanding the provisions of Article 3, in a contract of employment a choice of law made by the parties shall not have the result of depriving the employee of the protection afforded to him by the mandatory rules of the law which would be applicable under paragraph 2 in the absence of choice.

2. Notwithstanding the provisions of Article 4, a contract of employment shall, in the absence of choice in accordance with Article 3, be governed—
  (a) by the law of the country in which the employee habitually carries out his work in performance of the contract, even if he is temporarily employed in another country; or
  (b) if the employee does not habitually carry out his work in any one country, by the law of the country in which the place of business through which he was engaged is situated;
unless it appears from the circumstances as a whole that the contract is more closely connected with another country, in which case the contract shall be governed by the law of that country.

Article 7
Mandatory rules

1. When applying under this Convention the law of a country, effect may be given to the mandatory rules of the law of another country with which the situation has a close connection, if and in so far as, under the law of the latter country, those rules must be applied whatever the law applicable to the contract. In considering whether to give effect to these mandatory rules, regard shall be had to their nature and purpose and to the consequences of their application or non-application.

2. Nothing in this Convention shall restrict the application of the rules of the law of the forum in a situation where they are mandatory irrespective of the law otherwise applicable to the contract.

Article 8
Material validity

1. The existence and validity of a contract, or of any term of a contract, shall be determined by the law which would govern it under this Convention if the contract or term were valid.

2. Nevertheless a party may rely upon the law of the country in which he has his habitual residence to establish that he did not consent if it appears from the circumstances that it would not be reasonable to determine the effect of his conduct in accordance with the law specified in the preceding paragraph.

Article 9
Formal validity

1. A contract concluded between persons who are in the same country is formally valid if it satisfies the formal requirements of the law which governs it under this Convention or of the law of the country where it is concluded.

2. A contract concluded between persons who are in different countries is formally valid if it satisfies the formal requirements of the law which governs it under this Convention or of the law of one of those countries.

3. Where a contract is concluded by an agent, the country in which the agent acts is the relevant country for the purposes of paragraphs 1 and 2.

4. An act intended to have legal effect relating to an existing or contemplated contract is formally valid if it satisfies the formal requirements of the law which under this Convention governs or would govern the contract or of the law of the country where the act was done.

5. The provisions of the preceding paragraphs shall not apply to a contract to which Article 5 applies, concluded in the circumstances described in paragraph 2 of Article 5. The formal validity of such a contract is governed by the law of the country in which the consumer has his habitual residence.

6. Notwithstanding paragraphs 1 to 4 of this Article, a contract the subject matter of which is a right in immovable property or a right to use immovable property shall be subject to the mandatory requirements of form of the law of the country where the property is situated if by that law those requirements are imposed irrespective of the country where the contract is concluded and irrespective of the law governing the contract.

Article 10
Scope of the applicable law

1. The law applicable to a contract by virtue of Articles 3 to 6 and 12 of this Convention shall govern in particular—

- (a) interpretation;
- (b) performance;
- (c) within the limits of the powers conferred on the court by its procedural law, the consequences of breach, including the assessment of damages in so far as it is governed by rules of law;
- (d) the various ways of extinguishing obligations, and prescription and limitation of actions;
- (e) the consequences of nullity of the contract.

2. In relation to the manner of performance and the steps to be taken in the event of defective performance regard shall be had to the law of the country in which performance takes place.

Article 11
Incapacity

In a contract concluded between persons who are in the same country, a natural person who would have capacity under the law of that country may invoke his incapacity resulting from another law only if the other party to the contract was aware of this incapacity at the time of the conclusion of the contract or was not aware thereof as a result of negligence.

Article 12
Voluntary assignment

1. The mutual obligations of assignor and assignee under a voluntary assignment of a right against another person ("the debtor") shall be governed by the law which under this Convention applies to the contract between the assignor and assignee.

2. The law governing the right to which the assignment relates shall determine its assignability, the relationship between the assignee and the debtor, the conditions under which the assignment can be invoked against the debtor and any question whether the debtor's obligations have been discharged.

Article 13
Subrogation

1. Where a person ("the creditor") has a contractual claim upon another ("the debtor"), and a third person has a duty to satisfy the creditor, or has in fact satisfied the creditor in discharge of that duty, the law which governs the third person's duty to satisfy the creditor shall determine whether the third person is entitled to exercise against the debtor the rights which the creditor had against the debtor under the law governing their relationship and, if so, whether he may do so in full or only to a limited extent.

2. The same rule applies where several persons are subject to the same contractual claim and one of them has satisfied the creditor.

Article 14
Burden of proof, etc

1. The law governing the contract under this Convention applies to the extent that it contains, in the law of contract, rules which raise presumptions of law or determine the burden of proof.

2. A contract or an act intended to have legal effect may be proved by any mode of proof recognised by the law of the forum or by any of the laws referred to in Article 9 under which that contract or act is formally valid, provided that such mode of proof can be administered by the forum.

Article 15
Exclusion of renvoi

The application of the law of any country specified by this Convention means the application of the rules of law in force in that country other than its rules of private international law.

Article 16
"Ordre public"

The application of a rule of the law of any country specified by this Convention may be refused only if such application is manifestly incompatible with the public policy ("ordre public") of the forum.

Article 17
No retrospective effect

This Convention shall apply in a Contracting State to contracts made after the date on which this Convention has entered into force with respect to that State.

Article 18
Uniform interpretation

In the interpretation and application of the preceding uniform rules, regard shall be had to their international character and to the desirability of achieving uniformity in their interpretation and application.

Article 19
States with more than one legal system

1. Where a State comprises several territorial units each of which has its own rules of law in respect of contractual obligations, each territorial unit shall be considered as a country for the purposes of identifying the law applicable under this Convention.

2. A State within which different territorial units have their own rules of law in respect of contractual obligations shall not be bound to apply this Convention to conflicts solely between the laws of such units.

Article 20
Precedence of Community Law

This Convention shall not affect the application of provisions which, in relation to particular matters, lay down choice of law rules relating to contractual obligations and which are or will be contained in acts of the institutions of the European Communities or in national laws harmonised in implementation of such acts.

Article 21
Relationship with other conventions

This Convention shall not prejudice the application of international conventions to which a Contracting State is, or becomes, a party.

Article 22
Reservations

1. Any Contracting State may, at the time of signature, ratification, acceptance or approval, reserve the right not to apply—
    (a)   the provisions of Article 7(1);
    (b)   the provisions of Article 10(1)(e).

2. . . .

3. Any Contracting State may at any time withdraw a reservation which it has made; the reservation shall cease to have effect on the first day of the third calendar month after notification of the withdrawal.

TITLE III
FINAL PROVISIONS

Article 23

1. If, after the date on which this Convention has entered into force for a Contracting State, that State wishes to adopt any new choice of law rule in regard to any particular category of contract within the scope of this Convention, it shall communicate its intention to the other signatory States through the Secretary-General of the Council of the European Communities.

2. Any signatory State may, within six months from the date of the communication made to the Secretary-General, request him to arrange consultations between signatory States in order to reach agreement.

3. If no signatory State has requested consultations within this period or if within two years following the communication made to the Secretary-General no agreement is reached in the course of consultations, the Contracting State concerned may amend its law in the manner indicated. The measures taken by that State shall be brought to the knowledge of the other signatory States through the Secretary-General of the Council of the European Communities.

Article 24

1. If, after the date on which this Convention has entered into force with respect to a Contracting State, that State wishes to become a party to a multilateral convention whose principal aim or one of whose principal aims is to lay down rules of private international law concerning any of the matters governed by this Convention, the procedure set out in Article 23 shall apply. However, the period of two years, referred to in paragraph 3 of that Article, shall be reduced to one year.

2. The procedure referred to in the preceding paragraph need not be followed if a Contracting State or one of the European Communities is already a party to the multilateral convention, or if its object is to revise a convention to which the State concerned is already a party, or if it is a convention concluded within the framework of the Treaties establishing the European Communities.

Article 25

If a Contracting State considers that the unification achieved by this Convention is prejudiced by the conclusion of agreements not covered by Article 24(1), that State may request the Secretary-General of the Council of the European Communities to arrange consultations between the signatory States of this Convention.

Article 26

Any Contracting State may request the revision of this Convention. In this event a revision conference shall be convened by the President of the Council of the European Communities.

Article 27

. . .

Article 28

1. This Convention shall be open from 19 June 1980 for signature by the States party to the Treaty establishing the European Economic Community.

2. This Convention shall be subject to ratification, acceptance or approval by the signatory States. The instruments of ratification, acceptance or approval shall be deposited with the Secretary-General of the Council of the European Communities.

Article 29

1. This Convention shall enter into force on the first day of the third month following the deposit of the seventh instrument of ratification, acceptance or approval.

2. This Convention shall enter into force for each signatory State ratifying, accepting or approving at a later date on the first day of the third month following the deposit of its instrument of ratification, acceptance or approval.

Article 30

1. This Convention shall remain in force for 10 years from the date of its entry into force in accordance with Article 29(1), even for States for which it enters into force at a later date.

2. If there has been no denunciation it shall be renewed tacitly every five years.

3. A Contracting State which wishes to denounce shall, not less than six months before the expiration of the period of 10 or five years, as the case may be, give notice to the Secretary-General of the Council of the European Communities . . .

4. The denunciation shall have effect only in relation to the State which has notified it. The Convention will remain in force as between all other Contracting States.

Article 31

The Secretary-General of the Council of the European Communities shall notify the States party to the Treaty establishing the European Economic Community of—

(a)   the signatures;

(b)   the deposit of each instrument of ratification, acceptance or approval;

(c)   the date of entry into force of this Convention;

[(d)   communications made in pursuance of Articles 23, 24, 25, 26 and 30;]

(e)   the reservations and withdrawals of reservations referred to in Article 22.

Article 32

The Protocol annexed to this Convention shall form an integral part thereof.

Article 33

This Convention, drawn up in a single original in the Danish, Dutch, English, French, German, Irish and Italian languages, these texts being equally authentic, shall be deposited in the archives of the Secretariat of the Council of the European Communities. The Secretary-General shall transmit a certified copy thereof to the Government of each signatory State.

[PROTOCOL

The High Contracting Parties have agreed upon the following provision which shall be annexed to the Convention:

Notwithstanding the provisions of the Convention, Denmark, Sweden and Finland may retain national provisions concerning the law applicable to questions relating to the carriage of goods by sea and may amend such provisions without following the procedure provided for in Article 23 of the Convention of Rome. The national provisions applicable in this respect are the following:

—   in Denmark, paragraphs 252 and 321(3) and (4) of the "Sølov" (maritime law);

—   in Sweden, Chapter 13, Article 2(1) and (2), and Chapter 14, Article 1(3), of "sjölagen" (maritime law);

—   in Finland, Chapter 13, Article 2(1) and (2), and Chapter 14, Article 1(3) of "merilaki"/"sjölagen" (maritime law).]

NOTES

Articles 22.2, 27, and words omitted from Article 30.3 repealed, and Article 31(d) substituted, by the Contracts (Applicable Law) Act 1990 (Amendment) Order 1994, SI 1994/1900, arts 7, 8.

Protocol substituted by the Contracts (Applicable Law) Act 1990 (Amendment) Order 2000, SI 2000/1825, art 5.

SCHEDULE 2
THE LUXEMBOURG CONVENTION

Section 2

[1.1072]

The High Contracting Parties to the Treaty establishing the European Economic Community,

Considering that the Hellenic Republic, in becoming a Member of the Community, undertook to accede to the Convention on the law applicable to contractual obligations, opened for signature in Rome on 19 June 1980,

Have decided to conclude this Convention, and to this end have designated as their plenipotentiaries—

(designation of plenipotentiaries)

Who, meeting within the Council, having exchanged their full powers, found in good and due form,

HAVE AGREED AS FOLLOWS—

Article 1

The Hellenic Republic hereby accedes to the Convention on the law applicable to contractual obligations, opened for signature in Rome on 19 June 1980.

Article 2

The Secretary-General of the Council of the European Communities shall transmit a certified copy of the Convention on the law applicable to contractual obligations in the Danish, Dutch, English, French, German, Irish and Italian languages to the Government of the Hellenic Republic.

The text of the Convention on the law applicable to contractual obligations in the Greek language is annexed hereto. The text in the Greek language shall be authentic under the same conditions as the other texts of the Convention on the law applicable to contractual obligations.

Article 3

This Convention shall be ratified by the Signatory States. The instruments of ratification shall be deposited with the Secretary-General of the Council of the European Communities.

Article 4

This Convention shall enter into force, as between the States which have ratified it, on the first day of the third month following the deposit of the last instrument of ratification by the Hellenic Republic and seven States which have ratified the Convention on the law applicable to contractual obligations.

This Convention shall enter into force for each Contracting State which subsequently ratifies it on the first day of the third month following the deposit of its instrument of ratification.

Article 5

The Secretary-General of the Council of the European Communities shall notify the Signatory States of—
- (a) the deposit of each instrument of ratification;
- (b) the dates of entry into force of this Convention for the Contracting States.

Article 6

This Convention, drawn up in a single original in the Danish, Dutch, English, French, German, Greek, Irish and Italian languages, all eight texts being equally authentic, shall be deposited in the archives of the General Secretariat of the Council of the European Communities. The Secretary-General shall transmit a certified copy to the Government of each Signatory State.

SCHEDULE 3
THE BRUSSELS PROTOCOL

Section 2

[1.1073]
The High Contracting Parties to the Treaty establishing the European Economic Community,

Having regard to the Joint Declaration annexed to the Convention on the law applicable to contractual obligations, opened for signature in Rome on 19 June 1980,

Have decided to conclude a Protocol conferring jurisdiction on the Court of Justice of the European Communities to interpret that Convention, and to this end have designated as their Plenipotentiaries—

(designation of plenipotentiaries)

Who, meeting within the Council of the European Communities, having exchanged their full powers, found in good and due form,

HAVE AGREED AS FOLLOWS—

Article 1

The Court of Justice of the European Communities shall have jurisdiction to give rulings on the interpretation of—
- (a) the Convention on the law applicable to contractual obligations, opened for signature in Rome on 19 June 1980, hereinafter referred to as "the Rome Convention";
- (b) the Convention on accession to the Rome Convention by the States which have become Members of the European Communities since the date on which it was opened for signature;
- (c) this Protocol.

Article 2

Any of the courts referred to below may request the Court of Justice to give a preliminary ruling on a question raised in a case pending before it and concerning interpretation of the provisions contained in the instruments referred to in Article 1 if that court considers that a decision on the question is necessary to enable it to give judgment—
- (a) — in Belgium:
  la Cour de cassation (het Hof van Cassatie) and le Conseil d'Etat (de Raad van State),
  — in Denmark:
  Højesteret,
  — in the Federal Republic of Germany:

            die obersten Gerichtschöfe des Bundes,
—   in Greece:
            τα ανωτατα Δικαστηρια,
—   in Spain:
            el Tribunal Supremo,
—   in France:
            la Cour de cassation and le Conseil d'Etat,
—   in Ireland:
            the Supreme Court,
—   in Italy:
            la Corte suprema di cassazione and il Consiglio di Stato,
—   in Luxembourg:
            la Cour Supérieure de Justice, when sitting as Cour de cassation,
[—   in Austria:
            the Oberste Gerichtshof, the Verwaltungsgerichtshof and the Verfassungsgerichtshof,]
—   in the Netherlands:
            de Hoge Raad,
—   in Portugal:
            o Supremo Tribunal de Justiça and o Supremo Tribunal Administrativo,
[—   in Finland:
            korkein oikeus/högsta domstolen, korkein hallinto-oikeus/högsta förvaltningsdomstolen, markkinatuomioistuin/marknadsdomstolen and työtuomioistuin/arbetsdomstolen,
—   Sweden:
            Högsta domstolen, Regeringsrätten, Arbetsdomstolen and Marknadsdomstolen,]
—   in the United Kingdom:
            the House of Lords and other courts from which no further appeal is possible;
(b)   the courts of the Contracting States when acting as appeal courts.

Article 3

1. The competent authority of a Contracting State may request the Court of Justice to give a ruling on a question of interpretation of the provisions contained in the instruments referred to in Article 1 if judgments given by courts of that State conflict with the interpretation given either by the Court of Justice or in a judgment of one of the courts of another Contracting State referred to in Article 2. The provisions of this paragraph shall apply only to judgments which have become res judicata.

2. The interpretation given by the Court of Justice in response to such a request shall not affect the judgments which gave rise to the request for interpretation.

3. The Procurators-General of the Supreme Courts of Appeal of the Contracting States, or any other authority designated by a Contracting State, shall be entitled to request the Court of Justice for a ruling on interpretation in accordance with paragraph 1.

4. The Registrar of the Court of Justice shall give notice of the request to the Contracting States, to the Commission and to the Council of the European Communities; they shall then be entitled within two months of the notification to submit statements of case or written observations to the Court.

5. No fees shall be levied or any costs or expenses awarded in respect of the proceedings provided for in this Article.

Article 4

1. Except where this Protocol otherwise provides, the provisions of the Treaty establishing the European Economic Community and those of the Protocol on the Statute of the Court of Justice annexed thereto, which are applicable when the Court is requested to give a preliminary ruling, shall also apply to any proceedings for the interpretation of the instruments referred to in Article 1.

2. The Rules of Procedure of the Court of Justice shall, if necessary, be adjusted and supplemented in accordance with Article 188 of the Treaty establishing the European Economic Community.

Article 5

This Protocol shall be subject to ratification by the Signatory States. The instruments of ratification shall be deposited with the Secretary-General of the Council of the European Communities.

Article 6

1. To enter into force, this Protocol must be ratified by seven States in respect of which the Rome Convention is in force. This Protocol shall enter into force on the first day of the third month following the deposit of the instrument of ratification by the last such State to take this step. If, however, the Second Protocol conferring on the Court of Justice of the European Communities certain powers to interpret the Convention on the law applicable to contractual obligations, opened for signature in Rome on 19 June 1980, concluded in Brussels on 19 December 1988, enters into force on a later date, this Protocol shall enter into force on the date of entry into force of the Second Protocol.

2. Any ratification subsequent to the entry into force of this Protocol shall take effect on the first day of the third month following the deposit of the instrument of ratification provided that the ratification, acceptance or approval of the Rome Convention by the State in question has become effective.

Article 7

The Secretary-General of the Council of the European Communities shall notify the Signatory States of—
  (a) the deposit of each instrument of ratification;
  (b) the date of entry into force of this Protocol;
  (c) any designation communicated pursuant to Article 3(3);
  (d) any communication made pursuant to Article 8.

Article 8

The Contracting States shall communicate to the Secretary-General of the Council of the European Communities the texts of any provisions of their laws which necessitate an amendment to the list of courts in Article 2(a).

Article 9

This Protocol shall have effect for as long as the Rome Convention remains in force under the conditions laid down in Article 30 of that Convention.

Article 10

Any Contracting State may request the revision of this Protocol. In this event, a revision conference shall be convened by the President of the Council of the European Communities.

Article 11

This Protocol, drawn up in a single original in the Danish, Dutch, English, French, German, Greek, Irish, Italian, Portuguese and Spanish languages, all 10 texts being equally authentic, shall be deposited in the archives of the General Secretariat of the Council of the European Communities. The Secretary-General shall transmit a certified copy to the Government of each Signatory State.

NOTES

Art 2: in para (a) entries relating to Austria, Finland and Sweden inserted by the Contracts (Applicable Law) Act 1990 (Amendment) Order 2000, SI 2000/1825, art 6.

[SCHEDULE 3A
THE FUNCHAL CONVENTION

Section 2

[1.1074]
The High Contracting Parties to the Treaty establishing the European Economic Community.
  Considering that the Kingdom of Spain and the Portuguese Republic, in becoming Members of the Community, undertook to accede to the Convention on the law applicable to contractual obligations, opened for signature in Rome on 19th June 1980.
  Have decided to conclude this Convention, and to this end have designated as their plenipotentiaries—
  (designation of plenipotentiaries).
  Who, meeting within the Council, having exchanged their full powers, found in good and due form.

HAVE AGREED AS FOLLOWS—

Article 1

The Kingdom of Spain and the Portuguese Republic hereby accede to the Convention on the law applicable to contractual obligations, opened for signature in Rome on 19th June 1980.

Article 2

The Convention on the law applicable to contractual obligations is hereby amended as follows—
(1)   Article 22(2), Article 27 and the second sentence of Article 30(3) shall be deleted;
(2)   The reference to Article 27 in Article 31(d) shall be deleted.

Article 3

The Secretary-General of the Council of the European Communities shall transmit a certified copy of the Convention on the law applicable to contractual obligations in the Danish, Dutch, English, French, German, Greek, Irish and Italian languages to the Governments of the Kingdom of Spain and the Portuguese Republic.

Article 4

This Convention shall be ratified by the Signatory States. The instruments of ratification shall be deposited with the Secretary-General of the Council of the European Communities.

Article 5

This Convention shall enter into force, as between the States which have ratified it, on the first day of the third month following deposit of the last instrument of ratification by the Kingdom of Spain or the Portuguese Republic and by one State which has ratified the Convention on the law applicable to contractual obligations.

This Convention shall enter into force for each Contracting State which subsequently ratifies it on the first day of the third month following that of deposit of its instrument of ratification.

Article 6

The Secretary-General of the Council of the European Communities shall notify the Signatory States of—
(a)   the deposit of each instrument of ratification;
(b)   the dates of entry into force of this Convention for the Contracting States.

Article 7

This Convention, drawn up in a single original in the Danish, Dutch, English, French, German, Greek, Irish, Italian, Portuguese and Spanish languages, all ten texts being equally authentic, shall be deposited in the archives of the General Secretariat of the Council of the European Communities. The Secretary-General shall transmit a certified copy to the Government of each Signatory State.]

NOTES

Schedule inserted by the Contracts (Applicable Law) Act 1990 (Amendment) Order 1994, SI 1994/1900, art 9, Schedule.

[SCHEDULE 3B
THE 1996 ACCESSION CONVENTION

Section 2

[1.1075]

The High Contracting Parties to the Treaty establishing the European Community.

Considering that the Republic of Austria, the Republic of Finland and the Kingdom of Sweden, in becoming Members of the European Union, undertook to accede to the Convention on the Law applicable to Contractual Obligations, opened for signature in Rome on 19th June 1980, and to the First and Second Protocols on its interpretation by the Court of Justice,

HAVE AGREED AS FOLLOWS—

TITLE I
GENERAL PROVISIONS

Article 1

The Republic of Austria, the Republic of Finland and the Kingdom of Sweden hereby accede to—

(a) the Convention on the Law applicable to Contractual Obligations, opened for signature in Rome on 19th June 1980, hereinafter referred to as "the Convention of 1980", as it stands following incorporation of all the adjustments and amendments made thereto by—

— the Convention signed in Luxembourg on 10th April 1984, hereinafter referred to as "the Convention of 1984", on the accession of the Hellenic Republic to the Convention on the Law applicable to Contractual Obligations;

— the Convention signed in Funchal on 18th May 1992, hereinafter referred to as "the Convention of 1992", on the accession of the Kingdom of Spain and the Portuguese Republic to the Convention on the Law applicable to Contractual Obligations;

(b) the First Protocol, signed on 19th December 1988, hereinafter referred to as "the First Protocol of 1988", on the interpretation by the Court of Justice of the European Communities of the Convention on the Law applicable to Contractual Obligations;

(c) the Second Protocol, signed on 19th December 1988, hereinafter referred to as "the Second Protocol of 1988", conferring on the Court of Justice of the European Communities certain powers to interpret the Convention on the Law applicable to Contractual Obligations.

TITLE II
ADJUSTMENTS TO THE PROTOCOL ANNEXED TO THE CONVENTION OF 1980

Article 2

The Protocol annexed to the Convention of 1980 is hereby replaced by the following—

"Notwithstanding the provisions of the Convention, Denmark, Sweden and Finland may retain national provisions concerning the law applicable to questions relating to the carriage of goods by sea and may amend such provisions without following the procedure provided for in Article 23 of the Convention of Rome. The national provisions applicable in this respect are the following—

— in Denmark, paragraphs 252 and 321(3) and (4) of the "Sølov" (maritime law);
— in Sweden, Chapter 13, Article 2(1) and (2), and Chapter 14, Article 1(3), of "sjölagen" (maritime law);
— in Finland, Chapter 13, Article 2(1) and (2), and Chapter 14, Article 1(3), of "merilaki"/"sjölagn" (maritime law)."

TITLE III
ADJUSTMENTS TO THE FIRST PROTOCOL OF 1988

Article 3

The following indents shall be inserted in Article 2(a) of the First Protocol of 1988:

(a) between the tenth and eleventh indents:

"—in Austria:
the Oberste Gerichtshof, the Verwaltungsgerichtshof and the Verfassungsgerichtshof,"

(b) between the eleventh and twelfth indents:

"—in Finland:
Korkein oikeus/högsta domstolen, korkein hallinto-oikeus/högsta förvaltningsdomstolen, markkinatuomioistuin/ marknadsdomstolen and työtuomioistuin/arbetsdomstolen,
—in Sweden:
Högsta domstolen, Regeringsrätten, Arbetsdomstolen and Marknadsdomstolen,".

[TITLE IV
FINAL PROVISIONS

Article 4

1. The Secretary-General of the Council of the European Union shall transmit a certified copy of the Convention of 1980, the Convention of 1984, the First Protocol of 1988, the Second Protocol of 1988 and the Convention of 1992 in the Danish, Dutch, English, French, German, Greek, Irish, Italian, Spanish and Portuguese languages to the Governments of the Republic of Austria, the Republic of Finland and the Kingdom of Sweden.

2. The text of the Convention of 1980, the Convention of 1984, the First Protocol of 1988, the Second Protocol of 1988 and the Convention of 1992 in the Finnish and Swedish languages shall be authentic under the same conditions as the other texts of the Convention of 1980, the Convention of 1984, the First Protocol of 1988, the Second Protocol of 1988 and the Convention of 1992.

Article 5

This Convention shall be ratified by the Signatory States. The instruments of ratification shall be deposited with the Secretary-General of the Council of the European Union.

Article 6

1. This Convention shall enter into force, as between the States which have ratified it, on the first day of the third month following the deposit of the last instrument of ratification by the Republic of Austria, the Republic of Finland or the Kingdom of Sweden and by one Contracting State which has ratified the Convention on the Law applicable to Contractual Obligations.

2. This Convention shall enter into force for each Contracting State which subsequently ratifies it on the first day of the third month following the deposit of its instrument of ratification.

Article 7

The Secretary-General of the Council of the European Union shall notify the Signatory States of:
   (a)   the deposit of each instrument of ratification;
   (b)   the dates of entry into force of this Convention for the Contracting States.

Article 8

This Convention, drawn up in a single original in the Danish, Dutch, English, Finnish, French, German, Greek, Irish, Italian, Portuguese, Spanish and Swedish languages, all twelve texts being equally authentic, shall be deposited in the archives of the General Secretariat of the Council of the European Union. The Secretary-General shall transmit a certified copy to the Government of each Signatory State.]

NOTES
   Schedule inserted by the Contracts (Applicable Law) Act 1990 (Amendment) Order 2000, SI 2000/1825, art 7, Schedule.

SCHEDULE 4

(Sch 4 (consequential amendments) repealed in part; remainder outside the scope of this work.)

PROPERTY MISDESCRIPTIONS ACT 1991 (NOTE)

(1991 c 29)

[1.1076]

NOTES
   This Act was repealed by the Property Misdescriptions Act 1991 (Repeal) Order 2013, SI 2013/1575, art 2, as from 1 October 2013. Since the introduction of this Act, Directive 2005/29/EC of the European Parliament and of the Council concerning unfair business-to-consumer commercial practices (at **[4.345]**), and Directive 2006/114/EC of the European Parliament and of the Council concerning misleading and comparative advertising (at **[4.416]**) have been implemented in the UK. They provide the same protection for consumers as this Act but in a broader and more modern framework. This Act therefore become unnecessary and has been repealed.

EXPORT AND INVESTMENT GUARANTEES ACT 1991

(1991 c 67)

ARRANGEMENT OF SECTIONS

PART I
POWERS OF ECGD

PART II
TRANSFER OR DELEGATION OF ECGD FUNCTIONS

PART III
GENERAL

An Act to make new provision as to the functions exercisable by the Secretary of State through the Export Credits Guarantee Department; and make provision as to the delegation of any such functions and the transfer of property, rights and liabilities attributable to the exercise of any such functions

[22 October 1991]

PART I
POWERS OF ECGD

[1.1077]
1 [Arrangements for the support and development of supplies, etc]
[(1)   The Secretary of State may make arrangements under this section which the Secretary of State considers are conducive to supporting or developing (whether directly or indirectly) supplies or potential supplies by persons carrying on business in the United Kingdom of goods, services or intangible assets (including intellectual property) to persons carrying on business outside the United Kingdom.]
(2)   The Secretary of State may make arrangements under this section for the purpose of rendering economic assistance to countries outside the United Kingdom.
(3)   The Secretary of State may make arrangements under this section with a view to facilitating—
   (a)   the performance of obligations created or arising, directly or indirectly, in connection with matters as to which he has exercised his powers under this section or section 2 of this Act, or
   (b)   the reduction or avoidance of losses arising in connection with any failure to perform such obligations.
(4)   The arrangements that may be made under this section are arrangements for providing financial facilities or assistance for, or for the benefit of, persons carrying on business; and the facilities or assistance may be provided in any form, including guarantees, insurance, grants or loans.
[(5)   The arrangements that may be made under this section also include the provision of advice or information.]

NOTES
   Section heading: substituted by the Small Business, Enterprise and Employment Act 2015, s 11(1), (4).
   Sub-s (1): substituted for sub-ss (1), (1A) (as substituted for original sub-s (1) by the Industry and Exports (Financial Support) Act 2009, s 2(1)), by the Small Business, Enterprise and Employment Act 2015, s 11(1), (2).
   Sub-s (5): added by the Small Business, Enterprise and Employment Act 2015, s 11(1), (3).

[1.1078]
2 Insurance in connection with overseas investment
(1) The Secretary of State may make arrangements for insuring any person carrying on business in the United Kingdom against risks of losses arising—
  (a) in connection with any investment of resources by the insured in enterprises carried on outside the United Kingdom, or
  (b) in connection with guarantees given by the insured in respect of any investment of resources by others in such enterprises, being enterprises in which the insured has any interest,

being losses resulting directly or indirectly from war, expropriation, restrictions on remittances and other similar events.
(2) The Secretary of State may make arrangements for insuring persons providing such insurance.
(3) References in subsection (1) above to a person carrying on business in the United Kingdom and to the insured include any company controlled directly or indirectly by him.

[1.1079]
3 Financial management
(1) The Secretary of State may make any arrangements which, in his opinion, are in the interests of the proper financial management of the ECGD portfolio, or any part of it.
(2) In pursuance of arrangements under this section the Secretary of State may enter into any form of transaction, including—
  (a) lending, and
  (b) providing and taking out insurance and guarantees.
(3) The Secretary of State may not, in pursuance of such arrangements, enter into any transaction for the purpose of borrowing money but, subject to that, he is not precluded from entering into any transaction by reason of its involving borrowing.
(4) In pursuance of such arrangements the Secretary of State may—
  (a) alter any arrangements made under section 1 or 2 of this Act or the old law or make new arrangements in place of arrangements so made, or
  (b) make further arrangements in connection with arrangements so made.
(5) Arrangements under this section may be made in anticipation of further rights being acquired or liabilities being incurred by the Secretary of State.
(6) In this section the "ECGD portfolio" means the rights and liabilities to which the Secretary of State is entitled or subject by virtue of the exercise of his powers under this Act or the old law or in consequence of arrangements made in the exercise of those powers.
(7) The Secretary of State may certify that any transaction he has entered into or is entering into has been or, as the case may be, is entered into in the exercise of the powers conferred by this section and such a certificate shall be conclusive evidence of the matters stated in it.

[1.1080]
4 Provisions supplementary to sections 1 to 3
(1) Transactions entered into in pursuance of arrangements made under sections 1 to 3 of this Act may be on such terms and conditions as the Secretary of State considers appropriate.
(2) The powers of the Secretary of State under those sections are exercisable only with the consent of the Treasury and such consent may be given in relation to particular cases or in relation to such descriptions of cases as may be specified in the consent.
(3) In those sections—
  (a) "business" includes a profession,
  (b) "guarantee" includes indemnity,
  (c) references to persons carrying on business, in relation to things done outside the United Kingdom, include persons carrying on any other activities, and
  (d) references to things done in or outside the United Kingdom are to things done wholly or partly in or, as the case may be, outside the United Kingdom.
(4) References in this and those sections to the United Kingdom include the Isle of Man and the Channel Islands.

[1.1081]
5 Provision of services and information
(1) The Secretary of State may provide to any person—
  (a) information relating to credit or investment insurance,
  (b) services ancillary to the provision by that person of credit or investment insurance, and
  (c) such other goods or services as may be specified in an order under this section,
and may make such charges for doing so as he may determine.
(2) The power to make an order under this section is exercisable only with the consent of the Treasury.

[1.1082]
6 Commitment limits

(1) The aggregate amount of the Secretary of State's commitments at any time under arrangements relating to exports and insurance shall not exceed [67,700 million special drawing rights].

(2) In subsection (1) above, "arrangements relating to exports and insurance" means—

    (a)   arrangements under section 1 or 2 of this Act, other than arrangements for giving grants or arrangements under section 1(3), and

    (b)   arrangements under the old law, other than arrangements for giving grants.

(3) The aggregate amount of the Secretary of State's commitments at any time under section 3 of this Act shall not exceed [26,200 million special drawing rights].

(4) The Secretary of State may by order increase or further increase—

    (a)   [the limit] in subsection (1) above by a sum specified in the order not exceeding . . . 5,000 million special drawing rights

    (b)   [the limit] in subsection (3) above by a sum specified in the order not exceeding . . . 2,000 million special drawing rights,

. . . [after the commencement of section 12 of the Small Business, Enterprise and Employment Act 2015].

[(4A) The Secretary of State must not in respect of either limit mentioned in subsection (4) exercise the power to make an order on more than three occasions.]

(5) For the purposes of this section and section 7 of this Act—

    (a)   the commitments of the Secretary of State under any arrangements are his rights and liabilities relating to the arrangements,

    (b)   the amount of any commitments shall be ascertained in accordance with principles determined from time to time by the Secretary of State with the consent of the Treasury,

    (c), (d). . .

    (e)   the equivalent in special drawing rights of the amount of any commitments . . . shall be ascertained at intervals determined from time to time by the Secretary of State with the consent of the Treasury and in accordance with principles so determined.

(6) A determination under subsection (5)(e) above may provide for leaving out of account for the purposes of the limit in subsection [(1) or (3)] above any amount by which the limit would otherwise be exceeded to the extent that the amount is attributable to—

    (a)   a revaluation of commitments under subsection (5)(e) above, or

    (b)   the fulfilment of an undertaking which, had it been fulfilled when given, would not have caused the limit to be exceeded.

(7) Any power to make an order under this section is exercisable only with the consent of the Treasury.

NOTES

Sub-ss (1), (3), (6): words in square brackets substituted by the Small Business, Enterprise and Employment Act 2015, s 12(1)–(3), (8).

Sub-s (4): words in first and second pairs of square brackets substituted, words omitted repealed, and words in final pair of square brackets inserted by the Small Business, Enterprise and Employment Act 2015, s 12(1), (4), (5).

Sub-s (4A): inserted by the Small Business, Enterprise and Employment Act 2015, s 12(1), (6).

Sub-s (5): paras (c), (d) and words omitted from para (e) repealed by the Small Business, Enterprise and Employment Act 2015, s 12(1), (7).

Orders: the Export and Investment Guarantees (Limit on Foreign Currency Commitments) Order 2000, SI 2000/2087.

[1.1083]
7 Reports and returns

(1) The Secretary of State shall prepare an annual report on the discharge of his functions under sections 1 to 5 of this Act.

(2) The Secretary of State shall prepare, as soon as practicable after 31st March in each year, a return showing separately the aggregate amounts of the commitments . . . on that date for the purposes of the limits in section 6(1) and (3) of this Act.

(3) Any return under this section may also give such further information as to the amounts of his commitments for the purposes of those limits as the Secretary of State may determine for that return.

(4) . . .

(5) Reports and returns prepared under this section shall be laid before Parliament.

NOTES

Sub-s (2): words omitted repealed by the Small Business, Enterprise and Employment Act 2015, s 12(1), (9).

Sub-s (4): repealed by the Statute Law (Repeals) Act 2004.

PART II
TRANSFER OR DELEGATION OF ECGD FUNCTIONS

[1.1084]
8   Scheme of transfer

(1)   The Secretary of State may make a scheme or schemes for the transfer to any person or persons of such property, rights and liabilities as are specified in or determined in accordance with the scheme, being property, rights or liabilities—

   (a)   to which the Secretary of State (or, in the case of copyright, Her Majesty) is entitled or subject immediately before the day on which the scheme providing for the transfer comes into force, and

   (b)   which then subsisted for the purposes of or in connection with or are otherwise attributable (wholly or partly) to the exercise of functions under Part I of this Act or the old law.

(2)   Without prejudice to the generality of subsection (1)(b) above, any property, rights or liabilities shall be taken to fall within that subsection if the Secretary of State issues a certificate to that effect.

(3)   A scheme under this section may apply—

   (a)   to property wherever situated, and

   (b)   to property, rights and liabilities whether or not otherwise capable of being transferred or assigned by the Secretary of State or, as the case may be, Her Majesty.

(4)   A scheme under this section shall come into force on such day as may be specified in, or determined in accordance with, the scheme; and on that day the property, rights and liabilities to which the scheme applies shall be transferred and vest in accordance with the scheme.

(5)   A scheme under this section may contain such supplementary, incidental, consequential or transitional provisions as appear to the Secretary of State to be necessary or expedient.

(6)   The Schedule to this Act (scheme of transfer: supplementary provisions) shall have effect.

(7)   References below in this Act to a transferee are to any person to whom anything is transferred by virtue of a scheme under this section.

[1.1085]
9   Transferred staff

(1)   No scheme under section 8 of this Act shall provide for the transfer of any rights or liabilities relating to a person's employment, but the [Transfer of Undertakings (Protection of Employment) Regulations 2006] shall apply to the transfer of property, rights or liabilities by virtue of such a scheme whether or not the transfer would, apart from this subsection, be a relevant transfer for the purposes of those regulations.

(2)   Where, by reason of the operation of those regulations in relation to a transfer of property, rights or liabilities by virtue of such a scheme, a person ceases to be employed in the civil service of the State and becomes employed by a transferee—

   (a)   he shall not, on so ceasing, be treated for the purposes of any scheme under section 1 of the Superannuation Act 1972 as having retired on redundancy, and

   (b)   his ceasing to be employed in that service shall not be regarded as an occasion of redundancy for the purposes of the agreed redundancy procedures applicable to persons employed in that service.

NOTES

Sub-s (1): words in square brackets substituted, in relation to a relevant transfer that takes place on or after 6 April 2006, by the Transfer of Undertakings (Protection of Employment) Regulations 2006, SI 2006/246, reg 20(3), Sch 2, para 1(d), subject to transitional provisions and savings in reg 21 of those Regulations.

[1.1086]
10   Vehicle companies

(1)   In this section "vehicle company" means a company formed or acquired for the purpose of—

   (a)   becoming a transferee, or

   (b)   holding shares in a company formed or acquired for that purpose.

(2)   Subject to subsections (3) and (4) below, the Secretary of State may—

   (a)   subscribe for or otherwise acquire shares in or securities of a vehicle company, or acquire rights to subscribe for such shares or securities,

   (b)   by a direction given to a company formed or acquired for the purpose of becoming a transferee require it, in consequence of the transfer by virtue of a scheme under section 8 of this Act of property, rights or liabilities, to issue to him, or to such other person as may be specified in the direction, such shares or securities as may be so specified,

   (c)   from time to time by a direction given to a vehicle company require it to issue to him, or to such other person as may be specified in the direction, such shares or securities as may be so specified, or

   (d)   make loans to a vehicle company on such terms and conditions as he may determine.

(3)   A direction under subsection (2)(b) or (c) above may require any shares to which it relates to be issued as fully or partly paid up.

(4)   The Secretary of State shall not—

(a) subscribe for or otherwise acquire shares in or securities of a vehicle company, or acquire rights to subscribe for such shares or securities, unless all the relevant shares are to be held by or on behalf of the Crown, or

(b) at any time give a direction or make a loan to a vehicle company unless all the relevant shares are then held by or on behalf of the Crown.

(5) For the purposes of subsection (4) above—

(a) shares are held by or on behalf of the Crown where the Crown or any person acting on behalf of the Crown has a legal interest in them; and

(b) "relevant shares", in relation to a vehicle company, means the issued shares of that company or, if it is a subsidiary of another vehicle company, the issued shares of that other company.

(6) A scheme under section 8 of this Act may, as between any vehicle companies or as between a vehicle company and the Secretary of State, confer or impose rights and liabilities in connection with any of the matters as to which the Secretary of State may exercise his powers under this Act.

(7) The Secretary of State shall not exercise any of the powers conferred by the preceding provisions of this section or dispose of any shares in or securities of a vehicle company without the consent of the Treasury.

[1.1087]
11 Reinsurance

(1) The Secretary of State may make arrangements with any transferee under which the transferee insures the Secretary of State against risks of losses arising in consequence of arrangements made, before the day on which any scheme under section 8 of this Act comes into force, under Part I of this Act or the old law.

(2) The Secretary of State shall from time to time determine, in relation to such classes of risk determined by him as might be insured by him under section 1 of this Act, whether it is expedient in the national interest for him to exercise his powers under that section to make arrangements for reinsuring persons providing insurance for risks of that class.

(3) This section is without prejudice to any power of the Secretary of State under Part I of this Act.

[1.1088]
12 Delegation of assistance function

(1) The Secretary of State may make arrangements for any of the functions to which this section applies to be exercised on his behalf by any transferee or any other person, instead of through the Export Credits Guarantee Department, on such terms and conditions as he may determine.

(2) This section applies to the power of the Secretary of State to make arrangements under section 1 of this Act and to any functions of his under arrangements so made, or arrangements under the old law, including, so far as relating to any such arrangements, arrangements made by virtue of section 3(4) of this Act.

(3) This section does not affect any requirement for the consent of the Treasury.

PART III
GENERAL

[1.1089]
13 The Export Credits Guarantee Department and the Export Guarantees Advisory Council

(1) All the functions of the Secretary of State under Part I of this Act, except the power to make orders under section 5 or 6 of this Act, shall be exercised and performed through the Export Credits Guarantee Department, which shall continue to be a Department of the Secretary of State.

(2) There shall continue to be an Export Guarantees Advisory Council.

(3) The function of the Council shall be to give advice to the Secretary of State, at his request, in respect of ally matter relating to the exercise of his functions under this Act.

(4) . . .

NOTES

Sub-s (4): repealed by the Small Business, Enterprise and Employment Act 2015, s 12(1), (10).

[1.1090]
14 Expenses

(1) Any sums required by the Secretary of State for making payments or for defraying his administrative expenses under this Act shall be paid out of money provided by Parliament and any sums received by the Secretary of State by virtue of this Act shall be paid into the Consolidated Fund.

(2) If any sum required by the Secretary of State for fulfilling his liabilities under this Act is not paid out of money provided by Parliament, it shall be charged on and paid out of the Consolidated Fund.

[1.1091]
15   Short title, interpretation, commencement, etc
(1)   This Act may be cited as the Export and Investment Guarantees Act 1991.
(2)   In this Act "the old law" means the Export Guarantees and Overseas Investment Act 1978 and any earlier enactment from which any provision of that Act was derived.
(3)   Any power to make an order under section 5 or 6 of this Act shall be exercisable by statutory instrument and no such order shall be made unless a draft of it has been laid before and approved by resolution of the House of Commons.
(4)   . . .
(5)   Subsection (4) above does not affect any power exercisable by the Secretary of State in respect of arrangements made under the old law.
(6)   . . .

NOTES
Sub-s (4): repeals the Export Guarantees and Overseas Investment Act 1978.
Sub-s (6): repealed by the Statute Law (Repeals) Act 2004.
Orders: the Export and Investment Guarantees Act 1991 (Commencement) Order 1991, SI 1991/2430.

SCHEDULE
SCHEME OF TRANSFER: SUPPLEMENTARY PROVISIONS

Section 8

Certificate of vesting
[1.1092]
1.   A certificate by the Secretary of State that anything specified in the certificate has vested on any day in any person by virtue of a scheme under section 8 of this Act shall be conclusive evidence for all purposes of that fact.

Construction of agreements etc
2.   (1)   This paragraph applies to any agreement made, transaction effected or other thing (not contained in an enactment) which—
  (a)   has been made, effected or done by, to or in relation to the Secretary of State,
  (b)   relates to any property, right or liability transferred from the Secretary of State in accordance with the scheme, and
  (c)   is in force or effective immediately before the day on which the scheme comes into force.
(2)   The agreement, transaction or other thing shall have effect on and after that day as if made, effected or done by, to or in relation to the transferee.
(3)   Accordingly, references to the Secretary of State which relate to or affect any property, right or liability of the Secretary of State vesting by virtue of the scheme in the transferee and which are contained—
  (a)   in any agreement (whether or not in writing), deed, bond or instrument,
  (b)   in any process or other document issued, prepared or employed for the purpose of any proceeding before a court or other tribunal or authority, or
  (c)   in any other document whatever (other than an enactment) relating to or affecting any property, right or liability of the Secretary of State which vests by virtue of the scheme in the transferee,
shall be taken on and after that day to refer to the transferee.

CARRIAGE OF GOODS BY SEA ACT 1992

(1992 c 50)

ARRANGEMENT OF SECTIONS

An Act to replace the Bills of Lading Act 1855 with new provision with respect to bills of lading and certain other shipping documents

[16 July 1992]

[1.1093]
1   Shipping documents etc to which Act applies
(1)   This Act applies to the following documents, that is to say—

(a)   any bill of lading;
(b)   any sea waybill; and
(c)   any ship's delivery order.

(2)   References in this Act to a bill of lading—
  (a)   do not include references to a document which is incapable of transfer either by indorsement or, as a bearer bill, by delivery without indorsement; but
  (b)   subject to that, do include references to a received for shipment bill of lading.

(3)   References in this Act to a sea waybill are references to any document which is not a bill of lading but—
  (a)   is such a receipt for goods as contains or evidences a contract for the carriage of goods by sea; and
  (b)   identifies the person to whom delivery of the goods is to be made by the carrier in accordance with that contract.

(4)   References in this Act to a ship's delivery order are references to any document which is neither a bill of lading nor a sea waybill but contains an undertaking which—
  (a)   is given under or for the purposes of a contract for the carriage by sea of the goods to which the document relates, or of goods which include those goods; and
  (b)   is an undertaking by the carrier to a person identified in the document to deliver the goods to which the document relates to that person.

(5)   The Secretary of State may by regulations make provision for the application of this Act to cases where [an electronic communications network] or any other information technology is used for effecting transactions corresponding to—
  (a)   the issue of a document to which this Act applies;
  (b)   the indorsement, delivery or other transfer of such a document; or
  (c)   the doing of anything else in relation to such a document.

(6)   Regulations under subsection (5) above may—
  (a)   make such modifications of the following provisions of this Act as the Secretary of State considers appropriate in connection with the application of this Act to any case mentioned in that subsection; and
  (b)   contain supplemental, incidental, consequential and transitional provision;

and the power to make regulations under that subsection shall be exercisable by statutory instrument subject to annulment in pursuance of a resolution of either House of Parliament.

NOTES

Sub-s (5): words in square brackets substituted by the Communications Act 2003, s 406(1), Sch 17, para 119.

[1.1094]
2   Rights under shipping documents

(1)   Subject to the following provisions of this section, a person who becomes—
  (a)   the lawful holder of a bill of lading;
  (b)   the person who (without being an original party to the contract of carriage) is the person to whom delivery of the goods to which a sea waybill relates is to be made by the carrier in accordance with that contract; or
  (c)   the person to whom delivery of the goods to which a ship's delivery order relates is to be made in accordance with the undertaking contained in the order,

shall (by virtue of becoming the holder of the bill or, as the case may be, the person to whom delivery is to be made) have transferred to and vested in him all rights of suit under the contract of carriage as if he had been a party to that contract.

(2)   Where, when a person becomes the lawful holder of a bill of lading, possession of the bill no longer gives a right (as against the carrier) to possession of the goods to which the bill relates, that person shall not have any rights transferred to him by virtue of subsection (1) above unless he becomes the holder of the bill—
  (a)   by virtue of a transaction effected in pursuance of any contractual or other arrangements made before the time when such a right to possession ceased to attach to possession of the bill; or
  (b)   as a result of the rejection to that person by another person of goods or documents delivered to the other person in pursuance of any such arrangements.

(3)   The rights vested in any person by virtue of the operation of subsection (1) above in relation to a ship's delivery order—
  (a)   shall be so vested subject to the terms of the order; and
  (b)   where the goods to which the order relates form a part only of the goods to which the contract of carriage relates, shall be confined to rights in respect of the goods to which the order relates.

(4)   Where, in the case of any document to which this Act applies—
  (a)   a person with any interest or right in or in relation to goods to which the document relates sustains loss or damage in consequence of a breach of the contract of carriage; but
  (b)   subsection (1) above operates in relation to that document so that rights of suit in respect of that breach are vested in another person,

the other person shall be entitled to exercise those rights for the benefit of the person who sustained the loss or damage to the same extent as they could have been exercised if they had been vested in the person for whose benefit they are exercised.

(5) Where rights are transferred by virtue of the operation of subsection (1) above in relation to any document, the transfer for which that subsection provides shall extinguish any entitlement to those rights which derives—

    (a)   where that document is a bill of lading, from a person's having been an original party to the contract of carriage; or

    (b)   in the case of any document to which this Act applies, from the previous operation of that subsection in relation to that document;

but the operation of that subsection shall be without prejudice to any rights which derive from a person's having been an original party to the contract contained in, or evidenced by, a sea waybill and, in relation to a ship's delivery order, shall be without prejudice to any rights deriving otherwise than from the previous operation of that subsection in relation to that order.

[1.1095]
3 Liabilities under shipping documents
(1) Where subsection (1) of section 2 of this Act operates in relation to any document to which this Act applies and the person in whom rights are vested by virtue of that subsection—

    (a)   takes or demands delivery from the carrier of any of the goods to which the document relates;

    (b)   makes a claim under the contract of carriage against the carrier in respect of any of those goods; or

    (c)   is a person who, at a time before those rights were vested in him, took or demanded delivery from the carrier of any of those goods,

that person shall (by virtue of taking or demanding delivery or making the claim or, in a case falling within paragraph (c) above, of having the rights vested in him) become subject to the same liabilities under that contract as if he had been a party to that contract.

(2) Where the goods to which a ship's delivery order relates form a part only of the goods to which the contract of carriage relates, the liabilities to which any person is subject by virtue of the operation of this section in relation to that order shall exclude liabilities in respect of any goods to which the order does not relate.

(3) This section, so far as it imposes liabilities under any contract on any person, shall be without prejudice to the liabilities under the contract of any person as an original party to the contract.

[1.1096]
4 Representations in bills of lading
A bill of lading which—

    (a)   represents goods to have been shipped on board a vessel or to have been received for shipment on board a vessel; and

    (b)   has been signed by the master of the vessel or by a person who was not the master but had the express, implied or apparent authority of the carrier to sign bills of lading,

shall, in favour of a person who has become the lawful holder of the bill, be conclusive evidence against the carrier of the shipment of the goods or, as the case may be, of their receipt for shipment.

[1.1097]
5 Interpretation
(1) In this Act—

  "bill of lading", "sea waybill" and "ship's delivery order" shall be construed in accordance with section 1 above;

  "the contract of carriage"—

    (a)   in relation to a bill of lading or sea waybill, means the contract contained in or evidenced by that bill or waybill; and

    (b)   in relation to a ship's delivery order, means the contract under or for the purposes of which the undertaking contained in the order is given;

  "holder", in relation to a bill of lading, shall be construed in accordance with subsection (2) below;

  "information technology" includes any computer or other technology by means of which information or other matter may be recorded or communicated without being reduced to documentary form; . . .

   . . .

(2) References in this Act to the holder of a bill of lading are references to any of the following persons, that is to say—

    (a)   a person with possession of the bill who, by virtue of being the person identified in the bill, is the consignee of the goods to which the bill relates;

    (b)   a person with possession of the bill as a result of the completion, by delivery of the bill, of any indorsement of the bill or, in the case of a bearer bill, of any other transfer of the bill;

(c)   a person with possession of the bill as a result of any transaction by virtue of which he would have become a holder falling within paragraph (a) or (b) above had not the transaction been effected at a time when possession of the bill no longer gave a right (as against the carrier) to possession of the goods to which the bill relates;

and a person shall be regarded for the purposes of this Act as having become the lawful holder of a bill of lading wherever he has become the holder of the bill in good faith.

(3)   References in this Act to a person's being identified in a document include references to his being identified by a description which allows for the identity of the person in question to be varied, in accordance with the terms of the document, after its issue; and the reference in section 1(3)(b) of this Act to a document's identifying a person shall be construed accordingly.

(4)   Without prejudice to sections 2(2) and 4 above, nothing in this Act shall preclude its operation in relation to a case where the goods to which a document relates—

(a)   cease to exist after the issue of the document; or

(b)   cannot be identified (whether because they are mixed with other goods or for any other reason);

and references in this Act to the goods to which a document relates shall be construed accordingly.

(5)   The preceding provisions of this Act shall have effect without prejudice to the application, in relation to any case, of the rules (the Hague-Visby Rules) which for the time being have the force of law by virtue of section I of the Carriage of Goods by Sea Act 1971.

NOTES

Sub-s (1): definition "telecommunication system" (omitted) and the word "and" immediately preceding it repealed by the Communications Act 2003, s 406(7), Sch 19(1).

[1.1098]
6   Short title, repeal, commencement and extent
(1)   This Act may be cited as the Carriage of Goods by Sea Act 1992.
(2)   . . .
(3)   This Act shall come into force at the end of the period of two months beginning with the day on which it is passed; but nothing in this Act shall have effect in relation to any document issued before the coming into force of this Act.
(4)   This Act extends to Northern Ireland.

NOTES

Sub-s (2): repeals the Bills of Lading Act 1855.

REINSURANCE (ACTS OF TERRORISM) ACT 1993

(1993 c 18)

ARRANGEMENT OF SECTIONS

An Act to provide for the payment out of money provided by Parliament or into the Consolidated Fund of sums referable to reinsurance liabilities entered into by the Secretary of State in respect of loss or damage to property resulting from or consequential upon acts of terrorism and losses consequential on such loss or damage

[27 May 1993]

[1.1099]
1   Financing of reinsurance obligations of the [Treasury]
(1)   There shall be paid out of money provided by Parliament such sums as may be necessary to enable the [Treasury] to meet [their] obligations under—

(a)   any agreement of reinsurance which   . . .   is entered into (whether before or after the passing of this Act) pursuant to arrangements to which this Act applies, or

(b)   any guarantee which   . . .   is entered into (whether before or after that passing) pursuant to any such agreement.

(2)   As soon as practicable after the passing of this Act or, if it is later, after [they enter] into the agreement or guarantee, the [Treasury] shall lay before each House of Parliament a copy of any agreement or guarantee falling within subsection (1) above.

(3)   There shall be paid into the Consolidated Fund any sums received by the [Treasury] pursuant to any arrangements to which this Act applies.

NOTES

Words in square brackets substituted, and words omitted repealed, by the Transfer of Functions (Insurance) Order 1997, SI 1997/2781, art 8, Schedule, paras 120–122.

[1.1100]
2 Reinsurance arrangements to which this Act applies
(1)   This Act applies to arrangements under which the [Treasury] . . . [undertake] to any extent the liability of reinsuring risks against—
   (a)   loss of or damage to property in Great Britain resulting from or consequential upon acts of terrorism; and
   (b)   any loss which is consequential on loss or damage falling within paragraph (a) above;
and to the extent that the arrangements relate to events occurring before as well as after an agreement of reinsurance comes into being, the reference in section 1(1) above to the obligations of the [Treasury] shall be construed accordingly.
(2)   In this section "acts of terrorism" means acts of persons acting on behalf of, or in connection with, any organisation which carries out activities directed towards the overthrowing or influencing, by force or violence, of Her Majesty's government in the United Kingdom or any other government de jure or de facto.
(3)   In subsection (2) above "organisation" includes any association or combination of persons.

NOTES

Sub-s (1): words in square brackets substituted, and words omitted repealed, by the Transfer of Functions (Insurance) Order 1997, SI 1997/2781, art 8, Schedule, paras 120, 121, 123.

[1.1101]
3 Citation and extent
(1)   This Act may be cited as the Reinsurance (Acts of Terrorism) Act 1993.
(2)   This Act does not extend to Northern Ireland.

SUNDAY TRADING ACT 1994

(1994 c 20)

ARRANGEMENT OF SECTIONS

An Act to reform the law of England and Wales relating to Sunday trading; to make provision as to the rights of shop workers under the law of England and Wales in relation to Sunday working; and for connected purposes

[5 July 1994]

[1.1102]
1 Reform of law relating to Sunday trading
(1)   Schedules 1 and 2 to this Act shall come into force on such day as the Secretary of State may by order made by statutory instrument appoint (in this section referred to as "the appointed day").
(2)   . . .

NOTES

Sub-s (2): repeals the Shops Act 1950, ss 47–66, Schs 5–7.

[1.1103]

2   Loading and unloading at large shops on Sunday morning

(1)   A local authority may by resolution designate their area as a loading control area for the purposes of this section with effect from a date specified in the resolution, which must be a date at least one month after the date on which the resolution is passed.

(2)   A local authority may by resolution revoke any designation made by them under subsection (1) above.

(3)   It shall be the duty of a local authority, before making or revoking any designation under subsection (1) above, to consult persons appearing to the local authority to be likely to be affected by the proposed designation or revocation (whether as the occupiers of shops or as local residents) or persons appearing to the local authority to represent such persons.

(4)   Where a local authority make or revoke a designation under this section, they shall publish notice of the designation or revocation in such manner as they consider appropriate.

(5)   Schedule 3 to this Act (which imposes restrictions on loading and unloading on Sunday before 9 am at large shops in loading control areas) shall have effect.

[1.1104]

3   Construction of certain leases and agreements

(1)   Where any lease or agreement (however worded) entered into before the commencement of this section has the effect of requiring the occupier of a shop to keep the shop open for the serving of retail customers—

   (a)   during normal business hours, or

   (b)   during hours to be determined otherwise than by or with the consent of the occupier,

that lease or agreement shall not be regarded as requiring, or as enabling any person to require, the occupier to open the shop on Sunday for the serving of retail customers.

(2)   Subsection (1) above shall not affect any lease or agreement—

   (a)   to the extent that it relates specifically to Sunday and would (apart from this section) have the effect of requiring Sunday trading of a kind which before the commencement of this section would have been lawful by virtue of any provision of Part IV of the Shops Act 1950, or

   (b)   to the extent that it is varied by agreement after the commencement of this section.

(3)   In this section "retail customer" and "shop" have the same meaning as in Schedule 1 to this Act.

[1.1105]

4   Rights of shop workers as respects Sunday working

Schedule 4 to this Act shall have effect.

5   (*Repealed by the Deregulation and Contracting Out Act 1994, s 81(1), Sch 17.*)

[1.1106]

6   Consequential repeal or amendment of local Acts

(1)   The Secretary of State may by order made by statutory instrument—

   (a)   repeal any provision of a local Act passed before or in the same Session as this Act if it appears to him that the provision is inconsistent with or has become unnecessary in consequence of any provision of this Act, and

   (b)   amend any provision of such a local Act if it appears to him that the provision requires amendment in consequence of any provision of this Act or any repeal made by virtue of paragraph (a) above.

(2)   It shall be the duty of the Secretary of State, before he makes an order under subsection (1) above repealing or amending any provision of a local Act, to consult each local authority which he considers would be affected by the repeal or amendment of that provision.

(3)   A statutory instrument containing an order under subsection (1) above shall be subject to annulment in pursuance of a resolution of either House of Parliament.

[1.1107]

7   Expenses

There shall be paid out of money provided by Parliament any increase attributable to this Act in the sums payable out of such money under any other Act.

[1.1108]

8   Meaning of "local authority"

(1)   In this Act "local authority" means any unitary authority or any district council so far as they are not a unitary authority.

(2)   In subsection (1) above "unitary authority" means—

   (a)   the council of any county so far as they are the council for an area for which there are no district councils,

   (b)   the council of any district comprised in an area for which there is no county council,

   (c)   a county borough council,

   (d)   a London borough council,

(e)   the Common Council of the City of London, or

(f)   the Council of the Isles of Scilly.

(3)   Until 1st April 1996, the definition of "unitary authority" in subsection (2) above shall have effect with the omission of paragraph (c).

[1.1109]

9   Short title, repeals, commencement and extent

(1)   This Act may be cited as the Sunday Trading Act 1994.

(2)   The enactments mentioned in Schedule 5 to this Act are hereby repealed to the extent specified in the third column of that Schedule.

(3)   The following provisions of this Act—

sections 2 to 5,

subsection (2) of this section, and

Schedules 3, 4 and 5,

shall not come into force until the appointed day (as defined in section 1 above).

(4)   This Act extends to England and Wales only.

SCHEDULES

SCHEDULE 1
RESTRICTIONS ON SUNDAY OPENING OF LARGE SHOPS

Section 1(1)

Interpretation

[1.1110]

1. In this Schedule—

["alcohol" has the same meaning as in the Licensing Act 2003,]

"large shop" means a shop which has a relevant floor area exceeding 280 square metres,

"medicinal product" and "registered pharmacy" have the same meaning as in the Medicines Act 1968,

"relevant floor area", in relation to a shop, means the internal floor area of so much of the shop as consists of or is comprised in a building, but excluding any part of the shop which, throughout the week ending with the Sunday in question, is used neither for the serving of customers in connection with the sale of goods nor for the display of goods,

"retail customer" means a person who purchases goods retail,

"retail sale" means any sale other than a sale for use or resale in the course of a trade or business, and references to retail purchase shall be construed accordingly,

"sale of goods" does not include—

(a)   the sale of meals, refreshments or [alcohol] for consumption on the premises on which they are sold, or

(b)   the sale of meals or refreshments prepared to order for immediate consumption off those premises,

"shop" means any premises where there is carried on a trade or business consisting wholly or mainly of the sale of goods, and

"stand", in relation to an exhibition, means any platform, structure, space or other area provided for exhibition purposes;

["veterinary medicinal product" has the same meaning as in regulation 2 of the Veterinary Medicines Regulations 2006].

[Restrictions on Sunday opening hours of large shops]

2. (1) Subject to sub-paragraphs (2) and (3) below, a large shop shall not be open on Sunday for the serving of retail customers.

(2)   Sub-paragraph (1) above does not apply in relation to—

(a)   any of the shops mentioned in paragraph 3(1) below, or

(b)   any shop in respect of which a notice under paragraph 8(1) of Schedule 2 to this Act (shops occupied by persons observing the Jewish Sabbath) has effect.

[(3)   Sub-paragraph (1) above does not apply in relation to the opening of a large shop during any continuous period of six hours on a Sunday beginning no earlier than 10 am and ending no later than 6 pm, but this sub-paragraph has effect subject to sub-paragraph (4) below.]

(4)   The exemption conferred by sub-paragraph (3) above does not apply where the Sunday is Easter Day . . .

[(5)   Nothing in this paragraph applies where the Sunday is Christmas Day (the opening of large shops on Christmas Day being prohibited by section 1 of the Christmas Day (Trading) Act 2004).]

Exemptions

3. (1) The shops referred to in paragraph 2(2)(a) above are—

(a)   any shop which is at a farm and where the trade or business carried on consists wholly or mainly of the sale of produce from that farm,

(b) any shop where the trade or business carried on consists wholly or mainly of the sale of [alcohol],

(c) any shop where the trade or business carried on consists wholly or mainly of the sale of any one or more of the following—
  (i) motor supplies and accessories, and
  (ii) cycle supplies and accessories,

(d) any shop which—
  (i) is a registered pharmacy, and
  (ii) is not open for the retail sale of any goods other than medicinal products[, veterinary medicinal products] and medical and surgical appliances,

(e) any shop at a designated airport which is situated in a part of the airport to which sub-paragraph (3) below applies,

(f) any shop in a railway station,

(g) any shop at a service area within the meaning of the Highways Act 1980,

(h) any petrol filling station,

(j) any shop which is not open for the retail sale of any goods other than food, stores or other necessaries required by any person for a vessel or aircraft on its arrival at, or immediately before its departure from, a port, harbour or airport, and

(k) any stand used for the retail sale of goods during the course of an exhibition.

(2) In determining whether a shop falls within sub-paragraph (1)(a), (b) or (c) above, regard shall be had to the nature of the trade or business carried on there on weekdays as well as to the nature of the trade or business carried on there on Sunday.

(3) This sub-paragraph applies to every part of a designated airport, except any part which is not ordinarily used by persons travelling by air to or from the airport.

(4) In this paragraph "designated airport" means an airport designated for the purposes of this paragraph by an order made by the Secretary of State, as being an airport at which there appears to him to be a substantial amount of international passenger traffic.

(5) The power to make an order under sub-paragraph (4) above shall be exercisable by statutory instrument.

(6) Any order made under section 1(2) of the Shops (Airports) Act 1962 and in force at the commencement of this Schedule shall, so far as it relates to England and Wales, have effect as if made also under sub-paragraph (4) above, and may be amended or revoked as it has effect for the purposes of this paragraph by an order under sub-paragraph (4) above.

4, 5. . . .

Duty to display notice

6. At any time when—
  (a) a large shop is open on Sunday for the serving of retail customers, and
  (b) the prohibition in sub-paragraph (1) of paragraph 2 above is excluded only by sub-paragraph (3) of that paragraph,
a notice specifying [the Sunday opening hours] shall be displayed in a conspicuous position inside and outside the shop.

Offences

7. (1) If paragraph 2(1) above is contravened in relation to a shop, the occupier of the shop shall be liable on summary conviction to [a fine].

(2) If paragraph 6 above is contravened in relation to a shop, the occupier of the shop shall be liable on summary conviction to a fine not exceeding level 2 on the standard scale.

[**8.** Where a person is charged with having contravened paragraph 2(1) above, in relation to a large shop which was permitted to be open for the serving of retail customers on the Sunday in question, by reason of his having served a retail customer after the end of the period during which the shop is permitted to be open by virtue of paragraph 2(3) above, it shall be a defence to prove that the customer was in the shop before the end of that period and left not later than half an hour after the end of that period.]

9. . . .

<hr>

NOTES

Para 1: definition "alcohol" substituted, for original definition "intoxicating liquor", and in definition "sale of goods" word in square brackets in para (a) substituted by the Licensing Act 2003, s 198(1), Sch 6, para 110(1), (2); definition "veterinary medicinal product" inserted by the Veterinary Medicines Regulations 2006, SI 2006/2407, reg 44(3), Sch 9, Pt 1, para 9(a).

Para 2: heading and sub-para (3) substituted by the Regulatory Reform (Sunday Trading) Order 2004, SI 2004/470, art 2(1), (2)(a), (b); words omitted from sub-para (4) repealed and sub-para (5) inserted by the Christmas Day (Trading) Act 2004, s 4(1), (2).

Para 3: in sub-para (1)(b) word in square brackets substituted by the Licensing Act 2003, s 198(1), Sch 6, para 110(1), (3); in sub-para (1)(d)(ii) words in square brackets inserted by SI 2006/2407, reg 44(3), Sch 9, Pt 1, para 9(b).

Paras 4, 5, 9: repealed by SI 2004/470, art 2(1), (2)(c), (f).

Para 6: words in square brackets substituted by SI 2004/470, art 2(1), (2)(d).

Para 7: in sub-para (1) words in square brackets substituted by the Legal Aid, Sentencing and Punishment of Offenders Act 2012 (Fines on Summary Conviction) Regulations 2015, SI 2015/664, reg 4(1), Sch 4, Pt 1, para 26, for transitional provision and savings see reg 5(1) thereof.

Para 8: substituted by SI 2004/470, art 2(1), (2)(e).

See further, in relation to the disapplication of para 2(1) above to large shops in the terminal area of the Channel Tunnel: the Channel Tunnel (Sunday Trading Act 1994) (Disapplication) Order 1994, SI 1994/3286, art 3.

See further, in relation to the application of para 3(2) above and the definition "relevant floor area" in para 1 above, with modifications, for the purposes of the Christmas Day (Trading) Act 2004, s 1: the Christmas Day (Trading) Act 2004, s 1(4), (5) at **[1.1904]**.

SCHEDULE 2
SUPPLEMENTARY PROVISIONS

Section 1(1)

PART I
GENERAL ENFORCEMENT PROVISIONS

Duty to enforce Act

[1.1111]

1. It shall be the duty of every local authority to enforce within their area the provisions of Schedules 1 and 3 to this Act and Part II of this Schedule.

Inspectors

2. For the purposes of their duties under paragraph 1 above it shall be the duty of every local authority to appoint inspectors.

Powers of entry

3. *An inspector appointed by a local authority under paragraph 2 above shall, on producing if so required some duly authenticated document showing his authority, have a right at all reasonable hours—*

(a) *to enter any premises within the area of the local authority, with or without a constable, for the purpose of ascertaining whether there is or has been on the premises any contravention of the provisions of Schedules 1 and 3 to this Act,*

(b) *to require the production of, inspect and take copies of any records (in whatever form they are held) relating to any business carried on the premises which appear to him to be relevant for the purpose mentioned in paragraph (a) above,*

(c) *where those records are kept by means of a computer, to require the records to be produced in a form in which they may be taken away, and*

(d) *to take such measurements and photographs as he considers necessary for the purpose mentioned in paragraph (a) above.*

[Investigatory powers

[4A For the investigatory powers available to a local authority and the inspectors appointed by it under paragraph 2 for the purposes of the duty in paragraph 1, see Schedule 5 to the Consumer Rights Act 2015.]

Obstruction of inspectors

4. *Any person who intentionally obstructs an inspector appointed under paragraph 2 above acting in the execution of his duty shall be liable on summary conviction to a fine not exceeding level 3 on the standard scale.*

Offences due to fault of other person

5. Where the commission by any person of an offence under this Act is due to the act or default of some other person, that other person shall be guilty of the offence, and a person may be charged with and convicted of the offence by virtue of this paragraph whether or not proceedings are taken against the first-mentioned person.

Offences by bodies corporate

6. (1) Where an offence under this Act committed by a body corporate is proved to have been committed with the consent or connivance of, or to be attributable to any neglect on the part of, any director, manager, secretary or other similar officer of the body corporate, or any person who was purporting to act in any such capacity, he as well as the body corporate shall be guilty of the offence and shall be liable to be proceeded against and punished accordingly.

(2) Where the affairs of a body corporate are managed by its members, sub-paragraph (1) above shall apply in relation to the acts and defaults of a member in connection with his functions of management as if he were a director of the body corporate.

Defence of due diligence

7. (1)   In any proceedings for an offence under this Act it shall, subject to sub-paragraph (2) below, be a defence for the person charged to prove that he took all reasonable precautions and exercised all due diligence to avoid the commission of the offence by himself or by a person under his control.

(2)   If in any case the defence provided by sub-paragraph (1) above involves the allegation that the commission of the offence was due to the act or default of another person, the person charged shall not, without leave of the court, be entitled to rely on that defence unless, at least seven clear days before the hearing, he has served on the prosecutor a notice in writing giving such information identifying or assisting in the identification of that other person as was then in his possession.

NOTES

Paras 3, 4: repealed by the Consumer Rights Act 2015, s 77(2), Sch 6, para 58(1), (2), as from 1 October 2015 (for transitional provisions see the Consumer Rights Act 2015 (Commencement No 3, Transitional Provisions, Savings and Consequential Amendments) Order 2015, SI 2015/1630, arts 6–8 at **[2.1220]** et seq).

Para 4A: inserted by the Consumer Rights Act 2015, s 77(2), Sch 6, para 58(1), (3), as from 1 October 2015 (for transitional provisions see note above).

See further: in relation to the application of paras 3, 4 above, with modifications, for the purposes of the Christmas Day (Trading) Act 2004, s 3(2), see s 3(3) thereof at **[1.1906]**.

PART II
SHOPS OCCUPIED BY PERSONS OBSERVING THE JEWISH SABBATH

Shops occupied by persons of the Jewish religion

[1.1112]
8. (1)   A person of the Jewish religion who is the occupier of a large shop may give to the local authority for the area in which the shop is situated a notice signed by him stating—
   (a)   that he is a person of the Jewish religion, and
   (b)   that he intends to keep the shop closed for the serving of customers on the Jewish Sabbath.

(2)   For the purposes of this paragraph, a shop occupied by a partnership or company shall be taken to be occupied by a person of the Jewish religion if, and only if, the majority of the partners or of the directors, as the case may be, are persons of that religion.

(3)   A notice under sub-paragraph (1) above shall be accompanied by a certificate signed by an authorised person that the person giving the notice is a person of the Jewish religion.

(4)   Where the occupier of the shop is a partnership or company—
   (a)   any notice under sub-paragraph (1) above shall be given by the majority of the partners or directors and, if not given by all of them, shall specify the names of the other partners or directors, and
   (b)   a certificate under sub-paragraph (3) above is required in relation to each of the persons by whom such a notice is given.

(5)   Every local authority shall keep a register containing particulars of the name (if any) and address of every shop in respect of which a notice under sub-paragraph (1) above has effect.

(6)   Any register kept under this paragraph—
   (a)   shall be open to inspection by members of the public at all reasonable times, and
   (b)   may be kept by means of a computer.

(7)   If there is any change—
   (a)   in the occupation of a shop in respect of which a notice under sub-paragraph (1) above has effect, or
   (b)   in any partnership or among the directors of any company by which such a shop is occupied,
the notice shall be taken to be cancelled at the end of the period of 14 days beginning with the day on which the change occurred, unless during that period, or within such further time as may be allowed by the local authority, a fresh notice is given under sub-paragraph (1) above in respect of the shop.

(8)   Where a fresh notice is given under sub-paragraph (1) above by reason of a change of the kind mentioned in sub-paragraph (7) above, the local authority may dispense with the certificate required by sub-paragraph (3) above in the case of any person in respect of whom such a certificate has been provided in connection with a former notice in respect of that shop or any other shop in the area of the local authority.

(9)   A notice given under sub-paragraph (1) above in respect of any shop shall be cancelled on application in that behalf being made to the local authority by the occupier of the shop.

(10)   A person who, in a notice or certificate given for the purposes of this paragraph, makes a statement which is false in a material respect and which he knows to be false or does not believe to be true shall be liable on summary conviction to a fine not exceeding level 5 on the standard scale.

(11)   Where a person is convicted of an offence under sub-paragraph (10) above, the local authority may cancel any notice under sub-paragraph (1) above to which the offence relates.

(12) In this paragraph—

"authorised person", in relation to a notice under sub-paragraph (1) above, means—

(a) the Minister of the synagogue of which the person giving the notice is a member,

(b) the secretary of that synagogue, or

(c) any other person nominated for the purposes of this paragraph by the President of the London Committee of Deputies of the British Jews (otherwise known as the Board of Deputies of British Jews),

"large shop" and "shop" have the same meaning as in Schedule 1 to this Act, and

"secretary of a synagogue" has the same meaning as in Part IV of the Marriage Act 1949.

Members of other religious bodies observing the Jewish Sabbath

9. Paragraph 8 above shall apply to persons who are members of any religious body regularly observing the Jewish Sabbath as it applies to persons of the Jewish religion, and accordingly—

(a) references to persons of the Jewish religion shall be construed as including any person who is a member of such a body, and

(b) in the application of that paragraph to such persons "authorised person" means a Minister of the religious body concerned.

Transitional provisions

10. (1) Any shop which is registered under section 53 of the Shops Act 1950 at the commencement of this Schedule and is at that time a large shop within the meaning of Schedule 1 to this Act shall be taken to be a shop in respect of which a notice has been given under sub-paragraph (1) of paragraph 8 above by the person who was then registered as the occupier of the shop; and the provisions of that paragraph in relation to the cancellation of such a notice shall have effect accordingly.

(2) In paragraph 8(8) above, the reference to a certificate provided in connection with a former notice includes a reference to a statutory declaration provided under subsection (2) of section 53 of the Shops Act 1950 in connection with the registration of a shop under that section before the commencement of this Schedule.

SCHEDULE 3
LOADING AND UNLOADING AT LARGE SHOPS ON SUNDAY MORNING
Section 2

Shops to which Schedule applies

[1.1113]
1. This Schedule applies to any shop—

(a) which is a large shop, within the meaning of Schedule 1 to this Act, [that is permitted to be open on a Sunday by virtue of paragraph 2(3) of that Schedule and which the occupier opens on Sunday for the serving of retail customers], and

(b) which is situated in an area designated as a loading control area under section 2 of this Act.

Consent required for early Sunday loading and unloading

2. The occupier of a shop to which this Schedule applies shall not load or unload, or permit any other person to load or unload, goods from a vehicle at the shop before 9 am on Sunday in connection with the trade or business carried on in the shop, unless the loading or unloading is carried on—

(a) with the consent of the local authority for the area in which the shop is situated granted under this Schedule, and

(b) in accordance with any conditions subject to which that consent is granted.

3. (1) A consent under this Schedule may be granted subject to such conditions as the local authority consider appropriate.

(2) The local authority may at any time vary the conditions subject to which a consent is granted, and shall give notice of the variation to the person to whom the consent was granted.

Application for consent

4. An application for a consent under this Schedule shall be made in writing and shall contain such information as the local authority may reasonably require.

5. An applicant for a consent under this Schedule shall pay such reasonable fee in respect of his application as the local authority may determine.

6. (1) Where an application is duly made to the local authority for a consent under this Schedule, the authority shall grant the consent unless they are satisfied that the loading or unloading of goods from vehicles before 9 am on Sunday at the shop to which the application relates, in connection with the trade or business carried on at the shop, has caused, or would be likely to cause, undue annoyance to local residents.

(2)   The authority shall determine the application and notify the applicant in writing of their decision within the period of 21 days beginning with the day on which the application is received by the authority.

(3)   In a case where a consent is granted, the notification under sub-paragraph (2) above shall specify the conditions, if any, subject to which the consent is granted.

Revocation of consent

7. Where—
- (a)   the occupier of a shop in respect of which a consent under this Schedule is in force is convicted of an offence under paragraph 9 below by reason of his failure to comply with the conditions subject to which the consent was granted, or
- (b)   the local authority are satisfied that the loading or unloading authorised by virtue of a consent under this Schedule has caused undue annoyance to local residents,

the local authority may revoke the consent.

Publication of consent

8. Where a local authority grant a consent under this Schedule, the authority may cause a notice giving details of that consent to be published in a local newspaper circulating in their area.

Offence

9. A person who contravenes paragraph 2 above shall be liable on summary conviction to a fine not exceeding level 3 on the standard scale.

[Christmas Day

10.   Paragraph 2 does not apply where the Sunday is Christmas Day (loading and unloading at large shops on Christmas Day being regulated by section 2 of the Christmas Day (Trading) Act 2004).]

NOTES

Para 1: in sub-para (a) words in square brackets substituted by the Regulatory Reform (Sunday Trading) Order 2004, SI 2004/470, art 2(1), (3).

Para 10: inserted by the Christmas Day (Trading) Act 2004, s 4(1), (3).

See further, in relation to the application of paras 3–8 above, with modifications, for the purposes of the Christmas Day (Trading) Act 2004, s 2(1): the Christmas Day (Trading) Act 2004, s 2(2) at **[1.1905]**.

SCHEDULES 4 AND 5

(Schs 4, 5 outside the scope of this work.)

ARBITRATION ACT 1996

(1996 c 23)

ARRANGEMENT OF SECTIONS

PART I
ARBITRATION PURSUANT TO AN ARBITRATION AGREEMENT

SCHEDULES

An Act to restate and improve the law relating to arbitration pursuant to an arbitration agreement; to make other provision relating to arbitration and arbitration awards; and for connected purposes

[17 June 1996]

NOTES

Transfer of functions: functions under this Act, so far as exercisable in relation to Northern Ireland, are transferred to the Department of Justice by the Northern Ireland Act 1998 (Devolution of Policing and Justice Functions) Order 2010, SI 2010/976, arts 15(1), 28–31, Sch 17, para 13.

PART I
ARBITRATION PURSUANT TO AN ARBITRATION AGREEMENT
Introductory

[1.1114]
1   General principles
The provisions of this Part are founded on the following principles, and shall be construed accordingly—
(a)   the object of arbitration is to obtain the fair resolution of disputes by an impartial tribunal without unnecessary delay or expense;
(b)   the parties should be free to agree how their disputes are resolved, subject only to such safeguards as are necessary in the public interest;
(c)   in matters governed by this Part the court should not intervene except as provided by this Part.

[1.1115]
2   Scope of application of provisions
(1)   The provisions of this Part apply where the seat of the arbitration is in England and Wales or Northern Ireland.
(2)   The following sections apply even if the seat of the arbitration is outside England and Wales or Northern Ireland or no seat has been designated or determined—
(a)   sections 9 to 11 (stay of legal proceedings, &c), and
(b)   section 66 (enforcement of arbitral awards).
(3)   The powers conferred by the following sections apply even if the seat of the arbitration is outside England and Wales or Northern Ireland or no seat has been designated or determined—
(a)   section 43 (securing the attendance of witnesses), and
(b)   section 44 (court powers exercisable in support of arbitral proceedings);
but the court may refuse to exercise any such power if, in the opinion of the court, the fact that the seat of the arbitration is outside England and Wales or Northern Ireland, or that when designated or determined the seat is likely to be outside England and Wales or Northern Ireland, makes it inappropriate to do so.
(4)   The court may exercise a power conferred by any provision of this Part not mentioned in subsection (2) or (3) for the purpose of supporting the arbitral process where—
(a)   no seat of the arbitration has been designated or determined, and
(b)   by reason of a connection with England and Wales or Northern Ireland the court is satisfied that it is appropriate to do so.
(5)   Section 7 (separability of arbitration agreement) and section 8 (death of a party) apply where the law applicable to the arbitration agreement is the law of England and Wales or Northern Ireland even if the seat of the arbitration is outside England and Wales or Northern Ireland or has not been designated or determined.

[1.1116]
3   The seat of the arbitration
In this Part "the seat of the arbitration" means the juridical seat of the arbitration designated—
(a)   by the parties to the arbitration agreement, or
(b)   by any arbitral or other institution or person vested by the parties with powers in that regard, or
(c)   by the arbitral tribunal if so authorised by the parties,
or determined, in the absence of any such designation, having regard to the parties' agreement and all the relevant circumstances.

[1.1117]
4 Mandatory and non-mandatory provisions
(1) The mandatory provisions of this Part are listed in Schedule 1 and have effect notwithstanding any agreement to the contrary.
(2) The other provisions of this Part (the "non-mandatory provisions") allow the parties to make their own arrangements by agreement but provide rules which apply in the absence of such agreement.
(3) The parties may make such arrangements by agreeing to the application of institutional rules or providing any other means by which a matter may be decided.
(4) It is immaterial whether or not the law applicable to the parties' agreement is the law of England and Wales or, as the case may be, Northern Ireland.
(5) The choice of a law other than the law of England and Wales or Northern Ireland as the applicable law in respect of a matter provided for by a non-mandatory provision of this Part is equivalent to an agreement making provision about that matter.
    For this purpose an applicable law determined in accordance with the parties' agreement, or which is objectively determined in the absence of any express or implied choice, shall be treated as chosen by the parties.

[1.1118]
5 Agreements to be in writing
(1) The provisions of this Part apply only where the arbitration agreement is in writing, and any other agreement between the parties as to any matter is effective for the purposes of this Part only if in writing.
    The expressions "agreement", "agree" and "agreed" shall be construed accordingly.
(2) There is an agreement in writing—
    (a) if the agreement is made in writing (whether or not it is signed by the parties),
    (b) if the agreement is made by exchange of communications in writing, or
    (c) if the agreement is evidenced in writing.
(3) Where parties agree otherwise than in writing by reference to terms which are in writing, they make an agreement in writing.
(4) An agreement is evidenced in writing if an agreement made otherwise than in writing is recorded by one of the parties, or by a third party, with the authority of the parties to the agreement.
(5) An exchange of written submissions in arbitral or legal proceedings in which the existence of an agreement otherwise than in writing is alleged by one party against another party and not denied by the other party in his response constitutes as between those parties an agreement in writing to the effect alleged.
(6) References in this Part to anything being written or in writing include its being recorded by any means.

The arbitration agreement

[1.1119]
6 Definition of arbitration agreement
(1) In this Part an "arbitration agreement" means an agreement to submit to arbitration present or future disputes (whether they are contractual or not).
(2) The reference in an agreement to a written form of arbitration clause or to a document containing an arbitration clause constitutes an arbitration agreement if the reference is such as to make that clause part of the agreement.

[1.1120]
7 Separability of arbitration agreement
Unless otherwise agreed by the parties, an arbitration agreement which forms or was intended to form part of another agreement (whether or not in writing) shall not be regarded as invalid, non-existent or ineffective because that other agreement is invalid, or did not come into existence or has become ineffective, and it shall for that purpose be treated as a distinct agreement.

[1.1121]
8 Whether agreement discharged by death of a party
(1) Unless otherwise agreed by the parties, an arbitration agreement is not discharged by the death of a party and may be enforced by or against the personal representatives of that party.
(2) Subsection (1) does not affect the operation of any enactment or rule of law by virtue of which a substantive right or obligation is extinguished by death.

Stay of legal proceedings

[1.1122]
9 Stay of legal proceedings
(1) A party to an arbitration agreement against whom legal proceedings are brought (whether by way of claim or counterclaim) in respect of a matter which under the agreement is to be referred to arbitration may (upon notice to the other parties to the proceedings) apply to the court in which the proceedings have been brought to stay the proceedings so far as they concern that matter.

(2)   An application may be made notwithstanding that the matter is to be referred to arbitration only after the exhaustion of other dispute resolution procedures.

(3)   An application may not be made by a person before taking the appropriate procedural step (if any) to acknowledge the legal proceedings against him or after he has taken any step in those proceedings to answer the substantive claim.

(4)   On an application under this section the court shall grant a stay unless satisfied that the arbitration agreement is null and void, inoperative, or incapable of being performed.

(5)   If the court refuses to stay the legal proceedings, any provision that an award is a condition precedent to the bringing of legal proceedings in respect of any matter is of no effect in relation to those proceedings.

[1.1123]
10   Reference of interpleader issue to arbitration
(1)   Where in legal proceedings relief by way of interpleader is granted and any issue between the claimants is one in respect of which there is an arbitration agreement between them, the court granting the relief shall direct that the issue be determined in accordance with the agreement unless the circumstances are such that proceedings brought by a claimant in respect of the matter would not be stayed.

(2)   Where subsection (1) applies but the court does not direct that the issue be determined in accordance with the arbitration agreement, any provision that an award is a condition precedent to the bringing of legal proceedings in respect of any matter shall not affect the determination of that issue by the court.

[1.1124]
11   Retention of security where Admiralty proceedings stayed
(1)   Where Admiralty proceedings are stayed on the ground that the dispute in question should be submitted to arbitration, the court granting the stay may, if in those proceedings property has been arrested or bail or other security has been given to prevent or obtain release from arrest—

   (a)   order that the property arrested be retained as security for the satisfaction of any award given in the arbitration in respect of that dispute, or

   (b)   order that the stay of those proceedings be conditional on the provision of equivalent security for the satisfaction of any such award.

(2)   Subject to any provision made by rules of court and to any necessary modifications, the same law and practice shall apply in relation to property retained in pursuance of an order as would apply if it were held for the purposes of proceedings in the court making the order.

Commencement of arbitral proceedings

[1.1125]
12   Power of court to extend time for beginning arbitral proceedings, &c
(1)   Where an arbitration agreement to refer future disputes to arbitration provides that a claim shall be barred, or the claimant's right extinguished, unless the claimant takes within a time fixed by the agreement some step—

   (a)   to begin arbitral proceedings, or

   (b)   to begin other dispute resolution procedures which must be exhausted before arbitral proceedings can be begun,

the court may by order extend the time for taking that step.

(2)   Any party to the arbitration agreement may apply for such an order (upon notice to the other parties), but only after a claim has arisen and after exhausting any available arbitral process for obtaining an extension of time.

(3)   The court shall make an order only if satisfied—

   (a)   that the circumstances are such as were outside the reasonable contemplation of the parties when they agreed the provision in question, and that it would be just to extend the time, or

   (b)   that the conduct of one party makes it unjust to hold the other party to the strict terms of the provision in question.

(4)   The court may extend the time for such period and on such terms as it thinks fit, and may do so whether or not the time previously fixed (by agreement or by a previous order) has expired.

(5)   An order under this section does not affect the operation of the Limitation Acts (see section 13).

(6)   The leave of the court is required for any appeal from a decision of the court under this section.

[1.1126]
13   Application of Limitation Acts
(1)   The Limitation Acts apply to arbitral proceedings as they apply to legal proceedings.

(2)   The court may order that in computing the time prescribed by the Limitation Acts for the commencement of proceedings (including arbitral proceedings) in respect of a dispute which was the subject matter—

   (a)   of an award which the court orders to be set aside or declares to be of no effect, or

   (b)   of the affected part of an award which the court orders to be set aside in part, or declares to be in part of no effect, the period between the commencement of the arbitration and the date of the order referred to in paragraph (a) or (b) shall be excluded.

(3)   In determining for the purposes of the Limitation Acts when a cause of action accrued, any provision that an award is a condition precedent to the bringing of legal proceedings in respect of a matter to which an arbitration agreement applies shall be disregarded.

(4)   In this Part "the Limitation Acts" means—

(a)   in England and Wales, the Limitation Act 1980, the Foreign Limitation Periods Act 1984 and any other enactment (whenever passed) relating to the limitation of actions;

(b)   in Northern Ireland, the Limitation (Northern Ireland) Order 1989, the Foreign Limitation Periods (Northern Ireland) Order 1985 and any other enactment (whenever passed) relating to the limitation of actions.

[1.1127]
14   Commencement of arbitral proceedings
(1)   The parties are free to agree when arbitral proceedings are to be regarded as commenced for the purposes of this Part and for the purposes of the Limitation Acts.

(2)   If there is no such agreement the following provisions apply.

(3)   Where the arbitrator is named or designated in the arbitration agreement, arbitral proceedings are commenced in respect of a matter when one party serves on the other party or parties a notice in writing requiring him or them to submit that matter to the person so named or designated.

(4)   Where the arbitrator or arbitrators are to be appointed by the parties, arbitral proceedings are commenced in respect of a matter when one party serves on the other party or parties notice in writing requiring him or them to appoint an arbitrator or to agree to the appointment of an arbitrator in respect of that matter.

(5)   Where the arbitrator or arbitrators are to be appointed by a person other than a party to the proceedings, arbitral proceedings are commenced in respect of a matter when one party gives notice in writing to that person requesting him to make the appointment in respect of that matter.

The arbitral tribunal

[1.1128]
15   The arbitral tribunal
(1)   The parties are free to agree on the number of arbitrators to form the tribunal and whether there is to be a chairman or umpire.

(2)   Unless otherwise agreed by the parties, an agreement that the number of arbitrators shall be two or any other even number shall be understood as requiring the appointment of an additional arbitrator as chairman of the tribunal.

(3)   If there is no agreement as to the number of arbitrators, the tribunal shall consist of a sole arbitrator.

[1.1129]
16   Procedure for appointment of arbitrators
(1)   The parties are free to agree on the procedure for appointing the arbitrator or arbitrators, including the procedure for appointing any chairman or umpire.

(2)   If or to the extent that there is no such agreement, the following provisions apply.

(3)   If the tribunal is to consist of a sole arbitrator, the parties shall jointly appoint the arbitrator not later than 28 days after service of a request in writing by either party to do so.

(4)   If the tribunal is to consist of two arbitrators, each party shall appoint one arbitrator not later than 14 days after service of a request in writing by either party to do so.

(5)   If the tribunal is to consist of three arbitrators—

(a)   each party shall appoint one arbitrator not later than 14 days after service of a request in writing by either party to do so, and

(b)   the two so appointed shall forthwith appoint a third arbitrator as the chairman of the tribunal.

(6)   If the tribunal is to consist of two arbitrators and an umpire—

(a)   each party shall appoint one arbitrator not later than 14 days after service of a request in writing by either party to do so, and

(b)   the two so appointed may appoint an umpire at any time after they themselves are appointed and shall do so before any substantive hearing or forthwith if they cannot agree on a matter relating to the arbitration.

(7)   In any other case (in particular, if there are more than two parties) section 18 applies as in the case of a failure of the agreed appointment procedure.

[1.1130]
17   Power in case of default to appoint sole arbitrator
(1)   Unless the parties otherwise agree, where each of two parties to an arbitration agreement is to appoint an arbitrator and one party ("the party in default") refuses to do so, or fails to do so within the time specified, the other party, having duly appointed his arbitrator, may give notice in writing to the party in default that he proposes to appoint his arbitrator to act as sole arbitrator.

(2)   If the party in default does not within 7 clear days of that notice being given—

(a)   make the required appointment, and

    (b)   notify the other party that he has done so,
the other party may appoint his arbitrator as sole arbitrator whose award shall be binding on both parties as if he had been so appointed by agreement.

(3)   Where a sole arbitrator has been appointed under subsection (2), the party in default may (upon notice to the appointing party) apply to the court which may set aside the appointment.

(4)   The leave of the court is required for any appeal from a decision of the court under this section.

[1.1131]
18   Failure of appointment procedure

(1)   The parties are free to agree what is to happen in the event of a failure of the procedure for the appointment of the arbitral tribunal.

    There is no failure if an appointment is duly made under section 17 (power in case of default to appoint sole arbitrator), unless that appointment is set aside.

(2)   If or to the extent that there is no such agreement any party to the arbitration agreement may (upon notice to the other parties) apply to the court to exercise its powers under this section.

(3)   Those powers are—

    (a)   to give directions as to the making of any necessary appointments;

    (b)   to direct that the tribunal shall be constituted by such appointments (or any one or more of them) as have been made;

    (c)   to revoke any appointments already made;

    (d)   to make any necessary appointments itself.

(4)   An appointment made by the court under this section has effect as if made with the agreement of the parties.

(5)   The leave of the court is required for any appeal from a decision of the court under this section.

[1.1132]
19   Court to have regard to agreed qualifications

In deciding whether to exercise, and in considering how to exercise, any of its powers under section 16 (procedure for appointment of arbitrators) or section 18 (failure of appointment procedure), the court shall have due regard to any agreement of the parties as to the qualifications required of the arbitrators.

[1.1133]
20   Chairman

(1)   Where the parties have agreed that there is to be a chairman, they are free to agree what the functions of the chairman are to be in relation to the making of decisions, orders and awards.

(2)   If or to the extent that there is no such agreement, the following provisions apply.

(3)   Decisions, orders and awards shall be made by all or a majority of the arbitrators (including the chairman).

(4)   The view of the chairman shall prevail in relation to a decision, order or award in respect of which there is neither unanimity nor a majority under subsection (3).

[1.1134]
21   Umpire

(1)   Where the parties have agreed that there is to be an umpire, they are free to agree what the functions of the umpire are to be, and in particular—

    (a)   whether he is to attend the proceedings, and

    (b)   when he is to replace the other arbitrators as the tribunal with power to make decisions, orders and awards.

(2)   If or to the extent that there is no such agreement, the following provisions apply.

(3)   The umpire shall attend the proceedings and be supplied with the same documents and other materials as are supplied to the other arbitrators.

(4)   Decisions, orders and awards shall be made by the other arbitrators unless and until they cannot agree on a matter relating to the arbitration.

    In that event they shall forthwith give notice in writing to the parties and the umpire, whereupon the umpire shall replace them as the tribunal with power to make decisions, orders and awards as if he were sole arbitrator.

(5)   If the arbitrators cannot agree but fail to give notice of that fact, or if any of them fails to join in the giving of notice, any party to the arbitral proceedings may (upon notice to the other parties and to the tribunal) apply to the court which may order that the umpire shall replace the other arbitrators as the tribunal with power to make decisions, orders and awards as if he were sole arbitrator.

(6)   The leave of the court is required for any appeal from a decision of the court under this section.

[1.1135]
22 Decision-making where no chairman or umpire
(1)   Where the parties agree that there shall be two or more arbitrators with no chairman or umpire, the parties are free to agree how the tribunal is to make decisions, orders and awards.
(2)   If there is no such agreement, decisions, orders and awards shall be made by all or a majority of the arbitrators.

[1.1136]
23 Revocation of arbitrator's authority
(1)   The parties are free to agree in what circumstances the authority of an arbitrator may be revoked.
(2)   If or to the extent that there is no such agreement the following provisions apply.
(3)   The authority of an arbitrator may not be revoked except—
    (a)   by the parties acting jointly, or
    (b)   by an arbitral or other institution or person vested by the parties with powers in that regard.
(4)   Revocation of the authority of an arbitrator by the parties acting jointly must be agreed in writing unless the parties also agree (whether or not in writing) to terminate the arbitration agreement.
(5)   Nothing in this section affects the power of the court—
    (a)   to revoke an appointment under section 18 (powers exercisable in case of failure of appointment procedure), or
    (b)   to remove an arbitrator on the grounds specified in section 24.

[1.1137]
24 Power of court to remove arbitrator
(1)   A party to arbitral proceedings may (upon notice to the other parties, to the arbitrator concerned and to any other arbitrator) apply to the court to remove an arbitrator on any of the following grounds—
    (a)   that circumstances exist that give rise to justifiable doubts as to his impartiality;
    (b)   that he does not possess the qualifications required by the arbitration agreement;
    (c)   that he is physically or mentally incapable of conducting the proceedings or there are justifiable doubts as to his capacity to do so;
    (d)   that he has refused or failed—
        (i)   properly to conduct the proceedings, or
        (ii)   to use all reasonable despatch in conducting the proceedings or making an award,
        and that substantial injustice has been or will be caused to the applicant.
(2)   If there is an arbitral or other institution or person vested by the parties with power to remove an arbitrator, the court shall not exercise its power of removal unless satisfied that the applicant has first exhausted any available recourse to that institution or person.
(3)   The arbitral tribunal may continue the arbitral proceedings and make an award while an application to the court under this section is pending.
(4)   Where the court removes an arbitrator, it may make such order as it thinks fit with respect to his entitlement (if any) to fees or expenses, or the repayment of any fees or expenses already paid.
(5)   The arbitrator concerned is entitled to appear and be heard by the court before it makes any order under this section.
(6)   The leave of the court is required for any appeal from a decision of the court under this section.

[1.1138]
25 Resignation of arbitrator
(1)   The parties are free to agree with an arbitrator as to the consequences of his resignation as regards—
    (a)   his entitlement (if any) to fees or expenses, and
    (b)   any liability thereby incurred by him.
(2)   If or to the extent that there is no such agreement the following provisions apply.
(3)   An arbitrator who resigns his appointment may (upon notice to the parties) apply to the court—
    (a)   to grant him relief from any liability thereby incurred by him, and
    (b)   to make such order as it thinks fit with respect to his entitlement (if any) to fees or expenses or the repayment of any fees or expenses already paid.
(4)   If the court is satisfied that in all the circumstances it was reasonable for the arbitrator to resign, it may grant such relief as is mentioned in subsection (3)(a) on such terms as it thinks fit.
(5)   The leave of the court is required for any appeal from a decision of the court under this section.

[1.1139]
26 Death of arbitrator or person appointing him
(1)   The authority of an arbitrator is personal and ceases on his death.
(2)   Unless otherwise agreed by the parties, the death of the person by whom an arbitrator was appointed does not revoke the arbitrator's authority.

[1.1140]
27   Filling of vacancy, &c
(1)   Where an arbitrator ceases to hold office, the parties are free to agree—
   (a)   whether and if so how the vacancy is to be filled,
   (b)   whether and if so to what extent the previous proceedings should stand, and
   (c)   what effect (if any) his ceasing to hold office has on any appointment made by him (alone or jointly).
(2)   If or to the extent that there is no such agreement, the following provisions apply.
(3)   The provisions of sections 16 (procedure for appointment of arbitrators) and 18 (failure of appointment procedure) apply in relation to the filling of the vacancy as in relation to an original appointment.
(4)   The tribunal (when reconstituted) shall determine whether and if so to what extent the previous proceedings should stand.
   This does not affect any right of a party to challenge those proceedings on any ground which had arisen before the arbitrator ceased to hold office.
(5)   His ceasing to hold office does not affect any appointment by him (alone or jointly) of another arbitrator, in particular any appointment of a chairman or umpire.

[1.1141]
28   Joint and several liability of parties to arbitrators for fees and expenses
(1)   The parties are jointly and severally liable to pay to the arbitrators such reasonable fees and expenses (if any) as are appropriate in the circumstances.
(2)   Any party may apply to the court (upon notice to the other parties and to the arbitrators) which may order that the amount of the arbitrators' fees and expenses shall be considered and adjusted by such means and upon such terms as it may direct.
(3)   If the application is made after any amount has been paid to the arbitrators by way of fees or expenses, the court may order the repayment of such amount (if any) as is shown to be excessive, but shall not do so unless it is shown that it is reasonable in the circumstances to order repayment.
(4)   The above provisions have effect subject to any order of the court under section 24(4) or 25(3)(b) (order as to entitlement to fees or expenses in case of removal or resignation of arbitrator).
(5)   Nothing in this section affects any liability of a party to any other party to pay all or any of the costs of the arbitration (see sections 59 to 65) or any contractual right of an arbitrator to payment of his fees and expenses.
(6)   In this section references to arbitrators include an arbitrator who has ceased to act and an umpire who has not replaced the other arbitrators.

[1.1142]
29   Immunity of arbitrator
(1)   An arbitrator is not liable for anything done or omitted in the discharge or purported discharge of his functions as arbitrator unless the act or omission is shown to have been in bad faith.
(2)   Subsection (1) applies to an employee or agent of an arbitrator as it applies to the arbitrator himself.
(3)   This section does not affect any liability incurred by an arbitrator by reason of his resigning (but see section 25).

Jurisdiction of the arbitral tribunal

[1.1143]
30   Competence of tribunal to rule on its own jurisdiction
(1)   Unless otherwise agreed by the parties, the arbitral tribunal may rule on its own substantive jurisdiction, that is, as to—
   (a)   whether there is a valid arbitration agreement,
   (b)   whether the tribunal is properly constituted, and
   (c)   what matters have been submitted to arbitration in accordance with the arbitration agreement.
(2)   Any such ruling may be challenged by any available arbitral process of appeal or review or in accordance with the provisions of this Part.

[1.1144]
31   Objection to substantive jurisdiction of tribunal
(1)   An objection that the arbitral tribunal lacks substantive jurisdiction at the outset of the proceedings must be raised by a party not later than the time he takes the first step in the proceedings to contest the merits of any matter in relation to which he challenges the tribunal's jurisdiction.
   A party is not precluded from raising such an objection by the fact that he has appointed or participated in the appointment of an arbitrator.
(2)   Any objection during the course of the arbitral proceedings that the arbitral tribunal is exceeding its substantive jurisdiction must be made as soon as possible after the matter alleged to be beyond its jurisdiction is raised.

(3)   The arbitral tribunal may admit an objection later than the time specified in subsection (1) or (2) if it considers the delay justified.

(4)   Where an objection is duly taken to the tribunal's substantive jurisdiction and the tribunal has power to rule on its own jurisdiction, it may—

(a)   rule on the matter in an award as to jurisdiction, or

(b)   deal with the objection in its award on the merits.

If the parties agree which of these courses the tribunal should take, the tribunal shall proceed accordingly.

(5)   The tribunal may in any case, and shall if the parties so agree, stay proceedings whilst an application is made to the court under section 32 (determination of preliminary point of jurisdiction).

[1.1145]
32   Determination of preliminary point of jurisdiction

(1)   The court may, on the application of a party to arbitral proceedings (upon notice to the other parties), determine any question as to the substantive jurisdiction of the tribunal.

A party may lose the right to object (see section 73).

(2)   An application under this section shall not be considered unless—

(a)   it is made with the agreement in writing of all the other parties to the proceedings, or

(b)   it is made with the permission of the tribunal and the court is satisfied—

(i)   that the determination of the question is likely to produce substantial savings in costs,

(ii)   that the application was made without delay, and

(iii)   that there is good reason why the matter should be decided by the court.

(3)   An application under this section, unless made with the agreement of all the other parties to the proceedings, shall state the grounds on which it is said that the matter should be decided by the court.

(4)   Unless otherwise agreed by the parties, the arbitral tribunal may continue the arbitral proceedings and make an award while an application to the court under this section is pending.

(5)   Unless the court gives leave, no appeal lies from a decision of the court whether the conditions specified in subsection (2) are met.

(6)   The decision of the court on the question of jurisdiction shall be treated as a judgment of the court for the purposes of an appeal.

But no appeal lies without the leave of the court which shall not be given unless the court considers that the question involves a point of law which is one of general importance or is one which for some other special reason should be considered by the Court of Appeal.

The arbitral proceedings

[1.1146]
33   General duty of the tribunal

(1)   The tribunal shall—

(a)   act fairly and impartially as between the parties, giving each party a reasonable opportunity of putting his case and dealing with that of his opponent, and

(b)   adopt procedures suitable to the circumstances of the particular case, avoiding unnecessary delay or expense, so as to provide a fair means for the resolution of the matters falling to be determined.

(2)   The tribunal shall comply with that general duty in conducting the arbitral proceedings, in its decisions on matters of procedure and evidence and in the exercise of all other powers conferred on it.

[1.1147]
34   Procedural and evidential matters

(1)   It shall be for the tribunal to decide all procedural and evidential matters, subject to the right of the parties to agree any matter.

(2)   Procedural and evidential matters include—

(a)   when and where any part of the proceedings is to be held;

(b)   the language or languages to be used in the proceedings and whether translations of any relevant documents are to be supplied;

(c)   whether any and if so what form of written statements of claim and defence are to be used, when these should be supplied and the extent to which such statements can be later amended;

(d)   whether any and if so which documents or classes of documents should be disclosed between and produced by the parties and at what stage;

(e)   whether any and if so what questions should be put to and answered by the respective parties and when and in what form this should be done;

(f)   whether to apply strict rules of evidence (or any other rules) as to the admissibility, relevance or weight of any material (oral, written or other) sought to be tendered on any matters of fact or opinion, and the time, manner and form in which such material should be exchanged and presented;

(g)   whether and to what extent the tribunal should itself take the initiative in ascertaining the facts and the law;

(h)   whether and to what extent there should be oral or written evidence or submissions.

(3)   The tribunal may fix the time within which any directions given by it are to be complied with, and may if it thinks fit extend the time so fixed (whether or not it has expired).

[1.1148]

35   Consolidation of proceedings and concurrent hearings

(1)   The parties are free to agree—

(a)   that the arbitral proceedings shall be consolidated with other arbitral proceedings, or

(b)   that concurrent hearings shall be held,

on such terms as may be agreed.

(2)   Unless the parties agree to confer such power on the tribunal, the tribunal has no power to order consolidation of proceedings or concurrent hearings.

[1.1149]

36   Legal or other representation

Unless otherwise agreed by the parties, a party to arbitral proceedings may be represented in the proceedings by a lawyer or other person chosen by him.

[1.1150]

37   Power to appoint experts, legal advisers or assessors

(1)   Unless otherwise agreed by the parties—

(a)   the tribunal may—

    (i)   appoint experts or legal advisers to report to it and the parties, or

    (ii)   appoint assessors to assist it on technical matters,

    and may allow any such expert, legal adviser or assessor to attend the proceedings; and

(b)   the parties shall be given a reasonable opportunity to comment on any information, opinion or advice offered by any such person.

(2)   The fees and expenses of an expert, legal adviser or assessor appointed by the tribunal for which the arbitrators are liable are expenses of the arbitrators for the purposes of this Part.

[1.1151]

38   General powers exercisable by the tribunal

(1)   The parties are free to agree on the powers exercisable by the arbitral tribunal for the purposes of and in relation to the proceedings.

(2)   Unless otherwise agreed by the parties the tribunal has the following powers.

(3)   The tribunal may order a claimant to provide security for the costs of the arbitration.

This power shall not be exercised on the ground that the claimant is—

(a)   an individual ordinarily resident outside the United Kingdom, or

(b)   a corporation or association incorporated or formed under the law of a country outside the United Kingdom, or whose central management and control is exercised outside the United Kingdom.

(4)   The tribunal may give directions in relation to any property which is the subject of the proceedings or as to which any question arises in the proceedings, and which is owned by or is in the possession of a party to the proceedings—

(a)   for the inspection, photographing, preservation, custody or detention of the property by the tribunal, an expert or a party, or

(b)   ordering that samples be taken from, or any observation be made of or experiment conducted upon, the property.

(5)   The tribunal may direct that a party or witness shall be examined on oath or affirmation, and may for that purpose administer any necessary oath or take any necessary affirmation.

(6)   The tribunal may give directions to a party for the preservation for the purposes of the proceedings of any evidence in his custody or control.

[1.1152]

39   Power to make provisional awards

(1)   The parties are free to agree that the tribunal shall have power to order on a provisional basis any relief which it would have power to grant in a final award.

(2)   This includes, for instance, making—

(a)   a provisional order for the payment of money or the disposition of property as between the parties, or

(b)   an order to make an interim payment on account of the costs of the arbitration.

(3)   Any such order shall be subject to the tribunal's final adjudication; and the tribunal's final award, on the merits or as to costs, shall take account of any such order.

(4)   Unless the parties agree to confer such power on the tribunal, the tribunal has no such power.

This does not affect its powers under section 47 (awards on different issues, &c).

[1.1153]
40 General duty of parties
(1)   The parties shall do all things necessary for the proper and expeditious conduct of the arbitral proceedings.
(2)   This includes—
- (a)   complying without delay with any determination of the tribunal as to procedural or evidential matters, or with any order or directions of the tribunal, and
- (b)   where appropriate, taking without delay any necessary steps to obtain a decision of the court on a preliminary question of jurisdiction or law (see sections 32 and 45).

[1.1154]
41 Powers of tribunal in case of party's default
(1)   The parties are free to agree on the powers of the tribunal in case of a party's failure to do something necessary for the proper and expeditious conduct of the arbitration.
(2)   Unless otherwise agreed by the parties, the following provisions apply.
(3)   If the tribunal is satisfied that there has been inordinate and inexcusable delay on the part of the claimant in pursuing his claim and that the delay—
- (a)   gives rise, or is likely to give rise, to a substantial risk that it is not possible to have a fair resolution of the issues in that claim, or
- (b)   has caused, or is likely to cause, serious prejudice to the respondent,

the tribunal may make an award dismissing the claim.
(4)   If without showing sufficient cause a party—
- (a)   fails to attend or be represented at an oral hearing of which due notice was given, or
- (b)   where matters are to be dealt with in writing, fails after due notice to submit written evidence or make written submissions,

the tribunal may continue the proceedings in the absence of that party or, as the case may be, without any written evidence or submissions on his behalf, and may make an award on the basis of the evidence before it.
(5)   If without showing sufficient cause a party fails to comply with any order or directions of the tribunal, the tribunal may make a peremptory order to the same effect, prescribing such time for compliance with it as the tribunal considers appropriate.
(6)   If a claimant fails to comply with a peremptory order of the tribunal to provide security for costs, the tribunal may make an award dismissing his claim.
(7)   If a party fails to comply with any other kind of peremptory order, then, without prejudice to section 42 (enforcement by court of tribunal's peremptory orders), the tribunal may do any of the following—
- (a)   direct that the party in default shall not be entitled to rely upon any allegation or material which was the subject matter of the order;
- (b)   draw such adverse inferences from the act of non-compliance as the circumstances justify;
- (c)   proceed to an award on the basis of such materials as have been properly provided to it;
- (d)   make such order as it thinks fit as to the payment of costs of the arbitration incurred in consequence of the non-compliance.

Powers of court in relation to arbitral proceedings

[1.1155]
42 Enforcement of peremptory orders of tribunal
(1)   Unless otherwise agreed by the parties, the court may make an order requiring a party to comply with a peremptory order made by the tribunal.
(2)   An application for an order under this section may be made—
- (a)   by the tribunal (upon notice to the parties),
- (b)   by a party to the arbitral proceedings with the permission of the tribunal (and upon notice to the other parties), or
- (c)   where the parties have agreed that the powers of the court under this section shall be available.

(3)   The court shall not act unless it is satisfied that the applicant has exhausted any available arbitral process in respect of failure to comply with the tribunal's order.
(4)   No order shall be made under this section unless the court is satisfied that the person to whom the tribunal's order was directed has failed to comply with it within the time prescribed in the order or, if no time was prescribed, within a reasonable time.
(5)   The leave of the court is required for any appeal from a decision of the court under this section.

[1.1156]
43 Securing the attendance of witnesses
(1)   A party to arbitral proceedings may use the same court procedures as are available in relation to legal proceedings to secure the attendance before the tribunal of a witness in order to give oral testimony or to produce documents or other material evidence.
(2)   This may only be done with the permission of the tribunal or the agreement of the other parties.

(3) The court procedures may only be used if—
  (a) the witness is in the United Kingdom, and
  (b) the arbitral proceedings are being conducted in England and Wales or, as the case may be, Northern Ireland.

(4) A person shall not be compelled by virtue of this section to produce any document or other material evidence which he could not be compelled to produce in legal proceedings.

[1.1157]
44 Court powers exercisable in support of arbitral proceedings

(1) Unless otherwise agreed by the parties, the court has for the purposes of and in relation to arbitral proceedings the same power of making orders about the matters listed below as it has for the purposes of and in relation to legal proceedings.

(2) Those matters are—
  (a) the taking of the evidence of witnesses;
  (b) the preservation of evidence;
  (c) making orders relating to property which is the subject of the proceedings or as to which any question arises in the proceedings—
    (i) for the inspection, photographing, preservation, custody or detention of the property, or
    (ii) ordering that samples be taken from, or any observation be made of or experiment conducted upon, the property;
    and for that purpose authorising any person to enter any premises in the possession or control of a party to the arbitration;
  (d) the sale of any goods the subject of the proceedings;
  (e) the granting of an interim injunction or the appointment of a receiver.

(3) If the case is one of urgency, the court may, on the application of a party or proposed party to the arbitral proceedings, make such orders as it thinks necessary for the purpose of preserving evidence or assets.

(4) If the case is not one of urgency, the court shall act only on the application of a party to the arbitral proceedings (upon notice to the other parties and to the tribunal) made with the permission of the tribunal or the agreement in writing of the other parties.

(5) In any case the court shall act only if or to the extent that the arbitral tribunal, and any arbitral or other institution or person vested by the parties with power in that regard, has no power or is unable for the time being to act effectively.

(6) If the court so orders, an order made by it under this section shall cease to have effect in whole or in part on the order of the tribunal or of any such arbitral or other institution or person having power to act in relation to the subject-matter of the order.

(7) The leave of the court is required for any appeal from a decision of the court under this section.

[1.1158]
45 Determination of preliminary point of law

(1) Unless otherwise agreed by the parties, the court may on the application of a party to arbitral proceedings (upon notice to the other parties) determine any question of law arising in the course of the proceedings which the court is satisfied substantially affects the rights of one or more of the parties.

An agreement to dispense with reasons for the tribunal's award shall be considered an agreement to exclude the court's jurisdiction under this section.

(2) An application under this section shall not be considered unless—
  (a) it is made with the agreement of all the other parties to the proceedings, or
  (b) it is made with the permission of the tribunal and the court is satisfied—
    (i) that the determination of the question is likely to produce substantial savings in costs, and
    (ii) that the application was made without delay.

(3) The application shall identify the question of law to be determined and, unless made with the agreement of all the other parties to the proceedings, shall state the grounds on which it is said that the question should be decided by the court.

(4) Unless otherwise agreed by the parties, the arbitral tribunal may continue the arbitral proceedings and make an award while an application to the court under this section is pending.

(5) Unless the court gives leave, no appeal lies from a decision of the court whether the conditions specified in subsection (2) are met.

(6) The decision of the court on the question of law shall be treated as a judgment of the court for the purposes of an appeal.

But no appeal lies without the leave of the court which shall not be given unless the court considers that the question is one of general importance, or is one which for some other special reason should be considered by the Court of Appeal.

The award

[1.1159]
46 Rules applicable to substance of dispute

(1)   The arbitral tribunal shall decide the dispute—

    (a)   in accordance with the law chosen by the parties as applicable to the substance of the dispute, or

    (b)   if the parties so agree, in accordance with such other considerations as are agreed by them or determined by the tribunal.

(2)   For this purpose the choice of the laws of a country shall be understood to refer to the substantive laws of that country and not its conflict of laws rules.

(3)   If or to the extent that there is no such choice or agreement, the tribunal shall apply the law determined by the conflict of laws rules which it considers applicable.

[1.1160]
47 Awards on different issues, &c

(1)   Unless otherwise agreed by the parties, the tribunal may make more than one award at different times on different aspects of the matters to be determined.

(2)   The tribunal may, in particular, make an award relating—

    (a)   to an issue affecting the whole claim, or

    (b)   to a part only of the claims or cross-claims submitted to it for decision.

(3)   If the tribunal does so, it shall specify in its award the issue, or the claim or part of a claim, which is the subject matter of the award.

[1.1161]
48 Remedies

(1)   The parties are free to agree on the powers exercisable by the arbitral tribunal as regards remedies.

(2)   Unless otherwise agreed by the parties, the tribunal has the following powers.

(3)   The tribunal may make a declaration as to any matter to be determined in the proceedings.

(4)   The tribunal may order the payment of a sum of money, in any currency.

(5)   The tribunal has the same powers as the court—

    (a)   to order a party to do or refrain from doing anything;

    (b)   to order specific performance of a contract (other than a contract relating to land);

    (c)   to order the rectification, setting aside or cancellation of a deed or other document.

[1.1162]
49 Interest

(1)   The parties are free to agree on the powers of the tribunal as regards the award of interest.

(2)   Unless otherwise agreed by the parties the following provisions apply.

(3)   The tribunal may award simple or compound interest from such dates, at such rates and with such rests as it considers meets the justice of the case—

    (a)   on the whole or part of any amount awarded by the tribunal, in respect of any period up to the date of the award;

    (b)   on the whole or part of any amount claimed in the arbitration and outstanding at the commencement of the arbitral proceedings but paid before the award was made, in respect of any period up to the date of payment.

(4)   The tribunal may award simple or compound interest from the date of the award (or any later date) until payment, at such rates and with such rests as it considers meets the justice of the case, on the outstanding amount of any award (including any award of interest under subsection (3) and any award as to costs).

(5)   References in this section to an amount awarded by the tribunal include an amount payable in consequence of a declaratory award by the tribunal.

(6)   The above provisions do not affect any other power of the tribunal to award interest.

[1.1163]
50 Extension of time for making award

(1)   Where the time for making an award is limited by or in pursuance of the arbitration agreement, then, unless otherwise agreed by the parties, the court may in accordance with the following provisions by order extend that time.

(2)   An application for an order under this section may be made—

    (a)   by the tribunal (upon notice to the parties), or

    (b)   by any party to the proceedings (upon notice to the tribunal and the other parties),

but only after exhausting any available arbitral process for obtaining an extension of time.

(3)   The court shall only make an order if satisfied that a substantial injustice would otherwise be done.

(4)   The court may extend the time for such period and on such terms as it thinks fit, and may do so whether or not the time previously fixed (by or under the agreement or by a previous order) has expired.

(5)   The leave of the court is required for any appeal from a decision of the court under this section.

[1.1164]
51   Settlement
(1)   If during arbitral proceedings the parties settle the dispute, the following provisions apply unless otherwise agreed by the parties.
(2)   The tribunal shall terminate the substantive proceedings and, if so requested by the parties and not objected to by the tribunal, shall record the settlement in the form of an agreed award.
(3)   An agreed award shall state that it is an award of the tribunal and shall have the same status and effect as any other award on the merits of the case.
(4)   The following provisions of this Part relating to awards (sections 52 to 58) apply to an agreed award.
(5)   Unless the parties have also settled the matter of the payment of the costs of the arbitration, the provisions of this Part relating to costs (sections 59 to 65) continue to apply.

[1.1165]
52   Form of award
(1)   The parties are free to agree on the form of an award.
(2)   If or to the extent that there is no such agreement, the following provisions apply.
(3)   The award shall be in writing signed by all the arbitrators or all those assenting to the award.
(4)   The award shall contain the reasons for the award unless it is an agreed award or the parties have agreed to dispense with reasons.
(5)   The award shall state the seat of the arbitration and the date when the award is made.

[1.1166]
53   Place where award treated as made
Unless otherwise agreed by the parties, where the seat of the arbitration is in England and Wales or Northern Ireland, any award in the proceedings shall be treated as made there, regardless of where it was signed, despatched or delivered to any of the parties.

[1.1167]
54   Date of award
(1)   Unless otherwise agreed by the parties, the tribunal may decide what is to be taken to be the date on which the award was made.
(2)   In the absence of any such decision, the date of the award shall be taken to be the date on which it is signed by the arbitrator or, where more than one arbitrator signs the award, by the last of them.

[1.1168]
55   Notification of award
(1)   The parties are free to agree on the requirements as to notification of the award to the parties.
(2)   If there is no such agreement, the award shall be notified to the parties by service on them of copies of the award, which shall be done without delay after the award is made.
(3)   Nothing in this section affects section 56 (power to withhold award in case of non-payment).

[1.1169]
56   Power to withhold award in case of non-payment
(1)   The tribunal may refuse to deliver an award to the parties except upon full payment of the fees and expenses of the arbitrators.
(2)   If the tribunal refuses on that ground to deliver an award, a party to the arbitral proceedings may (upon notice to the other parties and the tribunal) apply to the court, which may order that—
   (a)   the tribunal shall deliver the award on the payment into court by the applicant of the fees and expenses demanded, or such lesser amount as the court may specify,
   (b)   the amount of the fees and expenses properly payable shall be determined by such means and upon such terms as the court may direct, and
   (c)   out of the money paid into court there shall be paid out such fees and expenses as may be found to be properly payable and the balance of the money (if any) shall be paid out to the applicant.
(3)   For this purpose the amount of fees and expenses properly payable is the amount the applicant is liable to pay under section 28 or any agreement relating to the payment of the arbitrators.
(4)   No application to the court may be made where there is any available arbitral process for appeal or review of the amount of the fees or expenses demanded.
(5)   References in this section to arbitrators include an arbitrator who has ceased to act and an umpire who has not replaced the other arbitrators.
(6)   The above provisions of this section also apply in relation to any arbitral or other institution or person vested by the parties with powers in relation to the delivery of the tribunal's award.
   As they so apply, the references to the fees and expenses of the arbitrators shall be construed as including the fees and expenses of that institution or person.

(7)   The leave of the court is required for any appeal from a decision of the court under this section.

(8)   Nothing in this section shall be construed as excluding an application under section 28 where payment has been made to the arbitrators in order to obtain the award.

[1.1170]
57   Correction of award or additional award
(1)   The parties are free to agree on the powers of the tribunal to correct an award or make an additional award.
(2)   If or to the extent there is no such agreement, the following provisions apply.
(3)   The tribunal may on its own initiative or on the application of a party—
   (a)   correct an award so as to remove any clerical mistake or error arising from an accidental slip or omission or clarify or remove any ambiguity in the award, or
   (b)   make an additional award in respect of any claim (including a claim for interest or costs) which was presented to the tribunal but was not dealt with in the award.
   These powers shall not be exercised without first affording the other parties a reasonable opportunity to make representations to the tribunal.
(4)   Any application for the exercise of those powers must be made within 28 days of the date of the award or such longer period as the parties may agree.
(5)   Any correction of an award shall be made within 28 days of the date the application was received by the tribunal or, where the correction is made by the tribunal on its own initiative, within 28 days of the date of the award or, in either case, such longer period as the parties may agree.
(6)   Any additional award shall be made within 56 days of the date of the original award or such longer period as the parties may agree.
(7)   Any correction of an award shall form part of the award.

[1.1171]
58   Effect of award
(1)   Unless otherwise agreed by the parties, an award made by the tribunal pursuant to an arbitration agreement is final and binding both on the parties and on any persons claiming through or under them.
(2)   This does not affect the right of a person to challenge the award by any available arbitral process of appeal or review or in accordance with the provisions of this Part.

Costs of the arbitration

[1.1172]
59   Costs of the arbitration
(1)   References in this Part to the costs of the arbitration are to—
   (a)   the arbitrators' fees and expenses,
   (b)   the fees and expenses of any arbitral institution concerned, and
   (c)   the legal or other costs of the parties.
(2)   Any such reference includes the costs of or incidental to any proceedings to determine the amount of the recoverable costs of the arbitration (see section 63).

[1.1173]
60   Agreement to pay costs in any event
An agreement which has the effect that a party is to pay the whole or part of the costs of the arbitration in any event is only valid if made after the dispute in question has arisen.

[1.1174]
61   Award of costs
(1)   The tribunal may make an award allocating the costs of the arbitration as between the parties, subject to any agreement of the parties.
(2)   Unless the parties otherwise agree, the tribunal shall award costs on the general principle that costs should follow the event except where it appears to the tribunal that in the circumstances this is not appropriate in relation to the whole or part of the costs.

[1.1175]
62   Effect of agreement or award about costs
Unless the parties otherwise agree, any obligation under an agreement between them as to how the costs of the arbitration are to be borne, or under an award allocating the costs of the arbitration, extends only to such costs as are recoverable.

[1.1176]
63   The recoverable costs of the arbitration
(1)   The parties are free to agree what costs of the arbitration are recoverable.
(2)   If or to the extent there is no such agreement, the following provisions apply.
(3)   The tribunal may determine by award the recoverable costs of the arbitration on such basis as it thinks fit.
   If it does so, it shall specify—

(a)   the basis on which it has acted, and
(b)   the items of recoverable costs and the amount referable to each.
(4)   If the tribunal does not determine the recoverable costs of the arbitration, any party to the arbitral proceedings may apply to the court (upon notice to the other parties) which may—
(a)   determine the recoverable costs of the arbitration on such basis as it thinks fit, or
(b)   order that they shall be determined by such means and upon such terms as it may specify.
(5)   Unless the tribunal or the court determines otherwise—
(a)   the recoverable costs of the arbitration shall be determined on the basis that there shall be allowed a reasonable amount in respect of all costs reasonably incurred, and
(b)   any doubt as to whether costs were reasonably incurred or were reasonable in amount shall be resolved in favour of the paying party.
(6)   The above provisions have effect subject to section 64 (recoverable fees and expenses of arbitrators).
(7)   Nothing in this section affects any right of the arbitrators, any expert, legal adviser or assessor appointed by the tribunal, or any arbitral institution, to payment of their fees and expenses.

[1.1177]
64   Recoverable fees and expenses of arbitrators
(1)   Unless otherwise agreed by the parties, the recoverable costs of the arbitration shall include in respect of the fees and expenses of the arbitrators only such reasonable fees and expenses as are appropriate in the circumstances.
(2)   If there is any question as to what reasonable fees and expenses are appropriate in the circumstances, and the matter is not already before the court on an application under section 63(4), the court may on the application of any party (upon notice to the other parties)—
(a)   determine the matter, or
(b)   order that it be determined by such means and upon such terms as the court may specify.
(3)   Subsection (1) has effect subject to any order of the court under section 24(4) or 25(3)(b) (order as to entitlement to fees or expenses in case of removal or resignation of arbitrator).
(4)   Nothing in this section affects any right of the arbitrator to payment of his fees and expenses.

[1.1178]
65   Power to limit recoverable costs
(1)   Unless otherwise agreed by the parties, the tribunal may direct that the recoverable costs of the arbitration, or of any part of the arbitral proceedings, shall be limited to a specified amount.
(2)   Any direction may be made or varied at any stage, but this must be done sufficiently in advance of the incurring of costs to which it relates, or the taking of any steps in the proceedings which may be affected by it, for the limit to be taken into account.

Powers of the court in relation to award

[1.1179]
66   Enforcement of the award
(1)   An award made by the tribunal pursuant to an arbitration agreement may, by leave of the court, be enforced in the same manner as a judgment or order of the court to the same effect.
(2)   Where leave is so given, judgment may be entered in terms of the award.
(3)   Leave to enforce an award shall not be given where, or to the extent that, the person against whom it is sought to be enforced shows that the tribunal lacked substantive jurisdiction to make the award.
    The right to raise such an objection may have been lost (see section 73).
(4)   Nothing in this section affects the recognition or enforcement of an award under any other enactment or rule of law, in particular under Part II of the Arbitration Act 1950 (enforcement of awards under Geneva Convention) or the provisions of Part III of this Act relating to the recognition and enforcement of awards under the New York Convention or by an action on the award.

[1.1180]
67   Challenging the award: substantive jurisdiction
(1)   A party to arbitral proceedings may (upon notice to the other parties and to the tribunal) apply to the court—
(a)   challenging any award of the arbitral tribunal as to its substantive jurisdiction; or
(b)   for an order declaring an award made by the tribunal on the merits to be of no effect, in whole or in part, because the tribunal did not have substantive jurisdiction.
    A party may lose the right to object (see section 73) and the right to apply is subject to the restrictions in section 70(2) and (3).
(2)   The arbitral tribunal may continue the arbitral proceedings and make a further award while an application to the court under this section is pending in relation to an award as to jurisdiction.
(3)   On an application under this section challenging an award of the arbitral tribunal as to its substantive jurisdiction, the court may by order—
(a)   confirm the award,
(b)   vary the award, or
(c)   set aside the award in whole or in part.

(4) The leave of the court is required for any appeal from a decision of the court under this section.

[1.1181]
68 Challenging the award: serious irregularity
(1) A party to arbitral proceedings may (upon notice to the other parties and to the tribunal) apply to the court challenging an award in the proceedings on the ground of serious irregularity affecting the tribunal, the proceedings or the award.

A party may lose the right to object (see section 73) and the right to apply is subject to the restrictions in section 70(2) and (3).
(2) Serious irregularity means an irregularity of one or more of the following kinds which the court considers has caused or will cause substantial injustice to the applicant—
- (a) failure by the tribunal to comply with section 33 (general duty of tribunal);
- (b) the tribunal exceeding its powers (otherwise than by exceeding its substantive jurisdiction: see section 67);
- (c) failure by the tribunal to conduct the proceedings in accordance with the procedure agreed by the parties;
- (d) failure by the tribunal to deal with all the issues that were put to it;
- (e) any arbitral or other institution or person vested by the parties with powers in relation to the proceedings or the award exceeding its powers;
- (f) uncertainty or ambiguity as to the effect of the award;
- (g) the award being obtained by fraud or the award or the way in which it was procured being contrary to public policy;
- (h) failure to comply with the requirements as to the form of the award; or
- (i) any irregularity in the conduct of the proceedings or in the award which is admitted by the tribunal or by any arbitral or other institution or person vested by the parties with powers in relation to the proceedings or the award.

(3) If there is shown to be serious irregularity affecting the tribunal, the proceedings or the award, the court may—
- (a) remit the award to the tribunal, in whole or in part, for reconsideration,
- (b) set the award aside in whole or in part, or
- (c) declare the award to be of no effect, in whole or in part.

The court shall not exercise its power to set aside or to declare an award to be of no effect, in whole or in part, unless it is satisfied that it would be inappropriate to remit the matters in question to the tribunal for reconsideration.
(4) The leave of the court is required for any appeal from a decision of the court under this section.

[1.1182]
69 Appeal on point of law
(1) Unless otherwise agreed by the parties, a party to arbitral proceedings may (upon notice to the other parties and to the tribunal) appeal to the court on a question of law arising out of an award made in the proceedings.

An agreement to dispense with reasons for the tribunal's award shall be considered an agreement to exclude the court's jurisdiction under this section.
(2) An appeal shall not be brought under this section except—
- (a) with the agreement of all the other parties to the proceedings, or
- (b) with the leave of the court.

The right to appeal is also subject to the restrictions in section 70(2) and (3).
(3) Leave to appeal shall be given only if the court is satisfied—
- (a) that the determination of the question will substantially affect the rights of one or more of the parties,
- (b) that the question is one which the tribunal was asked to determine,
- (c) that, on the basis of the findings of fact in the award—
  - (i) the decision of the tribunal on the question is obviously wrong, or
  - (ii) the question is one of general public importance and the decision of the tribunal is at least open to serious doubt, and
- (d) that, despite the agreement of the parties to resolve the matter by arbitration, it is just and proper in all the circumstances for the court to determine the question.

(4) An application for leave to appeal under this section shall identify the question of law to be determined and state the grounds on which it is alleged that leave to appeal should be granted.
(5) The court shall determine an application for leave to appeal under this section without a hearing unless it appears to the court that a hearing is required.
(6) The leave of the court is required for any appeal from a decision of the court under this section to grant or refuse leave to appeal.
(7) On an appeal under this section the court may by order—
- (a) confirm the award,
- (b) vary the award,

(c)   remit the award to the tribunal, in whole or in part, for reconsideration in the light of the court's determination, or

(d)   set aside the award in whole or in part.

The court shall not exercise its power to set aside an award, in whole or in part, unless it is satisfied that it would be inappropriate to remit the matters in question to the tribunal for reconsideration.

(8)   The decision of the court on an appeal under this section shall be treated as a judgment of the court for the purposes of a further appeal.

But no such appeal lies without the leave of the court which shall not be given unless the court considers that the question is one of general importance or is one which for some other special reason should be considered by the Court of Appeal.

[1.1183]
70   Challenge or appeal: supplementary provisions

(1)   The following provisions apply to an application or appeal under section 67, 68 or 69.

(2)   An application or appeal may not be brought if the applicant or appellant has not first exhausted—

(a)   any available arbitral process of appeal or review, and

(b)   any available recourse under section 57 (correction of award or additional award).

(3)   Any application or appeal must be brought within 28 days of the date of the award or, if there has been any arbitral process of appeal or review, of the date when the applicant or appellant was notified of the result of that process.

(4)   If on an application or appeal it appears to the court that the award—

(a)   does not contain the tribunal's reasons, or

(b)   does not set out the tribunal's reasons in sufficient detail to enable the court properly to consider the application or appeal,

the court may order the tribunal to state the reasons for its award in sufficient detail for that purpose.

(5)   Where the court makes an order under subsection (4), it may make such further order as it thinks fit with respect to any additional costs of the arbitration resulting from its order.

(6)   The court may order the applicant or appellant to provide security for the costs of the application or appeal, and may direct that the application or appeal be dismissed if the order is not complied with.

The power to order security for costs shall not be exercised on the ground that the applicant or appellant is—

(a)   an individual ordinarily resident outside the United Kingdom, or

(b)   a corporation or association incorporated or formed under the law of a country outside the United Kingdom, or whose central management and control is exercised outside the United Kingdom.

(7)   The court may order that any money payable under the award shall be brought into court or otherwise secured pending the determination of the application or appeal, and may direct that the application or appeal be dismissed if the order is not complied with.

(8)   The court may grant leave to appeal subject to conditions to the same or similar effect as an order under subsection (6) or (7).

This does not affect the general discretion of the court to grant leave subject to conditions.

[1.1184]
71   Challenge or appeal: effect of order of court

(1)   The following provisions have effect where the court makes an order under section 67, 68 or 69 with respect to an award.

(2)   Where the award is varied, the variation has effect as part of the tribunal's award.

(3)   Where the award is remitted to the tribunal, in whole or in part, for reconsideration, the tribunal shall make a fresh award in respect of the matters remitted within three months of the date of the order for remission or such longer or shorter period as the court may direct.

(4)   Where the award is set aside or declared to be of no effect, in whole or in part, the court may also order that any provision that an award is a condition precedent to the bringing of legal proceedings in respect of a matter to which the arbitration agreement applies, is of no effect as regards the subject matter of the award or, as the case may be, the relevant part of the award.

Miscellaneous

[1.1185]
72   Saving for rights of person who takes no part in proceedings

(1)   A person alleged to be a party to arbitral proceedings but who takes no part in the proceedings may question—

(a)   whether there is a valid arbitration agreement,

(b)   whether the tribunal is properly constituted, or

(c)   what matters have been submitted to arbitration in accordance with the arbitration agreement,

by proceedings in the court for a declaration or injunction or other appropriate relief.

(2)   He also has the same right as a party to the arbitral proceedings to challenge an award—

(a) by an application under section 67 on the ground of lack of substantive jurisdiction in relation to him, or

(b) by an application under section 68 on the ground of serious irregularity (within the meaning of that section) affecting him;

and section 70(2) (duty to exhaust arbitral procedures) does not apply in his case.

[1.1186]
73 Loss of right to object
(1) If a party to arbitral proceedings takes part, or continues to take part, in the proceedings without making, either forthwith or within such time as is allowed by the arbitration agreement or the tribunal or by any provision of this Part, any objection—

(a) that the tribunal lacks substantive jurisdiction,

(b) that the proceedings have been improperly conducted,

(c) that there has been a failure to comply with the arbitration agreement or with any provision of this Part, or

(d) that there has been any other irregularity affecting the tribunal or the proceedings,

he may not raise that objection later, before the tribunal or the court, unless he shows that, at the time he took part or continued to take part in the proceedings, he did not know and could not with reasonable diligence have discovered the grounds for the objection.

(2) Where the arbitral tribunal rules that it has substantive jurisdiction and a party to arbitral proceedings who could have questioned that ruling—

(a) by any available arbitral process of appeal or review, or

(b) by challenging the award,

does not do so, or does not do so within the time allowed by the arbitration agreement or any provision of this Part, he may not object later to the tribunal's substantive jurisdiction on any ground which was the subject of that ruling.

[1.1187]
74 Immunity of arbitral institutions, &c
(1) An arbitral or other institution or person designated or requested by the parties to appoint or nominate an arbitrator is not liable for anything done or omitted in the discharge or purported discharge of that function unless the act or omission is shown to have been in bad faith.

(2) An arbitral or other institution or person by whom an arbitrator is appointed or nominated is not liable, by reason of having appointed or nominated him, for anything done or omitted by the arbitrator (or his employees or agents) in the discharge or purported discharge of his functions as arbitrator.

(3) The above provisions apply to an employee or agent of an arbitral or other institution or person as they apply to the institution or person himself.

[1.1188]
75 Charge to secure payment of solicitors' costs
The powers of the court to make declarations and orders under section 73 of the Solicitors Act 1974 or Article 71H of the Solicitors (Northern Ireland) Order 1976 (power to charge property recovered in the proceedings with the payment of solicitors' costs) may be exercised in relation to arbitral proceedings as if those proceedings were proceedings in the court.

Supplementary

[1.1189]
76 Service of notices, &c
(1) The parties are free to agree on the manner of service of any notice or other document required or authorised to be given or served in pursuance of the arbitration agreement or for the purposes of the arbitral proceedings.

(2) If or to the extent that there is no such agreement the following provisions apply.

(3) A notice or other document may be served on a person by any effective means.

(4) If a notice or other document is addressed, pre-paid and delivered by post—

(a) to the addressee's last known principal residence or, if he is or has been carrying on a trade, profession or business, his last known principal business address, or

(b) where the addressee is a body corporate, to the body's registered or principal office,

it shall be treated as effectively served.

(5) This section does not apply to the service of documents for the purposes of legal proceedings, for which provision is made by rules of court.

(6) References in this Part to a notice or other document include any form of communication in writing and references to giving or serving a notice or other document shall be construed accordingly.

[1.1190]
77 Powers of court in relation to service of documents
(1) This section applies where service of a document on a person in the manner agreed by the parties, or in accordance with provisions of section 76 having effect in default of agreement, is not reasonably practicable.

(2)   Unless otherwise agreed by the parties, the court may make such order as it thinks fit—
(a)   for service in such manner as the court may direct, or
(b)   dispensing with service of the document.
(3)   Any party to the arbitration agreement may apply for an order, but only after exhausting any available arbitral process for resolving the matter.
(4)   The leave of the court is required for any appeal from a decision of the court under this section.

[1.1191]
78   Reckoning periods of time
(1)   The parties are free to agree on the method of reckoning periods of time for the purposes of any provision agreed by them or any provision of this Part having effect in default of such agreement.
(2)   If or to the extent there is no such agreement, periods of time shall be reckoned in accordance with the following provisions.
(3)   Where the act is required to be done within a specified period after or from a specified date, the period begins immediately after that date.
(4)   Where the act is required to be done a specified number of clear days after a specified date, at least that number of days must intervene between the day on which the act is done and that date.
(5)   Where the period is a period of seven days or less which would include a Saturday, Sunday or a public holiday in the place where anything which has to be done within the period falls to be done, that day shall be excluded.
   In relation to England and Wales or Northern Ireland, a "public holiday" means Christmas Day, Good Friday or a day which under the Banking and Financial Dealings Act 1971 is a bank holiday.

[1.1192]
79   Power of court to extend time limits relating to arbitral proceedings
(1)   Unless the parties otherwise agree, the court may by order extend any time limit agreed by them in relation to any matter relating to the arbitral proceedings or specified in any provision of this Part having effect in default of such agreement.
   This section does not apply to a time limit to which section 12 applies (power of court to extend time for beginning arbitral proceedings, &c).
(2)   An application for an order may be made—
(a)   by any party to the arbitral proceedings (upon notice to the other parties and to the tribunal), or
(b)   by the arbitral tribunal (upon notice to the parties).
(3)   The court shall not exercise its power to extend a time limit unless it is satisfied—
(a)   that any available recourse to the tribunal, or to any arbitral or other institution or person vested by the parties with power in that regard, has first been exhausted, and
(b)   that a substantial injustice would otherwise be done.
(4)   The court's power under this section may be exercised whether or not the time has already expired.
(5)   An order under this section may be made on such terms as the court thinks fit.
(6)   The leave of the court is required for any appeal from a decision of the court under this section.

[1.1193]
80   Notice and other requirements in connection with legal proceedings
(1)   References in this Part to an application, appeal or other step in relation to legal proceedings being taken "upon notice" to the other parties to the arbitral proceedings, or to the tribunal, are to such notice of the originating process as is required by rules of court and do not impose any separate requirement.
(2)   Rules of court shall be made—
(a)   requiring such notice to be given as indicated by any provision of this Part, and
(b)   as to the manner, form and content of any such notice.
(3)   Subject to any provision made by rules of court, a requirement to give notice to the tribunal of legal proceedings shall be construed—
(a)   if there is more than one arbitrator, as a requirement to give notice to each of them; and
(b)   if the tribunal is not fully constituted, as a requirement to give notice to any arbitrator who has been appointed.
(4)   References in this Part to making an application or appeal to the court within a specified period are to the issue within that period of the appropriate originating process in accordance with rules of court.
(5)   Where any provision of this Part requires an application or appeal to be made to the court within a specified time, the rules of court relating to the reckoning of periods, the extending or abridging of periods, and the consequences of not taking a step within the period prescribed by the rules, apply in relation to that requirement.
(6)   Provision may be made by rules of court amending the provisions of this Part—
(a)   with respect to the time within which any application or appeal to the court must be made,

(b) so as to keep any provision made by this Part in relation to arbitral proceedings in step with the corresponding provision of rules of court applying in relation to proceedings in the court, or

(c) so as to keep any provision made by this Part in relation to legal proceedings in step with the corresponding provision of rules of court applying generally in relation to proceedings in the court.

(7) Nothing in this section affects the generality of the power to make rules of court.

[1.1194]
81 Saving for certain matters governed by common law
(1) Nothing in this Part shall be construed as excluding the operation of any rule of law consistent with the provisions of this Part, in particular, any rule of law as to—
   (a) matters which are not capable of settlement by arbitration;
   (b) the effect of an oral arbitration agreement; or
   (c) the refusal of recognition or enforcement of an arbitral award on grounds of public policy.
(2) Nothing in this Act shall be construed as reviving any jurisdiction of the court to set aside or remit an award on the ground of errors of fact or law on the face of the award.

[1.1195]
82 Minor definitions
(1) In this Part—
   "arbitrator", unless the context otherwise requires, includes an umpire;
   "available arbitral process", in relation to any matter, includes any process of appeal to or review by an arbitral or other institution or person vested by the parties with powers in relation to that matter;
   "claimant", unless the context otherwise requires, includes a counterclaimant, and related expressions shall be construed accordingly;
   "dispute" includes any difference;
   "enactment" includes an enactment contained in Northern Ireland legislation;
   "legal proceedings" means civil proceedings [in England and Wales in the High Court or the county court or in Northern Ireland] in the High Court or a county court;
   "peremptory order" means an order made under section 41(5) or made in exercise of any corresponding power conferred by the parties;
   "premises" includes land, buildings, moveable structures, vehicles, vessels, aircraft and hovercraft;
   "question of law" means—
      (a) for a court in England and Wales, a question of the law of England and Wales, and
      (b) for a court in Northern Ireland, a question of the law of Northern Ireland;
   "substantive jurisdiction", in relation to an arbitral tribunal, refers to the matters specified in section 30(1)(a) to (c), and references to the tribunal exceeding its substantive jurisdiction shall be construed accordingly.
(2) References in this Part to a party to an arbitration agreement include any person claiming under or through a party to the agreement.

NOTES
Sub-s (1): in definition "legal proceedings" words in square brackets inserted by the Crime and Courts Act 2013, s 17(5), Sch 9, Pt 3, para 60(1).

[1.1196]
83 Index of defined expressions: Part I
In this Part the expressions listed below are defined or otherwise explained by the provisions indicated—

agreement, agree and agreed	section 5(1)
agreement in writing	section 5(2) to (5)
arbitration agreement	sections 6 and 5(1)
arbitrator	section 82(1)
available arbitral process	section 82(1)
claimant	section 82(1)
commencement (in relation to arbitral proceedings)	section 14
costs of the arbitration	section 59
the court	section 105
dispute	section 82(1)
enactment	section 82(1)
legal proceedings	section 82(1)
Limitation Acts	section 13(4)

notice (or other document)	section 76(6)
party—	
— in relation to an arbitration agreement	section 82(2)
— where section 106(2) or (3) applies	section 106(4)
peremptory order	section 82(1) (and see section 41(5))
premises	section 82(1)
question of law	section 82(1)
recoverable costs	sections 63 and 64
seat of the arbitration	section 3
serve and service (of notice or other document)	section 76(6)
substantive jurisdiction (in relation to an arbitral tribunal)	section 82(1) (and see section 30(1)(a) to (c))
upon notice (to the parties or the tribunal)	section 80
written and in writing	section 5(6)

[1.1197]
84 Transitional provisions
(1)   The provisions of this Part do not apply to arbitral proceedings commenced before the date on which this Part comes into force.
(2)   They apply to arbitral proceedings commenced on or after that date under an arbitration agreement whenever made.
(3)   The above provisions have effect subject to any transitional provision made by an order under section 109(2) (power to include transitional provisions in commencement order).

PART II
OTHER PROVISIONS RELATING TO ARBITRATION
Domestic arbitration agreements
[1.1198]
85 Modification of Part I in relation to domestic arbitration agreement
(1)   In the case of a domestic arbitration agreement the provisions of Part I are modified in accordance with the following sections.
(2)   For this purpose a "domestic arbitration agreement" means an arbitration agreement to which none of the parties is—
   (a)   an individual who is a national of, or habitually resident in, a state other than the United Kingdom, or
   (b)   a body corporate which is incorporated in, or whose central control and management is exercised in, a state other than the United Kingdom,
and under which the seat of the arbitration (if the seat has been designated or determined) is in the United Kingdom.
(3)   In subsection (2) "arbitration agreement" and "seat of the arbitration" have the same meaning as in Part I (see sections 3, 5(1) and 6).

NOTES
Commencement: to be appointed.

[1.1199]
86 Staying of legal proceedings
(1)   In section 9 (stay of legal proceedings), subsection (4) (stay unless the arbitration agreement is null and void, inoperative, or incapable of being performed) does not apply to a domestic arbitration agreement.
(2)   On an application under that section in relation to a domestic arbitration agreement the court shall grant a stay unless satisfied—
   (a)   that the arbitration agreement is null and void, inoperative, or incapable of being performed, or
   (b)   that there are other sufficient grounds for not requiring the parties to abide by the arbitration agreement.
(3)   The court may treat as a sufficient ground under subsection (2)(b) the fact that the applicant is or was at any material time not ready and willing to do all things necessary for the proper conduct of the arbitration or of any other dispute resolution procedures required to be exhausted before resorting to arbitration.
(4)   For the purposes of this section the question whether an arbitration agreement is a domestic arbitration agreement shall be determined by reference to the facts at the time the legal proceedings are commenced.

[1.1200]
87 Effectiveness of agreement to exclude court's jurisdiction
(1)   In the case of a domestic arbitration agreement any agreement to exclude the jurisdiction of the court under—
  (a)   section 45 (determination of preliminary point of law), or
  (b)   section 69 (challenging the award: appeal on point of law),
is not effective unless entered into after the commencement of the arbitral proceedings in which the question arises or the award is made.
(2)   For this purpose the commencement of the arbitral proceedings has the same meaning as in Part I (see section 14).
(3)   For the purposes of this section the question whether an arbitration agreement is a domestic arbitration agreement shall be determined by reference to the facts at the time the agreement is entered into.

[1.1201]
88 Power to repeal or amend sections 85 to 87
(1)   The Secretary of State may by order repeal or amend the provisions of sections 85 to 87.
(2)   An order under this section may contain such supplementary, incidental and transitional provisions as appear to the Secretary of State to be appropriate.
(3)   An order under this section shall be made by statutory instrument and no such order shall be made unless a draft of it has been laid before and approved by a resolution of each House of Parliament.

Consumer arbitration agreements

[1.1202]
89 Application of unfair terms regulations to consumer arbitration agreements
(1)   The following sections extend the application of *the Unfair Terms in Consumer Contracts Regulations 1994* in relation to a term which constitutes an arbitration agreement.
    For this purpose "arbitration agreement" means an agreement to submit to arbitration present or future disputes or differences (whether or not contractual).
(2)   *In those sections "the Regulations" means those regulations and includes any regulations amending or replacing those regulations.*
(3)   Those sections apply whatever the law applicable to the arbitration agreement.

[1.1203]
90   Regulations apply where consumer is a legal person
The Regulations apply where the consumer is a legal person as they apply where the consumer is a natural person.

[1.1204]
91 Arbitration agreement unfair where modest amount sought

(1) A term which constitutes an arbitration agreement is unfair for the purposes of the *Regulations* so far as it relates to a claim for a pecuniary remedy which does not exceed the amount specified by order for the purposes of this section.

(2) Orders under this section may make different provision for different cases and for different purposes.

(3) The power to make orders under this section is exercisable—

    (a)   for England and Wales, by the Secretary of State with the concurrence of the Lord Chancellor,

    (b)   for Scotland, by the Secretary of State . . . , and

    (c)   for Northern Ireland, by the Department of Economic Development for Northern Ireland with the concurrence of the Lord Chancellor.

(4) Any such order for England and Wales or Scotland shall be made by statutory instrument which shall be subject to annulment in pursuance of a resolution of either House of Parliament.

(5) Any such order for Northern Ireland shall be a statutory rule for the purposes of the Statutory Rules (Northern Ireland) Order 1979 and shall be subject to negative resolution, within the meaning of section 41(6) of the Interpretation Act (Northern Ireland) 1954.

NOTES

Sub-s (1): for the word in italics there is substituted the word "Part" by the Consumer Rights Act 2015, s 75, Sch 4, paras 30, 33, as from 1 October 2015 (for transitional provisions see the Consumer Rights Act 2015 (Commencement No 3, Transitional Provisions, Savings and Consequential Amendments) Order 2015, SI 2015/1630, arts 6–8 at **[2.1220]** et seq).

Sub-s (3): words omitted from para (b) repealed by the Transfer of Functions (Lord Advocate and Secretary of State) Order 1999, SI 1999/678, art 6.

Orders: the Unfair Arbitration Agreements (Specified Amount) Order 1999, SI 1999/2167.

Small claims arbitration in the county court

[1.1205]
92 Exclusion of Part I in relation to small claims arbitration in the county court

Nothing in Part I of this Act applies to arbitration under section 64 of the County Courts Act 1984.

Appointment of judges as arbitrators

[1.1206]
93 Appointment of judges as arbitrators

(1) A judge of the Commercial Court or an official referee may, if in all the circumstances he thinks fit, accept appointment as a sole arbitrator or as umpire by or by virtue of an arbitration agreement.

(2) A judge of the Commercial Court shall not do so unless the Lord Chief Justice has informed him that, having regard to the state of business in the High Court and the Crown Court, he can be made available.

(3) An official referee shall not do so unless the Lord Chief Justice has informed him that, having regard to the state of official referees' business, he can be made available.

(4) The fees payable for the services of a judge of the Commercial Court or official referee as arbitrator or umpire shall be taken in the High Court.

(5) In this section—

    "arbitration agreement" has the same meaning as in Part I; and

    "official referee" means a person nominated under section 68(1)(a) of the [Senior Courts Act 1981] to deal with official referees' business.

(6) The provisions of Part I of this Act apply to arbitration before a person appointed under this section with the modifications specified in Schedule 2.

NOTES

Sub-s (5): words in square brackets in definition "official referee" substituted by the Constitutional Reform Act 2005, s 59(5), Sch 11, Pt 1, para 1(2).

Statutory arbitrations

[1.1207]
94 Application of Part I to statutory arbitrations

(1) The provisions of Part I apply to every arbitration under an enactment (a "statutory arbitration"), whether the enactment was passed or made before or after the commencement of this Act, subject to the adaptations and exclusions specified in sections 95 to 98.

(2) The provisions of Part I do not apply to a statutory arbitration if or to the extent that their application—

    (a)   is inconsistent with the provisions of the enactment concerned, with any rules or procedure authorised or recognised by it, or

    (b)   is excluded by any other enactment.

(3) In this section and the following provisions of this Part "enactment"—

    (a)   in England and Wales, includes an enactment contained in subordinate legislation within the meaning of the Interpretation Act 1978;

(b)   in Northern Ireland, means a statutory provision within the meaning of section 1(f) of the Interpretation Act (Northern Ireland) 1954.

[1.1208]
95   General adaptation of provisions in relation to statutory arbitrations
(1)   The provisions of Part I apply to a statutory arbitration—
  (a)   as if the arbitration were pursuant to an arbitration agreement and as if the enactment were that agreement, and
  (b)   as if the persons by and against whom a claim subject to arbitration in pursuance of the enactment may be or has been made were parties to that agreement.
(2)   Every statutory arbitration shall be taken to have its seat in England and Wales or, as the case may be, in Northern Ireland.

[1.1209]
96   Specific adaptations of provisions in relation to statutory arbitrations
(1)   The following provisions of Part I apply to a statutory arbitration with the following adaptations.
(2)   In section 30(1) (competence of tribunal to rule on its own jurisdiction), the reference in paragraph (a) to whether there is a valid arbitration agreement shall be construed as a reference to whether the enactment applies to the dispute or difference in question.
(3)   Section 35 (consolidation of proceedings and concurrent hearings) applies only so as to authorise the consolidation of proceedings, or concurrent hearings in proceedings, under the same enactment.
(4)   Section 46 (rules applicable to substance of dispute) applies with the omission of subsection (1)(b) (determination in accordance with considerations agreed by parties).

[1.1210]
97   Provisions excluded from applying to statutory arbitrations
The following provisions of Part I do not apply in relation to a statutory arbitration—
  (a)   section 8 (whether agreement discharged by death of a party);
  (b)   section 12 (power of court to extend agreed time limits);
  (c)   sections 9(5), 10(2) and 71(4) (restrictions on effect of provision that award condition precedent to right to bring legal proceedings).

[1.1211]
98   Power to make further provision by regulations
(1)   The Secretary of State may make provision by regulations for adapting or excluding any provision of Part I in relation to statutory arbitrations in general or statutory arbitrations of any particular description.
(2)   The power is exercisable whether the enactment concerned is passed or made before or after the commencement of this Act.
(3)   Regulations under this section shall be made by statutory instrument which shall be subject to annulment in pursuance of a resolution of either House of Parliament.

PART III
RECOGNITION AND ENFORCEMENT OF CERTAIN FOREIGN AWARDS

Enforcement of Geneva Convention awards

[1.1212]
99   Continuation of Part II of the Arbitration Act 1950
Part II of the Arbitration Act 1950 (enforcement of certain foreign awards) continues to apply in relation to foreign awards within the meaning of that Part which are not also New York Convention awards.

Recognition and enforcement of New York Convention awards

[1.1213]
100   New York Convention awards
(1)   In this Part a "New York Convention award" means an award made, in pursuance of an arbitration agreement, in the territory of a state (other than the United Kingdom) which is a party to the New York Convention.
(2)   For the purposes of subsection (1) and of the provisions of this Part relating to such awards—
  (a)   "arbitration agreement" means an arbitration agreement in writing, and
  (b)   an award shall be treated as made at the seat of the arbitration, regardless of where it was signed, despatched or delivered to any of the parties.
    In this subsection "agreement in writing" and "seat of the arbitration" have the same meaning as in Part I.
(3)   If Her Majesty by Order in Council declares that a state specified in the Order is a party to the New York Convention, or is a party in respect of any territory so specified, the Order shall, while in force, be conclusive evidence of that fact.

(4) In this section "the New York Convention" means the Convention on the Recognition and Enforcement of Foreign Arbitral Awards adopted by the United Nations Conference on International Commercial Arbitration on 10th June 1958.

NOTES

Orders: by virtue of the Interpretation Act 1978, s 17(2)(b), the following Orders in Council have effect as if made under this section: the Arbitration (Foreign Awards) Order 1984, SI 1984/1168; the Arbitration (Foreign Awards) Order 1989, SI 1989/1348; the Arbitration (Foreign Awards) Order 1993, SI 1993/1256.

[1.1214]
101 Recognition and enforcement of awards

(1) A New York Convention award shall be recognised as binding on the persons as between whom it was made, and may accordingly be relied on by those persons by way of defence, set-off or otherwise in any legal proceedings in England and Wales or Northern Ireland.

(2) A New York Convention award may, by leave of the court, be enforced in the same manner as a judgment or order of the court to the same effect.

As to the meaning of "the court" see section 105.

(3) Where leave is so given, judgment may be entered in terms of the award.

[1.1215]
102 Evidence to be produced by party seeking recognition or enforcement

(1) A party seeking the recognition or enforcement of a New York Convention award must produce—

    (a)   the duly authenticated original award or a duly certified copy of it, and

    (b)   the original arbitration agreement or a duly certified copy of it.

(2) If the award or agreement is in a foreign language, the party must also produce a translation of it certified by an official or sworn translator or by a diplomatic or consular agent.

[1.1216]
103 Refusal of recognition or enforcement

(1) Recognition or enforcement of a New York Convention award shall not be refused except in the following cases.

(2) Recognition or enforcement of the award may be refused if the person against whom it is invoked proves—

    (a)   that a party to the arbitration agreement was (under the law applicable to him) under some incapacity;

    (b)   that the arbitration agreement was not valid under the law to which the parties subjected it or, failing any indication thereon, under the law of the country where the award was made;

    (c)   that he was not given proper notice of the appointment of the arbitrator or of the arbitration proceedings or was otherwise unable to present his case;

    (d)   that the award deals with a difference not contemplated by or not falling within the terms of the submission to arbitration or contains decisions on matters beyond the scope of the submission to arbitration (but see subsection (4));

    (e)   that the composition of the arbitral tribunal or the arbitral procedure was not in accordance with the agreement of the parties or, failing such agreement, with the law of the country in which the arbitration took place;

    (f)   that the award has not yet become binding on the parties, or has been set aside or suspended by a competent authority of the country in which, or under the law of which, it was made.

(3) Recognition or enforcement of the award may also be refused if the award is in respect of a matter which is not capable of settlement by arbitration, or if it would be contrary to public policy to recognise or enforce the award.

(4) An award which contains decisions on matters not submitted to arbitration may be recognised or enforced to the extent that it contains decisions on matters submitted to arbitration which can be separated from those on matters not so submitted.

(5) Where an application for the setting aside or suspension of the award has been made to such a competent authority as is mentioned in subsection (2)(f), the court before which the award is sought to be relied upon may, if it considers it proper, adjourn the decision on the recognition or enforcement of the award.

It may also on the application of the party claiming recognition or enforcement of the award order the other party to give suitable security.

[1.1217]
104 Saving for other bases of recognition or enforcement

Nothing in the preceding provisions of this Part affects any right to rely upon or enforce a New York Convention award at common law or under section 66.

PART IV
GENERAL PROVISIONS

[1.1218]
105 Meaning of "the court": jurisdiction of High Court and county court
(1) In this Act "the court" [in relation to England and Wales means the High Court or the county court and in relation to Northern Ireland] means the High Court or a county court, subject to the following provisions.
(2) The Lord Chancellor may by order make provision—
[(za) allocating proceedings under this Act in England and Wales to the High Court or the county court;]
(a) allocating proceedings under this Act [in Northern Ireland] to the High Court or to county courts; or
(b) specifying proceedings under this Act which may be commenced or taken only in the High Court or in [the county court or (as the case may be)] a county court.
(3) The Lord Chancellor may by order make provision requiring proceedings of any specified description under this Act in relation to which a county court [in Northern Ireland] has jurisdiction to be commenced or taken in one or more specified county courts.
Any jurisdiction so exercisable by a specified county court is exercisable throughout . . . Northern Ireland.
[(3A) The Lord Chancellor must consult the Lord Chief Justice of England and Wales or the Lord Chief Justice of Northern Ireland (as the case may be) before making an order under this section.
(3B) The Lord Chief Justice of England and Wales may nominate a judicial office holder (as defined in section 109(4) of the Constitutional Reform Act 2005) to exercise his functions under this section.
(3C) The Lord Chief Justice of Northern Ireland may nominate any of the following to exercise his functions under this section—
(a) the holder of one of the offices listed in Schedule 1 to the Justice (Northern Ireland) Act 2002;
(b) a Lord Justice of Appeal (as defined in section 88 of that Act).]
(4) An order under this section—
(a) may differentiate between categories of proceedings by reference to such criteria as the Lord Chancellor sees fit to specify, and
(b) may make such incidental or transitional provision as the Lord Chancellor considers necessary or expedient.
(5) An order under this section for England and Wales shall be made by statutory instrument which shall be subject to annulment in pursuance of a resolution of either House of Parliament.
(6) An order under this section for Northern Ireland shall be a statutory rule for the purposes of the Statutory Rules (Northern Ireland) Order 1979 which shall be subject to [negative resolution (within the meaning of section 41(6) of the Interpretation Act (Northern Ireland) 1954)].

NOTES
Sub-ss (1), (2): words in square brackets inserted by the Crime and Courts Act 2013, s 17(5), Sch 9, Pt 3, para 60(2)(a)–(d).
Sub-s (3): words in square brackets inserted, and words omitted repealed, by the Crime and Courts Act 2013, s 17(5), Sch 9, Pt 3, para 60(2)(e), (f).
Sub-ss (3A)–(3C): inserted by the Constitutional Reform Act 2005, s 15(1), Sch 4, Pt 1, para 250.
Sub-s (6): words in square brackets substituted by the Northern Ireland Act 1998 (Devolution of Policing and Justice Functions) Order 2010, SI 2010/976, art 15(5), Sch 18, Pt 1, para 50, subject to transitional provisions in arts 28–31 thereof.
Orders: the High Court and County Courts (Allocation of Arbitration Proceedings) Order 1996, SI 1996/3215; the High Court and County Courts (Allocation of Arbitration Proceedings) (Amendment) Order 1999, SI 1999/1010.

[1.1219]
106 Crown application
(1) Part I of this Act applies to any arbitration agreement to which Her Majesty, either in right of the Crown or of the Duchy of Lancaster or otherwise, or the Duke of Cornwall, is a party.
(2) Where Her Majesty is party to an arbitration agreement otherwise than in right of the Crown, Her Majesty shall be represented for the purposes of any arbitral proceedings—
(a) where the agreement was entered into by Her Majesty in right of the Duchy of Lancaster, by the Chancellor of the Duchy or such person as he may appoint, and
(b) in any other case, by such person as Her Majesty may appoint in writing under the Royal Sign Manual.
(3) Where the Duke of Cornwall is party to an arbitration agreement, he shall be represented for the purposes of any arbitral proceedings by such person as he may appoint.
(4) References in Part I to a party or the parties to the arbitration agreement or to arbitral proceedings shall be construed, where subsection (2) or (3) applies, as references to the person representing Her Majesty or the Duke of Cornwall.

[1.1220]
107   Consequential amendments and repeals
(1)   The enactments specified in Schedule 3 are amended in accordance with that Schedule, the amendments being consequential on the provisions of this Act.
(2)   The enactments specified in Schedule 4 are repealed to the extent specified.

[1.1221]
108   Extent
(1)   The provisions of this Act extend to England and Wales and, except as mentioned below, to Northern Ireland.
(2)   The following provisions of Part II do not extend to Northern Ireland—
     section 92 (exclusion of Part I in relation to small claims arbitration in the county court), and
     section 93 and Schedule 2 (appointment of judges as arbitrators).
(3)   Sections 89, 90 and 91 (consumer arbitration agreements) extend to Scotland and the provisions of Schedules 3 and 4 (consequential amendments and repeals) extend to Scotland so far as they relate to enactments which so extend, subject as follows.
(4)   The repeal of the Arbitration Act 1975 extends only to England and Wales and Northern Ireland.

[1.1222]
109   Commencement
(1)   The provisions of this Act come into force on such day as the Secretary of State may appoint by order made by statutory instrument, and different days may be appointed for different purposes.
(2)   An order under subsection (1) may contain such transitional provisions as appear to the Secretary of State to be appropriate.

NOTES
Orders: the Arbitration Act 1996 (Commencement No 1) Order 1996, SI 1996/3146.

[1.1223]
110   Short title
This Act may be cited as the Arbitration Act 1996.

SCHEDULES

SCHEDULE 1
MANDATORY PROVISIONS OF PART I
Section 4(1)

[1.1224]
     sections 9 to 11 (stay of legal proceedings);
     section 12 (power of court to extend agreed time limits);
     section 13 (application of Limitation Acts);
     section 24 (power of court to remove arbitrator);
     section 26(1) (effect of death of arbitrator);
     section 28 (liability of parties for fees and expenses of arbitrators);
     section 29 (immunity of arbitrator);
     section 31 (objection to substantive jurisdiction of tribunal);
     section 32 (determination of preliminary point of jurisdiction);
     section 33 (general duty of tribunal);
     section 37(2) (items to be treated as expenses of arbitrators);
     section 40 (general duty of parties);
     section 43 (securing the attendance of witnesses);
     section 56 (power to withhold award in case of non-payment);
     section 60 (effectiveness of agreement for payment of costs in any event);
     section 66 (enforcement of award);
     sections 67 and 68 (challenging the award: substantive jurisdiction and serious irregularity), and sections 70 and 71 (supplementary provisions; effect of order of court) so far as relating to those sections;
     section 72 (saving for rights of person who takes no part in proceedings);
     section 73 (loss of right to object);
     section 74 (immunity of arbitral institutions, &c);
     section 75 (charge to secure payment of solicitors' costs).

SCHEDULE 2
MODIFICATIONS OF PART I IN RELATION TO JUDGE-ARBITRATORS
Section 93(6)

Introductory

[1.1225]
1. In this Schedule "judge-arbitrator" means a judge of the Commercial Court or official referee appointed as arbitrator or umpire under section 93.

General

2. (1) Subject to the following provisions of this Schedule, references in Part I to the court shall be construed in relation to a judge-arbitrator, or in relation to the appointment of a judge-arbitrator, as references to the Court of Appeal.

(2) The references in sections 32(6), 45(6) and 69(8) to the Court of Appeal shall in such a case be construed as references to the [Supreme Court].

Arbitrator's fees

3. (1) The power of the court in section 28(2) to order consideration and adjustment of the liability of a party for the fees of an arbitrator may be exercised by a judge-arbitrator.

(2) Any such exercise of the power is subject to the powers of the Court of Appeal under sections 24(4) and 25(3)(b) (directions as to entitlement to fees or expenses in case of removal or resignation).

Exercise of court powers in support of arbitration

4. (1) Where the arbitral tribunal consists of or includes a judge-arbitrator the powers of the court under sections 42 to 44 (enforcement of peremptory orders, summoning witnesses, and other court powers) are exercisable by the High Court and also by the judge-arbitrator himself.

(2) Anything done by a judge-arbitrator in the exercise of those powers shall be regarded as done by him in his capacity as judge of the High Court and have effect as if done by that court.
   Nothing in this sub-paragraph prejudices any power vested in him as arbitrator or umpire.

Extension of time for making award

5. (1) The power conferred by section 50 (extension of time for making award) is exercisable by the judge-arbitrator himself.

(2) Any appeal from a decision of a judge-arbitrator under that section lies to the Court of Appeal with the leave of that court.

Withholding award in case of non-payment

6. (1) The provisions of paragraph 7 apply in place of the provisions of section 56 (power to withhold award in the case of non-payment) in relation to the withholding of an award for non-payment of the fees and expenses of a judge-arbitrator.

(2) This does not affect the application of section 56 in relation to the delivery of such an award by an arbitral or other institution or person vested by the parties with powers in relation to the delivery of the award.

7. (1) A judge-arbitrator may refuse to deliver an award except upon payment of the fees and expenses mentioned in section 56(1).

(2) The judge-arbitrator may, on an application by a party to the arbitral proceedings, order that if he pays into the High Court the fees and expenses demanded, or such lesser amount as the judge-arbitrator may specify—
   (a) the award shall be delivered,
   (b) the amount of the fees and expenses properly payable shall be determined by such means and upon such terms as he may direct, and
   (c) out of the money paid into court there shall be paid out such fees and expenses as may be found to be properly payable and the balance of the money (if any) shall be paid out to the applicant.

(3) For this purpose the amount of fees and expenses properly payable is the amount the applicant is liable to pay under section 28 or any agreement relating to the payment of the arbitrator.

(4) No application to the judge-arbitrator under this paragraph may be made where there is any available arbitral process for appeal or review of the amount of the fees or expenses demanded.

(5) Any appeal from a decision of a judge-arbitrator under this paragraph lies to the Court of Appeal with the leave of that court.

(6) Where a party to arbitral proceedings appeals under sub-paragraph (5), an arbitrator is entitled to appear and be heard.

Correction of award or additional award

8. Subsections (4) to (6) of section 57 (correction of award or additional award: time limit for application or exercise of power) do not apply to a judge-arbitrator.

Costs

9. Where the arbitral tribunal consists of or includes a judge-arbitrator the powers of the court under section 63(4) (determination of recoverable costs) shall be exercised by the High Court.

10. (1)   The power of the court under section 64 to determine an arbitrator's reasonable fees and expenses may be exercised by a judge-arbitrator.

(2)   Any such exercise of the power is subject to the powers of the Court of Appeal under sections 24(4) and 25(3)(b) (directions as to entitlement to fees or expenses in case of removal or resignation).

Enforcement of award

11. The leave of the court required by section 66 (enforcement of award) may in the case of an award of a judge-arbitrator be given by the judge-arbitrator himself.

Solicitors' costs

12. The powers of the court to make declarations and orders under the provisions applied by section 75 (power to charge property recovered in arbitral proceedings with the payment of solicitors' costs) may be exercised by the judge-arbitrator.

Powers of court in relation to service of documents

13. (1)   The power of the court under section 77(2) (powers of court in relation to service of documents) is exercisable by the judge-arbitrator.

(2)   Any appeal from a decision of a judge-arbitrator under that section lies to the Court of Appeal with the leave of that court.

Powers of court to extend time limits relating to arbitral proceedings

14. (1)   The power conferred by section 79 (power of court to extend time limits relating to arbitral proceedings) is exercisable by the judge-arbitrator himself.

(2)   Any appeal from a decision of a judge-arbitrator under that section lies to the Court of Appeal with the leave of that court.

NOTES

Para 2: words in square brackets in sub-para (2) substituted by the Constitutional Reform Act 2005, s 40(4), Sch 9, Pt 1, para 60.

SCHEDULES 3 AND 4

(Sch 3 (Consequential Amendments) and Sch 4 (Repeals) outside the scope of this work.)

LATE PAYMENT OF COMMERCIAL DEBTS (INTEREST) ACT 1998

(1998 c 20)

ARRANGEMENT OF SECTIONS

PART III
GENERAL AND SUPPLEMENTARY

An Act to make provision with respect to interest on the late payment of certain debts arising under commercial contracts for the supply of goods or services; and for connected purposes

[11 June 1998]

PART I
STATUTORY INTEREST ON QUALIFYING DEBTS

[1.1226]
1   Statutory interest

(1)   It is an implied term in a contract to which this Act applies that any qualifying debt created by the contract carries simple interest subject to and in accordance with this Part.

(2)   Interest carried under that implied term (in this Act referred to as "statutory interest") shall be treated, for the purposes of any rule of law or enactment (other than this Act) relating to interest on debts, in the same way as interest carried under an express contract term.

(3)   This Part has effect subject to Part II (which in certain circumstances permits contract terms to oust or vary the right to statutory interest that would otherwise be conferred by virtue of the term implied by subsection (1)).

[1.1227]
2   Contracts to which Act applies

(1)   This Act applies to a contract for the supply of goods or services where the purchaser and the supplier are each acting in the course of a business, other than an excepted contract.

(2)   In this Act "contract for the supply of goods or services" means—

    (a)   a contract of sale of goods; or

    (b)   a contract (other than a contract of sale of goods) by which a person does any, or any combination, of the things mentioned in subsection (3) for a consideration that is (or includes) a money consideration.

(3)   Those things are—

    (a)   transferring or agreeing to transfer to another the property in goods;

    (b)   bailing or agreeing to bail goods to another by way of hire or, in Scotland, hiring or agreeing to hire goods to another; and

    (c)   agreeing to carry out a service.

(4)   For the avoidance of doubt a contract of service or apprenticeship is not a contract for the supply of goods or services.

(5)   The following are excepted contracts—

    (a)   a consumer credit agreement;

    (b)   a contract intended to operate by way of mortgage, pledge, charge or other security; and

    (c)   . . .

(6)   . . .

(7)   In this section—

    "business" includes a profession and the activities of any government department or local or public authority;

    "consumer credit agreement" has the same meaning as in the Consumer Credit Act 1974;

    "contract of sale of goods" and "goods" have the same meaning as in the Sale of Goods Act 1979;

    ["government department" means any part of the Scottish Administration;]

    "property in goods" means the general property in them and not merely a special property.

NOTES

    Sub-s (5): para (c) repealed by the Late Payment of Commercial Debts Regulations 2002, SI 2002/1674, reg 2(1), (2), in relation to contracts made on or after 7 August 2002.

    Sub-s (6): repealed by SI 2002/1674, reg 2(1), (2), in relation to contracts made on or after 7 August 2002.

    Sub-s (7): definition "government department" inserted by the Scotland Act 1998 (Consequential Modifications) (No 2) Order 1999, SI 1999/1820, art 4, Sch 2, Pt I, para 132.

    Note: the repeals made by SI 2002/1674 as noted above apply to England, Wales and Northern Ireland. The same repeals are made in relation to Scotland by the Late Payment of Commercial Debts (Scotland) Regulations 2002, SSI 2002/335.

2A   (*Inserted in relation to Scotland only by the Late Payment of Commercial Debts (Scotland) Regulations 2002, SSI 2002/335.*)

[1.1228]

3 Qualifying debts

(1) A debt created by virtue of an obligation under a contract to which this Act applies to pay the whole or any part of the contract price is a "qualifying debt" for the purposes of this Act, unless (when created) the whole of the debt is prevented from carrying statutory interest by this section.

(2) A debt does not carry statutory interest if or to the extent that it consists of a sum to which a right to interest or to charge interest applies by virtue of any enactment (other than section 1 of this Act).

This subsection does not prevent a sum from carrying statutory interest by reason of the fact that a court, arbitrator or arbiter would, apart from this Act, have power to award interest on it.

(3) A debt does not carry (and shall be treated as never having carried) statutory interest if or to the extent that a right to demand interest on it, which exists by virtue of any rule of law, is exercised.

(4), (5) . . .

NOTES

Sub-ss (4), (5): repealed by the Late Payment of Commercial Debts Regulations 2002, SI 2002/1674, reg 2(1), (3), in relation to contracts made on or after 7 August 2002.

Note: the repeals made by SI 2002/1674 as noted above apply to England, Wales and Northern Ireland. The same repeals are made in relation to Scotland by the Late Payment of Commercial Debts (Scotland) Regulations 2002, SSI 2002/335.

[1.1229]

4 Period for which statutory interest runs

(1) Statutory interest runs in relation to a qualifying debt in accordance with this section (unless section 5 applies).

(2) Statutory interest starts to run on the day after the relevant day for the debt, at the rate prevailing under section 6 at the end of the relevant day.

[(2A) The relevant day for a debt is—
   (a) where there is an agreed payment day, that day, unless a different day is given by subsection (2D), (2E) or (2G);
   (b) where there is not an agreed payment day, the last day of the relevant 30-day period.

(2B) An "agreed payment day" is a date agreed between the supplier and the purchaser for payment of the debt (that is, the day on which the debt is to be created by the contract).

(2C) A date agreed for payment of a debt may be a fixed date or may depend on the happening of an event or the failure of an event to happen.

(2D) Where—
   (a) the purchaser is a public authority, and
   (b) the last day of the relevant 30-day period falls earlier than the agreed payment day,
the relevant day is the last day of the relevant 30-day period, unless subsection (2G) applies.

(2E) Where—
   (a) the purchaser is not a public authority, and
   (b) the last day of the relevant 60-day period falls earlier than the agreed payment day,
the relevant day is the last day of the relevant 60-day period, unless subsection (2G) applies.

(2F) But subsection (2E) does not apply (and so the relevant day is the agreed payment day, unless subsection (2G) applies) if the agreed payment day is not grossly unfair to the supplier (see subsection (7A)).

(2G) Where the debt relates to an obligation to make an advance payment, the relevant day is the day on which the debt is treated by section 11 as having been created (instead of the agreed payment day or the day given by subsection (2D) or (2E)).

(2H) "The relevant 30-day period" is the period of 30 days beginning with the later or latest of—
   (a) the day on which the obligation of the supplier to which the debt relates is performed;
   (b) the day on which the purchaser has notice of the amount of the debt or (where that amount is unascertained) the sum which the supplier claims is the amount of the debt;
   (c) where subsection (5A) applies, the day determined under subsection (5B).

(2I) "The relevant 60-day period" is the period of 60 days beginning with the later or latest of—
   (a) the day on which the obligation of the supplier to which the debt relates is performed;
   (b) the day on which the purchaser has notice of the amount of the debt or (where that amount is unascertained) the sum which the supplier claims is the amount of the debt;
   (c) where subsection (5A) applies, the day determined under subsection (5B).]

(3), (3A)–(3C), (4), (5) . . .

[(5A) This subsection applies where—
   (a) there is a procedure of acceptance or verification (whether provided for by an enactment or by the contract), under which the conforming of goods or services with the contract is to be ascertained, and
   (b) the purchaser has notice of the amount of the debt on or before the day on which the procedure is completed.

(5B) For the purposes of [subsections (2H)(c) and (2I)(c)], the day in question is the day . . . after the day on which the procedure is completed.

(5C)   Where, in a case where subsection (5A) applies, the procedure in question is completed after the end of the period of 30 days beginning with the day on which the obligation of the supplier to which the debt relates is performed, the procedure is to be treated for the purposes of subsection (5B) as being completed immediately after the end of that period.

(5D)   Subsection (5C) does not apply if—

(a)   the supplier and the purchaser expressly agree in the contract a period for completing the procedure in question that is longer than the period mentioned in that subsection, and

(b)   that longer period is not grossly unfair to the supplier (see subsection (7A)).]

(6)   Where the debt is created by virtue of an obligation to pay a sum due in respect of a period of hire of goods, [subsections (2H)(a) and (2I)(a) have effect as if they] referred to the last day of that period.

(7)   Statutory interest ceases to run when the interest would cease to run if it were carried under an express contract term.

[(7A)   In determining for the purposes of subsection [(2F)] or (5D) whether something is grossly unfair, all circumstances of the case shall be considered; and for that purpose, the circumstances of the case include in particular—

(a)   anything that is a gross deviation from good commercial practice and contrary to good faith and fair dealing,

(b)   the nature of the goods or services in question, and

(c)   whether the purchaser has any objective reason to deviate from the result which is provided for by subsection [(2E)] or (5C).]

[(8)   In this section—

"advance payment" has the same meaning as in section 11;

"enactment" includes an enactment contained in subordinate legislation (within the meaning of the Interpretation Act 1978);

"public authority" means a contracting authority (within the meaning of *regulation 3 of the Public Contracts Regulations 2006*).]

NOTES

Sub-ss (2A)–(2I): inserted, in relation to England, Wales and Northern Ireland, by the Late Payment of Commercial Debts (Amendment) Regulations 2015, SI 2015/1336, reg 2(1), (2) and in relation to Scotland by the Late Payment of Commercial Debts (Scotland) Regulations 2015, SSI 2015/226, reg 2(1), (2).

Sub-ss (3), (3A)–(3C), (4), (5): repealed, in relation to England, Wales and Northern Ireland, by SI 2015/1336, reg 2(1), (3) and in relation to Scotland by SSI 2015/226, reg 2(1), (3) (sub-ss (3A)–(3C) originally inserted, in relation to England, Wales and Northern Ireland, by the Late Payment of Commercial Debts Regulations 2013, SI 2013/395, reg 2(1), (2) and in relation to Scotland by the Late Payment of Commercial Debts (Scotland) Regulations 2013, SSI 2013/77, reg 2(1), (2)).

Sub-ss (5A)–(5D): inserted, in relation to England, Wales and Northern Ireland by SI 2013/395, reg 2(1), (4) and in relation to Scotland by SSI 2013/77, reg 2(1), (4).

Sub-s (5B): words in square brackets substituted, in relation to England, Wales and Northern Ireland, by SI 2015/1336, reg 2(1), (4) and in relation to Scotland by SSI 2015/226, reg 2(1), (4); words omitted repealed, in relation to England, Wales and Northern Ireland by the Late Payment of Commercial Debts (No 2) Regulations 2013, SI 2013/908, reg 2 and in relation to Scotland by the Late Payment of Commercial Debts (Scotland) (No 2) Regulations 2013, SSI 2013/131, reg 2.

Sub-s (6): words in square brackets substituted, in relation to England, Wales and Northern Ireland, by SI 2015/1336, reg 2(1), (5) and in relation to Scotland by SSI 2015/226, reg 2(1), (5).

Sub-s (7A): inserted, in relation to England, Wales and Northern Ireland, by the Late Payment of Commercial Debts Regulations 2013, SI 2013/395, reg 2(1), (5) and in relation to Scotland by the Late Payment of Commercial Debts (Scotland) Regulations 2013, SSI 2013/77, reg 2(1), (5); figures in square brackets substituted, in relation to England, Wales and Northern Ireland, by SI 2015/1336, reg 2(1), (6) and in relation to Scotland by SSI 2015/226, reg 2(1), (6).

Sub-s (8): substituted, in relation to England, Wales and Northern Ireland by SI 2013/395, reg 2(1), (6) and in relation to Scotland by SSI 2013/77, reg 2(1), (6); in definition "public authority" for the words in italics there are substituted the words "regulation 2(1) of the Public Contracts Regulations 2015", in relation to England and Wales, by the Public Contracts Regulations 2015, SI 2015/102, s 116(b), Sch 6, Pt 1, para 1.

[1.1230]

5   Remission of statutory interest

(1)   This section applies where, by reason of any conduct of the supplier, the interests of justice require that statutory interest should be remitted in whole or part in respect of a period for which it would otherwise run in relation to a qualifying debt.

(2)   If the interests of justice require that the supplier should receive no statutory interest for a period, statutory interest shall not run for that period.

(3)   If the interests of justice require that the supplier should receive statutory interest at a reduced rate for a period, statutory interest shall run at such rate as meets the justice of the case for that period.

(4)   Remission of statutory interest under this section may be required—

(a)   by reason of conduct at any time (whether before or after the time at which the debt is created); and

(b)   for the whole period for which statutory interest would otherwise run or for one or more parts of that period.

(5)   In this section "conduct" includes any act or omission.

[1.1231]
[5A   Compensation arising out of late payment
(1)   Once statutory interest begins to run in relation to a qualifying debt, the supplier shall be entitled to a fixed sum (in addition to the statutory interest on the debt).
(2)   That sum shall be—
    (a)   for a debt less than £1,000, the sum of £40;
    (b)   for a debt of £1,000 or more, but less than £10,000, the sum of £70;
    (c)   for a debt of £10,000 or more, the sum of £100.
[(2A)   If the reasonable costs of the supplier in recovering the debt are not met by the fixed sum, the supplier shall also be entitled to a sum equivalent to the difference between the fixed sum and those costs.]]
(3)   The obligation to pay [a sum] under this section in respect of a qualifying debt shall be treated as part of the term implied by section 1(1) in the contract creating the debt.
[(4)   Section 3(2)(b) of the Unfair Contract Terms Act 1977 (no reliance to be placed on certain contract terms) shall apply in cases where a contract term is not contained in written standard terms of the purchaser as well as in cases where the term is contained in such standard terms.
(5)   In this section "contract term" means a term of the contract relating to a sum due to the supplier under this section.]]

NOTES

Inserted by the Late Payment of Commercial Debts Regulations 2002, SI 2002/1674, reg 2(1), (4), in relation to contracts made on or after 7 August 2002.

Sub-s (2A), (4), (5): inserted and added in relation to England, Wales and Northern Ireland by the Late Payment of Commercial Debts Regulations 2013, SI 2013/395, reg 3(1), (2), (4) and in relation to Scotland by the Late Payment of Commercial Debts (Scotland) Regulations 2013, SSI 2013/77, reg 3(1), (2), (4).

Sub-s (3): words in square brackets substituted in relation to England, Wales and Northern Ireland by SI 2013/395, reg 3(1), (3) and in relation to Scotland by SSI 2013/77, reg 3(1), (3).

Note: this section as inserted by SI 2002/1674 as noted above applies to England, Wales and Northern Ireland. The same insertion is made in relation to Scotland by the Late Payment of Commercial Debts (Scotland) Regulations 2002, SSI 2002/335.

[1.1232]
6   Rate of statutory interest
(1)   The Secretary of State shall by order made with the consent of the Treasury set the rate of statutory interest by prescribing—
    (a)   a formula for calculating the rate of statutory interest; or
    (b)   the rate of statutory interest.
(2)   Before making such an order the Secretary of State shall, among other things, consider the extent to which it may be desirable to set the rate so as to—
    (a)   protect suppliers whose financial position makes them particularly vulnerable if their qualifying debts are paid late; and
    (b)   deter generally the late payment of qualifying debts.

NOTES

Orders: the Late Payment of Commercial Debts (Rate of Interest) (No 3) Order 2002, SI 2002/1675, which provides that the rate of interest for the purposes of this Act shall be 8 per cent per annum over the official dealing rate (ie, the rate announced from time to time by the Monetary Policy Committee of the Bank of England and for the time being in force as the official dealing rate, being the rate at which the Bank is willing to enter into transactions for providing short term liquidity in the money markets) in force on the 30 June (in respect of interest which starts to run between 1 July and 31 December) or the 31 December (in respect of interest which starts to run between 1 January and 30 June) immediately before the day on which statutory interest starts to run.

PART II
CONTRACT TERMS RELATING TO LATE PAYMENT OF QUALIFYING DEBTS

[1.1233]
7   Purpose of Part II
(1)   This Part deals with the extent to which the parties to a contract to which this Act applies may by reference to contract terms oust or vary the right to statutory interest that would otherwise apply when a qualifying debt created by the contract (in this Part referred to as "the debt") is not paid.
(2)   This Part applies to contract terms agreed before the debt is created; after that time the parties are free to agree terms dealing with the debt.
(3)   This Part has effect without prejudice to any other ground which may affect the validity of a contract term.

[1.1234]
8   Circumstances where statutory interest may be ousted or varied
(1)   Any contract terms are void to the extent that they purport to exclude the right to statutory interest in relation to the debt, unless there is a substantial contractual remedy for late payment of the debt.
(2)   Where the parties agree a contractual remedy for late payment of the debt that is a substantial remedy, statutory interest is not carried by the debt (unless they agree otherwise).

(3) The parties may not agree to vary the right to statutory interest in relation to the debt unless either the right to statutory interest as varied or the overall remedy for late payment of the debt is a substantial remedy.

(4) Any contract terms are void to the extent that they purport to—

    (a) confer a contractual right to interest that is not a substantial remedy for late payment of the debt, or

    (b) vary the right to statutory interest so as to provide for a right to statutory interest that is not a substantial remedy for late payment of the debt,

unless the overall remedy for late payment of the debt is a substantial remedy.

(5) Subject to this section, the parties are free to agree contract terms which deal with the consequences of late payment of the debt.

[1.1235]

9 Meaning of "substantial remedy"

(1) A remedy for the late payment of the debt shall be regarded as a substantial remedy unless—

    (a) the remedy is insufficient either for the purpose of compensating the supplier for late payment or for deterring late payment; and

    (b) it would not be fair or reasonable to allow the remedy to be relied on to oust or (as the case may be) to vary the right to statutory interest that would otherwise apply in relation to the debt.

(2) In determining whether a remedy is not a substantial remedy, regard shall be had to all the relevant circumstances at the time the terms in question are agreed.

(3) In determining whether subsection (1)(b) applies, regard shall be had (without prejudice to the generality of subsection (2)) to the following matters—

    (a) the benefits of commercial certainty;

    (b) the strength of the bargaining positions of the parties relative to each other;

    (c) whether the term was imposed by one party to the detriment of the other (whether by the use of standard terms or otherwise); and

    (d) whether the supplier received an inducement to agree to the term.

[1.1236]

10 Interpretation of Part II

(1) In this Part—

    "contract term" means a term of the contract creating the debt or any other contract term binding the parties (or either of them);

    "contractual remedy" means a contractual right to interest or any contractual remedy other than interest;

    "contractual right to interest" includes a reference to a contractual right to charge interest;

    "overall remedy", in relation to the late payment of the debt, means any combination of a contractual right to interest, a varied right to statutory interest or a contractual remedy other than interest;

    "substantial remedy" shall be construed in accordance with section 9.

(2) In this Part a reference (however worded) to contract terms which vary the right to statutory interest is a reference to terms altering in any way the effect of Part I in relation to the debt (for example by postponing the time at which interest starts to run or by imposing conditions on the right to interest).

(3) In this Part a reference to late payment of the debt is a reference to late payment of the sum due when the debt is created (excluding any part of that sum which is prevented from carrying statutory interest by section 3).

PART III
GENERAL AND SUPPLEMENTARY

[1.1237]

11 Treatment of advance payments of the contract price

(1) A qualifying debt created by virtue of an obligation to make an advance payment shall be treated for the purposes of this Act as if it was created on the day mentioned in subsection (3), (4) or (5) (as the case may be).

(2) In this section "advance payment" means a payment falling due before the obligation of the supplier to which the whole contract price relates ("the supplier's obligation") is performed, other than a payment of a part of the contract price that is due in respect of any part performance of that obligation and payable on or after the day on which that part performance is completed.

(3) Where the advance payment is the whole contract price, the debt shall be treated as created on the day on which the supplier's obligation is performed.

(4) Where the advance payment is a part of the contract price, but the sum is not due in respect of any part performance of the supplier's obligation, the debt shall be treated as created on the day on which the supplier's obligation is performed.

(5)   Where the advance payment is a part of the contract price due in respect of any part performance of the supplier's obligation, but is payable before that part performance is completed, the debt shall be treated as created on the day on which the relevant part performance is completed.

(6)   Where the debt is created by virtue of an obligation to pay a sum due in respect of a period of hire of goods, this section has effect as if—

   (a)   references to the day on which the supplier's obligation is performed were references to the last day of that period; and

   (b)   references to part performance of that obligation were references to part of that period.

(7)   For the purposes of this section an obligation to pay the whole outstanding balance of the contract price shall be regarded as an obligation to pay the whole contract price and not as an obligation to pay a part of the contract price.

[1.1238]
12   Conflict of laws

(1)   This Act does not have effect in relation to a contract governed by the law of a part of the United Kingdom by choice of the parties if—

   (a)   there is no significant connection between the contract and that part of the United Kingdom; and

   (b)   but for that choice, the applicable law would be a foreign law.

(2)   This Act has effect in relation to a contract governed by a foreign law by choice of the parties if—

   (a)   but for that choice, the applicable law would be the law of a part of the United Kingdom; and

   (b)   there is no significant connection between the contract and any country other than that part of the United Kingdom.

(3)   In this section—

   "contract" means a contract falling within section 2(1); and

   "foreign law" means the law of a country outside the United Kingdom.

[1.1239]
13   Assignments, etc

(1)   The operation of this Act in relation to a qualifying debt is not affected by—

   (a)   any change in the identity of the parties to the contract creating the debt; or

   (b)   the passing of the right to be paid the debt, or the duty to pay it (in whole or in part) to a person other than the person who is the original creditor or the original debtor when the debt is created.

(2)   Any reference in this Act to the supplier or the purchaser is a reference to the person who is for the time being the supplier or the purchaser or, in relation to a time after the debt in question has been created, the person who is for the time being the creditor or the debtor, as the case may be.

(3)   Where the right to be paid part of a debt passes to a person other than the person who is the original creditor when the debt is created, any reference in this Act to a debt shall be construed as (or, if the context so requires, as including) a reference to part of a debt.

(4)   A reference in this section to the identity of the parties to a contract changing, or to a right or duty passing, is a reference to it changing or passing by assignment or assignation, by operation of law or otherwise.

[1.1240]
14   Contract terms relating to the date for payment of the contract price

(1)   This section applies to any contract term which purports to have the effect of postponing the time at which a qualifying debt would otherwise be created by a contract to which this Act applies.

(2)   Sections 3(2)(b) and 17(1)(b) of the Unfair Contract Terms Act 1977 (no reliance to be placed on certain contract terms) shall apply in cases where such a contract term is not contained in written standard terms of the purchaser as well as in cases where the term is contained in such standard terms.

(3)   In this section "contract term" has the same meaning as in section 10(1).

[1.1241]
15   Orders and regulations

(1)   Any power to make an order or regulations under this Act is exercisable by statutory instrument.

(2)   Any statutory instrument containing an order or regulations under this Act, other than an order under section 17(2), shall be subject to annulment in pursuance of a resolution of either House of Parliament.

[1.1242]
16   Interpretation

(1)   In this Act—

   "contract for the supply of goods or services" has the meaning given in section 2(2);

   "contract price" means the price in a contract of sale of goods or the money consideration referred to in section 2(2)(b) in any other contract for the supply of goods or services;

"purchaser" means (subject to section 13(2)) the buyer in a contract of sale or the person who contracts with the supplier in any other contract for the supply of goods or services;

"qualifying debt" means a debt falling within section 3(1);

"statutory interest" means interest carried by virtue of the term implied by section 1(1); and

"supplier" means (subject to section 13(2)) the seller in a contract of sale of goods or the person who does one or more of the things mentioned in section 2(3) in any other contract for the supply of goods or services.

(2)   In this Act any reference (however worded) to an agreement or to contract terms includes a reference to both express and implied terms (including terms established by a course of dealing or by such usage as binds the parties).

[1.1243]

17   Short title, commencement and extent

(1)   This Act may be cited as the Late Payment of Commercial Debts (Interest) Act 1998.

(2)   This Act (apart from this section) shall come into force on such day as the Secretary of State may by order appoint; and different days may be appointed for different descriptions of contract or for other different purposes.

An order under this subsection may specify a description of contract by reference to any feature of the contract (including the parties).

(3)   The Secretary of State may by regulations make such transitional, supplemental or incidental provision (including provision modifying any provision of this Act) as the Secretary of State may consider necessary or expedient in connection with the operation of this Act while it is not fully in force.

(4)   This Act does not affect contracts of any description made before this Act comes into force for contracts of that description.

(5)   This Act extends to Northern Ireland.

NOTES

Orders: the Late Payment of Commercial Debts (Interest) Act 1998 (Commencement No 1) Order 1998, SI 1998/2479; the Late Payment of Commercial Debts (Interest) Act 1998 (Commencement No 2) Order 1999, SI 1999/1816; the Late Payment of Commercial Debts (Interest) Act 1998 (Commencement No 3) Order 2000, SI 2000/2225; the Late Payment of Commercial Debts (Interest) Act 1998 (Commencement No 4) Order 2000, SI 2000/2740; the Late Payment of Commercial Debts (Interest) Act 1998 (Commencement No 5) Order 2002, SI 2002/1673.

DATA PROTECTION ACT 1998

(1998 c 29)

ARRANGEMENT OF SECTIONS

PART I
PRELIMINARY

PART II
RIGHTS OF DATA SUBJECTS AND OTHERS

PART VI
MISCELLANEOUS AND GENERAL

General

SCHEDULES

An Act to make new provision for the regulation of the processing of information relating to individuals, including the obtaining, holding, use or disclosure of such information

[16 July 1998]

PART I
PRELIMINARY

[1.1244]
1 Basic interpretative provisions
(1) In this Act, unless the context otherwise requires—
"data" means information which—
- (a) is being processed by means of equipment operating automatically in response to instructions given for that purpose,
- (b) is recorded with the intention that it should be processed by means of such equipment,
- (c) is recorded as part of a relevant filing system or with the intention that it should form part of a relevant filing system, . . .
- (d) does not fall within paragraph (a), (b) or (c) but forms part of an accessible record as defined by section 68, [or
- (e) is recorded information held by a public authority and does not fall within any of paragraphs (a) to (d);]

"data controller" means, subject to subsection (4), a person who (either alone or jointly or in common with other persons) determines the purposes for which and the manner in which any personal data are, or are to be, processed;
"data processor", in relation to personal data, means any person (other than an employee of the data controller) who processes the data on behalf of the data controller;
"data subject" means an individual who is the subject of personal data;
"personal data" means data which relate to a living individual who can be identified—
- (a) from those data, or
- (b) from those data and other information which is in the possession of, or is likely to come into the possession of, the data controller,

and includes any expression of opinion about the individual and any indication of the intentions of the data controller or any other person in respect of the individual;
"processing", in relation to information or data, means obtaining, recording or holding the information or data or carrying out any operation or set of operations on the information or data, including—
- (a) organisation, adaptation or alteration of the information or data,
- (b) retrieval, consultation or use of the information or data,
- (c) disclosure of the information or data by transmission, dissemination or otherwise making available, or
- (d) alignment, combination, blocking, erasure or destruction of the information or data;

["public authority" means a public authority as defined by the Freedom of Information Act 2000 or a Scottish public authority as defined by the Freedom of Information (Scotland) Act 2002;]
"relevant filing system" means any set of information relating to individuals to the extent that, although the information is not processed by means of equipment operating automatically in response to instructions given for that purpose, the set is structured, either by reference to individuals or by reference to criteria relating to individuals, in such a way that specific information relating to a particular individual is readily accessible.
(2) In this Act, unless the context otherwise requires—
- (a) "obtaining" or "recording", in relation to personal data, includes obtaining or recording the information to be contained in the data, and
- (b) "using" or "disclosing", in relation to personal data, includes using or disclosing the information contained in the data.

(3) In determining for the purposes of this Act whether any information is recorded with the intention—
- (a) that it should be processed by means of equipment operating automatically in response to instructions given for that purpose, or

(b)   that it should form part of a relevant filing system,

it is immaterial that it is intended to be so processed or to form part of such a system only after being transferred to a country or territory outside the European Economic Area.

(4)   Where personal data are processed only for purposes for which they are required by or under any enactment to be processed, the person on whom the obligation to process the data is imposed by or under that enactment is for the purposes of this Act the data controller.

[(5)   In paragraph (e) of the definition of "data" in subsection (1), the reference to information "held" by a public authority shall be construed in accordance with section 3(2) of the Freedom of Information Act 2000 [or section 3(2), (4) and (5) of the Freedom of Information (Scotland) Act 2002].

(6)   Where—

[(a)]   section 7 of the Freedom of Information Act 2000 prevents Parts I to V of that Act [or

(b)   section 7(1) of the Freedom of Information (Scotland) Act 2002 prevents that Act,]

from applying to certain information held by a public authority, that information is not to be treated for the purposes of paragraph (e) of the definition of "data" in subsection (1) as held by a public authority.]

NOTES

Sub-s (1): in definition "data" word omitted from para (c) repealed, and para (e) and word immediately preceding it inserted by the Freedom of Information Act 2000, ss 68(1), (2)(a), 86, Sch 8, Pt III; definition "public authority" inserted by the Freedom of Information Act 2000, s 68(1), (2)(b), and substituted by the Freedom of Information (Scotland) Act 2002 (Consequential Modifications) Order 2004, SI 2004/3089, art 2(1), (2)(a).

Sub-s (5): added, together with sub-s (6), by the Freedom of Information Act 2000, s 68(1), (3); words in square brackets inserted by SI 2004/3089, art 2(1), (2)(b).

Sub-s (6): added as noted to sub-s (5); para (a) numbered as such and para (b) and the word immediately preceding it inserted by SI 2004/3089, art 2(1), (2)(c).

[1.1245]
2   Sensitive personal data
In this Act "sensitive personal data" means personal data consisting of information as to—
(a)   the racial or ethnic origin of the data subject,
(b)   his political opinions,
(c)   his religious beliefs or other beliefs of a similar nature,
(d)   whether he is a member of a trade union (within the meaning of the Trade Union and Labour Relations (Consolidation) Act 1992,
(e)   his physical or mental health or condition,
(f)   his sexual life,
(g)   the commission or alleged commission by him of any offence, or
(h)   any proceedings for any offence committed or alleged to have been committed by him, the disposal of such proceedings or the sentence of any court in such proceedings.

[1.1246]
3   The special purposes
In this Act "the special purposes" means any one or more of the following—
(a)   the purposes of journalism,
(b)   artistic purposes, and
(c)   literary purposes.

[1.1247]
4   The data protection principles
(1)   References in this Act to the data protection principles are to the principles set out in Part I of Schedule 1.
(2)   Those principles are to be interpreted in accordance with Part II of Schedule 1.
(3)   Schedule 2 (which applies to all personal data) and Schedule 3 (which applies only to sensitive personal data) set out conditions applying for the purposes of the first principle; and Schedule 4 sets out cases in which the eighth principle does not apply.
(4)   Subject to section 27(1), it shall be the duty of a data controller to comply with the data protection principles in relation to all personal data with respect to which he is the data controller.

[1.1248]
5   Application of Act
(1)   Except as otherwise provided by or under section 54, this Act applies to a data controller in respect of any data only if—
(a)   the data controller is established in the United Kingdom and the data are processed in the context of that establishment, or
(b)   the data controller is established neither in the United Kingdom nor in any other EEA State but uses equipment in the United Kingdom for processing the data otherwise than for the purposes of transit through the United Kingdom.
[(1A)   Subsection (1) is subject to regulation 50 of the Criminal Justice and Data Protection (Protocol No. 36) Regulations 2014.]

(2) A data controller falling within subsection (1)(b) must nominate for the purposes of this Act a representative established in the United Kingdom.

(3) For the purposes of subsections (1) and (2), each of the following is to be treated as established in the United Kingdom—

   (a) an individual who is ordinarily resident in the United Kingdom,

   (b) a body incorporated under the law of, or of any part of, the United Kingdom,

   (c) a partnership or other unincorporated association formed under the law of any part of the United Kingdom, and

   (d) any person who does not fall within paragraph (a), (b) or (c) but maintains in the United Kingdom—

      (i) an office, branch or agency through which he carries on any activity, or

      (ii) a regular practice;

and the reference to establishment in any other EEA State has a corresponding meaning.

NOTES

Sub-s (1A): inserted by the Criminal Justice and Data Protection (Protocol No 36) Regulations 2014, SI 2014/3141, reg 52(a).

[1.1249]

6 The Commissioner . . .

[(1) For the purposes of this Act and of the Freedom of Information Act 2000 there shall be an officer known as the Information Commissioner (in this Act referred to as "the Commissioner").]

(2) The Commissioner shall be appointed by Her Majesty by Letters Patent.

(3)–(6) . . .

(7) Schedule 5 has effect in relation to the Commissioner . . .

NOTES

Section heading: words omitted repealed by the Transfer of Tribunal Functions Order 2010, SI 2010/22, art 5(1), Sch 2, paras 24, 25(a), subject to transitional provisions in Sch 5 thereto.

Sub-s (1): substituted by the Freedom of Information Act 2000, s 18(4), Sch 2, Pt I, para 13(1), (2).

Sub-ss (3)–(6): repealed by SI 2010/22, art 5(1), Sch 2, paras 24, 25(b), subject to transitional provisions in Sch 5 thereto.

Sub-s (7): words omitted repealed by SI 2010/22, art 5(1), Sch 2, paras 24, 25(c), subject to transitional provisions in Sch 5 thereto.

PART II
RIGHTS OF DATA SUBJECTS AND OTHERS

[1.1250]

7 Right of access to personal data

(1) Subject to the following provisions of this section and to [sections 8, 9 and 9A], an individual is entitled—

   (a) to be informed by any data controller whether personal data of which that individual is the data subject are being processed by or on behalf of that data controller,

   (b) if that is the case, to be given by the data controller a description of—

      (i) the personal data of which that individual is the data subject,

      (ii) the purposes for which they are being or are to be processed, and

      (iii) the recipients or classes of recipients to whom they are or may be disclosed,

   (c) to have communicated to him in an intelligible form—

      (i) the information constituting any personal data of which that individual is the data subject, and

      (ii) any information available to the data controller as to the source of those data, and

   (d) where the processing by automatic means of personal data of which that individual is the data subject for the purpose of evaluating matters relating to him such as, for example, his performance at work, his creditworthiness, his reliability or his conduct, has constituted or is likely to constitute the sole basis for any decision significantly affecting him, to be informed by the data controller of the logic involved in that decision-taking.

(2) A data controller is not obliged to supply any information under subsection (1) unless he has received—

   (a) a request in writing, and

   (b) except in prescribed cases, such fee (not exceeding the prescribed maximum) as he may require.

[(3) Where a data controller—

   (a) reasonably requires further information in order to satisfy himself as to the identity of the person making a request under this section and to locate the information which that person seeks, and

   (b) has informed him of that requirement,

the data controller is not obliged to comply with the request unless he is supplied with that further information.]

(4)   Where a data controller cannot comply with the request without disclosing information relating to another individual who can be identified from that information, he is not obliged to comply with the request unless—

    (a)   the other individual has consented to the disclosure of the information to the person making the request, or

    (b)   it is reasonable in all the circumstances to comply with the request without the consent of the other individual.

(5)   In subsection (4) the reference to information relating to another individual includes a reference to information identifying that individual as the source of the information sought by the request; and that subsection is not to be construed as excusing a data controller from communicating so much of the information sought by the request as can be communicated without disclosing the identity of the other individual concerned, whether by the omission of names or other identifying particulars or otherwise.

(6)   In determining for the purposes of subsection (4)(b) whether it is reasonable in all the circumstances to comply with the request without the consent of the other individual concerned, regard shall be had, in particular, to—

    (a)   any duty of confidentiality owed to the other individual,

    (b)   any steps taken by the data controller with a view to seeking the consent of the other individual,

    (c)   whether the other individual is capable of giving consent, and

    (d)   any express refusal of consent by the other individual.

(7)   An individual making a request under this section may, in such cases as may be prescribed, specify that his request is limited to personal data of any prescribed description.

(8)   Subject to subsection (4), a data controller shall comply with a request under this section promptly and in any event before the end of the prescribed period beginning with the relevant day.

(9)   If a court is satisfied on the application of any person who has made a request under the foregoing provisions of this section that the data controller in question has failed to comply with the request in contravention of those provisions, the court may order him to comply with the request.

(10)   In this section—

    "prescribed" means prescribed by the [Secretary of State] by regulations;

    "the prescribed maximum" means such amount as may be prescribed;

    "the prescribed period" means forty days or such other period as may be prescribed;

    "the relevant day", in relation to a request under this section, means the day on which the data controller receives the request or, if later, the first day on which the data controller has both the required fee and the information referred to in subsection (3).

(11)   Different amounts or periods may be prescribed under this section in relation to different cases.

NOTES

Sub-s (1): words in square brackets substituted by the Freedom of Information Act 2000, s 69(1).

Sub-s (3): substituted by the Freedom of Information Act 2000, s 73, Sch 6, para 1.

Sub-s (10): in definition "prescribed" words in square brackets substituted by the Secretary of State for Constitutional Affairs Order 2003, SI 2003/1887, art 9, Sch 2, para 9(1)(a).

See further: the Criminal Justice and Data Protection (Protocol No 36) Regulations 2014, SI 2014/3141, reg 44(1), (2).

Regulations: the Data Protection (Subject Access) (Fees and Miscellaneous Provisions) Regulations 2000, SI 2000/191.

[1.1251]
8   Provisions supplementary to section 7

(1)   The [Secretary of State] may by regulations provide that, in such cases as may be prescribed, a request for information under any provision of subsection (1) of section 7 is to be treated as extending also to information under other provisions of that subsection.

(2)   The obligation imposed by section 7(1)(c)(i) must be complied with by supplying the data subject with a copy of the information in permanent form unless—

    (a)   the supply of such a copy is not possible or would involve disproportionate effort, or

    (b)   the data subject agrees otherwise;

and where any of the information referred to in section 7(1)(c)(i) is expressed in terms which are not intelligible without explanation the copy must be accompanied by an explanation of those terms.

(3)   Where a data controller has previously complied with a request made under section 7 by an individual, the data controller is not obliged to comply with a subsequent identical or similar request under that section by that individual unless a reasonable interval has elapsed between compliance with the previous request and the making of the current request.

(4)   In determining for the purposes of subsection (3) whether requests under section 7 are made at reasonable intervals, regard shall be had to the nature of the data, the purpose for which the data are processed and the frequency with which the data are altered.

(5)   Section 7(1)(d) is not to be regarded as requiring the provision of information as to the logic involved in any decision-taking if, and to the extent that, the information constitutes a trade secret.

(6)   The information to be supplied pursuant to a request under section 7 must be supplied by reference to the data in question at the time when the request is received, except that it may take account of any amendment or deletion made between that time and the time when the information is supplied, being an amendment or deletion that would have been made regardless of the receipt of the request.

(7)   For the purposes of section 7(4) and (5) another individual can be identified from the information being disclosed if he can be identified from that information, or from that and any other information which, in the reasonable belief of the data controller, is likely to be in, or to come into, the possession of the data subject making the request.

NOTES

Sub-s (1): words in square brackets substituted by the Secretary of State for Constitutional Affairs Order 2003, SI 2003/1887, art 9, Sch 2, para 9(1)(a).

See further: the Criminal Justice and Data Protection (Protocol No 36) Regulations 2014, SI 2014/3141, reg 44(1), (3).

Regulations: the Data Protection (Subject Access) (Fees and Miscellaneous Provisions) Regulations 2000, SI 2000/191.

[1.1252]
9   Application of section 7 where data controller is credit reference agency

(1)   Where the data controller is a credit reference agency, section 7 has effect subject to the provisions of this section.

(2)   An individual making a request under section 7 may limit his request to personal data relevant to his financial standing, and shall be taken to have so limited his request unless the request shows a contrary intention.

(3)   Where the data controller receives a request under section 7 in a case where personal data of which the individual making the request is the data subject are being processed by or on behalf of the data controller, the obligation to supply information under that section includes an obligation to give the individual making the request a statement, in such form as may be prescribed by the [Secretary of State] by regulations, of the individual's rights—

(a)   under section 159 of the Consumer Credit Act 1974, and

(b)   to the extent required by the prescribed form, under this Act.

NOTES

Sub-s (3): words in square brackets substituted by the Secretary of State for Constitutional Affairs Order 2003, SI 2003/1887, art 9, Sch 2, para 9(1)(a).

[1.1253]
[9A   Unstructured personal data held by public authorities

(1)   In this section "unstructured personal data" means any personal data falling within paragraph (e) of the definition of "data" in section 1(1), other than information which is recorded as part of, or with the intention that it should form part of, any set of information relating to individuals to the extent that the set is structured by reference to individuals or by reference to criteria relating to individuals.

(2)   A public authority is not obliged to comply with subsection (1) of section 7 in relation to any unstructured personal data unless the request under that section contains a description of the data.

(3)   Even if the data are described by the data subject in his request, a public authority is not obliged to comply with subsection (1) of section 7 in relation to unstructured personal data if the authority estimates that the cost of complying with the request so far as relating to those data would exceed the appropriate limit.

(4)   Subsection (3) does not exempt the public authority from its obligation to comply with paragraph (a) of section 7(1) in relation to the unstructured personal data unless the estimated cost of complying with that paragraph alone in relation to those data would exceed the appropriate limit.

(5)   In subsections (3) and (4) "the appropriate limit" means such amount as may be prescribed by the [Secretary of State] by regulations, and different amounts may be prescribed in relation to different cases.

(6)   Any estimate for the purposes of this section must be made in accordance with regulations under section 12(5) of the Freedom of Information Act 2000.]

NOTES

Inserted by the Freedom of Information Act 2000, s 69(2).

Sub-s (5): words in square brackets substituted by the Secretary of State for Constitutional Affairs Order 2003, SI 2003/1887, art 9, Sch 2, paras 9(1)(a), 12(1)(b).

Regulations: the Freedom of Information and Data Protection (Appropriate Limit and Fees) Regulations 2004, SI 2004/3244.

[1.1254]
10   Right to prevent processing likely to cause damage or distress

(1)   Subject to subsection (2), an individual is entitled at any time by notice in writing to a data controller to require the data controller at the end of such period as is reasonable in the circumstances to cease, or not to begin, processing, or processing for a specified purpose or in a specified manner, any personal data in respect of which he is the data subject, on the ground that, for specified reasons—

(a) the processing of those data or their processing for that purpose or in that manner is causing or is likely to cause substantial damage or substantial distress to him or to another, and

(b) that damage or distress is or would be unwarranted.

(2) Subsection (1) does not apply—

(a) in a case where any of the conditions in paragraphs 1 to 4 of Schedule 2 is met, or

(b) in such other cases as may be prescribed by the [Secretary of State] by order.

(3) The data controller must within twenty-one days of receiving a notice under subsection (1) ("the data subject notice") give the individual who gave it a written notice—

(a) stating that he has complied or intends to comply with the data subject notice, or

(b) stating his reasons for regarding the data subject notice as to any extent unjustified and the extent (if any) to which he has complied or intends to comply with it.

(4) If a court is satisfied, on the application of any person who has given a notice under subsection (1) which appears to the court to be justified (or to be justified to any extent), that the data controller in question has failed to comply with the notice, the court may order him to take such steps for complying with the notice (or for complying with it to that extent) as the court thinks fit.

(5) The failure by a data subject to exercise the right conferred by subsection (1) or section 11(1) does not affect any other right conferred on him by this Part.

NOTES

Sub-s (2): words in square brackets in para (b) substituted by the Secretary of State for Constitutional Affairs Order 2003, SI 2003/1887, art 9, Sch 2, para 9(1)(a).

[1.1255]
11 Right to prevent processing for purposes of direct marketing
(1) An individual is entitled at any time by notice in writing to a data controller to require the data controller at the end of such period as is reasonable in the circumstances to cease, or not to begin, processing for the purposes of direct marketing personal data in respect of which he is the data subject.

(2) If the court is satisfied, on the application of any person who has given a notice under subsection (1), that the data controller has failed to comply with the notice, the court may order him to take such steps for complying with the notice as the court thinks fit.

[(2A) This section shall not apply in relation to the processing of such data as are mentioned in paragraph (1) of regulation 8 of the Telecommunications (Data Protection and Privacy) Regulations 1999 (processing of telecommunications billing data for certain marketing purposes) for the purposes mentioned in paragraph (2) of that regulation.]

(3) In this section "direct marketing" means the communication (by whatever means) of any advertising or marketing material which is directed to particular individuals.

NOTES

Sub-s (2A): inserted by the Telecommunications (Data Protection and Privacy) Regulations 1999, SI 1999/2093, reg 3(3), Sch 1, Pt II, para 3.

[1.1256]
12 Rights in relation to automated decision-taking
(1) An individual is entitled at any time, by notice in writing to any data controller, to require the data controller to ensure that no decision taken by or on behalf of the data controller which significantly affects that individual is based solely on the processing by automatic means of personal data in respect of which that individual is the data subject for the purpose of evaluating matters relating to him such as, for example, his performance at work, his creditworthiness, his reliability or his conduct.

(2) Where, in a case where no notice under subsection (1) has effect, a decision which significantly affects an individual is based solely on such processing as is mentioned in subsection (1)—

(a) the data controller must as soon as reasonably practicable notify the individual that the decision was taken on that basis, and

(b) the individual is entitled, within twenty-one days of receiving that notification from the data controller, by notice in writing to require the data controller to reconsider the decision or to take a new decision otherwise than on that basis.

(3) The data controller must, within twenty-one days of receiving a notice under subsection (2)(b) ("the data subject notice") give the individual a written notice specifying the steps that he intends to take to comply with the data subject notice.

(4) A notice under subsection (1) does not have effect in relation to an exempt decision; and nothing in subsection (2) applies to an exempt decision.

(5) In subsection (4) "exempt decision" means any decision—

(a) in respect of which the condition in subsection (6) and the condition in subsection (7) are met, or

   (b)   which is made in such other circumstances as may be prescribed by the [Secretary of State] by order.

(6)   The condition in this subsection is that the decision—

   (a)   is taken in the course of steps taken—

      (i)   for the purpose of considering whether to enter into a contract with the data subject,

      (ii)   with a view to entering into such a contract, or

      (iii)   in the course of performing such a contract, or

   (b)   is authorised or required by or under any enactment.

(7)   The condition in this subsection is that either—

   (a)   the effect of the decision is to grant a request of the data subject, or

   (b)   steps have been taken to safeguard the legitimate interests of the data subject (for example, by allowing him to make representations).

(8)   If a court is satisfied on the application of a data subject that a person taking a decision in respect of him ("the responsible person") has failed to comply with subsection (1) or (2)(b), the court may order the responsible person to reconsider the decision, or to take a new decision which is not based solely on such processing as is mentioned in subsection (1).

(9)   An order under subsection (8) shall not affect the rights of any person other than the data subject and the responsible person.

NOTES

Sub-s (5): words in square brackets in para (b) substituted by the Secretary of State for Constitutional Affairs Order 2003, SI 2003/1887, art 9, Sch 2, para 9(1)(a).

[1.1257]
13   Compensation for failure to comply with certain requirements

(1)   An individual who suffers damage by reason of any contravention by a data controller of any of the requirements of this Act is entitled to compensation from the data controller for that damage.

(2)   An individual who suffers distress by reason of any contravention by a data controller of any of the requirements of this Act is entitled to compensation from the data controller for that distress if—

   (a)   the individual also suffers damage by reason of the contravention, or

   (b)   the contravention relates to the processing of personal data for the special purposes.

(3)   In proceedings brought against a person by virtue of this section it is a defence to prove that he had taken such care as in all the circumstances was reasonably required to comply with the requirement concerned.

[1.1258]
14   Rectification, blocking, erasure and destruction

(1)   If a court is satisfied on the application of a data subject that personal data of which the applicant is the subject are inaccurate, the court may order the data controller to rectify, block, erase or destroy those data and any other personal data in respect of which he is the data controller and which contain an expression of opinion which appears to the court to be based on the inaccurate data.

(2)   Subsection (1) applies whether or not the data accurately record information received or obtained by the data controller from the data subject or a third party but where the data accurately record such information, then—

   (a)   if the requirements mentioned in paragraph 7 of Part II of Schedule 1 have been complied with, the court may, instead of making an order under subsection (1), make an order requiring the data to be supplemented by such statement of the true facts relating to the matters dealt with by the data as the court may approve, and

   (b)   if all or any of those requirements have not been complied with, the court may, instead of making an order under that subsection, make such order as it thinks fit for securing compliance with those requirements with or without a further order requiring the data to be supplemented by such a statement as is mentioned in paragraph (a).

(3)   Where the court—

   (a)   makes an order under subsection (1), or

   (b)   is satisfied on the application of a data subject that personal data of which he was the data subject and which have been rectified, blocked, erased or destroyed were inaccurate,

it may, where it considers it reasonably practicable, order the data controller to notify third parties to whom the data have been disclosed of the rectification, blocking, erasure or destruction.

(4)   If a court is satisfied on the application of a data subject—

   (a)   that he has suffered damage by reason of any contravention by a data controller of any of the requirements of this Act in respect of any personal data, in circumstances entitling him to compensation under section 13, and

   (b)   that there is a substantial risk of further contravention in respect of those data in such circumstances,

the court may order the rectification, blocking, erasure or destruction of any of those data.

(5)   Where the court makes an order under subsection (4) it may, where it considers it reasonably practicable, order the data controller to notify third parties to whom the data have been disclosed of the rectification, blocking, erasure or destruction.

(6)   In determining whether it is reasonably practicable to require such notification as is mentioned in subsection (3) or (5) the court shall have regard, in particular, to the number of persons who would have to be notified.

[1.1259]
15   Jurisdiction and procedure
(1)   The jurisdiction conferred by sections 7 to 14 is exercisable [in England and Wales by the High Court or the county court or, in Northern Ireland,] by the High Court or a county court or, in Scotland, by the Court of Session or the sheriff.

(2)   For the purpose of determining any question whether an applicant under subsection (9) of section 7 is entitled to the information which he seeks (including any question whether any relevant data are exempt from that section by virtue of Part IV) a court may require the information constituting any data processed by or on behalf of the data controller and any information as to the logic involved in any decision-taking as mentioned in section 7(1)(d) to be made available for its own inspection but shall not, pending the determination of that question in the applicant's favour, require the information sought by the applicant to be disclosed to him or his representatives whether by discovery (or, in Scotland, recovery) or otherwise.

NOTES
Sub-s (1): words in square brackets inserted by the Crime and Courts Act 2013, s 17(5), Sch 9, Pt 3, para 77, for transitional provision see the Crime and Courts Act 2013 (Commencement No 10 and Transitional Provision) Order 2014, SI 2014/954, art 3.

16–50   ((*Pts III–V) Outside the scope of this work.*)

PART VI
MISCELLANEOUS AND GENERAL

51–62   (*Outside the scope of this work.*)

General

63–74   (*Outside the scope of this work.*)

[1.1260]
75   Short title, commencement and extent
(1)   This Act may be cited as the Data Protection Act 1998.
(2)   The following provisions of this Act—
  (a)   sections 1 to 3,
  (b)–(d)   (*outside the scope of this work.*)
  (e)   this section,
  (f)–(h)   (*outside the scope of this work.*)
  (i)   so much of any other provision of this Act as confers any power to make subordinate legislation,
shall come into force on the day on which this Act is passed.

(3)   The remaining provisions of this Act shall come into force on such day as the [Secretary of State] may by order appoint; and different days may be appointed for different purposes.

(4)   The day appointed under subsection (3) for the coming into force of section 56 must not be earlier than the first day on which [sections 112, 113A and 113B] of the Police Act 1997 (which provide for the issue . . . of criminal conviction certificates, criminal record certificates and enhanced criminal record certificates) are all in force.

[(4A)   Subsection (4) does not apply to section 56 so far as that section relates to a record containing information relating to—
  (a)   the Secretary of State's functions under the Safeguarding Vulnerable Groups Act 2006 [or the Safeguarding Vulnerable Groups (Northern Ireland) Order 2007],   . . .
  (b)   the [Independent Safeguarding Authority's] functions under that Act [or that Order][, or
  (c)   the Scottish Ministers' functions under Parts 1 and 2 of the Protection of Vulnerable Groups (Scotland) Act 2007 (asp 14)].]

(5)   Subject to [subsections (5A) and (6)], this Act extends to Northern Ireland.

[(5A)   In section 56(6) (prohibition of requirement as to production of certain records), paragraph (2)(e) of the Table in that section, insofar as it relates to Part 1 of the Welfare Reform Act 2007 [and Part 1 of the Welfare Reform Act 2012], extends to England and Wales and Scotland only.]

(6)   Any amendment, repeal or revocation made by Schedule 15 or 16 has the same extent as that of the enactment or instrument to which it relates.

NOTES
Sub-s (3): words in square brackets substituted by the Secretary of State for Constitutional Affairs Order 2003, SI 2003/1887, art 9, Sch 2, para 9(1)(a).

Sub-s (4): words in square brackets substituted by the Protection of Freedoms Act 2012, s 86; words omitted repealed by the Protection of Freedoms Act 2012 (Disclosure and Barring Service Transfer of Functions) Order 2012, SI 2012/3006, arts 72, 75.

Sub-s (4A): inserted by the Safeguarding Vulnerable Groups Act 2006, s 63(1), Sch 9, Pt 2, para 15(1), (3); words in square brackets in para (a) and words in second pair of square brackets in para (b) inserted by the Safeguarding Vulnerable Groups (Northern Ireland) Order 2007, SI 2007/1351, art 60(1), Sch 7, para 4(2); word omitted from para (a) repealed and para (c) inserted together with word immediately preceding it, by the Protection of Vulnerable Groups (Scotland) Act 2007 (Consequential Modifications) Order 2011, SI 2011/565, art 3(1), (3); words in first pair of square brackets in para (b) substituted by the Policing and Crime Act 2009, s 81(2), (3)(i).

Sub-s (5): words in square brackets substituted by the Social Security (Miscellaneous Amendments) (No 3) Regulations 2011, SI 2011/2425, reg 4(b)(i).

Sub-s (5A): inserted by SI 2011/2425, reg 4(b)(ii); words in square brackets inserted by the Universal Credit (Consequential, Supplementary, Incidental and Miscellaneous Provisions) Regulations 2013, SI 2013/630, reg 14(1), (3).

Orders: the Data Protection Act 1998 (Commencement) Order 2000, SI 2000/183; the Data Protection Act 1998 (Commencement No 2) Order 2008, SI 2008/1592; the Data Protection Act 1998 (Commencement No 3) Order 2011, SI 2011/601; the Data Protection Act 1998 (Commencement No 4) Order 2015, SI 2015/312.

SCHEDULES

SCHEDULE 1
THE DATA PROTECTION PRINCIPLES

Section 4(1) and (2)

PART I
THE PRINCIPLES

[1.1261]
1. Personal data shall be processed fairly and lawfully and, in particular, shall not be processed unless—
   (a)   at least one of the conditions in Schedule 2 is met, and
   (b)   in the case of sensitive personal data, at least one of the conditions in Schedule 3 is also met.

2. Personal data shall be obtained only for one or more specified and lawful purposes, and shall not be further processed in any manner incompatible with that purpose or those purposes.

3. Personal data shall be adequate, relevant and not excessive in relation to the purpose or purposes for which they are processed.

4. Personal data shall be accurate and, where necessary, kept up to date.

5. Personal data processed for any purpose or purposes shall not be kept for longer than is necessary for that purpose or those purposes.

6. Personal data shall be processed in accordance with the rights of data subjects under this Act.

7. Appropriate technical and organisational measures shall be taken against unauthorised or unlawful processing of personal data and against accidental loss or destruction of, or damage to, personal data.

8. Personal data shall not be transferred to a country or territory outside the European Economic Area unless that country or territory ensures an adequate level of protection for the rights and freedoms of data subjects in relation to the processing of personal data.

PART II
INTERPRETATION OF THE PRINCIPLES IN PART I

The first principle

[1.1262]
1. (1)   In determining for the purposes of the first principle whether personal data are processed fairly, regard is to be had to the method by which they are obtained, including in particular whether any person from whom they are obtained is deceived or misled as to the purpose or purposes for which they are to be processed.

(2)   Subject to paragraph 2, for the purposes of the first principle data are to be treated as obtained fairly if they consist of information obtained from a person who—
   (a)   is authorised by or under any enactment to supply it, or
   (b)   is required to supply it by or under any enactment or by any convention or other instrument imposing an international obligation on the United Kingdom.

2. (1)   Subject to paragraph 3, for the purposes of the first principle personal data are not to be treated as processed fairly unless—
   (a)   in the case of data obtained from the data subject, the data controller ensures so far as practicable that the data subject has, is provided with, or has made readily available to him, the information specified in sub-paragraph (3), and

(b) in any other case, the data controller ensures so far as practicable that, before the relevant time or as soon as practicable after that time, the data subject has, is provided with, or has made readily available to him, the information specified in sub-paragraph (3).

(2) In sub-paragraph (1)(b) "the relevant time" means—
  (a) the time when the data controller first processes the data, or
  (b) in a case where at that time disclosure to a third party within a reasonable period is envisaged—
     (i) if the data are in fact disclosed to such a person within that period, the time when the data are first disclosed,
     (ii) if within that period the data controller becomes, or ought to become, aware that the data are unlikely to be disclosed to such a person within that period, the time when the data controller does become, or ought to become, so aware, or
     (iii) in any other case, the end of that period.

(3) The information referred to in sub-paragraph (1) is as follows, namely—
  (a) the identity of the data controller,
  (b) if he has nominated a representative for the purposes of this Act, the identity of that representative,
  (c) the purpose or purposes for which the data are intended to be processed, and
  (d) any further information which is necessary, having regard to the specific circumstances in which the data are or are to be processed, to enable processing in respect of the data subject to be fair.

3. (1) Paragraph 2(1)(b) does not apply where either of the primary conditions in subparagraph (2), together with such further conditions as may be prescribed by the [Secretary of State] by order, are met.

(2) The primary conditions referred to in sub-paragraph (1) are—
  (a) that the provision of that information would involve a disproportionate effort, or
  (b) that the recording of the information to be contained in the data by, or the disclosure of the data by, the data controller is necessary for compliance with any legal obligation to which the data controller is subject, other than an obligation imposed by contract.

4. (1) Personal data which contain a general identifier falling within a description prescribed by the [Secretary of State] by order are not to be treated as processed fairly and lawfully unless they are processed in compliance with any conditions so prescribed in relation to general identifiers of that description.

(2) In sub-paragraph (1) "a general identifier" means any identifier (such as, for example, a number or code used for identification purposes) which—
  (a) relates to an individual, and
  (b) forms part of a set of similar identifiers which is of general application.

The second principle

5. The purpose or purposes for which personal data are obtained may in particular be specified—
  (a) in a notice given for the purposes of paragraph 2 by the data controller to the data subject, or
  (b) in a notification given to the Commissioner under Part III of this Act.

6. In determining whether any disclosure of personal data is compatible with the purpose or purposes for which the data were obtained, regard is to be had to the purpose or purposes for which the personal data are intended to be processed by any person to whom they are disclosed.

The fourth principle

7. The fourth principle is not to be regarded as being contravened by reason of any inaccuracy in personal data which accurately record information obtained by the data controller from the data subject or a third party in a case where—
  (a) having regard to the purpose or purposes for which the data were obtained and further processed, the data controller has taken reasonable steps to ensure the accuracy of the data, and
  (b) if the data subject has notified the data controller of the data subject's view that the data are inaccurate, the data indicate that fact.

The sixth principle

8. A person is to be regarded as contravening the sixth principle if, but only if—
  (a) he contravenes section 7 by failing to supply information in accordance with that section,
  (b) he contravenes section 10 by failing to comply with a notice given under subsection (1) of that section to the extent that the notice is justified or by failing to give a notice under subsection (3) of that section,
  (c) he contravenes section 11 by failing to comply with a notice given under subsection (1) of that section, or

(d)   he contravenes section 12 by failing to comply with a notice given under subsection (1) or (2)(b) of that section or by failing to give a notification under subsection (2)(a) of that section or a notice under subsection (3) of that section.

The seventh principle

9. Having regard to the state of technological development and the cost of implementing any measures, the measures must ensure a level of security appropriate to—

(a)   the harm that might result from such unauthorised or unlawful processing or accidental loss, destruction or damage as are mentioned in the seventh principle, and

(b)   the nature of the data to be protected.

10. The data controller must take reasonable steps to ensure the reliability of any employees of his who have access to the personal data.

11. Where processing of personal data is carried out by a data processor on behalf of a data controller, the data controller must in order to comply with the seventh principle—

(a)   choose a data processor providing sufficient guarantees in respect of the technical and organisational security measures governing the processing to be carried out, and

(b)   take reasonable steps to ensure compliance with those measures.

12. Where processing of personal data is carried out by a data processor on behalf of a data controller, the data controller is not to be regarded as complying with the seventh principle unless—

(a)   the processing is carried out under a contract—

(i)   which is made or evidenced in writing, and

(ii)   under which the data processor is to act only on instructions from the data controller, and

(b)   the contract requires the data processor to comply with obligations equivalent to those imposed on a data controller by the seventh principle.

The eighth principle

13. An adequate level of protection is one which is adequate in all the circumstances of the case, having regard in particular to—

(a)   the nature of the personal data,

(b)   the country or territory of origin of the information contained in the data,

(c)   the country or territory of final destination of that information,

(d)   the purposes for which and period during which the data are intended to be processed,

(e)   the law in force in the country or territory in question,

(f)   the international obligations of that country or territory,

(g)   any relevant codes of conduct or other rules which are enforceable in that country or territory (whether generally or by arrangement in particular cases), and

(h)   any security measures taken in respect of the data in that country or territory.

14. The eighth principle does not apply to a transfer falling within any paragraph of Schedule 4, except in such circumstances and to such extent as the [Secretary of State] may by order provide.

15. (1)   Where—

(a)   in any proceedings under this Act any question arises as to whether the requirement of the eighth principle as to an adequate level of protection is met in relation to the transfer of any personal data to a country or territory outside the European Economic Area, and

(b)   a Community finding has been made in relation to transfers of the kind in question,

that question is to be determined in accordance with that finding.

(2)   In sub-paragraph (1) "Community finding" means a finding of the European Commission, under the procedure provided for in Article 31(2) of the Data Protection Directive, that a country or territory outside the European Economic Area does, or does not, ensure an adequate level of protection within the meaning of Article 25(2) of the Directive.

NOTES

Paras 3, 4, 14: words in square brackets substituted by the Secretary of State for Constitutional Affairs Order 2003, SI 2003/1887, art 9, Sch 2, para 9(1)(b).

Orders: the Data Protection (Conditions under Paragraph 3 of Part II of Schedule 1) Order 2000, SI 2000/185.

SCHEDULE 2
CONDITIONS RELEVANT FOR PURPOSES OF THE FIRST PRINCIPLE: PROCESSING OF ANY PERSONAL DATA

Section 4(3)

[1.1263]

1. The data subject has given his consent to the processing.

2. The processing is necessary—

(a)   for the performance of a contract to which the data subject is a party, or

(b)   for the taking of steps at the request of the data subject with a view to entering into a contract.

3. The processing is necessary for compliance with any legal obligation to which the data controller is subject, other than an obligation imposed by contract.

4. The processing is necessary in order to protect the vital interests of the data subject.

5. The processing is necessary—
  (a)   for the administration of justice,
  [(aa) for the exercise of any functions of either House of Parliament,]
  (b)   for the exercise of any functions conferred on any person by or under any enactment,
  (c)   for the exercise of any functions of the Crown, a Minister of the Crown or a government department, or
  (d)   for the exercise of any other functions of a public nature exercised in the public interest by any person.

6. (1)   The processing is necessary for the purposes of legitimate interests pursued by the data controller or by the third party or parties to whom the data are disclosed, except where the processing is unwarranted in any particular case by reason of prejudice to the rights and freedoms or legitimate interests of the data subject.

(2)   The [Secretary of State] may by order specify particular circumstances in which this condition is, or is not, to be taken to be satisfied.

NOTES

Para 5: sub-para (aa) inserted by the Freedom of Information Act 2000, s 73, Sch 6, para 4.

Para 6: words in square brackets in sub-para (2) substituted by the Secretary of State for Constitutional Affairs Order 2003, SI 2003/1887, art 9, Sch 2, para 9(1)(b).

See further: the National Assembly for Wales Commission is treated as a government department for the purposes of para 5 above; see the National Assembly for Wales Commission (Crown Status) Order 2007, SI 2007/1118, art 5(1), (2)(b).

SCHEDULE 3
CONDITIONS RELEVANT FOR PURPOSES OF THE FIRST PRINCIPLE: PROCESSING OF SENSITIVE PERSONAL DATA

Section 4(3)

[1.1264]
1. The data subject has given his explicit consent to the processing of the personal data.

2. (1)   The processing is necessary for the purposes of exercising or performing any right or obligation which is conferred or imposed by law on the data controller in connection with employment.

(2)   The [Secretary of State] may by order—
  (a)   exclude the application of sub-paragraph (1) in such cases as may be specified, or
  (b)   provide that, in such cases as may be specified, the condition in subparagraph (1) is not to be regarded as satisfied unless such further conditions as may be specified in the order are also satisfied.

3. The processing is necessary—
  (a)   in order to protect the vital interests of the data subject or another person, in a case where—
    (i)   consent cannot be given by or on behalf of the data subject, or
    (ii)   the data controller cannot reasonably be expected to obtain the consent of the data subject, or
  (b)   in order to protect the vital interests of another person, in a case where consent by or on behalf of the data subject has been unreasonably withheld.

4. The processing—
  (a)   is carried out in the course of its legitimate activities by any body or association which—
    (i)   is not established or conducted for profit, and
    (ii)   exists for political, philosophical religious or trade-union purposes,
  (b)   is carried out with appropriate safeguards for the rights and freedoms of data subjects,
  (c)   relates only to individuals who either are members of the body or association or have regular contact with it in connection with its purposes, and
  (d)   does not involve disclosure of the personal data to a third party without the consent of the data subject.

5. The information contained in the personal data has been made public as a result of steps deliberately taken by the data subject.

6. The processing—

(a)   is necessary for the purpose of, or in connection with, any legal proceedings (including prospective legal proceedings),

(b)   is necessary for the purpose of obtaining legal advice, or

(c)   is otherwise necessary for the purposes of establishing, exercising or defending legal rights.

7. (1)   The processing is necessary—

(a)   for the administration of justice,

[(aa)   for the exercise of any functions of either House of Parliament,]

(b)   for the exercise of any functions conferred on any person by or under an enactment, or

(c)   for the exercise of any functions of the Crown, a Minister of the Crown or a government department.

(2)   The [Secretary of State] may by order—

(a)   exclude the application of sub-paragraph (1) in such cases as may be specified, or

(b)   provide that, in such cases as may be specified, the condition in subparagraph (1) is not to be regarded as satisfied unless such further conditions as may be specified in the order are also satisfied.

[7A. (1)   The processing—

(a)   is either—

     (i)   the disclosure of sensitive personal data by a person as a member of an anti-fraud organisation or otherwise in accordance with any arrangements made by such an organisation; or

     (ii)   any other processing by that person or another person of sensitive personal data so disclosed; and

(b)   is necessary for the purposes of preventing fraud or a particular kind of fraud.

(2)   In this paragraph "an anti-fraud organisation" means any unincorporated association, body corporate or other person which enables or facilitates any sharing of information to prevent fraud or a particular kind of fraud or which has any of these functions as its purpose or one of its purposes.]

8. (1)   The processing is necessary for medical purposes and is undertaken by—

(a)   a health professional, or

(b)   a person who in the circumstances owes a duty of confidentiality which is equivalent to that which would arise if that person were a health professional.

(2)   In this paragraph "medical purposes" includes the purposes of preventative medicine, medical diagnosis, medical research, the provision of care and treatment and the management of healthcare services.

9. (1)   The processing—

(a)   is of sensitive personal data consisting of information as to racial or ethnic origin,

(b)   is necessary for the purpose of identifying or keeping under review the existence or absence of equality of opportunity or treatment between persons of different racial or ethnic origins, with a view to enabling such equality to be promoted or maintained, and

(c)   is carried out with appropriate safeguards for the rights and freedoms of data subjects.

(2)   The [Secretary of State] may by order specify circumstances in which processing falling within sub-paragraph (1)(a) and (b) is, or is not, to be taken for the purposes of subparagraph (1)(c) to be carried out with appropriate safeguards for the rights and freedoms of data subjects.

10.   The personal data are processed in circumstances specified in an order made by the [Secretary of State] for the purposes of this paragraph.

NOTES

Paras 2, 9, 10: words in square brackets substituted by the Secretary of State for Constitutional Affairs Order 2003, SI 2003/1887, art 9, Sch 2, para 9(1)(b).

Para 7: sub-para (1)(aa) inserted by the Freedom of Information Act 2000, s 73, Sch 6, para 5; words in square brackets in sub-para (2) substituted by SI 2003/1887, art 9, Sch 2, para 9(1)(b).

Para 7A: inserted by the Serious Crime Act 2007, s 72.

Orders: the Data Protection (Processing of Sensitive Personal Data) Order 2000, SI 2000/417; the Data Protection (Processing of Sensitive Personal Data) (Elected Representatives) Order 2002, SI 2002/2905; the Data Protection (Processing of Sensitive Personal Data) Order 2006, SI 2006/2068; Data Protection (Processing of Sensitive Personal Data) Order 2009, SI 2009/1811; the Data Protection (Processing of Sensitive Personal Data) Order 2012, SI 2012/1978.

See further: the National Assembly for Wales Commission is treated as a government department for the purposes of para 7 above; see the National Assembly for Wales Commission (Crown Status) Order 2007, SI 2007/1118, art 5(1), (2)(c).

SCHEDULE 4

CASES WHERE THE EIGHTH PRINCIPLE DOES NOT APPLY

Section 4(3)

[1.1265]

1. The data subject has given his consent to the transfer.

2. The transfer is necessary—

    (a)   for the performance of a contract between the data subject and the data controller, or

    (b)   for the taking of steps at the request of the data subject with a view to his entering into a contract with the data controller.

3. The transfer is necessary—

    (a)   for the conclusion of a contract between the data controller and a person other than the data subject which—

        (i)   is entered into at the request of the data subject, or

        (ii)   is in the interests of the data subject, or

    (b)   for the performance of such a contract.

4. (1)   The transfer is necessary for reasons of substantial public interest.

(2)   The [Secretary of State] may by order specify—

    (a)   circumstances in which a transfer is to be taken for the purposes of sub-paragraph (1) to be necessary for reasons of substantial public interest, and

    (b)   circumstances in which a transfer which is not required by or under an enactment is not to be taken for the purpose of sub-paragraph (1) to be necessary for reasons of substantial public interest.

5. The transfer—

    (a)   is necessary for the purpose of, or in connection with, any legal proceedings (including prospective legal proceedings),

    (b)   is necessary for the purpose of obtaining legal advice, or

    (c)   is otherwise necessary for the purposes of establishing, exercising or defending legal rights.

6. The transfer is necessary in order to protect the vital interests of the data subject.

7. The transfer is of part of the personal data on a public register and any conditions subject to which the register is open to inspection are complied with by any person to whom the data are or may be disclosed after the transfer.

8. The transfer is made on terms which are of a kind approved by the Commissioner as ensuring adequate safeguards for the rights and freedoms of data subjects.

9. The transfer has been authorised by the Commissioner as being made in such a manner as to ensure adequate safeguards for the rights and freedoms of data subjects.

NOTES

    Para 4: words in square brackets in sub-para (2) substituted by the Secretary of State for Constitutional Affairs Order 2003, SI 2003/1887, art 9, Sch 2, para 9(1)(b).

SCHEDULES 5–16

(Schs 5–16 outside the scope of this work.)

COMPETITION ACT 1998

(1998 c 41)

ARRANGEMENT OF SECTIONS

PART I
COMPETITION

CHAPTER I
AGREEMENTS

SCHEDULES

An Act to make provision about competition and the abuse of a dominant position in the market; to confer powers in relation to investigations conducted in connection with [Article 81 or 82] of the treaty establishing the European Community; to amend the Fair Trading Act 1973 in relation to information which may be required in connection with investigations under that Act; to make provision with respect to the meaning of "supply of services" in the Fair Trading Act 1973; and for connected purposes

[9 November 1998]

NOTES

Long title: words in square brackets substituted by the Competition Act 1998 and Other Enactments (Amendment) Regulations 2004, SI 2004/1261, reg 4, Sch 1, para 1.

Director General of Fair Trading: the Enterprise Act 2002, s 2(1) provided that, as from the coming into force of that section (on 1 April 2003), the functions of the Director General of Fair Trading, his property, rights and liabilities were transferred to the Office of Fair Trading. Accordingly, (by virtue of s 2(2), (3) of the 2002 Act) the office of the Director was abolished, and any reference to the Director in any enactment, instrument or other document passed or made before the commencement of s 2(1) had, in so far as is necessary, effect as if it were a reference to the Office of Fair Trading (for transitional provisions in connection with the transfer, see Sch 24, para 6 to the 2002 Act). Section 2 of the 2002 Act was repealed by the Enterprise and Regulatory Reform Act 2013, s 26(3), Sch 5, Pt 4, para 229, as from 1 April 2014. Part 3 of the 2013 Act (ss 25–28) abolished the Office of Fair Trading (and the Competition Commission) and provided for the transfer of its functions to the newly created Competition and Markets Authority.

PART I
COMPETITION

CHAPTER I
AGREEMENTS

Introduction

[1.1266]
1   Enactments replaced
The following shall cease to have effect—
  (a)   the Restrictive Practices Court Act 1976 (c 33),
  (b)   the Restrictive Trade Practices Act 1976 (c 34),
  (c)   the Resale Prices Act 1976 (c 53), and
  (d)   the Restrictive Trade Practices Act 1977 (c 19).

NOTES

Commencement: 1 March 2000 (paras (b)–(d)); 10 March 2013 (para (a)).

The prohibition

[1.1267]
2 Agreements etc preventing, restricting or distorting competition
(1) Subject to section 3, agreements between undertakings, decisions by associations of undertakings or concerted practices which—
  (a) may affect trade within the United Kingdom, and
  (b) have as their object or effect the prevention, restriction or distortion of competition within the United Kingdom,
are prohibited unless they are exempt in accordance with the provisions of this Part.
(2) Subsection (1) applies, in particular, to agreements, decisions or practices which—
  (a) directly or indirectly fix purchase or selling prices or any other trading conditions;
  (b) limit or control production, markets, technical development or investment;
  (c) share markets or sources of supply;
  (d) apply dissimilar conditions to equivalent transactions with other trading parties, thereby placing them at a competitive disadvantage;
  (e) make the conclusion of contracts subject to acceptance by the other parties of supplementary obligations which, by their nature or according to commercial usage, have no connection with the subject of such contracts.
(3) Subsection (1) applies only if the agreement, decision or practice is, or is intended to be, implemented in the United Kingdom.
(4) Any agreement or decision which is prohibited by subsection (1) is void.
(5) A provision of this Part which is expressed to apply to, or in relation to, an agreement is to be read as applying equally to, or in relation to, a decision by an association of undertakings or a concerted practice (but with any necessary modifications).
(6) Subsection (5) does not apply where the context otherwise requires.
(7) In this section "the United Kingdom" means, in relation to an agreement which operates or is intended to operate only in a part of the United Kingdom, that part.
(8) The prohibition imposed by subsection (1) is referred to in this Act as "the Chapter I prohibition".

NOTES
  See further, in relation to the disapplication of this section to certain agreements concerning any part of a Core Competence: the Competition Act 1998 (Public Policy Exclusion) Order 2008, SI 2008/1820, art 4.
  See further, in relation to the disapplication of this section, for the purposes of the Competition Act 1998 (Public Policy Exclusion) Order 2012: the Competition Act 1998 (Public Policy Exclusion) Order 2012, SI 2012/710, art 4.

Excluded agreements

[1.1268]
3 Excluded agreements
(1) The Chapter I prohibition does not apply in any of the cases in which it is excluded by or as a result of—
  (a) Schedule 1 (mergers and concentrations);
  (b) Schedule 2 (competition scrutiny under other enactments);
  (c) Schedule 3 (planning obligations and other general exclusions); . . .
  (d) . . .
(2) The Secretary of State may at any time by order amend Schedule 1, with respect to the Chapter I prohibition, by—
  (a) providing for one or more additional exclusions; or
  (b) amending or removing any provision (whether or not it has been added by an order under this subsection).
(3) The Secretary of State may at any time by order amend Schedule 3, with respect to the Chapter I prohibition, by—
  (a) providing for one or more additional exclusions; or
  (b) amending or removing any provision—
    (i) added by an order under this subsection; or
    (ii) included in paragraph 1, 2, 8 or 9 of Schedule 3.
(4) The power under subsection (3) to provide for an additional exclusion may be exercised only if it appears to the Secretary of State that agreements which fall within the additional exclusion—
  (a) do not in general have an adverse effect on competition, or
  (b) are, in general, best considered under Chapter II or [the Enterprise Act 2002].
(5) An order under subsection (2)(a) or (3)(a) may include provision (similar to that made with respect to any other exclusion provided by the relevant Schedule) for the exclusion concerned to cease to apply to a particular agreement.
(6) Schedule 3 also gives the Secretary of State power to exclude agreements from the Chapter I prohibition in certain circumstances.

NOTES
  Sub-s (1): para (d) and the word immediately preceding it repealed by the Enterprise Act 2002, ss 207, 278(2), Sch 26 (subject to savings in Sch 24, para 20 to that Act).

Sub-s (4): words in square brackets substituted by the Enterprise Act 2002, s 278(1), Sch 25, para 38(1), (2) (for savings in relation to the merger of water and sewerage undertakers, see the Enterprise Act 2002 (Commencement No 3, Transitional and Transitory Provisions and Savings) Order 2003, SI 2003/1397, art 3, and the Enterprise Act 2002 (Commencement No 7 and Transitional Provisions and Savings) Order 2004, SI 2004/3233, arts 3–5).

Exemptions

4, 5   (*Repealed by the Competition Act 1998 and Other Enactments (Amendment) Regulations 2004, SI 2004/1261, reg 4, Sch 1, paras 2, 3 (for savings and transitional provisions see regs 6, 8, 10 of those Regulations).*)

[1.1269]

6   Block exemptions

(1)   If agreements which fall within a particular category of agreement are, in the opinion of the [CMA], likely to be [exempt agreements], the [CMA] may recommend that the Secretary of State make an order specifying that category for the purposes of this section.

(2)   The Secretary of State may make an order ("a block exemption order") giving effect to such a recommendation—

    (a)   in the form in which the recommendation is made; or

    (b)   subject to such modifications as he considers appropriate.

(3)   An agreement which falls within a category specified in a block exemption order is exempt from the Chapter I prohibition.

(4)   An exemption under this section is referred to in this Part as a block exemption.

(5)   A block exemption order may impose conditions or obligations subject to which a block exemption is to have effect.

(6)   A block exemption order may provide—

    (a)   that breach of a condition imposed by the order has the effect of cancelling the block exemption in respect of an agreement;

    (b)   that if there is a failure to comply with an obligation imposed by the order, the [CMA] may, by notice in writing, cancel the block exemption in respect of the agreement;

    (c)   that if the [CMA] considers that a particular agreement is not [an exempt agreement], [it] may cancel the block exemption in respect of that agreement.

(7)   A block exemption order may provide that the order is to cease to have effect at the end of a specified period.

[(8)   In this section—

    "exempt agreement" means an agreement which is exempt from the Chapter I prohibition as a result of section 9; and

    "specified" means specified in a block exemption order.]

NOTES

Sub-s (1): references in first and third pairs of square brackets substituted by the Enterprise and Regulatory Reform Act 2013, s 26(3), Sch 5, Pt 1, paras 1, 2. For various transitional provisions (including those relating to the abolition of the OFT and the Competition Commission, existing references to those bodies and provisions relating to continuity), see the Enterprise and Regulatory Reform Act 2013 (Commencement No 6, Transitional Provisions and Savings) Order 2014, SI 2014/416, Schedule at **[2.1126]**. Words in second pair of square brackets substituted by the Competition Act 1998 and Other Enactments (Amendment) Regulations 2004, SI 2004/1261, reg 4, Sch 1, para 4(1), (2).

Sub-s (6): words in second pair of square brackets substituted by SI 2004/1261, reg 4, Sch 1, para 4(1), (3).

Sub-s (8): substituted by SI 2004/1261, reg 4, Sch 1, para 4(1), (4).

References to the CMA, etc: as to the abolition of the office of the Director General of Fair Trading and the substitution of the original references to the Director (and related expressions), see the note preceding s 1 at **[1.1266]**.

Orders: the Competition Act 1998 (Public Transport Ticketing Schemes Block Exemption) Order 2001, SI 2001/319; the Competition Act 1998 (Public Transport Ticketing Schemes Block Exemption) (Amendment) Order 2005, SI 2005/3347; the Competition Act 1998 (Public Transport Ticketing Schemes Block Exemption) (Amendment) Order 2011, SI 2011/227.

---

7   (*Repealed by the Competition Act 1998 and Other Enactments (Amendment) Regulations 2004, SI 2004/1261, reg 4, Sch 1, para 5.*)

[1.1270]

8   Block exemptions: procedure

(1)   Before making a recommendation under section 6(1), the [CMA] must—

    (a)   publish details of [its] proposed recommendation in such a way as [it] thinks most suitable for bringing it to the attention of those likely to be affected; and

    (b)   consider any representations about it which are made to [it].

(2)   If the Secretary of State proposes to give effect to such a recommendation subject to modifications, he must inform the [CMA] of the proposed modifications and take into account any comments made by the [CMA].

(3)   If, in the opinion of the [CMA], it is appropriate to vary or revoke a block exemption order [it] may make a recommendation to that effect to the Secretary of State.

(4)   Subsection (1) also applies to any proposed recommendation under subsection (3).

(5)   Before exercising his power to vary or revoke a block exemption order (in a case where there has been no recommendation under subsection (3)), the Secretary of State must—

    (a)   inform the [CMA] of the proposed variation or revocation; and

(b)   take into account any comments made by the [CMA].

(6)   A block exemption order may provide for a block exemption to have effect from a date earlier than that on which the order is made.

NOTES

References to "CMA" in each place substituted (for references to "OFT" as substituted by the Enterprise Act 2002, s 278, Sch 25, para 38) by the Enterprise and Regulatory Reform Act 2013, s 26(3), Sch 5, Pt 1, paras 1, 3. For various transitional provisions (including those relating to the abolition of the OFT and the Competition Commission, existing references to those bodies and provisions relating to continuity), see the Enterprise and Regulatory Reform Act 2013 (Commencement No 6, Transitional Provisions and Savings) Order 2014, SI 2014/416, Schedule at **[2.1126]**. This section is also amended as follows:

Sub-s (1): words in second, third and fourth pairs of square brackets substituted by the Enterprise Act 2002, s 278, Sch 25, para 38.

Sub-s (3): word in second pair of square brackets substituted by the Enterprise Act 2002, s 278, Sch 25, para 38.

References to the CMA, etc: as to the abolition of the office of the Director General of Fair Trading and the substitution of the original references to the Director (and related expressions), see the note preceding s 1 at **[1.1266]**.

Orders: the Competition Act 1998 (Public Transport Ticketing Schemes Block Exemption) Order 2001, SI 2001/319; the Competition Act 1998 (Public Transport Ticketing Schemes Block Exemption) (Amendment) Order 2005, SI 2005/3347.

[1.1271]
9   [Exempt agreements]
[(1)]   [An agreement is exempt from the Chapter I prohibition if it]—
  (a)   contributes to—
     (i)   improving production or distribution, or
     (ii)   promoting technical or economic progress,
     while allowing consumers a fair share of the resulting benefit; [and]
  (b)   does not—
     (i)   impose on the undertakings concerned restrictions which are not indispensable to the attainment of those objectives; or
     (ii)   afford the undertakings concerned the possibility of eliminating competition in respect of a substantial part of the products in question.
[(2)   In any proceedings in which it is alleged that the Chapter I prohibition is being or has been infringed by an agreement, any undertaking or association of undertakings claiming the benefit of subsection (1) shall bear the burden of proving that the conditions of that subsection are satisfied.]

NOTES

Section heading: substituted by the Competition Act 1998 and Other Enactments (Amendment) Regulations 2004, SI 2004/1261, reg 4, Sch 1, para 6(5).

Sub-s (1): numbered as such and words in square brackets substituted by SI 2004/1261, reg 4, Sch 1, para 6(1)–(3).

Sub-s (2): added by SI 2004/1261, reg 4, Sch 1, para 6(4).

[1.1272]
10   Parallel exemptions
(1)   An agreement is exempt from the Chapter I prohibition if it is exempt from the Community prohibition—
  (a)   by virtue of a Regulation, [or
  (b)   because of a decision of the Commission under Article 10 of the EC Competition Regulation].
(2)   An agreement is exempt from the Chapter I prohibition if it does not affect trade between Member States but otherwise falls within a category of agreement which is exempt from the Community prohibition by virtue of a Regulation.
(3)   An exemption from the Chapter I prohibition under this section is referred to in this Part as a parallel exemption.
(4)   A parallel exemption—
  (a)   takes effect on the date on which the relevant exemption from the Community prohibition takes effect or, in the case of a parallel exemption under subsection (2), would take effect if the agreement in question affected trade between Member States; and
  (b)   ceases to have effect—
     (i)   if the relevant exemption from the Community prohibition ceases to have effect; or
     (ii)   on being cancelled by virtue of subsection (5) or (7).
(5)   In such circumstances and manner as may be specified in rules made under section 51, the [CMA] may—
  (a)   impose conditions or obligations subject to which a parallel exemption is to have effect;
  (b)   vary or remove any such condition or obligation;
  (c)   impose one or more additional conditions or obligations;
  (d)   cancel the exemption.
(6)   In such circumstances as may be specified in rules made under section 51, the date from which cancellation of an exemption is to take effect may be earlier than the date on which notice of cancellation is given.
(7)   Breach of a condition imposed by the [CMA] has the effect of cancelling the exemption.
(8)   In exercising [its] powers under this section, the [CMA] may require any person who is a party to the agreement in question to give [it] such information as [it] may require.

(9)   For the purpose of this section references to an agreement being exempt from the Community prohibition are to be read as including references to the prohibition being inapplicable to the agreement by virtue of a Regulation [other than the EC Competition Regulation] or a decision by the Commission.

(10)   In this section—

"the Community prohibition" means the prohibition contained in—

[(a)   [Article 101(1)];]

(b)   any corresponding provision replacing, or otherwise derived from, that provision;

(c)   such other Regulation as the Secretary of State may by order specify; and

"Regulation" means a Regulation adopted by the Commission or by the Council.

(11)   This section has effect in relation to the prohibition contained in paragraph 1 of Article 53 of the EEA Agreement (and the EFTA Surveillance Authority) as it has effect in relation to the Community prohibition (and the Commission) subject to any modifications which the Secretary of State may by order prescribe.

NOTES

References to "CMA" in each place substituted (for references to "OFT" as substituted by the Enterprise Act 2002, s 278, Sch 25, para 38) by the Enterprise and Regulatory Reform Act 2013, s 26(3), Sch 5, Pt 1, paras 1, 4. For various transitional provisions (including those relating to the abolition of the OFT and the Competition Commission, existing references to those bodies and provisions relating to continuity), see the Enterprise and Regulatory Reform Act 2013 (Commencement No 6, Transitional Provisions and Savings) Order 2014, SI 2014/416, Schedule at **[2.1126]**. This section is also amended as follows:

Sub-s (1): para (b) and the word immediately preceding it substituted (for original paras (b), (c)) by the Competition Act 1998 and Other Enactments (Amendment) Regulations 2004, SI 2004/1261, reg 4, Sch 1, para 7(1), (2) (for savings and transitional provisions see reg 7 of those Regulations).

Sub-s (8): words in first, third and fourth pairs of square brackets substituted by the Enterprise Act 2002, s 278, Sch 25, para 38.

Sub-s (9): words in square brackets inserted by SI 2004/1261, reg 4, Sch 1, para 7(1), (3).

Sub-s (10): in definition "the Community prohibition" para (a) substituted by SI 2004/1261, reg 4, Sch 1, para 7(1), (4); words in square brackets in that paragraph substituted by the Treaty of Lisbon (Changes in Terminology or Numbering) Order 2012, SI 2012/1809, art 3(1), Schedule, Pt 1 (note that the amendments made by this Order do not affect any provision in its application to things done before 1 December 2009 (the date on which the Treaty of Lisbon came into force)).

References to the CMA, etc: as to the abolition of the office of the Director General of Fair Trading and the substitution of the original references to the Director (and related expressions), see the note preceding s 1 at **[1.1266]**.

[1.1273]

11   Exemption for certain other agreements

(1)   The fact that a ruling may be given by virtue of [Article 104] of the Treaty on the question whether or not agreements of a particular kind are prohibited by [Article 101(1)] does not prevent such agreements from being subject to the Chapter I prohibition.

(2)   But the Secretary of State may by regulations make such provision as he considers appropriate for the purpose of granting an exemption from the Chapter I prohibition, in prescribed circumstances, in respect of such agreements.

(3)   An exemption from the Chapter I prohibition by virtue of regulations under this section is referred to in this Part as a section 11 exemption.

NOTES

Sub-s (1): words in square brackets substituted by the Treaty of Lisbon (Changes in Terminology or Numbering) Order 2012, SI 2012/1809, art 3, Schedule, Pt 1 (note that the amendments made by this Order do not affect any provision in its application to things done before 1 December 2009 (the date on which the Treaty of Lisbon came into force)).

Regulations: the Competition Act 1998 (Section 11 Exemption) Regulations 2001, SI 2001/2993.

12–16   *(Repealed by the Competition Act 1998 and Other Enactments (Amendment) Regula-tions 2004, SI 2004/1261, reg 4, Sch 1, para 9 (for savings and transitional provisions in relation to ss 13, 14 see reg 9 of those Regulations).)*

CHAPTER II

ABUSE OF DOMINANT POSITION

17   *(Repeals the Competition Act 1980, ss 2–10.)*

The prohibition

[1.1274]

18   Abuse of dominant position

(1)   Subject to section 19, any conduct on the part of one or more undertakings which amounts to the abuse of a dominant position in a market is prohibited if it may affect trade within the United Kingdom.

(2)   Conduct may, in particular, constitute such an abuse if it consists in—

(a)   directly or indirectly imposing unfair purchase or selling prices or other unfair trading conditions;

(b)   limiting production, markets or technical development to the prejudice of consumers;

(c)   applying dissimilar conditions to equivalent transactions with other trading parties, thereby placing them at a competitive disadvantage;

(d) making the conclusion of contracts subject to acceptance by the other parties of supplementary obligations which, by their nature or according to commercial usage, have no connection with the subject of the contracts.

(3) In this section—

"dominant position" means a dominant position within the United Kingdom; and

"the United Kingdom" means the United Kingdom or any part of it.

(4) The prohibition imposed by subsection (1) is referred to in this Act as "the Chapter II prohibition".

Excluded cases

[1.1275]
19 Excluded cases

(1) The Chapter II prohibition does not apply in any of the cases in which it is excluded by or as a result of—

    (a) Schedule 1 (mergers and concentrations); or

    (b) Schedule 3 (general exclusions).

(2) The Secretary of State may at any time by order amend Schedule 1, with respect to the Chapter II prohibition, by—

    (a) providing for one or more additional exclusions; or

    (b) amending or removing any provision (whether or not it has been added by an order under this subsection).

(3) The Secretary of State may at any time by order amend paragraph 8 of Schedule 3 with respect to the Chapter II prohibition.

(4) Schedule 3 also gives the Secretary of State power to provide that the Chapter II prohibition is not to apply in certain circumstances.

20–24 (*Repealed by the Competition Act 1998 and Other Enactments (Amendment) Regulations 2004, SI 2004/1261, reg 4, Sch 1, para 9.*)

CHAPTER III
INVESTIGATION AND ENFORCEMENT

Investigations

[1.1276]
[25 Power of [CMA] to investigate

(1) In any of the following cases, the [CMA] may conduct an investigation.

(2) The first case is where there are reasonable grounds for suspecting that there is an agreement which—

    (a) may affect trade within the United Kingdom; and

    (b) has as its object or effect the prevention, restriction or distortion of competition within the United Kingdom.

(3) The second case is where there are reasonable grounds for suspecting that there is an agreement which—

    (a) may affect trade between Member States; and

    (b) has as its object or effect the prevention, restriction or distortion of competition within the Community.

(4) The third case is where there are reasonable grounds for suspecting that the Chapter II prohibition has been infringed.

(5) The fourth case is where there are reasonable grounds for suspecting that the prohibition in [Article 102] has been infringed.

(6) The fifth case is where there are reasonable grounds for suspecting that, at some time in the past, there was an agreement which at that time—

    (a) may have affected trade within the United Kingdom; and

    (b) had as its object or effect the prevention, restriction or distortion of competition within the United Kingdom.

(7) The sixth case is where there are reasonable grounds for suspecting that, at some time in the past, there was an agreement which at that time—

    (a) may have affected trade between Member States; and

    (b) had as its object or effect the prevention, restriction or distortion of competition within the Community.

(8) Subsection (2) does not permit an investigation to be conducted in relation to an agreement if the [CMA]—

    (a) considers that the agreement is exempt from the Chapter I prohibition as a result of a block exemption or a parallel exemption; and

    (b) does not have reasonable grounds for suspecting that the circumstances may be such that it could exercise its power to cancel the exemption.

(9) Subsection (3) does not permit an investigation to be conducted if the [CMA]—

    (a) considers that the agreement is an agreement to which the prohibition in [Article 101(1)] is inapplicable by virtue of a regulation of the Commission ("the relevant regulation"); and

(b)   does not have reasonable grounds for suspecting that the conditions set out in Article 29(2) of the EC Competition Regulation for the withdrawal of the benefit of the relevant regulation may be satisfied in respect of that agreement.

(10)   Subsection (6) does not permit an investigation to be conducted in relation to any agreement if the [CMA] considers that, at the time in question, the agreement was exempt from the Chapter I prohibition as a result of a block exemption or a parallel exemption.

(11)   Subsection (7) does not permit an investigation to be conducted in relation to any agreement if the [CMA] considers that, at the time in question, the agreement was an agreement to which the prohibition in [Article 101(1)] was inapplicable by virtue of a regulation of the Commission.

(12)   It is immaterial for the purposes of subsection (6) or (7) whether the agreement in question remains in existence.]

NOTES

Substituted by the Competition Act 1998 and other enactments (Amendment) Regulations 2004, SI 2004/1261, reg 4, Sch 1, para 10.

References to "CMA" in each place substituted for original references to "OFT" by the Enterprise and Regulatory Reform Act 2013, s 26(3), Sch 5, Pt 1, paras 1, 5. For various transitional provisions (including those relating to the abolition of the OFT and the Competition Commission, existing references to those bodies and provisions relating to continuity), see the Enterprise and Regulatory Reform Act 2013 (Commencement No 6, Transitional Provisions and Savings) Order 2014, SI 2014/416, Schedule at **[2.1126]**.

Other words in square brackets in sub-ss (5), (9), (11) substituted by the Treaty of Lisbon (Changes in Terminology or Numbering) Order 2012, SI 2012/1809, art 3(1), Schedule, Pt 1 (note that the amendments made by this Order do not affect any provision in its application to things done before 1 December 2009 (the date on which the Treaty of Lisbon came into force)).

[1.1277]
[25A   Power of CMA to publish notice of investigation
(1)   Where the CMA decides to conduct an investigation it may publish a notice which may, in particular—
(a)   state its decision to do so;
(b)   indicate which of subsections (2) to (7) of section 25 the investigation falls under;
(c)   summarise the matter being investigated;
(d)   identify any undertaking whose activities are being investigated as part of the investigation;
(e)   identify the market which is or was affected by the matter being investigated.

(2)   Section 57 does not apply to a notice under subsection (1) to the extent that it includes information other than information mentioned in that subsection.

(3)   Subsection (4) applies if—
(a)   the CMA has published a notice under subsection (1) which identifies an undertaking whose activities are being investigated, and
(b)   the CMA subsequently decides (without making a decision within the meaning given by section 31(2)) to terminate the investigation of the activities of the undertaking so identified.

(4)   The CMA must publish a notice stating that the activities of the undertaking in question are no longer being investigated.]

NOTES

Commencement: 1 April 2014.

Inserted by the Enterprise and Regulatory Reform Act 2013, s 42(1), (2). For various transitional provisions (including those relating to the abolition of the OFT and the Competition Commission, existing references to those bodies and provisions relating to continuity), see the Enterprise and Regulatory Reform Act 2013 (Commencement No 6, Transitional Provisions and Savings) Order 2014, SI 2014/416, Schedule at **[2.1126]**.

[1.1278]
26   Powers when conducting investigations
(1)   For the purposes of an investigation . . . , the [CMA] may require any person to produce to [it] a specified document, or to provide [it] with specified information, which [it] considers relates to any matter relevant to the investigation.

(2)   The power conferred by subsection (1) is to be exercised by a notice in writing.

(3)   A notice under subsection (2) must indicate—
(a)   the subject matter and purpose of the investigation; and
(b)   the nature of the offences created by sections [43 and] 44.

(4)   In subsection (1) "specified" means—
(a)   specified, or described, in the notice; or
(b)   falling within a category which is specified, or described, in the notice.

(5)   The [CMA] may also specify in the notice—
(a)   the time and place at which any document is to be produced or any information is to be provided;
(b)   the manner and form in which it is to be produced or provided.

(6)   The power under this section to require a person to produce a document includes power—
(a)   if the document is produced—
(i)   to take copies of it or extracts from it;

(ii)   to require him, or any person who is a present or past officer of his, or is or was at any time employed by him, to provide an explanation of the document;

(b)   if the document is not produced, to require him to state, to the best of his knowledge and belief, where it is.

NOTES

References to "CMA" substituted (for references to "OFT" as substituted by the Enterprise Act 2002, s 278, Sch 25, para 38) by the Enterprise and Regulatory Reform Act 2013, s 26(3), Sch 5, Pt 1, paras 1, 6. For various transitional provisions (including those relating to the abolition of the OFT and the Competition Commission, existing references to those bodies and provisions relating to continuity), see the Enterprise and Regulatory Reform Act 2013 (Commencement No 6, Transitional Provisions and Savings) Order 2014, SI 2014/416, Schedule at **[2.1126]**. This section is also amended as follows:

Section heading substituted (for original words "Powers when conducting investigations"), by the Enterprise and Regulatory Reform Act 2013, s 39(1), (3), subject to transitional provisions in SI 2014/416 as noted above.

Sub-s (1): words omitted repealed by the Competition Act 1998 and other enactments (Amendment) Regulations 2004, SI 2004/1261, reg 4, Sch 1, para 11; words in second, third and fourth pairs of square brackets substituted by the Enterprise Act 2002, s 278, Sch 25, para 38.

Sub-s (3): words in square brackets substituted (for original words "42 to") by the Enterprise and Regulatory Reform Act 2013, s 57, Sch 15, paras 8, 9, subject to transitional provisions in SI 2014/416 as noted above.

References to the CMA, etc: as to the abolition of the office of the Director General of Fair Trading and the substitution of the original references to the Director (and related expressions), see the note preceding s 1 at **[1.1266]**.

[1.1279]
[26A Investigations: power to ask questions
(1) For the purposes of an investigation, the CMA may give notice to an individual who has a connection with a relevant undertaking requiring the individual to answer questions with respect to any matter relevant to the investigation—

(a)   at a place specified in the notice, and

(b)   either at a time so specified or on receipt of the notice.

(2) The CMA must give a copy of the notice under subsection (1) to each relevant undertaking with which the individual has a current connection at the time the notice is given to the individual.

(3) The CMA must take such steps as are reasonable in all the circumstances to comply with the requirement under subsection (2) before the time at which the individual is required to answer questions.

(4) Where the CMA does not comply with the requirement under subsection (2) before the time mentioned in subsection (3), it must comply with that requirement as soon as practicable after that time.

(5) A notice under subsection (1) must be in writing and must indicate—

(a)   the subject matter and purpose of the investigation, and

(b)   the nature of the offence created by section 44.

(6) For the purposes of this section—

(a)   an individual has a connection with an undertaking if he or she is or was—

    (i)   concerned in the management or control of the undertaking, or

    (ii)   employed by, or otherwise working for, the undertaking, and

(b)   an individual has a current connection with an undertaking if, at the time in question, he or she is so concerned, is so employed or is so otherwise working.

(7) In this section, a "relevant undertaking" means an undertaking whose activities are being investigated as part of the investigation in question.]

NOTES

Commencement: 1 April 2014.

Inserted by the Enterprise and Regulatory Reform Act 2013, s 39(1), (2). For various transitional provisions (including those relating to the abolition of the OFT and the Competition Commission, existing references to those bodies and provisions relating to continuity), see the Enterprise and Regulatory Reform Act 2013 (Commencement No 6, Transitional Provisions and Savings) Order 2014, SI 2014/416, Schedule at **[2.1126]**.

[1.1280]
27 [Power to enter business premises without a warrant]
(1) Any officer of the [CMA] who is authorised in writing by the [CMA] to do so ("an investigating officer") may enter [any business premises] in connection with an investigation . . .

(2) No investigating officer is to enter any premises in the exercise of his powers under this section unless he has given to the occupier of the premises a written notice which—

(a)   gives at least two working days' notice of the intended entry;

(b)   indicates the subject matter and purpose of the investigation; and

(c)   indicates the nature of the offences created by sections 42 to 44.

(3) Subsection (2) does not apply—

(a)   if the [CMA] has a reasonable suspicion that the premises are, or have been, occupied by—

    (i)   a party to an agreement which [it] is investigating under [section 25]; or

    (ii)   an undertaking the conduct of which [it] is investigating under [section 25]; or

(b)   if the investigating officer has taken all such steps as are reasonably practicable to give notice but has not been able to do so.

(4) In a case falling within subsection (3), the power of entry conferred by subsection (1) is to be exercised by the investigating officer on production of—

(a) evidence of his authorisation; and

(b) a document containing the information referred to in subsection (2)(b) and (c).

(5) An investigating officer entering any premises under this section may—

(a) take with him such equipment as appears to him to be necessary;

(b) require any person on the premises—

    (i) to produce any document which he considers relates to any matter relevant to the investigation; and

    (ii) if the document is produced, to provide an explanation of it;

(c) require any person to state, to the best of his knowledge and belief, where any such document is to be found;

(d) take copies of, or extracts from, any document which is produced;

(e) require any information which is [stored in any electronic form] and is accessible from the premises and which the investigating officer considers relates to any matter relevant to the investigation, to be produced in a form—

    (i) in which it can be taken away, and

    (ii) in which it is visible and legible [or from which it can readily be produced in a visible and legible form];

[(f) take any steps which appear to be necessary for the purpose of preserving or preventing interference with any document which he considers relates to any matter relevant to the investigation].

[(6) In this section "business premises" means premises (or any part of premises) not used as a dwelling.]

NOTES

References to "CMA" substituted (for references to "OFT" as substituted by the Enterprise Act 2002, s 278, Sch 25, para 38) by the Enterprise and Regulatory Reform Act 2013, s 26(3), Sch 5, Pt 1, paras 1, 7. For various transitional provisions (including those relating to the abolition of the OFT and the Competition Commission, existing references to those bodies and provisions relating to continuity), see the Enterprise and Regulatory Reform Act 2013 (Commencement No 6, Transitional Provisions and Savings) Order 2014, SI 2014/416, Schedule at **[2.1126]**. This section is also amended as follows—

Section heading: substituted by the Competition Act 1998 and Other Enactments (Amendment) Regulations 2004, SI 2004/1261, reg 4, Sch 1, para 12(1), (6).

Sub-s (1): words in final pair of square brackets substituted, and words omitted repealed, by SI 2004/1261, reg 4, Sch 1, para 12(1), (2).

Sub-s (3): words in second and fourth pairs of square brackets substituted by the Enterprise Act 2002, s 278, Sch 25, para 38; words "section 25" in both places that they occur substituted by SI 2004/1261, reg 4, Sch 1, para 12(1), (3).

Sub-s (5): words in first pair of square brackets in para (e) substituted, and words in second pair of square brackets in that paragraph added, by the Criminal Justice and Police Act 2001, s 70, Sch 2, Pt 2, para 21; para (f) added by SI 2004/1261, reg 4, Sch 1, para 12(1), (4).

Sub-s (6): added by SI 2004/1261, reg 4, Sch 1, para 12(1), (5).

References to the CMA, etc: as to the abolition of the office of the Director General of Fair Trading and the substitution of the original references to the Director (and related expressions), see the note preceding s 1 at **[1.1266]**.

[1.1281]

28   [Power to enter business premises under a warrant]

(1) [On an application made to it by the CMA, the court or the Tribunal may issue a warrant if it is satisfied that]—

(a) there are reasonable grounds for suspecting that there are on [any business premises] documents—

    (i) the production of which has been required under section 26 or 27; and

    (ii) which have not been produced as required;

(b) there are reasonable grounds for suspecting that—

    (i) there are on [any business premises] documents which the [CMA] has power under section 26 to require to be produced; and

    (ii) if the documents were required to be produced, they would not be produced but would be concealed, removed, tampered with or destroyed; or

(c) an investigating officer has attempted to enter premises in the exercise of his powers under section 27 but has been unable to do so and that there are reasonable grounds for suspecting that there are on the premises documents the production of which could have been required under that section.

(2) A warrant under this section shall authorise a named officer of the [CMA], and any other of [the [CMA's] officers whom the [CMA]] has authorised in writing to accompany the named officer—

(a) to enter the premises specified in the warrant, using such force as is reasonably necessary for the purpose;

(b) to search the premises and take copies of, or extracts from, any document appearing to be of a kind in respect of which the application under subsection (1) was granted ("the relevant kind");

(c) to take possession of any documents appearing to be of the relevant kind if—

      (i)   such action appears to be necessary for preserving the documents or preventing interference with them; or

      (ii)   it is not reasonably practicable to take copies of the documents on the premises;

(d)   to take any other steps which appear to be necessary for the purpose mentioned in paragraph (c)(i);

(e)   to require any person to provide an explanation of any document appearing to be of the relevant kind or to state, to the best of his knowledge and belief, where it may be found;

(f)   to require any information which is [stored in any electronic form] and is accessible from the premises and which the named officer considers relates to any matter relevant to the investigation, to be produced in a form—

      (i)   in which it can be taken away, and

      (ii)   in which it is visible and legible [or from which it can readily be produced in a visible and legible form].

(3)   If, in the case of a warrant under subsection (1)(b), [the court or (as the case may be) the Tribunal] is satisfied that it is reasonable to suspect that there are also on the premises other documents relating to the investigation concerned, the warrant shall also authorise action mentioned in subsection (2) to be taken in relation to any such document.

[(3A) A warrant under this section may authorise persons specified in the warrant to accompany the named officer who is executing it.]

(4)   Any person entering premises by virtue of a warrant under this section may take with him such equipment as appears to him to be necessary.

(5)   On leaving any premises which he has entered by virtue of a warrant under this section, the named officer must, if the premises are unoccupied or the occupier is temporarily absent, leave them as effectively secured as he found them.

(6)   A warrant under this section continues in force until the end of the period of one month beginning with the day on which it is issued.

(7)   Any document of which possession is taken under subsection (2)(c) may be retained for a period of three months.

[(7A) An application for a warrant under this section must be made—

   (a)   in the case of an application to the court, in accordance with rules of court;

   (b)   in the case of an application to the Tribunal, in accordance with Tribunal rules.]

[(8)   In this section "business premises" has the same meaning as in section 27.]

NOTES

Section heading: substituted by the Competition Act 1998 and Other Enactments (Amendment) Regulations 2004, SI 2004/1261, reg 4, Sch 1, para 13(1), (4).

Sub-s (1) is amended as follows:

Words in first pair of square brackets substituted for words "On an application made by the [OFT] to the court in accordance with rules of court, a judge may issue a warrant if he is satisfied that" by the Enterprise and Regulatory Reform Act 2013, s 41, Sch 13, paras 1, 2(1), (2). For various transitional provisions (including those relating to the abolition of the OFT and the Competition Commission, existing references to those bodies and provisions relating to continuity), see the Enterprise and Regulatory Reform Act 2013 (Commencement No 6, Transitional Provisions and Savings) Order 2014, SI 2014/416, Schedule at [**2.1126**].

Words "any business premises" in square brackets substituted by SI 2004/1261, reg 4, Sch 1, para 13(1), (2)(a).

Reference to "CMA" substituted (for reference to "OFT" as substituted by the Enterprise Act 2002, s 278, Sch 25, para 38) by the Enterprise and Regulatory Reform Act 2013, s 26(3), Sch 5, Pt 1, paras 1, 8(1), (2), subject to transitional provisions in SI 2014/416 as noted above.

Sub-s (2) is amended as follows:

References to "CMA" and "CMA's" substituted (for references to "OFT" and "OFT's" as substituted by the Enterprise Act 2002, s 278, Sch 25, para 38) by the Enterprise and Regulatory Reform Act 2013, s 26(3), Sch 5, Pt 1, paras 1, 8(1), (3), subject to transitional provisions in SI 2014/416 as noted above.

Words in second (outer) pair of square brackets substituted by the Enterprise Act 2002, s 278(1), Sch 25, para 38.

In para (f), words in first and second pairs of square brackets substituted and inserted respectively, by the Criminal Justice and Police Act 2001, s 70, Sch 2, Pt 2, para 21.

Sub-s (3): words in square brackets substituted for original words "the judge" by the Enterprise and Regulatory Reform Act 2013, s 41, Sch 13, paras 1, 2(1), subject to transitional provisions in SI 2014/416 as noted above.

Sub-s (3A): inserted by the Enterprise Act 2002, s 203(1), (2).

Sub-s (7A): inserted by the Enterprise and Regulatory Reform Act 2013, s 41, Sch 13, paras 1, 2(1), (4), subject to transitional provisions in SI 2014/416 as noted above.

Sub-s (8): added by SI 2004/1261, reg 4, Sch 1, para 13(1), (3).

References to the CMA, etc: as to the abolition of the office of the Director General of Fair Trading and the substitution of the original references to the Director (and related expressions), see the note preceding s 1 at [**1.1266**].

The power of seizure conferred by sub-s (2) is a power to which the Criminal Justice and Police Act 2001, s 50 applies (additional powers of seizure from premises); see s 50 of, and Sch 1, Pt 1, para 67 to, that Act. The Criminal Justice and Police Act 2001, ss 54 (obligation to return items subject to legal privilege), 59 (application to appropriate judicial authority), 62 (use of inextricably linked property), also apply to the powers of seizure conferred by sub-s (2) of this section.

[1.1282]

[28A Power to enter domestic premises under a warrant

(1)   [On an application made to it by the CMA, the court or the Tribunal may issue a warrant if it is satisfied that]—

(a) there are reasonable grounds for suspecting that there are on any domestic premises documents—
  (i) the production of which has been required under section 26; and
  (ii) which have not been produced as required; or
(b) there are reasonable grounds for suspecting that—
  (i) there are on any domestic premises documents which the [CMA] has power under section 26 to require to be produced; and
  (ii) if the documents were required to be produced, they would not be produced but would be concealed, removed, tampered with or destroyed.

(2) A warrant under this section shall authorise a named officer of the [CMA], and any other of its officers whom the [CMA] has authorised in writing to accompany the named officer—
(a) to enter the premises specified in the warrant, using such force as is reasonably necessary for the purpose;
(b) to search the premises and take copies of, or extracts from, any document appearing to be of a kind in respect of which the application under subsection (1) was granted ("the relevant kind");
(c) to take possession of any documents appearing to be of the relevant kind if—
  (i) such action appears to be necessary for preserving the documents or preventing interference with them; or
  (ii) it is not reasonably practicable to take copies of the documents on the premises;
(d) to take any other steps which appear to be necessary for the purpose mentioned in paragraph (c)(i);
(e) to require any person to provide an explanation of any document appearing to be of the relevant kind or to state, to the best of his knowledge and belief, where it may be found;
(f) to require any information which is stored in any electronic form and is accessible from the premises and which the named officer considers relates to any matter relevant to the investigation, to be produced in a form—
  (i) in which it can be taken away, and
  (ii) in which it is visible and legible or from which it can readily be produced in a visible and legible form.

(3) If, in the case of a warrant under subsection (1)(b), [the court or (as the case may be) the Tribunal] is satisfied that it is reasonable to suspect that there are also on the premises other documents relating to the investigation concerned, the warrant shall also authorise action mentioned in subsection (2) to be taken in relation to any such document.

(4) A warrant under this section may authorise persons specified in the warrant to accompany the named officer who is executing it.

(5) Any person entering premises by virtue of a warrant under this section may take with him such equipment as appears to him to be necessary.

(6) On leaving any premises which he has entered by virtue of a warrant under this section, the named officer must, if the premises are unoccupied or the occupier is temporarily absent, leave them as effectively secured as he found them.

(7) A warrant under this section continues in force until the end of the period of one month beginning with the day on which it is issued.

(8) Any document of which possession is taken under subsection (2)(c) may be retained for a period of three months.

[(8A) An application for a warrant under this section must be made—
(a) in the case of an application to the court, in accordance with rules of court;
(b) in the case of an application to the Tribunal, in accordance with Tribunal rules.]

(9) In this section, "domestic premises" means premises (or any part of premises) that are used as a dwelling and are—
(a) premises also used in connection with the affairs of an undertaking or association of undertakings; or
(b) premises where documents relating to the affairs of an undertaking or association of undertakings are kept.]

NOTES

Inserted by the Competition Act 1998 and Other Enactments (Amendment) Regulations 2004, SI 2004/1261, reg 4, Sch 1, para 14.

Sub-s (1): words in square brackets substituted for original words "On an application made by the OFT to the court in accordance with rules of court, a judge may issue a warrant if he is satisfied that" and "OFT" respectively, by the Enterprise and Regulatory Reform Act 2013, ss 26(3), 41, Sch 5, Pt 1, paras 1, 9, Sch 13, paras 1, 3(1), (4). For various transitional provisions (including those relating to the abolition of the OFT and the Competition Commission, existing references to those bodies and provisions relating to continuity), see the Enterprise and Regulatory Reform Act 2013 (Commencement No 6, Transitional Provisions and Savings) Order 2014, SI 2014/416, Schedule at **[2.1126]**.

Sub-s (2): references to "CMA" substituted (for original references to "OFT") by the Enterprise and Regulatory Reform Act 2013, s 26(3), Sch 5, Pt 1, paras 1, 9, subject to transitional provisions in SI 2014/416 as noted above.

Sub-s (3): words in square brackets substituted for original words "the judge" by the Enterprise and Regulatory Reform Act 2013, s 41, Sch 13, paras 1, 3(1), (3), subject to transitional provisions in SI 2014/416 as noted above.

Sub-s (8A): inserted by the Enterprise and Regulatory Reform Act 2013, s 41, Sch 13, paras 1, 3(1), (4), subject to transitional provisions in SI 2014/416 as noted above.

[1.1283]
29 Entry of premises under warrant: supplementary

(1)   A warrant issued under section 28 [or 28A] must indicate—
   (a)   the subject matter and purpose of the investigation;
   (b)   the nature of the offences created by sections 42 to 44.

(2)   The powers conferred by section 28 [or 28A] are to be exercised on production of a warrant issued under that section.

(3)   If there is no one at the premises when the named officer proposes to execute such a warrant he must, before executing it—
   (a)   take such steps as are reasonable in all the circumstances to inform the occupier of the intended entry; and
   (b)   if the occupier is informed, afford him or his legal or other representative a reasonable opportunity to be present when the warrant is executed.

(4)   If the named officer is unable to inform the occupier of the intended entry he must, when executing the warrant, leave a copy of it in a prominent place on the premises.

(5)   In this section—
"named officer" means the officer named in the warrant; and
"occupier", in relation to any premises, means a person whom the named officer reasonably
     believes is the occupier of those premises.

NOTES
  Sub-ss (1), (2): words in square brackets inserted by the Competition Act 1998 and Other Enactments (Amendment) Regulations 2004, SI 2004/1261, reg 4, Sch 1, para 15.

[1.1284]
30 Privileged communications

(1)   A person shall not be required, under any provision of this Part, to produce or disclose a privileged communication.

(2)   "Privileged communication" means a communication—
   (a)   between a professional legal adviser and his client, or
   (b)   made in connection with, or in contemplation of, legal proceedings and for the purposes of those proceedings,
which in proceedings in the High Court would be protected from disclosure on grounds of legal professional privilege.

(3)   In the application of this section to Scotland—
   (a)   references to the High Court are to be read as references to the Court of Session; and
   (b)   the reference to legal professional privilege is to be read as a reference to confidentiality of communications.

[1.1285]
[30A Use of statements in prosecution

[(1)]   A statement made by a person in response to a requirement imposed by virtue of any of sections [26 and 27 to 28A] may not be used in evidence against him on a prosecution for an offence under section 188 of the Enterprise Act 2002 unless, in the proceedings—
   (a)   in giving evidence, he makes a statement inconsistent with it, and
   (b)   evidence relating to it is adduced, or a question relating to it is asked, by him or on his behalf.

[(2)   A statement by an individual in response to a requirement imposed by virtue of section 26A (a "section 26A statement") may only be used in evidence against the individual—
   (a)   on a prosecution for an offence under section 44, or
   (b)   on a prosecution for some other offence in a case falling within subsection (3).

(3)   A prosecution falls within this subsection if, in the proceedings—
   (a)   in giving evidence, the individual makes a statement inconsistent with the section 26A statement, and
   (b)   evidence relating to the section 26A statement is adduced, or a question relating to it is asked, by or on behalf of the individual.

(4)   A section 26A statement may not be used in evidence against an undertaking with which the individual who gave the statement has a connection on a prosecution for an offence unless the prosecution is for an offence under section 44.

(5)   For the purposes of subsection (4), an individual has a connection with an undertaking if he or she is or was—
   (a)   concerned in the management or control of the undertaking, or
   (b)   employed by, or otherwise working for, the undertaking.]]

NOTES
  Inserted by the Enterprise Act 2002, s 198.
  Sub-s (1) numbered as such, and sub-ss (2)–(5) added, by the Enterprise and Regulatory Reform Act 2013, s 39(1), (4), (5), (7). For various transitional provisions (including those relating to the abolition of the OFT and the Competition Commission, existing references to those bodies and provisions relating to continuity), see the Enterprise and Regulatory Reform Act 2013 (Commencement No 6, Transitional Provisions and Savings) Order 2014, SI 2014/416, Schedule at **[2.1126]**.

Words in square brackets in sub-s (1) substituted (for words "26 [to 28A]" (as amended by the Competition Act 1998 and Other Enactments (Amendment) Regulations 2004, SI 2004/1261, reg 4, Sch 1, para 16)) by the Enterprise and Regulatory Reform Act 2013, s 39(1), (4), (6), subject to transitional provisions in SI 2014/416 as noted above.

[1.1286]
[31   Decisions following an investigation
(1)   If as a result of an investigation the [CMA] proposes to make a decision, the [CMA] must—
   (a)   give written notice to the person (or persons) likely to be affected by the proposed decision; and
   (b)   give that person (or those persons) an opportunity to make representations.
(2)   For the purposes of this section and sections 31A and 31B "decision" means a decision of the [CMA]—
   (a)   that the Chapter I prohibition has been infringed;
   (b)   that the Chapter II prohibition has been infringed;
   (c)   that the prohibition in [Article 101(1)] has been infringed; or
   (d)   that the prohibition in [Article 102] has been infringed.]

NOTES
Substituted by the Competition Act 1998 and Other Enactments (Amendment) Regulations 2004, SI 2004/1261, reg 4, Sch 1, para 17.
References to the "CMA" substituted (for original references to the "OFT") by the Enterprise and Regulatory Reform Act 2013, s 26(3), Sch 5, Pt 1, paras 1, 10. For various transitional provisions (including those relating to the abolition of the OFT and the Competition Commission, existing references to those bodies and provisions relating to continuity), see the Enterprise and Regulatory Reform Act 2013 (Commencement No 6, Transitional Provisions and Savings) Order 2014, SI 2014/416, Schedule at **[2.1126]**.
The words in square brackets in sub-s (2)(c), (d) were substituted by the Treaty of Lisbon (Changes in Terminology or Numbering) Order 2012, SI 2012/1809, art 3(1), Schedule, Pt 1 (note that the amendments made by this Order do not affect any provision in its application to things done before 1 December 2009 (the date on which the Treaty of Lisbon came into force)).

[1.1287]
[31A   Commitments
(1)   Subsection (2) applies in a case where the [CMA] has begun an investigation under section 25 but has not made a decision (within the meaning given by section 31(2)).
(2)   For the purposes of addressing the competition concerns it has identified, the [CMA] may accept from such person (or persons) concerned as it considers appropriate commitments to take such action (or refrain from taking such action) as it considers appropriate.
(3)   At any time when commitments are in force the [CMA] may accept from the person (or persons) who gave the commitments—
   (a)   a variation of them if it is satisfied that the commitments as varied will address its current competition concerns;
   (b)   commitments in substitution for them if it is satisfied that the new commitments will address its current competition concerns.
(4)   Commitments under this section—
   (a)   shall come into force when accepted; and
   (b)   may be released by the [CMA] where—
      (i)   it is requested to do so by the person (or persons) who gave the commitments; or
      (ii)   it has reasonable grounds for believing that the competition concerns referred to in subsection (2) or (3) no longer arise.
(5)   The provisions of Schedule 6A to this Act shall have effect with respect to procedural requirements for the acceptance, variation and release of commitments under this section.]

NOTES
Inserted, together with ss 31B–31E, by the Competition Act 1998 and Other Enactments (Amendment) Regulations 2004, SI 2004/1261, reg 4, Sch 1, para 18.
References to the "CMA" substituted (for original references to the "OFT") by the Enterprise and Regulatory Reform Act 2013, s 26(3), Sch 5, Pt 1, paras 1, 11. For various transitional provisions (including those relating to the abolition of the OFT and the Competition Commission, existing references to those bodies and provisions relating to continuity), see the Enterprise and Regulatory Reform Act 2013 (Commencement No 6, Transitional Provisions and Savings) Order 2014, SI 2014/416, Schedule at **[2.1126]**.

[1.1288]
[31B   Effect of commitments under section 31A
(1)   Subsection (2) applies if the [CMA] has accepted commitments under section 31A (and has not released them).
(2)   In such a case, the [CMA] shall not—
   (a)   continue the investigation,
   (b)   make a decision (within the meaning of section 31(2)), or
   (c)   give a direction under section 35,
in relation to the agreement or conduct which was the subject of the investigation (but this subsection is subject to subsections (3) and (4)).

(3) Nothing in subsection (2) prevents the [CMA] from taking any action in relation to competition concerns which are not addressed by commitments accepted by it.

(4) Subsection (2) also does not prevent the [CMA] from continuing the investigation, making a decision, or giving a direction where—

(a) it has reasonable grounds for believing that there has been a material change of circumstances since the commitments were accepted;

(b) it has reasonable grounds for suspecting that a person has failed to adhere to one or more of the terms of the commitments; or

(c) it has reasonable grounds for suspecting that information which led it to accept the commitments was incomplete, false or misleading in a material particular.

(5) If, pursuant to subsection (4), the [CMA] makes a decision or gives a direction the commitments are to be treated as released from the date of that decision or direction.]

NOTES

Inserted as noted to s 31A at **[1.1287]**.

References to the "CMA" substituted (for original references to the "OFT") by the Enterprise and Regulatory Reform Act 2013, s 26(3), Sch 5, Pt 1, paras 1, 12. For various transitional provisions (including those relating to the abolition of the OFT and the Competition Commission, existing references to those bodies and provisions relating to continuity), see the Enterprise and Regulatory Reform Act 2013 (Commencement No 6, Transitional Provisions and Savings) Order 2014, SI 2014/416, Schedule at **[2.1126]**.

[1.1289]
[31C Review of commitments

(1) Where the [CMA] is reviewing or has reviewed the effectiveness of commitments accepted under section 31A it must, if requested to do so by the Secretary of State, prepare a report of its findings.

(2) The [CMA] must—

(a) give any report prepared by it under subsection (1) to the Secretary of State; and

(b) publish the report.]

NOTES

Inserted as noted to s 31A at **[1.1287]**.

References to the "CMA" substituted (for original references to the "OFT") by the Enterprise and Regulatory Reform Act 2013, s 26(3), Sch 5, Pt 1, paras 1, 13. For various transitional provisions (including those relating to the abolition of the OFT and the Competition Commission, existing references to those bodies and provisions relating to continuity), see the Enterprise and Regulatory Reform Act 2013 (Commencement No 6, Transitional Provisions and Savings) Order 2014, SI 2014/416, Schedule at **[2.1126]**.

[1.1290]
[31D Guidance

(1) The [CMA] must prepare and publish guidance as to the circumstances in which it may be appropriate to accept commitments under section 31A.

(2) The [CMA] may at any time alter the guidance.

(3) If the guidance is altered, the [CMA] must publish it as altered.

(4) No guidance is to be published under this section without the approval of the Secretary of State.

(5) The [CMA] may, after consulting the Secretary of State, choose how it publishes its guidance.

(6) If the [CMA] is preparing or altering guidance under this section it must consult such persons as it considers appropriate.

(7) If the proposed guidance or alteration relates to a matter in respect of which a regulator exercises concurrent jurisdiction, those consulted must include that regulator.

(8) When exercising its discretion to accept commitments under section 31A, the [CMA] must have regard to the guidance for the time being in force under this section.]

NOTES

Inserted as noted to s 31A at **[1.1287]**.

References to the "CMA" substituted (for original references to the "OFT") by the Enterprise and Regulatory Reform Act 2013, s 26(3), Sch 5, Pt 1, paras 1, 14. For various transitional provisions (including those relating to the abolition of the OFT and the Competition Commission, existing references to those bodies and provisions relating to continuity), see the Enterprise and Regulatory Reform Act 2013 (Commencement No 6, Transitional Provisions and Savings) Order 2014, SI 2014/416, Schedule at **[2.1126]**.

[1.1291]
[31E Enforcement of commitments

(1) If a person from whom the [CMA] has accepted commitments fails without reasonable excuse to adhere to the commitments (and has not been released from them), the [CMA] may apply to the court for an order—

(a) requiring the defaulter to make good his default within a time specified in the order; or

(b) if the commitments relate to anything to be done in the management or administration of an undertaking, requiring the undertaking or any of its officers to do it.

(2)   An order of the court under subsection (1) may provide for all the costs of, or incidental to, the application for the order to be borne by—
(a)   the person in default; or
(b)   any officer of an undertaking who is responsible for the default.
(3)   In the application of subsection (2) to Scotland, the reference to "costs" is to be read as a reference to "expenses".]

NOTES
Inserted as noted to s 31A at **[1.1287]**.
Sub-s (1): references to the "CMA" substituted (for original references to the "OFT") by the Enterprise and Regulatory Reform Act 2013, s 26(3), Sch 5, Pt 1, paras 1, 15. For various transitional provisions (including those relating to the abolition of the OFT and the Competition Commission, existing references to those bodies and provisions relating to continuity), see the Enterprise and Regulatory Reform Act 2013 (Commencement No 6, Transitional Provisions and Savings) Order 2014, SI 2014/416, Schedule at **[2.1126]**.

[1.1292]
[31F   Power for Secretary of State to impose time-limits on investigations etc
(1)   The Secretary of State may by order impose time-limits in relation to—
(a)   the conduct by the CMA of investigations or investigations of a description specified in the order;
(b)   the making by the CMA of decisions (within the meaning given by section 31(2)) as a result of investigations or investigations of such a description.
(2)   Before making an order under subsection (1), the Secretary of State must consult the CMA and such other persons as the Secretary of State considers appropriate.]

NOTES
Commencement: 25 April 2013.
Inserted by the Enterprise and Regulatory Reform Act 2013, s 45.

Enforcement
[1.1293]
32   Directions in relation to agreements
(1)   If the [CMA] has made a decision that an agreement infringes the Chapter I prohibition [or that it infringes the prohibition in [Article 101(1)]], [it] may give to such person or persons as [it] considers appropriate such directions as [it] considers appropriate to bring the infringement to an end.
(2)   . . .
(3)   A direction under this section may, in particular, include provision—
(a)   requiring the parties to the agreement to modify the agreement; or
(b)   requiring them to terminate the agreement.
(4)   A direction under this section must be given in writing.

NOTES
Sub-s (1): reference in first pair of square brackets substituted (for reference to "OFT" as substituted by the Enterprise Act 2002, s 278, Sch 25, para 38) by the Enterprise and Regulatory Reform Act 2013, s 26(3), Sch 5, Pt 1, paras 1, 16. For various transitional provisions (including those relating to the abolition of the OFT and the Competition Commission, existing references to those bodies and provisions relating to continuity), see the Enterprise and Regulatory Reform Act 2013 (Commencement No 6, Transitional Provisions and Savings) Order 2014, SI 2014/416, Schedule at **[2.1126]**; words in second (outer) pair of square brackets inserted by the Competition Act 1998 and Other Enactments (Amendment) Regulations 2004, SI 2004/1261, reg 4, Sch 1, para 19(1), (2); words in third (inner) pair of square brackets substituted by the Treaty of Lisbon (Changes in Terminology or Numbering) Order 2012, SI 2012/1809, art 3(1), Schedule, Pt 1 (note that the amendments made by this Order do not affect any provision in its application to things done before 1 December 2009 (the date on which the Treaty of Lisbon came into force)); word "it" in square brackets (in each place that it occurs) substituted by the Enterprise Act 2002, s 278, Sch 25, para 38.
Sub-s (2): repealed by SI 2004/1261, reg 4, Sch 1, para 19(1), (3).
References to the CMA, etc: as to the abolition of the office of the Director General of Fair Trading and the substitution of the original references to the Director (and related expressions), see the note preceding s 1 at **[1.1266]**.

[1.1294]
33   Directions in relation to conduct
(1)   If the [CMA] has made a decision that conduct infringes the Chapter II prohibition [or that it infringes the prohibition in [Article 102]], [it] may give to such person or persons as [it] considers appropriate such directions as [it] considers appropriate to bring the infringement to an end.
(2)   . . .
(3)   A direction under this section may, in particular, include provision—
(a)   requiring the person concerned to modify the conduct in question; or
(b)   requiring him to cease that conduct.
(4)   A direction under this section must be given in writing.

NOTES
Sub-s (1): reference in first pair of square brackets substituted (for reference to "OFT" as substituted by the Enterprise Act 2002, s 278, Sch 25, para 38) by the Enterprise and Regulatory Reform Act 2013, s 26(3), Sch 5, Pt 1, paras 1, 17. For

various transitional provisions (including those relating to the abolition of the OFT and the Competition Commission, existing references to those bodies and provisions relating to continuity), see the Enterprise and Regulatory Reform Act 2013 (Commencement No 6, Transitional Provisions and Savings) Order 2014, SI 2014/416, Schedule at [**2.1126**]; words in second (outer) pair of square brackets inserted by the Competition Act 1998 and Other Enactments (Amendment) Regulations 2004, SI 2004/1261, reg 4, Sch 1, para 20(1), (2); words in third (inner) pair of square brackets substituted by the Treaty of Lisbon (Changes in Terminology or Numbering) Order 2012, SI 2012/1809, art 3(1), Schedule, Pt 1 (note that the amendments made by this Order do not affect any provision in its application to things done before 1 December 2009 (the date on which the Treaty of Lisbon came into force)); word "it" in square brackets (in each place that it occurs) substituted by the Enterprise Act 2002, s 278, Sch 25, para 38.

Sub-s (2): repealed by SI 2004/1261, reg 4, Sch 1, para 20(1), (3).

References to the CMA, etc: as to the abolition of the office of the Director General of Fair Trading and the substitution of the original references to the Director (and related expressions), see the note preceding s 1 at [**1.1266**].

[1.1295]
34 Enforcement of directions

(1)   If a person fails, without reasonable excuse, to comply with a direction under section 32 or 33, the [CMA] may apply to the court for an order—
  (a)   requiring the defaulter to make good his default within a time specified in the order; or
  (b)   if the direction related to anything to be done in the management or administration of an undertaking, requiring the undertaking or any of its officers to do it.

(2)   An order of the court under subsection (1) may provide for all of the costs of, or incidental to, the application for the order to be borne by—
  (a)   the person in default; or
  (b)   any officer of an undertaking who is responsible for the default.

(3)   In the application of subsection (2) to Scotland, the reference to "costs" is to be read as a reference to "expenses".

NOTES

Reference to "CMA" substituted (for reference to "OFT" as substituted by the Enterprise Act 2002, s 278, Sch 25, para 38) by the Enterprise and Regulatory Reform Act 2013, s 26(3), Sch 5, Pt 1, paras 1, 18. For various transitional provisions (including those relating to the abolition of the OFT and the Competition Commission, existing references to those bodies and provisions relating to continuity), see the Enterprise and Regulatory Reform Act 2013 (Commencement No 6, Transitional Provisions and Savings) Order 2014, SI 2014/416, Schedule at [**2.1126**].

References to the CMA, etc: as to the abolition of the office of the Director General of Fair Trading and the substitution of the original references to the Director (and related expressions), see the note preceding s 1 at [**1.1266**].

[1.1296]
35 Interim measures

[(1)   Subject to subsections (8) and (9), this section applies if the [CMA] has begun an investigation under section 25 and not completed it (but only applies so long as the [CMA] has power under section 25 to conduct that investigation).]

(2)   If the [CMA] considers that it is necessary for [it] to act under this section as a matter of urgency for the purpose—
  (a)   of preventing [significant damage] to a particular person or category of person, or
  (b)   of protecting the public interest,
[it] may give such directions as [it] considers appropriate for that purpose.

(3)   Before giving a direction under this section, the [CMA] must—
  (a)   give written notice to the person (or persons) to whom [it] proposes to give the direction; and
  (b)   give that person (or each of them) an opportunity to make representations.

(4)   A notice under subsection (3) must indicate the nature of the direction which the [CMA] is proposing to give and [its] reasons for wishing to give it.

[(5)   A direction given under this section may if the circumstances permit be replaced by—
  (a)   a direction under section 32 or (as appropriate) section 33, or
  (b)   commitments accepted under section 31A,
but, subject to that, has effect while this section applies.]

(6)   In the [cases mentioned in section 25(2), (3), (6) and (7)], sections 32(3) and 34 also apply to directions given under this section.

(7)   In the [cases mentioned in section 25(4) and (5)], sections 33(3) and 34 also apply to directions given under this section.

[(8)   In the case of an investigation conducted by virtue of section 25(2) or (6), this section does not apply if a person has produced evidence to the [CMA] in connection with the investigation that satisfies it on the balance of probabilities that, in the event of it reaching the basic infringement conclusion, it would also reach the conclusion that the suspected agreement is exempt from the Chapter I prohibition as a result of section 9(1); and in this subsection "the basic infringement conclusion" is the conclusion that there is an agreement which—
  (a)   may affect trade within the United Kingdom, and
  (b)   has as its object or effect the prevention, restriction or distortion of competition within the United Kingdom.

(9)   In the case of an investigation conducted by virtue of section 25(3) or (7), this section does not apply if a person has produced evidence to the [CMA] in connection with the investigation that satisfies it on the balance of probabilities that, in the event of it reaching the basic infringement conclusion, it would also reach the conclusion that the suspected agreement is an agreement to which the prohibition in [Article 101(1)] is inapplicable because the agreement satisfies the conditions in [Article 101(3)]; and in this subsection "the basic infringement conclusion" is the conclusion that there is an agreement which—

(a)   may affect trade between Member States, and

(b)   has as its object or effect the prevention, restriction or distortion of competition within the Community.]

NOTES

References to the "CMA" substituted (for original references to the "OFT") by the Enterprise and Regulatory Reform Act 2013, s 26(3), Sch 5, Pt 1, paras 1, 19. For various transitional provisions (including those relating to the abolition of the OFT and the Competition Commission, existing references to those bodies and provisions relating to continuity), see the Enterprise and Regulatory Reform Act 2013 (Commencement No 6, Transitional Provisions and Savings) Order 2014, SI 2014/416, Schedule at **[2.1126]**. This section is also amended as follows:

Sub-ss (1), (5): substituted by the Competition Act 1998 and Other Enactments (Amendment) Regulations 2004, SI 2004/1261, reg 4, Sch 1, para 21(1)–(3).

Sub-s (2): word "it" in square brackets (in each place that it occurs) substituted by the Enterprise Act 2002, s 278, Sch 25, para 38; words in square brackets in para (a) substituted (for original words "serious, irreparable damage") by the Enterprise and Regulatory Reform Act 2013, s 43, subject to transitional provisions in SI 2014/416 as noted above.

Sub-ss (3), (4): word in second pair of square brackets substituted by the Enterprise Act 2002, s 278, Sch 25, para 38.

Sub-ss (6), (7): words in square brackets substituted by SI 2004/1261, reg 4, Sch 1, para 21(1), (4), (5).

Sub-ss (8), (9): added by SI 2004/1261, reg 4, Sch 1, para 21(1), (6); words in square brackets in sub-s (9) substituted by the Treaty of Lisbon (Changes in Terminology or Numbering) Order 2012, SI 2012/1809, art 3(1), Schedule, Pt 1 (note that the amendments made by this Order do not affect any provision in its application to things done before 1 December 2009 (the date on which the Treaty of Lisbon came into force)).

References to the CMA, etc: as to the abolition of the office of the Director General of Fair Trading and the substitution of the original references to the Director (and related expressions), see the note preceding s 1 at **[1.1266]**.

[1.1297]
36   [Penalties]

(1)   On making a decision that an agreement has infringed the Chapter I prohibition [or that it has infringed the prohibition in [Article 101(1)]], the [CMA] may require an undertaking which is a party to the agreement to pay [the [CMA]] a penalty in respect of the infringement.

(2)   On making a decision that conduct has infringed the Chapter II prohibition [or that it has infringed the prohibition in [Article 102]], the [CMA] may require the undertaking concerned to pay [the [CMA]] a penalty in respect of the infringement.

(3)   The [CMA] may impose a penalty on an undertaking under subsection (1) or (2) only if [the [CMA]] is satisfied that the infringement has been committed intentionally or negligently by the undertaking.

(4)   Subsection (1) is subject to section 39 and does not apply [in relation to a decision that an agreement has infringed the Chapter I prohibition] if the [CMA] is satisfied that the undertaking acted on the reasonable assumption that that section gave it immunity in respect of the agreement.

(5)   Subsection (2) is subject to section 40 and does not apply [in relation to a decision that conduct has infringed the Chapter II prohibition] if the [CMA] is satisfied that the undertaking acted on the reasonable assumption that that section gave it immunity in respect of the conduct.

(6)   Notice of a penalty under this section must—

(a)   be in writing; and

(b)   specify the date before which the penalty is required to be paid.

(7)   The date specified must not be earlier than the end of the period within which an appeal against the notice may be brought under section 46.

[(7A)   In fixing a penalty under this section the CMA must have regard to—

(a)   the seriousness of the infringement concerned, and

(b)   the desirability of deterring both the undertaking on whom the penalty is imposed and others from—

(i)   entering into agreements which infringe the Chapter 1 prohibition or the prohibition in Article 81(1), or

(ii)   engaging in conduct which infringes the Chapter 2 prohibition or the prohibition in Article 82.]

(8)   No penalty fixed by the [CMA] under this section may exceed 10% of the turnover of the undertaking (determined in accordance with such provisions as may be specified in an order made by the Secretary of State).

(9)   Any sums received by the [CMA] under this section are to be paid into the Consolidated Fund.

NOTES

Section heading: substituted by the Competition Act 1998 and Other Enactments (Amendment) Regulations 2004, SI 2004/1261, reg 4, Sch 1, para 22(1), (6).

References to "CMA" substituted (for references to "OFT" as previously substituted, together with references to "the OFT" by the Enterprise Act 2002, s 278, Sch 25, para 38) by the Enterprise and Regulatory Reform Act 2013, s 26(3), Sch 5, Pt 1, paras 1, 20. For various transitional provisions (including those relating to the abolition of the OFT and the Competition Commission, existing references to those bodies and provisions relating to continuity), see the Enterprise and Regulatory Reform Act 2013 (Commencement No 6, Transitional Provisions and Savings) Order 2014, SI 2014/416, Schedule at [2.1126]. This section is also amended as follows:

Sub-ss (1), (2): words in first (outer) pair of square brackets inserted by SI 2004/1261, reg 4, Sch 1, para 22(1)–(3); words in second (inner) pair of square brackets substituted by the Treaty of Lisbon (Changes in Terminology or Numbering) Order 2012, SI 2012/1809, art 3(1), Schedule, Pt 1 (note that the amendments made by this Order do not affect any provision in its application to things done before 1 December 2009 (the date on which the Treaty of Lisbon came into force)).

Sub-ss (4), (5): words in first pair of square brackets inserted by SI 2004/1261, reg 4, Sch 1, para 22(1), (4), (5).

Sub-s (7A): inserted by the Enterprise and Regulatory Reform Act 2013, s 44(1), (2), subject to transitional provisions in SI 2014/416 as noted above. It is assumed that the references to Articles 81 and 82 should be references as Articles 101 and 102.

References to the CMA, etc: as to the abolition of the office of the Director General of Fair Trading and the substitution of the original references to the Director (and related expressions), see the note preceding s 1 at [1.1266].

Orders: the Competition Act 1998 (Determination of Turnover for Penalties) Order 2000, SI 2000/309 at [2.38]; the Competition Act 1998 (Determination of Turnover for Penalties) (Amendment) Order 2004, SI 2004/1259.

[1.1298]
37 Recovery of penalties

(1) If the specified date in a penalty notice has passed and—
  (a) the period during which an appeal against the imposition, or amount, of the penalty may be made has expired without an appeal having been made, or
  (b) such an appeal has been made and determined,

the [CMA] may recover from the undertaking, as a civil debt due to [the [CMA]], any amount payable under the penalty notice which remains outstanding.

(2) In this section—
  "penalty notice" means a notice given under section 36; and "specified date" means the date specified in the penalty notice.

NOTES

Sub-s (1): references to "CMA" substituted (for references to "OFT" as previously substituted, together with reference to "the OFT" by the Enterprise Act 2002, s 278, Sch 25, para 38) by the Enterprise and Regulatory Reform Act 2013, s 26(3), Sch 5, Pt 1, paras 1, 21. For various transitional provisions (including those relating to the abolition of the OFT and the Competition Commission, existing references to those bodies and provisions relating to continuity), see the Enterprise and Regulatory Reform Act 2013 (Commencement No 6, Transitional Provisions and Savings) Order 2014, SI 2014/416, Schedule at [2.1126].

References to the CMA, etc: as to the abolition of the office of the Director General of Fair Trading and the substitution of the original references to the Director (and related expressions), see the note preceding s 1 at [1.1266].

[1.1299]
38 The appropriate level of a penalty

(1) The [CMA] must prepare and publish guidance as to the appropriate amount of any penalty under this Part [in respect of an infringement of the Chapter 1 prohibition, the Chapter 2 prohibition, the prohibition in Article 81(1) or the prohibition in Article 82].

[(1A) The guidance must include provision about the circumstances in which, in determining [such a penalty], the [CMA] may take into account effects in another Member State of the agreement or conduct concerned.]

(2) The [CMA] may at any time alter the guidance.

(3) If the guidance is altered, the [CMA] must publish it as altered.

(4) No guidance is to be published under this section without the approval of the Secretary of State.

(5) The [CMA] may, after consulting the Secretary of State, choose how [it] publishes [its] guidance.

(6) If the [CMA] is preparing or altering guidance under this section [it] must consult such persons as [it] considers appropriate.

(7) If the proposed guidance or alteration relates to a matter in respect of which a regulator exercises concurrent jurisdiction, those consulted must include that regulator.

(8) When setting the amount of a penalty under this Part [in respect of an infringement of a kind mentioned in subsection (1)], the [CMA] [and the Tribunal] must have regard to the guidance for the time being in force under this section.

(9) If a penalty or a fine has been imposed by the Commission, or by a court or other body in another Member State, in respect of an agreement or conduct, the [CMA], [the Tribunal] or the appropriate court must take that penalty or fine into account when setting the amount of a penalty under this Part in relation to that agreement or conduct.

(10) In subsection (9) "the appropriate court" means—
  (a) in relation to England and Wales, the Court of Appeal;
  (b) in relation to Scotland, the Court of Session;
  (c) in relation to Northern Ireland, the Court of Appeal in Northern Ireland;
  [(d) the Supreme Court.]

NOTES

References to "CMA" substituted (for references to "OFT" as substituted by the Enterprise Act 2002, s 278, Sch 25, para 38) by the Enterprise and Regulatory Reform Act 2013, s 26(3), Sch 5, Pt 1, paras 1, 22. For various transitional provisions (including those relating to the abolition of the OFT and the Competition Commission, existing references to those bodies and provisions relating to continuity), see the Enterprise and Regulatory Reform Act 2013 (Commencement No 6, Transitional Provisions and Savings) Order 2014, SI 2014/416, Schedule at **[2.1126]**. This section is also amended as follows:

Sub-s (1): words in second pair of square brackets inserted by the Enterprise and Regulatory Reform Act 2013, s 40(1), (3), (4), subject to transitional provisions in SI 2014/416 as noted above (it is assumed that the references to Articles 81 and 82 should be references as Articles 101 and 102).

Sub-s (1A): inserted by the Competition Act 1998 and Other Enactments (Amendment) Regulations 2004, SI 2004/1261, reg 4, Sch 1, para 23; words in first pair of square brackets substituted (for original words "a penalty under this Part") by the Enterprise and Regulatory Reform Act 2013, s 40(1), (3), (5), subject to transitional provisions in SI 2014/416 as noted above.

Sub-ss (5), (6): words in second and third pairs of square brackets substituted by the Enterprise Act 2002, s 278, Sch 25, para 38.

Sub-s (8): words in first and third pairs of square brackets inserted by the Enterprise and Regulatory Reform Act 2013, ss 40(1), (3), (6), 44(1), (3), subject to transitional provisions in SI 2014/416 as noted above.

Sub-s (9): words in second pair of square brackets substituted (for original words "an appeal tribunal") by the Enterprise and Regulatory Reform Act 2013, s 57, Sch 15, paras 8, 10, subject to transitional provisions in SI 2014/416 as noted above.

Sub-s (10): para (d) substituted by the Constitutional Reform Act 2005, s 40(4), Sch 9, Pt 1, para 65(1), (2).

References to the CMA, etc: as to the abolition of the office of the Director General of Fair Trading and the substitution of the original references to the Director (and related expressions), see the note preceding s 1 at **[1.1266]**.

[1.1300]

39 [Limited immunity in relation to the Chapter I prohibition]

(1) In this section "small agreement" means an agreement—

   (a) which falls within a category prescribed for the purposes of this section; but

   (b) is not a price fixing agreement.

(2) The criteria by reference to which a category of agreement is prescribed may, in particular, include—

   (a) the combined turnover of the parties to the agreement (determined in accordance with prescribed provisions);

   (b) the share of the market affected by the agreement (determined in that way).

(3) A party to a small agreement is immune from the effect of section 36(1) [so far as that provision relates to decisions about infringement of the Chapter I prohibition]; but the [CMA] may withdraw that immunity under subsection (4).

(4) If the [CMA] has investigated a small agreement, [it] may make a decision withdrawing the immunity given by subsection (3) if, as a result of [its] investigation, [it] considers that the agreement is likely to infringe the Chapter I prohibition.

(5) The [CMA] must give each of the parties in respect of which immunity is withdrawn written notice of [its] decision to withdraw the immunity.

(6) A decision under subsection (4) takes effect on such date ("the withdrawal date") as may be specified in the decision.

(7) The withdrawal date must be a date after the date on which the decision is made.

(8) In determining the withdrawal date, the [CMA] must have regard to the amount of time which the parties are likely to require in order to secure that there is no further infringement of the Chapter I prohibition with respect to the agreement.

(9) In subsection (1) "price fixing agreement" means an agreement which has as its object or effect, or one of its objects or effects, restricting the freedom of a party to the agreement to determine the price to be charged (otherwise than as between that party and another party to the agreement) for the product, service or other matter to which the agreement relates.

NOTES

References to "CMA" substituted (for references to "OFT" as substituted by the Enterprise Act 2002, s 278, Sch 25, para 38) by the Enterprise and Regulatory Reform Act 2013, s 26(3), Sch 5, Pt 1, paras 1, 23. For various transitional provisions (including those relating to the abolition of the OFT and the Competition Commission, existing references to those bodies and provisions relating to continuity), see the Enterprise and Regulatory Reform Act 2013 (Commencement No 6, Transitional Provisions and Savings) Order 2014, SI 2014/416, Schedule at **[2.1126]**. This section is also amended as follows:

Section heading: substituted by the Competition Act 1998 and Other Enactments (Amendment) Regulations 2004, SI 2004/1261, reg 4, Sch 1, para 24(1), (3).

Sub-s (3): words in first pair of square brackets inserted by SI 2004/1261, reg 4, Sch 1, para 24(1), (2).

Sub-s (4): words in second, third and fourth pairs of square brackets substituted by the Enterprise Act 2002, s 278, Sch 25, para 38.

Sub-s (5): word in second pair of square brackets substituted by the Enterprise Act 2002, s 278, Sch 25, para 38.

References to the CMA, etc: as to the abolition of the office of the Director General of Fair Trading and the substitution of the original references to the Director (and related expressions), see the note preceding s 1 at **[1.1266]**.

Regulations: the Competition Act 1998 (Small Agreements and Conduct of Minor Significance) Regulations 2000, SI 2000/262 at **[2.32]**.

[1.1301]
40   Limited immunity in relation to the Chapter II prohibition
(1)   In this section "conduct of minor significance" means conduct which falls within a category prescribed for the purposes of this section.
(2)   The criteria by reference to which a category is prescribed may, in particular, include—
  (a)   the turnover of the person whose conduct it is (determined in accordance with prescribed provisions);
  (b)   the share of the market affected by the conduct (determined in that way).
(3)   A person is immune from the effect of section 36(2)[, so far as that provision relates to decisions about infringement of the Chapter II prohibition,] if his conduct is conduct of minor significance; but the [CMA] may withdraw that immunity under subsection (4).
(4)   If the [CMA] has investigated conduct of minor significance, [it] may make a decision withdrawing the immunity given by subsection (3) if, as a result of [its] investigation, [it] considers that the conduct is likely to infringe the Chapter II prohibition.
(5)   The [CMA] must give the person, or persons, whose immunity has been withdrawn written notice of [its] decision to withdraw the immunity.
(6)   A decision under subsection (4) takes effect on such date ("the withdrawal date") as may be specified in the decision.
(7)   The withdrawal date must be a date after the date on which the decision is made.
(8)   In determining the withdrawal date, the [CMA] must have regard to the amount of time which the person or persons affected are likely to require in order to secure that there is no further infringement of the Chapter II prohibition.

NOTES
   References to "CMA" substituted (for references to "OFT" as substituted by the Enterprise Act 2002, s 278, Sch 25, para 38) by the Enterprise and Regulatory Reform Act 2013, s 26(3), Sch 5, Pt 1, paras 1, 24. For various transitional provisions (including those relating to the abolition of the OFT and the Competition Commission, existing references to those bodies and provisions relating to continuity), see the Enterprise and Regulatory Reform Act 2013 (Commencement No 6, Transitional Provisions and Savings) Order 2014, SI 2014/416, Schedule at **[2.1126]**. This section is also amended as follows:
   Sub-s (3): words in first pair of square brackets inserted by the Competition Act 1998 and Other Enactments (Amendment) Regulations 2004, SI 2004/1261, reg 4, Sch 1, para 25.
   Sub-s (4): words in second, third and fourth pairs of square brackets substituted by the Enterprise Act 2002, s 278, Sch 25, para 38.
   Sub-s (5): word in second pair of square brackets substituted by the Enterprise Act 2002, s 278, Sch 25, para 38.
   References to the CMA, etc: as to the abolition of the office of the Director General of Fair Trading and the substitution of the original references to the Director (and related expressions), see the note preceding s 1 at **[1.1266]**.
   Regulations: the Competition Act 1998 (Small Agreements and Conduct of Minor Significance) Regulations 2000, SI 2000/262.

[Civil sanctions

[1.1302]
40A   Penalties: failure to comply with requirements
(1)   Where the CMA considers that a person has, without reasonable excuse, failed to comply with a requirement imposed on the person under section 26, 26A, 27, 28 or 28A, it may impose a penalty of such amount as it considers appropriate.
(2)   The amount may be—
  (a)   a fixed amount,
  (b)   an amount calculated by reference to a daily rate, or
  (c)   a combination of a fixed amount and an amount calculated by reference to a daily rate.
(3)   A penalty imposed under subsection (1) must not—
  (a)   in the case of a fixed amount, exceed such amount as the Secretary of State may by order specify;
  (b)   in the case of an amount calculated by reference to a daily rate, exceed such amount per day as the Secretary of State may so specify;
  (c)   in the case of a fixed amount and an amount calculated by reference to a daily rate, exceed such fixed amount and such amount per day as the Secretary of State may so specify.
(4)   The fixed amount specified for the purposes of subsection (3)(a) or (c) may not exceed £30,000.
(5)   The amount per day specified for the purposes of subsection (3)(b) or (c) may not exceed £15,000.
(6)   In imposing a penalty by reference to a daily rate—
  (a)   no account is to be taken of any days before the service of the notice under section 112 of the Enterprise Act 2002 (as applied by subsection (9)) on the person concerned, and
  (b)   unless the CMA determines an earlier date (whether before or after the penalty is imposed), the amount payable ceases to accumulate at the beginning of the earliest of the days mentioned in subsection (7).
(7)   The days are—
  (a)   the day on which the requirement concerned is satisfied;
  (b)   the day on which the CMA makes a decision (within the meaning given by section 31(2)) or terminates the investigation in question without making such a decision;

(c) if the Secretary of State has made an order under section 31F(1)(b) imposing a time-limit on the making of such a decision, the latest day on which such a decision may be made as a result of the investigation in question.

(8) Before making an order under subsection (3), the Secretary of State must consult the CMA and such other persons as the Secretary of State considers appropriate.

(9) Sections 112 to 115 of the Enterprise Act 2002 (supplementary provisions about penalties) apply in relation to a penalty imposed under subsection (1) as they apply in relation to a penalty imposed under section 110(1) of that Act.]

NOTES

Commencement: 25 April 2013 (for the purposes of enabling the exercise of any power to make provision by regulations, rules or order made by statutory instrument); 1 April 2014 (otherwise).

Inserted, together with the preceding heading and s 40B, by the Enterprise and Regulatory Reform Act 2013, s 40(1), (2). For various transitional provisions (including those relating to the abolition of the OFT and the Competition Commission, existing references to those bodies and provisions relating to continuity), see the Enterprise and Regulatory Reform Act 2013 (Commencement No 6, Transitional Provisions and Savings) Order 2014, SI 2014/416, Schedule at **[2.1126]**.

Orders: the Competition and Markets Authority (Penalties) Order 2014, SI 2014/559.

[1.1303]
[40B Statement of policy on penalties

(1) The CMA must prepare and publish a statement of policy in relation to the use of its powers under section 40A.

(2) The CMA must, in particular, include a statement about the considerations relevant to the determination of the nature and amount of any penalty imposed under section 40A.

(3) The CMA may revise its statement of policy and, where it does so, it must publish the revised statement.

(4) The CMA must consult such persons as it considers appropriate when preparing or revising its statement of policy.

(5) If the proposed statement of policy or revision relates to a matter in respect of which a regulator exercises concurrent jurisdiction, those consulted must include that regulator.

(6) In deciding whether and, if so, how to proceed under section 40A, the CMA must have regard to the statement of policy which was most recently published under this section at the time when the failure concerned occurred.]

NOTES

Commencement: 1 April 2014.

Inserted as noted to s 40A at **[1.1303]**.

41 (*Repealed by the Competition Act 1998 and Other Enactments (Amendment) Regulations 2004, SI 2004/1261, reg 4, Sch 1, para 26.*)

Offences

[1.1304]
42 Offences

(1)–(4) . . .

(5) A person is guilty of an offence if he intentionally obstructs an officer acting in the exercise of his powers under section 27.

(6) A person guilty of an offence under subsection . . . (5) is liable—

    (a) on summary conviction, to a fine not exceeding the statutory maximum;

    (b) on conviction on indictment, to a fine.

(7) A person who intentionally obstructs an officer in the exercise of his powers under a warrant issued under [section 28 or 28A] is guilty of an offence and liable—

    (a) on summary conviction, to a fine not exceeding the statutory maximum;

    (b) on conviction on indictment, to imprisonment for a term not exceeding two years or to a fine or to both.

NOTES

Sub-ss (1)–(4): repealed by the Enterprise and Regulatory Reform Act 2013, s 40(1), (7), (8). For various transitional provisions (including those relating to the abolition of the OFT and the Competition Commission, existing references to those bodies and provisions relating to continuity), see the Enterprise and Regulatory Reform Act 2013 (Commencement No 6, Transitional Provisions and Savings) Order 2014, SI 2014/416, Schedule at **[2.1126]**. Sub-ss (1)–(4) previously read as follows (with words in square brackets in sub-s (1) substituted by the Competition Act 1998 and Other Enactments (Amendment) Regulations 2004, SI 2004/1261, reg 4, Sch 1, para 27)—

"(1) A person is guilty of an offence if he fails to comply with a requirement imposed on him under section 26, 27[, 28 or 28A].

(2) If a person is charged with an offence under subsection (1) in respect of a requirement to produce a document, it is a defence for him to prove—

    (a) that the document was not in his possession or under his control; and

    (b) that it was not reasonably practicable for him to comply with the requirement.

(3) If a person is charged with an offence under subsection (1) in respect of a requirement—

    (a) to provide information,

(b) to provide an explanation of a document, or

(c) to state where a document is to be found,

it is a defence for him to prove that he had a reasonable excuse for failing to comply with the requirement.

(4) Failure to comply with a requirement imposed under section 26 or 27 is not an offence if the person imposing the requirement has failed to act in accordance with that section.".

Sub-s (6): words "(1) or" (omitted) repealed by the Enterprise and Regulatory Reform Act 2013, s 40(1), (7), (9), subject to transitional provisions in SI 2014/416 as noted above.

Sub-s (7): words in square brackets substituted by SI 2004/1261, reg 4, Sch 1, para 27(1), (3).

[1.1305]
43 Destroying or falsifying documents

(1) A person is guilty of an offence if, having been required to produce a document under section 26, 27[, 28 or 28A]—

(a) he intentionally or recklessly destroys or otherwise disposes of it, falsifies it or conceals it, or

(b) he causes or permits its destruction, disposal, falsification or concealment.

(2) A person guilty of an offence under subsection (1) is liable—

(a) on summary conviction, to a fine not exceeding the statutory maximum;

(b) on conviction on indictment, to imprisonment for a term not exceeding two years or to a fine or to both.

NOTES

Sub-s (1): words in square brackets substituted by the Competition Act 1998 and Other Enactments (Amendment) Regulations 2004, SI 2004/1261, reg 4, Sch 1, para 28.

[1.1306]
44 False or misleading information

(1) If information is provided by a person to the [CMA] in connection with any function of the [CMA] under this Part, that person is guilty of an offence if—

(a) the information is false or misleading in a material particular, and

(b) he knows that it is or is reckless as to whether it is.

(2) A person who—

(a) provides any information to another person, knowing the information to be false or misleading in a material particular, or

(b) recklessly provides any information to another person which is false or misleading in a material particular,

knowing that the information is to be used for the purpose of providing information to the [CMA] in connection with any of [its] functions under this Part, is guilty of an offence.

(3) A person guilty of an offence under this section is liable—

(a) on summary conviction, to a fine not exceeding the statutory maximum;

(b) on conviction on indictment, to imprisonment for a term not exceeding two years or to a fine or to both.

NOTES

References to "CMA" substituted (for references to "OFT" as substituted by the Enterprise Act 2002, s 278, Sch 25, para 38) by the Enterprise and Regulatory Reform Act 2013, s 26(3), Sch 5, Pt 1, paras 1, 25. For various transitional provisions (including those relating to the abolition of the OFT and the Competition Commission, existing references to those bodies and provisions relating to continuity), see the Enterprise and Regulatory Reform Act 2013 (Commencement No 6, Transitional Provisions and Savings) Order 2014, SI 2014/416, Schedule at **[2.1126]**.

Sub-s (2): word in second pair of square brackets substituted by the Enterprise Act 2002, s 278, Sch 25, para 38.

References to the CMA, etc: as to the abolition of the office of the Director General of Fair Trading and the substitution of the original references to the Director (and related expressions), see the note preceding s 1 at **[1.1266]**.

CHAPTER IV
[APPEALS, PROCEEDINGS BEFORE THE TRIBUNAL AND SETTLEMENTS RELATING TO INFRINGEMENTS OF COMPETITION LAW]

NOTES

Chapter heading: substituted by the Consumer Rights Act 2015, s 81, Sch 8, Pt 1, paras 1, 2.

The Commission

[1.1307]
45 *The Competition Commission*

(1) There is to be a body corporate known as the Competition Commission.

(2) The Commission is to have such functions as are conferred on it by or as a result of this Act.

(3) The Monopolies and Mergers Commission is dissolved and its functions are transferred to the Competition Commission.

(4) In any enactment, instrument or other document, any reference to the Monopolies and Mergers Commission which has continuing effect is to be read as a reference to the Competition Commission.

(5)   The Secretary of State may by order make such consequential, supplemental and incidental provision as he considers appropriate in connection with—

    (a)   the dissolution of the Monopolies and Mergers Commission; and

    (b)   the transfer of functions effected by subsection (3).

(6)   An order made under subsection (5) may, in particular, include provision—

    (a)   for the transfer of property, rights, obligations and liabilities and the continuation of proceedings, investigations and other matters; or

    (b)   amending any enactment which makes provision with respect to the Monopolies and Mergers Commission or any of its functions.

(7)   [Schedules 7 and 7A make] further provision about the Competition Commission.

[(8)   The Secretary of State may by order make such modifications in Part 2 of Schedule 7 and in Schedule 7A (performance of the Competition Commission's general functions) as he considers appropriate for improving the performance by the Competition Commission of its functions.]

NOTES

Repealed by the Enterprise and Regulatory Reform Act 2013, s 26(3), Sch 5, Pt 3, paras 218, 220. For various transitional provisions (including those relating to the abolition of the OFT and the Competition Commission, existing references to those bodies and provisions relating to continuity), see the Enterprise and Regulatory Reform Act 2013 (Commencement No 6, Transitional Provisions and Savings) Order 2014, SI 2014/416, Schedule at **[2.1126]**.

Sub-s (7): words in square brackets substituted by the Enterprise Act 2002, s 187(1).

Sub-s (8): added by the Enterprise Act 2002, s 278(1), Sch 25, para 38(1), (35).

Orders: the Competition Act 1998 (Competition Commission) Transitional, Consequential and Supplemental Provisions Order 1999, SI 1999/506; the Competition Act 1998 (Transitional, Consequential and Supplemental Provisions) Order 2000, SI 2000/311; the Competition Act 1998 (Consequential and Supplemental Provisions) Order 2000, SI 2000/2031.

[Appeals and proceedings before the Tribunal]

[1.1308]

46   Appealable decisions

(1)   Any party to an agreement in respect of which the [CMA] has made a decision may appeal to [the Tribunal] against, or with respect to, the decision.

(2)   Any person in respect of whose conduct the [CMA] has made a decision may appeal to [the Tribunal] against, or with respect to, the decision.

[(3)   In this section "decision" means a decision of the [CMA]—

    (a)   as to whether the Chapter I prohibition has been infringed,

    (b)   as to whether the prohibition in [Article 101(1)] has been infringed,

    (c)   as to whether the Chapter II prohibition has been infringed,

    (d)   as to whether the prohibition in [Article 102] has been infringed,

    (e)   cancelling a block or parallel exemption,

    (f)   withdrawing the benefit of a regulation of the Commission pursuant to Article 29(2) of the EC Competition Regulation,

    (g)   not releasing commitments pursuant to a request made under section 31A(4)(b)(i),

    (h)   releasing commitments under section 31A(4)(b)(ii),

    (i)   as to the imposition of any penalty under section 36 or as to the amount of any such penalty,

and includes a direction under section 32, 33 or 35 and such other decisions under this Part as may be prescribed.]

(4)   Except in the case of an appeal against the imposition, or the amount, of a penalty, the making of an appeal under this section does not suspend the effect of the decision to which the appeal relates.

(5)   Part I of Schedule 8 makes further provision about appeals.

NOTES

Cross-heading: substituted by the Consumer Rights Act 2015, s 81, Sch 8, Pt 1, paras 1, 3.

References to "CMA" substituted (for references to "OFT" as substituted by the Enterprise Act 2002, s 278, Sch 25, para 38) by the Enterprise and Regulatory Reform Act 2013, s 26(3), Sch 5, Pt 1, paras 1, 26. For various transitional provisions (including those relating to the abolition of the OFT and the Competition Commission, existing references to those bodies and provisions relating to continuity), see the Enterprise and Regulatory Reform Act 2013 (Commencement No 6, Transitional Provisions and Savings) Order 2014, SI 2014/416, Schedule at **[2.1126]**. This section is also amended as follows:

Sub-ss (1), (2): words in second pair of square brackets substituted by the Enterprise Act 2002, s 21, Sch 5, paras 1, 2(a); subject to transitional provisions as noted below.

Sub-s (3): substituted by the Competition Act 1998 and Other Enactments (Amendment) Regulations 2004, SI 2004/1261, reg 4, Sch 1, para 29 (for savings and transitional provisions see reg 8 of those Regulations); words in square brackets in paras (b), (d) substituted by the Treaty of Lisbon (Changes in Terminology or Numbering) Order 2012, SI 2012/1809, art 3(1), Schedule, Pt 1 (note that the amendments made by this Order do not affect any provision in its application to things done before 1 December 2009 (the date on which the Treaty of Lisbon came into force)).

Transitional provisions: for transitional provisions in relation to the constitution, etc, of the Tribunal, see the Enterprise Act 2002, Sch 24, paras 7–11 at **[1.432]**; and for transitional provisions in connection with an appeal made to the Competition Commission under ss 46 or 47 of this Act which has not been finally determined before 1 April 2003, see the Enterprise Act 2002 (Commencement No 2, Transitional and Transitory Provisions) Order 2003, SI 2003/766, art 3.

References to the CMA, etc: as to the abolition of the office of the Director General of Fair Trading and the substitution of the original references to the Director (and related expressions), see the note preceding s 1 at **[1.1266]**.

Regulations: the Competition Act 1998 (Appealable Decisions and Revocation of Notification of Excluded Agreements) Regulations 2004, SI 2004/1078.

[1.1309]
[47   Third party appeals
[(1)   A person who does not fall within section 46(1) or (2) may appeal to the Tribunal with respect to—
   (a)   a decision falling within paragraphs (a) to (f) of section 46(3);
   (b)   a decision falling within paragraph (g) of section 46(3);
   (c)   a decision of the [CMA] to accept or release commitments under section 31A, or to accept a variation of such commitments other than a variation which is not material in any respect;
   (d)   a decision of the [CMA] to make directions under section 35;
   (e)   a decision of the [CMA] not to make directions under section 35; or
   (f)   such other decision of the [CMA] under this Part as may be prescribed.]
(2)   A person may make an appeal under subsection (1) only if the Tribunal considers that he has a sufficient interest in the decision with respect to which the appeal is made, or that he represents persons who have such an interest.
(3)   The making of an appeal under this section does not suspend the effect of the decision to which the appeal relates.]

NOTES
Substituted by the Enterprise Act 2002, s 17 (for transitional provisions, see the note to s 46 at **[1.73]**, and the Enterprise Act 2002 (Commencement No 3, Transitional and Transitory Provisions and Savings) Order 2003, SI 2003/1397, art 5).
Sub-s (1): substituted by the Competition Act 1998 and Other Enactments (Amendment) Regulations 2004, SI 2004/1261, reg 4, Sch 1, para 30 (for savings and transitional provisions see reg 8 of those Regulations); references to "CMA" substituted (for original references to "OFT") by the Enterprise and Regulatory Reform Act 2013, s 26(3), Sch 5, Pt 1, paras 1, 27. For various transitional provisions (including those relating to the abolition of the OFT and the Competition Commission, existing references to those bodies and provisions relating to continuity), see the Enterprise and Regulatory Reform Act 2013 (Commencement No 6, Transitional Provisions and Savings) Order 2014, SI 2014/416, Schedule at **[2.1126]**.
Regulations: the Competition Act 1998 (Appealable Decisions and Revocation of Notification of Excluded Agreements) Regulations 2004, SI 2004/1078.

[1.1310]
[47A   Proceedings before the Tribunal: claims for damages etc
(1)   A person may make a claim to which this section applies in proceedings before the Tribunal, subject to the provisions of this Act and Tribunal rules.
(2)   This section applies to a claim of a kind specified in subsection (3) which a person who has suffered loss or damage may make in civil proceedings brought in any part of the United Kingdom in respect of an infringement decision or an alleged infringement of—
   (a)   the Chapter I prohibition,
   (b)   the Chapter II prohibition,
   (c)   the prohibition in Article 101(1), or
   (d)   the prohibition in Article 102.
(3)   The claims are—
   (a)   a claim for damages;
   (b)   any other claim for a sum of money;
   (c)   in proceedings in England and Wales or Northern Ireland, a claim for an injunction.
(4)   For the purpose of identifying claims which may be made in civil proceedings, any limitation rules or rules relating to prescription that would apply in such proceedings are to be disregarded.
(5)   The right to make a claim in proceedings under this section does not affect the right to bring any other proceedings in respect of the claim.
(6)   In this Part (except in section 49C) "infringement decision" means—
   (a)   a decision of the CMA that the Chapter I prohibition, the Chapter II prohibition, the prohibition in Article 101(1) or the prohibition in Article 102 has been infringed,
   (b)   a decision of the Tribunal on an appeal from a decision of the CMA that the Chapter I prohibition, the Chapter II prohibition, the prohibition in Article 101(1) or the prohibition in Article 102 has been infringed, or
   (c)   a decision of the Commission that the prohibition in Article 101(1) or the prohibition in Article 102 has been infringed.]

NOTES
Commencement: 1 October 2015.
Inserted by the Enterprise Act 2002, s 18(1), with effect in relation to claims arising before and after 20 June 2003 (see s 18(2) of the 2002 Act); substituted by the Consumer Rights Act 2015, s 81, Sch 8, Pt 1, paras 1, 4(1), with effect in relation to claims arising before and after 1 October 2015 (see Sch 8, Pt 1, para 4(2) of the 2015 Act).

[1.1311]
[47B Collective proceedings before the Tribunal

(1) Subject to the provisions of this Act and Tribunal rules, proceedings may be brought before the Tribunal combining two or more claims to which section 47A applies ("collective proceedings").

(2) Collective proceedings must be commenced by a person who proposes to be the representative in those proceedings.

(3) The following points apply in relation to claims in collective proceedings—

    (a)   it is not a requirement that all of the claims should be against all of the defendants to the proceedings,

    (b)   the proceedings may combine claims which have been made in proceedings under section 47A and claims which have not, and

    (c)   a claim which has been made in proceedings under section 47A may be continued in collective proceedings only with the consent of the person who made that claim.

(4) Collective proceedings may be continued only if the Tribunal makes a collective proceedings order.

(5) The Tribunal may make a collective proceedings order only—

    (a)   if it considers that the person who brought the proceedings is a person who, if the order were made, the Tribunal could authorise to act as the representative in those proceedings in accordance with subsection (8), and

    (b)   in respect of claims which are eligible for inclusion in collective proceedings.

(6) Claims are eligible for inclusion in collective proceedings only if the Tribunal considers that they raise the same, similar or related issues of fact or law and are suitable to be brought in collective proceedings.

(7) A collective proceedings order must include the following matters—

    (a)   authorisation of the person who brought the proceedings to act as the representative in those proceedings,

    (b)   description of a class of persons whose claims are eligible for inclusion in the proceedings, and

    (c)   specification of the proceedings as opt-in collective proceedings or opt-out collective proceedings (see subsections (10) and (11)).

(8) The Tribunal may authorise a person to act as the representative in collective proceedings—

    (a)   whether or not that person is a person falling within the class of persons described in the collective proceedings order for those proceedings (a "class member"), but

    (b)   only if the Tribunal considers that it is just and reasonable for that person to act as a representative in those proceedings.

(9) The Tribunal may vary or revoke a collective proceedings order at any time.

(10) "Opt-in collective proceedings" are collective proceedings which are brought on behalf of each class member who opts in by notifying the representative, in a manner and by a time specified, that the claim should be included in the collective proceedings.

(11) "Opt-out collective proceedings" are collective proceedings which are brought on behalf of each class member except—

    (a)   any class member who opts out by notifying the representative, in a manner and by a time specified, that the claim should not be included in the collective proceedings, and

    (b)   any class member who—

        (i)   is not domiciled in the United Kingdom at a time specified, and

        (ii)   does not, in a manner and by a time specified, opt in by notifying the representative that the claim should be included in the collective proceedings.

(12) Where the Tribunal gives a judgment or makes an order in collective proceedings, the judgment or order is binding on all represented persons, except as otherwise specified.

(13) The right to make a claim in collective proceedings does not affect the right to bring any other proceedings in respect of the claim.

(14) In this section and in section 47C, "specified" means specified in a direction made by the Tribunal.]

NOTES

    Commencement: 1 October 2015.

    Inserted by the Enterprise Act 2002, s 19; substituted by the Consumer Rights Act 2015, s 81, Sch 8, Pt 1, paras 1, 5(1), with effect in relation to claims arising before and after 1 October 2015 (see Sch 8, Pt 1, para 5(2) of the 2015 Act).

    Orders: the Specified Body (Consumer Claims) Order 2005, SI 2005/2365.

[1.1312]
[47C Collective proceedings: damages and costs

(1) The Tribunal may not award exemplary damages in collective proceedings.

(2) The Tribunal may make an award of damages in collective proceedings without undertaking an assessment of the amount of damages recoverable in respect of the claim of each represented person.

(3)   Where the Tribunal makes an award of damages in opt-out collective proceedings, the Tribunal must make an order providing for the damages to be paid on behalf of the represented persons to—
  (a)   the representative, or
  (b)   such person other than a represented person as the Tribunal thinks fit.
(4)   Where the Tribunal makes an award of damages in opt-in collective proceedings, the Tribunal may make an order as described in subsection (3).
(5)   Subject to subsection (6), where the Tribunal makes an award of damages in opt-out collective proceedings, any damages not claimed by the represented persons within a specified period must be paid to the charity for the time being prescribed by order made by the Lord Chancellor under section 194(8) of the Legal Services Act 2007.
(6)   In a case within subsection (5) the Tribunal may order that all or part of any damages not claimed by the represented persons within a specified period is instead to be paid to the representative in respect of all or part of the costs or expenses incurred by the representative in connection with the proceedings.
(7)   The Secretary of State may by order amend subsection (5) so as to substitute a different charity for the one for the time being specified in that subsection.
(8)   A damages-based agreement is unenforceable if it relates to opt-out collective proceedings.
(9)   In this section—
  (a)   "charity" means a body, or the trustees of a trust, established for charitable purposes only;
  (b)   "damages" (except in the term "exemplary damages") includes any sum of money which may be awarded by the Tribunal in collective proceedings (other than costs or expenses);
  (c)   "damages-based agreement" has the meaning given in section 58AA(3) of the Courts and Legal Services Act 1990.]

NOTES
Commencement: 1 October 2015.
Inserted by the Consumer Rights Act 2015, s 81, Sch 8, Pt 1, paras 1, 6.

[1.1313]
[47D   Proceedings under section 47A or collective proceedings: injunctions etc
(1)   An injunction granted by the Tribunal in proceedings under section 47A or in collective proceedings—
  (a)   has the same effect as an injunction granted by the High Court, and
  (b)   is enforceable as if it were an injunction granted by the High Court.
(2)   In deciding whether to grant an injunction in proceedings under section 47A or in collective proceedings, the Tribunal must—
  (a)   in proceedings in England and Wales, apply the principles which the High Court would apply in deciding whether to grant an injunction under section 37(1) of the Senior Courts Act 1981, and
  (b)   in proceedings in Northern Ireland, apply the principles that the High Court would apply in deciding whether to grant an injunction.
(3)   Subsection (2) is subject to Tribunal rules which make provision of the kind mentioned in paragraph 15A(3) of Schedule 4 to the Enterprise Act 2002 (undertakings as to damages in relation to claims subject to the fast-track procedure).]

NOTES
Commencement: 1 October 2015.
Inserted by the Consumer Rights Act 2015, s 81, Sch 8, Pt 1, paras 1, 7.

[1.1314]
[47E   Limitation or prescriptive periods for proceedings under section 47A and collective proceedings
(1)   Subsection (2) applies in respect of a claim to which section 47A applies, for the purposes of determining the limitation or prescriptive period which would apply in respect of the claim if it were to be made in—
  (a)   proceedings under section 47A, or
  (b)   collective proceedings at the commencement of those proceedings.
(2)   Where this subsection applies—
  (a)   in the case of proceedings in England and Wales, the Limitation Act 1980 applies as if the claim were an action in a court of law;
  (b)   in the case of proceedings in Scotland, the Prescription and Limitation (Scotland) Act 1973 applies as if the claim related to an obligation to which section 6 of that Act applies;
  (c)   in the case of proceedings in Northern Ireland, the Limitation (Northern Ireland) Order 1989 applies as if the claim were an action in a court established by law.
(3)   Where a claim is made in collective proceedings at the commencement of those proceedings ("the section 47B claim"), subsections (4) to (6) apply for the purpose of determining the limitation or prescriptive period which would apply in respect of the claim if it were subsequently to be made in proceedings under section 47A.

(4)   The running of the limitation or prescriptive period in respect of the claim is suspended from the date on which the collective proceedings are commenced.

(5)   Following suspension under subsection (4), the running of the limitation or prescriptive period in respect of the claim resumes on the date on which any of the following occurs—

(a)   the Tribunal declines to make a collective proceedings order in respect of the collective proceedings;

(b)   the Tribunal makes a collective proceedings order in respect of the collective proceedings, but the order does not provide that the section 47B claim is eligible for inclusion in the proceedings;

(c)   the Tribunal rejects the section 47B claim;

(d)   in the case of opt-in collective proceedings, the period within which a person may choose to have the section 47B claim included in the proceedings expires without the person having done so;

(e)   in the case of opt-out collective proceedings—

(i)   a person domiciled in the United Kingdom chooses (within the period in which such a choice may be made) to have the section 47B claim excluded from the collective proceedings, or

(ii)   the period within which a person not domiciled in the United Kingdom may choose to have the section 47B claim included in the collective proceedings expires without the person having done so;

(f)   the section 47B claim is withdrawn;

(g)   the Tribunal revokes the collective proceedings order in respect of the collective proceedings;

(h)   the Tribunal varies the collective proceedings order in such a way that the section 47B claim is no longer included in the collective proceedings;

(i)   the section 47B claim is settled with or without the Tribunal's approval;

(j)   the section 47B claim is dismissed, discontinued or otherwise disposed of without an adjudication on the merits.

(6)   Where the running of the limitation or prescriptive period in respect of the claim resumes under subsection (5) but the period would otherwise expire before the end of the period of six months beginning with the date of that resumption, the period is treated as expiring at the end of that six month period.

(7)   This section has effect subject to any provision in Tribunal rules which defers the date on which the limitation or prescriptive period begins in relation to claims in proceedings under section 47A or in collective proceedings.]

NOTES

Commencement: 1 October 2015.

Inserted by the Consumer Rights Act 2015, s 81, Sch 8, Pt 1, paras 1, 8(1), except in relation to claims arising before 1 October 2015 (see Sch 8, Pt 1, para 8(2) of the 2015 Act).

---

48   (*Repealed by the Enterprise Act 2002, ss 21, 278(2), Sch 5, paras 1, 3, Sch 26; for a saving in relation to rules made under this section, see s 276(1) of, and Sch 24, para 12 to, the 2002 Act.*)

[1.1315]
[49   Further appeals

(1)   An appeal lies to the appropriate court—

(a)   from a decision of the Tribunal as to the amount of a penalty under section 36; [and]

(b)   . . .

(c)   on a point of law arising from any other decision of the Tribunal on an appeal under section 46 or 47.

[(1A)   An appeal lies to the appropriate court on a point of law arising from a decision of the Tribunal in proceedings under section 47A or in collective proceedings—

(a)   as to the award of damages or other sum (other than a decision on costs or expenses), or

(b)   as to the grant of an injunction.

(1B)   An appeal lies to the appropriate court from a decision of the Tribunal in proceedings under section 47A or in collective proceedings as to the amount of an award of damages or other sum (other than the amount of costs or expenses).

(1C)   An appeal under subsection (1A) arising from a decision in respect of a stand-alone claim may include consideration of a point of law arising from a finding of the Tribunal as to an infringement of a prohibition listed in section 47A(2).

(1D)   In subsection (1C) "a stand-alone claim" is a claim—

(a)   in respect of an alleged infringement of a prohibition listed in section 47A(2), and

(b)   made in proceedings under section 47A or included in collective proceedings.]

(2)   An appeal under this section—

(a)   [except as provided by subsection (2A),] may be brought by a party to the proceedings before the Tribunal or by a person who has a sufficient interest in the matter; and

(b)   requires the permission of the Tribunal or the appropriate court.

[(2A)   An appeal from a decision of the Tribunal in respect of a claim included in collective proceedings may be brought only by the representative in those proceedings or by a defendant to that claim.]

(3)   In this section "the appropriate court" means the Court of Appeal or, in the case of an appeal from Tribunal proceedings in Scotland, the Court of Session.]

NOTES

Substituted by the Enterprise Act 2002, s 21, Sch 5, paras 1, 4b

Sub-s (1): word in para (a) inserted, and para (b) repealed, by the Consumer Rights Act 2015, s 81, Sch 8, Pt 1, paras 1, 9(1), (2).

Sub-ss (1A)–(1D), (2A): inserted by the Consumer Rights Act 2015, s 81, Sch 8, Pt 1, paras 1, 9(1), (3), (5).

Sub-s (2): words in para (a) inserted by the Consumer Rights Act 2015, s 81, Sch 8, Pt 1, paras 1, 9(1), (4).

[Settlements relating to infringements of competition law

[1.1316]
49A   Collective settlements: where a collective proceedings order has been made

(1)   The Tribunal may, in accordance with this section and Tribunal rules, make an order approving the settlement of claims in collective proceedings (a "collective settlement") where—
  (a)   a collective proceedings order has been made in respect of the claims, and
  (b)   the Tribunal has specified that the proceedings are opt-out collective proceedings.

(2)   An application for approval of a proposed collective settlement must be made to the Tribunal by the representative and the defendant in the collective proceedings.

(3)   The representative and the defendant must provide agreed details of the claims to be settled by the proposed collective settlement and the proposed terms of that settlement.

(4)   Where there is more than one defendant in the collective proceedings, "defendant" in subsections (2) and (3) means such of the defendants as wish to be bound by the proposed collective settlement.

(5)   The Tribunal may make an order approving a proposed collective settlement only if satisfied that its terms are just and reasonable.

(6)   On the date on which the Tribunal approves a collective settlement—
  (a)   if the period within which persons may opt out of or (in the case of persons not domiciled in the United Kingdom) opt in to the collective proceedings has expired, subsections (8) and (10) apply so as to determine the persons bound by the settlement;
  (b)   if that period has not yet expired, subsections (9) and (10) apply so as to determine the persons bound by the settlement.

(7)   If the period within which persons may opt out of the collective proceedings expires on a different date from the period within which persons not domiciled in the United Kingdom may opt in to the collective proceedings, the references in subsection (6) to the expiry of a period are to the expiry of whichever of those periods expires later.

(8)   Where this subsection applies, a collective settlement approved by the Tribunal is binding on all persons falling within the class of persons described in the collective proceedings order who—
  (a)   were domiciled in the United Kingdom at the time specified for the purposes of determining domicile in relation to the collective proceedings (see section 47B(11)(b)(i)) and did not opt out of those proceedings, or
  (b)   opted in to the collective proceedings.

(9)   Where this subsection applies, a collective settlement approved by the Tribunal is binding on all persons falling within the class of persons described in the collective proceedings order.

(10)   But a collective settlement is not binding on a person who—
  (a)   opts out by notifying the representative, in a manner and by a time specified, that the claim should not be included in the collective settlement, or
  (b)   is not domiciled in the United Kingdom at a time specified, and does not, in a manner and by a time specified, opt in by notifying the representative that the claim should be included in the collective settlement.

(11)   This section does not affect a person's right to offer to settle opt-in collective proceedings.

(12)   In this section and in section 49B, "specified" means specified in a direction made by the Tribunal.]

NOTES

Commencement: 1 October 2015.

Inserted, together with preceding cross-heading, by the Consumer Rights Act 2015, s 81, Sch 8, Pt 1, paras 1, 10(1), with effect in relation to claims arising before and after 1 October 2015 (see Sch 8, Pt 1, para 10(2) of the 2015 Act).

[1.1317]
[49B   Collective settlements: where a collective proceedings order has not been made

(1)   The Tribunal may, in accordance with this section and Tribunal rules, make an order approving the settlement of claims (a "collective settlement") where—
  (a)   a collective proceedings order has not been made in respect of the claims, but

(b)   if collective proceedings were brought, the claims could be made at the commencement of the proceedings (disregarding any limitation or prescriptive period applicable to a claim in collective proceedings).

(2)   An application for approval of a proposed collective settlement must be made to the Tribunal by—

    (a)   a person who proposes to be the settlement representative in relation to the collective settlement, and

    (b)   the person who, if collective proceedings were brought in respect of the claims, would be a defendant in those proceedings (or, where more than one person would be a defendant in those proceedings, such of those persons as wish to be bound by the proposed collective settlement).

(3)   The persons applying to the Tribunal under subsection (2) must provide agreed details of the claims to be settled by the proposed collective settlement and the proposed terms of that settlement.

(4)   The Tribunal may make an order approving a proposed collective settlement (see subsection (8)) only if it first makes a collective settlement order.

(5)   The Tribunal may make a collective settlement order only—

    (a)   if it considers that the person described in subsection (2)(a) is a person who, if the order were made, the Tribunal could authorise to act as the settlement representative in relation to the collective settlement in accordance with subsection (7), and

    (b)   in respect of claims which, if collective proceedings were brought, would be eligible for inclusion in the proceedings (see section 47B(6)).

(6)   A collective settlement order must include the following matters—

    (a)   authorisation of the person described in subsection (2)(a) to act as the settlement representative in relation to the collective settlement, and

    (b)   description of a class of persons whose claims fall within subsection (5)(b).

(7)   The Tribunal may authorise a person to act as the settlement representative in relation to a collective settlement—

    (a)   whether or not that person is a person falling within the class of persons described in the collective settlement order for that settlement, but

    (b)   only if the Tribunal considers that it is just and reasonable for that person to act as the settlement representative in relation to that settlement.

(8)   Where the Tribunal has made a collective settlement order, it may make an order approving a proposed collective settlement only if satisfied that its terms are just and reasonable.

(9)   A collective settlement approved by the Tribunal is binding on all persons falling within the class of persons described in the collective settlement order.

(10)   But a collective settlement is not binding on a person who—

    (a)   opts out by notifying the settlement representative, in a manner and by a time specified, that the claim should not be included in the collective settlement, or

    (b)   is not domiciled in the United Kingdom at a time specified, and does not, in a manner and by a time specified, opt in by notifying the settlement representative that the claim should be included in the collective settlement.

(11)   In this section, "settlement representative" means a person who is authorised by a collective settlement order to act in relation to a collective settlement.]

NOTES

Commencement: 1 October 2015.

Inserted by the Consumer Rights Act 2015, s 81, Sch 8, Pt 1, paras 1, 11(1), with effect in relation to claims arising before and after 1 October 2015 (see Sch 8, Pt 1, para 11(2) of the 2015 Act).

[1.1318]
[49C   Approval of redress schemes by the CMA

(1)   A person may apply to the CMA for approval of a redress scheme.

(2)   The CMA may consider an application before the infringement decision to which the redress scheme relates has been made, but may approve the scheme only—

    (a)   after that decision has been made, or

    (b)   in the case of a decision of the CMA, at the same time as that decision is made.

(3)   In deciding whether to approve a redress scheme, the CMA may take into account the amount or value of compensation offered under the scheme.

(4)   The CMA may approve a redress scheme under subsection (2)(b) subject to a condition or conditions requiring the provision of further information about the operation of the scheme (including about the amount or value of compensation to be offered under the scheme or how this will be determined).

(5)   If the CMA approves a redress scheme subject to such a condition, it may—

    (a)   approve the scheme subject to other conditions;

    (b)   withdraw approval from the scheme if any conditions imposed under subsection (4) or paragraph (a) are not met;

    (c)   approve a redress scheme as a replacement for the original scheme (but may not approve that scheme subject to conditions).

(6)   An approved scheme may not be varied by the CMA or the compensating party.

(7) But, where the CMA approves a redress scheme subject to a condition of the kind mentioned in subsection (4), subsection (6) does not prevent further information provided in accordance with the condition from forming part of the terms of the scheme.

(8) The Secretary of State may make regulations relating to the approval of redress schemes, and the regulations may in particular—

    (a) make provision as to the procedure governing an application for approval of a redress scheme, including the information to be provided with the application;

    (b) provide that the CMA may approve a redress scheme only if it has been devised according to a process specified in the regulations;

    (c) provide that the CMA may approve a redress scheme only if it is in a form, or contains terms, specified in the regulations (which may include terms requiring a settlement agreement under the scheme to be in a form, or contain terms, specified in the regulations);

    (d) provide that the CMA may approve a redress scheme only if (so far as the CMA can judge from facts known to it) the scheme is intended to be administered in a manner specified in the regulations;

    (e) describe factors which the CMA may or must take into account, or may not take into account, in deciding whether to approve a redress scheme.

(9) The CMA must publish guidance with regard to—

    (a) applications for approval of redress schemes,

    (b) the approval of redress schemes, and

    (c) the enforcement of approved schemes, and in particular as to the criteria which the CMA intends to adopt in deciding whether to bring proceedings under section 49E(4).

(10) Guidance under subsection (9) must be approved by the Secretary of State before it is published.

(11) In this section and sections 49D and 49E—

    "approved scheme" means a redress scheme approved by the CMA,

    "compensating party" means a person offering compensation under an approved scheme,

    "infringement decision" means—

        (a) a decision of the CMA that the Chapter I prohibition, the Chapter II prohibition, the prohibition in Article 101(1) or the prohibition in Article 102 has been infringed, or

        (b) a decision of the Commission that the prohibition in Article 101(1) or the prohibition in Article 102 has been infringed, and

    "redress scheme" means a scheme under which a person offers compensation in consequence of an infringement decision made in respect of that person.

    "approved scheme" means a redress scheme approved by the CMA,

    "compensating party" means a person offering compensation under an approved scheme,

    "infringement decision" means—

        (a) a decision of the CMA that the Chapter I prohibition, the Chapter II prohibition, the prohibition in Article 101(1) or the prohibition in Article 102 has been infringed, or

        (b) a decision of the Commission that the prohibition in Article 101(1) or the prohibition in Article 102 has been infringed, and

    "redress scheme" means a scheme under which a person offers compensation in consequence of an infringement decision made in respect of that person.

(12) For the purposes of this section and section 49E, "compensation"—

    (a) may be monetary or non-monetary, and

    (b) may be offered to persons who have not suffered a loss as a result of the infringement decision to which the redress scheme relates.]

NOTES

Commencement: 1 October 2015.

Inserted, together with ss 49D, 49E, by the Consumer Rights Act 2015, s 81, Sch 8, Pt 1, paras 1, 12.

[1.1319]
[49D Redress schemes: recovery of costs

(1) The CMA may require a person making an application for approval of a redress scheme to pay some or all of the CMA's reasonable costs relating to the application.

(2) A requirement to pay costs is imposed by giving that person written notice specifying—

    (a) the amount to be paid,

    (b) how that amount has been calculated, and

    (c) by when that amount must be paid.

(3) A person required to pay costs under this section may appeal to the Tribunal against the amount.

(4) Where costs required to be paid under this section relate to an approved scheme, the CMA may withdraw approval from that scheme if the costs have not been paid by the date specified in accordance with subsection (2)(c).

(5) Costs required to be paid under this section are recoverable by the CMA as a debt.]

NOTES

Commencement: 1 October 2015.

Inserted as noted to s 49C at **[1.1318]**.

[1.1320]
[49E   Enforcement of approved schemes
(1)   A compensating party is under a duty to comply with the terms of an approved scheme ("the duty").
(2)   The duty is owed to any person entitled to compensation under the terms of the approved scheme.
(3)   Where such a person suffers loss or damage as a result of a breach of the duty, the person may bring civil proceedings before the court for damages, an injunction or interdict or any other appropriate relief or remedy.
(4)   Where the CMA considers that the compensating party is in breach of the duty, the CMA may bring civil proceedings before the court for an injunction or interdict or any other appropriate relief or remedy.
(5)   Subsection (4) is without prejudice to any right that a person has to bring proceedings under subsection (3).
(6)   In any proceedings brought under subsection (3) or (4), it is a defence for the compensating party to show that it took all reasonable steps to comply with the duty.
(7)   Where the CMA considers that it is no longer appropriate for the compensating party to be subject to the duty, the CMA may give notice in writing to that party stating that it is released from the duty.
(8)   Where a person has entered into a settlement agreement with the compensating party, that agreement remains enforceable notwithstanding the release of the compensating party under subsection (7) from the duty.
(9)   In this section "the court" means—
   (a)   in England and Wales, the High Court or the county court,
   (b)   in Northern Ireland, the High Court or a county court,
   (c)   in Scotland, the Court of Session or the sheriff.]

NOTES
Commencement: 1 October 2015.
Inserted as noted to s 49C at **[1.1318]**.

CHAPTER V
MISCELLANEOUS

Vertical agreements and land agreements

[1.1321]
50   Vertical agreements and land agreements
(1)   The Secretary of State may by order provide for any provision of this Part to apply in relation to—
   (a)   vertical agreements, or
   (b)   land agreements,
with such modifications as may be prescribed.
(2)   An order may, in particular, provide for exclusions or exemptions, or otherwise provide for prescribed provisions not to apply, in relation to—
   (a)   vertical agreements, or land agreements, in general; or
   (b)   vertical agreements, or land agreements, of any prescribed description.
(3)   An order may empower the [CMA] to give directions to the effect that in prescribed circumstances an exclusion, exemption or modification is not to apply (or is to apply in a particular way) in relation to an individual agreement.
(4)   Subsections (2) and (3) are not to be read as limiting the powers conferred by section 71.
(5)   In this section—
   "land agreement" and "vertical agreement" have such meaning as may be prescribed; and
   "prescribed" means prescribed by an order.

NOTES
Sub-s (3): reference to "CMA" substituted (for reference to "OFT" as substituted by the Enterprise Act 2002, s 278, Sch 25, para 38) by the Enterprise and Regulatory Reform Act 2013, s 26(3), Sch 5, Pt 1, paras 1, 29. For various transitional provisions (including those relating to the abolition of the OFT and the Competition Commission, existing references to those bodies and provisions relating to continuity), see the Enterprise and Regulatory Reform Act 2013 (Commencement No 6, Transitional Provisions and Savings) Order 2014, SI 2014/416, Schedule at **[2.1126]**.
References to the CMA, etc: as to the abolition of the office of the Director General of Fair Trading and the substitution of the original references to the Director (and related expressions), see the note preceding s 1 at **[1.1266]**.
Orders: the Competition Act 1998 (Land Agreements Exclusion Revocation) Order 2010, SI 2010/1709.

[CMA's] rules, guidance and fees

[1.1322]
51 Rules
(1) The [CMA] may make such rules about procedural and other matters in connection with the carrying into effect of the provisions of this Part as [it] considers appropriate.
(2) Schedule 9 makes further provision about rules made under this section but is not to be taken as restricting the [CMA's] powers under this section.
(3) If the [CMA] is preparing rules under this section [it] must consult such persons as [it] considers appropriate.
(4) If the proposed rules relate to a matter in respect of which a regulator exercises concurrent jurisdiction, those consulted must include that regulator.
(5) No rule made by the [CMA] is to come into operation until it has been approved by an order made by the Secretary of State.
(6) The Secretary of State may approve any rule made by the [CMA]—
　(a)　in the form in which it is submitted; or
　(b)　subject to such modifications as he considers appropriate.
(7) If the Secretary of State proposes to approve a rule subject to modifications he must inform the [CMA] of the proposed modifications and take into account any comments made by the [CMA].
(8) Subsections (5) to (7) apply also to any alteration of the rules made by the [CMA].
(9) The Secretary of State may, after consulting the [CMA], by order vary or revoke any rules made under this section.
(10) If the Secretary of State considers that rules should be made under this section with respect to a particular matter he may direct the [CMA] to exercise [its] powers under this section and make rules about that matter.

NOTES
In this section and in the preceding heading, the references to "CMA" and "CMA's" were substituted (for references to "OFT" and "OFT's" as substituted by the Enterprise Act 2002, s 278, Sch 25, para 38) by the Enterprise and Regulatory Reform Act 2013, s 26(3), Sch 5, Pt 1, paras 1, 30, 31. For various transitional provisions (including those relating to the abolition of the OFT and the Competition Commission, existing references to those bodies and provisions relating to continuity), see the Enterprise and Regulatory Reform Act 2013 (Commencement No 6, Transitional Provisions and Savings) Order 2014, SI 2014/416, Schedule at **[2.1126]**.
The words "it" and "its" in square brackets (in every place that they occur) were substituted by the Enterprise Act 2002, s 278, Sch 25, para 38.
References to the CMA, etc: as to the abolition of the office of the Director General of Fair Trading and the substitution of the original references to the Director (and related expressions), see the note preceding s 1 at **[1.1266]**.
Orders: the Competition Act 1998 (Office of Fair Trading's Rules) Order 2004, SI 2004/2751.

[1.1323]
52 Advice and information
(1) [The CMA] must prepare and publish general advice and information about—
　(a)　the application of the Chapter I prohibition and the Chapter II prohibition, and
　(b)　the enforcement of those prohibitions.
[(1A) [The CMA] must prepare and publish general advice and information about—
　(a)　the application of the prohibitions in [Article 101(1) and Article 102]; and
　(b)　the enforcement by it of those prohibitions.]
(2) The [CMA] may at any time publish revised, or new, advice or information.
(3) Advice and information published under this section must be prepared with a view to—
　(a)　explaining provisions of this Part to persons who are likely to be affected by them; and
　(b)　indicating how the [CMA] expects such provisions to operate.
(4) Advice (or information) published by virtue of subsection (3)(b) may include advice (or information) about the factors which the [CMA] may take into account in considering whether, and if so how, to exercise a power conferred on [it] by Chapter I, II or III.
(5) Any advice or information published by the [CMA] under this section is to be published in such form and in such manner as [it] considers appropriate.
(6) If the [CMA] is preparing any advice or information under this section [it] must consult such persons as [it] considers appropriate.
(7) If the proposed advice or information relates to a matter in respect of which a regulator exercises concurrent jurisdiction, those consulted must include that regulator.
(8) In preparing any advice or information under this section about a matter in respect of which he may exercise functions under this Part, a regulator must consult—
　(a)　the [CMA];
　(b)　the other regulators; and
　(c)　such other persons as he considers appropriate.

NOTES
In sub-ss (2)–(6) and (8), references to "CMA" substituted (for references to "OFT" as substituted by the Enterprise Act 2002, s 278, Sch 25, para 38) by the Enterprise and Regulatory Reform Act 2013, s 26(3), Sch 5, Pt 1, paras 1, 32(1), (4). For various transitional provisions (including those relating to the abolition of the OFT and the Competition Commission,

existing references to those bodies and provisions relating to continuity), see the Enterprise and Regulatory Reform Act 2013 (Commencement No 6, Transitional Provisions and Savings) Order 2014, SI 2014/416, Schedule at **[2.1126]**. This section is also amended as follows:

Sub-s (1): words in square brackets substituted (for original words "As soon as is reasonably practicable after the passing of this Act, the Director") by the Enterprise and Regulatory Reform Act 2013, s 26(3), Sch 5, Pt 1, paras 1, 32(1), (2), subject to transitional provisions in SI 2014/416 as noted above.

Sub-s (1A): inserted by the Competition Act 1998 and Other Enactments (Amendment) Regulations 2004, SI 2004/1261, reg 4, Sch 1, para 31; words in first pair of square brackets substituted (for original words "As soon as is reasonably practicable after 1st May 2004, the OFT") by the Enterprise and Regulatory Reform Act 2013, s 26(3), Sch 5, Pt 1, paras 1, 32(1), (3), subject to transitional provisions in SI 2014/416 as noted above; words in second pair of square brackets substituted by the Treaty of Lisbon (Changes in Terminology or Numbering) Order 2012, SI 2012/1809, art 3(1), Schedule, Pt 1 (note that the amendments made by this Order do not affect any provision in its application to things done before 1 December 2009 (the date on which the Treaty of Lisbon came into force)).

Sub-s (4)–(6): word "it" in square brackets (in each place that it occurs) substituted by the Enterprise Act 2002, s 278, Sch 25, para 38.

References to the CMA, etc: as to the abolition of the office of the Director General of Fair Trading and the substitution of the original references to the Director (and related expressions), see the note preceding s 1 at **[1.1266]**.

---

53   (*Repealed by the Competition Act 1998 and Other Enactments (Amendment) Regulations 2004, SI 2004/1261, reg 4, Sch 1, para 32.*)

Regulators

[1.1324]
54   Regulators

(1)   In this Part "regulator" means[—
- [(a)   the Office of Communications;]
- (b)   the Gas and Electricity Markets Authority;
- (c)   . . .
- [(d)   the Water Services Regulation Authority;]
- (e)   [the Office of Rail and Road];
- [(f)   the Northern Ireland Authority for Utility Regulation;]
- (g)   the Civil Aviation Authority][; and
- (h)   Monitor];
- [(i)   the Payment Systems Regulator established under section 40 of the Financial Services (Banking Reform) Act 2013;]
- [(j)   the Financial Conduct Authority].

(2)   Parts II and III of Schedule 10 provide for functions of the [CMA] under this Part to be exercisable concurrently by regulators.

(3)   Parts IV and V of Schedule 10 make minor and consequential amendments in connection with the regulators' competition functions.

(4)   The Secretary of State may make regulations for the purpose of co-ordinating the performance of functions under this Part ("Part I functions") which are exercisable concurrently by two or more competent persons as a result of [any enactment (including any subordinate legislation) whenever passed or made].

(5)   The regulations may, in particular, make provision—
- (a)   as to the procedure to be followed by competent persons when determining who is to exercise Part I functions in a particular case;
- (b)   as to the steps which must be taken before a competent person exercises, in a particular case, such Part I functions as may be prescribed;
- (c)   as to the procedure for determining, in a particular case, questions arising as to which competent person is to exercise Part I functions in respect of the case;
- (d)   for Part I functions in a particular case to be exercised jointly—
  - (i)   by the [CMA] and one or more regulators, or
  - (ii)   by two or more regulators,
  - and as to the procedure to be followed in such cases;
- (e)   as to the circumstances in which the exercise by a competent person of such Part I functions as may be prescribed is to preclude the exercise of such functions by another such person;
- (f)   for cases in respect of which Part I functions are being, or have been, exercised by a competent person to be transferred to another such person;
- (g)   for the person ("A") exercising Part I functions in a particular case—
  - (i)   to appoint another competent person ("B") to exercise Part I functions on A's behalf in relation to the case; or
  - (ii)   to appoint officers of B (with B's consent) to act as officers of A in relation to the case;
- (h)   for notification as to who is exercising Part I functions in respect of a particular case.

(6)   Provision made by virtue of subsection (5)(c) may[—
- (a)   prescribe circumstances in which the CMA may decide that, in a particular case, it is to exercise Part 1 functions in respect of the case rather than a regulator;

(b)] provide for questions to be referred to and determined by the Secretary of State[, the CMA] or by such other person as may be prescribed.

[(6A) Where the regulations make provision as mentioned in subsection (6)(a), they must—

(a) include provision requiring the CMA to consult the regulator concerned before making a decision that the CMA is to exercise Part 1 functions in respect of a particular case, and

(b) provide that, in a case where a regulator has given notice under section 31(1) that it proposes to make a decision (within the meaning given by section 31(2)), the CMA may only decide that it is to exercise Part 1 functions in respect of the case rather than the regulator if the regulator consents.]

[(6B) The Secretary of State may by regulations make provision requiring arrangements to be made for the sharing of information between competent persons in connection with concurrent cases.

(6C) For the purposes of subsection (6B), "a concurrent case" is a case in respect of which—

(a) the CMA considers that Part 1 functions are, or (but for provision made under subsection (5)(e)) would be, exercisable by both it and any regulator;

(b) any regulator considers that Part 1 functions are, or (but for provision made under subsection (5)(e)) would be, exercisable by it.]

(7) "Competent person" means the [CMA] or any of the regulators.

[(8) In this section, "subordinate legislation" has the same meaning as in section 21(1) of the Interpretation Act 1978 (c 30) and includes an instrument made under—

(a) an Act of the Scottish Parliament;

(b) Northern Ireland legislation.]

NOTES

Sub-s (1) is amended as follows:

Paras (a)–(g) substituted by the Enterprise Act 2002, s 278(1), Sch 25, para 38(41)(a).

Para (a) further substituted by the Communications Act 2003, s 371(5)(a).

Para (c) repealed by the Enterprise and Regulatory Reform Act 2013, s 57, Sch 15, paras 8, 11(a). For various transitional provisions (including those relating to the abolition of the OFT and the Competition Commission, existing references to those bodies and provisions relating to continuity), see the Enterprise and Regulatory Reform Act 2013 (Commencement No 6, Transitional Provisions and Savings) Order 2014, SI 2014/416, Schedule at **[2.1126]**. Para (c) originally read as follows:

"(c) the Director General of Electricity Supply for Northern Ireland;".

Para (d) further substituted by the Water Act 2003, s 101(1), Sch 7, Pt 2, para 32(1), (2).

Words in square brackets in para (e) substituted by the Office of Rail Regulation (Change of Name) Regulations 2015, SI 2015/1682, reg 2(2), Schedule, Pt 1, para 4(m).

Para (f) substituted by the Enterprise and Regulatory Reform Act 2013, s 57, Sch 15, paras 8, 11(b), subject to transitional provisions in SI 2014/416 as noted above, and originally read as follows:

"(f) the Director General of Gas for Northern Ireland;".

Para (h) (and the preceding word) was added, by the Health and Social Care Act 2012, s 74(5).

Paras (i), (j) inserted by the Financial Services (Banking Reform) Act 2013, ss 67(2), s 129, Sch 8, Pt 2, para 9.

Sub-ss (2), (5), (7): references to "CMA" substituted (for references to "OFT" as substituted by the Enterprise Act 2002, s 278, Sch 25, para 38) by the Enterprise and Regulatory Reform Act 2013, s 26(3), Sch 5, Pt 1, paras 1, 33, subject to transitional provisions in SI 2014/416 as noted above.

Sub-s (4): words in square brackets substituted by the Competition Act 1998 and Other Enactments (Amendment) Regulations 2004, SI 2004/1261, reg 4, Sch 1, para 33(1), (2).

Sub-s (6): words in square brackets inserted by the Enterprise and Regulatory Reform Act 2013, s 51(1), (2).

Sub-ss (6A)–(6C): inserted by the Enterprise and Regulatory Reform Act 2013, s 51(1), (3), (4).

Sub-s (8): added by SI 2004/1261, reg 4, Sch 1, para 33(1), (3).

Regulations: the Competition Act 1998 (Concurrency) Regulations 2014, SI 2014/536 at **[2.47]**.

Confidentiality and immunity from defamation

55, 56 *(Repealed by the Enterprise Act 2002, ss 247(j), 278(2), Sch 26.)*

[1.1325]
57 Defamation

For the purposes of the law relating to defamation, absolute privilege attaches to any advice, guidance, notice or direction given, or decision made, by the [CMA] in the exercise of any of [its] functions under this Part.

NOTES

Reference to "CMA" substituted (for reference to "OFT" as substituted by the Enterprise Act 2002, s 278, Sch 25, para 38) by the Enterprise and Regulatory Reform Act 2013, s 26(3), Sch 5, Pt 1, paras 1, 34. For various transitional provisions (including those relating to the abolition of the OFT and the Competition Commission, existing references to those bodies and provisions relating to continuity), see the Enterprise and Regulatory Reform Act 2013 (Commencement No 6, Transitional Provisions and Savings) Order 2014, SI 2014/416, Schedule at **[2.1126]**.

Word "its" in square brackets substituted by the Enterprise Act 2002, s 278, Sch 25, para 38.

Findings of fact by [CMA]

[1.1326]
58   Findings of fact by [CMA]

(1)   Unless the court [or the Tribunal] directs . . . , [a CMA's] finding which is relevant to an issue arising in Part I proceedings is binding on the parties if—

    (a)   the time for bringing an appeal [under section 46 or 47] in respect of the finding has expired and the relevant party has not brought such an appeal; or

    (b)   the decision of [the Tribunal] on such an appeal has confirmed the finding.

(2)   In this section—

    ["[a CMA's] finding" means a finding of fact made by the [CMA] in the course of conducting an investigation;]

    ["Part I proceedings" means proceedings brought otherwise than by the [CMA]—

    [(za) in respect of an infringement decision;]

        (a)   in respect of an alleged infringement of the Chapter I prohibition or of the Chapter II prohibition; or

        (b)   in respect of an alleged infringement of the prohibitions in [Article 101(1) or Article 102];]

    "relevant party" means—

        (a)   in relation to the Chapter I prohibition [or the prohibition in [Article 101(1)]], a party to the agreement which [has been found to have infringed the prohibition or is alleged to have infringed the prohibition (as the case may be)]; and

        (b)   in relation to the Chapter II prohibition [or the prohibition in [Article 102]], the undertaking whose conduct [has been found to have infringed the prohibition or is alleged to have infringed the prohibition (as the case may be)].

(3)   Rules of court [or Tribunal rules] may make provision in respect of assistance to be given by the [CMA] to the court [or the Tribunal] in Part I proceedings.

[(4)   In this section "the court" means—

    (a)   in England and Wales or Northern Ireland, the High Court,

    (b)   in Scotland, the Court of Session or the sheriff.]

NOTES

In the section heading, preceding cross-heading and sub-s (3), references to "CMA" substituted (for references to "OFT" as substituted by the Enterprise Act 2002, s 278, Sch 25, para 38) by the Enterprise and Regulatory Reform Act 2013, s 26(3), Sch 5, Pt 1, paras 1, 35, 36(1), (4), (5). For various transitional provisions (including those relating to the abolition of the OFT and the Competition Commission, existing references to those bodies and provisions relating to continuity), see the Enterprise and Regulatory Reform Act 2013 (Commencement No 6, Transitional Provisions and Savings) Order 2014, SI 2014/416, Schedule at **[2.1126]**. This section is also amended as follows:

Sub-s (1): words in first pair of square brackets inserted by the Consumer Rights Act 2015, s 81, Sch 8, Pt 1, paras 1, 13(1), (2); words omitted repealed by the Competition Act 1998 and Other Enactments (Amendment) Regulations 2004, SI 2004/1261, reg 4, Sch 1, para 34(1), (2); words in second pair of square brackets substituted (for words "an OFT's" as substituted by the Enterprise Act 2002, s 278, Sch 25, para 38) by the Enterprise and Regulatory Reform Act 2013, s 26(3), Sch 5, Pt 1, paras 1, 36(1), (2), subject to transitional provisions in SI 2014/416 as noted above; words in third pair of square brackets inserted and words in final pair of square brackets substituted, by the Enterprise Act 2002, ss 21, 27, 83(1), Sch 5, paras 1, 5, Sch 25, para 38(1), (43)(b).

Sub-s (2) is amended as follows:

References to "a CMA's" and "CMA" substituted (for references to "an OFT's" and "OFT" respectively) by the Enterprise and Regulatory Reform Act 2013, s 26(3), Sch 5, Pt 1, paras 1, 36(1), (3), subject to transitional provisions in SI 2014/416 as noted above.

Definitions "a CMA's finding" and "Part I proceedings" substituted, and words in first (outer) and third (outer) pairs of square brackets in definition "relevant party" inserted, by SI 2004/1261, reg 4, Sch 1, para 34(1), (3).

In definition "Part I proceedings" para (za) inserted, and in definition "relevant party" words from "has been found" to "(as the case may be)" in square brackets in both places substituted, by the Consumer Rights Act 2015, s 81, Sch 8, Pt 1, paras 1, 13(1), (3).

The words "Article 101(1) or Article 102" in square brackets in the definition "Part I proceedings", and the words "Article 101(1)" and "Article 102" in square brackets in the definition "relevant party" were substituted by the Treaty of Lisbon (Changes in Terminology or Numbering) Order 2012, SI 2012/1809, art 3(1), Schedule, Pt 1 (note that the amendments made by this Order do not affect any provision in its application to things done before 1 December 2009 (the date on which the Treaty of Lisbon came into force)).

In sub-s (3) words "or Tribunal rules" and "or the Tribunal" in square brackets inserted, and sub-s (4) added, by the Consumer Rights Act 2015, s 81, Sch 8, Pt 1, paras 1, 13(1), (4), (5).

References to the CMA, etc: as to the abolition of the office of the Director General of Fair Trading and the substitution of the original references to the Director (and related expressions), see the note preceding s 1 at **[1.1266]**.

[Findings of infringements

[1.1327]
[58A   Findings of infringements

(1)   This section applies to proceedings before the court in which damages or any other sum of money is claimed in respect of an infringement of—

    (a)   the Chapter I prohibition;

    (b)   the Chapter II prohibition;

    (c)   the prohibition in [Article 101(1)] of the Treaty;

    (d)   the prohibition in [Article 102] of the Treaty.

(2)   In such proceedings, the court is bound by a decision mentioned in subsection (3) once any period specified in subsection (4) which relates to the decision has elapsed.

(3)   The decisions are—

    (a)   a decision of the [CMA] that the Chapter I prohibition or the Chapter II prohibition has been infringed;

    (b)   a decision of the [CMA] that the prohibition in [Article 101(1) or Article 102] of the Treaty has been infringed;

    (c)   a decision of the Tribunal (on an appeal from a decision of the [CMA]) that the Chapter I prohibition or the Chapter II prohibition has been infringed, or that the prohibition in [Article 101(1) or Article 102] of the Treaty has been infringed.

(4)   The periods mentioned in subsection (2) are—

    (a)   in the case of a decision of the [CMA], the period during which an appeal may be made to the Tribunal under section 46 or 47 . . . ;

    (b)   in the case of a decision of the Tribunal mentioned in subsection (3)(c), the period during which a further appeal may be made under section 49 . . . ;

    (c)   in the case of any decision which is the subject of a further appeal, the period during which an appeal may be made to the [Supreme Court] from a decision on the further appeal;

and, where any appeal mentioned in paragraph (a), (b) or (c) is made, the period specified in that paragraph includes the period before the appeal is determined.]

NOTES

Inserted, together with the preceding heading, by the Enterprise Act 2002, s 20(1); by s 20(2) of the 2002 Act, this section does not apply in relation to decisions made before the commencement of the said s 20.

References to "CMA" substituted (for original references to "OFT") by the Enterprise and Regulatory Reform Act 2013, s 26(3), Sch 5, Pt 1, paras 1, 37. For various transitional provisions (including those relating to the abolition of the OFT and the Competition Commission, existing references to those bodies and provisions relating to continuity), see the Enterprise and Regulatory Reform Act 2013 (Commencement No 6, Transitional Provisions and Savings) Order 2014, SI 2014/416, Schedule at **[2.1126]**. This section is also amended as follows:

Sub-s (1): words in square brackets substituted by the Treaty of Lisbon (Changes in Terminology or Numbering) Order 2012, SI 2012/1809, art 3(1), Schedule, Pt 1 (note that the amendments made by this Order do not affect any provision in its application to things done before 1 December 2009 (the date on which the Treaty of Lisbon came into force)).

Sub-s (3): words in second pair of square brackets in para (c) substituted by SI 2012/1809, art 3(1), Schedule, Pt 1 (note that the amendments made by this Order do not affect any provision in its application to things done before 1 December 2009 (the date on which the Treaty of Lisbon came into force)).

Sub-s (4): words omitted from paras (a), (b) repealed by the EC Competition Law (Articles 84 and 85) Enforcement (Revocation) Regulations 2007, SI 2007/1846, reg 3(1), Schedule; words in square brackets in para (c) substituted by the Constitutional Reform Act 2005, s 40(4), Sch 9, Pt 1, para 65(1), (4).

Section 58A is further substituted, except in relation to decisions made before 15 October 2015, by the Consumer Rights Act 2015, s 81, Sch 8, Pt 1, paras 1, 14, as follows:

  "58A   Infringement decisions

  (1)   This section applies to a claim in respect of an infringement decision which is brought in proceedings—

    (a)   before the court, or

    (b)   before the Tribunal under section 47A or 47B.

  (2)   The court or the Tribunal is bound by the infringement decision once it has become final.

  (3)   An infringement decision specified in section 47A(6)(a) or (b) becomes final—

    (a)   when the time for appealing against that decision expires without an appeal having been brought;

    (b)   where the decision is specified in section 47A(6)(a) and an appeal has been brought against the decision under section 46 or 47, when that appeal—

      (i)   has been withdrawn, dismissed or otherwise discontinued, or

      (ii)   has confirmed the infringement decision and the time for making any further appeal against that confirmatory decision expires without a further appeal having been brought;

    (c)   where an appeal has been brought in relation to the decision under section 49, when that appeal—

      (i)   in the case of an appeal against the infringement decision or against a decision which confirmed the infringement decision, has been withdrawn, dismissed or otherwise discontinued, or

      (ii)   has confirmed the infringement decision and the time for making any further appeal to the Supreme Court against that confirmatory decision expires without a further appeal having been brought; or

    (d)   where an appeal has been brought to the Supreme Court in relation to the decision, when that appeal—

      (i)   in the case of an appeal against a decision which confirmed the infringement decision, has been withdrawn, dismissed or otherwise discontinued, or

      (ii)   has confirmed the infringement decision.

  (4)   An infringement decision specified in section 47A(6)(c) becomes final—

    (a)   when the time for appealing against that decision in the European Court expires without an appeal having been brought; or

    (b)   where such an appeal has been brought against the decision, when that appeal—

      (i)   has been withdrawn, dismissed or otherwise discontinued, or

      (ii)   has confirmed the infringement decision.

  (5)   This section applies to the extent that the court or the Tribunal would not otherwise be bound by the infringement decision in question.

  (6)   In this section "the court" means—

    (a)   in England and Wales or Northern Ireland, the High Court,

    (b)   in Scotland, the Court of Session or the sheriff.".

Interpretation and governing principles

[1.1328]
59 [Interpretation of Part 1]
(1)   In this Part—
["agreement" is to be read with section 2(5) and (6);]
. . .

["Article 101(1)" means Article 101(1) of the Treaty;
"Article 101(3)" means Article 101(3) of the Treaty;
"Article 102" means Article 102 of the Treaty;]
"block exemption" has the meaning given in section 6(4);
"block exemption order" has the meaning given in section 6(2);
"the Chapter I prohibition" has the meaning given in section 2(8);
"the Chapter II prohibition" has the meaning given in section 18(4);
["class member" has the meaning given in section 47B(8)(a);]
["the CMA" means the Competition and Markets Authority;]
["collective proceedings" has the meaning given in section 47B(1);
"collective proceedings order" means an order made by the Tribunal authorising the continuance
       of collective proceedings;]
"the Commission"   . . .   means the European Commission;
"the Council" means the Council of the European Union;
"the court", except in sections [49E,] 58[, 58A] and 60 and the expression "European Court",
       means—
     (a)   in England and Wales, the High Court;
     (b)   in Scotland, the Court of Session; and
     (c)   in Northern Ireland, the High Court;

. . .
"document" includes information recorded in any form;
"the EEA Agreement" means the Agreement on the European Economic Area signed at Oporto
       on 2nd May 1992 as it has effect for the time being;
"the European Court" means the Court of Justice of the European Communities and includes the
       [General Court];
["the EC Competition Regulation" means Council Regulation (EC) No 1/2003 of 16th December
       2002 on the implementation of the rules on competition laid down in Articles 81 and 82 of
       the Treaty;]
. . .

["infringement decision", except in section 49C, has the meaning given in section 47A(6);]
"information" includes estimates and forecasts;
["injunction" includes an interim injunction;]
"investigating officer" has the meaning given in section 27(1);
["investigation" means an investigation under section 25;]
"Minister of the Crown" has the same meaning as in the Ministers of the Crown Act 1975;
["OFCOM" means the Office of Communications;]
"officer", in relation to a body corporate, includes a director, manager or secretary and, in
       relation to a partnership in Scotland, includes a partner;
["opt-in collective proceedings" has the meaning given in section 47B(10);
"opt-out collective proceedings" has the meaning given in section 47B(11);]
. . .
"parallel exemption" has the meaning given in section 10(3);
"person", in addition to the meaning given by the Interpretation Act 1978, includes any
       undertaking;
["premises" includes any land or means of transport;]
"prescribed" means prescribed by regulations made by the Secretary of State;
"regulator" has the meaning given by section 54;
["representative" means a person who is authorised by a collective proceedings order to bring
       collective proceedings;
"represented person" means a class member who—
     (a)   has opted in to opt-in collective proceedings,
     (b)   was domiciled in the United Kingdom at the time specified for the purposes of
           determining domicile (see section 47B(11)(b)(i)) and has not opted out of opt-out
           collective proceedings, or
     (c)   has opted in to opt-out collective proceedings;]
"section 11 exemption" has the meaning given in section 11(3); and
["the Treaty" means the treaty on the Functioning of the European Union;]
["the Tribunal" means the Competition Appeal Tribunal;
"Tribunal rules" means rules under section 15 of the Enterprise Act 2002];
["working day" means a day which is not—
     (a)   Saturday,
     (b)   Sunday,

    (c)   Christmas Day,

    (d)   Good Friday, or

    (e)   a day which is a bank holiday under the Banking and Financial Dealings Act 1971 (c 80) in any part of the United Kingdom].

[(1A)   In this Part, in respect of proceedings in Scotland, "defendant" is to be read as "defender".
(1B)   Sections 41, 42, 45 and 46 of the Civil Jurisdiction and Judgments Act 1982 apply for the purpose of determining whether a person is regarded as "domiciled in the United Kingdom" for the purposes of this Part.]

(2)   The fact that to a limited extent the Chapter I prohibition does not apply to an agreement, because of an exclusion provided by or under this Part or any other enactment, does not require those provisions of the agreement to which the exclusion relates to be disregarded when considering whether the agreement infringes the prohibition for other reasons.

(3)   For the purposes of this Part, the power to require information, in relation to information recorded otherwise than in a legible form, includes power to require a copy of it in a legible form.

(4)   Any power conferred on the [CMA] by this Part to require information includes power to require any document which [it] believes may contain that information.

NOTES

Section heading: substituted by the Competition Act 1998 and other enactments (Amendment) Regulations 2004, SI 2004/1261, reg 4, Sch 1, para 35(1), (3).

Sub-s (1) is amended as follows:

Definition "agreement" inserted by SI 2004/1261, reg 4, Sch 1, para 35(1), (2)(a).

Definition "appeal tribunal" (omitted) repealed by the Enterprise Act 2002, ss 21, 278(2), Sch 5, paras 1, 6(a), Sch 26.

Definitions "Article 101(1)", "Article 101(3)", "Article 102", and "the Treaty" substituted by the Treaty of Lisbon (Changes in Terminology or Numbering) Order 2012, SI 2012/1809, art 3(1), Schedule, Pt 1 (note that the amendments made by this Order do not affect any provision in its application to things done before 1 December 2009 (the date on which the Treaty of Lisbon came into force)).

Definitions "class member", "collective proceedings", "collective proceedings order", "infringement decision", "injunction", "opt-in collective proceedings", "opt-out collective proceedings", "representative" and "represented person", and figure in first pair of square brackets in the definition of "the court" inserted by the Consumer Rights Act 2015, s 81, Sch 8, Pt 1, paras 1, 15(1)–(3).

Definition "the CMA" inserted by the Enterprise and Regulatory Reform Act 2013, s 26(3), Sch 5, Pt 1, paras 1, 38(1), (2)(a).

Words "(except in relation to the Competition Commission)" omitted from the definition "the Commission" repealed by the Enterprise and Regulatory Reform Act 2013, s 26(3), Sch 5, Pt 3, paras 218, 221. For various transitional provisions (including those relating to the abolition of the OFT and the Competition Commission, existing references to those bodies and provisions relating to continuity), see the Enterprise and Regulatory Reform Act 2013 (Commencement No 6, Transitional Provisions and Savings) Order 2014, SI 2014/416, Schedule at **[2.1126]**.

Figure in second pair of square brackets in the definition "the court" inserted by the Enterprise Act 2002, s 20(3).

Definition "the Director" (omitted) repealed by the Enterprise Act 2002, s 278, Sch 25, para 38(1), (44)(a), Sch 26.

Words in square brackets in the definition "the European Court" substituted by SI 2012/1809, art 3(1), Schedule, Pt 1 (subject to the same exception as noted above)

Definition "the EC Competition Regulation" inserted by SI 2004/1261, reg 4, Sch 1, para 35(1), (2)(d).

Definition "individual exemption" (omitted) repealed by SI 2004/1261, reg 4, Sch 1, para 35(1), (2)(e).

Definition "investigation" inserted by SI 2004/1261, reg 4, Sch 1, para 35(1), (2)(f).

Definition "OFCOM" inserted by the Communications Act 2003, s 371(7).

Definition "the OFT" (omitted) inserted by the Enterprise Act 2002, s 278(1), Sch 25, para 38(1), (44)(a) and repealed by the Enterprise and Regulatory Reform Act 2013, s 26(3), Sch 5, Pt 1, paras 1, 38(1), (2)(b), subject to transitional provisions in SI 2014/416 as noted above, and originally read as follows—

    "["the OFT" means the Office of Fair Trading;]".

Definition "premises" substituted by SI 2004/1261, reg 4, Sch 1, para 35(1), (2)(g).

Definitions "the Tribunal" and "Tribunal rules" inserted by the Enterprise Act 2002, s 21, Sch 5, paras 1, 6(b).

Definition "working day" inserted by SI 2004/1261, reg 4, Sch 1, para 35(1), (2)(h).

Sub-ss (1A), (1B): inserted by the Consumer Rights Act 2015, s 81, Sch 8, Pt 1, paras 1, 15(1), (4).

Sub-s (4): reference to "CMA" substituted (for reference to "OFT" as substituted by the Enterprise Act 2002, s 278, Sch 25, para 38) by the Enterprise and Regulatory Reform Act 2013, s 26(3), Sch 5, Pt 1, paras 1, 38(1), (3), subject to transitional provisions in SI 2014/416 as noted above; word "it" in square brackets substituted by the Enterprise Act 2002, s 278, Sch 25, para 38.

Regulations: the Competition Act 1998 (Small Agreements and Conduct of Minor Significance) Regulations 2000, SI 2000/262; the Competition Act 1998 (Appealable Decisions and Revocation of Notification of Excluded Agreements) Regulations 2004, SI 2004/1078.

References to the CMA, etc: as to the abolition of the office of the Director General of Fair Trading and the substitution of the original references to the Director (and related expressions), see the note preceding s 1 at **[1.1266]**.

[1.1329]
60 Principles to be applied in determining questions

(1)   The purpose of this section is to ensure that so far as is possible (having regard to any relevant differences between the provisions concerned), questions arising under this Part in relation to competition within the United Kingdom are dealt with in a manner which is consistent with the treatment of corresponding questions arising in Community law in relation to competition within the Community.

(2)　At any time when the court determines a question arising under this Part, it must act (so far as is compatible with the provisions of this Part and whether or not it would otherwise be required to do so) with a view to securing that there is no inconsistency between—

    (a)　the principles applied, and decision reached, by the court in determining that question; and

    (b)　the principles laid down by the Treaty and the European Court, and any relevant decision of that Court, as applicable at that time in determining any corresponding question arising in Community law.

(3)　The court must, in addition, have regard to any relevant decision or statement of the Commission.

(4)　Subsections (2) and (3) also apply to—

    (a)　the [CMA]; and

    (b)　any person acting on behalf of the [CMA], in connection with any matter arising under this Part.

(5)　In subsections (2) and (3), "court" means any court or tribunal.

(6)　In subsections (2)(b) and (3), "decision" includes a decision as to—

    (a)　the interpretation of any provision of Community law;

    (b)　the civil liability of an undertaking for harm caused by its infringement of Community law.

NOTES

Sub-s (4): references to "CMA" substituted (for references to "OFT" as substituted by the Enterprise Act 2002, s 278, Sch 25, para 38) by the Enterprise and Regulatory Reform Act 2013, s 26(3), Sch 5, Pt 1, paras 1, 39. For various transitional provisions (including those relating to the abolition of the OFT and the Competition Commission, existing references to those bodies and provisions relating to continuity), see the Enterprise and Regulatory Reform Act 2013 (Commencement No 6, Transitional Provisions and Savings) Order 2014, SI 2014/416, Schedule at **[2.1126]**.

References to the CMA, etc: as to the abolition of the office of the Director General of Fair Trading and the substitution of the original references to the Director (and related expressions), see the note preceding s 1 at **[1.1266]**.

[PART 2
INSPECTIONS UNDER ARTICLES 20, 21 AND 22(2)

[1.1330]
61　Interpretation of Part 2
In this Part—

"Article 20 inspection" means an inspection ordered by a decision of the Commission under Article 20(4) of the EC Competition Regulation which is not an Article 22(2) inspection;

"Article 21 inspection" means an inspection ordered by a decision of the Commission under Article 21 of the EC Competition Regulation;

"Article 22(2) inspection" means an inspection requested by the Commission under Article 22(2) of the EC Competition Regulation;

"books and records" includes books and records stored on any medium;

["the CMA" means the Competition and Markets Authority;]

"the Commission" means the European Commission;

"the EC Competition Regulation" means Council Regulation (EC) No 1/2003 of 16th December 2002 on the implementation of the rules on competition laid down in Articles 81 and 82 of the Treaty;

. . . .

"premises" includes any land or means of transport;

["the Treaty" means the treaty on the Functioning of the European Union];

["the Tribunal" means the Competition Appeal Tribunal;

"Tribunal rules" means rules under section 15 of the Enterprise Act 2002].]

NOTES

Substituted, together with the preceding heading, by the Competition Act 1998 and other enactments (Amendment) Regulations 2004, SI 2004/1261, reg 4, Sch 1, para 36.

Definition "the CMA" inserted, and definition "the OFT" repealed, by the Enterprise and Regulatory Reform Act 2013, s 26(3), Sch 5, Pt 1, paras 1, 40. For various transitional provisions (including those relating to the abolition of the OFT and the Competition Commission, existing references to those bodies and provisions relating to continuity), see the Enterprise and Regulatory Reform Act 2013 (Commencement No 6, Transitional Provisions and Savings) Order 2014, SI 2014/416, Schedule at **[2.1126]**. The definition "the OFT" originally read as follows—

"the OFT" means the Office of Fair Trading;".

Definition "the Treaty" substituted by the Treaty of Lisbon (Changes in Terminology or Numbering) Order 2012, SI 2012/1809, art 3(1), Schedule, Pt 1 (note that the amendments made by this Order do not affect any provision in its application to things done before 1 December 2009 (the date on which the Treaty of Lisbon came into force)).

Definitions "the Tribunal" and "Tribunal rules" inserted by the Enterprise and Regulatory Reform Act 2013, s 41, Sch 13, paras 1, 4, subject to transitional provisions in SI 2014/416 as noted above.

[1.1331]
62　[Power to enter business premises under a warrant: Article 20 inspections]
(1)　A judge of the High Court [shall] issue a warrant if satisfied, on an application made to the High Court in accordance with rules of court by the [OFT], that—

[(a) the Commission has ordered an Article 20 inspection;

(b) the Article 20 inspection is being, or is likely to be, obstructed; and

(c) the measures that would be authorised by the warrant are neither arbitrary nor excessive having regard to the subject matter of the Article 20 inspection].

(2) [An Article 20 inspection] is being obstructed if—

(a) [a Commission official], exercising his power in accordance with [Article 20(3) of the EC Competition Regulation], has attempted to enter [any business premises] but has been unable to do so; and

(b) there are reasonable grounds for suspecting that there are [on any business premises] books or records . . . which the Commission official has power to examine.

(3) [An Article 20 inspection] is also being obstructed if there are reasonable grounds for suspecting that there are [on any business premises] books or records . . . —

(a) the production of which has been required by [a Commission official] exercising his power in accordance with [Article 20(3) of the EC Competition Regulation]; and

(b) which have not been produced as required.

(4) [An Article 20 inspection] is likely to be obstructed if—

(a)   . . .

(b) there are reasonable grounds for suspecting that there are [on any business premises] books or records . . . which [a Commission official] has power to examine; and

(c) there are also reasonable grounds for suspecting that, if the Commission official attempted to exercise his power to examine any of the books or records, they would not be produced but would be concealed, removed, tampered with or destroyed.

[(5) A warrant under this section shall authorise a named officer of the OFT and any other OFT officer, or Commission official, accompanying the named officer—

(a) to enter any business premises specified in the warrant using such force as is reasonably necessary for the purpose;

(b) to search for books and records which a Commission official has power to examine, using such force as is reasonably necessary for the purpose;

(c) to take or obtain copies of or extracts from such books and records;

(d) to seal the premises, any part of the premises or any books or records which a Commission official has power to seal, for the period and to the extent necessary for the inspection.]

[(5A) A warrant under this section may authorise persons specified in the warrant to accompany the named officer who is executing it.]

(6) Any person entering any premises by virtue of a warrant under this section may take with him such equipment as appears to him to be necessary.

(7) On leaving any premises entered by virtue of the warrant the named officer must, if the premises are unoccupied or the occupier is temporarily absent, leave them as effectively secured as he found them.

(8) A warrant under this section continues in force until the end of the period of one month beginning with the day on which it is issued.

(9) In the application of this section to Scotland, references to the High Court are to be read as references to the Court of Session.

[(10) In this section—

"business premises" means any premises of an undertaking or association of undertakings which a Commission official has under Article 20 of the EC Competition Regulation power to enter in the course of the Article 20 inspection;

"Commission official" means any of the persons authorised by the Commission to conduct the Article 20 inspection; and

"OFT officer" means any officer of the OFT whom the OFT has authorised in writing to accompany the named officer.

(11) In subsection (10), the reference in the definition of "business premises" to Article 20 of the EC Competition Regulation does not include a reference to that Article as applied by Article 21 of that Regulation.]

NOTES

Section heading: substituted by the Competition Act 1998 and other enactments (Amendment) Regulations 2004, SI 2004/1261, reg 4, Sch 1, para 37(1), (8).

Sub-s (1) is amended as follows:

Words in first pair of square brackets substituted (for the words "A judge of the High Court [shall] issue a warrant if satisfied, on an application made to the High Court in accordance with rules of court by the [OFT] that", with those words in square brackets substituted by the Enterprise Act 2002, s 278(1), Sch 25, para 38(1), (47)(a) and SI 2004/1261, reg 4, Sch 1, para 37(1), (2)(a)), by the Enterprise and Regulatory Reform Act 2013, s 41, Sch 13, paras 1, 5(1), (2). For various transitional provisions (including those relating to the abolition of the OFT and the Competition Commission, existing references to those bodies and provisions relating to continuity), see the Enterprise and Regulatory Reform Act 2013 (Commencement No 6, Transitional Provisions and Savings) Order 2014, SI 2014/416, Schedule at **[2.1126]**.

Paras (a)–(c) substituted by SI 2004/1261, reg 4, Sch 1, para 37(1), (2)(b).

Sub-s (2): words in first, second, third and fourth pairs of square brackets substituted, words in fifth pair of square brackets inserted, and words omitted repealed, by SI 2004/1261, reg 4, Sch 1, para 37(1), (3).

Sub-s (3): words in first, third and fourth pairs of square brackets substituted, words in second pair of square brackets inserted, and words omitted repealed, by SI 2004/1261, reg 4, Sch 1, para 37(1), (4).

Sub-s (4): words in first and third pairs of square brackets substituted, para (a) and words omitted from para (b) repealed, and words in second pair of square brackets inserted, by SI 2004/1261, reg 4, Sch 1, para 37(1), (5).

Sub-s (5): substituted by SI 2004/1261, reg 4, Sch 1, para 37(1), (6); references to "CMA" substituted (for references to "OFT") by the Enterprise and Regulatory Reform Act 2013, s 26(3), Sch 5, Pt 1, paras 1, 41, subject to transitional provisions in SI 2014/416 as noted above

Sub-s (5A): inserted by the Enterprise Act 2002, s 203(1), (3).

Sub-s (8A): inserted by the Enterprise and Regulatory Reform Act 2013, s 41, Sch 13, paras 1, 5(1), (3), subject to transitional provisions in SI 2014/416 as noted above.

Sub-ss (10), (11): added by SI 2004/1261, reg 4, Sch 1, para 37(1), (7); in sub-s (10), references to "CMA" substituted (for references to "OFT") by the Enterprise and Regulatory Reform Act 2013, s 26(3), Sch 5, Pt 1, paras 1, 41, subject to transitional provisions in SI 2014/416 as noted above.

References to the CMA, etc: as to the abolition of the office of the Director General of Fair Trading and the substitution of the original references to the Director (and related expressions), see the note preceding s 1 at **[1.1266]**.

[1.1332]

[62A   Power to enter non-business premises under a warrant: Article 21 inspections

(1)   [On an application made to it by the CMA, the High Court or the Tribunal must issue a warrant if it is satisfied that]—

   (a)   the Commission has ordered an Article 21 inspection; and

   (b)   the measures that would be authorised by the warrant are neither arbitrary nor excessive having regard in particular to the matters mentioned in subsection (2).

(2)   Those matters are—

   (a)   the seriousness of the suspected infringement of [Article 101(1) or 102] of the Treaty;

   (b)   the importance of the evidence sought;

   (c)   the involvement of the undertaking or association of undertakings concerned; and

   (d)   whether it is reasonably likely that business books and records relating to the subject matter of the Article 21 inspection are kept on the non-business premises that would be specified in the warrant.

(3)   A warrant under this section shall authorise a named officer of the [CMA] and any other [CMA] officer, or Commission official, accompanying the named officer to enter any non-business premises specified in the warrant.

(4)   A warrant under this section may authorise a named officer of the [CMA] and any other [CMA] officer, or Commission official, accompanying the named officer to search for books or records which a Commission official has power to examine.

(5)   A warrant under this section may authorise a named officer of the [CMA] and any other [CMA] officer, or Commission official, accompanying the named officer to take or obtain copies of books or records of which a Commission official has power to take or obtain copies.

(6)   A warrant granted under this section may authorise the use, for either or both of the purposes mentioned in subsections (3) and (4), of such force as is reasonably necessary.

(7)   A warrant under this section may authorise persons specified in the warrant to accompany the named officer who is executing it.

(8)   Any person entering any premises by virtue of a warrant under this section may take with him such equipment as appears to him to be necessary.

(9)   On leaving any premises entered by virtue of a warrant the named officer must, if the premises are unoccupied or the occupier is temporarily absent, leave them as effectively secured as he found them.

(10)   A warrant under this section continues in force until the end of the period of one month beginning with the day on which it is issued.

[(10A)   An application for a warrant under this section must be made—

   (a)   in the case of an application to the High Court, in accordance with rules of court;

   (b)   in the case of an application to the Tribunal, in accordance with Tribunal rules.]

(11)   In the application of this section to Scotland, references to the High Court are to be read as references to the Court of Session.

(12)   In this section—

   "non-business premises" means any premises to which a decision of the Commission ordering the Article 21 inspection relates;

   "Commission official" means any of the persons authorised by the Commission to conduct the Article 21 inspection; and

   "[CMA] officer" means any officer of the [CMA] whom the [CMA] has authorised in writing to accompany the named officer.]

NOTES

Inserted by the Competition Act 1998 and Other Enactments (Amendment) Regulations 2004, SI 2004/1261, reg 4, Sch 1, para 38.

Sub-s (1): words in square brackets substituted (for original words "A judge of the High Court shall issue a warrant if satisfied, on an application made to the High Court in accordance with the rules of court by the OFT, that") by the Enterprise and Regulatory Reform Act 2013, s 41, Sch 13, paras 1, 6(1), (2). For various transitional provisions (including those relating to the abolition of the OFT and the Competition Commission, existing references to those bodies and provisions relating to continuity), see the Enterprise and Regulatory Reform Act 2013 (Commencement No 6, Transitional Provisions and Savings) Order 2014, SI 2014/416, Schedule at **[2.1126]**.

Sub-s (2): words in square brackets in para (a) substituted by the Treaty of Lisbon (Changes in Terminology or Numbering) Order 2012, SI 2012/1809, art 3(1), Schedule, Pt 1 (note that the amendments made by this Order do not affect any provision in its application to things done before 1 December 2009 (the date on which the Treaty of Lisbon came into force)).

Sub-ss (3)–(5), (12): references to "CMA" substituted (for original references to "OFT") by the Enterprise and Regulatory Reform Act 2013, s 26(3), Sch 5, Pt 1, paras 1, 42, subject to transitional provisions in SI 2014/416 as noted above.

Sub-s (10A): inserted by the Enterprise and Regulatory Reform Act 2013, s 41, Sch 13, paras 1, 6(1), (3), subject to transitional provisions in SI 2014/416 as noted above.

[1.1333]
[62B Powers when conducting an Article 22(2) inspection

(1)   For the purposes of an Article 22(2) inspection, an authorised officer of the [CMA] has the powers specified in Article 20(2) of the EC Competition Regulation.

(2)   For the purposes of this section and section 63—

"authorised officer of the [CMA]" means any officer of the [CMA] to whom an authorisation has been given; and

"authorisation" means an authorisation given in writing by the [CMA] for the purposes of the Article 22(2) inspection which—

  (i)   identifies the officer;

  (ii)   indicates the subject matter and purpose of the inspection; and

  (iii)   draws attention to any penalties which a person may incur under the EC Competition Regulation in connection with the inspection.]

NOTES

Inserted by the Competition Act 1998 and Other Enactments (Amendment) Regulations 2004, SI 2004/1261, reg 4, Sch 1, para 39.

References to "CMA" substituted (for original references to "OFT") by the Enterprise and Regulatory Reform Act 2013, s 26(3), Sch 5, Pt 1, paras 1, 43. For various transitional provisions (including those relating to the abolition of the OFT and the Competition Commission, existing references to those bodies and provisions relating to continuity), see the Enterprise and Regulatory Reform Act 2013 (Commencement No 6, Transitional Provisions and Savings) Order 2014, SI 2014/416, Schedule at [2.1126].

[1.1334]
63 [Power to enter business premises under a warrant: Article 22(2) inspections]

(1)   [On an application made to it by the CMA, the High Court or the Tribunal must issue a warrant if it is satisfied that]—

  [(a)   the Commission has requested the [CMA] to conduct an Article 22(2) inspection which the Commission has ordered by a decision under Article 20(4) of the EC Competition Regulation;

  (b)   the Article 22(2) inspection is being, or is likely to be, obstructed; and

  (c)   the measures that would be authorised by the warrant are neither arbitrary nor excessive having regard to the subject matter of the Article 22(2) inspection].

(2)   [An Article 22(2) inspection] is being obstructed if—

  (a)   an authorised officer of the [CMA] has attempted to enter [any business] premises but has been unable to do so;

  (b)   the officer has produced his authorisation to the undertaking, or association of undertakings, concerned; and

  (c)   there are reasonable grounds for suspecting that there are [on any business premises] books or records . . . which the officer has power to examine.

(3)   [An Article 22(2) inspection] is also being obstructed if—

  (a)   there are reasonable grounds for suspecting that there are [on any business premises] books or records . . . which an authorised officer of the [CMA] has power to examine;

  (b)   the officer has produced his authorisation to the undertaking, or association of undertakings, and has required production of the books or records; and

  (c)   the books and records have not been produced as required.

(4)   [An Article 22(2) inspection] is likely to be obstructed if—

  (a)   there are reasonable grounds for suspecting that there are [on any business premises] books or records . . . which an authorised officer of the [CMA] has power to examine; and

  (b)   there are also reasonable grounds for suspecting that, if the officer attempted to exercise his power to examine any of the books or records, they would not be produced but would be concealed, removed, tampered with or destroyed.

[(5)   A warrant under this section shall authorise a named authorised officer of the [CMA] and any other authorised officer of the [CMA], or Commission official, accompanying the named authorised officer—

  (a)   to enter any business premises specified in the warrant using such force as is reasonably necessary for the purpose;

  (b)   to search for books and records which an authorised officer of the [CMA] has power to examine, using such force as is reasonably necessary for the purpose;

  (c)   to take or obtain copies of or extracts from such books and records; and

(d) to seal the premises, any part of the premises or any books or records which an authorised officer of the [CMA] has power to seal, for the period and to the extent necessary for the inspection.]

[(5A) A warrant under this section may authorise persons specified in the warrant to accompany the named authorised officer who is executing it.]

(6) Any person entering any premises by virtue of a warrant under this section may take with him such equipment as appears to him to be necessary.

(7) On leaving any premises which he has entered by virtue of the warrant the [named authorised officer] must, if the premises are unoccupied or the occupier is temporarily absent, leave them as effectively secured as he found them.

(8) A warrant under this section continues in force until the end of the period of one month beginning with the day on which it is issued.

[(8A) An application for a warrant under this section must be made—
(a) in the case of an application to the High Court, in accordance with rules of court;
(b) in the case of an application to the Tribunal, in accordance with Tribunal rules.]

(9) In the application of this section to Scotland, references to the High Court are to be read as references to the Court of Session.

[(10) In this section—
"business premises" means any premises of an undertaking or association of undertakings which an authorised officer of the [CMA] has power to enter in the course of the Article 22(2) inspection;
"Commission official" means any person authorised by the Commission to assist with the Article 22(2) inspection.]

NOTES

Section heading: substituted by the Competition Act 1998 and other enactments (Amendment) Regulations 2004, SI 2004/1261, reg 4, Sch 1, para 40(1), (9).

Sub-s (1): words in first pair of square brackets substituted (for words "A judge of the High Court [shall] issue a warrant if satisfied, on an application made to the High Court in accordance with rules of court by the [OFT, that]") and reference to "CMA" substituted (for original reference to "OFT") by the Enterprise and Regulatory Reform Act 2013, ss 26(3), 41, Sch 5, Pt 1, paras 1, 44, Sch 13, paras 1, 7(1), (2). For various transitional provisions (including those relating to the abolition of the OFT and the Competition Commission, existing references to those bodies and provisions relating to continuity), see the Enterprise and Regulatory Reform Act 2013 (Commencement No 6, Transitional Provisions and Savings) Order 2014, SI 2014/416, Schedule at [2.1126]; paras (a)–(c) substituted by SI 2004/1261, reg 4, Sch 1, para 40(1), (2)(b).

Sub-s (2): words in first pair of square brackets substituted, words in third and fourth pairs of square brackets inserted, and words omitted repealed, by SI 2004/1261, reg 4, Sch 1, para 40(1), (3); reference to "CMA" substituted (for reference to "OFT" as substituted by the Enterprise Act 2002, s 278, Sch 25, para 38) by the Enterprise and Regulatory Reform Act 2013, s 26(3), Sch 5, Pt 1, paras 1, 44, subject to transitional provisions in SI 2014/416 as noted above.

Sub-ss (3), (4): words in first pair of square brackets substituted, words in second pair of square brackets inserted, and word omitted repealed, by SI 2004/1261, reg 4, Sch 1, para 40(1), (4), (5); references to "CMA" substituted (for references to "OFT" as substituted by the Enterprise Act 2002, s 278, Sch 25, para 38) by the Enterprise and Regulatory Reform Act 2013, s 26(3), Sch 5, Pt 1, paras 1, 44, subject to transitional provisions in SI 2014/416 as noted above.

Sub-s (5): substituted by SI 2004/1261, reg 4, Sch 1, para 40(1), (6); references to "CMA" substituted (for original references to "OFT") by the Enterprise and Regulatory Reform Act 2013, s 26(3), Sch 5, Pt 1, paras 1, 44, subject to transitional provisions in SI 2014/416 as noted above.

Sub-s (5A): inserted by the Enterprise Act 2002, s 203(1), (4).

Sub-s (7): words in square brackets substituted by SI 2004/1261, reg 4, Sch 1, para 40(1), (7).

Sub-s (8A): inserted by the Enterprise and Regulatory Reform Act 2013, s 41, Sch 13, paras 1, 7(1), (3), subject to transitional provisions in SI 2014/416 as noted above.

Sub-s (10): added by SI 2004/1261, reg 4, Sch 1, para 40(1), (8); reference to "CMA" substituted (for original reference to "OFT") by the Enterprise and Regulatory Reform Act 2013, s 26(3), Sch 5, Pt 1, paras 1, 44, subject to transitional provisions in SI 2014/416 as noted above.

References to the CMA, etc: as to the abolition of the office of the Director General of Fair Trading and the substitution of the original references to the Director (and related expressions), see the note preceding s 1 at **[1.1266]**.

[1.1335]
64 Entry of premises under sections 62[, 62A] and 63: supplementary

(1) A warrant issued under section 62[, 62A] or 63 must indicate—
(a) the subject matter and purpose of the [inspection];
(b) the nature of the offence created by section 65.

(2) The powers conferred by section 62[, 62A] or 63 are to be exercised on production of a warrant issued under that section.

(3) If there is no one at the premises when the named officer proposes to execute such a warrant he must, before executing it—
(a) take such steps as are reasonable in all the circumstances to inform the occupier of the intended entry; and
(b) if the occupier is informed, afford him or his legal or other representative a reasonable opportunity to be present when the warrant is executed.

(4) If the named officer is unable to inform the occupier of the intended entry he must, when executing the warrant, leave a copy of it in a prominent place on the premises.

(5) In this section—
["named officer" means—

(a) for the purposes of a warrant issued under section 62 or 62A, the officer named in the warrant; and

(b) for the purposes of a warrant issued under section 63, the authorised officer named in the warrant;]

"occupier", in relation to any premises, means a person whom the named officer reasonably believes is the occupier of those premises.

NOTES

Section heading: number in square brackets inserted by the Competition Act 1998 and Other Enactments (Amendment) Regulations 2004, SI 2004/1261, reg 4, Sch 1, para 41(1), (4).

Sub-s (1): number in first pair of square brackets inserted and word in square brackets in para (a) substituted by SI 2004/1261, reg 4, Sch 1, para 41(1), (2), (4).

Sub-s (2): number in square brackets inserted by SI 2004/1261, reg 4, Sch 1, para 41(1), (4).

Sub-s (5): definition "named officer" substituted by SI 2004/1261, reg 4, Sch 1, para 41(1), (3).

[1.1336]
65 Offences

(1) A person is guilty of an offence if he intentionally obstructs any person in the exercise of his powers under a warrant issued under section 62[, 62A] or 63.

(2) A person guilty of an offence under subsection (1) is liable—

(a) on summary conviction, to a fine not exceeding the statutory maximum;

(b) on conviction on indictment, to imprisonment for a term not exceeding two years or to a fine or to both.

NOTES

Sub-s (1): number in square brackets inserted by the Competition Act 1998 and Other Enactments (Amendment) Regulations 2004, SI 2004/1261, reg 4, Sch 1, para 42.

[1.1337]
[65A Privileged communications: Article 22(2) inspections

(1) A person shall not be required, by virtue of any provision of section 62B or 63, to produce or disclose a privileged communication.

(2) "Privileged communication" means a communication—

(a) between a professional legal adviser and his client, or

(b) made in connection with, or in contemplation of, legal proceedings and for the purposes of those proceedings,

which in proceedings in the High Court would be protected from disclosure on grounds of legal professional privilege.

(3) In the application of this section to Scotland—

(a) the reference to the High Court is to be read as a reference to the Court of Session; and

(b) the reference to legal professional privilege is to be read as a reference to confidentiality of communications.]

NOTES

Inserted, together with s 65B, by the Competition Act 1998 and Other Enactments (Amendment) Regulations 2004, SI 2004/1261, reg 4, Sch 1, para 43.

[1.1338]
[65B Use of statements in prosecution: Article 22(2) inspections

A statement made by a person in response to a requirement imposed by virtue of section 62B or 63 may not be used in evidence against him on a prosecution for an offence under section 188 of the Enterprise Act 2002 unless, in the proceedings—

(a) in giving evidence, he makes a statement inconsistent with it, and

(b) evidence relating to it is adduced, or a question relating to it is asked, by him or on his behalf.]

NOTES

Inserted as noted to s 65A at **[1.1337]**.

[PART 2A
ARTICLE 22(1) INVESTIGATIONS

[1.1339]
65C Interpretation of Part 2A

(1) In this Part—

"Article 22(1) investigation" means an investigation conducted by the [CMA] on behalf and for the account of a competition authority of another Member State pursuant to Article 22(1) of the EC Competition Regulation;

"the Commission" means the European Commission;

"competition authority of another Member State" means a competition authority designated as such under Article 35 of the EC Competition Regulation by a Member State other than the United Kingdom;

"the EC Competition Regulation" means Council Regulation (EC) No 1/2003 of 16th December 2002 on the implementation of the rules on competition laid down in Articles 81 and 82 of the Treaty; and

"investigating officer" has the meaning given in section 65F(1).

(2) In this Part, the following expressions have the same meanings as in Part 1—

"[Article 101(1)]";

"[Article 102]";

["the CMA";]

"the court";

"document";

"information";

"officer";

. . .

"person";

"premises"

"the Treaty";

["the Tribunal";

"Tribunal rules";] and

"working day".

(3) For the purposes of this Part, the power to require information, in relation to information recorded otherwise than in a legible form, includes power to require a copy of it in a legible form.

(4) Any power conferred on the [CMA] by this Part to require information includes power to require any document which it believes may contain that information.]

NOTES

Part 2A (ss 65C–65N) inserted by the Competition Act 1998 and Other Enactments (Amendment) Regulations 2004, SI 2004/1261, reg 4, Sch 1, para 44.

Sub-ss (1), (4): references to "CMA" substituted (for references to "OFT") by the Enterprise and Regulatory Reform Act 2013, s 26(3), Sch 5, Pt 1, paras 1, 45(1), (2), (4). For various transitional provisions (including those relating to the abolition of the OFT and the Competition Commission, existing references to those bodies and provisions relating to continuity), see the Enterprise and Regulatory Reform Act 2013 (Commencement No 6, Transitional Provisions and Savings) Order 2014, SI 2014/416, Schedule at **[2.1126]**.

Sub-s (2): words in first and second pairs of square brackets substituted by the Treaty of Lisbon (Changes in Terminology or Numbering) Order 2012, SI 2012/1809, art 3(1), Schedule, Pt 1 (note that the amendments made by this Order do not affect any provision in its application to things done before 1 December 2009 (the date on which the Treaty of Lisbon came into force)); words in third, fourth and final pairs of square brackets inserted, and words ""the OFT";" (omitted) repealed, by the Enterprise and Regulatory Reform Act 2013, s 26(3), Sch 5, Pt 1, paras 1, 45(1), (3), (4), subject to transitional provisions in SI 2014/416 as noted above.

[1.1340]

[65D Power to conduct an Article 22(1) investigation

(1) In any of the following cases, the [CMA] may conduct an Article 22(1) investigation.

(2) The first case is where there are reasonable grounds for suspecting that there is an agreement which—

(a) may affect trade between Member States; and

(b) has as its object or effect the prevention, restriction or distortion of competition within the Community.

(3) The second case is where there are reasonable grounds for suspecting that the prohibition in [Article 102] has been infringed.

(4) The third case is where there are reasonable grounds for suspecting that, at some time in the past, there was an agreement which at that time—

(a) may have affected trade between Member States; and

(b) had as its object or effect the prevention, restriction or distortion of competition within the Community.

(5) It is immaterial for the purposes of subsection (4) whether the agreement in question remains in existence.

(6) A provision of this Part which is expressed to apply to, or in relation to, an agreement is to be read as applying equally to, or in relation to, a decision by an association of undertakings or a concerted practice.]

NOTES

Inserted as noted to s 65C at **[1.1339]**.

Sub-s (1): reference to "CMA" substituted (for original reference to "OFT") by the Enterprise and Regulatory Reform Act 2013, s 26(3), Sch 5, Pt 1, paras 1, 46. For various transitional provisions (including those relating to the abolition of the OFT and the Competition Commission, existing references to those bodies and provisions relating to continuity), see the Enterprise and Regulatory Reform Act 2013 (Commencement No 6, Transitional Provisions and Savings) Order 2014, SI 2014/416, Schedule at **[2.1126]**.

Sub-s (3): words in square brackets substituted by the Treaty of Lisbon (Changes in Terminology or Numbering) Order 2012, SI 2012/1809, art 3(1), Schedule, Pt 1 (note that the amendments made by this Order do not affect any provision in its application to things done before 1 December 2009 (the date on which the Treaty of Lisbon came into force)).

[1.1341]
[65E Powers when conducting Article 22(1) investigations

(1) For the purposes of an Article 22(1) investigation, the [CMA] may require any person to produce to it a specified document, or to provide it with specified information, which it considers relates to any matter relevant to the investigation.

(2) The power conferred by subsection (1) is to be exercised by a notice in writing.

(3) A notice under subsection (2) must indicate—
  (a) the subject matter and purpose of the Article 22(1) investigation; and
  (b) the nature of the offences created by sections 65L to 65N.

(4) In subsection (1) "specified" means—
  (a) specified, or described, in the notice; or
  (b) falling within a category which is specified, or described, in the notice.

(5) The [CMA] may also specify in the notice—
  (a) the time and place at which any document is to be produced or any information is to be provided;
  (b) the manner and form in which it is to be produced or provided.

(6) The power under this section to require a person to produce a document includes power—
  (a) if the document is produced—
    (i) to take copies of it or extracts from it;
    (ii) to require him, or any person who is a present or past officer of his, or is or was at any time employed by him, to provide an explanation of the document;
  (b) if the document is not produced, to require him to state, to the best of his knowledge and belief, where it is.]

NOTES
Inserted as noted to s 65C at **[1.1339]**.

Sub-ss (1), (5): references to "CMA" substituted (for original references to "OFT") by the Enterprise and Regulatory Reform Act 2013, s 26(3), Sch 5, Pt 1, paras 1, 47. For various transitional provisions (including those relating to the abolition of the OFT and the Competition Commission, existing references to those bodies and provisions relating to continuity), see the Enterprise and Regulatory Reform Act 2013 (Commencement No 6, Transitional Provisions and Savings) Order 2014, SI 2014/416, Schedule at **[2.1126]**.

[1.1342]
[65F Power to enter business premises without a warrant

(1) Any officer of the [CMA] who is authorised in writing by the [CMA] to do so ("an investigating officer") may enter any business premises in connection with an Article 22(1) investigation.

(2) No investigating officer is to enter any premises in the exercise of his powers under this section unless he has given to the occupier of the premises a written notice which—
  (a) gives at least two working days' notice of the intended entry;
  (b) indicates the subject matter and purpose of the Article 22(1) investigation; and
  (c) indicates the nature of the offences created by sections 65L to 65N.

(3) Subsection (2) does not apply—
  (a) if the [CMA] has a reasonable suspicion that the premises are, or have been, occupied by—
    (i) a party to an agreement which it is investigating under section 65D; or
    (ii) an undertaking the conduct of which it is investigating under section 65D; or
  (b) if the investigating officer has taken all such steps as are reasonably practicable to give notice but has not been able to do so.

(4) In a case falling within subsection (3), the power of entry conferred by subsection (1) is to be exercised by the investigating officer on production of—
  (a) evidence of his authorisation; and
  (b) a document containing the information referred to in subsection (2)(b) and (c).

(5) An investigating officer entering any premises under this section may—
  (a) take with him such equipment as appears to him to be necessary;
  (b) require any person on the premises—
    (i) to produce any document which he considers relates to any matter relevant to the investigation; and
    (ii) if the document is produced, to provide an explanation of it;
  (c) require any person to state, to the best of his knowledge and belief, where any such document is to be found;
  (d) take copies of, or extracts from, any document which is produced;
  (e) require any information which is stored in any electronic form and is accessible from the premises and which the investigating officer considers relates to any matter relevant to the investigation, to be produced in a form—
    (i) in which it can be taken away, and

    (ii)   in which it is visible and legible or from which it can readily be produced in a visible and legible form;
  (f)   take any steps which appear to be necessary for the purpose of preserving or preventing interference with any document which he consider relates to any matter relevant to the investigation.

(6)   In this section "business premises" means premises (or any part of premises) not used as a dwelling.]

NOTES

Inserted as noted to s 65C at **[1.1339]**.

Sub-ss (1), (3): references to "CMA" substituted (for original references to "OFT") by the Enterprise and Regulatory Reform Act 2013, s 26(3), Sch 5, Pt 1, paras 1, 48. For various transitional provisions (including those relating to the abolition of the OFT and the Competition Commission, existing references to those bodies and provisions relating to continuity), see the Enterprise and Regulatory Reform Act 2013 (Commencement No 6, Transitional Provisions and Savings) Order 2014, SI 2014/416, Schedule at **[2.1126]**.

[1.1343]
[65G   Power to enter business premises under a warrant
(1)   [On an application made to it by the CMA, the court or the Tribunal may issue a warrant if it is satisfied that]—
  (a)   there are reasonable grounds for suspecting that there are on any business premises documents—
    (i)   the production of which has been required under section 65E or 65F; and
    (ii)   which have not been produced as required;
  (b)   there are reasonable grounds for suspecting that—
    (i)   there are on any business premises documents which the [CMA] has power under section 65E to require to be produced; and
    (ii)   if the documents were required to be produced, they would not be produced but would be concealed, removed, tampered with or destroyed; or
  (c)   an investigating officer has attempted to enter premises in the exercise of his powers under section 65F but has been unable to do so and that there are reasonable grounds for suspecting that there are on the premises documents the production of which could have been required under that section.

(2)   A warrant under this section shall authorise a named officer of the [CMA] and any other of its officers whom the [CMA] has authorised in writing to accompany the named officer—
  (a)   to enter the premises specified in the warrant, using such force as is reasonably necessary for the purpose;
  (b)   to search the premises and take copies of, or extracts from, any document appearing to be of a kind in respect of which the application under subsection (1) was granted ("the relevant kind");
  (c)   to take possession of any documents appearing to be of the relevant kind if—
    (i)   such action appears to be necessary for preserving the documents or preventing interference with them; or
    (ii)   it is not reasonably practicable to take copies of the documents on the premises;
  (d)   to take any other steps which appear to be necessary for the purpose mentioned in paragraph (c)(i);
  (e)   to require any person to provide an explanation of any document appearing to be of the relevant kind or to state, to the best of his knowledge and belief, where it may be found;
  (f)   to require any information which is stored in any electronic form and is accessible from the premises and which the named officer considers relates to any matter relevant to the Article 22(1) investigation, to be produced in a form—
    (i)   in which it can be taken away, and
    (ii)   in which it is visible and legible or from which it can readily be produced in a visible and legible form.

(3)   If, in the case of a warrant under subsection (1)(b), [the court or (as the case may be) the Tribunal] is satisfied that it is reasonable to suspect that there are also on the premises other documents relating to the Article 22(1) investigation concerned, the warrant shall also authorise action mentioned in subsection (2) to be taken in relation to any such document.

(4)   A warrant under this section may authorise persons specified in the warrant to accompany the named officer who is executing it.

(5)   Any person entering premises by virtue of a warrant under this section may take with him such equipment as appears to him to be necessary.

(6)   On leaving any premises which he has entered by virtue of a warrant under this section, the named officer must, if the premises are unoccupied or the occupier is temporarily absent, leave them as effectively secured as he found them.

(7)   A warrant under this section continues in force until the end of the period of one month beginning with the day on which it is issued.

(8)   Any document of which possession is taken under subsection (2)(c) may be retained for a period of three months.

[(8A) An application for a warrant under this section must be made—
  (a) in the case of an application to the court, in accordance with rules of court;
  (b) in the case of an application to the Tribunal, in accordance with Tribunal rules.]
(9) In this section "business premises" has the same meaning as in section 65F.]

NOTES
Inserted as noted to s 65C at **[1.1339]**.
  Words in first pair of square brackets in sub-s (1) substituted (for original words "On an application made by the OFT to the court in accordance with rules of court, a judge may issue a warrant if he is satisfied that"), words in square brackets in sub-s (3) substituted (for original words "the judge") and sub-s (8A) inserted, by the Enterprise and Regulatory Reform Act 2013, s 41, Sch 13, paras 1, 9. For various transitional provisions (including those relating to the abolition of the OFT and the Competition Commission, existing references to those bodies and provisions relating to continuity), see the Enterprise and Regulatory Reform Act 2013 (Commencement No 6, Transitional Provisions and Savings) Order 2014, SI 2014/416, Schedule at **[2.1126]**.
  In sub-ss (1)(b)(i), (2) references to "CMA" substituted (for original references to "OFT") by the Enterprise and Regulatory Reform Act 2013, s 26(3), Sch 5, Pt 1, paras 1, 49, subject to transitional provisions in SI 2014/416 as noted above.

[1.1344]
[65H Power to enter domestic premises under a warrant
(1) [On an application made to it by the CMA, the court or the Tribunal may issue a warrant if it is satisfied that]—
  (a) there are reasonable grounds for suspecting that there are on any domestic premises documents—
    (i) the production of which has been required under section 65E; and
    (ii) which have not been produced as required; or
  (b) there are reasonable grounds for suspecting that—
    (i) there are on any domestic premises documents which the [CMA] has power under section 65E to require to be produced; and
    (ii) if the documents were required to be produced, they would not be produced but would be concealed, removed, tampered with or destroyed.
(2) A warrant under this section shall authorise a named officer of the [CMA], and any other of its officers whom the [CMA] has authorised in writing to accompany the named officer—
  (a) to enter the premises specified in the warrant, using such force as is reasonably necessary for the purpose;
  (b) to search the premises and take copies of, or extracts from, any document appearing to be of a kind in respect of which the application under subsection (1) was granted ("the relevant kind");
  (c) to take possession of any documents appearing to be of the relevant kind if—
    (i) such action appears to be necessary for preserving the documents or preventing interference with them; or
    (ii) it is not reasonably practicable to take copies of the documents on the premises;
  (d) to take any other steps which appear to be necessary for the purpose mentioned in paragraph (c)(i);
  (e) to require any person to provide an explanation of any document appearing to be of the relevant kind or to state, to the best of his knowledge or belief, where it may be found;
  (f) to require any information which is stored in any electronic form and is accessible from the premises and which the named officer considers relates to any matter relevant to the investigation, to be produced in a form—
    (i) in which it can be taken away; and
    (ii) in which it is visible and legible or from which it can readily be produced in a visible and legible form.
(3) If, in the case of a warrant under subsection (1)(b), [the court or (as the case may be) the Tribunal] is satisfied that it is reasonable to suspect that there are also on the premises other documents relating to the investigation concerned, the warrant shall also authorise action mentioned in subsection (2) to be taken in relation to any such document.
(4) A warrant under this section may authorise persons specified in the warrant to accompany the named officer who is executing it.
(5) Any person entering premises by virtue of a warrant under this section may take with him such equipment as appears to him to be necessary.
(6) On leaving any premises which he has entered by virtue of a warrant under this section, the named officer must, if the premises are unoccupied or the occupier is temporarily absent, leave them as effectively secured as he found them.
(7) A warrant under this section continues in force until the end of the period of one month beginning with the day on which it is issued.
(8) Any document of which possession is taken under subsection (2)(c) may be retained for a period of three months.
[(8A) An application for a warrant under this section must be made—
  (a) in the case of an application to the court, in accordance with rules of court;
  (b) in the case of an application to the Tribunal, in accordance with Tribunal rules.]

(9) In this section, "domestic premises" means premises (or any part of premises) that are used as a dwelling and are—

    (a) premises also used in connection with the affairs of an undertaking or association of undertakings; or

    (b) premises where documents relating to the affairs of an undertaking or association of undertakings are kept.]

NOTES

Inserted as noted to s 65C at **[1.1339]**.

Words in first pair of square brackets in sub-s (1) substituted (for original words "On an application made by the OFT to the court in accordance with rules of court, a judge may issue a warrant if he is satisfied that"), words in square brackets in sub-s (3) substituted (for original words "the judge") and sub-s (8A) inserted, by the Enterprise and Regulatory Reform Act 2013, s 41, Sch 13, paras 1, 10. For various transitional provisions (including those relating to the abolition of the OFT and the Competition Commission, existing references to those bodies and provisions relating to continuity), see the Enterprise and Regulatory Reform Act 2013 (Commencement No 6, Transitional Provisions and Savings) Order 2014, SI 2014/416, Schedule at **[2.1126]**.

In sub-ss (1)(b)(i), (2) references to "CMA" substituted (for original references to "OFT") by the Enterprise and Regulatory Reform Act 2013, s 26(3), Sch 5, Pt 1, paras 1, 50, subject to transitional provisions in SI 2014/416 as noted above.

[1.1345]

[65I   Entry of premises under a warrant: supplementary

(1) A warrant issued under section 65G or 65H must indicate—

    (a) the subject matter of the Article 22(1) investigation;

    (b) the nature of the offences created by sections 65L to 65N.

(2) The powers conferred by section 65G or 65H are to be exercised on production of a warrant issued under that section.

(3) If there is no one at the premises when the named officer proposes to execute such a warrant he must, before executing it—

    (a) take such steps as are reasonable in all the circumstances to inform the occupier of the intended entry; and

    (b) if the occupier is informed, afford him or his legal or other representative a reasonable opportunity to be present when the warrant is executed.

(4) If the named officer is unable to inform the occupier of the intended entry he must, when executing the warrant, leave a copy of it in a prominent place on the premises.

(5) In this section—

"named officer" means the officer named in the warrant; and

"occupier", in relation to any premises, means a person whom the named officer reasonably believes is the occupier of those premises.]

NOTES

Inserted as noted to s 65C at **[1.1339]**.

[1.1346]

[65J   Privileged communications

(1) A person shall not be required, under any provision of this Part, to produce or disclose a privileged communication.

(2) "Privileged communication" means a communication—

    (a) between a professional legal adviser and his client, or

    (b) made in connection with, or in contemplation of, legal proceedings and for the purposes of those proceedings,

which in proceedings in the High Court would be protected from disclosure on grounds of legal professional privilege.

(3) *(Applies to Scotland only.)*]

NOTES

Inserted as noted to s 65C at **[1.1339]**.

[1.1347]

[65K   Use of statements in prosecution

A statement made by a person in response to a requirement imposed by virtue of any of sections 65E to 65H may not be used in evidence against him on a prosecution for an offence under section 188 of the Enterprise Act 2002 unless, in the proceedings—

    (a) in giving evidence, he makes a statement inconsistent with it, and

    (b) evidence relating to it is adduced, or a question relating to it is asked, by him or on his behalf.]

NOTES

Inserted as noted to s 65C at **[1.1339]**.

[1.1348]
[65L   Offences
(1)   A person is guilty of an offence if he fails to comply with a requirement imposed on him under section 65E, 65F, 65G or 65H.
(2)   If a person is charged with an offence under subsection (1) in respect of a requirement to produce a document, it is a defence for him to prove—
  (a)   that the document was not in his possession or under his control; and
  (b)   that it was not reasonably practicable for him to comply with the requirement.
(3)   If a person is charged with an offence under subsection (1) in respect of a requirement—
  (a)   to provide information,
  (b)   to provide an explanation of a document, or
  (c)   to state where a document is to be found,
it is a defence for him to prove that he had a reasonable excuse for failing to comply with the requirement.
(4)   Failure to comply with a requirement imposed under section 65E or 65F is not an offence if the person imposing the requirement has failed to act in accordance with that section.
(5)   A person is guilty of an offence if he intentionally obstructs an officer acting in the exercise of his powers under section 65F.
(6)   A person guilty of an offence under subsection (1) or (5) is liable—
  (a)   on summary conviction, to a fine not exceeding the statutory maximum;
  (b)   on conviction on indictment, to a fine.
(7)   A person who intentionally obstructs an officer in the exercise of his powers under a warrant issued under section 65G or 65H is guilty of an offence and liable—
  (a)   on summary conviction, to a fine not exceeding the statutory maximum;
  (b)   on conviction on indictment, to imprisonment for a term not exceeding two years or to a fine or to both.]

NOTES
Inserted as noted to s 65C at **[1.1339]**.

[1.1349]
[65M   Destroying or falsifying documents
(1)   A person is guilty of an offence if, having been required to produce a document under section 65E, 65F, 65G or 65H—
  (a)   he intentionally or recklessly destroys or otherwise disposes of it, falsifies it or conceals it, or
  (b)   he causes or permits its destruction, disposal, falsification or concealment.
(2)   A person guilty of an offence under subsection (1) is liable—
  (a)   on summary conviction, to a fine not exceeding the statutory maximum;
  (b)   on conviction on indictment, to imprisonment for a term not exceeding two years or to a fine or to both.]

NOTES
Inserted as noted to s 65C at **[1.1339]**.

[1.1350]
[65N   False or misleading information
(1)   If information is provided by a person to the [CMA] in connection with any function of the [CMA] under this Part, that person is guilty of an offence if—
  (a)   the information is false or misleading in a material particular; and
  (b)   he knows that it is or is reckless as to whether it is.
(2)   A person who—
  (a)   provides any information to another person, knowing the information to be false or misleading in a material particular, or
  (b)   recklessly provides any information to another person which is false or misleading in a material particular,
knowing that the information is to be used for the purpose of providing information to the [CMA] in connection with any of its functions under this Part, is guilty of an offence.
(3)   A person guilty of an offence under this section is liable—
  (a)   on summary conviction, to a fine not exceeding the statutory maximum;
  (b)   on conviction on indictment, to imprisonment for a term not exceeding two years or to a fine or to both.]

NOTES
Inserted as noted to s 65C at **[1.1339]**.
References to "CMA" substituted (for original references to "OFT") by the Enterprise and Regulatory Reform Act 2013, s 26(3), Sch 5, Pt 1, paras 1, 51. For various transitional provisions (including those relating to the abolition of the OFT and the Competition Commission, existing references to those bodies and provisions relating to continuity), see the Enterprise and Regulatory Reform Act 2013 (Commencement No 6, Transitional Provisions and Savings) Order 2014, SI 2014/416, Schedule at **[2.1126]**.

66–69 ((*Pt III*) *ss 66, 67 repealed by the Enterprise Act 2002, s 278(2), Sch 26; s 68 inserts s 137(3A)–(3C) of the Fair Trading Act 1973 at* **[1.511]***; s 69 amends s 83 of the 1973 Act (repealed).*)

PART IV
SUPPLEMENTAL AND TRANSITIONAL

70   (*Repeals the Patents Act 1977, ss 44, 45.*)

[1.1351]
71   Regulations, orders and rules
(1)   Any power to make regulations or orders which is conferred by this Act is exercisable by statutory instrument.

(2)   The power to make rules which is conferred by section 48 is exercisable by statutory instrument.

(3)   Any statutory instrument made under this Act may—
    (a)   contain such incidental, supplemental, consequential and transitional provision as the Secretary of State considers appropriate; and
    (b)   make different provision for different cases.

(4)   No order is to be made under—
    (a)   section 3,
    (b)   section 19,
    (c)   section 36(8),
    [(ca)   section 45(8),]
    [(cb)   section 47C(7),]
    (d)   section 50, or
    (e)   paragraph 6(3) of Schedule 4,
unless a draft of the order has been laid before Parliament and approved by a resolution of each House.

(5)   Any statutory instrument made under this Act, apart from one made—
    (a)   under any of the provisions mentioned in subsection (4), or
    (b)   under section 76(3),
shall be subject to annulment by a resolution of either House of Parliament.

NOTES

Sub-s (4): para (ca) inserted by the Enterprise Act 2002, s 278(1), Sch 25, para 38(1), (49); para (cb) inserted by the Consumer Rights Act 2015, s 81, Sch 8, Pt 1, paras 1, 16.

[1.1352]
72   Offences by bodies corporate etc
(1)   This section applies to an offence under any of sections 42 to 44, [65 or 65L to 65N].

(2)   If an offence committed by a body corporate is proved—
    (a)   to have been committed with the consent or connivance of an officer, or
    (b)   to be attributable to any neglect on his part,
the officer as well as the body corporate is guilty of the offence and liable to be proceeded against and punished accordingly.

(3)   In subsection (2) "officer", in relation to a body corporate, means a director, manager, secretary or other similar officer of the body, or a person purporting to act in any such capacity.

(4)   If the affairs of a body corporate are managed by its members, subsection (2) applies in relation to the acts and defaults of a member in connection with his functions of management as if he were a director of the body corporate.

(5)   If an offence committed by a partnership in Scotland is proved—
    (a)   to have been committed with the consent or connivance of a partner, or
    (b)   to be attributable to any neglect on his part,
the partner as well as the partnership is guilty of the offence and liable to be proceeded against and punished accordingly.

(6)   In subsection (5) "partner" includes a person purporting to act as a partner.

NOTES

Sub-s (1): words in square brackets substituted by the Competition Act 1998 and Other Enactments (Amendment) Regulations 2004, SI 2004/1261, reg 4, Sch 1, para 45.

[1.1353]
73   Crown application
(1)   Any provision made by or under this Act binds the Crown except that—
    (a)   the Crown is not criminally liable as a result of any such provision;
    (b)   the Crown is not liable for any penalty under any such provision; and
    (c)   nothing in this Act affects Her Majesty in her private capacity.

(2)   Subsection (1)(a) does not affect the application of any provision of this Act in relation to persons in the public service of the Crown.

(3) Subsection (1)(c) is to be interpreted as if section 38(3) of the Crown Proceedings Act 1947 (interpretation of references in that Act to Her Majesty in her private capacity) were contained in this Act.

[(4) If an investigation is conducted under section 25 or 65D in respect of an agreement where none of the parties is the Crown or a person in the public service of the Crown, or in respect of conduct otherwise than by the Crown or such a person—

    (a)   the power conferred by section 27 or (as the case may be) section 65F may not be exercised in relation to land which is occupied by a government department, or otherwise for purposes of the Crown, without the written consent of the appropriate person; and

    (b)   none of sections 28, 28A, 65G and 65H applies in relation to land so occupied.]

(5) In any case in which consent is required under subsection (4), the person who is the appropriate person in relation to that case is to be determined in accordance with regulations made by the Secretary of State.

(6) Sections 62[, 62A] and 63 do not apply in relation to land which is occupied by a government department, or otherwise for purposes of the Crown, unless the matter being investigated is [an agreement to which the Crown or a person in the service of the Crown is a party, or conduct by the Crown or such a person].

[(6A) In subsections (4) and (6) "agreement" includes a suspected agreement and is to be read as applying equally to, or in relation to, a decision by an association of undertakings or a concerted practice; and "conduct" includes suspected conduct.]

(7)   . . .

(8) If the Secretary of State certifies that it appears to him to be in the interests of national security that the powers of entry—

    (a)   conferred by section 27 [or 65F], or

    (b)   that may be conferred by a warrant under [section 28, 28A, 62, 62A, 63, 65G or 65H],

should not be exercisable in relation to premises held or used by or on behalf of the Crown and which are specified in the certificate, those powers are not exercisable in relation to those premises.

(9) Any amendment, repeal or revocation made by this Act binds the Crown to the extent that the enactment amended, repealed or revoked binds the Crown.

NOTES

Sub-s (4): substituted by the Competition Act 1998 and Other Enactments (Amendment) Regulations 2004, SI 2004/1261, reg 4, Sch 1, para 46(1), (2).

Sub-s (6): words in first pair of square brackets inserted and words in second pair of square brackets substituted by SI 2004/1261, reg 4, Sch 1, para 46(1), (3).

Sub-s (6A): inserted by SI 2004/1261, reg 4, Sch 1, para 46(1), (4).

Sub-s (7): repealed by SI 2004/1261, reg 4, Sch 1, para 46(1), (5), subject to savings and transitional provision in reg 6(1), (2), (4) of those Regulations.

Sub-s (8): words in square brackets in para (a) inserted and words in square brackets in para (b) substituted by SI 2004/1261, reg 4, Sch 1, para 46(1), (6).

Regulations: the Competition Act 1998 (Definition of Appropriate Person) Regulations 1999, SI 1999/2282.

[1.1354]
74 Amendments, transitional provisions, savings and repeals

(1)   The minor and consequential amendments set out in Schedule 12 are to have effect.

(2)   The transitional provisions and savings set out in Schedule 13 are to have effect.

(3)   The enactments set out in Schedule 14 are repealed.

NOTES

9 November 1998 (certain purposes); 11 January 1999 (certain purposes); 10 November 1999 (certain purposes); 1 March 2000 (certain purposes); 10 March 2013 (otherwise).

[1.1355]
75 Consequential and supplementary provision

(1)   The Secretary of State may by order make such incidental, consequential, transitional or supplemental provision as he thinks necessary or expedient for the general purposes, or any particular purpose, of this Act or in consequence of any of its provisions or for giving full effect to it.

(2)   An order under subsection (1) may, in particular, make provision—

    (a)   for enabling any person by whom any powers will become exercisable, on a date specified by or under this Act, by virtue of any provision made by or under this Act to take before that date any steps which are necessary as a preliminary to the exercise of those powers;

    (b)   for making savings, or additional savings, from the effect of any repeal made by or under this Act.

(3)   Amendments made under this section shall be in addition, and without prejudice, to those made by or under any other provision of this Act.

(4)   No other provision of this Act restricts the powers conferred by this section.

NOTES

Orders: the Competition Act 1998 (Competition Commission) Transitional, Consequential and Supplemental Provisions Order 1999, SI 1999/506 at **[2.1]**; the Judicial Pensions (Qualifying Judicial Offices) (President of the Competition Commission

Appeal Tribunals) Order 1999, SI 1999/2283; the Competition Act 1998 (Transitional, Consequential and Supplemental Provisions) Order 2000, SI 2000/311; the Competition Act 1998 (Consequential and Supplemental Provisions) Order 2000, SI 2000/2031; the Competition Act 1998 (Public Transport Ticketing Schemes Block Exemption) Order 2001, SI 2001/319; the Competition Act 1998 (Consequential Provisions) Order 2013, SI 2013/294 (which provides for repeals and revocations consequential on the coming into force (on 10 March 2013) of provisions of this Act repealing the Restrictive Practices Court Act 1976).

[1.1356]
[75A   Rules in relation to Part 2 and Part 2A
(1)   The [CMA] may make such rules about procedural and other matters in connection with the carrying into effect of the provisions of Parts 2 and 2A as it considers appropriate.
(2)   If the [CMA] is preparing rules under this section it must consult such persons as it considers appropriate.
(3)   No rule made by the [CMA] is to come into operation until it has been approved by an order made by the Secretary of State.
(4)   The Secretary of State may approve any rule made by the [CMA]—
   (a)   in the form in which it is submitted; or
   (b)   subject to such modifications as he considers appropriate.
(5)   If the Secretary of State proposes to approve a rule subject to modifications he must inform the [CMA] of the proposed modifications and take into account any comments made by the [CMA].
(6)   Subsections (3) to (5) apply also to any alteration of the rules made by the [CMA].
(7)   The Secretary of State may, after consulting the [CMA], by order vary or revoke any rules made under this section.
(8)   If the Secretary of State considers that rules should be made under this section with respect to a particular matter he may direct the [CMA] to exercise its powers under this section and make rules about that matter.]

NOTES
Inserted by the Competition Act 1998 and Other Enactments (Amendment) Regulations 2004, SI 2004/1261, reg 4, Sch 1, para 47.
References to "CMA" substituted (for original references to "OFT") by the Enterprise and Regulatory Reform Act 2013, s 26(3), Sch 5, Pt 1, paras 1, 52. For various transitional provisions (including those relating to the abolition of the OFT and the Competition Commission, existing references to those bodies and provisions relating to continuity), see the Enterprise and Regulatory Reform Act 2013 (Commencement No 6, Transitional Provisions and Savings) Order 2014, SI 2014/416, Schedule at **[2.1126]**.
Rules: the Competition Act 1998 (Competition and Markets Authority's Rules) Order 2014, SI 2014/458 at **[2.21]**.

[1.1357]
76   Short title, commencement and extent
(1)   This Act may be cited as the Competition Act 1998.
(2)   Sections 71 and 75 and this section and paragraphs 1 to 7 and 35 of Schedule 13 come into force on the passing of this Act.
(3)   The other provisions of this Act come into force on such day as the Secretary of State may by order appoint; and different days may be appointed for different purposes.
(4)   This Act extends to Northern Ireland.

NOTES
Orders: the Competition Act 1998 (Commencement No 1) Order 1998, SI 1998/2750; the Competition Act 1998 (Commencement No 2) Order 1998, SI 1998/3166; the Competition Act 1998 (Commencement No 3) Order 1999, SI 1999/505; the Competition Act 1998 (Commencement No 4) Order 1999, SI 1999/2859; the Competition Act 1998 (Commencement No 5) Order 2000, SI 2000/344; the Competition Act 1998 (Commencement No 6) Order 2013, SI 2013/284.

SCHEDULES

SCHEDULE 1
EXCLUSIONS: MERGERS AND CONCENTRATIONS

Sections 3(1)(a) and 19(1)(a)

PART I
MERGERS

Enterprises ceasing to be distinct: the Chapter I prohibition
[1.1358]
1. (1)   To the extent to which an agreement (either on its own or when taken together with another agreement) results, or if carried out would result, in any two enterprises ceasing to be distinct enterprises for the purposes of [Part 3 of the Enterprise Act 2002 ("the 2002 Act")], the Chapter I prohibition does not apply to the agreement.
(2)   The exclusion provided by sub-paragraph (1) extends to any provision directly related and necessary to the implementation of the merger provisions.

(3)   In sub-paragraph (2) "merger provisions" means the provisions of the agreement which cause, or if carried out would cause, the agreement to have the result mentioned in sub-paragraph (1).

(4)   [Section 26 of the 2002 Act] applies for the purposes of this paragraph as if—
 (a)   in subsection (3) (circumstances in which a person or group of persons may be treated as having control of an enterprise), and
 (b)   in subsection (4) (circumstances in which a person or group of persons may be treated as bringing an enterprise under their control),
for "may" there were substituted "must".

Enterprises ceasing to be distinct: the Chapter II prohibition

2. (1)   To the extent to which conduct (either on its own or when taken together with other conduct)—
 (a)   results in any two enterprises ceasing to be distinct enterprises for the purposes of [Part 3 of the 2002 Act]), or
 (b)   is directly related and necessary to the attainment of the result mentioned in paragraph (a), the Chapter II prohibition does not apply to that conduct.

(2)   [Section 26 of the 2002 Act] applies for the purposes of this paragraph as it applies for the purposes of paragraph 1.

3.   . . .

Withdrawal of the paragraph 1 exclusion

4. (1)   The exclusion provided by paragraph 1 does not apply to a particular agreement if the [CMA] gives a direction under this paragraph to that effect.

(2)   If the [CMA] is considering whether to give a direction under this paragraph, [it] may by notice in writing require any party to the agreement in question to give [the [CMA]] such information in connection with the agreement as [it] may require.

(3)   The [CMA] may give a direction under this paragraph only as provided in sub-paragraph (4) or (5).

(4)   If at the end of such period as may be specified in rules under section 51 a person has failed, without reasonable excuse, to comply with a requirement imposed under sub-paragraph (2), the [CMA] may give a direction under this paragraph.

(5)   The [CMA] may also give a direction under this paragraph if—
 [(a)   it considers that the agreement will, if not excluded, infringe the Chapter I prohibition; and]
 (b)   the agreement is not a protected agreement.

(6)   . . .

(7)   A direction under this paragraph—
 (a)   must be in writing;
 (b)   may be made so as to have effect from a date specified in the direction (which may not be earlier than the date on which it is given).

Protected agreements

5.   An agreement is a protected agreement for the purposes of paragraph 4 if—
 [(a)   the [CMA] or (as the case may be) the Secretary of State has published its or his decision not to make a reference   . . .   under section 22, 33, 45 or 62 of the 2002 Act in connection with the agreement;
 (b)   the [CMA] or (as the case may be) the Secretary of State has made a reference   . . . under section 22, 33, 45 or 62 of the 2002 Act in connection with the agreement and [the CMA] has found that the agreement has given rise to, or would if carried out give rise to, a relevant merger situation or (as the case may be) a special merger situation;
 (c)   the agreement does not fall within paragraph (a) or (b) but has given rise to, or would if carried out give rise to, enterprises to which it relates being regarded under section 26 of the 2002 Act as ceasing to be distinct enterprises (otherwise than as the result of subsection (3) or (4)(b) of that section); or
 (d)   the [CMA] has made a reference   . . .   under section 32 of the Water Industry Act 1991 in connection with the agreement and [the CMA] has found that the agreement has given rise to, or would if carried out give rise to, a merger of any two or more water enterprises of the kind to which that section applies].

NOTES

Para 1: words in square brackets in sub-paras (1), (4) substituted by the Enterprise Act 2002, s 278(1), Sch 25, para 38(1), (50)(a) (for savings in relation the merger of water and sewerage undertakers, see the Enterprise Act 2002 (Commencement No 3, Transitional and Transitory Provisions and Savings) Order 2003, SI 2003/1397, art 3, and the Enterprise Act 2002 (Commencement No 7 and Transitional Provisions and Savings) Order 2004, SI 2004/3233, arts 3–5).

Para 2: words in square brackets in sub-paras (1)(a), (2) substituted by the Enterprise Act 2002, s 278(1), Sch 25, para 38(1), (50)(b) (for savings see the para 1 note above).

Para 3: repealed by the Communications Act 2003, s 406(7), Sch 19(1).

Para 4: references to "CMA" substituted (for references to "OFT" as substituted, together with references to "the OFT" by the Enterprise Act 2002, s 278, Sch 25, para 38) by the Enterprise and Regulatory Reform Act 2013, s 26(3), Sch 5, Pt 1, paras 1, 53(1), (2). For various transitional provisions (including those relating to the abolition of the OFT and the Competition Commission, existing references to those bodies and provisions relating to continuity), see the Enterprise and Regulatory Reform Act 2013 (Commencement No 6, Transitional Provisions and Savings) Order 2014, SI 2014/416, Schedule at **[2.1126]**; the words "it" in square brackets (in all places that they occur) were substituted by the Enterprise Act 2002, s 278(1), Sch 25, para 38(1), (50)(c) (for savings see the para 1 note above); sub-para (5)(a) was substituted, and sub-para (6) was repealed, by the Competition Act 1998 and Other Enactments (Amendment) Regulations 2004, SI 2004/1261, reg 4, Sch 1, para 48(1), (2).

Para 5: sub-paras (a)–(d) substituted by the Enterprise Act 2002, s 278(1), Sch 25, para 38(1), (50)(d); in sub-paras (a), (b), (d), the references to "CMA" are substituted (for original references to "OFT"), the words "to the Competition Commission" omitted from those sub-paras are repealed, and words "the CMA" in sub-paras (b), (d) are substituted for original words "the Commission", by the Enterprise and Regulatory Reform Act 2013, ss 26(3), 57, Sch 5, Pt 1, paras 1, 53(1), (3), Sch 15, paras 8, 12, subject to transitional provisions in SI 2014/416 as noted to para 4 above.

Modification: by virtue of the Enterprise Act 2002 (Protection of Legitimate Interests) Order 2003, SI 2003/1592, Sch 4, para 15(1)(a), (b), the following modifications of this Part of this Schedule apply: (a) in para 5(a), (b) above a reference to the Enterprise Act, s 62 includes a reference to art 5 of the 2003 Order; and (b) in para 5(b) above a reference to a "special merger situation" includes a reference to a "European relevant merger situation".

References to the CMA, etc: as to the abolition of the office of the Director General of Fair Trading and the substitution of the original references to the Director (and related expressions), see the note preceding s 1 at **[1.1266]**.

PART II
CONCENTRATIONS SUBJECT TO EC CONTROLS

[1.1359]

6. (1)   To the extent to which an agreement (either on its own or when taken together with another agreement) gives rise to, or would if carried out give rise to, a concentration, the Chapter I prohibition does not apply to the agreement if the Merger Regulation gives the Commission exclusive jurisdiction in the matter.

(2)   To the extent to which conduct (either on its own or when taken together with other conduct) gives rise to, or would if pursued give rise to, a concentration, the Chapter II prohibition does not apply to the conduct if the Merger Regulation gives the Commission exclusive jurisdiction in the matter.

(3)   In this paragraph—
"concentration" means a concentration with a Community dimension within the meaning of Articles 1 and 3 of the Merger Regulation; and
["Merger Regulation" means Council Regulation (EC) No 139/2004 of 20th January 2004 on the control of concentrations between undertakings].

NOTES

Para (3): definition "Merger Regulation" substituted by the EC Merger Control (Consequential Amendments) Regulations 2004, SI 2004/1079, reg 2, Schedule, para 1.

SCHEDULE 2

(Sch 2 outside the scope of this work.)

SCHEDULE 3
GENERAL EXCLUSIONS

Sections 3(1)(c) and 19(1)(b)

Planning obligations

[1.1360]

1. (1)   The Chapter I prohibition does not apply to an agreement—
   (a)   to the extent to which it is a planning obligation;
   (b)   which is made under section 75 (agreements regulating development or use of land) or 246 (agreements relating to Crown land) of the Town and Country Planning (Scotland) Act 1997; or
   (c)   which is made under Article 40 of the Planning (Northern Ireland) Order 1991.

(2)   In sub-paragraph (1)(a), "planning obligation" means—
   (a)   a planning obligation for the purposes of section 106 of the Town and Country Planning Act 1990; or
   (b)   a planning obligation for the purposes of section 299A of that Act.

2. . . . .

EEA Regulated Markets

3. (1)   The Chapter I prohibition does not apply to an agreement for the constitution of an EEA regulated market to the extent to which the agreement relates to any of the rules made, or guidance issued, by that market.

(2)   The Chapter I prohibition does not apply to a decision made by an EEA regulated market, to the extent to which the decision relates to any of the market's regulating provisions.

(3)   The Chapter I prohibition does not apply to—
   (a)   any practices of an EEA regulated market; or
   (b)   any practices which are trading practices in relation to an EEA regulated market.

(4)   The Chapter I prohibition does not apply to an agreement the parties to which are or include—
   (a)   an EEA regulated market, or
   (b)   a person who is subject to the rules of that market,
to the extent to which the agreement consists of provisions the inclusion of which is required or contemplated by the regulating provisions of that market.

(5)   In this paragraph—
   "EEA regulated market" is a market which—
      (a)   is listed by an EEA State other than the United Kingdom pursuant to [Article 47 of Directive 2004/39/EC of the European Parliament and of the Council of 21 April 2004 on markets in financial instruments]; and
      (b)   operates without any requirement that a person dealing on the market should have a physical presence in the EEA State from which any trading facilities are provided or on any trading floor that the market may have;
   "EEA State" means a State which is a contracting party to the EEA Agreement;
   "regulating provisions", in relation to an EEA regulated market, means—
      (a)   rules made, or guidance issued, by that market,
      (b)   practices of that market, or
      (c)   practices which, in relation to that market, are trading practices;
   "trading practices", in relation to an EEA regulated market, means practices of persons who are subject to the rules made by that market, and—
      (a)   which relate to business in respect of which those persons are subject to the rules of that market, and which are required or contemplated by those rules or by guidance issued by that market; or
      (b)   which are otherwise attributable to the conduct of that market as such.

Services of general economic interest etc

4. Neither the Chapter I prohibition nor the Chapter II prohibition applies to an undertaking entrusted with the operation of services of general economic interest or having the character of a revenue-producing monopoly in so far as the prohibition would obstruct the performance, in law or in fact, of the particular tasks assigned to that undertaking.

Compliance with legal requirements

5. (1)   The Chapter I prohibition does not apply to an agreement to the extent to which it is made in order to comply with a legal requirement.

(2)   The Chapter II prohibition does not apply to conduct to the extent to which it is engaged in an order to comply with a legal requirement.

(3)   In this paragraph "legal requirement" means a requirement—
   (a)   imposed by or under any enactment in force in the United Kingdom;
   (b)   imposed by or under the Treaty or the EEA Agreement and having legal effect in the United Kingdom without further enactment; or
   (c)   imposed by or under the law in force in another Member State and having legal effect in the United Kingdom.

Avoidance of conflict with international obligations

6. (1)   If the Secretary of State is satisfied that, in order to avoid a conflict between provisions of this Part and an international obligation of the United Kingdom, it would be appropriate for the Chapter I prohibition not to apply to—
   (a)   a particular agreement, or
   (b)   any agreement of a particular description,
he may by order exclude the agreement, or agreements of that description, from the Chapter I prohibition.

(2)   An order under sub-paragraph (1) may make provision for the exclusion of the agreement or agreements to which the order applies, or of such of them as may be specified, only in specified circumstances.

(3)   An order under sub-paragraph (1) may also provide that the Chapter I prohibition is to be deemed never to have applied in relation to the agreement or agreements, or in relation to such of them as may be specified.

(4)   If the Secretary of State is satisfied that, in order to avoid a conflict between provisions of this Part and an international obligation of the United Kingdom, it would be appropriate for the Chapter II prohibition not to apply in particular circumstances, he may by order provide for it not to apply in such circumstances as may be specified.

(5) An order under sub-paragraph (4) may provide that the Chapter II prohibition is to be deemed never to have applied in relation to specified conduct.

(6) An international arrangement relating to civil aviation and designated by an order made by the Secretary of State is to be treated as an international obligation for the purposes of this paragraph.

(7) In this paragraph and paragraph 7 "specified" means specified in the order.

Public policy

7. (1) If the Secretary of State is satisfied that there are exceptional and compelling reasons of public policy why the Chapter I prohibition ought not to apply to—

    (a) a particular agreement, or

    (b) any agreement of a particular description,

he may by order exclude the agreement, or agreements of that description, from the Chapter I prohibition.

(2) An order under sub-paragraph (1) may make provision for the exclusion of the agreement or agreements to which the order applies, or of such of them as may be specified, only in specified circumstances.

(3) An order under sub-paragraph (1) may also provide that the Chapter I prohibition is to be deemed never to have applied in relation to the agreement or agreements, or in relation to such of them as may be specified.

(4) If the Secretary of State is satisfied that there are exceptional and compelling reasons of public policy why the Chapter II prohibition ought not to apply in particular circumstances, he may by order provide for it not to apply in such circumstances as may be specified.

(5) An order under sub-paragraph (4) may provide that the Chapter II prohibition is to be deemed never to have applied in relation to specified conduct.

Coal and steel

8. (1) The Chapter I prohibition does not apply to an agreement which relates to a coal or steel product to the extent to which the ECSC Treaty gives the Commission exclusive jurisdiction in the matter.

(2) Sub-paragraph (1) ceases to have effect on the date on which the ECSC Treaty expires ("the expiry date").

(3) The Chapter II prohibition does not apply to conduct which relates to a coal or steel product to the extent to which the ECSC Treaty gives the Commission exclusive jurisdiction in the matter.

(4) Sub-paragraph (3) ceases to have effect on the expiry date.

(5) In this paragraph—

    "coal or steel product" means any product of a kind listed in Annex I to the ECSC Treaty; and

    "ECSC Treaty" means the Treaty establishing the European Coal and Steel Community.

Agricultural products

9. (1) The Chapter I prohibition does not apply to an agreement to the extent to which it relates to production of or trade in an agricultural product and—

    (a) forms an integral part of a national market organisation;

    (b) is necessary for the attainment of the objectives set out in [Article 39 of the Treaty on the Functioning of the European Union]; or

    (c) is an agreement of farmers or farmers' associations (or associations of such associations) belonging to a single member State which concerns—

        (i) the production or sale of agricultural products, or

        (ii) the use of joint facilities for the storage, treatment or processing of agricultural products,

    and under which there is no obligation to charge identical prices.

(2) If the Commission determines that an agreement does not fulfil the conditions specified by the provision for agricultural products for exclusion from [Article 101(1)], the exclusion provided by this paragraph ("the agriculture exclusion") is to be treated as ceasing to apply to the agreement on the date of the decision.

(3) The agriculture exclusion does not apply to a particular agreement if the [CMA] gives a direction under this paragraph to that effect.

(4) If the [CMA] is considering whether to give a direction under this paragraph, [it] may by notice in writing require any party to the agreement in question to give [the [CMA]] such information in connection with the agreement as [it] may require.

(5) The [CMA] may give a direction under this paragraph only as provided in sub-paragraph (6) or (7).

(6) If at the end of such period as may be specified in rules under section 51 a person has failed, without reasonable excuse, to comply with a requirement imposed under sub-paragraph (4), the [CMA] may give a direction under this paragraph.

(7)   The [CMA] may also give a direction under this paragraph if [it] considers that an agreement (whether or not [it] considers that it infringes the Chapter I prohibition) is likely, or is intended, substantially and unjustifiably to prevent, restrict or distort competition in relation to an agricultural product.

(8)   A direction under this paragraph—
   (a)   must be in writing;
   (b)   may be made so as to have effect from a date specified in the direction (which may not be earlier than the date on which it is given).

(9)   In this paragraph—
   "agricultural product" means any product of a kind listed in [Annex I] to the Treaty; and
   "provision for agricultural products" means Council Regulation (EEC) No 26/62 of 4th April 1962 applying certain rules of competition to production of and trade in agricultural products.

NOTES

Para 2: repealed by the Competition Act 1998 and Other Enactments (Amendment) Regulations 2004, SI 2004/1261, reg 4, Sch 1, para 50(a).

Para 3: in sub-para (5) in definition "EEA regulated market" words in square brackets in para (a) substituted by the Financial Services and Markets Act 2000 (Markets in Financial Instruments) Regulations 2007, SI 2007/126, reg 3(6), Sch 6, Pt 1, para 13.

Para 9: words in square brackets in sub-paras (1)(b) and (2) substituted by the Treaty of Lisbon (Changes in Terminology or Numbering) Order 2012, SI 2012/1809, art 3(1), Schedule, Pt 1 (note that the amendments made by this Order do not affect any provision in its application to things done before 1 December 2009 (the date on which the Treaty of Lisbon came into force)); references to "CMA" substituted (for original references to "OFT" as substituted, together with references to "the OFT" by the Enterprise Act 2002, s 278, Sch 25, para 38) by the Enterprise and Regulatory Reform Act 2013, s 26(3), Sch 5, Pt 1, paras 1, 55. For various transitional provisions (including those relating to the abolition of the OFT and the Competition Commission, existing references to those bodies and provisions relating to continuity), see the Enterprise and Regulatory Reform Act 2013 (Commencement No 6, Transitional Provisions and Savings) Order 2014, SI 2014/416, Schedule at [**2.1126**]; word "it" in square brackets in every place that it occurs in sub-paras (4), (7), substituted by the Enterprise Act 2002, s 278(1), Sch 25, para 38; words in square brackets in the definition "agricultural product" in sub-para (9) substituted by SI 2004/1261, reg 4, Sch 1, para 50(b).

Orders: the Competition Act 1998 (Public Policy Exclusion) Order 2006, SI 2006/605; the Competition Act 1998 (Public Policy Exclusion) Order 2008, SI 2008/1820; the Competition Act 1998 (Public Policy Exclusion) (Revocation) Order 2011, SI 2011/2886; the Competition Act 1998 (Public Policy Exclusion) Order 2012, SI 2012/710.

References to the CMA, etc: as to the abolition of the office of the Director General of Fair Trading and the substitution of the original references to the Director (and related expressions), see the note preceding s 1 at [**1.1266**].

Restrictive Trade Practices Act 1976: repealed by ss 1, 74(3) of, and Sch 14, Pt I to, this Act, subject to transitional provisions in Sch 13 at [**1.1370**].

SCHEDULES 4–6

(Sch 4 repealed by the Enterprise Act 2002, ss 207, 278(2), Sch 26; Schs 5, 6 repealed by the Competition Act 1998 and Other Enactments (Amendment) Regulations 2004, SI 2004/1261, reg 4, Sch 1, para 51.)

[SCHEDULE 6A
COMMITMENTS

Section 31A

PART 1
PROCEDURAL REQUIREMENTS FOR THE ACCEPTANCE AND VARIATION OF COMMITMENTS

[1.1361]

1.   Paragraph 2 applies where the [CMA] proposes to—
   (a)   accept any commitments under section 31A; or
   (b)   accept any variation of such commitments other than a variation which is not material in any respect.

2.   (1)   Before accepting the commitments or variation, the [CMA] must—
   (a)   give notice under this paragraph; and
   (b)   consider any representations made in accordance with the notice and not withdrawn.

   (2)   A notice under this paragraph must state—
   (a)   that the [CMA] proposes to accept the commitments or variation;
   (b)   the purpose of the commitments or variation and the way in which the commitments or variation would meet the [CMA's] competition concerns;
   (c)   any other facts which the [CMA] considers are relevant to the acceptance or variation of the commitments; and
   (d)   the period within which representations may be made in relation to the proposed commitments or variation.

(3)   The period stated for the purposes of sub-paragraph (2)(d) must be at least 11 working days starting with the date the notice is given or, if that date is not a working day, with the date of the first working day after that date.

3. (1)   The [CMA] must not accept the commitments or variation of which notice has been given under paragraph 2(1) with modifications unless it—
  (a)   gives notice under this paragraph of the proposed modifications; and
  (b)   considers any representations made in accordance with the notice and not withdrawn.

(2)   A notice under this paragraph must state—
  (a)   the proposed modifications;
  (b)   the reasons for them; and
  (c)   the period within which representations may be made in relation to the proposed modifications.

(3)   The period stated for the purposes of sub-paragraph (2)(c) must be at least 6 working days starting with the date the notice is given or, if that date is not a working day, with the date of the first working day after that date.

4. If, after giving notice under paragraph 2 or 3 the [CMA] decides—
  (a)   not to accept the commitments or variation concerned, and
  (b)   not to proceed by virtue of paragraph 5 or 6,
the [CMA] must give notice that it has so decided.

5. The requirements of paragraph 3 shall not apply if the [CMA]—
  (a)   has already given notice under paragraph 2 but not under paragraph 3; and
  (b)   considers that the modifications which are now being proposed are not material in any respect.

6. The requirements of paragraph 3 shall not apply if the [CMA]—
  (a)   has already given notices under paragraphs 2 and 3; and
  (b)   considers that the further modifications which are now being proposed are not material in any respect or do not differ in any material respect from the modifications in relation to which notice was last given under paragraph 3.

7. As soon as practicable after accepting commitments or a variation under section 31A the [CMA] must publish the commitments or the variation in such manner as the [CMA] considers appropriate.

8. A notice under paragraph 2 or 3 shall be given by—
  (a)   sending a copy of the notice to such person or persons as the [CMA] considers appropriate for the purpose of bringing the matter to which it relates to the attention of those likely to be affected by it; or
  (b)   publishing the notice in such manner as the [CMA] considers appropriate for the purpose of bringing the matter to which it relates to the attention of those likely to be affected by it.]

NOTES

  Schedule inserted by the Competition Act 1998 and Other Enactments (Amendment) Regulations 2004, SI 2004/1261, reg 4, Sch 1, para 52.

  References to the "CMA" and the "CMA's" substituted (for original references to the "OFT" and the "OFT's") by the Enterprise and Regulatory Reform Act 2013, s 26(3), Sch 5, Pt 1, paras 1, 56. For various transitional provisions (including those relating to the abolition of the OFT and the Competition Commission, existing references to those bodies and provisions relating to continuity), see the Enterprise and Regulatory Reform Act 2013 (Commencement No 6, Transitional Provisions and Savings) Order 2014, SI 2014/416, Schedule at **[2.1126]**.

[PART 2
PROCEDURAL REQUIREMENTS FOR THE RELEASE OF COMMITMENTS

[1.1362]
10. Paragraph 11 applies where the [CMA] proposes to release any commitments under section 31A.

11. (1)   Before releasing the commitments, the [CMA] must—
  (a)   give notice under this paragraph;
  (b)   send a copy of the notice to the person (or persons) who gave the commitments; and
  (c)   consider any representations made in accordance with the notice and not withdrawn.

(2)   A notice under this paragraph must state—
  (a)   the fact that a release is proposed;
  (b)   the reasons for it; and
  (c)   the period within which representations may be made in relation to the proposed release.

(3)   The period stated for the purposes of sub-paragraph (2)(c) must be at least 11 working days starting with the date the notice is given or, if that date is not a working day, with the date of the first working day after that date.

12. If after giving notice under paragraph 11 the [CMA] decides not to proceed with the release, it must—

   (a)   give notice that it has so decided; and

   (b)   send a copy of the notice to the person (or persons) who gave the commitments.

13. As soon as practicable after releasing the commitments, the [CMA] must—

   (a)   publish the release in such manner as it considers appropriate; and

   (b)   send a copy of the release to the person (or persons) who gave the commitments.

14. A notice under paragraph 11 or 12 shall be given by—

   (a)   sending a copy of the notice to such other person or persons as the [CMA] considers appropriate for the purpose of bringing the matter to which it relates to the attention of those likely to be affected by it; or

   (b)   publishing the notice in such manner as the [CMA] considers appropriate for the purpose of bringing the matter to which it relates to the attention of those likely to be affected by it.]

NOTES

Inserted as noted to Pt 1 at **[1.1361]**.

References to "CMA" substituted (for original references to "OFT") by the Enterprise and Regulatory Reform Act 2013, s 26(3), Sch 5, Pt 1, paras 1, 56. For various transitional provisions (including those relating to the abolition of the OFT and the Competition Commission, existing references to those bodies and provisions relating to continuity), see the Enterprise and Regulatory Reform Act 2013 (Commencement No 6, Transitional Provisions and Savings) Order 2014, SI 2014/416, Schedule at **[2.1126]**.

SCHEDULE 7
THE COMPETITION COMMISSION

Section 45(7)

PART I
GENERAL

Interpretation

[1.1363]

1. In this Schedule—

   "the 1973 Act" means the Fair Trading Act 1973;

   . . .

   "Chairman" means the chairman of the Commission;

   "the Commission" means the Competition Commission;

   "Council" has the meaning given in paragraph 5;

   "general functions" means any functions of the Commission other than functions—

      (a)   . . .

      (b)   which are to be discharged by the Council;

   "member" means a member of the Commission;

   "newspaper merger reference" means a [reference under section 45 of the Enterprise Act 2002 which specifies a newspaper public interest consideration (within the meaning of paragraph 20A of Schedule 8 to that Act) or a reference under section 62 of that Act which specifies a consideration specified in section 58(2A) or (2B) of that Act];

   ["newspaper panel member" means a member of the panel maintained under paragraph 22;]

   . . .

   "reporting panel member" means a member appointed under paragraph 2(1)(b);

   "secretary" means the secretary of the Commission appointed under paragraph 9; and

   "specialist panel member" means a member appointed under any of the provisions mentioned in paragraph 2(1)(d).

Membership of the Commission

2. (1)   The Commission is to consist of—

   (a)   . . .

   (b)   members appointed by the Secretary of State to form a panel for the purposes of the Commission's general functions;

   (c)   [the members of] the panel maintained under paragraph 22;

   (d)   members appointed by the Secretary of State under or by virtue of—

      (i)   . . .

      [(ii)   section 104 of the Utilities Act 2000;]

      [(iii)   section 194(1) of the Communications Act 2003;]

      (iv)   Article 15(9) of the Electricity (Northern Ireland) Order 1992;

   [(e)   one or more members appointed by the Secretary of State to serve on the Council].

[(1A)   A person may not be, at the same time, a member of the Commission and a member of the Tribunal.]

(2)   A person who is appointed as a member of a kind mentioned in one of paragraphs [(aa)] to (c) of sub-paragraph (3) may also be appointed as a member of either or both of the other kinds mentioned in those paragraphs.

(3)   The kinds of member are—
(a)   . . .
[(aa) a newspaper panel member;]
(b)   a reporting panel member;
(c)   a specialist panel member.

(4)   . . .

(5)   The validity of the Commission's proceedings is not affected by a defect in the appointment of a member.

Chairman and deputy chairmen

3. (1)   The Commission is to have a chairman appointed by the Secretary of State from among the reporting panel members.

(2)   The Secretary of State may appoint one or more of the reporting panel members to act as deputy chairman.

(3)   The Chairman, and any deputy chairman, may resign that office at any time by notice in writing addressed to the Secretary of State.

(4)   If the Chairman (or a deputy chairman) ceases to be a member he also ceases to be Chairman (or a deputy chairman).

(5)   If the Chairman is absent or otherwise unable to act, or there is no chairman, any of his functions may be performed—
(a)   if there is one deputy chairman, by him;
(b)   if there is more than one—
(i)   by the deputy chairman designated by the Secretary of State; or
(ii)   if no such designation has been made, by the deputy chairman designated by the deputy chairmen;
(c)   if there is no deputy chairman able to act—
(i)   by the member designated by the Secretary of State; or
(ii)   if no such designation has been made, by the member designated by the Commission.

4.   . . .

The Council

5. (1)   The   Commission   is   to   have   a   . . .   board   to   be   known   as the Competition Commission Council (but referred to in this Schedule as "the Council").

(2)   The Council is to consist of—
(a)   the Chairman [and any deputy chairmen of the Commission];
(b)   . . .
[(bb) the member or members appointed under paragraph 2(1)(e);]
(c)   such other members as the Secretary of State may appoint; and
(d)   the secretary.

(3)   In exercising its functions under paragraphs 3 and 7 to 12   . . . , the Commission is to act through the Council.

[(3A)   Without prejudice to the question whether any other functions of the Commission are to be so discharged, the functions of the Commission under sections 106, 116, and 171 of the Enterprise Act 2002 (and under section 116 as applied for the purposes of references under Part 4 of that Act by section 176 of that Act) are to be discharged by the Council.]

(4)   The Council may determine its own procedure including, in particular, its quorum.

(5)   The Chairman (and any person acting as Chairman) is to have a casting vote on any question being decided by the Council.

Term of office

6. (1)   Subject to the provisions of this Schedule, each member is to hold and vacate office in accordance with the terms of his appointment.

(2)   A person is not to be appointed as a member for more than [eight years (but this does not prevent a re-appointment for the purpose only of continuing to act as a member of a group selected under paragraph 15 before the end of his term of office)].

(3)   Any member may at any time resign by notice in writing addressed to the Secretary of State.

(4)   The Secretary of State may remove a member on the ground of incapacity or misbehaviour.

(5)   . . .

Expenses, remuneration and pensions

7. *(1)   The Secretary of State shall pay to the Commission such sums as he considers appropriate to enable it to perform its functions.*

(2)   The Commission may pay, or make provision for paying, to or in respect of each member such salaries or other remuneration and such pensions, allowances, fees, expenses or gratuities as the Secretary of State may determine.

(3)   If a person ceases to be a member otherwise than on the expiry of his term of office and it appears to the Secretary of State that there are special circumstances which make it right for him to receive compensation, the Commission may make a payment to him of such amount as the Secretary of State may determine.

(4)   . . .

[7A. The Commission may publish advice and information in relation to any matter connected with the exercise of its functions.]

The Commission's powers

8. *Subject to the provisions of this Schedule, the Commission has power to do anything (except borrow money)—*
   (a)   calculated to facilitate the discharge of its functions; or
   (b)   incidental or conducive to the discharge of its functions.

Staff

9. *(1)   The Commission is to have a secretary, appointed by the Secretary of State on such terms and conditions of service as he considers appropriate.*

(2)   . . .

(3)   Before appointing a person to be secretary, the Secretary of State must consult the Chairman . . .

(4)   Subject to obtaining the approval of [the Secretary of State as to numbers and terms and conditions of service] the Commission may appoint such staff as it thinks appropriate.

10. *. . .*

Application of seal and proof of instruments

11. *(1)   The application of the seal of the Commission must be authenticated by the signature of the secretary or of some other person authorised for the purpose.*

(2)   Sub-paragraph (1) does not apply in relation to any document which is or is to be signed in accordance with the law of Scotland.

(3)   A document purporting to be duly executed under the seal of the Commission—
   (a)   is to be received in evidence; and
   (b)   is to be taken to have been so executed unless the contrary is proved.

Accounts

12. *(1)   The Commission must—*
   (a)   keep proper accounts and proper records in relation to its accounts;
   (b)   prepare a statement of accounts in respect of each of its financial years; and
   (c)   send copies of the statement to the Secretary of State and to the Comptroller and Auditor General before the end of the month of August next following the financial year to which the statement relates.

(2)   The statement of accounts must comply with any directions given by the Secretary of State with the approval of the Treasury as to—
   (a)   the information to be contained in it,
   (b)   the manner in which the information contained in it is to be presented, or
   (c)   the methods and principles according to which the statement is to be prepared,
and must contain such additional information as the Secretary of State may with the approval of the Treasury require to be provided for informing Parliament.

(3)   The Comptroller and Auditor General must—
   (a)   examine, certify and report on each statement received by him as a result of this paragraph; and
   (b)   lay copies of each statement and of his report before each House of Parliament.

(4)   In this paragraph "financial year" means the period beginning with the date on which the Commission is established and ending with March 31st next, and each successive period of twelve months.

[Annual reports

12A. (1) The Commission shall make to the Secretary of State a report for each financial year on its activities during the year.

(2) The annual report must be made before the end of August next following the financial year to which it relates.

(3) The Secretary of State shall lay a copy of the annual report before Parliament and arrange for the report to be published.]

Status

13. (1) The Commission is not to be regarded as the servant or agent of the Crown or as enjoying any status, privilege or immunity of the Crown.

(2) The Commission's property is not to be regarded as property of, or held on behalf of, the Crown.

NOTES

Schedule repealed by the Enterprise and Regulatory Reform Act 2013, s 26(3), Sch 5, Pt 3, paras 218, 222. For various transitional provisions (including those relating to the abolition of the OFT and the Competition Commission, existing references to those bodies and provisions relating to continuity), see the Enterprise and Regulatory Reform Act 2013 (Commencement No 6, Transitional Provisions and Savings) Order 2014, SI 2014/416, Schedule at **[2.1126]**.

Para 1: definitions "appeal panel member" and "President" (omitted), and para (a) of definition "general functions" repealed, and definition "newspaper panel member" inserted, by the Enterprise Act 2002, ss 21, 185, 278(2), Sch 5, paras 1, 7(1), (2), Sch 11, paras 1, 2, Sch 26; words in square brackets in definition "newspaper merger reference" substituted by the Communications Act 2003, s 388.

Para 2: sub-paras (1)(a), (3)(a), (4) repealed, words in square brackets in sub-paras (1)(c), (2) substituted, and sub-paras (1)(e), (1A), (3)(aa) inserted, by the Enterprise Act 2002, ss 21, 185, 278(2), Sch 5, paras 1, 7(1), (3), Sch 11, paras 1, 3, Sch 26; sub-para (1)(d)(i) repealed by the Water Act 2003, s 101, Sch 7, Pt 2, para 32(1), (3), Sch 9, Pt 3; sub-para (1)(d)(ii) substituted by the Utilities Act 2000, s 104(3); sub-para (1)(d)(iii) substituted by the Communications Act 2003, s 406(1), Sch 17, para 153(1), (2) (note that s 406(7) of, and Sch 19 to, the 2003 Act, also purport to repeal para 2(1)(d)(iii)).

Para 4: repealed by the Enterprise Act 2002, ss 21, 278(2), Sch 5, paras 1, 7(1), (4), Sch 26.

Para 5: words omitted from sub-paras (1), (3) repealed, and sub-para (2)(b) repealed, and words in square brackets in sub-para (2)(a) and sub-paras (2)(bb), (3A) inserted, by the Enterprise Act 2002, ss 21, 185, 278(2), Sch 5, paras 1, 7(1), (5), Sch 11, paras 1, 4, Sch 26.

Para 6: words in square brackets in sub-para (2) substituted, and sub-para (5) repealed, by the Enterprise Act 2002, ss 185, 278(2), Sch 11, paras 1, 5, Sch 26, except in relation to the re-appointment as a member of any person who is a member on 1 April 2003 (see the Enterprise Act 2002 (Commencement No 2, Transitional and Transitory Provisions) Order 2003, SI 2003/766).

Para 7: sub-para (4) repealed by the Enterprise Act 2002, ss 185, 278(2), Sch 11, paras 1, 6, Sch 26.

Para 7A: inserted by the Enterprise Act 2002, s 185, Sch 11, paras 1, 7.

Para 9: sub-para (2), and words omitted from sub-para (3) repealed, and words in square brackets in sub-para (4) substituted, by the Enterprise Act 2002, ss 185, 278(2), Sch 11, paras 1, 8, Sch 26.

Para 10: repealed by the Enterprise Act 2002, ss 185, 278(2), Sch 11, paras 1, 9, Sch 26.

Para 12A: inserted by the Enterprise Act 2002, s 186.

Transitional provisions: for transitional provisions in relation to the constitution, etc, of the Competition Appeal Tribunal, see the Enterprise Act 2002, Sch 24, paras 7–12.

PART II
PERFORMANCE OF THE COMMISSION'S GENERAL FUNCTIONS

Interpretation

[1.1364]

14. In this Part of this Schedule "group" means a group selected under paragraph 15.

Discharge of certain functions by groups

15. (1) Except where sub-paragraph (7) [or (8)] gives the Chairman power to act on his own, any general function of the Commission must be performed through a group selected for the purpose by the Chairman.

(2) The group must consist of at least three persons one of whom may be the Chairman.

(3) In selecting the members of the group, the Chairman must comply with any requirement as to its constitution imposed by any enactment applying to specialist panel members.

(4) If the functions to be performed through the group relate to a newspaper merger reference, the group must, subject to sub-paragraph (5), consist of such reporting panel members as the Chairman may select.

[(5) The Chairman must select one or more newspaper panel members to be members of the group dealing with functions relating to a newspaper merger reference and, if he selects at least three such members, the group may consist entirely of those members.]

(6) Subject to sub-paragraphs (2) to (5), a group must consist of reporting panel members or specialist panel members selected by the Chairman.

(7) While a group is being constituted to perform a particular general function of the Commission, the Chairman may—

(a) take such steps (falling within that general function) as he considers appropriate to facilitate the work of the group when it has been constituted; . . .

(b) . . .

[(8) The Chairman may exercise the power conferred by section 37(1), 48(1) or 64(1) of the Enterprise Act 2002 while a group is being constituted to perform a relevant general function of the Commission or, when it has been so constituted, before it has held its first meeting.]

Chairmen of groups

16. The Chairman must appoint one of the members of a group to act as the chairman of the group.

Replacement of member of group

17. (1) If, during the proceedings of a group—

(a) a member of the group ceases to be a member of the Commission,

(b) the Chairman is satisfied that a member of the group will be unable for a substantial period to perform his duties as a member of the group, or

(c) it appears to the Chairman that because of a particular interest of a member of the group it is inappropriate for him to remain in the group,

the Chairman may appoint a replacement.

(2) The Chairman may also at any time appoint any reporting panel member to be an additional member of a group.

Attendance of other members

18. (1) At the invitation of the chairman of a group, any reporting panel member who is not a member of the group may attend meetings or otherwise take part in the proceedings of the group.

(2) But any person attending in response to such an invitation may not—

(a) vote in any proceedings of the group; or

(b) have a statement of his dissent from a conclusion of the group included in a report made by them.

(3) Nothing in sub-paragraph (1) is to be taken to prevent a group, or a member of a group, from consulting any member of the Commission with respect to any matter or question with which the group is concerned.

Procedure

19. (1) Subject to any special or general directions given by the Secretary of State, each group may determine its own procedure.

(2) Each group may, in particular, determine its quorum and determine—

(a) the extent, if any, to which persons interested or claiming to be interested in the subject-matter of the reference are allowed—

(i) to be present or to be heard, either by themselves or by their representatives;

(ii) to cross-examine witnesses; or

(iii) otherwise to take part; and

(b) the extent, if any, to which sittings of the group are to be held in public.

(3) In determining its procedure a group must have regard to any guidance issued by the Chairman.

(4) Before issuing any guidance for the purposes of this paragraph the Chairman must consult the members of the Commission.

[(5) This paragraph does not apply to groups for which rules must be made under paragraph 19A.]

[**19A.** (1) The Chairman must make rules of procedure in relation to merger reference groups, market reference groups and special reference groups.

(2) Schedule 7A makes further provision about rules made under this paragraph but is not to be taken as restricting the Chairman's powers under this paragraph.

(3) The Chairman must publish rules made under this paragraph in such manner as he considers appropriate for the purpose of bringing them to the attention of those likely to be affected by them.

(4) The Chairman must consult the members of the Commission and such other persons as he considers appropriate before making rules under this paragraph.

(5) Rules under this paragraph may—

(a) make different provision for different cases or different purposes;

(b) be varied or revoked by subsequent rules made under this paragraph.

(6) Subject to rules made under this paragraph, each merger reference group, market reference group and special reference group may determine its own procedure.

(7)   *In determining how to proceed in accordance with rules made under this paragraph and in determining its procedure under sub-paragraph (6), a group must have regard to any guidance issued by the Chairman.*

(8)   *Before issuing any guidance for the purposes of this paragraph the Chairman shall consult the members of the Commission and such other persons as he considers appropriate.*

(9)   *In this paragraph and in Schedule 7A—*

"*market reference group*" *means any group constituted in connection with a reference under section 131 or 132 of the Enterprise Act 2002 (including that section as it has effect by virtue of another enactment);*

"*merger reference group*" *means any group constituted in connection with a reference under . . . section 32 of the Water Industry Act 1991 (c 56) or section 22, 33, 45 or 62 of the Enterprise Act 2002; and*

"*special reference group*" *means any group constituted in connection with a reference . . . under—*

(a)   *section 11 of the Competition Act 1980 (c 21);*
(b)   *. . .*
(c)   *. . .*
(d)   *section . . . 41E of the Gas Act 1986 (c 44);*
(e)   *section . . . 56C of the Electricity Act 1989 (c 29);*
(f)   *. . .*
(g)   *section 12[, 14 or 17K] of the Water Industry Act 1991 (c 56);*
(h)   *article 15 of the Electricity (Northern Ireland) Order 1992 (SI 1992/231 (NI 1));*
(i)   *section 13 of, or Schedule 4A to, the Railways Act 1993 (c 43);*
(j)   *. . .*
(k)   *article 15 of the Gas (Northern Ireland) Order 1996 (SI 1996/275 (NI 2));*
(l)   *. . .*
(m)   *. . .*
(n)   *section 12 of the Transport Act 2000 (c 38); [. . .*
(o)   *section 193 of the Communications Act 2003;][or*
(p)   *article 3 of the Water Services etc (Scotland) Act 2005 (Consequential Provisions and Modifications) Order 2005].*

Effect of exercise of functions by group

20.   (1)   *Subject to [sub-paragraphs (2) to (9)], anything done by or in relation to a group in, or in connection with, the performance of functions to be performed by the group is to have the same effect as if done by or in relation to the Commission.*

[(2)   *For the purposes of Part 3 of the Enterprise Act 2002 (mergers) any decision of a group under section 35(1) or 36(1) of that Act (questions to be decided on non-public interest merger references) that there is an anti-competitive outcome is to be treated as a decision under that section that there is not an anti-competitive outcome if the decision is not that of at least two-thirds of the members of the group.*

(3)   *For the purposes of Part 3 of the Act of 2002, if the decision is not that of at least two-thirds of the members of the group—*

(a)   *any decision of a group under section 47 of that Act (questions to be decided on public interest merger references) that a relevant merger situation has been created is to be treated as a decision under that section that no such situation has been created;*
(b)   *any decision of a group under section 47 of that Act that the creation of a relevant merger situation has resulted, or may be expected to result, in a substantial lessening of competition within any market or markets in the United Kingdom for goods or services is to be treated as a decision under that section that the creation of that situation has not resulted, or may be expected not to result, in such a substantial lessening of competition;*
(c)   *any decision of a group under section 47 of that Act that arrangements are in progress or in contemplation which, if carried into effect, will result in the creation of a relevant merger situation is to be treated as a decision under that section that no such arrangements are in progress or in contemplation; and*
(d)   *any decision of a group under section 47 of that Act that the creation of such a situation as is mentioned in paragraph (c) may be expected to result in a substantial lessening of competition within any market or markets in the United Kingdom for goods or services is to be treated as a decision under that section that the creation of that situation may be expected not to result in such a substantial lessening of competition.*

(4)   *For the purposes of Part 3 of the Act of 2002, if the decision is not that of at least two-thirds of the members of the group—*

(a)   *any decision of a group under section 63 of that Act (questions to be decided on special public interest merger references) that a special merger situation has been created is to be treated as a decision under that section that no such situation has been created; and*

(b)   any decision of a group under section 63 of that Act that arrangements are in progress or in contemplation which, if carried into effect, will result in the creation of a special merger situation is to be treated as a decision under that section that no such arrangements are in progress or in contemplation.

(5)   For the purposes of Part 4 of the Act of 2002 (market investigations), if the decision is not that of at least two-thirds of the members of the group, any decision of a group under section 134 or 141 (questions to be decided on market investigation references) that a feature, or combination of features, of a relevant market prevents, restricts or distorts competition in connection with the supply or acquisition of any goods or services in the United Kingdom or a part of the United Kingdom is to be treated as a decision that the feature or (as the case may be) combination of features does not prevent, restrict or distort such competition.

(6)   Accordingly, for the purposes of Part 4 of the Act of 2002, a group is to be treated as having decided under section 134 or 141 that there is no adverse effect on competition if—

(a)   one or more than one decision of the group is to be treated as mentioned in sub-paragraph (5); and

(b)   there is no other relevant decision of the group.

(7)   In sub-paragraph (6) "relevant decision" means a decision which is not to be treated as mentioned in sub-paragraph (5) and which is that a feature, or combination of features, of a relevant market prevents, restricts or distorts competition in connection with the supply or acquisition of any goods or services in the United Kingdom or a part of the United Kingdom.

(8)   Expressions used in sub-paragraphs (2) to (7) shall be construed in accordance with Part 3 or (as the case may be) 4 of the Act of 2002.

(9)   Sub-paragraph (1) is also subject to specific provision made by or under other enactments about decisions which are not decisions of at least two-thirds of the members of a group.]

Casting votes

21.   The chairman of a group is to have a casting vote on any question to be decided by the group.

Newspaper merger references

22.   [There are to be members of the Commission appointed by the Secretary of State to form a panel of persons available] for selection as members of a group constituted in connection with a newspaper merger reference.

NOTES

Repealed as noted to Pt I of this Schedule at **[1.120]**.

Para 15: words in square brackets in sub-para (1), and sub-para (8) inserted, sub-para (7)(b) and the word preceding it repealed, and sub-para (5) substituted, by the Enterprise Act 2002, ss 185, 278(2), Sch 11, paras 1, 10, Sch 26.

Para 19: sub-para (5) added by the Enterprise Act 2002, s 187(2).

Para 19A: inserted by the Enterprise Act 2002, s 187(3); in sub-para (9) words omitted from the definition "merger reference group", and paras (b), (f) of the definition "special reference group", repealed by the Communications Act 2003, s 406(7), Sch 19; first words omitted from definition "special reference group" repealed, and para (m) of that definition repealed, by the Financial Services Act 2012, s 114(2), Sch 19; paras (c), (j) of the definition "special reference group repealed by the Civil Aviation Act 2012, s 76(4), Sch 9, para 9; words omitted from paras (d) and (e) of the definition "special reference group" repealed by the Electricity and Gas (Internal Markets) Regulations 2011, SI 2011/2704, reg 45(2); words in square brackets in para (g) of the definition "special reference group" substituted by the Water Act 2003, s 101(1), Sch 8, para 54; para (l) of the definition "special reference group" repealed by the Postal Services Act 2011, 91(1), (2), Sch 12, Pt 3 para 152; para (o) of the definition "special reference group" (and the word immediately preceding it) added by the Communications Act 2003, s 406(1), Sch 17, para 153(1), (3); para (p) of the definition "special reference group" (and the word immediately preceding it) added, and word omitted from para (n) repealed, by the Water Services etc (Scotland) Act 2005 (Consequential Provisions and Modifications) Order 2005, SI 2005/3172, art 11, Schedule, Pt 1, para 3(a).

Para 20: words in square brackets in sub-para (1) substituted, and sub-paras (2)–(9) substituted for original sub-para (2), by the Enterprise Act 2002, s 185, Sch 11, paras 1, 11.

Para 22: words in square brackets substituted by the Enterprise Act 2002, s 185, Sch 11, paras 1, 12.

(*Sch 7, Pt III repealed by the Enterprise Act 2002, ss 21, 278(2), Sch 5, paras 1, 7(6), Sch 26; Sch 7, Pt IV amended legislation outside the scope of this work and is repealed as noted to Pt I of this Schedule at* **[1.1363]**.)

PART V
TRANSITIONAL PROVISIONS

Interpretation

[1.1365]
30.   In this Part of this Schedule—

"*commencement date*" means the date on which section 45 comes into force; and

"*MMC*" means the Monopolies and Mergers Commission.

Chairman

31. (1)   The person who is Chairman of the MMC immediately before the commencement date is on that date to become both a member of the Commission and its chairman as if he had been duly appointed under paragraphs 2(1)(b) and 3.

(2)   He is to hold office as Chairman of the Commission for the remainder of the period for which he was appointed as Chairman of the MMC and on the terms on which he was so appointed.

Deputy chairmen

32.   The persons who are deputy chairmen of the MMC immediately before the commencement date are on that date to become deputy chairmen of the Commission as if they had been duly appointed under paragraph 3(2).

Reporting panel members

33. (1)   The persons who are members of the MMC immediately before the commencement date are on that date to become members of the Commission as if they had been duly appointed under paragraph 2(1)(b).

(2)   Each of them is to hold office as a member for the remainder of the period for which he was appointed as a member of the MMC and on the terms on which he was so appointed.

Specialist panel members

34. (1)   The persons who are members of the MMC immediately before the commencement date by virtue of appointments made under any of the enactments mentioned in paragraph 2(1)(d) are on that date to become members of the Commission as if they had been duly appointed to the Commission under the enactment in question.

(2)   Each of them is to hold office as a member for such period and on such terms as the Secretary of State may determine.

Secretary

35.   The person who is the secretary of the MMC immediately before the commencement date is on that date to become the secretary of the Commission as if duly appointed under paragraph 9, on the same terms and conditions.

Council

36. (1)   The members who become deputy chairmen of the Commission under paragraph 32 are also to become members of the Council as if they had been duly appointed under paragraph 5(2)(c).

(2)   Each of them is to hold office as a member of the Council for such period as the Secretary of State determines.

NOTES

Repealed as noted to Pt I of this Schedule at **[1.1363]**.

[SCHEDULE 7A
THE COMPETITION COMMISSION: PROCEDURAL RULES FOR MERGERS AND MARKET
REFERENCES ETC

[1.1366]

1. In this Schedule—

"market investigation" means an investigation carried out by a market reference group in connection with a reference under section 131 or 132 of the Enterprise Act 2002 (including that section as it has effect by virtue of another enactment);

"market reference group" has the meaning given by paragraph 19A(9) of Schedule 7 to this Act;

"merger investigation" means an investigation carried out by a merger reference group in connection with a reference under . . . section 32 of the Water Industry Act 1991 (c 56) or section 22, 33, 45 or 62 of the Act of 2002;

"merger reference group" has the meaning given by paragraph 19A(9) of Schedule 7 to this Act;

"relevant group" means a market reference group, merger reference group or special reference group;

"special investigation" means an investigation carried out by a special reference group—

    (a)   in connection with a reference under a provision mentioned in any of paragraphs (a) to (l) [and (n) to (p)] of the definition of "special reference group" in paragraph 19A(9) of Schedule 7 to this Act; or

    (b)   under a provision mentioned in paragraph (m) of that definition; and

"special reference group" has the meaning given by paragraph 19A(9) of Schedule 7 to this Act.

2.   Rules may make provision—

(a) for particular stages of a merger investigation, a market investigation or a special investigation to be dealt with in accordance with a timetable and for the revision of that timetable;

(b) as to the documents and information which must be given to a relevant group in connection with a merger investigation, a market investigation or a special investigation;

(c) as to the documents or information which a relevant group must give to other persons in connection with such an investigation.

3. *Rules made by virtue of paragraph 2(a) and (b) may, in particular, enable or require a relevant group to disregard documents or information given after a particular date.*

4. *Rules made by virtue of paragraph 2(c) may, in particular, make provision for the notification or publication of, and for consultation about, provisional findings of a relevant group.*

5. *Rules may make provision as to the quorum of relevant groups.*

6. *Rules may make provision—*

(a) as to the extent (if any) to which persons interested or claiming to be interested in a matter under consideration which is specified or described in the rules are allowed—

   (i) to be (either by themselves or by their representatives) present before a relevant group or heard by that group;

   (ii) to cross-examine witnesses; or

   (iii) otherwise to take part;

(b) as to the extent (if any) to which sittings of a relevant group are to be held in public; and

(c) generally in connection with any matters permitted by rules made under paragraph (a) or (b) (including, in particular, provision for a record of any hearings).

7. *Rules may make provision for—*

(a) the notification or publication of information in relation to merger investigations, market investigations or special investigations;

(b) consultation about such investigations.]

NOTES

Schedule inserted by the Enterprise Act 2002, s 187(4), Sch 12.

Repealed by the Enterprise and Regulatory Reform Act 2013, s 26(3), Sch 5, Pt 3, paras 218, 223. For various transitional provisions (including those relating to the abolition of the OFT and the Competition Commission, existing references to those bodies and provisions relating to continuity), see the Enterprise and Regulatory Reform Act 2013 (Commencement No 6, Transitional Provisions and Savings) Order 2014, SI 2014/416, Schedule at **[2.1126]**.

Para 1: in definition "merger investigation" words omitted repealed by the Communications Act 2003, s 406(7), Sch 19(1); in definition "special investigation" words in square brackets in para (a) substituted by the Water Services etc (Scotland) Act 2005 (Consequential Provisions and Modifications) Order 2005, SI 2005/3172, art 11, Schedule, Pt 1, para 3(b).

SCHEDULE 8
APPEALS

Sections 46(5) and 48(4)

PART I
GENERAL

[1.1367]
1. . . .

General procedure

2. (1) An appeal to the [Tribunal under section [46, 47 or 49D(3)] must be made by sending a notice of appeal to it] within the specified period.

(2) The notice of appeal must set out the grounds of appeal in sufficient detail to indicate—

(a) under which provision of this Act the appeal is brought;

(b) to what extent (if any) the appellant contends that the decision against, or with respect to which, the appeal is brought was based on an error of fact or was wrong in law; and

(c) to what extent (if any) the appellant is appealing against the [[CMA's] exercise of its] discretion in making the disputed decision.

(3) The [Tribunal] may give an appellant leave to amend the grounds of appeal identified in the notice of appeal.

[(4) In this paragraph references to the Tribunal are to the Tribunal as constituted (in accordance with section 14 of the Enterprise Act 2002) for the purposes of the proceedings in question.

(5) Nothing in this paragraph restricts the power under section 15 of the Enterprise Act 2002 (Tribunal rules) to make provision as to the manner of instituting proceedings before the Tribunal.]

Decisions of the [Tribunal]

3. [(A1) This paragraph applies to any appeal under section 46 or 47 other than—

(a)   an appeal under section 46 against, or with respect to, a decision of the kind specified in subsection (3)(g) or (h) of that section, and

(b)   an appeal under section 47(1)(b) or (c).]

(1)   The [Tribunal] must determine the appeal on the merits by reference to the grounds of appeal set out in the notice of appeal.

(2)   The [Tribunal] may confirm or set aside the decision which is the subject of the appeal, or any part of it, and may—

(a)   remit the matter to the [CMA],

(b)   impose or revoke, or vary the amount of, a penalty,

(c)   . . .

(d)   give such directions, or take such other steps, as the [CMA] could [itself] have given or taken, or

(e)   make any other decision which the [CMA] could [itself] have made.

(3)   Any decision of the [Tribunal] on an appeal has the same effect, and may be enforced in the same manner, as a decision of the [CMA].

(4)   If the [Tribunal] confirms the decision which is the subject of the appeal it may nevertheless set aside any finding of fact on which the decision was based.

[3A.   (1)   This paragraph applies to—

(a)   any appeal under section 46 against, or with respect to, a decision of the kind specified in subsection (3)(g) or (h) of that section, and

(b)   any appeal under section 47(1)(b) or (c).]

(2)   The Tribunal must, by reference to the grounds of appeal set out in the notice of appeal, determine the appeal by applying the same principles as would be applied by a court on an application for judicial review.

(3)   The Tribunal may—

(a)   dismiss the appeal or quash the whole or part of the decision to which it relates; and

(b)   where it quashes the whole or part of that decision, remit the matter back to the [CMA] with a direction to reconsider and make a new decision in accordance with the ruling of the Tribunal.]

[3B. (1)   This paragraph applies to an appeal under section 49D(3).

(2)   The Tribunal must determine the appeal on the merits by reference to the grounds of appeal set out in the notice of appeal.

(3)   The Tribunal may—

(a)   approve the amount of costs which is the subject of the appeal, or

(b)   impose a requirement to pay costs of a different amount.

(4)   The Tribunal may also give such directions, or take such other steps, as the CMA could itself have given or taken.

(5)   A requirement imposed by the Tribunal under sub-paragraph (3)(b) has the same effect, and may be enforced in the same manner, as a requirement imposed by the CMA under section 49D.]

4.   . . .

NOTES

Paras 1, 4: repealed by the Enterprise Act 2002, ss 21, 278(2), Sch 5, paras 1, 8(1), (2), (5), Sch 26.

Para 2: words in first (outer) pairs of square brackets in sub-paras (1), (2)(c), and words in square brackets in sub-para (3) substituted, and sub-paras (4), (5) added, by the Enterprise Act 2002, ss 21, 278(1), Sch 5, paras 1, 8(1), (3), Sch 25, para 38(1), (54)(b); words "46, 47 or 49D(3)" in square brackets substituted by the Consumer Rights Act 2015, s 81, Sch 8, Pt 1, paras 1, 17(1), (2); reference to the "CMA's" in sub-para (2)(c) substituted for reference to the "OFT's" by the Enterprise and Regulatory Reform Act 2013, s 26(3), Sch 5, Pt 1, paras 1, 57(1), (2). For various transitional provisions (including those relating to the abolition of the OFT and the Competition Commission, existing references to those bodies and provisions relating to continuity), see the Enterprise and Regulatory Reform Act 2013 (Commencement No 6, Transitional Provisions and Savings) Order 2014, SI 2014/416, Schedule at **[2.1126]**.

Para 3: sub-para (A1) inserted, and sub-para (2)(c) repealed, by the Competition Act 1998 and Other Enactments (Amendment) Regulations 2004, SI 2004/1261, reg 4, Sch 1, para 53(1)–(3) (for savings and transitional provisions see reg 8 of those Regulations); words "Tribunal" and "itself" in square brackets substituted by the Enterprise Act 2002, ss 21, 278(1), Sch 5, paras 1, 8(1), (4), Sch 25, para 38(1), (54)(c); references to "CMA" substituted (for references to "OFT" as substituted by the Enterprise Act 2002, s 278, Sch 25, para 38) by the Enterprise and Regulatory Reform Act 2013, s 26(3), Sch 5, Pt 1, paras 1, 57(1), (3), subject to transitional provisions in SI 2014/416 as noted above.

Para 3A: inserted by SI 2004/1261, reg 4, Sch 1, para 53(1), (4) (for savings and transitional provisions see reg 8 of those Regulations); reference to "CMA" in sub-para (3)(b) substituted (for original references to "OFT"; by the Enterprise and Regulatory Reform Act 2013, s 26(3), Sch 5, Pt 1, paras 1, 57(1) (4), subject to transitional provisions in SI 2014/416 as noted above.

Para 3B: inserted by the Consumer Rights Act 2015, s 81, Sch 8, Pt 1, paras 1, 17(1), (3).

Transitional provisions: for transitional provisions in relation to the constitution, etc, of the Tribunal, see the Enterprise Act 2002, Sch 24, paras 7–11 at **[1.432]**, and for transitional provisions in connection with existing appeals, see the Enterprise Act 2002 (Commencement No 2, Transitional and Transitory Provisions) Order 2003, SI 2003/766, art 3.

References to the CMA, etc: as to the abolition of the office of the Director General of Fair Trading and the substitution of the original references to the Director (and related expressions), see the note preceding s 1 at **[1.1266]**.

(Pt II repealed by the Enterprise Act 2002, ss 21, 278(2), Sch 5, paras 1, 8(1), (5), Sch 26.)

SCHEDULE 9
[CMA'S] RULES

Section 51(2)

General

[1.1368]
[1. In this Schedule "rules" means rules made by the [CMA] under section 51.]

[Delegation of functions

[1A. (1) Rules may provide for the exercise of a function of the CMA under this Part on its behalf—
  (a) by one or more members of the CMA Board (see Part 2 of Schedule 4 to the Enterprise and Regulatory Reform Act 2013);
  (b) by one or more members of the CMA panel (see Part 3 of that Schedule to that Act);
  (c) by one or more members of staff of the CMA;
  (d) jointly by one or more of the persons mentioned in paragraph (a), (b) or (c).

(2) Sub-paragraph (1) does not apply in relation to any function prescribed in regulations made under section 7(1) of the Civil Aviation Act 1982 (power for Secretary of State to prescribe certain functions of the Civil Aviation Authority which must not be performed on its behalf by any other person).]

2–4. . . . .

Decisions

5. (1) Rules may make provision as to—
  (a) the form and manner in which notice of any decision is to be given;
  (b) the person or persons to whom the notice is to be given;
  (c) the manner in which the [CMA] is to publish a decision;
  [(d) the procedure to be followed if—
    (i) the [CMA] takes further action with respect to an agreement after having decided that it does not infringe the Chapter I prohibition;
    (ii) the [CMA] takes further action with respect to an agreement after having decided that it does not infringe the prohibition in [Article 101(1)];
    (iii) the [CMA] takes further action with respect to conduct after having decided that it does not infringe the Chapter II prohibition; or
    (iv) the [CMA] takes further action with respect to conduct after having decided that it does not infringe the prohibition in [Article 102]].

[(2) In this paragraph "decision" means a decision of the [CMA]—
  (a) as to whether or not an agreement has infringed the Chapter I prohibition;
  (b) as to whether or not an agreement has infringed the prohibition in [Article 101(1)];
  (c) as to whether or not conduct has infringed the Chapter II prohibition; or
  (d) as to whether or not conduct has infringed the prohibition in [Article 102].]

6, 7. . . . .

Block exemptions

[8. Rules may make provision as to—
  (a) the procedure to be followed by the [CMA] if it cancels a block exemption;
  (b) the procedure to be followed by the [CMA] if it withdraws the benefit of a regulation of the Commission pursuant to Article 29(2) of the EC Competition Regulation.]

Parallel exemptions

9. Rules may make provision as to—
  (a) the circumstances in which the [CMA] may—
    (i) impose conditions or obligations in relation to a parallel exemption,
    (ii) vary or remove any such conditions or obligations,
    (iii) impose additional conditions or obligations, or
    (iv) cancel the exemption;
  (b) as to the procedure to be followed by the [CMA] if [it] is acting under section 10(5);
  (c) the form and manner in which notice of a decision to take any of the steps in sub-paragraph (a) is to be given;
  (d) the circumstances in which an exemption may be cancelled with retrospective effect.

Section 11 exemptions

10. Rules may, with respect to any exemption provided by regulations made under section 11, make provision similar to that made with respect to parallel exemptions by section 10 or by rules under paragraph 9.

Directions withdrawing exclusions

11. Rules may make provision as to the factors which the [CMA] may take into account when [it] is determining the date on which a direction given under paragraph 4(1) of Schedule 1 or paragraph . . . 9(3) of Schedule 3 is to have effect.

Disclosure of information

12. (1) Rules may make provision as to the circumstances in which the [CMA] is to be required, before disclosing information given to [it] by a third party in connection with the exercise of any of the [CMA's] functions under Part I, to give notice, and an opportunity to make representations, to the third party.

(2) In relation to the agreement (or conduct) concerned, "third party" means a person who is not a party to the agreement (or who has not engaged in the conduct).

Applications under section 47

13. Rules may make provision as to—
    (a)   the period within which an application under section 47(1) must be made;
    (b)   the procedure to be followed by the [CMA] in dealing with the application;
    (c)   the person or persons to whom notice of the [CMA's] response to the application is to be given.

[Oral hearings: procedure

13A. (1) Rules may make provision as to the procedure to be followed by the CMA in holding oral hearings as part of an investigation.

(2) Rules may, in particular, make provision as to the appointment of a person mentioned in sub-paragraph (3) who has not been involved in the investigation in question to—
    (a)   chair an oral hearing, and
    (b)   prepare a report following the hearing and give it to the person who is to exercise on behalf of the CMA its function of making a decision (within the meaning given by section 31(2)) as a result of the investigation.

(3) The persons are—
    (a)   a member of the CMA Board;
    (b)   a member of the CMA panel;
    (c)   a member of staff of the CMA.

(4) The report must—
    (a)   contain an assessment of the fairness of the procedure followed in holding the oral hearing, and
    (b)   identify any other concerns about the fairness of the procedure followed in the investigation which have been brought to the attention of the person preparing the report.]

[Procedural complaints

13B. (1) Rules may make provision as to arrangements to be made by the CMA for dealing with complaints about the conduct by the CMA of an investigation.

(2) Rules may, in particular, make provision as to—
    (a)   the appointment of a person mentioned in sub-paragraph (3) who has not been involved in the investigation in question to consider any such complaint;
    (b)   the time-table for the consideration of any such complaint.

(3) The persons are—
    (a)   a member of the CMA Board;
    (b)   a member of the CMA panel;
    (c)   a member of staff of the CMA.]

[Settling cases

13C. Rules may make provision as to the procedure to be followed in a case where, during an investigation, one or more persons notify the CMA that they accept that there has been an infringement of a kind to which the investigation relates.]

Enforcement

14. Rules may make provision as to the procedure to be followed when the [OFT] takes action under any of sections [32 to 40] with respect to the enforcement of the provisions of this Part.

NOTES
References to the "CMA" and the "CMA's" in each place substituted (for references to the "OFT" and the "OFT's" as substituted by the Enterprise Act 2002, s 278, Sch 25, para 38) by the Enterprise and Regulatory Reform Act 2013, s 26(3), Sch 5, Pt 1, paras 1, 58. For various transitional provisions (including those relating to the abolition of the OFT and the Competition Commission, existing references to those bodies and provisions relating to continuity), see the Enterprise and Regulatory Reform Act 2013 (Commencement No 6, Transitional Provisions and Savings) Order 2014, SI 2014/416, Schedule at **[2.1126]**. This Schedule is also amended as follows:

Paras 1, 8: substituted by the Competition Act 1998 and other enactments (Amendment) Regulations 2004, SI 2004/1261, reg 4, Sch 1, para 54(1), (2), (7).

Para 1A: inserted by the Enterprise and Regulatory Reform Act 2013, s 42(1), (3), (4), subject to transitional provisions in SI 2014/416 as noted above.

Paras 2–4, 6, 7: repealed by SI 2004/1261, reg 4, Sch 1, paras 54(1), (3), (6) (for savings and transitional provisions in relation to para 6, see reg 10 of those Regulations at).

Para 5: sub-paras (1)(d), (2) substituted by SI 2004/1261, reg 4, Sch 1, paras 54(1), (4), (5); words "Article 101(1)" and "Article 102" in square brackets substituted by the Treaty of Lisbon (Changes in Terminology or Numbering) Order 2012, SI 2012/1809, art 3(1), Schedule, Pt 1 (note that the amendments made by this Order do not affect any provision in its application to things done before 1 December 2009 (the date on which the Treaty of Lisbon came into force)).

Para 9: word in second pair of square brackets in sub-para (b) substituted by the Enterprise Act 2002, s 278, Sch 25, para 38.

Paras 11, 12: word in second pair of square brackets substituted by the Enterprise Act 2002, s 278, Sch 25, para 38; words omitted repealed by SI 2004/1261, reg 4, Sch 1, para 54(1), (8).

Paras 13A–13C: inserted by the Enterprise and Regulatory Reform Act 2013, s 42(3), (5)–(7), subject to transitional provisions in SI 2014/416 as noted above.

Para 14: words in second pair of square brackets substituted by SI 2004/1261, reg 4, Sch 1, para 54(1), (9).

References to the CMA, etc: as to the abolition of the office of the Director General of Fair Trading and the substitution of the original references to the Director (and related expressions), see the note preceding s 1 at **[1.1266]**.

SCHEDULE 10
REGULATORS

Sections 54 and 66(5)

(Pt I repealed by the Enterprise Act 2002, s 278(2), Sch 26.)

PART II
THE PROHIBITIONS

[1.1369]
2. . . .

Gas

3. (1)   In consequence of the repeal by this Act of provisions of the Competition Act 1980, the functions transferred by subsection (3) of section 36A of the Gas Act 1986 (functions with respect to competition) are no longer exercisable by the Director General of Gas Supply.
(2)–(11)   . . .

Electricity

4. (1)   In consequence of the repeal by this Act of provisions of the Competition Act 1980, the functions transferred by subsection (3) of section 43 of the Electricity Act 1989 (functions with respect to competition) are no longer exercisable by the Director General of Electricity Supply.
(2)–(9)   . . .

Water

5. (1)   In consequence of the repeal by this Act of provisions of the Competition Act 1980, the functions exercisable by virtue of subsection (3) of section 31 of the Water Industry Act 1991 (functions of Director with respect to competition) are no longer exercisable by the Director General of Water Services.
(2)–(13)   . . .

Railways

6. (1)   In consequence of the repeal by this Act of provisions of the Competition Act 1980, the functions transferred by subsection (3) of section 67 of the Railways Act 1993 (respective functions of the Regulator and the Director etc) are no longer exercisable by [the Office of Rail Regulation].
(2)–(9)   . . .

NOTES
Para 2: repealed by the Communications Act 2003, s 406(7), Sch 19(1) and the Enterprise Act 2002, s 278(2), Sch 26.

Para 3: sub-paras (2)–(11) amend the Gas Act 1986, ss 4, 36A; repealed in part by the Utilities Act 2000, s 108, Sch 8, and the Enterprise Act 2002, s 278(2), Sch 26.

Para 4: sub-paras (2)–(9) amend the Electricity Act 1989, ss 3, 43; repealed in part by the Utilities Act 2000, s 108, Sch 8, and the Enterprise Act 2002, s 278(2), Sch 26.

Para 5: sub-paras (2)–(13) amend the Water Industry Act 1991, ss 2, 31; repealed in part by the Water Act 2003, s 101, Sch 7, Pt 2, para 32(1), (4)(a), Sch 9, Pt 3 and the Enterprise Act 2002, s 278(2), Sch 26.

Para 6: words in square brackets in sub-para (1) substituted by virtue of the Railways and Transport Safety Act 2003, s 16(4), (5), Sch 3, para 4; sub-paras (2)–(9) amend the Railways Act 1993, ss 4, 67; repealed in part by the Enterprise Act 2002, s 278(2), Sch 26.

Director General of Gas Supply and the Director General of Electricity Supply: the functions of the Director General of Gas Supply and the Director General of Electricity Supply are transferred to the Gas and Electricity Markets Authority by virtue of the Utilities Act 2000, s 3(2). References in paras 3 and 4 above to either of those Directors should be construed accordingly.

The Director: ie, the Director General of Fair Trading. As to the transfer of the Director's functions, etc, see the note to Sch 13, Pt I to this Act at **[1.128]**).

(Pt III applies to Northern Ireland only; Pt IV (minor and consequential amendments), Pt V (minor and consequential amendments in relation to Northern Ireland) outside the scope of this work.)

SCHEDULES 11, 12

(Sch 11 repealed by the Enterprise Act 2002, ss 247(j), 278(2), Sch 26; Sch 12 (minor and consequential amendments) outside the scope of this work.)

SCHEDULE 13
TRANSITIONAL PROVISIONS AND SAVINGS

Section 74(2)

PART I
GENERAL

Interpretation

[1.1370]

1. (1) In this Schedule—

"RPA" means the Resale Prices Act 1976;

"RTPA" means the Restrictive Trade Practices Act 1976;

"continuing proceedings" has the meaning given by paragraph 15;

"the Court" means the Restrictive Practices Court;

"Director" means the Director General of Fair Trading;

"document" includes information recorded in any form;

"enactment date" means the date on which this Act is passed;

"information" includes estimates and forecasts;

"interim period" means the period beginning on the enactment date and ending immediately before the starting date;

"prescribed" means prescribed by an order made by the Secretary of State;

"regulator" means any person mentioned in paragraphs (a) to (g) of paragraph 1 of Schedule 10 [and the Civil Aviation Authority];

"starting date" means the date on which section 2 comes into force;

"transitional period" means the transitional period provided for in Chapters III and IV of Part IV of this Schedule.

(2) Sections 30, 44, 51, 53, 55, 56, 57 and 59(3) and (4) and paragraph 12 of Schedule 9 ("the applied provisions") apply for the purposes of this Schedule as they apply for the purposes of Part I of this Act.

(3) Section 2(5) applies for the purposes of any provisions of this Schedule which are concerned with the operation of the Chapter I prohibition as it applies for the purposes of Part I of this Act.

(4) In relation to any of the matters in respect of which a regulator may exercise powers as a result of paragraph 35(1), the applied provisions are to have effect as if references to the Director included references to the regulator.

(5) The fact that to a limited extent the Chapter I prohibition does not apply to an agreement, because a transitional period is provided by virtue of this Schedule, does not require those provisions of the agreement in respect of which there is a transitional period to be disregarded when considering whether the agreement infringes the prohibition for other reasons.

General power to make transitional provision and savings

2. (1) Nothing in this Schedule affects the power of the Secretary of State under section 75 to make transitional provisions or savings.

(2) An order under that section may modify any provision made by this Schedule.

Advice and information

3. (1) The Director may publish advice and information explaining provisions of this Schedule to persons who are likely to be affected by them.

(2)   Any advice or information published by the Director under this paragraph is to be published in such form and manner as he considers appropriate.

NOTES

Para 1: in sub-para (1) words in square brackets in definition "regulator" inserted by the Transport Act 2000, s 97, Sch 8, Pt IV, para 16(1), (2).

Director General of Fair Trading: the Enterprise Act 2002, s 2(1) provided that, as from the coming into force of that section (on 1 April 2003), the functions of the Director General of Fair Trading, his property, rights and liabilities were transferred to the Office of Fair Trading. Accordingly, (by virtue of s 2(2), (3) of the 2002 Act) the office of the Director was abolished, and any reference to the Director in any enactment, instrument or other document passed or made before the commencement of s 2(1) had, in so far as is necessary, effect as if it were a reference to the Office of Fair Trading (for transitional provisions in connection with the transfer, see Sch 24, para 6 to the 2002 Act). Section 2 of the 2002 Act was repealed by the Enterprise and Regulatory Reform Act 2013, s 26(3), Sch 5, Pt 4, para 229, as from 1 April 2014. Part 3 the 2013 Act (ss 25–28) abolished the Office of fair Trading (and the Competition Commission) and provided for the transfer of its functions to the newly created Competition and Markets Authority.

PART II
DURING THE INTERIM PERIOD

Block exemptions

[1.1371]

4. (1)   The Secretary of State may, at any time during the interim period, make one or more orders for the purpose of providing block exemptions which are effective on the starting date.

(2)   An order under this paragraph has effect as if properly made under section 6.

Certain agreements to be non-notifiable agreements

5. An agreement which—
   (a)   is made during the interim period, and
   (b)   satisfies the conditions set out in paragraphs (a), (c) and (d) of section 27A(1) of the RTPA, is to be treated as a non-notifiable agreement for the purposes of RTPA.

Application of RTPA during the interim period

6. In relation to agreements made during the interim period—
   (a)   the Director is no longer under the duty to take proceedings imposed by section 1(2)(c) of the RTPA but may continue to do so;
   (b)   section 21 of that Act has effect as if subsections (1) and (2) were omitted; and
   (c)   section 35(1) of that Act has effect as if the words "or within such further time as the Director may, upon application made within that time, allow" were omitted.

Guidance

7. (1)   Sub-paragraphs (2) to (4) apply in relation to agreements made during the interim period.

(2)   An application may be made to the Director in anticipation of the coming into force of section 13 in accordance with directions given by the Director and such an application is to have effect on and after the starting date as if properly made under section 13.

(3)   The Director may, in response to such an application—
   (a)   give guidance in anticipation of the coming into force of section 2; or
   (b)   on and after the starting date, give guidance under section 15 as if the application had been properly made under section 13.

(4)   Any guidance so given is to have effect on and after the starting date as if properly given under section 15.

NOTES

The Director: see note to Pt I of this Schedule at **[1.1370]**.

Note: references to the Director should be construed in accordance with the note preceding s 1 at **[1.1266]**.

PART III
ON THE STARTING DATE

Applications which fall

[1.1372]

8. (1)   Proceedings in respect of an application which is made to the Court under any of the provisions mentioned in sub-paragraph (2), but which is not determined before the starting date, cease on that date.

(2)   The provisions are—
   (a)   sections 2(2), 35(3), 37(1) and 40(1) of the RTPA and paragraph 5 of Schedule 4 to that Act;
   (b)   section 4(1) of the RTPA so far as the application relates to an order under section 2(2) of that Act; and

(c)   section 25(2) of the RPA.

(3)   The power of the Court to make an order for costs in relation to any proceedings is not affected by anything in this paragraph or by the repeals made by section 1.

Orders and approvals which fall

9. (1)   An order in force immediately before the starting date under—

(a)   section 2(2), 29(1), 30(1), 33(4), 35(3) or 37(1) of the RTPA; or

(b)   section 25(2) of the RPA,

ceases to have effect on that date.

(2)   An approval in force immediately before the starting date under section 32 of the RTPA ceases to have effect on that date.

PART IV
ON AND AFTER THE STARTING DATE

CHAPTER I
GENERAL

Duty of Director to maintain register etc

[1.1373]

10. (1)   This paragraph applies even though the relevant provisions of the RTPA are repealed by this Act.

(2)   The Director is to continue on and after the starting date to be under the duty imposed by section 1(2)(a) of the RTPA to maintain a register in respect of agreements—

(a)   particulars of which are, on the starting date, entered or filed on the register;

(b)   which fall within sub-paragraph (4);

(c)   which immediately before the starting date are the subject of proceedings under the RTPA which do not cease on that date by virtue of this Schedule; or

(d)   in relation to which a court gives directions to the Director after the starting date in the course of proceedings in which a question arises as to whether an agreement was, before that date—

     (i)   one to which the RTPA applied;

     (ii)   subject to registration under that Act;

     (iii) a non-notifiable agreement for the purposes of that Act.

(3)   The Director is to continue on and after the starting date to be under the duties imposed by section 1(2)(a) and (b) of the RTPA of compiling a register of agreements and entering or filing certain particulars in the register, but only in respect of agreements of a kind referred to in paragraph (b), (c) or (d) of sub-paragraph (2).

(4)   An agreement falls within this sub-paragraph if—

(a)   it is subject to registration under the RTPA but—

     (i)   is not a non-notifiable agreement within the meaning of section 27A of the RTPA, or

     (ii)   is not one to which paragraph 5 applies;

(b)   particulars of the agreement have been provided to the Director before the starting date; and

(c)   as at the starting date no entry or filing has been made in the register in respect of the agreement.

(5)   Sections 23 and 27 of the RTPA are to apply after the starting date in respect of the register subject to such modifications, if any, as may be prescribed.

(6)   In sub-paragraph (2)(d) "court" means—

(a)   the High Court;

(b)   the Court of Appeal;

(c)   the Court of Session;

(d)   the High Court or Court of Appeal in Northern Ireland; or

[(e)   the Supreme Court].

RTPA section 3 applications

11. (1)   Even though section 3 of the RTPA is repealed by this Act, its provisions (and so far as necessary that Act) are to continue to apply, with such modifications (if any) as may be prescribed—

(a)   in relation to a continuing application under that section; or

(b)   so as to allow an application to be made under that section on or after the starting date in respect of a continuing application under section 1(3) of the RTPA.

(2)   "Continuing application" means an application made, but not determined, before the starting date.

RTPA section 26 applications

12. (1) Even though section 26 of the RTPA is repealed by this Act, its provisions (and so far as necessary that Act) are to continue to apply, with such modifications (if any) as may be prescribed, in relation to an application which is made under that section, but not determined, before the starting date.

(2) If an application under section 26 is determined on or after the starting date, this Schedule has effect in relation to the agreement concerned as if the application had been determined immediately before that date.

Right to bring civil proceedings

13. (1) Even though section 35 of the RTPA is repealed by this Act, its provisions (and so far as necessary that Act) are to continue to apply in respect of a person who, immediately before the starting date, has a right by virtue of section 27ZA or 35(2) of that Act to bring civil proceedings in respect of an agreement (but only so far as that right relates to any period before the starting date or, where there are continuing proceedings, the determination of the proceedings).

(2) Even though section 25 of the RPA is repealed by this Act, the provisions of that section (and so far as necessary that Act) are to continue to apply in respect of a person who, immediately before the starting date, has a right by virtue of subsection (3) of that section to bring civil proceedings (but only so far as that right relates to any period before the starting date or, where there are continuing proceedings, the determination of the proceedings).

CHAPTER II
CONTINUING PROCEEDINGS
The general rule

14. (1) The Chapter I prohibition does not apply to an agreement at any time when the agreement is the subject of continuing proceedings under the RTPA.

(2) The Chapter I prohibition does not apply to an agreement relating to goods which are the subject of continuing proceedings under section 16 or 17 of the RPA to the extent to which the agreement consists of exempt provisions.

(3) In sub-paragraph (2) "exempt provisions" means those provisions of the agreement which would, disregarding section 14 of the RPA, be—

    (a)   void as a result of section 9(1) of the RPA; or

    (b)   unlawful as a result of section 9(2) or II of the RPA.

(4) If the Chapter I prohibition does not apply to an agreement because of this paragraph, the provisions of, or made under, the RTPA or the RPA are to continue to have effect in relation to the agreement.

(5) The repeals made by section 1 do not affect—

    (a)   continuing proceedings; or

    (b)   proceedings of the kind referred to in paragraph 11 or 12 of this Schedule which are continuing after the starting date.

Meaning of "continuing proceedings"

15. (1) For the purposes of this Schedule "continuing proceedings" means proceedings in respect of an application made to the Court under the RTPA or the RPA, but not determined, before the starting date.

(2) But proceedings under section 3 or 26 of the RTPA to which paragraph 11 or 12 applies are not continuing proceedings.

(3) The question whether (for the purposes of Part III, or this Part, of this Schedule) an application has been determined is to be decided in accordance with sub-paragraphs (4) and (5).

(4) If an appeal against the decision on the application is brought, the application is not determined until—

    (a)   the appeal is disposed of or withdrawn; or

    (b)   if as a result of the appeal the case is referred back to the Court—

        (i)   the expiry of the period within which an appeal ("the further appeal") in respect of the Court's decision on that reference could have been brought had this Act not been passed; or

        (ii)   if later, the date on which the further appeal is disposed of or withdrawn.

(5) Otherwise, the application is not determined until the expiry of the period within which any party to the application would have been able to bring an appeal against the decision on the application had this Act not been passed.

RTPA section 4 proceedings

16. Proceedings on an application for an order under section 4 of the RTPA are also continuing proceedings if—

(a)   leave to make the application is applied for before the starting date but the proceedings in respect of that application for leave are not determined before that date; or

(b)   leave to make an application for an order under that section is granted before the starting date but the application itself is not made before that date.

RPA section 16 or 17 proceedings

17. Proceedings on an application for an order under section 16 or 17 of the RPA are also continuing proceedings if—

(a)   leave to make the application is applied for before the starting date but the proceedings in respect of that application for leave are not determined before that date; or

(b)   leave to make an application for an order under section 16 or 17 of the RPA is granted before the starting date, but the application itself is not made before that date.

Continuing proceedings which are discontinued

18. (1)   On an application made jointly to the Court by all the parties to any continuing proceedings, the Court must, if it is satisfied that the parties wish it to do so, discontinue the proceedings.

(2)   If, on an application under sub-paragraph (1) or for any other reason, the Court orders the proceedings to be discontinued, this Schedule has effect (subject to paragraphs 21 and 22) from the date on which the proceedings are discontinued as if they had never been instituted.

CHAPTER III
THE TRANSITIONAL PERIOD

The general rule

19. (1)   Except where this Chapter or Chapter IV provides otherwise, there is a transitional period, beginning on the starting date and lasting for one year, for any agreement made before the starting date.

(2)   The Chapter I prohibition does not apply to an agreement to the extent to which there is a transitional period for the agreement.

(3)   The Secretary of State may by regulations provide for sections 13 to 16 and Schedule 5 to apply with such modifications (if any) as may be specified in the regulations, in respect of applications to the Director about agreements for which there is a transitional period.

Cases for which there is no transitional period

20. (1)   There is no transitional period for an agreement to the extent to which, immediately before the starting date, it is—

(a)   void under section 2(1) or 35(1)(a) of the RTPA;

(b)   the subject of an order under section 2(2) or 35(3) of the RTPA; or

(c)   unlawful under section 1, 2 or 11 of the RPA or void under section 9 of that Act.

(2)   There is no transitional period for an agreement to the extent to which, before the starting date, a person has acted unlawfully for the purposes of section 27ZA(2) or (3) of the RTPA in respect of the agreement.

(3)   There is no transitional period for an agreement to which paragraph 25(4) applies.

(4)   There is no transitional period for—

(a)   an agreement in respect of which there are continuing proceedings, or

(b)   an agreement relating to goods in respect of which there are continuing proceedings,

to the extent to which the agreement is, when the proceedings are determined, void or unlawful.

Continuing proceedings under the RTPA

21. In the case of an agreement which is the subject of continuing proceedings under the RTPA, the transitional period begins—

(a)   if the proceedings are discontinued, on the date of discontinuance;

(b)   otherwise, when the proceedings are determined.

Continuing proceedings under the RPA

22. (1)   In the case of an agreement relating to goods which are the subject of continuing proceedings under the RPA, the transitional period for the exempt provisions of the agreement begins—

(a)   if the proceedings are discontinued, on the date of discontinuance;

(b)   otherwise, when the proceedings are determined.

(2)   In sub-paragraph (1) "exempt provisions" has the meaning given by paragraph 14(3).

Provisions not contrary to public interest

23. (1) To the extent to which an agreement contains provisions which, immediately before the starting date, are provisions which the Court has found not to be contrary to the public interest, the transitional period lasts for five years.

(2) Sub-paragraph (1) is subject to paragraph 20(4).

(3) To the extent to which an agreement which on the starting date is the subject of continuing proceedings is, when the proceedings are determined, found by the Court not to be contrary to the public interest, the transitional period lasts for five years.

Goods

24. (1) In the case of an agreement relating to goods which, immediately before the starting date, are exempt under section 14 of the RPA, there is a transitional period for the agreement to the extent to which it consists of exempt provisions.

(2) Sub-paragraph (1) is subject to paragraph 20(4).

(3) In the case of an agreement relating to goods—
  (a) which on the starting date are the subject of continuing proceedings, and
  (b) which, when the proceedings are determined, are found to be exempt under section 14 of the RPA,
there is a transitional period for the agreement, to the extent to which it consists of exempt provisions.

(4) In each case, the transitional period lasts for five years.

(5) In sub-paragraphs (1) and (3) "exempt provisions" means those provisions of the agreement which would, disregarding section 14 of the RPA, be—
  (a) void as a result of section 9(1) of the RPA; or
  (b) unlawful as a result of section 9(2) or 11 of the RPA.

Transitional period for certain agreements

25. (1) This paragraph applies to agreements—
  (a) which are subject to registration under the RTPA but which—
      (i) are not non-notifiable agreements within the meaning of section 27A of the RTPA, or
      (ii) are not agreements to which paragraph 5 applies; and
  (b) in respect of which the time for furnishing relevant particulars as required by or under the RTPA expires on or after the starting date.

(2) "Relevant particulars" means—
  (a) particulars which are required to be furnished by virtue of section 24 of the RTPA; or
  (b) particulars of any variation of an agreement which are required to be furnished by virtue of sections 24 and 27 of the RTPA.

(3) There is a transitional period of one year for an agreement to which this paragraph applies if—
  (a) relevant particulars are furnished before the starting date; and
  (b) no person has acted unlawfully (for the purposes of section 27ZA(2) or (3) of the RTPA) in respect of the agreement.

(4) If relevant particulars are not furnished by the starting date, section 35(1)(a) of the RTPA does not apply in relation to the agreement (unless sub-paragraph (5) applies).

(5) This sub-paragraph applies if a person falling within section 27ZA(2) or (3) of the RTPA has acted unlawfully for the purposes of those subsections in respect of the agreement.

Special cases

26. (1) In the case of an agreement in respect of which—
  (a) . . .
  (b) a direction under section 194A(3) of the Broadcasting Act 1990 ("the 1990 Act") is in force immediately before the starting date,
the transitional period lasts for five years.

(2) . . .

(3) Sub-paragraphs (1) < . . . > do not affect the power of—
  (a) . . .
  (b) the Secretary of State to make a declaration under section 194A of the 1990 Act (as amended by Schedule 2 to this Act),
in respect of an agreement for which there is a transitional period.

CHAPTER IV
THE UTILITIES

General

27. In this Chapter "the relevant period" means the period beginning with the starting date and ending immediately before the fifth anniversary of that date.

Electricity

28. (1) For an agreement to which, immediately before the starting date, the RTPA does not apply by virtue of a section 100 order, there is a transitional period—
  (a) beginning on the starting date; and
  (b) ending at the end of the relevant period.

(2) For an agreement which is made at any time after the starting date and to which, had the RTPA not been repealed, that Act would not at the time at which the agreement is made have applied by virtue of a section 100 order, there is a transitional period—
  (a) beginning on the date on which the agreement is made; and
  (b) ending at the end of the relevant period.

(3) For an agreement (whether made before or after the starting date) which, during the relevant period, is varied at any time in such a way that it becomes an agreement which, had the RTPA not been repealed, would at that time have been one to which that Act did not apply by virtue of a section 100 order, there is a transitional period—
  (a) beginning on the date on which the variation is made; and
  (b) ending at the end of the relevant period.

(4) If an agreement for which there is a transitional period as a result of sub-paragraph (1), (2) or (3) is varied during the relevant period, the transitional period for the agreement continues if, had the RTPA not been repealed, the agreement would have continued to be one to which that Act did not apply by virtue of a section 100 order.

(5) But if an agreement for which there is a transitional period as a result of sub-paragraph (1), (2) or (3) ceases to be one to which, had it not been repealed, the RTPA would not have applied by virtue of a section 100 order, the transitional period ends on the date on which the agreement so ceases.

(6) Sub-paragraph (3) is subject to paragraph 20.

(7) In this paragraph and paragraph 29—
  "section 100 order" means an order made under section 100 of the Electricity Act 1989; and
  expressions which are also used in Part I of the Electricity Act 1989 have the same meaning as in that Part.

Electricity: power to make transitional orders

29. (1) There is a transitional period for an agreement (whether made before or after the starting date) relating to the generation, transmission or supply of electricity which—
  (a) is specified, or is of a description specified, in an order ("a transitional order") made by the Secretary of State (whether before or after the making of the agreement but before the end of the relevant period); and
  (b) satisfies such conditions as may be specified in the order.

(2) A transitional order may make provision as to when the transitional period in respect of such an agreement is to start or to be deemed to have started.

(3) The transitional period for such an agreement ends at the end of the relevant period.

(4) But if the agreement—
  (a) ceases to be one to which a transitional order applies, or
  (b) ceases to satisfy one or more of the conditions specified in the transitional order,
the transitional period ends on the date on which the agreement so ceases.

(5) Before making a transitional order, the Secretary of State must consult [the Gas and Electricity Markets Authority].

(6) The conditions specified in a transitional order may include conditions which refer any matter to the Secretary of State for determination after such consultation as may be so specified.

(7) In the application of this paragraph to Northern Ireland, the reference in sub-paragraph (5) to [the Gas and Electricity Markets Authority] is to be read as a reference to the Director General of Electricity Supply for Northern Ireland.

Gas

30. (1) For an agreement to which, immediately before the starting date, the RTPA does not apply by virtue of section 62 or a section 62 order, there is a transitional period—
  (a) beginning on the starting date; and
  (b) ending at the end of the relevant period.

(2) For an agreement which is made at any time after the starting date and to which, had the RTPA not been repealed, that Act would not at the time at which the agreement is made have applied by virtue of section 62 or a section 62 order, there is a transitional period—
  (a) beginning on the date on which the agreement is made; and
  (b) ending at the end of the relevant period.

(3) For an agreement (whether made before or after the starting date) which, during the relevant period, is varied at any time in such a way that it becomes an agreement which, had the RTPA not been repealed, would at that time have been one to which that Act did not apply by virtue of section 62 or a section 62 order, there is a transitional period—
  (a) beginning on the date on which the variation is made; and
  (b) ending at the end of the relevant period.

(4) If an agreement for which there is a transitional period as a result of sub-paragraph (1), (2) or (3) is varied during the relevant period, the transitional period for the agreement continues if, had the RTPA not been repealed, the agreement would have continued to be one to which that Act did not apply by virtue of section 62 or a section 62 order.

(5) But if an agreement for which there is a transitional period as a result of sub-paragraph (1), (2) or (3) ceases to be one to which, had it not been repealed, the RTPA would not have applied by virtue of section 62 or a section 62 order, the transitional period ends on the date on which the agreement so ceases.

(6) Sub-paragraph (3) also applies in relation to a modification which is treated as an agreement made on or after 28th November 1985 by virtue of section 62(4).

(7) Sub-paragraph (3) is subject to paragraph 20.

(8) In this paragraph and paragraph 31—
  "section 62" means section 62 of the Gas Act 1986;
  "section 62 order" means an order made under section 62.

Gas: power to make transitional orders

31. (1) There is a transitional period for an agreement of a description falling within section 62(2)(a) and (b) or section 62(2A)(a) and (b) which—
  (a) is specified, or is of a description specified, in an order ("a transitional order") made by the Secretary of State (whether before or after the making of the agreement but before the end of the relevant period); and
  (b) satisfies such conditions as may be specified in the order.

(2) A transitional order may make provision as to when the transitional period in respect of such an agreement is to start or to be deemed to have started.

(3) The transitional period for such an agreement ends at the end of the relevant period.

(4) But if the agreement—
  (a) ceases to be one to which a transitional order applies, or
  (b) ceases to satisfy one or more of the conditions specified in the transitional order,
the transitional period ends on the date when the agreement so ceases.

(5) Before making a transitional order, the Secretary of State must consult [the Gas and Electricity Markets Authority] and the Director.

(6) The conditions specified in a transitional order may include—
  (a) conditions which are to be satisfied in relation to a time before the coming into force of this paragraph;
  (b) conditions which refer any matter (which may be the general question whether the Chapter I prohibition should apply to a particular agreement) to the Secretary of State, the Director or [the Gas and Electricity Markets Authority] for determination after such consultation as may be so specified.

Gas: Northern Ireland

32. (1) For an agreement to which, immediately before the starting date, the RTPA does not apply by virtue of an Article 41 order, there is a transitional period—
  (a) beginning on the starting date; and
  (b) ending at the end of the relevant period.

(2) For an agreement which is made at any time after the starting date and to which, had the RTPA not been repealed, that Act would not at the time at which the agreement is made have applied by virtue of an Article 41 order, there is a transitional period—
  (a) beginning on the date on which the agreement is made; and
  (b) ending at the end of the relevant period.

(3) For an agreement (whether made before or after the starting date) which, during the relevant period, is varied at any time in such a way that it becomes an agreement which, had the RTPA not been repealed, would at that time have been one to which that Act did not apply by virtue of an Article 41 order, there is a transitional period—
  (a) beginning on the date on which the variation is made; and
  (b) ending at the end of the relevant period.

(4) If an agreement for which there is a transitional period as a result of sub-paragraph (1), (2) or (3) is varied during the relevant period, the transitional period for the agreement continues if, had the RTPA not been repealed, the agreement would have continued to be one to which that Act did not apply by virtue of an Article 41 order.

(5)   But if an agreement for which there is a transitional period as a result of sub-paragraph (1), (2) or (3) ceases to be one to which, had it not been repealed, the RTPA would not have applied by virtue of an Article 41 order, the transitional period ends on the date on which the agreement so ceases.

(6)   Sub-paragraph (3) is subject to paragraph 20.

(7)   In this paragraph and paragraph 33—
"Article 41 order" means an order under Article 41 of the Gas (Northern Ireland) Order 1996;
"Department" means the Department of Economic Development.

Gas: Northern Ireland—power to make transitional orders

33. (1)   There is a transitional period for an agreement of a description falling within Article 41(1) which—
- (a)   is specified, or is of a description specified, in an order ("a transitional order") made by the Department (whether before or after the making of the agreement but before the end of the relevant period); and
- (b)   satisfies such conditions as may be specified in the order.

(2)   A transitional order may make provision as to when the transitional period in respect of such an agreement is to start or to be deemed to have started.

(3)   The transitional period for such an agreement ends at the end of the relevant period.

(4)   But if the agreement—
- (a)   ceases to be one to which a transitional order applies, or
- (b)   ceases to satisfy one or more of the conditions specified in the transitional order,
the transitional period ends on the date when the agreement so ceases.

(5)   Before making a transitional order, the Department must consult the Director General of Gas for Northern Ireland and the Director.

(6)   The conditions specified in a transitional order may include conditions which refer any matter (which may be the general question whether the Chapter I prohibition should apply to a particular agreement) to the Department for determination after such consultation as may be so specified.

Railways

34. (1)   In this paragraph—
"section 131" means section 131 of the Railways Act 1993 ("the 1993 Act");
"section 131 agreement" means an agreement—
- (a)   to which the RTPA does not apply immediately before the starting date by virtue of section 131(1); or
- (b)   in respect of which a direction under section 131(3) is in force immediately before that date;
"non-exempt agreement" means an agreement relating to the provision of railway services (whether made before or after the starting date) which is not a section 131 agreement; and
"railway services" has the meaning given by section 82 of the 1993 Act.

(2)   For a section 131 agreement there is a transitional period of five years.

(3)   There is a transitional period for a non-exempt agreement to the extent to which the agreement is at any time before the end of the relevant period required or approved—
- (a)   by the Secretary of State or [the Office of Rail Regulation] in pursuance of any function assigned or transferred to him under or by virtue of any provision of the 1993 Act;
- (b)   by or under any agreement the making of which is required or approved by the Secretary of State or [the Office of Rail Regulation] in the exercise of any such function; or
- (c)   by or under a licence granted under Part I of the 1993 Act.

(4)   The transitional period conferred by sub-paragraph (3)—
- (a)   is to be taken to have begun on the starting date; and
- (b)   ends at the end of the relevant period.

(5)   Sub-paragraph (3) is subject to paragraph 20.

(6)   Any variation of a section 131 agreement on or after the starting date is to be treated, for the purposes of this paragraph, as a separate non-exempt agreement.

The regulators

35. (1)   Subject to sub-paragraph (3), each of the regulators may exercise, in respect of sectoral matters and concurrently with the Director, the functions of the Director under paragraph 3, 7, 19(3), 36, 37, 38 or 39.

(2)   In sub-paragraph (1) "sectoral matters" means—
- (a)   . . .
- (b)   in the case of [the Gas and Electricity Markets Authority], the matters referred to in section 36A(3) and (4) of the Gas Act 1986;
- (c)   in the case of [the Gas and Electricity Markets Authority], the matters referred to in section 43(3) of the Electricity Act 1989;

(d)   in the case of the Director General of Electricity Supply for Northern Ireland, the matters referred to in Article 46(3) of the Electricity (Northern Ireland) Order 1992;

(e)   in the case of the [Water Services Regulation Authority], the matters referred to in section 31(3) of the Water Industry Act 1991;

(f)   in the case of [the Office of Rail Regulation], the matters referred to in section 67(3) of the Railways Act 1993;

(g)   in the case of the Director General of Gas for Northern Ireland, the matters referred to in Article 23(3) of the Gas (Northern Ireland) Order 1996.

[(h)   in the case of the Civil Aviation Authority, the supply of air traffic services within the meaning given by section 98 of the Transport Act 2000.]

(3)   The power to give directions in paragraph 7(2) is exercisable by the Director only but if the Director is preparing directions which relate to a matter in respect of which a regulator exercises concurrent jurisdiction, he must consult that regulator.

(4)   Consultations conducted by the Director before the enactment date, with a view to preparing directions which have effect on or after that date, are to be taken to satisfy sub-paragraph (3).

(5)   References to enactments in sub-paragraph (2) are to the enactments as amended by or under this Act.

CHAPTER V
EXTENDING THE TRANSITIONAL PERIOD

36. (1)   A party to an agreement for which there is a transitional period may apply to the Director, not less than three months before the end of the period, for the period to be extended.

(2)   The Director may (on his own initiative or on an application under sub-paragraph (1))—

(a)   extend a one-year transitional period by not more than twelve months;

(b)   extend a transitional period of any period other than one year by not more than six months.

(3)   An application under sub-paragraph (1) must—

(a)   be in such form as may be specified; and

(b)   include such documents and information as may be specified.

(4)   If the Director extends the transitional period under this paragraph, he must give notice in such form, and to such persons, as may be specified.

(5)   The Director may not extend a transitional period more than once.

(6)   In this paragraph—

"person" has the same meaning as in Part I; and

"specified" means specified in rules made by the Director under section 51.

CHAPTER VI
TERMINATING THE TRANSITIONAL PERIOD

General

37. (1)   Subject to sub-paragraph (2), the Director may by a direction in writing terminate the transitional period for an agreement, but only in accordance with paragraph 38.

(2)   The Director may not terminate the transitional period, nor exercise any of the powers in paragraph 38, in respect of an agreement which is excluded from the Chapter I prohibition by virtue of any of the provisions of Part I of this Act other than paragraph 1 of Schedule 1 or paragraph 2 or 9 of Schedule 3 [or the Competition Act 1998 (Land and Vertical Agreements Exclusion) Order 2000].

Circumstances in which the Director may terminate the transitional period

38. (1)   If the Director is considering whether to give a direction under paragraph 37 ("a direction"), he may in writing require any party to the agreement concerned to give him such information in connection with that agreement as he may require.

(2)   If at the end of such period as may be specified in rules made under section 51, a person has failed, without reasonable excuse, to comply with a requirement imposed under sub-paragraph (1), the Director may give a direction.

(3)   The Director may also give a direction if he considers—

(a)   that the agreement would, but for the transitional period or a relevant exclusion, infringe the Chapter I prohibition; and

(b)   that he would not be likely to grant the agreement an unconditional individual exemption.

(4)   For the purposes of sub-paragraph (3) an individual exemption is unconditional if no conditions or obligations are imposed in respect of it under section 4(3)(a).

(5)   In this paragraph—

"person" has the same meaning as in Part I;

"relevant exclusion" means an exclusion under paragraph 1 of Schedule 1 or paragraph 2 or 9 of Schedule 3 [or the Competition Act 1998 (Land and Vertical Agreements Exclusion) Order 2000].

Procedural requirements on giving a paragraph 37 direction

39. (1) The Director must specify in a direction under paragraph 37 ("a direction") the date on which it is to have effect (which must not be less than 28 days after the direction is given).

(2) Copies of the direction must be given to—
    (a) each of the parties concerned, and
    (b) the Secretary of State,
not less than 28 days before the date on which the direction is to have effect.

(3) In relation to an agreement to which a direction applies, the transitional period (if it has not already ended) ends on the date specified in the direction unless, before that date, the direction is revoked by the Director or the Secretary of State.

(4) If a direction is revoked, the Director may give a further direction in respect of the same agreement only if he is satisfied that there has been a material change of circumstance since the revocation.

(5) If, as a result of paragraph 24(1) or (3), there is a transitional period in respect of provisions of an agreement relating to goods—
    (a) which immediately before the starting date are exempt under section 14 of the RPA, or
    (b) which, when continuing proceedings are determined, are found to be exempt under section 14 of the RPA,
the period is not affected by paragraph 37 or 38.

NOTES

Commencement: 9 November 1998 (para 35); 11 January 1999 (paras 10(5), 19(3), paras 11, 12(1) certain purposes); 1 March 2000 (paras 10(1)–(4), (6), 12(2), 13–18, 19(1), (2), 20–34, 36–39, para 12(1) remaining purposes); to be appointed (otherwise).

Para 10: sub-para (6)(e) substituted by the Constitutional Reform Act 2005, s 40(4), Sch 9, Pt 1, para 65(1), (5).

Para 26: words omitted repealed by the Financial Services Act 2012, s 114(2), Sch 19.

Para 29: words in square brackets in sub-paras (5), (7) substituted by virtue of the Utilities Act 2000, s 3(2).

Para 31: words in square brackets in sub-paras (5), (6)(b) substituted by virtue of the Utilities Act 2000, s 3(2).

Para 34: in sub-para (3) words in square brackets substituted by virtue of the Railways and Transport Safety Act 2003, s 16(4), (5), Sch 3, para 4.

Para 35: sub-para (a) repealed by the Communications Act 2003, s 406(7), Sch 19(1); words in square brackets in sub-para (2)(b), (c) substituted by virtue of the Utilities Act 2000, s 3(2)(2); words in square brackets in sub-para (2)(e) substituted by the Water Act 2003, s 101(1), Sch 7, Pt 2, para 32(1), (5); words in square brackets in sub-para (2)(f) substituted by virtue of the Railways and Transport Safety Act 2003, s 16(4), (5), Sch 3, para 4; sub-para (2)(h) added by the Transport Act 2000, s 97, Sch 8, Pt IV, para 16(1), (3).

Para 37: words in square brackets in sub-para (2) added by the Competition Act 1998 (Transitional, Consequential and Supplemental Provisions) Order 2000, SI 2000/311, art 2.

Para 38: words in square brackets in sub-para (5) inserted by the Competition Act 1998 (Consequential and Supplemental Provisions) Order 2000, SI 2000/2031, art 2.

The Director: see note to Pt I of this Schedule at **[1.1370]**.

Financial Services Act 1986, s 127: repealed.

Regulations: the Competition Act 1998 (Appealable Decisions and Revocation of Notification of Excluded Agreements) Regulations 2004, SI 2004/1078.

PART V
THE FAIR TRADING ACT 1973

References to the Monopolies and Mergers Commission

[1.1374]
40. (1) If, on the date on which the repeal by this Act of a provision mentioned in sub-paragraph (2) comes into force, the Monopolies and Mergers Commission has not completed a reference which was made to it before that date, continued consideration of the reference may include consideration of a question which could not have been considered if the provision had not been repealed.

(2) The provisions are—
    (a) sections 10(2), 54(5) and 78(3) and paragraph 3(1) and (2) of Schedule 8 to the Fair Trading Act 1973 (c 41);
    (b) section 11(8)(b) of the Competition Act 1980 (c 21);
    (c) section 14(2) of the Telecommunications Act 1984 (c 12);
    (d) section 45(3) of the Airports Act 1986 (c 31);
    (e) section 25(2) of the Gas Act 1986 (c 44);
    (f) section 13(2) of the Electricity Act 1989 (c 29);
    (g) section 15(2) of the Water Industry Act 1991 (c 56);
    (h) article 16(2) of the Electricity (Northern Ireland) Order 1992;
    (i) section 14(2) of the Railways Act 1993 (c 43);
    (j) article 36(3) of the Airports (Northern Ireland) Order 1994;
    (k) article 16(2) of the Gas (Northern Ireland) Order 1996.

Orders under Schedule 8

41. (1)   In this paragraph—

"the 1973 Act" means the Fair Trading Act 1973;

"agreement" means an agreement entered into before the date on which the repeal of the limiting provisions comes into force;

"the order" means an order under section 56 or 73 of the 1973 Act;

"the limiting provisions" means sub-paragraph (1) or (2) of paragraph 3 of Schedule 8 to the 1973 Act (limit on power to make orders under paragraph 1 or 2 of that Schedule) and includes any provision of the order included because of either of those sub-paragraphs; and

"transitional period" means the period which—

    (a)   begins on the day on which the repeal of the limiting provisions comes into force; and

    (b)   ends on the first anniversary of the starting date.

(2)   Sub-paragraph (3) applies to any agreement to the extent to which it would have been unlawful (in accordance with the provisions of the order) but for the limiting provisions.

(3)   As from the end of the transitional period, the order is to have effect in relation to the agreement as if the limiting provisions had never had effect.

Part III of the Act

42. (1)   The repeals made by section 1 do not affect any proceedings in respect of an application which is made to the Court under Part III of the Fair Trading Act 1973, but is not determined, before the starting date.

(2)   The question whether (for the purposes of sub-paragraph (1)) an application has been determined is to be decided in accordance with sub-paragraphs (3) and (4).

(3)   If an appeal against the decision on the application is brought, the application is not determined until—

    (a)   the appeal is disposed of or withdrawn; or

    (b)   if as a result of the appeal the case is referred back to the Court—

        (i)   the expiry of the period within which an appeal ("the further appeal") in respect of the Court's decision on that reference could have been brought had this Act not been passed; or

        (ii)   if later, the date on which the further appeal is disposed of or withdrawn.

(4)   Otherwise, the application is not determined until the expiry of the period within which any party to the application would have been able to bring an appeal against the decision on the application had this Act not been passed.

(5)   Any amendment made by Schedule 12 to this Act which substitutes references to a relevant Court for references to the Court is not to affect proceedings of the kind referred to in sub-paragraph (1).

PART VI
THE COMPETITION ACT 1980

Undertakings

[1.1375]

43. (1)   Subject to sub-paragraph (2), an undertaking accepted by the Director under section 4 or 9 of the Competition Act 1980 ceases to have effect on the coming into force of the repeal by this Act of that section.

(2)   If the undertaking relates to an agreement which on the starting date is the subject of continuing proceedings, the undertaking continues to have effect for the purposes of section 29 of the Competition Act 1980 until the proceedings are determined.

Application of sections 25 and 26

44.   The repeals made by section 1 do not affect—

   (a)   the operation of section 25 of the Competition Act 1980 in relation to an application under section 1(3) of the RTPA which is made before the starting date;

   (b)   an application under section 26 of the Competition Act 1980 which is made before the starting date.

NOTES

The Director: see note to Pt I of this Schedule at **[1.1370]**.

PART VII
MISCELLANEOUS

Disclosure of information

[1.1376]

45. (1) Section 55 of this Act applies in relation to information which, immediately before the starting date, is subject to section 41 of the RTPA as it applies in relation to information obtained under or as a result of Part I.

(2) But section 55 does not apply to any disclosure of information of the kind referred to in sub-paragraph (1) if the disclosure is made—

    (a)   for the purpose of facilitating the performance of functions of a designated person under the Control of Misleading Advertisements Regulations 1988; or

    (b)   for the purposes of any proceedings before the Court or of any other legal proceedings under the RTPA or the Fair Trading Act 1973 or the Control of Misleading Advertisements Regulations 1988.

(3) Section 56 applies in relation to information of the kind referred to in sub-paragraph (1) if particulars containing the information have been entered or filed on the special section of the register maintained by the Director under, or as a result of, section 27 of the RTPA or paragraph 10 of this Schedule.

(4) Section 55 has effect, in relation to the matters as to which section 41(2) of the RTPA had effect, as if it contained a provision similar to section 41(2).

The Court

46. If it appears to the Lord Chancellor that a person who ceases to be a non-judicial member of the Court as a result of this Act should receive compensation for loss of office, he may pay to him out of moneys provided by Parliament such sum as he may with the approval of the Treasury determine.

NOTES

The Director: see note to Pt I of this Schedule at **[1.1370]**.

SCHEDULE 14

(Sch 14 contains repeals and revocations.)

CONTRACTS (RIGHTS OF THIRD PARTIES) ACT 1999

(1999 c 31)

ARRANGEMENT OF SECTIONS

An Act to make provision for the enforcement of contractual terms by third parties

[11 November 1999]

[1.1377]
1   Right of third party to enforce contractual term
(1)   Subject to the provisions of this Act, a person who is not a party to a contract (a "third party") may in his own right enforce a term of the contract if—
   (a)   the contract expressly provides that he may, or
   (b)   subject to subsection (2), the term purports to confer a benefit on him.
(2)   Subsection (1)(b) does not apply if on a proper construction of the contract it appears that the parties did not intend the term to be enforceable by the third party.
(3)   The third party must be expressly identified in the contract by name, as a member of a class or as answering a particular description but need not be in existence when the contract is entered into.
(4)   This section does not confer a right on a third party to enforce a term of a contract otherwise than subject to and in accordance with any other relevant terms of the contract.
(5)   For the purpose of exercising his right to enforce a term of the contract, there shall be available to the third party any remedy that would have been available to him in an action for breach of contract if he had been a party to the contract (and the rules relating to damages, injunctions, specific performance and other relief shall apply accordingly).
(6)   Where a term of a contract excludes or limits liability in relation to any matter references in this Act to the third party enforcing the term shall be construed as references to his availing himself of the exclusion or limitation.
(7)   In this Act, in relation to a term of a contract which is enforceable by a third party—
   "the promisor" means the party to the contract against whom the term is enforceable by the third party, and
   "the promisee" means the party to the contract by whom the term is enforceable against the promisor.

[1.1378]
2   Variation and rescission of contract
(1)   Subject to the provisions of this section, where a third party has a right under section 1 to enforce a term of the contract, the parties to the contract may not, by agreement, rescind the contract, or vary it in such a way as to extinguish or alter his entitlement under that right, without his consent if—
   (a)   the third party has communicated his assent to the term to the promisor,
   (b)   the promisor is aware that the third party has relied on the term, or
   (c)   the promisor can reasonably be expected to have foreseen that the third party would rely on the term and the third party has in fact relied on it.
(2)   The assent referred to in subsection (1)(a)—
   (a)   may be by words or conduct, and
   (b)   if sent to the promisor by post or other means, shall not be regarded as communicated to the promisor until received by him.
(3)   Subsection (1) is subject to any express term of the contract under which—
   (a)   the parties to the contract may by agreement rescind or vary the contract without the consent of the third party, or
   (b)   the consent of the third party is required in circumstances specified in the contract instead of those set out in subsection (1)(a) to (c).
(4)   Where the consent of a third party is required under subsection (1) or (3), the court or arbitral tribunal may, on the application of the parties to the contract, dispense with his consent if satisfied—

(a)   that his consent cannot be obtained because his whereabouts cannot reasonably be ascertained, or

(b)   that he is mentally incapable of giving his consent.

(5)   The court or arbitral tribunal may, on the application of the parties to a contract, dispense with any consent that may be required under subsection (1)(c) if satisfied that it cannot reasonably be ascertained whether or not the third party has in fact relied on the term.

(6)   If the court or arbitral tribunal dispenses with a third party's consent, it may impose such conditions as it thinks fit, including a condition requiring the payment of compensation to the third party.

(7)   The jurisdiction conferred on the court by subsections (4) to (6) is exercisable [in England and Wales by both the High Court and the county court and in Northern Ireland] by both the High Court and a county court.

NOTES

Sub-s (7): words in square brackets inserted by the Crime and Courts Act 2013, s 17(5), Sch 9, Pt 3, para 71, for transitional provision see the Crime and Courts Act 2013 (Commencement No 10 and Transitional Provision) Order 2014, SI 2014/954, art 3.

[1.1379]
3   Defences etc available to promisor

(1)   Subsections (2) to (5) apply where, in reliance on section 1, proceedings for the enforcement of a term of a contract are brought by a third party.

(2)   The promisor shall have available to him by way of defence or setoff any matter that—

(a)   arises from or in connection with the contract and is relevant to the term, and

(b)   would have been available to him by way of defence or setoff if the proceedings had been brought by the promisee.

(3)   The promisor shall also have available to him by way of defence or setoff any matter if—

(a)   an express term of the contract provides for it to be available to him in proceedings brought by the third party, and

(b)   it would have been available to him by way of defence or setoff if the proceedings had been brought by the promisee.

(4)   The promisor shall also have available to him—

(a)   by way of defence or setoff any matter, and

(b)   by way of counterclaim any matter not arising from the contract,

that would have been available to him by way of defence or setoff or, as the case may be, by way of counterclaim against the third party if the third party had been a party to the contract.

(5)   Subsections (2) and (4) are subject to any express term of the contract as to the matters that are not to be available to the promisor by way of defence, setoff or counterclaim.

(6)   Where in any proceedings brought against him a third party seeks in reliance on section 1 to enforce a term of a contract (including, in particular, a term purporting to exclude or limit liability), he may not do so if he could not have done so (whether by reason of any particular circumstances relating to him or otherwise) had he been a party to the contract.

[1.1380]
4   Enforcement of contract by promisee

Section 1 does not affect any right of the promisee to enforce any term of the contract.

[1.1381]
5   Protection of party promisor from double liability

Where under section 1 a term of a contract is enforceable by a third party, and the promisee has recovered from the promisor a sum in respect of—

(a)   the third party's loss in respect of the term, or

(b)   the expense to the promisee of making good to the third party the default of the promisor,

then, in any proceedings brought in reliance on that section by the third party, the court or arbitral tribunal shall reduce any award to the third party to such extent as it thinks appropriate to take account of the sum recovered by the promisee.

[1.1382]
6   Exceptions

(1)   Section 1 confers no rights on a third party in the case of a contract on a bill of exchange, promissory note or other negotiable instrument.

(2)   Section 1 confers no rights on a third party in the case of any contract binding on a company and its members under [section 33 of the Companies Act 2006 (effect of company's constitution)].

[(2A)   Section 1 confers no rights on a third party in the case of any incorporation document of a limited liability partnership [or any agreement (express or implied) between the members of a limited liability partnership, or between a limited liability partnership and its members, that determines the mutual rights and duties of the members and their rights and duties in relation to the limited liability partnership].]

(3)   Section 1 confers no right on a third party to enforce—

(a)   any term of a contract of employment against an employee,

(b)   any term of a worker's contract against a worker (including a home worker), or

(c)   any term of a relevant contract against an agency worker.

(4)   In subsection (3)—

(a)   "contract of employment", "employee", "worker's contract", and "worker" have the meaning given by section 54 of the National Minimum Wage Act 1998,

(b)   "home worker" has the meaning given by section 35(2) of that Act,

(c)   "agency worker" has the same meaning as in section 34(1) of that Act, and

(d)   "relevant contract" means a contract entered into, in a case where section 34 of that Act applies, by the agency worker as respects work falling within subsection (1)(a) of that section.

(5)   Section 1 confers no rights on a third party in the case of—

(a)   a contract for the carriage of goods by sea, or

(b)   a contract for the carriage of goods by rail or road, or for the carriage of cargo by air, which is subject to the rules of the appropriate international transport convention,

except that a third party may in reliance on that section avail himself of an exclusion or limitation of liability in such a contract.

(6)   In subsection (5) "contract for the carriage of goods by sea" means a contract of carriage—

(a)   contained in or evidenced by a bill of lading, sea waybill or a corresponding electronic transaction, or

(b)   under or for the purposes of which there is given an undertaking which is contained in a ship's delivery order or a corresponding electronic transaction.

(7)   For the purposes of subsection (6)—

(a)   "bill of lading", "sea waybill" and "ship's delivery order" have the same meaning as in the Carriage of Goods by Sea Act 1992, and

(b)   a corresponding electronic transaction is a transaction within section 1(5) of that Act which corresponds to the issue, indorsement, delivery or transfer of a bill of lading, sea waybill or ship's delivery order.

(8)   In subsection (5) "the appropriate international transport convention" means—

(a)   in relation to a contract for the carriage of goods by rail, the Convention which has the force of law in the United Kingdom under [regulation 3 of the Railways (Convention on International Carriage by Rail) Regulations 2005],

(b)   in relation to a contract for the carriage of goods by road, the Convention which has the force of law in the United Kingdom under section 1 of the Carriage of Goods by Road Act 1965, and

(c)   in relation to a contract for the carriage of cargo by air—

(i)   the Convention which has the force of law in the United Kingdom under section 1 of the Carriage by Air Act 1961, or

(ii)   the Convention which has the force of law under section 1 of the Carriage by Air (Supplementary Provisions) Act 1962, or

(iii)   either of the amended Conventions set out in Part B of Schedule 2 or 3 to the Carriage by Air Acts (Application of Provisions) Order 1967.

NOTES

Sub-s (2): words in square brackets substituted by the Companies Act 2006 (Consequential Amendments, Transitional Provisions and Savings) Order 2009, SI 2009/1941, art 2(1), Sch 1, para 179(1), (2)(a).

Sub-s (2A): inserted by the Limited Liability Partnerships Regulations 2001, SI 2001/1090, reg 9(1), Sch 5, para 20; words in square brackets substituted by SI 2009/1941, art 2(1), Sch 1, para 179(1), (2)(b).

Sub-s (8): words in square brackets in para (a) substituted by the Railways (Convention on International Carriage by Rail) Regulations 2005, SI 2005/2092, reg 9(2), Sch 3, para 3.

[1.1383]

7   Supplementary provisions relating to third party

(1)   Section 1 does not affect any right or remedy of a third party that exists or is available apart from this Act.

(2)   Section 2(2) of the Unfair Contract Terms Act 1977 (restriction on exclusion etc of liability for negligence) shall not apply where the negligence consists of the breach of an obligation arising from a term of a contract and the person seeking to enforce it is a third party acting in reliance on section 1.

(3)   In sections 5 and 8 of the Limitation Act 1980 the references to an action founded on a simple contract and an action upon a specialty shall respectively include references to an action brought in reliance on section 1 relating to a simple contract and an action brought in reliance on that section relating to a specialty.

(4)   A third party shall not, by virtue of section 1(5) or 3(4) or (6), be treated as a party to the contract for the purposes of any other Act (or any instrument made under any other Act).

[1.1384]

8   Arbitration provisions

(1)   Where—

(a)   a right under section 1 to enforce a term ("the substantive term") is subject to a term providing for the submission of disputes to arbitration ("the arbitration agreement"), and

(b) the arbitration agreement is an agreement in writing for the purposes of Part I of the Arbitration Act 1996,

the third party shall be treated for the purposes of that Act as a party to the arbitration agreement as regards disputes between himself and the promisor relating to the enforcement of the substantive term by the third party.

(2) Where—

(a) a third party has a right under section 1 to enforce a term providing for one or more descriptions of dispute between the third party and the promisor to be submitted to arbitration ("the arbitration agreement"),

(b) the arbitration agreement is an agreement in writing for the purposes of Part I of the Arbitration Act 1996, and

(c) the third party does not fall to be treated under subsection (1) as a party to the arbitration agreement,

the third party shall, if he exercises the right, be treated for the purposes of that Act as a party to the arbitration agreement in relation to the matter with respect to which the right is exercised, and be treated as having been so immediately before the exercise of the right.

[1.1385]
9 Northern Ireland

(1) In its application to Northern Ireland, this Act has effect with the modifications specified in subsections (2) and (3).

(2) . . .

(3) In section 7, for subsection (3) there is substituted—

"(3) In Articles 4(a) and 15 of the Limitation (Northern Ireland) Order 1989, the references to an action founded on a simple contract and an action upon an instrument under seal shall respectively include references to an action brought in reliance on section 1 relating to a simple contract and an action brought in reliance on that section relating to a contract under seal.".

(4) . . .

_____

NOTES

Sub-s (2): repealed by the Companies Act 2006 (Consequential Amendments, Transitional Provisions and Savings) Order 2009, SI 2009/1941, art 2(1), Sch 1, para 179(1), (3).

Sub-s (4): amends the Law Reform (Husband and Wife) (Northern Ireland) Act 1964.

_____

[1.1386]
10 Short title, commencement and extent

(1) This Act may be cited as the Contracts (Rights of Third Parties) Act 1999.

(2) This Act comes into force on the day on which it is passed but, subject to subsection (3), does not apply in relation to a contract entered into before the end of the period of six months beginning with that day.

(3) The restriction in subsection (2) does not apply in relation to a contract which—

(a) is entered into on or after the day on which this Act is passed, and

(b) expressly provides for the application of this Act.

(4) This Act extends as follows—

(a) section 9 extends to Northern Ireland only;

(b) the remaining provisions extend to England and Wales and Northern Ireland only.

ELECTRONIC COMMUNICATIONS ACT 2000

(2000 c 7)

ARRANGEMENT OF SECTIONS

PART II
FACILITATION OF ELECTRONIC COMMERCE, DATA STORAGE, ETC

PART III
MISCELLANEOUS AND SUPPLEMENTAL

Supplemental

An Act to make provision to facilitate the use of electronic communications and electronic data storage; to make provision about the modification of licences granted under section 7 of the Telecommunications Act 1984; and for connected purposes

[25 May 2000]

1–6   ((*Pt I) repealed by virtue of s 16(4) of this Act at* **[1.1394]**.)

PART II
FACILITATION OF ELECTRONIC COMMERCE, DATA STORAGE, ETC

[1.1387]
7   Electronic signatures and related certificates
(1)   In any legal proceedings—
  (a)   an electronic signature incorporated into or logically associated with a particular electronic communication or particular electronic data, and
  (b)   the certification by any person of such a signature,
shall each be admissible in evidence in relation to any question as to the authenticity of the communication or data or as to the integrity of the communication or data.
(2)   For the purposes of this section an electronic signature is so much of anything in electronic form as—
  (a)   is incorporated into or otherwise logically associated with any electronic communication or electronic data; and
  (b)   purports to be so incorporated or associated for the purpose of being used in establishing the authenticity of the communication or data, the integrity of the communication or data, or both.
(3)   For the purposes of this section an electronic signature incorporated into or associated with a particular electronic communication or particular electronic data is certified by any person if that person (whether before or after the making of the communication) has made a statement confirming that—
  (a)   the signature,
  (b)   a means of producing, communicating or verifying the signature, or
  (c)   a procedure applied to the signature,
is (either alone or in combination with other factors) a valid means of establishing the authenticity of the communication or data, the integrity of the communication or data, or both.

[1.1388]
8   Power to modify legislation
(1)   Subject to subsection (3), the appropriate Minister may by order made by statutory instrument modify the provisions of—
  (a)   any enactment or subordinate legislation, or
  (b)   any scheme, licence, authorisation or approval issued, granted or given by or under any enactment or subordinate legislation,
in such manner as he may think fit for the purpose of authorising or facilitating the use of electronic communications or electronic storage (instead of other forms of communication or storage) for any purpose mentioned in subsection (2).
(2)   Those purposes are—
  (a)   the doing of anything which under any such provisions is required to be or may be done or evidenced in writing or otherwise using a document, notice or instrument;
  (b)   the doing of anything which under any such provisions is required to be or may be done by post or other specified means of delivery;
  (c)   the doing of anything which under any such provisions is required to be or may be authorised by a person's signature or seal, or is required to be delivered as a deed or witnessed;
  (d)   the making of any statement or declaration which under any such provisions is required to be made under oath or to be contained in a statutory declaration;
  (e)   the keeping, maintenance or preservation, for the purposes or in pursuance of any such provisions, of any account, record, notice, instrument or other document;
  (f)   the provision, production or publication under any such provisions of any information or other matter;
  (g)   the making of any payment that is required to be or may be made under any such provisions.
(3)   The appropriate Minister shall not make an order under this section authorising the use of electronic communications or electronic storage for any purpose, unless he considers that the authorisation is such that the extent (if any) to which records of things done for that purpose will be available will be no less satisfactory in cases where use is made of electronic communications or electronic storage than in other cases.
(4)   Without prejudice to the generality of subsection (1), the power to make an order under this section shall include power to make an order containing any of the following provisions—

(a) provision as to the electronic form to be taken by any electronic communications or electronic storage the use of which is authorised by an order under this section;

(b) provision imposing conditions subject to which the use of electronic communications or electronic storage is so authorised;

(c) provision, in relation to cases in which any such conditions are not satisfied, for treating anything for the purposes of which the use of such communications or storage is so authorised as not having been done;

(d) provision, in connection with anything so authorised, for a person to be able to refuse to accept receipt of something in electronic form except in such circumstances as may be specified in or determined under the order;

(e) provision, in connection with any use of electronic communications so authorised, for intermediaries to be used, or to be capable of being used, for the transmission of any data or for establishing the authenticity or integrity of any data;

(f) provision, in connection with any use of electronic storage so authorised, for persons satisfying such conditions as may be specified in or determined under the regulations to carry out functions in relation to the storage;

(g) provision, in relation to cases in which the use of electronic communications or electronic storage is so authorised, for the determination of any of the matters mentioned in subsection (5), or as to the manner in which they may be proved in legal proceedings;

(h) provision, in relation to cases in which fees or charges are or may be imposed in connection with anything for the purposes of which the use of electronic communications or electronic storage is so authorised, for different fees or charges to apply where use is made of such communications or storage;

(i) provision, in relation to any criminal or other liabilities that may arise (in respect of the making of false or misleading statements or otherwise) in connection with anything for the purposes of which the use of electronic communications or electronic storage is so authorised, for corresponding liabilities to arise in corresponding circumstances where use is made of such communications or storage;

(j) provision requiring persons to prepare and keep records in connection with any use of electronic communications or electronic storage which is so authorised;

(k) provision requiring the production of the contents of any records kept in accordance with an order under this section;

(l) provision for a requirement imposed by virtue of paragraph (j) or (k) to be enforceable at the suit or instance of such person as may be specified in or determined in accordance with the order;

(m) any such provision, in relation to electronic communications or electronic storage the use of which is authorised otherwise than by an order under this section, as corresponds to any provision falling within any of the preceding paragraphs that may be made where it is such an order that authorises the use of the communications or storage.

(5) The matters referred to in subsection (4)(g) are—

(a) whether a thing has been done using an electronic communication or electronic storage;

(b) the time at which, or date on which, a thing done using any such communication or storage was done;

(c) the place where a thing done using such communication or storage was done;

(d) the person by whom such a thing was done; and

(e) the contents, authenticity or integrity of any electronic data.

(6) An order under this section—

(a) shall not (subject to paragraph (b)) require the use of electronic communications or electronic storage for any purpose; but

(b) may make provision that a period of notice specified in the order must expire before effect is given to a variation or withdrawal of an election or other decision which—

(i) has been made for the purposes of such an order; and

(ii) is an election or decision to make use of electronic communications or electronic storage.

(7) The matters in relation to which provision may be made by an order under this section do not include any matter under the care and management of the Commissioners of Inland Revenue or any matter under the care and management of the Commissioners of Customs and Excise.

(8) In this section references to doing anything under the provisions of any enactment include references to doing it under the provisions of any subordinate legislation the power to make which is conferred by that enactment.

NOTES

Orders: the Local Government and Housing Act 1989 (Electronic Communications) (England) Order 2000, SI 2000/3056; the Companies Act 1985 (Electronic Communications) Order 2000, SI 2000/3373; the Local Government and Housing Act 1989 (Electronic Communications) (Wales) Order 2001, SI 2001/605; the Unsolicited Goods and Services Act 1971 (Electronic Communications) Order 2001, SI 2001/2778; the National Health Service (Pharmaceutical Services) and (Misuse of Drugs) (Electronic Communications) Order 2001, SI 2001/2888; the Public Records Act 1958 (Admissibility of Electronic Copies of Public Records) Order 2001, SI 2001/4058; the Building Societies Act 1986 (Electronic Communications) Order 2003, SI 2003/404; the Patents Act 1977 (Electronic Communications) Order 2003, SI 2003/512; the Town and Country Planning (Electronic Communications) (England) Order 2003, SI 2003/956; the Council Tax and Non-Domestic Rating

(Electronic Communications) (England) Order 2003, SI 2003/2604; the Social Security (Electronic Communications) (Carer's Allowance) Order 2003, SI 2003/2800; the Council Tax and Non-Domestic Rating (Electronic Communications) (England) (No 2) Order 2003, SI 2003/3052; the Education Act 1996 (Electronic Communications) Order 2004, SI 2004/2521; the Town and Country Planning (Electronic Communications) (Wales) (No 1) Order 2004, SI 2004/3156; the Town and Country Planning (Electronic Communications) (Wales) (No 2) Order 2004, SI 2004/3157; the Town and Country Planning (Electronic Communications) (Wales) (No 3) Order 2004, SI 2004/3172; the Consumer Credit Act 1974 (Electronic Communications) Order 2004, SI 2004/3236; the Social Security (Electronic Communications) (Miscellaneous Benefits) Order 2005, SI 2005/3321; the Non-Domestic Rating and Council Tax (Electronic Communications) (England) Order 2006, SI 2006/237; the Registered Designs Act 1949 and Patents Act 1977 (Electronic Communications) Order 2006, SI 2006/1229; the Transport Security (Electronic Communications) Order 2006, SI 2006/2190; the Registration of Births and Deaths (Electronic Communications and Electronic Storage) Order 2006, SI 2006/2809; the Housing Benefit and Council Tax Benefit (Electronic Communications) Order 2006, SI 2006/2968; the Income-related Benefits (Subsidy to Authorities) (Miscellaneous Amendments and Electronic Communications) Order 2007, SI 2007/26; the Council Tax (Electronic Communications) (England) Order 2008, SI 2008/316; the Building (Electronic Communications) Order 2008, SI 2008/2334; the Police Act 1997 (Criminal Records) (Electronic Communications) Order 2009, SI 2009/203; the Unit Trusts (Electronic Communications) Order 2009, SI 2009/555; the Council Tax and Non-Domestic Rating (Electronic Communications) (Wales) Order 2009, SI 2009/2706; the Registration of Marriages etc (Electronic Communications and Electronic Storage) Order 2009, SI 2009/2821; the Health and Social Care Act 2008 (Commencement No 13, Transitory and Transitional Provisions and Electronic Communications) Order 2009, SI 2009/3023; the Council Tax (Electronic Communications) (Wales) Order 2010, SI 2010/613; the Motor Vehicles (Electronic Communication of Certificates of Insurance) Order 2010, SI 2010/1117; the Mutual Societies (Electronic Communications) Order 2011, SI 2011/593; the Firearms (Electronic Communications) Order 2011, SI 2011/713; the Social Security (Electronic Communications) Order 2011, SI 2011/1498; the Social Security (Electronic Communications) (No 2) Order 2011, SI 2011/2943; the Non-Domestic Rating (Electronic Communications) (England) Order 2012, SI 2012/25; the Industrial and Provident Societies and Credit Unions (Electronic Communications) Order 2014, SI 2014/184; the Companies (Striking Off) (Electronic Communications) Order 2014, SI 2014/1602; the Local Government (Electronic Communications) (England) Order 2015, SI 2015/5; the Public Processions (Electronic Communication of Notices) (Northern Ireland) Order 2015, SI 2015/235.

[1.1389]
9   Section 8 orders

(1)   In this Part "the appropriate Minister" means (subject to subsections (2) and (7) and section 10(1))—

    (a)   in relation to any matter with which a department of the Secretary of State is concerned, the Secretary of State;

    (b)   in relation to any matter with which the Treasury is concerned, the Treasury; and

    (c)   in relation to any matter with which any Government department other than a department of the Secretary of State or the Treasury is concerned, the Minister in charge of the other department.

(2)   Where in the case of any matter—

    (a)   that matter falls within more than one paragraph of subsection (1),

    (b)   there is more than one such department as is mentioned in paragraph (c) of that subsection that is concerned with that matter, or

    (c)   both paragraphs (a) and (b) of this subsection apply,

references, in relation to that matter, to the appropriate Minister are references to any one or more of the appropriate Ministers acting (in the case of more than one) jointly.

(3)   Subject to subsection (4) and section 10(6), a statutory instrument containing an order under section 8 shall be subject to annulment in pursuance of a resolution of either House of Parliament.

(4)   Subsection (3) does not apply in the case of an order a draft of which has been laid before Parliament and approved by a resolution of each House.

(5)   An order under section 8 may—

    (a)   provide for any conditions or requirements imposed by such an order to be framed by reference to the directions of such persons as may be specified in or determined in accordance with the order;

    (b)   provide that any such condition or requirement is to be satisfied only where a person so specified or determined is satisfied as to specified matters.

(6)   The provision made by such an order may include—

    (a)   different provision for different cases;

    (b)   such exceptions and exclusions as the person making the order may think fit; and

    (c)   any such incidental, supplemental, consequential and transitional provision as he may think fit;

and the provision that may be made by virtue of paragraph (c) includes provision modifying any enactment or subordinate legislation or any scheme, licence, authorisation or approval issued, granted or given by or under any enactment or subordinate legislation.

(7)   In the case of any matter which is not one of the reserved matters within the meaning of the Scotland Act 1998 or in respect of which functions are, by virtue of section 63 of that Act, exercisable by the Scottish Ministers instead of by or concurrently with a Minister of the Crown, this section and section 8 shall apply to Scotland subject to the following modifications—

    (a)   subsections (1) and (2) of this section are omitted;

    (b)   any reference to the appropriate Minister is to be read as a reference to the Secretary of State;

(c)   any power of the Secretary of State, by virtue of paragraph (b), to make an order under section 8 may also be exercised by the Scottish Ministers with the consent of the Secretary of State; and

(d)   where the Scottish Ministers make an order under section 8—

  (i)   any reference to the Secretary of State (other than a reference in this subsection) shall be construed as a reference to the Scottish Ministers; and

  (ii)   any reference to Parliament or to a House of Parliament shall be construed as a reference to the Scottish Parliament.

NOTES

Orders: the Health and Social Care Act 2008 (Commencement No 13, Transitory and Transitional Provisions and Electronic Communications) Order 2009, SI 2009/3023; the Motor Vehicles (Electronic Communication of Certificates of Insurance) Order 2010, SI 2010/1117; the Mutual Societies (Electronic Communications) Order 2011, SI 2011/593; the Social Security (Electronic Communications) Order 2011, SI 2011/1498; the Social Security (Electronic Communications) (No 2) Order 2011, SI 2011/2943; the Industrial and Provident Societies and Credit Unions (Electronic Communications) Order 2014, SI 2014/184; the Local Government (Electronic Communications) (England) Order 2015, SI 2015/5; the Public Processions (Electronic Communication of Notices) (Northern Ireland) Order 2015, SI 2015/235.

[1.1390]
10   Modifications in relation to Welsh matters

(1)   For the purposes of the exercise of the powers conferred by section 8 in relation to any matter the functions in respect of which are exercisable by the National Assembly for Wales, the appropriate Minister is the Secretary of State.

(2)   Subject to the following provisions of this section, the powers conferred by section 8, so far as they fall within subsection (3), shall be exercisable by the National Assembly for Wales, as well as by the appropriate Minister.

(3)   The powers conferred by section 8 fall within this subsection to the extent that they are exercisable in relation to—

(a)   the provisions of any subordinate legislation made by the National Assembly for Wales;

(b)   so much of any other subordinate legislation as makes provision the power to make which is exercisable by that Assembly;

(c)   any power under any enactment to make provision the power to make which is so exercisable;

(d)   the giving, sending or production of any notice, account, record or other document or of any information to or by a body mentioned in subsection (4); or

(e)   the publication of anything by a body mentioned in subsection (4).

(4)   Those bodies are—

(a)   the National Assembly for Wales;

(b)   any body specified in Schedule 4 to the Government of Wales Act 1998 (Welsh public bodies subject to reform by that Assembly);

(c)   any other such body as may be specified for the purposes of this section by an order made by the Secretary of State with the consent of that Assembly.

(5)   The National Assembly for Wales shall not make an order under section 8 except with the consent of the Secretary of State.

(6)   Section 9(3) shall not apply to any order made under section 8 by the National Assembly for Wales.

(7)   Nothing in this section shall confer any power on the National Assembly for Wales to modify any provision of the Government of Wales Act 1998.

(8)   The power of the Secretary of State to make an order under subsection (4)(c)—

(a)   shall include power to make any such incidental, supplemental, consequential and transitional provision as he may think fit; and

(b)   shall be exercisable by statutory instrument subject to annulment in pursuance of a resolution of either House of Parliament.

NOTES

Orders: the Council Tax and Non-Domestic Rating (Electronic Communications) (Wales) Order 2009, SI 2009/2706; the Council Tax (Electronic Communications) (Wales) Order 2010, SI 2010/613.

PART III
MISCELLANEOUS AND SUPPLEMENTAL

11, 12   *(Repealed by the Communications Act 2003, s 406(7), Sch 19(1).)*

Supplemental

[1.1391]
13   Ministerial expenditure etc

There shall be paid out of money provided by Parliament—

(a)   any expenditure incurred by the Secretary of State for or in connection with the carrying out of his functions under this Act; and

(b) any increase attributable to this Act in the sums which are payable out of money so provided under any other Act.

[1.1392]
14 Prohibition on key escrow requirements

(1) Subject to subsection (2), nothing in this Act shall confer any power on any Minister of the Crown, on the Scottish Ministers, on the National Assembly for Wales or on any person appointed under section 3—

(a) by conditions of an approval under Part I, or

(b) by any regulations or order under this Act,

to impose a requirement on any person to deposit a key for electronic data with another person.

(2) Subsection (1) shall not prohibit the imposition by an order under section 8 of—

(a) a requirement to deposit a key for electronic data with the intended recipient of electronic communications comprising the data; or

(b) a requirement for arrangements to be made, in cases where a key for data is not deposited with another person, which otherwise secure that the loss of a key, or its becoming unusable, does not have the effect that the information contained in a record kept in pursuance of any provision made by or under any enactment or subordinate legislation becomes inaccessible or incapable of being put into an intelligible form.

(3) In this section "key", in relation to electronic data, means any code, password, algorithm, key or other data the use of which (with or without other keys)—

(a) allows access to the electronic data, or

(b) facilitates the putting of the electronic data into an intelligible form;

and references in this section to depositing a key for electronic data with a person include references to doing anything that has the effect of making the key available to that person.

[1.1393]
15 General interpretation

(1) In this Act, except in so far as the context otherwise requires—

"document" includes a map, plan, design, drawing, picture or other image;

"communication" includes a communication comprising sounds or images or both and a communication effecting a payment;

"electronic communication" means a communication transmitted (whether from one person to another, from one device to another or from a person to a device or vice versa)—

(a) by means of [an electronic communications network]; or

(b) by other means but while in an electronic form;

"enactment" includes—

(a) an enactment passed after the passing of this Act,

(b) an enactment comprised in an Act of the Scottish Parliament, and

(c) an enactment contained in Northern Ireland legislation,

but does not include an enactment contained in Part I or II of this Act;

"modification" includes any alteration, addition or omission, and cognate expressions shall be construed accordingly;

"record" includes an electronic record; and

"subordinate legislation" means—

(a) any subordinate legislation (within the meaning of the Interpretation Act 1978);

(b) any instrument made under an Act of the Scottish Parliament; or

(c) any statutory rules (within the meaning of the Statutory Rules (Northern Ireland) Order 1979).

(2) In this Act—

(a) references to the authenticity of any communication or data are references to any one or more of the following—

(i) whether the communication or data comes from a particular person or other source;

(ii) whether it is accurately timed and dated;

(iii) whether it is intended to have legal effect; and

(b) references to the integrity of any communication or data are references to whether there has been any tampering with or other modification of the communication or data.

(3) References in this Act to something's being put into an intelligible form include references to its being restored to the condition in which it was before any encryption or similar process was applied to it.

NOTES

Sub-s (1): in definition "electronic communication" words in square brackets substituted by the Communications Act 2003, s 406(1), Sch 17, para 158.

[1.1394]
16 Short title, commencement, extent

(1) This Act may be cited as the Electronic Communications Act 2000.

(2)   Part I of this Act and sections 7, 11 and 12 shall come into force on such day as the Secretary of State may by order made by statutory instrument appoint; and different days may be appointed under this subsection for different purposes.

(3)   An order shall not be made for bringing any of Part I of this Act into force for any purpose unless a draft of the order has been laid before Parliament and approved by a resolution of each House.

(4)   If no order for bringing Part I of this Act into force has been made under subsection (2) by the end of the period of five years beginning with the day on which this Act is passed, that Part shall, by virtue of this subsection, be repealed at the end of that period.

(5)   This Act extends to Northern Ireland.

NOTES

Orders: the Electronic Communications Act 2000 (Commencement No 1) Order 2000, SI 2000/1798.

FINANCIAL SERVICES AND MARKETS ACT 2000

(2000 c 8)

NOTES

Only provisions of this Act relevant to Commercial and Consumer law are reproduced. Provisions not reproduced are not annotated.

References to "the European Community", "Community", etc: see the Treaty of Lisbon (Changes in Terminology) Order 2011, SI 2011/1043, which provides that (as from 22 April 2011): (i) for references to the European Communities or to the European Community or the European Coal and Steel Community (including references to "the Communities", "the Community", "the EC" or "the EEC") substitute references to the European Union, and (ii) references to "EU" should be substituted for the word "Community" (subject to certain exceptions) in references to "Community treaties", "Community instrument", "Community obligation", "Community law", "Community legislation", etc.

ARRANGEMENT OF SECTIONS

PART 1A
THE REGULATORS

CHAPTER 1
THE FINANCIAL CONDUCT AUTHORITY

PART II
REGULATED AND PROHIBITED ACTIVITIES

PART V
PERFORMANCE OF REGULATED ACTIVITIES

Prohibition orders

Approval

Performance of controlled functions without approval

Certification of employees

Conduct of approved persons

Conduct of approved persons and others

Breach of statutory duty

"Relevant authorised person"

PART XXVI
NOTICES

Warning notices

Decision notices

Conclusion of proceedings

Publication

Third party rights and access to evidence

PART XXVIII
MISCELLANEOUS

Consumer redress schemes

PART XXX
SUPPLEMENTAL

SCHEDULES

An Act to make provision about the regulation of financial services and markets; to provide for the transfer of certain statutory functions relating to building societies, friendly societies, industrial and provident societies and certain other mutual societies; and for connected purposes

[14 June 2000]

[PART 1A
THE REGULATORS

NOTES

Transitional provisions etc in connection with the commencement of the Financial Services Act 2012: For transitional provisions in relation to the commencement of this Part, see the Financial Services Act 2012 (Transitional Provisions) (Miscellaneous Provisions) Order 2013, SI 2013/442. Part 2 of that Order contains transitional provisions in respect of the Financial Conduct Authority and the Prudential Regulation Authority. Article 2 makes provision in respect of the board of the Financial Services Authority (which is renamed as the Financial Conduct Authority by FSMA 2000 (as amended by the 2012 Act)). Article 3 makes provision in respect of the FCA's first annual report, and article 4 makes provision in respect of the PRA's first annual report. Articles 5 and 6 make provision in respect of the Consumer and Practitioner Panels. Article 7 makes provision in respect of references to "consumers" in certain provisions of FSMA 2000.

CHAPTER 1
THE FINANCIAL CONDUCT AUTHORITY

The Financial Conduct Authority

[1.1395]
1A   The Financial Conduct Authority
(1)   The body corporate previously known as the Financial Services Authority is renamed as the Financial Conduct Authority.
(2)   The Financial Conduct Authority is in this Act referred to as "the FCA".
(3)   The FCA is to have the functions conferred on it by or under this Act.
(4)   The FCA must comply with the requirements as to its constitution set out in Schedule 1ZA.
(5)   Schedule 1ZA also makes provision about the status of the FCA and the exercise of certain of its functions.
(6)   References in this Act or any other enactment to functions conferred on the FCA by or under this Act include references to functions conferred on the FCA by or under—
   (a)   the Insolvency Act 1986,
   (b)   the Banking Act 2009,
   (c)   the Financial Services Act 2012, . . .
   [(ca)   the Alternative Investment Fund Managers Regulations 2013, or]
   (d)   a qualifying EU provision that is specified, or of a description specified, for the purposes of this subsection by the Treasury by order.]

NOTES

Commencement: 24 January 2013 (sub-ss (2), (6), and sub-ss (4), (5) certain purposes); 1 April 2013 (otherwise).

This section was substituted (together with the rest of Part 1A (ie, ss 1A–1T, 2A–2O, 3A–3S) for the original Part I (ss 1–18)) by the Financial Services Act 2012, s 6(1), (for transitional provisions and savings in relation to the transfer of the FSA's functions, property, rights and liabilities, see s 119 of, and Schs 20, 21 to, the 2012 Act).

Sub-s (6): the word omitted from para (c) was repealed, and para (ca) was added, by the Alternative Investment Fund Managers Regulations 2013, SI 2013/1773, reg 80, Sch 1, Part 1, paras 1, 2, (for transitional provisions and savings see Part 9 of the 2013 Regulations).

Orders: the Financial Services and Markets Act 2000 (Qualifying EU Provisions) Order 2013, SI 2013/419; the Financial Services and Markets Act 2000 (Qualifying EU Provisions) (No 2) Order 2013, SI 2013/3116.

[The FCA's general duties

[1.1396]
1B   The FCA's general duties
(1)   In discharging its general functions the FCA must, so far as is reasonably possible, act in a way which—
   (a)   is compatible with its strategic objective, and
   (b)   advances one or more of its operational objectives.
(2)   The FCA's strategic objective is: ensuring that the relevant markets (see section 1F) function well.
(3)   The FCA's operational objectives are—
   (a)   the consumer protection objective (see section 1C);
   (b)   the integrity objective (see section 1D);
   (c)   the competition objective (see section 1E).
(4)   The FCA must, so far as is compatible with acting in a way which advances the consumer protection objective or the integrity objective, discharge its general functions in a way which promotes effective competition in the interests of consumers.
(5)   In discharging its general functions the FCA must have regard to—
   (a)   the regulatory principles in section 3B, and

(b)   the importance of taking action intended to minimise the extent to which it is possible for a business carried on—

    (i)   by an authorised person or a recognised investment exchange, or

    (ii)   in contravention of the general prohibition,

    to be used for a purpose connected with financial crime.

(6)   For the purposes of this Chapter, the FCA's general functions are—

(a)   its function of making rules under this Act (considered as a whole),

(b)   its function of preparing and issuing codes under this Act (considered as a whole),

(c)   its functions in relation to the giving of general guidance under this Act (considered as a whole), and

(d)   its function of determining the general policy and principles by reference to which it performs particular functions under this Act.

(7)   Except to the extent that an order under section 50 of the Financial Services Act 2012 (orders relating to mutual societies functions) so provides, the FCA's general functions do not include functions that are transferred functions within the meaning of section 52 of that Act.

[(7A)   The FCA's general functions do not include its general pensions guidance functions (see section 333O(3)).]

(8)   "General guidance" has the meaning given in section 139B(5).]

NOTES

    Commencement: 24 January 2013 (in so far as relevant to other provisions of the 2012 Act which are in force); 1 April 2013 (otherwise).

    Substituted as noted to s 1A at **[1.1395]**.

    Sub-s (7A): inserted by the Pension Schemes Act 2015, s 47, Sch 3, paras 1, 3.

    Note: sub-s (4) does not apply to certain credit-related rules made or guidance given by the FCA; see the Financial Services and Markets Act 2000 (Regulated Activities) (Amendment) (No 2) Order 2013, SI 2013/1881, art 61 at **[2.1042]**.

[1.1397]

[1C   The consumer protection objective

(1)   The consumer protection objective is: securing an appropriate degree of protection for consumers.

(2)   In considering what degree of protection for consumers may be appropriate, the FCA must have regard to—

(a)   the differing degrees of risk involved in different kinds of investment or other transaction;

(b)   the differing degrees of experience and expertise that different consumers may have;

(c)   the needs that consumers may have for the timely provision of information and advice that is accurate and fit for purpose;

(d)   the general principle that consumers should take responsibility for their decisions;

(e)   the general principle that those providing regulated financial services should be expected to provide consumers with a level of care that is appropriate having regard to the degree of risk involved in relation to the investment or other transaction and the capabilities of the consumers in question;

(f)   the differing expectations that consumers may have in relation to different kinds of investment or other transaction;

(g)   any information which the consumer financial education body has provided to the FCA in the exercise of the consumer financial education function;

(h)   any information which the scheme operator of the ombudsman scheme has provided to the FCA pursuant to section 232A.]

NOTES

    Commencement: 24 January 2013 (in so far as relevant to other provisions of the 2012 Act which are in force); 1 April 2013 (otherwise).

    Substituted as noted to s 1A at **[1.1395]**.

[1.1398]

[1D   The integrity objective

(1)   The integrity objective is: protecting and enhancing the integrity of the UK financial system.

(2)   The "integrity" of the UK financial system includes—

(a)   its soundness, stability and resilience,

(b)   its not being used for a purpose connected with financial crime,

(c)   its not being affected by behaviour that amounts to market abuse,

(d)   the orderly operation of the financial markets, and

(e)   the transparency of the price formation process in those markets.]

NOTES

    Commencement: 24 January 2013 (in so far as relevant to other provisions of the 2012 Act which are in force); 1 April 2013 (otherwise).

    Substituted as noted to s 1A at **[1.1395]**.

[1.1399]
[1E   The competition objective
(1)   The competition objective is: promoting effective competition in the interests of consumers in the markets for—
  (a)   regulated financial services, or
  (b)   services provided by a recognised investment exchange in carrying on regulated activities in respect of which it is by virtue of section 285(2) exempt from the general prohibition.
(2)   The matters to which the FCA may have regard in considering the effectiveness of competition in the market for any services mentioned in subsection (1) include—
  (a)   the needs of different consumers who use or may use those services, including their need for information that enables them to make informed choices,
  (b)   the ease with which consumers who may wish to use those services, including consumers in areas affected by social or economic deprivation, can access them,
  (c)   the ease with which consumers who obtain those services can change the person from whom they obtain them,
  (d)   the ease with which new entrants can enter the market, and
  (e)   how far competition is encouraging innovation.]

NOTES
Commencement: 24 January 2013 (in so far as relevant to other provisions of the 2012 Act which are in force); 1 April 2013 (otherwise).
Substituted as noted to s 1A at **[1.1395]**.

[Interpretation of terms used in relation to FCA's general duties

[1.1400]
1F   Meaning of "relevant markets" in strategic objective
In section 1B(2) "the relevant markets" means—
  (a)   the financial markets,
  (b)   the markets for regulated financial services (see section 1H(2)), and
  (c)   the markets for services that are provided by persons other than authorised persons in carrying on regulated activities but are provided without contravening the general prohibition.

NOTES
Commencement: 24 January 2013.
Substituted as noted to s 1A at **[1.1395]**.

[1.1401]
[1G   Meaning of "consumer"
(1)   In sections 1B to 1E "consumers" means persons who—
  (a)   use, have used or may use—
    (i)   regulated financial services, or
    (ii)   services that are provided by persons other than authorised persons but are provided in carrying on regulated activities,
  (b)   have relevant rights or interests in relation to any of those services,
  (c)   have invested, or may invest, in financial instruments, . . .
  (d)   have relevant rights or interests in relation to financial instruments[, or
  (e)   have rights, interests or obligations that are affected by the level of a regulated benchmark].
(2)   A person ("P") has a "relevant right or interest" in relation to any services within subsection (1)(a) if P has a right or interest—
  (a)   which is derived from, or is otherwise attributable to, the use of the services by others, or
  (b)   which may be adversely affected by the use of the services by persons acting on P's behalf or in a fiduciary capacity in relation to P.
(3)   If a person is providing a service within subsection (1)(a) as trustee, the persons who are, have been or may be beneficiaries of the trust are to be treated as persons who use, have used or may use the service.
(4)   A person who deals with another person ("B") in the course of B providing a service within subsection (1)(a) is to be treated as using the service.
(5)   A person ("P") has a "relevant right or interest" in relation to any financial instrument if P has—
  (a)   a right or interest which is derived from, or is otherwise attributable to, investment in the instrument by others, or
  (b)   a right or interest which may be adversely affected by the investment in the instrument by persons acting on P's behalf or in a fiduciary capacity in relation to P.]

NOTES
Commencement: 24 January 2013.
Substituted as noted to s 1A at **[1.1395]**.
Sub-s (1): the word omitted from para (c) was repealed, and para (e) (and the word immediately preceding it) was inserted, by the Financial Services and Markets Act 2000 (Regulated Activities) (Amendment) Order 2013, SI 2013/655, art 3(1), (2).

Note: the definition of "consumers" is extended for the purposes of this section by the Financial Services and Markets Act 2000 (Regulated Activities) (Amendment) (No 2) Order 2013, SI 2013/1881, art 65 at **[2.1046]**.

[1.1402]
[1H Further interpretative provisions for sections 1B to 1G
(1) The following provisions have effect for the interpretation of sections 1B to 1G.
(2) "Regulated financial services" means services provided—
  (a) by authorised persons in carrying on regulated activities;
  (b) . . .
  (c) by authorised persons in communicating, or approving the communication by others of, invitations to engage in investment activity;
  (d) by authorised persons who are investment firms, or credit institutions, in providing relevant ancillary services;
  (e) by persons acting as appointed representatives;
  (f) by payment service providers in providing payment services;
  (g) by electronic money issuers in issuing electronic money;
  (h) by sponsors to issuers of securities;
  (i) by primary information providers to persons who issue financial instruments.
(3) "Financial crime" includes any offence involving—
  (a) fraud or dishonesty,
  (b) misconduct in, or misuse of information relating to, a financial market,
  (c) handling the proceeds of crime, or
  (d) the financing of terrorism.
(4) "Offence" includes an act or omission which would be an offence if it had taken place in the United Kingdom.
(5) "Issuer", except in the expression "electronic money issuer", has the meaning given in section 102A(6).
(6) "Financial instrument" has the meaning given in section 102A(4).
(7) "Securities" has the meaning given in section 102A(2).
[(7A) "Regulated benchmark" means a benchmark, as defined in section 22(6), in relation to which any provision made under section 22(1A)(b) has effect.]
(8) In this section—
  . . .
  . . .
  "credit institution" means—
    (a) a credit institution authorised under the [capital requirements directive], or
    (b) an institution which would satisfy the requirements for authorisation as a credit institution under that directive if it had its registered office (or if it does not have a registered office, its head office) in an EEA State;
  "electronic money" has the same meaning as in the Electronic Money Regulations 2011;
  "electronic money issuer" means a person who is an electronic money issuer as defined in regulation 2(1) of the Electronic Money Regulations 2011 other than a person falling within paragraph (f), (g) or (j) of the definition;
  "engage in investment activity" has the meaning given in section 21;
  "financial instrument" has the meaning given in section 102A(4);
  "payment services" has the same meaning as in the Payment Services Regulations 2009;
  "payment service provider" means a person who is a payment service provider as defined in regulation 2(1) of the Payment Services Regulations 2009 other than a person falling within paragraph (g) or (h) of the definition;
  "primary information provider" has the meaning given in section 89P(2);
  "relevant ancillary service" means any service of a kind mentioned in Section B of Annex I to the markets in financial instruments directive the provision of which does not involve the carrying on of a regulated activity;
  "sponsor" has the meaning given in section 88(2).]

NOTES
Commencement: 24 January 2013.
Substituted as noted to s 1A at **[1.1395]**.
Para (b) of sub-s (2), and the definitions "accepting" and "consumer credit business" in sub-s (8), were repealed by the Financial Services and Markets Act 2000 (Regulated Activities) (Amendment) (No 2) Order 2013, SI 2013/1881, art 10(1), (2), (for transitional provisions see see Pt 8 thereof at **[2.1007]** et seq). Note that these amendments do not apply in so far as this section relates to, or applies for the purposes of, anything done under this Act concerning things done (or not done) before 1 April 2014 (see art 11(2) of the 2013 Order at **[2.1005]**).
Sub-s (7A) was inserted by the Financial Services and Markets Act 2000 (Regulated Activities) (Amendment) Order 2013, SI 2013/655, art 3(1), (3).
Words in square brackets in the definition "credit institution" in sub-s (8) substituted by the Capital Requirements Regulations 2013, SI 2013/3115, reg 46(1), Sch 2, Pt 1, paras 1, 2.

[1.1403]
[1I Meaning of "the UK financial system"
In this Act "the UK financial system" means the financial system operating in the United Kingdom and includes—
(a) financial markets and exchanges,
(b) regulated activities, and
(c) other activities connected with financial markets and exchanges.]

NOTES
Commencement: 24 January 2013.
Substituted as noted to s 1A at **[1.1395]**.

[Modifications applying if core activity not regulated by PRA

[1.1404]
1IA Modifications applying if core activity not regulated by PRA
(1) If and so long as any regulated activity is a core activity (see section 142B) without also being a PRA-regulated activity (see section 22A), the provisions of this Chapter are to have effect subject to the following modifications.
(2) Section 1B is to have effect as if—
(a) in subsection (3), after paragraph (c) there were inserted—
"(d) in relation to the matters mentioned in section 1EA(2), the continuity objective (see section 1EA).", and
(b) in subsection (4), for "or the integrity objective," there were substituted ", the integrity objective or (in relation to the matters mentioned in section 1EA(2)) the continuity objective,".
(3) After section 1E there is to be taken to be inserted—

"1EA Continuity objective
(1) In relation to the matters mentioned in subsection (2), the continuity objective is: protecting the continuity of the provision in the United Kingdom of core services (see section 142C).
(2) Those matters are—
(a) Part 9B (ring-fencing);
(b) ring-fenced bodies (see section 142A);
(c) any body corporate incorporated in the United Kingdom that has a ring-fenced body as a member of its group;
(d) applications under Part 4A which, if granted, would result, or would be capable of resulting, in a person becoming a ring-fenced body.
(3) The FCA's continuity objective is to be advanced primarily by—
(a) seeking to ensure that the business of ring-fenced bodies is carried on in a way that avoids any adverse effect on the continuity of the provision in the United Kingdom of core services,
(b) seeking to ensure that the business of ring-fenced bodies is protected from risks (arising in the United Kingdom or elsewhere) that could adversely affect the continuity of the provision in the United Kingdom of core services, and
(c) seeking to minimise the risk that the failure of a ring-fenced body or of a member of a ring-fenced body's group could adversely affect the continuity of the provision in the United Kingdom of core services.
(4) In subsection (3)(c), "failure" is to be read in accordance with section 2J(3) to (4)."]

NOTES
Commencement: to be appointed.
Inserted, together with the preceding heading, by the Financial Services (Banking Reform) Act 2013, s 2, as from a day to be appointed.

[Power to amend objectives

[1.1405]
1J Power to amend objectives
The Treasury may by order amend any of the following provisions—
(a) in section 1E(1), paragraphs (a) and (b),
(b) section 1G, and
(c) section 1H(2) and (5) to (8).]

NOTES
Commencement: 1 April 2013.
Substituted as noted to s 1A at **[1.1395]**.

[Guidance about objectives

[1.1406]
1K Guidance about objectives
(1) The general guidance given by the FCA under section 139A must include guidance about how it intends to advance its operational objectives in discharging its general functions in relation to different categories of authorised person or regulated activity.
(2) Before giving or altering any guidance complying with subsection (1), the FCA must consult the PRA.]

NOTES
Commencement: 1 April 2013.
Substituted as noted to s 1A at **[1.1395]**.

[Supervision, monitoring and enforcement

[1.1407]
1L Supervision, monitoring and enforcement
(1) The FCA must maintain arrangements for supervising authorised persons.
(2) The FCA must maintain arrangements designed to enable it to determine whether persons other than authorised persons are complying—
  (a) with requirements imposed on them by or under this Act, in cases where the FCA is the appropriate regulator for the purposes of Part 14 (disciplinary measures), . . .
  [(aa) with requirements imposed on them by the Alternative Investment Fund Managers Regulations 2013, or]
  (b) with requirements imposed on them by any qualifying EU provision that is specified, or of a description specified, for the purposes of this subsection by the Treasury by order.
(3) The FCA must also maintain arrangements for enforcing compliance by persons other than authorised persons with relevant requirements, within the meaning of Part 14, in cases where the FCA is the appropriate regulator for the purposes of any provision of that Part.]

NOTES
Commencement: 24 January 2013 (for the purposes of making orders); 1 April 2013 (otherwise).
Substituted as noted to s 1A at **[1.1395]**.
Sub-s (2): the word omitted from para (a) was repealed, and para (aa) was added, by the Alternative Investment Fund Managers Regulations 2013, SI 2013/1773, reg 80, Sch 1, Part 1, paras 1, 3, (for transitional provisions and savings see Part 9 of the 2013 Regulations).
Note: for the purposes of this section a requirement imposed by the FCA under the Electronic Commerce Directive (Financial Services and Markets) Regulations 2002, SI 2002/1775 upon an incoming provider is to be treated as imposed on him by or under this Act; see reg 12(2) of those Regulations.
Orders: the Financial Services and Markets Act 2000 (Qualifying EU Provisions) Order 2013, SI 2013/419; the Financial Services and Markets Act 2000 (Qualifying EU Provisions) (No 2) Order 2013, SI 2013/3116.

[Arrangements for consulting practitioners and consumers

[1.1407A]
1M The FCA's general duty to consult
The FCA must make and maintain effective arrangements for consulting practitioners and consumers on the extent to which its general policies and practices are consistent with its general duties under section 1B [and its duties under section 333O].]

NOTES
Commencement: 24 January 2013 (for the purposes of making orders); 1 April 2013 (otherwise).
Substituted as noted to s 1A at **[1.1395]**.
Words in square brackets inserted by the Pension Schemes Act 2015, s 47, Sch 3, paras 1, 4.

PART II
REGULATED AND PROHIBITED ACTIVITIES
The general prohibition

[1.1408]
19 The general prohibition
(1) No person may carry on a regulated activity in the United Kingdom, or purport to do so, unless he is—
  (a) an authorised person; or
  (b) an exempt person.
(2) The prohibition is referred to in this Act as the general prohibition.

Requirement for permission

[1.1409]
20 Authorised persons acting without permission
(1) If an authorised person [other than a PRA-authorised person] carries on a regulated activity in the United Kingdom, or purports to do so, otherwise than in accordance with permission—

[(a)   given to that person under Part 4A, or]

(b)   resulting from any other provision of this Act,

he is to be taken to have contravened a requirement imposed on him by the [FCA] under this Act. [(1A)   If a PRA-authorised person carries on a regulated activity in the United Kingdom, or purports to do so, otherwise than in accordance with permission given to the person under Part 4A or resulting from any other provision of this Act, the person is to be taken to have contravened—

(a)   a requirement imposed by the FCA, and

(b)   a requirement imposed by the PRA.]

[(2)   A contravention within subsection (1) or (1A)—

(a)   does not, except as provided by section 23(1A), make a person guilty of an offence,

(b)   does not, except as provided by section 26A, make any transaction void or unenforceable, and

(c)   does not, except as provided by subsection (3), give rise to any right of action for breach of statutory duty.]

(3)   In prescribed cases [a contravention within subsection (1) or (1A)] is actionable at the suit of a person who suffers loss as a result of the contravention, subject to the defences and other incidents applying to actions for breach of statutory duty.

[(4)   Subsections (1) and (1A) are subject to section 39(1D).]

(5)   References in this Act to an authorised person acting in contravention of this section are references to the person acting in a way that results in a contravention within subsection (1) or (1A).]

NOTES

Sub-s (1): words in first pair of square brackets inserted, and para (a) and the word "FCA" in square brackets substituted, by the Financial Services Act 2012, s 37(1), Sch 9, Pt 1, para 1, Pt 2, para 2(1), (2).

Sub-ss (1A), (4), (5): inserted and added respectively by the Financial Services Act 2012, s 37(1), Sch 9, Pt 1, para 1, Pt 2, para 2(1), (3), (6).

Sub-s (2): substituted by the Financial Services Act 2012, s 37(1), Sch 9, Pt 1, para 1, Pt 2, para 2(1), (4).

Sub-s (3): words in square brackets substituted by the Financial Services Act 2012, s 37(1), Sch 9, Pt 1, para 1, Pt 2, para 2(1), (5).

Regulations: the Financial Services and Markets Act 2000 (Rights of Action) Regulations 2001, SI 2001/2256.

Financial promotion

[1.1410]
21   Restrictions on financial promotion

(1)   A person ("A") must not, in the course of business, communicate an invitation or inducement to engage in investment activity.

(2)   But subsection (1) does not apply if—

(a)   A is an authorised person; or

(b)   the content of the communication is approved for the purposes of this section by an authorised person.

(3)   In the case of a communication originating outside the United Kingdom, subsection (1) applies only if the communication is capable of having an effect in the United Kingdom.

(4)   The Treasury may by order specify circumstances in which a person is to be regarded for the purposes of subsection (1) as—

(a)   acting in the course of business;

(b)   not acting in the course of business.

(5)   The Treasury may by order specify circumstances (which may include compliance with financial promotion rules) in which subsection (1) does not apply.

(6)   An order under subsection (5) may, in particular, provide that subsection (1) does not apply in relation to communications—

(a)   of a specified description;

(b)   originating in a specified country or territory outside the United Kingdom;

(c)   originating in a country or territory which falls within a specified description of country or territory outside the United Kingdom; or

(d)   originating outside the United Kingdom.

(7)   The Treasury may by order repeal subsection (3).

(8)   "Engaging in investment activity" means—

(a)   entering or offering to enter into an agreement the making or performance of which by either party constitutes a controlled activity; or

(b)   exercising any rights conferred by a controlled investment to acquire, dispose of, underwrite or convert a controlled investment.

(9)   An activity is a controlled activity if—

(a)   it is an activity of a specified kind or one which falls within a specified class of activity; and

(b)   it relates to an investment of a specified kind, or to one which falls within a specified class of investment.

(10)   An investment is a controlled investment if it is an investment of a specified kind or one which falls within a specified class of investment.

(11) Schedule 2 (except paragraph 26) applies for the purposes of subsections (9) and (10) with references to section 22 being read as references to each of those subsections.

(12) Nothing in Schedule 2, as applied by subsection (11), limits the powers conferred by subsection (9) or (10).

(13) "Communicate" includes causing a communication to be made.

(14) "Investment" includes any asset, right or interest.

(15) "Specified" means specified in an order made by the Treasury.

NOTES

Orders: the Financial Services and Markets Act 2000 (Miscellaneous Provisions) Order 2001, SI 2001/3650; the Financial Services and Markets Act 2000 (Financial Promotion and Miscellaneous Amendments) Order 2002, SI 2002/1310; the Financial Services and Markets Act 2000 (Commencement of Mortgage Regulation) (Amendment) Order 2002, SI 2002/1777; the Financial Services and Markets Act 2000 (Promotion of Collective Investment Schemes etc) (Exemptions) (Amendment) Order 2003, SI 2003/2067; the Financial Services and Markets Act 2000 (Financial Promotion and Promotion of Collective Investment Schemes) (Miscellaneous Amendments) Order 2005, SI 2005/270; the Financial Services and Markets Act 2000 (Financial Promotion) Order 2005, SI 2005/1529; the Financial Services and Markets Act 2000 (Financial Promotion) (Amendment) Order 2005, SI 2005/3392; the Financial Services and Markets Act 2000 (Financial Promotion) (Amendment) Order 2007, SI 2007/1083; the Financial Services and Markets Act 2000 (Financial Promotion) (Amendment No 2) Order 2007, SI 2007/2615; the Financial Services and Markets Act 2000 (Financial Promotion) (Amendment) Order 2010, SI 2010/905; the Financial Services and Markets Act 2000 (Miscellaneous Provisions) (No 2) Order 2015, SI 2015/352; the Financial Services and Markets Act 2000 (Miscellaneous Provisions) Order 2015, SI 2015/853; the Mortgage Credit Directive Order 2015, SI 2015/910 at **[2.1168]**.

Regulated activities

[1.1411]

22 [Regulated activities]

(1) An activity is a regulated activity for the purposes of this Act if it is an activity of a specified kind which is carried on by way of business and—

   (a) relates to an investment of a specified kind; or

   (b) in the case of an activity of a kind which is also specified for the purposes of this paragraph, is carried on in relation to property of any kind.

[(1A) An activity is also a regulated activity for the purposes of this Act if it is an activity of a specified kind which is carried on by way of business and relates to—

   (a) information about a person's financial standing, or

   (b) the setting of a specified benchmark.]

(2) Schedule 2 makes provision supplementing this section.

(3) Nothing in Schedule 2 limits the powers conferred by subsection (1) [or (1A)].

(4) "Investment" includes any asset, right or interest.

(5) "Specified" means specified in an order made by the Treasury.

[(6) "Benchmark" means an index, rate or price that—

   (a) is determined from time to time by reference to the state of the market,

   (b) is made available to the public (whether free of charge or on payment), and

   (c) is used for reference for purposes that include one or more of the following—

      (i) determining the interest payable, or other sums due, under loan agreements or under other contracts relating to investments;

      (ii) determining the price at which investments may be bought or sold or the value of investments;

      (iii) measuring the performance of investments.]

NOTES

Sub-ss (1A) and (6) were inserted and added respectively, the words in square brackets in sub-s (3) were inserted, and the section heading was substituted, by the Financial Services Act 2012, s 7(1).

See further, in relation to Orders made under this section, the Financial Services Act 2012, s 107, at **[1.2166]**

In sub-s (2) (as set out above) para (g) is repealed, and for the words in italics in sub-s (4) there are substituted the words "(2)(h) and (i)", by the Consumer Rights Act 2015, s 77, Sch 6, para 84, as from 1 October 2015 (for transitional provisions see the Consumer Rights Act 2015 (Commencement No 3, Transitional Provisions, Savings and Consequential Amendments) Order 2015, SI 2015/1630, arts 6–8 at **[2.1220]** et seq).

Investment of a specified kind: see the Gambling Act 2005, s 10, (Spread bets, &c) and s 38(3) which provides that an order under this section which has the effect that a class of bet becomes or ceases to be a regulated activity may, in particular, include transitional provision relating to the application of the 2005 Act to that class of bet.

Orders: the Financial Services and Markets Act 2000 (Regulated Activities) Order 2001, SI 2001/544 at **[2.168]**; the Financial Services and Markets Act 2000 (Regulated Activities) (Amendment) Order 2001, SI 2001/3544; the Financial Services and Markets Act 2000 (Regulated Activities) (Amendment) Order 2002, SI 2002/682; the Financial Services and Markets Act 2000 (Financial Promotion and Miscellaneous Amendments) Order 2002, SI 2002/1310; the Financial Services and Markets Act 2000 (Regulated Activities) (Amendment) (No 2) Order 2002, SI 2002/1776; the Financial Services and Markets Act 2000 (Commencement of Mortgage Regulation) (Amendment) Order 2002, SI 2002/1777; the Financial Services and Markets Act 2000 (Regulated Activities) (Amendment) (No 1) Order 2003, SI 2003/1475; the Financial Services and Markets Act 2000 (Regulated Activities) (Amendment) (No 2) Order 2003, SI 2003/1476; the Financial Services and Markets Act 2000 (Regulated Activities) (Amendment) (No 3) Order 2003, SI 2003/2822; the Financial Services and Markets Act 2000 (Regulated Activities) (Amendment) Order 2004, SI 2004/1610; the Financial Services and Markets Act 2000 (Regulated Activities) (Amendment) (No 2) Order 2004, SI 2004/2737; the Financial Services and Markets Act 2000 (Regulated Activities) (Amendment) Order 2005, SI 2005/593; the Financial Services and Markets Act 2000 (Regulated Activities) (Amendment) (No 2) Order 2005, SI 2005/1518; the Financial Services and Markets Act 2000 (Regulated Activities) (Amendment) Order 2006, SI 2006/1969; the

Financial Services and Markets Act 2000 (Regulated Activities) (Amendment) (No 2) Order 2006, SI 2006/2383; the Financial Services and Markets Act 2000 (Regulated Activities) (Amendment No 3) Order 2006, SI 2006/3384; the Financial Services and Markets Act 2000 (Regulated Activities) (Amendment) Order 2007, SI 2007/1339; the Financial Services and Markets Act 2000 (Reinsurance Directive) Order 2007, SI 2007/3254; the Financial Services and Markets Act 2000 (Regulated Activities) (Amendment) (No 2) Order 2007, SI 2007/3510; the Financial Services and Markets Act 2000 (Regulated Activities) (Amendment) Order 2009, SI 2009/1342; the Financial Services and Markets Act 2000 (Regulated Activities) (Amendment) (No 2) Order 2009, SI 2009/1389; the Financial Services and Markets Act 2000 (Regulated Activities) (Amendment) Order 2010, SI 2010/86; the Financial Services and Markets Act 2000 (Regulated Activities) (Amendment) Order 2011, SI 2011/133; the Financial Services and Markets Act 2000 (Regulated Activities) (Amendment) Order 2012, SI 2012/1906; the Financial Services and Markets Act 2000 (Regulated Activities) (Amendment) Order 2013, SI 2013/655; the Financial Services and Markets Act 2000 (Regulated Activities) (Amendment) (No 2) Order 2013, SI 2013/1881 at **[2.1004]**; the Financial Services and Markets Act 2000 (Regulated Activities) (Amendment) Order 2014, SI 2014/366 at **[2.1117]**; the Alternative Investment Fund Managers Order 2014, SI 2014/1292; the Alternative Investment Fund Managers (Amendment) Order 2014, SI 2014/1313; the Financial Services and Markets Act 2000 (Regulated Activities) (Amendment) (No 2) Order 2014, SI 2014/1448; the Financial Services and Markets Act 2000 (Regulated Activities) (Amendment) (No 3) Order 2014, SI 2014/1740; the Financial Services and Markets Act 2000 (Miscellaneous Provisions) (No 2) Order 2015, SI 2015/352; the Financial Services and Markets Act 2000 (Regulated Activities) (Amendment) Order 2015, SI 2015/369; the Financial Services and Markets Act 2000 (Regulated Activities) (Amendment) (Pensions Guidance Exclusions) Order 2015, SI 2015/489; the Financial Services and Markets Act 2000 (Regulated Activities) (Amendment) (No 2) Order 2015, SI 2015/731; the Electronic Commerce Directive (Financial Services and Markets) (Amendment) Order 2015, SI 2015/852; the Financial Services and Markets Act 2000 (Miscellaneous Provisions) Order 2015, SI 2015/853; the Mortgage Credit Directive Order 2015, SI 2015/910 at **[2.1168]**.

Offences

[1.1412]
23 Contravention of the general prohibition [or section 20(1) or (1A)]

(1) A person who contravenes the general prohibition is guilty of an offence and liable—

   (a) on summary conviction, to imprisonment for a term not exceeding six months or a fine not exceeding the statutory maximum, or both;

   (b) on conviction on indictment, to imprisonment for a term not exceeding two years or a fine, or both.

[(1A) An authorised person ("A") is guilty of an offence if A carries on a credit-related regulated activity in the United Kingdom, or purports to do so, otherwise than in accordance with permission—

   (a) given to that person under Part 4A, or

   (b) resulting from any other provision of this Act.

(1B) In this Act "credit-related regulated activity" means a regulated activity of a kind designated by the Treasury by order.

(1C) The Treasury may designate a regulated activity under subsection (1B) only if the activity involves a person—

   (a) entering into or administering an agreement under which the person provides another person with credit,

   (b) exercising or being able to exercise the rights of the lender under an agreement under which another person provides a third party with credit, or

   (c) taking steps to procure payment of debts due under an agreement under which another person is provided with credit.

(1D) But a regulated activity may not be designated under subsection (1B) if the agreement in question is one under which the obligation of the borrower is secured on land.

(1E) "Credit" includes any cash loan or other financial accommodation.

(1F) A person guilty of an offence under subsection (1A) is liable—

   (a) on summary conviction, to imprisonment for a term not exceeding the applicable maximum term or a fine not exceeding the statutory maximum, or both;

   (b) on conviction on indictment, to imprisonment for a term not exceeding two years, or a fine, or both.

(1G) The "applicable maximum term" is—

   (a) in England and Wales, 12 months (or 6 months, if the offence was committed before the commencement of section 154(1) of the Criminal Justice Act 2003);

   (b) in Scotland, 12 months;

   (c) in Northern Ireland, 6 months.]

(2) In this Act "an authorisation offence" means an offence under this section.

(3) In proceedings for an authorisation offence it is a defence for the accused to show that he took all reasonable precautions and exercised all due diligence to avoid committing the offence.

[(4) Subsection (1A) is subject to section 39(1D).

(5) No proceedings may be brought against a person in respect of an offence under subsection (1A) in a case where either regulator has taken action under section 205, 206 or 206A in relation to the alleged contravention within section 20(1) or (1A).]

NOTES

The words in square brackets in the section heading were added, and sub-ss (1A)–(1G) and sub-ss (4), (5) were inserted and added respectively, by the Financial Services Act 2012, s 37(1), Sch 9, Pt 1, para 1, Pt 2, para 3.

Deferred Prosecution Agreements: as to the application of Deferred Prosecution Agreements to an offence under this section and ss 25, 85, 346, 398 (ie, an agreement between a designated prosecutor and a person accused of a crime (P) whereby proceedings against P in respect of the alleged offence are automatically suspended as soon as they are instituted if P agrees to comply with certain requirements), see s 45 of, and Sch 17, Pt 1 and Sch 17, Pt 2, para 22 to, the Crime and Courts Act 2013.

    Orders: the Financial Services and Markets Act 2000 (Consumer Credit) (Designated Activities) Order 2014, SI 2014/334 at **[2.1115]**.

[1.1413]
24   False claims to be authorised or exempt

(1)   A person who is neither an authorised person nor, in relation to the regulated activity in question, an exempt person is guilty of an offence if he—

    (a)   describes himself (in whatever terms) as an authorised person;

    (b)   describes himself (in whatever terms) as an exempt person in relation to the regulated activity; or

    (c)   behaves, or otherwise holds himself out, in a manner which indicates (or which is reasonably likely to be understood as indicating) that he is—

        (i)   an authorised person; or

        (ii)   an exempt person in relation to the regulated activity.

(2)   In proceedings for an offence under this section it is a defence for the accused to show that he took all reasonable precautions and exercised all due diligence to avoid committing the offence.

(3)   A person guilty of an offence under this section is liable on summary conviction to imprisonment for a term not exceeding six months or a fine not exceeding level 5 on the standard scale, or both.

(4)   But where the conduct constituting the offence involved or included the public display of any material, the maximum fine for the offence is level 5 on the standard scale multiplied by the number of days for which the display continued.

NOTES
Sub-s (4): repealed by the Legal Aid, Sentencing and Punishment of Offenders Act 2012 (Fines on Summary Conviction) Regulations 2015, SI 2015/664, regs 4(4), 5, Sch 5, para 7, in relation to England and Wales only (except in relation to (a) fines for offences committed before 12 March 2015, (b) the operation of restrictions on fines that may be imposed on a person aged under 18, or (c) fines that may be imposed on a person convicted by a magistrates' court who is to be sentenced as if convicted on indictment).

[1.1414]
25   Contravention of section 21

(1)   A person who contravenes section 21(1) is guilty of an offence and liable—

    (a)   on summary conviction, to imprisonment for a term not exceeding six months or a fine not exceeding the statutory maximum, or both;

    (b)   on conviction on indictment, to imprisonment for a term not exceeding two years or a fine, or both.

(2)   In proceedings for an offence under this section it is a defence for the accused to show—

    (a)   that he believed on reasonable grounds that the content of the communication was prepared, or approved for the purposes of section 21, by an authorised person; or

    (b)   that he took all reasonable precautions and exercised all due diligence to avoid committing the offence.

NOTES
Deferred Prosecution Agreements: see the note to s 23 at **[1.1412]**.

Enforceability of agreements

[1.1415]
26   Agreements made by unauthorised persons

(1)   An agreement made by a person in the course of carrying on a regulated activity in contravention of the general prohibition is unenforceable against the other party.

(2)   The other party is entitled to recover—

    (a)   any money or other property paid or transferred by him under the agreement; and

    (b)   compensation for any loss sustained by him as a result of having parted with it.

(3)   "Agreement" means an agreement—

    (a)   made after this section comes into force; and

    (b)   the making or performance of which constitutes, or is part of, the regulated activity in question.

(4)   This section does not apply if the regulated activity is accepting deposits.

NOTES
Transitional provisions etc in connection with the original commencement of this Act: sub-ss (1), (2) above and s 27(1), (2) (and, subject to certain modifications, s 28 below) apply to certain agreements entered into in contravention of the Financial Services Act 1986, s 3 (repealed by the Financial Services and Markets Act 2000 (Consequential Amendments and Repeals) Order 2001, SI 2001/3649, art 3(1)(c)), or the Insurance Companies Act 1982, s 2 (repealed by art 3(1)(b) of that Order) as they apply to an agreement in contravention of the general prohibition; see the Financial Services and Markets Act 2000 (Transitional Provisions and Savings) (Civil Remedies, Discipline, Criminal Offences etc) (No 2) Order 2001, SI 2001/3083, art 5(1), (3), (4), (6).

[1.1416]
[26A   Agreements relating to credit
(1)   An agreement that is made by an authorised person in contravention of section 20 is unenforceable against the other party if the agreement is entered into in the course of carrying on a credit-related regulated activity involving matters falling within section 23(1C)(a).
(2)   The other party is entitled to recover—
   (a)   any money or other property paid or transferred by that party under the agreement, and
   (b)   compensation for any loss sustained by that party as a result of having parted with it.
(3)   In subsections (1) and (2) "agreement" means an agreement—
   (a)   which is made after this section comes into force, and
   (b)   the making or performance of which constitutes, or is part of, the credit-related regulated activity.
(4)   If the administration of an agreement involves the carrying on of a credit-related regulated activity, the agreement may not be enforced by a person for the time being exercising the rights of the lender under the agreement unless that person has permission, given under Part 4A or resulting from any other provision of this Act, in relation to that activity.
(5)   If the taking of steps to procure payment of debts due under an agreement involves the carrying on of a credit-related regulated activity, the agreement may not be enforced by a person for the time being exercising the rights of the lender under the agreement unless the agreement is enforced in accordance with permission—
   (a)   given under Part 4A to the person enforcing the agreement, or
   (b)   resulting from any other provision of this Act.]

NOTES
Commencement: 1 April 2013.
Inserted by the Financial Services Act 2012, s 37(1), Sch 9, Pt 1, para 1, Pt 2, para 5.

[1.1417]
27   Agreements made through unauthorised persons
[(1)   This section applies to an agreement that—
   (a)   is made by an authorised person ("the provider") in the course of carrying on a regulated activity,
   (b)   is not made in contravention of the general prohibition,
   (c)   if it relates to a credit-related regulated activity, is not made in contravention of section 20, and
   (d)   is made in consequence of something said or done by another person ("the third party") in the course of—
      (i)   a regulated activity carried on by the third party in contravention of the general prohibition, or
      (ii)   a credit-related regulated activity carried on by the third party in contravention of section 20.
(1A)   The agreement is unenforceable against the other party.]
(2)   The other party is entitled to recover—
   (a)   any money or other property paid or transferred by him under the agreement; and
   (b)   compensation for any loss sustained by him as a result of having parted with it.
(3)   "Agreement" means an agreement—
   (a)   made after this section comes into force; and
   (b)   the making or performance of which constitutes, or is part of, the regulated activity in question carried on by the provider.
(4)   This section does not apply if the regulated activity is accepting deposits.

NOTES
Sub-ss (1), (1A): substituted, for the original sub-s (1), by the Financial Services Act 2012, s 37(1), Sch 9, Pt 1, para 1, Pt 2, para 6.
Transitional provisions etc in connection with the original commencement of this Act: see the note to s 26 at **[1.1415]**.

[1.1418]
28   Agreements made unenforceable by section 26 or 27[: general cases]
(1)   This section applies to an agreement which is unenforceable because of section 26 or 27[, other than an agreement entered into in the course of carrying on a credit-related regulated activity].
(2)   The amount of compensation recoverable as a result of that section is—
   (a)   the amount agreed by the parties; or
   (b)   on the application of either party, the amount determined by the court.
(3)   If the court is satisfied that it is just and equitable in the circumstances of the case, it may allow—
   (a)   the agreement to be enforced; or
   (b)   money and property paid or transferred under the agreement to be retained.
(4)   In considering whether to allow the agreement to be enforced or (as the case may be) the money or property paid or transferred under the agreement to be retained the court must—

  (a) if the case arises as a result of section 26, have regard to the issue mentioned in subsection (5); or

  (b) if the case arises as a result of section 27, have regard to the issue mentioned in subsection (6).

(5) The issue is whether the person carrying on the regulated activity concerned reasonably believed that he was not contravening the general prohibition by making the agreement.

(6) The issue is whether the provider knew that the third party was (in carrying on the regulated activity) contravening the general prohibition.

(7) If the person against whom the agreement is unenforceable—

  (a) elects not to perform the agreement, or

  (b) as a result of this section, recovers money paid or other property transferred by him under the agreement,

he must repay any money and return any other property received by him under the agreement.

(8) If property transferred under the agreement has passed to a third party, a reference in section 26 or 27 or this section to that property is to be read as a reference to its value at the time of its transfer under the agreement.

(9) The commission of an authorisation offence does not make the agreement concerned illegal or invalid to any greater extent than is provided by section 26 or 27.

NOTES

Section heading, sub-s (1): words in square brackets inserted by the Financial Services Act 2012, s 37(1), Sch 9, Pt 1, para 1, Pt 2, para 7.

Transitional provisions etc in connection with the original commencement of this Act: see the note to s 26 at **[1.1415]**.

[1.1419]

[28A Credit-related agreements made unenforceable by section 26, 26A or 27

(1) This section applies to an agreement that—

  (a) is entered into in the course of carrying on a credit-related regulated activity, and

  (b) is unenforceable because of section 26, 26A or 27.

(2) The amount of compensation recoverable as a result of that section is—

  (a) the amount agreed by the parties, or

  (b) on the application of either party, the amount specified in a written notice given by the FCA to the applicant.

(3) If on application by the relevant firm the FCA is satisfied that it is just and equitable in the circumstances of the case, it may by written notice to the applicant allow—

  (a) the agreement to be enforced, or

  (b) money paid or property transferred under the agreement to be retained.

(4) In considering whether to allow the agreement to be enforced or (as the case may be) the money or property paid or transferred under the agreement to be retained the FCA must—

  (a) if the case arises as a result of section 26 or 26A, have regard to the issue mentioned in subsection (5), or

  (b) if the case arises as a result of section 27, have regard to the issue mentioned in subsection (6).

(5) The issue is whether the relevant firm reasonably believed that by making the agreement the relevant firm was neither contravening the general prohibition nor contravening section 20.

(6) The issue is whether the provider knew that the third party was (in carrying on the credit-related regulated activity) either contravening the general prohibition or contravening section 20.

(7) An application to the FCA under this section by the relevant firm may relate to specified agreements or to agreements of a specified description or made at a specified time.

(8) "The relevant firm" means—

  (a) in a case falling within section 26, the person in breach of the general prohibition;

  (b) in a case falling within section 26A or 27, the authorised person concerned.

(9) If the FCA thinks fit, it may when acting under subsection (2)(b) or (3)—

  (a) limit the determination in its notice to specified agreements, or agreements of a specified description or made at a specified time;

  (b) make the determination in its notice conditional on the doing of specified acts by the applicant.]

NOTES

Commencement: 1 April 2013.

Inserted, together with s 28B, by the Financial Services Act 2012, s 37(1), Sch 9, Pt 1, para 1, Pt 2, para 8.

[1.1420]

[28B Decisions under section 28A: procedure

(1) A notice under section 28A(2)(b) or (3) must—

  (a) give the FCA's reasons for its determination, and

  (b) give an indication of—

    (i) the right to have the matter referred to the Tribunal that is conferred by subsection (3), and

(ii)   the procedure on such a reference.

(2)   The FCA must, so far as it is reasonably practicable to do so, give a copy of the notice to any other person who appears to it to be affected by the determination to which the notice relates.

(3)   A person who is aggrieved by the determination of an application under section 28A(2)(b) or (3) may refer the matter to the Tribunal.]

NOTES
Commencement: 1 April 2013.
Inserted as noted to s 28A at **[1.1419]**.

[1.1421]
30   Enforceability of agreements resulting from unlawful communications

(1)   In this section—

"unlawful communication" means a communication in relation to which there has been a contravention of section 21(1);

"controlled agreement" means an agreement the making or performance of which by either party constitutes a controlled activity for the purposes of that section; and

"controlled investment" has the same meaning as in section 21.

(2)   If in consequence of an unlawful communication a person enters as a customer into a controlled agreement, it is unenforceable against him and he is entitled to recover—

(a)   any money or other property paid or transferred by him under the agreement; and

(b)   compensation for any loss sustained by him as a result of having parted with it.

(3)   If in consequence of an unlawful communication a person exercises any rights conferred by a controlled investment, no obligation to which he is subject as a result of exercising them is enforceable against him and he is entitled to recover—

(a)   any money or other property paid or transferred by him under the obligation; and

(b)   compensation for any loss sustained by him as a result of having parted with it.

(4)   But the court may allow—

(a)   the agreement or obligation to be enforced, or

(b)   money or property paid or transferred under the agreement or obligation to be retained,

if it is satisfied that it is just and equitable in the circumstances of the case.

(5)   In considering whether to allow the agreement or obligation to be enforced or (as the case may be) the money or property paid or transferred under the agreement to be retained the court must have regard to the issues mentioned in subsections (6) and (7).

(6)   If the applicant made the unlawful communication, the issue is whether he reasonably believed that he was not making such a communication.

(7)   If the applicant did not make the unlawful communication, the issue is whether he knew that the agreement was entered into in consequence of such a communication.

(8)   "Applicant" means the person seeking to enforce the agreement or obligation or retain the money or property paid or transferred.

(9)   Any reference to making a communication includes causing a communication to be made.

(10)   The amount of compensation recoverable as a result of subsection (2) or (3) is—

(a)   the amount agreed between the parties; or

(b)   on the application of either party, the amount determined by the court.

(11)   If a person elects not to perform an agreement or an obligation which (by virtue of subsection (2) or (3)) is unenforceable against him, he must repay any money and return any other property received by him under the agreement.

(12)   If (by virtue of subsection (2) or (3)) a person recovers money paid or property transferred by him under an agreement or obligation, he must repay any money and return any other property received by him as a result of exercising the rights in question.

(13)   If any property required to be returned under this section has passed to a third party, references to that property are to be read as references to its value at the time of its receipt by the person required to return it.

PART III
AUTHORISATION AND EXEMPTION

NOTES
Transitional provisions etc in connection with the original commencement of this Act: see the Financial Services and Markets Act 2000 (Transitional Provisions) (Authorised Persons etc) Order 2001, SI 2001/2636. That Order sets out the transitional arrangements for ensuring that people who had been authorised to carry on particular business under the various regulatory regimes replaced by this Act are treated as authorised persons with the appropriate permission for the purposes of this Act. The regulatory regimes covered by the Order are the Financial Services Act 1986, the Banking Act 1987, the Insurance Companies Act 1982, the Friendly Societies Act 1992, the Building Societies Act 1986, the Banking Coordination (Second Council Directive) Regulations 1992 (SI 1992/3218) and the Investment Services Regulations 1995 (SI 1995/3275).

Authorisation

[1.1422]
31   Authorised persons

(1)   The following persons are authorised for the purposes of this Act—

(a) a person who has a [Part 4A permission] to carry on one or more regulated activities;
(b) an EEA firm qualifying for authorisation under Schedule 3;
(c) a Treaty firm qualifying for authorisation under Schedule 4;
(d) a person who is otherwise authorised by a provision of, or made under, this Act.
(2) In this Act "authorised person" means a person who is authorised for the purposes of this Act.

NOTES

Sub-s (1): words in square brackets substituted by the Financial Services Act 2012, s 11(1).

[1.1423]
32 Partnerships and unincorporated associations
(1) If a firm is authorised—
  (a) it is authorised to carry on the regulated activities concerned in the name of the firm; and
  (b) its authorisation is not affected by any change in its membership.
(2) If an authorised firm is dissolved, its authorisation continues to have effect in relation to any [individual or] firm which succeeds to the business of the dissolved firm.
[(3) For the purposes of this section, an individual or firm is to be regarded as succeeding to the business of a dissolved firm only if succession is to the whole or substantially the whole of the business of the former firm.]
(4) "Firm" means—
  (a) a partnership; or
  (b) an unincorporated association of persons.
(5) "Partnership" does not include a partnership which is constituted under the law of any place outside the United Kingdom and is a body corporate.

NOTES

Para (2): words in square brackets inserted by the Regulatory Reform (Financial Services and Markets Act 2000) Order 2007, SI 2007/1973, arts 2, 3(a).
Para (3): substituted by SI 2007/1973, arts 2, 3(b).

Ending of authorisation

[1.1424]
33 Withdrawal of authorisation . . .
(1) This section applies if—
  (a) an authorised person's [Part 4A permission] is cancelled; and
  (b) as a result, there is no regulated activity for which he has permission.
(2) The [appropriate regulator] must give a direction withdrawing that person's status as an authorised person.
[(2A) In subsection (2) "the appropriate regulator" means—
  (a) in the case of a PRA-authorised person, the PRA, and
  (b) in any other case, the FCA.]

NOTES

The words omitted from the section heading were repealed, the words in square brackets in sub-ss (1), (2) were substituted, and sub-s (2A) was added, by the Financial Services Act 2012, s 114(1), Sch 18, Pt 1, paras 1, 2.

[1.1425]
34 EEA firms
(1) An EEA firm ceases to qualify for authorisation under Part II of Schedule 3 if it ceases to be an EEA firm as a result of—
  (a) having its EEA authorisation withdrawn; or
  (b) ceasing to have an EEA right in circumstances in which EEA authorisation is not required.
(2) At the request of an EEA firm, [the appropriate regulator] may give a direction cancelling its authorisation under Part II of Schedule 3.
[(2A) In subsection (2) "the appropriate regulator" means—
  (a) in the case of a PRA-authorised person, the PRA, and
  (b) in any other case, the FCA.]
(3) If an EEA firm has a [Part 4A permission], it does not cease to be an authorised person merely because it ceases to qualify for authorisation under Part II of Schedule 3.

NOTES

The words in square brackets in sub-ss (2), (3) were substituted, and sub-s (2A) was inserted, by the Financial Services Act 2012, s 12, Sch 4, Pt 3, para 27.
Transitional provisions etc in connection with the commencement of the Financial Services Act 2012: see the Financial Services Act 2012 (Transitional provisions) (Permission and Approval) Order 2013, SI 2013/440, art 16 (Ending of authorisation of an EEA firm).

[1.1426]
35   Treaty firms
(1)   A Treaty firm ceases to qualify for authorisation under Schedule 4 if its home State authorisation is withdrawn.
(2)   At the request of a Treaty firm, [the appropriate regulator] may give a direction cancelling its Schedule 4 authorisation.
[(2A)   In subsection (2) "the appropriate regulator" means—
   (a)   in the case of a PRA-authorised person, the PRA, and
   (b)   in any other case, the FCA.]
(3)   If a Treaty firm has a [Part 4A permission], it does not cease to be an authorised person merely because it ceases to qualify for authorisation under Schedule 4.

NOTES
The words in square brackets in sub-ss (2), (3) were substituted, and sub-s (2A) was inserted, by the Financial Services Act 2012, s 12, Sch 4, Pt 3, para 28.
Transitional provisions etc in connection with the commencement of the Financial Services Act 2012: see the Financial Services Act 2012 (Transitional provisions) (Permission and Approval) Order 2013, SI 2013/440, art 22 (Ending of authorisation of a Treaty firm).

Exemption

[1.1427]
38   Exemption orders
(1)   The Treasury may by order ("an exemption order") provide for—
   (a)   specified persons, or
   (b)   persons falling within a specified class,
to be exempt from the general prohibition.
(2)   But a person cannot be an exempt person as a result of an exemption order if he has a [Part 4A permission].
(3)   An exemption order may provide for an exemption to have effect—
   (a)   in respect of all regulated activities;
   (b)   in respect of one or more specified regulated activities;
   (c)   only in specified circumstances;
   (d)   only in relation to specified functions;
   (e)   subject to conditions.
(4)   "Specified" means specified by the exemption order.

NOTES
Sub-s (2): words in square brackets substituted by the Financial Services Act 2012, s 114(1), Sch 18, Pt 1, paras 1, 4.
Orders: the Financial Services and Markets Act 2000 (Exemption) Order 2001, SI 2001/1201; the Financial Services and Markets Act 2000 (Exemption) (Amendment) Order 2001, SI 2001/3623; the Financial Services and Markets Act 2000 (Financial Promotion and Miscellaneous Amendments) Order 2002, SI 2002/1310; the Financial Services and Markets Act 2000 (Exemption) (Amendment) Order 2003, SI 2003/47; the Financial Services and Markets Act 2000 (Exemption) (Amendment) (No 2) Order 2003, SI 2003/1675; the Financial Services and Markets Act 2000 (Exemption) (Amendment) Order 2005, SI 2005/592; the Financial Services and Markets Act 2000 (Exemption) (Amendment) Order 2007, SI 2007/125; the Financial Services and Markets Act 2000 (Exemption) (Amendment No 2) Order 2007, SI 2007/1821; the Financial Services and Markets Act 2000 (Exemption) (Amendment) Order 2008, SI 2008/682; the Financial Services and Markets Act 2000 (Exemption) (Amendment) Order 2009, SI 2009/118; the Financial Services and Markets Act 2000 (Exemption) (Amendment) Order 2009, SI 2009/264; the Financial Services and Markets Act 2000 (Exemption) (Amendment) Order 2011, SI 2011/1626; the Financial Services and Markets Act 2000 (Exemption) (Amendment No 2) Order 2011, SI 2011/2716; the Financial Services and Markets Act 2000 (Exemption) (Amendment) Order 2012, SI 2012/763; the Financial Services and Markets Act 2000 (Consumer Credit) (Miscellaneous Provisions) (No 2) Order 2014, SI 2014/506; the Financial Services and Markets Act 2000 (Miscellaneous Provisions) (No 2) Order 2015, SI 2015/352; the Financial Services and Markets Act 2000 (Exemption) (Amendment) Order 2015, SI 2015/447; the Mortgage Credit Directive Order 2015, SI 2015/910 at **[2.1168]**.

[1.1428]
39   Exemption of appointed representatives
(1)   If a person (other than an authorised person)—
   (a)   is a party to a contract with an authorised person ("his principal") which—
      (i)   permits or requires him to carry on business of a prescribed description, and
      (ii)   complies with such requirements as may be prescribed, and
   (b)   is someone for whose activities in carrying on the whole or part of that business his principal has accepted responsibility in writing,
he is exempt from the general prohibition in relation to any regulated activity comprised in the carrying on of that business for which his principal has accepted responsibility.
[(1ZA)   But a person is not exempt as a result of subsection (1) if subsection (1A) or (1BA) applies to the person.]
[(1A)   *But a person is not exempt as a result of subsection (1)—*
   (a)   if his principal is an investment firm or a credit institution, and
   (b)   so far as the business for which his principal has accepted responsibility is investment services business,
unless he is entered on the applicable register.

(1B)   The "applicable register" is—

(a)   in the case of a person established in an EEA State (other than the United Kingdom) which permits investment firms authorised by the competent authority of that State to appoint tied agents, the register of tied agents maintained in that State pursuant to Article 23 of the markets in financial instruments directive;

(b)   in the case of a person established in an EEA State which does not permit investment firms authorised as mentioned in paragraph (a) to appoint tied agents—

    (i)   if his principal has his relevant office in the United Kingdom, the record maintained by the [FCA] by virtue of section 347(1)(ha), and

    (ii)   if his principal is established in an EEA State (other than the United Kingdom) which permits investment firms authorised by the competent authority of the State to appoint tied agents, the register of tied agents maintained by that State pursuant to Article 23 of the markets in financial instruments directive; and

(c)   in any other case, the record maintained by the [FCA] by virtue of section 347(1)(ha).]

[(1BA)   This subsection applies to a person ("A")—

(a)   if A's principal is a mortgage intermediary, and

(b)   so far as the business for which A's principal has accepted responsibility is of a kind—

    (i)   specified in article 25A (arranging regulated mortgage contracts), article 36A (credit broking), article 53A (advising on regulated mortgage contracts) or article 53DA (advising on regulated credit agreements the purpose of which is to acquire land) of the Financial Services and Markets Act 2000 (Regulated Activities) Order 2001; and

    (ii)   to which the mortgages directive applies,

unless A meets the requirements of subsection (1BB).

(1BB)   The requirements of this subsection are—

(a)   that A is entered on the record maintained by the FCA by virtue of section 347(1)(hb);

(b)   that A's principal is a person who has a Part 4A permission to carry on one or more of the regulated activities mentioned in subsection (1BA)(b)(i); and

(c)   that A's principal is not a tied mortgage intermediary.]

[(1C)   Subsection (1D) applies where an authorised person ("A")—

(a)   has permission under Part 4A, or permission resulting from any other provision of this Act, only in relation to one or more qualifying activities,

(b)   is a party to a contract with another authorised person (A's "principal") which—

    (i)   permits or requires A to carry on business of a prescribed description ("the relevant business"), and

    (ii)   complies with such requirements as may be prescribed, and

(c)   is someone for whose activities in carrying on the whole or part of the relevant business A's principal has accepted responsibility in writing.

(1D)   Sections 20(1) and (1A) and 23(1A) do not apply in relation to the carrying on by A of a relevant additional activity.

(1E)   In subsections (1C) and (1D)—

(a)   "qualifying activity" means a regulated activity which is of a prescribed kind and relates—

    (i)   to rights under a contract of the kind mentioned in paragraph 23 of Schedule 2, other than one under which the obligation of the borrower to repay is secured on land, or

    (ii)   to rights under a contract of the kind mentioned in paragraph 23B of that Schedule;

(b)   "relevant additional activity" means a regulated activity which—

    (i)   is not one to which A's permission relates, and

    (ii)   is comprised in the carrying on of the business for which A's principal has accepted responsibility.]

[(2)   In this Act "appointed representative" means—

(a)   a person who is exempt as a result of subsection (1), or

(b)   a person carrying on a regulated activity in circumstances where, as a result of subsection (1D), sections 20(1) and (1A) and 23(1A) do not apply.]

(3)   The principal of an appointed representative is responsible, to the same extent as if he had expressly permitted it, for anything done or omitted by the representative in carrying on the business for which he has accepted responsibility.

[(4)   In determining whether an authorised person has complied with—

(a)   a provision contained in or made under this Act, or

(b)   a qualifying EU provision that is specified, or of a description specified, for the purposes of this subsection by the Treasury by order,

anything which a relevant person has done or omitted as respects business for which the authorised person has accepted responsibility is to be treated as having been done or omitted by the authorised person.]

(5)   "Relevant person" means a person who at the material time is or was an appointed representative by virtue of being a party to a contract with the authorised person.

(6)   Nothing in subsection (4) is to cause the knowledge or intentions of an appointed representative to be attributed to his principal for the purpose of determining whether the principal has committed an offence, unless in all the circumstances it is reasonable for them to be attributed to him.

[(7)   A person carries on "investment services business" if—

(a)   the business includes providing services or carrying on activities of the kind mentioned in Article 4.1.25 of the markets in financial instruments directive, and

(b)   as a result of providing such services or carrying on such activities he is a tied agent or would be if he were established in an EEA State.

(8)   In this section—

"competent authority" has the meaning given in Article 4.1.22 of the markets in financial instruments directive;

"credit institution" means—

(a)   a credit institution authorised under the [capital requirements directive], or

(b)   an institution which would satisfy the requirements for authorisation as a credit institution under that directive if it had its relevant office in an EEA State;

"relevant office" means—

(a)   in relation to a body corporate, its registered office or, if it has no registered office, its head office, and

(b)   in relation to a person other than a body corporate, the person's head office.]

NOTES

Sub-ss (1ZA), (1BA), (1BB): inserted by the Mortgage Credit Directive Order 2015, SI 2015/910, Sch 1, para 1(1), (2)(a), (c), as from 21 March 2016 (note that the 2015 Order also comes into force on 20 April 2015 and 21 December 2015 for limited other purposes, and for transitional provisions, see Part 4 of that Order at **[2.1194]** et seq).

Sub-ss (1A), (1B), (7), (8): inserted and added respectively by the Financial Services and Markets Act 2000 (Markets in Financial Instruments) Regulations 2007, SI 2007/126, reg 3(5), Sch 5, paras 1, 2(a), (c); for the words in italics in sub-s (1A) there are substituted the words "This subsection applies to a person" by SI 2015/910, Sch 1, para 1(1), (2)(b), as from 21 March 2016 (for further commencement details and transitional provisions, see the note relating to this Order above); words in square brackets in sub-s (1B) substituted by the Financial Services Act 2012, s 114(1), Sch 18, Pt 1, paras 1, 5(1), (2); words in square brackets in the definition "credit institution" in sub-s (8) substituted by the Capital Requirements Regulations 2013, SI 2013/3115, reg 46(1), Sch 2, Pt 1, paras 1, 4.

Sub-ss (1C)–(1E): inserted by the Financial Services Act 2012, s 10(1), (2).

Sub-s (2): substituted by the Financial Services Act 2012, s 10(1), (3).

Sub-s (4): substituted by the Financial Services Act 2012, s 114(1), Sch 18, Pt 1, paras 1, 5(1), (3).

Transitional provisions: see the Financial Services and Markets Act 2000 (Markets in Financial Instruments) Regulations 2007, SI 2007/126, reg 9 (transitional provision: appointed representatives and tied agents).

Regulations: the Financial Services and Markets Act 2000 (Appointed Representatives) Regulations 2001, SI 2001/1217; the Financial Services and Markets Act 2000 (Appointed Representatives) (Amendment) Regulations 2001, SI 2001/2508; the Financial Services and Markets Act 2000 (Appointed Representatives) (Amendment) Regulations 2004, SI 2004/453; the Financial Services and Markets Act 2000 (Appointed Representatives) (Amendment) Regulations 2006, SI 2006/3414; the Financial Services and Markets Act 2000 (Markets in Financial Instruments) (Amendment) Regulations 2007, SI 2007/763; the Financial Services and Markets Act 2000 (Appointed Representatives) (Amendment) Regulations 2014, SI 2014/206.

Orders: the Financial Services and Markets Act 2000 (Qualifying EU Provisions) Order 2013, SI 2013/419; the Financial Services and Markets Act 2000 (Qualifying EU Provisions) (No 2) Order 2013, SI 2013/3116; the Financial Services and Markets Act 2000 (Appointed Representatives) (Amendment) Regulations 2014, SI 2014/206.

[PART 4A
PERMISSION TO CARRY ON REGULATED ACTIVITIES

NOTES

Transitional provisions etc in connection with the commencement of the Financial Services Act 2012: For transitional provisions in relation to the commencement of this Part, see the Financial Services Act 2012 (Transitional Provisions) (Permission and Approval) Order 2013, SI 2013/440. Part 2 of that Order contains transitional provisions in relation to permission under this Act to carry on regulated activity, including (a) provision for things done by or in relation to the FSA before1 April 2013 to be treated as if done by or in relation to the PRA, or the PRA and the FCA, and (b) provision in respect of applications for permission, requirements on permission, variation of permission and cancellation of permission.

See also the Financial Services Act 2012 (Transitional Provisions) (Enforcement) Order 2013, SI 2013/441. Articles 26–29 contain transitional provisions in relation to various warning notices and decision notices given by the Financial Services Authority under the original Part IV of this Act before 1 April 2013.

See also the Financial Services Act 2012 (Transitional provisions) (Permission and Approval) Order 2013, SI 2013/440, art 14 (transitional provisions in relation to Lloyds).

Transitional provisions etc in connection with the original commencement of this Act: see the Financial Services and Markets Act 2000 (Transitional Provisions) (Authorised Persons etc) Order 2001, SI 2001/2636 which, inter alia, provides that persons who were authorised or exempted from the need for authorisation under provisions of the previous regulatory regimes were to be treated, as from 1 December 2001, as having permission under the original Pt IV of this Act (Permission to Carry on Regulated Activities) to carry on the activities they were lawfully able to carry on immediately before that date by reason of that authorisation or exemption. Note that the original Part IV was substituted by a new Part 4A by the Financial Services Act 2012.

See also the Financial Services and Markets Act 2000 (Interim Permissions) Order 2001, SI 2001/3374. This Order conferred an interim permission on certain applicants who applied to the FSA for permission under the original Part IV of the 2000 Act and whose application was pending on the date when the main provisions of the Act came into force (1 December 2001).

See also, the Financial Services and Markets Act 2000 (Consequential and Transitional Provisions) (Miscellaneous) (No 2) Order 2001, SI 2001/2659 (transitional provisions in consequence of the Financial Services and Markets Act 2000 (Commencement No 5) Order (SI 2001/2632). That Order brings into force the provisions of the Act relating to (among other things) the making of applications under the Act for permission or authorisation coming into force on 1 December 2001).

Transitional provisions (credit unions): see the Financial Services and Markets Act 2000 (Permission and Applications) (Credit Unions etc) Order 2002, SI 2002/704 (transitional provisions relating to the expiry, on 2 July 2002, of the transitional exemption of credit unions from the general prohibition imposed by s 19 of this Act (see the Financial Services and Markets Act 2000 (Exemption) Order 2001, SI 2001/1201, art 6).

See also the Financial Services and Markets Act 2000 (Permissions, Transitional Provisions and Consequential Amendments) (Northern Ireland Credit Unions) Order 2011, SI 2011/2832 which makes transitional provisions and consequential amendments relating to the revocation, on 31 March 2012, of the exemption for Northern Ireland credit unions from the general prohibition imposed by s 19 *ante*. The exemption, contained in para 24A of the Schedule to the Financial Services and Markets Act 2000 (Exemption) Order 2001 (SI 2001/1201), is revoked by SI 2011/2716.

Transitional provisions (newly regulated activities): as to interim permissions, interim approvals and the application of the this Act, subject to transitional provisions, to various activities that have become regulated activities following the amendment of the Regulated Activities Order, see the following:

— the Financial Services and Markets Act 2000 (Transitional Provisions) (Mortgages) Order 2004, SI 2004/2615 (in relation to certain mortgage mediation activities)

— the Financial Services and Markets Act 2000 (Regulated Activities) (Amendment) (No 2) Order 2004, SI 2004/2737 (in relation to advice on stakeholder products)

— the Financial Services and Markets Act 2000 (Transitional Provisions) (General Insurance Intermediaries) Order 2004, SI 2004/3351 (in relation to certain general insurance mediation activities)

— the Financial Services and Markets Act 2000 (Regulated Activities) (Amendment) Order 2006, SI 2006/1969 (in relation to establishing, operating or winding up a personal pension scheme, or activities which relate to the specified investment of rights under a personal pension scheme)

— the Financial Services and Markets Act 2000 (Regulated Activities) (Amendment) (No 2) Order 2006, SI 2006/2383 (in relation to administering, arranging or advising on regulated home reversion plans or regulated home purchase plans)

— the Financial Services and Markets Act 2000 (Regulated Activities) (Amendment) (No 2) Order 2007, SI 2007/3510 (in relation to provision of travel insurance in certain circumstances)

— the Financial Services and Markets Act 2000 (Regulated Activities) (Amendment) Order 2009, SI 2009/1342 (in relation to entering into, administering, arranging and advising on regulated sale and rent back agreements

— the Financial Services and Markets Act 2000 (Regulated Activities) (Amendment) Order 2013, SI 2013/655 and the Financial Services and Markets Act 2000 (Regulated Activities) (Amendment) Order 2015, SI 2015/369 (in relation to providing information in relation to and administering specified benchmarks)

— the Financial Services and Markets Act 2000 (Regulated Activities) (Amendment) (No 2) Order 2013, SI 2013/1881 at **[2.1004]** (in relation to credit broking, operating an electronic system in relation to lending, debt adjusting, debt-counselling, debt-collecting, debt administration, entering into etc a regulated credit agreement, entering into etc a regulated consumer hire agreement, providing credit information services and providing credit references).

— the Financial Services and Markets Act 2000 (Regulated Activities) (Amendment) (No 2) Order 2015, SI 2015/731, and the Financial Services and Markets Act 2000 (Regulated Activities) (Transitional Provisions) Order 2015, SI 2015/732 (in relation to advising on conversion or transfer of pension benefits).

See also the Mortgage Credit Directive Order 2015, SI 2015/910 at **[2.1168]** (interim permissions in relation to an activity of the kind specified by article 25A, 36A, 60B or 61 of this Order).

See also the Alternative Investment Fund Managers Order 2014, SI 2014/1292, art 7 which provides a process whereby fund managers that have applied for permission to carry on the new regulated activities of managing an AIF or managing a UCITS before 16 June 2014, and that will require permission to carry on insurance mediation activities after art 6 of that Order comes into force (ie, 22 July 2014), may notify the FCA of this fact and obtain such permission without the need to make a new application for a variation of permission.

See also Part 7 (reg 24) of the Collective Investment in Transferable Securities (Contractual Scheme) Regulations 2013, SI 2013/1388. That regulation contains transitional provisions in relation to depositaries of authorised contractual schemes. A person who already has permission under Part 4A of this Act to act as the trustee of an authorised unit trust scheme and as the depositary of an open-ended investment company, if that person gives the FCA notice in accordance with the regulation, is treated as having permission under this Part to act as the depositary of an authorised contractual scheme.

See also the Financial Services and Markets Act 2000 (Permissions, Transitional Provisions and Consequential Amendments) (Northern Ireland Credit Unions) Order 2011, SI 2011/2832 which makes transitional provisions and consequential amendments relating to the revocation, on 31 March 2012, of the exemption for Northern Ireland credit unions from the general prohibition imposed by s 19 *ante*. The exemption, contained in para 24A of the Schedule to the Financial Services and Markets Act 2000 (Exemption) Order 2001 (SI 2001/1201), is revoked by SI 2011/2716.

Application for permission

[1.1429]
55A Application for permission
(1) An application for permission to carry on one or more regulated activities may be made to the appropriate regulator by—
    (a) an individual,
    (b) a body corporate,
    (c) a partnership, or
    (d) an unincorporated association.
(2) "The appropriate regulator", in relation to an application under this section, means—
    (a) the PRA, in a case where—
        (i) the regulated activities to which the application relates consist of or include a PRA-regulated activity, or
        (ii) the applicant is a PRA-authorised person otherwise than by virtue of a Part 4A permission;
    (b) the FCA, in any other case.
(3) An authorised person who has a permission under this Part which is in force may not apply for permission under this section.
(4) An EEA firm may not apply for permission under this section to carry on a regulated activity which it is, or would be, entitled to carry on in exercise of an EEA right, whether through a United Kingdom branch or by providing services in the United Kingdom.
(5) A permission given by the appropriate regulator under this Part or having effect as if so given is referred to in this Act as "a Part 4A permission.]

NOTES
Commencement: 1 April 2013.
This section was substituted (together with the rest of Part 4A (ie, ss 55A–55Z4) for the original Part IV (ss 40–55)) by the Financial Services Act 2012, s 11(2).

[1.1430]
[55B   The threshold conditions
(1)   "The threshold conditions", in relation to a regulated activity, means the conditions set out in or specified under Schedule 6, as read with any threshold condition code made by either regulator under section 137O.
(2)   Any reference in this Part to the threshold conditions for which either regulator is responsible is to be read as a reference to the conditions set out in or specified under Schedule 6 that are expressed to be relevant to the discharge by that regulator of its functions, as read with any threshold condition code made by that regulator under section 137O.
(3)   In giving or varying permission, imposing or varying a requirement, or giving consent, under any provision of this Part, each regulator must ensure that the person concerned will satisfy, and continue to satisfy, in relation to all of the regulated activities for which the person has or will have permission, the threshold conditions for which that regulator is responsible.
(4)   But the duty imposed by subsection (3) does not prevent a regulator, having due regard to that duty, from taking such steps as it considers are necessary, in relation to a particular person, in order to advance—
    (a)   in the case of the FCA, any of its operational objectives;
    (b)   in the case of the PRA, any of its objectives.]

NOTES
Commencement: 1 April 2013.
Substituted as noted to s 55A at **[1.1429]**; for transitional provisions in relation to this section, see Sch 20, para 5 to the 2012 Act.

[1.1431]
[55C   Power to amend Schedule 6
(1)   The Treasury may by order amend Parts 1 and 2 of Schedule 6 by altering, adding or repealing provisions, or by substituting for those Parts as they have effect for the time being provisions specified in the order.
(2)   Different provision may be made under this section—
    (a)   in relation to the discharge of the functions of each regulator;
    (b)   in relation to different regulated activities;
    (c)   in relation to persons who carry on, or seek to carry on, activities that consist of or include a PRA-regulated activity and in relation to other persons.]

NOTES
Commencement: 24 January 2013 (for the purposes of making orders); 1 April 2013 (otherwise).
Substituted as noted to s 55A at **[1.1429]**; for transitional provisions in relation to this section, see Sch 20, para 5 to the 2012 Act.
Orders: the Financial Services and Markets Act 2000 (Threshold Conditions) Order 2013, SI 2013/555; the Financial Services and Markets Act 2000 (Miscellaneous Provisions) Order 2015, SI 2015/853.

[1.1432]
[55D   Firms based outside EEA
(1)   This section applies in relation to a person ("the non-EEA firm")—
    (a)   who is a body incorporated in, or formed under the law of, or is an individual who is a national of, any country or territory outside the EEA, and
    (b)   who is carrying on a regulated activity in any country or territory outside the United Kingdom in accordance with the law of that country or territory ("the overseas state").
(2)   In determining whether the non-EEA firm is satisfying or will satisfy, and continue to satisfy, any one or more of the threshold conditions for which a UK regulator is responsible, the UK regulator may have regard to any opinion notified to it by a regulatory authority in the overseas state ("the overseas regulator") which relates to the non-EEA firm and appears to the UK regulator to be relevant to compliance with those conditions.
(3)   In considering how much weight (if any) to attach to the opinion, the UK regulator must have regard to the nature and scope of the supervision exercised in relation to the non-EEA firm by the overseas regulator.
(4)   In this section "UK regulator" means the FCA or the PRA.]

NOTES
Commencement: 1 April 2013.
Substituted as noted to s 55A at **[1.1429]**.

[1.1433]
[55E Giving permission: the FCA
(1) This section applies where the FCA is the appropriate regulator in relation to an application for permission under section 55A.
(2) The FCA may give permission for the applicant to carry on the regulated activity or activities to which the application relates or such of them as may be specified in the permission.
(3) If the applicant is a member of a group which includes a PRA-authorised person, the FCA must consult the PRA before determining the application.
(4) If it gives permission, the FCA must specify the permitted regulated activity or activities, described in such manner as the FCA considers appropriate.
(5) The FCA may—
  (a) incorporate in the description of a regulated activity such limitations (for example as to circumstances in which the activity may, or may not, be carried on) as it considers appropriate;
  (b) specify a narrower or wider description of regulated activity than that to which the application relates;
  (c) give permission for the carrying on of a regulated activity which is not included among those to which the application relates and is not a PRA-regulated activity.]

NOTES
Commencement: 1 April 2013.
Substituted as noted to s 55A at **[1.1429]**.

[1.1434]
[55G   Giving permission: special cases
(1) "The applicant" means an applicant for permission under section 55A.
(2) If the applicant—
  (a) in relation to a particular regulated activity, is exempt from the general prohibition as a result of section 39(1) or an order made under section 38(1), but
  (b) has applied for permission in relation to another regulated activity,
the application is to be treated as relating to all the regulated activities which, if permission is given, the applicant will carry on.
(3) If the applicant—
  (a) in relation to a particular regulated activity, is exempt from the general prohibition as a result of [any of subsections (2) to (3C) of section 285], but
  (b) has applied for permission in relation to another regulated activity,
the application is to be treated as relating only to that other regulated activity.
(4) If the applicant—
  (a) is a person to whom, in relation to a particular regulated activity, the general prohibition does not apply as a result of Part 19, but
  (b) has applied for permission in relation to another regulated activity,
the application is to be treated as relating only to that other regulated activity.
(5) Subsection (6) applies where either regulator ("the responsible regulator") receives an application for permission under section 55A which is in the regulator's opinion similar to an application which was previously made to the other regulator and was either—
  (a) treated by the other regulator as not being a valid application to that regulator because of the regulated activities to which it related, or
  (b) refused by the other regulator after being considered.
(6) The responsible regulator must have regard to the desirability of minimising—
  (a) the additional work for the applicant in dealing with the new application, and
  (b) the time taken to deal with the new application.]

NOTES
Commencement: 1 April 2013.
Substituted as noted to s 55A at **[1.1429]**.
Sub-s (3): words in square brackets substituted by the Financial Services and Markets Act 2000 (Over the Counter Derivatives, Central Counterparties and Trade Repositories) Regulations 2013, SI 2013/504, reg 3(1), (2).

[Variation and cancellation of Part 4A permission

[1.1435]
55H   Variation by FCA at request of authorised person
(1) This section applies in relation to an authorised person who has a Part 4A permission but is not a PRA-authorised person.
(2) The FCA may, on the application of the authorised person, vary the permission by—
  (a) adding a regulated activity, other than a PRA-regulated activity, to those to which the permission relates;
  (b) removing a regulated activity from those to which the permission relates;
  (c) varying the description of a regulated activity to which the permission relates.
(3) The FCA may, on the application of the authorised person, cancel the permission.

(4)   The FCA may refuse an application under this section if it appears to it that it is desirable to do so in order to advance any of its operational objectives.

[(4A)   The FCA may also refuse an application under this section if it appears to the FCA that the authorised person would not comply with requirements in Part 5 of the Alternative Investment Fund Managers Regulations 2013 (AIFs which acquire control of non-listed companies and issuers) that would apply to the authorised person.]

(5)   If the applicant is a member of a group which includes a PRA-authorised person, the FCA must consult the PRA before determining the application.

(6)   If as a result of a variation of a Part 4A permission under this section there are no longer any regulated activities for which the authorised person concerned has permission, the FCA must, once it is satisfied that it is no longer necessary to keep the permission in force, cancel it.

(7)   The FCA's power to vary a Part 4A permission under this section extends to including in the permission as varied any provision that could be included if a fresh permission were being given by it in response to an application under section 55A.]

NOTES

Commencement: 1 April 2013.

Substituted as noted to s 55A at **[1.1429]**.

Sub-s (4A): inserted by the Alternative Investment Fund Managers Regulations 2013, SI 2013/1773, reg 80, Sch 1, Part 1, paras 1, 4, (for transitional provisions and savings see Part 9 of the 2013 Regulations).

[1.1436]

[55J   Variation or cancellation on initiative of regulator

(1)   Either regulator may exercise its power under this section in relation to an authorised person with a Part 4A permission ("A") if it appears to the regulator that—

(a)   A is failing, or is likely to fail, to satisfy the threshold conditions for which the regulator is responsible,

(b)   A has failed, during a period of at least 12 months, to carry on a regulated activity to which the Part 4A permission relates, . . .

(c)   it is desirable to exercise the power in order to advance—

(i)   in the case of the FCA, one or more of its operational objectives,

(ii)   in the case of the PRA, any of its objectives[; or

(d)   in the case of the FCA, A has failed to comply with a requirement in Part 5 of the Alternative Investment Fund Managers Regulations 2013 (AIFs which acquire control of non-listed companies and issuers), or it is for some other reason desirable to exercise the power for the purposes of ensuring compliance with such a requirement.]

(2)   The FCA's power under this section is the power—

(a)   to vary the Part 4A permission by—

(i)   adding a regulated activity other than a PRA-regulated activity to those to which the permission relates,

(ii)   removing a regulated activity from those to which the permission relates, or

(iii)   varying the description of a regulated activity to which the permission relates in a way which, if it is a PRA-regulated activity, does not, in the opinion of the FCA, widen the description, or

(b)   to cancel the Part 4A permission.

(3)   The PRA's power under this section is the power—

(a)   in the case of a PRA-authorised person, to vary the Part 4A permission in any of the ways mentioned in section 55I(1) or to cancel it;

(b)   in the case of an authorised person who is not a PRA-authorised person, to vary the Part 4A permission by adding a PRA-regulated activity to those to which the permission relates and, if the PRA does so, to vary the Part 4A permission in any of the other ways mentioned in section 55I(1).

(4)   The FCA—

(a)   must consult the PRA before exercising its power under this section in relation to—

(i)   a PRA-authorised person, or

(ii)   a member of a group which includes a PRA-authorised person, and

(b)   in the case of a PRA-authorised person, may exercise the power so as to add a new activity to those to which the permission relates or to widen the description of a regulated activity to which the permission relates, only with the consent of the PRA.

(5)   The PRA—

(a)   must consult the FCA before exercising its power under this section, and

(b)   may exercise the power so as to add a new activity to those to which the permission relates or to widen the description of a regulated activity to which the permission relates, only with the consent of the FCA.

(6)   Without prejudice to the generality of subsections (1) to (3), a regulator may, in relation to an authorised person who is an investment firm, exercise its power under this section to cancel the Part 4A permission if it appears to it that any of the conditions in section 55K is met.

[(6A)   Without prejudice to the generality of subsections (1) to (3), the FCA may, in relation to an authorised person who is a full-scope UK AIFM, exercise its power under this section to cancel the Part 4A permission if it appears to it that any of the following conditions is met—

(a)   the person has failed, during a period of at least six months, to carry on the regulated activity of managing an AIF;

(b)   the person obtained the Part 4A permission to carry on the regulated activity of managing an AIF by making a false statement or by any other irregular means;

(c)   in a case where the Part 4A permission includes permission to provide the discretionary portfolio management service referred to in Article 6.4(a) of the alternative investment fund managers directive, the person no longer complies with [the capital requirements regulation or the capital requirements directive];

(d)   the person no longer meets the conditions that a person must meet in order to obtain a Part 4A permission to carry on the regulated activity of managing an AIF;

(e)   the person has seriously or systematically infringed—

(i)   any provision of the Alternative Investment Fund Managers Regulations 2013;

(ii)   a provision of any directly applicable EU regulation made under the alternative investment fund managers directive; or

(iii)   any provision made by or under this Act which implements that directive.]

[(6B)   Without prejudice to the generality of subsections (1) to (3), the FCA may, in relation to an authorised person who is a mortgage intermediary and who has a Part 4A permission to carry on a relevant mortgage activity, exercise its power under this section to cancel the Part 4A permission or to vary the Part 4A permission by removing a relevant mortgage activity from the activities to which the permission relates, if it appears to the FCA that any of the following conditions is met—

(a)   during a period of at least six months, the person has not carried on a relevant mortgage activity;

(b)   the person obtained the Part 4A permission to carry on a relevant mortgage activity by making a false statement or by any other irregular means;

(c)   the person no longer meets the conditions which the person was, in accordance with Chapter 11 of the mortgages directive, required to meet in order to be granted a Part 4A permission to carry on a relevant mortgage activity; or

(d)   the person has seriously or systematically infringed any provision made by or under this Act which implements the operating conditions for mortgage intermediaries set out in the mortgages directive.

(6C)   In subsection (6B) "relevant mortgage activity" means—

(a)   an activity of a kind specified in article 25A (arranging regulated mortgage contracts), article 53A (advising on regulated mortgage contracts) or article 53DA (advising on regulated credit agreements the purpose of which is to acquire land) of the Financial Services and Markets Act 2000 (Regulated Activities) Order 2001, or

(b)   an activity of a kind specified in article 36A of that Order (credit broking) which is referred to in Article 33(1)(a) of the mortgages directive.]

(7)   Without prejudice to the generality of subsections (1) and (2), the FCA may, in relation to an authorised person who has permission to carry on the regulated activity specified in article 24A of the Financial Services and Markets Act 2000 (Regulated Activities) Order 2001 (which relates to bids in emission allowance auctions), exercise its power under this section to vary the Part 4A permission of the person concerned by removing that activity from those to which the permission relates if it appears to the FCA that the person has seriously and systematically infringed the provisions of paragraph 2 or 3 of Article 59 of the emission allowance auctioning regulation.

[(7A)   Without prejudice to the generality of subsections (1) and (3), if it appears to the PRA that there has been a serious failure by a PRA-authorised person who is an insurance undertaking or reinsurance undertaking to comply with requirements imposed by or under this Act in pursuance of the Solvency 2 Directive, the PRA may exercise its powers under this section to cancel the undertaking's Part 4A permission.

(7B)   If it appears to the PRA that the conditions in section 55KA are met in relation to a PRA-authorised person who is an insurance undertaking, reinsurance undertaking or third-country insurance undertaking, the PRA must—

(a)   in relation to the undertaking's Part 4A permission so far as the permission relates to the regulated activity of effecting contracts of insurance as principal ("activity A"), exercise the PRA's powers under this section by varying the permission—

(i)   where the permission relates to activity A in relation to both contracts of long-term insurance and contracts of general insurance and the conditions in section 55KA are met only in relation to the business of the undertaking so far as relating to contracts of one of those kinds, so as to remove activity A so far as relating to contracts of that kind from the regulated activities to which the permission relates, and

(ii)   in any other case, so as to remove activity A from the regulated activities to which the permission relates;

(b)   in relation to the undertaking's Part 4A permission so far as the permission relates to the regulated activity of carrying out contracts of insurance as principal ("activity B"), exercise the PRA's powers under this section, if it appears to the PRA to be necessary to do so to protect the interests of the undertaking's policyholders, by varying the Part 4A permission—

   (i)   where the permission relates to activity B in relation to both contracts of long-term insurance and contracts of general insurance and the conditions in section 55KA are met only in relation to the business of the undertaking so far as relating to contracts of one of the those kinds, so as to remove activity B so far as relating to contracts of that kind from the regulated activities to which the permission relates, and

   (ii)   in any other case, so as to remove activity B from the regulated activities to which the permission relates.

(7C)   If the effect of a variation required by subsection (7B) is to remove all the regulated activities to which the Part 4A permission relates, the PRA must instead cancel the permission.]

(8)   If, as a result of a variation of a Part 4A permission under this section, there are no longer any regulated activities for which the authorised person concerned has permission, the regulator responsible for the variation must, once it is satisfied that it is no longer necessary to keep the permission in force, cancel it.

(9)   Before cancelling under subsection (8) a Part 4A permission which relates to a person who (before the variation) was a PRA-authorised person, the regulator must consult the other regulator.

(10)   The power of either regulator to vary a Part 4A permission under this section extends to including in the permission as varied any provision that could be included if a fresh permission were being given in response to an application to that regulator under section 55A.

(11)   Consent given by one regulator for the purpose of subsection (4)(b) or (5)(b) may be conditional on the manner in which the other regulator exercises its powers under section 55E(4) and (5) or 55F(3) and (4) (as a result of subsection (10)).

(12)   The power of the FCA or the PRA under this section is referred to in this Part as its own-initiative variation power.]

NOTES

Commencement: 1 April 2013.

Substituted as noted to s 55A at **[1.1429]**.

The word omitted from sub-s (1)(b) was repealed, sub-s (1)(d) (and the preceding word) was inserted, and sub-s (6A) was inserted, by the Alternative Investment Fund Managers Regulations 2013, SI 2013/1773, reg 80, Sch 1, Part 1, para 5, (for transitional provisions and savings see Part 9 of the 2013 Regulations).

Words in square brackets in sub-s (6A) substituted by the Capital Requirements Regulations 2013, SI 2013/3115, reg 46(1), Sch 2, Pt 1, paras 1, 5.

Sub-ss (6B), (6C): inserted by the Mortgage Credit Directive Order 2015, SI 2015/910, Sch 1, para 1(1), (3), as from 21 March 2016 (note that the 2015 Order also comes into force on 20 April 2015 and 21 December 2015 for limited other purposes, and for transitional provisions, see Part 4 of that Order at **[2.1194]** et seq).

Sub-ss (7A)–(7C): inserted by the Solvency 2 Regulations 2015, SI 2015/575, reg 59, Sch 1, Pt 1, paras 1, 2, as from 1 January 2016.

[Imposition and variation of requirements

[1.1437]

55L   Imposition of requirements by FCA

(1)   Where a person has applied (whether to the FCA or the PRA) for a Part 4A permission or the variation of a Part 4A permission, the FCA may impose on that person such requirements, taking effect on or after the giving or variation of the permission, as the FCA considers appropriate.

(2)   The FCA may exercise its power under subsection (3) in relation to an authorised person with a Part 4A permission (whether given by it or by the PRA) ("A") if it appears to the FCA that—

   (a)   A is failing, or is likely to fail, to satisfy the threshold conditions for which the FCA is responsible,

   (b)   A has failed, during a period of at least 12 months, to carry on a regulated activity to which the Part 4A permission relates, or

   (c)   it is desirable to exercise the power in order to advance one or more of the FCA's operational objectives.

(3)   The FCA's power under this subsection is a power—

   (a)   to impose a new requirement,

   (b)   to vary a requirement imposed by the FCA under this section, or

   (c)   to cancel such a requirement.

(4)   The FCA's power under subsection (3) is referred to in this Part as its own-initiative requirement power.

(5)   The FCA may, on the application of an authorised person with a Part 4A permission—

   (a)   impose a new requirement,

   (b)   vary a requirement imposed by the FCA under this section, or

   (c)   cancel such a requirement.

(6)   The FCA may refuse an application under subsection (5) if it appears to it that it is desirable to do so in order to advance any of its operational objectives.

(7)   The FCA must consult the PRA before imposing or varying a requirement which relates to—

   (a)   a person who is, or will on the granting of an application for Part 4A permission be, a PRA-authorised person, or

(b)   a person who is a member of a group which includes a PRA-authorised person.]

NOTES
Commencement: 1 April 2013.
Substituted as noted to s 55A at **[1.1429]**.

[1.1438]
[55N   Requirements under section 55L or 55M: further provisions
(1)   A requirement may, in particular, be imposed—
  (a)   so as to require the person concerned to take specified action, or
  (b)   so as to require the person concerned to refrain from taking specified action.
(2)   A requirement may extend to activities which are not regulated activities.
(3)   A requirement may be imposed by reference to the person's relationship with—
  (a)   the person's group, or
  (b)   other members of the person's group.
(4)   A requirement may be expressed to expire at the end of such period as the regulator imposing it may specify, but the imposition of a requirement that expires at the end of a specified period does not affect the regulator's power to impose a new requirement.
(5)   A requirement may refer to the past conduct of the person concerned (for example, by requiring the person concerned to review or take remedial action in respect of past conduct).
(6)   In this section "requirement" means a requirement imposed under section 55L or 55M.]

NOTES
Commencement: 1 April 2013.
Substituted as noted to s 55A at **[1.1429]**.

[1.1439]
[55O   Imposition of requirements on acquisition of control
(1)   This section applies if it appears to the appropriate regulator that—
  (a)   a person has acquired control over a UK authorised person who has a Part 4A permission, but
  (b)   there are no grounds for exercising its own-initiative requirement power.
(2)   If it appears to the appropriate regulator that the likely effect of the acquisition of control on the UK authorised person, or on any of its activities, is uncertain, the appropriate regulator may—
  (a)   impose on the UK authorised person a requirement that could be imposed by that regulator under section 55L or 55M (as the case may be) on the giving of permission, or
  (b)   vary a requirement imposed by that regulator under that section on the UK authorised person.
(3)   "The appropriate regulator" means—
  (a)   in a case where the UK authorised person is a PRA-authorised person, the FCA or the PRA;
  (b)   in any other case, the FCA.
(4)   This section does not affect any duty of the appropriate regulator to consult or obtain the consent of the other regulator in connection with the imposition of the requirement.
(5)   Any reference to a person having acquired control is to be read in accordance with Part 12.]

NOTES
Commencement: 1 April 2013.
Substituted as noted to s 55A at **[1.1429]**.

[1.1440]
[55P   Prohibitions and restrictions
(1)   This section applies if—
  (a)   on a person being given a Part 4A permission, either regulator imposes an assets requirement on that person,
  (b)   an assets requirement is imposed on an authorised person, or
  (c)   an assets requirement previously imposed on such a person is varied.
(2)   A person on whom an assets requirement is imposed is referred to in this section as "A".
(3)   The "appropriate regulator" is the regulator which imposed the requirement.
(4)   "Assets requirement" means a requirement under section 55L or 55M—
  (a)   prohibiting the disposal of, or other dealing with, any of A's assets (whether in the United Kingdom or elsewhere) or restricting such disposals or dealings, or
  (b)   that all or any of A's assets, or all or any assets belonging to consumers but held by A or to A's order, must be transferred to and held by a trustee approved by the appropriate regulator.
(5)   If the appropriate regulator—
  (a)   imposes a requirement of the kind mentioned in subsection (4)(a), and
  (b)   gives notice of the requirement to any institution with whom A keeps an account,
the notice has the effects mentioned in subsection (6).
(6)   Those effects are that—

(a) the institution does not act in breach of any contract with A if, having been instructed by A (or on A's behalf) to transfer any sum or otherwise make any payment out of A's account, it refuses to do so in the reasonably held belief that complying with the instruction would be incompatible with the requirement, and

(b) if the institution complies with such an instruction, it is liable to pay to the appropriate regulator an amount equal to the amount transferred from, or otherwise paid out of, A's account in contravention of the requirement.

(7) If the appropriate regulator imposes a requirement of the kind mentioned in subsection (4)(b), no assets held by a person as trustee in accordance with the requirement may, while the requirement is in force, be released or dealt with except with the consent of the appropriate regulator.

(8) If, while a requirement of the kind mentioned in subsection (4)(b) is in force, A creates a charge over any assets of A held in accordance with the requirement, the charge is (to the extent that it confers security over the assets) void against the liquidator and any of A's creditors.

(9) Assets held by a person as trustee ("T") are to be taken to be held by T in accordance with any requirement mentioned in subsection (4)(b) only if—

(a) A has given T written notice that those assets are to be held by T in accordance with the requirement, or

(b) they are assets into which assets to which paragraph (a) applies have been transposed by T on the instructions of A.

(10) A person who contravenes subsection (7) is guilty of an offence and liable on summary conviction to a fine not exceeding level 5 on the standard scale.

(11) "Charge" includes a mortgage (or in Scotland a security over property).

(12) Subsections (7) and (9) do not affect any equitable interest or remedy in favour of a person who is a beneficiary of a trust as a result of a requirement of the kind mentioned in subsection (4)(b).]

NOTES

Commencement: 1 April 2013.

Substituted as noted to s 55A at **[1.1429]**.

[Connected persons

[1.1441]

55R Persons connected with an applicant

(1) In considering—

(a) an application for a Part 4A permission,

(b) whether to vary or cancel a Part 4A permission,

(c) whether to impose or vary a requirement under this Part, or

(d) whether to give any consent required by any provision of this Part,

the regulator concerned may have regard to any person appearing to it to be, or likely to be, in a relationship with the applicant or a person given permission which is relevant.

(2) Before—

(a) giving permission in response to an application under section 55A made by a person who is connected with an EEA firm (other than an EEA firm falling within paragraph 5(e) of Schedule 3 (insurance and reinsurance intermediaries)), or

(b) cancelling or varying a Part 4A permission given to such a person,

the regulator concerned must in prescribed circumstances consult the firm's home state regulator.

(3) A person ("A") is connected with an EEA firm if—

(a) A is a subsidiary undertaking of the firm, or

(b) A is a subsidiary undertaking of a parent undertaking of the firm.

[(4) Subsection (5) applies where—

(a) a credit institution ("B") makes an application for permission under section 55A; and

(b) B is controlled by a person who also controls a credit institution, insurance undertaking or investment firm authorised in another EEA State.

(5) Before granting B's application for permission, the regulator concerned must consult the competent authorities of the other EEA State.

(6) In subsections (4) and (5), "credit institution", "insurance undertaking" and "investment firm" have the meaning given in Article 4(1) of the capital requirements regulation.]]

NOTES

Commencement: 1 April 2013.

Substituted as noted to s 55A at **[1.1429]**.

Sub-ss (4)–(6): added by the Capital Requirements Regulations 2013, SI 2013/3115, reg 46(1), Sch 2, Pt 1, paras 1, 6.

Regulations: the Financial Services and Markets Act 2000 (Exercise of Powers under Part 4A) (Consultation with Home State Regulators) Regulations 2013, SI 2013/431.

[Additional permissions

[1.1442]

55S Duty of FCA or PRA to consider other permissions

(1) "Additional Part 4A permission"—

(a)   in relation to either regulator, means a Part 4A permission which is in force in relation to an EEA firm or a Treaty firm, and

(b)   in relation to the FCA, also includes a Part 4A permission which is in force in relation to a person authorised as a result of paragraph 1(1) of Schedule 5.

(2)   If either regulator is considering whether, and if so how, to exercise its own-initiative variation power or its own-initiative requirement power in relation to an additional Part 4A permission, it must take into account—

(a)   the home state authorisation of the authorised person concerned,

(b)   any relevant directive, and

(c)   relevant provisions of the Treaty.]

NOTES

Commencement: 1 April 2013.

Substituted as noted to s 55A at **[1.1429]**.

[Persons whose interests are protected

[1.1443]

55T   Persons whose interests are protected

For the purpose of any provision of this Part which refers to the FCA's operational objectives, or the PRA's objectives in relation to the exercise of a power in relation to a particular person, it does not matter whether there is a relationship between that person and the persons whose interests will be protected by the exercise of the power.]

NOTES

Commencement: 1 April 2013.

Substituted as noted to s 55A at **[1.1429]**.

[Procedure

[1.1444]

55U   Applications under this Part

(1)   An application for a Part 4A permission must—

(a)   contain a statement of the regulated activity or regulated activities which the applicant proposes to carry on and for which the applicant wishes to have permission, and

(b)   give the address of a place in the United Kingdom for service on the applicant of any notice or other document which is required or authorised to be served on the applicant under this Act.

(2)   An application for the variation of a Part 4A permission must contain a statement—

(a)   of the desired variation, and

(b)   of the regulated activity or regulated activities which the applicant proposes to carry on if the permission is varied.

(3)   An application for the variation of a requirement imposed under section 55L or 55M or for the imposition of a new requirement must contain a statement of the desired variation or requirement.

(4)   An application under this Part must—

(a)   be made in such manner as the regulator to which it is to be made may direct, and

(b)   contain, or be accompanied by, such other information as that regulator may reasonably require.

(5)   At any time after the application is received and before it is determined, the appropriate regulator may require the applicant to provide it with such further information as it reasonably considers necessary to enable it to determine the application or, as the case requires, to decide whether to give consent.

(6)   In subsection (5), the "appropriate regulator" means—

(a)   in a case where the application is made to the FCA, the FCA;

(b)   in a case where the application is made to the PRA, the FCA or the PRA.

(7)   Different directions may be given, and different requirements imposed, in relation to different applications or categories of application.

(8)   Each regulator may require an applicant to provide information which the applicant is required to provide to it under this section in such form, or to verify it in such a way, as the regulator may direct.

(9)   The PRA must consult the FCA before—

(a)   giving a direction under this section in relation to a class of applications, or

(b)   imposing a requirement under this section in relation to a class of applications.]

NOTES

Commencement: 24 January 2013 (in so far as relating to the giving of directions or the imposition of requirements); 1 April 2013 (otherwise).

Substituted as noted to s 55A at **[1.1429]**.

See further the Financial Services and Markets Act 2000 (Consumer Credit) (Miscellaneous Provisions) Order 2014, SI 2014/208, art 2 which provides that sub-ss (4), (5), (7) and (8) of this section apply to an application made under s 28A of this Act (credit-related agreements made unenforceable by ss 26, 26A or 27) as if the application were an application made to the FCA under Part 4A of this Act. It further provides that where a person ("A") has the right to exercise rights under an agreement entered into by another person ("B"), s 28A *ante* applies as if the references to the relevant firm in sub-ss (3) and (7) of that section include a reference to A. See also the Financial Services and Markets Act 2000 (Regulated Activities) (Amendment) Order 2014, SI 2014/366, art 4 which provides that those subsections also apply to an application made under the Consumer Credit Act 1974, ss 60(3), 64(4), 101(8) and 160.

[1.1445]
[55V Determination of applications
(1)   An application under this Part must be determined by the regulator to which it is required to be made ("the appropriate regulator") before the end of the period of 6 months beginning with the date on which it received the completed application.
(2)   The appropriate regulator may determine an incomplete application if it considers it appropriate to do so; and it must in any event determine such an application within 12 months beginning with the date on which it received the application.
(3)   Where the application cannot be determined by the appropriate regulator without the consent of the other regulator, the other regulator's decision must also be made within the period required by subsection (1) or (2).
(4)   The applicant may withdraw the application, by giving the appropriate regulator written notice, at any time before the appropriate regulator determines it.
(5)   If the appropriate regulator grants an application—
   (a)   for Part 4A permission,
   (b)   for the variation or cancellation of a Part 4A permission,
   (c)   for the variation or cancellation of a requirement imposed under section 55L or 55M, or
   (d)   for the imposition of a new requirement under either of those sections,
it must give the applicant written notice.
(6)   The notice must state the date from which the permission, variation, cancellation or requirement has effect.
(7)   A notice under this section which is given by the PRA and relates to the grant of an application for Part 4A permission or for the variation of a Part 4A permission must state that the FCA has given its consent to the grant of the application.
[(8)   In the case of an application for permission under this Part which—
   (a)   relates to the regulated activity of managing an AIF, and
   (b)   would if granted result in the applicant becoming a full-scope UK AIFM,
this section has effect subject to *regulation 5* of the Alternative Investment Fund Managers Regulations 2013 and, accordingly, subsections (1) to (3) do not apply.]

NOTES
Commencement: 1 April 2013.
Substituted as noted to s 55A at **[1.1429]**.
Sub-s (8): added by the Alternative Investment Fund Managers Regulations 2013, SI 2013/1773, reg 80, Sch 1, Part 1, paras 1, 6, (for transitional provisions and savings see Part 9 of the 2013 Regulations); for the words in italics there are substituted the words "regulations 5 and 5A" by the Alternative Investment Fund Managers (Amendment) Regulations 2013, SI 2013/1797, reg 3, Sch 1, para 1(1), (2), as from the date specified by the delegated act adopted by the European Commission pursuant to Article 67.6 of the Directive as the date when the rules set out in Articles 35 and 37 to 41 of the Directive become applicable (note also that ESMA is required to issue an opinion by 22 July 2015 and, if the Commission accepts their advice, a delegated act must be issued by 22 October 2015 specifying the date on which this provision will come into force).

[1.1446]
[55W   Applications under this Part: communications between regulators
The PRA must as soon as practicable notify the FCA of the receipt or withdrawal of—
   (a)   an application for permission under section 55A,
   (b)   an application under section 55I, or
   (c)   an application under section 55M(5).]

NOTES
Commencement: 1 April 2013.
Substituted as noted to s 55A at **[1.1429]**.

[1.1447]
[55X   Determination of applications: warning notices and decision notices
(1)   If a regulator proposes—
   (a)   to give a Part 4A permission but to exercise its power under section 55E(5)(a) or (b) or 55F(4)(a) or (b),
   (b)   to give a Part 4A permission but to exercise its power under section 55L(1) or 55M(1) in connection with the application for permission,
   (c)   to vary a Part 4A permission on the application of an authorised person but to exercise its power under section 55E(5)(a) or (b) or 55F(4)(a) or (b),
   (d)   to vary a Part 4A permission but to exercise its power under section 55L(1) or 55M(1) in connection with the application for variation, or
   (e)   in the case of the FCA, to exercise its power under section 55L(1) in connection with an application to the PRA for a Part 4A permission or the variation of a Part 4A permission,

it must give the applicant a warning notice.

(2) If a regulator proposes to refuse an application made under this Part, it must (unless subsection (3) applies) give the applicant a warning notice.

(3) This subsection applies if it appears to the regulator that—

    (a)   the applicant is an EEA firm, and

    (b)   the application is made with a view to carrying on a regulated activity in a manner in which the applicant is, or would be, entitled to carry on that activity in the exercise of an EEA right whether through a United Kingdom branch or by providing services in the United Kingdom.

(4) If a regulator decides—

    (a)   to give a Part 4A permission but to exercise its power under section 55E(5)(a) or (b) or 55F(4)(a) or (b),

    (b)   to give a Part 4A permission but to exercise its power under section 55L(1) or 55M(1) in connection with the giving of the permission,

    (c)   to vary a Part 4A permission on the application of an authorised person but to exercise its power under section 55E(5)(a) or (b) or 55F(4)(a) or (b),

    (d)   to vary a Part 4A permission on the application of an authorised person but to exercise its power under section 55L(1) or 55M(1) in connection with the variation,

    (e)   in the case of the FCA, to exercise its power under section 55L(1) in connection with an application to the PRA for a Part 4A permission or the variation of a Part 4A permission, or

    (f)   to refuse an application under this Part,

it must give the applicant a decision notice.]

NOTES

Commencement: 1 April 2013.

Substituted as noted to s 55A at **[1.1429]**.

[1.1448]

[55Y Exercise of own-initiative power: procedure

(1) This section applies to an exercise of either regulator's own-initiative variation power or own-initiative requirement power in relation to an authorised person ("A").

(2) A variation of a permission or the imposition or variation of a requirement takes effect—

    (a)   immediately, if the notice given under subsection (4) states that that is the case,

    (b)   on such date as may be specified in the notice, or

    (c)   if no date is specified in the notice, when the matter to which the notice relates is no longer open to review.

(3) A variation of a permission, or the imposition or variation of a requirement, may be expressed to take effect immediately (or on a specified date) only if the regulator concerned, having regard to the ground on which it is exercising its own-initiative variation power or own-initiative requirement power, reasonably considers that it is necessary for the variation, or the imposition or variation of the requirement, to take effect immediately (or on that date).

(4) If either regulator proposes to vary a Part 4A permission or to impose or vary a requirement, or varies a Part 4A permission or imposes or varies a requirement, with immediate effect, it must give A a written notice.

(5) The notice must—

    (a)   give details of the variation of the permission or the requirement or its variation,

    (b)   state the regulator's reasons for the variation of the permission or the imposition or variation of the requirement,

    (c)   inform A that A may make representations to the regulator within such period as may be specified in the notice (whether or not A has referred the matter to the Tribunal),

    (d)   inform A of when the variation of the permission or the imposition or variation of the requirement takes effect, and

    (e)   inform A of A's right to refer the matter to the Tribunal.

(6) The regulator may extend the period allowed under the notice for making representations.

(7) If, having considered any representations made by A, the regulator decides—

    (a)   to vary the permission, or impose or vary the requirement, in the way proposed, or

    (b)   if the permission has been varied or the requirement imposed or varied, not to rescind the variation of the permission or the imposition or variation of the requirement,

it must give A written notice.

(8) If, having considered any representations made by A, the regulator decides—

    (a)   not to vary the permission, or impose or vary the requirement, in the way proposed,

    (b)   to vary the permission or requirement in a different way, or impose a different requirement, or

    (c)   to rescind a variation or requirement which has effect,

it must give A written notice.

(9) A notice under subsection (7) must inform A of A's right to refer the matter to the Tribunal.

(10) A notice under subsection (8)(b) must comply with subsection (5).

(11) If a notice informs A of A's right to refer a matter to the Tribunal, it must give an indication of the procedure on such a reference.

(12) For the purposes of subsection (2)(c), whether a matter is open to review is to be determined in accordance with section 391(8).]

NOTES
Commencement: 1 April 2013.
Substituted as noted to s 55A at **[1.1429]**.

[1.1449]
[55Z Cancellation of Part 4A permission: procedure
(1) If a regulator proposes to cancel an authorised person's Part 4A permission otherwise than at the person's request, it must give the person a warning notice.
(2) If a regulator decides to cancel an authorised person's Part 4A permission otherwise than at the person's request, it must give the person a decision notice.]

NOTES
Commencement: 1 April 2013.
Substituted as noted to s 55A at **[1.1429]**.

[References to the Tribunal

[1.1450]
55Z3 Right to refer matters to the Tribunal
(1) An applicant who is aggrieved by the determination of an application made under this Part may refer the matter to the Tribunal.
(2) An authorised person who is aggrieved by the exercise by either regulator of its own-initiative variation power or its own-initiative requirement power may refer the matter to the Tribunal.]

NOTES
Commencement: 1 April 2013.
Substituted as noted to s 55A at **[1.1429]**.

[Interpretation

[1.1451]
55Z4 Interpretation of Part 4A
In this Part—
"own-initiative requirement power", in relation to the FCA or the PRA, is to be read in accordance with section 55L(4) or 55M(4);
"own-initiative variation power", in relation to the FCA or the PRA, is to be read in accordance with section 55J(12).]

NOTES
Commencement: 1 April 2013.
Substituted as noted to s 55A at **[1.1429]**.

PART V
PERFORMANCE OF REGULATED ACTIVITIES

NOTES
Transitional provisions etc in connection with the commencement of the Financial Services Act 2012: For transitional provisions in respect of the approval for a person to perform functions which are specified in rules made by a regulator, see the Financial Services Act 2012 (Transitional Provisions) (Permission and Approval) Order 2013, SI 2013/440, art 13 (Approval for particular arrangements). See also the Financial Services Act 2012 (Transitional Provisions) (Enforcement) Order 2013, SI 2013/441, which make provision for the imposition of penalties and disciplinary measures under this Act in relation to the performance of controlled functions before 1 April 2013 (see arts 2 and 3 of the 2013 Order).

Transitional provisions etc in connection with the original commencement of this Act: the Financial Services and Markets Act 2000 (Transitional Provisions) (Authorised Persons etc) Order 2001, SI 2001/2636, Pt VI makes transitional provisions for people working for authorised persons who will be covered by the regime for approved persons in Pt V of this Act after commencement. Where someone is working for an authorised person before commencement in a post for which they would need to be approved under Pt V after commencement, that person is treated has having been approved for the purpose of working in that post. This deemed approval applies unless the person was working before commencement in contravention of certain provisions of the regulatory rules or of rules made by a self-regulating organisation. The Part also carries forward approvals given under the Insurance Companies Act 1982 and the Banking Act 1987 where the person approved did not take up the appointment before commencement.

Other transitional and savings: see also the Financial Services (Banking Reform) Act 2013 (Transitional and Savings Provisions) Order 2015, SI 2015/492 which makes transitional and savings provisions in connection with the commencement of the Financial Services (Banking Reform) Act 2013, Part 4, which amends this Part. Article 2 makes provision about the conditions that must be met for a person who, before the 7 March 2016, has an approval to perform controlled functions in relation to a firm to continue to have approval on and after the 7 March 2016. Article 3 sets out additional conditions for the continuation of an approval. Article 4 makes provision about the treatment, on and after 7 March 2016, of a continuing approval for the purposes of this Part. In particular, it specifies what functions the approval is to be treated as relating to. Article 5 confers power on either regulator to impose further requirements about the form and content of a notice given in accordance with art 2. Article 6 requires a notice given in accordance with art 2 (or any revision of that notice) to be updated if there is a change relating to information given in, or accompanying, the notice. Article 7 makes provision to an authorised person to apply for the regulators to impose a condition on a continuing approval (or, if a condition has already been imposed, to vary or remove that condition). Article 8 requires that a statement of management responsibilities given under art 2 must be updated if there is any significant change in those responsibilities after 7 March 2016. Article 9 ensures that any steps taken by either regulator before 7 March 2016 in connection with the withdrawal of an approval continue to have effect on and after 7 March 2016. Article 10 suspends the period of time which the regulators have to consider such an application until the firm making the application has provided to the regulators a notice in accordance with art 11. Article 11 sets out the conditions for the continuation of an application on and after 7 March 2016, including provision of a notice referred to in art 10. Article 12 makes provision for the treatment of an application that continues on and after 7 March 2016. In particular, it specifies what functions the application is to be treated as relating to. Article 13 confers power on either regulator to impose further requirements about the form and content of an art 11 notice. Article 14 requires a notice given in accordance with art 11 to be updated if there is a change relating to information given in, or accompanying, the notice. Article 15 requires that a statement of responsibilities given under art 11 must be updated if there is any significant change in those responsibilities after 7 March 2016. Article 16 allows the PRA or the FCA, when determining an application which continues after 7 March 2016, to have regard to anything they could have had regard to if the application had been made on or after that date. Article 17 allows the regulators to specify which controlled functions that are specified on or after 7 March 2016 are, for the purposes of this Order, to be treated as equivalent to controlled functions that are specified before 7 March 2016. Article 18 provides that amendments made by the Financial Services (Banking Reform) Act 2013 to s 59 of this Act (or any rules made by the regulators) do not affect any prohibition made by either regulator before 7 March 2016 (and makes similar provision in relation to warning, decision and final notices given by a regulator in connection with a prohibition). Article 19 ensures that the regulators' powers to impose a penalty on a person for performing a controlled function without approval before 7th March 2016 is not affected by any rules made by the regulator which alter or replace the controlled function in question. Articles 20–23 contain miscellaneous provisions relating to rules and requirements imposed by a regulator under the Order, the giving of notices, consultation, and enforcement.

Prohibition orders

[1.1452]
56 Prohibition orders
[(1)   The FCA may make a prohibition order if it appears to it that an individual is not a fit and proper person to perform functions in relation to a regulated activity carried on by—
   (a)   an authorised person,
   (b)   a person who is an exempt person in relation to that activity, or
   (c)   a person to whom, as a result of Part 20, the general prohibition does not apply in relation to that activity.
(1A)   The PRA may make a prohibition order if it appears to it that an individual is not a fit and proper person to perform functions in relation to a regulated activity carried on by—
   (a)   a PRA-authorised person, or
   (b)   a person who is an exempt person in relation to a PRA-regulated activity carried on by the person.]
(2)   [A "prohibition order" is an order] prohibiting the individual from performing a specified function, any function falling within a specified description or any function.
(3)   A prohibition order may relate to—
   (a)   a specified regulated activity, any regulated activity falling within a specified description or all regulated activities;
   [(b)   all persons falling within subsection (3A) or a particular paragraph of that subsection or all persons within a specified class of person falling within a particular paragraph of that subsection.]
[(3A)   A person falls within this subsection if the person is—
   (a)   an authorised person,
   (b)   an exempt person, or
   (c)   a person to whom, as a result of Part 20, the general prohibition does not apply in relation to a regulated activity.]
(4)   An individual who performs or agrees to perform a function in breach of a prohibition order is guilty of an offence and liable on summary conviction to a fine not exceeding level 5 on the standard scale.
(5)   In proceedings for an offence under subsection (4) it is a defence for the accused to show that he took all reasonable precautions and exercised all due diligence to avoid committing the offence.
(6)   [A person falling within subsection (3A)] must take reasonable care to ensure that no function of his, in relation to the carrying on of a regulated activity, is performed by a person who is prohibited from performing that function by a prohibition order.
(7)   [The regulator that has made a prohibition order] may, on the application of the individual named in [the order], vary or revoke it.
[(7A)   If—
   (a)   the FCA proposes to vary or revoke a prohibition order, and
   (b)   as a result of the proposed variation or revocation, an individual—
      (i)   will no longer be prohibited from performing a function of interest to the PRA, or
      (ii)   will be prohibited from performing such a function,
the FCA must consult the PRA before varying or revoking the order.
(7B)   A function is of interest to the PRA if it is performed in relation to a regulated activity carried on by—
   (a)   a PRA-authorised person, or

    (b)   a person who is an exempt person in relation to a PRA-regulated activity carried on by the person.

(7C)   The PRA must consult the FCA before varying or revoking a prohibition order.]

(8)   . . .

(9)   "Specified" means specified in the prohibition order.

NOTES

   Sub-ss (1), (1A): substituted by the Financial Services Act 2012, s 13(1), (2),.
   Sub-ss (2), (6), (7): words in square brackets substituted by the Financial Services Act 2012, s 13(1), (3), (6), (7).
   Sub-s (3): para (b) substituted by the Financial Services Act 2012, s 13(1), (4).
   Sub-ss (3A), (7A)–(7C): inserted by the Financial Services Act 2012, s 13(1), (5), (8).
   Sub-s (8): repealed by the Financial Services Act 2012, s 13(1), (9).

[1.1453]
57 Prohibition orders: procedure and right to refer to Tribunal

(1)   If [a regulator] proposes to make a prohibition order it must give the individual concerned a warning notice.

(2)   The warning notice must set out the terms of the prohibition.

(3)   If [a regulator] decides to make a prohibition order it must give the individual concerned a decision notice.

(4)   The decision notice must—
    (a)   name the individual to whom the prohibition order applies;
    (b)   set out the terms of the order; and
    (c)   be given to the individual named in the order.

(5)   A person against whom a decision to make a prohibition order is made may refer the matter to the Tribunal.

[(6)   If—
    (a)   the FCA proposes to make a prohibition order, and
    (b)   as a result of the proposed order, an individual will be prohibited from performing a function of interest to the PRA,
the FCA must consult the PRA before giving a warning notice under this section.

(7)   A function is of interest to the PRA if it is performed in relation to a regulated activity carried on by—
    (a)   a PRA-authorised person, or
    (b)   a person who is an exempt person in relation to a PRA-regulated activity carried on by the person.

(8)   The PRA must consult the FCA before giving a warning notice under this section.]

NOTES

   Words in square brackets in sub-ss (1), (3) substituted, and sub-ss (6)–(8) added, by the Financial Services Act 2012, s 13(10)–(12).

[1.1454]
58 Applications relating to prohibitions: procedure and right to refer to Tribunal

(1)   This section applies to an application for the variation or revocation of a prohibition order.

(2)   If the [appropriate regulator] decides to grant the application, it must give the applicant written notice of its decision.

(3)   If the [appropriate regulator] proposes to refuse the application, it must give the applicant a warning notice.

(4)   If the [appropriate regulator] decides to refuse the application, it must give the applicant a decision notice.

(5)   If the [appropriate regulator] gives the applicant a decision notice, he may refer the matter to the Tribunal.

[(6)   The "appropriate regulator" means the regulator to which the application is made.]

NOTES

   Words in square brackets in sub-ss (2)–(5) substituted, and sub-s (6) added, by the Financial Services Act 2012, s 15, Sch 5, paras 1, 2.

Approval

[1.1455]
59 Approval for particular arrangements

(1)   An authorised person ("A") must take reasonable care to ensure that no person performs a controlled function under an arrangement entered into by A in relation to the carrying on by A of a regulated activity, unless *[the appropriate regulator]* approves the performance by that person of the controlled function to which the arrangement relates.

(2)   An authorised person ("A") must take reasonable care to ensure that no person performs a controlled function under an arrangement entered into by a contractor of A in relation to the carrying on by A of a regulated activity, unless *[the appropriate regulator]* approves the performance by that person of the controlled function to which the arrangement relates.

[(3)   Controlled function"—
  (a)   in relation to the carrying on of a regulated activity by a PRA-authorised person, means a function of a description specified in rules made by the FCA or the PRA, and
  (b)   in relation to the carrying on of a regulated activity by any other authorised person, means a function of a description specified in rules made by the FCA.
(4)   "The appropriate regulator"—
  (a)   in relation to a controlled function which is of a description specified in rules made by the FCA, means the FCA, and
  (b)   in relation to a controlled function which is of a description specified in rules made by the PRA, means the PRA with the consent of the FCA.
(5)   The FCA may specify a description of function under subsection (3)(a) or (b) only if, in relation to the carrying on of a regulated activity by an authorised person, it is satisfied that the function is—
  (a)   a customer-dealing function, or
  (b)   a significant-influence function.
(6)   The PRA may specify a description of function under subsection (3)(a) only if, in relation to the carrying on of a regulated activity by a PRA-authorised person, it is satisfied that the function is a significant-influence function.
[(6A)   If—
  (a)   a function of a description specified in rules made by the FCA under subsection (3)(a) or (b) is a controlled function in relation to the carrying on of a regulated activity by a relevant authorised person, and
  (b)   the FCA is satisfied that, in relation to the carrying on of a regulated activity by a relevant authorised person, the function is a senior management function as defined in section 59ZA,
the FCA must designate the function in the rules as a senior management function.
(6B)   If a function of a description specified in rules made by the PRA under subsection (3)(a) is a controlled function in relation to the carrying on of a regulated activity by a relevant authorised person, the PRA must designate the function in the rules as a senior management function.
(6C)   For the meaning of "relevant authorised person", see section 71A.]
(7)   In determining whether a function is a significant-influence function, the FCA or the PRA may take into account the likely consequences of a failure to discharge the function properly.
(7A)   "Customer-dealing function", in relation to the carrying on of a regulated activity by an authorised person ("A"), means a function that will involve the person performing it in dealing with—
  (a)   customers of A, or
  (b)   property of customers of A,
in a manner substantially connected with the carrying on of the activity.
(7B)   "Significant-influence function", in relation to the carrying on of a regulated activity by an authorised person, means a function that is likely to enable the person responsible for its performance to exercise a significant influence on the conduct of the authorised person's affairs, so far as relating to the activity.]
[(7C)   A regulator may not exercise the power in subsection (3) so as to provide for a function to be a controlled function in relation to the carrying on of the regulated activity of managing an AIF by an AIFM which—
  (a)   is also an AIF;
  (b)   does not manage any AIF other than itself;
  (c)   is a body corporate; and
  (d)   is not a collective investment scheme.]
(8)   Neither subsection (1) nor subsection (2) applies to an arrangement which allows a person to perform a function if the question of whether he is a fit and proper person to perform the function is reserved under any of the single market directives [or the emission allowance auctioning regulation] to an authority in a country or territory outside the United Kingdom.
(9)   . . .
(10)   "Arrangement"—
  (a)   means any kind of arrangement for the performance of a function of A which is entered into by A or any contractor of his with another person; and
  (b)   includes, in particular, that other person's appointment to an office, his becoming a partner or his employment (whether under a contract of service or otherwise).
(11)   "Customer", in relation to an authorised person, means a person who is using, or who is or may be contemplating using, any of the services provided by the authorised person.

NOTES

Words in square brackets in sub-ss (1), (2) substituted, and sub-ss (3)–(7B) substituted (for the original sub-ss (3)–(7)), by the Financial Services Act 2012, s 14(1).

For the words in italics in sub-ss (1) and (2) there are substituted the words "that person is acting in accordance with an approval given by the appropriate regulator under this section" by the Financial Services (Banking Reform) Act 2013, s 35, Sch 3, para 1, as from 7 March 2016.

Sub-ss (5), (7)–(7B) and (11) are repealed, sub-s (6) is substituted (as follows), and sub-ss (6A)–(6C) are inserted, by the Financial Services (Banking Reform) Act 2013, s 18, as from 25 July 2014 (for the purpose of the making of rules), and as from

7 March 2016 (otherwise)—

"(6) The PRA may specify a description of function under subsection (3)(a) only if, in relation to the carrying on of a regulated activity by a PRA-authorised person, it is satisfied that the function is a senior management function as defined in section 59ZA.".

Sub-s (7C) was inserted by the Alternative Investment Fund Managers Regulations 2013, SI 2013/1773, reg 80, Sch 1, Part 1, paras 1, 7, for transitional provisions and savings see Part 9 of the 2013 Regulations).

Sub-s (8): words in square brackets inserted by the Financial Services and Markets Act 2000 (Regulated Activities) (Amendment) Order 2012, SI 2012/1906, art 3(1), (4).

Sub-s (9): repealed by the Financial Services Act 2012, s 15, Sch 5, paras 1, 3.

[1.1456]
[59ZA Senior management functions

(1) This section has effect for determining whether a function is for the purposes of section 59(6) or (6A) a senior management function.

(2) A function is a "senior management function", in relation to the carrying on of a regulated activity by an authorised person, if—

    (a) the function will require the person performing it to be responsible for managing one or more aspects of the authorised person's affairs, so far as relating to the activity, and

    (b) those aspects involve, or might involve, a risk of serious consequences—

        (i) for the authorised person, or

        (ii) for business or other interests in the United Kingdom.

(3) In subsection (2)(a) the reference to managing one or more aspects of an authorised person's affairs includes a reference to taking decisions, or participating in the taking of decisions, about how one or more aspects of those affairs should be carried on.]

NOTES

Commencement: 25 July 2014.

Inserted by the Financial Services (Banking Reform) Act 2013, s 19.

[1.1457]
[59A Specifying functions as controlled functions: supplementary

(1) The FCA must—

    (a) keep under review the exercise of its power under section 59(3)(a) to specify any *significant-influence* function as a controlled function, and

    (b) exercise that power in a way that it considers will minimise the likelihood that approvals fall to be given by both the FCA and the PRA in respect of the performance by a person of *significant-influence* functions in relation to the carrying on of a regulated activity by the same PRA-authorised person.

(2) The FCA and the PRA must each consult the other before exercising any power under section 59(3)(a).

(3) Any reference in this section to the exercise of a power includes its exercise by way of amendment or revocation of provision previously made in the exercise of the power.

[(3A) Senior management function" has the meaning given by section 59ZA.]

(4) "Approval" means an approval under section 59.

(5) Any expression which is used both in this section and section 59 has the same meaning in this section as in that section.]

NOTES

Commencement: 1 April 2013.

Inserted, together with s 59B, by the Financial Services Act 2012, s 14(2).

For the words in italics in sub-s (1) there are substituted the words "senior management", and sub-s (3A) is inserted, by the Financial Services (Banking Reform) Act 2013, s 35, Sch 3, para 2, as from 25 July 2014 (for the purpose of the making of rules), and as from 7 March 2016 (otherwise).

[1.1458]
[59B Role of FCA in relation to PRA decisions

(1) The FCA may arrange with the PRA that in such cases as may be described in the arrangements the PRA may give approval under section 59 without obtaining the consent of the FCA.

(2) Arrangements under this section must be in writing, and must specify the date on which they come into force.

(3) The regulators must publish any arrangements under this section in such manner as they think fit.

(4) Section 59(4)(b) has effect subject to any arrangements in force under this section.]

NOTES

Commencement: 24 January 2013 (for the purpose of making arrangements); 1 April 2013 (otherwise).

Inserted as noted to s 59A at **[1.1457]**.

[1.1459]
60 Applications for approval

(1) An application for the [appropriate regulator's] approval under section 59 may be made by the authorised person concerned.

(2) The application must—
 (a) be made in such manner as the [appropriate regulator] may direct; and
 (b) contain, or be accompanied by, such information as the [appropriate regulator] may reasonably require.

[(2A) If—
 (a) the application is for the approval of a person to perform a designated senior management function, and
 (b) the authorised person concerned is a relevant authorised person (see section 71A),
the appropriate regulator must require the application to contain, or be accompanied by, a statement setting out the aspects of the affairs of the authorised person concerned which it is intended that the person will be responsible for managing in performing the function.

(2B) A statement provided under subsection (2A) is known as a "statement of responsibilities".

(2C) In subsection (2A) "designated senior management function" means a function designated as a senior management function under section 59(6A) or (6B).]

[(3) At any time after the application is received and before it is determined, the appropriate regulator may require the applicant to provide it with such further information as it reasonably considers necessary to enable it to determine the application or, as the case requires, to decide whether to give consent.]

(4) The [appropriate regulator] may require an applicant to present information which he is required to give under this section in such form, or to verify it in such a way, as the [appropriate regulator] may direct.

(5) Different directions may be given, and different requirements imposed, in relation to different applications or categories of application.

(6) "The authorised person concerned" includes a person who has applied for permission under [Part 4A] and will be the authorised person concerned if permission is given.

[(6A) Subsection (6) applies to references to a relevant authorised person as it applies to references to the authorised person concerned.]

[(7) The PRA must consult the FCA before—
 (a) giving a direction under subsection (2)(a) in relation to a class of applicants, or
 (b) imposing a requirement under subsection (2)(b) on a class of applicants.

(8) The PRA must as soon as practicable notify the FCA of the receipt or withdrawal of an application to the PRA, unless the case is one in which by virtue of arrangements under section 59B the consent of the FCA is not required.

(9) "The appropriate regulator"—
 (a) in relation to a controlled function which is of a description specified in rules made by the FCA, means the FCA;
 (b) in relation to a controlled function which is of a description specified in rules made by the PRA, means the PRA, and for the purposes of subsection (3) also includes the FCA in cases where the consent of the FCA is required.]

NOTES

Words in square brackets in sub-ss (1), (2), (4), (6) substituted, sub-s (3) substituted, and sub-ss (7)–(9) added, by the Financial Services Act 2012, s 15, Sch 5, paras 1, 4.

Sub-ss (2A)–(2C), (6A): inserted by the Financial Services (Banking Reform) Act 2013, s 20, as from 25 July 2014 (for the purpose of giving directions or imposing requirements), and as from 7 March 2016 (otherwise).

The authorised person concerned: as to the meaning of this, see also the Financial Services and Markets Act 2000 (EEA Passport Rights) Regulations 2001, SI 2001/2511, reg 10.

[1.1460]
[60A Vetting of candidates by relevant authorised persons

(1) Before a relevant authorised person may make an application for a regulator's approval under section 59, the authorised person must be satisfied that the person in respect of whom the application is made ("the candidate") is a fit and proper person to perform the function to which the application relates.

(2) In deciding that question, the authorised person must have regard, in particular, to whether the candidate, or any person who may perform a function on the candidate's behalf—
 (a) has obtained a qualification,
 (b) has undergone, or is undergoing, training,
 (c) possesses a level of competence, or
 (d) has the personal characteristics,
required by general rules made by the regulator in relation to persons performing functions of the kind to which the application relates.

(3) For the meaning of "relevant authorised person", see section 71A.]

NOTES
Commencement: 7 March 2016.

Inserted by the Financial Services (Banking Reform) Act 2013, s 21, as from 7 March 2016.

[1.1461]
61 Determination of applications
(1) [The regulator to which an application is made under section 60 may grant the application]
only if it is satisfied that the person in respect of whom the application is made ("the candidate")
is a fit and proper person to perform the function to which the application relates.
(2) In *deciding that question,* [the regulator] may have regard (among other things) to whether the
candidate, or any person who may perform a function on his behalf—
    (a)   has obtained a qualification,
    (b)   has undergone, or is undergoing, training, *or*
    (c)   possesses a level of competence, [or
    (d)   has the personal characteristics,]
required by general rules [made by that regulator] in relation to persons performing functions of the
kind to which the application relates.
[(2A)   Subsections (1) and (2) apply in relation to the giving by the FCA of any required consent
as they apply in relation to the grant of the application.]
[(2B)   The regulator to which a relevant senior management application is made under
section 60 may in particular—
    (a)   grant the application subject to any conditions that the regulator considers appropriate, and
    (b)   grant the application so as to give approval only for a limited period.
(2C)   A regulator may exercise the power under paragraph (a) or (b) of subsection (2B) only if—
    (a)   where the regulator is the FCA, it appears to the FCA that it is desirable to do so in order to
       advance one or more of its operational objectives, and
    (b)   where the regulator is the PRA, it appears to the PRA that it is desirable to do so in order to
       advance any of its objectives.
(2D)   Consent given by the FCA for the granting of the application may be conditional on the
manner in which the PRA exercises its power under subsection (2B).]
(3)   [The regulator to which an application is made under section 60 must, before the end of the
period for consideration, determine] whether—
    (a)   to grant the application; or
    (b)   to give a warning notice under section 62(2).
[(3ZA)   In the case of a relevant senior management application, the reference in subsection (3)(a)
to granting the application is a reference to granting it without imposing conditions or limiting the
period for which the approval has effect.]
[(3A)   The period for consideration"—
    (a)   in any case where the application under section 60 is made by a person applying for
       permission under Part 4A (see section 60(6)), means whichever ends last of—
       (i)   the period within which the application for that permission must be determined under
          section 55V(1) or (2), and
       (ii)   the period of 3 months beginning with the date on which the regulator receives the
          application under section 60, and
    (b)   in any other case, means the period of 3 months beginning with the date on which the
       regulator receives the application under section 60.]
(4)   If [a regulator] imposes a requirement under section 60(3), the period for consideration stops
running on the day on which the requirement is imposed but starts running again—
    (a)   on the day on which the required information is received by [a regulator]; or
    (b)   if the information is not provided on a single day, on the last of the days on which it is
       received by [a regulator].
(5)   A person who makes an application under section 60 may withdraw his application by giving
written notice to the [regulator to which the application was made] at any time before the
[regulator] determines it, but only with the consent of—
    (a)   the candidate; and
    (b)   the person by whom the candidate is to be retained to perform the function concerned, if
       not the applicant.
[(6)   In this section—
    (a)   "designated senior management function" means a function designated as a senior
       management function under section 59(6A) or (6B);
    (b)   any reference to a relevant authorised person includes a reference to a person who has
       applied for permission under Part 4A and will be a relevant authorised person if permission
       is given.
(7)   For the meaning of "relevant authorised person", see section 71A.]

NOTES
Sub-s (1): words in square brackets substituted by the Financial Services Act 2012, s 15, Sch 5, paras 1, 5(1), (2). This
subsection is substituted by the Financial Services (Banking Reform) Act 2013, s 23(1), (2), as from 7 March 2016, as follows—

"(1)   The regulator to which an application for approval is made under section 60 may grant the application only if—
    (a)   it is satisfied that the person in respect of whom the application is made ("the candidate") is a fit and proper
       person to perform the function to which the application relates, or

(b)   in a case where the application is for approval to perform a designated senior management function in relation to the carrying on of a regulated activity by a relevant authorised person (a "relevant senior management application"), it is satisfied that the condition in paragraph (a) will be met if the application is granted subject to one or more conditions (as to which, see subsection (2B)).".

Sub-s (2): for the first words in italics there are substituted the words "determining the application" by the Financial Services (Banking Reform) Act 2013, s 23(1), (3), as from 7 March 2016; words in first pair of square brackets substituted, and words in final pair of square brackets inserted, by the Financial Services Act 2012, s 15, Sch 5, paras 1, 5(1), (3); the word in italics in para (b) is repealed, and para (d) (and the preceding word) is inserted, by the Financial Services (Banking Reform) Act 2013, s 22, as from 7 March 2016.

Sub-ss (2A), (3A): inserted by the Financial Services Act 2012, s 15, Sch 5, paras 1, 5(1), (4), (6).

Sub-ss (2B)–(2D), (3ZA), (6), (7): inserted and added respectively by the Financial Services (Banking Reform) Act 2013, s 23(1), (4)–(6), as from 7 March 2016.

Sub-ss (3)–(5): words in square brackets substituted by the Financial Services Act 2012, s 15, Sch 5, paras 1, 5(1), (5), (7), (8).

[1.1462]
62   Applications for approval: procedure and right to refer to Tribunal
(1)   [If the regulator to which an application is made under section 60 ("an application") decides to grant the application, it] must give written notice of its decision to each of the interested parties.
(2)   If [the regulator to which an application is made] proposes to refuse [the application][, or to grant the application subject to conditions or for a limited period (or both)], it must give a warning notice to each of the interested parties.
(3)   If [the regulator to which an application is made] decides to refuse [the application][, or to grant the application subject to conditions or for a limited period (or both)], it must give a decision notice to each of the interested parties.
(4)   If [the regulator to which an application is made] decides to refuse [the application][, or to grant the application subject to conditions or for a limited period (or both)], each of the interested parties may refer the matter to the Tribunal.
(5)   "The interested parties", in relation to an application, are—
    (a)   the applicant;
    (b)   the person in respect of whom the application is made ("A"); and
    (c)   the person by whom A's services are to be retained, if not the applicant.

NOTES
The words ", or to grant the application subject to conditions or for a limited period (or both)" in square brackets in sub-ss (2)–(4) are inserted by the Financial Services (Banking Reform) Act 2013, s 23(7), as from 7 March 2016; all other words in square brackets in this section were substituted by the Financial Services Act 2012, s 15, Sch 5, paras 1, 6.

[1.1463]
[62A   Changes in responsibilities of senior managers
(1)   This section applies where—
    (a)   an authorised person has made an application to the appropriate regulator for approval under section 59 for a person to perform a designated senior management function,
    (b)   the application contained, or was accompanied by, a statement of responsibilities under section 60(2A), and
    (c)   the application has been granted.
(2)   If, since the granting of the application, there has been any significant change in the aspects of the authorised person's affairs which the person is responsible for managing in performing the function, the authorised person must provide the appropriate regulator with a revised statement of responsibilities.
(3)   The appropriate regulator may require the authorised person—
    (a)   to provide information which the person is required to give under this section in such form as the appropriate regulator may direct, or
    (b)   to verify such information in such a way as the appropriate regulator may direct.
(4)   In this section—
    "the appropriate regulator" has the same meaning as in section 60;
    "designated senior management function" means a function designated as a senior management function under section 59(6A) or (6B).]

NOTES
Commencement: 7 March 2016.
Inserted by the Financial Services (Banking Reform) Act 2013, s 24, as from 7 March 2016.

[1.1464]
63   Withdrawal of approval
[(1)   The FCA may withdraw an approval under section 59 given by the FCA or the PRA in relation to the performance by a person of a function if the FCA considers that the person is not a fit and proper person to perform the function.
(1A)   The PRA may withdraw an approval under section 59 in relation to the performance by a person ("A") of a function if—

(a)   the PRA gave the approval, or the FCA gave the approval and the function is a *significant-influence function* performed in relation to the carrying on by a PRA-authorised person of a regulated activity, and

(b)   the PRA considers that A is not a fit and proper person to perform the function.

(1B)   "Significant-influence function" has the same meaning as in section 59.

(1C)   Before one regulator withdraws an approval given by the other regulator, it must consult the other regulator.]

(2)   When considering whether to withdraw [an approval, the FCA or the PRA may take into account any matter which could be taken into account in] considering an application made under section 60 in respect of the performance of the function to which the approval relates [(on the assumption, if it is not the case, that the application was one falling to be considered by it)].

[(2A)   At least once a year each relevant authorised person must, in relation to every person in relation to whom an approval has been given on the application of the authorised person—

(a)   consider whether there are any grounds on which a regulator could withdraw the approval under this section, and

(b)   if the authorised person is of the opinion that there are such grounds, notify the regulator of those grounds.

(For the meaning of "relevant authorised person", see section 71A.)]

(3)   If [a regulator] proposes to withdraw [an approval], it must give each of the interested parties a warning notice.

(4)   If [a regulator] decides to withdraw [an approval], it must give each of the interested parties a decision notice.

(5)   If [a regulator] decides to withdraw [an approval], each of the interested parties may refer the matter to the Tribunal.

(6)   "The interested parties", in relation to an approval, are—

(a)   the person on whose application it was given ("A");

(b)   the person in respect of whom it was given ("B"); and

(c)   the person by whom B's services are retained, if not A.

NOTES

Sub-ss (1)–(1C): substituted (for the original sub-s (1)) by the Financial Services Act 2012, s 14(3). For the words in italics in sub-s (1A) there are substituted the words "relevant senior management function", and sub-s (1B) is substituted (as follows), by the Financial Services (Banking Reform) Act 2013, s 35, Sch 3, para 3, as from 7 March 2016—

"(1B)   In subsection (1A) "relevant senior management function" means a function which the PRA is satisfied is a senior management function as defined in section 59ZA (whether or not the function has been designated as such by the FCA).".

Sub-s (2): words in first pair of square brackets substituted, and words in second pair of square brackets inserted, by the Financial Services Act 2012, s 15, Sch 5, paras 1, 7(1), (2).

Sub-s (2A): inserted by the Financial Services (Banking Reform) Act 2013, s 25, as from 7 March 2016.

Sub-ss (3)–(5): words in square brackets substituted by the Financial Services Act 2012, s 15, Sch 5, paras 1, 7(1), (3).

[1.1465]
[63ZA   Variation of senior manager's approval at request of relevant authorised person

(1)   Where an application for approval under section 59 is granted subject to conditions, the authorised person concerned may apply to the appropriate regulator to vary the approval by—

(a)   varying a condition,

(b)   removing a condition, or

(c)   imposing a new condition.

(2)   "The appropriate regulator"—

(a)   in the case of an application for variation of an approval in a way described in subsection (1)(a) or (b), means whichever of the FCA or the PRA imposed the condition concerned;

(b)   in the case of an application for variation of an approval in the way described in subsection (1)(c), means the regulator who gave the approval.

(3)   The PRA must consult the FCA before determining an application under this section, unless the application relates to the variation or removal of a condition which was imposed by the PRA in exercise of its power under section 63ZB.

(4)   The regulator to which an application is made under this section must, before the end of the period for consideration, determine whether—

(a)   to grant the application; or

(b)   to give a warning notice under section 62(2).

(5)   "The period for consideration" means the period of 3 months beginning with the date on which the regulator receives the application.

(6)   The FCA may refuse an application under this section if it appears to the FCA that it is desirable to do so in order to advance one or more of its operational objectives.

(7)   The PRA may refuse an application under this section if it appears to the PRA that it is desirable to do so in order to advance any of its objectives.

(8)   The following provisions apply to an application made under this section for variation of an approval as they apply to an application for approval made under section 60—

section 60(2) to (8),

section 61(4) and (5),

section 62.]

NOTES
Commencement: 7 March 2016.
Inserted, together with ss 63ZB, 63ZC, by the Financial Services (Banking Reform) Act 2013, s 26, as from 7 March 2016.

[1.1466]
[63ZB Variation of senior manager's approval on initiative of regulator
(1)   The FCA may vary an approval under section 59 given by the FCA or the PRA for the performance of a designated senior management function in relation to the carrying on of a regulated activity by a relevant authorised person if the FCA considers that it is desirable to do so in order to advance one or more of its operational objectives.
(2)   The PRA may vary an approval under section 59 for the performance of a designated senior management function in relation to the carrying on of a regulated activity by a relevant authorised person if—
   (a)   either—
      (i)   the PRA gave the approval, or
      (ii) the FCA gave the approval and the relevant authorised person is a PRA-authorised person, and
   (b)   the PRA considers that it is desirable to do so in order to advance any of its objectives.
(3)   A regulator may vary an approval by—
   (a)   imposing a condition,
   (b)   varying a condition,
   (c)   removing a condition, or
   (d)   limiting the period for which the approval is to have effect.
(4)   Before one regulator varies an approval given by the other regulator, it must consult the other regulator.
(5)   In this section "designated senior management function" means a function designated as a senior management function under section 59(6A) or (6B).
(6)   For the meaning of "relevant authorised person", see section 71A.]

NOTES
Commencement: 7 March 2016.
Inserted as noted to s 63ZA at **[1.1465]**.

[1.1467]
[63ZC Exercise of power under section 63ZB: procedure
(1)   This section applies to an exercise, by either regulator, of the power to vary an approval under section 63ZB.
(2)   A variation takes effect—
   (a)   immediately, if the notice given under subsection (4) states that that is the case,
   (b)   on such date as is specified in the notice, or
   (c)   if no date is specified in the notice, when the matter to which the notice relates is no longer open to review.
(3)   A variation may be expressed to take effect immediately (or on a specified date) only if the regulator concerned, having regard to the ground on which it is exercising the power to vary, reasonably considers that it is necessary for the variation to take effect immediately (or on that date).
(4)   If either regulator proposes to vary an approval or varies an approval with immediate effect, it must give each of the interested parties written notice.
(5)   The notice must—
   (a)   give details of the variation,
   (b)   state the regulator's reasons for the variation,
   (c)   inform the interested parties that each of them may make representations to the regulator within such period as may be specified in the notice (whether or not any of the interested parties has referred the matter to the Tribunal),
   (d)   inform the interested parties of when the variation takes effect, and
   (e)   inform the interested parties of the right of each of them to refer the matter to the Tribunal.
(6)   "The interested parties", in relation to an approval, are—
   (a)   the person on whose application it was given ("A"),
   (b)   the person in respect of whom it was given ("B"), and
   (c)   the person by whom B's services are retained, if not A.
(7)   The regulator giving the notice may extend the period allowed under the notice for making representations.
(8)   If having considered the representations made by the interested parties, the regulator decides—
   (a)   to vary the approval, or
   (b)   if the variation has taken effect, not to rescind it,
it must give each of the interested parties written notice.

(9)   If having considered the representations made by the interested parties, the regulator decides—

(a)   not to vary the approval,

(b)   to vary the approval in a different way, or

(c)   if the variation has taken effect, to rescind it,

it must give each of the interested parties written notice.

(10)   A notice under subsection (8) must inform the interested parties of the right of each of them to refer the matter to the Tribunal.

(11)   A notice under subsection (9)(b) must comply with subsection (5).

(12)   If a notice informs the interested parties of the right to refer a matter to the Tribunal, it must give an indication of the procedure on such a reference.

(13)   For the purposes of subsection (2)(c), whether a matter is open to review is to be determined in accordance with section 391(8).

(14)   "Approval" means an approval under section 59.]

NOTES

Commencement: 7 March 2016.

Inserted as noted to s 63ZA at **[1.1465]**.

[1.1468]

[63ZD   Statement of policy relating to conditional approval and variation

(1)   Each regulator must prepare and issue a statement of its policy with respect to—

(a)   its giving of approval under section 59 subject to conditions or for a limited period only, and

(b)   its variation under section 63ZA or 63ZB of an approval given under section 59.

(2)   A regulator may at any time alter or replace a statement issued by it under this section.

(3)   If a statement issued under this section is altered or replaced by a regulator, the regulator must issue the altered or replacement statement.

(4)   A statement issued under this section must be published by the regulator concerned in the way appearing to the regulator to be best calculated to bring it to the attention of the public.

(5)   A regulator may charge a reasonable fee for providing a person with a copy of a statement published under this section.

(6)   A regulator must, without delay, give the Treasury a copy of any statement which it publishes under this section.]

NOTES

Commencement: 25 July 2014.

Inserted, together with s 63ZE, by the Financial Services (Banking Reform) Act 2013, s 27.

[1.1469]

[63ZE   Statement of policy: procedure

(1)   Before issuing a statement of policy under section 63ZD, a regulator ("the issuing regulator") must—

(a)   consult the other regulator, and

(b)   publish a draft of the proposed statement in the way appearing to the issuing regulator to be best calculated to bring it to the attention of the public.

(2)   The duty of the FCA to consult the PRA under subsection (1)(a) applies only in so far as the statement of policy applies to persons whose approval under section 59 relates to the performance of a function designated by the FCA as a senior management function under section 59(6A) in relation to the carrying on by PRA-authorised persons of regulated activities.

(3)   The draft must be accompanied by notice that representations about the proposal may be made to the issuing regulator within a specified time.

(4)   Before issuing the proposed statement, the issuing regulator must have regard to any representations made to it in accordance with subsection (3).

(5)   If the issuing regulator issues the proposed statement it must publish an account, in general terms, of—

(a)   the representations made to it in accordance with subsection (3), and

(b)   its response to them.

(6)   If the statement differs from the draft published under subsection (1) in a way which is in the opinion of the issuing regulator significant, the issuing regulator—

(a)   must before issuing it carry out any consultation required by subsection (1)(a), and

(b)   must (in addition to complying with subsection (5)) publish details of the difference.

(7)   The issuing regulator may charge a reasonable fee for providing a person with a draft published under subsection (1)(b).

(8)   This section also applies to a proposal to alter or replace a statement.]

NOTES

Commencement: 25 July 2014.

Inserted as noted to s 63ZD at **[1.1468]**.

[Performance of controlled functions without approval

[1.1470]
63A   Power to impose penalties
(1)   If the [appropriate regulator] is satisfied that—
   (a)   a person ("P") has at any time performed a controlled function without approval, and
   (b)   at that time P knew, or could reasonably be expected to have known, that P was performing a controlled function without approval,
it may impose a penalty on P of such amount as it considers appropriate.
(2)   For the purposes of this section P performs a controlled function without approval at any time if at that time—
   (a)   P performs a controlled function under an arrangement entered into by an authorised person ("A"), or by a contractor of A, in relation to the carrying on by A of a regulated activity; and
   (b)   *the performance by P of the function was not approved under section 59.*
(3)   The [appropriate regulator] may not impose a penalty under this section after the end of the limitation period unless, before the end of that period, it has given a warning notice to the person concerned under section 63B(1).
(4)   "The limitation period" means the [relevant period] beginning with the first day on which the [appropriate regulator] knew that the person concerned had performed a controlled function without approval.
(5)   For this purpose the [appropriate regulator] is to be treated as knowing that a person has performed a controlled function without approval if it has information from which that can reasonably be inferred.
[(5A)   The appropriate regulator"—
   (a)   in relation to a controlled function which is of a description specified in rules made by the FCA, means the FCA, and
   (b)   in relation to a controlled function which is of a description specified in rules made by the PRA, means the PRA.]
[(5B)   The relevant period" is—
   (a)   in relation to the performance of a controlled function without approval before the day on which this subsection comes into force, the period of 3 years, and
   (b)   in relation to the performance of a controlled function without approval on or after that day, the period of 6 years.]
(6)   Any [other] expression which is used both in this section and section 59 has the same meaning in this section as in that section.]

NOTES
Inserted, together with the preceding heading and ss 63B–63D, by the Financial Services Act 2010, s 11.
Words "appropriate regulator" in square brackets (in each place that they occur) substituted, and sub-s (5A) and the word in square brackets in sub-s (6) inserted, by the Financial Services Act 2012, s 15, Sch 5, paras 1, 8.
Sub-s (2)(b) substituted by the Financial Services (Banking Reform) Act 2013, s 35, Sch 3, para 4, as from 7 March 2016, as follows—

    "(b)   P, when performing the function, is not acting in accordance with an approval given under section 59.".

Words "relevant period" in square brackets in sub-s (4) substituted, and sub-s (5B) inserted, by the Financial Services (Banking Reform) Act 2013, s 28(1)–(3).

[1.1471]
[63B   Procedure and right to refer to Tribunal
(1)   If [a regulator] proposes to impose a penalty on a person under section 63A, it must give the person a warning notice.
(2)   A warning notice must state the amount of the penalty.
(3)   If [a regulator] decides to impose a penalty on a person under section 63A, it must give the person a decision notice.
(4)   A decision notice must state the amount of the penalty.
(5)   If [a regulator] decides to impose a penalty on a person under section 63A, the person may refer the matter to the Tribunal.]

NOTES
Inserted as noted to s 63A at **[1.1470]**.
Words in square brackets substituted by the Financial Services Act 2012, s 15, Sch 5, paras 1, 9.

[1.1472]
[63C   Statement of policy
(1)   [Each regulator] must prepare and issue a statement of its policy with respect to—
   (a)   the imposition of penalties under section 63A; and
   (b)   the amount of penalties under that section.
(2)   [Each regulator's] policy in determining whether a penalty should be imposed, and what the amount of a penalty should be, must include having regard to—
   (a)   the conduct of the person on whom the penalty is to be imposed;

(b)   the extent to which the person could reasonably be expected to have known that a controlled function was performed without approval;

(c)   the length of the period during which the person performed a controlled function without approval; and

(d)   whether the person on whom the penalty is to be imposed is an individual.

(3) [Each regulator's] policy in determining whether a penalty should be imposed on a person must also include having regard to the appropriateness of taking action against the person instead of, or in addition to, taking action against an authorised person.

(4) A statement issued under this section must include an indication of the circumstances in which [the regulator that has issued the statement] would expect to be satisfied that a person could reasonably be expected to have known that the person was performing a controlled function without approval.

(5) [A regulator] may at any time alter or replace a statement issued [by it] under this section.

(6) If a statement issued under this section is altered or [replaced by a regulator, the regulator] must issue the altered or replaced statement.

(7) [A regulator] must, without delay, give the Treasury a copy of any statement which it publishes under this section.

(8) A statement issued under this section [by a regulator] must be published by the [regulator] in the way appearing to the [regulator] to be best calculated to bring it to the attention of the public.

(9) The [regulator] may charge a reasonable fee for providing a person with a copy of the statement.

(10) In exercising, or deciding whether to exercise, its power under section 63A in the case of any particular person, [a regulator] must have regard to any statement of policy published [by it] under this section and in force at a time when the person concerned performed a controlled function without approval.]

NOTES

Inserted as noted to s 63A at [**1.1470**].

The words "by it" in square brackets in sub-ss (5) and (10) and the words "by a regulator" in square brackets in sub-s (8) were inserted, and all other words in square brackets in this section were substituted, by the Financial Services Act 2012, s 15, Sch 5, paras 1, 10.

[1.1473]
[63D Statement of policy: procedure

(1) Before [a regulator issues] a statement under section 63C, the [regulator] must publish a draft of the proposed statement in the way appearing to the [regulator] to be best calculated to bring it to the attention of the public.

(2) The draft must be accompanied by notice that representations about the proposal may be made to the [regulator] within a specified time.

(3) Before issuing the proposed statement, the [regulator] must have regard to any representations made to it in accordance with subsection (2).

(4) If the [regulator] issues the proposed statement it must publish an account, in general terms, of—

(a)   the representations made to it in accordance with subsection (2); and

(b)   its response to them.

(5) If the statement differs from the draft published under subsection (1) in a way which is, in the opinion of the [regulator], significant, the [regulator] must (in addition to complying with subsection (4)) publish details of the difference.

(6) [A regulator] may charge a reasonable fee for providing a person with a copy of a draft published [by it] under subsection (1).

(7) This section also applies to a proposal to alter or replace a statement.]

NOTES

Inserted as noted to s 63A at [**1.1470**].

The words "by it" in square brackets in sub-s (6) were inserted, and all other words in square brackets in this section were substituted, by the Financial Services Act 2012, s 15, Sch 5, paras 1, 11.

[Certification of employees

[1.1474]
63E Certification of employees by relevant authorised persons

(1) A relevant authorised person ("A") must take reasonable care to ensure that no employee of A performs a specified function under an arrangement entered into by A in relation to the carrying on by A of a regulated activity, unless the employee has a valid certificate issued by A under section 63F.

(2) "Specified function"—

(a)   in relation to the carrying on of a regulated activity by a PRA-authorised person, means a function of a description specified in rules made by the FCA or the PRA, and

(b)   in relation to the carrying on of a regulated activity by any other authorised person, means a function of a description specified in rules made by the FCA.

(3)   The FCA may specify a description of function under subsection (2)(a) or (b) only if, in relation to the carrying on of a regulated activity by a relevant authorised person of a particular description—

(a)   the function is not a controlled function in relation to the carrying on of that activity by a relevant authorised person of that description, but

(b)   the FCA is satisfied that the function is nevertheless a significant-harm function.

(4)   The PRA may specify a description of function under subsection (2)(a) only if, in relation to the carrying on of a regulated activity by a relevant PRA-authorised person of a particular description—

(a)   the function is not a controlled function in relation to the carrying on of that activity by a relevant PRA-authorised person of that description, but

(b)   the PRA is satisfied that the function is nevertheless a significant-harm function.

(5)   A function is a "significant-harm function", in relation to the carrying on of a regulated activity by an authorised person, if—

(a)   the function will require the person performing it to be involved in one or more aspects of the authorised person's affairs, so far as relating to the activity, and

(b)   those aspects involve, or might involve, a risk of significant harm to the authorised person or any of its customers.

(6)   Each regulator must—

(a)   keep under review the exercise of its power under subsection (2) to specify any significant-harm function as a specified function, and

(b)   exercise that power in a way that it considers will minimise the risk of employees of relevant authorised persons performing significant-harm functions which they are not fit and proper persons to perform.

(7)   Subsection (1) does not apply to an arrangement which allows an employee to perform a function if the question of whether the employee is a fit and proper person to perform the function is reserved under any of the single market directives or the emission allowance auctioning regulation to an authority in a country or territory outside the United Kingdom.

(8)   In this section—

"controlled function" has the meaning given by section 59(3);

"customer", in relation to an authorised person, means a person who is using, or who is or may be contemplating using, any of the services provided by the authorised person;

"relevant PRA-authorised person" means a PRA-authorised person that is a relevant authorised person.

(9)   In this section any reference to an employee of a person ("A") includes a reference to a person who—

(a)   personally provides, or is under an obligation personally to provide, services to A under an arrangement made between A and the person providing the services or another person, and

(b)   is subject to (or to the right of) supervision, direction or control by A as to the manner in which those services are provided.

(10)   For the meaning of "relevant authorised person", see section 71A.]

NOTES

Commencement: 25 July 2014 (for the purpose of the making of rules); 7 March 2016 (otherwise).

Inserted, together with the preceding heading and s 63F, by the Financial Services (Banking Reform) Act 2013, s 29.

[1.1475]
[63F   Issuing of certificates

(1)   A relevant authorised person may issue a certificate to a person under this section only if the authorised person is satisfied that the person is a fit and proper person to perform the function to which the certificate relates.

(2)   In deciding whether the person is a fit and proper person to perform the function, the relevant authorised person must have regard, in particular, to whether the person—

(a)   has obtained a qualification,

(b)   has undergone, or is undergoing, training,

(c)   possesses a level of competence, or

(d)   has the personal characteristics,

required by general rules made by the appropriate regulator in relation to employees performing functions of that kind.

(3)   In subsection (2) "the appropriate regulator" means—

(a)   in relation to employees of PRA-authorised persons, the FCA or the PRA, and

(b)   in relation to employees of any other authorised person, the FCA.

(4)   A certificate issued by a relevant authorised person to a person under this section must—

(a)   state that the authorised person is satisfied that the person is a fit and proper person to perform the function to which the certificate relates, and

(b)   set out the aspects of the affairs of the authorised person in which the person will be involved in performing the function.

(5)   A certificate issued under this section is valid for a period of 12 months beginning with the day on which it is issued.

(6) If, after having considered whether a person is a fit and proper person to perform a specified function, a relevant authorised person decides not to issue a certificate to the person under this section, the authorised person must give the person a notice in writing stating—

  (a) what steps (if any) the authorised person proposes to take in relation to the person as a result of the decision, and

  (b) the reasons for proposing to take those steps.

(7) A relevant authorised person must maintain a record of every employee who has a valid certificate issued by it under this section.

(8) Expressions used in this section and in section 63E have the same meaning in this section as they have in that section.]

NOTES

Commencement: 25 July 2014 (for the purpose of the making of rules); 7 March 2016 (otherwise).
Inserted as noted to s 63E at **[1.1470]**.

Conduct [of approved persons]

NOTES

Words in square brackets in the above heading added by the Financial Services Act 2010, s 24(1), (2), Sch 2, Pt 1, paras 1, 7.

[1.1476]
64 Conduct: statements and codes

[(1) *The FCA may issue statements of principle with respect to the conduct expected of persons in relation to whom either regulator has given its approval under section 59.*

(1A) *The PRA may issue statements of principle with respect to—*

  (a) *the conduct expected of persons in relation to whom it has given its approval under section 59, and*

  (b) *the conduct expected of persons in relation to whom the FCA has given its approval under section 59 in respect of the performance by them of significant-influence functions in relation to the carrying on by PRA-authorised persons of regulated activities.*

(1B) *A statement of principle issued by either regulator may relate to conduct expected of persons in relation to—*

  (a) *the performance by them of controlled functions, or*

  (b) *the performance by them of any other functions in relation to the carrying on by authorised persons of regulated activities.]*

(2) *If [a regulator] issues a statement of principle under subsection (1) [or (1A)], it must also issue a code of practice for the purpose of helping to determine whether or not a person's conduct complies with the statement of principle.*

(3) *A code issued under subsection (2) may specify—*

  (a) *descriptions of conduct which, in the opinion of the [regulator issuing the code], comply with a statement of principle;*

  (b) *descriptions of conduct which, in the opinion of the [regulator issuing the code], do not comply with a statement of principle;*

  (c) *factors which, in the opinion of the [regulator issuing the code], are to be taken into account in determining whether or not a person's conduct complies with a statement of principle.*

(4) *[A regulator] may at any time alter or replace a statement or code issued [by it] under this section.*

(5) *If a statement or code is altered or replaced [by a regulator], the altered or replacement statement or code must be issued by the [regulator].*

(6) *A statement or code issued under this section must be published by [the regulator that issued it] in the way appearing to [that regulator] to be best calculated to bring it to the attention of the public.*

(7) *A code published under this section and in force at the time when any particular conduct takes place may be relied on so far as it tends to establish whether or not that conduct complies with a statement of principle.*

(8) *Failure to comply with a statement of principle under this section does not of itself give rise to any right of action by persons affected or affect the validity of any transaction.*

(9) *A person is not to be taken to have failed to comply with a statement of principle if he shows that, at the time of the alleged failure, it or its associated code of practice had not been published.*

(10) *[A regulator] must, without delay, give the Treasury a copy of any statement or code which it publishes under this section.*

(11) *The power under this section to issue statements of principle and codes of practice—*

  (a) *includes power to make different provision in relation to persons, cases or circumstances of different descriptions; and*

  [(b) *is to be treated for the purposes of section 1B(6)(a) as part of the FCA's rule-making functions (where the power is exercisable by the FCA) and is to be treated for the purposes of section 2J(1)(a) as part of the PRA's rule-making functions (where the power is exercisable by the PRA)].*

(12)   [A regulator] may charge a reasonable fee for providing a person with a copy of a statement or code published [by it] under this section.

[(13)   Any expression which is used both in this section and section 59 has the same meaning in this section as in that section.]

NOTES

Repealed, together with the preceding heading and s 65, by the Financial Services (Banking Reform) Act 2013, s 30(1), (2), as from 25 July 2014 (for the purpose of the making of rules), and as from 7 March 2016 (otherwise).

Sub-ss (1)–(1B) were substituted (for the original sub-s (1)) by the Financial Services Act 2012, s 14(4).

Sub-ss (11)(b) and sub-s (13) were substituted, and all other words in square brackets in sub-ss (2)–(6), (10), (12) were substituted or inserted, by the Financial Services Act 2012, s 15, Sch 5, paras 1, 12.

[1.1477]
65   Statements and codes: procedure

[(1)   Before a regulator issues a statement or code under section 64, it must—
  (a)   consult the other regulator; and
  (b)   after doing so, publish a draft of the statement or code in the way appearing to it to be best calculated to bring the statement or code to the attention of the public.

(1A)   The duty of the FCA to consult the PRA under subsection (1)(a) applies only in so far as the statement or code applies to persons in relation to whom approval is given under section 59 in respect of the performance by them of significant-influence functions (within the meaning of that section) in relation to the carrying on by PRA-authorised persons of regulated activities.]

(2)   The draft must be accompanied by—
  (a)   a cost benefit analysis; and
  (b)   notice that representations about the proposal may be made to [the regulator publishing the draft] within a specified time.

(3)   Before [a regulator issues] the proposed statement or code, [it] must have regard to any representations made to it in accordance with subsection (2)(b).

(4)   If [a regulator] issues the proposed statement or code it must publish an account, in general terms, of—
  (a)   the representations made to it in accordance with subsection (2)(b); and
  (b)   its response to them.

(5)   If the statement or code differs from the draft published under subsection (1) in a way which is, in the opinion of [the regulator issuing the statement or code], significant—
  (a)   [the regulator] must (in addition to complying with subsection (4)) publish details of the difference; and
  (b)   those details must be accompanied by a cost benefit analysis.

(6)   Neither subsection (2)(a) nor subsection (5)(b) applies if [the regulator concerned] considers—
  (a)   that, making the appropriate comparison, there will be no increase in costs; or
  (b)   that, making that comparison, there will be an increase in costs but the increase will be of minimal significance.

[(7)   Subsections (1)(b) and (2) to (6) do not apply in relation to—
  (a)   a statement or code issued by the FCA if it considers that the delay involved in complying with them would be prejudicial to the interests of consumers, as defined in section 425A; or
  (b)   a statement or code issued by the PRA if it considers that the delay involved in complying with them would—
    (i)   be prejudicial to the safety and soundness of PRA-authorised persons, or
    (ii)   in a case where section 2C applies, be prejudicial to securing the appropriate degree of protection for policyholders.]

(8)   A statement or code must state that it is issued under section 64.

(9)   [A regulator] may charge a reasonable fee for providing a copy of a draft published [by it] under subsection (1).

(10)   This section also applies to a proposal to alter or replace a statement or code.

[(11)   Cost benefit analysis" means—
  (a)   an analysis of the costs together with an analysis of the benefits that will arise—
    (i)   if the proposed statement or code is issued, or
    (ii)   if subsection (5)(b) applies, from the statement or code that has been issued, and
  (b)   subject to subsection (11A), an estimate of those costs and of those benefits.

(11A)   If, in the opinion of the regulator concerned—
  (a)   the costs or benefits referred to in subsection (11) cannot reasonably be estimated, or
  (b)   it is not reasonably practicable to produce an estimate,
the cost benefit analysis need not estimate them, but must include a statement of the opinion of the regulator concerned and an explanation of it.]*

(12)   "The appropriate comparison" means—
  (a)   in relation to subsection (2)(a), a comparison between the overall position if the statement or code is issued and the overall position if it is not issued;
  (b)   in relation to subsection (5)(b), a comparison between the overall position after the issuing of the statement or code and the overall position before it was issued.

NOTES
Repealed as noted to s 64 at **[1.1476]**.
Sub-ss (1), (1A) were substituted (for the original sub-s (1)), sub-s (7) was substituted, sub-ss (11), (11A) were substituted (for the original sub-s (11)), the words "by it" in square brackets in sub-s (9) were inserted, and all other words in square brackets in this section were substituted, by the Financial Services Act 2012, s 15, Sch 5, paras 1, 13.

[Conduct of approved persons and others

[1.1478]
64A   Rules of conduct
(1)   If it appears to the FCA to be necessary or expedient for the purpose of advancing one or more of its operational objectives, the FCA may make rules about the conduct of the following persons—
   (a)   persons in relation to whom either regulator has given its approval under section 59;
   (b)   persons who are employees of relevant authorised persons (see section 71A).
(2)   If it appears to the PRA to be necessary or expedient for the purpose of advancing any of its objectives, the PRA may make rules about the conduct of the following persons—
   (a)   persons in relation to whom it has given its approval under section 59;
   (b)   persons in relation to whom the FCA has given its approval under section 59 in respect of the performance by them of a relevant senior management function in relation to the carrying on by a PRA-authorised person of a regulated activity;
   (c)   persons who are employees of relevant PRA-authorised persons.
(3)   In subsection (2)—
"relevant PRA-authorised person" means a PRA-authorised person that is a relevant authorised person (see section 71A), and
"relevant senior management function" means a function which the PRA is satisfied is a senior management function as defined in section 59ZA (whether or not the function has been designated as such by the FCA).
(4)   Rules made under this section must relate to the conduct of persons in relation to the performance by them of qualifying functions.
(5)   In subsection (4) "qualifying function", in relation to a person, means a function relating to the carrying on of activities (whether or not regulated activities) by—
   (a)   in the case of an approved person, the person on whose application approval was given, and
   (b)   in any other case, the person's employer.
(6)   In this section any reference to an employee of a person ("P") includes a reference to a person who—
   (a)   personally provides, or is under an obligation personally to provide, services to P under an arrangement made between P and the person providing the services or another person, and
   (b)   is subject to (or to the right of) supervision, direction or control by P as to the manner in which those services are provided,
and "employer" is to be read accordingly.]

NOTES
Commencement: 25 July 2014 (for the purpose of the making of rules); 7 March 2016 (otherwise).
Inserted, together with the preceding heading and s 64B, by the Financial Services (Banking Reform) Act 2013, s 30(3), as from 25 July 2014 (for the purpose of the making of rules), and as from 7 March 2016 (otherwise).

[1.1479]
[64B   Rules of conduct: responsibilities of relevant authorised persons
(1)   This section applies where a regulator makes rules under section 64A ("conduct rules").
(2)   Every relevant authorised person must—
   (a)   notify all relevant persons of the conduct rules that apply in relation to them, and
   (b)   take all reasonable steps to secure that those persons understand how those rules apply in relation to them.
(3)   The steps which a relevant authorised person must take to comply with subsection (2)(b) include, in particular, the provision of suitable training.
(4)   In this section "relevant person", in relation to an authorised person, means—
   (a)   any person in relation to whom an approval is given under section 59 on the application of the authorised person, and
   (b)   any employee of the authorised person.
(5)   If a relevant authorised person knows or suspects that a relevant person has failed to comply with any conduct rules, the authorised person must notify the regulator of that fact.
(6)   In this section "employee", in relation to an authorised person, has the same meaning as in section 64A.
(7)   For the meaning of "relevant authorised person", see section 71A.]

NOTES
Commencement: 25 July 2014 (for the purpose of the making of rules); 7 March 2016 (otherwise).
Inserted as noted to s 64A at **[1.1478]**.

[1.1480]

[64C   Requirement for relevant authorised persons to notify regulator of disciplinary action

(1)   If—

    (a)   a relevant authorised person takes disciplinary action in relation to a relevant person, and

    (b)   the reason, or one of the reasons, for taking that action is a reason specified in rules made by the appropriate regulator for the purposes of this section,

the relevant authorised person must notify that regulator of that fact.

(2)   "Disciplinary action", in relation to a person, means any of the following—

    (a)   the issuing of a formal written warning;

    (b)   the suspension or dismissal of the person;

    (c)   the reduction or recovery of any of the person's remuneration.

(3)   "The appropriate regulator" means—

    (a)   in relation to relevant authorised persons that are PRA-authorised persons, the FCA or the PRA;

    (b)   in relation to any other relevant authorised persons, the FCA.

(4)   "Relevant person" has the same meaning as in section 64B.

(5)   For the meaning of "relevant authorised person", see section 71A.]

NOTES

Commencement: 25 July 2014 (for the purpose of the making of rules); 7 March 2016 (otherwise).

Inserted by the Financial Services (Banking Reform) Act 2013, s 31, as from 25 July 2014 (for the purpose of the making of rules), and as from 7 March 2016 (otherwise).

[1.1481]

66   Disciplinary powers

(1)   [A regulator] may take action against a person under this section [(whether or not it has given its approval in relation to the person)] if—

    (a)   it appears to the [regulator] that he is guilty of misconduct; and

    (b)   the [regulator] is satisfied that it is appropriate in all the circumstances to take action against him.

[(1A)   For provision about when a person is guilty of misconduct for the purposes of action by a regulator—

    (a)   see section 66A, in the case of action by the FCA, and

    (b)   see section 66B, in the case of action by the PRA.]

[(2)   For the purposes of action by the FCA, a person is guilty of misconduct if, while an approved person—

    (a)   the person has failed to comply with a statement of principle issued by the FCA under section 64, or

    (b)   the person has been knowingly concerned in a contravention by the relevant authorised person of a requirement imposed on that authorised person—

        (i)   by or under this Act, . . .

        [(ia)   by the Alternative Investment Fund Managers Regulations 2013, or]

        (ii)   by any qualifying EU provision specified, or of a description specified, for the purposes of this subsection by the Treasury by order.

(2A)   For the purposes of action by the PRA, a person is guilty of misconduct if, while an approved person in respect of the performance of a significant-influence function in relation to the carrying on by a PRA-authorised person of a regulated activity—

    (a)   the person has failed to comply with a statement of principle issued by the PRA under section 64, or

    (b)   the person has been knowingly concerned in a contravention by the relevant authorised person of a requirement imposed on that authorised person—

        (i)   by or under this Act, or

        (ii)   by any qualifying EU provision specified, or of a description specified, for the purposes of this subsection by the Treasury by order.]

(3)   If the [regulator] is entitled to take action under this section against a person, [it may do one or more of the following]—

    (a)   impose a penalty on him of such amount as it considers appropriate;

    [(aa)   suspend, for such period as it considers appropriate, any approval of the performance by him of any function to which the approval relates;

    (ab)   impose, for such period as it considers appropriate, such limitations or other restrictions in relation to the performance by him of any function to which any approval relates as it considers appropriate;] or

    (b)   publish a statement of his misconduct.

[(3A)   The period for which a suspension or *restriction* is to have effect may not exceed two years.

(3B)   A suspension *or restriction* may have effect in relation to part of a function.

(3C)   A *restriction* may, in particular, be imposed so as to require any person to take, or refrain from taking, specified action.

(3D)   [The regulator taking action under this section] may—

    (a)   withdraw a suspension *or restriction*; or

(b)   vary a suspension or *restriction* so as to reduce the period for which it has effect or otherwise to limit its effect;

[(c)   vary a limitation so as to increase the period for which the approval is to have effect].]

(4)   [A regulator] may not take action under this section after the end of the [relevant period] beginning with the first day on which [the regulator] knew of the misconduct, unless proceedings in respect of it against the person concerned were begun before the end of that period.

(5)   For the purposes of subsection (4)—

(a)   [a regulator] is to be treated as knowing of misconduct if it has information from which the misconduct can reasonably be inferred; and

(b)   proceedings against a person in respect of misconduct are to be treated as begun when a warning notice is given to him under section 67(1).

[(5ZA)   The relevant period" is—

(a)   in relation to misconduct which occurs before the day on which this subsection comes into force, the period of 3 years, and

(b)   in relation to misconduct which occurs on or after that day, the period of 6 years.]

[(5A)   Approval" means an approval given under section 59.]

[(6)   *Approved person" means a person in relation to whom an approval is given under that section.]*

(7)   "Relevant authorised person", in relation to an approved person, means the person on whose application approval . . . was given.

[(8)   In relation to any time while a suspension is in force under subsection (3)(aa) in relation to part of a function, any reference in section 59 or 63A to the performance of a function includes the performance of part of a function.

(9)   If at any time a *restriction* imposed under subsection (3)(ab) is contravened, the approval in relation to the person concerned is to be treated for the purposes of sections 59 and 63A as if it had been withdrawn at that time.]

NOTES

Sub-s (1): words in square brackets substituted or inserted by the Financial Services Act 2012, s 15, Sch 5, paras 1, 14(1), (2).

Sub-s (1A): inserted by the Financial Services (Banking Reform) Act 2013, s 32(1)(a), as from 7 March 2016.

Sub-ss (2), (2A): substituted (for the original sub-s (2)) by the Financial Services Act 2012, s 15, Sch 5, paras 1, 14(1), (3); the word omitted from subs (2)(b)(i) was repealed, and sub-s (2)(b)(ia) was inserted, by the Alternative Investment Fund Managers Regulations 2013, SI 2013/1773, reg 80, Sch 1, Part 1, paras 1, 8, (for transitional provisions and savings see Part 9 of the 2013 Regulations). Both sub-ss (2), (2A) are repealed by the Financial Services (Banking Reform) Act 2013, s 32(1)(b), as from 7 March 2016.

Sub-s (3) is amended as follows:

Words in first pair of square brackets substituted by the Financial Services Act 2012, s 15, Sch 5, paras 1, 14(1), (4).

Words in second pair of square brackets substituted, and paras (aa), (ab) inserted, by the Financial Services Act 2010, s 12(1), (2).

Para (ab) substituted by the Financial Services (Banking Reform) Act 2013, s 35, Sch 3, para 5(1), (2), as from 7 March 2016, as follows—

"(ab)   impose, for such period as it considers appropriate, any conditions in relation to any such approval which it considers appropriate;

(ac)   limit the period for which any such approval is to have effect;".

Sub-ss (3A)–(3D): inserted by the Financial Services Act 2010, ss 12(1), (3), and subsequently amended as follows:

In sub-ss (3A), (3C) for the word in italics there is substituted the word "condition", and in sub-s (3B) for the words in italics there are substituted the words ", condition or limitation", by the Financial Services (Banking Reform) Act 2013, s 35, Sch 3, para 5(1), (3)–(5), as from 7 March 2016.

In sub-s (3D) for the first words in italics in para (a) there are substituted the words ", condition or limitation", the word "or" in italics at the end of that paragraph is repealed, for the word in italics in para (b) there is substituted the word "condition", and para (c) is added, by the Financial Services (Banking Reform) Act 2013, s 35, Sch 3, para 5(1), (6), as from 7 March 2016.

Words in square brackets in sub-s (3D) substituted by the Financial Services Act 2012, s 15, Sch 5, paras 1, 14(1), (5).

Sub-s (4): words in first and third pairs of square brackets substituted by the Financial Services Act 2012, s 15, Sch 5, paras 1, 14(1), (6); words in second pair of square brackets substituted by the Financial Services (Banking Reform) Act 2013, s 28(4), (5).

Sub-s (5): words in square brackets substituted by the Financial Services Act 2012, s 15, Sch 5, paras 1, 14(1), (7).

Sub-s (5ZA): inserted by the Financial Services (Banking Reform) Act 2013, s 28(4), (6).

Sub-s (5A): inserted by the Financial Services Act 2010, s 24(1), (2), Sch 2, Pt 1, paras 1, 8(1), (2).

Sub-s (6): substituted by the Financial Services Act 2012, s 15, Sch 5, paras 1, 14(1), (8); this subsection is repealed by the Financial Services (Banking Reform) Act 2013, s 32(1)(b), as from 7 March 2016.

Sub-s (7): words omitted repealed by the Financial Services Act 2010, s 24(1), (2), Sch 2, Pt 1, paras 1, 8(1), (3); this subsection is repealed by the Financial Services (Banking Reform) Act 2013, s 32(1)(b), as from 7 March 2016.

Sub-ss (8), (9): added by the Financial Services Act 2010, s 24(1), (2), Sch 2, Pt 1, paras 1, 8(1), (4); for the word in italics in sub-s (9) there is substituted the word "condition" by the Financial Services (Banking Reform) Act 2013, s 35, Sch 3, para 5(1), (7), as from 7 March 2016.

Note: see *Andrew Jeffery v The Financial Conduct Authority* FS/2010/0039 (7 Feb 2013) in relation to actions under this section and, in particular, sub-ss (4) and (5); although an application has been made to the Court of Appeal for review of the Upper Tribunal decision.

Orders: the Financial Services and Markets Act 2000 (Qualifying EU Provisions) Order 2013, SI 2013/419; the Financial Services and Markets Act 2000 (Qualifying EU Provisions) (No 2) Order 2013, SI 2013/3116.

[1.1482]

[66A   Misconduct: action by the FCA

(1)   For the purposes of action by the FCA under section 66, a person is guilty of misconduct if any of conditions A to C is met in relation to the person.

(2)   Condition A is that—

    (a)   the person has at any time failed to comply with rules made by the FCA under section 64A, and

    (b)   at that time the person was—

       (i)   an approved person, or

       (ii)   an employee of a relevant authorised person.

(3)   Condition B is that—

    (a)   the person has at any time been knowingly concerned in a contravention of a relevant requirement by an authorised person, and

    (b)   at that time the person was—

       (i)   an approved person in relation to the authorised person, or

       (ii)   in the case of a relevant authorised person, an employee of the authorised person.

(4)   In this section "relevant requirement" means a requirement—

    (a)   imposed by or under this Act, or

    (b)   imposed by any qualifying EU provision specified, or of a description specified, for the purposes of this subsection by the Treasury by order.

(5)   Condition C is that—

    (a)   the person has at any time been a senior manager in relation to a relevant authorised person,

    (b)   there has at that time been (or continued to be) a contravention of a relevant requirement by the authorised person, and

    (c)   the senior manager was at that time responsible for the management of any of the authorised person's activities in relation to which the contravention occurred.

(6)   But a person ("P") is not guilty of misconduct by virtue of subsection (5) if P satisfies the FCA that P had taken such steps as a person in P's position could reasonably be expected to take to avoid the contravention occurring (or continuing).

(7)   For the purposes of subsection (5)—

"senior manager", in relation to a relevant authorised person, means a person who has approval under section 59 to perform a designated senior management function in relation to the carrying on by the authorised person of a regulated activity;

"designated senior management function" means a function designated as a senior management function under section 59(6A) or (6B).

(8)   In this section—

"approved person"—

       (a)   means a person in relation to whom an approval is given under section 59, and

       (b)   in relation to an authorised person, means a person in relation to whom such approval is given on the application of the authorised person;

"employee", in relation to a person, has the same meaning as in section 64A.

(9)   For the meaning of "relevant authorised person", see section 71A.]

NOTES

Commencement: 7 March 2016.

Inserted, together with s 66B, by the Financial Services (Banking Reform) Act 2013, s 32(2), as from 7 March 2016.

[1.1483]

[66B   Misconduct: action by the PRA

(1)   For the purposes of action by the PRA under section 66, a person is guilty of misconduct if any of conditions A to C is met in relation to the person.

(2)   Condition A is that—

    (a)   the person has at any time failed to comply with rules made by the PRA under section 64A, and

    (b)   at that time the person was—

       (i)   an approved person, or

       (ii)   an employee of a relevant PRA-authorised person.

(3)   Condition B is that—

    (a)   the person has at any time been knowingly concerned in a contravention of a relevant requirement by a PRA-authorised person, and

    (b)   at that time the person was—

       (i)   an approved person in respect of the performance of a relevant senior management function in relation to the carrying on by the PRA-authorised person of a regulated activity, or

       (ii)   in the case of a relevant PRA-authorised person, an employee of the authorised person.

(4)   In this section "relevant requirement" means a requirement—

    (a)   imposed by or under this Act, or

(b) imposed by any qualifying EU provision specified, or of a description specified, for the purposes of this subsection by the Treasury by order.

(5) Condition C is that—

(a) the person has at any time been a senior manager in relation to a relevant PRA-authorised person,

(b) there has at that time been (or continued to be) a contravention of a relevant requirement by the authorised person, and

(c) the senior manager was at that time responsible for the management of any of the authorised person's activities in relation to which the contravention occurred.

(6) But a person ("P") is not guilty of misconduct by virtue of subsection (5) if P satisfies the PRA that P had taken such steps as a person in P's position could reasonably be expected to take to avoid the contravention occurring (or continuing).

(7) For the purposes of subsection (5)—

"senior manager", in relation to a relevant PRA-authorised person, means a person who has approval under section 59 to perform a designated senior management function in relation to the carrying on by the authorised person of a regulated activity;

"designated senior management function" means a function designated as a senior management function under section 59(6A) or (6B).

(8) In this section—

"approved person"—

(a) means a person in relation to whom—

(i) the PRA has given its approval under section 59, or

(ii) the FCA has given its approval under section 59 in respect of the performance by the person of a relevant senior management function in relation to the carrying on by a PRA-authorised person of a regulated activity, and

(b) in relation to an authorised person, means a person in relation to whom approval under section 59 is given on the application of the authorised person;

"employee", in relation to a person, has the same meaning as in section 64A;

"relevant PRA-authorised person" means a PRA-authorised person that is a relevant authorised person;

"relevant senior management function" means a function which the PRA is satisfied is a senior management function as defined in section 59ZA (whether or not the function has been designated as such by the FCA).

(9) For the meaning of "relevant authorised person", see section 71A.]

NOTES

Commencement: 7 March 2016.
Inserted as noted to s 66A at **[1.1482]**.

[1.1484]

67 Disciplinary measures: procedure and right to refer to Tribunal

(1) If [a regulator] proposes to take action against a person under section 66, it must give him a warning notice[; and if it proposes to take action under subsection (3)(aa) *or (ab)* of that section, it must also give each of the other interested parties a warning notice].

(2) A warning notice about a proposal to impose a penalty must state the amount of the penalty.

[(2A) A warning notice about a proposal—

(a) to suspend an approval, or

(b) to impose a *restriction* in relation to the performance of a function,

must state the period for which the suspension or *restriction* is to have effect.]

[(2B) A warning notice about a proposal to limit the period for which an approval is to have effect must state the length of that period.]

(3) A warning notice about a proposal to publish a statement must set out the terms of the statement.

(4) If [a regulator] decides to take action against a person under section 66, it must give him a decision notice[; and if it decides to take action under subsection (3)(aa) *or (ab)* of that section, it must also give each of the other interested parties a decision notice].

(5) A decision notice about the imposition of a penalty must state the amount of the penalty.

[(5A) A decision notice about—

(a) the suspension of an approval, or

(b) the imposition of a *restriction* in relation to the performance of a function,

must state the period for which the suspension or *restriction* is to have effect.]

[(5B) A decision notice about limiting the period for which an approval is to have effect must state the length of that period.]

(6) A decision notice about the publication of a statement must set out the terms of the statement.

(7) If [a regulator] decides to take action against a person under section 66, he may refer the matter to the Tribunal[; and if [the regulator] decides to take action under section 66(3)(aa) *or (ab)*, each of the other interested parties may also refer the matter to the Tribunal].

[(8) Approval" means an approval given under section 59.

(9)   "Other interested parties", in relation to [a person ("A") in relation to whom approval has been given], are—

   (a)   the person on whose application the approval was given ("B"); and

   (b)   the person by whom A's services are retained, if not B.

   . . .]

NOTES

Sub-ss (1), (4): words "a regulator" in square brackets substituted by the Financial Services Act 2012, s 15, Sch 5, paras 1, 15(1), (2); other words in square brackets added by the Financial Services Act 2010, s 24(1), (2), Sch 2, Pt 1, paras 1, 9(1), (2), (4); for the words in italics there are substituted the words ", (ab) or (ac)" by the Financial Services (Banking Reform) Act 2013, s 35, Sch 3, para 6(1), (2), (5), as from 7 March 2016.

Sub-ss (2A), (5A): inserted by the Financial Services Act 2010, s 24(1), (2), Sch 2, Pt 1, paras 1, 9(1), (3), (5); for the words "restriction" in italics (in each place that it occurs) there is substituted the word "condition" by the Financial Services (Banking Reform) Act 2013, s 35, Sch 3, para 6(1), (3), (6), as from 7 March 2016.

Sub-ss (2B), (5B): inserted by the Financial Services (Banking Reform) Act 2013, s 35, Sch 3, para 6(1), (4), (7), as from 7 March 2016.

Sub-s (7): words in first pair of square brackets and in third (inner) pair of square brackets substituted by the Financial Services Act 2012, s 15, Sch 5, paras 1, 15(1), (3); words in second (outer) pair of square brackets added by the Financial Services Act 2010, s 24(1), (2), Sch 2, Pt 1, paras 1, 9(1), (6); for the words in italics there are substituted the words ", (ab) or (ac)" by the Financial Services (Banking Reform) Act 2013, s 35, Sch 3, para 6(1), (8), as from 7 March 2016.

Sub-ss (8), (9): added by the Financial Services Act 2010, s 24(1), (2), Sch 2, Pt 1, paras 1, 9(1), (7); words in square brackets in sub-s (9) substituted, and words omitted repealed, by the Financial Services Act 2012, s 15, Sch 5, paras 1, 15(1), (4).

[1.1485]
68   Publication

After a statement under section 66 is published, [the regulator publishing it] must send a copy of it to the person concerned and to any person to whom a copy of the decision notice was given.

NOTES

Words in square brackets substituted by the Financial Services Act 2012, s 15, Sch 5, paras 1, 16.

[1.1486]
69   Statement of policy

(1)   [Each regulator must] prepare and issue a statement of its policy with respect to—

   [(a)   the imposition of penalties, suspensions[, conditions or limitations] under section 66;

   (b)   the amount of penalties under that section;   . . .

   (c)   the period for which suspensions or [conditions] under that section are to have effect][; and

   (d)   the period for which approvals under section 59 are to have effect as a result of a limitation under section 66].

(2)   [A regulator's] policy in determining what the amount of a penalty should be[, or what the period for which a suspension or restriction is to have effect should be,] must include having regard to—

   (a)   the seriousness of the misconduct in question in relation to the nature of the principle or requirement concerned;

   (b)   the extent to which that misconduct was deliberate or reckless; and

   (c)   whether [the person against whom action is to be taken] is an individual.

(3)   [A regulator] may at any time alter or replace a statement issued [by it] under this section.

(4)   If a statement issued under this section is altered or [replaced by a regulator, the regulator] must issue the altered or replacement statement.

(5)   [A regulator] must, without delay, give the Treasury a copy of any statement which it publishes under this section.

(6)   A statement issued under this section [by a regulator] must be published by [the regulator] in the way appearing to [the regulator] to be best calculated to bring it to the attention of the public.

(7)   The [regulator] may charge a reasonable fee for providing a person with a copy of the statement.

(8)   In exercising, or deciding whether to exercise, its power under section 66 in the case of any particular misconduct, [a regulator] must have regard to any statement of policy published [by it] under this section and in force at the time when the misconduct in question occurred.

NOTES

Sub-s (1)(a)–(c) were substituted (for the original sub-s (1)(a), (b)), the words ", or what the period for which a suspension or restriction is to have effect should be," in square brackets in sub-s (2) were inserted, and the words "the person against whom action is to be taken" in that subsection were substituted, by the Financial Services Act 2010, s 24(1), (2), Sch 2, Pt 1, paras 1, 10.

The words ", conditions or limitations" in square brackets in sub-s (1)(a) were substituted, the word omitted from sub-s (1)(b) was repealed, the word "conditions" in square brackets sub-s (1)(c) was substituted, and sub-s (1)(d) (and the preceding word) was inserted, by the Financial Services (Banking Reform) Act 2013, s 35, Sch 3, para 7.

All other words in square brackets in this section were substituted or inserted by the Financial Services Act 2012, s 15, Sch 5, paras 1, 17.

[1.1487]
70 Statements of policy: procedure
(1) Before [a regulator issues] a statement under section 69, the [regulator] must publish a draft of the proposed statement in the way appearing to the [regulator] to be best calculated to bring it to the attention of the public.
(2) The draft must be accompanied by notice that representations about the proposal may be made to the [regulator] within a specified time.
(3) Before issuing the proposed statement, the [regulator] must have regard to any representations made to it in accordance with subsection (2).
(4) If the [regulator] issues the proposed statement it must publish an account, in general terms, of—
  (a) the representations made to it in accordance with subsection (2); and
  (b) its response to them.
(5) If the statement differs from the draft published under subsection (1) in a way which is, in the opinion of the [regulator], significant, the [regulator] must (in addition to complying with subsection (4)) publish details of the difference.
(6) [A regulator] may charge a reasonable fee for providing a person with a copy of a draft published [by it] under subsection (1).
(7) This section also applies to a proposal to alter or replace a statement.

NOTES
Words in square brackets substituted by the Financial Services Act 2012, s 15, Sch 5, paras 1, 18.

Breach of statutory duty

[1.1488]
71 Actions for damages
(1) A contravention of section 56(6) or 59(1) or (2) is actionable at the suit of a private person who suffers loss as a result of the contravention, subject to the defences and other incidents applying to actions for breach of statutory duty.
(2) In prescribed cases, a contravention of that kind which would be actionable at the suit of a private person is actionable at the suit of a person who is not a private person, subject to the defences and other incidents applying to actions for breach of statutory duty.
(3) "Private person" has such meaning as may be prescribed.

NOTES
Regulations: the Financial Services and Markets Act 2000 (Rights of Action) Regulations 2001, SI 2001/2256.

["Relevant authorised person"

[1.1489]
71A Meaning of "relevant authorised person"
(1) In this Part "relevant authorised person" means a UK institution which—
  (a) meets condition A or B, and
  (b) is not an insurer.
(2) Condition A is that the institution has permission under Part 4A to carry on the regulated activity of accepting deposits.
(3) Condition B is that—
  (a) the institution is an investment firm,
  (b) it has permission under Part 4A to carry on the regulated activity of dealing in investments as principal, and
  (c) when carried on by it, that activity is a PRA-regulated activity.
(4) The Treasury may by order provide that authorised persons falling within any of the following descriptions are "relevant authorised persons" for the purposes of this Part—
  (a) non-UK institutions (or non-UK institutions of a specified description) that are credit institutions;
  (b) non-UK institutions that are investment firms of a specified description.
"Specified" means specified in the order.
(5) If the Treasury propose to make an order under subsection (4) they must consult—
  (a) the FCA,
  (b) the PRA,
  (c) any organisations that appear to them to be representative of interests substantially affected by the proposals, and
  (d) any other persons that they consider appropriate.
(6) In this section—
  (a) "UK institution" means an institution which is incorporated in, or formed under the law of any part of, the United Kingdom;
  (b) "non-UK institution" means an institution that is not a UK institution;
  (c) "credit institution" means any credit institution as defined in Article 4.1(1) of Regulation (EU) No 575/2013 of the European Parliament and of the Council;

(d)   "insurer" means an institution which is authorised under this Act to carry on the regulated activity of effecting or carrying out contracts of insurance as principal.

(7)   Subsections (2), (3) and (6)(d) are to be read in accordance with Schedule 2, taken with any order under section 22.]

NOTES

Commencement: 25 July 2014.

Inserted, together with the preceding heading, by the Financial Services (Banking Reform) Act 2013, s 33.

PART IX
HEARINGS AND APPEALS

NOTES

Transitional provisions etc in connection with the commencement of the Financial Services Act 2012: For transitional provisions in relation to hearings and appeals, see Part 4 of the Financial Services Act 2012 (Transitional Provisions) (Miscellaneous Provisions) Order 2013, SI 2013/442. Article 12 deals with proceedings before the Tribunal where appeals and references were made before 1 April 2013; art 13 deals with cases where they were made on or after that date; art 14 concerns decisions referred to the Tribunal.

Financial Services and Markets Tribunal: By the Tribunals, Courts and Enforcement Act 2007, Sch 6, Pt 3, the Financial Services and Markets Tribunal was a 'scheduled tribunal' for the purposes of ss 30, 36 of that Act. For the powers of the Lord Chancellor to transfer a function of a scheduled tribunal to the First-tier Tribunal, Upper Tribunal, etc, to abolish the scheduled tribunal and transfer members etc, see ss 30, 31 of the 2007 Act; for powers relating to the transfer of powers to make procedural rules, see s 36 of that Act. In relation to the Financial Services and Markets Tribunal, see the Transfer of Tribunal Functions Order 2010, SI 2010/22 and the amendments made by that Order to this Part. Note, in particular, that the 2010 Order abolishes the Financial Services and Markets Tribunal and transfers its functions to the Upper Tribunal (as from 6 April 2010). See also *Andrew Jeffrey v The Financial Services Authority*, Upper Tribunal (FS 010/0039, 5 December 2012); although an application has been made to the Court of Appeal for review of the Upper Tribunal decision.

[1.1490]
[133   Proceedings before Tribunal: general provision

(1)   This section applies in the case of a reference or appeal to the Tribunal (whether made under this or any other Act) in respect of—

(a)   a decision of [the FCA or the PRA];

(b)   a decision of the Bank of England; or

(c)   a decision of a person relating to the assessment of any compensation or consideration under the Banking (Special Provisions) Act 2008 or the Banking Act 2009.

(2)   In this section—

"relevant decision" means a decision mentioned in subsection (1)(a), (b) or (c); and

"the decision-maker", in relation to a relevant decision, means the person who made the relevant decision.

(3)   Tribunal Procedure Rules may make provision for the suspension of a relevant decision which has taken effect, pending determination of the reference or appeal.

(4)   The Tribunal may consider any evidence relating to the subject-matter of the reference or appeal, whether or not it was available to the decision-maker at the material time.

[(5)   In the case of a disciplinary reference or a reference under section 393(11), the Tribunal—

(a)   must determine what (if any) is the appropriate action for the decision-maker to take in relation to the matter; and

(b)   on determining the reference, must remit the matter to the decision-maker with such directions (if any) as the Tribunal considers appropriate for giving effect to its determination.

(6)   In any other case, the Tribunal must determine the reference or appeal by either—

(a)   dismissing it; or

(b)   remitting the matter to the decision-maker with a direction to reconsider and reach a decision in accordance with the findings of the Tribunal.

(6A)   The findings mentioned in subsection (6)(b) are limited to findings as to—

(a)   issues of fact or law;

(b)   the matters to be, or not to be, taken into account in making the decision; and

(c)   the procedural or other steps to be taken in connection with the making of the decision.]

(7)   The decision-maker must act in accordance with the determination of, and any direction given by, the Tribunal.

[(7A)   A reference is a "disciplinary reference" for the purposes of this section if it is in respect of any of the following decisions—

(a)   a decision to impose a penalty under section 63A;

(b)   a decision to take action under section 66;

(c)   a decision to take action under section 87M;

(d)   a decision to take action under section 88A;

(e)   a decision to take action under section 89K;

(f)   a decision to take action under section 89Q;

(g)   a decision to take action under section 91;

(h)   a decision to take action under section 123;

(i)   a decision to take action under section 131G;

[(ia) a decision to take action under section 142S;]

(j)   a decision to take action under section 192K;

(k)   a decision to publish a statement under section 205, impose a penalty under section 206 or suspend a permission or impose a restriction under section 206A;

(l)   a decision to take action under section 249 [or 261K];

(m) a decision to publish a statement under section 312E or impose a penalty under section 312F;

(n)   a decision to take action under section 345 or 345A];

[(o) a decision to take action under section 83ZR of the Banking Act 2009].

(8)   An order of the Tribunal may be enforced—

(a)   [in England and Wales, as if it were an order of the county court or, in Northern Ireland,] as if it were an order of a county court; or

(b)   in Scotland, as if it were an order of the Court of Session.]

NOTES

Substituted (together with new ss 133A, 133B) for the original s 133, by the Transfer of Tribunal Functions Order 2010, SI 2010/22, art 5(1), Sch 2, paras 44, 46, (for transitional provisions and savings in relation to existing cases and appeals from the Financial Services and Markets Tribunal, see Sch 5 to that Order).

Words in square brackets in sub-s (1)(a) substituted, sub-ss (5)–(6A) substituted (for the original sub-ss (5), (6)), and sub-s (7A) inserted, by the Financial Services Act 2012, s 23(1), (2).

Sub-s (7A)(ia) inserted by the Financial Services (Banking Reform) Act 2013, s 4(2), as from a day to be appointed.

Words in square brackets in sub-s (7A)(l) inserted by the Collective Investment in Transferable Securities (Contractual Scheme) Regulations 2013, SI 2013/1388, reg 3(1), (3).

Sub-s (7A)(o) inserted by the Bank Recovery and Resolution Order 2014, SI 2014/3329, arts 112, 116.

Words in square brackets in sub-s (8)(a) inserted by the Crime and Courts Act 2013, s 17, Sch 9, Pt 3, para 83.

Note: any reference in this section to this Act includes a reference to the Electronic Commerce Directive (Financial Services and Markets) Regulations 2002, SI 2002/1775; see reg 12(4) of the 2002 Regulations.

Rules: the Tribunal Procedure (Upper Tribunal) (Amendment) Rules 2010, SI 2010/747; Tribunal Procedure (Amendment No 2) Rules 2013, SI 2013/606.

[1.1491]
[133A   Proceedings before Tribunal: decision and supervisory notices, etc

(1)   In determining [in accordance with section 133(5)] a reference made (whether under this or any other Act) as a result of a decision notice [given by a body, the Tribunal may not direct the body to take action which it would] not, as a result of section 388(2), have had power to take when giving the notice.

(2), (3)   . . .

(4)   [The action specified in a decision notice must not be taken—]

(a)   during the period within which the matter to which the notice relates may be referred to the Tribunal (whether under this or any other Act); and

(b)   if the matter is so referred, until the reference, and any appeal against the Tribunal's determination, has been finally disposed of.

(5)   The Tribunal may, on determining a reference (whether made under this or any other Act) in respect of a decision of [the FCA or the PRA], make recommendations as to [its] regulating provisions or its procedures.]

NOTES

Substituted as noted to s 133 at **[1.1490]**.

The words "in accordance with section 133(5)" in square brackets in sub-s (1) were inserted, all other words in square brackets in this section were substituted, and sub-ss (2), (3) were repealed, by the Financial Services Act 2012, s 23(1), (3).

Note: any reference in this section to this Act includes a reference to the Electronic Commerce Directive (Financial Services and Markets) Regulations 2002, SI 2002/1775; see reg 12(4) of the 2002 Regulations.

[1.1492]
[133B   Offences

(1)   This section applies in the case of proceedings before the Tribunal in respect of—

(a)   a decision of [the FCA or the PRA];

(b)   a decision of the Bank of England; or

(c)   a decision of a person relating to the assessment of any compensation or consideration under the Banking (Special Provisions) Act 2008 or the Banking Act 2009.

(2)   A person is guilty of an offence if that person, without reasonable excuse—

(a)   refuses or fails—

(i)   to attend following the issue of a summons by the Tribunal; or

(ii)   to give evidence; or

(b)   alters, suppresses, conceals or destroys, or refuses to produce a document which he may be required to produce for the purposes of proceedings before the Tribunal.

(3)   A person guilty of an offence under subsection (2)(a) is liable on summary conviction to a fine not exceeding level 5 on the standard scale.

(4)   A person guilty of an offence under subsection (2)(b) is liable—

(a)   on summary conviction, to a fine not exceeding the statutory maximum;

   (b)   on conviction on indictment, to imprisonment for a term not exceeding two years or a fine or both.]

NOTES

Substituted as noted to s 133 at **[1.1490]**.

Sub-s (1): words in square brackets substituted by the Financial Services Act 2012, s 23(1), (4).

Legal assistance before the Tribunal

[1.1493]
134   Legal assistance scheme

(1)   The Lord Chancellor may by regulations establish a scheme governing the provision of legal assistance in connection with proceedings before the Tribunal.

(2)   If the Lord Chancellor establishes a scheme under subsection (1), it must provide that a person is eligible for assistance only if—

   (a)   he falls within subsection (3); and

   (b)   he fulfils such other criteria (if any) as may be prescribed as a result of section 135(1)(d).

(3)   A person falls within this subsection if he is an individual who has referred a matter to the Tribunal under section 127(4).

(4)   In this Part of this Act "the legal assistance scheme" means any scheme in force under subsection (1).

NOTES

Regulations: the Financial Services and Markets Tribunal (Legal Assistance) Regulations 2001, SI 2001/3632; the Financial Services and Markets Tribunal (Legal Assistance Scheme—Costs) Regulations 2001, SI 2001/3633.

[1.1494]
135   Provisions of the legal assistance scheme

(1)   The legal assistance scheme may, in particular, make provision as to—

   (a)   the kinds of legal assistance that may be provided;

   (b)   the persons by whom legal assistance may be provided;

   (c)   the manner in which applications for legal assistance are to be made;

   (d)   the criteria on which eligibility for legal assistance is to be determined;

   (e)   the persons or bodies by whom applications are to be determined;

   (f)   appeals against refusals of applications;

   (g)   the revocation or variation of decisions;

   (h)   its administration and the enforcement of its provisions.

(2)   Legal assistance under the legal assistance scheme may be provided subject to conditions or restrictions, including conditions as to the making of contributions by the person to whom it is provided.

NOTES

Regulations: the Financial Services and Markets Tribunal (Legal Assistance) Regulations 2001, SI 2001/3632; the Financial Services and Markets Tribunal (Legal Assistance Scheme—Costs) Regulations 2001, SI 2001/3633.

136, 137   (*S 136 outside the scope of this work; s 137 repealed by the Transfer of Tribunal Functions Order 2010, SI 2010/22, art 5(1), Sch 2, paras 43, 46..*)

[PART 9A
RULES AND GUIDANCE

CHAPTER 1
RULE-MAKING POWERS

General rule-making powers of the FCA and the PRA

[1.1495]
137A   The FCA's general rules

(1)   The FCA may make such rules applying to authorised persons—

   (a)   with respect to the carrying on by them of regulated activities, or

   (b)   with respect to the carrying on by them of activities which are not regulated activities,

as appear to the FCA to be necessary or expedient for the purpose of advancing one or more of its operational objectives.

(2)   Rules made under this section are referred to in this Act as the FCA's general rules.

(3)   The FCA's general rules may make provision applying to authorised persons even though there is no relationship between the authorised persons to whom the rules will apply and the persons whose interests will be protected by the rules.

(4)   The FCA's general rules may contain requirements which take into account, in the case of an authorised person who is a member of a group, any activity of another member of the group.

(5)   The FCA's general rules may not—

(a) make provision prohibiting an EEA firm from carrying on, or holding itself out as carrying on, any activity which it has permission conferred by Part 2 of Schedule 3 to carry on in the United Kingdom;

(b) make provision, as respects an EEA firm, about any matter for which responsibility is, under any of the single market directives or the emission allowance auctioning regulation, reserved to the firm's home state regulator.]

NOTES

Commencement: 24 January 2013 (for the purpose of making rules); 1 April 2013 (otherwise).

This section was substituted (together with the rest of Part 9A (ie, ss 137A–137T, 138A–138O, 139A, 139B, 140A–140H, 141A) for the original Part X (ss 138–164)) by the Financial Services Act 2012, s 24(1).

Note: the Industrial Assurance (Premium Receipt Books) Regulations 1948, SI 1948/2770 were originally made under the powers conferred by Industrial Assurance and Friendly Societies Act 1948, s 8(2). By virtue of the Financial Services and Markets Act 2000 (Transitional Provisions and Savings) (Rules) Order 2001, SI 2001/1534, they took effect (except in relation to the Channel Islands) as rules made by the FSA under s 138 of this Act and could be altered or revoked in accordance with that section (see s 8(2) of the 1948 as substituted in relation to existing policies by the Financial Services and Markets Act 2000 (Consequential Amendments and Savings) (Industrial Assurance) Order 2001, SI 2001/3647). Following the substitution of Part X (as noted above), the 1948 rules have effect as if made under this section.

[1.1496]
[137B FCA general rules: clients' money, right to rescind etc
(1) Rules relating to the handling of money held by an authorised person in specified circumstances ("clients' money") may—

(a) make provision which results in that clients' money being held on trust in accordance with the rules,

(b) treat 2 or more accounts as a single account for specified purposes (which may include the distribution of money held in the accounts),

(c) authorise the retention by the authorised person of interest accruing on the clients' money, and

(d) make provision as to the distribution of such interest which is not to be retained by the authorised person.

(2) An institution with which an account is kept in pursuance of rules relating to the handling of clients' money does not incur any liability as constructive trustee if the money is wrongfully paid from the account, unless the institution permits the payment—

(a) with knowledge that it is wrongful, or

(b) having deliberately failed to make enquiries in circumstances in which a reasonable and honest person would have done so.

(3) Rules may—

(a) confer rights on persons to rescind agreements with, or withdraw offers to, authorised persons within a specified period, and

(b) make provision, in respect of authorised persons and persons exercising those rights, for the restitution of property and the making or recovery of payments where those rights are exercised.

(4) "Rules" means general rules of the FCA.

(5) "Specified" means specified in the rules.]

NOTES

Commencement: 24 January 2013 (for the purpose of making rules); 1 April 2013 (otherwise).

Substituted as noted to s 137A at **[1.1495]**.

[1.1497]
[137C FCA general rules: cost of credit and duration of credit agreements
(1) The power of the FCA to make general rules includes power to make rules prohibiting authorised persons from—

(a) entering into a regulated credit agreement that provides for—

(i) the payment by the borrower of charges of a specified description, or

(ii) the payment by the borrower over the duration of the agreement of charges that, taken with the charges paid under one or more other agreements which are treated by the rules as being connected with it, exceed, or are capable of exceeding, a specified amount;

(b) imposing charges of a specified description or exceeding a specified amount on a person who is the borrower under a regulated credit agreement;

(c) entering into a regulated credit agreement that—

(i) is capable of remaining in force after the end of a specified period,

(ii) when taken with one or more other regulated credit agreements which are treated by the rules as being connected with it, would be capable of remaining in force after the end of a specified period, or

(iii) is treated by the rules as being connected with a number of previous regulated credit agreements that exceeds a specified maximum;

(d)   exercising the rights of the lender under a regulated credit agreement (as a person for the time being entitled to exercise them) in a way that enables the agreement to remain in force after the end of a specified period or enables the imposition on the borrower of charges within paragraph (a)(i) or (ii).

[(1A)   The FCA must make rules by virtue of subsection (1)(a)(ii) and (b) in relation to one or more specified descriptions of regulated credit agreement appearing to the FCA to involve the provision of high-cost short-term credit, with a view to securing an appropriate degree of protection for borrowers against excessive charges.

(1B)   Before the FCA publishes a draft of any rules to be made by virtue of subsection (1)(a)(ii) or (b), it must consult the Treasury.]

(2)   "Charges" means charges payable, by way of interest or otherwise, in connection with the provision of credit under the regulated credit agreement, whether or not the agreement itself makes provision for them and whether or not the person to whom they are payable is a party to the regulated credit agreement or an authorised person.

(3)   "The borrower" includes—
(a)   any person providing a guarantee or indemnity under the regulated credit agreement, and
(b)   a person to whom the rights and duties of the borrower under the regulated credit agreement or a person falling within paragraph (a) have passed by assignment or operation of law.

(4)   In relation to an agreement entered into or obligation imposed in contravention of the rules, the rules may—
(a)   provide for the agreement or obligation to be unenforceable against any person or specified person;
(b)   provide for the recovery of any money or other property paid or transferred under the agreement or other obligation by any person or specified person;
(c)   provide for the payment of compensation for any loss sustained by any person or specified person as a result of paying or transferring any money or other property under the agreement or obligation.

(5)   The provision that may be made as a result of subsection (4) includes provision corresponding to that made by section 30 (enforceability of agreements resulting from unlawful communications).

(6)   A credit agreement is a contract of the kind mentioned in paragraph 23 of Schedule 2, other than one under which the obligation of the borrower to repay is secured on land: and a credit agreement is a "regulated credit agreement" if any of the following is a regulated activity—
(a)   entering into or administering the agreement;
(b)   exercising or being able to exercise the rights of the lender under the agreement.

(7)   In this section—
(a)   "specified amount" means an amount specified in or determined in accordance with the rules;
(b)   "specified period" means a period of a duration specified in or determined in accordance with the rules;
(c)   "specified person" means a person of a description specified in the rules;
(d)   subject to that, "specified" means specified in the rules.]

NOTES

Commencement: 24 January 2013 (for the purpose of making rules); 1 April 2013 (otherwise).
Substituted as noted to s 137A at **[1.1495]**.
Sub-ss (1A), (1B): inserted by the Financial Services (Banking Reform) Act 2013, s 131(1).

137D–137T   *(Outside the scope of this work.)*

[CHAPTER 2
RULES: MODIFICATION, WAIVER, CONTRAVENTION AND
PROCEDURAL PROVISIONS

NOTES

Transitional provisions etc in connection with the commencement of the Financial Services Act 2012: see the Financial Services Act 2012 (Transitional Provisions) (Rules and Miscellaneous Provisions) Order 2013, SI 2013/161, arts 9–11. Article 9 makes transitional provision in respect of waivers and modifications of rules made under this Act; article 10 makes transitional provision in respect of applications for a waiver or modification or rules; and article 11 sets out definitions relevant for those purposes.

Modification or waiver of rules

[1.1498]
138A   Modification or waiver of rules
(1)   Either regulator may, on the application or with the consent of a person who is subject to rules made by that regulator, direct that all or any of those rules—
(a)   are not to apply to that person, or
(b)   are to apply to that person with such modifications as may be specified in the direction.
(2)   Subsection (1) does not apply to—
[(za) rules made by either regulator under section 64A (rules of conduct);]

(a) rules made by either regulator under section 137O (threshold condition code);

(b) rules made by the FCA under section 247 (trust scheme rules)[, section 248 (scheme particulars rules), section 261I (contractual scheme rules) or section 261J (contractual scheme particulars rules)].

(3) An application must be made in such manner as the regulator may direct.

(4) A regulator may not give a direction unless it is satisfied that—

(a) compliance by the person with the rules, or with the rules as unmodified, would be unduly burdensome or would not achieve the purpose for which the rules were made, and

(b) the direction would not adversely affect the advancement of any of the regulator's objectives.

(5) In subsection (4)(b) "objectives", in relation to the FCA, means operational objectives.

(6) A direction may be given subject to conditions.

(7) The regulator may—

(a) revoke a direction, or

(b) vary it on the application, or with the consent, of the person to whom it relates.

(8) "Direction" means a direction under this section.]

NOTES

[Commencement: 24 January 2013 (for the purpose of the giving of directions); 1 April 2013 (otherwise).

Substituted as noted to s 137A at **[1.1495]**.

Sub-s (2): para (za) inserted by the Financial Services (Banking Reform) Act 2013, s 35, Sch 3, para 8; words in square brackets in para (b) substituted by the Collective Investment in Transferable Securities (Contractual Scheme) Regulations 2013, SI 2013/1388, reg 3(1), (4).

[1.1499]
[138B Publication of directions under section 138A

(1) Subject to subsection (2), a direction must be published by the regulator concerned in the way appearing to the regulator to be best calculated for bringing it to the attention of—

(a) persons likely to be affected by it, and

(b) persons who are, in the opinion of the regulator, likely to make an application for a similar direction.

(2) Subsection (1) does not apply if the regulator is satisfied that it is inappropriate or unnecessary to publish the direction.

(3) In deciding whether it is satisfied as mentioned in subsection (2), the regulator must—

(a) consider whether the publication of the direction would be detrimental to the stability of the UK financial system,

(b) take into account whether the direction relates to a rule contravention of which is actionable in accordance with section 138D,

(c) consider whether publication of the direction would prejudice, to an unreasonable degree, the commercial interests of the person concerned or any other member of the person's immediate group, and

(d) consider whether its publication would be contrary to an international obligation of the United Kingdom.

(4) The FCA must consult the PRA before publishing or deciding not to publish a direction which relates to—

(a) a PRA-authorised person, or

(b) an authorised person who has as a member of its immediate group a PRA-authorised person.

(5) For the purposes of paragraphs (c) and (d) of subsection (3), the regulator must consider whether it would be possible to publish the direction without either of the consequences mentioned in those paragraphs by publishing it without disclosing the identity of the person concerned.

(6) "Direction" means a direction under section 138A.]

NOTES

Commencement: 24 January 2013 (for the purpose of the giving of directions under s 138A); 1 April 2013 (otherwise).

Substituted as noted to s 137A at **[1.1495]**.

[Contravention of rules

[1.1500]
138C Evidential provisions

(1) If a particular rule made by either regulator so provides, contravention of the rule does not give rise to any of the consequences provided for by other provisions of this Act.

(2) A rule made by a regulator which so provides must also provide—

(a) that contravention may be relied on as tending to establish contravention of such other rule made by that regulator as may be specified, or

(b) that compliance may be relied on as tending to establish compliance with such other rule made by that regulator as may be specified.

(3) A rule may include the provision mentioned in subsection (1) only if the regulator making the rule considers that it is appropriate for it also to include the provision required by subsection (2).

(4) In this section "rule" does not include a rule made under—

(a)   section 137O (threshold condition code);
(b)   section 192J (provision of information by parent undertakings).]

NOTES
Commencement: 24 January 2013 (for the purpose of making rules); 1 April 2013 (otherwise).
Substituted as noted to s 137A at **[1.1495]**.

[1.1501]
[138D   Actions for damages
(1)   A rule made by the PRA may provide that contravention of the rule is actionable at the suit of a private person who suffers loss as a result of the contravention, subject to the defences and other incidents applying to actions for breach of statutory duty.
(2)   A contravention by an authorised person of a rule made by the FCA is actionable at the suit of a private person who suffers loss as a result of the contravention, subject to the defences and other incidents applying to actions for breach of statutory duty.
(3)   If rules made by the FCA so provide, subsection (2) does not apply to a contravention of a specified provision of the rules.
(4)   In prescribed cases, a contravention of a rule which by virtue of subsection (1) or (2) would be actionable at the suit of a private person is actionable at the suit of a person who is not a private person, subject to the defences and other incidents applying to actions for breach of statutory duty.
(5)   In subsections (1), (2) and (3) "rule" does not include—
    [(za) rules made by either regulator under section 64A (rules of conduct);]
    (a)   Part 6 rules;
    (b)   rules under section 137O (threshold condition code);
    (c)   rules under section 192J (provision of information by parent undertakings);
    (d)   a rule requiring an authorised person to have or maintain financial resources.
(6)   "Private person" has such meaning as may be prescribed.]

NOTES
Commencement: 24 January 2013 (for the purpose of making rules); 1 April 2013 (otherwise).
Substituted as noted to s 137A at **[1.1495]**.
Sub-s (5): para (za) inserted by the Financial Services (Banking Reform) Act 2013, s 35, Sch 3, para 9.
Regulations: the Financial Services and Markets Act 2000 (Rights of Action) Regulations 2001, SI 2001/2256, and the Financial Services and Markets Act 2000 (Fourth Motor Insurance Directive) Regulations 2002, SI 2002/2706 have effect as if made under this section by virtue of the Interpretation Act 1978, s 17(2)(b).

[1.1502]
[138E   Limits on effect of contravening rules
(1)   A person is not guilty of an offence by reason of a contravention of a rule made by either regulator.
(2)   No such contravention makes any transaction void or unenforceable.
(3)   Subsection (2) does not apply in relation to—
    (a)   rules made by the FCA under section 137C, or
    (b)   product intervention rules made by the FCA under section 137D.]

NOTES
Commencement: 1 April 2013.
Substituted as noted to s 137A at **[1.1495]**.

[Procedural provisions

[1.1503]
138F   Notification of rules
[(1)]   If either regulator makes, alters or revokes any rules, that regulator must without delay give written notice—
    (a)   to the Treasury, and
    (b)   to the Bank of England.
[(2)   Subsection (1)(b) does not apply to rules made under or by virtue of section 137FB, 333Q or 333R.]]

NOTES
Commencement: 24 January 2013 (for the purpose of making rules); 1 April 2013 (otherwise).
Substituted as noted to s 137A at **[1.1495]**.
Sub-s (1) numbered as such, and sub-s (2) added, by the Pension Schemes Act 2015, s 47, Sch 3, paras 1, 7.

[1.1504]
[138G   Rule-making instruments
(1)   Any power conferred on either regulator to make rules is exercisable in writing.
(2)   An instrument by which rules are made by either regulator ("a rule-making instrument") must specify the provision under which the rules are made.
(3)   To the extent that a rule-making instrument does not comply with subsection (2), it is void.

(4) A rule-making instrument must be published by the regulator making the rule in the way appearing to that regulator to be best calculated to bring it to the attention of the public.

(5) The regulator making the rule may charge a reasonable fee for providing a person with a copy of a rule-making instrument.

(6) A person is not to be taken to have contravened any rule made by a regulator if the person shows that at the time of the alleged contravention the rule-making instrument concerned had not been made available in accordance with this section.]

NOTES

Commencement: 24 January 2013 (for the purpose of making rules); 1 April 2013 (otherwise).

Substituted as noted to s 137A at **[1.1495]**.

[1.1505]
[138H   Verification of rules

(1) The production of a printed copy of a rule-making instrument purporting to be made by a regulator—

  (a)   on which is endorsed a certificate signed by a member of staff of that regulator who is authorised by the regulator for that purpose, and

  (b)   which contains the required statements,

is evidence (or in Scotland sufficient evidence) of the facts stated in the certificate.

(2) The required statements are—

  (a)   that the instrument was made by the FCA or the PRA (as the case may be),

  (b)   that the copy is a true copy of the instrument, and

  (c)   that on a specified date the instrument was made available to the public in accordance with section 138G(4).

(3) A certificate purporting to be signed as mentioned in subsection (1) is to be taken to have been properly signed unless the contrary is shown.

(4) A person who wishes in any legal proceedings to rely on a rule-making instrument may require the regulator that made the rule to endorse a copy of the instrument with a certificate of the kind mentioned in subsection (1).]

NOTES

Commencement: 24 January 2013 (for the purpose of making rules); 1 April 2013 (otherwise).

Substituted as noted to s 137A at **[1.1495]**.

Rule-making instrument: designating instruments made in accordance with the Financial Services Act 2012 (Transitional Provisions) (Rules and Miscellaneous Provisions) Order 2013, SI 2013/161, art 3, and the Financial Services and Markets Act 2000 (Regulated Activities) (Amendment) (No 2) Order 2013, SI 2013/1881, art 64 (at **[2.1045]**) are to be treated as rule-making instruments for the purposes of this section.

138I–138O   (*Outside the scope of this work.*)

[CHAPTER 3
GUIDANCE

[1.1506]
139A   Power of the FCA to give guidance

(1) The FCA may give guidance consisting of such information and advice as it considers appropriate—

  (a)   with respect to the operation of specified parts of this Act and of any rules made by the FCA;

  (b)   with respect to any other matter relating to functions of the FCA;

  (c)   with respect to any other matters about which it appears to the FCA to be desirable to give information or advice.

[(1A) The FCA may not give guidance under this section relating to its functions under sections 333H, 333I, 333J, 333K and 333Q (see section 333P for provision about the giving of guidance relating to these functions).]

(2) The FCA may give financial or other assistance to persons giving information or advice of a kind which the FCA could give under this section.

(3) Subsection (5) applies where the FCA proposes to give guidance to FCA-regulated persons generally, or to a class of FCA-regulated persons, in relation to rules to which those persons are subject.

(4) Subsection (5) also applies in relation to guidance which the FCA proposes to give to persons generally, or to a class of person, in relation to its functions under the short selling regulation.

(5) Where this subsection applies, subsections (1), (2)(e) and (3) of section 138I (consultation) apply to the proposed guidance as they apply to proposed rules, unless the FCA considers that the delay in complying with those provisions would be prejudicial to the interests of consumers.

(6) The FCA may—

  (a)   publish its guidance,

  (b)   offer copies of its published guidance for sale at a reasonable price, and

(c)   if it gives guidance in response to a request made by any person, make a reasonable charge for that guidance.

(7)   In this Chapter, references to guidance given by the FCA include references to any recommendations made by the FCA to FCA-regulated persons generally, or to any class of FCA-regulated person.

(8)   "Consumers" has the meaning given in section 1G.

(9)   "FCA-regulated person" means—

(a)   an authorised person, or

(b)   any person who is otherwise subject to rules made by the FCA.]

NOTES

Commencement: 24 January 2013 (for the purpose of the giving of guidance under this section); 1 April 2013 (otherwise).
Substituted as noted to s 137A at **[1.1495]**.
Sub-s (1A): inserted by the Pension Schemes Act 2015, s 47, Sch 3, paras 1, 9.

139B, 140A–140H, 141A, 142A–142Z1   *(Outside the scope of this work.)*

PART XI
INFORMATION GATHERING AND INVESTIGATIONS

NOTES

Transitional provisions etc in connection with the commencement of the Financial Services Act 2012: For transitional provisions in relation to information gathering and investigations, and in respect of legally privileged information, see Part 5 of the Financial Services Act 2012 (Transitional Provisions) (Miscellaneous Provisions) Order 2013, SI 2013/442. Articles 15 and 16 contain transitional provisions in relation to cases where the FSA exercised its power to require information under s 165 or s 165A respectively before 1 April 2013; art 17 contains safeguards in respect of the exercise of the power under s 165A; art 18 deals with reports by skilled persons; art 19 concerns the appointment of persons to carry out investigations; art 20 deals with requests from overseas regulators made before 1 April 2013; art 21 concerns the power to enter premises under s 176; art 20 contains transitional provisions with regard to legal professional privilege.

Powers to gather information

[1.1507]
165   [Regulators'] power to require information[: authorised persons etc]

(1)   [Either regulator] may, by notice in writing given to an authorised person, require him—

(a)   to provide specified information or information of a specified description; or

(b)   to produce specified documents or documents of a specified description.

(2)   The information or documents must be provided or produced—

(a)   before the end of such reasonable period as may be specified; and

(b)   at such place as may be specified.

(3)   An officer who has written authorisation from the [regulator] to do so may require an authorised person without delay—

(a)   to provide the officer with specified information or information of a specified description; or

(b)   to produce to him specified documents or documents of a specified description.

(4)   This section applies only to information and documents reasonably required in connection with the exercise by [either regulator] of functions conferred on it by or under this Act.

(5)   [The regulator in question] may require any information provided under this section to be provided in such form as it may reasonably require.

(6)   [The regulator in question] may require—

(a)   any information provided, whether in a document or otherwise, to be verified in such manner, or

(b)   any document produced to be authenticated in such manner,

as it may reasonably require.

(7)   The powers conferred by subsections (1) and (3) may also be exercised—

(a)   by either regulator, to impose requirements on a person who is connected with an authorised person;

(b)   by the FCA, to impose requirements on an operator, trustee or depositary of a scheme recognised under section   . . .   272 who is not an authorised person;

(c)   by the FCA, to impose requirements on a recognised investment exchange;

(d)   by the FCA, to impose requirements on a person who is connected with a recognised investment exchange;]

[(e)   by either regulator, to impose requirements on a person who provides any service to an insurance undertaking, reinsurance undertaking or third-country insurance undertaking.]

(8)   "Authorised person" includes a person who was at any time an authorised person but who has ceased to be an authorised person.

(9)   "Officer" means an officer of [the regulator exercising the power] and includes a member of [that regulator's] staff or an agent of [that regulator].

(10)   "Specified" means—

(a)   in subsections (1) and (2), specified in the notice; and

(b)   in subsection (3), specified in the authorisation.

(11)   For the purposes of this section, a person is connected with [another person] ("A") if he is or has at any relevant time been—

    (a)   a member of A's group;

    (b)   a controller of A;

    (c)   any other member of a partnership of which A is a member; or

    (d)   in relation to A, a person mentioned in Part I of Schedule 15 [(reading references in that Part to the authorised person as references to A)].

NOTES

The words in the second pair of square brackets in the section heading were inserted by the Financial Services Act 2010, s 24(1), (2), Sch 2, Pt 1, paras 1, 15.

The words omitted from sub-s (7)(b) were repealed by the Alternative Investment Fund Managers Regulations 2013, SI 2013/1773, reg 80, Sch 1, Part 1, paras 1, 9, (for transitional provisions and savings see Part 9 of the 2013 Regulations).

Para (e) of sub-s (7) added by the Solvency 2 Regulations 2015, SI 2015/575, reg 59, Sch 1, Pt 1, paras 1, 7, as from 1 January 2016.

The final words in square brackets in sub-s (11) were added, and all other words in square brackets in this section were substituted, by the Financial Services Act 2012, s 41, Sch 12, Pt 1, para 1.

Authorised person: as from 1 April 2014, this section has effect as if each reference to "authorised person" (except in sub-s (7)) included a reference to a person who at any time held a standard licence under the Consumer Credit Act 1974; see the Financial Services and Markets Act 2000 (Regulated Activities) (Amendment) (No 2) Order 2013, SI 2013/1881, art 50(1) at **[2.1030]**.

Note: any reference in ss 165–168 and 176 to an authorised person includes a reference to an unauthorised incoming provider; see the Electronic Commerce Directive (Financial Services and Markets) Regulations 2002, SI 2002/1775, reg 12(3).

Note that the Banking Act 2009, s 250 provides that the PRA shall collect information that it thinks is or may be relevant to the stability of individual financial institutions, or one or more aspects of the financial systems of the UK. The Authority may perform that function by the exercise of the power in section 165 or 165A.

Transitional provisions etc in connection with the original commencement of this Act: this section and ss 166, 167 are modified by the Financial Services and Markets Act 2000 (Transitional Provisions and Savings) (Civil Remedies, Discipline, Criminal Offences etc) (No 2) Order 2001, SI 2001/3083, arts 15–17, so that the powers conferred by ss 165–167 are exercisable in respect of any person who was, before 1 December 2001, a regulated person but who is not, and never has been, an authorised person under this Act.

Transitional provisions (credit unions): see the Financial Services and Markets Act 2000 (Permissions, Transitional Provisions and Consequential Amendments) (Northern Ireland Credit Unions) Order 2011, SI 2011/2832 which enabled the Authority to exercise its powers under this section (from 31 December 2011) in relation to those credit unions which it has reasonable grounds to believe will be authorised persons at 31 March 2012.

Transitional provisions: see also the Financial Services and Markets Act 2000 (Consumer Credit) (Transitional Provisions) Order 2013, SI 2013/3128, art 4.

[1.1508]
[166   Reports by skilled persons
(1)   This section applies where either regulator has required or could require a person to whom subsection (2) applies ("the person concerned") to provide information or produce documents with respect to any matter ("the matter concerned").

(2)   This subsection applies to—

    (a)   an authorised person ("A"),

    (b)   any other member of A's group,

    (c)   a partnership of which A is a member, or

    (d)   a person who has at any relevant time been a person falling within paragraph (a), (b) or (c),

who is, or was at the relevant time, carrying on a business.

(3)   The regulator mentioned in subsection (1) may either—

    (a)   by notice in writing given to the person concerned, require the person concerned to provide the regulator with a report on the matter concerned, or

    (b)   itself appoint a person to provide the regulator with a report on the matter concerned.

(4)   When acting under subsection (3)(a), the regulator may require the report to be in such form as may be specified in the notice.

(5)   The regulator must give notice of an appointment under subsection (3)(b) to the person concerned.

(6)   The person appointed to make a report—

    (a)   must be a person appearing to the regulator to have the skills necessary to make a report on the matter concerned, and

    (b)   where the appointment is to be made by the person concerned, must be a person nominated or approved by the regulator.

(7)   It is the duty of—

    (a)   the person concerned, and

    (b)   any person who is providing (or who has at any time provided) services to the person concerned in relation to the matter concerned,

to give the person appointed to prepare a report all such assistance as the appointed person may reasonably require.

(8)   The obligation imposed by subsection (7) is enforceable, on the application of the regulator in question, by an injunction or, in Scotland, by an order for specific performance under section 45 of the Court of Session Act 1988.

(9)　A regulator may make rules providing for expenses incurred by it in relation to an appointment under subsection (3)(b) to be payable as a fee by the person concerned.

(10)　The powers conferred by this section may also be exercised by the FCA in relation to a person to whom subsection (11) applies, (and references to the person concerned are to be read accordingly).

(11)　This subsection applies to—
  (a)　a recognised investment exchange ("A"),
  (b)　any other member of A's group,
  (c)　a partnership of which A is a member, or
  (d)　a person who has at any time been a person falling within paragraph (a), (b) or (c),
who is, or was at the relevant time, carrying on a business.]

NOTES

Commencement: 24 January 2013 (for the purpose of making rules); 1 April 2013 (otherwise).
Substituted by the Financial Services Act 2012, s 41, Sch 12, Pt 1, para 5.
Note: any reference in ss 165–168 and 176 to an authorised person includes a reference to an unauthorised incoming provider; see the Electronic Commerce Directive (Financial Services and Markets) Regulations 2002, SI 2002/1775, reg 12(3).
Transitional provisions etc in connection with the original commencement of this Act: see the note to s 165 at **[1.1507]**.

[1.1509]
[166A　Appointment of skilled person to collect and update information

(1)　This section applies if either regulator considers that an authorised person has contravened a requirement in rules made by that regulator to collect, and keep up to date, information of a description specified in the rules.

(2)　The regulator may either—
  (a)　require the authorised person to appoint a skilled person to collect or update the information, or
  (b)　itself appoint a skilled person to do so.

(3)　References in this section to a skilled person are to a person—
  (a)　appearing to the regulator to have the skills necessary to collect or update the information in question, and
  (b)　where the appointment is to be made by the authorised person, nominated or approved by the regulator.

(4)　The regulator must give notice of an appointment under subsection (2)(b) to the authorised person.

(5)　The skilled person may require any person to provide all such assistance as the skilled person may reasonably require to collect or update the information in question.

(6)　A requirement imposed under subsection (5) is enforceable, on the application of the regulator in question, by an injunction or, in Scotland, by an order for specific performance under section 45 of the Court of Session Act 1988.

(7)　A contractual or other requirement imposed on a person ("P") to keep any information in confidence does not apply if—
  (a)　the information is or may be relevant to anything required to be done as a result of this section,
  (b)　an authorised person or a skilled person requests or requires P to provide the information for the purpose of securing that those things are done, and
  (c)　the regulator in question has approved the making of the request or the imposition of the requirement before it is made or imposed.

(8)　An authorised person may provide information (whether received under subsection (7) or otherwise) that would otherwise be subject to a contractual or other requirement to keep it in confidence if it is provided for the purposes of anything required to be done as a result of this section.

(9)　A regulator may make rules providing for expenses incurred by it in relation to an appointment under subsection (2)(b) to be payable as a fee by the authorised person.

(10)　In this section "authorised person", in relation to the PRA, means PRA-authorised person.]

NOTES

Commencement: 24 January 2013 (for the purposes of making rules); 1 April 2013 (otherwise).
Inserted by the Financial Services Act 2012, s 41, Sch 12, Pt 1, para 6.
Note: any reference in ss 165–168 and 176 to an authorised person includes a reference to an unauthorised incoming provider; see the Electronic Commerce Directive (Financial Services and Markets) Regulations 2002, SI 2002/1775, reg 12(3).

Appointment of investigators

[1.1510]
167　Appointment of persons to carry out general investigations

(1)　If it appears to [an investigating authority] that there is good reason for doing so, the investigating authority may appoint one or more competent persons to conduct an investigation on its behalf into—
  (a)　the nature, conduct or state of the business of [a recognised investment exchange or] an authorised person or of an appointed representative;

(b) a particular aspect of that business; or

(c) the ownership or control of [a recognised investment exchange or] an authorised person.

(2) If a person appointed under subsection (1) thinks it necessary for the purposes of his investigation, he may also investigate the business of a person who is or has at any relevant time been—

(a) a member of the group of which the person under investigation ("A") is part; *or*

(b) a partnership of which A is a member[; or;]

[(c) where A is an insurance undertaking, reinsurance undertaking or third-country insurance undertaking, a person who provides services to A].

(3) If a person appointed under subsection (1) decides to investigate the business of any person under subsection (2) he must give that person written notice of his decision.

[(3A) If a person appointed under subsection (1) decides under subsection (2)(c) to investigate a person located in an EEA State other than the United Kingdom the person appointed must inform the supervisory authority of that EEA State prior to conducting an on-site inspection.]

(4) The power conferred by this section may be exercised in relation to a former authorised person (or appointed representative) but only in relation to—

(a) business carried on at any time when he was an authorised person (or appointed representative); or

(b) the ownership or control of a former authorised person at any time when he was an authorised person.

(5) "Business" includes any part of a business even if it does not consist of carrying on regulated activities.

[(5A) Investigating authority" means—

(a) in relation to a recognised investment exchange, the Secretary of State or the FCA;

(b) in relation to an authorised person or former authorised person, the FCA or the PRA;

(c) in relation to an appointed representative or former appointed representative, the FCA or the PRA.]

[(6) References in subsection (1) to a recognised investment exchange do not include references to an overseas investment exchange (as defined by section 313(1)).]

NOTES

Sub-s (1): words in first pair of square brackets substituted by the Financial Services Act 2012, s 41, Sch 12, Pt 1, para 7(1), (2); words in second pair of square brackets inserted by the Financial Services and Markets Act 2000 (Markets in Financial Instruments) Regulations 2007, SI 2007/126, reg 3(5), Sch 5, paras 1, 7(a).

Sub-s (2): word in italics in para (a) repealed, and para (c) (and the preceding word in square brackets) inserted, by the Solvency 2 Regulations 2015, SI 2015/575, reg 59, Sch 1, Pt 1, paras 1, 8(1), (2), as from 1 January 2016.

Sub-s (3A): inserted by SI 2015/575, reg 59, Sch 1, Pt 1, paras 1, 8(1), (3), as from 1 January 2016.

Sub-s (5A): inserted by the Financial Services Act 2012, s 41, Sch 12, Pt 1, para 7(1), (3).

Sub-s (6): added by SI 2007/126, reg 3(5), Sch 5, paras 1, 7(b).

Note: any reference in ss 165–168 and 176 to an authorised person includes a reference to an unauthorised incoming provider; see the Electronic Commerce Directive (Financial Services and Markets) Regulations 2002, SI 2002/1775, reg 12(3).

Transitional provisions etc in connection with the original commencement of this Act: see the note to s 165 at [**1.1507**].

[1.1511]
168 Appointment of persons to carry out investigations in particular cases

(1) Subsection (3) applies if it appears to an investigating authority that there are circumstances suggesting that—

(a) . . .

(b) a person may be guilty of an offence under section 177, [191F], 346 or 398(1) or under Schedule 4.

(2) Subsection (3) also applies if it appears to an investigating authority that there are circumstances suggesting that—

(a) an offence under section 24(1) [or 333G] [or under Part 7 of the Financial Services Act 2012] or under Part V of the Criminal Justice Act 1993 may have been committed;

(b) there may have been a breach of the general prohibition;

[(ba) an authorised person may have contravened section 20 in relation to a credit-related regulated activity;]

(c) there may have been a contravention of section 21 or 238; or

(d) market abuse may have taken place.

(3) The investigating authority may appoint one or more competent persons to conduct an investigation on its behalf.

(4) Subsection (5) applies if it appears to [an investigating authority] that there are circumstances suggesting that—

(a) a person may have contravened section 20;

(b) a person may be guilty of an offence under prescribed regulations relating to money laundering;

[(ba) a person may be guilty of an offence under Schedule 7 to the Counter-Terrorism Act 2008 (terrorist financing or money laundering);]

(c) [a person] may have contravened a rule made by the [investigating authority];

[(ca) a recognised investment exchange may have contravened the recognition requirements (within the meaning of Part 18);]

(d)   an individual may not be a fit and proper person to perform functions in relation to a regulated activity carried on by an authorised or exempt person;

(e)   an individual may have performed or agreed to perform a function in breach of a prohibition order;

(f)   [a person] may have failed to comply with section 56(6);

(g)   an authorised person may have failed to comply with section 59(1) or (2);

(h)   a person in relation to whom [a regulator] has given its approval under section 59 may not be a fit and proper person to perform the function to which that approval relates;   . . .

[(ha) a person may have performed a controlled function without approval for the purposes of section 63A;]

(i)   a person may be guilty of misconduct for the purposes of section 66[;   . . .

(j)   a person may have contravened any provision made by or under this Act for the purpose of implementing the markets in financial instruments directive   . . .]; [. . .

[(ja) a person may have contravened—

     (i)   any provision made by or under this Act for the purpose of implementing the alternative investment fund managers directive; or

     (ii)   any provision made by the Alternative Investment Fund Managers Regulations 2013; or]

[(k)   a person may have contravened a qualifying EU provision that is specified, or of a description specified, for the purposes of this subsection by the Treasury by order].

(5)   The [investigating authority] may appoint one or more competent persons to conduct an investigation on its behalf.

[(6)   Investigating authority" means—

(a)   in subsections (1) to (3), the FCA, the PRA or the Secretary of State;

(b)   in subsections (4) and (5), the FCA or the PRA.]

NOTES

Sub-s (1): para (a) repealed, and figure in square brackets substituted, by the Financial Services Act 2012, s 41, Sch 12, Pt 1, para 8(1), (2).

Sub-s (2): words in first pair of square brackets in para (a) inserted by the Pension Schemes Act 2015, s 47, Sch 3, paras 1, 11; words in second pair of square brackets in para (a) substituted, and para (ba) inserted, by the Financial Services Act 2012, s 41, Sch 12, Pt 1, para 8(1), (3).

Sub-s (4) is amended as follows

Words "an investigating authority" in square brackets substituted by the Financial Services Act 2012, s 41, Sch 12, Pt 1, para 8(1), (4)(a).

Para (ba) inserted by the Counter-Terrorism Act 2008, s 62, Sch 7, Pt 7, para 33(3).

Words "a person" in square brackets in para (c) substituted, and para (ha) inserted, by the Financial Services Act 2010, s 24(1), (2), Sch 2, Pt 1, paras 1, 16.

Words "investigating authority" in square brackets in para (c) substituted by the Financial Services Act 2012, s 41, Sch 12, Pt 1, para 8(1), (4)(b).

Para (ca) inserted by the Financial Services Act 2012, s 41, Sch 12, Pt 1, para 8(1), (4)(c).

Words "a person" in square brackets in para (f) substituted by the Financial Services Act 2012, s 41, Sch 12, Pt 1, para 8(1), (4)(d).

Words "a regulator" in square brackets in para (h) substituted by the Financial Services Act 2012, s 41, Sch 12, Pt 1, para 8(1), (4)(e).

Word omitted from para (h) repealed, and para (j) and the word immediately preceding it inserted, by the Financial Services and Markets Act 2000 (Markets in Financial Instruments) Regulations 2007, SI 2007/126, reg 3(5), Sch 5, paras 1, 8.

Word omitted from para (i) repealed, and para (k) and the word immediately preceding it inserted, by the Financial Services and Markets Act 2000 (Short Selling) Regulations 2012, SI 2012/2554, reg 2(1), (11).

First words omitted from para (j) repealed by the Financial Services Act 2012, s 41, Sch 12, Pt 1, para 8(1), (4)(f).

The second word omitted from para (j) was repealed, and para (ja) was inserted, by the Alternative Investment Fund Managers Regulations 2013, SI 2013/1773, reg 80, Sch 1, Part 1, paras 1, 10, (for transitional provisions and savings see Part 9 of the 2013 Regulations).

Para (k) substituted by the Financial Services Act 2012, s 41, Sch 12, Pt 1, para 8(1), (4)(g).

Sub-s (5): words in square brackets substituted by the Financial Services Act 2012, s 41, Sch 12, Pt 1, para 8(1), (5).

Sub-s (6): substituted by the Financial Services Act 2012, s 41, Sch 12, Pt 1, para 8(1), (5).

Offence: as from 1 April 2014, this section applies as if sub-s (1) included a reference to an offence under the Consumer Credit Act 1974; see the Financial Services and Markets Act 2000 (Regulated Activities) (Amendment) (No 2) Order 2013, SI 2013/1881, art 50(2)(a) at **[2.1030]**.

Circumstances suggesting, etc (sub-s (4)): as from 1 April 2014, sub-s (4) has effect as if it included a reference to circumstances suggesting that a person may have, before that date, failed to comply with a requirement imposed on that person under the Consumer Credit Act 1974, ss 33A, 33B or 36A; see the Financial Services and Markets Act 2000 (Regulated Activities) (Amendment) (No 2) Order 2013, SI 2013/1881, art 50(2)(b) at **[2.1030]**.

Note: any reference in ss 165–168 and 176 to an authorised person includes a reference to an unauthorised incoming provider; see the Electronic Commerce Directive (Financial Services and Markets) Regulations 2002, SI 2002/1775, reg 12(3). Note also that the reference in sub-s (4)(c) to a rule made by the FCA includes a reference to a requirement imposed by the FCA under the 2002 Regulations; see reg 12(5).

Transitional provisions etc in connection with the original commencement of this Act: see the Financial Services and Markets Act 2000 (Transitional Provisions and Savings) (Civil Remedies, Discipline, Criminal Offences etc) (No 2) Order 2001, SI 2001/3083, art 18 which modifies this section so it applies where there are circumstances suggesting that a person has contravened, or committed an offence under, certain enactments, provisions or rules before commencement.

Note: the Money Laundering Regulations 2007, SI 2007/2157 are prescribed for the purposes of sub-s (4)(b) above by reg 1(2) of those Regulations (at **[2.464]**). The Transfer of Funds (Information on the Payer) Regulations 2007, SI 2007/3298 are also prescribed for the purposes of sub-s (4)(b) above by reg 1(2) of those Regulations.

Extension of powers (civil sanctions): where, by virtue of sub-s (4)(b) above, a Minister of the Crown (or the Welsh Ministers) has the power by statutory instrument to make provision creating a criminal offence and the power has been or is being exercised so as to create the offence, then that power is extended so as to include the power to confer on certain persons the power to impose civil sanctions in relation to the offence; see the Regulatory Enforcement and Sanctions Act 2008, s 62, Sch 7.

Regulations: the Money Laundering Regulations 2007, SI 2007/2157 at **[2.464]**; the Transfer of Funds (Information on the Payer) Regulations 2007, SI 2007/3298.

Orders: the Financial Services and Markets Act 2000 (Qualifying EU Provisions) Order 2013, SI 2013/419; the Financial Services and Markets Act 2000 (Qualifying EU Provisions) (No 2) Order 2013, SI 2013/3116.

Conduct of investigations

[1.1512]
170 Investigations: general
(1) This section applies if an investigating authority appoints one or more competent persons ("investigators") under section 167 or 168(3) or (5) to conduct an investigation on its behalf.
(2) The investigating authority must give written notice of the appointment of an investigator to the person who is the subject of the investigation ("the person under investigation").
(3) Subsections (2) and (9) do not apply if—
(a) the investigator is appointed as a result of section 168(1) or (4) and the investigating authority believes that the notice required by subsection (2) or (9) would be likely to result in the investigation being frustrated; or
(b) the investigator is appointed as a result of subsection (2) of section 168.
(4) A notice under subsection (2) must—
(a) specify the provisions under which, and as a result of which, the investigator was appointed; and
(b) state the reason for his appointment.
(5) Nothing prevents the investigating authority from appointing a person who is a member of its staff as an investigator.
(6) An investigator must make a report of his investigation to the investigating authority.
(7) The investigating authority may, by a direction to an investigator, control—
(a) the scope of the investigation;
(b) the period during which the investigation is to be conducted;
(c) the conduct of the investigation; and
(d) the reporting of the investigation.
(8) A direction may, in particular—
(a) confine the investigation to particular matters;
(b) extend the investigation to additional matters;
(c) require the investigator to discontinue the investigation or to take only such steps as are specified in the direction;
(d) require the investigator to make such interim reports as are so specified.
(9) If there is a change in the scope or conduct of the investigation and, in the opinion of the investigating authority, the person subject to investigation is likely to be significantly prejudiced by not being made aware of it, that person must be given written notice of the change.
(10) "Investigating authority", in relation to an investigator, means—
  [(a) the FCA, if the FCA appointed the investigator;
  (aa) the PRA, if the PRA appointed the investigator;
  (b) the Secretary of State, if the Secretary of State appointed the investigator].

NOTES
Sub-s (10): paras (a), (aa), (b) substituted (for the original paras (a), (b)) by the Financial Services Act 2012, s 41, Sch 12, Pt 1, para 10.

[1.1513]
171 Powers of persons appointed under section 167
(1) An investigator may require the person who is the subject of the investigation ("the person under investigation") or any person connected with the person under investigation—
(a) to attend before the investigator at a specified time and place and answer questions; or
(b) otherwise to provide such information as the investigator may require.
(2) An investigator may also require any person to produce at a specified time and place any specified documents or documents of a specified description.
(3) A requirement under subsection (1) or (2) may be imposed only so far as the investigator concerned reasonably considers the question, provision of information or production of the document to be relevant to the purposes of the investigation.
[(3A) Where the investigation relates to a recognised investment exchange, an investigator has the additional powers conferred by sections 172 and 173 (and for this purpose references in those sections to an investigator are to be read accordingly).]

(4)   For the purposes of this section and section 172, a person is connected with the person under investigation ("A") if he is or has at any relevant time been—
  (a)   a member of A's group;
  (b)   a controller of A;
  (c)   a partnership of which A is a member; or
  (d)   in relation to A, a person mentioned in Part I or II of Schedule 15.
(5)   "Investigator" means a person conducting an investigation under section 167.
(6)   "Specified" means specified in a notice in writing.
[(7)   The reference in subsection (3A) to a recognised investment exchange does not include a reference to an overseas investment exchange (as defined by section 313(1)).]

NOTES

Sub-ss (3A), (7): inserted and added respectively by the Financial Services and Markets Act 2000 (Markets in Financial Instruments) Regulations 2007, SI 2007/126, reg 3(5), Sch 5, paras 1, 9.

[1.1514]
172   Additional power of persons appointed as a result of section 168(1) or (4)
(1)   An investigator has the powers conferred by section 171.
(2)   An investigator may also require a person who is neither the subject of the investigation ("the person under investigation") nor a person connected with the person under investigation—
  (a)   to attend before the investigator at a specified time and place and answer questions; or
  (b)   otherwise to provide such information as the investigator may require for the purposes of the investigation.
(3)   A requirement may only be imposed under subsection (2) if the investigator is satisfied that the requirement is necessary or expedient for the purposes of the investigation.
(4)   "Investigator" means a person appointed as a result of subsection (1) or (4) of section 168.
(5)   "Specified" means specified in a notice in writing.

[1.1515]
173   Powers of persons appointed as a result of section 168(2)
(1)   Subsections (2) to (4) apply if an investigator considers that any person ("A") is or may be able to give information which is or may be relevant to the investigation.
(2)   The investigator may require A—
  (a)   to attend before him at a specified time and place and answer questions; or
  (b)   otherwise to provide such information as he may require for the purposes of the investigation.
(3)   The investigator may also require A to produce at a specified time and place any specified documents or documents of a specified description which appear to the investigator to relate to any matter relevant to the investigation.
(4)   The investigator may also otherwise require A to give him all assistance in connection with the investigation which A is reasonably able to give.
(5)   "Investigator" means a person appointed under subsection (3) of section 168 (as a result of subsection (2) of that section).

[1.1516]
174   Admissibility of statements made to investigators
(1)   A statement made to an investigator by a person in compliance with an information requirement is admissible in evidence in any proceedings, so long as it also complies with any requirements governing the admissibility of evidence in the circumstances in question.
(2)   But in criminal proceedings in which that person is charged with an offence to which this subsection applies or in proceedings in relation to action to be taken against that person under section 123—
  (a)   no evidence relating to the statement may be adduced, and
  (b)   no question relating to it may be asked,
by or on behalf of the prosecution or (as the case may be) [a regulator], unless evidence relating to it is adduced, or a question relating to it is asked, in the proceedings by or on behalf of that person.
(3)   Subsection (2) applies to any offence other than one—
  (a)   under section 177(4) or 398;
  (b)   under section 5 of the Perjury Act 1911 (false statements made otherwise than on oath);
  (c)   under section 44(2) of the Criminal Law (Consolidation) (Scotland) Act 1995 (false statements made otherwise than on oath); or
  (d)   under Article 10 of the Perjury (Northern Ireland) Order 1979.
(4)   "Investigator" means a person appointed under section 167 or 168(3) or (5).
(5)   "Information requirement" means a requirement imposed by an investigator under section 171, 172, 173 or 175.

NOTES

Sub-s (2): words in square brackets substituted by the Financial Services Act 2012, s 41, Sch 12, Pt 1, para 12.

[1.1517]
175 Information and documents: supplemental provisions

(1) If [either regulator] or an investigator has power under this Part to require a person to produce a document but it appears that the document is in the possession of a third person, that power may be exercised in relation to the third person.

(2) If a document is produced in response to a requirement imposed under this Part, the person to whom it is produced may—

   (a) take copies or extracts from the document; or
   (b) require the person producing the document, or any relevant person, to provide an explanation of the document.

[(2A) A document so produced may be retained for so long as the person to whom it is produced considers that it is necessary to retain it (rather than copies of it) for the purposes for which the document was requested.

(2B) If the person to whom a document is so produced has reasonable grounds for believing—

   (a) that the document may have to be produced for the purposes of any legal proceedings, and
   (b) that it might otherwise be unavailable for those purposes,

it may be retained until the proceedings are concluded.]

(3) If a person who is required under this Part to produce a document fails to do so, the [regulator] or an investigator may require him to state, to the best of his knowledge and belief, where the document is.

(4) A lawyer may be required under this Part to furnish the name and address of his client.

(5) No person may be required under this Part to disclose information or produce a document in respect of which he owes an obligation of confidence by virtue of carrying on the business of banking unless—

   (a) he is the person under investigation or a member of that person's group;
   (b) the person to whom the obligation of confidence is owed is the person under investigation or a member of that person's group;
   (c) the person to whom the obligation of confidence is owed consents to the disclosure or production; or
   (d) the imposing on him of a requirement with respect to such information or document has been specifically authorised by the investigating authority.

(6) If a person claims a lien on a document, its production under this Part does not affect the lien.

(7) "Relevant person", in relation to a person who is required to produce a document, means a person who—

   (a) has been or is or is proposed to be a director or controller of that person;
   (b) has been or is an auditor of that person;
   (c) has been or is an actuary, accountant or lawyer appointed or instructed by that person; or
   (d) has been or is an employee of that person.

(8) "Investigator" means a person appointed under section 167 or 168(3) or (5).

NOTES
Words in square brackets in sub-ss (1), (3) substituted, and sub-ss (2A), (2B) inserted, by the Financial Services Act 2012, s 41, Sch 12, Pt 1, para 13.

[1.1518]
176 Entry of premises under warrant

(1) A justice of the peace may issue a warrant under this section if satisfied on information on oath given by or on behalf of the Secretary of State, [either regulator] or an investigator that there are reasonable grounds for believing that the first, second or third set of conditions is satisfied.

(2) The first set of conditions is—

   (a) that a person on whom an information requirement has been imposed has failed (wholly or in part) to comply with it; and
   (b) that on the premises specified in the warrant—
       (i) there are documents which have been required; or
       (ii) there is information which has been required.

(3) The second set of conditions is—

   (a) that the premises specified in the warrant are premises of an authorised person or an appointed representative;
   (b) that there are on the premises documents or information in relation to which an information requirement could be imposed; and
   (c) that if such a requirement were to be imposed—
       (i) it would not be complied with; or
       (ii) the documents or information to which it related would be removed, tampered with or destroyed.

(4) The third set of conditions is—

   (a) that an offence mentioned in section 168 for which the maximum sentence on conviction on indictment is two years or more has been (or is being) committed by any person;
   (b) that there are on the premises specified in the warrant documents or information relevant to whether that offence has been (or is being) committed;

  (c)   that an information requirement could be imposed in relation to those documents or information; and

  (d)   that if such a requirement were to be imposed—

      (i)   it would not be complied with; or

      (ii)   the documents or information to which it related would be removed, tampered with or destroyed.

(5)   A warrant under this section shall authorise a constable—

  (a)   to enter the premises specified in the warrant;

  (b)   to search the premises and take possession of any documents or information appearing to be documents or information of a kind in respect of which a warrant under this section was issued ("the relevant kind") or to take, in relation to any such documents or information, any other steps which may appear to be necessary for preserving them or preventing interference with them;

  (c)   to take copies of, or extracts from, any documents or information appearing to be of the relevant kind;

  (d)   to require any person on the premises to provide an explanation of any document or information appearing to be of the relevant kind or to state where it may be found; and

  (e)   to use such force as may be reasonably necessary.

[(5A)   A warrant under this section may be executed by any constable.

(5B)   The warrant may authorise persons to accompany any constable who is executing it.

(5C)   The powers in subsection (5) may be exercised by a person authorised by the warrant to accompany a constable; but that person may exercise those powers only in the company of, and under the supervision of, a constable.]

(6)   In England and Wales, sections 15(5) to (8) and section [16(3) to (12)] of the Police and Criminal Evidence Act 1984 (execution of search warrants and safeguards) apply to warrants issued under this section.

(7)   In Northern Ireland, Articles 17(5) to (8) and [18(3) to (12)] of the Police and Criminal Evidence (Northern Ireland) Order 1989 apply to warrants issued under this section.

(8)   . . .

(9)   In the application of this section to Scotland—

  (a)   for the references to a justice of the peace substitute references to a justice of the peace or a sheriff; and

  (b)   for the references to information on oath substitute references to evidence on oath.

(10)   "Investigator" means a person appointed under section 167 or 168(3) or (5).

(11)   "Information requirement" means a requirement imposed—

  (a)   by [a regulator] under section [87C, 87J,] 165[, 165A, 169A] or 175; or

  (b)   by an investigator under section 171, 172, 173 or 175.

NOTES

The words in square brackets in sub-ss (1), (6), (7) were substituted, sub-ss (5A)–(5C) were inserted, sub-s (8) was repealed, and the words "a regulator" in square brackets in subs (11) were substituted, by the Financial Services Act 2012, s 41, Sch 12, Pt 1, para 14.

Figures "87C, 87J" in square brackets in sub-s (11)(a) inserted by the Prospectus Regulations 2005, SI 2005/1433, reg 2(1), Sch 1, para 12.

Figures ", 165A, 169A" in square brackets in sub-s (11)(a) inserted by the Financial Services Act 2010, s 24(1), (2), Sch 2, Pt 1, paras 1, 17.

Note: any reference in ss 165–168 and 176 to an authorised person includes a reference to an unauthorised incoming provider; see the Electronic Commerce Directive (Financial Services and Markets) Regulations 2002, SI 2002/1775, reg 12(3).

Additional powers of seizure: the power of seizure conferred by sub-s (5) above is a power of seizure to which the Criminal Justice and Police Act 2001, s 50 (additional powers of seizure from premises) applies; see s 50 of, and Sch 1, Pt 1, para 69 to, the 2001 Act.

[1.1519]

[176A   Retention of documents taken under section 176

(1)   Any document of which possession is taken under section 176 ("a seized document") may be retained so long as it is necessary to retain it (rather than copies of it) in the circumstances.

(2)   A person claiming to be the owner of a seized document may apply to a magistrates' court or (in Scotland) the sheriff for an order for the delivery of the document to the person appearing to the court or sheriff to be the owner.

(3)   If on an application under subsection (2) the court or (in Scotland) the sheriff cannot ascertain who is the owner of the seized document the court or sheriff (as the case may be) may make such order as the court or sheriff thinks fit.

(4)   An order under subsection (2) or (3) does not affect the right of any person to take legal proceedings against any person in possession of a seized document for the recovery of the document.

(5)   Any right to bring proceedings (as described in subsection (4)) may only be exercised within 6 months of the date of the order made under subsection (2) or (3).]

NOTES

Commencement: 1 April 2013.

Inserted by the Financial Services Act 2012, s 41, Sch 12, Pt 1, para 15.

Offences

[1.1520]
177 Offences
(1) If a person other than the investigator ("the defaulter") fails to comply with a requirement imposed on him under this Part the person imposing the requirement may certify that fact in writing to the court.
(2) If the court is satisfied that the defaulter failed without reasonable excuse to comply with the requirement, it may deal with the defaulter (and in the case of a body corporate, any director or [other] officer) as if he were in contempt[; and "officer", in relation to a limited liability partnership, means a member of the limited liability partnership].
(3) A person who knows or suspects that an investigation is being or is likely to be conducted under this Part is guilty of an offence if—
  (a) he falsifies, conceals, destroys or otherwise disposes of a document which he knows or suspects is or would be relevant to such an investigation, or
  (b) he causes or permits the falsification, concealment, destruction or disposal of such a document,
unless he shows that he had no intention of concealing facts disclosed by the documents from the investigator.
(4) A person who, in purported compliance with a requirement imposed on him under this Part—
  (a) provides information which he knows to be false or misleading in a material particular, or
  (b) recklessly provides information which is false or misleading in a material particular,
is guilty of an offence.
(5) A person guilty of an offence under subsection (3) or (4) is liable—
  (a) on summary conviction, to imprisonment for a term not exceeding six months or a fine not exceeding the statutory maximum, or both;
  (b) on conviction on indictment, to imprisonment for a term not exceeding two years or a fine, or both.
(6) Any person who intentionally obstructs the exercise of any rights conferred by a warrant under section 176 is guilty of an offence and liable on summary conviction to imprisonment for a term not exceeding *three months* or a fine not exceeding level 5 on the standard scale, or both.
(7) "Court" means—
  (a) the High Court;
  (b) in Scotland, the Court of Session.

NOTES
Sub-s (2): word in first pair of square brackets inserted by the Financial Services Act 2012, s 114(1), Sch 18, Pt 1, paras 1, 8; words in second pair of square brackets added by the Limited Liability Partnerships Regulations 2001, SI 2001/1090, reg 9, Sch 5, para 21.
Sub-s (6): for the words in italics there are substituted the words "51 weeks" by the Criminal Justice Act 2003, s 280(2), Sch 26, para 54(1), (2).

PART XIV
DISCIPLINARY MEASURES

NOTES
Extension of scope: section 404C of this Act (at **[1.1574]**) extends the scope of this Part (and so much of this Act that relates to any provision in this Part) to relevant firms which are not, or are no longer, authorised persons.
Transitional provisions etc in connection with the commencement of the Financial Services Act 2012: see the Financial Services Act 2012 (Transitional Provisions) (Enforcement) Order 2013, SI 2013/441. Article 11 makes transitional provision in relation to the exercise of disciplinary powers under this Act in relation to contravention of requirements occurring before 1 April 2013.

[1.1521]
[204A Meaning of "relevant requirement" and "appropriate regulator"
(1) The following definitions apply for the purposes of this Part.
(2) "Relevant requirement" means a requirement imposed—
  (a) by or under this Act, . . .
  (b) by a qualifying EU provision specified, or of a description specified, for the purposes of this subsection by the Treasury by order, [or
  (c) by the Alternative Investment Fund Managers Regulations 2013].
(3) The PRA is "the appropriate regulator" in the case of a contravention of—
  (a) a requirement that is imposed under any provision of this Act by the PRA;
  (b) a requirement under section 56(6) where the authorised person concerned is a PRA-authorised person and the prohibition order concerned is made by the PRA;
  (c) a requirement under section 59(1) or (2) where the authorised person concerned is a PRA-authorised person and the approval concerned falls to be given by the PRA.

(4)   In the case of a contravention of a requirement that is imposed by a qualifying EU provision, "the appropriate regulator" for the purpose of any provision of this Part is whichever of the PRA or the FCA (or both) is specified by the Treasury by order in relation to the qualifying EU provision for the purposes of that provision of this Part.

(5)   In the case of a contravention of a requirement where the contravention constitutes an offence, the "appropriate regulator" is whichever of the PRA or the FCA has power to prosecute the offence (see section 401).

(6)   The FCA is "the appropriate regulator" in the case of a contravention of any other requirement imposed by or under this Act.

(7)   The Treasury may by order amend the provisions defining "the appropriate regulator".]

NOTES

Commencement: 24 January 2013 (for the purposes of making orders); 1 April 2013 (otherwise).

Inserted by the Financial Services Act 2012, s 37(1), Sch 9, Pt 1, para 1, Pt 4, para 10.

Sub-s (2): the word omitted from para (a) was repealed, and para (c) (and the preceding word) was added, by the Alternative Investment Fund Managers Regulations 2013, SI 2013/1773, reg 80, Sch 1, Part 1, paras 1, 15, (for transitional provisions and savings see Part 9 of the 2013 Regulations).

Note: (1) for the purposes of ss 204A–209 and 384 a requirement imposed by the FCA under Part 3 of the Electronic Commerce Directive (Financial Services and Markets) Regulations 2002, SI 2002/1775 upon an authorised incoming provider is to be treated as imposed on that provider by or under this Act; (2) for the purposes of those sections, (a) a requirement imposed by a direction imposed by the FCA under reg 11B of the 2002 Regulations is to be treated as a requirement imposed by or under this Act, and (b) any reference in those sections to an authorised person includes a reference to an unauthorised incoming provider. See reg 12(1), (1A) of those Regulations.

Orders: the Financial Services and Markets Act 2000 (Qualifying EU Provisions) Order 2013, SI 2013/419; the Financial Services and Markets Act 2000 (Qualifying EU Provisions) (No 2) Order 2013, SI 2013/3116.

[1.1522]
205   Public censure
If the [appropriate regulator] considers that an authorised person has contravened [a relevant requirement imposed on the person, it may] publish a statement to that effect.

NOTES

Words in square brackets substituted by the Financial Services Act 2012, s 37(1), Sch 9, Pt 1, para 1, Pt 4, para 11.

Transitional provisions etc in connection with the original commencement of this Act: as to the exercise of the power conferred by this section in respect of: (a) certain contraventions of the Financial Services Act 1986 (repealed), before 1 December 2001; and (b) contraventions of the rules of self-regulating organisations before that date, see the Financial Services and Markets Act 2000 (Transitional Provisions and Savings) (Civil Remedies, Discipline, Criminal Offences etc) (No 2) Order 2001, SI 2001/3083, arts 6, 7.

Note: (1) for the purposes of ss 204A–209 and 384 a requirement imposed by the FCA under Part 3 of the Electronic Commerce Directive (Financial Services and Markets) Regulations 2002, SI 2002/1775 upon an authorised incoming provider is to be treated as imposed on that provider by or under this Act; (2) for the purposes of those sections, (a) a requirement imposed by a direction imposed by the FCA under reg 11B of the 2002 Regulations is to be treated as a requirement imposed by or under this Act, and (b) any reference in those sections to an authorised person includes a reference to an unauthorised incoming provider. See reg 12(1), (1A) of those Regulations.

[1.1523]
206   Financial penalties
(1)   If the [appropriate regulator] considers that an authorised person has contravened [a relevant requirement imposed on the person,] it may impose on him a penalty, in respect of the contravention, of such amount as it considers appropriate.

(2)   . . .

(3)   A penalty under this section is payable to the [regulator that imposed the penalty].

NOTES

Sub-ss (1), (3): words in square brackets substituted by the Financial Services Act 2012, s 37(1), Sch 9, Pt 1, Pt 4, para 12.

Sub-s (2): repealed by the Financial Services Act 2010, s 10.

Transitional provisions etc in connection with the original commencement of this Act: as to the exercise of the power conferred by this section in respect of contraventions of the rules of self-regulating organisations before 1 December 2001, see the Financial Services and Markets Act 2000 (Transitional Provisions and Savings) (Civil Remedies, Discipline, Criminal Offences etc) (No 2) Order 2001, SI 2001/3083, art 8.

Note: (1) for the purposes of ss 204A–209 and 384 a requirement imposed by the FCA under Part 3 of the Electronic Commerce Directive (Financial Services and Markets) Regulations 2002, SI 2002/1775 upon an authorised incoming provider is to be treated as imposed on that provider by or under this Act; (2) for the purposes of those sections, (a) a requirement imposed by a direction imposed by the FCA under reg 11B of the 2002 Regulations is to be treated as a requirement imposed by or under this Act, and (b) any reference in those sections to an authorised person includes a reference to an unauthorised incoming provider. See reg 12(1), (1A) of those Regulations.

[1.1524]
[206A   Suspending permission to carry on regulated activities etc
(1)   If the [appropriate regulator] considers that an authorised person has contravened a relevant requirement imposed on the person, it may—

(a)   suspend, for such period as it considers appropriate, any permission which the person has to carry on a regulated activity; or

(b)   impose, for such period as it considers appropriate, such limitations or other restrictions in relation to the carrying on of a regulated activity by the person as it considers appropriate.

[(1A)   The power conferred by subsection (1) is also exercisable by the FCA if it considers that an authorised person has contravened a requirement imposed on the person by—

(a)   the Payment Services Regulations 2009, or

(b)   the Electronic Money Regulations 2011.]

(2)   In subsection (1)—

"permission" means any permission that the authorised person has, whether given (or treated as given) by [the FCA or the PRA] or conferred by any provision of this Act;

. . .

(3)   The period for which a suspension or restriction is to have effect may not exceed 12 months.

(4)   A suspension may relate only to the carrying on of an activity in specified circumstances.

(5)   A restriction may, in particular, be imposed so as to require the person concerned to take, or refrain from taking, specified action.

(6)   The [appropriate regulator] may—

(a)   withdraw a suspension or restriction; or

(b)   vary a suspension or restriction so as to reduce the period for which it has effect or otherwise to limit its effect.

(7)   The power under this section may (but need not) be exercised so as to have effect in relation to all the regulated activities that the person concerned carries on.

(8)   Any one or more of the powers under—

(a)   subsection (1)(a) and (b) of this section, and

(b)   sections 205 and 206,

may be exercised in relation to the same contravention.]

NOTES

Inserted by the Financial Services Act 2010, s 9.

Sub-ss (1), (6): words in square brackets substituted by the Financial Services Act 2012, s 37(1), Sch 9, Pt 1, para 1, Pt 4, para 13(1), (2), (5).

Sub-s (1A): inserted by the Financial Services Act 2012, s 37(1), Sch 9, Pt 1, Pt 4, para 13(1), (3).

Sub-s (2): words in square brackets in the definition "permission" substituted, and the definition "relevant requirement" (omitted) repealed, by the Financial Services Act 2012, s 37(1), Sch 9, Pt 1, para 1, Pt 4, para 13(1), (4).

Transitional provisions etc in connection with the commencement of the Financial Services Act 2012: see the Financial Services Act 2012 (Transitional provisions) (Enforcement) Order 2013, SI 2013/441, arts 23–25.

Note: (1) for the purposes of ss 204A–209 and 384 a requirement imposed by the FCA under Part 3 of the Electronic Commerce Directive (Financial Services and Markets) Regulations 2002, SI 2002/1775 upon an authorised incoming provider is to be treated as imposed on that provider by or under this Act; (2) for the purposes of those sections, (a) a requirement imposed by a direction imposed by the FCA under reg 11B of the 2002 Regulations is to be treated as a requirement imposed by or under this Act, and (b) any reference in those sections to an authorised person includes a reference to an unauthorised incoming provider. See reg 12(1), (1A) of those Regulations.

[1.1525]
207   Proposal to take disciplinary measures

(1)   If [a regulator] proposes—

(a)   to publish a statement in respect of an authorised person (under section 205),   . . .

(b)   to impose a penalty on an authorised person (under section 206), [or

(c)   to suspend a permission of an authorised person or impose a restriction in relation to the carrying on of a regulated activity by an authorised person (under section 206A),]

it must give the authorised person a warning notice.

(2)   A warning notice about a proposal to publish a statement must set out the terms of the statement.

(3)   A warning notice about a proposal to impose a penalty, must state the amount of the penalty.

[(4)   A warning notice about a proposal to suspend a permission or impose a restriction must state the period for which the suspension or restriction is to have effect.]

NOTES

Sub-s (1): words in first pair of square brackets substituted by the Financial Services Act 2012, s 37(1), Sch 9, Pt 1, Pt 4, para 14; word omitted from para (a) repealed, and para (c) (and the word immediately preceding it) inserted, by the Financial Services Act 2010, s 24(1), (2), Sch 2, Pt 1, paras 1, 18(1), (2).

Sub-s (4): added by the Financial Services Act 2010, s 24(1), (2), Sch 2, Pt 1, paras 1, 18(1), (3).

Note: (1) for the purposes of ss 204A–209 and 384 a requirement imposed by the FCA under Part 3 of the Electronic Commerce Directive (Financial Services and Markets) Regulations 2002, SI 2002/1775 upon an authorised incoming provider is to be treated as imposed on that provider by or under this Act; (2) for the purposes of those sections, (a) a requirement imposed by a direction imposed by the FCA under reg 11B of the 2002 Regulations is to be treated as a requirement imposed by or under this Act, and (b) any reference in those sections to an authorised person includes a reference to an unauthorised incoming provider. See reg 12(1), (1A) of those Regulations.

[1.1526]
208   Decision notice

(1)   If [a regulator] decides—

(a)   to publish a statement under section 205 (whether or not in the terms proposed), . . .
(b)   to impose a penalty under section 206 (whether or not of the amount proposed), [or
(c)   to suspend a permission or impose a restriction under section 206A (whether or not in the manner proposed),]
it must without delay give the authorised person concerned a decision notice.
(2)   In the case of a statement, the decision notice must set out the terms of the statement.
(3)   In the case of a penalty, the decision notice must state the amount of the penalty.
[(3A)   In the case of a suspension or restriction, the decision notice must state the period for which the suspension or restriction is to have effect.]
(4)   If [a regulator] decides to—
(a)   publish a statement in respect of an authorised person under section 205, . . .
(b)   impose a penalty on an authorised person under section 206, [or
(c)   suspend a permission of an authorised person, or impose a restriction in relation to the carrying on of a regulated activity by an authorised person, under section 206A,]
the authorised person may refer the matter to the Tribunal.

NOTES

Sub-ss (1), (4): words in first pair of square brackets substituted by the Financial Services Act 2012, s 37(1), Sch 9, Pt 1, para 1, Pt 4, para 15; word omitted from para (a) repealed, and para (c) (and the word immediately preceding it) inserted, by the Financial Services Act 2010, s 24(1), (2), Sch 2, Pt 1, paras 1, 19(1), (2), (4).
Sub-s (3A): inserted by the Financial Services Act 2010, s 24(1), (2), Sch 2, Pt 1, paras 1, 19(1), (3).
Note: (1) for the purposes of ss 204A–209 and 384 a requirement imposed by the FCA under Part 3 of the Electronic Commerce Directive (Financial Services and Markets) Regulations 2002, SI 2002/1775 upon an authorised incoming provider is to be treated as imposed on that provider by or under this Act; (2) for the purposes of those sections, (a) a requirement imposed by a direction imposed by the FCA under reg 11B of the 2002 Regulations is to be treated as a requirement imposed by or under this Act, and (b) any reference in those sections to an authorised person includes a reference to an unauthorised incoming provider. See reg 12(1), (1A) of those Regulations.

[1.1527]
209   Publication
After a statement under section 205 is published, [the regulator concerned] must send a copy of it to the authorised person and to any person on whom a copy of the decision notice was given under section 393(4).

NOTES

Words in square brackets substituted by the Financial Services Act 2012, s 37(1), Sch 9, Pt 1, para 1, Pt 4, para 16.
Note: (1) for the purposes of ss 204A–209 and 384 a requirement imposed by the FCA under Part 3 of the Electronic Commerce Directive (Financial Services and Markets) Regulations 2002, SI 2002/1775 upon an authorised incoming provider is to be treated as imposed on that provider by or under this Act; (2) for the purposes of those sections, (a) a requirement imposed by a direction imposed by the FCA under reg 11B of the 2002 Regulations is to be treated as a requirement imposed by or under this Act, and (b) any reference in those sections to an authorised person includes a reference to an unauthorised incoming provider. See reg 12(1), (1A) of those Regulations.

[1.1528]
210   Statements of policy
(1)   [Each regulator] must prepare and issue a statement of its policy with respect to—
[(a)   the imposition of penalties, suspensions or restrictions under this Part;
(b)   the amount of penalties under this Part; and
(c)   the period for which suspensions or restrictions under this Part are to have effect].
[(1A)   Each regulator's policy with respect to the imposition of penalties, suspensions or restrictions under this Part must include policy with respect to their imposition in relation to conduct which constitutes or may constitute an offence by virtue of section 23(1A) (authorised persons carrying on credit-related regulated activities otherwise than in accordance with permission).]
(2)   [A regulator's] policy in determining what the amount of a penalty should be[, or what the period for which a suspension or restriction is to have effect should be,] must include having regard to—
(a)   the seriousness of the contravention in question in relation to the nature of the requirement contravened;
(b)   the extent to which that contravention was deliberate or reckless; and
(c)   whether [the person against whom action is to be taken] is an individual.
(3)   [A regulator] may at any time alter or replace a statement issued [by it] under this section.
(4)   If a statement issued under this section is altered or [replaced by a regulator, the regulator] must issue the altered or replacement statement.
(5)   [A regulator] must, without delay, give the Treasury a copy of any statement which it publishes under this section.
(6)   A statement issued under this section [by a regulator] must be published by the [regulator] in the way appearing to the [regulator] to be best calculated to bring it to the attention of the public.
(7)   In exercising, or deciding whether to exercise, its power under section 206 [or 206A] in the case of any particular contravention, [a regulator] must have regard to any statement published [by it] under this section and in force at the time when the contravention in question occurred.

(8) The [regulator] may charge a reasonable fee for providing a person with a copy of the statement.

NOTES
Sub-s (1)(a)–(c) were substituted (for the original sub-s(1)(a), (b)), the words in the second pair of square brackets in sub-s (2) were inserted, the words in the final pair of square brackets in that subsection were substituted, and the words "or 206A" in square brackets in sub-s (7) were inserted, by the Financial Services Act 2010, s 24(1), (2), Sch 2, Pt 1, paras 1, 20.
Sub-s (1A) was inserted, and all other words in square brackets in this section were substituted or inserted, by the Financial Services Act 2012, s 37(1), Sch 9, Pt 1, para 1, Pt 4, para 17.

[1.1529]
211 Statements of policy: procedure
(1) Before [a regulator issues] a statement under section 210, the [regulator] must publish a draft of the proposed statement in the way appearing to the [regulator] to be best calculated to bring it to the attention of the public.
(2) The draft must be accompanied by notice that representations about the proposal may be made to the [regulator] within a specified time.
(3) Before issuing the proposed statement, the [regulator] must have regard to any representations made to it in accordance with subsection (2).
(4) If the [regulator] issues the proposed statement it must publish an account, in general terms, of—
    (a) the representations made to it in accordance with subsection (2); and
    (b) its response to them.
(5) If the statement differs from the draft published under subsection (1) in a way which is, in the opinion of the [regulator], significant, the [regulator] must (in addition to complying with subsection (4)) publish details of the difference.
(6) [A regulator] may charge a reasonable fee for providing a person with a copy of a draft published under subsection (1).
(7) This section also applies to a proposal to alter or replace a statement.

NOTES
Words in square brackets substituted by the Financial Services Act 2012, s 37(1), Sch 9, Pt 1, para 1, Pt 4, para 18.

PART XVI
THE OMBUDSMAN SCHEME

NOTES
Transitional provisions etc in connection with the original commencement of this Act: see the Financial Services and Markets Act 2000 (Transitional Provisions) (Ombudsman Scheme and Complaints Scheme) Order 2001, SI 2001/2326. Arts 2–17 of that Order make transitional provisions in relation to the establishment of the ombudsman scheme by this Part. The Order provides for certain complaints relating to acts or omissions occurring before the commencement of this Part, which fell (or would have fallen) within the scope of one of the "former schemes", to be dealt with under the new scheme, subject to specified modifications set out in arts 4–7.
See also the Financial Services and Markets Act 2000 (Transitional Provisions) (Complaints Relating to General Insurance and Mortgages) Order 2004, SI 2004/454. The 2004 Order makes further provision in relation to the inclusion of the activities of arranging and advising on regulated mortgage contracts, and insurance mediation activities, as regulated activities for the purposes of this Act. It modifies this Part and provides that certain complaints relating to acts or omissions which would have fallen within the Mortgage Code Arbitration Scheme or the Dispute Resolution Facility established by the General Insurance Standards Council can be dealt with under the new scheme established by this Part.
Data protection: personal data processed for the purpose of discharging any function which is conferred by or under this Part on the body established for the purposes of this Part are exempt from the subject information provisions in any case to the extent to which the application of those provisions to the data would be likely to prejudice the proper discharge of the function; see the Data Protection Act 1998, s 31(4A).

The scheme

[1.1530]
225 The scheme and the scheme operator
(1) This Part provides for a scheme under which certain disputes may be resolved quickly and with minimum formality by an independent person.
(2) The scheme is to be administered by a body corporate ("the scheme operator").
(3) The scheme is to be operated under a name chosen by the scheme operator but is referred to in this Act as "the ombudsman scheme".
(4) Schedule 17 makes provision in connection with the ombudsman scheme and the scheme operator.

[1.1531]
226 Compulsory jurisdiction
(1) A complaint which relates to an act or omission of a person ("the respondent") in carrying on an activity to which compulsory jurisdiction rules apply is to be dealt with under the ombudsman scheme if the conditions mentioned in subsection (2) are satisfied.
(2) The conditions are that—

(a)   the complainant is eligible and wishes to have the complaint dealt with under the scheme;
(b)   the respondent was an authorised person [or an electronic money issuer within the meaning of the Electronic Money Regulations 2011][, or a payment service provider within the meaning of the Payment Services Regulations 2009,] at the time of the act or omission to which the complaint relates; and
(c)   the act or omission to which the complaint relates occurred at a time when compulsory jurisdiction rules were in force in relation to the activity in question.
(3)   "Compulsory jurisdiction rules" means rules—
(a)   made by the [FCA] for the purposes of this section; and
(b)   specifying the activities to which they apply.
(4)   Only activities which are regulated activities, or which could be made regulated activities by an order under section 22, may be specified.
(5)   Activities may be specified by reference to specified categories (however described).
(6)   A complainant is eligible, in relation to the compulsory jurisdiction of the ombudsman scheme, if he falls within a class of person specified in the rules as eligible.
(7)   The rules—
(a)   may include provision for persons other than individuals to be eligible; but
(b)   may not provide for authorised persons to be eligible except in specified circumstances or in relation to complaints of a specified kind.
(8)   The jurisdiction of the scheme which results from this section is referred to in this Act as the "compulsory jurisdiction".

NOTES

Sub-s (2): words in first pair of square brackets inserted by the Electronic Money Regulations 2011, SI 2011/99, reg 79, Sch 4, Pt 1, para 2(1), (3)(a); words in second pair of square brackets inserted by the Payment Services Regulations 2009, SI 2009/209, reg 126, Sch 6, Pt 1, para 1(1)(a).
Sub-s (3): word in square brackets substituted by the Financial Services Act 2012, s 39, Sch 11, para 1.
Transitional provisions: see the note relating to the repeal of s 226A *below*.

226A   (*Repealed by the Financial Services and Markets Act 2000 (Regulated Activities) (Amendment) (No 2) Order 2013, SI 2013/1881, art 10(1), (5), (for transitional provisions see see Pt 8 thereof at* **[2.1007]** *et seq). For transitional provisions in relation to complaints made under the ombudsman scheme before 1 April 2014, and in relation to complaints made after that date which relate to an act or omission which took place before that date, see art 11(5)–(9) of the 2013 Order at* **[2.1005]**.)

[1.1532]
227   Voluntary jurisdiction
(1)   A complaint which relates to an act or omission of a person ("the respondent") in carrying on an activity to which voluntary jurisdiction rules apply is to be dealt with under the ombudsman scheme if the conditions mentioned in subsection (2) are satisfied.
(2)   The conditions are that—
(a)   the complainant is eligible and wishes to have the complaint dealt with under the scheme;
(b)   at the time of the act or omission to which the complaint relates, the respondent was participating in the scheme;
(c)   at the time when the complaint is referred under the scheme, the respondent has not withdrawn from the scheme in accordance with its provisions;
(d)   the act or omission to which the complaint relates occurred at a time when voluntary jurisdiction rules were in force in relation to the activity in question; and
(e)   the complaint cannot be dealt with under the compulsory jurisdiction [. . .   ].
(3)   "Voluntary jurisdiction rules" means rules—
(a)   made by the scheme operator for the purposes of this section; and
(b)   specifying the activities to which they apply.
(4)   The only activities which may be specified in the rules are activities which are, or could be, specified in compulsory jurisdiction rules.
(5)   Activities may be specified by reference to specified categories (however described).
(6)   The rules require the [FCA's] approval.
(7)   A complainant is eligible, in relation to the voluntary jurisdiction of the ombudsman scheme, if he falls within a class of person specified in the rules as eligible.
(8)   The rules may include provision for persons other than individuals to be eligible.
(9)   A person qualifies for participation in the ombudsman scheme if he falls within a class of person specified in the rules in relation to the activity in question.
(10)   Provision may be made in the rules for persons other than authorised persons to participate in the ombudsman scheme.
(11)   The rules may make different provision in relation to complaints arising from different activities.
(12)   The jurisdiction of the scheme which results from this section is referred to in this Act as the "voluntary jurisdiction".
(13)   In such circumstances as may be specified in voluntary jurisdiction rules, a complaint—
(a)   which relates to an act or omission occurring at a time before the rules came into force, and

(b)   which could have been dealt with under a scheme which has to any extent been replaced by the voluntary jurisdiction,

is to be dealt with under the ombudsman scheme even though paragraph (b) or (d) of subsection (2) would otherwise prevent that.

(14)   In such circumstances as may be specified in voluntary jurisdiction rules, a complaint is to be dealt with under the ombudsman scheme even though—

(a)   paragraph (b) or (d) of subsection (2) would otherwise prevent that, and

(b)   the complaint is not brought within the scheme as a result of subsection (13),

but only if the respondent has agreed that complaints of that kind were to be dealt with under the scheme.

NOTES

Sub-s (2): words omitted originally inserted by the Consumer Credit Act 2006, s 61(2), and repealed by the Financial Services and Markets Act 2000 (Regulated Activities) (Amendment) (No 2) Order 2013, SI 2013/1881, art 10(1), (6), (for transitional provisions see see Pt 8 thereof at **[2.1007]** et seq).

Sub-s (6): word in square brackets substituted by the Financial Services Act 2012, s 39, Sch 11, para 3.

Determination of complaints

[1.1533]
228   Determination under the compulsory jurisdiction
(1)   This section applies only in relation to the compulsory jurisdiction [. . .].
(2)   A complaint is to be determined by reference to what is, in the opinion of the ombudsman, fair and reasonable in all the circumstances of the case.
(3)   When the ombudsman has determined a complaint he must give a written statement of his determination to the respondent and to the complainant.
(4)   The statement must—

(a)   give the ombudsman's reasons for his determination;

(b)   be signed by him; and

(c)   require the complainant to notify him . . . , before a date specified in the statement, whether he accepts or rejects the determination.

(5)   If the complainant notifies the ombudsman that he accepts the determination, it is binding on the respondent and the complainant and final.
(6)   If, by the specified date, the complainant has not notified the ombudsman of his acceptance or rejection of the determination he is to be treated as having rejected it.
[(6A)   But the complainant is not to be treated as having rejected the determination by virtue of subsection (6) if—

(a)   the complainant notifies the ombudsman after the specified date of the complainant's acceptance of the determination,

(b)   the complainant has not previously notified the ombudsman of the complainant's rejection of the determination, and

(c)   the ombudsman is satisfied that such conditions as may be prescribed by rules made by the scheme operator for the purposes of this section are satisfied.]

(7)   The ombudsman must notify the respondent of the outcome.
[(7A)   Where a determination is rejected by virtue of subsection (6), the notification under subsection (7) must contain a general description of the effect of subsection (6A).]
(8)   A copy of the determination on which appears a certificate signed by an ombudsman is evidence (or in Scotland sufficient evidence) that the determination was made under the scheme.
(9)   Such a certificate purporting to be signed by an ombudsman is to be taken to have been duly signed unless the contrary is shown.

NOTES

Sub-s (1): words omitted originally inserted by the Consumer Credit Act 2006, s 61(3), and repealed by the Financial Services and Markets Act 2000 (Regulated Activities) (Amendment) (No 2) Order 2013, SI 2013/1881, art 10(1), (7), (for transitional provisions see see Pt 8 thereof at **[2.1007]** et seq).

Sub-s (4): words omitted repealed by the Financial Services Act 2012, s 39, Sch 11, para 4(1), (2).

Sub-ss (6A), (7A):inserted by the Financial Services Act 2012, s 39, Sch 11, para 4(1), (3), (4).

[1.1534]
229   Awards
(1)   This section applies only in relation to the compulsory jurisdiction [. . .].
(2)   If a complaint which has been dealt with under the scheme is determined in favour of the complainant, the determination may include—

(a)   an award against the respondent of such amount as the ombudsman considers fair compensation for loss or damage (of a kind falling within subsection (3)) suffered by the complainant ("a money award");

(b)   a direction that the respondent take such steps in relation to the complainant as the ombudsman considers just and appropriate (whether or not a court could order those steps to be taken).

(3)   A money award may compensate for—

(a)   financial loss; or

(b)   any other loss, or any damage, of a specified kind.

(4)   The [FCA] may specify [for the purposes of the compulsory jurisdiction] the maximum amount which may be regarded as fair compensation for a particular kind of loss or damage specified under subsection (3)(b).

[(4A)   . . .]

(5)   A money award may not exceed the monetary limit; but the ombudsman may, if he considers that fair compensation requires payment of a larger amount, recommend that the respondent pay the complainant the balance.

(6)   The monetary limit is such amount as may be specified.

(7)   Different amounts may be specified in relation to different kinds of complaint.

(8)   A money award—

(a)   may provide for the amount payable under the award to bear interest at a rate and as from a date specified in the award; and

(b)   is enforceable by the complainant in accordance with Part III of Schedule 17 [. . .].

(9)   Compliance with a direction under subsection (2)(b)—

(a)   is enforceable by an injunction; or

(b)   in Scotland, is enforceable by an order under section 45 of the Court of Session Act 1988.

(10)   Only the complainant may bring proceedings for an injunction or proceedings for an order.

[[(11)   "Specified" means specified in compulsory jurisdiction rules.]

(12)   . . .]

NOTES

   Sub-ss (1), (8): words omitted originally inserted by the Consumer Credit Act 2006, s 61(3), (6), and repealed by the Financial Services and Markets Act 2000 (Regulated Activities) (Amendment) (No 2) Order 2013, SI 2013/1881, art 10(1), (8)(a), (c), (for transitional provisions see see Pt 8 thereof at **[2.1007]** et seq).

   Sub-s (4): word in first pair of square brackets substituted by the Financial Services Act 2012, s 39, Sch 11, para 5; words in second pair of square brackets inserted by the Consumer Credit Act 2006, s 61(4).

   Sub-ss (4A): originally inserted by the Consumer Credit Act 2006, s 61(5), and repealed by SI 2013/1881, art 10(1), (8)(b).

   Sub-ss (11), (12): substituted (for the original sub-s (11)) by the Consumer Credit Act 2006, s 61(7). Sub-s (11) was further substituted, and sub-s (12) was repealed, by SI 2013/1881, art 10(1), (8)(d), (e).

[1.1535]
230   Costs

(1)   The scheme operator may by rules ("costs rules") provide for an ombudsman to have power, on determining a complaint under the compulsory jurisdiction [. . .], to award costs in accordance with the provisions of the rules.

(2)   Costs rules require the approval of the [FCA].

(3)   Costs rules may not provide for the making of an award against the complainant in respect of the respondent's costs.

(4)   But they may provide for the making of an award against the complainant in favour of the scheme operator, for the purpose of providing a contribution to resources deployed in dealing with the complaint, if in the opinion of the ombudsman—

(a)   the complainant's conduct was improper or unreasonable; or

(b)   the complainant was responsible for an unreasonable delay.

(5)   Costs rules may authorise an ombudsman making an award in accordance with the rules to order that the amount payable under the award bears interest at a rate and as from a date specified in the order.

(6)   An amount due under an award made in favour of the scheme operator is recoverable as a debt due to the scheme operator.

(7)   Any other award made against the respondent is to be treated as a money award for the purposes of paragraph 16 of Schedule 17 [. . .].

NOTES

   Sub-ss (1), (7): words omitted originally inserted by the Consumer Credit Act 2006, s 61(8), and repealed by the Financial Services and Markets Act 2000 (Regulated Activities) (Amendment) (No 2) Order 2013, SI 2013/1881, art 10(1), (9), (for transitional provisions see see Pt 8 thereof at **[2.1007]** et seq).

   Sub-s (2): word in square brackets substituted by the Financial Services Act 2012, s 39, Sch 11, para 6.

[1.1536]
[230A   Reports of determinations

(1)   The scheme operator must publish a report of any determination made under this Part.

(2)   But if the ombudsman who makes the determination informs the scheme operator that, in the ombudsman's opinion, it is inappropriate to publish a report of that determination (or any part of it) the scheme operator must not publish a report of that determination (or that part).

(3)   Unless the complainant agrees, a report of a determination published by the scheme operator may not include the name of the complainant, or particulars which, in the opinion of the scheme operator, are likely to identify the complainant.

(4)   The scheme operator may charge a reasonable fee for providing a person with a copy of a report.]

NOTES
Commencement: 1 April 2013.
Inserted by the Financial Services Act 2012, s 39, Sch 11, para 7.

Information

[1.1537]
231 Ombudsman's power to require information

(1)   An ombudsman may, by notice in writing given to a party to a complaint, require that party—
  (a)   to provide specified information or information of a specified description; or
  (b)   to produce specified documents or documents of a specified description.
(2)   The information or documents must be provided or produced—
  (a)   before the end of such reasonable period as may be specified; and
  (b)   in the case of information, in such manner or form as may be specified.
(3)   This section applies only to information and documents the production of which the ombudsman considers necessary for the determination of the complaint.
(4)   If a document is produced in response to a requirement imposed under this section, the ombudsman may—
  (a)   take copies or extracts from the document; or
  (b)   require the person producing the document to provide an explanation of the document.
(5)   If a person who is required under this section to produce a document fails to do so, the ombudsman may require him to state, to the best of his knowledge and belief, where the document is.
(6)   If a person claims a lien on a document, its production under this Part does not affect the lien.
(7)   "Specified" means specified in the notice given under subsection (1).

[1.1538]
232 Powers of court where information required

(1)   If a person ("the defaulter") fails to comply with a requirement imposed under section 231, the ombudsman may certify that fact in writing to the court and the court may enquire into the case.
(2)   If the court is satisfied that the defaulter failed without reasonable excuse to comply with the requirement, it may deal with the defaulter (and, in the case of a body corporate, any director or [other] officer) as if he were in contempt[; and "officer", in relation to a limited liability partnership, means a member of the limited liability partnership].
(3)   "Court" means—
  (a)   the High Court;
  (b)   in Scotland, the Court of Session.

NOTES
Sub-s (2): word in first pair of square brackets inserted by the Financial Services Act 2012, s 39, Sch 11, para 8; words in second pair of square brackets added by the Limited Liability Partnerships Regulations 2001, SI 2001/1090, reg 9, Sch 5, para 21.

[1.1539]
[232A   Scheme operator's duty to provide information to FCA

If the scheme operator considers that it has information that, in its opinion, would or might be of assistance to the FCA in advancing one or more of the FCA's operational objectives, it must disclose that information to the FCA.]

NOTES
Commencement: 1 April 2013.
Inserted by the Financial Services Act 2012, s 39, Sch 11, para 9.

Funding

[1.1540]
234 Industry funding

(1)   For the purpose of funding—
  (a)   the establishment of the ombudsman scheme (whenever any relevant expense is incurred), and
  (b)   its operation in relation to the compulsory jurisdiction,
the [FCA] may make rules requiring the payment to it or to the scheme operator, by authorised persons or any class of authorised person[, any electronic money issuer within the meaning of the Electronic Money Regulations 2011] [or any payment service provider within the meaning of the Payment Services Regulations 2009] of specified amounts (or amounts calculated in a specified way).
(2)   "Specified" means specified in the rules.

NOTES
Sub-s (1): word "FCA" in square brackets substituted by the Financial Services Act 2012, s 39, Sch 11, para 10; words in second pair of square brackets inserted by the Electronic Money Regulations 2011, SI 2011/99, reg 79, Sch 4, Pt 1, para 2(1),

(3)(b); words in third pair of square brackets inserted by the Payment Services Regulations 2009, SI 2009/209, reg 126, Sch 6, Pt 1, para 1(1)(b).

PART XX
PROVISION OF FINANCIAL SERVICES BY MEMBERS OF THE PROFESSIONS

[1.1541]
326　Designation of professional bodies

(1)　The Treasury may by order designate bodies for the purposes of this Part.

(2)　A body designated under subsection (1) is referred to in this Part as a designated professional body.

(3)　The Treasury may designate a body under subsection (1) only if they are satisfied that—
  (a)　the basic condition, and
  (b)　one or more of the additional conditions,
are met in relation to it.

(4)　The basic condition is that the body has rules applicable to the carrying on by members of the profession in relation to which it is established of regulated activities which, if the body were to be designated, would be exempt regulated activities.

(5)　The additional conditions are that—
  (a)　the body has power under any enactment to regulate the practice of the profession;
  (b)　being a member of the profession is a requirement under any enactment for the exercise of particular functions or the holding of a particular office;
  (c)　the body has been recognised for the purpose of any enactment other than this Act and the recognition has not been withdrawn;
  (d)　the body is established in an EEA State other than the United Kingdom and in that State—
    (i)　the body has power corresponding to that mentioned in paragraph (a);
    (ii)　there is a requirement in relation to the body corresponding to that mentioned in paragraph (b); or
    (iii)　the body is recognised in a manner corresponding to that mentioned in paragraph (c).

(6)　"Enactment" includes an Act of the Scottish Parliament, Northern Ireland legislation and subordinate legislation (whether made under an Act, an Act of the Scottish Parliament or Northern Ireland legislation).

(7)　"Recognised" means recognised by—
  (a)　a Minister of the Crown;
  (b)　the Scottish Ministers;
  (c)　a Northern Ireland Minister;
  (d)　a Northern Ireland department or its head.

NOTES

Orders: the Financial Services and Markets Act 2000 (Designated Professional Bodies) Order 2001, SI 2001/1226, which, at the date of publication, designates the following bodies for the purposes of this Part: the Law Society, the Law Society of Scotland, the Law Society of Northern Ireland, the Institute of Chartered Accountants in England and Wales, the Institute of Chartered Accountants of Scotland, the Institute of Chartered Accountants in Ireland, the Association of Chartered Certified Accountants, the Institute of Actuaries, the Council for Licensed Conveyancers, and the Royal Institution of Chartered Surveyors. Note that the Council for Licensed Conveyancers was added by the Financial Services and Markets Act 2000 (Designated Professional Bodies) (Amendment) Order 2004, SI 2004/3352, as from 14 January 2005, and the Royal Institution of Chartered Surveyors was added by the Financial Services and Markets Act 2000 (Designated Professional Bodies) (Amendment) Order 2006, SI 2006/58, as from 10 February 2006 (both Orders also made under this section).

[1.1542]
327　Exemption from the general prohibition

(1)　The general prohibition does not apply to the carrying on of a regulated activity by a person ("P") if—
  (a)　the conditions set out in subsections (2) to (7) are satisfied; and
  (b)　there is not in force—
    (i)　a direction under section 328, or
    (ii)　an order under section 329,
    which prevents this subsection from applying to the carrying on of that activity by him.

(2)　P must be—
  (a)　a member of a profession; or
  (b)　controlled or managed by one or more such members.

(3)　P must not receive from a person other than his client any pecuniary reward or other advantage, for which he does not account to his client, arising out of his carrying on of any of the activities.

(4)　The manner of the provision by P of any service in the course of carrying on the activities must be incidental to the provision by him of professional services.

(5)　P must not carry on, or hold himself out as carrying on, a regulated activity other than—
  (a)　one which rules made as a result of section 332(3) allow him to carry on; or
  (b)　one in relation to which he is an exempt person.

(6)   The activities must not be of a description, or relate to an investment of a description, specified in an order made by the Treasury for the purposes of this subsection.

(7)   The activities must be the only regulated activities carried on by P (other than regulated activities in relation to which he is an exempt person).

(8)   "Professional services" means services—

(a)   which do not constitute carrying on a regulated activity, and

(b)   the provision of which is supervised and regulated by a designated professional body.

NOTES

Incidental: this Act does not define what is "incidental" for the purposes of sub-s (4) above, but the FCA Handbook provides guidance on what the FCA considers "incidental" and the factors that it considers relevant (PROF 2.1.14G).

Orders: the Financial Services and Markets Act 2000 (Professions) (Non-Exempt Activities) Order 2001, SI 2001/1227; the Financial Services and Markets Act 2000 (Miscellaneous Provisions) Order 2001, SI 2001/3650; the Financial Services and Markets Act 2000 (Commencement of Mortgage Regulation) (Amendment) Order 2002, SI 2002/1777.

[1.1543]
328   Directions in relation to the general prohibition

(1)   The [FCA] may direct that section 327(1) is not to apply to the extent specified in the direction.

(2)   A direction under subsection (1)—

(a)   must be in writing;

(b)   may be given in relation to different classes of person or different descriptions of regulated activity.

(3)   A direction under subsection (1) must be published in the way appearing to the [FCA] to be best calculated to bring it to the attention of the public.

(4)   The [FCA] may charge a reasonable fee for providing a person with a copy of the direction.

(5)   The [FCA] must, without delay, give the Treasury a copy of any direction which it gives under this section.

[(6)   The [FCA] may exercise the power conferred by subsection (1) only if it is satisfied either—

(a)   that it is desirable to do so in order to protect the interests of clients; or

(b)   that it is necessary to do so in order to comply with a Community obligation imposed by the insurance mediation directive [or Directive 2008/48/EC of the European Parliament and of the Council of 23 April 2008 on credit agreements for consumers and repealing Council Directive 87/102/EEC].]

(7)   In considering whether it is [satisfied of the matter specified in subsection (6)(a)], the [FCA] must have regard amongst other things to the effectiveness of any arrangements made by any designated professional body—

(a)   for securing compliance with rules made under section 332(1);

(b)   for dealing with complaints against its members in relation to the carrying on by them of exempt regulated activities;

(c)   in order to offer redress to clients who suffer, or claim to have suffered, loss as a result of misconduct by its members in their carrying on of exempt regulated activities;

(d)   for co-operating with the [FCA] under section 325(4).

(8)   In this Part "clients" means—

(a)   persons who use, have used or are or may be contemplating using, any of the services provided by a member of a profession in the course of carrying on exempt regulated activities;

(b)   persons who have rights or interests which are derived from, or otherwise attributable to, the use of any such services by other persons; or

(c)   persons who have rights or interests which may be adversely affected by the use of any such services by persons acting on their behalf or in a fiduciary capacity in relation to them.

(9)   If a member of a profession is carrying on an exempt regulated activity in his capacity as a trustee, the persons who are, have been or may be beneficiaries of the trust are to be treated as persons who use, have used or are or may be contemplating using services provided by that person in his carrying on of that activity.

NOTES

The word "FCA" in square brackets (in each place that it occurs) was substituted by the Financial Services Act 2012, s 46, Sch 16, para 2.

Sub-s (6) and the words in the first pair of square brackets in sub-s (7) were substituted by the Insurance Mediation Directive (Miscellaneous Amendments) Regulations 2003, SI 2003/1473, reg 9.

The words "or Directive 2008/48/EC of the European Parliament and of the Council of 23 April 2008 on credit agreements for consumers and repealing Council Directive 87/102/EEC" in sub-s (6) were added by the Financial Services and Markets Act 2000 (Regulated Activities) (Amendment) (No 2) Order 2013, SI 2013/1881, art 10(1), (12), (for transitional provisions see see Pt 8 thereof at **[2.1007]** et seq).

References to the European Community and related expressions: see the note "References to "the European Community", "Community", etc" in the introductory notes to this Act.

[1.1544]
329   Orders in relation to the general prohibition
(1)   Subsection (2) applies if it appears to the [FCA] that a person to whom, as a result of section 327(1), the general prohibition does not apply is not a fit and proper person to carry on regulated activities in accordance with that section.

(2)   The [FCA] may make an order disapplying section 327(1) in relation to that person to the extent specified in the order.

(3)   The [FCA] may, on the application of the person named in an order under subsection (1), vary or revoke it.

(4)   "Specified" means specified in the order.

(5)   If a partnership is named in an order under this section, the order is not affected by any change in its membership.

(6)   If a partnership named in an order under this section is dissolved, the order continues to have effect in relation to any partnership which succeeds to the business of the dissolved partnership.

(7)   For the purposes of subsection (6), a partnership is to be regarded as succeeding to the business of another partnership only if—
   (a)   the members of the resulting partnership are substantially the same as those of the former partnership; and
   (b)   succession is to the whole or substantially the whole of the business of the former partnership.

NOTES
   Word "FCA" in square brackets (in each place that it occurs) substituted by the Financial Services Act 2012, s 46, Sch 16, para 3.

[1.1545]
330   Consultation
(1)   Before giving a direction under section 328(1), the [FCA] must publish a draft of the proposed direction.

(2)   The draft must be accompanied by—
   (a)   a cost benefit analysis; and
   (b)   notice that representations about the proposed direction may be made to the [FCA] within a specified time.

(3)   Before giving the proposed direction, the [FCA] must have regard to any representations made to it in accordance with subsection (2)(b).

(4)   If the [FCA] gives the proposed direction it must publish an account, in general terms, of—
   (a)   the representations made to it in accordance with subsection (2)(b); and
   (b)   its response to them.

(5)   If the direction differs from the draft published under subsection (1) in a way which is, in the opinion of the [FCA], significant—
   (a)   the [FCA] must (in addition to complying with subsection (4)) publish details of the difference; and
   (b)   those details must be accompanied by a cost benefit analysis.

(6)   Subsections (1) to (5) do not apply if the [FCA] considers that the delay involved in complying with them would prejudice the interests of consumers.

(7)   Neither subsection (2)(a) nor subsection (5)(b) applies if the [FCA] considers—
   (a)   that, making the appropriate comparison, there will be no increase in costs; or
   (b)   that, making that comparison, there will be an increase in costs but the increase will be of minimal significance.

(8)   The [FCA] may charge a reasonable fee for providing a person with a copy of a draft published under subsection (1).

(9)   When the [FCA] is required to publish a document under this section it must do so in the way appearing to it to be best calculated to bring it to the attention of the public.

[(10)   Cost benefit analysis" means—
   (a)   an analysis of the costs together with an analysis of the benefits that will arise—
      (i)   if the proposed direction is given, or
      (ii)   if subsection (5)(b) applies, from the direction that has been given, and
   (b)   subject to subsection (10A), an estimate of those costs and of those benefits.

(10A)   If, in the opinion of the FCA—
   (a)   the costs or benefits referred to in subsection (10) cannot reasonably be estimated, or
   (b)   it is not reasonably practicable to produce an estimate,
the cost benefit analysis need not estimate them, but must include a statement of the FCA's opinion and an explanation of it.]

(11)   "The appropriate comparison" means—
   (a)   in relation to subsection (2)(a), a comparison between the overall position if the direction is given and the overall position if it is not given;
   (b)   in relation to subsection (5)(b), a comparison between the overall position after the giving of the direction and the overall position before it was given.

NOTES

The word "FCA" in square brackets (in each place that it occurs) was substituted, and sub-ss (10), (10A) were substituted (for the original sub-s (10)), by the Financial Services Act 2012, s 46, Sch 16, para 4.

[1.1546]
331 Procedure on making or varying orders under section 329
(1) If the [FCA] proposes to make an order under section 329, it must give the person concerned a warning notice.
(2) The warning notice must set out the terms of the proposed order.
(3) If the [FCA] decides to make an order under section 329, it must give the person concerned a decision notice.
(4) The decision notice must—
    (a)   name the person to whom the order applies;
    (b)   set out the terms of the order; and
    (c)   be given to the person named in the order.
(5) Subsections (6) to (8) apply to an application for the variation or revocation of an order under section 329.
(6) If the [FCA] decides to grant the application, it must give the applicant written notice of its decision.
(7) If the [FCA] proposes to refuse the application, it must give the applicant a warning notice.
(8) If the [FCA] decides to refuse the application, it must give the applicant a decision notice.
(9) A person—
    (a)   against whom the [FCA] have decided to make an order under section 329, or
    (b)   whose application for the variation or revocation of such an order the [FCA] had decided to refuse,
may refer the matter to the Tribunal.
(10) The [FCA] may not make an order under section 329 unless—
    (a)   the period within which the decision to make to the order may be referred to the Tribunal has expired and no such reference has been made; or
    (b)   if such a reference has been made, the reference has been determined.

NOTES

Word "FCA" in square brackets (in each place that it occurs) substituted by the Financial Services Act 2012, s 46, Sch 16, para 5.

[1.1547]
332 Rules in relation to persons to whom the general prohibition does not apply
(1) The [FCA] may make rules applicable to persons to whom, as a result of section 327(1), the general prohibition does not apply.
(2) The power conferred by subsection (1) is to be exercised for the purpose of ensuring that clients are aware that such persons are not authorised persons.
(3) A designated professional body must make rules—
    (a)   applicable to members of the profession in relation to which it is established who are not authorised persons; and
    (b)   governing the carrying on by those members of regulated activities (other than regulated activities in relation to which they are exempt persons).
(4) Rules made in compliance with subsection (3) must be designed to secure that, in providing a particular professional service to a particular client, the member carries on only regulated activities which arise out of, or are complementary to, the provision by him of that service to that client.
(5) Rules made by a designated professional body under subsection (3) require the approval of the [FCA].

NOTES

Word "FCA" in square brackets in sub-ss (1), (5) substituted by the Financial Services Act 2012, s 46, Sch 16, para 6.

[1.1548]
333 False claims to be a person to whom the general prohibition does not apply
(1) A person who—
    (a)   describes himself (in whatever terms) as a person to whom the general prohibition does not apply, in relation to a particular regulated activity, as a result of this Part, or
    (b)   behaves, or otherwise holds himself out, in a manner which indicates (or which is reasonably likely to be understood as indicating) that he is such a person,
is guilty of an offence if he is not such a person.
(2) In proceedings for an offence under this section it is a defence for the accused to show that he took all reasonable precautions and exercised all due diligence to avoid committing the offence.
(3) A person guilty of an offence under this section is liable on summary conviction to imprisonment for a term not exceeding six months or a fine not exceeding level 5 on the standard scale, or both.

(4)   But where the conduct constituting the offence involved or included the public display of any material, the maximum fine for the offence is level 5 on the standard scale multiplied by the number of days for which the display continued.

PART XXIII
PUBLIC RECORD, DISCLOSURE OF INFORMATION AND CO-OPERATION

The public record

[1.1549]
347   The record of authorised persons etc
(1)   The [FCA] must maintain a record of every—
  (a)   person who appears to the [FCA] to be an authorised person;
  (b)   authorised unit trust scheme;
  [(ba)   authorised contractual scheme;]
  (c)   authorised open-ended investment company;
  (d)   recognised scheme;
  (e)   recognised investment exchange;
  (f)   . . .
  (g)   individual to whom a prohibition order relates;
  (h)   approved person;   . . .
  [(ha)   person to whom subsection (2A) applies; *and*]
  [(hb)   appointed representative to whom subsection (2B) applies; and]
  (i)   person falling within such other class (if any) as the [FCA] may determine.
(2)   The record must include such information as the [FCA] considers appropriate and at least the following information—
  (a)   in the case of a person appearing to the [FCA] to be an authorised person—
    (i)   information as to the services which he holds himself out as able to provide; and
    (ii)   any address of which the [FCA] is aware at which a notice or other document may be served on him;
  (b)   in the case of an authorised unit trust scheme, the name and address of the manager and trustee of the scheme;
  [(ba)   in the case of an authorised contractual scheme, the name and address of the operator and depositary of the scheme;]
  (c)   in the case of an authorised open-ended investment company, the name and address of—
    (i)   the company;
    (ii)   if it has only one director, the director; and
    (iii)   its depositary (if any);
  (d)   in the case of a recognised scheme, the name and address of—
    (i)   the operator of the scheme; and
    (ii)   any representative of the operator in the United Kingdom;
  (e)   in the case of a recognised investment exchange   . . . , the name and address of the exchange   . . . ;
  (f)   in the case of an individual to whom a prohibition order relates—
    (i)   his name; and
    (ii)   details of the effect of the order;
  (g)   in the case of a person who is an approved person—
    (i)   his name;
    (ii)   the name of the *relevant authorised person*;
    (iii)   if the approved person is performing a controlled function under an arrangement with a contractor of the *relevant authorised person*, the name of the contractor;
    [(iv)   in a case where the authorised person concerned is a relevant authorised person, whether or not the person is a senior manager;]
  [(h)   in the case of an approved person who is a senior manager in relation to a relevant authorised person—
    (i)   whether a final notice has been given to the person under section 390; and
    (ii)   if so, any information about the matter to which the notice relates which has been published under section 391(4)];
  [(i)   in the case of a mortgage intermediary—
    (i)   the names of the persons within the management who are responsible for the activities specified by article 25A (arranging regulated mortgage contracts), article 36A (credit broking), article 53A (advising on regulated mortgage contracts) and article 53DA (advising on regulated credit agreements the purpose of which is to acquire land) of the Financial Services and Markets Act 2000 (Regulated Activities) Order 2001; and
    (ii)   whether the mortgage intermediary is a tied mortgage intermediary or not;
  (j)   in the case of an appointed representative to whom subsection (2B) applies, the name of the mortgage intermediary on whose behalf the appointed representative acts].
[(2A)   This subsection applies to—

(a) an appointed representative to whom subsection (1A) of section 39 applies for whom the applicable register (as defined by subsection (1B) of that section) is the record maintained by virtue of subsection (1)(ha) above;

(b) a person mentioned in subsection (1)(a) of section 39A if—

    (i) the contract with an authorised person to which he is party complies with the applicable requirements (as defined by subsection (7) of that section), and

    (ii) the authorised person has accepted responsibility in writing for the person's activities in carrying on investment services business (as defined by subsection (8) of that section); and

(c) any person not falling within paragraph (a) or (b) in respect of whom the [FCA] considers that a record must be maintained for the purpose of securing compliance with Article 23.3 of the markets in financial instruments directive (registration of tied agents).]

[(2B) This subsection applies to an appointed representative to whom section 39(1BA) applies or to whom that subsection would apply if the requirements of section 39(1BB) were not met.]

(3) If it appears to the [FCA] that a person in respect of whom there is an entry in the record as a result of one of the paragraphs of subsection (1) has ceased to be a person to whom that paragraph applies, the [FCA] may remove the entry from the record.

(4) But if the [FCA] decides not to remove the entry, it must—

(a) make a note to that effect in the record; and

(b) state why it considers that the person has ceased to be a person to whom that paragraph applies.

[(4A) If the FCA cancels or varies the Part 4A permission of a mortgage intermediary and as a result the person to whom the entry relates no longer has a Part 4A permission to carry on a relevant mortgage activity within the meaning of section 55J(6C), the FCA must delete mention of such permission from the record without undue delay.]

(5) The [FCA] must—

(a) make the record available for inspection by members of the public in a legible form at such times and in such place or places as the [FCA] may determine; and

(b) provide a certified copy of the record, or any part of it, to any person who asks for it—

    (i) on payment of the fee (if any) fixed by the [FCA]; and

    (ii) in a form (either written or electronic) in which it is legible to the person asking for it.

(6) The [FCA] may—

(a) publish the record, or any part of it;

(b) exploit commercially the information contained in the record, or any part of that information.

(7) "Authorised unit trust scheme", ["authorised contractual scheme",] "authorised open-ended investment company" and "recognised scheme" have the same meaning as in Part XVII, and associated expressions are to be read accordingly.

(8) "Approved person" means a person in relation to whom the [FCA or the PRA] has given its approval under section 59 and "controlled function" and "arrangement" have the same meaning as in that section.

[(8A) In this section—

"relevant authorised person" has the same meaning as in Part 5 (see section 71A),

"senior manager", in relation to a relevant authorised person, means a person who has approval under section 59 to perform a designated senior management function in relation to the carrying on by the authorised person of a regulated activity, and

"designated senior management function" means a function designated as a senior management function under section 59(6A) or (6B).]

(9) *"Relevant authorised person" has the meaning given in section 66.*

NOTES

The word omitted from sub-s (1)(h) was repealed, and sub-s (1)(ha) and sub-s (2A) were inserted, by the Financial Services and Markets Act 2000 (Markets in Financial Instruments) Regulations 2007, SI 2007/126, reg 3(5), Sch 5, paras 1, 12.

Sub-ss (1)(ba) and (2)(ba) were inserted, and the words in square brackets in sub-s (7) were inserted, by the Collective Investment in Transferable Securities (Contractual Scheme) Regulations 2013, SI 2013/1388, reg 3(1), (16).

Word in italics in sub-s (1)(ha) repealed, sub-s (2)(i), (j) and sub-ss (2B), (4A) inserted, by the Mortgage Credit Directive Order 2015, SI 2015/910, Sch 1, para 1(1), (7), as from 21 March 2016 (note that the 2015 Order also comes into force on 20 April 2015 and 21 December 2015 for limited other purposes, and for transitional provisions, see Part 4 of that Order at **[2.1194]** et seq).

For the words in italics in sub-s (2)(g)(ii), (iii) there are substituted the words "authorised person concerned" by the Financial Services (Banking Reform) Act 2013, s 35, Sch 3, para 11, as from 7 March 2016.

Sub-s (2)(g)(iv), (h) and sub-s (8A) are inserted, and sub-s (9) is substituted (as follows) by the Financial Services (Banking Reform) Act 2013, s 34, as from 7 March 2016—

"(9) "The authorised person concerned", in relation to an approved person, means the person on whose application approval was given.".

Sub-s (1)(f) and the words omitted from sub-s (2)(e) were repealed, and all other words in square brackets in this section were substituted, by the Financial Services Act 2012, s 41, Sch 12, Pt 2, para 16.

Disclosure of information

[1.1550]
348   Restrictions on disclosure of confidential information by [FCA, PRA] etc
(1)   Confidential information must not be disclosed by a primary recipient, or by any person obtaining the information directly or indirectly from a primary recipient, without the consent of—
   (a)   the person from whom the primary recipient obtained the information; and
   (b)   if different, the person to whom it relates.
(2)   In this Part "confidential information" means information which—
   (a)   relates to the business or other affairs of any person;
   (b)   was received by the primary recipient for the purposes of, or in the discharge of, any functions of the [FCA, the PRA] . . . or the Secretary of State under any provision made by or under this Act; and
   (c)   is not prevented from being confidential information by subsection (4).
(3)   It is immaterial for the purposes of subsection (2) whether or not the information was received—
   (a)   by virtue of a requirement to provide it imposed by or under this Act;
   (b)   for other purposes as well as purposes mentioned in that subsection.
(4)   Information is not confidential information if—
   (a)   it has been made available to the public by virtue of being disclosed in any circumstances in which, or for any purposes for which, disclosure is not precluded by this section; or
   (b)   it is in the form of a summary or collection of information so framed that it is not possible to ascertain from it information relating to any particular person.
(5)   Each of the following is a primary recipient for the purposes of this Part—
   [(a)   the FCA;
   (aa) the PRA;]
   (b)   . . .
   (c)   the Secretary of State;
   (d)   a person appointed [to collect or update information under section [166A] or] to make a report under section 166;
   (e)   any person who is or has been employed by a person mentioned in paragraphs (a) to (c);
   [(ea) a person who is or has been engaged to provide services to a person mentioned in those paragraphs;]
   (f)   any auditor or expert instructed by a person mentioned in those paragraphs.
(6)   In subsection (5)(f) "expert" includes—
   (a)   a competent person appointed by [the FCA] under section 97;
   (b)   a competent person appointed by the [FCA, the PRA] or the Secretary of State to conduct an investigation under Part XI;
   (c)   . . .
[(7)   Nothing in this section applies to information received by a primary recipient for the purposes of, or in the discharge of, any functions of the FCA under the Competition Act 1998 or the Enterprise Act 2002 by virtue of Part 16A of this Act.

NOTES
   The words in the first (outer) pair of square brackets in sub-s (5)(d) were inserted by the Financial Services Act 2010, s 24(1), (2), Sch 2, Pt 1, paras 1, 26.
   Sub-s (7) was added by the Financial Services (Banking Reform) Act 2013, s 129, Sch 8, Pt 1, para 5.
   All other words in square brackets in this section were substituted, and the words omitted were repealed, by the Financial Services Act 2012, s 41, Sch 12, Pt 2, para 18, (for transitional provisions in relation to disclosure by the FSA to the PRA and the Bank of England, see Sch 20, para 9 to the 2012 Act).
   Note: "primary recipient" includes the Bank of England for the purposes of the Financial Services and Markets Act 2000 (Confidential Information) (Bank of England) (Consequential Provisions) Order 2001, SI 2001/3648, art 3(4), and any person upon whom functions are conferred by, or under, the Financial Services and Markets Act 2000 (Disclosure of Confidential Information) (Amendment) (No 2) Regulations 2003, SI 2003/2174, with effect from 23 August 2003.
   Information relating to mutual societies: the following information is to be treated as confidential information for the purposes of this section and ss 349–353: (a) certain information relating to the business or other affairs of a building society or other body (see the Building Societies Act 1986, s 53A (disclosure of information)); (b) certain information relating to the business or other affairs of a friendly society, a registered branch of a friendly society or any other person (see the Friendly Societies Act 1992, s 63A (disclosure of information)).

[1.1551]
349   Exceptions from section 348
(1)   Section 348 does not prevent a disclosure of confidential information which is—
   (a)   made for the purpose of facilitating the carrying out of a public function; and
   (b)   permitted by regulations made by the Treasury under this section.
(2)   The regulations may, in particular, make provision permitting the disclosure of confidential information or of confidential information of a prescribed kind—
   (a)   by prescribed recipients, or recipients of a prescribed description, to any person for the purpose of enabling or assisting the recipient to discharge prescribed public functions;

(b) by prescribed recipients, or recipients of a prescribed description, to prescribed persons, or persons of prescribed descriptions, for the purpose of enabling or assisting those persons to discharge prescribed public functions;

(c) by the [FCA or the PRA] to the Treasury or the Secretary of State for any purpose;

(d) by any recipient if the disclosure is with a view to or in connection with prescribed proceedings.

(3) The regulations may also include provision—

(a) making any permission to disclose confidential information subject to conditions (which may relate to the obtaining of consents or any other matter);

(b) restricting the uses to which confidential information disclosed under the regulations may be put.

[(3A) Section 348 does not apply to—

(a) the disclosure by a recipient to which subsection (3B) applies of confidential information disclosed to it by the [FCA or the PRA] in reliance on subsection (1);

(b) the disclosure of such information by a person obtaining it directly or indirectly from a recipient to which subsection (3B) applies.

(3B) This subsection applies to—

(a) the Panel on Takeovers and Mergers;

(b) an authority designated as a supervisory authority for the purposes of Article 4.1 of the Takeovers Directive;

(c) any other person or body that exercises public functions, under legislation in an EEA State other than the United Kingdom, that are similar to the [functions of the FCA or the PRA] or those of the Panel on Takeovers and Mergers.]

(4) In relation to confidential information, each of the following is a "recipient"—

(a) a primary recipient;

(b) a person obtaining the information directly or indirectly from a primary recipient.

(5) "Public functions" includes—

(a) functions conferred by or in accordance with any provision contained in any enactment or subordinate legislation;

(b) functions conferred by or in accordance with any provision contained in the Community Treaties or any Community instrument;

(c) similar functions conferred on persons by or under provisions having effect as part of the law of a country or territory outside the United Kingdom;

(d) functions exercisable in relation to prescribed disciplinary proceedings.

(6) "Enactment" includes—

(a) an Act of the Scottish Parliament;

(b) Northern Ireland legislation.

(7) "Subordinate legislation" has the meaning given in the Interpretation Act 1978 and also includes an instrument made under an Act of the Scottish Parliament or under Northern Ireland legislation.

[(8) . . .]

NOTES

Sub-s (2): words in square brackets substituted by the Financial Services Act 2012, s 41, Sch 12, Pt 2, para 19(1), (2).

Sub-ss (3A), (3B): inserted by the Companies Act 2006, s 964(1), (4); words in square brackets substituted by the Financial Services Act 2012, s 41, Sch 12, Pt 2, para 19(1), (3), (4).

Sub-s (8): added by the Takeovers Directive (Interim Implementation) Regulations 2006, SI 2006/1183, reg 18(3), (5); repealed by the Companies Act 2006 (Commencement No 2, Consequential Amendments, Transitional Provisions and Savings) Order 2007, SI 2007/1093, art 7, Sch 5.

References to the European Community and related expressions: see the note "References to "the European Community", "Community", etc" in the introductory notes to this Act. Note that "Community Treaties" was defined by the European Communities Act 1972, s 1(2)–(4), Sch 1, Pt 1 (as originally enacted), as applied by the Interpretation Act 1978, s 5, Sch 1. See now, by virtue of the European Union (Amendment) Act 2008, s 3, Schedule, the definition "EU treaties" in s 1(2)–(4), Sch 1, Pt I of the 1972 Act, as applied by the Interpretation Act 1978, s 5, Sch 1.

Information relating to mutual societies: see the note to s 348 at [**1.1550**].

Regulations: the Financial Services and Markets Act 2000 (Disclosure of Confidential Information) Regulations 2001, SI 2001/2188; the Financial Services and Markets Act 2000 (Disclosure of Confidential Information) (Amendment) Regulations 2001, SI 2001/3437; the Financial Services and Markets Act 2000 (Disclosure of Confidential Information) (Amendment) (No 2) Regulations 2001, SI 2001/3624; the Electronic Commerce Directive (Financial Services and Markets) Regulations 2002, SI 2002/1775; the Financial Services and Markets Act 2000 (Disclosure of Confidential Information) (Amendment) Regulations 2003, SI 2003/693; the Insurance Mediation Directive (Miscellaneous Amendments) Regulations 2003, SI 2003/1473; the Collective Investment Schemes (Miscellaneous Amendments) Regulations 2003, SI 2003/2066; the Financial Services and Markets Act 2000 (Disclosure of Confidential Information) (Amendment) (No 2) Regulations 2003, SI 2003/2174; the Financial Services and Markets Act 2000 (Disclosure of Confidential Information) (Amendment) (No 3) Regulations 2003, SI 2003/2817; the Financial Services and Markets Act 2000 (Disclosure of Confidential Information) (Amendment) Regulations 2005, SI 2005/3071; the Financial Services and Markets Act 2000 (Disclosure of Confidential Information) (Amendment) Regulations 2006, SI 2006/3413; the Financial Services and Markets Act 2000 (Markets in Financial Instruments) (Amendment) Regulations 2007, SI 2007/763; the Financial Services and Markets Act 2000 (Reinsurance Directive) Regulations 2007, SI 2007/3255; the Financial Services and Markets Act 2000 (Disclosure of Confidential Information) (Amendment) Regulations 2009, SI 2009/2877; the Credit Rating Agencies Regulations 2010, SI 2010/906 at [**2.792**]; the Financial Services and Markets Act 2000 (Disclosure of Confidential Information) (Amendment) Regulations 2012, SI 2012/3019; the Alternative Investment Fund Managers Regulations 2013, SI 2013/1773; the Capital

Requirements Regulations 2013, SI 2013/3115; the Financial Services and Markets Act 2000 (Disclosure of Confidential Information) (Amendment) Regulations 2014, SI 2014/883.

[1.1552]
350   Disclosure of information by the Inland Revenue
[(1)   No obligation as to secrecy imposed by statute or otherwise prevents the disclosure of Revenue information to—
  (a)   the FCA or the PRA, if the disclosure is made for the purpose of assisting or enabling that regulator to discharge its functions under this or any other Act, or
  (b)   the Secretary of State, if the disclosure is made for the purpose of assisting in the investigation of a matter under section 168 or with a view to the appointment of an investigator under that section.]
(2)   A disclosure may only be made under subsection (1) by or under the authority of the Commissioners of Inland Revenue.
(3)   Section 348 does not apply to Revenue information.
(4)   Information obtained as a result of [subsection (1)] may not be used except—
  (a)   for the purpose of deciding whether to appoint an investigator under section 168;
  (b)   in the conduct of an investigation under section 168;
  (c)   in criminal proceedings brought against a person under this Act or the Criminal Justice Act 1993 as a result of an investigation under section 168;
  (d)   for the purpose of taking action under this Act against a person as a result of an investigation under section 168;
  (e)   in proceedings before the Tribunal as a result of action taken as mentioned in paragraph (d).
(5)   Information obtained as a result of subsection (1) may not be disclosed except—
  (a)   by or under the authority of the Commissioners of Inland Revenue;
  (b)   in proceedings mentioned in subsection (4)(c) or (e) or with a view to their institution.
(6)   Subsection (5) does not prevent the disclosure of information obtained as a result of subsection (1) to a person to whom it could have been disclosed under subsection (1).
(7)   "Revenue information" means information held by a person which it would be an offence under section 182 of the Finance Act 1989 for him to disclose.

NOTES
Sub-s (1) was substituted, and the words in square brackets in sub-s (4) were substituted, by the Financial Services Act 2012, s 41, Sch 12, Pt 2, para 20.
Information relating to mutual societies: see the note to s 348 at **[1.1550]**.
Commissioners of Inland Revenue: a reference to the Commissioners of Inland Revenue is now to be taken as a reference to the Commissioners for Her Majesty's Revenue and Customs; see the Commissioners for Revenue and Customs Act 2005, s 50(1), (7).
Application: the Commissioners for Her Majesty's Revenue and Customs may supply information in accordance with this section only if the information was obtained or is held in the exercise of a function relating to matters to which the Commissioners for Revenue and Customs Act 2005, s 7 applies; see s 17(6) of, and Sch 2, Pt 2, para 18 to, that Act

[1.1553]
352   Offences
(1)   A person who discloses information in contravention of section 348 or 350(5) is guilty of an offence.
(2)   A person guilty of an offence under subsection (1) is liable—
  (a)   on summary conviction, to imprisonment for a term not exceeding three months or a fine not exceeding the statutory maximum, or both;
  (b)   on conviction on indictment, to imprisonment for a term not exceeding two years or a fine, or both.
(3)   A person is guilty of an offence if, in contravention of any provision of regulations made under section 349, he uses information which has been disclosed to him in accordance with the regulations.
(4)   A person is guilty of an offence if, in contravention of subsection (4) of section 350, he uses information which has been disclosed to him in accordance with that section.
(5)   A person guilty of an offence under subsection (3) or (4) is liable on summary conviction to imprisonment for a term not exceeding *three months* or a fine not exceeding level 5 on the standard scale, or both.
(6)   In proceedings for an offence under this section it is a defence for the accused to prove—
  (a)   that he did not know and had no reason to suspect that the information was confidential information or that it had been disclosed in accordance with section 350;
  (b)   that he took all reasonable precautions and exercised all due diligence to avoid committing the offence.

NOTES
Sub-s (5): for the words in italics there are substituted the words "51 weeks" by the Criminal Justice Act 2003, s 280(2), Sch 26, para 54(1), (3), as from a day to be appointed.
Information relating to mutual societies: see the note to s 348 at **[1.1550]**.

[1.1554]
353 Removal of other restrictions on disclosure
(1) The Treasury may make regulations permitting the disclosure of any information, or of information of a prescribed kind—

(a) by prescribed persons for the purpose of assisting or enabling them to discharge prescribed functions under this Act or any rules or regulations made under it;

(b) by prescribed persons, or persons of a prescribed description, to the [FCA or the PRA] for the purpose of assisting or enabling [either of them] to discharge prescribed functions;

[(c) . . .].

(2) Regulations under this section may not make any provision in relation to the disclosure of confidential information by primary recipients or by any person obtaining confidential information directly or indirectly from a primary recipient.

(3) If a person discloses any information as permitted by regulations under this section the disclosure is not to be taken as a contravention of any duty to which he is subject.

NOTES
Sub-s (1): words in square brackets in para (b) substituted by the Financial Services Act 2012, s 41, Sch 12, Pt 2, para 23; para (c) originally inserted by the Consumer Credit Act 2006, s 61(9), and repealed by the Financial Services and Markets Act 2000 (Regulated Activities) (Amendment) (No 2) Order 2013, SI 2013/1881, art 10(1), (13), (for transitional provisions see see Pt 8 thereof at **[2.1007]** et seq).

Information relating to mutual societies: see the note to s 348 at **[1.1550]**.

Regulations: the Financial Services and Markets Act 2000 (Disclosure of Information by Prescribed Persons) Regulations 2001, SI 2001/1857; the Financial Services and Markets Act 2000 (Disclosure of Information by Prescribed Persons) (Amendment) Regulations 2005, SI 2005/272.

[Information received from Bank of England]

[1.1555]
353A Information received from Bank of England
(1) A regulator must not disclose to any person specially protected information.

(2) "Specially protected information" is information in relation to which the first and second conditions are met.

(3) The first condition is that the regulator received the information from—

(a) the Bank of England ("the Bank"), or

(b) the other regulator where that regulator had received the information from the Bank.

(4) The second condition is that the Bank notified the regulator to which it disclosed the information that the Bank held the information for the purpose of its functions with respect to any of the following—

(a) monetary policy;

(b) financial operations intended to support financial institutions for the purposes of maintaining stability;

(c) the provision of private banking services and related services.

(5) The notification referred to in subsection (4) must be—

(a) in writing, and

(b) given before, or at the same time as, the Bank discloses the information.

(6) The prohibition in subsection (1) does not apply—

(a) to disclosure by one regulator to the other regulator where the regulator making the disclosure informs the other regulator that the information is specially protected information by virtue of this section;

(b) where the Bank has consented to disclosure of the information;

(c) to information which has been made available to the public by virtue of being disclosed in any circumstances in which, or for any purposes for which, disclosure is not precluded by this section;

(d) to information which the regulator is required to disclose in pursuance of any EU obligation.

(7) In this section references to disclosure by or to a regulator or by the Bank include references to disclosure by or to—

(a) persons who are, or are acting as,—

(i) officers of, or members of the staff of, the regulator, or

(ii) officers, employees or agents of the Bank, or

(b) auditors, experts, contractors or investigators appointed by the regulator or the Bank under powers conferred by this Act or otherwise.

(8) References to disclosure by a regulator do not include references to disclosure between persons who fall within any paragraph of subsection (7)(a) or (b) in relation to that regulator.

(9) Each regulator must take such steps as are reasonable in the circumstances to prevent the disclosure of specially protected information, in cases not excluded by subsection (6), by those who are or have been—

(a) its officers or members of staff (including persons acting as its officers or members of staff);

(b)　auditors, experts, contractors or investigators appointed by the regulator under powers conferred by this Act or otherwise;

(c)　persons to whom the regulator has delegated any of its functions.]

NOTES
Commencement: 1 April 2013.
Inserted, together with the preceding heading, by the Financial Services Act 2012, s 41, Sch 12, Pt 2, para 24.

Co-operation

[1.1556]
[354A　FCA's duty to co-operate with others
(1)　The FCA must take such steps as it considers appropriate to co-operate with other persons (whether in the United Kingdom or elsewhere) who have functions—
(a)　similar to those of the FCA, or
(b)　in relation to the prevention or detection of financial crime.
(2)　The persons referred to in subsection (1) do not include the Bank of England or the PRA (but see sections 3D and 3Q).
[(2A)　Subsection (1) does not apply in relation to the Competition and Markets Authority in a case where the FCA has made a reference under section 131 of the Enterprise Act 2002 as a result of section 234I (but see section 234L).]
(3)　The FCA must take such steps as it considers appropriate to co-operate with—
(a)　the Panel on Takeovers and Mergers;
(b)　an authority designated as a supervisory authority for the purposes of Article 4.1 of the Takeovers Directive;
(c)　any other person or body that exercises functions of a public nature, under legislation in any country or territory outside the United Kingdom, that appear to the FCA to be similar to those of the Panel on Takeovers and Mergers.
(4)　Co-operation may include the sharing of information which the FCA is not prevented from disclosing.
(5)　"Financial crime" has the meaning given in section 1H(3).]

NOTES
Commencement: 1 April 2013.
Sections 354A–354C substituted (for the original s 354) by the Financial Services Act 2012, s 41, Sch 12, Pt 2, para 25.
Sub-s (2A): inserted by the Financial Services (Banking Reform) Act 2013, s 129, Sch 8, Pt 1, para 6.

PART XXV
INJUNCTIONS AND RESTITUTION

NOTES
Transitional provisions etc in connection with the commencement of the Financial Services Act 2012: see the Financial Services Act 2012 (Transitional Provisions) (Enforcement) Order 2013, SI 2013/441. Article 15 contains transitional provisions in relation to injunctions. Article 16 contains transitional provisions in relation to restitution orders. Article 17 contains transitional provisions in relation to the power to require restitution. Article 18 contains transitional provisions in relation to injunctions and restitution in respect of certain post-1 April 2013 contraventions.

Injunctions

[1.1557]
380　Injunctions
(1)　If, on the application of the [appropriate regulator] or the Secretary of State, the court is satisfied—
(a)　that there is a reasonable likelihood that any person will contravene a relevant requirement, or
(b)　that any person has contravened a relevant requirement and that there is a reasonable likelihood that the contravention will continue or be repeated,
the court may make an order restraining (or in Scotland an interdict prohibiting) the contravention.
(2)　If on the application of the [appropriate regulator] or the Secretary of State the court is satisfied—
(a)　that any person has contravened a relevant requirement, and
(b)　that there are steps which could be taken for remedying the contravention,
the court may make an order requiring that person, and any other person who appears to have been knowingly concerned in the contravention, to take such steps as the court may direct to remedy it.
(3)　If, on the application of the [appropriate regulator] or the Secretary of State, the court is satisfied that any person may have—
(a)　contravened a relevant requirement, or
(b)　been knowingly concerned in the contravention of such a requirement,
it may make an order restraining (or in Scotland an interdict prohibiting) him from disposing of, or otherwise dealing with, any assets of his which it is satisfied he is reasonably likely to dispose of or otherwise deal with.

(4)   The jurisdiction conferred by this section is exercisable by the High Court and the Court of Session.

(5)   In subsection (2), references to remedying a contravention include references to mitigating its effect.

(6)   "Relevant requirement"—

   (a)   in relation to an application by the [appropriate regulator], means a requirement—

      [(i)   which is imposed by or under this Act or by a qualifying EU provision specified, or of a description specified, for the purposes of this subsection by the Treasury by order];   . . .

      (ii)   which is imposed by or under any other Act and whose contravention constitutes an offence [mentioned in section 402(1)][;   . . .

      (iii)   which is imposed by the Alternative Investment Fund Managers Regulations 2013;][or

      (iv)   which is imposed by Part 7 of the Financial Services Act 2012 (offences relating to financial services) and whose contravention constitutes an offence under that Part;]

   (b)   in relation to an application by the Secretary of State, means a requirement which is imposed by or under this Act and whose contravention constitutes an offence which the Secretary of State has power to prosecute under this Act.

(7)   In the application of subsection (6) to Scotland—

   (a)   . . .

   (b)   in paragraph (b) omit "which the Secretary of State has power to prosecute under this Act".

[(8)   The PRA is the "appropriate regulator" in the case of a contravention of—

   (a)   a requirement that is imposed by the PRA under any provision of this Act,

   (b)   a requirement under section 56(6) where the authorised person concerned is a PRA-authorised person and the prohibition order concerned is made by the PRA, or

   (c)   a requirement under section 59(1) or (2) where the authorised person concerned is a PRA-authorised person and the approval concerned falls to be given by the PRA.

(9)   In the case of a contravention of a requirement that is imposed by a qualifying EU provision, "the appropriate regulator" is whichever of the PRA or the FCA (or both) is specified by the Treasury by order in relation to the qualifying EU provision for the purposes of this section.

(10)   In the case of a contravention of a requirement where the contravention constitutes an offence under this Act, the "appropriate regulator" is whichever of the PRA or the FCA has power to prosecute the offence (see section 401).

(11)   The FCA is the "appropriate regulator" in the case of a contravention of any other requirement.

(12)   The Treasury may by order amend the definition of "appropriate regulator".]

NOTES

Sub-ss (1)–(3): words in square brackets substituted by the Financial Services Act 2012, s 37(1), Sch 9, Pt 1, para 1, Pt 5, para 19(1), (2).

Sub-s (6) is amended as follows:

The word "or" omitted from sub-para (a)(i) was repealed, and sub-para (a)(iii) (and the preceding word) was inserted, by the Alternative Investment Fund Managers Regulations 2013, SI 2013/1773, reg 80, Sch 1, Part 1, paras 1, 27, (for transitional provisions and savings see Part 9 of the 2013 Regulations).

Sub-para (a)(iv) (and the preceding word) was inserted, and the word omitted from sub-para (a)(ii) was repealed, by the Financial Services (Banking Reform) Act 2013, s 141, Sch 10, para 3(1), (2).

Other words in square brackets substituted by the Financial Services Act 2012, s 37(1), Sch 9, Pt 1, para 1, Pt 5, para 19(1), (3).

Sub-s (7): para (a) repealed by the Financial Services Act 2012, s 37(1), Sch 9, Pt 1, para 1, Pt 5, para 19(1), (4).

Sub-ss (8)–(12): added by the Financial Services Act 2012, s 37(1), Sch 9, Pt 1, para 1, Pt 5, para 19(1), (5).

Transitional provisions in relation to the original commencement of this Act: any requirement, condition or prohibition imposed before 1 December 2001 by or under certain specified provisions is to be treated as a relevant requirement for the purposes of sub-s (2) above, and any restriction or requirement imposed by or under certain other provisions is to be treated as a relevant requirement for the purposes of sub-s (3)(a) above; see, in general, the Financial Services and Markets Act 2000 (Transitional Provisions and Savings) (Civil Remedies, Discipline, Criminal Offences etc) (No 2) Order 2001, SI 2001/3083, arts 2, 4.

Note: for the purposes of this section (i) a requirement imposed by the FCA under the Electronic Commerce Directive (Financial Services and Markets) Regulations 2002, SI 2002/1775 upon an incoming provider is to be treated as imposed on him by or under this Act (see reg 12(2) of those Regulations); (ii) a requirement imposed by the FCA under the Central Securities Depositories Regulations 2014, SI 2014/2879 is a "relevant requirement" for the purposes of this section (see reg 3(8) of those Regulations).

Orders: the Financial Services and Markets Act 2000 (Qualifying EU Provisions) Order 2013, SI 2013/419; the Financial Services and Markets Act 2000 (Qualifying EU Provisions) (No 2) Order 2013, SI 2013/3116.

Restitution orders

[1.1558]
382   Restitution orders

(1)   The court may, on the application of the [appropriate regulator] or the Secretary of State, make an order under subsection (2) if it is satisfied that a person has contravened a relevant requirement, or been knowingly concerned in the contravention of such a requirement, and—

   (a)   that profits have accrued to him as a result of the contravention; or

    (b)   that one or more persons have suffered loss or been otherwise adversely affected as a result of the contravention.

(2) The court may order the person concerned to pay to the [regulator concerned] such sum as appears to the court to be just having regard—

    (a)   in a case within paragraph (a) of subsection (1), to the profits appearing to the court to have accrued;

    (b)   in a case within paragraph (b) of that subsection, to the extent of the loss or other adverse effect;

    (c)   in a case within both of those paragraphs, to the profits appearing to the court to have accrued and to the extent of the loss or other adverse effect.

(3) Any amount paid to the [regulator concerned] in pursuance of an order under subsection (2) must be paid by it to such qualifying person or distributed by it among such qualifying persons as the court may direct.

(4) On an application under subsection (1) the court may require the person concerned to supply it with such accounts or other information as it may require for any one or more of the following purposes—

    (a)   establishing whether any and, if so, what profits have accrued to him as mentioned in paragraph (a) of that subsection;

    (b)   establishing whether any person or persons have suffered any loss or adverse effect as mentioned in paragraph (b) of that subsection and, if so, the extent of that loss or adverse effect; and

    (c)   determining how any amounts are to be paid or distributed under subsection (3).

(5) The court may require any accounts or other information supplied under subsection (4) to be verified in such manner as it may direct.

(6) The jurisdiction conferred by this section is exercisable by the High Court and the Court of Session.

(7) Nothing in this section affects the right of any person other than the [appropriate regulator] or the Secretary of State to bring proceedings in respect of the matters to which this section applies.

(8) "Qualifying person" means a person appearing to the court to be someone—

    (a)   to whom the profits mentioned in subsection (1)(a) are attributable; or

    (b)   who has suffered the loss or adverse effect mentioned in subsection (1)(b).

(9) "Relevant requirement"—

    (a)   in relation to an application by the [appropriate regulator], means a requirement—

        [(i)   which is imposed by or under this Act or by a qualifying EU provision specified, or of a description specified, for the purposes of this subsection by the Treasury by order]; . . .

        (ii)   which is imposed by or under any other Act and whose contravention constitutes an offence [mentioned in section 402(1)]; [. . .

        (iii)   which is imposed by the Alternative Investment Fund Managers Regulations 2013;][or

        (iv)   which is imposed by Part 7 of the Financial Services Act 2012 (offences relating to financial services) and whose contravention constitutes an offence under that Part;]

    (b)   in relation to an application by the Secretary of State, means a requirement which is imposed by or under this Act and whose contravention constitutes an offence which the Secretary of State has power to prosecute under this Act.

(10) In the application of subsection (9) to Scotland—

    (a)   . . .

    (b)   in paragraph (b) omit "which the Secretary of State has power to prosecute under this Act".

[(11) The PRA is the "appropriate regulator" in the case of a contravention of—

    (a)   a requirement that is imposed by the PRA under any provision of this Act,

    (b)   a requirement under section 56(6) where the authorised person concerned is a PRA-authorised person and the prohibition order concerned is made by the PRA, or

    (c)   a requirement under section 59(1) or (2) where the authorised person concerned is a PRA-authorised person and the approval concerned falls to be given by the PRA.

(12) In the case of a contravention of a requirement that is imposed by a qualifying EU provision, "the appropriate regulator" is whichever of the PRA or the FCA (or both) is specified by the Treasury by order in relation to the qualifying EU provision for the purposes of this section.

(13) In the case of a contravention of a requirement where the contravention constitutes an offence under this Act, the "appropriate regulator" is the regulator which has power to prosecute the offence (see section 401).

(14) The FCA is the "appropriate regulator" in the case of a contravention of any other requirement.

(15) The Treasury may by order amend the definition of "appropriate regulator".]

NOTES

Sub-ss (1)–(3), (7): words in square brackets substituted by the Financial Services Act 2012, s 37(1), Sch 9, Pt 1, para 1, Pt 5, para 21(1)–(4).

Sub-s (9) is amended as follows:

The word "or" omitted from sub-para (a)(i) was repealed, and sub-para (a)(iii) (and the preceding word) was inserted, by the Alternative Investment Fund Managers Regulations 2013, SI 2013/1773, reg 80, Sch 1, Part 1, paras 1, 27, (for transitional provisions and savings see Part 9 of the 2013 Regulations).

Sub-para (a)(iv) (and the preceding word) was inserted, and the word omitted from sub-para (a)(ii) was repealed, by the Financial Services (Banking Reform) Act 2013, s 141, Sch 10, para 3(1), (3).

Other words in square brackets substituted by the Financial Services Act 2012, s 37(1), Sch 9, Pt 1, para 1, Pt 5, para 21(1), (5).

Sub-s (10): para (a) repealed by the Financial Services Act 2012, s 37(1), Sch 9, Pt 1, para 1, Pt 5, para 21(1), (6).

Sub-ss (11)–(15): added by the Financial Services Act 2012, s 37(1), Sch 9, Pt 1, para 1, Pt 5, para 21(1), (7).

Transitional provisions in relation to the original commencement of this Act: any requirement, condition or prohibition imposed before 1 December 2001 by or under certain specified provisions is to be treated as a relevant requirement for the purposes of this section; see the Financial Services and Markets Act 2000 (Transitional Provisions and Savings) (Civil Remedies, Discipline, Criminal Offences etc) (No 2) Order 2001, SI 2001/3083, art 2.

Note: for the purposes of this section (i) a requirement imposed by the FCA under the Electronic Commerce Directive (Financial Services and Markets) Regulations 2002, SI 2002/1775 upon an incoming provider is to be treated as imposed on him by or under this Act (see reg 12(2) of those Regulations); (ii) a requirement imposed by the FCA under the Central Securities Depositories Regulations 2014, SI 2014/2879 is a "relevant requirement" for the purposes of this section (see reg 3(8) of those Regulations).

Note: see *Financial Conduct Authority v Anderson & Others* [2014 EWHC 3630] (5 November 2014).

Orders: the Financial Services and Markets Act 2000 (Qualifying EU Provisions) Order 2013, SI 2013/419; the Financial Services and Markets Act 2000 (Qualifying EU Provisions) (No 2) Order 2013, SI 2013/3116.

Restitution required by [FCA or PRA]

[1.1559]
384   Power of [FCA or PRA] to require restitution
(1)   [The appropriate regulator] may exercise the power in subsection (5) if it is satisfied that an authorised person [or recognised investment exchange] ("the person concerned") has contravened a relevant requirement, or been knowingly concerned in the contravention of such a requirement, and—
  (a)   that profits have accrued to him as a result of the contravention; or
  (b)   that one or more persons have suffered loss or been otherwise adversely affected as a result of the contravention.
(2)   The [FCA] may exercise the power in subsection (5) if it is satisfied that a person ("the person concerned")—
  (a)   has engaged in market abuse, or
  (b)   by taking or refraining from taking any action has required or encouraged another person or persons to engage in behaviour which, if engaged in by the person concerned, would amount to market abuse,
and the condition mentioned in subsection (3) is fulfilled,
(3)   The condition is—
  (a)   that profits have accrued to the person concerned as a result of the market abuse; or
  (b)   that one or more persons have suffered loss or been otherwise adversely affected as a result of the market abuse.
(4)   But the [FCA] may not exercise that power as a result of subsection (2) if, having considered any representations made to it in response to a warning notice, there are reasonable grounds for it to be satisfied that—
  (a)   the person concerned believed, on reasonable grounds, that his behaviour did not fall within paragraph (a) or (b) of that subsection; or
  (b)   he took all reasonable precautions and exercised all due diligence to avoid behaving in a way which fell within paragraph (a) or (b) of that subsection.
(5)   The power referred to in subsections (1) and (2) is a power to require the person concerned, in accordance with such arrangements as the [regulator exercising the power ("the regulator concerned")] considers appropriate, to pay to the appropriate person or distribute among the appropriate persons such amount as appears to the [regulator concerned] to be just having regard—
  (a)   in a case within paragraph (a) of subsection (1) or (3), to the profits appearing to the [regulator concerned] to have accrued;
  (b)   in a case within paragraph (b) of subsection (1) or (3), to the extent of the loss or other adverse effect;
  (c)   in a case within paragraphs (a) and (b) of subsection (1) or (3), to the profits appearing to the [regulator concerned] to have accrued and to the extent of the loss or other adverse effect.
(6)   "Appropriate person" means a person appearing to the [regulator concerned] to be someone—
  (a)   to whom the profits mentioned in paragraph (a) of subsection (1) or (3) are attributable; or
  (b)   who has suffered the loss or adverse effect mentioned in paragraph (b) of subsection (1) or (3).
(7)   "Relevant requirement" means—
  (a)   a requirement imposed by or under this Act [or by [a qualifying EU provision specified, or of a description specified, for the purposes of this subsection by the Treasury by order]]; . . .
  (b)   a requirement which is imposed by or under any other Act and whose contravention constitutes an offence [mentioned in section 402(1)][; . . .

(c)   a requirement imposed by the Alternative Investment Fund Managers Regulations 2013][or

(d)   a requirement which is imposed by Part 7 of the Financial Services Act 2012 (offences relating to financial services) and whose contravention constitutes an offence under that Part].

(8)   . . .

[(9)   The PRA is the "appropriate regulator" in the case of a contravention of—

(a)   a requirement that is imposed by the PRA under any provision of this Act,

(b)   a requirement under section 56(6) where the authorised person concerned is a PRA-authorised person and the prohibition order concerned is made by the PRA, or

(c)   a requirement under section 59(1) or (2) where the authorised person concerned is a PRA-authorised person and the approval concerned falls to be given by the PRA.

(10)   In the case of a contravention of a requirement that is imposed by a qualifying EU provision, "the appropriate regulator" is whichever of the PRA or the FCA (or both) is specified by the Treasury by order in relation to the qualifying EU provision for the purposes of this section.

(11)   In the case of a contravention of a requirement where the contravention constitutes an offence under this Act, the "appropriate regulator" is the regulator which has power to prosecute the offence (see section 401).

(12)   The FCA is the "appropriate regulator" in the case of a contravention of any other requirement.

(13)   The Treasury may by order amend the definition of "appropriate regulator".]

NOTES

In the heading preceding this section, and in the section heading, the words in square brackets were substituted by the Financial Services Act 2012, s 37(1), Sch 9, Pt 1, para 1, Pt 5, para 23(1), (9), (10).

Sub-s (1): word in first pair of square brackets substituted, and words in second pair of square brackets inserted, by the Financial Services Act 2012, s 37(1), Sch 9, Pt 1, para 1, Pt 5, para 23(1), (2).

Sub-ss (2), (4)–(6): words in square brackets substituted by the Financial Services Act 2012, s 37(1), Sch 9, Pt 1, para 1, Pt 5, para 23(1), (3)–(5).

Sub-s (7) is amended as follows:

Words in first (outer) pair of square brackets in para (a) inserted by the Financial Services and Markets Act 2000 (Markets in Financial Instruments) Regulations 2007, SI 2007/126, reg 3(5), Sch 5, paras 1, 15.

Words in second (inner) pair of square brackets in para (a), and words in square brackets in para (b), substituted by the Financial Services Act 2012, s 37(1), Sch 9, Pt 1, para 1, Pt 5, para 23(1), (6).

The word omitted from para (a) was repealed, and para (c) (and the preceding word) was inserted, by the Alternative Investment Fund Managers Regulations 2013, SI 2013/1773, reg 80, Sch 1, Part 1, paras 1, 29, (for transitional provisions and savings see Part 9 of the 2013 Regulations).

Para (d) (and the preceding word) was inserted, and the word omitted from para (b) was repealed, by the Financial Services (Banking Reform) Act 2013, s 141, Sch 10, para 3(4).

Sub-s (8): repealed by the Financial Services Act 2012, s 37(1), Sch 9, Pt 1, para 1, Pt 5, para 23(1), (7).

Sub-ss (9)–(13): added by the Financial Services Act 2012, s 37(1), Sch 9, Pt 1, para 1, Pt 5, para 23(1), (8).

Transitional provisions in relation to the original commencement of this Act: as to the power of the FSA under sub-s (5) in relation to certain conduct before 1 December 2001, see the Financial Services and Markets Act 2000 (Transitional Provisions and Savings) (Civil Remedies, Discipline, Criminal Offences etc) (No 2) Order 2001, SI 2001/3083, art 3.

Note: (1) for the purposes of ss 204A–209 and 384 a requirement imposed by the FCA under Part 3 of the Electronic Commerce Directive (Financial Services and Markets) Regulations 2002, SI 2002/1775 upon an authorised incoming provider is to be treated as imposed on that provider by or under this Act; (2) for the purposes of those sections, (a) a requirement imposed by a direction imposed by the FCA under reg 11B of the 2002 Regulations is to be treated as a requirement imposed by or under this Act, and (b) any reference in those sections to an authorised person includes a reference to an unauthorised incoming provider. See reg 12(1), (1A) of those Regulations.

Orders: the Financial Services and Markets Act 2000 (Qualifying EU Provisions) Order 2013, SI 2013/419; the Financial Services and Markets Act 2000 (Qualifying EU Provisions) (No 2) Order 2013, SI 2013/3116.

[1.1560]
385   Warning notices
(1)   If [a regulator] proposes to exercise the power under section 384(5) in relation to a person, it must give him a warning notice.

(2)   A warning notice under this section must specify the amount which [the regulator] proposes to require the person concerned to pay or distribute as mentioned in section 384(5).

NOTES

Words in square brackets substituted by the Financial Services Act 2012, s 37(1), Sch 9, Pt 1, para 1, Pt 5, para 24.

[1.1561]
386   Decision notices
(1)   If the [regulator] decides to exercise the power under section 384(5), it must give a decision notice to the person in relation to whom the power is exercised.

(2)   The decision notice must—

(a)   state the amount that he is to pay or distribute as mentioned in section 384(5);

(b)   identify the person or persons to whom that amount is to be paid or among whom that amount is to be distributed; and

(c)   state the arrangements in accordance with which the payment or distribution is to be made.

(3)   If the [regulator] decides to exercise the power under section 384(5), the person in relation to whom it is exercised may refer the matter to the Tribunal.

NOTES
Words in square brackets substituted by the Financial Services Act 2012, s 37(1), Sch 9, Pt 1, para 1, Pt 5, para 25.

PART XXVI
NOTICES

NOTES
Transitional provisions etc in connection with the commencement of the Financial Services Act 2012: See the Financial Services Act 2012 (Transitional Provisions) (Enforcement) Order 2013, SI 2013/441. Articles 19–32 make provision for various notices and other matters given or imposed by the Financial Services Authority before 1 April 2013 to be treated as if given or imposed by the Prudential Regulation Authority, or by the Prudential Regulation Authority and the Financial Conduct Authority. See, in particular, art 19 (warning notices), art 20 (written notices) and art 21 (decision notices). Article 33 disapplies provisions relating to the publication of warning notices under s 390 in relation to warning notices given before that date.

Warning notices

[1.1562]
387   Warning notices
(1)   A warning notice must—
   (a)   state the action which the [regulator giving the notice ("the regulator concerned")] proposes to take;
   (b)   be in writing;
   (c)   give reasons for the proposed action;
   (d)   state whether section 394 applies; and
   (e)   if that section applies, describe its effect and state whether any secondary material exists to which the person concerned must be allowed access under it.
[(1A)   Where the PRA is the regulator concerned and the FCA proposes to refuse consent for the purposes of section 55F, 55I or 59 or to give conditional consent as mentioned in section 55F(5) *or 55I(8)*, the warning notice given by the PRA must—
   (a)   state that fact, and
   (b)   give the reasons for the FCA's proposal.]
(2)   [A warning] notice must specify a reasonable period (which may not be less than [14 days]) within which the person to whom it is given may make representations to the [regulator concerned].
(3)   [The regulator concerned] may extend the period specified in the notice.
[(3A)   Where the PRA receives any representations in response to a warning notice given by it under section 55X(1) or (2) or 62(2) in a case falling within subsection (1A) it must—
   (a)   if the representations are in writing, give a copy to the FCA, or
   (b)   if they are not in writing and have not been given directly to the FCA by the person making them, provide the FCA with a record of them.]
(4)   [The regulator concerned] must then decide, within a reasonable period, whether to give the person concerned a decision notice.

NOTES
Sub-ss (1A), (3A) were inserted, and all other words in square brackets in this section were substituted, by the Financial Services Act 2012, s 37(1), Sch 9, Pt 1, para 1, Pt 6, para 26.
For the words in italics in sub-s (1A) there are substituted the words ", 55I(8) or 61(2D)" by the Financial Services (Banking Reform) Act 2013, s 35, Sch 3, para 12.
Note: "secondary material" is defined in s 394(6) at **[1.1570]**.
Not be less than 14 days: note that any provision of this Act (other than a provision of Part VI) authorising or requiring a person to do anything within a specified number of days must not take into account any day which is a public holiday in any part of the United Kingdom; see s 417(3).

Decision notices

[1.1563]
388   Decision notices
(1)   A decision notice must—
   (a)   be in writing;
   (b)   give [the reasons of the regulator giving the notice ("the regulator concerned")] for the decision to take the action to which the notice relates;
   (c)   state whether section 394 applies;
   (d)   if that section applies, describe its effect and state whether any secondary material exists to which the person concerned must be allowed access under it; and
   (e)   give an indication of—
      (i)   any right to have the matter referred to the Tribunal which is given by this Act; and
      (ii)   the procedure on such a reference.
[(1A)   Where the PRA is the regulator concerned and the FCA has decided to refuse consent for the purposes of section 55F, 55I or 59 or to give conditional consent as mentioned in section 55F(5) *or 55I(8)*, the decision notice given by the PRA must—

(a)   state that fact, and
(b)   give the reasons for the FCA's decision.]
(2)   If the decision notice was preceded by a warning notice, the action to which the decision notice relates must be action under the same Part as the action proposed in the warning notice.
(3)   [The regulator concerned] may, before it takes the action to which a decision notice ("the original notice") relates, give the person concerned a further decision notice which relates to different action in respect of the same matter.
(4)   [The regulator concerned] may give a further decision notice as a result of subsection (3) only if the person to whom the original notice was given consents.
(5)   If the person to whom a decision notice is given under subsection (3) had the right to refer the matter to which the original decision notice related to the Tribunal, he has that right as respects the decision notice under subsection (3).

NOTES
Words in square brackets in sub-ss (1), (3), (4) substituted, and sub-s (1A) inserted, by the Financial Services Act 2012, s 37(1), Sch 9, Pt 1, para 1, Pt 6, para 27.
For the words in italics in sub-s (1A) there are substituted the words ", 55I(8) or 61(2D)" by the Financial Services (Banking Reform) Act 2013, s 35, Sch 3, para 13, as from 7 March 2016.

Conclusion of proceedings

[1.1564]
389   Notices of discontinuance
(1)   If [a regulator] decides not to take—
(a)   the action proposed in a warning notice [given by it], or
(b)   the action to which a decision notice [given by it] relates,
it must give a notice of discontinuance to the person to whom the warning notice or decision notice was given.
(2)   But subsection (1) does not apply if the discontinuance of the proceedings concerned results in the granting of an application made by the person to whom the warning or decision notice was given.
(3)   A notice of discontinuance must identify the proceedings which are being discontinued.

NOTES
Words in first pair of square brackets in sub-s (1) substituted, and words in square brackets in paras (a), (b) of that subsection inserted, by the Financial Services Act 2012, s 37(1), Sch 9, Pt 1, para 1, Pt 6, para 28.

[1.1565]
390   Final notices
(1)   If [a regulator] has given a person a decision notice and the matter was not referred to the Tribunal within the [time required by Tribunal Procedure Rules], [the regulator] must, on taking the action to which the decision notice relates, give the person concerned and any person to whom the decision notice was copied a final notice.
(2)   If [a regulator] has given a person a decision notice and the matter was referred to the Tribunal, [the regulator] must, on taking action in accordance with any directions given by—
(a)   the Tribunal, or
[(b)   a court on an appeal against the decision of the Tribunal,]
give that person and any person to whom the decision notice was copied [the notice required by subsection (2A)].
[(2A)   The notice required by this subsection is—
(a)   in a case where the regulator is acting in accordance with a direction given by the Tribunal under section 133(6)(b), or by the court on an appeal from a decision by the Tribunal under section 133(6), a further decision notice, and
(b)   in any other case, a final notice.]
(3)   A final notice about a statement must—
(a)   set out the terms of the statement;
(b)   give details of the manner in which, and the date on which, the statement will be published.
(4)   A final notice about an order must—
(a)   set out the terms of the order;
(b)   state the date from which the order has effect.
(5)   A final notice about a penalty must—
(a)   state the amount of the penalty;
(b)   state the manner in which, and the period within which, the penalty is to be paid;
(c)   give details of the way in which the penalty will be recovered if it is not paid by the date stated in the notice.
(6)   A final notice about a requirement to make a payment or distribution in accordance with section 384(5) must state—
(a)   the persons to whom,
(b)   the manner in which, and
(c)   the period within which,
it must be made.

(7) In any other case, the final notice must—

(a) give details of the action being taken;

(b) state the date on which the action is to be taken.

(8) The period stated under subsection (5)(b) or (6)(c) may not be less than 14 days beginning with the date on which the final notice is given.

(9) If all or any of the amount of a penalty payable under a final notice is outstanding at the end of the period stated under subsection (5)(b), [the regulator giving the notice] may recover the outstanding amount as a debt due to it.

(10) If all or any of a required payment or distribution has not been made at the end of a period stated in a final notice under subsection (6)(c), the obligation to make the payment is enforceable, on the application of [the regulator giving the notice], by injunction or, in Scotland, by an order under section 45 of the Court of Session Act 1988.

NOTES

Sub-s (1): words in first and third pairs of square brackets substituted by the Financial Services Act 2012, s 37(1), Sch 9, Pt 1, para 1, Pt 6, para 29(1), (2); words in second pair of square brackets substituted by the Transfer of Tribunal Functions Order 2010, SI 2010/22, art 5(1), Sch 2, paras 43, 47(a), (for transitional provisions and savings in relation to existing cases and appeals from the Financial Services and Markets Tribunal, see Sch 5 to that Order).

Sub-s (2): words in first, second and final pairs of square brackets substituted by the Financial Services Act 2012, s 37(1), Sch 9, Pt 1, para 1, Pt 6, para 29(1), (3); para (b) substituted by SI 2010/22, art 5(1), Sch 2, paras 43, 47, (for transitional provisions and savings in relation to existing cases and appeals from the Financial Services and Markets Tribunal, see Sch 5 to that Order).

Sub-s (2A): inserted by the Financial Services Act 2012, s 37(1), Sch 9, Pt 1, para 1, Pt 6, para 29(1), (4).

Sub-ss (9), (10): words in square brackets substituted by the Financial Services Act 2012, s 37(1), Sch 9, Pt 1, para 1, Pt 6, para 29(1), (5).

Transitional provisions: see the Financial Services (Banking Reform) Act 2013 (Transitional and Savings Provisions) Order 2015, SI 2015/492, art 18 (Prohibition orders).

Not be less than 14 days: note that any provision of this Act (other than a provision of Part VI) authorising or requiring a person to do anything within a specified number of days must not take into account any day which is a public holiday in any part of the United Kingdom; see s 417(3) at **[1.722]**.

Publication

[1.1566]

391 Publication

[(1) In the case of a warning notice falling within subsection (1ZB)—

(a) neither the regulator giving the notice nor a person to whom it is given or copied may publish the notice,

(b) a person to whom the notice is given or copied may not publish any details concerning the notice unless the regulator giving the notice has published those details, and

(c) after consulting the persons to whom the notice is given or copied, the regulator giving the notice may publish such information about the matter to which the notice relates as it considers appropriate.

(1ZA) In the case of a warning notice not falling within subsection (1ZB), neither the regulator giving the notice nor a person to whom it is given or copied may publish the notice or any details concerning it.

(1ZB) A warning notice falls within this subsection if it is given under—

(a) section 63B;

(b) section 67;

(c) section 87M;

(d) section 88B;

(e) section 89K;

(f) section 89R;

(g) section 92;

(h) section 126;

(i) section 131H;

[(ia) section 142N;]

(j) section 192L;

(k) section 207;

(l) section 312G;

(m) section 345B (whether as a result of section 345(2) or 345A(3) or section 249(1) [or 261K(1)]).]

[(1A) A person to whom a decision notice is given or copied may not publish the notice or any details concerning it unless the [regulator giving the notice] has published the notice or those details.]

(2) A notice of discontinuance must state that, if the person to whom the notice is given consents, the [regulator giving the notice] may publish such information as it considers appropriate about the matter to which the discontinued proceedings related.

(3) A copy of a notice of discontinuance must be accompanied by a statement that, if the person to whom the notice is copied consents, the [regulator giving the notice] may publish such information as it considers appropriate about the matter to which the discontinued proceedings related, so far as relevant to that person.

(4) [The regulator giving a decision or final notice] must publish such information about the matter to which [the notice] relates as it considers appropriate.

[(4A) Subsection (4) is subject to section 391A.]

(5) When a supervisory notice takes effect, the [regulator giving the notice] must publish such information about the matter to which the notice relates as it considers appropriate.

[(5A) Subsection (5) does not apply in relation to a notice given in accordance with section 137S(5) or (8)(a) (but see section 137S(11)).]

[(6) The FCA may not publish information under this section if, in its opinion, publication of the information would be—

    (a)   unfair to the person with respect to whom the action was taken (or was proposed to be taken),

    (b)   prejudicial to the interests of consumers, or

    (c)   detrimental to the stability of the UK financial system.

(6A) The PRA may not publish information under this section if, in its opinion, publication of the information would be—

    (a)   unfair to the person with respect to whom the action was taken (or was proposed to be taken),

    (b)   prejudicial to the safety and soundness of PRA-authorised persons, or

    (c)   in a case where section 2C applies, prejudicial to securing the appropriate degree of protection for policyholders.]

(7) Information is to be published under this section in such manner as the [a regulator] considers appropriate.

[(7A) Where the [regulator] publishes information under subsection (4) or (5) in respect of a final notice or a supervisory notice which relates to a contravention of a requirement falling within subsection (7B) at the same time as it publishes the information it must notify ESMA that it has done so.

(7B) A requirement falls within this subsection if it is imposed—

    (a)   by or under any provision made by or under this Act which implements Directive 2003/6/EC of the European Parliament and of the Council of 28 January 2003 on insider dealing and market manipulation (market abuse),

    (b)   by any directly applicable EU regulation made under that directive,

    (c)   by or under any provision made by or under this Act which implements the markets in financial instruments directive, or

    (d)   by any directly applicable EU regulation made under the markets in financial instruments directive.]

(8) For the purposes of determining when a supervisory notice takes effect, a matter to which the notice relates is open to review if—

    (a)   the period during which any person may refer the matter to the Tribunal is still running;

    (b)   the matter has been referred to the Tribunal but has not been dealt with;

    (c)   the matter has been referred to the Tribunal and dealt with but the period during which an appeal may be brought against the Tribunal's decision is still running; or

    (d)   such an appeal has been brought but has not been determined.

[(8A) Where a decision notice or final notice relates to any decision or action under a provision of this Act in relation to the contravention of a requirement imposed by the CSD regulation or any directly applicable regulation made under the CSD regulation, this section has effect subject to Article 62 of the CSD regulation (publication of decisions).]

(9) "Notice of discontinuance" means a notice given under section 389.

(10) "Supervisory notice" has the same meaning as in section 395.

[(11) Section 425A (meaning of "consumers") applies for the purposes of this section.]

NOTES

Sub-ss (1)–(1ZB): substituted (for the original sub-s (1)) by the Financial Services Act 2012, s 37(1), Sch 9, Pt 1, para 1, Pt 6, para 30(1), (2); sub-s (1ZB)(ia) inserted by the Financial Services (Banking Reform) Act 2013, s 4(3), as from a day to be appointed; words in square brackets in sub-s (1ZB)(m) inserted by the Collective Investment in Transferable Securities (Contractual Scheme) Regulations 2013, SI 2013/1388, reg 3(1), (18).

Sub-s (1A): inserted by the Financial Services Act 2010, s 13(1), (3), (note that this subsection does not apply in relation to cases where a warning notice was given by the FSA under this Act before 12 October 2010); words in square brackets substituted by the Financial Services Act 2012, s 37(1), Sch 9, Pt 1, para 1, Pt 6, para 30(1), (3).

Sub-ss (2)–(5), (7): words in square brackets substituted by the Financial Services Act 2012, s 37(1), Sch 9, Pt 1, para 1, Pt 6, para 30(1), (3)–(5), (7).

Sub-s (4A): inserted by the Capital Requirements Regulations 2013, SI 2013/3115, reg 46(1), Sch 2, Pt 1, paras 1, 22.

Sub-s (5A): inserted by the Financial Services Act 2012, s 24(2).

Sub-ss (6), (6A): substituted (for the original sub-s (6)) by the Financial Services Act 2012, s 37(1), Sch 9, Pt 1, para 1, Pt 6, para 30(1), (6).

Sub-ss (7A), (7B): inserted by the Financial Services (Omnibus 1 Directive) Regulations 2012, SI 2012/916, reg 2(1), (13); words in square brackets in sub-s (7A) substituted by the Financial Services Act 2012, s 37(1), Sch 9, Pt 1, para 1, Pt 6, para 30(1), (8).

Sub-s (8A): inserted by the Central Securities Depositories Regulations 2014, SI 2014/2879, reg 6(1), (2).

Sub-s (11): substituted by the Financial Services Act 2010, s 24(1), (2), Sch 2, Pt 1, paras 1, 28, .

Note: the definition of "consumers" is extended for the purposes of this sub-s (6)(b) by the Financial Services and Markets Act 2000 (Regulated Activities) (Amendment) (No 2) Order 2013, SI 2013/1881, art 65 at **[2.1046]**.

Note that the Financial Services Act 2012, s 37(2)(a) provides that if the Treasury consider that it is in the public interest to do so, it may by order amend this section by substituting for subsections (1)–(1ZB) the following—

"(1)   Neither the regulator giving a warning notice nor a person to whom it is given or copied may publish the notice or any details concerning it.".

[1.1567]
[391A   Publication: special provisions relating to certain penalties

(1)   This section applies where a decision notice or final notice relates to the imposition of a penalty to which Article 68(1) of the capital requirements directive applies.

(2)   Where a regulator publishes information under section 391(4) about a matter to which a decision notice relates and the person to whom the notice is given refers the matter to the Tribunal, the regulator must, without undue delay, publish on its official website information about the status of the appeal and its outcome.

(3)   Subject to subsection (4), where a regulator gives a final notice, the regulator must publish information on the type and nature of the breach and the identity of the person on whom the penalty is imposed.

(4)   Information about a matter to which a final notice relates must be published anonymously where—

(a)   the penalty is imposed on an individual and, following an obligatory prior assessment, publication of personal data is found to be disproportionate;

(b)   publication would jeopardise the stability of financial markets or an ongoing criminal investigation; or

(c)   publication would cause, insofar as it can be determined, disproportionate damage to the persons involved.

(5)   Where subsection (4) applies, the regulator may make such arrangements as to the publication of information (including as to the timing of publication) as are necessary to preserve the anonymity of the person on whom the penalty is imposed.

(6)   Where a regulator publishes information in accordance with subsections (2) to (5), the regulator must—

(a)   publish the information on its official website;

(b)   ensure the information remains on its official website for at least five years, unless the information is personal data and the Data Protection Act 1998 requires the information to be retained for a different period; and

(c)   disclose to EBA any penalty imposed, any appeal against such a penalty and the outcome of the appeal, unless such a disclosure is not permitted by section 348.]

NOTES

Commencement: 1 January 2014.

Inserted by the Capital Requirements Regulations 2013, SI 2013/3115, reg 46(1), Sch 2, Pt 1, paras 1, 23.

Third party rights and access to evidence

[1.1568]
392   Application of sections 393 and 394

Sections 393 and 394 apply to—

(a)   a warning notice given in accordance with section [55Z(1)], 57(1), 63(3), [63B(1),] 67(1), 88(4)(b),[88B(1)], 92(1), 126(1), [131H(1),] [142T(1),] [192L(1),] 207(1), 255(1), [261V(1),] 280(1), [312G(1),] 331(1), [345B(1) (whether as a result of section 345(2), 345A(3)] or section 249(1) [or 261K(1)])[, 385(1) or 412B(4) or (8)];

(b)   a decision notice given in accordance with section[55Z(2)], 57(3), 63(4), [63B(3),] 67(4), 88(6)(b), [88B(5)], 92(4), 127(1), [131H(4),] [142T(4),] [192L(4),] 208(1), 255(2), [261V(2),] 280(2), [312H(1),] 331(3), [345B(4) (whether as a result of section 345(2), 345A(3)] or section 249(1) [or 261K(1)])[, 386(1) or 412B(5) or (9)].

NOTES

Figures "55Z(1)" and "55Z(2)" in square brackets substituted, and figures "192L(1)," and "192L(4)," in square brackets inserted, by the Financial Services Act 2012, s 37(1), Sch 9, Pt 1, para 1, Pt 6, para 31.

Figures "63B(1),", "131H(1),", "63B(3),", and "131H(4)," in square brackets inserted by the Financial Services Act 2010, s 24(1), (2), Sch 2, Pt 1, paras 1, 29.

Figures "88B(1)" and "88B(5)" in square brackets substituted by the Financial Services Act 2012, s 18(1), (5).

Figures "142T(1)," and "142T(4)," inserted by the Financial Services (Banking Reform) Act 2013, s 4(4), as from a day to be appointed.

Figures and words "261V(1),", "or 261K(1)", "261V(2)," and "or 261K(1)" in square brackets inserted by the Collective Investment in Transferable Securities (Contractual Scheme) Regulations 2013, SI 2013/1388, reg 3(1), (19).

Figures "312G(1)," and "312H(1)," in square brackets inserted by the Financial Services Act 2012, s 35, Sch 8, paras 1, 37.

Words "345B(1) (whether as a result of section 345(2), 345A(3)" and "345B(4) (whether as a result of section 345(2), 345A(3)" in square brackets substituted by the Financial Services Act 2012, s 42, Sch 13, para 8.

Words ", 385(1) or 412B(4) or (8)" and ", 386(1) or 412B(5) or (9)" in square brackets substituted by the Financial Services and Markets Act 2000 (Markets in Financial Instruments) Regulations 2007, SI 2007/126, reg 3(5), Sch 5, paras 1, 16.

[1.1569]
393   Third party rights

(1)   If any of the reasons contained in a warning notice to which this section applies relates to a matter which—

   (a)   identifies a person ("the third party") other than the person to whom the notice is given, and

   (b)   in the opinion of the [regulator giving the notice], is prejudicial to the third party,

a copy of the notice must be given to the third party.

(2)   Subsection (1) does not require a copy to be given to the third party if the [regulator giving the notice]—

   (a)   has given him a separate warning notice in relation to the same matter; or

   (b)   gives him such a notice at the same time as it gives the warning notice which identifies him.

(3)   The notice copied to a third party under subsection (1) must specify a reasonable period (which may not be less than [14 days]) within which he may make representations to [the regulator giving the notice].

(4)   If any of the reasons contained in a decision notice to which this section applies relates to a matter which—

   (a)   identifies a person ("the third party") other than the person to whom the decision notice is given, and

   (b)   in the opinion of [the regulator giving the notice], is prejudicial to the third party,

a copy of the notice must be given to the third party.

(5)   If the decision notice was preceded by a warning notice, a copy of the decision notice must (unless it has been given under subsection (4)) be given to each person to whom the warning notice was copied.

(6)   Subsection (4) does not require a copy to be given to the third party if [the regulator giving the notice]—

   (a)   has given him a separate decision notice in relation to the same matter; or

   (b)   gives him such a notice at the same time as it gives the decision notice which identifies him.

(7)   Neither subsection (1) nor subsection (4) requires a copy of a notice to be given to a third party if [the regulator giving the notice] considers it impracticable to do so.

(8)   Subsections (9) to (11) apply if the person to whom a decision notice is given has a right to refer the matter to the Tribunal.

(9)   A person to whom a copy of the notice is given under this section may refer to the Tribunal—

   (a)   the decision in question, so far as it is based on a reason of the kind mentioned in subsection (4); or

   (b)   any opinion expressed by [the regulator giving the notice] in relation to him.

(10)   The copy must be accompanied by an indication of the third party's right to make a reference under subsection (9) and of the procedure on such a reference.

(11)   A person who alleges that a copy of the notice should have been given to him, but was not, may refer to the Tribunal the alleged failure and—

   (a)   the decision in question, so far as it is based on a reason of the kind mentioned in subsection (4); or

   (b)   any opinion expressed by [the regulator giving the notice] in relation to him.

(12)   Section 394 applies to a third party as it applies to the person to whom the notice to which this section applies was given, in so far as the material [to which access must be given] under that section relates to the matter which identifies the third party.

(13)   A copy of a notice given to a third party under this section must be accompanied by a description of the effect of section 394 as it applies to him.

(14)   Any person to whom a warning notice or decision notice was copied under this section must be given a copy of a notice of discontinuance applicable to the proceedings to which the warning notice or decision notice related.

NOTES

  All words in square brackets in this section were substituted by the Financial Services Act 2012, s 37(1), Sch 9, Pt 1, para 1, Pt 6, para 32.

[1.1570]
394   Access to [FCA or PRA] material

(1)   If [a regulator] gives a person ("A") a notice to which this section applies, it must—

   (a)   allow him access to the material on which it relied in taking the decision which gave rise to the obligation to give the notice;

   (b)   allow him access to any secondary material which[, in the regulator's opinion,] might undermine that decision.

(2) But [the regulator giving the notice] does not have to allow A access to material under subsection (1) if the material is excluded material or it—
- (a) relates to a case involving a person other than A; and
- (b) was taken into account by [the regulator giving the notice] in A's case only for purposes of comparison with other cases.

(3) [The regulator giving the notice] may refuse A access to particular material which it would otherwise have to allow him access to if, in its opinion, allowing him access to the material—
- (a) would not be in the public interest; or
- (b) would not be fair, having regard to—
  - (i) the likely significance of the material to A in relation to the matter in respect of which he has been given a notice to which this section applies; and
  - (ii) the potential prejudice to the commercial interests of a person other than A which would be caused by the material's disclosure.

(4) If [the regulator giving the notice] does not allow A access to material because it is excluded material consisting of a protected item, it must give A written notice of—
- (a) the existence of the protected item; and
- (b) [the regulator's] decision not to allow him access to it.

(5) If [the regulator giving the notice] refuses under subsection (3) to allow A access to material, it must give him written notice of—
- (a) the refusal; and
- (b) the reasons for it.

(6) "Secondary material" means material, other than material falling within paragraph (a) of subsection (1) which—
- (a) was considered by [the regulator giving the notice] in reaching the decision mentioned in that paragraph; or
- (b) was obtained by [the regulator giving the notice in connection with the matter to which that notice] relates but which was not considered by it in reaching that decision.

(7) "Excluded material" means material which—
- [(a) is material the disclosure of which for the purposes of or in connection with any legal proceedings is prohibited by section 17 of the Regulation of Investigatory Powers Act 2000; or]
- (c) is a protected item (as defined in section 413).

NOTES

Sub-s (7)(a) was substituted (for original paras (a), (b)) by the Regulation of Investigatory Powers Act 2000, s 82(1), Sch 4, para 11.

All other words in square brackets in this section were substituted by the Financial Services Act 2012, s 37(1), Sch 9, Pt 1, para 1, Pt 6, para 33.

PART XXVIII
MISCELLANEOUS

[Consumer redress schemes

[1.1571]
404 Consumer redress schemes
(1) This section applies if—
- (a) it appears to the [FCA] that there may have been a widespread or regular failure by relevant firms to comply with requirements applicable to the carrying on by them of any activity;
- (b) it appears to it that, as a result, consumers have suffered (or may suffer) loss or damage in respect of which, if they brought legal proceedings, a remedy or relief would be available in the proceedings; and
- (c) it considers that it is desirable to make rules for the purpose of securing that redress is made to the consumers in respect of the failure (having regard to other ways in which consumers may obtain redress).

(2) "Relevant firms" means—
- (a) authorised persons; . . .
- (b) payment service providers; [or
- (c) electronic money issuers.]

(3) The [FCA] may make rules requiring each relevant firm (or each relevant firm of a specified description) which has carried on the activity on or after the specified date to establish and operate a consumer redress scheme.

(4) A "consumer redress scheme" is a scheme under which the firm is required to take one or more of the following steps in relation to the activity.

(5) The firm must first investigate whether, on or after the specified date, it has failed to comply with the requirements mentioned in subsection (1)(a) that are applicable to the carrying on by it of the activity.

(6) The next step is for the firm to determine whether the failure has caused (or may cause) loss or damage to consumers.

(7)   If the firm determines that the failure has caused (or may cause) loss or damage to consumers, it must then—

   (a)   determine what the redress should be in respect of the failure; and

   (b)   make the redress to the consumers.

(8)   A relevant firm is required to take the above steps in relation to any particular consumer even if, after the rules are made, a defence of limitation becomes available to the firm in respect of the loss or damage in question.

(9)   Before making rules under this section, the [FCA] must consult the scheme operator of the ombudsman scheme.

(10)   For the meaning of consumers, see section 404E.]

NOTES

Sections 404–404G (and the preceding heading) were substituted, for the original s 404, by the Financial Services Act 2010, s 14(1). Note that by s 14(2) of the 2010 Act, this substitution has effect in relation to failures occurring before 12 October 2010 (as well as in relation to failures occurring at or after that date).

Sub-ss (1), (3), (9): word "FCA" in square brackets substituted by the Financial Services Act 2012, s 114(1), Sch 18, Pt 1, paras 1, 18.

Sub-s (2): word omitted from para (a) repealed, and para (c) (and the preceding word) added, by the Electronic Money Regulations 2011, SI 2011/99, reg 79, Sch 4, Pt 1, para 2(1), (4)(a).

[1.1572]
[404A   Rules under s 404: supplementary

(1)   Rules under section 404 may make provision—

   (a)   specifying the activities and requirements in relation to which relevant firms are to carry out investigations under consumer redress schemes;

   (b)   setting out, in relation to any specified description of case, examples of things done, or omitted to be done, that are to be regarded as constituting a failure to comply with a requirement;

   (c)   setting out, in relation to any specified description of case, matters to be taken into account, or steps to be taken, by relevant firms for the purpose of—

      (i)   assessing evidence as to a failure to comply with a requirement; or

      (ii)   determining whether such a failure has caused (or may cause) loss or damage to consumers;

   (d)   as to the kinds of redress that are, or are not, to be made to consumers in specified descriptions of case and the way in which redress is to be determined in specified descriptions of case;

   (e)   as to the things that relevant firms are, or are not, to do in establishing and operating consumer redress schemes;

   (f)   securing that relevant firms are not required to investigate anything occurring after a specified date;

   (g)   specifying the times by which anything required to be done under any consumer redress scheme is to be done;

   (h)   requiring relevant firms to provide information to the [FCA];

   (i)   authorising one or more competent persons to do anything for the purposes of, or in connection with, the establishment or operation of any consumer redress scheme;

   (j)   for the nomination or approval by the [FCA] of persons authorised under paragraph (i);

   (k)   as to the circumstances in which, instead of a relevant firm, the [FCA] (or one or more competent persons acting on the [FCA's] behalf) may carry out the investigation and take the other relevant steps under any consumer redress scheme;

   (l)   as to the powers to be available to those carrying out an investigation by virtue of paragraph (k);

   (m)   as to the enforcement of any redress (for example, in the case of a money award, as a debt owed by a relevant firm).

(2)   The only examples that may be set out in the rules as a result of subsection (1)(b) are examples of things done, or omitted to be done, that have been, or would be, held by a court or tribunal to constitute a failure to comply with a requirement.

(3)   Matters may not be set out in the rules as a result of subsection (1)(c) if they have not been, or would not be, taken into account by a court or tribunal for the purpose mentioned there.

(4)   The [FCA] must exercise the power conferred as a result of subsection (1)(d) so as to secure that, in relation to any description of case, the only kinds of redress to be made are those which it considers to be just in relation to that description of case.

(5)   In acting under subsection (4), the [FCA] must have regard (among other things) to the nature and extent of the losses or damage in question.

(6)   The provision that may be made under subsection (1)(h) includes provision applying (with or without modifications)—

   (a)   any provision of section 165; or

   (b)   any provision of Part 11 relating to that section.

(7)   The reference in subsection (1)(k) to the other relevant steps under any consumer redress scheme is a reference to the [FCA] making the determinations mentioned in section 404(6) and (7) (with the firm still required to make the redress).

(8)   If the rules include provision under subsection (1)(k), they must also include provision for—

(a)   giving warning and decision notices, and

(b)   conferring rights on relevant firms to refer matters to the Tribunal,

in relation to any determination mentioned in section 404(6) and (7) made by the [FCA].

(9)   Nothing in this section is to be taken as limiting the power conferred by section 404.]

NOTES

Substituted as noted to s 404 at [**1.1571**].

Words "FCA" and "FCA's" in square brackets (in each place that they occur) substituted by the Financial Services Act 2012, s 114(1), Sch 18, Pt 1, paras 1, 19.

[1.1573]
[404B   Complaints to the ombudsman scheme

(1)   If—

(a)   a consumer makes a complaint under the ombudsman scheme in respect of an act or omission of a relevant firm, and

(b)   at the time the complaint is made, the subject-matter of the complaint falls to be dealt with (or has been dealt with) under a consumer redress scheme,

the way in which the complaint is to be determined by the ombudsman is to be as mentioned in subsection (4).

[(1A)   Subsection (1) does not apply if the consumer and the relevant firm agree that it should not apply.]

(2)   If a consumer—

(a)   is not satisfied with a determination made by a relevant firm under a consumer redress scheme, or

(b)   considers that a relevant firm has failed to make a determination in accordance with a consumer redress scheme,

the consumer may, in respect of that determination or failure, make a complaint under the ombudsman scheme.

[(2A)   The way in which a complaint mentioned in subsection (2) is to be determined by the ombudsman is to be as mentioned in subsection (4).

(2B)   Subsection (2A) does not apply if the consumer and the relevant firm agree that it should not apply.]

[(3)   In the following provisions of this section "relevant complaint" means—

(a)   a complaint mentioned in subsection (1) other than one in relation to which subsection (1A) applies, or

(b)   a complaint mentioned in subsection (2) other than one in relation to which subsection (2B) applies.]

(4)   A relevant complaint is to be determined by reference to what, in the opinion of the ombudsman, the determination under the consumer redress scheme should be or should have been (subject to subsection (5)).

(5)   If, in determining a relevant complaint, the ombudsman determines that the firm should make (or should have made) a payment of an amount to the consumer, the amount awarded by the ombudsman (a "money award") must not exceed the monetary limit (within the meaning of section 229).

(6)   But the ombudsman may recommend that the firm pay a larger amount.

(7)   A money award—

(a)   may specify the date by which the amount awarded is to be paid;

(b)   may provide for interest to be payable, at a rate specified in the award, on any amount which is not paid by that date; and

(c)   is enforceable by the consumer in accordance with Part 3 or 3A of Schedule 17 (as the case may be).

(8)   If, in determining a relevant complaint, the ombudsman determines that the firm should take (or should have taken) particular action in relation to the consumer, the ombudsman may direct the firm to take that action.

(9)   Compliance with a direction under subsection (8) is enforceable, on the application of the consumer, by an injunction or, in Scotland, by an order for specific performance under section 45 of the Court of Session Act 1988.

(10)   In consequence of the provision made by this section, sections 228(2) and 229 do not apply in relation to relevant complaints; but all other provision made by or under Part 16 applies in relation to those complaints.

(11)   The compulsory jurisdiction of the ombudsman scheme is to include the jurisdiction resulting from this section.

(12)   Nothing in subsection (1) is to be taken as requiring the ombudsman to determine a complaint in any case where (apart from that subsection) the complaint would not fall to be determined (whether as a result of rules made under Schedule 17 or otherwise).

(13)   Nothing in subsection (2) is to be taken as conferring an entitlement on a person who, for the purposes of the ombudsman scheme, is not an eligible complainant in relation to the subject-matter of the determination mentioned there.]

NOTES

Substituted as noted to s 404 at **[1.1571]**.

Sub-ss (1A), (2A), (2B) inserted, and sub-s (3) substituted, by the Alternative Dispute Resolution for Consumer Disputes (Competent Authorities and Information) Regulations 2015, SI 2015/542, reg 16, Sch 7, para 1(1), (2).

[1.1574]
[404C   Enforcement
The following provisions—
  (a)   Part 14 (disciplinary measures), and
  (b)   so much of this Act as relates to any provision of that Part,
(which apply only in relation to authorised persons) are also to apply in relation to relevant firms which are not (or are no longer) authorised persons.]

NOTES

Substituted as noted to s 404 at **[1.1571]**.

[1.1575]
[404D   Applications to Tribunal to quash rules or provision of rules
(1)   Any person may apply to the Tribunal for a review of any rules made under section 404.
(2)   The Tribunal may—
  (a)   dismiss the application; or
  (b)   make an order (a "quashing order") quashing any rules made under section 404 or any provision of those rules.
(3)   An application may be made only if permission to make it has first been obtained from the Tribunal.
(4)   The Tribunal may grant permission to make an application only if it considers that the applicant has a sufficient interest in the matter to which the application relates.
(5)   The general rule is that, in determining an application, the Tribunal is to apply the principles applicable on an application for judicial review.
(6)   If (or so far as) an application relates to an example set out in the rules as a result of section 404A(1)(b), the Tribunal may determine whether the example constitutes a failure to comply with the requirement in question.
(7)   If (or so far as) an application relates to a matter set out in the rules as a result of section 404A(1)(c), the Tribunal may determine whether the matter should be taken into account as mentioned in that provision.
(8)   In the case of an application within subsection (6) or (7), the Tribunal's jurisdiction under that subsection is in addition to its jurisdiction under subsection (5).
(9)   A quashing order may be enforced as if it were an order made, on an application for judicial review, by the High Court or, in Scotland, the Court of Session.
(10)   The Tribunal may award damages to the applicant if—
  (a)   the application includes a claim for damages arising from any matter to which the application relates; and
  (b)   the Tribunal is satisfied that an award would have been made by the High Court or, in Scotland, the Court of Session if the claim had been made in an action begun in that court by the applicant when making the application.
(11)   An award of damages under subsection (10) may be enforced as if it were an award made by the High Court or, in Scotland, the Court of Session.
(12)   In the case of any proceedings under this section, the judge presiding at the proceedings must be—
  (a)   a judge of the High Court or the Court of Appeal or a judge of the Court of Session; or
  (b)   such other person as may be agreed from time to time by—
    (i)   the Lord Chief Justice, the Lord President or the Lord Chief Justice of Northern Ireland (as the case may be); and
    (ii)   the Senior President of Tribunals.
(13)   Section 133 does not apply in the case of an application under this section, but—
  (a)   Tribunal Procedure Rules may make provision for the suspension of rules made under section 404 or of any provision of those rules, pending determination of the application; and
  (b)   in the case of an application within subsection (6) or (7), the Tribunal may consider any evidence relating to the application's subject-matter, whether or not it was available at the time the rules were made.
(14)   If—
  (a)   the Tribunal refuses to grant permission to make an application under this section, and
  (b)   on an appeal by the applicant, the Court of Appeal grants the permission,
the Court of Appeal may go on to decide the application under this section.]

NOTES
Substituted as noted to s 404 at **[1.1571]**.

[1.1576]
[404E   Meaning of "consumers"
(1)   For the purposes of sections 404 to 404B "consumers" means persons who—
    (a)   have used, or may have contemplated using, any of the services within subsection (2); or
    (b)   have relevant rights or interests in relation to any of the services within that subsection.
(2)   The services within this subsection are services provided by—
    (a)   authorised persons in carrying on regulated activities;
    (b)   . . .
    (c)   authorised persons in communicating, or approving the communication by others of, invitations or inducements to engage in investment activity;
    (d)   authorised persons who are investment firms, or credit institutions, in providing relevant ancillary services;
    (e)   persons acting as appointed representatives;   . . .
    (f)   payment service providers in providing payment services; [or
    (g)   electronic money issuers in issuing electronic money.]
(3)   A person ("P") has a "relevant right or interest" in relation to any services within subsection (2) if P has a right or interest—
    (a)   which is derived from, or is otherwise attributable to, the use of the services by others; or
    (b)   which may be adversely affected by the use of the services by persons acting on P's behalf or in a fiduciary capacity in relation to P.
(4)   If a person is providing a service within subsection (2) as a trustee, the persons who have been, or may have been, beneficiaries of the trust are to be treated as persons who have used, or may have contemplated using, the service.
(5)   A person who deals with another person ("B") in the course of B providing a service within subsection (2) is to be treated as using the service.
(6)   In this section—
    . . .
    . . .
    "credit institution" has the meaning given by section 138(1B);
    "engage in investment activity" has the meaning given by section 21;
    ["electronic money" has the same meaning as in the Electronic Money Regulations 2011 and any reference to issuing electronic money must be read accordingly;]
    "payment services" has the same meaning as in the Payment Services Regulations 2009;
    "payment service provider" means a person who is a payment service provider for the purposes of those regulations as a result of falling within any of paragraphs (a) to (e) of the definition in regulation 2(1);
    "relevant ancillary services" has the meaning given by section 138(1C).]

NOTES
Substituted as noted to s 404 at **[1.1571]**.
Sub-s (2): para (b) repealed by the Financial Services and Markets Act 2000 (Regulated Activities) (Amendment) (No 2) Order 2013, SI 2013/1881, art 10(1), (15)(a), (for transitional provisions see see Pt 8 thereof at **[2.1007]** et seq); word omitted from para (e) repealed, and para (g) (and the preceding word) added, by the Electronic Money Regulations 2011, SI 2011/99, reg 79, Sch 4, Pt 1, para 2(1), (4)(b)(i).
Sub-s (6): definitions "accepting" and "consumer credit business" (omitted) repealed by SI 2013/1881, art 10(1), (15)(b), (for transitional provisions, see the sub-s (2) note above); definition "electronic money" inserted by SI 2011/99, reg 79, Sch 4, Pt 1, para 2(1), (4)(b)(ii).
Note that the amendments made by the Financial Services and Markets Act 2000 (Regulated Activities) (Amendment) (No 2) Order 2013, SI 2013/1881 do not apply in so far as this section relates to, or applies for the purposes of, anything done under this Act concerning things done (or not done) before 1 April 2014 (see art 11(2) of the 2013 Order **[2.1005]**).

[1.1577]
[404F   Other definitions etc
(1)   For the purposes of sections 404 to 404B—
    "redress" includes—
        (a)   interest; and
        (b)   a remedy or relief which could not be awarded in legal proceedings;
    "specified" means specified in rules made under section 404.
(2)   In determining for the purposes of those sections whether an authorised person has failed to comply with a requirement, anything which an appointed representative has done or omitted as respects business for which the authorised person has accepted responsibility is to be treated as having been done or omitted by the authorised person.
(3)   References in those sections to the failure by a relevant firm to comply with a requirement applicable to the carrying on by it of any activity include anything done, or omitted to be done, by it in carrying on the activity—
    (a)   which is in breach of a duty or other obligation, prohibition or restriction; or

(b)   which otherwise gives rise to the availability of a remedy or relief in legal proceedings.

(4)   It does not matter whether—

(a)   the duty or other obligation, prohibition or restriction, or

(b)   the remedy or relief,

arises as a result of any provision made by or under this or any other Act, a rule of law or otherwise.

(5)   References in sections 404 to 404B to a relevant firm include—

(a)   a person who was at any time a relevant firm but has subsequently ceased to be one; and

(b)   a person who has assumed a liability (including a contingent one) incurred by a relevant firm in respect of a failure by the firm to comply with a requirement applicable to the carrying on by it of any activity.

(6)   References in those sections to the carrying on of an activity by a relevant firm are, accordingly, to be read in that case with the appropriate modifications.

[(6A)   References in sections 404 and 404E to an "electronic money issuer" are references to a person mentioned in paragraph (a), (b), (c), (d), (h) or (i) of the definition of "electronic money issuer" in regulation 2(1) of the Electronic Money Regulations 2011.]

(7)   If the [FCA] varies a permission or authorisation of a person so as to impose requirements on the person to establish and operate a scheme which corresponds to, or is similar to, a consumer redress scheme, the provision that may be included in the permission or authorisation as varied includes—

(a)   provision imposing requirements on the person corresponding to those that could be included in rules made under section 404; and

(b)   provision corresponding to section 404B.

(8)   In subsection (7) the reference to the variation of a permission or authorisation by the [FCA] is a reference to—

[(a)   the variation under section 55H or 55J of a Part 4A permission,

(aa) the imposition or variation of a requirement under section 55L, or]

(b)   the variation under regulation 8 or 11 of the Payment Services Regulations 2009 of an authorisation under those regulations; [or

(c)   the variation under regulation 8 or 11 of the Electronic Money Regulations 2011 of an authorisation under those regulations.]]

NOTES

Substituted as noted to s 404 at **[1.1571]**.

Sub-s (6A): inserted by the Electronic Money Regulations 2011, SI 2011/99, reg 79, Sch 4, Pt 1, para 2(1), (5)(i).

Sub-s (7): word "FCA" in square brackets substituted by the Financial Services Act 2012, s 114(1), Sch 18, Pt 1, paras 1, 20(1), (2).

Sub-s (8); word "FCA" in square brackets substituted, and paras (a), (aa) substituted (for the original para (a)), by the Financial Services Act 2012, s 114(1), Sch 18, Pt 1, paras 1, 20(1)–(3); para (c) (and the preceding word) added by SI 2011/99, reg 79, Sch 4, Pt 1, para 2(1), (5)(ii).

[1.1578]

[404G   Power to widen the scope of consumer redress schemes

(1)   The Treasury may by order amend the definition of "relevant firms" in section 404 or the definition of "consumers" in section 404E (or both).

(2)   An order under this section may make consequential amendments of any provision of sections 404 to 404F.]

NOTES

Substituted as noted to s 404 at **[1.1571]**.

PART XXX
SUPPLEMENTAL

[1.1579]

430   Extent

(1)   This Act, except Chapter IV of Part XVII, extends to Northern Ireland.

(2)   Except where Her Majesty by Order in Council provides otherwise, the extent of any amendment or repeal made by or under this Act is the same as the extent of the provision amended or repealed.

(3)   Her Majesty may by Order in Council provide for any provision of or made under this Act relating to a matter which is the subject of other legislation which extends to any of the Channel Islands or the Isle of Man to extend there with such modifications (if any) as may be specified in the Order.

[1.1580]

431   Commencement

(1)   The following provisions come into force on the passing of this Act—

(a)   this section;

(b)   sections 428, 430 and 433;

(c)   paragraphs 1 and 2 of Schedule 21.

(2) The other provisions of this Act come into force on such day as the Treasury may by order appoint; and different days may be appointed for different purposes.

NOTES

Orders: the Financial Services and Markets Act 2000 (Commencement No 1) Order 2001, SI 2001/516; the Financial Services and Markets Act 2000 (Commencement No 2) Order 2001, SI 2001/1282; the Financial Services and Markets Act 2000 (Commencement No 3) Order 2001, SI 2001/1820; the Financial Services and Markets Act 2000 (Commencement No 4 and Transitional Provision) Order 2001, SI 2001/2364; the Financial Services and Markets Act 2000 (Commencement No 5) Order 2001, SI 2001/2632; the Financial Services and Markets Act 2000 (Commencement No 6) Order 2001, SI 2001/3436; the Financial Services and Markets Act 2000 (Commencement No 7) Order 2001, SI 2001/3538.

[1.1581]
433   Short title
This Act may be cited as the Financial Services and Markets Act 2000.

SCHEDULES

[SCHEDULE 1ZA
THE FINANCIAL CONDUCT AUTHORITY

Section 1A

NOTES

Transitional provisions etc in connection with the commencement of the Financial Services Act 2012: for transitional provisions in relation to the commencement of this Schedule, see Part 2 of the Financial Services Act 2012 (Transitional Provisions) (Miscellaneous Provisions) Order 2013, SI 2013/442. See also the Financial Services Act 2012 (Transitional Provisions) (Rules and Miscellaneous Provisions) Order 2013, SI 2013/161, Part 3 (Exercise of functions by the FCA before commencement date). Article 5 provides for the FSA to appoint persons to discharge, before 1 April 2013, certain functions of the FCA. Article 6(1) specifies the functions that may be discharged by appointed persons; art 6(2) provides that certain functions exercisable by the FSA are to be treated as exercisable by the FCA. Article 7 provides for: (i) things done by appointed persons to be treated as if they had been done by the FCA acting through its governing body; (ii) certain duties on the FCA to consult various persons to be satisfied by consultation undertaken by the FSA; and (iii) for certain provisions relating to members of the governing body of the FCA also to apply to appointed persons. Article 8 sets aside procedural requirements for consultation in respect of rules made by the FCA where the rules replicate threshold conditions in Sch 6 to this Act.

PART 1
GENERAL

Interpretation

[1.1582]
1. In this Schedule—
   "the Bank" means the Bank of England;
   "functions", in relation to the FCA, means functions conferred on the FCA by or under any provision of this Act (see section 1A(6) which affects the meaning of references to such functions).

Constitution

2. (1)   The constitution of the FCA must provide for the FCA to have a governing body.

(2)   The governing body must consist of—
   (a)   a chair appointed by the Treasury,
   (b)   a chief executive appointed by the Treasury,
   (c)   the Bank's Deputy Governor for prudential regulation,
   (d)   2 members appointed jointly by the Secretary of State and the Treasury, and
   (e)   at least one other member appointed by the Treasury.

(3)   The members referred to in sub-paragraph (2)(a), (c) and (d) are to be non-executive members.

(4)   In exercising its powers under sub-paragraph (2)(e) to appoint executive or non-executive members, the Treasury must secure that the majority of members of the governing body are non-executive members.

(5)   An employee of the FCA may not be appointed as a non-executive member.

(6)   In the following provisions of this Schedule an "appointed member" means a member of the governing body appointed under sub-paragraph (2)(a), (b), (d) or (e).

3. (1)   The terms of service of the appointed members are to be determined by the Treasury.

(2)   In the case of a member appointed under paragraph 2(2)(d), the Treasury must consult the Secretary of State about the terms of service.

(3)   Before appointing a person as an appointed member, the Treasury (or as the case requires the Treasury and the Secretary of State) must consider whether the person has any financial or other interests that could have a material effect on the extent of the functions as member that it would be proper for the person to discharge.

(4) The terms of service of an appointed member ("M") must be such as—
  (a) to secure that M is not subject to direction by the Treasury or the Secretary of State,
  (b) to require M not to act in accordance with the directions of any other person, and
  (c) to prohibit M from acquiring any financial or other interests that have a material effect on the extent of the functions as member that it would be proper for M to discharge.

(5) If an appointed member is an employee of the FCA, the member's interest as employee is to be disregarded for the purposes of sub-paragraphs (3) and (4)(c) and paragraph 4(1)(b).

(6) A person who is an employee of the PRA is disqualified for appointment as an appointed member.

(7) The FCA may pay expenses to the Bank's Deputy Governor for prudential regulation in respect of that person's service as a member.

4. (1) The Treasury may remove an appointed member from office—
  (a) on the grounds of incapacity or serious misconduct, or
  (b) on the grounds that in all the circumstances the member's financial or other interests are such as to have a material effect on the extent of the functions as member that it would be proper for the person to discharge.

(2) Before removing from office a member appointed under paragraph 2(2)(d), the Treasury must consult the Secretary of State.

5. The validity of any act of the FCA is not affected—
  (a) by any vacancy in any of the offices mentioned in paragraph 2(2)(a), (b) or (c), or
  (b) by a defect in the appointment of a person—
    (i) to any of those offices, or
    (ii) as an appointed member.

6. The Bank's Deputy Governor for prudential regulation must not take part in any discussion by or decision of the FCA which relates to—
  (a) the exercise of the FCA's functions in relation to a particular person, or
  (b) a decision not to exercise those functions.

Remuneration

7. The FCA must pay to the appointed members such remuneration as may be determined—
  (a) in the case of the non-executive members, by the Treasury;
  (b) in the case of the executive members, by the FCA.

Arrangements for discharging functions

8. (1) The FCA may make arrangements for any of its functions to be discharged by a committee, sub-committee, officer or member of staff of the FCA, but subject to the following provisions.

(2) In exercising its legislative functions, the FCA must act through its governing body.

(3) For that purpose, the following are the FCA's legislative functions—
  (a) making rules;
  (b) issuing codes under section *64 or* 119;
  (c) issuing statements under—
    (i) section [63ZD,] 63C, *64,* 69, 88C, 89S, 93, 124, 131J, 138N, [142V,] 192H, 192N, 210[, 312J or 333K],
    (ii) section 345D (whether as a result of section 345(2)[, section 249(1) or 261K(1)]), or
    (iii) section 80 of the Financial Services Act 2012;
  (d) giving directions under section 316, 318 or 328;
  [(e) setting standards under section 333H].

(4) The function of issuing general guidance (as defined in section 139B(5) [or 333P(9)]) may not be discharged by an officer or member of staff of the FCA.

[(5) In respect of the exercise of a function under Part 1 of the Competition Act 1998, the power in sub-paragraph (1) is subject to provision in rules made under section 51 of that Act by virtue of paragraph 1A of Schedule 9 to that Act.]

Records

9. The FCA must maintain satisfactory arrangements for—
  (a) recording decisions made in the exercise of its functions, and
  (b) the safe-keeping of those records which it considers ought to be preserved.

Publication of record of meetings of governing body

10. (1) The FCA must publish a record of each meeting of its governing body—
  (a) before the end of the period of 6 weeks beginning with the day of the meeting, or
  (b) if no meeting of the governing body is subsequently held during that period, before the end of the period of 2 weeks beginning with the day of the next meeting.

(2)   The record must specify any decision taken at the meeting (including decisions to take no action) and must set out, in relation to each decision, a summary of the deliberations of the governing body.

(3)   Sub-paragraphs (1) and (2) do not require the publication of information whose publication within the time required by sub-paragraph (1) would in the opinion of the governing body be against the public interest.

(4)   Publication under this section is to be in such manner as the FCA thinks fit.

Annual report

11.   (1)   At least once a year the FCA must make a report to the Treasury on—
  (a)   the discharge of its functions,
  (b)   the extent to which, in its opinion, its operational objectives have been advanced,
  (c)   the extent to which, in its opinion, it has acted compatibly with its strategic objective,
  (d)   how, in its opinion, it has complied with the duty in section 1B(4),
  (e)   its consideration of the matter mentioned in section 1B(5)(b),
  (f)   its consideration of the principles in section 3B,
  (g)   how it has complied with section 3D,
  (h)   any direction received under section 3I or 3J during the period to which the report relates,
  [(ha) any rules that it has made as a result of section 137C during the period to which the report relates and the kinds of regulated credit agreement (within the meaning of that section) to which the rules apply,]
  [(hb) how, in its opinion, it has complied with its duties in section 333O,]
  (i)   how it has complied with section 354A(1) so far as relating to co-operation with persons outside the United Kingdom, and
  (j)   such other matters as the Treasury may from time to time direct.

(2)   Sub-paragraph (1) does not require the inclusion in the report of any information whose publication would in the opinion of the FCA be against the public interest.

(3)   The report must be accompanied by—
  (a)   a statement of the remuneration of the appointed members of the governing body of the FCA during the period to which the report relates, and
  (b)   such other reports or information, prepared by such persons, as the Treasury may from time to time direct.

(4)   The Treasury must lay before Parliament a copy of each report received by them under this paragraph.

Annual public meeting

12.   (1)   Not later than 3 months after making a report under paragraph 11, the FCA must hold a public meeting ("the annual meeting") for the purposes of enabling that report to be considered.

(2)   The FCA must organise the annual meeting so as to allow—
  (a)   a general discussion of the contents of the report which is being considered, and
  (b)   a reasonable opportunity for those attending the meeting to put questions to the FCA about the way in which it discharged, or failed to discharge, its functions during the period to which the report relates.

(3)   But otherwise the annual meeting is to be organised and conducted in such a way as the FCA considers appropriate.

(4)   The FCA must give reasonable notice of its annual meeting.

(5)   That notice must—
  (a)   give details of the time and place at which the meeting is to be held,
  (b)   set out the proposed agenda for the meeting,
  (c)   indicate the proposed duration of the meeting,
  (d)   give details of the FCA's arrangements for enabling persons to attend, and
  (e)   be published by the FCA in the way appearing to it to be best calculated to bring the notice to the attention of the public.

(6)   If the FCA proposes to alter any of the arrangements which have been included in the notice given under sub-paragraph (5), it must—
  (a)   give reasonable notice of the alteration, and
  (b)   publish that notice in the way appearing to the FCA to be best calculated to bring it to the attention of the public.

Report of annual meeting

13.   Not later than one month after its annual meeting, the FCA must publish a report of the proceedings of the meeting.

Accounts and audit

14.   (1)   The Treasury may—

(a)   require the FCA to comply with any provisions of the Companies Act 2006 about accounts and their audit which would not otherwise apply to it, or

(b)   direct that any provision of that Act about accounts and their audit is to apply to the FCA with such modifications as are specified in the direction, whether or not the provision would otherwise apply to the FCA.

(2)   Compliance with any requirement under sub-paragraph (1)(a) or (b) is enforceable by injunction or, in Scotland, an order for specific performance under section 45 of the Court of Session Act 1988.

(3)   Proceedings under sub-paragraph (2) may be brought only by the Treasury.

15. (1)   The FCA must send a copy of its annual accounts to the Comptroller and Auditor General as soon as is reasonably practicable.

(2)   The Comptroller and Auditor General must—

(a)   examine, certify and report on accounts received under this paragraph, and

(b)   send a copy of the certified accounts and the report to the Treasury.

(3)   The Treasury must lay the copy of the certified accounts and the report before Parliament.

(4)   Except as provided by paragraph 14(1), the FCA is exempt from the requirements of Part 16 of the Companies Act 2006 (audit), and its balance sheet must contain a statement to that effect.

(5)   In this paragraph "annual accounts" has the meaning given in section 471 of the Companies Act 2006.

NOTES

Commencement: 24 January 2013 (in so far as relating to the preparation of a scheme under para 21 of this Schedule or the making of rules); 19 February 2013 (paras 2, 3 for the purposes of making appointments); 1 April 2013 (otherwise).

This Schedule was substituted (together with Sch 1ZB for the original Sch 1) by the Financial Services Act 2012, s 6(2), Sch 3; for transitional provisions and savings in relation to the transfer of the FSA's functions, property, rights and liabilities, see s 119 of, and Schs 20, 21 to, the 2012 Act.

Para 8 is amended as follows:

The words and figure in italics in sub-paras (3)(b), (c)(i) are repealed, and the figure "63ZD," in square brackets in sub-para (3)(c)(i) is inserted, by the Financial Services (Banking Reform) Act 2013, s 35, Sch 3, para 16, as from 25 July 2014 (in so far as relating to the insertion of the figure "63ZD,"), and as from 7 March 2016 (otherwise).

The figure "142V," in square brackets in sub-para (3)(c)(i) is inserted by the Financial Services (Banking Reform) Act 2013, s 4(6), as from a day to be appointed.

The words ", 312J or 333K" in square brackets in sub-para (3)(c)(i) were substituted, sub-para (3)(e) was inserted, and the words in square brackets in sub-para (4) were inserted, by the Pension Schemes Act 2015, s 47, Sch 3, paras 1, 13.

The words in square brackets in sub-para (3)(c)(ii) were inserted by the Collective Investment in Transferable Securities (Contractual Scheme) Regulations 2013, SI 2013/1388, reg 3(1), (21).

Sub-para (5) added by the Financial Services (Banking Reform) Act 2013, s 129, Sch 8, Pt 1, para 7(1), (2).

Para 11: sub-para (1)(ha) inserted by the Financial Services (Banking Reform) Act 2013, s 131(2); sub-para (1)(hb) inserted by the Pension Schemes Act 2015, s 47, Sch 3, paras 1, 14.

Rule-making instrument: designating instruments made in accordance with the Financial Services Act 2012 (Transitional Provisions) (Rules and Miscellaneous Provisions) Order 2013, SI 2013/161, art 3 and the Financial Services and Markets Act 2000 (Regulated Activities) (Amendment) (No 2) Order 2013, SI 2013/1881 art 64, (at **[2.1045]**) are to be treated as rule-making instruments for the purposes of para 8(2) above.

**[PART 2
STATUS**

Status

[1.1583]

16.   In relation to any of its functions—

(a)   the FCA is not to be regarded as acting on behalf of the Crown, and

(b)   its members, officers and staff are not to be regarded as Crown servants.

Exemption from requirement for use of "limited" in name of FCA

17.   The FCA is to continue to be exempt from the requirements of the Companies Act 2006 relating to the use of "limited" as part of its name.

18.   If the Secretary of State is satisfied that any action taken by the FCA makes it inappropriate for the exemption given by paragraph 17 to continue, the Secretary of State may, after consulting the Treasury, give a direction removing it.]

NOTES

Commencement: 24 January 2013 (in so far as relating to the preparation of a scheme under para 21 of this Schedule or the making of rules); 1 April 2013 (otherwise).

Substituted as noted to Part 1 of this Schedule at **[1.1582]**.

[PART 3
PENALTIES AND FEES

Penalties

[1.1584]
19. In determining its policy with respect to the amounts of penalties to be imposed by it under this Act, the FCA must take no account of the expenses which it incurs, or expects to incur, in discharging its functions.

20. (1) The FCA must in respect of each of its financial years pay to the Treasury its penalty receipts after deducting its enforcement costs.

(2) The FCA's "penalty receipts" in respect of a financial year are any amounts received by it during the year by way of penalties imposed under this Act.

(3) The FCA's "enforcement costs" in respect of a financial year are the expenses incurred by it during the year in connection with—
  (a) the exercise, or consideration of the possible exercise, of any of its enforcement powers in particular cases, or
  (b) the recovery of penalties imposed under this Act [or under a provision mentioned in sub-paragraph (4A)].

(4) For this purpose the FCA's enforcement powers are—
  (a) its powers under any of the provisions mentioned in section 133(7A),
  (b) its powers under section 56 (prohibition orders),
  (c) its powers under Part 25 of this Act (injunctions and restitution),
  [(ca) its powers under the relevant competition provisions (as applied by Part 16A of this Act),]
  (d) its powers under any other enactment specified by the Treasury by order,
  (e) its powers in relation to the investigation of relevant offences, and
  (f) its powers in England and Wales or Northern Ireland in relation to the prosecution of relevant offences.

[(4A) The relevant competition provisions" are—
  (a) section 31E of the Competition Act 1998 (enforcement of commitments);
  (b) section 34 of that Act (enforcement of directions);
  (c) section 36 of that Act (penalties);
  (d) section 40A of that Act (penalties: failure to comply with requirements);
  (e) section 174A of the Enterprise Act 2002 (penalties).]

(5) "Relevant offences" are—
  (a) offences under [this Act],
  (b) offences under subordinate legislation made under [this Act],
  (c) offences falling within section 402(1) . . . ,
  [(ca) offences under Part 1 of the Competition Act 1998,
  (cb) offences under Part 4 of the Enterprise Act 2002,]
  (d) offences under Part 7 of the Financial Services Act 2012, and
  (e) any other offences specified by the Treasury by order.

(6) The Treasury may give directions to the FCA as to how the FCA is to comply with its duty under sub-paragraph (1).

(7) The directions may in particular—
  (a) specify descriptions of expenditure that are, or are not, to be regarded as incurred in connection with either of the matters mentioned in sub-paragraph (3),
  (b) relate to the calculation and timing of the deduction in respect of the FCA's enforcement costs, and
  (c) specify the time when any payment is required to be made to the Treasury.

(8) The directions may also require the FCA to provide the Treasury at specified times with specified information relating to—
  (a) penalties that the FCA has imposed under this Act, or
  (b) the FCA's enforcement costs.

(9) The Treasury must pay into the Consolidated Fund any sums received by them under this paragraph.

21. (1) The FCA must prepare and operate a scheme ("the financial penalty scheme") for ensuring that the amounts that, as a result of the deduction for which paragraph 20(1) provides, are retained by the FCA in respect of amounts paid to it by way of penalties imposed under this Act are applied for the benefit of regulated persons.

(2) "Regulated persons" means—
  (a) authorised persons,
  (b) recognised investment exchanges,
  (c) issuers of securities admitted to the official list, . . .
  (d) issuers who have requested or approved the admission of financial instruments to trading on a regulated market[, and

(e)　designated guidance providers].

(3)　The financial penalty scheme may, in particular, make different provision with respect to different classes of regulated person.

(4)　The financial penalty scheme must ensure that those who have become liable to pay a penalty to the FCA in any financial year of the FCA do not receive any benefit under the scheme in the following financial year.

(5)　Up-to-date details of the financial penalty scheme must be set out in a document ("the scheme details").

22.　(1)　The scheme details must be published by the FCA in the way appearing to it to be best calculated to bring them to the attention of the public.

(2)　Before making the financial penalty scheme, the FCA must publish a draft of the proposed scheme in the way appearing to the FCA to be best calculated to bring it to the attention of the public.

(3)　The draft must be accompanied by notice that representations about the proposals may be made to the FCA within a specified time.

(4)　Before making the scheme, the FCA must have regard to any representations made to it in accordance with sub-paragraph (3).

(5)　If the FCA makes the proposed scheme, it must publish an account, in general terms, of—
    (a)　the representations made to it in accordance with sub-paragraph (3), and
    (b)　its response to them.

(6)　If the scheme differs from the draft published under sub-paragraph (2) in a way which is, in the opinion of the FCA, significant, the FCA must (in addition to complying with sub-paragraph (5)) publish details of the difference.

(7)　The FCA must, without delay, give the Treasury a copy of any scheme details published by it.

(8)　The FCA may charge a reasonable fee for providing a person with a copy of—
    (a)　a draft published under sub-paragraph (2);
    (b)　scheme details.

(9)　Sub-paragraphs (2) to (6) and (8)(a) also apply to a proposal to alter or replace the financial penalty scheme.

Fees

23.　(1)　The FCA may make rules providing for the payment to it of such fees, in connection with the discharge of any of its qualifying functions, as it considers will (taking account of its expected income from fees and charges provided for by any other provision of this Act [other than sections 333Q and 333R]) enable it—
    (a)　to meet expenses incurred in carrying out its functions[, other than its excepted functions,] or for any incidental purpose,
    (b)　to repay the principal of, and pay any interest on, any relevant borrowing and to meet relevant commencement expenses, and
    (c)　to maintain adequate reserves.

(2)　The "qualifying functions" of the FCA are—
    (a)　its functions under or as a result of this Act or any of the [other enactments mentioned in section 1A(6)(a) to (ca)] [but not its excepted functions], and
    (b)　its functions under or as a result of a qualifying EU provision that is specified, or of a description specified, for the purposes of this sub-paragraph by the Treasury by order.

[(2ZA)　The "excepted functions" of the FCA are—
    (a)　its functions under sections 333E to 333Q, and
    (b)　its functions under section 333R so far as relating to the collection of payments.]

[(2A)　The functions referred to in sub-paragraph (1)(a) include functions of the FCA under the Competition Act 1998 or the Enterprise Act 2002 as a result of Part 16A of this Act; but this sub-paragraph is not to be regarded as limiting the effect of the definition of "functions" in paragraph 1.]

(3)　In sub-paragraph (1)(b)—
    "relevant borrowing" means any money borrowed by the FCA which has been used for the purpose of meeting expenses incurred in relation to its assumption of functions under this Act, and
    "relevant commencement expenses" means expenses incurred by the FCA—
        (a)　in preparation for the exercise of functions by the FCA under this Act, or
        (b)　for the purpose of facilitating the exercise by the FCA of those functions or otherwise in connection with their exercise by it.

(4)　Neither section 1A(6)(d) nor the definition of "functions" in paragraph 1 applies for the purposes of sub-paragraph (2).

(5) For the purposes of sub-paragraph (3) it is irrelevant when the borrowing of the money, the incurring of the expenses or the assumption of functions took place (and, in particular, it is irrelevant if any of those things were done at a time when the FCA was known as the Financial Services Authority).

(6) In the case of rules made under Part 6 of this Act, the rules may, in particular, require the payment of fees in respect of—

    (a)   the continued inclusion of securities or persons in any list or register required to be kept by the FCA as a result of any provision made by or under that Part,

    (b)   access to any list or register within paragraph (a), and

    (c)   the continued admission of financial instruments to trading on a regulated market.

(7) In fixing the amount of any fee which is to be payable to the FCA, no account is to be taken of any sums which the FCA receives, or expects to receive, by way of penalties imposed by it under this Act.

(8) Any fee which is owed to the FCA under any provision made by or under this Act may be recovered as a debt due to the FCA.

Services for which fees may not be charged

24. The power conferred by paragraph 23 may not be used to require—

    (a)   a fee to be paid in respect of the discharge of any of the FCA's functions under paragraph 13, 14, 19 or 20 of Schedule 3, or

    (b)   a fee to be paid by any person whose application for approval under section 59 has been granted.

NOTES

Commencement: 24 January 2013 (in so far as relating to the preparation of a scheme under para 21 of this Schedule or the making of rules, and in so far as relating to para 20 for the purposes of making orders); 1 April 2013 (otherwise).

Substituted as noted to Part 1 of this Schedule at **[1.1582]**.

Para 20: the words in square brackets in sub-para (3)(b) were inserted, sub-paras (4)(ca), (4A) and (5)(ca), (cb) were inserted, the words in square brackets in sub-paras (5)(a), (b) were substituted, and the words omitted from sub-para (5)(c) were repealed, by the Financial Services (Banking Reform) Act 2013, s 141, Sch 10, para 4.

Para 21: word omitted from sub-para (2)(c) repealed, and sub-para (2)(e) (and the preceding word) inserted, by the Pension Schemes Act 2015, s 47, Sch 3, paras 1, 15.

Para 23: words in square brackets in sub-para (1) inserted, words in second pair of square brackets in words in square brackets in sub-para (2)(a) inserted, and sub-para (2ZA) inserted, by the Pension Schemes Act 2015, s 47, Sch 3, paras 1, 16; words in first pair of square brackets in sub-para (2)(a) substituted by the Alternative Investment Fund Managers Regulations 2013, SI 2013/1773, reg 80, Sch 1, Part 1, paras 1, 33, (for transitional provisions and savings see Part 9 of the 2013 Regulations); sub-para (2A) inserted by the Financial Services (Banking Reform) Act 2013, s 129, Sch 8, Pt 1, para 7(1), (3).

Orders: the Payment to Treasury of Penalties (Enforcement Costs) Order 2013, SI 2013/418; the Financial Services and Markets Act 2000 (Qualifying EU Provisions) Order 2013, SI 2013/419; the Financial Services and Markets Act 2000 (Qualifying EU Provisions) (No 2) Order 2013, SI 2013/3116.

[PART 4
MISCELLANEOUS

Exemption from liability in damages

[1.1585]

25. (1) None of the following is to be liable in damages for anything done or omitted in the discharge, or purported discharge, of the FCA's functions—

    (a)   the FCA;

    (b)   any person ("P") who is, or is acting as, a member, officer or member of staff of the FCA;

    (c)   any person who could be held vicariously liable for things done or omitted by P, but only in so far as the liability relates to P's conduct.

[(1A) In sub-paragraph (1) the reference to the FCA's functions includes its functions under Part 5 of the Financial Services (Banking Reform) Act 2013 (regulation of payment systems).]

(2) Anything done or omitted by a person mentioned in sub-paragraph (1)(a) or (b) while acting, or purporting to act, as a result of an appointment under any of sections 166 to 169 is to be taken for the purposes of sub-paragraph (1) to have been done or omitted in the discharge, or as the case may be purported discharge, of the FCA's functions.

(3) Sub-paragraph (1) does not apply—

    (a)   if the act or omission is shown to have been in bad faith, or

    (b)   so as to prevent an award of damages made in respect of an act or omission on the ground that the act or omission was unlawful as a result of section 6(1) of the Human Rights Act 1998.

Accredited financial investigators

26. For the purposes of this Act anything done by an accredited financial investigator within the meaning of the Proceeds of Crime Act 2002 who—

    (a)   is, or is acting as, an officer of, or member of the staff of, the FCA, or

    (b)   is appointed by the FCA under section 97, 167 or 168 to conduct an investigation, is to be treated as done in the exercise or discharge of a function of the FCA.

Amounts required by rules to be paid to the FCA

27. Any amount (other than a fee) which is required by rules to be paid to the FCA may be recovered as a debt due to the FCA.]

NOTES

Commencement: 24 January 2013 (in so far as relating to the preparation of a scheme under para 21 of this Schedule or the making of rules); 1 April 2013 (otherwise).

Substituted as noted to Part 1 of this Schedule at **[1.1582]**.

Para 25: sub-para (1A) inserted by the Financial Services (Banking Reform) Act 2013, s 109(1).

SCHEDULES 1–5

(Schs 1–5 outside the scope of this work.)

SCHEDULE 6
THRESHOLD CONDITIONS

[Section 55B]

[PART 1
INTRODUCTION

[1.1586]

1A. (1)　In this Schedule—

"assets" includes contingent assets;

"consolidated supervision" has the same meaning as in section 3M;

"consumers" has the meaning given in section 425A;

"financial crime" is to be read with section 1H(3);

"functions", in relation to the FCA or the PRA, means functions conferred on that regulator by or under this Act;

"liabilities" includes contingent liabilities;

"relevant directives" has the same meaning as in section 3M;

"Society" means the society incorporated by Lloyd's Act 1871 by the name of Lloyd's;

"subsidiary undertaking" includes all the instances mentioned in Article 1(1) and (2) of the Seventh Company Law Directive in which an entity may be a subsidiary of an undertaking.

(2)　For the purposes of this Schedule, the "non-financial resources" of a person include any systems, controls, plans or policies that the person maintains, any information that the person holds and the human resources that the person has available.

(3)　In this Schedule, References to "integrity" of the UK financial system are to be read in accordance section 1D(2).

(4)　References to the failure of a person are to be read in accordance with section 2J(3) and (4).]

NOTES

Commencement: 1 April 2013.

The enabling authority of this Schedule was substituted (it was previously s 41) and Parts 1 and 1B–1G were substituted for the original Parts I, II, by the Financial Services and Markets Act 2000 (Threshold Conditions) Order 2013, SI 2013/555, art 2.

[PART 1B
PART 4A PERMISSION: AUTHORISED PERSONS WHO ARE NOT
PRA-AUTHORISED PERSONS

[1.1587]

2A.　Introduction

If the person concerned ("A") carries on, or is seeking to carry on, regulated activities which do not consist of or include a PRA-regulated activity, the threshold conditions that are relevant to the discharge by the FCA of its functions in relation to A are the conditions set out in paragraphs 2B to 2F.

2B.　Location of offices

(1)　Unless sub-paragraph (3)[, (4)(a) or (7)] applies, if A is a body corporate incorporated in the United Kingdom—

(a)　A's head office, and

(b)　if A has a registered office, that office,

must be in the United Kingdom.

(2)　If A is not a body corporate but A's head office is in the United Kingdom, A must carry on business in the United Kingdom.

(3)　If—

(a) A is seeking to carry on, or is carrying on, a regulated activity which is any of the investment services and activities,

(b) A is a body corporate with no registered office, and

(c) A's head office is in the United Kingdom,

A must carry on business in the United Kingdom.

(4) If A is seeking to carry on, or is carrying on, an insurance mediation activity—

(a) where A is a body corporate incorporated in the United Kingdom, A's registered office, or if A has no registered office, A's head office, must be in the United Kingdom;

(b) where A is an individual, A is to be treated for the purposes of sub-paragraph (2) as having a head office in the United Kingdom if A is resident in the United Kingdom.

(5) "Insurance mediation activity" means any of the following activities—

(a) dealing in rights under a contract of insurance as agent;

(b) arranging deals in rights under a contract of insurance;

(c) assisting in the administration and performance of a contract of insurance;

(d) advising on buying or selling rights under a contract of insurance;

(e) agreeing to do any of the activities specified in paragraphs (a) to (d).

(6) Sub-paragraph (5) must be read with—

(a) section 22,

(b) any relevant order under that section, and

(c) Schedule 2.

[(7) If A is seeking to carry on, or is carrying on, the regulated activity of managing an AIF and is, or upon being granted Part 4A permission to carry on that regulated activity would be, *a full-scope UK AIFM, A's head office and registered office must be in the United Kingdom.*]

2C. Effective supervision

(1) A must be capable of being effectively supervised by the FCA having regard to all the circumstances including—

(a) the nature (including the complexity) of the regulated activities that A carries on or seeks to carry on;

(b) the complexity of any products that A provides or will provide in carrying on those activities;

(c) the way in which A's business is organised;

(d) if A is a member of a group, whether membership of the group is likely to prevent the FCA's effective supervision of A;

(e) whether A is subject to consolidated supervision required under any of the relevant directives;

(f) if A has close links with another person ("CL")—

    (i) the nature of the relationship between A and CL,

    (ii) whether those links are or that relationship is likely to prevent the FCA's effective supervision of A, and

    (iii) if CL is subject to the laws, regulations or administrative provisions of a territory which is not an EEA State ("the foreign provisions"), whether those foreign provisions, or any deficiency in their enforcement, would prevent the FCA's effective supervision of A.

[(1A) Paragraphs (a), (b) and (e) of sub-paragraph (1) do not apply where the only regulated activities that the person carries on, or seeks to carry on, are—

(a) relevant credit activities, and

(b) if any, activities to which, by virtue of section 39(1D), sections 20(1) and (1A) and 23(1A) do not apply when carried on by the person.]

(2) A has close links with CL if—

(a) CL is a parent undertaking of A,

(b) CL is a subsidiary undertaking of A,

(c) CL is a parent undertaking of a subsidiary undertaking of A,

(d) CL is a subsidiary undertaking of a parent undertaking of A,

(e) CL owns or controls 20% or more of the voting rights or capital of A, or

(f) A owns or controls 20% or more of the voting rights or capital of CL.

2D. Appropriate resources

(1) The resources of A must be appropriate in relation to the regulated activities that A carries on or seeks to carry on.

(2) The matters which are relevant in determining whether A has appropriate resources include—

(a) the nature and scale of the business carried on, or to be carried on, by A;

(b) the risks to the continuity of the services provided by, or to be provided by, A;

(c) A's membership of a group and any effect which that membership may have.

(3) [Except in a case within sub-paragraph (3A), the matters] which are relevant in determining whether A has appropriate financial resources include—

    (a)   the provision A makes and, if A is a member of a group, which other members of the group make, in respect of liabilities;

    (b)   the means by which A manages and, if A is a member of a group, by which other members of the group manage, the incidence of risk in connection with A's business.

[(3A)   Where the only regulated activities that A carries on or seeks to carry on are—

    (a)   relevant credit activities, and

    (b)   if any, activities to which, by virtue of section 39(1D), sections 20(1) and (1A) and 23(1A) do not apply when carried on by A,

A has adequate financial resources if A is capable of meeting A's debts as they fall due.]

(4)   The matters which are relevant in determining whether A has appropriate non-financial resources include—

    (a)   the skills and experience of those who manage A's affairs;

    (b)   whether A's non-financial resources are sufficient to enable A to comply with—

        (i)   requirements imposed or likely to be imposed on A by the FCA in the exercise of its functions, or

        (ii)   any other requirement in relation to whose contravention the FCA would be the appropriate regulator for the purpose of any provision of Part 14 of this Act.

2E.   Suitability

A must be a fit and proper person having regard to all the circumstances, including—

    (a)   A's connection with any person;

    (b)   the nature (including the complexity) of the regulated activities that A carries on or seeks to carry on;

    (c)   the need to ensure that A's affairs are conducted in an appropriate manner, having regard in particular to the interests of consumers and the integrity of the UK financial system;

    (d)   whether A has complied and is complying with requirements imposed by the FCA in the exercise of its functions, or requests made by the FCA, relating to the provision of information to the FCA and, where A has so complied or is so complying, the manner of that compliance;

    (e)   whether those who manage A's affairs have adequate skills and experience and have acted and may be expected to act with probity;

    (f)   whether A's business is being, or is to be, managed in such a way as to ensure that its affairs will be conducted in a sound and prudent manner;

    (g)   the need to minimise the extent to which it is possible for the business carried on by A, or to be carried on by A, to be used for a purpose connected with financial crime.

2F.   Business model

(1)   A's business model (that is, A's strategy for doing business) must be suitable for a person carrying on the regulated activities that A carries on or seeks to carry on.

(2)   The matters which are relevant in determining whether A satisfies the condition in sub-paragraph (1) include—

    (a)   whether the business model is compatible with A's affairs being conducted, and continuing to be conducted, in a sound and prudent manner;

    (b)   the interests of consumers;

    (c)   the integrity of the UK financial system.

[(3)   This paragraph does not apply where the only regulated activities that the person carries on, or seeks to carry on, are—

    (a)   relevant credit activities, and

    (b)   if any, activities to which, by virtue of section 39(1D), sections 20(1) and (1A) and 23(1A) do not apply when carried on by the person.]

[2G.   Interpretation

(1)   In this Part of this Schedule, each of the following is a "relevant credit activity"—

    (a)   an activity of the kind specified by article 36A of the Regulated Activities Order (credit broking) when carried on in the case specified in sub-paragraph (3), (4) or (5),

    (b)   an activity of the kind specified by article 39D of that Order (debt adjusting) when carried on—

        (i)   in the case specified in sub-paragraph (3), by a person who also carries on an activity of the kind specified by paragraph (a),

        [(ii)   by a person in connection with an activity of the kind specified by paragraph (d) or (e) which the person also carries on,]

        (iii)   by a not-for-profit body,

    (c)   an activity of the kind specified by article 39E of that Order (debt-counselling) when carried on—

        (i)   in the case specified in sub-paragraph (3), by a person who also carries on an activity of the kind specified by paragraph (a),

        [(ii)   by a person in connection with an activity of the kind specified by paragraph (d) or (e) which the person also carries on,]

(iii) by a not-for-profit body,

(d) an activity of the kind specified by article 60B of that Order (regulated credit agreements) if—

    (i) it is carried on by a supplier,

    (ii) no charge (by way of interest or otherwise) is payable by the borrower in connection with the provision of credit under the regulated credit agreement, and

    (iii) the regulated credit agreement is not a hire-purchase agreement or a conditional sale agreement,

[(da) an activity of the kind specified by article 60B of that Order (regulated credit agreements) if carried on by a local authority,]

(e) an activity of the kind specified by article 60N of that Order (regulated consumer hire agreements),

(f) an activity of the kind specified by article 89A of that Order (providing credit information services) where carried on by a person [in connection with an activity of the kind specified by any of paragraphs (a) to (e) which the person also carries on], or

(g) an activity of the kind specified by article 64 of that Order (agreeing to carry on specified kinds of activity) so far as relevant to any of the activities specified in paragraphs (a) to (f).

(2) [Except where the activity is carried on by a not-for-profit body,] an activity is not a relevant credit activity for the purposes of—

(a) paragraph (a) to (e) of sub-paragraph (1), and

(b) paragraph (g) of that sub-paragraph so far at it relates to activities of the kind specified by any of those paragraphs,

if it relates to an agreement under which the obligation of the borrower to repay [or the hirer to pay] is secured, or is to be secured, by a legal mortgage on land.

(3) The case specified in this sub-paragraph is where a supplier (other than a domestic premises supplier) carries on the activity for the purposes of, or in connection with, the sale of goods or supply of services by the supplier to a customer (who need not be the borrower under the credit agreement or the hirer under the consumer hire agreement).

[(3A) For the purposes of sub-paragraph (3), "domestic premises supplier" means a supplier who—

(a) sells, offers to sell or agrees to sell goods, or

(b) offers to supply services or contracts to supply services,

to customers who are individuals while the supplier, or the supplier's representative, is physically present at the dwelling of the individual (but see sub-paragraph (3B)).

(3B) A supplier who acts as described in sub-paragraph (3A) on an occasional basis only will not be a domestic premises supplier unless the supplier indicates to the public at large, or any section of the public, the supplier's willingness to attend (in person or through a representative) the dwelling of potential customers in order to carry on any of the activities mentioned in sub-paragraph (3A)(a) or (b).]

(4) The case specified in this sub-paragraph is where the activity relates to a green deal plan.

[(5) The case specified in this sub-paragraph is where the activity relates to a consumer hire agreement or a hire-purchase agreement.]

(6) For the purposes of this paragraph—

"borrower" includes—

    (a) any person providing a guarantee or indemnity under an agreement, and

    (b) a person to whom the rights and duties of the borrower under an agreement or a person falling within paragraph (a) have passed by assignment or operation of law;

"conditional sale agreement" has the meaning given by article 60L of the Regulated Activities Order;

["consumer hire agreement" has the meaning given by article 60N(3) of the Regulated Activities Order;]

"customer" means a person to whom a supplier sells goods or supplies services or agrees to do so;

. . .

"green deal plan" has the meaning given by section 1 of the Energy Act 2011;

"hire-purchase agreement" has the meaning given by the Regulated Activities Order;

["local authority" means—

    (a) in England and Wales, a local authority within the meaning of the Local Government Act 1972, the Greater London Authority, the Common Council of the City of London or the Council of the Isles of Scilly;

    (b) in Scotland, a local authority within the meaning of the Local Government (Scotland) Act 1973; and

    (c) in Northern Ireland, a district council within the meaning of the Local Government Act (Northern Ireland) 1972;]

"not-for-profit body" means a body which, by virtue of its constitution or any enactment—

    (a) is required (after payment of outgoings) to apply the whole of its income and any capital it expends for charitable or public purposes, and

(b)   is prohibited from directly or indirectly distributing amongst its members any part of its assets (otherwise than for charitable or public purposes);

"Regulated Activities Order" means the Financial Services and Markets Act 2000 (Regulated Activities) Order 2001;

"regulated credit agreement" has the meaning given by the Regulated Activities Order;

"supplier" means a person whose main business is to sell goods or supply services and not to carry on a regulated activity, other than an activity of the kind specified by article 60N of the Regulated Activities Order (regulated consumer hire agreements).]]

NOTES

Commencement: 1 April 2013.

Substituted as noted to Part 1 of this Schedule at **[1.1586]**.

Para 2B: words in square brackets in sub-para (1) substituted, and sub-para (7) added, by the Alternative Investment Fund Managers Regulations 2013, SI 2013/1773, reg 80, Sch 1, Part 1, paras 1, 36, (for transitional provisions and savings see Part 9 of the 2013 Regulations); for the words in italics in sub-para (7) there are substituted the following words by the Alternative Investment Fund Managers (Amendment) Regulations 2013, SI 2013/1797, reg 3, Sch 1, para 1(1), (6), as from the date specified by the delegated act adopted by the European Commission pursuant to Article 67.6 of the Directive as the date when the rules set out in Articles 35 and 37 to 41 of the Directive become applicable (note also that ESMA is required to issue an opinion by 22 July 2015 and, if the Commission accepts their advice, a delegated act must be issued by 22 October 2015 specifying the date on which this provision will come into force)—

"a full-scope UK AIFM—
(a)   A's head office and registered office must be in the United Kingdom, or
(b)   A's registered office must be in a country that is not an EEA State.".

Para 2C: sub-para (1A) was originally inserted by the Financial Services and Markets Act 2000 (Regulated Activities) (Amendment) (No 2) Order 2013, SI 2013/1881, art 10(1), (19)(a), (for transitional provisions see see Pt 8 thereof at **[2.1007]** et seq). It was subsequently substituted by the Financial Services and Markets Act 2000 (Regulated Activities) (Amendment) Order 2014, SI 2014/366, art 5(1), (2).

Para 2D: words in square brackets in sub-para (3) substituted, and sub-para (3A) inserted, by SI 2013/1881, art 10(1), (19)(b), (as to transitional provisions, see the note relating to para 2C above). Sub-para (3A) was subsequently substituted by SI 2014/366, art 5(1), (3).

Para 2F: sub-para (3) added by SI 2013/1881, art 10(1), (19)(c), (as to transitional provisions, see the note relating to para 2C above). Sub-para (3) was subsequently substituted by SI 2014/366, art 5(1), (4).

Para 2G: added by SI 2013/1881, art 10(1), (19)(d), (as to transitional provisions, see the note relating to para 2C above); sub-paras (3A), (3B) inserted, sub-para (5) substituted, definition "consumer hire agreement" in sub-para (6) inserted, and definition "domestic premises supplier" (omitted) revoked, by the Financial Services and Markets Act 2000 (Miscellaneous Provisions) Order 2015, SI 2015/853, art 2; all other words in square brackets in para 2G were inserted or substituted by SI 2014/366, art 5(1), (5).

[PART 1C
PART 4A PERMISSION: CONDITIONS FOR WHICH FCA IS RESPONSIBLE IN RELATION TO PRA-AUTHORISED PERSONS

[1.1588]
3A.   Introduction

If the person concerned ("B") carries on, or is seeking to carry on, regulated activities which consist of or include a PRA-regulated activity, the threshold conditions which are relevant to the discharge by the FCA of its functions in relation to B are the conditions set out in paragraphs 3B to 3E.

3B.   Effective supervision

(1)   B must be capable of being effectively supervised by the FCA having regard to all the circumstances including—
(a)   the nature (including the complexity) of the regulated activities that B carries on or seeks to carry on;
(b)   the complexity of any products that B provides or will provide in carrying on those activities;
(c)   the way in which B's business is organised;
(d)   if B is a member of a group, whether membership of the group is likely to prevent the FCA's effective supervision of B;
(e)   whether B is subject to consolidated supervision required under any of the relevant directives;
(f)   if B has close links with another person ("CL")—
(i)   the nature of the relationship between B and CL,
(ii)   whether those links are or that relationship is likely to prevent the FCA's effective supervision of B, and
(iii)   if CL is subject to the laws, regulations or administrative provisions of a territory which is not an EEA State ("the foreign provisions"), whether those foreign provisions, or any deficiency in their enforcement, would prevent the FCA's effective supervision of B.

(2)   B has close links with CL if—
(a)   CL is a parent undertaking of B,

(b)   CL is a subsidiary undertaking of B,

(c)   CL is a parent undertaking of a subsidiary undertaking of B,

(d)   CL is a subsidiary undertaking of a parent undertaking of B,

(e)   CL owns or controls 20% or more of the voting rights or capital of B, or

(f)   B owns or controls 20% or more of the voting rights or capital of CL.

3C.   Appropriate non-financial resources

(1)   The non-financial resources of B must be appropriate in relation to the regulated activities that B carries on or seeks to carry on, having regard to the operational objectives of the FCA.

(2)   The matters which are relevant in determining whether the condition in sub-paragraph (1) is met include—

(a)   the nature and scale of the business carried on, or to be carried on, by B;

(b)   the risks to the continuity of the services provided by, or to be provided by, B;

(c)   B's membership of a group and any effect which that membership may have;

(d)   the skills and experience of those who manage B's affairs;

(e)   whether B's non-financial resources are sufficient to enable B to comply with—

    (i)   requirements imposed or likely to be imposed on B by the FCA in the exercise of its functions, or

    (ii)   any other requirement in relation to whose contravention the FCA would be the appropriate regulator for the purpose of any provision of Part 14 of this Act.

3D.   Suitability

(1)   B must be a fit and proper person, having regard to the operational objectives of the FCA.

(2)   The matters which are relevant in determining whether B satisfies the condition in sub-paragraph (1) include—

(a)   B's connection with any person;

(b)   the nature (including the complexity) of the regulated activities that B carries on or seeks to carry on;

(c)   the need to ensure that B's affairs are conducted in an appropriate manner, having regard in particular to the interests of consumers and the integrity of the UK financial system;

(d)   whether B has complied and is complying with requirements imposed by the FCA in the exercise its functions, or requests made by the FCA, relating to the provision of information to the FCA and, where B has so complied or is so complying, the manner of that compliance;

(e)   whether those who manage B's affairs have adequate skills and experience and have acted and may be expected to act with probity;

(f)   the need to minimise the extent to which it is possible for the business carried on by B, or to be carried on by B, to be used for a purpose connected with financial crime.

3E.   Business model

B's business model (that is, B's strategy for doing business) must be suitable for a person carrying on the regulated activities that B carries on or seeks to carry on, having regard to the FCA's operational objectives.]

NOTES

Commencement: 1 April 2013.

Substituted as noted to Part 1 of this Schedule at **[1.1586]**.

[PART 1D
PART 4A PERMISSION: CONDITIONS FOR WHICH THE PRA IS RESPONSIBLE IN RELATION TO INSURERS ETC

[1.1589]
4A.   Introduction

(1)   If the person concerned ("C") carries on, or is seeking to carry on, regulated activities which consist of or include a PRA-regulated activity relating to the effecting or carrying out of contracts of insurance, the threshold conditions which are relevant to the discharge by the PRA of its functions in relation to C are the conditions set out in paragraphs 4B to 4F.

(2)   If the person concerned ("C") carries on, or is seeking to carry on, regulated activities which consist of or include a PRA-regulated activity relating to managing the underwriting capacity of a Lloyd's syndicate as a managing agent at Lloyd's, the conditions which are relevant to the discharge by the PRA of its functions in relation to C are the conditions set out in paragraphs 4C to 4F except for sub-paragraphs (5)(d) and (5)(e) of paragraph 4D which are not relevant for that purpose.

(3)   If the person concerned ("C") carries on, or is seeking to carry on, regulated activities which consist of or include a PRA-regulated activity relating to the arranging, by the Society, of deals in contracts of insurance written at Lloyd's, the conditions which are relevant to the discharge by the PRA of its functions in relation to C are the conditions set out in paragraphs 4C to 4F, subject to sub-paragraph (4).

(4)   Paragraph 4D has effect in relation to persons of the kind specified by sub-paragraph (3) as if—

    (a)   for paragraph (d) and (e) of sub-paragraph (5) there were substituted—

        "(d)   the effect that the carrying on of business by C might be expected to have on the stability of the UK financial system or on those who are or may become policyholders of members of C;

        (e)   the effect that the failure of C might be expected to have on the stability of the UK financial system or on those who are or may become policyholders of members of C;", and

    (b)   sub-paragraph (6) were omitted.

4B.   Legal status

C must be—
    (a)   a body corporate (other than a limited liability partnership),
    (b)   a registered friendly society, or
    (c)   a member of Lloyd's.

4C.   Location of offices

(1)   If C is a body corporate incorporated in the United Kingdom—
    (a)   C's head office, and
    (b)   if C has a registered office, that office,
must be in the United Kingdom.

(2)   If C is not a body corporate but C's head office is in the United Kingdom, C must carry on business in the United Kingdom.

4D.   Business to be conducted in a prudent manner

(1)   The business of C must be conducted in a prudent manner.

(2)   To satisfy the condition in sub-paragraph (1), C must in particular have appropriate financial and non-financial resources.

(3)   To have appropriate financial resources C must satisfy the following conditions—
    (a)   C's assets must be appropriate given C's liabilities, and
    (b)   the liquidity of C's resources must be appropriate given C's liabilities and when they fall due or may fall due.

(4)   To have appropriate non-financial resources C must satisfy the following conditions—
    (a)   C must be willing and able to value C's assets and liabilities appropriately,
    (b)   C must have resources to identify, monitor, measure and take action to remove or reduce risks to the safety and soundness of C,
    (c)   C must have resources to identify, monitor, measure and take action to remove or reduce risks to the accuracy of C's valuation of C's assets and liabilities,
    (d)   the effectiveness with which C's business is managed must meet a reasonable standard of effectiveness, and
    (e)   C's non-financial resources must be sufficient to enable C to comply with—
        (i)   requirements imposed or likely to be imposed on C by the PRA in the exercise of its functions, and
        (ii)   any other requirement in relation to whose contravention the PRA would be the appropriate regulator for the purpose of any provision of Part 14 of this Act.

(5)   The matters which are relevant in determining whether C satisfies the condition in sub-paragraph (1) or (2) include—
    (a)   the nature (including the complexity) of the regulated activities that C carries on or seeks to carry on;
    (b)   the nature and scale of the business carried on or to be carried on by C;
    (c)   the risks to the continuity of the services provided by, or to be provided by, C;
    (d)   the effect that the carrying on of the business of effecting or carrying out contracts of insurance by C might be expected to have on the stability of the UK financial system or on those who are or may become C's policyholders;
    (e)   the effect that C's failure or C being closed to new business might be expected to have on the stability of the UK financial system or on those who are or may become C's policyholders;
    (f)   C's membership of a group and any effect which that membership may have.

(6)   C is "closed to new business" for the purposes of this paragraph if C has ceased to effect contracts of insurance or has substantially reduced the number of such contracts which C effects.

4E.   Suitability

(1)   C must be a fit and proper person, having regard to the PRA's objectives.

(2)   The matters which are relevant in determining whether C satisfies the condition in sub-paragraph (1) include—

(a) whether C has complied and is complying with requirements imposed by the PRA in the exercise of its functions, or requests made by the PRA relating to the provision of information to the PRA and, if C has so complied or is so complying, the manner of that compliance;

(b) whether those who manage C's affairs have adequate skills and experience and have acted and may be expected to act with probity.

4F. Effective supervision

(1) C must be capable of being effectively supervised by the PRA.

(2) The matters which are relevant in determining whether C satisfies the condition in sub-paragraph (1) include—

(a) the nature (including the complexity) of the regulated activities that C carries on or seeks to carry on;

(b) the complexity of any products that C provides or will provide in carrying on those activities;

(c) the way in which C's business is organised;

(d) if C is a member of a group, whether membership of the group is likely to prevent the PRA's effective supervision of C;

(e) whether C is subject to consolidated supervision required under any of the relevant directives;

(f) if C has close links with another person ("CL")—

    (i) the nature of the relationship between C and CL,

    (ii) whether those links are or that relationship is likely to prevent the PRA's effective supervision of C, and

    (iii) if CL is subject to the laws, regulations or administrative provisions of a territory which is not an EEA State ("the foreign provisions"), whether those foreign provisions, or any deficiency in their enforcement, would prevent the PRA's effective supervision of C.

(3) C has close links with CL if—

(a) CL is a parent undertaking of C,

(b) CL is a subsidiary undertaking of C,

(c) CL is a parent undertaking of a subsidiary undertaking of C,

(d) CL is a subsidiary undertaking of a parent undertaking of C,

(e) CL owns or controls 20% or more of the voting rights or capital of C, or

(f) C owns or controls 20% or more of the voting rights or capital of CL.]

NOTES

Commencement: 1 April 2013.

Substituted as noted to Part 1 of this Schedule at **[1.1586]**.

[PART 1E
PART 4A PERMISSION: CONDITIONS FOR WHICH THE PRA IS RESPONSIBLE IN RELATION TO OTHER PRA-AUTHORISED PERSONS

[1.1590]
5A. Introduction

If the person concerned ("D") carries on, or is seeking to carry on, PRA-regulated activities which do not consist of or include a regulated activity relating to—

(a) the effecting or carrying out of contracts of insurance,

(b) managing the underwriting capacity of a Lloyd's syndicate as a managing agent at Lloyds, or

(c) arranging, by the Society, of deals in contracts of insurance written at Lloyd's,

the threshold conditions which are relevant to the discharge by the PRA of its functions in relation to D are the conditions set out in paragraphs 5B to 5F.

5B. Legal status

If D carries on or is seeking to carry on a regulated activity which consists of or includes accepting deposits or issuing electronic money, D must be—

(a) a body corporate, or

(b) a partnership.

5C. Location of offices

(1) If D is a body corporate incorporated in the United Kingdom—

(a) D's head office, and

(b) if D has a registered office, that office,

must be in the United Kingdom.

(2) If D is not a body corporate but D's head office is in the United Kingdom, D must carry on business in the United Kingdom.

5D.   Business to be conducted in a prudent manner

(1)   The business of D must be conducted in a prudent manner.

(2)   To satisfy the condition in sub-paragraph (1), D must in particular have appropriate financial and non-financial resources.

(3)   To have appropriate financial resources D must satisfy the following conditions—
- (a)   D's assets must be appropriate given D's liabilities, and
- (b)   the liquidity of D's resources must be appropriate given D's liabilities and when they fall due or may fall due.

(4)   To have appropriate non-financial resources D must satisfy the following conditions—
- (a)   D must be willing and able to value D's assets and liabilities appropriately,
- (b)   D must have resources to identify, monitor, measure and take action to remove or reduce risks to the safety and soundness of D,
- (c)   D must have resources to identify, monitor, measure and take action to remove or reduce risks to the accuracy of D's valuation of D's assets and liabilities,
- (d)   the effectiveness with which D's business is managed must meet a reasonable standard of effectiveness, and
- (e)   D's non-financial resources must be sufficient to enable D to comply with—
  - (i)   requirements imposed or likely to be imposed on D by the PRA in the exercise of its functions, and
  - (ii)   any other requirement in relation to whose contravention the PRA would be the appropriate regulator for the purpose of any provision of Part 14 of this Act.

(5)   The matters which are relevant in determining whether D satisfies the condition in sub-paragraph (1) or (2) include—
- (a)   the nature (including the complexity) of the regulated activities that D carries on or seeks to carry on;
- (b)   the nature and scale of the business carried on or to be carried on by D;
- (c)   the risks to the continuity of the services provided or to be provided by D;
- (d)   the effect that the carrying on of the business carried on or to be carried on by D might be expected to have on the stability of the UK financial system;
- (e)   the effect that D's failure might be expected to have on the stability of the UK financial system;
- (f)   D's membership of a group and any effect which that membership may have.

5E.   Suitability

(1)   D must be a fit and proper person, having regard to the PRA's objectives.

(2)   The matters which are relevant in determining whether D satisfies the condition in sub-paragraph (1) include—
- (a)   whether D has complied and is complying with requirements imposed by the PRA in the exercise of its functions, or requests made by the PRA relating to the provision of information to the PRA and, if D has so complied or is so complying, the manner of that compliance;
- (b)   whether those who manage D's affairs have adequate skills and experience and have acted and may be expected to act with probity.

5F.   Effective supervision

(1)   D must be capable of being effectively supervised by the PRA.

(2)   The matters which are relevant in determining whether D satisfies the condition in sub-paragraph (1) include—
- (a)   the nature (including the complexity) of the regulated activities that D carries on or seeks to carry on;
- (b)   the complexity of any products that D provides or will provide in carrying on those activities;
- (c)   the way in which D's business is organised;
- (d)   if D is a member of a group, whether membership of the group is likely to prevent the PRA's effective supervision of D;
- (e)   whether D is subject to consolidated supervision required under any of the relevant directives;
- (f)   if D has close links with another person ("CL")—
  - (i)   the nature of the relationship between D and CL,
  - (ii)   whether those links are or that relationship is likely to prevent the PRA's effective supervision of D, and
  - (iii)   if CL is subject to the laws, regulations or administrative provisions of a territory which is not an EEA State ("the foreign provisions"), whether those foreign provisions, or any deficiency in their enforcement, would prevent the PRA's effective supervision of D.

(3)   D has close links with CL if—
- (a)   CL is a parent undertaking of D,

(b)   CL is a subsidiary undertaking of D,

(c)   CL is a parent undertaking of a subsidiary undertaking of D,

(d)   CL is a subsidiary undertaking of a parent undertaking of D,

(e)   CL owns or controls 20% or more of the voting rights or capital of D, or

(f)   D owns or controls 20% or more of the voting rights or capital of CL.]

NOTES
Commencement: 1 April 2013.
Substituted as noted to Part 1 of this Schedule at **[1.1586]**.

[PART 1F
AUTHORISATION UNDER SCHEDULE 3

[1.1591]
6A. (1)   In relation to an EEA firm qualifying for authorisation under Schedule 3 which carries on PRA-regulated activities which consist of or include a regulated activity relating to the effecting or carrying out of contracts of insurance—

(a)   the conditions in paragraphs 3B to 3E apply so far as relevant to the discharge by the FCA of its relevant functions, and

(b)   the conditions in paragraphs 4B, 4D, 4E and 4F apply so far as relevant to the discharge by the PRA of its relevant functions.

(2)   In relation to an EEA firm qualifying for authorisation under Schedule 3 which carries on PRA-regulated activities which do not consist of or include a regulated activity relating to the effecting or carrying out of contracts of insurance—

(a)   the conditions in paragraphs 3B to 3E apply so far as relevant to the discharge by the FCA of its relevant functions, and

(b)   the conditions in paragraphs 5B, 5D, 5E and 5F apply so far as relevant to the discharge by the PRA of its relevant functions.

(3)   In relation to an EEA firm qualifying for authorisation under Schedule 3 which carries on regulated activities which do not consist of or include a PRA-regulated activity, the conditions in paragraphs 2C, 2D, 2E and 2F apply so far as relevant to the discharge by the FCA of its relevant functions.

(4)   In this paragraph, "relevant functions", in relation to the FCA or the PRA, means functions of that regulator in relation to—

(a)   an application for permission under Part 4A, or

(b)   the exercise by that regulator of its own-initiative requirement power or own-initiative variation power in relation to a Part 4A permission.]

NOTES
Commencement: 1 April 2013.
Substituted as noted to Part 1 of this Schedule at **[1.1586]**.

[PART 1G
AUTHORISATION UNDER SCHEDULE 4

[1.1592]
7A. (1)   In relation to a person who qualifies for authorisation under Schedule 4 who carries on PRA-regulated activities which consist of or include a regulated activity relating to the effecting or carrying out of contracts of insurance—

(a)   the conditions in paragraphs 3B to 3E apply so far as relevant to the discharge by the FCA of its relevant functions, and

(b)   the conditions in paragraphs 4B, 4D, 4E and 4F apply so far as relevant to the discharge by the PRA of its relevant functions.

(2)   In relation to a person who qualifies for authorisation under Schedule 4 who carries on PRA-regulated activities which do not consist of or include a regulated activity relating to the effecting or carrying out of contracts of insurance—

(a)   the conditions in paragraphs 3B to 3E apply so far as relevant to the discharge by the FCA of its relevant functions, and

(b)   the conditions in paragraphs 5B, 5D, 5E and 5F apply so far as relevant to the discharge by the PRA of its relevant functions.

(3)   In relation to a person who qualifies for authorisation under Schedule 4 who carries on regulated activities which do not consist of or include a PRA-regulated activity, the conditions in paragraphs 2C, 2D, 2E and 2F apply so far as relevant to the discharge by the FCA of its relevant functions.

(4)   In this paragraph, "relevant functions", in relation to the FCA or the PRA, means functions of that regulator in relation to—

(a)   an application for an additional permission, or

(b)　the exercise by that regulator of its own-initiative requirement power or own-initiative variation power in relation to an additional permission.]

NOTES
Commencement: 1 April 2013.
Substituted as noted to Part 1 of this Schedule at **[1.1586]**.

PART III
ADDITIONAL CONDITIONS

[1.1593]
8.　(1)　If this paragraph applies to the person concerned, he must, for the purposes of such provisions of this Act as may be specified, satisfy specified additional conditions.

(2)　This paragraph applies to a person who—
(a)　has his head office outside the EEA; and
(b)　appears to [such of the FCA or the PRA as may be specified,] to be seeking to carry on a regulated activity relating to insurance business.

(3)　"Specified" means specified in, or in accordance with, an order made by the Treasury.

9. . . .

NOTES
Para 8: words in square brackets substituted by the Financial Services Act 2012, s 114(1), Sch 18, Pt 1, paras 1, 26.
Para 9: repealed by the Financial Services Act 2012, s 11(3).
Orders: the Financial Services and Markets Act 2000 (Variation of Threshold Conditions) Order 2001, SI 2001/2507; the Financial Services and Markets Act 2000 (Variation of Threshold Conditions) (Amendment) Order 2005, SI 2005/680.

SCHEDULE 17
THE OMBUDSMAN SCHEME

Section 225(4)

NOTES
Transitional provisions etc in connection with the original commencement of this Act: see the notes preceding s 225 at **[1.1530]**.

PART I
GENERAL

Interpretation

[1.1594]
1.　In this Schedule—
["ADR Directive" means Directive 2013/11/EU of the European Parliament and of the Council of 21 May 2013 on alternative dispute resolution for consumer disputes and amending Regulation (EC) No 2006/2004 and Directive 2009/22/EC;
"ADR entity" means any entity which is listed by a member State in accordance with Article 20(2) of the ADR Directive;]
"ombudsman" means a person who is a member of the panel; and
"the panel" means the panel established under paragraph 4.

NOTES
Para 1: definitions "ADR Directive" and "ADR entity" inserted by the Alternative Dispute Resolution for Consumer Disputes (Competent Authorities and Information) Regulations 2015, SI 2015/542, reg 16, Sch 7, para 1(1), (3)(a).

PART II
THE SCHEME OPERATOR

Establishment by the Authority

[1.1595]
[2. **[(1)]**　The FCA must take such steps as are necessary to ensure that the body corporate established by the Financial Services Authority under this Schedule as originally enacted is, at all times, capable of exercising the functions conferred on the scheme operator by or under this Act.]

[(2)　The FCA must exercise any function falling within sub-paragraph (3) in a way which is consistent with enabling the scheme operator, at all times, to qualify as an ADR entity and to meet the quality requirements in Chapter II of the ADR Directive.

(3)　The following functions of the FCA fall within this sub-paragraph—
(a)　making rules for the purposes of section 226;
(b)　approving rules made for the purposes of section 227;
(c)　specifying an amount under section 229(4);
(d)　approving rules made under section 230;
(e)　taking steps under sub-paragraph (1);

(f) appointing or removing members of the board under paragraph 3(2);
(g) taking steps under paragraph 3A(1);
(h) making rules under paragraph 7(3);
(i) making rules under paragraph 13;
(j) consenting to scheme rules under paragraph 14(7), other than rules relating to fees;
(k) approving the fixing, variation, addition or removal of standard terms under paragraph 18, other than terms relating to the making of payments to the scheme operator; and
(l) approving arrangements under paragraph 19(3).]

Constitution

3. (1) The constitution of the scheme operator must provide for it to have—
(a) a chairman; and
(b) a board (which must include the chairman) whose members are the scheme operator's directors.

(2) The chairman and other members of the board must be persons appointed, and liable to removal from office, by the [FCA] (acting, in the case of the chairman, with the approval of the Treasury).

(3) But the terms of their appointment (and in particular those governing removal from office) must be such as to secure their independence from the [FCA] in the operation of the scheme.

(4) The function of making voluntary jurisdiction rules under section 227 [. . .] and the functions conferred by paragraphs 4, 5, 7, 9[, 9A] or 14 may be exercised only by the board.

(5) The validity of any act of the scheme operator is unaffected by—
(a) a vacancy in the office of chairman; or
(b) a defect in the appointment of a person as chairman or as a member of the board.

[Relationship with FCA

3A. (1) The scheme operator and the FCA must each take such steps as it considers appropriate to co-operate with the other in the exercise of their functions under this Part of this Act.

(2) The scheme operator and the FCA must prepare and maintain a memorandum describing how they intend to comply with sub-paragraph (1).

(3) The scheme operator must ensure that the memorandum as currently in force is published in the way appearing to the scheme operator to be best calculated to bring it to the attention of the public.]

The panel of ombudsmen

4. (1) The scheme operator must appoint and maintain a panel of persons, appearing to it to have appropriate qualifications and experience, to act as ombudsmen for the purposes of the scheme.

(2) A person's appointment to the panel is to be on such terms (including terms as to the duration and termination of his appointment and as to remuneration) as the scheme operator considers—
(a) consistent with the independence of the person appointed; and
(b) otherwise appropriate.

The Chief Ombudsman

5. (1) The scheme operator must appoint one member of the panel to act as Chief Ombudsman.

(2) The Chief Ombudsman is to be appointed on such terms (including terms as to the duration and termination of his appointment) as the scheme operator considers appropriate.

Status

6. (1) The scheme operator is not to be regarded as exercising functions on behalf of the Crown.

(2) The scheme operator's . . . officers and staff are not to be regarded as Crown servants.

(3) Appointment as Chief Ombudsman or to the panel or as a deputy ombudsman does not confer the status of Crown servant.

Annual reports

7. (1) At least once a year—
(a) the scheme operator must make a report to the [FCA] on the discharge of its functions; and
(b) the Chief Ombudsman must make a report to the [FCA] on the discharge of his functions.

(2) Each report must distinguish between functions in relation to the scheme's compulsory jurisdiction [. . .] and functions in relation to its voluntary jurisdiction.

(3) Each report must also comply with any requirements specified in rules made by the [FCA].

(4) The scheme operator must publish each report in the way it considers appropriate.

[(5) The Treasury may—
(a) require the scheme operator to comply with any provisions of the Companies Act 2006 about accounts and their audit which would not otherwise apply to it, or

(b) direct that any provision of that Act about accounts and their audit is to apply to the scheme operator with such modifications as are specified in the direction, whether or not the provision would otherwise apply to the scheme manager.

(6) Compliance with any requirement under sub-paragraph (5)(a) or (b) is enforceable by injunction or, in Scotland, an order for specific performance under section 45 of the Court of Session Act 1988.

(7) Proceedings under sub-paragraph (6) may be brought only by the Treasury.]

[Audit of accounts

7A. (1) The scheme operator must send a copy of its annual accounts to the Comptroller and Auditor General as soon as is reasonably practicable.

(2) The Comptroller and Auditor General must—
(a) examine, certify and report on accounts received under this paragraph, and
(b) send a copy of the certified accounts and the report to the Treasury.

(3) The Treasury must lay the copy of the certified accounts and the report before Parliament.

(4) The scheme operator must send a copy of the certified accounts and the report to the FCA.

(5) Except as provided by paragraph 7(5), the scheme operator is exempt from the requirements of Part 16 of the Companies Act 2006 (audit), and its balance sheet must contain a statement to that effect.

(6) In this paragraph "annual accounts" has the meaning given by section 471 of the Companies Act 2006.]

[Information, advice and guidance]

8. The scheme operator may publish [such information, guidance or advice] as it considers appropriate and may charge for it or distribute it free of charge.

Budget

9. (1) The scheme operator must, before the start of each of its financial years, adopt an annual budget which has been approved by the [FCA].

(2) The scheme operator may, with the approval of the [FCA], vary the budget for a financial year at any time after its adoption.

(3) The annual budget must include an indication of—
(a) the distribution of resources deployed in the operation of the scheme, and
(b) the amounts of income of the scheme operator arising or expected to arise from the operation of the scheme,
distinguishing between the scheme's compulsory [. . . .] and voluntary jurisdiction.

[Annual plan

9A. (1) The scheme operator must in respect of each of its financial years prepare an annual plan.

(2) The plan must be prepared before the start of the financial year.

(3) An annual plan in respect of a financial year must make provision about the use of the resources of the scheme operator.

(4) The plan may include material relating to periods longer than the financial year in question.

(5) Before preparing an annual plan, the scheme operator must consult such persons (if any) as the scheme operator considers appropriate.

(6) The scheme operator must publish each annual plan in the way it considers appropriate.]

Exemption from liability in damages

10. (1) No person is to be liable in damages for anything done or omitted in the discharge, or purported discharge, of any functions under this Act in relation to the compulsory jurisdiction [. . .].

(2) Sub-paragraph (1) does not apply—
(a) if the act or omission is shown to have been in bad faith; or
(b) so as to prevent an award of damages made in respect of an act or omission on the ground that the act or omission was unlawful as a result of section 6(1) of the Human Rights Act 1998.

Privilege

11. For the purposes of the law relating to defamation, proceedings in relation to a complaint which is subject to the compulsory jurisdiction [. . .] are to be treated as if they were proceedings before a court.

NOTES
Para 2: substituted by the Financial Services Act 2012, s 39, Sch 11, paras 13, 14; sub-para (1) numbered as such, and sub-paras (2), (3) added, by the Alternative Dispute Resolution for Consumer Disputes (Competent Authorities and Information) Regulations 2015, SI 2015/542, reg 16, Sch 7, para 1(1), (3)(b).
Para 3: word "FCA" in square brackets in sub-paras (2), (3) substituted, and the figure ", 9A" in square brackets in sub-para (4) inserted, by the Financial Services Act 2012, s 39, Sch 11, paras 13, 15; words omitted from sub-para (4) originally inserted by the Consumer Credit Act 2006, s 61(10)(a) and repealed by the Financial Services and Markets Act 2000 (Regulated Activities) (Amendment) (No 2) Order 2013, SI 2013/1881, art 10(1), (17)(a), (for transitional provisions see see Pt 8 thereof at [**2.1007**] et seq).
Paras 3A, 7A, 9A: inserted by the Financial Services Act 2012, s 39, Sch 11, paras 13, 16, 19, 23.
Para 6: words omitted repealed by the Financial Services Act 2012, s 39, Sch 11, paras 13, 17.
Para 7: word "FCA" in square brackets (in each place that it occurs) substituted, and sub-paras (5)–(7) added, by the Financial Services Act 2012, s 39, Sch 11, paras 13, 18; words omitted from sub-para (2) originally inserted by the Consumer Credit Act 2006, s 61(10)(b), and repealed by SI 2013/1881, art 10(1), (17)(b).
Para 8: words in square brackets substituted by the Financial Services Act 2012, s 39, Sch 11, paras 13, 20, 21.
Para 9: word "FCA" in square brackets (in each place that it occurs) substituted by the Financial Services Act 2012, s 39, Sch 11, paras 13, 22; words omitted from sub-para (3) originally inserted by the Consumer Credit Act 2006, s 61(10)(c), and repealed by SI 2013/1881, art 10(1), (17)(c).
Paras 10, 11: words omitted originally inserted by the Consumer Credit Act 2006, s 61(10)(d), and repealed by SI 2013/1881, art 10(1), (17)(d), (e).

PART III
THE COMPULSORY JURISDICTION

Introduction

[1.1596]
12. This Part of this Schedule applies only in relation to the compulsory jurisdiction.

[FCA's] . . . rules

13. (1) The [FCA] must make rules providing that a complaint is not to be entertained unless[—
  (a)] the complainant has referred it under the ombudsman scheme before the applicable time limit (determined in accordance with the rules) has expired[, or
  (b) in the case of a complaint other than a relevant complaint within the meaning of section 404B, the respondent agrees that the complaint should be entertained despite the complainant having referred it under the ombudsman scheme after the applicable time limit has expired].

(2) The rules may provide that an ombudsman may extend that time limit in specified circumstances.

(3) The [FCA] may make rules providing that a complaint is not to be entertained (except in specified circumstances) if the complainant has not previously communicated its substance to the respondent and given him a reasonable opportunity to deal with it.

(4) The [FCA] may make rules requiring an authorised person, [an electronic money issuer within the meaning of the Electronic Money Regulations 2011][, or a payment service provider within the meaning of the Payment Services Regulations 2009,] who may become subject to the compulsory jurisdiction as a respondent to establish such procedures as the [FCA] considers appropriate for the resolution of complaints which—
  (a) may be referred to the scheme; and
  (b) arise out of activity to which the [FCA's] powers under [Part 9A] do not apply.

The scheme operator's rules

14. (1) The scheme operator must make rules, to be known as "scheme rules", which are to set out the procedure for reference of complaints and for their investigation, consideration and determination by an ombudsman.

(2) Scheme rules may, among other things—
  (a) specify matters which are to be taken into account in determining whether an act or omission was fair and reasonable;
  (b) provide that a complaint may, in specified circumstances, be dismissed without consideration of its merits;
  (c) provide for the reference of a complaint, in specified circumstances and with the consent of the complainant, to another body with a view to its being determined by that body instead of by an ombudsman;
  (d) make provision as to the evidence which may be required or admitted, the extent to which it should be oral or written and the consequences of a person's failure to produce any information or document which he has been required (under section 231 or otherwise) to produce;
  (e) allow an ombudsman to fix time limits for any aspect of the proceedings and to extend a time limit;

(f)   provide for certain things in relation to the reference, investigation or consideration (but not determination) of a complaint to be done by a member of the scheme operator's staff instead of by an ombudsman;

[(fa) allow the correction of any clerical mistake in the written statement of a determination made by an ombudsman;

(fb) provide that any irregularity arising from a failure to comply with any provisions of the scheme rules does not of itself render a determination void;]

(g)   make different provision in relation to different kinds of complaint.

(3)   The circumstances specified under sub-paragraph (2)(b) may include the following—

(a)   the ombudsman considers the complaint frivolous or vexatious;

(b)   legal proceedings have been brought concerning the subject-matter of the complaint and the ombudsman considers that the complaint is best dealt with in those proceedings; or

(c)   the ombudsman is satisfied that there are other compelling reasons why it is inappropriate for the complaint to be dealt with under the ombudsman scheme.

[(3A)   The scheme operator must exercise the function of making scheme rules in a way which is consistent with enabling the scheme operator to qualify as an ADR entity and to meet the quality requirements in Chapter II of the ADR Directive.]

(4)   If the scheme operator proposes to make any scheme rules it must publish a draft of the proposed rules in the way appearing to it to be best calculated to bring them to the attention of persons appearing to it to be likely to be affected.

(5)   The draft must be accompanied by a statement that representations about the proposals may be made to the scheme operator within a time specified in the statement.

(6)   Before making the proposed scheme rules, the scheme operator must have regard to any representations made to it under sub-paragraph (5).

(7)   The consent of the [FCA] is required before any scheme rules may be made.

Fees

15.   (1)   Scheme rules may require a respondent to pay to the scheme operator such fees as may be specified in the rules.

(2)   The rules may, among other things—

(a)   provide for the scheme operator to reduce or waive a fee in a particular case;

(b)   set different fees for different stages of the proceedings on a complaint;

(c)   provide for fees to be refunded in specified circumstances;

(d)   make different provision for different kinds of complaint.

Enforcement of money awards

16.   A money award, including interest, which has been registered in accordance with scheme rules may—

(a)   if [the county court] so orders in England and Wales, be recovered [under section 85 of the County Courts Act 1984] (or otherwise) as if it were payable under an order of that court;

(b)   be enforced in Northern Ireland as a money judgment under the Judgments Enforcement (Northern Ireland) Order 1981;

(c)   be enforced in Scotland by the sheriff, as if it were a judgment or order of the sheriff and whether or not the sheriff could himself have granted such judgment or order.

NOTES

Para 13 is amended as follows:

The word omitted from the heading preceding para 13 was repealed, "—(a)" in square brackets and sub-para (b) (and the preceding word) were inserted, by the Alternative Dispute Resolution for Consumer Disputes (Competent Authorities and Information) Regulations 2015, SI 2015/542, reg 16, Sch 7, para 1(1), (3)(c), (d).

Words "FCA" and "FCA's" in square brackets (in each place that they occur) substituted, and the words "Part 9A" in square brackets substituted, by the Financial Services Act 2012, s 39, Sch 11, paras 13, 24.

Words in second pair of square brackets in sub-para (4) inserted by the Electronic Money Regulations 2011, SI 2011/99, reg 79, Sch 4, Pt 1, para 2(1), (8).

Words in third pair of square brackets in sub-para (4) inserted by the Payment Services Regulations 2009, SI 2009/209, reg 126, Sch 6, Pt 1, para 1(2), (for the full commencement details of the 2009 Regulations, see reg 1 of those Regulations at **[2.629]**).

Para 14: sub-paras (2)(fa), (fb) inserted, and word in square brackets in sub-para (7) substituted, by the Financial Services Act 2012, s 39, Sch 11, paras 13, 25; sub-para (3A) inserted by the Alternative Dispute Resolution for Consumer Disputes (Competent Authorities and Information) Regulations 2015, SI 2015/542, reg 16, Sch 7, para 1(1), (3)(e).

Para 16: words in first pair of square brackets in sub-para (a) substituted by the Crime and Courts Act 2013, s 17, Sch 9, Pt 3, para 52; words in second pair of square brackets in sub-para (a) substituted by the Tribunals, Courts and Enforcement Act 2007, s 62(3), Sch 13, para 134.

[PART 3A

(*Originally inserted by the Consumer Credit Act 2006, s 59(2), Sch 2, and repealed by the Financial*

Services and Markets Act 2000 (Regulated Activities) (Amendment) (No 2) Order 2013, SI 2013/1881, art 10(1), (17)(f), (for transitional provisions see see Pt 8 thereof at **[2.1007]** *et seq).)*

PART IV
THE VOLUNTARY JURISDICTION

Introduction

[1.1597]
17. This Part of this Schedule applies only in relation to the voluntary jurisdiction.

Terms of reference to the scheme

18. (1) Complaints are to be dealt with and determined under the voluntary jurisdiction on standard terms fixed by the scheme operator with the approval of the [FCA].

(2) Different standard terms may be fixed with respect to different matters or in relation to different cases.

(3) The standard terms may, in particular—
   (a) require the making of payments to the scheme operator by participants in the scheme of such amounts, and at such times, as may be determined by the scheme operator;
   (b) make provision as to the award of costs on the determination of a complaint.

(4) The scheme operator may not vary any of the standard terms or add or remove terms without the approval of the [FCA].

(5) The standard terms may include provision to the effect that (unless acting in bad faith) none of the following is to be liable in damages for anything done or omitted in the discharge or purported discharge of functions in connection with the voluntary jurisdiction—
   (a) the scheme operator;
   (b) any member of its governing body;
   (c) any member of its staff;
   (d) any person acting as an ombudsman for the purposes of the scheme.

Delegation by and to other schemes

19. (1) The scheme operator may make arrangements with a relevant body—
   (a) for the exercise by that body of any part of the voluntary jurisdiction of the ombudsman scheme on behalf of the scheme; or
   (b) for the exercise by the scheme of any function of that body as if it were part of the voluntary jurisdiction of the scheme.

(2) A "relevant body" is one which the scheme operator is satisfied—
   (a) is responsible for the operation of a broadly comparable scheme (whether or not established by statute) for the resolution of disputes; and
   (b) in the case of arrangements under sub-paragraph (1)(a), will exercise the jurisdiction in question in a way compatible with the requirements imposed by or under this Act in relation to complaints of the kind concerned.

(3) Such arrangements require the approval of the [FCA].

Voluntary jurisdiction rules: procedure

20. (1) If the scheme operator makes voluntary jurisdiction rules, it must give a copy to the [FCA] without delay.

(2) If the scheme operator revokes any such rules, it must give written notice to the [FCA] without delay.

(3) The power to make voluntary jurisdiction rules is exercisable in writing.

(4) Immediately after making voluntary jurisdiction rules, the scheme operator must arrange for them to be printed and made available to the public.

(5) The scheme operator may charge a reasonable fee for providing a person with a copy of any voluntary jurisdiction rules.

Verification of the rules

21. (1) The production of a printed copy of voluntary jurisdiction rules purporting to be made by the scheme operator—
   (a) on which is endorsed a certificate signed by a member of the scheme operator's staff authorised by the scheme operator for that purpose, and
   (b) which contains the required statements,
is evidence (or in Scotland sufficient evidence) of the facts stated in the certificate.

(2) The required statements are—
   (a) that the rules were made by the scheme operator;
   (b) that the copy is a true copy of the rules; and
   (c) that on a specified date the rules were made available to the public in accordance with paragraph 20(4).

(3) A certificate purporting to be signed as mentioned in sub-paragraph (1) is to be taken to have been duly signed unless the contrary is shown.

Consultation

22. (1) If the scheme operator proposes to make voluntary jurisdiction rules, it must publish a draft of the proposed rules in the way appearing to it to be best calculated to bring them to the attention of the public.

(2) The draft must be accompanied by—
  (a) an explanation of the proposed rules; and
  (b) a statement that representations about the proposals may be made to the scheme operator within a specified time.

(3) Before making any voluntary jurisdiction rules, the scheme operator must have regard to any representations made to it in accordance with sub-paragraph (2)(b).

(4) If voluntary jurisdiction rules made by the scheme operator differ from the draft published under sub-paragraph (1) in a way which the scheme operator considers significant, the scheme operator must publish a statement of the difference.

NOTES

Paras 18–20: word "FCA" in square brackets (in each place that it occurs) substituted by the Financial Services Act 2012, s 39, Sch 11, paras 13, 28–30.

LIMITED LIABILITY PARTNERSHIPS ACT 2000

(2000 c 12)

ARRANGEMENT OF SECTIONS

Introductory

An Act to make provision for limited liability partnerships

                       [20 July 2000]

Introductory

[1.1598]
1 Limited liability partnerships
(1) There shall be a new form of legal entity to be known as a limited liability partnership.

(2) A limited liability partnership is a body corporate (with legal personality separate from that of its members) which is formed by being incorporated under this Act; and—

    (a) in the following provisions of this Act (except in the phrase "oversea limited liability partnership"), and

    (b) in any other enactment (except where provision is made to the contrary or the context otherwise requires),

references to a limited liability partnership are to such a body corporate.

(3) A limited liability partnership has unlimited capacity.

(4) The members of a limited liability partnership have such liability to contribute to its assets in the event of its being wound up as is provided for by virtue of this Act.

(5) Accordingly, except as far as otherwise provided by this Act or any other enactment, the law relating to partnerships does not apply to a limited liability partnership.

(6) The Schedule (which makes provision about the names and registered offices of limited liability partnerships) has effect.

Incorporation

[1.1599]
2 Incorporation document etc

(1) For a limited liability partnership to be incorporated—

    (a) two or more persons associated for carrying on a lawful business with a view to profit must have subscribed their names to an incorporation document,

    [(b) the incorporation document or a copy of it must have been delivered to the registrar, and]

    (c) there must have been so delivered a statement . . . made by either a solicitor engaged in the formation of the limited liability partnership or anyone who subscribed his name to the incorporation document, that the requirement imposed by paragraph (a) has been complied with.

(2) The incorporation document must—

    (a) . . .

    (b) state the name of the limited liability partnership,

    (c) state whether the registered office of the limited liability partnership is to be situated in England and Wales, in Wales[, in Scotland or in Northern Ireland],

    (d) state the address of that registered office,

    [(e) give the required particulars of each of the persons who are to be members of the limited liability partnership on incorporation, and]

    (f) either specify which of those persons are to be designated members or state that every person who from time to time is a member of the limited liability partnership is a designated member.

[(2ZA) The required particulars mentioned in subsection (2)(e) are the particulars required to be stated in the LLP's register of members and register of members' residential addresses.]

[(2A), (2B) . . .]

(3) If a person makes a false statement under subsection (1)(c) which he—

    (a) knows to be false, or

    (b) does not believe to be true,

he commits an offence.

(4) A person guilty of an offence under subsection (3) is liable—

    (a) on summary conviction, to imprisonment for a period not exceeding six months or a fine not exceeding the statutory maximum, or to both, or

    (b) on conviction on indictment, to imprisonment for a period not exceeding two years or a fine, or to both.

NOTES
Sub-s (1): para (b) substituted and words omitted from para (c) repealed by the Limited Liability Partnerships (Application of Companies Act 2006) Regulations 2009, SI 2009/1804, reg 85, Sch 3, Pt 1, para 1(1)–(3), except in relation to an obligation arising before 1 October 2009 to deliver a document to the registrar.

Sub-s (2): para (a) repealed, words in square brackets in para (c), and para (e) substituted by SI 2009/1804, reg 85, Sch 3, Pt 1, para 1(1), (4), except in relation to an obligation arising before 1 October 2009 to deliver a document to the registrar.

Sub-s (2ZA): inserted by SI 2009/1804, reg 85, Sch 3, Pt 1, para 1(1), (5), except in relation to an obligation arising before 1 October 2009 to deliver a document to the registrar.

Sub-ss (2A), (2B): inserted by the Limited Liability Partnerships (Particulars of Usual Residential Address) (Confidentiality Orders) Regulations 2002, SI 2002/915, reg 16, Sch 2, para 1; repealed by SI 2009/1804, reg 85, Sch 3, Pt 1, para 1(1), (6), except in relation to an obligation arising before 1 October 2009 to deliver a document to the registrar.

[1.1600]
3 Incorporation by registration

[(1) The registrar, if satisfied that the requirements of section 2 are complied with, shall—

    (a) register the documents delivered under that section, and

    (b) give a certificate that the limited liability partnership is incorporated.

(1A) The certificate must state—

    (a) the name and registered number of the limited liability partnership,

    (b) the date of its incorporation, and

(c)   whether the limited liability partnership's registered office is situated in England and Wales (or in Wales), in Scotland or in Northern Ireland.]

(2)   The registrar may accept the statement delivered under paragraph (c) of subsection (1) of section 2 as sufficient evidence that the requirement imposed by paragraph (a) of that subsection has been complied with.

(3)   The certificate shall either be signed by the registrar or be authenticated by his official seal.

(4)   The certificate is conclusive evidence that the requirements of section 2 are complied with and that the limited liability partnership is incorporated by the name specified in the incorporation document.

NOTES

Sub-ss (1), (1A): substituted for original sub-s (1) by the Limited Liability Partnerships (Application of Companies Act 2006) Regulations 2009, SI 2009/1804, reg 85, Sch 3, Pt 1, para 2, except in relation to an obligation arising before 1 October 2009 to deliver a document to the registrar.

Membership

[1.1601]
4   Members
(1)   On the incorporation of a limited liability partnership its members are the persons who subscribed their names to the incorporation document (other than any who have died or been dissolved).

(2)   Any other person may become a member of a limited liability partnership by and in accordance with an agreement with the existing members.

(3)   A person may cease to be a member of a limited liability partnership (as well as by death or dissolution) in accordance with an agreement with the other members or, in the absence of agreement with the other members as to cessation of membership, by giving reasonable notice to the other members.

(4)   A member of a limited liability partnership shall not be regarded for any purpose as employed by the limited liability partnership unless, if he and the other members were partners in a partnership, he would be regarded for that purpose as employed by the partnership.

[1.1602]
[4A   Minimum membership for carrying on business
(1)   This section applies where a limited liability partnership carries on business without having at least two members, and does so for more than 6 months.

(2)   A person who, for the whole or any part of the period that it so carries on business after those 6 months—

(a)   is a member of the limited liability partnership, and

(b)   knows that it is carrying on business with only one member,

is liable (jointly and severally with the limited liability partnership) for the payment of the limited liability partnership's debts contracted during the period or, as the case may be, that part of it.]

NOTES

Inserted by the Limited Liability Partnerships (Application of Companies Act 2006) Regulations 2009, SI 2009/1804, reg 85, Sch 3, Pt 1, para 3, except in relation to an obligation arising before 1 October 2009 to deliver a document to the registrar.

[1.1603]
5   Relationship of members etc
(1)   Except as far as otherwise provided by this Act or any other enactment, the mutual rights and duties of the members of a limited liability partnership, and the mutual rights and duties of a limited liability partnership and its members, shall be governed—

(a)   by agreement between the members, or between the limited liability partnership and its members, or

(b)   in the absence of agreement as to any matter, by any provision made in relation to that matter by regulations under section 15(c).

(2)   An agreement made before the incorporation of a limited liability partnership between the persons who subscribe their names to the incorporation document may impose obligations on the limited liability partnership (to take effect at any time after its incorporation).

[1.1604]
6   Members as agents
(1)   Every member of a limited liability partnership is the agent of the limited liability partnership.

(2)   But a limited liability partnership is not bound by anything done by a member in dealing with a person if—

(a)   the member in fact has no authority to act for the limited liability partnership by doing that thing, and

(b)   the person knows that he has no authority or does not know or believe him to be a member of the limited liability partnership.

(3)   Where a person has ceased to be a member of a limited liability partnership, the former member is to be regarded (in relation to any person dealing with the limited liability partnership) as still being a member of the limited liability partnership unless—

(a)   the person has notice that the former member has ceased to be a member of the limited liability partnership, or

(b)   notice that the former member has ceased to be a member of the limited liability partnership has been delivered to the registrar.

(4)   Where a member of a limited liability partnership is liable to any person (other than another member of the limited liability partnership) as a result of a wrongful act or omission of his in the course of the business of the limited liability partnership or with its authority, the limited liability partnership is liable to the same extent as the member.

[1.1605]
7   Ex-members
(1)   This section applies where a member of a limited liability partnership has either ceased to be a member or—

(a)   has died,

(b)   has become bankrupt or had his estate sequestrated or has been wound up,

(c)   has granted a trust deed for the benefit of his creditors, or

(d)   has assigned the whole or any part of his share in the limited liability partnership (absolutely or by way of charge or security).

(2)   In such an event the former member or—

(a)   his personal representative,

(b)   his trustee in bankruptcy or permanent or interim trustee (within the meaning of the Bankruptcy (Scotland) Act 1985) or liquidator,

(c)   his trustee under the trust deed for the benefit of his creditors, or

(d)   his assignee,

may not interfere in the management or administration of any business or affairs of the limited liability partnership.

(3)   But subsection (2) does not affect any right to receive an amount from the limited liability partnership in that event.

[1.1606]
8   Designated members
(1)   If the incorporation document specifies who are to be designated members—

(a)   they are designated members on incorporation, and

(b)   any member may become a designated member by and in accordance with an agreement with the other members,

and a member may cease to be a designated member in accordance with an agreement with the other members.

(2)   But if there would otherwise be no designated members, or only one, every member is a designated member.

(3)   If the incorporation document states that every person who from time to time is a member of the limited liability partnership is a designated member, every member is a designated member.

(4)   A limited liability partnership may at any time deliver to the registrar—

(a)   notice that specified members are to be designated members, or

(b)   notice that every person who from time to time is a member of the limited liability partnership is a designated member,

and, once it is delivered, subsection (1) (apart from paragraph (a)) and subsection (2), or subsection (3), shall have effect as if that were stated in the incorporation document.

(5)   . . .

(6)   A person ceases to be a designated member if he ceases to be a member.

NOTES
Sub-s (5): repealed by the Limited Liability Partnerships (Application of Companies Act 2006) Regulations 2009, SI 2009/1804, reg 85, Sch 3, Pt 1, para 4, except in relation to an obligation arising before 1 October 2009 to deliver a document to the registrar.

[1.1607]
9   Registration of membership changes
(1)   A limited liability partnership must ensure that—

(a)   where a person becomes or ceases to be a member or designated member, notice is delivered to the registrar within fourteen days, and

(b)   where there is any change in the [particulars contained in its register of members or its register of members' residential addresses], notice is delivered to the registrar within [14 days].

(2)   Where all the members from time to time of a limited liability partnership are designated members, subsection (1)(a) does not require notice that a person has become or ceased to be a designated member as well as a member.

[(3)   A notice delivered under subsection (1) that relates to a person becoming a member or designated member must contain—
  (a)   a statement that the member or designated member consents to acting in that capacity, and
  (b)   in the case of a person becoming a member, a statement of the particulars of the new member that are required to be included in the limited liability partnership's register of members and its register of residential addresses.]
[(3ZA)   Where—
  (a)   a limited liability partnership gives notice of a change of a member's service address as stated in its register of members, and
  (b)   the notice is not accompanied by notice of any resulting change in the particulars contained in its register of members' residential addresses,
the notice must be accompanied by a statement that no such change is required.]
[(3A), (3B)   . . .]
(4)   If a limited liability partnership fails to comply with [this section], the partnership and every designated member commits an offence.
(5)   But it is a defence for a designated member charged with an offence under subsection (4) to prove that he took all reasonable steps for securing that [this section] was complied with.
(6)   A person guilty of an offence under subsection (4) is liable on summary conviction to a fine not exceeding level 5 on the standard scale.

NOTES

Sub-s (1): words in square brackets substituted by the Limited Liability Partnerships (Application of Companies Act 2006) Regulations 2009, SI 2009/1804, reg 85, Sch 3, Pt 1, para 5(1), (2), except in relation to an obligation arising before 1 October 2009 to deliver a document to the registrar.

Sub-s (3): substituted by SI 2009/1804, reg 85, Sch 3, Pt 1, para 5(1), (3), except in relation to an obligation arising before 1 October 2009 to deliver a document to the registrar.

Sub-s (3ZA): inserted by SI 2009/1804, reg 85, Sch 3, Pt 1, para 5(1), (4), except in relation to an obligation arising before 1 October 2009 to deliver a document to the registrar.

Sub-ss (3A), (3B): inserted by the Limited Liability Partnerships (Particulars of Usual Residential Address) (Confidentiality Orders) Regulations 2002, SI 2002/915, reg 16, Sch 2, para 1; repealed by SI 2009/1804, reg 85, Sch 3, Pt 1, para 5(1), (5), except in relation to an obligation arising before 1 October 2009 to deliver a document to the registrar.

Sub-ss (4), (5): words in square brackets substituted by SI 2009/1804, reg 85, Sch 3, Pt 1, para 5(1), (6), except in relation to an obligation arising before 1 October 2009 to deliver a document to the registrar.

Taxation

10, 11   (*Outside the scope of this work.*)

[1.1608]
12   Stamp duty
(1)   Stamp duty shall not be chargeable on an instrument by which property is conveyed or transferred by a person to a limited liability partnership in connection with its incorporation within the period of one year beginning with the date of incorporation if the following two conditions are satisfied.
(2)   The first condition is that at the relevant time the person—
  (a)   is a partner in a partnership comprised of all the persons who are or are to be members of the limited liability partnership (and no-one else), or
  (b)   holds the property conveyed or transferred as nominee or bare trustee for one or more of the partners in such a partnership.
(3)   The second condition is that—
  (a)   the proportions of the property conveyed or transferred to which the persons mentioned in subsection (2)(a) are entitled immediately after the conveyance or transfer are the same as those to which they were entitled at the relevant time, or
  (b)   none of the differences in those proportions has arisen as part of a scheme or arrangement of which the main purpose, or one of the main purposes, is avoidance of liability to any duty or tax.
(4)   For the purposes of subsection (2) a person holds property as bare trustee for a partner if the partner has the exclusive right (subject only to satisfying any outstanding charge, lien or other right of the trustee to resort to the property for payment of duty, taxes, costs or other outgoings) to direct how the property shall be dealt with.
(5)   In this section "the relevant time" means—
  (a)   if the person who conveyed or transferred the property to the limited liability partnership acquired the property after its incorporation, immediately after he acquired the property, and
  (b)   in any other case, immediately before its incorporation.
(6)   An instrument in respect of which stamp duty is not chargeable by virtue of subsection (1) shall not be taken to be duly stamped unless—
  (a)   it has, in accordance with section 12 of the Stamp Act 1891, been stamped with a particular stamp denoting that it is not chargeable with any duty or that it is duly stamped, or
  (b)   it is stamped with the duty to which it would be liable apart from that subsection.

13   (*Outside the scope of this work.*)

Regulations

[1.1609]
14 Insolvency and winding up
(1) Regulations shall make provision about the insolvency and winding up of limited liability partnerships by applying or incorporating, with such modifications as appear appropriate[—

(a) in relation to a limited liability partnership registered in Great Britain, Parts 1 to 4, 6 and 7 of the Insolvency Act 1986;

(b) in relation to a limited liability partnership registered in Northern Ireland, Parts 2 to 5 and 7 of the Insolvency (Northern Ireland) Order 1989, and so much of Part 1 of that Order as applies for the purposes of those Parts].

(2) Regulations may make other provision about the insolvency and winding up of limited liability partnerships, and provision about the insolvency and winding up of oversea limited liability partnerships, by—

(a) applying or incorporating, with such modifications as appear appropriate, any law relating to the insolvency or winding up of companies or other corporations which would not otherwise have effect in relation to them, or

(b) providing for any law relating to the insolvency or winding up of companies or other corporations which would otherwise have effect in relation to them not to apply to them or to apply to them with such modifications as appear appropriate.

(3) In this Act "oversea limited liability partnership" means a body incorporated or otherwise established outside [the United Kingdom] and having such connection with [the United Kingdom], and such other features, as regulations may prescribe.

NOTES
Sub-s (1): words in square brackets substituted by the Limited Liability Partnerships (Application of Companies Act 2006) Regulations 2009, SI 2009/1804, reg 85, Sch 3, Pt 1, para 6(1), (2), except in relation to an obligation arising before 1 October 2009 to deliver a document to the registrar.

Sub-s (3): words in square brackets substituted by SI 2009/1804, reg 85, Sch 3, Pt 1, para 6(1), (3), except in relation to an obligation arising before 1 October 2009 to deliver a document to the registrar.

Regulations: the Limited Liability Partnerships Regulations 2001, SI 2001/1090.

[1.1610]
15 Application of company law etc
Regulations may make provision about limited liability partnerships and oversea limited liability partnerships (not being provision about insolvency or winding up) by—

(a) applying or incorporating, with such modifications as appear appropriate, any law relating to companies or other corporations which would not otherwise have effect in relation to them,

(b) providing for any law relating to companies or other corporations which would otherwise have effect in relation to them not to apply to them or to apply to them with such modifications as appear appropriate, or

(c) applying or incorporating, with such modifications as appear appropriate, any law relating to partnerships.

NOTES
Regulations: the Limited Liability Partnerships Regulations 2001, SI 2001/1090; the Companies (Registrar, Languages and Trading Disclosures) Regulations 2006, SI 2006/3429; the Companies (Late Filing Penalties) and Limited Liability Partnerships (Filing Periods and Late Filing Penalties) Regulations 2008, SI 2008/497; the Limited Liability Partnerships (Accounts and Audit) (Application of Companies Act 2006) Regulations 2008, SI 2008/1911; the Small Limited Liability Partnerships (Accounts) Regulations 2008, SI 2008/1912; the Large and Medium-sized Limited Liability Partnerships (Accounts) Regulations 2008, SI 2008/1913; the Limited Liability Partnerships (Application of Companies Act 2006) Regulations 2009, SI 2009/1804; the Limited Liability Partnerships (Amendment) Regulations 2009, SI 2009/1833; the Company, Limited Liability Partnership and Business Names (Miscellaneous Provisions) (Amendment) Regulations 2009, SI 2009/2404; the Companies Act 2006 and Limited Liability Partnerships (Transitional Provisions and Savings) (Amendment) Regulations 2009, SI 2009/2476; the Limited Liability Partnerships (Amendment) (No 2) Regulations 2009, SI 2009/2995; the Companies and Limited Liability Partnerships (Accounts and Audit Exemptions and Change of Accounting Framework) Regulations 2012, SI 2012/2301; the Limited Liability Partnerships (Application of Companies Act 2006) (Amendment) Regulations 2013, SI 2013/618; the Companies and Partnerships (Accounts and Audit) Regulations 2013, SI 2013/2005; the Reports on Payments to Governments Regulations 2014, SI 2014/3209.

[1.1611]
16 Consequential amendments
(1) Regulations may make in any enactment such amendments or repeals as appear appropriate in consequence of this Act or regulations made under it.
(2) The regulations may, in particular, make amendments and repeals affecting companies or other corporations or partnerships.

NOTES
Regulations: the Limited Liability Partnerships Regulations 2001, SI 2001/1090.

[1.1612]
17 General
(1) In this Act "regulations" means regulations made by the Secretary of State by statutory instrument.
(2) Regulations under this Act may in particular—
  (a) make provisions for dealing with non-compliance with any of the regulations (including the creation of criminal offences),
  (b) impose fees (which shall be paid into the Consolidated Fund), and
  (c) provide for the exercise of functions by persons prescribed by the regulations.
(3) Regulations under this Act may—
  (a) contain any appropriate consequential, incidental, supplementary or transitional provisions or savings, and
  (b) make different provision for different purposes.
(4) No regulations to which this subsection applies shall be made unless a draft of the statutory instrument containing the regulations (whether or not together with other provisions) has been laid before, and approved by a resolution of, each House of Parliament.
(5) Subsection (4) applies to—
  (a) regulations under section 14(2) not consisting entirely of the application or incorporation (with or without modifications) of provisions contained in or made under the Insolvency Act 1986 [or the Insolvency (Northern Ireland) Order 1989],
  [(b) regulations under section 15 not consisting entirely of the application or incorporation (with or without modifications) of provisions contained in or made under the following provisions of the Companies Act 2006 (c 46)—
    Part 4 (a company's capacity and related matters);
    Part 5 (a company's name);
    Part 6 (a company's registered office);
    Chapters 1 and 8 of Part 10 (register of directors);
    Part 15 (accounts and reports);
    Part 16 (audit);
    Part 19 (debentures);
    Part 21 (certification and transfer of securities);
    Part 24 (a company's annual return);
    Part 25 (company charges);
    Part 26 (arrangements and reconstructions);
    Part 29 (fraudulent trading);
    Part 30 (protection of members against unfair prejudice);
    Part 31 (dissolution and restoration to the register);
    Part 35 (the registrar of companies);
    Part 36 (offences under the Companies Acts);
    Part 37 (supplementary provisions);
    Part 38 (interpretation),]
  (c) regulations under section 14 or 15 making provision about oversea limited liability partnerships, and
  (d) regulations under section 16.
(6) A statutory instrument containing regulations under this Act shall (unless a draft of it has been approved by a resolution of each House of Parliament) be subject to annulment in pursuance of a resolution of either House of Parliament.

NOTES
Sub-s (5): words in square brackets in para (a) inserted and para (b) substituted by the Limited Liability Partnerships (Application of Companies Act 2006) Regulations 2009, SI 2009/1804, reg 85, Sch 3, Pt 1, para 7, except in relation to an obligation arising before 1 October 2009 to deliver a document to the registrar.
Regulations: the Companies (Registrar, Languages and Trading Disclosures) Regulations 2006, SI 2006/3429; the Limited Liability Partnerships (Accounts and Audit) (Application of Companies Act 2006) Regulations 2008, SI 2008/1911; the Small Limited Liability Partnerships (Accounts) Regulations 2008, SI 2008/1912; the Limited Liability Partnerships (Application of Companies Act 2006) Regulations 2009, SI 2009/1804.

Supplementary

[1.1613]
18 Interpretation
In this Act—
  . . .
  "business" includes every trade, profession and occupation,
  "designated member" shall be construed in accordance with section 8,
  "enactment" includes subordinate legislation (within the meaning of the Interpretation Act 1978),
  "incorporation document" shall be construed in accordance with section 2,
  "limited liability partnership" has the meaning given by section 1(2),
  "member" shall be construed in accordance with section 4,
  "modifications" includes additions and omissions,

"name", in relation to a member of a limited liability partnership, means—

    (a)   if an individual, his forename and surname (or, in the case of a peer or other person usually known by a title, his title instead of or in addition to either or both his forename and surname), and

    (b)   if a corporation or Scottish firm, its corporate or firm name,

"oversea limited liability partnership" has the meaning given by section 14(3),

["the registrar" means—

    (a)   if the registered office of the limited liability partnership is, or is to be, in England and Wales (or Wales), the registrar of companies for England and Wales,

    (b)   if the registered office of the limited liability partnership is, or is to be, in Scotland, the registrar of companies for Scotland, and

    (c)   if the registered office of the limited liability partnership is, or is to be, in Northern Ireland, the registrar of companies for Northern Ireland;] and

"regulations" has the meaning given by section 17(1).

NOTES

Definition "address" (omitted) repealed and definition "the registrar" substituted by the Limited Liability Partnerships (Application of Companies Act 2006) Regulations 2009, SI 2009/1804, reg 85, Sch 3, Pt 1, para 8, except in relation to an obligation arising before 1 October 2009 to deliver a document to the registrar.

[1.1614]
19 Commencement, extent and short title

(1) The preceding provisions of this Act shall come into force on such day as the Secretary of State may by order made by statutory instrument appoint; and different days may be appointed for different purposes.

(2) The Secretary of State may by order made by statutory instrument make any transitional provisions and savings which appear appropriate in connection with the coming into force of any provision of this Act.

(3) For the purposes of the Scotland Act 1998 this Act shall be taken to be a pre-commencement enactment within the meaning of that Act.

[(4) This Act extends to the whole of the United Kingdom.]

(5) This Act may be cited as the Limited Liability Partnerships Act 2000.

NOTES

Sub-s (4): substituted by the Limited Liability Partnerships (Application of Companies Act 2006) Regulations 2009, SI 2009/1804, reg 85, Sch 3, Pt 1, para 9, except in relation to an obligation arising before 1 October 2009 to deliver a document to the registrar.

Orders: the Limited Liability Partnerships Act 2000 (Commencement) Order 2000, SI 2000/3316.

SCHEDULE
NAMES AND REGISTERED OFFICES

Section 1

PART I
NAMES

[1.1615]
1. . . .

Name to indicate status

2. (1) The name of a limited liability partnership must end with—

    (a)   the expression "limited liability partnership", or

    (b)   the abbreviation "llp" or "LLP".

(2) But if the incorporation document for a limited liability partnership states that the registered office is to be situated in Wales, its name must end with—

    (a)   one of the expressions "limited liability partnership" and "partneriaeth atebolrwydd cyfyngedig", or

    (b)   one of the abbreviations "llp", "LLP", "pac" and "PAC".

3. . . .

Change of name

4. (1) A limited liability partnership may change its name at any time.

[(2) The name of a limited liability partnership may also be changed—

    (a)   on the determination of a new name by a company names adjudicator under section 73 of the Companies Act 2006 (C 46) as applied to limited liability partnerships (powers of adjudicator on upholding objection to name);

    (b)   on the determination of a new name by the court under section 74 of the Companies Act 2006 as so applied (appeal against decision of company names adjudicator);

(c)   under section 1033 as so applied (name on restoration to the register).]

Notification of change of name

5. (1)   Where a limited liability partnership changes its name it shall deliver notice of the change to the registrar.

(2)   . . .

(3)   Where the registrar receives [notice of a change of name] he shall (unless the new name is one by which a limited liability partnership may not be registered)—
     [(a)   enter the new name on the register in place of the former name, and]
     (b)   issue a certificate of the change of name.

(4)   The change of name has effect from the date on which the certificate is issued.

Effect of change of name

6. A change of name by a limited liability partnership does not—
     (a)   affect any of its rights or duties,
     (b)   render defective any legal proceedings by or against it,
and any legal proceedings that might have been commenced or continued against it by its former name may be commenced or continued against it by its new name.

Improper use of "limited liability partnership" etc

7. (1)   If any person carries on a business under a name or title which includes as the last words—
     (a)   the expression "limited liability partnership" or "partneriaeth atebolrwydd cyfyngedig", or
     (b)   any contraction or imitation of either of those expressions,
that person, unless a limited liability partnership or oversea limited liability partnership, commits an offence.

(2)   A person guilty of an offence under sub-paragraph (1) is liable on summary conviction to a fine not exceeding level 3 on the standard scale.

8.   . . .

NOTES

Para 1: repealed by the Companies Act 2006, s 1295, Sch 16.

Para 3: repealed by the Limited Liability Partnerships (Application of Companies Act 2006) Regulations 2009, SI 2009/1804, reg 85, Sch 3, Pt 1, para 10(1), (2), except in relation to an obligation arising before 1 October 2009 to deliver a document to the registrar.

Para 4: sub-para (2) substituted for original sub-paras (2)–(9) by SI 2009/1804, reg 85, Sch 3, Pt 1, para 10(1), (3), except in relation to an obligation arising before 1 October 2009 to deliver a document to the registrar.

Para 5: sub-para (2) repealed and words in square brackets in sub-para (3) substituted by SI 2009/1804, reg 85, Sch 3, Pt 1, para 10(1), (4), except in relation to an obligation arising before 1 October 2009 to deliver a document to the registrar.

Para 8: repealed by SI 2009/1804, reg 85, Sch 3, Pt 1, para 10(1), (5), except in relation to an obligation arising before 1 October 2009 to deliver a document to the registrar.

(*Pt II repealed by the Limited Liability Partnerships (Application of Companies Act 2006) Regulations 2009, SI 2009/1804, reg 85, Sch 3, Pt 1, para 10(1), (6), except in relation to an obligation arising before 1 October 2009 to deliver a document to the registrar.*)

REGULATION OF INVESTIGATORY POWERS ACT 2000

(2000 c 23)

ARRANGEMENT OF SECTIONS

PART I
COMMUNICATIONS

CHAPTER I
INTERCEPTION

Unlawful and authorised interception

PART IV

SCRUTINY ETC OF INVESTIGATORY POWERS AND OF THE FUNCTIONS
OF THE INTELLIGENCE SERVICES

Codes of practice

PART V

MISCELLANEOUS AND SUPPLEMENTAL

Supplemental

SCHEDULES

An Act to make provision for and about the interception of communications, the acquisition and disclosure of data relating to communications, the carrying out of surveillance, the use of covert human intelligence sources and the acquisition of the means by which electronic data protected by encryption or passwords may be decrypted or accessed; to provide for Commissioners and a tribunal with functions and jurisdiction in relation to those matters, to entries on and interferences with property or with wireless telegraphy and to the carrying out of their functions by the Security Service, the Secret Intelligence Service and the Government Communications Headquarters; and for connected purposes

[28 July 2000]

PART I

COMMUNICATIONS

CHAPTER I

INTERCEPTION

Unlawful and authorised interception

[1.1616]

1   Unlawful interception

(1)   It shall be an offence for a person intentionally and without lawful authority to intercept, at any place in the United Kingdom, any communication in the course of its transmission by means of—

(a)   a public postal service; or

(b)   a public telecommunication system.

[(1A)   The Interception of Communications Commissioner may serve a monetary penalty notice on a person if the Commissioner—

(a)   considers that the person—

(i)   has without lawful authority intercepted, at any place in the United Kingdom, any communication in the course of its transmission by means of a public telecommunication system, and

(ii)   was not, at the time of the interception, making an attempt to act in accordance with an interception warrant which might, in the opinion of the Commissioner, explain the interception concerned, and

(b)   does not consider that the person has committed an offence under subsection (1).

(1B)   Schedule A1 (which makes further provision about monetary penalty notices) has effect.]

(2)   It shall be an offence for a person—

(a)   intentionally and without lawful authority, and

(b)   otherwise than in circumstances in which his conduct is excluded by subsection (6) from criminal liability under this subsection,

to intercept, at any place in the United Kingdom, any communication in the course of its transmission by means of a private telecommunication system.

(3)   Any interception of a communication which is carried out at any place in the United Kingdom by, or with the express or implied consent of, a person having the right to control the operation or the use of a private telecommunication system shall be actionable at the suit or instance of the sender or recipient, or intended recipient, of the communication if it is without lawful authority and is either—

(a)   an interception of that communication in the course of its transmission by means of that private system; or

(b)   an interception of that communication in the course of its transmission, by means of a public telecommunication system, to or from apparatus comprised in that private telecommunication system.

(4)   Where the United Kingdom is a party to an international agreement which—
   (a)   relates to the provision of mutual assistance in connection with, or in the form of, the interception of communications,
   (b)   requires the issue of a warrant, order or equivalent instrument in cases in which assistance is given, and
   (c)   is designated for the purposes of this subsection by an order made by the Secretary of State,
it shall be the duty of the Secretary of State to secure that no request for assistance in accordance with the agreement is made on behalf of a person in the United Kingdom to the competent authorities of a country or territory outside the United Kingdom except with lawful authority.
(5)   Conduct has lawful authority for the purposes of this section if, and only if—
   (a)   it is authorised by or under section 3 or 4;
   (b)   it takes place in accordance with a warrant under section 5 ("an interception warrant"); or
   (c)   it is in exercise, in relation to any stored communication, of any statutory power that is exercised (apart from this section) for the purpose of obtaining information or of taking possession of any document or other property;
and conduct (whether or not prohibited by this section) which has lawful authority for the purposes of this section by virtue of paragraph (a) or (b) shall also be taken to be lawful for all other purposes.
(6)   The circumstances in which a person makes an interception of a communication in the course of its transmission by means of a private telecommunication system are such that his conduct is excluded from criminal liability under subsection (2) if—
   (a)   he is a person with a right to control the operation or the use of the system; or
   (b)   he has the express or implied consent of such a person to make the interception.
(7)   A person who is guilty of an offence under subsection (1) or (2) shall be liable—
   (a)   on conviction on indictment, to imprisonment for a term not exceeding two years or to a fine, or to both;
   (b)   on summary conviction, to a fine not exceeding the statutory maximum.
(8)   No proceedings for any offence which is an offence by virtue of this section shall be instituted—
   (a)   in England and Wales, except by or with the consent of the Director of Public Prosecutions;
   (b)   in Northern Ireland, except by or with the consent of the Director of Public Prosecutions for Northern Ireland.

NOTES
Sub-ss (1A), (1B): inserted by the Regulation of Investigatory Powers (Monetary Penalty Notices and Consents for Interceptions) Regulations 2011, SI 2011/1340, reg 2(1).
Orders: the Regulation of Investigatory Powers (Designation of an International Agreement) Order 2004, SI 2004/158.

[1.1617]
2   Meaning and location of "interception" etc
(1)   In this Act—
  "postal service" means any service which—
   (a)   consists in the following, or in any one or more of them, namely, the collection, sorting, conveyance, distribution and delivery (whether in the United Kingdom or elsewhere) of postal items; and
   (b)   is offered or provided as a service the main purpose of which, or one of the main purposes of which, is to make available, or to facilitate, a means of transmission from place to place of postal items containing communications;
  "private telecommunication system" means any telecommunication system which, without itself being a public telecommunication system, is a system in relation to which the following conditions are satisfied—
   (a)   it is attached, directly or indirectly and whether or not for the purposes of the communication in question, to a public telecommunication system; and
   (b)   there is apparatus comprised in the system which is both located in the United Kingdom and used (with or without other apparatus) for making the attachment to the public telecommunication system;
  "public postal service" means any postal service which is offered or provided to, or to a substantial section of, the public in any one or more parts of the United Kingdom;
  "public telecommunications service" means any telecommunications service which is offered or provided to, or to a substantial section of, the public in any one or more parts of the United Kingdom;
  "public telecommunication system" means any such parts of a telecommunication system by means of which any public telecommunications service is provided as are located in the United Kingdom;
  "telecommunications service" means any service that consists in the provision of access to, and of facilities for making use of, any telecommunication system (whether or not one provided by the person providing the service); and

"telecommunication system" means any system (including the apparatus comprised in it) which exists (whether wholly or partly in the United Kingdom or elsewhere) for the purpose of facilitating the transmission of communications by any means involving the use of electrical or electro-magnetic energy.

(2)   For the purposes of this Act, but subject to the following provisions of this section, a person intercepts a communication in the course of its transmission by means of a telecommunication system if, and only if, he—

(a)   so modifies or interferes with the system, or its operation,

(b)   so monitors transmissions made by means of the system, or

(c)   so monitors transmissions made by wireless telegraphy to or from apparatus comprised in the system,

as to make some or all of the contents of the communication available, while being transmitted, to a person other than the sender or intended recipient of the communication.

(3)   References in this Act to the interception of a communication do not include references to the interception of any communication broadcast for general reception.

(4)   For the purposes of this Act the interception of a communication takes place in the United Kingdom if, and only if, the modification, interference or monitoring or, in the case of a postal item, the interception is effected by conduct within the United Kingdom and the communication is either—

(a)   intercepted in the course of its transmission by means of a public postal service or public telecommunication system; or

(b)   intercepted in the course of its transmission by means of a private telecommunication system in a case in which the sender or intended recipient of the communication is in the United Kingdom.

(5)   References in this Act to the interception of a communication in the course of its transmission by means of a postal service or telecommunication system do not include references to—

(a)   any conduct that takes place in relation only to so much of the communication as consists in any traffic data comprised in or attached to a communication (whether by the sender or otherwise) for the purposes of any postal service or telecommunication system by means of which it is being or may be transmitted; or

(b)   any such conduct, in connection with conduct falling within paragraph (a), as gives a person who is neither the sender nor the intended recipient only so much access to a communication as is necessary for the purpose of identifying traffic data so comprised or attached.

(6)   For the purposes of this section references to the modification of a telecommunication system include references to the attachment of any apparatus to, or other modification of or interference with—

(a)   any part of the system; or

(b)   any wireless telegraphy apparatus used for making transmissions to or from apparatus comprised in the system.

(7)   For the purposes of this section the times while a communication is being transmitted by means of a telecommunication system shall be taken to include any time when the system by means of which the communication is being, or has been, transmitted is used for storing it in a manner that enables the intended recipient to collect it or otherwise to have access to it.

(8)   For the purposes of this section the cases in which any contents of a communication are to be taken to be made available to a person while being transmitted shall include any case in which any of the contents of the communication, while being transmitted, are diverted or recorded so as to be available to a person subsequently.

[(8A)   For the purposes of the definition of "telecommunications service" in subsection (1), the cases in which a service is to be taken to consist in the provision of access to, and of facilities for making use of, a telecommunication system include any case where a service consists in or includes facilitating the creation, management or storage of communications transmitted, or that may be transmitted, by means of such a system.]

(9)   In this section "traffic data", in relation to any communication, means—

(a)   any data identifying, or purporting to identify, any person, apparatus or location to or from which the communication is or may be transmitted,

(b)   any data identifying or selecting, or purporting to identify or select, apparatus through which, or by means of which, the communication is or may be transmitted,

(c)   any data comprising signals for the actuation of apparatus used for the purposes of a telecommunication system for effecting (in whole or in part) the transmission of any communication, and

(d)   any data identifying the data or other data as data comprised in or attached to a particular communication,

but that expression includes data identifying a computer file or computer program access to which is obtained, or which is run, by means of the communication to the extent only that the file or program is identified by reference to the apparatus in which it is stored.

(10)   In this section—

(a) references, in relation to traffic data comprising signals for the actuation of apparatus, to a telecommunication system by means of which a communication is being or may be transmitted include references to any telecommunication system in which that apparatus is comprised; and

(b) references to traffic data being attached to a communication include references to the data and the communication being logically associated with each other;

and in this section "data", in relation to a postal item, means anything written on the outside of the item.

(11) In this section "postal item" means any letter, postcard or other such thing in writing as may be used by the sender for imparting information to the recipient, or any packet or parcel.

NOTES

Sub-s (8A): inserted by the Data Retention and Investigatory Powers Act 2014, s 5; repealed by s 8(3) of that Act, as from 31 December 2016.

[1.1618]
3 Lawful interception without an interception warrant

(1) Conduct by any person consisting in the interception of a communication is authorised by this section if the communication is one which . . . . is both—

(a) a communication sent by a person who has consented to the interception; and

(b) a communication the intended recipient of which has so consented.

(2) Conduct by any person consisting in the interception of a communication is authorised by this section if—

(a) the communication is one sent by, or intended for, a person who has consented to the interception; and

(b) surveillance by means of that interception has been authorised under Part II.

(3) Conduct consisting in the interception of a communication is authorised by this section if—

(a) it is conduct by or on behalf of a person who provides a postal service or a telecommunications service; and

(b) it takes place for purposes connected with the provision or operation of that service or with the enforcement, in relation to that service, of any enactment relating to the use of postal services or telecommunications services.

[(3A) Conduct consisting in the interception of a communication in the course of its transmission by means of a public postal service is authorised by this section if it is conduct—

(a) under section 159 of the Customs and Excise Management Act 1979 as applied by virtue of—

(i) section 105 of the Postal Services Act 2000 (power to open postal items etc); or

(ii) that section 105 and another enactment; and

(b) by an officer of Revenue and Customs.]

[(3B) Conduct consisting in the interception of a communication in the course of its transmission by means of a public postal service is authorised by this section if it is conduct under paragraph 9 of Schedule 7 to the Terrorism Act 2000 (port and border controls).]

(4) Conduct by any person consisting in the interception of a communication in the course of its transmission by means of wireless telegraphy is authorised by this section if it takes place—

(a) with the authority of a designated person under [section 48 of the Wireless Telegraphy Act 2006 (interception and disclosure of wireless telegraphy messages)]; and

(b) for purposes connected with anything falling within subsection (5).

(5) Each of the following falls within this subsection—

[(a) the grant of wireless telegraphy licences under the Wireless Telegraphy Act 2006;]

(b) the prevention or detection of anything which constitutes interference with wireless telegraphy; and

(c) the enforcement of[—

(i) any provision of Part 2 (other than Chapter 2 and sections 27 to 31) or Part 3 of that Act, or

(ii) any enactment not falling within sub-paragraph (i),]

that relates to such interference.

NOTES

Sub-s (1): words omitted repealed by the Regulation of Investigatory Powers (Monetary Penalty Notices and Consents for Interceptions) Regulations 2011, SI 2011/1340, reg 3.

Sub-s (3A): inserted by the Policing and Crime Act 2009, s 100(1).

Sub-s (3B): inserted by the Counter-Terrorism and Security Act 2015, s 43, Sch 8, para 2.

Sub-s (4): words in square brackets in para (a) substituted by the Wireless Telegraphy Act 2006, s 123, Sch 7, paras 21, 22(1), (2).

Sub-s (5): paras (a), (c)(i), (ii) substituted by the Wireless Telegraphy Act 2006, s 123, Sch 7, paras 21, 22(1), (3).

[1.1619]
4 Power to provide for lawful interception

(1) Conduct by any person ("the interceptor") consisting in the interception of a communication in the course of its transmission by means of a telecommunication system is authorised by this section if—

    (a)   the interception is carried out for the purpose of obtaining information about the communications of a person who, or who the interceptor has reasonable grounds for believing, is in a country or territory outside the United Kingdom;

    (b)   the interception relates to the use of a telecommunications service provided to persons in that country or territory which is either—

        (i)   a public telecommunications service; or

        (ii)   a telecommunications service that would be a public telecommunications service if the persons to whom it is offered or provided were members of the public in a part of the United Kingdom;

    (c)   the person who provides that service (whether the interceptor or another person) is required by the law of that country or territory to carry out, secure or facilitate the interception in question;

    (d)   the situation is one in relation to which such further conditions as may be prescribed by regulations made by the Secretary of State are required to be satisfied before conduct may be treated as authorised by virtue of this subsection; and

    (e)   the conditions so prescribed are satisfied in relation to that situation.

(2) Subject to subsection (3), the Secretary of State may by regulations authorise any such conduct described in the regulations as appears to him to constitute a legitimate practice reasonably required for the purpose, in connection with the carrying on of any business, of monitoring or keeping a record of—

    (a)   communications by means of which transactions are entered into in the course of that business; or

    (b)   other communications relating to that business or taking place in the course of its being carried on.

(3) Nothing in any regulations under subsection (2) shall authorise the interception of any communication except in the course of its transmission using apparatus or services provided by or to the person carrying on the business for use wholly or partly in connection with that business.

(4) Conduct taking place in a prison is authorised by this section if it is conduct in exercise of any power conferred by or under any rules made under section 47 of the Prison Act 1952, section 39 of the Prisons (Scotland) Act 1989 or section 13 of the Prison Act (Northern Ireland) 1953 (prison rules).

(5) Conduct taking place in any hospital premises where high security psychiatric services are provided is authorised by this section if it is conduct in pursuance of, and in accordance with, any direction given under [[section 4(3A)(a) of the National Health Service Act 2006], or section 19 or 23 of the National Health Service (Wales) Act 2006] (directions as to the carrying out of their functions by health bodies) to the body providing those services at those premises.

(6) Conduct taking place in a state hospital is authorised by this section if it is conduct in pursuance of, and in accordance with, any direction given to the State Hospitals Board for Scotland under section 2(5) of the National Health Service (Scotland) Act 1978 (regulations and directions as to the exercise of their functions by health boards) as applied by Article 5(1) of and the Schedule to The State Hospitals Board for Scotland Order 1995 (which applies certain provisions of that Act of 1978 to the State Hospitals Board).

(7) In this section references to a business include references to any activities of a government department, of any public authority or of any person or office holder on whom functions are conferred by or under any enactment.

(8) In this section—

    "government department" includes any part of the Scottish Administration, a Northern Ireland department and [the Welsh Assembly Government];

    "high security psychiatric services" has the same meaning as in [section 4 of the National Health Service Act 2006];

    "hospital premises" has the same meaning as in section 4(3) of that Act; and

    "state hospital" has the same meaning as in the National Health Service (Scotland) Act 1978.

(9) In this section "prison" means—

    (a)   any prison, young offender institution, young offenders centre or remand centre which is under the general superintendence of, or is provided by, the Secretary of State under the Prison Act 1952 or the Prison Act (Northern Ireland) 1953, or

    (b)   any prison, young offenders institution or remand centre which is under the general superintendence of the Scottish Ministers under the Prisons (Scotland) Act 1989,

and includes any contracted out prison, within the meaning of Part IV of the Criminal Justice Act 1991 or section 106(4) of the Criminal Justice and Public Order Act 1994, and any legalised police cells within the meaning of section 14 of the Prisons (Scotland) Act 1989.

NOTES

Sub-s (5): words in first (outer) pair of square brackets substituted by the National Health Service (Consequential Provisions) Act 2006, s 2, Sch 1, paras 207, 208(a); words in second (inner) pair of square brackets substituted by the Health and Social Care Act 2012, s 55(2), Sch 5, para 98.

Sub-s (8): in definition "government department" words in square brackets substituted by the Government of Wales Act 2006 (Consequential Modifications and Transitional Provisions) Order 2007, SI 2007/1388, art 3, Sch 1, paras 76(1), (2); in definition "high security psychiatric services" words in square brackets substituted by the National Health Service (Consequential Provisions) Act 2006, s 2, Sch 1, paras 207, 208(b).

Regulations: the Telecommunications (Lawful Business Practice) (Interception of Communications) Regulations 2000, SI 2000/2699 at **[2.165]**; the Regulation of Investigatory Powers (Conditions for the Lawful Interception of Persons outside the United Kingdom) Regulations 2004, SI 2004/157.

5–56   (Ss 5–25, ss 26–56 (Pts II, III) *outside the scope of this work.*)

PART IV
SCRUTINY ETC OF INVESTIGATORY POWERS AND OF THE FUNCTIONS OF THE INTELLIGENCE SERVICES

57–70   (*Outside the scope of this work.*)

Codes of practice

[1.1620]
71 Issue and revision of codes of practice
(1)   The Secretary of State shall issue one or more codes of practice relating to the exercise and performance of the powers and duties mentioned in subsection (2).
(2)   Those powers and duties are those (excluding any power to make subordinate legislation [and subject to [subsections (10) and (11)]]) that are conferred or imposed otherwise than on the Surveillance Commissioners [or the relevant judicial authority (within the meaning of section 23A or 32A)] by or under—
   (a)   Parts I to III of this Act;
   (b)   section 5 of the Intelligence Services Act 1994 (warrants for interference with property or wireless telegraphy for the purposes of the intelligence services); . . .
   (c)   Part III of the Police Act 1997 (authorisation by the police or [Her Majesty's Revenue and Customs] of interference with property or wireless telegraphy).
   [(d)   section 1(1) to (6) of the Data Retention and Investigatory Powers Act 2014.]
[(2A)   A code of practice under subsection (1) that relates (expressly or otherwise) to the exercise and performance, in connection with the prevention or detection of serious crime, of powers and duties conferred or imposed by or under Part 1 of this Act—
   (a)   shall include provision designed to protect the public interest in the confidentiality of journalistic sources;
   (b)   shall not be issued unless the Secretary of State has first consulted the Interception of Communications Commissioner and considered any relevant report made to the Prime Minister under section 58.]
(3)   Before issuing a code of practice under subsection (1), the Secretary of State shall—
   (a)   prepare and publish a draft of that code; and
   (b)   consider any representations made to him about the draft;
and the Secretary of State may incorporate in the code finally issued any modifications made by him to the draft after its publication.
(4)   The Secretary of State shall lay before both Houses of Parliament every draft code of practice prepared and published by him under this section.
(5)   A code of practice issued by the Secretary of State under this section shall not be brought into force except in accordance with an order made by the Secretary of State.
(6)   An order under subsection (5) may contain such transitional provisions and savings as appear to the Secretary of State to be necessary or expedient in connection with the bringing into force of the code brought into force by that order.
(7)   The Secretary of State may from time to time—
   (a)   revise the whole or any part of a code issued under this section; and
   (b)   issue the revised code.
(8)   Subsections (3) to (6) shall apply (with appropriate modifications) in relation to the issue of any revised code under this section as they apply in relation to the first issue of such a code.
(9)   The Secretary of State shall not make an order containing provision for any of the purposes of this section unless a draft of the order has been laid before Parliament and approved by a resolution of each House.
[(10)   A code of practice under this section may not relate to any matter which is to be dealt with by guidance of the Interception of Communications Commissioner by virtue of paragraph 7 of Schedule A1.]
[(11)   The reference in subsection (2) to powers and duties conferred or imposed by or under section 1(1) to (6) of the Data Retention and Investigatory Powers Act 2014 does not include a reference to any such powers and duties which are conferred or imposed on the Secretary of State.]

NOTES

Sub-s (2): words in first (outer) pair of square brackets inserted by the Regulation of Investigatory Powers (Monetary Penalty Notices and Consents for Interceptions) Regulations 2011, SI 2011/1340, reg 2(2); words in second (inner) pair of square brackets substituted, word omitted from para (b) repealed and para (d) added, by the Data Retention Regulations 2014, SI 2014/2042, reg 10(1), (2); words in third pair of square brackets inserted by the Protection of Freedoms Act 2012, s 115(1), Sch 9, Pt 3, paras 6, 14; words in square brackets in para (c) substituted by the Serious Crime Act 2007, s 88, Sch 12, paras 5, 25.

Sub-s (2A): inserted by the Serious Crime Act 2015, s 83, for transitional and saving provisions see s 86(12) thereof.

Sub-s (10): added by SI 2011/1340, reg 2(3).

Sub-s (11): added by SI 2014/2042, reg 10(1), (3).

Orders: the Regulation of Investigatory Powers (Interception of Communications: Code of Practice) Order 2002, SI 2002/1693; the Regulation of Investigatory Powers (Covert Human Intelligence Sources: Code of Practice) Order 2002, SI 2002/1932; the Regulation of Investigatory Powers (Covert Surveillance: Code of Practice) Order 2002, SI 2002/1933; the Regulation of Investigatory Powers (Acquisition and Disclosure of Communications Data: Code of Practice) Order 2007, SI 2007/2197; the Regulation of Investigatory Powers (Investigation of Protected Electronic Information: Code of Practice) Order 2007, SI 2007/2200; the Regulation of Investigatory Powers (Covert Human Intelligence Sources: Code of Practice) Order 2010, SI 2010/462; the Regulation of Investigatory Powers (Covert Surveillance and Property Interference: Code of Practice) Order 2010, SI 2010/463; the Regulation of Investigatory Powers (Covert Surveillance and Property Interference: Code of Practice) Order 2014, SI 2014/3103; the Regulation of Investigatory Powers (Covert Human Intelligence Sources: Code of Practice) Order 2014, SI 2014/3119; the Retention of Communications Data (Code of Practice) Order 2015, SI 2015/926; the Regulation of Investigatory Powers (Acquisition and Disclosure of Communications Data: Code of Practice) Order 2015, SI 2015/927.

[1.1621]
72 Effect of codes of practice

(1) A person exercising or performing any power or duty in relation to which provision may be made by a code of practice under section 71 shall, in doing so, have regard to the provisions (so far as they are applicable) of every code of practice for the time being in force under that section.

(2) A failure on the part of any person to comply with any provision of a code of practice for the time being in force under section 71 shall not of itself render him liable to any criminal or civil proceedings.

(3) A code of practice in force at any time under section 71 shall be admissible in evidence in any criminal or civil proceedings.

(4) If any provision of a code of practice issued or revised under section 71 appears to—

  (a)   the court or tribunal conducting any civil or criminal proceedings,
  (b)   the Tribunal,
  (c)   a relevant Commissioner carrying out any of his functions under this Act,
  [(ca) the Information Commissioner carrying out any of the Commissioner's functions under Part 2 of the Data Retention Regulations 2014,]
  (d)   a Surveillance Commissioner carrying out his functions under this Act or the Police Act 1997, or
  (e)   any Assistant Surveillance Commissioner carrying out any functions of his under section 63 of this Act,

to be relevant to any question arising in the proceedings, or in connection with the exercise of that jurisdiction or the carrying out of those functions, in relation to a time when it was in force, that provision of the code shall be taken into account in determining that question.

(5) In this section "relevant Commissioner" means the Interception of Communications Commissioner, the Intelligence Services Commissioner or the Investigatory Powers Commissioner for Northern Ireland.

NOTES

Sub-s (4): para (ca) inserted by the Data Retention Regulations 2014, SI 2014/2042, reg 10(1), (4).

PART V
MISCELLANEOUS AND SUPPLEMENTAL

73–76A   (*Outside the scope of this work.*)

Supplemental

77–82   (*Outside the scope of this work.*)

[1.1622]
83 Short title, commencement and extent

(1) This Act may be cited as the Regulation of Investigatory Powers Act 2000.

(2) The provisions of this Act, other than this section, shall come into force on such day as the Secretary of State may by order appoint; and different days may be appointed under this subsection for different purposes.

(3) This Act extends to Northern Ireland.

NOTES

Orders: the Regulation of Investigatory Powers (Commencement No 1 and Transitional Provisions) Order 2000, SI 2000/2543; the Regulation of Investigatory Powers Act 2000 (Commencement No 2) Order 2001, SI 2001/2727; the

Regulation of Investigatory Powers Act 2000 (Commencement No 3) Order 2003, SI 2003/3140; the Regulation of Investigatory Powers Act 2000 (Commencement No 4) Order 2007, SI 2007/2196.

SCHEDULES

[SCHEDULE A1
MONETARY PENALTY NOTICES IN RELATION TO CERTAIN UNLAWFUL INTERCEPTIONS

PART 1
MONETARY PENALTY NOTICES

General

[1.1623]

1. (1)　A monetary penalty notice is a notice requiring the person on whom it is served to pay to the Interception of Communications Commissioner ("the Commissioner") a monetary penalty of an amount determined by the Commissioner and specified in the notice.

(2)　The amount determined by the Commissioner must not exceed £50,000.

(3)　The monetary penalty must be paid to the Commissioner within such period as is specified in the notice.

(4)　The period concerned must not be less than 28 days beginning with the day after the day on which the notice is served.

(5)　The notice must, in particular—
  (a)　state the name and address of the person on whom it is to be served,
  (b)　provide details of the notice of intent served on that person,
  (c)　state whether the Commissioner has received written representations in accordance with that notice,
  (d)　state the grounds on which the Commissioner serves the monetary penalty notice,
  (e)　state the grounds on which the Commissioner decided the amount of the monetary penalty,
  (f)　state the details of how the monetary penalty is to be paid,
  (g)　provide details of the rights of appeal of the person concerned under paragraph 5 in respect of the monetary penalty notice,
  (h)　provide details of the Commissioner's rights of enforcement under paragraph 6 in respect of the monetary penalty notice.

(6)　Any sum received by the Commissioner by virtue of a monetary penalty notice must be paid into the Consolidated Fund.

Enforcement obligations

2. (1)　The Commissioner may include one or more than one enforcement obligation in a monetary penalty notice if the Commissioner considers that the interception to which the notice relates is continuing.

(2)　Each of the following is an enforcement obligation—
  (a)　a requirement on the person on whom the notice is served to cease the interception concerned on such day, or within such period, as is specified in the notice,
  (b)　(where appropriate for achieving such a cessation) a requirement on the person to take within such period as is specified in the notice, or to refrain from taking after the end of such period as is so specified, such steps as are so specified.

(3)　No enforcement obligation is to have effect before the end of the period of 7 days beginning with the day after the day on which the notice is served.

(4)　Where an enforcement obligation is included in a monetary penalty notice under this paragraph, the notice must state what the obligation is and the grounds for including it.

Consultation requirements before service of notices

3. (1)　The Commissioner must proceed in accordance with sub-paragraphs (2) to (7) before serving a monetary penalty notice on a person.

(2)　The Commissioner must serve a notice of intent on the person.

(3)　A notice of intent is a notice that the Commissioner proposes to serve a monetary penalty notice on the person.

(4)　A notice of intent must, in particular—
  (a)　state the name and address of the person concerned,
  (b)　state the grounds on which the Commissioner proposes to serve the monetary penalty notice,
  (c)　provide an indication of the amount of the monetary penalty that the Commissioner proposes to impose and the Commissioner's grounds for deciding that amount,
  (d)　state whether the monetary penalty notice is to include any enforcement obligation and, if so, what the obligation is and the grounds for including it,

   (e)   state the date on which the Commissioner proposes to serve the monetary penalty notice,

   (f)   inform the person concerned that the person may make written representations in relation to the Commissioner's proposal within a period specified in the notice, and

   (g)   inform the person concerned that the person may, within a period specified in the notice, request an oral hearing before the Commissioner in order to make representations of the kind mentioned in sub-paragraph (6)(b).

(5)   No period specified as mentioned in sub-paragraph (4)(f) or (g) may be less than 21 days beginning with the day after the day on which the notice is served.

(6)   Where the person concerned has requested an oral hearing within the period specified for the purpose in the notice—

   (a)   the Commissioner must arrange such a hearing, and

   (b)   the person may make representations at the hearing about—

      (i)   any matter falling within section 1(1A)(a)(ii), or

      (ii)   any other matter relating to the Commissioner's proposal which, by virtue of section 17, the person would be unable to raise on an appeal under paragraph 5.

(7)   The Commissioner must consider any representations which have been made by the person concerned in accordance with the notice or sub-paragraph (6).

(8)   Subject to sub-paragraph (9), the Commissioner may not vary a notice of intent.

(9)   The Commissioner may vary a notice of intent by extending the period mentioned in sub-paragraph (4)(f) or (g).

(10)   Sub-paragraph (8) does not prevent the Commissioner from issuing a new notice of intent instead of varying such a notice.

(11)   The Commissioner may cancel a notice of intent.

(12)   A variation or cancellation of a notice of intent is effected by serving on the person on whom the notice was served a notice setting out the variation or cancellation.

(13)   Subject to sub-paragraph (14), the Commissioner must not serve a monetary penalty notice on a person in respect of an interception if any notice of intent in respect of that interception was served on the person more than 3 months earlier.

(14)   The Commissioner may serve a monetary penalty notice on a person where the service of the notice would otherwise be prevented by virtue of sub-paragraph (13) if the Commissioner—

   (a)   considers it reasonable to do so, and

   (b)   includes the reasons for doing so in the monetary penalty notice.

(15)   If the Commissioner decides not to serve a monetary penalty notice on a person as a result of any representations which have been made by the person in accordance with a notice of intent or sub-paragraph (6), the Commissioner must inform the person of that fact.

Variation or cancellation of notices

4. (1)   The Commissioner may, subject as follows, vary or cancel a monetary penalty notice.

(2)   The Commissioner may not vary a monetary penalty notice in a way that is detrimental to the person on whom it was served (whether by increasing the amount of the monetary penalty, by reducing the period specified in the notice as the period within which the penalty must be paid, by imposing a new enforcement obligation or making an existing enforcement obligation effective earlier or otherwise more onerous, or otherwise).

(3)   The Commissioner must—

   (a)   in the case of a variation which reduces the amount of a monetary penalty, repay any excess already paid in accordance with the notice, and

   (b)   in the case of a cancellation, repay any amount already paid in accordance with the notice.

(4)   A variation or cancellation of a monetary penalty notice is effected by serving on the person on whom the monetary penalty notice was served a notice setting out the variation or cancellation.

(5)   The Commissioner may not serve another monetary penalty notice on a person in respect of an interception if the Commissioner has cancelled a previous notice served on the person in respect of the same interception.

(6)   If the Commissioner refuses a request by a person to vary or cancel a monetary penalty notice which has been served on the person, the Commissioner must inform the person of that fact.

Appeals against notices

5. (1)   A person on whom a monetary penalty notice is served may appeal to the First-tier Tribunal against—

   (a)   the monetary penalty notice or any provision of it, or

   (b)   any refusal of a request by the person to issue a notice of variation or cancellation in relation to the monetary penalty notice.

(2) Where there is an appeal under sub-paragraph (1)(a) in relation to a monetary penalty notice or any provision of it, any requirement in the notice or (as the case may be) provision concerned which does not relate to the imposition of an enforcement obligation need not be complied with until the appeal is withdrawn or finally determined.

(3) Sub-paragraphs (4) to (6) apply in relation to an appeal under sub-paragraph (1)(a).

(4) The First-tier Tribunal must allow the appeal or substitute such other monetary penalty notice as could have been served by the Commissioner if the Tribunal considers—
    (a)   that the notice concerned is not in accordance with the law, or
    (b)   to the extent that the notice involved an exercise of discretion by the Commissioner, that the Commissioner ought to have exercised the discretion differently.

(5) In any other case, the First-tier Tribunal must dismiss the appeal.

(6) The First-tier Tribunal may review any determination of fact on which the notice concerned was based.

(7) Sub-paragraphs (8) to (10) apply in relation to an appeal under sub-paragraph (1)(b).

(8) The First-tier Tribunal must direct the Commissioner to issue, on such terms as the Tribunal considers appropriate, a notice of variation or cancellation in relation to the monetary penalty notice if the Tribunal considers that the monetary penalty notice ought to be varied or cancelled on those terms.

(9) In any other case, the First-tier Tribunal must dismiss the appeal.

(10) The First-tier Tribunal may review any determination of fact on which the refusal to issue the notice of variation or cancellation was based.

Enforcement of notices

6. (1) Sub-paragraphs (2) and (3) apply in relation to any penalty payable to the Commissioner by virtue of a monetary penalty notice.

(2) In England and Wales or Northern Ireland, the penalty is recoverable—
    (a)   if [the county court in England and Wales or a county court in Northern Ireland] so orders, as if it were payable under an order of that court,
    (b)   if the High Court so orders, as if it were payable under an order of that court.

(3) In Scotland, the penalty is recoverable as if it were payable under an extract registered decree arbitral bearing a warrant for execution issued by the sheriff for any sheriffdom in Scotland.

(4) The person on whom a monetary penalty notice containing an enforcement obligation is served must comply with the obligation; and that duty is enforceable by civil proceedings by the Commissioner for an injunction, or for specific performance of a statutory duty under section 45 of the Court of Session Act 1988, or for any other appropriate relief.

Guidance

7. (1) The Commissioner must prepare and issue guidance on how the Commissioner proposes to exercise the Commissioner's functions under section 1(1A) and (1B) and this Schedule.

(2) The guidance must, in particular, deal with—
    (a)   the manner in which the Commissioner is to deal with claims of a description specified in the guidance which may give rise to grounds for serving a monetary penalty notice,
    (b)   the circumstances in which the Commissioner would consider it appropriate to serve a monetary penalty notice,
    (c)   how the Commissioner will determine the amount of the penalty, and
    (d)   the circumstances in which the Commissioner would consider it appropriate to impose an enforcement obligation.

(3) The Commissioner may alter or replace the guidance.

(4) If the guidance is altered or replaced, the Commissioner must issue the altered or replacement guidance.

(5) The Commissioner must arrange for the publication, in such form and manner as the Commissioner considers appropriate, of any guidance issued under this paragraph.

Interpretation: Part 1

8. In this Part—
    "address" means—
        (a)   in the case of a registered company, the address of its registered office, and
        (b)   in the case of a person (other than a registered company) carrying on a business, the address of the person's principal place of business in the United Kingdom;
    "business" includes any trade or profession;
    "the Commissioner" has the meaning given by paragraph 1(1);
    "enforcement obligation" has the meaning given by paragraph 2(2);
    "monetary penalty notice" means a monetary penalty notice under section 1(1A);
    "notice" means notice in writing;
    "notice of intent" means a notice under paragraph 3(2) to (5);

"registered company" means a company registered under the enactments relating to companies for the time being in force in the United Kingdom.]

NOTES

Schedule inserted by the Regulation of Investigatory Powers (Monetary Penalty Notices and Consents for Interceptions) Regulations 2011, SI 2011/1340, reg 2(4), Schedule.

Para 6: in sub-para (2)(a) words in square brackets substituted by the Crime and Courts Act 2013, s 17(5), Sch 9, Pt 3, para 125, for transitional provision see the Crime and Courts Act 2013 (Commencement No 10 and Transitional Provision) Order 2014, SI 2014/954, art 3.

[PART 2
INFORMATION PROVISIONS

Information notices

[1.1624]

9. (1)   The Commissioner may by notice ("an information notice") request any person on whom the Commissioner is considering whether to serve a Part 1 notice of intent or a Part 1 monetary penalty notice to provide such information as the Commissioner reasonably requires for the purpose of deciding whether to serve the Part 1 notice concerned.

(2)   Where the Commissioner requests that documents be produced, the Commissioner may take copies of, or extracts from, any document so produced.

(3)   An information notice must—
  (a)   specify or describe the information to be provided,
  (b)   specify the manner in which, and the period within which, the information is to be provided,
  (c)   state that the Commissioner considers that the information is information which the Commissioner reasonably requires for the purpose of deciding whether to serve a Part 1 notice of intent or (as the case may be) a Part 1 monetary penalty notice,
  (d)   state the Commissioner's grounds for this view, and
  (e)   provide details of the rights of appeal under paragraph 10 in respect of the information notice.

(4)   For the purposes of sub-paragraph (3)(b)—
  (a)   specifying the manner in which the information is to be provided may include specifying the form in which it is to be provided, and
  (b)   the specified period within which the information is to be provided must not be less than 28 days beginning with the day after the day on which the information notice is served.

(5)   Subject to sub-paragraph (6), the Commissioner may not vary an information notice.

(6)   The Commissioner may vary an information notice by extending the period within which the information is to be provided if the person on whom the notice is served appeals under paragraph 10 in relation to the notice.

(7)   Sub-paragraph (5) does not prevent the Commissioner from issuing a new information notice instead of varying such a notice.

(8)   The Commissioner may cancel an information notice.

(9)   A variation or cancellation of an information notice is effected by serving on the person on whom the notice was served a notice setting out the variation or cancellation.

Appeals against notices

10. (1)   A person on whom an information notice is served may appeal to the First-tier Tribunal against—
  (a)   the information notice or any provision of it, or
  (b)   any refusal of a request by the person to issue a notice of variation or cancellation in relation to the information notice.

(2)   Subject to paragraph 9(6), an appeal under this paragraph does not affect the need to comply with the information notice while the appeal is not finally determined.

(3)   Sub-paragraphs (4) to (6) apply in relation to an appeal under sub-paragraph (1)(a).

(4)   The First-tier Tribunal must allow the appeal or substitute such other information notice as could have been served by the Commissioner if the Tribunal considers—
  (a)   that the notice concerned is not in accordance with the law, or
  (b)   to the extent that the notice involved an exercise of discretion by the Commissioner, that the Commissioner ought to have exercised the discretion differently.

(5)   In any other case, the First-tier Tribunal must dismiss the appeal.

(6)   The First-tier Tribunal may review any determination of fact on which the notice concerned was based.

(7)   Sub-paragraphs (8) to (10) apply in relation to an appeal under sub-paragraph (1)(b).

(8) The First-tier Tribunal must direct the Commissioner to issue, on such terms as the Tribunal considers appropriate, a notice of variation or cancellation in relation to the information notice if the Tribunal considers that the information notice ought to be varied or cancelled on those terms.

(9) In any other case, the First-tier Tribunal must dismiss the appeal.

(10) The First-tier Tribunal may review any determination of fact on which the refusal to issue the notice of variation or cancellation was based.

Enforcement of notices

11. (1) The Commissioner may serve a Part 2 monetary penalty notice on a person if the person—

    (a) without reasonable excuse refuses or fails to comply with an information notice, or

    (b) knowingly or recklessly gives any information which is false in a material particular in response to an information notice.

(2) Subject to sub-paragraphs (3) to (7), Part 1 of this Schedule applies in relation to a Part 2 monetary penalty notice and the penalty that relates to that notice as it applies in relation to a Part 1 monetary penalty notice and the penalty that relates to that notice.

(3) The amount of the monetary penalty determined by the Commissioner and specified in the Part 2 monetary penalty notice may be—

    (a) a fixed amount,

    (b) an amount calculated by reference to a daily rate, or

    (c) a fixed amount and an amount calculated by reference to a daily rate,

provided that the total amount payable does not exceed £10,000.

(4) In the case of an amount calculated by reference to a daily rate—

    (a) no account is to be taken of the day on which the Part 2 monetary penalty notice is served or any day before that day, and

    (b) the Part 2 monetary penalty notice must specify—

        (i) i)the day on which the amount first starts to accumulate and the circumstances in which it is to cease to accumulate, and

        (ii) the period or periods within which the amount, or any part or parts so far accumulated, must be paid to the Commissioner (provided that no such period ends less than 28 days beginning with the day after the day on which the notice is served).

(5) The provisions in Part 1 of this Schedule so far as relating to enforcement obligations do not apply in relation to a Part 2 monetary penalty notice.

(6) Paragraph 3 applies by virtue of sub-paragraph (2) above as if—

    (a) paragraph 3(6)(b)(i), the word "or" at the end of that sub-paragraph (i) and the word "other" in paragraph 3(6)(b)(ii) were omitted, and

    (b) in paragraph 3(13) the references to an interception were references to conduct falling within paragraph 11(1)(a) or (b).

(7) Paragraph 4(5) applies by virtue of sub-paragraph (2) above as if the references to an interception were references to conduct falling within paragraph 11(1)(a) or (b).

Technical assistance for the Commissioner

12. (1) OFCOM must comply with any reasonable request made by the Commissioner, in connection with the Commissioner's functions under section 1(1A) and (1B) and this Schedule, for advice on technical and similar matters relating to electronic communications.

(2) For this purpose, the Commissioner may disclose to OFCOM any information obtained by the Commissioner under this Schedule.

(3) In this paragraph "OFCOM" means the Office of Communications established by section 1 of the Office of Communications Act 2002.

Interpretation: Part 2

13. In this Part—

    "the Commissioner" has the meaning given by paragraph 1(1);

    "enforcement obligation" has the meaning given by paragraph 2(2);

    "information" includes documents; and any reference to providing or giving information includes a reference to producing a document;

    "information notice" has the meaning given by paragraph 9(1);

    "notice" means notice in writing;

    "Part 1 monetary penalty notice" means a monetary penalty notice under section 1(1A);

    "Part 2 monetary penalty notice" means a monetary penalty notice under paragraph 11; "Part 1 notice of intent" means a notice under paragraph 3(2) to (5) (but excluding those provisions as applied by paragraph 11).]

NOTES

Inserted as noted to Pt 1 of this Schedule at **[1.1623]**.

Part 1   Statutes

SCHEDULES 1–5

(Schs 1–5 outside the scope of this work.)

PROCEEDS OF CRIME ACT 2002

(2002 c 29)

ARRANGEMENT OF SECTIONS

PART 7
MONEY LAUNDERING

Offences

PART 8
INVESTIGATIONS

CHAPTER 1
INTRODUCTION

CHAPTER 2
ENGLAND AND WALES AND NORTHERN IRELAND

Judges and courts

Part 1 **Statutes**

An Act to establish the Assets Recovery Agency and make provision about the appointment of its Director and his functions (including Revenue functions), to provide for confiscation orders in relation to persons who benefit from criminal conduct and for restraint orders to prohibit dealing with property, to allow the recovery of property which is or represents property obtained through unlawful conduct or which is intended to be used in unlawful conduct, to make provision about money laundering, to make provision about investigations relating to benefit from criminal conduct or to property which is or represents property obtained through unlawful conduct or to money laundering, to make provision to give effect to overseas requests and orders made where property is found or believed to be obtained through criminal conduct, and for connected purposes

[24 July 2002]

1–326   *((Pts 1–6) outside the scope of this work.)*

PART 7
MONEY LAUNDERING

Offences

[1.1625]
327   Concealing etc
(1)   A person commits an offence if he—
  (a)   conceals criminal property;
  (b)   disguises criminal property;
  (c)   converts criminal property;
  (d)   transfers criminal property;
  (e)   removes criminal property from England and Wales or from Scotland or from Northern Ireland.
(2)   But a person does not commit such an offence if—
  (a)   he makes an authorised disclosure under section 338 and (if the disclosure is made before he does the act mentioned in subsection (1)) he has the appropriate consent;
  (b)   he intended to make such a disclosure but had a reasonable excuse for not doing so;
  (c)   the act he does is done in carrying out a function he has relating to the enforcement of any provision of this Act or of any other enactment relating to criminal conduct or benefit from criminal conduct.
[(2A)   Nor does a person commit an offence under subsection (1) if—
  (a)   he knows, or believes on reasonable grounds, that the relevant criminal conduct occurred in a particular country or territory outside the United Kingdom, and
  (b)   the relevant criminal conduct—
    (i)   was not, at the time it occurred, unlawful under the criminal law then applying in that country or territory, and
    (ii)   is not of a description prescribed by an order made by the Secretary of State.
(2B)   In subsection (2A) "the relevant criminal conduct" is the criminal conduct by reference to which the property concerned is criminal property.]
[(2C)   A deposit-taking body that does an act mentioned in paragraph (c) or (d) of subsection (1) does not commit an offence under that subsection if—
  (a)   it does the act in operating an account maintained with it, and
  (b)   the value of the criminal property concerned is less than the threshold amount determined under section 339A for the act.]
(3)   Concealing or disguising criminal property includes concealing or disguising its nature, source, location, disposition, movement or ownership or any rights with respect to it.

NOTES
  Sub-ss (2A), (2B): inserted by the Serious Organised Crime and Police Act 2005, s 102(1), (2).
  Sub-s (2C): inserted by the Serious Organised Crime and Police Act 2005, s 103(1), (2).
  Transitional provisions: by virtue of the Proceeds of Crime Act 2002 (Commencement No 4, Transitional Provisions and Savings) Order 2003, SI 2003/120, the new principal money laundering offences (ie, those contained in ss 327, 328 and 329 of this Act) do not have effect where the conduct constituting an offence under those provisions began before 24 February 2003 and ended on or after that date. In such a case, the old principal money laundering offences (ie, those contained in (i) the Criminal Justice Act 1988, ss 93A, 93B, 93C, (ii) the Criminal Justice (International Co-operation) Act 1990, s 14, (iii) the Drug Trafficking Act 1994, ss 49, 50, 51, (iv) the Criminal Law (Consolidation) (Scotland) Act 1995, ss 37, 38, and (v) the Proceeds of Crime (Northern Ireland) Order 1996, arts 45, 46, 47, continue to have effect.
  Deferred Prosecution Agreements: as to the application of Deferred Prosecution Agreements to an offence under this section and ss 328, 329, 330, 333A (ie, an agreement between a designated prosecutor and a person accused of a crime (P) whereby proceedings against P in respect of the alleged offence are automatically suspended as soon as they are instituted if P agrees to comply with certain requirements), see s 45 of, and Sch 17, Pt 1 and Sch 17, Pt 2, para 23 to, the Crime and Courts Act 2013.
  Serious crime prevention orders: a court may make a serious crime prevention order under the Serious Crime Act 2007, ss 1 or 19 if it is satisfied that a person has been involved in serious crime, and it has reasonable grounds to believe that the order would protect the public by preventing, restricting or disrupting involvement by the person in serious crime. By virtue of s 2 of, and Sch 1 to, the 2007 Act, the offence under this section (and ss 328, 329) is a serious crime.

Orders: the Proceeds of Crime Act 2002 (Money Laundering: Exceptions to Overseas Conduct Defence) Order 2006, SI 2006/1070.

[1.1626]
328 Arrangements
(1) A person commits an offence if he enters into or becomes concerned in an arrangement which he knows or suspects facilitates (by whatever means) the acquisition, retention, use or control of criminal property by or on behalf of another person.
(2) But a person does not commit such an offence if—
  (a) he makes an authorised disclosure under section 338 and (if the disclosure is made before he does the act mentioned in subsection (1)) he has the appropriate consent;
  (b) he intended to make such a disclosure but had a reasonable excuse for not doing so;
  (c) the act he does is done in carrying out a function he has relating to the enforcement of any provision of this Act or of any other enactment relating to criminal conduct or benefit from criminal conduct.
[(3) Nor does a person commit an offence under subsection (1) if—
  (a) he knows, or believes on reasonable grounds, that the relevant criminal conduct occurred in a particular country or territory outside the United Kingdom, and
  (b) the relevant criminal conduct—
    (i) was not, at the time it occurred, unlawful under the criminal law then applying in that country or territory, and
    (ii) is not of a description prescribed by an order made by the Secretary of State.
(4) In subsection (3) "the relevant criminal conduct" is the criminal conduct by reference to which the property concerned is criminal property.]
[(5) A deposit-taking body that does an act mentioned in subsection (1) does not commit an offence under that subsection if—
  (a) it does the act in operating an account maintained with it, and
  (b) the arrangement facilitates the acquisition, retention, use or control of criminal property of a value that is less than the threshold amount determined under section 339A for the act.]

NOTES
Sub-ss (3), (4): added by the Serious Organised Crime and Police Act 2005, s 102(1), (3).
Sub-s (5): added by the Serious Organised Crime and Police Act 2005, s 103(1), (3).
Transitional provisions: see the note to s 327 at **[1.1625]**.
Deferred Prosecution Agreements: see the note to s 327 at **[1.1625]**.
Serious crime prevention orders: see the note to s 327 at **[1.1625]**.
Orders: the Proceeds of Crime Act 2002 (Money Laundering: Exceptions to Overseas Conduct Defence) Order 2006, SI 2006/1070.

[1.1627]
329 Acquisition, use and possession
(1) A person commits an offence if he—
  (a) acquires criminal property;
  (b) uses criminal property;
  (c) has possession of criminal property.
(2) But a person does not commit such an offence if—
  (a) he makes an authorised disclosure under section 338 and (if the disclosure is made before he does the act mentioned in subsection (1)) he has the appropriate consent;
  (b) he intended to make such a disclosure but had a reasonable excuse for not doing so;
  (c) he acquired or used or had possession of the property for adequate consideration;
  (d) the act he does is done in carrying out a function he has relating to the enforcement of any provision of this Act or of any other enactment relating to criminal conduct or benefit from criminal conduct.
[(2A) Nor does a person commit an offence under subsection (1) if—
  (a) he knows, or believes on reasonable grounds, that the relevant criminal conduct occurred in a particular country or territory outside the United Kingdom, and
  (b) the relevant criminal conduct—
    (i) was not, at the time it occurred, unlawful under the criminal law then applying in that country or territory, and
    (ii) is not of a description prescribed by an order made by the Secretary of State.
(2B) In subsection (2A) "the relevant criminal conduct" is the criminal conduct by reference to which the property concerned is criminal property.]
[(2C) A deposit-taking body that does an act mentioned in subsection (1) does not commit an offence under that subsection if—
  (a) it does the act in operating an account maintained with it, and
  (b) the value of the criminal property concerned is less than the threshold amount determined under section 339A for the act.]
(3) For the purposes of this section—

(a)   a person acquires property for inadequate consideration if the value of the consideration is significantly less than the value of the property;

(b)   a person uses or has possession of property for inadequate consideration if the value of the consideration is significantly less than the value of the use or possession;

(c)   the provision by a person of goods or services which he knows or suspects may help another to carry out criminal conduct is not consideration.

NOTES

Sub-ss (2A), (2B): inserted by the Serious Organised Crime and Police Act 2005, s 102(1), (4).

Sub-s (2C): inserted by the Serious Organised Crime and Police Act 2005, s 103(1), (4).

Transitional provisions: see the note to s 327 at **[1.1625]**.

Deferred Prosecution Agreements: see the note to s 327 at **[1.1625]**.

Serious crime prevention orders: see the note to s 327 at **[1.1625]**.

Orders: the Proceeds of Crime Act 2002 (Money Laundering: Exceptions to Overseas Conduct Defence) Order 2006, SI 2006/1070.

[1.1628]
330   Failure to disclose: regulated sector

(1)   A person commits an offence if [the conditions in subsections (2) to (4) are satisfied].

(2)   The first condition is that he—
   (a)   knows or suspects, or
   (b)   has reasonable grounds for knowing or suspecting,
that another person is engaged in money laundering.

(3)   The second condition is that the information or other matter—
   (a)   on which his knowledge or suspicion is based, or
   (b)   which gives reasonable grounds for such knowledge or suspicion,
came to him in the course of a business in the regulated sector.

[(3A)   The third condition is—
   (a)   that he can identify the other person mentioned in subsection (2) or the whereabouts of any of the laundered property, or
   (b)   that he believes, or it is reasonable to expect him to believe, that the information or other matter mentioned in subsection (3) will or may assist in identifying that other person or the whereabouts of any of the laundered property.

(4)   The fourth condition is that he does not make the required disclosure to—
   (a)   a nominated officer, or
   (b)   a person authorised for the purposes of this Part by [the Director General of the National Crime Agency],
as soon as is practicable after the information or other matter mentioned in subsection (3) comes to him.

(5)   The required disclosure is a disclosure of—
   (a)   the identity of the other person mentioned in subsection (2), if he knows it,
   (b)   the whereabouts of the laundered property, so far as he knows it, and
   (c)   the information or other matter mentioned in subsection (3).

(5A)   The laundered property is the property forming the subject-matter of the money laundering that he knows or suspects, or has reasonable grounds for knowing or suspecting, that other person to be engaged in.

(6)   But he does not commit an offence under this section if—
   (a)   he has a reasonable excuse for not making the required disclosure,
   (b)   he is a professional legal adviser [or   . . .   relevant professional adviser] and—
      (i)   if he knows either of the things mentioned in subsection (5)(a) and (b), he knows the thing because of information or other matter that came to him in privileged circumstances, or
      (ii)   the information or other matter mentioned in subsection (3) came to him in privileged circumstances, or
   (c)   subsection (7) [or (7B)] applies to him.]

(7)   This subsection applies to a person if—
   (a)   he does not know or suspect that another person is engaged in money laundering, and
   (b)   he has not been provided by his employer with such training as is specified by the Secretary of State by order for the purposes of this section.

[(7A)   Nor does a person commit an offence under this section if—
   (a)   he knows, or believes on reasonable grounds, that the money laundering is occurring in a particular country or territory outside the United Kingdom, and
   (b)   the money laundering—
      (i)   is not unlawful under the criminal law applying in that country or territory, and
      (ii)   is not of a description prescribed in an order made by the Secretary of State.]

[(7B)   This subsection applies to a person if—
   (a)   he is employed by, or is in partnership with, a professional legal adviser or a relevant professional adviser to provide the adviser with assistance or support,
   (b)   the information or other matter mentioned in subsection (3) comes to the person in connection with the provision of such assistance or support, and

(c)   the information or other matter came to the adviser in privileged circumstances.]
(8)   In deciding whether a person committed an offence under this section the court must consider whether he followed any relevant guidance which was at the time concerned—
(a)   issued by a supervisory authority or any other appropriate body,
(b)   approved by the Treasury, and
(c)   published in a manner it approved as appropriate in its opinion to bring the guidance to the attention of persons likely to be affected by it.
(9)   A disclosure to a nominated officer is a disclosure which—
(a)   is made to a person nominated by the alleged offender's employer to receive disclosures under this section, and
(b)   is made in the course of the alleged offender's employment . . .
[(9A)   But a disclosure which satisfies paragraphs (a) and (b) of subsection (9) is not to be taken as a disclosure to a nominated officer if the person making the disclosure—
(a)   is a professional legal adviser [or . . . relevant professional adviser],
(b)   makes it for the purpose of obtaining advice about making a disclosure under this section, and
(c)   does not intend it to be a disclosure under this section.]
(10)   Information or other matter comes to a professional legal adviser [or . . . relevant professional adviser] in privileged circumstances if it is communicated or given to him—
(a)   by (or by a representative of) a client of his in connection with the giving by the adviser of legal advice to the client,
(b)   by (or by a representative of) a person seeking legal advice from the adviser, or
(c)   by a person in connection with legal proceedings or contemplated legal proceedings.
(11)   But subsection (10) does not apply to information or other matter which is communicated or given with the intention of furthering a criminal purpose.
(12)   Schedule 9 has effect for the purpose of determining what is—
(a)   a business in the regulated sector;
(b)   a supervisory authority.
(13)   An appropriate body is any body which regulates or is representative of any trade, profession, business or employment carried on by the alleged offender.
[(14)   A relevant professional adviser is an accountant, auditor or tax adviser who is a member of a professional body which is established for accountants, auditors or tax advisers (as the case may be) and which makes provision for—
(a)   testing the competence of those seeking admission to membership of such a body as a condition for such admission; and
(b)   imposing and maintaining professional and ethical standards for its members, as well as imposing sanctions for non-compliance with those standards.]

NOTES

Sub-s (1): words in square brackets substituted by the Serious Organised Crime and Police Act 2005, s 104(1), (2).

Sub-ss (3A), (5), (5A): substituted, together with sub-ss (4), (6), for original sub-ss (4)–(6), by the Serious Organised Crime and Police Act 2005, s 104(1), (3), subject to transitional provisions in the Serious Organised Crime and Police Act 2005 (Commencement No 1, Transitional and Transitory Provisions) Order 2005, SI 2005/1521, art 3(4).

Sub-s (4): substituted as noted above; words in square brackets substituted by the Crime and Courts Act 2013, s 15, Sch 8, Pt 2, paras 108, 129 (for general transitional provisions in connection with the abolition of SOCA, see Sch 8, Pt 1 to the 2013 Act).

Sub-s (6): substituted as noted above; words in square brackets in paras (b), (c) inserted by the Proceeds of Crime Act 2002 and Money Laundering Regulations 2003 (Amendment) Order 2006, SI 2006/308, art 2(1)–(3); word omitted from para (b) repealed by the Terrorism Act 2000 and Proceeds of Crime Act 2002 (Amendment) Regulations 2007, SI 2007/3398, reg 3, Sch 2, paras 1, 2.

Sub-s (7A): inserted by the Serious Organised Crime and Police Act 2005, s 102(1), (5).

Sub-s (7B): inserted by SI 2006/308, art 2(1), (4).

Sub-s (9): words omitted from para (b) repealed by the Serious Organised Crime and Police Act 2005, ss 105(1), (2), 174(2), Sch 17, Pt 2.

Sub-s (9A): inserted by the Serious Organised Crime and Police Act 2005, s 106(1), (2); in para (a) words in square brackets inserted by SI 2006/308, art 2(1), (2); word omitted from para (a) repealed by SI 2007/3398, reg 3, Sch 2, paras 1, 2.

Sub-s (10): words in square brackets inserted by SI 2006/308, art 2(1), (2); word omitted repealed by SI 2007/3398, reg 3, Sch 2, paras 1, 2.

Sub-s (14): added by SI 2006/308, art 2(1), (5).

Transitional provisions: by virtue of the Proceeds of Crime Act 2002 (Commencement No 4, Transitional Provisions and Savings) Order 2003, SI 2003/120, the new failure to disclose offences (ie, those contained in ss 330, 331 and 332 of this Act) do not have effect where the information or other matter on which knowledge or suspicion that another person is engaged in money laundering is based, or which gives reasonable grounds for such knowledge or suspicion, came to a person before 24 February 2003. In such a case, the old failure to disclose offences (ie, those contained in (i) the Drug Trafficking Act 1994, s 53, (ii) the Criminal Law (Consolidation) (Scotland) Act 1995, s 39, and (iii) the Proceeds of Crime (Northern Ireland) Order 1996, art 44, continue to have effect.

Transitional provisions: the Serious Crime Act 2007 (Commencement No 2 and Transitional and Transitory Provisions and Savings) Order 2008, SI 2008/755, arts 3–14 ensure that, notwithstanding the abolition of the Assets Recovery Agency ("the Agency") and its Director, the cases of the Agency or its Director in relation to Part 5 (civil recovery), Part 6 (revenue), Part 8 (investigations) and section 3 (accreditation and training of civilian financial investigators) will be continued by specified successors. The successors are the National Policing Improvement Agency in relation to accreditation and training of civilian financial investigators and the Serious Organised Crime Agency for all other cases. Cases being dealt with by the Agency and its Director concerning the confiscation of the proceeds of crime will be continued by the Serious Organised Crime Agency. The 2008 Order makes further transitional and transitory provision and savings in relation to the abolition of the Agency and its Director.

Deferred Prosecution Agreements: see the note to s 327 at **[1.1625]**.

Orders: the Proceeds of Crime Act 2002 (Failure to Disclose Money Laundering: Specified Training) Order 2003, SI 2003/171.

[1.1629]
331 Failure to disclose: nominated officers in the regulated sector
(1) A person nominated to receive disclosures under section 330 commits an offence if the conditions in subsections (2) to (4) are satisfied.
(2) The first condition is that he—
    (a) knows or suspects, or
    (b) has reasonable grounds for knowing or suspecting,
that another person is engaged in money laundering.
(3) The second condition is that the information or other matter—
    (a) on which his knowledge or suspicion is based, or
    (b) which gives reasonable grounds for such knowledge or suspicion,
came to him in consequence of a disclosure made under section 330.
[(3A) The third condition is—
    (a) that he knows the identity of the other person mentioned in subsection (2), or the whereabouts of any of the laundered property, in consequence of a disclosure made under section 330,
    (b) that that other person, or the whereabouts of any of the laundered property, can be identified from the information or other matter mentioned in subsection (3), or
    (c) that he believes, or it is reasonable to expect him to believe, that the information or other matter will or may assist in identifying that other person or the whereabouts of any of the laundered property.
(4) The fourth condition is that he does not make the required disclosure to a person authorised for the purposes of this Part by [the Director General of the National Crime Agency] as soon as is practicable after the information or other matter mentioned in subsection (3) comes to him.
(5) The required disclosure is a disclosure of—
    (a) the identity of the other person mentioned in subsection (2), if disclosed to him under section 330,
    (b) the whereabouts of the laundered property, so far as disclosed to him under section 330, and
    (c) the information or other matter mentioned in subsection (3).
(5A) The laundered property is the property forming the subject-matter of the money laundering that he knows or suspects, or has reasonable grounds for knowing or suspecting, that other person to be engaged in.
(6) But he does not commit an offence under this section if he has a reasonable excuse for not making the required disclosure.]
[(6A) Nor does a person commit an offence under this section if—
    (a) he knows, or believes on reasonable grounds, that the money laundering is occurring in a particular country or territory outside the United Kingdom, and
    (b) the money laundering—
        (i) is not unlawful under the criminal law applying in that country or territory, and
        (ii) is not of a description prescribed in an order made by the Secretary of State.]
(7) In deciding whether a person committed an offence under this section the court must consider whether he followed any relevant guidance which was at the time concerned—
    (a) issued by a supervisory authority or any other appropriate body,
    (b) approved by the Treasury, and
    (c) published in a manner it approved as appropriate in its opinion to bring the guidance to the attention of persons likely to be affected by it.
(8) Schedule 9 has effect for the purpose of determining what is a supervisory authority.
(9) An appropriate body is a body which regulates or is representative of a trade, profession, business or employment.

NOTES
Sub-ss (3A), (5), (5A), (6): substituted, together with sub-s (4), for original sub-ss (4)–(6), by the Serious Organised Crime and Police Act 2005, s 104(1), (4), subject to transitional provisions in the Serious Organised Crime and Police Act 2005 (Commencement No 1, Transitional and Transitory Provisions) Order 2005, SI 2005/1521, art 3(4).

Sub-s (4): substituted as noted above; words in square brackets substituted by the Crime and Courts Act 2013, s 15, Sch 8, Pt 2, paras 108, 130 (for general transitional provisions in connection with the abolition of SOCA, see Sch 8, Pt 1 to the 2013 Act).

Sub-s (6A): inserted by the Serious Organised Crime and Police Act 2005, s 102(1), (6).

Transitional provisions: see the notes to s 330 at **[1.1628]**.

[1.1630]
332 Failure to disclose: other nominated officers

(1) A person nominated to receive disclosures under section 337 or 338 commits an offence if the conditions in subsections (2) to (4) are satisfied.

(2) The first condition is that he knows or suspects that another person is engaged in money laundering.

(3) The second condition is that the information or other matter on which his knowledge or suspicion is based came to him in consequence of a disclosure made under [the applicable section].

[(3A) The third condition is—

   (a)   that he knows the identity of the other person mentioned in subsection (2), or the whereabouts of any of the laundered property, in consequence of a disclosure made under the applicable section,

   (b)   that that other person, or the whereabouts of any of the laundered property, can be identified from the information or other matter mentioned in subsection (3), or

   (c)   that he believes, or it is reasonable to expect him to believe, that the information or other matter will or may assist in identifying that other person or the whereabouts of any of the laundered property.

(4) The fourth condition is that he does not make the required disclosure to a person authorised for the purposes of this Part by [the Director General of the National Crime Agency] as soon as is practicable after the information or other matter mentioned in subsection (3) comes to him.

(5) The required disclosure is a disclosure of—

   (a)   the identity of the other person mentioned in subsection (2), if disclosed to him under the applicable section,

   (b)   the whereabouts of the laundered property, so far as disclosed to him under the applicable section, and

   (c)   the information or other matter mentioned in subsection (3).

(5A) The laundered property is the property forming the subject-matter of the money laundering that he knows or suspects that other person to be engaged in.

(5B) The applicable section is section 337 or, as the case may be, section 338.

(6) But he does not commit an offence under this section if he has a reasonable excuse for not making the required disclosure.]

[(7) Nor does a person commit an offence under this section if—

   (a)   he knows, or believes on reasonable grounds, that the money laundering is occurring in a particular country or territory outside the United Kingdom, and

   (b)   the money laundering—

      (i)   is not unlawful under the criminal law applying in that country or territory, and

      (ii) is not of a description prescribed in an order made by the Secretary of State.]

NOTES

Sub-s (3): words in square brackets substituted by the Serious Organised Crime and Police Act 2005, s 104(1), (5).

Sub-ss (3A), (4), (5), (5A), (5B), (6): substituted, for original sub-ss (4)–(6), by the Serious Organised Crime and Police Act 2005, s 104(1), (6).

Sub-s (4): substituted as noted above; words in square brackets substituted by the Crime and Courts Act 2013, s 15, Sch 8, Pt 2, paras 108, 131 (for general transitional provisions in connection with the abolition of SOCA, see Sch 8, Pt 1 to the 2013 Act).

Sub-s (7): added by the Serious Organised Crime and Police Act 2005, s 102(1), (7).

Transitional provisions: see the notes to s 330 at **[1.1628]**.

---

333 *(Repealed by the Terrorism Act 2000 and Proceeds of Crime Act 2002 (Amendment) Regulations 2007, SI 2007/3398, reg 3, Sch 2, paras 1, 3.)*

[1.1631]
[333A Tipping off: regulated sector

(1) A person commits an offence if—

   (a)   the person discloses any matter within subsection (2);

   (b)   the disclosure is likely to prejudice any investigation that might be conducted following the disclosure referred to in that subsection; and

   (c)   the information on which the disclosure is based came to the person in the course of a business in the regulated sector.

(2) The matters are that the person or another person has made a disclosure under this Part—

   (a)   to a constable,

   (b)   to an officer of Revenue and Customs,

   (c)   to a nominated officer, or

   (d)   to a [National Crime Agency officer] authorised for the purposes of this Part by the Director General of that Agency,

of information that came to that person in the course of a business in the regulated sector.

(3) A person commits an offence if—

   (a)   the person discloses that an investigation into allegations that an offence under this Part has been committed is being contemplated or is being carried out;

   (b)   the disclosure is likely to prejudice that investigation; and

   (c)   the information on which the disclosure is based came to the person in the course of a business in the regulated sector.

(4)   A person guilty of an offence under this section is liable—

   (a)   on summary conviction to imprisonment for a term not exceeding three months, or to a fine not exceeding level 5 on the standard scale, or to both;

   (b)   on conviction on indictment to imprisonment for a term not exceeding two years, or to a fine, or to both.

(5)   This section is subject to—

   (a)   section 333B (disclosures within an undertaking or group etc),

   (b)   section 333C (other permitted disclosures between institutions etc), and

   (c)   section 333D (other permitted disclosures etc).]

NOTES

Inserted, together with ss 333B–333E, by the Terrorism Act 2000 and Proceeds of Crime Act 2002 (Amendment) Regulations 2007, SI 2007/3398, reg 3, Sch 2, paras 1, 4.

Sub-s (2): words in square brackets substituted by the Crime and Courts Act 2013, s 15, Sch 8, Pt 2, paras 108, 132 (for general transitional provisions in connection with the abolition of SOCA, see Sch 8, Pt 1 to the 2013 Act).

Deferred Prosecution Agreements: see the note to s 327 at **[1.1628]**.

[1.1632]

[333B Disclosures within an undertaking or group etc

(1)   An employee, officer or partner of an undertaking does not commit an offence under section 333A if the disclosure is to an employee, officer or partner of the same undertaking.

(2)   A person does not commit an offence under section 333A in respect of a disclosure by a credit institution or a financial institution if—

   (a)   the disclosure is to a credit institution or a financial institution,

   (b)   the institution to whom the disclosure is made is situated in an EEA State or in a country or territory imposing equivalent money laundering requirements, and

   (c)   both the institution making the disclosure and the institution to whom it is made belong to the same group.

(3)   In subsection (2) "group" has the same meaning as in Directive 2002/87/EC of the European Parliament and of the Council of 16th December 2002 on the supplementary supervision of credit institutions, insurance undertakings and investment firms in a financial conglomerate.

(4)   A professional legal adviser or a relevant professional adviser does not commit an offence under section 333A if—

   (a)   the disclosure is to professional legal adviser or a relevant professional adviser,

   (b)   both the person making the disclosure and the person to whom it is made carry on business in an EEA State or in a country or territory imposing equivalent money laundering requirements, and

   (c)   those persons perform their professional activities within different undertakings that share common ownership, management or control.]

NOTES

Inserted as noted to s 333A at **[1.1631]**.

[1.1633]

[333C Other permitted disclosures between institutions etc

(1)   This section applies to a disclosure—

   (a)   by a credit institution to another credit institution,

   (b)   by a financial institution to another financial institution,

   (c)   by a professional legal adviser to another professional legal adviser, or

   (d)   by a relevant professional adviser of a particular kind to another relevant professional adviser of the same kind.

(2)   A person does not commit an offence under section 333A in respect of a disclosure to which this section applies if—

   (a)   the disclosure relates to—

      (i)   a client or former client of the institution or adviser making the disclosure and the institution or adviser to whom it is made,

      (ii)   a transaction involving them both, or

      (iii)   the provision of a service involving them both;

   (b)   the disclosure is for the purpose only of preventing an offence under this Part of this Act;

   (c)   the institution or adviser to whom the disclosure is made is situated in an EEA State or in a country or territory imposing equivalent money laundering requirements; and

   (d)   the institution or adviser making the disclosure and the institution or adviser to whom it is made are subject to equivalent duties of professional confidentiality and the protection of personal data (within the meaning of section 1 of the Data Protection Act 1998).]

NOTES

Inserted as noted to s 333A at **[1.1631]**.

Part 1 Statutes

[1.1634]
[333D   Other permitted disclosures etc
(1)   A person does not commit an offence under section 333A if the disclosure is—
   (a)   to the authority that is the supervisory authority for that person by virtue of the Money Laundering Regulations 2007 (SI 2007/2157); or
   (b)   for the purpose of—
      (i)   the detection, investigation or prosecution of a criminal offence (whether in the United Kingdom or elsewhere),
      (ii)   an investigation under this Act, or
      (iii)   the enforcement of any order of a court under this Act.
(2)   A professional legal adviser or a relevant professional adviser does not commit an offence under section 333A if the disclosure—
   (a)   is to the adviser's client, and
   (b)   is made for the purpose of dissuading the client from engaging in conduct amounting to an offence.
(3)   A person does not commit an offence under section 333A(1) if the person does not know or suspect that the disclosure is likely to have the effect mentioned in section 333A(1)(b).
(4)   A person does not commit an offence under section 333A(3) if the person does not know or suspect that the disclosure is likely to have the effect mentioned in section 333A(3)(b).]

NOTES
Inserted as noted to s 333A at **[1.1631]**.

[1.1635]
[333E   Interpretation of sections 333A to 333D
(1)   For the purposes of sections 333A to 333D, Schedule 9 has effect for determining—
   (a)   what is a business in the regulated sector, and
   (b)   what is a supervisory authority.
(2)   In those sections—
   "credit institution" has the same meaning as in Schedule 9;
   "financial institution" means an undertaking that carries on a business in the regulated sector by virtue of any of paragraphs (b) to (i) of paragraph 1(1) of that Schedule.
(3)   References in those sections to a disclosure by or to a credit institution or a financial institution include disclosure by or to an employee, officer or partner of the institution acting on its behalf.
(4)   For the purposes of those sections a country or territory imposes "equivalent money laundering requirements" if it imposes requirements equivalent to those laid down in Directive 2005/60/EC of the European Parliament and of the Council of 26th October 2005 on the prevention of the use of the financial system for the purpose of money laundering and terrorist financing.
(5)   In those sections "relevant professional adviser" means an accountant, auditor or tax adviser who is a member of a professional body which is established for accountants, auditors or tax advisers (as the case may be) and which makes provision for—
   (a)   testing the competence of those seeking admission to membership of such a body as a condition for such admission; and
   (b)   imposing and maintaining professional and ethical standards for its members, as well as imposing sanctions for non-compliance with those standards.]

NOTES
Inserted as noted to s 333A at **[1.1631]**.

[1.1636]
334   Penalties
(1)   A person guilty of an offence under section 327, 328 or 329 is liable—
   (a)   on summary conviction, to imprisonment for a term not exceeding six months or to a fine not exceeding the statutory maximum or to both, or
   (b)   on conviction on indictment, to imprisonment for a term not exceeding 14 years or to a fine or to both.
(2)   A person guilty of an offence under section 330, 331 [or 332] is liable—
   (a)   on summary conviction, to imprisonment for a term not exceeding six months or to a fine not exceeding the statutory maximum or to both, or
   (b)   on conviction on indictment, to imprisonment for a term not exceeding five years or to a fine or to both.
[(3)   A person guilty of an offence under section 339(1A) is liable on summary conviction to a fine not exceeding level 5 on the standard scale.]

NOTES
Sub-s (2): words in square brackets substituted by the Terrorism Act 2000 and Proceeds of Crime Act 2002 (Amendment) Regulations 2007, SI 2007/3398, reg 3, Sch 2, paras 1, 5.
Sub-s (3): added by the Serious Organised Crime and Police Act 2005, s 105(1), (3).

Consent

[1.1637]
335 Appropriate consent
(1) The appropriate consent is—
   (a)   the consent of a nominated officer to do a prohibited act if an authorised disclosure is made
         to the nominated officer;
   (b)   the consent of a constable to do a prohibited act if an authorised disclosure is made to a
         constable;
   (c)   the consent of a customs officer to do a prohibited act if an authorised disclosure is made
         to a customs officer.
(2) A person must be treated as having the appropriate consent if—
   (a)   he makes an authorised disclosure to a constable or a customs officer, and
   (b)   the condition in subsection (3) or the condition in subsection (4) is satisfied.
(3) The condition is that before the end of the notice period he does not receive notice from a
constable or customs officer that consent to the doing of the act is refused.
(4) The condition is that—
   (a)   before the end of the notice period he receives notice from a constable or customs officer
         that consent to the doing of the act is refused, and
   (b)   the moratorium period has expired.
(5) The notice period is the period of seven working days starting with the first working day after
the person makes the disclosure.
(6) The moratorium period is the period of 31 days starting with the day on which the person
receives notice that consent to the doing of the act is refused.
(7) A working day is a day other than a Saturday, a Sunday, Christmas Day, Good Friday or a day
which is a bank holiday under the Banking and Financial Dealings Act 1971 (c 80) in the part of the
United Kingdom in which the person is when he makes the disclosure.
(8) References to a prohibited act are to an act mentioned in section 327(1), 328(1) or 329(1) (as
the case may be).
(9) A nominated officer is a person nominated to receive disclosures under section 338.
(10) Subsections (1) to (4) apply for the purposes of this Part.

[1.1638]
336 Nominated officer: consent
(1) A nominated officer must not give the appropriate consent to the doing of a prohibited act
unless the condition in subsection (2), the condition in subsection (3) or the condition in
subsection (4) is satisfied.
(2) The condition is that—
   (a)   he makes a disclosure that property is criminal property to a person authorised for the
         purposes of this Part by [the Director General of the National Crime Agency], and
   (b)   such a person gives consent to the doing of the act.
(3) The condition is that—
   (a)   he makes a disclosure that property is criminal property to a person authorised for the
         purposes of this Part by [the Director General of the National Crime Agency], and
   (b)   before the end of the notice period he does not receive notice from such a person that
         consent to the doing of the act is refused.
(4) The condition is that—
   (a)   he makes a disclosure that property is criminal property to a person authorised for the
         purposes of this Part by [the Director General of the National Crime Agency],
   (b)   before the end of the notice period he receives notice from such a person that consent to the
         doing of the act is refused, and
   (c)   the moratorium period has expired.
   (a)   he gives consent to a prohibited act in circumstances where none of the conditions in
         subsections (2), (3) and (4) is satisfied, and
   (b)   he knows or suspects that the act is a prohibited act.
(6) A person guilty of such an offence is liable—
   (a)   on summary conviction, to imprisonment for a term not exceeding six months or to a fine
         not exceeding the statutory maximum or to both, or
   (b)   on conviction on indictment, to imprisonment for a term not exceeding five years or to a
         fine or to both.
(7) The notice period is the period of seven working days starting with the first working day after
the nominated officer makes the disclosure.
(8) The moratorium period is the period of 31 days starting with the day on which the nominated
officer is given notice that consent to the doing of the act is refused.
(9) A working day is a day other than a Saturday, a Sunday, Christmas Day, Good Friday or a day
which is a bank holiday under the Banking and Financial Dealings Act 1971 (c 80) in the part of the
United Kingdom in which the nominated officer is when he gives the appropriate consent.
(10) References to a prohibited act are to an act mentioned in section 327(1), 328(1) or 329(1) (as
the case may be).
(11) A nominated officer is a person nominated to receive disclosures under section 338.

NOTES

Sub-ss (2)–(4): words in square brackets substituted by the Crime and Courts Act 2013, s 15, Sch 8, Pt 2, paras 108, 133 (for general transitional provisions in connection with the abolition of SOCA, see Sch 8, Pt 1 to the 2013 Act).

Disclosures

[1.1639]
337 Protected disclosures
(1) A disclosure which satisfies the following three conditions is not to be taken to breach any restriction on the disclosure of information (however imposed).
(2) The first condition is that the information or other matter disclosed came to the person making the disclosure (the discloser) in the course of his trade, profession, business or employment.
(3) The second condition is that the information or other matter—
  (a) causes the discloser to know or suspect, or
  (b) gives him reasonable grounds for knowing or suspecting,
that another person is engaged in money laundering.
(4) The third condition is that the disclosure is made to a constable, a customs officer or a nominated officer as soon as is practicable after the information or other matter comes to the discloser.
[(4A) Where a disclosure consists of a disclosure protected under subsection (1) and a disclosure of either or both of—
  (a) the identity of the other person mentioned in subsection (3), and
  (b) the whereabouts of property forming the subject-matter of the money laundering that the discloser knows or suspects, or has reasonable grounds for knowing or suspecting, that other person to be engaged in,
the disclosure of the thing mentioned in paragraph (a) or (b) (as well as the disclosure protected under subsection (1)) is not to be taken to breach any restriction on the disclosure of information (however imposed).]
(5) A disclosure to a nominated officer is a disclosure which—
  (a) is made to a person nominated by the discloser's employer to receive disclosures under [section 330 or] this section, and
  (b) is made in the course of the discloser's employment   . . .

NOTES

Sub-s (4A): inserted by the Serious Organised Crime and Police Act 2005, s 104(1), (7).
Sub-s (5): in para (a) words in square brackets inserted and words omitted repealed by the Serious Organised Crime and Police Act 2005, ss 105(1), (2), 106(1), (3), 174(2), Sch 17, Pt 2.

[1.1640]
338 Authorised disclosures
(1) For the purposes of this Part a disclosure is authorised if—
  (a) it is a disclosure to a constable, a customs officer or a nominated officer by the alleged offender that property is criminal property,
  (b)   . . . and
  (c) the first[, second or third] condition set out below is satisfied.
(2) The first condition is that the disclosure is made before the alleged offender does the prohibited act.
[(2A) The second condition is that—
  (a) the disclosure is made while the alleged offender is doing the prohibited act,
  (b) he began to do the act at a time when, because he did not then know or suspect that the property constituted or represented a person's benefit from criminal conduct, the act was not a prohibited act, and
  (c) the disclosure is made on his own initiative and as soon as is practicable after he first knows or suspects that the property constitutes or represents a person's benefit from criminal conduct.]
(3) The [third] condition is that—
  (a) the disclosure is made after the alleged offender does the prohibited act,
  (b) [he has a reasonable excuse] for his failure to make the disclosure before he did the act, and
  (c) the disclosure is made on his own initiative and as soon as it is practicable for him to make it.
(4) An authorised disclosure is not to be taken to breach any restriction on the disclosure of information (however imposed).
[(4A) Where an authorised disclosure is made in good faith, no civil liability arises in respect of the disclosure on the part of the person by or on whose behalf it is made.]
(5) A disclosure to a nominated officer is a disclosure which—
  (a) is made to a person nominated by the alleged offender's employer to receive authorised disclosures, and
  (b) is made in the course of the alleged offender's employment   . . .

(6)   References to the prohibited act are to an act mentioned in section 327(1), 328(1) or 329(1) (as the case may be).

[1.1641]
339   Form and manner of disclosures
(1)   The Secretary of State may by order prescribe the form and manner in which a disclosure under section 330, 331, 332 or 338 must be made.
[(1A)   A person commits an offence if he makes a disclosure under section 330, 331, 332 or 338 otherwise than in the form prescribed under subsection (1) or otherwise than in the manner so prescribed.
(1B)   But a person does not commit an offence under subsection (1A) if he has a reasonable excuse for making the disclosure otherwise than in the form prescribed under subsection (1) or (as the case may be) otherwise than in the manner so prescribed.
(2)   The power under subsection (1) to prescribe the form in which a disclosure must be made includes power to provide for the form to include a request to a person making a disclosure that the person provide information specified or described in the form if he has not provided it in making the disclosure.
(3)   Where under subsection (2) a request is included in a form prescribed under subsection (1), the form must—
    (a)   state that there is no obligation to comply with the request, and
    (b)   explain the protection conferred by subsection (4) on a person who complies with the request.]
(4)   A disclosure made in pursuance of a request under subsection (2) is not to be taken to breach any restriction on the disclosure of information (however imposed).
(5), (6)   . . .
(7)   Subsection (2) does not apply to a disclosure made to a nominated officer.

[1.1642]
[339ZA   Disclosures to [the NCA]
Where a disclosure is made under this Part to a constable or an officer of Revenue and Customs, the constable or officer of Revenue and Customs must disclose it in full to a person authorised for the purposes of this Part by the [Director General of the National Crime Agency] as soon as practicable after it has been made.]

[Threshold amounts
[1.1643]
339A   Threshold amounts
(1)   This section applies for the purposes of sections 327(2C), 328(5) and 329(2C).
(2)   The threshold amount for acts done by a deposit-taking body in operating an account is £250 unless a higher amount is specified under the following provisions of this section (in which event it is that higher amount).
(3)   An officer of Revenue and Customs, or a constable, may specify the threshold amount for acts done by a deposit-taking body in operating an account—
    (a)   when he gives consent, or gives notice refusing consent, to the deposit-taking body's doing of an act mentioned in section 327(1), 328(1) or 329(1) in opening, or operating, the account or a related account, or
    (b)   on a request from the deposit-taking body.

(4)   Where the threshold amount for acts done in operating an account is specified under subsection (3) or this subsection, an officer of Revenue and Customs, or a constable, may vary the amount (whether on a request from the deposit-taking body or otherwise) by specifying a different amount.

(5)   Different threshold amounts may be specified under subsections (3) and (4) for different acts done in operating the same account.

(6)   The amount specified under subsection (3) or (4) as the threshold amount for acts done in operating an account must, when specified, not be less than the amount specified in subsection (2).

(7)   The Secretary of State may by order vary the amount for the time being specified in subsection (2).

(8)   For the purposes of this section, an account is related to another if each is maintained with the same deposit-taking body and there is a person who, in relation to each account, is the person or one of the persons entitled to instruct the body as respects the operation of the account.]

NOTES
Inserted, together with preceding cross-heading, by the Serious Organised Crime and Police Act 2005, s 103(1), (5).

Interpretation

[1.1644]
340   Interpretation
(1)   This section applies for the purposes of this Part.

(2)   Criminal conduct is conduct which—
   (a)   constitutes an offence in any part of the United Kingdom, or
   (b)   would constitute an offence in any part of the United Kingdom if it occurred there.

(3)   Property is criminal property if—
   (a)   it constitutes a person's benefit from criminal conduct or it represents such a benefit (in whole or part and whether directly or indirectly), and
   (b)   the alleged offender knows or suspects that it constitutes or represents such a benefit.

(4)   It is immaterial—
   (a)   who carried out the conduct;
   (b)   who benefited from it;
   (c)   whether the conduct occurred before or after the passing of this Act.

(5)   A person benefits from conduct if he obtains property as a result of or in connection with the conduct.

(6)   If a person obtains a pecuniary advantage as a result of or in connection with conduct, he is to be taken to obtain as a result of or in connection with the conduct a sum of money equal to the value of the pecuniary advantage.

(7)   References to property or a pecuniary advantage obtained in connection with conduct include references to property or a pecuniary advantage obtained in both that connection and some other.

(8)   If a person benefits from conduct his benefit is the property obtained as a result of or in connection with the conduct.

(9)   Property is all property wherever situated and includes—
   (a)   money;
   (b)   all forms of property, real or personal, heritable or moveable;
   (c)   things in action and other intangible or incorporeal property.

(10)   The following rules apply in relation to property—
   (a)   property is obtained by a person if he obtains an interest in it;
   (b)   references to an interest, in relation to land in England and Wales or Northern Ireland, are to any legal estate or equitable interest or power;
   (c)   references to an interest, in relation to land in Scotland, are to any estate, interest, servitude or other heritable right in or over land, including a heritable security;
   (d)   references to an interest, in relation to property other than land, include references to a right (including a right to possession).

(11)   Money laundering is an act which—
   (a)   constitutes an offence under section 327, 328 or 329,
   (b)   constitutes an attempt, conspiracy or incitement to commit an offence specified in paragraph (a),
   (c)   constitutes aiding, abetting, counselling or procuring the commission of an offence specified in paragraph (a), or
   (d)   would constitute an offence specified in paragraph (a), (b) or (c) if done in the United Kingdom.

(12)   For the purposes of a disclosure to a nominated officer—
   (a)   references to a person's employer include any body, association or organisation (including a voluntary organisation) in connection with whose activities the person exercises a function (whether or not for gain or reward), and
   (b)   references to employment must be construed accordingly.

(13)   References to a constable include references to a person authorised for the purposes of this Part by [the Director General of the National Crime Agency].

[(14)   "Deposit-taking body" means—

(a)   a business which engages in the activity of accepting deposits, or

(b)   the National Savings Bank.]

NOTES

Sub-s (13): words in square brackets substituted by the Crime and Courts Act 2013, s 15, Sch 8, Pt 2, paras 108, 135 (for general transitional provisions in connection with the abolition of SOCA, see Sch 8, Pt 1 to the 2013 Act).

Sub-s (14): added by the Serious Organised Crime and Police Act 2005, s 103(1), (6).

See further, in relation to England, Wales and Northern Ireland, the Serious Crime Act 2007, s 63(1), Sch 6, Pt 1, para 44(a), which provides that the reference in sub-s (11)(b) above to (or to conduct amounting to) the common law offence of inciting the commission of another offence, has effect (as from the day that offence is abolished) as a reference to (or to conduct amounting to) offences under the Serious Crime Act 2007, Pt 2.

PART 8
INVESTIGATIONS

CHAPTER 1
INTRODUCTION

[1.1645]
341   Investigations
(1)   For the purposes of this Part a confiscation investigation is an investigation into—

(a)   whether a person has benefited from his criminal conduct, *or*

(b)   the extent or whereabouts of his benefit from his criminal conduct, [or

(c)   the extent or whereabouts of realisable property available for satisfying a confiscation order made in respect of him].

[(2)   For the purposes of this Part a civil recovery investigation is an investigation for the purpose of identifying recoverable property or associated property and includes investigation into—

(a)   whether property is or has been recoverable property or associated property,

(b)   who holds or has held property,

(c)   what property a person holds or has held, or

(d)   the nature, extent or whereabouts of property.

(3)   But an investigation is not a civil recovery investigation to the extent that it relates to—

(a)   property in respect of which proceedings for a recovery order have been started,

(b)   property to which an interim receiving order applies,

(c)   property to which an interim administration order applies, or

(d)   property detained under section 295.]

[(3A)   For the purposes of this Part a detained cash investigation is [an investigation for the purposes of Chapter 3 of Part 5 into]—

(a)   . . .   the derivation of cash detained under [that Chapter] or a part of such cash, or

(b)   . . .   whether cash detained under [that Chapter], or a part of such cash, is intended by any person to be used in unlawful conduct.]

(4)   For the purposes of this Part a money laundering investigation is an investigation into whether a person has committed a money laundering offence.

[(5)   For the purposes of this Part an exploitation proceeds investigation is an investigation for the purposes of Part 7 of the Coroners and Justice Act 2009 (criminal memoirs etc) into—

(a)   whether a person is a qualifying offender,

(b)   whether a person has obtained exploitation proceeds from a relevant offence,

(c)   the value of any benefits derived by a person from a relevant offence, or

(d)   the available amount in respect of a person.

Paragraphs (a) to (d) are to be construed in accordance with that Part of that Act.]

NOTES

Sub-s (1): the word in italics in para (a) is repealed by the Serious Crime Act 2015, s 85, Sch 4, para 55, as from a day to be appointed; para (c) (and the preceding word) is inserted by s 38(1) of the 2015 Act, as from a day to be appointed.

Sub-ss (2), (3): substituted by the Crime and Courts Act 2013, s 49, Sch 19, Pt 1, paras 1, 2 (for savings see the final note below); the original subsections read as follows—

"(2)   For the purposes of this Part a civil recovery investigation is an investigation into—

(a)   whether property is recoverable property or associated property,

(b)   who holds the property, or

(c)   its extent or whereabouts.

(3)   But an investigation is not a civil recovery investigation if—

(a)   proceedings for a recovery order have been started in respect of the property in question,

(b)   an interim receiving order applies to the property in question,

(c)   an interim administration order applies to the property in question, or

(d)   the property in question is detained under section 295.!.

Sub-s (3A): inserted by the Serious Crime Act 2007, s 75(1); first words in square brackets inserted, and words omitted repealed, by the Crime and Courts Act 2013, s 49, Sch 19, Pt 2, paras 24, 25; second and final words in square brackets substituted by the Policing and Crime Act 2009, s 112, Sch 7, Pt 7, paras 99, 110.

Sub-s (5): added by the Coroners and Justice Act 2009, s 169, Sch 19, paras 1, 2.

Savings: the Crime and Courts Act 2013 (Commencement No 13 and Savings) Order 2015, SI 2015/964, art 3 provides as follows—

"3   Savings

(1)   Notwithstanding the commencement of section 49 of, and Part 1 of Schedule 19 to, the 2013 Act, this has no effect in relation to—

    (a)   any application for an order under Part 8 of the 2002 Act (investigations) relating to a civil recovery investigation made before 1st June 2015;

    (b)   any order made under Part 8 of the 2002 Act in relation to a civil recovery investigation—

        (i)   which is in existence on the coming into force of this Order; or

        (ii)   as the result of an application mentioned in sub-paragraph (a);

    (c)   any application for a search and seizure warrant under section 352 of the Proceeds of Crime Act 2002 in relation to a civil recovery investigation made before 1st June 2015;

    (d)   any search and seizure warrant issued under section 352 of the Proceeds of Crime Act 2002 in relation to a civil recovery investigation—

        (i)   which is in existence on the coming into force of this Order; or

        (ii)   as the result of an application mentioned in sub-paragraph (c);

    (e)   any power of seizure under a search and seizure warrant mentioned in sub-paragraph (d); and

    (f)   any proceedings arising in relation to—

        (i)   an application mentioned in sub-paragraphs (a) or (c);

        (ii)   an order mentioned in sub-paragraph (b);

        (iii)   a search and seizure warrant mentioned in sub-paragraph (d); or

        (iv)   a power of seizure mentioned in sub-paragraph (e).

(2)   The proceedings mentioned in paragraph (1)(f) are not to be regarded as concluded until there is no further possibility of any appeal in relation to those proceedings.".

Modification: this section is applied, with modifications, in so far as it relates to bank insolvency or administration under the Banking Act 2009, Pts 2, 3, by the Banking Act 2009 (Parts 2 and 3 Consequential Amendments) Order 2009, SI 2009/317, art 3, Schedule.

[1.1646]

[341A   Orders and warrants sought for civil recovery investigations

Where an application under this Part for an order or warrant specifies property that is subject to a civil recovery investigation, references in this Part to the investigation for the purposes of which the order or warrant is sought include investigation into—

    (a)   whether a person who appears to hold or to have held the specified property holds or has held other property,

    (b)   whether the other property is or has been recoverable property or associated property, and

    (c)   the nature, extent or whereabouts of the other property.]

NOTES

Commencement: 1 June 2015.

Inserted by the Crime and Courts Act 2013, s 49, Sch 19, Pt 1, paras 1, 3 (for savings see the note to s 341 at **[1.1645]**).

[1.1647]

342   Offences of prejudicing investigation

(1)   This section applies if a person knows or suspects that an appropriate officer or (in Scotland) a proper person is acting (or proposing to act) in connection with a confiscation investigation, a civil recovery investigation[, a detained cash investigation][, an exploitation proceeds investigation] or a money laundering investigation which is being or is about to be conducted.

(2)   The person commits an offence if—

    (a)   he makes a disclosure which is likely to prejudice the investigation, or

    (b)   he falsifies, conceals, destroys or otherwise disposes of, or causes or permits the falsification, concealment, destruction or disposal of, documents which are relevant to the investigation.

(3)   A person does not commit an offence under subsection (2)(a) if—

    (a)   he does not know or suspect that the disclosure is likely to prejudice the investigation,

    (b)   the disclosure is made in the exercise of a function under this Act or any other enactment relating to criminal conduct or benefit from criminal conduct or in compliance with a requirement imposed under or by virtue of this Act,

    [(ba)   the disclosure is of a matter within section 333A(2) or (3)(a) (money laundering: tipping off) and the information on which the disclosure is based came to the person in the course of a business in the regulated sector,]

    [(bb)   the disclosure is made in the exercise of a function under Part 7 of the Coroners and Justice Act 2009 (criminal memoirs etc) or in compliance with a requirement imposed under or by virtue of that Act,] or

    (c)   he is a professional legal adviser and the disclosure falls within subsection (4).

(4)   A disclosure falls within this subsection if it is a disclosure—

    (a)   to (or to a representative of) a client of the professional legal adviser in connection with the giving by the adviser of legal advice to the client, or

    (b)   to any person in connection with legal proceedings or contemplated legal proceedings.

(5)   But a disclosure does not fall within subsection (4) if it is made with the intention of furthering a criminal purpose.

(6) A person does not commit an offence under subsection (2)(b) if—
  (a) he does not know or suspect that the documents are relevant to the investigation, or
  (b) he does not intend to conceal any facts disclosed by the documents from any appropriate officer or (in Scotland) proper person carrying out the investigation.
(7) A person guilty of an offence under subsection (2) is liable—
  (a) on summary conviction, to imprisonment for a term not exceeding six months or to a fine not exceeding the statutory maximum or to both, or
  (b) on conviction on indictment, to imprisonment for a term not exceeding five years or to a fine or to both.
(8) For the purposes of this section—
  (a) "appropriate officer" must be construed in accordance with section 378;
  (b) "proper person" must be construed in accordance with section 412;
  [(c) Schedule 9 has effect for determining what is a business in the regulated sector].

NOTES
  Sub-s (1): words in first pair of square brackets inserted by the Serious Crime Act 2007, s 77, Sch 10, paras 1, 2; words in second pair of square brackets inserted by the Coroners and Justice Act 2009, s 169, Sch 19, paras 1, 3(a).
  Sub-s (3): para (ba) inserted by the Terrorism Act 2000 and Proceeds of Crime Act 2002 (Amendment) Regulations 2007, SI 2007/3398, reg 3, Sch 2, paras 1, 8(1), (2); para (bb) inserted by the Coroners and Justice Act 2009, s 169, Sch 19, paras 1, 3(b).
  Sub-s (8): para (c) added by SI 2007/3398, reg 3, Sch 2, paras 1, 8(1), (3).

CHAPTER 2
ENGLAND AND WALES AND NORTHERN IRELAND

Judges and courts

[1.1648]
343 Judges
(1) In this Chapter references to a judge in relation to an application must be construed in accordance with this section.
(2) In relation to an application for the purposes of a confiscation investigation[, a money laundering investigation or a detained cash investigation] a judge is—
  (a) in England and Wales, a judge entitled to exercise the jurisdiction of the Crown Court;
  (b) in Northern Ireland, a Crown Court judge.
(3) In relation to an application for the purposes of a civil recovery investigation [or an exploitation proceeds investigation] [. . .] a judge is a judge of the High Court.

NOTES
  Sub-s (2): words in square brackets by the Policing and Crime Act 2009, s 66(1), (2)(a).
  Sub-s (3): words in first pair of square brackets inserted by the Coroners and Justice Act 2009, s 169, Sch 19, paras 1, 4; words in second pair of square brackets (omitted) inserted by the Serious Crime Act 2007, s 77, Sch 10, paras 1, 3 and repealed by the Policing and Crime Act 2009, ss 66(1), (2)(b), 112(2), Sch 8, Pt 5.

[1.1649]
344 Courts
In this Chapter references to the court are to—
  (a) the Crown Court, in relation to an order for the purposes of a confiscation investigation[, a money laundering investigation or a detained cash investigation];
  (b) the High Court, in relation to an order for the purposes of a civil recovery investigation [or an exploitation proceeds investigation] [. . .].

NOTES
  Para (a): words in square brackets by the Policing and Crime Act 2009, s 66(1), (3)(a).
  Para (b): words in first pair of square brackets inserted by the Coroners and Justice Act 2009, s 169, Sch 19, paras 1, 5; words in second pair of square brackets (omitted) inserted by the Serious Crime Act 2007, s 77, Sch 10, paras 1, 4 and repealed by the Policing and Crime Act 2009, ss 66(1), (3)(b), 112(2), Sch 8, Pt 5.

Production orders

[1.1650]
345 Production orders
(1) A judge may, on an application made to him by an appropriate officer, make a production order if he is satisfied that each of the requirements for the making of the order is fulfilled.
(2) The application for a production order must state that—
  (a) a person specified in the application is subject to a confiscation investigation[, a civil recovery investigation][, an exploitation proceeds investigation] or a money laundering investigation, or
  (b) property specified in the application is subject to a civil recovery investigation [or a detained cash investigation].
(3) The application must also state that—
  (a) the order is sought for the purposes of the investigation;

(b)   the order is sought in relation to material, or material of a description, specified in the application;

(c)   a person specified in the application appears to be in possession or control of the material.

(4)   A production order is an order either—

(a)   requiring the person the application for the order specifies as appearing to be in possession or control of material to produce it to an appropriate officer for him to take away, or

(b)   requiring that person to give an appropriate officer access to the material,

within the period stated in the order.

(5)   The period stated in a production order must be a period of seven days beginning with the day on which the order is made, unless it appears to the judge by whom the order is made that a longer or shorter period would be appropriate in the particular circumstances.

NOTES

Sub-s (2): words in first pair of square brackets in para (a) inserted by the Crime and Courts Act 2013, s 49, Sch 19, Pt 1, paras 1, 4 (for savings see the note to s 341 at **[1.1645]**); words in second pair of square brackets in para (a) inserted by the Coroners and Justice Act 2009, s 169, Sch 19, paras 1, 6; words in square brackets in para (b) added by the Serious Crime Act 2007, s 75(2).

[1.1651]
346 Requirements for making of production order

(1)   These are the requirements for the making of a production order.

(2)   There must be reasonable grounds for suspecting that—

(a)   in the case of a confiscation investigation, the person the application for the order specifies as being subject to the investigation has benefited from his criminal conduct;

[(b)   in the case of a civil recovery investigation—

(i)   the person the application for the order specifies as being subject to the investigation holds recoverable property or associated property,

(ii)   that person has, at any time, held property that was recoverable property or associated property at the time, or

(iii)   the property the application for the order specifies as being subject to the investigation is recoverable property or associated property;]

[(ba)   in the case of a detained cash investigation into the derivation of cash, the property the application for the order specifies as being subject to the investigation, or a part of it, is recoverable property;

(bb)   in the case of a detained cash investigation into the intended use of cash, the property the application for the order specifies as being subject to the investigation, or a part of it, is intended by any person to be used in unlawful conduct;]

(c)   in the case of a money laundering investigation, the person the application for the order specifies as being subject to the investigation has committed a money laundering offence.

[(d)   in the case of an exploitation proceeds investigation, the person the application for the order specifies as being subject to the investigation is within subsection (2A)].

[(2A)   A person is within this subsection if, for the purposes of Part 7 of the Coroners and Justice Act 2009 (criminal memoirs etc), exploitation proceeds have been obtained by the person from a relevant offence by reason of any benefit derived by the person.

This subsection is to be construed in accordance with that Part.]

(3)   There must be reasonable grounds for believing that the person the application specifies as appearing to be in possession or control of the material so specified is in possession or control of it.

(4)   There must be reasonable grounds for believing that the material is likely to be of substantial value (whether or not by itself) to the investigation for the purposes of which the order is sought.

(5)   There must be reasonable grounds for believing that it is in the public interest for the material to be produced or for access to it to be given, having regard to—

(a)   the benefit likely to accrue to the investigation if the material is obtained;

(b)   the circumstances under which the person the application specifies as appearing to be in possession or control of the material holds it.

NOTES

Sub-s (2) is amended as follows:

Para (b) substituted by the Crime and Courts Act 2013, s 49, Sch 19, Pt 1, paras 1, 5 (for savings see the note to s 341 at **[1.1645]**); the original paragraph read as follows—

"(b)   in the case of a civil recovery investigation, the property the application for the order specifies as being subject to the investigation is recoverable property or associated property;".

Paras (ba), (bb) inserted by the Serious Crime Act 2007, s 75(3).

Para (d) inserted by the Coroners and Justice Act 2009, s 169, Sch 19, paras 1, 7(a).

Sub-s (2A): inserted by the Coroners and Justice Act 2009, s 169, Sch 19, paras 1, 7(b).

[1.1652]
347　Order to grant entry

(1)　This section applies if a judge makes a production order requiring a person to give an appropriate officer access to material on any premises.

(2)　The judge may, on an application made to him by an appropriate officer and specifying the premises, make an order to grant entry in relation to the premises.

(3)　An order to grant entry is an order requiring any person who appears to an appropriate officer to be entitled to grant entry to the premises to allow him to enter the premises to obtain access to the material.

[1.1653]
348　Further provisions

(1)　A production order does not require a person to produce, or give access to, privileged material.

(2)　Privileged material is any material which the person would be entitled to refuse to produce on grounds of legal professional privilege in proceedings in the High Court.

(3)　A production order does not require a person to produce, or give access to, excluded material.

(4)　A production order has effect in spite of any restriction on the disclosure of information (however imposed).

(5)　An appropriate officer may take copies of any material which is produced, or to which access is given, in compliance with a production order.

(6)　Material produced in compliance with a production order may be retained for so long as it is necessary to retain it (as opposed to copies of it) in connection with the investigation for the purposes of which the order was made.

(7)　But if an appropriate officer has reasonable grounds for believing that—

　(a)　the material may need to be produced for the purposes of any legal proceedings, and

　(b)　it might otherwise be unavailable for those purposes,

it may be retained until the proceedings are concluded.

[1.1654]
349　Computer information

(1)　This section applies if any of the material specified in an application for a production order consists of information contained in a computer.

(2)　If the order is an order requiring a person to produce the material to an appropriate officer for him to take away, it has effect as an order to produce the material in a form in which it can be taken away by him and in which it is visible and legible.

(3)　If the order is an order requiring a person to give an appropriate officer access to the material, it has effect as an order to give him access to the material in a form in which it is visible and legible.

[1.1655]
350　Government departments

(1)　A production order may be made in relation to material in the possession or control of an authorised government department.

(2)　An order so made may require any officer of the department (whether named in the order or not) who may for the time being be in possession or control of the material to comply with it.

(3)　An order containing such a requirement must be served as if the proceedings were civil proceedings against the department.

(4)　If an order contains such a requirement—

　(a)　the person on whom it is served must take all reasonable steps to bring it to the attention of the officer concerned;

　(b)　any other officer of the department who is in receipt of the order must also take all reasonable steps to bring it to the attention of the officer concerned.

(5)　If the order is not brought to the attention of the officer concerned within the period stated in the order (in pursuance of section 345(4)) the person on whom it is served must report the reasons for the failure to—

　(a)　a judge entitled to exercise the jurisdiction of the Crown Court or (in Northern Ireland) a Crown Court judge, in the case of an order made for the purposes of a confiscation investigation[, a money laundering investigation or a detained cash investigation];

　(b)　a High Court judge, in the case of an order made for the purposes of a civil recovery investigation [or an exploitation proceeds investigation] [. . .].

(6)　An authorised government department is a government department, or a Northern Ireland department, which is an authorised department for the purposes of the Crown Proceedings Act 1947 (c 44).

NOTES

Sub-s (5): words in square brackets in para (a) substituted by the Policing and Crime Act 2009, s 66(1), (4)(a); in para (b), words in first pair of square brackets inserted by the Coroners and Justice Act 2009, s 169, Sch 19, paras 1, 8; words in second pair of square brackets (omitted) inserted by the Serious Crime Act 2007, s 77, Sch 10, paras 1, 5 and repealed by the Policing and Crime Act 2009, ss 66(1), (4)(b), 112(2), Sch 8, Pt 5.

[1.1656]
351 Supplementary
(1) An application for a production order or an order to grant entry may be made ex parte to a judge in chambers.
(2) Rules of court may make provision as to the practice and procedure to be followed in connection with proceedings relating to production orders and orders to grant entry.
(3) An application to discharge or vary a production order or an order to grant entry may be made to the court by—
  (a) the person who applied for the order;
  (b) any person affected by the order.
(4) The court—
  (a) may discharge the order;
  (b) may vary the order.
(5) If an accredited financial investigator, [a [National Crime Agency officer]] a constable or [an officer of Revenue and Customs] [or an immigration officer] applies for a production order or an order to grant entry, an application to discharge or vary the order need not be by the same accredited financial investigator, [National Crime Agency officer] constable or [officer of Revenue and Customs] [or immigration officer].
(6) References to a person who applied for a production order or an order to grant entry must be construed accordingly.
(7) Production orders and orders to grant entry have effect as if they were orders of the court.
(8) Subsections (2) to (7) do not apply to orders made in England and Wales for the purposes of a civil recovery investigation [or an exploitation proceeds investigation] [. . .].

NOTES
Sub-s (5) is amended as follows:
The word "a" in the first (outer) pair of square brackets was inserted by virtue of the Serious Crime Act 2007, s 74(2)(d), Sch 8, Pt 4, paras 103, 104(a).
The words "National Crime Agency officer" (in both places they occur) were substituted by the Crime and Courts Act 2013, s 15, Sch 8, Pt 2, paras 108, 136 (for general transitional provisions in connection with the abolition of SOCA, see Sch 8, Pt 1 to the 2013 Act).
The words "an officer of Revenue and Customs" and "officer of Revenue and Customs" in square brackets were substituted by the Finance Act 2013, s 224, Sch 48, paras 1, 11.
The words "or an immigration officer" and "or immigration officer" in square brackets were inserted by the Crime and Courts Act 2013, s 55(14), Sch 21, Pt 1, paras 14, 30.
Sub-s (8): words in first pair of square brackets inserted by the Coroners and Justice Act 2009, s 169, Sch 19, paras 1, 9; words in second pair of square brackets (omitted) inserted by the Serious Crime Act 2007, s 77, Sch 10, paras 1, 6 and repealed by the Policing and Crime Act 2009, ss 66(1), (5), 112(2), Sch 8, Pt 5.
Transitional provisions: see the second note to s 330 at **[1.1628]**.
Rules: the Crown Court (Amendment) Rules 2003, SI 2003/422; the Criminal Procedure Rules 2014, SI 2014/1610.

Search and seizure warrants

[1.1657]
352 Search and seizure warrants
(1) A judge may, on an application made to him by an appropriate officer, issue a search and seizure warrant if he is satisfied that either of the requirements for the issuing of the warrant is fulfilled.
(2) The application for a search and seizure warrant must state that—
  (a) a person specified in the application is subject to a confiscation investigation[, a civil recovery investigation][, an exploitation proceeds investigation] or a money laundering investigation, or
  (b) property specified in the application is subject to a civil recovery investigation [or a detained cash investigation].
(3) The application must also state—
  (a) that the warrant is sought for the purposes of the investigation;
  (b) that the warrant is sought in relation to the premises specified in the application;
  (c) that the warrant is sought in relation to material specified in the application, or that there are reasonable grounds for believing that there is material falling within section 353(6), (7)[, (7A), (7B)] or (8) on the premises;
(4) A search and seizure warrant is a warrant authorising an appropriate person—
  (a) to enter and search the premises specified in the application for the warrant, and
  (b) to seize and retain any material found there which is likely to be of substantial value (whether or not by itself) to the investigation for the purposes of which the application is made.
(5) An appropriate person is—
  (a)   . . .
  (b) a [[National Crime Agency officer or a member] of the staff of the relevant Director], if the warrant is sought for the purposes of a civil recovery investigation;

[(c)   a constable[, an accredited financial investigator] or an officer of Revenue and Customs [or
        an immigration officer], if the warrant is sought for the purposes of a detained cash
        investigation[, a confiscation investigation or a money laundering investigation]];

[(d)   a [National Crime Agency officer], if the warrant is sought for the purposes of an
        exploitation proceeds investigation.]

[(5A)   In this Part "relevant Director"—

(a)   in relation to England and Wales, means the Director of Public Prosecutions . . . or the
        Director of the Serious Fraud Office; and

(b)   in relation to Northern Ireland, means the Director of the Serious Fraud Office or the
        Director of Public Prosecutions for Northern Ireland.]

(6)   The requirements for the issue of a search and seizure warrant are—

(a)   that a production order made in relation to material has not been complied with and there
        are reasonable grounds for believing that the material is on the premises specified in the
        application for the warrant, or

(b)   that section 353 is satisfied in relation to the warrant.

[(7)   The reference in paragraph . . . (c) of subsection (5) to an accredited financial investigator
is a reference to an accredited financial investigator who falls within a description specified in an
order made for the purposes of that paragraph by the Secretary of State under section 453.]

[(8)   Criminal Procedure Rules may make provision about proceedings under this section on an
application to a judge entitled to exercise the jurisdiction of the Crown Court in England and
Wales.]

NOTES

Sub-s (2): words in first pair of square brackets in para (a) inserted by the Crime and Courts Act 2013, s 49, Sch 19, Pt 1,
paras 1, 6 (for savings see the note to s 341 at **[1.1645]**); words in second pair of square brackets in para (a) inserted by
the Coroners and Justice Act 2009, s 169, Sch 19, paras 1, 10(a); words in square brackets in para (b) inserted by the Serious
Crime Act 2007, s 76(1).

Sub-s (3): words in square brackets in para (c) inserted by the Serious Crime Act 2007, s 77, Sch 10, paras 1, 7(1), (2).

Sub-s (5): para (a) repealed by the Finance Act 2013, s 224, Sch 48, paras 1, 12(1), (2)(a); words in first (outer) pair of square
brackets in para (b) substituted by the Serious Crime Act 2007, s 74(2), Sch 8, Pt 4, paras 103, 105(1), (2); words in second
(inner) pair of square brackets in para (b) substituted, and words in square brackets in para (d) substituted, by the Crime
and Courts Act 2013, s 15, Sch 8, Pt 2, paras 108, 137 (for general transitional provisions in connection with the abolition of
SOCA, see Sch 8, Pt 1 to the 2013 Act); para (c) was inserted by s 77 of, and Sch 10, para 7(1), (3) to, the 2007 Act; words
in first pair of square brackets in para (c) inserted by s 80(1)(b) of that Act; words in second pair of square brackets in para (c)
inserted by the Crime and Courts Act 2013, s 55, Sch 21, Pt 1, paras 14, 31; words in third pair of square brackets in para (c)
inserted by the Finance Act 2013, s 224, Sch 48, paras 1, 12(1), (2)(b); para (d) added by the Coroners and Justice Act 2009,
s 169, Sch 19, paras 1, 10(b).

Sub-s (5A): inserted by the Serious Crime Act 2007, s 74(2), Sch 8, Pt 4, paras 103, 105(1), (3); words omitted repealed by
the Public Bodies (Merger of the Director of Public Prosecutions and the Director of Revenue and Customs Prosecutions) Order
2014, SI 2014/834, art 3(3), Sch 2, paras 19, 26 (for general transitional provisions, etc, relating to the abolition of the Revenue
and Customs Prosecutions Office and the transfer of the functions of the Director of Revenue and Customs Prosecutions to the
Director of Public Prosecutions, see arts 4–10 of the 2014 Order).

Sub-s (7): added by the Serious Crime Act 2007, s 80(2); words omitted repealed by the Finance Act 2013, s 224, Sch 48,
paras 1, 12(1), (3).

Sub-s (8): added by the Deregulation Act 2015, s 82(6).

Transitional provisions: see the second note to s 330 at **[1.1628]**.

[1.1658]
353   Requirements where production order not available

(1)   This section is satisfied in relation to a search and seizure warrant if—

(a)   subsection (2) applies, and

(b)   either the first or the second set of conditions is complied with.

(2)   This subsection applies if there are reasonable grounds for suspecting that—

(a)   in the case of a confiscation investigation, the person specified in the application for the
        warrant has benefited from his criminal conduct;

[(b)   in the case of a civil recovery investigation—

    (i)   the person specified in the application for the warrant holds recoverable property or
            associated property,

    (ii)   that person has, at any time, held property that was recoverable property or
            associated property at the time, or

    (iii)   the property specified in the application for the warrant is recoverable property or
            associated property;]

[(ba)   in the case of a detained cash investigation into the derivation of cash, the property
        specified in the application for the warrant, or a part of it, is recoverable property;

(bb)   in the case of a detained cash investigation into the intended use of cash, the property
        specified in the application for the warrant, or a part of it, is intended by any person to be
        used in unlawful conduct;]

(c)   in the case of a money laundering investigation, the person specified in the application for
        the warrant has committed a money laundering offence;

[(d)   in the case of an exploitation proceeds investigation, the person specified in the application
        for the warrant is within section 346(2A).]

(3)   The first set of conditions is that there are reasonable grounds for believing that—

   (a)   any material on the premises specified in the application for the warrant is likely to be of substantial value (whether or not by itself) to the investigation for the purposes of which the warrant is sought,

   (b)   it is in the public interest for the material to be obtained, having regard to the benefit likely to accrue to the investigation if the material is obtained, and

   (c)   it would not be appropriate to make a production order for any one or more of the reasons in subsection (4).

(4)   The reasons are—

   (a)   that it is not practicable to communicate with any person against whom the production order could be made;

   (b)   that it is not practicable to communicate with any person who would be required to comply with an order to grant entry to the premises;

   (c)   that the investigation might be seriously prejudiced unless an appropriate person is able to secure immediate access to the material.

(5)   The second set of conditions is that—

   (a)   there are reasonable grounds for believing that there is material on the premises specified in the application for the warrant and that the material falls within subsection (6), (7)[, (7A), (7B)][, (8) or (8A)],

   (b)   there are reasonable grounds for believing that it is in the public interest for the material to be obtained, having regard to the benefit likely to accrue to the investigation if the material is obtained, and

   (c)   any one or more of the requirements in subsection (9) is met.

(6)   In the case of a confiscation investigation, material falls within this subsection if it cannot be identified at the time of the application but it—

   (a)   relates to the person specified in the application, the question whether he has benefited from his criminal conduct or any question as to the extent or whereabouts of his benefit from his criminal conduct [or of realisable property available for satisfying a confiscation order made in respect of him], and

   (b)   is likely to be of substantial value (whether or not by itself) to the investigation for the purposes of which the warrant is sought.

(7)   In the case of a civil recovery investigation, material falls within this subsection if it cannot be identified at the time of the application but it—

   [(a)   relates to the person or property specified in the application or to any of the questions listed in subsection (7ZA), and]

   (b)   is likely to be of substantial value (whether or not by itself) to the investigation for the purposes of which the warrant is sought.

[(7ZA)   Those questions are—

   (a)   where a person is specified in the application, any question as to—

      (i)   what property the person holds or has held,

      (ii)   whether the property is or has been recoverable property or associated property, or

      (iii)   the nature, extent or whereabouts of the property, and

   (b)   where property is specified in the application, any question as to—

      (i)   whether the property is or has been recoverable property or associated property,

      (ii)   who holds it or has held it,

      (iii)   whether a person who appears to hold or to have held it holds or has held other property,

      (iv)   whether the other property is or has been recoverable property or associated property, or

      (v)   the nature, extent or whereabouts of the specified property or the other property.]

[(7A)   In the case of a detained cash investigation into the derivation of cash, material falls within this subsection if it cannot be identified at the time of the application but it—

   (a)   relates to the property specified in the application, the question whether the property, or a part of it, is recoverable property or any other question as to its derivation, and

   (b)   is likely to be of substantial value (whether or not by itself) to the investigation for the purposes of which the warrant is sought.

(7B)   In the case of a detained cash investigation into the intended use of cash, material falls within this subsection if it cannot be identified at the time of the application but it—

   (a)   relates to the property specified in the application or the question whether the property, or a part of it, is intended by any person to be used in unlawful conduct, and

   (b)   is likely to be of substantial value (whether or not by itself) to the investigation for the purposes of which the warrant is sought.]

(8)   In the case of a money laundering investigation, material falls within this subsection if it cannot be identified at the time of the application but it—

   (a)   relates to the person specified in the application or the question whether he has committed a money laundering offence, and

   (b)   is likely to be of substantial value (whether or not by itself) to the investigation for the purposes of which the warrant is sought.

[(8A)   In the case of an exploitation proceeds investigation, material falls within this subsection if it cannot be identified at the time of the application but it—

(a)   relates to the person specified in the application, the question whether exploitation proceeds have been obtained from a relevant offence in relation to that person, any question as to the extent or whereabouts of any benefit as a result of which exploitation proceeds are obtained or any question about the person's available amount, and

(b)   is likely to be of substantial value (whether or not by itself) to the investigation for the purposes of which the warrant is sought.

This subsection is to be construed in accordance with Part 7 of the Coroners and Justice Act 2009 (criminal memoirs etc).]

(9)   The requirements are—

(a)   that it is not practicable to communicate with any person entitled to grant entry to the premises;

(b)   that entry to the premises will not be granted unless a warrant is produced;

(c)   that the investigation might be seriously prejudiced unless an appropriate person arriving at the premises is able to secure immediate entry to them.

(10)   An appropriate person is—

(a)   . . .

(b)   a [National Crime Agency officer or a member] [of the staff of the relevant Director], if the warrant is sought for the purposes of a civil recovery investigation;

[(c)   a constable[, an accredited financial [investigator,]] an officer of Revenue and Customs [or an immigration officer], if the warrant is sought for the purposes of a detained cash investigation[, a confiscation investigation or a money laundering investigation]];

[(d)   a [National Crime Agency officer], if the warrant is sought for the purposes of an exploitation proceeds investigation.]

[(11)   The reference in paragraph (a) or (c) of subsection (10) to an accredited financial investigator is a reference to an accredited financial investigator who falls within a description specified in an order made for the purposes of that paragraph by the Secretary of State under section 453.]

NOTES

Sub-s (2):

Para (b) substituted by the Crime and Courts Act 2013, s 49, Sch 19, Pt 1, paras 1, 7(1), (2) (for savings see the note to s 341 at [**1.1645**]); the original paragraph read as follows—

> (b)   in the case of a civil recovery investigation, the property specified in the application for the warrant is recoverable property or associated property;

Paras (ba), (bb) inserted by the Serious Crime Act 2007, s 76(2).

Para (d) inserted by the Coroners and Justice Act 2009, s 169, Sch 19, paras 1, 11(a).

Sub-s (5): reference in first pair of square brackets in para (a) inserted by the Serious Crime Act 2007, s 77, Sch 10, paras 1, 8(1), (2); reference in second pair of square brackets in para (a) substituted by the Coroners and Justice Act 2009, s 169, Sch 19, paras 1, 11(b).

Sub-s (6): words in square brackets inserted by the Serious Crime Act 2015, s 38(2), as from a day to be appointed.

Sub-s (7): para (a) substituted by the Crime and Courts Act 2013, s 49, Sch 19, Pt 1, paras 1, 7(1), (3) (for savings see the note to s 341 at [**1.1645**]); the original paragraph read as follows—

> "(a)   relates to the property specified in the application, the question whether it is recoverable property or associated property, the question as to who holds any such property, any question as to whether the person who appears to hold any such property holds other property which is recoverable property, or any question as to the extent or whereabouts of any property mentioned in this paragraph, and".

Sub-s (7ZA): inserted by the Crime and Courts Act 2013, s 49, Sch 19, Pt 1, paras 1, 7(1), (4) (for savings see the note to s 341 at [**1.1645**]).

Sub-ss (7A), (7B): inserted by the Serious Crime Act 2007, s 76(3).

Sub-s (8A): inserted by the Coroners and Justice Act 2009, s 169, Sch 19, paras 1, 11(c).

Sub-s (10) is amended as follows:

Para (a) repealed by the Finance Act 2013, s 224, Sch 48, paras 1, 13(1), (2)(a).

Words in first pair of square brackets in para (b) substituted, and words in square brackets in para (d) substituted, by the Crime and Courts Act 2013, s 15, Sch 8, Pt 2, paras 108, 138 (for general transitional provisions in connection with the abolition of SOCA, see Sch 8, Pt 1 to the 2013 Act).

Words in second pair of square brackets in para (b) substituted by the Serious Crime Act 2007, s 74(2), Sch 8, Pt 4, paras 103, 106.

Para (c) inserted by the Serious Crime Act 2007, s 77, Sch 10, para 8(1), (3).

Words in first (outer) pair of square brackets in para (c) inserted by the Serious Crime Act 2007, s 80(3)(b).

Word in second (inner) pair of square brackets in para (c) substituted, and words in third pair of square brackets inserted, by the Crime and Courts Act 2013, s 55, Sch 21, Pt 1, paras 14, 32(b).

Words in final pair of square brackets in para (c) inserted by the Finance Act 2013, s 224, Sch 48, paras 1, 13(1), (2)(b).

Para (d) added by the Coroners and Justice Act 2009, s 169, Sch 19, paras 1, 11(d).

Sub-s (11): added by the Serious Crime Act 2007, s 80(4).

Transitional provisions: see the second note to s 330 at [**1.1628**].

[1.1659]

354   Further provisions: general

(1)   A search and seizure warrant does not confer the right to seize privileged material.

(2)   Privileged material is any material which a person would be entitled to refuse to produce on grounds of legal professional privilege in proceedings in the High Court.

(3)   A search and seizure warrant does not confer the right to seize excluded material.

[1.1660]
355   Further provisions: confiscation and money laundering
(1)   This section applies to—
  (a)   search and seizure warrants sought for the purposes of a confiscation investigation[, a money laundering investigation or a detained cash investigation], and
  (b)   powers of seizure under them.
(2)   In relation to such warrants and powers, the Secretary of State may make an order which applies[, in relation to England and Wales,] the provisions to which [subsection (3) applies] subject to any specified modifications.
(3)   This subsection applies to the following provisions of the Police and Criminal Evidence Act 1984 (c 60)—
  (a)   section 15 (search warrants – safeguards);
  (b)   section 16 (execution of warrants);
  (c)   section 21 (access and copying);
  (d)   section 22 (retention).
[(3A)   In relation to such warrants and powers, the Department of Justice in Northern Ireland may make an order which applies, in relation to Northern Ireland, the provisions to which subsection (4) applies subject to any specified modifications.]
(4)   This subsection applies to the following provisions of the Police and Criminal Evidence (Northern Ireland) Order 1989 (SI 1989/1341 (NI 12))—
  (a)   Article 17 (search warrants -safeguards);
  (b)   Article 18 (execution of warrants);
  (c)   Article 23 (access and copying);
  (d)   Article 24 (retention).

NOTES
Sub-s (1): words in square brackets substituted by the Policing and Crime Act 2009, s 66(1), (6).
Sub-s (2): words in first pair of square brackets inserted and words in second pair of square brackets substituted by the Northern Ireland Act 1998 (Devolution of Policing and Justice Functions) Order 2010, SI 2010/976, art 12, Sch 14, paras 47, 66(1), (2), subject to transitional provisions in arts 28–31 thereof.
Sub-s (3A): inserted by SI 2010/976, art 12, Sch 14, paras 47, 66(1), (3), subject to transitional provisions in arts 28–31 thereof.
Orders: the Proceeds of Crime Act 2002 (Application of Police and Criminal Evidence Act 1984 and Police and Criminal Evidence (Northern Ireland) Order 1989) Order 2003, SI 2003/174; the Proceeds of Crime Act 2002 (Application of Police and Criminal Evidence Act 1984) Order 2015, SI 2015/759.

[1.1661]
356   Further provisions: civil recovery [. . .]
(1)   This section applies to search and seizure warrants sought for the purposes of civil recovery investigations [or exploitation proceeds investigations] [. . .].
(2)   An application for a warrant may be made ex parte to a judge in chambers.
(3)   A warrant may be issued subject to conditions.
(4)   A warrant continues in force until the end of the period of one month starting with the day on which it is issued.
(5)   A warrant authorises the person it names to require any information which is held in a computer and is accessible from the premises specified in the application for the warrant, and which the named person believes relates to any matter relevant to the investigation, to be produced in a form—
  (a)   in which it can be taken away, and
  (b)   in which it is visible and legible.
(6)   . . .
(7)   A warrant may include provision authorising a person who is exercising powers under it to do other things which—
  (a)   are specified in the warrant, and
  (b)   need to be done in order to give effect to it.
(8)   Copies may be taken of any material seized under a warrant.
(9)   Material seized under a warrant may be retained for so long as it is necessary to retain it (as opposed to copies of it) in connection with the investigation for the purposes of which the warrant was issued.
(10)   But [if an appropriate officer has reasonable] grounds for believing that—
  (a)   the material may need to be produced for the purposes of any legal proceedings, and
  (b)   it might otherwise be unavailable for those purposes,
it may be retained until the proceedings are concluded.
[(11)   . . .]
[(12)   . . .]

NOTES

Section heading: words in square brackets (omitted) inserted by the Serious Crime Act 2007, s 77, Sch 10, paras 1, 9(1), (2) and repealed by the Policing and Crime Act 2009, ss 66(1), (7)(a), 112(2), Sch 8, Pt 5.

Sub-s (1): words in first pair of square brackets inserted by the Coroners and Justice Act 2009, s 169, Sch 19, paras 1, 12; words in second pair of square brackets (omitted) inserted by the Serious Crime Act 2007, s 77, Sch 10, paras 1, 9(1), (3) and repealed by the Policing and Crime Act 2009, ss 66(1), (7)(b), 112(2), Sch 8, Pt 5.

Sub-s (6): repealed by the Serious Crime Act 2007, ss 74(2)(d), 92, Sch 8, Pt 4, paras 103, 107(1), (2), Sch 14.

Sub-s (10): words in square brackets substituted by the Policing and Crime Act 2009, s 66(1), (7)(c).

Sub-s (11): added by the Serious Crime Act 2007, s 77, Sch 10, paras 1, 9(1), (6); repealed by the Policing and Crime Act 2009, ss 66(1), (7)(d), 112(2), Sch 8, Pt 5.

Sub-s (12): added by the Serious Crime Act 2007, s 80(6); repealed by the Policing and Crime Act 2009, ss 66(1), (7)(d), 112(2), Sch 8, Pt 5.

Transitional provisions: see the second note to s 330 at **[1.1628]**.

Disclosure orders

[1.1662]

357   Disclosure orders

(1)   A judge may, on an application made to him by [an appropriate officer], make a disclosure order if he is satisfied that each of the requirements for the making of the order is fulfilled.

(2)   No application for a disclosure order may be made in relation to a [detained cash investigation or a] money laundering investigation.

[(2A)   The relevant authority may only make an application for a disclosure order in relation to a confiscation investigation if the relevant authority is in receipt of a request to do so from an appropriate officer.]

(3)   The application for a disclosure order must state that—

   (a)   a person specified in the application is subject to a confiscation investigation which is being carried out by [an appropriate officer] and the order is sought for the purposes of the investigation, or

   (b)   [a person specified in the application or] property specified in the application is subject to a civil recovery investigation and the order is sought for the purposes of the investigation;

   [(c)   a person specified in the application is subject to an exploitation proceeds investigation and the order is sought for the purposes of the investigation.]

(4)   A disclosure order is an order authorising [an appropriate officer] to give to any person [the appropriate officer] considers has relevant information notice in writing requiring him to do, with respect to any matter relevant to the investigation for the purposes of which the order is sought, any or all of the following—

   (a)   answer questions, either at a time specified in the notice or at once, at a place so specified;

   (b)   provide information specified in the notice, by a time and in a manner so specified;

   (c)   produce documents, or documents of a description, specified in the notice, either at or by a time so specified or at once, and in a manner so specified.

(5)   Relevant information is information (whether or not contained in a document) which [the appropriate officer concerned] considers to be relevant to the investigation.

(6)   A person is not bound to comply with a requirement imposed by a notice given under a disclosure order unless evidence of authority to give the notice is produced to him.

[(7)   In this Part "relevant authority" means—

   (a)   in relation to a confiscation investigation, a prosecutor; and

   (b)   in relation to a civil recovery investigation, a [National Crime Agency officer] or the relevant Director;

   [(c)   in relation to an exploitation proceeds investigation, a [National Crime Agency officer].]

(8)   For the purposes of subsection (7)(a) a prosecutor is—

   (a)   in relation to a confiscation investigation carried out by a [National Crime Agency officer], the relevant Director or any specified person;

   (b)   in relation to a confiscation investigation carried out by an accredited financial investigator, the Director of Public Prosecutions, the Director of Public Prosecutions for Northern Ireland or any specified person;

   (c)   in relation to a confiscation investigation carried out by a constable, the Director of Public Prosecutions, the Director of Public Prosecutions for Northern Ireland, the Director of the Serious Fraud Office or any specified person;   . . .

   (d)   in relation to a confiscation investigation carried out by an officer of Revenue and Customs, [the Director of Public Prosecutions], the Director of Public Prosecutions for Northern Ireland or any specified person[; and—

   (e)   in relation to a confiscation investigation carried out by an immigration officer, the Director of Public Prosecutions, the Director of Public Prosecutions for Northern Ireland or any specified person].

(9)   In subsection (8) "specified person" means any person specified, or falling within a description specified, by an order of the Secretary of State.]

NOTES

Sub-ss (1), (4), (5): words in square brackets substituted by the Serious Crime Act 2007, s 74(2), Sch 8, Pt 4, paras 103, 108(1), (2), (5), (6).

Sub-s (2): words in square brackets inserted by the Serious Crime Act 2007, s 77, Sch 10, paras 1, 10.

Sub-s (2A): inserted by the Serious Crime Act 2007, s 74(2)(d), Sch 8, Pt 4, paras 103, 107(1), (3).

Sub-s (3): words in square brackets in para (a) substituted by the Serious Crime Act 2007, s 74(2), Sch 8, Pt 4, paras 103, 108(1), (4); words in square brackets in para (b) inserted by the Crime and Courts Act 2013, s 49, Sch 19, Pt 1, paras 1, 8 (for savings see the note to s 341 at **[1.1645]**); para (c) added by the Coroners and Justice Act 2009, s 169, Sch 19, paras 1, 13(a).

Sub-s (7): added, together with sub-ss (8), (9), by the Serious Crime Act 2007, s 74(2), Sch 8, Pt 4, paras 103, 108(1), (7); para (c) added by the Coroners and Justice Act 2009, s 169, Sch 19, paras 1, 13(b); words in square brackets in paras (b), (c) substituted by the Crime and Courts Act 2013, s 15, Sch 8, Pt 2, paras 108, 139 (for general transitional provisions in connection with the abolition of SOCA, see Sch 8, Pt 1 to the 2013 Act).

Sub-s (8): added as noted above; words "the Director of Public Prosecutions" in square brackets in para (d) substituted by the Public Bodies (Merger of the Director of Public Prosecutions and the Director of Revenue and Customs Prosecutions) Order 2014, SI 2014/834, art 3(3), Sch 2, paras 19, 27 (for general transitional provisions, etc, relating to the abolition of the Revenue and Customs Prosecutions Office and the transfer of the functions of the Director of Revenue and Customs Prosecutions to the Director of Public Prosecutions, see arts 4–10 of the 2014 Order); words in square brackets in para (a) substituted by the Crime and Courts Act 2013, s 15, Sch 8, Pt 2, paras 108, 139 (for general transitional provisions in connection with the abolition of SOCA, see Sch 8, Pt 1 to the 2013 Act); the word omitted from para (c) was repealed, and para (e) and the word immediately preceding it were added, by s 55 of, and Sch 21, Pt 1, paras 14, 34 to, the 2013 Act.

Sub-s (9): added as noted above.

Transitional provisions: see the second note to s 330 at **[1.1628]**.

Orders: the Proceeds of Crime (Disclosure Orders: Confiscation Investigations) (Specified Person) Order 2014, SI 2014/3207.

[1.1663]
358 Requirements for making of disclosure order
(1)   These are the requirements for the making of a disclosure order.
(2)   There must be reasonable grounds for suspecting that—
   (a)   in the case of a confiscation investigation, the person specified in the application for the order has benefited from his criminal conduct;
   [(b)   in the case of a civil recovery investigation—
      (i)   the person specified in the application for the order holds recoverable property or associated property,
      (ii)   that person has, at any time, held property that was recoverable property or associated property at the time, or
      (iii)   the property specified in the application for the order is recoverable property or associated property;]
   [(c)   in the case of an exploitation proceeds investigation, the person specified in the application for the order is a person within section 346(2A)].
(3)   There must be reasonable grounds for believing that information which may be provided in compliance with a requirement imposed under the order is likely to be of substantial value (whether or not by itself) to the investigation for the purposes of which the order is sought.
(4)   There must be reasonable grounds for believing that it is in the public interest for the information to be provided, having regard to the benefit likely to accrue to the investigation if the information is obtained.

NOTES

Para (b) substituted by the Crime and Courts Act 2013, s 49, Sch 19, Pt 1, paras 1, 9 (for savings see the note to s 341 at **[1.1645]**); the original paragraph read as follows—

   "(b)   in the case of a civil recovery investigation, the property specified in the application for the order is recoverable property or associated property;".

Para (c) added by the Coroners and Justice Act 2009, s 169, Sch 19, paras 1, 14.

[1.1664]
359 Offences
(1)   A person commits an offence if without reasonable excuse he fails to comply with a requirement imposed on him under a disclosure order.
(2)   A person guilty of an offence under subsection (1) is liable on summary conviction to—
   (a)   imprisonment for a term not exceeding six months,
   (b)   a fine not exceeding level 5 on the standard scale, or
   (c)   both.
(3)   A person commits an offence if, in purported compliance with a requirement imposed on him under a disclosure order, he—
   (a)   makes a statement which he knows to be false or misleading in a material particular, or
   (b)   recklessly makes a statement which is false or misleading in a material particular.
(4)   A person guilty of an offence under subsection (3) is liable—
   (a)   on summary conviction, to imprisonment for a term not exceeding six months or to a fine not exceeding the statutory maximum or to both, or

(b)   on conviction on indictment, to imprisonment for a term not exceeding two years or to a fine or to both.

[1.1665]
360   Statements
(1)   A statement made by a person in response to a requirement imposed on him under a disclosure order may not be used in evidence against him in criminal proceedings.
(2)   But subsection (1) does not apply—
   (a)   in the case of proceedings under Part 2 or 4,
   (b)   on a prosecution for an offence under section 359(1) or (3),
   (c)   on a prosecution for an offence under section 5 of the Perjury Act 1911 (c 6) or Article 10 of the Perjury (Northern Ireland) Order 1979 (SI 1979/1714 (NI 19)) (false statements), or
   (d)   on a prosecution for some other offence where, in giving evidence, the person makes a statement inconsistent with the statement mentioned in subsection (1).
(3)   A statement may not be used by virtue of subsection (2)(d) against a person unless—
   (a)   evidence relating to it is adduced, or
   (b)   a question relating to it is asked,
by him or on his behalf in the proceedings arising out of the prosecution.

[1.1666]
361   Further provisions
(1)   A disclosure order does not confer the right to require a person to answer any privileged question, provide any privileged information or produce any privileged document, except that a lawyer may be required to provide the name and address of a client of his.
(2)   A privileged question is a question which the person would be entitled to refuse to answer on grounds of legal professional privilege in proceedings in the High Court.
(3)   Privileged information is any information which the person would be entitled to refuse to provide on grounds of legal professional privilege in proceedings in the High Court.
(4)   Privileged material is any material which the person would be entitled to refuse to produce on grounds of legal professional privilege in proceedings in the High Court.
(5)   A disclosure order does not confer the right to require a person to produce excluded material.
(6)   A disclosure order has effect in spite of any restriction on the disclosure of information (however imposed).
(7)   [An appropriate officer] may take copies of any documents produced in compliance with a requirement to produce them which is imposed under a disclosure order.
(8)   Documents so produced may be retained for so long as it is necessary to retain them (as opposed to a copy of them) in connection with the investigation for the purposes of which the order was made.
(9)   But if [an appropriate officer] has reasonable grounds for believing that—
   (a)   the documents may need to be produced for the purposes of any legal proceedings, and
   (b)   they might otherwise be unavailable for those purposes,
they may be retained until the proceedings are concluded.

NOTES
Sub-ss (7), (9): words in square brackets substituted by the Serious Crime Act 2007, s 74(2)(d), Sch 8, Pt 4, paras 103, 109.
Transitional provisions: see the second note to s 330 at **[1.1628]**.

[1.1667]
362   Supplementary
(1)   An application for a disclosure order may be made ex parte to a judge in chambers.
(2)   Rules of court may make provision as to the practice and procedure to be followed in connection with proceedings relating to disclosure orders.
(3)   An application to discharge or vary a disclosure order may be made to the court by—
   (a)   the [person who applied for the order];
   (b)   any person affected by the order.
(4)   The court—
   (a)   may discharge the order;
   (b)   may vary the order.
[(4A)   If a [National Crime Agency officer] staff or a person falling within a description of persons specified by virtue of section 357(9) applies for a disclosure order, an application to discharge or vary the order need not be by the same [National Crime Agency officer] or (as the case may be) the same person falling within that description.
(4B)   References to a person who applied for a disclosure order must be construed accordingly.]
(5)   Subsections (2) to [(4B)] do not apply to orders made in England and Wales for the purposes of a civil recovery investigation [or an exploitation proceeds investigation].

NOTES
Sub-s (3): words in square brackets in para (a) substituted by the Serious Crime Act 2007, s 74(2)(d), Sch 8, Pt 4, paras 103, 110(1), (2).

Part 1   Statutes

Sub-ss (4A), (4B): inserted by the Serious Crime Act 2007, s 74(2), Sch 8, Pt 4, paras 103, 110(1), (3); words in square brackets in sub-s (4A) substituted by the Crime and Courts Act 2013, s 15, Sch 8, Pt 2, paras 108, 140 (for general transitional provisions in connection with the abolition of SOCA, see Sch 8, Pt 1 to the 2013 Act).

Sub-s (5): reference in first pair of square brackets substituted by the Serious Crime Act 2007, s 74(2)(d), Sch 8, Pt 4, paras 103, 110(1), (4); words in second pair of square brackets added by the Coroners and Justice Act 2009, s 169, Sch 19, paras 1, 15.

Transitional provisions: see the second note to s 330 at **[1.1628]**.

Rules: the Crown Court (Amendment) Rules 2003, SI 2003/422; the Criminal Procedure Rules 2014, SI 2014/1610.

Customer information orders

[1.1668]
363   Customer information orders
(1)   A judge may, on an application made to him by an appropriate officer, make a customer information order if he is satisfied that each of the requirements for the making of the order is fulfilled.

[(1A)   No application for a customer information order may be made in relation to a detained cash investigation.]

(2)   The application for a customer information order must state that—
  (a)   a person specified in the application is subject to a confiscation investigation[, a civil recovery investigation][, an exploitation proceeds investigation] or a money laundering investigation, *or*
  (b)   *property specified in the application is subject to a civil recovery investigation and a person specified in the application appears to hold the property.*

(3)   The application must also state that—
  (a)   the order is sought for the purposes of the investigation;
  (b)   the order is sought against the financial institution or financial institutions specified in the application.

(4)   An application for a customer information order may specify—
  (a)   all financial institutions,
  (b)   a particular description, or particular descriptions, of financial institutions, or
  (c)   a particular financial institution or particular financial institutions.

(5)   A customer information order is an order that a financial institution covered by the application for the order must, on being required to do so by notice in writing given by an appropriate officer, provide any such customer information as it has relating to the person specified in the application.

(6)   A financial institution which is required to provide information under a customer information order must provide the information to an appropriate officer in such manner, and at or by such time, as an appropriate officer requires.

(7)   If a financial institution on which a requirement is imposed by a notice given under a customer information order requires the production of evidence of authority to give the notice, it is not bound to comply with the requirement unless evidence of the authority has been produced to it.

NOTES
Sub-s (1A): inserted by the Serious Crime Act 2007, s 77, Sch 10, paras 1, 11.

Sub-s (2): words in first pair of square brackets in para (a) inserted, and para (b) and word immediately preceding it repealed, by the Crime and Courts Act 2013, s 49, Sch 19, Pt 1, paras 1, 10 (for savings see the note to s 341 at **[1.1645]**); words in second pair of square brackets in para (a) inserted by the Coroners and Justice Act 2009, s 169, Sch 19, paras 1, 16.

[1.1669]
364   Meaning of customer information
(1)   "Customer information", in relation to a person and a financial institution, is information whether the person holds, or has held, an account or accounts [or any safe deposit box] at the financial institution (whether solely or jointly with another) and (if so) information as to—
  (a)   the matters specified in subsection (2) if the person is an individual;
  (b)   the matters specified in subsection (3) if the person is a company or limited liability partnership or a similar body incorporated or otherwise established outside the United Kingdom.

(2)   The matters referred to in subsection (1)(a) are—
  (a)   the account number or numbers [or the number of any safe deposit box];
  (b)   the person's full name;
  (c)   his date of birth;
  (d)   his most recent address and any previous addresses;
  (e)   [in the case of an account or accounts,] the date or dates on which he began to hold the account or accounts and, if he has ceased to hold the account or any of the accounts, the date or dates on which he did so;
  [(ee)   in the case of any safe deposit box, the date on which the box was made available to him and if the box has ceased to be available to him the date on which it so ceased;]
  (f)   such evidence of his identity as was obtained by the financial institution under or for the purposes of any legislation relating to money laundering;
  (g)   the full name, date of birth and most recent address, and any previous addresses, of any person who holds, or has held, an account at the financial institution jointly with him;

(h) the account number or numbers of any other account or accounts held at the financial institution to which he is a signatory and details of the person holding the other account or accounts.

(3) The matters referred to in subsection (1)(b) are—

(a) the account number or numbers [or the number of any safe deposit box];

(b) the person's full name;

(c) a description of any business which the person carries on;

(d) the country or territory in which it is incorporated or otherwise established and any number allocated to it under [the Companies Act 2006] or corresponding legislation of any country or territory outside the United Kingdom;

(e) any number assigned to it for the purposes of value added tax in the United Kingdom;

(f) its registered office, and any previous registered offices, under [the Companies Act 2006 (or corresponding earlier legislation)] or anything similar under corresponding legislation of any country or territory outside the United Kingdom;

(g) its registered office, and any previous registered offices, under the Limited Liability Partnerships Act 2000 (c 12) or anything similar under corresponding legislation of any country or territory outside Great Britain;

(h) [in the case of an account or accounts,] the date or dates on which it began to hold the account or accounts and, if it has ceased to hold the account or any of the accounts, the date or dates on which it did so;

[(hh) in the case of any safe deposit box, the date on which the box was made available to it and if the box has ceased to be available to it the date on which it so ceased;]

(i) such evidence of its identity as was obtained by the financial institution under or for the purposes of any legislation relating to money laundering;

(j) the full name, date of birth and most recent address and any previous addresses of any person who is a signatory to the account or any of the accounts.

(4) The Secretary of State may by order provide for information of a description specified in the order—

(a) to be customer information, or

(b) no longer to be customer information.

(5) Money laundering is an act which—

(a) constitutes an offence under section 327, 328 or 329 of this Act or section 18 of the Terrorism Act 2000 (c 11),

[(aa) constitutes an offence specified in section 415(1A) of this Act,] or

(b) would constitute an offence specified in paragraph (a) [or (aa)] if done in the United Kingdom.

[(6) A "safe deposit box" includes any procedure under which a financial institution provides a facility to hold items for safe keeping on behalf of another person.]

NOTES

Sub-s (1): words in square brackets inserted, in relation to Northern Ireland, by the Criminal Justice (Northern Ireland) Order 2005, SI 2005/1965, art 14(1), (2).

Sub-s (2): in paras (a), (e) words in square brackets inserted, and para (ee) inserted, in relation to Northern Ireland, by the Criminal Justice (Northern Ireland) Order 2005, SI 2005/1965, art 14(1), (3).

Sub-s (3): in paras (a), (h) words in square brackets inserted, and para (hh) inserted, in relation to Northern Ireland, by the Criminal Justice (Northern Ireland) Order 2005, SI 2005/1965, art 14(1), (4); words in square brackets in paras (d), (f) substituted by the Companies Act 2006 (Consequential Amendments, Transitional Provisions and Savings) Order 2009, SI 2009/1941, art 2(1), Sch 1, para 196(1), (2).

Sub-s (5): para (aa) inserted and words in square brackets in para (b) inserted by the Serious Organised Crime and Police Act 2005, s 107(1), (2).

Sub-s (6): inserted, in relation to Northern Ireland, by the Criminal Justice (Northern Ireland) Order 2005, SI 2005/1965, art 14(1), (5).

[1.1670]
365 Requirements for making of customer information order

(1) These are the requirements for the making of a customer information order.

(2) In the case of a confiscation investigation, there must be reasonable grounds for suspecting that the person specified in the application for the order has benefited from his criminal conduct.

[(3A) In the case of a civil recovery investigation, there must be reasonable grounds for suspecting that the person specified in the application—

(a) holds recoverable property or associated property, or

(b) has, at any time, held property that was recoverable property or associated property at the time.]

(4) In the case of a money laundering investigation, there must be reasonable grounds for suspecting that the person specified in the application for the order has committed a money laundering offence.

(5) In the case of any investigation, there must be reasonable grounds for believing that customer information which may be provided in compliance with the order is likely to be of substantial value (whether or not by itself) to the investigation for the purposes of which the order is sought.

(6) In the case of any investigation, there must be reasonable grounds for believing that it is in the public interest for the customer information to be provided, having regard to the benefit likely to accrue to the investigation if the information is obtained.

NOTES

Sub-s (3A): substituted (for the original sub-s (3)) by the Crime and Courts Act 2013, s 49, Sch 19, Pt 1, paras 1, 11 (for savings see the note to s 341 at **[1.1645]**); the original subsection read as follows—

"(3)   In the case of a civil recovery investigation, there must be reasonable grounds for suspecting that—
  (a)   the property specified in the application for the order is recoverable property or associated property;
  (b)   the person specified in the application holds all or some of the property.".

[1.1671]
366   Offences
(1)   A financial institution commits an offence if without reasonable excuse it fails to comply with a requirement imposed on it under a customer information order.
(2)   A financial institution guilty of an offence under subsection (1) is liable on summary conviction to a fine not exceeding level 5 on the standard scale.
(3)   A financial institution commits an offence if, in purported compliance with a customer information order, it—
  (a)   makes a statement which it knows to be false or misleading in a material particular, or
  (b)   recklessly makes a statement which is false or misleading in a material particular.
(4)   A financial institution guilty of an offence under subsection (3) is liable—
  (a)   on summary conviction, to a fine not exceeding the statutory maximum, or
  (b)   on conviction on indictment, to a fine.

[1.1672]
367   Statements
(1)   A statement made by a financial institution in response to a customer information order may not be used in evidence against it in criminal proceedings.
(2)   But subsection (1) does not apply—
  (a)   in the case of proceedings under Part 2 or 4,
  (b)   on a prosecution for an offence under section 366(1) or (3), or
  (c)   on a prosecution for some other offence where, in giving evidence, the financial institution makes a statement inconsistent with the statement mentioned in subsection (1).
(3)   A statement may not be used by virtue of subsection (2)(c) against a financial institution unless—
  (a)   evidence relating to it is adduced, or
  (b)   a question relating to it is asked,
by or on behalf of the financial institution in the proceedings arising out of the prosecution.

[1.1673]
368   Disclosure of information
A customer information order has effect in spite of any restriction on the disclosure of information (however imposed).

[1.1674]
369   Supplementary
(1)   An application for a customer information order may be made ex parte to a judge in chambers.
(2)   Rules of court may make provision as to the practice and procedure to be followed in connection with proceedings relating to customer information orders.
(3)   An application to discharge or vary a customer information order may be made to the court by—
  (a)   the person who applied for the order;
  (b)   any person affected by the order.
(4)   The court—
  (a)   may discharge the order;
  (b)   may vary the order.
(5)   If an accredited financial investigator, [a [National Crime Agency officer],] a constable or [an officer of Revenue and Customs] [or an immigration officer] applies for a customer information order, an application to discharge or vary the order need not be by the same accredited financial investigator, [National Crime Agency officer] constable or [officer of Revenue and Customs] [or immigration officer].
(6)   References to a person who applied for a customer information order must be construed accordingly.
(7)   An accredited financial investigator, [a [National Crime Agency officer],] a constable or [an officer of Revenue and Customs] [or an immigration officer] may not make an application for a customer information order or an application to vary such an order unless he is a senior appropriate officer or he is authorised to do so by a senior appropriate officer.
(8)   Subsections (2) to (6) do not apply to orders made in England and Wales for the purposes of a civil recovery investigation.

NOTES

Sub-s (5) is amended as follows:

Word "a" in first (outer) pair of square brackets inserted by virtue of the Serious Crime Act 2007, s 74(2)(d), Sch 8, Pt 4, paras 103, 111(1), (2)(a).

Word "National Crime Agency officer" (in both places they occur) substituted by the Crime and Courts Act 2013, s 15, Sch 8, Pt 2, paras 108, 141 (for general transitional provisions in connection with the abolition of SOCA, see Sch 8, Pt 1 to the 2013 Act.

Words "an officer of Revenue and Customs" and "officer of Revenue and Customs" in square brackets substituted by the Finance Act 2013, s 224, Sch 48, paras 1, 14(1), (2).

Words "or an immigration officer" and "or immigration officer" in square brackets inserted by the Crime and Courts Act 2013, s 55(14), Sch 21, Pt 1, paras 14, 35(1), (2).

Sub-s (7) is amended as follows:

Word "a" in first (outer) pair of square brackets inserted by virtue of the Serious Crime Act 2007, s 74(2)(d), Sch 8, Pt 4, paras 103, 111(1), (3).

Words "National Crime Agency officer" in second (inner) pair of square brackets substituted by the Crime and Courts Act 2013, s 15, Sch 8, Pt 2, paras 108, 141 (for general transitional provisions in connection with the abolition of SOCA, see Sch 8, Pt 1 to the 2013 Act.

Words "an officer of Revenue and Customs" in square brackets substituted by the Finance Act 2013, s 224, Sch 48, paras 1, 14(1), (3).

Words "or an immigration officer" in square brackets inserted by the Crime and Courts Act 2013, s 55(14), Sch 21, Pt 1, paras 14, 35(1), (3).

Transitional provisions: see the second note to s 330 at **[1.1628]**.

Rules: the Crown Court (Amendment) Rules 2003, SI 2003/422 (see the note to s 351 at **[2.365]**); the Criminal Procedure Rules 2014, SI 2014/1610.

Account monitoring orders

[1.1675]
370 Account monitoring orders

(1) A judge may, on an application made to him by an appropriate officer, make an account monitoring order if he is satisfied that each of the requirements for the making of the order is fulfilled.

[(1A) No application for an account monitoring order may be made in relation to a detained cash investigation.]

(2) The application for an account monitoring order must state that—
   (a) a person specified in the application is subject to a confiscation investigation[, a civil recovery investigation][, an exploitation proceeds investigation] or a money laundering investigation, . . .
   (b) . . .

(3) The application must also state that—
   (a) the order is sought for the purposes of the investigation;
   (b) the order is sought against the financial institution specified in the application in relation to account information of the description so specified.

(4) Account information is information relating to an account or accounts held at the financial institution specified in the application by the person so specified (whether solely or jointly with another).

(5) The application for an account monitoring order may specify information relating to—
   (a) all accounts held by the person specified in the application for the order at the financial institution so specified,
   (b) a particular description, or particular descriptions, of accounts so held, or
   (c) a particular account, or particular accounts, so held.

(6) An account monitoring order is an order that the financial institution specified in the application for the order must, for the period stated in the order, provide account information of the description specified in the order to an appropriate officer in the manner, and at or by the time or times, stated in the order.

(7) The period stated in an account monitoring order must not exceed the period of 90 days beginning with the day on which the order is made.

NOTES

Sub-s (1A): inserted by the Serious Crime Act 2007, s 77, Sch 10, paras 1, 12.

Sub-s (2): words in first pair of square brackets in para (a) inserted, and para (b) and word immediately preceding it (omitted) repealed, by the Crime and Courts Act 2013, s 49, Sch 19, Pt 1, paras 1, 12 (for savings see the note to s 341 at **[1.1645]**) words in second pair of square brackets in para (a) inserted by the Coroners and Justice Act 2009, s 169, Sch 19, paras 1, 17.

[1.1676]
371 Requirements for making of account monitoring order

(1) These are the requirements for the making of an account monitoring order.

(2) In the case of a confiscation investigation, there must be reasonable grounds for suspecting that the person specified in the application for the order has benefited from his criminal conduct.

[(3A) In the case of a civil recovery investigation, there must be reasonable grounds for suspecting that the person specified in the application holds recoverable property or associated property.]

(4) In the case of a money laundering investigation, there must be reasonable grounds for suspecting that the person specified in the application for the order has committed a money laundering offence.

(5) In the case of any investigation, there must be reasonable grounds for believing that account information which may be provided in compliance with the order is likely to be of substantial value (whether or not by itself) to the investigation for the purposes of which the order is sought.

(6) In the case of any investigation, there must be reasonable grounds for believing that it is in the public interest for the account information to be provided, having regard to the benefit likely to accrue to the investigation if the information is obtained.

NOTES

Sub-s (3A): substituted (for the original sub-s (3)) by the Crime and Courts Act 2013, s 49, Sch 19, Pt 1, paras 1, 13 (for savings see the note to s 341 at **[1.1645]**); the original subsection read as follows—

"(3) In the case of a civil recovery investigation, there must be reasonable grounds for suspecting that—
   (a)   the property specified in the application for the order is recoverable property or associated property;
   (b)   the person specified in the application holds all or some of the property.".

[1.1677]
372 Statements
(1) A statement made by a financial institution in response to an account monitoring order may not be used in evidence against it in criminal proceedings.
(2) But subsection (1) does not apply—
   (a)   in the case of proceedings under Part 2 or 4,
   (b)   in the case of proceedings for contempt of court, or
   (c)   on a prosecution for an offence where, in giving evidence, the financial institution makes a statement inconsistent with the statement mentioned in subsection (1).
(3) A statement may not be used by virtue of subsection (2)(c) against a financial institution unless—
   (a)   evidence relating to it is adduced, or
   (b)   a question relating to it is asked,
by or on behalf of the financial institution in the proceedings arising out of the prosecution.

[1.1678]
373 Applications
An application for an account monitoring order may be made ex parte to a judge in chambers.

[1.1679]
374 Disclosure of information
An account monitoring order has effect in spite of any restriction on the disclosure of information (however imposed).

[1.1680]
375 Supplementary
(1) Rules of court may make provision as to the practice and procedure to be followed in connection with proceedings relating to account monitoring orders.
(2) An application to discharge or vary an account monitoring order may be made to the court by—
   (a)   the person who applied for the order;
   (b)   any person affected by the order.
(3) The court—
   (a)   may discharge the order;
   (b)   may vary the order.
(4) If an accredited financial investigator, [a [National Crime Agency officer],] a constable or [an officer of Revenue and Customs] [or an immigration officer] applies for an account monitoring order, an application to discharge or vary the order need not be by the same accredited financial investigator, [National Crime Agency officer] constable or [officer of Revenue and Customs] [or immigration officer].
(5) References to a person who applied for an account monitoring order must be construed accordingly.
(6) Account monitoring orders have effect as if they were orders of the court.
(7) This section does not apply to orders made in England and Wales for the purposes of a civil recovery investigation.

NOTES

Sub-s (4) is amended as follows:

Word "a" in first (outer) pair of square brackets inserted by virtue of the Serious Crime Act 2007, s 74(2)(d), Sch 8, Pt 4, paras 103, 112.

Word "National Crime Agency officer" (in both places they occur) substituted by the Crime and Courts Act 2013, s 15, Sch 8, Pt 2, paras 108, 142 (for general transitional provisions in connection with the abolition of SOCA, see Sch 8, Pt 1 to the 2013 Act.

Words "an officer of Revenue and Customs" and "officer of Revenue and Customs" in square brackets substituted by the Finance Act 2013, s 224, Sch 48, paras 1, 15.

Words "or an immigration officer" and "or immigration officer" in square brackets inserted by the Crime and Courts Act 2013, s 55(14), Sch 21, Pt 1, paras 14, 36.

Transitional provisions: see the second note to s 330 at **[1.1628]**.

Rules: the Crown Court (Amendment) Rules 2003, SI 2003/422; the Criminal Procedure Rules 2014, SI 2014/1610.

Evidence overseas

[1.1681]
[375A Evidence overseas
(1) This section applies if a person or property is subject to a civil recovery investigation, a detained cash investigation or an exploitation proceeds investigation.
(2) A judge may request assistance under this section if—
   (a) an application is made by an appropriate officer or a person subject to the investigation, and
   (b) the judge thinks that there is relevant evidence in a country or territory outside the United Kingdom.
(3) The relevant Director or a senior appropriate officer may request assistance under this section if the Director or officer thinks that there is relevant evidence in a country or territory outside the United Kingdom.
(4) The assistance that may be requested under this section is assistance in obtaining outside the United Kingdom relevant evidence specified in the request.
(5) Relevant evidence is—
   (a) in relation to an application or request made for the purposes of a civil recovery investigation, evidence relevant for the purpose of identifying recoverable property or associated property, including evidence as to a matter described in section 341(2)(a) to (d);
   (b) in relation to an application or request made for the purposes of a detained cash investigation, evidence as to a matter described in section 341(3A)(a) or (b);
   (c) in relation to an application or request made for the purposes of an exploitation proceeds investigation, evidence as to a matter described in section 341(5)(a) to (d).
(6) A request for assistance under this section may be sent—
   (a) to a court or tribunal which is specified in the request and which exercises jurisdiction in the place where the evidence is to be obtained,
   (b) to the government of the country or territory concerned, or
   (c) to an authority recognised by the government of the country or territory concerned as the appropriate authority for receiving requests for assistance of that kind.
(7) Alternatively, a request for assistance under this section may be sent to the Secretary of State with a view to it being forwarded to a court, tribunal, government or authority mentioned in subsection (6).
(8) The Secretary of State must forward the request for assistance to the court, tribunal, government or authority.
(9) In a case of urgency, a request for assistance under this section may be sent to—
   (a) the International Criminal Police Organisation, or
   (b) any person competent to receive it under any provisions adopted under the EU Treaties, for forwarding to the court, tribunal, government or authority mentioned in subsection (6).
(10) Rules of court may make provision as to the practice and procedure to be followed in connection with proceedings relating to requests for assistance made by a judge under this section.
(11) "Evidence" includes documents, information in any other form and material.]

NOTES
Commencement: 22 November 2014 (sub-ss (5), (10), (11) so far as is necessary for the purpose of making rules of court); 1 June 2015 (otherwise).
Inserted by the Crime and Courts Act 2013, s 49, Sch 19, Pt 2, paras 24, 26.

[1.1682]
[375B Evidence overseas: restrictions on use
(1) This section applies to evidence obtained by means of a request for assistance under section 375A.
(2) The evidence must not be used for any purpose other than—
   (a) for the purposes of the investigation for which it was obtained, or
   (b) for the purposes of proceedings described in subsection (3) or any proceedings arising out of such proceedings.
(3) Those proceedings are—
   (a) if the request was made for the purposes of a civil recovery investigation, proceedings under Chapter 2 of Part 5 of this Act arising out of the investigation;
   (b) if the request was made for the purposes of a detained cash investigation, proceedings under Chapter 3 of Part 5 of this Act arising out of the investigation;

(c)   if the request was made for the purposes of an exploitation proceeds investigation, proceedings under Part 7 of the Coroners and Justice Act 2009 arising out of the investigation.

(4)   Subsection (2) does not apply if the court, tribunal, government or authority to whom the request for assistance was sent consents to the use.]

NOTES

Commencement: 1 June 2015.

Inserted by the Crime and Courts Act 2013, s 49, Sch 19, Pt 2, paras 24, 26.

[Officers of Revenue and Customs

[1.1683]

[375C Restriction on exercise of certain powers conferred on officers of Revenue and Customs

(1)   This section applies to the powers conferred on an officer of Revenue and Customs which are exercisable in connection with—

(a)   a production order made or to be made in relation to a confiscation investigation or a money laundering investigation,

(b)   a search and seizure warrant issued or to be issued in relation to a confiscation investigation or a money laundering investigation,

(c)   a customer information order, and

(d)   an account monitoring order.

(2)   The powers are exercisable by the officer only so far as the officer is exercising a function relating to a matter other than an excluded matter.

(3)   The reference in subsection (2) to an excluded matter is to a matter specified in section 54(4)(b) of, or in any of paragraphs 3, 5, 7, 10, 12 and 14 to 30 of Schedule 1 to, the Commissioners for Revenue and Customs Act 2005.]

NOTES

Commencement: 17 July 2013.

Inserted, together with the preceding heading, by the Finance Act 2013, s 224, Sch 48, paras 1, 16.

376   *(Repealed by the Serious Crime Act 2007, ss 74(2), 92, Sch 8, Pt 4, paras 103, 113, Sch 14, except in relation to confiscation investigations begun before 1 April 2008 and carried on by SOCA on or after that date.)*

Code of practice

[1.1684]

377   Code of practice [of Secretary of State etc]

(1)   The Secretary of State must prepare a code of practice as to the exercise by all of the following of functions they have under this Chapter—

[(a)   the Director General of the National Crime Agency;

(b)   other National Crime Agency officers;]

(c)   [in relation to England and Wales,] accredited financial investigators;

(d)   [in relation to England and Wales,] constables;

[(e)   officers of Revenue and Customs;]

[(f)   immigration officers].

(2)   After preparing a draft of the code the Secretary of State—

(a)   must publish the draft;

(b)   must consider any representations made to him about the draft;

(c)   may amend the draft accordingly.

(3)   After the Secretary of State has proceeded under subsection (2) he must lay the code before Parliament.

(4)   When he has done so the Secretary of State may bring the code into operation on such day as he may appoint by order.

(5)   A person specified in subsection (1)(a) to [(f)] must comply with a code of practice which is in operation under this section in the exercise of any function he has under this Chapter.

(6)   If such a person fails to comply with any provision of such a code of practice he is not by reason only of that failure liable in any criminal or civil proceedings.

(7)   But the code of practice is admissible in evidence in such proceedings and a court may take account of any failure to comply with its provisions in determining any question in the proceedings.

(8)   The Secretary of State may from time to time revise a code previously brought into operation under this section; and the preceding provisions of this section apply to a revised code as they apply to the code as first prepared.

(9)   . . .

NOTES

Section heading: words in square brackets inserted by the Serious Crime Act 2007, s 74(2)(d), Sch 8, Pt 4, paras 103, 114(1), (2).

Sub-s (1) is amended as follows:

Part 1   Statutes

Paras (a), (b) substituted by the Crime and Courts Act 2013, s 15, Sch 8, Pt 2, paras 108, 143 (for general transitional provisions in connection with the abolition of SOCA, see Sch 8, Pt 1 to the 2013 Act).

Words in square brackets in paras (c), (d) inserted by the Northern Ireland Act 1998 (Devolution of Policing and Justice Functions) Order 2010, SI 2010/976, art 12, Sch 14, paras 47, 67(1), (2).

Para (e) substituted by the Finance Act 2013, s 224, Sch 48, paras 1, 17.

Para (f) added by the Crime and Courts Act 2013, s 55, Sch 21, Pt 1, paras 14, 37(1), (2).

Sub-s (5): "(f)" in square brackets substituted by the Crime and Courts Act 2013, s 55, Sch 21, Pt 1, paras 14, 37(1), (3).

Sub-s (9): repealed by SI 2010/976, art 12, Sch 14, paras 47, 67(1), (3), subject to transitional provisions in arts 28–31 thereof.

Transitional provisions: see the second note to s 330 at **[1.1628]**.

Orders: the Proceeds of Crime Act 2002 (Investigations in England, Wales and Northern Ireland: Code of Practice) Order 2008, SI 2008/946; the Proceeds of Crime Act 2002 (Investigations: Code of Practice) (England and Wales) Order 2015, SI 2015/729.

[1.1685]
[377ZA   Code of practice (Northern Ireland)
(1)   The Department of Justice in Northern Ireland must prepare a code of practice as to the exercise, in relation to Northern Ireland, by constables and accredited financial investigators of functions they have under this Chapter.
(2)   After preparing a draft of the code the Department of Justice—
  (a)   must publish the draft;
  (b)   must consider any representations made to the Department of Justice about the draft;
  (c)   may amend the draft accordingly.
(3)   After the Department of Justice has proceeded under subsection (2) it must lay the code before the Northern Ireland Assembly.
(4)   When the Department of Justice has done so it may bring the code into operation on such day as the Department of Justice may appoint by order.
(5)   Section 41(3) of the Interpretation Act (Northern Ireland) 1954 applies for the purposes of subsection (3) in relation to the laying of a code as it applies in relation to the laying of a statutory document under an enactment.
(6)   A constable or accredited financial investigator must comply with a code of practice which is in operation under this section in the exercise of any function he has under this Chapter.
(7)   If a constable or accredited financial investigator fails to comply with any provision of such a code of practice he is not by reason only of that failure liable in any criminal or civil proceedings.
(8)   But the code of practice is admissible in evidence in such proceedings and a court may take account of any failure to comply with its provisions in determining any question in the proceedings.
(9)   The Department of Justice may from time to time revise a code previously brought into operation under this section; and the preceding provisions of this section apply to a revised code as they apply to the code as first prepared.]

NOTES
Inserted, together with s 377ZB, by the Northern Ireland Act 1998 (Devolution of Policing and Justice Functions) Order 2010, SI 2010/976, art 12, Sch 14, paras 47, 68, subject to transitional provisions in arts 28–31 thereof.

[1.1686]
[377ZB   Disapplication of PACE codes
The following provisions do not apply to an appropriate officer or the relevant authority in the exercise of any function either has under this Chapter—
  (a)   section 67(9) of the Police and Criminal Evidence Act 1984 (application of codes of practice under that Act to persons other than police officers);
  (b)   Article 66(8) of the Police and Criminal Evidence (Northern Ireland) Order 1989 (which makes similar provision for Northern Ireland).]

NOTES
Inserted as noted to s 377ZA at **[1.1685]**.

[1.1687]
[377A   Code of practice of Attorney General or Advocate General for Northern Ireland
(1)   The Attorney General must prepare a code of practice as to—
  (a)   the exercise by the Director of Public Prosecutions . . . and the Director of the Serious Fraud Office of functions they have under this Chapter; and
  (b)   the exercise by any other person, who is the relevant authority by virtue of section 357(9) in relation to a confiscation investigation, of functions he has under this Chapter in relation to England and Wales as the relevant authority.
(2)   The Advocate General for Northern Ireland must prepare a code of practice as to—
  (a)   the exercise by the Director of Public Prosecutions for Northern Ireland of functions he has under this Chapter; and
  (b)   the exercise by any other person, who is the relevant authority by virtue of section 357(9) in relation to a confiscation investigation, of functions he has under this Chapter in relation to Northern Ireland as the relevant authority.

(3)   After preparing a draft of the code the Attorney General or (as the case may be) the Advocate General for Northern Ireland—
 (a)   must publish the draft;
 (b)   must consider any representations made to him about the draft;
 (c)   may amend the draft accordingly.
(4)   After the Attorney General or the Advocate General for Northern Ireland has proceeded under subsection (3) he must lay the code before Parliament.
(5)   When the code has been so laid the Attorney General or (as the case may be) the Advocate General for Northern Ireland may bring the code into operation on such day as he may appoint by order.
(6)   A person specified in subsection (1)(a) or (b) or (2)(a) or (b) must comply with a code of practice which is in operation under this section in the exercise of any function he has under this Chapter to which the code relates.
(7)   If such a person fails to comply with any provision of such a code of practice the person is not by reason only of that failure liable in any criminal or civil proceedings.
(8)   But the code of practice is admissible in evidence in such proceedings and a court may take account of any failure to comply with its provisions in determining any question in the proceedings.
(9)   The Attorney General or (as the case may be) the Advocate General for Northern Ireland may from time to time revise a code previously brought into operation under this section; and the preceding provisions of this section apply to a revised code as they apply to the code as first prepared.
(10)   In this section references to the Advocate General for Northern Ireland are to be read, before the coming into force of section 27(1) of the Justice (Northern Ireland) Act 2002 (c 26), as references to the Attorney General for Northern Ireland.]

NOTES
Inserted by the Serious Crime Act 2007, s 74(2)(d), Sch 8, Pt 4, paras 103, 115.
Para (1): words omitted repealed by the Public Bodies (Merger of the Director of Public Prosecutions and the Director of Revenue and Customs Prosecutions) Order 2014, SI 2014/834, art 3(3), Sch 2, paras 19, 28 (for general transitional provisions, etc, relating to the abolition of the Revenue and Customs Prosecutions Office and the transfer of the functions of the Director of Revenue and Customs Prosecutions to the Director of Public Prosecutions, see arts 4–10 of the 2014 Order).
Transitional provisions: see the second note to s 330 at **[1.1628]**.
Orders: the Proceeds of Crime Act 2002 (Investigative Powers of Prosecutors in England, Wales and Northern Ireland: Code of Practice) Order 2008, SI 2008/1978; the Proceeds of Crime Act 2002 (Investigative Powers of Prosecutors: Code of Practice) (England and Wales) Order 2015, SI 2015/612.

Interpretation

[1.1688]
378   Officers
(1)   In relation to a confiscation investigation these are appropriate officers—
 [(a)   a National Crime Agency officer;]
 (b)   an accredited financial investigator;
 (c)   a constable;
 [(d)   an officer of Revenue and Customs;]
 [(e)   an immigration officer.]
(2)   In relation to a confiscation investigation these are senior appropriate officers—
 [(a)   a senior National Crime Agency officer;]
 (b)   a police officer who is not below the rank of superintendent;
 (c)   [an officer of Revenue and Customs] who is not below such grade as is designated by the Commissioners of Customs and Excise as equivalent to that rank;
 [(ca)   an immigration officer who is not below such grade as is designated by the Secretary of State as equivalent to that rank;]
 (d)   an accredited financial investigator who falls within a description specified in an order made for the purposes of this paragraph by the Secretary of State under section 453.
(3)   In relation to a civil recovery investigation[—
 (a)   a [National Crime Agency officer] or the relevant Director is an appropriate officer;
 (b)   a [senior National Crime Agency officer] is a senior appropriate officer.]
[(3A)   In relation to a detained cash investigation these are appropriate officers—
 (a)   a constable;
 [(ab)   an accredited financial investigator;]
 (b)   an officer of Revenue and Customs;]
 [(c)   an immigration officer.]
[(3AA)   In relation to a detained cash investigation these are senior appropriate officers—
 (a)   a police officer who is not below the rank of superintendent;
 (b)   an accredited financial investigator who falls within a description specified in an order made for the purposes of this paragraph by the Secretary of State under section 453;
 (c)   an officer of Revenue and Customs who is not below such grade as is designated by the Commissioners for Her Majesty's Revenue and Customs as equivalent to that rank;
 [(d)   an immigration officer who is not below such grade as is designated by the Secretary of State as equivalent to that rank.]]

[(3B) The reference in paragraph (ab) of subsection (3A) to an accredited financial investigator is a reference to an accredited financial investigator who falls within a description specified in an order made for the purposes of that paragraph by the Secretary of State under section 453.]

(4) In relation to a money laundering investigation these are appropriate officers—

    (a) an accredited financial investigator;

    (b) a constable;

    [(c) an officer of Revenue and Customs;]

    [(d) an immigration officer.]

(5) For the purposes of section 342, in relation to a money laundering investigation a person authorised for the purposes of money laundering investigations by [the [Director General of the National Crime Agency]] is also an appropriate officer.

(6) In relation to a money laundering investigation these are senior appropriate officers—

    (a) a police officer who is not below the rank of superintendent;

    (b) [an officer of Revenue and Customs] who is not below such grade as is designated by the Commissioners of Customs and Excise as equivalent to that rank;

    [(ba) an immigration officer who is not below such grade as is designated by the Secretary of State as equivalent to that rank;]

    (c) an accredited financial investigator who falls within a description specified in an order made for the purposes of this paragraph by the Secretary of State under section 453.

[(6A) In relation to an exploitation proceeds investigation[—

    (a)] [a National Crime Agency officer] is an appropriate officer

    [(b) a [senior National Crime Agency officer] is a senior appropriate officer].]

(7) . . .

[(8) For the purposes of this Part a [senior National Crime Agency officer] is—

    (a) the [Director General of the National Crime Agency]; or

    (b) any [other National Crime Agency officer] authorised by the Director General (whether generally or specifically) for this purpose.]

NOTES

Sub-s (1) is amended as follows:

Para (a) substituted by the Crime and Courts Act 2013, s 15, Sch 8, Pt 2, paras 108, 144(1), (2) (for general transitional provisions in connection with the abolition of SOCA, see Sch 8, Pt 1 to the 2013 Act).

Para (d) substituted by the Finance Act 2013, s 224, Sch 48, paras 1, 18(a).

Para (e) inserted by the Crime and Courts Act 2013, s 55(5)(a).

Sub-s (2): para (a) substituted by the Crime and Courts Act 2013, s 15, Sch 8, Pt 2, paras 108, 144(1), (3) (for general transitional provisions in connection with the abolition of SOCA, see Sch 8, Pt 1 to the 2013 Act); words in square brackets in para (c) substituted by the Finance Act 2013, s 224, Sch 48, paras 1, 18(b); para (ca) inserted by the Crime and Courts Act 2013, s 55(5)(b).

Sub-s (3): words in first (outer) pair of square brackets substituted by the Serious Crime Act 2007, s 74(2), Sch 8, Pt 4, paras 103, 116(1), (4); words in square brackets in paras (a), (b) substituted by the Crime and Courts Act 2013, s 15, Sch 8, Pt 2, paras 108, 144(1), (4) (for general transitional provisions in connection with the abolition of SOCA, see Sch 8, Pt 1 to the 2013 Act).

Sub-s (3A): inserted by the Serious Crime Act 2007, s 77, Sch 10, paras 1, 13; para (ab) inserted by s 80(7) of that Act; para (c) added by the Crime and Courts Act 2013, s 55(5)(c).

Sub-s (3AA): inserted by the Crime and Courts Act 2013, s 49, Sch 19, Pt 2, paras 24, 27(1), (2); para (d) added by s 49 of, and Sch 19, Pt 3, para 29 to, the 2013 Act.

Sub-s (3B): inserted by the Serious Crime Act 2007, s 80(8).

Sub-s (4): para (c) substituted by the Finance Act 2013, s 224, Sch 48, paras 1, 18(b); para (d) inserted by the Crime and Courts Act 2013, s 55(5)(d).

Sub-s (5): word in first (outer) pair of square brackets substituted by virtue of the Serious Organised Crime and Police Act 2005, s 59, Sch 4, paras 168, 175; words in second (inner) pair of square brackets substituted by the Crime and Courts Act 2013, s 15, Sch 8, Pt 2, paras 108, 144(1), (5) (for general transitional provisions in connection with the abolition of SOCA, see Sch 8, Pt 1 to the 2013 Act).

Sub-s (6): words in square brackets in para (b) substituted by the Finance Act 2013, s 224, Sch 48, paras 1, 18(b); para (ba) inserted by the Crime and Courts Act 2013, s 55(5)(e).

Sub-s (6A) was inserted by the Coroners and Justice Act 2009, s 169, Sch 19, paras 1, 18, and has been amended as follows:

Word "— (a)" in square brackets inserted, and para (b) inserted, by the Crime and Courts Act 2013, s 49, Sch 19, Pt 2, paras 24, 27(1), (3).

Words in square brackets in para (a) substituted by the Crime and Courts Act 2013, s 15, Sch 8, Pt 2, paras 108, 144(1), (6) (for general transitional provisions in connection with the abolition of SOCA, see Sch 8, Pt 1 to the 2013 Act).

Words in square brackets in para (b) substituted by the Crime and Courts Act 2013, s 49, Sch 19, Pt 3, para 30.

Sub-s (7): repealed by the Serious Crime Act 2007, ss 74(2), 92, Sch 8, Pt 4, paras 103, 116(1), (6), Sch 14.

Sub-s (8): added by the Serious Crime Act 2007, s 74(2), Sch 8, Pt 4, paras 103, 116(1), (7); words in square brackets substituted by the Crime and Courts Act 2013, s 15, Sch 8, Pt 2, paras 108, 144(1), (7) (for general transitional provisions in connection with the abolition of SOCA, see Sch 8, Pt 1 to the 2013 Act).

Transitional provisions: see the second note to s 330 at **[1.1628]**.

[1.1689]

379 Miscellaneous

"Document", "excluded material" and "premises" have the same meanings as in the Police and Criminal Evidence Act 1984 (c 60) or (in relation to Northern Ireland) the Police and Criminal Evidence (Northern Ireland) Order 1989 (SI 1989/1341 (NI 12)).

380–412 ((*Ch 3) outside the scope of this work.*)

CHAPTER 4
INTERPRETATION

[1.1690]
413 Criminal conduct
(1) Criminal conduct is conduct which—
  (a) constitutes an offence in any part of the United Kingdom, or
  (b) would constitute an offence in any part of the United Kingdom if it occurred there.
(2) A person benefits from conduct if he obtains property or a pecuniary advantage as a result of or in connection with the conduct.
(3) References to property or a pecuniary advantage obtained in connection with conduct include references to property or a pecuniary advantage obtained in both that connection and some other.
(4) If a person benefits from conduct his benefit is the property or pecuniary advantage obtained as a result of or in connection with the conduct.
(5) It is immaterial—
  (a) whether conduct occurred before or after the passing of this Act, and
  (b) whether property or a pecuniary advantage constituting a benefit from conduct was obtained before or after the passing of this Act.

[1.1691]
414 Property
(1) Property is all property wherever situated and includes—
  (a) money;
  (b) all forms of property, real or personal, heritable or moveable;
  (c) things in action and other intangible or incorporeal property.
(2) "Recoverable property" and "associated property" have the same meanings as in Part 5.
(3) The following rules apply in relation to property—
  (a) property is obtained by a person if he obtains an interest in it;
  (b) references to an interest, in relation to land in England and Wales or Northern Ireland, are to any legal estate or equitable interest or power;
  (c) references to an interest, in relation to land in Scotland, are to any estate, interest, servitude or other heritable right in or over land, including a heritable security;
  (d) references to an interest, in relation to property other than land, include references to a right (including a right to possession).

[1.1692]
415 Money laundering offences
(1) An offence under section 327, 328 or 329 is a money laundering offence.
[(1A) Each of the following is a money laundering offence—
  (a) an offence under section 93A, 93B or 93C of the Criminal Justice Act 1988;
  (b) an offence under section 49, 50 or 51 of the Drug Trafficking Act 1994;
  (c) an offence under section 37 or 38 of the Criminal Law (Consolidation) (Scotland) Act 1995;
  (d) an offence under article 45, 46 or 47 of the Proceeds of Crime (Northern Ireland) Order 1996.]
(2) Each of the following is a money laundering offence—
  (a) an attempt, conspiracy or incitement to commit an offence specified in subsection (1);
  (b) aiding, abetting, counselling or procuring the commission of an offence specified in subsection (1).

NOTES
Sub-s (1A): inserted by the Serious Organised Crime and Police Act 2005, s 107(1), (4).
See further, in relation to England, Wales and Northern Ireland, the Serious Crime Act 2007, s 63(1), Sch 6, Pt 1, para 44(b), which provides that the reference in sub-s (2)(a) above to (or to conduct amounting to) the common law offence of inciting the commission of another offence, has effect (as from the day that offence is abolished) as a reference to (or to conduct amounting to) offences under the Serious Crime Act 2007, Pt 2.
Criminal Justice Act 1988, ss 93A, 93B, 93C; Drug Trafficking Act 1994, ss 49, 50, 51; Criminal Law (Consolidation) (Scotland) Act 1995, ss 37, 38: repealed by ss 456, 457 of, and Sch 11, paras 17, 25, Sch 12 to, this Act.

[1.1693]
416 Other interpretative provisions
(1) These expressions are to be construed in accordance with these provisions of this Part—
  civil recovery investigation: section 341(2) and (3)
  confiscation investigation: section 341(1)
  [detained cash investigation: section 341(3A)]
  money laundering investigation: section 341(4).
(2) In the application of this Part to England and Wales and Northern Ireland, these expressions are to be construed in accordance with these provisions of this Part—

    account information: section 370(4)
    account monitoring order: section 370(6)
    appropriate officer: section 378
    customer information: section 364
    customer information order: section 363(5)
    disclosure order: section 357(4)
    document: section 379
    order to grant entry: section 347(3)
    production order: section 345(4)
    [relevant authority: section 357(7) to (9)
    relevant Director: section 352(5A)]
    search and seizure warrant: section 352(4)
    senior appropriate officer: section 378
    [senior [National Crime Agency officer]: section 378(8)].

(3)   In the application of this Part to Scotland, these expressions are to be construed in accordance with these provisions of this Part—
    account information: section 404(5)
    account monitoring order: section 404(7)
    customer information: section 398
    customer information order: section 397(6)
    disclosure order: section 391(4)
    production order: section 380(5)
    proper person: section 412
    search warrant: section 387(4).

[(3A)   The expressions "realisable property" and "confiscation order"—
    (a)   in the application of this Part to England and Wales, have the same meanings as in Part 2;
    (b)   in the application of this Part to Scotland, have the same meanings as in Part 3;
    (c)   in the application of this Part to Northern Ireland, have the same meanings as in Part 4.]

(4)   "Financial institution" means a person carrying on a business in the regulated sector.

(5)   But a person who ceases to carry on a business in the regulated sector (whether by virtue of paragraph 5 of Schedule 9 or otherwise) is to continue to be treated as a financial institution for the purposes of any requirement under—
    (a)   a customer information order, or
    (b)   an account monitoring order,
to provide information which relates to a time when the person was a financial institution.

(6)   References to a business in the regulated sector must be construed in accordance with Schedule 9.

(7)   "Recovery order", "interim receiving order" and "interim administration order" have the same meanings as in Part 5.

[(7A)   "Unlawful conduct" has the meaning given by section 241.]

(8)   References to notice in writing include references to notice given by electronic means.

(9)   This section and sections 413 to 415 apply for the purposes of this Part.

NOTES

Sub-s (1): words in square brackets inserted by the Serious Crime Act 2007, s 77, Sch 10, paras 1, 24(1), (2).

Sub-s (2): words in first and second (outer) pairs of square brackets inserted by the Serious Crime Act 2007, s 74(2)(d), Sch 8, Pt 4, paras 103, 117; words in second (inner) pair of square brackets substituted by the Crime and Courts Act 2013, s 15, Sch 8, Pt 2, paras 108, 145 (for general transitional provisions in connection with the abolition of SOCA, see Sch 8, Pt 1 to the 2013 Act).

Sub-s (3A): inserted by the Serious Crime Act 2015, s 85, Sch 4, para 56.

Sub-s (7A): inserted by the Serious Crime Act 2007, s 77, Sch 10, paras 1, 24(1), (3).

Transitional provisions: see the second note to s 330 at **[1.1628]**.

417–447   ((*Pts 9–11*) *outside the scope of this work.*)

PART 12
MISCELLANEOUS AND GENERAL

448–455   (*Outside the scope of this work.*)

General

456, 457   (*Outside the scope of this work.*)

[1.1694]
458   Commencement

(1)   The preceding provisions of this Act (except the provisions specified in subsection (3) [or (4)]) come into force in accordance with provision made by the Secretary of State by order.

(2)   But no order may be made [by the Secretary of State] which includes provision for the commencement of Part 5, 8 or 10 unless the Secretary of State has consulted the Scottish Ministers.

(3)   The following provisions come into force in accordance with provision made by the Scottish Ministers by order after consultation with the Secretary of State—

(a)   Part 3;
(b)   this Part, to the extent that it relates to Part 3.

[(4)   Any provision of this Act which provides for the repeal of any provision of the Proceeds of Crime (Northern Ireland) Order 1996 comes into force in accordance with provision made by the Department of Justice in Northern Ireland by order.]

NOTES

Sub-ss (1), (2): words in square brackets inserted by the Northern Ireland Act 1998 (Devolution of Policing and Justice Functions) Order 2010, SI 2010/976, art 12, Sch 14, paras 47, 73(a), (b), subject to transitional provisions in arts 28–31 thereof.

Sub-s (4): added by SI 2010/976, art 12, Sch 14, paras 47, 73(c), subject to transitional provisions in arts 28–31 thereof.

Orders: the commencement order relevant to the provisions of this Act reproduced in this work is the Proceeds of Crime Act 2002 (Commencement No 4, Transitional Provisions and Savings) Order 2003, SI 2003/120 (as amended by SI 2003/333).

459, 460   (*Outside the scope of this work.*)

[1.1695]
461   Extent
(1)   Part 2 extends to England and Wales only.
(2)   In Part 8, Chapter 2 extends to England and Wales and Northern Ireland only.
(3)   These provisions extend to Scotland only—
   (a)   Part 3;
   (b)   in Part 8, Chapter 3.
(4)   Part 4 extends to Northern Ireland only.
(5)   The amendments in Schedule 11 have the same extent as the provisions amended.
(6)   The repeals and revocations in Schedule 12 have the same extent as the provisions repealed or revoked.

[1.1696]
462   Short title
This Act may be cited as the Proceeds of Crime Act 2002.

SCHEDULES

SCHEDULES 1–8

(*Schs 1–8 outside the scope of this work.*)

SCHEDULE 9
REGULATED SECTOR AND SUPERVISORY AUTHORITIES

Section 330

[PART 1
REGULATED SECTOR

Business in the Regulated Sector

[1.1697]
1. (1)   A business is in the regulated sector to the extent that it consists of—
   (a)   the acceptance by a credit institution of deposits or other repayable funds from the public, or the granting by a credit institution of credits for its own account;
   (b)   the carrying on of one or more of the activities listed in points 2 to 12[, 14 and 15] of Annex 1 to the [Capital Requirements Regulation] by an undertaking other than—
      (i)   a credit institution; or
      (ii)   an undertaking whose only listed activity is trading for own account in one or more of the products listed in point 7 of Annex 1 to the [Capital Requirements Regulation] and which does not act on behalf of a customer (that is, a third party which is not a member of the same group as the undertaking);
   (c)   the carrying on of activities covered by *the Life Assurance Consolidation Directive* by an insurance company authorised in accordance with that Directive;
   (d)   the provision of investment services or the performance of investment activities by a person (other than a person falling within Article 2 of the Markets in Financial Instruments Directive) whose regular occupation or business is the provision to other persons of an investment service or the performance of an investment activity on a professional basis;
   (e)   the marketing or other offering of units or shares by a collective investment undertaking;
   (f)   the activities of an insurance intermediary as defined in Article 2(5) of the Insurance Mediation Directive, other than a tied insurance intermediary as mentioned in Article 2(7) of that Directive, in respect of contracts of long-term insurance within the meaning given by article 3(1) of, and Part II of Schedule 1 to, the Financial Services and Markets Act 2000 (Regulated Activities) Order 2001;

(g)   the carrying on of any of the activities mentioned in paragraphs (b) to (f) by a branch located in an EEA State of a person referred to in those paragraphs (or of an equivalent person in any other State), wherever its head office is located;

(h)   the activities of the National Savings Bank;

(i)   any activity carried on for the purpose of raising money authorised to be raised under the National Loans Act 1968 under the auspices of the Director of Savings;

(j)   the carrying on of statutory audit work within the meaning of section 1210 of the Companies Act 2006 (meaning of "statutory auditor" etc) by any firm or individual who is a statutory auditor within the meaning of Part 42 of that Act (statutory auditors);

(k)   the activities of a person appointed to act as an insolvency practitioner within the meaning of section 388 of the Insolvency Act 1986 (meaning of "act as insolvency practitioner") or article 3 of the Insolvency (Northern Ireland) Order 1989;

(l)   the provision to other persons of accountancy services by a firm or sole practitioner who by way of business provides such services to other persons;

(m)   the provision of advice about the tax affairs of other persons by a firm or sole practitioner who by way of business provides advice about the tax affairs of other persons;

(n)   the participation in financial or real property transactions concerning—
>   (i)   the buying and selling of real property (or, in Scotland, heritable property) or business entities;
>   (ii)   the managing of client money, securities or other assets;
>   (iii)   the opening or management of bank, savings or securities accounts;
>   (iv)   the organisation of contributions necessary for the creation, operation or management of companies; or
>   (v)   the creation, operation or management of trusts, companies or similar structures,
>
>   by a firm or sole practitioner who by way of business provides legal or notarial services to other persons;

(o)   the provision to other persons by way of business by a firm or sole practitioner of any of the services mentioned in sub-paragraph (4);

(p)   the carrying on of estate agency work . . . by a firm or a sole practitioner who carries on, or whose employees carry on, such work;

(q)   the trading in goods (including dealing as an auctioneer) whenever a transaction involves the receipt of a payment or payments in cash of at least 15,000 euros in total, whether the transaction is executed in a single operation or in several operations which appear to be linked, by a firm or sole trader who by way of business trades in goods;

(r)   operating a casino under a casino operating licence (within the meaning given by section 65(2) of the Gambling Act 2005 (nature of licence));

[(s)   the auctioning by an auction platform of two-day spot or five-day futures, within the meanings given by Article 3 of the Emission Allowance Auctioning Regulation];

[(t)   bidding directly, on behalf of clients, in auctions of emissions allowances in accordance with the Emission Allowance Auctioning Regulation].

(2)   For the purposes of sub-paragraph (1)(a) and (b) "credit institution" means—

(a)   a credit institution as defined in [Article 4(1)(1) of the Capital Requirements Regulation]; or

(b)   a branch (within the meaning of [Article 4(1)(17) of that Regulation]) located in an EEA state of an institution falling within paragraph (a) (or of an equivalent institution in any other State) wherever its head office is located.

(3)   For the purposes of sub-paragraph (1)(n) a person participates in a transaction by assisting in the planning or execution of the transaction or otherwise acting for or on behalf of a client in the transaction.

(4)   The services referred to in sub-paragraph (1)(o) are—

(a)   forming companies or other legal persons;

(b)   acting, or arranging for another person to act—
>   (i)   as a director or secretary of a company;
>   (ii)   as a partner of a partnership; or
>   (iii)   in a similar position in relation to other legal persons;

(c)   providing a registered office, business address, correspondence or administrative address or other related services for a company, partnership or any other legal person or arrangement;

(d)   acting, or arranging for another person to act, as—
>   (i)   a trustee of an express trust or similar legal arrangement; or
>   (ii)   a nominee shareholder for a person other than a company whose securities are listed on a regulated market.

(5)   For the purposes of sub-paragraph (4)(d) "regulated market"—

(a)   in relation to any EEA State, has the meaning given by point 14 of Article 4(1) of the Markets in Financial Instruments Directive; and

(b)   in relation to any other State, means a regulated financial market which subjects companies whose securities are admitted to trading to disclosure obligations which are contained in international standards and are equivalent to the specified disclosure obligations.

(6)   For the purposes of sub-paragraph (5) "the specified disclosure obligations" means disclosure requirements consistent with—

   (a)   Article 6(1) to (4) of Directive 2003/6/EC of the European Parliament and of the Council of 28th January 2003 on insider dealing and market manipulation;

   (b)   Articles 3, 5, 7, 8, 10, 14 and 16 of Directive 2003/71/EC of the European Parliament and of the Council of 4th November 2003 on the prospectuses to be published when securities are offered to the public or admitted to trading;

   (c)   Articles 4 to 6, 14, 16 to 19 and 30 of Directive 2004/109/EC of the European Parliament and of the Council of 15th December 2004 relating to the harmonisation of transparency requirements in relation to information about issuers whose securities are admitted to trading on a regulated market; or

   (d)   Community legislation made under the provisions mentioned in paragraphs (a) to (c).

[(6A)   For the purposes of sub-paragraph (1)(p) "estate agency work" is to be read in accordance with section 1 of the Estate Agents Act 1979 (estate agency work), but for those purposes references in that section to disposing of or acquiring an interest in land are (despite anything in section 2 of that Act) to be taken to include references to disposing of or acquiring an estate or interest in land outside the United Kingdom where that estate or interest is capable of being owned or held as a separate interest.]

(7)   For the purposes of sub-paragraph (1)(j) and (l) to (q) "firm" means any entity, whether or not a legal person, that is not an individual and includes a body corporate and a partnership or other unincorporated association.

(8)   For the purposes of sub-paragraph (1)(q) "cash" means notes, coins or travellers' cheques in any currency.

[(9)   For the purposes of sub-paragraph (1)(s) "auction platform" means a platform on which auctions of emissions allowances are held in accordance with the Emission Allowance Auctioning Regulation.]

Excluded Activities

2. (1)   A business is not in the regulated sector to the extent that it consists of—

   (a)   the issuing of withdrawable share capital within the limit set by [section 24 of the Co-operative and Community Benefit Societies Act 2014 (maximum interest in a society's withdrawable shares)], or the acceptance of deposits from the public within the limit set by [section 67(2) of that Act (registered society with withdrawable share capital not to carry on banking etc)], by [a registered society within the meaning of that Act];

   (b)   the issuing of withdrawable share capital within the limit set by section 6 of the Industrial and Provident Societies Act (Northern Ireland) 1969 (maximum shareholding in society), or the acceptance of deposits from the public within the limit set by section 7(3) of that Act (carrying on of banking by societies), by a society registered under that Act;

   (c)   the carrying on of any activity in respect of which a person who is (or falls within a class of persons) specified in any of paragraphs 2 to 23, 25 to 38 or 40 to 49 of the Schedule to the Financial Services and Markets Act 2000 (Exemption) Order 2001 is exempt;

   (d)   the exercise of the functions specified in section 45 of the Financial Services Act 1986 (miscellaneous exemptions) by a person who was an exempted person for the purposes of that section immediately before its repeal; [or]

   (e)   the engaging in financial activity which fulfils all of the conditions set out in paragraphs (a) to (g) of sub-paragraph (3) of this paragraph by a person whose main activity is that of a high value dealer; . . .

   (f)   . . .

(2)   For the purposes of sub-paragraph (1)(e) a "high value dealer" means a person mentioned in paragraph 1(1)(q) when carrying on the activities mentioned in that paragraph.

(3)   A business is not in the regulated sector to the extent that it consists of financial activity if—

   (a)   the person's total annual turnover in respect of the financial activity does not exceed £64,000;

   (b)   the financial activity is limited in relation to any customer to no more than one transaction exceeding 1,000 euros, whether the transaction is carried out in a single operation, or a series of operations which appear to be linked;

   (c)   the financial activity does not exceed 5% of the person's total annual turnover;

   (d)   the financial activity is ancillary to the person's main activity and directly related to that activity;

   (e)   the financial activity is not the transmission or remittance of money (or any representation of monetary value) by any means;

   (f)   the main activity of the person carrying on the financial activity is not an activity mentioned in paragraph 1(1)(a) to (p) or (r); and

   (g)   the financial activity is provided only to customers of the person's main activity and is not offered to the public.

(4)   A business is not in the regulated sector if it is carried on by—

   (a)   the Auditor General for Scotland;

(b)   the Auditor General for Wales;
(c)   the Bank of England;
(d)   the Comptroller and Auditor General;
(e)   the Comptroller and Auditor General for Northern Ireland;
(f)   the Official Solicitor to the Supreme Court, when acting as trustee in his official capacity; or
(g)   the Treasury Solicitor.

Interpretation

3. (1)   In this Part—

. . .

["the Capital Requirements Regulation" means Regulation (EU) No 575/2013 of the European Parliament and of the Council;]
["the Emission Allowance Auctioning Regulation" means Commission Regulation (EU) No 1031/2010 of 12 November 2010 on the timing, administration and other aspects of auctioning of greenhouse gas emission allowances pursuant to Directive 2003/87/EC of the European Parliament and of the Council establishing a scheme for greenhouse gas emission allowances trading within the Community;]
"the Insurance Mediation Directive" means directive 2002/92/EC of the European Parliament and of the Council of 9th December 2002 on insurance mediation;
"the Life Assurance Consolidation Directive" means directive 2002/83/EC of the European Parliament and of the Council of 5th November 2002 concerning life assurance; and
"the Markets in Financial Instruments Directive" means directive 2004/39/EC of the European Parliament and of the Council of 12th April 2004 on markets in financial instruments;
["the Solvency 2 Directive" means Directive 2009/138/EC of the European Parliament and of the Council of 25 November 2009 on the taking-up and pursuit of the business of Insurance and Reinsurance (Solvency II)].

(2)   In this Part references to amounts in euros include references to equivalent amounts in another currency.

(3)   Terms used in this Part and in the Banking Consolidation Directive or the Markets in Financial Instruments Directive have the same meaning in this Part as in those Directives.]

NOTES
Substituted by the Proceeds of Crime Act 2002 (Business in the Regulated Sector and Supervisory Authorities) Order 2007, SI 2007/3287, art 2.
Para 1 is amended as follows:
The words in the first pair of square brackets in sub-para (1)(b) were substituted by the Electronic Money Regulations 2011, SI 2011/99, reg 79, Sch 4, Pt 1, para 4.
The words in the second and third pairs of square brackets in sub-para (1)(b) were substituted, and the words in square brackets in sub-para (2) were substituted, by the Capital Requirements Regulations 2013, SI 2013/3115, reg 46(1), Sch 2, Pt 2, para 41(1)–(4).
For the words in italics in sub-para (1)(c) there are substituted the words "the Solvency 2 Directive" by the Solvency 2 Regulations 2015, SI 2015/575, reg 59, Sch 1, Pt 2, para 23(1), (2), as from 1 January 2016. Note that the amending provision actually provides "in paragraph 1(1)(c) for "the Life Assurance Directive" substitute "the Solvency 2 Directive""; it is assumed that this is an error and the intention is to substitute the words "the Life Assurance Consolidation Directive".
The words omitted from sub-para (1)(p) were repealed, and sub-para (6A) was inserted, by the Terrorism Act 2000 and Proceeds of Crime Act 2002 (Business in the Regulated Sector) (No 2) Order 2012, SI 2012/2299, art 3.
Sub-paras (1)(s) and (9) were added by the Terrorism Act 2000 and Proceeds of Crime Act 2002 (Business in the Regulated Sector) Order 2011, SI 2011/2701, art 3.
Sub-para (1)(t) inserted by the Terrorism Act 2000 and Proceeds of Crime Act 2002 (Business in the Regulated Sector) Order 2012, SI 2012/1534, art 2.
Para 2: words in square brackets in sub-para (1)(a) substituted by the Co-operative and Community Benefit Societies Act 2014, s 151, Sch 4, Pt 2, para 81; word in square brackets in sub-para (1)(d) added, and sub-para (1)(f) (and the word immediately preceding it) repealed, by the Localism Act 2011, ss 183, 237, Sch 18, para 2, Sch 25, Pt 29.
Para 3: definition "the Banking Consolidation Directive" (omitted) repealed, and definition "the Capital Requirements Regulation" inserted, by SI 2013/3115, reg 46(1), Sch 2, Pt 2, para 41(1), (5); definition "the Emission Allowance Auctioning Regulation" inserted by SI 2011/2701, art 3; definition "the Life Assurance Consolidation Directive" in italics repealed, and definition "the Solvency 2 Directive inserted, by SI 2015/575, reg 59, Sch 1, Pt 2, para 23(1), (3), as from 1 January 2016.

[PART 2
SUPERVISORY AUTHORITIES

[1.1698]
4. (1)   The following bodies are supervisory authorities—
(a)   the Commissioners for Her Majesty's Revenue and Customs;
(b)   the Department of Enterprise, Trade and Investment in Northern Ireland;
[(c)   Financial Conduct Authority;]
(d)   the Gambling Commission;
(e)   . . .
[(ea) Prudential Regulation Authority;]
(f)   the Secretary of State; and

(g)   the professional bodies listed in sub-paragraph (2).

(2)   The professional bodies referred to in sub-paragraph (1)(g) are—

    (a)   the Association of Accounting Technicians;
    (b)   the Association of Chartered Certified Accountants;
    (c)   the Association of International Accountants;
    (d)   the Association of Taxation Technicians;
    (e)   the Chartered Institute of Management Accountants;
    (f)   the Chartered Institute of Public Finance and Accountancy;
    (g)   the Chartered Institute of Taxation;
    (h)   the Council for Licensed Conveyancers;
    (i)   the Faculty of Advocates;
    (j)   the Faculty Office of the Archbishop of Canterbury;
    (k)   the General Council of the Bar;
    (l)   the General Council of the Bar of Northern Ireland;
    (m)   the Insolvency Practitioners Association;
    (n)   the Institute of Certified Bookkeepers;
    (o)   the Institute of Chartered Accountants in England and Wales;
    (p)   the Institute of Chartered Accountants in Ireland;
    (q)   the Institute of Chartered Accountants of Scotland;
    (r)   the Institute of Financial Accountants;
    (s)   the International Association of Book-keepers;
    (t)   the Law Society;
    (u)   the Law Society for Northern Ireland; and
    (v)   the Law Society of Scotland.]

NOTES

Substituted as noted to Pt 1 at **[1.1697]**.

Para 4: sub-para (1)(c) substituted, and sub-para (1)(ea) inserted, by the Financial Services Act 2012, s 114(1), Sch 18, Pt 2, para 94(1), (4); sub-para 4(1)(e) repealed by the Enterprise and Regulatory Reform Act 2013 (Competition) (Consequential, Transitional and Saving Provisions) Order 2014, SI 2014/892, art 2, Sch 1, Pt 2, para 159 (for transitional provisions in relation to the abolition of the OFT and the Competition Commission and the continuity of functions, etc, see art 3 of that Order).

PART 3
POWER TO AMEND

[1.1699]

5. The Treasury may by order amend Part 1 or 2 of this Schedule.

NOTES

Orders: the Proceeds of Crime Act 2002 (Business in the Regulated Sector and Supervisory Authorities) Order 2007, SI 2007/3287; the Terrorism Act 2000 and Proceeds of Crime Act 2002 (Business in the Regulated Sector) Order 2011, SI 2011/2701; the Terrorism Act 2000 and Proceeds of Crime Act 2002 (Business in the Regulated Sector) Order 2012, SI 2012/1534; the Terrorism Act 2000 and Proceeds of Crime Act 2002 (Business in the Regulated Sector) (No 2) Order 2012, SI 2012/2299.

SCHEDULES 10–12

(Schs 10–12 outside the scope of this work.)

ENTERPRISE ACT 2002

(2002 c 40)

ARRANGEMENT OF SECTIONS

PART 1
GENERAL FUNCTIONS OF THE CMA

General functions of CMA

PART 2
THE COMPETITION APPEAL TRIBUNAL

The Competition Appeal Tribunal

PART 4
MARKET INVESTIGATIONS

CHAPTER 1
MARKET INVESTIGATION REFERENCES

Market studies

Making of references

Determination of references

CHAPTER 2
PUBLIC INTEREST CASES

Intervention notices

Intervention notices under section 139(1)

Intervention notices under section 139(2)

Other

Establish and provide for the functions of the Office of Fair Trading, the Competition Appeal Tribunal and the Competition Service; to make provision about mergers and market structures and conduct; to amend the constitution and functions of the Competition Commission; to create an offence for those entering into certain anticompetitive agreements; to provide for the disqualification of directors of companies engaging in certain anticompetitive practices; to make other provision about competition law; to amend the law relating to the protection of the collective interests of consumers; to make further provision about the disclosure of information obtained under competition and consumer legislation; to amend the Insolvency Act 1986 and make other provision about insolvency; and for connected purposes

[7 November 2002]

PART 1
[GENERAL FUNCTIONS OF THE CMA]

NOTES

The Part heading (The Office of Fair Trading) was substituted by the Enterprise and Regulatory Reform Act 2013, s 26(3), Sch 5, Pt 2, paras 59, 65 (for transitional provisions relating to the abolition of the OFT (and the Competition Commission), including provisions relating to continuity of functions, see the Enterprise and Regulatory Reform Act 2013 (Commencement No 6, Transitional Provisions and Savings) Order 2014, SI 2014/416, Schedule at **[2.1126]**).

Transfer of consumer advice scheme function: the OFT's power under this Part to support a public consumer advice scheme was, so far as regards support of a scheme that takes the form of providing, or securing the provision of, an arrangement for giving advice without charge to individual consumers on matters personal to them, transferred to Citizens Advice and Citizens Advice Scotland: see the Public Bodies (The Office of Fair Trading Transfer of Consumer Advice Scheme Function and Modification of Enforcement Functions) Order 2013, SI 2013/783, art 2 at **[2.984]**.

1–4 (*Repealed by the Enterprise and Regulatory Reform Act 2013, s 26(3), Sch 5, Pt 4, para 229. For transitional provisions relating to the abolition of the OFT, including provisions relating to continuity of functions, see the Enterprise and Regulatory Reform Act 2013 (Commencement No 6, Transitional Provisions and Savings) Order 2014, SI 2014/416, Schedule at* **[2.1126]**. *See also the Enterprise and Regulatory Reform Act 2013 (Competition) (Consequential, Transitional and Saving Provisions) Order 2014, SI 2014/892, art 3(7) which provides that the repeal of s 2(3) does not apply in so far as that section creates references to the transferor to which art 3(5) or (6) are capable of applying (references to the transferor to be construed as references to the transferee).*)

General functions of [CMA]

[1.1700]
5   Acquisition of information etc
(1)   The [CMA] has the function of obtaining, compiling and keeping under review information about matters relating to the carrying out of its functions.

(2)   That function is to be carried out with a view to (among other things) ensuring that the [CMA] has sufficient information to take informed decisions and to carry out its other functions effectively.

(3)   In carrying out that function the [CMA] may carry out, commission or support (financially or otherwise) research.

NOTES

Words in square brackets (including the word in the preceding heading) substituted by the Enterprise and Regulatory Reform Act 2013, s 26(3), Sch 5, Pt 2, paras 59, 60 (for transitional provisions relating to the abolition of the OFT, including provisions relating to continuity of functions, see the Enterprise and Regulatory Reform Act 2013 (Commencement No 6, Transitional Provisions and Savings) Order 2014, SI 2014/416, Schedule at **[2.1126]**).

[1.1701]
6   Provision of information etc to the public
(1)   The [CMA] has the function of—

(a)   making the public aware of the ways in which competition may benefit consumers in, and the economy of, the United Kingdom; and

(b)   giving information or advice in respect of matters relating to any of its functions to the public.

(2)   In carrying out those functions the [CMA] may—

(a)   publish educational materials or carry out other educational activities; or

(b)   support (financially or otherwise) the carrying out by others of such activities or the provision by others of information or advice.

NOTES

Words in square brackets substituted by the Enterprise and Regulatory Reform Act 2013, s 26(3), Sch 5, Pt 2, paras 59, 61 (for transitional provisions relating to the abolition of the OFT, including provisions relating to continuity of functions, see the Enterprise and Regulatory Reform Act 2013 (Commencement No 6, Transitional Provisions and Savings) Order 2014, SI 2014/416, Schedule at [**2.1126**]).

[1.1702]
7   Provision of information and advice to Ministers etc
(1)   The [CMA] has the function of—

(a)   making proposals, or

(b)   giving other information or advice,

on matters relating to any of its functions to any Minister of the Crown or other public authority (including proposals, information or advice as to any aspect of the law or a proposed change in the law).

[(1A)   The CMA may, in particular, carry out the function under subsection (1)(a) by making a proposal in the form of a recommendation to a Minister of the Crown about the potential effect of a proposal for Westminster legislation on competition within any market or markets in the United Kingdom for goods or services

(1B)   The CMA must publish such a recommendation in such manner as the CMA considers appropriate for bringing the subject matter of the recommendation to the attention of those likely to be affected by it.]

(2)   A Minister of the Crown may request the [CMA] to make proposals or give other information or advice on any matter relating to any of its functions; and the [CMA] shall, so far as is reasonably practicable and consistent with its other functions, comply with the request.

[(3)   In this section—

"market in the United Kingdom" includes—

(a)   so far as it operates in the United Kingdom or a part of the United Kingdom, any market which operates there and in another country or territory or in a part of another country or territory; and

(b)   any market which operates only in a part of the United Kingdom;

and the reference to a market for goods or services includes a reference to a market for goods and services; and

"Westminster legislation" means—

(a)   an Act of Parliament, or

(b)   subordinate legislation (within the meaning given by section 21 of the Interpretation Act 1978).]

NOTES

Sub-ss (1A), (1B), (3): inserted and added respectively by the Small Business, Enterprise and Employment Act 2015, s 37.

Other words in square brackets substituted by the Enterprise and Regulatory Reform Act 2013, s 26(3), Sch 5, Pt 2, paras 59, 62 (for transitional provisions relating to the abolition of the OFT, including provisions relating to continuity of functions, see the Enterprise and Regulatory Reform Act 2013 (Commencement No 6, Transitional Provisions and Savings) Order 2014, SI 2014/416, Schedule at [**2.1126**]).

8   (*Repealed by the Enterprise and Regulatory Reform Act 2013, s 26(3), Sch 5, Pt 2, paras 59, 63. For general transitional provisions relating to the abolition of the OFT, including provisions relating to continuity of functions, see the Enterprise and Regulatory Reform Act 2013 (Commencement No 6, Transitional Provisions and Savings) Order 2014, SI 2014/416, Schedule at [**2.1126**].*)

[1.1703]
[8A   Exclusion of public consumer advice scheme
The [CMA] may not under this Part support a public consumer advice scheme, where that support of a scheme consists of providing, or securing the provision of, an arrangement for giving advice without charge to individual consumers on matters personal to them.]

NOTES

Commencement: 28 March 2013.

Inserted by the Public Bodies (The Office of Fair Trading Transfer of Consumer Advice Scheme Function and Modification of Enforcement Functions) Order 2013, SI 2013/783, art 3.

Word in square brackets substituted by the Enterprise and Regulatory Reform Act 2013 (Competition) (Consequential, Transitional and Saving Provisions) Order 2014, SI 2014/892, art 2, Sch 1, Pt 1, paras 1, 2 (for transitional provisions in relation to the abolition of the OFT and the Competition Commission and the continuity of functions, etc, see art 3 of that Order).

Miscellaneous

9   (*Repeals the Fair Trading Act 1973, s 12, and the Competition Act 1980, s 13.*)

[1.1704]

10   Part 2 of the 1973 Act

(1)   The following provisions of the 1973 Act shall cease to have effect—

- (a)   section 3 and Schedule 2 (which establish, and make provision with respect to, the Consumer Protection Advisory Committee);
- (b)   sections 13 to 21 (which relate to references made to, and reports of, that Committee); and
- (c)   section 22 (power of Secretary of State to make orders in pursuance of a report of that Committee).

(2)–(4)   . . .

NOTES

Sub-ss (2)–(4): repealed by the Consumer Protection from Unfair Trading Regulations 2008, SI 2008/1277, reg 30(1), (3), Sch 2, Pt 1, paras 68, 69, Sch 4, subject to savings in reg 30(2) of, and Sch 3 to, those Regulations at **[2.595]**, **[2.597]**.

[1.1705]

11   Super-complaints to [CMA]

(1)   This section applies where a designated consumer body makes a complaint to the [CMA] that any feature, or combination of features, of a market in the United Kingdom for goods or services is or appears to be significantly harming the interests of consumers.

(2)   The [CMA] must, within 90 days after the day on which it receives the complaint, publish a response stating how it proposes to deal with the complaint, and in particular—

- (a)   whether it has decided to take any action, or to take no action, in response to the complaint, and
- (b)   if it has decided to take action, what action it proposes to take.

(3)   The response must state the [CMA's] reasons for its proposals.

(4)   The Secretary of State may by order amend subsection (2) by substituting any period for the period for the time being specified there.

(5)   "Designated consumer body" means a body designated by the Secretary of State by order.

(6)   The Secretary of State—

- (a)   may designate a body only if it appears to him to represent the interests of consumers of any description, and
- (b)   must publish (and may from time to time vary) other criteria to be applied by him in determining whether to make or revoke a designation.

(7)   The [CMA]—

- (a)   must issue guidance as to the presentation by the complainant of a reasoned case for the complaint, and
- (b)   may issue such other guidance as appears to it to be appropriate for the purposes of this section.

(8)   An order under this section—

- (a)   shall be made by statutory instrument, and
- (b)   shall be subject to annulment in pursuance of a resolution of either House of Parliament.

(9)   In this section—

- (a)   references to a feature of a market in the United Kingdom for goods or services have the same meaning as if contained in Part 4, and
- (b)   "consumer" means an individual who is a consumer within the meaning of that Part.

NOTES

Section heading, sub-ss (1)–(3), (7): words in square brackets substituted by the Enterprise and Regulatory Reform Act 2013, s 26(3), Sch 5, Pt 2, paras 59, 64.

Orders: the Enterprise Act 2002 (Bodies Designated to make Super-complaints) Order 2004, SI 2004/1517; the Enterprise Act 2002 (Bodies Designated to make Super-complaints) (Amendment) Order 2009, SI 2009/2079.

PART 2
THE COMPETITION APPEAL TRIBUNAL

The Competition Appeal Tribunal

[1.1706]

12   The Competition Appeal Tribunal

(1)   There shall be a tribunal, to be called the Competition Appeal Tribunal (in this Part referred to as "the Tribunal").

(2)   The Tribunal shall consist of—

- (a)   a person appointed by the Lord Chancellor to preside over the Tribunal (in this Part referred to as "the President");
- [(aa)   such judges as are nominated from time to time by the Lord Chief Justice of England and Wales from the High Court of England and Wales;

(ab)   such judges as are nominated from time to time by the Lord President of the Court of Session from the judges of the Court of Session;

(ac)   such judges as are nominated from time to time by the Lord Chief Justice of Northern Ireland from the High Court in Northern Ireland;]

(b)   members appointed by the Lord Chancellor to form a panel of chairmen; and

(c)   members appointed by the Secretary of State to form a panel of ordinary members.

(3)   The Tribunal shall have a Registrar appointed by the Secretary of State.

(4)   The expenses of the Tribunal shall be paid by the Competition Service.

(5)   Schedule 2 (which makes further provision about the Tribunal) has effect.

NOTES

Sub-s (2): paras (aa)–(ac) inserted by the Consumer Rights Act 2015, s 82(1).

[1.1707]
13   The Competition Service
(1)   There shall be a body corporate called the Competition Service (in this Part referred to as "the Service").

(2)   The purpose of the Service is to fund, and provide support services to, the Competition Appeal Tribunal.

(3)   In subsection (2) "support services" includes the provision of staff, accommodation and equipment and any other services which facilitate the carrying out by the Tribunal of its functions.

(4)   The activities of the Service are not carried out on behalf of the Crown (and its property is not to be regarded as held on behalf of the Crown).

(5)   The Secretary of State shall pay to the Service such sums as he considers appropriate to enable it to fund the activities of the Tribunal and to carry out its other activities.

(6)   Schedule 3 (which makes further provision about the Service) has effect.

[1.1708]
14   Constitution of Tribunal for particular proceedings and its decisions
(1)   For the purposes of any proceedings before it[, including proceedings relating to the approval of a collective settlement under section 49A or 49B of the 1998 Act,] the Tribunal shall consist of a chairman and two other members.

[(1A)   But in the case of proceedings relating to a claim under section 47A of the 1998 Act which is subject to the fast-track procedure (as described in Tribunal rules), the Tribunal may consist of a chairman only.]

(2)   The chairman must be the President[, a judge within any of paragraphs (aa) to (ac) of section 12(2)] or a member of the panel of chairmen.

(3)   The other members may be chosen from [the judges within paragraphs (aa) to (ac) of section 12(2),] the panel of chairmen or the panel of ordinary members.

(4)   If the members of the Tribunal as constituted in accordance with this section are unable to agree on any decision, the decision is to be taken by majority vote.

(5)   This section has effect subject to [paragraphs 10A(1)(a) and 18] of Schedule 4 (consequences of a member of the Tribunal being unable to continue after the proceedings have begun to be heard).

(6)   Part 1 of Schedule 4 (which makes further provision about the decisions of the Tribunal and their enforcement) has effect.

NOTES

Sub-ss (1), (2): words in square brackets inserted by the Consumer Rights Act 2015, ss 81, 82(2)(a), Sch 8, Pt 2, paras 18, 19(1), (2).

Sub-s (1A): inserted by the Consumer Rights Act 2015, s 81, Sch 8, Pt 2, paras 18, 19(1), (3).

Sub-s (3): words in square brackets substituted by the Consumer Rights Act 2015, s 82(2)(b).

Sub-s (5): words in square brackets substituted by the Enterprise and Regulatory Reform Act 2013, s 48(6) (for transitional provisions relating to the abolition of the OFT, including provisions relating to continuity of functions, see the Enterprise and Regulatory Reform Act 2013 (Commencement No 6, Transitional Provisions and Savings) Order 2014, SI 2014/416, Schedule at **[2.1126]**).

[1.1709]
15   Tribunal rules
(1)   The Secretary of State may, after consulting the President and such other persons as he considers appropriate, make rules (in this Part referred to as "Tribunal rules") with respect to proceedings before the Tribunal[, including proceedings relating to the approval of a collective settlement under section 49A or 49B of the 1998 Act].

(2)   Tribunal rules may make provision with respect to matters incidental to or consequential upon appeals provided for by or under any Act to the Court of Appeal or the Court of Session in relation to a decision of the Tribunal.

(3)   Tribunal rules may—

(a)   specify qualifications for appointment as Registrar;

(b)   confer functions on the President or the Registrar in relation to proceedings before the Tribunal; and

(c)   contain incidental, supplemental, consequential or transitional provision.

(4)   The power to make Tribunal rules is exercisable by statutory instrument subject to annulment in pursuance of a resolution of either House of Parliament.

(5)   Part 2 of Schedule 4 (which makes further provision about the rules) has effect, but without prejudice to the generality of subsection (1).

NOTES

Sub-s (1): words in square brackets inserted by the Consumer Rights Act 2015, s 81, Sch 8, Pt 2, paras 18, 20.

Rules: the Competition Appeal Tribunal Rules 2003, SI 2003/1372; the Competition Appeal Tribunal (Amendment and Communications Act Appeals) Rules 2004, SI 2004/2068.

[1.1710]
16   Transfers of certain proceedings to and from Tribunal
(1)   The Lord Chancellor may by regulations—
  (a)   make provision enabling the court—
    (i)   to transfer to the Tribunal for its determination so much of any proceedings before the court as relates to an infringement issue; and
    (ii)   to give effect to the determination of that issue by the Tribunal; and
  (b)   make such incidental, supplementary, consequential, transitional or saving provision as the Lord Chancellor may consider appropriate.
(2)   The power to make regulations under subsection (1) is exercisable by statutory instrument subject to annulment in pursuance of a resolution of either House of Parliament.
(3)   Rules of court may prescribe the procedure to be followed in connection with a transfer mentioned in subsection (1).
(4)   The court may transfer to the Tribunal, in accordance with rules of court, so much of any proceedings before it as relates to a claim to which section 47A of the 1998 Act applies.
(5)   Rules of court may make provision in connection with the transfer from the Tribunal to the [court of all or any part of] a claim made in proceedings under section 47A of the 1998 Act.
(6)   In this section—
  "the court" means—
    (a)   the High Court [or the county court]; or
    (b)   the Court of Session or a sheriff court; and
  "infringement issue" means any question relating to whether or not an infringement of—
    (a)   the Chapter I prohibition or the Chapter II prohibition; or
    (b)   [Article 101 or 102] of the Treaty,
    has been or is being committed;
but otherwise any terms used in this section and Part 1 of the 1998 Act have the same meaning as they have in that Part.

NOTES

Sub-s (5): words in square brackets substituted by the Consumer Rights Act 2015, s 81, Sch 8, Pt 2, paras 18, 21.

Sub-s (6): in definition "the court" in para (a) words "or the county court" in square brackets substituted by the Crime and Courts Act 2013, s 17(5), Sch 9, Pt 3, para 81(a) (note that the amending provision inserts the words but this is considered to be an error); in definition "infringement issue" words in square brackets substituted by the Treaty of Lisbon (Changes in Terminology or Numbering) Order 2012, SI 2012/1809, art 3, Schedule, Pt 1.

17–130   (*S 17 substitutes the Competition Act 1998, s 47 at* **[1.1309]***; s 18 inserts s 47A of the 1998 Act at* **[1.1310]***; s 19 inserts s 47B of the 1998 Act at* **[1.1311]***; s 20 inserts s 58A of the 1998 Act at* **[1.1327]** *and amends 59(1) of that Act at* **[1.1328]***; s 21 introduces Sch 5 to this Act (further amendments of the 1998 Act); ss 22–130 (Pt 3: Mergers) outside the scope of this work.*)

PART 4
MARKET INVESTIGATIONS

CHAPTER 1
MARKET INVESTIGATION REFERENCES

[Market studies

[1.1711]
130A   Duty to publish market study notice
(1)   Where the CMA is proposing to carry out its functions under section 5 in relation to a matter for the purposes mentioned in subsection (2), the CMA must publish a notice under this section (referred to in this Part as a "market study notice").
(2)   The purposes are—
  (a)   to consider the extent to which a matter in relation to the acquisition or supply of goods or services of one or more than one description in the United Kingdom has or may have effects adverse to the interests of consumers; and
  (b)   to assess the extent to which steps can and should be taken to remedy, mitigate or prevent any such adverse effects.
(3)   A market study notice shall, in particular, specify—

(a) the matter in relation to which the CMA is proposing to carry out its functions under section 5;

(b) the period during which representations may be made to the CMA in relation to the matter; and

(c) the dates by which the CMA is required to comply with the requirements imposed on it by sections 131A and 131B.]

NOTES

Commencement: 1 April 2014.

Inserted, together with the preceding heading, by the Enterprise and Regulatory Reform Act 2013, s 38, Sch 12, para 1. For transitional provisions relating to the abolition of the OFT, including provisions relating to continuity of functions, see the Enterprise and Regulatory Reform Act 2013 (Commencement No 6, Transitional Provisions and Savings) Order 2014, SI 2014/416, Schedule at **[2.1126]**.

Making of references

[1.1712]
131 Power of [CMA] to make references

(1) [The CMA may, subject to subsection (4), make a reference to its chair for the constitution of a group under Schedule 4 to the Enterprise and Regulatory Reform Act 2013 if the CMA] has reasonable grounds for suspecting that any feature, or combination of features, of a market in the United Kingdom for goods or services prevents, restricts or distorts competition in connection with the supply or acquisition of any goods or services in the United Kingdom or a part of the United Kingdom.

(2) For the purposes of this Part any reference to a feature of a market in the United Kingdom for goods or services shall be construed as a reference to—

(a) the structure of the market concerned or any aspect of that structure;

(b) any conduct (whether or not in the market concerned) of one or more than one person who supplies or acquires goods or services in the market concerned; or

(c) any conduct relating to the market concerned of customers of any person who supplies or acquires goods or services.

[(2A) In a case where the feature or each of the features concerned falls within subsection (2)(b) or (c), a reference under subsection (1) may be made in relation to more than one market in the United Kingdom for goods or services.]

(3) In subsection (2) "conduct" includes any failure to act (whether or not intentional) and any other unintentional conduct.

(4) No reference shall be made under this section if—

(a) the making of the reference is prevented by [section 156(A1) or (1)]; or

(b) a reference has been made under section 132 [or 140A(6)] in relation to the same matter but has not been finally determined.

(5) References in this Part to a market investigation reference being finally determined shall be construed in accordance with section 183(3) to (6).

(6) In this Part—

["cross-market reference" means a reference under this section which falls within subsection (2A) or a reference under section 132 which falls within subsection (3A) of that section (and see section 140A);]

"market in the United Kingdom" includes—

(a) so far as it operates in the United Kingdom or a part of the United Kingdom, any market which operates there and in another country or territory or in a part of another country or territory; and

(b) any market which operates only in a part of the United Kingdom;

"market investigation reference" means a reference under this section or section 132 [or 140A(6)];

["ordinary reference" means a reference under this section or section 132 which is not a cross-market reference (and see section 140A);]

and references to a market for goods or services include references to a market for goods and services.

and references to a market for goods or services include references to a market for goods and services.

NOTES

Word in square brackets in the section heading, and words in square brackets in sub-s (1), substituted by the Enterprise and Regulatory Reform Act 2013, s 26(3), Sch 5, Pt 2, paras 59, 163 (for transitional provisions relating to the abolition of the OFT, including provisions relating to continuity of functions, see the Enterprise and Regulatory Reform Act 2013 (Commencement No 6, Transitional Provisions and Savings) Order 2014, SI 2014/416, Schedule at **[2.1126]**).

Sub-s (2A) inserted, the definitions "cross-market reference" and "ordinary reference" in sub-s (6) inserted, and words in square brackets in sub-s (4)(a) substituted, by the Enterprise and Regulatory Reform Act 2013, s 33 (as to transitional provisions etc, see the note above).

Words in square brackets in sub-s (4)(b) and in the definition "market investigation reference" in sub-s (6) inserted by the Enterprise and Regulatory Reform Act 2013, s 35(10), Sch 10, paras 1, 2 (as to transitional provisions etc, see the note above).

[1.1713]
[131A   Decisions about references under section 131: consultation
(1)   This section applies to a case where the CMA has published a market study notice and—
    (a)   the CMA is proposing to make a reference under section 131 in relation to the matter specified in the notice; or
    (b)   a representation has been made to the CMA within the period specified in the notice under section 130A(3)(b) to the effect that such a reference should be made but the CMA is proposing not to make such a reference.
(2)   The CMA shall—
    (a)   publish notice of the proposal concerned; and
    (b)   consult the relevant persons about the proposal, in such manner as it considers practicable, before deciding whether to make a reference.
(3)   The CMA may, for the purposes of subsection (1), ignore any representation which it considers to be frivolous or vexatious.
(4)   For the purposes of subsection (2), a person is a "relevant person" if the CMA considers that its decision whether to make a reference is likely to have a substantial impact on the person's interests.
(5)   In consulting a person for the purposes of this section, the CMA shall, so far as practicable, give its reasons for the proposal.
(6)   In considering what is practicable for the purposes of this section, the CMA shall, in particular, have regard to—
    (a)   the restrictions imposed by the time-table for making the decision (see section 131B); and
    (b)   any need to keep what is proposed, or the reasons for it, confidential.]

NOTES
Commencement: 1 April 2014.
Inserted, together with ss 131B, 131C, by the Enterprise and Regulatory Reform Act 2013, s 38, Sch 12, para 2 (for transitional provisions (including those relating to the abolition of the OFT and the continuity of functions), see the Enterprise and Regulatory Reform Act 2013 (Commencement No 6, Transitional Provisions and Savings) Order 2014, SI 2014/416, Schedule at **[2.1126]**).

[1.1714]
[131B   Market studies and the making of decisions to refer: time-limits
(1)   Where the CMA has published a market study notice in a case to which section 131A applies, the CMA shall, within the period of 6 months beginning with the date on which it publishes the notice—
    (a)   publish the notice under section 131A(2)(a); and
    (b)   begin the process of consultation under section 131A(2)(b) (but the CMA need not complete the process within that period).
(2)   Subsection (3) applies where—
    (a)   the CMA has published a market study notice;
    (b)   no representation has been made to the CMA within the period specified in the notice under section 130A(3)(b) to the effect that a reference under section 131 should be made in relation to the matter specified in the notice; and
    (c)   the CMA has decided not to make such a reference.
(3)   The CMA shall, within the period of 6 months beginning with the date on which it publishes the market study notice, publish notice of the decision not to make a reference.
(4)   Where the CMA has published a market study notice it shall, within the period of 12 months beginning with the date on which it publishes the notice, prepare and publish a report (referred to in this Part as a "market study report") which sets out—
    (a)   the findings of the CMA in relation to the matter specified in the notice; and
    (b)   the action (if any) which the CMA proposes to take in relation to the matter.
(5)   In a case to which section 131A applies, the market study report shall, in particular, contain—
    (a)   the decision of the CMA to make a reference under section 131 in relation to the matter specified in the market study notice, the decision to accept an undertaking under section 154 instead of making such a reference or (as the case may be) the decision otherwise not to make such a reference;
    (b)   the CMA's reasons for the decision; and
    (c)   such information as the CMA considers appropriate for facilitating a proper understanding of its reasons for the decision.
(6)   Where a market study report contains a decision of the CMA to make a reference under section 131 in relation to a matter, the CMA shall, at the same time as it publishes the report, make the reference.
(7)   This section is subject to section 140A (duty of Secretary of State to refer in public interest intervention cases).]

NOTES
Commencement: 1 April 2014.
Inserted as noted to s 131A at **[1.1713]**.

[1.1715]
[131C   Time-limits under section 131B: supplementary
(1)   The Secretary of State may by order amend section 131B so as to alter one or more of the following periods—
  (a)   the period of 6 months mentioned in subsection (1) or (3) or any period for the time being mentioned in either of those subsections in substitution for that period;
  (b)   the period of 12 months mentioned in subsection (4) or any period for the time being there mentioned in substitution for that period.
(2)   But no alteration may be made by virtue of subsection (1) which results in—
  (a)   the period for the time being mentioned in subsection (1) or (3) exceeding 6 months; or
  (b)   the period for the time being mentioned in subsection (4) exceeding 12 months.
(3)   Before making an order under this section the Secretary of State shall consult the CMA and such other persons as the Secretary of State considers appropriate.]

NOTES
  Commencement: 25 April 2013 (for the purposes of enabling the exercise of any power to make provision by regulations, rules or order made by statutory instrument); 1 April 2014 (otherwise).
  Inserted as noted to s 131A at **[1.1713]**.

[1.1716]
132   Ministerial power to make references
(1)   Subsection (3) applies where, in relation to any goods or services[—
  (a)]   the appropriate Minister is not satisfied with a decision of the [CMA] not to make a reference under section 131[; and
  (b)   in a case in which the CMA has published a market study notice under section 130A, the period permitted by section 131B for the preparation and publication by the CMA of the market study report has expired].
(2)   Subsection (3) also applies where, in relation to any goods or services, the appropriate Minister—
  (a)   has brought to the attention of the [CMA] information which the appropriate Minister considers to be relevant to the question of whether the [CMA] should make a reference under section 131; but
  (b)   is not satisfied that the [CMA] will decide, within such period as the appropriate Minister considers to be reasonable, whether [to publish a market study notice in relation to the matter concerned].
(3)   The appropriate Minister may, subject to subsection (4), make a reference to the [chair of the CMA for the constitution of a group under Schedule 4 to the Enterprise and Regulatory Reform Act 2013] if he has reasonable grounds for suspecting that any feature, or combination of features, of a market in the United Kingdom for goods or services prevents, restricts or distorts competition in connection with the supply or acquisition of any goods or services in the United Kingdom or a part of the United Kingdom.
[(3A)   In a case where the feature or each of the features concerned falls within section 131(2)(b) or (c), a reference under subsection (3) may be made in relation to more than one market in the United Kingdom for goods or services.]
(4)   No reference shall be made under this section if[—
  (a)]   the making of the reference is prevented by [section 156(A1) or (1)][; or
  (b)   a reference has been made under section 140A(6) in relation to the same matter but has not been finally determined].
(5)   In this Part "the appropriate Minister" means—
  (a)   the Secretary of State; or
  (b)   the Secretary of State and one or more than one other Minister of the Crown acting jointly.

NOTES
  The word "CMA" in square brackets (in each place that it occurs), and the words in square brackets in sub-s (3) were substituted, by the Enterprise and Regulatory Reform Act 2013, s 26(3), Sch 5, Pt 2, paras 59, 164 (for transitional provisions (including those relating to the abolition of the OFT and the Competition Commission and the continuity of functions), see the Enterprise and Regulatory Reform Act 2013 (Commencement No 6, Transitional Provisions and Savings) Order 2014, SI 2014/416, Schedule at **[2.1126]**).
  Words in first and final pairs of square brackets in sub-s (1) inserted, and words in final pair of square brackets in sub-s (2) substituted, by the Enterprise and Regulatory Reform Act 2013, s 38, Sch 12, paras 7, 10 (as to transitional provisions etc, see the note above).
  Sub-s (3A) inserted, and words "section 156(A1) or (1)" in square brackets in sub-s (4)(a) substituted, by the Enterprise and Regulatory Reform Act 2013, s 34(1)–(3) (as to transitional provisions etc, see the note above).
  Other words in square brackets in sub-s (4) inserted by the Enterprise and Regulatory Reform Act 2013, s 35(10), Sch 10, paras 1, 3 (as to transitional provisions etc, see the note above).

[1.1717]
133   Contents of references
(1)   A market investigation reference shall, in particular, specify—
  (a)   the enactment under which it is made;
  (b)   the date on which it is made; . . .

(c)   [in the case of an ordinary reference,] the description of goods or services to which the feature or combination of features concerned relates[; and

(d)   in the case of a cross-market reference, the feature or features concerned and the descriptions of goods or services to which it or they relate.]

(2)   A market investigation reference may be framed so as to require the [group constituted by the chair of the CMA in respect of the reference] to confine its investigation into the effects of features of markets in the United Kingdom for goods or services of a description specified in the reference to the effects of features of such of those markets as exist in connection with—

(a)   a supply [or, in the case of a cross-market reference, supplies], of a description specified in the reference, of the goods or services concerned; or

(b)   an acquisition [or, in the case of a cross-market reference, acquisitions], of a description specified in the reference, of the goods or services concerned.

(3)   A description of the kind mentioned in subsection (2)(a) or (b) may, in particular, be by reference to—

(a)   the place where the goods or services are supplied or acquired; or

(b)   the persons by or to whom they are supplied or by or from whom they are acquired.

NOTES

Sub-s (1): word omitted from para (b) repealed, words in square brackets in para (c) added, and para (d) (and the preceding word) added, by the Enterprise and Regulatory Reform Act 2013, s 34(4), Sch 9, paras 1, 2(1), (2) (for transitional provisions (including those relating to the abolition of the OFT and the Competition Commission and the continuity of functions), see the Enterprise and Regulatory Reform Act 2013 (Commencement No 6, Transitional Provisions and Savings) Order 2014, SI 2014/416, Schedule at **[2.1126]**).

Sub-s (2): words in first pair of square brackets substituted by the Enterprise and Regulatory Reform Act 2013, s 26(3), Sch 5, Pt 2, paras 59, 165 (as to transitional provisions etc, see the note above); words in square brackets in paras (a) and (b) inserted by s 34(4) of, and Sch 9, paras 1, 2(1), (3) to, the 2013 Act (as to transitional provisions etc, see the note above).

Determination of references

[1.1718]

[133A   Functions to be exercised by CMA groups

(1) Where a reference is made to the chair of the CMA under section 131, 132 or 140A for the constitution of a group under Schedule 4 to the Enterprise and Regulatory Reform Act 2013, the functions of the CMA under or by virtue of the following provisions of this Part in relation to the matter concerned are to be carried out on behalf of the CMA by the group so constituted—

(a)   sections 134 to 138B, except for section 135(1);

(b)   sections 140B to 145, 148, 148A and 151;

(c)   sections 157 and 158;

(d)   section 159;

(e)   section 160, except for subsection (6) of that section;

(f)   section 161, except for subsection (5) of that section;

(g)   section 162(4), so far as relating to an enforcement undertaking or enforcement order made on behalf of the CMA by the group;

(h)   section 164(2)(b), so far as relating to an enforcement order made on behalf of the CMA by the group;

(i)   section 167, so far as relating to an enforcement undertaking or enforcement order made on behalf of the CMA by the group;

(j)   section 168;

(k)   section 169, so far as relating to a decision mentioned in paragraph (a)(iii) of the definition of relevant decision in subsection (6) of that section;

(l)   section 172, so far as relating to anything done on behalf of the CMA by the group;

(m)   section 174, where the permitted purpose in question relates to a function that (by virtue of this section) is being or is to be carried out on behalf of the CMA by the group;

(n)   sections 174A to 174D, so far as relating to a notice given under section 174 on behalf of the CMA by the group;

(o)   section 179(5)(b), so far as relating to a decision of the group;

(p)   Schedule 10, so far as relating to an enforcement undertaking or enforcement order which the group is considering accepting or making, or which the group has accepted or made, on behalf of the CMA.

(2)   Nothing in subsection (1) prevents the CMA Board from carrying out a function of the CMA under or by virtue of the following provisions of this Part where the group constituted as mentioned in subsection (1) has ceased to exist—

(a)   section 160 and Schedule 10, so far as relating to the making of an order under section 160;

(b)   sections 159 to 161 and Schedule 10, so far as relating to the variation, supersession or release of enforcement undertakings or the variation or revocation of enforcement orders;

(c)   section 162(4);

(d)   section 164(2)(b);

(e)   section 167.]

NOTES

Commencement: 1 April 2014.

Inserted by the Enterprise and Regulatory Reform Act 2013, s 26(3), Sch 5, Pt 2, paras 59, 166 (for transitional provisions (including those relating to the abolition of the OFT and the Competition Commission and the continuity of functions), see the Enterprise and Regulatory Reform Act 2013 (Commencement No 6, Transitional Provisions and Savings) Order 2014, SI 2014/416, Schedule at **[2.1126]**).

[1.1719]
134 Questions to be decided on market investigation references

(1) The [CMA] shall, on [an ordinary] reference, decide whether any feature, or combination of features, of each relevant market prevents, restricts or distorts competition in connection with the supply or acquisition of any goods or services in the United Kingdom or a part of the United Kingdom.

[(1A) The CMA shall, on a cross-market reference, decide in relation to each feature and each combination of the features specified in the reference, whether the feature or combination of features, as it relates to goods or services of one or more than one of the descriptions so specified, prevents, restricts or distorts competition in connection with the supply or acquisition of any goods or services in the United Kingdom or a part of the United Kingdom.]

(2) For the purposes of this Part, in relation to [an ordinary] reference, there is an adverse effect on competition if any feature, or combination of features, of a relevant market prevents, restricts or distorts competition in connection with the supply or acquisition of any goods or services in the United Kingdom or a part of the United Kingdom.

[(2A) For the purposes of this Part, in relation to a cross-market reference, there is an adverse effect on competition if a feature or a combination of the features specified in the reference, as that feature or combination of features relates to goods or services of one or more than one of the descriptions so specified, prevents, restricts or distorts competition in connection with the supply or acquisition of any goods or services in the United Kingdom or a part of the United Kingdom.]

(3) In subsections (1) and (2) "relevant market" means—

   (a)   in the case of subsection (2) so far as it applies in connection with a possible reference, a market in the United Kingdom—

      (i)   for goods or services of a description to be specified in the reference; and

      (ii)   which would not be excluded from investigation by virtue of section 133(2); and

   (b)   in any other case, a market in the United Kingdom—

      (i)   for goods or services of a description specified in the reference concerned; and

      (ii)   which is not excluded from investigation by virtue of section 133(2).

(4) The [CMA] shall, if it has decided on a market investigation reference that there is an adverse effect on competition, decide the following additional questions—

   (a)   whether action should be taken by it under section 138 for the purpose of remedying, mitigating or preventing the adverse effect on competition concerned or any detrimental effect on customers so far as it has resulted from, or may be expected to result from, the adverse effect on competition;

   (b)   whether it should recommend the taking of action by others for the purpose of remedying, mitigating or preventing the adverse effect on competition concerned or any detrimental effect on customers so far as it has resulted from, or may be expected to result from, the adverse effect on competition; and

   (c)   in either case, if action should be taken, what action should be taken and what is to be remedied, mitigated or prevented.

(5) For the purposes of this Part, in relation to a market investigation reference, there is a detrimental effect on customers if there is a detrimental effect on customers or future customers in the form of—

   (a)   higher prices, lower quality or less choice of goods or services in any market in the United Kingdom (whether or not the market [or markets] to which the feature or features concerned relate); or

   (b)   less innovation in relation to such goods or services.

(6) In deciding the questions mentioned in subsection (4), the [CMA] shall, in particular, have regard to the need to achieve as comprehensive a solution as is reasonable and practicable to the adverse effect on competition and any detrimental effects on customers so far as resulting from the adverse effect on competition.

(7) In deciding the questions mentioned in subsection (4), the [CMA] may, in particular, have regard to the effect of any action on any relevant customer benefits of the feature or features of the market [or markets] concerned.

(8) For the purposes of this Part a benefit is a relevant customer benefit of a feature or features of a market if—

   (a)   it is a benefit to customers or future customers in the form of—

      (i)   lower prices, higher quality or greater choice of goods or services in any market in the United Kingdom (whether or not the market [or markets] to which the feature or features concerned relate); or

      (ii)   greater innovation in relation to such goods or services; and

(b)   the [CMA or (as the case may be) the Secretary of State] believes that—
     (i)   the benefit has accrued as a result (whether wholly or partly) of the feature or features concerned or may be expected to accrue within a reasonable period as a result (whether wholly or partly) of that feature or those features; and
     (ii)   the benefit was, or is, unlikely to accrue without the feature or features concerned.

NOTES

Word "CMA" in square brackets (in each place that they occur) substituted, and words in square brackets in sub-s (8)(b) substituted, by the Enterprise and Regulatory Reform Act 2013, s 26(3), Sch 5, Pt 2, paras 59, 167 (for transitional provisions (including those relating to the abolition of the OFT and the Competition Commission and the continuity of functions), see the Enterprise and Regulatory Reform Act 2013 (Commencement No 6, Transitional Provisions and Savings) Order 2014, SI 2014/416, Schedule at **[2.1126]**).

Words "an ordinary", in square brackets in sub-ss (1), (2) substituted, sub-ss (1A) and (2A) inserted, and words in square brackets in sub-ss (5)(a), (7), (8)(a) inserted, by the Enterprise and Regulatory Reform Act 2013, s 34(4), Sch 9, paras 1, 3 (as to transitional provisions etc, see the note above).

[1.1720]
135   Variation of market investigation references

(1)   The [CMA] or (as the case may be) the appropriate Minister may at any time vary a market investigation reference made [by it under section 131 or (as the case may be) by the appropriate Minister under section 132].

(2)   The . . . appropriate Minister shall consult the [CMA] before varying any such reference [made by him].

(3)   Subsection (2) shall not apply if the [CMA] has requested the variation concerned.

(4) . . .

NOTES

Sub-s (1): word "CMA" in square brackets substituted by the Enterprise and Regulatory Reform Act 2013, s 26(3), Sch 5, Pt 2, paras 59, 168(1), (2), (4) (for transitional provisions (including those relating to the abolition of the OFT and the Competition Commission and the continuity of functions), see the Enterprise and Regulatory Reform Act 2013 (Commencement No 6, Transitional Provisions and Savings) Order 2014, SI 2014/416, Schedule at **[2.1126]**); words in second pair of square brackets substituted by s 35(1) of, and Sch 10, paras 1, 4 to, the 2013 Act (as to transitional provisions etc, see the note above).

Sub-s (2): words omitted repealed, word "CMA" in square brackets substituted, and other words in square brackets inserted, by the Enterprise and Regulatory Reform Act 2013, s 26(3), Sch 5, Pt 2, paras 59, 168(1), (3) (as to transitional provisions etc, see the note above).

Sub-s (3): word "CMA" in square brackets substituted by the Enterprise and Regulatory Reform Act 2013, s 26(3), Sch 5, Pt 2, paras 59, 168(1), (2), (4) (as to transitional provisions etc, see the note above).

Sub-s (4): repealed by the Enterprise and Regulatory Reform Act 2013, s 38, Sch 12, paras 7, 11 (as to transitional provisions etc, see the note above).

[1.1721]
136   Investigations and reports on market investigation references

(1)   The [CMA] shall prepare and publish a report on a market investigation reference within the period permitted by section 137.

(2)   The report shall, in particular, contain—
   (a)   the decisions of the [CMA] on the questions which it is required to answer by virtue of section 134;
   (b)   its reasons for its decisions; and
   (c)   such information as the [CMA] considers appropriate for facilitating a proper understanding of those questions and of its reasons for its decisions.

(3)   The [CMA] shall carry out such investigations as it considers appropriate for the purposes of preparing a report under this section.

[(4)   Where a reference has been made by the appropriate Minister under section 132 the CMA shall, at the same time as the report under this section is published, give it to the appropriate Minister.]

(5)   Where a reference has been made by the [CMA] under section 131 or by the appropriate Minister under section 132 in circumstances in which a reference could have been made by a relevant sectoral regulator under section 131 as it has effect by virtue of a relevant sectoral enactment, the [CMA] shall, at the same time as the report under this section is published, give a copy of it to the relevant sectoral regulator concerned.

(6) . . .

(7)   In this Part "relevant sectoral enactment" means—
   (a) . . .
   (b)   in relation to the Gas and Electricity Markets Authority, section 36A of the Gas Act 1986 (c 44) or (as the case may be) section 43 of the Electricity Act 1989 (c 29);
   (c)   in relation to [the Water Services Regulation Authority], section 31 of the Water Industry Act 1991 (c 56);
   (d) . . .
   (e)   in relation to [the Office of Rail Regulation], section 67 of the Railways Act 1993 (c 43);

[(ea) in relation to the Financial Conduct Authority, section 234I of the Financial Services and Markets Act 2000;]

(f) . . .

(g) in relation to the Civil Aviation Authority, section 86 of the Transport Act 2000 (c 38) [or section 60 of the Civil Aviation Act 2012];

[(h) in relation to the Office of Communications, sections 370 and 371 of the Communications Act 2003];

[(h) in relation to the Northern Ireland Authority for Utility Regulation, Article 46 of the Electricity (Northern Ireland) Order 1992, Article 23 of the Gas (Northern Ireland) Order 1996 or Article 29 of the Water and Sewerage Services (Northern Ireland) Order 2006];

[(i) in relation to Monitor, section 73 of the Health and Social Care Act 2012];

[(j) in relation to the Payment Systems Regulator, section 59 of the Financial Services (Banking Reform) Act 2013].

(8) In this Part "relevant sectoral regulator" means . . . the Gas and Electricity Markets Authority, [the Water Services Regulation Authority], . . . ,[the Office of Rail Regulation], [the Financial Conduct Authority,] . . . [, the Civil Aviation Authority or the Office of [Communications,]] [the Northern Ireland Authority for Utility Regulation][, Monitor or the Payment Systems Regulator].

(9) The Secretary of State may by order modify subsection (7) or (8).

[(10) In this section "the Payment Systems Regulator" means the body established under section 40 of the Financial Services (Banking Reform) Act 2013.]

NOTES

Word "CMA" in square brackets (in each place that it occurs) substituted, sub-s (4) substituted, and sub-s (6) repealed, by the Enterprise and Regulatory Reform Act 2013, s 26(3), Sch 5, Pt 2, paras 59, 169 (for transitional provisions (including those relating to the abolition of the OFT and the Competition Commission and the continuity of functions), see the Enterprise and Regulatory Reform Act 2013 (Commencement No 6, Transitional Provisions and Savings) Order 2014, SI 2014/416, Schedule at **[2.1126]**).

Sub-s (7) is amended as follows:

Para (a) repealed, and first para (h) inserted, by the Communications Act 2003, s 406(1), (7), Sch 17, para 174(1), (4)(a), Sch 19.

Words in square brackets in para (c) substituted by the Water Act 2003, s 101(1), Sch 7, Pt 2, para 36(1), (2).

Paras (d), (f) repealed, and second para (h) inserted, by the Water and Sewerage Services (Northern Ireland) Order 2006, SI 2006/3336, art 308, Sch 12, para 46(1), Sch 13.

Words in square brackets in para (e) substituted by the Railways and Transport Safety Act 2003, s 16(5), Sch 2, Pt 2, para 19(u).

Para (ea) inserted by the Financial Services (Banking Reform) Act 2013, s 129, Sch 8, Pt 2, para 10(1), (2).

Words in square brackets in para (g) inserted by the Civil Aviation Act 2012, s 61(11).

Para (i) added by the Health and Social Care Act 2012, s 74(6)(a).

Para (j) added by the Financial Services (Banking Reform) Act 2013, s 67(3)(a).

Sub-s (8) is amended as follows:

First words omitted repealed, and words ", the Civil Aviation Authority or the Office of" in square brackets substituted, by the Communications Act 2003, s 406(7), Sch 19(1).

Words "the Water Services Regulation Authority" in square brackets substituted by the Water Act 2003, s 101(1), Sch 7, Pt 2, para 36(1), (2).

Second and third words omitted repealed, and words "or the Northern Ireland Authority for Utility Regulation" in square brackets inserted, by SI 2006/3336, art 308, Sch 12, para 46(2), Sch 13.

Words "the Office of Rail Regulation" in square brackets substituted by the Railways and Transport Safety Act 2003, s 16(5), Sch 2, Pt 2, para 19(u).

Words "the Financial Conduct Authority," in square brackets inserted by the Financial Services (Banking Reform) Act 2013, s 129, Sch 8, Pt 2, para 10(1), (3).

Word "Communications," in square brackets substituted by the Health and Social Care Act 2012, s 74(6)(b).

Words ", Monitor or the Payment Systems Regulator" in square brackets substituted by the Financial Services (Banking Reform) Act 2013, s 67(3)(b).

Sub-s (10): added by the Financial Services (Banking Reform) Act 2013, s 67(3)(c).

[1.1722]
137 Time-limits for market investigations and reports

(1) The [CMA] shall prepare and publish its report under section 136 within the period of [18 months] beginning with the date of the market investigation reference concerned.

(2) Subsection (1) is subject to section 151(3) and (5).

[(2A) The CMA may extend, by no more than 6 months, the period within which its report under section 136 is to be prepared and published if it considers that there are special reasons for doing so.

(2B) An extension under subsection (2A) shall come into force when published under section 172.

(2C) No more than one extension is possible under subsection (2A).]

[(3) The Secretary of State may by order amend this section so as to alter one or more of the following periods—

(a) the period of 18 months mentioned in subsection (1) or any period for the time being there mentioned in substitution for that period;

843 *Enterprise Act 2002, s 138A* **[1.1724]**

Part 1 Statutes

(b)   the period of 6 months mentioned in subsection (2A) or any period for the time being there mentioned in substitution for that period.

(4)   But no alteration shall be made by virtue of subsection (3) which results in—

(a)   the period for the time being mentioned in subsection (1) exceeding 18 months; or

(b)   the period for the time being mentioned in subsection (2A) exceeding 6 months.]

(5)   An order under subsection (3) shall not affect any period of time within which the [CMA] is under a duty to prepare and publish its report under section 136 in relation to a market investigation reference if the [CMA] is already under that duty in relation to that reference when the order is made.

(6)   Before making an order under subsection (3) the Secretary of State shall consult the [CMA] and such other persons as he considers appropriate.

(7)   References in this Part to the date of a market investigation reference shall be construed as references to the date specified in the reference as the date on which it is made.

NOTES

Word "CMA" in square brackets (in each place that it occurs) substituted by the Enterprise and Regulatory Reform Act 2013, s 26(3), Sch 5, Pt 2, paras 59, 170 (for transitional provisions (including those relating to the abolition of the OFT and the Competition Commission and the continuity of functions), see the Enterprise and Regulatory Reform Act 2013 (Commencement No 6, Transitional Provisions and Savings) Order 2014, SI 2014/416, Schedule at **[2.1126]**).

Words "18 months" in square brackets in sub-s (1) substituted, sub-ss (2A)–(2C) inserted, and sub-ss (3), (4) substituted, by the Enterprise and Regulatory Reform Act 2013, s 38, Sch 12, para 3 (as to transitional provisions etc, see the note above).

[1.1723]
138 Duty to remedy adverse effects

(1)   Subsection (2) applies where a report of the [CMA] has been prepared and published under section 136 within the period permitted by section 137 and contains the decision that there is one or more than one adverse effect on competition.

(2)   The [CMA] shall, [within the period permitted by section 138A,] in relation to each adverse effect on competition, take such action under section 159 or 161 as it considers to be reasonable and practicable—

(a)   to remedy, mitigate or prevent the adverse effect on competition concerned; and

(b)   to remedy, mitigate or prevent any detrimental effects on customers so far as they have resulted from, or may be expected to result from, the adverse effect on competition.

(3)   The decisions of the [CMA] under subsection (2) shall be consistent with its decisions as included in its report by virtue of section 134(4) unless there has been a material change of circumstances since the preparation of the report or the [CMA] otherwise has a special reason for deciding differently.

(4)   In making a decision under subsection (2), the [CMA] shall, in particular, have regard to the need to achieve as comprehensive a solution as is reasonable and practicable to the adverse effect on competition concerned and any detrimental effects on customers so far as resulting from the adverse effect on competition.

(5)   In making a decision under subsection (2), the [CMA] may, in particular, have regard to the effect of any action on any relevant customer benefits of the feature or features of the market [or markets] concerned.

(6)   The [CMA] shall take no action under subsection (2) to remedy, mitigate or prevent any detrimental effect on customers so far as it may be expected to result from the adverse effect on competition concerned if—

(a)   no detrimental effect on customers has resulted from the adverse effect on competition; and

(b)   the adverse effect on competition is not being remedied, mitigated or prevented.

NOTES

Word "CMA" in square brackets (in each place that it occurs) substituted by the Enterprise and Regulatory Reform Act 2013, s 26(3), Sch 5, Pt 2, paras 59, 171 (for transitional provisions (including those relating to the abolition of the OFT and the Competition Commission and the continuity of functions), see the Enterprise and Regulatory Reform Act 2013 (Commencement No 6, Transitional Provisions and Savings) Order 2014, SI 2014/416, Schedule at **[2.1126]**).

Words "within the period permitted by section 138A," in square brackets in sub-s (2) inserted by the Enterprise and Regulatory Reform Act 2013, s 38, Sch 12, para 4 (as to transitional provisions etc, see the note above).

Words "or markets" in square brackets in sub-s (5) inserted by the Enterprise and Regulatory Reform Act 2013, s 34(4), Sch 9, paras 1, 4 (as to transitional provisions etc, see the note above).

[1.1724]
[138A Time-limits for discharging duty under section 138

(1)   The CMA shall discharge its duty under section 138(2) within the period of 6 months beginning with the date on which it publishes the report concerned under section 136.

(2)   The CMA may extend, by no more than 4 months, the period within which its duty under section 138(2) is required to be discharged if it considers that there are special reasons for doing so.

(3)   The CMA may extend the period within which its duty under section 138(2) is required to be discharged if it considers that—

(a)   a person has failed (whether with or without reasonable excuse) to comply with any requirement of a notice under section 174 which was given in relation to the reference; and

(b)   the failure is preventing the CMA from properly discharging its duty under section 138(2).

(4)   An extension under subsection (2) or (3) shall come into force when published under section 172.

(5)   An extension under subsection (3) continues in force until—

(a)   the person concerned provides the information or documents to the satisfaction of the CMA or (as the case may be) appears as a witness in accordance with the requirements of the CMA; or

(b)   the CMA publishes its decision to cancel the extension.]

NOTES

Commencement: 1 April 2014.

Inserted by the Enterprise and Regulatory Reform Act 2013, s 38, Sch 12, para 5 (for transitional provisions (including those relating to the abolition of the OFT and the Competition Commission and the continuity of functions), see the Enterprise and Regulatory Reform Act 2013 (Commencement No 6, Transitional Provisions and Savings) Order 2014, SI 2014/416, Schedule at **[2.1126]**).

[1.1725]
[138B   Section 138A: supplementary

(1)   A period extended under section 138A(2) may also be extended under section 138A(3), and a period extended under section 138A(3) may also be extended under section 138A(2).

(2)   No more than one extension is possible under section 138A(2).

(3)   Where a period is extended or further extended under section 138A(2) or (3), the period as extended or (as the case may be) further extended shall, subject to subsections (4) and (5), be calculated by taking the period being extended and adding to it the period of the extension (whether or not those periods overlap in time).

(4)   Subsection (5) applies where—

(a)   the period within which the CMA shall discharge its duty under section 138(2) is further extended;

(b)   the further extension and at least one previous extension is made under section 138A(3); and

(c)   the same days or fractions of days are included in or comprise the further extension and are included in or comprise at least one such previous extension.

(5)   In calculating the period of the further extension, any days or fractions of days of the kind mentioned in subsection (4)(c) shall be disregarded.

(6)   The Secretary of State may by order amend section 138A so as to alter one or more of the following periods—

(a)   the period of 6 months mentioned in subsection (1) or any period for the time being there mentioned in substitution for that period;

(b)   the period of 4 months mentioned in subsection (2) or any period for the time being there mentioned in substitution for that period.

(7)   But no alteration shall be made by virtue of subsection (6) which results in—

(a)   the period for the time being mentioned in section 138A(1) exceeding 6 months; or

(b)   the period for the time being mentioned in section 138A(2) exceeding 4 months.

(8)   Before making an order under subsection (6) the Secretary of State shall consult the CMA and such other persons as the Secretary of State considers appropriate.]

NOTES

Commencement: 25 April 2013 (for the purposes of enabling the exercise of any power to make provision by order made by statutory instrument); 1 April 2014 (otherwise).

Inserted by the Enterprise and Regulatory Reform Act 2013, s 38, Sch 12, para 5 (for the purposes of enabling the exercise of any power to make provision by order made by statutory instrument), and as from 1 April 2014 (otherwise) (for transitional provisions (including those relating to the abolition of the OFT and the Competition Commission and the continuity of functions), see the Enterprise and Regulatory Reform Act 2013 (Commencement No 6, Transitional Provisions and Savings) Order 2014, SI 2014/416, Schedule at **[2.1126]**).

CHAPTER 2
PUBLIC INTEREST CASES

Intervention notices

[1.1726]
139   Public interest intervention by Secretary of State

[(A1)   This section applies where—

(a)   the CMA has published a market study notice in relation to a matter; or

(b)   the CMA has begun the process of consultation under section 169 in respect of a decision of the kind mentioned in subsection (6)(a)(i) of that section.

(1)   The Secretary of State may, within the permitted period, give a notice to the CMA if the Secretary of State believes that it is or may be the case that one or more than one public interest consideration is relevant to the matter.

(1A) For the purposes of subsection (1), the permitted period, in a case to which this section applies by virtue of paragraph (a) of subsection (A1), is the period beginning with the publication of the market study notice and ending with—

(a) the acceptance by the CMA of an undertaking under section 154 instead of the making of a reference under section 131 in relation to the matter;

(b) the publication of notice of the fact that the CMA has otherwise decided not to make such a reference in relation to the matter;

(c) the making of such a reference in relation to the matter; or

(d) in a case where the period permitted by section 131B for the preparation and publication by the CMA of the market study report in relation to the matter has expired and no such report has been prepared or published, the end of that period.

(1B) For the purposes of subsection (1), the permitted period, in a case to which this section applies by virtue of paragraph (b) of subsection (A1), is the period beginning with the date on which the CMA begins the process of consultation concerned and ending with—

(a) the acceptance by the CMA of an undertaking under section 154 instead of the making of a reference under section 131 in relation to the matter concerned;

(b) the publication of notice of the fact that the CMA has otherwise decided not to make such a reference in relation to the matter; or

(c) the making of such a reference in relation to the matter.]

(2) The Secretary of State may[, within the permitted period,] give a notice to the [CMA] if—

(a) the [CMA] is considering whether to accept—

  (i) an undertaking under section 154 instead of making a reference under section 131 [in relation to the matter]; or

  (ii) an undertaking varying or superseding any such undertaking;

(b) the [CMA] has published a notice under section 155(1) or (4); and

(c) the Secretary of State believes that it is or may be the case that one or more than one public interest consideration is relevant to the [proposal to accept the undertaking].

[(2A) For the purposes of subsection (2), the permitted period is—

(a) where the CMA publishes a notice under section 155(1), the period within which representations may be made in relation to the proposed undertaking (as to which, see section 155(2)(f));

(b) where the CMA publishes a notice under section 155(4), the period within which representations may be made in relation to the proposed modifications to the proposed undertaking (as to which, see section 155(5)(c)).]

(3) In this Part "intervention notice" means a notice under subsection (1) or (2).

[(4) No more than one intervention notice shall be given under subsection (1) in relation to the same matter.

(4A) An intervention notice shall not be given under subsection (2) in relation to a proposal to accept an undertaking if the proposal relates to a matter in respect of which an intervention notice under subsection (1) has already been given.

(4B) No more than one intervention notice shall be given under subsection (2) in relation to the same proposed undertaking or in relation to proposed undertakings which do not differ from each other in any material respect.]

[(4C) In this section, a reference to the acceptance of an undertaking shall, in a case where the CMA has accepted a group of undertakings under section 154, be treated as a reference to the acceptance of the last undertaking in the group; but undertakings which vary, supersede or revoke earlier undertakings shall be disregarded for the purposes of this section.]

(5) For the purposes of this Part a public interest consideration is a consideration which, at the time of the giving of the intervention notice concerned, is specified in section 153 or is not so specified but, in the opinion of the Secretary of State, ought to be so specified.

(6) Where the Secretary of State has given an intervention notice mentioning a public interest consideration which, at that time, is not finalised, he shall, as soon as practicable, take such action as is within his power to ensure that it is finalised.

(7) For the purposes of this Part a public interest consideration is finalised if—

(a) it is specified in section 153 otherwise than by virtue of an order under subsection (3) of that section; or

(b) it is specified in that section by virtue of an order under subsection (3) of that section and the order providing for it to be so specified has been laid before, and approved by, Parliament in accordance with subsection (6) of section 181 and within the period mentioned in that subsection.

NOTES

Sub-ss (A1)–(1B) were substituted (for the original sub-s (1)), the words in the first pair of square brackets in sub-s (2) were inserted, the words in the final pair of square brackets in that subsection were substituted, sub-ss (2A), (4C) were inserted, and sub-ss (4)–(4B) were substituted (for the original sub-s (4)), by the Enterprise and Regulatory Reform Act 2013, s 35(1)–(7) (for transitional provisions (including those relating to the abolition of the OFT and the Competition Commission and the continuity of functions), see the Enterprise and Regulatory Reform Act 2013 (Commencement No 6, Transitional Provisions and Savings) Order 2014, SI 2014/416, Schedule at **[2.1126]**).

The word "CMA" in square brackets (in each place that it occurs in sub-s (2)) was substituted by the Enterprise and Regulatory Reform Act 2013, s 26(3), Sch 5, Pt 2, paras 59, 172 (as to transitional provisions etc, see the note above).

Intervention notices under section 139(1)

[1.1727]
140 Intervention notices under section 139(1)
(1) An intervention notice under section 139(1) shall state—
  [(a) the matter to which the market study notice or (as the case may be) the consultation under section 169 concerned relates;
  (b) the date of publication of that notice or (as the case may be) on which the process of consultation began;]
  (c) the public interest consideration or considerations which are, or may be, relevant to the [matter]; and
  (d) where any public interest consideration concerned is not finalised, the proposed timetable for finalising it.
(2) Where the Secretary of State believes that it is or may be the case that two or more public interest considerations are relevant to the [matter], he may decide not to mention in the intervention notice such of those considerations as he considers appropriate.
(3) The Secretary of State may at any time revoke an intervention notice which has been given under section 139(1) and which is in force.
(4) An intervention notice under section 139(1) shall come into force when it is given and shall cease to be in force when the matter to which it relates is finally determined under this Chapter.
[(4A) An intervention notice under section 139(1) shall also cease to be in force if—
  (a) it mentions a public interest consideration which was not finalised on the giving of the notice or public interest considerations which, at that time, were not finalised;
  (b) no other public interest consideration is mentioned in the notice;
  (c) at least 24 weeks has elapsed since the giving of the notice;
  (d) the public interest consideration mentioned in the notice has not been finalised within that period of 24 weeks or (as the case may be) none of the public interest considerations mentioned in the notice has been finalised within that period of 24 weeks; and
  (e) the Secretary of State has not, by the end of that period of 24 weeks, made a reference under section 140A in relation to the matter.
(4B) Subsection (4D) applies in a case where—
  (a) an intervention notice ceases to be in force in accordance with subsection (4A);
  (b) the CMA has, before the time at which the notice ceases to be in force, prepared a market study report in relation to the matter within the period permitted by section 131B(4) and given it to the Secretary of State in accordance with section 140A(3)(b); and
  (c) the report contains the decision of the CMA that it should make a reference in relation to the matter concerned under section 131.
(4C) Subsection (4D) also applies in a case where—
  (a) an intervention notice ceases to be in force in accordance with subsection (4A); and
  (b) the CMA has, before the time at which the notice ceases to be in force—
    (i) decided that it should make an ordinary reference or a cross-market reference under section 131 in relation to the matter concerned; and
    (ii) given a document containing its decision, the reasons for it and such information as the CMA considers appropriate for facilitating a proper understanding of the reasons for its decision to the Secretary of State in accordance with section 140A(3)(c).
(4D) In a case to which this subsection applies—
  (a) the CMA shall, as soon as reasonably practicable, make a reference in relation to the matter under section 131; and
  (b) the reference is to be treated for the purposes of this Part as having been made in accordance with the requirements imposed by this Part.]
(5) For the purposes of subsection (4) a matter to which an intervention notice under section 139(1) relates is finally determined under this Chapter if—
  [(za) the CMA accepts an undertaking under section 154 instead of making a reference under section 131 in relation to the matter;
  (zb) the CMA publishes notice that it has otherwise decided not to make a reference under section 131 in relation to the matter;
  (zc) the period permitted for the preparation by the CMA of the market study report in relation to the matter and for the report to be published under section 131B(4) or (as the case may be) given to the Secretary of State under section 140A(3) has expired and no such report has been so prepared or no such action has been taken;
  (zd) the Secretary of State makes a reference under section 140A(5) in relation to the matter;]
  (a) the period permitted by section 144 for the preparation of the report of the [CMA] under section 142 and for action to be taken in relation to it under section 143(1) or (3) [or (as the case may be) 143A(2) or (3)] has expired and no such report has been so prepared or no such action has been taken;
  (b) the [CMA] decides under section 145(1) to terminate its investigation;

  (c)   the report of the [CMA] has been prepared under section 142 and published under section 143(1) [or (as the case may be) 143A(2)] within the period permitted by section 144;

  (d)   the Secretary of State fails to make and publish a decision under subsection (2) of section 146 within the period required by subsection (3) of that section [or (as the case may be) fails to make and publish a decision under subsection (2) of section 146A within the period required by subsection (6) of that section];

  (e)   the Secretary of State decides under section 146(2) that no eligible public interest consideration is relevant [or (as the case may be) decides under section 146A(2) to make no finding at all in relation to the matter];

  (f)   the Secretary of State decides under section 147(2) [or (as the case may be) 147A(2)] neither to accept an undertaking under section 159 nor to make an order under section 161;

  (g)   the Secretary of State accepts an undertaking under section 159 or makes an order under section 161; or

  (h)   the Secretary of State decides to revoke the intervention notice concerned.

(6)   For the purposes of subsections (4) and (5) the time when a matter to which an intervention notice under section 139(1) relates is finally determined under this Chapter is—

  [(za) in a case falling within subsection (5)(za), the acceptance of the undertaking concerned;

  (zb) in a case falling within subsection (5)(zb), the publication of the notice concerned;]

  (a)   in a case falling within subsection (5)[(zc),] (a) or (d), the expiry of the period concerned;

  [(aa) in a case falling within subsection (5)(zd), the making of the reference concerned;]

  (b)   in a case falling within subsection (5)(b), (e), (f) or (h), the making of the decision concerned;

  (c)   in a case falling within subsection (5)(c), the publication of the report concerned; and

  (d)   in a case falling within subsection (5)(g), the acceptance of the undertaking concerned or (as the case may be) the making of the order concerned.

[(6A) In subsection (6)(za) the reference to the acceptance of the undertaking concerned shall, in a case where the CMA has accepted a group of undertakings under section 154, be treated as a reference to the acceptance of the last undertaking in the group; but undertakings which vary, supersede or revoke earlier undertakings shall be disregarded for the purposes of subsections (5)(za) and (6)(za).]

(7)   In subsection (6)(d) the reference to the acceptance of the undertaking concerned or the making of the order concerned shall, in a case where the enforcement action under section 147(2) [or (as the case may be) 147A(2)] involves the acceptance of a group of undertakings, the making of a group of orders or the acceptance and making of a group of undertakings and orders, be treated as a reference to the acceptance or making of the last undertaking or order in the group; but undertakings or orders which vary, supersede or revoke earlier undertakings or orders shall be disregarded for the purposes of subsections (5)(g) and (6)(d).

NOTES

The word "CMA" in square brackets (in each place that it occurs) was substituted by the Enterprise and Regulatory Reform Act 2013, s 26(3), Sch 5, Pt 2, paras 59, 173 (for transitional provisions (including those relating to the abolition of the OFT and the Competition Commission and the continuity of functions), see the Enterprise and Regulatory Reform Act 2013 (Commencement No 6, Transitional Provisions and Savings) Order 2014, SI 2014/416, Schedule at **[2.1126]**).

All other words in square brackets in this section were substituted or inserted by the Enterprise and Regulatory Reform Act 2013, s 35(10), Sch 10, paras 1, 5 (as to transitional provisions etc, see the note above).

[1.1728]
[140A   Section 139(1) intervention notices: Secretary of State's duty to refer

(1)   This section applies where—

  (a)   the CMA has prepared a market study report in relation to a matter within the period permitted by section 131B(4);

  (b)   an intervention notice under section 139(1) is in force in relation to the matter at the time when the CMA would (but for this section) be required to publish the report; and

  (c)   the report contains the decision of the CMA that it should make an ordinary reference or a cross-market reference in relation to the matter under section 131.

(2)   This section also applies where—

  (a)   the CMA has conducted a consultation under section 169 in respect of a decision of the kind mentioned in subsection (6)(a)(i) of that section;

  (b)   the CMA has decided that it should make an ordinary reference or a cross-market reference in relation to the matter concerned under section 131; and

  (c)   an intervention notice under section 139(1) is in force in relation to the matter at the time when the CMA makes that decision.

(3)   The CMA—

  (a)   shall not exercise the power under section 131 to refer the matter;

  (b)   in a case falling within subsection (1), shall not publish the market study report under section 131B(4) and shall instead, within the period mentioned in section 131B(4), give the report to the Secretary of State; and

(c)   in a case falling within subsection (2), shall give to the Secretary of State a document containing—
  (i)   its decision and the reasons for its decision; and
  (ii)   such information as the CMA considers appropriate for facilitating a proper understanding of the reasons for its decision.
(4)   The Secretary of State shall decide whether any public interest consideration which was mentioned in the intervention notice is relevant to the matter in question.
(5)   Where the Secretary of State decides that there is no relevant public interest consideration—
  (a)   the Secretary of State shall (in accordance with the CMA's decision) make a reference in relation to the matter to the chair of the CMA for the constitution of a group under Schedule 4 to the Enterprise and Regulatory Reform Act 2013; and
  (b)   the reference is to be treated for the purposes of this Part as an ordinary reference or (as the case may be) a cross-market reference made under section 131 in accordance with the requirements imposed by this Part.
(6)   Where the Secretary of State decides that there is one or more than one relevant public interest consideration, the Secretary of State shall (in accordance with the CMA's decision) make a reference in relation to the matter to the chair of the CMA for the constitution of a group under Schedule 4 to the Enterprise and Regulatory Reform Act 2013.
(7)   The Secretary of State shall specify in a reference made under subsection (6)—
  (a)   the relevant public interest consideration or considerations; and
  (b)   whether the reference is a restricted PI reference or a full PI reference (as to which, see sections 141 and 141A respectively).
(8)   Where the Secretary of State makes a full PI reference under subsection (6), the reference shall also specify whether the Secretary of State proposes to appoint a public interest expert under section 141B.
(9)   For the purposes of this Part, a reference under subsection (6) is to be treated—
  (a)   in a case where the decision of the CMA was that it should make an ordinary reference, as an ordinary reference;
  (b)   in a case where the decision of the CMA was that it should make a cross-market reference, as a cross-market reference.
(10)   In a case falling within subsection (1), the Secretary of State shall publish the market study report concerned at the same time as the Secretary of State makes a reference under this section.
(11)   In a case falling within subsection (2), the Secretary of State shall publish the document given to the Secretary of State by the CMA under subsection (3)(c), at the same time as the Secretary of State makes a reference under this section.
(12)   In this Part—
  "full PI reference" means a reference made by the Secretary of State under subsection (6) which specifies that it is a full PI reference;
  "restricted PI reference" means a reference made by the Secretary of State under subsection (6) which specifies that it is a restricted PI reference.]

NOTES
Commencement: 1 April 2014.
Inserted by the Enterprise and Regulatory Reform Act 2013, s 35(1), (8) (for transitional provisions (including those relating to the abolition of the OFT and the Competition Commission and the continuity of functions), see the Enterprise and Regulatory Reform Act 2013 (Commencement No 6, Transitional Provisions and Savings) Order 2014, SI 2014/416, Schedule at **[2.1126]**).

[1.1729]
[140B   Variation of restricted PI references and full PI references
(1)   The Secretary of State may at any time vary a restricted PI reference or a full PI reference.
(2)   The Secretary of State shall consult the CMA before varying any such reference.
(3)   But subsection (2) does not apply if the CMA requested the variation concerned.
(4)   No variation under this section is capable of altering the public interest consideration or considerations specified in the reference.]

NOTES
Commencement: 1 April 2014.
Inserted by the Enterprise and Regulatory Reform Act 2013, s 35(10), Sch 10, paras 1, 6 (for transitional provisions (including those relating to the abolition of the OFT and the Competition Commission and the continuity of functions), see the Enterprise and Regulatory Reform Act 2013 (Commencement No 6, Transitional Provisions and Savings) Order 2014, SI 2014/416, Schedule at **[2.1126]**).

[1.1730]
141   [Restricted PI references: questions to be decided by CMA]
[(1)   This section applies where the Secretary of State makes a restricted PI reference.]
(2)   [CMA] shall[, on an ordinary reference,] decide whether any feature, or combination of features, of each relevant market (within the meaning given by section 134(3)) prevents, restricts or distorts competition in connection with the supply or acquisition of any goods or services in the United Kingdom or a part of the United Kingdom.

[(2A)   The CMA shall, on a cross-market reference, decide in relation to each feature and each combination of the features specified in the reference, whether the feature or combination of features, as it relates to goods or services of one or more than one of the descriptions so specified, prevents, restricts or distorts competition in connection with the supply or acquisition of any goods or services in the United Kingdom or a part of the United Kingdom.]

(3)   The [CMA] shall, if it has decided that there is an adverse effect on competition, decide the following additional questions—

    (a)   whether action should be taken by the Secretary of State under section 147 for the purpose of remedying, mitigating or preventing the adverse effect on competition concerned or any detrimental effect on customers so far as it has resulted from, or may be expected to result from, the adverse effect on competition;

    (b)   whether the [CMA] should recommend the taking of other action by the Secretary of State or action by persons other than itself and the Secretary of State for the purpose of remedying, mitigating or preventing the adverse effect on competition concerned or any detrimental effect on customers so far as it has resulted from, or may be expected to result from, the adverse effect on competition; and

    (c)   in either case, if action should be taken, what action should be taken and what is to be remedied, mitigated or prevented.

(4)   The [CMA] shall, if it has decided that there is an adverse effect on competition, also decide separately the following questions (on the assumption that it is proceeding as mentioned in section 148(1))—

    (a)   whether action should be taken by it under section 138 for the purpose of remedying, mitigating or preventing the adverse effect on competition concerned or any detrimental effect on customers so far as it has resulted from, or may be expected to result from, the adverse effect on competition;

    (b)   whether the [CMA] should recommend the taking of action by other persons for the purpose of remedying, mitigating or preventing the adverse effect on competition concerned or any detrimental effect on customers so far as it has resulted from, or may be expected to result from, the adverse effect on competition; and

    (c)   in either case, if action should be taken, what action should be taken and what is to be remedied, mitigated or prevented.

(5)   In deciding the questions mentioned in subsections (3) and (4), the [CMA] shall, in particular, have regard to the need to achieve as comprehensive a solution as is reasonable and practicable to the adverse effect on competition concerned and any detrimental effects on customers so far as resulting from the adverse effect on competition.

(6)   In deciding the questions mentioned in subsections (3) and (4), the [CMA] may, in particular, have regard to the effect of any action on any relevant customer benefits of the feature or features of the market [or markets] concerned.

NOTES

    The section heading and sub-s (1) were substituted by the Enterprise and Regulatory Reform Act 2013, s 35(10), Sch 10, paras 1, 7(1), (3) (for transitional provisions (including those relating to the abolition of the OFT and the Competition Commission and the continuity of functions), see the Enterprise and Regulatory Reform Act 2013 (Commencement No 6, Transitional Provisions and Savings) Order 2014, SI 2014/416, Schedule at **[2.1126]**).

    The word "CMA" in square brackets (in each place that it occurs) was substituted by the Enterprise and Regulatory Reform Act 2013, s 26(3), Sch 5, Pt 2, paras 59, 174 (as to transitional provisions etc, see the note above).

    The words ", on an ordinary reference," in square brackets in sub-s (2) and the words in "or markets" in square brackets in sub-s (6) were inserted, and sub-s (2A) was inserted, by the Enterprise and Regulatory Reform Act 2013, s 34(4), Sch 9, paras 1, 5 (as to transitional provisions etc, see the note above).

[1.1731]
[141A   Full PI references: questions to be decided by CMA

(1)   This section applies where the Secretary of State makes a full PI reference.

(2)   The CMA shall, on an ordinary reference, decide whether any feature, or combination of features, of each relevant market (within the meaning given by section 134(3)) prevents, restricts or distorts competition in connection with the supply or acquisition of any goods or services in the United Kingdom or a part of the United Kingdom.

(3)   The CMA shall, on a cross-market reference, decide in relation to each feature and each combination of the features specified in the reference, whether the feature or combination of features, as it relates to goods or services of one or more than one of the descriptions so specified, prevents, restricts or distorts competition in connection with the supply or acquisition of any goods or services in the United Kingdom or a part of the United Kingdom.

(4)   The CMA shall, if it has decided that there is an adverse effect on competition, decide whether, taking account only of any adverse effect on competition and the admissible public interest consideration or considerations concerned, any feature or combination of features which gave rise to an adverse effect on competition operates or may be expected to operate against the public interest.

(5)   The CMA shall, if it has decided that any such feature or combination of features operates or may be expected to operate against the public interest, also decide separately the following additional questions—

(a) whether action should be taken by the Secretary of State under section 147A for the purpose of remedying, mitigating or preventing any of the effects adverse to the public interest concerned;

(b) whether the CMA should recommend the taking of other action by the Secretary of State, or action by persons other than itself and the Secretary of State, for the purpose of remedying, mitigating or preventing any of the effects adverse to the public interest concerned; and

(c) in either case, if action should be taken, what action should be taken and what is to be remedied, mitigated or prevented.

(6) The CMA shall, if it has decided that there is an adverse effect on competition, also decide separately the following questions (on the assumption that it is proceeding as mentioned in section 148A(2))—

(a) whether action should be taken by it under section 138 for the purpose of remedying, mitigating or preventing the adverse effect on competition concerned or any detrimental effect on customers so far as it has resulted from, or may be expected to result from, the adverse effect on competition;

(b) whether the CMA should recommend the taking of action by other persons for the purpose of remedying, mitigating or preventing the adverse effect on competition concerned or any detrimental effect on customers so far as it has resulted from, or may be expected to result from, the adverse effect on competition; and

(c) in either case, if action should be taken, what action should be taken and what is to be remedied, mitigated or prevented.

(7) In a case where the Secretary of State has appointed a public interest expert under section 141B in relation to a full PI reference, the CMA shall, in deciding the questions mentioned in subsections (4) and (5), have regard, in particular, to the views of the expert.

(8) In deciding the questions mentioned in subsection (5), the CMA shall, in particular, have regard to—

(a) the need to achieve as comprehensive a solution as is reasonable and practicable to the effects adverse to the public interest concerned; and

(b) any detrimental effects on customers so far as resulting from those effects.

(9) In deciding the questions mentioned in subsection (6), the CMA shall, in particular, have regard to—

(a) the need to achieve as comprehensive a solution as is reasonable and practicable to the adverse effect on competition concerned; and

(b) any detrimental effects on customers so far as resulting from it.

(10) In deciding the questions mentioned in subsections (5) and (6), the CMA may, in particular, have regard to the effect of any action on any relevant customer benefits of the feature or features of the market or markets concerned.

(11) In this section, "admissible public interest consideration" means any public interest consideration specified in the reference concerned and which the CMA is not under a duty to disregard.

NOTES
Commencement: 1 April 2014.
Inserted, together with s 141B, by the Enterprise and Regulatory Reform Act 2013, s 35(1), (9) (for transitional provisions (including those relating to the abolition of the OFT and the Competition Commission and the continuity of functions), see the Enterprise and Regulatory Reform Act 2013 (Commencement No 6, Transitional Provisions and Savings) Order 2014, SI 2014/416, Schedule at **[2.1126]**).

[1.1732]
[141B Full PI references: power of Secretary of State to appoint expert
(1) This section applies where the Secretary of State makes a full PI reference.
(2) The Secretary of State may appoint one or more than one person to advise the CMA on the questions mentioned in subsections (4) and (5) of section 141A in relation to the reference.
(3) A person so appointed shall be a person who appears to the Secretary of State to have particular knowledge of, or expertise in, matters relating to a public interest consideration specified in the reference.
(4) Each person so appointed is referred to in this Part as a "public interest expert".
(5) The terms and conditions of appointment of a public interest expert (including, in particular, as to remuneration) are to be determined by the Secretary of State.
(6) Any appointment of a public interest expert under this section shall be made within the period of 2 months beginning with the date of the reference concerned.
(7) Before appointing a public interest expert the Secretary of State shall consult the chair of the CMA.]

NOTES
Commencement: 1 April 2014.
Inserted as noted to s 141A at **[1.1731]**.

[1.1733]
142 Investigations and reports by [CMA]
(1) [Where the Secretary of State makes a restricted PI reference or a full PI reference, the CMA] shall prepare a report on the reference and take action in relation to it under section 143(1) or (3) [or (as the case may be) 143A(2) or (3)] within the period permitted by section 144.
(2) The report shall, in particular, contain—
  (a) the decisions of the [CMA] on the questions which it is required to answer by virtue of section 141 [or (as the case may be) 141A];
  (b) its reasons for its decisions; . . .
  (c) such information as the [CMA] considers appropriate for facilitating a proper understanding of those questions and of its reasons for its decisions[; and
  (d) in the case of a report in relation to a full PI reference in respect of which the Secretary of State appointed a public interest expert, a summary of the views of the expert.]
[(2A) A summary of the views of a public interest expert in a report under this section shall be approved by the expert before action is taken in relation to the report under section 143A(2) or (3).]
(3) The [CMA] shall carry out such investigations as it considers appropriate for the purposes of preparing a report under this section.

NOTES
 The word "CMA" in square brackets (in each place that it occurs) was substituted by the Enterprise and Regulatory Reform Act 2013, s 26(3), Sch 5, Pt 2, paras 59, 175 (for transitional provisions (including those relating to the abolition of the OFT and the Competition Commission and the continuity of functions), see the Enterprise and Regulatory Reform Act 2013 (Commencement No 6, Transitional Provisions and Savings) Order 2014, SI 2014/416, Schedule at **[2.1126]**).
 All other words in square brackets in this section were substituted or inserted, and the word omitted from sub-s (2)(b) was repealed, by the Enterprise and Regulatory Reform Act 2013, s 35(10), Sch 10, paras 1, 8 (as to transitional provisions etc, see the note above).

[1.1734]
143 [Restricted PI references: publication etc of reports of CMA]
[(A1) This section applies in relation to a report prepared under section 142 in respect of a restricted PI reference.]
(1) The [CMA] shall publish [the report] if it contains—
  (a) the decision of the [CMA] that there is no adverse effect on competition; or
  (b) the decisions of the [CMA] that there is one or more than one adverse effect on competition but, on the question mentioned in section 141(4)(a) and in relation to each adverse effect on competition, that no action should be taken by it.
(2) . . .
(3) Where [the report] contains the decisions of the [CMA] that there is one or more than one adverse effect on competition and, on the question mentioned in section 141(4)(a) and in relation to at least one such adverse effect, that action should be taken by it, the [CMA] shall give the report to the Secretary of State.
(4) The Secretary of State shall publish, no later than publication of his decision under section 146(2) in relation to the case, a report of the [CMA] given to him under subsection (3) and not required to be published by virtue of section 148(2).
(5)–(8) . . .

NOTES
 The section heading was substituted, the words "the report" in square brackets in sub-ss (1), (3) were substituted, sub-s (A1) was inserted, and sub-ss (2), (5)–(8) were repealed, by the Enterprise and Regulatory Reform Act 2013, s 35(10), Sch 10, paras 1, 9 (for transitional provisions (including those relating to the abolition of the OFT and the Competition Commission and the continuity of functions), see the Enterprise and Regulatory Reform Act 2013 (Commencement No 6, Transitional Provisions and Savings) Order 2014, SI 2014/416, Schedule at **[2.1126]**).
 The word "CMA" in square brackets (in each place that it occurs) was substituted by the Enterprise and Regulatory Reform Act 2013, s 26(3), Sch 5, Pt 2, paras 59, 176 (as to transitional provisions etc, see the note above).

[1.1735]
[143A Full PI references: publication etc of reports of CMA
(1) This section applies in relation to a report prepared under section 142 in respect of a full PI reference.
(2) The CMA shall publish the report if it contains—
  (a) the decision of the CMA that there is no adverse effect on competition;
  (b) the decision of the CMA that there is an adverse effect on competition but that the feature or combination of features which gave rise to it does not operate and may not be expected to operate against the public interest; or
  (c) the decisions of the CMA that there is one or more than one adverse effect on competition and that one or more than one of the features or combinations of features which gave rise to an adverse effect on competition operates or may be expected to operate against the public interest but, on the question mentioned in section 141A(5)(a), and in relation to each effect adverse to the public interest concerned, that no action should be taken by the Secretary of State.

(3)   The CMA shall give the report to the Secretary of State if it contains the decisions of the CMA—
- (a)   that there is one or more than one adverse effect on competition and that one or more than one of the features or combinations of features which gave rise to an adverse effect on competition operates or may be expected to operate against the public interest; and
- (b)   in relation to at least one effect adverse to the public interest concerned, that action should be taken by the Secretary of State.

(4)   The Secretary of State shall publish, no later than publication of the Secretary of State's decision under section 146A(2) in relation to the case, a report of the CMA given to the Secretary of State under subsection (3) and not required to be published by virtue of section 148A(3).]

NOTES
Commencement: 1 April 2014.

Inserted by the Enterprise and Regulatory Reform Act 2013, s 35(10), Sch 10, paras 1, 10 (for transitional provisions (including those relating to the abolition of the OFT and the Competition Commission and the continuity of functions), see the Enterprise and Regulatory Reform Act 2013 (Commencement No 6, Transitional Provisions and Savings) Order 2014, SI 2014/416, Schedule at **[2.1126]**).

[1.1736]
144   Time-limits for investigations and reports: Part 4
(1)   The [CMA] shall, within the period of [18 months] beginning with [the relevant date], prepare its report under section 142 and [publish it under section 143(1) or 143A(2) or (as the case may be) give it to the Secretary of State in accordance with section 143(3) or 143A(3)].
[(1A)   For the purposes of subsection (1), the "relevant date" is—
- (a)   in the case of a report in relation to a restricted PI reference or to a full PI reference which specifies that the Secretary of State does not propose to appoint a public interest expert, the date of the reference;
- (b)   in the case of a report in relation to a full PI reference which specifies that the Secretary of State proposes to appoint a public interest expert, the earliest of the following—
  - (i)   the date of the appointment of the expert;
  - (ii)   the date on which the Secretary of State gives notice to the CMA that the Secretary of State no longer intends to appoint such an expert;
  - (iii)   the end of the period of 2 months beginning with the date of the reference.]
[(1B)   The CMA may extend, by no more than 6 months, the period within which its report under section 142 is to be prepared and action is to be taken in relation to it under section 143(1) or (3) or (as the case may be) 143A(2) or (3) if it considers that there are special reasons for doing so.
(1C)   An extension under subsection (1B) shall come into force when published under section 172.
(1D)   No more than one extension is possible under subsection (1B).]
(2)   The Secretary of State may by order amend[—
- (a)]   subsection (1) so as to alter the period of [18 months] mentioned in that subsection or any period for the time being mentioned in that subsection in substitution for that period;
- [(b)   subsection (1B) so as to alter the period of 6 months mentioned in that subsection or any period for the time being mentioned in that subsection in substitution for that period].
(3)   No alteration shall be made by virtue of subsection (2) which results in[—
- (a)]   the period for the time being mentioned in subsection (1) exceeding [18 months][; or
- (b)   the period for the time being mentioned in subsection (1B) exceeding 6 months].
(4)   An order under subsection (2) shall not affect any period of time within which, in relation to a market investigation reference, the [CMA] is under a duty to prepare its report under section 142 and take action in relation to it under section 143(1) or (3) [or (as the case may be) 143A(2) or (3)] if the [CMA] is already under that duty in relation to that reference when the order is made.
(5)   Before making an order under subsection (2) the Secretary of State shall consult the [CMA] and such other persons as he considers appropriate.

NOTES
The word "CMA" in square brackets (in each place that it occurs) was substituted by the Enterprise and Regulatory Reform Act 2013, s 26(3), Sch 5, Pt 2, paras 59, 177 (for transitional provisions (including those relating to the abolition of the OFT and the Competition Commission and the continuity of functions), see the Enterprise and Regulatory Reform Act 2013 (Commencement No 6, Transitional Provisions and Savings) Order 2014, SI 2014/416, Schedule at **[2.1126]**).

The words "18 months" in square brackets in sub-ss (1), (2), (3) were substituted, sub-ss (1B)–(1D) were inserted, and the other words in square brackets in sub-ss (2), (3) were inserted, by the Enterprise and Regulatory Reform Act 2013, s 38, Sch 12, para 6 (as to transitional provisions etc, see the note above).

Words in third and final pairs of square brackets in sub-s (1) were substituted, sub-s (1A) was inserted, and the words "or (as the case may be) 143A(2) or (3)" in square brackets in sub-s (4) were inserted, by the Enterprise and Regulatory Reform Act 2013, s 35(10), Sch 10, paras 1, 11 (as to transitional provisions etc, see the note above).

[1.1737]
145   Restrictions where public interest considerations not finalised: Part 4
(1)   The [CMA] shall terminate its investigation under section 142 if—

(a)   the intervention notice concerned mentions a public interest consideration which was not finalised on the giving of that notice or public interest considerations which, at that time, were not finalised;

(b)   no other public interest consideration is mentioned in the notice;

(c)   at least 24 weeks has elapsed since the giving of the notice; and

(d)   the public interest consideration mentioned in the notice has not been finalised within that period of 24 weeks or (as the case may be) none of the public interest considerations mentioned in the notice has been finalised within that period of 24 weeks.

(2)   Where the intervention notice concerned mentions a public interest consideration which is not finalised on the giving of the notice, the [CMA] shall not give its report under section 142 to the Secretary of State in accordance with section 143(3) [or (as the case may be) 143A(3)] unless the period of 24 weeks beginning with the giving of the intervention notice concerned has expired or the public interest consideration concerned has been finalised.

(3)   The [CMA] shall, in reporting on any of the questions mentioned in section 141(3) [or (as the case may be) 141A(4) and (5)], disregard any public interest consideration which has not been finalised before the giving of the report.

(4)   The [CMA] shall, in reporting on any of the questions mentioned in section 141(3) [or (as the case may be) 141A(4) and (5)], disregard any public interest consideration which was not finalised on the giving of the intervention notice concerned and has not been finalised within the period of 24 weeks beginning with the giving of the notice concerned.

(5)   Subsections (1) to (4) are without prejudice to the power of the [CMA] to carry out investigations in relation to any public interest consideration to which it might be able to have regard in its report.

NOTES

The word "CMA" in square brackets (in each place that it occurs) was substituted by the Enterprise and Regulatory Reform Act 2013, s 26(3), Sch 5, Pt 2, paras 59, 178 (for transitional provisions (including those relating to the abolition of the OFT and the Competition Commission and the continuity of functions), see the Enterprise and Regulatory Reform Act 2013 (Commencement No 6, Transitional Provisions and Savings) Order 2014, SI 2014/416, Schedule at **[2.1126]**).

The other words in square brackets in sub-ss (2)–(4) were inserted by the Enterprise and Regulatory Reform Act 2013, s 35(10), Sch 10, paras 1, 12 (as to transitional provisions etc, see the note above).

[1.1738]
146   [Restricted PI references:] decision of Secretary of State

(1)   Subsection (2) applies where the Secretary of State has received a [report of the CMA in relation to a restricted PI reference] which—

(a)   has been prepared under section 142;

(b)   contains the decisions that there is one or more than one adverse effect on competition and, on the question mentioned in section 141(4)(a) and in relation to at least one such adverse effect, that action should be taken by it; and

(c)   has been given to the Secretary of State as required by section 143(3).

(2)   The Secretary of State shall decide whether—

(a)   any eligible public interest consideration is relevant; or

(b)   any eligible public interest considerations are relevant;

to any action which is mentioned in the report by virtue of section 141(4)(a) and (c) and which the [CMA] should take for the purpose of remedying, mitigating or preventing any adverse effect on competition concerned or any detrimental effect on customers so far as it has resulted or may be expected to result from any adverse effect on competition.

(3)   The Secretary of State shall make and publish his decision under subsection (2) within the period of 90 days beginning with the receipt of the report of the [CMA] under section 142.

(4)   In this section "eligible public interest consideration" means a public interest consideration which—

(a)   was mentioned in the intervention notice concerned; and

(b)   was not disregarded by the [CMA] for the purposes of its report under section 142.

NOTES

The words in square brackets in the section heading were inserted, and the words in square brackets in sub-s (1) were substituted, by the Enterprise and Regulatory Reform Act 2013, s 35(10), Sch 10, paras 1, 13 (for transitional provisions (including those relating to the abolition of the OFT and the Competition Commission and the continuity of functions), see the Enterprise and Regulatory Reform Act 2013 (Commencement No 6, Transitional Provisions and Savings) Order 2014, SI 2014/416, Schedule at **[2.1126]**).

The word "CMA" in square brackets in sub-ss (2)–(4) was substituted by the Enterprise and Regulatory Reform Act 2013, s 26(3), Sch 5, Pt 2, paras 59, 179 (as to transitional provisions etc, see the note above).

[1.1739]
[146A   Full PI references: decision of Secretary of State

(1)   Subsection (2) applies where the Secretary of State has received a report of the CMA in relation to a full PI reference which—

(a)   has been prepared under section 142;

(b)   contains the decisions of the CMA that there is one or more than one adverse effect on competition and that one or more than one of the features or combinations of features that gave rise to an adverse effect on competition operates or may be expected to operate against the public interest and that, in relation to at least one effect adverse to the public interest concerned, action should be taken by the Secretary of State; and

(c)   has been given to the Secretary of State as required by section 143A(3).

(2)   The Secretary of State shall decide whether to make an adverse public interest finding in relation to the matter and whether to make no finding at all in the matter.

(3)   For the purposes of this Part, the Secretary of State makes an adverse public interest finding in relation to a matter if, in relation to that matter, the Secretary of State decides—

(a)   that there is an adverse effect on competition;

(b)   that there is one or more than one admissible public interest consideration which is relevant to the matter; and

(c)   taking account only of any adverse effect on competition and any relevant admissible public interest consideration or considerations, that any feature or combination of features which gave rise to an adverse effect on competition operates or may be expected to operate against the public interest.

(4)   The Secretary of State may make no finding at all in a matter only if the Secretary of State decides that there is no admissible public interest consideration which is relevant to a consideration of the matter concerned.

(5)   In deciding whether to make an adverse public interest finding under subsection (2), the Secretary of State shall accept the decision of the CMA as to whether there is an adverse effect on competition in relation to the matter.

(6)   The Secretary of State shall make and publish the decision under subsection (2) within the period of 90 days beginning with the receipt of the report of the CMA under section 142.

(7)   In this section "admissible public interest consideration" means a public interest consideration which—

(a)   was mentioned in the intervention notice concerned; and

(b)   was not disregarded by the CMA for the purposes of its report under section 142.]

NOTES

Commencement: 1 April 2014.

Inserted by the Enterprise and Regulatory Reform Act 2013, s 35(10), Sch 10, paras 1, 14 (for transitional provisions (including those relating to the abolition of the OFT and the Competition Commission and the continuity of functions), see the Enterprise and Regulatory Reform Act 2013 (Commencement No 6, Transitional Provisions and Savings) Order 2014, SI 2014/416, Schedule at [2.1126]).

[1.1740]
147   [Restricted PI references:] remedial action by Secretary of State

(1)   Subsection (2) applies where the Secretary of State—

(a)   has decided under subsection (2) of section 146 within the period required by subsection (3) of that section that an eligible public interest consideration is relevant as mentioned in subsection (2) of that section or eligible public interest considerations are so relevant; and

(b)   has published his decision within the period required by subsection (3) of that section.

(2)   The Secretary of State may, in relation to any adverse effect on competition identified in the report concerned, take such action under section 159 or 161 as he considers to be—

(a)   reasonable and practicable—

(i)   to remedy, mitigate or prevent the adverse effect on competition concerned; or

(ii)   to remedy, mitigate or prevent any detrimental effect on customers so far as it has resulted from, or may be expected to result from, the adverse effect on competition; and

(b)   appropriate in the light of the eligible public interest consideration concerned or (as the case may be) the eligible public interest considerations concerned.

(3)   In making a decision under subsection (2), the Secretary of State shall, in particular, have regard to—

(a)   the need to achieve as comprehensive a solution as is reasonable and practicable to the adverse effect on competition concerned and any detrimental effects on customers so far as resulting from the adverse effect on competition; and

(b)   the report of the [CMA] under section 142.

(4)   In having regard by virtue of subsection (3) to the report of the [CMA] under section 142, the Secretary of State shall not challenge the decision of the [CMA] contained in the report that there is one or more than one adverse effect on competition.

(5)   In making a decision under subsection (2), the Secretary of State may, in particular, have regard to the effect of any action on any relevant customer benefits of the feature or features of the market [or markets] concerned.

(6)   The Secretary of State shall take no action under subsection (2) to remedy, mitigate or prevent any detrimental effect on customers so far as it may be expected to result from the adverse effect on competition concerned if—

    (a)   no detrimental effect on customers has resulted from the adverse effect on competition; and

    (b)   the adverse effect on competition is not being remedied, mitigated or prevented.

(7)   In this section "eligible public interest consideration" has the same meaning as in section 146.

NOTES

Words in square brackets in the section heading inserted by the Enterprise and Regulatory Reform Act 2013, s 35(10), Sch 10, paras 1, 15 (for transitional provisions (including those relating to the abolition of the OFT and the Competition Commission and the continuity of functions), see the Enterprise and Regulatory Reform Act 2013 (Commencement No 6, Transitional Provisions and Savings) Order 2014, SI 2014/416, Schedule at **[2.1126]**).

The word "CMA" in square brackets in sub-ss (3), (4) was substituted by the Enterprise and Regulatory Reform Act 2013, s 26(3), Sch 5, Pt 2, paras 59, 180 (as to transitional provisions etc, see the note above).

Words in square brackets in sub-s (5) inserted by the Enterprise and Regulatory Reform Act 2013, s 34(4), Sch 9, paras 1, 6 (as to transitional provisions etc, see the note above).

[1.1741]

[147A   Full PI references: remedial action by Secretary of State

(1)   Subsection (2) applies where the Secretary of State has decided under subsection (2) of section 146A within the period required by subsection (6) of that section to make an adverse public interest finding in relation to a matter and has published the decision within the period so required.

(2)   The Secretary of State may take such action under section 159 or 161 as the Secretary of State considers to be reasonable and practicable to remedy, mitigate or prevent any of the effects adverse to the public interest which have resulted from, or may be expected to result from, the features or combinations of features in question.

(3)   In making a decision under subsection (2), the Secretary of State shall, in particular, have regard to the report of the CMA under section 142.

(4)   In making a decision under subsection (2), the Secretary of State may, in particular, have regard to—

    (a)   the need to achieve as comprehensive a solution as is reasonable and practicable to the effects adverse to the public interest concerned; and

    (b)   any detrimental effects on customers so far as resulting from those effects.]

NOTES

Commencement: 1 April 2014.

Inserted by the Enterprise and Regulatory Reform Act 2013, s 35(10), Sch 10, paras 1, 16 (for transitional provisions (including those relating to the abolition of the OFT and the Competition Commission and the continuity of functions), see the Enterprise and Regulatory Reform Act 2013 (Commencement No 6, Transitional Provisions and Savings) Order 2014, SI 2014/416, Schedule at **[2.1126]**).

[1.1742]

148   [Restricted PI references: reversion of the matter to CMA]

(1)   If—

    (a)   the Secretary of State fails to make and publish his decision under subsection (2) of section 146 within the period required by subsection (3) of that section; or

    (b)   the Secretary of State decides that no eligible public interest consideration is relevant as mentioned in subsection (2) of that section;

the [CMA] shall proceed under section 138 as if the report had been prepared and published under section 136 within the period permitted by section 137.

(2)   The [CMA] shall publish the report which has been prepared by it under section 142 (if still unpublished) as soon as it becomes able to proceed by virtue of subsection (1).

(3)–(5)   . . .

(6)   In relation to proceedings by virtue of subsection (1), the reference in section 138(3) to decisions of the [CMA] included in its report by virtue of section 134(4) shall be construed as a reference to decisions which were included in the report of the [CMA] by virtue of section 141(4).

(7)   Where the [CMA], in proceeding by virtue of subsection (1), intends to proceed in a way which is not consistent with its decisions as included in its report by virtue of section 141(4), it shall not so proceed without the consent of the Secretary of State.

(8)   The Secretary of State shall not withhold his consent under subsection (7) unless he believes that the proposed alternative way of proceeding will operate against the public interest.

(9)   For the purposes of subsection (8) a proposed alternative way of proceeding will operate against the public interest only if any eligible public interest consideration or considerations outweigh the considerations which have led the [CMA] to propose proceeding in that way.

(10)   In deciding whether to withhold his consent under subsection (7), the Secretary of State shall accept the [CMA's] view of what, if the only relevant consideration were how to remedy, mitigate or prevent the adverse effect on competition concerned or any detrimental effect on customers so far as resulting from the adverse effect on competition, would be the most appropriate way to proceed.

(11)   In this section "eligible public interest consideration" has the same meaning as in section 146.

NOTES

Section heading substituted, and sub-ss (3)–(5) repealed, by the Enterprise and Regulatory Reform Act 2013, s 35(10), Sch 10, paras 1, 17 (for transitional provisions (including those relating to the abolition of the OFT and the Competition Commission and the continuity of functions), see the Enterprise and Regulatory Reform Act 2013 (Commencement No 6, Transitional Provisions and Savings) Order 2014, SI 2014/416, Schedule at **[2.1126]**).

The words "CMA" and "CMA's" in square brackets (in each place that they occur) were substituted by the Enterprise and Regulatory Reform Act 2013, s 26(3), Sch 5, Pt 2, paras 59, 181 (as to transitional provisions etc, see the note above).

[1.1743]
[148A   Full PI references: reversion of the matter to CMA
(1)   This section applies if—
  (a)   the Secretary of State decides under section 146A(2) to make no finding at all in the matter; or
  (b)   the Secretary of State fails to make and publish the decision under subsection (2) of section 146A within the period required by subsection (6) of that section.
(2)   The CMA shall proceed under section 138 as if—
  (a)   a reference under section 131 had been made (in accordance with the requirements imposed by this Part) instead of a full PI reference; and
  (b)   its report had been prepared and published under section 136 within the period permitted by section 137.
(3)   The CMA shall publish the report which has been prepared by it under section 142 (if still unpublished) as soon as it becomes able to proceed by virtue of subsection (2).
(4)   In relation to proceedings by virtue of subsection (2), the reference in section 138(3) to decisions of the CMA included in its report by virtue of section 134(4) is to be construed as a reference to decisions which were included in the report of the CMA by virtue of section 141A(6).
(5)   Where the CMA becomes under a duty to proceed as mentioned in subsection (2), references in this Part to a reference under section 131, so far as necessary, are to be construed accordingly.
(6)   Where the CMA, in proceeding by virtue of subsection (2), intends to proceed in a way which is not consistent with its decisions as included in its report by virtue of section 141A(6), it shall not so proceed without the consent of the Secretary of State.
(7)   The Secretary of State shall not withhold consent under subsection (6) unless the Secretary of State believes that the proposed alternative way of proceeding will operate against the public interest.
(8)   For the purposes of subsection (7) a proposed alternative way of proceeding will operate against the public interest only if any admissible public interest consideration or considerations outweigh the considerations which have led the CMA to propose proceeding in that way.
(9)   In deciding whether to withhold consent under subsection (6), the Secretary of State shall accept the CMA's view of what, if the only relevant consideration were how to remedy, mitigate or prevent the adverse effect on competition concerned or any detrimental effect on customers so far as resulting from the adverse effect on competition, would be the most appropriate way to proceed.
(10)   In this section "admissible public interest consideration" has the same meaning as in section 146A.]

NOTES
Commencement: 1 April 2014.

Inserted by the Enterprise and Regulatory Reform Act 2013, s 35(10), Sch 10, paras 1, 18 (for transitional provisions (including those relating to the abolition of the OFT and the Competition Commission and the continuity of functions), see the Enterprise and Regulatory Reform Act 2013 (Commencement No 6, Transitional Provisions and Savings) Order 2014, SI 2014/416, Schedule at **[2.1126]**).

Intervention notices under section 139(2)

[1.1744]
149   Intervention notices under section 139(2)
(1)   An intervention notice under section 139(2) shall state—
  (a)   the proposed undertaking which may be accepted by the [CMA];
  (b)   the notice under section 155(1) or (4);
  (c)   the public interest consideration or considerations which are, or may be, relevant to the [proposal to accept the undertaking]; and
  (d)   where any public interest consideration concerned is not finalised, the proposed timetable for finalising it.
(2)   Where the Secretary of State believes that it is or may be the case that two or more public interest considerations are relevant to the *case*, he may decide not to mention in the intervention notice such of those considerations as he considers appropriate.
(3)   The Secretary of State may at any time revoke an intervention notice which has been given under section 139(2) and which is in force.
(4)   An intervention notice under section 139(2) shall come into force when it is given and shall cease to be in force on the occurrence of any of the events mentioned in subsection (5).
(5)   The events are—
  (a)   the acceptance by the [CMA] with the consent of the Secretary of State of an undertaking which is the same as the proposed undertaking mentioned in the intervention notice by virtue of subsection (1)(a) or which does not differ from it in any material respect;

(b) the decision of the [CMA] to proceed neither with the proposed undertaking mentioned in the intervention notice by virtue of subsection (1)(a) nor a proposed undertaking which does not differ from it in any material respect; or

(c) the decision of the Secretary of State to revoke the intervention notice concerned.

NOTES

The word "CMA" in square brackets (in each place that it occurs) was substituted by the Enterprise and Regulatory Reform Act 2013, s 26(3), Sch 5, Pt 2, paras 59, 182 (for transitional provisions (including those relating to the abolition of the OFT and the Competition Commission and the continuity of functions), see the Enterprise and Regulatory Reform Act 2013 (Commencement No 6, Transitional Provisions and Savings) Order 2014, SI 2014/416, Schedule at [2.1126]).

Words "proposal to accept the undertaking" in square brackets (in each place that they occur) substituted by the Enterprise and Regulatory Reform Act 2013, s 35(10), Sch 10, paras 1, 19 (as to transitional provisions etc, see the note above).

[1.1745]
150 Power of veto of Secretary of State
[(A1) Where an intervention notice under subsection 139(1) is in force, the CMA shall not, without the consent of the Secretary of State, accept any proposed undertaking under section 154 in relation to the matter concerned.]

(1) Where an intervention notice under section 139(2) is in force, the [CMA] shall not, without the consent of the Secretary of State, accept the proposed undertaking concerned or a proposed undertaking which does not differ from it in any material respect.

(2) The Secretary of State shall withhold his consent if he believes that it is or may be the case that the proposed undertaking will, if accepted, operate against the public interest.

(3) For the purposes of subsection (2) a proposed undertaking will, if accepted, operate against the public interest only if any public interest consideration which is mentioned in the intervention notice concerned and has been finalised, or any public interest considerations which are so mentioned and have been finalised, outweigh the considerations which have led the [CMA] to propose accepting the undertaking.

(4) In making his decision under subsection (2) the Secretary of State shall accept the [CMA's] view of what undertakings, if the only relevant consideration were how to remedy, mitigate or prevent the adverse effect on competition concerned or any detrimental effect on customers so far as resulting from the adverse effect on competition, would be most appropriate.

(5) Where a public interest consideration which is mentioned in the intervention notice concerned is not finalised on the giving of the notice, the Secretary of State shall not make his decision as to whether to give his consent under this section before—

(a) the end of the period of 24 weeks beginning with the giving of the intervention notice; or

(b) if earlier, the date on which the public interest consideration concerned has been finalised.

(6) Subject to subsections (2) to (5), the Secretary of State shall not withhold his consent under this section.

NOTES

Sub-s (A1): inserted by the Enterprise and Regulatory Reform Act 2013, s 35(10), Sch 10, paras 1, 20 (for transitional provisions (including those relating to the abolition of the OFT and the Competition Commission and the continuity of functions), see the Enterprise and Regulatory Reform Act 2013 (Commencement No 6, Transitional Provisions and Savings) Order 2014, SI 2014/416, Schedule at [2.1126]).

The words "CMA" and "CMA's" in square brackets (in each place that they occur) were substituted by the Enterprise and Regulatory Reform Act 2013, s 26(3), Sch 5, Pt 2, paras 59, 183 (as to transitional provisions etc, see the note above).

Other

[1.1746]
151 [Public interest intervention cases: interaction with general procedure]
[(1) Sections 134(1), (1A), (4), (6) and (7), 136(1) to (6), 137(1) to (6), 138 and 138A do not apply in relation to a restricted PI reference or a full PI reference.]

(2) Where the Secretary of State revokes an intervention notice which has been given under section 139(1) [at a time after the Secretary of State has made a restricted PI reference or a full PI reference, the CMA shall proceed as if the reference concerned had instead been made under section 131 (in accordance with the requirements imposed by this Part)].

(3) Where the [CMA] is proceeding by virtue of subsection (2), the period within which the [CMA] shall prepare and publish its report under section 136 shall be extended by an additional period of 20 days.

(4) Where the [CMA] terminates its investigation under section 145(1)[, the CMA shall proceed as if the restricted PI reference or (as the case may be) the full PI reference concerned had instead been made by the CMA under section 131 (in accordance with the requirements imposed by this Part)].

(5) Where the [CMA] is proceeding by virtue of subsection (4), the period within which the [CMA] shall prepare and publish its report under section 136 shall be extended by an additional period of 20 days.

(6) In determining the period of 20 days mentioned in subsection (3) or (5) no account shall be taken of—

(a) Saturday, Sunday, Good Friday and Christmas Day; and

(b)   any day which is a bank holiday in England and Wales.

NOTES

The section heading and sub-s (1) were substituted, the words in square brackets in sub-s (2) were substituted, and the words in the second pair of square brackets in sub-s (4) were substituted, by the Enterprise and Regulatory Reform Act 2013, s 35(10), Sch 10, paras 1, 21 (for transitional provisions (including those relating to the abolition of the OFT and the Competition Commission and the continuity of functions), see the Enterprise and Regulatory Reform Act 2013 (Commencement No 6, Transitional Provisions and Savings) Order 2014, SI 2014/416, Schedule at [**2.1126**]).

The word "CMA" in square brackets (in each place that it occurs) was substituted by the Enterprise and Regulatory Reform Act 2013, s 26(3), Sch 5, Pt 2, paras 59, 184 (as to transitional provisions etc, see the note above).

[1.1747]
152   Certain duties of [CMA]
(1)   The [CMA] shall, in considering whether to make a reference under section 131, bring to the attention of the Secretary of State any case which it believes raises any consideration specified in section 153 unless it believes that the Secretary of State would consider any such consideration immaterial in the context of the particular case.
(2)   . . .
(3)   The [CMA] shall bring to the attention of the Secretary of State any representations about exercising his power under section 153(3) which have been made to the [CMA].

NOTES

Sub-s (2) was repealed by the Enterprise and Regulatory Reform Act 2013, s 35(10), Sch 10, paras 1, 22 (for transitional provisions (including those relating to the abolition of the OFT and the Competition Commission and the continuity of functions), see the Enterprise and Regulatory Reform Act 2013 (Commencement No 6, Transitional Provisions and Savings) Order 2014, SI 2014/416, Schedule at [**2.1126**]).

The word "CMA" in square brackets (in each place that it occurs) was substituted by the Enterprise and Regulatory Reform Act 2013, s 26(3), Sch 5, Pt 2, paras 59, 185 (as to transitional provisions etc, see the note above).

[1.1748]
153   Specified considerations: Part 4
(1)   The interests of national security are specified in this section.
(2)   In subsection (1) "national security" includes public security; and in this subsection "public security" has the same meaning as in article [21(4) of Council Regulation (EC) No 139/2004 of 20th January 2004 on the control of concentrations between undertakings].
(3)   The Secretary of State may by order modify this section for the purpose of specifying in this section a new consideration or removing or amending any consideration which is for the time being specified in this section.
(4)   An order under this section may apply in relation to cases under consideration by the [CMA] [by the Secretary of State or] by the appropriate Minister (other than the Secretary of State acting alone)   . . .   before the making of the order as well as cases under consideration on or after the making of the order.

NOTES

Sub-s (2): words in square brackets substituted by the EC Merger Control (Consequential Amendments) Regulations 2004, SI 2004/1079, reg 2, Schedule, para 2(1), (27).

Sub-s (4): words in square brackets substituted, and words omitted repealed, by the Enterprise and Regulatory Reform Act 2013, s 26(3), Sch 5, Pt 2, paras 59, 186 (for transitional provisions (including those relating to the abolition of the OFT and the Competition Commission and the continuity of functions), see the Enterprise and Regulatory Reform Act 2013 (Commencement No 6, Transitional Provisions and Savings) Order 2014, SI 2014/416, Schedule at [**2.1126**]).

CHAPTER 3
ENFORCEMENT
Undertakings and orders

[1.1749]
154   Undertakings in lieu of market investigation references
(1)   Subsection (2) applies if the [CMA] considers that it has the power to make a reference under section 131 and otherwise intends to make such a reference.
(2)   The [CMA] may, instead of making such a reference and for the purpose of remedying, mitigating or preventing—
  (a)   any adverse effect on competition concerned; or
  (b)   any detrimental effect on customers so far as it has resulted from, or may be expected to result from, the adverse effect on competition;
accept, from such persons as it considers appropriate, undertakings to take such action as it considers appropriate.
(3)   In proceeding under subsection (2), the [CMA] shall, in particular, have regard to the need to achieve as comprehensive a solution as is reasonable and practicable to the adverse effect on competition concerned and any detrimental effects on customers so far as resulting from the adverse effect on competition.

(4)   In proceeding under subsection (2), the [CMA] may, in particular, have regard to the effect of any action on any relevant customer benefits of the feature or features of the market [or markets] concerned.

(5)   The [CMA] shall take no action under subsection (2) to remedy, mitigate or prevent any detrimental effect on customers so far as it may be expected to result from the adverse effect on competition concerned if—

    (a)   no detrimental effect on customers has resulted from the adverse effect on competition; and

    (b)   the adverse effect on competition is not being remedied, mitigated or prevented.

(6)   An undertaking under this section—

    (a)   shall come into force when accepted;

    (b)   may be varied or superseded by another undertaking; and

    (c)   may be released by the [CMA].

(7)   The [CMA] shall, as soon as reasonably practicable, consider any representations received by it in relation to varying or releasing an undertaking under this section.

(8)   This section is subject to sections 150 and 155.

NOTES

    The word "CMA" in square brackets (in each place that it occurs) was substituted by the Enterprise and Regulatory Reform Act 2013, s 26(3), Sch 5, Pt 2, paras 59, 187 (for transitional provisions (including those relating to the abolition of the OFT and the Competition Commission and the continuity of functions), see the Enterprise and Regulatory Reform Act 2013 (Commencement No 6, Transitional Provisions and Savings) Order 2014, SI 2014/416, Schedule at **[2.1126]**).

    Words "or markets" in square brackets in sub-s (4) inserted by the Enterprise and Regulatory Reform Act 2013, s 34(4), Sch 9, paras 1, 7 (as to transitional provisions etc, see the note above).

[1.1750]
155   Undertakings in lieu: procedural requirements

(1)   Before accepting an undertaking under section 154 (other than an undertaking under that section which varies an undertaking under that section but not in any material respect), the [CMA] shall—

    (a)   publish notice of the proposed undertaking; and

    (b)   consider any representations made in accordance with the notice and not withdrawn.

(2)   A notice under subsection (1) shall state—

    (a)   that the [CMA] proposes to accept the undertaking;

    (b)   the purpose and effect of the undertaking;

    (c)   the situation that the undertaking is seeking to deal with;

    (d)   any other facts which the [CMA] considers justify the acceptance of the undertaking;

    (e)   a means of gaining access to an accurate version of the proposed undertaking at all reasonable times; and

    (f)   the period (not less than 15 days starting with the date of publication of the notice) within which representations may be made in relation to the proposed undertaking.

(3)   The matters to be included in a notice under subsection (1) by virtue of subsection (2) shall, in particular, include—

    (a)   the terms of the reference under section 131 which the [CMA] considers that it has power to make and which it otherwise intends to make [or (but for the effect of section 140A(3)) it would have had power to make and which it would otherwise have intended to make]; and

    (b)   the adverse effect on competition, and any detrimental effect on customers so far as resulting from the adverse effect on competition, which the [CMA] has identified.

(4)   The [CMA] shall not accept the undertaking with modifications unless it—

    (a)   publishes notice of the proposed modifications; and

    (b)   considers any representations made in accordance with the notice and not withdrawn.

(5)   A notice under subsection (4) shall state—

    (a)   the proposed modifications;

    (b)   the reasons for them; and

    (c)   the period (not less than 7 days starting with the date of the publication of the notice under subsection (4)) within which representations may be made in relation to the proposed modifications.

(6)   If, after publishing notice under subsection (1) or (4), the [CMA] decides—

    (a)   not to accept the undertaking concerned; and

    (b)   not to proceed by virtue of subsection (8) or (9);

it shall publish notice of that decision.

(7)   As soon as practicable after accepting an undertaking to which this section applies, the [CMA] shall—

    (a)   serve a copy of the undertaking on any person by whom it is given; and

    (b)   publish the undertaking.

(8)   The requirements of subsection (4) (and those of subsection (1)) shall not apply if the [CMA]—

    (a)   has already published notice under subsection (1) but not subsection (4) in relation to the proposed undertaking; and

   (b)   considers that the modifications which are now being proposed are not material in any respect.

(9) The requirements of subsection (4) (and those of subsection (1)) shall not apply if the [CMA]—

   (a)   has already published notice under subsections (1) and (4) in relation to the matter concerned; and

   (b)   considers that the further modifications which are now being proposed do not differ in any material respect from the modifications in relation to which notice was last given under subsection (4).

(10) Paragraphs 6 to 8 (but not paragraph 9) of Schedule 10 (procedural requirements before terminating undertakings) shall apply in relation to the proposed release of undertakings under section 154 (other than in connection with accepting an undertaking under that section which varies or supersedes an undertaking under that section) as they apply in relation to the proposed release of undertakings under section 73.

<hr>

NOTES

   The word "CMA" in square brackets (in each place that it occurs) was substituted by the Enterprise and Regulatory Reform Act 2013, s 26(3), Sch 5, Pt 2, paras 59, 188 (for transitional provisions (including those relating to the abolition of the OFT and the Competition Commission and the continuity of functions), see the Enterprise and Regulatory Reform Act 2013 (Commencement No 6, Transitional Provisions and Savings) Order 2014, SI 2014/416, Schedule at **[2.1126]**).

   Words in second pair of square brackets in sub-s (3)(a) inserted by the Enterprise and Regulatory Reform Act 2013, s 35(10), Sch 10, paras 1, 23 (as to transitional provisions etc, see the note above).

<hr>

[1.1751]
156 Effect of undertakings under section 154

[(A1) No market investigation reference shall be made by the CMA or the appropriate Minister in relation to any feature, or combination of features, of a market in the United Kingdom for goods or services if—

   (a)   the CMA has accepted an undertaking or group of undertakings under section 154 within the previous 12 months;

   (b)   the feature or combination of features to which the undertaking or group of undertakings relates is the same as the feature or combination of features to which the reference would relate; and

   (c)   the goods or services to which the undertaking or group of undertakings relates are of the same description as the goods or services to which the reference would relate.]

(1) No [ordinary] reference shall be made by the [CMA] or the appropriate Minister in relation to any feature, or combination of features, of a market in the United Kingdom for goods or services if—

   (a)   the [CMA] has[, instead of making an ordinary reference,] accepted an undertaking or group of undertakings under section 154 within the previous 12 months; and

   (b)   the goods or services to which the undertaking or group of undertakings relates are of the same description as the goods or services to which [the reference would relate].

(2) [Subsections (A1) and (1) do] not prevent the making of a market investigation reference if—

   (a)   the [CMA] considers that any undertaking concerned has been breached and has given notice of that fact to the person responsible for giving the undertaking; or

   (b)   the person responsible for giving any undertaking concerned supplied, in connection with the matter, information to the [CMA] which was false or misleading in a material respect.

[(3) The expiry of the period mentioned in section 131B(4) does not prevent the making of a market investigation reference if the CMA has accepted an undertaking or group of undertakings under section 154 and—

   (a)   the CMA considers that any undertaking concerned has been breached and has given notice of that fact to the person responsible for giving the undertaking; or

   (b)   the person responsible for giving any undertaking concerned supplied, in connection with the matter, information to the OFT which was false or misleading in a material respect.]

<hr>

NOTES

   The word "CMA" in square brackets (in each place that it occurs) was substituted by the Enterprise and Regulatory Reform Act 2013, s 26(3), Sch 5, Pt 2, paras 59, 189 (for transitional provisions (including those relating to the abolition of the OFT and the Competition Commission and the continuity of functions), see the Enterprise and Regulatory Reform Act 2013 (Commencement No 6, Transitional Provisions and Savings) Order 2014, SI 2014/416, Schedule at **[2.1126]**).

   Sub-s (A1) was inserted, and the other words in square brackets in sub-ss (1) and (2) were inserted or substituted, by the Enterprise and Regulatory Reform Act 2013, s 34(4), Sch 9, paras 1, 8 (as to transitional provisions etc, see the note above).

   Sub-s (3) was added by the Enterprise and Regulatory Reform Act 2013, s 38, Sch 12, paras 7, 12 (as to transitional provisions etc, see the note above).

<hr>

[1.1752]
157 Interim undertakings: Part 4

(1) Subsection (2) applies where—

   (a)   a market investigation reference has been made;

(b)   a report has been published under section 136 within the period permitted by section 137 or (as the case may be) a report prepared under section 142 and given to the Secretary of State under section 143(3) [or (as the case may be) 143A(3)] within the period permitted by section 144 has been published; and

(c)   the market investigation reference concerned is not finally determined.

(2)   The relevant authority may, for the purpose of preventing pre-emptive action, accept, from such persons as the relevant authority considers appropriate, undertakings to take such action as the relevant authority considers appropriate.

[(2A)   Subsection (2B) applies where—

(a)   subsection (1)(a) to (c) applies; and

(b)   the relevant authority has reasonable grounds for suspecting that pre-emptive action has or may have been taken.

(2B)   The relevant authority may, for the purpose of restoring the position to what it would have been had the pre-emptive action not been taken or otherwise for the purpose of mitigating its effects, accept, from such persons as the relevant authority considers appropriate, undertakings to take such action as the relevant authority considers appropriate.]

[(2C)   A person may, with the consent of the relevant authority, take action of a particular description where the action would otherwise constitute a contravention of an undertaking accepted under this section.]

(3)   An undertaking under this section—

(a)   shall come into force when accepted;

(b)   may be varied or superseded by another undertaking; and

(c)   may be released by the relevant authority.

(4)   An undertaking under this section shall, if it has not previously ceased to be in force, cease to be in force when the market investigation reference is finally determined.

(5)   The relevant authority shall, as soon as reasonably practicable, consider any representations received by the relevant authority in relation to varying or releasing an undertaking under this section.

(6)   In this section and section 158—

"pre-emptive action" means action which might impede the taking of any action under section 138(2)[, 147(2) or (as the case may be) 147A(2)] in relation to the market investigation reference concerned; and

["the relevant authority" means—

(a)   in the case of a restricted PI reference or a full PI reference, the Secretary of State;

(b)   in any other case, the CMA.]

NOTES

Sub-s (1): words in square brackets inserted by the Enterprise and Regulatory Reform Act 2013, s 35(10), Sch 10, paras 1, 24(1), (2) (for transitional provisions (including those relating to the abolition of the OFT and the Competition Commission and the continuity of functions), see the Enterprise and Regulatory Reform Act 2013 (Commencement No 6, Transitional Provisions and Savings) Order 2014, SI 2014/416, Schedule at **[2.1126]**).

Sub-ss (2A)–(2C): inserted by the Enterprise and Regulatory Reform Act 2013, s 37(1)–(3) (as to transitional provisions etc, see the note above).

Sub-s (6): words in square brackets in the definition "pre-emptive action" substituted, and definition "relevant authority" substituted, by the Enterprise and Regulatory Reform Act 2013, s 35(10), Sch 10, paras 1, 24(1), (3) (as to transitional provisions etc, see the note above).

[1.1753]
158   Interim orders: Part 4

(1)   Subsection (2) applies where—

(a)   a market investigation reference has been made;

(b)   a report has been published under section 136 within the period permitted by section 137 or (as the case may be) a report prepared under section 142 and given to the Secretary of State under section 143(3) [or (as the case may be) 143A(3)] within the period permitted by section 144 has been published; and

(c)   the market investigation reference concerned is not finally determined.

(2)   The relevant authority may by order, for the purpose of preventing pre-emptive action—

(a)   prohibit or restrict the doing of things which the relevant authority considers would constitute pre-emptive action;

(b)   impose on any person concerned obligations as to the carrying on of any activities or the safeguarding of any assets;

(c)   provide for the carrying on of any activities or the safeguarding of any assets either by the appointment of a person to conduct or supervise the conduct of any activities (on such terms and with such powers as may be specified or described in the order) or in any other manner;

(d)   do anything which may be done by virtue of paragraph 19 of Schedule 8.

[(2A)   Subsection (2B) applies where—

(a)   subsection (1)(a) to (c) applies; and

(b)   the relevant authority has reasonable grounds for suspecting that pre-emptive action has or may have been taken.

(2B)   The relevant authority may by order, for the purpose of restoring the position to what it would have been had the pre-emptive action not been taken or otherwise for the purpose of mitigating its effects—

(a)   do anything mentioned in subsection (2)(b) to (d);

(b)   impose such other obligations, prohibitions or restrictions as it considers appropriate for that purpose.]

[(2C)   A person may, with the consent of the relevant authority, take action of a particular description where the action would otherwise constitute a contravention of an order under this section.]

(3)   An order under this section—

(a)   shall come into force at such time as is determined by or under the order; and

(b)   may be varied or revoked by another order.

(4)   An order under this section shall, if it has not previously ceased to be in force, cease to be in force when the market investigation reference is finally determined.

(5)   The relevant authority shall, as soon as reasonably practicable, consider any representations received by the relevant authority in relation to varying or revoking an order under this section.

NOTES

Sub-s (1): words in square brackets inserted by the Enterprise and Regulatory Reform Act 2013, s 35(10), Sch 10, paras 1, 25 (for transitional provisions (including those relating to the abolition of the OFT and the Competition Commission and the continuity of functions), see the Enterprise and Regulatory Reform Act 2013 (Commencement No 6, Transitional Provisions and Savings) Order 2014, SI 2014/416, Schedule at **[2.1126]**).

Sub-ss (2A)–(2C): inserted by the Enterprise and Regulatory Reform Act 2013, s 37(1), (4), (5) (as to transitional provisions etc, see the note above).

[1.1754]
159   Final undertakings: Part 4
(1)   The [CMA] may, in accordance with section 138, accept, from such persons as it considers appropriate, undertakings to take action specified or described in the undertakings.

(2)   The Secretary of State may, in accordance with section 147 [or (as the case may be) 147A], accept, from such persons as he considers appropriate, undertakings to take action specified or described in the undertakings.

(3)   An undertaking under this section shall come into force when accepted.

(4)   An undertaking under subsection (1) or (2) may be varied or superseded by another undertaking under that subsection.

(5)   An undertaking under subsection (1) may be released by the [CMA] and an undertaking under subsection (2) may be released by the Secretary of State.

(6)   The [CMA] or (as the case may be) the Secretary of State shall, as soon as reasonably practicable, consider any representations received by it or (as the case may be) him in relation to varying or releasing an undertaking under this section.

NOTES

Sub-ss (1), (5), (6): word "CMA" in square brackets substituted by the Enterprise and Regulatory Reform Act 2013, s 26(3), Sch 5, Pt 2, paras 59, 190 (for transitional provisions (including those relating to the abolition of the OFT and the Competition Commission and the continuity of functions), see the Enterprise and Regulatory Reform Act 2013 (Commencement No 6, Transitional Provisions and Savings) Order 2014, SI 2014/416, Schedule at **[2.1126]**).

Sub-s (2): words in square brackets inserted by the Enterprise and Regulatory Reform Act 2013, s 35(10), Sch 10, paras 1, 26 (as to transitional provisions etc, see the note above).

[1.1755]
160   Order-making power where final undertakings not fulfilled: Part 4
(1)   Subsection (2) applies where the relevant authority considers that—

(a)   an undertaking accepted by the relevant authority under section 159 has not been, is not being or will not be fulfilled; or

(b)   in relation to an undertaking accepted by the relevant authority under that section, information which was false or misleading in a material respect was given to [a relevant person] by the person giving the undertaking before the relevant authority decided to accept the undertaking.

[(1A)   In subsection (1), a "relevant person" means—

(a)   in a case where the relevant authority is the CMA, the CMA;

(b)   in a case where the relevant authority is the Secretary of State, the Secretary of State or the CMA.]

(2)   The relevant authority may, for any of the purposes mentioned in section 138(2)[, 147(2) or (as the case may be) 147A(2)], make an order under this section.

(3)   Subsections (3) to (6) of section 138 [or 147 or (as the case may be) subsections (3) and (4) of section 147A] shall apply for the purposes of subsection (2) above as they apply for the purposes of that section.

(4)   An order under this section may contain—

(a)   anything permitted by Schedule 8; and

(b)   such supplementary, consequential or incidental provision as the relevant authority considers appropriate.

(5)   An order under this section—
   (a)   shall come into force at such time as is determined by or under the order;
   (b)   may contain provision which is different from the provision contained in the undertaking concerned; and
   (c)   may be varied or revoked by another order.

(6)   [The Secretary of State shall not vary or revoke an order made by him under this section unless the CMA] advises that such a variation or revocation is appropriate by reason of a change of circumstances.

(7)   In this section "the relevant authority" means—
   (a)   in the case of an undertaking accepted under section 159 by the [CMA], the [CMA]; and
   (b)   in the case of an undertaking accepted under that section by the Secretary of State, the Secretary of State.

NOTES

Sub-ss (1), (6): words in square brackets substituted by the Enterprise and Regulatory Reform Act 2013, s 26(3), Sch 5, Pt 2, paras 59, 191(1), (2), (4) (for transitional provisions (including those relating to the abolition of the OFT and the Competition Commission and the continuity of functions), see the Enterprise and Regulatory Reform Act 2013 (Commencement No 6, Transitional Provisions and Savings) Order 2014, SI 2014/416, Schedule at [**2.1126**]).

Sub-s (1A): inserted by the Enterprise and Regulatory Reform Act 2013, s 26(3), Sch 5, Pt 2, paras 59, 191(1), (3) (as to transitional provisions etc, see the note above).

Sub-s (2), (3): words in square brackets substituted by the Enterprise and Regulatory Reform Act 2013, s 35(10), Sch 10, paras 1, 27 (as to transitional provisions etc, see the note above).

Sub-s (7): words in square brackets substituted by the Enterprise and Regulatory Reform Act 2013, s 26(3), Sch 5, Pt 2, paras 59, 191(1), (5) (as to transitional provisions etc, see the note above).

[1.1756]
161   Final orders: Part 4
(1)   The [CMA] may, in accordance with section 138, make an order under this section.
(2)   The Secretary of State may, in accordance with section 147 [or (as the case may be) 147A], make an order under this section.
(3)   An order under this section may contain—
   (a)   anything permitted by Schedule 8; and
   (b)   such supplementary, consequential or incidental provision as the person making it considers appropriate.
(4)   An order under this section—
   (a)   shall come into force at such time as is determined by or under the order; and
   (b)   may be varied or revoked by another order.
(5)   [The Secretary of State shall not vary or revoke an order made by him under this section unless the CMA] advises that such a variation or revocation is appropriate by reason of a change of circumstances.

NOTES

Sub-ss (1), (5): words in square brackets substituted by the Enterprise and Regulatory Reform Act 2013, s 26(3), Sch 5, Pt 2, paras 59, 192 (for transitional provisions (including those relating to the abolition of the OFT and the Competition Commission and the continuity of functions), see the Enterprise and Regulatory Reform Act 2013 (Commencement No 6, Transitional Provisions and Savings) Order 2014, SI 2014/416, Schedule at [**2.1126**]).

Sub-s (2): words in square brackets inserted by the Enterprise and Regulatory Reform Act 2013, s 35(10), Sch 10, paras 1, 28 (as to transitional provisions etc, see the note above).

[Undertakings and orders: monitoring, consultation and advice]

NOTES

The preceding heading was substituted by the Enterprise and Regulatory Reform Act 2013, s 26(3), Sch 5, Pt 2, paras 59, 193 (for transitional provisions (including those relating to the abolition of the OFT and the Competition Commission and the continuity of functions), see the Enterprise and Regulatory Reform Act 2013 (Commencement No 6, Transitional Provisions and Savings) Order 2014, SI 2014/416, Schedule at [**2.1126**]).

[1.1757]
162   Duty of [CMA] to monitor undertakings and orders: Part 4
(1)   The [CMA] shall keep under review the carrying out of any enforcement undertaking or any enforcement order.
(2)   The [CMA] shall, in particular, from time to time consider—
   (a)   whether an enforcement undertaking or enforcement order has been or is being complied with;
   (b)   whether, by reason of any change of circumstances, an enforcement undertaking is no longer appropriate and—
      (i)   one or more of the parties to it can be released from it; or
      (ii)   it needs to be varied or to be superseded by a new enforcement undertaking; and
   (c)   whether, by reason of any change of circumstances, an enforcement order is no longer appropriate and needs to be varied or revoked.

(3)   The [CMA] shall give . . .   the Secretary of State such advice as it considers appropriate in relation to—

    (a)   any possible variation or release by   . . .   the Secretary of State of an enforcement undertaking accepted by . . . him;

    (b)   any possible new enforcement undertaking to be accepted by . . . the Secretary of State so as to supersede another enforcement undertaking given to . . . the Secretary of State;

    (c)   any possible variation or revocation by . . . the Secretary of State of an enforcement order made by . . . the Secretary of State;

    (d)   any possible enforcement undertaking to be accepted by . . . the Secretary of State instead of an enforcement order or any possible enforcement order to be made by . . . the Secretary of State instead of an enforcement undertaking; or

    (e)   the enforcement by virtue of section [167(6) and (7)] of any enforcement undertaking or enforcement order.

(4)   The [CMA] shall take such action as it considers appropriate in relation to—

    (a)   any possible variation or release by it of an undertaking accepted by it under section 154;

    (b)   any possible new undertaking to be accepted by it under section 154 so as to supersede another undertaking given to it under that section;

  [(ba) any possible variation or release by it of an enforcement undertaking accepted by it;

  (bb) any possible new enforcement undertaking to be accepted by it so as to supersede another enforcement undertaking given to it;

  (bc) any possible variation or revocation by it of an enforcement order made by it;

  (bd) any possible enforcement undertaking to be accepted by it instead of an enforcement order or any possible enforcement order to be made by it instead of an enforcement undertaking;] or

    (c)   the enforcement by it by virtue of section 167(6) of any enforcement undertaking or enforcement order.

(5)   The [CMA] shall keep under review the effectiveness of enforcement undertakings accepted under this Part and enforcement orders made under this Part.

(6)   The [CMA] shall, whenever requested to do so by the Secretary of State and otherwise from time to time, prepare a report of its findings under subsection (5).

(7)   The [CMA] shall—

    (a)   . . .

    (b)   give a copy of [any report prepared by it under subsection (6)] to the Secretary of State; and

    (c)   publish the report.

(8)   In this Part—

    "enforcement order" means an order made under section 158, 160 or 161; and

    "enforcement undertaking" means an undertaking accepted under section 154, 157 or 159.

NOTES

   All words in square brackets in this section were substituted or inserted, and the words omitted were repealed, by the Enterprise and Regulatory Reform Act 2013, s 26(3), Sch 5, Pt 2, paras 59, 194 (for transitional provisions (including those relating to the abolition of the OFT and the Competition Commission and the continuity of functions), see the Enterprise and Regulatory Reform Act 2013 (Commencement No 6, Transitional Provisions and Savings) Order 2014, SI 2014/416, Schedule at [**2.1126**]).

[1.1758]
163   [Role of CMA in relation to undertakings and orders in public interest cases: Part 4]

(1)   Subsections (2) and (3) apply where   . . .   the Secretary of State   . . .   is considering whether to accept undertakings under section 157 or 159.

(2)   The [Secretary of State] may require the [CMA] to consult with such persons as the [Secretary of State] considers appropriate with a view to discovering whether they will offer undertakings which the [Secretary of State] would be prepared to accept under section 157 or (as the case may be) 159.

(3)   The [Secretary of State] may require the [CMA] to report to the [Secretary of State] on the outcome of the [CMA's] consultations within such period as the [Secretary of State] may require.

(4)   A report under subsection (3) shall, in particular, contain advice from the [CMA] as to whether any undertakings offered should be accepted by the [Secretary of State] under section 157 or (as the case may be) 159.

(5)   The powers conferred on the [Secretary of State] by subsections (1) to (4) are without prejudice to the power of the [Secretary of State] to consult the persons concerned . . .

(6)   If asked by the [Secretary of State] for advice in relation to the taking of enforcement action (whether or not by way of undertakings) in a particular case, the [CMA] shall give such advice as it considers appropriate.

NOTES

   All words in square brackets in this section were substituted, and the words omitted were repealed, by the Enterprise and Regulatory Reform Act 2013, s 26(3), Sch 5, Pt 2, paras 59, 194 (for transitional provisions (including those relating to the abolition of the OFT and the Competition Commission and the continuity of functions), see the Enterprise and Regulatory

Reform Act 2013 (Commencement No 6, Transitional Provisions and Savings) Order 2014, SI 2014/416, Schedule at **[2.1126]**).

Supplementary

[1.1759]

164 Enforcement undertakings and orders under this Part: general provisions

(1) The provision which may be contained in an enforcement undertaking is not limited to the provision which is permitted by Schedule 8.

(2) The following enactments in Part 3 shall apply in relation to enforcement orders under this Part as they apply in relation to enforcement orders under that Part—

  (a) section 86(1) to (5) (enforcement orders: general provisions); and

  (b) section 87 (power of directions conferred by enforcement order).

(3) An enforcement order under section 160 or 161 or any explanatory material accompanying the order shall state—

  (a) the actions that the persons or description of persons to whom the order is addressed must do or (as the case may be) refrain from doing;

  (b) the date on which the order comes into force;

  (c) the possible consequences of not complying with the order; and

  (d) the section of this Part under which a review can be sought in relation to the order.

[1.1760]

165 Procedural requirements for certain undertakings and orders: Part 4

Schedule 10 (procedural requirements for certain undertakings and orders), other than paragraph 9 of that Schedule, shall apply in relation to undertakings under section 159 and orders under section 160 or 161 as it applies in relation to undertakings under section 82 and orders under section 83 or 84.

[1.1761]

166 Register of undertakings and orders: Part 4

(1) The [CMA] shall compile and maintain a register for the purposes of this Part.

(2) The register shall be kept in such form as the [CMA] considers appropriate.

(3) The [CMA] shall ensure that the following matters are entered in the register—

  (a) the provisions of any enforcement undertaking accepted by virtue of this Part . . .

  (b) the provisions of any enforcement order made by virtue of this Part . . . ; and

  (c) the details of any variation, release or revocation of such an undertaking or order.

(4) The duty in subsection (3) does not extend to anything of which the [CMA] is unaware.

(5) The . . . Secretary of State and any relevant sectoral regulator shall inform the [CMA] of any matters which are to be included in the register by virtue of subsection (3) and which relate to enforcement undertakings accepted by them or enforcement orders made by them.

(6) The [CMA] shall ensure that the contents of the register are available to the public—

  (a) during (as a minimum) such hours as may be specified in an order made by the Secretary of State; and

  (b) subject to such reasonable fees (if any) as the [CMA] may determine.

(7) If requested by any person to do so and subject to such reasonable fees (if any) as the [CMA] may determine, the [CMA] shall supply the person concerned with a copy (certified to be true) of the register or of an extract from it.

NOTES

  Words in square brackets substituted, and words omitted repealed, by the Enterprise and Regulatory Reform Act 2013, s 26(3), Sch 5, Pt 2, paras 59, 196 (for transitional provisions (including those relating to the abolition of the OFT and the Competition Commission and the continuity of functions), see the Enterprise and Regulatory Reform Act 2013 (Commencement No 6, Transitional Provisions and Savings) Order 2014, SI 2014/416, Schedule at **[2.1126]**).

  Orders: the CMA Registers of Undertakings and Orders (Available Hours) Order 2014, SI 2014/558.

[1.1762]

167 Rights to enforce undertakings and orders under this Part

(1) This section applies to any enforcement undertaking or enforcement order.

(2) Any person to whom such an undertaking or order relates shall have a duty to comply with it.

(3) The duty shall be owed to any person who may be affected by a contravention of the undertaking or (as the case may be) order.

(4) Any breach of the duty which causes such a person to sustain loss or damage shall be actionable by him.

(5) In any proceedings brought under subsection (4) against a person to whom an enforcement undertaking or enforcement order relates it shall be a defence for that person to show that he took all reasonable steps and exercised all due diligence to avoid contravening the undertaking or (as the case may be) order.

(6) Compliance with an enforcement undertaking or an enforcement order shall also be enforceable by civil proceedings brought by the [CMA] for an injunction or for interdict or for any other appropriate relief or remedy.

(7) Compliance with an undertaking accepted [by the Secretary of State] under section 157 or 159, or an order [made by the Secretary of State] under section 158, 160 or 161, shall also be enforceable by civil proceedings brought by the [Secretary of State] for an injunction or for interdict or for any other appropriate relief or remedy.

(8) . . .

(9) Subsections [(6) and (7)] shall not prejudice any right that a person may have by virtue of subsection (4) to bring civil proceedings for contravention or apprehended contravention of an enforcement undertaking or an enforcement order.

NOTES

The words in square brackets in sub-ss (6), (7) and (9) were substituted or inserted, and sub-s (8) was repealed, by the Enterprise and Regulatory Reform Act 2013, s 26(3), Sch 5, Pt 2, paras 59, 197 (for transitional provisions (including those relating to the abolition of the OFT and the Competition Commission and the continuity of functions), see the Enterprise and Regulatory Reform Act 2013 (Commencement No 6, Transitional Provisions and Savings) Order 2014, SI 2014/416, Schedule at [**2.1126**]).

CHAPTER 4
SUPPLEMENTARY

Regulated markets

[1.1763]
168 Regulated markets
(1) Subsection (2) applies where the [CMA] or the Secretary of State is considering for the purposes of this Part whether relevant action would be reasonable and practicable for the purpose of remedying, mitigating or preventing an adverse effect on competition or any detrimental effect on customers so far as resulting from such an effect.

(2) The [CMA] or (as the case may be) the Secretary of State shall, in deciding whether such action would be reasonable and practicable, have regard to the relevant statutory functions of the sectoral regulator concerned.

(3) In this section "relevant action" means—
  (a), (b) . . .
  (c) modifying the conditions of a licence granted under section 7[, 7A or 7AB] of the Gas Act 1986 (c 44);
  (d) modifying the conditions of a licence granted under section 6 of the Electricity Act 1989 (c 29);
  (e) modifying networking arrangements (within the meaning given by [section 290 of the Communications Act 2003]);
  (f) modifying the conditions of a company's appointment under Chapter 1 of Part 2 of the Water Industry Act 1991 (c 56);
  [(ff) modifying the conditions of a licence granted under Chapter 1A of Part 2 of the Act of 1991 or modifying the terms and conditions of an agreement under section 66D [or 117E] of that Act;]
  (g) modifying the conditions of a licence granted under article 10 of the Electricity (Northern Ireland) Order 1992 (SI 1992/231 (NI 1));
  (h) modifying the conditions of a licence granted under section 8 of the Railways Act 1993 (c 43);
  [(hh) modifying the conditions of a SNRP issued pursuant to the Railways Infrastructure (Access, Management and Licensing of Railway Undertakings) Regulations (Northern Ireland) 2005;]
  (i) modifying an access agreement (within the meaning given by section 83(1) of the Act of 1993) or a franchise agreement (within the meaning given by section 23(3) of that Act);
  (j) modifying conditions in force under Part 4 of the Airports (Northern Ireland) Order 1994 (SI 1994/426 (NI 1)) other than any conditions imposed or modified in pursuance of article 40(3) or (4) of that Order;
  (k) modifying the conditions of a licence granted under article 8 of the Gas (Northern Ireland) Order 1996 (SI 1996/275 (NI 2));
  (l) . . .
  (m) modifying the conditions of a licence granted under section 5 of the Transport Act 2000 (c 38);
  [(n) modifying the conditions of a company's appointment under Chapter I of Part III of the Water and Sewerage Services (Northern Ireland) Order 2006];
  [(o) modifying regulatory conditions imposed under Part 3 of the Postal Services Act 2011];
  [(p) modifying the conditions of a licence issued under section 87 of the Health and Social Care Act 2012];
  [(q) modifying the conditions of a licence granted under Chapter 1 of Part 1 of the Civil Aviation Act 2012].
(4) In this section "relevant statutory functions" means—
  (a), (b) . . .

(c)   in relation to any licence granted under section 7[, 7A or 7AB] of the Gas Act 1986 (c 44), the objectives and duties of the Gas and Electricity Markets Authority under section 4AA and 4AB(2) of that Act;

(d)   in relation to any licence granted under section 6 of the Electricity Act 1989 (c 29), the objectives and duties of the Gas and Electricity Markets Authority under section 3A and 3B(2) of that Act;

[(e)   in relation to any networking arrangements (within the meaning given by section 290 of the Communications Act 2003), the duty of the Office of Communications under subsection (1) of section 3 of that Act to secure the matters mentioned in subsection (2)(c) of that section;]

(f)   in relation to a company's appointment under Chapter 1 of Part 2 of the Water Industry Act 1991 (c 56), the duties of [the Water Services Regulation Authority] under section 2 of that Act;

[(ff)   in relation to a licence granted under Chapter 1A of Part 2 of the Act of 1991 or an agreement under section 66D [or 117E] of that Act, the duties of the Authority under section 2 of that Act or under that section and section 66D [or 117E] of that Act (as the case may be);]

(g)   in relation to any licence granted under article 10 of the Electricity (Northern Ireland) Order 1992 (SI 1992/231 (NI 1)), the duty of the Director General of Electricity Supply for Northern Ireland under article 6 of that Order;

(h)   in relation to any licence granted under section 8 of the Railways Act 1993 (c 43) . . . the duties of [the Office of Rail Regulation] under section 4 of that Act;

[(hh)   in relation to a SNRP issued pursuant to the Railways Infrastructure (Access, Management and Licensing of Railway Undertakings) Regulations (Northern Ireland) 2005 where none of the conditions of the SNRP relate to consumer protection, the duties of the Department for Regional Development under regulation 36 of those Regulations;]

(i)   . . .

(j)   in relation to any access agreement (within the meaning given by section 83(1) of the Act of 1993), the duties of [the Office of Rail Regulation] under section 4 of the Act of 1993;

(k)   in relation to any franchise agreement (within the meaning given by section 23(3) of the Act of 1993), the duties of the [Secretary of State, the Scottish Ministers and the National Assembly for Wales under section 4 of the Act of 1993];

(l)   in relation to conditions in force under Part 4 of the Airports (Northern Ireland) Order 1994 (SI 1994/426 (NI 1)) other than any conditions imposed or modified in pursuance of article 40(3) or (4) of that Order, the duties of the Civil Aviation Authority under article 30(2) and (3) of that Order;

(m)   in relation to any licence granted under article 8 of the Gas (Northern Ireland) Order 1996 (SI 1996/275 (NI 2)), the duties of the Director General of Gas for Northern Ireland under article 5 of that Order;

(n)   . . .

(o)   in relation to any licence granted under section 5 of the Transport Act 2000, the duties of the Civil Aviation Authority under section 87 of that Act;

[(p)   in relation to a company's appointment under Chapter I of Part III of the Water and Sewerage Services (Northern Ireland) Order 2006, the duties of the Northern Ireland Authority for Utility Regulation under Article 6 of that Order];

[(q)   in relation to regulatory conditions imposed under Part 3 of the Postal Services Act 2011, the duty of the Office of Communications under section 29 of that Act];

[(r)   in relation to any licence issued under section 87 of the Health and Social Care Act 2012, the duties of Monitor under sections 62 and 66 of that Act];

[(s)   in relation to a licence granted under Chapter 1 of Part 1 of the Civil Aviation Act 2012, the duties of the Civil Aviation Authority under section 1 of that Act].

(5)   In this section "sectoral regulator" means—

(a)   the Civil Aviation Authority;

[(b)   the Northern Ireland Authority for Utility Regulation;]

(d)   . . .

[(e)   the Water Services Regulation Authority;]

(f)   the Gas and Electricity Markets Authority;

[(g)   the Office of Communications;]

(h)   . . .

(i)   [the Office of Rail Regulation]; . . .

[(ia)   [Monitor;]

[(j)   the Secretary of State;

(k)   the Scottish Ministers; or

(l)   the National Assembly for Wales].

(6)   Subsection (7) applies where the [CMA] or the Secretary of State is considering for the purposes of this Part whether modifying the conditions of a licence granted under section 7[, 7A or 7AB] of the Gas Act 1986 (c 44) or section 6 of the Electricity Act 1989 (c 29) would be reasonable and practicable for the purpose of remedying, mitigating or preventing an adverse effect on competition or any detrimental effect on customers so far as resulting from such an effect.

(7) The [CMA] or (as the case may be) the Secretary of State may, in deciding whether modifying the conditions of such a licence would be reasonable and practicable, have regard to those matters to which the Gas and Electricity Markets Authority may have regard by virtue of section 4AA(4) of the Act of 1986 or (as the case may be) section 3A(4) of the Act of 1989.

(8) The Secretary of State may by order modify subsection (3), (4), (5), (6) or (7).

(9) Part 2 of Schedule 9 (which makes provision for functions under this Part to be exercisable by various sectoral regulators) shall have effect.

NOTES

Sub-ss (1), (2), (7): word "CMA" in square brackets substituted by the Enterprise and Regulatory Reform Act 2013, s 26(3), Sch 5, Pt 2, paras 59, 198 (for transitional provisions (including those relating to the abolition of the OFT and the Competition Commission and the continuity of functions), see the Enterprise and Regulatory Reform Act 2013 (Commencement No 6, Transitional Provisions and Savings) Order 2014, SI 2014/416, Schedule at **[2.1126]**).

Sub-s (3) is amended as follows:

Para (a) repealed by the Communications Act 2003, s 406(7), Sch 19(1).

Para (b) repealed, and para (q) added, by the Civil Aviation Act 2012, s 76, Sch 9, paras 13, 14(1), (2).

Words in square brackets in para (c) substituted by the Electricity and Gas (Smart Meters Licensable Activity) Order 2012, SI 2012/2400, art 31.

Words in square brackets in para (e) substituted by the Communications Act 2003, s 406(1), Sch 17, para 174(1), (5)(a).

Para (ff) inserted by the Water Act 2003, s 101(1), Sch 8, para 55(1), (2)(a); words in square brackets inserted by the Water Act 2014, s 56, Sch 7, paras 128, 129(1), (2), as from a day to be appointed.

Para (hh) inserted by the Railways Infrastructure (Access, Management and Licensing of Railway Undertakings) Regulations (Northern Ireland) 2005, SR 2005/537, reg 45, Sch 5, para 4(a).

Para (l) repealed, and para (o) inserted, by the Postal Services Act 2011, s 91, Sch 12, Pt 3, para 164.

Para (n) inserted by the Water and Sewerage Services (Northern Ireland) Order 2006, SI 2006/3336, art 308(1), Sch 12, para 46(3).

Para (p) inserted by the Health and Social Care Act 2012, s 74(7)(a).

Sub-s (4) is amended as follows:

Para (a) repealed by the Communications Act 2003, s 406(7), Sch 19(1).

Para (b) repealed, and para (s) added, by the Civil Aviation Act 2012, s 76, Sch 9, paras 13, 14(1), (3).

Words in square brackets in para (c) substituted by SI 2012/2400, art 31.

Para (e) substituted by the Communications Act 2003, s 406(1), Sch 17, para 174(1), (5)(b).

Words in square brackets in para (f) substituted by the Water Act 2003, s 101(1), Sch 7, Pt 2, para 36(1), (3)(a).

Para (ff) added by the Water Act 2003, s 101(1), Sch 8, para 55(1), (2)(b); words in square brackets inserted by the Water Act 2014, s 56, Sch 7, paras 128, 129(1), (3), as from a day to be appointed.

Words omitted from para (h) repealed by the Railways Act 2005, s 59(1), (6), Sch 12, para 18(1), (2)(a), Sch 13, Pt 1; words in square brackets in para (h) substituted by the Railways and Transport Safety Act 2003, s 16(5), Sch 2, Pt 2, para 19(u).

Para (hh) inserted by the Railways Infrastructure (Access, Management and Licensing of Railway Undertakings) Regulations (Northern Ireland) 2005, SR 2005/537, reg 45, Sch 5, para 4(b).

Para (i) repealed by the Railways Act 2005, s 59(1), (6), Sch 12, para 18(1), (2)(b), Sch 13, Pt 1.

Words in square brackets in para (j) substituted by the Railways and Transport Safety Act 2003, s 16(5), Sch 2, Pt 2, para 19(u).

Words in square brackets in para (k) substituted by the Railways Act 2005, s 59(1), Sch 12, para 18(1), (2)(c).

Para (n) repealed, and para (q) inserted, by the Postal Services Act 2011, s 91, Sch 12, Pt 3, para 164.

Para (p) inserted by the Water and Sewerage Services (Northern Ireland) Order 2006, SI 2006/3336, art 308(1), Sch 12, para 46(4).

Para (r) inserted by the Health and Social Care Act 2012, s 74(7)(b).

Sub-s (5) is amended as follows:

Para (b) substituted, for the original paras (b), (c), by the Water and Sewerage Services (Northern Ireland) Order 2006, SI 2006/3336, art 308(1), Sch 12, para 46(5).

Para (d) repealed by the Communications Act 2003, s 406(7), Sch 19(1).

Para (e) substituted by the Water Act 2003, s 101(1), Sch 7, Pt 2, para 36(1), (3)(b).

Para (g) substituted by the Communications Act 2003, s 406(1), Sch 17, para 174(1), (5)(c).

Para (h) repealed by the Postal Services Act 2011, s 91, Sch 12, Pt 3, para 164.

Words in square brackets in para (i) substituted by the Railways and Transport Safety Act 2003, s 16(5), Sch 2, Pt 2, para 19(u); word omitted from that paragraph repealed by the Railways Act 2005, s 59(6), Sch 13, Pt 1 (in relation to England, Scotland and Wales), and by the Railways Infrastructure (Access, Management and Licensing of Railway Undertakings) Regulations (Northern Ireland) 2005, SR 2005/537, reg 45, Sch 5, para 4(c)(i) (in relation to Northern Ireland).

Para (ia) inserted by the Health and Social Care Act 2012, s 74(7)(c).

Paras (j)–(l) substituted (for the original para (j)) by the Railways Act 2005, s 59(1), Sch 12, para 18(1), (3) (in relation to England, Scotland and Wales). For a corresponding amendment in relation to Northern Ireland, see SR 2005/537, reg 45, Sch 5, para 4(c).

Sub-s (6): word in first pair of square brackets substituted by the Enterprise and Regulatory Reform Act 2013, s 26(3), Sch 5, Pt 2, paras 59, 198 (as to transitional provisions etc, see the first note above); words in second pair of square brackets substituted by SI 2012/2400, art 31.

Consultation, information and publicity

[1.1764]
169 Certain duties of relevant authorities to consult: Part 4

(1) Subsection (2) applies where the relevant authority is proposing to make a relevant decision in a way which the relevant authority considers is likely to have a substantial impact on the interests of any person.

(2) The relevant authority shall, so far as practicable, consult that person about what is proposed before making that decision.

(3)   In consulting the person concerned, the relevant authority shall, so far as practicable, give the reasons of the relevant authority for the proposed decision.

(4)   In considering what is practicable for the purposes of this section the relevant authority shall, in particular, have regard to—

   (a)   any restrictions imposed by any timetable for making the decision; and

   (b)   any need to keep what is proposed, or the reasons for it, confidential.

(5)   The duty under this section shall not apply in relation to the making of any decision so far as particular provision is made elsewhere by virtue of this Part for consultation before the making of that decision.

(6)   In this section—

   "the relevant authority" means the [CMA, the appropriate Minister] [or the Secretary of State]; and

   "relevant decision" means—

   (a)   in the case of the [CMA], any decision by the [CMA]—

      [(i)   to make a reference under section 131 in a case where the CMA has not published a market study notice under section 130A in relation to the matter concerned;

      (ia)   as to whether to accept undertakings under section 154 instead of making any reference under section 131;]

      (ii)   to vary under section 135 such a reference; [or

      (iii)   on the questions mentioned in section 134, 141 or 141A; and]

   (b)   in the case of the appropriate Minister [(other than the Secretary of State acting alone)], any decision by the appropriate Minister—

      (i)   . . . to make a reference under section 132; or

      (ii)   to vary under section 135 such a reference; . . .

   [(ba) in the case of the Secretary of State, any decision by the Secretary of State—

      (i)   to make a reference under section 132;

      (ii)   to vary under section 135 such a reference;

      (iii)   in a case where the Secretary of State is required to make a reference under section 140A, whether to make a reference under subsection (5) or (6) of that section; or

      (iv)   to vary under section 140B a reference made under section 140A(6).]

   (c)   . . .

NOTES

Sub-s (6) is amended as follows:

The words "CMA, the appropriate Minister" in square brackets in the definition "the relevant authority" were substituted by the Enterprise and Regulatory Reform Act 2013, s 26(3), Sch 5, Pt 2, paras 59, 199(a) (for transitional provisions (including those relating to the abolition of the OFT and the Competition Commission and the continuity of functions), see the Enterprise and Regulatory Reform Act 2013 (Commencement No 6, Transitional Provisions and Savings) Order 2014, SI 2014/416, Schedule at **[2.1126]**).

The words "or the Secretary of State" in square brackets in the definition "the relevant authority" were inserted by the Enterprise and Regulatory Reform Act 2013, s 35(10), Sch 10, paras 1, 29(a) (as to transitional provisions etc, see the note above).

The word "CMA" in square brackets in each place that it occurs in the definition "relevant decision" was substituted, sub-para (a)(iii) of that definition (and the preceding word) was added, and sub-para (c) (and the second word omitted from para (b)) was repealed, by the Enterprise and Regulatory Reform Act 2013, s 26(3), Sch 5, Pt 2, paras 59, 199(b)–(d) (as to transitional provisions etc, see the note above).

Para (a)(i) of the definition "relevant decision" was substituted, and the first words omitted from para (b) were repealed, by the Enterprise and Regulatory Reform Act 2013, s 38, Sch 12, paras 7, 13 (as to transitional provisions etc, see the note above).

The words "(other than the Secretary of State acting alone)" in square brackets in para (b) of the definition "relevant decision" were inserted, and para (ba) of that definition was inserted, by the Enterprise and Regulatory Reform Act 2013, s 35(10), Sch 10, paras 1, 29(b), (c) (as to transitional provisions etc, see the note above).

[1.1765]
170   General information duties

(1), (2)   . . .

(3)   The [CMA] shall give the Secretary of State or the appropriate Minister so far as he is not the Secretary of State acting alone—

   (a)   such information in [its possession] as the Secretary of State or (as the case may be) the appropriate Minister concerned may by direction reasonably require to enable him to carry out his functions under this Part; and

   (b)   any other assistance which the Secretary of State or (as the case may be) the appropriate Minister concerned may by direction reasonably require for the purpose of assisting him in carrying out his functions under this Part and which it is within the power of the [CMA] to give.

(4)   The [CMA] shall give the Secretary of State or the appropriate Minister so far as he is not the Secretary of State acting alone any information in its possession which has not been requested by the Secretary of State or (as the case may be) the appropriate Minister concerned but which, in the

opinion of the [CMA], would be appropriate to give to the Secretary of State or (as the case may be) the appropriate Minister concerned for the purpose of assisting him in carrying out his functions under this Part.

(5) [The Secretary of State] or (as the case may be) the appropriate Minister concerned shall have regard to any information given to him under subsection (3) or (4).

(6) Any direction given under subsection (3)—

(a) shall be in writing; and

(b) may be varied or revoked by a subsequent direction.

NOTES

Sub-ss (1), (2) were repealed, and the words in square brackets in sub-ss (3)–(5) were substituted, by the Enterprise and Regulatory Reform Act 2013, s 26(3), Sch 5, Pt 2, paras 59, 200 (for transitional provisions (including those relating to the abolition of the OFT and the Competition Commission and the continuity of functions), see the Enterprise and Regulatory Reform Act 2013 (Commencement No 6, Transitional Provisions and Savings) Order 2014, SI 2014/416, Schedule at **[2.1126]**).

[1.1766]
171   Advice and information: Part 4

(1) [The CMA] shall prepare and publish general advice and information about[—

(a) the making and consideration by it of market investigation references, and

(b) the way in which relevant customer benefits may affect the taking of enforcement action in relation to such references].

(2) The [CMA] may at any time publish revised, or new, advice or information.

(3), (4) . . .

(5) Advice and information published under this section shall be prepared with a view to—

(a) explaining relevant provisions of this Part to persons who are likely to be affected by them; and

(b) indicating how the [CMA] expects such provisions to operate.

(6) Advice and information published by virtue of subsection (1) . . . . shall include such advice and information about the effect of [EU] law, and anything done under or in accordance with it, on the provisions of this Part as the [CMA] considers appropriate.

(7) Advice (or information) published by virtue of subsection (1) . . . may include advice (or information) about the factors which the [CMA] may take into account in considering whether, and if so how, to exercise a function conferred by this Part.

(8) Any advice or information published by the [CMA] under this section shall be published in such manner as the [CMA] considers appropriate.

(9) In preparing any advice or information under this section, the [CMA shall consult such persons] as it considers appropriate.

(10) . . .

(11) In this section "[EU] law" means—

(a) all the rights, powers, liabilities, obligations and restrictions from time to time created or arising by or under the Community Treaties; and

(b) all the remedies and procedures from time to time provided for by or under the Community Treaties.

NOTES

Sub-ss (6), (11): references in square brackets substituted by the Treaty of Lisbon (Changes in Terminology) Order 2011, SI 2011/1043, art 6(1)(a), (2)(a).

All words in square brackets in this section were substituted, and all words omitted were repealed, by the Enterprise and Regulatory Reform Act 2013, s 26(3), Sch 5, Pt 2, paras 59, 201 (for transitional provisions (including those relating to the abolition of the OFT and the Competition Commission and the continuity of functions), see the Enterprise and Regulatory Reform Act 2013 (Commencement No 6, Transitional Provisions and Savings) Order 2014, SI 2014/416, Schedule at **[2.1126]**).

[1.1767]
172   Further publicity requirements: Part 4

(1) The [CMA] shall publish—

(a) any reference made by it under section 131[, other than a reference treated as so made by virtue of section 140A(5)(b)];

[(aa) any decision not to make a reference under section 131 following a consultation in relation to the matter concerned under section 169;]

(b) any variation made by it under section 135 of a reference under section 131;

(c) any decision of a kind mentioned in section 149(5)(b); and

(d) such information as it considers appropriate about any decision made by it under section 152(1) to bring a case to the attention of the Secretary of State.

(2) The [CMA shall also] publish—

[(za) any extension by it under section 137 of the period within which a report under section 136 is to be prepared and published;

(zb) any extension by it under section 138A of the period within which its duty under section 138(2) is to be discharged;]

(a) any decision made by it under section 138(2) neither to accept an undertaking under section 159 nor to make an order under section 161;

(b) any decision made by it that there has been a material change of circumstances as mentioned in section 138(3) or there is another special reason as mentioned in that section;

[(ba) any extension by it under section 144 of the period within which a report under section 142 is to be prepared and action is to be taken in relation to it;]

(c) any termination under section 145(1) of an investigation by it;

(d) . . .

(e) any enforcement undertaking accepted by it under section 157;

(f) any enforcement order made by it under section 158; and

(g) any variation, release or revocation of such an undertaking or order.

(3) The Secretary of State shall publish—

(a) any reference made by him under section 132;

(b) any variation made by him under section 135 of a reference under section 132;

(c) any intervention notice given by him;

(d) any decision made by him to revoke such a notice;

[(da) any reference made by him under section 140A(5) or (6);

(db) any variation made by him under section 140B of a reference under section 140A(6);]

(e) any decision made by him under section 147(2) [or (as the case may be) 147A(2)] neither to accept an undertaking under section 159 nor to make an order under section 161;

(f) any enforcement undertaking accepted by him under section 157;

(g) any variation or release of such an undertaking; and

(h) any direction given by him under section 170(3) in connection with the exercise by him of his functions under section 132(3).

(4) The appropriate Minister (other than the Secretary of State acting alone) shall publish—

(a) any reference made by him under section 132;

(b) any variation made by him under section 135 of a reference under section 132; and

(c) any direction given by him under section 170(3) in connection with the exercise by him of his functions under section 132(3).

(5) Where any person is under an obligation by virtue of subsection (1), (2), (3) or (4) to publish the result of any action taken by that person or any decision made by that person, the person concerned shall, subject to subsections (6) and (7), also publish that person's reasons for the action concerned or (as the case may be) the decision concerned.

(6) Such reasons need not, if it is not reasonably practicable to do so, be published at the same time as the result of the action concerned or (as the case may be) as the decision concerned.

(7) Subsections (5) and (6) shall not apply in relation to any case falling within subsection (1)(d) . . . .

[(7A) Subsection (6) shall not apply in relation to any case falling within subsection (1)(a) [or (3)(da)].]

(8) The Secretary of State shall publish his reasons for—

(a) any decision made by him under section 146(2) [or 146A(2)]; or

(b) any decision to make an order under section 153(3) or vary or revoke such an order.

(9) Such reasons may be published after—

(a) in the case of subsection (8)(a), the publication of the decision concerned; and

(b) in the case of subsection (8)(b), the making of the order or of the variation or revocation;

if it is not reasonably practicable to publish them at the same time as the publication of the decision or (as the case may be) the making of the order or variation or revocation.

(10) Where the Secretary of State has decided under section 147(2) [or 147A(2)] to accept an undertaking under section 159 or to make an order under section 161, he shall (after the acceptance of the undertaking or (as the case may be) the making of the order) lay details of his decision and his reasons for it, and the [CMA's] report under section 142, before each House of Parliament.

NOTES

Sub-s (1): word in first pair of square brackets substituted by the Enterprise and Regulatory Reform Act 2013, s 26(3), Sch 5, Pt 2, paras 59, 202(1), (2) (for transitional provisions (including those relating to the abolition of the OFT and the Competition Commission and the continuity of functions), see the Enterprise and Regulatory Reform Act 2013 (Commencement No 6, Transitional Provisions and Savings) Order 2014, SI 2014/416, Schedule at **[2.1126]**); words in square brackets in para (a) inserted by s 35(10) of, and Sch 10, paras 1, 30(1), (2) to, the 2013 Act (as to transitional provisions etc, see above); para (aa) inserted by s 38 of, and Sch 12, paras 7, 14(1), (2) to, the 2013 Act (as to transitional provisions etc, see above).

Sub-s (2): words in first pair of square brackets substituted by the Enterprise and Regulatory Reform Act 2013, s 26(3), Sch 5, Pt 2, paras 59, 202(1), (3) (as to transitional provisions etc, see the note above); paras (za), (zb), (ba) inserted by s 38 of, and Sch 12, paras 7, 14(1), (3) to, the 2013 Act (as to transitional provisions etc, see the note above); para (d) repealed by s 35(10) of, and Sch 10, paras 1, 30(1), (3) to, the 2013 Act (as to transitional provisions etc, see the note above).

Sub-s (3): paras (da), (db) inserted, and the words in square brackets in para (e) inserted, by the Enterprise and Regulatory Reform Act 2013, s 35(10), Sch 10, paras 1, 30(1), (4) (as to transitional provisions etc, see the note above).

Sub-s (7): words omitted repealed by the Enterprise and Regulatory Reform Act 2013, s 35(10), Sch 10, paras 1, 30(1), (5) (as to transitional provisions etc, see the note above).

Sub-s (7A): inserted by the Enterprise and Regulatory Reform Act 2013, s 38, Sch 12, paras 7, 14(1), (4) (as to transitional provisions etc, see the note above); words in square brackets inserted by s 35(10) of, and Sch 10, paras 1, 30(1), (6) to, the 2013 Act (as to transitional provisions etc, see the note above).

Sub-s (8): words in square brackets inserted by the Enterprise and Regulatory Reform Act 2013, s 35(10), Sch 10, paras 1, 30(1), (7) (as to transitional provisions etc, see the note above).

Sub-s (10): words "CMA's" in square brackets substituted by the Enterprise and Regulatory Reform Act 2013, s 26(3), Sch 5, Pt 2, paras 59, 202(1), (4) (as to transitional provisions etc, see the note above); other words in square brackets inserted by s 35(10) of, and Sch 10, paras 1, 30(1), (8) to, the 2013 Act (as to transitional provisions etc, see the note above).

[1.1768]
173 Defamation: Part 4
For the purposes of the law relating to defamation, absolute privilege attaches to any advice, guidance, notice or direction given, or decision or report made, by the [CMA], [by the Secretary of State or] by the appropriate Minister (other than the Secretary of State acting alone) . . . in the exercise of any of their functions under this Part.

NOTES
Words in square brackets substituted, and words omitted repealed, by the Enterprise and Regulatory Reform Act 2013, s 26(3), Sch 5, Pt 2, paras 59, 203 (for transitional provisions (including those relating to the abolition of the OFT and the Competition Commission and the continuity of functions), see the Enterprise and Regulatory Reform Act 2013 (Commencement No 6, Transitional Provisions and Savings) Order 2014, SI 2014/416, Schedule at **[2.1126]**).

Investigation powers

[1.1769]
174 [Attendance of witnesses and production of documents etc]
[(1)   For the purposes of this section, the permitted purposes are the following—
   (a)   assisting the CMA in carrying out its functions under section 5 in relation to a matter in a case where it has published a market study notice;
   (b)   assisting the CMA in carrying out any functions, including enforcement functions, exercisable by it under or by virtue of this Part in connection with a matter that is or has been the subject of a reference under section 131 or 132 or possible reference under section 131;
   (c)   assisting the CMA or the Secretary of State in carrying out any functions, including enforcement functions, of the CMA or (as the case may be) the Secretary of State under or by virtue of this Part in connection with a matter that is or has been the subject of a reference under section 140A(6) or possible reference under section 140A(5) or (6).
(2)   The CMA may exercise any of the powers in subsections (3) to (5) for a permitted purpose.]
(3)   The [CMA] may give notice to any person requiring him—
   (a)   to attend at a time and place specified in the notice; and
   (b)   to give evidence to the [CMA] or a person nominated by the [CMA] for the purpose.
(4)   The [CMA] may give notice to any person requiring him—
   (a)   to produce any documents which—
      (i)   are specified or described in the notice, or fall within a category of document which is specified or described in the notice; and
      (ii)   are in that person's custody or under his control; and
   (b)   to produce them at a time and place so specified and to a person so specified.
(5)   The [CMA] may give notice to any person who carries on any business requiring him—
   (a)   to supply to the [CMA] such estimates, forecasts, returns or other information as may be specified or described in the notice; and
   (b)   to supply it at a time and place, and in a form and manner, so specified and to a person so specified.
(6)   A notice under this section shall[—
   (a)   specify the permitted purpose for which the notice is given, including the function or functions in question; and
   (b)]   include information about the possible consequences of not complying with the notice.
[(6A)   The CMA or any person nominated by it for the purpose may, for a permitted purpose, take evidence on oath and for that purpose may administer oaths.]
(7)   The person to whom any document is produced in accordance with a notice under this section may, for [a permitted purpose], copy the document so produced.
(8)   No person shall be required under this section—
   (a)   to give any evidence or produce any documents which he could not be compelled to give or produce in civil proceedings before the court; or
   (b)   to supply any information which he could not be compelled to supply in evidence in such proceedings.
(9)   No person shall be required, in compliance with a notice under this section, to go more than 10 miles from his place of residence unless his necessary travelling expenses are paid or offered to him.
[(9A)   In subsection (1), "enforcement functions" means—
   (a)   in relation to the CMA—
      (i)   functions conferred by virtue of section 164(2)(b) on the CMA by enforcement orders;
      (ii)   functions of the CMA in relation to the variation, supersession or release of enforcement undertakings or the variation or revocation of enforcement orders;

(iii) functions of the CMA under or by virtue of section 160 or 162 in relation to enforcement undertakings or enforcement orders;

(b) in relation to the Secretary of State—

(i) functions conferred by virtue of section 164(2)(b) on the Secretary of State by enforcement orders;

(ii) functions of the Secretary of State in relation to the variation, supersession or release of enforcement undertakings or the variation or revocation of enforcement orders;

(iii) functions of the Secretary of State under or by virtue of section 160 in relation to enforcement undertakings or enforcement orders.]

(10) Any reference in this section to the production of a document includes a reference to the production of a legible and intelligible copy of information recorded otherwise than in legible form.

(11) In this section "the court" means—

(a) in relation to England and Wales or Northern Ireland, the High Court; and

(b) in relation to Scotland, the Court of Session.

NOTES

The section heading was substituted, sub-ss (1), (2) were substituted, the words in square brackets in sub-s (6) were inserted, sub-ss (6A) and (9A) were inserted, and the words in square brackets in sub-s (7) were substituted, by the Enterprise and Regulatory Reform Act 2013, s 36(1)–(7) (for transitional provisions (including those relating to the abolition of the OFT and the Competition Commission and the continuity of functions), see the Enterprise and Regulatory Reform Act 2013 (Commencement No 6, Transitional Provisions and Savings) Order 2014, SI 2014/416, Schedule at **[2.1126]**). See also the Enterprise and Regulatory Reform Act 2013 (Competition) (Consequential, Transitional and Saving Provisions) Order 2014, SI 2014/892, Sch 2, para 3 which provides that these amendments do not have effect in relation to this section as applied by or by virtue of (a) s 140D of the Financial Services and Markets Act 2000 and (b) s 57 of the Legal Services Act 2007, in relation to any notice given under this section before 1 April 2014.

The word "CMA" in square brackets (in each place that it occurs) was substituted by the Enterprise and Regulatory Reform Act 2013, s 26(3), Sch 5, Pt 2, paras 59, 204 (as to transitional provisions etc, see the note above).

[1.1770]

[174A Enforcement of powers under section 174: general

(1) Where the CMA considers that a person has, without reasonable excuse, failed to comply with any requirement of a notice under section 174, it may impose a penalty in accordance with section 174D.

(2) The CMA may proceed (whether at the same time or at different times) under subsection (1) and section 138A(3) in relation to the same failure.

(3) Where the CMA considers that a person has intentionally obstructed or delayed another person in the exercise of its powers under section 174(7), it may impose a penalty in accordance with section 174D.

(4) A person commits an offence if the person intentionally alters, suppresses or destroys any document which the person has been required to produce by a notice under section 174.

(5) But a person does not commit an offence under subsection (4) in relation to any act which constitutes a failure to comply with a notice under section 174 if the CMA has proceeded against the person under subsection (1) in relation to that failure.

(6) A person who commits an offence under subsection (4) is liable—

(a) on summary conviction, to a fine not exceeding the statutory maximum;

(b) on conviction on indictment, to imprisonment for a term not exceeding 2 years or to a fine or to both.

(7) The CMA shall not proceed against a person under subsection (1) in relation to an act which constitutes an offence under subsection (4) if that person has been found guilty of that offence.

(8) In deciding whether and, if so, how to proceed under subsection (1) or (3) or section 138A(3), the CMA shall have regard to the statement of policy which was most recently published under section 174E at the time the failure or (as the case may be) the obstruction or delay concerned occurred.

(9) In this section—

(a) the reference to the production of a document includes a reference to the production of a legible and intelligible copy of information recorded otherwise than in legible form; and

(b) the reference to suppressing a document includes a reference to destroying the means of reproducing information recorded otherwise than in legible form.]

NOTES

Commencement: 1 April 2014.

Inserted, together with ss 174B–174E, by the Enterprise and Regulatory Reform Act 2013, s 36(8), Sch 11, para 1 (for transitional provisions (including those relating to the abolition of the OFT and the Competition Commission and the continuity of functions), see the Enterprise and Regulatory Reform Act 2013 (Commencement No 6, Transitional Provisions and Savings) Order 2014, SI 2014/416, Schedule at **[2.1126]**).

[1.1771]
[174B   Restriction on powers to impose penalties under section 174A
(1)   No penalty shall be imposed by virtue of section 174A(1) or (3) if more than 4 weeks have passed since the day which is the relevant day in the case in question; but this subsection shall not apply in relation to any variation or substitution of the penalty which is permitted by virtue of this Part.
(2)   In the following provisions of this section, "the section 174 power" means the power under section 174 to which the failure or (as the case may be) the obstruction or delay in question relates.
(3)   Where the section 174 power is exercised for the purpose mentioned in section 174(1)(a), the relevant day is the day when the CMA finally concludes the carrying out of its section 5 functions.
(4)   Where the section 174 power is exercised in connection with an enforcement function (within the meaning of that section), the relevant day is the day when the enforcement undertaking concerned is superseded or released or (as the case may be) the enforcement order concerned is revoked.
(5)   Except where subsection (3) or (4) applies, the relevant day is the day determined in accordance with the following provisions of this section.
(6)   Where the section 174 power is exercised for the purpose mentioned in section 174(1)(b) in connection with a matter that is the subject of a possible reference under section 131, the relevant day is the day when the CMA finally decides whether to make the reference.
(7)   Where the section 174 power is exercised for the purpose mentioned in section 174(1)(b) in connection with a matter that is the subject of a reference under section 131 or 132, the relevant day is the day when the reference is finally determined (see section 183).
(8)   Where the section 174 power is exercised for the purpose mentioned in section 174(1)(c) in connection with a matter that is the subject of a possible reference under section 140A(5) or (6), the relevant day is the day when the Secretary of State makes the reference.
(9)   Where the section 174 power is exercised for the purpose mentioned in section 174(1)(c) in connection with a matter that is the subject of a reference under section 140A(6), the relevant day is the day when the reference is finally determined (see section 183).]

NOTES
   Commencement: 1 April 2014.
   Inserted as noted to s 174A at **[1.1770]**.

[1.1772]
[174C   Section 174B: supplementary provision
(1)   For the purpose of section 174B(3), the CMA finally concludes the carrying out of its section 5 functions if—
   (a)   the CMA publishes the market study report under section 131B(4) or (as the case may be) gives it to the Secretary of State under section 140A(3)(b); or
   (b)   the period permitted for the preparation by the CMA of the market study report and for the report to be published under section 131B(4) or (as the case may be) given to the Secretary of State under section 140A(3)(b) expires and no such report has been so prepared or no such action has been taken.
(2)   For the purpose of section 174B(3), the time when the CMA finally concludes the carrying out of its section 5 functions is—
   (a)   in a case falling within subsection (1)(a), the publication of the report or (as the case may be) the giving of it to the Secretary of State;
   (b)   in a case falling within subsection (1)(b), the expiry of the period concerned.
(3)   For the purpose of section 174B(6), the CMA finally decides whether to make a reference under section 131 if—
   (a)   the CMA makes such a reference;
   (b)   the CMA accepts an undertaking under section 154 instead of making such a reference;
   (c)   the CMA publishes notice that it has otherwise decided not to make such a reference; or
   (d)   the period permitted for the preparation by the CMA of a market study report in relation to the matter and for the report to be published under section 131B(4) has expired and no such report has been so prepared or published.
(4)   For the purpose of section 174B(6), the time when the CMA finally decides whether to make a reference under section 131 is—
   (a)   in a case falling within subsection (3)(a), the making of the reference;
   (b)   in a case falling within subsection (3)(b), the acceptance of the undertaking concerned;
   (c)   in a case falling within subsection (3)(c), the publication of the notice concerned;
   (d)   in a case falling within subsection (3)(d), the expiry of the period concerned.
(5)   In subsection (4)(b) the reference to the acceptance of the undertaking concerned shall, in a case where the CMA has accepted a group of undertakings under section 154, be treated as a reference to the acceptance of the last undertaking in the group; but undertakings which vary, supersede or revoke earlier undertakings shall be disregarded for the purposes of subsections (3)(b) and (4)(b).]

NOTES
Commencement: 1 April 2014.
Inserted as noted to s 174A at **[1.1770]**.

[1.1773]
[174D Penalties
(1) A penalty imposed under section 174A(1) or (3) shall be of such amount as the CMA considers appropriate.
(2) In the case of a penalty imposed under section 174A(1), the amount may be—
  (a) a fixed amount;
  (b) an amount calculated by reference to a daily rate; or
  (c) a combination of a fixed amount and an amount calculated by reference to a daily rate.
(3) In the case of a penalty imposed under section 174A(3), the amount shall be a fixed amount.
(4) A penalty imposed under section 174A(1) shall not—
  (a) in the case of a fixed amount, exceed such amount as the Secretary of State may by order specify;
  (b) in the case of an amount calculated by reference to a daily rate, exceed such amount per day as the Secretary of State may so specify; and
  (c) in the case of a fixed amount and an amount calculated by reference to a daily rate, exceed such fixed amount and such amount per day as the Secretary of State may so specify.
(5) A penalty imposed under section 174A(3) shall not exceed such amount as the Secretary of State may by order specify.
(6) An order under subsection (4) or (5) shall not specify—
  (a) in the case of a fixed amount, an amount exceeding £30,000;
  (b) in the case of an amount calculated by reference to a daily rate, an amount per day exceeding £15,000; and
  (c) in the case of a fixed amount and an amount calculated by reference to a daily rate, a fixed amount exceeding £30,000 and an amount per day exceeding £15,000.
(7) Before making an order under subsection (4) or (5), the Secretary of State shall consult—
  (a) the CMA; and
  (b) such other persons as the Secretary of State considers appropriate.
(8) In imposing a penalty by reference to a daily rate—
  (a) no account is to be taken of any days before the service on the person concerned of notice of the penalty under section 112 (as applied by subsection (10)); and
  (b) unless the CMA determines an earlier date (whether before or after the penalty is imposed), the amount payable ceases to accumulate at the beginning of the earliest of the days mentioned in subsection (9).
(9) Those days are—
  (a) the day on which the requirement of the notice concerned under section 174 is satisfied;
  (b) the day which is the relevant day in the case in question for the purposes of section 174B.
(10) Sections 112 to 115 apply in relation to a penalty imposed under section 174A(1) or (3) as they apply in relation to a penalty imposed under section 110(1) or (3).]

NOTES
Commencement: 25 April 2013 (for the purposes of enabling the exercise of any power to make provision by order made by statutory instrument); 1 April 2014 (otherwise).
Inserted as noted to s 174A at **[1.1770]**.

[1.1774]
[174E Statement of policy on penalties
(1) The CMA shall prepare and publish a statement of policy in relation to the enforcement of notices given under section 174.
(2) The statement shall, in particular, include a statement about the considerations relevant to the determination of the nature and amount of any penalty imposed under section 174A(1) or (3).
(3) The CMA may revise its statement of policy and, where it does so, it shall publish the revised statement.
(4) The CMA shall consult such persons as it considers appropriate when preparing or revising its statement of policy.]

NOTES
Commencement: 1 April 2014.
Inserted as noted to s 174A at **[1.1770]**.

175, 176 (*Repealed by the Enterprise and Regulatory Reform Act 2013, s 36(8), Sch 11, paras 2–4 (for transitional provisions (including those relating to the abolition of the OFT and the Competition Commission and the continuity of functions), see the Enterprise and Regulatory Reform Act 2013 (Commencement No 6, Transitional Provisions and Savings) Order 2014, SI 2014/416, Schedule at* **[2.1126]**). *See also the Enterprise and Regulatory Reform Act 2013 (Competition) (Consequential, Transitional and Saving Provisions) Order 2014, SI 2014/892, Sch 2, para 3 which* *provides that the repeal of s 175 does not have effect in relation to that section as applied by or by virtue of (a) s 140D of the Financial Services and Markets Act 2000 and (b) s 57 of the Legal Services Act 2007, in relation to any notice given under s 174 before 1 April 2014.)*

Reports

[1.1775]
177 Excisions from reports: Part 4
(1)   Subsection (2) applies where the Secretary of State is under a duty to publish a report of the [CMA] under section 142.
(2)   The Secretary of State may exclude a matter from the report if he considers that publication of the matter would be inappropriate.
(3)   In deciding what is inappropriate for the purposes of subsection (2) the Secretary of State shall have regard to the considerations mentioned in section 244.
(4)   The [CMA] shall advise the Secretary of State as to the matters (if any) which it considers should be excluded by him under subsection (2).
(5)   References in sections 136(4) to (6) . . . and 172(10) to the giving or laying of a report of the [CMA] shall be construed as references to the giving or laying of the report as published.

NOTES
    The word "CMA" in square brackets (in each place that it occurs) was substituted by the Enterprise and Regulatory Reform Act 2013, s 26(3), Sch 5, Pt 2, paras 59, 205 (for transitional provisions (including those relating to the abolition of the OFT and the Competition Commission and the continuity of functions), see the Enterprise and Regulatory Reform Act 2013 (Commencement No 6, Transitional Provisions and Savings) Order 2014, SI 2014/416, Schedule at **[2.1126]**).
    Words omitted from sub-s (5) repealed by the Enterprise and Regulatory Reform Act 2013, s 35(10), Sch 10, paras 1, 31 (as to transitional provisions etc, see the note above).

[1.1776]
178 Minority reports of [CMA]: Part 4
(1)   Subsection (2) applies where, on a market investigation reference, a member of a group constituted in connection with the reference . . . disagrees with any decisions contained in the report of the [CMA] under this Part as the decisions of the [CMA].
(2)   The report shall, if the member so wishes, include a statement of his disagreement and of his reasons for disagreeing.

NOTES
    The word "CMA" in square brackets (in each place that it occurs) was substituted, and the words omitted were repealed, by the Enterprise and Regulatory Reform Act 2013, s 26(3), Sch 5, Pt 2, paras 59, 206 (for transitional provisions (including those relating to the abolition of the OFT and the Competition Commission and the continuity of functions), see the Enterprise and Regulatory Reform Act 2013 (Commencement No 6, Transitional Provisions and Savings) Order 2014, SI 2014/416, Schedule at **[2.1126]**).

Other

[1.1777]
179 Review of decisions under Part 4
(1)   Any person aggrieved by a decision of the [CMA], the appropriate Minister [or the Secretary of State] in connection with a reference or possible reference under this Part may apply to the Competition Appeal Tribunal for a review of that decision.
(2)   For this purpose "decision"—
    [(za) does not include a decision whether to carry out functions under section 5 in a case where the CMA is, or would have been, required to publish a market study notice (see section 130A(1));]
    (a)   does not include a decision to impose a penalty under [section 174A(1) or (3)]; but
    (b)   includes a failure to take a decision permitted or required by this Part in connection with a reference or possible reference.
(3)   Except in so far as a direction to the contrary is given by the Competition Appeal Tribunal, the effect of the decision is not suspended by reason of the making of the application.
(4)   In determining such an application the Competition Appeal Tribunal shall apply the same principles as would be applied by a court on an application for judicial review.
(5)   The Competition Appeal Tribunal may—
    (a)   dismiss the application or quash the whole or part of the decision to which it relates; and
    (b)   where it quashes the whole or part of that decision, refer the matter back to the original decision maker with a direction to reconsider and make a new decision in accordance with the ruling of the Competition Appeal Tribunal.
(6)   An appeal lies on any point of law arising from a decision of the Competition Appeal Tribunal under this section to the appropriate court.
(7)   An appeal under subsection (6) requires the permission of the Tribunal or the appropriate court.
(8)   In this section—
    "the appropriate court" means the Court of Appeal or, in the case of Tribunal proceedings in Scotland, the Court of Session; and

"Tribunal rules" has the meaning given by section 15(1).

NOTES

Sub-s (1): words in square brackets substituted by the Enterprise and Regulatory Reform Act 2013, s 26(3), Sch 5, Pt 2, paras 59, 207 (for transitional provisions (including those relating to the abolition of the OFT and the Competition Commission and the continuity of functions), see the Enterprise and Regulatory Reform Act 2013 (Commencement No 6, Transitional Provisions and Savings) Order 2014, SI 2014/416, Schedule at **[2.1126]**).

Sub-s (2): para (za) inserted by the Enterprise and Regulatory Reform Act 2013, s 38, Sch 12, paras 7, 15 (as to transitional provisions etc, see the note above); words in square brackets in para (a) substituted by s 36(8) of, and Sch 11, paras 2, 5 to, the 2013 Act (as to transitional provisions etc, see the note above).

[1.1778]
180 Offences
(1) Sections 117 (false or misleading information) and 125 (offences by bodies corporate) shall apply, with the modifications mentioned in subsection (2) below, for the purposes of this Part as they apply for the purposes of Part 3.
(2) Section 117 shall, in its application by virtue of subsection (1) above, have effect as if references to the Secretary of State included references to the appropriate Minister so far as he is not the Secretary of State acting alone [and as if the references to OFCOM were omitted].

NOTES

Sub-s (2): words in square brackets added by the Communications Act 2003, s 389, Sch 16, para 26.

[1.1779]
181 Orders under Part 4
(1) Any power of the Secretary of State to make an order under this Part shall be exercisable by statutory instrument.
(2) Any power of the Secretary of State to make an order under this Part—
 (a) may be exercised so as to make different provision for different cases or different purposes;
 (b) includes power to make such incidental, supplementary, consequential, transitory, transitional or saving provision as the Secretary of State considers appropriate.
(3) The power of the Secretary of State under section [131C(1), 136(9), 137(3), 138B(6)], 144(2), 153(3) or 168(8) as extended by subsection (2) above may be exercised by modifying any enactment comprised in or made under this Act, or any other enactment.
(4) An order made by the Secretary of State under section [131C(1), 137(3), 138B(6)], 144(2), 158, 160[, 161, 174D(4) or (5), or under section 114(3)(b) or (4)(b) as applied by section 174D], shall be subject to annulment in pursuance of a resolution of either House of Parliament.
(5) No order shall be made by the Secretary of State under section 136(9) or 168(8), or section 128(6) as applied by section 183(2), unless a draft of it has been laid before, and approved by a resolution of, each House of Parliament.
(6) An order made by the Secretary of State under section 153(3) shall be laid before Parliament after being made and shall cease to have effect unless approved, within the period of 28 days beginning with the day on which it is made, by a resolution of each House of Parliament.
(7) In calculating the period of 28 days mentioned in subsection (6), no account shall be taken of any time during which Parliament is dissolved or prorogued or during which both Houses are adjourned for more than four days.
(8) If an order made by the Secretary of State ceases to have effect by virtue of subsection (6), any modification made by it of an enactment is repealed (and the previous enactment revived) but without prejudice to the validity of anything done in connection with that modification before the order ceased to have effect and without prejudice to the making of a new order.
(9) If, apart from this subsection, an order made by the Secretary of State under section 153(3) would be treated for the purposes of the standing orders of either House of Parliament as a hybrid instrument, it shall proceed in that House as if it were not such an instrument.
(10) References in this section to an order made under this Part include references to an order made under section . . . 114(3)(b) or (4)(b) as applied by section [174D] and an order made under section 128(6) as applied by section 183(2).

NOTES

Sub-s (3): figures in square brackets substituted by the Enterprise and Regulatory Reform Act 2013, s 38, Sch 12, paras 7, 16(1), (2) (for transitional provisions (including those relating to the abolition of the OFT and the Competition Commission and the continuity of functions), see the Enterprise and Regulatory Reform Act 2013 (Commencement No 6, Transitional Provisions and Savings) Order 2014, SI 2014/416, Schedule at **[2.1126]**).

Sub-s (4): figures in first pair of square brackets substituted by the Enterprise and Regulatory Reform Act 2013, s 38, Sch 12, paras 7, 16(1), (3) (as to transitional provisions etc, see the note above); words in second pair of square brackets substituted by s 36(8) of, and Sch 11, paras 2, 6(1), (2) to, the 2013 Act (as to transitional provisions etc, see the note above).

Sub-s (10): words omitted repealed, and figure in square brackets substituted by the Enterprise and Regulatory Reform Act 2013, s 36(8), Sch 11, paras 2, 6(1), (3) (as to transitional provisions etc, see the note above).

[1.1780]
182 Service of documents: Part 4
Section 126 shall apply for the purposes of this Part as it applies for the purposes of Part 3.

[1.1781]
183 Interpretation: Part 4

(1)   In this Part, unless the context otherwise requires—

"action" includes omission; and references to the taking of action include references to refraining from action;

"business" includes a professional practice and includes any other undertaking which is carried on for gain or reward or which is an undertaking in the course of which goods or services are supplied otherwise than free of charge;

"change of circumstances" includes any discovery that information has been supplied which is false or misleading in a material respect;

"consumer" means any person who is—

(a)   a person to whom goods are or are sought to be supplied (whether by way of sale or otherwise) in the course of a business carried on by the person supplying or seeking to supply them; or

(b)   a person for whom services are or are sought to be supplied in the course of a business carried on by the person supplying or seeking to supply them;

and who does not receive or seek to receive the goods or services in the course of a business carried on by him;

"customer" includes a customer who is not a consumer;

"enactment" includes an Act of the Scottish Parliament, Northern Ireland legislation and an enactment comprised in subordinate legislation, and includes an enactment whenever passed or made;

"goods" includes buildings and other structures, and also includes ships, aircraft and hovercraft;

"Minister of the Crown" means the holder of an office in Her Majesty's Government in the United Kingdom and includes the Treasury;

"modify" includes amend or repeal;

"notice" means notice in writing;

"subordinate legislation" has the same meaning as in the Interpretation Act 1978 (c 30) and also includes an instrument made under an Act of the Scottish Parliament and an instrument made under Northern Ireland legislation; and

"supply", in relation to the supply of goods, includes supply by way of sale, lease, hire or hire-purchase, and, in relation to buildings or other structures, includes the construction of them by a person for another person.

(2)   Sections 127(1)(b) and (4) to (6) and 128 shall apply for the purposes of this Part as they apply for the purposes of Part 3.

(3)   For the purposes of this Part a market investigation reference is finally determined if—

(a)   [where the reference is made under section 131 or 132—]

(i)   the period permitted by section 137 for preparing and publishing a report under section 136 has expired and no such report has been prepared and published;

(ii)   such a report has been prepared and published within the period permitted by section 137 and contains the decision that there is no adverse effect on competition;

(iii) the [CMA] has decided under section 138(2) neither to accept undertakings under section 159 nor to make an order under section 161; or

(iv)   the [CMA] has accepted an undertaking under section 159 or made an order under section 161;

(b)   [where the reference is a restricted PI reference or a full PI reference]

(i)   the period permitted by section 144 for the preparation of the report of the [CMA] under section 142 and for action to be taken in relation to it under section 143(1) or (3) [or (as the case may be) 143A(2) or (3)] has expired while the intervention notice is still in force and no such report has been so prepared or no such action has been taken;

(ii)   the [CMA] has terminated under section 145(1) its investigation and the reference is finally determined under paragraph (a) above . . . ;

(iii) the report of the [CMA] has been prepared under section 142 and published under section 143(1) [or (as the case may be) 143A(2)] within the period permitted by section 144;

(iv)   the intervention notice was revoked and the reference is finally determined under paragraph (a) above . . . ;

[(v)   the Secretary of State has failed to make and publish a decision under subsection (2) of section 146 within the period permitted by subsection (3) of that section or (as the case may be) under subsection (2) of section 146A within the period permitted by subsection (6) of that section and the reference is finally determined under paragraph (a) above;]

(vi)   the Secretary of State has decided under section 146(2) that no eligible public interest consideration is relevant and the reference is finally determined under paragraph (a) above . . . ;

[(via) the Secretary of State has made no finding at all under section 146A(2) and the reference is finally determined under paragraph (a) above;]

    (vii) the Secretary of State has decided under 146(2) that a public interest consideration is relevant but has decided under section 147(2) neither to accept an undertaking under section 159 nor to make an order under section 161; . . .

    [(viia)the Secretary of State has made an adverse public interest finding under section 146A(2) but has decided under section 147A(2) neither to accept an undertaking under section 159 nor to make an order under section 161;]

    (viii) the Secretary of State has decided under section 146(2) that a public interest consideration is relevant and has accepted an undertaking under section 159 or made an order under section 161[; or

    (ix) the Secretary of State has made an adverse public interest finding under section 146A(2) and has accepted an undertaking under section 159 or made an order under section 161].

(4) For the purposes of this Part the time when a market investigation reference is finally determined is—

    (a) in a case falling within subsection (3)(a)(i) or (b)(i), the expiry of the time concerned;

    (b) in a case falling within subsection (3)(a)(ii) or (b)(iii), the publication of the report;

    (c) in a case falling within subsection (3)(a)(iv) or (b)(viii) [or (ix)], the acceptance of the undertaking concerned or (as the case may be) the making of the order concerned; and

    (d) in any other case, the making of the decision or last decision concerned or the taking of the action concerned.

(5) The references in subsection (4) to subsections (3)(a)(i), (ii) and (iv) include those enactments as applied by subsection (3)(b)(ii), (iv), (v)[, (vi) or (via)].

(6) In subsection (4)(c) the reference to the acceptance of the undertaking concerned or the making of the order concerned shall, in a case where the enforcement action concerned involves the acceptance of a group of undertakings, the making of a group of orders or the acceptance and making of a group of undertakings and orders, be treated as a reference to the acceptance or making of the last undertaking or order in the group; but undertakings or orders which vary, supersede or revoke earlier undertakings or orders shall be disregarded for the purposes of subsections (3)(a)(iv) and (b)(viii) [and (ix)] and (4)(c).

(7) Any duty to publish which is imposed on a person by this Part shall, unless the context otherwise requires, be construed as a duty on that person to publish in such manner as that person considers appropriate for the purpose of bringing the matter concerned to the attention of those likely to be affected by it.

NOTES

Sub-s (3) is amended as follows:

Words in first pair of square brackets in para (a) substituted by the Enterprise and Regulatory Reform Act 2013, s 35(10), Sch 10, paras 1, 32(1), (2) (for transitional provisions (including those relating to the abolition of the OFT and the Competition Commission and the continuity of functions), see the Enterprise and Regulatory Reform Act 2013 (Commencement No 6, Transitional Provisions and Savings) Order 2014, SI 2014/416, Schedule at **[2.1126]**).

The word "CMA" in square brackets (in each place that it occurs) was substituted by the Enterprise and Regulatory Reform Act 2013, s 26(3), Sch 5, Pt 2, paras 59, 208 (as to transitional provisions etc, see the note above).

Words in first pair of square brackets in para (b) substituted by the Enterprise and Regulatory Reform Act 2013, s 35(10), Sch 10, paras 1, 32(1), (3)(a) (as to transitional provisions etc, see the note above).

Words in square brackets in paras (b)(i), (iii) inserted by the Enterprise and Regulatory Reform Act 2013, s 35(10), Sch 10, paras 1, 32(1), (3)(b), (d) (as to transitional provisions etc, see the note above).

Words omitted repealed by the Enterprise and Regulatory Reform Act 2013, s 35(10), Sch 10, paras 1, 32(1), (3)(c), (e), (g), (i) (as to transitional provisions etc, see the note above).

Para (b)(v) substituted by the Enterprise and Regulatory Reform Act 2013, s 35(10), Sch 10, paras 1, 32(1), (3)(f) (as to transitional provisions etc, see the note above).

Paras (b)(via), (viia), (ix) inserted (together with the word "or" preceding sub-para (ix)) by the Enterprise and Regulatory Reform Act 2013, s 35(10), Sch 10, paras 1, 32(1), (3)(h), (j), (k) (as to transitional provisions etc, see the note above).

Sub-ss (4), (6): words in square brackets inserted by the Enterprise and Regulatory Reform Act 2013, s 35(10), Sch 10, paras 1, 32(1), (4), (6) (as to transitional provisions etc, see the note above).

Sub-s (5): words in square brackets substituted by the Enterprise and Regulatory Reform Act 2013, s 35(10), Sch 10, paras 1, 32(1), (5) (as to transitional provisions etc, see the note above).

[1.1782]
184 Index of defined expressions: Part 4
In this Part, the expressions listed in the left-hand column have the meaning given by, or are to be interpreted in accordance with, the provisions listed in the right-hand column.

Expression	Provision of this Act
Action (and the taking of action)	Section 183(1)
Adverse effect on competition	Section 134(2) [and (2A)]
[Adverse public interest finding	Section 146A(3)]
Appropriate Minister	Section 132(5)
Business	Section 183(1)
[The CMA	Section 273]

Expression	Provision of this Act
Change of circumstances	Section 183(1)
. . .	. . .
Consumer	Section 183(1)
[Cross-market reference	Section 131(6)]
Customer	Section 183(1)
Date of market investigation reference	Section 137(7)
Detrimental effect on customers	Section 134(5)
Enactment	Section 183(1)
Enforcement order	Section 162(8)
Enforcement undertaking	Section 162(8)
Feature of a market	Section 131(2)
Final determination of market investigation reference	Section 183(3) to (6)
[Full PI reference	Section 140A(12)]
Goods	Section 183(1)
Intervention notice	Section 139(3)
Market for goods or services	Section 131(6)
Market in the United Kingdom	Section 131(6)
Market investigation reference	Section 131(6)
[Market study notice	Section 130A(1)]
[Market study report	Section 131B(4)]
Minister of the Crown	Section 183(1)
Modify	Section 183(1)
Notice	Section 183(1)
. . .	. . .
[Ordinary reference	Section 131(6)]
Public interest consideration	Section 139(5)
Public interest consideration being finalised	Section 139(7)
[Public interest expert	Section 141B(4)]
Publish	Section 183(7)
Relevant customer benefit	Section 134(8)
Relevant sectoral enactment	Section 136(7)
Relevant sectoral regulator	Section 136(8)
Reports of the [CMA]	Section 177(5)
[Restricted PI reference	Section 140A(12)]
Subordinate legislation	Section 183(1)
Supply (in relation to the supply of goods)	Section 183(1)
The supply of services (and a market for services etc)	Section 183(2)

NOTES

Words in square brackets in the entry "Adverse effect on competition" inserted, and entries "Cross-market reference" and "Ordinary reference" inserted, by the Enterprise and Regulatory Reform Act 2013, s 34(4), Sch 9, paras 1, 9 (for transitional provisions (including those relating to the abolition of the OFT and the Competition Commission and the continuity of functions), see the Enterprise and Regulatory Reform Act 2013 (Commencement No 6, Transitional Provisions and Savings) Order 2014, SI 2014/416, Schedule at **[2.1126]**).

Entries, "Adverse public interest finding", "Full PI reference", "Public interest expert", and "Restricted PI reference" inserted by the Enterprise and Regulatory Reform Act 2013, s 35(10), Sch 10, paras 1, 33 (as to transitional provisions etc, see the note above).

Entry "The CMA" inserted, entries "The Commission" and "The OFT" (omitted) repealed, and word in square brackets in the entry "Reports of the CMA" substituted, by the Enterprise and Regulatory Reform Act 2013, s 26(3), Sch 5, Pt 2, paras 59, 209 (as to transitional provisions etc, see the note above).

Entries "Market study notice" and "Market study report" inserted by the Enterprise and Regulatory Reform Act 2013, s 38, Sch 12, paras 7, 17 (as to transitional provisions etc, see the note above).

185–187   ((Pt 5) ss 185–187 repealed by the Enterprise and Regulatory Reform Act 2013, s 26(3), Sch 5, Pt 3, paras 224, 225 (for transitional provisions (including those relating to the abolition of the OFT and the Competition Commission and the continuity of functions), see the Enterprise and Regulatory Reform Act 2013 (Commencement No 6, Transitional Provisions and Savings) Order 2014, SI 2014/416, Schedule at **[2.1126]**.)

PART 6
CARTEL OFFENCE

Cartel offence

[1.1783]
188 Cartel offence
(1) An individual is guilty of an offence if he . . . . agrees with one or more other persons to make or implement, or to cause to be made or implemented, arrangements of the following kind relating to at least two undertakings (A and B).
(2) The arrangements must be ones which, if operating as the parties to the agreement intend, would—
  (a) directly or indirectly fix a price for the supply by A in the United Kingdom (otherwise than to B) of a product or service,
  (b) limit or prevent supply by A in the United Kingdom of a product or service,
  (c) limit or prevent production by A in the United Kingdom of a product,
  (d) divide between A and B the supply in the United Kingdom of a product or service to a customer or customers,
  (e) divide between A and B customers for the supply in the United Kingdom of a product or service, or
  (f) be bid-rigging arrangements.
(3) Unless subsection (2)(d), (e) or (f) applies, the arrangements must also be ones which, if operating as the parties to the agreement intend, would—
  (a) directly or indirectly fix a price for the supply by B in the United Kingdom (otherwise than to A) of a product or service,
  (b) limit or prevent supply by B in the United Kingdom of a product or service, or
  (c) limit or prevent production by B in the United Kingdom of a product.
(4) In subsections (2)(a) to (d) and (3), references to supply or production are to supply or production in the appropriate circumstances (for which see section 189).
(5) "Bid-rigging arrangements" are arrangements under which, in response to a request for bids for the supply of a product or service in the United Kingdom, or for the production of a product in the United Kingdom—
  (a) A but not B may make a bid, or
  (b) A and B may each make a bid but, in one case or both, only a bid arrived at in accordance with the arrangements.
(6) . . .
(7) "Undertaking" has the same meaning as in Part 1 of the 1998 Act.
[(8) This section is subject to section 188A.]

NOTES
  Sub-s (1): words omitted repealed by the Enterprise and Regulatory Reform Act 2013, s 47(1), (2) (for transitional provisions (including those relating to the abolition of the OFT and the Competition Commission and the continuity of functions), see s 47(8) of the 2013 Act and the Enterprise and Regulatory Reform Act 2013 (Commencement No 6, Transitional Provisions and Savings) Order 2014, SI 2014/416, Schedule at **[2.1126]**).
  Sub-s (6): repealed by the Enterprise and Regulatory Reform Act 2013, s 47(1), (3) (as to transitional provisions etc, see note above).
  Sub-s (8): added by the Enterprise and Regulatory Reform Act 2013, s 47(1), (4) (as to transitional provisions etc, see note above).

[1.1784]
[188A Circumstances in which cartel offence not committed
(1) An individual does not commit an offence under section 188(1) if, under the arrangements—
  (a) in a case where the arrangements would (operating as the parties intend) affect the supply in the United Kingdom of a product or service, customers would be given relevant information about the arrangements before they enter into agreements for the supply to them of the product or service so affected,
  (b) in the case of bid-rigging arrangements, the person requesting bids would be given relevant information about them at or before the time when a bid is made, or
  (c) in any case, relevant information about the arrangements would be published, before the arrangements are implemented, in the manner specified at the time of the making of the agreement in an order made by the Secretary of State.
(2) In subsection (1), "relevant information" means—
  (a) the names of the undertakings to which the arrangements relate,
  (b) a description of the nature of the arrangements which is sufficient to show why they are or might be arrangements of the kind to which section 188(1) applies,
  (c) the products or services to which they relate, and
  (d) such other information as may be specified in an order made by the Secretary of State.

(3) An individual does not commit an offence under section 188(1) if the agreement is made in order to comply with a legal requirement.

(4) In subsection (3), "legal requirement" has the same meaning as in paragraph 5 of Schedule 3 to the Competition Act 1998.

(5) A power to make an order under this section—

    (a) is exercisable by statutory instrument,

    (b) may be exercised so as to make different provision for different cases or different purposes, and

    (c) includes power to make such incidental, supplementary, consequential, transitory, transitional or saving provision as the Secretary of State considers appropriate.

(6) A statutory instrument containing an order under this section is subject to annulment in pursuance of a resolution of either House of Parliament.]

NOTES

Commencement: 25 April 2013 (for the purposes of enabling the exercise of any power to make provision by regulations, rules or order made by statutory instrument); 1 April 2014 (remaining purposes).

Inserted, together with s 188B, by the Enterprise and Regulatory Reform Act 2013, s 47(5) (for transitional provisions see s 47(8) of the 2013 Act).

[1.1785]
[188B   Defences to commission of cartel offence

(1) In a case where the arrangements would (operating as the parties intend) affect the supply in the United Kingdom of a product or service, it is a defence for an individual charged with an offence under section 188(1) to show that, at the time of the making of the agreement, he or she did not intend that the nature of the arrangements would be concealed from customers at all times before they enter into agreements for the supply to them of the product or service.

(2) It is a defence for an individual charged with an offence under section 188(1) to show that, at the time of the making of the agreement, he or she did not intend that the nature of the arrangements would be concealed from the CMA.

(3) It is a defence for an individual charged with an offence under section 188(1) to show that, before the making of the agreement, he or she took reasonable steps to ensure that the nature of the arrangements would be disclosed to professional legal advisers for the purposes of obtaining advice about them before their making or (as the case may be) their implementation.]

NOTES

Commencement: 1 April 2014.

Inserted as noted to s 188A at **[1.1785]**.

[1.1786]
189   Cartel offence: supplementary

(1) For section 188(2)(a), the appropriate circumstances are that A's supply of the product or service would be at a level in the supply chain at which the product or service would at the same time be supplied by B in the United Kingdom.

(2) For section 188(2)(b), the appropriate circumstances are that A's supply of the product or service would be at a level in the supply chain—

    (a) at which the product or service would at the same time be supplied by B in the United Kingdom, or

    (b) at which supply by B in the United Kingdom of the product or service would be limited or prevented by the arrangements.

(3) For section 188(2)(c), the appropriate circumstances are that A's production of the product would be at a level in the production chain—

    (a) at which the product would at the same time be produced by B in the United Kingdom, or

    (b) at which production by B in the United Kingdom of the product would be limited or prevented by the arrangements.

(4) For section 188(2)(d), the appropriate circumstances are that A's supply of the product or service would be at the same level in the supply chain as B's.

(5) For section 188(3)(a), the appropriate circumstances are that B's supply of the product or service would be at a level in the supply chain at which the product or service would at the same time be supplied by A in the United Kingdom.

(6) For section 188(3)(b), the appropriate circumstances are that B's supply of the product or service would be at a level in the supply chain—

    (a) at which the product or service would at the same time be supplied by A in the United Kingdom, or

    (b) at which supply by A in the United Kingdom of the product or service would be limited or prevented by the arrangements.

(7) For section 188(3)(c), the appropriate circumstances are that B's production of the product would be at a level in the production chain—

    (a) at which the product would at the same time be produced by A in the United Kingdom, or

    (b) at which production by A in the United Kingdom of the product would be limited or prevented by the arrangements.

[1.1787]
190 Cartel offence: penalty and prosecution
(1) A person guilty of an offence under section 188 is liable—
  (a) on conviction on indictment, to imprisonment for a term not exceeding five years or to a fine, or to both;
  (b) on summary conviction, to imprisonment for a term not exceeding six months or to a fine not exceeding the statutory maximum, or to both.
(2) In England and Wales and Northern Ireland, proceedings for an offence under section 188 may be instituted only—
  (a) by the Director of the Serious Fraud Office, or
  (b) by or with the consent of the [CMA].
(3) No proceedings may be brought for an offence under section 188 in respect of an agreement outside the United Kingdom, unless it has been implemented in whole or in part in the United Kingdom.
(4) Where, for the purpose of the investigation or prosecution of offences under section 188, the [CMA] gives a person written notice under this subsection, no proceedings for an offence under section 188 that falls within a description specified in the notice may be brought against that person in England and Wales or Northern Ireland except in circumstances specified in the notice.

NOTES
Sub-ss (1), (4): words in square brackets substituted by the Enterprise and Regulatory Reform Act 2013, s 26(3), Sch 5, Pt 2, paras 59, 210 (for transitional provisions (including those relating to the abolition of the OFT and the Competition Commission and the continuity of functions), see the Enterprise and Regulatory Reform Act 2013 (Commencement No 6, Transitional Provisions and Savings) Order 2014, SI 2014/416, Schedule at **[2.1126]**).

[1.1788]
[190A Cartel offence: prosecution guidance
(1) The CMA must prepare and publish guidance on the principles to be applied in determining, in any case, whether proceedings for an offence under section 188(1) should be instituted.
(2) The CMA may at any time issue revised or new guidance.
(3) Guidance published by the CMA under this section is to be published in such manner as it considers appropriate.
(4) In preparing guidance under this section the CMA must consult—
  (a) the Director of the Serious Fraud Office;
  (b) the Lord Advocate; and
  (c) such other persons as it considers appropriate.]

NOTES
Commencement: 1 April 2014.
Inserted by the Enterprise and Regulatory Reform Act 2013, s 47(7) (for transitional provisions (including those relating to the abolition of the OFT and the Competition Commission and the continuity of functions), see the Enterprise and Regulatory Reform Act 2013 (Commencement No 6, Transitional Provisions and Savings) Order 2014, SI 2014/416, Schedule at **[2.1126]**).

191 (*Repealed by the Extradition Act 2003, ss 219(1), 220, Sch 3, paras 1, 14, Sch 4.*)

Criminal investigations by [CMA]

[1.1789]
192 Investigation of offences under section 188
(1) The [CMA] may conduct an investigation if there are reasonable grounds for suspecting that an offence under section 188 has been committed.
(2) The powers of the [CMA] under sections 193 and 194 are exercisable, but only for the purposes of an investigation under subsection (1), in any case where it appears to the OFT that there is good reason to exercise them for the purpose of investigating the affairs, or any aspect of the affairs, of any person ("the person under investigation").

NOTES
Cross-heading, sub-ss (1), (2): words in square brackets substituted by, or by virtue of, the Enterprise and Regulatory Reform Act 2013, s 26(3), Sch 5, Pt 2, paras 59, 211 (for transitional provisions (including those relating to the abolition of the OFT and the Competition Commission and the continuity of functions), see the Enterprise and Regulatory Reform Act 2013 (Commencement No 6, Transitional Provisions and Savings) Order 2014, SI 2014/416, Schedule at **[2.1126]**).

[1.1790]
193 Powers when conducting an investigation
(1) The [CMA] may by notice in writing require the person under investigation, or any other person who it has reason to believe has relevant information, to answer questions, or otherwise provide information, with respect to any matter relevant to the investigation at a specified place and either at a specified time or forthwith.

(2)   The [CMA] may by notice in writing require the person under investigation, or any other person, to produce, at a specified place and either at a specified time or forthwith, specified documents, or documents of a specified description, which appear to the [CMA] to relate to any matter relevant to the investigation.

(3)   If any such documents are produced, the [CMA] may—
   (a)   take copies or extracts from them;
   (b)   require the person producing them to provide an explanation of any of them.

(4)   If any such documents are not produced, the [CMA] may require the person who was required to produce them to state, to the best of his knowledge and belief, where they are.

(5)   A notice under subsection (1) or (2) must indicate—
   (a)   the subject matter and purpose of the investigation; and
   (b)   the nature of the offences created by section 201.

NOTES

Words in square brackets substituted by the Enterprise and Regulatory Reform Act 2013, s 26(3), Sch 5, Pt 2, paras 59, 212 (for transitional provisions (including those relating to the abolition of the OFT and the Competition Commission and the continuity of functions), see the Enterprise and Regulatory Reform Act 2013 (Commencement No 6, Transitional Provisions and Savings) Order 2014, SI 2014/416, Schedule at [**2.1126**]).

[1.1791]
194   Power to enter premises under a warrant

(1)   [On an application made to it by the CMA or, in Scotland, the procurator fiscal, the appropriate body may issue a warrant if it is satisfied] that there are reasonable grounds for believing—
   (a)   that there are on any premises documents which the [CMA] has power under section 193 to require to be produced for the purposes of an investigation; and
   (b)   that—
      (i)   a person has failed to comply with a requirement under that section to produce the documents;
      (ii) it is not practicable to serve a notice under that section in relation to them; or
      (iii) the service of such a notice in relation to them might seriously prejudice the investigation.

[(1A)   In subsection (1), "appropriate body" means—
   (a)   in England and Wales and Northern Ireland, the High Court or the Competition Appeal Tribunal;
   (b)   in Scotland, the sheriff.]

(2)   A warrant under this section shall authorise a named officer of the [CMA], and any other officers of the [CMA] whom the [CMA] has authorised in writing to accompany the named officer—
   (a)   to enter the premises, using such force as is reasonably necessary for the purpose;
   (b)   to search the premises and—
      (i)   take possession of any documents appearing to be of the relevant kind, or
      (ii) take, in relation to any documents appearing to be of the relevant kind, any other steps which may appear to be necessary for preserving them or preventing interference with them;
   (c)   to require any person to provide an explanation of any document appearing to be of the relevant kind or to state, to the best of his knowledge and belief, where it may be found;
   (d)   to require any information which is stored in any electronic form and is accessible from the premises and which the named officer considers relates to any matter relevant to the investigation, to be produced in a form—
      (i)   in which it can be taken away, and
      (ii) in which it is visible and legible or from which it can readily be produced in a visible and legible form.

(3)   Documents are of the relevant kind if they are of a kind in respect of which the application under subsection (1) was granted.

(4)   A warrant under this section may authorise persons specified in the warrant to accompany the named officer who is executing it.

[(4A)   An application for a warrant under this section must be made—
   (a)   in the case of an application to the High Court or the sheriff, in accordance with rules of court;
   (b)   in the case of an application to the Competition Appeal Tribunal, in accordance with rules made under section 15.]

(5)   . . .

NOTES

Sub-ss (1), (2): words in square brackets substituted by the Enterprise and Regulatory Reform Act 2013, ss 26(3), 48(1), (2), Sch 5, Pt 2, paras 59, 212 (for transitional provisions (including those relating to the abolition of the OFT and the Competition Commission and the continuity of functions), see the Enterprise and Regulatory Reform Act 2013 (Commencement No 6, Transitional Provisions and Savings) Order 2014, SI 2014/416, Schedule at [**2.1126**]).

Sub-ss (1A), (4A): inserted by the Enterprise and Regulatory Reform Act 2013, s 48(1), (3), (4).

Sub-s (5): inserts the Criminal Justice and Police Act 2001, Sch 1, Pt 1, para 73A.

[1.1792]
195 Exercise of powers by authorised person
(1) The [CMA] may authorise any competent person who is not an officer of the [CMA] to exercise on its behalf all or any of the powers conferred by section 193 or 194.
(2) No such authority may be granted except for the purpose of investigating the affairs, or any aspect of the affairs, of a person specified in the authority.
(3) No person is bound to comply with any requirement imposed by a person exercising powers by virtue of any authority granted under this section unless he has, if required to do so, produced evidence of his authority.

NOTES
Sub-s (1): words in square brackets substituted by the Enterprise and Regulatory Reform Act 2013, s 26(3), Sch 5, Pt 2, paras 59, 214 (for transitional provisions (including those relating to the abolition of the OFT and the Competition Commission and the continuity of functions), see the Enterprise and Regulatory Reform Act 2013 (Commencement No 6, Transitional Provisions and Savings) Order 2014, SI 2014/416, Schedule at **[2.1126]**).

[1.1793]
196 Privileged information etc
(1) A person may not under section 193 or 194 be required to disclose any information or produce any document which he would be entitled to refuse to disclose or produce on grounds of legal professional privilege in proceedings in the High Court, except that a lawyer may be required to provide the name and address of his client.
(2) A person may not under section 193 or 194 be required to disclose any information or produce any document in respect of which he owes an obligation of confidence by virtue of carrying on any banking business unless—
    (a) the person to whom the obligation of confidence is owed consents to the disclosure or production; or
    (b) the [CMA] has authorised the making of the requirement.
(3) In the application of this section to Scotland, the reference in subsection (1)—
    (a) to proceedings in the High Court is to be read as a reference to legal proceedings generally; and
    (b) to an entitlement on grounds of legal professional privilege is to be read as a reference to an entitlement by virtue of any rule of law whereby—
        (i) communications between a professional legal adviser and his client, or
        (ii) communications made in connection with or in contemplation of legal proceedings and for the purposes of those proceedings,
    are in such proceedings protected from disclosure on the ground of confidentiality.

NOTES
Sub-s (2): word in square brackets substituted by the Enterprise and Regulatory Reform Act 2013, s 26(3), Sch 5, Pt 2, paras 59, 215 (for transitional provisions (including those relating to the abolition of the OFT and the Competition Commission and the continuity of functions), see the Enterprise and Regulatory Reform Act 2013 (Commencement No 6, Transitional Provisions and Savings) Order 2014, SI 2014/416, Schedule at **[2.1126]**).

[1.1794]
197 Restriction on use of statements in court
(1) A statement by a person in response to a requirement imposed by virtue of section 193 or 194 may only be used in evidence against him—
    (a) on a prosecution for an offence under section 201(2); or
    (b) on a prosecution for some other offence where in giving evidence he makes a statement inconsistent with it.
(2) However, the statement may not be used against that person by virtue of paragraph (b) of subsection (1) unless evidence relating to it is adduced, or a question relating to it is asked, by or on behalf of that person in the proceedings arising out of the prosecution.

198–200 (*S 198 inserts the Competition Act 1998, s 30A at* **[1.1285]**; *ss 199, 200 amend legislation outside the scope of this work.*)

[1.1795]
201 Offences
(1) Any person who without reasonable excuse fails to comply with a requirement imposed on him under section 193 or 194 is guilty of an offence and liable on summary conviction to imprisonment for a term not exceeding six months or to a fine not exceeding level 5 on the standard scale or to both.
(2) A person who, in purported compliance with a requirement under section 193 or 194—
    (a) makes a statement which he knows to be false or misleading in a material particular; or
    (b) recklessly makes a statement which is false or misleading in a material particular,
is guilty of an offence.

(3)   A person guilty of an offence under subsection (2) is liable—

  (a)   on conviction on indictment, to imprisonment for a term not exceeding two years or to a fine or to both; and

  (b)   on summary conviction, to imprisonment for a term not exceeding six months or to a fine not exceeding the statutory maximum, or to both.

(4)   Where any person—

  (a)   knows or suspects that an investigation by the Serious Fraud Office or the [CMA] into an offence under section 188 is being or is likely to be carried out; and

  (b)   falsifies, conceals, destroys or otherwise disposes of, or causes or permits the falsification, concealment, destruction or disposal of documents which he knows or suspects are or would be relevant to such an investigation,

he is guilty of an offence unless he proves that he had no intention of concealing the facts disclosed by the documents from the persons carrying out such an investigation.

(5)   A person guilty of an offence under subsection (4) is liable—

  (a)   on conviction on indictment, to imprisonment for a term not exceeding 5 years or to a fine or to both; and

  (b)   on summary conviction, to imprisonment for a term not exceeding six months or to a fine not exceeding the statutory maximum, or to both.

(6)   A person who intentionally obstructs a person in the exercise of his powers under a warrant issued under section 194 is guilty of an offence and liable—

  (a)   on conviction on indictment, to imprisonment for a term not exceeding 2 years or to a fine or to both; and

  (b)   on summary conviction, to a fine not exceeding the statutory maximum.

NOTES

  Sub-s (4): word in square brackets substituted by the Enterprise and Regulatory Reform Act 2013, s 26(3), Sch 5, Pt 2, paras 59, 216 (for transitional provisions (including those relating to the abolition of the OFT and the Competition Commission and the continuity of functions), see the Enterprise and Regulatory Reform Act 2013 (Commencement No 6, Transitional Provisions and Savings) Order 2014, SI 2014/416, Schedule at **[2.1126]**).

[1.1796]
202   Interpretation of sections 192 to 201
In sections 192 to 201—

  "documents" includes information recorded in any form and, in relation to information recorded otherwise than in a form in which it is visible and legible, references to its production include references to producing it in a form in which it is visible and legible or from which it can readily be produced in a visible and legible form;

  "person under investigation" has the meaning given in section 192(2).

PART 7
MISCELLANEOUS COMPETITION PROVISIONS

203, 204   (*S 203 amends the Competition Act 1998, ss 28, 62, 63 at* **[1.1281]**, **[1.1331]**, **[1.1334]**; *s 204 outside the scope of this work.*)

Miscellaneous

[1.1797]
205   Super-complaints to regulators other than [CMA]
(1)   The Secretary of State may by order provide that section 11 is to apply to complaints made to a specified regulator in relation to a market of a specified description as it applies to complaints made to the [CMA], with such modifications as may be specified.

(2)   An order under this section—

  (a)   shall be made by statutory instrument, and

  (b)   shall be subject to annulment in pursuance of a resolution of either House of Parliament.

(3)   In this section—

  "regulator" has the meaning given in section 54(1) of the 1998 Act; and

  "specified" means specified in the order.

NOTES

  Section heading, sub-s (1): words in square brackets substituted by the Enterprise and Regulatory Reform Act 2013 (Competition) (Consequential, Transitional and Saving Provisions) Order 2014, SI 2014/892, art 2, Sch 1, Pt 1, paras 1, 4.

  Orders: the Enterprise Act 2002 (Super-complaints to Regulators) Order 2003, SI 2003/1368; the Enterprise Act 2002 (Water Services Regulation Authority) Order 2006, SI 2006/522.

[1.1798]
206   Power to modify Schedule 8
(1)   The Secretary of State may by order made by statutory instrument modify Schedule 8.

(2)   An order under this section may make—

  (a)   different provision for different cases or different purposes;

(b) such incidental, supplementary, consequential, transitory, transitional or saving provision as the Secretary of State considers appropriate.

(3) An order under this section may, in particular, modify that Schedule in its application by virtue of Part 3 of this Act, in its application by virtue of Part 4 of this Act, in its application by virtue of any other enactment (whether by virtue of Part 4 of this Act as applied by that enactment or otherwise) or in its application by virtue of every enactment that applies it.

(4) An order under this section as extended by subsection (2) may modify any enactment comprised in or made under this Act, or any other enactment.

(5) No order shall be made under this section unless a draft of it has been laid before, and approved by a resolution of, each House of Parliament.

(6) No modification of Schedule 8 in its application by virtue of Part 3 of this Act shall be made by an order under this section if the modification relates to a relevant merger situation or (as the case may be) a special merger situation which has been created before the coming into force of the order.

(7) No modification shall be made by an order under this section of Schedule 8 in its application in relation to references made under section 22, 33, 45 or 62 before the coming into force of the order.

(8) No modification shall be made by an order under this section of Schedule 8 in its application in relation to references made under section 131 or 132 before the coming into force of the order (including references made under section 131 as applied by another enactment).

(9) Before making an order under this section, the Secretary of State shall consult the [CMA] and the Commission.

(10) Expressions used in this section which are also used in Part 3 of this Act have the same meaning in this section as in that Part.

NOTES

Sub-s (9): word in square brackets substituted by the Enterprise and Regulatory Reform Act 2013 (Competition) (Consequential, Transitional and Saving Provisions) Order 2014, SI 2014/892, art 2, Sch 1, Pt 1, paras 1, 5.

207, 208 (*S 207 repeals the Competition Act 1998, s 3(1)(d), Sch 4; s 208 repeals the Fair Trading Act 1973, ss 78–80.*)

[1.1799]
209 Reform of [EU competition law]
(1) The Secretary of State may by regulations make such modifications of the 1998 Act as he considers appropriate for the purpose of eliminating or reducing any differences between—
(a) the domestic provisions of the 1998 Act, and
(b) [EU competition law],
which result (or would otherwise result) from a relevant [EU] instrument made after the passing of this Act.
(2) In subsection (1)—
"the domestic provisions of the 1998 Act" means the provisions of the 1998 Act so far as they do not implement or give effect to a relevant [EU] instrument;
"[EU competition law]" includes any Act or subordinate legislation so far as it implements or gives effect to a relevant [EU] instrument;
"relevant [EU] instrument" means a regulation or directive under [Article 103 of the Treaty on the Functioning of the European Union].
(3) The Secretary of State may by regulations repeal or otherwise modify any provision of an Act (other than the 1998 Act) which excludes any matter from the Chapter I prohibition or the Chapter II prohibition (within the meaning of Part 1 of the 1998 Act).
(4) The power under subsection (3) may not be exercised—
(a) before the power under subsection (1) has been exercised; or
(b) so as to extend the scope of any exclusion that is not being removed by the regulations.
(5) Regulations under this section may—
(a) confer power to make subordinate legislation;
(b) make such consequential, supplementary, incidental, transitory, transitional or saving provision as the Secretary of State considers appropriate (including provision modifying any Act or subordinate legislation); and
(c) make different provision for different cases or circumstances.
(6) The power to make regulations under this section is exercisable by statutory instrument.
(7) No regulations may be made under this section unless a draft of them has been laid before and approved by a resolution of each House of Parliament.
(8) Paragraph 1(1)(c) of Schedule 2 to the European Communities Act 1972 (c 68) (restriction on powers to legislate) shall not apply to regulations which implement or give effect to a relevant [EU] instrument made after the passing of this Act.

NOTES

Section heading: words in square brackets substituted by the Treaty of Lisbon (Changes in Terminology or Numbering) Order 2012, SI 2012/1809, art 3, Schedule, Pt 1.

Sub-s (1): words in first pair of square brackets substituted by SI 2012/1809, art 3, Schedule, Pt 1; reference in second pair of square brackets substituted by the Treaty of Lisbon (Changes in Terminology) Order 2011, SI 2011/1043, art 6(1)(d).

Sub-s (2): references to "EU" in square brackets substituted by SI 2011/1043, art 6(1)(d); other words in square brackets substituted by SI 2012/1809, art 3, Schedule, Pt 1.

Sub-s (8): reference in square brackets substituted by SI 2011/1043, art 6(1)(d).

PART 8
ENFORCEMENT OF CERTAIN CONSUMER LEGISLATION

Introduction

[1.1800]

210 Consumers

(1)   In this Part references to consumers must be construed in accordance with this section.

(2)   In relation to a domestic infringement a consumer is an individual in respect of whom the first and second conditions are satisfied.

(3)   The first condition is that—

(a)   goods are or are sought to be supplied to the individual (whether by way of sale or otherwise) in the course of a business carried on by the person supplying or seeking to supply them, or

(b)   services are or are sought to be supplied to the individual in the course of a business carried on by the person supplying or seeking to supply them.

(4)   The second condition is that—

(a)   the individual receives or seeks to receive the goods or services otherwise than in the course of a business carried on by him, or

(b)   the individual receives or seeks to receive the goods or services with a view to carrying on a business but not in the course of a business carried on by him.

(5)   . . .

(6)   In relation to a Community infringement a consumer is a person who is a consumer for the purposes of—

(a)   the Injunctions Directive, and

(b)   the listed Directive [or the listed Regulation] concerned.

(7)   A Directive is a listed Directive—

(a)   if it is a Directive of the Council of the [European Union] or of the European Parliament and of the Council, and

(b)   if it is specified in Schedule 13 or to the extent that any of its provisions is so specified.

[(7A)   A Regulation is a listed Regulation—

(a)   if it is a Regulation of the Council of the [European Union] or of the European Parliament and of the Council, and

(b)   if it is specified in Schedule 13 or to the extent that any of its provisions is so specified.]

(8)   A business includes—

(a)   a professional practice;

(b)   any other undertaking carried on for gain or reward;

(c)   any undertaking in the course of which goods or services are supplied otherwise than free of charge.

(9)   The Secretary of State may by order modify Schedule 13.

(10)   An order under this section must be made by statutory instrument subject to annulment in pursuance of a resolution of either House of Parliament.

NOTES

Sub-s (5): repealed by the Consumer Rights Act 2015, s 79(1), Sch 7, paras 1, 2.

Sub-s (6): words in square brackets in para (b) inserted by the Enterprise Act 2002 (Amendment) Regulations 2006, SI 2006/3363, regs 3, 4.

Sub-s (7): words in square brackets substituted by the Treaty of Lisbon (Changes in Terminology) Order 2011, SI 2011/1043, art 4(1).

Sub-s (7A): inserted by SI 2006/3363, regs 3, 5; words in square brackets substituted by SI 2011/1043, art 4(1).

Orders: the Enterprise Act 2002 (Part 8 Community Infringements Specified UK Laws) Order 2003, SI 2003/1374; the Enterprise Act 2002 (Part 8 EU Infringements) Order 2014, SI 2014/2908.

[1.1801]

211 Domestic infringements

(1)   In this Part a domestic infringement is an act or omission which—

(a)   is done or made by a person in the course of a business,

(b)   falls within subsection (2), and

(c)   harms the collective interests of consumers . . . .

[(1A)   But an act or omission which satisfies the conditions in subsection (1) is a domestic infringement only if at least one of the following is satisfied—

(a)   the person supplying (or seeking to supply) goods or services has a place of business in the United Kingdom, or

(b)   the goods or services are supplied (or sought to be supplied) to or for a person in the United Kingdom (see section 232).]

(2)   An act or omission falls within this subsection if it is of a description specified by the Secretary of State by order and consists of any of the following—

(a)   a contravention of an enactment which imposes a duty, prohibition or restriction enforceable by criminal proceedings;

(b)   an act done or omission made in breach of contract;

(c)   an act done or omission made in breach of a non-contractual duty owed to a person by virtue of an enactment or rule of law and enforceable by civil proceedings;

(d)   an act or omission in respect of which an enactment provides for a remedy or sanction enforceable by civil proceedings;

(e)   an act done or omission made by a person supplying or seeking to supply goods or services as a result of which an agreement or security relating to the supply is void or unenforceable to any extent;

(f)   an act or omission by which a person supplying or seeking to supply goods or services purports or attempts to exercise a right or remedy relating to the supply in circumstances where the exercise of the right or remedy is restricted or excluded under or by virtue of an enactment;

(g)   an act or omission by which a person supplying or seeking to supply goods or services purports or attempts to avoid (to any extent) liability relating to the supply in circumstances where such avoidance is restricted or prevented under an enactment.

(3)   But an order under this section may provide that any description of act or omission falling within subsection (2) is not a domestic infringement.

(4)   For the purposes of subsection (2) it is immaterial—

(a)   whether or not any duty, prohibition or restriction exists in relation to consumers as such;

(b)   whether or not any remedy or sanction is provided for the benefit of consumers as such;

(c)   whether or not any proceedings have been brought in relation to the act or omission;

(d)   whether or not any person has been convicted of an offence in respect of the contravention mentioned in subsection (2)(a);

(e)   whether or not there is a waiver in respect of the breach of contract mentioned in subsection (2)(b).

(5)   References to an enactment include references to subordinate legislation (within the meaning of the Interpretation Act 1978 (c 30)).

(6)   The power to make an order under this section must be exercised by statutory instrument.

(7)   But no such order may be made unless a draft of it has been laid before Parliament and approved by a resolution of each House.

NOTES

Sub-s (1): words omitted from para (c) repealed by the Consumer Rights Act 2015, s 79(1), Sch 7, paras 1, 3(1), (2).

Sub-s (1A): inserted by the Consumer Rights Act 2015, s 79(1), Sch 7, paras 1, 3(1), (3).

Orders: the Enterprise Act 2002 (Part 8 Domestic Infringements) Order 2003, SI 2003/1593.

[1.1802]

212   Community infringements

(1)   In this Part a Community infringement is an act or omission which harms the collective interests of consumers and which—

(a)   contravenes a listed Directive as given effect by the laws, regulations or administrative provisions of an EEA State, . . .

(b)   contravenes such laws, regulations or administrative provisions which provide additional permitted protections,

[(c)   contravenes a listed Regulation, or

(d)   contravenes any laws, regulations or administrative provisions of an EEA State which give effect to a listed Regulation.]

(2)   The laws, regulations or administrative provisions of an EEA State which give effect to a listed Directive provide additional permitted protections if—

(a)   they provide protection for consumers which is in addition to the minimum protection required by the Directive concerned, and

(b)   such additional protection is permitted by that Directive.

(3)   The Secretary of State may by order specify for the purposes of this section the law in the United Kingdom which—

(a)   gives effect to the listed Directives;

(b)   provides additional permitted protections[; or]

[(c)   gives effect to a listed Regulation].

(4)   References to a listed Directive [or to a listed Regulation] must be construed in accordance with section 210.

[(5)   EEA State has the meaning given by Schedule 1 to the Interpretation Act 1978.]

(6)   An order under this section must be made by statutory instrument subject to annulment in pursuance of a resolution of either House of Parliament.

NOTES

Sub-s (1): word omitted repealed and paras (c), (d) added by the Enterprise Act 2002 (Amendment) Regulations 2006, SI 2006/3363, regs 3, 6, 7.

Sub-s (3): para (c) and word "or" immediately preceding it added by SI 2006/3363, regs 3, 8.

Sub-s (4): words in square brackets inserted by SI 2006/3363, regs 3, 9.

Sub-s (5): substituted by the Enterprise Act 2002 (EEA State) (Amendment) Regulations 2007, SI 2007/528, reg 2.

Orders: the Enterprise Act 2002 (Part 8 Community Infringements Specified UK Laws) Order 2003, SI 2003/1374; the Enterprise Act 2002 (Part 8 Community Infringements Specified UK Laws) Order 2006, SI 2006/3372; the Enterprise Act 2002 (Part 8 EU Infringements) Order 2014, SI 2014/2908; the Alternative Dispute Resolution for Consumer Disputes (Amendment) Regulations 2015, SI 2015/1392; the Enterprise Act 2002 (Part 8 Community Infringements and Specified UK Laws) (Amendment) Order 2015, SI 2015/1628.

[1.1803]
213 Enforcers
(1) Each of the following is a general enforcer—
  (a) the [CMA];
  (b) every local weights and measures authority in Great Britain;
  (c) the Department of Enterprise, Trade and Investment in Northern Ireland.
(2) A designated enforcer is any person or body (whether or not incorporated) which the Secretary of State—
  (a) thinks has as one of its purposes the protection of the collective interests of consumers, and
  (b) designates by order.
(3) The Secretary of State may designate a public body only if he is satisfied that it is independent.
(4) The Secretary of State may designate a person or body which is not a public body only if the person or body (as the case may be) satisfies such criteria as the Secretary of State specifies by order.
(5) A Community enforcer is a qualified entity for the purposes of the Injunctions Directive—
  (a) which is for the time being specified in the list published in the Official Journal of the [European Union] in pursuance of Article 4.3 of that Directive, but
  [(b) which is not a general enforcer, a designated enforcer or a CPC enforcer.]
[(5A) Each of the following (being bodies or persons designated by the Secretary of State under Article 4(1) or 4(2) of the CPC Regulation) is a CPC enforcer—
  (a) the [CMA];
  (b) the Civil Aviation Authority;
  (c) the [Financial Conduct Authority];
  (d) the Secretary of State for Health;
  (e) the Department of Health, Social Services and Public Safety in Northern Ireland;
  (f) the Office of Communications;
  (g) the Department of Enterprise, Trade and Investment in Northern Ireland;
  (h) every local weights and measures authority in Great Britain;
  [(i) an enforcement authority within the meaning of section 120(15) of the Communications Act 2003 (regulation of premium rate services);]
  [(j) the Information Commissioner].]
(6) An order under this section may designate an enforcer in respect of—
  (a) all infringements;
  (b) infringements of such descriptions as are specified in the order.
(7) An order under this section may make different provision for different purposes.
(8) The designation of a body by virtue of subsection (3) is conclusive evidence for the purposes of any question arising under this Part that the body is a public body.
(9) An order under this section must be made by statutory instrument subject to annulment in pursuance of a resolution of either House of Parliament.
(10) If requested to do so by a designated enforcer which is designated in respect of one or more Community infringements the Secretary of State must notify the Commission of the [European Union]—
  (a) of its name and purpose;
  (b) of the Community infringements in respect of which it is designated.
(11) The Secretary of State must also notify the Commission—
  (a) of the fact that a person or body in respect of which he has given notice under subsection (10) ceases to be a designated enforcer;
  (b) of any change in the name or purpose of a designated enforcer in respect of which he has given such notice;
  (c) of any change to the Community infringements in respect of which a designated enforcer is designated.

NOTES

Sub-s (1): word in square brackets substituted by the Enterprise and Regulatory Reform Act 2013 (Competition) (Consequential, Transitional and Saving Provisions) Order 2014, SI 2014/892, art 2, Sch 1, Pt 1, paras 1, 6.

Sub-s (5): words in square brackets in para (a) substituted by the Treaty of Lisbon (Changes in Terminology) Order 2011, SI 2011/1043, art 4(1); para (b) substituted by the Enterprise Act 2002 (Amendment) Regulations 2006, SI 2006/3363, regs 3, 10.

Sub-s (5A): inserted by SI 2006/3363, regs 3, 11; in para (a) word in square brackets substituted by SI 2014/892, art 2, Sch 1, Pt 1, paras 1, 6; in para (c) words in square brackets substituted by the Financial Services Act 2012, s 114(1), Sch 18, Pt 2, paras 95(1), (2); para (i) substituted by the Consumer Rights Act 2015, s 79(1), Sch 7, paras 1, 4; para (j) added by the Privacy and Electronic Communications (EC Directive) (Amendment) Regulations 2011, SI 2011/1208, reg 16(a).

Sub-s (10): words in square brackets substituted by SI 2011/1043, art 4(1).

Orders: the Enterprise Act 2002 (Part 8 Designated Enforcers: Criteria for Designation, Designation of Public Bodies as Designated Enforcers and Transitional Provisions) Order 2003, SI 2003/1399; the Enterprise Act 2002 (Part 8) (Designation of the Financial Services Authority as a Designated Enforcer) Order 2004, SI 2004/935; the Enterprise Act 2002 (Part 8) (Designation of the Consumers' Association) Order 2005, SI 2005/917; the Enterprise Act 2002 (Water Services Regulation Authority) Order 2006, SI 2006/522; the Enterprise Act 2002 (Part 8) (Designation of the Financial Conduct Authority as a Designated Enforcer) Order 2013, SI 2013/478.

Enforcement procedure

[1.1804]

214   Consultation

[(1)   An enforcer must not make an application for an enforcement order unless—
  (a)   the enforcer has engaged in appropriate consultation with the person against whom the enforcement order would be made, and
  (b)   if the enforcer is not the [CMA], the enforcer has given notice to the [CMA] of the enforcer's intention to apply for the enforcement order, and the appropriate minimum period has elapsed.

(1A)   The appropriate minimum period is—
  (a)   in the case of an enforcement order, 14 days beginning with the day on which notice under subsection (1)(b) is given;
  (b)   in the case of an interim enforcement order, seven days beginning with the day on which notice under subsection (1)(b) is given.]

(2)   Appropriate consultation is consultation for the purpose of—
  (a)   achieving the cessation of the infringement in a case where an infringement is occurring;
  (b)   ensuring that there will be no repetition of the infringement in a case where the infringement has occurred;
  (c)   ensuring that there will be no repetition of the infringement in a case where the cessation of the infringement is achieved under paragraph (a);
  (d)   ensuring that the infringement does not take place in the case of a Community infringement which the enforcer believes is likely to take place.

(3)   Subsection (1) does not apply if the [CMA] thinks that an application for an enforcement order should be made without delay.

(4)   [Subsection (1)(a)] ceases to apply—
  (a)   for the purposes of an application for an enforcement order at the end of the period of 14 days [or, where subsection (4A) applies, 28 days] beginning with the day after the person against whom the enforcement order would be made receives a request for consultation from the enforcer;
  (b)   for the purposes of an application for an interim enforcement order at the end of the period of seven days beginning with the day after the person against whom the interim enforcement order would be made receives a request for consultation from the enforcer.

[(4A)   This subsection applies where the person against whom the enforcement order would be made is a member of, or is represented by, a representative body, and that body operates a consumer code which has been approved by—
  (a)   an enforcer, other than a designated enforcer which is not a public body,
  (b)   a body which represents an enforcer mentioned in paragraph (a),
  (c)   a group of enforcers mentioned in paragraph (a), or
  (d)   a community interest company whose objects include the approval of consumer codes.

(4B)   In subsection (4A)—
  "consumer code" means a code of practice or other document (however described) intended, with a view to safeguarding or promoting the interests of consumers, to regulate by any means the conduct of persons engaged in the supply of goods or services to consumers (or the conduct of their employees or representatives), and
  "representative body" means an organisation established to represent the interests of two or more businesses in a particular sector or area, and for this purpose "business" has the meaning it bears in section 210.]

(5)   The Secretary of State may by order make rules in relation to consultation under this section.

(6)   Such an order must be made by statutory instrument subject to annulment in pursuance of a resolution of either House of Parliament.

(7)   In this section [(except subsections (1A) and (4))] and in sections 215 and 216 references to an enforcement order include references to an interim enforcement order.

NOTES

Sub-ss (1), (1A): substituted, for sub-s (1) as originally enacted, by the Public Bodies (The Office of Fair Trading Transfer of Consumer Advice Scheme Function and Modification of Enforcement Functions) Order 2013, SI 2013/783, art 9(1), (2); in sub-s (1)(b) words in square brackets substituted by the Enterprise and Regulatory Reform Act 2013 (Competition) (Consequential, Transitional and Saving Provisions) Order 2014, SI 2014/892, art 2, Sch 1, Pt 1, paras 1, 7.

Sub-s (3): word in square brackets substituted by SI 2014/892, art 2, Sch 1, Pt 1, paras 1, 7.

Sub-s (4): words in first pair of square brackets substituted by SI 2013/783, art 9(1), (3); words in square brackets in para (a) inserted by the Consumer Rights Act 2015, s 79(1), Sch 7, paras 1, 5(1), (2).

Sub-ss (4A), (4B): inserted by the Consumer Rights Act 2015, s 79(1), Sch 7, paras 1, 5(1), (3).

Sub-s (7): words in square brackets substituted by SI 2013/783, art 9(1), (4).

Orders: the Enterprise Act 2002 (Part 8 Request for Consultation) Order 2003, SI 2003/1375.

[1.1805]
215 Applications

(1)   An application for an enforcement order must name the person the enforcer thinks—
   (a)   has engaged or is engaging in conduct which constitutes a domestic or a Community infringement, or
   (b)   is likely to engage in conduct which constitutes a Community infringement.

(2)   A general enforcer may make an application for an enforcement order in respect of any infringement.

(3)   A designated enforcer may make an application for an enforcement order in respect of an infringement to which his designation relates.

(4)   A Community enforcer may make an application for an enforcement order in respect of a Community infringement.

[(4A)   A CPC enforcer may make an application for an enforcement order in respect of a Community infringement.]

(5)   The following courts have jurisdiction to make an enforcement order—
   [(za)   the High Court or the county court if the person against whom the order is sought carries on business or has a place of business in England and Wales;]
   (a)   the High Court or a county court if the person against whom the order is sought carries on business or has a place of business in . . .   Northern Ireland
   (b)   the Court of Session or the sheriff if the person against whom the order is sought carries on business or has a place of business in Scotland.

(6)   If an application for an enforcement order is made by a Community enforcer the court may examine whether the purpose of the enforcer justifies its making the application.

(7)   If the court thinks that the purpose of the Community enforcer does not justify its making the application the court may refuse the application on that ground alone.

(8)   The purpose of a Community enforcer must be construed by reference to the Injunctions Directive.

(9)   An enforcer which is not the [CMA] must notify the [CMA] of the result of an application under this section.

NOTES

Sub-s (4A): inserted by the Enterprise Act 2002 (Amendment) Regulations 2006, SI 2006/3363, regs 3, 12.

Sub-s (5): para (za) inserted, and words omitted from para (a) repealed, by the Crime and Courts Act 2013, s 17(5), Sch 9, Pt 3, para 81(b), (c), for transitional provision see the Crime and Courts Act 2013 (Commencement No 10 and Transitional Provision) Order 2014, SI 2014/954, art 3.

Sub-s (9): words in square brackets substituted by the Enterprise and Regulatory Reform Act 2013 (Competition) (Consequential, Transitional and Saving Provisions) Order 2014, SI 2014/892, art 2, Sch 1, Pt 1, paras 1, 8.

[1.1806]
216 Applications: directions by [CMA]

(1)   This section applies if the [CMA] believes that an enforcer other than the [CMA] intends to apply for an enforcement order.

(2)   In such a case the [CMA] may direct that if an application in respect of a particular infringement is to be made it must be made—
   (a)   only by the [CMA], or
   (b)   only by such other enforcer as the [CMA] directs.

(3)   If the [CMA] directs that only it may make an application that does not prevent—
   (a)   the [CMA] or any enforcer from accepting an undertaking under section 219, or
   (b)   the [CMA] from taking such other steps it thinks appropriate (apart from making an application) for the purpose of securing that the infringement is not committed, continued or repeated.

(4)   The [CMA] may vary or withdraw a direction given under this section.

(5)   The [CMA] must take such steps as it thinks appropriate to bring a direction (or a variation or withdrawal of a direction) to the attention of enforcers it thinks may be affected by it.

(6)   But this section does not prevent an application for an enforcement order being made by a Community enforcer.

NOTES

Sub-s (9): words in square brackets substituted by the Enterprise and Regulatory Reform Act 2013 (Competition) (Consequential, Transitional and Saving Provisions) Order 2014, SI 2014/892, art 2, Sch 1, Pt 1, paras 1, 9.

[1.1807]
217 Enforcement orders
(1)   This section applies if an application for an enforcement order is made under section 215 and the court finds that the person named in the application has engaged in conduct which constitutes the infringement.

(2)   This section also applies if such an application is made in relation to a Community infringement and the court finds that the person named in the application is likely to engage in conduct which constitutes the infringement.

(3)   If this section applies the court may make an enforcement order against the person.

(4)   In considering whether to make an enforcement order the court must have regard to whether the person named in the application—

(a)   has given an undertaking under section 219 in respect of conduct such as is mentioned in subsection (3) of that section;

(b)   has failed to comply with the undertaking.

(5)   An enforcement order must—

(a)   indicate the nature of the conduct to which the finding under subsection (1) or (2) relates, and

(b)   direct the person to comply with subsection (6).

(6)   A person complies with this subsection if he—

(a)   does not continue or repeat the conduct;

(b)   does not engage in such conduct in the course of his business or another business;

(c)   does not consent to or connive in the carrying out of such conduct by a body corporate with which he has a special relationship (within the meaning of section 222(3)).

(7)   But subsection (6)(a) does not apply in the case of a finding under subsection (2).

(8)   An enforcement order may require a person against whom the order is made to publish in such form and manner and to such extent as the court thinks appropriate for the purpose of eliminating any continuing effects of the infringement—

(a)   the order;

(b)   a corrective statement.

(9)   If the court makes a finding under subsection (1) or (2) it may accept an undertaking by the person—

(a)   to comply with subsection (6), or

(b)   to take steps which the court believes will secure that he complies with subsection (6).

(10)   An undertaking under subsection (9) may include a further undertaking by the person to publish in such form and manner and to such extent as the court thinks appropriate for the purpose of eliminating any continuing effects of the infringement—

(a)   the terms of the undertaking;

(b)   a corrective statement.

[(10A)   An enforcement order may require a person against whom the order is made to take enhanced consumer measures (defined in section 219A) within a period specified by the court.

(10B)   An undertaking under subsection (9) may include a further undertaking by the person to take enhanced consumer measures within a period specified in the undertaking.

(10C)   Subsections (10A) and (10B) are subject to section 219C in a case where the application for the enforcement order was made by a designated enforcer which is not a public body.

(10D)   Where a person is required by an enforcement order or an undertaking under this section to take enhanced consumer measures, the order or undertaking may include requirements as to the provision of information or documents to the court by the person in order that the court may determine if the person is taking those measures.]

(11)   If the court—

(a)   makes a finding under subsection (1) or (2), and

(b)   accepts an undertaking under subsection (9),

it must not make an enforcement order in respect of the infringement to which the undertaking relates.

(12)   An enforcement order made by a court in one part of the United Kingdom has effect in any other part of the United Kingdom as if made by a court in that part.

NOTES

Sub-ss (10A)–(10D): inserted by the Consumer Rights Act 2015, s 79(1), Sch 7, paras 1, 6.

[1.1808]
218 Interim enforcement order
(1)   The court may make an interim enforcement order against a person named in the application for the order if it appears to the court—

(a)   that it is alleged that the person is engaged in conduct which constitutes a domestic or Community infringement or is likely to engage in conduct which constitutes a Community infringement,

(b)   that if the application had been an application for an enforcement order it would be likely to be granted,

(c)   that it is expedient that the conduct is prohibited or prevented (as the case may be) immediately, and

(d)   if no notice of the application has been given to the person named in the application that it is appropriate to make an interim enforcement order without notice.

(2)   An interim enforcement order must—

(a)   indicate the nature of the alleged conduct, and

(b)   direct the person to comply with subsection (3).

(3)   A person complies with this subsection if he—

(a)   does not continue or repeat the conduct;

(b)   does not engage in such conduct in the course of his business or another business;

(c)   does not consent to or connive in the carrying out of such conduct by a body corporate with which he has a special relationship (within the meaning of section 222(3)).

(4)   But subsection (3)(a) does not apply in so far as the application is made in respect of an allegation that the person is likely to engage in conduct which constitutes a Community infringement.

(5)   An application for an interim enforcement order against a person may be made at any time before an application for an enforcement order against the person in respect of the same conduct is determined.

(6)   An application for an interim enforcement order must refer to all matters—

(a)   which are known to the applicant, and

(b)   which are material to the question whether or not the application is granted.

(7)   If an application for an interim enforcement order is made without notice the application must state why no notice has been given.

(8)   The court may vary or discharge an interim enforcement order on the application of—

(a)   the enforcer who applied for the order;

(b)   the person against whom it is made.

(9)   An interim enforcement order against a person is discharged on the determination of an application for an enforcement order made against the person in respect of the same conduct.

(10)   If it appears to the court as mentioned in subsection (1)(a) to (c) the court may instead of making an interim enforcement order accept an undertaking from the person named in the application—

(a)   to comply with subsection (3), or

(b)   to take steps which the court believes will secure that he complies with subsection (3).

(11)   An interim enforcement order made by a court in one part of the United Kingdom has effect in any other part of the United Kingdom as if made by a court in that part.

[1.1809]
[218A   Unfair commercial practices: substantiation of claims

(1)   This section applies where an application for an enforcement order or for an interim enforcement order is made in respect of a Community infringement involving a contravention of Directive 2005/29/EC of the European Parliament and of the Council of 11 May 2005 concerning unfair business-to-consumer commercial practices in the internal market.

(2)   For the purposes of considering the application the court may require the person named in the application to provide evidence as to the accuracy of any factual claim made as part of a commercial practice of that person if, taking into account the legitimate interests of that person and any other party to the proceedings, it appears appropriate in the circumstances.

(3)   If, having been required under subsection (2) to provide evidence as to the accuracy of a factual claim, a person—

(a)   fails to provide such evidence, or

(b)   provides evidence as to the accuracy of the factual claim that the court considers inadequate,

the court may consider that the factual claim is inaccurate.

(4)   In this section "commercial practice" has the meaning given by regulation 2 of the Consumer Protection from Unfair Trading Regulations 2008.]

NOTES

Inserted by the Consumer Protection from Unfair Trading Regulations 2008, SI 2008/1277, reg 27.

[1.1810]
219   Undertakings

(1)   This section applies if an enforcer has power to make an application under section 215.

(2)   In such a case the enforcer may accept from a person to whom subsection (3) applies an undertaking that the person will comply with subsection (4).

(3)   This subsection applies to a person who the enforcer believes—

(a)   has engaged in conduct which constitutes an infringement;

(b)   is engaging in such conduct;

(c)   is likely to engage in conduct which constitutes a Community infringement.

(4)   A person complies with this subsection if he—

(a)   does not continue or repeat the conduct;

(b)   does not engage in such conduct in the course of his business or another business;
(c)   does not consent to or connive in the carrying out of such conduct by a body corporate with
       which he has a special relationship (within the meaning of section 222(3)).
(5)   But subsection (4)(a) does not apply in the case of an undertaking given by a person in so far
as subsection (3) applies to him by virtue of paragraph (c).
[(5ZA)   An undertaking under this section may include a further undertaking by the person—
(a)   to take enhanced consumer measures (defined in section 219A) within a period specified in
       the undertaking, and
(b)   where such measures are included, to provide information or documents to the enforcer in
       order that the enforcer may determine if the person is taking those measures.
(5ZB)   Subsection (5ZA) is subject to section 219C in a case where the enforcer is a designated
enforcer which is not a public body.]
[(5A)   A CPC enforcer who has accepted an undertaking under this section may—
(a)   accept a further undertaking from the person concerned to publish the terms of the
       undertaking; or
(b)   take steps itself to publish the undertaking.
(5B)   In each case the undertaking shall be published in such form and manner and to such extent
as the CPC enforcer thinks appropriate for the purpose of eliminating any continuing effects of
the Community infringement.]
(6)   If an enforcer accepts an undertaking under this section it must notify the [CMA]—
(a)   of the terms of the undertaking;
(b)   of the identity of the person who gave it.

NOTES
  Sub-ss (5ZA), (5ZB): inserted by the Consumer Rights Act 2015, s 79(1), Sch 7, paras 1, 7.
  Sub-ss (5A), (5B): inserted by the Enterprise Act 2002 (Amendment) Regulations 2006, SI 2006/3363, regs 3, 13.
  Sub-s (6): words in square brackets substituted by the Enterprise and Regulatory Reform Act 2013 (Competition)
(Consequential, Transitional and Saving Provisions) Order 2014, SI 2014/892, art 2, Sch 1, Pt 1, paras 1, 10.

[1.1811]
[219A   Definition of enhanced consumer measures
(1)   In this Part, enhanced consumer measures are measures (not excluded by subsection (5))
falling within—
(a)   the redress category described in subsection (2),
(b)   the compliance category described in subsection (3), or
(c)   the choice category described in subsection (4).
(2)   The measures in the redress category are—
(a)   measures offering compensation or other redress to consumers who have suffered loss as a
       result of the conduct which has given rise to the enforcement order or undertaking,
(b)   where the conduct referred to in paragraph (a) relates to a contract, measures offering such
       consumers the option to terminate (but not vary) that contract,
(c)   where such consumers cannot be identified, or cannot be identified without
       disproportionate cost to the subject of the enforcement order or undertaking, measures
       intended to be in the collective interests of consumers.
(3)   The measures in the compliance category are measures intended to prevent or reduce the risk
of the occurrence or repetition of the conduct to which the enforcement order or undertaking relates
(including measures with that purpose which may have the effect of improving compliance with
consumer law more generally).
(4)   The measures in the choice category are measures intended to enable consumers to choose
more effectively between persons supplying or seeking to supply goods or services.
(5)   The following are not enhanced consumer measures—
(a)   a publication requirement included in an enforcement order as described in section 217(8),
(b)   a publication requirement included in an undertaking accepted by the court as described in
       section 217(10), or
(c)   a publication requirement included in an undertaking accepted by a CPC enforcer as
       described in section 219(5A)(a).]

NOTES
  Commencement: 1 October 2015.
  Inserted, together with ss 219B, 219C, by the Consumer Rights Act 2015, s 79(1), Sch 7, para 8.

[1.1812]
[219B   Inclusion of enhanced consumer measures etc
(1)   An enforcement order or undertaking may include only such enhanced consumer measures as
the court or enforcer (as the case may be) considers to be just and reasonable.
(2)   For the purposes of subsection (1) the court or enforcer must in particular consider whether
any proposed enhanced consumer measures are proportionate, taking into account—
(a)   the likely benefit of the measures to consumers,
(b)   the costs likely to be incurred by the subject of the enforcement order or undertaking, and
(c)   the likely cost to consumers of obtaining the benefit of the measures.

(3)   The costs referred to in subsection (2)(b) are—
   (a)   the cost of the measures, and
   (b)   the reasonable administrative costs associated with taking the measures.
(4)   An enforcement order or undertaking may include enhanced consumer measures in the redress category—
   (a)   only in a loss case, and
   (b)   only if the court or enforcer (as the case may be) is satisfied that the cost of such measures to the subject of the enforcement order or undertaking is unlikely to be more than the sum of the losses suffered by consumers as a result of the conduct which has given rise to the enforcement order or undertaking.
(5)   The cost referred to in subsection (4)(b) does not include the administrative costs associated with taking the measures.
(6)   Subsection (7) applies if an enforcement order or undertaking includes enhanced consumer measures offering compensation and a settlement agreement is entered into in connection with the payment of compensation.
(7)   A waiver of a person's rights in the settlement agreement is not valid if it is a waiver of the right to bring civil proceedings in respect of conduct other than the conduct which has given rise to the enforcement order or undertaking.
(8)   The following definitions apply for the purposes of subsection (4)(a).
(9)   In the case of an enforcement order or undertaking under section 217, "a loss case" means a case in which—
   (a)   subsection (1) of that section applies (a finding that a person has engaged in conduct which constitutes an infringement), and
   (b)   consumers have suffered loss as a result of that conduct.
(10)   In the case of an undertaking under section 219, "a loss case" means a case in which—
   (a)   subsection (3)(a) or (b) of that section applies (a belief that a person has engaged or is engaging in conduct which constitutes an infringement), and
   (b)   consumers have suffered loss as a result of that conduct.]

NOTES

Commencement: 1 October 2015.
Inserted as noted to s 219A at **[1.1811]**.

[1.1813]
[219C   Availability of enhanced consumer measures to private enforcers
(1)   An enforcement order made on the application of a designated enforcer which is not a public body may require a person to take enhanced consumer measures only if the following conditions are satisfied.
(2)   An undertaking given under section 217(9) following an application for an enforcement order made by a designated enforcer which is not a public body, or an undertaking given to such an enforcer under section 219, may include a further undertaking by a person to take enhanced consumer measures only if the following conditions are satisfied.
(3)   The first condition is that the enforcer is specified for the purposes of this section by order made by the Secretary of State.
(4)   The second condition is that the enhanced consumer measures do not directly benefit the enforcer or an associated undertaking.
(5)   Enhanced consumer measures which directly benefit an enforcer or an associated undertaking include, in particular, measures which—
   (a)   require a person to pay money to the enforcer or associated undertaking,
   (b)   require a person to participate in a scheme which is designed to recommend persons supplying or seeking to supply goods or services to consumers and which is administered by the the enforcer or associated undertaking, or
   (c)   would give the enforcer or associated undertaking a commercial advantage over any of its competitors.
(6)   The Secretary of State may make an order under subsection (3) specifying an enforcer only if the Secretary of State is satisfied that to do so is likely to—
   (a)   improve the availability to consumers of redress for infringements to which the enforcer's designation relates,
   (b)   improve the availability to consumers of information which enables them to choose more effectively between persons supplying or seeking to supply goods or services, or
   (c)   improve compliance with consumer law.
(7)   The Secretary of State may make an order under subsection (3) specifying an enforcer only if the functions of the enforcer under this Part have been specified under section 24 of the Legislative and Regulatory Reform Act 2006 (functions to which principles under section 21 and code of practice under section 22 apply), to the extent that they are capable of being so specified.
(8)   The power to make an order under subsection (3)—
   (a)   is exercisable by statutory instrument subject to annulment in pursuance of a resolution of either House of Parliament;

(b) includes power to make incidental, supplementary, consequential, transitional, transitory or saving provision.

(9) Subsection (10) applies if—

(a) an enforcer exercises a function in relation to a person by virtue of subsection (1) or (2),

(b) that function is a relevant function for the purposes of Part 2 (co-ordination of regulatory enforcement) of the Regulatory Enforcement and Sanctions Act 2008, and

(c) a primary authority (within the meaning of that Part) has given advice or guidance under section 27(1) of that Act—

(i) to that person in relation to that function, or

(ii) to other local authorities (within the meaning of that Part) with that function as to how they should exercise it in relation to that person.

(10) The enforcer must, in exercising the function in relation to that person, act consistently with that advice or guidance.

(11) In this section "associated undertaking", in relation to a designated enforcer, means—

(a) a parent undertaking or subsidiary undertaking of the enforcer, or

(b) a subsidiary undertaking of a parent undertaking of the enforcer,

and for this purpose "parent undertaking" and "subsidiary undertaking" have the meanings given by section 1162 of the Companies Act 2006.]

NOTES

Commencement: 1 October 2015.

Inserted as noted to s 219A at **[1.1811]**.

[1.1814]
220 Further proceedings

(1) This section applies if the court—

(a) makes an enforcement order under section 217,

(b) makes an interim enforcement order under section 218, or

(c) accepts an undertaking under either of those sections.

[(1A) This section does not apply in the case of a failure to comply with an order or undertaking which consists only of a failure to provide information or documents required by the order or undertaking as described in section 217(10D).]

(2) [Any CPC enforcer] has the same right to apply to the court in respect of a failure to comply with the order or undertaking as the enforcer who made the application for the order.

(3) An application to the court in respect of a failure to comply with an undertaking may include an application for an enforcement order or for an interim enforcement order.

(4) If the court finds that an undertaking is not being complied with it may make an enforcement order or an interim enforcement order (instead of making any other order it has power to make).

(5) In the case of an application for an enforcement order or for an interim enforcement order as mentioned in subsection (3) sections 214 and 216 must be ignored and [sections 215, 217 or 218 (as the case may be) and 219A, 219B and 219C] apply subject to the following modifications—

(a) section 215(1)(b) must be ignored;

(b) section 215(5) must be ignored and the application must be made to the court which accepted the undertaking;

[(c) section 217(9), (10), (10B) and (11) must be ignored, and section 217(10C) and (10D) must be ignored to the extent that they relate to an undertaking under section 217(9);]

(d) section 218(10) must be ignored.

[(e) sections 219A, 219B and 219C must be ignored to the extent that they relate to an undertaking under section 217(9) or 219.]

(6) If an enforcer which is not the [CMA] makes an application in respect of the failure of a person to comply with an enforcement order, an interim enforcement order or an undertaking given under section 217 or 218 the enforcer must notify the [CMA]—

(a) of the application;

(b) of any order made by the court on the application.

NOTES

Sub-s (1A): inserted by the Consumer Rights Act 2015, s 79(1), Sch 7, paras 1, 9(1), (2).

Sub-s (2): words in square brackets substituted by the Consumer Rights Act 2015, s 79(1), Sch 7, paras 1, 9(1), (3).

Sub-s (5): words in first pair of square brackets and para (c) substituted, and para (e) added, by the Consumer Rights Act 2015, s 79(1), Sch 7, paras 1, 9(1), (4).

Sub-s (6): words in square brackets substituted by the Enterprise and Regulatory Reform Act 2013 (Competition) (Consequential, Transitional and Saving Provisions) Order 2014, SI 2014/892, art 2, Sch 1, Pt 1, paras 1, 11.

[1.1815]
221 Community infringements: proceedings

(1) Subsection (2) applies to—

(a) every general enforcer;

(b) every designated enforcer which is a public body.

(2) An enforcer to which this subsection applies has power to take proceedings in EEA States other than the United Kingdom for the cessation or prohibition of a Community infringement.

(3)   Subsection (4) applies to—
  (a)   every general enforcer;
  (b)   every designated enforcer;
  [(c)   every CPC enforcer.]
(4)   An enforcer to which this subsection applies may co-operate with a Community enforcer—
  (a)   for the purpose of bringing proceedings mentioned in subsection (2);
  (b)   in connection with the exercise by the Community enforcer of its functions under this Part.
(5)   An EEA State is a State which is a contracting party to the Agreement on the European Economic Area signed at Oporto on 2nd May 1992 as adjusted by the Protocol signed at Brussels on 17th March 1993.

NOTES

Sub-s (3): para (c) added by the Enterprise Act 2002 (Amendment) Regulations 2006, SI 2006/3363, regs 3, 14.

[1.1816]
222   Bodies corporate: accessories
(1)   This section applies if the person whose conduct constitutes a domestic infringement or a Community infringement is a body corporate.
(2)   If the conduct takes place with the consent or connivance of a person (an accessory) who has a special relationship with the body corporate, the consent or connivance is also conduct which constitutes the infringement.
(3)   A person has a special relationship with a body corporate if he is—
  (a)   a controller of the body corporate, or
  (b)   a director, manager, secretary or other similar officer of the body corporate or a person purporting to act in such a capacity.
(4)   A person is a controller of a body corporate if—
  (a)   the directors of the body corporate or of another body corporate which is its controller are accustomed to act in accordance with the person's directions or instructions, or
  (b)   either alone or with an associate or associates he is entitled to exercise or control the exercise of one third or more of the voting power at any general meeting of the body corporate or of another body corporate which is its controller.
(5)   An enforcement order or an interim enforcement order may be made against an accessory in respect of an infringement whether or not such an order is made against the body corporate.
(6)   The court may accept an undertaking under section 217(9) or 218(10) from an accessory in respect of an infringement whether or not it accepts such an undertaking from the body corporate.
(7)   An enforcer may accept an undertaking under section 219 from an accessory in respect of an infringement whether or not it accepts such an undertaking from the body corporate.
(8)   Subsection (9) applies if—
  (a)   an order is made as mentioned in subsection (5), or
  (b)   an undertaking is accepted as mentioned in subsection (6) or (7).
(9)   In such a case for subsection (6) of section 217, subsection (3) of section 218 or subsection (4) of section 219 (as the case may be) there is substituted the following subsection—

  "()   A person complies with this subsection if he—
    (a)   does not continue or repeat the conduct;
    (b)   does not in the course of any business carried on by him engage in conduct such as that which constitutes the infringement committed by the body corporate mentioned in section 222(1);
    (c)   does not consent to or connive in the carrying out of such conduct by another body corporate with which he has a special relationship (within the meaning of section 222(3))."

(10)   A person is an associate of an individual if—
  (a)   he is the spouse [or civil partner] of the individual;
  (b)   he is a relative of the individual;
  (c)   he is a relative of the individual's spouse [or civil partner];
  (d)   he is the spouse [or civil partner] of a relative of the individual;
  (e)   he is the spouse [or civil partner] of a relative of the individual's spouse [or civil partner];
  (f)   he lives in the same household as the individual otherwise than merely because he or the individual is the other's employer, tenant, lodger or boarder;
  (g)   he is a relative of a person who is an associate of the individual by virtue of paragraph (f);
  (h)   he has at some time in the past fallen within any of paragraphs (a) to (g).
(11)   A person is also an associate of—
  (a)   an individual with whom he is in partnership;
  (b)   an individual who is an associate of the individual mentioned in paragraph (a);
  (c)   a body corporate if he is a controller of it or he is an associate of a person who is a controller of the body corporate.
(12)   A body corporate is an associate of another body corporate if—
  (a)   the same person is a controller of both;

(b)   a person is a controller of one and persons who are his associates are controllers of the other;

(c)   a person is a controller of one and he and persons who are his associates are controllers of the other;

(d)   a group of two or more persons is a controller of each company and the groups consist of the same persons;

(e)   a group of two or more persons is a controller of each company and the groups may be regarded as consisting of the same persons by treating (in one or more cases) a member of either group as replaced by a person of whom he is an associate.

(13)   A relative is a brother, sister, uncle, aunt, nephew, niece, lineal ancestor or lineal descendant.

NOTES

Sub-s (10): words in square brackets inserted by the Civil Partnership Act 2004, s 261(1), Sch 27, para 169.

[1.1817]
223   Bodies corporate: orders

(1)   This section applies if a court makes an enforcement order or an interim enforcement order against a body corporate and—

(a)   at the time the order is made the body corporate is a member of a group of interconnected bodies corporate,

(b)   at any time when the order is in force the body corporate becomes a member of a group of interconnected bodies corporate, or

(c)   at any time when the order is in force a group of interconnected bodies corporate of which the body corporate is a member is increased by the addition of one or more further members.

(2)   The court may direct that the order is binding upon all of the members of the group as if each of them were the body corporate against which the order is made.

(3)   A group of interconnected bodies corporate is a group consisting of two or more bodies corporate all of whom are interconnected with each other.

(4)   Any two bodies corporate are interconnected—

(a)   if one of them is a subsidiary of the other, or

(b)   if both of them are subsidiaries of the same body corporate.

[(5)   In this section "subsidiary" has the meaning given by section 1159 of the Companies Act 2006.]

NOTES

Sub-s (5): substituted by the Companies Act 2006 (Consequential Amendments, Transitional Provisions and Savings) Order 2009, SI 2009/1941, art 2(1), Sch 1, para 199(1), (4).

Information

[1.1818]
224   [CMA]

(1)   The [CMA] may for any of the purposes mentioned in subsection (2) give notice to any person requiring the person to provide it with the information specified in the notice.

(2)   The purposes are—

(a)   to enable the [CMA] to exercise or to consider whether to exercise any function it has under this Part;

(b)   to enable a designated enforcer to which section 225 does not apply to consider whether to exercise any function it has under this Part;

(c)   to enable a Community enforcer to consider whether to exercise any function it has under this Part;

(d)   to ascertain whether a person has complied with or is complying with an enforcement order, an interim enforcement order or an undertaking given under section 217(9), 218(10) or 219.

NOTES

Repealed by the Consumer Rights Act 2015, s 77(2), Sch 6, paras 67, 68, as from 1 October 2015 (for transitional provisions see the Consumer Rights Act 2015 (Commencement No 3, Transitional Provisions, Savings and Consequential Amendments) Order 2015, SI 2015/1630, arts 6–8 at **[2.1220]** et seq).

Words in square brackets substituted by the Enterprise and Regulatory Reform Act 2013 (Competition) (Consequential, Transitional and Saving Provisions) Order 2014, SI 2014/892, art 2, Sch 1, Pt 1, paras 1, 12.

[1.1819]
225   Other enforcers

(1)   This section applies to—

(a)   every general enforcer (other than the [CMA]);

(b)   every designated enforcer which is a public body;

[(c)   every CPC enforcer (other than the [CMA]).]

(2) An enforcer to which this section applies may for any of the purposes mentioned in subsection (3) give notice to any person requiring the person to provide the enforcer with the information specified in the notice.

(3) The purposes are—

   (a) to enable the enforcer to exercise or to consider whether to exercise any function it has under this Part;

   (b) to ascertain whether a person has complied with or is complying with an enforcement order or an interim enforcement order made on the application of the enforcer or an undertaking given under section 217(9) or 218(10) (as the case may be) following such an application or an undertaking given to the enforcer under section 219.

NOTES

Repealed by the Consumer Rights Act 2015, s 77(2), Sch 6, paras 67, 69, as from 1 October 2015 (for transitional provisions see the Consumer Rights Act 2015 (Commencement No 3, Transitional Provisions, Savings and Consequential Amendments) Order 2015, SI 2015/1630, arts 6–8 at **[2.1220]** et seq).

Sub-s (1): words in square brackets in paras (a), (c) substituted by the Enterprise and Regulatory Reform Act 2013 (Competition) (Consequential, Transitional and Saving Provisions) Order 2014, SI 2014/892, art 2, Sch 1, Pt 1, paras 1, 13; para (c) added by the Enterprise Act 2002 (Amendment) Regulations 2006, SI 2006/3363, regs 3, 15.

[1.1820]
226 Notices: procedure

(1) This section applies to a notice given under section 224 or 225.

(2) The notice must—

   (a) be in writing;

   (b) specify the purpose for which the information is required.

(3) If the purpose is as mentioned in section 224(2)(a), (b) or (c) or 225(3)(a) the notice must specify the function concerned.

(4) A notice may specify the time within which and manner in which it is to be complied with.

(5) A notice may require the production of documents or any description of documents.

(6) An enforcer may take copies of any documents produced in compliance with such a requirement.

[(6A) A notice may specify the form in which information is to be provided.]

(7) A notice may be varied or revoked by a subsequent notice.

(8) But a notice must not require a person to provide any information or produce any document which he would be entitled to refuse to provide or produce—

   (a) in proceedings in the High Court on the grounds of legal professional privilege;

   (b) in proceedings in the Court of Session on the grounds of confidentiality of communications.

NOTES

Repealed by the Consumer Rights Act 2015, s 77(2), Sch 6, paras 67, 70, as from 1 October 2015 (for transitional provisions see the Consumer Rights Act 2015 (Commencement No 3, Transitional Provisions, Savings and Consequential Amendments) Order 2015, SI 2015/1630, arts 6–8 at **[2.1220]** et seq).

Sub-s (6A): inserted by the Enterprise Act 2002 (Amendment) Regulations 2006, SI 2006/3363, regs 3, 16.

[1.1821]
227 Notices: enforcement

(1) If a person fails to comply with a notice given under section 224 or 225 the enforcer who gave the notice may make an application under this section.

(2) If it appears to the court that the person to whom the notice was given has failed to comply with the notice the court may make an order under this section.

(3) An order under this section may require the person to whom the notice was given to do anything the court thinks it is reasonable for him to do for any of the purposes mentioned in section 224 or 225 (as the case may be) to ensure that the notice is complied with.

(4) An order under this section may require the person to meet all the costs or expenses of the application.

(5) If the person is a company or association the court in proceeding under subsection (4) may require any officer of the company or association who is responsible for the failure to meet the costs or expenses.

(6) The court is a court which may make an enforcement order.

(7) In subsection (5) an officer of a company is a person who is a director, manager, secretary or other similar officer of the company.

NOTES

Repealed by the Consumer Rights Act 2015, s 77(2), Sch 6, paras 67, 71, as from 1 October 2015 (for transitional provisions see the Consumer Rights Act 2015 (Commencement No 3, Transitional Provisions, Savings and Consequential Amendments) Order 2015, SI 2015/1630, arts 6–8 at **[2.1220]** et seq).

[1.1822]
[227A   Power to enter premises without warrant
(1)   An officer of a CPC enforcer who reasonably suspects that there has been, or is likely to be, a Community infringement may for any purpose relating to the functions of the CPC enforcer under this Part enter any premises to investigate whether there has been, or is likely to be, such an infringement.
(2)   An officer of a CPC enforcer who reasonably suspects that there is, or has been, a failure to comply with a relevant enforcement measure may for any purpose relating to the functions of the CPC enforcer under this Part enter any premises to investigate whether a person is complying with, or has complied with, the relevant enforcement measure.
(3)   An appropriate notice must be given to the occupier of the premises before an officer of a CPC enforcer enters them under subsection (1) and (2).
(4)   An appropriate notice is a notice in writing given by an officer of a CPC enforcer which—
(a)   gives at least two working days' notice of entry on the premises;
(b)   sets out why the entry is necessary; and
(c)   indicates the nature of the offence created by section 227E.
(5)   Subsection (3) does not apply if such a notice cannot be given despite all reasonably practicable steps having been taken to do so.
(6)   In that case, the officer entering the premises must produce to any occupier that he finds on the premises a document setting out why the entry is necessary and indicating the nature of the offence created by section 227E.
(7)   In all cases, the officer entering the premises must produce to any occupier evidence of—
(a)   his identity; and
(b)   in the case of an authorised officer of a CPC enforcer, his authorisation;
if asked to do so.
(8)   In this section—
"give", in relation to the giving of a notice to the occupier of premises, includes delivering or leaving it at the premises or sending it there by post; and
"working day" means a day which is not—
(a)   Saturday or Sunday; or
(b)   Christmas Day, Good Friday or a day which is a bank holiday under the Banking and Financial Dealings Act 1971 in the part of the United Kingdom in which the premises are situated.
(9)   In this section and sections 227B to 227F—
"authorised officer of a CPC enforcer" means an officer of a CPC enforcer who is authorised by that enforcer for the purposes of this Part;
"occupier" means any person whom the officer concerned reasonably suspects to be the occupier;
"officer of a CPC enforcer" means—
(a)   an officer of a local weights and measures authority in Great Britain; or
(b)   an authorised officer of a CPC enforcer which is not a local weights and measures authority in Great Britain;
"premises" includes vehicles but does not include any premises which are used only as a dwelling; and
"relevant enforcement measure" means—
(a)   an enforcement order made under section 217 on the application of the CPC enforcer;
(b)   an interim enforcement order made under section 218 on the application of the CPC enforcer;
(c)   an undertaking under section 217(9) in connection with an application made by the CPC enforcer for an enforcement order under section 217;
(d)   an undertaking under section 218(10) in connection with an application made by the CPC enforcer for an interim enforcement order under section 218; or
(e)   an undertaking under section 219 to the CPC enforcer.]

NOTES
Inserted, together with ss 227B–227F, by the Enterprise Act 2002 (Amendment) Regulations 2006, SI 2006/3363, regs 3, 17.
Repealed by the Consumer Rights Act 2015, s 77(2), Sch 6, paras 67, 72, as from 1 October 2015 (for transitional provisions see the Consumer Rights Act 2015 (Commencement No 3, Transitional Provisions, Savings and Consequential Amendments) Order 2015, SI 2015/1630, arts 6–8 at **[2.1220]** et seq).

[1.1823]
[227B   Powers exercisable on the premises
(1)   An officer of a CPC enforcer may, in the exercise of his powers under section 227A—
(a)   observe the carrying on of a business on the premises;
(b)   inspect goods or documents on the premises;
(c)   require any person on the premises to produce goods or documents within such period as the officer considers to be reasonable;

(d) seize goods or documents to carry out tests on them on the premises or seize, remove and retain them to carry out tests on them elsewhere; or

(e) seize, remove and retain goods or documents which he reasonably suspects may be required as evidence of a Community infringement or a breach of a relevant enforcement measure.

(2) The power in subsection (1)(c) to require a person to produce goods or documents includes the power to require him—

(a) to state, to the best of his knowledge and belief, where the goods or documents are;

(b) to give an explanation of the goods or documents; and

(c) to secure that any goods or documents produced are authenticated or verified in such manner as the officer considers appropriate.

(3) An officer of a CPC enforcer may take copies of, or extracts from, any documents to which he has access by virtue of subsection (1).

(4) But nothing in this section authorises action to be taken in relation to anything which, in proceedings in the High Court, a person would be entitled to refuse to produce on the grounds of legal professional privilege.

(5) In this section document includes information recorded in any form.

(6) The reference in subsection (1)(c) to the production of documents is, in the case of a document which contains information recorded otherwise than in legible form, a reference to the production of a copy of the information in legible form.

(7) (Applies to Scotland only.)]

NOTES

Inserted as noted to s 227A at **[1.1822]**.

Repealed by the Consumer Rights Act 2015, s 77(2), Sch 6, paras 67, 73, as from 1 October 2015 (for transitional provisions see the Consumer Rights Act 2015 (Commencement No 3, Transitional Provisions, Savings and Consequential Amendments) Order 2015, SI 2015/1630, arts 6–8 at **[2.1220]** et seq).

[1.1824]
[227C   Power to enter premises with warrant
(1)   A justice of the peace may issue a warrant authorising an officer of a CPC enforcer to enter premises for purposes falling within section 227A(1) or (2) if the justice of the peace considers that there are reasonable grounds for believing that—

(a) condition A is met; and

(b) either condition B, C or D is met.

(2)   Condition A is that there are, on the premises, goods or documents to which an officer of a CPC enforcer would be entitled to have access under sections 227A and 227B.

(3)   Condition B is that an officer of a CPC enforcer acting under sections 227A and 227B has been, or would be likely to be, refused admission to the premises or access to the goods or documents.

(4)   Condition C is that the goods or documents would be likely to be concealed or interfered with if an appropriate notice were given under section 227A.

(5)   Condition D is that there is likely to be nobody at the premises capable of granting admission.

(6)   A warrant under this section authorises the officer of the CPC enforcer—

(a) to enter the premises specified in the warrant (using reasonable force if necessary);

(b) to do anything on the premises that an officer of the CPC enforcer would be able to do if he had entered the premises under section 227A;

(c) to search for goods or documents which he has required a person on the premises to produce where that person has failed to comply with such a requirement;

(d) to the extent that it is reasonably necessary to do so, to require any person to whom subsection (7) applies to break open a container and, if that person does not comply with the requirement, or if such a person cannot be identified after all reasonably practicable steps have been taken to identify such a person, to do so himself;

(e) to take any other steps which he considers to be reasonably necessary to preserve, or prevent interference with, goods or documents to which he would be entitled to have access under sections 227A and 227B.

(7)   This subsection applies to a person who is responsible for discharging any of the functions of the business being carried on at the premises under inspection.

(8)   A warrant under this section—

(a) is issued on information on oath given by an officer of a CPC enforcer;

(b) ceases to have effect at the end of the period of one month beginning with the day of issue; and

(c) must, on request, be produced to the occupier of the premises for inspection.

(9)   Any reference in this section to goods or documents being interfered with includes a reference to them being destroyed.

(10)   (Applies to Scotland only.)

(11)   In its application to Northern Ireland, this section has effect as if the references in subsection (1) to a justice of the peace were references to a lay magistrate.]

NOTES

Inserted as noted to s 227A at **[1.1822]**.

Repealed by the Consumer Rights Act 2015, s 77(2), Sch 6, paras 67, 74, as from 1 October 2015 (for transitional provisions see the Consumer Rights Act 2015 (Commencement No 3, Transitional Provisions, Savings and Consequential Amendments) Order 2015, SI 2015/1630, arts 6–8 at **[2.1220]** et seq).

[1.1825]
[227D　Ancillary provisions about powers of entry
(1)　An officer of a CPC enforcer who enters premises by virtue of section 227A may only do so at a reasonable time.
(2)　An officer of a CPC enforcer who enters premises by virtue of section 227A or 227C may take with him such persons and equipment as he considers appropriate.
(3)　An officer of a CPC enforcer who enters premises by virtue of section 227A or 227C must, if the premises are unoccupied or the occupier is temporarily absent, take reasonable steps to ensure that when he leaves the premises they are as secure as they were before he entered.]

NOTES

Inserted as noted to s 227A at **[1.1822]**.

Repealed by the Consumer Rights Act 2015, s 77(2), Sch 6, paras 67, 75, as from 1 October 2015 (for transitional provisions see the Consumer Rights Act 2015 (Commencement No 3, Transitional Provisions, Savings and Consequential Amendments) Order 2015, SI 2015/1630, arts 6–8 at **[2.1220]** et seq).

[1.1826]
[227E　Obstructing, or failing to co-operate with, powers of entry
(1)　A person commits an offence if, without reasonable excuse, he intentionally obstructs, or fails to co-operate with, an officer of a CPC enforcer who is exercising or seeking to exercise a power under sections 227A to 227D.
(2)　A person guilty of an offence under subsection (1) is liable, on summary conviction, to a fine not exceeding level 5 on the standard scale.]

NOTES

Inserted as noted to s 227A at **[1.1822]**.

Repealed by the Consumer Rights Act 2015, s 77(2), Sch 6, paras 67, 76, as from 1 October 2015 (for transitional provisions see the Consumer Rights Act 2015 (Commencement No 3, Transitional Provisions, Savings and Consequential Amendments) Order 2015, SI 2015/1630, arts 6–8 at **[2.1220]** et seq).

[1.1827]
[227F　Retention of documents and goods
(1)　No documents seized under sections 227A to 227D may be retained for a period of more than three months.
(2)　No goods seized under sections 227A to 227D may be retained for a period of more than three months unless they are reasonably required in connection with the exercise of any function of a CPC enforcer under this Part.
(3)　Where goods are so required they may be retained for as long as they are so required.]

NOTES

Inserted as noted to s 227A at **[1.1822]**.

Repealed by the Consumer Rights Act 2015, s 77(2), Sch 6, paras 67, 77, as from 1 October 2015 (for transitional provisions see the Consumer Rights Act 2015 (Commencement No 3, Transitional Provisions, Savings and Consequential Amendments) Order 2015, SI 2015/1630, arts 6–8 at **[2.1220]** et seq).

Miscellaneous
[1.1828]
[223A　Investigatory powers
For the investigatory powers available to enforcers for the purposes of enforcers' functions under this Part, see Schedule 5 to the Consumer Rights Act 2015.]

NOTES

Commencement: 1 October 2015.

Inserted by the Consumer Rights Act 2015, s 77(2), Sch 6, paras 67, 78, as from 1 October 2015 (for transitional provisions see the Consumer Rights Act 2015 (Commencement No 3, Transitional Provisions, Savings and Consequential Amendments) Order 2015, SI 2015/1630, arts 6–8 at **[2.1220]** et seq).

[1.1829]
228　Evidence
(1)　Proceedings under this Part are civil proceedings for the purposes of—
　(a)　section 11 of the Civil Evidence Act 1968 (c 64) (convictions admissible as evidence in civil proceedings);
　(b)　section 10 of the Law Reform (Miscellaneous Provisions) (Scotland) Act 1968 (c 70) (corresponding provision in Scotland);

(c) section 7 of the Civil Evidence Act (Northern Ireland) 1971 (c 36 (NI)) (corresponding provision in Northern Ireland).

(2) In proceedings under this Part any finding by a court in civil proceedings that an act or omission mentioned in section 211(2)(b), (c) or (d) or 212(1) has occurred—

(a) is admissible as evidence that the act or omission occurred;

(b) unless the contrary is proved, is sufficient evidence that the act or omission occurred.

(3) But subsection (2) does not apply to any finding—

(a) which has been reversed on appeal;

(b) which has been varied on appeal so as to negative it.

[(4) *This section does not apply to proceedings for an offence under section 227E.*]

NOTES

Sub-s (4): added by the Enterprise Act 2002 (Amendment) Regulations 2006, SI 2006/3363, regs 3, 18; repealed by the Consumer Rights Act 2015, s 77(2), Sch 6, paras 67, 79, as from 1 October 2015 (for transitional provisions see the Consumer Rights Act 2015 (Commencement No 3, Transitional Provisions, Savings and Consequential Amendments) Order 2015, SI 2015/1630, arts 6–8 at **[2.1220]** et seq).

[1.1830]
229 Advice and information

(1) [The CMA] must prepare and publish advice and information with a view to—

(a) explaining the provisions of this Part to persons who are likely to be affected by them, and

(b) indicating how the [CMA] expects such provisions to operate.

[(1A) As soon as is reasonably practicable after the commencement of Schedule 5 to the Consumer Rights Act 2015 (investigatory powers etc) the CMA must prepare and publish advice and information with a view to—

(a) explaining the provisions of that Schedule, so far as they relate to investigatory powers exercised for the purposes set out in paragraphs 13(2) and (3) and 19 of that Schedule, to persons who are likely to be affected by them, and

(b) indicating how the CMA expects such provisions to operate.]

(2) The [CMA] may at any time publish revised or new advice or information.

(3) Advice or information published in pursuance of subsection (1)(b) may include advice or information about the factors which the [CMA] may take into account in considering how to exercise the functions conferred on it by this Part.

(4) Advice or information published by the [CMA] under this section is to be published in such form and in such manner as it considers appropriate.

(5) In preparing advice or information under this section the [CMA] must consult such persons as it thinks are representative of persons affected by this Part.

(6) If any proposed advice or information relates to a matter in respect of which another general [or CPC] enforcer or a designated enforcer may act the persons to be consulted must include that enforcer.

NOTES

Sub-ss (1)–(5): words in square brackets substituted by the Enterprise and Regulatory Reform Act 2013 (Competition) (Consequential, Transitional and Saving Provisions) Order 2014, SI 2014/892, art 2, Sch 1, Pt 1, paras 1, 14.

Sub-s (1A): inserted by the Consumer Rights Act 2015, s 79(1), Sch 7, paras 1, 10.

Sub-s (6): words in square brackets inserted by the Enterprise Act 2002 (Amendment) Regulations 2006, SI 2006/3363, regs 3, 19.

[1.1831]
230 Notice to [CMA] of intended prosecution

(1) This section applies if a local weights and measures authority in England and Wales intends to start proceedings for an offence under an enactment or subordinate legislation specified by the Secretary of State by order for the purposes of this section.

(2) The authority must give the [CMA]—

(a) notice of its intention to start the proceedings;

(b) . . .

(3) The authority must not start the proceedings until whichever is the earlier of the following—

(a) the end of the period of 14 days starting with the day on which the authority gives the notice;

(b) the day on which it is notified by the [CMA] that the [CMA] has received the notice . . . given under subsection (2).

(4) The authority must also notify the [CMA] of the outcome of the proceedings after they are finally determined.

(5) But such proceedings are not invalid by reason only of the failure of the authority to comply with this section.

(6) Subordinate legislation has the same meaning as in section 21(1) of the Interpretation Act 1978 (c 30).

(7) An order under this section must be made by statutory instrument subject to annulment in pursuance of a resolution of either House of Parliament.

NOTES

Section heading, sub-ss (1)–(4): words in square brackets substituted and words omitted repealed by, or by virtue of, the Enterprise and Regulatory Reform Act 2013 (Competition) (Consequential, Transitional and Saving Provisions) Order 2014, SI 2014/892, art 2, Sch 1, Pt 1, paras 1, 15.

Orders: the Enterprise Act 2002 (Part 8 Notice to OFT of Intended Prosecution Specified Enactments, Revocation and Transitional Provision) Order 2003, SI 2003/1376; the Enterprise Act 2002 (Part 8 Notice to OFT of Intended Prosecution Specified Enactments) Order 2006, SI 2006/3371.

[1.1832]
231 Notice of convictions and judgments to [CMA]
(1) This section applies if—
- (a) a person is convicted of an offence by or before a court in the United Kingdom, or
- (b) a judgment is given against a person by a court in civil proceedings in the United Kingdom.

(2) The court may make arrangements to bring the conviction or judgment to the attention of the [CMA] if it appears to the court—
- (a) having regard to the functions of the [CMA] under this Part . . . that it is expedient for the conviction or judgment to be brought to the attention of the [CMA], and
- (b) without such arrangements the conviction or judgment may not be brought to the attention of the [CMA].

(3) For the purposes of subsection (2) it is immaterial that the proceedings have been finally disposed of by the court.

(4) Judgment includes an order or decree and references to the giving of the judgment must be construed accordingly.

NOTES

Section heading: word in square brackets substituted by the Enterprise and Regulatory Reform Act 2013 (Competition) (Consequential, Transitional and Saving Provisions) Order 2014, SI 2014/892, art 2, Sch 1, Pt 1, paras 1, 16.

Sub-s (2): words in square brackets substituted by the Enterprise and Regulatory Reform Act 2013 (Competition) (Consequential, Transitional and Saving Provisions) Order 2014, SI 2014/892, art 2, Sch 1, Pt 1, paras 1, 16; words omitted from para (a) repealed by the Public Bodies (Abolition of the National Consumer Council and Transfer of the Office of Fair Trading's Functions in relation to Estate Agents etc) Order 2014, SI 2014/631, art 5(3)(a), Sch 2, Pt 1, para 4 (for transitional provisions and savings see art 5(3)(a), Sch 2, Pt 4 thereof at **[2.1133]**, **[2.1134A]**).

Orders: the Enterprise Act 2002 (Part 8 Notice to OFT of Intended Prosecution Specified Enactments, Revocation and Transitional Provision) Order 2003, SI 2003/1376; the Enterprise Act 2002 (Part 8 Notice to OFT of Intended Prosecution Specified Enactments) Order 2006, SI 2006/3371.

Interpretation

[1.1833]
232 Goods and services
(1) References in this Part to goods and services must be construed in accordance with this section.
(2) Goods include—
- (a) buildings and other structures;
- (b) ships, aircraft and hovercraft.

(3) The supply of goods includes—
- (a) supply by way of sale, lease, hire or hire purchase;
- (b) in relation to buildings and other structures, construction of them by one person for another.

(4) Goods or services which are supplied wholly or partly outside the United Kingdom must be taken to be supplied to or for a person in the United Kingdom if they are supplied in accordance with arrangements falling within subsection (5).

(5) Arrangements fall within this subsection if they are made by any means and—
- (a) at the time the arrangements are made the person seeking the supply is in the United Kingdom, or
- (b) at the time the goods or services are supplied (or ought to be supplied in accordance with the arrangements) the person responsible under the arrangements for effecting the supply is in or has a place of business in the United Kingdom.

[1.1834]
233 Person supplying goods
(1) This section has effect for the purpose of references in this Part to a person supplying or seeking to supply goods under—
- (a) a hire-purchase agreement;
- (b) a credit-sale agreement;
- (c) a conditional sale agreement.

(2) The references include references to a person who conducts any antecedent negotiations relating to the agreement.

(3)   The following expressions must be construed in accordance with section 189 of the Consumer Credit Act 1974 (c 39)—

(a)   hire-purchase agreement;
(b)   credit-sale agreement;
(c)   conditional sale agreement;
(d)   antecedent negotiations.

[1.1835]
234   Supply of services
(1)   References in this Part to the supply of services must be construed in accordance with this section.
(2)   The supply of services does not include the provision of services under a contract of service or of apprenticeship whether it is express or implied and (if it is express) whether it is oral or in writing.
(3)   The supply of services includes—

(a)   performing for gain or reward any activity other than the supply of goods;
(b)   rendering services to order;
(c)   the provision of services by making them available to potential users.

(4)   The supply of services includes making arrangements for the use of computer software or for granting access to data stored in any form which is not readily accessible.
(5)   The supply of services includes making arrangements by means of a relevant agreement (within the meaning of [paragraph 29 of Schedule 2 to the Telecommunications Act 1984]) for sharing the use of telecommunications apparatus.
(6)   The supply of services includes permitting or making arrangements to permit the use of land in such circumstances as the Secretary of State specifies by order.
(7)   The power to make an order under subsection (6) must be exercised by statutory instrument.
(8)   But no such order may be made unless a draft of it has been laid before Parliament and approved by a resolution of each House.

NOTES
Sub-s (5): words in square brackets substituted by the Communications Act 2003, s 406(1), Sch 17, para 174(1), (6).
Orders: the Enterprise Act 2002 (Supply of Services) Order 2003, SI 2003/1594.

[1.1836]
235   Injunctions Directive
In this Part the Injunctions Directive is Directive 98/27/EC of the European Parliament and of the Council on injunctions for the protection of consumers' interests.

[1.1837]
[235A   CPC Regulation
In this Part—

(a)   the CPC Regulation is Regulation (EC) No 2006/2004 of the European Parliament and of the Council of 27 October 2004 on cooperation between national authorities responsible for the enforcement of consumer protection laws as amended by the Unfair Commercial Practices Directive;
(b)   the Unfair Commercial Practices Directive is Directive 2005/29/EC of the European Parliament and of the Council of 11 May 2005 concerning unfair business-to-consumer commercial practices in the internal market.]

NOTES
Inserted, together with s 235B, by the Enterprise Act 2002 (Amendment) Regulations 2006, SI 2006/3363, regs 3, 20.

[1.1838]
[235B   Dual enforcers
References in this Part to a general enforcer, a designated enforcer or a CPC enforcer are to be read, in the case of a person or body which is more than one kind of enforcer, as references to that person or body acting in its capacity as a general enforcer, designated enforcer or (as the case may be) CPC enforcer.]

NOTES
Inserted as noted to s 235A at **[1.1837]**.

Crown

[1.1839]
[236   Crown
(1)   This Part binds the Crown.
(2)   *But the powers conferred by sections 227A to 227D are not exercisable in relation to premises occupied by the Crown.*]

NOTES

Substituted by the Enterprise Act 2002 (Amendment) Regulations 2006, SI 2006/3363, regs 3, 21.

Sub-s (2): repealed by the Consumer Rights Act 2015, s 77(2), Sch 6, paras 67, 80, as from 1 October 2015 (for transitional provisions see the Consumer Rights Act 2015 (Commencement No 3, Transitional Provisions, Savings and Consequential Amendments) Order 2015, SI 2015/1630, arts 6–8 at **[2.1220]** et seq).

237–272   (*Ss 237–247 (Pt 9: Information); ss 248–272 (Pt 10: Insolvency) outside the scope of this work.*)

PART 11
SUPPLEMENTARY

[1.1840]
273   Interpretation
In this Act—
    "the 1973 Act" means the Fair Trading Act 1973 (c 41);
    "the 1998 Act" means the Competition Act 1998 (c 41);
    ["the CMA" means the Competition and Markets Authority;]
    "the Director" means the Director General of Fair Trading; and
    . . .

NOTES

Definition "the CMA" substituted (for original definition "the Commission") and definition "the OFT" (omitted) repealed by the Enterprise and Regulatory Reform Act 2013, s 26(3), Sch 5, Pt 2, paras 59, 217 (for transitional provisions (including those relating to the abolition of the OFT and the Competition Commission and the continuity of functions), see the Enterprise and Regulatory Reform Act 2013 (Commencement No 6, Transitional Provisions and Savings) Order 2014, SI 2014/416, Schedule at **[2.1126]**).

[1.1841]
274   Provision of financial assistance for consumer purposes
The Secretary of State may give financial assistance to any person for the purpose of assisting—
    (a)   activities which the Secretary of State considers are of benefit to consumers; or
    (b)   the provision of—
        (i)   advice or information about consumer matters;
        (ii)   educational materials relating to consumer matters; or
        (iii) advice or information to the Secretary of State in connection with the formulation of policy in respect of consumer matters.

[1.1842]
275   Financial provision
There shall be paid out of money provided by Parliament—
    (a)   any expenditure incurred by the OFT, the Secretary of State, any other Minister of the Crown or a government department by virtue of this Act; and
    (b)   any increase attributable to this Act in the sums payable out of money so provided by virtue of any other Act.

[1.1843]
276   Transitional or transitory provision and savings
(1)   Schedule 24 (which makes transitional and transitory provisions and savings) has effect.
(2)   The Secretary of State may by order made by statutory instrument make such transitional or transitory provisions and savings as he considers appropriate in connection with the coming into force of any provision of this Act.
(3)   An order under subsection (2) may modify any Act or subordinate legislation.
(4)   Schedule 24 does not restrict the power under subsection (2) to make other transitional or transitory provisions and savings.

NOTES

Orders: the Enterprise Act 2002 (Commencement No 2, Transitional and Transitory Provisions) Order 2003, SI 2003/766; the Enterprise Act 2002 (Commencement No 3, Transitional and Transitory Provisions and Savings) Order 2003, SI 2003/1397; the Enterprise Act 2002 (Part 8 Designated Enforcers: Criteria for Designation, Designation of Public Bodies as Designated Enforcers and Transitional Provisions) Order 2003, SI 2003/1399; the Enterprise Act 2002 (Commencement No 4 and Transitional Provisions and Savings) Order 2003, SI 2003/2093; the Enterprise Act 2002 (Transitional Provisions) (Insolvency) Order 2003, SI 2003/2332; the Enterprise Act 2002 (Commencement No 7 and Transitional Provisions and Savings) Order 2004, SI 2004/3233.

[1.1844]
277   Power to make consequential amendments etc
(1)   The Secretary of State may by order make such supplementary, incidental or consequential provision as he thinks appropriate—
    (a)   for the general purposes, or any particular purpose, of this Act; or

(b)　in consequence of any provision made by or under this Act or for giving full effect to it.

(2)　An order under this section may—

(a)　modify any Act or subordinate legislation (including this Act);

(b)　make incidental, supplementary, consequential, transitional, transitory or saving provision.

(3)　The power to make an order under this section is exercisable by statutory instrument subject to annulment in pursuance of a resolution of either House of Parliament.

(4)　The power conferred by this section is not restricted by any other provision of this Act.

NOTES

Orders: the Enterprise Act 2002 (Consequential and Supplemental Provisions) Order 2003, SI 2003/1398; the Enterprise Act 2002 (Insolvency) Order 2003, SI 2003/2096; the Enterprise Act 2002 and Media Mergers (Consequential Amendments) Order 2003, SI 2003/3180; the Enterprise Act 2002 (Part 9 Restrictions on Disclosure of Information) (Specification) Order 2004, SI 2004/693; the Enterprise Act 2002 (Insolvency) Order 2004, SI 2004/2312; the Enterprise Act 2002 (Enforcement Undertakings) Order 2006, SI 2006/354; the Enterprise Act 2002 (Enforcement Undertakings and Orders) Order 2006, SI 2006/355; the Enterprise Act 2002 (Enforcement Undertakings) (No 2) Order 2006, SI 2006/3095; the Enterprise Act 2002 (Part 8) (Designation of the Financial Conduct Authority as a Designated Enforcer) Order 2013, SI 2013/478.

278　(*Introduces Sch 25 (minor and consequential amendments) and Sch 26 (repeals and revocations).*)

[1.1845]
279　Commencement
The preceding provisions of this Act shall come into force on such day as the Secretary of State may by order made by statutory instrument appoint; and different days may be appointed for different purposes.

NOTES

Orders: the Enterprise Act 2002 (Commencement No 1) Order 2003, SI 2003/765; the Enterprise Act 2002 (Commencement No 2, Transitional and Transitory Provisions) Order 2003, SI 2003/766; the Enterprise Act 2002 (Commencement No 3, Transitional and Transitory Provisions and Savings) Order 2003, SI 2003/1397; the Enterprise Act 2002 (Commencement No 4 and Transitional Provisions and Savings) Order 2003, SI 2003/2093; the Enterprise Act 2002 (Commencement No 5 and Amendment) Order 2003, SI 2003/3340; the Enterprise Act 2002 (Commencement No 6) Order 2004, SI 2004/1866; the Enterprise Act 2002 (Commencement No 7 and Transitional Provisions and Savings) Order 2004, SI 2004/3233.

[1.1846]
280　Extent
(1)　Sections 256 to 265, 267, 269 and 272 extend only to England and Wales.

(2)　Sections 204, 248 to 255 and 270 extend only to England and Wales and Scotland (but subsection (3) of section 415A as inserted by section 270 extends only to England and Wales).

(3)　Any other modifications by this Act of an enactment have the same extent as the enactment being modified.

(4)　Otherwise, this Act extends to England and Wales, Scotland and Northern Ireland.

[1.1847]
281　Short title
This Act may be cited as the Enterprise Act 2002.

SCHEDULES

(*Sch 1 repealed by the Enterprise and Regulatory Reform Act 2013, s 26(3), Sch 5, Pt 4, para 229 (for transitional provisions (including those relating to the abolition of the OFT and the Competition Commission and the continuity of functions), see the Enterprise and Regulatory Reform Act 2013 (Commencement No 6, Transitional Provisions and Savings) Order 2014, SI 2014/416, Schedule at* **[2.1126]***).*)

SCHEDULE 2
THE COMPETITION APPEAL TRIBUNAL

Section 12

Appointment, etc of President and chairmen

[1.1848]
1. (1)　A person is not eligible for appointment as President unless—

[(a)　he satisfies the judicial-appointment eligibility condition on a 7-year basis;]

(b)　he is an advocate or solicitor in Scotland of at least [7] years' standing; or

(c)　he is a member of the Bar of Northern Ireland or [solicitor of the Court of Judicature of Northern Ireland] of at least [7] years' standing;

and he appears to the Lord Chancellor to have appropriate experience and knowledge of competition law and practice.

(2)　A person is not eligible for appointment as a chairman unless—

[(a)　he satisfies the judicial-appointment eligibility condition on a 5-year basis,]

(b)   he is an advocate or solicitor in Scotland of at least [5] years' standing; or

(c)   he is a member of the Bar of Northern Ireland or [solicitor of the Court of Judicature of Northern Ireland] of at least [5] years' standing;

and he appears to the Lord Chancellor to have appropriate experience and knowledge (either of competition law and practice or any other relevant law and practice).

(3)   Before appointing an advocate or solicitor in Scotland under this paragraph, the Lord Chancellor must consult the Lord President of the Court of Session.

(4)   . . .

[(5)   The Lord Chancellor may remove a person from office as President under sub-paragraph (4) only with the concurrence of all of the following—

(a)   the Lord Chief Justice of England and Wales;

(b)   the Lord President of the Court of Session;

(c)   the Lord Chief Justice of Northern Ireland.

(6)   The Lord Chancellor may remove a person from office as chairman under sub-paragraph (4) only with the concurrence of the appropriate senior judge.

(7)   The appropriate senior judge is the Lord Chief Justice of England and Wales, unless—

(a)   the person to be removed exercises functions wholly or mainly in Scotland, in which case it is the Lord President of the Court of Session, or

(b)   the person to be removed exercises functions wholly or mainly in Northern Ireland, in which case it is the Lord Chief Justice of Northern Ireland.]

2. (1)   The members appointed as President or as chairmen shall hold and vacate office in accordance with their terms of appointment, subject to the following provisions.

(2)   A person may not be a chairman for more than 8 years (but this does not prevent a temporary reappointment for the purpose of continuing to act as a member of the Tribunal as constituted for the purposes of any proceedings instituted before the end of his term of office).

(3)   The President and the chairmen may resign their offices by notice in writing to the Lord Chancellor.

(4)   The Lord Chancellor may remove a person from office as President or chairman on the ground of incapacity or misbehaviour.

3. If the President is absent or otherwise unable to act the Lord Chancellor may appoint as acting President any person qualified for appointment as a chairman.

Appointment, etc of ordinary members

4. (1)   Ordinary members shall hold and vacate office in accordance with their terms of appointment, subject to the following provisions.

(2)   A person may not be an ordinary member for more than 8 years (but this does not prevent a temporary reappointment for the purpose of continuing to act as a member of the Tribunal as constituted for the purposes of any proceedings instituted before the end of his term of office).

(3)   An ordinary member may resign his office by notice in writing to the Secretary of State.

(4)   The Secretary of State may remove a person from office as an ordinary member on the ground of incapacity or misbehaviour.

Remuneration etc for members

5. (1)   The Competition Service shall pay to the President, the chairmen and the ordinary members such remuneration (whether by way of salaries or fees), and such allowances, as the Secretary of State may determine.

(2)   The Competition Service shall, if required to do so by the Secretary of State—

(a)   pay such pension, allowances or gratuities as may be determined by the Secretary of State to or in respect of a person who holds or has held office as President, a chairman or an ordinary member; or

(b)   make such payments as may be so determined towards provision for the payment of a pension, allowance or gratuities to or in respect of such a person.

Compensation for loss of office

6. If, where any person ceases to hold office as President, a chairman or ordinary member, the Secretary of State determines that there are special circumstances which make it right that he should receive compensation, the Competition Service shall pay to him such amount by way of compensation as the Secretary of State may determine.

Staff, accommodation and property

7. Any staff, office accommodation or equipment required for the Tribunal shall be provided by the Competition Service.

Miscellaneous

8. The President must arrange such training for members of the Tribunal as he considers appropriate.

9. In this Schedule "chairman" and "ordinary member" mean respectively a member of the panel of chairmen, or a member of the panel of ordinary members, appointed under section 12.

10, 11. . . .

NOTES

Para 1: sub-paras (1)(a), (2)(a) and numbers in square brackets in sub-paras (1)(b), (c), (2)(b), (c) substituted and sub-para (4) repealed by the Tribunals, Courts and Enforcement Act 2007, ss 50, 146, Sch 10, Pt 1, para 36, Sch 23, Pt 2; words in square brackets in sub-paras (1)(c), (2)(c) substituted by the Constitutional Reform Act 2005, s 59(5), Sch 11, Pt 3, para 5.

Para 2: sub-paras (5)–(7) added by the Constitutional Reform Act 2005, s 15(1), Sch 4, Pt 1, paras 304, 306.

Paras 10, 11: amend the House of Commons Disqualification Act 1975, Sch 1, Pt II, and the Northern Ireland Assembly Disqualification Act 1975, Sch 1, Pt II.

SCHEDULES 3–26

(Schs 3–26 outside the scope of this work.)

FIREWORKS ACT 2003

(2003 c 22)

ARRANGEMENT OF SECTIONS

An Act to make provision about fireworks and other explosives

[18 September 2003]

Introductory

[1.1849]
1 Introduction
(1)   In this Act "fireworks" means devices which—
    (a)   are fireworks for the purposes of the British Standard Specification relating to fireworks published on 30th November 1988 (BS 7114) or any British Standard Specification replacing it, or
    (b)   would be fireworks for those purposes if they were intended as a form of entertainment.
(2)   The Secretary of State may by regulations substitute a new definition of "fireworks" for the definition in subsection (1).
(3)   References in this Act to supplying fireworks include—
    (a)   selling them,
    (b)   exchanging them for any consideration other than money, and
    (c)   giving them as a prize or otherwise making a gift of them,
but do not include supplying them otherwise than in the course of a business.

Fireworks regulations

[1.1850]
2 Power to make regulations about fireworks
(1)   The Secretary of State may by regulations ("fireworks regulations") make any provision which the Secretary of State considers appropriate—
    (a)   for securing that there is no risk that use of fireworks will have the consequences specified in subsection (2), or
    (b)   for securing that the risk that the use of fireworks will have those consequences is the minimum that is compatible with their being used.
(2)   The consequences are—
    (a)   death of persons or injury, alarm, distress or anxiety to persons,
    (b)   death of animals or injury or distress to animals, and
    (c)   destruction of, or damage to, property.
(3)   Before making fireworks regulations the Secretary of State must consult—
    (a)   [the Health and Safety Executive],
    (b)   organisations which appear to the Secretary of State to be representative of interests substantially affected by the proposal, and
    (c)   other persons whom the Secretary of State considers it appropriate to consult.

(4) Before making fireworks regulations the Secretary of State must issue a full regulatory impact assessment setting out details of the costs and benefits and the wider economic, social and environmental impact of the proposed regulations.

(5) But subsection (3) does not apply if the regulations are to—
  (a) cease to have effect at the end of the period of not more than twelve months beginning with the day on which they come into force, and
  (b) contain a statement that it appears to the Secretary of State that the need to protect the public requires that the regulations should be made without delay.

(6) The power to make fireworks regulations includes power—
  (a) to make different provision for different cases, and
  (b) to make any incidental, supplementary, consequential and transitional provision which the Secretary of State considers appropriate.

(7) Section 18 of the Consumer Protection Act 1987 (c 43) (power to require information for deciding whether to make, vary or revoke regulations under section 11 of that Act) applies in relation to fireworks regulations as in relation to regulations under section 11 of that Act.

(8) Nothing in this Act shall be construed as in any way limiting the provision that may be made in regulations under section 11 of the Consumer Protection Act 1987.

NOTES
Sub-s (3): words in square brackets substituted by the Legislative Reform (Health and Safety Executive) Order 2008, SI 2008/960, art 22, Sch 3, subject to transitional provisions in art 21 of, and Sch 2 to, that Order.
Regulations: the Fireworks Regulations 2004, SI 2004/1836; the Fireworks (Amendment) Regulations 2004, SI 2004/3262.

[1.1851]
3   Prohibition of supply etc to young persons
(1) Fireworks regulations may include provision prohibiting persons from—
  (a) supplying, or
  (b) offering or agreeing to supply,
fireworks, or fireworks of a description specified in the regulations, to persons who are below an age so specified.

(2) Fireworks regulations may include provision prohibiting the purchase or possession of fireworks, or fireworks of a description specified in the regulations, by persons who are below an age so specified.

(3) If fireworks regulations impose any prohibition by virtue of this section, they may contain—
  (a) exceptions from the prohibition, or
  (b) provision for the granting of dispensations from the prohibition.

NOTES
Regulations: the Fireworks Regulations 2004, SI 2004/1836.

[1.1852]
4   Prohibition of supply etc in certain circumstances
(1) Fireworks regulations may include provision prohibiting persons from supplying, purchasing, possessing or using fireworks, or fireworks of a description specified in the regulations, during hours of the day so specified.

(2) Fireworks regulations may include provision prohibiting persons from supplying, exposing for supply, purchasing, possessing or using fireworks, or fireworks of a description specified in the regulations—
  (a) in places or places of a description, or
  (b) in circumstances,
specified in the regulations.

(3) If fireworks regulations impose any prohibition by virtue of this section, they may contain—
  (a) exceptions from the prohibition, or
  (b) provision for the granting of dispensations from the prohibition.

NOTES
Regulations: the Fireworks Regulations 2004, SI 2004/1836; the Fireworks (Amendment) Regulations 2004, SI 2004/3262.

[1.1853]
5   Prohibition of supply etc of certain fireworks
(1) Fireworks regulations may include provision—
  (a) prohibiting persons from supplying, or offering or agreeing to supply, fireworks of a description specified in the regulations, or
  (b) prohibiting persons from supplying, or offering or agreeing to supply, fireworks of a description specified in the regulations to persons of a description so specified.

(2) Fireworks regulations may include provision—
  (a) prohibiting the purchase or possession of fireworks of a description specified in the regulations, or
  (b) prohibiting the purchase or possession of fireworks of a description specified in the regulations by persons of a description so specified.

(3)   Subsections (1) and (2) shall not apply to class I and class II fireworks.

(4)   The descriptions of persons which may be specified in fireworks regulations by virtue of subsection (1) or (2) include in particular persons who do not satisfy any conditions which are specified in the regulations and relate to any of the matters mentioned in subsection (5).

(5)   Those matters are—

   (a)   the satisfactory completion of a course, or courses, of training relating to fireworks and the means of proving the satisfactory completion of such a course or courses,

   (b)   proficiency or experience in the use of fireworks and the means of proving such proficiency or experience, and

   (c)   the possession of insurance cover against liability arising from the use of fireworks and the means of proving possession of such cover.

(6)   If fireworks regulations impose any prohibition by virtue of this section, they may contain—

   (a)   exceptions from the prohibition, or

   (b)   provision for the granting of dispensations from the prohibition.

NOTES

Regulations: the Fireworks Regulations 2004, SI 2004/1836.

[1.1854]
6   Public fireworks displays

(1)   Fireworks regulations may include provision prohibiting persons from operating a public fireworks display unless—

   (a)   notice of the display has been given in accordance with the regulations to any local or other authority to which the regulations require it to be given,

   (b)   any other information relating to the display which is required by the regulations to be given to any local or other authority has been so given,

   (c)   any fee imposed by any local or other authority in accordance with the regulations has been paid, and

   (d)   such other conditions relating to the holding of public fireworks displays as are specified in the regulations have been complied with.

(2)   Fireworks regulations may include provision prohibiting persons from operating public fireworks displays unless they satisfy—

   (a)   any conditions which are specified in the regulations and relate to the satisfactory completion of a course, or courses, of training relating to fireworks and to the means of proving the satisfactory completion of such a course or courses, or

   (b)   any other conditions which are so specified.

(3)   Fireworks regulations may include provision prohibiting persons from operating, or assisting in the operation of, public fireworks displays if they are below an age specified in the regulations.

(4)   If fireworks regulations impose any prohibition by virtue of this section, they may contain—

   (a)   exceptions from the prohibition, or

   (b)   provision for the granting of dispensations from the prohibition.

(5)   In this section "public fireworks display" means a fireworks display at which the public, or any section of the public, are present (whether or not they have paid to be).

[1.1855]
7   Licensing of suppliers

(1)   Fireworks regulations may include provision prohibiting persons, or persons of a description specified in the regulations, from supplying, exposing for supply or possessing for supply fireworks, or fireworks of a description so specified, unless—

   (a)   they are licensed in accordance with the regulations, and

   (b)   the fireworks are supplied, exposed for supply or kept at premises which are so licensed.

(2)   If fireworks regulations impose any prohibition by virtue of subsection (1), they may contain provision—

   (a)   specifying the local or other authority by which a licence relating to any person or premises may be granted, varied and revoked,

   (b)   relating to the grant, variation and revocation of licences,

   (c)   about conditions which may be attached to licences (including, in particular, conditions as to the time of year for which persons or premises are licensed),

   (d)   for the charging of fees for the grant or variation of licences, and

   (e)   about appeals against refusals to grant or vary, or variations of, licences.

(3)   The provision that may be contained in fireworks regulations by virtue of subsection (1) includes, in particular, provision that a person may not be licensed unless any conditions which are specified in the regulations are satisfied by the person or his employees (or both).

(4)   Those conditions may include conditions relating to the satisfactory completion of a course, or courses, of training about fireworks and the means of proving the satisfactory completion of such course or courses.

(5)   If fireworks regulations impose any prohibition by virtue of this section, they may contain—

   (a)   exceptions from the prohibition, or

   (b)   provision for the granting of dispensations from the prohibition.

NOTES

Regulations: the Fireworks Regulations 2004, SI 2004/1836; the Fireworks (Amendment) Regulations 2004, SI 2004/3262.

[1.1856]
8 Information about fireworks
(1) Fireworks regulations may include provision for securing that—
  (a) appropriate information is, and
  (b) inappropriate information is not,
given in relation to fireworks, or fireworks of a description specified in the regulations.
(2) The provision that may be contained in fireworks regulations by virtue of subsection (1) includes, in particular, provision—
  (a) requiring that a mark, warning or instruction relating to the fireworks be put on or accompany the fireworks, or
  (b) requiring that information specified in the regulations be given to any person so specified.
(3) If fireworks regulations impose any requirement by virtue of this section, they may contain—
  (a) exceptions from the requirement, or
  (b) provision for the granting of dispensations from the requirement.
(4) If fireworks regulations impose any requirement by virtue of this section, they may contain provision requiring the keeping of records by any person to whom information is given under the regulations.

NOTES

Regulations: the Fireworks Regulations 2004, SI 2004/1836; the Fireworks (Amendment) Regulations 2004, SI 2004/3262.

[1.1857]
9 Prohibition of importation etc of fireworks
(1) Fireworks regulations may include provision prohibiting persons from—
  (a) importing,
  (b) completing the manufacture of, or
  (c) placing on the market,
fireworks, or fireworks of a description specified in the regulations, unless they have complied with any requirement imposed by the regulations for the giving of information.
(2) If fireworks regulations impose any prohibition by virtue of subsection (1)(b) or (c), they shall specify the circumstances in which—
  (a) (if the prohibition is imposed by virtue of subsection (1)(b)) a person completes the manufacture of fireworks, or
  (b) (if the prohibition is imposed by virtue of subsection (1)(c)) a person places fireworks on the market.
(3) If fireworks regulations impose any prohibition by virtue of this section, they may contain—
  (a) exceptions from the prohibition, or
  (b) provision for the granting of dispensations from the prohibition.
(4) If fireworks regulations impose any prohibition by virtue of this section, they may contain provision requiring the keeping of records by any person to whom information is given under the regulations.

NOTES

Regulations: the Fireworks Regulations 2004, SI 2004/1836.

[1.1858]
10 Training courses
(1) If fireworks regulations specify conditions relating to the satisfactory completion of a course, or courses, of training about fireworks, they may make provision for courses to be provided by—
  (a) the Secretary of State,
  (b) a body or bodies established or recognised by the Secretary of State, or
  (c) licensed persons.
(2) If fireworks regulations make provision for courses to be provided by licensed persons, they may—
  (a) make provision for the licensing of persons by the Secretary of State or by any body or bodies established or recognised by the Secretary of State,
  (b) authorise the making by the Secretary of State of provision about the charging of fees for the grant or variation of licences, and
  (c) authorise the making by the Secretary of State, or by any such body or bodies, of provision about any of the matters mentioned in subsection (3).
(3) Those matters are—
  (a) the grant, variation and revocation of licences,
  (b) conditions which may be attached to licences, and
  (c) appeals against refusals to grant or vary, or variations of, licences.
(4) Fireworks regulations may authorise—

(a)   the making by the Secretary of State of provision about the charging of fees for attendance at courses of training about fireworks, and

(b)   the making by the Secretary of State, or by any body or bodies established or recognised by the Secretary of State under this section, of provision about any of the matters mentioned in subsection (5).

(5)   Those matters are—

(a)   the descriptions of persons who are to be eligible to attend courses of training about fireworks,

(b)   the subject matter to be covered by courses and the conduct of courses,

(c)   the criteria to be applied in determining whether persons have satisfactorily completed courses,

(d)   the form and content of certificates to be awarded to persons who have satisfactorily completed courses,

(e)   appeals against refusals to award certificates to persons who have attended courses, and

(f)   the keeping of records about persons who have attended courses.

NOTES

Commencement: to be appointed.

Supplementary

[1.1859]
11   Offences

(1)   Any person who contravenes a prohibition imposed by fireworks regulations is guilty of an offence.

(2)   Any person who fails to comply with a requirement imposed by or under fireworks regulations to give or not to give information is guilty of an offence.

(3)   Where a requirement to give information is imposed by or under fireworks regulations, a person is guilty of an offence if, in giving the information, he—

(a)   makes a statement which he knows is false in a material particular, or

(b)   recklessly makes a statement which is false in a material particular.

(4)   A person guilty of an offence under this section is liable on summary conviction to—

(a)   imprisonment for a term not exceeding six months, or

(b)   a fine not exceeding level 5 on the standard scale,

or to both.

(5)   Fireworks regulations may not provide for any contravention of the regulations to be an offence.

(6)   Paragraphs (c), (e) and (f) of section 11(3) of the Consumer Protection Act 1987 (c 43) (provision about offences which may be included in regulations) apply in relation to fireworks regulations as to regulations under section 11 of that Act, but as if references to an offence under section 12 of that Act were references to an offence under this section.

(7)   Section 39 of that Act (defence of due diligence) applies to offences under subsections (1) and (2) of this section; and section 40(1) of that Act (liability of persons other than the principal offender) has effect accordingly.

(8)   In proceedings against any person for an offence of contravening a prohibition imposed by fireworks regulations made by virtue of section 3(1) it is a defence for that person to show that he had no reason to suspect that the person to whom he supplied, offered to supply or agreed to supply the fireworks was below the age specified in the regulations.

(9)   Section 40(2) and (3) of the Consumer Protection Act 1987 (c 43) (offences by bodies corporate) applies to an offence under this section as to an offence under that Act.

NOTES

Commencement: 28 November 2003 (for the purposes of fireworks regulations made in exercise of powers conferred by the provisions of the Act brought into force on that date); 15 July 2004 (for the purposes of fireworks regulations made in exercise of powers conferred by the provisions of the Act brought into force on that date); to be appointed (otherwise).

11A, 11B   (*Inserted in relation to Scotland only by the Police, Public Order and Criminal Justice (Scotland) Act 2006, s 76.*)

[1.1860]
12   Enforcement

(1)   Section 27 of the Consumer Protection Act 1987 (enforcement authorities), apart from subsection (1)(b), applies in relation to fireworks regulations as to regulations under section 11 of that Act.

(2)   The following provisions of that Act—

(a)   *section 28(1)(a) and (2) to (4) (test purchases), apart from the references to forfeiture and suspension notices,*

(b)   section 29(1) to (5), (6)(a) and (7) and section 30(1) to (9) (powers of search etc), apart from the references to forfeiture and suspension notices,

(c)   section 32 (obstruction of officer),

(d)   section 33 (appeals against detention), apart from subsections (2)(a)(ii) and (3)(a)(ii),

(e)   section 34 (compensation for seizure and detention),
(f)   section 35 (recovery of enforcement expenses), apart from subsections (1)(b) and (2)(b),
(g)   section 37 (disclosure of information by Customs and Excise),
(h)   section 41 (civil proceedings), and
(i)   section 44 (service of documents),

apply in relation to fireworks regulations as to regulations under section 11 of that Act.

[(2A)   For the investigatory powers available to a person for the purposes of the duty to enforce imposed by virtue of subsection (1) (in addition to the powers in Part 4 of the Consumer Protection Act 1987), see Schedule 5 to the Consumer Rights Act 2015.]

(3)   . . .

NOTES

Commencement: 28 November 2003 (for the purposes of fireworks regulations made in exercise of powers conferred by the provisions of the Act brought into force on that date); 15 July 2004 (for the purposes of fireworks regulations made in exercise of powers conferred by the provisions of the Act brought into force on that date); to be appointed (otherwise).

Sub-s (2): para (a) repealed, and for the words in italics in para (b) there are substituted the words "29(4) and (7)", by the Consumer Rights Act 2015, s 77(2), Sch 6, para 82(1), (2), as from 1 October 2015 (for transitional provisions see the Consumer Rights Act 2015 (Commencement No 3, Transitional Provisions, Savings and Consequential Amendments) Order 2015, SI 2015/1630, arts 6–8 at **[2.1220]** et seq).

Sub-s (2A): inserted by the Consumer Rights Act 2015, s 77(2), Sch 6, para 82(1), (3), as from 1 October 2015 (for transitional provisions see note above).

Sub-s (3): amends the Enterprise Act 2002, Schs 14, 15.

[1.1861]
13   Savings for certain privileges
Section 47 of the Consumer Protection Act 1987 (savings for privileges) applies in relation to this Act.

NOTES

Commencement: 28 November 2003 (for the purposes of fireworks regulations made in exercise of powers conferred by the provisions of the Act brought into force on that date); 15 July 2004 (for the purposes of fireworks regulations made in exercise of powers conferred by the provisions of the Act brought into force on that date); to be appointed (otherwise).

[1.1862]
14   Prohibition of supply etc of other explosives
(1)   The power to make regulations under section 3 or 4(2) applies to explosives other than fireworks as to fireworks; and regulations made by virtue of this subsection are fireworks regulations for all the purposes of this Act.
(2)   In subsection (1) "explosives" has the same meaning as in [the Explosives Regulations 2014].
(3)   The Secretary of State may by regulations substitute a new definition of "explosives" for the definition in subsection (2).

NOTES

Commencement: to be appointed.

Sub-s (2): words in square brackets substituted by the Explosives Regulations 2014, SI 2014/1638, reg 48(1), Sch 13, Pt 1, para 7.

15   *(Introduces the Schedule to this Act (outside the scope of this work).)*

[1.1863]
16   Parliamentary procedure for regulations
(1)   Any power to make regulations under this Act is exercisable by statutory instrument.
(2)   Regulations under section 1(2) or 14(3) must not be made unless a draft of the statutory instrument containing them has been laid before Parliament and approved by a resolution of each House.
(3)   A statutory instrument containing fireworks regulations is subject to annulment in pursuance of a resolution of either House of Parliament.

NOTES

Commencement: 28 November 2003 (for the purposes of fireworks regulations made in exercise of powers conferred by the provisions of the Act brought into force on that date); 15 July 2004 (for the purposes of fireworks regulations made in exercise of powers conferred by the provisions of the Act brought into force on that date); to be appointed (otherwise).

[1.1864]
17   Financial provisions
(1)   There is to be paid out of money provided by Parliament—
    (a)   any expenses incurred by the Secretary of State in consequence of any provision of this Act, and
    (b)   any increase attributable to this Act in the sums payable out of money so provided under any other Act.
(2)   Any sums received by the Secretary of State by virtue of this Act are to be paid into the Consolidated Fund.

[1.1865]
18　Commencement
(1)　Sections 1 to 16 (and the Schedule) do not come into force until a day appointed by order made by the Secretary of State by statutory instrument; and different days may be appointed for different purposes.
(2)　The Secretary of State may by order made by statutory instrument make such transitional provision in connection with the coming into force of any provision of this Act as the Secretary of State considers appropriate.

NOTES
　Orders: the Fireworks Act 2003 (Commencement No 1) Order 2003, SI 2003/3084; the Fireworks Act 2003 (Commencement No 2) Order 2004, SI 2004/1831.

[1.1866]
19　Short title and extent
(1)　This Act may be cited as the Fireworks Act 2003.
(2)　This Act does not extend to Northern Ireland.

SCHEDULE

(Schedule (Repeals and Revocation) outside the scope of this work.)

DEALING IN CULTURAL OBJECTS (OFFENCES) ACT 2003

(2003 c 27)

ARRANGEMENT OF SECTIONS

An Act to provide for an offence of acquiring, disposing of, importing or exporting tainted cultural objects, or agreeing or arranging to do so; and for connected purposes

[30 October 2003]

[1.1867]
1　Offence of dealing in tainted cultural objects
(1)　A person is guilty of an offence if he dishonestly deals in a cultural object that is tainted, knowing or believing that the object is tainted.
(2)　It is immaterial whether he knows or believes that the object is a cultural object.
(3)　A person guilty of the offence is liable—
　(a)　on conviction on indictment, to imprisonment for a term not exceeding seven years or a fine (or both),
　(b)　on summary conviction, to imprisonment for a term not exceeding six months or a fine not exceeding the statutory maximum (or both).

[1.1868]
2　Meaning of "tainted cultural object"
(1)　"Cultural object" means an object of historical, architectural or archaeological interest.
(2)　A cultural object is tainted if, after the commencement of this Act—
　(a)　a person removes the object in a case falling within subsection (4) or he excavates the object, and
　(b)　the removal or excavation constitutes an offence.
(3)　It is immaterial whether—
　(a)　the removal or excavation was done in the United Kingdom or elsewhere,
　(b)　the offence is committed under the law of a part of the United Kingdom or under the law of any other country or territory.
(4)　An object is removed in a case falling within this subsection if—
　(a)　it is removed from a building or structure of historical, architectural or archaeological interest where the object has at any time formed part of the building or structure, or
　(b)　it is removed from a monument of such interest.
(5)　"Monument" means—
　(a)　any work, cave or excavation,

(b) any site comprising the remains of any building or structure or of any work, cave or excavation,

(c) any site comprising, or comprising the remains of, any vehicle, vessel, aircraft or other movable structure, or part of any such thing.

(6) "Remains" includes any trace or sign of the previous existence of the thing in question.

(7) It is immaterial whether—

(a) a building, structure or work is above or below the surface of the land,

(b) a site is above or below water.

(8) This section has effect for the purposes of section 1.

[1.1869]
3 Meaning of "deals in"

(1) A person deals in an object if (and only if) he—

(a) acquires, disposes of, imports or exports it,

(b) agrees with another to do an act mentioned in paragraph (a), or

(c) makes arrangements under which another person does such an act or under which another person agrees with a third person to do such an act.

(2) "Acquires" means buys, hires, borrows or accepts.

(3) "Disposes of" means sells, lets on hire, lends or gives.

(4) In relation to agreeing or arranging to do an act, it is immaterial whether the act is agreed or arranged to take place in the United Kingdom or elsewhere.

(5) This section has effect for the purposes of section 1.

[1.1870]
[4 Revenue and Customs prosecutions]

(1) Proceedings for an offence relating to the dealing in a tainted cultural object may be instituted [by [the Director of Public Prosecutions] or by order of the Commissioners for Her Majesty's Revenue and Customs] [if it appears to the Director or to the Commissioners] that the offence has involved the importation or exportation of such an object.

(2) An offence relates to the dealing in a tainted cultural object if it is—

(a) an offence under section 1, or

(b) an offence of inciting the commission of, or attempting or conspiring to commit, such an offence.

(3) Proceedings for an offence which are instituted [by order of the Commissioners] under subsection (1) are to be commenced in the name of an officer [of Revenue and Customs], but may be continued by another officer.

(4) Where the Commissioners . . . investigate, or propose to investigate, any matter with a view to determining—

(a) whether there are grounds for believing that a person has committed an offence which relates to the dealing in a tainted cultural object and which involves the importation or exportation of such an object, or

(b) whether a person should be prosecuted for such an offence,

the matter is to be treated as an assigned matter within the meaning of the Customs and Excise Management Act 1979 (c 2).

(5) Nothing in this section affects any powers of any person (including any officer) apart from this section.

(6)   . . .

NOTES

Section heading: substituted by the Commissioners for Revenue and Customs Act 2005, s 50(6), Sch 4, para 128(e).

Sub-s (1): words in first (outer) and final pairs of square brackets substituted by the Commissioners for Revenue and Customs Act 2005, s 50(6), Sch 4, para 128(a); words in second (inner) pair of square brackets substituted by the Public Bodies (Merger of the Director of Public Prosecutions and the Director of Revenue and Customs Prosecutions) Order 2014, SI 2014/834, art 3(3)(b), Sch 2, para 36.

Sub-s (3): words in square brackets inserted by the Commissioners for Revenue and Customs Act 2005, s 50(6), Sch 4, para 128(b).

Sub-s (4): words omitted repealed by the Commissioners for Revenue and Customs Act 2005, s 50(6), Sch 4, para 128(c).

Sub-s (6): repealed by the Commissioners for Revenue and Customs Act 2005, ss 50(6), 52(2), Sch 4, para 128(d), Sch 5.

See further, the Serious Crime Act 2007, s 63(1), Sch 6, Pt 1, para 45, which provides that the reference above to (or to conduct amounting to) the common law offence of inciting the commission of another offence, has effect (as from the day that offence is abolished) as a reference to (or to conduct amounting to) offences under the Serious Crime Act 2007, Pt 2.

[1.1871]
5 Offences by bodies corporate

(1) If an offence under section 1 committed by a body corporate is proved—

(a) to have been committed with the consent or connivance of an officer, or

(b) to be attributable to any neglect on his part,

he (as well as the body corporate) is guilty of the offence and liable to be proceeded against and punished accordingly.

(2) "Officer", in relation to a body corporate, means—

(a) a director, manager, secretary or other similar officer of the body,

(b)   a person purporting to act in any such capacity.

(3)   If the affairs of a body corporate are managed by its members, subsection (1) applies in relation to the acts and defaults of a member in connection with his functions of management as if he were a director of the body.

[1.1872]
6   Short title, commencement and extent
(1)   This Act may be cited as the Dealing in Cultural Objects (Offences) Act 2003.

(2)   This Act comes into force at the end of the period of two months beginning with the day on which it is passed.

(3)   This Act does not extend to Scotland.

GANGMASTERS (LICENSING) ACT 2004

(2004 c 11)

ARRANGEMENT OF SECTIONS

An Act to make provision for the licensing of activities involving the supply or use of workers in connection with agricultural work, the gathering of wild creatures and wild plants, the

Part 1   Statutes

harvesting of fish from fish farms, and certain processing and packaging; and for connected purposes

[8 July 2004]

The Gangmasters Licensing Authority

[1.1873]
1   The Gangmasters Licensing Authority
(1)   There shall be a body known as the Gangmasters Licensing Authority (in this Act referred to as "the Authority").
(2)   The functions of the Authority shall be—
    (a)   to carry out the functions relating to licensing that are conferred on it by this Act,
    (b)   to ensure the carrying out of such inspections as it considers necessary of persons holding licences under this Act,
    (c)   to keep under review generally the activities of persons acting as gangmasters,
    (d)   to supply information held by it to specified persons in accordance with the provisions of this Act,
    (e)   to keep under review the operation of this Act, and
    (f)   such other functions as may be prescribed in regulations made by the Secretary of State.
(3)   The Authority may do anything that it considers is calculated to facilitate, or is incidental or conducive to, the carrying out of any of its functions.
(4)   The Authority shall not be regarded—
    (a)   as the servant or agent of the Crown, or
    (b)   as enjoying any status, immunity or privilege of the Crown,
and the property of the Authority shall not be regarded as property of, or property held on behalf of, the Crown.
(5)   The Secretary of State may by regulations make provision as to—
    (a)   the status and constitution of the Authority,
    (b)   the appointment of its members,
    (c)   the payment of remuneration and allowances to its members, and
    (d)   such other matters in connection with its establishment and operation as he thinks fit.
(6)   Schedule 1 amends certain enactments in consequence of the establishment of the Authority.

NOTES
Regulations: the Gangmasters (Licensing Authority) Regulations 2015, SI 2015/805.

[1.1874]
2   Directions etc by the Secretary of State
(1)   In carrying out its functions the Authority shall comply with any general or specific directions given to it in writing by the Secretary of State.
(2)   Before giving any such directions the Secretary of State shall consult the Authority.
(3)   The Authority shall provide the Secretary of State with such information about its activities as he may request.

Scope of Act

[1.1875]
3   Work to which this Act applies
(1)   The work to which this Act applies is—
    (a)   agricultural work,
    (b)   gathering shellfish, and
    (c)   processing or packaging—
        (i)   any produce derived from agricultural work, or
        (ii)   shellfish, fish or products derived from shellfish or fish.
This is subject to any provision made by regulations under subsection (5) below and to section 5 (territorial scope of application).
(2)   In subsection (1)(a) "agricultural work" means work in agriculture.
(3)   In this Act "agriculture" includes—
    (a)   dairy-farming,
    (b)   the production for the purposes of any trade, business or other undertaking (whether carried on for profit or not) of consumable produce,
    (c)   the use of land as grazing, meadow or pasture land,
    (d)   the use of land as an orchard or as osier land or woodland, and
    (e)   the use of land for market gardens or nursery grounds.
In paragraph (b) "consumable produce" means produce grown for sale, consumption or other use after severance from the land on which it is grown.
(4)   In this Act "shellfish" means crustaceans and molluscs of any kind, and includes any part of a shellfish and any (or any part of any) brood, ware, halfware or spat of shellfish, and any spawn of shellfish, and the shell, or any part of the shell, of a shellfish.
(5)   The Secretary of State may by regulations make provision—
    (a)   excluding work of a prescribed description from being work to which this Act applies;

(b) including work of the following nature as being work to which this Act applies—
  (i) the gathering (by any manner) of wild creatures, or wild plants, of a prescribed description and the processing and packaging of anything so gathered, and
  (ii) the harvesting of fish from a fish farm (within the meaning of [the Salmon and Freshwater Fisheries Act 1975]).

NOTES

Sub-s (5): words in square brackets substituted in relation to England and Wales by the Aquatic Animal Health (England and Wales) Regulations 2009, SI 2009/463, reg 45, Sch 2, para 10 and in relation to Scotland by the Aquatic Animal Health (Scotland) Regulations 2009, SSI 2009/85, reg 48, Sch 2, para 11.

[1.1876]
4   Acting as a gangmaster
(1) This section defines what is meant in this Act by a person acting as a gangmaster.
(2) A person ("A") acts as a gangmaster if he supplies a worker to do work to which this Act applies for another person ("B").
(3) For the purposes of subsection (2) it does not matter—
  (a) whether the worker works under a contract with A or is supplied to him by another person,
  (b) whether the worker is supplied directly under arrangements between A and B or indirectly under arrangements involving one or more intermediaries,
  (c) whether A supplies the worker himself or procures that the worker is supplied,
  (d) whether the work is done under the control of A, B or an intermediary,
  (e) whether the work done for B is for the purposes of a business carried on by him or in connection with services provided by him to another person.
(4) A person ("A") acts as a gangmaster if he uses a worker to do work to which this Act applies in connection with services provided by him to another person.
(5) A person ("A") acts as a gangmaster if he uses a worker to do any of the following work to which this Act applies for the purposes of a business carried on by him—
  (a) harvesting or otherwise gathering agricultural produce following—
    (i) a sale, assignment or lease of produce to A, or
    (ii) the making of any other agreement with A,
    where the sale, assignment, lease or other agreement was entered into for the purpose of enabling the harvesting or gathering to take place;
  (b) gathering shellfish;
  (c) processing or packaging agricultural produce harvested or gathered as mentioned in paragraph (a).
  In this subsection "agricultural produce" means any produce derived from agriculture.
(6) For the purposes of subsection (4) or (5) A shall be treated as using a worker to do work to which this Act applies if he makes arrangements under which the worker does the work—
  (a) whether the worker works for A (or for another) or on his own account, and
  (b) whether or not he works under a contract (with A or another).
(7) Regulations under section 3(5)(b) may provide for the application of subsections (5) and (6) above in relation to work that is work to which this Act applies by virtue of the regulations.

[1.1877]
5   Territorial scope of application
(1) The work to which this Act applies is work—
  (a) in the United Kingdom,
  (b) on any portion of the shore or bed of the sea, or of an estuary or tidal river, adjacent to the United Kingdom, whether above or below (or partly above and partly below) the low water mark, or
  (c) in UK coastal waters.
(2) In subsection (1)(c) "UK coastal waters" means waters adjacent to the United Kingdom to a distance of six miles measured from the baselines from which the breadth of the territorial sea is measured.
  In this subsection "miles" means international nautical miles of 1,852 metres.
(3) The provisions of this Act apply where a person acts as a gangmaster, whether in the United Kingdom or elsewhere, in relation to work to which this Act applies.

Licensing

[1.1878]
6   Prohibition of unlicensed activities
(1) A person shall not act as a gangmaster except under the authority of a licence.
(2) Regulations made by the Secretary of State may specify circumstances in which a licence is not required.

NOTES

Regulations: the Gangmasters Licensing (Exclusions) Regulations 2013, SI 2013/2216.

[1.1879]
7 Grant of licence
(1)   The Authority may grant a licence if it thinks fit.
(2)   A licence shall describe the activities authorised by it and shall be granted for such period as the Authority thinks fit.
(3)   A licence authorises activities—
  (a)   by the holder of the licence, and
  (b)   by persons employed or engaged by the holder of the licence who are named or otherwise specified in the licence.
(4)   In the case of a licence held otherwise than by an individual, the reference in subsection (3)(a) to activities by the holder of the licence shall be read as a reference only to such activities as are mentioned in whichever of the following provisions applies—
     section 20(2) (body corporate);
     section 21(2) (unincorporated association);
     section 22(4) (partnership that is regarded as a legal person under the law of the country or territory under which it is formed).
(5)   A licence shall be granted subject to such conditions as the Authority considers appropriate.

[1.1880]
8 General power of Authority to make rules
(1)   The Authority may make such rules as it thinks fit in connection with the licensing of persons acting as gangmasters.
(2)   The rules may, in particular—
  (a)   prescribe the form and contents of applications for licences and other documents to be filed in connection with applications;
  (b)   regulate the procedure to be followed in connection with applications and authorise the rectification of procedural irregularities;
  (c)   prescribe time limits for doing anything required to be done in connection with an application and provide for the extension of any period so prescribed;
  (d)   prescribe the requirements which must be met before a licence is granted;
  (e)   provide for the manner in which the meeting of those requirements is to be verified;
  (f)   allow for the grant of licences on a provisional basis before it is determined whether the requirements for the grant of a licence are met and for the withdrawal of such licences (if appropriate) if it appears that those requirements are not met;
  (g)   prescribe the form of licences and the information to be contained in them;
  (h)   require the payment of such fees as may be prescribed or determined in accordance with the rules;
  (i)   provide that licences are to be granted subject to conditions requiring the licence holder—
     (i)   to produce, in prescribed circumstances, evidence in a prescribed form of his being licensed, and
     (ii)   to comply with any prescribed requirements relating to the recruitment, use and supply of workers.
(3)   The Authority must consult the Secretary of State before making any rules about fees.
(4)   In subsection (2) "prescribed" means prescribed by the rules.

NOTES
   Rules: the Gangmasters (Licensing Conditions) Rules 2009, SI 2009/307.

[1.1881]
9 Modification, revocation or transfer of licence
(1)   The Authority may by notice in writing to the licensee modify or revoke any licence granted to him (including any of the conditions of that licence)—
  (a)   with the consent of the licensee, or
  (b)   where it appears to him that a condition of the licence or any requirement of this Act has not been complied with.
(2)   The modifications that may be made include one suspending the effect of the licence for such period as the Authority may determine.
(3)   A licence may be transferred with the written consent of the Authority and in such other cases as may be determined by the Authority.

[1.1882]
10 Appeals
(1)   The Secretary of State shall by regulations make provision for an appeal against any decision of the Authority—
  (a)   to refuse an application for a licence,
  (b)   as to the conditions to which the grant of the licence is subject,
  (c)   to refuse consent to the transfer of a licence, or
  (d)   to modify or revoke a licence.
(2)   The regulations shall make provision—

(a)   for and in connection with the appointment of a person to hear and determine such appeals (including provision for the payment of remuneration and allowances to such a person), and

(b)   as to the procedure to be followed in connection with an appeal.

NOTES

Regulations: the Gangmasters (Appeals) Regulations 2006, SI 2006/662.

[1.1883]
11   Register of licences
(1)   The Authority shall establish and maintain a register of persons licensed under this Act.
(2)   The register shall contain such particulars as the Authority may determine of every person who for the time being holds a licence or whose activities are authorised by a licence (whether or not they are named in the licence).
(3)   The Authority shall ensure that appropriate arrangements are in force for allowing members of the public to inspect the contents of the register.

Offences
[1.1884]
12   Offences: acting as a gangmaster, being in possession of false documents etc
(1)   A person commits an offence if he acts as a gangmaster in contravention of section 6 (prohibition of unlicensed activities).
For this purpose a person acting as a gangmaster does not contravene section 6 by reason only of the fact that he breaches a condition of the licence which authorises him to so act.
(2)   A person commits an offence if he has in his possession or under his control—
   (a)   a relevant document that is false and that he knows or believes to be false,
   (b)   a relevant document that was improperly obtained and that he knows or believes to have been improperly obtained, or
   (c)   a relevant document that relates to someone else,
with the intention of inducing another person to believe that he or another person acting as a gangmaster in contravention of section 6 is acting under the authority of a licence.
(3)   A person guilty of an offence under subsection (1) or (2) is liable on summary conviction—
   (a)   in England and Wales, to imprisonment for a term not exceeding twelve months, or to a fine not exceeding the statutory maximum, or to both;
   (b)   in Scotland or Northern Ireland, to imprisonment for a term not exceeding six months, or to a fine not exceeding the statutory maximum, or to both.
In relation to an offence committed before the commencement of section 154(1) of the Criminal Justice Act 2003 (c 44), for "twelve months" in paragraph (a) substitute "six months".
(4)   A person guilty of an offence under subsection (1) or (2) is liable on conviction on indictment to imprisonment for a term not exceeding ten years, or to a fine, or to both.
(5)   For the purposes of this section—
   (a)   except in Scotland, a document is false only if it is false within the meaning of Part 1 of the Forgery and Counterfeiting Act 1981 (c 45) (see section 9(1) of that Act), and
   (b)   a document was improperly obtained if false information was provided, in or in connection with the application for its issue or an application for its modification, to the person who issued it or (as the case may be) to a person entitled to modify it,
and references to the making of a false document include references to the modification of a document so that it becomes false.
(6)   In this section "relevant document" means—
   (a)   a licence, or
   (b)   any document issued by the Authority in connection with a licence.

[1.1885]
13   Offences: entering into arrangements with gangmasters
(1)   A person commits an offence if—
   (a)   he enters into arrangements under which a person ("the gangmaster") supplies him with workers or services, and
   (b)   the gangmaster in supplying the workers or services contravenes section 6 (prohibition of unlicensed activities).
(2)   In proceedings against a person for an offence under subsection (1) it is a defence for him to prove that he—
   (a)   took all reasonable steps to satisfy himself that the gangmaster was acting under the authority of a valid licence, and
   (b)   did not know, and had no reasonable grounds for suspecting that the gangmaster was not the holder of a valid licence.
(3)   The Secretary of State may by regulations make provision as to what constitutes "reasonable steps" for the purposes of subsection (2)(a).
(4)   A person guilty of an offence under subsection (1) is liable—

(a) on summary conviction in England and Wales, to imprisonment for a term not exceeding 51 weeks, or to a fine not exceeding the statutory maximum, or to both,

(b) on summary conviction in Scotland or Northern Ireland, to imprisonment for a term not exceeding six months, or to a fine not exceeding the statutory maximum, or to both.

In relation to an offence committed before the commencement of section 281(5) of the Criminal Justice Act 2003 (c 44), for "51 weeks" in paragraph (a) substitute "six months".

[1.1886]
14 Offences: supplementary provisions

(1) An enforcement officer (see section 15) has the powers of arrest mentioned in subsection (2) (in addition to powers under [section 24A] of the Police and Criminal Evidence Act 1984 (c 60)) in relation to any of the following offences—

(a) an offence under section 12(1) or (2),

(b) conspiring to commit any such offence,

(c) attempting to commit any such offence,

(d) inciting, aiding, abetting, counselling or procuring the commission of any such offence.

(2) Those powers are as follows—

(a) if he has reasonable grounds for suspecting that such an offence has been committed, he may arrest without warrant anyone whom he has reasonable grounds for suspecting to be guilty of the offence;

(b) he may arrest without warrant—

(i) anyone who is about to commit such an offence;

(ii) anyone whom he has reasonable grounds for suspecting to be about to commit such an offence.

(3) Subsections (1) and (2) do not apply in Scotland.

(4) . . .

NOTES

Sub-s (1): words in square brackets substituted by the Serious Organised Crime and Police Act 2005, s 111, Sch 7, Pt 4, para 62(a).

Sub-s (4): amends the Proceeds of Crime Act 2002, Schs 2, 4, 5.

See further, in relation to England, Wales and Northern Ireland, the Serious Crime Act 2007, s 63(1), Sch 6, Pt 1, para 50, which provides that the reference above to (or to conduct amounting to) the common law offence of inciting the commission of another offence, has effect (as from the day that offence is abolished) as a reference to (or to conduct amounting to) offences under the Serious Crime Act 2007, Pt 2.

Enforcement

[1.1887]
15 Enforcement and compliance officers

(1) The Secretary of State may appoint officers ("enforcement officers") to act for the purposes of this Act—

(a) in enforcing the provisions of section 6 (prohibition of unlicensed activities), and

(b) in taking action in circumstances in which it appears that an offence under section 13 (persons entering into arrangements with gangmasters) has been, is being, or may be committed.

(2) The Secretary of State may, instead of or in addition to appointing enforcement officers under subsection (1), make arrangements with a relevant authority for officers of that authority to be enforcement officers.

(3) The following are relevant authorities for this purpose—

(a) the Authority,

(b) any Minister of the Crown or government department,

(c) the National Assembly for Wales,

(d) the Scottish Ministers,

(e) any body performing functions on behalf of the Crown.

(4) The Authority may appoint officers ("compliance officers") to act for the purposes of this Act in verifying, from time to time or in such circumstances as the Authority may determine, compliance by a licence holder with the conditions of the licence.

(5) When acting for the purposes of this Act, an enforcement officer or a compliance officer shall, if so required, produce some duly authenticated document showing his authority to act.

(6) If it appears to an enforcement officer or a compliance officer that any person with whom he is dealing while acting for the purposes of this Act does not know that he is an officer so acting, the officer shall identify himself as such to that person.

[(7) This section does not prevent the Secretary of State from making arrangements for ensuring that functions relating to the institution or conduct of proceedings in England and Wales for an offence under this Act are carried out by the Director of Public Prosecutions and, accordingly, the terms of appointments under subsection (1), or arrangements under subsection (2), may include provision, or be modified so as to include provision, for enforcement officers not to carry out such functions at any time when they are being carried out by the Director.]

Part 1 Statutes

NOTES

Sub-s (7): added by the Deregulation Act 2015, s 92, as from a day to be appointed.

[1.1888]
16 Powers of officers

(1) An enforcement officer or a compliance officer acting for the purposes of this Act shall have power for the performance of his duties—

 (a) to require the production by a relevant person of any records required to be kept by virtue of this Act, to inspect and examine those records, to remove those records from the premises where they are kept and to copy any material part of them,

 (b) to require a relevant person to furnish to him (either alone or in the presence of any other person, as the officer thinks fit) an explanation of any such records,

 (c) to require a relevant person to furnish to him (either alone or in the presence of any other person, as the officer thinks fit) any additional information known to the relevant person which might reasonably be needed in order to establish whether—

  (i) any provision of this Act, or

  (ii) any condition of any licence granted under it,

  is being complied with,

 (d) at all reasonable times to enter any relevant premises in order to exercise any power conferred on the officer by virtue of paragraphs (a) to (c).

(2) The powers conferred by subsection (1) include power, on reasonable written notice, to require a relevant person—

 (a) to produce any such records as are mentioned in paragraph (a) of that subsection to an officer at such time and place as may be specified in the notice, or

 (b) to attend before an officer at such time and place as may be specified in the notice to furnish any such explanation or additional information as is mentioned in paragraph (b) or (c) of that subsection.

(3) The power conferred by subsection (1)(a) includes, in relation to records which are kept by means of a computer, power to require the records to be produced in a form in which they are legible and can be taken away.

(4) A person authorised by virtue of subsection (1)(a) to inspect any records is entitled to have access to, and to check the operation of, any computer and any associated apparatus or material which is or has been in use in connection with the records in question.

(5) In this section "relevant person" means any person whom an officer acting for the purposes of this Act has reasonable cause to believe to be—

 (a) a person acting as a gangmaster,

 (b) a person supplied with workers or services by a person acting as a gangmaster,

 (c) any employee or agent of a person falling within paragraph (a) or (b).

(6) In this section and section 17—

 "relevant premises" means any premises which an officer acting for the purposes of this Act has reasonable cause to believe to be—

  (a) premises at which a person mentioned in subsection (5)(a) or (b) carries on business, and

  (b) premises which such a person uses in connection with his business,

 "premises" includes any place and, in particular, includes—

  (a) any vehicle, vessel, aircraft or hovercraft, and

  (b) any tent or movable structure.

[1.1889]
17 Entry by warrant

(1) If a justice of the peace is satisfied by written information on oath that there are reasonable grounds for an enforcement officer to enter relevant premises for the purpose of ascertaining whether there has been any contravention of section 6 (prohibition of unlicensed activities), and is also satisfied—

 (a) that admission to the premises has been refused, or that a refusal is expected, and (in either case) that notice of the intention to apply for a warrant has been given to the occupier,

 (b) that an application for admission, or the giving of such a notice, would defeat the object of the entry,

 (c) that the case is one of extreme urgency, or

 (d) that the premises are unoccupied or the occupier is temporarily absent,

the justice may issue a warrant authorising the enforcement officer to enter the premises, if necessary using reasonable force.

(2) An enforcement officer entering any premises by virtue of a warrant under this section may—

 (a) take with him when he enters those premises such other persons and such other equipment as he considers necessary,

 (b) carry out on those premises such inspections and examinations as he considers necessary for the purpose of ascertaining whether there has been any contravention of section 6, and

(c)   take possession of any book, document, data, record (in whatever form it is held) or product which is on the premises and retain it for as long as he considers necessary for that purpose.

(3)   On leaving any premises which an enforcement officer is authorised to enter by a warrant under this section, that officer shall, if the premises are unoccupied or the occupier is temporarily absent, leave the premises as effectively secured against trespassers as he found them.

(4)   Where by virtue of subsection (2)(c) an enforcement officer takes possession of any item, he shall leave on the premises from which the item was removed a statement giving particulars of what he has taken and stating that he has taken possession of it.

(5)   In the application of this section to Scotland—

(a)   the reference to a justice of the peace being satisfied by written information on oath, shall be read as a reference to a sheriff or a justice of the peace being satisfied; and

(b)   "the justice" shall be read as a reference to the sheriff, or as the case may be, to the justice.

[1.1890]
18   Obstruction of officers
(1)   A person commits an offence who—

(a)   intentionally obstructs an enforcement officer or compliance officer who is acting in the exercise of his functions under this Act, or

(b)   without reasonable cause, fails to comply with any requirement made of him by such an officer who is so acting.

(2)   A person who, in giving any information which is required of him by an enforcement officer or compliance officer, makes a statement which is false in a material particular commits an offence.

(3)   A person guilty of an offence under this section is liable—

(a)   on summary conviction in England and Wales, to imprisonment for a term not exceeding 51 weeks, or to a fine not exceeding the statutory maximum, or to both,

(b)   on summary conviction in Scotland or Northern Ireland, to imprisonment for a term not exceeding six months, or to a fine not exceeding the statutory maximum, or to both.

    In relation to an offence committed before the commencement of section 281(5) of the Criminal Justice Act 2003 (c 44), for "51 weeks" in paragraph (a) substitute "six months".

[1.1891]
19   Information relating to gangmasters
(1)   Information held by any person for the purposes of, or for any purpose connected with, the exercise of functions under this Act—

(a)   may be supplied to any other person for use for any such purpose, and

(b)   may be supplied to any person having functions in relation to—

(i)   the enforcement of any other enactment applying to the operations of a person acting as a gangmaster,

(ii)   the enforcement of any other enactment in connection with accommodation, meals or facilities provided to workers, or the conditions in which they work, or

(iii)   offences committed by workers in connection with or by reason of their doing work to which this Act applies,

    for use for the purposes of, or for any purpose connected with, those functions.

(2)   Information relating to the operations of a person acting as a gangmaster which is held by any person for the purposes of, or for any purpose connected with, such functions as are mentioned in subsection (1)(b) may be supplied to any person having functions under this Act for the purposes of, or for any purpose connected with, the exercise of those functions.

(3)   Information supplied under subsection (2) by or on behalf of the Commissioners of Inland Revenue or the Commissioners of Customs and Excise must not be supplied by the recipient to any other person without the consent of the Commissioners concerned.

(4)   This section—

(a)   has effect notwithstanding any restriction on the disclosure of information imposed by any enactment or rule of law, and

(b)   does not limit the circumstances in which information may be used or supplied apart from this section.

(5)   In this section "enactment" means an Act of Parliament, an Act of the Scottish Parliament or any Northern Ireland legislation or any instrument made under or having effect by virtue of an Act of Parliament, an Act of the Scottish Parliament or any Northern Ireland legislation.

(6)   References in this section to a person having functions of any description include references to any person providing, or employed in the provision of, services for that person in connection with those functions.

Supplementary

[1.1892]
20   Application of Act to bodies corporate
(1)   A licence under this Act may be granted to a body corporate.

(2)   A licence granted to a body corporate authorises activities carried on by the body through such persons representing, or acting on behalf of, the body as are named or otherwise specified in the licence.

(3)   If an offence under this Act committed by a body corporate is shown—
   (a)   to have been committed with the consent or connivance of an officer of the body corporate, or
   (b)   to be attributable to any neglect on his part,
the officer, as well as the body corporate, is guilty of the offence and liable to be proceeded against and punished accordingly.

(4)   In subsection (3) "officer" means—
   (a)   any director, manager, secretary or other similar officer of the body corporate, or
   (b)   any person purporting to act in any such capacity.

(5)   If the affairs of a body corporate are managed by its members, subsection (3) applies in relation to the acts and defaults of a member in connection with his functions of management as if he were a director of the body corporate.

[1.1893]
21   Application of Act to unincorporated associations

(1)   A licence under this Act may be granted to an unincorporated association (other than a partnership).

(2)   A licence granted to an unincorporated association authorises activities carried on by the association through such persons representing, or acting on behalf of, the association as are named or otherwise specified in the licence.

(3)   Proceedings for an offence under this Act alleged to have been committed by an unincorporated association may be brought against the association in the name of the association.

(4)   For the purposes of such proceedings—
   (a)   rules of court relating to the service of documents have effect as if the association were a body corporate, and
   (b)   the following provisions apply as they apply in relation to a body corporate—
      section 33 of the Criminal Justice Act 1925 (c 86) and Schedule 3 to the Magistrates' Courts Act 1980 (c 43),
      sections 70 and 143 of the Criminal Procedure (Scotland) Act 1995,
      section 18 of the Criminal Justice Act (Northern Ireland) 1945 (c 15 (NI)) and Schedule 4 to the Magistrates' Courts (Northern Ireland) Order 1981 (SI 1981/1675 (NI 26)).

(5)   A fine imposed on the association on its conviction of an offence shall be paid out of the funds of the association.

(6)   If an offence under this Act committed by an unincorporated association is shown—
   (a)   to have been committed with the consent or connivance of an officer of the association, or
   (b)   to be attributable to any neglect on his part,
the officer, as well as the association, is guilty of the offence and liable to be proceeded against and punished accordingly.

(7)   In subsection (6) "officer", in relation to any association, means—
   (a)   any officer of the association or any member of its governing body, or
   (b)   any person purporting to act in such a capacity.

[1.1894]
22   Application of Act to partnerships

(1)   A licence under this Act may be granted to a partnership in the firm name.

(2)   Where the partnership is not regarded as a legal person under the law of the country or territory under which it is formed, the grant of a licence to the partnership in the firm name—
   (a)   continues to have effect notwithstanding a change of partners, so long as at least one of the persons who was a partner before the change remains a partner after it; and
   (b)   has effect as the grant of a licence to those partners named in the licence.

(3)   If in the case of such a partnership an offence under this Act committed by a partner is shown—
   (a)   to have been committed with the consent or connivance of another partner, or
   (b)   to be attributable to any neglect on the part of another partner,
that other partner, as well as the first-mentioned partner, is guilty of the offence and liable to be proceeded against and punished accordingly.

(4)   A licence granted to a partnership that is regarded as a legal person under the law of the country or territory under which it is formed authorises activities carried on by the partnership through those partners named in the licence.

(5)   Proceedings for an offence under this Act alleged to have been committed by such a partnership may be brought against the partnership in the firm name.

(6)   For the purposes of such proceedings—
   (a)   rules of court relating to the service of documents have effect as if the partnership were a body corporate, and
   (b)   the following provisions apply as they apply in relation to a body corporate—

section 33 of the Criminal Justice Act 1925 (c 86) and Schedule 3 to the Magistrates' Courts Act 1980 (c 43),

sections 70 and 143 of the Criminal Procedure (Scotland) Act 1995,

section 18 of the Criminal Justice Act (Northern Ireland) 1945 (c 15 (NI)) and Schedule 4 to the Magistrates' Courts (Northern Ireland) Order 1981 (SI 1981/1675 (NI 26)).

(7)   A fine imposed on a partnership on its conviction of an offence shall be paid out of the funds of the partnership.

(8)   If an offence under this Act committed by a partnership is shown—

(a)   to have been committed with the consent or connivance of a partner, or

(b)   to be attributable to any neglect on the part of a partner,

the partner, as well as the partnership, is guilty of the offence and liable to be proceeded against and punished accordingly.

(9)   In subsections (3) and (8) "partner" includes a person purporting to act as a partner.

Miscellaneous and general

[1.1895]
23   Annual report
The Secretary of State shall each year lay a report before each House of Parliament on the operation of this Act.

[1.1896]
24   Financial provision
(1)   The Secretary of State may make payments to the Authority of such amounts, at such times and on such conditions (if any) as he considers appropriate.

(2)   The Authority shall (unless the Secretary of State directs otherwise) pay to the Secretary of State all sums received by it in the course of, or in connection with, the carrying out of its functions.

(3)   Any sums received by the Secretary of State under subsection (2) shall be paid into the Consolidated Fund.

[1.1897]
25   Regulations, rules and orders
(1)   In this Act, unless otherwise indicated, "prescribed" means prescribed by regulations made by the Secretary of State.

(2)   Any power to make regulations or rules under this Act includes power to make different provision for different cases.

(3)   Any power of the Secretary of State to make regulations or orders under this Act is exercisable by statutory instrument.

(4)   Any power of the Authority to make rules under this Act is exercisable by statutory instrument.

(5)   A statutory instrument containing regulations made by the Secretary of State under—

(a)   section 1(5) (regulations as to status, constitution, etc of the Authority), or

(b)   section 3(5)(b) (regulations extending work to which this Act applies),

must not be made unless a draft of the instrument has been laid before, and approved by a resolution of, each House of Parliament.

(6)   A statutory instrument containing—

(a)   regulations made by the Secretary of State under any other provision of this Act, or

(b)   rules made by the Authority under section 8 (general power of Authority to make rules),

is subject to annulment in pursuance of a resolution of either House of Parliament.

[1.1898]
26   Meaning of "worker"
(1)   In this Act "worker" means an individual who does work to which this Act applies.

(2)   A person is not prevented from being a worker for the purposes of this Act by reason of the fact that he has no right to be, or to work, in the United Kingdom.

[1.1899]
27   Exclusion of provisions relating to employment agencies and businesses
(1)   The Employment Agencies Act 1973 (c 35) does not apply to an employment agency or an employment business in so far as it consists of activities for which a licence is required under this Act.

(2)   In subsection (1) "employment agency" and "employment business" have the same meaning as in that Act.

[1.1900]
28   Application of Act to Northern Ireland
The provisions of Schedule 2 to this Act have effect with respect to the application of this Act to Northern Ireland.

[1.1901]
29 Commencement and transitional provision
(1) The provisions of this Act come into force on such day as the Secretary of State may by order appoint.

(2) Different days may be appointed for different purposes and for different areas.

(3) The Secretary of State may by order make such transitional provision as he considers appropriate in connection with the coming into force of any provision of this Act.

NOTES

Orders: the Gangmasters (Licensing) Act 2004 (Commencement No 1) Order 2004, SI 2004/2857; the Gangmasters (Licensing) Act 2004 (Commencement No 2) Order 2005, SI 2005/447; the Gangmasters (Licensing) Act 2004 (Commencement No 3) Order 2006, SI 2006/2406; the Gangmasters (Licensing) Act 2004 (Commencement No 4) Order 2006, SI 2006/2906; the Gangmasters (Licensing) Act 2004 (Commencement No 5) Order 2007, SI 2007/695.

[1.1902]
30 Short title and extent
(1) This Act may be cited as the Gangmasters (Licensing) Act 2004.

(2) This Act extends to England and Wales, Scotland and Northern Ireland.

SCHEDULES

SCHEDULE 1

(Sch 1 (Consequential Amendments) outside the scope of this work.)

SCHEDULE 2
APPLICATION OF ACT TO NORTHERN IRELAND
Section 28

Introduction

[1.1903]
1. (1) The following provisions have effect in relation to the application of this Act to Northern Ireland.

(2) For the purposes of this Schedule the relevant Northern Ireland department is the Department of Agriculture and Rural Development in Northern Ireland.

General

2. (1) References in this Schedule to "work in Northern Ireland" are to work—
  (a) in Northern Ireland,
  (b) on any portion of the shore or bed of the sea, or of an estuary or tidal river, adjacent to Northern Ireland, whether above or below (or partly above and partly below) the low water mark, or
  (c) in Northern Ireland coastal waters.

(2) In sub-paragraph (1)(c) "Northern Ireland coastal waters" means waters adjacent to Northern Ireland to a distance of six miles measured from the baselines from which the breadth of the territorial sea is measured.

  In this sub-paragraph "miles" means international nautical miles of 1,852 metres.

(3) The provisions of this Act relating to work in Northern Ireland apply where a person acts as a gangmaster, whether in Northern Ireland or elsewhere, in relation to work in Northern Ireland to which this Act applies.

(4) References in this Schedule to "Northern Ireland licences" are to licences under this Act in respect of activities as a gangmaster in relation to work in Northern Ireland.

Section 1: The Gangmasters Licensing Authority

3. In relation to persons acting as gangmasters in Northern Ireland or persons acting as gangmasters in relation to work in Northern Ireland, the reference to the Secretary of State in section 1(2)(f) (power to prescribe additional functions of Authority) shall be read as a reference to the relevant Northern Ireland department.

4. Before making any regulations under that provision, the relevant Northern Ireland department shall consult the Secretary of State.

5. Before making any regulations under section 1(5) (regulations as to status, constitution etc of the Authority), the Secretary of State shall consult the relevant Northern Ireland department.

Section 2: Directions etc by the Secretary of State

6. In relation to the Authority's functions in connection with persons acting as gangmasters in Northern Ireland or persons acting as gangmasters in relation to work in Northern Ireland, the references in section 2 to the Secretary of State shall be read as references to the relevant Northern Ireland department.

Section 3: Work to which this Act applies

7. In section 3(5) (power to make regulations excluding or including work) as it applies in relation to work in Northern Ireland—
  (a)   the reference to the Secretary of State shall be read as a reference to the relevant Northern Ireland department, and
  (b)   for the reference to the Diseases of Fish Act 1937 (c 33) substitute a reference to the Fisheries Act (NI) 1966 (c 17 (NI)).

Section 6: Prohibition of unlicensed activities

8. In section 6(2) (power to specify circumstances in which licence not required) as it applies in relation to work in Northern Ireland, the reference to the Secretary of State shall be read as a reference to the relevant Northern Ireland department.

Section 7: Grant of licences

9. The Authority shall grant separate licences in respect of activities as a gangmaster in relation to work in Northern Ireland.

Section 8: General power of Authority to make rules

10. (1)   Rules under section 8 (general power of Authority to make rules) may make different provision for Northern Ireland licences.
(2)   In section 8(3) as it applies in relation to rules requiring the payment of fees in connection with Northern Ireland licences, the reference to the Secretary of State shall be read as a reference to the relevant Northern Ireland department.

Section 10: Appeals

11. In section 10 as it applies in relation to decisions made in connection with Northern Ireland licences, the reference to the Secretary of State shall be read as a reference to the relevant Northern Ireland department.

Section 11: Register of licences

12. The Authority shall establish and maintain a separate register of Northern Ireland licences.

Section 13: Offences: entering into arrangements with gangmasters

13. In section 13(3) (power to make regulations as to what constitutes "reasonable steps") as it applies in relation to persons entering into arrangements with gangmasters in relation to work in Northern Ireland, the reference to the Secretary of State shall be read as a reference to the relevant Northern Ireland department.

Section 14: Offences: supplementary provisions

14. In section 14(1) (additional powers of arrest) the reference to [section 24A] of the Police and Criminal Evidence Act 1984 (c 60) shall be read as a reference to [Article 26A] of the Police and Criminal Evidence (Northern Ireland) Order 1989 (SI 1989/1341 (NI 12)).

Section 15: Enforcement and compliance officers

15. (1)   The relevant Northern Ireland department may appoint officers ("enforcement officers") to act for the purposes of this Act in Northern Ireland—
  (a)   in enforcing the provisions of section 6 (prohibition of unlicensed activities), and
  (b)   in taking action in circumstances in which it appears that an offence under section 13 (persons entering into arrangements with gangmasters) has been, is being, or may be committed.
(2)   The relevant Northern Ireland department may, instead of or in addition to appointing enforcement officers under sub-paragraph (1), make arrangements with a relevant authority for officers of that authority to be enforcement officers in Northern Ireland.
(3)   The following are relevant authorities for this purpose—
  (a)   the Authority,
  (b)   any Minister of the Crown or government department,
  (c)   any Minister within the meaning of the Northern Ireland Act 1998 (c 47) or Northern Ireland department,
  (d)   any body performing functions on behalf of the Crown.

Section 17: Entry by warrant

16. In section 17 the reference in subsection (1) to information on oath shall be read as a reference to a complaint on oath.

Section 23: Annual report

17. (1)   The Secretary of State shall send to the relevant Northern Ireland department a copy of every report laid by him before Parliament under section 23.

(2)   The relevant Northern Ireland department shall lay a copy of the report before the Northern Ireland Assembly.

Section 24: Financial provision

18. In relation to payments to the Authority with respect to its functions in connection with persons acting as gangmasters in Northern Ireland or persons acting as gangmasters in relation to work in Northern Ireland, the reference in section 24(1) to the Secretary of State shall be read as a reference to the relevant Northern Ireland department.

Section 25: Regulations, rules and orders

19. (1)   In section 25(1) (meaning of "prescribed") as it applies in relation to matters in relation to which the relevant Northern Ireland department has power to make regulations the reference to the Secretary of State shall be read as a reference to the relevant Northern Ireland department.

(2)   Regulations under this Act made by the relevant Northern Ireland department shall be made by statutory rule (for the purposes of the Statutory Rules (Northern Ireland) Order 1979 (SI 1979/1573 (NI 12)).

(3)   A statutory rule containing regulations under section 3(5)(b) (regulations extending work to which this Act applies) must not be made unless a draft of the rule has been laid before and approved by the Northern Ireland Assembly.

(4)   Any other power under this Act to make a statutory rule is subject to negative resolution.

In this sub-paragraph "negative resolution" shall be construed in accordance with section 41 of the Interpretation Act (Northern Ireland) 1954 (c 33 (NI)).

Section 27: Exclusion of provisions relating to employment agencies and businesses

20. In section 27 as it applies in relation to activities in relation to work in Northern Ireland, the references to the Employment Agencies Act 1973 (c 35) shall be read as references to Part 2 of the Employment (Miscellaneous Provisions) (Northern Ireland) Order 1981 (SI 1981/839 (NI 20)).

Section 29: Commencement and transitional provision

21. Before exercising the power under section 29(1) or (3) in relation to the coming into force of any provision of this Act in relation to persons acting as gangmasters in relation to work in Northern Ireland, the Secretary of State shall consult the relevant Northern Ireland department.

NOTES

Para 14: words in first pair of square brackets substituted by the Serious Organised Crime and Police Act 2005, s 111, Sch 7, Pt 4, para 62(b); words in second pair of square brackets substituted by the Police and Criminal Evidence (Amendment) (Northern Ireland) Order 2007, SI 2007/288, art 15(4), Sch 1, para 38.

CHRISTMAS DAY (TRADING) ACT 2004

(2004 c 26)

ARRANGEMENT OF SECTIONS

An Act to prohibit the opening of large shops on Christmas Day and to restrict the loading or unloading of goods at such shops on Christmas Day

[28 October 2004]

[1.1904]
1   Prohibition of opening of large shops on Christmas Day
(1)   A large shop must not be open on Christmas Day for the serving of retail customers.
(2)   Subsection (1) does not apply to any of the shops mentioned in paragraph 3(1) of Schedule 1 to the 1994 Act (shops exempt from restrictions on Sunday trading).

(3)   If subsection (1) is contravened in relation to a shop, the occupier of the shop is liable on summary conviction to [a fine].

(4)   In its application for the purposes of subsection (2), paragraph 3(2) of Schedule 1 to the 1994 Act (which relates to the interpretation of paragraph 3(1) of that Schedule) has effect as if—
  (a)   the reference to weekdays were a reference to days of the year other than Christmas Day, and
  (b)   the reference to Sunday were a reference to Christmas Day.

(5)   In this section—
  "large shop" has the same meaning as in Schedule 1 to the 1994 Act, except that for the purposes of this section the definition of "relevant floor area" in paragraph 1 of that Schedule is to be read as if the reference to the week ending with the Sunday in question were a reference to the period of seven days ending with the Christmas Day in question;
  "retail customer" and "shop" have the same meaning as in that Schedule.

NOTES

Sub-s (3): words in square brackets substituted by the Legal Aid, Sentencing and Punishment of Offenders Act 2012 (Fines on Summary Conviction) Regulations 2015, SI 2015/664, reg 4(1), Sch 4, Pt 1, para 36, for transitional provision and savings see reg 5(1) thereof.

[1.1905]
2   Loading and unloading early on Christmas Day
(1)   Where a shop which is prohibited by section 1 from opening on Christmas Day is located in a loading control area, the occupier of the shop must not load or unload, or permit any other person to load or unload, goods from a vehicle at the shop before 9am on Christmas Day in connection with the trade or business carried on in the shop, unless the loading or unloading is carried on—
  (a)   with the consent of the local authority for the area in which the shop is situated, granted in accordance with this section, and
  (b)   in accordance with any conditions subject to which that consent is granted.

(2)   The provisions of paragraphs 3 to 8 of Schedule 3 to the 1994 Act shall apply in relation to consent under subsection (1) as they apply in relation to consent under that Schedule, but as if—
  (a)   the reference in paragraph 6(1) to Sunday were a reference to Christmas Day, and
  (b)   the reference in paragraph 7(a) to an offence under paragraph 9 of that Schedule were a reference to an offence under subsection (3).

(3)   A person who contravenes subsection (1) is liable on summary conviction to a fine not exceeding level 3 on the standard scale.

(4)   In this section, "loading control area" means any area designated by a local authority as a loading control area in accordance with section 2 of the 1994 Act.

[1.1906]
3   Enforcement
(1)   It is the duty of every local authority to enforce within their area the provisions of sections 1 and 2.

(2)   For the purposes of their duties under subsection (1), it is the duty of every local authority to appoint inspectors, who may be the same persons as those appointed as inspectors by the local authority under paragraph 2 of Schedule 2 to the 1994 Act.

(3)   Paragraphs 3 and 4 of Schedule 2 to the 1994 Act (powers of entry and obstruction of inspectors) apply in respect of inspectors appointed under subsection (2) as they apply to inspectors appointed under paragraph 2 of that Schedule and, for the purposes of paragraph 3 of that Schedule as so applied, the reference in that paragraph to the provisions of Schedules 1 and 3 to the 1994 Act is to be taken to be a reference to the provisions of sections 1 and 2 of this Act.

[(3A)   For the powers available to a local authority and the inspectors appointed by it under subsection (3) for the purposes of the duty in subsection (1), see Schedule 5 to the Consumer Rights Act 2015.]

(4)   Paragraphs 5, 6 and 7 of Schedule 2 to the 1994 Act (offences due to fault of other person, offences by body corporate and defence of due diligence) apply in respect of the offences under sections 1 and 2 as they apply in respect of offences under the 1994 Act.

(5)   In this section "local authority" has the meaning given by section 8 of the 1994 Act.

NOTES

Sub-s (3): repealed by the Consumer Rights Act 2015, s 77(2), Sch 6, para 83(1), (2), as from 1 October 2015 (for transitional provisions see the Consumer Rights Act 2015 (Commencement No 3, Transitional Provisions, Savings and Consequential Amendments) Order 2015, SI 2015/1630, arts 6–8 at **[2.1220]** et seq).

Sub-s (3A): inserted by the Consumer Rights Act 2015, s 77(2), Sch 6, para 83(1), (3), as from 1 October 2015 (for transitional provisions see note above).

4   *(Amends the Sunday Trading Act 1994, Schs 1, 3 at* **[1.1110]**, **[1.1113]**.*)*

[1.1907]
5　Expenses
There is to be paid out of money provided by Parliament any increase attributable to this Act in the sums which under any other Act are payable out of money so provided.

[1.1908]
6　Short title, interpretation, commencement and extent
(1)　This Act may be cited as the Christmas Day (Trading) Act 2004.
(2)　In this Act "the 1994 Act" means the Sunday Trading Act 1994 (c 20).
(3)　This Act comes into force on such day as the Secretary of State may by order made by statutory instrument appoint.
(4)　This Act extends to England and Wales only.

NOTES
　　Orders: the Christmas Day (Trading) Act 2004 (Commencement) Order 2004, SI 2004/3235.

MENTAL CAPACITY ACT 2005

(2005 c 9)

ARRANGEMENT OF SECTIONS

PART 1
PERSONS WHO LACK CAPACITY

The principles

69   Short title . . . .[1.1937]

SCHEDULES

An Act to make new provision relating to persons who lack capacity; to establish a superior court of record called the Court of Protection in place of the office of the Supreme Court called by that name; to make provision in connection with the Convention on the International Protection of Adults signed at the Hague on 13th January 2000; and for connected purposes

[7 April 2005]

PART 1
PERSONS WHO LACK CAPACITY

The principles

[1.1909]
1   The principles
(1)   The following principles apply for the purposes of this Act.
(2)   A person must be assumed to have capacity unless it is established that he lacks capacity.
(3)   A person is not to be treated as unable to make a decision unless all practicable steps to help him to do so have been taken without success.
(4)   A person is not to be treated as unable to make a decision merely because he makes an unwise decision.
(5)   An act done, or decision made, under this Act for or on behalf of a person who lacks capacity must be done, or made, in his best interests.
(6)   Before the act is done, or the decision is made, regard must be had to whether the purpose for which it is needed can be as effectively achieved in a way that is less restrictive of the person's rights and freedom of action.

Preliminary

[1.1910]
2   People who lack capacity
(1)   For the purposes of this Act, a person lacks capacity in relation to a matter if at the material time he is unable to make a decision for himself in relation to the matter because of an impairment of, or a disturbance in the functioning of, the mind or brain.
(2)   It does not matter whether the impairment or disturbance is permanent or temporary.
(3)   A lack of capacity cannot be established merely by reference to—
  (a)   a person's age or appearance, or
  (b)   a condition of his, or an aspect of his behaviour, which might lead others to make unjustified assumptions about his capacity.
(4)   In proceedings under this Act or any other enactment, any question whether a person lacks capacity within the meaning of this Act must be decided on the balance of probabilities.
(5)   No power which a person ("D") may exercise under this Act—
  (a)   in relation to a person who lacks capacity, or
  (b)   where D reasonably thinks that a person lacks capacity,
is exercisable in relation to a person under 16.
(6)   Subsection (5) is subject to section 18(3).

[1.1911]
3   Inability to make decisions
(1)   For the purposes of section 2, a person is unable to make a decision for himself if he is unable—
  (a)   to understand the information relevant to the decision,
  (b)   to retain that information,
  (c)   to use or weigh that information as part of the process of making the decision, or
  (d)   to communicate his decision (whether by talking, using sign language or any other means).
(2)   A person is not to be regarded as unable to understand the information relevant to a decision if he is able to understand an explanation of it given to him in a way that is appropriate to his circumstances (using simple language, visual aids or any other means).
(3)   The fact that a person is able to retain the information relevant to a decision for a short period only does not prevent him from being regarded as able to make the decision.
(4)   The information relevant to a decision includes information about the reasonably foreseeable consequences of—
  (a)   deciding one way or another, or
  (b)   failing to make the decision.

[1.1912]
4   Best interests
(1)   In determining for the purposes of this Act what is in a person's best interests, the person making the determination must not make it merely on the basis of—
    (a)   the person's age or appearance, or
    (b)   a condition of his, or an aspect of his behaviour, which might lead others to make unjustified assumptions about what might be in his best interests.
(2)   The person making the determination must consider all the relevant circumstances and, in particular, take the following steps.
(3)   He must consider—
    (a)   whether it is likely that the person will at some time have capacity in relation to the matter in question, and
    (b)   if it appears likely that he will, when that is likely to be.
(4)   He must, so far as reasonably practicable, permit and encourage the person to participate, or to improve his ability to participate, as fully as possible in any act done for him and any decision affecting him.
(5)   Where the determination relates to life-sustaining treatment he must not, in considering whether the treatment is in the best interests of the person concerned, be motivated by a desire to bring about his death.
(6)   He must consider, so far as is reasonably ascertainable—
    (a)   the person's past and present wishes and feelings (and, in particular, any relevant written statement made by him when he had capacity),
    (b)   the beliefs and values that would be likely to influence his decision if he had capacity, and
    (c)   the other factors that he would be likely to consider if he were able to do so.
(7)   He must take into account, if it is practicable and appropriate to consult them, the views of—
    (a)   anyone named by the person as someone to be consulted on the matter in question or on matters of that kind,
    (b)   anyone engaged in caring for the person or interested in his welfare,
    (c)   any donee of a lasting power of attorney granted by the person, and
    (d)   any deputy appointed for the person by the court,
as to what would be in the person's best interests and, in particular, as to the matters mentioned in subsection (6).
(8)   The duties imposed by subsections (1) to (7) also apply in relation to the exercise of any powers which—
    (a)   are exercisable under a lasting power of attorney, or
    (b)   are exercisable by a person under this Act where he reasonably believes that another person lacks capacity.
(9)   In the case of an act done, or a decision made, by a person other than the court, there is sufficient compliance with this section if (having complied with the requirements of subsections (1) to (7)) he reasonably believes that what he does or decides is in the best interests of the person concerned.
(10)   "Life-sustaining treatment" means treatment which in the view of a person providing health care for the person concerned is necessary to sustain life.
(11)   "Relevant circumstances" are those—
    (a)   of which the person making the determination is aware, and
    (b)   which it would be reasonable to regard as relevant.

[1.1913]
[4A   Restriction on deprivation of liberty
(1)   This Act does not authorise any person ("D") to deprive any other person ("P") of his liberty.
(2)   But that is subject to—
    (a)   the following provisions of this section, and
    (b)   section 4B.
(3)   D may deprive P of his liberty if, by doing so, D is giving effect to a relevant decision of the court.
(4)   A relevant decision of the court is a decision made by an order under section 16(2)(a) in relation to a matter concerning P's personal welfare.
(5)   D may deprive P of his liberty if the deprivation is authorised by Schedule A1 (hospital and care home residents: deprivation of liberty).]

NOTES
Inserted, together with s 4B, by the Mental Health Act 2007, s 50(1), (2).

[1.1914]
[4B   Deprivation of liberty necessary for life-sustaining treatment etc
(1)   If the following conditions are met, D is authorised to deprive P of his liberty while a decision as respects any relevant issue is sought from the court.
(2)   The first condition is that there is a question about whether D is authorised to deprive P of his liberty under section 4A.

(3) The second condition is that the deprivation of liberty—
- (a) is wholly or partly for the purpose of—
  - (i) giving P life-sustaining treatment, or
  - (ii) doing any vital act, or
- (b) consists wholly or partly of—
  - (i) giving P life-sustaining treatment, or
  - (ii) doing any vital act.

(4) The third condition is that the deprivation of liberty is necessary in order to—
- (a) give the life-sustaining treatment, or
- (b) do the vital act.

(5) A vital act is any act which the person doing it reasonably believes to be necessary to prevent a serious deterioration in P's condition.]

NOTES

Inserted as noted to s 4A at **[1.1913]**.

[1.1915]
5 Acts in connection with care or treatment

(1) If a person ("D") does an act in connection with the care or treatment of another person ("P"), the act is one to which this section applies if—
- (a) before doing the act, D takes reasonable steps to establish whether P lacks capacity in relation to the matter in question, and
- (b) when doing the act, D reasonably believes—
  - (i) that P lacks capacity in relation to the matter, and
  - (ii) that it will be in P's best interests for the act to be done.

(2) D does not incur any liability in relation to the act that he would not have incurred if P—
- (a) had had capacity to consent in relation to the matter, and
- (b) had consented to D's doing the act.

(3) Nothing in this section excludes a person's civil liability for loss or damage, or his criminal liability, resulting from his negligence in doing the act.

(4) Nothing in this section affects the operation of sections 24 to 26 (advance decisions to refuse treatment).

[1.1916]
6 Section 5 acts: limitations

(1) If D does an act that is intended to restrain P, it is not an act to which section 5 applies unless two further conditions are satisfied.

(2) The first condition is that D reasonably believes that it is necessary to do the act in order to prevent harm to P.

(3) The second is that the act is a proportionate response to—
- (a) the likelihood of P's suffering harm, and
- (b) the seriousness of that harm.

(4) For the purposes of this section D restrains P if he—
- (a) uses, or threatens to use, force to secure the doing of an act which P resists, or
- (b) restricts P's liberty of movement, whether or not P resists.

(5) . . .

(6) Section 5 does not authorise a person to do an act which conflicts with a decision made, within the scope of his authority and in accordance with this Part, by—
- (a) a donee of a lasting power of attorney granted by P, or
- (b) a deputy appointed for P by the court.

(7) But nothing in subsection (6) stops a person—
- (a) providing life-sustaining treatment, or
- (b) doing any act which he reasonably believes to be necessary to prevent a serious deterioration in P's condition,

while a decision as respects any relevant issue is sought from the court.

NOTES

Sub-s (5): repealed by the Mental Health Act 2007, ss 50(1), (4)(a), 55, Sch 11, Pt 10.

[1.1917]
7 Payment for necessary goods and services

(1) If necessary goods or services are supplied to a person who lacks capacity to contract for the supply, he must pay a reasonable price for them.

(2) "Necessary" means suitable to a person's condition in life and to his actual requirements at the time when the goods or services are supplied.

[1.1918]
8 Expenditure

(1) If an act to which section 5 applies involves expenditure, it is lawful for D—
- (a) to pledge P's credit for the purpose of the expenditure, and

    (b)   to apply money in P's possession for meeting the expenditure.

(2)   If the expenditure is borne for P by D, it is lawful for D—

    (a)   to reimburse himself out of money in P's possession, or

    (b)   to be otherwise indemnified by P.

(3)   Subsections (1) and (2) do not affect any power under which (apart from those subsections) a person—

    (a)   has lawful control of P's money or other property, and

    (b)   has power to spend money for P's benefit.

Lasting powers of attorney

[1.1919]

9 Lasting powers of attorney

(1)   A lasting power of attorney is a power of attorney under which the donor ("P") confers on the donee (or donees) authority to make decisions about all or any of the following—

    (a)   P's personal welfare or specified matters concerning P's personal welfare, and

    (b)   P's property and affairs or specified matters concerning P's property and affairs,

and which includes authority to make such decisions in circumstances where P no longer has capacity.

(2)   A lasting power of attorney is not created unless—

    (a)   section 10 is complied with,

    (b)   an instrument conferring authority of the kind mentioned in subsection (1) is made and registered in accordance with Schedule 1, and

    (c)   at the time when P executes the instrument, P has reached 18 and has capacity to execute it.

(3)   An instrument which—

    (a)   purports to create a lasting power of attorney, but

    (b)   does not comply with this section, section 10 or Schedule 1,

confers no authority.

(4)   The authority conferred by a lasting power of attorney is subject to—

    (a)   the provisions of this Act and, in particular, sections 1 (the principles) and 4 (best interests), and

    (b)   any conditions or restrictions specified in the instrument.

[1.1920]

10 Appointment of donees

(1)   A donee of a lasting power of attorney must be—

    (a)   an individual who has reached 18, or

    (b)   if the power relates only to P's property and affairs, either such an individual or a trust corporation.

(2)   An individual who is bankrupt [or is a person in relation to whom a debt relief order is made] may not be appointed as donee of a lasting power of attorney in relation to P's property and affairs.

(3)   Subsections (4) to (7) apply in relation to an instrument under which two or more persons are to act as donees of a lasting power of attorney.

(4)   The instrument may appoint them to act—

    (a)   jointly,

    (b)   jointly and severally, or

    (c)   jointly in respect of some matters and jointly and severally in respect of others.

(5)   To the extent to which it does not specify whether they are to act jointly or jointly and severally, the instrument is to be assumed to appoint them to act jointly.

(6)   If they are to act jointly, a failure, as respects one of them, to comply with the requirements of subsection (1) or (2) or Part 1 or 2 of Schedule 1 prevents a lasting power of attorney from being created.

(7)   If they are to act jointly and severally, a failure, as respects one of them, to comply with the requirements of subsection (1) or (2) or Part 1 or 2 of Schedule 1—

    (a)   prevents the appointment taking effect in his case, but

    (b)   does not prevent a lasting power of attorney from being created in the case of the other or others.

(8)   An instrument used to create a lasting power of attorney—

    (a)   cannot give the donee (or, if more than one, any of them) power to appoint a substitute or successor, but

    (b)   may itself appoint a person to replace the donee (or, if more than one, any of them) on the occurrence of an event mentioned in section 13(6)(a) to (d) which has the effect of terminating the donee's appointment.

NOTES

Sub-s (2): words in square brackets inserted by the Tribunals, Courts and Enforcement Act 2007 (Consequential Amendments) Order 2012, SI 2012/2404, art 3(2), Sch 2, para 53(1), (2), for transitional provisions see art 5 thereof.

[1.1921]
11 Lasting powers of attorney: restrictions
(1) A lasting power of attorney does not authorise the donee (or, if more than one, any of them) to do an act that is intended to restrain P, unless three conditions are satisfied.
(2) The first condition is that P lacks, or the donee reasonably believes that P lacks, capacity in relation to the matter in question.
(3) The second is that the donee reasonably believes that it is necessary to do the act in order to prevent harm to P.
(4) The third is that the act is a proportionate response to—
    (a)   the likelihood of P's suffering harm, and
    (b)   the seriousness of that harm.
(5) For the purposes of this section, the donee restrains P if he—
    (a)   uses, or threatens to use, force to secure the doing of an act which P resists, or
    (b)   restricts P's liberty of movement, whether or not P resists,
or if he authorises another person to do any of those things.
(6) . . .
(7) Where a lasting power of attorney authorises the donee (or, if more than one, any of them) to make decisions about P's personal welfare, the authority—
    (a)   does not extend to making such decisions in circumstances other than those where P lacks, or the donee reasonably believes that P lacks, capacity,
    (b)   is subject to sections 24 to 26 (advance decisions to refuse treatment), and
    (c)   extends to giving or refusing consent to the carrying out or continuation of a treatment by a person providing health care for P.
(8) But subsection (7)(c)—
    (a)   does not authorise the giving or refusing of consent to the carrying out or continuation of life-sustaining treatment, unless the instrument contains express provision to that effect, and
    (b)   is subject to any conditions or restrictions in the instrument.

NOTES
Sub-s (6): repealed by the Mental Health Act 2007, ss 50(1), (4)(b), 55, Sch 11, Pt 10.

[1.1922]
12 Scope of lasting powers of attorney: gifts
(1) Where a lasting power of attorney confers authority to make decisions about P's property and affairs, it does not authorise a donee (or, if more than one, any of them) to dispose of the donor's property by making gifts except to the extent permitted by subsection (2).
(2) The donee may make gifts—
    (a)   on customary occasions to persons (including himself) who are related to or connected with the donor, or
    (b)   to any charity to whom the donor made or might have been expected to make gifts,
if the value of each such gift is not unreasonable having regard to all the circumstances and, in particular, the size of the donor's estate.
(3) "Customary occasion" means—
    (a)   the occasion or anniversary of a birth, a marriage or the formation of a civil partnership, or
    (b)   any other occasion on which presents are customarily given within families or among friends or associates.
(4) Subsection (2) is subject to any conditions or restrictions in the instrument.

[1.1923]
13 Revocation of lasting powers of attorney etc
(1) This section applies if—
    (a)   P has executed an instrument with a view to creating a lasting power of attorney, or
    (b)   a lasting power of attorney is registered as having been conferred by P,
and in this section references to revoking the power include revoking the instrument.
(2) P may, at any time when he has capacity to do so, revoke the power.
(3) P's bankruptcy[, or the making of a debt relief order (under Part 7A of the Insolvency Act 1986) in respect of P,] revokes the power so far as it relates to P's property and affairs.
(4) But where P is bankrupt merely because an interim bankruptcy restrictions order has effect in respect of him [or where P is subject to an interim debt relief restrictions order (under Schedule 4ZB of the Insolvency Act 1986)], the power is suspended, so far as it relates to P's property and affairs, for so long as the order has effect.
(5) The occurrence in relation to a donee of an event mentioned in subsection (6)—
    (a)   terminates his appointment, and
    (b)   except in the cases given in subsection (7), revokes the power.
(6) The events are—
    (a)   the disclaimer of the appointment by the donee in accordance with such requirements as may be prescribed for the purposes of this section in regulations made by the Lord Chancellor,

(b)   subject to subsections (8) and (9), the death or bankruptcy of the donee [or the making of a debt relief order (under Part 7A of the Insolvency Act 1986) in respect of the donee] or, if the donee is a trust corporation, its winding-up or dissolution,

(c)   subject to subsection (11), the dissolution or annulment of a marriage or civil partnership between the donor and the donee,

(d)   the lack of capacity of the donee.

(7)   The cases are—

(a)   the donee is replaced under the terms of the instrument,

(b)   he is one of two or more persons appointed to act as donees jointly and severally in respect of any matter and, after the event, there is at least one remaining donee.

(8)   The bankruptcy of a donee [or the making of a debt relief order (under Part 7A of the Insolvency Act 1986) in respect of a donee] does not terminate his appointment, or revoke the power, in so far as his authority relates to P's personal welfare.

(9)   Where the donee is bankrupt merely because an interim bankruptcy restrictions order has effect in respect of him [or where the donee is subject to an interim debt relief restrictions order (under Schedule 4ZB of the Insolvency Act 1986),], his appointment and the power are suspended, so far as they relate to P's property and affairs, for so long as the order has effect.

(10)   Where the donee is one of two or more appointed to act jointly and severally under the power in respect of any matter, the reference in subsection (9) to the suspension of the power is to its suspension in so far as it relates to that donee.

(11)   The dissolution or annulment of a marriage or civil partnership does not terminate the appointment of a donee, or revoke the power, if the instrument provided that it was not to do so.

NOTES

Sub-ss (3), (4), (6), (8), (8): words in square brackets inserted by the Tribunals, Courts and Enforcement Act 2007 (Consequential Amendments) Order 2012, SI 2012/2404, art 3(2), Sch 2, para 53(1), (3), for transitional provisions see art 5 thereof.

Regulations: the Lasting Powers of Attorney, Enduring Powers of Attorney and Public Guardian Regulations 2007, SI 2007/1253.

[1.1924]
14   Protection of donee and others if no power created or power revoked
(1)   Subsections (2) and (3) apply if—

(a)   an instrument has been registered under Schedule 1 as a lasting power of attorney, but

(b)   a lasting power of attorney was not created,

whether or not the registration has been cancelled at the time of the act or transaction in question.

(2)   A donee who acts in purported exercise of the power does not incur any liability (to P or any other person) because of the non-existence of the power unless at the time of acting he—

(a)   knows that a lasting power of attorney was not created, or

(b)   is aware of circumstances which, if a lasting power of attorney had been created, would have terminated his authority to act as a donee.

(3)   Any transaction between the donee and another person is, in favour of that person, as valid as if the power had been in existence, unless at the time of the transaction that person has knowledge of a matter referred to in subsection (2).

(4)   If the interest of a purchaser depends on whether a transaction between the donee and the other person was valid by virtue of subsection (3), it is conclusively presumed in favour of the purchaser that the transaction was valid if—

(a)   the transaction was completed within 12 months of the date on which the instrument was registered, or

(b)   the other person makes a statutory declaration, before or within 3 months after the completion of the purchase, that he had no reason at the time of the transaction to doubt that the donee had authority to dispose of the property which was the subject of the transaction.

(5)   In its application to a lasting power of attorney which relates to matters in addition to P's property and affairs, section 5 of the Powers of Attorney Act 1971 (c 27) (protection where power is revoked) has effect as if references to revocation included the cessation of the power in relation to P's property and affairs.

(6)   Where two or more donees are appointed under a lasting power of attorney, this section applies as if references to the donee were to all or any of them.

General powers of the court and appointment of deputies

[1.1925]
15   Power to make declarations
(1)   The court may make declarations as to—

(a)   whether a person has or lacks capacity to make a decision specified in the declaration;

(b)   whether a person has or lacks capacity to make decisions on such matters as are described in the declaration;

(c)   the lawfulness or otherwise of any act done, or yet to be done, in relation to that person.

(2)   "Act" includes an omission and a course of conduct.

[1.1926]
16 Powers to make decisions and appoint deputies: general

(1) This section applies if a person ("P") lacks capacity in relation to a matter or matters concerning—

   (a) P's personal welfare, or

   (b) P's property and affairs.

(2) The court may—

   (a) by making an order, make the decision or decisions on P's behalf in relation to the matter or matters, or

   (b) appoint a person (a "deputy") to make decisions on P's behalf in relation to the matter or matters.

(3) The powers of the court under this section are subject to the provisions of this Act and, in particular, to sections 1 (the principles) and 4 (best interests).

(4) When deciding whether it is in P's best interests to appoint a deputy, the court must have regard (in addition to the matters mentioned in section 4) to the principles that—

   (a) a decision by the court is to be preferred to the appointment of a deputy to make a decision, and

   (b) the powers conferred on a deputy should be as limited in scope and duration as is reasonably practicable in the circumstances.

(5) The court may make such further orders or give such directions, and confer on a deputy such powers or impose on him such duties, as it thinks necessary or expedient for giving effect to, or otherwise in connection with, an order or appointment made by it under subsection (2).

(6) Without prejudice to section 4, the court may make the order, give the directions or make the appointment on such terms as it considers are in P's best interests, even though no application is before the court for an order, directions or an appointment on those terms.

(7) An order of the court may be varied or discharged by a subsequent order.

(8) The court may, in particular, revoke the appointment of a deputy or vary the powers conferred on him if it is satisfied that the deputy—

   (a) has behaved, or is behaving, in a way that contravenes the authority conferred on him by the court or is not in P's best interests, or

   (b) proposes to behave in a way that would contravene that authority or would not be in P's best interests.

[1.1927]
[16A Section 16 powers: Mental Health Act patients etc

(1) If a person is ineligible to be deprived of liberty by this Act, the court may not include in a welfare order provision which authorises the person to be deprived of his liberty.

(2) If—

   (a) a welfare order includes provision which authorises a person to be deprived of his liberty, and

   (b) that person becomes ineligible to be deprived of liberty by this Act,

the provision ceases to have effect for as long as the person remains ineligible.

(3) Nothing in subsection (2) affects the power of the court under section 16(7) to vary or discharge the welfare order.

(4) For the purposes of this section—

   (a) Schedule 1A applies for determining whether or not P is ineligible to be deprived of liberty by this Act;

   (b) "welfare order" means an order under section 16(2)(a).]

NOTES

Inserted by the Mental Health Act 2007, s 50(1), (3).

[1.1928]
17 Section 16 powers: personal welfare

(1) The powers under section 16 as respects P's personal welfare extend in particular to—

   (a) deciding where P is to live;

   (b) deciding what contact, if any, P is to have with any specified persons;

   (c) making an order prohibiting a named person from having contact with P;

   (d) giving or refusing consent to the carrying out or continuation of a treatment by a person providing health care for P;

   (e) giving a direction that a person responsible for P's health care allow a different person to take over that responsibility.

(2) Subsection (1) is subject to section 20 (restrictions on deputies).

[1.1929]
18 Section 16 powers: property and affairs

(1) The powers under section 16 as respects P's property and affairs extend in particular to—

   (a) the control and management of P's property;

   (b) the sale, exchange, charging, gift or other disposition of P's property;

   (c)   the acquisition of property in P's name or on P's behalf;

   (d)   the carrying on, on P's behalf, of any profession, trade or business;

   (e)   the taking of a decision which will have the effect of dissolving a partnership of which P is a member;

   (f)   the carrying out of any contract entered into by P;

   (g)   the discharge of P's debts and of any of P's obligations, whether legally enforceable or not;

   (h)   the settlement of any of P's property, whether for P's benefit or for the benefit of others;

   (i)   the execution for P of a will;

   (j)   the exercise of any power (including a power to consent) vested in P whether beneficially or as trustee or otherwise;

   (k)   the conduct of legal proceedings in P's name or on P's behalf.

(2)   No will may be made under subsection (1)(i) at a time when P has not reached 18.

(3)   The powers under section 16 as respects any other matter relating to P's property and affairs may be exercised even though P has not reached 16, if the court considers it likely that P will still lack capacity to make decisions in respect of that matter when he reaches 18.

(4)   Schedule 2 supplements the provisions of this section.

(5)   Section 16(7) (variation and discharge of court orders) is subject to paragraph 6 of Schedule 2.

(6)   Subsection (1) is subject to section 20 (restrictions on deputies).

[1.1930]

19   Appointment of deputies

(1)   A deputy appointed by the court must be—

   (a)   an individual who has reached 18, or

   (b)   as respects powers in relation to property and affairs, an individual who has reached 18 or a trust corporation.

(2)   The court may appoint an individual by appointing the holder for the time being of a specified office or position.

(3)   A person may not be appointed as a deputy without his consent.

(4)   The court may appoint two or more deputies to act—

   (a)   jointly,

   (b)   jointly and severally, or

   (c)   jointly in respect of some matters and jointly and severally in respect of others.

(5)   When appointing a deputy or deputies, the court may at the same time appoint one or more other persons to succeed the existing deputy or those deputies—

   (a)   in such circumstances, or on the happening of such events, as may be specified by the court;

   (b)   for such period as may be so specified.

(6)   A deputy is to be treated as P's agent in relation to anything done or decided by him within the scope of his appointment and in accordance with this Part.

(7)   The deputy is entitled—

   (a)   to be reimbursed out of P's property for his reasonable expenses in discharging his functions, and

   (b)   if the court so directs when appointing him, to remuneration out of P's property for discharging them.

(8)   The court may confer on a deputy powers to—

   (a)   take possession or control of all or any specified part of P's property;

   (b)   exercise all or any specified powers in respect of it, including such powers of investment as the court may determine.

(9)   The court may require a deputy—

   (a)   to give to the Public Guardian such security as the court thinks fit for the due discharge of his functions, and

   (b)   to submit to the Public Guardian such reports at such times or at such intervals as the court may direct.

[1.1931]

20   Restrictions on deputies

(1)   A deputy does not have power to make a decision on behalf of P in relation to a matter if he knows or has reasonable grounds for believing that P has capacity in relation to the matter.

(2)   Nothing in section 16(5) or 17 permits a deputy to be given power—

   (a)   to prohibit a named person from having contact with P;

   (b)   to direct a person responsible for P's health care to allow a different person to take over that responsibility.

(3)   A deputy may not be given powers with respect to—

   (a)   the settlement of any of P's property, whether for P's benefit or for the benefit of others,

   (b)   the execution for P of a will, or

   (c)   the exercise of any power (including a power to consent) vested in P whether beneficially or as trustee or otherwise.

(4)   A deputy may not be given power to make a decision on behalf of P which is inconsistent with a decision made, within the scope of his authority and in accordance with this Act, by the donee of a lasting power of attorney granted by P (or, if there is more than one donee, by any of them).

(5)   A deputy may not refuse consent to the carrying out or continuation of life-sustaining treatment in relation to P.

(6)   The authority conferred on a deputy is subject to the provisions of this Act and, in particular, sections 1 (the principles) and 4 (best interests).

(7)   A deputy may not do an act that is intended to restrain P unless four conditions are satisfied.

(8)   The first condition is that, in doing the act, the deputy is acting within the scope of an authority expressly conferred on him by the court.

(9)   The second is that P lacks, or the deputy reasonably believes that P lacks, capacity in relation to the matter in question.

(10)   The third is that the deputy reasonably believes that it is necessary to do the act in order to prevent harm to P.

(11)   The fourth is that the act is a proportionate response to—
  (a)   the likelihood of P's suffering harm, [and]
  (b)   the seriousness of that harm.

(12)   For the purposes of this section, a deputy restrains P if he—
  (a)   uses, or threatens to use, force to secure the doing of an act which P resists, or
  (b)   restricts P's liberty of movement, whether or not P resists,
or if he authorises another person to do any of those things.

(13)   . . .

NOTES

Sub-s (11): word in square brackets in para (a) substituted by the Mental Health Act 2007, s 51.

Sub-s (13): repealed by the Mental Health Act 2007, ss 50(1), (4)(c), 55, Sch 11, Pt 10.

[1.1932]
21   Transfer of proceedings relating to people under 18
[(1)]   The [Lord Chief Justice, with the concurrence of the Lord Chancellor,] may by order make provision as to the transfer of proceedings relating to a person under 18, in such circumstances as are specified in the order—
  (a)   from the Court of Protection to a court having jurisdiction under the Children Act 1989 (c 41), or
  (b)   from a court having jurisdiction under that Act to the Court of Protection.
[(2)   The Lord Chief Justice may nominate any of the following to exercise his functions under this section—
  (a)   the President of the Court of Protection;
  (b)   a judicial office holder (as defined in section 109(4) of the Constitutional Reform Act 2005).]

NOTES

Sub-s (1): numbered as such and words in square brackets substituted by the Lord Chancellor (Transfer of Functions and Supplementary Provisions) (No 2) Order 2006, SI 2006/1016, art 2, Sch 1, paras 30, 31(1)–(3).

Sub-s (2): added by SI 2006/1016, art 2, Sch 1, paras 30, 31(1), (4).

Orders: the Mental Capacity Act 2005 (Transfer of Proceedings) Order 2007, SI 2007/1899.

[Powers of the court in relation to Schedule A1

[1.1933]
21A   Powers of court in relation to Schedule A1
(1)   This section applies if either of the following has been given under Schedule A1—
  (a)   a standard authorisation;
  (b)   an urgent authorisation.
(2)   Where a standard authorisation has been given, the court may determine any question relating to any of the following matters—
  (a)   whether the relevant person meets one or more of the qualifying requirements;
  (b)   the period during which the standard authorisation is to be in force;
  (c)   the purpose for which the standard authorisation is given;
  (d)   the conditions subject to which the standard authorisation is given.
(3)   If the court determines any question under subsection (2), the court may make an order—
  (a)   varying or terminating the standard authorisation, or
  (b)   directing the supervisory body to vary or terminate the standard authorisation.
(4)   Where an urgent authorisation has been given, the court may determine any question relating to any of the following matters—
  (a)   whether the urgent authorisation should have been given;
  (b)   the period during which the urgent authorisation is to be in force;
  (c)   the purpose for which the urgent authorisation is given.
(5)   Where the court determines any question under subsection (4), the court may make an order—
  (a)   varying or terminating the urgent authorisation, or

(b)   directing the managing authority of the relevant hospital or care home to vary or terminate the urgent authorisation.

(6)   Where the court makes an order under subsection (3) or (5), the court may make an order about a person's liability for any act done in connection with the standard or urgent authorisation before its variation or termination.

(7)   An order under subsection (6) may, in particular, exclude a person from liability.]

NOTES

Inserted, together with preceding cross-heading, by the Mental Health Act 2007, s 50(7), Sch 9, Pt 1, paras 1, 2.

Powers of the court in relation to lasting powers of attorney

[1.1934]
22   Powers of court in relation to validity of lasting powers of attorney
(1)   This section and section 23 apply if—
   (a)   a person ("P") has executed or purported to execute an instrument with a view to creating a lasting power of attorney, or
   (b)   an instrument has been registered as a lasting power of attorney conferred by P.
(2)   The court may determine any question relating to—
   (a)   whether one or more of the requirements for the creation of a lasting power of attorney have been met;
   (b)   whether the power has been revoked or has otherwise come to an end.
(3)   Subsection (4) applies if the court is satisfied—
   (a)   that fraud or undue pressure was used to induce P—
      (i)   to execute an instrument for the purpose of creating a lasting power of attorney, or
      (ii)   to create a lasting power of attorney, or
   (b)   that the donee (or, if more than one, any of them) of a lasting power of attorney—
      (i)   has behaved, or is behaving, in a way that contravenes his authority or is not in P's best interests, or
      (ii)   proposes to behave in a way that would contravene his authority or would not be in P's best interests.
(4)   The court may—
   (a)   direct that an instrument purporting to create the lasting power of attorney is not to be registered, or
   (b)   if P lacks capacity to do so, revoke the instrument or the lasting power of attorney.
(5)   If there is more than one donee, the court may under subsection (4)(b) revoke the instrument or the lasting power of attorney so far as it relates to any of them.
(6)   "Donee" includes an intended donee.

[1.1935]
23   Powers of court in relation to operation of lasting powers of attorney
(1)   The court may determine any question as to the meaning or effect of a lasting power of attorney or an instrument purporting to create one.
(2)   The court may—
   (a)   give directions with respect to decisions—
      (i)   which the donee of a lasting power of attorney has authority to make, and
      (ii)   which P lacks capacity to make;
   (b)   give any consent or authorisation to act which the donee would have to obtain from P if P had capacity to give it.
(3)   The court may, if P lacks capacity to do so—
   (a)   give directions to the donee with respect to the rendering by him of reports or accounts and the production of records kept by him for that purpose;
   (b)   require the donee to supply information or produce documents or things in his possession as donee;
   (c)   give directions with respect to the remuneration or expenses of the donee;
   (d)   relieve the donee wholly or partly from any liability which he has or may have incurred on account of a breach of his duties as donee.
(4)   The court may authorise the making of gifts which are not within section 12(2) (permitted gifts).
(5)   Where two or more donees are appointed under a lasting power of attorney, this section applies as if references to the donee were to all or any of them.

24–61   *(Ss 24–44, ss 45–61 (Pt 2) outside the scope of this work.)*

PART 3
MISCELLANEOUS AND GENERAL

62, 63   *(Outside the scope of this work.)*

General

64, 65   *(Outside the scope of this work.)*

[1.1936]
66   Existing receivers and enduring powers of attorney etc
(1)   The following provisions cease to have effect—
   (a)   Part 7 of the Mental Health Act,
   (b)   the Enduring Powers of Attorney Act 1985 (c 29).
(2)   No enduring power of attorney within the meaning of the 1985 Act is to be created after the commencement of subsection (1)(b).
(3)   Schedule 4 has effect in place of the 1985 Act in relation to any enduring power of attorney created before the commencement of subsection (1)(b).
(4)   Schedule 5 contains transitional provisions and savings in relation to Part 7 of the Mental Health Act and the 1985 Act.

67, 68   (*Outside the scope of this work.*)

[1.1937]
69   Short title
This Act may be cited as the Mental Capacity Act 2005.

SCHEDULES

SCHEDULE A1

(*Sch A1 outside the scope of this work.*)

SCHEDULE 1
LASTING POWERS OF ATTORNEY: FORMALITIES

Section 9

PART 1
MAKING INSTRUMENTS

General requirements as to making instruments

[1.1938]
1. (1)   An instrument is not made in accordance with this Schedule unless—
   (a)   it is in the prescribed form,
   (b)   it complies with paragraph 2, and
   (c)   any prescribed requirements in connection with its execution are satisfied.
(2)   Regulations may make different provision according to whether—
   (a)   the instrument relates to personal welfare or to property and affairs (or to both);
   (b)   only one or more than one donee is to be appointed (and if more than one, whether jointly or jointly and severally).
(3)   In this Schedule—
   (a)   "prescribed" means prescribed by regulations, and
   (b)   "regulations" means regulations made for the purposes of this Schedule by the Lord Chancellor.

Requirements as to content of instruments

2. (1)   The instrument must include—
   (a)   the prescribed information about the purpose of the instrument and the effect of a lasting power of attorney,
   (b)   a statement by the donor to the effect that he—
      (i)   has read the prescribed information or a prescribed part of it (or has had it read to him), and
      (ii)   intends the authority conferred under the instrument to include authority to make decisions on his behalf in circumstances where he no longer has capacity,
   (c)   a statement by the donor—
      (i)   naming a person or persons whom the donor wishes to be notified of any application for the registration of the instrument, or
      (ii)   stating that there are no persons whom he wishes to be notified of any such application,
   (d)   a statement by the donee (or, if more than one, each of them) to the effect that he—
      (i)   has read the prescribed information or a prescribed part of it (or has had it read to him), and
      (ii)   understands the duties imposed on a donee of a lasting power of attorney under sections 1 (the principles) and 4 (best interests), and
   (e)   a certificate by a person of a prescribed description that, in his opinion, at the time when the donor executes the instrument—

- (i) the donor understands the purpose of the instrument and the scope of the authority conferred under it,
- (ii) no fraud or undue pressure is being used to induce the donor to create a lasting power of attorney, and
- (iii) there is nothing else which would prevent a lasting power of attorney from being created by the instrument.

(2) Regulations may—
- (a) prescribe a maximum number of named persons;
- (b) provide that, where the instrument includes a statement under sub-paragraph (1)(c)(ii), two persons of a prescribed description must each give a certificate under sub-paragraph (1)(e).

(3) The persons who may be named persons do not include a person who is appointed as donee under the instrument.

(4) In this Schedule, "named person" means a person named under sub-paragraph (1)(c).

(5) A certificate under sub-paragraph (1)(e)—
- (a) must be made in the prescribed form, and
- (b) must include any prescribed information.

(6) The certificate may not be given by a person appointed as donee under the instrument.

Failure to comply with prescribed form

3. (1) If an instrument differs in an immaterial respect in form or mode of expression from the prescribed form, it is to be treated by the Public Guardian as sufficient in point of form and expression.

(2) The court may declare that an instrument which is not in the prescribed form is to be treated as if it were, if it is satisfied that the persons executing the instrument intended it to create a lasting power of attorney.

NOTES

Regulations: the Lasting Powers of Attorney, Enduring Powers of Attorney and Public Guardian (Amendment) Regulations 2007, SI 2007/2161; the Lasting Powers of Attorney, Enduring Powers of Attorney and Public Guardian (Amendment) Regulations 2009, SI 2009/1884; the Public Guardian (Fees, etc) (Amendment) Regulations 2011, SI 2011/2189; the Lasting Powers of Attorney, Enduring Powers of Attorney and Public Guardian (Amendment) Regulations 2013, SI 2013/506; the Lasting Powers of Attorney, Enduring Powers of Attorney and Public Guardian (Amendment) Regulations 2015, SI 2015/899.

PART 2
REGISTRATION

Applications and procedure for registration

[1.1939]

4. (1) An application to the Public Guardian for the registration of an instrument intended to create a lasting power of attorney—
- (a) must be made in the prescribed form, and
- (b) must include any prescribed information.

(2) The application may be made—
- (a) by the donor,
- (b) by the donee or donees, or
- (c) if the instrument appoints two or more donees to act jointly and severally in respect of any matter, by any of the donees.

(3) The application must be accompanied by—
- (a) the instrument, and
- (b) any fee provided for under section 58(4)(b).

(4) A person who, in an application for registration, makes a statement which he knows to be false in a material particular is guilty of an offence and is liable—
- (a) on summary conviction, to imprisonment for a term not exceeding 12 months or a fine not exceeding the statutory maximum or both;
- (b) on conviction on indictment, to imprisonment for a term not exceeding 2 years or a fine or both.

5. Subject to paragraphs 11 to 14, the Public Guardian must register the instrument as a lasting power of attorney at the end of the prescribed period.

Notification requirements

6. (1) A donor about to make an application under paragraph 4(2)(a) must notify any named persons that he is about to do so.

(2) The donee (or donees) about to make an application under paragraph 4(2)(b) or (c) must notify any named persons that he is (or they are) about to do so.

7. As soon as is practicable after receiving an application by the donor under paragraph 4(2)(a), the Public Guardian must notify the donee (or donees) that the application has been received.

8. (1) As soon as is practicable after receiving an application by a donee (or donees) under paragraph 4(2)(b), the Public Guardian must notify the donor that the application has been received.

(2) As soon as is practicable after receiving an application by a donee under paragraph 4(2)(c), the Public Guardian must notify—
- (a) the donor, and
- (b) the donee or donees who did not join in making the application,

that the application has been received.

9. (1) A notice under paragraph 6 must be made in the prescribed form.

(2) A notice under paragraph 6, 7 or 8 must include such information, if any, as may be prescribed.

Power to dispense with notification requirements

10. The court may—
- (a) on the application of the donor, dispense with the requirement to notify under paragraph 6(1), or
- (b) on the application of the donee or donees concerned, dispense with the requirement to notify under paragraph 6(2),

if satisfied that no useful purpose would be served by giving the notice.

Instrument not made properly or containing ineffective provision

11. (1) If it appears to the Public Guardian that an instrument accompanying an application under paragraph 4 is not made in accordance with this Schedule, he must not register the instrument unless the court directs him to do so.

(2) Sub-paragraph (3) applies if it appears to the Public Guardian that the instrument contains a provision which—
- (a) would be ineffective as part of a lasting power of attorney, or
- (b) would prevent the instrument from operating as a valid lasting power of attorney.

(3) The Public Guardian—
- (a) must apply to the court for it to determine the matter under section 23(1), and
- (b) pending the determination by the court, must not register the instrument.

(4) Sub-paragraph (5) applies if the court determines under section 23(1) (whether or not on an application by the Public Guardian) that the instrument contains a provision which—
- (a) would be ineffective as part of a lasting power of attorney, or
- (b) would prevent the instrument from operating as a valid lasting power of attorney.

(5) The court must—
- (a) notify the Public Guardian that it has severed the provision, or
- (b) direct him not to register the instrument.

(6) Where the court notifies the Public Guardian that it has severed a provision, he must register the instrument with a note to that effect attached to it.

Deputy already appointed

12. (1) Sub-paragraph (2) applies if it appears to the Public Guardian that—
- (a) there is a deputy appointed by the court for the donor, and
- (b) the powers conferred on the deputy would, if the instrument were registered, to any extent conflict with the powers conferred on the attorney.

(2) The Public Guardian must not register the instrument unless the court directs him to do so.

Objection by donee or named person

13. (1) Sub-paragraph (2) applies if a donee or a named person—
- (a) receives a notice under paragraph 6, 7 or 8 of an application for the registration of an instrument, and
- (b) before the end of the prescribed period, gives notice to the Public Guardian of an objection to the registration on the ground that an event mentioned in section 13(3) or (6)(a) to (d) has occurred which has revoked the instrument.

(2) If the Public Guardian is satisfied that the ground for making the objection is established, he must not register the instrument unless the court, on the application of the person applying for the registration—
- (a) is satisfied that the ground is not established, and
- (b) directs the Public Guardian to register the instrument.

(3) Sub-paragraph (4) applies if a donee or a named person—
- (a) receives a notice under paragraph 6, 7 or 8 of an application for the registration of an instrument, and

(b)   before the end of the prescribed period—
     (i)   makes an application to the court objecting to the registration on a prescribed ground, and
     (ii)   notifies the Public Guardian of the application.

(4)   The Public Guardian must not register the instrument unless the court directs him to do so.

Objection by donor

14. (1)   This paragraph applies if the donor—
   (a)   receives a notice under paragraph 8 of an application for the registration of an instrument, and
   (b)   before the end of the prescribed period, gives notice to the Public Guardian of an objection to the registration.

(2)   The Public Guardian must not register the instrument unless the court, on the application of the donee or, if more than one, any of them—
   (a)   is satisfied that the donor lacks capacity to object to the registration, and
   (b)   directs the Public Guardian to register the instrument.

Notification of registration

15.   Where an instrument is registered under this Schedule, the Public Guardian must give notice of the fact in the prescribed form to—
   (a)   the donor, and
   (b)   the donee or, if more than one, each of them.

Evidence of registration

16. (1)   A document purporting to be an office copy of an instrument registered under this Schedule is, in any part of the United Kingdom, evidence of—
   (a)   the contents of the instrument, and
   (b)   the fact that it has been registered.

(2)   Sub-paragraph (1) is without prejudice to—
   (a)   section 3 of the Powers of Attorney Act 1971 (c 27) (proof by certified copy), and
   (b)   any other method of proof authorised by law.

NOTES

Regulations: the Lasting Powers of Attorney, Enduring Powers of Attorney and Public Guardian (Amendment) Regulations 2007, SI 2007/2161; the Lasting Powers of Attorney, Enduring Powers of Attorney and Public Guardian (Amendment) Regulations 2009, SI 2009/1884; the Public Guardian (Fees, etc) (Amendment) Regulations 2011, SI 2011/2189; the Lasting Powers of Attorney, Enduring Powers of Attorney and Public Guardian (Amendment) Regulations 2013, SI 2013/506; the Lasting Powers of Attorney, Enduring Powers of Attorney and Public Guardian (Amendment) Regulations 2015, SI 2015/899.

PART 3
CANCELLATION OF REGISTRATION AND NOTIFICATION OF SEVERANCE

[1.1940]

17. (1)   The Public Guardian must cancel the registration of an instrument as a lasting power of attorney on being satisfied that the power has been revoked—
   (a)   as a result of the donor's bankruptcy, or
   (b)   on the occurrence of an event mentioned in section 13(6)(a) to (d).

(2)   If the Public Guardian cancels the registration of an instrument he must notify—
   (a)   the donor, and
   (b)   the donee or, if more than one, each of them.

18.   The court must direct the Public Guardian to cancel the registration of an instrument as a lasting power of attorney if it—
   (a)   determines under section 22(2)(a) that a requirement for creating the power was not met,
   (b)   determines under section 22(2)(b) that the power has been revoked or has otherwise come to an end, or
   (c)   revokes the power under section 22(4)(b) (fraud etc).

19. (1)   Sub-paragraph (2) applies if the court determines under section 23(1) that a lasting power of attorney contains a provision which—
   (a)   is ineffective as part of a lasting power of attorney, or
   (b)   prevents the instrument from operating as a valid lasting power of attorney.

(2)   The court must—
   (a)   notify the Public Guardian that it has severed the provision, or
   (b)   direct him to cancel the registration of the instrument as a lasting power of attorney.

20.   On the cancellation of the registration of an instrument, the instrument and any office copies of it must be delivered up to the Public Guardian to be cancelled.

NOTES

Regulations: the Lasting Powers of Attorney, Enduring Powers of Attorney and Public Guardian (Amendment) Regulations 2009, SI 2009/1884; the Public Guardian (Fees, etc) (Amendment) Regulations 2011, SI 2011/2189; the Lasting Powers of Attorney, Enduring Powers of Attorney and Public Guardian (Amendment) Regulations 2013, SI 2013/506; the Lasting Powers of Attorney, Enduring Powers of Attorney and Public Guardian (Amendment) Regulations 2015, SI 2015/899.

PART 4
RECORDS OF ALTERATIONS IN REGISTERED POWERS

Partial revocation or suspension of power as a result of bankruptcy

[1.1941]

21. If in the case of a registered instrument it appears to the Public Guardian that under section 13 a lasting power of attorney is revoked, or suspended, in relation to the donor's property and affairs (but not in relation to other matters), the Public Guardian must attach to the instrument a note to that effect.

Termination of appointment of donee which does not revoke power

22. If in the case of a registered instrument it appears to the Public Guardian that an event has occurred—
  (a)   which has terminated the appointment of the donee, but
  (b)   which has not revoked the instrument,
the Public Guardian must attach to the instrument a note to that effect.

Replacement of donee

23. If in the case of a registered instrument it appears to the Public Guardian that the donee has been replaced under the terms of the instrument the Public Guardian must attach to the instrument a note to that effect.

Severance of ineffective provisions

24. If in the case of a registered instrument the court notifies the Public Guardian under paragraph 19(2)(a) that it has severed a provision of the instrument, the Public Guardian must attach to it a note to that effect.

Notification of alterations

25. If the Public Guardian attaches a note to an instrument under paragraph 21, 22, 23 or 24 he must give notice of the note to the donee or donees of the power (or, as the case may be, to the other donee or donees of the power).

NOTES

Regulations: the Lasting Powers of Attorney, Enduring Powers of Attorney and Public Guardian (Amendment) Regulations 2009, SI 2009/1884; the Public Guardian (Fees, etc) (Amendment) Regulations 2011, SI 2011/2189; the Lasting Powers of Attorney, Enduring Powers of Attorney and Public Guardian (Amendment) Regulations 2013, SI 2013/506; the Lasting Powers of Attorney, Enduring Powers of Attorney and Public Guardian (Amendment) Regulations 2015, SI 2015/899.

SCHEDULES 1A–7

(Schs 1A–7 outside the scope of this work.)

CONSUMER CREDIT ACT 2006

(2006 c 14)

ARRANGEMENT OF SECTIONS

Final provisions

An Act to amend the Consumer Credit Act 1974; to extend the ombudsman scheme under the Financial Services and Markets Act 2000 to cover licensees under the Consumer Credit Act 1974; and for connected purposes

[30 March 2006]

1–65 (*Ss 1, 2, 5–25, 27, 51, 56(1), (3), 63, 64 amend the Consumer Credit Act 1974 at* **[1.520]** *et seq and amend other provisions outside the scope of this work; ss 3, 4, 26, 28–50, 52–54, 59, 60, 62, 65 repealed by the Financial Services and Markets Act 2000 (Regulated Activities) (Amendment) (No 2) Order 2013, SI 2013/1881, art 28, Schedule, Pt 1, para 10(a); ss 55, 56(2), 57, 58 repealed by the Transfer of Functions of the Consumer Credit Appeals Tribunal Order 2009, SI 2009/1835, art 4(3), Sch 3, subject to transitional provisions in Sch 4 thereto at* **[2.791]***; s 61 amended s 4 of the 1974 Act (repealed) and amends ss 227–230, 353 of, and Sch 17 to, the 2000 Act at* **[1.1532]–[1.1535], [1.1594]***.*)

Final provisions

[1.1942]
66 Financial provision
There shall be payable out of money provided by Parliament—
  (a) any expenditure incurred by a Minister of the Crown or the Office of Fair Trading by virtue of this Act; and
  (b) any increase attributable to this Act in the sums payable out of money so provided by virtue of any other Act.

[1.1943]
67 Interpretation
In this Act—
  "the 1974 Act" means the Consumer Credit Act 1974 (c 39);
  "the 2000 Act" means the Financial Services and Markets Act 2000 (c 8).

[1.1944]
68 Consequential amendments
(1) The Secretary of State may by order made by statutory instrument make such modifications of—
  (a) any Act or subordinate legislation (within the meaning of the Interpretation Act 1978 (c 30)), or
  (b) any Northern Ireland legislation or instrument made under such legislation,
as he thinks fit in consequence of any provision of this Act.
(2) An order under this section may include transitional or transitory provisions and savings.
(3) A statutory instrument containing an order under this section may not be made by the Secretary of State unless a draft has been laid before and approved by a resolution of each House of Parliament.

[1.1945]
69 Transitional provision and savings
(1) Schedule 3 (which sets out transitional provision and savings) has effect.
(2) The Secretary of State may by order made by statutory instrument make such transitional or transitory provisions and savings as he thinks fit in connection with the coming into force of any provision of this Act.
(3) An order under this section may (amongst other things)—
  (a) where a provision of this Act is brought into force for limited purposes only, make provision about how references in Schedule 3 to the commencement of that provision of this Act are to apply;
  (b) make provision for or in connection with the application of any provision of this Act in relation to—
    (i) things existing or done, or
    (ii) persons who have done something or in relation to whom something has been done,
    before the coming into force of that provision of this Act.
(4) An order under this section may—
  (a) modify any Act or any subordinate legislation (within the meaning of the Interpretation Act 1978);
  (b) modify any Northern Ireland legislation or any instrument made under such legislation;
  (c) make different provision for different cases.
(5) Schedule 3 does not restrict the power under this section to make transitional or transitory provisions or savings.

NOTES
  Orders: the Consumer Credit Act 2006 (Commencement No 2 and Transitional Provisions and Savings) Order 2007, SI 2007/123; the Consumer Credit Act 2006 (Commencement No 3) Order 2007, SI 2007/3300; the Consumer Credit Act 2006 (Commencement No 4 and Transitional Provisions) Order 2008, SI 2008/831.

70 (*Introduces Sch 4 (outside the scope of this work).*)

[1.1946]
71 Short title, commencement and extent
(1) This Act may be cited as the Consumer Credit Act 2006.
(2) This Act (apart from this section) shall come into force on such day as the Secretary of State may by order made by statutory instrument appoint; and different days may be appointed for different purposes.
(3) This Act extends to Northern Ireland.

NOTES
Orders: the Consumer Credit Act 2006 (Commencement No 1) Order 2006, SI 2006/1508; the Consumer Credit Act 2006 (Commencement No 2 and Transitional Provisions and Savings) Order 2007, SI 2007/123; the Consumer Credit Act 2006 (Commencement No 2 and Transitional Provisions and Savings) (Amendment) Order 2007, SI 2007/387; the Consumer Credit Act 2006 (Commencement No 3) Order 2007, SI 2007/3300; the Consumer Credit Act 2006 (Commencement No 4 and Transitional Provisions) Order 2008, SI 2008/831; the Consumer Credit Act 2006 (Commencement No 4 and Transitional Provisions) (Amendment) Order 2008, SI 2008/2444.

SCHEDULES

SCHEDULES 1 AND 2

(*Sch 1 repealed by the Transfer of Functions of the Consumer Credit Appeals Tribunal Order 2009, SI 2009/1835, art 4(3), Sch 3, subject to transitional provisions in Sch 4 thereto at* **[2.791]**; *Sch 2 repealed by the Financial Services and Markets Act 2000 (Regulated Activities) (Amendment) (No 2) Order 2013, SI 2013/1881, art 28, Schedule, Pt 1, para 10(b).*)

SCHEDULE 3
TRANSITIONAL PROVISION AND SAVINGS

Section 69

Interpretation

[1.1947]
1. (1) Expressions used in the 1974 Act have the same meaning in this Schedule (apart from paragraphs 14 to 16 and 26) as they have in that Act.
(2) For the purposes of this Schedule an agreement becomes a completed agreement once—
  (a) there is no sum payable under the agreement; and
  (b) there is no sum which will or may become so payable.

Statements to be provided in relation to regulated agreements

2. . . .

3. Regulations made under section 78(4A) of the 1974 Act may apply in relation to agreements regardless of when they were made.

4. (1) Section 7(3) of this Act shall have effect in relation to agreements whenever made.
(2) A dispensing notice given under section 185(2) of the 1974 Act which is operative immediately before the commencement of section 7(3)—
  (a) shall, on the commencement of section 7(3), be treated as having been given under section 185(2) as substituted by section 7(3); and
  (b) shall continue to be operative accordingly.

Default under regulated agreements

5. The OFT shall prepare, and give general notice of, the arrears information sheet and the default information sheet required under section 86A of the 1974 Act as soon as practicable after the commencement of section 8 of this Act.

6. (1) Section 86B of the 1974 Act applies in relation to agreements whenever made.
(2) In the application of section 86B in relation to an agreement made before the commencement of section 9 of this Act, the conditions under subsection (1) can be satisfied only if the two payments mentioned in paragraph (c) were not required to have been made before the commencement of section 9.
(3) In the case of an agreement within subsection (9) of section 86B, sub-paragraph (2) has effect as if for "two" there were substituted "four".

7. (1) Section 86C of the 1974 Act applies in relation to agreements whenever made.

(2) In the application of section 86C in relation to an agreement made before the commencement of section 10 of this Act, the conditions mentioned in subsection (1) can be satisfied only if the two payments mentioned in paragraph (b) were not required to have been made before the commencement of section 10.

8. Section 86E of the 1974 Act applies in relation to agreements whenever made but only as regards default sums which become payable after the commencement of section 12 of this Act.

9. (1) Section 86F of the 1974 Act applies in relation to agreements whenever made but only as regards default sums which become payable after the commencement of section 13 of this Act.

(2) Where section 86F applies in relation to an agreement made before the commencement of section 13, the agreement shall have effect as if any right of the creditor or owner to recover compound interest in connection with the default sum in question at a particular rate were a right to recover simple interest in that connection at that rate.

10. Section 14 of this Act shall have effect in relation to any default notice served after the commencement of that section, regardless of—
  (a) when the breach of the agreement in question occurred; or
  (b) when that agreement was made.

11. The repeal by this Act of—
  (a) the words "(subject to subsections (3) and (4))" in subsection (1) of section 127 of the 1974 Act,
  (b) subsections (3) to (5) of that section, and
  (c) the words "or 127(3)" in subsection (3) of section 185 of that Act,
has no effect in relation to improperly-executed agreements made before the commencement of section 15 of this Act.

12. A debtor or hirer under an agreement may make an application under section 129(1)(ba) of the 1974 Act regardless of when that agreement was made.

13. Section 130A of the 1974 Act applies in relation to agreements whenever made but only as regards sums that are required to be paid under judgments given after the commencement of section 17 of this Act.

Unfair relationships

14. (1) The court may make an order under section 140B of the 1974 Act in connection with a credit agreement made before the commencement of section 20 of this Act but only—
  (a) on an application of the kind mentioned in paragraph (a) of subsection (2) of section 140B made at a time after the end of the transitional period; or
  (b) at the instance of the debtor or a surety in any proceedings of the kind mentioned in paragraph (b) or (c) of that subsection which were commenced at such a time.

(2) But the court shall not make such an order in connection with such an agreement so made if the agreement—
  (a) became a completed agreement before the commencement of section 20; or
  (b) becomes a completed agreement during the transitional period.

(3) Expressions used in sections 140A to 140C of the 1974 Act have the same meaning in this paragraph as they have in those sections.

(4) In this paragraph "the transitional period" means the period of one year beginning with the day of the commencement of section 20.

(5) An order under section 69 of this Act may extend, or further extend, the transitional period.

15. (1) The repeal by this Act of sections 137 to 140 of the 1974 Act shall not affect the court's power to reopen an existing agreement under those sections as set out in this paragraph.

(2) The court's power to reopen an existing agreement which—
  (a) became a completed agreement before the commencement of section 22(3) of this Act, or
  (b) becomes a completed agreement during the transitional period,
is not affected at all.

(3) The court may also reopen an existing agreement—
  (a) on an application of the kind mentioned in paragraph (a) of subsection (1) of section 139 made at a time before the end of the transitional period; or
  (b) at the instance of the debtor or a surety in any proceedings of the kind mentioned in paragraph (b) or (c) of that subsection which were commenced at such a time.

(4) Nothing in section 16A or 16B of the 1974 Act shall affect the application of sections 137 to 140 (whether by virtue of this paragraph or otherwise).

(5) The repeal or revocation by this Act of the following provisions has no effect in relation to existing agreements so far as they may be reopened as set out in this paragraph—
  (a) section 16(7) of the 1974 Act;
  (b) in section 143(b) of that Act, the words ", 139(1)(a)";

   (c)   section 171(7) of that Act;

   (d)   in subsection (1) of section 181 of that Act, the words "139(5) and (7),";

   (e)   in subsection (2) of that section, the words "or 139(5) or (7)";

   (f)   in section 61(6) of the Bankruptcy (Scotland) Act 1985 (c 66), the words from the beginning to "but";

   (g)   in section 343(6) of the Insolvency Act 1986 (c 45), the words from the beginning to "But";

   (h)   Article 316(6) of the Insolvency (Northern Ireland) Order 1989 (SI 1989/2405 (NI 19)).

(6)   Expressions used in sections 137 to 140 of the 1974 Act have the same meaning in this paragraph as they have in those sections.

(7)   In this paragraph—

"existing agreement" means a credit agreement made before the commencement of section 22(3) of this Act;

"the transitional period" means the period of one year beginning with the day of the commencement of section 22(3).

(8)   An order under section 69 of this Act may extend, or further extend, the transitional period.

16. (1)   It is immaterial for the purposes of section 140C(4)(a) to (c) of the 1974 Act when (as the case may be) a credit agreement or a linked transaction was made or a security was provided.

(2)   In relation to an order made under section 140B of the 1974 Act during the transitional period in connection with a credit agreement—

   (a)   references in subsection (1) of that section to any related agreement shall not include references to a related agreement to which this sub-paragraph applies;

   (b)   the reference to a security in paragraph (d) of that subsection shall not include a reference to a security to which this sub-paragraph applies;

and the order shall not under paragraph (g) of that subsection direct accounts to be taken, or (in Scotland) an accounting to be made, between any persons in relation to a related agreement to which this sub-paragraph applies.

(3)   Sub-paragraph (2) applies to a related agreement or a security if—

   (a)   it was made or provided before the commencement of section 21 of this Act; and

   (b)   it ceased to have any operation before the order under section 140B is made.

(4)   In relation to an order made under section 140B after the end of the transitional period in connection with a credit agreement—

   (a)   references in subsection (1) of that section to any related agreement shall not include references to a related agreement to which this sub-paragraph applies;

   (b)   the reference to a security in paragraph (d) of that subsection shall not include a reference to a security to which this sub-paragraph applies;

and the order shall not under paragraph (g) of that subsection direct accounts to be taken, or (in Scotland) an accounting to be made, between any persons in relation to a related agreement to which this sub-paragraph applies.

(5)   Sub-paragraph (4) applies to a related agreement or a security if—

   (a)   it was made or provided before the commencement of section 21; and

   (b)   it ceased to have any operation before the end of the transitional period.

(6)   Expressions used in sections 140A to 140C of the 1974 Act have the same meanings in this paragraph as they have in those sections.

(7)   In this paragraph "the transitional period" means the period of one year beginning with the day of the commencement of section 21.

(8)   An order under section 69 of this Act may extend, or further extend, the transitional period.

17. Section 1 of this Act shall have no effect for the purposes of section 140C(1) of the 1974 Act in relation to agreements made before the commencement of section 1.

18., 19.   . . .

20.–22.   . . .

23., 24.   . . .

25. . . .

Appeals

26. (1)   A person who—

(a)   immediately before the commencement of section 55 of this Act is a member of a panel established under regulation 24 of the appeals regulations, and

(b)   at the time of his appointment to that panel fell within paragraph (2)(a) of that regulation, shall be treated as having been appointed to the panel of chairmen on the day of the commencement of section 55.

(2)   A person who—

(a)   immediately before the commencement of section 55 is a member of a panel established under regulation 24 of the appeals regulations, and

(b)   is not to be treated as having been appointed to the panel of chairmen in accordance with sub-paragraph (1),

shall be treated as having been appointed to the lay panel on the day of the commencement of section 55.

(3)   A person who is to be treated as having been appointed to the panel of chairmen or to the lay panel in accordance with this paragraph shall, subject to paragraph 4(2) and (3) of Schedule A1 to the 1974 Act, hold office as a member of the panel in question—

(a)   for the remainder of the period for which he was appointed under regulation 24 of the appeals regulations; and

(b)   on the terms on which he was so appointed (except as to the renewal of his appointment).

(4)   In this paragraph—

"appeals regulations" means the Consumer Credit Licensing (Appeals) Regulations 1998 (SI 1998/1203);

"lay panel" and "panel of chairmen" have the same meanings as in Schedule A1 to the 1974 Act.

27. (1)   Neither—

(a)   subsections (1) and (2) of section 56 of this Act, nor

(b)   the repeal by this Act of subsections (2) to (5) of section 41 of the 1974 Act,

has effect in relation to determinations of the OFT made before the commencement of section 56.

(2)   This Act, so far as it repeals section 11 of the Tribunals and Inquiries Act 1992 (c 53), has no effect in relation to such determinations so made.

(3)   The repeal by this Act of paragraph 27(2) of Schedule 25 to the Enterprise Act 2002 (c 40) has no effect in relation to such determinations so made.

28.   Neither subsection (1) nor (4)(a) of section 58 of this Act has effect in relation to determinations of the OFT made before the commencement of that section.

Ombudsman scheme

29.   Section 1 of this Act shall have no effect for the purposes of section 226A(4)(a) of the 2000 Act in relation to a complaint which relates to an act or omission occurring before the commencement of section 1.

NOTES

Para 2: repealed by the Legislative Reform (Consumer Credit) Order 2008, SI 2008/2826, art 6.

Paras 18–25: repealed by the Financial Services and Markets Act 2000 (Regulated Activities) (Amendment) (No 2) Order 2013, SI 2013/1881, art 28, Schedule, Pt 1, para 10(c).

SCHEDULE 4

(Sch 4 (Repeals) outside the scope of this work.)

COMPENSATION ACT 2006

(2006 c 29)

ARRANGEMENT OF SECTIONS

An Act to specify certain factors that may be taken into account by a court determining a claim in negligence or breach of statutory duty; to make provision about damages for mesothelioma; and to make provision for the regulation of claims management services

[25 July 2006]

PART 1
STANDARD OF CARE

[1.1948]
1 Deterrent effect of potential liability
A court considering a claim in negligence or breach of statutory duty may, in determining whether the defendant should have taken particular steps to meet a standard of care (whether by taking precautions against a risk or otherwise), have regard to whether a requirement to take those steps might—
   (a) prevent a desirable activity from being undertaken at all, to a particular extent or in a particular way, or
   (b) discourage persons from undertaking functions in connection with a desirable activity.

[1.1949]
2 Apologies, offers of treatment or other redress
An apology, an offer of treatment or other redress, shall not of itself amount to an admission of negligence or breach of statutory duty.

[1.1950]
3 Mesothelioma: damages
(1) This section applies where—
   (a) a person ("the responsible person") has negligently or in breach of statutory duty caused or permitted another person ("the victim") to be exposed to asbestos,
   (b) the victim has contracted mesothelioma as a result of exposure to asbestos,
   (c) because of the nature of mesothelioma and the state of medical science, it is not possible to determine with certainty whether it was the exposure mentioned in paragraph (a) or another exposure which caused the victim to become ill, and
   (d) the responsible person is liable in tort, by virtue of the exposure mentioned in paragraph (a), in connection with damage caused to the victim by the disease (whether by reason of having materially increased a risk or for any other reason).
(2) The responsible person shall be liable—
   (a) in respect of the whole of the damage caused to the victim by the disease (irrespective of whether the victim was also exposed to asbestos—
       (i)   other than by the responsible person, whether or not in circumstances in which another person has liability in tort, or
       (ii) by the responsible person in circumstances in which he has no liability in tort), and
   (b) jointly and severally with any other responsible person.
(3) Subsection (2) does not prevent—
   (a) one responsible person from claiming a contribution from another, or
   (b) a finding of contributory negligence.
(4) In determining the extent of contributions of different responsible persons in accordance with subsection (3)(a), a court shall have regard to the relative lengths of the periods of exposure for which each was responsible; but this subsection shall not apply—
   (a) if or to the extent that responsible persons agree to apportion responsibility amongst themselves on some other basis, or
   (b) if or to the extent that the court thinks that another basis for determining contributions is more appropriate in the circumstances of a particular case.
(5) In subsection (1) the reference to causing or permitting a person to be exposed to asbestos includes a reference to failing to protect a person from exposure to asbestos.
(6) In the application of this section to Scotland—
   (a) a reference to tort shall be taken as a reference to delict, and
   (b) a reference to a court shall be taken to include a reference to a jury.
(7) The Treasury may make regulations about the provision of compensation to a responsible person where—
   (a) he claims, or would claim, a contribution from another responsible person in accordance with subsection (3)(a), but
   (b) he is unable or likely to be unable to obtain the contribution, because an insurer of the other responsible person is unable or likely to be unable to satisfy the claim for a contribution.
(8) The regulations may, in particular—
   (a) . . .
   (b) replicate or apply (with or without modification) a transitional compensation provision;
   (c) provide for a specified person to assess and pay compensation;

(d)   provide for expenses incurred (including the payment of compensation) to be met out of levies collected in accordance with section 213(3)(b) of the Financial Services and Markets Act 2000 (c 8) (the Financial Services Compensation Scheme);

(e)   modify the effect of a transitional compensation provision;

(f)   enable the [Financial Conduct Authority or the Prudential Regulation Authority] to amend the Financial Services Compensation Scheme;

(g)   modify the Financial Services and Markets Act 2000 in its application to an amendment pursuant to paragraph (f);

(h)   make, or require the making of, provision for the making of a claim by a responsible person for compensation whether or not he has already satisfied claims in tort against him;

(i)   make, or require the making of, provision which has effect in relation to claims for contributions made on or after the date on which this Act is passed.

(9)   . . .

(10)   In subsections (7) and (8)—

(a)   a reference to a responsible person includes a reference to an insurer of a responsible person, and

(b)   "transitional compensation provision" means a provision of an enactment which is made under the Financial Services and Markets Act 2000 and—

     (i)   preserves the effect of the Policyholders Protection Act 1975 (c 75), or

     (ii)   applies the Financial Services Compensation Scheme in relation to matters arising before its establishment.

(11)   Regulations under subsection (7)—

(a)   may include consequential or incidental provision,

(b)   may make provision which has effect generally or only in relation to specified cases or circumstances,

(c)   may make different provision for different cases or circumstances,

(d)   shall be made by statutory instrument, and

(e)   may not be made unless a draft has been laid before and approved by resolution of each House of Parliament.

NOTES

Sub-s (8): para (a) repealed, and in para (f) words in square brackets substituted by the Financial Services Act 2012, s 114(1), Sch 18, Pt 2, paras 109(1), (2).

Sub-s (9): repealed by the Financial Services Act 2012, s 114(1), Sch 18, Pt 2, paras 109(1), (3).

Regulations: the Compensation Act 2006 (Contribution for Mesothelioma Claims) Regulations 2006, SI 2006/3259.

4–15   ((*Pt 2) Outside the scope of this work.*)

PART 3
GENERAL

16, 17   (*Outside the scope of this work.*)

[1.1951]
18   Short title
This Act may be cited as the Compensation Act 2006.

SCHEDULE

(*Schedule outside the scope of this work.*)

FRAUD ACT 2006

(2006 c 35)

ARRANGEMENT OF SECTIONS

Fraud

An Act to make provision for, and in connection with, criminal liability for fraud and obtaining services dishonestly

[8 November 2006]

Fraud

[1.1952]
1 Fraud
(1)   A person is guilty of fraud if he is in breach of any of the sections listed in subsection (2) (which provide for different ways of committing the offence).
(2)   The sections are—
   (a)   section 2 (fraud by false representation),
   (b)   section 3 (fraud by failing to disclose information), and
   (c)   section 4 (fraud by abuse of position).
(3)   A person who is guilty of fraud is liable—
   (a)   on summary conviction, to imprisonment for a term not exceeding 12 months or to a fine not exceeding the statutory maximum (or to both);
   (b)   on conviction on indictment, to imprisonment for a term not exceeding 10 years or to a fine (or to both).
(4)   Subsection (3)(a) applies in relation to Northern Ireland as if the reference to 12 months were a reference to 6 months.

[1.1953]
2 Fraud by false representation
(1)   A person is in breach of this section if he—
   (a)   dishonestly makes a false representation, and
   (b)   intends, by making the representation—
      (i)   to make a gain for himself or another, or
      (ii)   to cause loss to another or to expose another to a risk of loss.
(2)   A representation is false if—
   (a)   it is untrue or misleading, and
   (b)   the person making it knows that it is, or might be, untrue or misleading.
(3)   "Representation" means any representation as to fact or law, including a representation as to the state of mind of—
   (a)   the person making the representation, or
   (b)   any other person.
(4)   A representation may be express or implied.
(5)   For the purposes of this section a representation may be regarded as made if it (or anything implying it) is submitted in any form to any system or device designed to receive, convey or respond to communications (with or without human intervention).

[1.1954]
3 Fraud by failing to disclose information
A person is in breach of this section if he—
   (a)   dishonestly fails to disclose to another person information which he is under a legal duty to disclose, and
   (b)   intends, by failing to disclose the information—
      (i)   to make a gain for himself or another, or
      (ii)   to cause loss to another or to expose another to a risk of loss.

[1.1955]
4 Fraud by abuse of position
(1)   A person is in breach of this section if he—
   (a)   occupies a position in which he is expected to safeguard, or not to act against, the financial interests of another person,
   (b)   dishonestly abuses that position, and
   (c)   intends, by means of the abuse of that position—
      (i)   to make a gain for himself or another, or
      (ii)   to cause loss to another or to expose another to a risk of loss.

(2)   A person may be regarded as having abused his position even though his conduct consisted of an omission rather than an act.

[1.1956]
5   "Gain" and "loss"
(1)   The references to gain and loss in sections 2 to 4 are to be read in accordance with this section.
(2)   "Gain" and "loss"—
   (a)   extend only to gain or loss in money or other property;
   (b)   include any such gain or loss whether temporary or permanent;
and "property" means any property whether real or personal (including things in action and other intangible property).
(3)   "Gain" includes a gain by keeping what one has, as well as a gain by getting what one does not have.
(4)   "Loss" includes a loss by not getting what one might get, as well as a loss by parting with what one has.

[1.1957]
6   Possession etc of articles for use in frauds
(1)   A person is guilty of an offence if he has in his possession or under his control any article for use in the course of or in connection with any fraud.
(2)   A person guilty of an offence under this section is liable—
   (a)   on summary conviction, to imprisonment for a term not exceeding 12 months or to a fine not exceeding the statutory maximum (or to both);
   (b)   on conviction on indictment, to imprisonment for a term not exceeding 5 years or to a fine (or to both).
(3)   Subsection (2)(a) applies in relation to Northern Ireland as if the reference to 12 months were a reference to 6 months.

[1.1958]
7   Making or supplying articles for use in frauds
(1)   A person is guilty of an offence if he makes, adapts, supplies or offers to supply any article—
   (a)   knowing that it is designed or adapted for use in the course of or in connection with fraud, or
   (b)   intending it to be used to commit, or assist in the commission of, fraud.
(2)   A person guilty of an offence under this section is liable—
   (a)   on summary conviction, to imprisonment for a term not exceeding 12 months or to a fine not exceeding the statutory maximum (or to both);
   (b)   on conviction on indictment, to imprisonment for a term not exceeding 10 years or to a fine (or to both).
(3)   Subsection (2)(a) applies in relation to Northern Ireland as if the reference to 12 months were a reference to 6 months.

[1.1959]
8   "Article"
(1)   For the purposes of—
   (a)   sections 6 and 7, and
   (b)   the provisions listed in subsection (2), so far as they relate to articles for use in the course of or in connection with fraud,
"article" includes any program or data held in electronic form.
(2)   The provisions are—
   (a)   section 1(7)(b) of the Police and Criminal Evidence Act 1984 (c 60),
   (b)   section 2(8)(b) of the Armed Forces Act 2001 (c 19), and
   (c)   Article 3(7)(b) of the Police and Criminal Evidence (Northern Ireland) Order 1989 (SI 1989/1341 (NI 12));
(meaning of "prohibited articles" for the purposes of stop and search powers).

[1.1960]
9   Participating in fraudulent business carried on by sole trader etc
(1)   A person is guilty of an offence if he is knowingly a party to the carrying on of a business to which this section applies.
(2)   This section applies to a business which is carried on—
   (a)   by a person who is outside the reach of [section 993 of the Companies Act 2006] (offence of fraudulent trading), and
   (b)   with intent to defraud creditors of any person or for any other fraudulent purpose.
(3)   The following are within the reach of [that section]—
   (a)   a company [(as defined in section 1(1) of the Companies Act 2006)];
   (b)   a person to whom that section applies (with or without adaptations or modifications) as if the person were a company;
   (c)   a person exempted from the application of that section.
(4)   . . .

(5) "Fraudulent purpose" has the same meaning as in [that section].

(6) A person guilty of an offence under this section is liable—

(a) on summary conviction, to imprisonment for a term not exceeding 12 months or to a fine not exceeding the statutory maximum (or to both);

(b) on conviction on indictment, to imprisonment for a term not exceeding 10 years or to a fine (or to both).

(7) Subsection (6)(a) applies in relation to Northern Ireland as if the reference to 12 months were a reference to 6 months.

NOTES

Sub-s (2): words in square brackets substituted by the Companies Act 2006 (Commencement No 3, Consequential Amendments, Transitional Provisions and Savings) Order 2007, SI 2007/2194, art 10(1), (2), Sch 4, Pt 3, para 111(1), (2), in relation to an offence if any act, omission or other event (including any result of one or more acts or omissions), proof of which is required for conviction of the offence, occurs on or after 1 October 2007.

Sub-s (3): words in first pair of square brackets substituted by SI 2007/2194, art 10(1), (2), Sch 4, Pt 3, para 111(1), (3)(a), in relation to an offence if any act, omission or other event (including any result of one or more acts or omissions), proof of which is required for conviction of the offence, occurs on or after 1 October 2007; words in square brackets in para (a) substituted by the Companies Act 2006 (Consequential Amendments, Transitional Provisions and Savings) Order 2009, SI 2009/1941, art 2(1), Sch 1, para 257.

Sub-s (4): repealed by SI 2007/2194, art 10, Sch 4, Pt 3, para 111(1), (4), Sch 5, in relation to an offence if any act, omission or other event (including any result of one or more acts or omissions), proof of which is required for conviction of the offence, occurs on or after 1 October 2007.

Sub-s (5): words in square brackets substituted by SI 2007/2194, art 10(1), (2), Sch 4, Pt 3, para 111(1), (5), in relation to an offence if any act, omission or other event (including any result of one or more acts or omissions), proof of which is required for conviction of the offence, occurs on or after 1 October 2007.

10 (*Repealed by the Companies Act 2006 (Consequential Amendments, Transitional Provisions and Savings) Order 2009, SI 2009/1941, art 2(2), Sch 2.*)

Obtaining services dishonestly

[1.1961]
11 Obtaining services dishonestly

(1) A person is guilty of an offence under this section if he obtains services for himself or another—

(a) by a dishonest act, and

(b) in breach of subsection (2).

(2) A person obtains services in breach of this subsection if—

(a) they are made available on the basis that payment has been, is being or will be made for or in respect of them,

(b) he obtains them without any payment having been made for or in respect of them or without payment having been made in full, and

(c) when he obtains them, he knows—

(i) that they are being made available on the basis described in paragraph (a), or

(ii) that they might be,

but intends that payment will not be made, or will not be made in full.

(3) A person guilty of an offence under this section is liable—

(a) on summary conviction, to imprisonment for a term not exceeding 12 months or to a fine not exceeding the statutory maximum (or to both);

(b) on conviction on indictment, to imprisonment for a term not exceeding 5 years or to a fine (or to both).

(4) Subsection (3)(a) applies in relation to Northern Ireland as if the reference to 12 months were a reference to 6 months.

Supplementary

[1.1962]
12 Liability of company officers for offences by company

(1) Subsection (2) applies if an offence under this Act is committed by a body corporate.

(2) If the offence is proved to have been committed with the consent or connivance of—

(a) a director, manager, secretary or other similar officer of the body corporate, or

(b) a person who was purporting to act in any such capacity,

he (as well as the body corporate) is guilty of the offence and liable to be proceeded against and punished accordingly.

(3) If the affairs of a body corporate are managed by its members, subsection (2) applies in relation to the acts and defaults of a member in connection with his functions of management as if he were a director of the body corporate.

[1.1963]
13 Evidence

(1) A person is not to be excused from—

(a) answering any question put to him in proceedings relating to property, or

(b) complying with any order made in proceedings relating to property, on the ground that doing so may incriminate him or his spouse or civil partner of an offence under this Act or a related offence.

(2)   But, in proceedings for an offence under this Act or a related offence, a statement or admission made by the person in—

    (a)   answering such a question, or

    (b)   complying with such an order,

is not admissible in evidence against him or (unless they married or became civil partners after the making of the statement or admission) his spouse or civil partner.

(3)   "Proceedings relating to property" means any proceedings for—

    (a)   the recovery or administration of any property,

    (b)   the execution of a trust, or

    (c)   an account of any property or dealings with property,

and "property" means money or other property whether real or personal (including things in action and other intangible property).

(4)   "Related offence" means—

    (a)   conspiracy to defraud;

    (b)   any other offence involving any form of fraudulent conduct or purpose.

[1.1964]
14   Minor and consequential amendments etc

(1)   Schedule 1 contains minor and consequential amendments.

(2)   Schedule 2 contains transitional provisions and savings.

(3)   Schedule 3 contains repeals and revocations.

[1.1965]
15   Commencement and extent

(1)   This Act (except this section and section 16) comes into force on such day as the Secretary of State may appoint by an order made by statutory instrument; and different days may be appointed for different purposes.

(2)   Subject to subsection (3), sections 1 to 9 and 11 to 13 extend to England and Wales and Northern Ireland only.

(3)   Section 8, so far as it relates to the Armed Forces Act 2001 (c 19), extends to any place to which that Act extends.

(4)   Any amendment in section 10 or Schedule 1, and any related provision in section 14 or Schedule 2 or 3, extends to any place to which the provision which is the subject of the amendment extends.

NOTES

    Orders: the Fraud Act 2006 (Commencement) Order 2006, SI 2006/3200.

[1.1966]
16   Short title

This Act may be cited as the Fraud Act 2006.

SCHEDULES

SCHEDULE 1

(Sch 1 (Minor and Consequential Amendments) outside the scope of this work.)

SCHEDULE 2
TRANSITIONAL PROVISIONS AND SAVINGS

Section 14(2)

Maximum term of imprisonment for offences under this Act

[1.1967]
1.   In relation to an offence committed before the commencement of section 154(1) of the Criminal Justice Act 2003 (c 44), the references to 12 months in sections 1(3)(a), 6(2)(a), 7(2)(a), 9(6)(a) and 11(3)(a) are to be read as references to 6 months.

Increase in penalty for fraudulent trading

2.   Section 10 does not affect the penalty for any offence committed before that section comes into force.

Abolition of deception offences

3. (1)   Paragraph 1 of Schedule 1 does not affect any liability, investigation, legal proceeding or penalty for or in respect of any offence partly committed before the commencement of that paragraph.

(2)   An offence is partly committed before the commencement of paragraph 1 of Schedule 1 if—

    (a)   a relevant event occurs before its commencement, and

    (b)   another relevant event occurs on or after its commencement.

(3) "Relevant event", in relation to an offence, means any act, omission or other event (including any result of one or more acts or omissions) proof of which is required for conviction of the offence.

Scope of offences relating to stolen goods under the Theft Act 1968 (c 60)

4. Nothing in paragraph 6 of Schedule 1 affects the operation of section 24 of the Theft Act 1968 in relation to goods obtained in the circumstances described in section 15(1) of that Act where the obtaining is the result of a deception made before the commencement of that paragraph.

Dishonestly retaining a wrongful credit under the Theft Act 1968

5. Nothing in paragraph 7 of Schedule 1 affects the operation of section 24A(7) and (8) of the Theft Act 1968 in relation to credits falling within section 24A(3) or (4) of that Act and made before the commencement of that paragraph.

Scope of offences relating to stolen goods under the Theft Act (Northern Ireland) 1969 (c 16 (NI))

6. Nothing in paragraph 11 of Schedule 1 affects the operation of section 23 of the Theft Act (Northern Ireland) 1969 in relation to goods obtained in the circumstances described in section 15(1) of that Act where the obtaining is the result of a deception made before the commencement of that paragraph.

Dishonestly retaining a wrongful credit under the Theft Act (Northern Ireland) 1969

7. Nothing in paragraph 12 of Schedule 1 affects the operation of section 23A(7) and (8) of the Theft Act (Northern Ireland) 1969 in relation to credits falling within section 23A(3) or (4) of that Act and made before the commencement of that paragraph.

Limitation periods under the Limitation Act 1980 (c 58)

8. Nothing in paragraph 18 of Schedule 1 affects the operation of section 4 of the Limitation Act 1980 in relation to chattels obtained in the circumstances described in section 15(1) of the Theft Act 1968 where the obtaining is a result of a deception made before the commencement of that paragraph.

Limitation periods under the Limitation (Northern Ireland) Order 1989 (SI 1989/1339 (NI 11))

9. Nothing in paragraph 22 of Schedule 1 affects the operation of Article 18 of the Limitation (Northern Ireland) Order 1989 in relation to chattels obtained in the circumstances described in section 15(1) of the Theft Act (Northern Ireland) 1969 where the obtaining is a result of a deception made before the commencement of that paragraph.

Scheduled offences under the Terrorism Act 2000 (c 11)

10. Nothing in paragraph 30 of Schedule 1 affects the operation of Part 7 of the Terrorism Act 2000 in relation to an offence under section 15(1) of the Theft Act (Northern Ireland) 1969 where the obtaining is a result of a deception made before the commencement of that paragraph.

Powers of arrest under Asylum and Immigration (Treatment of Claimants, etc) Act 2004 (c 19)

11. (1)   Nothing in paragraph 35 of Schedule 1 affects the power of arrest conferred by section 14 of the Asylum and Immigration (Treatment of Claimants, etc) Act 2004 in relation to an offence partly committed before the commencement of that paragraph.

(2) An offence is partly committed before the commencement of paragraph 35 of Schedule 1 if—

    (a)   a relevant event occurs before its commencement, and

    (b)   another relevant event occurs on or after its commencement.

(3) "Relevant event", in relation to an offence, means any act, omission or other event (including any result of one or more acts or omissions) proof of which is required for conviction of the offence.

SCHEDULE 3

(Sch 3 (Repeals and Revocations) outside the scope of this work.)

COMPANIES ACT 2006

(2006 c 46)

ARRANGEMENT OF SECTIONS

PART 41
BUSINESS NAMES

CHAPTER 1
RESTRICTED OR PROHIBITED NAMES

An Act to reform company law and restate the greater part of the enactments relating to companies; to make other provision relating to companies and other forms of business organisation; to make provision about directors' disqualification, business names, auditors and actuaries; to amend Part 9 of the Enterprise Act 2002; and for connected purposes

[8 November 2006]

1–1191   *((Pts 1–40) Outside the scope of this work.)*

PART 41
BUSINESS NAMES

CHAPTER 1
RESTRICTED OR PROHIBITED NAMES

Introductory

[1.1968]
1192 Application of this Chapter
(1) This Chapter applies to any person carrying on business in the United Kingdom.
(2) The provisions of this Chapter do not prevent—
  (a) an individual carrying on business under a name consisting of his surname without any addition other than a permitted addition, or
  (b) individuals carrying on business in partnership under a name consisting of the surnames of all the partners without any addition other than a permitted addition.
(3) The following are the permitted additions—
  (a) in the case of an individual, his forename or initial;
  (b) in the case of a partnership—
      (i) the forenames of individual partners or the initials of those forenames, or
      (ii) where two or more individual partners have the same surname, the addition of "s" at the end of that surname;
  (c) in either case, an addition merely indicating that the business is carried on in succession to a former owner of the business.

Sensitive words or expressions

[1.1969]
1193 Name suggesting connection with government or public authority
(1) A person must not, without the approval of the Secretary of State, carry on business in the United Kingdom under a name that would be likely to give the impression that the business is connected with—
  (a) Her Majesty's Government, any part of the Scottish administration[, the Welsh Assembly Government] or Her Majesty's Government in Northern Ireland,
  (b) any local authority, or
  (c) any public authority specified for the purposes of this section by regulations made by the Secretary of State.
(2) For the purposes of this section—
  "local authority" means—
      (a) a local authority within the meaning of the Local Government Act 1972 (c 70), the Common Council of the City of London or the Council of the Isles of Scilly,
      (b) a council constituted under section 2 of the Local Government etc (Scotland) Act 1994 (c 39), or
      (c) a district council in Northern Ireland;
  "public authority" includes any person or body having functions of a public nature.
(3) Regulations under this section are subject to affirmative resolution procedure.
(4) A person who contravenes this section commits an offence.
(5) Where an offence under this section is committed by a body corporate, an offence is also committed by every officer of the body who is in default.
(6) A person guilty of an offence under this section is liable on summary conviction to a fine not exceeding level 3 on the standard scale and, for continued contravention, a daily default fine not exceeding one-tenth of level 3 on the standard scale.

NOTES
  Sub-s (1): words in square brackets inserted by the Government of Wales Act 2006 (Consequential Modifications, Transitional Provisions and Saving) Order 2009, SI 2009/2958, arts 8, 11.
  Regulations: the Company, Limited Liability Partnership and Business (Names and Trading Disclosures) Regulations 2015, SI 2015/17.

[1.1970]
1194 Other sensitive words or expressions
(1) A person must not, without the approval of the Secretary of State, carry on business in the United Kingdom under a name that includes a word or expression for the time being specified in regulations made by the Secretary of State under this section.
(2) Regulations under this section are subject to approval after being made.
(3) A person who contravenes this section commits an offence.
(4) Where an offence under this section is committed by a body corporate, an offence is also committed by every officer of the body who is in default.
(5) A person guilty of an offence under this section is liable on summary conviction to a fine not exceeding level 3 on the standard scale and, for continued contravention, a daily default fine not exceeding one-tenth of level 3 on the standard scale.

NOTES
Regulations: the Company, Limited Liability Partnership and Business Names (Sensitive Words and Expressions) Regulations 2014, SI 2014/3140.

[1.1971]
1195   Requirement to seek comments of government department or other relevant body

(1)   The Secretary of State may by regulations under—
  (a)   section 1193 (name suggesting connection with government or public authority), or
  (b)   section 1194 (other sensitive words or expressions),
require that, in connection with an application for the approval of the Secretary of State under that section, the applicant must seek the view of a specified Government department or other body.

(2)   Where such a requirement applies, the applicant must request the specified department or other body (in writing) to indicate whether (and if so why) it has any objections to the proposed name.

(3)   He must submit to the Secretary of State a statement that such a request has been made and a copy of any response received from the specified body.

(4)   If these requirements are not complied with, the Secretary of State may refuse to consider the application for approval.

(5)   In this section "specified" means specified in the regulations.

NOTES
Regulations: the Company, Limited Liability Partnership and Business Names (Sensitive Words and Expressions) Regulations 2014, SI 2014/3140; the Company, Limited Liability Partnership and Business (Names and Trading Disclosures) Regulations 2015, SI 2015/17.

[1.1972]
1196   Withdrawal of Secretary of State's approval

(1)   This section applies to approval given for the purposes of—
  section 1193 (name suggesting connection with government or public authority), or
  section 1194 (other sensitive words or expressions).

(2)   If it appears to the Secretary of State that there are overriding considerations of public policy that require such approval to be withdrawn, the approval may be withdrawn by notice in writing given to the person concerned.

(3)   The notice must state the date as from which approval is withdrawn.

Misleading names

[1.1973]
1197   Name containing inappropriate indication of company type or legal form

(1)   The Secretary of State may make provision by regulations prohibiting a person from carrying on business in the United Kingdom under a name consisting of or containing specified words, expressions or other indications—
  (a)   that are associated with a particular type of company or form of organisation, or
  (b)   that are similar to words, expressions or other indications associated with a particular type of company or form of organisation.

(2)   The regulations may prohibit the use of words, expressions or other indications—
  (a)   in a specified part, or otherwise than in a specified part, of a name;
  (b)   in conjunction with, or otherwise than in conjunction with, such other words, expressions or indications as may be specified.

(3)   In this section "specified" means specified in the regulations.

(4)   Regulations under this section are subject to negative resolution procedure.

(5)   A person who uses a name in contravention of regulations under this section commits an offence.

(6)   Where an offence under this section is committed by a body corporate, an offence is also committed by every officer of the body who is in default.

(7)   A person guilty of an offence under this section is liable on summary conviction to a fine not exceeding level 3 on the standard scale and, for continued contravention, a daily default fine not exceeding one-tenth of level 3 on the standard scale.

NOTES
Regulations: the Company, Limited Liability Partnership and Business (Names and Trading Disclosures) Regulations 2015, SI 2015/17.

[1.1974]
1198   Name giving misleading indication of activities

(1)   A person must not carry on business in the United Kingdom under a name that gives so misleading an indication of the nature of the activities of the business as to be likely to cause harm to the public.

(2)   A person who uses a name in contravention of this section commits an offence.

(3)   Where an offence under this section is committed by a body corporate, an offence is also committed by every officer of the body who is in default.

(4)   A person guilty of an offence under this section is liable on summary conviction to a fine not exceeding level 3 on the standard scale and, for continued contravention, a daily default fine not exceeding one-tenth of level 3 on the standard scale.

Supplementary

[1.1975]
1199   Savings for existing lawful business names
(1)   This section has effect in relation to—
sections 1192 to 1196 (sensitive words or expressions), and
section 1197 (inappropriate indication of company type or legal form).
(2)   Those sections do not apply to the carrying on of a business by a person who—
  (a)   carried on the business immediately before the date on which this Chapter came into force, and
  (b)   continues to carry it on under the name that immediately before that date was its lawful business name.
(3)   Where—
  (a)   a business is transferred to a person on or after the date on which this Chapter came into force, and
  (b)   that person carries on the business under the name that was its lawful business name immediately before the transfer,
those sections do not apply in relation to the carrying on of the business under that name during the period of twelve months beginning with the date of the transfer.
(4)   In this section "lawful business name", in relation to a business, means a name under which the business was carried on without contravening—
  (a)   section 2(1) of the Business Names Act 1985 (c 7) or Article 4(1) of the Business Names (Northern Ireland) Order 1986 (SI 1986/1033 NI 7)), or
  (b)   after this Chapter has come into force, the provisions of this Chapter.

CHAPTER 2
DISCLOSURE REQUIRED IN CASE OF INDIVIDUAL OR PARTNERSHIP

Introductory

[1.1976]
1200   Application of this Chapter
(1)   This Chapter applies to an individual or partnership carrying on business in the United Kingdom under a business name.
References in this Chapter to "a person to whom this Chapter applies" are to such an individual or partnership.
(2)   For the purposes of this Chapter a "business name" means a name other than—
  (a)   in the case of an individual, his surname without any addition other than a permitted addition;
  (b)   in the case of a partnership—
    (i)   the surnames of all partners who are individuals, and
    (ii)   the corporate names of all partners who are bodies corporate,
    without any addition other than a permitted addition.
(3)   The following are the permitted additions—
  (a)   in the case of an individual, his forename or initial;
  (b)   in the case of a partnership—
    (i)   the forenames of individual partners or the initials of those forenames, or
    (ii)   where two or more individual partners have the same surname, the addition of "s" at the end of that surname;
  (c)   in either case, an addition merely indicating that the business is carried on in succession to a former owner of the business.

[1.1977]
[1201   Information required to be disclosed
(1)   The "information required by this Chapter" is—
  (a)   in the case of an individual, the individual's name;
  (b)   in the case of a partnership, the name of each member of the partnership;
and, in relation to each person so named, an address at which service of any document relating in any way to the business will be effective.
(2)   If the individual or partnership has a place of business in the United Kingdom, the address must be in the United Kingdom.
(3)   If the individual or partnership does not have a place of business in the United Kingdom, the address must be an address at which service of documents can be effected by physical delivery and the delivery of documents is capable of being recorded by the obtaining of an acknowledgement of delivery.]

NOTES

Substituted by the Companies Act 2006 (Substitution of Section 1201) Regulations 2009, SI 2009/3182, reg 2.

Disclosure requirements

[1.1978]

1202   Disclosure required: business documents etc

(1)   A person to whom this Chapter applies must state the information required by this Chapter, in legible characters, on all—

    (a)   business letters,

    (b)   written orders for goods or services to be supplied to the business,

    (c)   invoices and receipts issued in the course of the business, and

    (d)   written demands for payment of debts arising in the course of the business.

This subsection has effect subject to section 1203 (exemption for large partnerships if certain conditions met).

(2)   A person to whom this Chapter applies must secure that the information required by this Chapter is immediately given, by written notice, to any person with whom anything is done or discussed in the course of the business and who asks for that information.

(3)   The Secretary of State may by regulations require that such notices be given in a specified form.

(4)   Regulations under this section are subject to negative resolution procedure.

[1.1979]

1203   Exemption for large partnerships if certain conditions met

(1)   Section 1202(1) (disclosure required in business documents) does not apply in relation to a document issued by a partnership of more than 20 persons if the following conditions are met.

(2)   The conditions are that—

    (a)   the partnership maintains at its principal place of business a list of the names of all the partners,

    (b)   no partner's name appears in the document, except in the text or as a signatory, and

    (c)   the document states in legible characters the address of the partnership's principal place of business and that the list of the partners' names is open to inspection there.

(3)   Where a partnership maintains a list of the partners' names for the purposes of this section, any person may inspect the list during office hours.

(4)   Where an inspection required by a person in accordance with this section is refused, an offence is committed by any member of the partnership concerned who without reasonable excuse refused the inspection or permitted it to be refused.

(5)   A person guilty of an offence under subsection (4) is liable on summary conviction to a fine not exceeding level 3 on the standard scale and, for continued contravention, a daily default fine not exceeding one-tenth of level 3 on the standard scale.

[1.1980]

1204   Disclosure required: business premises

(1)   A person to whom this Chapter applies must, in any premises—

    (a)   where the business is carried on, and

    (b)   to which customers of the business or suppliers of goods or services to the business have access,

display in a prominent position, so that it may easily be read by such customers or suppliers, a notice containing the information required by this Chapter.

(2)   The Secretary of State may by regulations require that such notices be displayed in a specified form.

(3)   Regulations under this section are subject to negative resolution procedure.

Consequences of failure to make required disclosure

[1.1981]

1205   Criminal consequences of failure to make required disclosure

(1)   A person who without reasonable excuse fails to comply with the requirements of—

    section 1202 (disclosure required: business documents etc), or

    section 1204 (disclosure required: business premises),

commits an offence.

(2)   Where an offence under this section is committed by a body corporate, an offence is also committed by every officer of the body who is in default.

(3)   A person guilty of an offence under this section is liable on summary conviction to a fine not exceeding level 3 on the standard scale and, for continued contravention, a daily default fine not exceeding one-tenth of level 3 on the standard scale.

(4)   References in this section to the requirements of section 1202 or 1204 include the requirements of regulations under that section.

[1.1982]
1206   Civil consequences of failure to make required disclosure
(1)   This section applies to any legal proceedings brought by a person to whom this Chapter applies to enforce a right arising out of a contract made in the course of a business in respect of which he was, at the time the contract was made, in breach of section 1202(1) or (2) (disclosure in business documents etc) or section 1204(1) (disclosure at business premises).
(2)   The proceedings shall be dismissed if the defendant (in Scotland, the defender) to the proceedings shows—
   (a)   that he has a claim against the claimant (pursuer) arising out of the contract that he has been unable to pursue by reason of the latter's breach of the requirements of this Chapter, or
   (b)   that he has suffered some financial loss in connection with the contract by reason of the claimant's (pursuer's) breach of those requirements,
unless the court before which the proceedings are brought is satisfied that it is just and equitable to permit the proceedings to continue.
(3)   References in this section to the requirements of this Chapter include the requirements of regulations under this Chapter.
(4)   This section does not affect the right of any person to enforce such rights as he may have against another person in any proceedings brought by that person.

CHAPTER 3
SUPPLEMENTARY

[1.1983]
1207   Application of general provisions about offences
The provisions of sections 1121 to 1123 (liability of officer in default) and 1125 to 1131 (general provisions about offences) apply in relation to offences under this Part as in relation to offences under the Companies Acts.

[1.1984]
1208   Interpretation
In this Part—
   "business" includes a profession;
   "initial" includes any recognised abbreviation of a name;
   "partnership" means—
      (a)   a partnership within the Partnership Act 1890 (c 39), or
      (b)   a limited partnership registered under the Limited Partnerships Act 1907 (c 24),
      or a firm or entity of a similar character formed under the law of a country or territory outside the United Kingdom;
   "surname", in relation to a peer or person usually known by a British title different from his surname, means the title by which he is known.

1209–1297   *((Pts 42–46) Outside the scope of this work.)*

PART 47
FINAL PROVISIONS

[1.1985]
1298   Short title
The short title of this Act is the Companies Act 2006.

[1.1986]
1299   Extent
Except as otherwise provided (or the context otherwise requires), the provisions of this Act extend to the whole of the United Kingdom.

[1.1987]
1300   Commencement
(1)   The following provisions come into force on the day this Act is passed—
   (a)–(c)   *(outside the scope of this work)*
   (d)   this Part.
(2)   The other provisions of this Act come into force on such day as may be appointed by order of the Secretary of State or the Treasury.

NOTES
   Orders: the Companies Act 2006 (Commencement No 1, Transitional Provisions and Savings) Order 2006, SI 2006/3428; the Companies Act 2006 (Commencement No 2, Consequential Amendments, Transitional Provisions and Savings) Order 2007, SI 2007/1093; the Companies Act 2006 (Commencement No 3, Consequential Amendments, Transitional Provisions and Savings) Order 2007, SI 2007/2194; the Companies Act 2006 (Commencement No 4 and Commencement No 3 (Amendment)) Order 2007, SI 2007/2607; the Companies Act 2006 (Commencement No 5, Transitional Provisions and Savings) Order 2007, SI 2007/3495; the Companies Act 2006 (Commencement No 6, Saving and Commencement Nos 3 and 5 (Amendment))

Order 2008, SI 2008/674; the Companies Act 2006 (Commencement No 7, Transitional Provisions and Savings) Order 2008, SI 2008/1886; the Companies Act 2006 (Commencement No 8, Transitional Provisions and Savings) Order 2008, SI 2008/2860; the Companies Act 2006 (Consequential Amendments, Transitional Provisions and Savings) Order 2009, SI 2009/1941; the Companies Act 2006 and Limited Liability Partnerships (Transitional Provisions and Savings) (Amendment) Regulations 2009, SI 2009/2476; the Companies and Limited Liability Partnerships (Forms, etc) Amendment Regulations 2013, SI 2013/1947.

SCHEDULES

SCHEDULES 1–16

(Schs 1–16 outside the scope of this work.)

INVESTMENT EXCHANGES AND CLEARING HOUSES ACT 2006

(2006 c 55)

An Act to confer power on the Financial Services Authority to disallow excessive regulatory provision by recognised investment exchanges and clearing houses; and for connected purposes

[19 December 2006]

1–4 *(S 1 inserts the Financial Services and Markets Act 2000, s 300A; s 2 inserts ss 300B–300E of the 2000 Act; s 3 repealed by s 3(8) of this Act; s 4 inserts s 290A of the 2000 Act.)*

[1.1988]
5 Short title and commencement
(1) The short title of this Act is the Investment Exchanges and Clearing Houses Act 2006.
(2) This Act comes into force on the day after that on which it is passed.
(3) Sections 300A to 300E of the Financial Services and Markets Act 2000 (c 8) (as inserted by this Act)—
  (a) do not apply to regulatory provision made before that day, and
  (b) apply to regulatory provision proposed on or after that day, whenever originally proposed.
  Expressions used in this subsection that are defined for the purposes of those sections have the same meaning as in those sections.

CONSUMERS, ESTATE AGENTS AND REDRESS ACT 2007

(2007 c 17)

ARRANGEMENT OF SECTIONS

PART 1
THE CONSUMER ADVOCACY BODIES

An Act to make provision for the establishment of the National Consumer Council and its functions; to make provision for the abolition of other consumer bodies; to make provision about the handling of consumer complaints by certain providers; to make provision requiring certain providers to be members of redress schemes in respect of consumer complaints; to amend the Estate Agents Act 1979; to make provision about the cancellation of certain contracts concluded away from business premises; and for connected purposes

[19 July 2007]

PART 1
[THE CONSUMER ADVOCACY BODIES]

NOTES
  Part heading: substituted by the Public Bodies (Abolition of the National Consumer Council and Transfer of the Office of Fair Trading's Functions in relation to Estate Agents etc) Order 2014, SI 2014/631, arts 3, 4, Sch 1, Pt 1, para 12(1), (2), for transitional provisions see arts 3, 4, Sch 1, Pt 5 thereof at **[2.1131]**, **[2.1132]**, **[2.1134]**.

[The Consumer Advocacy Bodies]

[1.1989]
[1   The consumer advocacy bodies
(1)   In this Act—
  "Citizens Advice" means the National Association of Citizens Advice Bureaux;
  "Citizens Advice Scotland" means the Scottish Association of Citizens Advice Bureaux;
  "the GCCNI" means the General Consumer Council for Northern Ireland.
(2)   Except where this Act otherwise provides, a reference in this Act to a consumer advocacy body is a reference to—
  (a)   Citizens Advice,
  (b)   Citizens Advice Scotland, or
  (c)   the GCCNI.
(3)   Except where this Act otherwise provides, Citizens Advice and Citizens Advice Scotland may jointly carry out a function conferred by or under this Act on Citizens Advice or Citizens Advice Scotland, and each may if the other agrees carry out on behalf of the other a function conferred on the other by or under this Act.
(4)   A function conferred on the GCCNI by this Act may be exercised by the GCCNI only in relation to consumer matters that relate to postal services in Northern Ireland.]

NOTES
  Cross-heading: substituted by the Public Bodies (Abolition of the National Consumer Council and Transfer of the Office of Fair Trading's Functions in relation to Estate Agents etc) Order 2014, SI 2014/631, arts 3, 4, Sch 1, Pt 1, para 12(1), (3), for transitional provisions see arts 3, 4, Sch 1, Pt 5 thereof at **[2.1131]**, **[2.1132]**, **[2.1134]**.
  Substituted by SI 2014/631, arts 3, 4, Sch 1, Pt 1, para 12(1), (4), for transitional provisions see note above.

2   (*Repealed by the Public Bodies (Abolition of the National Consumer Council and Transfer of the Office of Fair Trading's Functions in relation to Estate Agents etc) Order 2014, SI 2014/631, arts 3, 4, Sch 1, Pt 1, para 12(1), (5), for transitional provisions see arts 3, 4, Sch 1, Pt 5 thereof at* **[2.1131]**, **[2.1132]**, **[2.1134]**.*)*

"Consumer", "consumer matters" and "designated consumers"

[1.1990]
3   "Consumer" and "consumer matters"
(1)   In this Part "consumer" and "consumer matters" have the meaning given by this section.
(2)   "Consumer" means—
  (a)   a person who purchases, uses or receives, in Great Britain, goods or services which are supplied in the course of a business carried on by the person supplying or seeking to supply them, or
  (b)   a person who purchases, uses or receives [postal services] in Northern Ireland.
(3)   "Consumer" includes both an existing consumer and a future consumer.
(4)   For the purposes of subsection (2)—
  (a)   a person who uses services includes, in relation to [postal services], an addressee;
  (b)   "goods" includes land or an interest in land;

(c) "business" includes a profession and the activities of any government department, local or public authority or other public body.

(5) "Consumer matters" means—

(a) the interests of consumers, and

(b) any matter connected with those interests.

NOTES

Sub-ss (2), (4): words in square brackets substituted by the Postal Services Act 2011, s 91(1), (2), Sch 12, Pt 3, paras 175, 176.

[1.1991]
4 "Designated consumers"

(1) In this Part "designated consumers" means—

(a) consumers in relation to gas conveyed through pipes or electricity conveyed by distribution systems or transmission systems, and

(b) consumers in relation to [postal services].

(2) The Secretary of State may, by order, amend subsection (1) so as—

(a) to make any description of consumers within subsection (3) "designated consumers" for the purposes of this Part;

(b) to provide for any description of consumers to cease to be "designated consumers" for those purposes.

(3) The consumers within this subsection are consumers in England and Wales in relation to services provided by a water undertaker, a sewerage undertaker *or a licensed water supplier*, in *its capacity* as such.

(4) Before making an order under subsection (2), the Secretary of State must consult—

[(a) except in the case of an order which relates only to consumers in Northern Ireland, Citizens Advice,

(aa) in the case of a relevant order other than one relating only to consumers in Northern Ireland or consumers within subsection (3), Citizens Advice Scotland,

(ab) in the case of an order which relates to consumers in Northern Ireland in relation to postal services, the GCCNI,]

(b) in the case of a relevant order, the Scottish Ministers,

(c) the Welsh Ministers, and

(d) such other persons as the Secretary of State considers appropriate.

(5) For this purpose a "relevant order" is an order which relates to any description of—

(a) consumers in relation to gas conveyed through pipes or electricity conveyed by distribution systems or transmission systems, or

(b) consumers in relation to [postal services].

NOTES

Sub-ss (1), (5): words in square brackets in para (b) substituted by the Postal Services Act 2011, s 91(1), (2), Sch 12, Pt 3, paras 175, 176.

Sub-s (3): for the words in italics there are substituted the words ", a water supply licensee or a sewerage licensee" and "the undertaker's or licensee's capacity" respectively by the Water Act 2014, s 56, Sch 7, paras 136, 137, as from a day to be appointed.

Sub-s (4): paras (a), (aa), (ab) substituted, for original para (a), by the Public Bodies (Abolition of the National Consumer Council and Transfer of the Office of Fair Trading's Functions in relation to Estate Agents etc) Order 2014, SI 2014/631, arts 3, 4, Sch 1, Pt 1, para 12(1), (6), for transitional provisions see arts 3, 4, Sch 1, Pt 5 thereof at [**2.1131**], [**2.1132**], [**2.1134**].

Determining priorities

[1.1992]
5 Forward work programmes [of the GCCNI]

(1) [The GCCNI] must [before each programme year] publish a document (the "forward work programme") containing—

(a) a statement of any priorities of [the GCCNI] for the year in relation to designated consumers generally or any description of designated consumers;

(b) a general description of the main activities (including any projects) which it plans to undertake during the year in relation to designated consumers generally or any description of designated consumers;

(c) a statement of any other priorities of [the GCCNI] for the year;

(d) a general description of any other projects which it plans to undertake during the year (other than those comprising routine activities in the exercise of its functions).

(2) The description of a project under subsection (1)(b) or (d) must include the objectives of the project.

(3) The forward work programme for any year must also include—

(a) an estimate of the overall expenditure which [the GCCNI] expects to incur during the year in the exercise of its functions, and

(b) an estimate of the expenditure (if any) which [the GCCNI] expects to incur during the year in the exercise of its functions in relation to designated consumers.

(4)   . . .

[(4A)   In preparing a draft of the forward work programme for any year, the GCCNI must consult—

    (a)   Citizens Advice, and

    (b)   Citizens Advice Scotland.]

(5)   Before publishing the forward work programme for any year, [the GCCNI] must publish a notice—

    (a)   containing a draft of the forward work programme, and

    (b)   specifying the period within which representations about the proposals contained in it may be made,

and must consider any representations which are duly made and not withdrawn.

(6)   The notice under subsection (5) must be published by [the GCCNI in such manner as it considers appropriate for the purpose of bringing the matters contained in the notice to the attention of persons likely to have an interest in them.

(7)   [The GCCNI] must send a copy of any notice given by it under subsection (5) to—

    (a)   the Secretary of State,

    (b), (c). . . .

    (d)   the Office of Fair Trading, and

    (e)   any regulatory body which [the GCCNI] considers might have an interest in the content of the notice.

[(8)   References in this section to "designated consumers" are references to designated consumers who are consumers in relation to postal services in Northern Ireland.

(9)   In this section "programme year" means—

    (a)   the period beginning on 1st April 2014 and ending with the next following 31st March, and

    (b)   each successive period of 12 months.]

NOTES

    Section heading: words in square brackets added by the Public Bodies (Abolition of the National Consumer Council and Transfer of the Office of Fair Trading's Functions in relation to Estate Agents etc) Order 2014, SI 2014/631, arts 3, 4, Sch 1, Pt 1, para 12(1), (7)(a), for transitional provisions see arts 3, 4, Sch 1, Pt 5 thereof at **[2.1131]**, **[2.1132]**, **[2.1134]**.

    Sub-ss (1), (3), (5), (6): words in square brackets substituted by SI 2014/631, arts 3, 4, Sch 1, Pt 1, para 12(1), (7)(b), (c), (f), (g), for transitional provisions see note above.

    Sub-s (4): repealed by SI 2014/631, arts 3, 4, Sch 1, Pt 1, para 12(1), (7)(d), for transitional provisions see note above.

    Sub-ss (4A), (8), (9): inserted and added respectively by SI 2014/631, arts 3, 4, Sch 1, Pt 1, para 12(1), (7)(e), (i), for transitional provisions see note above.

    Sub-s (7): words in square brackets substituted, and paras (b), (c) repealed, by SI 2014/631, arts 3, 4, Sch 1, Pt 1, para 12(1), (7)(h), for transitional provisions see note above.

[1.1993]

6   General provision about functions [of the GCCNI]

(1)   In exercising its functions [the GCCNI] must comply with the requirements of this section.

(2)   [The GCCNI] must have regard to the forward work programme published under section 5.

(3)   [The GCCNI] must have regard to the interests of consumers in different areas.

(4)   [The GCCNI] must have regard to the interests of consumers that are one or more of the following—

    (a)   disabled or chronically sick individuals;

    (b)   individuals of pensionable age;

    (c)   individuals with low incomes;

    (d)   individuals residing in rural areas.

(5)   But nothing in subsection (4) is to be taken as implying that regard may not be had to the interests of other descriptions of consumers.

(6)   [The GCCNI] must have regard to the need to use its resources in the most efficient and economic way.

(7)   In discharging the duty imposed by subsection (6), [the GCCNI] must take account of the existence of any other public bodies with the same functions as, or similar functions to, those of [the GCCNI] and the activities carried on by such bodies.

(8)   [The GCCNI] must exercise its functions in the manner which it considers is best calculated to contribute to the achievement of sustainable development.

(9)   . . .

(10)   A person is of pensionable age for the purposes of this section if—

    (a)   the person has attained pensionable age (within the meaning given by the rules in paragraph 1 of Schedule 4 to the Pensions Act 1995 (c 26)), or

    (b)   in the case of a man born before [6 December 1953], he is the same age as a woman who has attained pensionable age (within the meaning so given).

NOTES

    Section heading: words in square brackets added by the Public Bodies (Abolition of the National Consumer Council and Transfer of the Office of Fair Trading's Functions in relation to Estate Agents etc) Order 2014, SI 2014/631, arts 3, 4, Sch 1, Pt 1, para 12(1), (8)(a), for transitional provisions see arts 3, 4, Sch 1, Pt 5 thereof at **[2.1131]**, **[2.1132]**, **[2.1134]**.

    Sub-ss (1)–(4), (6)–(8): words in square brackets substituted by SI 2014/631, arts 3, 4, Sch 1, Pt 1, para 12(1), (8)(b), (c), for transitional provisions see note above.

Sub-s (9): repealed by SI 2014/631, arts 3, 4, Sch 1, Pt 1, para 12(1), (8)(d), for transitional provisions see note above.
Sub-s (10): words in square brackets in para (b) substituted by the Pensions Act 2011, s 1(7), Sch 1, para 7.

[1.1994]
[6A Exercise of functions of consumer advocacy bodies
Subject to section 13 (investigation of complaints relating to the disconnection of gas or electricity), nothing in this Part imposes on a consumer advocacy body a duty to exercise any of its functions on behalf of or at the request of a particular consumer.]

NOTES
Commencement: 1 April 2014.
Inserted by the Public Bodies (Abolition of the National Consumer Council and Transfer of the Office of Fair Trading's Functions in relation to Estate Agents etc) Order 2014, SI 2014/631, arts 3, 4, Sch 1, Pt 1, para 12(1), (9), for transitional provisions see arts 3, 4, Sch 1, Pt 5 thereof at **[2.1131]**, **[2.1132]**, **[2.1134]**.

7, 7A *(Repealed by the Public Bodies (Abolition of the National Consumer Council and Transfer of the Office of Fair Trading's Functions in relation to Estate Agents etc) Order 2014, SI 2014/631, arts 3, 4, Sch 1, Pt 1, para 12(1), (10), (11), for transitional provisions see arts 3, 4, Sch 1, Pt 5 thereof at* **[2.1131]**, **[2.1132]**, **[2.1134]** *(s 7A as inserted by the Public Services Reform (Scotland) Act 2010, s 3(6), Sch 2, Pt 1, paras 15, 17).)*

The core functions

[1.1995]
8 The representative function
(1) [The GCCNI] may—
  (a) provide advice and information to persons within subsection (2) about consumer matters,
  (b) make proposals to such persons about consumer matters, and
  (c) represent the views of consumers on consumer matters to such persons.
(2) Those persons are—
  (a) any Minister of the Crown or government department;
  (b) the Scottish Ministers;
  (c) the Welsh Ministers;
  (d) any regulatory body established by or under an enactment;
  (e) the European Commission or any other international organisation;
  (f) any other person whom [the GCCNI] considers might have an interest in the matter in question.
(3) In this section "enactment" means—
  (a) an Act of Parliament,
  (b) an Act of the Scottish Parliament,
  (c) a Measure or Act of the National Assembly for Wales, or
  (d) Northern Ireland legislation,
whenever passed or made.

NOTES
Sub-ss (1), (2): words in square brackets substituted by the Public Bodies (Abolition of the National Consumer Council and Transfer of the Office of Fair Trading's Functions in relation to Estate Agents etc) Order 2014, SI 2014/631, arts 3, 4, Sch 1, Pt 1, para 12(1), (12), for transitional provisions see arts 3, 4, Sch 1, Pt 5 thereof at **[2.1131]**, **[2.1132]**, **[2.1134]**.

[1.1996]
9 The research function
[The GCCNI] may obtain and keep under review—
  (a) information about consumer matters,
  (b) information about the views of consumers on consumer matters, and
  (c) information of such other description as may be prescribed by the Secretary of State by order.

NOTES
Words in square brackets substituted by the Public Bodies (Abolition of the National Consumer Council and Transfer of the Office of Fair Trading's Functions in relation to Estate Agents etc) Order 2014, SI 2014/631, arts 3, 4, Sch 1, Pt 1, para 12(1), (13), for transitional provisions see arts 3, 4, Sch 1, Pt 5 thereof at **[2.1131]**, **[2.1132]**, **[2.1134]**.

[1.1997]
10 The information function
(1) [The GCCNI] may facilitate the dissemination to consumers of advice and information—
  (a) about [the GCCNI] and its functions,
  (b) about consumer matters, and
  (c) about such other matters as may be prescribed by the Secretary of State by order.
(2) In exercising the power conferred by subsection (1) [the GCCNI] may (among other things)—
  (a) publish or otherwise make available information in any manner [the GCCNI] thinks appropriate for the purpose of bringing it to the attention of those likely to be interested;
  (b) support (financially or otherwise), facilitate or co-ordinate the activities of other persons.

NOTES

Words in square brackets substituted by the Public Bodies (Abolition of the National Consumer Council and Transfer of the Office of Fair Trading's Functions in relation to Estate Agents etc) Order 2014, SI 2014/631, arts 3, 4, Sch 1, Pt 1, para 12(1), (14), for transitional provisions see arts 3, 4, Sch 1, Pt 5 thereof at **[2.1131]**, **[2.1132]**, **[2.1134]**.

Powers of investigation

[1.1998]
11 General powers of investigation
(1) [The GCCNI] may investigate—
- (a)   a complaint made by or on behalf of a consumer which appears to [the GCCNI] to raise one or more issues of general relevance [concerning consumer matters that relate to postal services in Northern Ireland];
- (b)   any matter which appears to [the GCCNI] to be, or to be related to, a problem which affects or may affect [consumers of postal services in Northern Ireland.]

(2) For this purpose, a complaint raises an issue of general relevance if it raises—
- (a)   a novel issue which affects or may affect consumers generally or consumers of a particular description, or
- (b)   any other issue which has or may have an important effect on consumers generally or consumers of a particular description.

NOTES

Sub-s (1): words in first, second, fourth and final pairs of square brackets substituted, and words in third pair of square brackets inserted, by the Public Bodies (Abolition of the National Consumer Council and Transfer of the Office of Fair Trading's Functions in relation to Estate Agents etc) Order 2014, SI 2014/631, arts 3, 4, Sch 1, Pt 1, para 12(1), (15), for transitional provisions see arts 3, 4, Sch 1, Pt 5 thereof at **[2.1131]**, **[2.1132]**, **[2.1134]**.

[1.1999]
12 Investigation of complaints made by vulnerable designated consumers
(1) Subsection (3) applies to a complaint which is made—
- (a)   by or on behalf of a vulnerable person in that person's capacity as a designated consumer ("the designated consumer"),
- (b)   against a person ("the supplier") who in the course of a business carried on by the supplier supplies or seeks to supply, or refuses to supply, goods or services to the designated consumer, and
- (c)   in respect of a matter connected with the supply of goods or services by the supplier to the designated consumer or a refusal by the supplier to supply goods or services to the designated consumer.

(2) For this purpose a person is "vulnerable" if [the consumer advocacy body to which the complaint is referred] is satisfied that it is not reasonable to expect that person to pursue the complaint on that person's own behalf.

(3) Where a complaint to which this subsection applies is referred to [a consumer advocacy body] by or on behalf of the designated consumer, [that consumer advocacy body] may investigate the complaint for the purpose of determining whether it is appropriate to take any action under subsection (4).

(4) Where it appears to [a consumer advocacy body] to be appropriate to do so with a view to assisting in reaching a satisfactory resolution of a complaint referred to it under this section, [that consumer advocacy body] may—
- (a)   provide advice to the designated consumer or, if the complaint was made by another person on the designated consumer's behalf, that person;
- (b)   make representations on behalf of the designated consumer to the supplier about anything to which the complaint relates.

[(5)   Where a complaint is referred to Citizens Advice or Citizens Advice Scotland, those bodies may agree that the complaint is to be treated as having been referred to the other of them.

(6)   If Citizens Advice and Citizens Advice Scotland so agree in a particular case, subsections (3) and (4) and sections 14(2) to (4) and 15(1) are to have effect accordingly.]

NOTES

Sub-ss (2)–(4): words in square brackets substituted by the Public Bodies (Abolition of the National Consumer Council and Transfer of the Office of Fair Trading's Functions in relation to Estate Agents etc) Order 2014, SI 2014/631, arts 3, 4, Sch 1, Pt 1, para 12(1), (16)(a)–(c), for transitional provisions see arts 3, 4, Sch 1, Pt 5 thereof at **[2.1131]**, **[2.1132]**, **[2.1134]**.

Sub-ss (5), (6): added by SI 2014/631, arts 3, 4, Sch 1, Pt 1, para 12(1), (16)(d), for transitional provisions see note above.

[1.2000]
13 Investigation of complaints relating to disconnection of gas or electricity
(1) This section applies to—
- (a)   a complaint by a gas consumer against a gas transporter, in respect of the disconnection of, or a threat to disconnect, the consumer's premises by the gas transporter;
- (b)   a complaint by a gas consumer against a gas transporter, following such a disconnection, in respect of a refusal by the gas transporter to reconnect the premises;

   (c)   a complaint by a gas consumer against a gas supplier, in respect of the cutting off of, or a threat to cut off, a supply of gas to the consumer's premises by the gas supplier;

   (d)   a complaint by a gas consumer against a gas supplier, following such a cutting off, in respect of a refusal by the gas supplier to restore the supply to the premises;

   (e)   a complaint by a gas consumer against a gas supplier, in respect of the failure of a prepayment system;

   (f)   a complaint by an electricity consumer against an electricity supplier, an electricity distributor or a transmission licence holder, in respect of the disconnection of, or a threat to disconnect, the consumer's premises by the electricity supplier, electricity distributor or licence holder;

   (g)   a complaint by an electricity consumer against an electricity supplier, electricity distributor or transmission licence holder, following such a disconnection by the supplier, distributor or licence holder, in respect of a refusal by the supplier, distributor or licence holder to reconnect the premises;

   (h)   a complaint by an electricity consumer against an electricity supplier, in respect of the failure of a prepayment system.

(2)   Where a complaint to which this section applies is referred to [a consumer advocacy body] by or on behalf of the complainant, [that consumer advocacy body] must investigate the complaint for the purpose of determining whether it is appropriate to take any action under subsection (3).

(3)   Where it appears to [a consumer advocacy body] to be appropriate to do so with a view to assisting in reaching a satisfactory resolution of a complaint referred to it under this section, [that consumer advocacy body] must—

   (a)   provide advice to the complainant, or

   (b)   make representations on behalf of the complainant to the person against whom the complaint is made about anything to which the complaint relates.

(4)   [A consumer advocacy body] may refuse to investigate a complaint, or part of a complaint, if—

   (a)   the complaint or part appears to [the consumer advocacy body] to be frivolous or vexatious;

   (b)   the complaint or part falls within a class of matter which a regulatory body is under a duty (whether imposed by or under an enactment or otherwise) to investigate;

   (c)   the complaint or part is being dealt with, or [the consumer advocacy body] is satisfied that it would be better dealt with, under an ombudsman scheme or any other redress scheme or in legal proceedings;

   (d)   [the consumer advocacy body] considers that there has been undue delay in the making of the complaint or part, or the provision of evidence to support it;

   (e)   [the consumer advocacy body] considers that there are other compelling reasons why it is inappropriate for the complaint or part to be investigated by [the consumer advocacy body].

(5)   [A consumer advocacy body] may refuse to investigate a complaint until the complainant has taken such steps as appear to [the consumer advocacy body] to be reasonable for the purpose of giving the person against whom the complaint is made a reasonable opportunity to deal with it.

[(5A)   Where a complaint is referred to Citizens Advice or Citizens Advice Scotland, those bodies may agree that the complaint is to be treated as having been referred to the other of them.

(5B)   If Citizens Advice or Citizens Advice Scotland so agree in a particular case, subsections (2) to (5) and section 14(2) to (4) are to have effect accordingly.]

(6)   In subsection (1)—

   (a)   in paragraphs (a) and (b) "disconnection" in relation to any premises, means disconnection from a main of a gas transporter or the discontinuation of the conveyance of gas to the premises;

   (b)   in paragraphs (b), (d) and (g), the references to a gas consumer or electricity consumer are references to a person who was such a consumer at the time the disconnection of, or cutting off of the supply to, the premises occurred;

   (c)   in paragraphs (e) and (h), references to the failure of a prepayment system are references to—

     (i)   a failure in the facilities for payment for the supply of gas or electricity which results in a consumer with a prepayment meter being unable to make a payment for the supply of gas or electricity, or

     (ii)   where a payment has been made for the supply of gas or electricity through a prepayment meter, a case where the supply is not given through the prepayment meter because of a defect in the meter or in the facilities for payment.

(6A)   In this section, a reference to a consumer advocacy body does not include a reference to the GCCNI.]

(7)   In this section—

"electricity consumer" means an individual who is a consumer in relation to electricity supplied by an authorised supplier;

"enactment" means—

   (a)   an Act of Parliament,

   (b)   an Act of the Scottish Parliament, or

(c)   a Measure or Act of the National Assembly for Wales,
whenever passed or made;
"gas consumer" means an individual who is a consumer in relation to gas supplied by an
authorised supplier;
"the consumer's premises"—
(a)   in relation to an electricity consumer, means the premises to which the electricity
supplied to the consumer by the authorised supplier is supplied;
(b)   in relation to a gas consumer, means the premises to which the gas supplied to the
consumer is conveyed by the gas transporter;
"redress scheme" means a scheme under which complaints may be made to, and investigated and
determined by, an independent person.

NOTES

Sub-ss (2)–(5): words in square brackets substituted by the Public Bodies (Abolition of the National Consumer Council and
Transfer of the Office of Fair Trading's Functions in relation to Estate Agents etc) Order 2014, SI 2014/631, arts 3, 4, Sch 1,
Pt 1, para 12(1), (17)(a)–(d), for transitional provisions see arts 3, 4, Sch 1, Pt 5 thereof at **[2.1131]**, **[2.1132]**, **[2.1134]**.

Sub-ss (5A), (5B), (6A): inserted by SI 2014/631, arts 3, 4, Sch 1, Pt 1, para 12(1), (17)(e), (f), for transitional provisions see
note above.

[1.2001]
14   Reference of matters to the Gas and Electricity Markets Authority
(1)   In this section references to a complaint are to a complaint within section 11(1)(a) or to which
section 12(3) or 13 applies.
(2)   Where it appears to [the consumer advocacy body in question] that a complaint relates to a
matter in respect of which any of the Authority's enforcement functions may be exercisable, [that
body] must refer the complaint to the Authority unless it is satisfied that the Authority is already
aware of the matter.
(3)   Where a complaint to which section 13 applies is referred to the Authority under
subsection (2), [the consumer advocacy body in question] is not required to investigate the
complaint under subsection (2) of that section until the Authority has had a reasonable opportunity
to exercise its enforcement functions in relation to the matter to which the complaint relates.
(4)   On investigating a complaint, [the consumer advocacy body in question] must inform the
complainant if it considers that the complaint relates to a matter of a kind which can be referred by
the complainant to the Authority under any provision of the Gas Act 1986 (c 44) or the Electricity
Act 1989 (c 29).
[(4A)   In this section, a reference to a consumer advocacy body does not include a reference to the
GCCNI.]
(5)   In this section—
"the Authority" means the Gas and Electricity Markets Authority;
"enforcement function", in relation to the Authority, means any of its functions under section 28
or 30A of the Gas Act 1986 or section 25 or 27A of the Electricity Act 1989.

NOTES

Sub-ss (2)–(4): words in square brackets substituted by the Public Bodies (Abolition of the National Consumer Council and
Transfer of the Office of Fair Trading's Functions in relation to Estate Agents etc) Order 2014, SI 2014/631, arts 3, 4, Sch 1,
Pt 1, para 12(1), (18)(a)–(c), for transitional provisions see arts 3, 4, Sch 1, Pt 5 thereof at **[2.1131]**, **[2.1132]**, **[2.1134]**.

Sub-s (4A): inserted by SI 2014/631, arts 3, 4, Sch 1, Pt 1, para 12(1), (18)(d), for transitional provisions see note above.

[1.2002]
[15   Reference of postal matters to OFCOM]
(1)   [A consumer advocacy body] must refer any complaint within section 11(1)(a), or to which
section 12(3) applies, to [the Office of Communications ("OFCOM")] if [that consumer advocacy
body] considers that—
(a)   the subject matter of the complaint indicates that [a regulatory condition imposed under
Part 3 of the Postal Services Act 2011 (c 5)] has been contravened,
(b)   the subject matter of the complaint is a referable matter, or
(c)   it is appropriate to do so.
(2)   [The consumer advocacy bodies] and [OFCOM] must, from time to time, agree the
descriptions of matters which are to be referred to [OFCOM] and, for the purposes of
subsection (1)(b), a matter is a "referable matter" if it is of a description for the time being so
agreed.

NOTES

Section heading: substituted by the Postal Services Act 2011, s 91(1), (2), Sch 12, Pt 3, paras 175, 177(1), (2).

Sub-s (1): words in first and final pairs of square brackets substituted by the Public Bodies (Abolition of the
National Consumer Council and Transfer of the Office of Fair Trading's Functions in relation to Estate Agents etc) Order 2014,
SI 2014/631, arts 3, 4, Sch 1, Pt 1, para 12(1), (19)(a), for transitional provisions see arts 3, 4, Sch 1, Pt 5 thereof at **[2.1131]**,
[2.1132], **[2.1134]**; words in second pair of square brackets substituted by the Postal Services Act 2011, s 91(1), (2), Sch 12,
Pt 3, paras 175, 177(1), (3), (4).

Sub-s (2): words in first pair of square brackets substituted by SI 2014/631, arts 3, 4, Sch 1, Pt 1, para 12(1), (19)(b), for transitional provisions see note above; word in second pair of square brackets substituted by the Postal Services Act 2011, s 91(1), (2), Sch 12, Pt 3, paras 175, 177(1), (3), (4).

[1.2003]
16   Investigations relating to public post offices
[(1)   Without prejudice to the generality of section 11—
   (a)   Citizens Advice and Citizens Advice Scotland may investigate any matter relating to the number and location of public post offices in England, Wales and Scotland;
   (b)   the GCCNI may investigate any matter relating to the number and location of public post offices in Northern Ireland.]
(2)   In this section "public post office" has the same meaning as in the Postal Services Act 2000 (c 26) (see [section 125(1)] of that Act).

NOTES
Sub-s (1): substituted by the Public Bodies (Abolition of the National Consumer Council and Transfer of the Office of Fair Trading's Functions in relation to Estate Agents etc) Order 2014, SI 2014/631, arts 3, 4, Sch 1, Pt 1, para 12(1), (20), for transitional provisions see arts 3, 4, Sch 1, Pt 5 thereof at **[2.1131]**, **[2.1132]**, **[2.1134]**.

Other functions of [the consumer advocacy bodies]
[1.2004]
17   Reports by [the GCCNI]
(1)   [The GCCNI] may prepare a report in relation to any matter falling within the scope of its functions [under this Act].
(2)   [The GCCNI] may publish any report prepared under this section.

NOTES
Cross-heading, section heading, sub-s (2): words in square brackets substituted by the Public Bodies (Abolition of the National Consumer Council and Transfer of the Office of Fair Trading's Functions in relation to Estate Agents etc) Order 2014, SI 2014/631, arts 3, 4, Sch 1, Pt 1, para 12(1), (21), (22)(a), (c), for transitional provisions see arts 3, 4, Sch 1, Pt 5 thereof at **[2.1131]**, **[2.1132]**, **[2.1134]**.
Sub-s (1): words in first pair of square brackets substituted, and words in second pair of square brackets added, by SI 2014/631, arts 3, 4, Sch 1, Pt 1, para 12(1), (22)(b), for transitional provisions see note above.

[1.2005]
18   Secretary of State's power to require reports
(1)   The Secretary of State may direct [the GCCNI] to prepare, and submit to the Secretary of State within a specified period, a report in respect of any matter specified in the direction which relates to consumer matters [which relate to postal services in Northern Ireland].
(2)   The Secretary of State may publish any report submitted under this section.

NOTES
Sub-s (1): words in first pair of square brackets substituted, and words in second pair of square brackets added, by the Public Bodies (Abolition of the National Consumer Council and Transfer of the Office of Fair Trading's Functions in relation to Estate Agents etc) Order 2014, SI 2014/631, arts 3, 4, Sch 1, Pt 1, para 12(1), (23), for transitional provisions see arts 3, 4, Sch 1, Pt 5 thereof at **[2.1131]**, **[2.1132]**, **[2.1134]**.

[1.2006]
19   Advice, information and guidance
(1)   [The GCCNI] may issue advice or guidance to any person with a view to improving standards of service and promoting best practice in connection with the handling of complaints made by consumers or any other matter affecting the interests of consumers.
(2)   [The GCCNI] may publish advice or information about consumer matters if it appears to [the GCCNI] that its publication would promote the interests of consumers.
(3)   For this purpose "information about consumer matters" includes information about the views of consumers on consumer matters.

NOTES
Sub-ss (1), (2): words in square brackets substituted by the Public Bodies (Abolition of the National Consumer Council and Transfer of the Office of Fair Trading's Functions in relation to Estate Agents etc) Order 2014, SI 2014/631, arts 3, 4, Sch 1, Pt 1, para 12(1), (24), for transitional provisions see arts 3, 4, Sch 1, Pt 5 thereof at **[2.1131]**, **[2.1132]**, **[2.1134]**.

[1.2007]
[19A   Guidance for energy consumers
(1)   [A consumer advocacy body] must prepare, and keep under review—
   (a)   guidance for energy consumers (the "energy consumer guidance"), and
   (b)   a summary prepared in accordance with subsection (4) (the "concise guidance").
(2)   The energy consumer guidance must address the matters included in any document published by the European Commission pursuant to Article 3(16) of the Electricity Directive or Article 3(12) of the Gas Directive.

(3)   The energy consumer guidance may include any other information relating to the rights of energy consumers which [the consumer advocacy body in question] thinks appropriate.

(4)   The concise guidance must—

(a)   summarise any information in the energy consumer guidance which [in the view of the consumer advocacy body in question] is particularly relevant to the interests of energy consumers, and

(b)   state where a copy of the energy consumer guidance can be obtained.

(5)   In preparing and reviewing [its energy consumer guidance and its concise guidance] [a consumer advocacy body] must consult—

(a)   the Secretary of State,

(b)   the Gas and Electricity Markets Authority, and

(c)   any other person [the consumer advocacy body in question] considers appropriate.

[(6)   A consumer advocacy body must publish the first version of its energy consumer guidance and its concise guidance on its website.]

(7)   If, following a review, [a consumer advocacy body] considers it necessary to amend [its energy consumer guidance and its concise guidance], [the consumer advocacy body] must, as soon as is reasonably practicable—

(a)   publish the amended version on its website, and

(b)   inform any person it consulted in accordance with subsection (5) that it has done so.

(8)   [A consumer advocacy body] may also make the first and any amended version of [its energy consumer guidance and its concise guidance] available in any other manner [the consumer advocacy body] thinks appropriate for the purpose of bringing that guidance to the attention of those likely to be interested.

[(8A)   Until a consumer advocacy body has published the first version of its energy consumer guidance and its concise guidance, it must—

(a)   publish on its website, and

(b)   make available in any other manner that it thinks appropriate for the purpose of bringing them to the attention of those likely to be interested,

the last version of the energy consumer guidance and the concise guidance to be published by the National Consumer Council under this section (as it had effect immediately before the amendments made to this Act by the Public Bodies (Abolition of the National Consumer Council and Transfer of the Office of Fair Trading's Functions in relation to Estate Agents etc) Order 2014 (SI 2014/ . . .) came into force.

(8B)   Nothing in this section prevents a consumer advocacy body from publishing its energy consumer guidance or its concise summary in a document that includes the energy consumer guidance or, as the case may be, the concise summary of another consumer advocacy body.

(8C)   In this section, a reference to a consumer advocacy body does not include a reference to the GCCNI.]

(9)   In this section—

"the Electricity Directive" means Directive 2009/72/EC of the European Parliament and of the Council of 13 July 2009 concerning common rules for the internal market in electricity and repealing Directive 2003/54/EC;

"energy consumer" means an individual who is—

(a)   a consumer in relation to gas supplied by an authorised supplier for consumption by the consumer's own household;

(b)   a consumer in relation to electricity supplied by an authorised supplier for consumption by the consumer's own household;

"the Gas Directive" means Directive 2009/73/EC of the European Parliament and of the Council of 13 July 2009 concerning common rules for the internal market in natural gas and repealing Directive 2003/55/EC.]

NOTES

Inserted by the Electricity and Gas (Internal Markets) Regulations 2011, SI 2011/2704, reg 3(1), (2).

Sub-ss (1), (3)–(5), (7), (8): words in square brackets substituted by the Public Bodies (Abolition of the National Consumer Council and Transfer of the Office of Fair Trading's Functions in relation to Estate Agents etc) Order 2014, SI 2014/631, arts 3, 4, Sch 1, Pt 1, para 12(1), (25)(a)–(d), (f), (g)(i)–(iii), for transitional provisions see arts 3, 4, Sch 1, Pt 5 thereof at **[2.1131]**, **[2.1132]**, **[2.1134]**.

Sub-s (6): inserted by SI 2014/631, arts 3, 4, Sch 1, Pt 1, para 12(1), (25)(e), for transitional provisions see note above.

Sub-ss (8A)–(8C): inserted by SI 2014/631, arts 3, 4, Sch 1, Pt 1, para 12(1), (25)(g)(iv), for transitional provisions see note above.

20, 20A, 21–23   *(Repealed by the Public Bodies (Abolition of the National Consumer Council and Transfer of the Office of Fair Trading's Functions in relation to Estate Agents etc) Order 2014, SI 2014/631, arts 3, 4, Sch 1, Pt 1, para 12(1), (26), for transitional provisions see arts 3, 4, Sch 1, Pt 5 at* **[2.1131]**, **[2.1132]**, **[2.1134]***) (s 20A as inserted in relation to Scotland only by the Public Services Reform (Scotland) Act 2010, s 3(6), Sch 2, Pt 1, paras 15, 18.)*

Information

[1.2008]

24   Provision of information to [the consumer advocacy bodies]

(1)   [A consumer advocacy body] may, by notice, require a person within subsection (3) to supply it with such information as is specified or described in the notice within such reasonable period as is so specified.

(2)   [In the case of the GCCNI, the] information specified or described in a notice under subsection (1) must be information [the GCCNI] requires for the purpose of exercising its functions.

[(2A)   In the case of Citizens Advice or Citizens Advice Scotland, the information specified or described in a notice under subsection (1) must be information it requires—

    (a)   for the purpose of exercising a function conferred on it by or under an enactment, or

    (b)   for the purpose of exercising a function it has that—

        (i)   is not conferred by or under an enactment, and

        (ii)   corresponds to a function conferred on the GCCNI under section 8, 9, 10, 11 or 19, disregarding for these purposes the limitations relating to postal services in Northern Ireland in sections 1(4) and 11(1).

(2B)   For the purposes of subsection (2A) "enactment" means an Act, an Act of the Scottish Parliament, a measure or Act of the National Assembly for Wales or Northern Ireland legislation.]

(3)   The persons referred to in subsection (1) are—

    (a)   the Office of Fair Trading;

    (b)   a designated regulator;

    (c)   any person who supplies goods or services in the course of a business carried on by that person;

    (d)   any other person specified or of a description specified by the Secretary of State by order for the purposes of this subsection.

(4)   A notice under subsection (1) may specify the manner and form in which any information is to be provided.

(5)   Before giving a notice under subsection (1), or specifying the manner or form in which any information is to be provided, [a consumer advocacy body] must have regard to the desirability of minimising the costs, or any other detriment, to the person to whom the notice is to be given.

(6)   If a person within subsection (3)(a) or (b) fails to comply with a notice under subsection (1), the person must, if so required by [the consumer advocacy body in question], give notice to [that body] of the reasons for the failure.

(7)   An order under subsection (3)(d) may provide either—

    (a)   that subsection (6) is to apply in relation to a person specified or of a description specified by the order as it applies to a person within subsection (3)(a) or (b), or

    (b)   that section 26 is to apply in relation to such a person.

(8)   [A consumer advocacy body] may publish any notice received under subsection (6).

[(8A)   Information provided to a consumer advocacy body because of a notice under subsection (1) may be provided by that body to the other consumer advocacy bodies.]

(9)   In this section—

"designated regulator" means—

    (a)   the Gas and Electricity Markets Authority;

    [(b)   the Office of Communications;]

    (c)   the Water Services Regulation Authority;

    [(ca)   the Water Industry Commission for Scotland;]

    (d)   any other person prescribed by the Secretary of State by order for the purposes of this subsection;

"goods" includes land or an interest in land.

NOTES

Section heading, sub-ss (1), (2), (5), (6), (8): words in square brackets substituted by the Public Bodies (Abolition of the National Consumer Council and Transfer of the Office of Fair Trading's Functions in relation to Estate Agents etc) Order 2014, SI 2014/631, arts 3, 4, Sch 1, Pt 1, para 12(1), (27)(a)–(c), (e)–(g), for transitional provisions see arts 3, 4, Sch 1, Pt 5 thereof at **[2.1131]**, **[2.1132]**, **[2.1134]**.

Sub-ss (2A), (2B), (8A): inserted by SI 2014/631, arts 3, 4, Sch 1, Pt 1, para 12(1), (27)(d), (h), for transitional provisions see note above.

Sub-s (9): in definition "designated regulator" para (b) substituted by the Postal Services Act 2011, s 91(1), (2), Sch 12, Pt 3, paras 175, 179; para (ca) inserted in relation to Scotland only by the Public Services Reform (Scotland) Act 2010, s 3(6), Sch 2, Pt 1, paras 15, 19.

[1.2009]

25   Enforcement by regulator of section 24 notice

(1)   Where a regulated provider fails to comply with a notice under section 24(1), [the consumer advocacy body in question] may refer the failure to—

    (a)   a person prescribed by the Secretary of State by order for the purposes of this section, or

    (b)   if no person has been so prescribed, the relevant regulator.

(2) Subsection (1) applies only to the extent that the notice relates to information which is held or may be obtained by the regulated provider in *its capacity* as a regulated provider.

(3) For the purposes of this section—

"designated investigator", in relation to a failure to comply with a notice under section 24(1), means the person to whom the failure is referred under subsection (1);

"regulated provider" means a person listed in the first column of the following table;

"relevant regulator", in relation to a regulated provider, means the body listed in relation to the regulated provider in the second column of that table.

TABLE

Regulated provider	*Relevant regulator*
A person holding a licence under section 7, 7ZA[, 7A or 7AB] of the Gas Act 1986 (c 44).	The Gas and Electricity Markets Authority.
A person holding a licence under section 6 of the Electricity Act 1989 (c 29).	The Gas and Electricity Markets Authority.
[A postal operator.	The Office of Communications.]
[Scottish Water.	The Water Industry Commission for Scotland.]
A water undertaker, sewerage undertaker *or licensed water supplier.*	The Water Services Regulation Authority.

(4) Where a failure is referred under subsection (1), the designated investigator must—

    (a)   consider any representations made by [the consumer advocacy body] or the regulated provider, and

    (b)   determine whether the regulated provider is entitled to refuse to comply with the notice by virtue of provision made under section 28 (exemptions from requirements to provide information).

(5) If the designated investigator determines that the regulated provider is not entitled to refuse to comply with the notice, the designated investigator must direct the regulated provider to comply with it.

(6) The designated investigator must give [the consumer advocacy body] and the regulated provider notice of—

    (a)   a determination under subsection (4)(b) and the reasons for it, and

    (b)   any direction under subsection (5).

[(6A) An obligation imposed by virtue of subsection (5) on a postal operator is enforceable by OFCOM under Schedule 7 to the Postal Services Act 2011 (enforcement of regulatory requirements).]

(7) An obligation imposed by virtue of subsection (5) on a water undertaker, sewerage undertaker *or licensed water supplier* is enforceable by the Water Services Regulation Authority under section 18 of the Water Industry Act 1991 (c 56) (orders for securing compliance).

(8) Schedule 2 makes provision about the enforcement of obligations imposed by virtue of subsection (5) on other regulated providers.

NOTES

Sub-ss (1), (4), (6): words in square brackets substituted by the Public Bodies (Abolition of the National Consumer Council and Transfer of the Office of Fair Trading's Functions in relation to Estate Agents etc) Order 2014, SI 2014/631, arts 3, 4, Sch 1, Pt 1, para 12(1), (28), for transitional provisions see arts 3, 4, Sch 1, Pt 5 thereof at **[2.1131]**, **[2.1132]**, **[2.1134]**.

Sub-s (2): for the words in italics there are substituted the words "the person's capacity" by the Water Act 2014, s 56, Sch 7, paras 136, 138(1), (2), as from a day to be appointed.

Sub-s (3): in the Table, in entry relating to the Gas Act 1986, words in square brackets substituted by the Electricity and Gas (Smart Meters Licensable Activity) Order 2012, SI 2012/2400, art 32; entry relating to "A postal operator" substituted by the Postal Services Act 2011, s 91(1), (2), Sch 12, Pt 3, paras 175, 180(1), (2), and entry relating to "Scottish Water" inserted in relation to Scotland only by the Public Services Reform (Scotland) Act 2010, s 3(6), Sch 2, Pt 1, paras 15, 20; for the words in italics there are substituted the words ", water supply licensee or sewerage licensee" by the Water Act 2014, s 56, Sch 7, paras 136, 138(1), (3), as from a day to be appointed.

Sub-s (6A): inserted by the Postal Services Act 2011, s 91(1), (2), Sch 12, Pt 3, paras 175, 180(1), (3).

Sub-s (7): for the words in italics there are substituted the words ", water supply licensee or sewerage licensee" by the Water Act 2014, s 56, Sch 7, paras 136, 138(1), (4), as from a day to be appointed.

[1.2010]

26 Enforcement by court of section 24 notice

(1) This section applies where a person ("the defaulter") refuses, or otherwise fails, to comply with a notice given to the defaulter under section 24(1) and the defaulter is—

    (a)   within section 24(3)(c), or

    (b)   a person in relation to whom this section applies by virtue of provision made under section 24(7)(b).

(2)   But this section does not apply in relation to a notice if, or to the extent that, section 25(1) applies in relation to the notice.

(3)   [The consumer advocacy body in question] may apply to the court for an order requiring the defaulter to comply with the notice or with such directions for the like purpose as may be contained in the order.

(4)   An order under this section may, in particular, provide that all the costs or expenses of and incidental to the application are to be borne—

(a)   by the defaulter, or

(b)   if officers of a company or other association are responsible for the failure to comply with the notice, by those officers.

(5)   In this section "the court"—

(a)   in relation to England and Wales or Northern Ireland, means the High Court, and

(b)   in relation to Scotland, means the Court of Session.

NOTES

Sub-s (3): words in square brackets substituted by the Public Bodies (Abolition of the National Consumer Council and Transfer of the Office of Fair Trading's Functions in relation to Estate Agents etc) Order 2014, SI 2014/631, arts 3, 4, Sch 1, Pt 1, para 12(1), (29), for transitional provisions see arts 3, 4, Sch 1, Pt 5 thereof at **[2.1131]**, **[2.1132]**, **[2.1134]**.

[1.2011]
27   Provision of information by [a consumer advocacy body]
[(1)   An authorised person may, by notice, require—

(a)   the GCCNI to supply it with such information in relation to consumer matters that relate to postal services in Northern Ireland, as is specified or described in the notice within such reasonable period as is so specified, or

(b)   Citizens Advice or Citizens Advice Scotland to supply it with such information relating to its functions conferred by or under section 24 or any other enactment as is specified or described in the notice within such reasonable period as is so specified.

(1A)   For the purpose of subsection (1)(b), "enactment" means any provision of an Act, Act of the Scottish Parliament, a Measure or Act of the National Assembly for Wales or Northern Ireland legislation.]

(2)   The information specified or described in a notice under subsection (1) must be information the authorised person requires for the purpose of exercising its functions.

(3)   "Authorised person" means—

(a)   the Office of Fair Trading;

(b)   a designated regulator (within the meaning of section 24(9);

(c)   any person specified or of a description specified by the Secretary of State by order.

(4)   A notice under subsection (1) may specify the manner and form in which any information is to be provided.

(5)   Before giving a notice under subsection (1) or specifying the manner or form in which any information is to be provided, an authorised person must have regard to the desirability of minimising the costs, or any other detriment, to [the consumer advocacy body in question].

(6)   If [a consumer advocacy body] fails to comply with a notice under subsection (1), it must, if so required by the authorised person which gave that notice, give notice to the authorised person of the reasons for the failure.

(7)   An authorised person may publish any notice received by it under subsection (6).

NOTES

Section heading, sub-ss (5), (6): words in square brackets substituted by the Public Bodies (Abolition of the National Consumer Council and Transfer of the Office of Fair Trading's Functions in relation to Estate Agents etc) Order 2014, SI 2014/631, arts 3, 4, Sch 1, Pt 1, para 12(1), (30)(a), (c), (d), for transitional provisions see arts 3, 4, Sch 1, Pt 5 thereof at **[2.1131]**, **[2.1132]**, **[2.1134]**.

Sub-ss (1), (1A): substituted, for original sub-s (1), by SI 2014/631, arts 3, 4, Sch 1, Pt 1, para 12(1), (30)(b), for transitional provisions see note above.

[1.2012]
28   Exemptions from requirements to provide information
(1)   The Secretary of State may make regulations prescribing—

(a)   descriptions of persons to whom [a consumer advocacy body] may not give a notice under section 24(1);

(b)   descriptions of information which a person may refuse to supply in accordance with a notice under section 24(1) or 27(1);

(c)   circumstances in which a person may refuse to comply with such a notice.

(2)   No person may be required by a notice under section 24(1) or 27(1) or a court order under section 26—

(a)   to provide any information which that person could not be compelled to supply in evidence in civil proceedings before the High Court or the Court of Session, or

(b)   to produce any document which that person could not be compelled to produce in such proceedings.

NOTES

Sub-s (1): words in square brackets substituted by the Public Bodies (Abolition of the National Consumer Council and Transfer of the Office of Fair Trading's Functions in relation to Estate Agents etc) Order 2014, SI 2014/631, arts 3, 4, Sch 1, Pt 1, para 12(1), (31), for transitional provisions see arts 3, 4, Sch 1, Pt 5 thereof at **[2.1131]**, **[2.1132]**, **[2.1134]**.

[1.2013]
29   Disclosure of information

(1), (2)   . . .

(3)   For the purposes of Part 9 of the Enterprise Act 2002 (c 40) (information) the following information is to be regarded as "specified information" within the meaning of that Part—

    (a)   information obtained by [Citizens Advice or Citizens Advice Scotland] under or by virtue of Part 1 of the Gas Act 1986 (c 44), Part 1 of the Electricity Act 1989 (c 29) or the Utilities Act 2000 (c 27);

    (b)   information obtained by [the consumer advocacy bodies] under or by virtue of [the Postal Services Act 2011].

[(3A)   Citizens Advice and Citizens Advice Scotland are to be treated as public authorities for the purposes of section 238(1) of the Enterprise Act 2002 only so far as regards functions conferred on the body in question under or by virtue of—

    (a)   the enactments mentioned in subsection (3), or

    (b)   this Act.

(3B)   If and so far as a relevant function is exercisable by Citizens Advice or Citizens Advice Scotland it is to be regarded as a function of that body under this Act for the purpose of enabling that body to receive information under section 241(3) of the Enterprise Act 2002 (disclosure to facilitate the exercise of another person's function).

(3C)   "Relevant function" means a function that—

    (a)   is not conferred by or under an enactment, and

    (b)   corresponds to a function conferred on the GCCNI under section 8, 9, 10, 11 or 19, disregarding for these purposes the limitations relating to postal services in Northern Ireland in sections 1(4) and 11(1).]

(4)   Part 9 of the Enterprise Act 2002 (which among other things restricts the disclosure of certain information) does not limit the information which may be—

    (a)   made available by [the GCCNI] under section 8 or 10,

    (b)   included in, or made public as part of, a report of [the GCCNI] under any provision of this Part,

    (c)   published by [the GCCNI] under section 19(2) . . . ,

    [(ca) published or made available by [Citizens Advice or Citizens Advice Scotland] under [subsection (7) or (8)] of section 19A,

    (cb) published by [Citizens Advice or Citizens Advice Scotland] under section 24(8),]

    (d)   published by an authorised person under section 27(7),

    (e)   published by [a consumer advocacy body] under section 45, or

    (f)   published by [Citizens Advice or Citizens Advice Scotland] under section 33DA of the Gas Act 1986 or section 42AA of the Electricity Act 1989.

(5)   Before disclosing any specified information by virtue of subsection (4) (other than by publishing it as mentioned in subsection (4)(e) or (f)), [the consumer advocacy body in question or the] or authorised person must consult—

    (a)   if the information relates to the affairs of an individual, that individual, and

    (b)   if the information relates to the business of an undertaking, the person for the time being carrying on the business.

(6)   Before disclosing any specified information by virtue of subsection (4) (other than by publishing it as mentioned in subsection (4)(e) or (f)), [the consumer advocacy body in question or the] authorised person must also have regard to the considerations set out in subsections (2) to (4) of section 244 of the Enterprise Act 2002.

For this purpose, references to "the authority" in those subsections are to be read as references to [the consumer advocacy body in question or the] authorised person, as appropriate.

(7)   In this section—

    "authorised person" has the same meaning as in section 27;

    "specified information" has the meaning given by section 238(1) of the Enterprise Act 2002.

NOTES

Sub-ss (1), (2): amend the Enterprise Act 2002, Schs 14, 15.

Sub-s (3): words in first and second pairs of square brackets substituted by the Public Bodies (Abolition of the National Consumer Council and Transfer of the Office of Fair Trading's Functions in relation to Estate Agents etc) Order 2014, SI 2014/631, arts 3, 4, Sch 1, Pt 1, para 12(1), (32)(a), for transitional provisions see arts 3, 4, Sch 1, Pt 5 thereof at **[2.1131]**, **[2.1132]**, **[2.1134]**; words in final pair of square brackets substituted by the Postal Services Act 2011, s 91(1), (2), Sch 12, Pt 3, paras 175, 181.

Sub-ss (3A)–(3C): inserted by SI 2014/631, arts 3, 4, Sch 1, Pt 1, para 12(1), (32)(b), for transitional provisions see note above.

Sub-s (4): words in square brackets substituted by SI 2014/631, arts 3, 4, Sch 1, Pt 1, para 12(1), (32)(c), for transitional provisions see note above; words omitted from para (c) repealed and paras (ca), (cb) inserted by the Electricity and Gas (Internal Markets) Regulations 2011, SI 2011/2704, reg 3(1), (3).

Sub-ss (5), (6): words in square brackets substituted by SI 2014/631, arts 3, 4, Sch 1, Pt 1, para 12(1), (32)(d), (e), for transitional provisions see note above.

Abolition of consumer bodies

[1.2014]
30   Abolition of "Energywatch" and "Postwatch"
(1)   The Gas and Electricity Consumer Council is abolished.
(2)   The Consumer Council for Postal Services is abolished.
(3)   Subject to any modifications made by this Act—
   (a)   the functions of the Gas and Electricity Consumer Council under the Gas Act 1986 (c 44), the Electricity Act 1989 (c 29) and the Utilities Act 2000 (c 27), and
   (b)   the functions of the Consumer Council for Postal Services under the Postal Services Act 2000 (c 26),
are transferred by this section to the Council.
(4)   . . .
(5)   Schedule 3 contains transitional provisions.

NOTES
Sub-s (4): amends the Gas Act 1986, s 66, the Electricity Act 1989, s 111(1), the Postal Services Act 2000, s 125(1), the Utilities Act 2000, s 106(1).

[1.2015]
31   Designation of the Consumer Council for Water for abolition
(1)   The Secretary of State may by order designate the Consumer Council for Water for abolition.
(2)   An order under this section must specify the earliest date on which a transfer order or an abolition order under section 32 may take effect in respect of the Consumer Council for Water.
(3)   Before making an order under this section the Secretary of State must consult—
   (a)   the Consumer Council for Water,
   (b)   [Citizens Advice], and
   (c)   such other persons as the Secretary of State considers appropriate.
(4)   An order under this section may only be made with the consent of the Welsh Ministers.

NOTES
Sub-s (3): words in square brackets substituted by the Public Bodies (Abolition of the National Consumer Council and Transfer of the Office of Fair Trading's Functions in relation to Estate Agents etc) Order 2014, SI 2014/631, arts 3, 4, Sch 1, Pt 1, para 12(1), (33), for transitional provisions see arts 3, 4, Sch 1, Pt 5 thereof at **[2.1131]**, **[2.1132]**, **[2.1134]**.

[1.2016]
32   Transfer orders and abolition orders
(1)   Where the Consumer Council for Water is designated for abolition under section 31, the Secretary of State may make in respect of it—
   (a)   one or more transfer orders;
   (b)   an abolition order.
(2)   A transfer order is an order which provides for the transfer to [Citizens Advice] of any function of the Consumer Council for Water.
(3)   An abolition order is an order which provides for the abolition of the Consumer Council for Water.
(4)   No provision of an order under this section may take effect before the date specified under section 31(2).
[(4A)   A transfer order may be made only with the consent of Citizens Advice.]
(5)   A transfer order or abolition order may be made only with the consent of the Welsh Ministers.

NOTES
Sub-s (3): words in square brackets substituted by the Public Bodies (Abolition of the National Consumer Council and Transfer of the Office of Fair Trading's Functions in relation to Estate Agents etc) Order 2014, SI 2014/631, arts 3, 4, Sch 1, Pt 1, para 12(1), (34)(a), for transitional provisions see arts 3, 4, Sch 1, Pt 5 thereof at **[2.1131]**, **[2.1132]**, **[2.1134]**.
Sub-s (4A): inserted by SI 2014/631, arts 3, 4, Sch 1, Pt 1, para 12(1), (34)(b), for transitional provisions see note above.

[1.2017]
33   Supplementary provision about transfer and abolition orders
(1)   This section applies where the Consumer Council for Water has been designated for abolition under section 31.
(2)   In this section "payment conditions" means—
   (a)   in the case of an appointment under Chapter 1 of Part 2 of the Water Industry Act 1991 (c 56), conditions included in the appointment by virtue of section 11(1)(c) of that Act, and
   (b)   in the case of a water supply licence under Chapter 1A of that Part, conditions included in the licence by virtue of section 17G(1)(b) of that Act.

(3) The payment conditions of such an appointment or licence may (without prejudice to the generality of sections 11(1)(c) and 17G(1)(b) of that Act) require the payment by the company holding the appointment or licence of sums relating to any of the expenses mentioned in subsection (4).

(4) Those expenses are—
- (a) the appropriate proportion of the expenses of [Citizens Advice] (other than those expenses within paragraph (b) and [any expenses which relate to taking on functions transferred from the Consumer Council for Water]);
- (b) any expenses of [Citizens Advice], the Secretary of State or the Consumer Council for Water which relate to a transfer scheme made in respect of the Consumer Council for Water under section 35(2)(a) or (7);
- (c) the expenses of the Secretary of State which relate to the abolition of the Consumer Council for Water;
- (d) the expenses of [Citizens Advice] expanding [a qualifying consumer advice scheme] to enable it to cater for water consumers;
- (e) the appropriate proportion of the expenses of [Citizens Advice] on, or in connection with, the support of [a qualifying consumer advice scheme].

(5) The "appropriate proportion" of any relevant expenses means such proportion of the expenses as the Secretary of State considers is reasonable having regard to—
- (a) in the case of expenses within subsection (4)(a), the functions exercisable by [Citizens Advice] in relation to water consumers;
- (b) in the case of expenses within subsection (4)(e), the functions under [a qualifying consumer advice scheme] which are exercisable in relation to water consumers.

(6) The Authority may, in accordance with this section, modify any payment conditions where it considers it necessary or expedient to do so in consequence of, or of preparations for—
- (a) the abolition of the Consumer Council for Water, or
- (b) a transfer order or abolition order under section 32.

(7) The Authority may, in accordance with this section, make such incidental or consequential modifications of the other conditions which are included in—
- (a) an appointment under Chapter 1 of Part 2 of the Water Industry Act 1991 (c 56), or
- (b) a water supply licence under Chapter 1A of that Part,

as it considers necessary or expedient in consequence of, or of preparations for, an event mentioned in subsection (6)(a) or (b).

(8) Before modifying under subsection (6) or (7) the conditions included in an appointment or licence, the Authority must consult the company holding the appointment or licence.

(9) The Secretary of State may, after consulting the Welsh Ministers, give directions to the Authority for the purpose of securing that sums relating to any of the expenses mentioned in subsection (4) are included in the sums payable by virtue of payment conditions; and the Authority must comply with any such direction.

[(9A) For the purposes of this section a qualifying public consumer advice scheme is a scheme that is supported by Citizens Advice or Citizens Advice Scotland, or by them jointly, in a manner that the Office of Fair Trading is prohibited from supporting by section 8A of the Enterprise Act 2002.]

(10) In this section—
"the Authority" means the Water Services Regulation Authority;
. . .
"water consumers" means consumers in relation to services provided by a water undertaker, a sewerage undertaker *or a licensed water supplier*, in *its capacity* as such.

NOTES

Sub-ss (4), (5): words in square brackets substituted by the Public Bodies (Abolition of the National Consumer Council and Transfer of the Office of Fair Trading's Functions in relation to Estate Agents etc) Order 2014, SI 2014/631, arts 3, 4, Sch 1, Pt 1, para 12(1), (35)(a), (b), for transitional provisions see arts 3, 4, Sch 1, Pt 5 thereof at **[2.1131]**, **[2.1132]**, **[2.1134]**.

Sub-s (9A): inserted by SI 2014/631, arts 3, 4, Sch 1, Pt 1, para 12(1), (35)(c), for transitional provisions see note above.

Sub-s (10): definition "OFT scheme" (omitted) repealed by SI 2014/631, arts 3, 4, Sch 1, Pt 1, para 12(1), (35)(d), for transitional provisions see note above; for the words in italics there are substituted the words ", a water supply licensee or sewerage licensee" and "the undertaker's or licensee's capacity" respectively by the Water Act 2014, s 56, Sch 7, paras 136, 139, as from a day to be appointed.

Abolition: supplementary provision

[1.2018]
34 Compensation for loss of office
(1) The Secretary of State may pay such sums as the Secretary of State may, with the approval of the Treasury, determine by way of compensation to any person who—
- (a) ceases to be a member of the Consumer Council for Postal Services, the Gas and Electricity Consumer Council, or the Consumer Council for Water by virtue of the abolition of the body in question by or under this Part, or
- (b) ceases to be a member of the company called the National Consumer Council (a company limited by guarantee and registered under the Companies Acts) by virtue of its dissolution.

(2)   The compensation is payable in respect of loss of office, or loss or diminution of pension rights.

[1.2019]
35   Transfer of property etc
(1)   This section applies to—
  (a), (b). . .
  (c)   if a transfer order has been made under section 32 (whether or not it has taken effect), the Consumer Council for Water;
  (d)   . . .
(2)   The Secretary of State may direct a body to which this section applies—
  (a)   to make a scheme or schemes for the transfer of its property, rights and liabilities to [Citizens Advice];
  (b)   to transfer such property, rights or obligations as are specified in the direction to a person (other than [Citizens Advice]) so specified ("the specified transferee").
(3)   Before giving, varying or revoking a direction under subsection (2), the Secretary of State must consult—
  (a)   the body to which the direction is to be or has been given,
  (b)   [Citizens Advice], and
  (c)   in the case of a direction under subsection (2)(b), the specified transferee.
(4)   A body given a direction under subsection (2)(a) must consult [Citizens Advice] before making a transfer scheme.
(5)   A transfer scheme made pursuant to a direction under subsection (2)(a) has effect—
  (a)   only if approved by the Secretary of State, and
  (b)   subject to any modifications made by the Secretary of State.
(6)   Before making any modifications the Secretary of State must consult the body to which the direction was given.
(7)   The Secretary of State may make a scheme or schemes for the transfer to [Citizens Advice] of the property, rights and liabilities of a body to which this section applies.
(8)   Schedule 4 makes further provision about transfer schemes.
(9)   In this section "transfer scheme" means a scheme made under or by virtue of subsection (2)(a) or (7).

_____

NOTES
Sub-s (1): paras (a), (b), (d) repealed by the Public Bodies (Abolition of the National Consumer Council and Transfer of the Office of Fair Trading's Functions in relation to Estate Agents etc) Order 2014, SI 2014/631, arts 3, 4, Sch 1, Pt 1, para 12(1), (36)(a), for transitional provisions see arts 3, 4, Sch 1, Pt 5 thereof at **[2.1131]**, **[2.1132]**, **[2.1134]**.
Sub-ss (2)–(4), (7): words in square brackets substituted by SI 2014/631, arts 3, 4, Sch 1, Pt 1, para 12(1), (36)(b)–(e), for transitional provisions see note above.

_____

[1.2020]
36   Directions
(1)   The Secretary of State may direct a body to which section 35 applies to supply to the Secretary of State such information specified or described in the direction as the Secretary of State may require in relation to—
  (a)   the body's property, rights or liabilities, or
  (b)   the exercise by the body of its functions.
(2)   A direction under subsection (1)—
  (a)   must specify the period within which the information is to be provided, and
  (b)   may require the information to be supplied in a specified form.
(3)   A body given a direction under subsection (1) must comply with it within the specified period.
(4)   The Secretary of State may direct a body to which section 35 applies not to take any action of a specified kind, or in specified circumstances.
(5)   Before giving, varying or revoking a direction under this section, the Secretary of State must consult—
  (a)   the body to which the direction is to be or has been given, and
  (b)   [Citizens Advice].
(6)   In this section "specified" means specified in the direction given by the Secretary of State.

_____

NOTES
Sub-s (5): words in square brackets substituted by the Public Bodies (Abolition of the National Consumer Council and Transfer of the Office of Fair Trading's Functions in relation to Estate Agents etc) Order 2014, SI 2014/631, arts 3, 4, Sch 1, Pt 1, para 12(1), (37), for transitional provisions see arts 3, 4, Sch 1, Pt 5 thereof at **[2.1131]**, **[2.1132]**, **[2.1134]**.

Alteration of [the functions of Citizens Advice and Citizens Advice Scotland]

[1.2021]
37   [Extension of the functions of Citizens Advice and Citizens Advice Scotland]
(1)   The Secretary of State may, by order, confer on [Citizens Advice or Citizens Advice Scotland] any other function or functions if the Secretary of State considers that it is in the interests of consumers generally, or consumers of a particular description, to do so.

(2)   The Secretary of State may only confer a function on [Citizens Advice or Citizens Advice Scotland] under this section if the function appears to the Secretary of State to be connected (directly or indirectly) to an existing or former function of the Council.

(3)   Before making an order under subsection (1), the Secretary of State must consult—

   (a)   [the body on which the Secretary of State proposes to confer a function or functions],

   (b)   if it appears to the Secretary of State that the exercise of any function conferred by the order might affect Wales in relation to any matter as respects which functions are exercisable by the Welsh Ministers, those Ministers, and

   (c)   such other persons as the Secretary of State considers appropriate.

[(3A)   An order under this section may not—

   (a)   confer a function on Citizens Advice or Citizens Advice Scotland, or

   (b)   modify a function conferred on Citizens Advice or Citizens Advice Scotland by an order under this section,

unless that body consents to the conferring or modifying of the function.]

(4)   An order under this section may not make provision which would be within the legislative competence of the Scottish Parliament if it were contained in an Act of that Parliament.

(5)   An order under this section which makes provision which would be within the legislative competence of the National Assembly for Wales if it were contained in a Measure of the Assembly (or, if the order is made after the Assembly Act provisions come into force, an Act of the Assembly) may only be made with the consent of the Assembly.

(6)   In subsection (5) "the Assembly Act provisions" has the meaning given by section 103(8) of the Government of Wales Act 2006 (c 32).

NOTES

Cross-heading, section heading, sub-ss (1)–(3): words in square brackets substituted by the Public Bodies (Abolition of the National Consumer Council and Transfer of the Office of Fair Trading's Functions in relation to Estate Agents etc) Order 2014, SI 2014/631, arts 3, 4, Sch 1, Pt 1, para 12(1), (38), (39)(a)–(d), for transitional provisions see arts 3, 4, Sch 1, Pt 5 thereof at **[2.1131]**, **[2.1132]**, **[2.1134]**.

Sub-s (3A): inserted by SI 2014/631, arts 3, 4, Sch 1, Pt 1, para 12(1), (38), (39)(e), for transitional provisions see note above.

38–40   (*S 38 repealed by the Public Bodies (Abolition of the National Consumer Council and Transfer of the Office of Fair Trading's Functions in relation to Estate Agents etc) Order 2014, SI 2014/631, arts 3, 4, Sch 1, Pt 1, para 12(1), (40), for transitional provisions see arts 3, 4, Sch 1, Pt 5 thereof at* **[2.1131]**, **[2.1132]**, **[2.1134]***; s 39 repealed by the Financial Services Act 2012, s 114(2), Sch 19; s 40 outside the scope of this work.*)

[Provision about consumer advocacy bodies

[1.2022]

40A   Grants to consumer advocacy bodies

(1)   The Secretary of State, or any other Minister of the Crown may, from time to time make grants to a consumer advocacy body in connection with functions conferred on it by or by virtue of this Act or any other enactment.

(2)   In the case of the GCCNI, grants under paragraph (1) may only be made in relation to consumer matters that relate to postal services in Northern Ireland.

(3)   In this section "enactment" means—

   (a)   an Act of Parliament,

   (b)   an Act of the Scottish Parliament,

   (c)   a Measure or Act of the National Assembly for Wales, or

   (d)   Northern Ireland legislation.]

NOTES

Commencement: 1 April 2014.

Inserted, together with preceding cross-heading and s 40B, by the Public Bodies (Abolition of the National Consumer Council and Transfer of the Office of Fair Trading's Functions in relation to Estate Agents etc) Order 2014, SI 2014/631, arts 3, 4, Sch 1, Pt 1, para 12(1), (41), for transitional provisions see arts 3, 4, Sch 1, Pt 5 thereof at **[2.1131]**, **[2.1132]**, **[2.1134]**.

[1.2023]

[40B   Exemption from liability in damages

(1)   A person listed in paragraph (2) is not liable in damages for anything done or omitted to be done in the exercise or purported exercise of any of the functions conferred by this or any other relevant enactment.

(2)   The persons referred to in paragraph (1) are—

   (a)   Citizens Advice and Citizens Advice Scotland;

   (b)   an employee of Citizens Advice or Citizens Advice Scotland;

   (c)   a person contracted to work for Citizens Advice or Citizens Advice Scotland;

   (d)   a charity trustee of Citizens Advice or Citizens Advice Scotland.

(3)   Paragraph (1) does not apply—

   (a)   if it is shown that the act or omission was in bad faith, or

(b)   so as to prevent an award of damages made in respect of an act or omission on the ground that the act or omission was unlawful as a result of section 6(1) of the Human Rights Act 1998.

(4)   In this section—

"charity trustee" in relation to Citizens Advice, has the meaning given by section 177 of the Charities Act 2011 and in relation to Citizens Advice Scotland, has the meaning given by section 106 of the Charities and Trustee Investment (Scotland) Act 2005;

"relevant enactment" means a provision of—

(a)   the Gas Act 1986;
(b)   the Electricity Act 1989;
(c)   The Postal Services Act 2000;
(d)   the Utilities Act 2000;
(e)   the Warm Homes and Energy Conservation Act 2000;
(f)   the Communications Act 2003;
(g)   the Postal Services Act 2011;
(h)   The Water Industry (Scotland) Act 2002;
(i)   the Water Services etc (Scotland) Act 2005;
(j)   this Act.]

NOTES

Commencement: 1 April 2014.
Inserted as noted to s 40A at **[1.2022]**.

Interpretation

[1.2024]
41   Interpretation of Part 1

(1)   In this Part—

"distribution system" has the meaning given by section 4(4) of the Electricity Act 1989 (c 29);

. . .

"functions" includes powers and duties;

"gas" has the meaning given by section 48(1) of the Gas Act 1986 (c 44);

"licensed water supplier" means a company holding a water supply licence under Chapter 1A of Part 2 of the Water Industry Act 1991 (c 56);

"modify" includes amend, add to, revoke or repeal (and references to "modification" are to be read accordingly);

["postal operator" has the same meaning as in Part 3 of the Postal Services Act 2011 (see section 65 of that Act);]

"postal services" has the same meaning as in [Part 3 of the Postal Services Act 2011 (see section 65 of that Act)];

"regulatory body" means a person who exercises regulatory functions in relation to a particular description of persons with a view to ensuring compliance with particular standards of conduct (whether statutory or non-statutory) by those persons;

. . .

["sewerage licensee" means a person holding a sewerage licence under Chapter 1A of Part 2 of the Water Industry Act 1991;

"water supply licensee" means a person holding a water supply licence under Chapter 1A of Part 2 of the Water Industry Act 1991.]

(2)   In this Part—

(a)   expressions used, as regards matters relating to gas, which are defined in section 48 of the Gas Act 1986 have the same meaning as in Part 1 of that Act, and
(b)   expressions used, as regards matters relating to electricity, which are defined in section 64 of the Electricity Act 1989, have the same meaning as in Part 1 of that Act.

NOTES

Sub-s (1): definition "financial year" (omitted) repealed by the Public Bodies (Abolition of the National Consumer Council and Transfer of the Office of Fair Trading's Functions in relation to Estate Agents etc) Order 2014, SI 2014/631, arts 3, 4, Sch 1, Pt 1, para 12(1), (42), for transitional provisions see arts 3, 4, Sch 1, Pt 5 thereof at **[2.1131]**, **[2.1132]**, **[2.1134]**; definition "licensed water supplier" repealed, and definitions "sewerage licensee" and "water supply licensee" added, by the Water Act 2014, s 56, Sch 7, paras 136, 140, as from a day to be appointed; definition "postal operator" inserted, words in square brackets in definition "postal services" substituted and definition "relevant postal services" (omitted) repealed by the Postal Services Act 2011, s 91(1), (2), Sch 12, Pt 3, paras 175, 182.

Modification: for the purposes of s 5 of this Act, para (a) of the definition "financial year" has effect as if it referred to the period beginning with 1 October 2008 and ending with 31 March 2010: see the Consumers, Estate Agents and Redress Act 2007 (Commencement No 3 and Supplementary Provision) Order 2008, SI 2008/1262, art 4.

PART 2
COMPLAINTS HANDLING AND REDRESS SCHEMES
Introductory

[1.2025]
42 Interpretation of Part 2
(1) In this Part—

"regulated provider" means a person within an entry in column 1 of the table;

"relevant consumer", in relation to a regulated provider, means a person within the corresponding entry in column 2 of the table;

"relevant regulator", in relation to a regulated provider, means the body specified in the corresponding entry in column 3 of the table.

TABLE

Regulated provider	Relevant consumer	Relevant regulator
A person holding a licence under section 7A(1) of the Gas Act 1986 (c 44) (supply licences).	A person who is a consumer in relation to gas supplied by a gas supplier (within the meaning of Part 1 of that Act).	The Gas and Electricity Markets Authority.
A person holding a licence under section 7(2) of the Gas Act 1986 (transportation licences).	A person (other than a gas licensee) who is a consumer in relation to services provided by a gas transporter (within the meaning of Part 1 of that Act).	The Gas and Electricity Markets Authority.
A person holding a licence under section 6(1)(d) of the Electricity Act 1989 (c 29) (supply licences).	A person who is a consumer in relation to electricity supplied by an electricity supplier (within the meaning of Part 1 of that Act).	The Gas and Electricity Markets Authority.
A person holding a licence under section 6(1)(c) of the Electricity Act 1989 (distribution licences).	A person (other than an electricity licensee) who is a consumer in relation to services provided by an electricity distributor (within the meaning of Part 1 of that Act).	The Gas and Electricity Markets Authority.
. . .	. . .	. . .
A water undertaker, sewerage undertaker *or licensed water supplier*.	A person who is a consumer in relation to services provided by a water undertaker, sewerage undertaker *or licensed water supplier in its capacity* as such.	The Water Services Regulation Authority.

(2) In this Part—

"consumer" has the same meaning as in Part 1;

"consumer complaint" means a complaint which is made against a regulated provider by or on behalf of a person in that person's capacity as a relevant consumer in relation to the regulated provider;

"licensed water supplier" has the same meaning as in Part 1;

"regulator" means a body listed in column 3 of the table.

(3) In this Part references to a regulator's regulated providers are to the regulated providers in relation to which the regulator is the relevant regulator.

(4) In this section—

"electricity licensee" means—

    (a) an electricity supplier (within the meaning of Part 1 of the Electricity Act 1989);

    (b) an electricity distributor (within the meaning of that Part);

    (c) the holder of a licence under section 6(1)(a), (b) or (e) of that Act (generation licences, transmission licences and interconnector licences), except where the holder is acting otherwise than for purposes connected with the carrying on of activities authorised by the licence;

"gas licensee" means—

    (a) a gas supplier (within the meaning of Part 1 of the Gas Act 1986 (c 44));

    (b) a gas transporter (within the meaning of that Part);

    (c) a gas shipper (within the meaning of that Part);

(d)   the holder of a licence under section 7ZA of that Act (licences for operation of gas interconnectors), except where the holder is acting otherwise than for purposes connected with the carrying on of activities authorised by the licence.

["sewerage licensee" means a person holding a sewerage licence under Chapter 1A of Part 2 of the Water Industry Act 1991;

"water supply licensee" means a person holding a water supply licence under Chapter 1A of Part 2 of the Water Industry Act 1991.]

NOTES

Sub-s (1): entry omitted from the Table repealed by the Postal Services Act 2011, s 91(1), (2), Sch 12, Pt 3, paras 175, 183; for the words in italics in column 1 there are substituted the words " , water supply licensee or sewerage licensee" and for the words in italics in column 2 there are substituted the words " , water supply licensee or sewerage licensee in the undertaker's or licensee's capacity" respectively by the Water Act 2014, s 56, Sch 7, paras 136, 141(1), (2), as from a day to be appointed.

Sub-s (2): definition "licensed water supplier" repealed, and definitions "sewerage licensee" and "water supply licensee" added by the Water Act 2014, s 56, Sch 7, paras 136, 141(1), (3), as from a day to be appointed.

Standards for handling complaints

[1.2026]

43 Standards for handling complaints

(1)   A regulator must by regulations prescribe standards for the handling by its regulated providers of consumer complaints made to them.

(2)   The regulations may prescribe standards in relation to all consumer complaints, or consumer complaints of a kind specified in the regulations.

(3)   In particular, the regulations may specify a kind of consumer complaint by reference to the subject-matter of a complaint, or the description of person making a complaint.

(4)   Regulations under this section may be made only with the consent of the Secretary of State.

(5)   A regulator must make arrangements for securing that regulations made by it under this section are available to the public, by whatever means it considers appropriate.

(6)   If a date is prescribed in relation to a regulator for the purposes of this subsection, from that date subsection (1) has effect in relation to that regulator as if, in that subsection, for "must" there were substituted "may".

(7)   In subsection (6) "prescribed" means prescribed by order made by the Secretary of State under this section.

(8)   Before prescribing a date in relation to a regulator for the purposes of subsection (6), the Secretary of State must consult—

(a)   the regulator,

[(b)   Citizens Advice,

(ba) Citizens Advice Scotland, and]

(c)   such other persons as the Secretary of State considers appropriate.

(9)   This section does not apply to the Water Services Regulation Authority.

NOTES

Sub-s (8): paras (b), (ba) substituted, for original para (b), by the Public Bodies (Abolition of the National Consumer Council and Transfer of the Office of Fair Trading's Functions in relation to Estate Agents etc) Order 2014, SI 2014/631, arts 3, 4, Sch 1, Pt 1, para 12(1), (43), for transitional provisions see arts 3, 4, Sch 1, Pt 5 thereof at **[2.1131]**, **[2.1132]**, **[2.1134]**.

Regulations: the Gas and Electricity (Consumer Complaints Handling Standards) Regulations 2008, SI 2008/1898.

[1.2027]

44 Requirements for making regulations under section 43

(1)   Before making regulations under section 43 a regulator must—

(a)   arrange for such research as it considers appropriate with a view to discovering the views of a representative sample of persons likely to be affected, and consider the results,

(b)   publish a notice of its proposals (a "proposals notice") in such manner as the regulator considers appropriate for bringing it to the attention of those likely to be affected by the proposals,

(c)   consider any representations duly made, and

(d)   consult persons or bodies appearing to it to be representative of persons likely to be affected by the proposals.

(2)   The proposals notice must—

(a)   set out the standards the regulator proposes to prescribe,

(b)   give the reasons why the regulator proposes to prescribe those standards,

(c)   explain how the standards will be enforced, and

(d)   specify a time (not being earlier than the end of the period of 30 days beginning with the day on which the notice is published) before which representations may be made.

(3)   The requirements of subsection (1) may be satisfied by action taken before the commencement of this section or the passing of this Act.

NOTES

Regulations: the Gas and Electricity (Consumer Complaints Handling Standards) Regulations 2008, SI 2008/1898.

[1.2028]
45 Information with respect to compliance with complaints handling standards

(1) This section applies in relation to standards prescribed by a regulator by regulations under section 43 in relation to its regulated providers (or some of them).

[(1A) This section also applies in relation to standards for the handling of complaints made about postal operators by users of their services which are contained in consumer protection conditions imposed under Part 3 of the Postal Services Act 2011.]

(2) [Citizens Advice and Citizens Advice Scotland] must publish such statistical information as [Citizens Advice or, as the case may be, Citizens Advice Scotland consider] appropriate relating to the levels of compliance with the standards which those regulated providers [or postal operators] have achieved.

[(2A) The GCCNI must publish such statistical information as it considers appropriate relating to the levels of compliance with the standards which those postal operators have achieved.]

(3) That information must be published in such form and manner, and with such frequency, as [the consumer advocacy body in question] thinks appropriate.

(4) Schedule 5 makes further provision with respect to information about compliance with complaints handling standards.

NOTES

Sub-s (1A): inserted by the Postal Services Act 2011, s 91(1), (2), Sch 12, Pt 3, paras 175, 184(1), (2).

Sub-s (2): words in first and second pairs of square brackets substituted by the Public Bodies (Abolition of the National Consumer Council and Transfer of the Office of Fair Trading's Functions in relation to Estate Agents etc) Order 2014, SI 2014/631, arts 3, 4, Sch 1, Pt 1, para 12(1), (44)(a), for transitional provisions see arts 3, 4, Sch 1, Pt 5 thereof at **[2.1131]**, **[2.1132]**, **[2.1134]**; words in final pair of square brackets inserted by the Postal Services Act 2011, s 91(1), (2), Sch 12, Pt 3, paras 175, 184(1), (3).

Sub-s (2A): inserted by SI 2014/631, arts 3, 4, Sch 1, Pt 1, para 12(1), (44)(b), for transitional provisions see note above.

Sub-s (3): words in square brackets substituted by SI 2014/631, arts 3, 4, Sch 1, Pt 1, para 12(1), (44)(c), for transitional provisions see note above.

[1.2029]
46 Supply of information to consumers

(1) A regulator may make regulations requiring each of its regulated providers in relation to which standards are prescribed under section 43 to give to the provider's relevant consumers such information as may be specified or described in the regulations about—
    (a) the standards, and
    (b) the levels of compliance with those standards achieved by the provider.

(2) Regulations under this section may include provision specifying the form and manner in which, and the frequency with which, information is to be given.

NOTES

Regulations: the Gas and Electricity (Consumer Complaints Handling Standards) Regulations 2008, SI 2008/1898.

Requirements relating to redress schemes

[1.2030]
47 Membership of redress scheme

(1) The Secretary of State may by order require regulated providers to be members of a redress scheme which is—
    (a) approved by their relevant regulator in accordance with section 49, or
    (b) administered by the Secretary of State (or a person appointed by the Secretary of State) and designated by the Secretary of State as an appropriate redress scheme in relation to them.

(2) The order may provide that the requirement applies only in relation to consumer complaints of a kind specified in the order.

(3) In particular, the order may specify a kind of consumer complaint by reference to the subject-matter of a complaint, or the description of person making a complaint.

(4) Before making an order under this section the Secretary of State must consult—
    (a) each relevant regulator (in relation to regulated providers to which the order will apply), and
    (b) other persons appearing to the Secretary of State to be representative of persons who have an interest in the matter.

(5) The requirements of subsection (4) may be satisfied by consultation undertaken before the commencement of this section or the passing of this Act.

(6) An order under this section which applies to a water undertaker or sewerage undertaker for an area which is wholly or mainly in Wales may be made only with the consent of the Welsh Ministers.

(7) The Secretary of State may not make an order under this section unless satisfied, in relation to each regulated provider to which the order will apply, that—
    (a) there is at least one qualifying redress scheme which the provider is eligible to join and membership of which will satisfy the requirement imposed by the order, or
    (b) there will be such a scheme when the order comes into force.

(8)   The Secretary of State may not designate a scheme in relation to regulated providers under subsection (1)(b) unless the Secretary of State is satisfied that the scheme is one which could be approved by their relevant regulator in accordance with section 49.

(9)   The Secretary of State may establish or administer a scheme for the purposes of subsection (1)(b), or provide financial assistance to a person who establishes or administers such a scheme; and such a scheme may provide for fees to be payable by members of the scheme.

NOTES

Orders: the Gas and Electricity Regulated Providers (Redress Scheme) Order 2008, SI 2008/2268; the the Gas and Electricity Regulated Providers (Redress Scheme) (Amendment) Order 2014, SI 2014/2378.

[1.2031]
48   Membership of redress schemes: supplementary
(1)   In this Part—
   "qualifying redress scheme" means a redress scheme within paragraph (a) or (b) of section 47(1);
   "redress scheme" means a scheme under which consumer complaints may be made to, and investigated and determined by, an independent person ("the independent person");
   "scheme administrator", in relation to a redress scheme, means the person who administers the scheme,
and references to approval of a redress scheme are to approval of the scheme for the purposes of section 47(1)(a).

(2)   In the definition of "redress scheme", "independent", in relation to a consumer complaint, means independent of—
   (a)   the regulated provider against whom the complaint is made, and
   (b)   the regulator who is the relevant regulator in relation to the regulated provider.

(3)   Nothing in this Part prevents a qualifying redress scheme providing—
   (a)   for membership to be open to persons who are not subject to any duty to belong to a qualifying redress scheme;
   (b)   for the investigation and determination of complaints other than those in relation to which such a duty applies, made against members who have voluntarily accepted the jurisdiction of the scheme over such complaints.

(4)   For the purposes of the law relating to defamation, proceedings under a qualifying redress scheme (in relation to a consumer complaint and a regulated provider to which an order under section 47 applies) are to be treated in the same way as proceedings before a court.

[1.2032]
49   Approval of redress schemes
(1)   In deciding whether to approve a redress scheme, a regulator must have regard to—
   (a)   the provisions of the scheme;
   (b)   the manner in which the scheme will be operated (so far as that can be judged from the facts known to the regulator);
   (c)   the interests of relevant consumers (in relation to the regulator's regulated providers);
   (d)   such principles as—
      (i)   in the opinion of the regulator constitute generally accepted principles of best practice in relation to schemes for providing redress to consumers, and
      (ii)   it is reasonable to regard as applicable to the scheme.

(2)   In considering the interests of relevant consumers under subsection (1)(c), the regulator must in particular have regard to the number of other redress schemes applying to its regulated providers which are (or are likely to become) qualifying redress schemes.

(3)   A regulator must not approve a redress scheme unless—
   (a)   membership of the scheme is open to all the regulator's regulated providers, and those regulated providers may not be expelled from membership of the scheme,
   (b)   if, at the time the approval is given, any of the regulator's regulated providers are required under section 47 to be a member of a redress scheme (or would be so required but for the fact that an order which has been made under that section is not yet in force), the scheme covers all the consumer complaints to which the requirement applies,
   (c)   the independent person may require regulated providers to provide complainants with the types of redress listed in subsection (6) (whether or not other types of redress are available), and
   (d)   the regulator considers that the scheme makes satisfactory provision about the matters listed in subsection (7).

(4)   Subsection (3)(a) does not prevent the Gas and Electricity Markets Authority approving—
   (a)   a scheme which is open to all regulated gas providers, but not regulated electricity providers,
   (b)   a scheme which is open to all regulated electricity providers, but not regulated gas providers,
and, in the case of such a scheme, subsection (3)(b) applies as if the reference to the regulator's regulated providers were to the regulated gas providers or, as the case may be, regulated electricity providers.

(5) For this purpose—

"regulated electricity provider" means a person holding a licence under section 6(1)(c) or (d) of the Electricity Act 1989 (c 29);

"regulated gas provider" means a person holding a licence under section 7(2) or 7A(1) of the Gas Act 1986 (c 44).

(6) The types of redress mentioned in subsection (3)(c) are—

(a) providing an apology or explanation,

(b) paying compensation, and

(c) taking such other action in the interests of the complainant as the independent person may specify.

(7) The matters mentioned in subsection (3)(d) are—

(a) the matters about which complaints may be made (which may include non-compliance with a code of practice or other document);

(b) the independent person's duties and powers in relation to the investigation and determination of complaints (which may include power to decide not to investigate or determine a complaint);

(c) the enforcement of any requirement to provide redress imposed on a regulated provider in accordance with the scheme;

(d) the provision of information by the independent person to the regulator and to persons within subsection (8);

(e) the provision of information by the independent person—

   [(i) to Citizens Advice Scotland, for the purposes of any qualifying public consumer advice scheme supported by it (on its own or jointly with Citizens Advice), and

   (ii) to persons who operate a qualifying public consumer advice scheme supported by Citizens Advice or Citizens Advice Scotland, or by them jointly, for the purposes of that scheme;]

(f) the acceptance and handling of complaints transferred from redress schemes which have their approval withdrawn under section 51.

(8) The persons within this subsection are—

(a) any other body having regulatory functions in relation to the regulated providers to which the scheme applies;

(b) persons exercising functions under other redress schemes which apply to the regulator's regulated providers;

[(c) Citizens Advice;

(ca) so far as regards schemes to be approved by the Gas and Electricity Markets Authority, Citizens Advice Scotland;]

(d) the Secretary of State.

[(9) For the purposes of this section a qualifying public consumer advice scheme is a scheme that is supported by Citizens Advice or Citizens Advice Scotland, or by them jointly, in a manner that the Office of Fair Trading is prohibited from supporting by section 8A of the Enterprise Act 2002.]

NOTES

Sub-s (7): paras (e)(i), (ii) substituted by the Public Bodies (Abolition of the National Consumer Council and Transfer of the Office of Fair Trading's Functions in relation to Estate Agents etc) Order 2014, SI 2014/631, arts 3, 4, Sch 1, Pt 1, para 12(1), (45)(a), for transitional provisions see arts 3, 4, Sch 1, Pt 5 thereof at **[2.1131]**, **[2.1132]**, **[2.1134]**.

Sub-s (8): paras (c), (ca) substituted, for original para (c), by SI 2014/631, arts 3, 4, Sch 1, Pt 1, para 12(1), (45)(b), for transitional provisions see note above.

Sub-s (9): added by SI 2014/631, arts 3, 4, Sch 1, Pt 1, para 12(1), (45)(c), for transitional provisions see note above.

[1.2033]

50 Approval of redress schemes: supplementary

(1) An application for approval of a redress scheme must be made in such manner, and accompanied by such information, as the regulator to which the application is made may determine.

(2) Section 51 applies if the regulator is minded to refuse an application for approval.

(3) The scheme administrator of a redress scheme approved by a regulator must notify the regulator of any change to the scheme before the end of the period of 14 days beginning with the day on which the change is made.

(4) A regulator may, in accordance with section 51, withdraw its approval of a redress scheme, and may do so generally or in relation to consumer complaints of a description specified by the regulator.

(5) In particular, a regulator may withdraw its approval in relation to consumer complaints made on or after a date specified by the regulator.

[1.2034]

51 Procedure for refusing or withdrawing approval

(1) Before refusing or withdrawing its approval of a redress scheme, the regulator must give the scheme administrator a notice—

(a) stating that the regulator proposes to refuse or withdraw its approval,

(b) giving the reasons for the proposed refusal or withdrawal, and

    (c)   specifying a time (not being earlier than the end of the period of 30 days beginning with the day on which the notice is given to the scheme administrator) before which representations about the proposed refusal or withdrawal may be made.

(2)   The regulator must give notice to the scheme administrator of—

    (a)   the regulator's decision on a proposal to refuse or withdraw approval, and

    (b)   the reasons for its decision.

(3)   In the case of a decision to withdraw approval, the regulator must also give notice of its decision and the reasons for it to the Secretary of State.

(4)   The scheme administrator must give a copy of the notice under subsection (2) to each member of the scheme.

(5)   If the regulator decides to withdraw approval, the withdrawal has effect in accordance with, and from the date specified in, the notice under subsection (2).

(6)   Where a redress scheme designated under section 47(1)(b) is administered by a person appointed by the Secretary of State, this section (other than subsection (3)) applies in relation to a revocation by the Secretary of State of that person's appointment as it applies in relation to a withdrawal by a regulator of the approval of a redress scheme.

Enforcement

[1.2035]

52   Enforcement of requirements imposed under Part 2

(1), (2)   . . .

(3)   A requirement imposed under section 47 on a water undertaker, sewerage undertaker *or licensed water supplier* is enforceable by the Water Services Regulation Authority under section 18 of the Water Industry Act 1991 (c 56) (orders for securing compliance).

(4)   . . .

NOTES

Sub-s (1): amends the Gas Act 1986, s 28.

Sub-s (2): amends the Electricity Act 1989, s 25.

Sub-s (3): for the words in italics there are substituted the words ", water supply licensee or sewerage licensee" by the Water Act 2014, s 56, Sch 7, paras 136, 142, as from a day to be appointed.

Sub-s (4): repealed by the Postal Services Act 2011, s 91(1), (2), Sch 12, Pt 3, paras 175, 185.

53–58   ((Pt 3) S 53(1) introduces Sch 6; s 53(2) amends the Estate Agents Act 1979, s 3 at **[1.788]**; s 53(3) repeals the Housing Act 2004, ss 172–174; s 54 inserts s 21A of the 1979 Act at **[1.807]** and amends s 3 of that Act at **[1.788]**; s 55 amends ss 3, 5 of, and Sch 1 to, the 1979 Act at **[1.788]**, **[1.790]**, **[1.824]**; s 56 amends s 4 of the 1979 Act at **[1.789]**; s 57 amends s 11 of the 1979 Act at **[1.796]**; s 58 inserts s 11A of the 1979 Act at **[1.797]** and amends ss 3, 9, 27 of the 1979 Act at **[1.788]**, **[1.794]**, **[1.815]**.)

PART 4
MISCELLANEOUS AND GENERAL

Contracts concluded away from business premises

[1.2036]

59   Contracts concluded away from business premises

(1)   The Secretary of State may make regulations entitling a consumer who is a party to a protected contract to cancel the contract.

(2)   A protected contract is a contract between a consumer and a trader which is for the supply of goods or services to the consumer by a trader and is made—

    (a)   during a solicited visit by a trader to the consumer's home or place of work, or to the home of another individual, or

    (b)   after an offer made by the consumer during such a visit.

(3)   A visit is solicited if it is made at the express request of the consumer.

(4)   Regulations made under this section may make any provision which may be made by regulations under section 2(2) of the European Communities Act 1972 (c 68) (by virtue of section 2(4) of that Act).

(5)   The regulations may in particular make provision—

    (a)   as to the circumstances in which the consumer may cancel the contract and the effect of such a cancellation;

    (b)   requiring the trader to inform the consumer of the matters within paragraph (a);

    (c)   for the enforcement of any requirement imposed by virtue of paragraph (b).

(6)   For the purposes of this section, "consumer" and "trader" in relation to a contract have the same meaning as they have for the purposes of the relevant Directive in relation to transactions within that Directive.

(7)   "The relevant Directive" means—

    (a)   Council Directive 85/577/EEC to protect the consumer in respect of contracts negotiated away from business premises, as it has effect from time to time, or

    (b)   if that Directive is repealed and re-enacted (with or without modification), that Directive as re-enacted.

NOTES

Regulations: the Cancellation of Contracts made in a Consumer's Home or Place of Work etc Regulations 2008, SI 2008/1816 at **[2.602]**.

Subordinate legislation

[1.2037]
60 Orders and regulations

(1)   An order or regulations under this Act must be made by statutory instrument.

(2)   The Statutory Instruments Act 1946 (c 36) is to apply in relation to any power of a regulator to make regulations under section 43 or 46 as if the regulator were a Minister of the Crown.

(3)   Any order or regulations under this Act may—

    (a)   make provision generally or subject to exceptions or in relation to specified cases or descriptions of case;

    (b)   make different provision for different cases or circumstances or for different purposes;

    (c)   provide for a person to exercise a discretion in dealing with any matter;

    (d)   make incidental, supplementary, consequential, transitory and transitional provision and savings.

(4)   A provision of this Act which permits regulations or orders to make provision of a specified kind is without prejudice to the generality of subsection (3).

(5)   In the case of an order or regulations made by the Secretary of State, the provision which may be made by virtue of subsection (3)(d) includes provision modifying any provision made by or under any enactment.

(6)   For this purpose—

"enactment" means—

    (a)   an Act of Parliament (including, in the case of an order under section 32, this Act),

    (b)   an Act of the Scottish Parliament,

    (c)   a Measure or Act of the National Assembly for Wales, or

    (d)   Northern Ireland legislation,

whenever passed or made;

"modify" has the same meaning as in Part 1.

(7)   Nothing in this section authorises an order or regulations under this Act to make provision which would be within the legislative competence of the Scottish Parliament if it were contained in an Act of that Parliament.

(8)   The Documentary Evidence Act 1868 (c 37) (proof of order and regulations etc) has effect as if—

    (a)   the regulators were included in column 1 of the Schedule to that Act, and

    (b)   the entry in column 2 of that Schedule corresponding to each regulator mentioned the regulator and persons authorised to act on the regulator's behalf.

(9)   Nothing in this section applies in relation to a court order under section 26.

(10)   In this section "regulator" means—

    (a)   the Gas and Electricity Markets Authority, . . .

    (b)   . . .

NOTES

Sub-s (10): para (b) and word immediately preceding it (omitted) repealed by the Postal Services Act 2011, s 91(1), (2), Sch 12, Pt 3, paras 175, 186.

[1.2038]
61 Directions

(1)   A requirement or power under this Act to give a notice (or to notify) is a requirement or power to give notice in writing.

(2)   A requirement or power under this Act to give a direction (or to direct) is a requirement or power to give a direction in writing.

(3)   Any power conferred by this Act to give a direction includes power to vary or revoke the direction.

[1.2039]
62 Parliamentary control of orders and regulations

(1)   Any instrument to which this subsection applies is subject to annulment in pursuance of a resolution of either House of Parliament.

(2)   Subsection (1) applies to any order or regulations made by the Secretary of State under any provision of this Act except—

    (a)   an order or regulations to which subsection (3) applies, or

    (b)   an order under section 66 (commencement).

(3)   An order or regulations containing (whether alone or with other provision) provision made under or by virtue of any of the following provisions may not be made unless a draft of the order or regulations has been laid before, and approved by a resolution of, each House of Parliament—

    (a)   section 4 ("designated consumers");

(b) section 24(3)(d) (power to specify persons from whom [the consumer advocacy bodies] may require information);

(c) section 31 (designation of the Consumer Council for Water for abolition);

(d) section 37(1) (conferral of additional functions on [Citizens Advice or Citizens Advice Scotland]);

(e) . . .

(f) section 59 (contracts concluded away from business premises), so far as it enables provision to be made modifying an Act of Parliament;

(g) section 60(5) (consequential provision etc), so far as it enables such provision to be made;

(h) section 63(2) (consequential provision etc), so far as it enables such provision to be made.

(4) In subsection (3), "modify" has the same meaning as in Part 1.

NOTES

Sub-s (3): words in square brackets substituted, and para (e) repealed, by the Public Bodies (Abolition of the National Consumer Council and Transfer of the Office of Fair Trading's Functions in relation to Estate Agents etc) Order 2014, SI 2014/631, arts 3, 4, Sch 1, Pt 1, para 12(1), (46), for transitional provisions see arts 3, 4, Sch 1, Pt 5 thereof at **[2.1131]**, **[2.1132]**, **[2.1134]**.

Amendments, transitional provision and repeals

[1.2040]
63 Minor, consequential and transitional provision
(1) Schedule 7 contains minor and consequential amendments.
(2) The Secretary of State may by order make such consequential, supplementary, incidental, transitory or transitional provision or savings (including provision modifying any provision made by or under an enactment) as the Secretary of State considers necessary or expedient in connection with the coming into force of any provision made by or under this Act.
(3) An order under this section may make such adaptations of provisions of this Act brought into force as appear to be necessary or expedient in consequence of other provisions of this Act not yet having come into force.
(4) In this section—
    "enactment" means—
        (a) an Act of Parliament,
        (b) an Act of the Scottish Parliament,
        (c) a Measure or Act of the National Assembly for Wales, or
        (d) Northern Ireland legislation,
        whenever passed or made;
    "modify" has the same meaning as in Part 1.
(5) An order under this section may not make provision which would be within the legislative competence of the Scottish Parliament if it were contained in an Act of that Parliament.

NOTES

Commencement: 21 December 2007 (sub-s (1) certain purposes; sub-ss (2)–(5)); 1 October 2008 (sub-s (1), certain purposes); to be appointed (otherwise).

Orders: the Consumers, Estate Agents and Redress Act 2007 (Commencement No 3 and Supplementary Provision) Order 2008, SI 2008/1262.

64 (*Introduces Sch 8 (outside the scope of this work).*)

General

[1.2041]
65 Extent
(1) Subject to subsections (2) to (6), this Act extends to England and Wales, Scotland and Northern Ireland.
(2) The following provisions extend to England and Wales and Scotland only—
    (a) section 13 (investigation of complaints relating to disconnection of gas or electricity);
    (b) section 14 (reference of matters to Gas and Electricity Markets Authority);
    [(ba) section 19A (guidance for energy consumers);]
    (c) section 37 (extension of [the functions of Citizens Advice and Citizens Advice Scotland]).
(3) Sections 31 to 33 (abolition of Consumer Council for Water) extend to England and Wales only.
(4), (5) . . .
(6) Any amendment or repeal made by this Act has the same extent as the enactment to which it relates.
(7) . . .

NOTES

Sub-s (2): para (ba) inserted by the Electricity and Gas (Internal Markets) Regulations 2011, SI 2011/2704, reg 3(1), (4); words in square brackets in para (c) substituted by the Public Bodies (Abolition of the National Consumer Council and Transfer of the Office of Fair Trading's Functions in relation to Estate Agents etc) Order 2014, SI 2014/631, arts 3, 4, Sch 1, Pt 1, para 12(1), (47)(a), for transitional provisions see arts 3, 4, Sch 1, Pt 5 thereof at **[2.1131]**, **[2.1132]**, **[2.1134]**.

Sub-ss (4), (5): repealed by the Postal Services Act 2011, s 91(1), (2), Sch 12, Pt 3, paras 175, 187.

Sub-s (7): repealed by SI 2014/631, arts 3, 4, Sch 1, Pt 1, para 12(1), (47)(b), for transitional provisions see note above.

[1.2042]
66   Commencement
(1)   This section and sections 60 to 62, 65 and 67 come into force on the day this Act is passed.
(2)   Subject to that, the provisions of this Act come into force on such day as may be appointed by order of the Secretary of State.

NOTES
Orders: the Consumers, Estate Agents and Redress Act 2007 (Commencement No 1) Order 2007, SI 2007/2934; the Consumers, Estate Agents and Redress Act 2007 (Commencement No 2) Order 2007, SI 2007/3546; the Consumers, Estate Agents and Redress Act 2007 (Commencement No 4) Order 2008, SI 2008/905; the Consumers, Estate Agents and Redress Act 2007 (Commencement No 3 and Supplementary Provision) Order 2008, SI 2008/1262; the Consumers, Estate Agents and Redress Act 2007 (Commencement No 5 and Savings and Transitional Provisions) Order 2008, SI 2008/2550.

[1.2043]
67   Short title
This Act may be cited as the Consumers, Estate Agents and Redress Act 2007.

SCHEDULES

SCHEDULES 1, 2

(Sch 1 repealed by the Public Bodies (Abolition of the National Consumer Council and Transfer of the Office of Fair Trading's Functions in relation to Estate Agents etc) Order 2014, SI 2014/631, arts 3, 4, Sch 1, Pt 1, para 12(1), (48), for transitional provisions see arts 3, 4, Sch 1, Pt 5 thereof at **[2.1131]**, **[2.1132]**, **[2.1134]**; *Sch 2 outside the scope of this work.)*

SCHEDULE 3
ABOLITION OF CONSUMER BODIES: TRANSITIONAL PROVISION
Section 30

Complaints and investigations functions of Gas and Electricity Consumer Council
[1.2044]
1. (1)   This paragraph applies to—
(a)   any complaint to which section 32(1) of the Gas Act 1986 (c 44) applies which is referred to the Gas and Electricity Consumer Council before the appointed day;
(b)   any matter under investigation by the Gas and Electricity Consumer Council under section 33 of that Act immediately before the appointed day.
(2)   The functions of the Gas and Electricity Consumer Council under section 32 or 33 of the Gas Act 1986 are exercisable by the Council in relation to the complaint or matter, but as if in section 32(8) of that Act the reference to the Utilities Act 2000 (c 27) or the Gas Act 1986 included a reference to this Act and to Part 9 of the Enterprise Act 2002 (c 40).
(3)   Sub-paragraph (2) applies—
(a)   notwithstanding the repeal of sections 32 and 33 of the Gas Act 1986 by this Act, and
(b)   whether or not the complaint is within section 11, 12 or 13, or the matter is within section 11.
(4)   "The appointed day" is the day on which section 30(1) comes into force.

2. (1)   This paragraph applies to—
(a)   any complaint to which section 46(1) of the Electricity Act 1989 (c 29) applies which is referred to the Gas and Electricity Consumer Council before the appointed day;
(b)   any matter under investigation by the Gas and Electricity Consumer Council under section 46A of that Act immediately before the appointed day.
(2)   The functions of the Gas and Electricity Consumer Council under section 46 or 46A of the Electricity Act 1989 are exercisable by the Council in relation to the complaint or matter, but as if in section 46(8) of that Act the reference to the Utilities Act 2000 or the Electricity Act 1989 included a reference to this Act and Part 9 of the Enterprise Act 2002.
(3)   Sub-paragraph (2) applies—
(a)   notwithstanding the repeal of sections 46 and 46A of the Electricity Act 1989 by this Act, and
(b)   whether or not the complaint is within section 11, 12 or 13, or the matter is within section 11.
(4)   "The appointed day" is the day on which section 30(1) comes into force.

Annual reports of the Gas and Electricity Consumer Council

3. (1)   After the abolition of the Gas and Electricity Consumer Council under section 30(1), any duty of the Gas and Electricity Consumer Council to make an annual report, in relation to any financial year for which such a report has not been made, is to be discharged by the Council.

(2)   The period between the abolition of the Gas and Electricity Consumer Council and the end of the preceding financial year (if less than 12 months) is to be treated as its financial year for which the last annual report is required.

(3)   If that period is 9 months or longer the Council must make the last annual report as soon as practicable after the end of that period.

(4)   If that period is shorter than 9 months the last annual report must be made no later than the first report of the Council under section 7.

(5)   In this paragraph—
"annual report" means a report required by paragraph 6 of Schedule 2 to the Utilities Act 2000 (c 27);
"financial year" means a year ending with 31 March.

Complaints and investigations functions of Consumer Council for Postal Services

4. (1)   This paragraph applies to any matter which, immediately before the appointed day, is under investigation by the Consumer Council for Postal Services under—
   (a)   section 56(1) of the Postal Services Act 2000 (c 26) (complaints referred to the Consumer Council for Postal Services), or
   (b)   section 57 of that Act (power of that Council to investigate other matters).

(2)   The functions of the Consumer Council for Postal Services under section 56 or 57 of the Postal Services Act 2000 are exercisable by the Council in relation to the matter, and any agreement between the Consumer Council for Postal Services and the Commission under section 56(3) of that Act has effect as if agreed between the Council and the Commission.

(3)   Sub-paragraph (2) applies—
   (a)   notwithstanding the repeal of sections 56 and 57 of the Postal Services Act 2000 by this Act;
   (b)   whether or not the matter is within section 11 or 16.

(4)   "The appointed day" is the day on which section 30(2) comes into force.

Annual reports of the Consumer Council for Postal Services

5. (1)   After the abolition of the Consumer Council for Postal Services under section 30(2), any duty of the Consumer Council for Postal Services to make an annual report, in relation to any financial year for which such a report has not been made, is to be discharged by the Council.

(2)   The period between the abolition of the Consumer Council for Postal Services and the end of the preceding financial year (if less than 12 months) is to be treated as the financial year for which the last annual report is required.

(3)   If that period is 9 months or longer the Council must make the last annual report as soon as practicable after the end of that period.

(4)   If that period is shorter than 9 months the last annual report must be made no later than the first report of the Council under section 7.

(5)   In this paragraph—
"annual report" means a report required by section 55(1) of the Postal Services Act 2000 (c 26);
"financial year" means a year ending with 31 March.

SCHEDULE 4
TRANSFER OF PROPERTY ETC TO COUNCIL

Section 35

Preliminary

[1.2045]
1. In this Schedule—
"transfer scheme" has the meaning given by section 35;
"transferor" means the body to which section 35 applies and to which the transfer scheme relates.

Contents of transfer schemes

2. (1)   The property, rights and liabilities that may be transferred by a transfer scheme include property, rights and liabilities that would not otherwise be capable of being transferred or assigned.

(2)   The transfers authorised by sub-paragraph (1) include transfers of interests and rights that are to take effect in accordance with the scheme as if there were—
   (a)   no such requirement to obtain a person's consent or concurrence,
   (b)   no such liability in respect of a contravention of any other requirement, and
   (c)   no such interference with any interest or right,

as there would otherwise be by reason of a provision within sub-paragraph (3).

(3) A provision is within this sub-paragraph to the extent that it has effect (whether under an enactment or agreement or otherwise) in relation to the terms on which the transferor is entitled or subject to anything to which the transfer relates.

3. A transfer scheme may define the property, rights and liabilities to be transferred by specifying them or describing them.

4. A transfer scheme may contain supplementary, incidental, transitional and consequential provision.

Effect of transfers

5. (1) On the day appointed by a transfer scheme the property, rights and liabilities which are the subject of the scheme are transferred to [Citizens Advice] in accordance with the provisions of the scheme.

(2) Sub-paragraph (1) has effect in relation to property, rights or liabilities to which it applies in spite of any provision (of whatever nature) which would prevent or restrict the transfer of the property, rights or liabilities otherwise than by virtue of that sub-paragraph.

6. (1) So far as is appropriate in consequence of the transfer, anything done by the transferor for the purposes of or in connection with anything transferred which is in effect immediately before it is transferred is to be treated as if done by [Citizens Advice].

(2) A transfer does not affect the validity of anything done by or in relation to the transferor before the transfer takes effect.

(3) There may be continued by or in relation to [Citizens Advice] anything (including legal proceedings) relating to anything transferred which is in the process of being done by or in relation to the transferor immediately before it is transferred.

(4) So far as is appropriate in consequence of the transfer, [Citizens Advice] is substituted for the transferor in any agreement, instrument or other document relating to anything transferred.

Staff

7. The Transfer of Undertakings (Protection of Employment) Regulations 2006 (SI 2006/246) apply to a transfer which relates to rights or liabilities under a contract of employment whether or not the transfer would, apart from this paragraph, be a relevant transfer for the purposes of those regulations.

8. Where an employee of the transferor becomes an employee of [Citizens Advice] by virtue of a transfer scheme—
  (a) a period of employment with the transferor is to be treated as a period of employment with [Citizens Advice], and
  (b) the transfer to [Citizens Advice] is not to be treated as a break in service.

Chargeable gains: asset to be treated as disposed of without a gain or loss

9. For the purposes of the Taxation of Chargeable Gains Act 1992 (c 12), a transfer of an asset by a transfer scheme is to be treated as a disposal of that asset to [Citizens Advice] for a consideration of such amount as would secure that, on the disposal, neither a gain nor a loss accrues to the transferor.

Continuity in relation to transfer of intangible assets

10. (1) For the purposes of Schedule 29 to the Finance Act 2002 (c 23)—
  (a) a transfer by a transfer scheme of a chargeable intangible asset of the transferor is to be treated as a tax-neutral transfer, and
  (b) an intangible fixed asset which is an existing asset of the transferor at the time of the transfer is to be treated, on and after the transfer, as an existing asset in the hands of the Council.

(2) Expressions used in this paragraph and in that Schedule have the same meanings in this paragraph as in that Schedule.

Corporation Tax Acts

11. So far as it relates to corporation tax, this Schedule is to be construed as one with the Corporation Tax Acts.

Modification of transfer schemes after appointed day

12. (1) If, after the day appointed by a transfer scheme, the transferor and [Citizens Advice] so agree in writing, the scheme shall for all purposes be deemed to have come into force on that day with such modifications as may be agreed.

(2)   An agreement under this paragraph may, in connection with giving effect to modifications to the scheme, include supplementary, incidental, transitional and consequential provision.

NOTES

Words in square brackets substituted by the Public Bodies (Abolition of the National Consumer Council and Transfer of the Office of Fair Trading's Functions in relation to Estate Agents etc) Order 2014, SI 2014/631, arts 3, 4, Sch 1, Pt 1, para 12(1), (49), for transitional provisions see arts 3, 4, Sch 1, Pt 5 thereof at **[2.1131]**, **[2.1132]**, **[2.1134]**.

SCHEDULES 5–8

*(Schs 5, 7, 8 outside the scope of this work; Sch 6 inserts the Estate Agents Act 1979, ss 23A–23C at **[1.810]**–**[1.812]** and inserts Schs 3, 4 to that Act at **[1.827]**, **[1.828]**.)*

CORPORATE MANSLAUGHTER AND CORPORATE HOMICIDE ACT 2007

(2007 c 19)

ARRANGEMENT OF SECTIONS

Corporate manslaughter and corporate homicide

An Act to create a new offence that, in England and Wales or Northern Ireland, is to be called corporate manslaughter and, in Scotland, is to be called corporate homicide; and to make provision in connection with that offence

[26 July 2007]

Corporate manslaughter and corporate homicide

[1.2046]
1   The offence
(1)   An organisation to which this section applies is guilty of an offence if the way in which its activities are managed or organised—
   (a)   causes a person's death, and
   (b)   amounts to a gross breach of a relevant duty of care owed by the organisation to the deceased.
(2)   The organisations to which this section applies are—
   (a)   a corporation;
   (b)   a department or other body listed in Schedule 1;
   (c)   a police force;
   (d)   a partnership, or a trade union or employers' association, that is an employer.
(3)   An organisation is guilty of an offence under this section only if the way in which its activities are managed or organised by its senior management is a substantial element in the breach referred to in subsection (1).

(4)   For the purposes of this Act—

   (a)   "relevant duty of care" has the meaning given by section 2, read with sections 3 to 7;

   (b)   a breach of a duty of care by an organisation is a "gross" breach if the conduct alleged to amount to a breach of that duty falls far below what can reasonably be expected of the organisation in the circumstances;

   (c)   "senior management", in relation to an organisation, means the persons who play significant roles in—

     (i)   the making of decisions about how the whole or a substantial part of its activities are to be managed or organised, or

     (ii)   the actual managing or organising of the whole or a substantial part of those activities.

(5)   The offence under this section is called—

   (a)   corporate manslaughter, in so far as it is an offence under the law of England and Wales or Northern Ireland;

   (b)   corporate homicide, in so far as it is an offence under the law of Scotland.

(6)   An organisation that is guilty of corporate manslaughter or corporate homicide is liable on conviction on indictment to a fine.

(7)   The offence of corporate homicide is indictable only in the High Court of Justiciary.

Relevant duty of care

[1.2047]
2   Meaning of "relevant duty of care"
(1)   A "relevant duty of care", in relation to an organisation, means any of the following duties owed by it under the law of negligence—

   (a)   a duty owed to its employees or to other persons working for the organisation or performing services for it;

   (b)   a duty owed as occupier of premises;

   (c)   a duty owed in connection with—

     (i)   the supply by the organisation of goods or services (whether for consideration or not),

     (ii)   the carrying on by the organisation of any construction or maintenance operations,

     (iii)   the carrying on by the organisation of any other activity on a commercial basis, or

     (iv)   the use or keeping by the organisation of any plant, vehicle or other thing;

   (d)   a duty owed to a person who, by reason of being a person within subsection (2), is someone for whose safety the organisation is responsible.

(2)   A person is within this subsection if—

   (a)   he is detained at a custodial institution or in a custody area at a court[, a police station or customs premises];

   [(aa)   he is detained in service custody premises;]

   (b)   he is detained at a removal centre[, a short-term holding facility or in pre-departure accommodation];

   (c)   he is being transported in a vehicle, or being held in any premises, in pursuance of prison escort arrangements or immigration escort arrangements;

   (d)   he is living in secure accommodation in which he has been placed;

   (e)   he is a detained patient.

(3)   Subsection (1) is subject to sections 3 to 7.

(4)   A reference in subsection (1) to a duty owed under the law of negligence includes a reference to a duty that would be owed under the law of negligence but for any statutory provision under which liability is imposed in place of liability under that law.

(5)   For the purposes of this Act, whether a particular organisation owes a duty of care to a particular individual is a question of law.

The judge must make any findings of fact necessary to decide that question.

(6)   For the purposes of this Act there is to be disregarded—

   (a)   any rule of the common law that has the effect of preventing a duty of care from being owed by one person to another by reason of the fact that they are jointly engaged in unlawful conduct;

   (b)   any such rule that has the effect of preventing a duty of care from being owed to a person by reason of his acceptance of a risk of harm.

(7)   In this section—

"construction or maintenance operations" means operations of any of the following descriptions—

   (a)   construction, installation, alteration, extension, improvement, repair, maintenance, decoration, cleaning, demolition or dismantling of—

     (i)   any building or structure,

     (ii)   anything else that forms, or is to form, part of the land, or

     (iii)   any plant, vehicle or other thing;

   (b)   operations that form an integral part of, or are preparatory to, or are for rendering complete, any operations within paragraph (a);

"custodial institution" means a prison, a young offender institution, a secure training centre, [a secure college,] a young offenders institution, a young offenders centre, a juvenile justice centre or a remand centre;

["customs premises" means premises wholly or partly occupied by persons designated under section 3 (general customs officials) or 11 (customs revenue officials) of the Borders, Citizenship and Immigration Act 2009;]

"detained patient" means—

    (a)   a person who is detained in any premises under—

        (i)   Part 2 or 3 of the Mental Health Act 1983 (c 20) ("the 1983 Act"), or

        (ii)   Part 2 or 3 of the Mental Health (Northern Ireland) Order 1986 (SI 1986/595 (NI 4)) ("the 1986 Order");

    (b)   a person who (otherwise than by reason of being detained as mentioned in paragraph (a)) is deemed to be in legal custody by—

        (i)   section 137 of the 1983 Act,

        (ii)   Article 131 of the 1986 Order, or

        (iii)   article 11 of the Mental Health (Care and Treatment) (Scotland) Act 2003 (Consequential Provisions) Order 2005 (SI 2005/2078);

    (c)   a person who is detained in any premises, or is otherwise in custody, under the Mental Health (Care and Treatment) (Scotland) Act 2003 (asp 13) or Part 6 of the Criminal Procedure (Scotland) Act 1995 (c 46) or who is detained in a hospital under section 200 of that Act of 1995;

"immigration escort arrangements" means arrangements made under section 156 of the Immigration and Asylum Act 1999 (c 33);

"the law of negligence" includes—

    (a)   in relation to England and Wales, the Occupiers' Liability Act 1957 (c 31), the Defective Premises Act 1972 (c 35) and the Occupiers' Liability Act 1984 (c 3);

    (b)   in relation to Scotland, the Occupiers' Liability (Scotland) Act 1960 (c 30);

    (c)   in relation to Northern Ireland, the Occupiers' Liability Act (Northern Ireland) 1957 (c 25), the Defective Premises (Northern Ireland) Order 1975 (SI 1975/1039 (NI 9)), the Occupiers' Liability (Northern Ireland) Order 1987 (SI 1987/1280 (NI 15)) and the Defective Premises (Landlord's Liability) Act (Northern Ireland) 2001 (c 10);

"prison escort arrangements" means arrangements made under section 80 of the Criminal Justice Act 1991 (c 53) or under section 102 or 118 of the Criminal Justice and Public Order Act 1994 (c 33);

"removal centre"[, "short-term holding facility" and "pre-departure accommodation"] have the meaning given by section 147 of the Immigration and Asylum Act 1999;

"secure accommodation" means accommodation, not consisting of or forming part of a custodial institution, provided for the purpose of restricting the liberty of persons under the age of 18;

["service custody premises" has the meaning given by section 300(7) of the Armed Forces Act 2006].

NOTES

Sub-s (2): words in square brackets in para (a) substituted, and para (aa) inserted, by the Corporate Manslaughter and Corporate Homicide Act 2007 (Amendment) Order 2011, SI 2011/1868, art 2(1)–(3); words in square brackets in para (b) substituted by the Immigration Act 2014, s 73(6), Sch 9, Pt 2, para 15(a).

Sub-s (7): in definition "custodial institution" words in square brackets inserted by the Criminal Justice and Courts Act 2015, s 38(3), Sch 9, para 23; definitions "customs premises" and "service custody premises" inserted by SI 2011/1868, art 2(1), (4), in definition ""removal centre", "short-term holding facility" and "pre-departure accommodation"" words in square brackets substituted by the Immigration Act 2014, s 73(6), Sch 9, Pt 2, para 15(b).

[1.2048]
3 Public policy decisions, exclusively public functions and statutory inspections

(1) Any duty of care owed by a public authority in respect of a decision as to matters of public policy (including in particular the allocation of public resources or the weighing of competing public interests) is not a "relevant duty of care".

(2) Any duty of care owed in respect of things done in the exercise of an exclusively public function is not a "relevant duty of care" unless it falls within section 2(1)(a), (b) or (d).

(3) Any duty of care owed by a public authority in respect of inspections carried out in the exercise of a statutory function is not a "relevant duty of care" unless it falls within section 2(1)(a) or (b).

(4) In this section—

"exclusively public function" means a function that falls within the prerogative of the Crown or is, by its nature, exercisable only with authority conferred—

    (a)   by the exercise of that prerogative, or

    (b)   by or under a statutory provision;

"statutory function" means a function conferred by or under a statutory provision.

[1.2049]
4 Military activities

(1) Any duty of care owed by the Ministry of Defence in respect of—
- (a) operations within subsection (2),
- (b) activities carried on in preparation for, or directly in support of, such operations, or
- (c) training of a hazardous nature, or training carried out in a hazardous way, which it is considered needs to be carried out, or carried out in that way, in order to improve or maintain the effectiveness of the armed forces with respect to such operations,

is not a "relevant duty of care".

(2) The operations within this subsection are operations, including peacekeeping operations and operations for dealing with terrorism, civil unrest or serious public disorder, in the course of which members of the armed forces come under attack or face the threat of attack or violent resistance.

(3) Any duty of care owed by the Ministry of Defence in respect of activities carried on by members of the special forces is not a "relevant duty of care".

(4) In this section "the special forces" means those units of the armed forces the maintenance of whose capabilities is the responsibility of the Director of Special Forces or which are for the time being subject to the operational command of that Director.

[1.2050]
5 Policing and law enforcement

(1) Any duty of care owed by a public authority in respect of—
- (a) operations within subsection (2),
- (b) activities carried on in preparation for, or directly in support of, such operations, or
- (c) training of a hazardous nature, or training carried out in a hazardous way, which it is considered needs to be carried out, or carried out in that way, in order to improve or maintain the effectiveness of officers or employees of the public authority with respect to such operations,

is not a "relevant duty of care".

(2) Operations are within this subsection if—
- (a) they are operations for dealing with terrorism, civil unrest or serious disorder,
- (b) they involve the carrying on of policing or law-enforcement activities, and
- (c) officers or employees of the public authority in question come under attack, or face the threat of attack or violent resistance, in the course of the operations.

(3) Any duty of care owed by a public authority in respect of other policing or law-enforcement activities is not a "relevant duty of care" unless it falls within section 2(1)(a), (b) or (d).

(4) In this section "policing or law-enforcement activities" includes—
- (a) activities carried on in the exercise of functions that are—
  - (i) functions of police forces, or
  - (ii) functions of the same or a similar nature exercisable by public authorities other than police forces;
- (b) activities carried on in the exercise of functions of constables employed by a public authority;
- (c) activities carried on in the exercise of functions exercisable under Chapter 4 of Part 2 of the Serious Organised Crime and Police Act 2005 (c 15) (protection of witnesses and other persons);
- (d) activities carried on to enforce any provision contained in or made under the Immigration Acts.

[1.2051]
6 Emergencies

(1) Any duty of care owed by an organisation within subsection (2) in respect of the way in which it responds to emergency circumstances is not a "relevant duty of care" unless it falls within section 2(1)(a) or (b).

(2) The organisations within this subsection are—
- (a) a fire and rescue authority in England and Wales;
- [(b) the Scottish Fire and Rescue Service;]
- (c) the Northern Ireland Fire and Rescue Service Board;
- (d) any other organisation providing a service of responding to emergency circumstances either—
  - (i) in pursuance of arrangements made with an organisation within paragraph (a), (b) or (c), or
  - (ii) (if not in pursuance of such arrangements) otherwise than on a commercial basis;
- (e) a relevant NHS body;
- (f) an organisation providing ambulance services in pursuance of arrangements—
  - (i) made by, or at the request of, a relevant NHS body, or
  - (ii) made with the Secretary of State or with the Welsh Ministers;
- (g) an organisation providing services for the transport of organs, blood, equipment or personnel in pursuance of arrangements of the kind mentioned in paragraph (f);
- (h) an organisation providing a rescue service;

(i) the armed forces.

(3) For the purposes of subsection (1), the way in which an organisation responds to emergency circumstances does not include the way in which—

(a) medical treatment is carried out, or

(b) decisions within subsection (4) are made.

(4) The decisions within this subsection are decisions as to the carrying out of medical treatment, other than decisions as to the order in which persons are to be given such treatment.

(5) Any duty of care owed in respect of the carrying out, or attempted carrying out, of a rescue operation at sea in emergency circumstances is not a "relevant duty of care" unless it falls within section 2(1)(a) or (b).

(6) Any duty of care owed in respect of action taken—

(a) in order to comply with a direction under Schedule 3A to the Merchant Shipping Act 1995 (c 21) (safety directions), or

(b) by virtue of paragraph 4 of that Schedule (action in lieu of direction),

is not a "relevant duty of care" unless it falls within section 2(1)(a) or (b).

(7) In this section—

"emergency circumstances" means circumstances that are present or imminent and—

(a) are causing, or are likely to cause, serious harm or a worsening of such harm, or

(b) are likely to cause the death of a person;

"medical treatment" includes any treatment or procedure of a medical or similar nature;

"relevant NHS body" means—

[(za) the National Health Service Commissioning Board;]

(a) [a clinical commissioning group,] *a Strategic Health Authority, Primary Care Trust, NHS trust,* Special Health Authority or NHS foundation trust in England;

(b) a Local Health Board, NHS trust or Special Health Authority in Wales;

(c) a Health Board or Special Health Board in Scotland, or the Common Services Agency for the Scottish Health Service;

(d) a Health and Social Services trust or Health and Social Services Board in Northern Ireland;

"serious harm" means—

(a) serious injury to or the serious illness (including mental illness) of a person;

(b) serious harm to the environment (including the life and health of plants and animals);

(c) serious harm to any building or other property.

(8) A reference in this section to emergency circumstances includes a reference to circumstances that are believed to be emergency circumstances.

NOTES

Sub-s (2): para (b) substituted in relation to Scotland by the Police and Fire Reform (Scotland) Act 2012, s 128(1), Sch 7, Pt 2, para 71, for supplementary, transitional, transitory and saving provision see SSI 2013/121, and in relation to England and Wales by the Police and Fire Reform (Scotland) Act 2012 (Consequential Provisions and Modifications) Order 2013, SI 2013/602, art 25, Sch 1, para 9, for transitional provisions and savings see art 27, Sch 3 thereof.

Sub-s (7): in definition "relevant NHS body", para (za) and words in square brackets in para (a) inserted by the Health and Social Care Act 2012, s 55(2), Sch 5, para 147(a), (b)(i); words in italics repealed by the Health and Social Care Act 2012, ss 55(2), 179(6), Sch 5, Pt 1, para 147(b)(ii), (iii), Sch 14, Part 2, para 102, as from a day to be appointed.

[1.2052]
7 Child-protection and probation functions

(1) A duty of care to which this section applies is not a "relevant duty of care" unless it falls within section 2(1)(a), (b) or (d).

(2) This section applies to any duty of care that a local authority or other public authority owes in respect of the exercise by it of functions conferred by or under—

(a) Parts 4 and 5 of the Children Act 1989 (c 41),

(b) Part 2 of the Children (Scotland) Act 1995 (c 36),

[(ba) the Children's Hearings (Scotland) Act 2011,] or

(c) Parts 5 and 6 of the Children (Northern Ireland) Order 1995 (SI 1995/755 (NI 2)).

(3) This section also applies to any duty of care that a local probation board[, a provider of probation services] or other public authority owes in respect of the exercise by it of functions conferred by or under—

(a) Chapter 1 of Part 1 of the Criminal Justice and Court Services Act 2000 (c 43),

[(aa) section 13 of the Offender Management Act 2007 (c 21)]

(b) section 27 of the Social Work (Scotland) Act 1968 (c 49), or

(c) Article 4 of the Probation Board (Northern Ireland) Order 1982 (SI 1982/713 (NI 10)).

[(4) This section also applies to any duty of care that a provider of probation services owes in respect of the carrying out by it of activities in pursuance of arrangements under section 3 of the Offender Management Act 2007.]

NOTES

Sub-s (2): para (ba) inserted by the Children's Hearings (Scotland) Act 2011 (Consequential and Transitional Provisions and Savings) Order 2013, SI 2013/1465, art 17(1), Sch 1, Pt 1, para 11.

Sub-s (3): words in first pair of square brackets and para (aa) inserted by the Offender Management Act 2007 (Consequential Amendments) Order 2008, SI 2008/912, art 3, Sch 1, para 25(1), (2).

Sub-s (4): added by SI 2008/912, art 3, Sch 1, para 25(1), (3).

Gross breach

[1.2053]
8   Factors for jury
(1)   This section applies where—
   (a)   it is established that an organisation owed a relevant duty of care to a person, and
   (b)   it falls to the jury to decide whether there was a gross breach of that duty.
(2)   The jury must consider whether the evidence shows that the organisation failed to comply with any health and safety legislation that relates to the alleged breach, and if so—
   (a)   how serious that failure was;
   (b)   how much of a risk of death it posed.
(3)   The jury may also—
   (a)   consider the extent to which the evidence shows that there were attitudes, policies, systems or accepted practices within the organisation that were likely to have encouraged any such failure as is mentioned in subsection (2), or to have produced tolerance of it;
   (b)   have regard to any health and safety guidance that relates to the alleged breach.
(4)   This section does not prevent the jury from having regard to any other matters they consider relevant.
(5)   In this section "health and safety guidance" means any code, guidance, manual or similar publication that is concerned with health and safety matters and is made or issued (under a statutory provision or otherwise) by an authority responsible for the enforcement of any health and safety legislation.

Remedial orders and publicity orders

[1.2054]
9   Power to order breach etc to be remedied
(1)   A court before which an organisation is convicted of corporate manslaughter or corporate homicide may make an order (a "remedial order") requiring the organisation to take specified steps to remedy—
   (a)   the breach mentioned in section 1(1) ("the relevant breach");
   (b)   any matter that appears to the court to have resulted from the relevant breach and to have been a cause of the death;
   (c)   any deficiency, as regards health and safety matters, in the organisation's policies, systems or practices of which the relevant breach appears to the court to be an indication.
(2)   A remedial order may be made only on an application by the prosecution specifying the terms of the proposed order.
Any such order must be on such terms (whether those proposed or others) as the court considers appropriate having regard to any representations made, and any evidence adduced, in relation to that matter by the prosecution or on behalf of the organisation.
(3)   Before making an application for a remedial order the prosecution must consult such enforcement authority or authorities as it considers appropriate having regard to the nature of the relevant breach.
(4)   A remedial order—
   (a)   must specify a period within which the steps referred to in subsection (1) are to be taken;
   (b)   may require the organisation to supply to an enforcement authority consulted under subsection (3), within a specified period, evidence that those steps have been taken.
A period specified under this subsection may be extended or further extended by order of the court on an application made before the end of that period or extended period.
(5)   An organisation that fails to comply with a remedial order is guilty of an offence, and liable on conviction on indictment to a fine.

[1.2055]
10   Power to order conviction etc to be publicised
(1)   A court before which an organisation is convicted of corporate manslaughter or corporate homicide may make an order (a "publicity order") requiring the organisation to publicise in a specified manner—
   (a)   the fact that it has been convicted of the offence;
   (b)   specified particulars of the offence;
   (c)   the amount of any fine imposed;
   (d)   the terms of any remedial order made.
(2)   In deciding on the terms of a publicity order that it is proposing to make, the court must—
   (a)   ascertain the views of such enforcement authority or authorities (if any) as it considers appropriate, and
   (b)   have regard to any representations made by the prosecution or on behalf of the organisation.
(3)   A publicity order—

(a) must specify a period within which the requirements referred to in subsection (1) are to be complied with;

(b) may require the organisation to supply to any enforcement authority whose views have been ascertained under subsection (2), within a specified period, evidence that those requirements have been complied with.

(4) An organisation that fails to comply with a publicity order is guilty of an offence, and liable on conviction on indictment to a fine.

11–14 (*Outside the scope of this work.*)

Miscellaneous

15, 16 (*Outside the scope of this work.*)

[1.2056]
17 DPP's consent required for proceedings
Proceedings for an offence of corporate manslaughter—

(a) may not be instituted in England and Wales without the consent of the Director of Public Prosecutions;

(b) may not be instituted in Northern Ireland without the consent of the Director of Public Prosecutions for Northern Ireland.

[1.2057]
18 No individual liability
(1) An individual cannot be guilty of aiding, abetting, counselling or procuring the commission of an offence of corporate manslaughter.

[(1A) An individual cannot be guilty of an offence under Part 2 of the Serious Crime Act 2007 (encouraging or assisting crime) by reference to an offence of corporate manslaughter.]

(2) An individual cannot be guilty of aiding, abetting, counselling or procuring, or being art and part in, the commission of an offence of corporate homicide.

NOTES
Sub-s (1A): inserted, in relation to England, Wales and Northern Ireland, by the Serious Crime Act 2007, s 62.

[1.2058]
19 Convictions under this Act and under health and safety legislation
(1) Where in the same proceedings there is—

(a) a charge of corporate manslaughter or corporate homicide arising out of a particular set of circumstances, and

(b) a charge against the same defendant of a health and safety offence arising out of some or all of those circumstances,

the jury may, if the interests of justice so require, be invited to return a verdict on each charge.
(2) An organisation that has been convicted of corporate manslaughter or corporate homicide arising out of a particular set of circumstances may, if the interests of justice so require, be charged with a health and safety offence arising out of some or all of those circumstances.
(3) In this section "health and safety offence" means an offence under any health and safety legislation.

[1.2059]
20 Abolition of liability of corporations for manslaughter at common law
The common law offence of manslaughter by gross negligence is abolished in its application to corporations, and in any application it has to other organisations to which section 1 applies.

General and supplemental

21–28 (*Outside the scope of this work.*)

[1.2060]
29 Short title
This Act may be cited as the Corporate Manslaughter and Corporate Homicide Act 2007.

SCHEDULES

SCHEDULES 1, 2

(*Schs 1, 2 outside the scope of this work.*)

THIRD PARTIES (RIGHTS AGAINST INSURERS) ACT 2010

(2010 c 10)

ARRANGEMENT OF SECTIONS

Transfer of rights to third parties

An Act to make provision about the rights of third parties against insurers of liabilities to third parties in the case where the insured is insolvent, and in certain other cases.

[25 March 2010]

Transfer of rights to third parties

[1.2061]
1   Rights against insurer of insolvent person etc
(1)   This section applies if—
  (a)   a relevant person incurs a liability against which that person is insured under a contract of
      insurance, or
  (b)   a person who is subject to such a liability becomes a relevant person.
(2)   The rights of the relevant person under the contract against the insurer in respect of the liability are transferred to and vest in the person to whom the liability is or was incurred (the "third party").
(3)   The third party may bring proceedings to enforce the rights against the insurer without having established the relevant person's liability; but the third party may not enforce those rights without having established that liability.
(4)   For the purposes of this Act, a liability is established only if its existence and amount are established; and, for that purpose, "establish" means establish—
  (a)   by virtue of a declaration under section 2 or a declarator under section 3,
  (b)   by a judgment or decree,
  (c)   by an award in arbitral proceedings or by an arbitration, or

(d) by an enforceable agreement.

(5) In this Act—

    (a) references to an "insured" are to a person who incurs or who is subject to a liability to a third party against which that person is insured under a contract of insurance;

    (b) references to a "relevant person" are to a person within sections 4 to 7 [(and see also paragraph 1A of Schedule 3)];

    (c) references to a "third party" are to be construed in accordance with subsection (2);

    (d) references to "transferred rights" are to rights under a contract of insurance which are transferred under this section.

NOTES

Commencement: to be appointed.

Sub-s (5): in para (b) words in square brackets added by the Insurance Act 2015, s 20, Sch 2, paras 1, 4, as from a day to be appointed.

[1.2062]

2 Establishing liability in England and Wales and Northern Ireland

(1) This section applies where a person (P)—

    (a) claims to have rights under a contract of insurance by virtue of a transfer under section 1, but

    (b) has not yet established the insured's liability which is insured under that contract.

(2) P may bring proceedings against the insurer for either or both of the following—

    (a) a declaration as to the insured's liability to P;

    (b) a declaration as to the insurer's potential liability to P.

(3) In such proceedings P is entitled, subject to any defence on which the insurer may rely, to a declaration under subsection (2)(a) or (b) on proof of the insured's liability to P or (as the case may be) the insurer's potential liability to P.

(4) Where proceedings are brought under subsection (2)(a) the insurer may rely on any defence on which the insured could rely if those proceedings were proceedings brought against the insured in respect of the insured's liability to P.

(5) Subsection (4) is subject to section 12(1).

(6) Where the court makes a declaration under this section, the effect of which is that the insurer is liable to P, the court may give the appropriate judgment against the insurer.

(7) Where a person applying for a declaration under subsection (2)(b) is entitled or required, by virtue of the contract of insurance, to do so in arbitral proceedings, that person may also apply in the same proceedings for a declaration under subsection (2)(a).

(8) In the application of this section to arbitral proceedings, subsection (6) is to be read as if "tribunal" were substituted for "court" and "make the appropriate award" for "give the appropriate judgment".

(9) When bringing proceedings under subsection (2)(a), P may also make the insured a defendant to those proceedings.

(10) If (but only if) the insured is a defendant to proceedings under this section (whether by virtue of subsection (9) or otherwise), a declaration under subsection (2) binds the insured as well as the insurer.

(11) In this section, references to the insurer's potential liability to P are references to the insurer's liability in respect of the insured's liability to P, if established.

NOTES

Commencement: to be appointed.

3 (*Applies to Scotland only.*)

Relevant persons

[1.2063]

4 Individuals

(1) An individual is a relevant person if any of the following is in force in respect of that individual in England and Wales—

    (a) a deed of arrangement registered in accordance with the Deeds of Arrangement Act 1914,

    (b) an administration order made under Part 6 of the County Courts Act 1984,

    (c) an enforcement restriction order made under Part 6A of that Act,

    (d) subject to subsection (4), a debt relief order made under Part 7A of the Insolvency Act 1986,

    (e) a voluntary arrangement approved in accordance with Part 8 of that Act, or

    (f) a bankruptcy order made under Part 9 of that Act.

(2) An individual is a relevant person if any of the following is in force in respect of that individual (or, in the case of paragraph (a) or (b), that individual's estate) in Scotland—

    (a) an award of sequestration made under section 5 of the Bankruptcy (Scotland) Act 1985,

    (b) a protected trust deed within the meaning of that Act, or

    (c) a composition approved in accordance with Schedule 4 to that Act.

(3)   An individual is a relevant person if any of the following is in force in respect of that individual in Northern Ireland—

(a)   an administration order made under Part 6 of the Judgments Enforcement (Northern Ireland) Order 1981 (SI 1981/226 (NI 6)),

(b)   a deed of arrangement registered in accordance with Chapter 1 of Part 8 of the Insolvency (Northern Ireland) Order 1989 (SI 1989/2405 (NI 19)),

[(ba) subject to subsection (4), a debt relief order made under Part 7A of that Order,]

(c)   a voluntary arrangement approved under Chapter 2 of Part 8 of that Order, or

(d)   a bankruptcy order made under Part 9 of that Order.

(4)   If an individual is a relevant person by virtue of subsection (1)(d) [or (3)(ba)], that person is a relevant person for the purposes of section 1(1)(b) only.

(5)   Where an award of sequestration made under section 5 of the Bankruptcy (Scotland) Act 1985 is recalled or reduced, any rights which were transferred under section 1 as a result of that award are re-transferred to and vest in the person who became a relevant person as a result of the award.

(6)   Where an order discharging an individual from an award of sequestration made under section 5 of the Bankruptcy (Scotland) Act 1985 is recalled or reduced under paragraph 17 or 18 of Schedule 4 to that Act, the order is to be treated for the purposes of this section as never having been made.

NOTES

Commencement: to be appointed.

Sub-s (3): para (ba) inserted by the Insurance Act 2015, s 20, Sch 2, paras 1, 2(1), (2), as from a day to be appointed.

Sub-s (4): words in square brackets inserted by the Insurance Act 2015, s 20, Sch 2, paras 1, 2(1), (3), as from a day to be appointed.

[1.2064]
5   Individuals who die insolvent

(1)   An individual who dies insolvent is a relevant person for the purposes of section 1(1)(b) only.

(2)   For the purposes of this section an individual (D) is to be regarded as having died insolvent if, following D's death—

(a)   D's estate falls to be administered in accordance with an order under section 421 of the Insolvency Act 1986 or Article 365 of the Insolvency (Northern Ireland) Order 1989 (SI 1989/2405 (NI 19)),

(b)   an award of sequestration is made under section 5 of the Bankruptcy (Scotland) Act 1985 in respect of D's estate and the award is not recalled or reduced, or

(c)   a judicial factor is appointed under section 11A of the Judicial Factors (Scotland) Act 1889 in respect of D's estate and the judicial factor certifies that the estate is absolutely insolvent within the meaning of the Bankruptcy (Scotland) Act 1985.

(3)   Where a transfer of rights under section 1 takes place as a result of an insured person being a relevant person by virtue of this section, references in this Act to an insured are, where the context so requires, to be read as references to the insured's estate.

NOTES

Commencement: to be appointed.

[1.2065]
6   Corporate bodies etc

(1)   A body corporate or an unincorporated body is a relevant person if—

(a)   a compromise or arrangement between the body and its creditors (or a class of them) is in force, having been sanctioned in accordance with section 899 of the Companies Act 2006, or

(b)   the body has been dissolved under section 1000, 1001 or 1003 of that Act, and the body has not been—

(i)   restored to the register by virtue of section 1025 of that Act, or

(ii)   ordered to be restored to the register by virtue of section 1031 of that Act.

(2)   A body corporate or an unincorporated body is a relevant person if, in England and Wales or Scotland—

(a)   a voluntary arrangement approved in accordance with Part 1 of the Insolvency Act 1986 is in force in respect of it,

(b)   an administration order made under Part 2 of that Act is in force in respect of it,

(c)   there is a person appointed in accordance with Part 3 of that Act who is acting as receiver or manager of the body's property (or there would be such a person so acting but for a temporary vacancy),

(d)   the body is, or is being, wound up voluntarily in accordance with Chapter 2 of Part 4 of that Act,

(e)   there is a person appointed under section 135 of that Act who is acting as provisional liquidator in respect of the body (or there would be such a person so acting but for a temporary vacancy), or

(f) the body is, or is being, wound up by the court following the making of a winding-up order under Chapter 6 of Part 4 of that Act or Part 5 of that Act.

(3) A body corporate or an unincorporated body is a relevant person if, in Scotland—

(a) an award of sequestration has been made under section 6 of the Bankruptcy (Scotland) Act 1985 in respect of the body's estate, and the body has not been discharged under that Act,

(b) the body has been dissolved and an award of sequestration has been made under that section in respect of its estate,

(c) a protected trust deed within the meaning of the Bankruptcy (Scotland) Act 1985 is in force in respect of the body's estate, or

(d) a composition approved in accordance with Schedule 4 to that Act is in force in respect of the body.

(4) A body corporate or an unincorporated body is a relevant person if, in Northern Ireland—

(a) a voluntary arrangement approved in accordance with Part 2 of the Insolvency (Northern Ireland) Order 1989 (SI 1989/2405 (NI 19)) is in force in respect of the body,

(b) *an administration order made under Part 3 of that Order is in force in respect of the body,*

(c) there is a person appointed in accordance with Part 4 of that Order who is acting as receiver or manager of the body's property (or there would be such a person so acting but for a temporary vacancy),

(d) the body is, or is being, wound up voluntarily in accordance with Chapter 2 of Part 5 of that Order,

(e) there is a person appointed under Article 115 of that Order who is acting as provisional liquidator in respect of the body (or there would be such a person so acting but for a temporary vacancy), or

(f) the body is, or is being, wound up by the court following the making of a winding-up order under Chapter 6 of Part 5 of that Order or Part 6 of that Order.

(5) A body within subsection (1)(a) is not a relevant person in relation to a liability that is transferred to another body by the order sanctioning the compromise or arrangement.

(6) Where a body is a relevant person by virtue of subsection (1)(a), section 1 has effect to transfer rights only to a person on whom the compromise or arrangement is binding.

(7) Where an award of sequestration made under section 6 of the Bankruptcy (Scotland) Act 1985 is recalled or reduced, any rights which were transferred under section 1 as a result of that award are re-transferred to and vest in the person who became a relevant person as a result of the award.

(8) Where an order discharging a body from an award of sequestration made under section 6 of the Bankruptcy (Scotland) Act 1985 is recalled or reduced under paragraph 17 or 18 of Schedule 4 to that Act, the order is to be treated for the purposes of this section as never having been made.

(9) In this section—

(a) a reference to a person appointed in accordance with Part 3 of the Insolvency Act 1986 includes a reference to a person appointed under section 101 of the Law of Property Act 1925;

(b) a reference to a receiver or manager of a body's property includes a reference to a receiver or manager of part only of the property and to a receiver only of the income arising from the property or from part of it;

(c) for the purposes of subsection (3) "body corporate or unincorporated body" includes any entity, other than a trust, the estate of which may be sequestrated under section 6 of the Bankruptcy (Scotland) Act 1985;

(d) a reference to a person appointed in accordance with Part 4 of the Insolvency (Northern Ireland) Order 1989 (SI 1989/2405 (NI 19)) includes a reference to a person appointed under section 19 of the Conveyancing Act 1881.

NOTES

Commencement: to be appointed.

Sub-s (2): para (b) substituted as follows by the Insurance Act 2015, s 20, Sch 2, paras 1, 3(1), (2), as from a day to be appointed:

"(b) the body is in administration under Schedule B1 to that Act,".

Sub-s (4): para (b) substituted as follows by the Insurance Act 2015, s 20, Sch 2, paras 1, 3(1), (3), as from a day to be appointed:

"(b) the body is in administration under Schedule B1 to that Order,".

[1.2066]
7 Scottish trusts

(1) A trustee of a Scottish trust is, in respect of a liability of that trustee that falls to be met out of the trust estate, a relevant person if—

(a) an award of sequestration has been made under section 6 of the Bankruptcy (Scotland) Act 1985 in respect of the trust estate, and the trust has not been discharged under that Act,

(b) a protected trust deed within the meaning of that Act is in force in respect of the trust estate, or

(c)   a composition approved in accordance with Schedule 4 to that Act is in force in respect of the trust estate.

(2)   Where an award of sequestration made under section 6 of the Bankruptcy (Scotland) Act 1985 is recalled or reduced any rights which were transferred under section 1 as a result of that award are re-transferred to and vest in the person who became a relevant person as a result of the award.

(3)   Where an order discharging an individual, body or trust from an award of sequestration made under section 6 of the Bankruptcy (Scotland) Act 1985 is recalled or reduced under paragraph 17 or 18 of Schedule 4 to that Act, the order is to be treated for the purposes of this section as never having been made.

(4)   In this section "Scottish trust" means a trust the estate of which may be sequestrated under section 6 of the Bankruptcy (Scotland) Act 1985.

NOTES

Commencement: to be appointed.

Transferred rights: supplemental

[1.2067]
8   Limit on rights transferred

Where the liability of an insured to a third party is less than the liability of the insurer to the insured (ignoring the effect of section 1), no rights are transferred under that section in respect of the difference.

NOTES

Commencement: to be appointed.

[1.2068]
9   Conditions affecting transferred rights

(1)   This section applies where transferred rights are subject to a condition (whether under the contract of insurance from which the transferred rights are derived or otherwise) that the insured has to fulfil.

(2)   Anything done by the third party which, if done by the insured, would have amounted to or contributed to fulfilment of the condition is to be treated as if done by the insured.

(3)   The transferred rights are not subject to a condition requiring the insured to provide information or assistance to the insurer if that condition cannot be fulfilled because the insured is—
   (a)   an individual who has died, or
   (b)   a body corporate that has been dissolved.

(4)   A condition requiring the insured to provide information or assistance to the insurer does not include a condition requiring the insured to notify the insurer of the existence of a claim under the contract of insurance.

(5)   The transferred rights are not subject to a condition requiring the prior discharge by the insured of the insured's liability to the third party.

(6)   In the case of a contract of marine insurance, subsection (5) applies only to the extent that the liability of the insured is a liability in respect of death or personal injury.

(7)   In this section—
   "contract of marine insurance" has the meaning given by section 1 of the Marine Insurance Act 1906;
   "dissolved" means dissolved under—
   (a)   Chapter 9 of Part 4 of the Insolvency Act 1986,
   (b)   section 1000, 1001 or 1003 of the Companies Act 2006, or
   (c)   Chapter 9 of Part 5 of the Insolvency (Northern Ireland) Order 1989 (SI 1989/2405 (NI 19));
   "personal injury" includes any disease and any impairment of a person's physical or mental condition.

NOTES

Commencement: to be appointed.

[1.2069]
10   Insurer's right of set off

(1)   This section applies if—
   (a)   rights of an insured under a contract of insurance have been transferred to a third party under section 1,
   (b)   the insured is under a liability to the insurer under the contract ("the insured's liability"), and
   (c)   if there had been no transfer, the insurer would have been entitled to set off the amount of the insured's liability against the amount of the insurer's own liability to the insured.

(2)   The insurer is entitled to set off the amount of the insured's liability against the amount of the insurer's own liability to the third party in relation to the transferred rights.

Provision of information etc

[1.2070]
11   Information and disclosure for third parties
Schedule 1 (information and disclosure for third parties) has effect.

Enforcement of transferred rights

[1.2071]
12   Limitation and prescription
(1)   Subsection (2) applies where a person brings proceedings for a declaration under section 2(2)(a), or for a declarator under section 3(2)(a), and the proceedings are started or, in Scotland, commenced—
    (a)   after the expiry of a period of limitation applicable to an action against the insured to enforce the insured's liability, or of a period of prescription applicable to that liability, but
    (b)   while such an action is in progress.
(2)   The insurer may not rely on the expiry of that period as a defence unless the insured is able to rely on it in the action against the insured.
(3)   For the purposes of subsection (1), an action is to be treated as no longer in progress if it has been concluded by a judgment or decree, or by an award, even if there is an appeal or a right of appeal.
(4)   Where a person who has already established an insured's liability to that person brings proceedings under this Act against the insurer, nothing in this Act is to be read as meaning—
    (a)   that, for the purposes of the law of limitation in England and Wales, that person's cause of action against the insurer arose otherwise than at the time when that person established the liability of the insured,
    (b)   that, for the purposes of the law of prescription in Scotland, the obligation in respect of which the proceedings are brought became enforceable against the insurer otherwise than at that time, or
    (c)   that, for the purposes of the law of limitation in Northern Ireland, that person's cause of action against the insurer arose otherwise than at the time when that person established the liability of the insured.

[1.2072]
13   Jurisdiction within the United Kingdom
(1)   Where a person (P) domiciled in a part of the United Kingdom is entitled to bring proceedings under this Act against an insurer domiciled in another part, P may do so in the part where P is domiciled or in the part where the insurer is domiciled (whatever the contract of insurance may stipulate as to where proceedings are to be brought).
(2)   The following provisions of the Civil Jurisdiction and Judgments Act 1982 (relating to determination of domicile) apply for the purposes of subsection (1)—
    (a)   section 41(2), (3), (5) and (6) (individuals);
    (b)   section 42(1), (3), (4) and (8) (corporations and associations);
    (c)   section 45(2) and (3) (trusts);
    (d)   section 46(1), (3) and (7) (the Crown).
(3)   . . .

Enforcement of insured's liability

[1.2073]
14   Effect of transfer on insured's liability
(1)   Where rights in respect of an insured's liability to a third party are transferred under section 1, the third party may enforce that liability against the insured only to the extent (if any) that it exceeds the amount recoverable from the insurer by virtue of the transfer.
(2)   Subsection (3) applies if a transfer of rights under section 1 occurs because the insured person is a relevant person by virtue of—
    (a)   section 4(1)(a) or (e), (2)(b) or (3)(b) or (c),
    (b)   section 6(1)(a), (2)(a), (3)(c) or (4)(a), or

(c)   section 7(1)(b).

(3)   If the liability is subject to the arrangement, trust deed or compromise by virtue of which the insured is a relevant person, the liability is to be treated as subject to that arrangement, trust deed or compromise only to the extent that the liability exceeds the amount recoverable from the insurer by virtue of the transfer.

(4)   Subsection (5) applies if a transfer of rights under section 1 occurs in respect of a liability which, after the transfer, becomes one that is subject to a composition approved in accordance with Schedule 4 to the Bankruptcy (Scotland) Act 1985.

(5)   The liability is to be treated as subject to the composition only to the extent that the liability exceeds the amount recoverable from the insurer by virtue of the transfer.

(6)   For the purposes of this section the amount recoverable from the insurer does not include any amount that the third party is unable to recover as a result of—

(a)   a shortage of assets on the insurer's part, in a case where the insurer is a relevant person, or

(b)   a limit set by the contract of insurance on the fund available to meet claims in respect of a particular description of liability of the insured.

(7)   Where a third party is eligible to make a claim in respect of the insurer's liability under or by virtue of rules made under Part 15 of the Financial Services and Markets Act 2000 (the Financial Services Compensation Scheme)—

(a)   subsection (6)(a) applies only if the third party has made such a claim, and

(b)   the third party is to be treated as being able to recover from the insurer any amount paid to, or due to, the third party as a result of the claim.

NOTES
Commencement: to be appointed.

Application of Act

[1.2074]
15   Reinsurance
This Act does not apply to a case where the liability referred to in section 1(1) is itself a liability incurred by an insurer under a contract of insurance.

NOTES
Commencement: to be appointed.

[1.2075]
16   Voluntarily-incurred liabilities
It is irrelevant for the purposes of section 1 whether or not the liability of the insured is or was incurred voluntarily.

NOTES
Commencement: to be appointed.

[1.2076]
17   Avoidance
(1)   A contract of insurance to which this section applies is of no effect in so far as it purports, whether directly or indirectly, to avoid or terminate the contract or alter the rights of the parties under it in the event of the insured—

(a)   becoming a relevant person, or

(b)   dying insolvent (within the meaning given by section 5(2)).

(2)   A contract of insurance is one to which this section applies if the insured's rights under it are capable of being transferred under section 1.

NOTES
Commencement: to be appointed.

[1.2077]
18   Cases with a foreign element
Except as expressly provided, the application of this Act does not depend on whether there is a connection with a part of the United Kingdom; and in particular it does not depend on—

(a)   whether or not the liability (or the alleged liability) of the insured to the third party was incurred in, or under the law of, England and Wales, Scotland or Northern Ireland;

(b)   the place of residence or domicile of any of the parties;

(c)   whether or not the contract of insurance (or a part of it) is governed by the law of England and Wales, Scotland or Northern Ireland;

(d)   the place where sums due under the contract of insurance are payable.

NOTES
Commencement: to be appointed.

Supplemental

[1.2078]
[19 Power to change the meaning of "relevant person"

(1) The Secretary of State may by regulations make provision adding or removing circumstances in which a person is a "relevant person" for the purposes of this Act, subject to subsection (2).

(2) Regulations under this section may add circumstances only if, in the Secretary of State's opinion, the additional circumstances—

    (a)   involve actual or anticipated dissolution of a body corporate or an unincorporated body,

    (b)   involve actual or anticipated insolvency or other financial difficulties for an individual, a body corporate or an unincorporated body, or

    (c)   are similar to circumstances for the time being described in sections 4 to 7.

(3) Regulations under this section may make provision about—

    (a)   the persons to whom, and the extent to which, rights are transferred under section 1 in the circumstances added or removed by the regulations (the "affected circumstances"),

    (b)   the re-transfer of rights transferred under section 1 where the affected circumstances change, and

    (c)   the effect of a transfer of rights under section 1 on the liability of the insured in the affected circumstances.

(4) Regulations under this section which add or remove circumstances involving actual or anticipated dissolution of a body corporate or unincorporated body may change the cases in which the following provisions apply so that they include or exclude cases involving that type of dissolution or any other type of dissolution of a body—

    (a)   section 9(3) (cases in which transferred rights are not subject to a condition requiring the insured to provide information or assistance to the insurer), and

    (b)   paragraph 3 of Schedule 1 (notices requiring disclosure).

(5) Regulations under this section which add circumstances may provide that section 1 of this Act applies in cases involving those circumstances in which either or both of the following occurred in relation to a person before the day on which the regulations come into force—

    (a)   the circumstances arose in relation to the person;

    (b)   a liability against which the person was insured under an insurance contract was incurred.

(6) Regulations under this section which—

    (a)   add circumstances, and

    (b)   provide that section 1 of this Act applies in a case involving those circumstances in which both of the events mentioned in subsection (5)(a) and (b) occurred in relation to a person before the day on which the regulations come into force,

must provide that, in such a case, the person is to be treated for the purposes of this Act as not having become a relevant person until that day or a later day specified in the regulations.

(7) Regulations under this section which remove circumstances may provide that section 1 of this Act does not apply in cases involving those circumstances in which one of the events mentioned in subsection (5)(a) and (b) (but not both) occurred in relation to a person before the day on which the regulations come into force.

(8) Regulations under this section may—

    (a)   include consequential, incidental, supplementary, transitional, transitory or saving provision,

    (b)   make different provision for different purposes, and

    (c)   make provision by reference to an enactment as amended, extended or applied from time to time,

(and subsections (3) to (7) are without prejudice to the generality of this subsection).

(9) Regulations under this section may amend an enactment, whenever passed or made, including this Act.

(10) Regulations under this section are to be made by statutory instrument.

(11) Regulations under this section may not be made unless a draft of the statutory instrument containing the regulations has been laid before, and approved by a resolution of, each House of Parliament.]

NOTES

    Commencement: 12 April 2015.

    Substituted by the Insurance Act 2015, s 19.

[1.2079]
[19A Interpretation

(1) The references to enactments in sections 4 to 7, 9(7) and 14(4) and paragraph 3(2)(b), (4) and (5) of Schedule 1 are to be treated as including references to those enactments as amended, extended or applied by another enactment, whenever passed or made, unless the contrary intention appears.

(2) In this Act, "enactment" means an enactment contained in, or in an instrument made under, any of the following—

    (a)   an Act;

    (b)   an Act or Measure of the National Assembly for Wales;

(c)   an Act of the Scottish Parliament;
(d)   Northern Ireland legislation.]

NOTES
Commencement: to be appointed.
Inserted by the Insurance Act 2015, s 20, Sch 2, paras 1, 6, as from a day to be appointed.

[1.2080]
20   Amendments, transitionals, repeals, etc
(1)   Schedule 2 (amendments) has effect.
(2)   Schedule 3 (transitory, transitional and saving provisions) has effect.
(3)   Schedule 4 (repeals and revocations) has effect.

NOTES
Commencement: to be appointed.

[1.2081]
21   Short title, commencement and extent
(1)   This Act may be cited as the Third Parties (Rights against Insurers) Act 2010.
(2)   This Act comes into force on such day as the Secretary of State may by order made by statutory instrument appoint.
(3)   This Act extends to England and Wales, Scotland and Northern Ireland, subject as follows.
(4)   Section 2 and paragraphs 3 and 4 of Schedule 1 do not extend to Scotland.
(5)   Section 3 extends to Scotland only.
(6)   Any amendment, repeal or revocation made by this Act has the same extent as the provision to which it relates.

NOTES
Commencement: to be appointed.

SCHEDULES

SCHEDULE 1
INFORMATION AND DISCLOSURE FOR THIRD PARTIES

Section 11

Notices requesting information

[1.2082]
1. (1)   If a person (A) reasonably believes that—
   (a)   another person (B) has incurred a liability to A, and
   (b)   B is a relevant person,
A may, by notice in writing, request from B such information falling within sub-paragraph (3) as the notice specifies.
(2)   If a person (A) reasonably believes that—
   (a)   a liability has been incurred to A,
   (b)   the person who incurred the liability is insured against it under a contract of insurance,
   (c)   rights of that person under the contract have been transferred to A under section 1, and
   (d)   there is a person (C) who is able to provide information falling within sub-paragraph (3),
A may, by notice in writing, request from C such information falling within that sub-paragraph as the notice specifies.
(3)   The following is the information that falls within this sub-paragraph—
   (a)   whether there is a contract of insurance that covers the supposed liability or might reasonably be regarded as covering it;
   (b)   if there is such a contract—
     (i)   who the insurer is;
     (ii)   what the terms of the contract are;
     (iii)   whether the insured has been informed that the insurer has claimed not to be liable under the contract in respect of the supposed liability;
     (iv)   whether there are or have been any proceedings between the insurer and the insured in respect of the supposed liability and, if so, relevant details of those proceedings;
     (v)   in a case where the contract sets a limit on the fund available to meet claims in respect of the supposed liability and other liabilities, how much of it (if any) has been paid out in respect of other liabilities;
     (vi)   whether there is a fixed charge to which any sums paid out under the contract in respect of the supposed liability would be subject.
(4)   For the purpose of sub-paragraph (3)(b)(iv), relevant details of proceedings are—
   (a)   in the case of court proceedings—
     (i)   the name of the court;
     (ii)   the case number;

        (iii)   the contents of all documents served in the proceedings in accordance with rules of court or orders made in the proceedings, and the contents of any such orders;
    (b)   in the case of arbitral proceedings or, in Scotland, an arbitration—
        (i)   the name of the arbitrator;
        (ii)   information corresponding with that mentioned in paragraph (a)(iii).

(5)   In sub-paragraph (3)(b)(vi), in its application to Scotland, "fixed charge" means a fixed security within the meaning given by section 47(1) of the Bankruptcy and Diligence etc (Scotland) Act 2007 (asp 3).

(6)   A notice given by a person under this paragraph must include particulars of the facts on which that person relies as entitlement to give the notice.

Provision of information where notice given under paragraph 1

2. (1)   A person (R) who receives a notice under paragraph 1 must, within the period of 28 days beginning with the day of receipt of the notice—
    (a)   provide to the person who gave the notice any information specified in it that R is able to provide;
    (b)   in relation to any such information that R is not able to provide, notify that person why R is not able to provide it.

(2)   Where—
    (a)   a person (R) receives a notice under paragraph 1,
    (b)   there is information specified in the notice that R is not able to provide because it is contained in a document that is not in R's control,
    (c)   the document was at one time in R's control, and
    (d)   R knows or believes that it is now in another person's control,
R must, within the period of 28 days beginning with the day of receipt of the notice, provide the person who gave the notice with whatever particulars R can as to the nature of the information and the identity of that other person.

(3)   If R fails to comply with a duty imposed on R by this paragraph, the person who gave R the notice may apply to court for an order requiring R to comply with the duty.

(4)   No duty arises by virtue of this paragraph in respect of information as to which a claim to legal professional privilege or, in Scotland, to confidentiality as between client and professional legal adviser could be maintained in legal proceedings.

Notices requiring disclosure: defunct bodies

3. (1)   If—
    (a)   a person (P) has started proceedings under this Act against an insurer in respect of a liability that P claims has been incurred to P by a body corporate, and
    (b)   the body is defunct,
P may by notice in writing require a person to whom sub-paragraph (2) applies to disclose to P any documents that are relevant to that liability.

(2)   This sub-paragraph applies to a person if—
    (a)   immediately before the time of the alleged transfer under section 1, that person was an officer or employee of the body, or
    (b)   immediately before the body became defunct, that person was—
        (i)   acting as an insolvency practitioner in relation to the body (within the meaning given by section 388(1) of the Insolvency Act 1986 or Article 3 of the Insolvency (Northern Ireland) Order 1989 (SI 1989/2405 NI 19)), or
        (ii)   acting as the official receiver in relation to the winding up of the body.

(3)   A notice under this paragraph must be accompanied by—
    (a)   a copy of the particulars of claim required to be served in connection with the proceedings mentioned in sub-paragraph (1), or
    (b)   where those proceedings are arbitral proceedings, the particulars of claim that would be required to be so served if they were court proceedings.

(4)   For the purposes of this paragraph a body corporate is defunct if, subject to sub-paragraph (5), it has been dissolved under—
    (a)   Chapter 9 of Part 4 of the Insolvency Act 1986,
    (b)   Chapter 9 of Part 5 of the Insolvency (Northern Ireland) Order 1989 (SI 1989/2405 NI 19)), or
    (c)   section 1000, 1001 or 1003 of the Companies Act 2006.

(5)   But a body corporate is not defunct for the purposes of this paragraph if the body has been—
    (a)   restored to the register by virtue of section 1025 of the Companies Act 2006, or
    (b)   ordered to be restored to the register by virtue of section 1031 of that Act.

Disclosure and inspection where notice given under paragraph 3

4. (1)   Subject to the provisions of this paragraph and to any necessary modifications—
    (a)   the duties of disclosure of a person who receives a notice under paragraph 3, and

(b)   the rights of inspection of the person giving the notice,
are the same as the corresponding duties and rights under Civil Procedure Rules of parties to court proceedings in which an order for standard disclosure has been made.

(2)   In sub-paragraph (1), in its application to Northern Ireland—
  (a)   the reference to Civil Procedure Rules is—
    (i)   in the case of proceedings in the High Court, to be read as a reference to the Rules of the Court of Judicature (Northern Ireland) 1980 (SR 1980 No 346), and
    (ii)   in the case of proceedings in the county court, to be read as a reference to the County Court Rules (Northern Ireland) 1981 (SR 1981 No 225), and
  (b)   the reference to an order for standard disclosure is to be read as a reference to an order for discovery.

(3)   A person who by virtue of sub-paragraph (1) or (2) has to serve a list of documents must do so within the period of 28 days beginning with the day of receipt of the notice.

(4)   A person who has received a notice under paragraph 3 and has served a list of documents in response to it is not under a duty of disclosure by reason of that notice in relation to documents that the person did not have when the list was served.

Avoidance

5. A contract of insurance is of no effect in so far as it purports, whether directly or indirectly—
  (a)   to avoid or terminate the contract or alter the rights of the parties under it in the event of a person providing information, or giving disclosure, that the person is required to provide or give by virtue of a notice under paragraph 1 or 3, or
  (b)   otherwise to prohibit, prevent or restrict a person from providing such information or giving such disclosure.

Other rights to information etc

6. Rights to information, or to inspection of documents, that a person has by virtue of paragraph 1 or 3 are in addition to any such rights as the person has apart from that paragraph.

Interpretation

7. For the purposes of this Schedule—
  (a)   a person is able to provide information only if—
    (i)   that person can obtain it without undue difficulty from a document that is in that person's control, or
    (ii)   where that person is an individual, the information is within that person's knowledge;
  (b)   a document is in a person's control if it is in that person's possession or if that person has a right to possession of it or to inspect or take copies of it.

NOTES

Commencement: to be appointed.

SCHEDULE 2

(Sch 2 contains amendments outside the scope of this work.)

SCHEDULE 3
TRANSITORY, TRANSITIONAL AND SAVING PROVISIONS

Section 20

[Application of this Act]

[1.2083]
1. (1)   Section 1(1)(a) applies where the insured became a relevant person before, as well as when the insured becomes such a person on or after, commencement day.

(2)   Section 1(1)(b) applies where the liability was incurred before, as well as where it is incurred on or after, commencement day.

[Relevant persons

1A. (1)   An individual, company or limited liability partnership not within sections 4 to 7 is to be treated as a relevant person for the purposes of this Act in the following cases.

(2)   The first case is where an individual—
  (a)   became bankrupt before commencement day, and
  (b)   has not been discharged from that bankruptcy.

(3)   The second case is where—
  (a)   an individual made a composition or arrangement with his or her creditors before commencement day, and
  (b)   the composition or arrangement remains in force.

(4) The third case is where—
   (a) a winding-up order was made, or a resolution for a voluntary winding-up was passed, with respect to a company or limited liability partnership before commencement day, and
   (b) the company or partnership is still wound up.

(5) The fourth case is where a company or limited liability partnership—
   (a) entered administration before commencement day, and
   (b) is still in administration.

(6) The fifth case is where—
   (a) a receiver or manager of the business or undertaking of a company or limited liability partnership was appointed before commencement day, and
   (b) the appointment remains in force.

(7) In those cases, the person is a relevant person only in relation to liabilities under a contract of insurance under which the person was insured at the time of the event mentioned in sub-paragraph (2)(a), (3)(a), (4)(a), (5)(a) or (6)(a) (as appropriate).]

[Bankruptcy and Diligence etc (Scotland) Act 2007]

2. Until the coming into force of section 47(1) of the Bankruptcy and Diligence etc (Scotland) Act 2007 (asp 3), the reference to that provision in paragraph 1(5) of Schedule 1 is to be read as a reference to section 486(1) of the Companies Act 1985.

[Application of 1930 Acts]

3. Despite its repeal by this Act, the Third Parties (Rights against Insurers) Act 1930 continues to apply in relation to—
   (a) cases where the event referred to in subsection (1) of section 1 of that Act and the incurring of the liability referred to in that subsection both happened before commencement day;
   (b) cases where the death of the deceased person referred to in subsection (2) of that section happened before that day.

4. Despite its repeal by this Act, the Third Parties (Rights against Insurers) Act (Northern Ireland) 1930 continues to apply in relation to—
   (a) cases where the event referred to in subsection (1) of section 1 of that Act and the incurring of the liability referred to in that subsection both happened before commencement day;
   (b) cases where the death of the deceased person referred to in subsection (2) of that section happened before that day.

[Interpretation]

5. In this Schedule "commencement day" means the day on which this Act comes into force.

NOTES
   Commencement: to be appointed.
   Paras 1–3, 5: cross-headings inserted by the Insurance Act 2015, s 20, Sch 2, paras 1, 5(1), (2), (4)–(6), as from a day to be appointed.
   Para 1A: inserted, together with preceding cross-heading, by the Insurance Act 2015, s 20, Sch 2, paras 1, 5(1), (3), as from a day to be appointed.

SCHEDULE 4

(Sch 4 contains repeals and revocations outside the scope of this work.)

EQUALITY ACT 2010

(2010 c 15)

ARRANGEMENT OF SECTIONS

PART 1
SOCIO-ECONOMIC INEQUALITIES

PART 2
EQUALITY: KEY CONCEPTS

CHAPTER 1
PROTECTED CHARACTERISTICS

CHAPTER 2
PROHIBITED CONDUCT

Discrimination

Adjustments for disabled persons

Discrimination: supplementary

Other prohibited conduct

PART 3
SERVICES AND PUBLIC FUNCTIONS

Preliminary

Provision of services, etc

Supplementary

PART 16
GENERAL AND MISCELLANEOUS

Final provisions

An Act to make provision to require Ministers of the Crown and others when making strategic decisions about the exercise of their functions to have regard to the desirability of reducing socio-economic inequalities; to reform and harmonise equality law and restate the greater part of the enactments relating to discrimination and harassment related to certain personal characteristics; to enable certain employers to be required to publish information about the differences in pay between male and female employees; to prohibit victimisation in certain circumstances; to require the exercise of certain functions to be with regard to the need to eliminate discrimination and other prohibited conduct; to enable duties to be imposed in relation to the exercise of public procurement functions; to increase equality of opportunity; to amend the law relating to rights and responsibilities in family relationships; and for connected purposes

[8 April 2010]

PART 1
SOCIO-ECONOMIC INEQUALITIES

[1.2084]
1 Public sector duty regarding socio-economic inequalities
(1)   An authority to which this section applies must, when making decisions of a strategic nature about how to exercise its functions, have due regard to the desirability of exercising them in a way that is designed to reduce the inequalities of outcome which result from socio-economic disadvantage.

(2)   In deciding how to fulfil a duty to which it is subject under subsection (1), an authority must take into account any guidance issued by a Minister of the Crown.

(3)   The authorities to which this section applies are—
  (a)   a Minister of the Crown;
  (b)   a government department other than the Security Service, the Secret Intelligence Service or the Government Communications Head-quarters;
  (c)   a county council or district council in England;
  (d)   the Greater London Authority;
  (e)   a London borough council;
  (f)   the Common Council of the City of London in its capacity as a local authority;
  (g)   the Council of the Isles of Scilly;
  (h)–(j) . . .
  (k)   a [police and crime commissioner] established for an area in England.

(4), (5)   . . .

(6)   The reference to inequalities in subsection (1) does not include any inequalities experienced by a person as a result of being a person subject to immigration control within the meaning given by section 115(9) of the Immigration and Asylum Act 1999.

NOTES
Commencement: to be appointed.
Sub-s (3) is amended as follows:
Paras (h), (i) repealed by the Health and Social Care Act 2012, s 55(2), Sch 5, paras 180, 181.
Para (j) repealed by the Public Bodies Act 2011, s 30(3), Sch 6.
Words in square brackets in para (k) substituted by the Police Reform and Social Responsibility Act 2011, s 99, Sch 16, Pt 3, paras 380, 381 (for general transitional provisions relating to police reform and the abolition of existing police authorities, see Sch 15 to the 2011 Act).
Sub-ss (4), (5): repealed by the Deregulation Act 2015, s 100(2)(g).

[1.2085]
2 Power to amend section 1
(1)   A Minister of the Crown may by regulations amend section 1 so as to—
  (a)   add a public authority to the authorities that are subject to the duty under subsection (1) of that section;
  (b)   remove an authority from those that are subject to the duty;
  (c)   make the duty apply, in the case of a particular authority, only in relation to certain functions that it has;
  (d)   in the case of an authority to which the application of the duty is already restricted to certain functions, remove or alter the restriction.

(2)   In subsection (1) "public authority" means an authority that has functions of a public nature.

(3)   Provision made under subsection (1) may not impose a duty on an authority in relation to any devolved Scottish functions or devolved Welsh functions.

(4)   The Scottish Ministers or the Welsh Ministers may by regulations amend section 1 so as to—
  (a)   add a relevant authority to the authorities that are subject to the duty under subsection (1) of that section;
  (b)   remove a relevant authority from those that are subject to the duty;
  (c)   make the duty apply, in the case of a particular relevant authority, only in relation to certain functions that it has;
  (d)   in the case of a relevant authority to which the application of the duty is already restricted to certain functions, remove or alter the restriction.

(5)   For the purposes of the power conferred by subsection (4) on the Scottish Ministers, "relevant authority" means an authority whose functions—
  (a)   are exercisable only in or as regards Scotland,
  (b)   are wholly or mainly devolved Scottish functions, and
  (c)   correspond or are similar to those of an authority for the time being specified in section 1(3).

(6)   For the purposes of the power conferred by subsection (4) on the Welsh Ministers, "relevant authority" means an authority whose functions—

    (a)   are exercisable only in or as regards Wales,

    (b)   are wholly or mainly devolved Welsh functions, and

    (c)   correspond or are similar to those of an authority for the time being specified in subsection (3) of section 1 or referred to in subsection (4) of that section.

(7)   Before making regulations under this section, the Scottish Ministers or the Welsh Ministers must consult a Minister of the Crown.

(8)   Regulations under this section may make any amendments of section 1 that appear to the Minister or Ministers to be necessary or expedient in consequence of provision made under subsection (1) or (as the case may be) subsection (4).

(9)   Provision made by the Scottish Ministers or the Welsh Ministers in reliance on subsection (8) may, in particular, amend section 1 so as to—

    (a)   confer on the Ministers a power to issue guidance;

    (b)   require a relevant authority to take into account any guidance issued under a power conferred by virtue of paragraph (a);

    (c)   disapply section 1(2) in consequence of the imposition of a requirement by virtue of paragraph (b).

(10)   Before issuing guidance under a power conferred by virtue of subsection (9)(a), the Ministers must—

    (a)   take into account any guidance issued by a Minister of the Crown under section 1;

    (b)   consult a Minister of the Crown.

(11)   For the purposes of this section—

    (a)   a function is a devolved Scottish function if it is exercisable in or as regards Scotland and it does not relate to reserved matters (within the meaning of the Scotland Act 1998);

    (b)   a function is a devolved Welsh function if it relates to a matter in respect of which functions are exercisable by the Welsh Ministers, the First Minister for Wales or the Counsel General to the Welsh Assembly Government, or to a matter within the legislative competence of the National Assembly for Wales.

NOTES

Commencement: to be appointed.

[1.2086]

3   Enforcement

A failure in respect of a performance of a duty under section 1 does not confer a cause of action at private law.

NOTES

Commencement: to be appointed.

PART 2

EQUALITY: KEY CONCEPTS

CHAPTER 1

PROTECTED CHARACTERISTICS

[1.2087]

4   The protected characteristics

The following characteristics are protected characteristics—

    age;

    disability;

    gender reassignment;

    marriage and civil partnership;

    pregnancy and maternity;

    race;

    religion or belief;

    sex;

    sexual orientation.

[1.2088]

5   Age

(1)   In relation to the protected characteristic of age—

    (a)   a reference to a person who has a particular protected characteristic is a reference to a person of a particular age group;

    (b)   a reference to persons who share a protected characteristic is a reference to persons of the same age group.

(2)   A reference to an age group is a reference to a group of persons defined by reference to age, whether by reference to a particular age or to a range of ages.

[1.2089]
6 Disability
(1) A person (P) has a disability if—
  (a)   P has a physical or mental impairment, and
  (b)   the impairment has a substantial and long-term adverse effect on P's ability to carry out normal day-to-day activities.
(2) A reference to a disabled person is a reference to a person who has a disability.
(3) In relation to the protected characteristic of disability—
  (a)   a reference to a person who has a particular protected characteristic is a reference to a person who has a particular disability;
  (b)   a reference to persons who share a protected characteristic is a reference to persons who have the same disability.
(4) This Act (except Part 12 and section 190) applies in relation to a person who has had a disability as it applies in relation to a person who has the disability; accordingly (except in that Part and that section)—
  (a)   a reference (however expressed) to a person who has a disability includes a reference to a person who has had the disability, and
  (b)   a reference (however expressed) to a person who does not have a disability includes a reference to a person who has not had the disability.
(5) A Minister of the Crown may issue guidance about matters to be taken into account in deciding any question for the purposes of subsection (1).
(6) Schedule 1 (disability: supplementary provision) has effect.

NOTES
  Orders: the Equality Act 2010 (Guidance on the Definition of Disability) Appointed Day Order 2011, SI 2011/1159.

[1.2090]
7 Gender reassignment
(1) A person has the protected characteristic of gender reassignment if the person is proposing to undergo, is undergoing or has undergone a process (or part of a process) for the purpose of reassigning the person's sex by changing physiological or other attributes of sex.
(2) A reference to a transsexual person is a reference to a person who has the protected characteristic of gender reassignment.
(3) In relation to the protected characteristic of gender reassignment—
  (a)   a reference to a person who has a particular protected characteristic is a reference to a transsexual person;
  (b)   a reference to persons who share a protected characteristic is a reference to transsexual persons.

[1.2091]
8 Marriage and civil partnership
(1) A person has the protected characteristic of marriage and civil partnership if the person is married or is a civil partner.
(2) In relation to the protected characteristic of marriage and civil partnership—
  (a)   a reference to a person who has a particular protected characteristic is a reference to a person who is married or is a civil partner;
  (b)   a reference to persons who share a protected characteristic is a reference to persons who are married or are civil partners.

[1.2092]
9 Race
(1) Race includes—
  (a)   colour;
  (b)   nationality;
  (c)   ethnic or national origins.
(2) In relation to the protected characteristic of race—
  (a)   a reference to a person who has a particular protected characteristic is a reference to a person of a particular racial group;
  (b)   a reference to persons who share a protected characteristic is a reference to persons of the same racial group.
(3) A racial group is a group of persons defined by reference to race; and a reference to a person's racial group is a reference to a racial group into which the person falls.
(4) The fact that a racial group comprises two or more distinct racial groups does not prevent it from constituting a particular racial group.
(5) A Minister of the Crown . . . —
  (a)   [must by order] amend this section so as to provide for caste to be an aspect of race;
  (b)   [may by order] amend this Act so as to provide for an exception to a provision of this Act to apply, or not to apply, to caste or to apply, or not to apply, to caste in specified circumstances.

(6) The power under section 207(4)(b), in its application to subsection (5), includes power to amend this Act.

NOTES

Sub-s (5): words omitted repealed, and words in square brackets in paras (a), (b) inserted, by the Enterprise and Regulatory Reform Act 2013, s 97(1)–(4).

Review: as to the review of the effect of sub-s (5) of this section (and orders made under it) and whether it remains appropriate, see the Enterprise and Regulatory Reform Act 2013, s 97(5)–(10).

[1.2093]
10 Religion or belief
(1) Religion means any religion and a reference to religion includes a reference to a lack of religion.
(2) Belief means any religious or philosophical belief and a reference to belief includes a reference to a lack of belief.
(3) In relation to the protected characteristic of religion or belief—
  (a) a reference to a person who has a particular protected characteristic is a reference to a person of a particular religion or belief;
  (b) a reference to persons who share a protected characteristic is a reference to persons who are of the same religion or belief.

[1.2094]
11 Sex
In relation to the protected characteristic of sex—
  (a) a reference to a person who has a particular protected characteristic is a reference to a man or to a woman;
  (b) a reference to persons who share a protected characteristic is a reference to persons of the same sex.

[1.2095]
12 Sexual orientation
(1) Sexual orientation means a person's sexual orientation towards—
  (a) persons of the same sex,
  (b) persons of the opposite sex, or
  (c) persons of either sex.
(2) In relation to the protected characteristic of sexual orientation—
  (a) a reference to a person who has a particular protected characteristic is a reference to a person who is of a particular sexual orientation;
  (b) a reference to persons who share a protected characteristic is a reference to persons who are of the same sexual orientation.

CHAPTER 2
PROHIBITED CONDUCT

Discrimination

[1.2096]
13 Direct discrimination
(1) A person (A) discriminates against another (B) if, because of a protected characteristic, A treats B less favourably than A treats or would treat others.
(2) If the protected characteristic is age, A does not discriminate against B if A can show A's treatment of B to be a proportionate means of achieving a legitimate aim.
(3) If the protected characteristic is disability, and B is not a disabled person, A does not discriminate against B only because A treats or would treat disabled persons more favourably than A treats B.
(4) If the protected characteristic is marriage and civil partnership, this section applies to a contravention of Part 5 (work) only if the treatment is because it is B who is married or a civil partner.
(5) If the protected characteristic is race, less favourable treatment includes segregating B from others.
(6) If the protected characteristic is sex—
  (a) less favourable treatment of a woman includes less favourable treatment of her because she is breast-feeding;
  (b) in a case where B is a man, no account is to be taken of special treatment afforded to a woman in connection with pregnancy or childbirth.
(7) Subsection (6)(a) does not apply for the purposes of Part 5 (work).
(8) This section is subject to sections 17(6) and 18(7).

[1.2097]
14   Combined discrimination: dual characteristics
(1)   A person (A) discriminates against another (B) if, because of a combination of two relevant protected characteristics, A treats B less favourably than A treats or would treat a person who does not share either of those characteristics.
(2)   The relevant protected characteristics are—
   (a)   age;
   (b)   disability;
   (c)   gender reassignment;
   (d)   race
   (e)   religion or belief;
   (f)   sex;
   (g)   sexual orientation.
(3)   For the purposes of establishing a contravention of this Act by virtue of subsection (1), B need not show that A's treatment of B is direct discrimination because of each of the characteristics in the combination (taken separately).
(4)   But B cannot establish a contravention of this Act by virtue of subsection (1) if, in reliance on another provision of this Act or any other enactment, A shows that A's treatment of B is not direct discrimination because of either or both of the characteristics in the combination.
(5)   Subsection (1) does not apply to a combination of characteristics that includes disability in circumstances where, if a claim of direct discrimination because of disability were to be brought, it would come within section 116 (special educational needs).
(6)   A Minister of the Crown may by order amend this section so as to—
   (a)   make further provision about circumstances in which B can, or in which B cannot, establish a contravention of this Act by virtue of subsection (1);
   (b)   specify other circumstances in which subsection (1) does not apply.
(7)   The references to direct discrimination are to a contravention of this Act by virtue of section 13.

NOTES
   Commencement: to be appointed.

[1.2098]
15   Discrimination arising from disability
(1)   A person (A) discriminates against a disabled person (B) if—
   (a)   A treats B unfavourably because of something arising in consequence of B's disability, and
   (b)   A cannot show that the treatment is a proportionate means of achieving a legitimate aim.
(2)   Subsection (1) does not apply if A shows that A did not know, and could not reasonably have been expected to know, that B had the disability.

[1.2099]
16   Gender reassignment discrimination: cases of absence from work
(1)   This section has effect for the purposes of the application of Part 5 (work) to the protected characteristic of gender reassignment.
(2)   A person (A) discriminates against a transsexual person (B) if, in relation to an absence of B's that is because of gender reassignment, A treats B less favourably than A would treat B if—
   (a)   B's absence was because of sickness or injury, or
   (b)   B's absence was for some other reason and it is not reasonable for B to be treated less favourably.
(3)   A person's absence is because of gender reassignment if it is because the person is proposing to undergo, is undergoing or has undergone the process (or part of the process) mentioned in section 7(1).

[1.2100]
17   Pregnancy and maternity discrimination: non-work cases
(1)   This section has effect for the purposes of the application to the protected characteristic of pregnancy and maternity of—
   (a)   Part 3 (services and public functions);
   (b)   Part 4 (premises);
   (c)   Part 6 (education);
   (d)   Part 7 (associations).
(2)   A person (A) discriminates against a woman if A treats her unfavourably because of a pregnancy of hers.
(3)   A person (A) discriminates against a woman if, in the period of 26 weeks beginning with the day on which she gives birth, A treats her unfavourably because she has given birth.
(4)   The reference in subsection (3) to treating a woman unfavourably because she has given birth includes, in particular, a reference to treating her unfavourably because she is breast-feeding.
(5)   For the purposes of this section, the day on which a woman gives birth is the day on which—
   (a)   she gives birth to a living child, or

(b)   she gives birth to a dead child (more than 24 weeks of the pregnancy having passed).

(6)   Section 13, so far as relating to sex discrimination, does not apply to anything done in relation to a woman in so far as—

     (a)   it is for the reason mentioned in subsection (2), or

     (b)   it is in the period, and for the reason, mentioned in subsection (3).

[1.2101]
18   Pregnancy and maternity discrimination: work cases

(1)   This section has effect for the purposes of the application of Part 5 (work) to the protected characteristic of pregnancy and maternity.

(2)   A person (A) discriminates against a woman if, in the protected period in relation to a pregnancy of hers, A treats her unfavourably—

     (a)   because of the pregnancy, or

     (b)   because of illness suffered by her as a result of it.

(3)   A person (A) discriminates against a woman if A treats her unfavourably because she is on compulsory maternity leave.

(4)   A person (A) discriminates against a woman if A treats her unfavourably because she is exercising or seeking to exercise, or has exercised or sought to exercise, the right to ordinary or additional maternity leave.

(5)   For the purposes of subsection (2), if the treatment of a woman is in implementation of a decision taken in the protected period, the treatment is to be regarded as occurring in that period (even if the implementation is not until after the end of that period).

(6)   The protected period, in relation to a woman's pregnancy, begins when the pregnancy begins, and ends—

     (a)   if she has the right to ordinary and additional maternity leave, at the end of the additional maternity leave period or (if earlier) when she returns to work after the pregnancy;

     (b)   if she does not have that right, at the end of the period of 2 weeks beginning with the end of the pregnancy.

(7)   Section 13, so far as relating to sex discrimination, does not apply to treatment of a woman in so far as—

     (a)   it is in the protected period in relation to her and is for a reason mentioned in paragraph (a) or (b) of subsection (2), or

     (b)   it is for a reason mentioned in subsection (3) or (4).

[1.2102]
19   Indirect discrimination

(1)   A person (A) discriminates against another (B) if A applies to B a provision, criterion or practice which is discriminatory in relation to a relevant protected characteristic of B's.

(2)   For the purposes of subsection (1), a provision, criterion or practice is discriminatory in relation to a relevant protected characteristic of B's if—

     (a)   A applies, or would apply, it to persons with whom B does not share the characteristic,

     (b)   it puts, or would put, persons with whom B shares the characteristic at a particular disadvantage when compared with persons with whom B does not share it,

     (c)   it puts, or would put, B at that disadvantage, and

     (d)   A cannot show it to be a proportionate means of achieving a legitimate aim.

(3)   The relevant protected characteristics are—

age;

disability;

gender reassignment;

marriage and civil partnership;

race;

religion or belief;

sex;

sexual orientation.

Adjustments for disabled persons

[1.2103]
20   Duty to make adjustments

(1)   Where this Act imposes a duty to make reasonable adjustments on a person, this section, sections 21 and 22 and the applicable Schedule apply; and for those purposes, a person on whom the duty is imposed is referred to as A.

(2)   The duty comprises the following three requirements.

(3)   The first requirement is a requirement, where a provision, criterion or practice of A's puts a disabled person at a substantial disadvantage in relation to a relevant matter in comparison with persons who are not disabled, to take such steps as it is reasonable to have to take to avoid the disadvantage.

(4)   The second requirement is a requirement, where a physical feature puts a disabled person at a substantial disadvantage in relation to a relevant matter in comparison with persons who are not disabled, to take such steps as it is reasonable to have to take to avoid the disadvantage.

(5)   The third requirement is a requirement, where a disabled person would, but for the provision of an auxiliary aid, be put at a substantial disadvantage in relation to a relevant matter in comparison with persons who are not disabled, to take such steps as it is reasonable to have to take to provide the auxiliary aid.

(6)   Where the first or third requirement relates to the provision of information, the steps which it is reasonable for A to have to take include steps for ensuring that in the circumstances concerned the information is provided in an accessible format.

(7)   A person (A) who is subject to a duty to make reasonable adjustments is not (subject to express provision to the contrary) entitled to require a disabled person, in relation to whom A is required to comply with the duty, to pay to any extent A's costs of complying with the duty.

(8)   A reference in section 21 or 22 or an applicable Schedule to the first, second or third requirement is to be construed in accordance with this section.

(9)   In relation to the second requirement, a reference in this section or an applicable Schedule to avoiding a substantial disadvantage includes a reference to—

   (a)   removing the physical feature in question,

   (b)   altering it, or

   (c)   providing a reasonable means of avoiding it.

(10)   A reference in this section, section 21 or 22 or an applicable Schedule (apart from paragraphs 2 to 4 of Schedule 4) to a physical feature is a reference to—

   (a)   a feature arising from the design or construction of a building,

   (b)   a feature of an approach to, exit from or access to a building,

   (c)   a fixture or fitting, or furniture, furnishings, materials, equipment or other chattels, in or on premises, or

   (d)   any other physical element or quality.

(11)   A reference in this section, section 21 or 22 or an applicable Schedule to an auxiliary aid includes a reference to an auxiliary service.

(12)   A reference in this section or an applicable Schedule to chattels is to be read, in relation to Scotland, as a reference to moveable property.

(13)   The applicable Schedule is, in relation to the Part of this Act specified in the first column of the Table, the Schedule specified in the second column.

Part of this Act	Applicable Schedule
Part 3 (services and public functions)	Schedule 2
Part 4 (premises)	Schedule 4
Part 5 (work)	Schedule 8
Part 6 (education)	Schedule 13
Part 7 (associations)	Schedule 15
Each of the Parts mentioned above	Schedule 21

[1.2104]
21   Failure to comply with duty

(1)   A failure to comply with the first, second or third requirement is a failure to comply with a duty to make reasonable adjustments.

(2)   A discriminates against a disabled person if A fails to comply with that duty in relation to that person.

(3)   A provision of an applicable Schedule which imposes a duty to comply with the first, second or third requirement applies only for the purpose of establishing whether A has contravened this Act by virtue of subsection (2); a failure to comply is, accordingly, not actionable by virtue of another provision of this Act or otherwise.

[1.2105]
22   Regulations

(1)   Regulations may prescribe—

   (a)   matters to be taken into account in deciding whether it is reasonable for A to take a step for the purposes of a prescribed provision of an applicable Schedule;

   (b)   descriptions of persons to whom the first, second or third requirement does not apply.

(2)   Regulations may make provision as to—

   (a)   circumstances in which it is, or in which it is not, reasonable for a person of a prescribed description to have to take steps of a prescribed description;

   (b)   what is, or what is not, a provision, criterion or practice;

   (c)   things which are, or which are not, to be treated as physical features;

   (d)   things which are, or which are not, to be treated as alterations of physical features;

   (e)   things which are, or which are not, to be treated as auxiliary aids.

(3)   Provision made by virtue of this section may amend an applicable Schedule.

NOTES

   Regulations: the Equality Act 2010 (Disability) Regulations 2010, SI 2010/2128.

Discrimination: supplementary

[1.2106]
23 Comparison by reference to circumstances
(1) On a comparison of cases for the purposes of section 13, 14, or 19 there must be no material difference between the circumstances relating to each case.

(2) The circumstances relating to a case include a person's abilities if—
 (a) on a comparison for the purposes of section 13, the protected characteristic is disability;
 (b) on a comparison for the purposes of section 14, one of the protected characteristics in the combination is disability.

(3) If the protected characteristic is sexual orientation, the fact that one person (whether or not the person referred to as B) is a civil partner while another is married [to a person of the opposite sex] is not a material difference between the circumstances relating to each case.

[(4) If the protected characteristic is sexual orientation, the fact that one person (whether or not the person referred to as B) is married to a person of the same sex while another is married to a person of the opposite sex is not a material difference between the circumstances relating to each case.]

NOTES
Words in square brackets in sub-s (3) inserted, and sub-s (4) added, by the Marriage (Same Sex Couples) Act 2013, s 17(4), Sch 7, Pt 2, paras 42, 43.

[1.2107]
24 Irrelevance of alleged discriminator's characteristics
(1) For the purpose of establishing a contravention of this Act by virtue of section 13(1), it does not matter whether A has the protected characteristic.

(2) For the purpose of establishing a contravention of this Act by virtue of section 14(1), it does not matter—
 (a) whether A has one of the protected characteristics in the combination;
 (b) whether A has both.

[1.2108]
25 References to particular strands of discrimination
(1) Age discrimination is—
 (a) discrimination within section 13 because of age;
 (b) discrimination within section 19 where the relevant protected characteristic is age.

(2) Disability discrimination is—
 (a) discrimination within section 13 because of disability;
 (b) discrimination within section 15;
 (c) discrimination within section 19 where the relevant protected characteristic is disability;
 (d) discrimination within section 21.

(3) Gender reassignment discrimination is—
 (a) discrimination within section 13 because of gender reassignment;
 (b) discrimination within section 16;
 (c) discrimination within section 19 where the relevant protected characteristic is gender reassignment.

(4) Marriage and civil partnership discrimination is—
 (a) discrimination within section 13 because of marriage and civil partnership;
 (b) discrimination within section 19 where the relevant protected characteristic is marriage and civil partnership.

(5) Pregnancy and maternity discrimination is discrimination within section 17 or 18.

(6) Race discrimination is—
 (a) discrimination within section 13 because of race;
 (b) discrimination within section 19 where the relevant protected characteristic is race.

(7) Religious or belief-related discrimination is—
 (a) discrimination within section 13 because of religion or belief;
 (b) discrimination within section 19 where the relevant protected characteristic is religion or belief.

(8) Sex discrimination is—
 (a) discrimination within section 13 because of sex;
 (b) discrimination within section 19 where the relevant protected characteristic is sex.

(9) Sexual orientation discrimination is—
 (a) discrimination within section 13 because of sexual orientation;
 (b) discrimination within section 19 where the relevant protected characteristic is sexual orientation.

Other prohibited conduct

[1.2109]
26 Harassment
(1) A person (A) harasses another (B) if—

    (a)   A engages in unwanted conduct related to a relevant protected characteristic, and

    (b)   the conduct has the purpose or effect of—

        (i)   violating B's dignity, or

        (ii)   creating an intimidating, hostile, degrading, humiliating or offensive environment for B.

(2)   A also harasses B if—

    (a)   A engages in unwanted conduct of a sexual nature, and

    (b)   the conduct has the purpose or effect referred to in subsection (1)(b).

(3)   A also harasses B if—

    (a)   A or another person engages in unwanted conduct of a sexual nature or that is related to gender reassignment or sex,

    (b)   the conduct has the purpose or effect referred to in subsection (1)(b), and

    (c)   because of B's rejection of or submission to the conduct, A treats B less favourably than A would treat B if B had not rejected or submitted to the conduct.

(4)   In deciding whether conduct has the effect referred to in subsection (1)(b), each of the following must be taken into account—

    (a)   the perception of B;

    (b)   the other circumstances of the case;

    (c)   whether it is reasonable for the conduct to have that effect.

(5)   The relevant protected characteristics are—

age;

disability;

gender reassignment;

race;

religion or belief;

sex;

sexual orientation.

[1.2110]
27 Victimisation

(1)   A person (A) victimises another person (B) if A subjects B to a detriment because—

    (a)   B does a protected act, or

    (b)   A believes that B has done, or may do, a protected act.

(2)   Each of the following is a protected act—

    (a)   bringing proceedings under this Act;

    (b)   giving evidence or information in connection with proceedings under this Act;

    (c)   doing any other thing for the purposes of or in connection with this Act;

    (d)   making an allegation (whether or not express) that A or another person has contravened this Act.

(3)   Giving false evidence or information, or making a false allegation, is not a protected act if the evidence or information is given, or the allegation is made, in bad faith.

(4)   This section applies only where the person subjected to a detriment is an individual.

(5)   The reference to contravening this Act includes a reference to committing a breach of an equality clause or rule.

PART 3
SERVICES AND PUBLIC FUNCTIONS

Preliminary

[1.2111]
28 Application of this Part

(1)   This Part does not apply to the protected characteristic of—

    (a)   age, so far as relating to persons who have not attained the age of 18;

    (b)   marriage and civil partnership.

(2)   This Part does not apply to discrimination, harassment or victimisation—

    (a)   that is prohibited by Part 4 (premises), 5 (work) or 6 (education), or

    (b)   that would be so prohibited but for an express exception.

(3)   This Part does not apply to—

    (a)   a breach of an equality clause or rule;

    (b)   anything that would be a breach of an equality clause or rule but for section 69 or Part 2 of Schedule 7;

    (c)   a breach of a non-discrimination rule.

NOTES

Commencement: 1 October 2010 (certain purposes); 1 October 2012 (otherwise).

Provision of services, etc

[1.2112]

29 Provision of services, etc

(1) A person (a "service-provider") concerned with the provision of a service to the public or a section of the public (for payment or not) must not discriminate against a person requiring the service by not providing the person with the service.

(2) A service-provider (A) must not, in providing the service, discriminate against a person (B)—

    (a)   as to the terms on which A provides the service to B;

    (b)   by terminating the provision of the service to B;

    (c)   by subjecting B to any other detriment.

(3) A service-provider must not, in relation to the provision of the service, harass—

    (a)   a person requiring the service, or

    (b)   a person to whom the service-provider provides the service.

(4) A service-provider must not victimise a person requiring the service by not providing the person with the service.

(5) A service-provider (A) must not, in providing the service, victimise a person (B)—

    (a)   as to the terms on which A provides the service to B;

    (b)   by terminating the provision of the service to B;

    (c)   by subjecting B to any other detriment.

(6) A person must not, in the exercise of a public function that is not the provision of a service to the public or a section of the public, do anything that constitutes discrimination, harassment or victimisation.

(7) A duty to make reasonable adjustments applies to—

    (a)   a service-provider (and see also section 55(7));

    (b)   a person who exercises a public function that is not the provision of a service to the public or a section of the public.

(8) In the application of section 26 for the purposes of subsection (3), and subsection (6) as it relates to harassment, neither of the following is a relevant protected characteristic—

    (a)   religion or belief;

    (b)   sexual orientation.

(9) In the application of this section, so far as relating to race or religion or belief, to the granting of entry clearance (within the meaning of the Immigration Act 1971), it does not matter whether an act is done within or outside the United Kingdom.

(10) Subsection (9) does not affect the application of any other provision of this Act to conduct outside England and Wales or Scotland.

NOTES

    Commencement: 1 October 2010 (certain purposes); 1 October 2012 (otherwise).

Supplementary

[1.2113]

30 Ships and hovercraft

(1) This Part (subject to subsection (2)) applies only in such circumstances as are prescribed in relation to—

    (a)   transporting people by ship or hovercraft;

    (b)   a service provided on a ship or hovercraft.

(2) Section 29(6) applies in relation to the matters referred to in paragraphs (a) and (b) of subsection (1); but in so far as it relates to disability discrimination, section 29(6) applies to those matters only in such circumstances as are prescribed.

(3) It does not matter whether the ship or hovercraft is within or outside the United Kingdom.

(4) "Ship" has the same meaning as in the Merchant Shipping Act 1995.

(5) "Hovercraft" has the same meaning as in the Hovercraft Act 1968.

(6) Nothing in this section affects the application of any other provision of this Act to conduct outside England and Wales or Scotland.

NOTES

    Commencement: 1 October 2010 (certain purposes); 1 October 2012 (otherwise).

[1.2114]

31 Interpretation and exceptions

(1) This section applies for the purposes of this Part.

(2) A reference to the provision of a service includes a reference to the provision of goods or facilities.

(3) A reference to the provision of a service includes a reference to the provision of a service in the exercise of a public function.

(4) A public function is a function that is a function of a public nature for the purposes of the Human Rights Act 1998.

(5) Where an employer arranges for another person to provide a service only to the employer's employees—

(a) the employer is not to be regarded as the service-provider, but

(b) the employees are to be regarded as a section of the public.

(6) A reference to a person requiring a service includes a reference to a person who is seeking to obtain or use the service.

(7) A reference to a service-provider not providing a person with a service includes a reference to—

(a) the service-provider not providing the person with a service of the quality that the service-provider usually provides to the public (or the section of it which includes the person), or

(b) the service-provider not providing the person with the service in the manner in which, or on the terms on which, the service-provider usually provides the service to the public (or the section of it which includes the person).

(8) In relation to the provision of a service by either House of Parliament, the service-provider is the Corporate Officer of the House concerned; and if the service involves access to, or use of, a place in the Palace of Westminster which members of the public are allowed to enter, both Corporate Officers are jointly the service-provider.

(9) Schedule 2 (reasonable adjustments) has effect.

(10) Schedule 3 (exceptions) has effect.

NOTES

Commencement: 1 October 2010 (certain purposes); 1 September 2012 (certain purposes); 1 October 2012 (remaining purposes).

32–201 ((*Pts 4–15*) *Outside the scope of this work.*)

PART 16
GENERAL AND MISCELLANEOUS

202–214 (*Outside the scope of this work.*)

Final provisions

215 (*Outside the scope of this work.*)

[1.2115]
216 Commencement
(1) The following provisions come into force on the day on which this Act is passed—

(a) (*outside the scope of this work*)

(b) this Part (except sections 202 (civil partnerships on religious premises), 206 (information society services) and 211 (amendments, etc)).

(2) (*Outside the scope of this work.*)

(3) The other provisions of this Act come into force on such day as a Minister of the Crown may by order appoint.

NOTES

Orders: the Equality Act 2010 (Commencement No 1) Order 2010, SI 2010/1736; the Equality Act 2010 (Commencement No 2) Order 2010, SI 2010/1966; the Equality Act 2010 (Commencement No 3) Order 2010, SI 2010/2191; the Equality Act 2010 (Consequential Amendments, Saving and Supplementary Provisions) Order 2010, SI 2010/2279; the Equality Act 2010 (Commencement No 4, Savings, Consequential, Transitional, Transitory and Incidental Provisions and Revocation) Order 2010, SI 2010/2317; the Equality Act 2010 (Commencement No 5) Order 2011, SI 2011/96; the Equality Act 2010 (Commencement No 6) Order 2011, SI 2011/1066; the Equality Act 2010 (Commencement No 7) Order 2011, SI 2011/1636; the Equality Act 2010 (Commencement No 8) Order 2011, SI 2011/2646; the Equality Act 2010 (Commencement No 9) Order 2012, SI 2012/1569; the Equality Act 2010 (Commencement No 10) Order 2012, SI 2012/2184.

[1.2116]
217 Extent
(1) This Act forms part of the law of England and Wales.

(2) This Act, apart from section 190 (improvements to let dwelling houses) and Part 15 (family property), forms part of the law of Scotland.

(3) (*Outside the scope of this work.*)

[1.2117]
218 Short title
This Act may be cited as the Equality Act 2010.

SCHEDULES

SCHEDULES 1–28

(*Schs 1–28 outside the scope of this work.*)

BRIBERY ACT 2010

(2010 c 23)

ARRANGEMENT OF SECTIONS

An Act to make provision about offences relating to bribery; and for connected purposes.

[8 April 2010]

General bribery offences

[1.2118]
1   Offences of bribing another person

(1)   A person ("P") is guilty of an offence if either of the following cases applies.
(2)   Case 1 is where—
    (a)   P offers, promises or gives a financial or other advantage to another person, and
    (b)   P intends the advantage—
       (i)   to induce a person to perform improperly a relevant function or activity, or
       (ii)   to reward a person for the improper performance of such a function or activity.
(3)   Case 2 is where—
    (a)   P offers, promises or gives a financial or other advantage to another person, and
    (b)   P knows or believes that the acceptance of the advantage would itself constitute the improper performance of a relevant function or activity.
(4)   In case 1 it does not matter whether the person to whom the advantage is offered, promised or given is the same person as the person who is to perform, or has performed, the function or activity concerned.
(5)   In cases 1 and 2 it does not matter whether the advantage is offered, promised or given by P directly or through a third party.

NOTES

Deferred Prosecution Agreements: as to the application of Deferred Prosecution Agreements to an offence under this section and ss 2, 6, 7, (ie, an agreement between a designated prosecutor and a person accused of a crime (P) whereby proceedings against P in respect of the alleged offence are automatically suspended as soon as they are instituted if P agrees to comply with certain requirements), see s 45 of, and Sch 17, Pt 1 and Sch 17, Pt 2, para 26 to, the Crime and Courts Act 2013.

[1.2119]
2   Offences relating to being bribed

(1)   A person ("R") is guilty of an offence if any of the following cases applies.

(2) Case 3 is where R requests, agrees to receive or accepts a financial or other advantage intending that, in consequence, a relevant function or activity should be performed improperly (whether by R or another person).

(3) Case 4 is where—

   (a) R requests, agrees to receive or accepts a financial or other advantage, and
   (b) the request, agreement or acceptance itself constitutes the improper performance by R of a relevant function or activity.

(4) Case 5 is where R requests, agrees to receive or accepts a financial or other advantage as a reward for the improper performance (whether by R or another person) of a relevant function or activity.

(5) Case 6 is where, in anticipation of or in consequence of R requesting, agreeing to receive or accepting a financial or other advantage, a relevant function or activity is performed improperly—

   (a) by R, or
   (b) by another person at R's request or with R's assent or acquiescence.

(6) In cases 3 to 6 it does not matter—

   (a) whether R requests, agrees to receive or accepts (or is to request, agree to receive or accept) the advantage directly or through a third party,
   (b) whether the advantage is (or is to be) for the benefit of R or another person.

(7) In cases 4 to 6 it does not matter whether R knows or believes that the performance of the function or activity is improper.

(8) In case 6, where a person other than R is performing the function or activity, it also does not matter whether that person knows or believes that the performance of the function or activity is improper.

NOTES

Deferred Prosecution Agreements: see the note to s 1 at **[1.2118]**.

[1.2120]

3 Function or activity to which bribe relates

(1) For the purposes of this Act a function or activity is a relevant function or activity if—

   (a) it falls within subsection (2), and
   (b) meets one or more of conditions A to C.

(2) The following functions and activities fall within this subsection—

   (a) any function of a public nature,
   (b) any activity connected with a business,
   (c) any activity performed in the course of a person's employment,
   (d) any activity performed by or on behalf of a body of persons (whether corporate or unincorporate).

(3) Condition A is that a person performing the function or activity is expected to perform it in good faith.

(4) Condition B is that a person performing the function or activity is expected to perform it impartially.

(5) Condition C is that a person performing the function or activity is in a position of trust by virtue of performing it.

(6) A function or activity is a relevant function or activity even if it—

   (a) has no connection with the United Kingdom, and
   (b) is performed in a country or territory outside the United Kingdom.

(7) In this section "business" includes trade or profession.

[1.2121]

4 Improper performance to which bribe relates

(1) For the purposes of this Act a relevant function or activity—

   (a) is performed improperly if it is performed in breach of a relevant expectation, and
   (b) is to be treated as being performed improperly if there is a failure to perform the function or activity and that failure is itself a breach of a relevant expectation.

(2) In subsection (1) "relevant expectation"—

   (a) in relation to a function or activity which meets condition A or B, means the expectation mentioned in the condition concerned, and
   (b) in relation to a function or activity which meets condition C, means any expectation as to the manner in which, or the reasons for which, the function or activity will be performed that arises from the position of trust mentioned in that condition.

(3) Anything that a person does (or omits to do) arising from or in connection with that person's past performance of a relevant function or activity is to be treated for the purposes of this Act as being done (or omitted) by that person in the performance of that function or activity.

[1.2122]
5   Expectation test

(1)   For the purposes of sections 3 and 4, the test of what is expected is a test of what a reasonable person in the United Kingdom would expect in relation to the performance of the type of function or activity concerned.

(2)   In deciding what such a person would expect in relation to the performance of a function or activity where the performance is not subject to the law of any part of the United Kingdom, any local custom or practice is to be disregarded unless it is permitted or required by the written law applicable to the country or territory concerned.

(3)   In subsection (2) "written law" means law contained in—

  (a)   any written constitution, or provision made by or under legislation, applicable to the country or territory concerned, or

  (b)   any judicial decision which is so applicable and is evidenced in published written sources.

Bribery of foreign public officials

[1.2123]
6   Bribery of foreign public officials

(1)   A person ("P") who bribes a foreign public official ("F") is guilty of an offence if P's intention is to influence F in F's capacity as a foreign public official.

(2)   P must also intend to obtain or retain—

  (a)   business, or

  (b)   an advantage in the conduct of business.

(3)   P bribes F if, and only if—

  (a)   directly or through a third party, P offers, promises or gives any financial or other advantage—

    (i)   to F, or

    (ii)   to another person at F's request or with F's assent or acquiescence, and

  (b)   F is neither permitted nor required by the written law applicable to F to be influenced in F's capacity as a foreign public official by the offer, promise or gift.

(4)   References in this section to influencing F in F's capacity as a foreign public official mean influencing F in the performance of F's functions as such an official, which includes—

  (a)   any omission to exercise those functions, and

  (b)   any use of F's position as such an official, even if not within F's authority.

(5)   "Foreign public official" means an individual who—

  (a)   holds a legislative, administrative or judicial position of any kind, whether appointed or elected, of a country or territory outside the United Kingdom (or any subdivision of such a country or territory),

  (b)   exercises a public function—

    (i)   for or on behalf of a country or territory outside the United Kingdom (or any subdivision of such a country or territory), or

    (ii)   for any public agency or public enterprise of that country or territory (or subdivision), or

  (c)   is an official or agent of a public international organisation.

(6)   "Public international organisation" means an organisation whose members are any of the following—

  (a)   countries or territories,

  (b)   governments of countries or territories,

  (c)   other public international organisations,

  (d)   a mixture of any of the above.

(7)   For the purposes of subsection (3)(b), the written law applicable to F is—

  (a)   where the performance of the functions of F which P intends to influence would be subject to the law of any part of the United Kingdom, the law of that part of the United Kingdom,

  (b)   where paragraph (a) does not apply and F is an official or agent of a public international organisation, the applicable written rules of that organisation,

  (c)   where paragraphs (a) and (b) do not apply, the law of the country or territory in relation to which F is a foreign public official so far as that law is contained in—

    (i)   any written constitution, or provision made by or under legislation, applicable to the country or territory concerned, or

    (ii)   any judicial decision which is so applicable and is evidenced in published written sources.

(8)   For the purposes of this section, a trade or profession is a business.

NOTES

Deferred Prosecution Agreements: see the note to s 1 at **[1.2118]**.

Failure of commercial organisations to prevent bribery

[1.2124]
7   Failure of commercial organisations to prevent bribery
(1)   A relevant commercial organisation ("C") is guilty of an offence under this section if a person ("A") associated with C bribes another person intending—
    (a)   to obtain or retain business for C, or
    (b)   to obtain or retain an advantage in the conduct of business for C.
(2)   But it is a defence for C to prove that C had in place adequate procedures designed to prevent persons associated with C from undertaking such conduct.
(3)   For the purposes of this section, A bribes another person if, and only if, A—
    (a)   is, or would be, guilty of an offence under section 1 or 6 (whether or not A has been prosecuted for such an offence), or
    (b)   would be guilty of such an offence if section 12(2)(c) and (4) were omitted.
(4)   See section 8 for the meaning of a person associated with C and see section 9 for a duty on the Secretary of State to publish guidance.
(5)   In this section—
  "partnership" means—
    (a)   a partnership within the Partnership Act 1890, or
    (b)   a limited partnership registered under the Limited Partnerships Act 1907,
    or a firm or entity of a similar character formed under the law of a country or territory outside the United Kingdom,
  "relevant commercial organisation" means—
    (a)   a body which is incorporated under the law of any part of the United Kingdom and which carries on a business (whether there or elsewhere),
    (b)   any other body corporate (wherever incorporated) which carries on a business, or part of a business, in any part of the United Kingdom,
    (c)   a partnership which is formed under the law of any part of the United Kingdom and which carries on a business (whether there or elsewhere), or
    (d)   any other partnership (wherever formed) which carries on a business, or part of a business, in any part of the United Kingdom,
and, for the purposes of this section, a trade or profession is a business.

NOTES
  Deferred Prosecution Agreements: see the note to s 1 at **[1.2118]**.

[1.2125]
8   Meaning of associated person
(1)   For the purposes of section 7, a person ("A") is associated with C if (disregarding any bribe under consideration) A is a person who performs services for or on behalf of C.
(2)   The capacity in which A performs services for or on behalf of C does not matter.
(3)   Accordingly A may (for example) be C's employee, agent or subsidiary.
(4)   Whether or not A is a person who performs services for or on behalf of C is to be determined by reference to all the relevant circumstances and not merely by reference to the nature of the relationship between A and C.
(5)   But if A is an employee of C, it is to be presumed unless the contrary is shown that A is a person who performs services for or on behalf of C.

[1.2126]
9   Guidance about commercial organisations preventing bribery
(1)   The Secretary of State must publish guidance about procedures that relevant commercial organisations can put in place to prevent persons associated with them from bribing as mentioned in section 7(1).
(2)   The Secretary of State may, from time to time, publish revisions to guidance under this section or revised guidance.
(3)   The Secretary of State must consult the Scottish Ministers [and the Department of Justice in Northern Ireland] before publishing anything under this section.
(4)   Publication under this section is to be in such manner as the Secretary of State considers appropriate.
(5)   Expressions used in this section have the same meaning as in section 7.

NOTES
  Sub-s (3): words in square brackets inserted by the Northern Ireland Act 1998 (Devolution of Policing and Justice Functions) Order 2012, SI 2012/2595, art 19(1), (2) (for general transitional provisions in relation to continuity and the transfer of functions etc, see arts 24–29 of that Order).

Prosecution and penalties

[1.2127]

10   Consent to prosecution

(1)   No proceedings for an offence under this Act may be instituted in England and Wales except by or with the consent of—

    (a)   the Director of Public Prosecutions, [or]

    (b)   the Director of the Serious Fraud Office, . . .

    (c)   . . .

(2)   No proceedings for an offence under this Act may be instituted in Northern Ireland except by or with the consent of—

    (a)   the Director of Public Prosecutions for Northern Ireland, or

    (b)   the Director of the Serious Fraud Office.

(3)   No proceedings for an offence under this Act may be instituted in England and Wales or Northern Ireland by a person—

    (a)   who is acting—

        (i)   under the direction or instruction of the Director of Public Prosecutions [or the Director of the Serious Fraud Office], or

        (ii)   on behalf of such a Director, or

    (b)   to whom such a function has been assigned by such a Director,

except with the consent of the Director concerned to the institution of the proceedings.

(4)   The Director of Public Prosecutions [and the Director of the Serious Fraud Office] must exercise personally any function under subsection (1), (2) or (3) of giving consent.

(5)   The only exception is if—

    (a)   the Director concerned is unavailable, and

    (b)   there is another person who is designated in writing by the Director acting personally as the person who is authorised to exercise any such function when the Director is unavailable.

(6)   In that case, the other person may exercise the function but must do so personally.

(7)   Subsections (4) to (6) apply instead of any other provisions which would otherwise have enabled any function of the Director of Public Prosecutions [or the Director of the Serious Fraud Office] under subsection (1), (2) or (3) of giving consent to be exercised by a person other than the Director concerned.

(8)   No proceedings for an offence under this Act may be instituted in Northern Ireland by virtue of section 36 of the Justice (Northern Ireland) Act 2002 (delegation of the functions of the Director of Public Prosecutions for Northern Ireland to persons other than the Deputy Director) except with the consent of the Director of Public Prosecutions for Northern Ireland to the institution of the proceedings.

(9)   The Director of Public Prosecutions for Northern Ireland must exercise personally any function under subsection (2) or (8) of giving consent unless the function is exercised personally by the Deputy Director of Public Prosecutions for Northern Ireland by virtue of section 30(4) or (7) of the Act of 2002 (powers of Deputy Director to exercise functions of Director).

(10)   Subsection (9) applies instead of section 36 of the Act of 2002 in relation to the functions of the Director of Public Prosecutions for Northern Ireland and the Deputy Director of Public Prosecutions for Northern Ireland under, or (as the case may be) by virtue of, subsections (2) and (8) above of giving consent.

NOTES

The word in square brackets in sub-s (1) was inserted, the words omitted from that subsection were repealed, and the words in square brackets in sub-ss (3), (4) and (7) were substituted, by the Public Bodies (Merger of the Director of Public Prosecutions and the Director of Revenue and Customs Prosecutions) Order 2014, SI 2014/834, art 3(3), Sch 2, para 74 (for general transitional provisions, etc, relating to the abolition of the Revenue and Customs Prosecutions Office and the transfer of the functions of the Director of Revenue and Customs Prosecutions to the Director of Public Prosecutions, see arts 4–10 of the 2014 Order).

[1.2128]

11   Penalties

(1)   An individual guilty of an offence under section 1, 2 or 6 is liable—

    (a)   on summary conviction, to imprisonment for a term not exceeding 12 months, or to a fine not exceeding the statutory maximum, or to both,

    (b)   on conviction on indictment, to imprisonment for a term not exceeding 10 years, or to a fine, or to both.

(2)   Any other person guilty of an offence under section 1, 2 or 6 is liable—

    (a)   on summary conviction, to a fine not exceeding the statutory maximum,

    (b)   on conviction on indictment, to a fine.

(3)   A person guilty of an offence under section 7 is liable on conviction on indictment to a fine.

(4)   The reference in subsection (1)(a) to 12 months is to be read—

    (a)   in its application to England and Wales in relation to an offence committed before the commencement of section 154(1) of the Criminal Justice Act 2003, and

    (b)   in its application to Northern Ireland,

as a reference to 6 months.

Other provisions about offences

[1.2129]
12 Offences under this Act: territorial application

(1) An offence is committed under section 1, 2 or 6 in England and Wales, Scotland or Northern Ireland if any act or omission which forms part of the offence takes place in that part of the United Kingdom.

(2) Subsection (3) applies if—

    (a) no act or omission which forms part of an offence under section 1, 2 or 6 takes place in the United Kingdom,

    (b) a person's acts or omissions done or made outside the United Kingdom would form part of such an offence if done or made in the United Kingdom, and

    (c) that person has a close connection with the United Kingdom.

(3) In such a case—

    (a) the acts or omissions form part of the offence referred to in subsection (2)(a), and

    (b) proceedings for the offence may be taken at any place in the United Kingdom.

(4) For the purposes of subsection (2)(c) a person has a close connection with the United Kingdom if, and only if, the person was one of the following at the time the acts or omissions concerned were done or made—

    (a) a British citizen,

    (b) a British overseas territories citizen,

    (c) a British National (Overseas),

    (d) a British Overseas citizen,

    (e) a person who under the British Nationality Act 1981 was a British subject,

    (f) a British protected person within the meaning of that Act,

    (g) an individual ordinarily resident in the United Kingdom,

    (h) a body incorporated under the law of any part of the United Kingdom,

    (i) a Scottish partnership.

(5) An offence is committed under section 7 irrespective of whether the acts or omissions which form part of the offence take place in the United Kingdom or elsewhere.

(6) Where no act or omission which forms part of an offence under section 7 takes place in the United Kingdom, proceedings for the offence may be taken at any place in the United Kingdom.

(7) Subsection (8) applies if, by virtue of this section, proceedings for an offence are to be taken in Scotland against a person.

(8) Such proceedings may be taken—

    (a) in any sheriff court district in which the person is apprehended or in custody, or

    (b) in such sheriff court district as the Lord Advocate may determine.

(9) In subsection (8) "sheriff court district" is to be read in accordance with section 307(1) of the Criminal Procedure (Scotland) Act 1995.

[1.2130]
13 Defence for certain bribery offences etc

(1) It is a defence for a person charged with a relevant bribery offence to prove that the person's conduct was necessary for—

    (a) the proper exercise of any function of an intelligence service, or

    (b) the proper exercise of any function of the armed forces when engaged on active service.

(2) The head of each intelligence service must ensure that the service has in place arrangements designed to ensure that any conduct of a member of the service which would otherwise be a relevant bribery offence is necessary for a purpose falling within subsection (1)(a).

(3) The Defence Council must ensure that the armed forces have in place arrangements designed to ensure that any conduct of—

    (a) a member of the armed forces who is engaged on active service, or

    (b) a civilian subject to service discipline when working in support of any person falling within paragraph (a),

which would otherwise be a relevant bribery offence is necessary for a purpose falling within subsection (1)(b).

(4) The arrangements which are in place by virtue of subsection (2) or (3) must be arrangements which the Secretary of State considers to be satisfactory.

(5) For the purposes of this section, the circumstances in which a person's conduct is necessary for a purpose falling within subsection (1)(a) or (b) are to be treated as including any circumstances in which the person's conduct—

    (a) would otherwise be an offence under section 2, and

    (b) involves conduct by another person which, but for subsection (1)(a) or (b), would be an offence under section 1.

(6) In this section—

    "active service" means service in—

        (a) an action or operation against an enemy,

        (b) an operation outside the British Islands for the protection of life or property, or

        (c) the military occupation of a foreign country or territory,

    "armed forces" means Her Majesty's forces (within the meaning of the Armed Forces Act 2006), "civilian subject to service discipline" and "enemy" have the same meaning as in the Act of 2006,

"GCHQ" has the meaning given by section 3(3) of the Intelligence Services Act 1994,

"head" means—

    (a)   in relation to the Security Service, the Director General of the Security Service,

    (b)   in relation to the Secret Intelligence Service, the Chief of the Secret Intelligence Service, and

    (c)   in relation to GCHQ, the Director of GCHQ,

"intelligence service" means the Security Service, the Secret Intelligence Service or GCHQ,

"relevant bribery offence" means—

    (a)   an offence under section 1 which would not also be an offence under section 6,

    (b)   an offence under section 2,

    (c)   an offence committed by aiding, abetting, counselling or procuring the commission of an offence falling within paragraph (a) or (b),

    (d)   an offence of attempting or conspiring to commit, or of inciting the commission of, an offence falling within paragraph (a) or (b), or

    (e)   an offence under Part 2 of the Serious Crime Act 2007 (encouraging or assisting crime) in relation to an offence falling within paragraph (a) or (b).

[1.2131]

14   Offences under sections 1, 2 and 6 by bodies corporate etc

(1)   This section applies if an offence under section 1, 2 or 6 is committed by a body corporate or a Scottish partnership.

(2)   If the offence is proved to have been committed with the consent or connivance of—

    (a)   a senior officer of the body corporate or Scottish partnership, or

    (b)   a person purporting to act in such a capacity,

the senior officer or person (as well as the body corporate or partnership) is guilty of the offence and liable to be proceeded against and punished accordingly.

(3)   But subsection (2) does not apply, in the case of an offence which is committed under section 1, 2 or 6 by virtue of section 12(2) to (4), to a senior officer or person purporting to act in such a capacity unless the senior officer or person has a close connection with the United Kingdom (within the meaning given by section 12(4)).

(4)   In this section—

"director", in relation to a body corporate whose affairs are managed by its members, means a member of the body corporate,

"senior officer" means—

    (a)   in relation to a body corporate, a director, manager, secretary or other similar officer of the body corporate, and

    (b)   in relation to a Scottish partnership, a partner in the partnership.

[1.2132]

15   Offences under section 7 by partnerships

(1)   Proceedings for an offence under section 7 alleged to have been committed by a partnership must be brought in the name of the partnership (and not in that of any of the partners).

(2)   For the purposes of such proceedings—

    (a)   rules of court relating to the service of documents have effect as if the partnership were a body corporate, and

    (b)   the following provisions apply as they apply in relation to a body corporate—

        (i)   section 33 of the Criminal Justice Act 1925 and Schedule 3 to the Magistrates' Courts Act 1980,

        (ii)   section 18 of the Criminal Justice Act (Northern Ireland) 1945 (c 15 (NI)) and Schedule 4 to the Magistrates' Courts (Northern Ireland) Order 1981 (SI 1981/1675 (NI 26)),

        (iii)   section 70 of the Criminal Procedure (Scotland) Act 1995.

(3)   A fine imposed on the partnership on its conviction for an offence under section 7 is to be paid out of the partnership assets.

(4)   In this section "partnership" has the same meaning as in section 7.

Supplementary and final provisions

[1.2133]

16   Application to Crown

This Act applies to individuals in the public service of the Crown as it applies to other individuals.

[1.2134]

17   Consequential provision

(1)   The following common law offences are abolished—

    (a)   the offences under the law of England and Wales and Northern Ireland of bribery and embracery,

    (b)   the offences under the law of Scotland of bribery and accepting a bribe.

(2)   Schedule 1 (which contains consequential amendments) has effect.

(3) Schedule 2 (which contains repeals and revocations) has effect.

(4) The relevant national authority may by order make such supplementary, incidental or consequential provision as the relevant national authority considers appropriate for the purposes of this Act or in consequence of this Act.

(5) The power to make an order under this section—
  (a) is exercisable by statutory instrument [(subject to subsection (9A))],
  (b) includes power to make transitional, transitory or saving provision,
  (c) may, in particular, be exercised by amending, repealing, revoking or otherwise modifying any provision made by or under an enactment (including any Act passed in the same Session as this Act).

(6) Subject to subsection (7), a statutory instrument containing an order of the Secretary of State under this section may not be made unless a draft of the instrument has been laid before, and approved by a resolution of, each House of Parliament.

(7) A statutory instrument containing an order of the Secretary of State under this section which does not amend or repeal a provision of a public general Act or of devolved legislation is subject to annulment in pursuance of a resolution of either House of Parliament.

(8) Subject to subsection (9), a statutory instrument containing an order of the Scottish Ministers under this section may not be made unless a draft of the instrument has been laid before, and approved by a resolution of, the Scottish Parliament.

(9) A statutory instrument containing an order of the Scottish Ministers under this section which does not amend or repeal a provision of an Act of the Scottish Parliament or of a public general Act is subject to annulment in pursuance of a resolution of the Scottish Parliament.

[(9A) The power of the Department of Justice in Northern Ireland to make an order under this section is exercisable by statutory rule for the purposes of the Statutory Rules (Northern Ireland) Order 1979 (and not by statutory instrument).

(9B) Subject to subsection (9C), an order of the Department of Justice in Northern Ireland made under this section is subject to affirmative resolution (within the meaning of section 41(4) of the Interpretation Act (Northern Ireland) 1954).

(9C) An order of the Department of Justice in Northern Ireland made under this section which does not amend or repeal a provision of an Act of the Northern Ireland Assembly or of a public general Act is subject to negative resolution (within the meaning of section 41(6) of the Interpretation Act (Northern Ireland) 1954).]

(10) In this section—
  "devolved legislation" means an Act of the Scottish Parliament, a Measure of the National Assembly for Wales or an Act of the Northern Ireland Assembly,
  "enactment" includes an Act of the Scottish Parliament and Northern Ireland legislation,
  "relevant national authority" means—
  (a) in the case of provision which would be within the legislative competence of the Scottish Parliament if it were contained in an Act of that Parliament, the Scottish Ministers, . . .
  [(aa) in the case of provision which could be made by an Act of the Northern Ireland Assembly without the consent of the Secretary of State (see sections 6 to 8 of the Northern Ireland Act 1998), the Department of Justice in Northern Ireland, and]
  (b) in any other case, the Secretary of State.

NOTES

The words in square brackets in sub-s (5)(a) were inserted, sub-ss (9A)–(9C) were inserted, the word omitted from para (a) of the definition "relevant national authority" was repealed, and para (aa) of that definition was inserted, by the Northern Ireland Act 1998 (Devolution of Policing and Justice Functions) Order 2012, SI 2012/2595, art 19(1), (3) (for general transitional provisions in relation to continuity and the transfer of functions etc, see arts 24–29 of that Order).

Orders: the Bribery Act 2010 (Consequential Amendments) Order 2011, SI 2011/1441.

[1.2135]
18 Extent

(1) Subject as follows, this Act extends to England and Wales, Scotland and Northern Ireland.

(2) Subject to subsections (3) to (5), any amendment, repeal or revocation made by Schedule 1 or 2 has the same extent as the provision amended, repealed or revoked.

(3) The amendment of, and repeals in, the Armed Forces Act 2006 do not extend to the Channel Islands.

(4) The amendments of the International Criminal Court Act 2001 extend to England and Wales and Northern Ireland only.

(5) Subsection (2) does not apply to the repeal in the Civil Aviation Act 1982.

[1.2136]
19 Commencement and transitional provision etc

(1) Subject to subsection (2), this Act comes into force on such day as the Secretary of State may by order made by statutory instrument appoint.

(2) Sections 16, 17(4) to (10) and 18, this section (other than subsections (5) to (7)) and section 20 come into force on the day on which this Act is passed.

(3) An order under subsection (1) may—

(a) appoint different days for different purposes,

(b) make such transitional, transitory or saving provision as the Secretary of State considers appropriate in connection with the coming into force of any provision of this Act.

(4) The Secretary of State must consult the Scottish Ministers before making an order under this section in connection with any provision of this Act which would be within the legislative competence of the Scottish Parliament if it were contained in an Act of that Parliament.

(5) This Act does not affect any liability, investigation, legal proceeding or penalty for or in respect of—

(a) a common law offence mentioned in subsection (1) of section 17 which is committed wholly or partly before the coming into force of that subsection in relation to such an offence, or

(b) an offence under the Public Bodies Corrupt Practices Act 1889 or the Prevention of Corruption Act 1906 committed wholly or partly before the coming into force of the repeal of the Act by Schedule 2 to this Act.

(6) For the purposes of subsection (5) an offence is partly committed before a particular time if any act or omission which forms part of the offence takes place before that time.

(7) Subsections (5) and (6) are without prejudice to section 16 of the Interpretation Act 1978 (general savings on repeal).

NOTES

Orders: the Bribery Act 2010 (Commencement) Order 2011, SI 2011/1418.

[1.2137]
20 Short title
This Act may be cited as the Bribery Act 2010.

SCHEDULES

SCHEDULES 1, 2

(*Schs 1, 2 contain amendments, repeals and revocations outside the scope of this work.*)

FINANCIAL SERVICES ACT 2010

(2010 c 28)

ARRANGEMENT OF SECTIONS

Measures to protect consumers

An Act to make provision amending the Financial Services and Markets Act 2000, including provision about financial education, and other provision about financial services and markets; and to make provision for the administration of court funds by the Director of Savings

[8 April 2010]

1–13 (*Outside the scope of this work.*)

Measures to protect consumers

14 (*Amends provisions of the Financial Services and Markets Act 2000 which are outside the scope of this work.*)

[1.2138]
15 Restrictions on provision of credit card cheques
(1)–(3) . . .
(4) An offence under section 51A of the CCA 1974 is to be treated for the purposes of Part 3 of the Regulatory Enforcement and Sanctions Act 2008 (civil sanctions) as contained in the CCA 1974 immediately before the day on which that Act of 2008 was passed.

NOTES

Commencement: to be appointed.

Sub-ss (1)–(3): inserted the Consumer Credit Act 1974, ss 51A, 51B (repealed) and amend Sch 1 to that Act at **[1.689]**.

16, 17 (*Amends provisions of the Financial Services and Markets Act 2000 which are outside the scope of this work.*)

Powers to require information

18 (*Amends provisions of the Financial Services and Markets Act 2000 which are outside the scope of this work.*)

[1.2139]
19 Asset protection scheme etc
(1)   The Treasury may, by notice in writing, require a person who participates (or is proposing to participate) in the asset protection scheme or a qualifying scheme—
 (a)   to provide such information, or
 (b)   to produce such documents,
as they may reasonably require for the purposes of, or in connection with, the scheme or a relevant scheme agreement.
(2)   "The asset protection scheme" means the scheme known as the Asset Protection Scheme that was the subject of a statement made by the Chancellor of the Exchequer on 26 February 2009.
(3)   "Qualifying scheme" means a scheme specified in an order made by the Treasury.
(4)   "Relevant scheme agreement" means an agreement entered into (or proposed to be entered into) under the asset protection scheme or a qualifying scheme.
(5)   The information or documents must be provided or produced at such times, and at such place, as the Treasury may specify in the notice.
(6)   The Treasury may require the information to be provided in such form as they may reasonably require.
(7)   A requirement imposed on a person as a result of this section is enforceable by an injunction or, in Scotland, by an order for specific performance under section 45 of the Court of Session Act 1988.
(8)   The Treasury may specify a scheme in an order under subsection (3) only if it appears to them that the purpose of the scheme corresponds to, or is connected with, the purpose of the asset protection scheme.
(9)   An order under subsection (3) is subject to negative resolution procedure.

20–22   (*Outside the scope of this work.*)

General

23, 24   (*Outside the scope of this work.*)

[1.2140]
25 Extent
This Act extends to England and Wales, Scotland and Northern Ireland.

[1.2141]
26 Commencement
(1)   The following provisions of this Act come into force on the day on which this Act is passed—
 (a)–(e)   (*outside the scope of this work*)
 (f)   sections 19 to 23,
 (g)   (*outside the scope of this work*)
 (h)   section 25,
 (i)   this section,
 (j)   section 27,
 (k), (l)   (*outside the scope of this work.*)
(2)   (*Outside the scope of this work.*)
(3)   The other provisions of this Act come into force on such day as the Treasury or the Secretary of State may by order appoint (and different days may be appointed for different purposes).
(4)   The Treasury or the Secretary of State may by order make such provision as they consider necessary or expedient for transitory, transitional or saving purposes in connection with the commencement of any provision made by this Act.

NOTES

Orders: the Financial Services Act 2010 (Commencement No 1 and Transitional Provision) Order 2010, SI 2010/2480.

[1.2142]
27 Short title
This Act may be cited as the Financial Services Act 2010.

SCHEDULES

SCHEDULES 1, 2

(Schs 1, 2 outside the scope of this work.)

CONSUMER INSURANCE (DISCLOSURE AND REPRESENTATIONS) ACT 2012

(2012 c 6)

ARRANGEMENT OF SECTIONS

An Act to make provision about disclosure and representations in connection with consumer insurance contracts.

[8 March 2012]

Main definitions

[1.2143]
1   Main definitions
In this Act—
   "consumer insurance contract" means a contract of insurance between—
    (a)   an individual who enters into the contract wholly or mainly for purposes unrelated to the individual's trade, business or profession, and
    (b)   a person who carries on the business of insurance and who becomes a party to the contract by way of that business (whether or not in accordance with permission for the purposes of the Financial Services and Markets Act 2000);
   "consumer" means the individual who enters into a consumer insurance contract, or proposes to do so;
   "insurer" means the person who is, or would become, the other party to a consumer insurance contract.

Pre-contract and pre-variation information

[1.2144]
2   Disclosure and representations before contract or variation
(1)   This section makes provision about disclosure and representations by a consumer to an insurer before a consumer insurance contract is entered into or varied.
(2)   It is the duty of the consumer to take reasonable care not to make a misrepresentation to the insurer.
(3)   A failure by the consumer to comply with the insurer's request to confirm or amend particulars previously given is capable of being a misrepresentation for the purposes of this Act (whether or not it could be apart from this subsection).
(4)   The duty set out in subsection (2) replaces any duty relating to disclosure or representations by a consumer to an insurer which existed in the same circumstances before this Act applied.
(5)   *Accordingly—*
  (a)   *any rule of law to the effect that a consumer insurance contract is one of the utmost good faith is modified to the extent required by the provisions of this Act, and*
  (b)   *the application of section 17 of the Marine Insurance Act 1906 (contracts of marine insurance are of utmost good faith), in relation to a contract of marine insurance which is a consumer insurance contract, is subject to the provisions of this Act.*

NOTES
Commencement: 6 April 2013.
Sub-s (5): repealed by the Insurance Act 2015, s 14(4), as from 12 August 2016.

[1.2145]
3   Reasonable care
(1)   Whether or not a consumer has taken reasonable care not to make a misrepresentation is to be determined in the light of all the relevant circumstances.
(2)   The following are examples of things which may need to be taken into account in making a determination under subsection (1)—
  (a)   the type of consumer insurance contract in question, and its target market,
  (b)   any relevant explanatory material or publicity produced or authorised by the insurer,
  (c)   how clear, and how specific, the insurer's questions were,
  (d)   in the case of a failure to respond to the insurer's questions in connection with the renewal or variation of a consumer insurance contract, how clearly the insurer communicated the importance of answering those questions (or the possible consequences of failing to do so),
  (e)   whether or not an agent was acting for the consumer.
(3)   The standard of care required is that of a reasonable consumer: but this is subject to subsections (4) and (5).
(4)   If the insurer was, or ought to have been, aware of any particular characteristics or circumstances of the actual consumer, those are to be taken into account.
(5)   A misrepresentation made dishonestly is always to be taken as showing lack of reasonable care.

NOTES
Commencement: 6 April 2013.

Qualifying misrepresentations

[1.2146]
4   Qualifying misrepresentations: definition and remedies
(1)   An insurer has a remedy against a consumer for a misrepresentation made by the consumer before a consumer insurance contract was entered into or varied only if—
  (a)   the consumer made the misrepresentation in breach of the duty set out in section 2(2), and
  (b)   the insurer shows that without the misrepresentation, that insurer would not have entered into the contract (or agreed to the variation) at all, or would have done so only on different terms.
(2)   A misrepresentation for which the insurer has a remedy against the consumer is referred to in this Act as a "qualifying misrepresentation".
(3)   The only such remedies available are set out in Schedule 1.

NOTES
Commencement: 6 April 2013.

[1.2147]
5   Qualifying misrepresentations: classification and presumptions
(1)   For the purposes of this Act, a qualifying misrepresentation (see section 4(2)) is either—
  (a)   deliberate or reckless, or
  (b)   careless.
(2)   A qualifying misrepresentation is deliberate or reckless if the consumer—

(a)   knew that it was untrue or misleading, or did not care whether or not it was untrue or misleading, and

(b)   knew that the matter to which the misrepresentation related was relevant to the insurer, or did not care whether or not it was relevant to the insurer.

(3)   A qualifying misrepresentation is careless if it is not deliberate or reckless.

(4)   It is for the insurer to show that a qualifying misrepresentation was deliberate or reckless.

(5)   But it is to be presumed, unless the contrary is shown—

(a)   that the consumer had the knowledge of a reasonable consumer, and

(b)   that the consumer knew that a matter about which the insurer asked a clear and specific question was relevant to the insurer.

NOTES
Commencement: 6 April 2013.

Specific issues

[1.2148]
6   Warranties and representations

(1)   This section applies to representations made by a consumer—

(a)   in connection with a proposed consumer insurance contract, or

(b)   in connection with a proposed variation to a consumer insurance contract.

(2)   Such a representation is not capable of being converted into a warranty by means of any provision of the consumer insurance contract (or of the terms of the variation), or of any other contract (and whether by declaring the representation to form the basis of the contract or otherwise).

NOTES
Commencement: 6 April 2013.

[1.2149]
7   Group insurance

(1)   This section applies where—

(a)   a contract of insurance is entered into by a person ("A") in order to provide cover for another person ("C"), or is varied or extended so as to do so,

(b)   C is not a party to the contract,

(c)   so far as the cover for C is concerned, the contract would have been a consumer insurance contract if entered into by C rather than by A, and

(d)   C provided information directly or indirectly to the insurer before the contract was entered into, or before it was varied or extended to provide cover for C.

(2)   So far as the cover for C is concerned—

(a)   sections 2 and 3 apply in relation to disclosure and representations by C to the insurer as if C were proposing to enter into a consumer insurance contract for the relevant cover with the insurer, and

(b)   subject to subsections (3) to (5) and the modifications in relation to the insurer's remedies set out in Part 3 of Schedule 1, the remainder of this Act applies in relation to the cover for C as if C had entered into a consumer insurance contract for that cover with the insurer.

(3)   Section 4(1)(b) applies as if it read as follows—

"(b)   the insurer shows that without the misrepresentation, that insurer would not have agreed to provide cover for C at all, or would have done so only on different terms."

(4)   If there is more than one C, a breach on the part of one of them of the duty imposed (by virtue of subsection (2)(a)) by section 2(2) does not affect the contract so far as it relates to the others.

(5)   Nothing in this section affects any duty owed by A to the insurer, or any remedy which the insurer may have against A for breach of such a duty.

NOTES
Commencement: 6 April 2013.

[1.2150]
8   Insurance on life of another

(1)   This section applies in relation to a consumer insurance contract for life insurance on the life of an individual ("L") who is not a party to the contract.

(2)   If this section applies—

(a)   information provided to the insurer by L is to be treated for the purposes of this Act as if it were provided by the person who is the party to the contract, but

(b)   in relation to such information, if anything turns on the state of mind, knowledge, circumstances or characteristics of the individual providing the information, it is to be determined by reference to L and not the party to the contract.

NOTES
Commencement: 6 April 2013.

[1.2151]
9 Agents
Schedule 2 applies for determining, for the purposes of this Act only, whether an agent through whom a consumer insurance contract is effected is the agent of the consumer or of the insurer.

NOTES
Commencement: 6 April 2013.

[1.2152]
10 Contracting out
(1) A term of a consumer insurance contract, or of any other contract, which would put the consumer in a worse position as respects the matters mentioned in subsection (2) than the consumer would be in by virtue of the provisions of this Act is to that extent of no effect.
(2) The matters are—
    (a) disclosure and representations by the consumer to the insurer before the contract is entered into or varied, and
    (b) any remedies for qualifying misrepresentations (see section 4(2)).
(3) This section does not apply in relation to a contract for the settlement of a claim arising under a consumer insurance contract.

NOTES
Commencement: 6 April 2013.

Final provision

[1.2153]
11 Consequential provision
(1) Any rule of law to the same effect as the following is abolished in relation to consumer insurance contracts—
    (a) section 18 of the Marine Insurance Act 1906 (disclosure by assured),
    (b) section 19 of that Act (disclosure by agent effecting insurance),
    (c) section 20 of that Act (representations pending negotiation of contract).
(2)–(4) . . .

NOTES
Commencement: 6 April 2013.
Sub-ss (1), (2): repealed by the Insurance Act 2015, s 21(6), as from 12 August 2016.
Sub-s (2): amends the Marine Insurance Act 1906, ss 18–20 at **[1.264]**–**[1.266]**.
Sub-ss (3), (4): amend legislation outside the scope of this work.

[1.2154]
12 Short title, commencement, application and extent
(1) This Act may be cited as the Consumer Insurance (Disclosure and Representations) Act 2012.
(2) Section 1 and this section come into force on the day on which this Act is passed, but otherwise this Act comes into force on such day as the Treasury may by order made by statutory instrument appoint.
(3) An order under subsection (2) may not appoint a day sooner than the end of the period of 1 year beginning with the day on which this Act is passed.
(4) This Act applies only in relation to consumer insurance contracts entered into, and variations to consumer insurance contracts agreed, after the Act comes into force.
In the case of group insurance (see section 7), that includes the provision of cover for C by means of an insurance contract entered into by A after the Act comes into force, or varied or extended so as to do so after the Act comes into force.
(5) Nothing in this Act affects the circumstances in which a person is bound by the acts or omissions of that person's agent.
(6) Apart from the provisions listed in subsection (7), this Act extends to England and Wales, Scotland and Northern Ireland.
(7) In section 11—
    (a) subsection (3) extends to England and Wales and Scotland only;
    (b) subsection (4) extends to Northern Ireland only.

NOTES
Orders: the Consumer Insurance (Disclosure and Representations) Act 2012 (Commencement) Order 2013, SI 2013/450.

SCHEDULES

SCHEDULE 1
INSURERS' REMEDIES FOR QUALIFYING MISREPRESENTATIONS
Section 4(3)

PART 1
CONTRACTS

General

[1.2155]

1 This Part of this Schedule applies in relation to qualifying misrepresentations made in connection with consumer insurance contracts (for variations to them, see Part 2).

Deliberate or reckless misrepresentations

2 If a qualifying misrepresentation was deliberate or reckless, the insurer—
  (a) may avoid the contract and refuse all claims, and
  (b) need not return any of the premiums paid, except to the extent (if any) that it would be unfair to the consumer to retain them.

Careless misrepresentations—claims

3 If the qualifying misrepresentation was careless, paragraphs 4 to 8 apply in relation to any claim.

4 The insurer's remedies are based on what it would have done if the consumer had complied with the duty set out in section 2(2), and paragraphs 5 to 8 are to be read accordingly.

5 If the insurer would not have entered into the consumer insurance contract on any terms, the insurer may avoid the contract and refuse all claims, but must return the premiums paid.

6 If the insurer would have entered into the consumer insurance contract, but on different terms (excluding terms relating to the premium), the contract is to be treated as if it had been entered into on those different terms if the insurer so requires.

7 In addition, if the insurer would have entered into the consumer insurance contract (whether the terms relating to matters other than the premium would have been the same or different), but would have charged a higher premium, the insurer may reduce proportionately the amount to be paid on a claim.

8 "Reduce proportionately" means that the insurer need pay on the claim only X% of what it would otherwise have been under an obligation to pay under the terms of the contract (or, if applicable, under the different terms provided for by virtue of paragraph 6), where—
    $X = $ (Premium actually charged/Higher premium) $\times 100$

Careless misrepresentations—treatment of contract for the future

9 (1) This paragraph—
  (a) applies if the qualifying misrepresentation was careless, but
  (b) does not relate to any outstanding claim.

(2) Paragraphs 5 and 6 (as read with paragraph 4) apply as they apply where a claim has been made.

(3) Paragraph 7 (as read with paragraph 4) applies in relation to a claim yet to be made as it applies in relation to a claim which has been made.

(4) If by virtue of sub-paragraph (2) or (3), the insurer would have either (or both) of the rights conferred by paragraph 6 or 7, the insurer may—
  (a) give notice to that effect to the consumer, or
  (b) terminate the contract by giving reasonable notice to the consumer.

(5) But the insurer may not terminate a contract under sub-paragraph (4)(b) if it is wholly or mainly one of life insurance.

(6) If the insurer gives notice to the consumer under sub-paragraph (4)(a), the consumer may terminate the contract by giving reasonable notice to the insurer.

(7) If either party terminates the contract under this paragraph, the insurer must refund any premiums paid for the terminated cover in respect of the balance of the contract term.

(8) Termination of the contract under this paragraph does not affect the treatment of any claim arising under the contract in the period before termination.

(9) Nothing in this paragraph affects any contractual right to terminate the contract.

NOTES

Commencement: 6 April 2013.

PART 2
VARIATIONS

[1.2156]

10 This Part of this Schedule applies in relation to qualifying misrepresentations made in connection with variations to consumer insurance contracts.

11 If the subject-matter of a variation can reasonably be treated separately from the subject-matter of the rest of the contract, Part 1 of this Schedule applies (with any necessary modifications) in relation to the variation as it applies in relation to a contract.

12 Otherwise, Part 1 applies (with any necessary modifications) as if the qualifying misrepresentation had been made in relation to the whole contract (for this purpose treated as including the variation) rather than merely in relation to the variation.

NOTES

Commencement: 6 April 2013.

PART 3
MODIFICATIONS FOR GROUP INSURANCE

[1.2157]

13 Part 1 is to be read subject to the following modifications in relation to cover provided for C under a group insurance contract as mentioned in section 7 (and in this Part "A" and "C" mean the same as in that section).

14 References to the consumer insurance contract (however described) are to that part of the contract which provides for cover for C.

15 References to claims and premiums are to claims and premiums in relation to that cover.

16 The reference to the consumer is to be read—
   (a)   in paragraph 2(b), as a reference to whoever paid the premiums, or the part of them that related to the cover for C,
   (b)   in paragraph 9(4) and (6), as a reference to A.

NOTES

Commencement: 6 April 2013.

PART 4
SUPPLEMENTARY

[1.2158]

17 Section 84 of the Marine Insurance Act 1906 (return of premium for failure of consideration) is to be read subject to the provisions of this Schedule in relation to contracts of marine insurance which are consumer insurance contracts.

NOTES

Commencement: 6 April 2013.

SCHEDULE 2
RULES FOR DETERMINING STATUS OF AGENTS

Section 9

[1.2159]

1   This Schedule sets out rules for determining, for the purposes of this Act only, whether an agent through whom a consumer insurance contract is effected is acting as the agent of the consumer or of the insurer.

2   The agent is to be taken as the insurer's agent in each of the following cases—
   (a)   when the agent does something in the agent's capacity as the appointed representative of the insurer for the purposes of the Financial Services and Markets Act 2000 (see section 39 of that Act),
   (b)   when the agent collects information from the consumer, if the insurer had given the agent express authority to do so as the insurer's agent,
   (c)   when the agent enters into the contract as the insurer's agent, if the insurer had given the agent express authority to do so.

3   (1)   In any other case, it is to be presumed that the agent is acting as the consumer's agent unless, in the light of all the relevant circumstances, it appears that the agent is acting as the insurer's agent.

(2)   Some factors which may be relevant are set out below.

(3) Examples of factors which may tend to confirm that the agent is acting for the consumer are—
   (a) the agent undertakes to give impartial advice to the consumer,
   (b) the agent undertakes to conduct a fair analysis of the market,
   (c) the consumer pays the agent a fee.

(4) Examples of factors which may tend to show that the agent is acting for the insurer are—
   (a) the agent places insurance of the type in question with only one of the insurers who provide insurance of that type,
   (b) the agent is under a contractual obligation which has the effect of restricting the number of insurers with whom the agent places insurance of the type in question,
   (c) the insurer provides insurance of the type in question through only a small proportion of the agents who deal in that type of insurance,
   (d) the insurer permits the agent to use the insurer's name in providing the agent's services,
   (e) the insurance in question is marketed under the name of the agent,
   (f) the insurer asks the agent to solicit the consumer's custom.

4 (1) If it appears to the Treasury that the list of factors in sub-paragraph (3) or (4) of paragraph 3 has become outdated, the Treasury may by order made by statutory instrument bring the list up to date by amending the sub-paragraph so as to add, omit or alter any factor.

(2) A statutory instrument containing an order under sub-paragraph (1) may not be made unless a draft of the instrument has been laid before and approved by a resolution of each House of Parliament.

NOTES

Commencement: 6 April 2013.

FINANCIAL SERVICES ACT 2012

(2012 c 21)

NOTES

Only provisions of this Act relevant to Commercial and Consumer law are reproduced. Provisions not reproduced are not annotated.

ARRANGEMENT OF SECTIONS

PART 7
OFFENCES RELATING TO FINANCIAL SERVICES

An Act to amend the Bank of England Act 1998, the Financial Services and Markets Act 2000 and the Banking Act 2009; to make other provision about financial services and markets; to make provision about the exercise of certain statutory functions relating to building societies, friendly societies and other mutual societies; to amend section 785 of the Companies Act 2006; to make provision enabling the Director of Savings to provide services to other public bodies; and for connected purposes

[19 December 2012]

PART 7
OFFENCES RELATING TO FINANCIAL SERVICES

[1.2160]
89 Misleading statements
(1) Subsection (2) applies to a person ("P") who—
   (a) makes a statement which P knows to be false or misleading in a material respect,
   (b) makes a statement which is false or misleading in a material respect, being reckless as to whether it is, or

(c)   dishonestly conceals any material facts whether in connection with a statement made by P or otherwise.

(2)   P commits an offence if P makes the statement or conceals the facts with the intention of inducing, or is reckless as to whether making it or concealing them may induce, another person (whether or not the person to whom the statement is made)—

(a)   to enter into or offer to enter into, or to refrain from entering or offering to enter into, a relevant agreement, or

(b)   to exercise, or refrain from exercising, any rights conferred by a relevant investment.

(3)   In proceedings for an offence under subsection (2) brought against a person to whom that subsection applies as a result of paragraph (a) of subsection (1), it is a defence for the person charged ("D") to show that the statement was made in conformity with—

(a)   price stabilising rules,

(b)   control of information rules, or

(c)   the relevant provisions of Commission Regulation (EC) No 2273/2003 of 22 December 2003 implementing Directive 2003/6/EC of the European Parliament and of the Council as regards exemptions for buy-back programmes and stabilisation of financial instruments.

(4)   Subsections (1) and (2) do not apply unless—

(a)   the statement is made in or from, or the facts are concealed in or from, the United Kingdom or arrangements are made in or from the United Kingdom for the statement to be made or the facts to be concealed,

(b)   the person on whom the inducement is intended to or may have effect is in the United Kingdom, or

(c)   the agreement is or would be entered into or the rights are or would be exercised in the United Kingdom.

NOTES

Commencement: 1 April 2013.

[1.2161]
90   Misleading impressions

(1)   A person ("P") who does any act or engages in any course of conduct which creates a false or misleading impression as to the market in or the price or value of any relevant investments commits an offence if—

(a)   P intends to create the impression, and

(b)   the case falls within subsection (2) or (3) (or both).

(2)   The case falls within this subsection if P intends, by creating the impression, to induce another person to acquire, dispose of, subscribe for or underwrite the investments or to refrain from doing so or to exercise or refrain from exercising any rights conferred by the investments.

(3)   The case falls within this subsection if—

(a)   P knows that the impression is false or misleading or is reckless as to whether it is, and

(b)   P intends by creating the impression to produce any of the results in subsection (4) or is aware that creating the impression is likely to produce any of the results in that subsection.

(4)   Those results are—

(a)   the making of a gain for P or another, or

(b)   the causing of loss to another person or the exposing of another person to the risk of loss.

(5)   References in subsection (4) to gain or loss are to be read in accordance with subsections (6) to (8).

(6)   "Gain" and "loss"—

(a)   extend only to gain or loss in money or other property of any kind;

(b)   include such gain or loss whether temporary or permanent.

(7)   "Gain" includes a gain by keeping what one has, as well as a gain by getting what one does not have.

(8)   "Loss" includes a loss by not getting what one might get, as well as a loss by parting with what one has.

(9)   In proceedings brought against any person ("D") for an offence under subsection (1) it is a defence for D to show—

(a)   to the extent that the offence results from subsection (2), that D reasonably believed that D's conduct would not create an impression that was false or misleading as to the matters mentioned in subsection (1),

(b)   that D acted or engaged in the conduct—

(i)   for the purpose of stabilising the price of investments, and

(ii)   in conformity with price stabilising rules,

(c)   that D acted or engaged in the conduct in conformity with control of information rules, or

(d)   that D acted or engaged in the conduct in conformity with the relevant provisions of Commission Regulation (EC) No 2273/2003 of 22 December 2003 implementing Directive 2003/6/EC of the European Parliament and of the Council as regards exemptions for buy-back programmes and stabilisation of financial instruments.

(10)   This section does not apply unless—

(a)   the act is done, or the course of conduct is engaged in, in the United Kingdom, or

(b)   the false or misleading impression is created there.

NOTES
Commencement: 1 April 2013.

[1.2162]
91   Misleading statements etc in relation to benchmarks
(1)   A person ("A") who makes to another person ("B") a false or misleading statement commits an offence if—
(a)   A makes the statement in the course of arrangements for the setting of a relevant benchmark,
(b)   A intends that the statement should be used by B for the purpose of the setting of a relevant benchmark, and
(c)   A knows that the statement is false or misleading or is reckless as to whether it is.
(2)   A person ("C") who does any act or engages in any course of conduct which creates a false or misleading impression as to the price or value of any investment or as to the interest rate appropriate to any transaction commits an offence if—
(a)   C intends to create the impression,
(b)   the impression may affect the setting of a relevant benchmark,
(c)   C knows that the impression is false or misleading or is reckless as to whether it is, and
(d)   C knows that the impression may affect the setting of a relevant benchmark.
(3)   In proceedings for an offence under subsection (1), it is a defence for the person charged ("D") to show that the statement was made in conformity with—
(a)   price stabilising rules,
(b)   control of information rules, or
(c)   the relevant provisions of Commission Regulation (EC) No 2273/2003 of 22 December 2003 implementing Directive 2003/6/EC of the European Parliament and of the Council as regards exemptions for buy-back programmes and stabilisation of financial instruments.
(4)   In proceedings brought against any person ("D") for an offence under subsection (2) it is a defence for D to show—
(a)   that D acted or engaged in the conduct—
(i)   for the purpose of stabilising the price of investments, and
(ii)   in conformity with price stabilising rules,
(b)   that D acted or engaged in the conduct in conformity with control of information rules, or
(c)   that D acted or engaged in the conduct in conformity with the relevant provisions of Commission Regulation (EC) No 2273/2003 of 22 December 2003 implementing Directive 2003/6/EC of the European Parliament and of the Council as regards exemptions for buy-back programmes and stabilisation of financial instruments.
(5)   Subsection (1) does not apply unless the statement is made in or from the United Kingdom or to a person in the United Kingdom.
(6)   Subsection (2) does not apply unless—
(a)   the act is done, or the course of conduct is engaged in, in the United Kingdom, or
(b)   the false or misleading impression is created there.

NOTES
Commencement: 1 April 2013.

[1.2163]
92   Penalties
(1)   A person guilty of an offence under this Part is liable—
(a)   on summary conviction, to imprisonment for a term not exceeding the applicable maximum term or a fine not exceeding the statutory maximum, or both;
(b)   on conviction on indictment, to imprisonment for a term not exceeding 7 years or a fine, or both.
(2)   For the purpose of subsection (1)(a) "the applicable maximum term" is—
(a)   in England and Wales, 12 months (or 6 months, if the offence was committed before the commencement of section 154(1) of the Criminal Justice Act 2003);
(b)   in Scotland, 12 months;
(c)   in Northern Ireland, 6 months.

NOTES
Commencement: 1 April 2013.

[1.2164]
93   Interpretation of Part 7
(1)   This section has effect for the interpretation of this Part.
(2)   "Investment" includes any asset, right or interest.
(3)   "Relevant agreement" means an agreement—

(a) the entering into or performance of which by either party constitutes an activity of a kind specified in an order made by the Treasury, and

(b) which relates to a relevant investment.

(4) "Relevant benchmark" means a benchmark of a kind specified in an order made by the Treasury.

(5) "Relevant investment" means an investment of a kind specified in an order made by the Treasury.

(6) Schedule 2 to FSMA 2000 (except paragraphs 25 and 26) applies for the purposes of subsections (3) and (5) with references to section 22 of that Act being read as references to each of those subsections.

(7) Nothing in Schedule 2 to FSMA 2000, as applied by subsection (6), limits the power conferred by subsection (3) or (5).

(8) "Price stabilising rules" and "control of information rules" have the same meaning as in FSMA 2000.

(9) In this section "benchmark" has the meaning given in section 22(6) of FSMA 2000.

NOTES

Commencement: 24 January 2013.

Orders: the Financial Services Act 2012 (Misleading Statements and Impressions) Order 2013, SI 2013/637; the Financial Services and Markets Act 2000 (Regulated Activities) (Amendment) Order 2015, SI 2015/369.

[1.2165]
94 Affirmative procedure for certain orders

(1) This section applies to the first order made under section 93.

(2) This section also applies to any subsequent order made under that section which contains a statement by the Treasury that the effect of the proposed order would include one or more of the following—

(a) that an activity which is not specified for the purposes of subsection (3)(a) of that section would become one so specified,

(b) that an investment which is not a relevant investment would become a relevant investment;

(c) that a benchmark which is not a relevant benchmark would become a relevant benchmark.

(3) A statutory instrument containing (alone or with other provisions) an order to which this section applies may not be made unless a draft of the instrument has been laid before Parliament and approved by a resolution of each House.

NOTES

Commencement: 24 January 2013.

95 Consequential repeal

(*Repeals FSMA 2000, s 397 (which related to misleading statements and practices and is superseded by the provisions of this Part).*)

PART 9
MISCELLANEOUS

Consumer credit

[1.2166]
107 Power to make further provision about regulation of consumer credit

(1) Subsection (2) applies on or at any time after the making, after the passing of this Act, of an order under section 22 of FSMA 2000 which has the effect that an activity (a "transferred activity")—

(a) ceases to be an activity in respect of which a licence under section 21 of CCA 1974 is required or would be required but for the exemption conferred by subsection (2), (3) or (4) of that section or paragraph 15(3) of Schedule 3 to FSMA 2000, and

(b) becomes a regulated activity for the purposes of FSMA 2000.

(2) The Treasury may by order do any one or more of the following—

(a) transfer to the FCA functions of the OFT under any provision of CCA 1974 that remains in force;

(b) provide that any specified provision of FSMA 2000 which relates to the powers or duties of the FCA in connection with the failure of any person to comply with a requirement imposed by or under FSMA 2000 is to apply, subject to any specified modifications, in connection with the failure of any person to comply with a requirement imposed by or under a specified provision of CCA 1974;

(c) require the FCA to issue a statement of policy in relation to the exercise of powers conferred on it by virtue of paragraph (b);

(d) in connection with provision made by virtue of paragraph (b), provide that failure to comply with a specified provision of CCA 1974 no longer constitutes an offence or that a person may not be convicted of an offence under a specified provision of CCA 1974 in respect of an act or omission in a case where the FCA has exercised specified powers in relation to that person in respect of that act or omission;

(e)   provide for the transfer to the Treasury of any functions under CCA 1974 previously exercisable by the Secretary of State;

(f)   provide that functions of the Secretary of State under CCA 1974 are exercisable concurrently with the Treasury;

(g)   *provide for any provision of sections 162 to 165 and 174A of CCA 1974 which relates to—*

     (i)   *the powers of a local weights and measures authority in Great Britain or the Department of Enterprise, Trade and Investment in Northern Ireland in relation to compliance with any provision made by or under CCA 1974,*

     (ii)   *the powers of such an authority or that Department in relation to the commission or suspected commission of offences under any provision made by or under CCA 1974,*

     (iii)   *the powers that may be conferred by warrant on an officer of such an authority or that Department, or*

     (iv)   *things done in the exercise of any of those powers,*

     to apply in relation to compliance with FSMA 2000 so far as relating to relevant regulated activities, in relation to the commission or suspected commission of a relevant offence or in relation to things done in the exercise of any of those powers as applied by the order;

(h)   enable local weights and measures authorities to institute proceedings in England and Wales for a relevant offence;

(i)   enable the Department of Enterprise, Trade and Investment in Northern Ireland to institute proceedings in Northern Ireland for a relevant offence;

(j)   provide that references in a specified enactment to the FCA's functions under FSMA 2000 include references to its functions resulting from any order under this section.

(3)   If an order under this section makes provision by virtue of subsection (2)(b) enabling the FCA to exercise any of its powers under sections 205 to 206A of FSMA 2000 (disciplinary measures) by reference to an act or omission that constitutes an offence under CCA 1974, the order must also make provision by virtue of subsection (2)(d) ensuring that a person in respect of whom the power has been exercised cannot subsequently be convicted of the offence by reference to the same act or omission.

(4)   In subsection *(2)(g) to (i)*—

(a)   "relevant regulated activity" means an activity that is a regulated activity for the purposes of FSMA 2000 by virtue of—

     (i)   an order made under section 22(1) of that Act in relation to an investment of a kind falling within paragraph 23 or 23B of Schedule 2 to that Act, or

     (ii)   an order made under section 22(1A)(a) of that Act;

(b)   "relevant offence" means an offence under FSMA 2000 committed in relation to such an activity.

(5)   The Treasury may make provision by virtue of subsection (2)(i) only with the consent of the Department of Enterprise, Trade and Investment in Northern Ireland.

(6)   On or at any time after the making of an order under section 22 of FSMA 2000 of the kind mentioned in subsection (1), the Treasury may by order—

(a)   exclude the application of any provision of CCA 1974 in relation to a transferred activity, or

(b)   repeal any provision of CCA 1974 which relates to a transferred activity.

(7)   In exercising their powers under this section, the Treasury must have regard to—

(a)   the importance of securing an appropriate degree of protection for consumers, and

(b)   the principle that a burden or restriction which is imposed on a person, or on the carrying on of an activity, should be proportionate to the benefits, considered in general terms, which are expected to result from the imposition of that burden or restriction.

(8)   The additional powers conferred by section 115(2) on a person making an order under this Act include power for the Treasury, when making an order under this section—

(a)   to make such consequential provision as the Treasury consider appropriate;

(b)   to amend any enactment, including any provision of, or made under, this Act.

(9)   The provisions of this section do not limit—

(a)   the powers conferred by section 118 or by section 22 of FSMA 2000, or

(b)   the powers exercisable under Schedule 21 in connection with the transfer of functions from the OFT.

(10)   In this section—

     "CCA 1974" means the Consumer Credit Act 1974;

     "consumers" has the meaning given in section 1G of FSMA 2000;

     "the OFT" means the Office of Fair Trading.

NOTES

Commencement: 1 April 2013.

In sub-s (2) para (g) is repealed, and for the words in italics in sub-s (4) there are substituted the words "(2)(h) and (i)", by the Consumer Rights Act 2015, s 77, Sch 6, para 84, as from 1 October 2015 (for transitional provisions see the Consumer Rights Act 2015 (Commencement No 3, Transitional Provisions, Savings and Consequential Amendments) Order 2015, SI 2015/1630, arts 6–8 at **[2.1220]** et seq).

Office of Fair Trading: as to the abolition of the OFT, see the Enterprise and Regulatory Reform Act 2013, s 26. The OFT (and the Competition Commission) was replaced by the Competition and Markets Authority as from 1 April 2014. See also the Enterprise and Regulatory Reform Act 2013 (Commencement No 6, Transitional Provisions and Savings) Order 2014, SI 2014/416 (at **[2.1125]**). The Schedule to that Order contains various transitional provisions relating to the abolition of the OFT, including provisions relating to continuity, and provisions relating to existing references to the OFT.

Orders: the Financial Services Act 2012 (Consumer Credit) Order 2013, SI 2013/1882 at **[2.1048]**. As to Orders made under this section, see also the Financial Services and Markets Act 2000 (Regulated Activities) (Amendment) (No 2) Order 2013, SI 2013/1881, art 66 at **[2.1004]**.

---

108 Suspension of licences under Part 3 of Consumer Credit Act 1974
(*Amends the Consumer Credit Act 1974, ss 32, 33, 33A, 34A, 41, and inserts ss 32A, 32B and 34ZA (see the 1974 Act at* **[1.520]** *et seq). Note that sub-s (8) of this section provides that nothing in this section affects the powers conferred by s 22 of FSMA 2000 or s 107 of this Act.*)

SCRAP METAL DEALERS ACT 2013

(2013 c 10)

ARRANGEMENT OF SECTIONS

Licensing of scrap metal dealers

SCHEDULES

An Act to amend the law relating to scrap metal dealers; and for connected purposes

[28 February 2013]

Licensing of scrap metal dealers

[1.2167]
1   Requirement for licence to carry on business as scrap metal dealer
(1)   No person may carry on business as a scrap metal dealer unless authorised by a licence under this Act (a "scrap metal licence").
(2)   See section 21 for the meaning of "carry on business as a scrap metal dealer".

(3) A person who carries on business as a scrap metal dealer in breach of subsection (1) is guilty of an offence and is liable on summary conviction to a fine not exceeding level 5 on the standard scale.

NOTES

Commencement: 1 October 2013 (sub-ss (1), (2)); 1 December 2013 (otherwise).

Transitional provisions: the Scrap Metal Dealers Act 2013 (Commencement and Transitional Provisions) Order 2013, SI 2013/1966, art 5 provides as follows—

"**5   Transitional provisions**

(1) A scrap metal dealer who, immediately before 1st October 2013, was registered under either section 1 of the Scrap Metal Dealers Act 1964 or section 1 of the Vehicles (Crime) Act 2001 shall be deemed to be authorised by a licence under section 1 of the 2013 Act, and references in this article to a "deemed licence" shall be construed accordingly.

(2) Subject to paragraphs (3) and (5), a deemed licence has effect from 1st October 2013 until the local authority to whom he applies for a licence either issues him with a licence or gives him a notice of the decision to refuse him a licence.

(3) If a scrap metal dealer who was so previously registered fails to submit an application for a licence on or before 15th October 2013, his deemed licence will lapse on 16th October 2013.

(4) The lapsing of the deemed licence on 16th October 2013 shall not be treated as a revocation of the deemed licence, and does not give rise to a right of appeal under paragraph 9(2)(b) of Schedule 1 to the 2013 Act.

(5) Where a scrap metal dealer who was so previously registered applies for a licence on or before 15th October, and the local authority refuses his application for a licence, this refusal shall only come into effect when no appeal under paragraph 9 of Schedule 1 to the 2013 Act is possible in relation to the refusal, or when any such appeal is finally determined or withdrawn.

(6) Pending an appeal against the refusal of an application for a licence, if the authority considers that the deemed licence should not continue in force without conditions, it may, by notice, provide that until the refusal comes into effect, the deemed licence is subject to one or both of the conditions set out in section 3(8) of the 2013 Act.

(7) The obligations of the Environment Agency and Natural Resources Body for Wales in section 7(1) to (3) of the 2013 Act (register of licences) do not apply in relation to deemed licences.

(8) The obligations in section 10 (display of licence) do not apply to deemed licences."

[1.2168]
2   Form and effect of licence

(1) A scrap metal licence is to be issued by a local authority.

(2) A licence must be one of the following types—

   (a)   a site licence, or

   (b)   a collector's licence.

(3) A site licence authorises the licensee to carry on business at any site in the authority's area which is identified in the licence.

(4) A site licence must—

   (a)   name the licensee,

   (b)   name the authority,

   (c)   identify all the sites in the authority's area at which the licensee is authorised to carry on business,

   (d)   name the site manager of each site, and

   (e)   state the date on which the licence is due to expire.

(5) A collector's licence authorises the licensee to carry on business as a mobile collector in the authority's area.

(6) A collector's licence must—

   (a)   name the licensee,

   (b)   name the authority, and

   (c)   state the date on which the licence is due to expire.

(7) A licence is to be in a form which—

   (a)   complies with subsection (4) or (6), and

   (b)   enables the licensee to comply with section 10 (display of licence).

(8) The Secretary of State may in regulations prescribe further requirements as to the form and content of licences.

(9) A person may hold more than one licence issued by different local authorities, but may not hold more than one licence issued by any one authority.

NOTES

Commencement: 1 October 2013.

[1.2169]
3   Issue of licence

(1) A local authority must not issue or renew a scrap metal licence unless it is satisfied that the applicant is a suitable person to carry on business as a scrap metal dealer.

(2) In determining whether the applicant is a suitable person, the authority may have regard to any information which it considers to be relevant, including in particular—

   (a)   whether the applicant or any site manager has been convicted of any relevant offence;

   (b)   whether the applicant or any site manager has been the subject of any relevant enforcement action;

(c)   any previous refusal of an application for the issue or renewal of a scrap metal licence (and the reasons for the refusal);

(d)   any previous refusal of an application for a relevant environmental permit or registration (and the reasons for the refusal);

(e)   any previous revocation of a scrap metal licence (and the reasons for the revocation);

(f)   whether the applicant has demonstrated that there will be in place adequate procedures to ensure that the provisions of this Act are complied with.

(3)   In this section—

(a)   "site manager" means an individual proposed to be named in the licence as a site manager,

(b)   "relevant offence" means an offence which is prescribed for the purposes of this section in regulations made by the Secretary of State, and

(c)   "relevant enforcement action" means enforcement action which is so prescribed.

(4)   In determining whether a company is a suitable person to carry on business as a scrap metal dealer, a local authority is to have regard, in particular, to whether any of the following is a suitable person—

(a)   any director of the company;

(b)   any secretary of the company;

(c)   any shadow director of the company (that is to say, any person in accordance with whose directions or instructions the directors of the company are accustomed to act).

(5)   In determining whether a partnership is a suitable person to carry on business as a scrap metal dealer, a local authority is to have regard, in particular, to whether each of the partners is a suitable person.

(6)   The authority must also have regard to any guidance on determining suitability which is issued from time to time by the Secretary of State.

(7)   The authority may consult other persons regarding the suitability of an applicant, including in particular—

(a)   any other local authority;

(b)   the Environment Agency;

(c)   the Natural Resources Body for Wales;

(d)   an officer of a police force.

(8)   If the applicant or any site manager has been convicted of a relevant offence, the authority may include in the licence one or both of the following conditions—

(a)   that the dealer must not receive scrap metal except between 9 am and 5 pm on any day;

(b)   that all scrap metal received must be kept in the form in which it is received for a specified period, not exceeding 72 hours, beginning with the time when it is received.

(9)   "Specified" means specified in the condition.

NOTES

Commencement: 1 October 2013.

Transitional provisions: see the note to s 1 at **[1.2167]**.

Regulations: the Scrap Metal Dealers Act 2013 (Prescribed Relevant Offences and Relevant Enforcement Action) Regulations 2013, SI 2013/2258.

[1.2170]

4 Revocation of licence and imposition of conditions

(1)   The authority may revoke a scrap metal licence if it is satisfied that the licensee does not carry on business at any of the sites identified in the licence.

(2)   The authority may revoke a licence if it is satisfied that a site manager named in the licence does not act as site manager at any of the sites identified in the licence.

(3)   The authority may revoke a licence if it is no longer satisfied that the licensee is a suitable person to carry on business as a scrap metal dealer.

(4)   Section 3(2) to (7) apply for the purposes of subsection (3).

(5)   If the licensee or any site manager named in a licence is convicted of a relevant offence, the authority may vary the licence by adding one or both of the conditions set out in section 3(8).

(6)   A revocation or variation under this section comes into effect when no appeal under paragraph 9 of Schedule 1 is possible in relation to the revocation or variation, or when any such appeal is finally determined or withdrawn.

(7)   But if the authority considers that the licence should not continue in force without conditions, it may by notice provide—

(a)   that, until a revocation under this section comes into effect, the licence is subject to one or both of the conditions set out in section 3(8), or

(b)   that a variation under this section comes into effect immediately.

(8)   In this section "the authority" means the local authority which issued the licence.

NOTES

Commencement: 1 October 2013.

[1.2171]
5 Further provision about licences
Schedule 1 (which makes further provision about licences) has effect.

NOTES
Commencement: 1 September 2013 (certain purposes); 1 October 2013 (otherwise).

[1.2172]
6 Supply of information by authority
(1)   This section applies to information which has been supplied to a local authority under this Act and relates to a scrap metal licence or to an application for or relating to a licence.

(2)   The local authority must supply any such information to any of the following persons who requests it for purposes relating to this Act—

   (a)   any other local authority;

   (b)   the Environment Agency;

   (c)   the Natural Resources Body for Wales;

   (d)   an officer of a police force.

(3)   This section does not limit any other power the authority has to supply that information.

NOTES
Commencement: 1 October 2013.

[1.2173]
7 Register of licences
(1)   The Environment Agency must maintain a register of scrap metal licences issued by authorities in England.

(2)   The Natural Resources Body for Wales must maintain a register of scrap metal licences issued by authorities in Wales.

(3)   Each entry in the registers must record—

   (a)   the name of the authority which issued the licence,

   (b)   the name of the licensee,

   (c)   any trading name of the licensee,

   (d)   the address of any site identified in the licence,

   (e)   the type of licence, and

   (f)   the date on which the licence is due to expire.

(4)   The registers are to be open for inspection to the public.

(5)   The Environment Agency or the Natural Resources Body for Wales may combine its register with any other register maintained by it.

NOTES
Commencement: 1 October 2013.
Transitional provisions: see the note to s 1 at **[1.2167]**.

[1.2174]
8 Notification requirements
(1)   An applicant for a scrap metal licence, or for the renewal or variation of a licence, must notify the authority to which the application was made of any changes which materially affect the accuracy of the information which the applicant has provided in connection with the application.

(2)   A licensee who is not carrying on business as a scrap metal dealer in the area of the authority which issued the licence must notify the authority of that fact.

(3)   Notification under subsection (2) must be given within 28 days of the beginning of the period in which the licensee is not carrying on business in that area while licensed.

(4)   If a licensee carries on business under a trading name, the licensee must notify the authority which issued the licence of any change to that name.

(5)   Notification under subsection (4) must be given within 28 days of the change occurring.

(6)   An authority must notify the relevant environment body of—

   (a)   any notification given to the authority under subsection (2) or (4),

   (b)   any variation made by the authority under paragraph 3 of Schedule 1 (variation of type of licence or matters set out in licence), and

   (c)   any revocation by the authority of a licence.

(7)   Notification under subsection (6) must be given within 28 days of the notification, variation or revocation in question.

(8)   Where an authority notifies the relevant environment body under subsection (6), the body must amend the register under section 7 accordingly.

(9)   An applicant or licensee who fails to comply with this section is guilty of an offence and is liable on summary conviction to a fine not exceeding level 3 on the standard scale.

(10)   It is a defence for a person charged with an offence under this section to prove that the person took all reasonable steps to avoid committing the offence.

(11)   In this section "the relevant environment body" means—

(a)   for an authority in England, the Environment Agency;
(b)   for an authority in Wales, the Natural Resources Body for Wales.

NOTES
Commencement: 1 October 2013 (sub-ss (1)–(8), (11)); 1 December 2013 (otherwise).

[1.2175]
9   Closure of unlicensed sites
Schedule 2 (which makes provision for the closure of sites at which a scrap metal business is being carried on without a licence) has effect.

NOTES
Commencement: 1 December 2013.

Conduct of business

[1.2176]
10   Display of licence
(1)   A scrap metal dealer who holds a site licence must display a copy of the licence at each site identified in the licence.
(2)   The copy must be displayed in a prominent place in an area accessible to the public.
(3)   A scrap metal dealer who holds a collector's licence must display a copy of the licence on any vehicle that is being used in the course of the dealer's business.
(4)   The copy must be displayed in a manner which enables it easily to be read by a person outside the vehicle.
(5)   A scrap metal dealer who fails to comply with this section is guilty of an offence and is liable on summary conviction to a fine not exceeding level 3 on the standard scale.

NOTES
Commencement: 1 October 2013 (sub-ss (1)–(4)); 1 December 2013 (otherwise).
Transitional provisions: see the note to s 1 at **[1.2167]**.

[1.2177]
11   Verification of supplier's identity
(1)   A scrap metal dealer must not receive scrap metal from a person without verifying the person's full name and address.
(2)   That verification must be by reference to documents, data or other information obtained from a reliable and independent source.
(3)   The Secretary of State may prescribe in regulations—
    (a)   documents, data or other information which are sufficient for the purpose of subsection (2);
    (b)   documents, data or other information which are not sufficient for that purpose.
(4)   If a scrap metal dealer receives scrap metal in breach of subsection (1), each of the following is guilty of an offence—
    (a)   the scrap metal dealer;
    (b)   if the metal is received at a site, the site manager;
    (c)   any person who, under arrangements made by a person within paragraph (a) or (b), has responsibility for verifying the name and address.
(5)   It is a defence for a person within subsection (4)(a) or (b) who is charged with an offence under subsection (4) to prove that the person—
    (a)   made arrangements to ensure that the metal was not received in breach of subsection (1), and
    (b)   took all reasonable steps to ensure that those arrangements were complied with.
(6)   A person guilty of an offence under subsection (4) is liable on summary conviction to a fine not exceeding level 3 on the standard scale.
(7)   A person who, on delivering scrap metal to a scrap metal dealer, gives a false name or false address is guilty of an offence and is liable on summary conviction to a fine not exceeding level 3 on the standard scale.

NOTES
Commencement: 1 October 2013 (sub-ss (1)–(3)); 1 December 2013 (otherwise).
Regulations: Scrap Metal Dealers Act 2013 (Prescribed Documents and Information for Verification of Name and Address) Regulations 2013, SI 2013/2276.

[1.2178]
12   Offence of buying scrap metal for cash etc
(1)   A scrap metal dealer must not pay for scrap metal except—
    (a)   by a cheque which under section 81A of the Bills of Exchange Act 1882 is not transferable, or
    (b)   by an electronic transfer of funds (authorised by credit or debit card or otherwise).
(2)   The Secretary of State may by order amend subsection (1) to permit other methods of payment.

(3)　In this section paying includes paying in kind (with goods or services).

(4)　If a scrap metal dealer pays for scrap metal in breach of subsection (1), each of the following is guilty of an offence—

    (a)　the scrap metal dealer;

    (b)　if the payment is made at a site, the site manager;

    (c)　any person who makes the payment acting for the dealer.

(5)　It is a defence for a person within subsection (4)(a) or (b) who is charged with an offence under this section to prove that the person—

    (a)　made arrangements to ensure that the payment was not made in breach of subsection (1), and

    (b)　took all reasonable steps to ensure that those arrangements were complied with.

(6)　A person guilty of an offence under this section is liable on summary conviction to a fine not exceeding level 5 on the standard scale.

NOTES

    Commencement: 1 October 2013.

[1.2179]

13　Records: receipt of metal

(1)　This section applies if a scrap metal dealer receives any scrap metal in the course of the dealer's business.

(2)　The dealer must record the following information—

    (a)　the description of the metal, including its type (or types if mixed), form, condition, weight and any marks identifying previous owners or other distinguishing features;

    (b)　the date and time of its receipt;

    (c)　if the metal is delivered in or on a vehicle, the registration mark (within the meaning of section 23 of the Vehicle Excise and Registration Act 1994) of the vehicle;

    (d)　if the metal is received from a person, the full name and address of that person;

    (e)　if the dealer pays for the metal, the full name of the person who makes the payment acting for the dealer.

(3)　If the dealer receives the metal from a person, the dealer must keep a copy of any document which the dealer uses to verify the name or address of that person.

(4)　If the dealer pays for the metal by cheque, the dealer must keep a copy of the cheque.

(5)　If the dealer pays for the metal by electronic transfer—

    (a)　the dealer must keep the receipt identifying the transfer, or

    (b)　if no receipt identifying the transfer was obtained, the dealer must record particulars identifying the transfer.

NOTES

    Commencement: 1 October 2013.

[1.2180]

14　Records: disposal of metal

(1)　This section applies if a scrap metal dealer disposes of any scrap metal in the course of the dealer's business.

(2)　For these purposes metal is disposed of—

    (a)　whether or not it is in the same form in which it was received;

    (b)　whether or not the disposal is to another person;

    (c)　whether or not the metal is despatched from a site.

(3)　Where the disposal is in the course of business under a site licence, the dealer must record the following information—

    (a)　the description of the metal, including its type (or types if mixed), form and weight;

    (b)　the date and time of its disposal;

    (c)　if the disposal is to another person, the full name and address of that person;

    (d)　if the dealer receives payment for the metal (whether by way of sale or exchange), the price or other consideration received.

(4)　Where the disposal is in the course of business under a collector's licence, the dealer must record the following information—

    (a)　the date and time of the disposal;

    (b)　if the disposal is to another person, the full name and address of that person.

NOTES

    Commencement: 1 October 2013.

[1.2181]

15　Records: supplementary

(1)　The information mentioned in sections 13(2) and (5) and 14(3) and (4) must be recorded in a manner which allows the information and the scrap metal to which it relates to be readily identified by reference to each other.

(2)   The records mentioned in section 13(3) and (4) must be marked so as to identify the scrap metal to which they relate.

(3)   The dealer must keep the information and other records mentioned in sections 13(2) to (5) and 14(3) and (4) for a period of 3 years beginning with the day on which the metal is received or (as the case may be) disposed of.

(4)   If a scrap metal dealer fails to fulfil a requirement under section 13 or 14 or this section, each of the following is guilty of an offence—

    (a)   the scrap metal dealer;

    (b)   if the metal is received at or (as the case may be) despatched from a site, the site manager;

    (c)   any person who, under arrangements made by a person within paragraph (a) or (b), has responsibility for fulfilling the requirement.

(5)   It is a defence for a person within subsection (4)(a) or (b) who is charged with an offence under this section to prove that the person—

    (a)   made arrangements to ensure that the requirement was fulfilled, and

    (b)   took all reasonable steps to ensure that those arrangements were complied with.

(6)   A person guilty of an offence under this section is liable on summary conviction to a fine not exceeding level 5 on the standard scale.

NOTES

Commencement: 1 October 2013 (sub-s (1)–(3)); 1 December 2013 (otherwise).

Supplementary

[1.2182]
16   Right to enter and inspect
(1)   A constable or an officer of a local authority may enter and inspect a licensed site at any reasonable time on notice to the site manager.

(2)   A constable or an officer of a local authority may enter and inspect a licensed site at any reasonable time, otherwise than on notice to the site manager, if—

    (a)   reasonable attempts to give such notice have been made and have failed, or

    (b)   entry to the site is reasonably required for the purpose of ascertaining whether the provisions of this Act are being complied with or investigating offences under it and (in either case) the giving of notice would defeat that purpose.

(3)   Subsections (1) and (2) do not apply to residential premises.

(4)   A constable or an officer of a local authority is not entitled to use force to enter premises in the exercise of the powers under subsections (1) and (2).

(5)   A justice of the peace may issue a warrant authorising entry (in accordance with subsection (7)) to any premises within subsection (6) if the justice is satisfied by information on oath that there are reasonable grounds for believing that entry to the premises is reasonably required for the purpose of—

    (a)   securing compliance with the provisions of this Act, or

    (b)   ascertaining whether those provisions are being complied with.

(6)   Premises are within this subsection if—

    (a)   the premises are a licensed site, or

    (b)   the premises are not a licensed site but there are reasonable grounds for believing that the premises are being used by a scrap metal dealer in the course of business.

(7)   The warrant is a warrant signed by the justice which—

    (a)   specifies the premises concerned, and

    (b)   authorises a constable or an officer of a local authority to enter and inspect the premises at any time within one month from the date of the warrant.

(8)   A constable or an officer of a local authority may, if necessary, use reasonable force in the exercise of the powers under a warrant under subsection (5).

(9)   A constable or an officer of a local authority may—

    (a)   require production of, and inspect, any scrap metal kept at any premises mentioned in subsection (1) or (2) or in a warrant under subsection (5);

    (b)   require production of, and inspect, any records kept in accordance with section 13 or 14 and any other records relating to payment for scrap metal;

    (c)   take copies of or extracts from any such records.

(10)   Subsection (11) applies if a constable or an officer of a local authority ("the officer") seeks to exercise powers under this section in relation to any premises.

(11)   If the owner, occupier or other person in charge of the premises requires the officer to produce—

    (a)   evidence of the officer's identity, or

    (b)   evidence of the officer's authority to exercise those powers,

the officer must produce that evidence.

(12)   In the case of an officer of a local authority, the powers under this section are exercisable only in relation to premises in the area of the authority.

(13)   A person who—

    (a)   obstructs the exercise of a right of entry or inspection under this section, or

    (b)   fails to produce a record required to be produced under this section, is guilty of an offence and is liable on summary conviction to a fine not exceeding level 3 on the standard scale.

NOTES

Commencement: 1 October 2013.

[1.2183]
17 Offences by bodies corporate
(1)   Where an offence under this Act is committed by a body corporate and is proved—
  (a)   to have been committed with the consent or connivance of a director, manager, secretary or other similar officer, or
  (b)   to be attributable to any neglect on the part of any such individual,
the individual as well as the body corporate is guilty of the offence and is liable to be proceeded against and punished accordingly.
(2)   Where the affairs of a body corporate are managed by its members, subsection (1) applies in relation to the acts and omissions of a member in connection with that management as if the member were a director of the body corporate.

NOTES

Commencement: 1 October 2013.

[1.2184]
18 Review of Act
(1)   Before the end of 5 years beginning with the day on which section 1 comes into force, the Secretary of State must—
  (a)   carry out a review of this Act, and
  (b)   publish a report of the conclusions of the review.
(2)   The report must in particular—
  (a)   set out the objectives intended to be achieved by this Act,
  (b)   assess the extent to which those objectives have been achieved, and
  (c)   assess whether it is appropriate to retain or repeal the Act or any of its provisions in order to achieve those objectives.

NOTES

Commencement: 1 October 2013.

19   (*Repeals the Scrap Metal Dealers Act 1964, and contains amendments to the Local Government (Wales) Act 1994, the Vehicle Excise and Registration Act 1994, the Vehicles (Crime) Act 2001, the Legal Aid, Sentencing and Punishment of Offenders Act 2012, the Communications Act 2003, and the Regulatory Enforcement and Sanctions Act 2008.*)

[1.2185]
20 Orders and regulations
(1)   Any power to make an order or regulations under this Act is exercisable by statutory instrument.
(2)   A statutory instrument containing an order or regulations under this Act, other than an order under section 12(2), 21(8) or 23(2), is subject to annulment in pursuance of a resolution of either House of Parliament.
(3)   A statutory instrument containing an order under section 12(2) or 21(8) may not be made unless a draft of the instrument has been laid before and approved by a resolution of each House of Parliament.
(4)   Any power to make an order or regulations under this Act—
  (a)   may be exercised so as to make different provision for different purposes;
  (b)   includes power to make such incidental, supplementary, consequential, transitory, transitional or saving provision as the Secretary of State considers appropriate.

NOTES

Commencement: 28 February 2013.

[1.2186]
21 "Carrying on business as a scrap metal dealer" and "scrap metal"
(1)   The following provisions apply for the purposes of this Act.
(2)   A person carries on business as a scrap metal dealer if the person—
  (a)   carries on a business which consists wholly or partly in buying or selling scrap metal, whether or not the metal is sold in the form in which it was bought, or
  (b)   carries on business as a motor salvage operator (so far as that does not fall within paragraph (a)).
(3)   For the purposes of subsection (2)(a), a person who manufactures articles is not to be regarded as selling scrap metal if that person sells scrap metal only as a by-product of manufacturing articles or as surplus materials not required for manufacturing them.

(4)   For the purposes of subsection (2)(b), a person carries on business as a motor salvage operator if the person carries on a business which consists—

    (a)   wholly or partly in recovering salvageable parts from motor vehicles for re-use or sale and subsequently selling or otherwise disposing of the rest of the vehicle for scrap,

    (b)   wholly or mainly in buying written-off vehicles and subsequently repairing and reselling them,

    (c)   wholly or mainly in buying or selling motor vehicles which are to be the subject (whether immediately or on a subsequent re-sale) of any of the activities mentioned in paragraphs (a) and (b), or

    (d)   wholly or mainly in activities falling within paragraphs (b) and (c).

(5)   "Scrap metal dealer" means a person who is for the time being carrying on business as a scrap metal dealer, whether or not authorised by a licence.

(6)   "Scrap metal" includes—

    (a)   any old, waste or discarded metal or metallic material, and

    (b)   any product, article or assembly which is made from or contains metal and is broken, worn out or regarded by its last holder as having reached the end of its useful life.

(7)   But the following are not scrap metal—

    (a)   gold,

    (b)   silver, and

    (c)   any alloy of which 2 per cent or more by weight is attributable to gold or silver.

(8)   The Secretary of State may by order amend the definition of "scrap metal" for the purposes of this Act (whether by amending subsection (6) or (7) or otherwise).

NOTES

Commencement: 1 October 2013.

[1.2187]
22   Other definitions

(1)   The following provisions apply for the purposes of this Act.

(2)   "Licensed site" means a site identified in a scrap metal licence.

(3)   "Local authority" means—

    (a)   in relation to England, the council of a district, the Common Council of the City of London or the council of a London borough;

    (b)   in relation to Wales, the council of a county or a county borough.

(4)   "Mobile collector" means a person who—

    (a)   carries on business as a scrap metal dealer otherwise than at a site, and

    (b)   regularly engages, in the course of that business, in collecting waste materials and old, broken, worn out or defaced articles by means of visits from door to door.

(5)   "Officer of a police force" includes a constable of the British Transport Police Force.

(6)   "Premises" includes any land or other place (whether enclosed or not).

(7)   "Relevant environmental permit or registration", in relation to an application made to a local authority, means—

    (a)   any environmental permit under regulation 13 of the Environmental (Permitting) Regulations 2010 (SI 2010/675) authorising any operation by the applicant in the local authority's area;

    (b)   any registration of the applicant under Schedule 2 to those Regulations in relation to an exempt waste operation (within the meaning of regulation 5 of those Regulations) carried on in that area;

    (c)   any registration of the applicant under Part 8 of the Waste (England and Wales) Regulations 2011 (SI 2011/988) (carriers, brokers and dealers of controlled waste).

(8)   "Relevant offence" and "relevant enforcement action" have the meaning given by section 3(3).

(9)   "Site" means any premises used in the course of carrying on business as a scrap metal dealer (whether or not metal is kept there).

(10)   "Site manager", in relation to a site at which a scrap metal dealer carries on business, means the individual who exercises day-to-day control and management of activities at the site.

(11)   An individual may be named in a licence as site manager at more than one site; but no site may have more than one site manager named in relation to it.

(12)   "Trading name" means a name, other than that stated in the licence under section 2(4)(a) or (6)(a), under which a licensee carries on business as a scrap metal dealer.

NOTES

Commencement: 1 October 2013.

[1.2188]
23   Extent, commencement and short title

(1)   This Act extends to England and Wales.

(2)   The provisions of this Act, except section 20 and this section, come into force on such day as the Secretary of State may appoint by order.

(3)   Different days may be appointed for different purposes.

(4)   This Act may be cited as the Scrap Metal Dealers Act 2013.

NOTES

Commencement: 28 February 2013.
Orders: Scrap Metal Dealers Act 2013 (Commencement and Transitional Provisions) Order 2013, SI 2013/1966.

SCHEDULES

SCHEDULE 1
FURTHER PROVISION ABOUT LICENCES

Section 5

Term of licence

[1.2189]

1. (1)   A licence expires at the end of the period of 3 years beginning with the day on which it is issued.

(2)   But if an application to renew a licence is received before the licence expires, the licence continues in effect and—

    (a)   if the application is withdrawn, the licence expires at the end of the day on which the application is withdrawn;

    (b)   if the application is refused, the licence expires when no appeal under paragraph 9 is possible in relation to the refusal or any such appeal is finally determined or withdrawn;

    (c)   if the licence is renewed, it expires at the end of the period of 3 years beginning with the day on which it is renewed or (if renewed more than once) the day on which it is last renewed.

(3)   Sub-paragraphs (1) and (2) are subject to section 4 (revocation of licence).

(4)   The Secretary of State may by order substitute different periods for the periods specified in sub-paragraphs (1) and (2)(c).

Applications

2. (1)   A licence is to be issued or renewed on an application, which must be accompanied by—

    (a)   if the applicant is an individual, the full name, date of birth and usual place of residence of the applicant,

    (b)   if the applicant is a company, the name and registered number of the applicant and the address of the applicant's registered office,

    (c)   if the applicant is a partnership, the full name, date of birth and usual place of residence of each partner,

    (d)   any proposed trading name,

    (e)   the telephone number and e-mail address (if any) of the applicant,

    (f)   the address of any site in the area of any other local authority at which the applicant carries on business as a scrap metal dealer or proposes to do so,

    (g)   details of any relevant environmental permit or registration in relation to the applicant,

    (h)   details of any other scrap metal licence issued (whether or not by the local authority) to the applicant within the period of 3 years ending with the date of the application,

    (i)   details of the bank account which is proposed to be used in order to comply with section 12 (scrap metal not to be bought for cash etc), and

    (j)   details of any conviction of the applicant for a relevant offence, or any relevant enforcement action taken against the applicant.

(2)   If the application relates to a site licence, it must also be accompanied by—

    (a)   the address of each site proposed to be identified in the licence (or, in the case of an application to renew, of each site identified in the licence whose renewal is sought), and

    (b)   the full name, date of birth and usual place of residence of each individual proposed to be named in the licence as a site manager (other than the applicant).

(3)   If the application relates to a site licence, the references in sub-paragraph (1)(g), (h) and (j) to the applicant are to be read as including any individual proposed to be named in the licence as a site manager.

(4)   The Secretary of State may by order amend sub-paragraph (1) or (2) to alter the requirements as to what information must accompany an application.

Variation of licence

3. (1)   A local authority may, on an application, vary a licence by changing it from one type to the other.

(2)   If there is a change in any of the matters mentioned in section 2(4)(a), (c) or (d) or (6)(a), the licensee must make an application to vary the licence accordingly.

(3)   But the power to amend the name of the licensee does not include the power to transfer the licence from one person to another.

(4)   An application under this paragraph—

(a)   is to be made to the authority which issued the licence, and

(b)   must contain particulars of the changes to be made to the licence.

(5)   A licensee who fails to comply with sub-paragraph (2) is guilty of an offence and is liable on summary conviction to a fine not exceeding level 3 on the standard scale.

(6)   It is a defence for a person charged with an offence under this paragraph to prove that the person took all reasonable steps to avoid committing the offence.

Further information

4. (1)   The local authority may request (either when the application is made or later) that the applicant provide such further information as the authority considers relevant for the purpose of considering the application.

(2)   If an applicant fails to provide information requested under sub-paragraph (1), the authority may decline to proceed with the application.

Offence of making false statement

5.   An applicant who in an application or in response to a request under paragraph 4(1)—

(a)   makes a statement knowing it be false in a material particular, or

(b)   recklessly makes a statement which is false in a material particular,

is guilty of an offence and is liable on summary conviction to a fine not exceeding level 3 on the standard scale.

Fee

6. (1)   An application must be accompanied by a fee set by the authority.

(2)   In setting a fee under this paragraph, the authority must have regard to any guidance issued from time to time by the Secretary of State with the approval of the Treasury.

Right to make representations

7. (1)   If a local authority proposes—

(a)   to refuse an application made under paragraph 2 or 3, or

(b)   to revoke or vary a licence under section 4,

the authority must give the applicant or licensee a notice which sets out what the authority proposes to do and the reasons for it.

(2)   In this paragraph and paragraph 8 the applicant or licensee is referred to as "A".

(3)   A notice under sub-paragraph (1) must also state that, within the period specified in the notice, A may either—

(a)   make representations about the proposal, or

(b)   inform the authority that A wishes to do so.

(4)   The period specified in the notice must be not less than 14 days beginning with the date on which the notice is given to A.

(5)   The authority may refuse the application, or revoke or vary the licence under section 4, if—

(a)   within the period specified in the notice, A informs the authority that A does not wish to make representations, or

(b)   the period specified in the notice expires and A has neither made representations nor informed the authority that A wishes to do so.

(6)   If, within the period specified in the notice, A informs the authority that A wishes to make representations, the authority—

(a)   must allow A a further reasonable period to make representations, and

(b)   may refuse the application, or revoke or vary the licence under section 4, if A fails to make representations within that period.

(7)   If A makes representations (either within the period specified in the notice under sub-paragraph (1) or within the further period under sub-paragraph (6)), the authority must consider the representations.

(8)   If A informs the authority that A wishes to make oral representations, the authority must give A the opportunity of appearing before, and being heard by, a person appointed by the authority.

Notice of decision

8. (1)   If the authority refuses the application, or revokes or varies the licence under section 4, it must give A a notice setting out the decision and the reasons for it.

(2)   A notice under this paragraph must also state—

(a)   that A may appeal under paragraph 9 against the decision,

(b)   the time within which such an appeal may be brought, and

(c)   in the case of a revocation or variation under section 4, the date on which the revocation or variation is to take effect.

Appeals

9. (1) An applicant may appeal to a magistrates' court against the refusal of an application made under paragraph 2 or 3.

(2) A licensee may appeal to a magistrates' court against—
  (a) the inclusion in a licence of a condition under section 3(8), or
  (b) the revocation or variation of a licence under section 4.

(3) An appeal under this paragraph is to be made within the period of 21 days beginning with the day on which notice of the decision to refuse the application, to include the condition, or to revoke or vary the licence under section 4, was given.

(4) The procedure on an appeal under this paragraph is to be by way of complaint for an order and in accordance with the Magistrates' Courts Act 1980.

(5) For the purposes of the time limit for making an appeal under this paragraph, the making of the complaint is to be treated as the making of the appeal.

(6) On an appeal under this paragraph, the magistrates' court may—
  (a) confirm, vary or reverse the authority's decision, and
  (b) give such directions as it considers appropriate having regard to the provisions of this Act.

(7) The authority must comply with any directions given by the magistrates' court under sub-paragraph (6).

(8) But the authority need not comply with any such directions—
  (a) until the time for making an application under section 111 of the Magistrates' Courts Act 1980 (application by way of case stated) has passed, or
  (b) if such an application is made, until the application is finally determined or withdrawn.

NOTES

Commencement: 1 September 2013 (para 6); 1 October 2013 (paras 1, 2, 3(1)–(4), 4, 7–9); 1 December 2013 (otherwise). Transitional provisions: see the note to s 1 at **[1.2167]**.

SCHEDULE 2
CLOSURE OF UNLICENSED SITES

Section 9

Interpretation

[1.2190]
1. (1) For the purposes of this Schedule, a person has an interest in premises if the person is the owner, leaseholder or occupier of the premises.

(2) In the case of a local authority, the powers conferred by this Schedule are exercisable only in relation to premises in the authority's area; and "the local authority", in relation any premises, is to read accordingly.

Closure notice

2. (1) This paragraph applies if a constable or the local authority is satisfied—
  (a) that premises are being used by a scrap metal dealer in the course of business, and
  (b) that the premises are not a licensed site.

(2) But this paragraph does not apply if the premises are residential premises.

(3) The constable or authority may issue a notice (a "closure notice") which—
  (a) states that the constable or authority is satisfied as mentioned in sub-paragraph (1),
  (b) gives the reasons for that,
  (c) states that the constable or authority may apply to the court for a closure order (see paragraphs 4 and 5), and
  (d) specifies the steps which may be taken to ensure that the alleged use of the premises ceases.

(4) The constable or authority must give the closure notice to—
  (a) the person who appears to the constable or authority to be the site manager of the premises, and
  (b) any person (other than the person in paragraph (a)) who appears to the constable or authority to be a director, manager or other officer of the business in question.

(5) The constable or authority may also give the notice to any person who has an interest in the premises.

(6) Sub-paragraph (7) applies where—
  (a) a person occupies another part of any building or structure of which the premises form part, and
  (b) the constable or authority reasonably believes, at the time of giving the notice under sub-paragraph (4), that the person's access to that other part would be impeded if a closure order were made in respect of the premises.

(7) The constable or authority must give the notice to that person.

Cancellation of closure notice

3. (1)   A closure notice may be cancelled by a notice (a "cancellation notice") issued by a constable or the local authority.

(2)   A cancellation notice takes effect when it is given to any one of the persons to whom the closure notice was given.

(3)   The cancellation notice must also be given to any other person to whom the closure notice was given.

Application for closure order

4. (1)   Where a closure notice has been given under paragraph 2(4), a constable or the local authority may make a complaint to a justice of the peace for a closure order (see paragraph 5).

(2)   A complaint under this paragraph may not be made—
  (a)   less than 7 days after the date on which the closure notice was given, or
  (b)   more than 6 months after that date.

(3)   A complaint under this paragraph may not be made if the constable or authority is satisfied that—
  (a)   the premises are not (or are no longer) being used by a scrap metal dealer in the course of business, and
  (b)   there is no reasonable likelihood that the premises will be so used in the future.

(4)   Where a complaint has been made under this paragraph, the justice may issue a summons to answer to the complaint.

(5)   The summons must be directed to any person to whom the closure notice was given under paragraph 2(4).

(6)   If a summons is issued under sub-paragraph (4), notice of the date, time and place at which the complaint will be heard must be given to all the persons to whom the closure notice was given under paragraph 2(5) and (7).

(7)   The procedure on a complaint under this paragraph is to be in accordance with the Magistrates' Courts Act 1980.

Closure order

5. (1)   This paragraph applies if, on hearing a complaint under paragraph 4, the court is satisfied that the closure notice was given under paragraph 2(4) and that—
  (a)   the premises continue to be used by a scrap metal dealer in the course of business, or
  (b)   there is a reasonable likelihood that the premises will be so used in the future.

(2)   The court may make such order as it considers appropriate for the closure of the premises (a "closure order").

(3)   A closure order may, in particular, require—
  (a)   that the premises be closed immediately to the public and remain closed until a constable or the local authority makes a certificate under paragraph 6;
  (b)   that the use of the premises by a scrap metal dealer in the course of business be discontinued immediately;
  (c)   that any defendant pay into court such sum as the court determines and that the sum will not be released by the court to that person until the other requirements of the order are met.

(4)   A closure order including a requirement mentioned in sub-paragraph (3)(a) may, in particular, include such conditions as the court considers appropriate relating to—
  (a)   the admission of persons onto the premises;
  (b)   the access by persons to another part of any building or other structure of which the premises form part.

(5)   A closure order may include such provision as the court considers appropriate for dealing with the consequences if the order should cease to have effect under paragraph 6.

(6)   As soon as practicable after a closure order is made, the complainant must fix a copy of it in a conspicuous position on the premises in respect of which it was made.

(7)   A sum which has been ordered to be paid into court under a closure order is to be paid to the designated officer for the court.

Termination of closure order by certificate of constable or authority

6. (1)   This paragraph applies where—
  (a)   a closure order has been made, but
  (b)   a constable or the local authority is satisfied that the need for the order has ceased.

(2)   The constable or authority may make a certificate to that effect.

(3)   The closure order ceases to have effect when the certificate is made.

(4)   If the closure order includes a requirement under paragraph 5(3)(c), any sum paid into court under the order is to be released by the court to the defendant (whether or not the court has made provision to that effect under paragraph 5(5)).

(5) As soon as practicable after making a certificate, the constable or authority must—

 (a) give a copy of it to any person against whom the closure order was made,

 (b) give a copy of it to the designated officer for the court which made the order, and

 (c) fix a copy of it in a conspicuous position on the premises in respect of which the order was made.

(6) The constable or authority must give a copy of the certificate to any person who requests one.

Discharge of closure order by court

7. (1) Any of the following persons may make a complaint to a justice of the peace for an order that a closure order be discharged (a "discharge order")—

 (a) any person to whom the relevant closure notice was given under paragraph 2;

 (b) any person who has an interest in the premises but to whom the closure notice was not given.

(2) The court may not make a discharge order unless it is satisfied that there is no longer a need for the closure order.

(3) Where a complaint has been made under this paragraph, the justice may issue a summons directed to—

 (a) such constable as the justice considers appropriate, or

 (b) the local authority,

requiring that person to appear before the magistrates' court to answer to the complaint.

(4) If a summons is issued under sub-paragraph (3), notice of the date, time and place at which the complaint will be heard must be given to all the persons to whom the closure notice was given under paragraph 2 (other than the complainant).

(5) The procedure on a complaint under this paragraph is to be in accordance with the Magistrates' Courts Act 1980.

Appeals

8. (1) An appeal may be made to the Crown Court against—

 (a) a closure order;

 (b) a decision not to make a closure order;

 (c) a discharge order;

 (d) a decision not to make a discharge order.

(2) Any appeal under this paragraph must be made before the end of the period of 21 days beginning with the day on which the order or the decision in question was made.

(3) An appeal under this paragraph against a closure order or a decision not to make a discharge order may be made by—

 (a) any person to whom the relevant closure notice was given under paragraph 2;

 (b) any person who has an interest in the premises but to whom the closure notice was not given.

(4) An appeal under this paragraph against a decision not to make a closure order or against a discharge order may be made by a constable or (as the case may be) the local authority.

(5) On an appeal under this paragraph the Crown Court may make such order as it considers appropriate.

Enforcement of closure order

9. (1) A person is guilty of an offence if the person, without reasonable excuse,—

 (a) permits premises to be open in contravention of a closure order, or

 (b) otherwise fails to comply with, or does an act in contravention of, a closure order.

(2) If a closure order has been made in respect of any premises, a constable or an authorised person may (if necessary using reasonable force)—

 (a) enter the premises at any reasonable time, and

 (b) having entered the premises, do anything reasonably necessary for the purpose of securing compliance with the order.

(3) Sub-paragraph (4) applies if a constable or an authorised person ("the officer") seeks to exercise powers under this paragraph in relation to any premises.

(4) If the owner, occupier or other person in charge of the premises requires the officer to produce—

 (a) evidence of the officer's identity, or

 (b) evidence of the officer's authority to exercise those powers,

the officer must produce that evidence.

(5) A person who intentionally obstructs a constable or an authorised person in the exercise of powers under this paragraph is guilty of an offence.

(6) A person guilty of an offence under this paragraph is liable on summary conviction to a fine not exceeding level 5 on the standard scale.

(7)   In this paragraph "an authorised person" is a person authorised for the purposes of this paragraph by the local authority.

NOTES
  Commencement: 1 December 2013.

ENTERPRISE AND REGULATORY REFORM ACT 2013

(2013 c 24)

NOTES
  Only provisions of this Act relevant to Commercial and Consumer law are reproduced. Provisions not reproduced are not annotated.

ARRANGEMENT OF SECTIONS

PART3
THE COMPETITION AND MARKETS AUTHORITY

SCHEDULES

An Act to make provision about the UK Green Investment Bank; to make provision about employment law; to establish and make provision about the Competition and Markets Authority and to abolish the Competition Commission and the Office of Fair Trading; to amend the Competition Act 1998 and the Enterprise Act 2002; to make provision for the reduction of legislative burdens; to make provision about copyright and rights in performances; to make provision about payments to company directors; to make provision about redress schemes relating to lettings agency work and property management work; to make provision about the supply of customer data; to make provision for the protection of essential supplies in cases of insolvency; to make provision about certain bodies established by Royal Charter; to amend section 9(5) of the Equality Act 2010; and for connected purposes.

[25 April 2013]

PART 3
THE COMPETITION AND MARKETS AUTHORITY

[1.2191]
25   The Competition and Markets Authority
(1)   There is to be a body corporate known as the Competition and Markets Authority.
(2)   In this Part that body is referred to as "the CMA".
(3)   The CMA must seek to promote competition, both within and outside the United Kingdom, for the benefit of consumers.
(4)   Schedule 4 (which makes provision about the CMA) has effect.

NOTES
  Commencement: 1 October 2013 (sub-ss (1), (2), (4)); 1 April 2014 (sub-s (3)).
  For transitional provisions and savings in connection with the abolition of the OFT and the establishment of the CMA, see Enterprise and Regulatory Reform Act 2013 (Commencement No 6, Transitional Provisions and Savings) Order 2014, SI 2014/416, Schedule at **[2.1126]**.

[1.2192]
26   Abolition of the Competition Commission and the OFT
(1)   The Competition Commission is abolished.
(2)   The Office of Fair Trading is abolished.
(3)   Schedule 5 (which amends the Competition Act 1998 and the Enterprise Act 2002 to make provision for the transfer of certain functions from the Competition Commission and the Office of Fair Trading to the CMA and to make other minor and consequential amendments) has effect.
(4)   Schedule 6 (which amends other enactments to make provision for the transfer of certain functions from the Competition Commission and the Office of Fair Trading to the CMA) has effect.

[1.2193]
27   Transfer schemes

(1)   The Secretary of State may make one or more transfer schemes in connection with—
  (a)   the establishment of the CMA under this Act,
  (b)   the transfer of functions under or by virtue of this Act from the Competition Commission or the Office of Fair Trading to the CMA, or
  (c)   the abolition of that Commission or that Office under this Act.

(2)   A transfer scheme is a scheme for the transfer of property, rights and liabilities of the Competition Commission or the Office of Fair Trading to—
  (a)   the CMA, or
  (b)   a Minister of the Crown (as defined by section 8 of the Ministers of the Crown Act 1975).

(3)   The things that may be transferred under a transfer scheme include—
  (a)   property, rights and liabilities that could not otherwise be transferred;
  (b)   property acquired, and rights and liabilities arising, after the making of the scheme.

(4)   A transfer scheme may make consequential, supplementary, incidental or transitional provision and may in particular—
  (a)   create rights, or impose liabilities, in relation to property or rights transferred;
  (b)   make provision about the continuing effect of things done by the transferor in respect of anything transferred;
  (c)   make provision about the continuation of things (including legal proceedings) in the process of being done by, on behalf of, or in relation to the transferor in respect of anything transferred;
  (d)   make provision for references to the transferor in an instrument or other document in respect of anything transferred to be treated as references to the transferee;
  (e)   make provision for the shared ownership or use of property;
  (f)   make provision that is the same as or similar to the TUPE regulations.

(5)   A transfer scheme may provide—
  (a)   for the scheme to be modified by agreement after it comes into effect;
  (b)   for modifications to have effect from the date when the scheme first came into effect.

(6)   For the purposes of this section—
  (a)   an individual who holds employment in the civil service is to be treated as employed by virtue of a contract of employment, and
  (b)   the terms of the individual's employment in the civil service are to be regarded as constituting the terms of the contract of employment.

(7)   In this section—
  "civil service" means the civil service of the State;
  "TUPE regulations" means the Transfer of Undertakings (Protection of Employment) Regulations 2006 (SI 2006/246);
  references to rights and liabilities include rights and liabilities relating to a contract of employment;
  references to the transfer of property include references to the grant of a lease.

[1.2194]
28   Transitional provision: consultation

(1)   This section applies in relation to a provision of this Act under or by virtue of which the CMA has a function of consulting another person in preparing rules, statements of policy, guidance or general advice or information.

(2)   At any time before the provision comes into force, the Office of Fair Trading or the Competition Commission or both bodies acting jointly—
  (a)   may carry out any consultation that the CMA would have power to carry out after the provision comes into force, and
  (b)   for that purpose, may prepare drafts of any documents to which the consultation relates.

(3)   At any time after the provision comes into force, the CMA may elect to treat any consultation carried out or other thing done under subsection (2) by the Office of Fair Trading or the Competition Commission (or by both bodies acting jointly) as carried out or done by the CMA.

(4)   The Secretary of State may direct the Office of Fair Trading or the Competition Commission, or both of them acting jointly, to exercise a power conferred by subsection (2).

NOTES
Commencement: 25 April 2013.

SCHEDULES

SCHEDULE 4
THE COMPETITION AND MARKETS AUTHORITY

Section 25(4)

PART 1
GENERAL

Membership

[1.2195]

1. (1)   The CMA is to consist of—
  (a)   a person appointed by the Secretary of State to chair the CMA and the CMA Board (the "chair"), and
  (b)   other persons appointed by the Secretary of State to membership of—
    (i)   the CMA Board (see Part 2);
    (ii)   the CMA panel (see Part 3);
    (iii)   both the CMA Board and the CMA panel.

(2)   The Secretary of State must consult the chair before making an appointment under sub-paragraph (1)(b).

(3)   At least five of the members appointed under sub-paragraph (1)(b) must be appointed to membership of the CMA Board.

(4)   At least one of the members appointed under sub-paragraph (1)(b) must be appointed to membership of the CMA Board and to membership of the CMA panel.

(5)   Of the persons appointed to membership of the CMA Board under sub-paragraph (1)(b), no more than half may be members of staff of the CMA.

(6)   In this Schedule, references to members of the CMA are to persons appointed under sub-paragraph (1).

(7)   A person holding office as a member of the Competition Appeal Tribunal is ineligible for appointment under this paragraph.

Terms and conditions

2. (1)   The members of the CMA are to hold and vacate office in accordance with the terms and conditions of their appointments.

(2)   Those terms and conditions are to be determined by the Secretary of State.

Term of appointment

3. (1)   Appointment to membership of the CMA Board under paragraph 1(1)(b) is to be for a term of not more than five years.

(2)   Appointment to membership of the CMA panel under paragraph 1(1)(b) is to be for a term of not more than eight years.

(3)   Appointment as the chair is to be for a term of not more than five years.

Re-appointment

4. (1)   A person who has been appointed to membership of the CMA panel may be re-appointed to membership of the CMA panel only for the purpose of continuing to act as a member of a group constituted under paragraph 36 before the expiry of his or her term of office.

(2)   Subject to sub-paragraph (1), a person's previous appointment under paragraph 1 does not affect eligibility for a subsequent appointment under that paragraph.

Remuneration etc of members

5. (1)   The CMA must pay to its members such remuneration, allowances and expenses as the Secretary of State may determine.

(2)   The CMA must pay or make provision for the payment of such pension, allowances or gratuities as the Secretary of State may determine to or in respect of a current or former member.

(3)   If a person ceases to hold an office to which he or she has been appointed under paragraph 1, and the Secretary of State decides that there are special circumstances which mean that the person should be compensated, the CMA must pay compensation to the person of such amount as the Secretary of State may determine.

Resignation

6. (1)   The chair may at any time resign from membership of the CMA by giving written notice to this effect to the Secretary of State.

(2)   A person who is a member of either the CMA Board or the CMA panel (but not of both) may at any time resign from membership of the CMA by giving written notice to this effect to the Secretary of State.

(3)   A person who is a member of both the CMA Board and the CMA panel may at any time, by giving written notice to this effect to the Secretary of State—
- (a)   resign from membership of either the CMA Board or the CMA panel, or
- (b)   resign from membership of the CMA.

Termination of membership

7. The Secretary of State may at any time remove a person from office as a member of the CMA on any of the following grounds—
- (a)   incapacity;
- (b)   misbehaviour;
- (c)   failure to carry out his or her duties.

Status

8. The CMA is to perform its functions on behalf of the Crown.

Chief executive and other staff

9. (1)   The CMA is to have a chief executive appointed by the Secretary of State (the "chief executive").

(2)   The chief executive may also be a member of the CMA, but must not be—
- (a)   the chair, or
- (b)   a member of the CMA panel.

(3)   Before appointing the chief executive, the Secretary of State must consult the chair.

(4)   The appointment—
- (a)   is to be for a term of not more than five years;
- (b)   subject to that, is to be on such terms and conditions as the Secretary of State considers fit.

(5)   The chief executive holds that office as a member of the staff of the CMA.

(6)   A previous appointment as chief executive does not affect a person's eligibility for re-appointment.

10. (1)   The CMA may appoint other members of staff.

(2)   A person appointed as a member of the CMA's staff under sub-paragraph (1) may also be a member of the CMA, but must not be—
- (a)   the chair, or
- (b)   a member of the CMA panel.

(3)   The following are to be determined by the CMA with the approval of the Minister for the Civil Service—
- (a)   the number of members of staff appointed under sub-paragraph (1);
- (b)   their conditions of service.

11. A person holding office as a member of the Competition Appeal Tribunal is ineligible for appointment under paragraph 9 or 10.

Annual plan

12. (1)   The CMA must prepare an annual plan for each financial year.

(2)   The plan must—
- (a)   set out the CMA's main objectives for the year and indicate the relative priorities of each of those objectives;
- (b)   provide a summary of the proposed allocation of the CMA's financial resources to the activities to be carried on in connection with those objectives.

(3)   The CMA must arrange for the plan to be laid before Parliament.

(4)   The CMA must publish the plan, in whatever way it considers appropriate, before the start of the financial year in question.

13. (1)   Before finalising an annual plan, the CMA must draw up proposals for it.

(2)   The CMA must arrange for the proposals to be laid before Parliament.

(3)   The CMA must—
- (a)   publish the proposals in whatever way it considers appropriate, and
- (b)   make arrangements to consult with the public about them.

(4)   Arrangements made under sub-paragraph (3)(b) may provide for consultation with the public to be effected in whatever way the CMA considers appropriate.

Performance report

14. (1)   As soon as practicable after the end of each financial year, the CMA must prepare and send to the Secretary of State an annual report on its activities and performance during the year.

(2)   The report must include—
   (a)   a survey of developments, during the year, in matters relating to the CMA's functions;
   (b)   an assessment of the extent to which the CMA's objectives for the year, as set out in the plan published under paragraph 12, have been met;
   (c)   a summary of the significant decisions, investigations or other activities made or carried out by the CMA during the year;
   (d)   a summary of the allocation of the CMA's financial resources to its various activities during the year;
   (e)   an assessment of the CMA's performance and practices, during the year, in relation to its enforcement functions.

(3)   The CMA must—
   (a)   arrange for the report to be laid before Parliament;
   (b)   publish the report in whatever way it considers appropriate.

15.   The CMA may—
   (a)   prepare other reports about matters relating to any of its functions;
   (b)   publish a report prepared under this paragraph.

Concurrency report

16. (1)   As soon as practicable after the end of each financial year, the CMA must prepare a report containing an assessment of how the concurrency arrangements have operated during the year.

(2)   The concurrency arrangements are the arrangements for co-operation between the CMA and the sectoral regulators in respect of functions which are exercisable concurrently by the CMA and one or more of the regulators under Part 1 of the Competition Act 1998 (the "1998 Act") and Part 4 of the Enterprise Act 2002 (the "2002 Act").

(3)   The report must, in particular, include information about—
   (a)   the exercise during the year by the CMA of its functions under Part 1 of the 1998 Act or Part 4 of the 2002 Act in cases in which the functions are or were exercisable concurrently by one or more sectoral regulators,
   (b)   the exercise during the year by each sectoral regulator of its functions under Part 1 of the 1998 Act or Part 4 of the 2002 Act, and
   (c)   any decision made during the year by a sectoral regulator, in respect of a case in relation to which the regulator considers that its functions under Part 1 of the 1998 Act were exercisable, that it was more appropriate for it to proceed by exercising functions other than those it has under that Part of that Act.

(4)   The CMA is not required to include information in a report under this paragraph if it considers that doing so would, or would be likely to, prejudice the exercise of any of the functions of the CMA or a sectoral regulator.

(5)   In preparing a report under this paragraph, the CMA must consult each sectoral regulator.

(6)   The CMA must publish a report prepared under this paragraph in whatever way it considers appropriate.

(7)   Each of the following is a sectoral regulator—
   (a)   the Office of Communications;
   (b)   the Gas and Electricity Markets Authority;
   (c)   the Water Services Regulation Authority;
   (d)   the Office of Rail Regulation;
   (e)   the Northern Ireland Authority for Utility Regulation;
   (f)   the Civil Aviation Authority;
   (g)   Monitor;
   [(h)   the Payment Systems Regulator established under section 40 of the Financial Services (Banking Reform) Act 2013];
   [(i)   the Financial Conduct Authority].

Documents

17. (1)   The application of the CMA's seal must be authenticated by the signature of—
   (a)   a person who is a member of the CMA Board, or
   (b)   a person authorised (generally or specifically) for that purpose by the CMA.

(2)   A document purporting to be duly executed under the CMA's seal or signed on its behalf—
   (a)   is to be received in evidence;

(b)   is to be taken to be duly signed or sealed unless the contrary is shown.

(3)   But this paragraph does not apply in relation to a document which is, or is to be, signed in accordance with the law of Scotland.

Membership of committees and sub-committees

18. (1)   The members of a committee or sub-committee of the CMA may include persons who are not members of the CMA.

(2)   A sub-committee may include persons who are not members of the committee that established it.

Additional powers

19. The CMA may—
  (a)   if so requested by the Secretary of State, represent the government of the United Kingdom in matters relating to international relations in any field connected to its functions, and
  (b)   promote good practice outside the United Kingdom in the carrying on of activities which may affect the economic interests of consumers in the United Kingdom.

20. (1)   The CMA may do anything that is calculated to facilitate, or is conducive or incidental to, the performance of its functions.

(2)   The power in sub-paragraph (1) is subject to any restrictions imposed by or under any enactment.

21–26 *(Amend the Public Records Act 1958, the Parliamentary Commissioner Act 1967, the House of Commons Disqualification Act 1975, the Northern Ireland Assembly Disqualification Act 1975, the Freedom of Information Act 2000, and Equality Act 2010.)*

NOTES

Commencement: 1 October 2013 (paras 1–18, 20–26); 1 April 2014 (otherwise).

Para 16: sub-para (7)(h) inserted by the Financial Services (Banking Reform) Act 2013, s 67(5); sub-para (7)(i) inserted by s 129 of, and Sch 8, Pt 2, para 12 to, the 2013 Act.

Transitional provisions: see the Enterprise and Regulatory Reform Act 2013 (Commencement No 3, Transitional Provisions and Savings) Order 2013, SI 2013/2227, art 3 which provides for transitional provisions in connection with the terms of office of members of the Competition Commission. See also, in connection with the abolition of the OFT and the establishment of the CMA, Enterprise and Regulatory Reform Act 2013 (Commencement No 6, Transitional Provisions and Savings) Order 2014, SI 2014/416, Schedule at **[2.1126]**.

PART 2
THE CMA BOARD

Membership

[1.2196]
27. The CMA Board is to consist of—
  (a)   the chair;
  (b)   the members appointed under paragraph 1(1)(b) to membership of the CMA Board.

Functions

28. Except where otherwise provided by or under any enactment, the functions of the CMA are exercisable by the CMA Board on behalf of the CMA.

Delegation

29. (1)   Anything that the CMA Board is required or permitted to do (including conferring authorisation under this sub-paragraph) may be done by—
  (a)   a member of the CMA Board, or a member of staff of the CMA, who has been authorised for that purpose by the CMA Board, whether generally or specifically;
  (b)   a committee or sub-committee of the CMA Board that has been so authorised.

(2)   Sub-paragraph (1) does not apply to the functions of deciding—
  (a)   whether the duty to publish a market study notice under section 130A of the Enterprise Act 2002 applies;
  (b)   whether to propose to make, or to make, a reference under section 131 of that Act;
  (c)   for the purposes of the requirement imposed by section 131A(2)(b) of that Act, whether the CMA is proposing to make a decision as to whether to make a reference under section 131 of that Act in a way that is likely to have a substantial impact on the interests of any person;
  (d)   whether section 140A of that Act applies in respect of a particular case;
  (e)   whether to accept an undertaking under section 154 of that Act, or to vary or supersede or release an undertaking under that section;
  (f)   for the purposes of the requirement imposed by section 169(2) of that Act, whether the CMA is proposing to make a decision to make a reference under section 131 of that Act in a way that is likely to have a substantial impact on the interests of any person.

(3) Sub-paragraph (1)(b) does not apply to a committee or sub-committee whose members include any person who is not a member of the CMA or of its staff.

30. Paragraph 29(1) is subject to provision in rules made under section 51 of the Competition Act 1998, by virtue of paragraph 1A of Schedule 9 to that Act, in respect of the exercise of a function of the CMA under Part 1 of that Act.

Proceedings

31. (1) The CMA Board may regulate its own proceedings.

(2) The CMA Board must consult the Secretary of State before making or revising rules and procedures, under sub-paragraph (1), for dealing with—
   (a) conflicts of interest, or
   (b) quorum.

Validity

32. The validity of anything done by the CMA Board is not affected by—
   (a) a vacancy;
   (b) a defective appointment.

Reference of matter to the chair

33. (1) This paragraph applies where the CMA Board is to consider whether a matter should be referred to the chair for the constitution of a group under this Schedule.

(2) Before the CMA Board considers whether to refer the matter to the chair, the chair must determine whether a person who is a member of the CMA Board might reasonably be expected to be a member of a group constituted in connection with the matter.

(3) If the chair determines that a person who is a member of the CMA Board might reasonably be expected to be a member of such a group, that person is not to participate in the CMA Board's consideration of whether to refer the matter to the chair.

NOTES

Commencement: 1 October 2013 (paras 27, 28, 29(1), 31, 32); 1 April 2014 (otherwise).
Transitional provisions: see the note to Part 1 of this Schedule at **[1.2195]**.

PART 3
THE CMA PANEL

The CMA panel

[1.2197]
34. The CMA panel is a panel of persons available for selection as members of a group constituted in accordance with this Part of this Schedule.

Membership of CMA panel

35. (1) The CMA panel is to consist of—
   (a) at least one person (a "newspaper panel member") appointed to the CMA panel under paragraph 1(1)(b) for the purpose of being available for selection as a member of a group constituted to carry out functions on behalf of the CMA with respect to a newspaper merger reference (a "newspaper merger reference group");
   (b) at least three persons ("specialist communications panel members") appointed to the CMA panel under paragraph 1(1)(b) for the purpose of being available for selection as members of a group constituted to carry out functions on behalf of the CMA with respect to a specialist communications reference (a "specialist communications reference group");
   (c) at least six persons ("specialist utility panel members") appointed to the CMA panel under paragraph 1(1)(b) for the purpose of being available for selection as a member of a group constituted to carry out specialist utility functions on behalf of the CMA (a "specialist utility group");
   [(ca) at least one person (a "payment systems panel member") appointed to the CMA panel under paragraph 1(1)(b) for the purpose of being available for selection as a member of a group constituted to carry out functions on behalf of the CMA with respect to an appeal made in accordance with section 79 of the Financial Services (Banking Reform) Act 2013 (a "specialist payment systems group");]
   (d) at least one person (a "reporting panel member") appointed to the CMA panel under paragraph 1(1)(b) for the purpose of being available for selection as a member of any group constituted to carry out functions on behalf of the CMA;
   (e) any persons who are appointed to the CMA panel under paragraph 1(1)(b) for the purpose of being available for selection as members of a group constituted to carry out functions with respect to a reference under article 15 of the Electricity (Northern Ireland) Order 1992 (SI 1992/231 (NI 1)).

(2) A person who is appointed to the CMA panel as a member of a kind mentioned in one of paragraphs (a) to (e) of sub-paragraph (1) may also be appointed as a member of one or more of the other kinds mentioned in those paragraphs.

(3) For the purposes of this paragraph and paragraph 38—

a "newspaper merger reference" is—

    (a)   a reference under section 45 of the Enterprise Act 2002 that specifies a newspaper public interest consideration (within the meaning of paragraph 20A of Schedule 8 to that Act);

    (b)   a reference under section 62 of that Act that specifies a consideration specified in section 58(2A) or (2B) of that Act;

a "specialist communications reference" is a reference under section 193 of the Communications Act 2003;

"specialist utility functions" are functions with respect to—

    (a)   an appeal under section 23B, or a reference under section 41E, of the Gas Act 1986;

    (b)   an appeal under section 11C, or a reference under section 56C, of the Electricity Act 1989;

    (c)   a reference under section 12, 14 or 17K of the Water Industry Act 1991;

    (d)   the giving of a direction or the making of modifications under section 16A or 17P of that Act;

    (e)   an appeal under section 173 of the Energy Act 2004;

    (f)   a reference under article 3 of the Water Services etc (Scotland) Act 2005 (Consequential Provisions and Modifications) Order 2005 (SI 2005/3172);

    (g)   the giving of a direction or the making of modifications under article 9 of that Order.

Constitution of CMA groups

36. Where the chair is, by or under any enactment, required to constitute a group under this Schedule (a "CMA group"), the chair must constitute the group in accordance with this Part of this Schedule.

Membership of CMA groups

37. (1) The members of a CMA group are to be selected by the chair.

(2) In selecting the members of a CMA group, the chair must comply with any requirements imposed by or under any enactment.

(3) Subject to that, paragraph 38 has effect for the purposes of the membership of a CMA group.

38. (1) Each CMA group is to consist of at least three members of the CMA panel.

(2) Subject to sub-paragraphs (3) to (6), those members are to be such persons as the chair may select.

(3) In the case of a newspaper merger reference group—

    (a)   the group must include at least one newspaper panel member;

    (b)   the members of the group (if any) who are not newspaper panel members must be reporting panel members.

(4) In the case of a specialist communications reference group, the group must include at least one, but not more than three, of the specialist communications panel members.

(5) In the case of a specialist utility group, the group must include at least one of the specialist utility panel members.

[(5A) In the case of a specialist payment systems group, the group must include at least one payment systems member.]

(6) A newspaper panel member is not to be selected as a member of a CMA group that is not a newspaper merger reference group.

(7) The chair may at any time appoint a reporting panel member to be an additional member of a CMA group.

(8) The chair must appoint one of the members of a CMA group to chair the group (the "group chair").

39. The validity of anything done by a CMA group is not affected by—

    (a)   a vacancy;

    (b)   a defective appointment.

Termination of person's membership of a CMA group

40. A member of the CMA panel may at any time resign from a CMA group by giving written notice to this effect to the chair.

41. (1) Sub-paragraph (2) applies if the chair considers that—

    (a)   a member of a CMA group will be unable, for a substantial period, to perform his or her duties as a member of the group, or

(b)   because of a particular interest of a member of a CMA group, it is inappropriate for him or her to remain a member of the group.

(2)   The chair may remove the person in question from membership of the group.

42. A person ceases to be a member of a CMA group on ceasing to be a member of the CMA panel.

Replacement of a member of a CMA group

43. (1) Sub-paragraph (2) applies if a person ceases to be a member of a CMA group, whether by being removed under paragraph 41, or otherwise.

(2)   The chair may select a replacement member of the group from the CMA panel.

Continuity on removal or replacement

44. (1) A person's ceasing to be a member of a CMA group, whether by being removed under paragraph 41, or otherwise, does not prevent—
(a)   the group from continuing with anything begun before the person ceased to be a member of it;
(b)   any decision made or direction given by the person while a member of the group from having effect after he or she has ceased to be a member of the group.

(2)   Sub-paragraph (1)—
(a)   applies whether or not a replacement member of the group is selected under paragraph 43;
(b)   does not affect any requirements imposed by or under any enactment with respect to the constitution of a CMA group.

Attendance of other members

45. (1) At the invitation of the group chair of a CMA group, any reporting panel member who is not a member of the group may attend its meetings or otherwise take part in its proceedings.

(2)   But a person attending in response to such an invitation may not—
(a)   vote in any proceedings of the group, or
(b)   have a statement of his or her dissent from a conclusion of the group included in a report made by the group.

(3)   Nothing in sub-paragraph (1) is to be taken to prevent a CMA group from consulting any member of the CMA panel with respect to any matter or question with which the group is concerned.

Powers of chair pending group's constitution and first meeting

46. (1) While a CMA group is being constituted, the chair may take such steps as he or she considers appropriate to facilitate the work of the group once it has been constituted.

(2)   The steps taken must be steps that it would be within the power of the group to take, had it already been constituted.

47. (1) The chair may, on behalf of the CMA, exercise the power conferred by section 37(1), 48(1) or 64(1) of the Enterprise Act 2002 in respect of the reference of a matter—
(a)   while a CMA group is being constituted in connection with the reference;
(b)   after a CMA group has been so constituted, but before it has held its first meeting.

(2)   Sections 34C, 46D and 62A of the Enterprise Act 2002 have effect subject to sub-paragraph (1).

Performance of functions of chair with respect to constitution etc of CMA group

48. (1) A function of the chair that is specified in sub-paragraph (4) may, with the consent of the CMA Board, be exercised on behalf of the chair by—
(a)   a person who is a member of both the CMA panel and the CMA Board, or
(b)   a member of the CMA panel designated by the Secretary of State (whether generally or specifically) for the purposes of this paragraph.

(2)   The consent referred to in sub-paragraph (1) must specify the identity of the person by whom a function of the chair is to be exercised.

(3)   It may be given—
(a)   by reference generally to functions specified in sub-paragraph (4);
(b)   by reference to specific functions, or functions of a particular description;
(c)   by reference generally to CMA groups;
(d)   by reference to specific matters or specific CMA groups, or by reference to matters or CMA groups of a particular description.

(4)   The functions are—
(a)   the chair's functions under paragraph 33 and under this Part of this Schedule;
(b)   the chair's functions by or under any other enactment in respect of the constitution of a CMA group;

(c)   the chair's functions under—
    (i)   Schedule 4A to the Gas Act 1986;
    (ii)   Schedule 5A to the Electricity Act 1989;
    (iii)   Schedule 22 to the Energy Act 2004;
    (iv)   Schedule 2 to the Civil Aviation Act 2012;
    [(iv)   Schedule 5 to the Financial Services (Banking Reform) Act 2013].

Independence of groups

49. (1)   In making decisions that they are required or permitted to make by virtue of any enactment, CMA groups must act independently of the CMA Board.

(2)   Nothing in sub-paragraph (1) prevents—
    (a)   the CMA Board from giving information in its possession to a CMA group, or
    (b)   a CMA group giving information in its possession to the CMA Board.

Casting votes

50.   If a CMA group's vote on any decision is tied, the group chair is to have a casting vote.

Requirement to make rules of procedure for certain groups

51. (1)   The CMA Board must make rules of procedure for merger reference groups, market reference groups, and special reference groups.

(2)   Those rules are subject to any provision made by or under any enactment in respect of the procedure of a CMA group.

(3)   Before making rules under this paragraph, the CMA Board must consult such persons as it considers appropriate.

(4)   The CMA Board must publish rules made under this paragraph in whatever manner it considers appropriate for bringing them to the attention of those likely to be affected by them.

(5)   Subject to rules made under this paragraph, and to any provision made by or under any enactment, a CMA group of a type referred to in sub-paragraph (1) may determine its own procedure.

(6)   In this paragraph and paragraph 53—
    (a)   "market reference group" means a CMA group constituted in connection with a reference under section 131, 132 or 140A of the Enterprise Act 2002;
    (b)   "merger reference group" means a CMA group constituted in connection with a reference under section 32 of the Water Industry Act 1991 or section 22, 33, 45, or 62 of the Enterprise Act 2002;
    (c)   "special reference group" means a CMA group constituted in connection with a reference under—
       (i)   section 11 of the Competition Act 1980;
       (ii)   section 41E of the Gas Act 1986;
       (iii)   section 56C of the Electricity Act 1989;
       (iv)   section 12, 14 or 17K of the Water Industry Act 1991;
       (v)   article 15 of the Electricity (Northern Ireland) Order 1992 (SI 1992/231 (NI 1));
       (vi)   section 13 of, or Schedule 4A to, the Railways Act 1993;
       (vii)   article 15 of the Gas (Northern Ireland) Order 1996 (SI 1996/275 (NI 2));
       (viii) section 12 of the Transport Act 2000;
       (ix)   section 193 of the Communications Act 2003;
       (x)   article 3 of the Water Services etc (Scotland) Act 2005 (Consequential Provisions and Modifications) Order 2005 (SI 2005/3172).

52. (1)   In determining how to proceed in accordance with rules made for it by the CMA Board under paragraph 51(1), and in determining its own procedure under paragraph 51(5), a group must have regard to any guidance issued by the CMA Board.

(2)   Before issuing guidance for the purposes of this paragraph, or amending or revoking it, the CMA Board must consult such persons as it considers appropriate.

53. (1)   Rules made under paragraph 51 may—
    (a)   make different provision for different cases or different purposes;
    (b)   be varied or revoked by rules subsequently made under that paragraph.

(2)   They may in particular make provision—
    (a)   for particular stages of a merger investigation, market investigation, or special investigation to be dealt with in accordance with a timetable and for revision of that timetable;
    (b)   as to the documents and information that must be given to a relevant group in connection with a merger investigation, market investigation or special investigation;
    (c)   as to the documents and information that a relevant group must give to other persons in connection with such an investigation.

(3) Rules making provision as described in sub-paragraph (2)(a) or (2)(b) may, in particular, permit or require a relevant group to disregard documents or information given after a particular date.

(4) Rules making provision as described in sub-paragraph (2)(c) may in particular make provision for the notification or publication of, and for consultation about, provisional findings of a relevant group.

(5) Rules made under paragraph 51 may make provision as to the quorum of relevant groups.

(6) They may make provision—
  (a) as to the extent (if any) to which persons interested or claiming to be interested in a matter under consideration that is specified or described in the rules are allowed—
    (i) to be present before or heard by a relevant group, either by themselves or by their representatives;
    (ii) to cross-examine witnesses;
    (iii) otherwise to take part;
  (b) as to the extent (if any) to which sittings of a relevant group are to be held in public;
  (c) generally in connection with any matters permitted by rules making provision as described in paragraph (a) or (b) (including, in particular, provision for a record of any hearings).

(7) Rules made under paragraph 51 may make provision for—
  (a) the notification or publication of information relating to merger investigations, market investigations or special investigations;
  (b) consultation about such investigations.

(8) Rules made under paragraph 51 for market reference groups may make provision as to the involvement of any public interest expert in the market investigation in connection with the reference under section 140A of the Enterprise Act 2002 in relation to which the expert was appointed.

(9) For the purposes of this paragraph—
  "market investigation" means an investigation carried out by a market reference group in connection with a reference under section 131, 132 or 140A of the Enterprise Act 2002;
  "merger investigation" means an investigation carried out by a merger reference group in connection with a reference under section 32 of the Water Industry Act 1991 or section 22, 33, 45, or 62 of the Enterprise Act 2002;
  "public interest expert" means a person appointed under section 141B of the Enterprise Act 2002 in relation to a reference under section 140A(6) of that Act;
  "relevant group" means a market reference group, a merger reference group, or a special reference group;
  "special investigation" means an investigation carried out by a special reference group in connection with a provision listed in paragraph 51(6)(c).

Procedure of other CMA groups

54. (1) Subject to any special or general directions given by the Secretary of State, and to any provision made by or under any enactment, a CMA group that is not a group of a type referred to in paragraph 51(1) may determine its own procedure.

(2) It may, in particular, determine its quorum, and determine—
  (a) the extent (if any) to which persons interested or claiming to be interested in a matter under consideration are allowed—
    (i) to be present before or heard by it, either by themselves or by their representatives;
    (ii) to cross-examine witnesses;
    (iii) otherwise to take part;
  (b) the extent (if any) to which its sittings are to be held in public.

(3) In determining its procedure under sub-paragraph (1), a CMA group must have regard to any guidance issued by the CMA Board.

CMA group decision: requirement for two thirds majority

55. For the purposes of paragraphs 56 to 58, a "qualifying majority decision" is a decision made by a CMA group which is that of at least two-thirds of the members of the group.

56. (1) This paragraph applies for the purposes of Part 3 of the Enterprise Act 2002.

(2) Where a decision of a CMA group under section 35(1) or 36(1) of that Act that there is an anti-competitive outcome is not a qualifying majority decision, it is to be treated as a decision under that section that there is not an anti-competitive outcome.

(3) Where a decision of a CMA group under section 47 of that Act is not a qualifying majority decision—
  (a) in the case of a decision that a relevant merger situation has been created, it is to be treated as a decision under section 47 that no such situation has been created;
  (b) in the case of a decision that the creation of a relevant merger situation has resulted, or may be expected to result, in a substantial lessening of competition within any market or

markets in the United Kingdom for goods and services, it is to be treated as a decision under section 47 that the creation of that situation has not resulted, or may be expected not to result, in such a substantial lessening of competition;

(c)   in the case of a decision that arrangements are in progress or in contemplation which, if carried into effect, will result in the creation of a relevant merger situation, it is to be treated as a decision under section 47 that no such arrangements are in progress or in contemplation;

(d)   in the case of a decision that the creation of such a situation as is mentioned in paragraph (c) may be expected to result in a substantial lessening of competition within any market or markets in the United Kingdom for goods and services, it is to be treated as a decision under section 47 that the creation of that situation may be expected not to result in such a substantial lessening of competition.

(4)   Where a decision of a CMA group under section 63 of that Act is not a qualifying majority decision—

(a)   in the case of a decision that a special merger situation has been created, it is to be treated as a decision under section 63 that no such situation has been created;

(b)   in the case of a decision that arrangements are in progress or in contemplation which, if carried into effect, will result in the creation of a special merger situation, it is to be treated as a decision under section 63 that no such arrangements are in progress or in contemplation.

(5)   Expressions used in this paragraph are to be construed in accordance with Part 3 of the Enterprise Act 2002.

57. (1)   This paragraph applies for the purposes of Part 4 of the Enterprise Act 2002.

(2)   Where a decision under section 134, 141 or 141A of that Act is not a qualifying majority decision—

(a)   in the case of a decision on an ordinary reference that a feature or combination of features of a relevant market prevents, restricts or distorts competition in connection with the supply or acquisition of any goods or services in the United Kingdom or a part of the United Kingdom, it is to be treated as a decision that the feature or (as the case may be) combination of features of that relevant market does not prevent, restrict or distort such competition;

(b)   in the case of a decision on a cross-market reference that a feature or a combination of the features specified in the reference, as that feature or combination of features relates to goods or services of one or more than one of the descriptions so specified, prevents, restricts or distorts competition in connection with the supply or acquisition of any goods or services in the United Kingdom or a part of the United Kingdom, it is to be treated as a decision that that feature or (as the case may be) combination of features as it relates to goods or services of those descriptions does not prevent, restrict or distort such competition.

(3)   Accordingly, a CMA group is to be treated as having decided under section 134, 141 or 141A that there is no adverse effect on competition in relation to an ordinary reference or a cross-market reference if—

(a)   one or more than one decision of the group, in relation to the reference, is to be treated as mentioned in sub-paragraph (2)(a) or (as the case may be) (b), and

(b)   there is, in relation to the reference, no other relevant decision of the group.

(4)   "Relevant decision", in sub-paragraph (3)(b), means—

(a)   in relation to an ordinary reference, a decision that is not to be treated as mentioned in sub-paragraph (2)(a), and which is that a feature or combination of features of a relevant market prevents, restricts or distorts competition in connection with the supply or acquisition of any goods or services in the United Kingdom or a part of the United Kingdom;

(b)   in relation to a cross-market reference, a decision that is not to be treated as mentioned in sub-paragraph (2)(b), and which is that a feature or a combination of the features specified in the reference, as that feature or combination of features relates to goods or services of one or more than one of the descriptions so specified, prevents, restricts or distorts competition in connection with the supply or acquisition of any goods or services in the United Kingdom or a part of the United Kingdom.

(5)   Where a decision of a CMA group under section 141A of that Act is not a qualifying majority decision, in the case of a decision under section 141A(4) that the feature or combination of features in question operates or may be expected to operate against the public interest, it is to be treated as a decision under section 141A that the feature or combination of features in question does not operate nor may be expected to operate against the public interest.

(6)   Expressions used in this paragraph are to be construed in accordance with Part 4 of the Enterprise Act 2002.

58. A decision made by a CMA group is also subject to any other provision made by or under any enactment about decisions that are not qualifying majority decisions.

NOTES
Commencement: 1 October 2013 (paras 34, 35, paras 51, 53 (for the purposes of making and publishing rules of procedure), para 52 (for the purposes of preparing and issuing guidance)); 1 April 2014 (otherwise).
Paras 35(1)(ca), 38(5A) and 38(4)(c)(v) were inserted by the Financial Services (Banking Reform) Act 2013, s 79(8), Sch 5, para 2.
Transitional provisions: see the note to Part 1 of this Schedule at **[1.2195]**.

PART 4
INTERPRETATION AND TRANSITIONAL AND TRANSITORY PROVISION

Interpretation

[1.2198]

59. (1) In this Schedule, "enactment" means—

(a) an enactment contained in this or any other Act;

(b) an enactment comprised in subordinate legislation within the meaning of the Interpretation Act 1978;

(c) an enactment contained in, or in an instrument made under, an Act of the Scottish Parliament;

(d) a Measure or Act of the National Assembly for Wales;

(e) an enactment contained in, or in an instrument made under, Northern Ireland legislation (within the meaning of the Interpretation Act 1978).

(2) Any reference in this Schedule to an enactment includes a reference to an enactment whenever passed or made.

60. References in this Schedule to the commencement date are to the date on which section 25(3) comes into force.

Members of the Competition Commission

61. (1) This paragraph applies—

(a) in relation to any appointments under paragraph 1(1)(b) to the CMA panel that are made before the abolition of the Competition Commission under section 26, to any person who is a panel member of the Competition Commission and whose term of office as such is not due to expire before the abolition of the Competition Commission under that section;

(b) in relation to any other appointment under paragraph 1(1)(b) to the CMA panel, to a person who was a panel member of the Competition Commission immediately prior to its abolition under section 26.

(2) A person to whom this paragraph applies may be appointed under paragraph 1(1)(b) as a member of the CMA panel.

(3) But the terms of the person's appointment as a member of the CMA panel must not be such that the sum of the period of his or her office as a member of the CMA panel, and of the period of his or her office as a panel member of the Competition Commission (excluding any period when he or she also holds office as a member of the CMA panel), exceeds eight years.

(4) Paragraph 4(1) applies for the purposes of the person's re-appointment as a member of the CMA panel as it does for the purposes of the re-appointment of a CMA panel member to whom this paragraph does not apply.

(5) The power conferred by section 100 includes power to make provision for the appointment of panel members of the Competition Commission as members of the CMA panel, or for the re-appointment of persons who are appointed as members of the CMA panel by virtue of sub-paragraph (2), for the purpose of enabling anything in the process of being done by or on behalf of the Competition Commission immediately prior to its abolition to be completed by or on behalf of the CMA; and nothing in sub-paragraphs (1) to (4) restricts the provision that may be made for that purpose.

62. Except as provided for by paragraph 61, a person who holds or has held office as a panel member of the Competition Commission at any time prior to its abolition may not be appointed under paragraph 1(1)(b) as a member of the CMA panel.

63. References in paragraphs 61 and 62 to a panel member of the Competition Commission are to a person appointed as a member of the Competition Commission of a kind mentioned in paragraph 2(3) of Schedule 7 to the Competition Act 1998.

Financial years of the CMA

64. (1) If the duration of the period beginning with the commencement date and ending with the next 31 March is six months or more, the first financial year of the CMA is that period.

(2) But if the duration of that period is less than six months, the first financial year of the CMA is the period beginning with the commencement date, and ending with the 31 March in the year following the next 31 March after the commencement date.

(3)   The subsequent financial years of the CMA are each successive period of 12 months.

First annual plan of the CMA

65. (1)   The CMA is to publish its first annual plan within the period of three months beginning with the commencement date.

(2)   The first annual plan is to relate to the period beginning with the date of publication of the plan, and ending with the date on which the CMA's first financial year ends.

NOTES

Commencement: 1 October 2013 (paras 59, 60, 61(1)–(4), 62–65); 1 April 2014 (otherwise).

Orders: the Enterprise and Regulatory Reform Act 2013 (Commencement No 3, Transitional Provisions and Savings) Order 2013, SI 2013/2227.

Transitional provisions: see the note to Part 1 of this Schedule at **[1.2195]**.

INSURANCE ACT 2015

(2015 c 4)

ARRANGEMENT OF SECTIONS

An Act to make new provision about insurance contracts; to amend the Third Parties (Rights against Insurers) Act 2010 in relation to the insured persons to whom that Act applies; and for connected purposes.

[12 February 2015]

PART 1
INSURANCE CONTRACTS: MAIN DEFINITIONS

[1.2199]
1 Insurance contracts: main definitions
In this Act (apart from Part 6)—
   "consumer insurance contract" has the same meaning as in the Consumer Insurance (Disclosure and Representations) Act 2012;
   "non-consumer insurance contract" means a contract of insurance that is not a consumer insurance contract;
   "insured" means the party to a contract of insurance who is the insured under the contract, or would be if the contract were entered into;
   "insurer" means the party to a contract of insurance who is the insurer under the contract, or would be if the contract were entered into;
   "the duty of fair presentation" means the duty imposed by section 3(1).

NOTES
Commencement: 12 August 2016.

PART 2
THE DUTY OF FAIR PRESENTATION

[1.2200]
2 Application and interpretation
(1)   This Part applies to non-consumer insurance contracts only.
(2)   This Part applies in relation to variations of non-consumer insurance contracts as it applies to contracts, but—
   (a)   references to the risk are to be read as references to changes in the risk relevant to the proposed variation, and
   (b)   references to the contract of insurance are to the variation.

NOTES
Commencement: 12 August 2016.

[1.2201]
3 The duty of fair presentation
(1)   Before a contract of insurance is entered into, the insured must make to the insurer a fair presentation of the risk.
(2)   The duty imposed by subsection (1) is referred to in this Act as "the duty of fair presentation".
(3)   A fair presentation of the risk is one—
   (a)   which makes the disclosure required by subsection (4),
   (b)   which makes that disclosure in a manner which would be reasonably clear and accessible to a prudent insurer, and
   (c)   in which every material representation as to a matter of fact is substantially correct, and every material representation as to a matter of expectation or belief is made in good faith.
(4)   The disclosure required is as follows, except as provided in subsection (5)—
   (a)   disclosure of every material circumstance which the insured knows or ought to know, or
   (b)   failing that, disclosure which gives the insurer sufficient information to put a prudent insurer on notice that it needs to make further enquiries for the purpose of revealing those material circumstances.
(5)   In the absence of enquiry, subsection (4) does not require the insured to disclose a circumstance if—
   (a)   it diminishes the risk,
   (b)   the insurer knows it,
   (c)   the insurer ought to know it,
   (d)   the insurer is presumed to know it, or
   (e)   it is something as to which the insurer waives information.
(6)   Sections 4 to 6 make further provision about the knowledge of the insured and of the insurer, and section 7 contains supplementary provision.

NOTES
Commencement: 12 August 2016.

[1.2202]
4   Knowledge of insured
(1)   This section provides for what an insured knows or ought to know for the purposes of section 3(4)(a).

(2)   An insured who is an individual knows only—
    (a)   what is known to the individual, and
    (b)   what is known to one or more of the individuals who are responsible for the insured's insurance.

(3)   An insured who is not an individual knows only what is known to one or more of the individuals who are—
    (a)   part of the insured's senior management, or
    (b)   responsible for the insured's insurance.

(4)   An insured is not by virtue of subsection (2)(b) or (3)(b) taken to know confidential information known to an individual if—
    (a)   the individual is, or is an employee of, the insured's agent; and
    (b)   the information was acquired by the insured's agent (or by an employee of that agent) through a business relationship with a person who is not connected with the contract of insurance.

(5)   For the purposes of subsection (4) the persons connected with a contract of insurance are—
    (a)   the insured and any other persons for whom cover is provided by the contract, and
    (b)   if the contract re-insures risks covered by another contract, the persons who are (by virtue of this subsection) connected with that other contract.

(6)   Whether an individual or not, an insured ought to know what should reasonably have been revealed by a reasonable search of information available to the insured (whether the search is conducted by making enquiries or by any other means).

(7)   In subsection (6) "information" includes information held within the insured's organisation or by any other person (such as the insured's agent or a person for whom cover is provided by the contract of insurance).

(8)   For the purposes of this section—
    (a)   "employee", in relation to the insured's agent, includes any individual working for the agent, whatever the capacity in which the individual acts,
    (b)   an individual is responsible for the insured's insurance if the individual participates on behalf of the insured in the process of procuring the insured's insurance (whether the individual does so as the insured's employee or agent, as an employee of the insured's agent or in any other capacity), and
    (c)   "senior management" means those individuals who play significant roles in the making of decisions about how the insured's activities are to be managed or organised.

NOTES
Commencement: 12 August 2016.

[1.2203]
5   Knowledge of insurer
(1)   For the purposes of section 3(5)(b), an insurer knows something only if it is known to one or more of the individuals who participate on behalf of the insurer in the decision whether to take the risk, and if so on what terms (whether the individual does so as the insurer's employee or agent, as an employee of the insurer's agent or in any other capacity).

(2)   For the purposes of section 3(5)(c), an insurer ought to know something only if—
    (a)   an employee or agent of the insurer knows it, and ought reasonably to have passed on the relevant information to an individual mentioned in subsection (1), or
    (b)   the relevant information is held by the insurer and is readily available to an individual mentioned in subsection (1).

(3)   For the purposes of section 3(5)(d), an insurer is presumed to know—
    (a)   things which are common knowledge, and
    (b)   things which an insurer offering insurance of the class in question to insureds in the field of activity in question would reasonably be expected to know in the ordinary course of business.

NOTES
Commencement: 12 August 2016.

[1.2204]
6   Knowledge: general
(1)   For the purposes of sections 3 to 5, references to an individual's knowledge include not only actual knowledge, but also matters which the individual suspected, and of which the individual would have had knowledge but for deliberately refraining from confirming them or enquiring about them.

(2)   Nothing in this Part affects the operation of any rule of law according to which knowledge of a fraud perpetrated by an individual ("F") either on the insured or on the insurer is not to be attributed to the insured or to the insurer (respectively), where—

  (a)   if the fraud is on the insured, F is any of the individuals mentioned in section 4(2)(b) or (3), or

  (b)   if the fraud is on the insurer, F is any of the individuals mentioned in section 5(1).

NOTES

  Commencement: 12 August 2016.

[1.2205]

7   Supplementary

(1)   A fair presentation need not be contained in only one document or oral presentation.

(2)   The term "circumstance" includes any communication made to, or information received by, the insured.

(3)   A circumstance or representation is material if it would influence the judgement of a prudent insurer in determining whether to take the risk and, if so, on what terms.

(4)   Examples of things which may be material circumstances are—

  (a)   special or unusual facts relating to the risk,

  (b)   any particular concerns which led the insured to seek insurance cover for the risk,

  (c)   anything which those concerned with the class of insurance and field of activity in question would generally understand as being something that should be dealt with in a fair presentation of risks of the type in question.

(5)   A material representation is substantially correct if a prudent insurer would not consider the difference between what is represented and what is actually correct to be material.

(6)   A representation may be withdrawn or corrected before the contract of insurance is entered into.

NOTES

  Commencement: 12 August 2016.

[1.2206]

8   Remedies for breach

(1)   The insurer has a remedy against the insured for a breach of the duty of fair presentation only if the insurer shows that, but for the breach, the insurer—

  (a)   would not have entered into the contract of insurance at all, or

  (b)   would have done so only on different terms.

(2)   The remedies are set out in Schedule 1.

(3)   A breach for which the insurer has a remedy against the insured is referred to in this Act as a "qualifying breach".

(4)   A qualifying breach is either—

  (a)   deliberate or reckless, or

  (b)   neither deliberate nor reckless.

(5)   A qualifying breach is deliberate or reckless if the insured—

  (a)   knew that it was in breach of the duty of fair presentation, or

  (b)   did not care whether or not it was in breach of that duty.

(6)   It is for the insurer to show that a qualifying breach was deliberate or reckless.

NOTES

  Commencement: 12 August 2016.

PART 3

WARRANTIES AND OTHER TERMS

[1.2207]

9   Warranties and representations

(1)   This section applies to representations made by the insured in connection with—

  (a)   a proposed non-consumer insurance contract, or

  (b)   a proposed variation to a non-consumer insurance contract.

(2)   Such a representation is not capable of being converted into a warranty by means of any provision of the non-consumer insurance contract (or of the terms of the variation), or of any other contract (and whether by declaring the representation to form the basis of the contract or otherwise).

NOTES

  Commencement: 12 August 2016.

[1.2208]

10   Breach of warranty

(1)   Any rule of law that breach of a warranty (express or implied) in a contract of insurance results in the discharge of the insurer's liability under the contract is abolished.

(2)　An insurer has no liability under a contract of insurance in respect of any loss occurring, or attributable to something happening, after a warranty (express or implied) in the contract has been breached but before the breach has been remedied.

(3)　But subsection (2) does not apply if—

    (a)　because of a change of circumstances, the warranty ceases to be applicable to the circumstances of the contract,

    (b)　compliance with the warranty is rendered unlawful by any subsequent law, or

    (c)　the insurer waives the breach of warranty.

(4)　Subsection (2) does not affect the liability of the insurer in respect of losses occurring, or attributable to something happening—

    (a)　before the breach of warranty, or

    (b)　if the breach can be remedied, after it has been remedied.

(5)　For the purposes of this section, a breach of warranty is to be taken as remedied—

    (a)　in a case falling within subsection (6), if the risk to which the warranty relates later becomes essentially the same as that originally contemplated by the parties,

    (b)　in any other case, if the insured ceases to be in breach of the warranty.

(6)　A case falls within this subsection if—

    (a)　the warranty in question requires that by an ascertainable time something is to be done (or not done), or a condition is to be fulfilled, or something is (or is not) to be the case, and

    (b)　that requirement is not complied with.

(7)　In the Marine Insurance Act 1906—

    (a)　in section 33 (nature of warranty), in subsection (3), the second sentence is omitted,

    (b)　section 34 (when breach of warranty excused) is omitted.

NOTES
Commencement: 12 August 2016.

[1.2209]
11　Terms not relevant to the actual loss

(1)　This section applies to a term (express or implied) of a contract of insurance, other than a term defining the risk as a whole, if compliance with it would tend to reduce the risk of one or more of the following—

    (a)　loss of a particular kind,

    (b)　loss at a particular location,

    (c)　loss at a particular time.

(2)　If a loss occurs, and the term has not been complied with, the insurer may not rely on the non-compliance to exclude, limit or discharge its liability under the contract for the loss if the insured satisfies subsection (3).

(3)　The insured satisfies this subsection if it shows that the non-compliance with the term could not have increased the risk of the loss which actually occurred in the circumstances in which it occurred.

(4)　This section may apply in addition to section 10.

NOTES
Commencement: 12 August 2016.

PART 4
FRAUDULENT CLAIMS

[1.2210]
12　Remedies for fraudulent claims

(1)　If the insured makes a fraudulent claim under a contract of insurance—

    (a)　the insurer is not liable to pay the claim,

    (b)　the insurer may recover from the insured any sums paid by the insurer to the insured in respect of the claim, and

    (c)　in addition, the insurer may by notice to the insured treat the contract as having been terminated with effect from the time of the fraudulent act.

(2)　If the insurer does treat the contract as having been terminated—

    (a)　it may refuse all liability to the insured under the contract in respect of a relevant event occurring after the time of the fraudulent act, and

    (b)　it need not return any of the premiums paid under the contract.

(3)　Treating a contract as having been terminated under this section does not affect the rights and obligations of the parties to the contract with respect to a relevant event occurring before the time of the fraudulent act.

(4)　In subsections (2)(a) and (3), "relevant event" refers to whatever gives rise to the insurer's liability under the contract (and includes, for example, the occurrence of a loss, the making of a claim, or the notification of a potential claim, depending on how the contract is written).

NOTES
Commencement: 12 August 2016.

[1.2211]
13 Remedies for fraudulent claims: group insurance

(1) This section applies where—

(a) a contract of insurance is entered into with an insurer by a person ("A"),

(b) the contract provides cover for one or more other persons who are not parties to the contract ("the Cs"), whether or not it also provides cover of any kind for A or another insured party, and

(c) a fraudulent claim is made under the contract by or on behalf of one of the Cs ("CF").

(2) Section 12 applies in relation to the claim as if the cover provided for CF were provided under an individual insurance contract between the insurer and CF as the insured; and, accordingly—

(a) the insurer's rights under section 12 are exercisable only in relation to the cover provided for CF, and

(b) the exercise of any of those rights does not affect the cover provided under the contract for anyone else.

(3) In its application by virtue of subsection (2), section 12 is subject to the following particular modifications—

(a) the first reference to "the insured" in subsection (1)(b) of that section, in respect of any particular sum paid by the insurer, is to whichever of A and CF the insurer paid the sum to; but if a sum was paid to A and passed on by A to CF, the reference is to CF,

(b) the second reference to "the insured" in subsection (1)(b) is to A or CF,

(c) the reference to "the insured" in subsection (1)(c) is to both CF and A,

(d) the reference in subsection (2)(b) to the premiums paid under the contract is to premiums paid in respect of the cover for CF.

NOTES
Commencement: 12 August 2016.

PART 5
GOOD FAITH AND CONTRACTING OUT

Good faith

[1.2212]
14 Good faith

(1) Any rule of law permitting a party to a contract of insurance to avoid the contract on the ground that the utmost good faith has not been observed by the other party is abolished.

(2) Any rule of law to the effect that a contract of insurance is a contract based on the utmost good faith is modified to the extent required by the provisions of this Act and the Consumer Insurance (Disclosure and Representations) Act 2012.

(3) Accordingly—

(a) (*Amends the Marine Insurance Act 1906, s 17 at* **[1.263]**.)

(b) the application of that section (as so amended) is subject to the provisions of this Act and the Consumer Insurance (Disclosure and Representations) Act 2012.

(4) (*Repeals the Consumer Insurance (Disclosure and Representations) Act 2012, s 2(5) at* **[1.2144]**.)

NOTES
Commencement: 12 August 2016.

Contracting out

[1.2213]
15 Contracting out: consumer insurance contracts

(1) A term of a consumer insurance contract, or of any other contract, which would put the consumer in a worse position as respects any of the matters provided for in Part 3 or 4 of this Act than the consumer would be in by virtue of the provisions of those Parts (so far as relating to consumer insurance contracts) is to that extent of no effect.

(2) In subsection (1) references to a contract include a variation.

(3) This section does not apply in relation to a contract for the settlement of a claim arising under a consumer insurance contract.

NOTES
Commencement: 12 August 2016.

[1.2214]
16   Contracting out: non-consumer insurance contracts

(1)   A term of a non-consumer insurance contract, or of any other contract, which would put the insured in a worse position as respects representations to which section 9 applies than the insured would be in by virtue of that section is to that extent of no effect.

(2)   A term of a non-consumer insurance contract, or of any other contract, which would put the insured in a worse position as respects any of the other matters provided for in Part 2, 3 or 4 of this Act than the insured would be in by virtue of the provisions of those Parts (so far as relating to non-consumer insurance contracts) is to that extent of no effect, unless the requirements of section 17 have been satisfied in relation to the term.

(3)   In this section references to a contract include a variation.

(4)   This section does not apply in relation to a contract for the settlement of a claim arising under a non-consumer insurance contract.

NOTES
Commencement: 12 August 2016.

[1.2215]
17   The transparency requirements

(1)   In this section, "the disadvantageous term" means such a term as is mentioned in section 16(2).

(2)   The insurer must take sufficient steps to draw the disadvantageous term to the insured's attention before the contract is entered into or the variation agreed.

(3)   The disadvantageous term must be clear and unambiguous as to its effect.

(4)   In determining whether the requirements of subsections (2) and (3) have been met, the characteristics of insured persons of the kind in question, and the circumstances of the transaction, are to be taken into account.

(5)   The insured may not rely on any failure on the part of the insurer to meet the requirements of subsection (2) if the insured (or its agent) had actual knowledge of the disadvantageous term when the contract was entered into or the variation agreed.

NOTES
Commencement: 12 August 2016.

[1.2216]
18   Contracting out: group insurance contracts

(1)   This section applies to a contract of insurance referred to in section 13(1)(a); and in this section—

"A" and "the Cs" have the same meaning as in section 13,

"consumer C" means an individual who is one of the Cs, where the cover provided by the contract for that individual would have been a consumer insurance contract if entered into by that person rather than by A, and

"non-consumer C" means any of the Cs who is not a consumer C.

(2)   A term of the contract of insurance, or any other contract, which puts a consumer C in a worse position as respects any matter dealt with in section 13 than that individual would be in by virtue of that section is to that extent of no effect.

(3)   A term of the contract of insurance, or any other contract, which puts a non-consumer C in a worse position as respects any matter dealt with in section 13 than that person would be in by virtue of that section is to that extent of no effect, unless the requirements of section 17 have been met in relation to the term.

(4)   Section 17 applies in relation to such a term as it applies to a term mentioned in section 16(2), with references to the insured being read as references to A rather than the non-consumer C.

(5)   In this section references to a contract include a variation.

(6)   This section does not apply in relation to a contract for the settlement of a claim arising under a contract of insurance to which this section applies.

NOTES
Commencement: 12 August 2016.

PART 6
AMENDMENT OF THE THIRD PARTIES (RIGHTS AGAINST INSURERS) ACT 2010

19   *(This section substitutes the Third Parties (Rights against Insurers) Act 2010, s 19 at* **[1.2078]***).*

[1.2217]
20   Other amendments

Schedule 2 amends the Third Parties (Rights against Insurers) Act 2010 in relation to the insured persons to whom the Act applies.

NOTES

Commencement: to be appointed.

PART 7
GENERAL

21 *(This section repeals the Marine Insurance Act 1906, ss 18, 19, 20 and provides that any rule of law to the same effect as any of those provisions is abolished; repeals the Consumer Insurance (Disclosure and Representations) Act 2012, s 11(1), (2) at* **[1.2153]** *and contains other amendments that are outside the scope of this work.)*

[1.2218]
22 Application etc of Parts 2 to 5

(1) Part 2 (and section 21) and section 14 apply only in relation to—
  (a) contracts of insurance entered into after the end of the relevant period, and
  (b) variations, agreed after the end of the relevant period, to contracts of insurance entered into at any time.

(2) Parts 3 and 4 of this Act apply only in relation to contracts of insurance entered into after the end of the relevant period, and variations to such contracts.

(3) In subsections (1) and (2) "the relevant period" means the period of 18 months beginning with the day on which this Act is passed.

(4) Unless the contrary intention appears, references in Parts 2 to 5 to something being done by or in relation to the insurer or the insured include its being done by or in relation to that person's agent.

NOTES

Commencement: 12 August 2016.

[1.2219]
23 Extent, commencement and short title

(1) This Act extends to England and Wales, Scotland and Northern Ireland, except for—
  (a) section 21(4), which does not extend to Northern Ireland; and
  (b) section 21(5), which extends to Northern Ireland only.

(2) This Act (apart from Part 6 and this section) comes into force at the end of the period of 18 months beginning with the day on which it is passed.

(3) In Part 6—
  (a) section 19 comes into force at the end of the period of two months beginning with the day on which this Act is passed; and
  (b) section 20 and Schedule 2 come into force on the day appointed under section 21(2) of the Third Parties (Rights against Insurers) Act 2010 for the coming into force of that Act.

(4) This section comes into force on the day on which this Act is passed.

(5) This Act may be cited as the Insurance Act 2015.

NOTES

Commencement: 12 February 2015.

SCHEDULES

SCHEDULE 1
INSURERS' REMEDIES FOR QUALIFYING BREACHES

Section 8(2)

PART 1
CONTRACTS

General

[1.2220]
1. This Part of this Schedule applies to qualifying breaches of the duty of fair presentation in relation to non-consumer insurance contracts (for variations to them, see Part 2).

Deliberate or reckless breaches

2. If a qualifying breach was deliberate or reckless, the insurer—
  (a) may avoid the contract and refuse all claims, and
  (b) need not return any of the premiums paid.

Other breaches

3. Paragraphs 4 to 6 apply if a qualifying breach was neither deliberate nor reckless.

4. If, in the absence of the qualifying breach, the insurer would not have entered into the contract on any terms, the insurer may avoid the contract and refuse all claims, but must in that event return the premiums paid.

5. If the insurer would have entered into the contract, but on different terms (other than terms relating to the premium), the contract is to be treated as if it had been entered into on those different terms if the insurer so requires.

6. (1) In addition, if the insurer would have entered into the contract (whether the terms relating to matters other than the premium would have been the same or different), but would have charged a higher premium, the insurer may reduce proportionately the amount to be paid on a claim.

(2) In sub-paragraph (1), "reduce proportionately" means that the insurer need pay on the claim only X% of what it would otherwise have been under an obligation to pay under the terms of the contract (or, if applicable, under the different terms provided for by virtue of paragraph 5), where—

X = (Premium actually charged / Higher premium) x 100

NOTES

Commencement: 12 August 2016.

PART 2
VARIATIONS
General

[1.2221]
7. This Part of this Schedule applies to qualifying breaches of the duty of fair presentation in relation to variations to non-consumer insurance contracts.

Deliberate or reckless breaches

8. If a qualifying breach was deliberate or reckless, the insurer—
(a) may by notice to the insured treat the contract as having been terminated with effect from the time when the variation was made, and
(b) need not return any of the premiums paid.

Other breaches

9. (1) This paragraph applies if—
(a) a qualifying breach was neither deliberate nor reckless, and
(b) the total premium was increased or not changed as a result of the variation.

(2) If, in the absence of the qualifying breach, the insurer would not have agreed to the variation on any terms, the insurer may treat the contract as if the variation was never made, but must in that event return any extra premium paid.

(3) If sub-paragraph (2) does not apply—
(a) if the insurer would have agreed to the variation on different terms (other than terms relating to the premium), the variation is to be treated as if it had been entered into on those different terms if the insurer so requires, and
(b) paragraph 11 also applies if (in the case of an increased premium) the insurer would have increased the premium by more than it did, or (in the case of an unchanged premium) the insurer would have increased the premium.

10. (1) This paragraph applies if—
(a) a qualifying breach was neither deliberate nor reckless, and
(b) the total premium was reduced as a result of the variation.

(2) If, in the absence of the qualifying breach, the insurer would not have agreed to the variation on any terms, the insurer may treat the contract as if the variation was never made, and paragraph 11 also applies.

(3) If sub-paragraph (2) does not apply—
(a) if the insurer would have agreed to the variation on different terms (other than terms relating to the premium), the variation is to be treated as if it had been entered into on those different terms if the insurer so requires, and
(b) paragraph 11 also applies if the insurer would have increased the premium, would not have reduced the premium, or would have reduced it by less than it did.

Proportionate reduction

11. (1) If this paragraph applies, the insurer may reduce proportionately the amount to be paid on a claim arising out of events after the variation.

(2) In sub-paragraph (1), "reduce proportionately" means that the insurer need pay on the claim only Y% of what it would otherwise have been under an obligation to pay under the terms of the contract (whether on the original terms, or as varied, or under the different terms provided for by virtue of paragraph 9(3)(a) or 10(3)(a), as the case may be), where—

Y = (Total premium actually charged / P) x 100

(3) In the formula in sub-paragraph (2), "P"—
   (a) in a paragraph 9(3)(b) case, is the total premium the insurer would have charged,
   (b) in a paragraph 10(2) case, is the original premium,
   (c) in a paragraph 10(3)(b) case, is the original premium if the insurer would not have changed it, and otherwise the increased or (as the case may be) reduced total premium the insurer would have charged.

NOTES
  Commencement: 12 August 2016.

PART 3
SUPPLEMENTARY

Relationship with section 84 of the Marine Insurance Act 1906

[1.2222]
12 Section 84 of the Marine Insurance Act 1906 (return of premium for failure of consideration) is to be read subject to the provisions of this Schedule in relation to contracts of marine insurance which are non-consumer insurance contracts.

NOTES
  Commencement: 12 August 2016.

SCHEDULE 2
RIGHTS OF THIRD PARTIES AGAINST INSURERS: RELEVANT INSURED PERSONS

*(Sch 2 amends the Third Parties (Rights against Insurers) Act 2010 at **[1.2061]** et seq.)*

CONSUMER RIGHTS ACT 2015

(2015 c 15)

ARRANGEMENT OF SECTIONS

PART 1
CONSUMER CONTRACTS FOR GOODS, DIGITAL CONTENT AND SERVICES

CHAPTER 1
INTRODUCTION

CHAPTER 2
GOODS

What Goods Contracts are Covered?

What Statutory Rights are There under a Goods Contract?

What Remedies are There if Statutory Rights under a Goods Contract are not Met?

CHAPTER 3
DIGITAL CONTENT

CHAPTER 4
SERVICES

CHAPTER 5
GENERAL AND SUPPLEMENTARY PROVISIONS

SCHEDULES

An Act to amend the law relating to the rights of consumers and protection of their interests; to make provision about investigatory powers for enforcing the regulation of traders; to make provision about private actions in competition law and the Competition Appeal Tribunal; and for connected purposes.

[26 March 2015]

NOTES

Commencement: the commencement of this Act is provided for by s 100. See that section at **[1.2318]** and the Orders made under it, ie: the Consumer Rights Act 2015 (Commencement) (England) Order 2015, SI 2015/965 at **[2.1172]**; the Consumer Rights Act 2015 (Commencement No 1) Order 2015, SI 2015/1333 at **[2.1204]**; the Consumer Rights Act 2015 (Commencement No 2 and Transitional Provision) (England) Order 2015, SI 2015/1575 at **[2.1206]**; the Consumer Rights Act 2015 (Commencement No 2) Order 2015, SI 2015/1584 at **[2.1209]**; the Consumer Rights Act 2015 (Commencement No 1 and Transitional Provision) (Wales) Order 2015, SI 2015/1605 at **[2.1212]**; the Consumer Rights Act 2015 (Commencement No 3, Transitional Provisions, Savings and Consequential Amendments) Order 2015, SI 2015/1630 at **[2.1215]**. Note, in particular, the transitional provisions relating to the commencement of this Act in the Consumer Rights Act 2015 (Commencement No 2 and Transitional Provision) (England) Order 2015, SI 2015/1575, the Consumer Rights Act 2015 (Commencement No 1 and Transitional Provision) (Wales) Order 2015, SI 2015/1605, and the Consumer Rights Act 2015 (Commencement No 3, Transitional Provisions, Savings and Consequential Amendments) Order 2015, SI 2015/1630.

PART 1
CONSUMER CONTRACTS FOR GOODS, DIGITAL CONTENT AND SERVICES

CHAPTER 1
INTRODUCTION

[1.2223]
1 Where Part 1 applies
(1)   This Part applies where there is an agreement between a trader and a consumer for the trader to supply goods, digital content or services, if the agreement is a contract.
(2)   It applies whether the contract is written or oral or implied from the parties' conduct, or more than one of these combined.
(3)   Any of Chapters 2, 3 and 4 may apply to a contract—
  (a)   if it is a contract for the trader to supply goods, see Chapter 2;
  (b)   if it is a contract for the trader to supply digital content, see Chapter 3 (also, subsection (6));
  (c)   if it is a contract for the trader to supply a service, see Chapter 4 (also, subsection (6)).
(4)   In each case the Chapter applies even if the contract also covers something covered by another Chapter (a mixed contract).
(5)   Two or all three of those Chapters may apply to a mixed contract.
(6)   For provisions about particular mixed contracts, see—
  (a)   section 15 (goods and installation);
  (b)   section 16 (goods and digital content).
(7)   For other provision applying to contracts to which this Part applies, see Part 2 (unfair terms).

NOTES
Commencement: 1 October 2015.

[1.2224]
2 Key definitions
(1)   These definitions apply in this Part (as well as the definitions in section 59).
(2)   "Trader" means a person acting for purposes relating to that person's trade, business, craft or profession, whether acting personally or through another person acting in the trader's name or on the trader's behalf.

(3) "Consumer" means an individual acting for purposes that are wholly or mainly outside that individual's trade, business, craft or profession.

(4) A trader claiming that an individual was not acting for purposes wholly or mainly outside the individual's trade, business, craft or profession must prove it.

(5) For the purposes of Chapter 2, except to the extent mentioned in subsection (6), a person is not a consumer in relation to a sales contract if—
    (a) the goods are second hand goods sold at public auction, and
    (b) individuals have the opportunity of attending the sale in person.

(6) A person is a consumer in relation to such a contract for the purposes of—
    (a) sections 11(4) and (5), 12, 28 and 29, and
    (b) the other provisions of Chapter 2 as they apply in relation to those sections.

(7) "Business" includes the activities of any government department or local or public authority.

(8) "Goods" means any tangible moveable items, but that includes water, gas and electricity if and only if they are put up for supply in a limited volume or set quantity.

(9) "Digital content" means data which are produced and supplied in digital form.

NOTES
Commencement: 1 October 2015.

CHAPTER 2
GOODS

What Goods Contracts are Covered?

[1.2225]
3 Contracts covered by this Chapter
(1) This Chapter applies to a contract for a trader to supply goods to a consumer.

(2) It applies only if the contract is one of these (defined for the purposes of this Part in sections 5 to 8)—
    (a) a sales contract;
    (b) a contract for the hire of goods;
    (c) a hire-purchase agreement;
    (d) a contract for transfer of goods.

(3) It does not apply—
    (a) to a contract for a trader to supply coins or notes to a consumer for use as currency;
    (b) to a contract for goods to be sold by way of execution or otherwise by authority of law;
    (c) to a contract intended to operate as a mortgage, pledge, charge or other security;
    (d) in relation to England and Wales or Northern Ireland, to a contract made by deed and for which the only consideration is the presumed consideration imported by the deed;
    (e) in relation to Scotland, to a gratuitous contract.

(4) A contract to which this Chapter applies is referred to in this Part as a "contract to supply goods".

(5) Contracts to supply goods include—
    (a) contracts entered into between one part owner and another;
    (b) contracts for the transfer of an undivided share in goods;
    (c) contracts that are absolute and contracts that are conditional.

(6) Subsection (1) is subject to any provision of this Chapter that applies a section or part of a section to only some of the kinds of contracts listed in subsection (2).

(7) A mixed contract (see section 1(4)) may be a contract of any of those kinds.

NOTES
Commencement: 1 October 2015.

[1.2226]
4 Ownership of goods
(1) In this Chapter ownership of goods means the general property in goods, not merely a special property.

(2) For the time when ownership of goods is transferred, see in particular the following provisions of the Sale of Goods Act 1979 (which relate to contracts of sale)—

section 16:	goods must be ascertained
section 17:	property passes when intended to pass
section 18:	rules for ascertaining intention
section 19:	reservation of right of disposal
section 20A:	undivided shares in goods forming part of a bulk
section 20B:	deemed consent by co-owner to dealings in bulk goods

NOTES
Commencement: 1 October 2015.

[1.2227]
5   Sales contracts
(1)   A contract is a sales contract if under it—
   (a)   the trader transfers or agrees to transfer ownership of goods to the consumer, and
   (b)   the consumer pays or agrees to pay the price.
(2)   A contract is a sales contract (whether or not it would be one under subsection (1)) if under the contract—
   (a)   goods are to be manufactured or produced and the trader agrees to supply them to the consumer,
   (b)   on being supplied, the goods will be owned by the consumer, and
   (c)   the consumer pays or agrees to pay the price.
(3)   A sales contract may be conditional (see section 3(5)), but in this Part "conditional sales contract" means a sales contract under which—
   (a)   the price for the goods or part of it is payable by instalments, and
   (b)   the trader retains ownership of the goods until the conditions specified in the contract (for the payment of instalments or otherwise) are met;
and it makes no difference whether or not the consumer possesses the goods.

NOTES
Commencement: 1 October 2015.

[1.2228]
6   Contracts for the hire of goods
(1)   A contract is for the hire of goods if under it the trader gives or agrees to give the consumer possession of the goods with the right to use them, subject to the terms of the contract, for a period determined in accordance with the contract.
(2)   But a contract is not for the hire of goods if it is a hire-purchase agreement.

NOTES
Commencement: 1 October 2015.

[1.2229]
7   Hire-purchase agreements
(1)   A contract is a hire-purchase agreement if it meets the two conditions set out below.
(2)   The first condition is that under the contract goods are hired by the trader in return for periodical payments by the consumer (and "hired" is to be read in accordance with section 6(1)).
(3)   The second condition is that under the contract ownership of the goods will transfer to the consumer if the terms of the contract are complied with and—
   (a)   the consumer exercises an option to buy the goods,
   (b)   any party to the contract does an act specified in it, or
   (c)   an event specified in the contract occurs.
(4)   But a contract is not a hire-purchase agreement if it is a conditional sales contract.

NOTES
Commencement: 1 October 2015.

[1.2230]
8   Contracts for transfer of goods
A contract to supply goods is a contract for transfer of goods if under it the trader transfers or agrees to transfer ownership of the goods to the consumer and—
   (a)   the consumer provides or agrees to provide consideration otherwise than by paying a price, or
   (b)   the contract is, for any other reason, not a sales contract or a hire-purchase agreement.

NOTES
Commencement: 1 October 2015.

What Statutory Rights are There under a Goods Contract?

[1.2231]
9   Goods to be of satisfactory quality
(1)   Every contract to supply goods is to be treated as including a term that the quality of the goods is satisfactory.
(2)   The quality of goods is satisfactory if they meet the standard that a reasonable person would consider satisfactory, taking account of—
   (a)   any description of the goods,

(b)   the price or other consideration for the goods (if relevant), and
(c)   all the other relevant circumstances (see subsection (5)).
(3)   The quality of goods includes their state and condition; and the following aspects (among others) are in appropriate cases aspects of the quality of goods—
    (a)   fitness for all the purposes for which goods of that kind are usually supplied;
    (b)   appearance and finish;
    (c)   freedom from minor defects;
    (d)   safety;
    (e)   durability.
(4)   The term mentioned in subsection (1) does not cover anything which makes the quality of the goods unsatisfactory—
    (a)   which is specifically drawn to the consumer's attention before the contract is made,
    (b)   where the consumer examines the goods before the contract is made, which that examination ought to reveal, or
    (c)   in the case of a contract to supply goods by sample, which would have been apparent on a reasonable examination of the sample.
(5)   The relevant circumstances mentioned in subsection (2)(c) include any public statement about the specific characteristics of the goods made by the trader, the producer or any representative of the trader or the producer.
(6)   That includes, in particular, any public statement made in advertising or labelling.
(7)   But a public statement is not a relevant circumstance for the purposes of subsection (2)(c) if the trader shows that—
    (a)   when the contract was made, the trader was not, and could not reasonably have been, aware of the statement,
    (b)   before the contract was made, the statement had been publicly withdrawn or, to the extent that it contained anything which was incorrect or misleading, it had been publicly corrected, or
    (c)   the consumer's decision to contract for the goods could not have been influenced by the statement.
(8)   In a contract to supply goods a term about the quality of the goods may be treated as included as a matter of custom.
(9)   See section 19 for a consumer's rights if the trader is in breach of a term that this section requires to be treated as included in a contract.

___

NOTES
Commencement: 1 October 2015.

___

[1.2232]
10   Goods to be fit for particular purpose
(1)   Subsection (3) applies to a contract to supply goods if before the contract is made the consumer makes known to the trader (expressly or by implication) any particular purpose for which the consumer is contracting for the goods.
(2)   Subsection (3) also applies to a contract to supply goods if—
    (a)   the goods were previously sold by a credit-broker to the trader,
    (b)   in the case of a sales contract or contract for transfer of goods, the consideration or part of it is a sum payable by instalments, and
    (c)   before the contract is made, the consumer makes known to the credit-broker (expressly or by implication) any particular purpose for which the consumer is contracting for the goods.
(3)   The contract is to be treated as including a term that the goods are reasonably fit for that purpose, whether or not that is a purpose for which goods of that kind are usually supplied.
(4)   Subsection (3) does not apply if the circumstances show that the consumer does not rely, or it is unreasonable for the consumer to rely, on the skill or judgment of the trader or credit-broker.
(5)   In a contract to supply goods a term about the fitness of the goods for a particular purpose may be treated as included as a matter of custom.
(6)   See section 19 for a consumer's rights if the trader is in breach of a term that this section requires to be treated as included in a contract.

___

NOTES
Commencement: 1 October 2015.

___

[1.2233]
11   Goods to be as described
(1)   Every contract to supply goods by description is to be treated as including a term that the goods will match the description.
(2)   If the supply is by sample as well as by description, it is not sufficient that the bulk of the goods matches the sample if the goods do not also match the description.
(3)   A supply of goods is not prevented from being a supply by description just because—
    (a)   the goods are exposed for supply, and
    (b)   they are selected by the consumer.

(4) Any information that is provided by the trader about the goods and is information mentioned in paragraph (a) of Schedule 1 or 2 to the Consumer Contracts (Information, Cancellation and Additional Charges) Regulations 2013 (SI 2013/3134) (main characteristics of goods) is to be treated as included as a term of the contract.

(5) A change to any of that information, made before entering into the contract or later, is not effective unless expressly agreed between the consumer and the trader.

(6) See section 2(5) and (6) for the application of subsections (4) and (5) where goods are sold at public auction.

(7) See section 19 for a consumer's rights if the trader is in breach of a term that this section requires to be treated as included in a contract.

NOTES

Commencement: 1 October 2015.

[1.2234]
12 Other pre-contract information included in contract

(1) This section applies to any contract to supply goods.

(2) Where regulation 9, 10 or 13 of the Consumer Contracts (Information, Cancellation and Additional Charges) Regulations 2013 (SI 2013/3134) required the trader to provide information to the consumer before the contract became binding, any of that information that was provided by the trader other than information about the goods and mentioned in paragraph (a) of Schedule 1 or 2 to the Regulations (main characteristics of goods) is to be treated as included as a term of the contract.

(3) A change to any of that information, made before entering into the contract or later, is not effective unless expressly agreed between the consumer and the trader.

(4) See section 2(5) and (6) for the application of this section where goods are sold at public auction.

(5) See section 19 for a consumer's rights if the trader is in breach of a term that this section requires to be treated as included in the contract.

NOTES

Commencement: 1 October 2015.

[1.2235]
13 Goods to match a sample

(1) This section applies to a contract to supply goods by reference to a sample of the goods that is seen or examined by the consumer before the contract is made.

(2) Every contract to which this section applies is to be treated as including a term that—

    (a) the goods will match the sample except to the extent that any differences between the sample and the goods are brought to the consumer's attention before the contract is made, and

    (b) the goods will be free from any defect that makes their quality unsatisfactory and that would not be apparent on a reasonable examination of the sample.

(3) See section 19 for a consumer's rights if the trader is in breach of a term that this section requires to be treated as included in a contract.

NOTES

Commencement: 1 October 2015.

[1.2236]
14 Goods to match a model seen or examined

(1) This section applies to a contract to supply goods by reference to a model of the goods that is seen or examined by the consumer before entering into the contract.

(2) Every contract to which this section applies is to be treated as including a term that the goods will match the model except to the extent that any differences between the model and the goods are brought to the consumer's attention before the consumer enters into the contract.

(3) See section 19 for a consumer's rights if the trader is in breach of a term that this section requires to be treated as included in a contract.

NOTES

Commencement: 1 October 2015.

[1.2237]
15 Installation as part of conformity of the goods with the contract

(1) Goods do not conform to a contract to supply goods if—

    (a) installation of the goods forms part of the contract,

    (b) the goods are installed by the trader or under the trader's responsibility, and

    (c) the goods are installed incorrectly.

(2) See section 19 for the effect of goods not conforming to the contract.

NOTES

Commencement: 1 October 2015.

[1.2238]
16 Goods not conforming to contract if digital content does not conform

(1)   Goods (whether or not they conform otherwise to a contract to supply goods) do not conform to it if—

    (a)   the goods are an item that includes digital content, and

    (b)   the digital content does not conform to the contract to supply that content (for which see section 42(1)).

(2)   See section 19 for the effect of goods not conforming to the contract.

NOTES

Commencement: 1 October 2015.

[1.2239]
17 Trader to have right to supply the goods etc

(1)   Every contract to supply goods, except one within subsection (4), is to be treated as including a term—

    (a)   in the case of a contract for the hire of goods, that at the beginning of the period of hire the trader must have the right to transfer possession of the goods by way of hire for that period,

    (b)   in any other case, that the trader must have the right to sell or transfer the goods at the time when ownership of the goods is to be transferred.

(2)   Every contract to supply goods, except a contract for the hire of goods or a contract within subsection (4), is to be treated as including a term that—

    (a)   the goods are free from any charge or encumbrance not disclosed or known to the consumer before entering into the contract,

    (b)   the goods will remain free from any such charge or encumbrance until ownership of them is to be transferred, and

    (c)   the consumer will enjoy quiet possession of the goods except so far as it may be disturbed by the owner or other person entitled to the benefit of any charge or encumbrance so disclosed or known.

(3)   Every contract for the hire of goods is to be treated as including a term that the consumer will enjoy quiet possession of the goods for the period of the hire except so far as the possession may be disturbed by the owner or other person entitled to the benefit of any charge or encumbrance disclosed or known to the consumer before entering into the contract.

(4)   This subsection applies to a contract if the contract shows, or the circumstances when they enter into the contract imply, that the trader and the consumer intend the trader to transfer only—

    (a)   whatever title the trader has, even if it is limited, or

    (b)   whatever title a third person has, even if it is limited.

(5)   Every contract within subsection (4) is to be treated as including a term that all charges or encumbrances known to the trader and not known to the consumer were disclosed to the consumer before entering into the contract.

(6)   Every contract within subsection (4) is to be treated as including a term that the consumer's quiet possession of the goods—

    (a)   will not be disturbed by the trader, and

    (b)   will not be disturbed by a person claiming through or under the trader, unless that person is claiming under a charge or encumbrance that was disclosed or known to the consumer before entering into the contract.

(7)   If subsection (4)(b) applies (transfer of title that a third person has), the contract is also to be treated as including a term that the consumer's quiet possession of the goods—

    (a)   will not be disturbed by the third person, and

    (b)   will not be disturbed by a person claiming through or under the third person, unless the claim is under a charge or encumbrance that was disclosed or known to the consumer before entering into the contract.

(8)   In the case of a contract for the hire of goods, this section does not affect the right of the trader to repossess the goods where the contract provides or is to be treated as providing for this.

(9)   See section 19 for a consumer's rights if the trader is in breach of a term that this section requires to be treated as included in a contract.

NOTES

Commencement: 1 October 2015.

[1.2240]
18 No other requirement to treat term about quality or fitness as included

(1)   Except as provided by sections 9, 10, 13 and 16, a contract to supply goods is not to be treated as including any term about the quality of the goods or their fitness for any particular purpose, unless the term is expressly included in the contract.

(2)   Subsection (1) is subject to provision made by any other enactment (whenever passed or made).

NOTES
Commencement: 1 October 2015.

What Remedies are There if Statutory Rights under a Goods Contract are not Met?

[1.2241]
19   Consumer's rights to enforce terms about goods
(1)   In this section and sections 22 to 24 references to goods conforming to a contract are references to—
  (a)   the goods conforming to the terms described in sections 9, 10, 11, 13 and 14,
  (b)   the goods not failing to conform to the contract under section 15 or 16, and
  (c)   the goods conforming to requirements that are stated in the contract.
(2)   But, for the purposes of this section and sections 22 to 24, a failure to conform as mentioned in subsection (1)(a) to (c) is not a failure to conform to the contract if it has its origin in materials supplied by the consumer.
(3)   If the goods do not conform to the contract because of a breach of any of the terms described in sections 9, 10, 11, 13 and 14, or if they do not conform to the contract under section 16, the consumer's rights (and the provisions about them and when they are available) are—
  (a)   the short-term right to reject (sections 20 and 22);
  (b)   the right to repair or replacement (section 23); and
  (c)   the right to a price reduction or the final right to reject (sections 20 and 24).
(4)   If the goods do not conform to the contract under section 15 or because of a breach of requirements that are stated in the contract, the consumer's rights (and the provisions about them and when they are available) are—
  (a)   the right to repair or replacement (section 23); and
  (b)   the right to a price reduction or the final right to reject (sections 20 and 24).
(5)   If the trader is in breach of a term that section 12 requires to be treated as included in the contract, the consumer has the right to recover from the trader the amount of any costs incurred by the consumer as a result of the breach, up to the amount of the price paid or the value of other consideration given for the goods.
(6)   If the trader is in breach of the term that section 17(1) (right to supply etc) requires to be treated as included in the contract, the consumer has a right to reject (see section 20 for provisions about that right and when it is available).
(7)   Subsections (3) to (6) are subject to section 25 and subsections (3)(a) and (6) are subject to section 26.
(8)   Section 28 makes provision about remedies for breach of a term about the time for delivery of goods.
(9)   This Chapter does not prevent the consumer seeking other remedies—
  (a)   for a breach of a term that this Chapter requires to be treated as included in the contract,
  (b)   on the grounds that, under section 15 or 16, goods do not conform to the contract, or
  (c)   for a breach of a requirement stated in the contract.
(10)   Those other remedies may be ones—
  (a)   in addition to a remedy referred to in subsections (3) to (6) (but not so as to recover twice for the same loss), or
  (b)   instead of such a remedy, or
  (c)   where no such remedy is provided for.
(11)   Those other remedies include any of the following that is open to the consumer in the circumstances—
  (a)   claiming damages;
  (b)   seeking specific performance;
  (c)   seeking an order for specific implement;
  (d)   relying on the breach against a claim by the trader for the price;
  (e)   for breach of an express term, exercising a right to treat the contract as at an end.
(12)   It is not open to the consumer to treat the contract as at an end for breach of a term that this Chapter requires to be treated as included in the contract, or on the grounds that, under section 15 or 16, goods do not conform to the contract, except as provided by subsections (3), (4) and (6).
(13)   In this Part, treating a contract as at an end means treating it as repudiated.
(14)   For the purposes of subsections (3)(b) and (c) and (4), goods which do not conform to the contract at any time within the period of six months beginning with the day on which the goods were delivered to the consumer must be taken not to have conformed to it on that day.
(15)   Subsection (14) does not apply if—
  (a)   it is established that the goods did conform to the contract on that day, or
  (b)   its application is incompatible with the nature of the goods or with how they fail to conform to the contract.

NOTES
Commencement: 1 October 2015.

Part 1   Statutes

[1.2242]
20 Right to reject
(1)   The short-term right to reject is subject to section 22.

(2)   The final right to reject is subject to section 24.

(3)   The right to reject under section 19(6) is not limited by those sections.

(4)   Each of these rights entitles the consumer to reject the goods and treat the contract as at an end, subject to subsections (20) and (21).

(5)   The right is exercised if the consumer indicates to the trader that the consumer is rejecting the goods and treating the contract as at an end.

(6)   The indication may be something the consumer says or does, but it must be clear enough to be understood by the trader.

(7)   From the time when the right is exercised—
   (a)   the trader has a duty to give the consumer a refund, subject to subsection (18), and
   (b)   the consumer has a duty to make the goods available for collection by the trader or (if there is an agreement for the consumer to return rejected goods) to return them as agreed.

(8)   Whether or not the consumer has a duty to return the rejected goods, the trader must bear any reasonable costs of returning them, other than any costs incurred by the consumer in returning the goods in person to the place where the consumer took physical possession of them.

(9)   The consumer's entitlement to receive a refund works as follows.

(10)   To the extent that the consumer paid money under the contract, the consumer is entitled to receive back the same amount of money.

(11)   To the extent that the consumer transferred anything else under the contract, the consumer is entitled to receive back the same amount of what the consumer transferred, unless subsection (12) applies.

(12)   To the extent that the consumer transferred under the contract something for which the same amount of the same thing cannot be substituted, the consumer is entitled to receive back in its original state whatever the consumer transferred.

(13)   If the contract is for the hire of goods, the entitlement to a refund extends only to anything paid or otherwise transferred for a period of hire that the consumer does not get because the contract is treated as at an end.

(14)   If the contract is a hire-purchase agreement or a conditional sales contract and the contract is treated as at an end before the whole of the price has been paid, the entitlement to a refund extends only to the part of the price paid.

(15)   A refund under this section must be given without undue delay, and in any event within 14 days beginning with the day on which the trader agrees that the consumer is entitled to a refund.

(16)   If the consumer paid money under the contract, the trader must give the refund using the same means of payment as the consumer used, unless the consumer expressly agrees otherwise.

(17)   The trader must not impose any fee on the consumer in respect of the refund.

(18)   There is no entitlement to receive a refund—
   (a)   if none of subsections (10) to (12) applies,
   (b)   to the extent that anything to which subsection (12) applies cannot be given back in its original state, or
   (c)   where subsection (13) applies, to the extent that anything the consumer transferred under the contract cannot be divided so as to give back only the amount, or part of the amount, to which the consumer is entitled.

(19)   It may be open to a consumer to claim damages where there is no entitlement to receive a refund, or because of the limits of the entitlement, or instead of a refund.

(20)   Subsection (21) qualifies the application in relation to England and Wales and Northern Ireland of the rights mentioned in subsections (1) to (3) where—
   (a)   the contract is a severable contract,
   (b)   in relation to the final right to reject, the contract is a contract for the hire of goods, a hire-purchase agreement or a contract for transfer of goods, and
   (c)   section 26(3) does not apply.

(21)   The consumer is entitled, depending on the terms of the contract and the circumstances of the case—
   (a)   to reject the goods to which a severable obligation relates and treat that obligation as at an end (so that the entitlement to a refund relates only to what the consumer paid or transferred in relation to that obligation), or
   (b)   to exercise any of the rights mentioned in subsections (1) to (3) in respect of the whole contract.

NOTES
Commencement: 1 October 2015.

[1.2243]
21 Partial rejection of goods
(1)   If the consumer has any of the rights mentioned in section 20(1) to (3), but does not reject all of the goods and treat the contract as at an end, the consumer—
   (a)   may reject some or all of the goods that do not conform to the contract, but

(b)   may not reject any goods that do conform to the contract.

(2) If the consumer is entitled to reject the goods in an instalment, but does not reject all of those goods, the consumer—

    (a)   may reject some or all of the goods in the instalment that do not conform to the contract, but

    (b)   may not reject any goods in the instalment that do conform to the contract.

(3) If any of the goods form a commercial unit, the consumer cannot reject some of those goods without also rejecting the rest of them.

(4) A unit is a "commercial unit" if division of the unit would materially impair the value of the goods or the character of the unit.

(5) The consumer rejects goods under this section by indicating to the trader that the consumer is rejecting the goods.

(6) The indication may be something the consumer says or does, but it must be clear enough to be understood by the trader.

(7) From the time when a consumer rejects goods under this section—

    (a)   the trader has a duty to give the consumer a refund in respect of those goods (subject to subsection (10)), and

    (b)   the consumer has a duty to make those goods available for collection by the trader or (if there is an agreement for the consumer to return rejected goods) to return them as agreed.

(8) Whether or not the consumer has a duty to return the rejected goods, the trader must bear any reasonable costs of returning them, other than any costs incurred by the consumer in returning those goods in person to the place where the consumer took physical possession of them.

(9) Section 20(10) to (17) apply to a consumer's right to receive a refund under this section (and in section 20(13) and (14) references to the contract being treated as at an end are to be read as references to goods being rejected).

(10) That right does not apply—

    (a)   if none of section 20(10) to (12) applies,

    (b)   to the extent that anything to which section 20(12) applies cannot be given back in its original state, or

    (c)   to the extent that anything the consumer transferred under the contract cannot be divided so as to give back only the amount, or part of the amount, to which the consumer is entitled.

(11) It may be open to a consumer to claim damages where there is no right to receive a refund, or because of the limits of the right, or instead of a refund.

(12) References in this section to goods conforming to a contract are to be read in accordance with section 19(1) and (2), but they also include the goods conforming to the terms described in section 17.

(13) Where section 20(21)(a) applies the reference in subsection (1) to the consumer treating the contract as at an end is to be read as a reference to the consumer treating the severable obligation as at an end.

NOTES

Commencement: 1 October 2015.

[1.2244]
22   Time limit for short-term right to reject

(1) A consumer who has the short-term right to reject loses it if the time limit for exercising it passes without the consumer exercising it, unless the trader and the consumer agree that it may be exercised later.

(2) An agreement under which the short-term right to reject would be lost before the time limit passes is not binding on the consumer.

(3) The time limit for exercising the short-term right to reject (unless subsection (4) applies) is the end of 30 days beginning with the first day after these have all happened—

    (a)   ownership or (in the case of a contract for the hire of goods, a hire-purchase agreement or a conditional sales contract) possession of the goods has been transferred to the consumer,

    (b)   the goods have been delivered, and

    (c)   where the contract requires the trader to install the goods or take other action to enable the consumer to use them, the trader has notified the consumer that the action has been taken.

(4) If any of the goods are of a kind that can reasonably be expected to perish after a shorter period, the time limit for exercising the short-term right to reject in relation to those goods is the end of that shorter period (but without affecting the time limit in relation to goods that are not of that kind).

(5) Subsections (3) and (4) do not prevent the consumer exercising the short-term right to reject before something mentioned in subsection (3)(a), (b) or (c) has happened.

(6) If the consumer requests or agrees to the repair or replacement of goods, the period mentioned in subsection (3) or (4) stops running for the length of the waiting period.

(7) If goods supplied by the trader in response to that request or agreement do not conform to the contract, the time limit for exercising the short-term right to reject is then either—

    (a)   7 days after the waiting period ends, or

    (b)   if later, the original time limit for exercising that right, extended by the waiting period.

(8) The waiting period—
    (a) begins with the day the consumer requests or agrees to the repair or replacement of the goods, and
    (b) ends with the day on which the consumer receives goods supplied by the trader in response to the request or agreement.

NOTES
Commencement: 1 October 2015.

[1.2245]
23 Right to repair or replacement
(1) This section applies if the consumer has the right to repair or replacement (see section 19(3) and (4)).
(2) If the consumer requires the trader to repair or replace the goods, the trader must—
    (a) do so within a reasonable time and without significant inconvenience to the consumer, and
    (b) bear any necessary costs incurred in doing so (including in particular the cost of any labour, materials or postage).
(3) The consumer cannot require the trader to repair or replace the goods if that remedy (the repair or the replacement)—
    (a) is impossible, or
    (b) is disproportionate compared to the other of those remedies.
(4) Either of those remedies is disproportionate compared to the other if it imposes costs on the trader which, compared to those imposed by the other, are unreasonable, taking into account—
    (a) the value which the goods would have if they conformed to the contract,
    (b) the significance of the lack of conformity, and
    (c) whether the other remedy could be effected without significant inconvenience to the consumer.
(5) Any question as to what is a reasonable time or significant inconvenience is to be determined taking account of—
    (a) the nature of the goods, and
    (b) the purpose for which the goods were acquired.
(6) A consumer who requires or agrees to the repair of goods cannot require the trader to replace them, or exercise the short-term right to reject, without giving the trader a reasonable time to repair them (unless giving the trader that time would cause significant inconvenience to the consumer).
(7) A consumer who requires or agrees to the replacement of goods cannot require the trader to repair them, or exercise the short-term right to reject, without giving the trader a reasonable time to replace them (unless giving the trader that time would cause significant inconvenience to the consumer).
(8) In this Chapter, "repair" in relation to goods that do not conform to a contract, means making them conform.

NOTES
Commencement: 1 October 2015.

[1.2246]
24 Right to price reduction or final right to reject
(1) The right to a price reduction is the right—
    (a) to require the trader to reduce by an appropriate amount the price the consumer is required to pay under the contract, or anything else the consumer is required to transfer under the contract, and
    (b) to receive a refund from the trader for anything already paid or otherwise transferred by the consumer above the reduced amount.
(2) The amount of the reduction may, where appropriate, be the full amount of the price or whatever the consumer is required to transfer.
(3) Section 20(10) to (17) applies to a consumer's right to receive a refund under subsection (1)(b).
(4) The right to a price reduction does not apply—
    (a) if what the consumer is (before the reduction) required to transfer under the contract, whether or not already transferred, cannot be divided up so as to enable the trader to receive or retain only the reduced amount, or
    (b) if anything to which section 20(12) applies cannot be given back in its original state.
(5) A consumer who has the right to a price reduction and the final right to reject may only exercise one (not both), and may only do so in one of these situations—
    (a) after one repair or one replacement, the goods do not conform to the contract;
    (b) because of section 23(3) the consumer can require neither repair nor replacement of the goods; or
    (c) the consumer has required the trader to repair or replace the goods, but the trader is in breach of the requirement of section 23(2)(a) to do so within a reasonable time and without significant inconvenience to the consumer.

(6)　There has been a repair or replacement for the purposes of subsection (5)(a) if—
   (a)　the consumer has requested or agreed to repair or replacement of the goods (whether in relation to one fault or more than one), and
   (b)　the trader has delivered goods to the consumer, or made goods available to the consumer, in response to the request or agreement.

(7)　For the purposes of subsection (6) goods that the trader arranges to repair at the consumer's premises are made available when the trader indicates that the repairs are finished.

(8)　If the consumer exercises the final right to reject, any refund to the consumer may be reduced by a deduction for use, to take account of the use the consumer has had of the goods in the period since they were delivered, but this is subject to subsections (9) and (10).

(9)　No deduction may be made to take account of use in any period when the consumer had the goods only because the trader failed to collect them at an agreed time.

(10)　No deduction may be made if the final right to reject is exercised in the first 6 months (see subsection (11)), unless—
   (a)　the goods consist of a motor vehicle, or
   (b)　the goods are of a description specified by order made by the Secretary of State by statutory instrument.

(11)　In subsection (10) the first 6 months means 6 months beginning with the first day after these have all happened—
   (a)　ownership or (in the case of a contract for the hire of goods, a hire-purchase agreement or a conditional sales contract) possession of the goods has been transferred to the consumer,
   (b)　the goods have been delivered, and
   (c)　where the contract requires the trader to install the goods or take other action to enable the consumer to use them, the trader has notified the consumer that the action has been taken.

(12)　In subsection (10)(a) "motor vehicle"—
   (a)　in relation to Great Britain, has the same meaning as in the Road Traffic Act 1988 (see sections 185 to 194 of that Act);
   (b)　in relation to Northern Ireland, has the same meaning as in the Road Traffic (Northern Ireland) Order 1995 (SI 1995/2994 (NI 18)) (see Parts I and V of that Order).

(13)　But a vehicle is not a motor vehicle for the purposes of subsection (10)(a) if it is constructed or adapted—
   (a)　for the use of a person suffering from some physical defect or disability, and
   (b)　so that it may only be used by one such person at any one time.

(14)　An order under subsection (10)(b)—
   (a)　may be made only if the Secretary of State is satisfied that it is appropriate to do so because of significant detriment caused to traders as a result of the application of subsection (10) in relation to goods of the description specified by the order;
   (b)　may contain transitional or transitory provision or savings.

(15)　No order may be made under subsection (10)(b) unless a draft of the statutory instrument containing it has been laid before, and approved by a resolution of, each House of Parliament.

NOTES
Commencement: 1 October 2015.

Other Rules about Remedies under Goods Contracts

[1.2247]
25　Delivery of wrong quantity
(1)　Where the trader delivers to the consumer a quantity of goods less than the trader contracted to supply, the consumer may reject them, but if the consumer accepts them the consumer must pay for them at the contract rate.

(2)　Where the trader delivers to the consumer a quantity of goods larger than the trader contracted to supply, the consumer may accept the goods included in the contract and reject the rest, or may reject all of the goods.

(3)　Where the trader delivers to the consumer a quantity of goods larger than the trader contracted to supply and the consumer accepts all of the goods delivered, the consumer must pay for them at the contract rate.

(4)　Where the consumer is entitled to reject goods under this section, any entitlement for the consumer to treat the contract as at an end depends on the terms of the contract and the circumstances of the case.

(5)　The consumer rejects goods under this section by indicating to the trader that the consumer is rejecting the goods.

(6)　The indication may be something the consumer says or does, but it must be clear enough to be understood by the trader.

(7)　Subsections (1) to (3) do not prevent the consumer claiming damages, where it is open to the consumer to do so.

(8)　This section is subject to any usage of trade, special agreement, or course of dealing between the parties.

NOTES
Commencement: 1 October 2015.

[1.2248]
26 Instalment deliveries

(1)   Under a contract to supply goods, the consumer is not bound to accept delivery of the goods by instalments, unless that has been agreed between the consumer and the trader.

(2)   The following provisions apply if the contract provides for the goods to be delivered by stated instalments, which are to be separately paid for.

(3)   If the trader makes defective deliveries in respect of one or more instalments, the consumer, apart from any entitlement to claim damages, may be (but is not necessarily) entitled—

(a)   to exercise the short-term right to reject or the right to reject under section 19(6) (as applicable) in respect of the whole contract, or

(b)   to reject the goods in an instalment.

(4)   Whether paragraph (a) or (b) of subsection (3) (or neither) applies to a consumer depends on the terms of the contract and the circumstances of the case.

(5)   In subsection (3), making defective deliveries does not include failing to make a delivery in accordance with section 28.

(6)   If the consumer neglects or refuses to take delivery of or pay for one or more instalments, the trader may—

(a)   be entitled to treat the whole contract as at an end, or

(b)   if it is a severable breach, have a claim for damages but not a right to treat the whole contract as at an end.

(7)   Whether paragraph (a) or (b) of subsection (6) (or neither) applies to a trader depends on the terms of the contract and the circumstances of the case.

NOTES
Commencement: 1 October 2015.

[1.2249]
27 Consignation, or payment into court, in Scotland

(1)   Subsection (2) applies where—

(a)   a consumer has not rejected goods which the consumer could have rejected for breach of a term mentioned in section 19(3) or (6),

(b)   the consumer has chosen to treat the breach as giving rise only to a claim for damages or to a right to rely on the breach against a claim by the trader for the price of the goods, and

(c)   the trader has begun proceedings in court to recover the price or has brought a counter-claim for the price.

(2)   The court may require the consumer—

(a)   to consign, or pay into court, the price of the goods, or part of the price, or

(b)   to provide some other reasonable security for payment of the price.

NOTES
Commencement: 1 October 2015.

Other Rules about Goods Contracts

[1.2250]
28 Delivery of goods

(1)   This section applies to any sales contract.

(2)   Unless the trader and the consumer have agreed otherwise, the contract is to be treated as including a term that the trader must deliver the goods to the consumer.

(3)   Unless there is an agreed time or period, the contract is to be treated as including a term that the trader must deliver the goods—

(a)   without undue delay, and

(b)   in any event, not more than 30 days after the day on which the contract is entered into.

(4)   In this section—

(a)   an "agreed" time or period means a time or period agreed by the trader and the consumer for delivery of the goods;

(b)   if there is an obligation to deliver the goods at the time the contract is entered into, that time counts as the "agreed" time.

(5)   Subsections (6) and (7) apply if the trader does not deliver the goods in accordance with subsection (3) or at the agreed time or within the agreed period.

(6)   If the circumstances are that—

(a)   the trader has refused to deliver the goods,

(b)   delivery of the goods at the agreed time or within the agreed period is essential taking into account all the relevant circumstances at the time the contract was entered into, or

    (c)   the consumer told the trader before the contract was entered into that delivery in accordance with subsection (3), or at the agreed time or within the agreed period, was essential,

then the consumer may treat the contract as at an end.

(7)   In any other circumstances, the consumer may specify a period that is appropriate in the circumstances and require the trader to deliver the goods before the end of that period.

(8)   If the consumer specifies a period under subsection (7) but the goods are not delivered within that period, then the consumer may treat the contract as at an end.

(9)   If the consumer treats the contract as at an end under subsection (6) or (8), the trader must without undue delay reimburse all payments made under the contract.

(10)   If subsection (6) or (8) applies but the consumer does not treat the contract as at an end—

    (a)   that does not prevent the consumer from cancelling the order for any of the goods or rejecting goods that have been delivered, and

    (b)   the trader must without undue delay reimburse all payments made under the contract in respect of any goods for which the consumer cancels the order or which the consumer rejects.

(11)   If any of the goods form a commercial unit, the consumer cannot reject or cancel the order for some of those goods without also rejecting or cancelling the order for the rest of them.

(12)   A unit is a "commercial unit" if division of the unit would materially impair the value of the goods or the character of the unit.

(13)   This section does not prevent the consumer seeking other remedies where it is open to the consumer to do so.

(14)   See section 2(5) and (6) for the application of this section where goods are sold at public auction.

NOTES

Commencement: 1 October 2015.

[1.2251]
29 Passing of risk
(1)   A sales contract is to be treated as including the following provisions as terms.

(2)   The goods remain at the trader's risk until they come into the physical possession of—

    (a)   the consumer, or

    (b)   a person identified by the consumer to take possession of the goods.

(3)   Subsection (2) does not apply if the goods are delivered to a carrier who—

    (a)   is commissioned by the consumer to deliver the goods, and

    (b)   is not a carrier the trader named as an option for the consumer.

(4)   In that case the goods are at the consumer's risk on and after delivery to the carrier.

(5)   Subsection (4) does not affect any liability of the carrier to the consumer in respect of the goods.

(6)   See section 2(5) and (6) for the application of this section where goods are sold at public auction.

NOTES

Commencement: 1 October 2015.

[1.2252]
30 Goods under guarantee
(1)   This section applies where—

    (a)   there is a contract to supply goods, and

    (b)   there is a guarantee in relation to the goods.

(2)   "Guarantee" here means an undertaking to the consumer given without extra charge by a person acting in the course of the person's business (the "guarantor") that, if the goods do not meet the specifications set out in the guarantee statement or in any associated advertising—

    (a)   the consumer will be reimbursed for the price paid for the goods, or

    (b)   the goods will be repaired, replaced or handled in any way.

(3)   The guarantee takes effect, at the time the goods are delivered, as a contractual obligation owed by the guarantor under the conditions set out in the guarantee statement and in any associated advertising.

(4)   The guarantor must ensure that—

    (a)   the guarantee sets out in plain and intelligible language the contents of the guarantee and the essential particulars for making claims under the guarantee,

    (b)   the guarantee states that the consumer has statutory rights in relation to the goods and that those rights are not affected by the guarantee, and

    (c)   where the goods are offered within the territory of the United Kingdom, the guarantee is written in English.

(5)   The contents of the guarantee to be set out in it include, in particular—

    (a)   the name and address of the guarantor, and

    (b)   the duration and territorial scope of the guarantee.

(6)   The guarantor and any other person who offers to supply to consumers the goods which are the subject of the guarantee must, on request by the consumer, make the guarantee available to the consumer within a reasonable time, in writing and in a form accessible to the consumer.

(7)   What is a reasonable time is a question of fact.

(8)   If a person fails to comply with a requirement of this section, the enforcement authority may apply to the court for an injunction or (in Scotland) an order of specific implement against that person requiring that person to comply.

(9)   On an application the court may grant an injunction or (in Scotland) an order of specific implement on such terms as it thinks appropriate.

(10)   In this section—

  "court" means—

    (a)   in relation to England and Wales, the High Court or the county court,

    (b)   in relation to Northern Ireland, the High Court or a county court, and

    (c)   in relation to Scotland, the Court of Session or the sheriff;

  "enforcement authority" means—

    (a)   the Competition and Markets Authority,

    (b)   a local weights and measures authority in Great Britain, and

    (c)   the Department of Enterprise, Trade and Investment in Northern Ireland.

NOTES

Commencement: 1 October 2015.

Can a Trader Contract out of Statutory Rights and Remedies under a Goods Contract?

[1.2253]

31   Liability that cannot be excluded or restricted

(1)   A term of a contract to supply goods is not binding on the consumer to the extent that it would exclude or restrict the trader's liability arising under any of these provisions—

    (a)   section 9 (goods to be of satisfactory quality);

    (b)   section 10 (goods to be fit for particular purpose);

    (c)   section 11 (goods to be as described);

    (d)   section 12 (other pre-contract information included in contract);

    (e)   section 13 (goods to match a sample);

    (f)   section 14 (goods to match a model seen or examined);

    (g)   section 15 (installation as part of conformity of the goods with the contract);

    (h)   section 16 (goods not conforming to contract if digital content does not conform);

    (i)   section 17 (trader to have right to supply the goods etc);

    (j)   section 28 (delivery of goods);

    (k)   section 29 (passing of risk).

(2)   That also means that a term of a contract to supply goods is not binding on the consumer to the extent that it would—

    (a)   exclude or restrict a right or remedy in respect of a liability under a provision listed in subsection (1),

    (b)   make such a right or remedy or its enforcement subject to a restrictive or onerous condition,

    (c)   allow a trader to put a person at a disadvantage as a result of pursuing such a right or remedy, or

    (d)   exclude or restrict rules of evidence or procedure.

(3)   The reference in subsection (1) to excluding or restricting a liability also includes preventing an obligation or duty arising or limiting its extent.

(4)   An agreement in writing to submit present or future differences to arbitration is not to be regarded as excluding or restricting any liability for the purposes of this section.

(5)   Subsection (1)(i), and subsection (2) so far as it relates to liability under section 17, do not apply to a term of a contract for the hire of goods.

(6)   But an express term of a contract for the hire of goods is not binding on the consumer to the extent that it would exclude or restrict a term that section 17 requires to be treated as included in the contract, unless it is inconsistent with that term (and see also section 62 (requirement for terms to be fair)).

(7)   See Schedule 3 for provision about the enforcement of this section.

NOTES

Commencement: 1 October 2015.

[1.2254]

32   Contracts applying law of non-EEA State

(1)   If—

    (a)   the law of a country or territory other than an EEA State is chosen by the parties to be applicable to a sales contract, but

    (b)   the sales contract has a close connection with the United Kingdom,

this Chapter, except the provisions in subsection (2), applies despite that choice.

(2) The exceptions are—
  (a) sections 11(4) and (5) and 12;
  (b) sections 28 and 29;
  (c) section 31(1)(d), (j) and (k).

(3) For cases where those provisions apply, or where the law applicable has not been chosen or the law of an EEA State is chosen, see Regulation (EC) No 593/2008 of the European Parliament and of the Council of 17 June 2008 on the law applicable to contractual obligations.

NOTES
Commencement: 1 October 2015.

CHAPTER 3
DIGITAL CONTENT

What Digital Content Contracts are Covered?

[1.2255]
33 Contracts covered by this Chapter
(1) This Chapter applies to a contract for a trader to supply digital content to a consumer, if it is supplied or to be supplied for a price paid by the consumer.
(2) This Chapter also applies to a contract for a trader to supply digital content to a consumer, if—
  (a) it is supplied free with goods or services or other digital content for which the consumer pays a price, and
  (b) it is not generally available to consumers unless they have paid a price for it or for goods or services or other digital content.
(3) The references in subsections (1) and (2) to the consumer paying a price include references to the consumer using, by way of payment, any facility for which money has been paid.
(4) A trader does not supply digital content to a consumer for the purposes of this Part merely because the trader supplies a service by which digital content reaches the consumer.
(5) The Secretary of State may by order provide for this Chapter to apply to other contracts for a trader to supply digital content to a consumer, if the Secretary of State is satisfied that it is appropriate to do so because of significant detriment caused to consumers under contracts of the kind to which the order relates.
(6) An order under subsection (5)—
  (a) may, in particular, amend this Act;
  (b) may contain transitional or transitory provision or savings.
(7) A contract to which this Chapter applies is referred to in this Part as a "contract to supply digital content".
(8) This section, other than subsection (4), does not limit the application of section 46.
(9) The power to make an order under subsection (5) is exercisable by statutory instrument.
(10) No order may be made under subsection (5) unless a draft of the statutory instrument containing it has been laid before, and approved by a resolution of, each House of Parliament.

NOTES
Commencement: 1 October 2015.

What Statutory Rights are There under a Digital Content Contract?

[1.2256]
34 Digital content to be of satisfactory quality
(1) Every contract to supply digital content is to be treated as including a term that the quality of the digital content is satisfactory.
(2) The quality of digital content is satisfactory if it meets the standard that a reasonable person would consider satisfactory, taking account of—
  (a) any description of the digital content,
  (b) the price mentioned in section 33(1) or (2)(b) (if relevant), and
  (c) all the other relevant circumstances (see subsection (5)).
(3) The quality of digital content includes its state and condition; and the following aspects (among others) are in appropriate cases aspects of the quality of digital content—
  (a) fitness for all the purposes for which digital content of that kind is usually supplied;
  (b) freedom from minor defects;
  (c) safety;
  (d) durability.
(4) The term mentioned in subsection (1) does not cover anything which makes the quality of the digital content unsatisfactory—
  (a) which is specifically drawn to the consumer's attention before the contract is made,
  (b) where the consumer examines the digital content before the contract is made, which that examination ought to reveal, or
  (c) where the consumer examines a trial version before the contract is made, which would have been apparent on a reasonable examination of the trial version.

(5)   The relevant circumstances mentioned in subsection (2)(c) include any public statement about the specific characteristics of the digital content made by the trader, the producer or any representative of the trader or the producer.

(6)   That includes, in particular, any public statement made in advertising or labelling.

(7)   But a public statement is not a relevant circumstance for the purposes of subsection (2)(c) if the trader shows that—

    (a)   when the contract was made, the trader was not, and could not reasonably have been, aware of the statement,

    (b)   before the contract was made, the statement had been publicly withdrawn or, to the extent that it contained anything which was incorrect or misleading, it had been publicly corrected, or

    (c)   the consumer's decision to contract for the digital content could not have been influenced by the statement.

(8)   In a contract to supply digital content a term about the quality of the digital content may be treated as included as a matter of custom.

(9)   See section 42 for a consumer's rights if the trader is in breach of a term that this section requires to be treated as included in a contract.

NOTES

    Commencement: 1 October 2015.

[1.2257]
35   Digital content to be fit for particular purpose

(1)   Subsection (3) applies to a contract to supply digital content if before the contract is made the consumer makes known to the trader (expressly or by implication) any particular purpose for which the consumer is contracting for the digital content.

(2)   Subsection (3) also applies to a contract to supply digital content if—

    (a)   the digital content was previously sold by a credit-broker to the trader,

    (b)   the consideration or part of it is a sum payable by instalments, and

    (c)   before the contract is made, the consumer makes known to the credit-broker (expressly or by implication) any particular purpose for which the consumer is contracting for the digital content.

(3)   The contract is to be treated as including a term that the digital content is reasonably fit for that purpose, whether or not that is a purpose for which digital content of that kind is usually supplied.

(4)   Subsection (3) does not apply if the circumstances show that the consumer does not rely, or it is unreasonable for the consumer to rely, on the skill or judgment of the trader or credit-broker.

(5)   A contract to supply digital content may be treated as making provision about the fitness of the digital content for a particular purpose as a matter of custom.

(6)   See section 42 for a consumer's rights if the trader is in breach of a term that this section requires to be treated as included in a contract.

NOTES

    Commencement: 1 October 2015.

[1.2258]
36   Digital content to be as described

(1)   Every contract to supply digital content is to be treated as including a term that the digital content will match any description of it given by the trader to the consumer.

(2)   Where the consumer examines a trial version before the contract is made, it is not sufficient that the digital content matches (or is better than) the trial version if the digital content does not also match any description of it given by the trader to the consumer.

(3)   Any information that is provided by the trader about the digital content that is information mentioned in paragraph (a), (j) or (k) of Schedule 1 or paragraph (a), (v) or (w) of Schedule 2 (main characteristics, functionality and compatibility) to the Consumer Contracts (Information, Cancellation and Additional Charges) Regulations 2013 (SI 2013/3134) is to be treated as included as a term of the contract.

(4)   A change to any of that information, made before entering into the contract or later, is not effective unless expressly agreed between the consumer and the trader.

(5)   See section 42 for a consumer's rights if the trader is in breach of a term that this section requires to be treated as included in a contract.

NOTES

    Commencement: 1 October 2015.

[1.2259]
37   Other pre-contract information included in contract

(1)   This section applies to any contract to supply digital content.

(2) Where regulation 9, 10 or 13 of the Consumer Contracts (Information, Cancellation and Additional Charges) Regulations 2013 (SI 2013/3134) required the trader to provide information to the consumer before the contract became binding, any of that information that was provided by the trader other than information about the digital content and mentioned in paragraph (a), (j) or (k) of Schedule 1 or paragraph (a), (v) or (w) of Schedule 2 to the Regulations (main characteristics, functionality and compatibility) is to be treated as included as a term of the contract.

(3) A change to any of that information, made before entering into the contract or later, is not effective unless expressly agreed between the consumer and the trader.

(4) See section 42 for a consumer's rights if the trader is in breach of a term that this section requires to be treated as included in a contract.

NOTES

Commencement: 1 October 2015.

[1.2260]

38 No other requirement to treat term about quality or fitness as included

(1) Except as provided by sections 34 and 35, a contract to supply digital content is not to be treated as including any term about the quality of the digital content or its fitness for any particular purpose, unless the term is expressly included in the contract.

(2) Subsection (1) is subject to provision made by any other enactment, whenever passed or made.

NOTES

Commencement: 1 October 2015.

[1.2261]

39 Supply by transmission and facilities for continued transmission

(1) Subsection (2) applies where there is a contract to supply digital content and the consumer's access to the content on a device requires its transmission to the device under arrangements initiated by the trader.

(2) For the purposes of this Chapter, the digital content is supplied—

    (a) when the content reaches the device, or

    (b) if earlier, when the content reaches another trader chosen by the consumer to supply, under a contract with the consumer, a service by which digital content reaches the device.

(3) Subsections (5) to (7) apply where—

    (a) there is a contract to supply digital content, and

    (b) after the trader (T) has supplied the digital content, the consumer is to have access under the contract to a processing facility under arrangements made by T.

(4) A processing facility is a facility by which T or another trader will receive digital content from the consumer and transmit digital content to the consumer (whether or not other features are to be included under the contract).

(5) The contract is to be treated as including a term that the processing facility (with any feature that the facility is to include under the contract) must be available to the consumer for a reasonable time, unless a time is specified in the contract.

(6) The following provisions apply to all digital content transmitted to the consumer on each occasion under the facility, while it is provided under the contract, as they apply to the digital content first supplied—

    (a) section 34 (quality);

    (b) section 35 (fitness for a particular purpose);

    (c) section 36 (description).

(7) Breach of a term treated as included under subsection (5) has the same effect as breach of a term treated as included under those sections (see section 42).

NOTES

Commencement: 1 October 2015.

[1.2262]

40 Quality, fitness and description of content supplied subject to modifications

(1) Where under a contract a trader supplies digital content to a consumer subject to the right of the trader or a third party to modify the digital content, the following provisions apply in relation to the digital content as modified as they apply in relation to the digital content as supplied under the contract—

    (a) section 34 (quality);

    (b) section 35 (fitness for a particular purpose);

    (c) section 36 (description).

(2) Subsection (1)(c) does not prevent the trader from improving the features of, or adding new features to, the digital content, as long as—

    (a) the digital content continues to match the description of it given by the trader to the consumer, and

(b) the digital content continues to conform to the information provided by the trader as mentioned in subsection (3) of section 36, subject to any change to that information that has been agreed in accordance with subsection (4) of that section.

(3) A claim on the grounds that digital content does not conform to a term described in any of the sections listed in subsection (1) as applied by that subsection is to be treated as arising at the time when the digital content was supplied under the contract and not the time when it is modified.

NOTES

Commencement: 1 October 2015.

[1.2263]
41 Trader's right to supply digital content
(1) Every contract to supply digital content is to be treated as including a term—
   (a) in relation to any digital content which is supplied under the contract and which the consumer has paid for, that the trader has the right to supply that content to the consumer;
   (b) in relation to any digital content which the trader agrees to supply under the contract and which the consumer has paid for, that the trader will have the right to supply it to the consumer at the time when it is to be supplied.

(2) See section 42 for a consumer's rights if the trader is in breach of a term that this section requires to be treated as included in a contract.

NOTES

Commencement: 1 October 2015.

What Remedies are There if Statutory Rights under a Digital Content Contract are not Met?
[1.2264]
42 Consumer's rights to enforce terms about digital content
(1) In this section and section 43 references to digital content conforming to a contract are references to the digital content conforming to the terms described in sections 34, 35 and 36.

(2) If the digital content does not conform to the contract, the consumer's rights (and the provisions about them and when they are available) are—
   (a) the right to repair or replacement (see section 43);
   (b) the right to a price reduction (see section 44).

(3) Section 16 also applies if an item including the digital content is supplied.

(4) If the trader is in breach of a term that section 37 requires to be treated as included in the contract, the consumer has the right to recover from the trader the amount of any costs incurred by the consumer as a result of the breach, up to the amount of the price paid for the digital content or for any facility within section 33(3) used by the consumer.

(5) If the trader is in breach of the term that section 41(1) (right to supply the content) requires to be treated as included in the contract, the consumer has the right to a refund (see section 45 for provisions about that right and when it is available).

(6) This Chapter does not prevent the consumer seeking other remedies for a breach of a term to which any of subsections (2), (4) or (5) applies, instead of or in addition to a remedy referred to there (but not so as to recover twice for the same loss).

(7) Those other remedies include any of the following that is open to the consumer in the circumstances—
   (a) claiming damages;
   (b) seeking to recover money paid where the consideration for payment of the money has failed;
   (c) seeking specific performance;
   (d) seeking an order for specific implement;
   (e) relying on the breach against a claim by the trader for the price.

(8) It is not open to the consumer to treat the contract as at an end for breach of a term to which any of subsections (2), (4) or (5) applies.

(9) For the purposes of subsection (2), digital content which does not conform to the contract at any time within the period of six months beginning with the day on which it was supplied must be taken not to have conformed to the contract when it was supplied.

(10) Subsection (9) does not apply if—
   (a) it is established that the digital content did conform to the contract when it was supplied, or
   (b) its application is incompatible with the nature of the digital content or with how it fails to conform to the contract.

NOTES

Commencement: 1 October 2015.

[1.2265]
43   Right to repair or replacement
(1)   This section applies if the consumer has the right to repair or replacement.
(2)   If the consumer requires the trader to repair or replace the digital content, the trader must—
   (a)   do so within a reasonable time and without significant inconvenience to the consumer; and
   (b)   bear any necessary costs incurred in doing so (including in particular the cost of any labour, materials or postage).
(3)   The consumer cannot require the trader to repair or replace the digital content if that remedy (the repair or the replacement)—
   (a)   is impossible, or
   (b)   is disproportionate compared to the other of those remedies.
(4)   Either of those remedies is disproportionate compared to the other if it imposes costs on the trader which, compared to those imposed by the other, are unreasonable, taking into account—
   (a)   the value which the digital content would have if it conformed to the contract,
   (b)   the significance of the lack of conformity, and
   (c)   whether the other remedy could be effected without significant inconvenience to the consumer.
(5)   Any question as to what is a reasonable time or significant inconvenience is to be determined taking account of—
   (a)   the nature of the digital content, and
   (b)   the purpose for which the digital content was obtained or accessed.
(6)   A consumer who requires or agrees to the repair of digital content cannot require the trader to replace it without giving the trader a reasonable time to repair it (unless giving the trader that time would cause significant inconvenience to the consumer).
(7)   A consumer who requires or agrees to the replacement of digital content cannot require the trader to repair it without giving the trader a reasonable time to replace it (unless giving the trader that time would cause significant inconvenience to the consumer).
(8)   In this Chapter, "repair" in relation to digital content that does not conform to a contract, means making it conform.

NOTES
Commencement: 1 October 2015.

[1.2266]
44   Right to price reduction
(1)   The right to a price reduction is the right to require the trader to reduce the price to the consumer by an appropriate amount (including the right to receive a refund for anything already paid above the reduced amount).
(2)   The amount of the reduction may, where appropriate, be the full amount of the price.
(3)   A consumer who has that right may only exercise it in one of these situations—
   (a)   because of section 43(3)(a) the consumer can require neither repair nor replacement of the digital content, or
   (b)   the consumer has required the trader to repair or replace the digital content, but the trader is in breach of the requirement of section 43(2)(a) to do so within a reasonable time and without significant inconvenience to the consumer.
(4)   A refund under this section must be given without undue delay, and in any event within 14 days beginning with the day on which the trader agrees that the consumer is entitled to a refund.
(5)   The trader must give the refund using the same means of payment as the consumer used to pay for the digital content, unless the consumer expressly agrees otherwise.
(6)   The trader must not impose any fee on the consumer in respect of the refund.

NOTES
Commencement: 1 October 2015.

[1.2267]
45   Right to a refund
(1)   The right to a refund gives the consumer the right to receive a refund from the trader of all money paid by the consumer for the digital content (subject to subsection (2)).
(2)   If the breach giving the consumer the right to a refund affects only some of the digital content supplied under the contract, the right to a refund does not extend to any part of the price attributable to digital content that is not affected by the breach.
(3)   A refund must be given without undue delay, and in any event within 14 days beginning with the day on which the trader agrees that the consumer is entitled to a refund.
(4)   The trader must give the refund using the same means of payment as the consumer used to pay for the digital content, unless the consumer expressly agrees otherwise.
(5)   The trader must not impose any fee on the consumer in respect of the refund.

NOTES
Commencement: 1 October 2015.

Compensation for Damage to Device or to other Digital Content

[1.2268]
46   Remedy for damage to device or to other digital content
(1)   This section applies if—
  (a)   a trader supplies digital content to a consumer under a contract,
  (b)   the digital content causes damage to a device or to other digital content,
  (c)   the device or digital content that is damaged belongs to the consumer, and
  (d)   the damage is of a kind that would not have occurred if the trader had exercised reasonable care and skill.
(2)   If the consumer requires the trader to provide a remedy under this section, the trader must either—
  (a)   repair the damage in accordance with subsection (3), or
  (b)   compensate the consumer for the damage with an appropriate payment.
(3)   To repair the damage in accordance with this subsection, the trader must—
  (a)   repair the damage within a reasonable time and without significant inconvenience to the consumer, and
  (b)   bear any necessary costs incurred in repairing the damage (including in particular the cost of any labour, materials or postage).
(4)   Any question as to what is a reasonable time or significant inconvenience is to be determined taking account of—
  (a)   the nature of the device or digital content that is damaged, and
  (b)   the purpose for which it is used by the consumer.
(5)   A compensation payment under this section must be made without undue delay, and in any event within 14 days beginning with the day on which the trader agrees that the consumer is entitled to the payment.
(6)   The trader must not impose any fee on the consumer in respect of the payment.
(7)   A consumer with a right to a remedy under this section may bring a claim in civil proceedings to enforce that right.
(8)   The Limitation Act 1980 and the Limitation (Northern Ireland) Order 1989 (SI 1989/1339 (NI 11)) apply to a claim under this section as if it were an action founded on simple contract.
(9)   The Prescription and Limitation (Scotland) Act 1973 applies to a right to a remedy under this section as if it were an obligation to which section 6 of that Act applies.

NOTES
Commencement: 1 October 2015.

Can a Trader Contract out of Statutory Rights and Remedies under a Digital Content Contract?
[1.2269]
47   Liability that cannot be excluded or restricted
(1)   A term of a contract to supply digital content is not binding on the consumer to the extent that it would exclude or restrict the trader's liability arising under any of these provisions—
  (a)   section 34 (digital content to be of satisfactory quality),
  (b)   section 35 (digital content to be fit for particular purpose),
  (c)   section 36 (digital content to be as described),
  (d)   section 37 (other pre-contract information included in contract), or
  (e)   section 41 (trader's right to supply digital content).
(2)   That also means that a term of a contract to supply digital content is not binding on the consumer to the extent that it would—
  (a)   exclude or restrict a right or remedy in respect of a liability under a provision listed in subsection (1),
  (b)   make such a right or remedy or its enforcement subject to a restrictive or onerous condition,
  (c)   allow a trader to put a person at a disadvantage as a result of pursuing such a right or remedy, or
  (d)   exclude or restrict rules of evidence or procedure.
(3)   The reference in subsection (1) to excluding or restricting a liability also includes preventing an obligation or duty arising or limiting its extent.
(4)   An agreement in writing to submit present or future differences to arbitration is not to be regarded as excluding or restricting any liability for the purposes of this section.
(5)   See Schedule 3 for provision about the enforcement of this section.
(6)   For provision limiting the ability of a trader under a contract within section 46 to exclude or restrict the trader's liability under that section, see section 62.

NOTES
Commencement: 1 October 2015.

CHAPTER 4
SERVICES

What Services Contracts are Covered?

[1.2270]
48   Contracts covered by this Chapter
(1)   This Chapter applies to a contract for a trader to supply a service to a consumer.
(2)   That does not include a contract of employment or apprenticeship.
(3)   In relation to Scotland, this Chapter does not apply to a gratuitous contract.
(4)   A contract to which this Chapter applies is referred to in this Part as a "contract to supply a service".
(5)   The Secretary of State may by order made by statutory instrument provide that a provision of this Chapter does not apply in relation to a service of a description specified in the order.
(6)   The power in subsection (5) includes power to provide that a provision of this Chapter does not apply in relation to a service of a description specified in the order in the circumstances so specified.
(7)   An order under subsection (5) may contain transitional or transitory provision or savings.
(8)   No order may be made under subsection (5) unless a draft of the statutory instrument containing it has been laid before, and approved by a resolution of, each House of Parliament.

NOTES
Commencement: 26 March 2015 (sub-ss (5)–(8)); 1 October 2015 (sub-ss (1)–(4) except for the purpose of a contract to supply a consumer transport service); 6 April 2016 (sub-ss (1)–(4) otherwise).

What Statutory Rights are There under a Services Contract?

[1.2271]
49   Service to be performed with reasonable care and skill
(1)   Every contract to supply a service is to be treated as including a term that the trader must perform the service with reasonable care and skill.
(2)   See section 54 for a consumer's rights if the trader is in breach of a term that this section requires to be treated as included in a contract.

NOTES
Commencement: 1 October 2015 (except for the purpose of a contract to supply a consumer transport service); 6 April 2016 (otherwise).

[1.2272]
50   Information about the trader or service to be binding
(1)   Every contract to supply a service is to be treated as including as a term of the contract anything that is said or written to the consumer, by or on behalf of the trader, about the trader or the service, if—
  (a)   it is taken into account by the consumer when deciding to enter into the contract, or
  (b)   it is taken into account by the consumer when making any decision about the service after entering into the contract.
(2)   Anything taken into account by the consumer as mentioned in subsection (1)(a) or (b) is subject to—
  (a)   anything that qualified it and was said or written to the consumer by the trader on the same occasion, and
  (b)   any change to it that has been expressly agreed between the consumer and the trader (before entering into the contract or later).
(3)   Without prejudice to subsection (1), any information provided by the trader in accordance with regulation 9, 10 or 13 of the Consumer Contracts (Information, Cancellation and Additional Charges) Regulations 2013 (SI 2013/3134) is to be treated as included as a term of the contract.
(4)   A change to any of the information mentioned in subsection (3), made before entering into the contract or later, is not effective unless expressly agreed between the consumer and the trader.
(5)   See section 54 for a consumer's rights if the trader is in breach of a term that this section requires to be treated as included in a contract.

NOTES
Commencement: 1 October 2015 (except for the purpose of a contract to supply a consumer transport service); 6 April 2016 (otherwise).

[1.2273]
51   Reasonable price to be paid for a service
(1)   This section applies to a contract to supply a service if—
  (a)   the consumer has not paid a price or other consideration for the service,
  (b)   the contract does not expressly fix a price or other consideration, and does not say how it is to be fixed, and
  (c)   anything that is to be treated under section 50 as included in the contract does not fix a price or other consideration either.

(2)   In that case the contract is to be treated as including a term that the consumer must pay a reasonable price for the service, and no more.

(3)   What is a reasonable price is a question of fact.

NOTES

Commencement: 1 October 2015 (except for the purpose of a contract to supply a consumer transport service); 6 April 2016 (otherwise).

[1.2274]
52   Service to be performed within a reasonable time

(1)   This section applies to a contract to supply a service, if—

(a)   the contract does not expressly fix the time for the service to be performed, and does not say how it is to be fixed, and

(b)   information that is to be treated under section 50 as included in the contract does not fix the time either.

(2)   In that case the contract is to be treated as including a term that the trader must perform the service within a reasonable time.

(3)   What is a reasonable time is a question of fact.

(4)   See section 54 for a consumer's rights if the trader is in breach of a term that this section requires to be treated as included in a contract.

NOTES

Commencement: 1 October 2015 (except for the purpose of a contract to supply a consumer transport service); 6 April 2016 (otherwise).

[1.2275]
53   Relation to other law on contract terms

(1)   Nothing in this Chapter affects any enactment or rule of law that imposes a stricter duty on the trader.

(2)   This Chapter is subject to any other enactment which defines or restricts the rights, duties or liabilities arising in connection with a service of any description.

NOTES

Commencement: 1 October 2015 (except for the purpose of a contract to supply a consumer transport service); 6 April 2016 (otherwise).

What Remedies are There if Statutory Rights under a Services Contract are not Met?

[1.2276]
54   Consumer's rights to enforce terms about services

(1)   The consumer's rights under this section and sections 55 and 56 do not affect any rights that the contract provides for, if those are not inconsistent.

(2)   In this section and section 55 a reference to a service conforming to a contract is a reference to—

(a)   the service being performed in accordance with section 49, or

(b)   the service conforming to a term that section 50 requires to be treated as included in the contract and that relates to the performance of the service.

(3)   If the service does not conform to the contract, the consumer's rights (and the provisions about them and when they are available) are—

(a)   the right to require repeat performance (see section 55);

(b)   the right to a price reduction (see section 56).

(4)   If the trader is in breach of a term that section 50 requires to be treated as included in the contract but that does not relate to the service, the consumer has the right to a price reduction (see section 56 for provisions about that right and when it is available).

(5)   If the trader is in breach of what the contract requires under section 52 (performance within a reasonable time), the consumer has the right to a price reduction (see section 56 for provisions about that right and when it is available).

(6)   This section and sections 55 and 56 do not prevent the consumer seeking other remedies for a breach of a term to which any of subsections (3) to (5) applies, instead of or in addition to a remedy referred to there (but not so as to recover twice for the same loss).

(7)   Those other remedies include any of the following that is open to the consumer in the circumstances—

(a)   claiming damages;

(b)   seeking to recover money paid where the consideration for payment of the money has failed;

(c)   seeking specific performance;

(d)   seeking an order for specific implement;

(e)   relying on the breach against a claim by the trader under the contract;

(f)   exercising a right to treat the contract as at an end.

Part 1   Statutes

NOTES

Commencement: 1 October 2015 (except for the purpose of a contract to supply a consumer transport service); 6 April 2016 (otherwise).

[1.2277]
55   Right to repeat performance
(1)   The right to require repeat performance is a right to require the trader to perform the service again, to the extent necessary to complete its performance in conformity with the contract.

(2)   If the consumer requires such repeat performance, the trader—
  (a)   must provide it within a reasonable time and without significant inconvenience to the consumer; and
  (b)   must bear any necessary costs incurred in doing so (including in particular the cost of any labour or materials).

(3)   The consumer cannot require repeat performance if completing performance of the service in conformity with the contract is impossible.

(4)   Any question as to what is a reasonable time or significant inconvenience is to be determined taking account of—
  (a)   the nature of the service, and
  (b)   the purpose for which the service was to be performed.

NOTES

Commencement: 1 October 2015 (except for the purpose of a contract to supply a consumer transport service); 6 April 2016 (otherwise).

[1.2278]
56   Right to price reduction
(1)   The right to a price reduction is the right to require the trader to reduce the price to the consumer by an appropriate amount (including the right to receive a refund for anything already paid above the reduced amount).

(2)   The amount of the reduction may, where appropriate, be the full amount of the price.

(3)   A consumer who has that right and the right to require repeat performance is only entitled to a price reduction in one of these situations—
  (a)   because of section 55(3) the consumer cannot require repeat performance; or
  (b)   the consumer has required repeat performance, but the trader is in breach of the requirement of section 55(2)(a) to do it within a reasonable time and without significant inconvenience to the consumer.

(4)   A refund under this section must be given without undue delay, and in any event within 14 days beginning with the day on which the trader agrees that the consumer is entitled to a refund.

(5)   The trader must give the refund using the same means of payment as the consumer used to pay for the service, unless the consumer expressly agrees otherwise.

(6)   The trader must not impose any fee on the consumer in respect of the refund.

NOTES

Commencement: 1 October 2015 (except for the purpose of a contract to supply a consumer transport service); 6 April 2016 (otherwise).

Can a Trader Contract out of Statutory Rights and Remedies under a Services Contract?

[1.2279]
57   Liability that cannot be excluded or restricted
(1)   A term of a contract to supply services is not binding on the consumer to the extent that it would exclude the trader's liability arising under section 49 (service to be performed with reasonable care and skill).

(2)   Subject to section 50(2), a term of a contract to supply services is not binding on the consumer to the extent that it would exclude the trader's liability arising under section 50 (information about trader or service to be binding).

(3)   A term of a contract to supply services is not binding on the consumer to the extent that it would restrict the trader's liability arising under any of sections 49 and 50 and, where they apply, sections 51 and 52 (reasonable price and reasonable time), if it would prevent the consumer in an appropriate case from recovering the price paid or the value of any other consideration. (If it would not prevent the consumer from doing so, Part 2 (unfair terms) may apply.)

(4)   That also means that a term of a contract to supply services is not binding on the consumer to the extent that it would —
  (a)   exclude or restrict a right or remedy in respect of a liability under any of sections 49 to 52,
  (b)   make such a right or remedy or its enforcement subject to a restrictive or onerous condition,
  (c)   allow a trader to put a person at a disadvantage as a result of pursuing such a right or remedy, or
  (d)   exclude or restrict rules of evidence or procedure.

(5)   The references in subsections (1) to (3) to excluding or restricting a liability also include preventing an obligation or duty arising or limiting its extent.

(6)   An agreement in writing to submit present or future differences to arbitration is not to be regarded as excluding or restricting any liability for the purposes of this section.

(7)   See Schedule 3 for provision about the enforcement of this section.

NOTES

Commencement: 1 October 2015 (except for the purpose of a contract to supply a consumer transport service); 6 April 2016 (otherwise).

CHAPTER 5
GENERAL AND SUPPLEMENTARY PROVISIONS

[1.2280]
58   Powers of the court

(1)   In any proceedings in which a remedy is sought by virtue of section 19(3) or (4), 42(2) or 54(3), the court, in addition to any other power it has, may act under this section.

(2)   On the application of the consumer the court may make an order requiring specific performance or, in Scotland, specific implement by the trader of any obligation imposed on the trader by virtue of section 23, 43 or 55.

(3)   Subsection (4) applies if—

   (a)   the consumer claims to exercise a right under the relevant remedies provisions, but
   (b)   the court decides that those provisions have the effect that exercise of another right is appropriate.

(4)   The court may proceed as if the consumer had exercised that other right.

(5)   If the consumer has claimed to exercise the final right to reject, the court may order that any reimbursement to the consumer is reduced by a deduction for use, to take account of the use the consumer has had of the goods in the period since they were delivered.

(6)   Any deduction for use is limited as set out in section 24(9) and (10).

(7)   The court may make an order under this section unconditionally or on such terms and conditions as to damages, payment of the price and otherwise as it thinks just.

(8)   The "relevant remedies provisions" are—

   (a)   where Chapter 2 applies, sections 23 and 24;
   (b)   where Chapter 3 applies, sections 43 and 44;
   (c)   where Chapter 4 applies, sections 55 and 56.

NOTES

Commencement: 1 October 2015 (except for the purpose of a contract to supply a consumer transport service); 6 April 2016 (otherwise).

[1.2281]
59   Interpretation

(1)   These definitions apply in this Part (as well as the key definitions in section 2)—

   "conditional sales contract" has the meaning given in section 5(3);

   "Consumer Rights Directive" means Directive 2011/83/EU of the European Parliament and of the Council of 25 October 2011 on consumer rights, amending Council Directive 93/13/EEC and Directive 1999/44/EC of the European Parliament and of the Council and repealing Council Directive 85/577/EEC and Directive 97/7/EC of the European Parliament and of the Council;

   "credit-broker" means a person acting in the course of a business of credit brokerage carried on by that person;

   "credit brokerage" means—

   (a)   introducing individuals who want to obtain credit to persons carrying on any business so far as it relates to the provision of credit,
   (b)   introducing individuals who want to obtain goods on hire to persons carrying on a business which comprises or relates to supplying goods under a contract for the hire of goods, or
   (c)   introducing individuals who want to obtain credit, or to obtain goods on hire, to other persons engaged in credit brokerage;

   "delivery" means voluntary transfer of possession from one person to another;

   "enactment" includes—

   (a)   an enactment contained in subordinate legislation within the meaning of the Interpretation Act 1978,
   (b)   an enactment contained in, or in an instrument made under, a Measure or Act of the National Assembly for Wales,
   (c)   an enactment contained in, or in an instrument made under, an Act of the Scottish Parliament, and
   (d)   an enactment contained in, or in an instrument made under, Northern Ireland legislation;

"producer", in relation to goods or digital content, means—

    (a)   the manufacturer,

    (b)   the importer into the European Economic Area, or

    (c)   any person who purports to be a producer by placing the person's name, trade mark or other distinctive sign on the goods or using it in connection with the digital content.

(2)   References in this Part to treating a contract as at an end are to be read in accordance with section 19(13).

NOTES

Commencement: 1 October 2015 (except for the purpose of a contract to supply a consumer transport service); 6 April 2016 (otherwise).

[1.2282]
60   Changes to other legislation

Schedule 1 (amendments consequential on this Part) has effect.

NOTES

Commencement: 1 October 2015.

PART 2
UNFAIR TERMS

What Contracts and Notices are Covered by this Part?

[1.2283]
61   Contracts and notices covered by this Part

(1)   This Part applies to a contract between a trader and a consumer.

(2)   This does not include a contract of employment or apprenticeship.

(3)   A contract to which this Part applies is referred to in this Part as a "consumer contract".

(4)   This Part applies to a notice to the extent that it—

    (a)   relates to rights or obligations as between a trader and a consumer, or

    (b)   purports to exclude or restrict a trader's liability to a consumer.

(5)   This does not include a notice relating to rights, obligations or liabilities as between an employer and an employee.

(6)   It does not matter for the purposes of subsection (4) whether the notice is expressed to apply to a consumer, as long as it is reasonable to assume it is intended to be seen or heard by a consumer.

(7)   A notice to which this Part applies is referred to in this Part as a "consumer notice".

(8)   In this section "notice" includes an announcement, whether or not in writing, and any other communication or purported communication.

NOTES

Commencement: 1 October 2015.

What are the General Rules about Fairness of Contract Terms and Notices?

[1.2284]
62   Requirement for contract terms and notices to be fair

(1)   An unfair term of a consumer contract is not binding on the consumer.

(2)   An unfair consumer notice is not binding on the consumer.

(3)   This does not prevent the consumer from relying on the term or notice if the consumer chooses to do so.

(4)   A term is unfair if, contrary to the requirement of good faith, it causes a significant imbalance in the parties' rights and obligations under the contract to the detriment of the consumer.

(5)   Whether a term is fair is to be determined—

    (a)   taking into account the nature of the subject matter of the contract, and

    (b)   by reference to all the circumstances existing when the term was agreed and to all of the other terms of the contract or of any other contract on which it depends.

(6)   A notice is unfair if, contrary to the requirement of good faith, it causes a significant imbalance in the parties' rights and obligations to the detriment of the consumer.

(7)   Whether a notice is fair is to be determined—

    (a)   taking into account the nature of the subject matter of the notice, and

    (b)   by reference to all the circumstances existing when the rights or obligations to which it relates arose and to the terms of any contract on which it depends.

(8)   This section does not affect the operation of—

    (a)   section 31 (exclusion of liability: goods contracts),

    (b)   section 47 (exclusion of liability: digital content contracts),

    (c)   section 57 (exclusion of liability: services contracts), or

    (d)   section 65 (exclusion of negligence liability).

NOTES
Commencement: 1 October 2015.

[1.2285]
63 Contract terms which may or must be regarded as unfair
(1) Part 1 of Schedule 2 contains an indicative and non-exhaustive list of terms of consumer contracts that may be regarded as unfair for the purposes of this Part.
(2) Part 1 of Schedule 2 is subject to Part 2 of that Schedule; but a term listed in Part 2 of that Schedule may nevertheless be assessed for fairness under section 62 unless section 64 or 73 applies to it.
(3) The Secretary of State may by order made by statutory instrument amend Schedule 2 so as to add, modify or remove an entry in Part 1 or Part 2 of that Schedule.
(4) An order under subsection (3) may contain transitional or transitory provision or savings.
(5) No order may be made under subsection (3) unless a draft of the statutory instrument containing it has been laid before, and approved by a resolution of, each House of Parliament.
(6) A term of a consumer contract must be regarded as unfair if it has the effect that the consumer bears the burden of proof with respect to compliance by a distance supplier or an intermediary with an obligation under any enactment or rule implementing the Distance Marketing Directive.
(7) In subsection (6)—
"the Distance Marketing Directive" means Directive 2002/65/EC of the European Parliament and of the Council of 23 September 2002 concerning the distance marketing of consumer financial services and amending Council Directive 90/619/EEC and Directives 97/7/EC and 98/27/EC;
"distance supplier" means—
    (a) a supplier under a distance contract within the meaning of the Financial Services (Distance Marketing) Regulations 2004 (SI 2004/2095), or
    (b) a supplier of unsolicited financial services within the meaning of regulation 15 of those regulations;
"enactment" includes an enactment contained in subordinate legislation within the meaning of the Interpretation Act 1978;
"intermediary" has the same meaning as in the Financial Services (Distance Marketing) Regulations 2004;
"rule" means a rule made by the Financial Conduct Authority or the Prudential Regulation Authority under the Financial Services and Markets Act 2000 or by a designated professional body within the meaning of section 326(2) of that Act.

NOTES
Commencement: 1 October 2015.

[1.2286]
64 Exclusion from assessment of fairness
(1) A term of a consumer contract may not be assessed for fairness under section 62 to the extent that—
    (a) it specifies the main subject matter of the contract, or
    (b) the assessment is of the appropriateness of the price payable under the contract by comparison with the goods, digital content or services supplied under it.
(2) Subsection (1) excludes a term from an assessment under section 62 only if it is transparent and prominent.
(3) A term is transparent for the purposes of this Part if it is expressed in plain and intelligible language and (in the case of a written term) is legible.
(4) A term is prominent for the purposes of this section if it is brought to the consumer's attention in such a way that an average consumer would be aware of the term.
(5) In subsection (4) "average consumer" means a consumer who is reasonably well-informed, observant and circumspect.
(6) This section does not apply to a term of a contract listed in Part 1 of Schedule 2.

NOTES
Commencement: 1 October 2015.

[1.2287]
65 Bar on exclusion or restriction of negligence liability
(1) A trader cannot by a term of a consumer contract or by a consumer notice exclude or restrict liability for death or personal injury resulting from negligence.
(2) Where a term of a consumer contract, or a consumer notice, purports to exclude or restrict a trader's liability for negligence, a person is not to be taken to have voluntarily accepted any risk merely because the person agreed to or knew about the term or notice.
(3) In this section "personal injury" includes any disease and any impairment of physical or mental condition.

(4) In this section "negligence" means the breach of—
- (a) any obligation to take reasonable care or exercise reasonable skill in the performance of a contract where the obligation arises from an express or implied term of the contract,
- (b) a common law duty to take reasonable care or exercise reasonable skill,
- (c) the common duty of care imposed by the Occupiers' Liability Act 1957 or the Occupiers' Liability Act (Northern Ireland) 1957, or
- (d) the duty of reasonable care imposed by section 2(1) of the Occupiers' Liability (Scotland) Act 1960.

(5) It is immaterial for the purposes of subsection (4)—
- (a) whether a breach of duty or obligation was inadvertent or intentional, or
- (b) whether liability for it arises directly or vicariously.

(6) This section is subject to section 66 (which makes provision about the scope of this section).

NOTES
Commencement: 1 October 2015.

[1.2288]
66 Scope of section 65
(1) Section 65 does not apply to—
- (a) any contract so far as it is a contract of insurance, including a contract to pay an annuity on human life, or
- (b) any contract so far as it relates to the creation or transfer of an interest in land.

(2) Section 65 does not affect the validity of any discharge or indemnity given by a person in consideration of the receipt by that person of compensation in settlement of any claim the person has.

(3) Section 65 does not—
- (a) apply to liability which is excluded or discharged as mentioned in section 4(2)(a) (exception to liability to pay damages to relatives) of the Damages (Scotland) Act 2011, or
- (b) affect the operation of section 5 (discharge of liability to pay damages: exception for mesothelioma) of that Act.

(4) Section 65 does not apply to the liability of an occupier of premises to a person who obtains access to the premises for recreational purposes if—
- (a) the person suffers loss or damage because of the dangerous state of the premises, and
- (b) allowing the person access for those purposes is not within the purposes of the occupier's trade, business, craft or profession.

NOTES
Commencement: 1 October 2015.

[1.2289]
67 Effect of an unfair term on the rest of a contract
Where a term of a consumer contract is not binding on the consumer as a result of this Part, the contract continues, so far as practicable, to have effect in every other respect.

NOTES
Commencement: 1 October 2015.

[1.2290]
68 Requirement for transparency
(1) A trader must ensure that a written term of a consumer contract, or a consumer notice in writing, is transparent.

(2) A consumer notice is transparent for the purposes of subsection (1) if it is expressed in plain and intelligible language and it is legible.

NOTES
Commencement: 1 October 2015.

[1.2291]
69 Contract terms that may have different meanings
(1) If a term in a consumer contract, or a consumer notice, could have different meanings, the meaning that is most favourable to the consumer is to prevail.

(2) Subsection (1) does not apply to the construction of a term or a notice in proceedings on an application for an injunction or interdict under paragraph 3 of Schedule 3.

NOTES
Commencement: 1 October 2015.

How are the General Rules Enforced?

[1.2292]
70 Enforcement of the law on unfair contract terms
(1)   Schedule 3 confers functions on the Competition and Markets Authority and other regulators in relation to the enforcement of this Part.
(2)   For provision about the investigatory powers that are available to those regulators for the purposes of that Schedule, see Schedule 5.

NOTES
    Commencement: 1 October 2015.

Supplementary Provisions

[1.2293]
71 Duty of court to consider fairness of term
(1)   Subsection (2) applies to proceedings before a court which relate to a term of a consumer contract.
(2)   The court must consider whether the term is fair even if none of the parties to the proceedings has raised that issue or indicated that it intends to raise it.
(3)   But subsection (2) does not apply unless the court considers that it has before it sufficient legal and factual material to enable it to consider the fairness of the term.

NOTES
    Commencement: 1 October 2015.

[1.2294]
72 Application of rules to secondary contracts
(1)   This section applies if a term of a contract ("the secondary contract") reduces the rights or remedies or increases the obligations of a person under another contract ("the main contract").
(2)   The term is subject to the provisions of this Part that would apply to the term if it were in the main contract.
(3)   It does not matter for the purposes of this section—
    (a)   whether the parties to the secondary contract are the same as the parties to the main contract, or
    (b)   whether the secondary contract is a consumer contract.
(4)   This section does not apply if the secondary contract is a settlement of a claim arising under the main contract.

NOTES
    Commencement: 1 October 2015.

[1.2295]
73 Disapplication of rules to mandatory terms and notices
(1)   This Part does not apply to a term of a contract, or to a notice, to the extent that it reflects—
    (a)   mandatory statutory or regulatory provisions, or
    (b)   the provisions or principles of an international convention to which the United Kingdom or the EU is a party.
(2)   In subsection (1) "mandatory statutory or regulatory provisions" includes rules which, according to law, apply between the parties on the basis that no other arrangements have been established.

NOTES
    Commencement: 1 October 2015.

[1.2296]
74 Contracts applying law of non-EEA State
(1)   If—
    (a)   the law of a country or territory other than an EEA State is chosen by the parties to be applicable to a consumer contract, but
    (b)   the consumer contract has a close connection with the United Kingdom,
this Part applies despite that choice.
(2)   For cases where the law applicable has not been chosen or the law of an EEA State is chosen, see Regulation (EC) No 593/2008 of the European Parliament and of the Council of 17 June 2008 on the law applicable to contractual obligations.

NOTES
    Commencement: 1 October 2015.

[1.2297]
75 Changes to other legislation
Schedule 4 (amendments consequential on this Part) has effect.

NOTES

Commencement: 1 October 2015.

[1.2298]
76 Interpretation of Part 2

(1) In this Part—
"consumer contract" has the meaning given by section 61(3);
"consumer notice" has the meaning given by section 61(7);
"transparent" is to be construed in accordance with sections 64(3) and 68(2).

(2) The following have the same meanings in this Part as they have in Part 1—
"trader" (see section 2(2));
"consumer" (see section 2(3));
"goods" (see section 2(8));
"digital content" (see section 2(9)).

(3) Section 2(4) (trader who claims an individual is not a consumer must prove it) applies in relation to this Part as it applies in relation to Part 1.

NOTES

Commencement: 1 October 2015.

PART 3
MISCELLANEOUS AND GENERAL

CHAPTER 1
ENFORCEMENT ETC

[1.2299]
77 Investigatory powers etc

(1) Schedule 5 (investigatory powers etc) has effect.
(2) Schedule 6 (investigatory powers: consequential amendments) has effect.

NOTES

Commencement: 26 March 2015 (certain purposes); 27 May 2015 (certain purposes); 1 October 2015 (otherwise).

78 *(This section amends the Weights and Measures (Packaged Goods) Regulations 2006, SI 2006/659, Sch 5. It further provides that use of this Act to make amendments to the 2006 Regulations has no effect on the availability of any power in the Weights and Measures Act 1985 to amend or revoke those Regulations. It also amends the Weights and Measures (Packaged Goods) Regulations (Northern Ireland) 2011, SR 2011/331 and provides that the use of this Act to make amendments to the 2011 Regulations has no effect on the availability of any power in the Weights and Measures (Northern Ireland) Order 1981, SI 1981/231.)*

[1.2300]
79 Enterprise Act 2002: enhanced consumer measures and other enforcement

(1) Schedule 7 contains amendments of Part 8 of the Enterprise Act 2002 (enforcement of certain consumer legislation).
(2) The amendments have effect only in relation to conduct which occurs, or which is likely to occur, after the commencement of this section.

NOTES

Commencement: 1 October 2015.

80 *(Amends the Communications Act 2003, ss 120(3), 121(5), 123.*

CHAPTER 2
COMPETITION

[1.2301]
81 Private actions in competition law

Schedule 8 (private actions in competition law) has effect.

NOTES

Commencement: 3 August 2015 (certain purposes); 1 October 2015 (otherwise).

82 *(Amends the Enterprise Act 2002, ss 12, 14, Sch 4.*

CHAPTER 3
DUTY OF LETTING AGENTS TO PUBLICISE FEES ETC

[1.2302]
83 Duty of letting agents to publicise fees etc
(1) A letting agent must, in accordance with this section, publicise details of the agent's relevant fees.
(2) The agent must display a list of the fees—
  (a) at each of the agent's premises at which the agent deals face-to-face with persons using or proposing to use services to which the fees relate, and
  (b) at a place in each of those premises at which the list is likely to be seen by such persons.
(3) The agent must publish a list of the fees on the agent's website (if it has a website).
(4) A list of fees displayed or published in accordance with subsection (2) or (3) must include—
  (a) a description of each fee that is sufficient to enable a person who is liable to pay it to understand the service or cost that is covered by the fee or the purpose for which it is imposed (as the case may be),
  (b) in the case of a fee which tenants are liable to pay, an indication of whether the fee relates to each dwelling-house or each tenant under a tenancy of the dwelling-house, and
  (c) the amount of each fee inclusive of any applicable tax or, where the amount of a fee cannot reasonably be determined in advance, a description of how that fee is calculated.
(5) Subsections (6) and (7) apply to a letting agent engaging in letting agency or property management work in relation to dwelling-houses in England.
(6) If the agent holds money on behalf of persons to whom the agent provides services as part of that work, the duty imposed on the agent by subsection (2) or (3) includes a duty to display or publish, with the list of fees, a statement of whether the agent is a member of a client money protection scheme.
(7) If the agent is required to be a member of a redress scheme for dealing with complaints in connection with that work, the duty imposed on the agent by subsection (2) or (3) includes a duty to display or publish, with the list of fees, a statement—
  (a) that indicates that the agent is a member of a redress scheme, and
  (b) that gives the name of the scheme.
(8) The appropriate national authority may by regulations specify—
  (a) other ways in which a letting agent must publicise details of the relevant fees charged by the agent or (where applicable) a statement within subsection (6) or (7);
  (b) the details that must be given of fees publicised in that way.
(9) In this section—
  "client money protection scheme" means a scheme which enables a person on whose behalf a letting agent holds money to be compensated if all or part of that money is not repaid to that person in circumstances where the scheme applies;
  "redress scheme" means a redress scheme for which provision is made by order under section 83 or 84 of the Enterprise and Regulatory Reform Act 2013.

NOTES
Commencement: 26 March 2015 (in so far as it confers powers to make regulations); 27 May 2015 (in relation to England, for all other purposes); to be appointed (otherwise).

[1.2303]
84 Letting agents to which the duty applies
(1) In this Chapter "letting agent" means a person who engages in letting agency work (whether or not that person engages in other work).
(2) A person is not a letting agent for the purposes of this Chapter if the person engages in letting agency work in the course of that person's employment under a contract of employment.
(3) A person is not a letting agent for the purposes of this Chapter if—
  (a) the person is of a description specified in regulations made by the appropriate national authority;
  (b) the person engages in work of a description specified in regulations made by the appropriate national authority.

NOTES
Commencement: 26 March 2015 (in so far as it confers powers to make regulations); 27 May 2015 (in relation to England, for all other purposes); to be appointed (otherwise).
Regulations: the Duty of Letting Agents to Publicise Fees etc (Exclusion) (England) Regulations 2015, SI 2015/951.

[1.2304]
85 Fees to which the duty applies
(1) In this Chapter "relevant fees", in relation to a letting agent, means the fees, charges or penalties (however expressed) payable to the agent by a landlord or tenant—
  (a) in respect of letting agency work carried on by the agent,
  (b) in respect of property management work carried on by the agent, or
  (c) otherwise in connection with—

    (i)   an assured tenancy of a dwelling-house, or

    (ii)   a dwelling-house that is, has been or is proposed to be let under an assured tenancy.

(2)   Subsection (1) does not apply to—

    (a)   the rent payable to a landlord under a tenancy,

    (b)   any fees, charges or penalties which the letting agent receives from a landlord under a tenancy on behalf of another person,

    (c)   a tenancy deposit within the meaning of section 212(8) of the Housing Act 2004, or

    (d)   any fees, charges or penalties of a description specified in regulations made by the appropriate national authority.

NOTES

Commencement: 26 March 2015 (in so far as it confers powers to make regulations); 27 May 2015 (in relation to England, for all other purposes); to be appointed (otherwise).

[1.2305]
86   Letting agency work and property management work

(1)   In this Chapter "letting agency work" means things done by a person in the course of a business in response to instructions received from—

    (a)   a person ("a prospective landlord") seeking to find another person wishing to rent a dwelling-house under an assured tenancy and, having found such a person, to grant such a tenancy, or

    (b)   a person ("a prospective tenant") seeking to find a dwelling-house to rent under an assured tenancy and, having found such a dwelling-house, to obtain such a tenancy of it.

(2)   But "letting agency work" does not include any of the following things when done by a person who does nothing else within subsection (1)—

    (a)   publishing advertisements or disseminating information;

    (b)   providing a means by which a prospective landlord or a prospective tenant can, in response to an advertisement or dissemination of information, make direct contact with a prospective tenant or a prospective landlord;

    (c)   providing a means by which a prospective landlord and a prospective tenant can communicate directly with each other.

(3)   "Letting agency work" also does not include things done by a local authority.

(4)   In this Chapter "property management work", in relation to a letting agent, means things done by the agent in the course of a business in response to instructions received from another person where—

    (a)   that person wishes the agent to arrange services, repairs, maintenance, improvements or insurance in respect of, or to deal with any other aspect of the management of, premises on the person's behalf, and

    (b)   the premises consist of a dwelling-house let under an assured tenancy.

NOTES

Commencement: 26 March 2015 (in so far as it confers powers to make regulations); 27 May 2015 (in relation to England, for all other purposes); to be appointed (otherwise).

[1.2306]
87   Enforcement of the duty

(1)   It is the duty of every local weights and measures authority in England and Wales to enforce the provisions of this Chapter in its area.

(2)   If a letting agent breaches the duty in section 83(3) (duty to publish list of fees etc on agent's website), that breach is taken to have occurred in each area of a local weights and measures authority in England and Wales in which a dwelling-house to which the fees relate is located.

(3)   Where a local weights and measures authority in England and Wales is satisfied on the balance of probabilities that a letting agent has breached a duty imposed by or under section 83, the authority may impose a financial penalty on the agent in respect of that breach.

(4)   A local weights and measures authority in England and Wales may impose a penalty under this section in respect of a breach which occurs in England and Wales but outside that authority's area (as well as in respect of a breach which occurs within that area).

(5)   But a local weights and measures authority in England and Wales may impose a penalty in respect of a breach which occurs outside its area and in the area of a local weights and measures authority in Wales only if it has obtained the consent of that authority.

(6)   Only one penalty under this section may be imposed on the same letting agent in respect of the same breach.

(7)   The amount of a financial penalty imposed under this section—

    (a)   may be such as the authority imposing it determines, but

    (b)   must not exceed £5,000.

(8)   Schedule 9 (procedure for and appeals against financial penalties) has effect.

(9)   A local weights and measures authority in England must have regard to any guidance issued by the Secretary of State about—

    (a)   compliance by letting agents with duties imposed by or under section 83;

   (b)   the exercise of its functions under this section or Schedule 9.

(10)   A local weights and measures authority in Wales must have regard to any guidance issued by the Welsh Ministers about—

   (a)   compliance by letting agents with duties imposed by or under section 83;

   (b)   the exercise of its functions under this section or Schedule 9.

(11)   The Secretary of State may by regulations made by statutory instrument—

   (a)   amend any of the provisions of this section or Schedule 9 in their application in relation to local weights and measures authorities in England;

   (b)   make consequential amendments to Schedule 5 in its application in relation to such authorities.

(12)   The Welsh Ministers may by regulations made by statutory instrument—

   (a)   amend any of the provisions of this section or Schedule 9 in their application in relation to local weights and measures authorities in Wales;

   (b)   make consequential amendments to Schedule 5 in its application in relation to such authorities.

NOTES

Commencement: 26 March 2015 (in so far as it confers powers to make regulations); 27 May 2015 (in relation to England, for all other purposes); to be appointed (otherwise).

[1.2307]
88 Supplementary provisions

(1)   In this Chapter—

   "the appropriate national authority" means—

      (a)   in relation to England, the Secretary of State, and

      (b)   in relation to Wales, the Welsh Ministers;

   "assured tenancy" means a tenancy which is an assured tenancy for the purposes of the Housing Act 1988 except where—

      (a)   the landlord is—

         (i)   a private registered provider of social housing,

         (ii)   a registered social landlord, or

         (iii)   a fully mutual housing association, or

      (b)   the tenancy is a long lease;

   "dwelling-house" may be a house or part of a house;

   "fully mutual housing association" has the same meaning as in Part 1 of the Housing Associations Act 1985 (see section 1(1) and (2) of that Act);

   "landlord" includes a person who proposes to be a landlord under a tenancy and a person who has ceased to be a landlord under a tenancy because the tenancy has come to an end;

   "long lease" means a lease which—

      (a)   is a long lease for the purposes of Chapter 1 of Part 1 of the Leasehold Reform, Housing and Urban Development Act 1993, or

      (b)   in the case of a shared ownership lease (within the meaning given by section 7(7) of that Act), would be a lease within paragraph (a) of this definition if the tenant's total share (within the meaning given by that section) were 100%;

   "registered social landlord" means a body registered as a social landlord under Chapter 1 of Part 1 of the Housing Act 1996;

   "tenant" includes a person who proposes to be a tenant under a tenancy and a person who has ceased to be a tenant under a tenancy because the tenancy has come to an end.

(2)   In this Chapter "local authority" means—

   (a)   a county council,

   (b)   a county borough council,

   (c)   a district council,

   (d)   a London borough council,

   (e)   the Common Council of the City of London in its capacity as local authority, or

   (f)   the Council of the Isles of Scilly.

(3)   References in this Chapter to a tenancy include a proposed tenancy and a tenancy that has come to an end.

(4)   References in this Chapter to anything which is payable, or which a person is liable to pay, to a letting agent include anything that the letting agent claims a person is liable to pay, regardless of whether the person is in fact liable to pay it.

(5)   Regulations under this Chapter are to be made by statutory instrument.

(6)   A statutory instrument containing (whether alone or with other provision) regulations made by the Secretary of State under section 87(11) is not to be made unless a draft of the instrument has been laid before, and approved by a resolution of, each House of Parliament.

(7)   A statutory instrument containing (whether alone or with other provision) regulations made by the Welsh Ministers under section 87(12) is not to be made unless a draft of the instrument has been laid before, and approved by a resolution of, the National Assembly for Wales.

(8) A statutory instrument containing regulations made by the Secretary of State under this Chapter other than one to which subsection (6) applies is subject to annulment in pursuance of a resolution of either House of Parliament.

(9) A statutory instrument containing regulations made by the Welsh Ministers under this Chapter other than one to which subsection (7) applies is subject to annulment in pursuance of a resolution of the National Assembly for Wales.

(10) Regulations under this Chapter—
    (a)   may make different provision for different purposes;
    (b)   may make provision generally or in relation to specific cases.

(11) Regulations under this Chapter may include incidental, supplementary, consequential, transitional, transitory or saving provision.

NOTES

Commencement: 26 March 2015 (sub-ss (5)–(11)); 27 May 2015 (in relation to England, for all other purposes); to be appointed (otherwise).

CHAPTER 4
STUDENT COMPLAINTS SCHEME

89   *(Amends the Higher Education Act 2004, ss 11, 12).*

CHAPTER 5
SECONDARY TICKETING

[1.2308]
90   Duty to provide information about tickets

(1) This section applies where a person ("the seller") re-sells a ticket for a recreational, sporting or cultural event in the United Kingdom through a secondary ticketing facility.

(2) The seller and each operator of the facility must ensure that the person who buys the ticket ("the buyer") is given the information specified in subsection (3), where this is applicable to the ticket.

(3) That information is—
    (a)   where the ticket is for a particular seat or standing area at the venue for the event, the information necessary to enable the buyer to identify that seat or standing area,
    (b)   information about any restriction which limits use of the ticket to persons of a particular description, and
    (c)   the face value of the ticket.

(4) The reference in subsection (3)(a) to information necessary to enable the buyer to identify a seat or standing area at a venue includes, so far as applicable—
    (a)   the name of the area in the venue in which the seat or standing area is located (for example the name of the stand in which it is located),
    (b)   information necessary to enable the buyer to identify the part of the area in the venue in which the seat or standing area is located (for example the block of seats in which the seat is located),
    (c)   the number, letter or other distinguishing mark of the row in which the seat is located, and
    (d)   the number, letter or other distinguishing mark of the seat.

(5) The reference in subsection (3)(c) to the face value of the ticket is to the amount stated on the ticket as its price.

(6) The seller and each operator of the facility must ensure that the buyer is given the information specified in subsection (7), where the seller is—
    (a)   an operator of the secondary ticketing facility,
    (b)   a person who is a parent undertaking or a subsidiary undertaking in relation to an operator of the secondary ticketing facility,
    (c)   a person who is employed or engaged by an operator of the secondary ticketing facility,
    (d)   a person who is acting on behalf of a person within paragraph (c), or
    (e)   an organiser of the event or a person acting on behalf of an organiser of the event.

(7) That information is a statement that the seller of the ticket is a person within subsection (6) which specifies the ground on which the seller falls within that subsection.

(8) Information required by this section to be given to the buyer must be given—
    (a)   in a clear and comprehensible manner, and
    (b)   before the buyer is bound by the contract for the sale of the ticket.

(9) This section applies in relation to the re-sale of a ticket through a secondary ticketing facility only if the ticket is first offered for re-sale through the facility after the coming into force of this section.

NOTES
Commencement: 26 May 2015.

[1.2309]
91 Prohibition on cancellation or blacklisting
(1)   This section applies where a person ("the seller") re-sells, or offers for re-sale, a ticket for a recreational, sporting or cultural event in the United Kingdom through a secondary ticketing facility.
(2)   An organiser of the event must not cancel the ticket merely because the seller has re-sold the ticket or offered it for re-sale unless—
    (a)   a term of the original contract for the sale of the ticket—
        (i)   provided for its cancellation if it was re-sold by the buyer under that contract,
        (ii)   provided for its cancellation if it was offered for re-sale by that buyer, or
        (iii)   provided as mentioned in sub-paragraph (i) and (ii), and
    (b)   that term was not unfair for the purposes of Part 2 (unfair terms).
(3)   An organiser of the event must not blacklist the seller merely because the seller has re-sold the ticket or offered it for re-sale unless—
    (a)   a term of the original contract for the sale of the ticket—
        (i)   provided for the blacklisting of the buyer under that contract if it was re-sold by that buyer,
        (ii)   provided for the blacklisting of that buyer if it was offered for re-sale by that buyer, or
        (iii)   provided as mentioned in sub-paragraph (i) and (ii), and
    (b)   that term was not unfair for the purposes of Part 2 (unfair terms).
(4)   In subsections (2) and (3) "the original contract" means the contract for the sale of the ticket by an organiser of the event to a person other than an organiser of the event.
(5)   For the purposes of this section an organiser of an event cancels a ticket if the organiser takes steps which result in the holder for the time being of the ticket no longer being entitled to attend that event.
(6)   For the purposes of this section an organiser of an event blacklists a person if the organiser takes steps—
    (a)   to prevent the person from acquiring a ticket for a recreational, sporting or cultural event in the United Kingdom, or
    (b)   to restrict the person's opportunity to acquire such a ticket.
(7)   Part 2 (unfair terms) may apply to a term of a contract which, apart from that Part, would permit the cancellation of a ticket for a recreational, sporting or cultural event in the United Kingdom, or the blacklisting of the seller of such a ticket, in circumstances other than those mentioned in subsection (2) or (3).
(8)   Before the coming into force of Part 2, references to that Part in this section are to be read as references to the Unfair Terms in Consumer Contracts Regulations 1999 (SI 1999/2083).
(9)   This section applies in relation to a ticket that is re-sold or offered for re-sale before or after the coming into force of this section; but the prohibition in this section applies only to things done after its coming into force.

NOTES
   Commencement: 26 May 2015.

[1.2310]
92 Duty to report criminal activity
(1)   This section applies where—
    (a)   an operator of a secondary ticketing facility knows that a person has used or is using the facility in such a way that an offence has been or is being committed, and
    (b)   the offence relates to the re-sale of a ticket for a recreational, sporting or cultural event in the United Kingdom.
(2)   The operator must, as soon as the operator becomes aware that a person has used or is using the facility as mentioned in subsection (1), disclose the matters specified in subsection (3) to—
    (a)   an appropriate person, and
    (b)   an organiser of the event (subject to subsection (5)).
(3)   Those matters are—
    (a)   the identity of the person mentioned in subsection (1), if this is known to the operator, and
    (b)   the fact that the operator knows that an offence has been or is being committed as mentioned in that subsection.
(4)   The following are appropriate persons for the purposes of this section—
    (a)   a constable of a police force in England and Wales,
    (b)   a constable of the police service of Scotland, and
    (c)   a police officer within the meaning of the Police (Northern Ireland) Act 2000.
(5)   This section does not require an operator to make a disclosure to an organiser of an event if the operator has reasonable grounds for believing that to do so will prejudice the investigation of any offence.
(6)   References in this section to an offence are to an offence under the law of any part of the United Kingdom.

(7) This section applies only in relation to an offence of which an operator becomes aware after the coming into force of this section.

NOTES
Commencement: 26 May 2015.

[1.2311]
93 Enforcement of this Chapter
(1) A local weights and measures authority in Great Britain may enforce the provisions of this Chapter in its area.
(2) The Department of Enterprise, Trade and Investment may enforce the provisions of this Chapter in Northern Ireland.
(3) Each of the bodies referred to in subsections (1) and (2) is an "enforcement authority" for the purposes of this Chapter.
(4) Where an enforcement authority is satisfied on the balance of probabilities that a person has breached a duty or prohibition imposed by this Chapter, the authority may impose a financial penalty on the person in respect of that breach.
(5) But in the case of a breach of a duty in section 90 or a prohibition in section 91 an enforcement authority may not impose a financial penalty on a person ("P") if the authority is satisfied on the balance of probabilities that—
    (a) the breach was due to—
        (i) a mistake,
        (ii) reliance on information supplied to P by another person,
        (iii) the act or default of another person,
        (iv) an accident, or
        (v) another cause beyond P's control, and
    (b) P took all reasonable precautions and exercised all due diligence to avoid the breach.
(6) A local weights and measures authority in England and Wales may impose a penalty under this section in respect of a breach which occurs in England and Wales but outside that authority's area (as well as in respect of a breach which occurs within that area).
(7) A local weights and measures authority in Scotland may impose a penalty under this section in respect of a breach which occurs in Scotland but outside that authority's area (as well as in respect of a breach which occurs within that area).
(8) Only one penalty under this section may be imposed on the same person in respect of the same breach.
(9) The amount of a financial penalty imposed under this section—
    (a) may be such as the enforcement authority imposing it determines, but
    (b) must not exceed £5,000.
(10) Schedule 10 (procedure for and appeals against financial penalties) has effect.
(11) References in this section to this Chapter do not include section 94.

NOTES
Commencement: 26 May 2015.

[1.2312]
94 Duty to review measures relating to secondary ticketing
(1) The Secretary of State must—
    (a) review, or arrange for a review of, consumer protection measures applying to the re-sale of tickets for recreational, sporting or cultural events in the United Kingdom through secondary ticketing facilities,
    (b) prepare a report on the outcome of the review or arrange for such a report to be prepared, and
    (c) publish that report.
(2) The report must be published before the end of the period of 12 months beginning with the day on which this section comes into force.
(3) The Secretary of State must lay the report before Parliament.
(4) In this section "consumer protection measures" includes such legislation, rules of law, codes of practice and guidance as the Secretary of State considers relate to the rights of consumers or the protection of their interests.

NOTES
Commencement: 26 May 2015.

[1.2313]
95 Interpretation of this Chapter
(1) In this Chapter—
    "enforcement authority" has the meaning given by section 93(3);
    "operator", in relation to a secondary ticketing facility, means a person who—
        (a) exercises control over the operation of the facility, and

(b)   receives revenue from the facility,

but this is subject to regulations under subsection (2);

"organiser", in relation to an event, means a person who—

(a)   is responsible for organising or managing the event, or

(b)   receives some or all of the revenue from the event;

"parent undertaking" has the meaning given by section 1162 of the Companies Act 2006;

"secondary ticketing facility" means an internet-based facility for the re-sale of tickets for recreational, sporting or cultural events;

"subsidiary undertaking" has the meaning given by section 1162 of the Companies Act 2006;

"undertaking" has the meaning given by section 1161(1) of the Companies Act 2006.

(2)   The Secretary of State may by regulations provide that a person of a description specified in the regulations is or is not to be treated for the purposes of this Chapter as an operator in relation to a secondary ticketing facility.

(3)   Regulations under subsection (2)—

(a)   are to be made by statutory instrument;

(b)   may make different provision for different purposes;

(c)   may include incidental, supplementary, consequential, transitional, transitory or saving provision.

(4)   A statutory instrument containing regulations under subsection (2) is not to be made unless a draft of the instrument has been laid before, and approved by a resolution of, each House of Parliament.

NOTES

Commencement: 26 May 2015.

CHAPTER 6
GENERAL

[1.2314]
96   Power to make consequential provision

(1)   The Secretary of State may by order made by statutory instrument make provision in consequence of this Act.

(2)   The power conferred by subsection (1) includes power—

(a)   to amend, repeal, revoke or otherwise modify any provision made by an enactment or an instrument made under an enactment (including an enactment passed or instrument made in the same Session as this Act);

(b)   to make transitional, transitory or saving provision.

(3)   A statutory instrument containing (whether alone or with other provision) an order under this section which amends, repeals, revokes or otherwise modifies any provision of primary legislation is not to be made unless a draft of the instrument has been laid before, and approved by a resolution of, each House of Parliament.

(4)   A statutory instrument containing an order under this section which does not amend, repeal, revoke or otherwise modify any provision of primary legislation is subject to annulment in pursuance of a resolution of either House of Parliament.

(5)   In this section—

"enactment" includes an Act of the Scottish Parliament, a Measure or Act of the National Assembly for Wales and Northern Ireland legislation;

"primary legislation" means—

(a)   an Act of Parliament,

(b)   an Act of the Scottish Parliament,

(c)   a Measure or Act of the National Assembly for Wales, and

(d)   Northern Ireland legislation.

NOTES

Commencement: 26 March 2015.

[1.2315]
97   Power to make transitional, transitory and saving provision

(1)   The Secretary of State may by order made by statutory instrument make transitional, transitory or saving provision in connection with the coming into force of any provision of this Act other than the coming into force of Chapter 3 or 4 of this Part in relation to Wales.

(2)   The Welsh Ministers may by order made by statutory instrument make transitional, transitory or saving provision in connection with the coming into force of Chapter 3 or 4 of this Part in relation to Wales.

NOTES

Commencement: 26 March 2015.

[1.2316]
98   Financial provision
There is to be paid out of money provided by Parliament—
    (a)   any expenses incurred by a Minister of the Crown or a government department under this Act, and
    (b)   any increase attributable to this Act in the sums payable under any other Act out of money so provided.

NOTES
Commencement: 26 March 2015.

[1.2317]
99   Extent
(1)   The amendment, repeal or revocation of any provision by this Act has the same extent as the provision concerned.
(2)   Section 27 extends only to Scotland.
(3)   Chapter 3 of this Part extends only to England and Wales.
(4)   Subject to that, this Act extends to England and Wales, Scotland and Northern Ireland.

NOTES
Commencement: 26 March 2015.

[1.2318]
100   Commencement
(1)   The provisions of this Act listed in subsection (2) come into force on the day on which this Act is passed.
(2)   Those provisions are—
    (a)   section 48(5) to (8),
    (b)   Chapter 3 of this Part in so far as it confer powers to make regulations,
    (c)   section 88(5) to (11),
    (d)   this Chapter, and
    (e)   paragraph 12 of Schedule 5.
(3)   Chapters 3 and 4 of this Part come into force—
    (a)   in relation to England, on such day as the Secretary of State may appoint by order made by statutory instrument;
    (b)   in relation to Wales, on such day as the Welsh Ministers may appoint by order made by statutory instrument.
(4)   Chapter 5 of this Part comes into force at the end of the period of two months beginning with the day on which this Act is passed.
(5)   The other provisions of this Act come into force on such day as the Secretary of State may appoint by order made by statutory instrument.
(6)   An order under this section may appoint different days for different purposes.

NOTES
Commencement: 26 March 2015.
Orders: the Consumer Rights Act 2015 (Commencement) (England) Order 2015, SI 2015/965 at **[2.1172]**; the Consumer Rights Act 2015 (Commencement No 1) Order 2015, SI 2015/1333 at **[2.1204]**; the Consumer Rights Act 2015 (Commencement No 2 and Transitional Provision) (England) Order 2015, SI 2015/1575 at **[2.1206]**; the Consumer Rights Act 2015 (Commencement No 2) Order 2015, SI 2015/1584 at **[2.1209]**; the Consumer Rights Act 2015 (Commencement No 1 and Transitional Provision) (Wales) Order 2015, SI 2015/1605 at **[2.1212]**; the Consumer Rights Act 2015 (Commencement No 3, Transitional Provisions, Savings and Consequential Amendments) Order 2015, SI 2015/1630 at **[2.1215]**.

[1.2319]
101   Short title
This Act may be cited as the Consumer Rights Act 2015.

NOTES
Commencement: 26 March 2015.

SCHEDULES

SCHEDULE 1
AMENDMENTS CONSEQUENTIAL ON PART 1

(*Sch 1 amends the Supply of Goods (Implied Terms) Act 1973 at* **[1.490]** *et seq; the Sale of Goods Act 1979 at* **[1.829]** *et seq; the Supply of Goods and Services Act 1982 at* **[1.921]** *et seq; the Sale and Supply of Goods Act 1994; the Regulatory Enforcement and Sanctions Act 2008; the Consumer Protection from Unfair Trading Regulations 2008, SI 2008/1277 at* **[2.555]** *et seq; and revokes the Sale and Supply of Goods to Consumers Regulations 2002, SI 2002/3045 at* **[2.253]**.)

SCHEDULE 2
CONSUMER CONTRACT TERMS WHICH MAY BE REGARDED AS UNFAIR

Section 63

PART 1
LIST OF TERMS

[1.2320]

1 A term which has the object or effect of excluding or limiting the trader's liability in the event of the death of or personal injury to the consumer resulting from an act or omission of the trader.

2 A term which has the object or effect of inappropriately excluding or limiting the legal rights of the consumer in relation to the trader or another party in the event of total or partial non-performance or inadequate performance by the trader of any of the contractual obligations, including the option of offsetting a debt owed to the trader against any claim which the consumer may have against the trader.

3 A term which has the object or effect of making an agreement binding on the consumer in a case where the provision of services by the trader is subject to a condition whose realisation depends on the trader's will alone.

4 A term which has the object or effect of permitting the trader to retain sums paid by the consumer where the consumer decides not to conclude or perform the contract, without providing for the consumer to receive compensation of an equivalent amount from the trader where the trader is the party cancelling the contract.

5 A term which has the object or effect of requiring that, where the consumer decides not to conclude or perform the contract, the consumer must pay the trader a disproportionately high sum in compensation or for services which have not been supplied.

6 A term which has the object or effect of requiring a consumer who fails to fulfil his obligations under the contract to pay a disproportionately high sum in compensation.

7 A term which has the object or effect of authorising the trader to dissolve the contract on a discretionary basis where the same facility is not granted to the consumer, or permitting the trader to retain the sums paid for services not yet supplied by the trader where it is the trader who dissolves the contract.

8 A term which has the object or effect of enabling the trader to terminate a contract of indeterminate duration without reasonable notice except where there are serious grounds for doing so.

9 A term which has the object or effect of automatically extending a contract of fixed duration where the consumer does not indicate otherwise, when the deadline fixed for the consumer to express a desire not to extend the contract is unreasonably early.

10 A term which has the object or effect of irrevocably binding the consumer to terms with which the consumer has had no real opportunity of becoming acquainted before the conclusion of the contract.

11 A term which has the object or effect of enabling the trader to alter the terms of the contract unilaterally without a valid reason which is specified in the contract.

12 A term which has the object or effect of permitting the trader to determine the characteristics of the subject matter of the contract after the consumer has become bound by it.

13 A term which has the object or effect of enabling the trader to alter unilaterally without a valid reason any characteristics of the goods, digital content or services to be provided.

14 A term which has the object or effect of giving the trader the discretion to decide the price payable under the contract after the consumer has become bound by it, where no price or method of determining the price is agreed when the consumer becomes bound.

15 A term which has the object or effect of permitting a trader to increase the price of goods, digital content or services without giving the consumer the right to cancel the contract if the final price is too high in relation to the price agreed when the contract was concluded.

16 A term which has the object or effect of giving the trader the right to determine whether the goods, digital content or services supplied are in conformity with the contract, or giving the trader the exclusive right to interpret any term of the contract.

17 A term which has the object or effect of limiting the trader's obligation to respect commitments undertaken by the trader's agents or making the trader's commitments subject to compliance with a particular formality.

18 A term which has the object or effect of obliging the consumer to fulfil all of the consumer's obligations where the trader does not perform the trader's obligations.

19 A term which has the object or effect of allowing the trader to transfer the trader's rights and obligations under the contract, where this may reduce the guarantees for the consumer, without the consumer's agreement.

20 A term which has the object or effect of excluding or hindering the consumer's right to take legal action or exercise any other legal remedy, in particular by—
   (a)   requiring the consumer to take disputes exclusively to arbitration not covered by legal provisions,
   (b)   unduly restricting the evidence available to the consumer, or
   (c)   imposing on the consumer a burden of proof which, according to the applicable law, should lie with another party to the contract.

NOTES
Commencement: 1 October 2015.

PART 2
SCOPE OF PART 1

Financial services

[1.2321]
21 Paragraph 8 (cancellation without reasonable notice) does not include a term by which a supplier of financial services reserves the right to terminate unilaterally a contract of indeterminate duration without notice where there is a valid reason, if the supplier is required to inform the consumer of the cancellation immediately.

22 Paragraph 11 (variation of contract without valid reason) does not include a term by which a supplier of financial services reserves the right to alter the rate of interest payable by or due to the consumer, or the amount of other charges for financial services without notice where there is a valid reason, if—
   (a)   the supplier is required to inform the consumer of the alteration at the earliest opportunity, and
   (b)   the consumer is free to dissolve the contract immediately.

Contracts which last indefinitely

23 Paragraphs 11 (variation of contract without valid reason), 12 (determination of characteristics of goods etc after consumer bound) and 14 (determination of price after consumer bound) do not include a term under which a trader reserves the right to alter unilaterally the conditions of a contract of indeterminate duration if—
   (a)   the trader is required to inform the consumer with reasonable notice, and
   (b)   the consumer is free to dissolve the contract.

Sale of securities, foreign currency etc

24 Paragraphs 8 (cancellation without reasonable notice), 11 (variation of contract without valid reason), 14 (determination of price after consumer bound) and 15 (increase in price) do not apply to—
   (a)   transactions in transferable securities, financial instruments and other products or services where the price is linked to fluctuations in a stock exchange quotation or index or a financial market rate that the trader does not control, and
   (b)   contracts for the purchase or sale of foreign currency, traveller's cheques or international money orders denominated in foreign currency.

Price index clauses

25 Paragraphs 14 (determination of price after consumer bound) and 15 (increase in price) do not include a term which is a price-indexation clause (where otherwise lawful), if the method by which prices vary is explicitly described.

NOTES
Commencement: 1 October 2015.

SCHEDULE 3
ENFORCEMENT OF THE LAW ON UNFAIR CONTRACT TERMS AND NOTICES
Section 70

Application of Schedule

[1.2322]
1 This Schedule applies to—
   (a)   a term of a consumer contract,

    (b)   a term proposed for use in a consumer contract,

    (c)   a term which a third party recommends for use in a consumer contract, or

    (d)   a consumer notice.

Consideration of complaints

2 (1)   A regulator may consider a complaint about a term or notice to which this Schedule applies (a "relevant complaint").

(2)   If a regulator other than the CMA intends to consider a relevant complaint, it must notify the CMA that it intends to do so, and must then consider the complaint.

(3)   If a regulator considers a relevant complaint, but decides not to make an application under paragraph 3 in relation to the complaint, it must give reasons for its decision to the person who made the complaint.

Application for injunction or interdict

3 (1)   A regulator may apply for an injunction or (in Scotland) an interdict against a person if the regulator thinks that—

    (a)   the person is using, or proposing or recommending the use of, a term or notice to which this Schedule applies, and

    (b)   the term or notice falls within any one or more of sub-paragraphs (2), (3) or (5).

(2)   A term or notice falls within this sub-paragraph if it purports to exclude or restrict liability of the kind mentioned in—

    (a)   section 31 (exclusion of liability: goods contracts),

    (b)   section 47 (exclusion of liability: digital content contracts),

    (c)   section 57 (exclusion of liability: services contracts), or

    (d)   section 65(1) (business liability for death or personal injury resulting from negligence).

(3)   A term or notice falls within this sub-paragraph if it is unfair to any extent.

(4)   A term within paragraph 1(1)(b) or (c) (but not within paragraph 1(1)(a)) is to be treated for the purposes of section 62(4) and (5) (assessment of fairness) as if it were a term of a contract.

(5)   A term or notice falls within this sub-paragraph if it breaches section 68 (requirement for transparency).

(6)   A regulator may apply for an injunction or interdict under this paragraph in relation to a term or notice whether or not it has received a relevant complaint about the term or notice.

Notification of application

4 (1)   Before making an application under paragraph 3, a regulator other than the CMA must notify the CMA that it intends to do so.

(2)   The regulator may make the application only if—

    (a)   the period of 14 days beginning with the day on which the regulator notified the CMA has ended, or

    (b)   before the end of that period, the CMA agrees to the regulator making the application.

Determination of application

5 (1)   On an application for an injunction under paragraph 3, the court may grant an injunction on such conditions, and against such of the respondents, as it thinks appropriate.

(2)   On an application for an interdict under paragraph 3, the court may grant an interdict on such conditions, and against such of the defenders, as it thinks appropriate.

(3)   The injunction or interdict may include provision about—

    (a)   a term or notice to which the application relates, or

    (b)   any term of a consumer contract, or any consumer notice, of a similar kind or with a similar effect.

(4)   It is not a defence to an application under paragraph 3 to show that, because of a rule of law, a term to which the application relates is not, or could not be, an enforceable contract term.

(5)   If a regulator other than the CMA makes the application, it must notify the CMA of—

    (a)   the outcome of the application, and

    (b)   if an injunction or interdict is granted, the conditions on which, and the persons against whom, it is granted.

Undertakings

6 (1)   A regulator may accept an undertaking from a person against whom it has applied, or thinks it is entitled to apply, for an injunction or interdict under paragraph 3.

(2)   The undertaking may provide that the person will comply with the conditions that are agreed between the person and the regulator about the use of terms or notices, or terms or notices of a kind, specified in the undertaking.

(3)   If a regulator other than the CMA accepts an undertaking, it must notify the CMA of—

    (a)   the conditions on which the undertaking is accepted, and

   (b)   the person who gave it.

Publication, information and advice

7 (1)   The CMA must arrange the publication of details of—
   (a)   any application it makes for an injunction or interdict under paragraph 3,
   (b)   any injunction or interdict under this Schedule, and
   (c)   any undertaking under this Schedule.

(2)   The CMA must respond to a request whether a term or notice, or one of a similar kind or with a similar effect, is or has been the subject of an injunction, interdict or undertaking under this Schedule.

(3)   Where the term or notice, or one of a similar kind or with a similar effect, is or has been the subject of an injunction or interdict under this Schedule, the CMA must give the person making the request a copy of the injunction or interdict.

(4)   Where the term or notice, or one of a similar kind or with a similar effect, is or has been the subject of an undertaking under this Schedule, the CMA must give the person making the request—
   (a)   details of the undertaking, and
   (b)   if the person giving the undertaking has agreed to amend the term or notice, a copy of the amendments.

(5)   The CMA may arrange the publication of advice and information about the provisions of this Part.

(6)   In this paragraph—
   (a)   references to an injunction or interdict under this Schedule are to an injunction or interdict granted on an application by the CMA under paragraph 3 or notified to it under paragraph 5, and
   (b)   references to an undertaking are to an undertaking given to the CMA under paragraph 6 or notified to it under that paragraph.

Meaning of "regulator"

8 (1)   In this Schedule "regulator" means—
   (a)   the CMA,
   (b)   the Department of Enterprise, Trade and Investment in Northern Ireland,
   (c)   a local weights and measures authority in Great Britain,
   (d)   the Financial Conduct Authority,
   (e)   the Office of Communications,
   (f)   the Information Commissioner,
   (g)   the Gas and Electricity Markets Authority,
   (h)   the Water Services Regulation Authority,
   (i)   the Office of Rail Regulation,
   (j)   the Northern Ireland Authority for Utility Regulation, or
   (k)   the Consumers' Association.

(2)   The Secretary of State may by order made by statutory instrument amend sub-paragraph (1) so as to add, modify or remove an entry.

(3)   An order under sub-paragraph (2) may amend sub-paragraph (1) so as to add a body that is not a public authority only if the Secretary of State thinks that the body represents the interests of consumers (or consumers of a particular description).

(4)   The Secretary of State must publish (and may from time to time vary) other criteria to be applied by the Secretary of State in deciding whether to add an entry to, or remove an entry from, sub-paragraph (1).

(5)   An order under sub-paragraph (2) may make consequential amendments to this Schedule (including with the effect that any of its provisions apply differently, or do not apply, to a body added to sub-paragraph (1)).

(6)   An order under sub-paragraph (2) may contain transitional or transitory provision or savings.

(7)   No order may be made under sub-paragraph (2) unless a draft of the statutory instrument containing it has been laid before, and approved by a resolution of, each House of Parliament.

(8)   In this paragraph "public authority" has the same meaning as in section 6 of the Human Rights Act 1998.

Other definitions

9 In this Schedule—
    "the CMA" means the Competition and Markets Authority;
    "injunction" includes an interim injunction;
    "interdict" includes an interim interdict.

The Financial Conduct Authority

10 The functions of the Financial Conduct Authority under this Schedule are to be treated as functions of the Authority under the Financial Services and Markets Act 2000.

NOTES

Commencement: 1 October 2015.

SCHEDULE 4
AMENDMENTS CONSEQUENTIAL ON PART 2

(Sch 4 amends the Misrepresentation Act 1967 at **[1.419]** *et seq; the Unfair Contract Terms Act 1977 at* **[1.731]** *et seq; the Sale of Goods Act 1979 at* **[1.829]** *et seq; the Companies Act 1985; the Merchant Shipping Act 1995; the Arbitration Act 1996 at* **[1.1114]** *et seq; the Enterprise Act 2002 at* **[1.1700]** *et seq; the Companies Act 2006 at* **[1.1968]** *et seq; and revokes the Unfair Terms in Consumer Contracts Regulations 1999, SI 1999/2083, at* **[2.121]** *et seq).*

SCHEDULE 5
INVESTIGATORY POWERS ETC

Section 77

PART 1
BASIC CONCEPTS

Overview

[1.2323]
1 (1)   This Schedule confers investigatory powers on enforcers and specifies the purposes for which and the circumstances in which those powers may be exercised.

(2)   Part 1 of this Schedule contains interpretation provisions; in particular paragraphs 2 to 6 explain what is meant by an "enforcer".

(3)   Part 2 of this Schedule explains what is meant by "the enforcer's legislation".

(4)   Part 3 of this Schedule contains powers in relation to the production of information; paragraph 13 sets out which enforcers may exercise those powers, and the purposes for which they may do so.

(5)   Part 4 of this Schedule contains further powers; paragraphs 19 and 20 set out which enforcers may exercise those powers, and the purposes for which they may do so.

(6)   Part 5 of this Schedule contains provisions that are supplementary to the powers in Parts 3 and 4 of this Schedule.

(7)   Part 6 of this Schedule makes provision about the exercise of functions by certain enforcers outside their area or district and the bringing of proceedings in relation to conduct outside an enforcer's area or district.

Enforcers

2 (1)   In this Schedule "enforcer" means—
   (a)   a domestic enforcer,
   (b)   an EU enforcer,
   (c)   a public designated enforcer, or
   (d)   an unfair contract terms enforcer.

(2)   But in Part 4 and paragraphs 38 and 41 of this Schedule "enforcer" means—
   (a)   a domestic enforcer, or
   (b)   an EU enforcer.

(3)   In paragraphs 13, 19 and 20 of this Schedule, a reference to an enforcer exercising a power includes a reference to an officer of the enforcer exercising that power.

Domestic enforcers

3 (1)   In this Schedule "domestic enforcer" means—
   (a)   the Competition and Markets Authority,
   (b)   a local weights and measures authority in Great Britain,
   (c)   a district council in England,
   (d)   the Department of Enterprise, Trade and Investment in Northern Ireland,
   (e)   a district council in Northern Ireland,
   (f)   the Secretary of State,
   (g)   the Gas and Electricity Markets Authority,
   (h)   the British Hallmarking Council,
   (i)   an assay office within the meaning of the Hallmarking Act 1973, or

(j)   any other person to whom the duty in subsection (1) of section 27 of the Consumer Protection Act 1987 (duty to enforce safety provisions) applies by virtue of regulations under subsection (2) of that section.

(2)   But the Gas and Electricity Markets Authority is not a domestic enforcer for the purposes of Part 4 of this Schedule.

(3)   The reference to the Department of Enterprise, Trade and Investment in Northern Ireland includes a person with whom the Department has made arrangements, under paragraph 3(1) of Schedule 15 to the Lifts Regulations 1997 (SI 1997/831) for enforcement of those regulations.

EU enforcers

4   In this Schedule "EU enforcer" means—

(a)   the Competition and Markets Authority,

(b)   a local weights and measures authority in Great Britain,

(c)   the Department of Enterprise, Trade and Investment in Northern Ireland,

(d)   the Financial Conduct Authority,

(e)   the Civil Aviation Authority,

(f)   the Secretary of State,

(g)   the Department of Health, Social Services and Public Safety in Northern Ireland,

(h)   the Office of Communications,

(i)   an enforcement authority within the meaning of section 120(15) of the Communications Act 2003 (regulation of premium rate services), or

(j)   the Information Commissioner.

Public designated enforcers

5   In this Schedule "public designated enforcer" means a person or body which—

(a)   is designated by order under subsection (2) of section 213 of the Enterprise Act 2002, and

(b)   has been designated by virtue of subsection (3) of that section (which provides that the Secretary of State may designate a public body only if satisfied that it is independent).

Unfair contract terms enforcer

6   In this Schedule "unfair contract terms enforcer" means a person or body which—

(a)   is for the time being listed in paragraph 8(1) of Schedule 3 (persons or bodies that may enforce provisions about unfair contract terms), and

(b)   is a public authority within the meaning of section 6 of the Human Rights Act 1998.

Officers

7   (1)   In this Schedule "officer", in relation to an enforcer, means—

(a)   an inspector appointed by the enforcer to exercise powers under this Schedule, or authorised to do so,

(b)   an officer of the enforcer appointed by the enforcer to exercise powers under this Schedule, or authorised to do so,

(c)   an employee of the enforcer (other than an inspector or officer) appointed by the enforcer to exercise powers under this Schedule, or authorised to do so, or

(d)   a person (other than an inspector, officer or employee of the enforcer) authorised by the enforcer to exercise powers under this Schedule.

(2)   But references in this Schedule to an officer in relation to a particular power only cover a person within sub-paragraph (1) if and to the extent that the person has been appointed or authorised to exercise that power.

(3)   A person who, immediately before the coming into force of this Schedule, was appointed or authorised to exercise a power replaced by a power in this Schedule is to be treated as having been appointed or authorised to exercise the new power.

(4)   In this paragraph "employee", in relation to the Secretary of State, means a person employed in the civil service of the State.

Interpretation of other terms

8   In this Schedule—

"Community infringement" has the same meaning as in section 212 of the Enterprise Act 2002;

"document" includes information recorded in any form;

"enforcement order" means an order under section 217 of the Enterprise Act 2002;

"interim enforcement order" means an order under section 218 of that Act;

"the Regulation on Accreditation and Market Surveillance" means Regulation (EC) No 765/2008 of the European Parliament and of the Council of 9 July 2008 setting out the requirements for accreditation and market surveillance relating to the marketing of products and repealing Regulation (EEC) No 339/93.

NOTES

Commencement: 27 May 2015 (in so far as relating to Chapter 3 of Part 3, in relation to England; and in so far as relating to Chapter 5 of Part 3); 1 October 2015 (otherwise).

PART 2
THE ENFORCER'S LEGISLATION

Enforcer's legislation

[1.2324]

9 (1) In this Schedule "the enforcer's legislation", in relation to a domestic enforcer, means—

(a) legislation or notices which, by virtue of a provision listed in paragraph 10, the domestic enforcer has a duty or power to enforce, and

(b) where the domestic enforcer is listed in an entry in the first column of the table in paragraph 11, the legislation listed in the corresponding entry in the second column of that table.

(2) References in this Schedule to a breach of or compliance with the enforcer's legislation include a breach of or compliance with a notice issued under—

(a) the enforcer's legislation, or

(b) legislation under which the enforcer's legislation is made.

(3) References in this Schedule to a breach of or compliance with the enforcer's legislation are to be read, in relation to the Lifts Regulations 1997 (SI 1997/831), as references to a breach of or compliance with the Regulations as they apply to relevant products (within the meaning of Schedule 15 to the Regulations) for private use or consumption.

Enforcer's legislation: duties and powers mentioned in paragraph 9(1)(a)

10 The duties and powers mentioned in paragraph 9(1)(a) are those arising under any of the following provisions—

section 26(1) or 40(1)(b) of the Trade Descriptions Act 1968 (including as applied by regulation 8(3) of the Crystal Glass (Descriptions) Regulations 1973 (SI 1973/1952) and regulation 10(2) of the Footwear (Indication of Composition) Labelling Regulations 1995 (SI 1995/2489));

section 9(1) or (6) of the Hallmarking Act 1973;

paragraph 6 of the Schedule to the Prices Act 1974 (including as read with paragraph 14(1) of that Schedule);

section 161(1) of the Consumer Credit Act 1974;

section 26(1) of the Estate Agents Act 1979;

Article 39 of the Weights and Measures (Northern Ireland) Order 1981 (SI 1981/231 (NI 10));

section 16A(1) or (4) of the Video Recordings Act 1984;

section 27(1) of the Consumer Protection Act 1987 (including as applied by section 12(1) of the Fireworks Act 2003 to fireworks regulations under that Act);

section 215(1) of the Education Reform Act 1988;

section 107A(1) or (3) or 198A(1) or (3) of the Copyright, Designs and Patents Act 1988;

paragraph 3(a) of Schedule 5 to the Simple Pressure Vessels (Safety) Regulations 1991 (SI 1991/2749);

paragraph 1 of Schedule 3 to the Package Travel, Package Holidays and Package Tours Regulations 1992 (SI 1992/3288);

section 30(4) or (7) or 31(4)(a) of the Clean Air Act 1993;

paragraph 1 of Schedule 2 to the Sunday Trading Act 1994;

section 93(1) or (3) of the Trade Marks Act 1994;

section 8A(1) or (3) of the Olympic Symbol etc (Protection) Act 1995;

paragraph 2(a) or 3(1) of Schedule 15 to the Lifts Regulations 1997 (SI 1997/831);

paragraph 2(a) or 3(3)(a) of Schedule 8 to the Pressure Equipment Regulations 1999 (SI 1999/2001);

regulation 5C(5) of the Motor Fuel (Composition and Content) Regulations 1999 (SI 1999/3107);

paragraph 1(1)(b) or (2)(b) or 2 of Schedule 9 to the Radio Equipment and Telecommunications Terminal Equipment Regulations 2000 (SI 2000/730);

paragraph 1(a) of Schedule 10 to the Personal Protective Equipment Regulations 2002 (SI 2002/1144);

. . .

section 3(1) of the Christmas Day Trading Act 2004;

regulation 10(1) of the General Product Safety Regulations 2005 (SI 2005/1803);

regulation 10(1) of the Weights and Measures (Packaged Goods) Regulations 2006 (SI 2006/659);

regulation 17 of the Measuring Instruments (Automatic Discontinuous Totalisers) Regulations

2006 (SI 2006/1255);

regulation 18 of the Measuring Instruments (Automatic Rail-weighbridges) Regulations 2006 (SI 2006/1256);

regulation 20 of the Measuring Instruments (Automatic Catchweighers) Regulations 2006 (SI 2006/1257);

regulation 18 of the Measuring Instruments (Automatic Gravimetric Filling Instruments) Regulations 2006 (SI 2006/1258);

regulation 18 of the Measuring Instruments (Beltweighers) Regulations 2006 (SI 2006/1259);

regulation 16 of the Measuring Instruments (Capacity Serving Measures) Regulations 2006 (SI 2006/1264);

regulation 17 of the Measuring Instruments (Liquid Fuel and Lubricants) Regulations 2006 (SI 2006/1266);

regulation 16 of the Measuring Instruments (Material Measures of Length) Regulations 2006 (SI 2006/1267);

regulation 17 of the Measuring Instruments (Cold-water Meters) Regulations 2006 (SI 2006/1268);

regulation 18 of the Measuring Instruments (Liquid Fuel delivered from Road Tankers) Regulations 2006 (SI 2006/1269);

regulation 37(1)(a)(ii) or (b)(ii) of the Electromagnetic Compatibility Regulations 2006 (SI 2006/3418);

regulation 13(1) or (1A) of the Business Protection from Misleading Marketing Regulations 2008 (SI 2008/1276);

regulation 19(1) or (1A) of the Consumer Protection from Unfair Trading Regulations 2008 (SI 2008/1277);

paragraph 2 or 5 of Schedule 5 to the Supply of Machinery (Safety) Regulations 2008 (SI 2008/1597);

regulation 32(2) or (3) of the Timeshare, Holiday Products, Resale and Exchange Contracts Regulations 2010 (SI 2010/2960);

regulation 10(1) of the Weights and Measures (Packaged Goods) Regulations (Northern Ireland) 2011 (SR 2011/331);

regulation 11 of the Textile Products (Labelling and Fibre Composition) Regulations 2012 (SI 2012/1102);

regulation 6(1) of the Cosmetic Products Enforcement Regulations 2013 (SI 2013/1478);

[regulation 23(1) of the Consumer Contracts (Information, Cancellation and Additional Charges) Regulations 2013 (SI 2013/3134);]

section 87(1) of this Act;

section 93(1) or (2) of this Act.

[regulation 7(1) of the Packaging (Essential Requirements) Regulations 2015].

Enforcer's legislation: legislation mentioned in paragraph 9(1)(b)

11 Here is the table mentioned in paragraph 9(1)(b)—

Enforcer	Legislation
A local weights and measures authority in Great Britain or the Department of Enterprise, Trade and Investment in Northern Ireland	Section 35ZA of the Registered Designs Act 1949
A local weights and measures authority in Great Britain or the Department of Enterprise, Trade and Investment in Northern Ireland	The Measuring Container Bottles (EEC Requirements) Regulations 1977 (SI 1977/932)
The Secretary of State	The Alcoholometers and Alcohol Hydrometers (EEC Requirements) Regulations 1977 (SI 1977/1753)
A local weights and measures authority in Great Britain	The Weights and Measures Act 1985 and regulations and orders made under that Act
A local weights and measures authority in Great Britain or the Department of Enterprise, Trade and Investment in Northern Ireland	The Measuring Instruments (EEC Requirements) Regulations 1988 (SI 1988/186)
A local weights and measures authority in Great Britain or the Department of Enterprise, Trade and Investment in Northern Ireland	The Financial Services and Markets Act 2000 so far as it relates to a relevant regulated activity within the meaning of section 107(4)(a) of the Financial Services Act 2012
A local weights and measures authority in Great Britain or the Department of Enterprise, Trade and Investment in Northern Ireland	The Non-Automatic Weighing Instruments Regulations 2000 (SI 2000/3236)

Powers to amend paragraph 10 or 11

12 (1) The Secretary of State may by order made by statutory instrument—

    (a) amend paragraph 10 or the table in paragraph 11 by adding, modifying or removing any entry in it;

    (b) in consequence of provision made under paragraph (a), amend, repeal or revoke any other legislation (including this Act) whenever passed or made.

(2) The Secretary of State may not make an order under this paragraph that has the effect that a power of entry, or an associated power, contained in legislation other than this Act is replaced by a power of entry, or an associated power, contained in this Schedule unless the Secretary of State thinks that the condition in sub-paragraph (3) is met.

(3) That condition is that, on and after the changes made by the order, the safeguards applicable to the new power, taken together, provide a greater level of protection than any safeguards applicable to the old power.

(4) In sub-paragraph (2) "power of entry" and "associated power" have the meanings given by section 46 of the Protection of Freedoms Act 2012.

(5) An order under this paragraph may contain transitional or transitory provision or savings.

(6) A statutory instrument containing an order under this paragraph that amends or repeals primary legislation may not be made unless a draft of the instrument containing the order has been laid before, and approved by a resolution of, each House of Parliament.

(7) Any other statutory instrument containing an order under this paragraph is subject to annulment in pursuance of a resolution of either House of Parliament.

(8) In this paragraph "primary legislation" means—

    (a) an Act of Parliament,

    (b) an Act of the Scottish Parliament,

    (c) an Act or Measure of the National Assembly for Wales, or

    (d) Northern Ireland legislation.

NOTES

Commencement: 26 March 2015 (para 12); 27 May 2015 (paras 9–11 in so far as relating to Chapter 3 of Part 3, in relation to England; and in so far as relating to Chapter 5 of Part 3));1 October 2015 (otherwise).

Para 10: entry omitted repealed, and entry relating to the Packaging (Essential Requirements) Regulations 2015 added, by the Packaging (Essential Requirements) Regulations 2015, SI 2015/1640, reg 15; entry relating to the Consumer Contracts (Information, Cancellation and Additional Charges) Regulations 2013 inserted by the Consumer Rights Act 2015 (Consequential Amendments) Order 2015, SI 2015/1726, art 2, Schedule, Pt 1, para 6.

PART 3
POWERS IN RELATION TO THE PRODUCTION OF INFORMATION

Exercise of powers in this Part

[1.2325]

13 (1) An enforcer of a kind mentioned in this paragraph may exercise a power in this Part of this Schedule only for the purposes and in the circumstances mentioned in this paragraph in relation to that kind of enforcer.

(2) The Competition and Markets Authority may exercise the powers in this Part of this Schedule for any of the following purposes—

    (a) to enable the Authority to exercise or to consider whether to exercise any function it has under Part 8 of the Enterprise Act 2002;

    (b) to enable a private designated enforcer to consider whether to exercise any function it has under that Part;

    (c) to enable a Community enforcer to consider whether to exercise any function it has under that Part;

    (d) to ascertain whether a person has complied with or is complying with an enforcement order or an interim enforcement order;

    (e) to ascertain whether a person has complied with or is complying with an undertaking given under section 217(9), 218(10) or 219 of the Enterprise Act 2002.

(3) A public designated enforcer, a local weights and measures authority in Great Britain, the Department of Enterprise, Trade and Investment in Northern Ireland or an EU enforcer other than the Competition and Markets Authority may exercise the powers in this Part of this Schedule for any of the following purposes—

    (a) to enable that enforcer to exercise or to consider whether to exercise any function it has under Part 8 of the Enterprise Act 2002;

    (b) to ascertain whether a person has complied with or is complying with an enforcement order or an interim enforcement order made on the application of that enforcer;

    (c) to ascertain whether a person has complied with or is complying with an undertaking given under section 217(9) or 218(10) of the Enterprise Act 2002 following such an application;

    (d) to ascertain whether a person has complied with or is complying with an undertaking given to that enforcer under section 219 of that Act.

(4) A domestic enforcer may exercise the powers in this Part of this Schedule for the purpose of ascertaining whether there has been a breach of the enforcer's legislation.

(5) But a domestic enforcer may not exercise the power in paragraph 14 (power to require the production of information) for the purpose in sub-paragraph (4) unless an officer of the enforcer reasonably suspects a breach of the enforcer's legislation.

(6) Sub-paragraph (5) does not apply if the enforcer is a market surveillance authority within the meaning of Article 2(18) of the Regulation on Accreditation and Market Surveillance and the power is exercised for the purpose of market surveillance within the meaning of Article 2(17) of that Regulation.

(7) An unfair contract terms enforcer may exercise the powers in this Part of this Schedule for either of the following purposes—
  (a)   to enable the enforcer to exercise or to consider whether to exercise any function it has under Schedule 3 (enforcement of the law on unfair contract terms and notices);
  (b)   to ascertain whether a person has complied with or is complying with an injunction or interdict (within the meaning of that Schedule) granted under paragraph 5 of that Schedule or an undertaking given under paragraph 6 of that Schedule.

(8) But an unfair contract terms enforcer may not exercise the power in paragraph 14 for a purpose mentioned in sub-paragraph (7)(a) unless an officer of the enforcer reasonably suspects that a person is using, or proposing or recommending the use of, a contractual term or notice within paragraph 3 of Schedule 3.

(9) A local weights and measures authority in Great Britain may exercise the powers in this Part of this Schedule for either of the following purposes—
  (a)   to enable it to determine whether to make an order under section 3 or 4 of the Estate Agents Act 1979;
  (b)   to enable it to exercise any of its functions under section 5, 6, 8, 13 or 17 of that Act.

(10) In this paragraph—
  "Community enforcer" has the same meaning as in the Enterprise Act 2002 (see section 213(5) of that Act);
  "private designated enforcer" means a person or body which—
    (a)   is designated by order under subsection (2) of section 213 of that Act, and
    (b)   has been designated by virtue of subsection (4) of that section (which provides that the Secretary of State may designate a person or body which is not a public body only if it satisfies criteria specified by order).

Power to require the production of information

14 An enforcer or an officer of an enforcer may give notice to a person requiring the person to provide the enforcer with the information specified in the notice.

Procedure for notice under paragraph 14

15 (1) A notice under paragraph 14 must be in writing and specify the purpose for which the information is required.

(2) If the purpose is to enable a person to exercise or to consider whether to exercise a function, the notice must specify the function concerned.

(3) The notice may specify—
  (a)   the time within which and the manner in which the person to whom it is given must comply with it;
  (b)   the form in which information must be provided.

(4) The notice may require—
  (a)   the creation of documents, or documents of a description, specified in the notice, and
  (b)   the provision of those documents to the enforcer or an officer of the enforcer.

(5) A requirement to provide information or create a document is a requirement to do so in a legible form.

(6) A notice under paragraph 14 does not require a person to provide any information or create any documents which the person would be entitled to refuse to provide or produce—
  (a)   in proceedings in the High Court on the grounds of legal professional privilege, or
  (b)   in proceedings in the Court of Session on the grounds of confidentiality of communications.

(7) In sub-paragraph (6) "communications" means—
  (a)   communications between a professional legal adviser and the adviser's client, or
  (b)   communications made in connection with or in contemplation of legal proceedings or for the purposes of those proceedings.

Enforcement of notice under paragraph 14

16 (1) If a person fails to comply with a notice under paragraph 14, the enforcer or an officer of the enforcer may make an application under this paragraph to the court.

(2)   If it appears to the court that the person has failed to comply with the notice, it may make an order under this paragraph.

(3)   An order under this paragraph is an order requiring the person to do anything that the court thinks it is reasonable for the person to do, for any of the purposes for which the notice was given, to ensure that the notice is complied with.

(4)   An order under this paragraph may require the person to meet the costs or expenses of the application.

(5)   If the person is a company, partnership or unincorporated association, the court in acting under sub-paragraph (4) may require an official who is responsible for the failure to meet the costs or expenses.

(6)   In this paragraph—
   "the court" means—
      (a)   the High Court,
      (b)   in relation to England and Wales, the county court,
      (c)   in relation to Northern Ireland, a county court,
      (d)   the Court of Session, or
      (e)   the sheriff;
   "official" means—
      (a)   in the case of a company, a director, manager, secretary or other similar officer,
      (b)   in the case of a limited liability partnership, a member,
      (c)   in the case of a partnership other than a limited liability partnership, a partner, and
      (d)   in the case of an unincorporated association, a person who is concerned in the management or control of its affairs.

Limitations on use of information provided in response to a notice under paragraph 14

17 (1)   This paragraph applies if a person provides information in response to a notice under paragraph 14.

(2)   This includes information contained in a document created by a person in response to such a notice.

(3)   In any criminal proceedings against the person—
   (a)   no evidence relating to the information may be adduced by or on behalf of the prosecution, and
   (b)   no question relating to the information may be asked by or on behalf of the prosecution.

(4)   Sub-paragraph (3) does not apply if, in the proceedings—
   (a)   evidence relating to the information is adduced by or on behalf of the person providing it, or
   (b)   a question relating to the information is asked by or on behalf of that person.

(5)   Sub-paragraph (3) does not apply if the proceedings are for—
   (a)   an offence under paragraph 36 (obstruction),
   (b)   an offence under section 5 of the Perjury Act 1911 (false statutory declarations and other false statements without oath),
   (c)   an offence under section 44(2) of the Criminal Law (Consolidation) (Scotland) Act 1995 (false statements and declarations), or
   (d)   an offence under Article 10 of the Perjury (Northern Ireland) Order 1979 (SI 1979/1714 (NI 19)) (false statutory declarations and other false unsworn statements).

Application to Crown

18 In its application in relation to—
   (a)   an enforcer acting for a purpose within paragraph 13(2) or (3), or
   (b)   an enforcer acting for the purpose of ascertaining whether there has been a breach of the Consumer Protection from Unfair Trading Regulations 2008 (SI 2008/1277),
this Part binds the Crown.

NOTES
   Commencement: 27 May 2015 (in so far as relating to Chapter 3 of Part 3, in relation to England; and in so far as relating to Chapter 5 of Part 3); 1 October 2015 (otherwise).

PART 4
FURTHER POWERS EXERCISABLE BY DOMESTIC ENFORCERS AND EU ENFORCERS

Exercise of powers in this Part: domestic enforcers

[1.2326]
19 (1)   A domestic enforcer may exercise a power in this Part of this Schedule only for the purposes and in the circumstances mentioned in this paragraph in relation to that power.

(2)   A domestic enforcer may exercise any power in paragraphs 21 to 26 and 31 to 34 for the purpose of ascertaining compliance with the enforcer's legislation.

(3)   A domestic enforcer may exercise the power in paragraph 27 (power to require the production of documents) for either of the following purposes—

(a)   subject to sub-paragraph (4), to ascertain compliance with the enforcer's legislation;

(b)   to ascertain whether the documents may be required as evidence in proceedings for a breach of, or under, the enforcer's legislation.

(4)   A domestic enforcer may exercise the power in paragraph 27 for the purpose mentioned in sub-paragraph (3)(a) only if an officer of the enforcer reasonably suspects a breach of the enforcer's legislation, unless—

(a)   the power is being exercised in relation to a document that the trader is required to keep by virtue of a provision of the enforcer's legislation, or

(b)   the enforcer is a market surveillance authority within the meaning of Article 2(18) of the Regulation on Accreditation and Market Surveillance and the power is exercised for the purpose of market surveillance within the meaning of Article 2(17) of that Regulation.

(5)   A domestic enforcer may exercise the power in paragraph 28 (power to seize and detain goods) in relation to—

(a)   goods which an officer of the enforcer reasonably suspects may disclose (by means of testing or otherwise) a breach of the enforcer's legislation,

(b)   goods which an officer of the enforcer reasonably suspects are liable to forfeiture under that legislation, and

(c)   goods which an officer of the enforcer reasonably suspects may be required as evidence in proceedings for a breach of, or under, that legislation.

(6)   A domestic enforcer may exercise the power in paragraph 29 (power to seize documents required as evidence) in relation to documents which an officer of the enforcer reasonably suspects may be required as evidence—

(a)   in proceedings for a breach of the enforcer's legislation, or

(b)   in proceedings under the enforcer's legislation.

(7)   A domestic enforcer may exercise the power in paragraph 30 (power to decommission or switch off fixed installations)—

(a)   if an officer of the enforcer reasonably suspects a breach of the Electromagnetic Compatibility Regulations 2006 (SI 2006/3418), and

(b)   for the purpose of ascertaining (by means of testing or otherwise) whether there has been such a breach.

(8)   For purposes of the enforcement of the Estate Agents Act 1979—

(a)   the references in sub-paragraphs (2) and (3)(a) to ascertaining compliance with the enforcer's legislation include ascertaining whether a person has engaged in a practice mentioned in section 3(1)(d) of that Act (practice in relation to estate agency work declared undesirable by the Secretary of State), and

(b)   the references in sub-paragraph (4) and paragraphs 23(6)(a) and 32(3)(a) to a breach of the enforcer's legislation include references to a person's engaging in such a practice.

Exercise of powers in this Part: EU enforcers

20 (1)   Any power in this Part of this Schedule which is conferred on an EU enforcer may be exercised by such an enforcer only for the purposes and in the circumstances mentioned in this paragraph in relation to that power.

(2)   If the condition in sub-paragraph (3) is met, an EU enforcer may exercise any power conferred on it by paragraphs 21 to 25 and 31 to 34 for any purpose relating to the functions that the enforcer has under Part 8 of the Enterprise Act 2002 in its capacity as a CPC enforcer under that Part.

(3)   The condition is that an officer of the EU enforcer reasonably suspects—

(a)   that there has been, or is likely to be, a Community infringement,

(b)   a failure to comply with an enforcement order or an interim enforcement order made on the application of that enforcer,

(c)   a failure to comply with an undertaking given under section 217(9) or 218(10) of the Enterprise Act 2002 following such an application, or

(d)   a failure to comply with an undertaking given to that enforcer under section 219 of that Act.

(4)   An EU enforcer may exercise the power in paragraph 27 (power to require the production of documents) for either of the following purposes—

(a)   the purpose mentioned in sub-paragraph (2), if the condition in sub-paragraph (3) is met;

(b)   to ascertain whether the documents may be required as evidence in proceedings under Part 8 of the Enterprise Act 2002.

(5)   An EU enforcer may exercise the power in paragraph 28 (power to seize and detain goods) in relation to goods which an officer of the enforcer reasonably suspects—

(a)   may disclose (by means of testing or otherwise) a Community infringement or a failure to comply with a measure specified in sub-paragraph (3)(b), (c) or (d), or (b)　may be required as evidence in proceedings under Part 8 of the Enterprise Act 2002.

(6)　An EU enforcer may exercise the power in paragraph 29 (power to seize documents required as evidence) in relation to documents which an officer of the enforcer reasonably suspects may be required as evidence in proceedings under Part 8 of the Enterprise Act 2002.

Power to purchase products

21 (1)　An officer of an enforcer may—
(a)　make a purchase of a product, or
(b)　enter into an agreement to secure the provision of a product.

(2)　For the purposes of exercising the power in sub-paragraph (1), an officer may—
(a)　at any reasonable time, enter premises to which the public has access (whether or not the public has access at that time), and
(b)　inspect any product on the premises which the public may inspect.

(3)　The power of entry in sub-paragraph (2) may be exercised without first giving notice or obtaining a warrant.

Power to observe carrying on of business etc

22 (1)　An officer of an enforcer may enter premises to which the public has access in order to observe the carrying on of a business on those premises.

(2)　The power in sub-paragraph (1) may be exercised at any reasonable time (whether or not the public has access at that time).

(3)　The power of entry in sub-paragraph (1) may be exercised without first giving notice or obtaining a warrant.

Power to enter premises without warrant

23 (1)　An officer of an enforcer may enter premises at any reasonable time.

(2)　Sub-paragraph (1) does not authorise the entry into premises used wholly or mainly as a dwelling.

(3)　In the case of a routine inspection, the power of entry in sub-paragraph (1) may only be exercised if a notice has been given to the occupier of the premises in accordance with the requirements in sub-paragraph (4), unless sub-paragraph (5) applies.

(4)　Those requirements are that—
(a)　the notice is in writing and is given by an officer of the enforcer,
(b)　the notice sets out why the entry is necessary and indicates the nature of the offence under paragraph 36 (obstruction), and
(c)　there are at least two working days between the date of receipt of the notice and the date of entry.

(5)　A notice need not be given if the occupier has waived the requirement to give notice.

(6)　In this paragraph "routine inspection" means an exercise of the power in sub-paragraph (1) other than where—
(a)　the power is exercised by an officer of a domestic enforcer who reasonably suspects a breach of the enforcer's legislation,
(b)　the officer reasonably considers that to give notice in accordance with sub-paragraph (3) would defeat the purpose of the entry,
(c)　it is not reasonably practicable in all the circumstances to give notice in accordance with that sub-paragraph, in particular because the officer reasonably suspects that there is an imminent risk to public health or safety, or
(d)　the enforcer is a market surveillance authority within the meaning of Article 2(18) of the Regulation on Accreditation and Market Surveillance and the entry is for the purpose of market surveillance within the meaning of Article 2(17) of that Regulation.

(7)　If an officer of an enforcer enters premises under sub-paragraph (1) otherwise than in the course of a routine inspection, and finds one or more occupiers on the premises, the officer must provide to that occupier or (if there is more than one) to at least one of them a document that—
(a)　sets out why the entry is necessary, and
(b)　indicates the nature of the offence under paragraph 36 (obstruction).

(8)　If an officer of an enforcer enters premises under sub-paragraph (1) and finds one or more occupiers on the premises, the officer must produce evidence of the officer's identity and authority to that occupier or (if there is more than one) to at least one of them.

(9)　An officer need not comply with sub-paragraph (7) or (8) if it is not reasonably practicable to do so.

(10)　Proceedings resulting from the exercise of the power under sub-paragraph (1) are not invalid merely because of a failure to comply with sub-paragraph (7) or (8).

(11)　An officer entering premises under sub-paragraph (1) may be accompanied by such persons, and may take onto the premises such equipment, as the officer thinks necessary.

(12)　In this paragraph—

"give", in relation to the giving of a notice to the occupier of premises, includes delivering or leaving it at the premises or sending it there by post;

"working day" means a day other than—

    (a)   Saturday or Sunday,

    (b)   Christmas Day or Good Friday, or

    (c)   a day which is a bank holiday under the Banking and Financial Dealings Act 1971 in the part of the United Kingdom in which the premises are situated.

Application of paragraphs 25 to 31

24 Paragraphs 25 to 31 apply if an officer of an enforcer has entered any premises under the power in paragraph 23(1) or under a warrant under paragraph 32.

Power to inspect products etc

25 (1)   The officer may inspect any product on the premises.

(2)   The power in sub-paragraph (3) is also available to an officer of a domestic enforcer acting pursuant to the duty in section 27(1) of the Consumer Protection Act 1987 or regulation 10(1) of the General Product Safety Regulations 2005 (SI 2005/1803).

(3)   The officer may examine any procedure (including any arrangements for carrying out a test) connected with the production of a product.

(4)   The powers in sub-paragraph (5) are also available to an officer of a domestic enforcer acting pursuant to—

    (a)   the duty in regulation 10(1) of the Weights and Measures (Packaged Goods) Regulations 2006 (SI 2006/659) ("the ("2006 Regulations"), or

    (b)   the duty in regulation 10(1) of the Weights and Measures (Packaged Goods) Regulations (Northern Ireland) 2011 (SR 2011/331) ("the 2011 Regulations").

(5)   The officer may inspect and take copies of, or of anything purporting to be—

    (a)   a record of a kind mentioned in regulation 5(2) or 9(1), or

    (b)   evidence of a kind mentioned in regulation 9(3).

(6)   The references in sub-paragraph (5) to regulations are to regulations in the 2006 Regulations in the case of a domestic enforcer in Great Britain or the 2011 Regulations in the case of a domestic enforcer in Northern Ireland.

(7)   The powers in sub-paragraph (8) are also available to an officer of a domestic enforcer acting pursuant to the duty in regulation 37(1)(a)(ii) or (b)(ii) of the Electromagnetic Compatibility Regulations 2006 (SI 2006/3418).

(8)   The officer may—

    (a)   inspect any apparatus or fixed installation (as defined in those Regulations), or

    (b)   examine any procedure (including any arrangements for carrying out a test) connected with the production of apparatus.

Power to test equipment

26 (1)   An officer of a domestic enforcer may test any weighing or measuring equipment—

    (a)   which is, or which the officer has reasonable cause to believe may be, used for trade or in the possession of any person or on any premises for such use, or

    (b)   which has been, or which the officer has reasonable cause to believe to have been, passed by an approved verifier, or by a person purporting to act as such a verifier, as fit for such use.

(2)   Expressions used in sub-paragraph (1) have the same meaning—

    (a)   as in the Weights and Measures Act 1985, in the case of a domestic enforcer in Great Britain;

    (b)   as in the Weights and Measures (Northern Ireland) Order 1981 (SI 1981/231 (NI 10)), in the case of a domestic enforcer in Northern Ireland.

(3)   The powers in sub-paragraph (4) are available to an officer of a domestic enforcer acting pursuant to—

    (a)   the duty in regulation 10(1) of the Weights and Measures (Packaged Goods) Regulations 2006 (SI 2006/659) ("the 2006 Regulations"), or

    (b)   the duty in regulation 10(1) of the Weights and Measures (Packaged Goods) Regulations (Northern Ireland) 2011 (SR 2011/331) ("the 2011 Regulations").

(4)   The officer may test any equipment which the officer has reasonable cause to believe is used in—

    (a)   making up packages (as defined in regulation 2) in the United Kingdom, or

    (b)   carrying out a check mentioned in paragraphs (1) and (3) of regulation 9.

(5)   The references in sub-paragraph (4) to regulations are to regulations in the 2006 Regulations in the case of a domestic enforcer in Great Britain or the 2011 Regulations in the case of a domestic enforcer in Northern Ireland.

Power to require the production of documents

27 (1) The officer may, at any reasonable time—
  (a) require a trader occupying the premises, or a person on the premises acting on behalf of such a trader, to produce any documents relating to the trader's business to which the trader has access, and
  (b) take copies of, or of any entry in, any such document.

(2) The power in sub-paragraph (1) is available regardless of whether—
  (a) the purpose for which the documents are required relates to the trader or some other person, or
  (b) the proceedings referred to in paragraph 19(3)(b) or 20(4)(b) could be taken against the trader or some other person.

(3) That power includes power to require the person to give an explanation of the documents.

(4) Where a document required to be produced under sub-paragraph (1) contains information recorded electronically, the power in that sub-paragraph includes power to require the production of a copy of the document in a form in which it can easily be taken away and in which it is visible and legible.

(5) This paragraph does not permit an officer to require a person to create a document other than as described in sub-paragraph (4).

(6) This paragraph does not permit an officer to require a person to produce any document which the person would be entitled to refuse to produce—
  (a) in proceedings in the High Court on the grounds of legal professional privilege, or
  (b) in proceedings in the Court of Session on the grounds of confidentiality of communications.

(7) In sub-paragraph (6) "communications" means—
  (a) communications between a professional legal adviser and the adviser's client, or
  (b) communications made in connection with or in contemplation of legal proceedings or for the purposes of those proceedings.

(8) In this paragraph "trader" has the same meaning as in Part 1 of this Act.

Power to seize and detain goods

28 (1) The officer may seize and detain goods other than documents (for which see paragraph 29).

(2) An officer seizing goods under this paragraph from premises which are occupied must produce evidence of the officer's identity and authority to an occupier of the premises before seizing them.

(3) The officer need not comply with sub-paragraph (2) if it is not reasonably practicable to do so.

(4) An officer seizing goods under this paragraph must take reasonable steps to—
  (a) inform the person from whom they are seized that they have been seized, and
  (b) provide that person with a written record of what has been seized.

(5) If, under this paragraph, an officer seizes any goods from a vending machine, the duty in sub-paragraph (4) also applies in relation to—
  (a) the person whose name and address are on the vending machine as the owner of the machine, or
  (b) if there is no such name and address on the machine, the occupier of the premises on which the machine stands or to which it is fixed.

(6) In determining the steps to be taken under sub-paragraph (4), an officer exercising a power under this paragraph in England and Wales or Northern Ireland must have regard to any relevant provision about the seizure of property made by—
  (a) a code of practice under section 66 of the Police and Criminal Evidence Act 1984, or
  (b) a code of practice under Article 65 of the Police and Criminal Evidence (Northern Ireland) Order 1989 (SI 1989/1341 (NI 12)),
(as the case may be).

(7) Goods seized under this paragraph (except goods seized for a purpose mentioned in paragraph 19(5)(b)) may not be detained—
  (a) for a period of more than 3 months beginning with the day on which they were seized, or
  (b) where the goods are reasonably required to be detained for a longer period by the enforcer for a purpose for which they were seized, for longer than they are required for that purpose.

Power to seize documents required as evidence

29 (1) The officer may seize and detain documents.

(2) An officer seizing documents under this paragraph from premises which are occupied must produce evidence of the officer's identity and authority to an occupier of the premises before seizing them.

(3) The officer need not comply with sub-paragraph (2) if it is not reasonably practicable to do so.

(4) An officer seizing documents under this paragraph must take reasonable steps to—
  (a) inform the person from whom they are seized that they have been seized, and

(b)   provide that person with a written record of what has been seized.

(5)   In determining the steps to be taken under sub-paragraph (4), an officer exercising a power under this paragraph in England and Wales or Northern Ireland must have regard to any relevant provision about the seizure of property made by—

     (a)   a code of practice under section 66 of the Police and Criminal Evidence Act 1984, or

     (b)   a code of practice under Article 65 of the Police and Criminal Evidence (Northern Ireland) Order 1989 (SI 1989/1341 (NI 12)),

(as the case may be).

(6)   This paragraph does not confer any power on an officer to seize from a person any document which the person would be entitled to refuse to produce—

     (a)   in proceedings in the High Court on the grounds of legal professional privilege, or

     (b)   in proceedings in the Court of Session on the grounds of confidentiality of communications.

(7)   In sub-paragraph (6) "communications" means—

     (a)   communications between a professional legal adviser and the adviser's client, or

     (b)   communications made in connection with or in contemplation of legal proceedings or for the purposes of those proceedings.

(8)   Documents seized under this paragraph may not be detained—

     (a)   for a period of more than 3 months beginning with the day on which they were seized, or

     (b)   where the documents are reasonably required to be detained for a longer period by the enforcer for the purposes of the proceedings for which they were seized, for longer than they are required for those purposes.

Power to decommission or switch off fixed installations

30 (1)   The power in sub-paragraph (2) is available to an officer of a domestic enforcer acting pursuant to the duty in regulation 37(1)(a)(ii) or (b)(ii) of the Electromagnetic Compatibility Regulations 2006 (SI 2006/3418).

(2)   The officer may decommission or switch off any fixed installation (as defined in those Regulations) or part of such an installation.

Power to break open container etc

31 (1)   The officer may, for the purpose of exercising any of the powers in paragraphs 28 to 30, require a person with authority to do so to—

     (a)   break open any container,

     (b)   open any vending machine, or

     (c)   access any electronic device in which information may be stored or from which it may be accessed.

(2)   Where a requirement under sub-paragraph (1) has not been complied with, the officer may, for the purpose of exercising any of the powers in paragraphs 28 to 30—

     (a)   break open the container,

     (b)   open the vending machine, or

     (c)   access the electronic device.

(3)   Sub-paragraph (1) or (2) applies if and to the extent that the exercise of the power in that sub-paragraph is reasonably necessary for the purposes for which that power may be exercised.

(4)   In this paragraph "container" means anything in which goods may be stored.

Power to enter premises with warrant

32 (1)   A justice of the peace may issue a warrant authorising an officer of an enforcer to enter premises if satisfied, on written information on oath given by such an officer, that there are reasonable grounds for believing that—

     (a)   condition A or B is met, and

     (b)   condition C, D or E is met.

(2)   Condition A is that on the premises there are—

     (a)   products which an officer of the enforcer has power to inspect under paragraph 25, or

     (b)   documents which an officer of the enforcer could require a person to produce under paragraph 27.

(3)   Condition B is that, on the premises—

     (a)   in the case of a domestic enforcer, there has been or is about to be a breach of the enforcer's legislation,

     (b)   in the case of an EU enforcer, there has been or is about to be a Community infringement as defined in section 212 of the Enterprise Act 2002, or

     (c)   in the case of an EU enforcer, there has been a failure to comply with a measure specified in paragraph 20(3)(b), (c) or (d).

(4)   Condition C is that—

     (a)   access to the premises has been or is likely to be refused, and

(b) notice of the enforcer's intention to apply for a warrant under this paragraph has been given to the occupier of the premises.

(5) Condition D is that it is likely that products or documents on the premises would be concealed or interfered with if notice of entry on the premises were given to the occupier of the premises.

(6) Condition E is that—

(a) the premises are unoccupied, or

(b) the occupier of the premises is absent, and it might defeat the purpose of the entry to wait for the occupier's return.

(7) In the application of this paragraph to Scotland—

(a) the reference in sub-paragraph (1) to a justice of the peace is to be read as a reference to a sheriff, and

(b) the reference in that sub-paragraph to information on oath is to be read as a reference to evidence on oath.

(8) In the application of this paragraph to Northern Ireland—

(a) the reference in sub-paragraph (1) to a justice of the peace is to be read as a reference to a lay magistrate, and

(b) the reference in that sub-paragraph to written information is to be read as a reference to a written complaint.

Entry to premises under warrant

33 (1) A warrant under paragraph 32 authorises an officer of the enforcer to enter the premises at any reasonable time, using reasonable force if necessary.

(2) A warrant under that paragraph ceases to have effect at the end of the period of one month beginning with the day it is issued.

(3) An officer entering premises under a warrant under paragraph 32 may be accompanied by such persons, and may take onto the premises such equipment, as the officer thinks necessary.

(4) If the premises are occupied when the officer enters them, the officer must produce the warrant for inspection to an occupier of the premises.

(5) Sub-paragraph (6) applies if the premises are unoccupied or the occupier is temporarily absent.

(6) On leaving the premises the officer must—

(a) leave a notice on the premises stating that the premises have been entered under a warrant under paragraph 32, and

(b) leave the premises as effectively secured against trespassers as the officer found them.

Power to require assistance from person on premises

34 (1) If an officer of an enforcer has entered premises under the power in paragraph 23(1) or under a warrant under paragraph 32, the officer may require any person on the premises to provide such assistance or information as the officer reasonably considers necessary.

(2) Sub-paragraph (3) applies if an officer of a domestic enforcer has entered premises under the power in paragraph 23(1) or under a warrant under paragraph 32 for the purposes of the enforcement of—

(a) the Weights and Measures (Packaged Goods) Regulations 2006 (SI 2006/659), or

(b) the Weights and Measures (Packaged Goods) Regulations (Northern Ireland) 2011 (SR 2011/331).

(3) The officer may, in particular, require any person on the premises to provide such information as the person possesses about the name and address of the packer and of any importer of a package which the officer finds on the premises.

(4) In sub-paragraph (3) "importer", "package" and "packer" have the same meaning as in—

(a) the Weights and Measures (Packaged Goods) Regulations 2006 (see regulation 2), in the case of a domestic enforcer in Great Britain, or

(b) the Weights and Measures (Packaged Goods) Regulations (Northern Ireland) 2011 (see regulation 2), in the case of a domestic enforcer in Northern Ireland.

Definitions for purposes of this Part

35 In this Part of this Schedule—

"goods" has the meaning given by section 2(8);

"occupier", in relation to premises, means any person an officer of an enforcer reasonably suspects to be the occupier of the premises;

"premises" includes any stall, vehicle, vessel or aircraft;

"product" means—

(a) goods,

(b) a service,

(c) digital content, as defined in section 2(9),

(d) immovable property, or

(e)   rights or obligations.

NOTES

Commencement: 27 May 2015 (in so far as relating to Chapter 3 of Part 3, in relation to England; and in so far as relating to Chapter 5 of Part 3); 1 October 2015 (otherwise).

PART 5
PROVISIONS SUPPLEMENTARY TO PARTS 3 AND 4

Offence of obstruction

[1.2327]

36 (1)   A person commits an offence if the person—

(a)   intentionally obstructs an enforcer or an officer of an enforcer who is exercising or seeking to exercise a power under Part 4 of this Schedule in accordance with that Part,

(b)   intentionally fails to comply with a requirement properly imposed by an enforcer or an officer of an enforcer under Part 4 of this Schedule, or

(c)   without reasonable cause fails to give an enforcer or an officer of an enforcer any other assistance or information which the enforcer or officer reasonably requires of the person for a purpose for which the enforcer or officer may exercise a power under Part 4 of this Schedule.

(2)   A person commits an offence if, in giving information of a kind referred to in sub-paragraph (1)(c), the person—

(a)   makes a statement which the person knows is false or misleading in a material respect, or

(b)   recklessly makes a statement which is false or misleading in a material respect.

(3)   A person who is guilty of an offence under sub-paragraph (1) or (2) is liable on summary conviction to a fine not exceeding level 3 on the standard scale.

(4)   Nothing in this paragraph requires a person to answer any question or give any information if to do so might incriminate that person.

Offence of purporting to act as officer

37 (1)   A person who is not an officer of an enforcer commits an offence if the person purports to act as such under Part 3 or 4 of this Schedule.

(2)   A person who is guilty of an offence under sub-paragraph (1) is liable on summary conviction to a fine not exceeding level 5 on the standard scale.

(3)   If section 85(1) of the Legal Aid, Sentencing and Punishment of Offenders Act 2012 comes into force on or before the day on which this Act is passed—

(a)   section 85 of that Act (removal of limit on certain fines on conviction by magistrates' court) applies in relation to the offence in this paragraph as if it were a relevant offence (as defined in section 85(3) of that Act), and

(b)   regulations described in section 85(11) of that Act may amend or otherwise modify sub-paragraph (2).

Access to seized goods and documents

38 (1)   This paragraph applies where anything seized by an officer of an enforcer under Part 4 of this Schedule is detained by the enforcer.

(2)   If a request for permission to be granted access to that thing is made to the enforcer by a person who had custody or control of it immediately before it was seized, the enforcer must allow that person access to it under the supervision of an officer of the enforcer.

(3)   If a request for a photograph or copy of that thing is made to the enforcer by a person who had custody or control of it immediately before it was seized, the enforcer must—

(a)   allow that person access to it under the supervision of an officer of the enforcer for the purpose of photographing or copying it, or

(b)   photograph or copy it, or cause it to be photographed or copied.

(4)   Where anything is photographed or copied under sub-paragraph (3), the photograph or copy must be supplied to the person who made the request within a reasonable time from the making of the request.

(5)   This paragraph does not require access to be granted to, or a photograph or copy to be supplied of, anything if the enforcer has reasonable grounds for believing that to do so would prejudice the investigation for the purposes of which it was seized.

(6)   An enforcer may recover the reasonable costs of complying with a request under this paragraph from the person by whom or on whose behalf it was made.

(7)   References in this paragraph to a person who had custody or control of a thing immediately before it was seized include a representative of such a person.

Notice of testing of goods

39 (1) Sub-paragraphs (3) and (4) apply where goods purchased by an officer of a domestic enforcer under paragraph 21 are submitted to a test and as a result—

    (a)   proceedings are brought for a breach of, or under, the enforcer's legislation or for the forfeiture of the goods by the enforcer, or

    (b)   a notice is served by the enforcer preventing a person from doing any thing.

(2) Sub-paragraphs (3) and (4) also apply where goods seized by an officer of a domestic enforcer under paragraph 28 are submitted to a test.

(3) The enforcer must inform the relevant person of the results of the test.

(4) The enforcer must allow a relevant person to have the goods tested if it is reasonably practicable to do so.

(5) In sub-paragraph (3) "relevant person" means the person from whom the goods were purchased or seized or, where the goods were purchased or seized from a vending machine—

    (a)   the person whose name and address are on the vending machine as the owner of the machine, or

    (b)   if there is no such name and address on the machine, the occupier of the premises on which the machine stands or to which it is fixed.

(6) In sub-paragraph (4) "relevant person" means—

    (a)   a person within sub-paragraph (5),

    (b)   in a case within sub-paragraph (1)(a), a person who is a party to the proceedings, and

    (c)   in a case within sub-paragraph (1)(b), a person with an interest in the goods.

Appeals against detention of goods and documents

40 (1) This paragraph applies where goods or documents are being detained as the result of the exercise of a power in Part 4 of this Schedule.

(2) A person with an interest in the goods or documents may apply for an order requiring them to be released to that or another person.

(3) An application under this paragraph may be made in England and Wales or Northern Ireland—

    (a)   to any magistrates' court in which proceedings have been brought for an offence as the result of the investigation in the course of which the goods or documents were seized,

    (b)   to any magistrates' court in which proceedings have been brought for the forfeiture of the goods or documents or (in the case of seized documents) any goods to which the documents relate, or

    (c)   if no proceedings within paragraph (a) or (b) have been brought, by way of complaint to a magistrates' court.

(4) An application under this paragraph may be made in Scotland by summary application to the sheriff.

(5) On an application under this paragraph, the court or sheriff may make an order requiring goods to be released only if satisfied that condition A or B is met.

(6) Condition A is that—

    (a)   no proceedings have been brought—

        (i)   for an offence as the result of the investigation in the course of which the goods or documents were seized, or

        (ii)   for the forfeiture of the goods or documents or (in the case of seized documents) any goods to which the documents relate, and

    (b)   the period of 6 months beginning with the date the goods or documents were seized has expired.

(7) Condition B is that—

    (a)   proceedings of a kind mentioned in sub-paragraph (6)(a) have been brought, and

    (b)   those proceedings have been concluded without the goods or documents being forfeited.

(8) A person aggrieved by an order made under this paragraph by a magistrates' court, or by the decision of a magistrates' court not to make such an order, may appeal against the order or decision—

    (a)   in England and Wales, to the Crown Court;

    (b)   in Northern Ireland, to a county court.

(9) An order made under this paragraph by a magistrates' court may contain such provision as the court thinks appropriate for delaying its coming into force pending the making and determination of any appeal.

(10) In sub-paragraph (9) "appeal" includes an application under section 111 of the Magistrates' Courts Act 1980 or Article 146 of the Magistrates' Courts (Northern Ireland) Order 1981 (SI 1981/1675 (NI 26)) (statements of case).

Compensation

41 (1)   This paragraph applies where an officer of an enforcer has seized and detained goods under Part 4 of this Schedule for a purpose within paragraph 19(5)(a) or 20(5)(a).

(2)   The enforcer must pay compensation to any person with an interest in the goods in respect of any loss or damage caused by the seizure and detention, if the condition in sub-paragraph (3) or (4) that is relevant to the enforcer is met.

(3)   The condition that is relevant to a domestic enforcer is that—
    (a)   the goods have not disclosed a breach of the enforcer's legislation, and
    (b)   the power to seize and detain the goods was not exercised as a result of any neglect or default of the person seeking the compensation.

(4)   The condition that is relevant to an EU enforcer is that—
    (a)   the goods have not disclosed a Community infringement or a failure to comply with a measure specified in paragraph 20(3)(b), (c) or (d), and
    (b)   the power to seize and detain the goods was not exercised as a result of any neglect or default of the person seeking the compensation.

(5)   Any dispute about the right to or amount of any compensation payable under this paragraph is to be determined—
    (a)   in England and Wales or Northern Ireland, by arbitration, or
    (b)   in Scotland, by a single arbitrator appointed by the parties or, if there is no agreement between the parties as to that appointment, by the sheriff.

Meaning of "goods" in this Part

42 In this Part of this Schedule "goods" does not include a document.

NOTES

Commencement: 27 May 2015 (in so far as relating to Chapter 3 of Part 3, in relation to England; and in so far as relating to Chapter 5 of Part 3); 1 October 2015 (otherwise).

PART 6
EXERCISE OF ENFORCEMENT FUNCTIONS BY AREA ENFORCERS

Interpretation of this Part

[1.2328]

43 In this Part, "area enforcer" means—
    (a)   a local weights and measures authority in Great Britain,
    (b)   a district council in England, or
    (c)   a district council in Northern Ireland.

Investigatory powers

44 (1)   Sub-paragraphs (3) to (6) apply in relation to an area enforcer's exercise, in accordance with this Schedule, of a power in Part 3 or 4 of this Schedule.

(2)   Sub-paragraphs (3) to (6) also apply in relation to an area enforcer's exercise of an investigatory power—
    (a)   conferred by legislation which, by virtue of a provision listed in paragraph 10 of this Schedule, the area enforcer has a duty or power to enforce, or conferred by legislation under which such legislation is made, or
    (b)   conferred by legislation listed in the second column of the table in paragraph 11 of this Schedule,

for the purpose of ascertaining whether there has been a breach of that legislation or of any notice issued by the area enforcer under that legislation.

(3)   A local weights and measures authority in England or Wales may exercise the power in a part of England or Wales which is outside that authority's area.

(4)   A local weights and measures authority in Scotland may exercise the power in a part of Scotland which is outside that authority's area.

(5)   A district council in England may exercise the power in a part of England which is outside that council's district.

(6)   A district council in Northern Ireland may exercise the power in a part of Northern Ireland which is outside that council's district.

Civil proceedings

45 (1)   Sub-paragraphs (4) to (7) apply in relation to civil proceedings which may be brought by an area enforcer under—
    (a)   Part 8 of the Enterprise Act 2002,
    (b)   Schedule 3 to this Act,

(c) legislation which, by virtue of a provision listed in paragraph 10 of this Schedule, the area enforcer has a duty or power to enforce,

(d) legislation under which legislation mentioned in paragraph (c) is made, or

(e) legislation listed in the second column of the table in paragraph 11 of this Schedule.

(2) Sub-paragraphs (4) to (7) also apply in relation to an application for forfeiture which may be made by an area enforcer, in circumstances where there are no related criminal proceedings,—

(a) under section 35ZC of the Registered Designs Act 1949,

(b) under section 16 of the Consumer Protection Act 1987,

(c) under section 97 of the Trade Marks Act 1994 (including as applied by section 11 of the Olympic Symbol etc (Protection) Act 1995), or

(d) under legislation which, by virtue of a provision listed in paragraph 10 of this Schedule, the area enforcer has a duty or power to enforce.

(3) In sub-paragraphs (4), (5), (6) and (7), the reference to civil proceedings includes a reference to an application mentioned in sub-paragraph (2).

(4) A local weights and measures authority in England or Wales may bring civil proceedings in respect of conduct in a part of England or Wales which is outside that authority's area.

(5) A local weights and measures authority in Scotland may bring civil proceedings in respect of conduct in a part of Scotland which is outside that authority's area.

(6) A district council in England may bring civil proceedings in respect of conduct in a part of England which is outside that council's district.

(7) A district council in Northern Ireland may bring civil proceedings in respect of conduct in a part of Northern Ireland which is outside that council's district.

Criminal proceedings

46 (1) A local weights and measures authority in England or Wales may bring proceedings for a consumer offence allegedly committed in a part of England or Wales which is outside that authority's area.

(2) In sub-paragraph (1) "a consumer offence" means—

(a) an offence under legislation which, by virtue of a provision listed in paragraph 10 of this Schedule, a local weights and measures authority in England or Wales has a duty or power to enforce,

(b) an offence under legislation under which legislation within paragraph (a) is made,

(c) an offence under legislation listed in the second column of the table in paragraph 11 of this Schedule in relation to which a local weights and measures authority is listed in the corresponding entry in the first column of the table as an enforcer,

(d) an offence originating from an investigation into a breach of legislation mentioned in paragraph (a), (b) or (c), or

(e) an offence described in paragraph 36 or 37 of this Schedule.

(3) A district council in England may bring proceedings for a consumer offence allegedly committed in a part of England which is outside that council's district.

(4) In sub-paragraph (3) "a consumer offence" means—

(a) an offence under legislation which, by virtue of a provision listed in paragraph 10 of this Schedule, a district council in England has a duty or power to enforce,

(b) an offence under legislation under which legislation within paragraph (a) is made,

(c) an offence originating from an investigation into a breach of legislation mentioned in paragraph (a) or (b), or

(d) an offence described in paragraph 36 or 37 of this Schedule.

(5) A district council in Northern Ireland may bring proceedings for a consumer offence allegedly committed in a part of Northern Ireland which is outside that council's district.

(6) In sub-paragraph (5) "a consumer offence" means—

(a) an offence under legislation which, by virtue of a provision listed in paragraph 10 of this Schedule, a district council in Northern Ireland has a duty or power to enforce,

(b) an offence under legislation under which legislation within paragraph (a) is made,

(c) an offence originating from an investigation into a breach of legislation mentioned in paragraph (a) or (b), or

(d) an offence described in paragraph 36 or 37 of this Schedule.

NOTES

Commencement: 27 May 2015 (in so far as relating to Chapter 3 of Part 3, in relation to England; and in so far as relating to Chapter 5 of Part 3); to be appointed (otherwise).

SCHEDULE 6
INVESTIGATORY POWERS: CONSEQUENTIAL AMENDMENTS

(Sch 6 amends the Trade Descriptions Act 1968 at **[1.431]** *et seq; the Prices Act 1974 at* **[1.515]** *et seq; the Consumer Credit Act 1974 at* **[1.520]** *et seq; the Estate Agents Act 1979, at* **[1.786]** *et seq;*

the Weights and Measures Act 1985, at **[1.942]** *et seq; the Consumer Protection Act 1987 at* **[1.985]** *et seq; the Sunday Trading Act 1994 at* **[1.1102]** *et seq; the Enterprise Act 2002 at* **[1.1700]** *et seq; the Fireworks Act 2003 at* **[1.1849]** *et seq; the Christmas Day (Trading) Act 2004 at* **[1.1904]** *et seq; the Consumer Protection from Unfair Trading Regulations 2008, SI 2008/1277, at* **[2.555]** *et seq; the Timeshare, Holiday Products, Resale and Exchange Contracts Regulations 2010, SI 2010/2960 at* **[2.841]** *et seq; and contains various other amendments to enactments that are outside the scope of this work.)*

SCHEDULE 7
ENTERPRISE ACT 2002: ENHANCED CONSUMER MEASURES AND OTHER ENFORCEMENT

(Sch 7 amends the Enterprise Act 2002 at **[1.1700]** *et seq.)*

SCHEDULE 8
PRIVATE ACTIONS IN COMPETITION LAW

(Sch 8 amends the Courts and Legal Services Act 1990; the Competition Act 1998 at **[1.1266]** *et seq; and the Enterprise Act 2002 at* **[1.1700]** *et seq).*

Section 81

SCHEDULE 9
DUTY OF LETTING AGENTS TO PUBLICISE FEES: FINANCIAL PENALTIES

Section 87

Notice of intent

[1.2329]

1 (1) Before imposing a financial penalty on a letting agent for a breach of a duty imposed by or under section 83, a local weights and measures authority must serve a notice on the agent of its proposal to do so (a "notice of intent").

(2) The notice of intent must be served before the end of the period of 6 months beginning with the first day on which the authority has sufficient evidence of the agent's breach, subject to sub-paragraph (3).

(3) If the agent is in breach of the duty on that day, and the breach continues beyond the end of that day, the notice of intent may be served—

    (a)   at any time when the breach is continuing, or

    (b)   within the period of 6 months beginning with the last day on which the breach occurs.

(4) The notice of intent must set out—

    (a)   the amount of the proposed financial penalty,

    (b)   the reasons for proposing to impose the penalty, and

    (c)   information about the right to make representations under paragraph 2.

Right to make representations

2 The letting agent may, within the period of 28 days beginning with the day after that on which the notice of intent was sent, make written representations to the local weights and measures authority about the proposal to impose a financial penalty on the agent.

Final notice

3 (1) After the end of the period mentioned in paragraph 2 the local weights and measures authority must—

    (a)   decide whether to impose a financial penalty on the letting agent, and

    (b)   if it decides to do so, decide the amount of the penalty.

(2) If the authority decides to impose a financial penalty on the agent, it must serve a notice on the agent (a "final notice") imposing that penalty.

(3) The final notice must require the penalty to be paid within the period of 28 days beginning with the day after that on which the notice was sent.

(4) The final notice must set out—

    (a)   the amount of the financial penalty,

    (b)   the reasons for imposing the penalty,

    (c)   information about how to pay the penalty,

    (d)   the period for payment of the penalty,

    (e)   information about rights of appeal, and

    (f)   the consequences of failure to comply with the notice.

Withdrawal or amendment of notice

4 (1) A local weights and measures authority may at any time—

(a) withdraw a notice of intent or final notice, or

(b) reduce the amount specified in a notice of intent or final notice.

(2) The power in sub-paragraph (1) is to be exercised by giving notice in writing to the letting agent on whom the notice was served.

Appeals

5 (1) A letting agent on whom a final notice is served may appeal against that notice to—

(a) the First-tier Tribunal, in the case of a notice served by a local weights and measures authority in England, or

(b) the residential property tribunal, in the case of a notice served by a local weights and measures authority in Wales.

(2) The grounds for an appeal under this paragraph are that—

(a) the decision to impose a financial penalty was based on an error of fact,

(b) the decision was wrong in law,

(c) the amount of the financial penalty is unreasonable, or

(d) the decision was unreasonable for any other reason.

(3) An appeal under this paragraph to the residential property tribunal must be brought within the period of 28 days beginning with the day after that on which the final notice was sent.

(4) If a letting agent appeals under this paragraph, the final notice is suspended until the appeal is finally determined or withdrawn.

(5) On an appeal under this paragraph the First-tier Tribunal or (as the case may be) the residential property tribunal may quash, confirm or vary the final notice.

(6) The final notice may not be varied under sub-paragraph (5) so as to make it impose a financial penalty of more than £5,000.

Recovery of financial penalty

6 (1) This paragraph applies if a letting agent does not pay the whole or any part of a financial penalty which, in accordance with this Schedule, the agent is liable to pay.

(2) The local weights and measures authority which imposed the financial penalty may recover the penalty or part on the order of the county court as if it were payable under an order of that court.

(3) In proceedings before the county court for the recovery of a financial penalty or part of a financial penalty, a certificate which is—

(a) signed by the chief finance officer of the local weights and measures authority which imposed the penalty, and

(b) states that the amount due has not been received by a date specified in the certificate,

is conclusive evidence of that fact.

(4) A certificate to that effect and purporting to be so signed is to be treated as being so signed unless the contrary is proved.

(5) A local weights and measures authority may use the proceeds of a financial penalty for the purposes of any of its functions (whether or not the function is expressed to be a function of a local weights and measures authority).

(6) In this paragraph "chief finance officer" has the same meaning as in section 5 of the Local Government and Housing Act 1989.

NOTES

Commencement: 27 May 2015 (in relation to England)); to be appointed (otherwise).

SCHEDULE 10
SECONDARY TICKETING: FINANCIAL PENALTIES

Section 93

Notice of intent

[1.2330]

1 (1) Before imposing a financial penalty on a person for a breach of a duty or prohibition imposed by Chapter 5 of Part 3, an enforcement authority must serve a notice on the person of its proposal to do so (a "notice of intent").

(2) The notice of intent must be served before the end of the period of 6 months beginning with the first day on which the authority has sufficient evidence of the person's breach, subject to sub-paragraph (3).

(3) If the person is in breach of the duty or prohibition on that day, and the breach continues beyond the end of that day, the notice of intent may be served—

(a) at any time when the breach is continuing, or

(b) within the period of 6 months beginning with the last day on which the breach occurs.

(4) The notice of intent must set out—

(a) the amount of the proposed financial penalty,

(b) the reasons for proposing to impose the penalty, and

(c)   information about the right to make representations under paragraph 2.

Right to make representations

2   A person on whom a notice of intent is served may, within the period of 28 days beginning with the day after that on which the notice was sent, make written representations to the enforcement authority about the proposal to impose a financial penalty on the person.

Final notice

3   (1)   After the end of the period mentioned in paragraph 2 the enforcement authority must—
     (a)   decide whether to impose a financial penalty on the person, and
     (b)   if it decides to do so, decide the amount of the penalty.

(2)   If the authority decides to impose a financial penalty on the person, it must serve a notice on the person (a "final notice") imposing that penalty.

(3)   The final notice must require the penalty to be paid within the period of 28 days beginning with the day after that on which the notice was sent.

(4)   The final notice must set out—
     (a)   the amount of the financial penalty,
     (b)   the reasons for imposing the penalty,
     (c)   information about how to pay the penalty,
     (d)   the period for payment of the penalty,
     (e)   information about rights of appeal, and
     (f)   the consequences of failure to comply with the notice.

Withdrawal or amendment of notice

4   (1)   The enforcement authority may at any time—
     (a)   withdraw a notice of intent or final notice, or
     (b)   reduce the amount specified in a notice of intent or final notice.

(2)   The power in sub-paragraph (1) is to be exercised by giving notice in writing to the person on whom the notice was served.

Appeals

5   (1)   A person on whom a final notice is served may appeal against that notice—
     (a)   in England and Wales and Scotland, to the First-tier Tribunal;
     (b)   in Northern Ireland, to a county court.

(2)   The grounds for an appeal under this paragraph are that—
     (a)   the decision to impose a financial penalty was based on an error of fact,
     (b)   the decision was wrong in law,
     (c)   the amount of the financial penalty is unreasonable, or
     (d)   the decision was unreasonable for any other reason.

(3)   If a person appeals under this paragraph, the final notice is suspended until the appeal is finally determined or withdrawn.

(4)   On an appeal under this paragraph the First-tier Tribunal or the court may quash, confirm or vary the final notice.

(5)   The final notice may not be varied under sub-paragraph (4) so as to make it impose a financial penalty of more than £5,000.

Recovery of financial penalty

6   (1)   This paragraph applies if a person does not pay the whole or any part of a financial penalty which, in accordance with this Schedule, the person is liable to pay.

(2)   In England and Wales the local weights and measures authority which imposed the financial penalty may recover the penalty or part on the order of the county court as if it were payable under an order of that court.

(3)   In Scotland the penalty may be enforced in the same manner as an extract registered decree arbitral bearing a warrant for execution issued by the sheriff court of any sheriffdom in Scotland.

(4)   In Northern Ireland the Department of Enterprise, Trade and Investment may recover the penalty or part on the order of a county court as if it were payable under an order of that court.

(5)   In proceedings before the court for the recovery of a financial penalty or part of a financial penalty, a certificate which is—
     (a)   signed by the chief finance officer of the local weights and measures authority which imposed the penalty or (as the case may be) issued by the Department of Enterprise, Trade and Investment, and
     (b)   states that the amount due has not been received by a date specified in the certificate,
is conclusive evidence of that fact.

(6)   A certificate to that effect and purporting to be so signed or issued is to be treated as being so signed or issued unless the contrary is proved.

(7) A local weights and measures authority may use the proceeds of a financial penalty for the purposes of any of its functions (whether or not the function is expressed to be a function of a local weights and measures authority).

(8) In this paragraph "chief finance officer" has the same meaning as in section 5 of the Local Government and Housing Act 1989.

NOTES

Commencement: 26 May 2015.

PART 2
STATUTORY INSTRUMENTS

CONSUMER CREDIT (TOTAL CHARGE FOR CREDIT) REGULATIONS 1980

(SI 1980/51)

NOTES

Made: 17 January 1980.

Authority: Consumer Credit Act 1974, ss 20, 182(2).

Commencement: 28 April 1980.

These Regulations were revoked by the Financial Services and Markets Act 2000 (Regulated Activities) (Amendment) (No 2) Order 2013, SI 2013/1881, art 21(d), for transitional provisions see Pt 8 thereof at **[2.1007]** et seq, and are reproduced here for reference only.

ARRANGEMENT OF REGULATIONS

PART I
GENERAL

[2.1]

1   Citation, commencement, interpretation and revocation

(1) These Regulations may be cited as the Consumer Credit (Total Charge for Credit) Regulations 1980 and shall come into operation on 28th April 1980.

(2) In these Regulations—

"the Act" means the Consumer Credit Act 1974;

"agreement" means a consumer credit agreement;

["land-related agreement" means an agreement which is—

> *(a)   intended primarily to finance the acquisition or retention of land, or*
>
> *(b)   intended to finance the renovation or improvement of a building,*
>
> *or any other agreement secured by a mortgage on land or, in Scotland, by a standard security within the meaning of the Conveyancing and Feudal Reform (Scotland) Act 1970;]*

["period rate of charge" means a percentage rate of charge for a period, comprising all charges included in the total charge for credit determined in accordance with Part II of these Regulations;]

"the relevant date" means, in a case where a date is specified in or determinable under an agreement at the date of its making as that on which the debtor is entitled to require provision of anything the subject of the agreement, the earliest such date and, in any other case, the date of the making of the agreement; and

"*transaction*", *except in regulation 5(1)(c) below, means an agreement, any transaction which is a linked transaction by virtue of section 19(1)(a) of the Act, any contract for the provision of security relating to the agreement[, any credit brokerage contract relating to the agreement] and any other contract to which the debtor or a relative of his is a party and which the creditor requires to be made or maintained as a condition of the making of the agreement,*

and, except where the contrary intention appears, other expressions used in these Regulations have the same respective meanings as in the Act.

(3)   *For the purposes of these Regulations, references to the period for which credit is provided,—*

   (a)   *in the case of an agreement under which the period for which credit is to be provided is ascertainable at the date of the making of the agreement, are references to the period beginning with the relevant date and ending with the end of the period for which credit is to be provided;*

   (b)   *in the case of an agreement under which the period for which credit is to be provided can be ascertained at the relevant date if the assumption set out in regulation 13 below is applied, are references to the period beginning with the relevant date and ending with the end of the period for which credit would be provided under the agreement if the amount given by that assumption were the amount of the credit so provided; and*

   (c)   *in any other case, are references to the period of one year referred to in regulation 14 below.*

(4)   *References in these Regulations to repayment of the credit under an agreement and of the total charge for credit include references to any repayment or payment, as the case may require, of any part of the credit and of the total charge for credit.*

(5)   *. . .*

NOTES

Revoked as noted to the start of these Regulations.

Para (2): definition "land-related agreement" inserted, and definition "period rate of charge" substituted, by the Consumer Credit (Total Charge for Credit, Agreements and Advertisements) (Amendment) Regulations 1999, SI 1999/3177, reg 3(a); in definition "transaction" words in square brackets inserted by the Consumer Credit (Total Charge for Credit and Rebate on Early Settlement) (Amendment) Regulations 1989, SI 1989/596, reg 2(a).

Para (5): revokes the Consumer Credit (Total Charge for Credit) Regulations 1977, SI 1977/327.

[2.2]
[1A   Application

These Regulations apply to regulated consumer credit agreements which are secured on land or to prospective regulated consumer credit agreements which are to be secured on land except to the extent that the Consumer Credit (Disclosure of Information) Regulations 2010 apply to such agreements.]

NOTES

Revoked as noted to the start of these Regulations.

Inserted by the Consumer Credit (EU Directive) Regulations 2010, SI 2010/1010, reg 50, with effect in relation to certain agreements entered into before 1 February 2011, as provided for in regs 101, 101A of the 2010 Regulations at **[2.804]**, **[2.805]**.

[2.3]
2   General provisions about calculation

(1)   *Any calculation under these Regulations shall be made on the following assumptions—*

   (a)   *the assumption that the debtor will not be entitled to any income tax relief relating to the transaction other than relief under section 19 of the Income and Corporation Taxes Act 1970 and Schedule 4 to the Finance Act 1976 (which afford relief in respect of premiums under certain policies of insurance) without any deduction under section 21 of the said Act of 1970;*

   (b)   *the assumption that no assistance is given under the Home Purchase Assistance and Housing Corporation Guarantee Act 1978;*

   (c)

      (i)   *in the case of a transaction which provides for repayment of the credit or of the total charge for credit at or not later than a specified time or times, the assumption that the creditor will not exercise any right under the transaction to require repayment at any other time or times; and*

      (ii)   *in any other case, the assumption that the creditor will not exercise any right under the transaction to require repayment;*
      the debtor, in any case, performing all his obligations under the transaction;   . . .

   (d)   *[subject to sub-paragraph (e) below,] in the case of a transaction which provides for variation of the rate or amount of any item included in the total charge for credit in consequence of the occurrence after the relevant date of any event, the assumption that the event will not occur; and, in this sub-paragraph, "event" means an act or omission of the debtor or of the creditor or any other event (including where the transaction makes provision for variation upon the continuation of any circumstance, the continuation of that circumstance) but does not include an event which is certain to occur and of which the date of occurrence, or the earliest date of occurrence, can be ascertained at the date of the making of the agreement[; and]*

[(e)   in the case of a land-related agreement which provides for the possibility of any variation of the rate of interest in consequence of the occurrence after the relevant date of any event (being an event which is certain to occur and of which the date of occurrence, or the earliest date of occurrence, can be ascertained at the date of the making of the agreement), the assumption that such a variation will, when the event occurs, take place.]

(2)   For the purposes of these Regulations—
(a)   subject to sub-paragraph (b) below and regulation 18 below, in the case of any agreement each provision of credit and each repayment of the credit and of the total charge for credit shall be taken to be made—
(i)   at the earliest time provided under the transaction, and
(ii)   in a case where any such provision or repayment is to be made at or not later than a specified time, at that time
and, where any such repayment is to be made before the relevant date, it shall be taken to be made on the relevant date;
(b)   where under an agreement for running-account credit or an agreement for fixed-sum credit where the credit is not repayable at specified intervals or in specified amounts a constant period rate of charge in respect of periods of equal or of nearly equal length is charged, it shall be assumed for the purposes of calculations under these Regulations, notwithstanding regulation 17 below, that—
(i)   the amount of credit outstanding at the beginning of a period is to remain outstanding throughout the period;
(ii)   the amount of any credit provided during a period is provided immediately after the end of the period; and
(iii)   any repayment of credit or of the total charge for credit made during a period is made immediately after the end of the period; and
(c)   the assumption that the amount of any repayment of credit or of the total charge for credit will, at the time when the repayment is made, be the smallest for which the agreement provides.

(3)   In determining the amount of the total of the interest on the credit which may be provided under the agreement, any subsidy receivable by any person under Part II of the Housing Subsidies Act 1967 shall be deducted.

NOTES
Revoked as noted to the start of these Regulations.
Para (1): word omitted from sub-para (c) revoked, in sub-para (d) words in first pair of square brackets inserted, and word in second pair of square brackets substituted, and sub-para (e) added, by the Consumer Credit (Total Charge for Credit, Agreements and Advertisements) (Amendment) Regulations 1999, SI 1999/3177, reg 3(b)–(d).

PART II
TOTAL CHARGE FOR CREDIT

[2.4]
3   Total charge for credit
For the purposes of the Act, the total charge for the credit which may be provided under an actual or prospective agreement shall be the total of the amounts determined as at the date of the making of the agreement of such of the charges specified in regulation 4 below as apply in relation to the agreement but excluding the amount of the charges specified in regulation 5 below.

NOTES
Revoked as noted to the start of these Regulations.

[2.5]
4   Items included in total charge for credit
Except as provided in regulation 5 below, the amounts of the following charges are included in the total charge for credit in relation to an agreement—
(a)   the total of the interest on the credit which may be provided under the agreement; . . .
(b)   other charges at any time payable under the transaction by or on behalf of the debtor or a relative of his whether to the creditor or any other person[; and]
[(c)   a premium under a contract of insurance, payable under the transaction by the debtor or a relative of his, where the making or maintenance of the contract of insurance is required by the creditor—
(i)   as a condition of making the agreement, and
(ii)   for the sole purpose of ensuring complete or partial repayment of the credit, and complete or partial payment to the creditor of such of those charges included in the

> *total charge for credit as are payable to him under the transaction, in the event of the death, invalidity, illness or unemployment of the debtor,]*

notwithstanding that the whole or part of the charge may be repayable at any time or that the consideration therefor may include matters not within the transaction or subsisting at a time not within the duration of the agreement.

NOTES

Revoked as noted to the start of these Regulations.

Word omitted from para (a) revoked, in para (b) word in square brackets substituted, and para (c) inserted, by the Consumer Credit (Total Charge for Credit, Agreements and Advertisements) (Amendment) Regulations 1999, SI 1999/3177, reg 3(e), (f).

[2.6]

5 *Items excluded from total charge for credit*

(1) The amounts of the following items are not included in the total charge for credit in relation to an agreement—

(a) any charge payable under the transaction to the creditor upon failure by the debtor or a relative of his to do or to refrain from doing anything which he is required to do or to refrain from doing, as the case may be;

(b) any charge—
  (i) which is payable by the creditor to any person upon failure by the debtor or a relative of his to do or to refrain from doing anything which he is required under the transaction to do or to refrain from doing, as the case may be, and
  (ii) which the creditor may under the transaction require the debtor or a relative of his to pay to him or to another person on his behalf;

(c) any charge relating to an agreement which is an agreement to finance a transaction of a description referred to in paragraph (a) or (b) of section 11(1) of the Act, being a charge which would be payable if the transaction were for cash;

(d) any charge [(other than a fee or commission charged by a credit-broker)] not within sub-paragraph (c) above—
  (i) of a description which relates to services or benefits incidental to the agreement and also to other services or benefits which may be supplied to the debtor, and
  (ii) which is payable pursuant to an obligation incurred by the debtor under arrangements effected before he applies to enter into the agreement, not being arrangements under which the debtor is bound to enter into any personal credit agreement;

(e) subject to paragraph (2) below, any charge under arrangements for the care, maintenance or protection of any land or goods;

(f) charges for money transmission services relating to an arrangement for a current account whereby the debtor may, by cheques or similar orders payable to himself or to any other person, obtain or have the use of money held or made available by the creditor and which records alterations in the financial relationship between the creditor and debtor, being charges which vary with the use made by the debtor of the arrangement.

[(g) any charge for a guarantee other than a guarantee—
  (i) which is required by the creditor as a condition of making the agreement, and
  (ii) the purpose of which is to ensure complete or partial repayment of the credit, and complete or partial payment to the creditor of such of those charges included in the total charge for credit as are payable to him under the transaction, in the event of the death, invalidity, illness or unemployment of the debtor;]

(h) charges for the transfer of funds (other than charges within sub-paragraph (f) above) and charges for keeping an account intended to receive payments towards the repayment of the credit and the payment of interest and other charges, except where the debtor does not have reasonable freedom of choice in the matter and where such charges are abnormally high; but this sub-paragraph does not exclude from the total charge for credit charges for collection of the payments to which it refers, whether such payments are made in cash or otherwise;

(i) a premium under a contract of insurance other than a contract of insurance referred to in regulation 4(c) above.]

(2) Paragraph (1) above has effect only—

(a) in the case of a charge within sub-paragraph (e), where, in pursuance of the arrangements—
  (i) the services are to be performed if, after the date of the making of the agreement, the condition of the land or goods becomes or is in immediate danger of becoming such that the land or goods cannot reasonably be enjoyed or used, and
  (ii) the charge will not accrue unless the services are performed; and

(b) in the case of any other charge within sub-paragraph (e) . . . —
  (i) where provision of substantially the same description as that to which the arrangements . . . relate is available under comparable arrangements from a person who is not the creditor or a supplier or a credit-broker who introduced the debtor and the creditor, and

> (ii)   *where the arrangements . . .   are made with a person chosen by the debtor, and*
> (iii) *if, in accordance with the transaction, the consent of the creditor or of a supplier or of the credit-broker who introduced the debtor and the creditor is required to the making of the arrangements . . . , where the transaction provides that such consent may not be unreasonably withheld whether because no incidental benefit will or may accrue to the creditor or to the supplier or to the credit-broker or on any other ground;*

and references in this paragraph to the creditor, a supplier and a credit-broker include references to his near relative, his partner and a member of a group of which he is a member, to any person nominated by him or any such person in relation to the arrangements . . . , and to a near relative of his partner; and "near relative" means, in relation to any person, the husband, wife, father, mother, brother, sister, son or daughter of that person and "group" means the person (including a company) having control of a company together with all the companies directly or indirectly controlled by him.

NOTES

Revoked as noted to the start of these Regulations.

Para (1): in sub-para (d) words in square brackets inserted by the Consumer Credit (Total Charge for Credit and Rebate on Early Settlement) (Amendment) Regulations 1989, SI 1989/596, reg 2(b); sub-paras (g)–(i) substituted, for original sub-paras (g)–(l), by the Consumer Credit (Total Charge for Credit, Agreements and Advertisements) (Amendment) Regulations 1999, SI 1999/3177, reg 3(g).

Para (2): words omitted revoked by SI 1999/3177, reg 3(h).

PART III
RATE OF TOTAL CHARGE FOR CREDIT

[2.7]
6   Rate of total charge for credit

The rate of the total charge for credit in the case of an actual or prospective agreement shall be the annual percentage rate of charge determined in accordance with the following provisions of this Part of these Regulations and [(where it has more than one decimal place) rounded to one decimal place in accordance with regulation 6A below].

NOTES

Revoked as noted to the start of these Regulations.

Words in square brackets substituted by the Consumer Credit (Total Charge for Credit, Agreements and Advertisements) (Amendment) Regulations 1999, SI 1999/3177, reg 3(i).

[2.8]
[6A

The annual percentage rate of charge referred to in regulation 6 above shall be rounded to one decimal place as follows—

> (a)   *where the figure at the second decimal place is greater than or equal to 5, the figure at the first decimal place shall be increased by one and the decimal place (or places) following the first decimal place shall be disregarded; and*
> (b)   *where the figure at the second decimal place is less than 5, that decimal place and any decimal places following it shall be disregarded.]*

NOTES

Inserted by the Consumer Credit (Total Charge for Credit, Agreements and Advertisements) (Amendment) Regulations 1999, SI 1999/3177, reg 3(j), and revoked as noted to the start of these Regulations.

[2.9]
[7   Calculation where a period rate is charged

(1)   Subject to paragraph (4) below, the annual percentage rate of charge is the rate for i which satisfies the equation set out in paragraph (2) below, expressed as a percentage.

(2)   The equation referred to in paragraph (1) above is—

$$\sum_{K=1}^{K=m} \frac{A_K}{(1+i)^{t_K}} = \sum_{K'=1}^{K'=m'} \frac{A'_{K'}}{(1+i)^{t_{K'}}}$$

[where
> *K is the number identifying a particular advance of credit;*
> *K' is the number identifying a particular instalment;*
> *A_K is the amount of advance K;*
> *$A'_{K'}$ is the amount of instalment K';*
> *$\sum$ represents the sum of all the terms indicated;*
> *m is the number of advances of credit;*
> *m' is the total number of instalments;*

'K is the interval, expressed in years, between the relevant date and the date of the second advance and those of any subsequent advances numbered three to m; and

'K' is the interval, expressed in years, between the relevant date and the dates of instalments numbered one to m'.

(3)   In paragraph (2) above, references to instalments are references to any payment made by or on behalf of the debtor or a relative of his which comprises—

(a)   *a repayment of all or part of the credit under the agreement;*

(b)   *a payment of all or part of the total charge for credit; or*

(c)   *both a repayment of all or part of the credit and a payment of all or part of the total charge for credit.*

(4)   Where more than one rate is given under paragraph (1) above, the annual percentage rate of charge is the positive rate nearest to zero or, if no positive rate is so given, the negative rate nearest to zero.]

NOTES

Substituted, for original regs 7–9, by the Consumer Credit (Total Charge for Credit, Agreements and Advertisements) (Amendment) Regulations 1999, SI 1999/3177, reg 3(k), and revoked as noted to the start of these Regulations.

10   *(Revoked by the Consumer Credit (Total Charge for Credit, Agreements and Advertisements) (Amendment) Regulations 1999, SI 1999/3177, reg 3(l).)*

[2.10]
11   Computation of time

(1)   This regulation has effect for determining the length of any period for the purposes of calculations under this Part of these Regulations.

(2)   A period which is not a whole number of calendar months or a whole number of weeks shall be counted in years and days.

(3)   Subject to paragraph (4) below, a period which is a whole number of calendar months or a whole number of weeks shall be counted in calendar months or in weeks, as the case may be.

(4)   Where a period is both a whole number of calendar months and a whole number of weeks and—

(a)   *one repayment only is to be made, the period shall be counted in calendar months, or*

(b)   *more than one repayment is to be made,—*

(i)   *if all such repayments are to be made at intervals from the relevant date of one or more weeks, the period shall be counted in weeks, and*

(ii)   *in any other case, the period shall be counted in calendar months.*

(5)   A period which is to be counted—

(a)   *in calendar months shall be taken to be of a length equal to the relevant number of twelfth parts of a year, and*

(b)   *in weeks, shall be taken to be of a length equal to the relevant number of fifty-second parts of a year.*

[(6)   A day may be taken to be either—

(a)   *one three hundred and sixty-fifth part of a year or, if it is a leap year, one three hundred and sixty-sixth part of a year; or*

(b)   *1/365.25 of a year.]*

(7)   Every day shall be taken to be a working day.

NOTES

Revoked as noted to the start of these Regulations.

Para (6): substituted by the Consumer Credit (Total Charge for Credit, Agreements and Advertisements) (Amendment) Regulations 1999, SI 1999/3177, reg 3(m).

PART IV
ASSUMPTIONS FOR CALCULATIONS

[2.11]
12   Effect of Part IV

(1)   The provisions of this Part of these Regulations shall have effect as the case may require for the purpose of the calculation of the total charge for credit under Part II above and of the rate of such charge under Part III above in relation to any actual or prospective agreement in respect of matters necessary for the calculation which cannot be ascertained by the creditor at the date of the making of the agreement.

(2)   In a case where apart from this paragraph regulation 13 below and one or more other provisions of this Part would fall to be applied the said regulation 13 shall be applied first.

NOTES

Revoked as noted to the start of these Regulations.

[2.12]
13   Assumption about the amount of credit
Where the amount of the credit to be provided under the agreement cannot be ascertained at the date of the making of the agreement,—
- *(a)   in the case of an agreement for running-account credit under which there is a credit limit, that amount shall be taken to be such credit limit; and*
- *(b)   in any other case, that amount shall be taken to be £100.*

NOTES
Revoked as noted to the start of these Regulations.

[2.13]
14   Assumption about period for which credit is provided
Where the period for which credit is to be provided is not ascertainable at the date of the making of the agreement, it shall be assumed that credit is provided for one year beginning with the relevant date.

NOTES
Revoked as noted to the start of these Regulations.

[2.14]
15   Assumption about index-linked rates and amounts
[Subject to regulation 15A below,] where the rate or amount of any item included in the total charge for credit or the amount of any repayment of credit under a transaction falls to be ascertained thereunder by reference to the level of any index or other factor in accordance with any formula specified therein, the rate or amount, as the case may be, shall be taken to be the rate or amount so ascertained, the formula being applied as if the level of such index or other factor subsisting at the date of the making of the agreement were that subsisting at the date by reference to which the formula is to be applied.

NOTES
Revoked as noted to the start of these Regulations.
Words in square brackets inserted by the Consumer Credit (Total Charge for Credit, Agreements and Advertisements) (Amendment) Regulations 1999, SI 1999/3177, reg 3(n).

[2.15]
[15A   Assumptions about variations of interest rates in land-related agreements
(1)   This regulation applies to any land-related agreement which provides for the possibility of any variation of the rate of interest if it is to be assumed, by virtue of regulation 2(1)(e) above, that the variation will take place but the amount of the variation cannot be ascertained at the date of the making of the agreement.

(2)   In this regulation—
  "initial standard variable rate" means—
- *(a)   the standard variable rate of interest which would be applied by the creditor to the agreement on the date of the making of the agreement if the agreement provided for interest to be paid at the creditor's standard variable rate with effect from that date, or*
- *(b)   if there is no such rate, the standard variable rate of interest applied by the creditor on the date of the making of the agreement in question to other land-related agreements or, where there is more than one such rate, the highest such rate,*
  taking no account (for the avoidance of doubt) of any discount or other reduction to which the debtor would or might be entitled; and
  "varied rate" means any rate of interest charged when a variation of the rate of interest is to be assumed to take place by virtue of regulation 2(1)(e) above.

(3)   Where a land-related agreement provides a formula for calculating a varied rate by reference to a standard variable rate of interest applied by the creditor, or any other fluctuating rate of interest, but does not enable the varied rate to be ascertained at the date of the making of the agreement because it is not known on that date what the standard variable rate will be or (as the case may be) at what level the fluctuating rate will be fixed when the varied rate falls to be calculated, it shall be assumed that that rate or level will be the same as the initial standard variable rate.

(4)   Where a land-related agreement provides for the possibility of any variation in the rate of interest (other than a variation referred to in paragraph (3) above) which it is to be assumed, by virtue of regulation 2(1)(e) above, will take place but does not enable the amount of that variation to be ascertained at the date of the making of the agreement, it shall be assumed that the varied rate will be the same as the initial standard variable rate.]

NOTES
Inserted by the Consumer Credit (Total Charge for Credit, Agreements and Advertisements) (Amendment) Regulations 1999, SI 1999/3177, reg 3(n), and revoked as noted to the start of these Regulations.

[2.16]
16   Assumption about changes in charges
Where—
   (a)   *the period for which the credit or any part thereof is to be or may be provided cannot be ascertained at the date of the making of the agreement; and*
   (b)   *the rate or amount of any item included in the total charge for credit will change at a time provided in the transaction within one year beginning with the relevant date,*
the rate or amount shall be taken to be the highest rate or amount at any time obtaining under the transaction in that year.

NOTES
Revoked as noted to the start of these Regulations.

[2.17]
17   Assumption about time of provision of credit
Where the earliest date on which credit is to be provided cannot be ascertained at the date of the making of the agreement, it shall be assumed that credit is provided on that date.

NOTES
Revoked as noted to the start of these Regulations.

[2.18]
18   Assumptions about time of payment of charges
In the case of any transaction it shall be assumed—
   (a)   *that a charge payable at a time which cannot be ascertained at the date of the making of the agreement shall be payable on the relevant date or, where it may reasonably be expected that a debtor will not make payment on that date, on the earliest date at which it may reasonably be expected that he will make payment; or*
   (b)   *where more than one payment of a charge of the same description falls to be made at times which cannot be ascertained at the date of the making of the agreement, that the first such payment will be payable on the relevant date (or, where it may reasonably be expected that a debtor will not make payment on that date, at the earliest date on which it may reasonably be expected that he will make payment), that the last such payment will be payable at the end of the period for which credit is provided and that all other such payments (if any) will be payable at equal intervals between such times,*
as the case may require.

NOTES
Revoked as noted to the start of these Regulations.

SUPPLY OF SERVICES (EXCLUSION OF IMPLIED TERMS) ORDER 1982

(SI 1982/1771)

NOTES
Made: 8 December 1982.
Authority: Supply of Goods and Services Act 1982, s 12(4).
Commencement: 4 July 1983.

[2.19]
1
This Order may be cited as the Supply of Services (Exclusion of Implied Terms) Order 1982 and shall come into operation on 4th July 1983.

[2.20]
2
Section 13 of the Supply of Goods and Services Act 1982 (which provides that, in a contract for the supply of a service where the supplier is acting in the course of a business, there is an implied term that the supplier will carry out the service with reasonable care and skill) shall not apply to the following services—

(1)   the services of an advocate in court or before any tribunal, inquiry or arbitrator and in carrying out preliminary work directly affecting the conduct of the hearing;

(2)   the services rendered to a company by a director of the company in his capacity as such.

SUPPLY OF SERVICES (EXCLUSION OF IMPLIED TERMS) ORDER 1983

(SI 1983/902)

NOTES
Made: 24 June 1983.
Authority: Supply of Goods and Services Act 1982, s 12(4).
Commencement: 4 July 1983.

[2.21]
1

This Order may be cited as the Supply of Services (Exclusion of Implied Terms) Order 1983 and shall come into operation on 4th July 1983.

[2.22]
2

(1)   Section 13 of the Supply of Goods and Services Act 1982 (which provides that, in a contract for the supply of a service where the supplier is acting in the course of a business, there is an implied term that the supplier will carry out the service with reasonable care and skill) shall not apply to the following services—

(a)   the services rendered to a building society by a director of the society in his capacity as such;

(b)   the services rendered to a society registered or deemed to be registered under the Industrial and Provident Societies Act 1965 or the Industrial and Provident Societies Act (Northern Ireland) 1969 by any member of the committee of management or other directing body of such a society in his capacity as such.

(2)   In this Article, "building society" and "director" shall have the same meaning as in the Building Societies Act 1962 or the Building Societies Act (Northern Ireland) 1967.

NOTES
Industrial and Provident Societies Act 1965: repealed by the Co-operative and Community Benefit Societies Act 2014, s 151(4), Sch 7.

CONSUMER CREDIT (AGREEMENTS) REGULATIONS 1983

(SI 1983/1553)

NOTES
Made: 19 January 2004.
Authority: Consumer Credit Act 1974, ss 60, 61(1)(a), 105(9), 114(1), 127(3), 182(2), 189(1).
Commencement: 19 May 1985; see reg 1(1).

ARRANGEMENT OF REGULATIONS

SCHEDULES

Part 2   Statutory Instruments

[2.23]
1 Citation, commencement and interpretation

(1) These Regulations may be cited as the Consumer Credit (Agreements) Regulations 1983 and shall come into operation on 19th May 1985.

(2) In these Regulations, unless the context otherwise requires—

"the Act" means the Consumer Credit Act 1974;

"advance payment" includes any deposit and in relation to a regulated consumer credit agreement includes also any part-exchange allowance in respect of any goods agreed in antecedent negotiations to be taken by the creditor in part-exchange but does not include a repayment of credit or any insurance premium or any amount entering into the total charge for credit;

"the APR" means the annual percentage rate of charge for credit determined in accordance with the [total charge for credit rules] and Schedule 7 to, these Regulations and, in the case of modifying agreements, Regulation 7 of, and Part I of Schedule 8 to, these Regulations;

"cancellable agreement" includes an agreement which is a modifying agreement treated under section 82(5) of the Act as a cancellable agreement;

"cash price" in relation to any goods, services, land or other things means the price or charge at which the goods, services, land or other things may be purchased by, or supplied to, the debtor for cash;

[. . .]

["contract of shortfall insurance" means anything in writing which contains or purports to contain some promise or assurance (however worded or presented) that if a sum payable under a contract of insurance against loss of or damage to goods is less than the amount necessary to defray—

(a)   any amount of credit provided to finance the purchase of those goods; and

(b)   any other amount included in the total charge for that credit,

to the extent that these remain unpaid at the date of the loss or damage, a sum up to but not exceeding that shortfall will be paid;]

"earlier credit agreement" means an earlier agreement for the provision of credit;

"earlier hire agreement" means an earlier agreement for the bailment or the hiring of goods;

["guarantee of goods" means anything in writing which contains or purports to contain some promise or assurance (however worded or presented) that defects in goods will be made good by complete or partial replacement, or by repair, monetary compensation or otherwise;]

"hire payment" means any payment to be made by the hirer in relation to any period in consideration of the bailment or hiring to him of goods under a regulated consumer hire agreement;

"lettering" includes figures and symbols;

"modified agreement" means an earlier agreement as varied or supplemented by a modifying agreement, which is treated as—

(a)   revoking the earlier agreement, and

(b)   containing provisions reproducing the combined effect of the two agreements;

["the relevant date" means—

(a)   where a date is specified in or determinable under an agreement at the date of its making as that on which the debtor is entitled to require the provision of anything under the agreement, the earliest such date, or

(b)   where no such date is specified or determinable, the date of the making of the agreement;]

"total charge for credit" shall be determined in accordance with the [total charge for credit rules] [and Schedule 7 to these Regulations] and, in the case of modifying agreements, Regulation 7 of, and Part I of Schedule 8 to, these Regulations; and

["the total charge for credit rules" means rules made by the Financial Conduct Authority under article 60M of the Financial Services and Markets Act 2000 (Regulated Activities) Order 2001 for the purposes of Chapter 14A of Part 2 of that Order;]

[(2A) References in these Regulations to contracts of insurance must be read with—
(a) section 22 of the Financial Services and Markets Act 2000;
(b) any relevant order under that section; and
(c) Schedule 2 to that Act.]

(3) In these Regulations, any reference to a repayment is a reference to—
(a) a repayment of the whole or any part of the credit;
(b) a payment of the whole or any part of the total charge for credit; or
(c) a combination of such repayments and payments.

NOTES

Para (2): in definition "the APR" words in square brackets, in definition "total charge for credit" words in first pair of square brackets, and definition "the total charge for credit rules", substituted, for original definition "the Total Charge for Credit Regulations", by the Financial Services and Markets Act 2000 (Regulated Activities) (Amendment) (No 2) Order 2013, SI 2013/1881, art 23(1)–(3), for transitional provisions see Pt 8 thereof at **[2.1007]**; definition "contract of insurance" (omitted) inserted by the Consumer Credit (Agreements) (Amendment) Regulations 1984, SI 1984/1600, reg 2(a) and revoked by the Financial Services and Markets Act 2000 (Consequential Amendments and Repeals) Order 2001, SI 2001/3649, art 375(1); definition "contract of shortfall insurance" and words in second pair of square brackets in definition "total charge for credit" inserted by the Consumer Credit (Agreements) (Amendment) Regulations 2004, SI 2004/1482, regs 2, 3; definition "guarantee of goods" inserted by SI 1984/1600, reg 2(a); definition "the relevant date" substituted by the Consumer Credit (EU Directive) Regulations 2010, SI 2010/1010, regs 51, 52(a) (as substituted by the Consumer Credit (Amendment) Regulations 2010, SI 2010/1969, regs 4, 12), with effect in relation to certain agreements entered into before 1 February 2011, as provided for in regs 101, 101A of SI 2010/1010 at **[2.804]**, **[2.805]**.

Para (2A): inserted by SI 2001/3649, art 375(2).

[2.24]
[2 Form and content of regulated consumer credit agreements

(1) Subject to paragraphs (2) and (9) below, documents embodying regulated consumer credit agreements (other than modifying agreements) shall contain the information set out in Column 2 of Schedule 1 to these Regulations in so far as it relates to the type of agreement referred to in Column 1.

(2) Where any information about financial and related particulars set out in paragraphs 9 to 11 of Schedule 1 to these Regulations cannot be exactly ascertained by the creditor, estimated information based on the assumptions referred to in paragraph 10 of that Schedule, where applicable, and otherwise such assumptions as the creditor may reasonably make in all the circumstances of the case and a statement of the assumptions made shall be included in documents embodying regulated consumer credit agreements.

(3) Subject to paragraph (9) below, documents embodying regulated consumer credit agreements, other than agreements of the description specified in the Schedule to the Consumer Credit (Notices of Cancellation Rights) (Exemptions) Regulations 1983 in relation to which there are no charges forming part of the total charge for credit (in this regulation referred to as "exempted agreements"), shall contain statements of the protection and remedies available to debtors under the Act, in the Form numbered in Column 1 of Part 1 of Schedule 2 to these Regulations and set out in Column 3, in so far as they relate to the type of agreement referred to in Column 2.

(4) Subject to paragraphs (5) and (9) below, the information, statements of the protection and remedies, signature and separate boxes which this regulation requires documents embodying regulated consumer credit agreements to contain, shall be set out in the order given by paragraphs (a) to (f) below under, where applicable, the headings specified below—
(a) the nature of the agreement as set out in paragraph 1 of Schedule 1 to these Regulations;
(b) the parties to the agreement as set out in paragraph 2 of Schedule 1 to these Regulations;
[(c) under the heading "Key Financial Information", the financial and related particulars set out in paragraphs 6 to 8B, 11 to 14 and 15 to 17 of Schedule 1 to these Regulations;]
(d) under the heading "Other Financial Information", the financial and related particulars set out in paragraphs 3 to 5, 9, 10, 14A and 18 to 19A of Schedule 1 to these regulations;
(e) under the heading "Key Information"—
(i) the information set out in paragraphs 20 to 24 of Schedule 1 to these Regulations; and
(ii) the statements of protection and remedies set out in Schedule 2 to these Regulations; and
(f) the signature box and, where applicable, the separate box required by paragraph (7)(b) below;

and such information, statements of protection and remedies, signature and separate boxes shall be shown together as a whole and shall not be preceded by any information apart from trade names, logos or the reference number of the agreement or interspersed with any other information or

Part 2 Statutory Instruments

wording apart from subtotals of total amounts and cross references to the terms of the agreement.

(5)   In the case of documents embodying restricted-use debtor-creditor-supplier agreements for fixed-sum credit to finance a transaction comprising the acquisition of goods, services, land or other things specified in the agreement or identified and agreed on at the time the agreement is made and relating to more than one description of goods, services, land or other things, the cash prices, and the total cash price, referred to in paragraph 4 of Schedule 1 to these Regulations may be shown in a schedule to such document together with each description of the goods, services, land or other things, provided that the total cash price and a reference to the schedule to such document are shown together with the information required by paragraph (4)(d) above.

(6)   The APR referred to in paragraphs 15 to 17 of Schedule 1 to these Regulations shall in documents embodying regulated consumer credit agreements, other than exempted agreements—

    (a)   be denoted as "APR" or "annual percentage rate" or "annual percentage rate of the total charge for credit; and

    (b)   where it is subject to change, be accompanied by the word "variable".

(7)   Documents embodying regulated consumer credit agreements other than exempted agreements shall, subject to paragraph (9) below, contain a signature box in the Form numbered in Column 1 of Part 1 of Schedule 5 to these Regulations and set out in Column 3 in so far as it relates to the type of agreement referred to in Column 2 and shall—

    (a)   if—

        (i)   the documents embody a principal agreement and subsidiary agreement to which paragraph (9) below applies; or

        (ii)   at the time of entering into the agreement the debtor is also purchasing an optional contract of insurance which will be financed by credit advanced under that agreement,

    contain a form of consent in the Form set out in Part III of Schedule 5 immediately below the signature box required by this paragraph; and

    (b)   if the agreement is one to which section 58(1) of the Act applies, is a cancellable agreement or is an agreement under which a person takes any article in pawn and under which the pawn-receipt is not separate from the document embodying the agreement, contain a separate box immediately above, below or adjacent to the signature box in which shall be included the appropriate statements specified in Forms 1 and 4 to 6 of Part 1, and in Part II, of Schedule 2.

(8)   Paragraph (9) applies to documents embodying a debtor-creditor-supplier agreement falling within section 12(a) of the Act or a debtor-creditor agreement (in this paragraph and paragraph (9) in either case referred to as "the principal agreement") and also embodying, or containing the option of, a debtor-creditor-supplier agreement falling within section 12(b) of the Act (in this paragraph and paragraph (9) referred to as "the subsidiary agreement") where the subsidiary agreement is to finance a premium under one or more of—

    (a)   a contract of insurance to provide a sum payable in the event of the death of a debtor or a debtor suffering one or more of the following—

        (i)   accident;

        (ii)   sickness; and

        (iii)   unemployment,

    at any time before the credit under the principal agreement and the subsidiary agreement has been repaid, where the sum payable does not exceed the amount sufficient to defray the sums payable to the creditor in respect of that credit and of the total charge for credit and where the policy monies payable under the contract of insurance are to be used for a repayment under the principal agreement and the subsidiary agreement;

    (b)   a contract of shortfall insurance; and

    (c)   a contract of insurance in so far as it relates to the guarantee of goods.

(9)   Documents to which this paragraph applies may contain instead of the headings specified in paragraph 1 of Schedules 1 or 8 to these Regulations, statements of protection and remedies available to debtors under the Act and signature boxes that would otherwise apply—

    (a)   a heading and signature box in so far as they relate to the principal agreement;

    (b)   a statement in Form 14 of Part I of Schedule 2 to these Regulations; and

    (c)   other statements (other than in Form 16 of Part I of Schedule 2) of the protection and remedies available to debtors under the Act in so far as they relate to the principal agreement.

(10)   Documents embodying regulated consumer credit agreements shall embody any security provided in relation to the regulated agreement by the debtor.]

NOTES

Substituted by the Consumer Credit (Agreements) (Amendment) Regulations 2004, SI 2004/1482, regs 2, 4 (as amended by SI 2004/2619, reg 2(1), (2)).

[2.25]
3   Form and content of regulated consumer hire agreements

(1)   Subject to paragraph (2) below, documents embodying regulated consumer hire agreements (other than modifying agreements) shall contain the information set out in Column 2 of Schedule 3 to these Regulations in so far as it relates to the type of agreement referred to in Column 1.

(2)   Where any information about financial and related particulars set out in paragraphs 5 and 6 of Schedule 3 to these Regulations cannot be exactly ascertained by the owner, estimated information based on such assumptions as the owner may reasonably make in all the circumstances of the case and an indication of the assumptions made shall be included in documents embodying regulated consumer hire agreements.

(3)   Documents embodying regulated consumer hire agreements shall contain statements of the protection and remedies available to hirers under the Act, in the Form numbered in Column 1 of Schedule 4 to these Regulations and set out in Column 3, in so far as they relate to the type of agreement referred to in Column 2.

[(4)   Subject to paragraph (5) below the information, statements of the protection and remedies, signature and separate boxes which this regulation requires documents embodying regulated consumer hire agreements to contain, shall be set out in the order given by paragraphs (a) to (e) below under, where applicable, the headings specified below—

   (a)   the nature of the agreement as set out in paragraph 1 of Schedule 3 to these Regulations;
   (b)   the parties to the agreement as set out in paragraph 2 of Schedule 3 to these Regulations;
   (c)   under the heading "Key Financial Information", the financial and related particulars set out in paragraphs 3 to 8 of Schedule 3 to these Regulations;
   (d)   under the heading "Key Information"—
      (i)   the information set out in paragraphs 9 to 11 of Schedule 3 to these Regulations; and
      (ii)   the statements of protection and remedies set out in Schedule 4 to these Regulations; and
   (e)   the signature box and, where applicable, the separate box required by paragraph (6) below,
and such information, statements of protection and remedies, signature and separate boxes shall be shown together as a whole and shall not be preceded by any information apart from trade names, logos or the reference number of the agreement or interspersed with any other information or wording apart from subtotals of total amounts and cross references to the terms of the agreement.]

(5)   In the case of documents embodying consumer hire agreements relating to more than one description of goods to be bailed or hired under the agreement, the list or other description of the goods referred to in paragraph 3 of Schedule 3 to these Regulations may be shown in a schedule to such document, provided that a reference to the schedule to such document is shown together with the remaining financial and related particulars specified in [paragraph (4)(c) above].

(6)   Documents embodying regulated consumer hire agreements shall contain a signature box in the Form numbered in Column 1 of Part II of Schedule 5 to these Regulations and set out in Column 3, so far as it relates to the type of agreement referred to in Column 2 and shall, if the agreement is one to which section 58(1) of the Act applies or is a cancellable agreement, contain a separate box immediately above, below or adjacent to the signature box in which shall be included the appropriate statements specified in [Forms 1, 4 and 5] of Schedule 4.

(7)   Documents embodying regulated consumer hire agreements shall embody any security provided in relation to the regulated agreement by the hirer.

NOTES
   Para (4): substituted by the Consumer Credit (Agreements) (Amendment) Regulations 2004, SI 2004/1482, regs 2, 5(1), (2).
   Para (5): in square brackets substituted by SI 2004/1482, regs 2, 5(1), (3).
   Para (6): in square brackets substituted by SI 2004/1482, regs 2, 5(1), (4) (as amended by SI 2004/2619, reg 2(1), (3)).

[2.26]
4   Pawn-receipts

Where a pawn-receipt is given under section 114(1) of the Act, by a person who takes any article in pawn under a regulated consumer credit agreement or a modifying agreement varying or supplementing an earlier credit agreement which is, or is treated under section 82(3) of the Act as, a regulated agreement, and where the pawn-receipt is not separate from any document embodying such an agreement, it shall—

   (a)   contain the information set out in paragraphs 1, 2 and 20 of Schedule 1 to these Regulations, or, in the case of a modifying agreement varying or supplementing an earlier credit agreement, in paragraphs 1, 2 and 20 of Part I of Schedule 8; and
   (b)   contain a notice in the Form [numbered 18] in Column 1 of Part II of Schedule 2 to these Regulations and set out in Column 3.

NOTES
   Para (b): words in square brackets substituted by the Consumer Credit (Agreements) (Amendment) Regulations 2004, SI 2004/1482, regs 2, 6.

Part 2   Statutory Instruments

[2.27]
5   Statutory Forms

(1)   The wording of any Form specified in Schedules 2, 4 and 5 to these Regulations shall be reproduced in documents embodying regulated agreements without any alteration or addition, except that—

    (a)   the words "the creditor" or "the owner" may be replaced by the name of the creditor or owner, by the expression by which the creditor or owner is referred to in the agreement or by an appropriate pronoun, and any consequential changes to pronouns and verbs or other consequential grammatical changes may be made;

    (b)   the word "DEBTOR" may be replaced by "BORROWER" or "CUSTOMER" and the word "Debtor(s)" may be replaced by "Borrower(s)" or "Customer(s)"; and

    (c)   every Form shall be completed in accordance with any footnote.

(2)   Any such footnote shall not be treated as part of any Form specified in the said Schedules and may be reproduced in addition to any such Form.

(3)   Where any such footnote requires any words to be omitted, those words shall be omitted or deleted.

(4)   Where words are shown in capital letters in any Form specified in Schedule 2, 4 or 5 to these Regulations, and are reproduced in documents embodying regulated agreements, they shall be afforded more prominence (whether by capital letters, underlining, larger or bold print or otherwise) than any other lettering in that Form except lettering inserted in accordance with paragraph (1)(c) above and no less prominence than that given to any other information in the document apart from the heading to the document, . . . trade names, names of parties to the agreement or lettering in the document inserted in handwriting.

NOTES

   Para (4): words omitted revoked by the Consumer Credit (Agreements) (Amendment) Regulations 2004, SI 2004/1482, regs 2, 7.

[2.28]
6   Signing of agreement

(1)   The terms specified in Column 2 of Schedule 6 to these Regulations in relation to the type of regulated agreement referred to in Column 1 (and no other terms) are hereby prescribed for the purposes of section 61(1)(a) of the Act (the terms which must be contained in a document if a regulated agreement is not to be improperly executed) and of section 127(3) (the terms which must be contained in a document before any enforcement order can be made under section 65(1), if section 61(1)(a) was not complied with).

[(2)   The lettering of the terms of the agreement included in the document referred to in section 61(1)(a) of the Act, containing all the prescribed terms of the regulated agreement, and of the information contained in that document for the purpose of conforming to these Regulations shall—

    (a)   apart from any signature, be easily legible and, where applicable, be of a colour which is readily distinguishable from the background medium upon which the information is displayed; and

    (b)   apart from that inserted in handwriting, be of equal prominence, except that headings, trade names and names of parties to the agreement may be afforded more prominence whether by capital letters, underlining, larger or bold print or otherwise.]

(3)   The signature of the said document shall be made in the following manner—

    (a)   by the debtor or hirer, or by or on behalf of the debtor or hirer in the case of a partnership or an unincorporated body of persons, in the space in the document indicated for the purpose, and, subject to sub-paragraph (c) below, the date of the signature shall be inserted in the space in the document indicated for the purpose;

    (b)   by the creditor or owner, or by a person on his behalf, outside any signature box in which the debtor or hirer may sign and, subject to sub-paragraph (c) below, the date of the signature shall be inserted outside any such signature box;

    (c)   in the case of a regulated agreement which is not a cancellable agreement, the date on which the unexecuted agreement becomes an executed agreement may be inserted in the document and in such a case any other date specified in paragraphs (a) and (b) above need not be inserted; and

    (d)   nothing in this Regulation shall prohibit the inclusion in the said document, near to any such signature, of the signature by any witness outside any signature box in which the debtor or hirer may sign.

(4)   In Scotland any provision in paragraph (3) above requiring the said document to be signed shall be complied with by a body corporate if the document is properly executed in accordance with the law of Scotland.

[(5)   Where an agreement is intended to be concluded by the use of an electronic communication nothing in this Regulation shall prohibit the inclusion in the signature box of information about the process or means of providing, communicating or verifying the signature to be made by the debtor or hirer.]

NOTES

Para (2): substituted by the Consumer Credit (Agreements) (Amendment) Regulations 2004, SI 2004/1482, regs 2, 8.

Para (5): inserted by the Consumer Credit Act 1974 (Electronic Communications) Order 2004, SI 2004/3236, art 4(1), (2)(b).

S 127(3): repealed, subject to transitional provisions and savings, by the Consumer Credit Act 2006, ss 15, 69(1), 70, Sch 3, paras 1, 11(b), Sch 4.

[2.29]
7   Modifying agreements which are, or are treated as, regulated agreements

(1)   The provisions of these Regulations shall apply to modifying agreements which vary or supplement earlier credit agreements or earlier hire agreements and which are, or are treated under section 82(3) of the Act as, regulated agreements, subject as hereinafter mentioned.

(2)   Subject to paragraphs (3) and (12) below, documents embodying modifying agreements varying or supplementing earlier credit agreements shall contain the information set out in Column 2 of Part I of Schedule 8 to these Regulations in so far as it relates to the type of modifying agreement referred to in Column 1.

[(3)   Where any information about financial and related particulars set out in paragraphs 8 to 10 of Part 1 of Schedule 8 to these Regulations cannot be exactly ascertained by the creditor, estimated information based on the assumptions referred to in paragraph 9 of that Schedule, where applicable, and otherwise such assumptions as the creditor may reasonably make in all the circumstances of the case and a statement of the assumptions made shall be included in documents embodying modifying agreements varying or supplementing earlier credit agreements.]

[(4)   Subject to paragraph (5) below and regulation 2(9), the information, statements of the protection and remedies, signature and separate boxes which under these Regulations must be contained in documents embodying modifying agreements varying or supplementing earlier credit agreements in relation to the credit being provided under the modifying agreement, shall be set out in the order given by paragraphs (a) to (f) below under, where applicable, the headings specified below—

   (a)   the nature of the agreement as set out in paragraph 1 of Part 1 of Schedule 8 to these Regulations;

   (b)   parties to the agreement as set out in paragraph 2 of Part 1 of Schedule 8 to these Regulations;

   (c)   under the heading "Key Financial Information", the financial and related particulars set out in paragraphs 5 to 7B, 10 to 13 and 14 to 17 of Part 1 of Schedule 8 to these Regulations;

   (d)   under the heading "Other Financial Information", the financial and related particulars set out in paragraphs 3, 4, 8, 9, 13A and 18 to 19A of Part 1 of Schedule 8 to these Regulations;

   (e)   under the heading "Key Information"—

      (i)   the information set out in paragraphs 20 to 24 of Part 1 of Schedule 8 to these Regulations; and

      (ii)   the statements of protection and remedies set out in Schedule 2 to these Regulations; and

   (f)   the signature box and, where applicable, separate box required by regulation 2(7)(b),

and such information, statements of protection and remedies, signature and separate boxes shall be shown together as a whole and shall not be preceded by any information apart from trade names, logos or the reference number of the agreement or interspersed with any other information or wording apart from subtotals of total amounts and cross references to the terms of the agreement.]

(5)   In the case of documents embodying modifying agreements varying or supplementing earlier restricted-use debtor-creditor-supplier agreements for fixed-sum credit which were to finance a transaction comprising the acquisition of goods, services, land or other things specified in the earlier agreement or identified and agreed on at the time the earlier agreement was made and relating to more than one description of goods, services, land or other things, the cash prices, and the total cash price, referred to in paragraph 3 of Part I of Schedule 8 to these Regulations may be shown in a schedule to such document together with each description of the goods, services, land or other things, provided that the total cash price and a reference to the schedule to such document are shown together with the [the information required by paragraph (4)(d) above].

(6)   The APR referred to in paragraphs 14 to 17 of Part I of Schedule 8 to these Regulations shall in documents embodying agreements varying or supplementing earlier credit agreements—

   (a)   be denoted as "APR" or "annual percentage rate" or "annual percentage rate of the total charge for credit"; and

   [(b)   where it is subject to change, be accompanied by the word "variable"].

(7)   For the purposes of Part I of Schedule 8 to these Regulations, in calculating—

   (a)   the amount of repayments or of any capital outstanding under an earlier agreement;

Part 2   Statutory Instruments

(b)   the total charge for credit (or any items included in it) in relation to the credit to be provided under the modified agreement; or

(c)   the APR in relation to the modified agreement,

the relevant date shall be determined by reference to the date of the modifying agreement.

(8)   For the purposes of Part I of Schedule 8 to these Regulations, the total cash price under the modified agreement shall be taken to be the total of—

(a)   the total amount of the capital outstanding under the earlier agreement on the relevant date within the meaning of paragraph 5 of Part I of Schedule 8; and

(b)   the cash price in relation to each list or other description of any additional goods, services, land or other things the acquisition of which is to be financed by credit under the modifying agreement.

(9)   Subject to paragraphs (10), (12) and (15) below, documents embodying modifying agreements varying or supplementing earlier hire agreements shall contain the information set out in Column 2 of Part II of Schedule 8 to these Regulations in so far as it relates to the type of modifying agreement referred to in Column 1.

(10)   Where any information about financial and related particulars set out in paragraphs 5 and 6 of Part II of Schedule 8 to these Regulations cannot be exactly ascertained by the owner, estimated information based on such assumptions as the owner may reasonably make in all the circumstances of the case and an indication of the assumptions made shall be included in documents embodying modifying agreements varying or supplementing earlier hire agreements.

[(11)   The information, statements of the protection and remedies, signature and separate boxes which under these Regulations must be contained in documents embodying modifying agreements varying or supplementing earlier hire agreements in relation to the goods to be bailed or hired under the modifying agreement, shall be set out in the order given by paragraphs (a) to (e) below under, where applicable, the headings specified below—

(a)   the nature of the agreement as set out in paragraph 1 of Part II of Schedule 8 to these Regulations;

(b)   the parties to the agreement as set out in paragraph 2 of Part II of Schedule 8 to these Regulations;

(c)   under the heading "Key Financial Information", the financial and related particulars set out in paragraphs 3 to 8 of Part II of Schedule 8 to these Regulations;

(d)   under the heading "Key Information"—

   (i)   the information set out in paragraphs 9 to 11 of Part II of Schedule 8 to these Regulations; and

   (ii)   the information set out in Schedule 4 to these Regulations; and

(e)   the signature box and, where applicable, separate box required by regulation 3(6)

and such information, statements of protection and remedies, signature and separate boxes shall be shown together as a whole and shall not be preceded by any information apart from trade names, logos or the reference number of the agreement or interspersed with any other information or wording apart from subtotals of total amounts and cross references to the terms of the agreement.]

(12)   Where any information about financial and related particulars set out in paragraphs 3 to 19 of Schedule 1 to these Regulations and paragraphs 3 to 8 of Schedule 3 is contained in any document embodying an earlier agreement, nothing in the preceding provisions of this Regulation shall require the information to be contained in any document embodying a modifying agreement varying or supplementing an earlier agreement except as mentioned in Schedule 8 if the information is not varied or supplemented by the modifying agreement and the document contains a statement to this effect.

(13)   Documents embodying modifying agreements shall identify clearly the terms and financial and related particulars of earlier agreements varied or supplemented by modifying agreements.

(14)   In the application of Regulation 6(1) above and Schedule 6 to these Regulations to modifying agreements, which are, or are treated under section 82(3) of the Act as, regulated agreements—

(a)   for any reference to the type of agreement referred to in Column 1 of Schedule 6 there shall be substituted a reference to modifying agreements which vary or supplement the type of agreement referred to in Column 1 of Schedule 6;

(b)   any reference in Column 2 of Schedule 6 to an agreement, or a term, shall be a reference to a modified agreement, or a term of a modified agreement, as the case may be; and

(c)   any term referred to in Column 2 of Schedule 6 in relation to the type of modifying agreement referred to in sub-paragraph (a) above shall not be a prescribed term for the purposes of sections 61(1)(a) and 127(3) of the Act, if the term was a term of the earlier agreement and has not been varied or supplemented by the modifying agreement.

(15)   Where a modifying agreement varies or supplements an earlier hire agreement and the modified agreement is, or is treated as, a restricted-use debtor-creditor-supplier agreement, the provisions of this Regulation shall apply to any document embodying the modifying agreement as though it varied or supplemented an earlier restricted-use debtor-creditor-supplier agreement, except that its heading shall be "Agreement modifying a Hire Agreement and regulated by the Consumer Credit Act 1974".

NOTES

Para (3): substituted by the Consumer Credit (Agreements) (Amendment) Regulations 2004, SI 2004/1482, regs 2, 9(1), (2).

Para (4): substituted by SI 2004/1482, regs 2, 9(1), (3) (as amended by SI 2004/2619, reg 2(1), (4)).

Paras (5), (6): words in square brackets substituted by SI 2004/1482, regs 2, 9(1), (4), (5).

Para (11): substituted by SI 2004/1482, regs 2, 9(1), (6).

S 127(3) of the Act: Repealed, subject to transitional provisions and savings, by the Consumer Credit Act 2006, ss 15, 69(1), 70, Sch 3, paras 1, 11(b), Sch 4.

[2.30]
8   Application of Regulations

(1)   Subject to [paragraphs (1A) to (2) and (4)] below, Regulations 1 to 3 and 5 to 7 shall apply to regulated agreements, and modifying agreements treated under section 82(3) of the Act as regulated agreements, made on or after 19th May 1985.

[(1A)   Where an agreement is a regulated consumer credit agreement these Regulations apply where that agreement is——
   (a)   an agreement secured on land;
   (b)   *an agreement under which the creditor provides the debtor with credit exceeding £60,260; or*
   (c)   an agreement entered into by the debtor wholly or predominantly for the purposes of a business carried on, or intended to be carried on, by him.
except to the extent that the Consumer Credit (Agreements) Regulations 2010 apply to such agreements.

[(1B)   Article 60C(5) and (6) of the Financial Services and Markets Act 2000 (Regulated Activities) Order 2001 applies for the purposes of paragraph (1A)(c).]]

(2)   In the case of a modifying agreement of a type specified in paragraphs 3 to 19 of Part I and 3 to 8 of Part II of Schedule 8 to these Regulations made on or after 19th May 1985 which varies or supplements an earlier credit agreement or an earlier hire agreement made before that date, nothing in these Regulations shall require the information about financial and related particulars specified in those paragraphs to be contained in any document embodying the modifying agreement if no term of the earlier agreement relating to such financial and related particulars has been varied or supplemented by the modifying agreement.

(3)   Nothing in these Regulations applies to a regulated agreement which purports to bind a person to enter as debtor or hirer into a prospective regulated agreement and which is excluded from the operation of section 59(1) of the Act by the Consumer Credit (Agreements to enter Prospective Agreements) (Exemptions) Regulations 1983.

[(4)   These Regulations do not apply to an agreement entered into on or after 26th August 2010 and before 1st February 2011 where—
   (a)   that agreement is an agreement secured on land to which section 58 of the Act applies, and
   (b)   the Consumer Credit (Agreements) Regulations 2010 apply to that agreement.]

NOTES

Para (1): words in square brackets substituted by the Consumer Credit (EU Directive) Regulations 2010, SI 2010/1010, regs 51, 53(a) (as substituted by SI 2010/1969, regs 4, 13), with effect in relation to certain agreements before 1 February 2011, as provided for in regs 101, 101A of SI 2010/1010 at **[2.804]**, **[2.805]**.

Para (1A): inserted, together with para (1B), by SI 2010/1010, regs 51, 53(b) (as substituted by SI 2010/1969, regs 4, 13), with effect in relation to certain agreements entered into before 1 February 2011, as provided for in regs 101, 101A of SI 2010/1010 at **[2.804]**, **[2.805]**; sub-para (b) substituted by the Mortgage Credit Directive (Amendment) Order 2015, SI 2015/1557, art 3, as from 21 March 2016, as follows:

   "(b)   an agreement under which the creditor provides the debtor with credit exceeding £60,260 other than a residential renovation agreement, or".

Para (1B): inserted as noted above; substituted by the Financial Services and Markets Act 2000 (Regulated Activities) (Amendment) (No 2) Order 2013, SI 2013/1881, art 23(1), (4), for transitional provisions see Pt 8 thereof at **[2.1007]** et seq.

Para (4): added by SI 2010/1969, reg 2(1), (2)(b).

SCHEDULES

SCHEDULE 1
INFORMATION TO BE CONTAINED IN DOCUMENTS EMBODYING REGULATED CONSUMER CREDIT AGREEMENTS OTHER THAN MODIFYING AGREEMENTS

Regulation 2(1)

[2.31]

TYPE OF AGREEMENT (1)	INFORMATION (2)
Nature of agreement	
[1 All types.	(1) Subject to paragraph (2) below, a heading in one of the following forms of words—
	(a) "Hire-Purchase Agreement regulated by the Consumer Credit Act 1974";
	(b) "Conditional Sale Agreement regulated by the Consumer Credit Act 1974";
	(c) "Fixed-Sum Loan Agreement regulated by the Consumer Credit Act 1974"; or
	(d) "Credit Card Agreement regulated by the Consumer Credit Act 1974",
	as the case may require.
	(2) If none of the headings in 1(a) to (d) above are applicable a heading in the following form of words—"Credit Agreement regulated by the Consumer Credit Act 1974".
	(3) Where the document and a pawn-receipt are combined, the words ", and Pawn-Receipt," shall be inserted in the heading after the word "Agreement".
	(4) Where the document embodies an agreement of which at least one part is a credit agreement not regulated by the Act, the word "partly" shall be inserted before "regulated" unless the regulated and unregulated parts of the agreement are clearly separate.
	(5) Where the credit is being secured on land the words "secured on" followed by the address of the land shall be inserted at the end of the heading.]
Parties to agreement	
2 All types.	(1) The name[, postal address and, where appropriate, any other address] of the creditor.
	(2) The name[, postal address and, where appropriate, any other address] of the debtor.
FINANCIAL AND RELATED PARTICULARS	
Description of goods, services, land etc	
3 Restricted-use debtor-creditor-supplier agreements for fixed-sum credit to finance a transaction comprising the acquisition of goods, services, land or other things specified in the agreement or identified and agreed on at the time the agreement is made.	A list or other description of the goods, services or other things and, in the case of land, a general description of the land, the acquisition of which is to be financed by credit under the agreement.
Cash price	
4 Agreements falling within paragraph 3.	The cash price in relation to each list or other description of goods, services, land or other things, to be shown under paragraph 3 above, and the total cash price.

TYPE OF AGREEMENT (1)	INFORMATION (2)
Advance payments	
5 All types in relation to which any advance payment is to be made by the debtor (whether under the agreement or as a condition precedent to the making of the agreement) before he is provided with credit under the agreement or, as the case may be, before he enters into the agreement.	The amount of the advance payments to be made by the debtor and, in the case of a cancellable agreement, the nature of such payments.
Amount of credit	
6 Agreements falling within paragraph 3 except agreements under which both— (a) the total amount payable by the debtor is not greater than the total cash price referred to in paragraph 4; and (b) there is no advance payment falling within paragraph 5.	The amount of the credit to be provided under the agreement, namely the difference between the total cash price to be shown under paragraph 4 above and the total of any advance payments to be shown under paragraph 5 above.
7 Agreements for fixed-sum credit not falling within paragraph 3.	The amount of the credit to be provided under the agreement.
Credit limit	
8 Agreements for running-account credit.	The credit limit expressed as— (a) a sum of money; (b) a statement that the credit limit will be determined by the creditor from time to time under the agreement and that notice of it will be given by him to the debtor; (c) a sum of money together with a statement that the creditor may vary the credit limit to such sum as he may from time to time determine under the agreement and that notice of it will be given by him to the debtor; or (d) in a case not falling within head (a), (b) or (c) above, either a statement indicating the manner in which the credit limit will be determined and that notice of it will be given by the creditor to the debtor or a statement indicating that there is no credit limit.
[Term of the agreement	
8A Agreements of fixed duration for running-account credit.	The duration of the agreement.
8B Agreements for fixed-sum credit.	The duration or minimum duration of the agreement.]
Total charge for credit, rate of interest, etc	
[9 Agreements for fixed-sum credit except agreements— (a) which do not specify either the intervals between repayments or the amounts of repayments or both the intervals and the amounts; (b) under which the total amount payable by the debtor to discharge his indebtedness in respect of the amount of credit provided may vary according to any formula specified in the agreement having effect by reference to movements in the level of any index or to any other factor;	(1) The total charge for credit, with a list of its constituent parts. (2) The rate of interest on the credit to be provided under the agreement or, where more than one such rate applies, all the rates in all cases quoted on a per annum basis with details of when each rate applies. (3) A statement explaining how and when interest charges are calculated and applied under the agreement.]

TYPE OF AGREEMENT (1)	INFORMATION (2)
(c) which provide for a variation of, or permit the creditor to vary, (whether or not by reference to any index) the amount or rate of any item included in the total charge for credit after the relevant date; or	
(d) under which the total amount payable by the debtor is not greater than the total cash price referred to in paragraph 4.	
[10 Agreements for— (a) running-account credit; and (b) fixed-sum credit falling within the exceptions in paragraph 9(a) to (c).	(1) The total charge for credit with a list of its constituent parts and in the case of running-account credit, the total charge for credit shall be calculated on the same assumptions as are set out in paragraph 1 of Schedule 7 for the purpose of calculating the APR in place of the assumptions in . . . the [total charge for credit rules] that might otherwise apply.
	(2) The rate of interest on the credit to be provided under the agreement or, where more than one such rate applies, all the rates in all cases quoted on a per annum basis with details of when each rate applies.
	(3) A statement whether any interest rate to be shown under (2) above is fixed or variable.
	(4) A statement explaining how and when interest charges are calculated and applied under the agreement.]
Total amount payable	
11 Agreements falling within paragraph 9.	The total amount payable, being the total of any amounts to be shown under paragraphs 5, 6 or 7, and 9 above.
Timing of repayments	
12 All types	The timing of repayments to be made under the agreement expressed by reference to one or more of the following—
	(a) the dates on which each repayment is to be made;
	(b) the frequency and number of the repayments and the date of the first repayment or a statement indicating the manner in which that date will be determined;
	(c) a statement indicating the manner in which the dates of the repayments will be determined.
Amounts of repayments	
13 All types except those falling within paragraph 14.	The amount of each repayment to be made under the agreement expressed as—
	(a) a sum of money;
	(b) a specified proportion of a specified amount (including the amount outstanding from time to time);
	(c) a combination of heads (a) and (b) above; or
	(d) in a case where the amount of any repayment cannot be expressed in accordance with head (a), (b) or (c) above, a statement indicating the manner in which the amount will be determined.
14 Agreements where— (i) the credit to be provided is repayable by two or more instalments; and (ii) the interest on the credit is of a type to which section 26 of, and Schedule 7 to, the Finance Act 1982 apply.	The amount of each repayment to be made under the agreement (with or without the equivalent repayment after deduction of tax in accordance with section 26 of, and Schedule 7 to, the Finance Act 1982), expressed as—

TYPE OF AGREEMENT (1)	INFORMATION (2)
	(a) a sum of money;
	(b) a specified proportion of a specified amount (including the amount outstanding from time to time);
	(c) a combination of heads (a) and (b) above; or
	(d) in a case where the amount of any repayment cannot be expressed in accordance with head (a), (b) or (c) above, a statement indicating the manner in which the amount will be determined:
	Provided that, where the amounts to be paid by the debtor after deduction of tax in accordance with section 26 of, and Schedule 7 to, the Finance Act 1982 are the same, the requirements of this paragraph may be satisfied by a statement indicating the lowest and highest amounts of the repayments to be made under the agreement before deduction of tax.
[14A All types where different interest rates or different charges or both are or will be at any time during the term of the agreement payable in respect of—	A statement of the order or proportions in which any amount paid by the debtor which is not sufficient to discharge the total debt then due under the agreement will be applied or appropriated by the creditor towards the discharge of the sums due—
(a) credit provided under the agreement for different purposes; or	(a) in respect of the amounts of credit provided for different purposes, or
(b) under each of the different parts of the agreement,	(b) different parts of the agreement,
whether or not the agreement is a multiple agreement.	as the case may be.]
	APR
15 All types except those referred to in paragraph 16.	The APR in relation to the agreement or a statement indicating that the total amount payable under the agreement is not greater than the total cash price of the goods, services, land or other things the acquisition of which is to be financed by credit under the agreement.
16 Debtor-creditor-supplier agreements for running-account credit under which—	(1) The APR in relation to the agreement calculated on the assumptions specified in sub-paragraphs (2) and (3) below.
(a) the debtor agrees to pay the creditor an amount specified in the agreement on specified occasions;	(2) The first assumption referred to in sub-paragraph (1) above is the assumption that—
(b) there is a credit limit; and	
(c) charges for credit are either—	(a) the debtor is provided with an amount of credit at the date of the making of the agreement which, taken with the amount of the charge for that credit ascertained at that date, is equal to the credit limit; and
(i) a fixed amount in respect of each transaction, or	(b) the debtor repays the sum of the amounts referred to in head (a) above by payments of the amounts specified in the agreement on the occasions specified in the agreement and makes no other payment and obtains no further credit in relation to the account.
(ii) calculated as a proportion of the price payable under a transaction financed by the credit.	
	(3) The second assumption referred to in sub-paragraph (1) above is the like assumption as in sub-paragraph (2) above save that the sum of the amounts referred to in head (a) thereof shall be taken to be one third of the credit limit.

Part 2   Statutory Instruments

TYPE OF AGREEMENT (1)	INFORMATION (2)
	A statement indicating that it has been assumed in the calculation of the APR in relation to the agreement that relief may be available under section 19 of the Income and Corporation Taxes Act 1970 and Schedule 4 to the Finance Act 1976 in respect of premiums under certain policies of insurance without any deduction under section 21 of the said Act of 1970.
17 Agreements where the APR is based on a total charge for credit which is calculated to take account of relief available under section 19 of the Income and Corporation Taxes Act 1970 and Schedule 4 to the Finance Act 1976.	A statement indicating that it has been assumed in the calculation of the APR in relation to the agreement that relief may be available under section 19 of the Income and Corporation Taxes Act 1970 and Schedule 4 to the Finance Act 1976 in respect of premiums under certain policies of insurance without any deduction under section 21 of the said Act of 1970.

Variable rates or items

18 Agreements under which the rate or amount of any item included in the total charge for credit will or may be varied (other than a variation in consequence of an event which is certain to occur).	A statement indicating that in calculating the APR no account has been taken of any variation which may occur under the agreement of the rate or amount of any item entering into that calculation.
19 Agreements falling within paragraph 18.	A statement indicating the circumstances in which any variation referred to in paragraph 18 above may occur and where that information is ascertainable at the time at which the document referred to in section 61(1) of the Act is presented or sent to the debtor for signature, the time at which any such variation may occur.

[[Land-related agreements]

19A [Agreements which—	The initial standard variable rate within the meaning of [the total charge for credit rules] together with a statement explaining—
(a) are intended primarily to finance the acquisition or retention of land or the renovation or improvement of a building or any other agreement secured by a mortgage on land or, in Scotland, by a standard security within the meaning of the Conveyancing and Feudal Reform (Scotland) Act 1970, and	(a) what that rate is; and
(b) provide for the possibility of any variation of the rate of interest if it is to be assumed, by virtue of the total charge for credit rules, that the variation will take place but the amount of the variation cannot be ascertained at the date of the making of the agreement.]	(b) that it has been taken into account in calculating the APR.]

OTHER INFORMATION
Security provided by the debtor

20 Agreements, to which section 114 of the Act applies, under which a person takes any article in pawn and where no separate pawn-receipt is given.	A statement indicating that an article has been taken in pawn under the agreement and a description of the article sufficient to identify it.
21 All types except those referred to in paragraph 20 in relation to which any security is to be provided by the debtor to secure the carrying out of the obligations of the debtor under the agreement.	A description of the security to be provided by the debtor in relation to the agreement sufficient to identify it and—
	(a) a general description of any stocks and shares (including any right to become a stockholder or shareholder) to which it relates; and
	(b) in any other case a description of the subject matter to which it relates.

TYPE OF AGREEMENT (1)	INFORMATION (2)
[Charges	
22 All types.	(1) A list of any charges payable under the agreement to the creditor upon failure by the debtor or a relative of his to do or refrain from doing anything which he is required to do or refrain from doing, as the case may be.
	(2) A statement indicating any term of the agreement which provides for charges—
	(a) not required to be shown under (1) above; or
	(b) not included in the total charge for credit.]
[Cancellation rights	
23 Agreements that cannot be cancelled by the debtor under the Act, the Timeshare Act 1992 or the Financial Services (Distance Marketing) Regulations 2004.	A statement that the debtor has no right to cancel the agreement under the Consumer Credit Act 1974, the Timeshare Act 1992 or the Financial Services (Distance Marketing) Regulations 2004.]
[Right of withdrawal	
23A Agreements falling within regulation 8(1A)(c)	A statement providing details of the debtor's right under section 66A of the Act to withdraw from the consumer credit agreement including—
	(1) the right to withdraw within 14 days without the debtor having to give any reason;
	(2) when that period of withdrawal begins and ends;
	(3) the requirement of the debtor to notify the creditor of his intention to withdraw, in writing or orally;
	(4) contact details of the person/creditor whom he must notify of this intention to withdraw from the agreement;
	(5) the requirement to repay the credit without delay and no later than 30 calendar days of giving notice of withdrawal;
	(6) the requirement to pay, without delay and no later than 30 calendar days of giving notice of withdrawal, the interest accrued from the date of drawing down the credit to the date of repaying it; and
	(7) the amount of interest payable per day expressed as a sum of money;
	Paragraph (7) does not apply [in respect of agreements for running account credit] where it is not practicable for the creditor to state the amount of interest payable per day. In such cases, the agreement shall state that where credit is drawn down during the withdrawal period, the creditor shall inform the debtor, on request, without delay, of the amount of interest payable per day.]
[Amount payable on early settlement	
24 Agreements for fixed-sum credit [secured on land] for a term of more than one month.	(1) Examples based on the amount of credit to be provided under the agreement or the nominal amount of either £1000 or £100, showing the amount that would be payable if the debtor exercised the right under section 94 of the Act to discharge his indebtedness on the date when—
	(a) a quarter of the term of the agreement elapses;
	(b) half of the term elapses; and
	(c) three quarters of the term elapses.
	or on the first repayment date after each of those dates.

TYPE OF AGREEMENT (1)	INFORMATION (2)
	(2) A statement explaining that, in calculating the amounts shown, no account has been taken of any variation which might occur under the agreement, and that the amounts are accordingly only illustrative.]
[24A Agreements falling within regulation 8(1A)(b) and (c)	A statement providing details of the debtor's right of early repayment under section 94 of the Act including—
	(1) the fact that the debtor has a right to repay early in full or part,
	(2) the procedure for early repayment, and
	(3) where applicable details of the creditor's right to compensation under [sections 95A and 95B] of the Act and the manner in which that compensation shall be determined.]

NOTES

Paras 1, 9, 22: substituted by the Consumer Credit (Agreements) (Amendment) Regulations 2004, SI 2004/1482, regs 2, 10(1), (2), (4), (7).

Para 2: words in square brackets substituted by the Consumer Credit Act 1974 (Electronic Communications) Order 2004, SI 2004/3236, art 4(1), (3).

Paras 8A, 8B, 14A: inserted by SI 2004/1482, regs 2, 10(1), (3), (6).

Para 10: substituted by SI 2004/1482, regs 2, 10(1), (5); words omitted revoked and words in square brackets substituted by the Financial Services and Markets Act 2000 (Regulated Activities) (Amendment) (No 2) Order 2013, SI 2013/1881, art 23(1), (3), (5)(a), for transitional provisions see Pt 8 thereof at **[2.1007]** et seq.

Para 19A: inserted by the Consumer Credit (Total Charge for Credit, Agreements and Advertisements) (Amendment) Regulations 1999, SI 1999/3177, reg 4(a); year in square brackets in both places inserted by SI 2010/1010, regs 51, 54(zb) (as inserted by SI 2010/1969, regs 4, 14), with effect in relation to certain agreements entered into before 1 February 2011, as provided for in regs 101, 101A of SI 2010/1010 at **[2.804]**, **[2.805]**; preceding heading inserted, and words in square brackets substituted, by SI 2013/1881, art 23(1), (5)(b), (c), for transitional provisions see Pt 8 thereof at **[2.1007]** et seq.

Para 23: inserted by SI 2004/1482, regs 2, 10(1), (8) (as amended by SI 2004/2619, reg 2(1), (5)).

Paras 23A, 24A: inserted by SI 2010/1010, regs 51, 54(a), (c), with effect in relation to certain agreements entered into before 1 February 2011, as provided for in regs 101, 101A of the 2010 Regulations at **[2.804]**, **[2.805]**; in para 24A in column (2), words in square brackets substituted by the Consumer Credit (Green Deal) Regulations 2012, SI 2012/2798, reg 5, Schedule, para 1(1), (2).

Para 24: inserted by SI 2004/1482, regs 2, 10(1), (8) (as amended by SI 2004/2619, reg 2(1), (5)); words in square brackets inserted by SI 2010/1010, regs 51, 54(b), with effect in relation to certain agreements entered into before 1 February 2011, as provided for in regs 101, 101A of the 2010 Regulations at **[2.804]**, **[2.805]**.

[SCHEDULE 2

PART I

FORMS OF STATEMENT OF PROTECTION AND REMEDIES AVAILABLE UNDER THE CONSUMER CREDIT ACT 1974 TO DEBTORS UNDER REGULATED CONSUMER CREDIT AGREEMENTS

Regulation 2(3)

[2.32]

[FORM NO (1)	TYPE OF AGREEMENT (2)	FORM OF STATEMENT (3)
1	Agreement to which section 58(1) of the Act applies.	YOUR RIGHTS
		Under the Consumer Credit Act 1974, you should have been given a copy of this agreement at least seven days ago so you could consider whether you wanted to go ahead. If the creditor did not give you a copy of this agreement he can only enforce it with a court order.
2	All types.	MISSING PAYMENTS
		Missing payments could have severe consequences and make obtaining credit more difficult.
3	All agreements which are secured on land.	YOUR HOME MAY BE REPOSSESSED

[FORM NO (1)	TYPE OF AGREEMENT (2)	FORM OF STATEMENT (3)
		Your home may be repossessed if you do not keep up repayments on a mortgage or other debt secured on it.
4	Cancellable agreements to which section 68(b) of the Act applies.	YOUR RIGHT TO CANCEL
		You can cancel this agreement within FOUR-TEEN days (starting the day after you signed it) by giving WRITTEN notice to*.
		If you intend to cancel, you should not use any goods you have under the agreement and you should keep them safe. You can wait for them to be collected and you do not need to hand them over until you receive a written request for them. . . .
		Notes:
		*Creditor or agent to insert the name and address of person to whom the notice may be given or an indication of the person to whom a notice may be given with clear reference to the place in the document embodying the agreement where his name and address appear.
5	Cancellable agreements not included in paragraphs [4 or 6].	YOUR RIGHT TO CANCEL
		Once you have signed this agreement, you will have a short time in which you can cancel [it]* [that part of this agreement which is regulated by the Consumer Credit Act 1974]*. The creditor will send you exact details of how and when you can do this.
		Notes:
		*Creditor to omit passage in square brackets which does not apply to the agreement.
6	Modifying agreements treated under section 82(5) of the Act as cancellable agreements.	YOUR RIGHT TO CANCEL
		This agreement modifies an earlier agreement. Once you have signed this agreement your right to cancel [that part of]* the earlier agreement [which was regulated by the Consumer Credit Act 1974]* will be widened to cover the [regulated]* agreement as modified. The cancellation period itself will be unchanged. Details of how to cancel are given in your copy of this agreement.
		Notes:
		*Creditor to omit passages in square brackets except in the case of an agreement of which at least one part is a credit agreement not regulated by the Act.
7	Hire purchase and conditional sale agreements relating to goods, not included in paragraph 8.	TERMINATION: YOUR RIGHTS

Part 2   Statutory Instruments

[FORM NO (1)	TYPE OF AGREEMENT (2)	FORM OF STATEMENT (3)
		You have a right to end this agreement. To do so, you should write to the person you make your payments to. They will then be entitled to the return of the goods and to [the cost of installing the goods plus half the rest of the total amount payable under this agreement, that is] [half the total amount payable under this agreement, that is]* £x**. If you have already paid at least this amount plus any overdue instalments and have taken reasonable care of the goods, you will not have to pay any more.
		Notes:
		*Creditor to insert the appropriate passage in square brackets where the amount calculated in accordance with the provisions of section 100 of the Act applies. If the agreement provides for a sum below the minimum prescribed in the Act, both passages in square brackets are to be omitted.
		**Creditor to insert the amount calculated in accordance with the provisions of section 100 of the Act or such lesser sum as the agreement may provide.
8	Agreements modifying hire-purchase and conditional sale agreements relating to goods.	TERMINATION: YOUR RIGHTS
		You have a right to end this agreement. To do so, write to the person you make your payments to. They will then be entitled to the return of the goods and to [the cost of installing the goods plus half the total amount yet to be paid under the earlier agreement as modified by this agreement, that is] [half the total amount payable under the earlier agreement as modified by this agreement, that is]* £x**. If you have already paid at least this amount, plus any overdue instalments and have taken reasonable care of the goods, you will not have to pay any more.
		Notes:
		*Creditor to insert the appropriate passage in square brackets where the amount calculated in accordance with the provisions of section 100 of the Act applies. If the modified agreement provides for a sum below the minimum prescribed in the Act, both passages in square brackets are to be omitted.
		**Creditor to insert the amount calculated in accordance with the provisions of section 100 of the Act or such lesser sum as the agreement may provide.
9	Conditional sale agreements relating to land, not included in paragraph 10.	TERMINATION: YOUR RIGHTS
		Until the title to the land has passed to you, you have a right to end this agreement. To do so write to the person you make your payments to. They will then be entitled to the return of the land and to [half the total amount payable under this agreement, that is]* £x.** If, at the time you end this agreement, you have already paid at least this amount plus any overdue instalments and you have taken reasonable care of the land, you will not have to pay any more.

[FORM NO (1)	TYPE OF AGREEMENT (2)	FORM OF STATEMENT (3)
		Notes:
		*Creditor to insert the passage in square brackets where the amount calculated in accordance with the provisions of section 100 of the Act applies. If the agreement provides for a sum below the minimum prescribed in the Act, the passage in square brackets is to be omitted.
		**Creditor to insert the amount calculated in accordance with the provisions of section 100 of the Act or such lesser sum as the agreement may provide.
10	Agreements modifying conditional sale agreements relating to land.	TERMINATION: YOUR RIGHTS
		Until the title to the land has passed to you, you have a right to end this agreement. To do so write to the person you make your payments to. They will then be entitled to the return of the land and to [half the total amount payable under your earlier agreement as modified by this agreement, that is]* £x**. If you have already paid at least this amount plus any overdue instalments and taken reasonable care of the land, you will not have to pay any more.
		Notes:
		*Creditor to insert the passage in square brackets where the amount calculated in accordance with the provisions of section 100 of the Act applies. If the modified agreement provides for a sum below the minimum prescribed in the Act, the passage in square brackets is to be omitted.
		**Creditor to insert the amount calculated in accordance with the provisions of section 100 of the Act or such lesser sum as the modified agreement may provide.
11	Hire-purchase and conditional sale agreements relating to goods, not included in paragraph 12.	REPOSSESSION: YOUR RIGHTS
		If you do not keep your side of this agreement but you have paid at least [the cost of installing the goods plus one third of the rest of the total amount payable under this agreement, that is] [one third of the total amount payable under this agreement, that is]* £x** the creditor may not take back the goods against your wishes unless he gets a court order. (In Scotland he may need to get a court order at any time.) If he does take the goods without your consent or a court order, you have the right to get back any money that you have paid under this agreement.
		Notes:
		*Creditor to insert the appropriate passage in square brackets.
		**Creditor to insert the amount calculated in accordance with the provisions of section 90 of the Act.
12	Agreements modifying hire-purchase and conditional sale agreements relating to goods.	REPOSSESSION: YOUR RIGHTS

[FORM NO (1)	TYPE OF AGREEMENT (2)	FORM OF STATEMENT (3)
		If you do not keep to your side of this agreement [but you have paid at least £x*]** the creditor may not take back the goods against your wishes unless he gets a court order. (In Scotland he may need to get a court order at any time.) If he does take the goods without your consent or a court order, you have the right to get back all the money you have paid under this agreement.
		Notes:
		*Creditor to insert the amount calculated in accordance with the provisions of section 90 of the Act.
		**Creditor to omit both passages in square brackets in the case of a modifying agreement where the goods are protected at the time the modifying agreement is made.
13	Agreements, to which section 114 of the Act applies, under which a person takes any article in pawn.	IMPORTANT—READ THIS CAREFULLY TO FIND OUT ABOUT YOUR RIGHTS
		The Consumer Credit Act 1974 lays down certain requirements for your protection which should have been complied with when this agreement was made. If they were not, the creditor cannot enforce this agreement without getting a court order.
		The Act also gives you a number of rights. In particular you should read the NOTICE TO DEBTOR [in this agreement]* [in your pawn receipt].**
		If you would like to know more about your rights under the Act, contact either your local Trading Standards Department or your nearest Citizens' Advice Bureau.
		Notes:
		*Phrase in square brackets to be included by creditor in agreements where any document embodying the agreement is not separate from the pawn-receipt. Creditor to omit "in your pawn receipt".
		** Phrase in square brackets to be included by creditor in agreements where a separate pawn-receipt is given to the debtor. Creditor to omit "in this agreement".
14	Debtor-creditor-supplier agreements falling within section 12(b) and (c) of the Act, and multiple agreements not falling within paragraph 15 of which at least one part is a debtor-creditor-supplier agreement falling within section 12(b) or (c) of the Act.	IMPORTANT—READ THIS CAREFULLY TO FIND OUT ABOUT YOUR RIGHTS
		The Consumer Credit Act 1974 lays down certain requirements for your protection which should have been complied with when this agreement was made. If they were not, the creditor cannot enforce this agreement without getting a court order.
		The Act also gives you a number of rights:

[FORM NO (1)	TYPE OF AGREEMENT (2)	FORM OF STATEMENT (3)
		[1] You can settle this agreement at any time by giving notice [in writing]* and paying off the amount you owe under the agreement [which may be reduced by a rebate]** [Examples indicating the amount you have to pay appear in the agreement.]***
		[2] You can settle this agreement in part at any time by giving notice and paying off some of the amount you owe.]****
		[3] If you received unsatisfactory goods or services paid for under this agreement [, apart from any bought with a cash loan,]***** you may have a right to sue the supplier, the creditor or both.
		4) If the contract is not fulfilled, perhaps because the supplier has gone out of business, you may still be able to sue the creditor.]******
		If you would like to know more about your rights under the Act, contact either your local Trading Standards Department or your nearest Citizens' Advice Bureau.
		Notes:
		* Creditor to insert phrase in square brackets where agreement is secured on land
		** Creditor to insert phrase in square brackets in any agreement where rebate would be payable on early settlement under the agreement or the Consumer Credit (Early Settlement) Regulations 2004.
		*** Creditor to insert phrase in second pair of square brackets in any agreement for fixed-sum credit for a term of more than one month that is an agreement secured on land.
		**** Creditor to delete where agreement is secured on land.
		***** Creditor to insert phrase in square brackets in any multiple agreement, of which at least one part is a debtor-creditor-supplier agreement falling within section 12(b) or (c) of the Act and at least one part is a debtor-creditor agreement falling within section 13(c) of the Act.
		****** Creditor may delete text in 3) and 4) where agreement is a debtor-creditor-supplier agreement for running-account credit—
		(i) which provides for the making of payments by the debtor in relation to specified periods which, in the case of an agreement which is not secured on land, do not exceed three months, and
		(ii) which requires that the number of payments to be made by the debtor in repayments of the whole amount of credit provided in such period shall not exceed one.]
15	Multiple agreements of which at least one part is a credit agreement not regulated by the Act.	IMPORTANT—READ THIS CAREFULLY TO FIND OUT ABOUT YOUR RIGHTS

Part 2   Statutory Instruments

[FORM NO (1)	TYPE OF AGREEMENT (2)	FORM OF STATEMENT (3)
		That part of this agreement which deals with [. . . . .]* is a regulated agreement under the Consumer Credit Act 1974. As a result certain requirements for your protection should have been complied with when it was made. If they were not, the creditor cannot enforce this agreement without a court order.
		The Act also gives you a number of rights. [You can settle the regulated agreement at any time by giving notice [in writing]** and paying off the amount you owe under this agreement [which may be reduced by a rebate]*** [Examples indicating the amount you have to pay appear in the agreement.]****
		[You can settle this agreement in part at any time by giving notice and paying off some of the amount you owe.]***** If you would like to know more about your rights under the Act, contact either your local Trading Standards Department or your nearest Citizens' Advice Bureau.
		Notes:
		* Creditor to insert description of regulated agreement example, "the cash advance facility". ** Creditor to insert phrase in square brackets where agreement is secured on land
		*** Creditor to insert phrase in square brackets in any agreement where rebate would be payable on early settlement under the agreement or the Consumer Credit (Early Settlement) Regulations 2004.
		**** Creditor to insert phrase in second pair of square brackets in any agreement for fixed-sum credit for a term of more than one month that is an agreement secured on land.
		***** Creditor to delete where agreement is secured on land.]
16	All types not included in paragraphs 13,14 and 15.	IMPORTANT—READ THIS CAREFULLY TO FIND OUT ABOUT YOUR RIGHTS
		The Consumer Credit Act 1974 lays down certain requirements for your protection which should have been complied with when this agreement was made. If they were not, the creditor cannot enforce this agreement without getting a court order.
		The Act also gives you a number of rights. [You can settle this agreement at any time by giving notice [in writing]* and paying off the amount you owe under the agreement [which may be reduced by a rebate]**. [Examples indicating the amount you might have to pay appear in the agreement.]***
		[You can settle this agreement in part at any time by giving notice and paying off some of the amount you owe.]**** If you would like to know more about your rights under the Act, contact either your local Trading Standards Department or your nearest Citizens' Advice Bureau.
		Notes: * Creditor to insert phrase in square brackets where agreement is secured on land

[FORM NO (1)	TYPE OF AGREEMENT (2)	FORM OF STATEMENT (3)
		** Creditor to insert phrase in square brackets in any agreement where rebate would be payable on early settlement under the agreement or the Consumer Credit (Early Settlement) Regulations 2004.
		*** Creditor to insert phrase in second pair of square brackets in any agreement for fixed sum credit for a term of more than one month that is an agreement secured on land.
		**** Creditor to delete where agreement is secured on land.]
17	Credit-token agreements which make debtors liable for loss to the creditor resulting from the misuse of credit-tokens by other persons.	THEFT, LOSS OR MISUSE OF CREDIT-TOKEN*
		If your credit-token* is lost, stolen or misused by someone without your permission, you may have to pay up to £x** of any loss to the creditor. If it is misused with your permission you will probably be liable for ALL losses. You will not be liable to the creditor for losses which take place after you have told the creditor about the theft, etc [as long as you confirm this in writing within seven days]. ***[However, the credit-token* can also be used under an agreement to which this protection does not apply. As a result, there may be circumstances under which you may have to pay for all the losses to the creditor.]****
		Notes:
		*Creditor may insert specific designation or trade name of credit-token for example, credit card instead of "credit-token".
		**Creditor to insert the extent of the liability laid down in section 84(1) of the Act or the credit limit if lower or such lower figure as he may decide.
		***Creditor to omit phrase in square brackets if written confirmation is not required under the credit-token agreement.
		****Creditor to omit passage in square brackets if inapplicable.]

NOTES

Substituted by the Consumer Credit (Agreements) (Amendment) Regulations 2004, SI 2004/1482, regs 2, 11 (as amended by SI 2004/2619).

Form 14: in column 3, words in square brackets beginning with "1)" to the end of that form substituted by the Consumer Credit (EU Directive) Regulations 2010, SI 2010/1010, regs 51, 55(a) (as substituted by the Consumer Credit (Amendment) Regulations 2011, SI 2011/11, regs 2, 4), with effect in relation to certain agreements entered into before 1 February 2011, as provided for in regs 101, 101A of SI 2010/1010 at **[2.804]**, **[2.805]**.

Form 15: in column 3, words in square brackets beginning "You can settle" to the end of that form substituted by SI 2010/1010, regs 51, 55(b) (as substituted by SI 2011/11, regs 2, 4), with effect in relation to certain agreements entered into before 1 February 2011, as provided for regs 101, 101A of SI 2010/1010 at **[2.804]**, **[2.805]**.

Form 16: in column 3, words in square brackets beginning "You can settle" to the end of that form substituted by SI 2010/1010, regs 51, 55(c) (as substituted by SI 2011/11, regs 2, 4), with effect in relation to certain agreements entered into before 1 February 2011, as provided for in regs 101, 101A of SI 2010/1010 at **[2.804]**, **[2.805]**.

Part 2   Statutory Instruments

[PART II
NOTICE TO BE CONTAINED IN DOCUMENTS EMBODYING
A COMBINED CONSUMER CREDIT AGREEMENT AND PAWN-RECEIPT]

Regulation 4

[2.33]

FORM NO (1)	TYPE OF AGREEMENT (2)	FORM OF STATEMENT (3)
18	Agreements, to which section 114 of the Act applies, under which a person takes any article in pawn and where any document embodying the agreement is not separate from the pawn-receipt.	**NOTICE TO THE DEBTOR IMPORTANT—YOU SHOULD READ THIS CAREFULLY** **Right to Redeem Articles** If you hand in this agreement (which is also your pawn-receipt) and pay the amount you owe, you may redeem the article(s) in pawn at any time within 6 months of the date of this agreement or any longer time agreed with the creditor ("the redemption period"). IF YOU DO NOT REDEEM THE ARTICLE(S) ON OR BEFORE * YOU MAY LOSE YOUR RIGHT TO REDEEM IT (THEM). Loss of Receipt If you lose your receipt you may provide either a statutory declaration or, if the credit (or credit limit) is not more than £x** and the creditor agrees, a signed statement instead. The creditor may provide the form to be used and may charge for doing so. Unredeemed Articles An article not redeemed within the redemption period becomes the creditor's property if the credit (or credit limit) is not more than £x**** and the redemption period is 6 months. In any other case it may be sold by the creditor, but it continues to be redeemable until it is sold. Interest is payable until the actual date of redemption. Where the credit (or credit limit) is more than £x**** the creditor must give you 14 days notice of his intention to sell. When an article has been sold you will receive information about the sale. If the proceeds (less expenses) are more that the amount that would have been payable to redeem the article on the date of the sale you will be entitled to receive the extra amount. If the proceeds are less than the amount you will owe the creditor the shortfall. Your goods will not be insured by the creditor while they are in pawn. ***** Notes: *Creditor to insert the date at the end of the redemption period. **Creditor to insert the amount specified in section 118(1)(b) of the Act. ***Creditor to insert the amount specified in section 120(1)(a) of the Act. ****Creditor to insert the amount specified in the Consumer Credit (Realisation of Pawn) Regulations 1983

FORM NO (1)	TYPE OF AGREEMENT (2)	FORM OF STATEMENT (3)
		*****Creditor to omit this paragraph if inapplicable.]

NOTES

Substituted by the Consumer Credit (Agreements) (Amendment) Regulations 2004, SI 2004/1482, regs 2, 11.

SCHEDULE 3

INFORMATION TO BE CONTAINED IN DOCUMENTS EMBODYING REGULATED CONSUMER HIRE AGREEMENTS OTHER THAN MODIFYING AGREEMENTS

Regulation 3(1)

[2.34]

TYPE OF AGREEMENT (1)	INFORMATION (2)
	[Nature of agreement
1 All types.	(1) A heading in the following form of words— "Hire Agreement regulated by the Consumer Credit Act 1974".
	(2) Where the agreement to hire is being secured on land the words "secured on" and the address of the land shall be inserted at the end of the heading.]
	Parties to agreement
2 All types.	(1) The name[, postal address and, where appropriate, any other address] of the owner.
	(2) The name[, postal address and, where appropriate, any other address] of the hirer.
	FINANCIAL AND RELATED PARTICULARS
	Description of goods
3 All types.	A list or other description of the goods to be bailed or hired under the agreement.
	Advance payments
4 All types in relation to which any advance payment is to be made by the hirer (whether under the agreement or as a condition precedent to the making of the agreement) before he is to take possession of the goods to be bailed or hired under the agreement or, as the case may be, before he enters into the agreement.	The amount of the advance payments to be made by the hirer and, in the case of a cancellable agreement, the nature of such payments.
	Hire payments
5 All types.	(1) The amount of each hire payment, other than an advance payment to be shown under paragraph 4 above
	(2) The timing of such payments to be made under the agreement expressed by reference to one or more of the following—
	(a) the dates on which each payment is to be made;
	(b) the frequency and number of the payments and the date of the first payment or a statement indicating the manner in which that date will be determined.
	(c) a statement indicating the manner in which the dates of the payments will be determined.

TYPE OF AGREEMENT (1)	INFORMATION (2)
	Other payments
6 All types including provisions for payments other than advance payments and hire payments.	(1) The amount (or a statement indicating the manner in which the amount will be determined) of each of the following descriptions of payments (not being an advance payment to be shown under paragraph 4 above or a hire payment to be shown under paragraph 5) to be made under the agreement by, or on behalf of,' the hirer, or a relative of his, to the owner, that is to say,—
	(a) any payment under arrangements for the installation, care, maintenance or protection of any goods;
	(b) any premium under a contract of insurance; or
	(c) any payment payable on termination of the agreement (other than a payment on default to be shown under paragraph 10 below).
	(2) The timing of such payments expressed by reference to one or more of the following—
	(a) the dates on which each payment is to be made;
	(b) the frequency and number of the payments and the date of the first payment or a statement indicating the manner in which that date will be determined;
	(c) a statement indicating the manner in which the dates of the payments will be determined.
	(3) References in this paragraph to the owner include references to his near relative, his partner and a member of a group of which he is a member to any person nominated by him or by any such person in relation to the arrangements, the contract of insurance or the termination of the agreement, and to a near relative of his partner; and "near relative" means, in relation to any person, the husband, wife, father, mother, brother, sister, son or daughter of that person and "group" means the person (including a company) having control of a company together with all the companies directly or indirectly controlled by him.
	Variable payments
7 All types including provisions for variation of hire or other payments, where the amount of any such payment following any variation cannot be ascertained at the time of the making of the agreement.	(1) Subject to sub-paragraph (2) below, a statement indicating the circumstances in which any hire payment to be shown under paragraph 5 above or any other payment to be shown under paragraph 6 may be varied under the agreement and, where that information is ascertainable at the time at which the document referred to in section 61(1) of the Act is presented or sent to the hirer for signature, the time at which any such variation may occur.
	(2) Sub-paragraph (1) above does not apply to a variation under the agreement which takes account only of a change in value added tax.
	(3) References in sub-paragraph (2) above to a change in value added tax include references to a change to or from no tax being charged.
	Duration of hire
8 All types including a provision that goods are to be bailed or hired for a fixed period or a minimum period.	A statement indicating that goods are to be bailed or hired under the agreement for a fixed period or a minimum period, as the case may be, and the duration of that period.

TYPE OF AGREEMENT (1)	INFORMATION (2)
OTHER INFORMATION	
Security provided by the hirer	
9 All types in relation to which any security is to be provided by the hirer to secure the carrying out of the obligations of the hirer under the agreement.	A description of the security to be provided by the hirer in relation to the agreement sufficient to identify it and a description of the subject matter to which it relates.
[Charges	
10 All types.	(1) A list of any charges payable under the agreement to the owner upon failure by the hirer or a relative of his to do or refrain from doing anything which he is required to do or refrain from doing, as the case may be.
	(2) A statement indicating any term of the agreement which provides for charges not required to be shown under (1) above.]
[Cancellation rights	
11. Agreements that are not cancellable agreements.	A statement that the agreement is not cancellable.]

NOTES

Paras 1, 10: substituted by the Consumer Credit (Agreements) (Amendment) Regulations 2004, SI 2004/1482, regs 2, 12(1)–(3).

Para 2: words in square brackets substituted by the Consumer Credit Act 1974 (Electronic Communications) Order 2004, SI 2004/3236, art 4(1), (5).

Para 11: inserted by SI 2004/1482, regs 2, 12(1), (4).

[SCHEDULE 4
FORMS OF STATEMENT OF PROTECTION AND REMEDIES AVAILABLE UNDER THE CONSUMER CREDIT ACT 1974 TO HIRERS UNDER REGULATED CONSUMER HIRE AGREEMENTS

Regulation 3(3)

[2.35]

FORM (1)	TYPE OF AGREEMENT (2)	FORM OF STATEMENT (3)
1	Agreement to which section 58(1) of the Act applies.	YOUR RIGHTS Under the Consumer Credit Act 1974, you should have been given a copy of this agreement at least seven days ago so you could consider whether to go ahead. If the owner did not give you a copy this agreement can only be enforced with a court order.
2	All types.	MISSING PAYMENTS Missing payments could have severe consequences and may make obtaining credit more difficult.
3	All agreements which are secured on property.	YOUR HOME MAY BE REPOSSESSED Your home may be repossessed if you do not keep up repayments on a hire agreement secured by a mortgage or other security on your home.
4	All cancellable agreements not included in paragraph 5.	YOUR RIGHT TO CANCEL Once you have signed this agreement you have a short time in which you can cancel it. Details of how to cancel it will be sent to you by the owner.

FORM (1)	TYPE OF AGREEMENT (2)	FORM OF STATEMENT (3)
5	Modifying agreements treated under section 82(5) of the Act as cancellable agreements.	YOUR RIGHT TO CANCEL This agreement modifies an earlier agreement. Once you have signed it, your right to cancel the earlier agreement will cover this modified agreement. The cancellation period itself is unchanged. Details of how you can cancel can be found in the copy of this agreement.
6	Agreements to which the hirer is entitled to terminate by notice under section 101(1) of the Act and which provides for the bailment or hiring of goods for at least 18 months after the making of the agreement.	IMPORTANT—READ THIS CAREFULLY TO FIND OUT ABOUT YOUR RIGHTS] The Consumer Credit Act 1974 lays down certain requirements for your protection which should have been complied with when this agreement was made. If they were not, the owner cannot enforce this agreement without getting a court order. The Act also gives you a number of rights. You can end this agreement by writing to the person you make your payments to and giving at least * notice. In order to do this the agreement must have been allowed to run for at least 18 months [from the date of the original agreement]** though this may include the period of notice. You will have to make all payments and pay any amounts you owe until the date the agreement comes to an end. If you would like to know more about your rights under the Act, contact either your local Trading Standards Department or your nearest Citizens' Advice Bureau. Notes: *Owner to insert minimum period of notice as determined by section 101. **Owner to omit passage in square brackets except where this notice appears in a modifying agreement.
7	Agreements not included in paragraph 6.	IMPORTANT—READ THIS CAREFULLY TO FIND OUT ABOUT YOUR RIGHTS The Consumer Credit Act 1974 covers this agreement and lays down certain requirements for your protection which should have been complied with when this agreement was made. If they were not, the owner cannot enforce this agreement against you without getting a court order. If you would like to know more about your rights under the Act, contact either your local Trading Standards Department or your nearest Citizens' Advice Bureau.]

NOTES

Substituted by the Consumer Credit (Agreements) (Amendment) Regulations 2004, SI 2004/1482, regs 2, 13.

SCHEDULE 5
FORMS OF SIGNATURE BOX

PART I
REGULATED CONSUMER CREDIT AGREEMENTS

Regulation 2(7)

[2.36]

FORM NO (1)	TYPE OF AGREEMENT (2)	FORM OF SIGNATURE BOX (3)
1	Hire-purchase agreements.	This is a Hire-Purchase Agreement regulated by the Consumer Credit Act 1974. Sign it only if you want to be legally bound by its terms.
		Signature(s)
		of Debtor(s)
		Date(s) of signature(s)*
		The goods will not become your property until you have made all the payments. You must not sell them before then.
		Note:
		* Creditor may omit "Date(s) of signature(s)" where, by virtue of Regulation 6(3)(c), the date is not required.
2	Conditional sale agreements relating to land.	This is a Conditional Sale Agreement regulated by the Consumer Credit Act 1974. Sign it only if you want to be legally bound by its terms.
		Signature(s)
		of Debtor(s)
		Date(s) of signature(s)*
		The land will not become your property until you have made** payments. You must not sell it before then.
		Notes:
		* Creditor may omit "Date(s) of signature(s)" where, by virtue of Regulation 6(3)(c) the date is not required.
		** Creditor to insert "all the" or the number of payments as appropriate.
3	Conditional sale agreements relating to goods.	This is a Conditional Sale Agreement regulated by the Consumer Credit Act 1974. Sign it only if you want to be legally bound by its terms.
		Signature(s)
		of Debtor(s)
		Date(s) of signature(s)*
		The goods will not become your property until you have made** payments. You must not sell them before then.
		Notes:
		* Creditor may omit "Date(s) of signature(s)" where, by virtue of Regulation 6(3)(c), the date is not required.
		** Creditor to insert "all the" or the number of payments as appropriate.
4	Agreements under which a person takes any article in pawn and where the agreement is not separate from the pawn-receipt.	This is a Credit Agreement regulated by the Consumer Credit Act 1974. Sign it only if you want to be legally bound by its terms.
		Signature(s)*
		of Debtor(s)
		Date(s) of signature(s)*

		This document is also your PAWN-RECEIPT. Keep it safely.
		Note:
		* Creditor may omit "Date(s) of signature(s)" where, by virtue of Regulation 6(3)(c), the date is not required.
5	Multiple agreements of which at least one part is a credit agreement not regulated by the Act.	This is a Credit Agreement partly regulated by the Consumer Credit Act 1974. Sign it only if you want to be legally bound by its terms.
		Signature(s)
		of Debtor(s)
		Date(s) of signature(s)*
		Note:
		* Creditor may omit "Date(s) of signature(s)" where, by virtue of Regulation 6(3)(c), the date is not required.
6	Agreements not included in paragraphs 1–5 or 7–8.	This is a Credit Agreement regulated by the Consumer Credit Act 1974. Sign it only if you want to be legally bound by its terms.
		Signature(s)
		of Debtor(s)
		Date(s) of signature(s)*
		Note:
		* Creditor may omit "Date(s) of signature(s)" where, by virtue of Regulation 6(3)(c), the date is not required.
7	Modifying agreements varying or supplementing earlier multiple agreements of which at least one part was a credit agreement not regulated by the Act and where at least one part of the modified agreement is not regulated.	This Agreement varies and/or supplements a Credit Agreement and is partly regulated by the Consumer Credit Act 1974. Sign it only if you want to be legally bound by the new terms.
		Signature(s)
		Debtor(s)
		Date(s) of signature(s)*
		Note:
		* Creditor may omit "Date(s) of signature(s)" where, by virtue of Regulation 6(3)(c), the date is not required.
8	Modifying agreements other than those included in paragraph 7.	This Agreement varies and/or supplements a* Agreement regulated by the Consumer Credit Act 1974. Sign it only if you want to be legally bound by the new terms.
		Signature(s)
		of Debtor(s)
		Date(s) of signature(s)**
		Notes:
		* Creditor to insert "Hire-Purchase" or "Conditional Sale" or "Credit" as appropriate
		** Creditor may omit "Date(s) of signature(s)" where, by virtue of Regulation 6(3)(c), the date is not required.

PART II
REGULATED CONSUMER HIRE AGREEMENTS

Regulation 3(6)

[2.37]

FORM NO	TYPE OF AGREEMENT	FORM OF SIGNATURE BOX
(1)	(2)	(3)
9	All types not included in paragraph 10.	This is a Hire Agreement regulated by the Consumer Credit Act 1974. Sign it only if you want to be legally bound by its terms. (Signature(s) of Hirer(s) Date(s) of signature(s)* Under this agreement the goods do not become your property and you must not sell them. Note: * Owner may omit "Date(s) of signature(s)" where, by virtue of Regulation 6(3)(c), the date is not required.
10	Modifying agreements.	This Agreement varies and/or supplements a Hire Agreement regulated by the Consumer Credit Act 1974. Sign it only if you want to be legally bound by the new terms. (Signature(s) of Hirer(s) Date(s) of signature(s)* Note: * Owner may omit "Date(s) of signature(s)" where, by virtue of Regulation 6(3)(c), the date is not required.

[PART III
AGREEMENTS UNDER WHICH A SEPARATE FORM OF CONSENT IS REQUIRED]

[Regulation 2(7)]

[2.38]

[1	TYPE OF AGREEMENT	FORM OF CONSENT
(1)	(2)	(3)
	Agreements under which a separate form of consent is required.	I wish to purchase [. . . . .] * / ** I understand that I am purchasing the product(s) ticked above on credit provided by you and that the terms relating to the credit for the products can be found [. . . . .]*** in this agreement. Your signature(s): Notes: * Creditor to list the products being offered to the debtor for purchase. ** Debtor to indicate which products they wish to purchase by putting a tick next to the name(s) of the product(s). *** Creditor to insert the cross-references to the terms of the agreement containing the terms relating to the credit for the products being purchased.]

NOTES

Inserted by the Consumer Credit (Agreements) (Amendment) Regulations 2004, SI 2004/1482, regs 2, 14.

Part 2   **Statutory Instruments**

SCHEDULE 6
PRESCRIBED TERMS FOR THE PURPOSES OF SECTIONS 61(1)(A) AND 127(3) OF THE CONSUMER CREDIT ACT 1974

Regulation 6(1)

[2.39]

TYPE OF AGREEMENT (1)	PRESCRIBED TERMS (2)
Amount of credit	
1 Restricted-use debtor-creditor-supplier agreements for fixed-sum credit—	A term stating the amount of the credit, which may be expressed as the total cash price of the goods, services, land or other things, the acquisition of which is to be financed by credit under the agreement.
(a) to finance a transaction comprising the acquisition of goods, services, land or other things specified in the agreement or identified and agreed on at the time the agreement is made;	
(b) under which the total amount payable by the debtor is not greater than the total cash price; and	
(c) under which there is no advance payment.	
2 Agreements for fixed-sum credit not falling within paragraph 1.	A term stating the amount of the credit.
Credit limit	
3 Agreements for running-account credit.	A term stating the credit limit or the manner in which it will be
Rate of interest	
4 Agreements for—	A term stating the rate of any interest on the credit to be provided under the agreement.
(a) running-account credit; and	
(b) fixed-sum credit falling within the exceptions in paragraph 9(a) to (c) of Schedule 1 to these Regulations.	
Repayments	
5 Consumer credit agreements.	A term stating how the debtor is to discharge his obligations under the agreement to make the repayments, which may be expressed by reference to a combination of any of the following—
	(a) number of repayments;
	(b) amount of repayments;
	(c) frequency and timing of repayments;
	(d) dates of repayments;
	(e) the manner in which any of the above may be determined;
	or in any other way, and any power of the creditor to vary what is payable.
6 Consumer hire agreements.	A term stating how the hirer is to discharge his obligations under the agreement to pay the hire payments, which may be expressed by reference to a combination of any of the following—
	(a) number of payments;
	(b) amount of payments;
	(c) frequency and timing of payments;
	(d) dates of payments;
	(e) the manner in which any of the above may be determined;

TYPE OF AGREEMENT	PRESCRIBED TERMS
(1)	**(2)**
	or in any other way, and any power of the owner to vary what is payable.

NOTES

Consumer Credit Act 1974, s 127(3): Repealed, subject to transitional provisions and savings, by the Consumer Credit Act 2006, ss 15, 69(1), 70, Sch 3, paras 1, 11(b), Sch 4.

SCHEDULE 7
PROVISIONS RELATING TO DISCLOSURE OF THE APR

Regulation 1(2)

[2.40]
[1   Assumptions about running-account credit

In the case of an agreement for running-account credit, the following assumptions shall have effect for the purpose of calculating the APR in place of the assumptions in . . . the [total charge for credit rules] that might otherwise apply—

(1)   in any case where there will be a credit limit but that limit is not known at the date of making the agreement the amount of the credit to be provided shall be taken to be £1,500 or, in a case where the credit limit will be less than £1,500, an amount equal to that limit;

(2)   it shall be assumed that the credit is provided for a period of one year beginning with the relevant date;

(3)   it shall be assumed that the credit is provided in full on the relevant date;

(4)   where the rate of interest will change at a time provided in the agreement within a period of three years beginning with the date of the making of the agreement, the rate shall be taken to be the highest rate at any time obtaining under the agreement in that period;

(5)   where the agreement provides credit to finance the purchase of goods, services, land or other things and also provides one or more of—

    (a)   cash loans;

    (b)   credit to refinance existing indebtedness of the debtor's, whether to the creditor or another person; and

    (c)   credit for any other purpose,

and either or both different rates of interest and different charges are payable in relation to the credit provided for all or some of these purposes, it shall be assumed that the rate of interest and charges payable in relation to the whole of the credit are those applicable to the provision of credit for the purchase of goods, services, land or other things;

(6)   it shall be assumed that the credit is repaid—

    (a)   in twelve equal instalments, and

    (b)   at monthly intervals, beginning one month after the relevant date.

1A   Permissible tolerances in disclosure of the APR

For the purposes of these Regulations, it shall be sufficient compliance with the requirement to show the APR if there is included in the document—

(1)   a rate which exceed the APR by not more than one; or

(2)   a rate which falls short of the APR by not more than 0.1; or

(3)   in a case to which either of paragraphs 2 or 3 below applies, a rate determined in accordance with the paragraph or such of them as apply to that case.]

2   Tolerance where repayments are nearly equal

In the case of an agreement under which all repayments but one are equal and that one repayment does not differ from any other repayment by more whole pence than there are repayments, there may be included in the document a rate found under . . . the [total charge for credit rules] as if that one repayment were equal to the other repayments.

3   Tolerance where interval between relevant date and first repayment is greater than interval between repayments

In the case of an agreement under which—

    (a)   three or more repayments are to be made at equal intervals; and

    (b)   the interval between the relevant date and the first repayment is greater than the interval between the repayments,

there may be included in the document a rate found under . . . the [total charge for credit rules] as if the interval between the relevant date and the first repayment were shortened so as to be equal to the interval between the repayments.

4, 5 . . .

NOTES

Para 1: substituted together with para 1A, for original para 1, by the Consumer Credit (Agreements) (Amendment) Regulations 2004, SI 2004/1482, regs 2, 15; words omitted revoked and words in square brackets substituted, by the Financial Services and Markets Act 2000 (Regulated Activities) (Amendment) (No 2) Order 2013, SI 2013/1881, art 23(1), (3), (6)(a), for transitional provisions see Pt 8 thereof at **[2.1007]** et seq.

Para 1A: substituted as noted to para 1 above.

Paras 2, 3: words omitted revoked and words in square brackets substituted by SI 2013/1881, art 23(1), (3), (6)(b), for transitional provisions see Pt 8 thereof at **[2.1007]** et seq.

Paras 4, 5: revoked by the Consumer Credit (Total Charge for Credit, Agreements and Advertisements) (Amendment) Regulations 1999, SI 1999/3177, reg 4(d).

SCHEDULE 8
REGULATED MODIFYING AGREEMENTS

Regulation 7(2)

PART I
INFORMATION TO BE CONTAINED IN DOCUMENTS EMBODYING REGULATED MODIFYING AGREEMENTS VARYING OR SUPPLANTING EARLIER CREDIT AGREEMENTS

[2.41]

TYPE OF MODIFYING AGREEMENT (1)	INFORMATION (2)
Nature of modifying agreement	
[1 All types.	(1) A heading in one of the following forms of words—
	(a) "Agreement modifying a Hire-Purchase Agreement and regulated by the Consumer Credit Act 1974";
	(b) "Agreement modifying a Conditional Sale Agreement and regulated by the Consumer Credit Act 1974"; or
	(c) "Agreement modifying a Fixed-Sum Loan Agreement and regulated by the Consumer Credit Act 1974";
	(d) "Agreement modifying a Credit Card Agreement and regulated by the Consumer Credit Act 1974"; or
	(e) "Agreement modifying a Credit Agreement and regulated by the Consumer Credit Act 1974";
	as the case may require.
	(2) Where the document and a pawn-receipt are combined, the words ", and Pawn-Receipt," shall be inserted in the heading after the word "Agreement" in the second place that it occurs.
	(3) Where the document embodies an agreement of which at least one part is a credit agreement not regulated by the Act, the word "partly" shall be inserted before "regulated" unless the regulated and unregulated parts of the agreement are clearly separate.
	(4) Where the loan is being secured on land the words "secured on" and the address of the land shall be inserted at the end of the heading.]
Parties to modifying agreement	
2 All types	(1) The name[, postal address and, where appropriate, any other address] of the creditor.
	(2) The name[, postal address and, where appropriate, any other address] of the debtor.

TYPE OF MODIFYING AGREEMENT (1)	INFORMATION (2)
FINANCIAL AND RELATED PARTICULARS	
Description of goods, services, land etc and cash price	
3 Modifying agreements under which—	(1) A list or other description of the goods, services or other things and, in the case of land, a general description of the land (whether or not varied or supplemented under the modifying agreement) the acquisition of which is to be financed by credit under the modified agreement and the cash price (whether or not so varied or supplemented) in relation to each such list or other description:
(a) goods, services, land or other things, the acquisition of which was to be comprised in a transaction to be financed by an earlier restricted-use debtor-creditor-supplier agreement for fixed-sum credit and which were specified in the earlier agreement or identified and agreed on at the time the earlier agreement was made, are varied or supplemented; or	
(b) the cash price of goods, services, land or other things, the acquisition of which was to be comprised in a transaction to be financed by an earlier restricted-use debtor-creditor-supplier agreement for fixed-sum credit and which were specified in the earlier agreement or identified and agreed on at the time the earlier agreement was made, is varied but the goods, services, land or other things are not varied or supplemented.	Provided that, where both the description and the cash price of all the goods, services, land or other things the acquisition of which was to be comprised in a transaction to be financed by the earlier agreement are unchanged, the requirements of this paragraph may be satisfied in relation to such goods, services, land or other things by a statement clearly indicating that the descriptions and cash prices in the earlier agreement are unchanged.
	(2) The total cash price under the modified agreement.
Advance payments	
4 Modifying agreements in relation to which any advance payment is to be made by the debtor additional to any made in relation to an earlier agreement (whether under the modifying agreement or as a condition precedent to the making of that agreement) before he is provided with additional credit under that agreement, or, as the case may be, before he enters into that agreement.	The amount of the additional advance payments to be made by the debtor in relation to the modifying agreement, and, where the modifying agreement is a cancellable agreement, the nature of such payments.
Amount of credit	
5 Modifying agreements under which any charge included in the total charge for credit in relation to an earlier agreement for fixed-sum credit is varied or supplemented or under which the amount of the credit to be provided under such an earlier agreement is varied or supplemented, except—	(1) The total amount of the credit to be provided under the modified agreement calculated as follows, namely the total amount of the capital outstanding under the earlier agreement on the relevant date calculated in accordance with sub-paragraph (2) below, increased or reduced, as the case may require, by—
(a) modifying agreements falling within paragraph 3 under which both—	(a) the amount of any additional credit to be provided under the modifying agreement.
(i) the total amount payable by the debtor under the modified agreement is not greater than the total cash price under the agreement; and	(b) the amount of any reduction of credit to be effected under the modifying agreement.
(ii) there is no advance payment under the modifying agreement;	(2) The total amount of the capital outstanding referred to in sub-paragraph (1) above shall be the difference between—
[(b) modifying agreements where the earlier agreement is an agreement excluded from the scope of the Consumer Credit (Early Settlement) Regulations 2004 by regulation 2(2) of these Regulations.]	(a) the total amount of the repayments outstanding under the earlier agreement at the relevant date (whether or not due at that date); and
	(b) the total amount of the charges on the credit not yet accrued under the earlier agreement calculated in accordance with sub-paragraph (3) below.

Part 2   Statutory Instruments

TYPE OF MODIFYING AGREEMENT (1)	INFORMATION (2)
	[(3) The total amount of the charges on the credit not yet accrued referred to in sub-paragraph (2) above shall be the amount of a notional rebate calculated in accordance with the Consumer Credit (Early Settlement) Regulations 2004 as if early settlement had taken place and as if the settlement date were the relevant date disregarding any deferment of the settlement date under regulation 6 of those Regulations.]
[6 Modifying agreements both under which the amount of credit to be provided under an earlier agreement for fixed-sum credit is varied or supplemented and where the earlier agreement is an agreement excluded from the scope of the Consumer Credit (Early Settlement) Regulations 2004 by regulation 2(2) of those Regulations.	The total amount of the credit to be provided under the modified agreement calculated as follows, namely the total of— (a) the balance of the credit outstanding under the earlier agreement at the relevant date; (b) any charges thereon (included in the total charge for credit in relation to the credit to be provided under the earlier agreement) due and unpaid at the relevant date; (c) the amount of any additional credit to be provided under the modifying agreement, with a list of its constituent parts.]
Credit limit	
7 Modifying agreements under which the provisions relating to any credit limit under an earlier agreement for running-account credit are varied, including a change to or from there being no credit limit.	The varied credit limit under the modified agreement expressed as— (a) a sum of money; (b) a statement that the credit limit will be determined by the creditor from time to time under that agreement and that notice of it will be given by him to the debtor; (c) a sum of money together with a statement that the creditor may vary the credit limit to such sum as he may from time to time determine under that agreement and that notice of it will be given by him to the debtor; or (d) in a case not falling within head (a), (b) or (c) above, either a statement indicating the manner in which the credit limit will be determined and that notice of it will be given by the creditor to the debtor or a statement indicating that there is no credit limit.
[Term of the agreement	
7A. Modifying agreements under which the duration of an earlier agreement for running account credit of fixed duration is varied.	The duration of the modified agreement.
7B. Modifying agreements under which the duration of an earlier agreement for fixed-sum credit is varied.	The duration or minimum duration of the modified agreement.]
Total charge for credit, rate of interest, etc	
[8 Modifying agreements under which any charge included in the total charge for credit in relation to an earlier agreement for fixed-sum credit is varied or supplemented, except modifying agreements— (a) which do not specify either the intervals between repayments under the modified agreement or the amounts of repayments or both the intervals and the amounts;	(1) The total charge for credit in relation to the credit to be provided under the modified agreement, with a list of its constituent parts. (2) The varied or supplemented rates of any interest on the credit to be provided under the modified agreement quoted on a per annum basis, or a statement that the rates of interest under the earlier agreement are unchanged.

TYPE OF MODIFYING AGREEMENT (1)	INFORMATION (2)
(b) under which the total amount payable by the debtor under the modified agreement to discharge his indebtedness in respect of the amount of credit provided may vary according to any formula specified in such agreement having effect by reference to movements in the level of any index or to any other factor;	(3) A statement explaining how and when interest charges are calculated and applied under the modified agreement.]
(c) which provide for a variation of, or permit the creditor to vary, (whether or not by reference to any index) the amount or rate of any item included in the total charge for credit in relation to the modified agreement after the relevant date; or	
(d) under which the total amount payable by the debtor under the modified agreement is not greater than the total cash price under that agreement.	
[9 Modifying agreements under which—	(1) The total charge for credit in relation to the credit to be provided under the modified agreement with a list of its constituent parts and in the case of running-account credit, the total charge for credit shall be calculated on the same assumptions as are set out in paragraph 1 of Schedule 7 for the purpose of calculating the APR in place of the assumptions in . . . the [total charge for credit rules] that might otherwise apply.
(a) any charge included in the total charge for credit in relation to an earlier agreement for fixed-sum credit is varied or supplemented and which fall within the exceptions in paragraph 8(a) to (c); or	
(b) the rate of any other charge included in the total charge for credit in relation to an earlier agreement for running-account credit is varied or supplemented.	
	(2) The varied or supplemented rates of any interest on the credit to be provided under the modified agreement quoted on a per annum basis, or a statement that the rates of interest under the earlier agreement are unchanged.
	(3) A statement whether the interest rates to be shown under (2) above are fixed or variable.
	(4) A statement explaining how and when interest charges are calculated and applied under the modified agreement.]
Total amount payable	
10 Modifying agreements falling within paragraph 8.	The total amount payable under the modified agreement, being the total of any amounts to be shown under paragraphs 4, 5 or 6, and 8 above.
Timing of repayments	
11 Modifying agreements under which—	The timing of repayments to be made under the modified agreement expressed by reference to one or more of the following—
(i) the amount of the credit to be provided under an earlier agreement for fixed-sum credit is varied or supplemented;	(a) the dates on which each repayment is to be made;
(ii) the repayment provisions of an earlier agreement for fixed-sum or for running-account credit are varied or supplemented; or	(b) the frequency and number of the repayments and the date of the first repayment or a statement indicating the manner in which that date will be determined;
(iii) any charge included in the total charge for credit in relation to an earlier agreement for fixed-sum or for running-account credit is varied or supplemented.	(c) a statement indicating the manner in which the dates of the repayments will be determined.
Amount of repayments	
12 Modifying agreements falling within paragraph 11 but not falling within paragraph 13.	The amount of each repayment to be made under the modified agreement expressed as—

TYPE OF MODIFYING AGREEMENT (1)	INFORMATION (2)
	(a) a sum of money;
	(b) a specified proportion of a specified amount (including the amount outstanding from time to time);
	(c) a combination of heads (a) and (b) above; or
	(d) in a case where the amount of any repayment cannot be expressed in accordance with head (a), (b) or (c) above, a statement indicating the manner in which the amount will be determined.
13 Modifying agreements falling within paragraph 11 where—	The amount of each repayment to be made under the modified agreement (with or without the equivalent repayment after deduction of tax in accordance with section 26 of, and Schedule 7 to, the Finance Act 1982) expressed as—
(i) the credit to be provided under the modified agreement is repayable by two or more instalments; and	(a) a sum of money;
(ii) the interest on such credit is of a type to which section 26 of, and Schedule 7 to, the Finance Act 1982 apply.	(b) a specified proportion of a specified amount (including the amount outstanding from time to time);
	(c) a combination of heads (a) and (b) above; or
	(d) in a case where the amount of any repayment cannot be expressed in accordance with head (a), (b) or (c) above, a statement indicating the manner in which the amount will be determined:
	Provided that, where the amounts to be paid by the debtor after deduction of tax in accordance with section 26 of, and Schedule 7 to, the Finance Act 1982 are the same, the requirements of this paragraph may be satisfied by a statement indicating the lowest and highest amounts of the repayments to be made under the modified agreement before deduction of tax.
[13A Modifying agreements under which—	A statement of the order or proportions in which any amount paid by the debtor which is not sufficient to discharge the total debt then due under the agreement will be applied or appropriated by the creditor towards the discharge of the sums due—
(a) an earlier agreement is varied or supplemented so that different interest rates or different charges forming part of the total charge for credit or both are payable in respect of—	
(i) credit provided under the agreement for different purposes; or	(a) in respect of the amounts of credit provided for different purposes, or
(ii) different parts of the agreement,	(b) under each of the different parts of the agreement,
whether or not the agreement is a multiple agreement; or	as the case may be.]
(b) an earlier agreement is varied by varying the order or proportions in which any amount paid by the debtor which is not sufficient to discharge the total debt then due under the agreement will be applied or appropriated by the creditor towards the discharge of the sums due—	
(i) in respect of the amounts of credit provided for different purposes, or	
(ii) under each of the different parts of the agreement,	
as the case may require.	

TYPE OF MODIFYING AGREEMENT (1)	INFORMATION (2)
	APR
14 Modifying agreements under which— (a) the amount of the credit to be provided under an earlier agreement for fixed-sum credit is varied or supplemented; (b) the repayment provisions of such an agreement are varied or supplemented; or (c) any charge included in the total charge for credit in relation to such an agreement is varied or supplemented.	The APR in relation to the modified agreement or a statement indicating that the total amount payable under the modified agreement is not greater than the total cash price of the goods, services, land or other things, the acquisition of which is to be financed by credit under that agreement.
15 Modifying agreements not falling within paragraph 16 under which— (a) the provisions relating to any credit limit under an earlier agreement for running-account credit are varied, including a change to or from there being no credit limit; (b) the repayment provisions of such an agreement are varied or supplemented; or (c) any charge included in the total charge for credit in relation to such an agreement is varied or supplemented.	The APR in relation to the modified agreement.
16 (a) Modifying agreements under which— (i) the provisions relating to the credit limit under an earlier debtor-creditor-supplier agreement for running-account credit which fulfils all the criteria in sub-paragraph (b) below are varied; (ii) the repayment provisions of such an agreement are varied or supplemented; or (iii) any charge included in the total charge for credit in relation to such an agreement is varied or supplemented.	(1) The APR in relation to the modified agreement calculated on the assumptions specified in sub-paragraphs (2) and (3) below. (2) The first assumption referred to in sub-paragraph (1) above is the assumption that— (a) the debtor is provided with an amount of credit at the date of the making of the modifying agreement which, taken with the amount of the charge for that credit ascertained at that date under the provisions of the modified agreement, is equal to the credit limit under the modified agreement; and
(b) The criteria referred to in sub-paragraph (a) above are that— (i) the debtor agrees to pay the creditor an amount specified in the agreement on specified occasions; (ii) there is a credit limit; and (iii) charges for credit are either— (aa) a fixed amount in respect of each transaction; or	(b) the debtor repays the sum of the amounts referred to in head (a) above by payments of the amounts specified in the modified agreement on the occasions specified in that agreement and makes no other payment and obtains no further credit in relation to the account.
(bb) calculated as a proportion of the price payable under a transaction financed by the credit.	(3) The second assumption referred to in sub-paragraph (1) above is the like assumption as in sub-paragraph (2) above save that the sum of the amounts referred to in head (a) thereof shall be taken to be one third of the credit limit under the modified agreement.
17 Modifying agreements which are required under paragraph 14, 15 or 16 to disclose an APR in relation to the modified agreement and where the APR is based on a total charge for credit which is calculated to take account of relief available under section 19 of the Income and Corporation Taxes Act 1970 and Schedule 4 to the Finance Act 1976.	A statement indicating that it has been assumed in the calculation of the APR in relation to the modified agreement that relief may be available under section 19 of the Income and Corporation Taxes Act 1970 and Schedule 4 to the Finance Act 1976 in respect of premiums under certain policies of insurance without any deduction under section 21 of the said Act of 1970.

TYPE OF MODIFYING AGREEMENT (1)	INFORMATION (2)
Variable rates or items	
18 Modifying agreements which are required under paragraph 14, 15 or 16 to disclose an APR in relation to the modified agreement and under which the rate or amount of any item included in the total charge for credit in relation to the modified agreement will or may be varied (other than a variation in consequence of an event which is certain to occur).	A statement indicating that in calculating the APR in relation to the credit to be provided under the modified agreement no account has been taken of any variation which may occur under that agreement of the rate or amount of any item entering into that calculation.
19 Modifying agreements falling within paragraph 18.	A statement indicating the circumstances in which any variation referred to in paragraph 18 above may occur and, where that information is ascertainable at the time at which the document referred to in section 61(1) of the Act is presented or sent to the debtor for signature, the time at which any such variation may occur.
[[Land-related agreements]	
19A Modifying agreements which are required under paragraph 14, 15 or 16 to disclose an APR in relation to the modified agreement and under which the provisions of an earlier agreement are varied or supplemented with the result that the modified agreement is an agreement to which [paragraph 19A of Schedule 1] applies.	The initial standard variable rate (within the meaning of [the total charge for credit rules]) in relation to the modified agreement, together with a statement explaining— (a) what that rate is; and (b) that it has been taken into account in calculating the APR in relation to the modified agreement.]
OTHER INFORMATION	
Security provided by the debtor	
20 Modifying agreements (to which section 114 of the Act applies) under which an article taken in pawn by any person under an earlier agreement is varied or supplemented and where no separate pawn-receipt is given.	A statement indicating that an article has been taken in pawn under the modified agreement and a description of the article, unless unchanged from that in the earlier agreement, sufficient to identify it.
21 Modifying agreements (except those referred to in paragraph 20) under which— (a) any provisions for security provided by the debtor in relation to an earlier agreement to secure the carrying out of the obligations of the debtor under the earlier agreement are varied (including a variation to or from there being no security provided by the debtor); or (b) new or additional security is to be provided by the debtor.	A description of the new, additional or varied security to be provided by the debtor in relation to the modified agreement and of the subject matter to which it relates, sufficient to identify the new, additional or varied security, or a statement indicating that the debtor is no longer providing any security in relation to that agreement.
[Charges	
22 Modifying agreements under which any provision for charges under an earlier agreement are varied, including a variation to or from there being no such charges.	(1) A list of any charges payable under the modified agreement to the creditor upon failure by the debtor or a relative of his to do or refrain from doing anything which he is required to do or refrain from doing, as the case may be, or a statement indicating that no such charges are payable as the case may be. (2) A statement indicating any term of the modified agreement which provides for charges (a) not required to be shown under (1) above; or (b) included in the total charge for credit.]
[Cancellation rights	
23 Modifying agreements that are not treated as cancellable agreements under section 82(5) of the Act.	A statement that the modifying agreement is not cancellable.

TYPE OF MODIFYING AGREEMENT (1)	INFORMATION (2)
Amount payable on early settlement	
24 Agreements for fixed sum credit [secured on land] for a term of more than one month.	(1) Examples based on the amount of credit to be provided under the agreement or the nominal amount of either £1000 or £100, showing the amount that would be payable if the debtor exercised the right under section 94 of the Act to discharge his indebtedness on the date when—
	(a) a quarter of the term of the agreement elapses;
	(b) half of the term elapses; and
	(c) three quarters of the term elapses,
	or on the first repayment date after each of those dates.
	(2) A statement explaining that, in calculating the amounts shown, no account has been taken of any variation which might occur under the agreement, and that the amounts are accordingly only illustrative.]
[24A Modifying agreements falling within regulation 8(1A)(b) or (c)	A statement providing details of the debtor's right of early repayment under section 94 of the Act including—
	(1) the fact that the debtor has a right to repay early in full or part;
	(2) the procedure for early repayment, and
	(3) where applicable details of the creditor's right to compensation under [sections 95A and 95B] of the Act and the manner in which that compensation shall be determined.]

NOTES

Paras 1, 6, 8, 22: substituted by the Consumer Credit (Agreements) (Amendment) Regulations 2004, SI 2004/1482, regs 2, 16(1), (2), (4), (6), (9).

Para 2: words in brackets substituted by the Consumer Credit Act 1974 (Electronic Communications) Order 2004, SI 2004/3236, art 4(1), (7).

Para 5: words in square brackets substituted by SI 2004/1482, regs 2, 16(1), (3).

Paras 7A, 7B, 13A: inserted by SI 2004/1482, regs 2, 16(1), (5), (8).

Para 9: substituted by SI 2004/1482, regs 2, 16(1), (7); in column 2, words omitted revoked and words in square brackets substituted, by the Financial Services and Markets Act 2000 (Regulated Activities) (Amendment) (No 2) Order 2013, SI 2013/1881, art 23(1), (3), (7)(a), for transitional provisions see Pt 8 thereof at **[2.1007]** et seq.

Para 19A: inserted by the Consumer Credit (Total Charge for Credit, Agreements and Advertisements) (Amendment) Regulations 1999, SI 1999/3177, reg 4(e); years in square brackets inserted by SI 2010/1010, regs 51, 56(zb) (as inserted by SI 2010/1969, regs 4, 17), with effect in relation to certain agreements entered into before 1 February 2011, as provided for in regs 101, 101A of SI 2010/1010 at **[2.804]**, **[2.805]**; preceding heading inserted, and words in square brackets substituted, by SI 2013/1881, art 23(1), (7)(b), (c), for transitional provisions see Pt 8 thereof at **[2.1007]** et seq.

Para 23: inserted by SI 2004/1482, regs 2, 16(1), (10).

Para 24: inserted by SI 2004/1482, regs 2, 16(1), (10); words in square brackets inserted by SI 2010/1010, regs 51, 56(a), with effect in relation to certain agreements entered into before 1 February 2011, as provided for in regs 101, 101A of the 2010 Regulations at **[2.804]**, **[2.805]**.

Para 24A: inserted by SI 2010/1010, regs 51, 56(b), with effect in relation to certain agreements entered into before 1 February 2011, as provided for in regs 101, 101A of the 2010 Regulations at **[2.804]**, **[2.805]**; in para 24A in column (2), words in square brackets substituted by the Consumer Credit (Green Deal) Regulations 2012, SI 2012/2798, reg 5, Schedule, para 1(1), (3).

Part 2 Statutory Instruments

PART II
INFORMATION TO BE CONTAINED IN DOCUMENTS EMBODYING REGULATED MODIFYING AGREEMENTS VARYING OR SUPPLEMENTING EARLIER HIRE AGREEMENTS

Regulation 7(9)

[2.42]

TYPE OF MODIFYING AGREEMENT (1)	INFORMATION (2)
Nature of modifying agreement	
[1 All types.	(1) A heading in the following form of words—
	"Agreement modifying a Hire Agreement and regulated by the Consumer Credit Act 1974".
	(2) Where the credit is being secured on land the words "secured on" followed by the address of the land shall be inserted at the end of the heading.]
Parties to modifying agreement	
2 All types.	(1) The name[, postal address and, where appropriate, any other address] of the owner.
	(2) The name[, postal address and, where appropriate, any other address] of the hirer.
FINANCIAL AND RELATED PARTICULARS	
Description of goods	
3 Modifying agreements under which—	A list or other description of the goods to be bailed or hired under the modified agreement (whether or not varied or supplemented under the modifying agreement);
(a) goods to be bailed or hired under an earlier agreement are varied or supplemented; or	
(b) any provision of an earlier agreement relating to advance, hire or other payments is varied but the goods to be bailed or hired under the earlier agreement are not varied or supplemented.	Provided that, where the description of all goods to be bailed or hired under the earlier agreement is unchanged, the requirements of this paragraph may be satisfied in relation to such goods by a statement clearly indicating that the descriptions in the earlier agreement are unchanged.
Advance payments	
4 Modifying agreements in relation to which any advance payment is to be made by the hirer additional to any made in relation to an earlier agreement (whether under the modifying agreement or as a condition precedent to the making of that agreement) before he is to take possession of any additional goods to be bailed or hired under that agreement or, as the case may be, before he enters into that agreement.	The amount of the additional advance payments to be made by the hirer in relation to the modifying agreement, and, where the modifying agreement is a cancellable agreement, the nature of such payments.
Hire payments	
5 Modifying agreements under which any provisions of an earlier agreement relating to hire payments, other than advance payments, are varied or supplemented.	(1) The amount of each hire payment (other than an advance payment) to be made by the hirer under the modified agreement in relation to any period on or after the date of the modifying agreement.
	(2) The timing of such payments expressed by reference to one or more of the following—
	(a) the dates on which each payment is to be made;
	(b) the frequency and number of payments and the date of the first payment or a statement indicating the manner in which that date will be determined
	(c) a statement indicating the manner in which the dates of the payments will be determined.

TYPE OF MODIFYING AGREEMENT (1)	INFORMATION (2)
Other payments	
6 Modifying agreements under which any provisions of an earlier agreement relating to payments other than advance payments and hire payments are varied or supplemented, including a change to or from there being no such other payments.	(1) The amount (or a statement indicating the manner in which the amount will be determined) of each of the following descriptions of payments (not being an advance payment or a hire payment) to be made under the modified agreement by, or on behalf of, the hirer, or a relative of his, to the owner in relation to any period on or after the date of the modifying agreement, that is to say,—
	(a) any payment under arrangements for the installation, care, maintenance or protection of any goods;
	(b) any premium under a contract of insurance; or
	(c) any payment payable on termination of the modified agreement (other than a payment on default to be shown under paragraph 10 below).
	(2) The timing of such payments to be made under the modified agreement expressed by reference to one or more of the following—
	(a) the dates on which each payment is to be made;
	(b) the frequency and number of the payments and the date of the first payment or a statement indicating the manner in which that date will be determined; or
	(c) a statement indicating the manner in which the dates of the payments will be determined.
	(3) References in this paragraph to the owner include references to his near relative, his partner and a member of a group of which he is a member, to any person nominated by him or by any such person in relation to the arrangements, the contract of insurance or the termination of the modified agreement, and to a near relative of his partner; and "near relative" means, in relation to any person, the husband, wife, father, mother, brother, sister, son or daughter of that person and "group" means the person (including a company) having control of a company together with all the companies directly or indirectly controlled by him.
Variable payments	
7 Modifying agreements including provisions for variation of hire or other payments, where the amount of any such payment following any variation cannot be ascertained at the time of the making of the modifying agreement.	(1) Subject to sub-paragraph (2) below, a statement indicating the circumstances in which any hire payment to be shown under paragraph 5 above or any other payment to be shown under paragraph 6 may be varied under the modified agreement and, where that information is ascertainable at the time at which the document referred to in section 61(1) of the Act is presented or sent to the hirer for signature, the time at which any such variation may occur.
	(2) Sub-paragraph (1) above does not apply to a variation under the modified agreement which takes account only of a change in value added tax.
	(3) References in sub-paragraph (2) above to a change in value added tax include references to a change to or from no tax being charged.

TYPE OF MODIFYING AGREEMENT (1)	INFORMATION (2)
Duration of hire	
8 Modifying agreements under which— (a) additional goods are to be bailed or hired for a fixed period or a minimum period; or (b) any provisions of any earlier agreement that goods are to be bailed or hired for a fixed period or a minimum period are varied, including a variation to or from there being no such fixed or minimum period.	A statement indicating that goods are to be bailed or hired under the modified agreement for a fixed-period or a minimum period, as the case may be, and the duration of that period.
OTHER INFORMATION	
Security provided by the hirer	
9 Modifying agreements under which— (a) any provisions for security provided by the hirer in relation to an earlier agreement to secure the carrying out of the obligations of the hirer under the earlier agreement are varied (including a variation to or from there being no security provided by the hirer); or (b) new or additional security is to be provided by the hirer.	A description of the new, additional or varied security to be provided by the hirer in relation to the modified agreement and of the subject matter to which it relates, sufficient to identify the new, additional or varied security, or a statement indicating that the hirer is no longer providing any security in relation to that agreement.
Charges on default	
10 Modifying agreements under which any provisions for charges on default under an earlier agreement are varied, including a variation to or from there being no such charges.	[A list of all] charges payable under the modified agreement to the owner upon failure by the hirer or a relative of his to do or refrain from doing, as the case may be, or a statement indicating that no such charges are payable under that agreement.
[Cancellation rights	
11. Modifying agreements that are not treated as cancellable agreements under section 82(5) of the Act.	A statement that the modifying agreement is not cancellable.]

NOTES

Para 1: substituted by the Consumer Credit (Agreements) (Amendment) Regulations 2004, SI 2004/1482, regs 2, 17(1), (2).
Para 2: words in brackets substituted by the Consumer Credit Act 1974 (Electronic Communications) Order 2004, SI 2004/3236, art 4(1), (8).
Para 10: in column (2) words in square brackets substituted by SI 2004/1482, regs 2, 17(1), (3).
Para 11: inserted by SI 2004/1482, regs 2, 17(1), (4).

CONSUMER CREDIT (LINKED TRANSACTIONS) (EXEMPTIONS) REGULATIONS 1983

(SI 1983/1560)

NOTES

Made: 24 October 1983.
Authority: Consumer Credit Act 1974, ss 19(4), 69(5), 96(3), 189(1).
Commencement: 19 May 1985.

[2.43]
1 Citation, commencement and interpretation

(1) These Regulations may be cited as the Consumer Credit (Linked Transactions) (Exemptions) Regulations 1983 and shall come into operation on 19th May 1985.

(2) In these Regulations—

"the Act" means the Consumer Credit Act 1974;

. . .

. . . and

"guarantee of goods" means anything in writing which contains or purports to contain some promise of assurance (however worded or presented) that defects in goods will be made good by complete or partial replacement, or by repair, monetary compensation or otherwise.

[(2A) References in these Regulations to contracts of insurance and to deposits must be read with—

    (a)   section 22 of the Financial Services and Markets Act 2000;

    (b)   any relevant order under that section; and

    (c)   Schedule 2 to that Act.]

NOTES

Para (2): definitions omitted revoked by the Financial Services and Markets Act 2000 (Consequential Amendments and Repeals) Order 2001, SI 2001/3649, art 376(1).

Para (2A): added by SI 2001/3649, art 376(2).

[2.44]

2   Exempted linked transactions

(1) The linked transactions of the descriptions specified in paragraph (2) below shall be excluded from—

    (a)   the operation of section 19(3) of the Act (which provides that a linked transaction entered into before the making of the regulated consumer credit agreement or regulated consumer hire agreement to which it relates has no effect until such time (if any) as that agreement is made);

    (b)   section 69(1)(i) and (ii) (which provides that a notice of cancellation served by the debtor or hirer under a cancellable agreement shall operate to cancel any linked transaction and to withdraw any offer by the debtor or hirer, or his relative, to enter into a linked transaction); and

    (c)   the operation of section 96(1) (which provides that where the indebtedness of the debtor under a regulated consumer credit agreement is discharged before the time fixed by the agreement, he, and any relative of his, shall be discharged from any liability under a linked transaction, other than a debt which has already become payable).

(2) The linked transactions referred to in paragraph (1) above are as follows—

    (a)   contracts of insurance;

    (b)   other contracts in so far as they contain a guarantee of goods; or

    (c)   transactions comprising or effected under—

        (i)   any agreement for the operation of any account (including any savings account) for the deposit of money; or

        (ii)   any agreement for the operation of a current account, under which the customer may, by means of cheques or similar orders payable to himself or to any other person, obtain or have the use of money held or made available by the person with whom the account is kept and which records alterations in the financial relationship between the said person and the customer.

SUPPLY OF SERVICES (EXCLUSION OF IMPLIED TERMS) ORDER 1985

(SI 1985/1)

NOTES

Made: 4 January 1985.

Authority: Supply of Goods and Services Act 1982, s 12(4).

Commencement: 1 March 1985.

[2.45]

1

This Order may be cited as the Supply of Services (Exclusion of Implied Terms) Order 1985 and shall come into operation on 1st March 1985.

[2.46]

2

Section 13 of the Supply of Goods and Services Act 1982 (which provides that, in a contract for the supply of a service where the supplier is acting in the course of a business, there is an implied term that the supplier will carry out the service with reasonable care and skill) shall not apply to the services rendered by an arbitrator (including an umpire) in his capacity as such.

PROPERTY MISDESCRIPTIONS (SPECIFIED MATTERS) ORDER 1992

(SI 1992/2834)

NOTES
Made: 11 November 1992.
Authority: Property Misdescriptions Act 1991, s 1.
Commencement: 4 April 1993.

[2.47]
1

This Order may be cited as the Property Misdescriptions (Specified Matters) Order 1992 and shall come into force on 4th April 1993.

[2.48]
2

The matters contained in the Schedule to this Order are hereby specified to the extent described in that Schedule for the purposes of section 1(1) of the Property Misdescriptions Act 1991.

SCHEDULE
SPECIFIED MATTERS

Article 2

[2.49]
1. Location or address.

2. Aspect, view, outlook or environment.

3. Availability and nature of services, facilities or amenities.

4. Proximity to any services, places, facilities or amenities.

5. Accommodation, measurements or sizes.

6. Fixtures and fittings.

7. Physical or structural characteristics, form of construction or condition.

8. Fitness for any purpose or strength of any buildings or other structures on land or of land itself.

9. Treatments, processes, repairs or improvements or the effects thereof.

10. Conformity or compliance with any scheme, standard, test or regulations or the existence of any guarantee.

11. Survey, inspection, investigation, valuation or appraisal by any person or the results thereof.

12. The grant or giving of any award or prize for design or construction.

13. History, including the age, ownership or use of land or any building or fixture and the date of any alterations thereto.

14. Person by whom any building, (or part of any building), fixture or component was designed, constructed, built, produced, treated, processed, repaired, reconditioned or tested.

15. The length of time during which land has been available for sale either generally or by or through a particular person.

16. Price (other than the price at which accommodation or facilities are available and are to be provided by means of the creation or disposal of an interest in land in the circumstances specified in section 23(1)(a) and (b) of the Consumer Protection Act 1987 or Article 16(1)(a) and (b) of the Consumer Protection (NI) Order 1987 (which relate to the creation or disposal of certain interests in new dwellings)) and previous price.

17. Tenure or estate.

18. Length of any lease or of the unexpired term of any lease and the terms and conditions of a lease (and, in relation to land in Northern Ireland, any fee farm grant creating the relation of landlord and tenant shall be treated as a lease).

19. Amount of any ground-rent, rent or premium and frequency of any review.

20. Amount of any rent-charge.

21. Where all or any part of any land is let to a tenant or is subject to a licence, particulars of the tenancy or licence, including any rent, premium or other payment due and frequency of any review.

22. Amount of any service or maintenance charge or liability for common repairs.

23. Council tax payable in respect of a dwelling within the meaning of section 3, or in Scotland section 72, of the Local Government Finance Act 1992 or the basis or any part of the basis on which that tax is calculated.

24. Rates payable in respect of a non-domestic hereditament within the meaning of section 64 of the Local Government Finance Act 1988 or, in Scotland, in respect of lands and heritages shown on a valuation roll or the basis or any part of the basis on which those rates are calculated.

25. Rates payable in respect of a hereditament within the meaning of the Rates (Northern Ireland) Order 1977 or the basis or any part of the basis on which those rates are calculated.

26. Existence or nature of any planning permission or proposals for development, construction or change of use.

27. In relation to land in England and Wales, the passing or rejection of any plans of proposed building work in accordance with section 16 of the Building Act 1984 and the giving of any completion certificate in accordance with regulation 15 of the Building Regulations 1991.

28. In relation to land in Scotland, the granting of a warrant under section 6 of the Building (Scotland) Act 1959 or the granting of a certificate of completion under section 9 of that Act.

29. In relation to land in Northern Ireland, the passing or rejection of any plans of proposed building work in accordance with Article 13 of the Building Regulations (Northern Ireland) Order 1979 and the giving of any completion certificate in accordance with building regulations made under that Order.

30. Application of any statutory provision which restricts the use of land or which requires it to be preserved or maintained in a specified manner.

31. Existence or nature of any restrictive covenants, or of any restrictions on resale, restrictions on use, or pre-emption rights and, in relation to land in Scotland, (in addition to the matters mentioned previously in this paragraph) the existence or nature of any reservations or real conditions.

32. Easements, servitudes or wayleaves.

33. Existence and extent of any public or private right of way.

PACKAGE TRAVEL, PACKAGE HOLIDAYS AND PACKAGE TOURS REGULATIONS 1992

(SI 1992/3288)

NOTES
Made: 22 December 1992.
Authority: European Communities Act 1972, s 2(2).
Commencement: 23 December 1992.

ARRANGEMENT OF REGULATIONS

Part 2   Statutory Instruments

SCHEDULES

[2.50]
1   Citation and commencement
These Regulations may be cited as the Package Travel, Package Holidays and Package Tours Regulations 1992 and shall come into force on the day after the day on which they are made.

[2.51]
2   Interpretation
(1)   In these Regulations—
    "brochure" means any brochure in which packages are offered for sale;
    "contract" means the agreement linking the consumer to the organiser or to the retailer, or to
        both, as the case may be;
    "the Directive" means Council Directive 90/314/EEC on package travel, package holidays and
        package tours;
    ["member State" means a member State of the European Community or another State in the
        European Economic Area;]
    "offer" includes an invitation to treat whether by means of advertising or otherwise, and cognate
        expressions shall be construed accordingly;
    "organiser" means the person who, otherwise than occasionally, organises packages and sells or
        offers them for sale, whether directly or through a retailer;
    "the other party to the contract" means the party, other than the consumer, to the contract, that is,
        the organiser or the retailer, or both, as the case may be;
    "package" means the pre-arranged combination of at least two of the following components
        when sold or offered for sale at an inclusive price and when the service covers a period of
        more than twenty-four hours or includes overnight accommodation—
        (a)   transport;
        (b)   accommodation;
        (c)   other tourist services not ancillary to transport or accommodation and accounting for
                a significant proportion of the package, and
            (i)   the submission of separate accounts for different components shall not cause
                    the arrangements to be other than a package;
            (ii)   the fact that a combination is arranged at the request of the consumer and in
                    accordance with his specific instructions (whether modified or not) shall not of
                    itself cause it to be treated as other than pre-arranged; and
    "retailer" means the person who sells or offers for sale the package put together by the organiser.
(2)   In the definition of "contract" in paragraph (1) above, "consumer" means the person who takes
or agrees to take the package ("the principal contractor") and elsewhere in these Regulations
"consumer" means, as the context requires, the principal contractor, any person on whose behalf the
principal contractor agrees to purchase the package ("the other beneficiaries") or any person to
whom the principal contractor or any of the other beneficiaries transfers the package ("the
transferee").

NOTES
    Para (1): definition "member State" inserted by the Package Travel, Package Holidays and Package Tours (Amendment)
Regulations 1995, SI 1995/1648, reg 2(a).

[2.52]
3   Application of Regulations

(1)   These Regulations apply to packages sold or offered for sale in the territory of the United Kingdom.

(2)   Regulations 4 to 15 apply to packages so sold or offered for sale on or after 31st December 1992.

(3)   Regulations 16 to 22 apply to contracts which, in whole or part, remain to be performed on 31st December 1992.

[2.53]
4   Descriptive matter relating to packages must not be misleading

(1)   No organiser or retailer shall supply to a consumer any descriptive matter concerning a package, the price of a package or any other conditions applying to the contract which contains any misleading information.

(2)   If an organiser or retailer is in breach of paragraph (1) he shall be liable to compensate the consumer for any loss which the consumer suffers in consequence.

[2.54]
5   Requirements as to brochures

(1)   Subject to paragraph (4) below, no organiser shall make available a brochure to a possible consumer unless it indicates in a legible, comprehensible and accurate manner the price and adequate information about the matters specified in Schedule 1 to these Regulations in respect of the packages offered for sale in the brochure to the extent that those matters are relevant to the packages so offered.

(2)   Subject to paragraph (4) below, no retailer shall make available to a possible consumer a brochure which he knows or has reasonable cause to believe does not comply with the requirements of paragraph (1).

(3)   An organiser who contravenes paragraph (1) of this regulation and a retailer who contravenes paragraph (2) thereof shall be guilty of an offence and liable—
   (a)   on summary conviction, to a fine not exceeding level 5 on the standard scale; and
   (b)   on conviction on indictment, to a fine.

(4)   Where a brochure was first made available to consumers generally before 31st December 1992 no liability shall arise under this regulation in respect of an identical brochure being made available to a consumer at any time.

[2.55]
6   Circumstances in which particulars in brochure are to be binding

(1)   Subject to paragraphs (2) and (3) of this regulation, the particulars in the brochure (whether or not they are required by regulation 5(1) above to be included in the brochure) shall constitute implied warranties (or, as regards Scotland, implied terms) for the purposes of any contract to which the particulars relate.

(2)   Paragraph (1) of this regulation does not apply—
   (a)   in relation to information required to be included by virtue of paragraph 9 of Schedule 1 to these Regulations; or
   (b)   where the brochure contains an express statement that changes may be made in the particulars contained in it before a contract is concluded and changes in the particulars so contained are clearly communicated to the consumer before a contract is concluded.

(3)   Paragraph (1) of this regulation does not apply when the consumer and the other party to the contract agree after the contract has been made that the particulars in the brochure, or some of those particulars, should not form part of the contract.

[2.56]
7   Information to be provided before contract is concluded

(1)   Before a contract is concluded, the other party to the contract shall provide the intending consumer with the information specified in paragraph (2) below in writing or in some other appropriate form.

(2)   The information referred to in paragraph (1) is—
   (a)   general information about passport and visa requirements which apply to [nationals of the member State or States concerned] who purchase the package in question, including information about the length of time it is likely to take to obtain the appropriate passports and visas;
   (b)   information about health formalities required for the journey and the stay; and
   (c)   the arrangements for security for the money paid over and (where applicable) for the repatriation of the consumer in the event of insolvency.

(3)   If the intending consumer is not provided with the information required by paragraph (1) in accordance with that paragraph the other party to the contract shall be guilty of an offence and liable—

    (a)   on summary conviction, to a fine not exceeding level 5 on the standard scale; and

    (b)   on conviction on indictment, to a fine.

NOTES

Para (2): words in square brackets substituted by the Package Travel, Package Holidays and Package Tours (Amendment) Regulations 1998, SI 1998/1208, reg 5.

[2.57]
8   Information to be provided in good time

(1)   The other party to the contract shall in good time before the start of the journey provide the consumer with the information specified in paragraph (2) below in writing or in some other appropriate form.

(2)   The information referred to in paragraph (1) is the following—

    (a)   the times and places of intermediate stops and transport connections and particulars of the place to be occupied by the traveller (for example, cabin or berth on ship, sleeper compartment on train);

    (b)   the name, address and telephone number—

        (i)   of the representative of the other party to the contract in the locality where the consumer is to stay,

    or, if there is no such representative,

        (ii)   of an agency in that locality on whose assistance a consumer in difficulty would be able to call,

    or, if there is no such representative or agency, a telephone number or other information which will enable the consumer to contact the other party to the contract during the stay; and

    (c)   in the case of a journey or stay abroad by a child under the age of 16 on the day when the journey or stay is due to start, information enabling direct contact to be made with the child or the person responsible at the place where he is to stay; and

    (d)   except where the consumer is required as a term of the contract to take out an insurance policy in order to cover the cost of cancellation by the consumer or the cost of assistance, including repatriation, in the event of accident or illness, information about an insurance policy which the consumer may, if he wishes, take out in respect of the risk of those costs being incurred.

(3)   If the consumer is not provided with the information required by paragraph (1) in accordance with that paragraph the other party to the contract shall be guilty of an offence and liable—

    (a)   on summary conviction, to a fine not exceeding level 5 on the standard scale; and

    (b)   on conviction on indictment, to a fine.

[2.58]
9   Contents and form of contract

(1)   The other party to the contract shall ensure that—

    (a)   depending on the nature of the package being purchased, the contract contains at least the elements specified in Schedule 2 to these Regulations;

    (b)   subject to paragraph (2) below, all the terms of the contract are set out in writing or such other form as is comprehensible and accessible to the consumer and are communicated to the consumer before the contract is made; and

    (c)   a written copy of these terms is supplied to the consumer.

(2)   Paragraph (1)(b) above does not apply when the interval between the time when the consumer approaches the other party to the contract with a view to entering into a contract and the time of departure under the proposed contract is so short that it is impracticable to comply with the sub-paragraph.

(3)   It is an implied condition (or, as regards Scotland, an implied term) of the contract that the other party to the contract complies with the provisions of paragraph (1).

(4)   (*Applies to Scotland only.*)

[2.59]
10   Transfer of bookings

(1)   In every contract there is an implied term that where the consumer is prevented from proceeding with the package the consumer may transfer his booking to a person who satisfies all the conditions applicable to the package, provided that the consumer gives reasonable notice to the other party to the contract of his intention to transfer before the date when departure is due to take place.

(2)   Where a transfer is made in accordance with the implied term set out in paragraph (1) above, the transferor and the transferee shall be jointly and severally liable to the other party to the contract for payment of the price of the package (or, if part of the price has been paid, for payment of the balance) and for any additional costs arising from such transfer.

[2.60]
11   Price revision

(1)   Any term in a contract to the effect that the prices laid down in the contract may be revised shall be void and of no effect unless the contract provides for the possibility of upward or downward revision and satisfies the conditions laid down in paragraph (2) below.

(2)   The conditions mentioned in paragraph (1) are that—
   (a)   the contract states precisely how the revised price is to be calculated;
   (b)   the contract provides that price revisions are to be made solely to allow for variations in—
      (i)   transportation costs, including the cost of fuel,
      (ii)   dues, taxes or fees chargeable for services such as landing taxes or embarkation or disembarkation fees at ports and airports, or
      (iii) the exchange rates applied to the particular package; and

(3)   Notwithstanding any terms of a contract,
   (i)   no price increase may be made in a specified period which may not be less than 30 days before the departure date stipulated; and
   (ii)   as against an individual consumer liable under the contract, no price increase may be made in respect of variations which would produce an increase of less than 2 per cent, or such greater percentage as the contract may specify, ("non-eligible variations") and that the non-eligible variations shall be left out of account in the calculation.

[2.61]
12   Significant alterations to essential terms

In every contract there are implied terms to the effect that—
   (a)   where the organiser is constrained before the departure to alter significantly an essential term of the contract, such as the price (so far as regulation 11 permits him to do so), he will notify the consumer as quickly as possible in order to enable him to take appropriate decisions and in particular to withdraw from the contract without penalty or to accept a rider to the contract specifying the alterations made and their impact on the price; and
   (b)   the consumer will inform the organiser or the retailer of his decision as soon as possible.

[2.62]
13   Withdrawal by consumer pursuant to regulation 12 and cancellation by organiser

(1)   The terms set out in paragraphs (2) and (3) below are implied in every contract and apply where the consumer withdraws from the contract pursuant to the term in it implied by virtue of regulation 12(a), or where the organiser, for any reason other than the fault of the consumer, cancels the package before the agreed date of departure.

(2)   The consumer is entitled—
   (a)   to take a substitute package of equivalent or superior quality if the other party to the contract is able to offer him such a substitute; or
   (b)   to take a substitute package of lower quality if the other party to the contract is able to offer him one and to recover from the organiser the difference in price between the price of the package purchased and that of the substitute package; or
   (c)   to have repaid to him as soon as possible all the monies paid by him under the contract.

(3)   The consumer is entitled, if appropriate, to be compensated by the organiser for non-performance of the contract except where—
   (a)   the package is cancelled because the number of persons who agree to take it is less than the minimum number required and the consumer is informed of the cancellation, in writing, within the period indicated in the description of the package; or
   (b)   the package is cancelled by reason of unusual and unforeseeable circumstances beyond the control of the party by whom this exception is pleaded, the consequences of which could not have been avoided even if all due care had been exercised.

(4)   Overbooking shall not be regarded as a circumstance falling within the provisions of sub-paragraph (b) of paragraph (3) above.

[2.63]
14   Significant proportion of services not provided

(1)   The terms set out in paragraphs (2) and (3) below are implied in every contract and apply where, after departure, a significant proportion of the services contracted for is not provided or the organiser becomes aware that he will be unable to procure a significant proportion of the services to be provided.

(2)   The organiser will make suitable alternative arrangements, at no extra cost to the consumer, for the continuation of the package and will, where appropriate, compensate the consumer for the difference between the services to be supplied under the contract and those supplied.

(3)   If it is impossible to make arrangements as described in paragraph (2), or these are not accepted by the consumer for good reasons, the organiser will, where appropriate, provide the consumer with equivalent transport back to the place of departure or to another place to which the consumer has agreed and will, where appropriate, compensate the consumer.

[2.64]
15   Liability of other party to the contract for proper performance of obligations under contract

(1)   The other party to the contract is liable to the consumer for the proper performance of the obligations under the contract, irrespective of whether such obligations are to be performed by that other party or by other suppliers of services but this shall not affect any remedy or right of action which that other party may have against those other suppliers of services.

(2)   The other party to the contract is liable to the consumer for any damage caused to him by the failure to perform the contract or the improper performance of the contract unless the failure or the improper performance is due neither to any fault of that other party nor to that of another supplier of services, because—

    (a)   the failures which occur in the performance of the contract are attributable to the consumer;

    (b)   such failures are attributable to a third party unconnected with the provision of the services contracted for, and are unforeseeable or unavoidable; or

    (c)   such failures are due to—

        (i)   unusual and unforeseeable circumstances beyond the control of the party by whom this exception is pleaded, the consequences of which could not have been avoided even if all due care had been exercised; or

        (ii)   an event which the other party to the contract or the supplier of services, even with all due care, could not foresee or forestall.

(3)   In the case of damage arising from the non-performance or improper performance of the services involved in the package, the contract may provide for compensation to be limited in accordance with the international conventions which govern such services.

(4)   In the case of damage other than personal injury resulting from the non-performance or improper performance of the services involved in the package, the contract may include a term limiting the amount of compensation which will be paid to the consumer, provided that the limitation is not unreasonable.

(5)   Without prejudice to paragraph (3) and paragraph (4) above, liability under paragraphs (1) and (2) above cannot be excluded by any contractual term.

(6)   The terms set out in paragraphs (7) and (8) below are implied in every contract.

(7)   In the circumstances described in paragraph (2)(b) and (c) of this regulation, the other party to the contract will give prompt assistance to a consumer in difficulty.

(8)   If the consumer complains about a defect in the performance of the contract, the other party to the contract, or his local representative, if there is one, will make prompt efforts to find appropriate solutions.

(9)   The contract must clearly and explicitly oblige the consumer to communicate at the earliest opportunity, in writing or any other appropriate form, to the supplier of the services concerned and to the other party to the contract any failure which he perceives at the place where the services concerned are supplied.

[2.65]
16   Security in event of insolvency—requirements and offences

(1)   The other party to the contract shall at all times be able to provide sufficient evidence of security for the refund of money paid over and for the repatriation of the consumer in the event of insolvency.

(2)   Without prejudice to paragraph (1) above, and subject to paragraph (4) below, save to the extent that—

    (a)   the package is covered by measures adopted or retained by the member State where he is established for the purpose of implementing Article 7 of the Directive; or

    (b)   the package is one in respect of which he is required to hold a licence under the Civil Aviation (Air Travel Organisers' Licensing) Regulations 1972 or the package is one that is covered by the arrangements he has entered into for the purposes of those Regulations,

the other party to the contract shall at least ensure that there are in force arrangements as described in regulations 17, 18, 19 or 20 or, if that party is acting otherwise than in the course of business, as described in any of those regulations or in regulation 21.

(3)   Any person who contravenes paragraph (1) or (2) of this regulation shall be guilty of an offence and liable—

    (a)   on summary conviction to a fine not exceeding level 5 on the standard scale; and

(b)   on conviction on indictment, to a fine.

(4)   A person shall not be guilty of an offence under paragraph (3) above by reason only of the fact that arrangements such as are mentioned in paragraph (2) above are not in force in respect of any period before 1 April 1993 unless money paid over is not refunded when it is due or the consumer is not repatriated in the event of insolvency.

(5)   For the purposes of regulations 17 to 21 below a contract shall be treated as having been fully performed if the package or, as the case may be, the part of the package has been completed irrespective of whether the obligations under the contract have been properly performed for the purposes of regulation 15.

[2.66]
17   Bonding

(1)   The other party to the contract shall ensure that a bond is entered into by an authorised institution under which the institution binds itself to pay to an approved body of which that other party is a member a sum calculated in accordance with paragraph (3) below in the event of the insolvency of that other party.

(2)   Any bond entered into pursuant to paragraph (1) above shall not be expressed to be in force for a period exceeding eighteen months.

(3)   The sum referred to in paragraph (1) above shall be such sum as may reasonably be expected to enable all monies paid over by consumers under or in contemplation of contracts for relevant packages which have not been fully performed to be repaid and shall not in any event be a sum which is less than the minimum sum calculated in accordance with paragraph (4) below.

(4)   The minimum sum for the purposes of paragraph (3) above shall be a sum which represents—
   (a)   not less than 25 per cent of all the payments which the other party to the contract estimates that he will receive under or in contemplation of contracts for relevant packages in the twelve month period from the date of entry into force of the bond referred to in paragraph (1) above; or
   (b)   the maximum amount of all the payments which the other party to the contract expects to hold at any one time, in respect of contracts which have not been fully performed,
whichever sum is the smaller.

(5)   Before a bond is entered into pursuant to paragraph (1) above, the other party to the contract shall inform the approved body of which he is a member of the minimum sum which he proposes for the purposes of paragraphs (3) and (4) above and it shall be the duty of the approved body to consider whether such sum is sufficient for the purpose mentioned in paragraph (3) and, if it does not consider that this is the case, it shall be the duty of the approved body so to inform the other party to the contract and to inform him of the sum which, in the opinion of the approved body, is sufficient for that purpose.

(6)   Where an approved body has informed the other party to the contract of a sum pursuant to paragraph (5) above, the minimum sum for the purposes of paragraphs (3) and (4) above shall be that sum.

(7)   In this regulation—
   "approved body" means a body which is for the time being approved by the Secretary of State for the purposes of this regulation;
   "authorised institution" means a person authorised under the law of a member State[, of the Channel Islands or of the Isle of Man] to carry on the business of entering into bonds of the kind required by this regulation.

NOTES

   Para (7): words in square brackets in definition "authorised institution" inserted by the Package Travel, Package Holidays and Package Tours (Amendment) Regulations 1995, SI 1995/1648, reg 2(b).

[2.67]
18   Bonding where approved body has reserve fund or insurance

(1)   The other party to the contract shall ensure that a bond is entered into by an authorised institution, under which the institution agrees to pay to an approved body of which that other party is a member a sum calculated in accordance with paragraph (3) below in the event of the insolvency of that other party.

(2)   Any bond entered into pursuant to paragraph (1) above shall not be expressed to be in force for a period exceeding eighteen months.

(3)   The sum referred to in paragraph (1) above shall be such sum as may be specified by the approved body as representing the lesser of—
   (a)   the maximum amount of all the payments which the other party to the contract expects to hold at any one time in respect of contracts which have not been fully performed; or
   (b)   the minimum sum calculated in accordance with paragraph (4) below.

(4)   The minimum sum for the purposes of paragraph (3) above shall be a sum which represents not less than 10 per cent of all the payments which the other party to the contract estimates that he will receive under or in contemplation of contracts for relevant packages in the twelve month period from the date of entry referred to in paragraph (1) above.

(5)   In this regulation "approved body" means a body which is for the time being approved by the Secretary of State for the purposes of this regulation and no such approval shall be given unless the conditions mentioned in paragraph (6) below are satisfied in relation to it.

(6)   A body may not be approved for the purposes of this regulation unless—

(a)   it has a reserve fund or insurance cover with an insurer authorised in respect of such business in a member State[, the Channel Islands or the Isle of Man] of an amount in each case which is designed to enable all monies paid over to a member of the body of consumers under or in contemplation of contracts for relevant packages which have not been fully performed to be repaid to those consumers in the event of the insolvency of the member; and

(b)   where it has a reserve fund, it agrees that the fund will be held by persons and in a manner approved by the Secretary of State.

(7)   In this regulation, authorised institution has the meaning given to that expression by paragraph (7) of regulation 17.

NOTES

Para (6): words in square brackets in sub-para (a) inserted by the Package Travel, Package Holidays and Package Tours (Amendment) Regulations 1995, SI 1995/1648, reg 2(c).

[2.68]
19   Insurance

(1)   The other party to the contract shall have insurance under one or more appropriate policies with an insurer authorised in respect of such business in a member State under which the insurer agrees to indemnify consumers, who shall be insured persons under the policy, against the loss of money paid over by them under or in contemplation of contracts for packages in the event of the insolvency of the contractor.

(2)   The other party to the contract shall ensure that it is a term of every contract with a consumer that the consumer acquires the benefit of a policy of a kind mentioned in paragraph (1) above in the event of the insolvency of the other party to the contract.

(3)   In this regulation:

"appropriate policy" means one which does not contain a condition which provides (in whatever terms) that no liability shall arise under the policy, or that any liability so arising shall cease—

(i)   in the event of some specified thing being done or omitted to be done after the happening of the event giving rise to a claim under the policy;

(ii)   in the event of the policy holder not making payments under or in connection with other policies; or

(iii)   unless the policy holder keeps specified records or provides the insurer with or makes available to him information therefrom.

[2.69]
20   Monies in trust

(1)   The other party to the contract shall ensure that all monies paid over by a consumer under or in contemplation of a contract for a relevant package are held in the United Kingdom by a person as trustee for the consumer until the contract has been fully performed or any sum of money paid by the consumer in respect of the contract has been repaid to him or has been forfeited on cancellation by the consumer.

(2)   The costs of administering the trust mentioned in paragraph (1) above shall be paid for by the other party to the contract.

(3)   Any interest which is earned on the monies held by the trustee pursuant to paragraph (1) shall be held for the other party to the contract and shall be payable to him on demand.

(4)   Where there is produced to the trustee a statement signed by the other party to the contract to the effect that—

(a)   a contract for a package the price of which is specified in that statement has been fully performed;

(b)   the other party to the contract has repaid to the consumer a sum of money specified in that statement which the consumer had paid in respect of a contract for a package; or

(c)   the consumer has on cancellation forfeited a sum of money specified in that statement which he had paid in respect of a contract for a relevant package,

the trustee shall (subject to paragraph (5) below) release to the other party to the contract the sum specified in the statement.

(5)   Where the trustee considers it appropriate to do so, he may require the other party to the contract to provide further information or evidence of the matters mentioned in sub-paragraph (a), (b) or (c) of paragraph (4) above before he releases any sum to that other party pursuant to that paragraph.

(6)   Subject to paragraph (7) below, in the event of the insolvency of the other party to the contract the monies held in trust by the trustee pursuant to paragraph (1) of this regulation shall be applied to meet the claims of consumers who are creditors of that other party in respect of contracts for packages in respect of which the arrangements were established and which have not been fully performed and, if there is a surplus after those claims have been met, it shall form part of the estate of that insolvent other party for the purposes of insolvency law.

(7)   If the monies held in trust by the trustee pursuant to paragraph (1) of this regulation are insufficient to meet the claims of consumers as described in paragraph (6), payments to those consumers shall be made by the trustee on a pari passu basis.

[2.70]
21   Monies in trust where other party to contract is acting otherwise than in the course of business
(1)   The other party to the contract shall ensure that all monies paid over by a consumer under or in contemplation of a contract for a relevant package are held in the United Kingdom by a person as trustee for the consumer for the purpose of paying for the consumer's package.

(2)   The costs of administering the trust mentioned in paragraph (1) shall be paid for out of the monies held in trust and the interest earned on those monies.

(3)   Where there is produced to the trustee a statement signed by the other party to the contract to the effect that—
   (a)   the consumer has previously paid over a sum of money specified in that statement in respect of a contract for a package and that sum is required for the purpose of paying for a component (or part of a component) of the package;
   (b)   the consumer has previously paid over a sum of money specified in that statement in respect of a contract for a package and the other party to the contract has paid that sum in respect of a component (or part of a component) of the package;
   (c)   the consumer requires the repayment to him of a sum of money specified in that statement which was previously paid over by the consumer in respect of a contract for a package; or
   (d)   the consumer has on cancellation forfeited a sum of money specified in that statement which he had paid in respect of a contract for a package,
the trustee shall (subject to paragraph (4) below) release to the other party to the contract the sum specified in the statement.

(4)   Where the trustee considers it appropriate to do so, he may require the other party to the contract to provide further information or evidence of the matters mentioned in sub-paragraph (a), (b), (c) or (d) of paragraph (3) above before he releases to that other party any sum from the monies held in trust for the consumer.

(5)   Subject to paragraph (6) below, in the event of the insolvency of the other party to the contract and of contracts for packages not being fully performed (whether before or after the insolvency) the monies held in trust by the trustee pursuant to paragraph (1) of this regulation shall be applied to meet the claims of consumers who are creditors of that other party in respect of amounts paid over by them and remaining in the trust fund after deductions have been made in respect of amounts released to that other party pursuant to paragraph (3) and, if there is a surplus after those claims have been met, it shall be divided amongst those consumers pro rata.

(6)   If the monies held in trust by the trustee pursuant to paragraph (1) of this regulation are insufficient to meet the claims of consumers as described in paragraph (5) above, payments to those consumers shall be made by the trustee on a pari passu basis.

(7)   Any sums remaining after all the packages in respect of which the arrangements were established have been fully performed shall be dealt with as provided in the arrangements or, in default of such provision, may be paid to the other party to the contract.

[2.71]
22   Offences arising from breach of regulations 20 and 21
(1)   If the other party to the contract makes a false statement under paragraph (4) of regulation 20 or paragraph (3) of regulation 21 he shall be guilty of an offence.

(2)   If the other party to the contract applies monies released to him on the basis of a statement made by him under regulation 21(3)(a) or (c) for a purpose other than that mentioned in the statement he shall be guilty of an offence.

(3)   If the other party to the contract is guilty of an offence under paragraph (1) or (2) of this regulation shall be liable—
   (a)   on summary conviction to a fine not exceeding level 5 on the standard scale; and
   (b)   on conviction on indictment, to a fine.

Part 2   Statutory Instruments

[2.72]
23 Enforcement

Schedule 3 to these Regulations (which makes provision about the enforcement of regulations 5, 7, 8, 16 and 22 of these Regulations) shall have effect.

[2.73]
24 Due diligence defence

(1)   Subject to the following provisions of this regulation, in proceedings against any person for an offence under regulation 5, 7, 8, 16 or 22 of these Regulations, it shall be a defence for that person to show that he took all reasonable steps and exercised all due diligence to avoid committing the offence.

(2)   Where in any proceedings against any person for such an offence the defence provided by paragraph (1) above involves an allegation that the commission of the offence was due—
  (a)   to the act or default of another; or
  (b)   to reliance on information given by another,
that person shall not, without the leave of the court, be entitled to rely on the defence unless, not less than seven clear days before the hearing of the proceedings, or, in Scotland, the trial diet, he has served a notice under paragraph (3) below on the person bringing the proceedings.

(3)   A notice under this paragraph shall give such information identifying or assisting in the identification of the person who committed the act or default or gave the information as is in the possession of the person serving the notice at the time he serves it.

(4)   It is hereby declared that a person shall not be entitled to rely on the defence provided by paragraph (1) above by reason of his reliance on information supplied by another, unless he shows that it was reasonable in all the circumstances for him to have relied on the information, having regard in particular—
  (a)   to the steps which he took, and those which might reasonably have been taken, for the purpose of verifying the information; and
  (b)   to whether he had any reason to disbelieve the information.

[2.74]
25 Liability of persons other than principal offender

(1)   Where the commission by any person of an offence under regulation 5, 7, 8, 16 or 22 of these Regulations is due to an act or default committed by some other person in the course of any business of his, the other person shall be guilty of the offence and may be proceeded against and punished by virtue of this paragraph whether or not proceedings are taken against the first-mentioned person.

(2)   Where a body corporate is guilty of an offence under any of the provisions mentioned in paragraph (1) above (including where it is so guilty by virtue of the said paragraph (1)) in respect of any act or default which is shown to have been committed with the consent or connivance of, or to be attributable to any neglect on the part of, any director, manager, secretary or other similar officer of the body corporate or any person who was purporting to act in any such capacity he, as well as the body corporate, shall be guilty of that offence and shall be liable to be proceeded against and punished accordingly.

(3)   Where the affairs of a body corporate are managed by its members, paragraph (2) above shall apply in relation to the acts and defaults of a member in connection with his functions of management as if he were a director of the body corporate.

(4)   *(Applies to Scotland only.)*

(5)   On proceedings for an offence under regulation 5 by virtue of paragraph (1) above committed by the making available of a brochure it shall be a defence for the person charged to prove that he is a person whose business it is to publish or arrange for the publication of brochures and that he received the brochure for publication in the ordinary course of business and did not know and had no reason to suspect that its publication would amount to an offence under these Regulations.

[2.75]
26 Prosecution time limit

(1)   No proceedings for an offence under regulation 5, 7, 8, 16 or 22 of these Regulations or under paragraphs 5(3), 6 or 7 of Schedule 3 thereto shall be commenced after—
  (a)   the end of the period of three years beginning with the date of the commission of the offence; or
  (b)   the end of the period of one year beginning with the date of the discovery of the offence by the prosecutor,
whichever is the earlier.

(2)   For the purposes of this regulation a certificate signed by or on behalf of the prosecutor and stating the date on which the offence was discovered by him shall be conclusive evidence of that fact; and a certificate stating that matter and purporting to be so signed shall be treated as so signed unless the contrary is proved.

(3)   *(Applies to Scotland only.)*

[2.76]
27 Saving for civil consequences

No contract shall be void or unenforceable, and no right of action in civil proceedings in respect of any loss shall arise, by reason only of the commission of an offence under regulations 5, 7, 8, 16 or 22 of these Regulations.

[2.77]
28 Terms implied in contract

Where it is provided in these Regulations that a term (whether so described or whether described as a condition or warranty) is implied in the contract it is so implied irrespective of the law which governs the contract.

SCHEDULES

SCHEDULE 1
INFORMATION TO BE INCLUDED (IN ADDITION TO THE PRICE) IN BROCHURES WHERE RELEVANT TO PACKAGES OFFERED

Regulation 5

[2.78]
1. The destination and the means, characteristics and categories of transport used.

2. The type of accommodation, its location, category or degree of comfort and its main features and, where the accommodation is to be provided in a member State, its approval or tourist classification under the rules of that member State.

3. The meals which are included in the package.

4. The itinerary.

5. General information about passport and visa requirements which apply for [nationals of the member State or States in which the brochure is made available] and health formalities required for the journey and the stay.

6. Either the monetary amount or the percentage of the price which is to be paid on account and the timetable for payment of the balance.

7. Whether a minimum number of persons is required for the package to take place and, if so, the deadline for informing the consumer in the event of cancellation.

8. The arrangements (if any) which apply if consumers are delayed at the outward or homeward points of departure.

9. The arrangements for security for money paid over and for the repatriation of the consumer in the event of insolvency.

NOTES

Para 5: words in square brackets substituted by the Package Travel, Package Holidays and Package Tours (Amendment) Regulations 1998, SI 1998/1208, reg 4.

SCHEDULE 2
ELEMENTS TO BE INCLUDED IN THE CONTRACT IF RELEVANT TO THE PARTICULAR PACKAGE

Regulation 9

[2.79]
1. The travel destination(s) and, where periods of stay are involved, the relevant periods, with dates.

2. The means, characteristics and categories of transport to be used and the dates, times and points of departure and return.

3. Where the package includes accommodation, its location, its tourist category or degree of comfort, its main features and, where the accommodation is to be provided in a member State, its compliance with the rules of that member State.

4. The meals which are included in the package.

5. Whether a minimum number of persons is required for the package to take place and, if so, the deadline for informing the consumer in the event of cancellation.

6. The itinerary.

7. Visits, excursions or other services which are included in the total price agreed for the package.

8. The name and address of the organiser, the retailer and, where appropriate, the insurer.

9. The price of the package, if the price may be revised in accordance with the term which may be included in the contract under regulation 11, an indication of the possibility of such price revisions, and an indication of any dues, taxes or fees chargeable for certain services (landing, embarkation or disembarkation fees at ports and airports and tourist taxes) where such costs are not included in the package.

10. The payment schedule and method of payment.

11. Special requirements which the consumer has communicated to the organiser or retailer when making the booking and which both have accepted.

12. The periods within which the consumer must make any complaint about the failure to perform or the inadequate performance of the contract.

SCHEDULE 3
ENFORCEMENT

Regulation 23

Enforcement authority

[2.80]
1. (1) Every local weights and measures authority in Great Britain shall be an enforcement authority for the purposes of regulations 5, 7, 8, 16 and 22 of these Regulations ("the relevant regulations"), and it shall be the duty of each such authority to enforce those provisions within their area.

(2) The Department of Economic Development in Northern Ireland shall be an enforcement authority for the purposes of the relevant regulations, and it shall be the duty of the Department to enforce those provisions within Northern Ireland.

2. . . .

Powers of officers of enforcement authority
3 (1) If a duly authorised officer of an enforcement authority has reasonable grounds for suspecting that an offence has been committed under any of the relevant regulations, he may—
  (a)   require a person whom he believes on reasonable grounds to be engaged in the organisation or retailing of packages to produce any book or document relating to the activity and take copies of it or any entry in it, or
  (b)   require such a person to produce in a visible and legible documentary form any information so relating which is contained in a computer, and take copies of it,
for the purpose of ascertaining whether such an offence has been committed.
(2)   Such an officer may inspect any goods for the purpose of ascertaining whether such an offence has been committed.
(3)   If such an officer has reasonable grounds for believing that any documents or goods may be required as evidence in proceedings for such an offence, he may seize and detain them.
(4)   An officer seizing any documents or goods in the exercise of his power under sub-paragraph (3) above shall inform the person from whom they are seized.
(5)   The powers of an officer under this paragraph may be exercised by him only at a reasonable hour and on production (if required) of his credentials.
(6)   Nothing in this paragraph—
  (a)   requires a person to produce a document if he would be entitled to refuse to produce it in proceedings in a court on the ground that it is the subject of legal professional privilege or, in Scotland, that it contains a confidential communication made by or to an advocate or a solicitor in that capacity; or
  (b)   authorises the taking possession of a document which is in the possession of a person who would be so entitled.

4. (1)   A duly authorised officer of an enforcement authority may, at a reasonable hour and on production (if required) of his credentials, enter any premises for the purpose of ascertaining whether an offence under any of the relevant regulations has been committed.
(2)   If a justice of the peace, or in Scotland a justice of the peace or a sheriff, is satisfied—
  (a)   that any relevant books, documents or goods are on, or that any relevant information contained in a computer is available from, any premises, and that production or inspection is likely to disclose the commission of an offence under the relevant regulations; or
  (b)   that any such an offence has been, is being or is about to be committed on any premises, and that any of the conditions specified in sub-paragraph (3) below is met, he may by warrant under his hand authorise an officer of an enforcement authority to enter the premises, if need be by force.
(3)   The conditions referred to in sub-paragraph (2) above are—

(a)   that admission to the premises has been or is likely to be refused and that notice of intention to apply for a warrant under that sub-paragraph has been given to the occupier;

(b)   that an application for admission, or the giving of such a notice, would defeat the object of the entry;

(c)   that the premises are unoccupied; and

(d)   that the occupier is temporarily absent and it might defeat the object of the entry to await his return.

(4)   In sub-paragraph (2) above "relevant", in relation to books, documents, goods or information, means books, documents, goods or information which, under paragraph 3 above, a duly authorised officer may require to be produced or may inspect.

(5)   A warrant under sub-paragraph (2) above may be issued only if—

(a)   in England and Wales, the justice of the peace is satisfied as required by that sub-paragraph by written information on oath;

(b)   in Scotland, the justice of the peace or sheriff is so satisfied by evidence on oath; or

(c)   in Northern Ireland, the justice of the peace is so satisfied by complaint on oath.

(6)   A warrant under sub-paragraph (2) above shall continue in force for a period of one month.

(7)   An officer entering any premises by virtue of this paragraph may take with him such other persons as may appear to him necessary.

(8)   On leaving premises which he has entered by virtue of a warrant under sub-paragraph (2) above, an officer shall, if the premises are unoccupied or the occupier is temporarily absent, leave the premises as effectively secured against trespassers as he found them.

(9)   In this paragraph "premises" includes any place (including any vehicle, ship or aircraft) except premises used only as a dwelling.

Obstruction of officers

5.   (1)   A person who—

(a)   intentionally obstructs an officer of an enforcement authority acting in pursuance of this Schedule;

(b)   without reasonable excuse fails to comply with a requirement made of him by such an officer under paragraph 3(1) above; or

(c)   without reasonable excuse fails to give an officer of an enforcement authority acting in pursuance of this Schedule any other assistance or information which the officer may reasonably require of him for the purpose of the performance of the officer's functions under this Schedule,

shall be guilty of an offence.

(2)   A person guilty of an offence under sub-paragraph (1) above shall be liable on summary conviction to a fine not exceeding level 5 on the standard scale.

(3)   If a person, in giving any such information as is mentioned in sub-paragraph (1)(c) above,—

(a)   makes a statement which he knows is false in a material particular; or

(b)   recklessly makes a statement which is false in a material particular,

he shall be guilty of an offence.

(4)   A person guilty of an offence under sub-paragraph (3) above shall be liable—

(a)   on summary conviction, to a fine not exceeding level 5 on the standard scale; and

(b)   on conviction on indictment, to a fine.

Impersonation of officers

6.   (1)   If a person who is not a duly authorised officer of an enforcement authority purports to act as such under this Schedule he shall be guilty of an offence.

(2)   A person guilty of an offence under sub-paragraph (1) above shall be liable—

(a)   on summary conviction, to a fine not exceeding level 5 on the standard scale; and

(b)   on conviction on indictment, to a fine.

7.   . . .

Privilege against self-incrimination

8.   Nothing in this Schedule requires a person to answer any question or give any information if to do so might incriminate him.

COMMERCIAL AGENTS (COUNCIL DIRECTIVE) REGULATIONS 1993

(SI 1993/3053)

NOTES
Made: 7 December 1993.
Authority: European Communities Act 1972, s 2(2).
Commencement: 1 January 1994.

ARRANGEMENT OF REGULATIONS

PART I
GENERAL

[2.81]
1 Citation, commencement and applicable law

(1) These Regulations may be cited as the Commercial Agents (Council Directive) Regulations 1993 and shall come into force on 1st January 1994.

(2) These Regulations govern the relations between commercial agents and their principals and, subject to paragraph (3), apply in relation to the activities of commercial agents in Great Britain.

[(3) A court or tribunal shall—

   (a) apply the law of the other member State concerned in place of regulations 3 to 22 where the parties have agreed that the agency contract is to be governed by the law of that member State;

(b)   (whether or not it would otherwise be required to do so) apply these regulations where the law of another member State corresponding to these regulations enables the parties to agree that the agency contract is to be governed by the law of a different member State and the parties have agreed that it is to be governed by the law of England and Wales or Scotland.]

NOTES

Para (3): substituted by the Commercial Agents (Council Directive) (Amendment) Regulations 1998, SI 1998/2868, reg 2(a).

[2.82]
2 Interpretation, application and extent

(1)   In these Regulations—

"commercial agent" means a self-employed intermediary who has continuing authority to negotiate the sale or purchase of goods on behalf of another person (the "principal"), or to negotiate and conclude the sale or purchase of goods on behalf of and in the name of that principal; but shall be understood as not including in particular:

(i)   a person who, in his capacity as an officer of a company or association, is empowered to enter into commitments binding on that company or association;

(ii)   a partner who is lawfully authorised to enter into commitments binding on his partners;

(iii)   a person who acts as an insolvency practitioner (as that expression is defined in section 388 of the Insolvency Act 1986) or the equivalent in any other jurisdiction;

"commission" means any part of the remuneration of a commercial agent which varies with the number or value of business transactions;

["EEA Agreement" means the Agreement on the European Economic Area signed at Oporto on 2nd May 1992 as adjusted by the Protocol signed at Brussels on 17th March 1993;

"member State" includes a State which is a contracting party to the EEA Agreement;]

"restraint of trade clause" means an agreement restricting the business activities of a commercial agent following termination of the agency contract.

(2)   These Regulations do not apply to—

(a)   commercial agents whose activities are unpaid;

(b)   commercial agents when they operate on commodity exchanges or in the commodity market;

(c)   the Crown Agents for Overseas Governments and Administrations, as set up under the Crown Agents Act 1979, or its subsidiaries.

(3)   The provisions of the Schedule to these Regulations have effect for the purpose of determining the persons whose activities as commercial agents are to be considered secondary.

(4)   These Regulations shall not apply to the persons referred to in paragraph (3) above.

(5)   These Regulations do not extend to Northern Ireland.

NOTES

Para (1): definitions "EEA Agreement" and "member State" inserted by the Commercial Agents (Council Directive) (Amendment) Regulations 1998, SI 1998/2868, reg 2(b).

PART II
RIGHTS AND OBLIGATIONS

[2.83]
3 Duties of a commercial agent to his principal

(1)   In performing his activities a commercial agent must look after the interests of his principal and act dutifully and in good faith.

(2)   In particular, a commercial agent must—

(a)   make proper efforts to negotiate and where appropriate conclude the transactions he is instructed to take care of;

(b)   communicate to his principal all the necessary information available to him;

(c)   comply with reasonable instructions given by his principal.

[2.84]
4 Duties of a principal to his commercial agent

(1)   In his relations with his commercial agent a principal must act dutifully and in good faith.

(2)   In particular, a principal must—

(a)   provide his commercial agent with the necessary documentation relating to the goods concerned;

(b)   obtain for his commercial agent the information necessary for the performance of the agency contract, and in particular notify his commercial agent within a reasonable period once he anticipates that the volume of commercial transactions will be significantly lower than that which the commercial agent could normally have expected.

(3) A principal shall, in addition, inform his commercial agent within a reasonable period of his acceptance or refusal of, and of any non-execution by him of, a commercial transaction which the commercial agent has procured for him.

[2.85]
5 Prohibition on derogation from regulations 3 and 4 and consequence of breach

(1) The parties may not derogate from regulations 3 and 4 above.

(2) The law applicable to the contract shall govern the consequence of breach of the rights and obligations under regulations 3 and 4 above.

PART III
REMUNERATION

[2.86]
6 Form and amount of remuneration in absence of agreement

(1) In the absence of any agreement as to remuneration between the parties, a commercial agent shall be entitled to the remuneration that commercial agents appointed for the goods forming the subject of his agency contract are customarily allowed in the place where he carries on his activities and, if there is no such customary practice, a commercial agent shall be entitled to reasonable remuneration taking into account all the aspects of the transaction.

(2) This regulation is without prejudice to the application of any enactment or rule of law concerning the level of remuneration.

(3) Where a commercial agent is not remunerated (wholly or in part) by commission, regulations 7 to 12 below shall not apply.

[2.87]
7 Entitlement to commission on transactions concluded during agency contract

(1) A commercial agent shall be entitled to commission on commercial transactions concluded during the period covered by the agency contract—
  (a) where the transaction has been concluded as a result of his action; or
  (b) where the transaction is concluded with a third party whom he has previously acquired as a customer for transactions of the same kind.

(2) A commercial agent shall also be entitled to commission on transactions concluded during the period covered by the agency contract where he has an exclusive right to a specific geographical area or to a specific group of customers and where the transaction has been entered into with a customer belonging to that area or group.

[2.88]
8 Entitlement to commission on transactions concluded after agency contract has terminated

Subject to regulation 9 below, a commercial agent shall be entitled to commission on commercial transactions concluded after the agency contract has terminated if—
  (a) the transaction is mainly attributable to his efforts during the period covered by the agency contract and if the transaction was entered into within a reasonable period after that contract terminated; or
  (b) in accordance with the conditions mentioned in regulation 7 above, the order of the third party reached the principal or the commercial agent before the agency contract terminated.

[2.89]
9 Apportionment of commission between new and previous commercial agents

(1) A commercial agent shall not be entitled to the commission referred to in regulation 7 above if that commission is payable, by virtue of regulation 8 above, to the previous commercial agent, unless it is equitable because of the circumstances for the commission to be shared between the commercial agents.

(2) The principal shall be liable for any sum due under paragraph (1) above to the person entitled to it in accordance with that paragraph, and any sum which the other commercial agent receives to which he is not entitled shall be refunded to the principal.

[2.90]
10 When commission due and date for payment

(1) Commission shall become due as soon as, and to the extent that, one of the following circumstances occurs:
  (a) the principal has executed the transaction; or
  (b) the principal should, according to his agreement with the third party, have executed the transaction; or
  (c) the third party has executed the transaction.

(2)   Commission shall become due at the latest when the third party has executed his part of the transaction or should have done so if the principal had executed his part of the transaction, as he should have.

(3)   The commission shall be paid not later than on the last day of the month following the quarter in which it became due, and, for the purposes of these Regulations, unless otherwise agreed between the parties, the first quarter period shall run from the date the agency contract takes effect, and subsequent periods shall run from that date in the third month thereafter or the beginning of the fourth month, whichever is the sooner.

(4)   Any agreement to derogate from paragraphs (2) and (3) above to the detriment of the commercial agent shall be void.

[2.91]
11   Extinction of right to commission
(1)   The right to commission can be extinguished only if and to the extent that—
   (a)   it is established that the contract between the third party and the principal will not be executed; and
   (b)   that fact is due to a reason for which the principal is not to blame.

(2)   Any commission which the commercial agent has already received shall be refunded if the right to it is extinguished.

(3)   Any agreement to derogate from paragraph (1) above to the detriment of the commercial agent shall be void.

[2.92]
12   Periodic supply of information as to commission due and right of inspection of principal's books
(1)   The principal shall supply his commercial agent with a statement of the commission due, not later than the last day of the month following the quarter in which the commission has become due, and such statement shall set out the main components used in calculating the amount of the commission.

(2)   A commercial agent shall be entitled to demand that he be provided with all the information (and in particular an extract from the books) which is available to his principal and which he needs in order to check the amount of the commission due to him.

(3)   Any agreement to derogate from paragraphs (1) and (2) above shall be void.

(4)   Nothing in this regulation shall remove or restrict the effect of, or prevent reliance upon, any enactment or rule of law which recognises the right of an agent to inspect the books of a principal.

PART IV
CONCLUSION AND TERMINATION OF THE AGENCY CONTRACT

[2.93]
13   Right to signed written statement of terms of agency contract
(1)   The commercial agent and principal shall each be entitled to receive from the other on request, a signed written document setting out the terms of the agency contract including any terms subsequently agreed.

(2)   Any purported waiver of the right referred to in paragraph (1) above shall be void.

[2.94]
14   Conversion of agency contract after expiry of fixed period
An agency contract for a fixed period which continues to be performed by both parties after that period has expired shall be deemed to be converted into an agency contract for an indefinite period.

[2.95]
15   Minimum periods of notice for termination of agency contract
(1)   Where an agency contract is concluded for an indefinite period either party may terminate it by notice.

(2)   The period of notice shall be—
   (a)   1 month for the first year of the contract;
   (b)   2 months for the second year commenced;
   (c)   3 months for the third year commenced and for the subsequent years;
and the parties may not agree on any shorter periods of notice.

(3)   If the parties agree on longer periods than those laid down in paragraph (2) above, the period of notice to be observed by the principal must not be shorter than that to be observed by the commercial agent.

(4)   Unless otherwise agreed by the parties, the end of the period of notice must coincide with the end of a calendar month.

(5)   The provisions of this regulation shall also apply to an agency contract for a fixed period where it is converted under regulation 14 above into an agency contract for an indefinite period subject to the proviso that the earlier fixed period must be taken into account in the calculation of the period of notice.

[2.96]
16   Savings with regard to immediate termination
These Regulations shall not affect the application of any enactment or rule of law which provides for the immediate termination of the agency contract—
  (a)   because of the failure of one party to carry out all or part of his obligations under that contract; or
  (b)   where exceptional circumstances arise.

[2.97]
17   Entitlement of commercial agent to indemnity or compensation on termination of agency contract
(1)   This regulation has effect for the purpose of ensuring that the commercial agent is, after termination of the agency contract, indemnified in accordance with paragraphs (3) to (5) below or compensated for damage in accordance with paragraphs (6) and (7) below.
(2)   Except where the agency [contract] otherwise provides, the commercial agent shall be entitled to be compensated rather than indemnified.
(3)   Subject to paragraph (9) and to regulation 18 below, the commercial agent shall be entitled to an indemnity if and to the extent that—
  (a)   he has brought the principal new customers or has significantly increased the volume of business with existing customers and the principal continues to derive substantial benefits from the business with such customers; and
  (b)   the payment of this indemnity is equitable having regard to all the circumstances and, in particular, the commission lost by the commercial agent on the business transacted with such customers.
(4)   The amount of the indemnity shall not exceed a figure equivalent to an indemnity for one year calculated from the commercial agent's average annual remuneration over the preceding five years and if the contract goes back less than five years the indemnity shall be calculated on the average for the period in question.
(5)   The grant of an indemnity as mentioned above shall not prevent the commercial agent from seeking damages.
(6)   Subject to paragraph (9) and to regulation 18 below, the commercial agent shall be entitled to compensation for the damage he suffers as a result of the termination of his relations with his principal.
(7)   For the purpose of these Regulations such damage shall be deemed to occur particularly when the termination takes place in either or both of the following circumstances, namely circumstances which—
  (a)   deprive the commercial agent of the commission which proper performance of the agency contract would have procured for him whilst providing his principal with substantial benefits linked to the activities of the commercial agent; or
  (b)   have not enabled the commercial agent to amortize the costs and expenses that he had incurred in the performance of the agency contract on the advice of his principal.
(8)   Entitlement to the indemnity or compensation for damage as provided for under paragraphs (2) to (7) above shall also arise where the agency contract is terminated as a result of the death of the commercial agent.
(9)   The commercial agent shall lose his entitlement to the indemnity or compensation for damage in the instances provided for in paragraphs (2) to (8) above if within one year following termination of his agency contract he has not notified his principal that he intends pursuing his entitlement.

NOTES
  Para (2): word in square brackets substituted by the Commercial Agents (Council Directive) (Amendment) Regulations 1998, SI 1998/2868, reg 2(c).

[2.98]
18   Grounds for excluding payment of indemnity or compensation under regulation 17
The [indemnity or] compensation referred to in regulation 17 above shall not be payable to the commercial agent where—
  (a)   the principal has terminated the agency contract because of default attributable to the commercial agent which would justify immediate termination of the agency contract pursuant to regulation 16 above; or
  (b)   the commercial agent has himself terminated the agency contract, unless such termination is justified—
    (i)   by circumstances attributable to the principal, or

    (ii)   on grounds of the age, infirmity or illness of the commercial agent in consequence of which he cannot reasonably be required to continue his activities; or

  (c)   the commercial agent, with the agreement of his principal, assigns his rights and duties under the agency contract to another person.

NOTES

Words in square brackets inserted by the Commercial Agents (Council Directive) (Amendment) Regulations 1993, SI 1993/3173, reg 2.

[2.99]
19 Prohibition on derogation from regulations 17 and 18

The parties may not derogate from regulations 17 and 18 to the detriment of the commercial agent before the agency contract expires.

[2.100]
20 Restraint of trade clauses

(1) A restraint of trade clause shall be valid only if and to the extent that—
  (a)   it is concluded in writing; and
  (b)   it relates to the geographical area or the group of customers and the geographical area entrusted to the commercial agent and to the kind of goods covered by his agency under the contract.

(2) A restraint of trade clause shall be valid for not more than two years after termination of the agency contract.

(3) Nothing in this regulation shall affect any enactment or rule of law which imposes other restrictions on the validity or enforceability of restraint of trade clauses or which enables a court to reduce the obligations on the parties resulting from such clauses.

PART V
MISCELLANEOUS AND SUPPLEMENTAL

[2.101]
21 Disclosure of information

Nothing in these Regulations shall require information to be given where such disclosure would be contrary to public policy.

[2.102]
22 Service of notice etc

(1) Any notice, statement or other document to be given or supplied to a commercial agent or to be given or supplied to the principal under these Regulations may be so given or supplied:
  (a)   by delivering it to him;
  (b)   by leaving it at his proper address addressed to him by name;
  (c)   by sending it by post to him addressed either to his registered address or to the address of his registered or principal office;
or by any other means provided for in the agency contract.

(2) Any such notice, statement or document may—
  (a)   in the case of a body corporate, be given or served on the secretary or clerk of that body;
  (b)   in the case of a partnership, be given to or served on any partner or on any person having the control or management of the partnership business.

[2.103]
23 Transitional provisions

(1) Notwithstanding any provision in an agency contract made before 1st January 1994, these Regulations shall apply to that contract after that date and, accordingly any provision which is inconsistent with these Regulations shall have effect subject to them.

(2) Nothing in these Regulations shall affect the rights and liabilities of a commercial agent or a principal which have accrued before 1st January 1994.

SCHEDULE

Regulation 2(3)

[2.104]
1. The activities of a person as a commercial agent are to be considered secondary where it may reasonably be taken that the primary purpose of the arrangement with his principal is other than as set out in paragraph 2 below.

2. An arrangement falls within this paragraph if—
  (a)   the business of the principal is the sale, or as the case may be purchase, of goods of a particular kind; and

Part 2 Statutory Instruments

(b) the goods concerned are such that—
  (i) transactions are normally individually negotiated and concluded on a commercial basis, and
  (ii) procuring a transaction on one occasion is likely to lead to further transactions in those goods with that customer on future occasions, or to transactions in those goods with other customers in the same geographical area or among the same group of customers, and
  that accordingly it is in the commercial interests of the principal in developing the market in those goods to appoint a representative to such customers with a view to the representative devoting effort, skill and expenditure from his own resources to that end.

3. The following are indications that an arrangement falls within paragraph 2 above, and the absence of any of them is an indication to the contrary—
(a) the principal is the manufacturer, importer or distributor of the goods;
(b) the goods are specifically identified with the principal in the market in question rather than, or to a greater extent than, with any other person;
(c) the agent devotes substantially the whole of his time to representative activities (whether for one principal or for a number of principals whose interests are not conflicting);
(d) the goods are not normally available in the market in question other than by means of the agent;
(e) the arrangement is described as one of commercial agency.

4. The following are indications that an arrangement does not fall within paragraph 2 above—
(a) promotional material is supplied direct to potential customers;
(b) persons are granted agencies without reference to existing agents in a particular area or in relation to a particular group;
(c) customers normally select the goods for themselves and merely place their orders through the agent.

5. The activities of the following categories of persons are presumed, unless the contrary is established, not to fall within paragraph 2 above—
  Mail order catalogue agents for consumer goods.
  Consumer credit agents.

TRADING SCHEMES REGULATIONS 1997

(SI 1997/30)

NOTES
  Made: 13 January 1997.
  Authority: Fair Trading Act 1973, s 119.
  Commencement: 6 February 1997.

ARRANGEMENT OF REGULATIONS

[2.105]
1 Citation, commencement and application

(1) These Regulations may be cited as the Trading Schemes Regulations 1997 and shall come into force on 6th February 1997.

(2) Subject to paragraph (3) below, these Regulations shall apply—

(a) from the date of their coming into force to any trading scheme to which Part XI of the Fair Trading Act 1973 applies and which came into existence on or after the date of coming into force of these Regulations, and to any agreement made under such a trading scheme;

(b) after a period of six months from the date of their coming into force to any trading scheme in existence prior to the coming into force of the Act and to which Part XI of the Fair Trading Act 1973 did not apply prior to that date.

(3) Where an agreement is made after the date of coming into force of these Regulations but prior to the expiry of a six months period after that date under a trading scheme to which Part XI of the Fair Trading Act 1973 applied prior to the coming into force of the Act such agreement shall comply either with the 1989 Regulations or these Regulations.

(4) Subject to paragraph (3) above the 1989 Regulations shall not apply to any trading scheme coming into operation after the date of the coming into force of these Regulations or to any agreement made after that date under any trading scheme to which Part XI of the Fair Trading Act 1973 applies.

[2.106]
2 Interpretation

In these Regulations—

"the Act" means the Trading Schemes Act 1996;

"advertisement" means any advertisement, document, prospectus, circular or notice, whether transmitted in electronic or any other form, which promotes a trading scheme;

"the 1989 Regulations" means the Pyramid Selling Schemes Regulations 1989;

"the 1990 Regulations" means the Pyramid Selling Schemes (Amendment) Regulations 1990;

"participant" has the same meaning as in Part XI of the Fair Trading Act 1973;

"security" means a mortgage, charge, pledge, bond, debenture, indemnity, guarantee, bill, note or other right provided by the participant, or at his request (expressed or implied), to secure the carrying out of the obligations of the participant under an agreement referred to in regulation 4.

"trading scheme" has the same meaning as in Part XI of the Fair Trading Act 1973.

[2.107]
3 Contents of advertisements

(1) Subject to paragraph (2) of this regulation, a promoter of, or a participant in, a trading scheme shall not issue, circulate or distribute any advertisement which contains information likely to lead directly or indirectly to persons becoming participants in a trading scheme by any means unless such advertisement

(a) states the name and address of the promoter, or in the case of a scheme promoted by more than one person, the names and addresses of all of the promoters;

(b) describes the goods or services acquired or supplied under the trading scheme; and

(c) contains the words set out in Schedule 1 to these Regulations which must
   (i) not appear at the beginning or the end of the advertisement;
   (ii) insofar as the advertisement contains any information as to the sources of income for participants from participation in the trading scheme, appear together with such information and be given no less prominence than such information;
   (iii) be easily legible or audible; and
   (iv) be afforded no less prominence than that given to any other information in the advertisement apart from the heading of the advertisement.

(2) This regulation does not apply to any advertisement which—
(a) forms part of a newspaper or magazine; or
(b) is transmitted by way of a radio or television broadcast.

[2.108]
4 Pre-performance requirements

(1) Save where the requirements set out in paragraph (2) below are satisfied, no promoter of, nor participant in, a trading scheme shall—

(a) supply goods or services to a participant in the trading scheme;

(b) provide any goods or services under a transaction effected by such a participant;

(c) be a party to any arrangement under which goods or services are supplied or provided as aforesaid; or

(d) accept from any such participant any payment or undertaking to make a payment in respect of any goods or services supplied or provided as mentioned in any of the preceding paragraphs (a) to (c) above or in respect of any goods or services to be so supplied or provided.

(2) The requirements referred to in paragraph (1) above are that—

(a) the arrangements with a participant do not include a statement or promise that the participant will receive a payment or benefit in respect of the continued participation of another person in the trading scheme to which such arrangements relate or in any other trading scheme;

(b) the promoter or a participant and the participant joining the trading scheme shall have signed a written agreement which contains all the terms under which the participant joining the trading scheme is participating in the trading scheme and which complies with regulation 5;

(c) a copy of that agreement shall have been furnished to the participant joining the trading scheme.

[2.109]
5 Contents of contracts

The agreement referred to in regulation 4 shall include—

(a) the name and address of the promoter or, in the case of a scheme promoted by more than one person, the names and addresses of all the promoters;

(b) a description of the goods or services to be acquired by or supplied to the participant by the promoter or promoters, other participants or suppliers nominated by the promoter or promoters or any other person under the trading scheme;

(c) a statement describing the capacity in which the participant shall act for the purposes of any transaction which he may effect under the trading scheme;

(d) a statement describing the financial obligation of the participant during the period of twelve months from the commencement date of the agreement. The promoter shall give to the participant at least 60 days advance written notice of any subsequent changes in such financial obligation;

(e) a statement describing the right of the participant to cancel the agreement—

    (i) within 14 days of entering into the agreement without penalty and with the right to recover any monies which he had paid to or for the benefit of the promoter or any of the promoters or any other participant in connection with his participation in the trading scheme or paid to any other participant in accordance with the provisions of the trading scheme and the manner in which that cancellation and recovery shall be effected;

    (ii) within 14 days of entering into the agreement the right to return to an address specified in the agreement which must be an address in the United Kingdom, any goods the participant has purchased within that period under the trading scheme and which remain unsold provided that such unsold goods remain in the condition in which they were in at the time of purchase, whether or not their external wrappings have been broken and to recover any monies paid in respect of such goods;

    (iii) within 14 days of entering into the agreement the right to cancel any services ordered within that period under the trading scheme and to recover any monies paid in respect of such services not yet supplied to the participant;

    and that the promoter or any other person who has supplied goods to the participant under the trading scheme shall not be entitled to make a handling charge in respect of goods returned under sub-paragraph (ii) above or services cancelled under sub-paragraph (iii) above;

(f) a statement describing the rights of the participant to terminate the agreement at any time without penalty by giving 14 days written notice to the promoter or any of the promoters at an address which is specified in the agreement;

(g) a statement describing the rights of the participant following termination of the agreement by the promoter or the participant as set out in these Regulations;

(h) the written warnings in the form set out in Part I and Part II of Schedule 2 hereto which comply with the following—

    (i) the words are easily legible; and

    (ii) the words in Part II are printed immediately above the space for the participant's signature;

(i) a statement setting out the conditions under which the participant shall be entitled to return goods to the promoter or any promoters or any other participant which shall include at least the rights conferred on the participant by regulation 6 below and which must include an address in the United Kingdom to which such goods can be returned;

(j) a statement setting out the conditions when commission already paid by the promoter or another participant will be recoverable from the participant which shall include at least the rights conferred on the participant by regulation 9;

(k) where the agreement comprises more than one document, a statement setting out all documents which form part of the contract between the parties and that those documents form the entire agreement between the parties.

[2.110]
6 Right to return goods to promoter on termination

(1) The rights referred to in regulation 5(i) are, that if a participant or the promoter or any of the promoters terminates an agreement referred to in regulation 4 or any agreement entered into in consequence of such an agreement with a participant, the participant shall, subject to subsection (2) below, have the right to be released from all future contractual obligations and to return to the

promoter or any of the promoters or any other participant any goods the participant has purchased within a period of 90 days prior to such termination under the scheme and which remain unsold and to recover from the promoter or such other participant who supplied the goods—

    (a)   where the participant has terminated the agreement, the price (inclusive of Value Added Tax) which the participant paid for them less—

        (i)   in the case of any goods the condition of which has deteriorated due to an act or default on the part of the participant, an amount equal to the diminution in their value resulting from such deterioration; and

        (ii)   a reasonable handling charge;

    (b)   where the promoter or any of the promoters or any other participant has terminated the agreement the price (inclusive of Value Added Tax) which the participant paid for them together with any costs incurred by the participant for returning the goods to the promoter or any other participant;

    (c)   on terms whereby the purchase price is payable upon delivery of the goods or, if the goods are already held by the promoter or any of the promoters, forthwith, and

    (d)   on terms whereby the goods not already held by the promoter or any of the promoters will be delivered within 21 days of such termination at the promoter's expense to the address stated in the agreement.

(2)   Where an agreement referred to in regulation 4 contains an obligation on the participant not to compete with the business of the promoter after termination of such agreement, such non-competition provision shall continue in force after the date of termination.

[2.111]

7　Securities and guarantees

A promoter of, or a participant in, a trading scheme shall not accept from a participant any guarantee or security in whatever form in respect of goods or services supplied or to be supplied or in respect of the payment of the price for goods or services supplied or to be supplied or an undertaking to provide such a guarantee or such security unless the creditor or a promoter or other supplier who is not a creditor has agreed in writing to refund the amount of that payment to the debtor upon his returning the relevant goods in an undamaged condition to the creditor or to any promoter or supplier.

[2.112]

8　Supply of goods and services

A promoter of, or a participant in, a trading scheme shall not make a supply of goods or services to the participant unless, in respect of every supply of goods or services under a trading scheme, such promoter or participant has provided the participant to whom the goods are supplied or to be supplied with an adequate record of the transaction in respect of which payment is due from that participant. For the purposes of this regulation an itemised order form, invoice or receipt shall constitute an adequate record.

[2.113]

9　Recovery of commission

The rights referred to in regulation 5(j) are the right to retain, after termination of an agreement referred to in regulation 4 or any agreement made thereunder, any commission paid to the participant under a trading scheme unless—

    (a)   the commission was paid in respect of goods returned to the promoter or another participant who paid the commission;

    (b)   the promoter has refunded all monies due to the participant under the agreement referred to in regulation 4 in respect of goods returned to him by the participant;

    (c)   the commission payment is claimed within 120 days of the date of having been made; and

    (d)   the promoter has entered into an agreement with the participant that complies with the requirements in regulation 5 and that agreement and any subsequent agreement contains a statement describing when commission becomes repayable to the promoter and the terms upon which recovery of that payment may be made; and

    (e)   the promoter recovers the commission payment in accordance with the terms referred to in paragraph (d) above.

[2.114]

10　£200 liability limit

A promoter of, or a participant in, a trading scheme shall not accept from a participant joining the trading scheme any payment or an undertaking to make a payment of any sum exceeding £200 unless 7 days have expired from the making of the agreement relating to goods or services supplied or to be supplied under that agreement to the participant by the promoter or any other participant under the trading scheme.

[2.115]

11   Civil consequences of contraventions

(1)   Where a participant makes a payment to or for the benefit of a promoter of, or to a participant in, a trading scheme and the acceptance of that payment involves a contravention of these Regulations, that contravention shall be actionable at the suit of the participant who suffers loss as a result of the contravention subject to the defences and other incidents applying to actions for breach of statutory duty.

(2)   No undertaking to make any payment given by a participant in a trading scheme involving a contravention of sub-paragraph (d) of paragraph (1) of regulation 4 or regulation 10 shall be enforceable against him in any civil proceedings or recoverable in any other way.

(3)   A participant in a trading scheme shall be under no liability to pay for any goods or services as the case may be—

(a)   supplied to him in circumstances involving a contravention of regulations 4 to 10; or

(b)   unless it was clearly explained to him by a promoter or a participant supplying or seeking to supply goods or services under the trading scheme, before he purchased the goods or services, that he had a free choice whether or not to purchase those goods or services and the purchase price for those goods or services and his annual financial obligation under the agreement was clearly stated.

SCHEDULES

SCHEDULE 1

Regulation 3(1)(c)

[2.116]

Warning for use in advertisements—

1. It is illegal for a promoter or a participant in a trading scheme to persuade anyone to make a payment by promising benefits from getting others to join a scheme.

2. Do not be misled by claims that high earnings are easily achieved.

SCHEDULE 2

Regulation 5

[2.117]

Warning for use in contracts—

PART I

1. It is illegal for a promoter or a participant in a trading scheme to persuade anyone to make a payment by promising benefits from getting others to join a scheme.

2. Do not be misled by claims that high earnings are easily achieved.

PART II

3. If you sign this contract, you have 14 days in which to cancel and get your money back.

TRADING SCHEMES (EXCLUSION) REGULATIONS 1997

(SI 1997/31)

NOTES

Made: 13 January 1997.

Authority: Fair Trading Act 1973, s 118(6)(b).

Commencement: 6 February 1997.

[2.118]

1   Citation and Commencement

These Regulations may be cited as the Trading Schemes (Exclusion) Regulations 1997 and shall come into force on 6th February 1997.

[2.119]

2   Interpretation

In these Regulations—

"the Act" means the Fair Trading Act 1973.

"annual profit of the trading scheme" means for each financial year the net profit of the promoter or promoters of the trading scheme as shown in the accounts of the trading scheme.

"chain letter" means any trading scheme under which a letter is sent to participants or prospective participants directly or indirectly instructing or requesting them to—

  (a) send monies or other benefits to at least one of the individuals on a list of individuals, shown with their mailing addresses, which is contained in or accompanying that letter; and

  (b) carry on the chain by sending copies of the letter to other individuals not on the list and removing from the list any one name and address and adding their own to it.

"participant" has the same meaning as in section 118(8) of the Act.

"single tier trading scheme" means a trading scheme the only members of which are the promoter or promoters and one or more participants and under which, in the United Kingdom, either a single promoter or a single participant operates at one level and any other participant or participants of the trading scheme operate at the same level below such promoter or participant aforesaid.

"trading scheme" has the same meaning as in section 118(8) of the Act.

[2.120]
3   Disapplication of Part XI of the Act

For the purpose of section 118(6)(b) of the Act the Secretary of State hereby prescribes trading schemes of the following description, that is to say—

  (a) [any trading scheme which is a single tier trading scheme under which a participant operating at a level immediately below that of the promoter or single participant in the UK, who introduces another participant to the scheme at that level,] does not receive any payment or benefit, or can only receive a single benefit or payment, in respect of the introduction of that participant, such payment or benefit not exceeding £50 and can receive no other benefit or payment in respect of or flowing directly or indirectly from the membership or activities of that participant in that or any other trading scheme, unless such other benefit or payment results from—

     (i) a sharing of expenses of the operation of the trading scheme;

    (ii) a share in the annual profit of the trading scheme; or

   (iii) the sale of the participant's business, being a business in respect of which a registration under the Value Added Taxes Act 1994 was in force at the date of sale.

  [(b) any trading scheme all of the participants in which are making or have the intention of making taxable supplies in the UK and are registered for Value Added Tax; or]

  (c) any trading scheme which is a chain letter provided there is no requirement on the participant to send monies or other benefits

     (i) to a central address or the promoter of the trading scheme for onward distribution; or

    (ii) to any person or organisation other than or additional to the person whose name and address is to be deleted from the list when the participant sends the letter to others; or

   (iii) to an organisation or person for onward transmission to a participant (whether or not that participant is identified on the list); and

where the promoter does not benefit from the provision of any other service or facilities offered or provided either by him or any other person or organisation to participants.

NOTES

Words in square brackets substituted by the Trading Schemes (Exclusion) (Amendment) Regulations 1997, SI 1997/1887, reg 2.

UNFAIR TERMS IN CONSUMER CONTRACTS REGULATIONS 1999

(SI 1999/2083)

NOTES

Made: 22 July 1999.

Authority: European Communities Act 1972, s 2(2).

Commencement: 1 October 1999.

These regulations were revoked by the Consumer Rights Act 2015, s 75, Sch 4, para 34, as from 1 October 2015 (for transitional provisions see the Consumer Rights Act 2015 (Commencement No 3, Transitional Provisions, Savings and Consequential Amendments) Order 2015, SI 2015/1630, arts 6–8 at **[2.1220]** et seq).

ARRANGEMENT OF REGULATIONS

[2.121]
1   Citation and commencement
*These Regulations may be cited as the Unfair Terms in Consumer Contracts Regulations 1999 and
shall come into force on 1st October 1999.*

NOTES
Revoked by the Consumer Rights Act 2015, s 75, Sch 4, para 34, as from 1 October 2015, subject to transitional provisions
as noted in the introductory notes to this Order *ante*.

2   (Revokes the Unfair Terms in Consumer Contracts Regulations 1994, SI 1994/3159.)

[2.122]
3   Interpretation
(1)   In these Regulations—
. . .
    ["the CMA" means the Competition and Markets Authority;]
    ["complaint" means a complaint that any contract term drawn up for general use is unfair;]
    *"consumer" means any natural person who, in contracts covered by these Regulations, is acting
        for purposes which are outside his trade, business or profession;*
    *"court" in relation to England and Wales and Northern Ireland means a county court or the
        High Court, and in relation to Scotland, the Sheriff or the Court of Session;*
    ["DETINI" means the Department of Enterprise, Trade and Investment in Northern Ireland;]
. . .
    *"EEA Agreement" means the Agreement on the European Economic Area signed at Oporto on
        2nd May 1992 as adjusted by the protocol signed at Brussels on 17th March 1993;*
    *["a local weights and measures authority" means a local weights and measures authority in
        Great Britain (within the meaning of section 69 of the Weights and Measures Act 1985);]*
    "Member State" means a State which is a contracting party to the EEA Agreement;
    "notified" means notified in writing;
    "qualifying body" means a person specified in Schedule 1;
    *"seller or supplier" means any natural or legal person who, in contracts covered by these
        Regulations, is acting for purposes relating to his trade, business or profession, whether
        publicly owned or privately owned;*
    "unfair terms" means the contractual terms referred to in regulation 5.
[(1A)   The references—
    (a)   in regulation 4(1) to a seller or a supplier, and
    (b)   in regulation 8(1) to a seller or supplier,
include references to a distance supplier and to an intermediary.
(1B)   In paragraph (1A) and regulation 5(6)—
    "distance supplier" means—
        *(a)   a supplier under a distance contract within the meaning of the Financial Services
            (Distance Marketing) Regulations 2004, or*
        *(b)   a supplier of unsolicited financial services within regulation 15 of those Regulations;
            and*
    "intermediary" has the same meaning as in those Regulations.]
(2)   (Applies to Scotland only.)

NOTES
Revoked as noted to reg 1 at **[2.121]**.

Para (1): definition "the Community" (omitted) spent following the amendments made to these Regulations by the Treaty of Lisbon (Changes in Terminology) Order 2011, SI 2011/1043, art 4(1); definition "the CMA" inserted, and definition "OFT" (previously "Director") (omitted) revoked, by the Enterprise and Regulatory Reform Act 2013 (Competition) (Consequential, Transitional and Saving Provisions) (No 2) Order 2014, SI 2014/549, art 2, Sch 1, Pt 2, para 26(1), (2) (for transitional provisions in relation to the continuity of functions, etc, see art 3 of the 2014 Order); definitions "complaint", "DETINI" and "a local weights and measures authority" inserted by the Public Bodies (The Office of Fair Trading Transfer of Consumer Advice Scheme Function and Modification of Enforcement Functions) Order 2013, SI 2013/783, art 10(1), (2).

Paras (1A), (1B): inserted by the Financial Services (Distance Marketing) Regulations 2004, SI 2004/2095, reg 24(1), (2).

Director General of Fair Trading: the Enterprise Act 2002, s 2(1), provided that, as from the coming into force of that section (on 1 April 2003), the functions of the Director General of Fair Trading, his property, rights and liabilities were transferred to the Office of Fair Trading. Accordingly, (by virtue of s 2(2), (3) of the 2002 Act) the office of the Director was abolished, and any reference to the Director in any enactment, instrument or other document passed or made before the commencement of s 2(1) had, in so far as is necessary, effect as if it were a reference to the Office of Fair Trading (for transitional provisions in connection with the transfer, see Sch 24, para 6 to the 2002 Act). Section 2 of the 2002 Act was repealed by the Enterprise and Regulatory Reform Act 2013, s 26(3), Sch 5, Pt 4, para 229, as from 1 April 2014. Part 3 the 2013 Act (ss 25–28) abolished the Office of fair Trading (and the Competition Commission) and provided for the transfer of its functions to the newly created Competition and Markets Authority.

[2.123]
4   Terms to which these Regulations apply

(1)   These Regulations apply in relation to unfair terms in contracts concluded between a seller or a supplier and a consumer.

(2)   These Regulations do not apply to contractual terms which reflect—

  (a)   mandatory statutory or regulatory provisions (including such provisions under the law of any Member State or in [EU] legislation having effect in the United Kingdom without further enactment);

  (b)   the provisions or principles of international conventions to which the Member States or the [European Union] are party.

NOTES
Revoked as noted to reg 1 at **[2.121]**.
Para (2): words in square brackets substituted by the Treaty of Lisbon (Changes in Terminology) Order 2011, SI 2011/1043, arts 4(1), 6(2)(b).

[2.124]
5   Unfair Terms

(1)   A contractual term which has not been individually negotiated shall be regarded as unfair if, contrary to the requirement of good faith, it causes a significant imbalance in the parties' rights and obligations arising under the contract, to the detriment of the consumer.

(2)   A term shall always be regarded as not having been individually negotiated where it has been drafted in advance and the consumer has therefore not been able to influence the substance of the term.

(3)   Notwithstanding that a specific term or certain aspects of it in a contract has been individually negotiated, these Regulations shall apply to the rest of a contract if an overall assessment of it indicates that it is a pre-formulated standard contract.

(4)   It shall be for any seller or supplier who claims that a term was individually negotiated to show that it was.

(5)   Schedule 2 to these Regulations contains an indicative and non-exhaustive list of the terms which may be regarded as unfair.

[(6)   Any contractual term providing that a consumer bears the burden of proof in respect of showing whether a distance supplier or an intermediary complied with any or all of the obligations placed upon him resulting from the Directive and any rule or enactment implementing it shall always be regarded as unfair.

(7)   In paragraph (6)—

  "the Directive" means Directive 2002/65/EC of the European Parliament and of the Council of 23 September 2002 concerning the distance marketing of consumer financial services and amending Council Directive 90/619/EEC and Directives 97/7/EC and 98/27/EC; and

  "rule" means a rule made by the [Financial Conduct Authority or the Prudential Regulation Authority] under the Financial Services and Markets Act 2000 or by a designated professional body within the meaning of section 326(2) of that Act.]

NOTES
Revoked as noted to reg 1 at **[2.121]**.
Para (6): added, together with para (7), by the Financial Services (Distance Marketing) Regulations 2004, SI 2004/2095, reg 24(1), (3).
Para (7): added as noted above; in definition "rule" words in square brackets substituted by the Financial Services Act 2012 (Consequential Amendments and Transitional Provisions) Order 2013, SI 2013/472, art 3, Sch 2, para 26(a).

[2.125]
6 Assessment of unfair terms

(1)   Without prejudice to regulation 12, the unfairness of a contractual term shall be assessed, taking into account the nature of the goods or services for which the contract was concluded and by referring, at the time of conclusion of the contract, to all the circumstances attending the conclusion of the contract and to all the other terms of the contract or of another contract on which it is dependent.

(2)   In so far as it is in plain intelligible language, the assessment of fairness of a term shall not relate—

(a)   *to the definition of the main subject matter of the contract, or*

(b)   *to the adequacy of the price or remuneration, as against the goods or services supplied in exchange.*

NOTES
Revoked as noted to reg 1 at **[2.121]**.

[2.126]
7 Written contracts

(1)   A seller or supplier shall ensure that any written term of a contract is expressed in plain, intelligible language.

(2)   If there is doubt about the meaning of a written term, the interpretation which is most favourable to the consumer shall prevail but this rule shall not apply in proceedings brought under regulation 12.

NOTES
Revoked as noted to reg 1 at **[2.121]**.

[2.127]
8 Effect of unfair term

(1)   An unfair term in a contract concluded with a consumer by a seller or supplier shall not be binding on the consumer.

(2)   The contract shall continue to bind the parties if it is capable of continuing in existence without the unfair term.

[(3)   This regulation does not apply to anything that is governed by Article 6 of Regulation (EU) No 181/2011 of the European Parliament and of the Council of 16 February 2011 concerning the rights of passengers in bus and coach transport and amending Regulation (EC) No 2006/2004.]

NOTES
Revoked as noted to reg 1 at **[2.121]**.
Para (3): added by the Rights of Passengers in Bus and Coach Transport (Exemptions and Enforcement) Regulations 2013, SI 2013/1865, reg 13(6).

[2.128]
9 Choice of law clauses

These Regulations shall apply notwithstanding any contract term which applies or purports to apply the law of a non-Member State, if the contract has a close connection with the territory of the Member States.

NOTES
Revoked as noted to reg 1 at **[2.121]**.

[2.129]
[10 Complaints—consideration by [the CMA] and qualifying bodies

(1)   The following bodies may consider complaints—

(a)   *the [CMA];*

(b)   *a qualifying body.*

(2)   Where the [CMA] agrees to consider a complaint, it shall be under a duty to consider that complaint.

(3)   Where a qualifying body agrees to consider a complaint, it shall—

(a)   *be under a duty to consider that complaint; and*

(b)   *notify the [CMA] of its agreement to consider that complaint.*

(4)   The [CMA], or as the case may be, a qualifying body shall give reasons for its decision to apply or not to apply for an injunction under regulation 12 in relation to any complaints which these Regulations require it to consider.

(5)   In deciding whether or not to apply for an injunction in respect of a term which the [CMA] or a qualifying body considers to be unfair, the [CMA] or the qualifying body may, if it considers it appropriate to do so, have regard to any undertakings given to it by or on behalf of any person as to the continued use of such a term in contracts concluded with consumers.]

NOTES

Commencement: 28 March 2013.

Substituted by the Public Bodies (The Office of Fair Trading Transfer of Consumer Advice Scheme Function and Modification of Enforcement Functions) Order 2013, SI 2013/783, art 10(1), (3) and revoked as noted to reg 1 at **[2.121]**.

Words in square brackets substituted by the Enterprise and Regulatory Reform Act 2013 (Competition) (Consequential, Transitional and Saving Provisions) (No 2) Order 2014, SI 2014/549, art 2, Sch 1, Pt 2, para 26(1), (3) (for transitional provisions in relation to the continuity of functions, etc, see art 3 of the 2014 Order).

References to the CMA, etc: as to the abolition of the office of the Director General of Fair Trading and the substitution of the original references to the Director (and related expressions), see the note to reg 3 at **[2.122]**.

11   (Revoked by the Public Bodies (The Office of Fair Trading Transfer of Consumer Advice Scheme Function and Modification of Enforcement Functions) Order 2013, SI 2013/783, art 10(1), (4).)

[2.130]
12   Injunctions to prevent continued use of unfair terms
(1)   The [CMA] or, subject to paragraph (2), any qualifying body may apply for an injunction (including an interim injunction) against any person appearing to the [CMA] or that body to be using, or recommending use of, an unfair term drawn up for general use in contracts concluded with consumers.

(2)   A qualifying body may apply for an injunction only where—
  (a)   it has notified the [CMA] of its intention to apply at least fourteen days before the date on which the application is made, beginning with the date on which the notification was given; or
  (b)   the [CMA] consents to the application being made within a shorter period.

(3)   The court on an application under this regulation may grant an injunction on such terms as it thinks fit.

(4)   An injunction may relate not only to use of a particular contract term drawn up for general use but to any similar term, or a term having like effect, used or recommended for use by any person.

NOTES

Revoked as noted to reg 1 at **[2.121]**.

Paras (1), (2): words in square brackets substituted by the Enterprise and Regulatory Reform Act 2013 (Competition) (Consequential, Transitional and Saving Provisions) (No 2) Order 2014, SI 2014/549, art 2, Sch 1, Pt 2, para 26(1), (4) (for transitional provisions in relation to the continuity of functions, etc, see art 3 of the 2014 Order).

References to the CMA, etc: as to the abolition of the office of the Director General of Fair Trading and the substitution of the original references to the Director (and related expressions), see the note to reg 3 at **[2.122]**.

[2.131]
13   Powers of the [CMA] and qualifying bodies to obtain documents and information
(1)   The [CMA][, a local weights and measures authority or DETINI] may exercise the power conferred by this regulation for the purpose of—
  (a)   facilitating [its] consideration of a complaint . . . ; or
  (b)   ascertaining whether a person has complied with an undertaking or court order as to the continued use, or recommendation for use, of a term in contracts concluded with consumers.

(2)   A qualifying body specified in Part One of Schedule 1 [(other than a local weights and measures authority or DETINI),] may exercise the power conferred by this regulation for the purpose of—
  (a)   facilitating its consideration of a complaint . . . ; or
  (b)   ascertaining whether a person has complied with—
    (i)   an undertaking given to it or to the court following an application by that body, or
    (ii)   a court order made on an application by that body,
    as to the continued use, or recommendation for use, of a term in contracts concluded with consumers.

(3)   The [CMA] may require any person to supply to [it], and a qualifying body specified in Part One of Schedule 1 may require any person to supply to it—
  (a)   a copy of any document which that person has used or recommended for use, at the time the notice referred to in paragraph (4) below is given, as a pre-formulated standard contract in dealings with consumers;
  (b)   information about the use, or recommendation for use, by that person of that document or any other such document in dealings with consumers.

(4)   The power conferred by this regulation is to be exercised by a notice in writing which may—

Part 2   Statutory Instruments

(a) specify the way in which and the time within which it is to be complied with; and

(b) be varied or revoked by a subsequent notice.

(5) Nothing in this regulation compels a person to supply any document or information which he would be entitled to refuse to produce or give in civil proceedings before the court.

(6) If a person makes default in complying with a notice under this regulation, the court may, on the application of the [CMA] or of the qualifying body, make such order as the court thinks fit for requiring the default to be made good, and any such order may provide that all the costs or expenses of and incidental to the application shall be borne by the person in default or by any officers of a company or other association who are responsible for its default.

NOTES

Revoked as noted to reg 1 at **[2.121]**.

Heading: word in square brackets substituted by the Enterprise and Regulatory Reform Act 2013 (Competition) (Consequential, Transitional and Saving Provisions) (No 2) Order 2014, SI 2014/549, art 2, Sch 1, Pt 2, para 26(1), (5)(d) (for transitional provisions in relation to the continuity of functions, etc, see art 3 of the 2014 Order).

Para (1): words in first and third pairs of square brackets substituted by SI 2014/549, art 2, Sch 1, Pt 2, para 26(1), (5)(a) (for transitional provisions in relation to the continuity of functions, etc, see art 3 of the 2014 Order); words in second pair of square brackets substituted, and words omitted revoked, by the Public Bodies (The Office of Fair Trading Transfer of Consumer Advice Scheme Function and Modification of Enforcement Functions) Order 2013, SI 2013/783, art 10(1), (5)(a), (b).

Para (2): words in square brackets inserted, and words omitted revoked, by SI 2013/783, art 10(1), (5)(b), (c).

Paras (3), (6): words in square brackets substituted by SI 2014/549, art 2, Sch 1, Pt 2, para 26(1), (5)(b), (e) (for transitional provisions in relation to the continuity of functions, etc, see art 3 of the 2014 Order).

References to the CMA, etc: as to the abolition of the office of the Director General of Fair Trading and the substitution of the original references to the Director (and related expressions), see the note to reg 3 at **[2.122]**.

[2.132]

14 Notification of undertakings and orders to [the CMA]

A qualifying body shall notify the [CMA]—

(a) of any undertaking given to it by or on behalf of any person as to the continued use of a term which that body considers to be unfair in contracts concluded with consumers;

(b) of the outcome of any application made by it under regulation 12, and of the terms of any undertaking given to, or order made by, the court;

(c) of the outcome of any application made by it to enforce a previous order of the court.

NOTES

Revoked as noted to reg 1 at **[2.121]**.

Words in square brackets substituted by the Enterprise and Regulatory Reform Act 2013 (Competition) (Consequential, Transitional and Saving Provisions) (No 2) Order 2014, SI 2014/549, art 2, Sch 1, Pt 2, para 26(1), (6) (for transitional provisions in relation to the continuity of functions, etc, see art 3 of the 2014 Order).

References to the CMA, etc: as to the abolition of the office of the Director General of Fair Trading and the substitution of the original references to the Director (and related expressions), see the note to reg 3 at **[2.122]**.

[2.133]

15 Publication, information and advice

(1) The [CMA] shall arrange for the publication in such form and manner as [it] considers appropriate, of—

(a) details of any undertaking or order notified to [it] under regulation 14;

(b) details of any undertaking given to [it] by or on behalf of any person as to the continued use of a term which the [CMA] considers to be unfair in contracts concluded with consumers;

(c) details of any application made by [it] under regulation 12, and of the terms of any undertaking given to, or order made by, the court;

(d) details of any application made by the [CMA] to enforce a previous order of the court.

(2) The [CMA] shall inform any person on request whether a particular term to which these Regulations apply has been—

(a) the subject of an undertaking given to the [CMA] or notified to [it] by a qualifying body; or

(b) the subject of an order of the court made upon application by [it] or notified to [it] by a qualifying body;

and shall give that person details of the undertaking or a copy of the order, as the case may be, together with a copy of any amendments which the person giving the undertaking has agreed to make to the term in question.

(3) The [CMA] may arrange for the dissemination in such form and manner as [it] considers appropriate of such information and advice concerning the operation of these Regulations as may appear to [it] to be expedient to give to the public and to all persons likely to be affected by these Regulations.

NOTES

Revoked as noted to reg 1 at **[2.121]**.

Words in square brackets substituted by the Enterprise and Regulatory Reform Act 2013 (Competition) (Consequential, Transitional and Saving Provisions) (No 2) Order 2014, SI 2014/549, art 2, Sch 1, Pt 2, para 26(1), (7) (for transitional provisions in relation to the continuity of functions, etc, see art 3 of the 2014 Order).

References to the CMA, etc: as to the abolition of the office of the Director General of Fair Trading and the substitution of the original references to the Director (and related expressions), see the note to reg 3 at **[2.122]**.

[2.134]
[16 The functions of the [Financial Conduct Authority]

The functions of the [Financial Conduct Authority] under these Regulations shall be treated as functions of the [Financial Conduct Authority] under the [Financial Services and Markets Act 2000].]

NOTES
Inserted by the Unfair Terms in Consumer Contracts (Amendment) Regulations 2001, SI 2001/1186, reg 2(a), and revoked as noted to reg 1 at **[2.121]**.

Words in first, second and third pairs of square brackets substituted by the Financial Services Act 2012 (Consequential Amendments and Transitional Provisions) Order 2013, SI 2013/472, art 3, Sch 2, para 26(b); words in final pair of square brackets substituted by the Financial Services and Markets Act 2000 (Consequential Amendments and Repeals) Order 2001, SI 2001/3649, art 583.

SCHEDULES
SCHEDULE 1
QUALIFYING BODIES

Regulation 3

PART ONE

[2.135]
[1. The Information Commissioner.

2. The Gas and Electricity Markets Authority.

3. The Director General of Electricity Supply for Northern Ireland.

4. The Director General of Gas for Northern Ireland.

5. [The Office of Communications].

6. [The Water Services Regulation Authority].

7. [The Office of Rail Regulation].

8. Every weights and measures authority in Great Britain.

9. The Department of Enterprise, Trade and Investment in Northern Ireland.

10. [The Financial Conduct Authority].]

NOTES
Substituted by the Unfair Terms in Consumer Contracts (Amendment) Regulations 2001, SI 2001/1186, reg 2(b).

Revoked as noted to reg 1 at **[2.121]**.

Entry 5 relating to "The Office of Communications" substituted by the Communications Act 2003 (Consequential Amendments No 2) Order 2003, SI 2003/3182, art 2; entry 6 relating to "The Water Services Regulation Authority" substituted by the Unfair Terms in Consumer Contracts (Amendment) and Water Act 2003 (Transitional Provision) Regulations 2006, SI 2006/523, reg 2, subject to transitional provisions in reg 3 of those Regulations; entry 7 relating to "The Office of Rail Regulation" in square brackets substituted by virtue of the Railways and Transport Safety Act 2003, s 16(4), (5), Sch 3, para 4; words in square brackets in para 10 substituted by the Financial Services Act 2012 (Consequential Amendments and Transitional Provisions) Order 2013, SI 2013/472, art 3, Sch 2, para 26(c).

PART TWO

[2.136]
11. Consumers' Association.

NOTES
Revoked as noted to reg 1 at **[2.121]**.

SCHEDULE 2
INDICATIVE AND NON-EXHAUSTIVE LIST OF TERMS WHICH MAY BE REGARDED AS UNFAIR

Regulation 5(5)

[2.137]
1. Terms which have the object or effect of—

    (a)   *excluding or limiting the legal liability of a seller or supplier in the event of the death of a consumer or personal injury to the latter resulting from an act or omission of that seller or supplier;*

    (b)   *inappropriately excluding or limiting the legal rights of the consumer vis-à-vis the seller or supplier or another party in the event of total or partial non-performance or inadequate performance by the seller or supplier of any of the contractual obligations, including the option of offsetting a debt owed to the seller or supplier against any claim which the consumer may have against him;*

    (c)   *making an agreement binding on the consumer whereas provision of services by the seller or supplier is subject to a condition whose realisation depends on his own will alone;*

    (d)   *permitting the seller or supplier to retain sums paid by the consumer where the latter decides not to conclude or perform the contract, without providing for the consumer to receive compensation of an equivalent amount from the seller or supplier where the latter is the party cancelling the contract;*

    (e)   *requiring any consumer who fails to fulfil his obligation to pay a disproportionately high sum in compensation;*

    (f)   *authorising the seller or supplier to dissolve the contract on a discretionary basis where the same facility is not granted to the consumer, or permitting the seller or supplier to retain the sums paid for services not yet supplied by him where it is the seller or supplier himself who dissolves the contract;*

    (g)   *enabling the seller or supplier to terminate a contract of indeterminate duration without reasonable notice except where there are serious grounds for doing so;*

    (h)   *automatically extending a contract of fixed duration where the consumer does not indicate otherwise, when the deadline fixed for the consumer to express his desire not to extend the contract is unreasonably early;*

    (i)   *irrevocably binding the consumer to terms with which he had no real opportunity of becoming acquainted before the conclusion of the contract;*

    (j)   *enabling the seller or supplier to alter the terms of the contract unilaterally without a valid reason which is specified in the contract;*

    (k)   *enabling the seller or supplier to alter unilaterally without a valid reason any characteristics of the product or service to be provided;*

    (l)   *providing for the price of goods to be determined at the time of delivery or allowing a seller of goods or supplier of services to increase their price without in both cases giving the consumer the corresponding right to cancel the contract if the final price is too high in relation to the price agreed when the contract was concluded;*

    (m)   *giving the seller or supplier the right to determine whether the goods or services supplied are in conformity with the contract, or giving him the exclusive right to interpret any term of the contract;*

    (n)   *limiting the seller's or supplier's obligation to respect commitments undertaken by his agents or making his commitments subject to compliance with a particular formality;*

    (o)   *obliging the consumer to fulfil all his obligations where the seller or supplier does not perform his;*

    (p)   *giving the seller or supplier the possibility of transferring his rights and obligations under the contract, where this may serve to reduce the guarantees for the consumer, without the latter's agreement;*

    (q)   *excluding or hindering the consumer's right to take legal action or exercise any other legal remedy, particularly by requiring the consumer to take disputes exclusively to arbitration not covered by legal provisions, unduly restricting the evidence available to him or imposing on him a burden of proof which, according to the applicable law, should lie with another party to the contract.*

2.   *Scope of paragraphs 1(g), (j) and (l)*

    (a)   *Paragraph 1(g) is without hindrance to terms by which a supplier of financial services reserves the right to terminate unilaterally a contract of indeterminate duration without notice where there is a valid reason, provided that the supplier is required to inform the other contracting party or parties thereof immediately.*

    (b)   *Paragraph 1(j) is without hindrance to terms under which a supplier of financial services reserves the right to alter the rate of interest payable by the consumer or due to the latter, or the amount of other charges for financial services without notice where there is a valid reason, provided that the supplier is required to inform the other contracting party or parties thereof at the earliest opportunity and that the latter are free to dissolve the contract immediately.*

           Paragraph 1(j) is also without hindrance to terms under which a seller or supplier reserves the right to alter unilaterally the conditions of a contract of indeterminate duration, provided that he is required to inform the consumer with reasonable notice and that the consumer is free to dissolve the contract.

    (c)   *Paragraphs 1(g), (j) and (l) do not apply to:*

     —   *transactions in transferable securities, financial instruments and other products or services where the price is linked to fluctuations in a stock exchange quotation or index or a financial market rate that the seller or supplier does not control;*

     —   *contracts for the purchase or sale of foreign currency, traveller's cheques or international money orders denominated in foreign currency.*

     (d)   Paragraph 1(1) is without hindrance to price indexation clauses, where lawful, provided that the method by which prices vary is explicitly described.

NOTES

Revoked as noted to reg 1 at **[2.121]**.

CONSUMER PROTECTION (DISTANCE SELLING) REGULATIONS 2000

(SI 2000/2334)

NOTES

Made: 31 August 2000.
Authority: European Communities Act 1972, s 2(2).
Commencement: 31 October 2000.

ARRANGEMENT OF REGULATIONS

[2.138]
1   Title, commencement and extent

(1)   These Regulations may be cited as the Consumer Protection (Distance Selling) Regulations 2000 and shall come into force on 31st October 2000.

(2)   These Regulations extend to Northern Ireland.

NOTES

These Regulations are superseded by the Consumer Contracts (Information, Cancellation and Additional Charges) Regulations 2013, SI 2013/3134, reg 2(a), in relation to contracts entered into on or after 13 June 2014.

2   *(Revokes the Mail Order Transactions (Information) Order 1976, SI 1976/1812.)*

[2.139]
3 Interpretation

(1) In these Regulations—

["*the 2000 Act*" *means the Financial Services and Markets Act 2000;*

"*appointed representative*" *has the same meaning as in section 39(2) of the 2000 Act;*

"*authorised person*" *has the same meaning as in section 31(2) of the 2000 Act;*]

"*breach*" *means contravention by a supplier of a prohibition in, or failure to comply with a requirement of, these Regulations;*

"*business*" *includes a trade or profession;*

["*CMA*" *means Competition and Markets Authority;*]

"*consumer*" *means any natural person who, in contracts to which these Regulations apply, is acting for purposes which are outside his business;*

"*court*" *in relation to England and Wales and Northern Ireland means a county court or the High Court, and in relation to Scotland means the Sheriff Court or the Court of Session;*

"*credit*" *includes a cash loan and any other form of financial accommodation, and for this purpose* "*cash*" *includes money in any form;*

. . .

"*distance contract*" *means any contract concerning goods or services concluded between a supplier and a consumer under an organised distance sales or service provision scheme run by the supplier who, for the purpose of the contract, makes exclusive use of one or more means of distance communication up to and including the moment at which the contract is concluded;*

"*EEA Agreement*" *means the Agreement on the European Economic Area signed at Oporto on 2 May 1992 as adjusted by the Protocol signed at Brussels on 17 March 1993;*

"*enactment*" *includes an enactment comprised in, or in an instrument made under, an Act of the Scottish Parliament;*

"*enforcement authority*" *means* . . . , *every weights and measures authority in Great Britain, and the Department of Enterprise, Trade and Investment in Northern Ireland;*

"*excepted contract*" *means a contract such as is mentioned in regulation 5(1);*

["*financial service*" *means any service of a banking, credit, insurance, personal pension, investment or payment nature;*]

"*means of distance communication*" *means any means which, without the simultaneous physical presence of the supplier and the consumer, may be used for the conclusion of a contract between those parties; and an indicative list of such means is contained in Schedule 1;*

"*Member State*" *means a State which is a contracting party to the EEA Agreement;*

"*operator of a means of communication*" *means any public or private person whose business involves making one or more means of distance communication available to suppliers;*

"*period for performance*" *has the meaning given by regulation 19(2);*

"*personal credit agreement*" *has the meaning given by regulation 14(8);*

["*regulated activity*" *has the same meaning as in section 22 of the 2000 Act;*]

"*related credit agreement*" *has the meaning given by regulation 15(5);*

"*supplier*" *means any person who, in contracts to which these Regulations apply, is acting in his commercial or professional capacity; and*

"*working days*" *means all days other than Saturdays, Sundays and public holidays.*

(2) (Applies to Scotland only.)

NOTES

Superseded as noted to reg 1 at **[2.138]**.

Para (1): definitions "the 2000 Act", "appointed representative", "authorised person", "financial service" and "regulated activity" inserted by the Financial Services (Distance Marketing) Regulations 2004, SI 2004/2095, reg 25(1), (2); definition "CMA" inserted, and definition "OFT" (previously "Director") (omitted) revoked, by the Enterprise and Regulatory Reform Act 2013 (Competition) (Consequential, Transitional and Saving Provisions) (No 2) Order 2014, SI 2014/549, art 2, Sch 1, Pt 2, para 28(1), (2) (for transitional provisions in relation to the continuity of functions, etc, see art 3 of the 2014 Order); words omitted from definition "enforcement authority" revoked by the Public Bodies (The Office of Fair Trading Transfer of Consumer Advice Scheme Function and Modification of Enforcement Functions) Order 2013, SI 2013/783, art 11(1), (2).

Director General of Fair Trading: the Enterprise Act 2002, s 2(1) provided that, as from the coming into force of that section (on 1 April 2003), the functions of the Director General of Fair Trading, his property, rights and liabilities were transferred to the Office of Fair Trading. Accordingly, (by virtue of s 2(2), (3) of the 2002 Act) the office of the Director was abolished, and any reference to the Director in any enactment, instrument or other document passed or made before the commencement of s 2(1) had, in so far as is necessary, effect as if it were a reference to the Office of Fair Trading (for transitional provisions in connection with the transfer, see Sch 24, para 6 to the 2002 Act). Section 2 of the 2002 Act was repealed by the Enterprise and Regulatory Reform Act 2013, s 26(3), Sch 5, Pt 4, para 229, as from 1 April 2014. Part 3 of the 2013 Act (ss 25–28) abolished the Office of fair Trading (and the Competition Commission) and provided for the transfer of its functions to the newly created Competition and Markets Authority.

[2.140]
4 Contracts to which these Regulations apply

These Regulations apply, subject to regulation 6, to distance contracts other than excepted contracts.

NOTES
Superseded as noted to reg 1 at **[2.138]**.

[2.141]
5 Excepted contracts
(1) The following are excepted contracts, namely any contract—
  (a) for the sale or other disposition of an interest in land except for a rental agreement;
  (b) for the construction of a building where the contract also provides for a sale or other disposition of an interest in land on which the building is constructed, except for a rental agreement;
  (c) relating to financial services . . . ;
  (d) concluded by means of an automated vending machine or automated commercial premises;
  (e) concluded with a telecommunications operator through the use of a public pay-phone;
  (f) concluded at an auction.
(2) References in paragraph (1) to a rental agreement—
  (a) if the land is situated in England and Wales, are references to any agreement which does not have to be made in writing (whether or not in fact made in writing) because of section 2(5)(a) of the Law of Property (Miscellaneous Provisions) Act 1989;
  (b) (applies to Scotland only); and
  (c) if the land is situated in Northern Ireland, are references to any agreement which is not one to which section II of the Statute of Frauds, (Ireland) 1695 applies.
(3) Paragraph (2) shall not be taken to mean that a rental agreement in respect of land situated outside the United Kingdom is not capable of being a distance contract to which these Regulations apply.

NOTES
Superseded as noted to reg 1 at **[2.138]**.
Para (1): words omitted from sub-para (c) revoked by the Financial Services (Distance Marketing) Regulations 2004, SI 2004/2095, reg 25(1), (3).

[2.142]
6 Contracts to which only part of these Regulations apply
[(1) Regulations 7 to 20 shall not apply to a contract which is a regulated contract within the meaning of the Timeshare, Holiday Products, Resale and Exchange Contracts Regulations 2010.]
(2) Regulations 7 to 19(1) shall not apply to—
  (a) contracts for the supply of food, beverages or other goods intended for everyday consumption supplied to the consumer's residence or to his workplace by regular roundsmen; or
  (b) contracts for the provision of accommodation, transport, catering or leisure services, where the supplier undertakes, when the contract is concluded, to provide these services on a specific date or within a specific period.
(3) Regulations 19(2) to (8) and 20 do not apply to a contract for a "package" within the meaning of the Package Travel, Package Holidays and Package Tours Regulations 1992 which is sold or offered for sale in the territory of the Member States.
[(4) Regulations 7 to 14, 17 to 20 and 25 do not apply to any contract which is made, and regulation 24 does not apply to any unsolicited services which are supplied, by an authorised person where the making or performance of that contract or the supply of those services, as the case may be, constitutes or is part of a regulated activity carried on by him.
(5) Regulations 7 to 9, 17 to 20 and 25 do not apply to any contract which is made, and regulation 24 does not apply to any unsolicited services which are supplied, by an appointed representative where the making or performance of that contract or the supply of those services, as the case may be, constitutes or is part of a regulated activity carried on by him.]

NOTES
Superseded as noted to reg 1 at **[2.138]**.
Para (1): substituted by the Timeshare, Holiday Products, Resale and Exchange Contracts Regulations 2010, SI 2010/2960, reg 36(3), Sch 6, para 6.
Paras (4), (5): added by the Financial Services (Distance Marketing) Regulations 2004, SI 2004/2095, reg 25(1), (4).

[2.143]
7 Information required prior to the conclusion of the contract
(1) Subject to paragraph (4), in good time prior to the conclusion of the contract the supplier shall—
  (a) provide to the consumer the following information—
    (i) the identity of the supplier and, where the contract requires payment in advance, the supplier's address;
    (ii) a description of the main characteristics of the goods or services;

Part 2   Statutory Instruments

    (iii)   *the price of the goods or services including all taxes;*

    (iv)   *delivery costs where appropriate;*

    (v)   *the arrangements for payment, delivery or performance;*

    (vi)   *the existence of a right of cancellation except in the cases referred to in regulation 13;*

    (vii)   *the cost of using the means of distance communication where it is calculated other than at the basic rate;*

    (viii)   *the period for which the offer or the price remains valid; and*

    (ix)   *where appropriate, the minimum duration of the contract, in the case of contracts for the supply of goods or services to be performed permanently or recurrently;*

(b)   *inform the consumer if he proposes, in the event of the goods or services ordered by the consumer being unavailable, to provide substitute goods or services (as the case may be) of equivalent quality and price; and*

(c)   *inform the consumer that the cost of returning any such substitute goods to the supplier in the event of cancellation by the consumer would be met by the supplier.*

(2)   The supplier shall ensure that the information required by paragraph (1) is provided in a clear and comprehensible manner appropriate to the means of distance communication used, with due regard in particular to the principles of good faith in commercial transactions and the principles governing the protection of those who are unable to give their consent such as minors.

(3)   Subject to paragraph (4), the supplier shall ensure that his commercial purpose is made clear when providing the information required by paragraph (1).

(4)   In the case of a telephone communication, the identity of the supplier and the commercial purpose of the call shall be made clear at the beginning of the conversation with the consumer.

NOTES

Superseded as noted to reg 1 at **[2.138]**.

[2.144]
8   Written and additional information

(1)   Subject to regulation 9, the supplier shall provide to the consumer in writing, or in another durable medium which is available and accessible to the consumer, the information referred to in paragraph (2), either—

(a)   *prior to the conclusion of the contract, or*

(b)   *thereafter, in good time and in any event—*

    (i)   *during the performance of the contract, in the case of services; and*

    (ii)   *at the latest at the time of delivery where goods not for delivery to third parties are concerned.*

(2)   The information required to be provided by paragraph (1) is—

(a)   *the information set out in paragraphs (i) to (vi) of Regulation 7(1)(a);*

(b)   *information about the conditions and procedures for exercising the right to cancel under regulation 10, including—*

    (i)   *where a term of the contract requires (or the supplier intends that it will require) that the consumer shall return the goods to the supplier in the event of cancellation, notification of that requirement; . . .*

    (ii)   *information as to whether the consumer or the supplier would be responsible under these Regulations for the cost of returning any goods to the supplier, or the cost of his recovering them, if the consumer cancels the contract under regulation 10;*

    [(iii)   *in the case of a contract for the supply of services, information as to how the right to cancel may be affected by the consumer agreeing to performance of the services beginning before the end of the seven working day period referred to in regulation 12;]*

(c)   *the geographical address of the place of business of the supplier to which the consumer may address any complaints;*

(d)   *information about any after-sales services and guarantees; and*

(e)   *the conditions for exercising any contractual right to cancel the contract, where the contract is of an unspecified duration or a duration exceeding one year.*

(3)   Subject to regulation 9, prior to the conclusion of a contract for the supply of services, the supplier shall inform the consumer in writing or in another durable medium which is available and accessible to the consumer that, unless the parties agree otherwise, he will not be able to cancel the contract under regulation 10 once the performance of the services has begun with his agreement.

NOTES

Superseded as noted to reg 1 at **[2.138]**.

Para (2): word omitted and sub-para (b)(iii) added by the Consumer Protection (Distance Selling) (Amendment) Regulations 2005, SI 2005/689, reg 2, Schedule, para 1(1), (2).

Para (3): revoked by SI 2005/689, reg 2, Schedule, para 1(1), (3).

[2.145]
9 Services performed through the use of a means of distance communication

(1)   Regulation 8 shall not apply to a contract for the supply of services which are performed through the use of a means of distance communication, where those services are supplied on only one occasion and are invoiced by the operator of the means of distance communication.

(2)   But the supplier shall take all necessary steps to ensure that a consumer who is a party to a contract to which paragraph (1) applies is able to obtain the supplier's geographical address and the place of business to which the consumer may address any complaints.

NOTES
Superseded as noted to reg 1 at **[2.138]**.

[2.146]
10 Right to cancel

(1)   Subject to regulation 13, if within the cancellation period set out in regulations 11 and 12, the consumer gives a notice of cancellation to the supplier, or any other person previously notified by the supplier to the consumer as a person to whom notice of cancellation may be given, the notice of cancellation shall operate to cancel the contract.

(2)   Except as otherwise provided by these Regulations, the effect of a notice of cancellation is that the contract shall be treated as if it had not been made.

(3)   For the purposes of these Regulations, a notice of cancellation is a notice in writing or in another durable medium available and accessible to the supplier (or to the other person to whom it is given) which, however expressed, indicates the intention of the consumer to cancel the contract.

(4)   A notice of cancellation given under this regulation by a consumer to a supplier or other person is to be treated as having been properly given if the consumer—

   (a)   leaves it at the address last known to the consumer and addressed to the supplier or other person by name (in which case it is to be taken to have been given on the day on which it was left);

   (b)   sends it by post to the address last known to the consumer and addressed to the supplier or other person by name (in which case, it is to be taken to have been given on the day on which it was posted);

   (c)   sends it by facsimile to the business facsimile number last known to the consumer (in which case it is to be taken to have been given on the day on which it is sent); or

   (d)   sends it by electronic mail, to the business electronic mail address last known to the consumer (in which case it is to be taken to have been given on the day on which it is sent).

(5)   Where a consumer gives a notice in accordance with paragraph (4)(a) or (b) to a supplier who is a body corporate or a partnership, the notice is to be treated as having been properly given if—

   (a)   in the case of a body corporate, it is left at the address of, or sent to, the secretary or clerk of that body; or

   (b)   in the case of a partnership, it is left with or sent to a partner or a person having control or management of the partnership business.

NOTES
Superseded as noted to reg 1 at **[2.138]**.

[2.147]
11 Cancellation period in the case of contracts for the supply of goods

(1)   For the purposes of regulation 10, the cancellation period in the case of contracts for the supply of goods begins with the day on which the contract is concluded and ends as provided in paragraphs (2) to (5).

(2)   Where the supplier complies with regulation 8, the cancellation period ends on the expiry of the period of seven working days beginning with the day after the day on which the consumer receives the goods.

(3)   Where a supplier who has not complied with regulation 8 provides to the consumer the information referred to in regulation 8(2), and does so in writing or in another durable medium available and accessible to the consumer, within the period of three months beginning with the day after the day on which the consumer receives the goods, the cancellation period ends on the expiry of the period of seven working days beginning with the day after the day on which the consumer receives the information.

(4)   Where neither paragraph (2) nor (3) applies, the cancellation period ends on the expiry of the period of three months and seven working days beginning with the day after the day on which the consumer receives the goods.

(5)   In the case of contracts for goods for delivery to third parties, paragraphs (2) to (4) shall apply as if the consumer had received the goods on the day on which they were received by the third party.

[2.148]
12   Cancellation period in the case of contracts for the supply of services

(1)   For the purposes of regulation 10, the cancellation period in the case of contracts for the supply of services begins with the day on which the contract is concluded and ends as provided in paragraphs (2) to (4).

(2)   Where the supplier complies with regulation 8 on or before the day on which the contract is concluded, the cancellation period ends on the expiry of the period of seven working days beginning with the day after the day on which the contract is concluded.

(3)   [Subject to paragraph (3A)] where a supplier who has not complied with regulation 8 on or before the day on which the contract is concluded provides to the consumer the information referred to in regulation 8(2) . . . , and does so in writing or in another durable medium available and accessible to the consumer, within the period of three months beginning with the day after the day on which the contract is concluded, the cancellation period ends on the expiry of the period of seven working days beginning with the day after the day on which the consumer receives the information.

[(3A)   Where the performance of the contract has begun with the consumer's agreement before the expiry of the period of seven working days beginning with the day after the day on which the contract was concluded and the supplier has not complied with regulation 8 on or before the day on which performance began, but provides to the consumer the information referred to in regulation 8(2) in good time during the performance of the contract, the cancellation period ends—

 (a)   *on the expiry of the period of seven working days beginning with the day after the day on which the consumer receives the information; or*

 (b)   *if the performance of the contract is completed before the expiry of the period referred to in sub-paragraph (a), on the day when the performance of the contract is completed.]*

(4)   Where [none of paragraphs (2) to (3A) applies], the cancellation period ends on the expiry of the period of three months and seven working days beginning with the day after the day on which the contract is concluded.

NOTES
Superseded as noted to reg 1 at [**2.138**].
Para (3): words in square brackets inserted and words omitted revoked by the Consumer Protection (Distance Selling) (Amendment) Regulations 2005, SI 2005/689, reg 2, Schedule, para 2(1), (2).
Para (3A): inserted by SI 2005/689, reg 2, Schedule, para 2(1), (3).
Para (4): words in square brackets substituted by SI 2005/689, reg 2, Schedule, para 2(1), (4).

[2.149]
13   Exceptions to the right to cancel

(1)   Unless the parties have agreed otherwise, the consumer will not have the right to cancel the contract by giving notice of cancellation pursuant to regulation 10 in respect of contracts—

 [(a)   for the supply of services if the performance of the contract has begun with the consumer's agreement—
   (i)   *before the end of the cancellation period applicable under regulation 12(2); and*
   (ii)   *after the supplier has provided the information referred to in regulation 8(2).]*

 (b)   *for the supply of goods or services the price of which is dependent on fluctuations in the financial market which cannot be controlled by the supplier;*

 (c)   *for the supply of goods made to the consumer's specifications or clearly personalised or which by reason of their nature cannot be returned or are liable to deteriorate or expire rapidly;*

 (d)   *for the supply of audio or video recordings or computer software if they are unsealed by the consumer;*

 (e)   *for the supply of newspapers, periodicals or magazines; or*

 (f)   *for gaming, betting or lottery services.*

NOTES
Superseded as noted to reg 1 at [**2.138**].
Para (a) substituted by the Consumer Protection (Distance Selling) (Amendment) Regulations 2005, SI 2005/689, reg 2, Schedule, para 3.

[2.150]
14   Recovery of sums paid by or on behalf of the consumer on cancellation, and return of security

(1)   On the cancellation of a contract under regulation 10, the supplier shall reimburse any sum paid by or on behalf of the consumer under or in relation to the contract to the person by whom it was made free of any charge, less any charge made in accordance with paragraph (5).

(2) The reference in paragraph (1) to any sum paid on behalf of the consumer includes any sum paid by a creditor who is not the same person as the supplier under a personal credit agreement with the consumer.

(3) The supplier shall make the reimbursement referred to in paragraph (1) as soon as possible and in any case within a period not exceeding 30 days beginning with the day on which the notice of cancellation was given.

(4) Where any security has been provided in relation to the contract, the security (so far as it is so provided) shall, on cancellation under regulation 10, be treated as never having had effect and any property lodged with the supplier solely for the purposes of the security as so provided shall be returned by him forthwith.

(5) Subject to paragraphs (6) and (7), the supplier may make a charge, not exceeding the direct costs of recovering any goods supplied under the contract, where a term of the contract provides that the consumer must return any goods supplied if he cancels the contract under regulation 10 but the consumer does not comply with this provision or returns the goods at the expense of the supplier.

(6) Paragraph (5) shall not apply where—
  (a)   the consumer cancels in circumstances where he has the right to reject the goods under a term of the contract, including a term implied by virtue of any enactment, or
  (b)   the term requiring the consumer to return any goods supplied if he cancels the contract is an "unfair term" within the meaning of the Unfair Terms in Consumer Contracts Regulations 1999.

(7) Paragraph (5) shall not apply to the cost of recovering any goods which were supplied as substitutes for the goods ordered by the consumer.

(8) For the purposes of these Regulations, a personal credit agreement is an agreement between the consumer and any other person ("the creditor") by which the creditor provides the consumer with credit of any amount.

NOTES

Superseded as noted to reg 1 at **[2.138]**.

[2.151]
15 *Automatic cancellation of a related credit agreement*

(1) Where a notice of cancellation is given under regulation 10 which has the effect of cancelling the contract, the giving of the notice shall also have the effect of cancelling any related credit agreement.

(2) Where a related credit agreement is cancelled by virtue of paragraph (1), the supplier shall, if he is not the same person as the creditor under that agreement, forthwith on receipt of the notice of cancellation inform the creditor that the notice has been given.

(3) Where a related credit agreement is cancelled by virtue of paragraph (1)—
  (a)   any sum paid by or on behalf of the consumer under, or in relation to, the credit agreement which the supplier is not obliged to reimburse under regulation 14(1) shall be reimbursed, except for any sum which, if it had not already been paid, would have to be paid under sub-paragraph (b);
  (b)   the agreement shall continue in force so far as it relates to repayment of the credit and payment of interest, subject to regulation 16; and
  (c)   subject to sub-paragraph (b), the agreement shall cease to be enforceable.

(4) Where any security has been provided under a related credit agreement, the security, so far as it is so provided, shall be treated as never having had effect and any property lodged with the creditor solely for the purposes of the security as so provided shall be returned by him forthwith.

(5) For the purposes of this regulation and regulation 16, a "related credit agreement" means an agreement under which fixed sum credit which fully or partly covers the price under a contract cancelled under regulation 10 is granted—
  (a)   by the supplier, or
  (b)   by another person, under an arrangement between that person and the supplier.

(6) For the purposes of this regulation and regulation 16—
  (a)   "creditor" is a person who grants credit under a related credit agreement;
  (b)   "fixed sum credit" has the same meaning as in section 10 of the Consumer Credit Act 1974;
  (c)   "repayment" in relation to credit means repayment of money received by the consumer, and cognate expressions shall be construed accordingly; and
  (d)   "interest" means interest on money so received.

NOTES

Superseded as noted to reg 1 at **[2.138]**.

[2.152]

16   Repayment of credit and interest after cancellation of a related credit agreement

(1)   This regulation applies following the cancellation of a related credit agreement by virtue of regulation 15(1).

(2)   If the consumer repays the whole or a portion of the credit—

    (a)   before the expiry of one month following the cancellation of the credit agreement, or

    (b)   in the case of a credit repayable by instalments, before the date on which the first instalment is due,

no interest shall be payable on the amount repaid.

(3)   If the whole of a credit repayable by instalments is not repaid on or before the date referred to in paragraph (2)(b), the consumer shall not be liable to repay any of the credit except on receipt of a request in writing, signed by the creditor, stating the amounts of the remaining instalments (recalculated by the creditor as nearly as may be in accordance with the agreement and without extending the repayment period), but excluding any sum other than principal and interest.

(4)   Where any security has been provided under a related credit agreement the duty imposed on the consumer to repay credit and to pay interest shall not be enforceable before the creditor has discharged any duty imposed on him by regulation 15(4) to return any property lodged with him as security on cancellation.

NOTES

Superseded as noted to reg 1 at **[2.138]**.

[2.153]

17   Restoration of goods by consumer after cancellation

(1)   This regulation applies where a contract is cancelled under regulation 10 after the consumer has acquired possession of any goods under the contract other than any goods mentioned in regulation 13(1)(b) to (e).

(2)   The consumer shall be treated as having been under a duty throughout the period prior to cancellation—

    (a)   to retain possession of the goods, and

    (b)   to take reasonable care of them.

(3)   On cancellation, the consumer shall be under a duty to restore the goods to the supplier in accordance with this regulation, and in the meanwhile to retain possession of the goods and take reasonable care of them.

(4)   The consumer shall not be under any duty to deliver the goods except at his own premises and in pursuance of a request in writing, or in another durable medium available and accessible to the consumer, from the supplier and given to the consumer either before, or at the time when, the goods are collected from those premises.

(5)   If the consumer—

    (a)   delivers the goods (whether at his own premises or elsewhere) to any person to whom, under regulation 10(1), a notice of cancellation could have been given; or

    (b)   sends the goods at his own expense to such a person,

he shall be discharged from any duty to retain possession of the goods or restore them to the supplier.

(6)   Where the consumer delivers the goods in accordance with paragraph (5)(a), his obligation to take care of the goods shall cease; and if he sends the goods in accordance with paragraph (5)(b), he shall be under a duty to take reasonable care to see that they are received by the supplier and not damaged in transit, but in other respects his duty to take care of the goods shall cease when he sends them.

(7)   Where, at any time during the period of 21 days beginning with the day notice of cancellation was given, the consumer receives such a request as is mentioned in paragraph (4), and unreasonably refuses or unreasonably fails to comply with it, his duty to retain possession and take reasonable care of the goods shall continue until he delivers or sends the goods as mentioned in paragraph (5), but if within that period he does not receive such a request his duty to take reasonable care of the goods shall cease at the end of that period.

(8)   Where—

    (a)   a term of the contract provides that if the consumer cancels the contract, he must return the goods to the supplier, and

    (b)   the consumer is not otherwise entitled to reject the goods under the terms of the contract or by virtue of any enactment,

paragraph (7) shall apply as if for the period of 21 days there were substituted the period of 6 months.

(9)   Where any security has been provided in relation to the cancelled contract, the duty to restore goods imposed on the consumer by this regulation shall not be enforceable before the supplier has discharged any duty imposed on him by regulation 14(4) to return any property lodged with him as security on cancellation.

(10)   Breach of a duty imposed by this regulation on a consumer is actionable as a breach of statutory duty.

NOTES
Superseded as noted to reg 1 at **[2.138]**.

[2.154]
18   Goods given in part-exchange

(1)   This regulation applies on the cancellation of a contract under regulation 10 where the supplier agreed to take goods in part-exchange (the "part-exchange goods") and those goods have been delivered to him.

(2)   Unless, before the end of the period of 10 days beginning with the date of cancellation, the part-exchange goods are returned to the consumer in a condition substantially as good as when they were delivered to the supplier, the consumer shall be entitled to recover from the supplier a sum equal to the part-exchange allowance.

(3)   In this regulation the part-exchange allowance means the sum agreed as such in the cancelled contract, or if no such sum was agreed, such sum as it would have been reasonable to allow in respect of the part-exchange goods if no notice of cancellation had been served.

(4)   Where the consumer recovers from the supplier a sum equal to the part-exchange allowance, the title of the consumer to the part-exchange goods shall vest in the supplier (if it has not already done so) on recovery of that sum.

NOTES
Superseded as noted to reg 1 at **[2.138]**.

[2.155]
19   Performance

(1)   Unless the parties agree otherwise, the supplier shall perform the contract within a maximum of 30 days beginning with the day after the day the consumer sent his order to the supplier.

(2)   Subject to paragraphs (7) and (8), where the supplier is unable to perform the contract because the goods or services ordered are not available, within the period for performance referred to in paragraph (1) or such other period as the parties agree ("the period for performance"), he shall—

    (a)   inform the consumer; and

    (b)   reimburse any sum paid by or on behalf of the consumer under or in relation to the contract to the person by whom it was made.

(3)   The reference in paragraph (2)(b) to any sum paid on behalf of the consumer includes any sum paid by a creditor who is not the same person as the supplier under a personal credit agreement with the consumer.

(4)   The supplier shall make the reimbursement referred to in paragraph (2)(b) as soon as possible and in any event within a period of 30 days beginning with the day after the day on which the period for performance expired.

(5)   A contract which has not been performed within the period for performance shall be treated as if it had not been made, save for any rights or remedies which the consumer has under it as a result of the non-performance.

(6)   Where any security has been provided in relation to the contract, the security (so far as it is so provided) shall, where the supplier is unable to perform the contract within the period for performance, be treated as never having had any effect and any property lodged with the supplier solely for the purposes of the security as so provided shall be returned by him forthwith.

(7)   Where the supplier is unable to supply the goods or services ordered by the consumer, the supplier may perform the contract for the purposes of these Regulations by providing substitute goods or services (as the case may be) of equivalent quality and price provided that—

    (a)   this possibility was provided for in the contract;

    (b)   prior to the conclusion of the contract the supplier gave the consumer the information required by regulation 7(1)(b) and (c) in the manner required by regulation 7(2).

(8)   In the case of outdoor leisure events which by their nature cannot be rescheduled, paragraph 2(b) shall not apply where the consumer and the supplier so agree.

NOTES
Superseded as noted to reg 1 at **[2.138]**.

[2.156]
20   Effect of non-performance on related credit agreement

Where a supplier is unable to perform the contract within the period for performance—

    (a)   regulations 15 and 16 shall apply to any related credit agreement as if the consumer had given a valid notice of cancellation under regulation 10 on the expiry of the period for performance; and

(b) the reference in regulation 15(3)(a) to regulation 14(1) shall be read, for the purposes of this regulation, as a reference to regulation 19(2).

NOTES
Superseded as noted to reg 1 at **[2.138]**.

21–23 (Reg 21 revoked by the Payment Services Regulations 2009, SI 2009/209, reg 126, Sch 6, Pt 2, para 3; reg 22 repeals the Unsolicited Goods and Services Act 1971, s 1 and amends s 2 of that Act at **[1.483]**; reg 23 outside the scope of this work (regs 22, 23 superseded as noted to reg 1 at **[2.138]**.)

[2.157]
24 Inertia Selling

(1) Paragraphs (2) and (3) apply if—
(a) unsolicited goods are sent to a person ("the recipient") with a view to his acquiring them;
(b) the recipient has no reasonable cause to believe that they were sent with a view to their being acquired for the purposes of a business; and
(c) the recipient has neither agreed to acquire nor agreed to return them.

(2) The recipient may, as between himself and the sender, use, deal with or dispose of the goods as if they were an unconditional gift to him.

(3) The rights of the sender to the goods are extinguished.

(4), (5)   . . .

(6) In this regulation—
"acquire" includes hire;
"send" includes deliver;
"sender", in relation to any goods, includes—
(a) any person on whose behalf or with whose consent the goods are sent;
(b) any other person claiming through or under the sender or any person mentioned in paragraph (a); and
(c) any person who delivers the goods; and
"unsolicited" means, in relation to goods sent or services supplied to any person, that they are sent or supplied without any prior request made by or on behalf of the recipient.

(7)–(9)   . . .

(10) This regulation applies only to goods sent and services supplied after the date on which it comes into force.

NOTES
Superseded as noted to reg 1 at **[2.138]**.
Paras (4), (5), (7)–(9): revoked by the Consumer Protection from Unfair Trading Regulations 2008, SI 2008/1277, reg 30(1), (3), Sch 2, Pt 2, para 96, Sch 4.

[2.158]
25 No contracting-out

(1) A term contained in any contract to which these Regulations apply is void if, and to the extent that, it is inconsistent with a provision for the protection of the consumer contained in these Regulations.

(2) Where a provision of these Regulations specifies a duty or liability of the consumer in certain circumstances, a term contained in a contract to which these Regulations apply, other than a term to which paragraph (3) applies, is inconsistent with that provision if it purports to impose, directly or indirectly, an additional duty or liability on him in those circumstances.

(3) This paragraph applies to a term which requires the consumer to return any goods supplied to him under the contract if he cancels it under regulation 10.

(4) A term to which paragraph (3) applies shall, in the event of cancellation by the consumer under regulation 10, have effect only for the purposes of regulation 14(5) and 17(8).

(5) These Regulations shall apply notwithstanding any contract term which applies or purports to apply the law of a non-Member State if the contract has a close connection with the territory of a Member State.

NOTES
Superseded as noted to reg 1 at **[2.138]**.

[2.159]
26 Consideration of complaints

(1) It shall be the duty of an enforcement authority to consider any complaint made to it about a breach unless—
(a) the complaint appears to the authority to be frivolous or vexatious;   . . .

(b)   another enforcement authority has notified the [CMA] that it agrees to consider the complaint [or

(c)   the [CMA] has agreed to consider the complaint.]

(2)   If an enforcement authority notifies the [CMA] that it agrees to consider a complaint made to another enforcement authority, the first mentioned authority shall be under a duty to consider the complaint.

(3)   An enforcement authority which is under a duty to consider a complaint shall give reasons for its decision to apply or not to apply, as the case may be, for an injunction under regulation 27.

(4)   In deciding whether or not to apply for an injunction in respect of a breach an enforcement authority may, if it considers it appropriate to do so, have regard to any undertaking given to it or another enforcement authority by or on behalf of any person as to compliance with these Regulations.

NOTES

Superseded as noted to reg 1 at **[2.138]**.

Para (1): word omitted revoked, and para (c) and word immediately preceding it added, by the Public Bodies (The Office of Fair Trading Transfer of Consumer Advice Scheme Function and Modification of Enforcement Functions) Order 2013, SI 2013/783, art 11(1), (3); words in first and third (inner) pairs of square brackets substituted by the Enterprise and Regulatory Reform Act 2013 (Competition) (Consequential, Transitional and Saving Provisions) (No 2) Order 2014, SI 2014/549, art 2, Sch 1, Pt 2, para 28(1), (3) (for transitional provisions in relation to the continuity of functions, etc, see art 3 of the 2014 Order).

Para (2): word in square brackets substituted by SI 2014/549, art 2, Sch 1, Pt 2, para 28(1), (3)(a) (for transitional provisions in relation to the continuity of functions, etc, see art 3 of the 2014 Order).

References to the CMA, etc: as to the abolition of the office of the Director General of Fair Trading and the substitution of the original references to the Director (and related expressions), see the note to reg 3 at **[2.139]**.

[2.160]
[26A   Complaints—consideration by the [CMA]

(1)   If the [CMA] agrees to consider a complaint made to it about a breach it shall be under a duty to consider that complaint.

(2)   Paragraphs (3) and (4) of regulation 26 shall apply to the [CMA] when it is under a duty to consider a complaint as they apply to an enforcement authority.]

NOTES

Commencement: 28 March 2013.

Inserted by the Public Bodies (The Office of Fair Trading Transfer of Consumer Advice Scheme Function and Modification of Enforcement Functions) Order 2013, SI 2013/783, art 11(1), (4).

Superseded as noted to reg 1 at **[2.138]**.

Words in square brackets substituted by the Enterprise and Regulatory Reform Act 2013 (Competition) (Consequential, Transitional and Saving Provisions) (No 2) Order 2014, SI 2014/549, art 2, Sch 1, Pt 2, para 28(1), (4) (for transitional provisions in relation to the continuity of functions, etc, see art 3 of the 2014 Order).

References to the CMA, etc: as to the abolition of the office of the Director General of Fair Trading and the substitution of the original references to the Director (and related expressions), see the note to reg 3 at **[2.139]**.

[2.161]
27   *Injunctions to secure compliance with these Regulations*

(1)   The [OFT] or, subject to paragraph (2), [an] enforcement authority may apply for an injunction (including an interim injunction) against any person who appears to the [OFT] or that authority to be responsible for a breach.

(2)   An enforcement authority . . . may apply for an injunction only where—

(a)   it has notified the [OFT] of its intention to apply at least fourteen days before the date on which the application is to be made, beginning with the date on which the notification was given; or

(b)   the [OFT] consents to the application being made within a shorter period.

(3)   The court on an application under this regulation may grant an injunction on such terms as it thinks fit to secure compliance with these Regulations.

NOTES

Superseded as noted to reg 1 at **[2.138]**.

Para (1): words in first and third pairs of square brackets substituted by the Enterprise and Regulatory Reform Act 2013 (Competition) (Consequential, Transitional and Saving Provisions) (No 2) Order 2014, SI 2014/549, art 2, Sch 1, Pt 2, para 28(1), (5) (for transitional provisions in relation to the continuity of functions, etc, see art 3 of the 2014 Order); word in second pair of square brackets substituted by the Public Bodies (The Office of Fair Trading Transfer of Consumer Advice Scheme Function and Modification of Enforcement Functions) Order 2013, SI 2013/783, art 11(1), (5)(a).

Para (2): words omitted revoked by SI 2013/783, art 11(1), (5)(b); words in square brackets substituted by SI 2014/549, art 2, Sch 1, Pt 2, para 28(1), (5) (for transitional provisions in relation to the continuity of functions, etc, see art 3 of the 2014 Order).

References to the CMA, etc: as to the abolition of the office of the Director General of Fair Trading and the substitution of the original references to the Director (and related expressions), see the note to reg 3 at **[2.139]**.

[2.162]
28 Notification of undertakings and orders to the [CMA]

An enforcement authority . . . shall notify the [CMA]—

(a)   *of any undertaking given to it by or on behalf of any person who appears to it to be responsible for a breach;*

(b)   *of the outcome of any application made by it under regulation 27 and of the terms of any undertaking given to or order made by the court;*

(c)   *of the outcome of any application made by it to enforce a previous order of the court.*

NOTES

Superseded as noted to reg 1 at **[2.138]**.

Words in square brackets substituted by the Enterprise and Regulatory Reform Act 2013 (Competition) (Consequential, Transitional and Saving Provisions) (No 2) Order 2014, SI 2014/549, art 2, Sch 1, Pt 2, para 28(1), (6) (for transitional provisions in relation to the continuity of functions, etc, see art 3 of the 2014 Order); words omitted revoked by the Public Bodies (The Office of Fair Trading Transfer of Consumer Advice Scheme Function and Modification of Enforcement Functions) Order 2013, SI 2013/783, art 11(1), (6).

References to the OFT, etc: as to the abolition of the office of the Director General of Fair Trading and the substitution of the original references to the Director (and related expressions), see the note to reg 3 at **[2.139]**.

[2.163]
29 Publication, information and advice

(1)   The [CMA] shall arrange for the publication in such form and manner as [it] considers appropriate of—

(a)   *details of any undertaking or order notified to [it] under regulation 28;*

(b)   *details of any undertaking given to [it] by or on behalf of any person as to compliance with these Regulations;*

(c)   *details of any application made by [it] under regulation 27, and of the terms of any undertaking given to, or order made by, the court;*

(d)   *details of any application made by the [CMA] to enforce a previous order of the court.*

(2)   The [CMA] [or an enforcement authority] may arrange for the dissemination in such form and manner as [it] considers appropriate of such information and advice concerning the operation of these Regulations as it may appear to [it] to be expedient to give to the public and to all persons likely to be affected by these Regulations.

NOTES

Superseded as noted to reg 1 at **[2.138]**.

Para (1): words in square brackets substituted by the Enterprise and Regulatory Reform Act 2013 (Competition) (Consequential, Transitional and Saving Provisions) (No 2) Order 2014, SI 2014/549, art 2, Sch 1, Pt 2, para 28(1), (7) (for transitional provisions in relation to the continuity of functions, etc, see art 3 of the 2014 Order).

Para (2): words in first, third and final pairs of square brackets substituted by SI 2014/549, art 2, Sch 1, Pt 2, para 28(1), (7) (for transitional provisions in relation to the continuity of functions, etc, see art 3 of the 2014 Order); words in second pair of square brackets inserted by the Public Bodies (The Office of Fair Trading Transfer of Consumer Advice Scheme Function and Modification of Enforcement Functions) Order 2013, SI 2013/783, art 11(1), (7).

References to the CMA, etc: as to the abolition of the office of the Director General of Fair Trading and the substitution of the original references to the Director (and related expressions), see the note to reg 3 at **[2.139]**.

SCHEDULES

SCHEDULE 1
INDICATIVE LIST OF MEANS OF DISTANCE COMMUNICATION

Regulation 3

[2.164]
1.   Unaddressed printed matter.

2.   Addressed printed matter.

3.   Letter.

4.   Press advertising with order form.

5.   Catalogue.

6.   Telephone with human intervention.

7.   Telephone without human intervention (automatic calling machine, audiotext).

8.   Radio.

9.   Videophone (telephone with screen).

10.   Videotext (microcomputer and television screen) with keyboard or touch screen.

11.   Electronic mail.

12. *Facsimile machine (fax).*

13. *Television (teleshopping).*

NOTES
Superseded as noted to reg 1 at **[2.138]**.

SCHEDULE 2

(Sch 2 revoked by the Financial Services (Distance Marketing) Regulations 2004, SI 2004/2095, reg 25(1), (5).)

TELECOMMUNICATIONS (LAWFUL BUSINESS PRACTICE) (INTERCEPTION OF COMMUNICATIONS) REGULATIONS 2000

(SI 2000/2699)

NOTES
Made: 2 October 2000.
Authority: Regulation of Investigatory Powers Act 2000, ss 4(2), 78(5).
Commencement: 24 October 2000.

[2.165]
1   Citation and commencement

These Regulations may be cited as the Telecommunications (Lawful Business Practice) (Interception of Communications) Regulations 2000 and shall come into force on 24th October 2000.

[2.166]
2   Interpretation

In these Regulations—
  (a) references to a business include references to activities of a government department, of any public authority or of any person or office holder on whom functions are conferred by or under any enactment;
  (b) a reference to a communication as relevant to a business is a reference to—
    (i) a communication—
      (aa) by means of which a transaction is entered into in the course of that business, or
      (bb) which otherwise relates to that business, or
    (ii) a communication which otherwise takes place in the course of the carrying on of that business;
  (c) "regulatory or self-regulatory practices or procedures" means practices or procedures—
    (i) compliance with which is required or recommended by, under or by virtue of—
      (aa) any provision of the law of a member state or other state within the European Economic Area, or
      (bb) any standard or code of practice published by or on behalf of a body established in a member state or other state within the European Economic Area which includes amongst its objectives the publication of standards or codes of practice for the conduct of business, or
    (ii) which are otherwise applied for the purpose of ensuring compliance with anything so required or recommended;
  (d) "system controller" means, in relation to a particular telecommunication system, a person with a right to control its operation or use.

[2.167]
3   Lawful interception of a communication

(1)   For the purpose of section 1(5)(a) of the Act, conduct is authorised, subject to paragraphs (2) and (3) below, if it consists of interception of a communication, in the course of its transmission by means of a telecommunication system, which is effected by or with the express   . . .   consent of the system controller for the purpose of—
  (a) monitoring or keeping a record of communications—
    (i) in order to—
      (aa) establish the existence of facts, or
      (bb) ascertain compliance with regulatory or self-regulatory practices or procedures which are—**applicable to the system controller in the carrying on of his**

business orapplicable to another person in the carrying on of his business where that person is supervised by the system controller in respect of those practices or procedures, or

    (cc)   ascertain or demonstrate the standards which are achieved or ought to be achieved by persons using the system in the course of their duties, or

  (ii)   in the interests of national security, or

  (iii) for the purpose of preventing or detecting crime, or

  (iv) for the purpose of investigating or detecting the unauthorised use of that or any other telecommunication system, or

  (v)   where that is undertaken—

    (aa) in order to secure, or

    (bb) as an inherent part of,

the effective operation of the system (including any monitoring or keeping of a record which would be authorised by section 3(3) of the Act if the conditions in paragraphs (a) and (b) thereof were satisfied); or

(b)   monitoring communications for the purpose of determining whether they are communications relevant to the system controller's business which fall within regulation 2(b)(i) above; or

(c)   monitoring communications made to a confidential voice-telephony counselling or support service which is free of charge (other than the cost, if any, of making a telephone call) and operated in such a way that users may remain anonymous if they so choose.

(2)   Conduct is authorised by paragraph (1) of this regulation only if—

(a)   the interception in question is effected solely for the purpose of monitoring or (where appropriate) keeping a record of communications relevant to the system controller's business;

(b)   the telecommunication system in question is provided for use wholly or partly in connection with that business;

(c)   the system controller has made all reasonable efforts to inform every person who may use the telecommunication system in question that communications transmitted by means thereof may be intercepted; and

(d)   in a case falling within—

  (i)   paragraph (1)(a)(ii) above, the person by or on whose behalf the interception is effected is a person specified in section 6(2)(a) to (i) of the Act;

  (ii) paragraph (1)(b) above, the communication is one which is intended to be received (whether or not it has been actually received) by a person using the telecommunication system in question.

[(3)   Conduct falling within paragraph (1)(a)(i) above is authorised only to the extent that Article 5 of Directive 2002/58/EC of the European Parliament and of the Council of 12 July 2002 concerning the processing of personal data and the protection of privacy in the electronic communications sector so permits [as amended by Directive 2009/136/EC of the European Parliament and of the Council of 25 November 2009 amending Directive 2002/22/EC on universal service and users' rights relating to electronic communications networks and services, Directive 2002/58/EC concerning the processing of personal data and the protection of privacy in the electronic communications sector and Regulation (EC) No 2006/2004 on cooperation between national authorities responsible for the enforcement of consumer protection laws.]]

NOTES

   Para (1): words omitted revoked by the Privacy and Electronic Communications (EC Directive) (Amendment) Regulations 2011, SI 2011/1208, reg 15(a).

   Para (3): substituted by the Privacy and Electronic Communications (EC Directive) Regulations 2003, SI 2003/2426, reg 34; words in square brackets inserted by SI 2011/1208, reg 15(b).

FINANCIAL SERVICES AND MARKETS ACT 2000 (REGULATED ACTIVITIES) ORDER 2001

(SI 2001/544)

NOTES

   Made: 26 February 2001.

   Authority: Financial Services and Markets Act 2000, ss 22(1), (5), 426, 428(3), Sch 2, para 25.

   Commencement: see art 2.

   References to "the European Community", "Community", etc: see the Treaty of Lisbon (Changes in Terminology) Order 2011, SI 2011/1043, which provides that (as from 22 April 2011): (i) for references to the European Communities or to the European Community or the European Coal and Steel Community (including references to "the Communities", "the Community", "the EC" or "the EEC") substitute references to the European Union, and (ii) references to "EU" should be substituted for the word "Community" (subject to certain exceptions) in references to "Community treaties", "Community instrument", "Community obligation", "Community law", "Community legislation", etc.

Transitional provisions (interim permissions and interim approvals): see the Financial Services and Markets Act 2000 (Interim Permissions) Order 2001, SI 2001/3374. This Order conferred an interim permission on certain applicants who applied to the FSA for permission under the original Part IV of the 2000 Act and whose application was pending on the date when the main provisions of the Act came into force (1 December 2001). Note that the original Part IV of the 2000 Act has now been substituted by a new Part 4A by the Financial Services Act 2012. See the notes to Part 4A (preceding s 55A of the 2000 Act at **[1.1429]**) with regard to transitional provisions etc relating to the commencement of the 2012 Act.

For transitional provisions relating to interim permissions and interim approvals to various activities that have become regulated activities following the amendment of this Order, see below:

— the Financial Services and Markets Act 2000 (Transitional Provisions) (Mortgages) Order 2004, SI 2004/2615 (in relation to certain mortgage mediation activities)

— the Financial Services and Markets Act 2000 (Regulated Activities) (Amendment) (No 2) Order 2004, SI 2004/2737 (in relation to advice on stakeholder products)

— the Financial Services and Markets Act 2000 (Transitional Provisions) (General Insurance Intermediaries) Order 2004, SI 2004/3351 (in relation to certain general insurance mediation activities)

— the Financial Services and Markets Act 2000 (Regulated Activities) (Amendment) Order 2006, SI 2006/1969 (in relation to establishing, operating or winding up a personal pension scheme, or activities which relate to the specified investment of rights under a personal pension scheme)

— the Financial Services and Markets Act 2000 (Regulated Activities) (Amendment) (No 2) Order 2006, SI 2006/2383 (in relation to administering, arranging or advising on regulated home reversion plans or regulated home purchase plans)

— the Financial Services and Markets Act 2000 (Regulated Activities) (Amendment) (No 2) Order 2007, SI 2007/3510 (in relation to provision of travel insurance in certain circumstances)

— the Financial Services and Markets Act 2000 (Regulated Activities) (Amendment) Order 2009, SI 2009/1342 (in relation to entering into, administering, arranging and advising on regulated sale and rent back agreements

— the Financial Services and Markets Act 2000 (Regulated Activities) (Amendment) Order 2013, SI 2013/655 and the Financial Services and Markets Act 2000 (Regulated Activities) (Amendment) Order 2015, SI 2015/369 in relation to providing information in relation to and administering specified benchmarks)

— the Financial Services and Markets Act 2000 (Regulated Activities) (Amendment) (No 2) Order 2013, SI 2013/1881 (in relation to credit broking, operating an electronic system in relation to lending, debt adjusting, debt-counselling, debt-collecting, debt administration, entering into etc a regulated credit agreement, entering into etc a regulated consumer hire agreement, providing credit information services and providing credit references).

— the Financial Services and Markets Act 2000 (Regulated Activities) (Amendment) (No 2) Order 2015, SI 2015/731, and the Financial Services and Markets Act 2000 (Regulated Activities) (Transitional Provisions) Order 2015, SI 2015/732 (in relation to advising on conversion or transfer of pension benefits).

See also the Mortgage Credit Directive Order 2015, SI 2015/910 (interim permissions in relation to an activity of the kind specified by article 25A, 36A, 53A, 60B or 61 of this Order).

See article 7 (reg 24) of the Collective Investment in Transferable Securities (Contractual Scheme) Regulations 2013, SI 2013/1388. That regulation contains transitional provisions in relation to depositaries of authorised contractual schemes. A person who already has permission under Part 4A of the 2000 Act to act as the trustee of an authorised unit trust scheme and as the depositary of an open-ended investment company, if that person gives the FCA notice in accordance with the regulation, is treated as having permission under that Part to act as the depositary of an authorised contractual scheme.

See also the Alternative Investment Fund Managers Order 2014, SI 2014/1292, art 7 which provides a process whereby fund managers that have applied for permission to carry on the new regulated activities of managing an AIF or managing a UCITS before 16 June 2014, and that will require permission to carry on insurance mediation activities after art 6 of that Order comes into force (ie, 22 July 2014), may notify the FCA of this fact and obtain such permission without the need to make a new application for a variation of permission. Note that art 6 of the 2014 Order amends art 4(4A)(b) of this Order *post*.

See the Financial Services and Markets Act 2000 (Permission and Applications) (Credit Unions etc) Order 2002, SI 2002/704 (transitional provisions relating to the expiry, on 2 July 2002, of the transitional exemption of credit unions from the general prohibition imposed by s 19 of the 2000 Act (see the Financial Services and Markets Act 2000 (Exemption) Order 2001, SI 2001/1201, art 6).

See also the Financial Services and Markets Act 2000 (Permissions, Transitional Provisions and Consequential Amendments) (Northern Ireland Credit Unions) Order 2011, SI 2011/2832 which makes transitional provisions and consequential amendments relating to the revocation, on 31 March 2012, of the exemption for Northern Ireland credit unions from the general prohibition imposed by s 19 *ante*. The exemption, contained in para 24A of the Schedule to the Financial Services and Markets Act 2000 (Exemption) Order 2001 (SI 2001/1201), is revoked by SI 2011/2716.

See also the Financial Services and Markets Act 2000 (Regulated Activities) (Green Deal) (Amendment) Order 2014, SI 2014/1850, art 12. That article contains transitional provisions in connection with the application of the provisions of the Consumer Credit Act 1974 to a green deal plan which (a) is made in the period starting with 1 April 2014 and ending on 14 July 2014, and (b) is not a regulated credit agreement for the purposes of Chapter 14A of this Order at the time it is made, but (c) becomes on the coming into force of the 2014 Order a regulated credit agreement for those purposes in consequence of provision made by the 2014 Order (an "interim plan"). In such circumstances: (a) ss 55, 55C, 60, 61, 61A, 62, 63, 64, 65, 66A, 67–73, 75A, 80, 94–97A, 102, 105–107, 129–130, 136 and 173 of the 1974 Act do not apply to an interim plan; (b) ss 76, 86, 87 and 98 do not apply in respect of an entitlement of the creditor to take a step or action which arises in connection with an interim plan before 15 July 2014; (c) ss 77, 77B and 110 do not apply to an interim plan in respect of a request which is received by the creditor before that date; (d) s 78A does not apply to an interim plan in respect of a change in interest rate which takes effect before that date; (e) s 82(1)–(1E) does not apply to a variation to an interim plan which takes effect before that date; (f) ss 86E, 86F and 93 do not apply to an interim plan in respect of a sum which first becomes payable before that date; and (g) s 130A does not apply to an interim plan in respect of a sum that is required to be paid under a judgment given before that date.

PART II
SPECIFIED ACTIVITIES

CHAPTER I
General

CHAPTER 6A
CREDIT BROKING

The activity

Exclusions

CHAPTER 6B
OPERATING AN ELECTRONIC SYSTEM IN RELATION TO LENDING

The activity

Exclusions

Supplemental

CHAPTER 7B
ACTIVITIES IN RELATION TO DEBT

The Activities

Exclusions

Supplemental

CHAPTER 14A
REGULATED CREDIT AGREEMENTS

The activities

Exclusions

PART I
GENERAL

[2.168]
1   Citation
This Order may be cited as the Financial Services and Markets Act 2000 (Regulated Activities)
Order 2001.

2   (*Outside the scope of this work.*)

[2.169]
3   Interpretation
(1)   In this Order—
    "the Act" means the Financial Services and Markets Act 2000;

["acting as an insolvency practitioner" is to be read with section 388 of the Insolvency Act 1986 or, as the case may be, article 3 of the Insolvency (Northern Ireland) Order 1989 and, in any provision of this Order which provides for activities to be excluded from a specified activity, references to things done by a person acting—
- (a) as an insolvency practitioner, or
- (b) in reasonable contemplation of that person's appointment as an insolvency practitioner,

include anything done by the person's firm in connection with that person so acting;]

["AIFM" has the meaning given by regulation 4 of the Alternative Investment Fund Managers Regulations 2013;]

["agreement provider" has the meaning given by article 63J(3);

"agreement seller" has the meaning given by article 63J(3);]

["aircraft operator" has the same meaning as in the emission allowance trading directive;]

"annuities on human life" does not include superannuation allowances and annuities payable out of any fund applicable solely to the relief and maintenance of persons engaged, or who have been engaged, in any particular profession, trade or employment, or of the dependants of such persons;

["assignment", in relation to a credit agreement, has the meaning given by article 60L;]

["auction platform" means a platform on which auctions of greenhouse gas emissions allowances are held in accordance with the emission allowance auctioning regulation;]

["borrower"—
- (a) in relation to a credit agreement other than a regulated mortgage contract[,] an article 36H agreement (within the meaning given by article 36H) [or an agreement that is a green deal plan], has the meaning given by article 60L;
- (b) in relation to an article 36H agreement (within the meaning given by that article) other than a regulated mortgage contract, is to be read with article 36H(4);
- [(c) in relation to a credit agreement that is a green deal plan, has the meaning given by article 60LB].]

"buying" includes acquiring for valuable consideration;

"close relative" in relation to a person means—
- (a) his spouse [or civil partner];
- (b) his children and step children, his parents and step-parents, his brothers and sisters and his step-brothers and step-sisters; and
- (c) the spouse [or civil partner] of any person within sub-paragraph (b);

["the Commission Regulation" means Commission Regulation 1287/2006 of 10 August 2006;]

["consumer hire agreement" has the meaning given by article 60N;]

"contract of general insurance" means any contract falling within Part I of Schedule 1;

"contract of insurance" means any contract of insurance which is a contract of long-term insurance or a contract of general insurance, and includes—
- (a) fidelity bonds, performance bonds, administration bonds, bail bonds, customs bonds or similar contracts of guarantee, where these are—
  - (i)   effected or carried out by a person not carrying on a banking business;
  - (ii) not effected merely incidentally to some other business carried on by the person effecting them; and
  - (iii) effected in return for the payment of one or more premiums;
- (b) tontines;
- (c) capital redemption contracts or pension fund management contracts, where these are effected or carried out by a person who—
  - (i)   does not carry on a banking business; and
  - (ii) otherwise carries on a regulated activity of the kind specified by article 10(1) or (2);
- (d) contracts to pay annuities on human life;
- (e) contracts of a kind referred to in *article 1(2)(e) of the first life insurance directive (collective insurance etc)*; and
- (f) contracts of a kind referred to in *article 1(3) of the first life insurance directive (social insurance)*;

but does not include a funeral plan contract (or a contract which would be a funeral plan contract but for the exclusion in article 60);

"contract of long-term insurance" means any contract falling within Part II of Schedule 1;

"contractually based investment" means—
- (a) rights under a qualifying contract of insurance;
- (b) any investment of the kind specified by any of articles 83, 84, 85 and 87; or
- (c) any investment of the kind specified by article 89 so far as relevant to an investment falling within (a) or (b);

["credit agreement"—
- (a) in relation to an agreement other than a green deal plan, has the meaning given by article 60B;
- (b) in relation to a green deal plan, has the meaning given by article 60LB;]

["credit institution" means—

  (a)   a credit institution authorised under the [capital requirements directive] other than an institution to which Article 2.1 of the markets in financial instruments directive (the text of which is set out in Schedule 3) applies, or

  (b)   an institution which would satisfy the requirements for authorisation as a credit institution under that directive (other than an institution to which Article 2.1 of the markets in financial instruments directive would apply) if it had its registered office (or if it does not have a registered office, its head office) in an EEA State;]

"deposit" has the meaning given by article 5 [except where the definition given in article 60L applies];

["designated guidance provider" has the meaning given by section 333E(1) of the Act;]

["EEA AIFM" has the meaning given by regulation 2(1) of the Alternative Investment Fund Managers Regulations 2013;]

["electronic money" has the meaning given by regulation 2(1) of the Electronic Money Regulations 2011;]

["emission allowance trading directive" means Directive 2003/87/EC of the European Parliament and of the Council of 13 October 2003 establishing a scheme for greenhouse gas emission allowances trading within the Community;]

["emission allowance auctioning regulation" means Commission Regulation (EU) No 1031/2010 of 12 November 2010 on the timing, administration and other aspects of auctioning of greenhouse gas emission allowances pursuant to the emission allowance trading directive;]

["financial instrument" means any instrument listed in Section C of Annex I to the markets in financial instruments directive (the text of which is set out in Part 1 of Schedule 2) read with Chapter VI of the Commission Regulation (the text of which is set out in Part 2 of Schedule 2);]

["full-scope UK AIFM" has the meaning given by regulation 2(1) of the Alternative Investment Fund Managers Regulations 2013;]

"funeral plan contract" has the meaning given by article 59;

["green deal plan" has the meaning given by section 1 of the Energy Act 2011;]

["greenhouse gas emissions allowances" mean "allowances" as defined in Article 3(a) of the emission allowance trading directive;]

["hire-purchase agreement" has the meaning given by article 60L;]

["hirer" is to be read with the definition of "consumer hire agreement" in article 60N;]

["home Member State", in relation to an investment firm, has the meaning given by Article 4.1.20 of the markets in financial instruments directive, and in relation to a credit institution, has the meaning given by [Article 4(1)(43) of the capital requirements regulation][, and, in relation to a mortgage intermediary, has the meaning given by Article 4(19) of the mortgages directive];]

["home purchase provider" has the meaning given by article 63F(3);

"home purchaser" has the meaning given by article 63F(3);]

"instrument" includes any record whether or not in the form of a document;

["investment firm" means a person whose regular occupation or business is the provision or performance of investment services and activities on a professional basis but does not include—

  (a)   a person to whom the markets in financial instruments directive does not apply by virtue of Article 2 of that directive (the text of which is set out in Schedule 3);

  (b)   a person whose home Member State is an EEA State other than the United Kingdom and to whom, by reason of the fact that the State has given effect to Article 3 of that directive, that directive does not apply by virtue of that Article;

  (c)   a person who does not have a home Member State and to whom (if he had his registered office in an EEA State, or, being a person other than a body corporate or a body corporate not having a registered office, if he had his head office in an EEA State) the markets in financial instruments directive would not apply by virtue of Article 2 of that directive;]

["investment services and activities" means—

  (a)   any service provided to third parties listed in Section A of Annex 1 to the markets in financial instruments directive (the text of which is set out in Part 3 of Schedule 2) read with Article 52 of Commission Directive 2006/73/EC of 10 August 2006 (the text of which is set out in Part 4 of Schedule 2), including the reception, transmission or submission of a bid by an investment firm or credit institution on any auction platform, in relation to any financial instrument; or

  (b)   any activity listed in Section A of Annex 1 to that directive, in relation to any financial instrument;]

"joint enterprise" means an enterprise into which two or more persons ("the participators") enter for commercial purposes related to a business or businesses (other than the business of engaging in a regulated activity) carried on by them; and, where a participator is a member of a group, each other member of the group is also to be regarded as a participator in the enterprise;

["lender"—

(a) in relation to a credit agreement other than a regulated mortgage contract[,] an article 36H agreement (within the meaning given by article 36H) [or an agreement that is a green deal plan], has the meaning given by article 60L;

(b) in relation to an article 36H agreement (within the meaning given by that article) other than a regulated mortgage contract, is to be read with article 36H(4);

[(c) in relation to a credit agreement that is a green deal plan, has the meaning given by article 60LB;]]

"local authority" means—

(a) in England and Wales, a local authority within the meaning of the Local Government Act 1972, the Greater London Authority, the Common Council of the City of London or the Council of the Isles of Scilly;

(b) in Scotland, a local authority within the meaning of the Local Government (Scotland) Act 1973;

(c) in Northern Ireland, a district council within the meaning of the Local Government Act (Northern Ireland) 1972;

["management company" has the meaning given by Article 2.1(b) of the UCITS directive;]

"managing agent" means a person who is permitted by the Council of Lloyd's in the conduct of his business as an underwriting agent to perform for a member of Lloyd's one or more of the following functions—

(a) underwriting contracts of insurance at Lloyd's;

(b) reinsuring such contracts in whole or in part;

(c) paying claims on such contracts;

["market operator" means a market operator within the meaning of Article 4.1.13 of the markets in financial instruments directive, or a person who would be a market operator if he had his registered office, or if he does not have a registered office his head office, in an EEA State, but does not include—

(a) a person to whom the markets in financial instruments directive does not apply by virtue of Article 2 of that directive (the text of which is set out in Schedule 3);

(b) a person who does not have a home Member State to whom (if he had his registered office, or if he does not have a registered office his head office, in an EEA State) the markets in financial instruments directive would not apply by virtue of Article 2 of that directive;]

["multilateral trading facility" means—

(a) a multilateral trading facility (within the meaning of Article 4.1.15 of the markets in financial instruments directive) operated by an investment firm, a credit institution or a market operator, or

(b) a facility which—

(i) is operated by an investment firm, a credit institution or market operator which does not have a home Member State, and

(ii) if its operator had a home Member State, would be a multilateral trading facility within the meaning of Article 4.1.15 of the markets in financial instruments directive;]

["occupational pension scheme" has the meaning given by section 1 of the Pension Schemes Act 1993 but with paragraph (b) of the definition omitted;]

["operator" has the same meaning as in the emission allowance trading directive;]

"overseas person" means a person who—

(a) carries on activities of the kind specified by any of articles 14, 21, 25, [25A,] [25B, 25C,] [25D,] [25E,] 37[, 39A], 40, 45, [51ZA, 51ZB, 51ZC, 51ZD, 51ZE], 52[, 53, 53A[, 53B, 53C, [53D,] 61, 63B[, 63F and 63J]]] or, so far as relevant to any of those articles, article 64 (or activities of a kind which would be so specified but for the exclusion in article 72); but

(b) does not carry on any such activities, or offer to do so, from a permanent place of business maintained by him in the United Kingdom;

["owner", in relation to a hire purchase agreement, has the meaning given by article 60N;]

"pension fund management contract" means a contract to manage the investments of pension funds (other than funds solely for the benefit of the officers or employees of the person effecting or carrying out the contract and their dependants or, in the case of a company, partly for the benefit of officers and employees and their dependants of its subsidiary or holding company or a subsidiary of its holding company); and for the purposes of this definition, "subsidiary" and "holding company" are to be construed in accordance with [section 1159 of the Companies Act 2006];

["the person's firm", in relation to a person acting as an insolvency practitioner or in reasonable contemplation of that person's appointment as an insolvency practitioner, means—

(a) the person's employer;

(b) where the person is a partner in a partnership other than a limited liability partnership, that partnership;

(c) where the person is a member of a limited liability partnership, that partnership;]

["personal pension scheme" means a scheme or arrangement which is not an occupational pension scheme or a stakeholder pension scheme and which is comprised in one or more instruments or agreements, having or capable of having effect so as to provide benefits to or in respect of people—
  (a)   on retirement,
  (b)   on having reached a particular age, or
  (c)   on termination of service in an employment;]
["plan provider" has the meaning given by paragraph (3) of article 63B, read with paragraphs (7) and (8) of that article;]
"property" includes currency of the United Kingdom or any other country or territory;
"qualifying contract of insurance" means a contract of long-term insurance which is not—
  (a)   a reinsurance contract; nor
  (b)   a contract in respect of which the following conditions are met—
        (i)   the benefits under the contract are payable only on death or in respect of incapacity due to injury, sickness or infirmity;
        (ii)   . . .
        (iii)   the contract has no surrender value, or the consideration consists of a single premium and the surrender value does not exceed that premium; and
        (iv)   the contract makes no provision for its conversion or extension in a manner which would result in it ceasing to comply with any of the above conditions;
["reception", "transmission" and "submission" have the same meaning in relation to a bid at an auction for an investment of the kind specified in article 82A as in the emission allowance auctioning regulation;]
["regulated consumer hire agreement" has the meaning given by article 60N;]
["regulated credit agreement" has the meaning given by article 60B;]
["regulated home purchase plan" has the meaning given by article 63F(3);]
"regulated home reversion plan" has the meaning given by article 63B(3);]
"regulated mortgage contract" has the meaning given by article 61(3);
["regulated sale and rent back agreement" has the meaning given by article 63J(3);]
["relevant investment" means—
  (a)   rights under a qualifying contract of insurance;
  (b)   rights under any other contract of insurance;
  (c)   any investment of the kind specified by any of articles 83, 84, 85 and 87; or
  (d)   any investment of the kind specified by article 89 so far as relevant to an investment falling within (a) or (c);]
["relevant recipient of credit" has the meaning given by article 60L;]
["restricted-use credit agreement" has the meaning given in article 60L;]
["reversion seller" has the meaning given by article 63B(3);]
"security" means (except where the context otherwise requires) any investment of the kind specified by any of articles 76 to 82 or, so far as relevant to any such investment, article 89;
"selling", in relation to any investment, includes disposing of the investment for valuable consideration, and for these purposes "disposing" includes—
  (a)   in the case of an investment consisting of rights under a contract—
        (i)   surrendering, assigning or converting those rights; or
        (ii)   assuming the corresponding liabilities under the contract;
  (b)   in the case of an investment consisting of rights under other arrangements, assuming the corresponding liabilities under the arrangements; and
  (c)   in the case of any other investment, issuing or creating the investment or granting the rights or interests of which it consists;
["small registered UK AIFM" has the meaning given by regulation 2(1) of the Alternative Investment Fund Managers Regulations 2013;]
"stakeholder pension scheme" has the meaning given by section 1 of the Welfare Reform and Pensions Act 1999 [in relation to Great Britain and has the meaning given by article 3 of the Welfare Reform and Pensions (Northern Ireland) Order 1999 in relation to Northern Ireland];
"syndicate" means one or more persons, to whom a particular syndicate number has been assigned by or under the authority of the Council of Lloyd's, carrying out or effecting contracts of insurance written at Lloyd's;
["trade repository" means a person registered with ESMA under Article 55 of Regulation (EU) 648/2012 of the European Parliament and of the Council of 4 July 2012 on OTC derivatives, central counterparties and trade repositories or a person recognised by ESMA under Article 77 of that Regulation;]
["UCITS" has the meaning given by Article 1.2 of the UCITS directive;]
["UK AIF" has the meaning given by regulation 2(1) of the Alternative Investment Fund Managers Regulations 2013;]
"voting shares", in relation to a body corporate, means shares carrying voting rights attributable to share capital which are exercisable in all circumstances at any general meeting of that body corporate.

Part 2   Statutory Instruments

(2)   For the purposes of this Order, a transaction is entered into through a person if he enters into it as agent or arranges, in a manner constituting the carrying on of an activity of the kind specified by article 25(1)[, 25A(1), 25B(1)[, 25C(1) or 25E(1)]], for it to be entered into by another person as agent or principal.

(3)   For the purposes of this Order, a contract of insurance is to be treated as falling within Part II of Schedule 1, notwithstanding the fact that it contains related and subsidiary provisions such that it might also be regarded as falling within Part I of that Schedule, if its principal object is that of a contract falling within Part II and it is effected or carried out by an authorised person who has permission to effect or carry out contracts falling within paragraph I of Part II of Schedule 1.

NOTES

Para (1) is amended as follows:

Definitions "acting as an insolvency practitioner" and "the person's firm" inserted by the Financial Services and Markets Act 2000 (Regulated Activities) (Amendment) Order 2014, SI 2014/366, art 2(1), (2).

Definitions "AIFM", "EEA AIFM", "full-scope UK AIFM", "small registered UK AIFM", "UCITS" and "UK AIF" inserted by the Alternative Investment Fund Managers Regulations 2013, SI 2013/1773, reg 81, Sch 2, Part 1, para 1(1), (2) (for transitional provisions and savings see Part 9 of the 2013 Regulations).

Definitions "agreement provider", "agreement seller", and "regulated sale and rent back agreement" inserted by the Financial Services and Markets Act 2000 (Regulated Activities) (Amendment) Order 2009, SI 2009/1342, arts 2, 3(1)(a), (b).

Definitions "aircraft operator", "auction platform", "emission allowance trading directive", "emission allowance auctioning regulation", "greenhouse gas emissions allowances", "operator", "reception", "transmission" and "submission" inserted by the Financial Services and Markets Act 2000 (Regulated Activities) (Amendment) Order 2012, SI 2012/1906, art 2(1), (2)(b).

Definitions "assignment", "borrower", "consumer hire agreement", "credit agreement", "hire-purchase agreement", "hirer", "lender", "owner", "regulated consumer hire agreement", "regulated credit agreement", "relevant recipient of credit", and "restricted-use credit agreement" inserted, and words in square brackets in definition "deposit" inserted, by the Financial Services and Markets Act 2000 (Regulated Activities) (Amendment) (No 2) Order 2013, SI 2013/1881, arts 2, 3(1), (2), for transitional provisions see Pt 8 thereof at **[2.1007]** et seq.

In the definitions "borrower" and "lender", the comma in square brackets was substituted and the other words in square brackets were inserted, by the Financial Services and Markets Act 2000 (Regulated Activities) (Green Deal) (Amendment) Order 2014, SI 2014/1850, arts 2, 3(1), (2), (5) (except in relation to a green deal plan (within the meaning of the Energy Act 2011, s 1) made before 28 February 2014). With regard to the definition "lender", note that the original insertion by SI 2013/1881 as noted above, contained paragraphs (c) and (d) rather than paragraphs (a) and (b). It was assumed that this was a typographical error and the paragraphs have been numbered as (a) and (b) in the definition set out above. Note also that SI 2014/1850, art 3 did not correct this error but instead provided that a new paragraph (e) should be inserted after the existing paragraph (d). This new paragraph has been numbered as paragraph (c) in the above definition.

For the words in italics in para (e) of the definition "contract of insurance" there are substituted the words "Article 2(3)(b)(v) of the Solvency 2 Directive", and for the words in italics in para (f) of that definition there are substituted the words "Article 2(3)(c) of the Solvency 2 Directive", by the Solvency 2 Regulations 2015, SI 2015/575, reg 60, Sch 2, para 11(1), (2), as from 1 January 2016.

Definition "credit agreement" substituted, and definition "green deal plan" inserted, by SI 2014/1850, arts 2, 3(1), (3), (4) (except in relation to a green deal plan (within the meaning of the Energy Act 2011, s 1) made before 28 February 2014).

Words in square brackets in the definition "close relative" inserted by the Civil Partnership Act 2004 (Amendments to Subordinate Legislation) Order 2005, SI 2005/2114, art 2(16), Sch 16, Pt 1, para 1(1), (2).

Definitions "the Commission Regulation", "credit institution", "financial instrument", "home Member State", "investment firm", "management company", "market operator", and "multilateral trading facility" inserted by the Financial Services and Markets Act 2000 (Regulated Activities) (Amendment No 3) Order 2006, SI 2006/3384, arts 2, 3(b).

Words in square brackets in definitions "credit institution" and "home Member State" substituted by the Capital Requirements Regulations 2013, SI 2013/3115, reg 46(1), Sch 2, Pt 3, para 55(1), (2).

Definition "designated guidance provider" inserted by the Financial Services and Markets Act 2000 (Regulated Activities) (Amendment) (Pensions Guidance Exclusions) Order 2015, SI 2015/489, art 2(1), (2).

Definition "electronic money" inserted by the Financial Services and Markets Act 2000 (Regulated Activities) (Amendment) Order 2002, SI 2002/682, art 2, and substituted by SI 2011/99, reg 79, Sch 4, Pt 2, para 12(a)(ii).

Definition "investment services and activities" inserted by SI 2006/3384, arts 2, 3(b), subsequently substituted by SI 2012/1906, art 2(1), (2)(a).

In definition "home Member State" words in square brackets inserted by the Mortgage Credit Directive Order 2015, SI 2015/910, Sch 1, Pt 2, para 4(2), as from 21 March 2016 (note that the 2015 Order also comes into force on 20 April 2015 and 21 December 2015 for limited other purposes, and for transitional provisions, see Part 4 of that Order at **[2.1194]** et seq).

Definitions "home purchase provider", "home purchaser", "plan provider", "regulated home purchase plan", "regulated home reversion plan", and "reversion seller" inserted by the Financial Services and Markets Act 2000 (Regulated Activities) (Amendment) (No 2) Order 2006, SI 2006/2383, arts 2, 3(1)(a), (c)–(e), (for transitional provisions and effect see arts 36–40 of, and the Schedule to, the 2006 Order).

Definition "management company" substituted by the Undertakings for Collective Investment in Transferable Securities Regulations 2011, SI 2011/1613, reg 16, Schedule, para 1(1), (2).

Definition "occupational pension scheme" substituted by the Financial Services and Markets Act 2000 (Regulated Activities) (Amendment) Order 2006, SI 2006/1969, art 2(1), (2)(a), for transitional provisions and effect see arts 3–7 of, and the Schedule to, the 2006 Order.

Definition "overseas person" is amended as follows:

Figure "25A," in square brackets inserted by the Financial Services and Markets Act 2000 (Regulated Activities) (Amendment) (No 1) Order 2003, SI 2003/1475, art 3(a), (for transitional provisions see arts 26–29 of the 2003 Order).

Figures "25B, 25C," in square brackets inserted by SI 2006/2383, arts 2, 3(1)(b)(i).

Figure "25D," in square brackets inserted by SI 2006/3384, arts 2, 3(a).

Figure "25E," in square brackets inserted by SI 2009/1342, arts 2, 3(1)(c)(i).

Figure ", 39A" in square brackets inserted by SI 2003/1476, arts 2, 3(1)(a) (for transitional provisions see arts 22–27 of that Order).

Figures "51ZA, 51ZB, 51ZC, 51ZD, 51ZE" in square brackets substituted by SI 2013/1773, reg 81(1), Sch 2, Pt 1, para 1(1), (2)(a).

Words in square brackets beginning with the figures ", 53, 53A" substituted by SI 2003/1475, art 3(b) (for transitional provisions see arts 26–29).

Words in square brackets beginning with the figures ", 53B, 53C" substituted by SI 2006/2383, arts 2, 3(1)(b)(ii).

Figure "53D," in square brackets inserted by SI 2009/1342, arts 2, 3(1)(c)(ii).

Words ", 63F and 63J" in square brackets substituted by SI 2009/1342, arts 2, 3(1)(c)(iii).

Words in square brackets in definition "pension fund management contract" substituted by the Companies Act 2006 (Consequential Amendments and Transitional Provisions) Order 2011, SI 2011/1265, art 13(1), (2).

Definition "personal pension scheme" inserted by SI 2006/1969, art 2(1), (2)(a).

In definition "qualifying contract of insurance" sub-para (b)(ii) revoked by the Financial Services and Markets Act 2000 (Regulated Activities) (Amendment) Order 2007, SI 2007/1339, arts 2, 3.

Definition "relevant investment" inserted by SI 2003/1476, art 3(1)(b), (for transitional provisions see arts 22–27 of that Order).

Words in square brackets in definition "stakeholder pension scheme" added by SI 2005/593, art 2(1), (2)(b).

Definition "trade repository" inserted by the Financial Services and Markets Act 2000 (Over the Counter Derivatives, Central Counterparties and Trade Repositories) Regulations 2013, SI 2013/504, reg 33(1), (2).

Para (2): words in first (outer) pair of square brackets inserted by SI 2006/2383, arts 2, 3(2); words in second (inner) pair of square brackets substituted by SI 2009/1342, arts 2, 3(2).

Step-children, etc: as to the meaning of this and related expressions, see the Civil Partnership Act 2004, s 246 (as applied to this Order by the Civil Partnership Act 2004 (Relationships Arising Through Civil Partnership) Order 2005, SI 2005/3137, art 3, Schedule).

PART II
SPECIFIED ACTIVITIES

CHAPTER I
GENERAL

[2.170]
4   Specified activities: general

(1)   The following provisions of this Part specify kinds of activity for the purposes of [section 22(1)] of the Act (and accordingly any activity of one of those kinds, which is carried on by way of business, and relates to an investment of a kind specified by any provision of Part III and applicable to that activity, is a regulated activity for the purposes of the Act).

(2)   The kinds of activity specified by articles [[51ZA, 51ZB, 51ZC, 51ZD, 51ZE], 52 and 63N] are also specified for the purposes of section 22(1)(b) of the Act (and accordingly any activity of one of those kinds, when carried on by way of business, is a regulated activity when carried on in relation to property of any kind).

[(2A)   The kinds of activity specified by Part 3A are specified for the purposes of section 22(1A)(a) of the Act (and accordingly any activity of one of those kinds, when carried on by way of business, is a regulated activity).]

(3)   Subject to paragraph (4), each provision specifying a kind of activity is subject to the exclusions applicable to that provision (and accordingly any reference in this Order to an activity of the kind specified by a particular provision is to be read subject to any such exclusions).

[(4)   Where an investment firm or credit institution—
   (a)   provides or performs investment services and activities on a professional basis, and
   (b)   in doing so would be treated as carrying on an activity of a kind specified by a provision of this Part but for an exclusion in any of articles 15, 16, 19, 22, 23, 29, 38, 67, 68, 69, 70 and 72E,
that exclusion is to be disregarded and, accordingly, the investment firm or credit institution is to be treated as carrying on an activity of the kind specified by the provision in question.]

[(4A)   Where a person, other than a person specified by Article 1.2 of the insurance mediation directive (the text of which is set out in Part 1 of Schedule 4)—
   (a)   for remuneration, takes up or pursues insurance mediation or reinsurance mediation in relation to a risk or commitment located in an EEA State, and
   (b)   in doing so would be treated as carrying on an activity of a kind specified by a provision of this Part but for an exclusion in any of articles 30, 66[, 67 and 72AA],
that exclusion is to be disregarded (and accordingly that person is to be treated as carrying on an activity of the kind specified by the provision in question).]

[(4B)   Where—
   (a)   a person is a mortgage creditor or a mortgage intermediary; and
   (b)   in acting as a mortgage creditor or a mortgage intermediary, that person would be treated as carrying on an activity of a kind specified by article 25A (arranging regulated mortgage contracts), 36A (credit broking), 53A (advising on regulated mortgage contracts), 53DA (advising on regulated credit agreements for the acquisition of land), 60B (regulated credit agreements) or 61 (entering into and administering regulated mortgage contracts), but for an exclusion or exemption provided for by this Order,
that exclusion or exemption is to be disregarded (and accordingly that person is to be treated as carrying on an activity of the kind specified by the provision in question) to the extent that such exclusion or exemption does not fall within Article 3(2) or (3) of the mortgages directive.]

(5) In this article—

. . .

["insurance mediation" has the meaning given by Article 2.3 of the insurance mediation directive, the text of which is set out in Part II of Schedule 4;]

. . .

["reinsurance mediation" has the meaning given by Article 2.4 of the insurance mediation directive, the text of which is set out in Part III of Schedule 4.]

NOTES

Para (1): words in square brackets substituted by the Financial Services and Markets Act 2000 (Regulated Activities) (Amendment) (No 2) Order 2013, SI 2013/1881, arts 2, 3(3)(a), for transitional provisions see Pt 8 thereof at **[2.1007]** et seq).

Para (2): words in first (outer) square brackets substituted by the Financial Services and Markets Act 2000 (Regulated Activities) (Amendment) (No 2) Order 2009, SI 2009/1389, arts 2, 3; figures in second (inner) pair of square brackets substituted by the Alternative Investment Fund Managers Regulations 2013, SI 2013/1773, reg 81, Sch 2, Part 1, para 1(1), (3), (for transitional provisions and savings see Part 9 of the 2013 Regulations).

Para (2A): inserted by SI 2013/1881, arts 2, 3(3)(b), for transitional provisions see Pt 8 thereof at **[2.1007]** et seq.

Para (4): substituted by the Financial Services and Markets Act 2000 (Regulated Activities) (Amendment No 3) Order 2006, SI 2006/3384, arts 2, 4(a).

Para (4A): inserted by the Financial Services and Markets Act 2000 (Regulated Activities) (Amendment) (No 2) Order 2003, SI 2003/1476, art 3(2)(a), for transitional provisions see arts 22–27 of that Order; words in square brackets substituted by the Alternative Investment Fund Managers Order 2014, SI 2014/1292, art 6.

Para (4B): inserted by the Mortgage Credit Directive Order 2015, SI 2015/910, Sch 1, Pt 2, para 4(3), as from 21 March 2016 (note that the 2015 Order also comes into force on 20 April 2015 and 21 December 2015 for limited other purposes, and for transitional provisions, see Part 4 of that Order at **[2.1194]** et seq).

Para (5): definitions "insurance mediation" and "reinsurance mediation" inserted by SI 2003/1476, art 3(2)(b), for transitional provisions see arts 22–27 of that Order; definitions "core investment service" and "investment firm" (omitted) revoked by SI 2006/3384, arts 2, 4(a).

5–36 (*(Chapters II–VI) outside the scope of this work.*)

[CHAPTER 6A
CREDIT BROKING

The Activity

[2.171]
36A   Credit broking

(1) Each of the following is a specified kind of activity—
  (a)   effecting an introduction of an individual or relevant recipient of credit who wishes to enter into a credit agreement to a person ("P") with a view to P entering into by way of business as lender a regulated credit agreement (or an agreement which would be a regulated credit agreement but for any of the relevant provisions);
  (b)   effecting an introduction of an individual or relevant recipient of credit who wishes to enter into a consumer hire agreement to a person ("P") with a view to P entering into by way of business as owner a regulated consumer hire agreement or an agreement which would be a regulated consumer hire agreement but for article 60O (exempt agreements: exemptions relating to the nature of the agreement) or 60Q (exempt agreements: exemptions relating to the nature of the hirer);
  (c)   effecting an introduction of an individual or relevant recipient of credit who wishes to enter into a credit agreement or consumer hire agreement (as the case may be) to a person who carries on an activity of the kind specified in sub-paragraph (a) or (b) by way of business;
  (d)   presenting or offering an agreement which would (if entered into) be a regulated credit agreement (or an agreement which would be a regulated credit agreement but for any of the relevant provisions);
  (e)   assisting an individual or relevant recipient of credit by undertaking preparatory work with a view to that person entering into a regulated credit agreement (or an agreement which would be a regulated credit agreement but for any of the relevant provisions);
  (f)   entering into a regulated credit agreement (or an agreement which would be a regulated credit agreement but for any of the relevant provisions) on behalf of a lender.

(2) Paragraph (1) does not apply in so far as the activity is an activity of the kind specified by article 36H (operating an electronic system in relation to lending).

(3) For the purposes of paragraph (1) it is immaterial whether the credit agreement or consumer hire agreement is subject to the law of a country outside the United Kingdom.

(4) For the purposes of this article, the "relevant provisions" are the following provisions—
  (a)   article 60C (exempt agreements: exemptions relating to the nature of the agreement);
  (b)   article 60D (exempt agreements: exemptions relating to the purchase of land for non-residential purposes);
  (c)   article 60E (exempt agreements: exemptions relating to the nature of the lender)[, except for paragraph (5) of that article];
  (d)   article 60G (exempt agreements: exemptions relating to the total charge for credit);
  (e)   article 60H (exempt agreements: exemptions relating to the nature of the borrower).]

NOTES

Commencement: 26 July 2013 (certain purposes); 1 April 2014 (otherwise).

Chapter 6A (arts 36A–36G) was inserted by the Financial Services and Markets Act 2000 (Regulated Activities) (Amendment) (No 2) Order 2013, SI 2013/1881, arts 2, 4, for transitional provisions see art 12 of that Order at **[2.1006]** (Obligations of certain credit brokers who are not authorised persons), and Pt 8 thereof at **[2.1007]** et seq.

Para (4): words in square brackets in sub-para (c) inserted by the Financial Services and Markets Act 2000 (Regulated Activities) (Amendment) (No 2) Order 2014, SI 2014/1448, art 2.

[Exclusions

[2.172]
36B   Introducing by individuals in the course of canvassing off trade premises

(1)   There are excluded from article 36A activities carried on by an individual by canvassing off trade premises—
   (a)   a restricted-use credit agreement used to finance a transaction between the lender or a member of the lender's group and the borrower whether forming part of that agreement or not, or
   (b)   a regulated consumer hire agreement.

(2)   But paragraph (1) does not apply if A carries on any other activity of a kind specified by article 36A(1)(a) to (c).

(3)   A canvasses a restricted-use credit agreement or a regulated consumer hire agreement off trade premises for the purposes of this article if—
   (a)   A solicits the entry of an individual or relevant recipient of credit ("B") into such an agreement by making oral representations to B during a visit by A to any place (not excluded by paragraph (4)) where B is, and
   (b)   that visit is made by A for the purpose of making such oral representations.

(4)   A place is excluded from paragraph (3) if it is a place where a business is carried on (whether on a permanent or temporary basis) by—
   (a)   the lender or owner,
   (b)   the supplier under the restricted-use credit agreement,
   (c)   A,
   (d)   a person who employs A or has appointed A as an agent, or
   (e)   B.]

NOTES

Commencement: 26 July 2013 (certain purposes); 1 April 2014 (otherwise).
Inserted as noted to art 36A at **[2.171]**.

[2.173]
[36C   Activities for which no fee is paid

(1)   There are excluded from sub-paragraphs (d), (e) and (f) of article 36A(1) activities carried on by a person for which that person does not receive a fee.

(2)   For the purposes of this article, "fee" includes pecuniary consideration or any other form of financial consideration.]

NOTES

Commencement: 26 July 2013 (certain purposes); 1 April 2014 (otherwise).
Inserted as noted to art 36A at **[2.171]**.

[2.174]
[36D   Transaction to which the broker is a party

There are excluded from article 36A activities in relation to a regulated credit agreement (or an agreement which would be a regulated credit agreement but for the exclusions in articles 60C to 60H) or a regulated consumer hire agreement (or an agreement which would be a regulated consumer hire agreement but for the exclusions in articles 60O to 60Q) into which the person carrying on the activity enters or is to enter as lender or owner.]

NOTES

Commencement: 26 July 2013 (certain purposes); 1 April 2014 (otherwise).
Inserted as noted to art 36A at **[2.171]**.

[2.175]
[36E   Activities in relation to certain agreements relating to land

(1)   There are excluded from article 36A activities carried on with a view to an individual or relevant recipient of credit entering into a regulated mortgage contract if the person carrying on the activity is an authorised person who has permission to—
   (a)   enter into such a contract as lender, or

(b) make an introduction to an authorised person who has permission to enter into such a contract as lender.

(2) There are excluded from article 36A activities carried on with a view to an individual or relevant recipient of credit entering into a regulated home purchase plan if the person carrying on the activity is an authorised person who has permission to—

(a) enter into such a plan as home purchase provider, or

(b) make arrangements for another person ("the client") to enter into such a plan by introducing the client to an authorised person who has permission to enter into such a plan as home purchase provider.]

NOTES

Commencement: 26 July 2013 (certain purposes); 1 April 2014 (otherwise).

Inserted as noted to art 36A at **[2.171]**.

This article is substituted by the Mortgage Credit Directive Order 2015, SI 2015/910, Sch 1, para 4(1), (7), as from 21 March 2016 (as follows) (note that the 2015 Order also comes into force on 20 April 2015 and 21 December 2015 for limited other purposes, and for transitional provisions, see Part 4 of that Order at **[2.1194]** et seq)—

"36E   Activities in relation to certain agreements relating to land

(1)   There are excluded from article 36A activities carried on with a view to an individual or a relevant recipient of credit entering into an investment property loan, as defined in article 61A(6) (mortgage contracts which are not regulated mortgage contracts).

(2)   There are excluded from article 36A activities of a kind specified by article 25A (arranging regulated mortgage contracts) or 25C (arranging regulated home purchase plans).

(3)   There are excluded from article 36A other activities not excluded by paragraph (1) or (2) which consist of effecting an introduction with a view to an individual or relevant recipient of credit entering into a relevant agreement, if the person to whom the introduction is made is an authorised person who has permission to—

(a)   enter into such an agreement as lender or home purchase provider (as the case may be), or

(b)   make an introduction to an authorised person who has permission to enter into such an agreement as lender or home purchase provider (as the case may be).

(4)   In paragraph (3) "relevant agreement" means a regulated mortgage contract or a regulated home purchase plan.".

[2.176]
[36F   Activities carried on by members of the legal profession etc

(1)   There are excluded from article 36A (credit broking) activities carried on by—

(a)   a barrister or advocate acting in that capacity;

(b)   a solicitor (within the meaning of the Solicitors Act 1974) in the course of providing advocacy services or litigation services;

(c)   a solicitor (within the meaning of the Solicitors (Scotland) Act 1980) in the course of providing advocacy services or litigation services;

(d)   a solicitor (within the meaning of the Solicitors (Northern Ireland) Order 1976) in the course of providing advocacy services or litigation services;

(e)   a relevant person (other than a person falling within sub-paragraph (a) to (d)) in the course of providing advocacy services or litigation services.

(2)   In paragraph (1)—

"advocacy services" means any services which it would be reasonable to expect a person who is exercising, or contemplating exercising, a right of audience in relation to any proceedings, or contemplated proceedings, to provide for the purpose of those proceedings or contemplated proceedings;

"litigation services" means any services which it would be reasonable to expect a person who is exercising, or contemplating exercising, a right to conduct litigation in relation to any proceedings, or contemplated proceedings, to provide for the purpose of those proceedings or contemplated proceedings;

"relevant person" means a person who, for the purposes of the Legal Services Act 2007, is an authorised person in relation to an activity which constitutes the exercise of a right of audience or the conduct of litigation (within the meaning of that Act).]

NOTES

Commencement: 24 March 2015.

Inserted as noted to art 36A at **[2.171]**; subsequently substituted by the Financial Services and Markets Act 2000 (Miscellaneous Provisions) Order 2015, SI 2015/853, art 3(1), (2).

[2.177]
[36G   [Other exclusions]

Article 36A is also subject to *the exclusion in article 72A (information society services) [and the exclusion in article 72G (local authorities)].*]

NOTES

Commencement: 26 July 2013 (certain purposes); 1 April 2014 (otherwise).

Inserted as noted to art 36A at **[2.171]**.

Article heading substituted, and words in square brackets inserted, by the Financial Services and Markets Act 2000 (Regulated Activities) (Amendment) Order 2014, SI 2014/366, art 2(1), (7), (8).

For the words in italics there are substituted the words "the exclusions in articles 72A (information society services), 72G (local authorities) and 72I (registered consumer buy-to-let mortgage firms)" by the Mortgage Credit Directive Order 2015, SI 2015/910, Sch 1, Pt 2, para 4(8), as from 21 March 2016 (note that the 2015 Order also comes into force on 20 April 2015 and 21 December 2015 for limited other purposes, and for transitional provisions, see Part 4 of that Order at **[2.1194]** et seq).

[CHAPTER 6B
OPERATING AN ELECTRONIC SYSTEM IN RELATION TO LENDING

The Activity

[2.178]
36H   Operating an electronic system in relation to lending

(1)   Where the [conditions in paragraphs (2), (2A) and (2C) are] satisfied, operating an electronic system which enables the operator ("A") to facilitate persons ("B" and "C") becoming the lender and borrower under an article 36H agreement is a specified kind of activity.

(2)   The condition [in this paragraph] is that the system operated by A is capable of determining which agreements should be made available to each of B and C (whether in accordance with general instructions provided to A by B or C or otherwise).

[(2A)   The condition in this paragraph is that A, or another person ("X") acting under an arrangement with A or at A's direction, undertakes to—
(a)   receive payments in respect of interest and capital due under the article 36H agreement from C, and
(b)   make payments in respect of interest and capital due under the article 36H agreement to B.

(2B)   For the purposes of paragraph (2A)—
(a)   an agreement by A to appoint X to perform the activities in that paragraph is to be treated as an undertaking by A within the meaning of that paragraph;
(b)   it is immaterial that—
    (i)   payments may be subject to conditions;
    (ii)   A, or X, may be entitled to retain a portion or the entirety of any payment received from C.

(2C)   The condition in this paragraph is that A, or another person ("X") acting under an arrangement with A or at A's direction, undertakes to perform, or A undertakes to appoint or direct another person to perform either or both of the following activities—
(a)   taking steps to procure the payment of a debt under the article 36H agreement;
(b)   exercising or enforcing rights under the article 36H agreement on behalf of B.]

(3)   The following are specified kinds of activities if carried on by A in the course of, or in connection with, the carrying on by A of the activity specified by paragraph (1)—
(a)   presenting or offering article 36H agreements to B and C with a view to B becoming the lender under the article 36H agreement and C becoming the borrower under the article 36H agreement,
(b)   furnishing information relevant to the financial standing of a person ("Y") with a view to assisting in the determination as to whether another person should—
    (i)   enter into, as the lender, an article 36H agreement with Y, or
    (ii)   assume the rights of the lender under an article 36H agreement under which Y is the borrower,
(c)   taking steps to procure the payment of a debt due under an article 36H agreement,
(d)   performing duties, or exercising or enforcing rights under an article 36H agreement on behalf of the lender,
(e)   ascertaining whether a credit information agency (within the meaning given by article 89A(6)) holds information relevant to the financial standing of an individual or relevant person,
(f)   ascertaining the contents of such information,
(g)   securing the correction of, the omission of anything from, or the making of any other kind of modification of, such information, or
(h)   securing that a credit information agency which holds such information—
    (i)   stops holding the information, or
    (ii)   does not provide it to any other person.

(4)   An "article 36H agreement" is an agreement between one person ("the borrower") and another person ("the lender") by which the lender provides the borrower with credit (within the meaning given by article 60L) and in relation to which the condition in either paragraph (5) or (6) is satisfied.

(5)   The condition in this paragraph is that the lender is an individual or relevant person.

(6)   The condition in this paragraph is that the borrower is an individual or relevant person and—
(a)   the lender provides the borrower with credit less than or equal to £25,000, or
(b)   the agreement is not entered into by the borrower wholly or predominantly for the purposes of a business carried on, or intended to be carried on, by the borrower.

(7)   Paragraphs (5) and (6) of article 60C (exempt agreements: exemptions relating to the nature of the agreement) apply for the purposes of paragraph (6)(b).

(8)   It is immaterial for the purposes of this article whether the lender is carrying on a regulated activity.

(9)   In this article, "relevant person" means—
  (a)   a partnership consisting of two or three persons not all of whom are bodies corporate, or
  (b)   an unincorporated body of persons which does not consist entirely of bodies corporate and is not a partnership.

[(10)   For the purposes of the application of section 22(1) of the Act (regulated activities) to an activity of a kind specified by this article, article 88D (credit agreement), and article 73 (investments: general) in so far as it relates to that article, has effect as if the reference to a credit agreement in article 88D includes a reference to an article 36H agreement.]]

NOTES
Commencement: 26 July 2013 (certain purposes); 1 April 2014 (otherwise).
Chapter 6B (arts 36H–36J) was inserted by the Financial Services and Markets Act 2000 (Regulated Activities) (Amendment) (No 2) Order 2013, SI 2013/1881, arts 2, 4, for transitional provisions see Pt 8 thereof at **[2.1007]** et seq.
Words in square brackets in para (1) substituted, words in square brackets in para (2) inserted, and paras (2A)–(2C) and (10) inserted and added respectively, by the Financial Services and Markets Act 2000 (Regulated Activities) (Amendment) Order 2014, SI 2014/366, art 2(1), (9).

[Exclusion

[2.179]
36I   Information society services
Article 36H is subject to the exclusion in article 72A (information society services).]

NOTES
Commencement: 26 July 2013 (certain purposes); 1 April 2014 (otherwise).
Inserted as noted to art 36H at **[2.178]**.

[2.180]
[36IA   Activities in relation to debentures and bonds
There is excluded from article 36H (operating an electronic system in relation to lending) any activity of a kind specified by article 14 (dealing in investments as principal), 25 (arranging deals in investments), 37 (managing investments) or 53 (advising on investments).]

NOTES
Commencement: 1 April 2014.
Inserted by the Financial Services and Markets Act 2000 (Regulated Activities) (Amendment) Order 2014, SI 2014/366, art 2(1), (10).

[Supplemental

[2.181]
36J   Meaning of "consumer"
(1)   For the purposes of sections 1G, 404E and 425A of the Act (meaning of "consumer"), a person ("C") is only to be regarded as a person who uses, may use, has, may have used or has or may have contemplated using, services provided by authorised persons in carrying on a regulated activity of the kind specified by article 36H or article 64 in so far as relevant to that activity if—
  (a)   C is, may be, has been or may have been the lender under a relevant agreement and is an individual or relevant person, or
  (b)   C is, may be, has been or may have been the borrower under a relevant agreement, C is an individual or relevant person and one of the conditions in paragraph (2) is satisfied, or
  (c)   C meets the following conditions—
    (i)   C is, was or would be the lender under a relevant agreement, and
    (ii)   C is not, was not or would not be, as a result, carrying on a regulated activity.

(2)   The conditions in this paragraph are that—
  (a)   the lender provides, provided or would provide the borrower with credit (within the meaning given by article 60L) less than or equal to £25,000, or
  (b)   the agreement is not, was not or would not be entered into by the borrower wholly or predominantly for the purposes of a business carried on, or intended to be carried on, by the borrower.

(3)   Paragraphs (5) and (6) of article 60C (exempt agreements: exemptions relating to the nature of the agreement) apply for the purposes of paragraph (2)(b).

(4)   In paragraph (1)—
  "relevant agreement" means an agreement between one person ("the borrower") and another person ("the lender") by which the lender provides the borrower with credit (within the meaning given by article 60L);
  "relevant person" has the meaning given in article 36H.]

NOTES
Commencement: 26 July 2013 (certain purposes); 1 April 2014 (otherwise).

Inserted as noted to art 36H at **[2.178]**.

37–39C   ((*Chapters VII, VIIA outside the scope of this work.*)

[CHAPTER 7B
ACTIVITIES IN RELATION TO DEBT

The Activities

[2.182]
39D   Debt adjusting

(1)   When carried on in relation to debts due under a credit agreement—
   (a)   negotiating with the lender, on behalf of the borrower, terms for the discharge of a debt,
   (b)   taking over, in return for payments by the borrower, that person's obligation to discharge a debt, or
   (c)   any similar activity concerned with the liquidation of a debt,
is a specified kind of activity.

(2)   When carried on in relation to debts due under a consumer hire agreement—
   (a)   negotiating with the owner, on behalf of the hirer, terms for the discharge of a debt,
   (b)   taking over, in return for payments by the hirer, that person's obligation to discharge a debt, or
   (c)   any similar activity concerned with the liquidation of a debt,
is a specified kind of activity.]

NOTES

Commencement: 26 July 2013 (certain purposes); 1 April 2014 (otherwise).

Chapter 7B (arts 39D–39M) was inserted by the Financial Services and Markets Act 2000 (Regulated Activities) (Amendment) (No 2) Order 2013, SI 2013/1881, arts 2, 5, for transitional provisions see Pt 8 thereof at **[2.1007]** et seq.

[2.183]
[39E   Debt-counselling

(1)   Giving advice to a borrower about the liquidation of a debt due under a credit agreement is a specified kind of activity.

(2)   Giving advice to a hirer about the liquidation of a debt due under a consumer hire agreement is a specified kind of activity.]

NOTES

Commencement: 26 July 2013 (certain purposes); 1 April 2014 (otherwise).
Inserted as noted to art 39D at **[2.182]**.

[2.184]
[39F   Debt-collecting

(1)   Taking steps to procure the payment of a debt due under a credit agreement or a relevant article 36H agreement is a specified kind of activity.

(2)   Taking steps to procure the payment of a debt due under a consumer hire agreement is a specified kind of activity.

(3)   Paragraph (1) does not apply in so far as the activity is an activity of the kind specified by article 36H (operating an electronic system in relation to lending).

(4)   In this article, "relevant article 36H agreement" means an article 36H agreement (within the meaning of article 36H) which has been entered into with the facilitation of an authorised person with permission to carry on a regulated activity of the kind specified by that article.]

NOTES

Commencement: 26 July 2013 (certain purposes); 1 April 2014 (otherwise).
Inserted as noted to art 39D at **[2.182]**.

[2.185]
[39G   Debt administration

(1)   Subject to paragraph (3), taking steps—
   (a)   to perform duties under a credit agreement or relevant article 36H agreement on behalf of the lender, or
   (b)   to exercise or enforce rights under such an agreement on behalf of the lender,
is a specified kind of activity

(2)   Subject to paragraph (3), taking steps—
   (a)   to perform duties under a consumer hire agreement on behalf of the owner, or
   (b)   to exercise or enforce rights under such an agreement on behalf of the owner,
is a specified kind of activity.

(3)   Paragraphs (1) and (2) do not apply in so far as the activity is an activity of the kind specified by article 36H (operating an electronic system in relation to lending) or article 39F (debt-collecting).

(4)   In this article, "relevant article 36H agreement" means an article 36H agreement (within the meaning of article 36H) which has been entered into with the facilitation of an authorised person with permission to carry on a regulated activity of the kind specified by that article.]

NOTES

Commencement: 26 July 2013 (certain purposes); 1 April 2014 (otherwise).
Inserted as noted to art 39D at [**2.182**].

[Exclusions

[2.186]
39H   Activities where person has a connection to the agreement

(1)   There are excluded from articles 39D(1), 39E(1) and 39F(1) activities carried on by a person who is—
  (a)   the lender under the agreement,
  (b)   the supplier in relation to that agreement,
  (c)   a person carrying on an activity of the kind specified by article 36A by way of business and who has acquired the business of the person who was the supplier in relation to the agreement, or
  (d)   a person who would be carrying on an activity of the kind specified by article 36A by way of business but for the exclusion in article 36B where the agreement was made in consequence of an introduction (by that person or another person) to which article 36B applies.

(2)   There are excluded from articles 39D(2), 39E(2) and 39F(2) activities carried on by a person who is—
  (a)   the owner under the consumer hire agreement, or
  (b)   a person who would be carrying on an activity of the kind specified by article 36A by way of business but for the exclusion in article 36B where the agreement was made in consequence of an introduction (by that person or another person) to which article 36B applies.

(3)   There is excluded from article 39G(1) steps taken under or in relation to an agreement [by] a person who is, in relation to that agreement, a person falling within paragraph (1)(a) to (d).

(4)   There is excluded from article 39G(2) steps taken under or in relation to a consumer hire agreement [by] a person who is, in relation to that agreement, a person falling within paragraph (2)(a) or (b).

(5)   In paragraph (1), "supplier", in relation to an agreement, means—
  (a)   a person, other than the lender, whose transaction with the borrower is, or is to be, financed by the agreement, or
  (b)   a person to whom the rights and duties of a person falling within sub-paragraph (a) have been passed by assignment or operation of law.]

NOTES

Commencement: 26 July 2013 (certain purposes); 1 April 2014 (otherwise).
Inserted as noted to art 39D at [**2.182**].
Paras (3), (4): words in square brackets substituted by the Financial Services and Markets Act 2000 (Regulated Activities) (Amendment) Order 2014, SI 2014/366, art 2(1), (13).

[2.187]
[39I   Activities carried on by certain energy suppliers

(1)   There are excluded from articles 39D, 39E, 39F and 39G activities carried on by a relevant energy supplier acting in that capacity in relation to debts due under a green deal plan associated with the supplier.

(2)   A green deal plan is associated with a supplier if the payments under the plan are to be made to the supplier.

(3)   In this article—
  (a)   . . .
  (b)   "relevant energy supplier" has the meaning given in regulations made for the purpose of section 2(9) of [the Energy Act 2011].]

NOTES

Commencement: 26 July 2013 (certain purposes); 1 April 2014 (otherwise).
Inserted as noted to art 39D at [**2.182**].
Para (3): sub-para (a) revoked, and words in square brackets in sub-para (b) substituted, by the Financial Services and Markets Act 2000 (Regulated Activities) (Green Deal) (Amendment) Order 2014, SI 2014/1850, arts 2, 4 (except in relation to a green deal plan (within the meaning of the Energy Act 2011, s 1) made before 28 February 2014).

[2.188]
[39J   Activities carried on in relation to a relevant agreement in relation to land

There [is] excluded from articles 39D, 39E, 39F and 39G [any activity that relates] to a regulated mortgage contract or a regulated home purchase plan [to the extent that the activity constitutes an activity of the kind specified by a provision of Part 2 of this Order other than articles 39D, 39E, 39F and 39G, where entering into that contract as lender constitutes an activity of the kind specified by article 61 or entering into that plan as home purchase provider constitutes an activity of the kind under article 63F].]

NOTES
Commencement: 26 July 2013 (certain purposes); 1 April 2014 (otherwise).
Inserted as noted to art 39D at **[2.182]**.
Words in first and second pairs of square brackets substituted, and words in third pair of square brackets inserted, by the Financial Services and Markets Act 2000 (Regulated Activities) (Amendment) Order 2014, SI 2014/366, art 2(1), (14).

[2.189]
[39K   Activities carried on by members of the legal profession etc

(1)   There are excluded from articles 39D, 39E, 39F and 39G activities carried on by—
   (a)   a barrister or advocate acting in that capacity;
   (b)   a solicitor (within the meaning of the Solicitors Act 1974) in the course of providing advocacy services or litigation services;
   (c)   a solicitor (within the meaning of the Solicitors (Scotland) Act 1980) in the course of providing advocacy services or litigation services;
   (d)   a solicitor (within the meaning of the Solicitors (Northern Ireland) Order 1976) in the course of providing advocacy services or litigation services;
   (e)   a relevant person (other than a person falling within sub-paragraph (a) to (d)) in the course of providing advocacy services or litigation services.

(2)   In paragraph (1)—
"advocacy services" means any services which it would be reasonable to expect a person who is exercising, or contemplating exercising, a right of audience in relation to any proceedings, or contemplated proceedings, to provide for the purpose of those proceedings or contemplated proceedings;
"litigation services" means any services which it would be reasonable to expect a person who is exercising, or contemplating exercising, a right to conduct litigation in relation to any proceedings, or contemplated proceedings, to provide for the purpose of those proceedings or contemplated proceedings;
"relevant person" means a person who, for the purposes of the Legal Services Act 2007, is an authorised person in relation to an activity which constitutes the exercise of a right of audience or the conduct of litigation (within the meaning of that Act).]

NOTES
Commencement: 24 March 2015.
Inserted as noted to art 39D at **[2.182]**; subsequently substituted by the Financial Services and Markets Act 2000 (Miscellaneous Provisions) Order 2015, SI 2015/853, art 3(1), (3).

[2.190]
[39KA   Activities carried on by reason of providing pensions guidance under Part 20A of the Act

(1)   There are excluded from article 39E activities carried on by reason of providing pensions guidance under arrangements made with the Treasury pursuant to section 333B of the Act.

(2)   For the purposes of paragraph (1), pensions guidance given by a designated guidance provider is given under arrangements made with the Treasury.]

NOTES
Commencement: 26 March 2015.
Inserted by the Financial Services and Markets Act 2000 (Regulated Activities) (Amendment) (Pensions Guidance Exclusions) Order 2015, SI 2015/489, art 2(1), (4).

[2.191]
[39L   [Other exclusions]

Articles 39D, 39E, 39F and 39G are also subject to the [exclusions] in article 72A (information society services)[, article 72G (local authorities) and article 72H (insolvency practitioners)].]

NOTES
Commencement: 26 July 2013 (certain purposes); 1 April 2014 (otherwise).
Inserted as noted to art 39D at **[2.182]**.
Article heading and word in first pair of square brackets substituted, and words in second pair of square brackets inserted, by the Financial Services and Markets Act 2000 (Regulated Activities) (Amendment) Order 2014, SI 2014/366, art 2(1), (15), (16).

Part 2   Statutory Instruments

[Supplemental

[2.192]
39M Meaning of "consumer" etc

(1) For the purposes of sections 1G, 404E and 425A of the Act (meaning of "consumer"), in so far as those provisions relate to a person ("A") carrying on a regulated activity of the kind specified by article 39F (debt-collecting) or 39G (debt administration), or article 64 (agreeing to carry on specified kinds of activity) so far as relevant to that activity the following are to be treated as a "consumer"—

(a) the borrower under the agreement or the hirer under the consumer hire agreement;
(b) someone who has been the borrower or hirer under that agreement;
(c) a person who is treated by A as a person falling within sub-paragraph (a) or (b).

(2) For the purposes of section 328(8) of the Act (meaning of "clients") in so far as that provision relates to a person ("A") carrying on a regulated activity of the kind specified by article 39F or 39G, the following are to be treated as a "client"—

(a) the borrower under the agreement or the hirer under the consumer hire agreement;
(b) someone who has been the borrower or hirer under that agreement;
(c) a person who is treated by A as a person falling within sub-paragraph (a) or (b).

(3) In this article, "borrower" includes (in addition to those persons included in the definition in article 60L)—

(a) any person providing a guarantee or indemnity under the agreement, and
(b) a person to whom the rights and duties of a person falling within sub-paragraph (a) have passed by assignment or operation of law.]

NOTES
Commencement: 26 July 2013 (certain purposes); 1 April 2014 (otherwise).
Inserted as noted to art 39D at **[2.182]**.

40–60A *((Chapters VIII–XIV) outside the scope of this work.)*

[CHAPTER 14A
REGULATED CREDIT AGREEMENTS

The Activities

[2.193]
60B Regulated credit agreements

(1) Entering into a regulated credit agreement as lender is a specified kind of activity.

(2) It is a specified kind of activity for the lender or another person to exercise, or to have the right to exercise, the lender's rights and duties under a regulated credit agreement.

(3) In this article—
["credit agreement"—
(a) in relation to an agreement other than a green deal plan, means an agreement between an individual or relevant recipient of credit ("A") and any other person ("B") under which B provides A with credit of any amount;
(b) in relation to a green deal plan, has the meaning given by article 60LB;]
["exempt agreement" means a credit agreement which is an exempt agreement under articles 60C to 60H, but where only part of a credit agreement falls within a provision of articles 60C to 60H, only that part is an exempt agreement under those articles;]
"regulated credit agreement" means any credit agreement which is not an exempt agreement.]

NOTES
Commencement: 26 July 2013 (certain purposes); 1 April 2014 (otherwise).
Chapter 14A (originally arts 60B–60J, 60K, 60L, 60M) was inserted by the Financial Services and Markets Act 2000 (Regulated Activities) (Amendment) (No 2) Order 2013, SI 2013/1881, arts 2, 6, for transitional provisions see Pt 8 thereof at **[2.1007]** et seq.
Para (3): definition "credit agreement" substituted by the Financial Services and Markets Act 2000 (Regulated Activities) (Green Deal) (Amendment) Order 2014, SI 2014/1850, arts 2, 5 (except in relation to a green deal plan (within the meaning of the Energy Act 2011, s 1) made before 28 February 2014); definition "exempt agreement" substituted by the Financial Services and Markets Act 2000 (Miscellaneous Provisions) Order 2015, SI 2015/853, art 3(1), (4).

[2.194]
[60C Exempt agreements: exemptions relating to the nature of the agreement

(1) A credit agreement is an exempt agreement for the purposes of this Chapter in the following cases.

(2) A credit agreement is an exempt agreement if it is a regulated mortgage contract or *a regulated home purchase plan*.

(3) A credit agreement is an exempt agreement if—
(a) the lender provides the borrower with credit exceeding £25,000, and

(b)   the agreement is entered into by the borrower wholly or predominantly for the purposes of a business carried on, or intended to be carried on, by the borrower.

(4)   A credit agreement is an exempt agreement if—
    (a)   the lender provides the borrower with credit of £25,000 or less,
    (b)   the agreement is entered into by the borrower wholly for the purposes of a business carried on, or intended to be carried on, by the borrower, and
    [(c)   the agreement is a green deal plan made in relation to a property that is not a domestic property (as defined by article 60LB).]

(5)   For the purposes of paragraph (3), if an agreement includes a declaration which—
    (a)   is made by the borrower,
    (b)   provides that the agreement is entered into by the borrower wholly or predominantly for the purposes of a business carried on, or intended to be carried on, by the borrower, and
    (c)   complies with rules made by the FCA for the purpose of this article,
the agreement is to be presumed to have been entered into by the borrower wholly or predominantly for the purposes specified in sub-paragraph (b) unless paragraph (6) applies.

(6)   This paragraph applies if, when the agreement is entered into—
    (a)   the lender (or, if there is more than one lender, any of the lenders), or
    (b)   any person who has acted on behalf of the lender (or, if there is more than one lender, any of the lenders) in connection with the entering into of the agreement,
knows or has reasonable cause to suspect that the agreement is not entered into by the borrower wholly or predominantly for the purposes of a business carried on, or intended to be carried on, by the borrower.

(7)   Paragraphs (5) and (6) also apply for the purposes of paragraph (4) but with the omission of the words "or predominantly".

(8)   A credit agreement is an exempt agreement if it is made in connection with trade in goods or services—
    (a)   between the United Kingdom and a country outside the United Kingdom,
    (b)   within a country [outside the United Kingdom], or
    (c)   between countries outside the United Kingdom, and
the credit is provided to the borrower in the course of a business carried on by the borrower.]

NOTES

Commencement: 26 July 2013 (certain purposes); 1 April 2014 (otherwise).

Inserted as noted to art 60B at **[2.193]**.

Para (2): for the words in italics there are substituted the words "if it is of a type described in article 61A(1) or (2) (mortgage contracts which are not regulated mortgage contracts)" by the Mortgage Credit Directive Order 2015, SI 2015/910, Sch 1, Pt 2, para 4(13), as from 21 March 2016 (note that the 2015 Order also comes into force on 20 April 2015 and 21 December 2015 for limited other purposes, and for transitional provisions, see Part 4 of that Order at **[2.1194]** et seq).

Para (4): sub-para (c) substituted by the Financial Services and Markets Act 2000 (Regulated Activities) (Green Deal) (Amendment) Order 2014, SI 2014/1850, arts 2, 6 (except in relation to a green deal plan (within the meaning of the Energy Act 2011, s 1) made before 28 February 2014).

Para (8): words in square brackets in sub-para (b) inserted by the Financial Services and Markets Act 2000 (Regulated Activities) (Amendment) Order 2014, SI 2014/366, art 2(1), (24).

[2.195]
[60D Exempt agreements: exemption relating to the purchase of land for non-residential purposes

(1)   A credit agreement is an exempt agreement for the purposes of this Chapter if, at the time it is entered into, any sums due under it are secured by a legal [or equitable] mortgage on land and the condition in paragraph (2) is satisfied.

(2)   The condition is that less than 40% of the land is used, or is intended to be used, as or in connection with a dwelling—
    (a)   by the borrower or a related person of the borrower, or
    (b)   in the case of credit provided to trustees, by an individual who is a beneficiary of the trust or a related person of a beneficiary.

(3)   For the purposes of paragraph (2)—
    (a)   the area of any land which comprises a building or other structure containing two or more storeys is to be taken to be the aggregate of the floor areas of each of those stories;
    (b)   "related person" in relation to a person ("B") who is the borrower or (in the case of credit provided to trustees) a beneficiary of the trust, means—
       (i)   B's spouse or civil partner,
       (ii)   a person (whether or not of the opposite sex) whose relationship with B has the characteristics of the relationship between husband and wife, or
       (iii)   B's parent, brother, sister, child, grandparent or grandchild.

[(4)   This article does not apply to an agreement of the type described in Article 3(1)(b) of the mortgages directive.]]

Part 2   Statutory Instruments

NOTES

Commencement: 26 July 2013 (certain purposes); 1 April 2014 (otherwise).

Inserted as noted to art 60B at **[2.193]**.

Para (1): words in square brackets inserted by the Financial Services and Markets Act 2000 (Regulated Activities) (Amendment) Order 2014, SI 2014/366, art 2(1), (25).

Para (4): added by the Mortgage Credit Directive Order 2015, SI 2015/910, Sch 1, Pt 2, para 4(1), (14), as from 21 March 2016 (note that the 2015 Order also comes into force on 20 April 2015 and 21 December 2015 for limited other purposes, and for transitional provisions, see Part 4 of that Order at **[2.1194]** et seq).

[2.196]
[60E Exempt agreements: exemptions relating to the nature of the lender

(1) A credit agreement is an exempt agreement for the purposes of this Chapter in the following cases.

(2) A *relevant credit agreement* relating to the purchase of land is an exempt agreement if the lender is—

(a) specified, or of a description specified, in rules made by the FCA under paragraph (3), or

(b) a local authority.

(3) The FCA may make rules specifying any of the following for the purpose of paragraph (2)—

(a) an authorised person with permission to effect or carry out contracts of insurance;

(b) a friendly society;

(c) an organisation of employers or organisation of workers;

(d) a charity;

(e) an improvement company (within the meaning given by section 7 of the Improvement of Land Act 1899);

(f) a body corporate named or specifically referred to in any public general Act;

(g) a body corporate named or specifically referred to in, or in an order made under, a relevant housing provision;

(h) a building society (within the meaning of the Building Societies Act 1986);

(i) an authorised person with permission to accept deposits.

(4) Rules under paragraph (3) may—

(a) specify a particular person or class of persons;

(b) be limited so as to apply only to agreements or classes of agreement specified in the rules.

(5) A *credit agreement* is an exempt agreement if it is—

(a) secured by a legal [or equitable] mortgage on land,

(b) that land is used or is intended to be used as or in connection with a dwelling, and

(c) the lender is a housing authority.

(6) A credit agreement is an exempt agreement if—

(a) the lender is an investment firm or a credit institution, and

(b) the agreement is entered into for the purpose of allowing the borrower to carry out a transaction relating to one or more financial instruments.

(7) In this article—

"housing authority" means—

(a) in England and Wales, the Homes and Communities Agency, the Welsh Ministers[, a company which is a wholly-owned subsidiary of the Welsh Ministers,] or a private registered provider (within the meaning of Part 2 of the Housing and Regeneration Act 2008);

(b) in Scotland, the Scottish Ministers or a registered social landlord (within the meaning of the Housing (Scotland) Act 2010;

(c) in Northern Ireland, the Northern Ireland Housing Executive;

"relevant credit agreement relating to the purchase of land" means—

(a) a borrower-lender-supplier agreement financing—

(i) the purchase of land, or

(ii) provision of dwellings on land,

and secured by a legal [or equitable] mortgage on that land,

(b) a borrower-lender agreement secured by a legal mortgage on land, or

(c) a borrower-lender-supplier agreement financing a transaction which is a linked transaction in relation to—

(i) an agreement falling within sub-paragraph (a), or

(ii) an agreement falling within sub-paragraph (b) financing—

(aa) the purchase of land,

(bb) the provision of dwellings on land,

and secured by a legal mortgage on the land referred to in sub-paragraph (a) or the land referred to in paragraph (ii);

"relevant housing provision" means any of the following—

(a) section 156(4) or 447(2)(a) of the Housing Act 1985,

(b)   section 156(4) of that Act as it has effect by virtue of section 17 of the Housing Act 1996 (the right to acquire), or

(c)   article 154(1)(a) of the Housing (Northern Ireland) Order 1981.

[(7A)   In paragraph (7), in the definition of "housing authority", in paragraph (a), "wholly-owned subsidiary" has the same meaning as in section 1159 (meaning of "subsidiary" etc) of the Companies Act 2006.

(7B)   For the purpose of paragraph (7A), the Welsh Ministers are to be treated as a body corporate.]

(8)   For the purposes of the definition of "relevant credit agreement relating to the purchase of land", a transaction is, unless paragraph (9) applies, a "linked transaction" in relation to a credit agreement ("the principal agreement") if—

(a)   it is (or will be) entered into by the borrower under the principal agreement or by a relative of the borrower,

(b)   it does not relate to the provision of security,

(c)   it does not form part of the principal agreement, and

(d)   one of the following conditions is satisfied—

    (i)   the transaction is entered into in compliance with a term of the principal agreement;

    (ii)   the principal agreement is a borrower-lender-supplier agreement and the transaction is financed, or to be financed, by the principal agreement;

    (iii)   the following conditions are met—

        (aa)   the other party is a person to whom paragraph (10) applies,

        (bb)   the other party initiated the transaction by suggesting it to the borrower or the relative of the borrower, and

        (cc)   the borrower or the relative of the borrower enters into the transaction to induce the lender to enter into the principal agreement or for another purpose related to the principal agreement or to a transaction financed or to be financed by the principal agreement.

(9)   This paragraph applies if the transaction is—

(a)   a contract of insurance,

(b)   a contract which contains a guarantee of goods, or

(c)   a transaction which comprises, or is effected under—

    (i)   an agreement for the operation of an account (including any savings account) for the deposit of money, or

    (ii)   an agreement for the operation of a current account, under which the customer ("C") may, by means of cheques or similar orders payable to C or to any other person, obtain or have the use of money held or made available by the person with whom the account is kept.

(10)   The persons to whom this paragraph applies are—

(a)   the lender;

(b)   the lender's associate;

(c)   a person who, in the negotiation of the transaction, is represented by a person who carries on an activity of the kind specified by article 36A (credit broking) by way of business who is or was also a negotiator in negotiations for the principal agreement;

(d)   a person who, at the time the transaction is initiated, knows that the principal agreement has been made or contemplates that it might be made.]

NOTES

Commencement: 26 July 2013 (certain purposes); 1 April 2014 (otherwise).

Inserted as noted to art 60B at **[2.193]**.

For the words in italics in paras (2), (5) there are substituted the words "Subject to article 60HA, a relevant credit agreement" by the Mortgage Credit Directive Order 2015, SI 2015/910, Sch 1, Pt 2, para 4(15), as from 21 March 2016 (note that the 2015 Order also comes into force on 20 April 2015 and 21 December 2015 for limited other purposes, and for transitional provisions, see Part 4 of that Order at **[2.1194]** et seq).

The words in square brackets in para (5), and the words "or equitable" in square brackets in the definition "relevant credit agreement relating to the purchase of land" in para (7), were inserted by the Financial Services and Markets Act 2000 (Regulated Activities) (Amendment) Order 2014, SI 2014/366, art 2(1), (26).

The words ", a company which is a wholly-owned subsidiary of the Welsh Ministers" in square brackets in the definition "housing authority" in para (7) were inserted, and paras (7A), (7B) were inserted, by the Financial Services and Markets Act 2000 (Regulated Activities) (Amendment) (No 3) Order 2014, SI 2014/1740, art 2.

[2.197]

[60F   Exempt agreements: exemptions relating to number of repayments to be made

(1)   A credit agreement is an exempt agreement for the purposes of this Chapter in the following cases.

(2)   A credit agreement is an exempt agreement if—

(a)   the agreement is a borrower-lender-supplier agreement for fixed-sum credit[, other than a green deal plan],

(b)   the number of payments to be made by the borrower is not more than [twelve],

    (c)   those payments are required to be made within a period of 12 months or less (beginning on the date of the agreement),

    (d)   the credit is—

        (i)   secured on land, or

        (ii)   provided without interest or other . . . charges, and

    (e)   paragraph (7) does not apply to the agreement.

(3) A credit agreement is an exempt agreement if—

    (a)   the agreement is a borrower-lender-supplier agreement for running-account credit,

    (b)   the borrower is to make payments in relation to specified periods which must be, unless the agreement is secured on land, of 3 months or less,

    (c)   the number of payments to be made by the borrower in repayment of the whole amount of credit provided in each such period is not more than one,

    (d)   the credit is—

        (i)   secured on land, or

        (ii)   provided without interest or other significant charges, and

    (e)   paragraph (7) does not apply to the agreement.

(4) *A credit agreement* is an exempt agreement if—

    (a)   the agreement is a borrower-lender-supplier agreement financing the purchase of land,

    (b)   the number of payments to be made by the borrower is not more than four, and

    (c)   the credit is—

        (i)   secured on land, or

        (ii)   provided without interest or other charges.

(5) A credit agreement is an exempt agreement if—

    (a)   the agreement is a borrower-lender-supplier agreement for fixed-sum credit,

    (b)   the credit is to finance a premium under a contract of insurance relating to land or anything on land,

    (c)   the lender is the lender under a credit agreement secured by a legal [or equitable] mortgage on that land,

    (d)   the credit is to be repaid within the period (which must be 12 months or less) to which the premium relates,

    (e)   in the case of an agreement secured on land, there is no charge forming part of the total charge for credit under the agreement other than interest at a rate not exceeding the rate of interest from time to time payable under the agreement mentioned at sub-paragraph (c),

    (f)   in the case of an agreement which is not secured on land, the credit is provided without interest or other charges, and

    (g)   the number of payments to be made by the borrower is not more than twelve.

(6) A credit agreement is an exempt agreement if—

    (a)   the agreement is a borrower-lender-supplier agreement for fixed-sum credit,

    (b)   the lender is the lender under a credit agreement secured by a legal [or equitable] mortgage on land,

    (c)   the agreement is to finance a premium under a contract of whole life insurance which provides, in the event of the death of the person on whose life the contract is effected before the credit referred to in sub-paragraph (b) has been repaid, for payment of a sum not exceeding the amount sufficient to meet the amount which, immediately after that credit has been advanced, would be payable to the lender in respect of that credit (including interest from time to time payable under that agreement),

    (d)   in the case of an agreement secured on land, there is no charge forming part of the total charge for credit under the agreement other than interest at a rate not exceeding the rate of interest from time to time payable under the agreement mentioned at sub-paragraph (b),

    (e)   in the case of an agreement which is not secured on land, the credit is provided without interest or other charges, and

    (f)   the number of payments to be made by the borrower is not more than twelve.

(7) This paragraph applies to—

    (a)   agreements financing the purchase of land;

    (b)   agreements which are conditional sale agreements or hire-purchase agreements;

    (c)   agreements secured by a pledge (other than a pledge of documents of title or of bearer bonds).

[(8) In this article, "payment" means any payment which comprises or includes—

    (a)   the repayment of capital, or

    (b)   the payment of interest or any other charge which forms part of the total charge for credit.]

NOTES

Commencement: 26 July 2013 (certain purposes); 1 April 2014 (otherwise).

Inserted as noted to art 60B at **[2.193]**.

Words in square brackets in para (2)(a) inserted by the Financial Services and Markets Act 2000 (Regulated Activities) (Green Deal) (Amendment) Order 2014, SI 2014/1850, arts 2, 7 (except in relation to a green deal plan (within the meaning of the Energy Act 2011, s 1) made before 28 February 2014).

Word in square brackets in para (2)(b) substituted by the Financial Services and Markets Act 2000 (Miscellaneous Provisions) (No 2) Order 2015, SI 2015/352, art 2(a).

The word omitted from para (2)(d)(ii) was revoked, and the words in square brackets in paras (5)(c), (6)(b) were inserted, by the Financial Services and Markets Act 2000 (Regulated Activities) (Amendment) Order 2014, SI 2014/366, art 2(1), (27).

For the words in italics in para (4) there are substituted the words "Subject to article 60HA, a credit agreement" by the Mortgage Credit Directive Order 2015, SI 2015/910, Sch 1, Pt 2, para 4(16), as from 21 March 2016 (note that the 2015 Order also comes into force on 20 April 2015 and 21 December 2015 for limited other purposes, and for transitional provisions, see Part 4 of that Order at **[2.1194]** et seq).

Para (8) was substituted by the Financial Services and Markets Act 2000 (Miscellaneous Provisions) Order 2015, SI 2015/853, art 3(1), (5).

[2.198]
[60G   Exempt agreements: exemptions relating to the total charge for credit

(1)   A credit agreement is an exempt agreement for the purposes of this Chapter in the following cases.

(2)   A credit agreement is an exempt agreement if—
   (a)   it is a borrower-lender agreement, *and*
   (b)   the lender is a credit union and the rate of the total charge for credit does not exceed 42.6 per cent[, and.
   (c)   paragraph (2A) applies to the agreement.]

[(2A)   This paragraph applies to the agreement if—
   (a)   the agreement is not of a type described in Article 3(1) of the mortgages directive; or
   (b)   the agreement is of such a type and—
      (i)   the agreement is of a kind to which the mortgages directive does not apply by virtue of Article 3(2) of that directive,
      (ii)   the agreement is a bridging loan within the meaning of Article 4(23) of the mortgages directive, or
      (iii)   in relation to the agreement—
         (aa)   the borrower receives timely information on the main features, risks and costs of the agreement at the pre-contractual stage, and
         (bb)   any advertising of the agreement is fair, clear and not misleading.]

(3)   *A credit agreement* is an exempt agreement if—
   (a)   it is a borrower-lender agreement,
   (b)   it is an agreement of a kind offered to a particular class of individual or relevant recipient of credit and not offered to the public generally,
   (c)   it provides that the only charge included in the total charge for credit is interest,
   (d)   interest under the agreement may not at any time be more than the sum of one per cent and the highest of the base rates published by the banks specified in paragraph (7) on the date 28 days before the date on which the interest is charged, and
   (e)   paragraph (5) does not apply to the agreement.

(4)   *A credit agreement* is an exempt agreement if—
   (a)   it is a borrower-lender agreement,
   (b)   it is an agreement of a kind offered to a particular class of individual or relevant recipient of credit and not offered to the public generally,
   (c)   it does not provide for or permit an increase in the rate or amount of any item which is included in the total charge for credit,
   (d)   the total charge for credit under the agreement is not more than the sum of one per cent and the highest of the base rates published by the banks specified in paragraph (7) on the date 28 days before the date on which the charge is imposed, and
   (e)   paragraph (5) does not apply to the agreement.

(5)   This paragraph applies to an agreement if—
   (a)   the total amount to be repaid by the borrower to discharge the borrower's indebtedness may vary according to a formula which is specified in the agreement and which has effect by reference to movements in the level of any index or other factor, or
   [(b)   the agreement—
      (i)   is not—
         (aa)   secured on land, or
         [(bb)   offered by a lender to a borrower as an incident of the borrower's employment with the lender or with an undertaking in the same group as the lender;] and
      (ii)   does not meet the general interest test.]

(6)   For the purposes of *paragraph (5)*, an agreement meets the general interest test if—
   (a)   the agreement is offered under an enactment with a general interest purpose, and
   (b)   the terms on which the credit is provided are more favourable to the borrower than those prevailing on the market, either because the rate of interest is lower than that prevailing on the market, or because the rate of interest is no higher than that prevailing on the market but the other terms on which credit is provided are more favourable to the borrower.

(7)   The banks specified in this paragraph are—

    (a)   the Bank of England;
    (b)   Bank of Scotland;
    (c)   Barclays Bank plc;
    (d)   Clydesdale Bank plc;
    (e)   Co-operative Bank Public Limited Company;
    (f)   Coutts & Co;
    (g)   National Westminster Bank Public Limited Company;
    (h)   the Royal Bank of Scotland plc.]

[(8)   A credit agreement of a type described in Article 3(1) of the mortgages directive is an exempt agreement pursuant to paragraph (3) or (4) only if—
    (a)   the agreement meets the general interest test;
    (b)   the borrower receives timely information on the main features, risks and costs of the agreement at the pre-contractual stage; and
    (c)   any advertising of the agreement is fair, clear and not misleading.]

NOTES

Commencement: 26 July 2013 (certain purposes); 1 April 2014 (otherwise).

Inserted as noted to art 60B at **[2.193]**.

In para (2) word in italics revoked and sub-para (c) and word immediately preceding it added, paras (2A), (8) inserted and added respectively, for the words in italics in paras (3), (4) there are substituted the words "Subject to paragraph (8), a credit agreement", and for the words in italics in para (6) there are substituted the words "paragraphs (5) and (8)" by the Mortgage Credit Directive Order 2015, SI 2015/910, Sch 1, Pt 2, para 4(17), as from 21 March 2016 (note that the 2015 Order also comes into force on 20 April 2015 and 21 December 2015 for limited other purposes, and for transitional provisions, see Part 4 of that Order at **[2.1194]** et seq).

Para (5): sub-para (b) substituted by the Financial Services and Markets Act 2000 (Regulated Activities) (Amendment) Order 2014, SI 2014/366, art 2(1), (28); sub-para (b)(i)(bb) further substituted by the Financial Services and Markets Act 2000 (Miscellaneous Provisions) (No 2) Order 2015, SI 2015/352, art 2(b).

[2.199]

[60H   Exempt agreements: exemptions relating to the nature of the borrower

[(1)]   *A credit agreement* is an exempt agreement for the purposes of this Chapter if—
    (a)   the borrower is an individual,
    (b)   the agreement is either—
        (i)   secured on land, or
       (ii)   *for credit which exceeds £60,260,*
    (c)   the agreement includes a declaration made by the borrower which provides that the borrower agrees to forgo the protection and remedies that would be available to the borrower if the agreement were a regulated credit agreement and which complies with rules made by the FCA for the purposes of this paragraph,
    (d)   a statement has been made in relation to the income or assets of the borrower which complies with rules made by the FCA for the purposes of this paragraph,
    (e)   the connection between the statement and the agreement complies with any rules made by the FCA for the purposes of this paragraph (including as to the period of time between the making of the statement and the agreement being entered into), and
    (f)   a copy of the statement was provided to the lender before the agreement was entered into.]

[(2)   Where a credit agreement would be an exempt agreement pursuant to this article but for paragraph (1)(b)(ii)(bb) or article 60HA, the FCA may treat the agreement as an exempt agreement except for the purpose of the application of the requirements of the mortgages directive.]

NOTES

Commencement: 26 July 2013 (certain purposes); 1 April 2014 (otherwise).

Inserted as noted to art 60B at **[2.193]**.

Para (1) numbered as such and para (2) added, for the words in italics in para (a) there are substituted the words "Subject to article 60HA, a credit agreement" and sub-para (b)(ii) substituted as follows, by the Mortgage Credit Directive Order 2015, SI 2015/910, Sch 1, Pt 2, para 4(18), as from 21 March 2016 (note that the 2015 Order also comes into force on 20 April 2015 and 21 December 2015 for limited other purposes, and for transitional provisions, see Part 4 of that Order at **[2.1194]** et seq)—

        "(ii)   for credit which exceeds £60,260 and is for a purpose other than—
            (aa)   the renovation of residential property, or
            (bb)   to acquire or retain property rights in land or in an existing or projected building,".

[2.200]

[60HA   Exempt agreements: exemptions not permitted under the mortgages directive

(1)   A credit agreement is not an exempt agreement pursuant to article 60E(2) or (5), 60F(4) or 60H(1) if—
    (a)   the agreement is of a type described in Article 3(1) of the mortgages directive, and
    (b)   paragraph (2) does not apply.

(2)   This paragraph applies if—
    (a)   the agreement is of a kind to which the mortgages directive does not apply by virtue of Article 3(2) of that directive;
    (b)   the agreement is a bridging loan within the meaning of Article 4(23) of that directive; or

(c)   the agreement is a restricted public loan in respect of which—
    (i)   the borrower receives timely information on the main features, risks and costs at the pre-contractual stage; and
    (ii)   any advertising is fair, clear and not misleading.

(3)   In paragraph (2)(c) "restricted public loan" means a credit agreement that is—
(a)   offered to a particular class of borrower and not offered to the public generally;
(b)   offered under an enactment with a general interest purpose; and
(c)   provided on terms which are more favourable to the borrower than those prevailing on the market, because it meets one of the following conditions—
    (i)   it is interest free;
    (ii)   the rate of interest is lower than that prevailing on the market; or
    (iii)   the rate of interest is no higher than that prevailing on the market but the other terms on which credit is provided are more favourable to the borrower.]

NOTES

Commencement: see below.
Inserted by the Mortgage Credit Directive Order 2015, SI 2015/910, Sch 1, Pt 2, para 4(1), (19), as from 21 March 2016 (note that the 2015 Order also comes into force on 20 April 2015 and 21 December 2015 for limited other purposes, and for transitional provisions, see Part 4 of that Order at **[2.1194]** et seq).

[Exclusions

[2.201]
60I   Arranging administration by authorised person

A person ("A") who is not an authorised person does not carry on an activity of the kind specified by article 60B(2) in relation to a regulated credit agreement where A—
(a)   arranges for another person, who is an authorised person with permission to carry on an activity of that kind, to exercise or to have the right to exercise the lender's rights and duties under the agreement, or
(b)   exercises or has the right to exercise the lender's rights and duties under the agreement during a period of not more than one month beginning with the day on which any such arrangement comes to an end.]

NOTES

Commencement: 26 July 2013 (certain purposes); 1 April 2014 (otherwise).
Inserted as noted to art 60B at **[2.193]**.

[2.202]
[60J   Administration pursuant to agreement with authorised person

A person who is not an authorised person does not carry on an activity of the kind specified by article 60B(2) in relation to regulated credit agreement if that person exercises or has the right to exercise the lender's rights and duties under the agreement pursuant to an agreement with an authorised person who has permission to carry on an activity of the kind specified by article 60B(2).]

NOTES

Commencement: 26 July 2013 (certain purposes); 1 April 2014 (otherwise).
Inserted as noted to art 60B at **[2.193]**.

[2.203]
[60JA   Payment institutions

(1)   There are excluded from article 60B activities carried on by a person who is an EEA authorised payment institution exercising passport rights in the United Kingdom in accordance with Article 16(3) of the payment services directive.

(2)   Terms used in this article have the meanings given in Payment Services Regulations 2009.]

NOTES

Commencement: 1 April 2014.
Inserted, together with art 60JB, by the Financial Services and Markets Act 2000 (Regulated Activities) (Amendment) Order 2014, SI 2014/366, art 2(1), (29).

[2.204]
[60JB   Electronic money institutions

(1)   There are excluded from article 60B activities carried on by a person who is an EEA authorised electronic money institution exercising passport rights in the United Kingdom in accordance with Article 16(3) of the payment services directive as applied by Article 6 of the electronic money directive.

(2)   Terms used in this article have the meanings given in the Electronic Money Regulations 2011.]

NOTES

Commencement: 1 April 2014.

Inserted as noted to art 60JA at **[2.203]**.

[2.205]
[60K   [Other exclusions]

Article 60B is also subject to *the exclusion in article 72A (information society services) [and the exclusion in article 72G (local authorities)].*]

NOTES

Commencement: 26 July 2013 (certain purposes); 1 April 2014 (otherwise).

Inserted as noted to art 60B at **[2.193]**.

Article heading substituted, and words in square brackets inserted, by the Financial Services and Markets Act 2000 (Regulated Activities) (Amendment) Order 2014, SI 2014/366, art 2(1), (30), (31).

For the words in italics there are substituted the words "the exclusions in articles 72A (information society services), 72G (local authorities) and 72I (registered consumer buy-to-let mortgage firms)" by the Mortgage Credit Directive Order 2015, SI 2015/910, Sch 1, Pt 2, para 4(20), as from 21 March 2016 (note that the 2015 Order also comes into force on 20 April 2015 and 21 December 2015 for limited other purposes, and for transitional provisions, see Part 4 of that Order at **[2.1194]** et seq).

[Supplemental

[2.206]
60L   Interpretation of Chapter 14A etc

(1)   In this Chapter—

"assignment", in relation to Scotland, means assignation;

"associate" means, in relation to a person ("P")—

    (a)   where P is an individual, any person who is or who has been—

        (i)   P's spouse or P's civil partner;

        (ii)   a relative of P, of P's spouse or of P's civil partner;

        (iii)   the spouse or civil partner of a relative of P or P's spouse or civil partner;

        (iv)   if P is a member of a partnership, any of P's partners and the spouse or civil partner of any such person;

    (b)   where P is a body corporate—

        (i)   any person who is a controller ("C") of P, and

        (ii)   any other person for whom C is a controller;

"borrower" means [(except in relation to green deal plans: see instead article 60LB)] a person who receives credit under a credit agreement or a person to whom the rights and duties of a borrower under a credit agreement have passed by assignment or operation of law;

"borrower-lender agreement" means—

    (a)   a credit agreement—

        (i)   to finance a transaction between the borrower and a person ("the supplier") other than the lender, and

        (ii)   which is not made by the lender under pre-existing arrangements, or in contemplation of future arrangements, between the lender and the supplier,

    (b)   a credit agreement to refinance any existing indebtedness of the borrower, whether to the lender or another person, or

    (c)   a credit agreement which is—

        (i)   an unrestricted-use credit agreement, and

        (ii)   not made by the lender—

            (aa)   under pre-existing arrangements between the lender and a person other than the borrower ("the supplier"), and

           (bb)   in the knowledge that the credit is to be used to finance a transaction between the borrower and the supplier;

"borrower-lender-supplier agreement" means—

    (a)   a credit agreement to finance a transaction between the borrower and the lender, whether forming part of that agreement or not;

    (b)   a credit agreement—

        (i)   to finance a transaction between the borrower and a person ("the supplier") other than the lender, and

        (ii)   which is made by the lender under pre-existing arrangements, or in contemplation of future arrangements, between the lender and the supplier, or

    (c)   a credit agreement which is—

        (i)   an unrestricted-use credit agreement, and

        (ii)   made by the lender under pre-existing arrangements between the lender and a person ("the supplier") other than the borrower in the knowledge that the credit is to be used to finance a transaction between the borrower and the supplier;

"conditional sale agreement" means an agreement for the sale of goods or land under which the purchase price or part of it is payable by instalments, and the property in the goods or land is to remain with the seller (notwithstanding that the buyer is to be in possession of the goods or land) until such conditions as to the payment of instalments or otherwise as may be specified in the agreement are fulfilled;

"credit" includes a cash loan and any other form of financial accommodation;

["credit agreement"—

    (a)   in relation to an agreement other than a green deal plan, has the meaning given by article 60B;

    (b)   in relation to a green deal plan, has the meaning given by article 60LB;]

"credit union" means a credit union within the meaning of—

    (a)   the Credit Unions Act 1979;

    (b)   the Credit Unions (Northern Ireland) Order 1985;

"deposit" (except where specified otherwise) means any sum payable by a borrower by way of deposit or down-payment, or credited or to be credited to the borrower on account of any deposit or down-payment, whether the sum is to be or has been paid to the lender or any other person, or is to be or has been discharged by a payment of money or a transfer or delivery of goods or other means;

"exempt agreement" has the meaning given by article 60B;

"finance" includes financing in whole or in part, and "refinance" is to be read accordingly;

"fixed-sum credit" means a facility under a credit agreement whereby the borrower is enabled to receive credit (whether in one amount or by instalments) but which is not running-account credit;

"hire-purchase agreement" means an agreement—

    (a)   which is not a conditional sale agreement,

    (b)   under which goods are bailed or (in Scotland) hired to a person ("P") in return for periodical payments by P, and

    (c)   the property in the goods will pass to P if the terms of the agreement are complied with and one or more of the following occurs—

        (i)   the exercise by P of an option to purchase the goods;

        (ii)   the doing by any party to the agreement of any other act specified in the agreement;

        (iii)   the happening of any event specified in the agreement;

"legal [or equitable] mortgage" includes [a legal or equitable] charge and, in Scotland, a heritable security;

"lender" means [(except in relation to green deal plans: see instead article 60LB)]—

    (a)   the person providing credit under a credit agreement, or

    (b)   a person who exercises or has the right to exercise the rights and duties of a person who provided credit under such an agreement;

"payment" (except in article 60F) means a payment comprising or including an amount in respect of credit;

"regulated credit agreement" has the meaning given by article 60B;

"relative" means brother, sister, uncle, aunt, nephew, niece, lineal ancestor or lineal descendent;

"relevant recipient of credit" means—

    (a)   a partnership consisting of two or three persons not all of whom are bodies corporate, or

    (b)   an unincorporated body of persons which does not consist entirely of bodies corporate and is not a partnership;

"restricted-use credit agreement" means a credit agreement—

    (a)   to finance a transaction between the borrower and the lender, whether forming part of that agreement or not,

    (b)   to finance a transaction between the borrower and a person ("the supplier") other than the lender, or

    (c)   to refinance any existing indebtedness of the borrower's, whether to the lender or another person;

"running-account credit" means a facility under a credit agreement under which the borrower or another person is enabled to receive from time to time from the lender or a third party cash, goods or services to an amount or value such that, taking into account payments made by or to the credit of the borrower, the credit limit (if any) is not at any time exceeded;

"security" in relation to a credit agreement, means a mortgage, charge, pledge, bond, debenture, indemnity, guarantee, bill, note or other right provided by the borrower or at the implied or express request of the borrower to secure the carrying out of the obligations of the borrower under the agreement;

"total charge for credit" has the meaning given in rules made by the FCA under article 60M;

"total price" means the total sum payable by the debtor under a hire-purchase agreement, including any sum payable on the exercise of an option to purchase but excluding any sum payable as a penalty or as compensation or damages for a breach of the agreement;

"unrestricted-use credit agreement" means a credit agreement which is not a restricted-use credit agreement.

[(1A) For the purposes of this Chapter, a credit agreement that is a green deal plan is to be treated as—

(a) a borrower-lender-supplier agreement falling within paragraph (a) of the definition of "borrower-lender-supplier agreement";

(b) a restricted-use credit agreement falling within paragraph (a) of the definition of "restricted-use credit agreement".]

(2) For the purposes of the definition of "restricted-use credit agreement"—

(a) a credit agreement does not fall within the definition if the credit is in fact provided in such a way as to leave the borrower free to use it as the borrower chooses, even though certain uses would contravene that or any other agreement; and

(b) an agreement may fall within paragraph (b) of the definition even though the identity of the supplier is unknown at the time the agreement is made.

(3) For the purposes of the definition of "borrower-lender agreement" [and the definition of "borrower-lender-supplier agreement"], a credit agreement is, subject to paragraph (6), entered into under pre-existing arrangements between a lender and a supplier if it is entered into in accordance with, or in connection with, arrangements previously made between the lender (or the lender's associate) and the supplier (or the supplier's associate) unless the arrangements fall within paragraph (5).

(4) For the purposes of the definition of "borrower-lender agreement" [and the definition of "borrower-lender-supplier agreement"], a credit agreement is entered into in contemplation of future arrangements between a lender and a supplier if it is entered into in the expectation that arrangements will subsequently be made between the lender (or the lender's associate) and the supplier (or the supplier's associate) for the supply of cash, goods or services to be financed by the credit agreement unless the arrangements fall within paragraph (5).

(5) Arrangements fall within this paragraph if they are—

(a) for the making, in circumstances specified in the credit agreement, of payments to the supplier by the lender ("L") and L indicates that L is willing to make, in such circumstances, payments of the kind to suppliers generally, or

(b) for the electronic transfer of funds from a current account held with an authorised person with permission to accept deposits (within the meaning given by article 3).

(6) If a lender is an associate of the supplier's, the credit agreement is to be treated as entered into under pre-existing arrangements between the lender and the supplier unless the lender can show that this is not the case.

(7) For the purposes of the definition of "running-account credit", "credit limit" means, as respects any period, the maximum debit balance which, under a credit agreement, is allowed to stand on the account during that period, disregarding any term of the agreement allowing that maximum to be exceeded on a temporary basis.

(8) For the purposes of this Chapter, a person by whom goods are bailed or (in Scotland) hired to an individual or relevant recipient of credit under a hire-purchase agreement is to be taken to be providing that individual or person with fixed-sum credit to finance the transaction of an amount equal to the total price of the goods less the aggregate of the deposit (if any) and the total charge for credit.

(9) For the purposes of this Chapter, where credit is provided otherwise than in sterling, it is to be treated as provided in sterling of an equivalent amount.

[(10) For the purposes of this Chapter, where a provision specifies an amount of credit, running-account credit shall be taken not to exceed the amount specified in that provision ("the specified amount") if—

(a) the credit limit does not exceed the specified amount; or

(b) the credit limit exceeds the specified amount, or there is no credit limit, and—

(i) the borrower is not enabled to draw at any one time an amount which, so far as it represents credit, exceeds the specified amount; or

(ii) the agreement provides that, if the debit balance rises above a given amount (not exceeding the specified amount), the rate of the total charge for credit increases or any other condition favouring the lender or the lender's associate comes into operation; or

(iii) at the time the agreement is made it is probable, having regard to the terms of the agreement and any other relevant considerations, that the debit balance will not at any time rise above the specified amount.

(11) For the purposes of this Chapter, an item entering into the total charge for credit is not to be treated as credit even though time is allowed for its payment.]]

NOTES

Commencement: 26 July 2013 (certain purposes); 1 April 2014 (otherwise).

Inserted as noted to art 60B at **[2.193]**.

The words "(except in relation to green deal plans: see instead article 60LB)" in the definitions "borrower" and "lender" in para (1) were inserted, the definition "credit agreement" in that paragraph was substituted, and para (1A) was inserted, by the Financial Services and Markets Act 2000 (Regulated Activities) (Green Deal) (Amendment) Order 2014, SI 2014/1850, arts 2, 8 (except in relation to a green deal plan (within the meaning of the Energy Act 2011, s 1) made before 28 February 2014).

The other words in square brackets in para (1), and the words in square brackets in paras (3), (4), were inserted by the Financial Services and Markets Act 2000 (Regulated Activities) (Amendment) Order 2014, SI 2014/366, art 2(1), (32).

Paras (10), (11) were added by the Financial Services and Markets Act 2000 (Miscellaneous Provisions) Order 2015, SI 2015/853, art 3(1), (6).

[2.207]
[60LA   Meaning of consumer etc

(1)   For the purposes of sections 1G, 404E and 425A of the Act (meaning of "consumer"), in so far as those provisions relate to a person ("A") carrying on a regulated activity of the kind specified by—

(a)   article 60B (regulated credit agreements), or

(b)   article 64 (agreeing to carry on specified kinds of activity) in so far as that article relates to article 60B,

a person who is treated by A as a person who is or has been the borrower under a regulated credit agreement is to be treated as a "consumer".

(2)   For the purposes of section 328(8) of the Act (meaning of "clients") in so far as that provision relates to a person ("A") carrying on a regulated activity of the kind specified by—

(a)   article 60B (regulated credit agreements), or

(b)   article 64 (agreeing to carry on specified kinds of activity) in so far as that article relates to article 60B,

a person who is treated by A as a person who is or has been the borrower under a regulated credit agreement is to be treated as a "client".

(3)   In this article, "borrower" includes (in addition to those persons included in the definition in article 60L [or, where the credit agreement is a green deal plan, article 60LB])—

(a)   any person providing a guarantee or indemnity under a regulated credit agreement, and

(b)   a person to whom the rights and duties of a person falling within sub-paragraph (a) have passed by assignment or operation of law.]

NOTES

Commencement: 1 April 2014.

Inserted by the Financial Services and Markets Act 2000 (Regulated Activities) (Amendment) Order 2014, SI 2014/366, art 2(1), (33).

Para (3): words in square brackets inserted by the Financial Services and Markets Act 2000 (Regulated Activities) (Green Deal) (Amendment) Order 2014, SI 2014/1850, arts 2, 9 (except in relation to a green deal plan (within the meaning of the Energy Act 2011, s 1) made before 28 February 2014).

[2.208]
[60LB   Green deal plans

(1)   A green deal plan is to be treated as a credit agreement for the purposes of this Order if (and only if)—

(a)   the property in relation to the plan is a domestic property at the time when the plan is commenced, or

(b)   if sub-paragraph (a) does not apply, the occupier or owner of the property who makes the arrangement for the plan is an individual or relevant recipient of credit.

(2)   In the application of this Order to a green deal credit agreement—

(a)   the lender is to be treated as being—

(i)   the green deal provider (within the meaning of Chapter 1 of Part 1 of the Energy Act 2011) for the plan, or

(ii)   a person who exercises or has the right to exercise the rights and duties of the green deal provider under the plan,

(b)   credit is to be treated as advanced under the agreement of an amount equal to the amount of the improvement costs, and

(c)   the advance of credit is to be treated as made on the completion of the installation of the energy efficiency improvements to the property (but this sub-paragraph is subject to any term of the green deal plan providing that part of the advance is to be treated as made on completion of any part of the installation).

(3)   A reference in a provision of this Order listed in the first column of the table in Schedule 4A to the borrower is, in the application of the provision in relation to a green deal credit agreement, to be read as a reference to—

(a)   a person who at the relevant time falls (or fell) within the description or descriptions specified in the corresponding entry in the second column of the table, or

(b)   if more than one description is specified and at the relevant time different persons fall (or fell) within the descriptions, each of those persons,

and except as provided by this paragraph, a person is not and is not to be treated as the borrower in relation to the agreement.

(4) References in Schedule 4A to the "improver", "first bill payer", "current bill payer" and "previous bill payer" are to be read as follows—

(a) a person is the "improver" if the person—
   (i) is the owner or occupier of the property, and
   (ii) is the person who makes (or has made or proposes to make) the arrangement for the green deal plan;

(b) a person is the "first bill payer" if the person is liable to pay the energy bills for the property at the time when the green deal plan is commenced;

(c) a person is the "current bill payer" if the person is liable by virtue of section 1(6)(a) of the Energy Act 2011 to pay instalments under the plan as a result of being for the time being liable to pay the energy bills for the property;

(d) a person is a "previous bill payer" if, as a result of previously falling within sub-paragraph (c) for an earlier period, the person has an outstanding payment liability under the plan in respect of that period.

(5) In this article—

"domestic property" means a building or part of a building that is occupied as a dwelling or (if not occupied) is intended to be occupied as a dwelling;

"energy bill" has the same meaning as in section 1 of the Energy Act 2011;

"energy efficiency improvements" has the meaning given by section 2(4) of the Energy Act 2011;

"green deal credit agreement" means a green deal plan that is to be treated as a credit agreement for the purposes of this Order by virtue of paragraph (1);

"improvement costs", in relation to a green deal plan, are the costs of the energy efficiency improvements to the property which are to be paid by instalments under the plan after the time when credit is to be treated as being advanced by virtue of paragraph (2) (but ignoring any interest or other charges for credit in determining those costs);

"occupier" and "owner" have the same meanings as in Chapter 1 of Part 1 of the Energy Act 2011;

"property", in relation to a green deal plan, means the property to which the energy efficiency improvements under the plan are or are intended to be made.

(6) For the purposes of this article—

(a) a green deal plan is commenced when—
   (i) the occupier or owner of the property signs in the prescribed manner a document in relation to the plan in accordance with section 61(1) of the Consumer Credit Act 1974 (requirements as to form and content of regulated agreements), or
   (ii) if the occupier or owner of the property does not sign such a document, the green deal plan is made;

(b) a person is liable to pay the energy bills for a property at any time if the person would be treated as the bill payer for the property at that time for the purposes of Chapter 1 of Part 1 of the Energy Act 2011 (see section 2(3) and (10)).".

NOTES

Commencement: 15 July 2014.

Inserted by the Financial Services and Markets Act 2000 (Regulated Activities) (Green Deal) (Amendment) Order 2014, SI 2014/1850, arts 2, 10 (except in relation to a green deal plan (within the meaning of the Energy Act 2011, s 1) made before 28 February 2014).

[2.209]
[60M   Total charge for credit

(1) The FCA may make rules specifying how the total charge for credit to the borrower under a credit agreement is to be determined for the purposes of this Chapter.

(2) Rules made under paragraph (1) may in particular—

(a) specify how the total charge for credit to a person who is, or is to become, the borrower under a credit agreement is to be determined;

(b) specify what items are to be included in determining the total charge for credit and how the value of those items is to be determined;

(c) specify the method of calculating the rate of the total charge for credit;

(d) provide for the whole or part of the amount payable by the borrower or a relative of the borrower under a linked transaction (within the meaning given by article 60E(8)) to be included in the total charge for credit, whether or not the lender is a party to the transaction or derives a benefit from it.]

NOTES

Commencement: 26 July 2013 (certain purposes); 1 April 2014 (otherwise).

Inserted as noted to art 60B at **[2.193]**.

[CHAPTER 14B
REGULATED CONSUMER HIRE AGREEMENTS

The Activities

[2.210]
60N   Regulated consumer hire agreements

(1)   Entering into a regulated consumer hire agreement as owner is a specified kind of activity.

(2)   It is a specified kind of activity for the owner or another person to exercise, or to have the right to exercise, the owner's rights and duties under a regulated consumer hire agreement.

(3)   In this Chapter—

"consumer hire agreement" means an agreement between a person ("the owner") and an individual or relevant recipient of credit ("the hirer") for the bailment or, in Scotland, the hiring, of goods to the hirer which—
    (a)   is not a hire-purchase agreement, and
    (b)   is capable of subsisting for more than three months;

"exempt agreement" means a consumer hire agreement which is an exempt agreement under articles 60O to 60Q;

"owner" means—
    (a)   the person who bails or, in Scotland, hires, goods under a . . . consumer hire agreement, or
    (b)   a person who exercises or has the right to exercise the rights and duties of a person who bailed or, in Scotland, hired, goods under such an agreement;

"regulated consumer hire agreement" means a consumer hire agreement which is not an exempt agreement.]

NOTES

Commencement: 26 July 2013 (certain purposes); 1 April 2014 (otherwise).

Chapter 14B (originally arts 60N–60R) was inserted by the Financial Services and Markets Act 2000 (Regulated Activities) (Amendment) (No 2) Order 2013, SI 2013/1881, arts 2, 6, for transitional provisions see Pt 8 thereof at **[2.1007]** et seq.

Para (3): word omitted from the definition "owner" revoked by the Financial Services and Markets Act 2000 (Regulated Activities) (Amendment) Order 2014, SI 2014/366, art 2(1), (34).

[2.211]
[60O   Exempt agreements: exemptions relating to nature of agreement

(1)   An agreement is an exempt agreement for the purposes of this Chapter if—
    (a)   the hirer is required by the agreement to make payments exceeding £25,000, and
    (b)   the agreement is entered into by the hirer wholly or predominantly for the purposes of a business carried on, or intended to be carried on, by the hirer.

(2)   For the purposes of paragraph (1), if an agreement includes a declaration which—
    (a)   is made by the hirer,
    (b)   provides that the agreement is entered into by the hirer wholly or predominantly for the purposes of a business carried on, or intended to be carried on, by the hirer, and
    (c)   complies with rules made by the FCA for the purposes of this article,
the agreement is to be presumed to have been entered into by the hirer wholly or predominantly for the purpose in sub-paragraph (b) unless paragraph (3) applies.

(3)   This paragraph applies if, when the agreement is entered into—
    (a)   the owner (or, if there is more than one owner, any of the owners), or
    (b)   any person who has acted on behalf of the owner (or, if there is more than one owner, any of the owners), in connection with the entering into of the agreement,
knows or has reasonable cause to suspect that the agreement is not entered into by the hirer wholly or predominantly for the purposes of a business carried on, or intended to be carried on, by the hirer.

(4)   For the purposes of this article, where credit is provided otherwise than in sterling, it is to be treated as provided in sterling of an equivalent amount.]

NOTES

Commencement: 26 July 2013 (certain purposes); 1 April 2014 (otherwise).
Inserted as noted to art 60N at **[2.210]**.

[2.212]
[60P   Exempt agreements: exemptions relating to supply of essential services

An agreement is an exempt agreement for the purposes of this Chapter if—
    (a)   the owner is a body corporate which is authorised by or under an enactment to supply gas, electricity or water, and
    (b)   the subject of the agreement is a meter or metering equipment which is used (or is to be used) in connection with the supply of gas, electricity or water.]

NOTES

Commencement: 26 July 2013 (certain purposes); 1 April 2014 (otherwise).

Inserted as noted to art 60N at [**2.210**].

[2.213]
[60Q Exempt agreements: exemptions relating to the nature of the hirer

An agreement is an exempt agreement for the purposes of this Chapter if—

(a) the hirer is an individual,

(b) the agreement includes a declaration made by the hirer which provides that the hirer agrees to forgo the protection and remedies that would be available to the hirer if the agreement were a regulated consumer hire agreement and which complies with rules made by the FCA for the purposes of this paragraph,

(c) a statement has been made in relation to the income or assets of the hirer which complies with rules made by the FCA for the purposes of this paragraph,

(d) the connection between the statement and the agreement complies with any rules made by the FCA for the purposes of this paragraph (including as to the period of time between the making of the statement and the agreement being entered into), and

(e) a copy of the statement was provided to the owner before the agreement was entered into.]

NOTES

Commencement: 26 July 2013 (certain purposes); 1 April 2014 (otherwise).
Inserted as noted to art 60N at [**2.210**].

[Exclusion

[2.214]
60R [Other exclusions]

Article 60N is subject to the exclusion in article 72A (information society services) [and the exclusion in article 72G (local authorities)].]

NOTES

Commencement: 26 July 2013 (certain purposes); 1 April 2014 (otherwise).
Inserted as noted to art 60N at [**2.210**].
Article heading substituted, and words in square brackets inserted, by the Financial Services and Markets Act 2000 (Regulated Activities) (Amendment) Order 2014, SI 2014/366, art 2(1), (35), (36).

[Supplemental

[2.215]
60S Meaning of consumer etc

(1) For the purposes of sections 1G, 404E and 425A of the Act (meaning of "consumer"), in so far as those provisions relate to a person ("A") carrying on a regulated activity of the kind specified by—

(a) article 60N (regulated consumer hire agreements), or

(b) article 64 (agreeing to carry on specified kinds of activity) in so far as that article relates to article 60N,

a person who is treated by A as a person who is or has been the hirer under a regulated consumer hire agreement is to be treated as a "consumer".

(2) For the purposes of section 328(8) of the Act (meaning of "clients") in so far as that provision relates to a person ("A") carrying on a regulated activity of the kind specified by—

(a) article 60N (regulated consumer hire agreements), or

(b) article 64 (agreeing to carry on specified kinds of activity) in so far as that article relates to article 60N,

a person who is treated by A as a person who is or has been the hirer under a regulated consumer hire agreement is to be treated as a "client".

(3) In this article, "hirer" includes (in addition to those persons defined as "the hirer" in the definition of "consumer hire agreement" in article 60N(3))—

(a) any person providing a guarantee or indemnity under a consumer hire agreement, and

(b) a person to whom the rights and duties of a person falling within sub-paragraph (a) have passed by assignment or operation of law.]

NOTES

Commencement: 1 April 2014.
Inserted, together with the preceding heading, by the Financial Services and Markets Act 2000 (Regulated Activities) (Amendment) Order 2014, SI 2014/366, art 2(1), (37).

CHAPTER XV
REGULATED MORTGAGE CONTRACTS
The activities

[2.216]
61   Regulated mortgage contracts

(1)   Entering into a regulated mortgage contract as lender is a specified kind of activity.

(2)   Administering a regulated mortgage contract is also a specified kind of activity, where the contract was entered into [by way of business] after the coming into force of this article.

(3)   In this Chapter—

[(a)   a contract is a "regulated mortgage contract" if, at the time it is entered into, the following conditions are met—

(i)   *the contract is one under which a person ("the lender") provides credit to an individual or to trustees ("the borrower");*

(ii)   *the contract provides for the obligation of the borrower to repay to be secured by a first legal mortgage on land (other than timeshare accommodation) in the United Kingdom;*

(iii)   *at least 40% of that land is used, or is intended to be used, as or in connection with a dwelling by the borrower or (in the case of credit provided to trustees) by an individual who is a beneficiary of the trust, or by a related person;*

[but such a contract is not a regulated mortgage contract if it *is a regulated home purchase plan;*]]

(b)   "administering" a regulated mortgage contract means either or both of—

(i)   notifying the borrower of changes in interest rates or payments due under the contract, or of other matters of which the contract requires him to be notified; and

(ii)   taking any necessary steps for the purposes of collecting or recovering payments due under the contract from the borrower;

but a person is not to be treated as administering a regulated mortgage contract merely because he has, or exercises, a right to take action for the purposes of enforcing the contract (or to require that such action is or is not taken);

(c)   "credit" includes a cash loan, and any other form of financial accommodation.

(4)   For the purposes of [paragraph 3(a)]—

(a)   *a "first legal mortgage" means a legal mortgage ranking in priority ahead of all other mortgages (if any) affecting the land in question, where "mortgage" includes charge and (in Scotland) a heritable security;*

(b)   the area of any land which comprises a building or other structure containing two or more storeys is to be taken to be the aggregate of the floor areas of each of those storeys;

(c)   "related person", in relation to the borrower or (in the case of credit provided to trustees) a beneficiary of the trust, means—

(i)   that person's spouse [or civil partner];

(ii)   a person (whether or not of the opposite sex) whose relationship with that person has the characteristics of the relationship between husband and wife; or

(iii)   that person's parent, brother, sister, child, grandparent or grandchild; *and*

[(d)   *"timeshare accommodation" means overnight accommodation which is the subject of a timeshare contract within the meaning of the Timeshare, Holiday Products, Resale and Exchange Contracts Regulations 2010.]*

NOTES

Para (2): words in square brackets inserted by the Financial Services and Markets Act 2000 (Regulated Activities) (Amendment) Order 2001, SI 2001/3544, arts 2, 8(a).

Para (3): sub-para (a) substituted by SI 2001/3544, arts 2, 8(b); words in second pair of square brackets inserted by the Financial Services and Markets Act 2000 (Regulated Activities) (Amendment) (No 2) Order 2006, SI 2006/2383, arts 2, 17 (for transitional provisions and effect see arts 36–40 of, and the Schedule to, the 2006 Order); sub-paras (a)(i)–(iii) further substituted as follows, and for the words in italics there are substituted the words "falls within article 61A(1) or (2)", by the Mortgage Credit Directive Order 2015, SI 2015/910, Sch 1, Pt 2, para 4(21)(a), as from 21 March 2016 (note that the 2015 Order also comes into force on 20 April 2015 and 21 December 2015 for limited other purposes, and for transitional provisions, see Part 4 of that Order at **[2.1194]** et seq)—

"(i)   the contract is one under which a person ("the lender") provides credit to an individual or to trustees ("the borrower");

(ii)   the contract provides for the obligation of the borrower to repay to be secured by a mortgage on land in the EEA;

(iii)   at least 40% of that land is used, or is intended to be used—

(aa)   in the case of credit provided to an individual, as or in connection with a dwelling; or

(bb)   in the case of credit provided to a trustee which is not an individual, as or in connection with a dwelling by an individual who is a beneficiary of the trust, or by a related person".

Para (4): words in first pair of square brackets substituted by SI 2001/3544, arts 2, 8(c); words in second pair of square brackets inserted by the Civil Partnership Act 2004 (Amendments to Subordinate Legislation) Order 2005, SI 2005/2114, art 2(16), Sch 16, Pt 1, para 1(1), (3); sub-para (d) substituted by the Timeshare, Holiday Products, Resale and Exchange Contracts Regulations 2010, SI 2010/2960, reg 36(3), Sch 6, para 7(1), (2); sub-para (a) substituted as follows, and sub-para (d) and word immediately preceding it revoked, by SI 2015/910, Sch 1, Pt 2, para 4(21)(b), (c), as from 21 March 2016 (note that the 2015 Order also comes into force on 20 April 2015 and 21 December 2015 for limited other purposes, and for transitional provisions, see Part 4 of that Order at **[2.1194]** et seq)—

> "(a) "mortgage" includes a charge and (in Scotland) a heritable security;".

[2.217]
[61A Mortgage contracts which are not regulated mortgage contracts

(1) A contract falls within this paragraph if it is—
    (a) a regulated home purchase plan;
    (b) a limited payment second charge bridging loan;
    (c) a second charge business loan;
    (d) an investment property loan; or
    (e) an exempt consumer buy-to-let mortgage contract.

(2) A contract falls within this paragraph if—
    (a) it is a limited interest second charge credit union loan;
    (b) the borrower receives timely information on the main features, risks and costs of the contract at the pre-contractual stage; and
    (c) any advertising of the contract is fair, clear and not misleading.

(3) For the purposes of this article, if an agreement includes a declaration which—
    (a) is made by the borrower, and
    (b) includes—
        (i) a statement that the agreement is entered into by the borrower wholly or predominantly for the purposes of a business carried on, or intended to be carried on, by the borrower,
        (ii) a statement that the borrower understands that the borrower will not have the benefit of the protection and remedies that would be available to the borrower under the Act if the agreement were a regulated mortgage contract under the Act, and
        (iii) a statement that the borrower is aware that if the borrower is in any doubt as to the consequences of the agreement not being regulated by the Act, then the borrower should seek independent legal advice,

the agreement is to be presumed to have been entered into by the borrower wholly or predominantly for the purposes specified in sub-paragraph (b)(i) unless paragraph (4) applies.

(4) This paragraph applies if, when the agreement is entered into—
    (a) the lender (or, if there is more than one lender, any of the lenders), or
    (b) any person who has acted on behalf of the lender (or, if there is more than one lender, any of the lenders) in connection with the entering into of the agreement,

knows or has reasonable cause to suspect that the agreement is not entered into by the borrower wholly or predominantly for the purposes of a business carried on, or intended to be carried on, by the borrower.

(5) For the purposes of this article a borrower is to be regarded as entering into an agreement for the purposes of a business carried on, or intended to be carried on, by the borrower if the agreement is a buy-to-let mortgage contract and—
    (a)
        (i) the borrower previously purchased, or is entering into the contract in order to finance the purchase by the borrower of, the land subject to the mortgage;
        (ii) at the time of the purchase the borrower intended that the land would be occupied as a dwelling on the basis of a rental agreement and would not at any time be occupied as a dwelling by the borrower or by a related person, or where the borrower has not yet purchased the land the borrower has such an intention at the time of entering into the contract; and
        (iii) where the borrower has purchased the land, since the time of the purchase the land has not at any time been occupied as a dwelling by the borrower or by a related person; or
    (b) the borrower is the owner of land, other than the land subject to the mortgage, which is—
        (i) occupied as a dwelling on the basis of a rental agreement and is not occupied as a dwelling by the borrower or by a related person; or
        (ii) secured by a mortgage under a buy-to-let mortgage contract.

(6) For the purposes of this article—
    "borrower" and "lender" have the meaning set out in article 61(3) (regulated mortgage contracts);
    "borrower-lender agreement", "borrower-lender-supplier agreement", "credit union" and "total charge for credit" have the meanings set out in article 60L (interpretation of Chapter 14A);
    "bridging loan" has the meaning given by Article 4(23) of the mortgages directive;
    "buy-to-let mortgage contract" has the meaning given in article 4 of the Mortgage Credit Directive Order 2015 (interpretation of Part 3);

"exempt consumer buy-to-let mortgage contract" is a contract that, at the time it is entered into, is a consumer buy-to-let mortgage contract within the meaning of article 4 of the Mortgage Credit Directive Order 2015 and—

  (a)   is of a kind to which the mortgages directive does not apply by virtue of Article 3(2) of that directive; or

  (b)   is a bridging loan;

"investment property loan" is a contract that, at the time it is entered into, meets the conditions in paragraphs (i) to (iii) of article 61(3)(a) and the following conditions—

  (a)   less than 40% of the land subject to the mortgage is used, or intended to be used, as or in connection with a dwelling by the borrower or (in the case of credit provided to trustees) by an individual who is a beneficiary of the trust, or by a related person; and

  (b)   the agreement is entered into by the borrower wholly or predominantly for the purposes of a business carried on, or intended to be carried on, by the borrower;

"limited payment second charge bridging loan" is a contract that, at the time it is entered into, meets the conditions in paragraphs (i) to (iii) of article 61(3)(a) and the following conditions—

  (a)   it is a borrower-lender-supplier agreement financing the purchase of land;

  (b)   it is used by the borrower as a temporary financing solution while transitioning to another financial arrangement for the land subject to the mortgage;

  (c)   the mortgage ranks in priority behind one or more other mortgages affecting the land in question; and

  (d)   the number of payments to be made by the borrower under the contract is not more than four;

"limited interest second charge credit union loan" is a contract that, at the time it is entered into, meets the conditions in paragraphs (i) to (iii) of article 61(3)(a) and the following conditions—

  (a)   it is a borrower-lender agreement;

  (b)   the mortgage ranks in priority behind one or more other mortgages affecting the land in question;

  (c)   the lender is a credit union; and

  (d)   the rate of the total charge for credit does not exceed 42.6 per cent;

"payment" has the meaning set out in article 60F(8) (exempt agreement: exemptions relating to number of repayments to be made);

"regulated home purchase plan" has the meaning set out in article 63F(3)(a) (entering into and administering regulated home purchase plans);

"related person" in relation to the borrower or (in the case of credit provided to trustees) a beneficiary of the trust, means—

  (a)   that person's spouse or civil partner;

  (b)   a person (whether or not of the opposite sex) whose relationship with that person has the characteristics of the relationship between husband and wife; or

  (c)   that person's parent, brother, sister, child, grandparent or grandchild;

"second charge business loan" is a contract that, at the time it is entered into, meets the conditions in paragraphs (i) to (iii) of article 61(3)(a) and the following conditions—

  (a)   the lender provides the borrower with credit exceeding £25,000;

  (b)   the mortgage ranks in priority behind one or more other mortgages affecting the land in question; and

  (c)   the agreement is entered into by the borrower wholly or predominantly for the purposes of a business carried on, or intended to be carried on, by the borrower.]

NOTES

Commencement: see below.

Inserted by the Mortgage Credit Directive Order 2015, SI 2015/910, Sch 1, Pt 2, para 4(1), (22), as from 21 March 2016 (note that the 2015 Order also comes into force on 20 April 2015 and 21 December 2015 for limited other purposes, and for transitional provisions, see Part 4 of that Order at **[2.1194]** et seq).

Exclusions

[2.218]

62   Arranging administration by authorised person

A person who is not an authorised person does not carry on an activity of the kind specified by article 61(2) in relation to a regulated mortgage contract where he—

  (a)   arranges for another person, being an authorised person with permission to carry on an activity of that kind, to administer the contract; or

  (b)   administers the contract himself during a period of not more than one month beginning with the day on which any such arrangement comes to an end.

[2.219]
63 Administration pursuant to agreement with authorised person

A person who is not an authorised person does not carry on an activity of the kind specified by article 61(2) in relation to a regulated mortgage contract where he administers the contract pursuant to an agreement with an authorised person who has permission to carry on an activity of that kind.

[2.220]
[63A Other exclusions

Article 61 is also subject to the exclusions in articles 66 (trustees etc), 72 (overseas persons)[, 72A (information society services)[, 72AA (managers of UCITS and AIFs) *and 72G (local authorities)*]].]

NOTES

Inserted by the Financial Services and Markets Act 2000 (Regulated Activities) (Amendment) (No 2) Order 2002, SI 2002/1776, art 3(1), (16); substituted by the Financial Services and Markets Act 2000 (Regulated Activities) (Amendment) (No 1) Order 2003, SI 2003/1475, art 17 (for transitional provisions see arts 26–29); words in first (outer) pair of square brackets substituted by the Alternative Investment Fund Managers Regulations 2013, SI 2013/1773, reg 81, Sch 2, Part 1, para 1(1), (6) (for transitional provisions and savings see Part 9 of the 2013 Regulations); words in second (inner) pair of square brackets substituted by the Financial Services and Markets Act 2000 (Regulated Activities) (Amendment) Order 2014, SI 2014/366, art 2(1), (38); for the words in italics there are substituted the words ", 72G (local authorities) and 72I (registered consumer buy-to-let mortgage firms)" by the Mortgage Credit Directive Order 2015, SI 2015/910, Sch 1, Pt 2, para 4(23), as from 21 March 2016 (note that the 2015 Order also comes into force on 20 April 2015 and 21 December 2015 for limited other purposes, and for transitional provisions, see Part 4 of that Order at **[2.1194]** et seq).

63B–65 (*Chapters XVA–15E outside the scope of this work.*)

CHAPTER XVII
EXCLUSIONS APPLYING TO SEVERAL SPECIFIED KINDS OF ACTIVITY

66–72 (*Outside the scope of this work.*)

[2.221]
[72A Information society services

(1) There is excluded from this Part any activity consisting of the provision of an information society service from an EEA State other than the United Kingdom.

(2) The exclusion in paragraph (1) does not apply to the activity of effecting or carrying out a contract of insurance as principal, where—

(a) *the activity is carried on by an undertaking which has received official authorisation in accordance with [Article 4 of the life assurance consolidation directive] or the first non-life insurance directive, and*

(b) *the insurance falls within the scope of any of the insurance directives.*

[(3) The exclusion in paragraph (1) does not apply to an activity carried on by a person ("P") if—

(a) *the FCA has given a final notice to P under section 390 of the Act, as applied by regulation 11C of the Electronic Commerce Directive (Financial Services and Markets) Regulations 2002, in relation to that activity; and*

(b) *a determination made by that notice is in effect.*]]

NOTES

Inserted by the Financial Services and Markets Act 2000 (Regulated Activities) (Amendment) (No 2) Order 2002, SI 2002/1776, art 2.

Para (2): words in square brackets in para (a) substituted by the Life Assurance Consolidation Directive (Consequential Amendments) Regulations 2004, SI 2004/3379, reg 17; paras (a), (b) repealed, and the words "the insurance falls within the scope of the Solvency 2 Directive" are inserted at the end of para (2), by the Solvency 2 Regulations 2015, SI 2015/575, reg 60, Sch 2, para 11(1), (4), as from 1 January 2016.

Para (3): added by the Electronic Commerce Directive (Financial Services and Markets) (Amendment) Order 2015, SI 2015/852, art 4.

72AA (*Outside the scope of this work.*)

[2.222]
[72B Activities carried on by a provider of relevant goods or services

(1) In this article—
"connected contract of insurance" means a contract of insurance which—

(a) is not a contract of long-term insurance;

(b) has a total duration (or would have a total duration were any right to renew conferred by the contract exercised) of five years or less;

(c) has an annual premium (or, where the premium is paid otherwise than by way of annual premium, the equivalent of an annual premium) of 500 euro or less, or the equivalent amount in sterling or other currency;

(d) covers the risk of—

> (i)   breakdown, loss of, or damage to, non-motor goods supplied by the provider; or
>
> [(ii)   damage to, or loss of, baggage and other risks linked to the travel booked with the provider ("travel risks") in circumstances where—
>
> > (aa)   the travel booked with the provider relates to attendance at an event organised or managed by that provider and the party seeking insurance is not an individual (acting in his private capacity) or a small business; or
> >
> > (bb)   the travel booked with the provider is only the hire of an aircraft, vehicle or vessel which does not provide sleeping accommodation];

(e)   does not cover any liability risks (except, in the case of a contract which covers travel risks, where that cover is ancillary to the main cover provided by the contract);

(f)   is complementary to the non-motor goods being supplied or service being provided by the provider; and

(g)   is of such a nature that the only information that a person requires in order to carry on an activity of the kind specified by article 21, 25, 39A or 53 in relation to it is the cover provided by the contract;

"non-motor goods" means goods which are not mechanically propelled road vehicles;

"provider" means a person who supplies non-motor goods or provides services related to travel in the course of carrying on a profession or business which does not otherwise consist of the carrying on of regulated activities.

[For these purposes, the transfer of possession of an aircraft, vehicle or vessel under an agreement for hire which is not—

(a)   a hire-purchase agreement   . . . , or

(b)   any other agreement which contemplates that the property in those goods will also pass at some time in the future,

is the provision of a service related to travel, not a supply of goods];

["small business" means—

(a)   subject to paragraph (b) a sole trader, body corporate, partnership or an unincorporated association which had a turnover in the last financial year of less than £1,000,000;

(b)   where the business concerned is a member of a group within the meaning of [section 474(1) of the Companies Act 2006], reference to its turnover means the combined turnover of the group;

"turnover" means the amounts derived from the provision of goods and services falling within the business's ordinary activities, after deduction of trade discounts, value added tax and any other taxes based on the amounts so derived].

(2)   There is excluded from article 21 any transaction for the sale or purchase of a connected contract of insurance into which a provider enters as agent.

(3)   There are excluded from article 25(1) and (2) any arrangements made by a provider for, or with a view to, a transaction for the sale or purchase of a connected contract of insurance.

(4)   There is excluded from article 39A any activity carried on by a provider where the contract of insurance in question is a connected contract of insurance.

(5)   There is excluded from article 53 the giving of advice by a provider in relation to a transaction for the sale or purchase of a connected contract of insurance.

(6)   For the purposes of this article, a contract of insurance which covers travel risks is not to be treated as a contract of long-term insurance, notwithstanding the fact that it contains related and subsidiary provisions such that it might be regarded as a contract of long-term insurance, if the cover to which those provisions relate is ancillary to the main cover provided by the contract.]

NOTES

Inserted, together with arts 72C, 72D, by the Financial Services and Markets Act 2000 (Regulated Activities) (Amendment) (No 2) Order 2003, SI 2003/1476, art 11; for transitional provisions see arts 22–27 of that Order.

Para (1) is amended as follows:

In definition "connected contract of insurance" sub-para (d)(ii) substituted by the Financial Services and Markets Act 2000 (Regulated Activities) (Amendment) (No 2) Order 2007, SI 2007/3510, art 2(1), (2).

Words in square brackets in the definition "provider" inserted, and definitions "small business" and "turnover" added, by SI 2007/3510, art 2(1), (3).

The words omitted from the definition "provider" were revoked by the Financial Services and Markets Act 2000 (Regulated Activities) (Amendment) (No 2) Order 2013, SI 2013/1881, arts 2, 9(1), for transitional provisions see Pt 8 thereof at **[2.1007]** et seq).

Words in square brackets in definition "small business" substituted by the Companies Act 2006 (Consequential Amendments and Transitional Provisions) Order 2011, SI 2011/1265, art 13(1), (5).

See further, in relation to the definition of "provider" in para (1) above, the Financial Services and Markets Act 2000 (Regulated Activities) (Amendment) (No 2) Order 2013, SI 2013/1881, art 59A.

72C–72H   (*Outside the scope of this work.*)

[PART 3A
SPECIFIED ACTIVITIES IN RELATION TO INFORMATION

The Activities

[2.223]
89A Providing credit information services

(1) Taking any of the steps in paragraph (3) on behalf of an individual or relevant recipient of credit is a specified kind of activity.

(2) Giving advice to an individual or relevant recipient of credit in relation to the taking of any of the steps specified in paragraph (3) is a specified kind of activity.

(3) Subject to paragraph (4), the steps specified in this paragraph are steps taken with a view to—
   (a) ascertaining whether a credit information agency holds information relevant to the financial standing of an individual or relevant recipient of credit;
   (b) ascertaining the contents of such information;
   (c) securing the correction of, the omission of anything from, or the making of any other kind of modification of, such information;
   (d) securing that a credit information agency which holds such information—
      (i) stops holding the information, or
      (ii) does not provide it to any other person.

(4) Steps taken by a credit information agency in relation to information held by that agency are not steps specified in paragraph (3).

(5) Paragraphs (1) and (2) do not apply to an activity of the kind specified by article 36H (operating an electronic system in relation to lending).

(6) "Credit information agency" means a person who carries on by way of business an activity of the kind specified by any of the following—
   (a) article 36A (credit broking);
   (b) article 39D (debt adjusting);
   (c) article 39E (debt-counselling);
   (d) article 39F (debt-collecting);
   (e) article 39G (debt administration);
   (f) article 60B (regulated credit agreements) disregarding the effect of article 60F;
   (g) article 60N (regulated consumer hire agreements) disregarding the effect of article 60P;
   (h) article 89B (providing credit references).]

NOTES
Commencement: 26 July 2013 (certain purposes); 1 April 2014 (otherwise).
Part 3A (arts 89A–89E) was inserted by the Financial Services and Markets Act 2000 (Regulated Activities) (Amendment) (No 2) Order 2013, SI 2013/1881, arts 2, 8(2), for transitional provisions see Pt 8 thereof at **[2.1007]** et seq).

[2.224]
[89B Providing credit references

(1) Furnishing of persons with information relevant to the financial standing of individuals or relevant recipients of credit is a specified kind of activity if the person has collected the information for that purpose.

(2) There are excluded from paragraph (1) activities carried on in the course of a business which does not primarily consist of activities of the kind specified by paragraph (1).

(3) Paragraph (1) does not apply to an activity of the kind specified by article 36H (operating an electronic system in relation to lending).]

NOTES
Commencement: 26 July 2013 (certain purposes); 1 April 2014 (otherwise).
Inserted as noted to art 89A at **[2.223]**.

[Exclusions

[2.225]
89C Activities carried on by members of the legal profession etc

(1) There are excluded from articles 89A and 89B activities carried on by—
   (a) a barrister or advocate acting in that capacity;
   (b) a solicitor (within the meaning of the Solicitors Act 1974) in the course of providing advocacy services or litigation services;
   (c) a solicitor (within the meaning of the Solicitors (Scotland) Act 1980) in the course of providing advocacy services or litigation services;
   (d) a solicitor (within the meaning of the Solicitors (Northern Ireland) Order 1976) in the course of providing advocacy services or litigation services;
   (e) a relevant person (other than a person falling within sub-paragraph (a) to (d)) in the course of providing advocacy services or litigation services.

(2) In paragraph (1)—

"advocacy services" means any services which it would be reasonable to expect a person who is exercising, or contemplating exercising, a right of audience in relation to any proceedings, or contemplated proceedings, to provide for the purpose of those proceedings or contemplated proceedings;

"litigation services" means any services which it would be reasonable to expect a person who is exercising, or contemplating exercising, a right to conduct litigation in relation to any proceedings, or contemplated proceedings, to provide for the purpose of those proceedings or contemplated proceedings;

"relevant person" means a person who, for the purposes of the Legal Services Act 2007, is an authorised person in relation to an activity which constitutes the exercise of a right of audience or the conduct of litigation (within the meaning of that Act).]

NOTES

Commencement: 24 March 2015.

Inserted as noted to art 89A at **[2.223]**; subsequently substituted by the Financial Services and Markets Act 2000 (Miscellaneous Provisions) Order 2015, SI 2015/853, art 3(1), (7).

[2.226]
[89D   [Other exclusions]

[(1)]   Articles 89A and 89B are subject to the exclusion in article 72A (information society services).

[(2)   Article 89A is also subject to the exclusions in articles 72G (local authorities) and 72H (insolvency practitioners).]]

NOTES

Commencement: 26 July 2013 (certain purposes); 1 April 2014 (otherwise).

Inserted as noted to art 89A at **[2.223]**.

Article heading substituted, para (1) numbered as such, and para (2) added, by the Financial Services and Markets Act 2000 (Regulated Activities) (Amendment) Order 2014, SI 2014/366, art 2(1), (44), (45).

[Supplemental

[2.227]
89E   Meaning of "consumer" etc

(1)   For the purposes of sections 1G, 404E and 425A of the Act (meaning of "consumer")—

   (a)   an individual or a relevant recipient of credit who is, may be, has been or may have been the subject of the information referred to in article 89A, and

   (b)   an individual or a relevant recipient of credit who is, may be, has been or may have been the subject of information furnished in the course of a person carrying on an activity of the kind specified by article 89B, [or article 64 (agreeing to carry on specified kinds of activity) in so far as that article relates to article 89B,]

is to be treated as a "consumer".

(2)   For the purposes of section 328(8) of the Act (meaning of "clients")—

   (a)   an individual or a relevant recipient of credit who is, may be, has been or may have been the subject of the information referred to in article 89A, and

   (b)   an individual or a relevant recipient of credit who is, may be, has been or may have been the subject of information furnished in the course of a person carrying on an activity of the kind specified by article 89B, [or article 64 (agreeing to carry on specified kinds of activity) in so far as that article relates to article 89B,]

is to be treated as a "client".]

NOTES

Commencement: 26 July 2013 (certain purposes); 1 April 2014 (otherwise).

Inserted as noted to art 89A at **[2.223]**.

Words in square brackets inserted by the Financial Services and Markets Act 2000 (Regulated Activities) (Amendment) Order 2014, SI 2014/366, art 2(1), (46).

90–97   *((Pts IV–6) outside the scope of this work.)*

(Schedules 1–8 are outside the scope of this work.)

Part 2   Statutory Instruments

LATE PAYMENT OF COMMERCIAL DEBTS REGULATIONS 2002

(SI 2002/1674)

NOTES
Made: 22 June 2002.
Authority: European Communities Act 1972, s 2(2).
Commencement: 7 August 2002.

[2.228]
1 Citation, commencement and extent

(1) These Regulations may be cited as the Late Payment of Commercial Debts Regulations 2002 and shall come into force on 7th August 2002.

(2) These Regulations extend to England and Wales and Northern Ireland.

2 (*Amends the Late Payment of Commercial Debts (Interest) Act 1998, ss 2, 3 at* **[1.1227]**, **[1.1228]**, *and inserts s 5A thereof at* **[1.1231]**.)

[2.229]
3 Proceedings restraining use of grossly unfair terms

(1) In this regulation:

(a) "small and medium-sized enterprises" means those enterprises defined in Annex 1 to Commission Regulation (EC) No 70/2001 of 12th January 2001 on the application of Articles 87 and 88 of the EC Treaty to State aid to small and medium-sized enterprises;

(b) "representative body" means an organisation established to represent the collective interests of small and medium-sized enterprises in general or in a particular sector or area.

(2) This regulation applies where a person acting in the course of a business has written standard terms on which he enters (or intends to enter) as purchaser into contracts to which the Late Payment of Commercial Debts (Interest) Act 1998 applies which include a term purporting to oust or vary the right to statutory interest in relation to qualifying debts created by those contracts.

(3) If it appears to the High Court that in all or any circumstances the purported use of such a term in a relevant contract would be void under the Late Payment of Commercial Debts (Interest) Act 1998, the court on the application of a representative body may grant an injunction against that person restraining him in those circumstances from using the offending term, on such terms as the court may think fit.

(4) Only a representative body may apply to the High Court under this regulation.

4 (*Revokes the Late Payment of Commercial Debts (Interest) (Legal Aid Exceptions) Order 1998, SI 1998/2482.*)

[2.230]
5 Saving for existing contracts

These Regulations do not affect contracts made before 7th August 2002.

ELECTRONIC COMMERCE (EC DIRECTIVE) REGULATIONS 2002

(SI 2002/2013)

NOTES
Made: 30 July 2002.
Authority: European Communities Act 1972, s 2(2).
Commencement: 21 August 2002 (regs 1–15, 17–22, Schedule); 23 October 2002 (reg 16).

ARRANGEMENT OF REGULATIONS

[2.231]
1 Citation and commencement
(1) These Regulations may be cited as the Electronic Commerce (EC Directive) Regulations 2002 and except for regulation 16 shall come into force on 21st August 2002.

(2) Regulation 16 shall come into force on 23rd October 2002.

[2.232]
2 Interpretation
(1) In these Regulations and in the Schedule—
    "commercial communication" means a communication, in any form, designed to promote, directly or indirectly, the goods, services or image of any person pursuing a commercial, industrial or craft activity or exercising a regulated profession, other than a communication—
        (a) consisting only of information allowing direct access to the activity of that person including a geographic address, a domain name or an electronic mail address; or
        (b) relating to the goods, services or image of that person provided that the communication has been prepared independently of the person making it (and for this purpose, a communication prepared without financial consideration is to be taken to have been prepared independently unless the contrary is shown);
    "the Commission" means the Commission of the [European Union];
    "consumer" means any natural person who is acting for purposes other than those of his trade, business or profession;
    "coordinated field" means requirements applicable to information society service providers or information society services, regardless of whether they are of a general nature or specifically designed for them, and covers requirements with which the service provider has to comply in respect of—
        (a) the taking up of the activity of an information society service, such as requirements concerning qualifications, authorisation or notification, and
        (b) the pursuit of the activity of an information society service, such as requirements concerning the behaviour of the service provider, requirements regarding the quality or content of the service including those applicable to advertising and contracts, or requirements concerning the liability of the service provider,
    but does not cover requirements such as those applicable to goods as such, to the delivery of goods or to services not provided by electronic means;
    "the Directive" means Directive 2000/31/EC of the European Parliament and of the Council of 8 June 2000 on certain legal aspects of information society services, in particular electronic commerce, in the Internal Market (Directive on electronic commerce);
    ["EEA Agreement" has the meaning given by Schedule 1 to the Interpretation Act 1978;]
    "enactment" includes an enactment comprised in Northern Ireland legislation and comprised in, or an instrument made under, an Act of the Scottish Parliament;
    "enforcement action" means any form of enforcement action including, in particular—
        (a) in relation to any legal requirement imposed by or under any enactment, any action taken with a view to or in connection with imposing any sanction (whether criminal or otherwise) for failure to observe or comply with it; and
        (b) in relation to a permission or authorisation, anything done with a view to removing or restricting that permission or authorisation;
    "enforcement authority" does not include courts but, subject to that, means any person who is authorised, whether by or under an enactment or otherwise, to take enforcement action;
    "established service provider" means a service provider who is a national of a member State or a company or firm as mentioned in [Article 54] of the Treaty and who effectively pursues an economic activity by virtue of which he is a service provider using a fixed establishment in a member State for an indefinite period, but the presence and use of the technical means and technologies required to provide the information society service do not, in themselves, constitute an establishment of the provider; in cases where it cannot be determined from

which of a number of places of establishment a given service is provided, that service is to be regarded as provided from the place of establishment where the provider has the centre of his activities relating to that service; references to a service provider being established or to the establishment of a service provider shall be construed accordingly;

"information society services" (which is summarised in recital 17 of the Directive as covering "any service normally provided for remuneration, at a distance, by means of electronic equipment for the processing (including digital compression) and storage of data, and at the individual request of a recipient of a service") has the meaning set out in Article 2(a) of the Directive, (which refers to Article 1(2) of Directive 98/34/EC of the European Parliament and of the Council of 22 June 1998 laying down a procedure for the provision of information in the field of technical standards and regulations, as amended by Directive 98/48/EC of 20 July 1998);

"member State" includes a State which is a contracting party to the EEA Agreement;

"recipient of the service" means any person who, for professional ends or otherwise, uses an information society service, in particular for the purposes of seeking information or making it accessible;

"regulated profession" means any profession within the meaning of either Article 1(d) of Council Directive 89/48/EEC of 21 December 1988 on a general system for the recognition of higher-education diplomas awarded on completion of professional education and training of at least three years' duration or of Article 1(f) of Council Directive 92/51/EEC of 18 June 1992 on a second general system for the recognition of professional education and training to supplement Directive 89/48/EEC;

"service provider" means any person providing an information society service;

"the Treaty" means [the Treaty on the Functioning of the European Union].

(2)   In regulation 4 and 5, "requirement" means any legal requirement under the law of the United Kingdom, or any part of it, imposed by or under any enactment or otherwise.

(3)   Terms used in the Directive other than those in paragraph (1) above shall have the same meaning as in the Directive.

NOTES

Para (1): in definition "the Commission" words in square brackets substituted by the Treaty of Lisbon (Changes in Terminology) Order 2011, SI 2011/1043, art 4(1); definition "EEA Agreement" substituted by the Broadcasting and Communications (Amendment) Regulations 2013, SI 2013/2217, reg 8; words in square brackets in definitions "established service provider" and "the Treaty" substituted by the Treaty of Lisbon (Changes in Terminology or Numbering) Order 2012, SI 2012/1809, art 3, Schedule, Pt 2.

[2.233]
3   Exclusions

(1)   Nothing in these Regulations shall apply in respect of—

   (a)   the field of taxation;
   (b)   questions relating to information society services covered by the Data Protection Directive and the Telecommunications Data Protection Directive and Directive 2002/58/EC of the European Parliament and of the Council of 12th July 2002 concerning the processing of personal data and the protection of privacy in the electronic communications sector (Directive on privacy and electronic communications);
   (c)   questions relating to agreements or practices governed by cartel law; and
   (d)   the following activities of information society services—
      (i)   the activities of a public notary or equivalent professions to the extent that they involve a direct and specific connection with the exercise of public authority,
      (ii)   the representation of a client and defence of his interests before the courts, and
      (iii)   betting, gaming or lotteries which involve wagering a stake with monetary value.

[(2)   These Regulations shall not apply in relation to any Act passed on or after the date these Regulations are made or in relation to the exercise of a power to legislate after that date.]

(3)   In this regulation—

"cartel law" means so much of the law relating to agreements between undertakings, decisions by associations of undertakings or concerted practices as relates to agreements to divide the market or fix prices;

"Data Protection Directive" means Directive 95/46/EC of the European Parliament and of the Council of 24 October 1995 on the protection of individuals with regard to the processing of personal data and on the free movement of such data; and

"Telecommunications Data Protection Directive" means Directive 97/66/EC of the European Parliament and of the Council of 15 December 1997 concerning the processing of personal data and the protection of privacy in the telecommunications sector.

NOTES

Para (2): substituted by the Electronic Commerce (EC Directive) (Extension) Regulations 2004, SI 2004/1178, reg 3.

[2.234]

4   Internal market

(1)   Subject to paragraph (4) below, any requirement which falls within the coordinated field shall apply to the provision of an information society service by a service provider established in the United Kingdom irrespective of whether that information society service is provided in the United Kingdom or another member State.

(2)   Subject to paragraph (4) below, an enforcement authority with responsibility in relation to any requirement in paragraph (1) shall ensure that the provision of an information society service by a service provider established in the United Kingdom complies with that requirement irrespective of whether that service is provided in the United Kingdom or another member State and any power, remedy or procedure for taking enforcement action shall be available to secure compliance.

(3)   Subject to paragraphs (4), (5) and (6) below, any requirement shall not be applied to the provision of an information society service by a service provider established in a member State other than the United Kingdom for reasons which fall within the coordinated field where its application would restrict the freedom to provide information society services to a person in the United Kingdom from that member State.

(4)   Paragraphs (1), (2) and (3) shall not apply to those fields in the annex to the Directive set out in the Schedule.

(5)   The reference to any requirements the application of which would restrict the freedom to provide information society services from another member State in paragraph (3) above does not include any requirement maintaining the level of protection for public health and consumer interests established by Community acts.

(6)   To the extent that anything in these Regulations creates any new criminal offence, it shall not be punishable with imprisonment for more than two years or punishable on summary conviction with imprisonment for more than three months or with a fine of more than level 5 on the standard scale (if not calculated on a daily basis) or with a fine of more than £100 a day.

[2.235]

5   Derogations from Regulation 4

(1)   Notwithstanding regulation 4(3), an enforcement authority may take measures, including applying any requirement which would otherwise not apply by virtue of regulation 4(3) in respect of a given information society service, where those measures are necessary for reasons of—

    (a)   public policy, in particular the prevention, investigation, detection and prosecution of criminal offences, including the protection of minors and the fight against any incitement to hatred on grounds of race, sex, religion or nationality, and violations of human dignity concerning individual persons;

    (b)   the protection of public health;

    (c)   public security, including the safeguarding of national security and defence, or

    (d)   the protection of consumers, including investors,

and proportionate to those objectives.

(2)   Notwithstanding regulation 4(3), in any case where an enforcement authority with responsibility in relation to the requirement in question is not party to the proceedings, a court may, on the application of any person or of its own motion, apply any requirement which would otherwise not apply by virtue of regulation 4(3) in respect of a given information society service, if the application of that enactment or requirement is necessary for and proportionate to any of the objectives set out in paragraph (1) above.

(3)   Paragraphs (1) and (2) shall only apply where the information society service prejudices or presents a serious and grave risk of prejudice to an objective in paragraph (1)(a) to (d).

(4)   Subject to paragraphs (5) and (6), an enforcement authority shall not take the measures in paragraph (1) above, unless it—

    (a)   asks the member State in which the service provider is established to take measures and the member State does not take such measures or they are inadequate; and

    (b)   notifies the Commission and the member State in which the service provider is established of its intention to take such measures.

(5)   Paragraph (4) shall not apply to court proceedings, including preliminary proceedings and acts carried out in the course of a criminal investigation.

(6)   If it appears to the enforcement authority that the matter is one of urgency, it may take the measures under paragraph (1) without first asking the member State in which the service provider is established to take measures and notifying the Commission and the member State in derogation from paragraph (4).

(7)   In a case where a measure is taken pursuant to paragraph (6) above, the enforcement authority shall notify the measures taken to the Commission and to the member State concerned in the shortest possible time thereafter and indicate the reasons for urgency.

(8)   In paragraph (2), "court" means any court or tribunal.

Part 2   Statutory Instruments

[2.236]
6 General information to be provided by a person providing an information society service

(1)   A person providing an information society service shall make available to the recipient of the service and any relevant enforcement authority, in a form and manner which is easily, directly and permanently accessible, the following information—

(a)   the name of the service provider;

(b)   the geographic address at which the service provider is established;

(c)   the details of the service provider, including his electronic mail address, which make it possible to contact him rapidly and communicate with him in a direct and effective manner;

(d)   where the service provider is registered in a trade or similar register available to the public, details of the register in which the service provider is entered and his registration number, or equivalent means of identification in that register;

(e)   where the provision of the service is subject to an authorisation scheme, the particulars of the relevant supervisory authority;

(f)   where the service provider exercises a regulated profession—

   (i)   the details of any professional body or similar institution with which the service provider is registered;

   (ii)   his professional title and the member State where that title has been granted;

   (iii)   a reference to the professional rules applicable to the service provider in the member State of establishment and the means to access them; and

(g)   where the service provider undertakes an activity that is subject to value added tax, the identification number referred to in Article 22(1) of the sixth Council Directive 77/388/EEC of 17 May 1977 on the harmonisation of the laws of the member States relating to turnover taxes—Common system of value added tax: uniform basis of assessment.

(2)   Where a person providing an information society service refers to prices, these shall be indicated clearly and unambiguously and, in particular, shall indicate whether they are inclusive of tax and delivery costs.

[2.237]
7   Commercial communications

A service provider shall ensure that any commercial communication provided by him and which constitutes or forms part of an information society service shall—

(a)   be clearly identifiable as a commercial communication;

(b)   clearly identify the person on whose behalf the commercial communication is made;

(c)   clearly identify as such any promotional offer (including any discount, premium or gift) and ensure that any conditions which must be met to qualify for it are easily accessible, and presented clearly and unambiguously; and

(d)   clearly identify as such any promotional competition or game and ensure that any conditions for participation are easily accessible and presented clearly and unambiguously.

[2.238]
8   Unsolicited commercial communications

A service provider shall ensure that any unsolicited commercial communication sent by him by electronic mail is clearly and unambiguously identifiable as such as soon as it is received.

[2.239]
9   Information to be provided where contracts are concluded by electronic means

(1)   Unless parties who are not consumers have agreed otherwise, where a contract is to be concluded by electronic means a service provider shall, prior to an order being placed by the recipient of a service, provide to that recipient in a clear, comprehensible and unambiguous manner the information set out in (a) to (d) below—

(a)   the different technical steps to follow to conclude the contract;

(b)   whether or not the concluded contract will be filed by the service provider and whether it will be accessible;

(c)   the technical means for identifying and correcting input errors prior to the placing of the order; and

(d)   the languages offered for the conclusion of the contract.

(2)   Unless parties who are not consumers have agreed otherwise, a service provider shall indicate which relevant codes of conduct he subscribes to and give information on how those codes can be consulted electronically.

(3)   Where the service provider provides terms and conditions applicable to the contract to the recipient, the service provider shall make them available to him in a way that allows him to store and reproduce them.

(4)   The requirements of paragraphs (1) and (2) above shall not apply to contracts concluded exclusively by exchange of electronic mail or by equivalent individual communications.

[2.240]
10   Other information requirements

Regulations 6, 7, 8 and 9(1) have effect in addition to any other information requirements in legislation giving effect to [EU] law.

NOTES
Reference in square brackets substituted by the Treaty of Lisbon (Changes in Terminology) Order 2011, SI 2011/1043, art 6(2)(a).

[2.241]
11   Placing of the order

(1)   Unless parties who are not consumers have agreed otherwise, where the recipient of the service places his order through technological means, a service provider shall–
    (a)   acknowledge receipt of the order to the recipient of the service without undue delay and by electronic means; and
    (b)   make available to the recipient of the service appropriate, effective and accessible technical means allowing him to identify and correct input errors prior to the placing of the order.

(2)   For the purposes of paragraph (1)(a) above—
    (a)   the order and the acknowledgement of receipt will be deemed to be received when the parties to whom they are addressed are able to access them; and
    (b)   the acknowledgement of receipt may take the form of the provision of the service paid for where that service is an information society service.

(3)   The requirements of paragraph (1) above shall not apply to contracts concluded exclusively by exchange of electronic mail or by equivalent individual communications.

[2.242]
12   Meaning of the term "order"

Except in relation to regulation 9(1)(c) and regulation 11(1)(b) where "order" shall be the contractual offer, "order" may be but need not be the contractual offer for the purposes of regulations 9 and 11.

[2.243]
13   Liability of the service provider

The duties imposed by regulations 6, 7, 8, 9(1) and 11(1)(a) shall be enforceable, at the suit of any recipient of a service, by an action against the service provider for damages for breach of statutory duty.

[2.244]
14   Compliance with Regulation 9(3)

Where on request a service provider has failed to comply with the requirement in regulation 9(3), the recipient may seek an order from any court having jurisdiction in relation to the contract requiring that service provider to comply with that requirement.

[2.245]
15   Right to rescind contract

Where a person—
    (a)   has entered into a contract to which these Regulations apply, and
    (b)   the service provider has not made available means of allowing him to identify and correct input errors in compliance with regulation 11(1)(b),
he shall be entitled to rescind the contract unless any court having jurisdiction in relation to the contract in question orders otherwise on the application of the service provider.

16   (*Amends the Stop Now Orders (EC Directive) Regulations 2001, SI 2001/1422, reg 2, Sch 1.*)

[2.246]
17   Mere conduit

(1)   Where an information society service is provided which consists of the transmission in a communication network of information provided by a recipient of the service or the provision of access to a communication network, the service provider (if he otherwise would) shall not be liable for damages or for any other pecuniary remedy or for any criminal sanction as a result of that transmission where the service provider—
    (a)   did not initiate the transmission;
    (b)   did not select the receiver of the transmission; and
    (c)   did not select or modify the information contained in the transmission.

(2)   The acts of transmission and of provision of access referred to in paragraph (1) include the automatic, intermediate and transient storage of the information transmitted where—
    (a)   this takes place for the sole purpose of carrying out the transmission in the communication network, and

Part 2   Statutory Instruments

(b) the information is not stored for any period longer than is reasonably necessary for the transmission.

[2.247]
18 Caching

Where an information society service is provided which consists of the transmission in a communication network of information provided by a recipient of the service, the service provider (if he otherwise would) shall not be liable for damages or for any other pecuniary remedy or for any criminal sanction as a result of that transmission where—

(a) the information is the subject of automatic, intermediate and temporary storage where that storage is for the sole purpose of making more efficient onward transmission of the information to other recipients of the service upon their request, and

(b) the service provider—
  (i) does not modify the information;
  (ii) complies with conditions on access to the information;
  (iii) complies with any rules regarding the updating of the information, specified in a manner widely recognised and used by industry;
  (iv) does not interfere with the lawful use of technology, widely recognised and used by industry, to obtain data on the use of the information; and
  (v) acts expeditiously to remove or to disable access to the information he has stored upon obtaining actual knowledge of the fact that the information at the initial source of the transmission has been removed from the network, or access to it has been disabled, or that a court or an administrative authority has ordered such removal or disablement.

[2.248]
19 Hosting

Where an information society service is provided which consists of the storage of information provided by a recipient of the service, the service provider (if he otherwise would) shall not be liable for damages or for any other pecuniary remedy or for any criminal sanction as a result of that storage where—

(a) the service provider—
  (i) does not have actual knowledge of unlawful activity or information and, where a claim for damages is made, is not aware of facts or circumstances from which it would have been apparent to the service provider that the activity or information was unlawful; or
  (ii) upon obtaining such knowledge or awareness, acts expeditiously to remove or to disable access to the information, and

(b) the recipient of the service was not acting under the authority or the control of the service provider.

[2.249]
20 Protection of rights

(1) Nothing in regulations 17, 18 and 19 shall—
(a) prevent a person agreeing different contractual terms; or
(b) affect the rights of any party to apply to a court for relief to prevent or stop infringement of any rights.

(2) Any power of an administrative authority to prevent or stop infringement of any rights shall continue to apply notwithstanding regulations 17, 18 and 19.

[2.250]
21 Defence in Criminal Proceedings: burden of proof

(1) This regulation applies where a service provider charged with an offence in criminal proceedings arising out of any transmission, provision of access or storage falling within regulation 17, 18 or 19 relies on a defence under any of regulations 17, 18 and 19.

(2) Where evidence is adduced which is sufficient to raise an issue with respect to that defence, the court or jury shall assume that the defence is satisfied unless the prosecution proves beyond reasonable doubt that it is not.

[2.251]
22 Notice for the purposes of actual knowledge

In determining whether a service provider has actual knowledge for the purposes of regulations 18(b)(v) and 19(a)(i), a court shall take into account all matters which appear to it in the particular circumstances to be relevant and, among other things, shall have regard to—

(a) whether a service provider has received a notice through a means of contact made available in accordance with regulation 6(1)(c), and

(b) the extent to which any notice includes—
  (i) the full name and address of the sender of the notice;

(ii) details of the location of the information in question; and

(iii) details of the unlawful nature of the activity or information in question.

SCHEDULE

Regulation 4(4)

[2.252]

1. Copyright, neighbouring rights, rights referred to in Directive 87/54/EEC and Directive 96/9/EC and industrial property rights.

2. The freedom of the parties to a contract to choose the applicable law.

3. Contractual obligations concerning consumer contracts.

4. Formal validity of contracts creating or transferring rights in real estate where such contracts are subject to mandatory formal requirements of the law of the member State where the real estate is situated.

5. The permissibility of unsolicited commercial communications by electronic mail.

SALE AND SUPPLY OF GOODS TO CONSUMERS REGULATIONS 2002

(SI 2002/3045)

NOTES

Made: 10 December 2002.

Authority: European Communities Act 1972, s 2(2).

Commencement: 31 March 2003.

These Regulations were revoked by the Consumer Rights Act 2015, s 60, Sch 1, para 53, as from 1 October 2015, subject to transitional provisions in relation to the amendments made by these Regulations; see the Consumer Rights Act 2015 (Commencement No 3, Transitional Provisions, Savings and Consequential Amendments) Order 2015, SI 2015/1630, art 6(3) at **[2.1220]**.

[2.253]

1   Title, commencement and extent

(1)   These Regulations may be cited as the Sale and Supply of Goods to Consumers Regulations 2002 and shall come into force on 31st March 2003.

(2)   These Regulations extend to Northern Ireland.

NOTES

Revoked by the Consumer Rights Act 2015, s 60, Sch 1, para 53, as from 1 October 2015, subject to transitional provisions as noted in the introductory notes to this Order *ante*.

[2.254]

2   Interpretation

In these Regulations—

  "consumer" means any natural person who, in the contracts covered by these Regulations, is acting for purposes which are outside his trade, business or profession;

  "consumer guarantee" means any undertaking to a consumer by a person acting in the course of his business, given without extra charge, to reimburse the price paid or to replace, repair or handle consumer goods in any way if they do not meet the specifications set out in the guarantee statement or in the relevant advertising;

  "court" in relation to England and Wales and Northern Ireland means a county court or the High Court, and in relation to Scotland, the sheriff or the Court of Session;

  "enforcement authority" means [the Competition and Markets Authority], every local weights and measures authority in Great Britain and the Department of Enterprise, Trade and Investment for Northern Ireland;

  "goods" has the same meaning as in section 61 of the Sale of Goods Act 1979;

  "guarantor" means a person who offers a consumer guarantee to a consumer; and

  "supply" includes supply by way of sale, lease, hire or hire-purchase.

NOTES

Revoked as noted to reg 1 at **[2.253]**.

In definition "enforcement authority" words in square brackets substituted by the Enterprise and Regulatory Reform Act 2013 (Competition) (Consequential, Transitional and Saving Provisions) (No 2) Order 2014, SI 2014/549, art 2, Sch 1, Pt 1, para 7 (for transitional provisions in relation to the continuity of functions, etc, see art 3 of the 2014 Order).

3–14 (*Revoked as noted to reg 1 at* [2.253]; *reg 3 amends the Sale of Goods Act 1979, s 14 at* [1.842]; *reg 4 amends s 20 of the 1979 Act, at* [1.849]; *reg 5 inserts Pt 5A of the 1979 Act at* [1.880]; *reg 6 amends s 61(1) of the 1979 Act at* [1.897]; *reg 7 amends s 4 of the Supply of Goods and Services Act 1982; reg 8 amends s 11D of the 1982 Act; reg 9 inserts Pt 1B of the 1982 Act; reg 10 amends s 9 of the 1982 Act at* [1.924]; *reg 11 amends s 11J of the 1982 Act; reg 12 amends s 18(1) of the 1982 Act at* [1.939]; *reg 13 amends s 10 of the Supply of Goods (Implied Terms) Act 1973 at* [1.492]; *reg 14 amends ss 12, 25 of the Unfair Contract Terms Act 1977 at* [1.741]).

[2.255]
15   Consumer guarantees

(1)   Where goods are sold or otherwise supplied to a consumer which are offered with a consumer guarantee, the consumer guarantee takes effect at the time the goods are delivered as a contractual obligation owed by the guarantor under the conditions set out in the guarantee statement and the associated advertising.

(2)   The guarantor shall ensure that the guarantee sets out in plain intelligible language the contents of the guarantee and the essential particulars necessary for making claims under the guarantee, notably the duration and territorial scope of the guarantee as well as the name and address of the guarantor.

[(2A)   The guarantor shall also ensure that the guarantee contains a statement that the consumer has statutory rights in relation to the goods which are sold or supplied and that those rights are not affected by the guarantee.]

(3)   On request by the consumer to a person to whom paragraph (4) applies, the guarantee shall within a reasonable time be made available in writing or in another durable medium available and accessible to him.

(4)   This paragraph applies to the guarantor and any other person who offers to consumers the goods which are the subject of the guarantee for sale or supply.

(5)   Where consumer goods are offered with a consumer guarantee, and where those goods are offered within the territory of the United Kingdom, then the guarantor shall ensure that the consumer guarantee is written in English.

(6)   If the guarantor fails to comply with the provisions of paragraphs (2) or (5) above, or a person to whom paragraph (4) applies fails to comply with paragraph (3) then the enforcement authority may apply for an injunction or (in Scotland) an order of specific implement against that person requiring him to comply.

(7)   The court on application under this Regulation may grant an injunction or (in Scotland) an order of specific implement on such terms as it thinks fit.

NOTES
Revoked as noted to reg 1 at [2.253].
Para (2A): inserted by the Consumer Protection from Unfair Trading Regulations 2008, SI 2008/1277, reg 30(1), Sch 2, Pt 2, para 97.

PRIVACY AND ELECTRONIC COMMUNICATIONS (EC DIRECTIVE) REGULATIONS 2003

(SI 2003/2426)

NOTES
Made: 18 September 2003.
Authority: European Communities Act 1972, s 2(2).
Commencement: 11 December 2003.

ARRANGEMENT OF ARTICLES

SCHEDULES

[2.256]
1   Citation and commencement
These Regulations may be cited as the Privacy and Electronic Communications (EC Directive)
Regulations 2003 and shall come into force on 11th December 2003.

[2.257]
2   Interpretation
(1)   In these Regulations—
   "bill" includes an invoice, account, statement or other document of similar character and
        "billing" shall be construed accordingly;
   "call" means a connection established by means of a telephone service available to the public
        allowing two-way communication in real time;
   "communication" means any information exchanged or conveyed between a finite number of
        parties by means of a public electronic communications service, but does not include
        information conveyed as part of a programme service, except to the extent that such
        information can be related to the identifiable subscriber or user receiving the information;
   "communications provider" has the meaning given by section 405 of the Communications
        Act 2003;
   "corporate subscriber" means a subscriber who is—
        (a)   a company within the meaning of section 735(1) of the Companies Act 1985;
        (b)   a company incorporated in pursuance of a royal charter or letters patent;
        (c)   a partnership in Scotland;
        (d)   a corporation sole; or
        (e)   any other body corporate or entity which is a legal person distinct from its members;
   "the Directive" means Directive 2002/58/EC of the European Parliament and of the Council of
        12 July 2002 concerning the processing of personal data and the protection of privacy in
        the electronic communications sector (Directive on privacy and electronic
        communications);

"electronic communications network" has the meaning given by section 32 of the Communications Act 2003;

"electronic communications service" has the meaning given by section 32 of the Communications Act 2003;

"electronic mail" means any text, voice, sound or image message sent over a public electronic communications network which can be stored in the network or in the recipient's terminal equipment until it is collected by the recipient and includes messages sent using a short message service;

"enactment" includes an enactment comprised in, or in an instrument made under, an Act of the Scottish Parliament;

"individual" means a living individual and includes an unincorporated body of such individuals;

"the Information Commissioner" and "the Commissioner" both mean the Commissioner appointed under section 6 of the Data Protection Act 1998;

"information society service" has the meaning given in regulation 2(1) of the Electronic Commerce (EC Directive) Regulations 2002;

"location data" means any data processed in an electronic communications network [or by an electronic communications service] indicating the geographical position of the terminal equipment of a user of a public electronic communications service, including data relating to—

    (f) the latitude, longitude or altitude of the terminal equipment;

    (g) the direction of travel of the user; or

    (h) the time the location information was recorded;

"OFCOM" means the Office of Communications as established by section 1 of the Office of Communications Act 2002;

["personal data breach" means a breach of security leading to the accidental or unlawful destruction, loss, alteration, unauthorised disclosure of, or access to, personal data transmitted, stored or otherwise processed in connection with the provision of a public electronic communications service;]

"programme service" has the meaning given in section 201 of the Broadcasting Act 1990;

"public communications provider" means a provider of a public electronic communications network or a public electronic communications service;

"public electronic communications network" has the meaning given in section 151 of the Communications Act 2003;

"public electronic communications service" has the meaning given in section 151 of the Communications Act 2003;

"subscriber" means a person who is a party to a contract with a provider of public electronic communications services for the supply of such services;

"traffic data" means any data processed for the purpose of the conveyance of a communication on an electronic communications network or for the billing in respect of that communication and includes data relating to the routing, duration or time of a communication;

"user" means any individual using a public electronic communications service; and

"value added service" means any service which requires the processing of traffic data or location data beyond that which is necessary for the transmission of a communication or the billing in respect of that communication.

(2) Expressions used in these Regulations that are not defined in paragraph (1) and are defined in the Data Protection Act 1998 shall have the same meaning as in that Act.

(3) Expressions used in these Regulations that are not defined in paragraph (1) or the Data Protection Act 1998 and are defined in the Directive shall have the same meaning as in the Directive.

(4) Any reference in these Regulations to a line shall, without prejudice to paragraph (3), be construed as including a reference to anything that performs the function of a line, and "connected", in relation to a line, is to be construed accordingly.

NOTES

Para (1): words in square brackets in definition "location data" inserted and definition "personal data breach" inserted by the Privacy and Electronic Communications (EC Directive) (Amendment) Regulations 2011, SI 2011/1208, regs 2, 3.

3 (*Revokes the Telecommunications (Data Protection and Privacy) Regulations 1999, SI 1999/2093, and the amending SI 2000/157.*)

[2.258]

4 Relationship between these Regulations and the Data Protection Act 1998

Nothing in these Regulations shall relieve a person of his obligations under the Data Protection Act 1998 in relation to the processing of personal data.

[2.259]
5   Security of public electronic communications services

(1)   Subject to paragraph (2), a provider of a public electronic communications service ("the service provider") shall take appropriate technical and organisational measures to safeguard the security of that service.

[(1A)   The measures referred to in paragraph (1) shall at least—
   (a)   ensure that personal data can be accessed only by authorised personnel for legally authorised purposes;
   (b)   protect personal data stored or transmitted against accidental or unlawful destruction, accidental loss or alteration, and unauthorised or unlawful storage, processing, access or disclosure; and
   (c)   ensure the implementation of a security policy with respect to the processing of personal data.]

(2)   If necessary, the measures required by paragraph (1) may be taken by the service provider in conjunction with the provider of the electronic communications network by means of which the service is provided, and that network provider shall comply with any reasonable requests made by the service provider for these purposes.

(3)   Where, notwithstanding the taking of measures as required by paragraph (1), there remains a significant risk to the security of the public electronic communications service, the service provider shall inform the subscribers concerned of—
   (a)   the nature of that risk;
   (b)   any appropriate measures that the subscriber may take to safeguard against that risk; and
   (c)   the likely costs to the subscriber involved in the taking of such measures.

(4)   For the purposes of paragraph (1), a measure shall only be taken to be appropriate if, having regard to—
   (a)   the state of technological developments, and
   (b)   the cost of implementing it,
it is proportionate to the risks against which it would safeguard.

(5)   Information provided for the purposes of paragraph (3) shall be provided to the subscriber free of any charge other than the cost to the subscriber of receiving or collecting the information.

[(6)   The Information Commissioner may audit the measures taken by a provider of a public electronic communications service to safeguard the security of that service.]

NOTES
   Para (1A): inserted by the Privacy and Electronic Communications (EC Directive) (Amendment) Regulations 2011, SI 2011/1208, regs 2, 4(1).
   Para (6): added by SI 2011/1208, regs 2, 4(2).

[2.260]
[5A   Personal data breach

(1)   In this regulation and in regulations 5B and 5C, "service provider" has the meaning given in regulation 5(1).

(2)   If a personal data breach occurs, the service provider shall, without undue delay, notify that breach to the Information Commissioner.

(3)   Subject to paragraph (6), if a personal data breach is likely to adversely affect the personal data or privacy of a subscriber or user, the service provider shall also, without undue delay, notify that breach to the subscriber or user concerned.

(4)   The notification referred to in paragraph (2) shall contain at least a description of—
   (a)   the nature of the breach;
   (b)   the consequences of the breach; and
   (c)   the measures taken or proposed to be taken by the provider to address the breach.

(5)   The notification referred to the paragraph (3) shall contain at least—
   (a)   a description of the nature of the breach;
   (b)   information about contact points within the service provider's organisation from which more information may be obtained; and
   (c)   recommendations of measures to allow the subscriber to mitigate the possible adverse impacts of the breach.

(6)   The notification referred to in paragraph (3) is not required if the service provider has demonstrated, to the satisfaction of the Information Commissioner that—
   (a)   it has implemented appropriate technological protection measures which render the data unintelligible to any person who is not authorised to access it, and
   (b)   that those measures were applied to the data concerned in that breach.

(7)   If the service provider has not notified the subscriber or user in compliance with paragraph (3), the Information Commissioner may, having considered the likely adverse effects of the breach, require it to do so.

(8)   Service providers shall maintain an inventory of personal data breaches comprising—

    (a)   the facts surrounding the breach,

    (b)   the effects of that breach, and

    (c)   remedial action taken

which shall be sufficient to enable the Information Commissioner to verify compliance with the provisions of this regulation. The inventory shall only include information necessary for this purpose.]

NOTES

   Inserted, together with regs 5B, 5C, by the Privacy and Electronic Communications (EC Directive) (Amendment) Regulations 2011, SI 2011/1208, regs 2, 5.

[2.261]

[5B   Personal data breach: audit

The Information Commissioner may audit the compliance of service providers with the provisions of regulation 5A.]

NOTES

   Inserted as noted to reg 5A at **[2.260]**.

[2.262]

[5C   Personal data breach: enforcement

(1)   If a service provider fails to comply with the notification requirements of regulation 5A, the Information Commissioner may issue a fixed monetary penalty notice in respect of that failure.

(2)   The amount of a fixed monetary penalty under this regulation shall be £1,000.

(3)   Before serving such a notice, the Information Commissioner must serve the service provider with a notice of intent.

(4)   The notice of intent must—

    (a)   state the name and address of the service provider;

    (b)   state the nature of the breach;

    (c)   indicate the amount of the fixed monetary penalty;

    (d)   include a statement informing the service provider of the opportunity to discharge liability for the fixed monetary penalty;

    (e)   indicate the date on which the Information Commissioner proposes to serve the fixed monetary penalty notice; and

    (f)   inform the service provider that he may make written representations in relation to the proposal to serve a fixed monetary penalty notice within the period of 21 days from the service of the notice of intent.

(5)   A service provider may discharge liability for the fixed monetary penalty if he pays to the Information Commissioner the amount of £800 within 21 days of receipt of the notice of intent.

(6)   The Information Commissioner may not serve a fixed monetary penalty notice until the time within which representations may be made has expired.

(7)   The fixed monetary penalty notice must state—

    (a)   the name and address of the service provider;

    (b)   details of the notice of intent served on the service provider;

    (c)   whether there have been any written representations;

    (d)   details of any early payment discounts;

    (e)   the grounds on which the Information Commissioner imposes the fixed monetary penalty;

    (f)   the date by which the fixed monetary penalty is to be paid; and

    (g)   details of, including the time limit for, the service provider's right of appeal against the imposition of the fixed monetary penalty.

(8)   A service provider on whom a fixed monetary penalty is served may appeal to the Tribunal against the issue of the fixed monetary penalty notice.

(9)   Any sum received by the Information Commissioner by virtue of this regulation must be paid into the Consolidated Fund.

(10)   In England and Wales and Northern Ireland, the penalty is recoverable—

    (a)   if a county court so orders, as if it were payable under an order of that court;

    (b)   if the High Court so orders, as if it were payable under an order of that court.

(11)   In Scotland, the penalty may be enforced in the same manner as an extract registered decree arbitral bearing a warrant for execution issued by the sheriff court of any sheriffdom in Scotland.]

NOTES

   Inserted as noted to reg 5A at **[2.260]**.

[2.263]

6   Confidentiality of communications

(1)   Subject to paragraph (4), a person shall not [store or] gain access to information stored, in the terminal equipment of a subscriber or user unless the requirements of paragraph (2) are met.

(2)   The requirements are that the subscriber or user of that terminal equipment—

(a)   is provided with clear and comprehensive information about the purposes of the storage of, or access to, that information; and

[(b)   has given his or her consent.]

(3)   Where an electronic communications network is used by the same person to store or access information in the terminal equipment of a subscriber or user on more than one occasion, it is sufficient for the purposes of this regulation that the requirements of paragraph (2) are met in respect of the initial use.

[(3A)   For the purposes of paragraph (2), consent may be signified by a subscriber who amends or sets controls on the internet browser which the subscriber uses or by using another application or programme to signify consent.]

(4)   Paragraph (1) shall not apply to the technical storage of, or access to, information—

(a)   for the sole purpose of carrying out . . .   the transmission of a communication over an electronic communications network; or

(b)   where such storage or access is strictly necessary for the provision of an information society service requested by the subscriber or user.

NOTES

Para (1): words in square brackets substituted by the Privacy and Electronic Communications (EC Directive) (Amendment) Regulations 2011, SI 2011/1208, regs 2, 6(1), (2).

Para (2): sub-para (b) substituted by SI 2011/1208, regs 2, 6(1), (3).

Para (3A): inserted by SI 2011/1208, regs 2, 6(1), (4).

Para (4): words omitted revoked by SI 2011/1208, regs 2, 6(1), (5).

[2.264]
7   Restrictions on the processing of certain traffic data

(1)   Subject to paragraphs (2) and (3), traffic data relating to subscribers or users which are processed and stored by a public communications provider shall, when no longer required for the purpose of the transmission of a communication, be—

(a)   erased;

(b)   in the case of an individual, modified so that they cease to constitute personal data of that subscriber or user; or

(c)   in the case of a corporate subscriber, modified so that they cease to be data that would be personal data if that subscriber was an individual.

(2)   Traffic data held by a public communications provider for purposes connected with the payment of charges by a subscriber or in respect of interconnection payments may be processed and stored by that provider until the time specified in paragraph (5).

(3)   Traffic data relating to a subscriber or user may be processed and stored by a provider of a public electronic communications service if—

(a)   such processing and storage are for the purpose of marketing electronic communications services, or for the provision of value added services to that subscriber or user; and

(b)   the subscriber or user to whom the traffic data relate has [previously notified the provider that he consents] to such processing or storage; and

(c)   such processing and storage are undertaken only for the duration necessary for the purposes specified in subparagraph (a).

(4)   Where a user or subscriber has given his consent in accordance with paragraph (3), he shall be able to withdraw it at any time.

(5)   The time referred to in paragraph (2) is the end of the period during which legal proceedings may be brought in respect of payments due or alleged to be due or, where such proceedings are brought within that period, the time when those proceedings are finally determined.

(6)   Legal proceedings shall not be taken to be finally determined—

(a)   until the conclusion of the ordinary period during which an appeal may be brought by either party (excluding any possibility of an extension of that period, whether by order of a court or otherwise), if no appeal is brought within that period; or

(b)   if an appeal is brought, until the conclusion of that appeal.

(7)   References in paragraph (6) to an appeal include references to an application for permission to appeal.

NOTES

Para (3): words in square brackets in sub-para (b) substituted by the Privacy and Electronic Communications (EC Directive) (Amendment) Regulations 2011, SI 2011/1208, regs 2, 7.

Part 2   Statutory Instruments

[2.265]

8   Further provisions relating to the processing of traffic data under regulation 7

(1)   Processing of traffic data in accordance with regulation 7(2) or (3) shall not be undertaken by a public communications provider unless the subscriber or user to whom the data relate has been provided with information regarding the types of traffic data which are to be processed and the duration of such processing and, in the case of processing in accordance with regulation 7(3), he has been provided with that information before his consent has been obtained.

(2)   Processing of traffic data in accordance with regulation 7 shall be restricted to what is required for the purposes of one or more of the activities listed in paragraph (3) and shall be carried out only by the public communications provider or by a person acting under his authority.

(3)   The activities referred to in paragraph (2) are activities relating to—
    (a)   the management of billing or traffic;
    (b)   customer enquiries;
    (c)   the prevention or detection of fraud;
    (d)   the marketing of electronic communications services; or
    (e)   the provision of a value added service.

(4)   Nothing in these Regulations shall prevent the furnishing of traffic data to a person who is a competent authority for the purposes of any provision relating to the settling of disputes (by way of legal proceedings or otherwise) which is contained in, or made by virtue of, any enactment.

[2.266]

9   Itemised billing and privacy

(1)   At the request of a subscriber, a provider of a public electronic communications service shall provide that subscriber with bills that are not itemised.

(2)   OFCOM shall have a duty, when exercising their functions under Chapter 1 of Part 2 of the Communications Act 2003, to have regard to the need to reconcile the rights of subscribers receiving itemised bills with the rights to privacy of calling users and called subscribers, including the need for sufficient alternative privacy-enhancing methods of communications or payments to be available to such users and subscribers.

[2.267]

10   Prevention of calling line identification—outgoing calls

(1)   This regulation applies, subject to regulations 15 and 16, to outgoing calls where a facility enabling the presentation of calling line identification is available.

(2)   The provider of a public electronic communications service shall provide users originating a call by means of that service with a simple means to prevent presentation of the identity of the calling line on the connected line as respects that call.

(3)   The provider of a public electronic communications service shall provide subscribers to the service, as respects their line and all calls originating from that line, with a simple means of preventing presentation of the identity of that subscriber's line on any connected line.

(4)   The measures to be provided under paragraphs (2) and (3) shall be provided free of charge.

[2.268]

11   Prevention of calling or connected line identification—incoming calls

(1)   This regulation applies to incoming calls.

(2)   Where a facility enabling the presentation of calling line identification is available, the provider of a public electronic communications service shall provide the called subscriber with a simple means to prevent, free of charge for reasonable use of the facility, presentation of the identity of the calling line on the connected line.

(3)   Where a facility enabling the presentation of calling line identification prior to the call being established is available, the provider of a public electronic communications service shall provide the called subscriber with a simple means of rejecting incoming calls where the presentation of the calling line identification has been prevented by the calling user or subscriber.

(4)   Where a facility enabling the presentation of connected line identification is available, the provider of a public electronic communications service shall provide the called subscriber with a simple means to prevent, without charge, presentation of the identity of the connected line on any calling line.

(5)   In this regulation "called subscriber" means the subscriber receiving a call by means of the service in question whose line is the called line (whether or not it is also the connected line).

[2.269]

12   Publication of information for the purposes of regulations 10 and 11

Where a provider of a public electronic communications service provides facilities for calling or connected line identification, he shall provide information to the public regarding the availability of such facilities, including information regarding the options to be made available for the purposes of regulations 10 and 11.

[2.270]
13   Co-operation of communications providers for the purposes of regulations 10 and 11

For the purposes of regulations 10 and 11, a communications provider shall comply with any reasonable requests made by the provider of the public electronic communications service by means of which facilities for calling or connected line identification are provided.

[2.271]
14   Restrictions on the processing of location data

(1)   This regulation shall not apply to the processing of traffic data.

(2)   Location data relating to a user or subscriber of a public electronic communications network or a public electronic communications service may only be processed—
    (a)   where that user or subscriber cannot be identified from such data; or
    (b)   where necessary for the provision of a value added service, with the consent of that user or subscriber.

(3)   Prior to obtaining the consent of the user or subscriber under paragraph (2)(b), the public communications provider in question must provide the following information to the user or subscriber to whom the data relate—
    (a)   the types of location data that will be processed;
    (b)   the purposes and duration of the processing of those data; and
    (c)   whether the data will be transmitted to a third party for the purpose of providing the value added service.

(4)   A user or subscriber who has given his consent to the processing of data under paragraph (2)(b) shall—
    (a)   be able to withdraw such consent at any time, and
    (b)   in respect of each connection to the public electronic communications network in question or each transmission of a communication, be given the opportunity to withdraw such consent, using a simple means and free of charge.

(5)   Processing of location data in accordance with this regulation shall—
    (a)   only be carried out by—
        (i)   the public communications provider in question;
        (ii)   the third party providing the value added service in question; or
        (iii)   a person acting under the authority of a person falling within (i) or (ii); and
    (b)   where the processing is carried out for the purposes of the provision of a value added service, be restricted to what is necessary for those purposes.

[2.272]
15   Tracing of malicious or nuisance calls

(1)   A communications provider may override anything done to prevent the presentation of the identity of a calling line where—
    (a)   a subscriber has requested the tracing of malicious or nuisance calls received on his line; and
    (b)   the provider is satisfied that such action is necessary and expedient for the purposes of tracing such calls.

(2)   Any term of a contract for the provision of public electronic communications services which relates to such prevention shall have effect subject to the provisions of paragraph (1).

(3)   Nothing in these Regulations shall prevent a communications provider, for the purposes of any action relating to the tracing of malicious or nuisance calls, from storing and making available to a person with a legitimate interest data containing the identity of a calling subscriber which were obtained while paragraph (1) applied.

[2.273]
16   Emergency calls

(1)   For the purposes of this regulation, "emergency calls" means calls to either the national emergency call number 999 or the single European emergency call number 112.

(2)   In order to facilitate responses to emergency calls—
    (a)   all such calls shall be excluded from the requirements of regulation 10;
    (b)   no person shall be entitled to prevent the presentation on the connected line of the identity of the calling line; and
    (c)   the restriction on the processing of location data under regulation 14(2) shall be disregarded.

[2.274]
[16A   Emergency alerts

(1)   A relevant public communications provider (P) may, for the purpose of providing an emergency alert service, disregard the restrictions on the processing of data relating to users or subscribers set out in paragraph (2) if the conditions set out in paragraph (3) are met.

(2)   The restrictions are—

Part 2   Statutory Instruments

   (a)   the restrictions on the processing of traffic data under regulations 7(1) and 8(2); and

   (b)   the restrictions on the processing of location data under regulations 14(2) and 14(5).

(3)   The conditions are—

   (a)   P is notified by a relevant public authority that—

      (i)   an emergency within the meaning of section 1(1) of the Civil Contingencies Act 2004 has occurred, is occurring or is about to occur; and

      (ii)   it is expedient to use an emergency alert service;

   (b)   P is directed by the relevant public authority to convey a specified communication over a specified time period to users or subscribers of P's public electronic communications network whom P considers—

      (i)   are in one or more specified places in the United Kingdom which is or may be affected by the emergency; or

      (ii)   have been in a specified place affected by the emergency since the emergency occurred but are no longer in the place; and

   (c)   P complies with that direction.

(4)   P may, for the purpose of testing an emergency alert service, disregard the restrictions on the processing of data relating to users or subscribers set out in paragraph (2) if the conditions set out in paragraph (5) are met.

(5)   The conditions are—

   (a)   P is notified by a Minister of the Crown that, in the Minister's opinion, it is necessary to test an emergency alert service for the purpose of ensuring that the service is maintained in good working order and is an effective means of communicating with users and subscribers in an emergency;

   (b)   the Minister gives directions as to how the test is to be conducted; and

   (c)   P complies with the directions in sub-paragraph (b).

(6)   Traffic data or location data which relate to users or subscribers of a public electronic communications network and are processed in accordance with this regulation must, within 7 days of the expiry of the time period specified by the relevant public authority pursuant to paragraph (3)(b) or, as the case may be, within 48 hours of receipt of the Minister's directions pursuant to paragraph (5)(b), be—

   (a)   erased; or

   (b)

      (i)   in the case of an individual, modified so that they cease to constitute personal data of that user or subscriber; or

      (ii)   in the case of a corporate subscriber, modified so that they cease to be data that would be personal data if that user or subscriber was an individual.

(7)   The processing of traffic data or location data in accordance with this regulation shall be carried out only by P or by a person acting under P's authority.

(8)   For the purposes of this regulation—

   (a)   "emergency alert service" means a service comprising one or more communications to mobile telecommunications devices over a public electronic communications network to warn, advise or inform users or subscribers in relation to an aspect or effect of an emergency which may affect or have affected them by reason of their location;

   (b)   "relevant public authority" means—

      (i)   a Minister of the Crown;

      (ii)   the Scottish Ministers;

      (iii) the Welsh Ministers;

      (iv) a Northern Ireland department;

      (v)   a chief officer of police within the meaning of section 101(1) of the Police Act 1996;

      (vi) the chief constable of the Police Service of Scotland;

      (vii) the chief constable of the Police Service of Northern Ireland;

      (viii) the chief constable of the British Transport Police Force;

      (ix) the Environment Agency;

      (x)   the Scottish Environment Protection Agency;

      (xi) the Natural Resources Body for Wales;

   (c)   "relevant public communications provider" means a person who—

      (i)   provides a public electronic communications network;

      (ii)   provides cellular mobile electronic communications services; and

      (iii) holds a wireless telegraphy licence granted under section 8 of the Wireless Telegraphy Act 2006.]

NOTES

Commencement: 6 April 2015.

  Inserted by the Privacy and Electronic Communications (EC Directive) (Amendment) Regulations 2015, SI 2015/355, reg 2(1), (2).

[2.275]
17   Termination of automatic call forwarding

(1)   Where—
   (a)   calls originally directed to another line are being automatically forwarded to a subscriber's line as a result of action taken by a third party, and
   (b)   the subscriber requests his provider of electronic communications services ("the subscriber's provider") to stop the forwarding of those calls,

the subscriber's provider shall ensure, free of charge, that the forwarding is stopped without any avoidable delay.

(2)   For the purposes of paragraph (1), every other communications provider shall comply with any reasonable requests made by the subscriber's provider to assist in the prevention of that forwarding.

[2.276]
18   Directories of subscribers

(1)   This regulation applies in relation to a directory of subscribers, whether in printed or electronic form, which is made available to members of the public or a section of the public, including by means of a directory enquiry service.

(2)   The personal data of an individual subscriber shall not be included in a directory unless that subscriber has, free of charge, been—
   (a)   informed by the collector of the personal data of the purposes of the directory in which his personal data are to be included, and
   (b)   given the opportunity to determine whether such of his personal data as are considered relevant by the producer of the directory should be included in the directory.

(3)   Where personal data of an individual subscriber are to be included in a directory with facilities which enable users of that directory to obtain access to that data solely on the basis of a telephone number—
   (a)   the information to be provided under paragraph (2)(a) shall include information about those facilities; and
   (b)   for the purposes of paragraph (2)(b), the express consent of the subscriber to the inclusion of his data in a directory with such facilities must be obtained.

(4)   Data relating to a corporate subscriber shall not be included in a directory where that subscriber has advised the producer of the directory that it does not want its data to be included in that directory.

(5)   Where the data of an individual subscriber have been included in a directory, that subscriber shall, without charge, be able to verify, correct or withdraw those data at any time.

(6)   Where a request has been made under paragraph (5) for data to be withdrawn from or corrected in a directory, that request shall be treated as having no application in relation to an edition of a directory that was produced before the producer of the directory received the request.

(7)   For the purposes of paragraph (6), an edition of a directory which is revised after it was first produced shall be treated as a new edition.

(8)   In this regulation, "telephone number" has the same meaning as in section 56(5) of the Communications Act 2003 but does not include any number which is used as an internet domain name, an internet address or an address or identifier incorporating either an internet domain name or an internet address, including an electronic mail address.

[2.277]
19   Use of automated calling systems

(1)   A person shall neither transmit, nor instigate the transmission of, communications comprising recorded matter for direct marketing purposes by means of an automated calling [or communication] system except in the circumstances referred to in paragraph (2).

(2)   Those circumstances are where the called line is that of a subscriber who has previously notified the caller that for the time being he consents to such communications being sent by, or at the instigation of, the caller on that line.

(3)   A subscriber shall not permit his line to be used in contravention of paragraph (1).

(4)   For the purposes of this regulation, an automated calling system is a system which is capable of—
   (a)   automatically initiating a sequence of calls to more than one destination in accordance with instructions stored in that system; and
   (b)   transmitting sounds which are not live speech for reception by persons at some or all of the destinations so called.

NOTES

Para (1): words in square brackets inserted by the Privacy and Electronic Communications (EC Directive) (Amendment) Regulations 2011, SI 2011/1208, regs 2, 8.

[2.278]
20 Use of facsimile machines for direct marketing purposes

(1) A person shall neither transmit, nor instigate the transmission of, unsolicited communications for direct marketing purposes by means of a facsimile machine where the called line is that of—
  (a) an individual subscriber, except in the circumstances referred to in paragraph (2);
  (b) a corporate subscriber who has previously notified the caller that such communications should not be sent on that line; or
  (c) a subscriber and the number allocated to that line is listed in the register kept under regulation 25.

(2) The circumstances referred to in paragraph (1)(a) are that the individual subscriber has previously notified the caller that he consents for the time being to such communications being sent by, or at the instigation of, the caller.

(3) A subscriber shall not permit his line to be used in contravention of paragraph (1).

(4) A person shall not be held to have contravened paragraph (1)(c) where the number allocated to the called line has been listed on the register for less than 28 days preceding that on which the communication is made.

(5) Where a subscriber who has caused a number allocated to a line of his to be listed in the register kept under regulation 25 has notified a caller that he does not, for the time being, object to such communications being sent on that line by that caller, such communications may be sent by that caller on that line, notwithstanding that the number allocated to that line is listed in the said register.

(6) Where a subscriber has given a caller notification pursuant to paragraph (5) in relation to a line of his—
  (a) the subscriber shall be free to withdraw that notification at any time, and
  (b) where such notification is withdrawn, the caller shall not send such communications on that line.

(7) The provisions of this regulation are without prejudice to the provisions of regulation 19.

[2.279]
21 Unsolicited calls for direct marketing purposes

(1) A person shall neither use, nor instigate the use of, a public electronic communications service for the purposes of making unsolicited calls for direct marketing purposes where—
  (a) the called line is that of a subscriber who has previously notified the caller that such calls should not for the time being be made on that line; or
  (b) the number allocated to a subscriber in respect of the called line is one listed in the register kept under regulation 26.

(2) A subscriber shall not permit his line to be used in contravention of paragraph (1).

(3) A person shall not be held to have contravened paragraph (1)(b) where the number allocated to the called line has been listed on the register for less than 28 days preceding that on which the call is made.

(4) Where a subscriber who has caused a number allocated to a line of his to be listed in the register kept under regulation 26 has notified a caller that he does not, for the time being, object to such calls being made on that line by that caller, such calls may be made by that caller on that line, notwithstanding that the number allocated to that line is listed in the said register.

(5) Where a subscriber has given a caller notification pursuant to paragraph (4) in relation to a line of his—
  (a) the subscriber shall be free to withdraw that notification at any time, and
  (b) where such notification is withdrawn, the caller shall not make such calls on that line.

[2.280]
22 Use of electronic mail for direct marketing purposes

(1) This regulation applies to the transmission of unsolicited communications by means of electronic mail to individual subscribers.

(2) Except in the circumstances referred to in paragraph (3), a person shall neither transmit, nor instigate the transmission of, unsolicited communications for the purposes of direct marketing by means of electronic mail unless the recipient of the electronic mail has previously notified the sender that he consents for the time being to such communications being sent by, or at the instigation of, the sender.

(3) A person may send or instigate the sending of electronic mail for the purposes of direct marketing where—
  (a) that person has obtained the contact details of the recipient of that electronic mail in the course of the sale or negotiations for the sale of a product or service to that recipient;
  (b) the direct marketing is in respect of that person's similar products and services only; and

(c)   the recipient has been given a simple means of refusing (free of charge except for the costs of the transmission of the refusal) the use of his contact details for the purposes of such direct marketing, at the time that the details were initially collected, and, where he did not initially refuse the use of the details, at the time of each subsequent communication.

(4)   A subscriber shall not permit his line to be used in contravention of paragraph (2).

[2.281]
23   Use of electronic mail for direct marketing purposes where the identity or address of the sender is concealed

A person shall neither transmit, nor instigate the transmission of, a communication for the purposes of direct marketing by means of electronic mail—
(a)   where the identity of the person on whose behalf the communication has been sent has been disguised or concealed; . . .
(b)   where a valid address to which the recipient of the communication may send a request that such communications cease has not been provided;
[(c)   where that electronic mail would contravene regulation 7 of the Electronic Commerce (EC Directive) Regulations 2002; or
(d)   where that electronic mail encourages recipients to visit websites which contravene that regulation.]

NOTES
Word omitted from para (a) revoked and paras (c), (d) added by the Privacy and Electronic Communications (EC Directive) (Amendment) Regulations 2011, SI 2011/1208, regs 2, 9.

[2.282]
24   Information to be provided for the purposes of regulations 19, 20 and 21

(1)   Where a public electronic communications service is used for the transmission of a communication for direct marketing purposes the person using, or instigating the use of, the service shall ensure that the following information is provided with that communication—
(a)   in relation to a communication to which regulations 19 (automated calling systems) and 20 (facsimile machines) apply, the particulars mentioned in paragraph (2)(a) and (b);
(b)   in relation to a communication to which regulation 21 (telephone calls) applies, the particulars mentioned in paragraph (2)(a) and, if the recipient of the call so requests, those mentioned in paragraph (2)(b).

(2)   The particulars referred to in paragraph (1) are—
(a)   the name of the person;
(b)   either the address of the person or a telephone number on which he can be reached free of charge.

[2.283]
25   Register to be kept for the purposes of regulation 20

(1)   For the purposes of regulation 20 OFCOM shall maintain and keep up-to-date, in printed or electronic form, a register of the numbers allocated to subscribers, in respect of particular lines, who have notified them (notwithstanding, in the case of individual subscribers, that they enjoy the benefit of regulation 20(1)(a) and (2)) that they do not for the time being wish to receive unsolicited communications for direct marketing purposes by means of facsimile machine on the lines in question.

(2)   OFCOM shall remove a number from the register maintained under paragraph (1) where they have reason to believe that it has ceased to be allocated to the subscriber by whom they were notified pursuant to paragraph (1).

(3)   On the request of—
(a)   a person wishing to send, or instigate the sending of, such communications as are mentioned in paragraph (1), or
(b)   a subscriber wishing to permit the use of his line for the sending of such communications,
for information derived from the register kept under paragraph (1), OFCOM shall, unless it is not reasonably practicable so to do, on the payment to them of such fee as is, subject to paragraph (4), required by them, make the information requested available to that person or that subscriber.

(4)   For the purposes of paragraph (3) OFCOM may require different fees—
(a)   for making available information derived from the register in different forms or manners, or
(b)   for making available information derived from the whole or from different parts of the register,
but the fees required by them shall be ones in relation to which the Secretary of State has notified OFCOM that he is satisfied that they are designed to secure, as nearly as may be and taking one year with another, that the aggregate fees received, or reasonably expected to be received, equal the costs incurred, or reasonably expected to be incurred, by OFCOM in discharging their duties under paragraphs (1), (2) and (3).

(5) The functions of OFCOM under paragraphs (1), (2) and (3), other than the function of determining the fees to be required for the purposes of paragraph (3), may be discharged on their behalf by some other person in pursuance of arrangements made by OFCOM with that other person.

[2.284]
26 Register to be kept for the purposes of regulation 21

(1) For the purposes of regulation 21 OFCOM shall maintain and keep up-to-date, in printed or electronic form, a register of the numbers allocated to . . . subscribers, in respect of particular lines, who have notified them that they do not for the time being wish to receive unsolicited calls for direct marketing purposes on the lines in question.

[(1A) Notifications to OFCOM made for the purposes of paragraph (1) by corporate subscribers shall be in writing.]

(2) OFCOM shall remove a number from the register maintained under paragraph (1) where they have reason to believe that it has ceased to be allocated to the subscriber by whom they were notified pursuant to paragraph (1).

[(2A) Where a number allocated to a corporate subscriber is listed in the register maintained under paragraph (1), OFCOM shall, within the period of 28 days following each anniversary of the date of that number being first listed in the register, send to the subscriber a written reminder that the number is listed in the register.]

(3) On the request of—
  (a) a person wishing to make, or instigate the making of, such calls as are mentioned in paragraph (1), or
  (b) a subscriber wishing to permit the use of his line for the making of such calls,
for information derived from the register kept under paragraph (1), OFCOM shall, unless it is not reasonably practicable so to do, on the payment to them of such fee as is, subject to paragraph (4), required by them, make the information requested available to that person or that subscriber.

(4) For the purposes of paragraph (3) OFCOM may require different fees—
  (a) for making available information derived from the register in different forms or manners, or
  (b) for making available information derived from the whole or from different parts of the register,
but the fees required by them shall be ones in relation to which the Secretary of State has notified OFCOM that he is satisfied that they are designed to secure, as nearly as may be and taking one year with another, that the aggregate fees received, or reasonably expected to be received, equal the costs incurred, or reasonably expected to be incurred, by OFCOM in discharging their duties under paragraphs (1), (2) and (3).

(5) The functions of OFCOM under paragraphs (1), (2)[, (2A)] and (3), other than the function of determining the fees to be required for the purposes of paragraph (3), may be discharged on their behalf by some other person in pursuance of arrangements made by OFCOM with that other person.

NOTES
  Para (1): word omitted revoked by the Privacy and Electronic Communications (EC Directive) (Amendment) Regulations 2004, SI 2004/1039, reg 2(1), (2).
  Para (1A): inserted by SI 2004/1039, reg 2(1), (3).
  Para (2A): inserted by SI 2004/1039, reg 2(1), (4).
  Para (5): reference in square brackets inserted by SI 2004/1039, reg 2(1), (5).

[2.285]
27 Modification of contracts
To the extent that any term in a contract between a subscriber to and the provider of a public electronic communications service or such a provider and the provider of an electronic communications network would be inconsistent with a requirement of these Regulations, that term shall be void.

[2.286]
28 National security
(1) Nothing in these Regulations shall require a communications provider to do, or refrain from doing, anything (including the processing of data) if exemption from the requirement in question is required for the purpose of safeguarding national security.

(2) Subject to paragraph (4), a certificate signed by a Minister of the Crown certifying that exemption from any requirement of these Regulations is or at any time was required for the purpose of safeguarding national security shall be conclusive evidence of that fact.

(3) A certificate under paragraph (2) may identify the circumstances in which it applies by means of a general description and may be expressed to have prospective effect.

(4) Any person directly affected by the issuing of a certificate under paragraph (2) may appeal to the Tribunal against the issuing of the certificate.

(5)   If, on an appeal under paragraph (4), the Tribunal finds that, applying the principles applied by a court on an application for judicial review, the Minister did not have reasonable grounds for issuing the certificate, the Tribunal may allow the appeal and quash the certificate.

(6)   Where, in any proceedings under or by virtue of these Regulations, it is claimed by a communications provider that a certificate under paragraph (2) which identifies the circumstances in which it applies by means of a general description applies in the circumstances in question, any other party to the proceedings may appeal to the Tribunal on the ground that the certificate does not apply in those circumstances and, subject to any determination under paragraph (7), the certificate shall be conclusively presumed so to apply.

(7)   On any appeal under paragraph (6), the Tribunal may determine that the certificate does not so apply.

(8)   In this regulation—

  [(a)   "the Tribunal", in relation to any appeal under this regulation, means—

    (i)   the Upper Tribunal, in any case where it is determined by or under Tribunal Procedure Rules that the Upper Tribunal is to hear the appeal; or

    (ii)   the First-tier Tribunal, in any other case;]

  (b)   Subsections (8), (9), (10) and (12) of section 28 of and Schedule 6 to that Act apply for the purposes of this regulation as they apply for the purposes of section 28;

  (c)   section 58 of that Act shall apply for the purposes of this regulation as if the reference in that section to the functions of the Tribunal under that Act included a reference to the functions of the Tribunal under paragraphs (4) to (7) of this regulation; and

  (d)   subsections (1), (2) and (5)(f) of section 67 of that Act shall apply in respect of the making of rules relating to the functions of the Tribunal under this regulation.

NOTES

  Para (8): sub-para (a) substituted by the Transfer of Tribunal Functions Order 2010, SI 2010/22, art 5(2), Sch 3, para 40, subject to transitional provisions and savings in Sch 5 thereto.

[2.287]
29   Legal requirements, law enforcement etc

(1)   Nothing in these Regulations shall require a communications provider to do, or refrain from doing, anything (including the processing of data)—

  (a)   if compliance with the requirement in question—

    (i)   would be inconsistent with any requirement imposed by or under an enactment or by a court order; or

    (ii)   would be likely to prejudice the prevention or detection of crime or the apprehension or prosecution of offenders; or

  (b)   if exemption from the requirement in question—

    (i)   is required for the purposes of, or in connection with, any legal proceedings (including prospective legal proceedings);

    (ii)   is necessary for the purposes of obtaining legal advice; or

    (iii)   is otherwise necessary for the purposes of establishing, exercising or defending legal rights.

[2.288]
[29A

(1)   Where regulations 28 and 29 apply, communications providers must establish and maintain internal procedures for responding to requests for access to users' personal data.

(2)   Communications providers shall on demand provide the Information Commissioner with information about—

  (a)   those procedures;

  (b)   the number of requests received;

  (c)   the legal justification for the request; and

  (d)   the communications provider's response.]

NOTES

  Inserted by the Privacy and Electronic Communications (EC Directive) (Amendment) Regulations 2011, SI 2011/1208, regs 2, 10.

[2.289]
30   Proceedings for compensation for failure to comply with requirements of the Regulations

(1)   A person who suffers damage by reason of any contravention of any of the requirements of these Regulations by any other person shall be entitled to bring proceedings for compensation from that other person for that damage.

(2)   In proceedings brought against a person by virtue of this regulation it shall be a defence to prove that he had taken such care as in all the circumstances was reasonably required to comply with the relevant requirement.

(3)   The provisions of this regulation are without prejudice to those of regulation 31.

[2.290]
31   Enforcement—extension of Part V of the Data Protection Act 1998

(1)   The provisions of Part V [and sections 55A to 55E] of the Data Protection Act 1998 and of Schedules 6 and 9 to that Act are extended for the purposes of these Regulations and, for those purposes, shall have effect subject to the modifications set out in Schedule 1.

(2)   In regulations 32 and 33, "enforcement functions" means the functions of the Information Commissioner under the provisions referred to in paragraph (1) as extended by that paragraph [and the functions set out in regulations 31A and 31B].

(3)   The provisions of this regulation are without prejudice to those of regulation 30.

NOTES
Para (1): words in square brackets inserted by the Privacy and Electronic Communications (EC Directive) (Amendment) Regulations 2011, SI 2011/1208, regs 2, 11(a).
Para (2): words in square brackets added by SI 2011/1208, regs 2, 11(b).

[2.291]
[31A   Enforcement: third party information notices

(1)   The Information Commissioner may require a communications provider (A) to provide information to the Information Commissioner by serving on A a notice ("a third party information notice").

(2)   The third party information notice may require A to release information held by A about another person's use of an electronic communications network or an electronic communications service where the Information Commissioner believes that the information requested is relevant information.

(3)   Relevant information is information which the Information Commissioner considers is necessary to investigate the compliance of any person with these Regulations.

(4)   The notice shall set out—
   (a)   the information requested,
   (b)   the form in which the information must be provided;
   (c)   the time limit within which the information must be provided; and
   (d)   information about the rights of appeal conferred by these Regulations.

(5)   The time limit referred to in paragraph (4)(c) shall not expire before the end of the period in which an appeal may be brought. If an appeal is brought, the information requested need not be provided pending the determination or withdrawal of the appeal.

(6)   In an urgent case, the Commissioner may include in the notice—
   (a)   a statement that the case is urgent; and
   (b)   a statement of his reasons for reaching that conclusion,
in which case paragraph (5) shall not apply.

(7)   Where paragraph (6) applies, the communications provider shall have a minimum of 7 days (beginning on the day on which the notice is served) to provide the information requested.

(8)   A person shall not be required by virtue of this regulation to disclose any information in respect of—
   (a)   any communication between a professional legal adviser and the adviser's client in connection with the giving of legal advice with respect to the client's obligations, liabilities or rights under these Regulations, or
   (b)   any communication between a professional legal adviser and the adviser's client, or between such an adviser or the adviser's client and any other person, made in connection with or in contemplation of proceedings under or arising out of these Regulations (including proceedings before the Tribunal) and for the purposes of such proceedings.]

NOTES
Inserted, together with reg 31B, by the Privacy and Electronic Communications (EC Directive) (Amendment) Regulations 2011, SI 2011/1208, regs 2, 12.

[2.292]
[31B   Enforcement: appeals

(1)   A communications provider on whom a third party information notice has been served may appeal to the Tribunal against the notice.

(2)   Appeals shall be determined in accordance with section 49 of and Schedule 6 to the Data Protection Act 1998 as modified by Schedule 1 to these Regulations.]

NOTES
Inserted as noted to reg 31A at **[2.291]**.

[2.293]
32   Request that the Commissioner exercise his enforcement functions
Where it is alleged that there has been a contravention of any of the requirements of these Regulations either OFCOM or a person aggrieved by the alleged contravention may request the Commissioner to exercise his enforcement functions in respect of that contravention, but those functions shall be exercisable by the Commissioner whether or not he has been so requested.

[2.294]
33   Technical advice to the Commissioner
OFCOM shall comply with any reasonable request made by the Commissioner, in connection with his enforcement functions, for advice on technical and similar matters relating to electronic communications.

34, 35 *(Reg 34 amends the Telecommunications (Lawful Business Practice) (Interception of Communications) Regulations 2000, SI 2000/2699, reg 3 at* **[2.165]***; reg 35 amends the Electronic Communications (Universal Service) Order 2003, SI 2003/1904).*

[2.295]
36   Transitional provisions
The provisions in Schedule 2 shall have effect.

[2.296]
[37   Review of implementation
(1)   Before the end of each review period, the Secretary of State must—
   (a)   carry out a review of the implementation in the United Kingdom of the Directive;
   (b)   set out the conclusions of the review in a report; and
   (c)   publish the report.
(2)   In carrying out the review the Secretary of State must, so far as is reasonable, have regard to how the Directive is implemented in other member States.
(3)   The report must in particular—
   (a)   set out the objectives intended to be achieved by the implementation in the United Kingdom of the Directive;
   (b)   assess the extent to which those objectives are achieved; and
   (c)   assess whether those objectives remain appropriate and, if so, the extent to which they could be achieved with a system that imposes less regulation.
(4)   "Review period" means—
   (a)   the period of five years beginning with the 26th May 2011; and
   (b)   subject to paragraph (5), each successive period of 5 years.
(5)   If a report under this regulation is published before the last day of the review period to which it relates, the following review period is to being with the day on which that report is published.]

NOTES
   Inserted by the Privacy and Electronic Communications (EC Directive) (Amendment) Regulations 2011, SI 2011/1208, regs 2, 13.

SCHEDULES

SCHEDULE 1
MODIFICATIONS FOR THE PURPOSES OF THESE REGULATIONS TO PART V
[AND SECTIONS 55A TO 55E] OF THE DATA PROTECTION ACT 1998 AND
SCHEDULES 6 AND 9 TO THAT ACT AS EXTENDED BY REGULATION 31
Regulation 31

[2.297]
1. In section 40—
   (a)   in subsection (1), for the words "data controller" there shall be substituted the word "person", for the words "data protection principles" there shall be substituted the words "requirements of the Privacy and Electronic Communications (EC Directive) Regulations 2003 (in this Part referred to as "the relevant requirements")" and for the words "principle or principles" there shall be substituted the words "requirement or requirements";
   (b)   in subsection (2), the words "or distress" shall be omitted;
   (c)   subsections (3), (4), (5), (9) and (10) shall be omitted; and
   (d)   in subsection (6)(a), for the words "data protection principle or principles" there shall be substituted the words "relevant requirement or requirements."

2. In section 41(1) and (2), for the words "data protection principle or principles", in both places where they occur, there shall be substituted the words "relevant requirement or requirements".

[2A. Sections 41A to 41C shall be omitted.]

3. Section 42 shall be omitted.

4. In section 43—
  (a) for subsections (1) and (2) there shall be substituted the following provisions—

> "(1) If the Commissioner reasonably requires any information for the purpose of determining whether a person has complied or is complying with the relevant requirements, he may serve that person with a notice (in this Act referred to as "an information notice") requiring him, within such time as is specified in the notice, to furnish the Commissioner, in such form as may be so specified, with such information relating to compliance with the relevant requirements as is so specified.
> (2) An information notice must contain a statement that the Commissioner regards the specified information as relevant for the purpose of determining whether the person has complied or is complying with the relevant requirements and his reason for regarding it as relevant for that purpose."

  (b) in subsection (6)(a), after the word "under" there shall be inserted the words "the Privacy and Electronic Communications (EC Directive) Regulations 2003 or";
  (c) in subsection (6)(b), after the words "arising out of" there shall be inserted the words "the said Regulations or";
  [(d) in subsection (8), for "under this Act" there shall be substituted "under the Privacy and Electronic Communications (EC Directive) Regulations 2003";
  (e) in subsection (8B), for "under this Act (other than an offence under section 47)" there shall be substituted "under the Privacy and Electronic Communications (EC Directive) Regulations 2003"; and
  (f) subsection (10) shall be omitted.]

5. Sections 44, 45 and 46 shall be omitted.

[6. In section 47—
  (a) in subsection (1), "special information notice" there shall be substituted "third party information notice"; and
  (b) in subsection (2), for "special information notice" there shall be substituted "third party information notice".]

7. In section 48—
  (a) in subsections (1) and (3), for the words "an information notice or a special information notice", in both places where they occur, there shall be substituted the words "or an information notice";
  (b) in subsection (3) for the words "43(5) or 44(6)" there shall be substituted the words "or 43(5)"; and
  (c) subsection (4) shall be omitted.

8. In section 49 subsection (5) shall be omitted.

[8A. [Except where paragraph 8AA applies, in section 55A—]
  (a) in subsection (1)—
      (i) for "data controller" there shall be substituted "person", and
      (ii) for "of section 4(4) by the data controller" there shall be substituted "of the requirements of the Privacy and Electronic Communications (EC Directive) Regulations 2003";
  (b) in subsection (3), for "data controller" there shall be substituted "person";
  (c) subsection (3A) shall be omitted;
  (d) in subsection (4), for "data controller" there shall be substituted "person";
  (e) in subsection (9), the definition of "data controller" shall be omitted.

[8AA In section 55A, when applied to regulations 19 to 24 of these Regulations—
  (a) in subsection (1)—
      (i) for "data controller" there shall be substituted "person";
      (ii) in paragraph (a), for "of section 4(4) by the data controller" there shall be substituted "of the requirements of the Privacy and Electronic Communications (EC Directive) Regulations 2003, and
      (iii) for paragraphs (b) and (c) there shall be substituted—
          "(b) subsection (2) or (3) applies."
  (b) in subsection (3)—
      (i) for "data controller" there shall be substituted "person"; and
      (ii) for paragraph (a) substitute—
          "(a) knew or ought to have known that there was a risk that the contravention would occur, but";
  (c) subsection (3A) shall be omitted;

(d)   in subsection (4), for "data controller" there shall be substituted "person"; and
(e)   in subsection (9), the definition of "data controller" shall be omitted.]

8B. In section 55B, for the words "data controller" (in subsections (1), (3) and (4)), there shall be substituted the word "person".]

[8C In section 55E, for the words "data controller" in subsection (2), there shall be substituted the word "person".]

9. In paragraph 4(1) of [Schedule 6], for the words "(2) or (4)" there shall be substituted the words "or (2)".

10. In paragraph 1 of Schedule 9—
(a)   for subparagraph (1)(a) there shall be substituted the following provision—

> "(a)   that a person has contravened or is contravening any of the requirements of the Privacy and Electronic Communications (EC Directive) Regulations 2003 (in this Schedule referred to as "the 2003 Regulations") or"; . . .

[(b)   in subparagraph (1A) for "data controller" there shall be substituted "person", and for "requirement imposed by an assessment notice" there shall be substituted "the audit provisions in regulations 5 and 5B of the 2003 Regulations";
(c)   in subparagraph (1B)—
    (i)   for "data controller" there shall be substituted "person";
    (ii)   for "data protection principles" there shall be substituted "the requirements of the 2003 Regulations";
    (iii)   for "assessment notice" there shall be substituted "audit notice"; and
    (iv)   the words "subparagraph (2) and" shall be omitted;
(d)   subparagraph (2) shall be omitted;
(e)   in subparagraphs (3)(d)(ii) and (3)(f) for the words "data controller" there shall be substituted "person", and for the words "the data protection principles" there shall be substituted "the requirements of the 2003 Regulations".]

[10A. In paragraph 2(1A) of Schedule 9 for "assessment notice" there shall be substituted "audit notice".]

11. In paragraph 9 of Schedule 9—
(a)   in subparagraph (1)(a) after the words "rights under" there shall be inserted the words "the 2003 Regulations or"; and
(b)   in subparagraph (1)(b) after the words "arising out of" there shall be inserted the words "the 2003 Regulations or".

NOTES

Schedule heading: words in square brackets inserted by the Privacy and Electronic Communications (EC Directive) (Amendment) Regulations 2011, SI 2011/1208, regs 2, 14(a).
Paras 2A, 8A, 8B, 10A: inserted by SI 2011/1208, regs 2, 14(b), (e), (h).
Para 4: words in square brackets substituted by SI 2011/1208, regs 2, 14(c).
Para 6: substituted by SI 2011/1208, regs 2, 14(d).
Para 8A: words in square brackets substituted by the Privacy and Electronic Communications (EC Directive) (Amendment) Regulations 2015, SI 2015/355, reg 2(1), (3).
Paras 8AA, 8C: inserted by SI 2015/355, reg 2(1), (4), (5).
Para 9: words in square brackets substituted by SI 2011/1208, regs 2, 14(f).
Para 10: word omitted revoked and words in square brackets substituted by SI 2011/1208, regs 2, 14(g).

SCHEDULE 2
TRANSITIONAL PROVISIONS

Regulation 36

Interpretation

[2.298]
1. In this Schedule "the 1999 Regulations" means the Telecommunications (Data Protection and Privacy) Regulations 1999 and "caller" has the same meaning as in regulation 21 of the 1999 Regulations.

Directories

2. (1)   Regulation 18 of these Regulations shall not apply in relation to editions of directories first published before 11th December 2003.

(2)   Where the personal data of a subscriber have been included in a directory in accordance with Part IV of the 1999 Regulations, the personal data of that subscriber may remain included in that directory provided that the subscriber—
(a)   has been provided with information in accordance with regulation 18 of these Regulations; and
(b)   has not requested that his data be withdrawn from that directory.

(3)   Where a request has been made under subparagraph (2) for data to be withdrawn from a directory, that request shall be treated as having no application in relation to an edition of a directory that was produced before the producer of the directory received the request.

(4)   For the purposes of subparagraph (3), an edition of a directory, which is revised after it was first produced, shall be treated as a new edition.

Notifications

3. (1)   A notification of consent given to a caller by a subscriber for the purposes of regulation 22(2) of the 1999 Regulations is to have effect on and after 11th December 2003 as a notification given by that subscriber for the purposes of regulation 19(2) of these Regulations.

(2)   A notification given to a caller by a corporate subscriber for the purposes of regulation 23(2)(a) of the 1999 Regulations is to have effect on and after 11th December 2003 as a notification given by that subscriber for the purposes of regulation 20(1)(b) of these Regulations.

(3)   A notification of consent given to a caller by an individual subscriber for the purposes of regulation 24(2) of the 1999 Regulations is to have effect on and after 11th December 2003 as a notification given by that subscriber for the purposes of regulation 20(2) of these Regulations.

(4)   A notification given to a caller by an individual subscriber for the purposes of regulation 25(2)(a) of the 1999 Regulations is to have effect on and after the 11th December 2003 as a notification given by that subscriber for the purposes of regulation 21(1) of these Regulations.

Registers Kept Under Regulations 25 and 26

4. (1)   A notification given by a subscriber pursuant to regulation 23(4)(a) of the 1999 Regulations to the Director General of Telecommunications (or to such other person as is discharging his functions under regulation 23(4) of the 1999 Regulations on his behalf by virtue of an arrangement made under regulation 23(6) of those Regulations) is to have effect on or after 11th December 2003 as a notification given pursuant to regulation 25(1) of these Regulations.

(2)   A notification given by a subscriber who is an individual pursuant to regulation 25(4)(a) of the 1999 Regulations to the Director General of Telecommunications (or to such other person as is discharging his functions under regulation 25(4) of the 1999 Regulations on his behalf by virtue of an arrangement made under regulation 25(6) of those Regulations) is to have effect on or after 11th December 2003 as a notification given pursuant to regulation 26(1) of these Regulations.

References in these Regulations to OFCOM

5. In relation to times before an order made under section 411 of the Communications Act 2003 brings any of the provisions of Part 2 of Chapter 1 of that Act into force for the purpose of conferring on OFCOM the functions contained in those provisions, references to OFCOM in these Regulations are to be treated as references to the Director General of Telecommunications.

PRICE MARKING ORDER 2004

(SI 2004/102)

NOTES
   Made: 19 January 2004.
   Authority: Prices Act 1974, s 4.
   Commencement: 22 July 2004.

ARRANGEMENT OF ARTICLES

SCHEDULES

[2.299]

1 Citation, commencement and interpretation

(1) This Order may be cited as the Price Marking Order 2004 and shall come into force on 22nd July 2004.

(2) In this Order—

"advertisement" means any form of advertisement which is made in order to promote the sale of a product but does not include any advertisement by means of which the trader intends to encourage a consumer to enter into a distance contract, a catalogue, a price list, a container or a label;

"consumer" means any individual who buys a product for purposes that do not fall within the sphere of his commercial or professional activity;

"cosmetic products" means any substance or preparation intended to be placed in contact with an external part of the human body, or with the teeth, inside of the mouth or throat with a view exclusively or mainly to one or more of the following purposes: cleaning, perfuming, changing the appearance of, protecting, and keeping in good condition it or them or correcting body odour;

"distance contract" means any contract concerning products concluded between a trader and a consumer, by any means, without the simultaneous physical presence of the trader and the consumer;

"itinerant trader" means any trader who, as a pedestrian, or from a train, aircraft, vessel, vehicle, stall, barrow, or other mobile sales unit, offers products to consumers other than by means of pre-printed material;

"liquid medium" has the meaning given for the purposes of [the second subparagraph of point 5 of Annex IX to Regulation (EU) No 1169/2011 of the European Parliament and of the Council on the provision of food information to consumers;];

"make-up products" means cosmetic products solely intended temporarily to change the appearance of the face or nails, including (but not limited to) lipsticks, mascaras, eye shadows, blushers and concealers;

"net drained weight" means the weight of a solid food product when it is presented in a liquid medium;

"precious metal" means gold, silver or platinum, or any other metal to which by an order under section 17 of the Hallmarking Act 1973 the provisions of that Act are applied;

"products sold from bulk" means products which are not pre-packaged and are weighed or measured at the request of the consumer;

"relevant floor area" in relation to a shop means the internal floor area of the shop excluding any area not used for the retail sale of products or for the display of such products for retail sale;

"selling price" means the final price for a unit of a product, or a given quantity of a product, including VAT and all other taxes;

"shop" includes a store, kiosk and a franchise or concession within a shop;

"small shop" means any shop which has a "relevant floor area" not exceeding 280 square metres;

"standard of fineness" means any one of the standards of fineness specified in column (2) of paragraph 2 of Schedule 2 to the Hallmarking Act 1973;

"trader" means any person who sells or offers or exposes for sale products which fall within his commercial or professional activity;

"unit price" means the final price, including VAT and all other taxes, for one kilogram, one litre, one metre, one square metre or one cubic metre of a product, except (i) in respect of the products specified in Schedule 1, where unit price means the final price including VAT and all other taxes for the corresponding units of quantity set out in that Schedule; and (ii) in respect of products sold by number, where unit price means the final price including VAT and all other taxes for an individual item of the product.

NOTES

Para (2): in definition "liquid medium" words in square brackets substituted by the Food Information Regulations 2014, SI 2014/1855, reg 14, Sch 7, Pt 2, paras 40, 41.

2 (*Revokes the Price Marking Order 1999, SI 1999/3042.*)

[2.300]

3 Scope of application of the Order

(1) This Order shall not apply:

   (a) to products which are supplied in the course of the provision of a service; or

   (b) to sales by auction or sales of works of art or antiques.

(2) The Electronic Commerce (EC Directive) Regulations 2002 shall apply to this Order notwithstanding Regulation 3(2) of those Regulations.

Part 2   Statutory Instruments

[2.301]

4 Obligation to indicate selling price

(1) Subject to paragraph (2) and articles 9 and 10, where a trader indicates that any product is or may be for sale to a consumer, he shall indicate the selling price of that product in accordance with the provisions of this Order.

(2) The requirement in paragraph (1) above shall not apply in respect of:

   (a)   products sold from bulk; or

   (b)   an advertisement for a product.

[2.302]

5 Obligation to indicate unit price

(1) Subject to paragraph (2), (3) and (4) and article 9, where a trader indicates that any product is or may be for sale to a consumer, he shall indicate the unit price of that product in accordance with the provisions of this Order.

(2) The requirement in paragraph (1) only applies in respect of products sold from bulk or required by or under Parts IV or V of the Weights and Measures Act 1985 to be:

   (a)   marked with an indication of quantity; or

   (b)   made up in a quantity prescribed by or under that Act.

(3) The requirement in paragraph (1) shall not apply in relation to:

   (a)   any product which falls within Schedule 2;

   (b)   any product the unit price of which is identical to its selling price;

   (c)   bread made up in a prescribed quantity which is or may be for sale in a small shop, by an itinerant trader or from a vending machine; or

   (d)   any product which is pre-packaged in a constant quantity which is or may be for sale in a small shop, by an itinerant trader or from a vending machine.

(4) The requirement in paragraph (1) applies in relation to an advertisement for a product only where the selling price of the product is indicated in the advertisement.

[2.303]

6 Manner of indication of selling price and unit price

(1) The indication of selling price and unit price shall be in sterling.

(2) If a trader indicates his willingness to accept foreign currency in payment for a product, he shall, in addition to the required price indications in sterling:

   (a)   give an indication of the selling price and any unit price required for the product in the foreign currency in question together with any commission to be charged; or

   (b)   clearly identify the conversion rate on the basis of which the foreign currency price will be calculated together with any commission to be charged; and

indicate that such selling price, unit price or conversion rate as the case may be does not apply to transactions via a payment card to be applied to accounts denominated in currencies other than sterling, the conversion rate for which will be that applied by the relevant payment scheme which processes the transaction.

[2.304]

7

(1) An indication of selling price, unit price, commission, conversion rate or a change in the rate or coverage of value added tax given in accordance with article 11 shall be—

   (a)   unambiguous, easily identifiable and clearly legible;

   (b)   subject to paragraph 2, given in proximity to:

      (i)   the product; or

      (ii)   in the case of distance contracts and advertisements, a visual or written description of the product; and

   (c)   so placed as to be available to consumers without the need for them to seek assistance from the trader or someone on his behalf in order to ascertain it.

(2) Paragraph (1)(b)(i) does not apply to an indication given in relation to any item of jewellery, item of precious metal, or watch displayed in a window of the premises where it is or may be for sale and the selling price of which is in excess of £3,000.

(3) The indication of any charges for postage, package or delivery of a product shall be unambiguous, easily identifiable and clearly legible.

(4) Where, in addition to a unit price, a price per quantity is indicated in relation to a supplementary indication of quantity the unit price shall predominate and the price per supplementary indication of quantity shall be expressed in characters no larger than the unit price.

(5) In paragraph (4) "supplementary indication of quantity" refers to an indication of quantity expressed in a unit of measurement other than a metric unit as authorised by section 8(5A) of the Weights and Measures Act 1985.

[2.305]
8

In the case of a pre-packaged solid food product presented in a liquid medium, the unit price shall refer to the net drained weight of the product. Where a unit price is also given with reference to the net weight of the product, it shall be clearly indicated which unit price relates to net drained weight and which to net weight.

[2.306]
9 Special provisions relating to general reductions

Where a trader proposes to sell products to which this Order applies at less than the selling price or the unit price previously applicable and indicated in accordance with article 7(1), he may comply with the obligations specified in articles 4(1) (to indicate the selling price) and 5(1) (to indicate the unit price) by indicating by a general notice or any other visible means that the products are or may be for sale at a reduction, provided that the details of the reduction are prominently displayed, unambiguous, easily identifiable and clearly legible.

[2.307]
10 Special provisions relating to precious metals

In the case of products the selling price of which varies from day to day according to the price of the precious metals contained in them the obligation to indicate the selling price referred to in article 4(1) may be complied with by indicating in a manner which is unambiguous, easily identifiable and clearly legible:
(a)   the weight, type and standard of fineness of each precious metal contained in the product; and
(b)   any element of the selling price which is not referable to weight,
accompanied by a clearly legible and prominent notice stating the price per unit of weight for the type and standard of fineness of each precious metal contained in the product.

[2.308]
11 Change in Value Added Tax etc

Where there is a change in the rate or coverage of VAT or any other tax, a trader who adjusts his prices in consequence may comply with the provisions of this Order—
(a)   by means of a general notice or notices for a period of [28] days from the date any such change takes effect, indicating that any products subject to that change are not for sale at the price indicated and that such price will be adjusted to take account of the change; and
(b)   if he continues to distribute any catalogue or sales literature printed or ordered to be printed before a change is announced and there is firmly attached to it a label which prominently states that some or all of the prices printed in it are to be adjusted to reflect the change, and:
    (i)   the label includes sufficient information to enable consumers to establish the adjusted price of any product listed, or
    (ii)   the label refers to and is accompanied by a supplement which enables them to do so.

NOTES
Number in square brackets substituted by the Price Marking (Amendment) Order 2009, SI 2009/3231, art 2.

[2.309]
12 Decimal places and rounding of unit prices

Where the unit price of a product falls below £1 it shall be expressed to the nearest 0.1p. Where the figure denoting one hundredths of one penny in the unit price is 5 or higher, it shall be rounded up and where it is 4 or lower it shall be rounded down.

[2.310]
13

Where the unit price of a product falls above £1 it may be expressed to the nearest:
(a)   1p, in which case where the figure denoting tenths of one penny in the unit price is 5 or higher, it shall be rounded up and where it is 4 or lower it shall be rounded down; or
(b)   0.1p, in which case where the figure denoting one hundredths of one penny in the unit price is 5 or higher it shall be rounded up and where it is 4 or lower it shall be rounded down.

[2.311]
14 Units of Quantity

For the purposes of Schedule 1, the figure denoting the relevant units of quantity in the second column of the table for the corresponding product in the first column of the table refers, as indicated by or under the Weights and Measures Act 1985, and unless specified otherwise to:
(a)   grams where the product is sold by weight;
(b)   millilitres where the product is sold by volume; and
(c)   either grams or millilitres, as indicated by the manufacturer of the product, where the product is permitted to be sold by either weight or volume.

[2.312]

15   Enforcement

For the purpose of ascertaining whether any trader enjoys exemption from unit pricing under article 5(3)(c) or (d) in respect of a small shop, a local weights and measures authority may require that trader to produce such documentary evidence relating to the shop in question as it considers necessary.

NOTES

Revoked by the Consumer Rights Act 2015 (Commencement No 3, Transitional Provisions, Savings and Consequential Amendments) Order 2015, SI 2015/1630, art 5, Sch 2, para 44, as from 1 October 2015 (for transitional provisions see arts 6–8 thereof at **[2.1220]** et seq).

SCHEDULES

SCHEDULE 1
RELEVANT UNITS OF QUANTITY FOR SPECIFIED PRODUCTS FOR THE PURPOSE OF THE DEFINITION OF "UNIT PRICE"

Articles 1(2) and 14

[2.313]

Product	Units of Quantity
Flavouring essences	10
Food colourings	10
Herbs	10
Make-up Products	10 (except where sold by number)
Seeds other than pea, bean, grass and wild bird seeds	10
Spices	10
Biscuits and shortbread	100 (except where sold by number)
Bread	100 (except where sold by number)
Breakfast cereal products	100 (except where required to be quantity marked by number)
Chocolate confectionery and sugar confectionery	100
Coffee	100
Cooked or ready-to-eat fish, seafoods and crustacea	100
Cooked or ready-to-eat meat including game and poultry	100
Cosmetic products other than make-up products	100
Cream and non-dairy alternatives to cream	100
Dips and spreads excluding edible fats	100
Dry sauce mixes	100
Fresh processed salad	100
Fruit juices, soft drinks	100
Handrolling and pipe tobacco	100
Ice cream and frozen desserts	100
Lubricating oils other than oils for internal combustion engines	100
Pickles	100
Pies, pasties, sausage rolls, puddings and flans indicating net quantity	100 (except where sold by number)
Potato crisps and similar products commonly known as snack foods	100
Preserves including honey	100
Ready to eat desserts	100
Sauces, edible oils	100
Soups	100
Tea and other beverages prepared with liquid	100
Waters, including spa waters and aerated waters	100
Wines, sparkling wine, liqueur wine, fortified wine	75 cl

Product	Units of Quantity
Coal, where sold by the kilogram	50 kg
Ballast, where sold by the kilogram	1,000 kg

SCHEDULE 2
PRODUCTS IN RESPECT OF WHICH A TRADER IS EXEMPT FROM THE REQUIREMENT TO UNIT PRICE

Article 5(3)

[2.314]

1. Any product which is offered by traders to consumers by means of an advertisement which is:
- (a)   purely aural;
- (b)   broadcast on television;
- (c)   shown at a cinema; or
- (d)   inside a small shop.

2. Any product the price of which has been reduced from the usual price at which it is sold, on account of:
- (a)   its damaged condition; or
- (b)   the danger of its deterioration.

3. Any product which comprises an assortment of different items sold in a single package.

4. Any product the unit price of which is 0.0p as a result of article 12 (Decimal places and rounding of unit prices) of this Order.

CONSUMER CREDIT (DISCLOSURE OF INFORMATION) REGULATIONS 2004

(SI 2004/1481)

NOTES
Made: 5 June 2004.
Authority: Consumer Credit Act 1974, ss 55(1), 182(2), 189(1).
Commencement: 31 May 2005.

[2.315]
1   Citation, commencement and interpretation

(1)   These Regulations may be cited as the Consumer Credit (Disclosure of Information) Regulations 2004 and shall come into force on 31st May 2005.

(2)   In these Regulations—
["the Act" means the Consumer Credit Act 1974;]
"the Agreements Regulations" mean the Consumer Credit (Agreements) Regulations 1983;
"distance contract" means any regulated agreement made under an organised distance sales or service-provision scheme run by the creditor or owner or by an intermediary of the creditor or owner who, in any such case, for the purpose of that agreement makes exclusive use of one or more means of distance communication up to and including the time at which the agreement is made and for this purpose any means of communication is a means of distance communication if, without the simultaneous physical presence of the creditor or owner or any intermediary of the creditor or owner and of the debtor or hirer, it may be used for the distance marketing of a regulated agreement between the parties to that agreement;
"durable medium" means any instrument which enables the debtor or hirer to store information addressed personally to him in a way accessible for future reference for a period of time adequate for the purposes of the information and which allows the unchanged reproduction of the information stored.

NOTES
Para (2): definition "the Act" inserted by the Consumer Credit (EU Directive) Regulations 2010, SI 2010/1010, regs 73, 74, with effect in relation to certain agreements entered into before 1 February 2011, as provided for in regs 101, 101A of the 2010 Regulations at **[2.804]**, **[2.805]**.

[2.316]
[2   Agreements to which these Regulations apply

(1)   Subject to paragraph (3) these Regulations apply in respect of the following regulated agreements—

Part 2   Statutory Instruments

(a) consumer credit agreements secured on land except those to which section 58 of the Act (opportunity for withdrawal from prospective land mortgage) applies,

(b) consumer hire agreements,

(c) consumer credit agreements under which the creditor provides the debtor with credit which exceeds £60,260 [other than residential renovation agreements],

(d) consumer credit agreements entered into by the debtor wholly or predominantly for the purposes of a business carried on, or intended to be carried on, by him, and

(e) small debtor-creditor-supplier agreements for restricted-use credit,

except to the extent the Consumer Credit (Disclosure of Information) Regulations 2010 apply to such agreements.

(2) Subsections (2) to (5) of section 16B of the Act (declaration by the debtor as to the purposes of the agreement) apply for the purposes of paragraph (1)(d).

(3) These Regulations do not apply to—

(a) a distance contract;

(b) an authorised non-business overdraft agreement;

(c) an agreement which would be an authorised non-business overdraft agreement but for the fact that the credit is not repayable on demand or within three months.]

NOTES

Substituted by the Consumer Credit (EU Directive) Regulations 2010, SI 2010/1010, regs 73, 75 (as amended by the Consumer Credit (Amendment) Regulations 2010, SI 2010/1969, regs 4, 24), with effect in relation to certain agreements entered into before 1 February 2011, as provided for in regs 101, 101A of SI 2010/1010 at **[2.804]**, **[2.805]**.

Para (1): words in square brackets in sub-para (c) added by the Mortgage Credit Directive Order 2015, SI 2015/910, art 3, Sch 1, Pt 2, para 11, as from 21 March 2016 (note that the 2015 Order also comes into force on 20 April 2015 and 21 December 2015 for limited other purposes, and for transitional provisions, see Part 4 of that Order at **[2.1194]** et seq).

[2.317]
3 Information to be disclosed to a debtor or hirer before a regulated agreement is made

(1) Before a regulated agreement ("the relevant agreement") is made, the creditor or owner must disclose to the debtor or hirer in the manner set out in regulation 4 the information and statements of protection and remedies that are required to be given—

(a) in the case of a regulated consumer credit agreement, under regulation 2 of the Agreements Regulations;

(b) in the case of a regulated consumer hire agreement, under regulation 3 of the Agreements Regulations;

(c) in the case of a modifying agreement which is, or is treated as, a regulated consumer credit agreement, under regulations 2(3) and 7(2) of the Agreements Regulations;

(d) in the case of a modifying agreement which is or is treated as a regulated consumer hirer agreement, under regulations 3(3) and 7(9) of the Agreements Regulations.

[(1A) In the case of an agreement falling within regulation 2(1)(c), (d) or (e), the creditor shall provide, in addition to the information specified in paragraph (1), a statement that if he decided not to proceed with a prospective regulated consumer credit agreement on the basis of information from a credit reference agency, he will, when informing the debtor of that decision, inform the debtor that the decision has been reached on the basis of information from a credit reference agency and of the particulars of that agency (in compliance with section 157(A1) of the Act.]

(2) The information and statements of protection required to be disclosed under paragraph (1) shall be the information and statements that will be included in the document embodying the relevant agreement save that, where any of the information is not known at the time of disclosure, the creditor or owner shall disclose estimated information based on such assumptions as he may reasonably make in all the circumstances of the case.

NOTES

Para (1A): inserted by the Consumer Credit (EU Directive) Regulations 2010, SI 2010/1010, regs 73, 76 (as amended by the Consumer Credit (Amendment) Regulations 2010, SI 2010/1969, regs 4, 25), with effect in relation to certain agreements entered into before 1 February 2011, as provided for in regs 101, 101A of SI 2010/1010 at **[2.804]**, **[2.805]**.

[2.318]
4 Manner of disclosure

The information and statements of protection and remedies required to be disclosed under regulation 3 must be—

(a) easily legible and, where applicable, of a colour which is readily distinguishable from the background medium upon which they are displayed;

(b) not interspersed with any other information or wording apart from subtotals of total amounts and cross references to the terms of the agreement;

(c) of equal prominence except that headings may be afforded more prominence whether by capital letters, underlining, larger or bold print or otherwise; and

(d) contained in a document which:

(i) is separate from the document embodying the relevant agreement (within the meaning of regulation 3) and any other document referred to in the document embodying that agreement;

(ii) is headed with the words "Pre-contract Information";

(iii) does not contain any other information or wording apart from the heading referred to in sub-paragraph (ii);

(iv) is on paper or on another durable medium which is available and accessible to the debtor or hirer; and

(v) is of a nature that enables the debtor or hirer to remove it from the place where it is disclosed to him.

CONSUMER CREDIT (EARLY SETTLEMENT) REGULATIONS 2004

(SI 2004/1483)

NOTES

Made: 5 June 2004.

Authority: Consumer Credit Act 1974, ss 95, 97(1), 182(2), 189(1).

Commencement: 31 May 2005.

ARRANGEMENT OF REGULATIONS

[2.319]
1 Citation, commencement and interpretation

(1) These Regulations may be cited as the Consumer Credit (Early Settlement) Regulations 2004, and shall come into force on 31st May 2005.

(2) In these Regulations—

"the Act" means the Consumer Credit Act 1974;

"the APR" means the annual percentage rate of charge for credit determined in accordance with the [total charge for credit rules], subject to regulation 3(2) below;

"early settlement" shall be construed in accordance with [regulation 2(1A)] below;

["green deal plan" has the meaning given in section 1 of the Energy Act 2011;]

"rebate" means a rebate of charges for credit included in the total charge for credit;

"the relevant date" [means—

(a) where a date is specified in or determinable under an agreement at the date of its making as that on which the debtor is entitled to require the provision of anything under the agreement, the earliest such date, or

(b) where no such date is specified or determinable, the date of making of the agreement;]

"the settlement date", means the settlement date provided for in regulation 5 and, where applicable, regulation 6;

"the total charge for credit" shall be determined in accordance with the [total charge for credit rules], subject to regulations 3(2) and 7 below; and

["the total charge for credit rules" means rules made by the Financial Conduct Authority under article 60M of the Financial Services and Markets Act 2000 (Regulated Activities) Order 2001 for the purposes of Chapter 14A of Part 2 of that Order;]

(3) . . .

(4) In these Regulations, references to repayment of credit are references to repayment of credit with any amount included in the total charge for credit payable at the same time.

NOTES

Para (2): words in square brackets in definitions "the APR" and "the total charge for credit", and definition "the total charge for credit rules" substituted by the Financial Services and Markets Act 2000 (Regulated Activities) (Amendment) (No 2) Order 2013, SI 2013/1881, art 24, for transitional provisions see Pt 8 thereof at **[2.1007]** et seq; words in square brackets in definitions "early settlement" and "the relevant date" substituted by the Consumer Credit (EU Directive) Regulations 2010, SI 2010/1010, regs 77, 78(a)(i), (ii) (as amended by the Consumer Credit (Amendment) Regulations 2010, SI 2010/1969, regs 4, 26), with effect in relation to certain agreements entered into before 1 February 2011, as provided for in regs 100–101A of SI 2010/1010 at **[2.803]–[2.805]**; definition "green deal plan" inserted by the Consumer Credit (Green Deal) Regulations 2012, SI 2012/2798, reg 5, Schedule, para 3(1), (2).

Para (3): revoked by SI 2010/1010, regs 77, 78(b), with effect in relation to certain agreements entered into before 1 February 2011, as provided for in regs 100–101A of the 2010 Regulations at **[2.803]–[2.805]**.

[2.320]
2 Entitlement to rebate

[(1) Where early settlement takes place the creditor shall, subject to the following provisions of this regulation, allow to the debtor under a regulated consumer credit agreement a rebate at least equal to that calculated in accordance with the following provisions of these Regulations.]

[(1A) Early settlement takes place under paragraph (1) where—
(a) the indebtedness of the debtor is discharged or becomes payable before the time fixed by the agreement—
(i) under section 94(1) of the Act,
(ii) on refinancing,
(iii) on breach of the agreement, or
(iv) for any other reason,
(b) the indebtedness of the debtor is discharged in part under section 94(3) of the Act, or
(c) any sum becomes payable by the debtor before the time fixed by the agreement.]

(2) Paragraph (1) does not apply in the case of agreements of the following descriptions—
(a) agreements under which no payments of items included in the total charge for credit are required to be made in respect of the period of time commencing on the settlement date;
(b) agreements for running-account credit;
(c) land mortgages under which no instalment repayments secured by the mortgage on the debtor's home, and no payment of interest on the credit (other than interest charged when all or part of the credit is repaid voluntarily by the debtor), are due or capable of becoming due while the debtor continues to occupy the mortgaged land as his main residence.

(3) Paragraph (1) does not apply where a hire-purchase or conditional sale agreement is terminated by the debtor under section 99 of the Act.

(4) Where a sum less than the total remaining indebtedness of the debtor is required to be paid before the time fixed by the agreement, no consequential payment of any subsequent instalment required to be paid under the agreement, or under a modifying agreement not relating to the provision of additional credit or an increase in the total charge for credit, shall entitle the debtor to a rebate.

NOTES
Para (1): substituted by the Consumer Credit (EU Directive) Regulations 2010, SI 2010/1010, regs 77, 79(a), with effect in relation to certain agreements entered into before 1 February 2011, as provided for in regs 100–101A of the 2010 Regulations at **[2.803]–[2.805]**.
Para (1A): inserted by SI 2010/1010, regs 77, 79(b), with effect in relation to certain agreements entered into before 1 February 2011, as provided for in regs 100–101A of the 2010 Regulations at **[2.803]–[2.805]**.

[2.321]
3 Items included in the calculation of rebate

(1) Subject to paragraph (2), the rebate shall be calculated by reference to all sums paid or payable by the debtor or a relative of his under or in connection with the agreement (whether to the creditor or any other person) and included in the total charge for credit.

(2) There may be excluded from the calculation of the rebate—
(a) [so much of the amount of] taxes, duties, fees and charges payable under or by virtue of any statute or payable to the Secretary of State or any other Minister or government department (including for this purpose a Northern Ireland department or a government department in any country outside the United Kingdom) or to a local authority or similar body outside the United Kingdom [as is attributable to the period before the settlement date];
(b) sums paid or payable under linked transactions, except sums paid before the settlement date in respect of cash, goods or services to be supplied under the transaction wholly or partly after that date;
(c) sums payable under linked transactions excluded under regulations made under section 96(3) of the Act from the operation of section 96(1);
(d) [so much of] any fee or commission paid by the debtor or a relative of his under a credit brokerage contract relating to the agreement [as is attributable to the period before the settlement date] . . .

[(3) In relation to a regulated consumer credit agreement secured on land—
(a) paragraph (2)(a) shall apply as if the words "so much of the amount of" and "as is attributable to the period before the settlement date" were omitted; and

(b)   paragraph (2)(d) shall apply as if the words "so much of" and "as is attributable to the period before the settlement date" were omitted.]

[2.322]
4   Calculation of the amount of rebate

[(A1)   This regulation provides for the calculation of the amount of the rebate where early settlement takes place as provided in regulation 2(1A)(a) or (c) and the debtor pays the amount or sum by the time specified in regulation 5(1).]

(1)   The amount of the rebate is the difference between the total amount of the repayments of credit that would fall due for payment after the settlement date if early settlement did not take place and the amount given by the following formula—

$$\sum_{i=1}^{m} A_i(1+r)^{a_i} \quad \text{minus} \quad \sum_{j=1}^{n} B_j(1+r)^{b_j}$$

where:
     A_i = the amount of the *ith* advance of credit,
     B_j = the amount of the *jth* repayment of credit,
     r = the periodic rate equivalent of the APR/100,
     m = the number of advances of credit made before the settlement date,
     n = the number of repayments of credit made before the settlement date,
     a_i = the time between the *ith* advance of credit and the settlement date, expressed in periods,
     b_j = the time between the *jth* repayment of credit and the settlement date, expressed in periods, and
     Σ represents the sum of all the terms indicated.

(2)   In calculating the rebate, where the creditor so elects, any repayment of credit [not] made at a time or a rate . . . provided for in the agreement [(other than one made under section 94(3) of the Act)] shall be taken to have been made at the time or rate provided for.

(3)   . . .

[2.323]
[4A   Calculation of the amount of rebate (indebtedness discharged in part)

(1)   This regulation provides for the calculation of the amount of the rebate where early settlement takes place as provided in regulation 2(1A)(b) and the debtor pays the amount by the time specified in regulation 5(2).

(2)   The amount of the rebate is the amount given by the following formula—

$F - K - P$

where:
     F = the total amount of repayments of credit that would fall due for payment after the settlement date if early settlement did not take place,
     K = the total amount of repayments of credit that will fall due for payment after the settlement date if early settlement takes place; in calculating K—
         (i)   the amount of the credit outstanding from the debtor and the amount of the accrued charges remaining unpaid by the debtor under the agreement on the settlement date if early settlement takes place are to be determined in accordance with the formula given in regulation 4(1), and
         (ii)   the amount paid by the debtor to the creditor where early settlement takes place shall be treated as though it were reduced by the amount (if any) which the creditor may claim under section 95A(2) [or 95B(2)] of the Act,

and

P = the amount paid by the debtor to the creditor where early settlement takes place.

(3)   In calculating the rebate, where the creditor so elects, any repayment of credit not made at a time or a rate provided for in the agreement (other than one made under section 94(3) of the Act) shall be taken to have been made at the time or rate provided for.]

NOTES

Inserted by the Consumer Credit (EU Directive) Regulations 2010, SI 2010/1010, regs 77, 82, with effect in relation to certain agreements entered into before 1 February 2011, as provided for in regs 100–101A of the 2010 Regulations at **[2.803]–[2.805]**.

Para (2): in definition "K" figure in square brackets inserted by the Consumer Credit (Green Deal) Regulations 2012, SI 2012/2798, reg 5, Schedule, para 3(1), (3).

[2.324]
5   Settlement date

[(1)]   The settlement date for calculation of the rebate [in regulation 4] shall be taken to be—
  (a)   where the debtor has given notice under [section 94(1)] of the Act with a view to discharging his indebtedness under the agreement, the date falling 28 days after the date on which the notice was received by the creditor, or any later date specified as the date of early settlement in the notice, if the debtor pays the amount in question (less any rebate allowable under these Regulations) not later than that date;
  (b)   the date specified as the date for payment of any sum by the debtor involving early settlement in any notice served under section 76(1) of the Act, any default notice or any notice served under section 98(1), if the debtor pays the amount in question (less any rebate allowable under these Regulations) not later than that date;
  (c)   in any other case, the date on which the debtor pays any sum involving early settlement.
[(2)   The settlement date for the calculation of the rebate in regulation 4A shall be taken to be the date falling 28 days after the date on which the notice under section 94(4)(a) of the Act was received by the creditor, or any later date specified as the date of early settlement in the notice, if the debtor pays the amount in question not later than that date.]

NOTES

Para (1): original provision renumbered as such, words in first pair of square brackets inserted and words in square brackets in sub-para (a) substituted by the Consumer Credit (EU Directive) Regulations 2010, SI 2010/1010, regs 77, 83(a), (b), with effect in relation to certain agreements entered into before 1 February 2011, as provided for in regs 100–101A of the 2010 Regulations at **[2.803]–[2.805]**.

Para (2): added by SI 2010/1010, regs 77, 83(c), with effect in relation to certain agreements entered into before 1 February 2011, as provided for in regs 100–101A of the 2010 Regulations at **[2.803]–[2.805]**.

[2.325]
6   Deferment of settlement date

[(1)]   Where the agreement provides for the credit to be repaid over, or at the end of, a period which is more than a year after the relevant date, the settlement date for calculation of the rebate may be deferred by—
  (a)   one month, or
  (b)   where the length of a month's deferment would be more or less than 30 days and the creditor so elects, 30 days.
[(2)   Paragraph (1) does not apply where the agreement is a green deal plan and the creditor under that plan is claiming a payment under section 95B(2) of the Act.]

NOTES

Para (1) numbered as such and para (2) added by the Consumer Credit (Green Deal) Regulations 2012, SI 2012/2798, reg 5, Schedule, para 3(1), (4).

[2.326]
7   Variation of rates and amounts

Where, under a power contained in the agreement, the rate or amount of any item included in the total charge for credit, the amount of any instalment of repayment of credit or the time fixed by the agreement for the debtor's indebtedness to be discharged is or can be varied, the rate or amount, as the case may be, of any item to be included in the total charge for credit or the amount of any instalment of repayment of credit or the time fixed by the agreement for the debtor's indebtedness to be discharged for the purpose of calculation of the rebate shall be taken to be, in respect of any period of time commencing on or after the settlement date, the rate or amount or time subsisting at that date.

[2.327]
8   Revocation of Regulations

Subject to regulation 10, the Consumer Credit (Rebate on Early Settlement) Regulations 1983 are revoked.

[2.328]
9 Amendment of Regulations

(1) Subject to regulation 10, the Consumer Credit (Settlement Information) Regulations 1983 are amended as follows.

(2) In regulation 3 (which determines the settlement date to be taken for the purposes of the Regulations)—

    (a) paragraph (1) (which applies in the case of an agreement for credit to be repaid in instalments) is omitted, and

    (b) in paragraph (2) (which applies in all other cases), the words "Where paragraph (1) does not apply" are omitted.

(3) In regulation 4 (which prescribes the number of working days within which a creditor is required to respond to a request for a statement indicating the amount required to discharge a debt), for "12" there is substituted "7".

(4) In paragraph 7(a) of the Schedule (which provides for the statement to indicate, where any rebate is due, that the rebate has been calculated having regard to Regulations), for "the Consumer Credit (Rebate on Early Settlement) Regulations 1983" there is substituted "the Consumer Credit (Early Settlement) Regulations 2004".

[2.329]
10 Savings

(1) The Regulations referred to in regulation 8 continue to apply, in place of regulations 1–7 of these Regulations, and the amendments in regulation 9 do not apply, in the case of a regulated consumer credit agreement entered into before the date on which these Regulations come into force—

    (a) until 31st May 2007, if the agreement is for a term of 10 years or less;

    (b) until 31st May 2010, if the agreement is for a term of more than 10 years.

(2) For the purposes of paragraph (1), the term of an agreement is the term originally provided for, or, in the case where the term was varied before the date on which these Regulations are made, the term provided for on that date.

SCHEDULE

(*Schedule revoked by the Consumer Credit (EU Directive) Regulations 2010, SI 2010/1010, regs 77, 84, with effect in relation to certain agreements entered into before 1 February 2011, as provided for in regs 100–101A of the 2010 Regulations at* **[2.803]**–**[2.805]**.)

FINANCIAL SERVICES (DISTANCE MARKETING) REGULATIONS 2004

(SI 2004/2095)

NOTES
Made: 4 August 2004.
Authority: European Communities Act 1972, s 2(2).
Commencement: 31 October 2004.

ARRANGEMENT OF REGULATIONS

[2.330]
1   Citation, commencement and extent
These Regulations may be cited as the Financial Services (Distance Marketing) Regulations 2004 and come into force on 31st October 2004.

[2.331]
2   Interpretation
(1)   In these Regulations—
  "the 1974 Act" means the Consumer Credit Act 1974;
  "the 2000 Act" means the Financial Services and Markets Act 2000;
  "the Authority" means the [Financial Conduct Authority];
  "appointed representative" has the same meaning as in section 39(2) of the 2000 Act (exemption of appointed representatives);
  ["authorised non-business overdraft agreement" has the same meaning as in section 189 of the 1974 Act;]
  "authorised person" has the same meaning as in . . . the 2000 Act (authorised persons);
  "breach" means a contravention by a supplier of a prohibition in, or a failure by a supplier to comply with a requirement of, these Regulations;
  "business" includes a trade or profession;
  ["the CMA" means the Competition and Markets Authority;]
  "consumer" means any individual who, in contracts to which these Regulations apply, is acting for purposes which are outside any business he may carry on;
  ["consumer credit agreement" has the same meaning as in section 189 of the 1974 Act;]
  "court" in relation to England and Wales and Northern Ireland means a county court or the High Court, and in relation to Scotland means the Sheriff Court or the Court of Session;
  "credit" includes a cash loan and any other form of financial accommodation, and for this purpose "cash" includes money in any form;
  "designated professional body" has the same meaning as in section 326(2) of the 2000 Act (designation of professional bodies);
  "the Directive" means Directive 2002/65/EC of the European Parliament and of the Council of 23 September 2002 concerning the distance marketing of consumer financial services and amending Council Directive 90/619/EEC and Directives 97/7/EC and 98/27/EC;
  ["the Disclosure of Information Regulations" means the Consumer Credit (Disclosure of Information) Regulations 2010;]
  "distance contract" means any contract concerning one or more financial services concluded between a supplier and a consumer under an organised distance sales or service-provision scheme run by the supplier or by an intermediary, who, for the purpose of that contract, makes exclusive use of one or more means of distance communication up to and including the time at which the contract is concluded;
  "durable medium" means any instrument which enables a consumer to store information addressed personally to him in a way accessible for future reference for a period of time adequate for the purposes of the information and which allows the unchanged reproduction of the information stored;
  ["the European Consumer Credit Information form" means the form set out in schedule 3 to the Disclosure of Information Regulations;]
  "EEA supplier" means a supplier who is a national of an EEA State, or a company or firm (within the meaning of [Article 54 of the Treaty on the Functioning of the European Union]) formed in accordance with the law of an EEA State;
  ["EEA State" has the meaning given by Schedule 1 to the Interpretation Act 1978;]
  "exempt regulated activity" has the same meaning as in section 325(2) of the 2000 Act;
  "financial service" means any service of a banking, credit, insurance, personal pension, investment or payment nature;
  "means of distance communication" means any means which, without the simultaneous physical presence of the supplier and the consumer, may be used for the marketing of a service between those parties;
  . . .
  "regulated activity" has the same meaning as in section 22 of the 2000 Act (the classes of activity and categories of investment);

"Regulated Activities Order" means the Financial Services and Markets Act 2000 (Regulated Activities) Order 2001;

["regulated consumer credit agreement" means a consumer credit agreement [which is a regulated agreement (within the meaning given by section 189 of the 1974 Act)];]

["the relevant regulator" means—

    (a)   in relation to a specified contract (within the meaning given in regulation 17) or any alleged breach concerning such a contract, the Authority; and

    (b)   in relation to any other contract or any alleged breach concerning such a contract, the CMA;]

"rule" means a rule—

    (a)   made by the Authority under the 2000 Act, or

    (b)   made by a designated professional body, and approved by the Authority, under section 332 of the 2000 Act,

    as the context requires;

"supplier" means any person who, acting in his commercial or professional capacity, is the contractual provider of services.

(2)   In these Regulations, subject to paragraph (1), any expression used in these Regulations which is also used in the Directive has the same meaning as in the Directive.

NOTES

Para (1): in definition "the Authority" words in square brackets substituted, and words omitted from definition "authorised person" revoked, by the Financial Services Act 2012 (Consequential Amendments and Transitional Provisions) Order 2013, SI 2013/472, art 3, Sch 2, para 97; definitions "authorised non-business overdraft agreement", "consumer credit agreement", "the Disclosure of Information Regulations", "the European Consumer Credit Information form" and "regulated consumer credit agreement" inserted by the Consumer Credit (EU Directive) Regulations 2010, SI 2010/1010, regs 85, 86, with effect in relation to certain agreements entered into before 1 February 2011, as provided for in regs 101, 101A of the 2010 Regulations at **[2.804]**, **[2.805]**; definitions "the CMA" and "the relevant regulator" inserted, and definition "the OFT" (omitted) revoked, by the Financial Services and Markets Act 2000 (Consumer Credit) (Miscellaneous Provisions) Order 2014, SI 2014/208, art 3(1), (2); definition "EEA State" substituted by the Financial Services (EEA State) Regulations 2007, SI 2007/108, reg 10; in definition "EEA supplier" words in square brackets substituted by the Treaty of Lisbon (Changes in Terminology or Numbering) Order 2012, SI 2012/1809, art 3, Schedule, Pt 2; in definition "regulated consumer credit agreement" words in square brackets substituted by the Financial Services and Markets Act 2000 (Regulated Activities) (Amendment) (No 2) Order 2013, SI 2013/1881, art 28, Schedule, Pt 2, para 26(a), for transitional provisions see Pt 8 thereof at **[2.1007]** et seq.

[2.332]
3 Scope of these Regulations

(1)   Regulations 7 to 14 apply, subject to regulations 4 and 5, in relation to distance contracts made on or after 31st October 2004.

(2)   Regulation 15 applies in relation to financial services supplied on or after 31st October 2004 under an organised distance sales or service-provision scheme run by the supplier or by an intermediary, who, for the purpose of that supply, makes exclusive use of one or more means of distance communication up to and including the time at which the financial services are supplied.

[2.333]
4

(1)   Where an EEA State, other than the United Kingdom, has transposed the Directive or has obligations in its domestic law corresponding to those provided for in the Directive—

    (a)   regulations 7 to 14 do not apply in relation to any contract made between an EEA supplier contracting from an establishment in that EEA State and a consumer in the United Kingdom, and

    (b)   regulation 15 does not apply to any supply of financial services by an EEA supplier from an establishment in that EEA State to a consumer in the United Kingdom,

if the provisions by which that State has transposed the Directive, or the obligations in the domestic law of that State corresponding to those provided for in the Directive, as the case may be, apply to that contract or that supply.

(2)   Subject to paragraph (5) and regulation 6(3) and (4)—

    (a)   regulations 7 to 11 do not apply in relation to any contract made by a supplier who is an authorised person, the making or performance of which constitutes or is part of a regulated activity carried on by him;

    (b)   regulation 15 does not apply to any supply of financial services by a supplier who is an authorised person, where that supply constitutes or is part of a regulated activity carried on by him.

(3)   Subject to regulation 6(3) and (4)—

    (a)   regulations 7 and 8 do not apply in relation to any contract made by a supplier who is an appointed representative, the making or performance of which constitutes or is part of a regulated activity (other than an exempt regulated activity) carried on by him;

    (b)   regulation 15 does not apply to any supply of financial services by a supplier who is an appointed representative, where that supply constitutes or is part of a regulated activity (other than an exempt regulated activity) carried on by him.

(4)   Subject to regulation 6(3) and (4)—

   (a)   regulations 7 and 8 do not apply in relation to any contract where—

      (i)   the supplier is bound, or is controlled or managed by one or more persons who are bound, by rules of a designated professional body which are equivalent to those regulations, and

      (ii)   the making or performance of that contract constitutes or is part of an exempt regulated activity carried on by the supplier;

   (b)   regulation 15 does not apply to any supply of financial services where—

      (i)   the supplier is bound, or is controlled or managed by one or more persons who are bound, by rules of a designated professional body which are equivalent to that regulation, and

      (ii)   that supply constitutes or is part of an exempt regulated activity carried on by the supplier.

(5)   Paragraph (2) does not apply in relation to any contract or supply of financial services made by a supplier who is the operator, trustee or depositary of a scheme which is a recognised scheme by virtue of section 264 of the 2000 Act (schemes constituted in other EEA States), where the making or performance of the contract or the supply of the financial services constitutes or is part of a regulated activity for which he has permission in that capacity.

(6)   In paragraph (5)—

"the operator", "trustee" and "depositary" each has the same meaning as in section 237(2) of the 2000 Act (other definitions); and

"permission" has the same meaning as in section 266 of that Act (disapplication of rules).

[2.334]

5

(1)   Where a consumer and a supplier enter an initial service agreement and—

   (a)   successive operations of the same nature, or

   (b)   a series of separate operations of the same nature,

are subsequently performed between them over time and within the framework of that agreement, then, if any of regulations 7 to 14 apply, they apply only to the initial service agreement.

(2)   Where a consumer and a supplier do not enter an initial service agreement and—

   (a)   successive operations of the same nature, or

   (b)   a series of separate operations of the same nature,

are performed between them over time, then, if regulations 7 and 8 apply, they apply only—

      (i)   when the first operation is performed, and

      (ii)   to any operation which is performed more than one year after the previous operation.

(3)   For the purposes of this regulation, "initial service agreement" includes, for example, an agreement for the provision of—

   (a)   a bank account;

   (b)   a credit card; or

   (c)   portfolio management services.

(4)   For the purposes of this regulation, "operations" includes, for example—

   (a)   deposits to or withdrawals from a bank account;

   (b)   payments by a credit card;

   (c)   transactions carried out within the framework of an initial service agreement for portfolio management services; and

   (d)   subscriptions to new units of the same collective investment fund,

but does not include adding new elements to an existing initial service agreement, for example adding the possibility of using an electronic payment instrument together with an existing bank account.

[2.335]

6   Financial services marketed by an intermediary

(1)   This regulation applies where a financial service is marketed by an intermediary.

(2)   These Regulations have effect as if—

   (a)   each reference to a supplier in the definition of "breach" in regulation 2(1) were a reference to a supplier or an intermediary;

   (b)   the reference to the supplier in the definition of "means of distance communication" in regulation 2(1), each reference to the supplier in regulations 7, 8(1) and (2), 10 and 11(3)(b), and the first reference to the supplier in regulation 8(4), were a reference to the intermediary;

   (c)   the reference to the supplier in regulation 8(3) were a reference to the supplier or the intermediary;

   (d)   for regulation 11(2) there were substituted—

"(2)   Paragraph (1) does not apply to a distance contract if the intermediary has not complied with regulation 8(1) (and the supplier has not done what the intermediary was required to do by regulation 8(1)), unless—

    (a)   the circumstances fall within regulation 8(1)(b); and

    (b)   either—

        (i)   the intermediary has complied with regulation 7(1) and (2) or, if applicable, regulation 7(4)(b), and with regulation 7(5), or

        (ii)   the supplier has done what the intermediary was required to do by regulation 7(1) and (2) or, if applicable, regulation 7(4)(b), and by regulation 7(5).";

    (e)   the reference to a supplier in regulation 22(1) were a reference to an intermediary; and

    (f)   each reference to the supplier in paragraphs 2, 4, 5 and 19 of Schedule 1 were a reference to the supplier and the intermediary.

(3)   Notwithstanding paragraphs (2) to (4) of regulation 4, regulations 7 and 8 apply in relation to the intermediary unless—

    (a)   the intermediary is an authorised person and the marketing of the financial service constitutes or is part of a regulated activity carried on by him;

    (b)   the intermediary is an appointed representative and the marketing of the financial service constitutes or is part of a regulated activity (other than an exempt regulated activity) carried on by him; or

    (c)   the intermediary is not an authorised person, but—

        (i)   he is bound, or is controlled or managed by one or more persons who are bound, by rules of a designated professional body which are equivalent to regulations 7 and 8, and

        (ii)   the marketing of the financial service constitutes or is part of an exempt regulated activity carried on by him.

(4)   Notwithstanding paragraphs (2) to (4) of regulation 4, regulation 15 applies to the intermediary unless—

    (a)   the intermediary is an authorised person and is acting in the course of a regulated activity carried on by him;

    (b)   the intermediary is an appointed representative and is acting in the course of a regulated activity (other than an exempt regulated activity) carried on by him; or

    (c)   the intermediary is not an authorised person, but—

        (i)   he is bound, or is controlled or managed by one or more persons who are bound, by rules of a designated professional body which are equivalent to regulation 15, and

        (ii)   he is acting in the course an exempt regulated activity carried on by him.

[2.336]

7   Information required prior to the conclusion of the contract

(1)   Subject to [paragraphs (1A), (4), (6) and (7)], in good time prior to the consumer being bound by any distance contract, the supplier shall provide to the consumer the information specified in Schedule 1.

[(1A)   Where a distance contract to which paragraph (1) applies is also a contract for payment services to which the Payment Services Regulations 2009 apply, the supplier is required to provide to the consumer only the information specified in paragraphs 8 to 13, 16, 17 and 21 of Schedule 1.]

(2)   The supplier shall provide the information specified in Schedule 1 in a clear and comprehensible manner appropriate to the means of distance communication used, with due regard in particular to the principles of good faith in commercial transactions and the principles governing the protection of those who are unable to give their consent such as minors.

(3)   Subject to paragraph (4), the supplier shall make clear his commercial purpose when providing the information specified in Schedule 1.

(4)   In the case of a voice telephone communication—

    (a)   the supplier shall make clear his identity and the commercial purpose of any call initiated by him at the beginning of any conversation with the consumer; and

    (b)   if the consumer explicitly consents, only the information specified in Schedule 2 need be given.

(5)   The supplier shall ensure that the information he provides to the consumer pursuant to this regulation, regarding the contractual obligations which would arise if the distance contract were concluded, accurately reflects the contractual obligations which would arise under the law presumed to be applicable to that contract.

[(6)   This regulation shall not apply to a distance contract which is also a consumer credit agreement (other than an authorised non-business overdraft agreement) in respect of which the supplier has disclosed the pre-contract credit information required by regulations 3, 4 or 5, as the case may be, and 7, of the Disclosure of Information Regulations (information to be disclosed to a debtor before a regulated consumer credit agreement is made) in accordance with those Regulations.

(7)   This regulation shall not apply to a distance contract which is also an authorised non-business overdraft agreement in respect of which—

Part 2   Statutory Instruments

(a) the supplier has disclosed the information required by regulation 10(2) of the Disclosure of Information Regulations (authorised non-business overdraft agreements) by means of the European Consumer Credit Information form in accordance with those Regulations; or

(b) in the case of a voice telephone communication, the supplier has—
    (i) disclosed the information required by regulation 10(5) of the Disclosure of Information Regulations in accordance with those Regulations; and
    (ii) provided a copy of the written agreement in accordance with section 61B(2)(b) of the Consumer Credit Act 1974; or

(c) in the case of an agreement made using a means of distance communication, other than voice telephone communication, such that the supplier is unable to provide the information required by regulation 10(2) of the Disclosure of Information Regulations, the supplier has—
    (i) provided a copy of the written agreement in accordance with section 61B(2)(c) of the Consumer Credit Act 1974, and
    (ii) in relation to the contractual obligations which would arise if the distance contract were concluded, provided information which accurately reflects the contractual obligations which would arise under the law presumed to be applicable to that contract.]

NOTES

Para (1): words in square brackets substituted by the Consumer Credit (EU Directive) Regulations 2010, SI 2010/1010, regs 85, 87(a), with effect in relation to certain agreements entered into before 1 February 2011, as provided for in regs 101, 101A of the 2010 Regulations at **[2.804]**, **[2.805]**.

Para (1A): inserted by the Payment Services Regulations 2009, SI 2009/209, reg 126, Sch 6, Pt 2, para 5(a)(ii).

Paras (6), (7): added by SI 2010/1010, regs 85, 87(b), with effect in relation to certain agreements entered into before 1 February 2011, as provided for in regs 101, 101A of the 2010 Regulations at **[2.804]**, **[2.805]**.

[2.337]
8 Written and additional information

(1) [Subject to [paragraphs (1A) to (1C)],] the supplier under a distance contract shall communicate to the consumer on paper, or in another durable medium which is available and accessible to the consumer, all the contractual terms and conditions and the information specified in Schedule 1, either—
    (a) in good time prior to the consumer being bound by that distance contract; or
    (b) immediately after the conclusion of the contract, where the contract has been concluded at the consumer's request using a means of distance communication which does not enable provision in accordance with sub-paragraph (a) of the contractual terms and conditions and the information specified in Schedule 1.

[(1A) Where a distance contract to which paragraph (1) applies is also a contract for payment services to which the Payment Services Regulations 2009 apply, the supplier is required to communicate to the consumer all the contractual terms and conditions and the information specified in paragraphs 8 to 13, 16, 17 and 21 of Schedule 1.]

[(1B) Paragraph (1) shall not apply to a distance contract which is also a consumer credit agreement (other than an authorised non-business overdraft agreement) in respect of which the supplier has disclosed the pre-contract credit information required by regulations 3, 4 or 5, as the case may be, and 7 of the Disclosure of Information Regulations in accordance with those Regulations.

(1C) Paragraph (1) shall not apply to a distance contract which is also an authorised non-business overdraft agreement in respect of which—
    (a) the supplier has—
        (i) disclosed the information required by regulation 10(2) of the Disclosure of Information Regulations (authorised non-business overdraft agreements) by means of the European Consumer Credit Information form in accordance with those Regulations; and
        (ii) provided a copy of the contractual terms and conditions, or
    (b) in the case of a voice telephone communication the supplier has—
        (i) disclosed the information required by regulation 10(5) of the Disclosure of Information Regulations in accordance with those Regulations; and
        (ii) provided a copy of the written agreement in accordance with section 61B(2)(b) of the Consumer Credit Act 1974; or
    (c) in the case of an agreement made using a means of distance communication, other than voice telephone communication, such that the supplier is unable to provide the information required by regulation 10(2) of the Disclosure of Information Regulations, the supplier has provided a copy of the written agreement in accordance with section 61B(2)(c) of the Consumer Credit Act 1974.]

(2) The supplier shall communicate the contractual terms and conditions to the consumer on paper, if the consumer so requests at any time during their contractual relationship.

(3) Paragraph (2) does not apply if the supplier has already communicated the contractual terms and conditions to the consumer on paper during that contractual relationship, and those terms and conditions have not changed since they were so communicated.

(4) The supplier shall change the means of distance communication with the consumer if the consumer so requests at any time during his contractual relationship with the supplier, unless that is incompatible with the distance contract or the nature of the financial service provided to the consumer.

NOTES

Para (1): words in first (outer) pair of square brackets inserted by the Payment Services Regulations 2009, SI 2009/209, reg 126, Sch 6, Pt 2, para 5(b)(i); words in second (inner) pair of square brackets substituted by the Consumer Credit (EU Directive) Regulations 2010, SI 2010/1010, regs 85, 88(a), with effect in relation to certain agreements entered into before 1 February 2011, as provided for in regs 101, 101A of the 2010 Regulations at **[2.804]**, **[2.805]**.

Para (1A): inserted by SI 2009/209, reg 126, Sch 6, Pt 2, para 5(b)(ii).

Paras (1B), (1C): inserted by SI 2010/1010, regs 85, 88(b), with effect in relation to certain agreements entered into before 1 February 2011, as provided for in regs 101, 101A of the 2010 Regulations at **[2.804]**, **[2.805]**.

[2.338]
9   Right to cancel

(1) Subject to regulation 11, if within the cancellation period set out in regulation 10 notice of cancellation is properly given by the consumer to the supplier, the notice of cancellation shall operate to cancel the distance contract.

(2) Cancelling the contract has the effect of terminating the contract at the time at which the notice of cancellation is given.

(3) For the purposes of these Regulations, a notice of cancellation is a notification given—
    (a) orally (where the supplier has informed the consumer that notice of cancellation may be given orally),
    (b) in writing, or
    (c) in another durable medium available and accessible to the supplier,
which, however expressed, indicates the intention of the consumer to cancel the contract by that notification.

(4) Notice of cancellation given under this regulation by a consumer to a supplier is to be treated as having been properly given if the consumer—
    (a) gives it orally to the supplier (where the supplier has informed the consumer that notice of cancellation may be given orally);
    (b) leaves it at the address of the supplier last known to the consumer and addressed to the supplier by name (in which case it is to be taken to have been given on the day on which it was left);
    (c) sends it by post to the address of the supplier last known to the consumer and addressed to the supplier by name (in which case it is to be taken to have been given on the day on which it was posted);
    (d) sends it by facsimile to the business facsimile number of the supplier last known to the consumer (in which case it is to be taken to have been given on the day on which it was sent);
    (e) sends it by electronic mail to the business electronic mail address of the supplier last known to the consumer (in which case it is to be taken to have been given on the day on which it is sent); or
    (f) by other electronic means—
        (i)   sends it to an internet address or web-site which the supplier has notified the consumer may be used for the purpose, or
        (ii) indicates it on such a web-site in accordance with instructions which are on the web-site or which the supplier has provided to the consumer,
    (in which case it is to be taken to have been given on the day on which it is sent to that address or web-site or indicated on that web-site).

(5) The references in paragraph (4)(b) and (c) to the address of the supplier shall, in the case of a supplier which is a body corporate, be treated as including a reference to the address of the secretary or clerk of that body.

(6) The references in paragraph (4)(b) and (c) to the address of the supplier shall, in the case of a supplier which is a partnership, be treated as including a reference to the address of a partner or a person having control or management of the partnership business.

(7) In this regulation—
    (a) every reference to the supplier includes a reference to any other person previously notified by or on behalf of the supplier to the consumer as a person to whom notice of cancellation may be given;
    (b) the references to giving notice of cancellation orally include giving such notice by voice telephone communication, where the supplier has informed the consumer that notice of cancellation may be given in that way; and

(c)   "electronic mail" has the same meaning as in regulation 2(1) of the Privacy and Electronic Communications (EC Directive) Regulations 2003 (interpretation).

[2.339]
10   Cancellation period

(1)   For the purposes of regulation 9, the cancellation period begins on the day on which the distance contract is concluded ("conclusion day") and ends as provided for in paragraphs (2) to (5).

(2)   Where the supplier complies with regulation 8(1) on or before conclusion day, the cancellation period ends on the expiry of fourteen calendar days beginning with the day after conclusion day.

(3)   Where the supplier does not comply with regulation 8(1) on or before conclusion day, but subsequently communicates to the consumer on paper, or in another durable medium which is available and accessible to the consumer, all the contractual terms and conditions and the information required under regulation 8(1), the cancellation period ends on the expiry of fourteen calendar days beginning with the day after the day on which the consumer receives the last of those terms and conditions and that information.

[(3A)   Where the distance contract is also an authorised non-business overdraft agreement the cancellation period ends on the expiry of fourteen calendar days beginning with the day after the relevant day.

(3B)   For the purposes of paragraph (3A) the relevant day is whichever is the latest of the following—
(a)   the conclusion day;
(b)   where the supplier is required to inform the consumer of the credit limit under the distance contract the day on which the supplier first does so;
(c)   in the case of an agreement to which regulation 8(1C)(a) is relevant the day on which the consumer receives the information and the contractual terms and conditions referred to in that regulation;
(d)   in the case of an agreement to which regulation 8(1C)(b) or (c) is relevant the day on which the consumer receives the information and the written agreement or, as applicable, the written agreement referred to in that regulation.]

(4)   In the case of a distance contract relating to life insurance, for the references to conclusion day in paragraphs (2) and (3) there are substituted references to the day on which the consumer is informed that the distance contract has been concluded.

(5)   In the case of a distance contract relating to life insurance or a personal pension, for the references to fourteen calendar days in paragraphs (2) and (3) there are substituted references to thirty calendar days.

NOTES
Paras (3A), (3B): inserted by the Consumer Credit (EU Directive) Regulations 2010, SI 2010/1010, reg 88A (as inserted by the Consumer Credit (Amendment) Regulations 2011, SI 2011/11, regs 2, 6), with effect in relation to certain agreements entered into before 1 February 2011, as provided for in regs 101, 101A of the 2010 Regulations at **[2.804]**, **[2.805]**.

[2.340]
11   Exceptions to the right to cancel

(1)   Subject to paragraphs (2) and (3), regulation 9 does not confer on a consumer a right to cancel a distance contract which is—
(a)   a contract for a financial service where the price of that service depends on fluctuations in the financial market outside the supplier's control, which may occur during the cancellation period, such as services related to—
(i)   foreign exchange,
(ii)   money market instruments,
(iii)   transferable securities,
(iv)   units in collective investment undertakings,
(v)   financial-futures contracts, including equivalent cash-settled instruments,
(vi)   forward interest-rate agreements,
(vii)   interest-rate, currency and equity swaps,
(viii) options to acquire or dispose of any instruments referred to in sub-paragraphs (i) to (vii), including cash-settled instruments and options on currency and on interest rates;
(b)   a contract whose performance has been fully completed by both parties at the consumer's express request before the consumer gives notice of cancellation;
(c)   a contract which—
(i)   is a connected contract of insurance within the meaning of article 72B(1) of the Regulated Activities Order (activities carried on by a provider of relevant goods or services),
(ii)   covers travel risks within the meaning of article 72B(1)(d)(ii) of that Order, and
(iii)   has a total duration of less than one month;
(d)   a contract under which a supplier provides credit to a consumer and the consumer's obligation to repay is secured by a legal mortgage on land;

[(e)   a credit agreement terminated under regulation 38(1) of the Consumer Contracts (Information, Cancellation and Additional Charges) Regulations 2013 (automatic termination of related agreements)]

[(f)   a credit agreement cancelled under regulation 23 of the Timeshare, Holiday Products, Resale and Exchange Contracts Regulations 2010 (automatic termination of credit agreement);]

(g)   a restricted-use credit agreement (within the meaning of the 1974 Act) to finance the purchase of land or an existing building, or an agreement for a bridging loan in connection with the purchase of land or an existing building;

[(h)   a regulated consumer credit agreement to which the right of withdrawal applies under section 66A of the 1974 Act;]

(2)   Paragraph (1) does not apply to a distance contract if the supplier has not complied with regulation 8(1), unless—

(a)   the circumstances fall within regulation 8(1)(b); and

(b)   the supplier has complied with regulation 7(1) and (2) or, if applicable, regulation 7(4)(b), and with regulation 7(5).

(3)   Where—

(a)   the conditions in sub-paragraphs (a) and (b) of paragraph (2) are satisfied in relation to a distance contract falling within paragraph (1),

(b)   the supplier has not complied with regulation 8(1), and

(c)   the consumer has not, by the end of the sixth day after the day on which the distance contract is concluded, received all the contractual terms and conditions and the information required under regulation 8(1),

the consumer may cancel the contract under regulation 9 during the period beginning on the seventh day after the day on which the distance contract is concluded and ending when he receives the last of the contractual terms and conditions and the information required under regulation 8(1).

NOTES

Para (1): sub-para (e) substituted by the Consumer Contracts (Information, Cancellation and Additional Charges) Regulations 2013, SI 2013/3134, reg 47, Sch 4, para 4 (as amended by SI 2014/870, reg 9(1), (5)(a)), in relation to contracts entered into on or after 13 June 2014; the original text read as follows—

"(e)   a credit agreement cancelled under regulation 15(1) of the Consumer Protection (Distance Selling) Regulations 2000 (automatic cancellation of a related credit agreement)".

; sub-para (f) substituted by the Timeshare, Holiday Products, Resale and Exchange Contracts Regulations 2010, SI 2010/2960, reg 36(3), Sch 6, para 13; sub-para (h) added by the Consumer Credit (EU Directive) Regulations 2010, SI 2010/1010, regs 85, 89, and substituted by the Financial Services and Markets Act 2000 (Regulated Activities) (Amendment) (No 2) Order 2013, SI 2013/1881, art 28, Schedule, Pt 2, para 26(b), for transitional provisions see Pt 8 thereof at **[2.1007]** et seq.

[2.341]
12   Automatic cancellation of an attached distance contract

(1)   For the purposes of this regulation, where there is a distance contract for the provision of a financial service by a supplier to a consumer ("the main contract") and there is a further distance contract ("the secondary contract") for the provision to that consumer of a further financial service by—

(a)   the same supplier, or

(b)   a third party, the further financial service being provided pursuant to an agreement between the third party and the supplier under the main contract,

then the secondary contract (referred to in these Regulations as an "attached contract") is attached to the main contract if any of the conditions in paragraph (2) are satisfied.

(2)   The conditions referred to in paragraph (1) are—

(a)   the secondary contract is entered into in compliance with a term of the main contract;

(b)   the main contract is, or is to be, financed by the secondary contract;

(c)   the main contract is a debtor-creditor-supplier agreement within the meaning of the 1974 Act, and the secondary contract is, or is to be, financed by the main contract;

(d)   the secondary contract is entered into by the consumer to induce the supplier to enter into the main contract;

(e)   performance of the secondary contract requires performance of the main contract.

(3)   Where a main contract is cancelled by a notice of cancellation given under regulation 9—

(a)   the cancellation of the main contract also operates to cancel, at the time at which the main contract is cancelled, any attached contract which is not a contract or agreement of a type listed in regulation 11(1); and

(b)   the supplier under the main contract shall, if he is not the supplier under the attached contract, forthwith on receipt of the notice of cancellation inform the supplier under the attached contract.

Part 2   Statutory Instruments

(4)   Paragraph (3)(a) does not apply to an attached contract if, at or before the time at which the notice of cancellation in respect of the main contract is given, the consumer has given and not withdrawn a notice to the supplier under the main contract that cancellation of the main contract is not to operate to cancel that attached contract.

(5)   Where a main contract made by an authorised person, the making or performance of which constitutes or is part of a regulated activity carried on by him, is cancelled under rules made by the Authority corresponding to regulation 9—

(a)   the cancellation of the main contract also operates to cancel, at the time at which the main contract is cancelled, any attached contract which is not a contract or agreement of a type listed in regulation 11(1); and

(b)   the supplier under the main contract shall, if he is not the supplier under the attached contract, inform the supplier under the attached contract forthwith on receiving notification of the consumer's intention to cancel the main contract by that notification.

(6)   Paragraph (5)(a) does not apply to an attached contract if, at or before the time at which the consumer gives notification of his intention to cancel the main contract by that notification, the consumer has given and not withdrawn a notice to the supplier under the main contract that cancellation of the main contract is not to operate to cancel that attached contract.

[2.342]
13   Payment for services provided before cancellation

(1)   This regulation applies where a cancellation event occurs in relation to a distance contract.

(2)   In this regulation, "cancellation event" means the cancellation of a distance contract under regulation 9 or 12.

(3)   The supplier shall refund any sum paid by or on behalf of the consumer under or in relation to the contract to the person by whom it was paid, less any charge made in accordance with paragraph (6), as soon as possible and in any event within a period not exceeding 30 calendar days beginning with—

(a)   the day on which the cancellation event occurred; or

(b)   if the supplier proves that this is later—

(i)   in the case of a contract cancelled under regulation 9, the day on which the supplier in fact received the notice of cancellation, or

(ii)   in the case of an attached contract under which the supplier is not the supplier under the main contract, the day on which, pursuant to regulation 12(3)(b) or (5)(b), he was in fact informed by the supplier under the main contract of the cancellation of the main contract.

(4)   The reference in paragraph (3) to any sum paid on behalf of the consumer includes any sum paid by any other person ("the creditor"), who is not the supplier, under an agreement between the consumer and the creditor by which the creditor provides the consumer with credit of any amount.

(5)   Where any security has been provided in relation to the contract, the security (so far as it has been provided) shall, on cancellation under regulation 9 or 12, be treated as never having had effect; and any property lodged solely for the purposes of the security as so provided shall be returned forthwith by the person with whom it is lodged.

(6)   Subject to paragraphs (7), (8) and (9), the supplier may make a charge for any service actually provided by the supplier in accordance with the contract.

(7)   The charge shall not exceed an amount which is in proportion to the extent of the service provided to the consumer prior to the time at which the cancellation event occurred (including the service of arranging to provide the financial service) in comparison with the full coverage of the contract, and in any event shall not be such that it could be construed as a penalty.

(8)   The supplier may not make any charge unless he can prove on the balance of probabilities that the consumer was informed about the amount payable in accordance with—

(a)   regulation 7(1) and paragraph 13 of Schedule 1,

(b)   regulation 7(4) and paragraph 5 of Schedule 2, or

(c)   rules corresponding to those provisions,

as the case may be.

(9)   The supplier may not make any charge if, without the consumer's prior request, he commenced performance of the contract prior to the expiry of the relevant cancellation period.

(10)   In paragraph (9), the relevant cancellation period is the cancellation period which—

(a)   in the case of a main contract, is applicable to that contract, or

(b)   in the case of an attached contract, would be applicable to that contract if that contract were a main contract,

under regulation 10, or under rules corresponding to that regulation, as the case may be.

(11)   The consumer shall, as soon as possible and in any event within a period not exceeding 30 calendar days beginning with the day on which the cancellation event occurred—

(a)   refund any sum paid by or on behalf of the supplier under or in relation to that contract to the person by whom it was paid; and

(b)   either restore to the supplier any property of which he has acquired possession under that contract, or deliver or send that property to any person to whom, under regulation 9, a notice of cancellation could have been given in respect of that contract.

(12)   Breach of a duty imposed by paragraph (11) on a consumer is actionable as a breach of statutory duty.

14   *(Revoked by the Payment Services Regulations 2009, SI 2009/209, reg 126, Sch 6, Pt 2, para 5(c).)*

[2.343]
15   Unsolicited services

(1)   A person ("the recipient") who receives unsolicited financial services for purposes other than those of his business from another person who supplies those services in the course of his business, shall not thereby become subject to any obligation (to make payment, or otherwise).

(2), (3)   . . .

(4)   In this regulation, "unsolicited" means, in relation to financial services supplied to any person, that they are supplied without any prior request made by or on behalf of that person.

(5)–(7)   . . .

(8)   This regulation is without prejudice to any right a supplier may have at any time, by contract or otherwise, to renew a distance contract with a consumer without any request made by or on behalf of that consumer prior to the renewal of that contract.

NOTES
   Paras (2), (3), (5)–(7): revoked by the Consumer Protection from Unfair Trading Regulations 2008, SI 2008/1277, reg 30(1), (3), Sch 2, Pt 2, para 110(1), (2), Sch 4.

[2.344]
16   Prevention of contracting-out

(1)   A term contained in any contract is void if, and to the extent that, it is inconsistent with the application of a provision of these Regulations to a distance contract or the application of regulation 15 to a supply of unsolicited financial services.

(2)   Where a provision of these Regulations specifies a duty or liability of the consumer in certain circumstances, a term contained in a contract is inconsistent with that provision if it purports to impose, directly or indirectly, an additional or greater duty or liability on him in those circumstances.

(3)   These Regulations apply notwithstanding any contract term which applies or purports to apply the law of a State which is not an EEA State if the contract or supply has a close connection with the territory of an EEA State.

[2.345]
17   Enforcement authorities

(1)   For the purposes of regulations 18 to 21—
   (a)   in relation to any alleged breach concerning a specified contract[—
       (i)   the Authority, and
       (ii)   where the contract is a consumer credit contract—
           (aa)   in Great Britain, every local weights and measures authority, and
           (bb)   in Northern Ireland, the Department of Enterprise, Trade and Investment,
   is an enforcement authority.]
   (b)   in relation to any alleged breach concerning a contract under which the supplier is a local authority, but which is not a specified contract, the [CMA] is the enforcement authority;
   (c)   in relation to any other alleged breach—
       (i)   the [CMA], and
       (ii)   in Great Britain every local weights and measures authority, and in Northern Ireland the Department of Enterprise, Trade and Investment,
       is an enforcement authority.

(2)   For the purposes of paragraph (1) and regulation 22(6), each of the following is a specified contract—
   (a)   a contract the making or performance of which constitutes or is part of a regulated activity carried on by the supplier [or an activity which would constitute a regulated activity carried on by the supplier but for any of articles 60C to 60H of the Regulated Activities Order];
   (b)   a contract for the provision of a debit card;
   (c)   a contract relating to the issuing of electronic money by [an electronic money institution within the meaning of the Electronic Money Regulations 2011 . . . .] . . . . ;
   (d)   a contract the effecting or carrying out of which is excluded from article 10(1) or (2) of the Regulated Activities Order (effecting and carrying out contracts of insurance) by article 12 of that order (breakdown insurance), where the supplier is a person who does not otherwise carry on an activity of the kind specified by article 10 of that order;

(e) a contract under which a supplier provides credit to a consumer and the obligation of the consumer to repay is secured by a first legal mortgage on land;

(f) a contract, made before 14th January 2005, for insurance mediation activity other than in respect of a contract of long-term care insurance.

[(2A) For the purposes of paragraph (1) and regulation 22(6), a "consumer credit contract" means a contract the making or performance of which constitutes or is part of a regulated activity of the kind specified by a provision of the Regulated Activities Order listed in paragraph (2B) carried on by the supplier.

(2B) The provisions are—
  (a) article 36A (credit broking);
  (b) article 36H (operating an electronic system in relation to lending);
  (c) article 39D (debt adjusting);
  (d) article 39E (debt-counselling);
  (e) article 39F (debt-collecting);
  (f) article 39G (debt administration);
  (g) article 60B (regulated credit agreements);
  (h) article 60N (regulated consumer hire agreements);
  (i) article 89A (providing credit information services);
  (j) article 89B (providing credit references);
  (k) article 64 (agreeing to carry on specified kinds of activity) in so far as it relates to an activity of the kind specified by a provision listed in sub-paragraphs (a) to (j).]

(3) For the purposes of the application of this regulation and regulations 18 to 22 in relation to breaches of, and offences under, regulation 15, "contract"—
  (a) wherever it appears in this regulation other than in the expression "contract of long-term care insurance", and
  (b) in regulation 22(6),
is to be taken to mean "supply of financial services".

(4) For the purposes of this regulation—
  "contract of long-term care insurance" has the same meaning as in the Financial Services and Markets Act 2000 (Regulated Activities) (Amendment) (No 2) Order 2003;
  "insurance mediation activity" means any activity which is not a regulated activity at the time the contract is made but will be a regulated activity of the kind specified by article 21, 25(1) or (2), 39A or 53 of the Regulated Activities Order when the amendments to that order made by the Financial Services and Markets Act 2000 (Regulated Activities) (Amendment) (No 2) Order 2003 come into force;
  "local authority" means—
  (a) in England and Wales, a local authority within the meaning of the Local Government Act 1972, the Greater London Authority, the Common Council of the City of London or the Council of the Isles of Scilly,
  (b) in Scotland, a council constituted under section 2 of the Local Government etc (Scotland) Act 1994, and
  (c) in Northern Ireland, a district council within the meaning of the Local Government Act (Northern Ireland) 1972.

NOTES
Para (1): words in square brackets substituted by the Financial Services and Markets Act 2000 (Consumer Credit) (Miscellaneous Provisions) Order 2014, SI 2014/208, art 3(1), (3)(a).
Para (2): words in square brackets in sub-para (a) added, and words omitted from sub-para (c) revoked, by SI 2014/208, art 3(1), (3)(b); words in square brackets in sub-para (c) inserted by the Electronic Money Regulations 2011, SI 2011/99, reg 79, Sch 4, Pt 2, para 15.
Paras (2A), (2B): inserted by SI 2014/208, art 3(1), (3)(c).

[2.346]
18 Consideration of complaints

(1) An enforcement authority shall consider any complaint made to it about a breach unless—
  (a) the complaint appears to that authority to be frivolous or vexatious; or
  (b) that authority is aware that another enforcement authority [has agreed, by notifying that authority or the relevant regulator,] to consider the complaint.

(2) If an enforcement authority notifies [another enforcement authority or the relevant regulator] that it agrees to consider a complaint made to another enforcement authority, the first mentioned authority shall be under a duty to consider the complaint.

NOTES
Words in square brackets substituted by the Financial Services and Markets Act 2000 (Consumer Credit) (Miscellaneous Provisions) Order 2014, SI 2014/208, art 3(1), (4).

[2.347]
19 Injunctions to secure compliance with these Regulations

(1) Subject to paragraph (2), an enforcement authority may apply for an injunction (including an interim injunction) against any person who appears to that authority to be responsible for a breach.

(2) An enforcement authority, other than the [relevant regulator] . . . , may apply for an injunction only where—

   (a) that authority has notified the [relevant regulator], at least fourteen days before the date on which the application is to be made, of its intention to apply; or

   (b) the [relevant regulator] consents to the application being made within a shorter period.

(3) On an application made under this regulation, the court may grant an injunction on such terms as it thinks fit to secure compliance with these Regulations.

(4) An enforcement authority which has a duty under regulation 18 to consider a complaint shall give reasons for its decision to apply or not to apply, as the case may be, for an injunction.

(5) In deciding whether or not to apply for an injunction in respect of a breach, an enforcement authority may, if it considers it appropriate to do so, have regard to any undertaking as to compliance with these Regulations given to it or to another enforcement authority by or on behalf of any person.

(6) In the application of this regulation to Scotland, for references to an "injunction" or an "interim injunction" there are substituted references to an "interdict" or an "interim interdict" respectively.

NOTES

   Para (2): words in square brackets substituted, and words omitted revoked, by the Financial Services and Markets Act 2000 (Consumer Credit) (Miscellaneous Provisions) Order 2014, SI 2014/208, art 3(1), (5).

[2.348]
20 Notification of undertakings and orders to the [relevant regulator]

An enforcement authority, other than the [relevant regulator] . . . , shall notify the [relevant regulator] of—

   (a) any undertaking given to it by or on behalf of any person who appears to it to be responsible for a breach;

   (b) the outcome of any application made by it under regulation 19 and the terms of any undertaking given to, or order made by, the court; and

   (c) the outcome of any application made by it to enforce a previous order of the court.

NOTES

   Words in square brackets substituted, and words omitted revoked, by the Financial Services and Markets Act 2000 (Consumer Credit) (Miscellaneous Provisions) Order 2014, SI 2014/208, art 3(1), (6), (7).

[2.349]
21 Publication, information and advice

(1) The [relevant regulator] shall arrange for the publication, in such form and manner as it considers appropriate, of details of any undertaking or order notified to it under regulation 20.

(2) Each of the [relevant regulator] shall arrange for the publication in such form and manner as it considers appropriate of—

   (a) details of any undertaking as to compliance with these Regulations given to it by or on behalf of any person;

   (b) details of any application made by it under regulation 19, and of the terms of any undertaking given to, or order made by, the court; and

   (c) details of any application made by it to enforce a previous order of the court.

(3) Each of the [relevant regulator] may arrange for the dissemination, in such form and manner as it considers appropriate, of such information and advice concerning the operation of these Regulations as may appear to it to be expedient to give to the public and to all persons likely to be affected by these Regulations.

NOTES

   Words in square brackets substituted by the Financial Services and Markets Act 2000 (Consumer Credit) (Miscellaneous Provisions) Order 2014, SI 2014/208, art 3(1), (8).

[2.350]
22 Offences

(1) A supplier under a distance contract who fails to comply with regulation 7(3) or (4)(a) or regulation 8(2) or (4) is guilty of an offence and liable, on summary conviction, to a fine not exceeding level 3 on the standard scale.

(2) If an offence under paragraph (1) . . . committed by a body corporate is shown—

(a) to have been committed with the consent or connivance of any director, manager, secretary or other similar officer of the body corporate, or any person who was purporting to act in any such capacity, or

(b) to be attributable to any neglect on his part,

he as well as the body corporate is guilty of the offence and liable to be proceeded against and punished accordingly.

(3) If the affairs of a body corporate are managed by its members, paragraph (2) applies in relation to the acts and defaults of a member in connection with his functions of management as if he were a director of the body.

(4) If an offence under paragraph (1) . . . committed by a partnership is shown—

(a) to have been committed with the consent or connivance of any partner, or any person who was purporting to act as a partner, or

(b) to be attributable to any neglect on his part,

he as well as the partnership is guilty of an offence and liable to be proceeded against and punished accordingly.

(5) If an offence under paragraph (1) . . . committed by an unincorporated association (other than a partnership) is shown—

(a) to have been committed with the consent or connivance of an officer of the association or a member of its governing body, or any person who was purporting to act in any such capacity, or

(b) to be attributable to any neglect on his part,

he as well as the association is guilty of an offence and liable to be proceeded against and punished accordingly.

(6) Except in Scotland—

(a) the Authority may institute proceedings for an offence under these Regulations which relates to a specified contract;

[(aa) in Great Britain, every local weights and measures authority and, in Northern Ireland, the Department of Enterprise, Trade and Investment may institute proceedings for an offence under these Regulations which relates to a consumer credit contract;]

(b) the [CMA], and—

(i) in Great Britain, every local weights and measures authority,

(ii) in Northern Ireland, the Department of Enterprise, Trade and Investment,

may institute proceedings for any other offence under these Regulations.

NOTES

Paras (2), (4), (5): words omitted revoked by the Consumer Protection from Unfair Trading Regulations 2008, SI 2008/1277, reg 30(1), (3), Sch 2, Pt 2, para 110(1), (3), Sch 4.

Para (6): sub-para (aa) inserted, and word in square brackets in sub-para (b) substituted, by the Financial Services and Markets Act 2000 (Consumer Credit) (Miscellaneous Provisions) Order 2014, SI 2014/208, art 3(1), (9).

[2.351]
23 Functions of the Authority
The functions conferred on the Authority by these Regulations shall be treated as if they were conferred by the 2000 Act.

24–28 (*Reg 24 amends the Unfair Terms in Consumer Contracts Regulations 1999, SI 1999/2083, regs 3, 5 at* **[2.122]**, **[2.124]**; *reg 25 amends the Consumer Protection (Distance Selling) Regulations 2000, SI 2000/2334, regs 3, 5, 6 at* **[2.139]**, **[2.141]**, **[2.142]** *and repeals Sch 2 to those Regulations; regs 26–28 amend provisions outside the scope of this work.*)

[2.352]
29 Transitional provisions
(1) In relation to any contract made before 31st May 2005 which is a consumer credit agreement within the meaning of the 1974 Act and a regulated agreement within the meaning of that Act—

(a) regulations 7, 8, 10 and 11 apply subject to the modifications in paragraphs (2) to (5); and

(b) references in these Regulations to regulations 7, 8, 10 and 11 or to provisions contained in them shall be construed accordingly.

(2) In regulation 7—

(a) in paragraphs (1) to (3), before "Schedule 1" at each place where it occurs insert "paragraph 13 of"; and

(b) in paragraph (4)(b), before "Schedule 2" insert "paragraph 5 of".

(3) In regulation 8(1), for "contractual terms and conditions and the information specified in" at each place where it occurs substitute "information specified in paragraph 13 of".

(4) In regulation 10(3), omit—

(a) "the contractual terms and conditions and"; and

(b) "those terms and conditions and".

(5) In regulation 11(3), omit "the contractual terms and conditions and" at each place where it occurs.

SCHEDULES

SCHEDULE 1
INFORMATION REQUIRED PRIOR TO THE CONCLUSION OF THE CONTRACT

Regulations 7(1) and 8(1)

[2.353]

1. The identity and the main business of the supplier, the geographical address at which the supplier is established and any other geographical address relevant to the consumer's relations with the supplier.

2. Where the supplier has a representative established in the consumer's State of residence, the identity of that representative and the geographical address relevant to the consumer's relations with him.

3. Where the consumer's dealings are with any professional other than the supplier, the identity of that professional, the capacity in which he is acting with respect to the consumer, and the geographical address relevant to the consumer's relations with that professional.

4. Where the supplier is registered in a trade or similar public register, the particulars of the register in which the supplier is entered and his registration number or an equivalent means of identification in that register.

5. Where the supplier's activity is subject to an authorisation scheme, the particulars of the relevant supervisory authority.

6. A description of the main characteristics of the financial service.

7. The total price to be paid by the consumer to the supplier for the financial service, including all related fees, charges and expenses, and all taxes paid via the supplier or, where an exact price cannot be indicated, the basis for the calculation of the price enabling the consumer to verify it.

8. Where relevant, notice indicating that: (i) the financial service is related to instruments involving special risks related to their specific features or the operations to be executed or whose price depends on fluctuations in the financial markets outside the supplier's control; and (ii) historical performances are no indicators for future performances.

9. Notice of the possibility that other taxes or costs may exist that are not paid via the supplier or imposed by him.

10. Any limitations of the period for which the information provided is valid.

11. The arrangements for payment and for performance.

12. Any specific additional cost for the consumer of using the means of distance communication, if such additional cost is charged.

13. Whether or not there is a right of cancellation and, where there is a right of cancellation, its duration and the conditions for exercising it, including information on the amount which the consumer may be required to pay in accordance with regulation 13, as well as the consequences of not exercising that right.

14. The minimum duration of the distance contract in the case of financial services to be performed indefinitely or recurrently.

15. Information on any rights the parties may have to terminate the distance contract early or unilaterally by virtue of the terms of the contract, including any penalties imposed by the contract in such cases.

16. Practical instructions for exercising the right to cancel in accordance with regulation 9 indicating, among other things, the address at which the notice of cancellation should be left or to which it should be sent by post, and any facsimile number or electronic mail address to which it should be sent.

17. The EEA State or States whose laws are taken by the supplier as a basis for the establishment of relations with the consumer prior to the conclusion of the distance contract.

18. Any contractual clause on the law applicable to the distance contract or on the competent court.

19. In which language, or languages: (i) the contractual terms and conditions, and the prior information specified in this Schedule, are supplied; and (ii) the supplier, with the agreement of the consumer, undertakes to communicate during the duration of the distance contract.

20. Whether or not there is an out-of-court complaint and redress mechanism for the consumer and, if so, the methods for having access to it.

21. The existence of guarantee funds or other compensation arrangements, except to the extent that they are required by Directive 94/19/EC of the European Parliament and of the Council of 30 May 1994 on deposit guarantee schemes or Directive 97/9/EC of the European Parliament and of the Council of 3 March 1997 on investor compensation schemes.

SCHEDULE 2
INFORMATION REQUIRED IN THE CASE OF VOICE
TELEPHONE COMMUNICATIONS

Regulation 7(4)(b)

[2.354]

1. The identity of the person in contact with the consumer and his link with the supplier.

2. A description of the main characteristics of the financial service.

3. The total price to be paid by the consumer to the supplier for the financial service including all taxes paid via the supplier or, if an exact price cannot be indicated, the basis for the calculation of the price enabling the consumer to verify it.

4. Notice of the possibility that other taxes or costs may exist that are not paid via the supplier or imposed by him.

5. Whether or not there is a right to cancel and, where there is such a right, its duration and the conditions for exercising it, including information on the amount which the consumer may be required to pay in accordance with regulation 13, as well as the consequences of not exercising that right.

6. That other information is available on request and the nature of that information.

GENERAL PRODUCT SAFETY REGULATIONS 2005

(SI 2005/1803)

NOTES
Made: 30 June 2005.
Authority: European Communities Act 1972, s 2(2).
Commencement: see reg 1(1) at **[2.355]**.

ARRANGEMENT OF REGULATIONS

PART 1
GENERAL

PART 2
OBLIGATIONS OF PRODUCERS AND DISTRIBUTORS

PART 3
ENFORCEMENT

PART 1
GENERAL

[2.355]
1 Citation, commencement and revocation

(1)   These Regulations may be cited as the General Product Safety Regulations 2005 and shall come into force on 1st October 2005 with the exception of the reference to a civil partner in regulation 43(2) which shall come into force on 5th December 2005.

(2)   The General Product Safety Regulations 1994 are hereby revoked.

[2.356]
2 Interpretation

In these Regulations—
   "the 1987 Act" means the Consumer Protection Act 1987;
   "Community law" includes a law in any part of the United Kingdom which implements
      a Community obligation [and does not include Regulation (EC) No 765/2008 of the
      European Parliament and the Council setting out the requirements for accreditation and
      market surveillance relating to the marketing of products and repealing Regulation (EEC)
      No 339/93];
   "contravention" includes a failure to comply and cognate expressions shall be construed
      accordingly;
   "dangerous product" means a product other than a safe product;
   "distributor" means a professional in the supply chain whose activity does not affect the safety
      properties of a product;
   "enforcement authority" means the Secretary of State, any other Minister of the Crown in charge
      of a government department, any such department and any authority or council mentioned
      in regulation 10;
   "general safety requirement" means the requirement that only safe products should be placed on
      the market;
   "the GPS Directive" means Directive 2001/95/EC of the European Parliament and of the Council
      of 3 December 2001 on general product safety;
   "magistrates' court" in relation to Northern Ireland, means a court of summary jurisdiction;
   "Member State" means a member State, Norway, Iceland or Liechtenstein;
   "notice" means a notice in writing;
   "officer", in relation to an enforcement authority, means a person authorised in writing to assist
      the authority in carrying out its functions under or for the purposes of the enforcement of
      these Regulations and safety notices, except in relation to an enforcement authority which
      is a government department where it means an officer of that department;
   "producer" means—

(a)   the manufacturer of a product, when he is established in a Member State and any other person presenting himself as the manufacturer by affixing to the product his name, trade mark or other distinctive mark, or the person who reconditions the product;

(b)   when the manufacturer is not established in a Member State—

    (i)   if he has a representative established in a Member State, the representative,

    (ii)   in any other case, the importer of the product from a state that is not a Member State into a Member State;

(c)   other professionals in the supply chain, insofar as their activities may affect the safety properties of a product;

"product" means a product which is intended for consumers or likely, under reasonably foreseeable conditions, to be used by consumers even if not intended for them and which is supplied or made available, whether for consideration or not, in the course of a commercial activity and whether it is new, used or reconditioned and includes a product that is supplied or made available to consumers for their own use in the context of providing a service. "product" does not include equipment used by service providers themselves to supply a service to consumers, in particular equipment on which consumers ride or travel which is operated by a service provider;

"recall" means any measure aimed at achieving the return of a dangerous product that has already been supplied or made available to consumers;

"recall notice" means a notice under regulation 15;

"record" includes any book or document and any record in any form;

"requirement to mark" means a notice under regulation 12;

"requirement to warn" means a notice under regulation 13;

"safe product" means a product which, under normal or reasonably foreseeable conditions of use including duration and, where applicable, putting into service, installation and maintenance requirements, does not present any risk or only the minimum risks compatible with the product's use, considered to be acceptable and consistent with a high level of protection for the safety and health of persons. In determining the foregoing, the following shall be taken into account in particular—

(a)   the characteristics of the product, including its composition, packaging, instructions for assembly and, where applicable, instructions for installation and maintenance,

(b)   the effect of the product on other products, where it is reasonably foreseeable that it will be used with other products,

(c)   the presentation of the product, the labelling, any warnings and instructions for its use and disposal and any other indication or information regarding the product, and

(d)   the categories of consumers at risk when using the product, in particular children and the elderly.

The feasibility of obtaining higher levels of safety or the availability of other products presenting a lesser degree of risk shall not constitute grounds for considering a product to be a dangerous product;

"safety notice" means a suspension notice, a requirement to mark, a requirement to warn, a withdrawal notice or a recall notice;

"serious risk" means a serious risk, including one the effects of which are not immediate, requiring rapid intervention;

"supply" in relation to a product includes making it available, in the context of providing a service, for use by consumers;

"suspension notice" means a notice under regulation 11;

"withdrawal" means any measure aimed at preventing the distribution, display or offer of a dangerous product to a consumer;

"withdrawal notice" means a notice under regulation 14.

NOTES

Words in square brackets in definition "Community law" inserted by the Toys (Safety) Regulations 2011, SI 2011/1881, reg 57.

[2.357]

3 Application

(1)   Each provision of these Regulations applies to a product in so far as there are no specific provisions with the same objective in rules of Community law governing the safety of the product other than the GPS Directive.

(2)   Where a product is subject to specific safety requirements imposed by rules of Community law other than the GPS Directive, these Regulations shall apply only to the aspects and risks or category of risks not covered by those requirements. This means that:

(a)   the definition of "safe product" and "dangerous product" in regulation 2 and regulations 5 and 6 shall not apply to such a product in so far as concerns the risks or category of risks covered by the specific rules, and

(b)   the remainder of these Regulations shall apply except where there are specific provisions governing the aspects covered by those regulations with the same objective.

[2.358]
4

These Regulations do not apply to a second-hand product supplied as a product to be repaired or reconditioned prior to being used, provided the supplier clearly informs the person to whom he supplies the product to that effect.

PART 2
OBLIGATIONS OF PRODUCERS AND DISTRIBUTORS

[2.359]
5   General safety requirement

(1)   No producer shall place a product on the market unless the product is a safe product.

(2)   No producer shall offer or agree to place a product on the market or expose or possess a product for placing on the market unless the product is a safe product.

(3)   No producer shall offer or agree to supply a product or expose or possess a product for supply unless the product is a safe product.

(4)   No producer shall supply a product unless the product is a safe product.

[2.360]
6   Presumption of conformity

(1)   Where, in the absence of specific provisions in rules of Community law governing the safety of a product, the product conforms to the specific rules of the law of part of the United Kingdom laying down the health and safety requirements which the product must satisfy in order to be marketed in the United Kingdom, the product shall be deemed safe so far as concerns the aspects covered by such rules.

(2)   Where a product conforms to a voluntary national standard of the United Kingdom giving effect to a European standard the reference of which has been published in the Official Journal of the European Union in accordance with Article 4 of the GPS Directive, the product shall be presumed to be a safe product so far as concerns the risks and categories of risk covered by that national standard. The Secretary of State shall publish the reference number of such national standards in such manner as he considers appropriate.

(3)   In circumstances other than those referred to in paragraphs (1) and (2), the conformity of a product to the general safety requirement shall be assessed taking into account—
    (a)   any voluntary national standard of the United Kingdom giving effect to a European standard, other than one referred to in paragraph (2),
    (b)   other national standards drawn up in the United Kingdom,
    (c)   recommendations of the European Commission setting guidelines on product safety assessment,
    (d)   product safety codes of good practice in the sector concerned,
    (e)   the state of the art and technology, and
    (f)   reasonable consumer expectations concerning safety.

(4)   Conformity of a product with the criteria designed to ensure the general safety requirement is complied with, in particular the provisions mentioned in paragraphs (1) to (3), shall not bar an enforcement authority from exercising its powers under these Regulations in relation to that product where there is evidence that, despite such conformity, it is dangerous.

[2.361]
7   Other obligations of producers

(1)   Within the limits of his activities, a producer shall provide consumers with the relevant information to enable them—
    (a)   to assess the risks inherent in a product throughout the normal or reasonably foreseeable period of its use, where such risks are not immediately obvious without adequate warnings, and
    (b)   to take precautions against those risks.

(2)   The presence of warnings does not exempt any person from compliance with the other requirements of these Regulations.

(3)   Within the limits of his activities, a producer shall adopt measures commensurate with the characteristics of the products which he supplies to enable him to—
    (a)   be informed of the risks which the products might pose, and
    (b)   take appropriate action including, where necessary to avoid such risks, withdrawal, adequately and effectively warning consumers as to the risks or, as a last resort, recall.

(4)   The measures referred to in paragraph (3) include—
    (a)   except where it is not reasonable to do so, an indication by means of the product or its packaging of—

      (i)   the name and address of the producer, and

      (ii)   the product reference or where applicable the batch of products to which it belongs; and

  (b)   where and to the extent that it is reasonable to do so—

      (i)   sample testing of marketed products,

      (ii)   investigating and if necessary keeping a register of complaints concerning the safety of the product, and

      (iii) keeping distributors informed of the results of such monitoring where a product presents a risk or may present a risk.

[2.362]
8 Obligations of distributors

(1) A distributor shall act with due care in order to help ensure compliance with the applicable safety requirements and in particular he—

  (a)   shall not expose or possess for supply or offer or agree to supply, or supply, a product to any person which he knows or should have presumed, on the basis of the information in his possession and as a professional, is a dangerous product; and

  (b)   shall, within the limits of his activities, participate in monitoring the safety of a product placed on the market, in particular by—

      (i)   passing on information on the risks posed by the product,

      (ii)   keeping the documentation necessary for tracing the origin of the product,

      (iii) producing the documentation necessary for tracing the origin of the product, and cooperating in action taken by a producer or an enforcement authority to avoid the risks.

(2) Within the limits of his activities, a distributor shall take measures enabling him to cooperate efficiently in the action referred to in paragraph (1)(b)(iii).

[2.363]
9 Obligations of producers and distributors

(1) Subject to paragraph (2), where a producer or a distributor knows that a product he has placed on the market or supplied poses risks to the consumer that are incompatible with the general safety requirement, he shall forthwith notify an enforcement authority in writing of that information and—

  (a)   the action taken to prevent risk to the consumer; and

  (b)   where the product is being or has been marketed or otherwise supplied to consumers outside the United Kingdom, of the identity of each Member State in which, to the best of his knowledge, it is being or has been so marketed or supplied.

(2) Paragraph (1) shall not apply—

  (a)   in the case of a second-hand product supplied as an antique or as a product to be repaired or reconditioned prior to being used, provided the supplier clearly informed the person to whom he supplied the product to that effect,

  (b)   in conditions concerning isolated circumstances or products.

(3) In the event of a serious risk the notification under paragraph (1) shall include the following—

  (a)   information enabling a precise identification of the product or batch of products in question,

  (b)   a full description of the risks that the product presents,

  (c)   all available information relevant for tracing the product, and

  (d)   a description of the action undertaken to prevent risks to the consumer.

(4) Within the limits of his activities, a person who is a producer or a distributor shall co-operate with an enforcement authority (at the enforcement authority's request) in action taken to avoid the risks posed by a product which he supplies or has supplied. Every enforcement authority shall maintain procedures for such co-operation, including procedures for dialogue with the producers and distributors concerned on issues related to product safety.

PART 3
ENFORCEMENT

[2.364]
10 Enforcement

(1) It shall be the duty of every authority to which paragraph (4) applies to enforce within its area these Regulations and safety notices.

(2) An authority in England or Wales to which paragraph (4) applies shall have the power to investigate and prosecute for an alleged contravention of any provision imposed by or under these Regulations which was committed outside its area in any part of England and Wales.

(3) A district council in Northern Ireland shall have the power to investigate and prosecute for an alleged contravention of any provision imposed by or under these Regulations which was committed outside its area in any part of Northern Ireland.

(4) The authorities to which this paragraph applies are:

  (a)   in England, a county council, district council, London Borough Council, the Common Council of the City of London in its capacity as a local authority and the Council of the Isles of Scilly,

  (b)   in Wales, a county council or a county borough council,

  (c)   in Scotland, a council constituted under section 2 of the Local Government etc (Scotland) Act 1994,

  (d)   in Northern Ireland any district council.

(5) An enforcement authority shall in enforcing these Regulations act in a manner proportionate to the seriousness of the risk and shall take due account of the precautionary principle. In this context, it shall encourage and promote voluntary action by producers and distributors. Notwithstanding the foregoing, an enforcement authority may take any action under these Regulations urgently and without first encouraging and promoting voluntary action if a product poses a serious risk.

[2.365]
11 Suspension notices

(1) Where an enforcement authority has reasonable grounds for suspecting that a requirement of these Regulations has been contravened in relation to a product, the authority may, for the period needed to organise appropriate safety evaluations, checks and controls, serve a notice ("a suspension notice") prohibiting the person on whom it is served from doing any of the following things without the consent of the authority, that is to say—

  (a)   placing the product on the market, offering to place it on the market, agreeing to place it on the market or exposing it for placing on the market, or

  (b)   supplying the product, offering to supply it, agreeing to supply it or exposing it for supply.

(2) A suspension notice served by an enforcement authority in relation to a product may require the person on whom it is served to keep the authority informed of the whereabouts of any such product in which he has an interest.

(3) A consent given by the enforcement authority for the purposes of paragraph (1) may impose such conditions on the doing of anything for which the consent is required as the authority considers appropriate.

[2.366]
12 Requirements to mark

(1) Where an enforcement authority has reasonable grounds for believing that a product is a dangerous product in that it could pose risks in certain conditions, the authority may serve a notice ("a requirement to mark") requiring the person on whom the notice is served at his own expense to undertake either or both of the following, as specified in the notice—

  (a)   to ensure that the product is marked in accordance with requirements specified in the notice with warnings as to the risks it may present,

  (b)   to make the marketing of the product subject to prior conditions as specified in the notice so as to ensure the product is a safe product.

(2) The requirements referred to in paragraph (1)(a) shall be such as to ensure that the product is marked with a warning which is suitable, clearly worded and easily comprehensible.

[2.367]
13 Requirements to warn

Where an enforcement authority has reasonable grounds for believing that a product is a dangerous product in that it could pose risks for certain persons, the authority may serve a notice ("a requirement to warn") requiring the person on whom the notice is served at his own expense to undertake one or more of the following, as specified in the notice—

  (a)   where and to the extent it is practicable to do so, to ensure that any person who could be subject to such risks and who has been supplied with the product be given warning of the risks in good time and in a form specified in the notice,

  (b)   to publish a warning of the risks in such form and manner as is likely to bring those risks to the attention of any such person,

  (c)   to ensure that the product carries a warning of the risks in a form specified in the notice.

[2.368]
14 Withdrawal notices

(1) Where an enforcement authority has reasonable grounds for believing that a product is a dangerous product, the authority may serve a notice ("a withdrawal notice") prohibiting the person on whom it is served from doing any of the following things without the consent of the authority, that is to say—

  (a)   placing the product on the market, offering to place it on the market, agreeing to place it on the market or exposing it for placing on the market, or

  (b)   supplying the product, offering to supply it, agreeing to supply it or exposing it for supply.

(2) A withdrawal notice may require the person on whom it is served to take action to alert consumers to the risks that the product presents.

(3)   In relation to a product that is already on the market, a withdrawal notice may only be served by an enforcement authority where the action being undertaken by the producer or the distributor concerned in fulfilment of his obligations under these Regulations is unsatisfactory or insufficient to prevent the risks concerned to the health and safety of persons.

(4)   Paragraph (3) shall not apply in the case of a product posing a serious risk requiring, in the view of the enforcement authority, urgent action.

(5)   A withdrawal notice served by an enforcement authority in relation to a product may require the person on whom it is served to keep the authority informed of the whereabouts of any such product in which he has an interest.

(6)   A consent given by the enforcement authority for the purposes of paragraph (1) may impose such conditions on the doing of anything for which the consent is required as the authority considers appropriate.

[2.369]
15   Recall notices

(1)   Subject to paragraph (4), where an enforcement authority has reasonable grounds for believing that a product is a dangerous product and that it has already been supplied or made available to consumers, the authority may serve a notice ("a recall notice") requiring the person on whom it is served to use his reasonable endeavours to organise the return of the product from consumers to that person or to such other person as is specified in the notice.

(2)   A recall notice may require—
- (a)   the recall to be effected in accordance with a code of practice applicable to the product concerned, or
- (b)   the recipient of the recall notice to—
  - (i)   contact consumers who have purchased the product in order to inform them of the recall, where and to the extent it is practicable to do so,
  - (ii)   publish a notice in such form and such manner as is likely to bring to the attention of purchasers of the product the risk the product poses and the fact of the recall, or
  - (iii)   make arrangements for the collection or return of the product from consumers who have purchased it or for its disposal,

and may impose such additional requirements on the recipient of the notice as are reasonable and practicable with a view to achieving the return of the product from consumers to the person specified in the notice or its disposal.

(3)   In determining what requirements to include in a recall notice, the enforcement authority shall take into consideration the need to encourage distributors, users and consumers to contribute to its implementation.

(4)   A recall notice may only be issued by an enforcement authority where—
- (a)   other action which it may require under these Regulations would not suffice to prevent the risks concerned to the health and safety of persons,
- (b)   the action being undertaken by the producer or the distributor concerned in fulfilment of his obligations under these Regulations is unsatisfactory or insufficient to prevent the risks concerned to the health and safety of persons, and
- (c)   the authority has given not less than [ten] days notice to the person on whom the recall notice is to be served of its intention to serve such a notice and where that person has before the expiry of that period by notice required the authority to seek the advice of such person as the Institute determines on the questions of—
  - (i)   whether the product is a dangerous product,
  - (ii)   whether the issue of a recall notice is proportionate to the seriousness of the risk, and the authority has taken account of such advice.

(5)   Paragraphs (4)(b) and (c) shall not apply in the case of a product posing a serious risk requiring, in the view of the enforcement authority, urgent action.

(6)   Where a person requires an enforcement authority to seek advice as referred to in paragraph (4)(c), that person shall be responsible for the fees, costs and expenses of the Institute and of the person appointed by the Institute to advise the authority.

(7)   In paragraphs 4(c) and (6) "the Institute" means the charitable organisation with registered number 803725 and known as the Chartered Institute of Arbitrators.

(8)   A recall notice served by an enforcement authority in relation to a product may require the person on whom it is served to keep the authority informed of the whereabouts of any such product to which the recall notice relates, so far as he is able to do so.

(9)   Where the conditions in paragraph (1) for serving a recall notice are satisfied and either the enforcement authority has been unable to identify any person on whom to serve a recall notice, or the person on whom such a notice has been served has failed to comply with it, then the authority may itself take such action as could have been required by a recall notice.

(10)   Where—
- (a)   an authority has complied with the requirements of paragraph (4); and

(b) the authority has exercised its powers under paragraph (9) to take action following the failure of the person on whom the recall notice has been served to comply with that notice,

then the authority may recover from the person on whom the notice was served summarily as a civil debt, any costs or expenses reasonably incurred by it in undertaking the action referred to in sub-paragraph (b).

(11) A civil debt recoverable under the preceding paragraph may be recovered—

(a) in England and Wales by way of complaint (as mentioned in section 58 of the Magistrates' Courts Act 1980,

(b) in Northern Ireland in proceedings under Article 62 of the Magistrate's Court (Northern Ireland) Order 1981.

NOTES

Para (4): word in square brackets in sub-para (c) substituted by the Customs Disclosure of Information and Miscellaneous Amendments Regulations 2012, SI 2012/1848, reg 6.

[2.370]
16 Supplementary provisions relating to safety notices

(1) Whenever feasible, prior to serving a safety notice the authority shall give an opportunity to the person on whom the notice is to be served to submit his views to the authority. Where, due to the urgency of the situation, this is not feasible the person shall be given an opportunity to submit his views to the authority after service of the notice.

(2) A safety notice served by an enforcement authority in respect of a product shall—

(a) describe the product in a manner sufficient to identify it;

(b) state the reasons on which the notice is based;

(c) indicate the rights available to the recipient of the notice under these Regulations and (where applicable) the time limits applying to their exercise; and

(d) in the case of a suspension notice, state the period of time for which it applies.

(3) A safety notice shall have effect throughout the United Kingdom.

(4) Where an enforcement authority serves a suspension notice in respect of a product, the authority shall be liable to pay compensation to a person having an interest in the product in respect of any loss or damage suffered by reason of the notice if—

(a) there has been no contravention of any requirement of these Regulations in relation to the product; and

(b) the exercise by the authority of the power to serve the suspension notice was not attributable to any neglect or default by that person.

(5) Where an enforcement authority serves a withdrawal notice in respect of a product, the authority shall be liable to pay compensation to a person having an interest in the product in respect of any loss or damage suffered by reason of the notice if—

(a) the product was not a dangerous product; and

(b) the exercise by the authority of the power to serve the withdrawal notice was not attributable to any neglect or default by that person.

(6) Where an enforcement authority serves a recall notice in respect of a product, the authority shall be liable to pay compensation to the person on whom the notice was served in respect of any loss or damage suffered by reason of the notice if—

(a) the product was not a dangerous product; and

(b) the exercise by the authority of the power to serve the recall notice was not attributable to any neglect or default by that person.

(7) An enforcement authority may vary or revoke a safety notice which it has served provided that the notice is not made more restrictive for the person on whom it is served or more onerous for that person to comply with.

(8) Wherever feasible prior to varying a safety notice the authority shall give an opportunity to the person on whom the original notice was served to submit his views to the authority.

[2.371]
17 Appeals against safety notices

(1) A person on whom a safety notice has been served and a person having an interest in a product in respect of which a safety notice (other than a recall notice) has been served may, before the end of the period of 21 days beginning with the day on which the notice was served, apply for an order to vary or set aside the terms of the notice.

(2) On an application under paragraph (1) the court or the sheriff, as the case may be, shall make an order setting aside the notice only if satisfied that—

(a) in the case of a suspension notice, there has been no contravention in relation to the product of any requirement of these Regulations,

(b) in the case of a requirement to mark or a requirement to warn, the product is not a dangerous product,

(c) in the case of a withdrawal notice—

(i) the product is not a dangerous product, or

Part 2 Statutory Instruments

    (ii)   where applicable, regulation 14(3) has not been complied with by the enforcement authority concerned,

(d)   in the case of a recall notice—

    (i)   the product is not a dangerous product, or

    (ii)   regulation 15(4) has not been complied with,

(e)   in any case, the serving of the safety notice concerned was not proportionate to the seriousness of the risk.

(3)   On an application concerning the period of time specified in a suspension notice as the period for which it applies, the court or the sheriff, as the case may be, may reduce the period to such period as it considers sufficient for organising appropriate safety evaluations, checks and controls.

(4)   On an application to vary the terms of a notice, the court or the sheriff, as the case may be, may vary the requirements specified in the notice as it considers appropriate.

(5)   A person on whom a recall notice has been served and who proposes to make an application under paragraph (1) in relation to the notice may, before the end of the period of seven days beginning with the day on which the notice was served, apply to the court or the sheriff for an order suspending the effect of the notice and the court or the sheriff may, in any case where it considers it appropriate to do so, make an order suspending the effect of the notice.

(6)   If the court or the sheriff makes an order suspending the effect of a recall notice under paragraph (5) in the absence of the enforcement authority, the enforcement authority may apply for the revocation of such order.

(7)   An order under paragraph (5) shall take effect from the time it is made until—

(a)   it is revoked under paragraph (6),

(b)   where no application is made under paragraph (1) in respect of the recall notice within the time specified in that paragraph, the expiration of that time,

(c)   where such an application is made but is withdrawn or dismissed for want of prosecution, the date of dismissal or withdrawal of the application, or

(d)   where such an application is made and is not withdrawn or dismissed for want of prosecution, the determination of the application.

(8)   Subject to paragraph (6), in Scotland the sheriff's decision under paragraph (5) shall be final.

(9)   An application under this regulation may be made—

(a)   by way of complaint to any magistrates' court in which proceedings have been brought in England and Wales or Northern Ireland—

    (i)   in respect of a contravention in relation to the product of a requirement imposed by or under these Regulations; or

    (ii)   for the forfeiture of the product under regulation 18;

(b)   where no such proceedings have been brought, by way of complaint to any magistrates' court; or

(c)   in Scotland, by summary application to the sheriff.

(10)   A person aggrieved by an order made pursuant to an application under paragraph (1) by a magistrates' court in England, Wales or Northern Ireland, or by a decision of such a court not to make such an order, may appeal against that order or decision—

(a)   in England and Wales, to the Crown Court;

(b)   in Northern Ireland, to the county court.

[2.372]
18 Forfeiture: England and Wales and Northern Ireland

(1)   An enforcement authority in England and Wales or Northern Ireland may apply for an order for the forfeiture of a product on the grounds that the product is a dangerous product.

(2)   An application under paragraph (1) may be made—

(a)   where proceedings have been brought in a magistrates' court for an offence in respect of a contravention in relation to the product of a requirement imposed by or under these Regulations, to that court,

(b)   where an application with respect to the product has been made to a magistrates' court under regulation 17 (appeals against safety notices) or 25 (appeals against detention of products and records) to that court, and

(c)   otherwise, by way of complaint to a magistrates' court.

(3)   An enforcement authority making an application under paragraph (1) shall serve a copy of the application on any person appearing to it to be the owner of, or otherwise to have an interest in, the product to which the application relates, together with a notice giving him the opportunity to appear at the hearing of the application to show cause why the product should not be forfeited.

(4)   A person on whom notice is served under paragraph (3) and any other person claiming to be the owner of, or otherwise to have an interest in, the product to which the application relates shall be entitled to appear at the hearing of the application and show cause why the product should not be forfeited.

(5)   The court shall not make an order for the forfeiture of a product—

(a)   if any person on whom notice is served under paragraph (3) does not appear, unless service of the notice on that person is proved, or

(b)   if no notice under paragraph (3) has been served, unless the court is satisfied that in the circumstances it was reasonable not to serve notice on any person.

(6)   The court may make an order for the forfeiture of a product only if it is satisfied that the product is a dangerous product.

(7)   Any person aggrieved by an order made by a magistrates' court for the forfeiture of a product, or by a decision of such a court not to make such an order, may appeal against that order or decision—

(a)   in England and Wales, to the Crown Court;

(b)   in Northern Ireland, to the county court.

(8)   An order for the forfeiture of a product shall not take effect until the later of—

(i)   the end of the period within which an appeal under paragraph (7) may be brought or within which an application under section 111 of the Magistrates' Courts Act 1980 or article 146 of the Magistrates' Courts (Northern Ireland) Order 1981 (statement of case) may be made, or

(ii)   if an appeal or an application is so made, when the appeal or application is determined or abandoned.

(9)   Subject to the following paragraph, where a product is forfeited it shall be destroyed in accordance with such directions as the court may give.

(10)   On making an order for forfeiture of a product a magistrates' court may, if it considers it appropriate to do so, direct that the product shall (instead of being destroyed) be delivered up to such person as the court may specify, on condition that the person—

(a)   does not supply the product to any person otherwise than as mentioned in paragraph (11), and

(b)   on condition, if the court considers it appropriate, that he complies with any order to pay costs or expenses (including any order under regulation 28) which has been made against him in the proceedings for the order for forfeiture.

(11)   The supplies which may be permitted under the preceding paragraph are—

(a)   a supply to a person who carries on a business of buying products of the same description as the product concerned and repairing or reconditioning them,

(b)   a supply to a person as scrap (that is to say, for the value of materials included in the product rather than for the value of the product itself),

(c)   a supply to any person, provided that being so supplied the product is repaired by or on behalf of the person to whom the product was delivered up by direction of the court and that following such repair it is not a dangerous product.

19   *(Applies to Scotland only.)*

[2.373]
20   Offences

(1)   A person who contravenes regulations 5 or 8(1)(a) shall be guilty of an offence and liable on conviction on indictment to imprisonment for a term not exceeding 12 months or to a fine not exceeding £20,000 or to both, or on summary conviction to imprisonment for a term not exceeding three months or to a fine not exceeding the statutory maximum or to both.

(2)   A person who contravenes regulation 7(1), 7(3) (by failing to take any of the measures specified in regulation 7(4)), 8(1)(b)(i), (ii) or (iii) or 9(1) shall be guilty of an offence and liable on summary conviction to imprisonment for a term not exceeding three months or to a fine not exceeding level 5 on the standard scale or to both.

(3)   A producer or distributor who does not give notice to an enforcement authority under regulation 9(1) in respect of a product he has placed on the market or supplied commits an offence where it is proved that he ought to have known that the product poses risks to consumers that are incompatible with the general safety requirement and he shall be liable on summary conviction to imprisonment for a term not exceeding three months or to a fine not exceeding level 5 on the standard scale or to both.

(4)   A person who contravenes a safety notice shall be guilty of an offence and liable on conviction on indictment to imprisonment for a term not exceeding 12 months or to a fine not exceeding £20,000 or to both, or on summary conviction to imprisonment for a term not exceeding three months or to a fine not exceeding the statutory maximum or to both.

[2.374]
21   Test purchases

(1)   An enforcement authority shall have power to organise appropriate checks on the safety properties of a product, on an adequate scale, up to the final stage of use or consumption and for that purpose may make a purchase of a product or authorise an officer of the authority to make a purchase of a product.

(2)   Where a product purchased under paragraph (1) is submitted to a test and the test leads to—

Part 2   Statutory Instruments

(a) the bringing of proceedings for an offence in respect of a contravention in relation to the product of any requirement imposed by or under these Regulations or for the forfeiture of the product under regulation 18 or 19, or

(b) the serving of a safety notice in respect of the product, and

(c) the authority is requested to do so and it is practicable for the authority to comply with the request,

then the authority shall allow the person from whom the product was purchased, a person who is a party to the proceedings, on whom the notice was served or who has an interest in the product to which the notice relates, to have the product tested.

NOTES

Revoked, together with regs 22–26, by the Consumer Rights Act 2015 (Commencement No 3, Transitional Provisions, Savings and Consequential Amendments) Order 2015, SI 2015/1630, art 5, Sch 2, para 45, as from 1 October 2015 (for transitional provisions see arts 6–8 thereof at **[2.1220]** et seq).

[2.375]
22 Powers of entry and search etc

(1) An officer of an enforcement authority may at any reasonable hour and on production, if required, of his credentials exercise any of the powers conferred by the following provisions of this regulation.

(2) The officer may, for the purposes of ascertaining whether there has been a contravention of a requirement imposed by or under these Regulations, enter any premises other than premises occupied only as a person's residence and inspect any record or product.

(3) The officer may, for the purpose of ascertaining whether there has been a contravention of a requirement imposed by or under these Regulations, examine any procedure (including any arrangements for carrying out a test) connected with the production of a product.

(4) If the officer has reasonable grounds for suspecting that the product has not been placed on the market or supplied in the United Kingdom since it was manufactured or imported he may for the purpose of ascertaining whether there has been a contravention in relation to the product of a requirement imposed by or under these Regulations—

(a) require a person carrying on a commercial activity, or employed in connection with a commercial activity, to supply all necessary information relating to the activity, including by the production of records,

(b) require any record which is stored in an electronic form and is accessible from the premises to be produced in a form—
   (i) in which it can be taken away, and
   (ii) in which it is visible and legible.

(c) for the purpose of ascertaining (by testing or otherwise) whether there has been any such contravention, seize and detain samples of the product,

(d) take copies of, or of an entry in, any records produced by virtue of sub-paragraph (a).

(5) If the officer has reasonable grounds for suspecting that there has been a contravention in relation to a product of a requirement imposed by or under these Regulations, he may—

(a) for the purpose of ascertaining whether there has been any such contravention, require a person carrying on a commercial activity, or employed in connection with a commercial activity, to supply all necessary information relating to the activity, including by the production of records,

(b) for the purpose of ascertaining whether there has been any such contravention, require any record which is stored in an electronic form and is accessible from the premises to be produced in a form—
   (i) in which it can be taken away, and
   (ii) in which it is visible and legible,

(c) for the purpose of ascertaining (by testing or otherwise) whether there has been any such contravention, seize and detain samples of the product,

(d) take copies of, or of an entry in, any records produced by virtue of sub-paragraph (a).

(6) The officer may seize and detain any products or records which he has reasonable grounds for believing may be required as evidence in proceedings for an offence in respect of a contravention of any requirement imposed by or under these Regulations.

(7) If and to the extent that it is reasonably necessary to do so to prevent a contravention of any requirement imposed by or under these Regulations, the officer may, for the purpose of exercising his power under paragraphs (4) to (6) to seize products or records—

(a) require any person having authority to do so to open any container or to open any vending machine; and

(b) himself open or break open any such container or machine where a requirement made under sub-paragraph (a) in relation to the container or machine has not been complied with.

NOTES

Revoked as noted to reg 21 at **[2.374]**.

[2.376]
23   Provisions supplemental to regulation 22 and search warrants etc

(1)   An officer seizing any products or records shall, before he leaves the premises, provide to the person from whom they were seized a written notice—

    (a)   specifying the products (including the quantity thereof) and records seized,

    (b)   stating the reasons for their seizure, and

    (c)   explaining the right of appeal under regulation 25.

(2)   References in paragraph (1) and regulation 25 to the person from whom something has been seized, in relation to a case in which the power of seizure was exercisable by reason of the product having been found on any premises, are references to the occupier of the premises at the time of the seizure.

(3)   If a justice of the peace—

    (a)   is satisfied by written information on oath that there are reasonable grounds for believing either—

        (i)   that any products or records which an officer has power to inspect under regulation 22 are on any premises and that their inspection is likely to disclose evidence that there has been a contravention of any requirement imposed by or under these Regulations, or

        (ii)   that such a contravention has taken place, is taking place or is about to take place on any premises, and

    (b)   is also satisfied by such information either—

        (i)   that admission to the premises has been or is likely to be refused and that notice of the intention to apply for a warrant under this paragraph has been given to the occupier, or

        (ii)   that an application for admission, or the giving of such a notice, would defeat the object of the entry or that the premises are unoccupied or that the occupier is temporarily absent and it might defeat the object of the entry to await his return.

the justice may by warrant under his hand, which shall continue in force for a period of one month, authorise any officer of an enforcement authority to enter the premises, if need be by force.

(4)   An officer entering premises by virtue of regulation 22 or a warrant under paragraph (3) may take him such other persons and equipment as may appear to him necessary.

(5)   On leaving any premises which a person is authorised to enter by a warrant under paragraph (3), that person shall, if the premises are unoccupied or the occupier is temporarily absent—

    (a)   leave the premises as effectively secured against trespassers as he found them,

    (b)   attach a notice such as is mentioned in paragraph (1) in a prominent place at the premises.

(6)   Where a product seized by an officer of an enforcement authority under regulation 22 or 23 is submitted to a test, the authority shall inform the person mentioned in paragraph (1) of the result of the test and, if—

    (a)   proceedings are brought for an offence in respect of a contravention in relation to the product of any requirement imposed by or under these Regulations or for the forfeiture of the product under regulation 18 or 19; or

    (b)   a safety notice is served in respect of the product; and

    (c)   the authority is requested to do so and it is practicable for him to comply with the request,

then the authority shall allow a person who is a party to the proceedings or, on whom the notice was served or who has an interest in the product to which the notice relates to have the product tested.

(7)   If a person who is not an officer of an enforcement authority purports to act as such under regulation 22 or under this regulation he shall be guilty of an offence and liable on summary conviction to a fine not exceeding level 5 on the standard scale.

(8)   (Applies to Scotland only.)

(9)   In the application of this section to Northern Ireland, the reference in paragraph (3) to a justice of the peace shall include a reference to a lay magistrate and the references to an information on oath shall be construed as a reference to a complaint on oath.

NOTES

   Revoked as noted to reg 21 at **[2.374]**.

[2.377]
24   Obstruction of officers

(1)   A person who—

    (a)   intentionally obstructs an officer of an enforcement authority who is acting in pursuance of any provision of regulations 22 or 23; or

    (b)   intentionally fails to comply with a requirement made of him by an officer of an enforcement authority under any provision of those regulations; or

Part 2   Statutory Instruments

(c)   without reasonable cause fails to give an officer of an enforcement authority who is so acting any other assistance or information which the officer may reasonably require of him for the purposes of the exercise of the officer's functions under any provision of those regulations,

shall be guilty of an offence and liable on summary conviction to a fine not exceeding level 5 on the standard scale.

(2)   A person shall be guilty of an offence if, in giving any information which is required by him by virtue of paragraph (1)(c)—

(a)   he makes a statement which he knows is false in a material particular; or

(b)   he recklessly makes a statement which is false in a material particular.

(3)   A person guilty of an offence under paragraph (2) shall be liable—

(a)   on conviction on indictment, to a fine;

(b)   on summary conviction, to a fine not exceeding the statutory maximum.

NOTES

Revoked as noted to reg 21 at [**2.374**].

[2.378]
25   Appeals against detention of products and records

(1)   A person referred to in regulation 23(1) may apply for an order requiring any product or record which is for the time being detained under regulation 22 or 23 by an enforcement authority or by an officer of such an authority to be released to him or to another person.

(2)   An application under the preceding paragraph may be made—

(a)   to any magistrates' court in which proceedings have been brought in England and Wales or Northern Ireland—

(i)   for an offence in respect of a contravention in relation to the product of a requirement imposed by or under these Regulation, or

(ii)   for the forfeiture of the product under regulation 18,

(b)   where no such proceedings have been brought, by way of complaint to a magistrates' court;

(c)   in Scotland, by summary application to the sheriff.

(3)   On an application under paragraph (1) to a magistrates' court or to the sheriff, the court or the sheriff may make an order requiring a product or record to be released only if the court or sheriff is satisfied—

(a)   that proceedings

(i)   for an offence in respect of any contravention in relation to the product or, in the case of a record, the product to which the record relates, of any requirement imposed by or under these Regulations; or

(ii)   for the forfeiture of the product or, in the case of a record, the product to which the record relate, under regulation 18 or 19,

have not been brought or, having been brought, have been concluded without the product being forfeited; and

(b)   where no such proceedings have been brought, that more than six months have elapsed since the product or records was seized.

(4)   In determining whether to make an order under this regulation requiring the release of a product or record the court or sheriff shall take all the circumstances into account including the results of any tests on the product which have been carried out by or on behalf of the enforcement authority and any statement made by the enforcement authority to the court or sheriff as to its intention to bring proceedings for an offence in respect of a contravention in relation to the product of any requirement imposed by or under these Regulations.

(5)   Where—

(a)   more than 12 months have elapsed since a product or records were seized and the enforcement authority has not commenced proceedings for an offence in respect of a contravention in relation to the product (or, in the case of records, the product to which the records relate) of any requirement imposed by or under these Regulations or for the forfeiture of the product under regulation 18 or 19, or

(b)   an enforcement authority has brought proceedings for an offence as mentioned in sub-paragraph (a) and the proceedings were dismissed and all rights of appeal have been exercised or the time for appealing has expired,

the authority shall be under a duty to return the product or records detained under regulation 22 or 23 to the person from whom they were seized.

(6)   Where the authority is satisfied that some other person has a better right to a product or record than the person from whom they were seized, the authority shall, instead of the duty in paragraph (5), be under a duty to return it to that other person or, as the case may be, to the person appearing to the authority to have the best right to the product or record in question.

(7)   *Where different persons claim to be entitled to the return of a product or record that is required to be returned under paragraph (5), then it may be retained for as long as it reasonably necessary for the determination in accordance with paragraph (6) of the person to whom it must be returned.*

(8)   *A person aggrieved by an order made under this regulation by a magistrates' court in England and Wales or Northern Ireland, or by a decision of such a court not to make such an order, may appeal against that order or decision—*

     (a)   *in England and Wales, to the Crown Court;*

     (b)   *in Northern Ireland, to the county court;*

and an order so made may contain such provision as appears to the court to be appropriate for delaying the coming into force of the order pending the making and determination of any appeal (including any application under section 111 of the Magistrates' Courts Act 1980 or article 146 of the Magistrates' Courts (Northern Ireland) Order 1981 (statement of case)).

NOTES

Revoked as noted to reg 21 at **[2.374]**.

[2.379]

26   Compensation for seizure and detention

Where an officer of an enforcement authority exercises any power under regulation 22 or 23 to seize and detain a product, the enforcement authority shall be liable to pay compensation to any person having an interest in the product in respect of any loss or damage caused by reason of the exercise of the power if—

     (a)   *there has been no contravention in relation to the product of any requirement imposed by or under these Regulations, and*

     (b)   *the exercise of the power is not attributable to any neglect or default by that person.*

NOTES

Revoked as noted to reg 21 at **[2.374]**.

[2.380]

27   Recovery of expenses of enforcement

(1)   This regulation shall apply where a court—

     (a)   convicts a person of an offence in respect of a contravention in relation to a product of any requirement imposed by or under these Regulations, or

     (b)   makes an order under regulation 18 or 19 for the forfeiture of a product.

(2)   The court may (in addition to any other order it may make as to costs or expenses) order the person convicted or, as the case may be, any person having an interest in the product to reimburse an enforcement authority for any expenditure which has been or may be incurred by that authority—

     (a)   in connection with any seizure or detention of the product by or on behalf of the authority, or

     (b)   in connection with any compliance by the authority with directions given by the court for the purposes of any order for the forfeiture of the product.

[2.381]

28   Power of Secretary of State to obtain information

(1)   If the Secretary of State considers that, for the purposes of deciding whether to serve a safety notice, or to vary or revoke a safety notice which he has already served, he requires information or a sample of a product he may serve on a person a notice requiring him:

     (a)   to furnish to the Secretary of State, within a period specified in the notice, such information as is specified;

     (b)   to produce such records as are specified in the notice at a time and place so specified (and to produce any such records which are stored in any electronic form in a form in which they are visible and legible) and to permit a person appointed by the Secretary of State for that purpose to take copies of the records at that time and place;

     (c)   to produce such samples of a product as are specified in the notice at a time and place so specified.

(2)   A person shall be guilty of an offence if he—

     (a)   fails, without reasonable cause, to comply with a notice served on him under paragraph (1); or

     (b)   in purporting to comply with a requirement which by virtue of paragraph (1)(a) or (b) is contained in such a notice—

         (i)   furnishes information or records which he knows are false in a material particular, or

         (ii)   recklessly furnishes information or records which are false in a material particular.

(3)   A person guilty of an offence under paragraph (2) shall—

     (a)   in the case of an offence under sub-paragraph (a) of that paragraph, be liable on summary conviction to a fine not exceeding level 5 on the standard scale; and

(b)   in the case of an offence under sub-paragraph (b) of that paragraph, be liable—
    (i)   on conviction on indictment, to a fine;
    (ii)   on summary conviction, to a fine not exceeding the statutory maximum.

[2.382]
29   Defence of due diligence

(1)   Subject to the following provisions of this regulation, in proceedings against a person for an offence under these Regulations it shall be a defence for that person to show that he took all reasonable steps and exercised all due diligence to avoid committing the offence.

(2)   Where in any proceedings against any person for such an offence the defence provided by paragraph (1) involves an allegation that the commission of the offence was due—
    (a)   to the act or default of another, or
    (b)   to reliance on information given by another,
that person shall not, without the leave of the court, be entitled to rely on the defence unless, not less than seven clear days before, in England, Wales and Northern Ireland, the hearing of the proceedings or, in Scotland, the trial diet, he has served a notice under paragraph (3) on the person bringing the proceedings.

(3)   A notice under this paragraph shall give such information identifying or assisting in the identification of the person who—
    (a)   committed the act or default, or
    (b)   gave the information,
as is in the possession of the person serving the notice at the time he serves it.

(4)   A person may not rely on the defence provided by paragraph (1) by reason of his reliance on information supplied by another, unless he shows that it was reasonable in all the circumstances to have relied on the information, having regard in particular—
    (a)   to the steps which he took, and those which might reasonably have been taken, for the purpose of verifying the information; and
    (b)   to whether he had any reason to disbelieve the information.

[2.383]
30   Defence in relation to antiques

(1)   This regulation shall apply in proceedings against any person for an offence under regulation 20(1) in respect of the supply, offer or agreement to supply or exposure or possession for supply of second hand products supplied as antiques.

(2)   It shall be a defence for that person to show that the terms on which he supplied the product or agreed or offered to supply the product or, in the case of a product which he exposed or possessed for supply, the terms on which he intended to supply the product, contemplated the acquisition of an interest in the product by the person supplied or to be supplied.

(3)   Paragraph (2) applies only if the producer or distributor clearly informed the person to whom he supplied the product, or offered or agreed to supply the product or, in the case of a product which he exposed or possessed for supply, he intended to so inform that person, that the product is an antique.

[2.384]
31   Liability of person other than principal offender

(1)   Where the commission by a person of an offence under these Regulations is due to an act or default committed by some other person in the course of a commercial activity of his, the other person shall be guilty of the offence and may be proceeded against and punished by virtue of this paragraph whether or not proceedings are taken against the first-mentioned person.

(2)   Where a body corporate is guilty of an offence under these Regulations (including where it is so guilty by virtue of paragraph (1)) in respect of any act or default which is shown to have been committed with the consent or connivance of, or to be attributable to any neglect on the part of, any director, manager, secretary or other similar officer of the body corporate or any person who was purporting to act in any such capacity he, as well as the body corporate, shall be guilty of that offence and shall be liable to be proceeded against and punished accordingly.

(3)   Where the affairs of a body corporate are managed by its members, paragraph (2) shall apply in relation to the acts and defaults of a member in connection with his functions of management as if he were a director of the body corporate.

(4)   Where a Scottish partnership is guilty of an offence under these Regulations (including where it is so guilty by virtue of paragraph (1)) in respect of any act or default which is shown to have been committed with the consent or connivance of, or to be attributable to any neglect on the part of, a partner in the partnership, he, as well as the partnership, shall be guilty of that offence and shall be liable to be proceeded against and punished accordingly.

PART 4
MISCELLANEOUS

[2.385]
32   Reports

(1)   It shall be the duty of the Secretary of State to lay before each House of Parliament a report on the exercise during the period to which the report relates of the functions which are exercisable by enforcement authorities under these Regulations.

(2)   The first such report shall relate to the period beginning on the day on which these Regulations come into force and ending on 31 March 2008 and subsequent reports shall relate to a period of not more than five years beginning on the day after the day on which the period to which the previous report relates ends.

(3)   The Secretary of State may from time to time prepare and lay before each House of Parliament such other reports on the exercise of those functions as he considers appropriate.

(4)   The Secretary of State may direct an enforcement authority to report at such intervals as he may specify in the direction on the discharge by that authority of the functions exercisable by it under these Regulations.

(5)   A report under paragraph (4) shall be in such form and shall contain such particulars as are specified in the direction of the Secretary of State.

[2.386]
33   Duty to notify Secretary of State and Commission

(1)   An enforcement authority which has received a notification under regulation 9(1) shall immediately pass the same on to the Secretary of State, who shall immediately pass it on to the competent authorities appointed for the purpose in the Member States where the product in question is or has been marketed or otherwise supplied to consumers.

(2)   Where an enforcement authority takes a measure which restricts the placing on the market of a product, or requires its withdrawal or recall, it shall immediately notify the Secretary of State, specifying its reasons for taking the action. It shall also immediately notify the Secretary of State of any modification or lifting of such a measure.

(3)   On receiving a notification under paragraph (2), or if he takes a measure which restricts the placing on the market of a product, or requires its withdrawal or recall, the Secretary of State shall (to the extent that such notification is not required under article 12 of the GPS Directive or any other Community legislation) immediately notify the European Commission of the measure taken, specifying the reasons for taking it. The Secretary of State shall also immediately notify the European Commission of any modification or lifting of such a measure. If the Secretary of State considers that the effects of the risk do not or cannot go beyond the territory of the United Kingdom, he shall notify the European Commission of the measure concerned insofar as it involves information likely to be of interest to Member States from the product safety standpoint, and in particular if it is in response to a new risk which has not yet been reported in other notifications.

(4)   Where an enforcement authority adopts or decides to adopt, recommend or agree with producers and distributors, whether on a compulsory or voluntary basis, a measure or action to prevent, restrict or impose specific conditions on the possible marketing or use of a product (other than a pharmaceutical product) by reason of a serious risk, it shall immediately notify the Secretary of State. It shall also immediately notify the Secretary of State of any modification or withdrawal of any such measure or action.

(5)   On receiving a notification under paragraph (4), or if he adopts or decides to adopt, recommend or agree with producers and distributors, whether on a compulsory or voluntary basis, a measure or action to prevent, restrict or impose specific conditions on the possible marketing or use of a product (other than a pharmaceutical product) by reason of a serious risk, the Secretary of State shall immediately notify the European Commission of it through the Community Rapid Information System, known as RAPEX. The Secretary of State shall also inform the European Commission without delay of any modification or withdrawal of any such measure or action.

(6)   If the Secretary of State considers that the effects of the risk do not or cannot go beyond the territory of the United Kingdom, he shall notify the European Commission of the measures or action concerned insofar as they involve information likely to be of interest to Member States of the European Union from the product safety standpoint, and in particular if they are in response to a new risk which has not been reported in other notifications.

(7)   Before deciding to adopt such a measure or take such an action as is referred to in paragraph (5), the Secretary of State may pass on to the European Commission any information in his possession regarding the existence of a serious risk. Where he does so, he must inform the European Commission, within 45 days of the day of passing the information to it, whether he confirms or modifies that information.

(8)   Upon receipt of a notification from the European Commission under article 12(2) of the GPS Directive, the Secretary of State shall notify the Commission of the following—

(a) whether the product the subject of the notification has been marketed in the United Kingdom;

(b) what measure concerning the product the enforcement authorities in the United Kingdom may be adopting, stating the reasons, including any differing assessment of risk or any other special circumstance justifying the decision as to the measure, in particular lack of action or follow-up; and

(c) any relevant supplementary information he has obtained on the risk involved, including the results of any test or analysis carried out.

(9) The Secretary of State shall notify the European Commission without delay of any modification or withdrawal of any measures notified to it under paragraph (8)(b).

(10) In this regulation—

(a) references to a product excludes a second hand product supplied as an antique or as a product to be repaired or reconditioned prior to being used, provided the supplier clearly informs the person to whom he supplies the product to that effect;

(b) "pharmaceutical product" means a product falling within Council Directive 2001/83/EC of the European Parliament and of the Council on the Community code relating to medicinal products for human use [as amended by Directive 2002/98/EC of the European Parliament and of the Council setting standards of quality and safety for the collection, testing, processing, storage and distribution of human blood and blood components, Commission Directive 2003/63/EC amending Directive 2001/83/EC on the Community code relating to medicinal products for human use, Directive 2004/24/EC of the European Parliament and of the Council amending, as regards traditional herbal medicinal products, Directive 2001/83/EC on the Community code relating to medicinal products for human use and Directive 2004/27/EC of the European Parliament and of the Council amending Directive 2001/83/EC on the Community code relating to medicinal products for human use].

NOTES

Para (10): words in square brackets in sub-para (b) inserted by the Medicines (Marketing Authorisations Etc) Amendment Regulations 2005, SI 2005/2759, reg 4, Schedule, para 18.

[2.387]
34 Provisions supplemental to regulation 33

(1) A notification under regulation 33(2) to (6), (8) or (9) to the Secretary of State or the Commission shall be in writing and shall provide all available details and at least the following information—

(a) information enabling the product to be identified,

(b) a description of the risk involved, including a summary of the results of any test or analysis and of their conclusions which are relevant to assessing the level of risk,

(c) the nature and the duration of the measures or action taken or decided on, if applicable,

(d) information on supply chains and distribution of the product, in particular on destination countries.

(2) Where a measure notified to the Commission under regulation 33 seeks to limit the marketing or use of a chemical substance or preparation, the Secretary of State shall provide to the Commission as soon as possible either a summary or the references of the relevant data relating to the substance or preparation considered and to known and available substitutes, where such information is available. The Secretary of State shall also notify the Commission of the anticipated effects of the measure on consumer health and safety together with the assessment of the risk carried out in accordance with the general principles for the risk evaluation of chemical substances as referred to in article 10(4) of Council Regulation (EEC) No 793/93 of 23 March 1993 on the evaluation and control of the risks of existing substances, in the case of an existing substance, or in article 3(2) of Council Directive 67/548/EEC on the approximation of laws, regulations and administrative provisions relating to the classification, packaging and labelling of dangerous substances in the case of a new substance.

(3) Where the Commission carries out an investigation under paragraph 5 of Annex II to the GPS Directive, the Secretary of State shall supply the Commission with such information as it requests, to the best of his ability.

[2.388]
35 Implementation of Commission decisions

(1) This regulation applies where the Commission adopts a decision pursuant to article 13 of the GPS Directive.

(2) The Secretary of State shall—

(a) take such action under these Regulations, or

(b) direct another enforcement authority to take such action under these Regulations

as is necessary to comply with the decision.

(3)   Where an enforcement authority serves a safety notice pursuant to paragraph (2), the following provisions of these Regulations shall not apply in relation to that notice, namely regulations 14(3), 15(4) to (6) and 16(1), 16(2)(c) and (d), 16(5) to (7) and 17.

(4)   Unless the Commission's decision provides otherwise, export from the Community of a dangerous product which is the subject of such a decision is prohibited with effect from the date the decision comes into force.

(5)   The enforcement of the prohibition in paragraph (4) shall be treated as an assigned matter within the meaning of section 1(1) of the Customs and Excise Management Act 1979.

(6)   The measures necessary to implement the decision shall be taken within 20 days, unless the decision specifies a different period.

(7)   The Secretary of State or, where the Secretary of State has directed another enforcement authority to take action under paragraph (2)(b), that enforcement authority shall, within one month, give the parties concerned an opportunity to submit their views and shall inform the Commission accordingly.

[2.389]
36   Market surveillance

In order to ensure a high level of consumer health and safety protection, enforcement authorities shall within the limits of their responsibility and to the extent of their ability undertake market surveillance of products employing appropriate means and procedures and co-operating with other enforcement authorities and competent authorities of other Member States which may include:

  (a)   establishment, periodical updating and implementation of sectoral surveillance programmes by categories of products or risks and the monitoring of surveillance activities, findings and results,

  (b)   follow-up and updating of scientific and technical knowledge concerning the safety of products,

  (c)   the periodical review and assessment of the functioning of the control activities and their effectiveness and, if necessary revision of the surveillance approach and organisation put in place.

[2.390]
37   Complaints procedures

An enforcement authority shall maintain and publish a procedure by which complaints may be submitted by any person on product safety and on surveillance and control activities, which complaints shall be followed up as appropriate.

[2.391]
38   Co-operation between enforcement authorities

(1)   It shall be the duty of an enforcement authority to co-operate with other enforcement authorities in carrying out the functions conferred on them by these Regulations. In particular—

  (a)   enforcement authorities shall share their expertise and best practices with each other;

  (b)   enforcement authorities shall undertake collaborative working where they have a shared interest.

(2)   The Secretary of State shall inform the European Commission as to the arrangements for the enforcement of these Regulations, including which bodies are enforcement authorities.

[2.392]
39   Information

(1)   An enforcement authority shall in general make available to the public such information as is available to it on the following matters relating to the risks to consumer health and safety posed by a product—

  (a)   the nature of the risk,

  (b)   the product identification,

and the measures taken in respect of the risk, without prejudice to the need not to disclose information for effective monitoring and investigation activities.

(2)   Paragraph (1) shall not apply to any information obtained by an enforcement authority for the purposes of these Regulations which, by its nature, is covered by professional secrecy, unless the circumstances require such information to be made public in order to protect the health and safety of consumers.

(3)   . . .

NOTES
  Para (3): amends the Enterprise Act 2002 (Part 9 Restrictions on Disclosure of Information) (Amendment and Specification) Order 2003, SI 2003/1400.

Part 2   Statutory Instruments

[2.393]
40 Service of documents

(1)   A document required or authorised by virtue of these Regulations to be served on a person may be so served—

   (a)   on an individual by delivering it to him or by leaving it at his proper address or by sending it by post to him at that address;

   (b)   on a body corporate other than a limited liability partnership, by serving it in accordance with sub-paragraph (a) on the secretary of the body;

   (c)   on a limited liability partnership, by serving it in accordance with sub-paragraph (a) on a member of the partnership; or

   (d)   on a partnership, by serving it in accordance with sub-paragraph (a) on a partner or a person having the control or management of the partnership business;

   (e)   on any other person by leaving it at his proper address or by sending it by post to him at that address.

(2)   For the purposes of paragraph (1), and for the purposes of section 7 of the Interpretation Act 1978 (which relates to the service of documents by post) in its application to that paragraph, the proper address of a person on whom a document is to be served by virtue of these Regulations shall be his last known address except that—

   (a)   in the case of a body corporate (other than a limited liability partnership) or its secretary, it shall be the address of the registered or principal office of the body;

   (b)   in the case of a limited liability partnership or a member of the partnership, it shall be the address of the registered or principal office of the partnership;

   (c)   in the case of a partnership or a partner or a person having the control or management of a partnership business, it shall be the address of the principal office of the partnership,

and for the purposes of this paragraph the principal officer of a company constituted under the law of a country or territory outside the United Kingdom or of a partnership carrying on business outside the United Kingdom is its principal office within the United Kingdom.

(3)   A document required or authorised by virtue of these Regulations to be served on a person may also be served by transmitting the request by any means of electronic communication to an electronic address (which includes a fax number and an e-mail address) being an address which the person has held out as an address at which he or it can be contacted for the purposes of receiving such documents.

(4)   A document transmitted by any means of electronic communication in accordance with the preceding paragraph is, unless the contrary is proved, deemed to be received on the business day after the notice was transmitted over a public electronic communications network.

[2.394]
41 Extension of time for bringing summary proceedings

(1)   Notwithstanding section 127 of the Magistrates' Courts Act 1980 or article 19 of the Magistrates' Courts (Northern Ireland) Order 1981, in England, Wales and Northern Ireland a magistrates' court may try an information (in the case of England and Wales) or a complaint (in the case of Northern Ireland) in respect of an offence under these Regulations if (in the case of England and Wales) the information is laid or (in the case of Northern Ireland) the complaint is made within three years from the date of the offence or within one year from the discovery of the offence by the prosecutor whichever is the earlier.

(2)   Notwithstanding section 136 of the Criminal Procedure (Scotland) Act 1995, in Scotland summary proceedings for an offence under these Regulations may be commenced within three years from the date of the offence or within one year from the discovery of the offence by the prosecutor whichever is the earlier.

(3)   For the purposes of paragraph (2), section 136(3) of the Criminal Procedure (Scotland) Act 1995 shall apply as it applies for the purposes of that section.

[2.395]
42 Civil proceedings

These Regulations shall not be construed as conferring any right of action in civil proceedings in respect of any loss or damage suffered in consequence of a contravention of these Regulations.

[2.396]
43 Privileged information

(1)   Nothing in these Regulations shall be taken as requiring a person to produce any records if he would be entitled to refuse to produce those records in any proceedings in any court on the grounds that they are the subject of legal professional privilege or, in Scotland, that they contain a confidential communication made by or to an advocate or solicitor in that capacity, or as authorising a person to take possession of any records which are in the possession of a person who would be so entitled.

(2) Nothing in these Regulations shall be construed as requiring a person to answer any question or give any information if to do so would incriminate that person or that person's spouse or civil partner.

[2.397]
44   Evidence in proceedings for offence relating to regulation 9(1)

(1) This regulation applies where a person has given a notification to an enforcement authority pursuant to regulation 9(1).

(2) No evidence relating to that statement may be adduced and no question relating to it may be asked by the prosecution in any criminal proceedings (other than proceedings in which that person is charged with an offence under regulation 20 for a contravention of regulation 9(1)), unless evidence relating to it is adduced, or a question relating to it is asked, in the proceedings by or on behalf of that person.

[2.398]
45   Transitional provisions

Where, in relation to a product, a suspension notice (within the meaning of the 1987 Act) has (by virtue of regulation 11(b) of the General Product Safety Regulations 1994) been served under section 14 of the 1987 Act and is in force immediately prior to the coming into force of these Regulations, it shall continue in force notwithstanding the revocation of the General Product Safety Regulations 1994 by these Regulations, and those Regulations shall continue to apply accordingly.

46, 47   *(Reg 46 repeals the Consumer Protection Act 1987, s 10 and amends ss 11, 13, 19, 39, 45 of that Act at* **[1.994]**, **[1.996]**, **[1.1001]**, **[1.1012]**, **[1.1018]**; *reg 47 amends the Gas Act 1995, Sch 4 and the Criminal Justice and Police Act 2001, s 66, Schs 1, 2.)*

CONSUMER CREDIT (INFORMATION REQUIREMENTS AND DURATION OF LICENCES AND CHARGES) REGULATIONS 2007

(SI 2007/1167)

NOTES
   Made: 31 March 2007.
   Authority: Consumer Credit Act 1974, ss 22(1B), (1E), 28A(3)(b), (6), 77A(2), 78(4A), 86B(8), 86C(6), 86E(2), (7)(b), 88(1), (4), 130A(6), 182(2), 189(1).
   Commencement: in accordance with reg 1(2), (3).

ARRANGEMENT OF REGULATIONS

[2.399]
1 Citation and commencement

(1) These Regulations may be cited as the Consumer Credit (Information Requirements and Duration of Licences and Charges) Regulations 2007.

(2) This regulation and regulations 2 and 42 to 44 shall come into force on 6th April 2008.

(3) The remaining regulations shall come into force on 1st October 2008.

[2.400]
[1A Application

The following do not apply in relation to Northern Ireland—

(a) regulation 4(aa) and (ba);

(b) regulation 10A;

(c) regulation 10B;

(d) regulation 10C;

(e) regulation 41A;

(f) paragraph 3A of Part 1 of Schedule 1.]

NOTES

Commencement: 26 September 2014.

Inserted by the Consumer Credit (Information Requirements and Duration of Licences and Charges) (Amendment) Regulations 2014, SI 2014/2369, reg 2(1), (2).

[2.401]
2 Interpretation

In these Regulations—

"the 1974 Act" means the Consumer Credit Act 1974;

"agreement to aggregate" means an agreement (whether arising by conduct or otherwise) made between the creditor and the debtor—

    (a) concerning two or more agreements for fixed-sum credit between the creditor and the debtor where at least one such agreement is a regulated credit agreement; and

    (b) which permits or requires the debtor to aggregate all individual payments under the agreements mentioned in paragraph (a) and pay them at the same time; and

["current bill payer" means a person who is liable by virtue of section 1(6)(a) of the Energy Act 2011, whether alone or jointly with one or more other persons, to pay instalments under a green deal plan as a result of being for the time being liable to pay the energy bills for the property to which the plan relates;

"energy bill" has the meaning given in regulation 4(2) of the Green Deal Framework (Disclosure, Acknowledgment, Redress etc) Regulations 2012;

"energy efficiency improvement" has the meaning given by section 2(4) of the Energy Act 2011;

"green deal consumer credit agreement" means a green deal plan that is to be treated as a consumer credit agreement for the purposes of the 1974 Act by virtue of section 189B(1) of that Act;]

["green deal plan" has the meaning given in section 1 of the Energy Act 2011;]

"home credit loan agreement" means a debtor-creditor agreement which satisfies either or both of the following conditions—

    (a) the agreement provides that all or most of the sums payable by the debtor are to be collected by or on behalf of the creditor at the debtor's home or at the home of a natural person who makes payments to the creditor on the debtor's behalf (or, in either case, to be so collected if the debtor so wishes);

(b)   at the time the agreement is entered into, the debtor could reasonably expect, from representations made by or on behalf of the creditor at or before that time, that all or most of the sums payable would be collected as specified in paragraph (a) (or, in either case would be so collected if the debtor so wished).

["prepayment meter" has the meaning given in regulation 2 of the Electricity (Prepayment Meter) Regulations 2006;

"property", in relation to a green deal plan, means the property to which the energy efficiency improvements under the green deal plan are, or are intended to be, made;

"relevant energy supplier" has the meaning given in regulation 4(2) of the Green Deal Framework (Disclosure, Acknowledgment, Redress etc) Regulations 2012].

NOTES

Definitions "current bill payer", "energy bill" , "energy efficiency improvement", "green deal consumer credit agreement", "prepayment meter", "property" and "relevant energy supplier" inserted and added by the Consumer Credit (Information Requirements and Duration of Licences and Charges) (Amendment) Regulations 2014, SI 2014/2369, reg 2(1), (3).

Definition "green deal plan" inserted by the Consumer Credit (Green Deal) Regulations 2012, SI 2012/2798, reg 5, Schedule, para 4(1), (2).

[2.402]
3   Content of statements provided in relation to fixed-sum credit agreements

Regulations 4 to 11 shall apply to a statement given under section 77A of the 1974 Act (statements to be provided in relation to fixed-sum credit agreements).

[2.403]
4

Subject to regulations 5 to 9, [10A, 10B and 10C, as appropriate,] the statement shall contain—

(a)   [except where paragraph (aa) applies,] the information set out in Part 1 of Schedule 1;

[(aa)   where the statement relates to a green deal plan made before 28th February 2014 and the creditor knows, or has reasonable cause to believe, that the debtor is not the current bill payer, the information set out in paragraphs 1, 2, 3(a), 3(b) and 3(e) of Part 1 of Schedule 1, and Part 1A of Schedule 1;]

(b)   [except where . . . paragraph (ba) applies,] each of the forms of wording set out in Part 2 of Schedule 1;

[(ba)   where the statement relates to a green deal plan [made before 28th February 2014 or a green deal consumer credit agreement], each of the forms of wording set out in Part 2A of Schedule 1;]]

(c)   subject to paragraph (d),

     (i)   where the statement relates to a hire-purchase or conditional sale agreement, the first form of wording in paragraph 5 of Schedule 1; and

     (ii)   where the statement relates to a hire-purchase or conditional sale agreement and the debtor purchased a contract of insurance as referred to in regulation 2(8) of the Consumer Credit (Agreement) Regulations 1983 (information requirements in relation to credit and insurance finance agreements), each form of wording set out in paragraph 5 of Schedule 1;

(d)   where the statement referred to in paragraph (c) is required to be given after the final payment under the agreement has fallen due, the statement need not include either of the forms of wording set out in paragraph 5 of Schedule 1.

NOTES

Words in first, second and sixth (inner) pairs of square brackets, and para (aa) inserted, and word omitted revoked, by the Consumer Credit (Information Requirements and Duration of Licences and Charges) (Amendment) Regulations 2014, SI 2014/2369, reg 2(1), (4); in para (b) words in square brackets, and para (ba) inserted, by the Consumer Credit (Green Deal) Regulations 2012, SI 2012/2798, reg 5, Schedule, para 4(1), (3), (4).

[2.404]
5

The creditor shall indicate in the statement which of the two pieces of information referred to in each of paragraphs 3(d) and 3(e) of Schedule 1 it has included in the statement.

[2.405]
6

Where the rate or rates of interest provided for under the agreement are not applicable on a per annum basis, paragraph 3(h) of Schedule 1 shall not require amounts [and dates] of interest which become due during the period to which the statement relates to be set out separately in the statement.

NOTES

Words in square brackets inserted by the Consumer Credit (Information Requirements and Duration of Licences and Charges) (Amendment) Regulations 2008, SI 2008/1751, reg 2(a).

[2.406]
7

Subject to regulations 8 and 9, where the creditor and the debtor have entered into an agreement to aggregate—

[(za) the reference to opening balance in paragraph 3(f) of Schedule 1 may be construed as a reference to the aggregated opening balance;]

(a) the reference to payments made in paragraph 3(g) of Schedule 1 may be construed as a reference to the aggregated payments which the debtor is permitted or required to make;

(b) the reference to interest and charges which became due in paragraph 3(h) of Schedule 1 may be construed as the aggregated interest and charges which became due;

(c) the reference to movements in paragraph 3(i) of Schedule 1 may be construed as a reference to the aggregated movements in all the accounts maintained by the creditor in relation to the agreements to which the agreement to aggregate relates;

[(cc) the reference to balance in paragraph 3(j) of Schedule 1 may be construed as a reference to the aggregated balance;]

(d) where any of the forms of wording set out in Parts 2 and 3 of Schedule 1 do not apply to all the agreements to which the agreement to aggregate relates the creditor shall identify for each form of wording which does not so apply the regulated agreement or agreements to which it relates;

(e) the information required under paragraphs 1, 2, 3(c), 3(d) and 3(e) of Schedule 1 need only be shown once where the information which would otherwise have to be included for the agreements to which the agreement to aggregate relates is the same for each agreement.

NOTES

Paras (za), (cc) inserted by the Consumer Credit (Information Requirements and Duration of Licences and Charges) (Amendment) Regulations 2008, SI 2008/1751, reg 2(b).

[2.407]
8

Subject to regulation 9, where not all the sums permitted to be shown in the statement as an aggregated figure under regulation 7 are so shown the creditor shall indicate where each figure for payment made or interest or charges which became due or the movement which occurred is an aggregated figure.

[2.408]
9

(1) Paragraphs (2) to (4) shall apply where the agreement to aggregate concerns agreements to which regulation 2(8) of the Consumer Credit (Agreements) Regulations 1983 applies.

[(2) Where the statement is not the first statement given under section 77A of the 1974 Act in relation to the agreements to which the agreement to aggregate relates, the reference to the amount of credit in paragraph 3(b) of Schedule 1 may be construed as a reference to the aggregated amount of credit provided, and where applicable, to be provided under those agreements.]

(3) . . . .

(4) The creditor shall not be required to comply with regulation 8.

NOTES

Para (2): substituted by the Consumer Credit (Information Requirements and Duration of Licences and Charges) (Amendment) Regulations 2008, SI 2008/1751, reg 2(c)(i).
Para (3): revoked by SI 2008/1751, reg 2(c)(ii).

[2.409]
10

Where the creditor and the debtor have entered into an arrangement under which interest or charges payable under a fixed-sum credit agreement are applied to an account which is separate from the account to which payments referred to in paragraph 3(g) of Schedule 1 are applied, the statement shall include a form of wording referring to that arrangement [and the information referred to in paragraph 3(h) of Schedule 1 may be omitted from the statement].

NOTES

Words in square brackets added by the Consumer Credit (Information Requirements and Duration of Licences and Charges) (Amendment) Regulations 2008, SI 2008/1751, reg 2(d).

[2.410]
[10A

(1) This regulation applies to a statement provided in relation to a green deal consumer credit agreement.

(2)   The statement must not include information relating to a person who, at the time the statement is produced, is no longer a current bill payer, and must only show payments into, and movements in, the account of the current bill payer relating to the agreement.

(3)   The balances required by paragraphs 3(f) and 3(j) of Part 1 of Schedule 1 are to be calculated or based on the assumption that any liability which fell due for payment before the current bill payer became the current bill payer, was paid on time.

(4)   In any case where—

    (a)   there was more than one current bill payer in the period to which a previous statement related; and

    (b)   any one or more of them is no longer a current bill payer;

the balances required by paragraphs 3(f) and 3(j) of Part 1 of Schedule 1 are to be calculated or based on the assumption that any liability which fell due for payment by a person who is no longer a current bill payer, was paid on time.

(5)   In any case where a current bill payer switched relevant energy supplier during the period to which the statement relates—

    (a)   the balances required by paragraphs 3(f) and 3(j) of Part 1 of Schedule 1 are to be calculated or based on the assumption that any liability which fell due for payment before the date of the switch, was paid on time; and

    (b)   the statement must include a form of wording informing the current bill payer that any liability owing before the date of the switch is not shown on the statement but remains owing to the creditor, and will be collected by the previous relevant energy supplier.]

NOTES

Commencement: 26 September 2014.

Inserted, together with regs 10B, 10C, by the Consumer Credit (Information Requirements and Duration of Licences and Charges) (Amendment) Regulations 2014, SI 2014/2369, reg 2(1), (5).

[2.411]
[10B

(1)   This regulation applies to a statement provided in relation to a green deal plan made before 28th February 2014.

(2)   The statement must not include information relating to a person other than the debtor, and must only show payments into, and movements in, the account of the debtor relating to the agreement.

(3)   The balances required by paragraphs 3(f) and 3(j) of Part 1 of Schedule 1 are to be calculated or based on the assumption that any liability which fell due for payment before the debtor became the debtor, was paid on time.

(4)   In any case where—

    (a)   there was more than one debtor in the period to which a previous statement related; and

    (b)   any one or more of them is no longer the debtor;

the balances required by paragraphs 3(f) and 3(j) of Part 1 of Schedule 1 are to be calculated or based on the assumption that any liability which fell due for payment by a person who is no longer the debtor, was paid on time.

(5)   In any case where the debtor switched relevant energy supplier during the period to which the statement relates—

    (a)   the balances required by paragraphs 3(f) and 3(j) of Part 1 of Schedule 1 are to be calculated or based on the assumption that any liability which fell due for payment before the date of the switch, was paid on time; and

    (b)   the statement must include a form of wording informing the debtor that any liability owing before the date of the switch is not shown on the statement but remains owing to the creditor, and will be collected by the previous relevant energy supplier.]

NOTES

Commencement: 26 September 2014.

Inserted as noted to reg 10A at **[2.410]**.

[2.412]
[10C

(1)   This regulation applies to a statement provided in relation to a green deal plan made before 28th February 2014 or a green deal consumer credit agreement, where—

    (a)   the creditor has been informed by the relevant energy supplier that the current bill payer has taken his supply of electricity through a prepayment meter during part or all of the period to which the statement relates; and

    (b)   the creditor has not been informed of either or both of the following—

        (i)   the date on which a payment is made into the account of the current bill payer relating to the agreement;

        (ii)   the amount of a payment made into that account.

(2)   The following information in Part 1 of Schedule 1 may, to the extent necessary as a result of the creditor not being informed of any of the information referred to in paragraph (1)(b), be based on the assumption that the current bill payer paid the amount accruing under the green deal plan during the period to which the statement relates—

    (a)   in paragraph 3(g), dates and amounts of payments;

    (b)   in paragraph 3(h), interest or other charges;

    (c)   in paragraph 3(j), the balance under the agreement at the end of the period to which the statement relates.

(3)   The information required by paragraph 3(f) of Part 1 of Schedule 1 may, to the extent necessary as a result of the creditor not being informed of any of the information referred to in paragraph (1)(b), be based on the assumption that the person who was the current bill payer for the period preceding the period to which the statement relates paid the amount accruing under the green deal plan during that preceding period.

(4)   The information mentioned in paragraph (2)(a), and the information mentioned in paragraph (2)(b), may be aggregated in each case on a monthly basis.

(5)   Where a statement is produced in reliance on paragraphs (2), (3) or (4), the statement must include a form of wording informing the current bill payer of this, and clearly explaining the effect of the paragraph, or paragraphs, relied on.

(6)   For the purposes of this regulation, where a payment is made into the account of the current bill payer with the relevant energy supplier, that payment is to be treated as made into the account of the current bill payer with the creditor.]

NOTES

    Commencement: 26 September 2014.

    Inserted as noted to reg 10A at **[2.410]**.

11   (*Revoked by the Legislative Reform (Consumer Credit) Order 2008, SI 2008/2826, art 7.*)

[2.413]
12   Additional information in statements provided in relation to certain fixed-sum credit agreements

(1)   A statement given under section 77A of the 1974 Act in relation to a home credit loan agreement shall include—

    (a)   the total charge for credit provided under the agreement; and

    (b)   a statement in the following form:

        "You are entitled to request one free statement per quarter or one per loan (whichever allows for more requests). We are required to provide you with a statement free of charge within seven days of receiving your request.".

(2)   Such a statement, if given during a period when any relevant website is being [operated], shall also contain the statement—"You can compare our loans with other home credit loans available in your area by accessing the website", followed by the location of the website in question.

[(3)   For the purposes of paragraph (2), "relevant website" has the same meaning as in article 14 of the Home Credit Market Investigation Order 2007.]

NOTES

    Para (2): word in square brackets substituted by the Consumer Credit (Information Requirements and Duration of Licences and Charges) (Amendment) Regulations 2008, SI 2008/1751, reg 2(e)(i).

    Para (3): substituted by SI 2008/1751, reg 2(e)(ii).

[2.414]
13   Additional information in statements provided in relation to running-account credit agreements

Regulations 14 to 18 shall apply to a statement given under section 78(4) of the 1974 Act (duty to give information to debtor under running-account credit agreement).

[2.415]
[14

Subject to regulations 17 and 18, where the agreement to which the statement relates requires the payment each month of a minimum sum, the statement shall include the forms of wording set out in paragraphs 1 and 4 of Schedule 2, and in paragraph 2 of that Schedule if applicable, and the information set out in paragraph 3 of that Schedule.]

NOTES

    Substituted by the Consumer Credit (Information Requirements and Duration of Licences and Charges) (Amendment) Regulations 2008, SI 2008/1751, reg 2(f).

15   (*Revoked by the Consumer Credit (Information Requirements and Duration of Licences and Charges) (Amendment) Regulations 2008, SI 2008/1751, reg 2(g).*)

[2.416]
[16

Where the agreement to which the statement relates does not require the payment each month of a minimum sum, and the creditor has at any time during the period to which the statement relates required the debtor to repay sums which are due under the agreement, only the second form of wording set out in paragraph 4 of Schedule 2 shall be given.]

NOTES

Substituted by the Consumer Credit (Information Requirements and Duration of Licences and Charges) (Amendment) Regulations 2008, SI 2008/1751, reg 2(h).

[2.417]
17

For the purposes of regulations [14] and 16, "minimum sum" means a sum which is less than the total sum due under the agreement at the time the duty to give the notice arises.

NOTES

Number in square brackets substituted by the Consumer Credit (Information Requirements and Duration of Licences and Charges) (Amendment) Regulations 2008, SI 2008/1751, reg 2(i).

[2.418]
18

(1) Subject to paragraph (2), the form of wording in paragraph 2 of Schedule 2 need not be included in a statement where the total amount which the debtor has failed to pay in relation to all the payments due under the running-account credit agreement during the period to which the statement relates does not exceed £1.

(2) Paragraph (1) shall not apply where, at the date on which the duty to give the statement arose, a default sum or other charge has become payable as a result of the debtors failure to pay sums not exceeding £1 as set out in paragraph (1).

[2.419]
19   Content of notices of sums in arrears under fixed-sum credit agreements etc

(1) Subject to regulations 20 to 23, a notice given under section 86B of the 1974 Act (notice of sums in arrears under fixed-sum credit agreements etc) shall contain—

(a)   a form of wording to the effect that the notice is given in compliance with the 1974 Act because the debtor or hirer is behind with [the sums payable] under the agreement;

(b)   a form of wording encouraging the debtor or the hirer to discuss the state of his account with the creditor or owner;

(c)   the information required by paragraphs 1 to 3 of Schedule 3;

(d)   statements in the form specified in paragraphs 4 and 5 of Schedule 3 as applicable; and

(e)   a statement in the form specified in Part 5 of Schedule 3.

(2) In addition, where the notice is required to be given under section 86B(2)(a) of the 1974 Act—

(a)   it shall include the information set out in Part 2 of Schedule 3;

(b)   the creditor or owner shall within fifteen working days of receiving the debtor's or hirer's request for further information about the shortfall which gave rise to the duty to give the notice, give the debtor or hirer in relation to each of the sums which comprise the shortfall, notice of—

     (i)   the amount of the sums due which comprise the shortfall;

     (ii)   the date on which the sums became due; and

     (iii)   the amounts the debtor or hirer paid in respect of the sums due and the dates of those payments;

(c)   it shall, except where it contains all the information specified in regulation [19(2)(b)], include a statement in the following form:

"If you want more information about which payments you failed to make please get in touch with us. We are required to give you this information within fifteen working days of receiving your request for it.";

(d)   where the creditor or owner and the debtor or hirer have entered into an agreement to aggregate, the references to sums due and the reference to amounts paid in sub-paragraph (b) may be construed as a reference to the aggregated sums due to the creditor or owner and the aggregated amounts paid by the debtor or hirer in accordance with the terms of that agreement.

(3) [Subject to paragraph (3A),] where the notice is required to be given under section 86B(2)(b) of the 1974 Act it shall also include the information set out in Part 3 of Schedule 3 and the statement in paragraph 4(1) of that Schedule shall be amended as specified in paragraph 13 of that Schedule.

[(3A)   Where the rate or rates of interest provided for under the agreement are not applicable on a per annum basis, paragraph 9 of Schedule 3 shall not require amounts and dates of interest which became due during the period to which the notice relates to be set out separately in the notice.]

(4)   Where the notice includes a form of wording to the effect that it is not a demand for immediate payment, the creditor or owner shall include wording explaining why it is not such a demand.

(5)   Subject to regulation 20(3)(c), the reference to the account in paragraphs 8 and 10 of Schedule 3 shall be construed as a reference to all accounts maintained by the creditor or owner which relate to the agreement with the debtor or hirer.

NOTES
Para (1): words in square brackets substituted by the Consumer Credit (Information Requirements and Duration of Licences and Charges) (Amendment) Regulations 2008, SI 2008/1751, reg 2(j)(i).
Para (2): figure in square brackets substituted by SI 2008/1751, reg 2(j)(ii).
Para (3): words in square brackets inserted by SI 2008/1751, reg 2(j)(iii).
Para (3A): inserted by SI 2008/1751, reg 2(j)(iv).

[2.420]
20

(1)   Where the creditor and the debtor have entered into an agreement to aggregate and an arrears notice is required to be given in relation to two or more of the agreements to which the agreement to aggregate relates—
  (a)   the information required under paragraphs 1 and 2 of Schedule 3 need only be shown once where the information which would otherwise have to be included for the agreements to which the agreement to aggregate relates is the same for each agreement;
  (b)   where any of the forms of wording set out in paragraphs 4, 5 and 13 of that Schedule do not apply to all the agreements to which the agreement to aggregate relates the creditor shall identify for each such form of wording which does not so apply the regulated agreement or agreements to which it relates.

(2)   Where the creditor and the debtor have entered into an agreement to aggregate and the notice is required to be given under section 86B(2)(a) of the 1974 Act, the reference to the amount which comprises the shortfall in Part 2 of Schedule 3 may be construed as a reference to the aggregated shortfall due under the agreements to which the agreement to aggregate relates.

(3)   Subject to regulation 22, where the creditor and the debtor have entered into an agreement to aggregate and the notice is required to be given under section 86B(2)(b) of the 1974 Act—
  [(a)   the reference to sums paid in paragraph 8 of Schedule 3 may be construed as a reference to the aggregated sums which the debtor is permitted or required to pay;]
  (b)   the reference to interest or other charges in paragraph 9 of that Schedule may be construed as a reference to the aggregated interest or other charges which became due during the period to which the notice relates; and
  (c)   the reference to movements in paragraph 10 of that Schedule may be construed as a reference to the aggregated movements in all the accounts maintained by the creditor in relation to the agreements to which the agreement to aggregate relates.

NOTES
Para (3): sub-para (a) substituted by the Consumer Credit (Information Requirements and Duration of Licences and Charges) (Amendment) Regulations 2008, SI 2008/1751, reg 2(k).

[2.421]
21

Subject to regulation 22(c), where not all the sums permitted to be shown in the notice as an aggregated figure under regulation 20(3) are so shown, the creditor shall indicate where each figure for [a sum paid] or interest or charges which became due or the movement in the account which occurred is an aggregated figure.

NOTES
Words in square brackets substituted by the Consumer Credit (Information Requirements and Duration of Licences and Charges) (Amendment) Regulations 2008, SI 2008/1751, reg 2(l).

[2.422]
22

Where the agreement to aggregate concerns agreements to which regulation 2(8) of the Consumer Credit (Agreements) Regulations 1983 applies and the notice is required to be given under [section 86B(2)] of the 1974 Act—
  (a)   the references to—
    (i)   the opening balance in paragraph 3(b) of Schedule 3;
    [(ia) the amount of the shortfall in paragraph 6 of that Schedule; and]
    (ii)   the opening balance in paragraph 7 of that Schedule,
    may be construed as references to, respectively, the aggregated opening balance[, the

aggregated amount of the shortfall] and the aggregated opening balance of those sums to which paragraph 7 refers, under the agreements to which the agreement to aggregate relates;

(b)   the reference to the balance under the agreement at the end of the period to which the notice relates may be construed as a reference to the aggregated balance under the agreements to which the agreement to aggregate relates at the end of that period; and

(c)   the creditor shall not be required to comply with regulation 21.

NOTES

Words in first pair of square brackets substituted, word omitted revoked and words in second and third pairs of square brackets inserted by the Consumer Credit (Information Requirements and Duration of Licences and Charges) (Amendment) Regulations 2008, SI 2008/1751, reg 2(m).

[2.423]
23

Where all the sums payable under two or more agreements made between the creditor and the debtor at least one of which is a regulated fixed-sum credit agreement have become due and the creditor aggregates the sums due under those agreements for the purpose of recovering those sums—

(a)   the reference to the opening balance in paragraph 3(b) of Schedule 3 may be construed as a reference to the aggregated opening balance under those agreements;

(b)   the reference to opening balance in paragraph 7 of that Schedule may be construed as a reference to a sum equal to the aggregated parts of the opening balance under those agreements which the debtor has failed to pay in full when they became due;

[(c)   the reference to sums paid in paragraph 8 of that Schedule may be construed as a reference to the aggregated sums which the debtor is permitted or required to pay;]

(d)   the reference to interest and other charges becoming due to the creditor in paragraph 9 of that Schedule may be construed as a reference to the aggregated interest and other charges becoming due;

(e)   the reference to movements in paragraph 10 of that Schedule may be construed as a reference to the aggregated movements in all the accounts maintained by the creditor in relation to those agreements;

(f)   the reference to the balance in paragraph 11 of that Schedule may be construed as a reference to the aggregated balance under those agreements;

(g)   the reference to the balance in paragraph 12 of that Schedule may be construed as a reference to a sum equal to the aggregated balance under those agreements which the debtor has failed to pay in full when it became due and which remains unpaid at the end of the period to which the notice relates;

(h)   the information required under paragraphs 1 and 2 of Schedule 3 need only to be shown once where the information which would otherwise have to be included for those agreements is the same for each agreement; and

(i)   where any of the forms of wording set out in paragraphs 4, 5 and 13 of that Schedule do not apply to all those agreements the creditor shall identify for each form of wording which does not so apply the regulated agreement or agreements to which it relates.

NOTES

Para (c): substituted by the Consumer Credit (Information Requirements and Duration of Licences and Charges) (Amendment) Regulations 2008, SI 2008/1751, reg 2(n).

[2.424]
24   Content of notices of sums in arrears under running-account credit agreements

(1)   Subject to regulations 25 and 26, a notice given under section 86C of the 1974 Act (notice of sums in arrears under running-account credit agreements) ("the regulation 24 notice") shall contain—

(a)   a form of wording to the effect that it is given in compliance with the 1974 Act because the debtor is behind with his payments under the agreement;

(b)   a form of wording encouraging the debtor to discuss the state of his account with the creditor;

(c)   the information required by paragraphs 14 to 17 of Schedule 3;

(d)   a statement in the form set out in paragraph 18 of Schedule 3 and the appropriate statement specified in paragraph 19 of that Schedule; and

(e)   a statement in the form specified in Part 5 of Schedule 3.

(2)   Where a regulation 24 notice includes wording to the effect that it is not a demand for immediate payment the creditor shall include wording explaining why it is not such a demand.

[2.425]
25

Where a regulation 24 notice is incorporated into another notice or statement which the creditor gives the debtor in relation to the agreement by virtue of another provision of the 1974 Act ("the other notice"), the regulation 24 notice need not contain so much of the information required under paragraphs 14 to 17 of Schedule 3 as is required to be included in the other notice by or under the provision of the 1974 Act under which the other notice is given.

[2.426]
26

(1) Subject to paragraphs (2) and (3), where the total amount which the debtor has failed to pay in relation to the last two payments due under the agreement prior to the date on which the creditor came under a duty to give the debtor a regulation 24 notice is not more than £2, the notice—

    (a)   need not include any of the information or statements referred to in regulation 24;

    (b)   but in that event shall contain a statement in the following form—

        "You have failed to make two minimum payments

        Failing to make minimum payments can mean that you have broken the terms of this credit agreement. This could result in your having to pay additional costs. A copy of the [Financial Conduct Authority] Arrears information sheet is enclosed, which contains more information about what to do when you get behind with your payments.".

(2) Paragraph (1) shall not apply where at the date on which the duty to give notice arose a default sum or other charge has become payable as a result of the debtor's failure to pay sums as set out in paragraph (1).

(3) Where a regulation 24 notice is incorporated into a statement which the creditor is required to give the debtor under section 78(4) of the 1974 Act, the statement shall not contain the wording specified in paragraph 2 of Schedule 2.

NOTES

Words in square brackets substituted by the Financial Services and Markets Act 2000 (Regulated Activities) (Amendment) Order 2014, SI 2014/366, art 11(1), (2).

[2.427]
27 Giving of notices of default sums

Regulations 28 to 32 shall apply to a notice of default sums given under section 86E of the 1974 Act (notice of default sums) ("the regulation 27 notice").

[2.428]
28

A regulation 27 notice shall be given to the debtor or hirer by the creditor or owner within 35 days of a default sum becoming payable by the debtor or hirer.

[2.429]
29 Content of notices of default sums

A regulation 27 notice shall contain a form of wording to the effect that it relates to default sums and is given in compliance with the 1974 Act.

[2.430]
30

A regulation 27 notice shall contain the information and the form of wording set out in Part 1 of Schedule 4.

[2.431]
31

If a regulation 27 notice is given in relation to an agreement which provides that interest is payable in connection with default sums it shall contain the appropriate form of wording set out in Part 2 of Schedule 4.

[2.432]
32

Where a regulation 27 notice is incorporated into another notice or statement which the creditor gives the debtor in relation to the agreement by virtue of another provision of the 1974 Act ("the other notice"), the regulation 27 notice need not contain such of the information required under paragraphs 1 to 3 of Schedule 4 as is required to be included in the other notice by the provision of the 1974 Act under which the other notice is given.

33 (*Amends the Consumer Credit (Enforcement, Default and Termination Notices) Regulations 1983, SI 1983/1561, reg 2, Sch 2.*)

[2.433]
34 Content of notices of intention to recover post-judgment interest

Subject to regulation 35, a notice given under section 130A(1) of the 1974 Act (notice of intention to recover post-judgment interest in connection with a judgment sum) shall contain:

   (a)   if the notice is the first required notice—
       (i)   the information listed and forms of wording set out in Part 1 of Schedule 5; and
      (ii)   the form of wording set out in Part 3 of Schedule 5;
   (b)   if the notice is not the first required notice, the information and forms of wording set out in Part 1 of and the information set out in Part 2 of Schedule 5.

[2.434]
35

The creditor may, instead of including in the notice the form of wording set out in paragraph 6 of Schedule 5, include the wording which concerns advice and information available to consumers which is contained in the default information sheet referred to in section 86A of the 1974 Act and which is in effect in accordance with subsection (5) of that section at the time the duty to give the notice arose.

[2.435]
36   Form of notices and statements required under these Regulations

The wording required by regulations 10, 19(1)(a) and (b) and (4), 24(1)(a) and (b) and (2), 29 and 48(c) to be included in a notice or statement to be given under the 1974 Act shall be expressed in plain, intelligible language.

[2.436]
37

(1)   Subject to paragraph (2), the first form of wording set out in paragraph 4 of Schedule 1 and the first form of wording set out in paragraph 5 of that Schedule shall appear together as a whole and shall not be interspersed with any other information or wording.

(2)   The first form of wording set out in paragraph 4 of Schedule 1 and the first form of wording set out in paragraph 5 of that Schedule may be interspersed with the second form of wording set out in paragraph 5 of that Schedule.

[2.437]
38

(1)   The first form of wording set out in paragraph 4 of Schedule 2 and the closing balance shall be shown together as a whole and not interspersed with any other information or wording.

(2)   For the purposes of this regulation—
   (a)   . . .
   (b)   closing balance means, in relation to a statement required to be given under section 78(4) of the 1974 Act, the balance at the end of the period to which the statement relates which is required to be included in the statement under paragraph 1 of the Schedule to the Consumer Credit (Running-Account) Credit Information Regulations 1983.

NOTES
   Para (2): sub-para (a) revoked by the Consumer Credit (Information Requirements and Duration of Licences and Charges) (Amendment) Regulations 2008, SI 2008/1751, reg 2(o).

[2.438]
39

The lettering of the information and wording required by these Regulations to be included in a statement or notice and any figures and symbols forming part of that information or wording shall be easily legible and of a colour which is readily distinguishable from the background medium upon which it is or they are displayed.

[2.439]
40

(1)   Subject to paragraph (2), the information and wording required by these Regulations[, other than regulation 33,] to be included in a statement or notice to be given under the 1974 Act shall be no less prominent than any other information and wording included in the document in which that notice or statement is embodied.

(2)   But—
   (a)   the date of the notice or statement, trade names and names of parties to the agreement, logos, headings or the reference number of the agreement may be more prominent; and
   (b)   the form of wording set out in paragraph 2 of Schedule 2 shall be more prominent,
than any such other information and wording, whether prominence is achieved by capital letters, underlining, larger or bold print or otherwise.

NOTES
   Para (1): words in square brackets inserted by the Consumer Credit (Information Requirements and Duration of Licences and Charges) (Amendment) Regulations 2008, SI 2008/1751, reg 2(p).

[2.440]
41   Errors and omissions
Where a notice or statement contains an error or omission which does not affect the substance of the information or forms of wording which it is required by these Regulations to contain, that notice or statement shall not breach these Regulations on this ground alone.

[2.441]
[41A
(1)   Where a statement relates to a green deal plan made before 28th February 2014, or a green deal consumer credit agreement, and the statement contains an error or omission which arises as a result of one or more of the grounds specified in paragraph (2)—
    (a)   the statement shall not breach these Regulations on this ground alone; and
    (b)   paragraphs (3) to (5) apply.
(2)   The grounds specified in this paragraph are—
    (a)   a failure to provide information to the creditor by, or on behalf of, the relevant energy supplier;
    (b)   an error or omission in the information provided to the creditor by, or on behalf of, the relevant energy supplier;
    (c)   an error or omission in the information held by the creditor not falling within sub-paragraph (b);
where, at the time of providing the statement, the creditor did not know, and could not reasonably have been expected to know, that the relevant energy supplier had failed to provide information, or provided incorrect information, or that there was an error or omission in the information held by them (as the case may be).
(3)   Where the error or omission resulted in an error in the closing balance of the previous statement, the first statement provided after the creditor becomes aware of the error or omission must include—
    (a)   a balance carried forward, which is the closing balance from the previous statement;
    (b)   the amount and date of any payment which was omitted from the previous statement in error;
    (c)   the amount and date of any adjustment to—
        (i)   a payment;
        (ii)   an interest or other charge;
        (iii)   any other movement in the account of the debtor or the current bill payer relating to the agreement;
    which was incorrectly shown in the previous statement;
    (d)   an opening balance, which is the amount required by sub-paragraph (a) adjusted, as necessary, to take account of the amounts required to be included by virtue of sub-paragraphs (b) and (c).
(4)   Subject to regulation 41, where the error or omission did not result in an error in the closing balance of the previous statement, the first statement provided after the creditor becomes aware of the error or omission must identify and correct that error or omission (as the case may be).
(5)   Where a statement is produced in reliance on paragraphs (3) or (4), the statement must include a form of wording clearly explaining the effect of paragraph (3), or (4) (as the case may be).]

NOTES
Commencement: 26 September 2014.
Inserted by the Consumer Credit (Information Requirements and Duration of Licences and Charges) (Amendment) Regulations 2014, SI 2014/2369, reg 2(1), (6).

42–44   (*Regs 42, 43 revoked by the Financial Services and Markets Act 2000 (Regulated Activities) (Amendment) (No 2) Order 2013, SI 2013/1881, art 25, for transitional provisions see arts 29–66 of that Order at* **[2.1007]** *et seq; reg 44 revokes the Consumer Credit (Period of Standard Licence) Regulations 1975, SI 1975/2124.*)

[2.442]
45   Transitional provisions
Regulations 46 to 50 shall apply where a statement is given under section 77A of the 1974 Act in relation to a fixed-sum credit agreement made before 1 October 2008.

[2.443]
46
A statement to which this regulation applies need not include the information under paragraphs 3(b), 3(c)(ii), 3(d) and 3(e) of Schedule 1.

[2.444]
47

(1) Where the conditions set out in paragraph (2) are met and the statement includes the information under paragraph 3(b) of Schedule 1, regulation 9(2) shall apply to that statement as if the words "Where the statement is not the first statement given under section 77A of the 1974 Act in relation to the agreements to which the agreement to aggregate relates" were omitted.

(2) Those conditions are—
    (a)   a statement to which this regulation applies is the first given on or after 1 October 2008;
    (b)   the creditor and the debtor have entered into an agreement to aggregate;
    (c)   the agreement to aggregate was entered into prior to 1 October 2008; and
    (d)   regulation 9 applies to that agreement to aggregate.

[2.445]
48

Where a statement to which this regulation applies does not include some or all of the information referred to in regulation 46—
    (a)   the creditor shall give the debtor in writing such of the information referred to in regulation 46 as was omitted from the statement within fifteen working days of receipt of the debtor's request for that information;
    (b)   the statement shall contain the following wording:

    "**More information**
    This statement does not contain all the information which you are entitled to receive from us about your agreement. If you would like to receive this extra information please get in touch with us to obtain it. We are required to provide you with this information within fifteen working days of receiving your request for it.";

    (c)   the creditor shall include a form of words that identifies which pieces of the information referred to in regulation 46 it has not included in the statement;
    (d)   where the debtor requests some but not all of the information which the creditor has omitted from the statement in accordance with regulation 46 (whether or not the information requested amounts to all the information which the creditor has so omitted) paragraph (a) shall only require the creditor to give the debtor the information requested; and
    (e)   where it is not clear from the debtor's request which pieces of the information so omitted the debtor has requested, the creditor shall give the debtor all the information so omitted.

[2.446]
49

Regulations 45 to 48 shall apply until 30 September 2018.

[2.447]
50

(1) Subject to paragraph (2), where a notice of sums in arrears is given pursuant to section 86B of the 1974 Act in relation to a regulated agreement for fixed-sum credit or a regulated consumer hire agreement made before 1 October 2008 the notice may contain pre-commencement information.

[(2) Where pre-commencement information is included in a notice to which section 86(B)(2) applies it may be aggregated with—
    (a)   the amount of the shortfall in paragraph 6 of Schedule 3;
    (b)   the sum required to be included in the notice under paragraph 7 of that Schedule; or
    (c)   the sum required to be included in the notice under paragraph 12 of that Schedule.]

(3) For the purposes of this regulation, "pre-commencement information" means any sum which—
    (a)   became due before 1 October 2008;
    (b)   the debtor or hirer failed to pay in full when it became due under the agreement; and
    (c)   remains unpaid at the date the duty to give the notice arose.

NOTES
    Para (2): substituted by the Consumer Credit (Information Requirements and Duration of Licences and Charges) (Amendment) Regulations 2008, SI 2008/1751, reg 2(q).

SCHEDULES

SCHEDULE 1

PART 1
INFORMATION TO BE INCLUDED IN STATEMENTS RELATING TO FIXED-SUM CREDIT AGREEMENTS

Regulation 4(a)

[2.448]
1. The period to which the statement relates.

2. (1)   The name, telephone number or numbers, postal address and, where appropriate, any other address of the creditor.

(2)   Where the creditor and the debtor have entered into an arrangement under which the creditor has given the debtor details of a particular employee or category of employee of the creditor whom the debtor is entitled to contact in relation to all his dealings with the creditor, the creditor may, instead of including the telephone number or numbers referred to in sub-paragraph (1), refer to that arrangement.

3. Information specific to the agreement—
- (a)   a description of the agreement sufficient to identify it;
- (b)   the amount of credit provided and, where applicable, to be provided under the agreement (shown as one figure);
- (c)
  - (i)   any rate or rates of interest applicable on a per annum basis which applied during the period to which the statement relates and—
    - (aa)   the periods during which each rate applied; and
    - (bb)   if applicable, the element of the credit to which each rate applied; or
  - (ii)   where the rate or rates of interest are not applicable on a per annum basis, the rate or rates of interest on the credit provided under the agreement, in each case quoted on a per annum basis and a statement explaining how and when interest charges are calculated and applied under the agreement;
- (d)
  - (i)   the date on which the agreement became an executed agreement; or
  - (ii)   the date of first movement on the account;
- (e)
  - (i)   the duration; or
  - (ii)   the minimum duration,
  - of the agreement as provided in the agreement;
- (f)   any opening balance under the agreement at the beginning of the period to which the statement relates;
- (g)   the amount and date of any payment made into the account by, or to the credit of, the debtor during the period to which the statement relates;
- (h)   the amount and date of any interest or other charges payable by the debtor which became due during the period to which the statement relates, whether or not the interest or other charges relate only to that period;
- (i)   the amount and date of any movement in the account during the period to which the statement relates which is not required to be included in the statement under sub-paragraphs (g) and (h); and
- (j)   the balance under the agreement at the end of the period to which the statement relates.

[3A In this Part, where a statement relates to a green deal consumer credit agreement, a payment made into the account of the current bill payer with the relevant energy supplier, is to be treated as made into the account of the current bill payer with the creditor relating to the agreement.]

NOTES

Para 3A: added, together with para 3B and preceding Part heading, by the Consumer Credit (Information Requirements and Duration of Licences and Charges) (Amendment) Regulations 2014, SI 2014/2369, reg 2(1), (7)(a).

[PART 1A
ADDITIONAL INFORMATION TO BE INCLUDED IN STATEMENTS RELATING TO GREEN DEAL PLANS MADE BEFORE 28TH FEBRUARY 2014

[2.449]
3B The balance under the agreement at the end of the period to which the statement relates, which is to be based on the assumption that all liabilities which fell due during the period to which the statement relates have been paid.]

NOTES
Commencement: 26 September 2014.
Part 1A: inserted as noted to para 3A at **[2.448]**.

PART 2
FORMS OF WORDING TO BE INCLUDED IN STATEMENTS RELATING TO FIXED-SUM CREDIT AGREEMENTS

Regulation 4(b)

[2.450]
4. Each of the following forms of wording shall be contained in a statement under this Part:

"Settling your credit agreement early
You can settle this agreement [in full] at any time by giving us notice . . . and paying off the amount you owe. If you wish to settle early you should contact us for a final settlement figure.";
[[You can also settle this agreement in part at any time by giving notice and paying off some of the amount you owe.] [NOTE 1]
NOTE 1: Delete where agreement is secured on land.]];
"Dispute resolution
If you have a problem with your agreement, please try to resolve it with us in the first instance. If you are not happy with the way in which we handled your complaint or the result, you may be able to complain to the Financial Ombudsman Service. If you do not take up your problem with us first you will not be entitled to complain to the Ombudsman. We can provide details of how to contact the Ombudsman.";
"Paying less than the agreed sum:
If you pay less than your agreed payment in most cases it is likely to take you longer and may cost you more to pay off the debt under the agreement.
If you have difficulties making payments under your credit agreement please contact us if you have not already done so to discuss terms for the rest of the agreement. You may also want to seek advice on what to do from an independent free advice agency such as the Citizens Advice Bureau.".

NOTES
Words in first pair of square brackets inserted, words omitted revoked and words from "[You can also" to "secured on land.]" in square brackets inserted by the Consumer Credit (EU Directive) Regulations 2010, SI 2010/1010, reg 91A (as inserted by the Consumer Credit (Amendment) Regulations 2010, SI 2010/1969, regs 4, 27), with effect in relation to certain agreements entered into before 1 February 2011, as provided for in regs 100–101A of the 2010 Regulations at **[2.803]–[2.805]**.

[PART 2A
ADDITIONAL INFORMATION TO BE INCLUDED IN STATEMENTS RELATING TO GREEN DEAL PLANS MADE BEFORE 28TH FEBRUARY 2014 AND GREEN DEAL CONSUMER CREDIT AGREEMENTS]

[2.451]
4A Each of the following forms of wording shall be contained in a statement under this Part—
["Your Green Deal Plan
This credit agreement is part of a Green Deal Plan. Regular instalments are therefore collected through the electricity bill for this property. To keep this credit agreement up to date, it is important that your electricity bill is paid on time and as agreed with your electricity supplier. The bill payer or bill payers remain free to change the payment method and payment schedule of the electricity bill in line with the electricity supplier's policies, without any penalty or extra charges. If you wish to change payment frequency, you are advised to contact the electricity supplier directly."]
"Settling your Green Deal Plan early
You can settle your Green Deal Plan in full at any time by giving us notice and paying off the amount you owe. If you wish to settle early in full you should contact us for a final settlement figure.
You can also settle your Green Deal Plan in part at any time by giving notice and paying off some of the amount you owe.";
"Dispute resolution
If you have a problem with any aspect of your Green Deal Plan, please try to resolve it with us in the first instance. If you are not happy with the way in which we handled your complaint or the result, you may be able to complain to the Financial Ombudsman or the [Green Deal] Ombudsman. If you do not take up your problem with us first you will not be entitled to complain to either Ombudsman. We can provide details of how to contact both Ombudsmen."
"Paying less than the agreed sum

If you do not pay your electricity bill in full, you will be behind with payments due under both your Green Deal Plan and your electricity bill and, in most cases, it is likely to take you longer and [could] cost you more to pay off what you owe under your Green Deal Plan.

If you have difficulties paying your electricity bill please contact your electricity supplier. You may also want to seek advice on what to do from an independent free advice agency such as the Citizens Advice service."

[**"Payments**

This statement may not include a payment, or payments, made recently to the electricity supplier which has not yet been passed on to us.";

"Previous bill payers' payments and arrears

This statement does not contain information about payments made and arrears incurred by previous bill payers before the date on which the current bill payer or bill payers became liable for payments."].]

NOTES

Commencement: 26 September 2014.

Inserted by the Consumer Credit (Green Deal) Regulations 2012, SI 2012/2798, reg 5, Schedule, para 4(1), (5).

Part heading substituted, and entries relating to "Your Green Deal Plan", "Payments" and "Previous bill payers' payments and arrears" inserted and added, by the Consumer Credit (Information Requirements and Duration of Licences and Charges) (Amendment) Regulations 2014, SI 2014/2369, reg 2(1), (7)(b), (c)(i), (iv).

Entry relating to "Dispute resolution": words in square brackets substituted by SI 2014/2369, reg 2(1), (7)(c)(ii).

Entry relating to "Paying less than the agreed sum": word in square brackets inserted by SI 2014/2369, reg 2(1), (7)(c)(iii).

PART 3
FORMS OF WORDING TO BE INCLUDED IN FIXED-SUM CREDIT STATEMENTS RELATING TO HIRE-PURCHASE OR CONDITIONAL SALE AGREEMENTS

Regulation 4(c)

[2.452]

5. The following forms of wording shall be included, as appropriate, in a statement under this Part:

"**Termination: Your rights**

You also have the right to end this agreement early in accordance with section 99 of the Consumer Credit Act 1974. You will not have to pay all the sums due under the agreement but you will not be entitled to retain the goods if you do this. Details were set out in your credit agreement. If you wish to terminate the agreement you should contact us for further information including any amount payable on termination.".

"If you wish we can provide you with separate settlement figures for your [hire purchase] [conditional sale] [NOTE 1] agreement and for your insurance finance agreement. Please contact us in writing to obtain this.".

NOTE 1: Delete as applicable.

SCHEDULE 2
FORMS OF WORDING AND INFORMATION TO BE INCLUDED IN STATEMENTS RELATING TO RUNNING-ACCOUNT CREDIT AGREEMENTS

Regulation 14

[2.453]

1. The following form of wording shall be contained in a statement under this Part—

"**Minimum payments**

If you make only the minimum payment each month, it will take you longer and cost you more to clear your balance.".

2. If at the end of the period to which the statement relates, the debtor has paid less than the minimum payment required to be paid by him in accordance with the agreement, the statement shall contain the following form of wording—

"**You have failed to make a minimum payment**

Failing to make your minimum payment can mean that you have broken the terms of this credit agreement and could result in us taking legal action against you. It could lead to your having to pay additional costs and make it more difficult for you to obtain credit in future.".

3. The following information shall be contained in the statement—

A statement of the order or proportions in which any amount paid by the debtor which is not sufficient to discharge the total debt then due under the agreement will be applied or appropriated by the creditor towards the discharge of the sums due in respect of:

(a)   the amounts of credit provided for different purposes; or

(b)   different parts of the agreement.

4. The following forms of wording shall be contained in the statement—

"If you do not pay off the full amount outstanding, we will allocate your payment to the outstanding balance in a specific order, which is set out [NOTE 1]. The way in which payments are allocated can make a significant difference to the amount of interest you will pay until the balance is cleared completely.";

NOTE 1: state where in relation to this form of wording this information is located on the statement;

"Dispute resolution

If you have a problem with your agreement, please try to resolve it with us in the first instance. If you are not happy with the way in which we handled your complaint or the result, you may be able to complain to the Financial Ombudsman Service. If you do not take up your problem with us first you will not be entitled to complain to the Ombudsman. We can provide details of how to contact the Ombudsman.".

SCHEDULE 3

PART 1
INFORMATION AND STATEMENTS TO BE INCLUDED IN NOTICES OF SUMS IN ARREARS UNDER FIXED-SUM CREDIT AGREEMENTS ETC
Regulation 19(1)(c), (d)

[2.454]
1. The date of the notice.

2. (1)   The name, telephone number or numbers, the postal address, and, where appropriate, any other address of the creditor or owner.

(2)   Where the creditor and the debtor or the owner and the hirer have entered into an arrangement under which the debtor or the hirer has been given details of a particular employee or category of employee of the creditor or owner whom the debtor or hirer is entitled to contact in relation to all his dealings with the creditor or owner, the creditor or owner may, instead of including the telephone number or numbers referred to in sub-paragraph (1), refer to that arrangement.

3. Information specific to the agreement:
   (a)   a description of the agreement sufficient to identify it; and
   (b)   the opening balance under the agreement at the date on which the duty to give the notice arose.

4. (1)   Where default sums or interest (other than any set out in the notice) may be payable in connection with the amounts set out in the notice, a statement in the following form—

   "Default sums and interest
   You may have to pay default sums and interest in relation to the missed or partly made payments referred to in this notice. Please contact us if you would like further details. This notice does not take account of any payments received after the date of the notice.".

(2)   In any other case, a statement in the following form—

   "Default sums and interest
   You will not incur any default sums or extra interest in relation to the missed or partly made payments referred to in this notice. This notice does not take account of any payments received after the date of the notice.".

5. A statement in the following form:

   "Notices
   For so long as you continue to be behind with your payments by any amount, you will be sent notices about this at least every six months. We are not required to send you notices more frequently than this, even if you get further behind with your payments in between notices.".

PART 2
INFORMATION TO BE INCLUDED IN FIRST REQUIRED NOTICES OF SUMS IN ARREARS UNDER FIXED-SUM CREDIT AGREEMENTS ETC
Regulation 19(2)(a)

[2.455]
6. The amount of the shortfall under the agreement which gave rise to the duty to give the notice.

PART 3

INFORMATION AND STATEMENT TO BE INCLUDED IN ALL NOTICES OF SUMS IN ARREARS UNDER FIXED-SUM CREDIT AGREEMENTS ETC EXCEPT FIRST REQUIRED NOTICES

Regulation 19(3)

[2.456]

7. That part of the opening balance referred to in paragraph 3(b) of this Schedule which comprises any sum which the debtor or hirer has failed to pay in full when it became due under the agreement, whether or not such sums have been included in a previous notice.

8. The amount and date of any [sums paid] into the account by, or to the credit of, the debtor or hirer during the period to which the notice relates.

9. The amount and date of any interest or other charges payable by the debtor or hirer which became due during the period to which the notice relates, whether or not the interest or other charges relate only to that period.

10. The amount and date of any movement in the account during the period to which the notice relates which is not required to be included in the notice under paragraphs 8 [and 9].

11. The balance under the agreement at the end of the period to which the notice relates.

12. That part of the balance referred to in paragraph 11 which comprises any sum which the debtor or hirer has failed to pay in full when it became due under the agreement and which remains unpaid at the end of the period to which the notice relates, whether or not such a sum has been included in a previous notice.

13. Add the following words to the end of the first sentence of the statement in paragraph 4(1): "(in addition to any default sums and interest included in this notice).".

NOTES

Para 8: words in square brackets substituted by the Consumer Credit (Information Requirements and Duration of Licences and Charges) (Amendment) Regulations 2008, SI 2008/1751, reg 2(r)(i).

Para 10: words in square brackets added by SI 2008/1751, reg 2(r)(ii).

PART 4

INFORMATION AND STATEMENTS TO BE INCLUDED IN NOTICES OF SUMS IN ARREARS UNDER RUNNING-ACCOUNT CREDIT AGREEMENTS

Regulation 24(1)(c) and (d)

[2.457]

14. The date of the notice.

15. A description of the agreement sufficient to identify it.

16. (1) The name, telephone number, postal address and, where appropriate, any other address of the creditor.

(2) Where the creditor and the debtor have entered into an arrangement under which the creditor has given the debtor details of a particular employee or category of employee of the creditor whom the debtor is entitled to contact in relation to all his dealings with the creditor, the creditor may, instead of including the telephone number or numbers referred to in sub-paragraph (1), refer to that arrangement.

17. In relation to each of the last two payments which the debtor is required under the agreement to have made and which have not been paid or not fully paid:

  (a) the amount payable;

  (b) the date on which that amount became due;

  (c) in the event that the debtor has paid part of that amount, the amount he has paid and the date on which that payment was made; and

  (d) the nature of the amount due,

together with the aggregate of the amounts payable as shown under sub-paragraph (a) less the aggregate of the amounts paid as shown under sub-paragraph (c).

18. A statement in the following form—

    "Missed and partly made payments

    This notice does not give details of missed or partly made payments previously notified whether or not they remain unpaid.".

19. (1) Where default sums or interest (other than any set out in the notice) may be payable in connection with the amounts set out in the notice, a statement in the following form—

"Default sums and Interest
You may have to pay default sums and interest in relation to the missed or partly made payments indicated above in addition to any default sums and interest already included in this notice. Please contact us if you would like further details. This notice does not take account of any payments received after the date of the notice.".

(2)   In any other case, a statement in the following form—

"Default sums and Interest
You will not incur any default sums or extra interest in relation to the missed or partly made payments indicated above. This notice does not take account of any payments received after the date of the notice.".

PART 5
STATEMENT TO BE INCLUDED IN NOTICES OF SUMS IN ARREARS UNDER FIXED-SUM CREDIT AGREEMENTS ETC AND RUNNING-ACCOUNT CREDIT AGREEMENTS

Regulation 19(1)(e) and 24(1)(e)

[2.458]
A statement in the following form shall be contained in a notice under this Part—

"[Financial Conduct Authority] Information Sheet
This notice should include a copy of the current information sheet on arrears prepared by the [Financial Conduct Authority]. This contains important information about your rights and where to go for support and advice, for example on applying for a Time Order as well as our right to charge you interest. If it is not included you should contact us to get one. Please refer to the [Financial Conduct Authority] information sheet for more information about how to get advice on dealing with your debt.".

NOTES
    Words in square brackets substituted by the Financial Services and Markets Act 2000 (Regulated Activities) (Amendment) Order 2014, SI 2014/366, art 11(1), (3).

SCHEDULE 4

PART 1
INFORMATION AND FORM OF WORDING TO BE INCLUDED IN NOTICES OF DEFAULT SUMS

Regulation 30

[2.459]
1. The date of the notice.

2. A description of the agreement sufficient to identify it.

3. (1)   The name, telephone number, postal address and, where appropriate, any other address of the creditor or owner.

(2)   Where the creditor and the debtor or the owner and the hirer have entered into an arrangement under which the debtor or the hirer has been given details of a particular employee or category of employee of the creditor or owner whom the debtor or hirer is entitled to contact in relation to all his dealings with the creditor or owner, the creditor or owner may, instead of including the telephone number or numbers referred to in sub-paragraph (1), refer to that arrangement.

4. The amount and nature of each default sum payable under the agreement which has not been the subject of a previous notice of default sums.

5. The date upon which each default sum referred to in the notice became payable under the agreement.

6. The following statement:

    "This Notice does not take account of default sums which we have already told you about in another default sum notice, whether or not those sums remain unpaid.".

7. The total amount of all the default sums included in the notice.

PART 2
FORMS OF WORDING TO BE INCLUDED IN NOTICES OF DEFAULT SUMS WHERE INTEREST IS PAYABLE ON DEFAULT SUMS

Regulation 31

[2.460]

8. Where the interest rate which applies to the default sum in the event that it is not paid or not paid in full when it falls due is a variable rate the following form of wording shall be contained in a notice under this Part—

"**Interest**
We are not entitled to charge you interest on the default sums for the first 28 days after we have given you this notice. However if the sums are not paid in full by that date interest will be charged at the rate of . . . .[NOTE 1]. Since this interest rate is a variable rate, the rate which we will apply to the default sum once the 28 days have passed may be different.".

NOTE 1: Insert the interest rate applicable at the date of the notice.

9. Where the interest rate which applies to the default sum in the event that it is not paid or not paid in full when it falls due is a fixed rate the following form of wording shall be contained in the notice—

"**Interest**
We are not entitled to charge you interest on the default sums for the first 28 days after we have given you this notice. However if the sum is not paid in full by that date interest will be charged at the rate of . . . .[NOTE 1].".

NOTE 1: Insert applicable interest rate.

SCHEDULE 5

PART 1
INFORMATION AND STATEMENT TO BE INCLUDED IN ALL NOTICES UNDER SECTION 130A OF THE 1974 ACT

Regulation 34(a)(i) and (b)

[2.461]

1. The date of the notice.

2. A description of the agreement sufficient to identify it and the claim number of the judgment given in relation to the agreement.

3. (1) The name, telephone number, postal address and, where appropriate, any other address of the creditor or owner.

(2) Where the creditor and the debtor or the owner and the hirer have entered into an arrangement under which the debtor or the hirer has been given details of a particular employee or category of employee of the creditor or owner whom the debtor or hirer is entitled to contact in relation to all his dealings with the creditor or owner, the creditor or owner may, instead of including the telephone number or numbers referred to in sub-paragraph (1), refer to that arrangement.

4. The amount on which post-judgment interest is or will be charged at the date of the notice.

5. A statement in the following form—

"If you are having problems making repayments you should contact us in the first instance. If we cannot help you resolve the problem and if you are making payments under an instalment order you may be able to apply to the court to have the terms of the instalment order varied. If you do so you may also ask the court to reduce the amount of interest payable on the judgment debt.".

[6. A statement in the following form—

'**Advice and information**
You can also obtain advice and information about dealing with your debt issues from Citizens Advice, Consumer Credit Counselling Service, National Debtline, Consumer Direct, Consumerline and Community Legal Advice. [NOTE 1].'.

NOTE 1: Insert the contact details for the organisations referred to which are contained in the current [Financial Conduct Authority] Default information sheet.]

NOTES
Para 6: substituted by the Consumer Credit (Information Requirements and Duration of Licences and Charges) (Amendment) Regulations 2008, SI 2008/1751, reg 2(s); words in square brackets substituted by the Financial Services and Markets Act 2000 (Regulated Activities) (Amendment) Order 2014, SI 2014/366, art 11(1), (4).

PART 2
INFORMATION AND STATEMENT TO BE INCLUDED IN ALL EXCEPT FIRST REQUIRED NOTICE UNDER SECTION 130A OF THE 1974 ACT

Regulation 34(b)

[2.462]
7. The total amount of post-judgment interest charged since the date of the last notice given under section130A in relation to the agreement.

8. The date or dates on which post-judgment interest has been charged since that date.

9. The rate or rates at which post-judgment interest was charged. Where the rate is a variable rate it shall be stated to be variable.

PART 3
FORM OF WORDING TO BE INCLUDED IN FIRST REQUIRED NOTICE

Regulation 34(a)(ii)

[2.463]
"Interest payable after a judgment
This notice is being given to you because a court judgment has been obtained against you in relation to the agreement. Under the agreement we are allowed to continue to charge you interest on all the sums which the judgment states you owe us.
This notice is to advise you that we intend to charge interest. The rate of interest payable will be . . . . [NOTE 1] (variable) [NOTE 2].
Interest will be charged from the day you were given this notice (i.e. when the notice is deemed to have been delivered to you in the ordinary course of post) onwards.
This means that even if you pay off the whole amount of the judgment, you may still have a further sum to pay.
For so long as we intend to charge interest on the monies which the judgment states you owe us, you will be given a notice about this at least every six months. This will also include information about the amount of interest that has been charged since the previous notice was given.
If you are not given such a notice within 6 months starting with the day after the previous notice was given to you then we will not be able to charge further interest until you are given such a notice."

NOTE 1: Insert interest rate or rates. Where the rate is variable insert the rate applicable at the date of the notice.

NOTE 2: Delete where the rate or rates are fixed.

MONEY LAUNDERING REGULATIONS 2007

(SI 2007/2157)

NOTES
Made: 24 July 2007.
Authority: European Communities Act 1972, s 2(2); Financial Services and Markets Act 2000, ss 168(4)(b), 402(1)(b), 417(1), 428(3).
Commencement: 15 December 2007.
References to "the European Community", "Community", etc: see the Treaty of Lisbon (Changes in Terminology) Order 2011, SI 2011/1043, which provides that (as from 22 April 2011): (i) for references to the European Communities or to the European Community or the European Coal and Steel Community (including references to "the Communities", "the Community", "the EC" or "the EEC") substitute references to the European Union, and (ii) references to "EU" should be substituted for the word "Community" (subject to certain exceptions) in references to "Community treaties", "Community instrument", "Community obligation", "Community law", "Community legislation", etc.
Transfer of functions and transitional provisions: the Public Bodies (Abolition of the National Consumer Council and Transfer of the Office of Fair Trading's Functions in relation to Estate Agents etc) Order 2014, SI 2014/631, art 5(2) provides that the functions exercisable by the OFT under these Regulations by virtue of its role as the supervisory authority for estate agents pursuant to reg 23(1)(b)(ii) *post* (prior to its amendment by the 2014 Order) are transferred to the Commissioners for Her Majesty's Revenue and Customs. For transitional provisions see Sch 3 to that Order at **[2.1134B]**.

ARRANGEMENT OF REGULATIONS

PART 1
GENERAL

PART 1
GENERAL

[2.464]
1 Citation, commencement etc

(1) These Regulations may be cited as the Money Laundering Regulations 2007 and come into force on 15th December 2007.

(2) These Regulations are prescribed for the purposes of sections 168(4)(b) (appointment of persons to carry out investigations in particular cases) and 402(1)(b) (power of the Authority to institute proceedings for certain other offences) of the 2000 Act.

(3) . . .

NOTES
Para (3): revokes the Money Laundering Regulations 2003, SI 2003/3075.

[2.465]
2 Interpretation

(1) In these Regulations—
    "the 2000 Act" means the Financial Services and Markets Act 2000;
    "Annex I financial institution" has the meaning given by regulation 22(1);
    ["auction platform" has the meaning given by regulation 3(13A);]
    "auditor", except in regulation 17(2)(c) and (d), has the meaning given by regulation 3(4) and (5);
    "authorised person" means a person who is authorised for the purposes of the 2000 Act;
    "the Authority" means the [Financial Conduct Authority];
    "beneficial owner" has the meaning given by regulation 6;
    ["bill payment service provider" means an undertaking which provides a payment service enabling the payment of utility and other household bills;]
    "business relationship" means a business, professional or commercial relationship between a relevant person and a customer, which is expected by the relevant person, at the time when contact is established, to have an element of duration;
    ["the capital requirements directive" means Directive 2013/36/EU of the European Parliament and of the Council of 26 June 2013 relating to the activity of credit institutions and the prudential supervision of credit institutions and investment firms, amending Directive 2002/87/EC and repealing Directives 2006/48/EC and 2006/49/EC;

Part 2   Statutory Instruments

"the capital requirements regulation" means Regulation (EU) 575/2013 of the European Parliament and of the Council of 26 June 2013 on prudential requirements for credit institutions and investment firms and amending Regulation (EU) No 648/2012;]

"cash" means notes, coins or travellers' cheques in any currency;

"casino" has the meaning given by regulation 3(13);

"the Commissioners" means the Commissioners for Her Majesty's Revenue and Customs;

. . .

"credit institution" has the meaning given by regulation 3(2);

"customer due diligence measures" has the meaning given by regulation 5;

"DETI" means the Department of Enterprise, Trade and Investment in Northern Ireland;

["the electronic money directive" means Directive 2009/110/EC of the European Parliament and of the Council of 16th September 2009 on the taking up, pursuit and prudential supervision of the business of electronic money institutions;

"electronic money institution" has the meaning given by regulation 2(1) of the Electronic Money Regulations 2011;]

"estate agent" has the meaning given by regulation 3(11);

["the emission allowance auctioning regulation" means Commission Regulation (EU) No 1031/2010 of 12 November 2010 on the timing, administration and other aspects of auctioning of greenhouse gas emission allowances pursuant to Directive 2003/87/EC of the European Parliament and of the Council establishing a scheme for greenhouse gas emission allowances trading within the Community;]

"external accountant" has the meaning given by regulation 3(7);

"financial institution" has the meaning given by regulation 3(3);

"firm" means any entity, whether or not a legal person, that is not an individual and includes a body corporate and a partnership or other unincorporated association;

"high value dealer" has the meaning given by regulation 3(12);

"the implementing measures directive" means Commission Directive 2006/70/EC of 1st August 2006 laying down implementing measures for the money laundering directive;

"independent legal professional" has the meaning given by regulation 3(9);

"insolvency practitioner", except in regulation 17(2)(c) and (d), has the meaning given by regulation 3(6);

"the life assurance consolidation directive" means Directive 2002/83/EC of the European Parliament and of the Council of 5th November 2002 concerning life assurance;

"local weights and measures authority" has the meaning given by section 69 of the Weights and Measures Act 1985 (local weights and measures authorities);

"the markets in financial instruments directive" means Directive 2004/39/EC of the European Parliament and of the Council of 12th April 2004 on markets in financial instruments;

"money laundering" means an act which falls within section 340(11) of the Proceeds of Crime Act 2002;

"the money laundering directive" means Directive 2005/60/EC of the European Parliament and of the Council of 26th October 2005 on the prevention of the use of the financial system for the purpose of money laundering and terrorist financing;

"money service business" means an undertaking which by way of business operates a currency exchange office, transmits money (or any representations of monetary value) by any means or cashes cheques which are made payable to customers;

"nominated officer" means a person who is nominated to receive disclosures under Part 7 of the Proceeds of Crime Act 2002 (money laundering) or Part 3 of the Terrorism Act 2000 (terrorist property);

"non-EEA state" means a state that is not an EEA state;

"notice" means a notice in writing;

"occasional transaction" means a transaction (carried out other than as part of a business relationship) amounting to 15,000 euro or more, whether the transaction is carried out in a single operation or several operations which appear to be linked;

. . .

"ongoing monitoring" has the meaning given by regulation 8(2);

["payment services" has the meaning given by regulation 2(1) of the Payment Services Regulations 2009;]

["person who has a qualifying relationship with a PRA-authorised person" is to be read with section 415B(4) of the 2000 Act;

"the PRA" means the Prudential Regulation Authority;

"PRA-authorised person" has the meaning given in section 2B(5) of the 2000 Act;]

"regulated market"—

    (a)   within the EEA, has the meaning given by point 14 of Article 4(1) of the markets in financial instruments directive; and

    (b)   outside the EEA, means a regulated financial market which subjects companies whose securities are admitted to trading to disclosure obligations which are contained in international standards and are equivalent to the specified disclosure obligations;

"relevant person" means a person to whom, in accordance with regulations 3 and 4, these Regulations apply;

["the Solvency 2 Directive" means Directive 2009/138/EC of the European Parliament and of the Council of 25 November 2009 on the taking-up and pursuit of the business of Insurance and Reinsurance (Solvency II);]

"the specified disclosure obligations" means disclosure requirements consistent with—

   (a)   Article 6(1) to (4) of Directive 2003/6/EC of the European Parliament and of the Council of 28th January 2003 on insider dealing and market manipulation;

   (b)   Articles 3, 5, 7, 8, 10, 14 and 16 of Directive 2003/71/EC of the European Parliament and of the Council of 4th November 2003 on the prospectuses to be published when securities are offered to the public or admitted to trading;

   (c)   Articles 4 to 6, 14, 16 to 19 and 30 of Directive 2004/109/EC of the European Parliament and of the Council of 15th December 2004 relating to the harmonisation of transparency requirements in relation to information about issuers whose securities are admitted to trading on a regulated market; or

   (d)   Community legislation made under the provisions mentioned in sub-paragraphs (a) to (c);

"supervisory authority" in relation to any relevant person means the supervisory authority specified for such a person by regulation 23;

"tax adviser" (except in regulation 11(3)) has the meaning given by regulation 3(8);

["telecommunication, digital and IT payment service provider" means an undertaking which provides payment services falling within paragraph 1(g) of Schedule 1 to the Payment Services Regulations 2009;]

"terrorist financing" means an offence under—

   (a)   section 15 (fund-raising), 16 (use and possession), 17 (funding arrangements), 18 (money laundering) or 63 (terrorist finance: jurisdiction) of the Terrorism Act 2000;

   (b)   paragraph 7(2) or (3) of Schedule 3 to the Anti-Terrorism, Crime and Security Act 2001 (freezing orders);

   (c)   . . .

   [(d)   regulation 10 of the Al-Qaida (Asset-Freezing) Regulations 2011; or]

   [(e)   section 11, 12, 13, 14, 15 or 18 of the Terrorist Asset-Freezing etc Act 2010 (offences relating to the freezing of funds etc of designated persons);]

"trust or company service provider" has the meaning given by regulation 3(10).

(2) In these Regulations, references to amounts in euro include references to equivalent amounts in another currency.

(3) Unless otherwise defined, expressions used in these Regulations and the money laundering directive have the same meaning as in the money laundering directive and expressions used in these Regulations and in the implementing measures directive have the same meaning as in the implementing measures directive.

NOTES

Para (1) is amended as follows:

Definitions "auction platform" and "the emission allowance auctioning regulation" inserted by the Recognised Auction Platforms Regulations 2011, SI 2011/2699, reg 11(1), (2).

Words in square brackets in definition "the Authority" substituted, and definitions "person who has a qualifying relationship with a PRA-authorised person", "the PRA", and "PRA-authorised person" inserted, by the Financial Services Act 2012 (Consequential Amendments and Transitional Provisions) Order 2013, SI 2013/472, art 3, Sch 2, para 129(a).

Definition "the banking consolidation directive (omitted) revoked, and definitions "the capital requirements directive" and "the capital requirements regulation" inserted, by the Capital Requirements Regulations 2013, SI 2013/3115, reg 46(1), Sch 2, Pt 3, para 68(1), (2).

Definitions "bill payment service provider", "payment services", and "telecommunication, digital and IT payment service provider" inserted by the Payment Services Regulations 2009, SI 2009/209, reg 126, Sch 6, Pt 2, para 6(a).

Definitions "consumer credit financial institution" and "the OFT" (omitted) revoked by the Financial Services and Markets Act 2000 (Regulated Activities) (Amendment) (No 2) Order 2013, SI 2013/1881, art 28, Schedule, Pt 1, para 31(1), (2), for transitional provisions see arts 29–66 of that Order at **[2.1007]** et seq.

Definitions "the electronic money directive" and "electronic money institution" substituted (for the original definition "the electronic money directive") by the Electronic Money Regulations 2011, SI 2011/99, reg 79, Sch 4, Pt 2, para 19(a).

Definition "the life assurance consolidation directive" revoked, and definition "the Solvency 2 Directive" inserted, by the Solvency 2 Regulations 2015, SI 2015/575, reg 60, Sch 2, para 25(1), (2)(a), (b), as from 1 January 2016.

In the definition "terrorist financing" para (c) revoked, and para (e) substituted, by the Terrorist Asset-Freezing etc Act 2010, s 45, Sch 1, Pt 1, para 6, Sch 2, Pt 1; para (d) substituted by the Al-Qaida (Asset-Freezing) Regulations 2011, SI 2011/2742, reg 21, Sch 2, para 2; para (e) was originally added by the Terrorism (United Nations Measures) Order (Consequential Amendments) Regulations 2009, SI 2009/1912, art 2.

References to the European Community and related expressions: see the note "References to "the European Community", "Community", etc" in the introductory notes to these Regulations.

[2.466]

3 Application of the Regulations

(1) Subject to regulation 4, these Regulations apply to the following persons acting in the course of business carried on by them in the United Kingdom ("relevant persons")—

   (a)   credit institutions;

(b) financial institutions;

(c) auditors, insolvency practitioners, external accountants and tax advisers;

(d) independent legal professionals;

(e) trust or company service providers;

(f) estate agents;

(g) high value dealers;

(h) casinos.

[(1A) Regulations 2, 20, 21, 23, 24, 35 to 42, and 44 to 48 apply to an auction platform acting in the course of business carried on by it in the United Kingdom, and such an auction platform is a relevant person for the purposes of those provisions.]]

(2) "Credit institution" means—

(a) a credit institution as defined in [Article 4(1)(1) of the capital requirements regulation]; or

(b) a branch (within the meaning of [Article 4(1)(17) of that regulation]) located in an EEA state of an institution falling within sub-paragraph (a) (or an equivalent institution whose head office is located in a non-EEA state) wherever its head office is located,

when it accepts deposits or other repayable funds from the public or grants credits for its own account (within the meaning of the banking consolidation directive)[, or when it bids directly in auctions in accordance with the emission allowance auctioning regulation on behalf of its clients].

(3) "Financial institution" means—

(a) an undertaking, including a money service business, when it carries out one or more of the activities listed in points 2 to 12[, 14 and 15] of Annex 1 to the [capital requirements directive] (the relevant text of which is set out in Schedule 1 to these Regulations), other than—

  (i) a credit institution;

  [(ii) an undertaking whose only listed activity is as a creditor under an agreement which—

    (aa) falls within section 12(a) of the Consumer Credit Act 1974 (debtor-creditor-supplier agreements),

    (bb) provides fixed sum credit (within the meaning given in section 10 of the Consumer Credit Act 1974 (running-account credit and fixed-sum credit)) in relation to the provision of services, and

    (cc) provides financial accommodation by way of deferred payment or payment by instalments over a period not exceeding 12 months;]

  [(iii)] an undertaking whose only listed activity is trading for own account in one or more of the products listed in point 7 of Annex 1 to the [capital requirements directive] where the undertaking does not have a customer,

  and, for this purpose, "customer" means a third party which is not a member of the same group as the undertaking;

(b) an insurance company duly authorised in accordance with *the life assurance consolidation directive*, when it carries out *activities covered by that directive*;

[(c) a person, other than a person falling within Article 2 of the markets in financial instruments directive, whose regular occupation or business is the provision to other persons of an investment activity on a professional basis, when providing or performing investment services or activities (within the meaning of that directive) or when bidding directly in auctions in accordance with the emission allowance auctioning regulation on behalf of clients;]

[(ca) a person falling within Article 2(1)(i) of the markets in financial instruments directive, when bidding directly in auctions in accordance with the emission allowance auctioning regulation on behalf of clients of the person's main business;]

(d) a collective investment undertaking, when marketing or otherwise offering its units or shares;

(e) an insurance intermediary as defined in Article 2(5) of Directive 2002/92/EC of the European Parliament and of the Council of 9th December 2002 on insurance mediation, with the exception of a tied insurance intermediary as mentioned in Article 2(7) of that Directive, when it acts in respect of contracts of long-term insurance within the meaning given by article 3(1) of, and Part II of Schedule 1 to, the Financial Services and Markets Act 2000 (Regulated Activities) Order 2001;

(f) a branch located in an EEA state of a person referred to in sub-paragraphs (a) to (e) (or an equivalent person whose head office is located in a non-EEA state), wherever its head office is located, when carrying out any activity mentioned in sub-paragraphs (a) to (e);

(g) the National Savings Bank;

(h) the Director of Savings, when money is raised under the auspices of the Director under the National Loans Act 1968.

(4) "Auditor" means any firm or individual who is a statutory auditor within the meaning of Part 42 of the Companies Act 2006 (statutory auditors), when carrying out statutory audit work within the meaning of section 1210 of that Act.

(5) Before the entry into force of Part 42 of the Companies Act 2006 the reference in paragraph (4) to—

    (a)   a person who is a statutory auditor shall be treated as a reference to a person who is eligible for appointment as a company auditor under section 25 of the Companies Act 1989 (eligibility for appointment) or article 28 of the Companies (Northern Ireland) Order 1990; and

    (b)   the carrying out of statutory audit work shall be treated as a reference to the provision of audit services.

(6) "Insolvency practitioner" means any person who acts as an insolvency practitioner within the meaning of section 388 of the Insolvency Act 1986 (meaning of "act as insolvency practitioner") or article 3 of the Insolvency (Northern Ireland) Order 1989.

(7) "External accountant" means a firm or sole practitioner who by way of business provides accountancy services to other persons, when providing such services.

(8) "Tax adviser" means a firm or sole practitioner who by way of business provides advice about the tax affairs of other persons, when providing such services.

(9) "Independent legal professional" means a firm or sole practitioner who by way of business provides legal or notarial services to other persons, when participating in financial or real property transactions concerning—

    (a)   the buying and selling of real property or business entities;

    (b)   the managing of client money, securities or other assets;

    (c)   the opening or management of bank, savings or securities accounts;

    (d)   the organisation of contributions necessary for the creation, operation or management of companies; or

    (e)   the creation, operation or management of trusts, companies or similar structures,

and, for this purpose, a person participates in a transaction by assisting in the planning or execution of the transaction or otherwise acting for or on behalf of a client in the transaction.

(10) "Trust or company service provider" means a firm or sole practitioner who by way of business provides any of the following services to other persons—

    (a)   forming companies or other legal persons;

    (b)   acting, or arranging for another person to act—

        (i)   as a director or secretary of a company;

        (ii)   as a partner of a partnership; or

        (iii)   in a similar position in relation to other legal persons;

    (c)   providing a registered office, business address, correspondence or administrative address or other related services for a company, partnership or any other legal person or arrangement;

    (d)   acting, or arranging for another person to act, as—

        (i)   a trustee of an express trust or similar legal arrangement; or

        (ii)   a nominee shareholder for a person other than a company whose securities are listed on a regulated market,

        when providing such services.

(11) "Estate agent" means—

    (a)   a firm; or

    (b)   sole practitioner,

who, or whose employees, carry out estate agency work . . . , when in the course of carrying out such work.

[(11A) For the purposes of paragraph (11) "estate agency work" is to be read in accordance with section 1 of the Estate Agents Act 1979 (estate agency work), but for those purposes references in that section to disposing of or acquiring an interest in land are (despite anything in section 2 of that Act) to be taken to include references to disposing of or acquiring an estate or interest in land outside the United Kingdom where that estate or interest is capable of being owned or held as a separate interest.]

(12) "High value dealer" means a firm or sole trader who by way of business trades in goods (including an auctioneer dealing in goods), when he receives, in respect of any transaction, a payment or payments in cash of at least 15,000 euros in total, whether the transaction is executed in a single operation or in several operations which appear to be linked.

(13) "Casino" means the holder of a casino operating licence and, for this purpose, a "casino operating licence" has the meaning given by section 65(2) of the Gambling Act 2005 (nature of licence).

[(13A) "Auction platform" means a platform which auctions two-day spot or five-day futures, within the meanings given by Article 3(4) and (5) of the emission allowance auctioning regulation, when it carries out activities covered by that regulation.].

(14) In the application of this regulation to Scotland, for "real property" in paragraph (9) substitute "heritable property".

NOTES

Paras (1A), (13A): inserted by the Recognised Auction Platforms Regulations 2011, SI 2011/2699, reg 11(1), (3).

Paras (2), (3) are amended as follows:

Part 2 Statutory Instruments

The words in square brackets in sub-para (2)(a), (b) were substituted, and the words "capital requirements directive" in each place that they occur in para (3) were substituted, by the Capital Requirements Regulations 2013, SI 2013/3115, reg 46(1), Sch 2, Pt 3, para 68(1), (3).

The words ", 14 and 15" in square brackets in sub-para (3)(a) were substituted by the Electronic Money Regulations 2011, SI 2011/99, reg 79, Sch 4, Pt 2, para 19(b).

Sub-para (3)(a)(ii) was inserted, and the original sub-para (3)(a)(ii) was renumbered as sub-para (3)(a)(iii), by the Money Laundering (Amendment) Regulations 2012, SI 2012/2298, regs, 2, 3(a).

For the first words in italics in sub-para (3)(b) there are substituted the words "the Solvency 2 Directive", and for the second words in italics there are substituted the words "any activities or operations referred to in Article 2(3) of that Directive", by the Solvency 2 Regulations 2015, SI 2015/575, reg 60, Sch 2, para 25(1), (2)(c), as from 1 January 2016.

Other words in square brackets substituted or inserted by the Financial Services and Markets Act 2000 (Regulated Activities) (Amendment) Order 2012, SI 2012/1906, art 7.

Para (11): words omitted revoked by SI 2012/2298, regs, 2, 3(b).

Para (11A): inserted by SI 2012/2298, regs, 2, 3(c).

[2.467]
4 Exclusions

(1) These Regulations do not apply to the following persons when carrying out any of the following activities—

(a) a society registered under the Industrial and Provident Societies Act 1965, when it—
   (i) issues withdrawable share capital within the limit set by section 6 of that Act (maximum shareholding in society); or
   (ii) accepts deposits from the public within the limit set by section 7(3) of that Act (carrying on of banking by societies);

(b) a society registered under the Industrial and Provident Societies Act (Northern Ireland) 1969, when it—
   (i) issues withdrawable share capital within the limit set by section 6 of that Act (maximum shareholding in society); or
   (ii) accepts deposits from the public within the limit set by section 7(3) of that Act (carrying on of banking by societies);

(c) a person who is (or falls within a class of persons) specified in any of paragraphs 2 to 23, 25 to 38 or 40 to 49 of the Schedule to the Financial Services and Markets Act 2000 (Exemption) Order 2001, when carrying out any activity in respect of which he is exempt;

[(ca) a local authority within the meaning given in article 3 of the Financial Services and Markets Act 2000 (Regulated Activities) Order 2001, when carrying on an activity which would be a regulated activity for the purposes of the Financial Services and Markets Act 2000 but for article 72G of that Order;]

(d) a person who was an exempted person for the purposes of section 45 of the Financial Services Act 1986 (miscellaneous exemptions) immediately before its repeal, when exercising the functions specified in that section;

(e) a person whose main activity is that of a high value dealer, when he engages in financial activity on an occasional or very limited basis as set out in paragraph 1 of Schedule 2 to these Regulations; or

[(f) a person, when he prepares a home report].

(2) These Regulations do not apply to a person who falls within regulation 3 solely as a result of his engaging in financial activity on an occasional or very limited basis as set out in paragraph 1 of Schedule 2 to these Regulations.

(3) Parts 2 to 5 of these Regulations do not apply to—
(a) the Auditor General for Scotland;
(b) the Auditor General for Wales;
(c) the Bank of England;
(d) the Comptroller and Auditor General;
(e) the Comptroller and Auditor General for Northern Ireland;
(f) the Official Solicitor to the Supreme Court, when acting as trustee in his official capacity;
(g) the Treasury Solicitor.

[(4) In paragraph (1)(f), "home report" means the documents prescribed for the purposes of section 98, 99(1) or 101(2) of the Housing (Scotland) Act 2006.]

NOTES

Sub-para (1)(f) and para (4) were substituted by the Money Laundering (Amendment) Regulations 2012, SI 2012/2298, regs, 2, 4.

Sub-para (1)(ca) was inserted by the Financial Services and Markets Act 2000 (Consumer Credit) (Miscellaneous Provisions) (No 2) Order 2014, SI 2014/506, art 4.

Industrial and Provident Societies Act 1965: repealed by the Co-operative and Community Benefit Societies Act 2014.

PART 2
CUSTOMER DUE DILIGENCE

[2.468]
5   Meaning of customer due diligence measures

"Customer due diligence measures" means—
- (a)   identifying the customer and verifying the customer's identity on the basis of documents, data or information obtained from a reliable and independent source;
- (b)   identifying, where there is a beneficial owner who is not the customer, the beneficial owner and taking adequate measures, on a risk-sensitive basis, to verify his identity so that the relevant person is satisfied that he knows who the beneficial owner is, including, in the case of a legal person, trust or similar legal arrangement, measures to understand the ownership and control structure of the person, trust or arrangement; and
- (c)   obtaining information on the purpose and intended nature of the business relationship.

[2.469]
6   Meaning of beneficial owner

(1)   In the case of a body corporate, "beneficial owner" means any individual who—
- (a)   as respects any body other than a company whose securities are listed on a regulated market, ultimately owns or controls (whether through direct or indirect ownership or control, including through bearer share holdings) more than 25% of the shares or voting rights in the body; or
- (b)   as respects any body corporate, otherwise exercises control over the management of the body.

(2)   In the case of a partnership (other than a limited liability partnership), "beneficial owner" means any individual who—
- (a)   ultimately is entitled to or controls (whether the entitlement or control is direct or indirect) more than a 25% share of the capital or profits of the partnership or more than 25% of the voting rights in the partnership; or
- (b)   otherwise exercises control over the management of the partnership.

(3)   In the case of a trust, "beneficial owner" means—
- (a)   any individual who is entitled to a specified interest in at least 25% of the capital of the trust property;
- (b)   as respects any trust other than one which is set up or operates entirely for the benefit of individuals falling within sub-paragraph (a), the class of persons in whose main interest the trust is set up or operates;
- (c)   any individual who has control over the trust.

(4)   In paragraph (3)—
"specified interest" means a vested interest which is—
-     (a)   in possession or in remainder or reversion (or, in Scotland, in fee); and
-     (b)   defeasible or indefeasible;

"control" means a power (whether exercisable alone, jointly with another person or with the consent of another person) under the trust instrument or by law to—
-     (a)   dispose of, advance, lend, invest, pay or apply trust property;
-     (b)   vary the trust;
-     (c)   add or remove a person as a beneficiary or to or from a class of beneficiaries;
-     (d)   appoint or remove trustees;
-     (e)   direct, withhold consent to or veto the exercise of a power such as is mentioned in sub-paragraph (a), (b), (c) or (d).

(5)   For the purposes of paragraph (3)—
- (a)   where an individual is the beneficial owner of a body corporate which is entitled to a specified interest in the capital of the trust property or which has control over the trust, the individual is to be regarded as entitled to the interest or having control over the trust; and
- (b)   an individual does not have control solely as a result of—
  - (i)   his consent being required in accordance with section 32(1)(c) of the Trustee Act 1925 (power of advancement);
  - (ii)   any discretion delegated to him under section 34 of the Pensions Act 1995 (power of investment and delegation);
  - (iii)   the power to give a direction conferred on him by section 19(2) of the Trusts of Land and Appointment of Trustees Act 1996 (appointment and retirement of trustee at instance of beneficiaries); or
  - (iv)   the power exercisable collectively at common law to vary or extinguish a trust where the beneficiaries under the trust are of full age and capacity and (taken together) absolutely entitled to the property subject to the trust (or, in Scotland, have a full and unqualified right to the fee).

(6)   In the case of a legal entity or legal arrangement which does not fall within paragraph (1), (2) or (3), "beneficial owner" means—

(a) where the individuals who benefit from the entity or arrangement have been determined, any individual who benefits from at least 25% of the property of the entity or arrangement;

(b) where the individuals who benefit from the entity or arrangement have yet to be determined, the class of persons in whose main interest the entity or arrangement is set up or operates;

(c) any individual who exercises control over at least 25% of the property of the entity or arrangement.

(7) For the purposes of paragraph (6), where an individual is the beneficial owner of a body corporate which benefits from or exercises control over the property of the entity or arrangement, the individual is to be regarded as benefiting from or exercising control over the property of the entity or arrangement.

(8) In the case of an estate of a deceased person in the course of administration, "beneficial owner" means—

(a) in England and Wales and Northern Ireland, the executor, original or by representation, or administrator for the time being of a deceased person;

(b) in Scotland, the executor for the purposes of the Executors (Scotland) Act 1900.

(9) In any other case, "beneficial owner" means the individual who ultimately owns or controls the customer or on whose behalf a transaction is being conducted.

(10) In this regulation—

"arrangement", "entity" and "trust" means an arrangement, entity or trust which administers and distributes funds;

"limited liability partnership" has the meaning given by the Limited Liability Partnerships Act 2000.

[2.470]
7 Application of customer due diligence measures

(1) Subject to regulations 9, 10, 12, 13, 14, 16(4) and 17, a relevant person must apply customer due diligence measures when he—

(a) establishes a business relationship;

(b) carries out an occasional transaction;

(c) suspects money laundering or terrorist financing;

(d) doubts the veracity or adequacy of documents, data or information previously obtained for the purposes of identification or verification.

(2) Subject to regulation 16(4), a relevant person must also apply customer due diligence measures at other appropriate times to existing customers on a risk-sensitive basis.

(3) A relevant person must—

(a) determine the extent of customer due diligence measures on a risk-sensitive basis depending on the type of customer, business relationship, product or transaction; and

(b) be able to demonstrate to his supervisory authority that the extent of the measures is appropriate in view of the risks of money laundering and terrorist financing.

(4) Where—

(a) a relevant person is required to apply customer due diligence measures in the case of a trust, legal entity (other than a body corporate) or a legal arrangement (other than a trust); and

(b) the class of persons in whose main interest the trust, entity or arrangement is set up or operates is identified as a beneficial owner,

the relevant person is not required to identify all the members of the class.

(5) Paragraph (3)(b) does not apply to the National Savings Bank or the Director of Savings.

[2.471]
8 Ongoing monitoring

(1) A relevant person must conduct ongoing monitoring of a business relationship.

(2) "Ongoing monitoring" of a business relationship means—

(a) scrutiny of transactions undertaken throughout the course of the relationship (including, where necessary, the source of funds) to ensure that the transactions are consistent with the relevant person's knowledge of the customer, his business and risk profile; and

(b) keeping the documents, data or information obtained for the purpose of applying customer due diligence measures up-to-date.

(3) Regulation 7(3) applies to the duty to conduct ongoing monitoring under paragraph (1) as it applies to customer due diligence measures.

[2.472]
9 Timing of verification

(1) This regulation applies in respect of the duty under regulation 7(1)(a) and (b) to apply the customer due diligence measures referred to in regulation 5(a) and (b).

(2)   Subject to paragraphs (3) to (5) and regulation 10, a relevant person must verify the identity of the customer (and any beneficial owner) before the establishment of a business relationship or the carrying out of an occasional transaction.

(3)   Such verification may be completed during the establishment of a business relationship if—
   (a)   this is necessary not to interrupt the normal conduct of business; and
   (b)   there is little risk of money laundering or terrorist financing occurring,
provided that the verification is completed as soon as practicable after contact is first established.

(4)   The verification of the identity of the beneficiary under a life insurance policy may take place after the business relationship has been established provided that it takes place at or before the time of payout or at or before the time the beneficiary exercises a right vested under the policy.

(5)   The verification of the identity of a bank account holder may take place after the bank account has been opened provided that there are adequate safeguards in place to ensure that—
   (a)   the account is not closed; and
   (b)   transactions are not carried out by or on behalf of the account holder (including any payment from the account to the account holder),
before verification has been completed.

[2.473]
10   Casinos

(1)   A casino must establish and verify the identity of—
   (a)   all customers to whom the casino makes facilities for gaming available—
      (i)   before entry to any premises where such facilities are provided; or
      (ii)   where the facilities are for remote gaming, before access is given to such facilities; or
   (b)   if the specified conditions are met, all customers who, in the course of any period of 24 hours—
      (i)   purchase from, or exchange with, the casino chips with a total value of 2,000 euro or more;
      (ii)   pay the casino 2,000 [euro] or more for the use of gaming machines; or
      (iii)   pay to, or stake with, the casino 2,000 euro or more in connection with facilities for remote gaming.

(2)   The specified conditions are—
   (a)   the casino verifies the identity of each customer before or immediately after such purchase, exchange, payment or stake takes place, and
   (b)   the Gambling Commission is satisfied that the casino has appropriate procedures in place to monitor and record—
      (i)   the total value of chips purchased from or exchanged with the casino;
      (ii)   the total money paid for the use of gaming machines; or
      (iii)   the total money paid or staked in connection with facilities for remote gaming,
   by each customer.

(3)   In this regulation—
   "gaming", "gaming machine", "remote operating licence" and "stake" have the meanings given by, respectively, sections 6(1) (gaming & game of chance), 235 (gaming machine), 67 (remote gambling) and 353(1) (interpretation) of the Gambling Act 2005;
   "premises" means premises subject to—
      (a)   a casino premises licence within the meaning of section 150(1)(a) of the Gambling Act 2005 (nature of licence); or
      (b)   a converted casino premises licence within the meaning of paragraph 65 of Part 7 of Schedule 4 to the Gambling Act 2005 (Commencement No 6 and Transitional Provisions) Order 2006;
   "remote gaming" means gaming provided pursuant to a remote operating licence.

NOTES

  Para (1): word in square brackets in sub-para (b)(ii) inserted by the Money Laundering (Amendment) Regulations 2007, SI 2007/3299, reg 2(a).

[2.474]
11   Requirement to cease transactions etc

(1)   Where, in relation to any customer, a relevant person is unable to apply customer due diligence measures in accordance with the provisions of this Part, he—
   (a)   must not carry out a transaction with or for the customer through a bank account;
   (b)   must not establish a business relationship or carry out an occasional transaction with the customer;
   (c)   must terminate any existing business relationship with the customer;
   (d)   must consider whether he is required to make a disclosure by Part 7 of the Proceeds of Crime Act 2002 or Part 3 of the Terrorism Act 2000.

(2) Paragraph (1) does not apply where a lawyer or other professional adviser is in the course of ascertaining the legal position for his client or performing his task of defending or representing that client in, or concerning, legal proceedings, including advice on the institution or avoidance of proceedings.

(3) In paragraph (2), "other professional adviser" means an auditor, accountant or tax adviser who is a member of a professional body which is established for any such persons and which makes provision for—

    (a) testing the competence of those seeking admission to membership of such a body as a condition for such admission; and

    (b) imposing and maintaining professional and ethical standards for its members, as well as imposing sanctions for non-compliance with those standards.

[2.475]
12 Exception for trustees of debt issues

(1) A relevant person—

    (a) who is appointed by the issuer of instruments or securities specified in paragraph (2) as trustee of an issue of such instruments or securities; or

    (b) whose customer is a trustee of an issue of such instruments or securities,

is not required to apply the customer due diligence measure referred to in regulation 5(b) in respect of the holders of such instruments or securities.

(2) The specified instruments and securities are—

    (a) instruments which fall within article 77 [or 77A] of the Financial Services and Markets Act 2000 (Regulated Activities) Order 2001; and

    (b) securities which fall within article 78 of that Order.

NOTES

Para (2): words in square brackets in sub-para (a) inserted by the Financial Services and Markets Act 2000 (Regulated Activities) (Amendment) Order 2010, SI 2010/86, art 4, Schedule, para 10.

[2.476]
13 Simplified due diligence

(1) A relevant person is not required to apply customer due diligence measures in the circumstances mentioned in regulation 7(1)(a), (b) or (d) where he has reasonable grounds for believing that the customer, transaction or product related to such transaction, falls within any of the following paragraphs.

(2) The customer is—

    (a) a credit or financial institution which is subject to the requirements of the money laundering directive; or

    (b) a credit or financial institution (or equivalent institution) which—

        (i) is situated in a non-EEA state which imposes requirements equivalent to those laid down in the money laundering directive; and

        (ii) is supervised for compliance with those requirements.

(3) The customer is a company whose securities are listed on a regulated market subject to specified disclosure obligations.

(4) The customer is an independent legal professional and the product is an account into which monies are pooled, provided that—

    (a) where the pooled account is held in a non-EEA state—

        (i) that state imposes requirements to combat money laundering and terrorist financing which are consistent with international standards; and

        (ii) the independent legal professional is supervised in that state for compliance with those requirements; and

    (b) information on the identity of the persons on whose behalf monies are held in the pooled account is available, on request, to the institution which acts as a depository institution for the account.

(5) The customer is a public authority in the United Kingdom.

(6) The customer is a public authority which fulfils all the conditions set out in paragraph 2 of Schedule 2 to these Regulations.

(7) The product is—

    (a) a life insurance contract where the annual premium is no more than 1,000 euro or where a single premium of no more than 2,500 euro is paid;

    (b) an insurance contract for the purposes of a pension scheme where the contract contains no surrender clause and cannot be used as collateral;

    (c) a pension, superannuation or similar scheme which provides retirement benefits to employees, where contributions are made by an employer or by way of deduction from an employee's wages and the scheme rules do not permit the assignment of a member's interest under the scheme (other than an assignment permitted by section 44 of the Welfare Reform and Pensions Act 1999 (disapplication of restrictions on alienation) or section 91(5)(a) of the Pensions Act 1995 (inalienability of occupational pension)); or

(d)   electronic money, within the meaning of [Article 2(2)] of the electronic money directive, where—

   (i)   if the device cannot be recharged, the maximum amount stored in the device is no more than [250 euro or, in the case of electronic money used to carry out payment transactions within the United Kingdom, 500 euro]; or

   (ii)   if the device can be recharged, a limit of 2,500 euro is imposed on the total amount transacted in a calendar year, except when an amount of 1,000 euro or more is redeemed in the same calendar year [by the electronic money holder (within the meaning of Article 11 of the electronic money directive).]

(8)   The product and any transaction related to such product fulfils all the conditions set out in paragraph 3 of Schedule 2 to these Regulations.

(9)   The product is a child trust fund within the meaning given by section 1(2) of the Child Trust Funds Act 2004.

[(10)   The product is a junior ISA within the meaning given by regulation 2B of the Individual Savings Account Regulations 1998.]

NOTES

Para (7): words in square brackets in sub-para (d) substituted by the Electronic Money Regulations 2011, SI 2011/99, reg 79, Sch 4, Pt 2, para 19(c).

Para (10): added by the Money Laundering (Amendment) Regulations 2011, SI 2011/1781, reg 2.

[2.477]
14   Enhanced customer due diligence and ongoing monitoring

(1)   A relevant person must apply on a risk-sensitive basis enhanced customer due diligence measures and enhanced ongoing monitoring—

(a)   in accordance with paragraphs (2) to (4);

(b)   in any other situation which by its nature can present a higher risk of money laundering or terrorist financing.

(2)   Where the customer has not been physically present for identification purposes, a relevant person must take specific and adequate measures to compensate for the higher risk, for example, by applying one or more of the following measures—

(a)   ensuring that the customer's identity is established by additional documents, data or information;

(b)   supplementary measures to verify or certify the documents supplied, or requiring confirmatory certification by a credit or financial institution which is subject to the money laundering directive;

(c)   ensuring that the first payment is carried out through an account opened in the customer's name with a credit institution.

(3)   A credit institution ("the correspondent") which has or proposes to have a correspondent banking relationship with a respondent institution ("the respondent") from a non-EEA state must—

(a)   gather sufficient information about the respondent to understand fully the nature of its business;

(b)   determine from publicly-available information the reputation of the respondent and the quality of its supervision;

(c)   assess the respondent's anti-money laundering and anti-terrorist financing controls;

(d)   obtain approval from senior management before establishing a new correspondent banking relationship;

(e)   document the respective responsibilities of the respondent and correspondent; and

(f)   be satisfied that, in respect of those of the respondent's customers who have direct access to accounts of the correspondent, the respondent—

   (i)   has verified the identity of, and conducts ongoing monitoring in respect of, such customers; and

   (ii)   is able to provide to the correspondent, upon request, the documents, data or information obtained when applying customer due diligence measures and ongoing monitoring.

(4)   A relevant person who proposes to have a business relationship or carry out an occasional transaction with a politically exposed person must—

(a)   have approval from senior management for establishing the business relationship with that person;

(b)   take adequate measures to establish the source of wealth and source of funds which are involved in the proposed business relationship or occasional transaction; and

(c)   where the business relationship is entered into, conduct enhanced ongoing monitoring of the relationship.

(5)   In paragraph (4), "a politically exposed person" means a person who is—

(a)   an individual who is or has, at any time in the preceding year, been entrusted with a prominent public function by—
   (i)   a state other than the United Kingdom;
   (ii) a Community institution; or
   (iii) an international body,
   including a person who falls in any of the categories listed in paragraph 4(1)(a) of Schedule 2;

(b)   an immediate family member of a person referred to in sub-paragraph (a), including a person who falls in any of the categories listed in paragraph 4(1)(c) of Schedule 2; or

(c)   a known close associate of a person referred to in sub-paragraph (a), including a person who falls in either of the categories listed in paragraph 4(1)(d) of Schedule 2.

(6)   For the purpose of deciding whether a person is a known close associate of a person referred to in paragraph (5)(a), a relevant person need only have regard to information which is in his possession or is publicly known.

NOTES

References to the European Community and related expressions: see the note "References to "the European Community", "Community", etc" in the introductory notes to these Regulations.

[2.478]
15   Branches and subsidiaries

(1)   A credit or financial institution must require its branches and subsidiary undertakings which are located in a non-EEA state to apply, to the extent permitted by the law of that state, measures at least equivalent to those set out in these Regulations with regard to customer due diligence measures, ongoing monitoring and record-keeping.

(2)   Where the law of a non-EEA state does not permit the application of such equivalent measures by the branch or subsidiary undertaking located in that state, the credit or financial institution must—
   (a)   inform its supervisory authority accordingly; and
   (b)   take additional measures to handle effectively the risk of money laundering and terrorist financing.

(3)   In this regulation "subsidiary undertaking"—
   (a)   except in relation to an incorporated friendly society, has the meaning given by section 1162 of the Companies Act 2006 (parent and subsidiary undertakings) and, in relation to a body corporate in or formed under the law of an EEA state other than the United Kingdom, includes an undertaking which is a subsidiary undertaking within the meaning of any rule of law in force in that state for purposes connected with implementation of the European Council Seventh Company Law Directive 83/349/EEC of 13th June 1983 on consolidated accounts;
   (b)   in relation to an incorporated friendly society, means a body corporate of which the society has control within the meaning of section 13(9)(a) or (aa) of the Friendly Societies Act 1992 (control of subsidiaries and other bodies corporate).

(4)   Before the entry into force of section 1162 of the Companies Act 2006 the reference to that section in paragraph (3)(a) shall be treated as a reference to section 258 of the Companies Act 1985 (parent and subsidiary undertakings).

[2.479]
16   Shell banks, anonymous accounts etc

(1)   A credit institution must not enter into, or continue, a correspondent banking relationship with a shell bank.

(2)   A credit institution must take appropriate measures to ensure that it does not enter into, or continue, a corresponding banking relationship with a bank which is known to permit its accounts to be used by a shell bank.

(3)   A credit or financial institution carrying on business in the United Kingdom must not set up an anonymous account or an anonymous passbook for any new or existing customer.

(4)   As soon as reasonably practicable on or after 15th December 2007 all credit and financial institutions carrying on business in the United Kingdom must apply customer due diligence measures to, and conduct ongoing monitoring of, all anonymous accounts and passbooks in existence on that date and in any event before such accounts or passbooks are used.

(5)   A "shell bank" means a credit institution, or an institution engaged in equivalent activities, incorporated in a jurisdiction in which it has no physical presence involving meaningful decision-making and management, and which is not part of a financial conglomerate or third-country financial conglomerate.

(6)   In this regulation, "financial conglomerate" and "third-country financial conglomerate" have the meanings given by regulations 1(2) and 7(1) respectively of the Financial Conglomerates and Other Financial Groups Regulations 2004.

[2.480]
17 Reliance

(1) A relevant person may rely on a person who falls within paragraph (2) (or who the relevant person has reasonable grounds to believe falls within paragraph (2)) to apply any customer due diligence measures provided that—

    (a)   the other person consents to being relied on; and

    (b)   notwithstanding the relevant person's reliance on the other person, the relevant person remains liable for any failure to apply such measures.

(2) The persons are—

    (a)   a credit or financial institution which is an authorised person;

    [(aa) . . .]

    (b)   a relevant person who is—

        (i)   an auditor, insolvency practitioner, external accountant, tax adviser or independent legal professional; and

        (ii)   supervised for the purposes of these Regulations by one of the bodies listed in . . . Schedule 3;

    (c)   a person who carries on business in another EEA state who is—

        (i)   a credit or financial institution, auditor, insolvency practitioner, external accountant, tax adviser or independent legal professional;

        (ii)   subject to mandatory professional registration recognised by law; and

        (iii)   supervised for compliance with the requirements laid down in the money laundering directive in accordance with section 2 of Chapter V of that directive; or

    (d)   a person who carries on business in a non-EEA state who is—

        (i)   a credit or financial institution (or equivalent institution), auditor, insolvency practitioner, external accountant, tax adviser or independent legal professional;

        (ii)   subject to mandatory professional registration recognised by law;

        (iii)   subject to requirements equivalent to those laid down in the money laundering directive; and

        (iv)   supervised for compliance with those requirements in a manner equivalent to section 2 of Chapter V of the money laundering directive.

(3) In paragraph (2)(c)(i) and (d)(i), "auditor" and "insolvency practitioner" includes a person situated in another EEA state or a non-EEA state who provides services equivalent to the services provided by an auditor or insolvency practitioner.

(4) Nothing in this regulation prevents a relevant person applying customer due diligence measures by means of an outsourcing service provider or agent provided that the relevant person remains liable for any failure to apply such measures.

[(5) In this regulation, "financial institution" excludes—

    (a)   any money service business;

    (b)   any authorised payment institution, EEA authorised payment institution or small payment institution (within the meaning of the Payment Services Regulations 2009) which provides payment services mainly falling within paragraph 1(f) of Schedule 1 to those Regulations[; and

    (c)   any electronic money institution or EEA authorised electronic money institution (within the meaning of the Electronic Money Regulations 2011) which provides payment services mainly falling within paragraph 1(f) of Schedule 1 to the Payment Services Regulations 2009].]

NOTES

    Para (2): sub-para (aa) originally inserted, and words omitted from sub-para (b)(ii) revoked, by the Money Laundering (Amendment) Regulations 2012, SI 2012/2298, regs, 2, 5; sub-para (aa) subsequently revoked by the Financial Services and Markets Act 2000 (Regulated Activities) (Amendment) (No 2) Order 2013, SI 2013/1881, art 28, Schedule, Pt 1, para 31(1), (3), for transitional provisions see arts 29–66 of that Order at **[2.1007]** et seq.

    Para (5): substituted by the Payment Services Regulations 2009, SI 2009/209, reg 126, Sch 6, Pt 2, para 6(b); sub-para (c) (and the preceding word) added by the Electronic Money Regulations 2011, SI 2011/99, reg 79, Sch 4, Pt 2, para 19(d).

18 *(Revoked by the Money Laundering (Amendment) Regulations 2012, SI 2012/2298, regs, 2, 6.)*

PART 3
RECORD-KEEPING, PROCEDURES AND TRAINING

[2.481]
19 Record-keeping

(1) Subject to paragraph (4), a relevant person must keep the records specified in paragraph (2) for at least the period specified in paragraph (3).

(2) The records are—

    (a)   a copy of, or the references to, the evidence of the customer's identity obtained pursuant to regulation 7, 8, 10, 14 or 16(4);

(b)   the supporting records (consisting of the original documents or copies) in respect of a business relationship or occasional transaction which is the subject of customer due diligence measures or ongoing monitoring.

(3)   The period is five years beginning on—
   (a)   in the case of the records specified in paragraph (2)(a), the date on which—
       (i)   the occasional transaction is completed; or
       (ii)   the business relationship ends; or
   (b)   in the case of the records specified in paragraph (2)(b)—
       (i)   where the records relate to a particular transaction, the date on which the transaction is completed;
       (ii)   for all other records, the date on which the business relationship ends.

(4)   A relevant person who is relied on by another person must keep the records specified in paragraph (2)(a) for five years beginning on the date on which he is relied on for the purposes of regulation 7, 10, 14 or 16(4) in relation to any business relationship or occasional transaction.

(5)   A person referred to in regulation 17(2)(a) or (b) who is relied on by a relevant person must, if requested by the person relying on him within the period referred to in paragraph (4)—
   (a)   as soon as reasonably practicable make available to the person who is relying on him any information about the customer (and any beneficial owner) which he obtained when applying customer due diligence measures; and
   (b)   as soon as reasonably practicable forward to the person who is relying on him copies of any identification and verification data and other relevant documents on the identity of the customer (and any beneficial owner) which he obtained when applying those measures.

(6)   A relevant person who relies on a person referred to in regulation 17(2)(c) or (d) (a "third party") to apply customer due diligence measures must take steps to ensure that the third party will, if requested by the relevant person within the period referred to in paragraph (4)—
   (a)   as soon as reasonably practicable make available to him any information about the customer (and any beneficial owner) which the third party obtained when applying customer due diligence measures; and
   (b)   as soon as reasonably practicable forward to him copies of any identification and verification data and other relevant documents on the identity of the customer (and any beneficial owner) which the third party obtained when applying those measures.

(7)   Paragraphs (5) and (6) do not apply where a relevant person applies customer due diligence measures by means of an outsourcing service provider or agent.

(8)   For the purposes of this regulation, a person relies on another person where he does so in accordance with regulation 17(1).

[2.482]
20   Policies and procedures
(1)   A relevant person must establish and maintain appropriate and risk-sensitive policies and procedures relating to—
   (a)   customer due diligence measures and ongoing monitoring;
   (b)   reporting;
   (c)   record-keeping;
   (d)   internal control;
   (e)   risk assessment and management;
   (f)   the monitoring and management of compliance with, and the internal communication of, such policies and procedures,
in order to prevent activities related to money laundering and terrorist financing.

(2)   The policies and procedures referred to in paragraph (1) include policies and procedures—
   (a)   which provide for the identification and scrutiny of—
       (i)   complex or unusually large transactions;
       (ii)   unusual patterns of transactions which have no apparent economic or visible lawful purpose; and
       (iii) any other activity which the relevant person regards as particularly likely by its nature to be related to money laundering or terrorist financing;
   (b)   which specify the taking of additional measures, where appropriate, to prevent the use for money laundering or terrorist financing of products and transactions which might favour anonymity;
   (c)   to determine whether a customer is a politically exposed person;
   (d)   under which—
       (i)   an individual in the relevant person's organisation is a nominated officer under Part 7 of the Proceeds of Crime Act 2002 and Part 3 of the Terrorism Act 2000;
       (ii)   anyone in the organisation to whom information or other matter comes in the course of the business as a result of which he knows or suspects or has reasonable grounds for knowing or suspecting that a person is engaged in money laundering or terrorist financing is required to comply with Part 7 of the Proceeds of Crime Act 2002 or, as the case may be, Part 3 of the Terrorism Act 2000; and

    (iii) where a disclosure is made to the nominated officer, he must consider it in the light of any relevant information which is available to the relevant person and determine whether it gives rise to knowledge or suspicion or reasonable grounds for knowledge or suspicion that a person is engaged in money laundering or terrorist financing.

(3) Paragraph (2)(d) does not apply where the relevant person is an individual who neither employs nor acts in association with any other person.

(4) A credit or financial institution [and an auction platform] must establish and maintain systems which enable it to respond fully and rapidly to enquiries from financial investigators accredited under section 3 of the Proceeds of Crime Act 2002 (accreditation and training), persons acting on behalf of the Scottish Ministers in their capacity as an enforcement authority under that Act, officers of Revenue and Customs or constables as to—

    (a) whether it maintains, or has maintained during the previous five years, a business relationship with any person; and

    (b) the nature of that relationship.

(5) A credit or financial institution [and an auction platform] must communicate where relevant the policies and procedures which it establishes and maintains in accordance with this regulation to its branches and subsidiary undertakings which are located outside the United Kingdom.

[(5A) A relevant person who is an issuer of electronic money must appoint an individual to monitor and manage compliance with, and the internal communication of, the policies and procedures relating to the matters referred to in paragraph (1)(a) to (e), and in particular to—

    (a) identify any situations of higher risk of money laundering or terrorist financing;

    (b) maintain a record of its policies and procedures, risk assessment and risk management including the application of such policies and procedures;

    (c) apply measures to ensure that such policies and procedures are taken into account in all relevant functions including in the development of new products, dealing with new customers and in changes to business activities; and

    (d) provide information to senior management about the operation and effectiveness of such policies and procedures at least annually.]

(6) In this regulation—

    "politically exposed person" has the same meaning as in regulation 14(4);

    "subsidiary undertaking" has the same meaning as in regulation 15.

NOTES

Paras (4), (5): words in square brackets inserted by the Recognised Auction Platforms Regulations 2011, SI 2011/2699, reg 11(1), (4).

Para (5A): inserted by the Electronic Money Regulations 2011, SI 2011/99, reg 79, Sch 4, Pt 2, para 19(e).

[2.483]
21 Training

A relevant person must take appropriate measures so that all relevant employees of his are—

    (a) made aware of the law relating to money laundering and terrorist financing; and

    (b) regularly given training in how to recognise and deal with transactions and other activities which may be related to money laundering or terrorist financing.

PART 4
SUPERVISION AND REGISTRATION

Interpretation

[2.484]
22 Interpretation

(1) In this Part—

    "Annex I financial institution" means any undertaking which falls within regulation 3(3)(a) other than—

        (a) . . .

        (b) a money service business; . . .

        (c) an authorised person;

        [(d) a bill payment service provider; or

        (e) a telecommunication, digital and IT payment service provider;]

  . . .

    ["recognised investment exchange" has the same meaning as in section 285 of the 2000 Act (exemption for recognised investment exchanges and clearing houses).]

(2) . . .

NOTES

Para (1) is amended as follows:

Para (a) of the definition "Annex I financial institution" revoked by the Financial Services and Markets Act 2000 (Regulated Activities) (Amendment) (No 2) Order 2013, SI 2013/1881, art 28, Schedule, Pt 1, para 26(1), (4)(a)(i), for transitional provisions see arts 29–66 of that Order at **[2.1007]** et seq; the word omitted from the end of sub-para (b) of that definition was revoked, and sub-para (d), (e) were added, by the Payment Services Regulations 2009, SI 2009/209, reg 126, Sch 6, Pt 2, para 6(c).

Definition "consumer credit financial institution" (omitted) revoked by SI 2013/1881, art 28, Schedule, Pt 1, para 26(1), (4)(a)(ii), for transitional provisions, see the note relating to this Order above.

Definition "recognised investment exchange" added by the Money Laundering (Amendment) Regulations 2012, SI 2012/2298, regs, 2, 7.

Para (2): revoked by SI 2013/1881, art 28, Schedule, Pt 1, para 26(1), (4)(b), for transitional provisions, see the note relating to this Order above.

Supervision

[2.485]
23 Supervisory authorities

(1)   Subject to paragraph (2), the following bodies are supervisory authorities—
   (a)   the Authority is the supervisory authority for—
      (i)   credit and financial institutions which are authorised persons [but not excluded money service businesses];
      (ii)   trust or company service providers which are authorised persons;
      (iii)   Annex I financial institutions;
      [(iv)   electronic money institutions;]
      [(v)   auction platforms;]
      [(vi)   credit unions in Northern Ireland;]
      [(vii) recognised investment exchanges;]
   (b)   . . .
   (c)   each of the professional bodies listed in Schedule 3 is the supervisory authority for relevant persons who are regulated by it;
   (d)   the Commissioners are the supervisory authority for—
      (i)   high value dealers;
      (ii)   money service businesses which are not supervised by the Authority;
      (iii)   trust or company service providers which are not supervised by the Authority or one of the bodies listed in Schedule 3;
      (iv)   auditors, external accountants and tax advisers who are not supervised by one of the bodies listed in Schedule 3;
      [(v)   bill payment service providers which are not supervised by the Authority;
      (vi)   telecommunication, digital and IT payment service providers which are not supervised by the Authority];
      [(vii) estate agents].
   (e)   the Gambling Commission is the supervisory authority for casinos;
   (f)   DETI is the supervisory authority for—
      (i)   . . .
      (ii)   insolvency practitioners authorised by it under article 351 of the Insolvency (Northern Ireland) Order 1989;
   (g)   *the Secretary of State is the supervisory authority for insolvency practitioners authorised by him under section 393 of the Insolvency Act 1986 (grant, refusal and withdrawal of authorisation).*

(2)   Where under paragraph (1) there is more than one supervisory authority for a relevant person, the supervisory authorities may agree that one of them will act as the supervisory authority for that person.

(3)   Where an agreement has been made under paragraph (2), the authority which has agreed to act as the supervisory authority must notify the relevant person or publish the agreement in such manner as it considers appropriate.

(4)   Where no agreement has been made under paragraph (2), the supervisory authorities for a relevant person must cooperate in the performance of their functions under these Regulations.

[(5)   For the purposes of this regulation, a money service business is an "excluded money service business" if it is an authorised person who has permission under the 2000 Act which relates to or is connected with a contract of the kind mentioned in paragraph 23 or paragraph 23B of Schedule 2 to that Act (credit agreements and contracts for hire of goods) but does not have permission to carry on any other kind of regulated activity.

(6)   Paragraph (5) must be read with—
   (a)   section 22 of the 2000 Act,
   (b)   any relevant order under that section, and
   (c)   Schedule 2 to that Act.]

NOTES

Para (1) is amended as follows:

Words in square brackets in sub-para (a)(i) inserted, and sub-para (b) revoked, by the Financial Services and Markets Act 2000 (Regulated Activities) (Amendment) (No 2) Order 2013, SI 2013/1881, art 28, Schedule, Pt 1, para 35(1), (5)(a), for transitional provisions see arts 29–66 of that Order at **[2.1007]** et seq.

Sub-para (a)(iv) inserted by the Electronic Money Regulations 2011, SI 2011/99, reg 79, Sch 4, Pt 2, para 19(f).

Sub-para (a)(v) inserted by the Recognised Auction Platforms Regulations 2011, SI 2011/2699, reg 11(1), (5).

Sub-para (a)(vi) inserted, and sub-para (f)(i) revoked, by the Money Laundering (Amendment No 2) Regulations 2011, SI 2011/2833, reg 2(a).

Sub-para (a)(vii) added by the Money Laundering (Amendment) Regulations 2012, SI 2012/2298, regs, 2, 8.

Sub-para (d)(vii) added by the Public Bodies (Abolition of the National Consumer Council and Transfer of the Office of Fair Trading's Functions in relation to Estate Agents etc) Order 2014, SI 2014/631, art 5(3), Sch 3, Pt 1, para 2(1), (2) (see further the note "Transfer of functions and transitional provisions" in the introductory notes to these Regulations).

Sub-paras (d)(v), (vi) inserted by the Payment Services Regulations 2009, SI 2009/209, reg 126, Sch 6, Pt 2, para 6(d).

Sub-para (g) revoked by the Deregulation Act 2015 (Insolvency) (Consequential Amendments and Transitional and Savings Provisions) Order 2015, SI 2015/1641, art 4, Sch 1, para 6, subject to transitional provisions as noted below.

Transitional provisions: SI 2015/1641, arts 8, 9 provide as follows:

"**8.** (1)   Subject to paragraph (2), the amendments made by article 4 of, and Schedule 1 to, this Order have no effect for the duration of the transitional period in relation to an individual who before the 1st October 2015—

(a)   has applied for authorisation to act as an insolvency practitioner under section 392 of the 1986 Act and that application has not been granted, refused or withdrawn; or

(b)   holds an authorisation so to act granted under section 393 of the 1986 Act.

(2)   The reference in paragraph (1) to Schedule 1 to this Order does not include paragraphs 3(2), 4(3), 5(3) and 5(5) of that Schedule.

9. (1)   Where during the transitional period section 393(3A) of the Insolvency 1986 Act applies to an authorisation to act as an insolvency practitioner by virtue of paragraph 23(2) of Schedule 6 to the Act, and the insolvency practitioner has not requested or consented to a withdrawal of the authorisation, the revocation of regulation 11 of the Insolvency Practitioners Regulations 2005 by article 4 of, and paragraphs 5(1) and (5) of Schedule 1 to, this Order shall have no effect.

(2)   During the transitional period the Secretary of State may request that the holder of an authorisation granted by the Secretary of State to act as an insolvency practitioner provide any information relating to any matters of the kind referred to in paragraph (1) of regulation 11 of the Insolvency Practitioners Regulations 2005 and any such request must be complied with within one month of its receipt or within such longer period as the Secretary of State may allow.".

Paras (5), (6): added by SI 2013/1881, art 28, Schedule, Pt 1, para 35(1), (5)(b), for transitional provisions, see the note relating to this Order above.

[2.486]
24 Duties of supervisory authorities

(1)   A supervisory authority must effectively monitor the relevant persons for whom it is the supervisory authority and take necessary measures for the purpose of securing compliance by such persons with the requirements of these Regulations.

[(1A)   The Authority, when carrying out its supervisory functions in relation to an auction platform—

(a)   must effectively monitor the auction platform's compliance with—

(i)   the customer due diligence requirements of Articles 19 and 20(6) of the emission allowance auctioning regulation;

(ii)   the monitoring and record keeping requirements of Article 54 of the emission allowance auctioning regulation; and

(iii)   the notification requirements of Article 55(2) and (3) of the emission allowance auctioning regulation; and

(b)   may monitor the auction platform's compliance with regulations 20 and 21 of these Regulations.]

(2)   A supervisory authority which, in the course of carrying out any of its functions under these Regulations, knows or suspects that a person is or has engaged in money laundering or terrorist financing must promptly inform the [National Crime Agency].

(3)   A disclosure made under paragraph (2) is not to be taken to breach any restriction, however imposed, on the disclosure of information.

(4)   The functions of the Authority under these Regulations shall be treated for the purposes of Parts 1, 2 and 4 of [Schedule 1ZA] to the 2000 Act [(the Financial Conduct Authority)] as functions conferred on the Authority under that Act.

[(5)   The functions of the PRA under these Regulations shall be treated for the purposes of Parts 1, 2 and 4 of Schedule 1ZB to the 2000 Act (the Prudential Regulation Authority) as functions conferred on the PRA under that Act.]

NOTES

Para (1A): inserted by the Recognised Auction Platforms Regulations 2011, SI 2011/2699, reg 11(1), (6).

Sub-s (2): words in square brackets substituted by virtue of the Crime and Courts Act 2013, s 15(3), Sch 8, Pt 4, para 190 (for transitional provisions in connection with the creation of the NCA and the abolition of SOCA, see Sch 8, Part 1 to the 2013 Act).

Para (4): words in square brackets substituted by the Financial Services Act 2012 (Consequential Amendments and Transitional Provisions) Order 2013, SI 2013/472, art 3, Sch 2, para 129(b)(i).

Para (5): added by SI 2013/472, art 3, Sch 2, para 129(b)(ii).

[2.487]
[24A Disclosure by supervisory authorities

(1)   A supervisory authority may disclose to another supervisory authority information it holds relevant to its functions under these Regulations, provided the disclosure is made for purposes connected with the effective exercise of the functions of either supervisory authority under these Regulations.

(2)   Information disclosed to a supervisory authority under paragraph (1) may not be further disclosed by that authority, except—
  (a)   in accordance with paragraph (1);
  [(aa) by the Authority to the PRA, where the information concerns a PRA-authorised person or a person who has a qualifying relationship with a PRA-authorised person;]
  (b)   with a view to the institution of, or otherwise for the purposes of, any criminal or other enforcement proceedings; or
  (c)   as otherwise required by law.]

NOTES
Commencement: 1 October 2012.
Inserted by the Money Laundering (Amendment) Regulations 2012, SI 2012/2298, regs, 2, 9.
Para (2): sub-para (aa) inserted by the Financial Services Act 2012 (Consequential Amendments and Transitional Provisions) Order 2013, SI 2013/472, art 3, Sch 2, para 129(c).

Registration of high value dealers, money service businesses
and trust or company service providers

[2.488]
25   Duty to maintain registers

(1)   The Commissioners must maintain registers of—
  (a)   high value dealers;
  (b)   money service businesses for which they are the supervisory authority;   . . .
  (c)   trust or company service providers for which they are the supervisory authority.
  [(d)   bill payment service providers for which they are the supervisory authority; and
  (e)   telecommunication, digital and IT payment service providers for which they are the supervisory authority.]

(2)   The Commissioners may keep the registers in any form they think fit.

(3)   The Commissioners may publish or make available for public inspection all or part of a register maintained under this regulation.

NOTES
Para (1): word omitted from sub-para (b) revoked and sub-paras (d), (e) inserted by the Payment Services Regulations 2009, SI 2009/209, reg 126, Sch 6, Pt 2, para 6(e).

[2.489]
26   Requirement to be registered

(1)   A person in respect of whom the Commissioners are required to maintain a register under regulation 25 must not act as a—
  (a)   high value dealer;
  (b)   money service business;   . . .
  (c)   trust or company service provider,
  [(d)   bill payment service provider; or
  (e)   telecommunication, digital and IT payment service provider,]
unless he is included in the register.

(2)   Paragraph (1) and regulation 29 are subject to the transitional provisions set out in regulation 50.

NOTES
Para (1): word omitted from sub-para (b) revoked and sub-paras (d), (e) inserted by the Payment Services Regulations 2009, SI 2009/209, reg 126, Sch 6, Pt 2, para 6(f).

[2.490]
27   Applications for registration in a register maintained under regulation 25

(1)   An applicant for registration in a register maintained under regulation 25 must make an application in such manner and provide such information as the Commissioners may specify.

(2)   The information which the Commissioners may specify includes—
  (a)   the applicant's name and (if different) the name of the business;
  (b)   the nature of the business;
  (c)   the name of the nominated officer (if any);
  (d)   in relation to a money service business or trust or company service provider—
    (i)   the name of any person who effectively directs or will direct the business and any beneficial owner of the business; and

     (ii)   information needed by the Commissioners to decide whether they must refuse the application pursuant to regulation 28.

(3)   At any time after receiving an application and before determining it, the Commissioners may require the applicant to provide, within 21 days beginning with the date of being requested to do so, such further information as they reasonably consider necessary to enable them to determine the application.

(4)   If at any time after the applicant has provided the Commissioners with any information under paragraph (1) or (3)—

    (a)   there is a material change affecting any matter contained in that information; or

    (b)   it becomes apparent to that person that the information contains a significant inaccuracy,

he must provide the Commissioners with details of the change or, as the case may be, a correction of the inaccuracy within 30 days beginning with the date of the occurrence of the change (or the discovery of the inaccuracy) or within such later time as may be agreed with the Commissioners.

(5)   The obligation in paragraph (4) applies also to material changes or significant inaccuracies affecting any matter contained in any supplementary information provided pursuant to that paragraph.

(6)   Any information to be provided to the Commissioners under this regulation must be in such form or verified in such manner as they may specify.

[2.491]
28 Fit and proper test

(1)   The Commissioners must refuse to register an applicant as a money service business or trust or company service provider if they are satisfied that—

    (a)   the applicant;

    (b)   a person who effectively directs, or will effectively direct, the business or service provider;

    (c)   a beneficial owner of the business or service provider; or

    (d)   the nominated officer of the business or service provider,

is not a fit and proper person [with regard to the risk of money laundering or terrorist financing].

(2), (3)   . . .

NOTES

The words in square brackets in para (1) were inserted, and paras (2), (3) were revoked, by the Money Laundering (Amendment) Regulations 2012, SI 2012/2298, regs, 2, 10.

[2.492]
29 Determination of applications under regulation 27

(1)   Subject to regulation 28, the Commissioners may refuse to register an applicant for registration in a register maintained under regulation 25 only if—

    (a)   any requirement of, or imposed under, regulation 27 has not been complied with;

    (b)   it appears to the Commissioners that any information provided pursuant to regulation 27 is false or misleading in a material particular; or

    (c)   the applicant has failed to pay a charge imposed by them under regulation 35(1).

(2)   The Commissioners must within 45 days beginning either with the date on which they receive the application or, where applicable, with the date on which they receive any further information required under regulation 27(3), give the applicant notice of—

    (a)   their decision to register the applicant; or

    (b)   the following matters—

     (i)   their decision not to register the applicant;

     (ii)   the reasons for their decision;

     [(iii)   the right to a review under regulation 43A; and]

     (iv)   the right to appeal under regulation [43].

(3)   The Commissioners must, as soon as practicable after deciding to register a person, include him in the relevant register.

NOTES

Para (2): number in square brackets in sub-para (b)(iv) substituted, and sub-para (b)(iii) substituted, by the Transfer of Tribunal Functions and Revenue and Customs Appeals Order 2009, SI 2009/56, art 3, Sch 2, paras 168, 169 (note that art 6 of, and Sch 3 to, the 2009 Order make general transitional and saving provisions for the treatment of cases which would previously have been dealt with by the existing tribunals from which the functions are transferred following the coming into force of the Order).

[2.493]
30 Cancellation of registration in a register maintained under regulation 25

(1)   The Commissioners must cancel the registration of a money service business or trust or company service provider in a register maintained under regulation 25(1) if, at any time after registration, they are satisfied that he or any person mentioned in regulation 28(1)(b), (c) or (d) is not a fit and proper person within the meaning of regulation [28].

Part 2 Statutory Instruments

[(2)   The Commissioners may cancel a person's registration in a register maintained by them under regulation 25 if, at any time after registration—
  (a)   it appears to them that any condition in regulation 29(1) is met; or
  (b)   the person has failed to comply with any requirement of a notice given under regulation 37.]

[(2A)   The Commissioners may cancel the registration of a money service business in a register maintained under regulation 25(1)(b) where the money service business—
  (a)   is providing a payment service in the United Kingdom, or is purporting to do so;
  (b)   is not included in the register of payment service providers maintained by the Authority under regulation 4(1) of the Payment Service Regulations 2009; and
  (c)   is not a person mentioned in paragraphs (c) to (h) of the definition of a payment service provider in regulation 2(1) of the Payment Services Regulations 2009, or a person to whom regulation 3 or 121 of those Regulations applies.]

(3)   Where the Commissioners decide to cancel a person's registration they must give him notice of—
  (a)   their decision and, subject to paragraph (4), the date from which the cancellation takes effect;
  (b)   the reasons for their decision;
  [(c)   the right to a review under regulation 43A; and]
  (d)   the right to appeal under regulation [43].

(4)   If the Commissioners—
  (a)   consider that the interests of the public require the cancellation of a person's registration to have immediate effect; and
  (b)   include a statement to that effect and the reasons for it in the notice given under paragraph (3),
the cancellation takes effect when the notice is given to the person.

NOTES

Para (1): number in square brackets substituted by the Money Laundering (Amendment) Regulations 2012, SI 2012/2298, regs, 2, 11(a).

Para (2): substituted by SI 2012/2298, regs, 2, 11(b).

Para (2A): inserted by the Payment Services Regulations 2012, SI 2012/1791, reg 2.

Para (3): number in square brackets in sub-para (d) substituted, and sub-para (c) substituted, by the Transfer of Tribunal Functions and Revenue and Customs Appeals Order 2009, SI 2009/56, art 3, Sch 2, paras 168, 170 (note that art 6 of, and Sch 3 to, the 2009 Order make general transitional and saving provisions for the treatment of cases which would previously have been dealt with by the existing tribunals from which the functions are transferred following the coming into force of the Order).

Requirement to inform the authority

[2.494]
31   Requirement on authorised person to inform the Authority

(1)   An authorised person whose supervisory authority is the Authority must, before acting as a money service business or a trust or company service provider or within 28 days of so doing, inform the Authority that he intends, or has begun, to act as such.

(2)   Paragraph (1) does not apply to an authorised person who—
  (a)   immediately before 15th December 2007 was acting as a money service business or a trust or company service provider and continues to act as such after that date; and
  (b)   before 15th January 2008 informs the [Financial Services] Authority that he is or was acting as such.

(3)   Where an authorised person whose supervisory authority is the Authority ceases to act as a money service business or a trust or company service provider, he must immediately inform the Authority.

(4)   Any requirement imposed by this regulation is to be treated as if it were a requirement imposed by or under the 2000 Act.

(5)   Any information to be provided to the Authority under this regulation must be in such form or verified in such manner as it may specify.

NOTES

Para (2): words in square brackets inserted by the Financial Services Act 2012 (Consequential Amendments and Transitional Provisions) Order 2013, SI 2013/472, art 3, Sch 2, para 129(d).

Registration of Annex I financial institutions, estate agents etc

[2.495]
32   Power to maintain registers

(1)   The supervisory authorities mentioned in paragraph (2), (3) or (4) may, in order to fulfil their duties under regulation 24, maintain a register under this regulation.

(2)   The Authority may maintain a register of Annex I financial institutions.

(3)   . . .

(4)   The Commissioners may maintain registers of—
    (a)   auditors;
    (b)   external accountants; and
    (c)   tax advisers,
who are not supervised by the Secretary of State, DETI or any of the professional bodies listed in Schedule 3.

[(4A)   The Commissioners may maintain a register of estate agents.]

(5)   Where a supervisory authority decides to maintain a register under this regulation, it must take reasonable steps to bring its decision to the attention of those relevant persons in respect of whom the register is to be established.

(6)   A supervisory authority may keep a register under this regulation in any form it thinks fit.

(7)   A supervisory authority may publish or make available to public inspection all or part of a register maintained by it under this regulation.

NOTES

    Para (3): revoked by the Financial Services and Markets Act 2000 (Regulated Activities) (Amendment) (No 2) Order 2013, SI 2013/1881, art 28, Schedule, Pt 1, para 35(1), (6), for transitional provisions see arts 29–66 of that Order at **[2.1007]** et seq.

    Para (4A): inserted by the Public Bodies (Abolition of the National Consumer Council and Transfer of the Office of Fair Trading's Functions in relation to Estate Agents etc) Order 2014, SI 2014/631, art 5(3), Sch 3, Pt 1, para 2(1), (3) (see further the note "Transfer of functions and transitional provisions" in the introductory notes to these Regulations).

[2.496]
33   Requirement to be registered

Where a supervisory authority decides to maintain a register under regulation 32 in respect of any description of relevant persons and establishes a register for that purpose, a relevant person of that description may not carry on the business or profession in question for a period of more than six months beginning on the date on which the supervisory authority establishes the register unless he is included in the register.

[2.497]
34   Applications for and cancellation of registration in a register maintained under regulation 32

(1)   Regulations 27, 29 (with the omission of the words "Subject to regulation 28" in regulation 29(1)) and 30(2), (3) and (4) apply to registration in a register maintained by the Commissioners under regulation 32 as they apply to registration in a register maintained under regulation 25.

(2)   Regulation 27 applies to registration in a register maintained by the Authority . . . under regulation 32 as it applies to registration in a register maintained under regulation 25 and, for this purpose, references to the Commissioners are to be treated as references to the Authority . . .

(3)   The Authority . . . may refuse to register an applicant for registration in a register maintained under regulation 32 only if—
    (a)   any requirement of, or imposed under, regulation 27 has not been complied with;
    (b)   it appears to the Authority . . . that any information provided pursuant to regulation 27 is false or misleading in a material particular; or
    (c)   the applicant has failed to pay a charge imposed by the Authority . . . under regulation 35(1).

(4)   The Authority . . . must, within 45 days beginning either with the date on which it receives an application or, where applicable, with the date on which it receives any further information required under regulation 27(3), give the applicant notice of—
    (a)   its decision to register the applicant; or
    (b)   the following matters—
        (i)   that it is minded not to register the applicant;
        (ii)   the reasons for being minded not to register him; and
        (iii)   the right to make representations to it within a specified period (which may not be less than 28 days).

(5)   The Authority . . . must then decide, within a reasonable period, whether to register the applicant and it must give the applicant notice of—
    (a)   its decision to register the applicant; or
    (b)   the following matters—
        (i)   its decision not to register the applicant;
        (ii)   the reasons for its decision; and
        (iii)   the right to appeal under regulation 44(1)(b).

(6)   The Authority . . . must, as soon as reasonably practicable after deciding to register a person, include him in the relevant register.

[(7)   The Authority . . . may cancel a person's registration in a register maintained by them under regulation 32 if, at any time after registration—
    (a)   it appears to them that any condition in paragraph (3) is met; or

(b)   the person has failed to comply with any requirement of a notice given under regulation 37.]

(8)   Where the Authority . . . proposes to cancel a person's registration, it must give him notice of—
(a)   its proposal to cancel his registration;
(b)   the reasons for the proposed cancellation; and
(c)   the right to make representations to it within a specified period (which may not be less than 28 days).

(9)   The Authority . . . must then decide, within a reasonable period, whether to cancel the person's registration and it must give him notice of—
(a)   its decision not to cancel his registration; or
(b)   the following matters—
    (i)   its decision to cancel his registration and, subject to paragraph (10), the date from which cancellation takes effect;
    (ii)   the reasons for its decision; and
    (iii)   the right to appeal under regulation 44(1)(b).

(10)   If the Authority . . . —
(a)   considers that the interests of the public require the cancellation of a person's registration to have immediate effect; and
(b)   includes a statement to that effect and the reasons for it in the notice given under paragraph (9)(b),
the cancellation takes effect when the notice is given to the person.

(11)   In paragraphs (3) and (4), references to regulation 27 are to be treated as references to that paragraph as applied by paragraph (2) of this regulation.

NOTES

Words omitted revoked by the Financial Services and Markets Act 2000 (Regulated Activities) (Amendment) (No 2) Order 2013, SI 2013/1881, art 28, Schedule, Pt 1, para 35(1), (7), for transitional provisions see arts 29–66 of that Order at **[2.1007]** et seq.

Para (7) substituted by the Money Laundering (Amendment) Regulations 2012, SI 2012/2298, regs, 2, 12.

See further the note "Transfer of functions and transitional provisions" in the introductory notes to these Regulations.

Financial provisions

[2.498]
35   Costs of supervision
(1)   The Authority . . . and the Commissioners may impose charges—
(a)   on applicants for registration;
(b)   on relevant persons supervised by them.

(2)   Charges levied under paragraph (1) must not exceed such amount as the Authority . . . or the Commissioners (as the case may be) consider will enable them to meet any expenses reasonably incurred by them in carrying out their functions under these Regulations or for any incidental purpose.

(3)   Without prejudice to the generality of paragraph (2), a charge may be levied in respect of each of the premises at which a person carries on (or proposes to carry on) business.

[(4)   The Authority must pay to the Treasury any amounts received by the Financial Services Authority during the financial year beginning with 1st April 2012 year by way of penalties imposed under regulation 42 after deducting any amounts the Financial Services Authority has, prior to 1st April 2013, applied towards expenses incurred by it in carrying out its functions under these Regulations or for any incidental purpose.

(4A)   The Authority must in respect of the financial year beginning with 1st April 2013 and each subsequent financial year pay to the Treasury any amounts received by it during the year by way of penalties imposed under regulation 42.

(4B)   The Treasury may give directions to the Authority as to how the Authority is to comply with its duties under paragraphs (4) and (4A).

(4C)   The directions may in particular—
(a)   specify the time when any payment is required to be made to the Treasury, and
(b)   require the Authority to provide the Treasury at specified times with information relating to penalties that the Authority has imposed under regulation 42.

(4D)   The Treasury must pay into the Consolidated Fund any sums received by them under this regulation.]

(5)   In paragraph (2), "expenses" in relation to the [Authority] includes expenses incurred by a local weights and measures authority or DETI pursuant to arrangements made for the purposes of these Regulations with the [Authority]—
(a)   by or on behalf of the authority; or
(b)   by DETI.

NOTES

   Paras (1), (2): words omitted revoked by the Financial Services and Markets Act 2000 (Regulated Activities) (Amendment) (No 2) Order 2013, SI 2013/1881, art 28, Schedule, Pt 1, para 35(1), (8)(a), for transitional provisions see arts 29–66 of that Order at **[2.1007]** et seq.

   Paras (4)–(4D): substituted (for the original para (4)) by the Payment to Treasury of Penalties Regulations 2013, SI 2013/429, reg 2(1).

   Para (5): words in square brackets substituted by SI 2013/1881, art 28, Schedule, Pt 1, para 35(1), (8)(b), for transitional provisions, see the note relating to this Order above.

PART 5
ENFORCEMENT

Powers of designated authorities

[2.499]
36   Interpretation

In this Part—
   "designated authority" means—
      (a)   the Authority; [and]
      (b)   the Commissioners; [. . .]
      (c), (d). . .
   "officer", except in regulations 40(3), 41 and 47 means—
      (a)   an officer of the Authority, including a member of the Authority's staff or an agent of the Authority;
      (b)   an officer of Revenue and Customs; [or]
      (c)   . . .
      (d)   a relevant officer; . . .
      (e)   . . .
   "recorded information" includes information recorded in any form and any document of any nature;
   "relevant officer" means—
      (a)   in Great Britain, an officer of a local weights and measures authority;
      (b)   in Northern Ireland, an officer of DETI acting pursuant to arrangements made with the [Authority] for the purposes of these Regulations.

NOTES

   Word in square brackets in para (a) of the definition "designated authority" inserted, and para (c) of that definition (and the word omitted from para (b)) revoked, by the Financial Services and Markets Act 2000 (Regulated Activities) (Amendment) (No 2) Order 2013, SI 2013/1881, art 28, Schedule, Pt 1, para 35(1), (9)(a), for transitional provisions see arts 29–66 of that Order at **[2.1007]** et seq; word omitted from para (b) of that definition originally inserted, and para (d) (and the preceding word) revoked, by the Money Laundering (Amendment No 2) Regulations 2011, SI 2011/2833, reg 2(b), (c).

   Word in square brackets in para (b) of the definition "officer" inserted, and para (c) of that definition revoked, by SI 2013/1881, art 28, Schedule, Pt 1, para 35(1), (9)(b), for transitional provisions, see the note relating to this Order above; para (e) (and the preceding word) revoked, by the Money Laundering (Amendment No 2) Regulations 2011, SI 2011/2833, reg 2(b), (c).

   Word in square brackets in the definition "relevant officer" substituted by SI 2013/1881, art 28, Schedule, Pt 1, para 35(1), (9)(c), for transitional provisions, see the note relating to this Order above.

[2.500]
37   Power to require information from, and attendance of, relevant and connected persons

(1)   An officer may, by notice to a relevant person or to a person connected with a relevant person, require the relevant person or the connected person, as the case may be—
   (a)   to provide such information as may be specified in the notice;
   (b)   to produce such recorded information as may be so specified; or
   (c)   to attend before an officer at a time and place specified in the notice and answer questions.

[(2)   For the purposes of paragraph (1)—
   (a)   "relevant person" includes a person whom a designated authority believes, or has reasonable grounds to suspect, is or has at any time been a relevant person; and
   (b)   a person is connected with a relevant person if the person is, or has at any time been, in relation to the relevant person, a person listed in Schedule 4 to these Regulations.]

(3)   An officer may exercise powers under this regulation only if the information sought to be obtained as a result is reasonably required in connection with the exercise by the designated authority for whom he acts of its functions under these Regulations.

(4)   Where an officer requires information to be provided or produced pursuant to paragraph (1)(a) or (b)—
   (a)   the notice must set out the reasons why the officer requires the information to be provided or produced; and
   (b)   such information must be provided or produced—
      (i)   before the end of such reasonable period as may be specified in the notice; and

Part 2   Statutory Instruments

    (ii)   at such place as may be so specified.

(5)   In relation to information recorded otherwise than in legible form, the power to require production of it includes a power to require the production of a copy of it in legible form or in a form from which it can readily be produced in visible and legible form.

(6)   The production of a document does not affect any lien which a person has on the document.

(7)   A person may not be required under this regulation to provide or produce information or to answer questions which he would be entitled to refuse to provide, produce or answer on grounds of legal professional privilege in proceedings in the High Court, except that a lawyer may be required to provide the name and address of his client.

(8)   Subject to paragraphs (9) and (10), a statement made by a person in compliance with a requirement imposed on him under paragraph (1)(c) is admissible in evidence in any proceedings, so long as it also complies with any requirements governing the admissibility of evidence in the circumstances in question.

(9)   In criminal proceedings in which a person is charged with an offence to which this paragraph applies—
    (a)   no evidence relating to the statement may be adduced; and
    (b)   no question relating to it may be asked,
by or on behalf of the prosecution unless evidence relating to it is adduced, or a question relating to it is asked, in the proceedings by or on behalf of that person.

(10)   Paragraph (9) applies to any offence other than one under—
    (a)   section 5 of the Perjury Act 1911 (false statements without oath);
    (b)   section 44(2) of the Criminal Law (Consolidation) (Scotland) Act 1995 (false statements and declarations); or
    (c)   Article 10 of the Perjury (Northern Ireland) Order 1979 (false unsworn statements).

(11)   In the application of this regulation to Scotland, the reference in paragraph (7) to—
    (a)   proceedings in the High Court is to be read as a reference to legal proceedings generally; and
    (b)   an entitlement on grounds of legal professional privilege is to be read as a reference to an entitlement on the grounds of confidentiality of communications[—
        (i)   between a professional legal adviser and his client; or
        (ii)   made in connection with or in contemplation of legal proceedings and for the purposes of those proceedings].

NOTES

Para (2): substituted by the Money Laundering (Amendment) Regulations 2012, SI 2012/2298, regs, 2, 13.
Para (11): sub-paras (b)(i), (ii) inserted by the Money Laundering (Amendment) Regulations 2007, SI 2007/3299, reg 2(b).

[2.501]
38   Entry, inspection without a warrant etc

(1)   Where an officer has reasonable cause to believe that any premises are being used by a relevant person in connection with his business or professional activities, he may on producing evidence of his authority at any reasonable time—
    (a)   enter the premises;
    (b)   inspect the premises;
    (c)   observe the carrying on of business or professional activities by the relevant person;
    (d)   inspect any recorded information found on the premises;
    (e)   require any person on the premises to provide an explanation of any recorded information or to state where it may be found;
    (f)   in the case of a money service business or a high value dealer, inspect any cash found on the premises.

(2)   An officer may take copies of, or make extracts from, any recorded information found under paragraph (1).

(3)   Paragraphs (1)(d) and (e) and (2) do not apply to recorded information which the relevant person would be entitled to refuse to disclose on grounds of legal professional privilege in proceedings in the High Court, except that a lawyer may be required to provide the name and address of his client and, for this purpose, regulation 37(11) applies to this paragraph as it applies to regulation 37(7).

(4)   An officer may exercise powers under this regulation only if the information sought to be obtained as a result is reasonably required in connection with the exercise by the designated authority for whom he acts of its functions under these Regulations.

(5)   In this regulation, "premises" means any premises other than premises used only as a dwelling.

[2.502]
39 Entry to premises under warrant

(1) A justice may issue a warrant under this paragraph if satisfied on information on oath given by an officer that there are reasonable grounds for believing that the first, second or third set of conditions is satisfied.

(2) The first set of conditions is—
  (a) that there is on the premises specified in the warrant recorded information in relation to which a requirement could be imposed under regulation 37(1)(b); and
  (b) that if such a requirement were to be imposed—
    (i) it would not be complied with; or
    (ii) the recorded information to which it relates would be removed, tampered with or destroyed.

(3) The second set of conditions is—
  (a) that a person on whom a requirement has been imposed under regulation 37(1)(b) has failed (wholly or in part) to comply with it; and
  (b) that there is on the premises specified in the warrant recorded information which has been required to be produced.

(4) The third set of conditions is—
  (a) that an officer has been obstructed in the exercise of a power under regulation 38; and
  (b) that there is on the premises specified in the warrant recorded information or cash which could be inspected under regulation 38(1)(d) or (f).

(5) A justice may issue a warrant under this paragraph if satisfied on information on oath given by an officer that there are reasonable grounds for suspecting that—
  (a) an offence under these Regulations has been, is being or is about to be committed by a relevant person; and
  (b) there is on the premises specified in the warrant recorded information relevant to whether that offence has been, or is being or is about to be committed.

(6) A warrant issued under this regulation shall authorise an officer—
  (a) to enter the premises specified in the warrant;
  (b) to search the premises and take possession of any recorded information or anything appearing to be recorded information specified in the warrant or to take, in relation to any such recorded information, any other steps which may appear to be necessary for preserving it or preventing interference with it;
  (c) to take copies of, or extracts from, any recorded information specified in the warrant;
  (d) to require any person on the premises to provide an explanation of any recorded information appearing to be of the kind specified in the warrant or to state where it may be found;
  (e) to use such force as may reasonably be necessary.

(7) Where a warrant is issued by a justice under paragraph (1) or (5) on the basis of information [on oath] given by an officer of the Authority, for "an officer" in paragraph (6) substitute "a constable".

(8) In paragraphs (1), (5) and (7), "justice" means—
  (a) in relation to England and Wales, a justice of the peace;
  (b) in relation to Scotland, a justice within the meaning of section 307 of the Criminal Procedure (Scotland) Act 1995 (interpretation);
  (c) in relation to Northern Ireland, a lay magistrate.

(9) In the application of this regulation to Scotland, the references in paragraphs [(1), (5) and (7)] to information on oath are to be read as references to evidence on oath.

NOTES
  Para (7): words in square brackets inserted by the Money Laundering (Amendment) Regulations 2007, SI 2007/3299, reg 2(c)(i).
  Para (9): words in square brackets substituted by SI 2007/3299, reg 2(c)(ii).

[2.503]
40 Failure to comply with information requirement

(1) If, on an application made by—
  (a) a designated authority; or
  (b) a local weights and measures authority or DETI pursuant to arrangements made with the [Authority]—
    (i) by or on behalf of the authority; or
    (ii) by DETI,
it appears to the court that a person (the "information defaulter") has failed to do something that he was required to do under regulation 37(1), the court may make an order under this regulation.

(2) An order under this regulation may require the information defaulter—
  (a) to do the thing that he failed to do within such period as may be specified in the order;

(b) otherwise to take such steps to remedy the consequences of the failure as may be so specified.

(3) If the information defaulter is a body corporate, a partnership or an unincorporated body of persons which is not a partnership, the order may require any officer of the body corporate, partnership or body, who is (wholly or partly) responsible for the failure to meet such costs of the application as are specified in the order.

(4) In this regulation, "court" means—
(a) in England and Wales and Northern Ireland, the High Court or the county court;
(b) in Scotland, the Court of Session or the sheriff [court].

NOTES

Para (1): word in square brackets substituted by the Financial Services and Markets Act 2000 (Regulated Activities) (Amendment) (No 2) Order 2013, SI 2013/1881, art 28, Schedule, Pt 1, para 35(1), (10), for transitional provisions see arts 29–66 of that Order at **[2.1007]** et seq.

Para (4): word in square brackets in sub-para (b) inserted by the Money Laundering (Amendment) Regulations 2007, SI 2007/3299, reg 2(d).

[2.504]
41 Powers of relevant officers

(1) A relevant officer may only exercise powers under regulations 37 to 39 pursuant to arrangements made with the [Authority]—
(a) by or on behalf of the local weights and measures authority of which he is an officer ("his authority"); or
(b) by DETI.

(2) Anything done or omitted to be done by, or in relation to, a relevant officer in the exercise or purported exercise of a power in this Part shall be treated for all purposes as having been done or omitted to be done by, or in relation to, an officer of the [Authority].

(3) Paragraph (2) does not apply for the purposes of any criminal proceedings brought against the relevant officer, his authority, DETI or the [Authority], in respect of anything done or omitted to be done by the officer.

(4) A relevant officer shall not disclose to any person other than the [Authority] and his authority or, as the case may be, DETI information obtained by him in the exercise of such powers unless—
(a) he has the approval of the [Authority] to do so; or
(b) he is under a duty to make the disclosure.

NOTES

Word "Authority" in square brackets (in each place that it occurs) substituted by the Financial Services and Markets Act 2000 (Regulated Activities) (Amendment) (No 2) Order 2013, SI 2013/1881, art 28, Schedule, Pt 1, para 35(1), (11), for transitional provisions see arts 29–66 of that Order at **[2.1007]** et seq.

Civil penalties, review and appeals

[2.505]
42 Power to impose civil penalties

(1) A designated authority may impose a penalty of such amount as it considers appropriate on a . . . person [(except an auction platform)] who fails to comply with any requirement in regulation 7(1), (2) or (3), 8(1) or (3), 9(2), 10(1), 11(1), 14(1), 15(1) or (2), 16(1), (2), (3) or (4), 19(1), (4), (5) or (6), 20(1), (4) or (5), 21, 26, 27(4) or 33 . . . .

[(1A) A designated authority may impose a penalty of such amount as it considers appropriate on an auction platform which fails to comply with—
(a) the customer due diligence requirements of Article 19 or 20(6) of the emission allowance auctioning regulation;
(b) the monitoring and record keeping requirements of Article 54 of the emission allowance auctioning regulation; or
(c) regulation 20(1), (4) or (5) or 21 of these Regulations;
. . .]

[(1B) A designated authority may impose a penalty of such amount as it considers appropriate on a person who fails to comply with any requirement of a notice given under regulation 37(1).

(1C) In paragraphs (1), (1A) and (1B), "appropriate" means effective, proportionate and dissuasive.]

(2) The designated authority must not impose a penalty on a person under paragraph (1)[, (1A) or (1B)] where there are reasonable grounds for it to be satisfied that the person took all reasonable steps and exercised all due diligence to ensure that the requirement would be complied with.

(3) In deciding whether a person has failed to comply with a requirement of these Regulations, the designated authority must consider whether he followed any relevant guidance which was at the time—
(a) issued by a supervisory authority or any other appropriate body;
(b) approved by the Treasury; and

(c)   published in a manner approved by the Treasury as suitable in their opinion to bring the guidance to the attention of persons likely to be affected by it.

(4)   In paragraph (3), an "appropriate body" means any body which regulates or is representative of any trade, profession, business or employment carried on by the [person].

[(4A) Where the Authority proposes to impose a penalty under this regulation on a PRA-authorised person or on a person who has a qualifying relationship with a PRA-authorised person, it must consult the PRA.]

(5)   Where the Commissioners decide to impose a penalty under this regulation, they must give the person notice of—
(a)   their decision to impose the penalty and its amount;
(b)   the reasons for imposing the penalty;
(c)   the right to a review under regulation [43A]; and
(d)   the right to appeal under regulation [43].

(6)   Where the Authority . . . or DETI proposes to impose a penalty under this regulation, it must give the person notice of—
(a)   its proposal to impose the penalty and the proposed amount;
(b)   the reasons for imposing the penalty; and
(c)   the right to make representations to it within a specified period (which may not be less than 28 days).

(7)   The Authority . . . or DETI, as the case may be, must then decide, within a reasonable period, whether to impose a penalty under this regulation and it must give the person notice of—
(a)   its decision not to impose a penalty; or
(b)   the following matters—
    (i)   its decision to impose a penalty and the amount;
    (ii)   the reasons for its decision; and
    (iii) the right to appeal under regulation 44(1)(b).

(8)   A penalty imposed under this regulation is payable to the designated authority which imposes it.

NOTES

Para (1): words omitted revoked by the Money Laundering (Amendment) Regulations 2012, SI 2012/2298, regs, 2, 14(a); words in square brackets inserted by the Recognised Auction Platforms Regulations 2011, SI 2011/2699, reg 11(1), (7)(a).
Para (1A): inserted by SI 2011/2699, reg 11(1), (7)(b); words omitted revoked by SI 2012/2298, regs, 2, 14(b).
Paras (1B), (1C): inserted by SI 2012/2298, regs, 2, 14(c).
Para (2): words in square brackets originally inserted by the Recognised Auction Platforms Regulations 2011, SI 2011/2699, reg 11(1), (7)(a), (c), and subsequently substituted by SI 2012/2298, regs, 2, 14(d).
Para (4): word in square brackets substituted by the Money Laundering (Amendment) Regulations 2007, SI 2007/3299, reg 2(e).
Para (4A): inserted by the Financial Services Act 2012 (Consequential Amendments and Transitional Provisions) Order 2013, SI 2013/472, art 3, Sch 2, para 129(e).
Para (5): numbers in square brackets substituted by the Transfer of Tribunal Functions and Revenue and Customs Appeals Order 2009, SI 2009/56, art 3, Sch 2, paras 168, 171 (note that art 6 of, and Sch 3 to, the 2009 Order make general transitional and saving provisions for the treatment of cases which would previously have been dealt with by the existing tribunals from which the functions are transferred following the coming into force of the Order).
Paras (6), (7): words omitted revoked by the Financial Services and Markets Act 2000 (Regulated Activities) (Amendment) (No 2) Order 2013, SI 2013/1881, art 28, Schedule, Pt 1, para 35(1), (12), for transitional provisions see arts 29–66 of that Order at **[2.1007]** et seq.
See further the note "Transfer of functions and transitional provisions" in the introductory notes to these Regulations.

[2.506]
43 [Appeals against decisions of the Commissioners]

(1)   This regulation applies to decisions of the Commissioners made under—
  [(za) regulation 28, to the effect that a person is not a fit and proper person;]
(a)   regulation 29, to refuse to register an applicant;
(b)   regulation 30, to cancel the registration of a registered person; and
(c)   regulation 42, to impose a penalty.

(2)   Any person who is the subject of a decision to which this regulation applies may [appeal to the tribunal in accordance with regulation 43F].

[(3) The provisions of Part 5 of the Value Added Tax Act 1994 (appeals), subject to the modifications set out in paragraph 1 of Schedule 5 to these Regulations, apply in respect of appeals to a tribunal made under this regulation as they apply in respect of appeals made to the tribunal under section 83 (appeals) of that Act.

(4)   A tribunal hearing an appeal under paragraph (2) has the power to—
(a)   quash or vary any decision of the supervisory authority, including the power to reduce any penalty to such amount (including nil) as it thinks proper, and
(b)   substitute its own decision for any decision quashed on appeal.

(5)   The modifications in Schedule 5 have effect for the purposes of appeals made under this regulation.

(6) For the purposes of appeals under this regulation, the meaning of "tribunal" is as defined in section 82 of the Value Added Tax Act 1994.]

NOTES

The words in square brackets in the regulation heading and in para (2) were substituted, and paras (3)–(6) were substituted (for the original paras (3)–(5)), by the Transfer of Tribunal Functions and Revenue and Customs Appeals Order 2009, SI 2009/56, art 3, Sch 2, paras 168, 172 (note that art 6 of, and Sch 3 to, the 2009 Order make general transitional and saving provisions for the treatment of cases which would previously have been dealt with by the existing tribunals from which the functions are transferred following the coming into force of the Order).

In para (1), sub-para (za) was inserted by the Money Laundering (Amendment) Regulations 2012, SI 2012/2298, regs, 2, 15.

See further the note "Transfer of functions and transitional provisions" in the introductory notes to these Regulations.

[2.507]
[43A Offer of review

(1) The Commissioners must offer a person (P) a review of a decision that has been notified to P if an appeal lies under regulation 43 in respect of the decision.

(2) The offer of the review must be made by notice given to P at the same time as the decision is notified to P.

(3) This regulation does not apply to the notification of the conclusions of a review.]

NOTES

Inserted, together with regs 43B–43F, by the Transfer of Tribunal Functions and Revenue and Customs Appeals Order 2009, SI 2009/56, art 3, Sch 2, paras 168, 173 (note that art 6 of, and Sch 3 to, the 2009 Order make general transitional and saving provisions for the treatment of cases which would previously have been dealt with by the existing tribunals from which the functions are transferred following the coming into force of the Order).

See further the note "Transfer of functions and transitional provisions" in the introductory notes to these Regulations.

[2.508]
[43B Review by the Commissioners

(1) The Commissioners must review a decision if—
   (a) they have offered a review of the decision under regulation 43A, and
   (b) P notifies the Commissioners accepting the offer within 30 days from the date of the document containing the notification of the offer.

(2) But P may not notify acceptance of the offer if P has already appealed to the tribunal under regulation 43F.

(3) The Commissioners shall not review a decision if P has appealed to the tribunal under regulation 43F in respect of the decision.]

NOTES

Inserted as noted to reg 43A at **[2.507]**.

See further the note "Transfer of functions and transitional provisions" in the introductory notes to these Regulations.

[2.509]
[43C Extensions of time

(1) If under regulation 43A, the Commissioners have offered P a review of a decision, the Commissioners may within the relevant period notify P that the relevant period is extended.

(2) If notice is given the relevant period is extended to the end of 30 days from—
   (a) the date of the notice, or
   (b) any other date set out in the notice or a further notice.

(3) In this regulation "relevant period" means—
   (a) the period of 30 days referred to in regulation 43B(1)(b), or
   (b) if notice has been given under paragraph (1) that period as extended (or as most recently extended) in accordance with paragraph (2).]

NOTES

Inserted as noted to reg 43A at **[2.507]**.

See further the note "Transfer of functions and transitional provisions" in the introductory notes to these Regulations.

[2.510]
[43D Review out of time

(1) This regulation applies if—
   (a) the Commissioners have offered a review of a decision under regulation 43A, and
   (b) P does not accept the offer within the time allowed under regulation 43B(1)(b) or 43C(2).

(2) The Commissioners must review the decision under regulation 43B if—
   (a) after the time allowed, P notifies the Commissioners in writing requesting a review out of time,
   (b) the Commissioners are satisfied that P had a reasonable excuse for not accepting the offer or requiring review within the time allowed, and

   (c)   the Commissioners are satisfied that P made the request without unreasonable delay after the excuse had ceased to apply.

(3)   The Commissioners shall not review a decision if P has appealed to the tribunal under regulation 43F in respect of the decision.]

NOTES

Inserted as noted to reg 43A at **[2.507]**.

See further the note "Transfer of functions and transitional provisions" in the introductory notes to these Regulations.

[2.511]
[43E   Nature of review etc

(1)   This regulation applies if the Commissioners are required to undertake a review under regulation 43B or 43D.

(2)   The nature and extent of the review are to be such as appear appropriate to the Commissioners in the circumstances.

(3)   For the purpose of paragraph (2), the Commissioners must, in particular, have regard to steps taken before the beginning of the review—
   (a)   by the Commissioners in reaching the decision, and
   (b)   by any person in seeking to resolve disagreement about the decision.

(4)   The review must take account of any representations made by P at a stage which gives the Commissioners a reasonable opportunity to consider them.

(5)   The review may conclude that the decision is to be—
   (a)   upheld,
   (b)   varied, or
   (c)   cancelled.

(6)   The Commissioners must give P notice of the conclusions of the review and their reasoning within—
   (a)   a period of 45 days beginning with the relevant date, or
   (b)   such other period as the Commissioners and P may agree.

(7)   In paragraph (6) "relevant date" means—
   (a)   the date the Commissioners received P's notification accepting the offer of a review (in a case falling within regulation 43A), or
   (b)   the date on which the Commissioners decided to undertake the review (in a case falling within regulation 43D).

(8)   Where the Commissioners are required to undertake a review but do not give notice of the conclusions within the time period specified in paragraph (6), the review is to be treated as having concluded that the decision is upheld.

(9)   If paragraph (8) applies, the Commissioners must notify P of the conclusion which the review is treated as having reached.]

NOTES

Inserted as noted to reg 43A at **[2.507]**.

See further the note "Transfer of functions and transitional provisions" in the introductory notes to these Regulations.

[2.512]
[43F   Bringing of appeals against decisions of the Commissioners

(1)   An appeal under regulation 43 is to be made to the tribunal before—
   (a)   the end of the period of 30 days beginning with the date of the document notifying the decision to which the appeal relates, or
   (b)   if later, the end of the relevant period (within the meaning of regulation 43C).

(2)   But that is subject to paragraphs (3) to (5).

(3)   In a case where the Commissioners are required to undertake a review under regulation 43B—
   (a)   an appeal may not be made until the conclusion date, and
   (b)   any appeal is to be made within the period of 30 days beginning with the conclusion date.

[(4)   In a case where the Commissioners are requested to undertake a review in accordance with regulation 43D—
   (a)   an appeal may not be made—
      (i)   unless the Commissioners have notified P as to whether or not a review will be undertaken, and
      (ii)   if the Commissioners have notified P that a review will be undertaken, until the conclusion date;
   (b)   any appeal where sub-paragraph (a)(ii) applies is to be made within the period of 30 days beginning with the conclusion date;
   (c)   if the Commissioners have notified P that a review will not be undertaken, an appeal may be made only if the tribunal gives permission to do so.]

(5)   In a case where regulation 43E(8) applies, an appeal may be made at any time from the end of the period specified in regulation 43E(6) to the date 30 days after the conclusion date.

(6)   An appeal may be made after the end of the period specified in paragraph (1), (3)(b), (4)(b) or (5) if the tribunal gives permission to do so.

(7)   In this regulation "conclusion date" means the date of the document notifying the conclusions of the review.]

NOTES

Inserted as noted to reg 43A at **[2.507]**.

Para (4): substituted by the Revenue and Customs (Amendment of Appeal Provisions for Out of Time Reviews) Order 2014, SI 2014/1264, art 11, in relation to requests for a review out of time notified to HMRC on or after 1 June 2014. The original paragraph read as follows—

"(4)   In a case where the Commissioners are requested to undertake a review in accordance with regulation 43D—
  (a)   an appeal may not be made—
    (i)   unless the Commissioners have decided whether or not to undertake a review, and
    (ii)   if the Commissioners decide to undertake a review, until the conclusion date; and
  (b)   any appeal is to be made within the period of 30 days beginning with—
    (i)   the conclusion date (if the Commissioners decide to undertake a review), or
    (ii)   the date on which the Commissioners decide not to undertake a review.".

See further the note "Transfer of functions and transitional provisions" in the introductory notes to these Regulations.

[2.513]
44   Appeals

(1)   A person may appeal from a decision by—
  (a)   . . .
  (b)   the Authority . . . or DETI under regulation 34 or 42.

(2)   An appeal from a decision by—
  (a)   . . .
  (b)   the Authority is to the [Upper Tribunal];
  (c)   . . .
  (d)   DETI is to the High Court.

(3)   . . .

(4)   The provisions of Part 9 of the 2000 Act (hearings and appeals), subject to the modifications set out in paragraph 2 of Schedule 5, apply in respect of appeals to the [Upper Tribunal] made under this regulation as they apply in respect of references made to that Tribunal under that Act.

(5), (6)   . . .

(7)   . . .

(8)   The modifications in Schedule 5 have effect for the purposes of appeals made under this regulation.

NOTES

Paras (1)(a), (2)(a), (3), (6) were revoked by the Transfer of Tribunal Functions and Revenue and Customs Appeals Order 2009, SI 2009/56, art 3, Sch 2, paras 168, 174 (note that art 6 of, and Sch 3 to, the 2009 Order make general transitional and saving provisions for the treatment of cases which would previously have been dealt with by the existing tribunals from which the functions are transferred following the coming into force of the Order).

The words omitted from para (1)(b) were revoked, and paras (2)(c) and (7) were revoked, by the Financial Services and Markets Act 2000 (Regulated Activities) (Amendment) (No 2) Order 2013, SI 2013/1881, art 28, Schedule, Pt 1, para 35(1), (13), for transitional provisions see arts 29–66 of that Order at **[2.1007]** et seq.

The words in square brackets in paras (2)(b), (4) were substituted by the Transfer of Tribunal Functions Order 2010, SI 2010/22, art 5(2), Sch 3, paras 140, 141 (for transitional provisions and savings in relation to existing cases and appeals from the Financial Services and Markets Tribunal, see Sch 5 to that Order).

Para (5) was revoked by the Transfer of Functions of the Consumer Credit Appeals Tribunal Order 2009, SI 2009/1835, art 4(2), Sch 2, para 1 (for general transitional provisions in connection with the transfer of the functions of the Consumer Credit Appeals Tribunal to the First-tier Tribunal, see Sch 4 to that Order).

See further the note "Transfer of functions and transitional provisions" in the introductory notes to these Regulations.

Criminal offences

[2.514]
45   Offences

(1)   A person [(except an auction platform)] who fails to comply with any requirement in regulation 7(1), (2) or (3), 8(1) or (3), 9(2), 10(1), 11(1)(a), (b) or (c), 14(1), 15(1) or (2), 16(1), (2), (3) or (4), 19(1), (4), (5) or (6), 20(1), (4) or (5), 21, 26, 27(4) or 33 . . . is guilty of an offence and liable—
  (a)   on summary conviction, to a fine not exceeding the statutory maximum;
  (b)   on conviction on indictment, to imprisonment for a term not exceeding two years, to a fine or to both.

[(1A) An auction platform which fails to comply with the customer due diligence requirements of Article 19 or 20(6) of the emission allowance auctioning regulation, the monitoring and record keeping requirements of Article 54 of that regulation, or regulation 20(1), (4) or (5) or 21 of these Regulations, is guilty of an offence and liable—

    (a)   on summary conviction, to a fine not exceeding the statutory maximum;

    (b)   on conviction on indictment, to imprisonment for a term not exceeding two years, to a fine or to both.]

(2) In deciding whether a person has committed an offence under paragraph (1) [or (1A)], the court must consider whether he followed any relevant guidance which was at the time—

    (a)   issued by a supervisory authority or any other appropriate body;

    (b)   approved by the Treasury; and

    (c)   published in a manner approved by the Treasury as suitable in their opinion to bring the guidance to the attention of persons likely to be affected by it.

(3) In paragraph (2), an "appropriate body" means any body which regulates or is representative of any trade, profession, business or employment carried on by the alleged offender.

(4) A person is not guilty of an offence under this regulation if he took all reasonable steps and exercised all due diligence to avoid committing the offence.

(5) Where a person is convicted of an offence under this regulation, he shall not also be liable to a penalty under regulation 42.

NOTES

Words in square brackets in paras (1), (2) inserted, and para (1A) inserted, by the Recognised Auction Platforms Regulations 2011, SI 2011/2699, reg 11(1), (8).

Words omitted from para (1) revoked by the Money Laundering (Amendment) Regulations 2012, SI 2012/2298, regs, 2, 16.

Deferred Prosecution Agreements: as to the application of Deferred Prosecution Agreements to offences under this regulation (ie, an agreement between a designated prosecutor and a person accused of a crime (P) whereby proceedings against P in respect of the alleged offence are automatically suspended as soon as they are instituted if P agrees to comply with certain requirements), see s 45 of, and Sch 17, Pt 1 and Sch 17, Pt 2, para 27 to, the Crime and Courts Act 2013.

[2.515]
46 Prosecution of offences

(1) Proceedings for an offence under regulation 45 may be instituted by—

    (a)   . . . order of the Commissioners;

    (b)   . . .

    (c)   a local weights and measures authority;

    (d)   DETI;

    (e)   the Director of Public Prosecutions; or

    (f)   the Director of Public Prosecutions for Northern Ireland.

(2) Proceedings for an offence under regulation 45 may be instituted only against a relevant person or, where such a person is a body corporate, a partnership or an unincorporated association, against any person who is liable to be proceeded against under regulation 47.

(3) Where proceedings under paragraph (1) are instituted by order of the Commissioners, the proceedings must be brought in the name of an officer of Revenue and Customs.

(4), (5) . . .

(6) A local weights and measures authority must, whenever the [Authority] requires, report in such form and with such particulars as the [Authority] requires on the exercise of its functions under these Regulations.

(7) Where the Commissioners investigate, or propose to investigate, any matter with a view to determining—

    (a)   whether there are grounds for believing that an offence under regulation 45 has been committed by any person; or

    (b)   whether such a person should be prosecuted for such an offence,

that matter is to be treated as an assigned matter within the meaning of section 1(1) of the Customs and Excise Management Act 1979.

(8) Paragraphs (1) and (3) to (6) do not extend to Scotland.

[(9) In its application to the Commissioners acting in Scotland, paragraph (7)(b) shall be read as referring to the Commissioners determining whether to refer the matter to the Crown Office and Procurator Fiscal Service with a view to the Procurator Fiscal determining whether a person should be prosecuted for such an offence.]

NOTES

Words omitted from para (1)(a) revoked by the Public Bodies (Merger of the Director of Public Prosecutions and the Director of Revenue and Customs Prosecutions) Order 2014, SI 2014/834, art 3(3), Sch 3, para 21 (for general transitional provisions, etc, relating to the abolition of the Revenue and Customs Prosecutions Office and the transfer of the functions of the Director of Revenue and Customs Prosecutions to the Director of Public Prosecutions, see arts 4–10 of the 2014 Order).

Paras (1)(b), (4), (5) revoked, and word "Authority" in square brackets (in each place that it occurs in para (6)) substituted, by the Financial Services and Markets Act 2000 (Regulated Activities) (Amendment) (No 2) Order 2013, SI 2013/1881, art 28, Schedule, Pt 1, para 31(1), (14), for transitional provisions see arts 29–66 of that Order at **[2.1007]** et seq.

Para (9) was added by the Money Laundering (Amendment) Regulations 2007, SI 2007/3299, reg 2(f).

[2.516]
47 Offences by bodies corporate etc

(1) If an offence under regulation 45 committed by a body corporate is shown—
   (a)   to have been committed with the consent or the connivance of an officer of the body corporate; or
   (b)   to be attributable to any neglect on his part,
the officer as well as the body corporate is guilty of an offence and liable to be proceeded against and punished accordingly.

(2) If an offence under regulation 45 committed by a partnership is shown—
   (a)   to have been committed with the consent or the connivance of a partner; or
   (b)   to be attributable to any neglect on his part,
the partner as well as the partnership is guilty of an offence and liable to be proceeded against and punished accordingly.

(3) If an offence under regulation 45 committed by an unincorporated association (other than a partnership) is shown—
   (a)   to have been committed with the consent or the connivance of an officer of the association; or
   (b)   to be attributable to any neglect on his part,
that officer as well as the association is guilty of an offence and liable to be proceeded against and punished accordingly.

(4) If the affairs of a body corporate are managed by its members, paragraph (1) applies in relation to the acts and defaults of a member in connection with his functions of management as if he were a director of the body.

(5) Proceedings for an offence alleged to have been committed by a partnership or an unincorporated association must be brought in the name of the partnership or association (and not in that of its members).

(6) A fine imposed on the partnership or association on its conviction of an offence is to be paid out of the funds of the partnership or association.

(7) Rules of court relating to the service of documents are to have effect as if the partnership or association were a body corporate.

(8) In proceedings for an offence brought against the partnership or association—
   (a)   section 33 of the Criminal Justice Act 1925 (procedure on charge of offence against corporation) and Schedule 3 to the Magistrates' Courts Act 1980 (corporations) apply as they do in relation to a body corporate;
   (b)   section 70 (proceedings against bodies corporate) of the Criminal Procedure (Scotland) Act 1995 applies as it does in relation to a body corporate;
   (c)   section 18 of the Criminal Justice (Northern Ireland) Act 1945 (procedure on charge) and Schedule 4 to the Magistrates' Courts (Northern Ireland) Order 1981 (corporations) apply as they do in relation to a body corporate.

(9) In this regulation—
   "officer"—
      (a)   in relation to a body corporate, means a director, manager, secretary, chief executive, member of the committee of management, or a person purporting to act in such a capacity; and
      (b)   in relation to an unincorporated association, means any officer of the association or any member of its governing body, or a person purporting to act in such capacity; and
   "partner" includes a person purporting to act as a partner.

PART 6
MISCELLANEOUS

[2.517]
48 Recovery of charges and penalties through the court

Any charge or penalty imposed on a person by a supervisory authority under regulation 35(1) or 42(1) is a debt due from that person to the authority, and is recoverable accordingly.

[2.518]
49 Obligations on public authorities

(1) The following bodies and persons must, if they know or suspect or have reasonable grounds for knowing or suspecting that a person is or has engaged in money laundering or terrorist financing, as soon as reasonably practicable inform the [National Crime Agency]—
   (a)   the Auditor General for Scotland;
   (b)   the Auditor General for Wales;
   (c)   the Authority;

(d) the Bank of England;

(e) the Comptroller and Auditor General;

(f) the Comptroller and Auditor General for Northern Ireland;

(g) the Gambling Commission;

(h) . . .

(i) the Official Solicitor to the Supreme Court;

(j) the Pensions Regulator;

[(ja) the PRA;]

(k) the Public Trustee;

(l) the Secretary of State, in the exercise of his functions under enactments relating to companies and insolvency;

(m) the Treasury, in the exercise of their functions under the 2000 Act;

(n) the Treasury Solicitor;

(o) a designated professional body for the purposes of Part 20 of the 2000 Act (provision of financial services by members of the professions);

(p) a person or inspector appointed under section 65 (investigations on behalf of Authority) or 66 (inspections and special meetings) of the Friendly Societies Act 1992;

(q) an inspector appointed under section 49 of the Industrial and Provident Societies Act 1965 (appointment of inspectors) or section 18 of the Credit Unions Act 1979 (power to appoint inspector);

(r) an inspector appointed under section 431 (investigation of a company on its own application), 432 (other company investigations), 442 (power to investigate company ownership) or [446D (appointment of replacement inspectors)] of the Companies Act 1985 . . .

(s) a person or inspector appointed under section 55 (investigations on behalf of Authority) or 56 (inspections and special meetings) of the Building Societies Act 1986;

(t) a person appointed under section 167 (appointment of persons to carry out investigations), 168(3) or (5) (appointment of persons to carry out investigations in particular cases), 169(1)(b) (investigations to support overseas regulator) or 284 (power to investigate affairs of a scheme) of the 2000 Act, or under regulations made under section 262(2)(k) (open-ended investment companies) of that Act, to conduct an investigation; and

(u) a person authorised to require the production of documents under section 447 of the Companies Act 1985 (Secretary of State's power to require production of documents), Article 440 of the Companies (Northern Ireland) Order 1986 or section 84 of the Companies Act 1989 (exercise of powers by officer).

(2) A disclosure made under paragraph (1) is not to be taken to breach any restriction on the disclosure of information however imposed.

NOTES

Para (1): words in first pair of square brackets substituted by virtue of the Crime and Courts Act 2013, s 15(3), Sch 8, Pt 4, para 190 (for transitional provisions in connection with the creation of the NCA and the abolition of SOCA, see Sch 8, Part 1 to the 2013 Act); sub-para (h) revoked by the Financial Services and Markets Act 2000 (Regulated Activities) (Amendment) (No 2) Order 2013, SI 2013/1881, art 28, Schedule, Pt 1, para 31(1), (15), for transitional provisions see arts 29–66 of that Order at **[2.1007]** et seq; sub-para (ja) inserted by the Financial Services Act 2012 (Consequential Amendments and Transitional Provisions) Order 2013, SI 2013/472, art 3, Sch 2, para 129(f); words in square brackets in sub-para (r) substituted, and words omitted from that sub-paragraph revoked, by the Companies Act 2006 (Consequential Amendments and Transitional Provisions) Order 2011, SI 2011/1265, art 30.

Industrial and Provident Societies Act 1965: repealed by the Co-operative and Community Benefit Societies Act 2014.

[2.519]

[49A Disclosure by the Commissioners

(1) The Commissioners may disclose to the Authority information held in connection with their functions under these Regulations if the disclosure is made for the purpose of enabling or assisting the Authority to discharge any of its functions under the Payment Services Regulations 2009 [or the Electronic Money Regulations 2011].

(2) Information disclosed to the Authority under subsection (1) may not be disclosed by the Authority or any person who receives the information directly or indirectly from the Authority except—

(a) to, or in accordance with authority given by, the Commissioners;

(b) with a view to the institution of, or otherwise for the purposes of, any criminal proceedings;

(c) with a view to the institution of any other proceedings by the Authority, for the purposes of any such proceedings instituted by the Authority, or for the purposes of any reference to the Tribunal under the Payment Services Regulations 2009; or

(d) in the form of a summary or collection of information so framed as not to enable information relating to any particular person to be ascertained from it.

(3) Any person who discloses information in contravention of subsection (2) is guilty of an offence and liable—

(a) on summary conviction, to imprisonment for a term not exceeding three months, to a fine not exceeding the statutory maximum, or to both;

(b) on conviction on indictment, to imprisonment for a term not exceeding two years to a fine, or to both.

(4) It is a defence for a person charged with an offence under this regulation of disclosing information to prove that they reasonably believed

(a) that the disclosure was lawful; or

(b) that the information had already and lawfully been made available to the public.]

NOTES

Inserted by the Payment Services Regulations 2009, SI 2009/209, reg 126, Sch 6, Pt 2, para 6(g).

Para (1): words in square brackets inserted by the Electronic Money Regulations 2011, SI 2011/99, reg 79, Sch 4, Pt 2, para 19(g).

[2.520]
50 Transitional provisions: requirement to be registered

(1) Regulation 26 does not apply to an existing money service business, an existing trust or company service provider[, an existing high value dealer, an existing bill payment service provider or an existing telecommunication, digital and IT payment service provider] until—

(a) where it has applied in accordance with regulation 27 before the specified date for registration in a register maintained under regulation 25(1) (a "new register")—

(i) the date it is included in a new register following the determination of its application by the Commissioners; or

(ii) where the Commissioners give it notice under regulation 29(2)(b) of their decision not to register it, the date on which the Commissioners state that the decision takes effect or, where a statement is included in accordance with paragraph (3)(b), the time at which the Commissioners give it such notice;

(b) in any other case, the specified date.

(2) The specified date is—

(a) in the case of an existing money service business, 1st February 2008;

(b) in the case of an existing trust or company service provider, 1st April 2008;

(c) in the case of an existing high value dealer, the first anniversary which falls on or after 1st January 2008 of the date of its registration in a register maintained under regulation 10 of the Money Laundering Regulations 2003;

[(d) in the case of an existing bill payment service provider or an existing telecommunication, digital and IT payment service provider, 1st March 2010.]

(3) In the case of an application for registration in a new register made before the specified date by an existing money service business, an existing trust or company service provider[, an existing high value dealer, an existing bill payment service provider or an existing telecommunication, digital and IT payment service provider], the Commissioners must include in a notice given to it under regulation 29(2)(b)—

(a) the date on which their decision is to take effect; or

(b) if the Commissioners consider that the interests of the public require their decision to have immediate effect, a statement to that effect and the reasons for it.

(4) In the case of an application for registration in a new register made before the specified date by an existing money services business or an existing trust or company service provider, the Commissioners must give it a notice under regulation 29(2) by—

(a) in the case of an existing money service business, 1st June 2008;

(b) in the case of an existing trust or company service provider, 1st July 2008; or

(c) where applicable, 45 days beginning with the date on which they receive any further information required under regulation 27(3).

(5) In this regulation—

["existing bill payment service provider" and "existing telecommunication, digital and IT payment service provider" mean a bill payment service provider or a telecommunication, digital and IT payment service provider carrying on business in the United Kingdom immediately before 1st November 2009;]

"existing money service business" and an "existing high value dealer" mean a money service business or a high value dealer which, immediately before 15th December 2007, was included in a register maintained under regulation 10 of the Money Laundering Regulations 2003;

"existing trust or company service provider" means a trust or company service provider carrying on business in the United Kingdom immediately before 15th December 2007.

NOTES

Para (1): words in square brackets substituted by the Payment Services Regulations 2009, SI 2009/209, reg 126, Sch 6, Pt 2, para 6(h)(i).

Para (2): sub-para (d) inserted by SI 2009/209, reg 126, Sch 6, Pt 2, para 6(h)(ii).

Para (3): words in square brackets substituted by SI 2009/209, reg 126, Sch 6, Pt 2, para 6(h)(iii).

Para (5): definition "existing bill payment service provider" and "existing telecommunication, digital and IT payment service provider" inserted by SI 2009/209, reg 126, Sch 6, Pt 2, para 6(h)(iv).

51 (*Introduces Sch 6 (outside the scope of this work).*)

SCHEDULES

SCHEDULE 1
[ACTIVITIES LISTED IN POINTS 2 TO 12, 14 AND 15 OF ANNEX 1 TO THE CAPITAL REQUIREMENTS DIRECTIVE]

Regulation 3(3)(a)

[2.521]

2. Lending including, inter alia: consumer credit, mortgage credit, factoring, with or without recourse, financing of commercial transactions (including forfeiting).

3. Financial leasing.

[4. Payment services as defined in Article 4(3) of Directive 2007/64/EC of the European Parliament and of the Council of 13 November 2007 on payment services in the internal market.

5. Issuing and administering other means of payment (including travellers' cheques and bankers' drafts) insofar as this activity is not covered by point 4.]

6. Guarantees and commitments.

7. Trading for own account or for account of customers in:
    (a)   money market instruments (cheques, bills, certificates of deposit, etc);
    (b)   foreign exchange;
    (c)   financial futures and options;
    (d)   exchange and interest-rate instruments; or
    (e)   transferable securities.

8. Participation in securities issues and the provision of services related to such issues.

9. Advice to undertakings on capital structure, industrial strategy and related questions and advice as well as services relating to mergers and the purchase of undertakings.

10. Money broking.

11. Portfolio management and advice.

12. Safekeeping and administration of securities.

14. Safe custody services.

[15. Issuing electronic money.]

NOTES

Schedule heading: substituted by the Capital Requirements Regulations 2013, SI 2013/3115, reg 46(1), Sch 2, Pt 3, para 68(1), (4).
Paras 4, 5: substituted by the Payment Services Regulations 2009, SI 2009/209, reg 126, Sch 6, Pt 2, para 6(i).
Para 15: added by SI 2011/99, reg 79, Sch 4, Pt 2, para 19(h)(ii).

SCHEDULE 2
FINANCIAL ACTIVITY, SIMPLIFIED DUE DILIGENCE AND POLITICALLY EXPOSED PERSONS

Regulations 4(1)(e) and (2), 13(6) and (8) and 14(5)

[2.522]
1   Financial activity on an occasional or very limited basis

For the purposes of regulation 4(1)(e) and (2), a person is to be considered as engaging in financial activity on an occasional or very limited basis if all the following conditions are fulfilled—
    (a)   the person's total annual turnover in respect of the financial activity does not exceed £64,000;
    (b)   the financial activity is limited in relation to any customer to no more than one transaction exceeding 1,000 euro, whether the transaction is carried out in a single operation, or a series of operations which appear to be linked;
    (c)   the financial activity does not exceed 5% of the person's total annual turnover;
    (d)   the financial activity is ancillary and directly related to the person's main activity;
    (e)   the financial activity is not the transmission or remittance of money (or any representation of monetary value) by any means;
    (f)   the person's main activity is not that of a person falling within regulation 3(1)(a) to (f) or (h);

Part 2   Statutory Instruments

    (g)   the financial activity is provided only to customers of the person's main activity and is not offered to the public.

2   Simplified due diligence

For the purposes of regulation 13(6), the conditions are—

    (a)   the authority has been entrusted with public functions pursuant to the [Treaty on European Union, the Treaty on the Functioning of the European Union or EU secondary legislation];

    (b)   the authority's identity is publicly available, transparent and certain;

    (c)   the activities of the authority and its accounting practices are transparent;

    (d)   either the authority is accountable to a Community institution or to the authorities of an EEA state, or otherwise appropriate check and balance procedures exist ensuring control of the authority's activity.

3 For the purposes of regulation 13(8), the conditions are—

    (a)   the product has a written contractual base;

    (b)   any related transaction is carried out through an account of the customer with a credit institution which is subject to the money laundering directive or with a credit institution situated in a non-EEA state which imposes requirements equivalent to those laid down in that directive;

    (c)   the product or related transaction is not anonymous and its nature is such that it allows for the timely application of customer due diligence measures where there is a suspicion of money laundering or terrorist financing;

    (d)   the product is within the following maximum threshold—

        (i)   in the case of insurance policies or savings products of a similar nature, the annual premium is no more than 1,000 euro or there is a single premium of no more than 2,500 euro;

        (ii)   in the case of products which are related to the financing of physical assets where the legal and beneficial title of the assets is not transferred to the customer until the termination of the contractual relationship (whether the transaction is carried out in a single operation or in several operations which appear to be linked), the annual payments do not exceed 15,000 euro;

        (iii)   in all other cases, the maximum threshold is 15,000 euro;

    (e)   the benefits of the product or related transaction cannot be realised for the benefit of third parties, except in the case of death, disablement, survival to a predetermined advanced age, or similar events;

    (f)   in the case of products or related transactions allowing for the investment of funds in financial assets or claims, including insurance or other kinds of contingent claims—

        (i)   the benefits of the product or related transaction are only realisable in the long term;

        (ii)   the product or related transaction cannot be used as collateral; and

        (iii)   during the contractual relationship, no accelerated payments are made, surrender clauses used or early termination takes place.

4   Politically exposed persons

(1)   For the purposes of regulation 14(5)—

    (a)   individuals who are or have been entrusted with prominent public functions include the following—

        (i)   heads of state, heads of government, ministers and deputy or assistant ministers;

        (ii)   members of parliaments;

        (iii)   members of supreme courts, of constitutional courts or of other high-level judicial bodies whose decisions are not generally subject to further appeal, other than in exceptional circumstances;

        (iv)   members of courts of auditors or of the boards of central banks;

        (v)   ambassadors, chargés d'affaires and high-ranking officers in the armed forces; and

        (vi)   members of the administrative, management or supervisory bodies of state-owned enterprises;

    (b)   the categories set out in paragraphs (i) to (vi) of sub-paragraph (a) do not include middle-ranking or more junior officials;

    (c)   immediate family members include the following—

        (i)   a spouse;

        (ii)   a partner;

        (iii)   children and their spouses or partners; and

        (iv)   parents;

    (d)   persons known to be close associates include the following—

        (i)   any individual who is known to have joint beneficial ownership of a legal entity or legal arrangement, or any other close business relations, with a person referred to in regulation 14(5)(a); and

        (ii)   any individual who has sole beneficial ownership of a legal entity or legal arrangement which is known to have been set up for the benefit of a person referred to in regulation 14(5)(a).

(2)   In paragraph (1)(c), "partner" means a person who is considered by his national law as equivalent to a spouse.

NOTES

Para 2: words in square brackets substituted by the Treaty of Lisbon (Changes in Terminology or Numbering) Order 2012, SI 2012/1809, art 3, Schedule, Pt 2.

References to the European Community and related expressions: see the note "References to "the European Community", "Community", etc" in the introductory notes to these Regulations.

[SCHEDULE 3
PROFESSIONAL BODIES

Regulations 17(2)(b), 23(1)(c) and 32(4)

[2.523]

1   Association of Accounting Technicians

2   Association of Chartered Certified Accountants

3   Association of International Accountants

4   Association of Taxation Technicians

[4A Chartered Institute of Legal Executives]

5   Chartered Institute of Management Accountants

6   . . .

7   Chartered Institute of Taxation

8   Council for Licensed Conveyancers

9   Faculty of Advocates

10 Faculty Office of the Archbishop of Canterbury

11 General Council of the Bar

12 General Council of the Bar of Northern Ireland

13 Insolvency Practitioners Association

14 Institute of Certified Bookkeepers

15 Institute of Chartered Accountants in England and Wales

16 Institute of Chartered Accountants in Ireland

17 Institute of Chartered Accountants of Scotland

18 Institute of Financial Accountants

19 International Association of Book-keepers

20 Law Society

21 Law Society of Northern Ireland

22 Law Society of Scotland]

NOTES

Substituted by the Money Laundering (Amendment) Regulations 2012, SI 2012/2298, regs, 2, 17, Schedule.
Para 4A inserted, and para 6 revoked, by the Money Laundering (Amendment) Regulations 2015, SI 2015/11, regs, 2, 3.

SCHEDULE 4
CONNECTED PERSONS

Regulation 37(2)

Corporate bodies

[2.524]

1. If the relevant person is a body corporate ("BC"), a person who is or has been—

(a)   an officer or manager of BC or of a parent undertaking of BC;

(b)   an employee of BC;

(c)   an agent of BC or of a parent undertaking of BC

Partnerships

2. If the relevant person is a partnership, a person who is or has been a member, manager, employee or agent of the partnership.

Unincorporated associations

3. If the relevant person is an unincorporated association of persons which is not a partnership, a person who is or has been an officer, manager, employee or agent of the association.

Individuals

4. If the relevant person is an individual, a person who is or has been an employee or agent of that individual.

SCHEDULE 5
MODIFICATIONS IN RELATION TO APPEALS

Regulation 44(8)

PART 1
PRIMARY LEGISLATION

[2.525]
1   The Value Added Tax Act 1994 (c 23)
[Part 5 of the Value Added Tax Act 1994 (appeals) is modified by omitting sections 83A to 84, 85A and 85B.]

2   The Financial Services and Markets Act 2000 (c 8)
Part 9 of the 2000 Act (hearings and appeals) is modified as follows—
   (a)   in the application of [sections 133 to 133B] to any appeal commenced before the coming into force of section 55 of the Consumer Credit Act 2006, for all the references to "the Authority", substitute "the Authority or the OFT (as the case may be)";
  [(aa) in section 133(7A), after paragraph (n), insert—

      "(o) a decision to impose a penalty under regulation 42 of the Money Laundering Regulations 2007.]

   (b)   . . .
   [(c) in section 133A omit subsections (1), (2), (3) and (5);] and
   (d)   in [section 133A(4)] for "decision notice" in both places where it occurs substitute "notice under regulation 34(5) or (9) or 42(7) of the Money Laundering Regulations 2007".

NOTES
Para 1: substituted by the Transfer of Tribunal Functions and Revenue and Customs Appeals Order 2009, SI 2009/56, art 3, Sch 2, paras 168, 175, subject to transitional provisions and savings in Sch 3 to the 2009 Order.
Para 2: words in square brackets in sub-paras (a), (d) and sub-para (c) substituted, and sub-para (b) revoked, by the Transfer of Tribunal Functions Order 2010, SI 2010/22, art 5(2), Sch 3, paras 140, 142(a), subject to transitional provisions and savings in Sch 5 thereto; sub-para (aa) inserted by the Financial Services Act 2012 (Consequential Amendments and Transitional Provisions) Order 2013, SI 2013/472, art 3, Sch 2, para 129(g).
Note: the Consumer Credit Act 2006, s 55 came into force for certain purposes on 1 December 2007 and 6 April 2008 (see the Consumer Credit Act 2006 (Commencement No 3) Order 2007, SI 2007/3300). Note also that it was repealed by SI 2009/1835, as from 1 September 2009.

(Sch 5, Pt 2 revoked by the Transfer of Tribunal Functions Order 2010, SI 2010/22, art 5(2), Sch 3, paras 140, 142(b), subject to transitional provisions and savings in Sch 5 thereto.)

SCHEDULE 6

(Sch 6 (Minor and Consequential Amendments) outside the scope of this work.)

BUSINESS PROTECTION FROM MISLEADING MARKETING
REGULATIONS 2008

(SI 2008/1276)

NOTES
Made: 8 May 2008.
Authority: European Communities Act 1972, s 2(2).
Commencement: 26 May 2008.

ARRANGEMENT OF REGULATIONS

PART 1
DEFINITIONS AND PROHIBITIONS

PART 1
DEFINITIONS AND PROHIBITIONS

[2.526]
1   Citation and Commencement

These Regulations may be cited as the Business Protection from Misleading Marketing Regulations 2008 and shall come into force on 26th May 2008.

[2.527]
2   Interpretation

(1)   In these Regulations—

"advertising" means any form of representation which is made in connection with a trade, business, craft or profession in order to promote the supply or transfer of a product and "advertiser" shall be construed accordingly;

["CMA" means the Competition and Markets Authority;]

"code owner" means a trader or a body responsible for—

(a)   the formulation and revision of a code of conduct; or

(b)   monitoring compliance with the code by those who have undertaken to be bound by it;

"comparative advertising" means advertising which in any way, either explicitly or by implication, identifies a competitor or a product offered by a competitor;

"court", in relation to England and Wales and Northern Ireland, means a county court or the High Court, and, in relation to Scotland, the sheriff or the Court of Session;

Part 2   Statutory Instruments

["DETINI" means the Department of Enterprise, Trade and Investment in Northern Ireland;]

["enforcement authority" means the [CMA], every local weights and measures authority, DETINI and GEMA;]

["GEMA" means the Gas and Electricity Markets Authority;]

"goods" includes ships, aircraft, animals, things attached to land and growing crops;

["local weights and measures authority" means a local weights and measures authority in Great Britain (within the meaning of section 69 of the Weights and Measures Act 1985);]

. . .

"premises" includes any place and any stall, vehicle, ship or aircraft;

"product" means any goods or services and includes immovable property, rights and obligations;

"ship" includes any boat and any other description of vessel used in navigation; and

"trader" means any person who is acting for purposes relating to his trade, craft, business or profession and anyone acting in the name of or on behalf of a trader.

(2) (*Applies to Scotland only.*)

NOTES

Para (1): definition "CMA" inserted, in definition "enforcement authority" reference in square brackets substituted, and definition "OFT" (omitted) revoked by the Enterprise and Regulatory Reform Act 2013 (Competition) (Consequential, Transitional and Saving Provisions) (No 2) Order 2014, SI 2014/549, art 2, Sch 1, Pt 2, para 34(1), (2) (for transitional provisions in relation to the continuity of functions, etc, see art 3 of the 2014 Order); definitions "DETINI" and "local weights and measures authority" inserted by the Public Bodies (The Office of Fair Trading Transfer of Consumer Advice Scheme Function and Modification of Enforcement Functions) Order 2013, SI 2013/783, art 12(1), (2)(a), (c); definition "enforcement authority" substituted, and definition "GEMA" inserted, by the Business Protection from Misleading Marketing (Amendment) Regulations 2013, SI 2013/2701, regs 2, 3.

[2.528]
3 Prohibition of advertising which misleads traders

(1) Advertising which is misleading is prohibited.

(2) Advertising is misleading which—
- (a) in any way, including its presentation, deceives or is likely to deceive the traders to whom it is addressed or whom it reaches; and by reason of its deceptive nature, is likely to affect their economic behaviour; or
- (b) for those reasons, injures or is likely to injure a competitor.

(3) In determining whether advertising is misleading, account shall be taken of all its features, and in particular of any information it contains concerning—
- (a) the characteristics of the product (as defined in paragraph (4));
- (b) the price or manner in which the price is calculated;
- (c) the conditions on which the product is supplied or provided; and
- (d) the nature, attributes and rights of the advertiser (as defined in paragraph (5)).

(4) In paragraph (3)(a) the "characteristics of the product" include—
- (a) availability of the product;
- (b) nature of the product;
- (c) execution of the product;
- (d) composition of the product;
- (e) method and date of manufacture of the product;
- (f) method and date of provision of the product;
- (g) fitness for purpose of the product;
- (h) uses of the product;
- (i) quantity of the product;
- (j) specification of the product;
- (k) geographical or commercial origin of the product;
- (l) results to be expected from use of the product; or
- (m) results and material features of tests or checks carried out on the product.

(5) In paragraph (3)(d) the "nature, attributes and rights" of the advertiser include the advertiser's—
- (a) identity;
- (b) assets;
- (c) qualifications;
- (d) ownership of industrial, commercial or intellectual property rights; or
- (e) awards and distinctions.

[2.529]
4 Comparative advertising

Comparative advertising shall, as far as the comparison is concerned, be permitted only when the following conditions are met—
- (a) it is not misleading under regulation 3;

(b)   it is not a misleading action under regulation 5 of the Consumer Protection from Unfair Trading Regulations 2008 or a misleading omission under regulation 6 of those Regulations;

(c)   it compares products meeting the same needs or intended for the same purpose;

(d)   it objectively compares one or more material, relevant, verifiable and representative features of those products, which may include price;

(e)   it does not create confusion among traders—
    (i)   between the advertiser and a competitor, or
    (ii)   between the trade marks, trade names, other distinguishing marks or products of the advertiser and those of a competitor;

(f)   it does not discredit or denigrate the trade marks, trade names, other distinguishing marks, products, activities, or circumstances of a competitor;

(g)   for products with designation of origin, it relates in each case to products with the same designation;

(h)   it does not take unfair advantage of the reputation of a trade mark, trade name or other distinguishing marks of a competitor or of the designation of origin of competing products;

(i)   it does not present products as imitations or replicas of products bearing a protected trade mark or trade name.

[2.530]
5   Promotion of misleading advertising and comparative advertising which is not permitted
A code owner shall not promote in a code of conduct—
    (a)   advertising which is misleading under regulation 3; or
    (b)   comparative advertising which is not permitted under regulation 4.

PART 2
OFFENCES

[2.531]
6   Misleading advertising
A trader is guilty of an offence if he engages in advertising which is misleading under regulation 3.

[2.532]
7   Penalty for offence under regulation 6
A person guilty of an offence under regulation 6 shall be liable—
    (a)   on summary conviction, to a fine not exceeding the statutory maximum; or
    (b)   on conviction on indictment, to a fine or imprisonment for a term not exceeding two years or both.

[2.533]
8   Offences committed by bodies of persons
(1)   Where an offence under these Regulations committed by a body corporate is proved—
    (a)   to have been committed with the consent or connivance of an officer of the body, or
    (b)   to be attributable to any neglect on his part,
the officer as well as the body corporate is guilty of the offence and liable to be proceeded against and punished accordingly.

(2)   In paragraph (1) a reference to an officer of a body corporate includes a reference to—
    (a)   a director, manager, secretary or other similar officer; and
    (b)   a person purporting to act as a director, manager, secretary or other similar officer.

(3)   Where an offence under these Regulations committed by a Scottish partnership is proved—
    (a)   to have been committed with the consent or connivance of a partner, or
    (b)   to be attributable to any neglect on his part,
the partner as well as the partnership is guilty of the offence and liable to be proceeded against and punished accordingly.

(4)   In paragraph (3) a reference to a partner includes a person purporting to act as a partner.

[2.534]
9   Offence due to the default of another person
(1)   This regulation applies where a person "X"—
    (a)   commits an offence under regulation 6, or
    (b)   would have committed an offence under regulation 6 but for a defence under regulation 11 or 12,
and the commission of the offence, or of what would have been an offence but for X being able to rely on a defence under regulations 11 or 12, is due to the act or default of some other person "Y".

(2)   Where this regulation applies Y shall be guilty of the offence subject to regulations 11 and 12 whether or not Y is a trader and whether or not Y's act or default is advertising.

(3)   Y may be charged with and convicted of the offence by virtue of paragraph (2) whether or not proceedings are taken against X.

[2.535]
10   Time limit for prosecution

(1)   No proceedings for an offence under these Regulations shall be commenced after—
  (a)   the end of the period of three years beginning with the date of the commission of the offence; or
  (b)   the end of the period of one year beginning with the date of discovery of the offence by the prosecutor,
whichever is earlier.

(2)   For the purposes of paragraph (1)(b) a certificate signed by or on behalf of the prosecutor and stating the date on which the offence was discovered by him shall be conclusive evidence of that fact and a certificate stating that matter and purporting to be so signed shall be treated as so signed unless the contrary is proved.

(3)   Notwithstanding anything in section 127(1) of the Magistrates' Courts Act 1980, an information relating to an offence under these Regulations which is triable by a magistrates' court in England and Wales may be so tried if it is laid at any time before the end of the period of twelve months beginning with the date of the commission of the offence.

(4)   Notwithstanding anything in section 136 of the Criminal Procedure (Scotland) Act 1995 summary proceedings in Scotland for an offence under these Regulations may be commenced at any time before the end of the period of twelve months beginning with the date of the commission of the offence.

(5)   For the purposes of paragraph (4), section 136(3) of the Criminal Procedure (Scotland) Act 1995 shall apply as it applies for the purposes of that section.

(6)   Notwithstanding anything in Article 19(1) of the Magistrates' Courts (Northern Ireland) Order 1981 a complaint charging an offence under these Regulations which is triable by a magistrates' court in Northern Ireland may be so tried if it is made at any time before the end of the period of twelve months beginning with the date of the commission of the offence.

[2.536]
11   Due diligence defence

(1)   In any proceedings against a person for an offence under regulation 6 it is a defence for that person to prove—
  (a)   that the commission of the offence was due to—
    (i)   a mistake;
    (ii)   reliance on information supplied to him by another person;
    (iii)   the act or default of another person;
    (iv)   an accident; or
    (v)   another cause beyond his control;
    and
  (b)   that he took all reasonable precautions and exercised all due diligence to avoid the commission of such an offence by himself or any person under his control.

(2)   A person shall not be entitled to rely on the defence provided by paragraph (1) by reason of the matters referred to in paragraph (ii) or (iii) of paragraph (1)(a) without the leave of the court unless—
  (a)   he has served on the prosecutor a notice in writing giving such information identifying or assisting in the identification of that other person as was in his possession; and
  (b)   the notice is served on the prosecutor at least seven clear days before the date of the hearing.

[2.537]
12   Innocent publication defence

In any proceedings against a person for an offence under regulation 6 committed by the publication of advertising it is a defence for that person to prove that—
  (a)   he is a person whose business it is to publish or to arrange for the publication of advertising;
  (b)   he received the advertising for publication in the ordinary course of business; and
  (c)   he did not know and had no reason to suspect that its publication would amount to an offence under regulation 6.

PART 3
ENFORCEMENT

[2.538]
13   [Duty and power to enforce]

[(1)   It shall be the duty of every local weights and measures authority and DETINI to enforce these Regulations.

[(1A)   Each of the following may also enforce these Regulations—
  (a)   the [CMA];

(b)   GEMA.]]

(2)   Where an enforcement authority is a local weights and measures authority the duty referred to in paragraph (1) shall apply to the enforcement of these Regulations within the authority's area.

(3)   Where the enforcement authority is the Department of Enterprise, Trade and Investment in Northern Ireland the duty referred to in paragraph (1) shall apply to the enforcement of these Regulations within Northern Ireland.

(4)   [In determining how to comply with paragraph (1), or as the case may be, paragraph (1A)] every enforcement authority shall have regard to the desirability of encouraging control of advertising which is misleading under regulation 3 and comparative advertising which is not permitted under regulation 4 by such established means as it considers appropriate having regard to all the circumstances of the particular case.

[(4A)   Nothing in this regulation shall authorise GEMA to bring proceedings for an offence.]

(5)   Nothing in this regulation shall authorise any enforcement authority to bring proceedings in Scotland for an offence.

NOTES

Provision heading substituted by the Public Bodies (The Office of Fair Trading Transfer of Consumer Advice Scheme Function and Modification of Enforcement Functions) Order 2013, SI 2013/783, art 12(1), (3).

Para (1): substituted, together with para (1A), for para (1) as originally enacted, by SI 2013/783, art 12(1), (4).

Para (1A): substituted as noted above, further substituted by the Business Protection from Misleading Marketing (Amendment) Regulations 2013, SI 2013/2701, regs 2, 4(a); in sub-para (a) reference in square brackets substituted by the Enterprise and Regulatory Reform Act 2013 (Competition) (Consequential, Transitional and Saving Provisions) (No 2) Order 2014, SI 2014/549, SI 2014/549, art 2, Sch 1, Pt 2, para 34(1), (3) (for transitional provisions in relation to the continuity of functions, etc, see art 3 of the 2014 Order).

Para (4): words in square brackets substituted by SI 2013/783, art 12(1), (5).

Para (4A): inserted by SI 2013/2701, regs 2, 4(b).

[2.539]
14   Notice to [CMA] of intended prosecution

(1)   Where an enforcement authority is a local weights and measures authority in England and Wales it may bring proceedings for an offence under regulation 6 only if—

(a)   it has notified the [CMA] of its intention to bring proceedings at least fourteen days before the date on which proceedings are brought; or

(b)   the [CMA] consents to proceedings being brought in a shorter period.

(2)   The enforcement authority must also notify the [CMA] of the outcome of the proceedings after they are finally determined.

(3)   Such proceedings are not invalid by reason only of the failure to comply with this regulation.

NOTES

References in square brackets substituted by the Enterprise and Regulatory Reform Act 2013 (Competition) (Consequential, Transitional and Saving Provisions) (No 2) Order 2014, SI 2014/549, art 2, Sch 1, Pt 2, para 34(1), (4) (for transitional provisions in relation to the continuity of functions, etc, see art 3 of the 2014 Order).

[2.540]
15   Injunctions to secure compliance with the Regulations

(1)   This regulation applies where an enforcement authority considers that there has been or is likely to be a breach of regulation 3, 4 or 5.

(2)   Where this regulation applies an enforcement authority may, subject to paragraph (3), if it thinks it appropriate to do so, bring proceedings for an injunction (in which proceedings it may also apply for an interim injunction) against any person appearing to it to be concerned or likely to be concerned with the breach.

(3)   Where the enforcement authority is a local weights and measures authority in Great Britain [or GEMA] it may apply for an injunction only if—

(a)   it has notified the [CMA] of its intention to apply for an injunction at least fourteen days before the date on which the application is made; or

(b)   the [CMA] consents to the application for an injunction being made within a shorter period.

(4)   Proceedings referred to in paragraph (2) are not invalid by reason only of the failure to comply with paragraph (3).

NOTES

Para (3): words in first pair of square brackets inserted by the Business Protection from Misleading Marketing (Amendment) Regulations 2013, SI 2013/2701, regs 2, 5; references in second and final pairs of square brackets substituted by the Enterprise and Regulatory Reform Act 2013 (Competition) (Consequential, Transitional and Saving Provisions) (No 2) Order 2014, SI 2014/549, art 2, Sch 1, Pt 2, para 34(1), (5) (for transitional provisions in relation to the continuity of functions, etc, see art 3 of the 2014 Order).

Part 2   Statutory Instruments

[2.541]
16 Undertakings

Where an enforcement authority considers that there has been or is likely to be a breach of regulation 3, 4 or 5 it may accept from the person concerned or likely to be concerned with the breach an undertaking that he will comply with those regulations.

[2.542]
17 Co-ordination

[(1) If more than one enforcement authority in Great Britain is contemplating bringing proceedings under regulation 15 in any particular case, the [CMA] may direct which enforcement authority is to bring the proceedings or decide that only it may do so.]

(2) Where the [CMA] directs that only it may bring such proceedings it may take into account whether compliance with regulation 3, 4 or 5 could be achieved by other means in deciding whether to bring proceedings.

NOTES

Para (1): substituted by the Business Protection from Misleading Marketing (Amendment) Regulations 2013, SI 2013/2701, regs 2, 6; reference in square brackets substituted by the Enterprise and Regulatory Reform Act 2013 (Competition) (Consequential, Transitional and Saving Provisions) (No 2) Order 2014, SI 2014/549, art 2, Sch 1, Pt 2, para 34(1), (6) (for transitional provisions in relation to the continuity of functions, etc, see art 3 of the 2014 Order).

Para (2): reference in square brackets substituted by SI 2014/549, art 2, Sch 1, Pt 2, para 34(1), (6) (for transitional provisions in relation to the continuity of functions, etc, see art 3 of the 2014 Order).

[2.543]
18 Powers of the court

(1) The court on an application by an enforcement authority may grant an injunction on such terms as it may think fit to secure compliance with regulation 3, 4 or 5.

(2) Before granting an injunction the court shall have regard to all the interests involved and in particular the public interest.

(3) An injunction may relate not only to particular advertising but to any advertising in similar terms or likely to convey a similar impression.

(4) The court may also require any person against whom an injunction (other than an interim injunction) is granted to publish in such form and manner and to such extent as the court thinks appropriate for the purpose of eliminating any continuing effects of the advertising—
  (a) the injunction; and
  (b) a corrective statement.

(5) In considering an application for an injunction the court may require the person named in the application to provide evidence as to the accuracy of any factual claim made as part of the advertising of that person if, taking into account the legitimate interests of that person and any other party to the proceedings, it appears appropriate in the circumstances.

(6) If, having been required under paragraph (5) to provide evidence as to the accuracy of a factual claim, a person—
  (a) fails to provide such evidence, or
  (b) provides evidence as to the accuracy of the factual claim that the court considers inadequate,
the court may consider that the factual claim is inaccurate.

(7) The court may grant an injunction even where there is no evidence of proof of actual loss or damage or of intention or negligence on the part of the advertiser.

[2.544]
19 Notifications of undertakings and orders to the [CMA]

An enforcement authority, other than the [CMA], shall notify the [CMA]—
  (a) of any undertaking given to it under regulation 16;
  (b) of the outcome of any application made by it under regulation 15 and the terms of any order made by the court; and
  (c) of the outcome of any application made by it to enforce a previous order of the court.

NOTES

References in square brackets substituted by the Enterprise and Regulatory Reform Act 2013 (Competition) (Consequential, Transitional and Saving Provisions) (No 2) Order 2014, SI 2014/549, art 2, Sch 1, Pt 2, para 34(1), (7) (for transitional provisions in relation to the continuity of functions, etc, see art 3 of the 2014 Order).

[2.545]
20 Publication, information and advice

(1) The [CMA] must arrange for the publication, in such form and manner as it considers appropriate, of—
  (a) details of any undertaking or order notified to it under regulation 19;
  (b) details of any undertaking given to it under regulation 16;

(c)   details of any application made by it under regulation 15 and of the terms of any undertaking given to, or order made by, the court;

(d)   details of any application made by it to enforce a previous order of the court.

(2)   [An enforcement authority] may arrange for the dissemination, in such form and manner as it considers appropriate, of such information and advice concerning the operation of these Regulations as appear to it to be expedient to give to the public and to all persons likely to be affected by these Regulations.

NOTES

Para (1): reference in square brackets substituted by the Enterprise and Regulatory Reform Act 2013 (Competition) (Consequential, Transitional and Saving Provisions) (No 2) Order 2014, SI 2014/549, art 2, Sch 1, Pt 2, para 34(1), (8) (for transitional provisions in relation to the continuity of functions, etc, see art 3 of the 2014 Order).

Para (2): words in square brackets substituted by the Public Bodies (The Office of Fair Trading Transfer of Consumer Advice Scheme Function and Modification of Enforcement Functions) Order 2013, SI 2013/783, SI 2013/783, art 12(1), (6).

PART 4
INVESTIGATION POWERS

[2.546]
21   Powers of Enforcement Authorities to obtain information
(1)   For the purpose of determining whether to bring proceedings for an injunction under regulation 15, an enforcement authority may by notice in writing require a person to provide to it such information as may be specified or described in the notice or to produce to it any documents so specified or described.

(2)   A notice under paragraph (1) may—
(a)   specify the way in which and the time within which it is to be complied with; and
(b)   be varied or revoked by a subsequent notice.

(3)   Nothing in this regulation gives an enforcement authority any power to require another person to provide or produce any information or document which the other person would be entitled to refuse to provide or produce in proceedings in the High Court on the grounds of legal professional privilege or (in Scotland) in proceedings in the Court of Session on the grounds of confidentiality of communications.

(4)   In paragraph (3) "communications" means—
(a)   communications between a professional legal adviser and his client; or
(b)   communications made in connection with or in contemplation of legal proceedings and for the purposes of those proceedings.

(5)   Nothing in this regulation shall be construed as requiring a person to provide information if to do so might incriminate him.

(6)   If a person does not comply with a notice under paragraph (1) the court may, on the application of an enforcement authority, make such order as the court thinks fit for requiring the default to be made good, and any such order may provide that all the costs or expenses of and incidental to the application shall be borne by the person in default or by any officers of a company or other association who are responsible for its default.

NOTES

Revoked, together with regs 22–27, by the Consumer Rights Act 2015 (Commencement No 3, Transitional Provisions, Savings and Consequential Amendments) Order 2015, SI 2015/1630, art 5, Sch 2, paras 111, 112, as from 1 October 2015 (for transitional provisions see arts 6–8 thereof at **[2.1220]** et seq).

[2.547]
22   Power to make test purchases
An enforcement authority[, other than GEMA,] may or may authorise any of its officers on its behalf to—
(a)   make a purchase of a product; or
(b)   enter into an agreement to secure the provision of a product,
for the purposes of determining whether these Regulations are being complied with.

NOTES

Revoked as noted to reg 21 at **[2.546]**.

Words in square brackets inserted by the Business Protection from Misleading Marketing (Amendment) Regulations 2013, SI 2013/2701, regs 2, 7.

[2.548]
23   Power of entry and investigation, etc
(1)   A duly authorised officer of an enforcement authority[, other than GEMA,] may at all reasonable hours exercise the following powers—

Part 2   Statutory Instruments

(a) he may, for the purpose of ascertaining whether a breach of these Regulations has been committed, inspect any goods and enter any premises other than premises used only as a dwelling;

(b) if he has reasonable cause to suspect that a breach of these Regulations has been committed, he may, for the purpose of ascertaining whether it has been committed, require any trader to produce any documents relating to his trade, business, craft or profession and may take copies of, or of any entry in, any such document;

(c) if he has reasonable cause to believe that a breach of these Regulations has been committed, he may seize and detain any goods for the purpose of ascertaining, by testing or otherwise, whether the breach has been committed; and

(d) he may seize and detain goods or documents which he has reason to believe may be required as evidence in proceedings for a breach of these Regulations.

(2) If and to the extent that it is reasonably necessary to do so to secure that the provisions of these Regulations are observed, the officer may for the purpose of exercising his powers under paragraphs (1) (c) and (d) to seize goods or documents—

(a) require any person having authority to do so to break open any container or open any vending machine; and

(b) himself open or break open any such container or open any vending machine where a requirement made under sub-paragraph (a) in relation to the container or vending machine has not been complied with.

(3) An officer seizing any goods or documents in exercise of his powers under this regulation shall—

(a) inform the person from whom they are seized; and

(b) where goods are seized from a vending machine, inform—

(i) the person whose name and address are stated on the vending machine as being the proprietor's, or

(ii) if there is no such name or address stated on the vending machine, the occupier of the premises on which the machine stands or to which it is affixed,

that the goods or documents have been so seized.

(4) In this regulation "document" includes information recorded in any form.

(5) The reference in paragraph (1)(b) to the production of documents is, in the case of a document which contains information recorded otherwise than in legible form, a reference to the production of a copy of the information in legible form.

(6) An officer seeking to exercise a power under this regulation must produce evidence of his identity and authority to a person (if there is one) who appears to the officer to be the occupier of the premises.

(7) Where an officer seizes goods or documents in exercise of a power under this regulation they may not be detained—

(a) for a period of more than 3 months; or

(b) where the goods or documents are reasonably required by the enforcement authority in connection with the enforcement of these Regulations, for longer than they are so required.

(8) An officer entering any premises under this regulation may take with him such other persons and such equipment as may appear to him to be necessary.

(9) Nothing in this regulation or in regulation 24 gives any power to an officer of an enforcement authority—

(a) to require any person to produce, or

(b) to seize from another person,

any document which the other person would be entitled to refuse to produce in proceedings in the High Court on the grounds of legal professional privilege or (in Scotland) in proceedings in the Court of Session on the grounds of confidentiality of communications.

(10) In paragraph (9) "communications" means—

(a) communications between a professional legal adviser and his client; or

(b) communications made in connection with or in contemplation of legal proceedings and for the purposes of those proceedings.

(11) If any person who is not an officer of an enforcement authority purports to act as such under this regulation or regulation 24 he shall be guilty of an offence and liable on summary conviction to a fine not exceeding level 5 on the standard scale.

NOTES

Revoked as noted to reg 21 at [**2.546**].

Para (1): words in square brackets inserted by the Business Protection from Misleading Marketing (Amendment) Regulations 2013, SI 2013/2701, regs 2, 8.

[**2.549**]

24 Power to enter premises with a warrant

(1) If a justice of the peace by a written information on oath is satisfied—

(a) that there are reasonable grounds for believing that Condition A or B is met, and

(b)   that Condition C, D or E is met,

the justice may by warrant under his hand authorise an officer of an enforcement authority[, other than GEMA,] to enter the premises at all reasonable times, if necessary by force.

(2)   Condition A is that there are on any premises goods or documents which a duly authorised officer of the enforcement authority has power under regulation 23(1) to inspect and that their inspection is likely to disclose evidence of a breach of these Regulations.

(3)   Condition B is that a breach of these Regulations has occurred, is occurring or is about to occur on any premises.

(4)   Condition C is that the admission to the premises has been or is likely to be refused and that notice of intention to apply for a warrant under this regulation has been given to the occupier.

(5)   Condition D is that an application for admission, or the giving of a notice of intention to apply for a warrant, would defeat the object of the entry.

(6)   Condition E is that the premises are unoccupied or that the occupier is absent and it might defeat the object of the entry to await his return.

(7)   A warrant under paragraph (1)—
(a)   ceases to have effect at the end of the period of one month beginning with the day it is issued;
(b)   must be produced for inspection to the person (if there is one) who appears to the officer to be the occupier of the premises.

(8)   An officer entering any premises under this regulation may take with him such other persons and such equipment as may appear to him to be necessary.

(9)   On leaving any premises which an officer is authorised to enter by warrant under this regulation the officer shall, if the premises are unoccupied or the occupier is temporarily absent, leave the premises as effectively secured against trespassers as he found them.

(10)   In its application to Scotland, this regulation has effect as if—
(a)   the references in paragraph (1) to a justice of the peace included references to a sheriff; and
(b)   the reference in paragraph (1) to information on oath were a reference to evidence on oath.

(11)   In its application to Northern Ireland, this regulation has effect as if the references in paragraph (1) to a justice of the peace were references to a lay magistrate.

NOTES

Revoked as noted to reg 21 at **[2.546]**.

Para (1): words in square brackets inserted by the Business Protection from Misleading Marketing (Amendment) Regulations 2013, SI 2013/2701, regs 2, 9.

[2.550]
25   Obstruction of authorised officers

(1)   Any person who—
(a)   intentionally obstructs an officer of an enforcement authority acting in pursuance of these Regulations;
(b)   intentionally fails to comply with any requirement properly made of him by such an officer under regulation 23; or
(c)   without reasonable cause fails to give such an officer any other assistance or information which he may reasonably require of him for the purpose of the performance of his functions under these Regulations,

is guilty of an offence and liable, on summary conviction, to a fine not exceeding level 5 on the standard scale.

(2)   Any person who, in giving any information which is required of him under paragraph (1)(c), makes any statement which he knows to be false in a material particular is guilty of an offence and liable—
(a)   on summary conviction, to a fine not exceeding the statutory maximum; or
(b)   on conviction on indictment, to a fine or imprisonment for a term not exceeding two years or both.

(3)   Nothing in this regulation shall be construed as requiring a person to answer any question or give any information if to do so might incriminate him.

(4)   Paragraph (1)(a) does not apply in relation to the exercise by an enforcement authority of its power to require information under regulation 21.

NOTES

Revoked as noted to reg 21 at **[2.546]**.

[2.551]
26 Notice of test and intended proceedings

(1)   Where goods purchased by an officer pursuant to regulation 22 are submitted to a test and the test leads to the institution of any proceedings for a breach of these Regulations the officer shall inform—

   (a)   the person from whom the goods were purchased; or

   (b)   where the goods were sold through a vending machine, the person mentioned in regulation 23(3)(b);

of the result of the test.

(2)   Where goods seized by an officer pursuant to regulation 23 are submitted to a test then the officer shall inform the person mentioned in regulation 23(3) of the result of the test.

(3)   Where, as a result of the test, proceedings for a breach of these Regulations are taken against any person, the officer shall allow him to have the goods tested on his behalf if it is reasonably practicable to do so.

NOTES
Revoked as noted to reg 21 at **[2.546]**.

[2.552]
27 Compensation

(1)   Where an officer of an enforcement authority seizes and detains goods in exercise of the powers under regulation 23 the enforcement authority shall be liable to pay compensation to any person having an interest in the goods in respect of any loss or damage caused by reason of the exercise of the power if—

   (a)   there has been no breach of these Regulations in relation to the goods, and

   (b)   the exercise of that power is not attributable to any neglect or default by that person.

(2)   Any disputed question as to the right to or the amount of any compensation payable under this provision shall be determined by arbitration or, in Scotland, by a single arbiter appointed, failing agreement between the parties, by the sheriff.

NOTES
Revoked as noted to reg 21 at **[2.546]**.

[2.553]
28 Crown

(1)   The powers conferred by regulations 23 and 24 are not exercisable in relation to premises occupied by the Crown.

(2)   The Crown is not criminally liable as a result of any provision of these Regulations.

(3)   Paragraph (2) does not affect the application of any provision of these Regulations in relation to a person in the public service of the Crown.

NOTES
Para (1): revoked by the Consumer Rights Act 2015 (Commencement No 3, Transitional Provisions, Savings and Consequential Amendments) Order 2015, SI 2015/1630, art 5, Sch 2, paras 111, 113, as from 1 October 2015 (for transitional provisions see arts 6–8 thereof at **[2.1220]** et seq).

[2.554]
29 Validity of agreements

An agreement shall not be void or unenforceable by reason only of a breach of these Regulations.

CONSUMER PROTECTION FROM UNFAIR TRADING
REGULATIONS 2008

(SI 2008/1277)

NOTES
Made: 8 May 2008.
Authority: European Communities Act 1972, s 2(2).
Commencement: 26 May 2008.

ARRANGEMENT OF REGULATIONS

PART 1
GENERAL

PART 2
PROHIBITIONS

PART 3
OFFENCES

PART 4
ENFORCEMENT

PART 4A
CONSUMERS' RIGHTS TO REDRESS

PART 5
SUPPLEMENTARY

SCHEDULES

PART 1
GENERAL

[2.555]
1   Citation and commencement
These Regulations may be cited as the Consumer Protection from Unfair Trading Regulations 2008 and shall come into force on 26th May 2008.

[2.556]
2   Interpretation
(1)   In these Regulations—
   "average consumer" shall be construed in accordance with paragraphs (2) to (6);
   "business" includes[—

Part 2   Statutory Instruments

(a)] a trade, craft or profession[, and

(b) the activities of any government department or local or public authority];

"code of conduct" means an agreement or set of rules (which is not imposed by legal or administrative requirements), which defines the behaviour of traders who undertake to be bound by it in relation to one or more commercial practices or business sectors;

"code owner" means a trader or a body responsible for—

(a) the formulation and revision of a code of conduct; or

(b) monitoring compliance with the code by those who have undertaken to be bound by it;

"commercial practice" means any act, omission, course of conduct, representation or commercial communication (including advertising and marketing) by a trader, which is directly connected with the promotion, sale or supply of a product to or from consumers, whether occurring before, during or after a commercial transaction (if any) in relation to a product;

["CMA" means the Competition and Markets Authority;]

["consumer" means an individual acting for purposes that are wholly or mainly outside that individual's business;]

["digital content" means data which are produced and supplied in digital form;]

["DETINI" means "the Department of Enterprise, Trade and Investment in Northern Ireland;]

["enforcement authority" means the [CMA], every local weights and measures authority and DETINI;]

["goods" means any tangible moveable items, but that includes water, gas and electricity if and only if they are put up for sale in a limited volume or set quantity;]

"invitation to purchase" means a commercial communication which indicates characteristics of the product and the price in a way appropriate to the means of that commercial communication and thereby enables the consumer to make a purchase;

["local weights and measures authority" means a local weights and measures authority in Great Britain (within the meaning of section 69 of the Weights and Measures Act 1985);]

"materially distort the economic behaviour" means in relation to an average consumer, appreciably to impair the average consumer's ability to make an informed decision thereby causing him to take a transactional decision that he would not have taken otherwise;

. . .

"premises" includes any place and any stall, vehicle, ship or aircraft;

["product" means—

(a) goods,

(b) a service,

(c) digital content,

(d) immoveable property,

(e) rights or obligations, or

(f) a product of the kind mentioned in paragraphs (1A) and (1B),

but the application of this definition to Part 4A is subject to regulations 27C and 27D;]

"professional diligence" means the standard of special skill and care which a trader may reasonably be expected to exercise towards consumers which is commensurate with either—

(a) honest market practice in the trader's field of activity, or

(b) the general principle of good faith in the trader's field of activity;

"ship" includes any boat and any other description of vessel used in navigation;

["trader"—

(a) means a person acting for purposes relating to that person's business, whether acting personally or through another person acting in the trader's name or on the trader's behalf, and

(b) except in Part 4A, includes a person acting in the name of or on behalf of a trader;]

"transactional decision" means any decision taken by a consumer, whether it is to act or to refrain from acting, concerning—

(a) whether, how and on what terms to purchase, make payment in whole or in part for, retain or dispose of a product; or

(b) whether, how and on what terms to exercise a contractual right in relation to a product [(but the application of this definition to regulations 5 and 7 as they apply for the purposes of Part 4A is subject to regulation 27B(2))].

[(1A) A trader ("T") who demands payment from a consumer ("C") in full or partial settlement of C's liabilities or purported liabilities to T is to be treated for the purposes of these Regulations as offering to supply a product to C.

(1B) In such a case the product that T offers to supply comprises the full or partial settlement of those liabilities or purported liabilities.]

(2) In determining the effect of a commercial practice on the average consumer where the practice reaches or is addressed to a consumer or consumers account shall be taken of the material characteristics of such an average consumer including his being reasonably well informed, reasonably observant and circumspect.

(3)   Paragraphs (4) and (5) set out the circumstances in which a reference to the average consumer shall be read as in addition referring to the average member of a particular group of consumers.

(4)   In determining the effect of a commercial practice on the average consumer where the practice is directed to a particular group of consumers, a reference to the average consumer shall be read as referring to the average member of that group.

(5)   In determining the effect of a commercial practice on the average consumer—

  (a)   where a clearly identifiable group of consumers is particularly vulnerable to the practice or the underlying product because of their mental or physical infirmity, age or credulity in a way which the trader could reasonably be expected to foresee, and

  (b)   where the practice is likely to materially distort the economic behaviour only of that group, a reference to the average consumer shall be read as referring to the average member of that group.

(6)   Paragraph (5) is without prejudice to the common and legitimate advertising practice of making exaggerated statements which are not meant to be taken literally.

NOTES

Para (1): in definitions "business" and "transactional decision" words in square brackets inserted, definitions "consumer", "goods", "product" and "trader" substituted, and definition "digital content" inserted, by the Consumer Protection (Amendment) Regulations 2014, SI 2014/870, reg 2(1)–(8), in relation to contracts entered into, or payments made, on or after 1 October 2014; original definitions "consumer", "goods", "product" and "trader" read as follows—

> ""consumer" means any individual who in relation to a commercial practice is acting for purposes which are outside his business;
> "goods" includes ships, aircraft, animals, things attached to land and growing crops;
> "product" means any goods or service and includes immovable property, rights and obligations;
> "trader" means any person who in relation to a commercial practice is acting for purposes relating to his business, and anyone acting in the name of or on behalf of a trader;"

; definition "CMA" inserted, in definition "enforcement authority" reference in square brackets substituted, definition "OFT" (omitted) revoked, and definition "CMA" inserted, by the Enterprise and Regulatory Reform Act 2013 (Competition) (Consequential, Transitional and Saving Provisions) (No 2) Order 2014, SI 2014/549, art 2, Sch 1, Pt 2 , para 35 (for transitional provisions in relation to the continuity of functions, etc, see art 3 of the 2014 Order); definitions "DETINI" and "local weights and measures authority" inserted, and definition "enforcement authority" substituted by the Public Bodies (The Office of Fair Trading Transfer of Consumer Advice Scheme Function and Modification of Enforcement Functions) Order 2013, SI 2013/783, art 13(1), (2).

Paras (1A), (1B): inserted by SI 2014/870, reg 2(1), (9), in relation to contracts entered into, or payments made, on or after 1 October 2014.

PART 2
PROHIBITIONS

[2.557]
3   Prohibition of unfair commercial practices

(1)   Unfair commercial practices are prohibited.

(2)   Paragraphs (3) and (4) set out the circumstances when a commercial practice is unfair.

(3)   A commercial practice is unfair if—
  (a)   it contravenes the requirements of professional diligence; and
  (b)   it materially distorts or is likely to materially distort the economic behaviour of the average consumer with regard to the product.

(4)   A commercial practice is unfair if—
  (a)   it is a misleading action under the provisions of regulation 5;
  (b)   it is a misleading omission under the provisions of regulation 6;
  (c)   it is aggressive under the provisions of regulation 7; or
  (d)   it is listed in Schedule 1.

[2.558]
4   Prohibition of the promotion of unfair commercial practices

The promotion of any unfair commercial practice by a code owner in a code of conduct is prohibited.

[2.559]
5   Misleading actions

(1)   A commercial practice is a misleading action if it satisfies the conditions in either paragraph (2) or paragraph (3).

(2)   A commercial practice satisfies the conditions of this paragraph—
  (a)   if it contains false information and is therefore untruthful in relation to any of the matters in paragraph (4) or if it or its overall presentation in any way deceives or is likely to deceive the average consumer in relation to any of the matters in that paragraph, even if the information is factually correct; and
  (b)   it causes or is likely to cause the average consumer to take a transactional decision he would not have taken otherwise.

(3)   A commercial practice satisfies the conditions of this paragraph if—
- (a)   it concerns any marketing of a product (including comparative advertising) which creates confusion with any products, trade marks, trade names or other distinguishing marks of a competitor; or
- (b)   it concerns any failure by a trader to comply with a commitment contained in a code of conduct which the trader has undertaken to comply with, if—
    - (i)   the trader indicates in a commercial practice that he is bound by that code of conduct, and
    - (ii)   the commitment is firm and capable of being verified and is not aspirational,

and it causes or is likely to cause the average consumer to take a transactional decision he would not have taken otherwise, taking account of its factual context and of all its features and circumstances.

(4)   The matters referred to in paragraph (2)(a) are—
- (a)   the existence or nature of the product;
- (b)   the main characteristics of the product (as defined in paragraph 5);
- (c)   the extent of the trader's commitments;
- (d)   the motives for the commercial practice;
- (e)   the nature of the sales process;
- (f)   any statement or symbol relating to direct or indirect sponsorship or approval of the trader or the product;
- (g)   the price or the manner in which the price is calculated;
- (h)   the existence of a specific price advantage;
- (i)   the need for a service, part, replacement or repair;
- (j)   the nature, attributes and rights of the trader (as defined in paragraph 6);
- (k)   the consumer's rights or the risks he may face.

(5)   In paragraph (4)(b), the "main characteristics of the product" include—
- (a)   availability of the product;
- (b)   benefits of the product;
- (c)   risks of the product;
- (d)   execution of the product;
- (e)   composition of the product;
- (f)   accessories of the product;
- (g)   after-sale customer assistance concerning the product;
- (h)   the handling of complaints about the product;
- (i)   the method and date of manufacture of the product;
- (j)   the method and date of provision of the product;
- (k)   delivery of the product;
- (l)   fitness for purpose of the product;
- (m)   usage of the product;
- (n)   quantity of the product;
- (o)   specification of the product;
- (p)   geographical or commercial origin of the product;
- (q)   results to be expected from use of the product; and
- (r)   results and material features of tests or checks carried out on the product.

(6)   In paragraph (4)(j), the "nature, attributes and rights" as far as concern the trader include the trader's—
- (a)   identity;
- (b)   assets;
- (c)   qualifications;
- (d)   status;
- (e)   approval;
- (f)   affiliations or connections;
- (g)   ownership of industrial, commercial or intellectual property rights; and
- (h)   awards and distinctions.

(7)   In paragraph (4)(k) "consumer's rights" include rights the consumer may have under *Part 5A of the Sale of Goods Act 1979 or Part 1B of the Supply of Goods and Services Act 1982.*

NOTES

Para (7): for the words in italics there are substituted the words "sections 19 and 23 or 24 of the Consumer Rights Act 2015" by the Consumer Rights Act 2015 (Commencement No 3, Transitional Provisions, Savings and Consequential Amendments) Order 2015, SI 2015/1630, art 5, Sch 1, para 3, as from 1 October 2015 (for transitional provisions see arts 6–8 thereof at **[2.1220]** et seq).

[2.560]
6   Misleading omissions

(1)   A commercial practice is a misleading omission if, in its factual context, taking account of the matters in paragraph (2)—
- (a)   the commercial practice omits material information,

   (b)   the commercial practice hides material information,

   (c)   the commercial practice provides material information in a manner which is unclear, unintelligible, ambiguous or untimely, or

   (d)   the commercial practice fails to identify its commercial intent, unless this is already apparent from the context,

and as a result it causes or is likely to cause the average consumer to take a transactional decision he would not have taken otherwise.

(2)   The matters referred to in paragraph (1) are—

   (a)   all the features and circumstances of the commercial practice;

   (b)   the limitations of the medium used to communicate the commercial practice (including limitations of space or time); and

   (c)   where the medium used to communicate the commercial practice imposes limitations of space or time, any measures taken by the trader to make the information available to consumers by other means.

(3)   In paragraph (1) "material information" means—

   (a)   the information which the average consumer needs, according to the context, to take an informed transactional decision; and

   (b)   any information requirement which applies in relation to a commercial communication as a result of [an] [EU] obligation.

(4)   Where a commercial practice is an invitation to purchase, the following information will be material if not already apparent from the context in addition to any other information which is material information under paragraph (3)—

   (a)   the main characteristics of the product, to the extent appropriate to the medium by which the invitation to purchase is communicated and the product;

   (b)   the identity of the trader, such as his trading name, and the identity of any other trader on whose behalf the trader is acting;

   (c)   the geographical address of the trader and the geographical address of any other trader on whose behalf the trader is acting;

   (d)   either—

       (i)   the price, including any taxes; or

       (ii)   where the nature of the product is such that the price cannot reasonably be calculated in advance, the manner in which the price is calculated;

   (e)   where appropriate, either—

       (i)   all additional freight, delivery or postal charges; or

       (ii)   where such charges cannot reasonably be calculated in advance, the fact that such charges may be payable;

   (f)   the following matters where they depart from the requirements of professional diligence—

       (i)   arrangements for payment,

       (ii)   arrangements for delivery,

       (iii)   arrangements for performance,

       (iv)   complaint handling policy;

   (g)   for products and transactions involving a right of withdrawal or cancellation, the existence of such a right.

NOTES

   Para (3): words in square brackets in sub-para (b) substituted by the Treaty of Lisbon (Changes in Terminology) Order 2011, SI 2011/1043, art 6(1)(e), (3).

[2.561]
7   Aggressive commercial practices

(1)   A commercial practice is aggressive if, in its factual context, taking account of all of its features and circumstances—

   (a)   it significantly impairs or is likely significantly to impair the average consumer's freedom of choice or conduct in relation to the product concerned through the use of harassment, coercion or undue influence; and

   (b)   it thereby causes or is likely to cause him to take a transactional decision he would not have taken otherwise.

(2)   In determining whether a commercial practice uses harassment, coercion or undue influence account shall be taken of—

   (a)   its timing, location, nature or persistence;

   (b)   the use of threatening or abusive language or behaviour;

   (c)   the exploitation by the trader of any specific misfortune or circumstance of such gravity as to impair the consumer's judgment, of which the trader is aware, to influence the consumer's decision with regard to the product;

   (d)   any onerous or disproportionate non-contractual barrier imposed by the trader where a consumer wishes to exercise rights under the contract, including rights to terminate a contract or to switch to another product or another trader; and

   (e)   any threat to take any action which cannot legally be taken.

(3)   In this regulation—
  (a)   "coercion" includes the use of physical force; and
  (b)   "undue influence" means exploiting a position of power in relation to the consumer so as to apply pressure, even without using or threatening to use physical force, in a way which significantly limits the consumer's ability to make an informed decision.

PART 3
OFFENCES

[2.562]
8   Offences relating to unfair commercial practices

(1)   A trader is guilty of an offence if—
  (a)   he knowingly or recklessly engages in a commercial practice which contravenes the requirements of professional diligence under regulation 3(3)(a); and
  (b)   the practice materially distorts or is likely to materially distort the economic behaviour of the average consumer with regard to the product under regulation 3(3)(b).

(2)   For the purposes of paragraph (1)(a) a trader who engages in a commercial practice without regard to whether the practice contravenes the requirements of professional diligence shall be deemed recklessly to engage in the practice, whether or not the trader has reason for believing that the practice might contravene those requirements.

[2.563]
9

A trader is guilty of an offence if he engages in a commercial practice which is a misleading action under regulation 5 otherwise than by reason of the commercial practice satisfying the condition in regulation 5(3)(b).

[2.564]
10

A trader is guilty of an offence if he engages in a commercial practice which is a misleading omission under regulation 6.

[2.565]
11

A trader is guilty of an offence if he engages in a commercial practice which is aggressive under regulation 7.

[2.566]
12

A trader is guilty of an offence if he engages in a commercial practice set out in any of paragraphs 1 to 10, 12 to 27 and 29 to 31 of Schedule 1.

[2.567]
13   Penalty for offences

A person guilty of an offence under regulation 8, 9, 10, 11 or 12 shall be liable—
  (a)   on summary conviction, to a fine not exceeding the statutory maximum; or
  (b)   on conviction on indictment, to a fine or imprisonment for a term not exceeding two years or both.

[2.568]
14   Time limit for prosecution

(1)   No proceedings for an offence under these Regulations shall be commenced after—
  (a)   the end of the period of three years beginning with the date of the commission of the offence, or
  (b)   the end of the period of one year beginning with the date of discovery of the offence by the prosecutor,
whichever is earlier.

(2)   For the purposes of paragraph (1)(b) a certificate signed by or on behalf of the prosecutor and stating the date on which the offence was discovered by him shall be conclusive evidence of that fact and a certificate stating that matter and purporting to be so signed shall be treated as so signed unless the contrary is proved.

(3)   Notwithstanding anything in section 127(1) of the Magistrates' Courts Act 1980, an information relating to an offence under these Regulations which is triable by a magistrates' court in England and Wales may be so tried if it is laid at any time before the end of the period of twelve months beginning with the date of the commission of the offence.

(4) Notwithstanding anything in section 136 of the Criminal Procedure (Scotland) Act 1995 summary proceedings in Scotland for an offence under these Regulations may be commenced at any time before the end of the period of twelve months beginning with the date of the commission of the offence.

(5) For the purposes of paragraph (4), section 136(3) of the Criminal Procedure (Scotland) Act 1995 shall apply as it applies for the purposes of that subsection.

(6) Notwithstanding anything in Article 19(1) of the Magistrates' Courts (Northern Ireland) Order 1981 a complaint charging an offence under these Regulations which is triable by a magistrates' court in Northern Ireland may be so tried if it is made at any time before the end of the period of twelve months beginning with the date of the commission of the offence.

[2.569]
15 Offences committed by bodies of persons

(1) Where an offence under these Regulations committed by a body corporate is proved—
    (a) to have been committed with the consent or connivance of an officer of the body, or
    (b) to be attributable to any neglect on his part,
the officer as well as the body corporate is guilty of the offence and liable to be proceeded against and punished accordingly.

(2) In paragraph (1) a reference to an officer of a body corporate includes a reference to—
    (a) a director, manager, secretary or other similar officer; and
    (b) a person purporting to act as a director, manager, secretary or other similar officer.

(3) Where an offence under these Regulations committed by a Scottish partnership is proved—
    (a) to have been committed with the consent or connivance of a partner, or
    (b) to be attributable to any neglect on his part,
the partner as well as the partnership is guilty of the offence and liable to be proceeded against and punished accordingly.

(4) In paragraph (3) a reference to a partner includes a person purporting to act as a partner.

[2.570]
16 Offence due to the default of another person

(1) This regulation applies where a person "X"—
    (a) commits an offence under regulation 9, 10, 11 or 12, or
    (b) would have committed an offence under those regulations but for a defence under regulation 17 or 18,
and the commission of the offence, or of what would have been an offence but for X being able to rely on a defence under regulation 17 or 18, is due to the act or default of some other person "Y".

(2) Where this regulation applies Y is guilty of the offence, subject to regulations 17 and 18, whether or not Y is a trader and whether or not Y's act or default is a commercial practice.

(3) Y may be charged with and convicted of the offence by virtue of paragraph (2) whether or not proceedings are taken against X.

[2.571]
17 Due diligence defence

(1) In any proceedings against a person for an offence under regulation 9, 10, 11 or 12 it is a defence for that person to prove—
    (a) that the commission of the offence was due to—
        (i) a mistake;
        (ii) reliance on information supplied to him by another person;
        (iii) the act or default of another person;
        (iv) an accident; or
        (v) another cause beyond his control; and
    (b) that he took all reasonable precautions and exercised all due diligence to avoid the commission of such an offence by himself or any person under his control.

(2) A person shall not be entitled to rely on the defence provided by paragraph (1) by reason of the matters referred to in paragraph (ii) or (iii) of paragraph (1)(a) without leave of the court unless—
    (a) he has served on the prosecutor a notice in writing giving such information identifying or assisting in the identification of that other person as was in his possession; and
    (b) the notice is served on the prosecutor at least seven clear days before the date of the hearing.

[2.572]
18 Innocent publication of advertisement defence

(1) In any proceedings against a person for an offence under regulation 9, 10, 11 or 12 committed by the publication of an advertisement it shall be a defence for a person to prove that—
    (a) he is a person whose business it is to publish or to arrange for the publication of advertisements;

(b)   he received the advertisement for publication in the ordinary course of business; and

(c)   he did not know and had no reason to suspect that its publication would amount to an offence under the regulation to which the proceedings relate.

(2)   In paragraph (1) "advertisement" includes a catalogue, a circular and a price list.

PART 4
ENFORCEMENT

[2.573]
19   [Duty and power to enforce]

[(1)   It shall be the duty of every local weights and measures authority and DETINI to enforce these Regulations [(other than Part 4A)].

(1A)   The [CMA] may also enforce these Regulations.]

(2)   Where the enforcement authority is a local weights and measures authority the duty referred to in paragraph (1) shall apply to the enforcement of these Regulations within the authority's area.

(3)   Where the enforcement authority is [DETINI] the duty referred to in paragraph (1) shall apply to the enforcement of these Regulations within Northern Ireland.

(4)   [In determining how to comply with paragraph (1), or as the case may be, paragraph (1A),] every enforcement authority shall have regard to the desirability of encouraging control of unfair commercial practices by such established means as it considers appropriate having regard to all the circumstances of the particular case.

(5)   Nothing in this regulation shall authorise any enforcement authority to bring proceedings in Scotland for an offence.

NOTES

Provision heading: substituted by the Public Bodies (The Office of Fair Trading Transfer of Consumer Advice Scheme Function and Modification of Enforcement Functions) Order 2013, SI 2013/783, art 13(1), (3).

Para (1): substituted, together with para (1A), for para (1) as originally enacted, by SI 2013/783, art 13(1), (4); words in square brackets added by the Consumer Protection (Amendment) Regulations 2014, SI 2014/870, reg 4(1), in relation to contracts entered into, or payments made, on or after 1 October 2014.

Para (1A): substituted as noted above; reference in square brackets substituted by the Enterprise and Regulatory Reform Act 2013 (Competition) (Consequential, Transitional and Saving Provisions) (No 2) Order 2014, SI 2014/549, art 2, Sch 1, Pt 2, para 35(1), (3) (for transitional provisions in relation to the continuity of functions, etc, see art 3 of the 2014 Order).

Paras (3), (4): words in square brackets substituted by SI 2013/783, art 13(1), (5), (6).

[2.574]
20   *Power to make test purchases*

An enforcement authority may or may authorise any of its officers on its behalf to—

  (a)   make a purchase of a product, or

  (b)   enter into an agreement to secure the provision of a product,

for the purposes of determining whether these Regulations are being complied with.

NOTES

Revoked, together with regs 21–25, by the Consumer Rights Act 2015 (Commencement No 3, Transitional Provisions, Savings and Consequential Amendments) Order 2015, SI 2015/1630, art 5, Sch 2, paras 114, 115, as from 1 October 2015 (for transitional provisions see arts 6–8 thereof at **[2.1220]** et seq).

[2.575]
21   *Power of entry and investigation, etc*

(1)   A duly authorised officer of an enforcement authority may at all reasonable hours exercise the following powers—

  (a)   he may, for the purposes of ascertaining whether a breach of these Regulations has been committed, inspect any goods and enter any premises other than premises used only as a dwelling;

  (b)   if he has reasonable cause to suspect that a breach of these Regulations has been committed, he may, for the purpose of ascertaining whether it has been committed, require any trader to produce any documents relating to his business and may take copies of, or of any entry in, any such document;

  (c)   if he has reasonable cause to believe that a breach of these Regulations has been committed, he may seize and detain any goods for the purpose of ascertaining, by testing or otherwise, whether the breach has been committed; and

  (d)   he may seize and detain goods or documents which he has reason to believe may be required as evidence in proceedings for a breach of these Regulations.

(2)   If and to the extent that it is reasonably necessary to secure that the provisions of these Regulations are observed, the officer may for the purpose of exercising his powers under paragraphs (1)(c) and (d) to seize goods or documents—

  (a)   require any person having authority to do so to break open any container or open any vending machine; and

(b)   *himself open or break open any such container or open any vending machine where a requirement made under sub-paragraph (a) in relation to the container or vending machine has not been complied with.*

(3)   *An officer seizing any goods or documents in exercise of his powers under this regulation shall—*

   (a)   *inform the person from whom they are seized, and,*

   (b)   *where goods are seized from a vending machine, inform—*

     (i)   *the person whose name and address are stated on the machine as being the proprietor's; or*

     (ii)   *if there is no such name or address stated on the machine the occupier of the premises on which the machine stands or to which it is affixed,*

   that the goods or documents have been so seized.

(4)   *In this regulation "document" includes information recorded in any form.*

(5)   *The reference in paragraph (1)(b) to the production of documents is, in the case of a document which contains information recorded otherwise than in legible form, a reference to the production of a copy of the information in legible form.*

(6)   *An officer seeking to exercise a power under this regulation must produce evidence of his identity and authority to a person (if there is one) who appears to the officer to be the occupier of the premises.*

(7)   *Where an officer seizes goods or documents in exercise of a power under this regulation they may not be detained—*

   (a)   *for a period of more than 3 months; or*

   (b)   *where the goods or documents are reasonably required by the enforcement authority in connection with the enforcement of these Regulations, for longer than they are so required.*

(8)   *An officer entering any premises under this regulation may take with him such other persons and such equipment as may appear to him to be necessary.*

(9)   *Nothing in this regulation or in regulation 22 gives any power to an officer of an enforcement authority—*

   (a)   *to require any person to produce, or*

   (b)   *to seize from another person,*

any document which the other person would be entitled to refuse to produce in proceedings in the High Court on the grounds of legal professional privilege or (in Scotland) in proceedings in the Court of Session on the grounds of confidentiality of communications.

(10)   *In paragraph (9) "communications" means—*

   (a)   *communications between a professional legal adviser and his client; or*

   (b)   *communications made in connection with or in contemplation of legal proceedings and for the purposes of those proceedings.*

(11)   *If any person who is not an officer of an enforcement authority purports to act as such under this regulation or under regulation 22 he shall be guilty of an offence and liable on summary conviction to a fine not exceeding level 5 on the standard scale.*

NOTES

Revoked as noted to reg 20 at **[2.574]**.

[2.576]

22   Power to enter premises with a warrant

(1)   *If a justice of the peace by any written information on oath is satisfied—*

   (a)   *that there are reasonable grounds for believing that Condition A or B is met, and*

   (b)   *that Condition C, D or E is met,*

the justice may by warrant under his hand authorise an officer of an enforcement authority to enter the premises at all reasonable times, if necessary by force.

(2)   *Condition A is that there are on any premises goods or documents which a duly authorised officer of the enforcement authority has power under regulation 21(1) to inspect and that their inspection is likely to disclose evidence of a breach of these Regulations.*

(3)   *Condition B is that a breach of these Regulations has been, is being or is about to be committed on any premises.*

(4)   *Condition C is that the admission to the premises has been or is likely to be refused and that notice of intention to apply for a warrant under this regulation has been given to the occupier.*

(5)   *Condition D is that an application for admission, or the giving of a notice of intention to apply for a warrant, would defeat the object of the entry.*

(6)   *Condition E is that the premises are unoccupied or that the occupier is absent and it might defeat the object of the entry to await his return.*

(7)   *A warrant under paragraph (1)—*

   (a)   *ceases to have effect at the end of the period of one month beginning with the day it is issued;*

    (b)   must be produced for inspection to the person (if there is one) who appears to the officer to be the occupier of the premises.

(8)   An officer entering any premises under this regulation may take with him such other persons and such equipment as may appear to him to be necessary.

(9)   On leaving any premises which an officer is authorised to enter by warrant under this regulation the officer shall, if the premises are unoccupied or the occupier is temporarily absent, leave the premises as effectively secured against trespassers as he found them.

(10)   (Applies to Scotland only.)

(11)   In its application to Northern Ireland, this regulation has effect as if the references in paragraph (1) to a justice of the peace were references to a lay magistrate.

NOTES
Revoked as noted to reg 20 at **[2.574]**.

[2.577]
23 *Obstruction of authorised officers*

(1)   Any person who—
    (a)   intentionally obstructs an officer of an enforcement authority acting in pursuance of these Regulations,
    (b)   intentionally fails to comply with any requirement properly made of him by such an officer under regulation 21, or
    (c)   without reasonable cause fails to give such an officer any other assistance or information which he may reasonably require of him for the purpose of the performance of his functions under these Regulations,
is guilty of an offence and liable, on summary conviction, to a fine not exceeding level 5 on the standard scale.

(2)   Any person who, in giving any information which is required of him under paragraph (1)(c), makes any statement which he knows to be false in a material particular is guilty of an offence and liable—
    (a)   on summary conviction, to a fine not exceeding the statutory maximum; or
    (b)   on conviction on indictment, to a fine or imprisonment for a term not exceeding two years or both.

(3)   Nothing in this regulation shall be construed as requiring a person to answer any question or give any information if to do so might incriminate him.

NOTES
Revoked as noted to reg 20 at **[2.574]**.

[2.578]
24 *Notice of test and intended proceedings*

(1)   Where goods purchased by an officer pursuant to regulation 20 are submitted to a test and the test leads to the institution of any proceedings for a breach of these Regulations the officer shall inform—
    (a)   the person from whom the goods were purchased, or
    (b)   where the goods were sold through a vending machine, the person mentioned in regulation 21(3)(b),
of the result of the test.

(2)   Where goods seized by an officer pursuant to regulation 21 are submitted to a test then the officer shall inform the person mentioned in regulation 21(3) of the result of the test.

(3)   Where, as a result of the test, any proceedings in respect of a breach of these Regulations are taken against any person, the officer shall allow him to have the goods tested on his behalf if it is reasonably practicable to do so.

NOTES
Revoked as noted to reg 20 at **[2.574]**.

[2.579]
25 *Compensation*

(1)   Where an officer of an enforcement authority seizes and detains goods in exercise of the powers under regulation 21 the enforcement authority shall be liable to pay compensation to any person having an interest in the goods in respect of any loss or damage caused by reason of the exercise of the power if—
    (a)   there has been no breach of these Regulations in relation to the goods, and
    (b)   the exercise of that power is not attributable to any neglect or default by that person.

(2)   Any disputed question as to the right to or the amount of any compensation payable under this provision shall be determined by arbitration or, in Scotland, by a single arbiter appointed, failing agreement between the parties, by the sheriff.

Part 2　Statutory Instruments

NOTES

Revoked as noted to reg 20 at **[2.574]**.

26, 27　(*Reg 26 amends the Enterprise Act 2002, Sch 13; reg 27 inserts s 218A of the 2002 Act at* **[1.1809]**.)

[PART 4A
CONSUMERS' RIGHTS TO REDRESS

[2.580]

27A　When does a consumer have a right to redress?

(1)　A consumer has a right to redress under this Part if—

   (a)　the conditions in this regulation are met, and

   (b)　the conditions (if any) in the following provisions of this Part for the availability of that right are met.

(2)　The first condition is that—

   (a)　the consumer enters into a contract with a trader for the sale or supply of a product by the trader (a "business to consumer contract"),

   (b)　the consumer enters into a contract with a trader for the sale of goods to the trader (a "consumer to business contract"), or

   (c)　the consumer makes a payment to a trader for the supply of a product (a "consumer payment").

(3)　Paragraph (2)(b) does not apply if, under the contract, the trader supplies or agrees to supply a product to the consumer as well as paying or agreeing to pay the consumer.

(4)　The second condition is that—

   (a)　the trader engages in a prohibited practice in relation to the product, or

   (b)　in a case where a consumer enters into a business to consumer contract for goods or digital content—

      (i)　a producer engages in a prohibited practice in relation to the goods or digital content, and

      (ii)　when the contract is entered into, the trader is aware of the commercial practice that constitutes the prohibited practice or could reasonably be expected to be aware of it.

(5)　In paragraph (4)(b) "producer" means—

   (a)　a manufacturer of the goods or digital content,

   (b)　an importer of the goods or digital content into the European Economic Area, or

   (c)　a person who purports to be a producer by placing the person's name, trade mark or other distinctive sign on the goods or using it in connection with the digital content,

and includes a producer acting personally or through another person acting in the producer's name or on the producer's behalf.

(6)　The third condition is that the prohibited practice is a significant factor in the consumer's decision to enter into the contract or make the payment.]

NOTES

Commencement: 1 October 2014.

Part 4A (regs 27A–27L) inserted by the Consumer Protection (Amendment) Regulations 2014, SI 2014/870, reg 3, in relation to contracts entered into, or payments made, on or after 1 October 2014.

[2.581]

[27B　What does "prohibited practice" mean in this Part?

(1)　In this Part "prohibited practice" means a commercial practice that—

   (a)　is a misleading action under regulation 5, or

   (b)　is aggressive under regulation 7.

(2)　Regulations 5 and 7 apply for the purposes of this Part as if for the definition of "transactional decision" in regulation 2(1) there were substituted—

   ""transactional decision" means any decision taken by a consumer to enter into a contract with a trader for the sale or supply of a product by the trader, or for the sale of goods to the trader, or to make a payment to a trader for the supply of a product.".]

NOTES

Commencement: 1 October 2014.

Inserted as noted to reg 27A at **[2.580]**.

[2.582]

[27C　What immoveable property is covered by this Part?

(1)　In this Part "product" does not include immoveable property other than a relevant lease.

(2)　In this regulation "relevant lease" in relation to England and Wales means—

   (a)　an assured tenancy within the meaning of Part 1 of the Housing Act 1988, or

    (b)   a lease under which accommodation is let as holiday accommodation.

(3) But none of the following are relevant leases for the purposes of paragraph (2)(a)—
    (a)   a lease granted by—
        (i)   a private registered provider of social housing, or
        (ii)   a registered social landlord within the meaning of Part 1 of the Housing Act 1996;
    (b)   a lease of a dwelling-house or part of a dwelling-house—
        (i)   granted on payment of a premium calculated by reference to a percentage of the value of the dwelling-house or part or of the cost of providing it, or
        (ii)   under which the lessee (or the lessee's personal representatives) will or may be entitled to a sum calculated by reference, directly or indirectly, to the value of the dwelling-house or part;
    (c)   a lease granted to a person as a result of the exercise by a local housing authority within the meaning of the Housing Act 1996 of its functions under Part 7 (homelessness) of that Act.

(4) In this regulation "relevant lease" in relation to Scotland means—
    (a)   an assured tenancy within the meaning of Part 2 of the Housing (Scotland) Act 1988, or
    (b)   a lease under which accommodation is let as holiday accommodation.

(5) In this regulation "relevant lease" in relation to Northern Ireland means—
    (a)   a private tenancy within the meaning of Article 3 of the Private Tenancies (Northern Ireland) Order 2006, or
    (b)   a lease under which accommodation is let as holiday accommodation.

(6) But neither of the following are relevant leases for the purposes of paragraph (5)(a)—
    (a)   a lease of a dwelling-house or part of a dwelling-house—
        (i)   granted on payment of a premium calculated by reference to a percentage of the value of the dwelling-house or part or of the cost of providing it, or
        (ii)   under which the lessee (or the lessee's personal representatives) will or may be entitled to a sum calculated by reference, directly or indirectly, to the value of the dwelling-house or part;
    (b)   a private tenancy resulting from the exercise by the Northern Ireland Housing Executive of its functions under Part 2 (homelessness) of the Housing (Northern Ireland) Order 1988.]

NOTES

Commencement: 1 October 2014.

Inserted as noted to reg 27A at **[2.580]**.

[2.583]
[27D What financial services are covered by this Part?

(1) In this Part "product" does not include a service provided in the course of carrying on a regulated activity within the meaning of section 22 of the Financial Services and Markets Act 2000, other than a service to which paragraph (2) applies.

(2) This paragraph applies to a service consisting of the provision of credit under an agreement which is a restricted-use credit agreement within paragraph (a) or (b) of the definition of that term in article 60L(1) of the Financial Services and Markets Act 2000 (Regulated Activities) Order 2001.

(3) But paragraph (2) does not apply to an agreement under which the obligation of the borrower to repay is secured by a legal or equitable mortgage on land (other than timeshare accommodation).

(4) In paragraph (3)—
    "mortgage" includes a charge and (in Scotland) a heritable security;
    "timeshare accommodation" means overnight accommodation which is the subject of a timeshare contract within the meaning of the Timeshare, Holiday Products, Resale and Exchange Contracts Regulations 2010.

(5) The fact that the supply of a product within regulation 2(1A) and (1B) may constitute an activity within article 39F (debt-collecting) of the Financial Services and Markets Act 2000 (Regulated Activities) Order 2001 does not prevent this Part from applying in relation to that supply.]

NOTES

Commencement: 1 October 2014.

Inserted as noted to reg 27A at **[2.580]**.

[2.584]
[27E When does the right to unwind apply to a business to consumer contract?

(1) A consumer has the right to unwind in respect of a business to consumer contract if the consumer indicates to the trader that the consumer rejects the product, and does so—
    (a)   within the relevant period, and
    (b)   at a time when the product is capable of being rejected.

(2) An indication under paragraph (1) may be something that the consumer says or does, but it must be clear.

(3) In paragraph (1)(a) "the relevant period" means the period of 90 days beginning with the later of—
   (a) the day on which the consumer enters into the contract, and
   (b) the relevant day.

(4) In this Part "the relevant day" means the day on which—
   (a) the goods are first delivered,
   (b) the performance of the service begins,
   (c) the digital content is first supplied,
   (d) the lease begins, or
   (e) the right is first exercisable,
(as the case may be).

(5) But in the case of a mixed contract, "the relevant day" means the latest of the days mentioned in paragraph (4) that is relevant to the contract.

(6) In this Part "mixed contract" means a contract relating to a product which consists of any two or more of goods, a service, digital content, immoveable property or rights.

(7) For the purposes of this Part, where the consumer's access to digital content on a device requires its transmission to the device under arrangements initiated by the trader, the day on which the digital content is first provided is—
   (a) the day on which it reaches the device, or
   (b) if earlier, the day on which it reaches another trader chosen by the consumer to supply, under a contract with the consumer, a service by which digital content reaches the device.

(8) For the purposes of paragraph (1)(b), a product remains capable of being rejected only if—
   (a) the goods have not been fully consumed,
   (b) the service has not been fully performed,
   (c) the digital content has not been fully consumed,
   (d) the lease has not expired, or
   (e) the right has not been fully exercised,
(as the case may be).

(9) For the purposes of paragraph (8)—
   (a) goods have been fully consumed only if nothing is left of them, and
   (b) digital content has been fully consumed only if the digital content was available to the consumer for a fixed period and that period has expired.

(10) A consumer does not have the right to unwind in respect of a business to consumer contract if the consumer has exercised the right to a discount in respect of that contract and the same prohibited practice.]

NOTES

Commencement: 1 October 2014.
Inserted as noted to reg 27A at **[2.580]**.

[2.585]
[27F How does the right to unwind work in the case of a business to consumer contract?
(1) Where a consumer has the right to unwind in respect of a business to consumer contract—
   (a) the contract comes to an end so that the consumer and the trader are released from their obligations under it,
   (b) the trader has a duty to give the consumer a refund (subject as follows), and
   (c) if the contract was wholly or partly for the sale or supply of goods the consumer must make the goods available for collection by the trader.

(2) The consumer's entitlement to a refund works as follows.

(3) To the extent that the consumer paid money under the contract, the consumer is entitled to receive back the same amount of money (but see paragraphs (7) to (10)).

(4) To the extent that the consumer transferred anything else under the contract, the consumer is entitled to receive back the same amount of what the consumer transferred, unless paragraph (5) applies.

(5) To the extent that the consumer transferred under the contract something for which the same amount of the same thing cannot be substituted—
   (a) the consumer is entitled to receive back in its original state whatever the consumer transferred, or
   (b) if it cannot be given back in its original state, the consumer is entitled to be paid its market price as at the time when the product was rejected.

(6) There is no entitlement to a refund if none of paragraphs (3) to (5) applies.

(7) The consumer's entitlement to receive back the same amount of money as the consumer paid is qualified by paragraphs (8) to (10) if—
   (a) the contract was for the sale or supply of a product on a regular or continuous basis, and
   (b) the period beginning with the relevant day and ending with the day on which the consumer rejected the product exceeds one month.

(8)   In that case the consumer is only entitled to receive back the amount (if any) found by deducting the market price, when the consumer rejected the product, of the product supplied up to that time from the amount the consumer paid for it.

(9)   But paragraph (8) does not apply if it is not appropriate to apply that deduction having regard to—
    (a)   the behaviour of the person who engaged in the prohibited practice, and
    (b)   the impact of the practice on the consumer.

(10)   Where the product supplied up to the time when the consumer rejected it consists wholly or partly of goods, their market price is only to be taken into account under paragraph (8) to the extent that they have been consumed.]

NOTES

Commencement: 1 October 2014.
Inserted as noted to reg 27A at [**2.580**].

[2.586]
[27G   How does the right to unwind work in the case of a consumer to business contract?
(1)   A consumer who has a right to redress in respect of a consumer to business contract has the right to unwind in respect of that contract.

(2)   Where paragraph (1) applies—
    (a)   the consumer has the right to treat the contract as at an end so that the trader and the consumer are released from their obligations under it, and
    (b)   the consumer has the right within paragraph (5) or (6).

(3)   To treat the contract as at an end, the consumer must indicate to the trader that the contract is ended.

(4)   An indication under paragraph (3) may be something that the consumer says or does, but it must be clear.

(5)   If the trader is able to return the goods to the consumer in the condition they were in when sold by the consumer—
    (a)   the consumer has a right to the return of the goods, and
    (b)   the consumer must repay to the trader the amount (if any) that the trader has paid for the goods.

(6)   If paragraph (5) does not apply, the consumer has a right to a payment from the trader of the amount (if any) by which the market price of the goods when the trader paid for them exceeds what the trader paid for them.]

NOTES

Commencement: 1 October 2014.
Inserted as noted to reg 27A at [**2.580**].

[2.587]
[27H   How does the right to unwind work if payments are demanded which are not due?
(1)   A consumer has the right to unwind in respect of a consumer payment for a product within regulation 2(1A) and (1B) if the consumer was not required to make all or part of the payment.

(2)   Where paragraph (1) applies, the consumer has the right to receive back from the trader—
    (a)   the same amount of money as the consumer paid to the trader, or
    (b)   in a case where the consumer was required to make part of the payment, an amount equal to the part of the payment the consumer was not required to make.]

NOTES

Commencement: 1 October 2014.
Inserted as noted to reg 27A at [**2.580**].

[2.588]
[27I   How does the right to a discount work?
[(1)   A consumer has the right to a discount in respect of a business to consumer contract if—
    (a)   the consumer has made one or more payments for the product to the trader or one or more payments under the contract have not been made, and
    (b)   the consumer has not exercised the right to unwind in respect of the contract.

(2)   If the consumer has made one or more payments, the consumer has the right to receive back from the trader the relevant percentage of the payment or payments.

(3)   If one or more payments have not been made, the consumer has the right—
    (a)   to reduce by the relevant percentage as many of those payments as is appropriate having regard to the seriousness of the prohibited practice, or
    (b)   in a case within paragraph (6), to reduce all of those payments by the relevant percentage.

(4)   Subject to paragraph (6), the relevant percentage is as follows—
    (a)   if the prohibited practice is more than minor, it is 25%,

(b)   if the prohibited practice is significant, it is 50%,
(c)   if the prohibited practice is serious, it is 75%, and
(d)   if the prohibited practice is very serious, it is 100%.

(5)   The seriousness of the prohibited practice is to be assessed by reference to—
   (a)   the behaviour of the person who engaged in the practice,
   (b)   the impact of the practice on the consumer, and
   (c)   the time that has elapsed since the prohibited practice took place.

(6)   *Paragraph (5)* does not apply if—
   (a)   the amount payable for the product under the contract exceeds £5,000,
   (b)   the market price of the product, at the time that the consumer entered into the contract, is lower than the amount payable for it under the contract, and
   (c)   there is clear evidence of the difference between the market price of the product and the amount payable for it under the contract.

(7)   In such a case, the relevant percentage is the percentage difference between the market price of the product and the amount payable for it under the contract.

(8)   The application of this regulation does not affect any of the other rights and liabilities under the contract.]

NOTES

Commencement: 1 October 2014.
Inserted as noted to reg 27A at **[2.580]**.
Para (6): for the words in italics there are substituted the words "Paragraph (4)" by the Consumer Contracts (Amendment) Regulations 2015, SI 2015/1629, regs 2, 9, in relation to contracts entered into on or after 1 October 2015.

[2.589]
[27J   How does the right to damages work?

(1)   Subject as follows, a consumer has the right to damages if the consumer—
   (a)   has incurred financial loss which the consumer would not have incurred if the prohibited practice in question had not taken place, or
   (b)   has suffered alarm, distress or physical inconvenience or discomfort which the consumer would not have suffered if the prohibited practice in question had not taken place.

(2)   The right to damages is the right to be paid damages by the trader for the loss or the alarm, distress or physical inconvenience or discomfort in question.

(3)   The right to be paid damages for financial loss does not include the right to be paid damages in respect of the difference between the market price of a product and the amount payable for it under a contract.

(4)   The right to be paid damages under this regulation is a right to be paid only damages in respect of loss that was reasonably foreseeable at the time of the prohibited practice.

(5)   A consumer does not have the right to damages if the trader proves that—
   (a)   the occurrence of the prohibited practice in question was due to—
      (i)   a mistake,
      (ii)   reliance on information supplied to the trader by another person,
      (iii)   the act or default of a person other than the trader,
      (iv)   an accident, or
      (v)   another cause beyond the trader's control, and
   (b)   the trader took all reasonable precautions and exercised all due diligence to avoid the occurrence of the prohibited practice.]

NOTES

Commencement: 1 October 2014.
Inserted as noted to reg 27A at **[2.580]**.

[2.590]
[27K   How can a consumer enforce the rights to redress?

(1)   A consumer with a right to redress under this Part may bring a claim in civil proceedings to enforce that right.

(2)   In Scotland, proceedings to enforce the right to unwind may be brought before the sheriff or in the Court of Session.

(3)   Paragraph (4) applies if in proceedings under this regulation the consumer establishes that the consumer has—
   (a)   the right to unwind,
   (b)   the right to a discount, or
   (c)   the right to damages.

(4)   The court must make an order that gives effect to—
   (a)   that right, and
   (b)   any associated obligations of the consumer under this Part.

(5) The Limitation Act 1980 applies to a claim under this regulation in England and Wales as if it were an action founded on simple contract.

(6) The Limitation (Northern Ireland) Order 1989 applies to a claim under this regulation in Northern Ireland as if it were an action founded on simple contract.]

NOTES

Commencement: 1 October 2014.
Inserted as noted to reg 27A at **[2.580]**.

[2.591]
[27L How does this Part relate to the existing law?

(1) Nothing in this Part affects the ability of a consumer to make a claim under a rule of law or equity, or under an enactment, in respect of conduct constituting a prohibited practice.

(2) But a consumer may not—
  (a) make a claim to be compensated under a rule of law or equity, or under an enactment, in respect of such conduct if the consumer has been compensated under this Part in respect of the conduct, or
  (b) make a claim to be compensated under this Part in respect of such conduct if the consumer has been compensated under a rule of law or equity, or under an enactment, in respect of the conduct.

(3) In this regulation "enactment" includes—
  (a) an enactment contained in subordinate legislation within the meaning of the Interpretation Act 1978,
  (b) an enactment contained in, or in an instrument made under, a Measure or Act of the National Assembly for Wales,
  (c) an enactment contained in, or in an instrument made under, an Act of the Scottish Parliament, and
  (d) an enactment contained in, or in an instrument made under, Northern Ireland legislation.]

NOTES

Commencement: 1 October 2014.
Inserted as noted to reg 27A at **[2.580]**.

[2.592]
[[27M Inertia selling

(1) This regulation applies where a trader engages in the unfair commercial practice described in paragraph 29 of Schedule 1 (inertia selling).

(2) The consumer is exempted from any obligation to provide consideration for the products supplied by the trader.

(3) The absence of a response from the consumer following the supply does not constitute consent to the provision of consideration for, or the return or safekeeping of, the products.

(4) In the case of an unsolicited supply of goods, the consumer may, as between the consumer and the trader, use, deal with or dispose of the goods as if they were an unconditional gift to the consumer.]

NOTES

Commencement: 1 October 2014.
Inserted (as reg 27A) by the Consumer Contracts (Information, Cancellation and Additional Charges) Regulations 2013, SI 2013/3134, reg 39, with effect in relation to contracts entered into on or after 13 June 2014; renumbered as reg 27M by the Consumer Protection (Amendment) Regulations 2014, SI 2014/870, reg 4(2), in relation to contracts entered into, or payments made, on or after 1 October 2014.

PART 5
SUPPLEMENTARY

[2.593]
28 Crown

(1) The powers conferred by regulations 21 and 22 are not exercisable in relation to premises occupied by the Crown.

(2) The Crown is not criminally liable as a result of any provision of these Regulations.

(3) Paragraph (2) does not affect the application of any provision of these Regulations in relation to a person in the public service of the Crown.

NOTES

Para (1): revoked by the Consumer Rights Act 2015 (Commencement No 3, Transitional Provisions, Savings and Consequential Amendments) Order 2015, SI 2015/1630, art 5, Sch 2, paras 114, 116, as from 1 October 2015 (for transitional provisions see arts 6–8 thereof at **[2.1220]** et seq).

[2.594]
29   Validity of agreements

[Except as provided by Part 4A,] an agreement shall not be void or unenforceable by reason only of a breach of these Regulations.

NOTES

Words in square brackets inserted by the Consumer Protection (Amendment) Regulations 2014, SI 2014/870, reg 4(3), in relation to contracts entered into, or payments made, on or after 1 October 2014.

[2.595]
30   Amendments, repeals and transitional and saving provisions

(1)   Schedule 2 (which contains amendments) shall have effect.

(2)   Schedule 3 (which contains transitional and saving provisions) shall have effect.

(3)   Schedule 4 (which contains repeals and revocations) shall have effect.

SCHEDULES

SCHEDULE 1
COMMERCIAL PRACTICES WHICH ARE IN ALL
CIRCUMSTANCES CONSIDERED UNFAIR

Regulation 3(4)(d)

[2.596]
1. Claiming to be a signatory to a code of conduct when the trader is not.

2. Displaying a trust mark, quality mark or equivalent without having obtained the necessary authorisation.

3. Claiming that a code of conduct has an endorsement from a public or other body which it does not have.

4. Claiming that a trader (including his commercial practices) or a product has been approved, endorsed or authorised by a public or private body when the trader, the commercial practices or the product have not or making such a claim without complying with the terms of the approval, endorsement or authorisation.

5. Making an invitation to purchase products at a specified price without disclosing the existence of any reasonable grounds the trader may have for believing that he will not be able to offer for supply, or to procure another trader to supply, those products or equivalent products at that price for a period that is, and in quantities that are, reasonable having regard to the product, the scale of advertising of the product and the price offered (bait advertising).

6. Making an invitation to purchase products at a specified price and then—
   (a)   refusing to show the advertised item to consumers,
   (b)   refusing to take orders for it or deliver it within a reasonable time, or
   (c)   demonstrating a defective sample of it,
with the intention of promoting a different product (bait and switch).

7. Falsely stating that a product will only be available for a very limited time, or that it will only be available on particular terms for a very limited time, in order to elicit an immediate decision and deprive consumers of sufficient opportunity or time to make an informed choice.

8. Undertaking to provide after-sales service to consumers with whom the trader has communicated prior to a transaction in a language which is not an official language of the EEA State where the trader is located and then making such service available only in another language without clearly disclosing this to the consumer before the consumer is committed to the transaction.

9. Stating or otherwise creating the impression that a product can legally be sold when it cannot.

10. Presenting rights given to consumers in law as a distinctive feature of the trader's offer.

11. Using editorial content in the media to promote a product where a trader has paid for the promotion without making that clear in the content or by images or sounds clearly identifiable by the consumer (advertorial).

12. Making a materially inaccurate claim concerning the nature and extent of the risk to the personal security of the consumer or his family if the consumer does not purchase the product.

13. Promoting a product similar to a product made by a particular manufacturer in such a manner as deliberately to mislead the consumer into believing that the product is made by that same manufacturer when it is not.

Part 2   Statutory Instruments

14. Establishing, operating or promoting a pyramid promotional scheme where a consumer gives consideration for the opportunity to receive compensation that is derived primarily from the introduction of other consumers into the scheme rather than from the sale or consumption of products.

15. Claiming that the trader is about to cease trading or move premises when he is not.

16. Claiming that products are able to facilitate winning in games of chance.

17. Falsely claiming that a product is able to cure illnesses, dysfunction or malformations.

18. Passing on materially inaccurate information on market conditions or on the possibility of finding the product with the intention of inducing the consumer to acquire the product at conditions less favourable than normal market conditions.

19. Claiming in a commercial practice to offer a competition or prize promotion without awarding the prizes described or a reasonable equivalent.

20. Describing a product as 'gratis', 'free', 'without charge' or similar if the consumer has to pay anything other than the unavoidable cost of responding to the commercial practice and collecting or paying for delivery of the item.

21. Including in marketing material an invoice or similar document seeking payment which gives the consumer the impression that he has already ordered the marketed product when he has not.

22. Falsely claiming or creating the impression that the trader is not acting for purposes relating to his trade, business, craft or profession, or falsely representing oneself as a consumer.

23. Creating the false impression that after-sales service in relation to a product is available in an EEA State other than the one in which the product is sold.

24. Creating the impression that the consumer cannot leave the premises until a contract is formed.

25. Conducting personal visits to the consumer's home ignoring the consumer's request to leave or not to return, except in circumstances and to the extent justified to enforce a contractual obligation.

26. Making persistent and unwanted solicitations by telephone, fax, e-mail or other remote media except in circumstances and to the extent justified to enforce a contractual obligation.

27. Requiring a consumer who wishes to claim on an insurance policy to produce documents which could not reasonably be considered relevant as to whether the claim was valid, or failing systematically to respond to pertinent correspondence, in order to dissuade a consumer from exercising his contractual rights.

28. Including in an advertisement a direct exhortation to children to buy advertised products or persuade their parents or other adults to buy advertised products for them.

29. Demanding immediate or deferred payment for or the return or safekeeping of products supplied by the trader, but not solicited by the consumer, *except where the product is a substitute supplied in accordance with regulation 19(7) of the Consumer Protection (Distance Selling) Regulations 2000 (inertia selling).*

30. Explicitly informing a consumer that if he does not buy the product or service, the trader's job or livelihood will be in jeopardy.

31. Creating the false impression that the consumer has already won, will win, or will on doing a particular act win, a prize or other equivalent benefit, when in fact either—
    (a)   there is no prize or other equivalent benefit, or
    (b)   taking any action in relation to claiming the prize or other equivalent benefit is subject to the consumer paying money or incurring a cost.

NOTES
    Words in italics revoked by the Consumer Contracts (Information, Cancellation and Additional Charges) Regulations 2013, SI 2013/3134, reg 47, Sch 4, para 9, with effect in relation to contracts entered into on or after 13 June 2014.

(*Schedule 2 (Amendments) outside the scope of this work.*)

SCHEDULE 3
TRANSITIONAL AND SAVING PROVISIONS

Regulation 30(2)

[2.597]
1.   Trade Descriptions Act 1968
Notwithstanding the repeal by these Regulations of section 5 of the Trade Descriptions Act 1968—
    (a)   section 5(3) shall continue to apply for the purposes of section 1(8) of the Hallmarking Act 1973 as it applied before that repeal, and

(b)   section 5 shall continue to apply for the purposes of regulation 8(1) of the Crystal Glass (Descriptions) Regulations 1973 as it applied before that repeal.

2. The repeal of section 19(4)(b) and (c) of the Trade Descriptions Act 1968 shall not have effect in relation to the references to section 19 in—
(a)   regulation 8(2) of the Crystal Glass (Descriptions) Regulations 1973;
(b)   regulation 11(1) of the Textile Products (Indications of Fibre Content) Regulations 1986;
(c)   regulation 4(1) of the Electro-medical Equipment (EEC Requirements) Regulations 1988; and
(d)   regulation 10(1) of the Footwear (Indication of Composition) Labelling Regulations 1995.

3. The repeal of section 24(3) of the Trade Descriptions Act 1968 shall not have effect in relation to the references to section 24 in—
(a)   regulation 8(2) of the Crystal Glass (Descriptions) Regulations 1973;
(b)   regulation 11(1) of the Textile Products (Indications of Fibre Content) Regulations 1986;
(c)   regulation 4(1) of the Electro-medical Equipment (EEC Requirements) Regulations 1988; and
(d)   regulation 10(1) of the Footwear (Indication of Composition) Labelling Regulations 1995.

4. Notwithstanding the repeal by these Regulations of section 39(2) of the Trade Descriptions Act 1968, that subsection shall continue to apply for the purposes of section 1 of the Hallmarking Act 1973 as it applied before that repeal.

5.   Application of the Consumer Protection Act 1987 to the Price Indications (Bureaux de Change) (No 2) Regulations 1992

(1)   Despite the repeal by these Regulations of section 26 of the Consumer Protection Act 1987, the Price Indications (Bureaux de Change) (No 2) Regulations 1992 shall continue in force, and that section shall continue to have effect as it had effect immediately before the coming into force of these Regulations for the purposes of amending or revoking those Regulations.

(2)   Where these Regulations repeal a provision of the Consumer Protection Act 1987 that, immediately before the coming into force of these Regulations, was applied by the Price Indications (Bureaux de Change) (No 2) Regulations 1992 to an offence under those Regulations, that provision shall continue to apply to that offence as it applied immediately before the coming into force of these Regulations, notwithstanding that repeal.

6. Notwithstanding the repeals and amendments made by these Regulations to the provisions of Parts 4 and 5 of the Consumer Protection Act 1987 those provisions shall continue to apply in relation to the Price Indications (Bureaux de Change) (No 2) Regulations 1992 as they applied before the coming into force of these Regulations.

7.   Application of the Consumer Protection (Northern Ireland) Order 1987 to the Price Indications (Bureaux de Change) Regulations (Northern Ireland) 1992

(1)   Despite the repeal by these Regulations of Article 19 of the Consumer Protection (Northern Ireland) Order 1987, the Price Indications (Bureaux de Change) Regulations (Northern Ireland) 1992 shall continue in force, and that Article shall continue to have effect as it had effect immediately before the coming into force of these Regulations for the purpose of amending or revoking those Regulations.

(2)   Where these Regulations repeal a provision of the Consumer Protection (Northern Ireland) Order 1987 that, immediately before the coming into force of these Regulations, was applied by the Price Indications (Bureaux de Change) Regulations (Northern Ireland) 1992 to an offence under that Order, that provision shall continue to apply to that offence as it applied immediately before the coming into force of these Regulations, notwithstanding that repeal.

8. Notwithstanding the repeals and amendments made by these Regulations to the provisions of Parts IV and V of the Consumer Protection (Northern Ireland) Order 1987 those provisions shall continue to apply in relation to the Price Indications (Bureaux de Change) Regulations (Northern Ireland) 1992 as they applied before the coming into force of these Regulations.

9.   Enterprise Act 2002 (Part 8 Notice to OFT of Intended Prosecution, Specified Enactments, Revocation and Transitional Provision) Order 2003

(1)   This paragraph applies to offences under the following provisions—
(a)   Part 3 of the Consumer Protection Act 1987;
(b)   section 23 of the Fair Trading Act 1973;
(c)   the Mock Auctions Act 1961;
(d)   section 29 of the Weights and Measures Act 1985.

(2)   Notwithstanding the omission of the references to these provisions in the Enterprise Act 2002 (Part 8 Notice to OFT of Intended Prosecution, Specified Enactments, Revocation and Transitional Provision) Order 2003 by these Regulations section 230 of the Enterprise Act 2002 shall continue to apply in relation to an intention by a local weights and measures authority in England and Wales to start proceedings for an offence to which paragraph (1) applies.

10. Notwithstanding the amendments made by these Regulations to the Enterprise Act 2002 (Part 8 Notice to OFT of Intended Prosecution, Specified Enactments, Revocation and Transitional Provision) Order 2003 that Order shall continue to apply in relation to the Price Indications (Bureaux de Change) (No 2) Regulations 1992 as it applied before the coming into force of these Regulations.

11.   Enterprise Act 2002 (Part 8 Domestic Infringements) Order 2003

(1)   This paragraph applies to an act or omission which immediately before the date on which these Regulations come into force is a domestic infringement under section 211 of the Enterprise Act 2002 in respect of the provisions of—

    (a)   the Business Advertisements (Disclosure) Order 1977;

    (b)   Part 3 of the Consumer Protection Act 1987;

    (c)   Part III of the Consumer Protection (Northern Ireland) Order 1987;

    (d)   the Consumer Transactions (Restrictions on Statements) Order 1976;

    (e)   the Control of Misleading Advertisements Regulations 1988;

    (f)   the Mock Auctions Act 1961;

    (g)   section 29 of the Weights and Measures Act 1985;

    (h)   Article 22(2) of the Weights and Measures (Northern Ireland) Order 1981.

(2)   Notwithstanding the omission of the references to these provisions in the Enterprise Act 2002 (Part 8 Domestic Infringements) Order 2003 by these Regulations an act or omission to which paragraph (1) applies shall continue to be a domestic infringement.

12. Notwithstanding the amendments made by these Regulations to the Enterprise Act 2002 (Part 8 Domestic Infringements) Order 2003 that Order shall continue to apply in relation to the Price Indications (Bureaux de Change) (No 2) Regulations 1992 as it applied before the coming into force of these Regulations.

13.   Enterprise Act 2002 (Part 8 Community Infringements Specified UK Laws) Order 2003

(1)   This paragraph applies to an act or omission which immediately before the date on which these Regulations come into force is a Community infringement under section 212 of the Enterprise Act 2002 by contravening the provisions of—

    (a)   Council Directive 84/450/EEC of 10 September 1984 relating to the approximation of the laws, regulations and administrative provisions of the Member States concerning misleading advertising;

    (b)   the Control of Misleading Advertisements Regulations 1988 except regulation 4A (comparative advertisements); or

    (c)   regulation 4 or 5 of the Consumer Transactions (Restrictions on Statements) Order 1976.

(2)   Notwithstanding the omission of the references to these provisions in the Enterprise Act 2002 (Part 8 Community Infringements Specified UK Laws) Order 2003 by these Regulations an act or omission to which paragraph (1) applies shall continue to be a Community infringement.

14.   Enterprise Act 2002 (Part 8 Community Infringements Specified UK Laws) Order 2006

(1)   This paragraph applies to an act or omission which immediately before the date on which these Regulations come into force is a Community infringement under section 212 of the Enterprise Act 2002 by contravening the provisions of—

    (a)   Directive 97/55/EC of the European Parliament and of the Council of 6 October 1997 amending Directive 84/450/EEC concerning misleading advertising so as to include comparative advertising; or

    (b)   regulation 4A of the Control of Misleading Advertisements Regulations 1988.

(2)   Notwithstanding the omission of the reference to these provisions in the Enterprise Act 2002 (Part 8 Community Infringements Specified UK Laws) Order 2006 by these Regulations an act or omission to which paragraph (1) applies shall continue to be a Community infringement.

15.   Disclosure of information

(1)   This paragraph applies in relation to information which immediately before the date on which these Regulations come into force was subject to the provisions of any enactment which permitted the disclosure of information for the purposes of any function under, or proceedings brought under or by virtue of—

    (a)   the Control of Misleading Advertisements Regulations 1988; or

    (b)   Part 2 of the Fair Trading Act 1973.

(2)   Notwithstanding the repeal of such provisions by these Regulations such disclosure shall continue to be permitted.

(**Schedule 4** *(Repeals and Revocations) outside the scope of this work.*)

ESTATE AGENTS (REDRESS SCHEME) ORDER 2008

(SI 2008/1712)

NOTES
Made: 28 June 2008.
Authority: Estate Agents Act 1979, s 23A.
Commencement: 1 October 2008.

[2.598]
1 Citation and Commencement
This Order may be cited as the Estate Agents (Redress Scheme) Order 2008 and shall come into force on 1st October 2008.

[2.599]
2 Requirement to belong to an approved redress scheme
Every person who engages in relevant estate agency work shall be required to be a member of an approved redress scheme.

ESTATE AGENTS (REDRESS SCHEME) (PENALTY CHARGE) REGULATIONS 2008

(SI 2008/1713)

NOTES
Made: 28 June 2008.
Authority: Estate Agents Act 1979, Sch 4, para 2.
Commencement: 1 October 2008.

[2.600]
1 Citation and Commencement
These Regulations may be cited as the Estate Agents (Redress Scheme) (Penalty Charge) Regulations 2008 and shall come into force on 1st October 2008.

[2.601]
2 Level of the penalty charge
The amount of the penalty charge specified in a notice given to a person under section 23B(1) of the Estate Agents Act 1979 shall be £1000.

CANCELLATION OF CONTRACTS MADE IN A CONSUMER'S HOME OR PLACE OF WORK ETC REGULATIONS 2008

(SI 2008/1816)

NOTES
Made: 8 July 2008.
Authority: European Communities Act 1972, s 2(2); Consumers, Estate Agents and Redress Act 2007, s 59.
Commencement: 1 October 2008.
These Regulations re-implemented Council Directive 85/577/EEC which was repealed and replaced by European Parliament and Council Directive 2011/83/EU (the Consumer Rights Directive) at **[4.523]**. The 1985 Directive was originally implemented in the UK by the Consumer Protection (Cancellation of Contracts Concluded away from Business Premises) Regulations 1987, SI 1987/2117 (revoked).
See further, in relation to the disapplication of these Regulations, to contracts entered into on or after 13 June 2014: the Consumer Contracts (Information, Cancellation and Additional Charges) Regulations 2013, SI 2013/3134, reg 2(b).

ARRANGEMENT OF REGULATIONS

Part 2   Statutory Instruments

[2.602]
1 Citation and commencement
These Regulations may be cited as the Cancellation of Contracts made in a Consumer's Home or Place of Work etc Regulations 2008 and shall come into force on 1st October 2008.

[2.603]
2 Interpretation
(1) In these Regulations:
"the 1974 Act" means the Consumer Credit Act 1974;
"cancellable agreement" has the same meaning as in section 189(1) of the 1974 Act;
"cancellation notice" means a notice in writing given by the consumer which indicates that he wishes to cancel the contract;
"cancellation period" means the period of 7 days starting with the date of receipt by the consumer of a notice of the right to cancel;
"consumer" means a natural person who in making a contract to which these Regulations apply is acting for purposes which can be regarded as outside his trade or profession;
"consumer credit agreement" means an agreement between the consumer and any other person by which the other person provides the consumer with credit of any amount;
"credit" includes a cash loan and any other form of financial accommodation, and for this purpose "cash" includes money in any form;
"enforcement authority" means any person mentioned in regulation 21;
"fixed sum credit" has the same meaning as in section 10(1) of the 1974 Act;
"notice of the right to cancel" means a notice given in accordance with regulation 7;
"related credit agreement" means a consumer credit agreement under which fixed sum credit which fully or partly covers the price under a contract which may be cancelled under regulation 7 is granted—
    (i)   by the trader; or
    (ii)   by another person, under an arrangement made between that person and the trader;
["regulated agreement" has the meaning given by section 189 of the 1974 Act;]
"solicited visit" has the meaning given in regulation 6(3);
"specified contract" has the meaning given in regulation 9; and
"trader" means a person who, in making a contract to which these Regulations apply, is acting in his commercial or professional capacity and anyone acting in the name or on behalf of a trader.
(2) Paragraph 8(2) of Schedule 3 has effect for the purposes of paragraphs 7 and 8(1).

NOTES
Para (1): definition "regulated agreement" inserted by the Financial Services and Markets Act 2000 (Regulated Activities) (Amendment) (No 2) Order 2013, SI 2013/1881, art 28, Schedule, Pt 2, para 38(a).

[2.604]
3 Consequential amendments, revocations and saving
Schedule 1 (Consequential Amendments) shall have effect.

[2.605]

4

(1)   Schedule 2 (Revocations) shall have effect.

(2)   The Consumer Protection (Cancellation of Contracts Concluded away from Business Premises) Regulations 1987 ("the 1987 Regulations") shall continue to have effect in relation to a contract to which they applied before their revocation by these Regulations.

(3)   These Regulations shall not apply to a contract to which the 1987 Regulations applied before their revocation.

[2.606]

5   Scope of application

These Regulations apply to a contract, including a consumer credit agreement, between a consumer and a trader which is for the supply of goods or services to the consumer by a trader and which is made—

    (a)   during a visit by the trader to the consumer's home or place of work, or to the home of another individual;

    (b)   during an excursion organised by the trader away from his business premises; or

    (c)   after an offer made by the consumer during such a visit or excursion.

[2.607]

6

(1)   These Regulations do not apply to—

    (a)   any contracts listed in Schedule 3 (Excepted Contracts);

    (b)   a cancellable agreement;

    (c)   a consumer credit agreement which may be cancelled by the consumer in accordance with the terms of the agreement conferring upon him similar rights as if the agreement were a cancellable agreement;

  [(ca)   a consumer credit agreement [which is a regulated agreement] to which the right of withdrawal applies under section 66A of [the 1974 Act];]

    (d)   a contract made during a solicited visit or a contract made after an offer made by a consumer during a solicited visit where the contract is—

        (i)   a regulated mortgage, home purchase plan or home reversion plan if the making or performance of such a contract constitutes a regulated activity for the purposes of the Financial Services and Markets Act 2000;

      [(ii)   a consumer credit agreement secured on land which is—

        (aa)   a regulated agreement;

        (bb)   an exempt agreement (within the meaning given by article 60B of the Financial Services and Markets Act 2000 (Regulated Activities) Order 2001); or

        (iii)   any other regulated agreement].

(2)   Where any agreement referred to in paragraph (1)(b), [(c), (ca) or (d)(iii)] is a related credit agreement the provisions of regulations 11 and 12 shall apply to the cancellation of that agreement.

(3)   A solicited visit means a visit by a trader, whether or not he is the trader who supplies the goods or services, to a consumer's home or place of work or to the home of another individual, which is made at the express request of the consumer but does not include—

    (a)   a visit by a trader which is made after he, or a person acting in his name or on his behalf—

        (i)   telephones the consumer (otherwise than at the consumer's express request) and indicates during the course of the telephone call (either expressly or by implication) that he, or the trader in whose name or on whose behalf he is acting, is willing to visit the consumer; or

        (ii)   visits the consumer (otherwise than at the consumer's express request) and indicates during the course of that visit (either expressly or by implication) that he, or the trader in whose name or on whose behalf he is acting, is willing to make a subsequent visit to the consumer; or

    (b)   a visit during which the contract which is made relates to goods and services other than those concerning which the consumer requested the visit of the trader, provided that when the visit was requested the consumer did not know, or could not reasonably have known, that the supply of such goods or services formed part of the trader's commercial or professional activities.

NOTES

Para (1): sub-para (ca) inserted by the Consumer Credit (EU Directive) Regulations 2010, SI 2010/1010, regs 94, 95(a), with effect in relation to certain agreements entered into before 1 February 2011, as provided for in regs 101, 101A of the 2010 Regulations at **[2.804]**, **[2.805]**; words in square brackets in sub-para (ca), and sub-para (d)(ii), (iii) substituted, by the Financial Services and Markets Act 2000 (Regulated Activities) (Amendment) (No 2) Order 2013, SI 2013/1881, art 28, Schedule, Pt 2, para 38.

Para (2): words in square brackets substituted by SI 2010/1010, regs 94, 95(b), with effect in relation to certain agreements entered into before 1 February 2011, as provided for in regs 101, 101A of the 2010 Regulations at **[2.804]**, **[2.805]**.

[2.608]

7 Right to cancel a contract to which these Regulations apply

(1) A consumer has the right to cancel a contract to which these Regulations apply within the cancellation period.

(2) The trader must give the consumer a written notice of his right to cancel the contract and such notice must be given at the time the contract is made except in the case of a contract to which regulation 5(c) applies in which case the notice must be given at the time the offer is made by the consumer.

(3) The notice must—

    (a) be dated;

    (b) indicate the right of the consumer to cancel the contract within the cancellation period;

    (c) be easily legible;

    (d) contain—

        (i) the information set out in Part I of Schedule 4; and

        (ii) a cancellation form in the form set out in Part II of that Schedule provided as a detachable slip and completed by or on behalf of the trader in accordance with the notes; and

    (e) indicate if applicable—

        (i) that the consumer may be required to pay for the goods or services supplied if the performance of the contract has begun with his written agreement before the end of the cancellation period;

        (ii) that a related credit agreement will be automatically cancelled if the contract for goods or services is cancelled.

(4) Where the contract is wholly or partly in writing the notice must be incorporated in the same document.

(5) If incorporated in the contract or another document the notice of the right to cancel must—

    (a) be set out in a separate box with the heading "Notice of the Right to Cancel"; and

    (b) have as much prominence as any other information in the contract or document apart from the heading and the names of the parties to the contract and any information inserted in handwriting.

(6) A contract to which these Regulations apply shall not be enforceable against the consumer unless the trader has given the consumer a notice of the right to cancel and the information required in accordance with this regulation.

[2.609]

8 Exercise of the right to cancel a contract

(1) If the consumer serves a cancellation notice within the cancellation period then the contract is cancelled.

(2) A contract which is cancelled shall be treated as if it had never been entered into by the consumer except where these Regulations provide otherwise.

(3) The cancellation notice must indicate the intention of the consumer to cancel the contract and does not need to follow the form of cancellation notice set out in Part II of Schedule 4.

(4) The cancellation notice must be served on the trader or another person specified in the notice of the right to cancel as a person to whom the cancellation notice may be given.

(5) A cancellation notice sent by post is taken to have been served at the time of posting, whether or not it is actually received.

(6) Where a cancellation notice is sent by electronic mail it is taken to have been served on the day on which it is sent.

[2.610]

9 Cancellation of specified contracts commenced before expiry of the right to cancel

(1) Where the consumer enters into a specified contract and he wishes the performance of the contract to begin before the end of the cancellation period, he must request this in writing.

(2) Where the consumer cancels a specified contract in accordance with regulation 8 he shall be under a duty to pay in accordance with the reasonable requirements of the cancelled contract for goods or services that were supplied before the cancellation.

(3) If the consumer fails to provide the request in writing referred to in paragraph (1) then—

    (a) the trader is not obliged to begin performance of the specified contract before the end of the cancellation period; and

    (b) the consumer is not bound by the duty referred to in paragraph (2) if he cancels the contract in accordance with regulation 8.

(4) For the purposes of this regulation and regulation 13, a "specified contact" means a contract for any of the following—

    (a) the supply of newspapers, periodicals or magazines;

    (b) advertising in any medium;

(c)   the supply of goods the price of which is dependent on fluctuations in the financial markets which cannot be controlled by the trader;

(d)   the supply of goods to meet an emergency;

(e)   the supply of goods made to a customer's specifications or clearly personalised and any services in connection with the provision of such goods;

(f)   the supply of perishable goods;

(g)   the supply of goods which by their nature are consumed by use and which, before the cancellation, were so consumed;

(h)   the supply of goods which, before the cancellation, had become incorporated in any land or thing not comprised in the cancelled contract;

(i)   the supply of goods or services relating to a funeral; or

(j)   the supply of services of any other kind.

[2.611]
10   Recovery of money paid by consumer

(1)   On the cancellation of a contract under regulation 8 any sum paid by or on behalf of the consumer in respect of the contract shall become repayable except where these Regulations provide otherwise.

(2)   If the consumer or any person on his behalf is in possession of any goods under the terms of the cancelled contract then he shall have a lien on them for any sum repayable to him under paragraph (1).

(3)   Where any security has been provided in relation to the cancelled contract, the security shall be treated as never having had effect for that purpose and the trader must immediately return any property lodged with him solely as security for the purposes of the cancelled contract.

[2.612]
11   Automatic cancellation of related credit agreement

(1)   A cancellation notice which cancels a contract for goods or services shall have the effect of cancelling any related credit agreement.

(2)   Subject to paragraphs (3) and (4), where a related credit agreement has been cancelled under paragraph (1)—

(a)   the trader must, if he is not the same person as the creditor under that agreement, immediately on receipt of the cancellation notice inform the creditor that the notice has been given;

(b)   any sum paid by or on behalf of the consumer in relation to the credit agreement must be reimbursed, except for any sum which would have to be paid under sub-paragraph (c);

(c)   the agreement shall continue in force so far as it relates to repayment of the credit and payment of interest in accordance with regulation 12, but shall otherwise cease to be enforceable; and

(d)   any security provided under the related credit agreement shall be treated as never having had effect for that purpose and the creditor must immediately return any property lodged with him solely as security for the purposes of the related credit agreement.

(3)   Where a related credit agreement is a cancellable agreement—

(a)   its cancellation under paragraph (1) shall take effect as if a notice of cancellation within the meaning of the 1974 Act had been served;

(b)   that Act shall apply in respect of the consequences of such cancellation;

(c)   paragraph (2)(b) to (d) and regulation 12 shall not apply in respect of its cancellation; and

(d)   regulations 13 and 14 shall not apply in respect of the cancellation of the related contract for goods or services.

(4)   Where a related credit agreement of a kind referred to in regulation 6(1)(c) is cancelled under paragraph (1)—

(a)   paragraph (2)(b) to (d) and regulation 12 shall not apply in respect of its cancellation; and

(b)   regulations 13 and 14 shall not apply in respect of the cancellation of the related contract for goods or services.

(5)   Where a related credit agreement of a kind referred to in [regulation 6(1)(ca) or 6(1)(d)(iii)] is cancelled under paragraph (1)—

(a)   the provisions of this regulation and regulation 12 shall apply in respect of its cancellation; and

(b)   the provisions of regulations 13 and 14 shall apply in respect of the cancellation of the related contract for goods or services.

(6)   For the purposes of this regulation and regulation 12 "creditor" is the person who grants credit under a related credit agreement.

NOTES

Para (5): words in square brackets substituted by the Consumer Credit (EU Directive) Regulations 2010, SI 2010/1010, regs 94, 96, with effect in relation to certain agreements entered into before 1 February 2011, as provided for in regs 101, 101A of the 2010 Regulations at **[2.804]**, **[2.805]**.

[2.613]

12 Repayment of credit and interest

(1) Where—

   (a)   a contract under which credit is provided to the consumer is cancelled under regulation 8; or

   (b)   a related credit agreement (other than a cancellable agreement or an agreement of a kind referred to in regulation 6(1)(c)) is cancelled as a result of the cancellation of a contract for goods or services,

the contract or agreement shall continue in force so far as it relates to repayment of the credit and payment of interest.

(2) If, following the cancellation of a contract or related credit agreement to which paragraph (1) applies, the consumer repays the whole or a portion of the credit—

   (a)   before the expiry of one month following service of the cancellation notice; or

   (b)   in the case of a credit repayable by instalments, before the date on which the first instalment is due,

no interest shall be payable on the amount repaid.

(3) If the whole of a credit repayable by instalments is not repaid on or before the date specified in paragraph (2)(b), the consumer shall not be liable to repay any of the credit except on receipt of a request in writing signed by the trader stating the amounts of the remaining instalments (recalculated by the trader as nearly as may be in accordance with the contract and without extending the repayment period), but excluding any sum other than principal and interest.

(4) Repayment of a credit, or payment of interest, under a cancelled contract or related credit agreement shall be treated as duly made if it is made to any person on whom, under regulation 8(4), a cancellation notice could have been served.

(5) Where any security has been provided in relation to the contract or consumer credit agreement, the duty imposed on the consumer by this regulation shall not be enforceable before the trader or creditor has discharged any duty imposed on him by regulation 10(3) or 11(2)(d) respectively.

[2.614]

13 Return of goods by consumer after cancellation

(1) A consumer who has acquired possession of any goods by virtue of the contract shall on the cancellation of that contract be under a duty, subject to any lien, to restore the goods to the trader and meanwhile to retain possession of the goods and take reasonable care of them.

(2) The consumer shall not be under a duty to restore goods supplied under a specified contract in circumstances where—

   (a)   he is required to pay, in accordance with the reasonable requirements of the cancelled contract, for the supply of such goods before cancellation; or

   (b)   the trader has begun performance of the contract before the end of the cancellation period without a prior request in writing by the consumer.

(3) The consumer shall not be under any duty to deliver the goods except at his own premises and following a request in writing signed by the trader and served on the consumer either before, or at the time when, the goods are collected from those premises.

(4) If the consumer—

   (a)   delivers the goods (whether at his own premises or elsewhere) to any person on whom, under regulation 8(4), a cancellation notice could have been served; or

   (b)   sends the goods at his own expense to such a person,

he shall be discharged from any duty to retain possession of the goods or restore them to the trader.

(5) Where the consumer delivers the goods as mentioned in paragraph (4)(a), his obligation to take care of the goods shall cease; and if he send the goods as mentioned in paragraph (4)(b), he shall be under a duty to take reasonable care to see that they are received by the trader and not damaged in transit, but in other respects his duty to take care of the goods shall cease.

(6) Where, at any time during the period of 21 days following the cancellation, the consumer receives such a request as is mentioned in paragraph (3) and unreasonably refuses or unreasonably fails to comply with it, his duty to retain possession and take reasonable care of the goods shall continue until he delivers or sends the goods as mentioned in paragraph (4); but if within that period he does not receive such a request his duty to take reasonable care of the goods shall cease at the end of that period.

(7) Where any security has been provided in relation to the cancelled contract, the duty imposed on the consumer to restore goods shall not be enforceable before the trader has discharged any duty imposed on him by regulation 10(3).

(8) Breach of a duty imposed on a consumer by this regulation is actionable as a breach of statutory duty.

[2.615]
14   Goods given in part-exchange

(1)   This regulation applies on the cancellation of a contract where the trader agreed to take goods in part-exchange (the "part-exchange goods") and those goods have been delivered to him.

(2)   Unless, before the end of the period of ten days beginning with the date of cancellation, the part-exchange goods are returned to the consumer in a condition substantially as good as when they were delivered to the trader, the consumer shall be entitled to recover from the trader a sum equal to the part-exchange allowance.

(3)   During the period of ten days beginning with the date of cancellation, the consumer, if he is in possession of goods to which the cancelled contract relates, shall have a lien on them for—
    (a)   delivery of the part-exchange goods in a condition substantially as good as when they were delivered to the trader; or
    (b)   a sum equal to the part-exchange allowance,
and if the lien continues to the end of that period it shall thereafter subsist only as a lien for a sum equal to the part-exchange allowance.

(4)   In this regulation the part-exchange allowance means the sum agreed as such in the cancelled contract, or if no such sum was agreed, such sum as it would have been reasonable to allow in respect of the part-exchange goods if no notice of cancellation had been served.

[2.616]
15   No contracting-out of contracts to which these Regulations apply

(1)   A term contained in a contract is void if, and to the extent that, it is inconsistent with a provision for the protection of the consumer contained in these Regulations.

(2)   Where a provision of these Regulations specifies the duty or liability of the consumer in certain circumstances, a term contained in a contract is inconsistent with that provision if it purports to impose, directly or indirectly, an additional or different duty or liability on the consumer in those circumstances.

[2.617]
16   Service of documents

(1)   A document to be served under these Regulations on a person may be so served—
    (a)   by delivering it to him, or by leaving it at his proper address or by sending it to him at that address;
    (b)   if the person is a body corporate, by serving it in accordance with sub-paragraph (a) on the secretary or clerk of that body;
    (c)   if the person is a partnership, by serving it in accordance with sub-paragraph (a) on a partner or on a person having the control or management of the partnership business; and
    (d)   if the person is an unincorporated body, by serving it in accordance with sub-paragraph (a) on a person having control or management of that body.

(2)   For the purposes of paragraph (1), the proper address of any person on whom a document is to be served under these Regulations is his last known address except that—
    (a)   in the case of service on a body corporate or its secretary or clerk, it is the address of the registered or principal office of the body corporate in the United Kingdom; and
    (b)   in the case of service on a partnership or partner or person having the control or management of a partnership business, it is the partnership's principal place of business in the United Kingdom.

(3)   A person's electronic mail address may also be his proper address for the purposes of paragraph (1).

Enforcement

[2.618]
17   Offence relating to the failure to give notice of the right to cancel

(1)   A trader is guilty of an offence if he enters into a contract to which these Regulations apply but fails to give the consumer a notice of the right to cancel in accordance with regulation 7.

(2)   A person who is guilty of an offence under paragraph (1) shall be liable on summary conviction to a fine not exceeding level 5 on the standard scale.

[2.619]
18   Defence of due diligence

(1)   In any proceedings against a person for an offence under regulation 17 it is a defence for that person to prove—
    (a)   that the commission of the offence was due to—
        (i)   the act or default of another, or
        (ii)   reliance on information given by another, and
    (b)   that he took all reasonable precautions and exercised all due diligence to avoid the commission of such an offence by himself or any person under his control.

Part 2   Statutory Instruments

(2)   A person shall not be entitled to rely on the defence provided by paragraph (1) without leave of the court unless—

(a)   he has served on the prosecutor a notice in writing giving such information identifying or assisting in the identification of that other person as was in his possession; and

(b)   the notice is served on the prosecutor not less than seven clear days before the hearing of the proceedings or, in Scotland, the diet of trial.

[2.620]
19   Liability of persons other than the principal offender
Where the commission by a person of an offence under regulation 17 is due to the act or default of another person, that other person is guilty of the offence and may be proceeded against and punished whether or not proceedings are taken against the first person.

[2.621]
20   Offences committed by bodies of persons
(1)   Where an offence under regulation 17 committed by a body corporate is proved—

(a)   to have been committed with the consent or connivance of an officer of the body corporate or

(b)   to be attributable to any neglect on his part,

the officer, as well as the body corporate shall be guilty of the offence and liable to be proceeded against and punished accordingly.

(2)   In paragraph (1) a reference to an officer of a body corporate includes a reference to—

(a)   a director, manager, secretary or other similar officer; and

(b)   a person purporting to act as a director, manager, secretary or other similar officer.

(3)   Where an offence under regulation 17 committed in Scotland by a Scottish partnership is proved—

(a)   to have been committed with the consent or connivance of a partner; or

(b)   to be attributable to any neglect on his part,

that partner, as well as the partnership shall be guilty of the offence and liable to be proceeded against and punished accordingly.

(4)   In paragraph (3) a reference to a partner includes a person purporting to act as a partner.

[2.622]
21   Duty to enforce
(1)   Subject to paragraphs (2) and (3)—

(a)   it shall be the duty of every weights and measures authority in Great Britain to enforce regulation 17 within its area; and

(b)   it shall be the duty of the Department of Enterprise Trade and Investment in Northern Ireland to enforce regulation 17 within Northern Ireland.

(2)   No proceedings for an offence under these Regulations may be instituted in England and Wales except by or on behalf of an enforcement authority.

(3)   Nothing in paragraph (1) shall authorise any weights and measures authority to bring proceedings in Scotland for an offence.

[2.623]
22   Powers of investigation
(1)   If a duly authorised officer of an enforcement authority has reasonable grounds for suspecting that an offence has been committed under regulation 17, he may require a person carrying on or employed in a business to produce any document relating to the business, and take copies of it or any entry in it for the purposes of ascertaining whether such an offence has been committed.

(2)   If the officer has reasonable grounds for believing that any documents may be required as evidence in proceedings for such an offence, he may seize and detain them and shall, if he does so, inform the person from whom they are seized.

(3)   In this regulation "document" includes information recorded in any form.

(4)   The reference in paragraph (1) to production of documents is, in the case of a document which contains information recorded otherwise than in a legible form, a reference to the production of a copy of the information in a legible form.

(5)   An officer seeking to exercise a power under this regulation must do so only at a reasonable hour and on production (if required) of his identification and authority.

(6)   Nothing in this regulation requires a person to produce, or authorises the taking from a person of, a document which the other person would be entitled to refuse to produce in proceedings in the High Court on the grounds of legal professional privilege or (in Scotland) in the Court of Session on the grounds of confidentiality of communications.

(7)   In paragraph (6) "communications" means—

(a)   communications between a professional legal adviser and his client; or

(b)   communications made in connection with, or in contemplation of legal proceedings and for the purpose of those proceedings.

[2.624]
23 Obstruction of authorised officers
(1)   A person is guilty of an offence if he—
(a)   intentionally obstructs an officer of an enforcement authority acting in pursuance of his functions under these Regulations;
(b)   without reasonable cause fails to comply with any requirement properly made of him by such an officer under regulation 22; or
(c)   without reasonable cause fails to give such an officer any other assistance or information which he may reasonably require of him for the purpose of the performance of his functions under these Regulations.

(2)   A person is guilty of an offence if, in giving any information which is required of him under paragraph (1)(c), he makes any statement which he knows to be false in a material particular.

(3)   A person guilty of an offence under paragraph (1) or (2) shall be liable on summary conviction to a fine not exceeding level 3 on the standard scale.

[2.625]
24

Nothing in regulation 22 or 23 shall be construed as requiring a person to answer any question or give any information if to do so might incriminate him.

SCHEDULES

SCHEDULES 1, 2

(Sch 1 amends the Consumer Credit Act 1974, s 74 at **[1.561]** *and amends other legislation outside the scope of this work; Sch 2 revokes the Consumer Protection (Cancellation of Contracts Concluded away from Business Premises) Regulations 1987, SI 1987/2117 and revokes other legislation outside the scope of this work.)*

SCHEDULE 3
EXCEPTED CONTRACTS
Regulations 2(2) and 6(1)(a)

[2.626]
1. A contract for the construction, sale or rental of immovable property or a contract concerning other rights relating to immovable property other than—
(a)   a contract for the construction of extensions, patios, conservatories or driveways;
(b)   a contract for the supply of goods and their incorporation in immovable property; and
(c)   a contract for the repair, refurbishment or improvement of immovable property.

2. A contract for the supply of foodstuffs or beverages or other goods intended for current consumption in the household and supplied by a regular roundsman.

3. A contract for the supply of goods or services provided that each of the following conditions is met:
(a)   the contract is concluded on the basis of a trader's catalogue which the consumer has a proper opportunity of reading in the absence of the trader's representative;
(b)   there is intended to be continuity of contact between the trader's representative and the consumer in relation to that or any subsequent transaction; and
(c)   both the catalogue and the contract contain a prominent notice informing the consumer of his rights to return goods to the supplier within a period of not less than seven days of receipt or otherwise to cancel the contract within that period without obligation of any kind other than to take reasonable care of the goods.

4. A contract of insurance.

5. Any contract under which credit within the meaning of the 1974 Act is provided not exceeding £35 other than a hire purchase or conditional sale agreement.

6. Any contract not falling within paragraph 5 under which the total payments to be made by the consumer do not exceed £35.

7. Any agreement the making or performance of which by either party constitutes a relevant regulated activity.

8. (1)   For the purposes of paragraph 7—
(a)   "a relevant regulated activity" means an activity of the following kind—
(i)   dealing in investments, as principal or as agent;

     (ii)   arranging deals in investments;

     (iii) operating a multilateral trading facility;

     (iv) managing investments;

     (v)   safeguarding and administering investments;

     (vi) establishing, operating or winding up a collective investment scheme; and

  (b) for these purposes "investment" means—

     (i)   shares;

     (ii) instruments creating or acknowledging indebtedness;

     (iii) instruments giving entitlement to investments

     (iv) certificates representing securities;

     (v)   units in a collective investment scheme;

     (vi) options;

     (vii) futures;

     (viii) contracts for differences; and

     (ix) rights to or interests in investments.

(2)   Paragraph 7 and this paragraph must be read with—

  (a) section 22 of the Financial Services and Markets Act 2000;

  (b) any relevant order under that section; and

  (c) Schedule 2 to that Act,

but any restriction on or exclusion from the meaning of a regulated activity for the purposes of paragraph 7 which arises from the identity of the person carrying on such activity is to be disregarded.

SCHEDULE 4
NOTICE OF THE RIGHT TO CANCEL

Regulation 7(3)

PART I
INFORMATION TO BE CONTAINED IN NOTICE OF THE RIGHT TO CANCEL

[2.627]

1. The identity of the trader including trading name if any.

2. The trader's reference number, code or other details to enable the contract or offer to be identified.

3. A statement that the consumer has a right to cancel the contract if he wishes and that this right can be exercised by delivering, or sending (including by electronic mail) a cancellation notice to the person mentioned in the next paragraph at any time within the period of 7 days starting with the day of receipt of a notice in writing of the right to cancel the contract.

4. The name and address, (including any electronic mail address as well as the postal address), of a person to whom a cancellation notice may be given.

5. A statement that notice of cancellation is deemed to be served as soon as it is posted or sent to a trader or in the case of an electronic communication from the day it is sent to the trader.

6. A statement that the consumer can use the cancellation form provided if he wishes.

PART II
CANCELLATION NOTICE TO BE INCLUDED IN NOTICE OF THE RIGHT TO CANCEL

[2.628]

If you wish to cancel the contract you MUST DO SO IN WRITING and deliver personally or send (which may be by electronic mail) this to the person named below. You may use this form if you want to but you do not have to.

(Complete, detach and return this form ONLY IF YOU WISH TO CANCEL THE CONTRACT).

To:. . . . . [trader to insert name and address of person to whom notice may be given.]

I/We (delete as appropriate) hereby give notice that I/we (delete as appropriate) wish to cancel my/our (delete as appropriate) contract . .[trader to insert reference number, code and other details to enable the contract or offer to be identified. He may also insert the name and address of the consumer.]

Signed

Name and Address

Date

PAYMENT SERVICES REGULATIONS 2009

(SI 2009/209)

NOTES

Made: 9 February 2009.

Authority: European Communities Act 1972, s 2(2).

Commencement: 2 March 2009 (for the purposes specified in reg 1(2)(a)), 1 May 2009 (for the purposes specified in reg 1(2)(b)), and 1 November 2009 (otherwise).

References to "the European Community", "Community", etc: see the Treaty of Lisbon (Changes in Terminology) Order 2011, SI 2011/1043, which provides that (as from 22 April 2011): (i) for references to the European Communities or to the European Community or the European Coal and Steel Community (including references to "the Communities", "the Community", "the EC" or "the EEC") substitute references to the European Union, and (ii) references to "EU" should be substituted for the word "Community" (subject to certain exceptions) in references to "Community treaties", "Community instrument", "Community obligation", "Community law", "Community legislation", etc.

ARRANGEMENT OF REGULATIONS

Part 2   Statutory Instruments

PART 1
INTRODUCTORY PROVISIONS

[2.629]

1   Citation and commencement

(1)   These Regulations may be cited as the Payment Services Regulations 2009.

(2)   These Regulations come into force—

    (a)   on 2nd March 2009 for the purposes of regulations 25, 80, 92 to 94, 95 in respect of paragraphs 5 and 10 of Schedule 5, 119 and 126 in respect of paragraphs 1 and 6(g) of Schedule 6;

    (b)   on 1st May 2009 for the purposes of—

        (i)   enabling applications for authorisation as a payment institution and the variation of an authorisation to be made under regulation 5 and the Authority to determine such applications in accordance with regulations 6 to 9;

        (ii)   enabling applications for registration as a small payment institution and the variation of a registration to be made under regulation 12 and the Authority to determine such applications in accordance with regulation 13 and regulations 7 to 9 (as applied by regulation 14);

        (iii)   enabling applications for an agent to be included on the register under regulation 29 and the Authority to determine such applications in accordance with that regulation;

        (iv)   enabling the Authority to give directions as to the manner in which an application under regulation 5(1) or (2), 12(1) or (2) or 29(3) is to be made and enabling the Authority to require the applicant to provide further information in accordance with regulation 5(4), 12(4) or 29(3)(a)(iv), as the case may be;

        (v)   enabling the Authority to cancel an authorisation or registration or vary an authorisation or registration on its own initiative in accordance with regulation 10 or 11 (as applied, in the case of a registration, by regulation 14);

        (vi)   requiring a person who has made an application under regulation 5(1) or (2) or 12(1) or (2) to provide information to the Authority in accordance with regulation 16 and enabling the Authority to give directions under that regulation;

        (vii)   enabling a person to make a reference to the [Upper Tribunal] under regulation 9(9), 10(4), 11(5), 24(4) or 29(11);

    (viii) enabling an applicant for authorisation as a payment institution to give the Authority a notice of intention under regulation 23(1) and the Authority to give directions as to the manner in which such a notice is to be given and to inform the host state competent authority in accordance with regulation 23(2);

    (ix) enabling the Authority to decide whether to register an EEA branch, or to cancel such a registration, under regulation 24(1);

    (x) enabling the Authority to give directions under regulation 82 to a person whose application under regulation 5(1) or 12(1) has been granted before 1st November 2009 in respect of—

        (aa) its provision as from that date of payment services; and

        (bb) its compliance as from that date with requirements imposed by or under Parts 2 to 6 of these Regulations;

    (xi) enabling the Authority to give directions under paragraph 7, 11, 12 or 16(3) of Schedule 3 to a person whose application under regulation 5(1) has been granted before 1st November 2009;

    (xii) requiring a person whose application under regulation 5(1), 12(1) or 29(3) has been granted before 1st November 2009 to provide information to the Authority in accordance with regulation 32 and enabling the Authority to give directions under that regulation;

    (xiii) regulations 95 in respect of paragraphs 2 and 7 to 9 of Schedule 5, 114 to 118, and 121, 124 and 125; and

  (c) for all other purposes on 1st November 2009.

NOTES

Para (2): words in square brackets in sub-para (b)(vii) substituted by the Transfer of Tribunal Functions Order 2010, SI 2010/22, art 5(2), Sch 3, paras 177, 178, subject to transitional provisions and savings in Sch 5 thereto.

[2.630]
2   Interpretation

(1) In these Regulations—

"the 2000 Act" means the Financial Services and Markets Act 2000;

"agent" means a person who acts on behalf of an authorised payment institution or a small payment institution in the provision of payment services;

"authorised payment institution" means—

  (a) a person included by the Authority in the register as an authorised payment institution pursuant to regulation 4(1)(a); or

  (b) a person deemed to have been granted authorisation by the Authority by virtue of regulation 121;

"the Authority" means the [Financial Conduct Authority];

"branch" means a place of business of an authorised payment institution, a small payment institution, or an EEA authorised payment institution, other than its head office, which forms a legally dependent part of the institution and which carries out directly all or some of the transactions inherent in its business; and, for the purposes of these Regulations, all places of business set up in the same EEA State other than the United Kingdom by an authorised payment institution are to be regarded as a single branch;

"business day" means any day on which the relevant payment service provider is open for business as required for the execution of a payment transaction;

["the capital requirements directive" means Directive 2013/36/EU of the European Parliament and of the Council of 26 June 2013 relating to the activity of credit institutions and the prudential supervision of credit institutions and investment firms, amending Directive 2002/87/EC and repealing Directives 2006/48/EC and 2006/49/EC;

"the capital requirements regulation" means Regulation (EU) 575/2013 of the European Parliament and of the Council of 26 June 2013 on prudential requirements for credit institutions and investment firms and amending Regulation (EU) No 648/2012;]

"charity" means a body whose annual income is less than £1 million and is—

  (c) in England and Wales, a charity as defined by section 1(1) of the Charities Act 2006;

  (d) in Scotland, a charity as defined by section 106 of the Charities and Trustee Investment (Scotland) Act 2005;

  (e) in Northern Ireland, a charity as defined by section 1(1) of the Charities Act (Northern Ireland) 2008 or, until that section comes into force, a body which is recognised as a charity for tax purposes by Her Majesty's Revenue and Customs;

[. . . .]

"the Commissioners" means the Commissioners for Her Majesty's Revenue and Customs;

"consumer" means an individual who, in contracts for payment services to which these Regulations apply, is acting for purposes other than a trade, business or profession;

"credit institution" has the meaning given in [Article 4(1)(1) of the capital requirements regulation];

"direct debit" means a payment service for debiting the payer's payment account where a payment transaction is initiated by the payee on the basis of consent given by the payer to the payee, to the payee's payment service provider or to the payer's own payment service provider;

"durable medium" means any instrument which enables the payment service user to store information addressed personally to them in a way accessible for future reference for a period of time adequate for the purposes of the information and which allows the unchanged reproduction of the information stored;

"the EEA" means the European Economic Area;

"EEA agent" means an agent through which an authorised payment institution, in the exercise of its passport rights, provides payment services in an EEA State other than the United Kingdom;

"EEA authorised payment institution" means a person authorised in an EEA State other than the United Kingdom to provide payment services in accordance with the payment services directive;

"EEA branch" means a branch established by an authorised payment institution, in the exercise of its passport rights, to carry out payment services in an EEA State other than the United Kingdom;

["the electronic money directive" means Directive 2009/110/EC of the European Parliament and of the Council of 16th September 2009 on the taking up, pursuit and prudential supervision of the business of electronic money institutions;]

"electronic money institution" has the meaning given in [Article 2(1)] of the electronic money directive;

"framework contract" means a contract for payment services which governs the future execution of individual and successive payment transactions and which may contain the obligation and conditions for setting up a payment account;

"funds" means banknotes and coins, scriptural money, and electronic money as defined in [Article 2(2)] of the electronic money directive;

"group" means a group of undertakings which consists of a parent undertaking, its subsidiary undertakings and the entities in which the parent undertaking or its subsidiary undertakings have a holding, as well as undertakings linked to each other by a relationship referred to in Article 12(1) of the Seventh Council Directive 83/349/EEC of 13th June 1983 based on Article 54(3)(g) of the Treaty on consolidated accounts;

"home state competent authority" means the competent authority designated in accordance with Article 20 of the payment services directive as being responsible for the authorisation and prudential supervision of an EEA authorised payment institution which is exercising (or intends to exercise) its passport rights in the United Kingdom;

"host state competent authority" means the competent authority designated in accordance with Article 20 of the payment services directive in an EEA State in which an authorised payment institution exercises (or intends to exercise) its passport rights;

"means of distance communication" means any means which, without the simultaneous physical presence of the payment service provider and the payment service user, may be used for the conclusion of a contract for payment services between those parties;

"micro-enterprise" means an enterprise which, at the time at which the contract for payment services is entered into, is an enterprise as defined in Article 1 and Article 2(1) and (3) of the Annex to Recommendation 2003/361/EC;

"the money laundering directive" means Directive 2005/60/EC of the European Parliament and of the Council of 26th October 2005 on the prevention of the use of the financial system for the purpose of money laundering and terrorist financing;

"money remittance" means a service for the transmission of money (or any representation of monetary value), without any payment accounts being created in the name of the payer or the payee, where—

(a) funds are received from a payer for the sole purpose of transferring a corresponding amount to a payee or to another payment service provider acting on behalf of the payee; or

(b) funds are received on behalf of, and made available to, the payee;

"notice" means a notice in writing;
. . .

"parent undertaking" has the same meaning as in the Companies Acts (see section 1162 of, and Schedule 7 to, the Companies Act 2006);

"passport right" (except for the purposes of regulation 26(1)) means the entitlement of a person to establish a branch or provide services in an EEA State other than that in which they are authorised to provide payment services—

(a) in accordance with [the Treaty on the Functioning of the European Union] as applied in the EEA; and

(b) subject to the conditions of the payment services directive;

"payee" means a person who is the intended recipient of funds which have been the subject of a payment transaction;

"payer" means—

(a)   a person who holds a payment account and initiates, or consents to the initiation of, a payment order from that payment account; or

(b)   where there is no payment account, a person who gives a payment order;

"payment account" means an account held in the name of one or more payment service users which is used for the execution of payment transactions;

"payment instrument" means any—

(a)   personalised device; or

(b)   personalised set of procedures agreed between the payment service user and the payment service provider,

used by the payment service user in order to initiate a payment order;

"payment order" means any instruction by—

(a)   a payer; or

(b)   a payee,

to their respective payment service provider requesting the execution of a payment transaction;

"payment services" means any of the activities specified in Part 1 of Schedule 1 when carried out as a regular occupation or business activity, other than any of the activities specified in Part 2 of that Schedule;

"payment services directive" means Directive 2007/64/EC of the European Parliament and of the Council of 13th November 2007 on payment services in the internal market;

"payment service provider" means any of the following persons when they carry out payment services—

(a)   authorised payment institutions;

(b)   small payment institutions;

(c)   EEA authorised payment institutions;

(d)   credit institutions;

(e)   electronic money institutions;

(f)   the Post Office Limited;

(g)   the Bank of England, the European Central Bank and the national central banks of EEA States other than the United Kingdom, other than when acting in their capacity as a monetary authority or carrying out other functions of a public nature; and

(h)   government departments and local authorities, other than when carrying out functions of a public nature;

"payment service user" means a person when making use of a payment service in the capacity of either payer or payee, or both;

"payment system" means a funds transfer system with formal and standardised arrangements and common rules for the processing, clearing and settlement of payment transactions;

["the Payment Systems Regulator" means the body established under section 40 of the Financial Services (Banking Reform) Act 2013;]

"payment transaction" means an act, initiated by the payer or payee, of placing, transferring or withdrawing funds, irrespective of any underlying obligations between the payer and payee;

"qualifying holding" has the meaning given in [Article 4(1)(36) of the capital requirements regulation];

"reference exchange rate" means the exchange rate which is used as the basis to calculate any currency exchange and which is made available by the payment service provider or comes from a publicly available source;

"reference interest rate" means the interest rate which is used as the basis for calculating any interest to be applied and which comes from a publicly available source which can be verified by both parties to a contract for payment services;

"the register" means the register maintained by the Authority under regulation 4;

"regulated agreement" has the meaning given by section 189(1) of the Consumer Credit Act 1974 (definitions);

"single payment service contract" means a contract for a single payment transaction not covered by a framework contract;

"small payment institution" means a person included by the Authority in the register pursuant to regulation 4(1)(b);

"subsidiary undertaking" has the same meaning as in the Companies Acts (see section 1162 of, and Schedule 7 to, the Companies Act 2006);

. . .

"unique identifier" means a combination of letters, numbers or symbols specified to the payment service user by the payment service provider and to be provided by the payment service user in relation to a payment transaction in order to identify unambiguously one or both of—

(a)   the other payment service user who is a party to the payment transaction;

(b)   the other payment service user's payment account;

"value date" means a reference time used by a payment service provider for the calculation of interest on the funds debited from or credited to a payment account.

Part 2   Statutory Instruments

(2)   In these Regulations references to amounts in euro include references to equivalent amounts in another currency.

(3)   Unless otherwise defined, expressions used in these Regulations which are also used in the payment services directive have the same meaning as in that directive.

(4)   Expressions used in these Regulations and in a modification to a provision in primary or secondary legislation applied by these Regulations have the same meaning as in these Regulations.

NOTES

Para (1) is amended as follows:

Words in square brackets in the definition "the Authority" substituted by the Financial Services Act 2012 (Consequential Amendments and Transitional Provisions) Order 2013, SI 2013/472, art 3, Sch 2, para 155(1), (2).

Definition "the banking consolidation directive" (omitted) revoked, definitions "the capital requirements directive" and "the capital requirements regulation" inserted, and words in square brackets in the definitions "credit institution" and "qualifying holding" substituted, by the Capital Requirements Regulations 2013, SI 2013/3115, reg 46(1), Sch 2, Pt 3, para 70(1), (2).

Definition "the CMA" (omitted) originally inserted by the Enterprise and Regulatory Reform Act 2013 (Competition) (Consequential, Transitional and Saving Provisions) (No 2) Order 2014, SI 2014/549, art 2, Schedule, Pt 2, para 36(1), (2) (for transitional provisions in relation to the continuity of functions, etc, see art 3 of the 2014 Order), and revoked by the Payment Services (Amendment) Regulations 2015, SI 2015/422, reg 2(1), (2).

Words in square brackets in the definitions "electronic money institution" and "funds" substituted by SI 2011/99, reg 79, Sch 4, Pt 2, para 21(a)(ii), (iv), (v).

Definition "the electronic money directive" substituted by SI 2011/99, reg 79, Sch 4, Pt 2, para 21(a)(iii).

Definition "the OFT" (omitted) revoked by SI 2014/549, art 2, Schedule, Pt 2, para 36(1), (2) (for transitional provisions in relation to the continuity of functions, etc, see art 3 of the 2014 Order).

Words in square brackets in the definition "passport right" substituted by the Treaty of Lisbon (Changes in Terminology or Numbering) Order 2012, SI 2012/1809, art 3, Schedule, Pt 2.

Definition "the Payment Systems Regulator" inserted by SI 2015/422, reg 2(1), (2).

Definition "the Tribunal" (omitted) revoked by the Transfer of Tribunal Functions Order 2010, SI 2010/22, art 5(2), Sch 3, paras 177, 179 (for transitional provisions and savings in relation to existing cases and appeals from the Financial Services and Markets Tribunal, see Sch 5 to that Order).

[2.631]
3   Exemption for certain bodies

(1)   Subject to paragraph (2) and regulation 4(1)(d), these Regulations do not apply to the following persons—

    (a)   credit unions;

    (b)   municipal banks; and

    (c)   the National Savings Bank.

(2)   Where municipal banks provide or propose to provide payment services they must give notice to the Authority.

(3)   In this regulation—

"credit union" means a credit union within the meaning of—

    (a)   the Credit Unions Act 1979;

    (b)   the Credit Unions (Northern Ireland) Order 1985;

"municipal bank" means a company which, immediately before 1st December 2001, fell within the definition in section 103 of the Banking Act 1987.

PART 2
REGISTRATION

The register

[2.632]
4   The register of certain payment service providers

(1)   The Authority must maintain a register of—

    (a)   authorised payment institutions and their EEA branches;

    (b)   small payment institutions;

    (c)   agents of authorised payment institutions and small payment institutions required to be registered under regulation 29; and

    (d)   the persons specified in regulation 3(1) where they provide payment services.

(2)   The Authority may include on the register any of the persons mentioned in paragraphs (c) to (h) of the definition of a payment service provider in regulation 2(1) where such persons provide payment services.

(3)   Where a person mentioned in paragraph (f), (g) or (h) of the definition of a payment service provider in regulation 2(1)—

    (a)   is not included on the register; and

    (b)   provides, or proposes to provide, payment services,

the person must give notice to the Authority.

(4)   The Authority may—

    (a)   keep the register in any form it thinks fit;

(b)   include on it such information as the Authority considers appropriate, provided that the register identifies the payment services for which an institution is authorised or registered under this Part; and

(c)   exploit commercially the information contained in the register, or any part of that information.

(5)   The Authority must—

(a)   publish the register online and make it available for public inspection;

(b)   update the register on a regular basis; and

(c)   provide a certified copy of the register, or any part of it, to any person who asks for it—

(i)   on payment of the fee (if any) fixed by the Authority; and

(ii)   in a form (either written or electronic) in which it is legible to the person asking for it.

Authorisation as a payment institution

[2.633]
5   Application for authorisation as a payment institution or variation of an existing authorisation

(1)   An application for authorisation as a payment institution must contain or be accompanied by the information specified in Schedule 2.

(2)   An application for the variation of an authorisation as a payment institution must—

(a)   contain a statement of the proposed variation;

(b)   contain a statement of the payment services which the applicant proposes to carry on if the authorisation is varied; and

(c)   contain, or be accompanied by, such other information as the Authority may reasonably require.

(3)   An application under paragraph (1) or (2) must be made in such manner as the Authority may direct.

(4)   At any time after receiving an application and before determining it, the Authority may require the applicant to provide it with such further information as it reasonably considers necessary to enable it to determine the application.

(5)   Different directions may be given, and different requirements imposed, in relation to different applications or categories of application.

[2.634]
6   Conditions for authorisation as a payment institution

(1)   The Authority may refuse to grant all or part of an application for authorisation as a payment institution only if any of the conditions set out in paragraphs (2) to (8) is not met.

(2)   The application must comply with the requirements of, and any requirements imposed under, regulation 5.

(3)   The applicant must immediately before the time of authorisation hold the amount of initial capital required in accordance with Part 1 of Schedule 3.

(4)   The applicant must be a body corporate constituted under the law of a part of the United Kingdom having—

(a)   its head office, and

(b)   if it has a registered office, that office,

in the United Kingdom.

(5)   The applicant must satisfy the Authority that, taking into account the need to ensure the sound and prudent conduct of the affairs of the institution, it has—

(a)   robust governance arrangements for its payment service business, including a clear organisational structure with well-defined, transparent and consistent lines of responsibility;

(b)   effective procedures to identify, manage, monitor and report any risks to which it might be exposed;

(c)   adequate internal control mechanisms, including sound administrative, risk management and accounting procedures,

which are comprehensive and proportionate to the nature, scale and complexity of the payment services to be provided by the institution.

(6)   The applicant must satisfy the Authority that—

(a)   any persons having a qualifying holding in it are fit and proper persons having regard to the need to ensure the sound and prudent conduct of the affairs of an authorised payment institution;

(b)   the directors and persons responsible for the management of the institution and, where relevant, the persons responsible for the management of payment services, are of good repute and possess appropriate knowledge and experience to provide payment services;

    (c)   it has a business plan (including, for the first three years, a forecast budget calculation) under which appropriate and proportionate systems, resources and procedures will be employed by the institution to operate soundly; and

    (d)   it has taken adequate measures for the purpose of safeguarding payment service users' funds in accordance with regulation 19.

(7)   The applicant must comply with a requirement of the Money Laundering Regulations 2007 to be included in a register maintained under those Regulations where such a requirement applies to the applicant.

(8)   If the applicant has close links with another person ("CL") the applicant must satisfy the Authority—

    (a)   that those links are not likely to prevent the Authority's effective supervision of the applicant; and

    (b)   if it appears to the Authority that CL is subject to the laws, regulations or administrative provisions of a territory which is not an EEA State ("the foreign provisions"), that neither the foreign provisions, nor any deficiency in their enforcement, would prevent the Authority's effective supervision of the applicant.

(9)   For the purposes of paragraph (8), an applicant has close links with CL if—

    (a)   CL is a parent undertaking of the applicant;

    (b)   CL is a subsidiary undertaking of the applicant;

    (c)   CL is a parent undertaking of a subsidiary undertaking of the applicant;

    (d)   CL is a subsidiary undertaking of a parent undertaking of the applicant;

    (e)   CL owns or controls 20% or more of the voting rights or capital of the applicant; or

    (f)   the applicant owns or controls 20% or more of the voting rights or capital of CL.

[2.635]
7   Imposition of requirements

(1)   The Authority may include in an authorisation such requirements as it considers appropriate.

(2)   A requirement may, in particular, be imposed so as to require the person concerned to—

    (a)   take a specified action;

    (b)   refrain from taking a specified action.

(3)   A requirement may be imposed by reference to the person's relationship with its group or other members of its group.

(4)   Where—

    (a)   an applicant for authorisation as a payment institution intends to carry on business activities other than the provision of payment services; and

    (b)   the Authority considers that the carrying on of such other business activities will impair, or is likely to impair—

        (i)   the financial soundness of the applicant, or

        (ii)   the Authority's effective supervision of the applicant,

the Authority may require the applicant to establish a separate body corporate to carry on the payment service business.

(5)   A requirement expires at the end of such period as the Authority may specify in the authorisation.

(6)   Paragraph (5) does not affect the Authority's powers under regulation 8 or 11.

[2.636]
8   Variation etc at request of authorised payment institution

The Authority may, on the application of an authorised payment institution, vary that person's authorisation by—

    (a)   adding a payment service to those for which it has granted authorisation;

    (b)   removing a payment service from those for which it has granted authorisation;

    (c)   imposing a requirement such as may, under regulation 7, be included in an authorisation;

    (d)   cancelling a requirement included in the authorisation or previously imposed under paragraph (c); or

    (e)   varying such a requirement,

provided that the conditions set out in regulation 6(4) to (8) and, if applicable, the requirement in regulation 18(1) to maintain own funds, will continue to be met.

[2.637]
9   Determination of application for authorisation or variation of authorisation

(1)   The Authority must determine an application for authorisation or the variation of an authorisation before the end of the period of three months beginning with the date on which it received the completed application.

(2)   The Authority may determine an incomplete application if it considers it appropriate to do so, and it must in any event determine any such application within 12 months beginning with the date on which it received the application.

(3)   The applicant may withdraw its application, by giving the Authority notice, at any time before the Authority determines it.

(4)   The Authority may grant authorisation to carry out the payment services to which the application relates or such of them as may be specified in the grant of the authorisation.

(5)   If the Authority decides to grant an application for authorisation, or for the variation of an authorisation, it must give the applicant notice of its decision specifying—

(a)   the payment services for which authorisation has been granted; or

(b)   the variation granted,

described in such manner as the Authority considers appropriate.

(6)   The notice must state the date on which the authorisation or variation takes effect.

(7)   If the Authority proposes to refuse an application or to impose a requirement it must give the applicant a warning notice.

(8)   The Authority must, having considered any representations made in response to the warning notice—

(a)   if it decides to refuse the application or to impose a requirement, give the applicant a decision notice; or

(b)   if it grants the application without imposing a requirement, give the applicant notice of its decision, stating the date on which the authorisation or variation takes effect.

(9)   If the Authority decides to refuse the application or to impose a requirement the applicant may refer the matter to the [Upper Tribunal].

(10)   If the Authority decides to authorise the applicant, or vary its authorisation, it must update the register as soon as practicable.

NOTES

Para (9): words in square brackets substituted by the Transfer of Tribunal Functions Order 2010, SI 2010/22, art 5(2), Sch 3, paras 177, 180, subject to transitional provisions and savings in Sch 5 thereto.

[2.638]
10   Cancellation of authorisation

(1)   The Authority may cancel a person's authorisation and remove the person from the register where—

(a)   the person does not provide payment services within 12 months beginning with the date on which the authorisation took effect;

(b)   the person requests, or consents to, the cancellation of the authorisation;

(c)   the person ceases to engage in business activity for more than six months;

(d)   the person has obtained authorisation through false statements or any other irregular means;

(e)   the person no longer meets, or is unlikely to continue to meet, any of the conditions set out in regulation 6(4) to (8) or, if applicable, the requirement in regulation 18(1) to maintain own funds;

(f)   the person has provided payment services other than in accordance with the authorisation granted to it;

(g)   the person would constitute a threat to the stability of a payment system by continuing its payment services business;

(h)   the cancellation is desirable in order to protect the interests of consumers; or

(i)   the person's provision of payment services is otherwise unlawful.

(2)   Where the Authority proposes to cancel a person's authorisation, other than at the person's request, it must give the person a warning notice.

(3)   The Authority must, having considered any representations made in response to the warning notice—

(a)   if it decides to cancel the authorisation, give the person a decision notice; or

(b)   if it decides not to cancel the authorisation, give the person notice of its decision.

(4)   If the Authority decides to cancel the authorisation, other than at the person's request, the person may refer the matter to the [Upper Tribunal].

(5)   Where the period for a reference to the [Upper Tribunal] has expired without a reference being made, the Authority must as soon as practicable update the register accordingly.

NOTES

Paras (4), (5): words in square brackets substituted by the Transfer of Tribunal Functions Order 2010, SI 2010/22, art 5(2), Sch 3, paras 177, 181, subject to transitional provisions and savings in Sch 5 thereto.

[2.639]
[10A   Request for cancellation of authorisation

(1)   A request for cancellation of a person's authorisation under regulation 10(1)(b) must be made in such manner as the Authority may direct.

(2) At any time after receiving a request and before determining it, the Authority may require the person making the request to provide it with such further information as it reasonably considers necessary to enable it to determine the request.

(3) Different directions may be given and different requirements imposed, in relation to different requests or categories of request.]

NOTES

Inserted by the Payment Services (Amendment) Regulations 2009, SI 2009/2475, regs 2, 3.

[2.640]
11 Variation of authorisation on Authority's own initiative

(1) The Authority may vary a person's authorisation in any of the ways mentioned in regulation 8 if it appears to the Authority that—

(a) the person no longer meets, or is unlikely to continue to meet, any of the conditions set out in regulation 6(4) to (8) or, if applicable, the requirement in regulation 18(1) to maintain own funds;

(b) the person has provided a particular payment service or payment services other than in accordance with the authorisation granted to it;

(c) the person would constitute a threat to the stability of a payment system by continuing to provide a particular payment service or payment services;

(d) the variation is desirable in order to protect the interests of consumers; or

(e) the person's provision of a particular payment service or payment services is otherwise unlawful.

(2) A variation under this regulation takes effect—

(a) immediately, if the notice given under paragraph (6) states that that is the case;

(b) on such date as may be specified in the notice; or

(c) if no date is specified in the notice, when the matter to which the notice relates is no longer open to review.

(3) A variation may be expressed to take effect immediately or on a specified date only if the Authority, having regard to the ground on which it is exercising the power under paragraph (1), reasonably considers that it is necessary for the variation to take effect immediately or, as the case may be, on that date.

(4) The Authority must as soon as practicable after the variation takes effect update the register accordingly.

(5) A person who is aggrieved by the variation of their authorisation under this regulation may refer the matter to the [Upper Tribunal].

(6) Where the Authority proposes to vary a person's authorisation under this regulation, it must give the person notice.

(7) The notice must—

(a) give details of the variation;

(b) state the Authority's reasons for the variation and for its determination as to when the variation takes effect;

(c) inform the person that they may make representations to the Authority within such period as may be specified in the notice (whether or not the person has referred the matter to the [Upper Tribunal]);

(d) inform the person of the date on which the variation takes effect; and

(e) inform the person of their right to refer the matter to the [Upper Tribunal] and the procedure for such a reference.

(8) The Authority may extend the period allowed under the notice for making representations.

(9) If, having considered any representations made by the person, the Authority decides—

(a) to vary the authorisation in the way proposed, or

(b) if the authorisation has been varied, not to rescind the variation,

it must give the person notice.

(10) If, having considered any representations made by the person, the Authority decides—

(a) not to vary the authorisation in the way proposed,

(b) to vary the authorisation in a different way, or

(c) to rescind a variation which has taken effect,

it must give the person notice.

(11) A notice given under paragraph (9) must inform the person of their right to refer the matter to the [Upper Tribunal] and the procedure for such a reference.

(12) A notice under paragraph (10)(b) must comply with paragraph (7).

(13) For the purposes of paragraph (2)(c), paragraphs (a) to (d) of section 391(8) of the 2000 Act (publication) apply to determine whether a matter is open to review.

Part 2 Statutory Instruments

NOTES

Paras (5), (7), (11): words in square brackets substituted by the Transfer of Tribunal Functions Order 2010, SI 2010/22, art 5(2), Sch 3, paras 177, 182, subject to transitional provisions and savings in Sch 5 thereto.

Registration as a small payment institution

[2.641]

12 Application for registration as a small payment institution or variation of an existing registration

(1)   An application for registration as a small payment institution must contain, or be accompanied by, such information as the Authority may reasonably require.

(2)   An application for the variation of a registration as a small payment institution must—

   (a)   contain a statement of the proposed variation;

   (b)   contain a statement of the payment services which the applicant proposes to carry on if the registration is varied; and

   (c)   contain, or be accompanied by, such other information as the Authority may reasonably require.

(3)   An application under paragraph (1) or (2) must be made in such manner as the Authority may direct.

(4)   At any time after receiving an application and before determining it, the Authority may require the applicant to provide it with such further information as it reasonably considers necessary to enable it to determine the application.

(5)   Different directions may be given, and different requirements imposed, in relation to different applications or categories of application.

[2.642]

13 Conditions for registration as a small payment institution

(1)   The Authority may refuse to register an applicant as a small payment institution only if any of the conditions set out in paragraphs (2) to (6) is not met.

(2)   The application must comply with the requirements of, and any requirements imposed under, regulation 12.

(3)   The monthly average over the period of 12 months preceding the application of the total amount of payment transactions executed by the applicant, including any of its agents in the United Kingdom, must not exceed 3 million euros.

(4)   None of the individuals responsible for the management or operation of the business has been convicted of—

   (a)   an offence under Part 7 of the Proceeds of Crime Act 2002 (money laundering) or under the Money Laundering Regulations 2007;

   (b)   an offence under section 15 (fund-raising), 16 (use and possession), 17 (funding arrangements), 18 (money laundering) or 63 (terrorist finance: jurisdiction) of the Terrorism Act 2000;

   (c)   an offence under the 2000 Act;

   [(d)   an offence under regulation 3, 4 or 6 of the Al-Qaida and Taliban (Asset-Freezing) Regulations 2010, or regulation 10 of the Al-Qaida (Asset-Freezing) Regulations 2011;]

   [(da) an offence under section 11, 12, 13, 14, 15 or 18 of the Terrorist Asset-Freezing etc Act 2010 (offences relating to the freezing of funds etc of designated persons);]

   (e)   an offence under these Regulations [or the Electronic Money Regulations 2011]; or

   (f)   any other financial crimes.

[(4A)   Where the applicant is a partnership, an unincorporated association or a body corporate, the applicant must satisfy the Authority that any persons having a qualifying holding in it are fit and proper persons having regard to the need to ensure the sound and prudent conduct of the affairs of a small payment institution.

(4B)   The applicant must satisfy the Authority that—

   (a)   where the applicant is a body corporate, the directors;

   (b)   the persons responsible for the management of the institution; and

   (c)   where relevant, the persons responsible for the management of payment services,

are of good repute and possess appropriate knowledge and experience to provide payment services.

(4C)   If the applicant is a body corporate which has close links with another person ("CL") the applicant must satisfy the Authority—

   (a)   that those links are not likely to prevent the Authority's effective supervision of the applicant; and

   (b)   if it appears to the Authority that CL is subject to the laws, regulations or administrative provisions of a territory which is not an EEA State ("the foreign provisions"), that neither the foreign provisions, nor any deficiency in their enforcement, would prevent the Authority's effective supervision of the applicant.

(4D)   Regulation 6(9) applies for the purposes of paragraph (4C) of this regulation as it applies for the purposes of regulation 6(8).]

(5)   The applicant's head office, registered office or place of residence, as the case may be, must be in the United Kingdom.

(6)   The applicant must comply with a requirement of the Money Laundering Regulations 2007 to be included in a register maintained under those Regulations where such a requirement applies to the applicant.

(7)   For the purposes of paragraph (3), where the applicant has yet to commence the provision of payment services, or has been providing payment services for less than 12 months, the monthly average may be based on the projected total amount of payment transactions over a 12 month period.

(8)   In paragraph (4) "financial crime" includes any offence involving fraud or dishonesty and, for this purpose, "offence" includes any act or omission which would be an offence if it had taken place in the United Kingdom.

NOTES

Para (4): sub-para (d) substituted by the Al-Qaida (Asset-Freezing) Regulations 2011, SI 2011/2742, reg 21, Sch 2, para 4; sub-para (da) (as originally inserted by the Terrorism (United Nations Measures) Order (Consequential Amendments) Regulations 2009, SI 2009/1912, reg 4) substituted by the Terrorist Asset-Freezing etc Act 2010, ss 45(1), 52(1), Sch 1, Pt 1, para 8; words in square brackets in sub-para (e) inserted by the Electronic Money Regulations 2011, SI 2011/99, reg 79, Sch 4, Pt 2, para 21(b).

Paras (4A)–(4D): inserted by the Payment Services Regulations 2012, SI 2012/1791, reg 3(1), (2).

[2.643]
14   Supplementary provisions
Regulations 7 to 11 apply to registration as a small payment institution as they apply to authorisation as a payment institution with the following modifications—
  (a)   references to authorisation are to be treated as references to registration;
  (b)   omit regulation 7(4);
  (c)   in regulation 8 for "an authorised payment institution" substitute "small payment institution" and for "provided that" to the end substitute—
      "provided that the conditions set out in regulation 13(4) to (6) [are] met and that the monthly average over any period of 12 months of the total amount of payment transactions executed by the institution, including any of its agents in the United Kingdom, continues not to exceed 3 million euro ("the financial limit").";

  [(d)   in regulation 10(1)—
      (i)   for sub-paragraph (e) substitute—
          "(e)   the person does not meet, or is unlikely to meet, any of the conditions set out in regulation 13(4) to (6) or the financial limit referred to in regulation 8;"; and
      (ii)   after sub-paragraph (i) insert—
      "or
          (j)   the person has failed to comply with paragraph (2) or (3) of regulation 125A.]

  (e)   in regulation 11 for paragraph (1)(a) substitute—
      "(a)   the person [does not meet], or is unlikely to . . . meet, any of the conditions set out in regulation 13(4) to (6) or the financial limit referred to in regulation 8;".

NOTES

Para (c): word in square brackets substituted by the Payment Services Regulations 2012, SI 2012/1791, reg 3(1), (3)(a).
Para (d): substituted by SI 2012/1791, reg 3(1), (3)(b).
Para (e): words in square brackets substituted and words omitted revoked by SI 2012/1791, reg 3(1), (3)(c).

[2.644]
15   Application for authorisation as a payment institution where the financial limit is exceeded
Where the financial limit referred to in regulation 8 (as applied by regulation 14(c)) is exceeded, the institution concerned must, within 30 days of becoming aware of the change in circumstances, apply for authorisation as a payment institution under regulation 5 if it intends to continue providing payment services in the United Kingdom.

Common provisions
[2.645]
16   Duty to notify changes
(1)   If at any time after an applicant has provided the Authority with any information under regulation 5(1), (2), or (4), or 12(1), (2) or (4) and before the Authority has determined the application—

    (a)   there is, or is likely to be, a material change affecting any matter contained in that information; or

    (b)   it becomes apparent to the applicant that the information is incomplete or contains a material inaccuracy,

the applicant must provide the Authority with details of the change, the complete information or a correction of the inaccuracy (as the case may be) without undue delay, or, in the case of a material change which has not yet taken place, the applicant must provide details of the likely change as soon as the applicant is aware of such change.

(2)   The obligation in paragraph (1) also applies to material changes or significant inaccuracies affecting any matter contained in any supplementary information provided pursuant to that paragraph.

(3)   Any information to be provided to the Authority under this regulation must be in such form or verified in such manner as it may direct.

[2.646]
17   Authorised payment institutions and small payment institutions acting without permission

If an authorised payment institution or a small payment institution carries on a payment service in the United Kingdom, or purports to do so, other than in accordance with an authorisation or registration granted, or deemed to be granted under regulation 121, to it by the Authority under these Regulations, it is to be taken to have contravened a requirement imposed on it under these Regulations.

PART 3
AUTHORISED PAYMENT INSTITUTIONS

[2.647]
18   Capital requirements

(1)   Subject to paragraph (2), an authorised payment institution must maintain at all times own funds as defined for the purposes of Part 2 of Schedule 3 equal to or in excess of—

    (a)   the amount of initial capital specified in Part 1 of Schedule 3, or

    (b)   the amount of the own funds requirement calculated in accordance with paragraph 11 of Schedule 3 subject to any adjustment directed by the Authority under paragraph 12 of that Schedule,

whichever is greater.

(2)   Paragraph (1) does not apply to an authorised payment institution—

    (a)   which is included in the consolidated supervision of a parent credit institution pursuant to the [capital requirements directive]; and

    (b)   in respect of which all of the conditions specified in [Article 7(1) of the capital requirements regulation] are met.

NOTES

Para (2): words in square brackets substituted by the Capital Requirements Regulations 2013, SI 2013/3115, reg 46(1), Sch 2, Pt 3, para 70(1), (3).

[2.648]
19   Safeguarding requirements

(1)   For the purposes of this regulation "relevant funds" comprise the following—

    (a)   sums received from, or for the benefit of, a payment service user for the execution of a payment transaction; and

    (b)   sums received from a payment service provider for the execution of a payment transaction on behalf of a payment service user.

(2)   Where—

    (a)   only a portion of the sums referred to in paragraph (1)(a) or (b) is to be used for the execution of a payment transaction (with the remainder being used for non-payment services); and

    (b)   the precise portion attributable to the execution of the payment transaction is variable or unknown in advance,

the relevant funds are such amount as may be reasonably estimated, on the basis of historical data and to the satisfaction of the Authority, to be representative of the portion attributable to the execution of the payment transaction.

(3)   Where the relevant funds in respect of a payment transaction exceed £50, an authorised payment institution must safeguard such funds in accordance with either—

    (a)   paragraphs (4) to (8); or

    (b)   paragraphs (9) and (10).

(4)   An authorised payment institution must keep relevant funds segregated from any other funds that it holds.

Part 2   Statutory Instruments

(5)   Where the authorised payment institution continues to hold the relevant funds at the end of the business day following the day on which they were received it must—

(a)   place them in a separate account that it holds with an authorised credit institution; or

(b)   invest the relevant funds in such secure, liquid assets as the Authority may approve ("relevant assets") and place those assets in a separate account with an authorised custodian.

(6)   An account in which relevant funds or relevant assets are placed under paragraph (5) must—

(a)   be designated in such a way as to show that it is an account which is held for the purpose of safeguarding relevant funds or relevant assets in accordance with this regulation; and

(b)   be used only for holding those funds or assets.

(7)   No person other than the authorised payment institution may have any interest in or right over the relevant funds or relevant assets placed in an account in accordance with paragraph (5)(a) or (b) except as provided by this regulation.

(8)   The authorised payment institution must keep a record of—

(a)   any relevant funds segregated in accordance with paragraph (4);

(b)   any relevant funds placed in an account in accordance with paragraph (5)(a); and

(c)   any relevant assets placed in an account in accordance with paragraph (5)(b).

(9)   The authorised payment institution must ensure that—

(a)   any relevant funds are covered by—

(i)   an insurance policy with an authorised insurer;

(ii)   a guarantee from an authorised insurer; or

(iii) a guarantee from an authorised credit institution; and

(b)   the proceeds of any such insurance policy or guarantee are payable upon an insolvency event into a separate account held by the authorised payment institution which must—

(i)   be designated in such a way as to show that it is an account which is held for the purpose of safeguarding relevant funds in accordance with this regulation; and

(ii)   be used only for holding such proceeds.

(10)   No person other than the authorised payment institution may have any interest in or right over the proceeds placed in an account in accordance with paragraph (9)(b) except as provided by this regulation.

(11)   Subject to paragraph (12), where there is an insolvency event—

(a)   the claims of payment service users are to be paid from the asset pool in priority to all other creditors; and

(b)   until all the claims of payment service users have been paid, no right of set-off or security right may be exercised in respect of the asset pool except to the extent that the right of set-off relates to fees and expenses in relation to operating an account held in accordance with paragraph (5)(a) or (b) or (9)(b).

(12)   The claims referred to in paragraph (11)(a) shall not be subject to the priority of expenses of an insolvency proceeding except in respect of the costs of distributing the asset pool.

(13)   Paragraphs (11) and (12) shall apply to any relevant funds which a small payment institution (or an authorised payment institution in relation to relevant funds of £50 or less) voluntarily safeguards in accordance with either paragraphs (4) to (8) or paragraphs (9) and (10).

(14)   An authorised payment institution (and any small payment institution which voluntarily safeguards relevant funds) must maintain organisational arrangements sufficient to minimise the risk of the loss or diminution of relevant funds or relevant assets through fraud, misuse, negligence or poor administration.

(15)   In this regulation—

"asset pool" means—

(a)   any relevant funds segregated in accordance with paragraph (4);

(b)   any relevant funds held in an account in accordance with paragraph (5)(a);

(c)   any relevant assets held in an account in accordance with paragraph (5)(b); and

(d)   any proceeds of an insurance policy or guarantee held in an account in accordance with paragraph (9)(b);

"authorised insurer" means a person authorised for the purposes of the 2000 Act to effect and carry out a contract of general insurance as principal or otherwise authorised in accordance with *Article 6 of the First Council Directive 73/239/EEC of 24th July 1973 on the business of direct insurance other than life insurance*, other than a person in the same group as the authorised payment institution;

"authorised credit institution" means a person authorised for the purposes of the 2000 Act to accept deposits or otherwise authorised as a credit institution in accordance with [Article 8 of the capital requirements directive] other than a person in the same group as the authorised payment institution;

"authorised custodian" means a person authorised for the purposes of the 2000 Act to safeguard and administer investments or authorised as an investment firm under Article 5 of Directive 2004/39/EC of 12th April 2004 on markets in financial instruments which holds those investments under regulatory standards at least equivalent to those set out under Article 13 of that directive;

"insolvency event" means any of the following procedures in relation to an authorised payment institution or small payment institution—

(e) the making of a winding-up order;

(f) the passing of a resolution for voluntary winding-up;

(g) the entry of the institution into administration;

(h) the appointment of a receiver or manager of the institution's property;

(i) the approval of a proposed voluntary arrangement (being a composition in satisfaction of debts or a scheme of arrangement);

(j) the making of a bankruptcy order;

(k) in Scotland, the award of sequestration;

(l) the making of any deed of arrangement for the benefit of creditors or, in Scotland, the execution of a trust deed for creditors;

(m) the conclusion of any composition contract with creditors; or

(n) the making of an insolvency administration order or, in Scotland, sequestration, in respect of the estate of a deceased person;

"insolvency proceeding" means—

(o) winding-up, administration, receivership, bankruptcy or, in Scotland, sequestration;

(p) a voluntary arrangement, deed of arrangement or trust deed for the benefit of creditors; or

(q) the administration of the insolvent estate of a deceased person;

"security right" means—

(r) security for a debt owed by an authorised payment institution or a small payment institution and includes any charge, lien, mortgage or other security over the asset pool or any part of the asset pool; and

(s) any charge arising in respect of the expenses of a voluntary arrangement.

NOTES

Para (15): words in square brackets in the definition "authorised credit institution" substituted by the Capital Requirements Regulations 2013, SI 2013/3115, reg 46(1), Sch 2, Pt 3, para 70(1), (4); for the words in italics in the definition "authorised insurer" there are substituted the words "Article 14 of Directive 2009/138/EC of the European Parliament and of the Council of 25 November 2009 on the taking-up and pursuit of the business of Insurance and Reinsurance (Solvency II) to carry out non-life insurance activities as referred to in Article 2(2) of that Directive" by the Solvency 2 Regulations 2015, SI 2015/575, reg 60, Sch 2, para 28, as from 1 January 2016.

[2.649]
20 Accounting and statutory audit

(1) Where an authorised payment institution carries on activities other than the provision of payment services, it must provide to the Authority separate accounting information in respect of its provision of payment services.

(2) Such accounting information must be subject, where relevant, to an auditor's report prepared by the institution's statutory auditors or an audit firm (within the meaning of Directive 2006/43/EC of the European Parliament and of the Council of 17th May 2006 on statutory audits of annual accounts and consolidated accounts).

(3) A statutory auditor or audit firm ("the auditor") must, in any of the circumstances referred to in paragraph (4), communicate to the Authority information on, or its opinion on, matters—

(a) of which it has become aware in its capacity as auditor of an authorised payment institution or of a person with close links to an authorised payment institution; and

(b) which relate to payment services provided by that institution.

(4) The circumstances are that—

(a) the auditor reasonably believes that—

(i) there is or has been, or may be or may have been, a contravention of any requirement imposed on the authorised payment institution by or under these Regulations; and

(ii) the contravention may be of material significance to the Authority in determining whether to exercise, in relation to that institution, any functions conferred on the Authority by these Regulations;

(b) the auditor reasonably believes that the information on, or his opinion on, those matters may be of material significance to the Authority in determining whether the institution meets or will continue to meet the conditions set out in regulation 6(4) to (8) and, if applicable, the requirement in regulation 18(1) to maintain own funds;

(c) the auditor reasonably believes that the institution is not, may not be or may cease to be, a going concern;

(d) the auditor is precluded from stating in his report that the annual accounts have been properly prepared in accordance with the Companies Act 2006;

(e) the auditor is precluded from stating in his report, where applicable, that the annual accounts give a true and fair view of the matters referred to in section 495 of the Companies Act 2006 (auditor's report on company's annual accounts) including as it is applied and modified by regulation 39 of the Limited Liability Partnerships (Accounts and Audit) (Application of Companies Act 2006) Regulations 2008 ("the LLP Regulations"); or

(f)   the auditor is required to state in his report in relation to the person concerned any of the facts referred to in subsection (2), (3) or (5) of section 498 of the Companies Act 2006 (duties of auditor) or, in the case of limited liability partnerships, subsection (2), (3) or (4) of section 498 as applied and modified by regulation 40 of the LLP Regulations.

(5)   In this regulation a person has close links with an authorised payment institution ("A") if that person is—

(a)   a parent undertaking of A;

(b)   a subsidiary undertaking of A;

(c)   a parent undertaking of a subsidiary undertaking of A; or

(d)   a subsidiary undertaking of a parent undertaking of A.

[2.650]
21 Outsourcing

(1)   An authorised payment institution must notify the Authority of its intention to enter into a contract with another person under which that other person will carry out any operational function relating to its provision of payment services ("outsourcing").

(2)   Where an authorised payment institution intends to outsource any important operational function, all of the following conditions must be met—

(a)   the outsourcing is not undertaken in such a way as to impair—

    (i)   the quality of the authorised payment institution's internal control; or

    (ii)   the ability of the Authority to monitor the authorised payment institution's compliance with these Regulations;

(b)   the outsourcing does not result in any delegation by the senior management of the authorised payment institution of responsibility for complying with the requirements imposed by or under these Regulations;

(c)   the relationship and obligations of the authorised payment institution towards its payment service users under these Regulations is not substantially altered;

(d)   compliance with the conditions which the authorised payment institution must observe in order to be authorised and remain so is not adversely affected; and

(e)   none of the conditions of the payment institution's authorisation requires removal or variation.

(3)   For the purposes of paragraph (2), an operational function is important if a defect or failure in its performance would materially impair—

(a)   compliance by the authorised payment institution with these Regulations and any requirements of its authorisation;

(b)   the financial performance of the authorised payment institution; or

(c)   the soundness or continuity of the authorised payment institution's payment services.

[2.651]
22 Record keeping

(1)   An authorised payment institution must maintain relevant records and keep them for at least five years from the date on which the record was created.

(2)   For the purposes of paragraph (1), records are relevant where they relate to the authorised payment institution's compliance with this Part and, in particular, would enable the Authority to supervise effectively such compliance.

Exercise of passport rights

[2.652]
23 Notice of intention

(1)   Where an authorised payment institution intends to exercise its passport rights for the first time in a particular EEA State it must give the Authority, in such manner as the Authority may direct, notice of its intention to do so ("a notice of intention") which—

(a)   identifies the payment services which it seeks to carry on in exercise of those rights in that State;

(b)   gives the names of those responsible for the management of a proposed EEA branch, if any; and

(c)   provides details of the organisational structure of a proposed EEA branch, if any.

(2)   The Authority must, within one month beginning with the date on which it receives the notice of intention, inform the host state competent authority of—

(a)   the name and address of the authorised payment institution; and

(b)   the information contained in the notice of intention.

(3)   Where an authorised payment institution intends to exercise its passport rights through an EEA agent, the provisions of regulation 29 apply.

[2.653]

24 Registration of EEA branch

(1) If the Authority, taking into account any information received from the host state competent authority, has reasonable grounds to suspect that, in connection with the establishment of an EEA branch by an authorised payment institution—

(a) money laundering or terrorist financing within the meaning of the money laundering directive is taking place, has taken place, or has been attempted; or

(b) the risk of such activities taking place would be increased,

the Authority may refuse to register the EEA branch or cancel any such registration already made and remove the branch from the register.

(2) If the Authority proposes to refuse to register, or cancel the registration of, an EEA branch, it must give the relevant authorised payment institution a warning notice.

(3) The Authority must, having considered any representations made in response to the warning notice—

(a) if it decides not to register the branch, or to cancel its registration, give the authorised payment institution a decision notice; or

(b) if it decides to register the branch, or not to cancel the registration, give the authorised payment institution notice of its decision.

(4) If the Authority decides not to register the branch, or to cancel its registration, the authorised payment institution may refer the matter to the [Upper Tribunal].

(5) If the Authority decides to register an EEA branch, it must update the register as soon as practicable.

(6) If the Authority decides to cancel the registration, the Authority must, where the period for a reference to the [Upper Tribunal] has expired without a reference being made, as soon as practicable update the register accordingly.

NOTES

Paras (4), (6): words in square brackets substituted by the Transfer of Tribunal Functions Order 2010, SI 2010/22, art 5(2), Sch 3, paras 177, 183, subject to transitional provisions and savings in Sch 5 thereto.

[2.654]

25 Supervision of firms exercising passport rights

(1) Without prejudice to the generality of regulation 119, the Authority must co-operate with the relevant host state competent authority or home state competent authority, as the case may be, in relation to the exercise of passport rights by any authorised payment institution or EEA authorised payment institution.

(2) The Authority must, in particular—

(a) notify the host state competent authority whenever it intends to carry out an on-site inspection in the host state competent authority's territory; and

(b) provide the host state competent authority or home state competent authority, as the case may be—

(i) on request, with all relevant information; and

(ii) on its own initiative, with all essential information,

relating to the exercise of passport rights by an authorised payment institution or EEA authorised payment institution, including where there is an infringement or suspected infringement of these Regulations or of the provisions of the payment services directive by an agent, branch or entity carrying out activities on behalf of such an institution.

(3) Where the Authority and the home state competent authority agree, the Authority may carry out on-site inspections on behalf of the home state competent authority in respect of payment services provided by an EEA authorised payment institution exercising its passport rights.

(4) If the Authority has reasonable grounds to suspect that, in connection with the proposed establishment of a branch or the proposed provision of services by an EEA authorised payment institution—

(a) money laundering or terrorist financing within the meaning of the Money Laundering Regulations 2007 is taking place, has taken place, or has been attempted; or

(b) the risk of such activities taking place would be increased,

it must inform the relevant home state competent authority of its grounds for suspicion.

26 (*Revoked by the Financial Services and Markets Act 2000 (Regulated Activities) (Amendment) (No 2) Order 2013, SI 2013/1881, art 28, Schedule, Pt 1, para 40(a); and for transitional provisions see arts 29–66 of that Order*).

PART 4
PROVISIONS APPLICABLE TO AUTHORISED PAYMENT INSTITUTIONS AND SMALL PAYMENT INSTITUTIONS

[2.655]
27 Additional activities

(1)   Authorised payment institutions and small payment institutions may, in addition to providing payment services, engage in the following activities—
   (a)   the provision of operational and closely related ancillary services, including—
      (i)   ensuring the execution of payment transactions;
      (ii)   foreign exchange services;
      (iii)   safe-keeping activities; and
      (iv)   the storage and processing of data;
   (b)   the operation of payment systems; and
   (c)   business activities other than the provision of payment services, subject to any relevant Community or national law.

(2)   Authorised payment institutions and small payment institutions may grant credit in relation to the provision of the payment services specified in paragraph 1(d), (e) and (g) of Schedule 1 only if—
   (a)   such credit is ancillary and granted exclusively in connection with the execution of a payment transaction;
   (b)   such credit is not granted from the funds received or held for the purposes of executing payment transactions;
   (c)   in cases where such credit is granted by an authorised payment institution exercising its passport rights, there is an obligation upon the payment service user to repay the credit within a period not exceeding 12 months; and
   (d)   in relation to an authorised payment institution, in the opinion of the Authority the institution's own funds (comprising the items specified in paragraph 3(a) to (j) of Schedule 3) are, and continue to be, adequate in the light of the overall amount of credit granted.

NOTES

   References to the European Community and related expressions: see the note "References to "the European Community", "Community", etc" in the introductory notes to these Regulations.

[2.656]
28 Payment accounts and sums received for the execution of payment transactions

Any payment account held by an authorised payment institution or a small payment institution must be used only in relation to payment transactions.

[2.657]
29 Use of agents

(1)   Authorised payment institutions and small payment institutions may not provide payment services in the United Kingdom through an agent unless the agent is included on the register.

(2)   Authorised payment institutions may not provide payment services in the exercise of their passport rights through an EEA agent unless the agent is included on the register.

(3)   An application for an agent to be included on the register must—
   (a)   contain, or be accompanied by, the following information—
      (i)   the name and address of the agent;
      (ii)   where relevant, a description of the internal control mechanisms that will be used by the agent—
         (aa)   in the case of an agent in the United Kingdom, to comply with the Money Laundering Regulations 2007; and
         (bb)   in the case of an EEA agent, to comply with provisions of the money laundering directive; and
      (iii)   . . . the identity of the directors and persons responsible for the management of the agent and evidence that they are fit and proper persons; and
      (iv)   such other information as the Authority may reasonably require; and
   (b)   be made in such manner as the Authority may direct.

(4)   Different directions may be given, and different requirements imposed, in relation to different applications or categories of application.

(5)   At any time after receiving an application and before determining it, the Authority may require the applicant to provide it with such further information as it reasonably considers necessary to enable it to determine the application.

(6)   The Authority may refuse to include the agent on the register only if—
   (a)   it has not received the information referred to in paragraph (3)(a), or is not satisfied that such information is correct;

(b)   it is not satisfied that the directors and persons responsible for the management of the agent are fit and proper persons;

(c)   it has reasonable grounds to suspect that, in connection with the provision of services through the agent—

(i)   money laundering or terrorist financing within the meaning of the money laundering directive (or, in the United Kingdom, the Money Laundering Regulations 2007) is taking place, has taken place, or has been attempted; or

(ii)   the risk of such activities taking place would be increased.

(7)   Where—

(a)   an authorised payment institution intends to provide payment services through an EEA agent; and

(b)   the Authority proposes to include the EEA agent on the register,

the Authority must inform the host state competent authority and take account of its opinion (if provided within such reasonable period as the Authority specifies) on any of the matters referred to in paragraph (6)(b) or (c).

(8)   The Authority must decide whether to include the agent on the register within a reasonable period of it having received a completed application.

(9)   If the Authority proposes to refuse to include the agent on the register, it must give the authorised payment institution or the small payment institution, as the case may be, a warning notice.

(10)   The Authority must, having considered any representations made in response to the warning notice—

(a)   if it decides not to include the agent on the register, give the applicant a decision notice; or

(b)   if it decides to include the agent on the register, give the applicant notice of its decision, stating the date on which the registration takes effect.

(11)   If the Authority decides not to include the agent on the register the applicant may refer the matter to the [Upper Tribunal].

(12)   If the Authority decides to include the agent on the register, it must update the register as soon as practicable.

(13)   An application under paragraph (3) may be combined with an application under regulation 5 or 12, in which case the application must be determined in the manner set out in regulation 9 (if relevant, as applied by regulation 14).

(14)   An authorised payment institution or a small payment institution must ensure that agents acting on its behalf inform payment service users of the agency arrangement.

NOTES

Para (3): words omitted revoked by the Payment Services Regulations 2012, SI 2012/1791, reg 3(1), (4).

Para (11): words in square brackets substituted by the Transfer of Tribunal Functions Order 2010, SI 2010/22, art 5(2), Sch 3, paras 177, 184, subject to transitional provisions and savings in Sch 5 thereto.

[2.658]
30   Removal of agent from register

(1)   The Authority may remove an agent of an authorised payment institution or small payment institution from the register where—

(a)   the authorised payment institution or small payment institution requests, or consents to, the agent's removal from the register;

(b)   the authorised payment institution or small payment institution has obtained registration through false statements or any other irregular means;

(c)   regulation 29(6)(b) or (c) applies;

(d)   the removal is desirable in order to protect the interests of consumers; or

(e)   the agent's provision of payment services is otherwise unlawful.

(2)   Where the Authority proposes to remove an agent from the register, other than at the request of the authorised payment institution or small payment institution, it must give the authorised payment institution or small payment institution a warning notice.

(3)   The Authority must, having considered any representations made in response to the warning notice—

(a)   if it decides to remove the agent, give the authorised payment institution or small payment institution a decision notice; or

(b)   if it decides not to remove the agent, give the authorised payment institution or small payment institution notice of its decision.

(4)   If the Authority decides to remove the agent, other than at the request of the authorised payment institution or small payment institution, the institution concerned may refer the matter to the [Upper Tribunal].

(5)   Where the period for a reference to the [Upper Tribunal] has expired without a reference being made, the Authority must as soon as practicable update the register accordingly.

NOTES

Paras (4), (5): words in square brackets substituted by the Transfer of Tribunal Functions Order 2010, SI 2010/22, art 5(2), Sch 3, paras 177, 185, subject to transitional provisions and savings in Sch 5 thereto.

[2.659]

31 Reliance

(1)   Where an authorised payment institution or a small payment institution relies on a third party for the performance of operational functions it must take all reasonable steps to ensure that these Regulations are complied with.

(2)   Without prejudice to paragraph (1), an authorised payment institution or a small payment institution is responsible, to the same extent as if it had expressly permitted it, for anything done or omitted by any of its employees, any agent or branch providing payment services on its behalf, or any entity to which activities are outsourced.

[2.660]

32 Duty to notify change in circumstance

(1)   Where it becomes apparent to an authorised payment institution or a small payment institution that there is, or is likely to be, a significant change in circumstances which is relevant to—

   (a)   in the case of an authorised payment institution—
      (i)   its fulfilment of any of the conditions set out in regulation 6(4) to (8) and, if applicable, the requirement in regulation 18(1) to maintain own funds;
      (ii)   the payment services which it seeks to carry on in exercise of its passport rights;
   (b)   in the case of a small payment institution, its fulfilment of any of the conditions set out in regulation 13(4) to (6) and compliance with the financial limit referred to in regulation 8 (as applied by regulation 14(c)); and
   (c)   in the case of the use of an agent to provide payment services, the matters referred to in regulation 29(6)(b) and (c),

it must provide the Authority with details of the change without undue delay, or, in the case of a substantial change in circumstances which has not yet taken place, details of the likely change a reasonable period before it takes place.

(2)   Any information to be provided to the Authority under this regulation must be in such form or verified in such manner as it may direct.

PART 5
INFORMATION REQUIREMENTS FOR PAYMENT SERVICES

Application

[2.661]

33 Application of Part 5

(1)   This Part applies to a contract for payment services where—

   (a)   the services are provided from an establishment maintained by a payment service provider or its agent in the United Kingdom;
   (b)   the payment service providers of both the payer and the payee are located within the EEA; and
   (c)   the payment services are carried out either in euro or in the currency of an EEA State that has not adopted the euro as its currency.

(2)   Regulations 36 to 39 apply to payment services provided under a single payment service contract.

(3)   Regulations 40 to 46 apply to payment services provided under a framework contract.

(4)   Except where the payment service user is—

   (a)   a consumer,
   (b)   a micro-enterprise, or
   (c)   a charity,

the parties may agree that any or all of the provisions of this Part do not apply to a contract for payment services.

[2.662]

34 Disapplication of certain regulations in the case of consumer credit agreements

Where the contract under which a payment service is provided is, or would be, when entered into, a regulated agreement—

   (a)   regulations 41, 42 and 43 do not apply;
   (b)   the payment service provider is only required under regulation 40(1) to provide the information specified in paragraph 3(b) of Schedule 4; and
   (c)   the payment service provider is only required under regulation 45(1) to provide the information specified in paragraph (2)(d) of regulation 45.

[2.663]

35 Disapplication of certain regulations in the case of low-value payment instruments

(1) This regulation applies in respect of payment instruments which, under the framework contract governing their use—

 (a) can be used only to execute individual payment transactions of 30 euro or less, or in relation to payment transactions executed wholly within the United Kingdom, 60 euro or less;

 (b) have a spending limit of 150 euro, or where payment transactions must be executed wholly within the United Kingdom, 300 euro; or

 (c) store funds that do not exceed 500 euro at any time.

(2) Where this regulation applies—

 (a) regulations 40 and 44 do not apply and the payment service provider is only required to provide the payer with information about the main characteristics of the payment service, including—

  (i) the way in which the payment instrument can be used;

  (ii) the liability of the payer, as set out in regulation 62;

  (iii) charges levied;

  (iv) any other material information the payer might need to take an informed decision; and

  (v) an indication of where the information specified in Schedule 4 is made available in an easily accessible manner;

 (b) the parties may agree that regulations 45 and 46 do not apply and instead—

  (i) the payment service provider must provide or make available a reference enabling the payment service user to identify—

   (aa) the payment transaction;

   (bb) the amount of the payment transaction;

   (cc) any charges payable in respect of the payment transaction;

  (ii) in the case of several payment transactions of the same kind made to the same payee, the payment service provider must provide or make available to the payment service user information about the total amount of the payment transactions and any charges for those payment transactions; or

  (iii) where the payment instrument is used anonymously or the payment service provider is not otherwise technically able to provide or make available the information specified in paragraph (i) or (ii), the payment service provider must enable the payer to verify the amount of funds stored; and

 (c) the parties may agree that regulation 47(1) does not apply to information provided or made available in accordance with regulation 42.

Single payment service contracts

[2.664]

36 Information required prior to the conclusion of a single payment service contract

(1) A payment service provider must provide or make available to the payment service user the information specified in paragraph (2), whether by supplying a copy of the draft single payment service contract or supplying a copy of the draft payment order or otherwise, either—

 (a) before the payment service user is bound by the single payment service contract; or

 (b) immediately after the execution of the payment transaction, where the contract is concluded at the payment service user's request using a means of distance communication which does not enable provision of such information in accordance with sub-paragraph (a).

(2) The information referred to in paragraph (1) is—

 (a) the information or unique identifier that has to be provided by the payment service user in order for a payment order to be properly executed;

 (b) the maximum time in which the payment service will be executed;

 (c) the charges payable by the payment service user to the user's payment service provider and, where applicable, a breakdown of the amounts of such charges;

 (d) where applicable, the actual or reference exchange rate to be applied to the payment transaction; and

 (e) such of the information specified in Schedule 4 as is relevant to the single payment service contract in question.

[2.665]

37 Information required after receipt of the payment order

(1) The payer's payment service provider must, immediately after receipt of the payment order, provide or make available to the payer the information specified in paragraph (2).

(2) The information referred to in paragraph (1) is—

 (a) a reference enabling the payer to identify the payment transaction and, where appropriate, information relating to the payee;

 (b) the amount of the payment transaction in the currency used in the payment order;

(c) the amount of any charges for the payment transaction payable by the payer and, where applicable, a breakdown of the amounts of such charges;

(d) where an exchange rate is used in the payment transaction and the actual rate used in the payment transaction differs from the rate provided in accordance with regulation 36(2)(d), the actual rate used or a reference to it, and the amount of the payment transaction after that currency conversion; and

(e) the date on which the payment service provider received the payment order.

[2.666]
38 Information for the payee after execution

(1) The payee's payment service provider must, immediately after the execution of the payment transaction, provide or make available to the payee the information specified in paragraph (2).

(2) The information referred to in paragraph (1) is—

(a) a reference enabling the payee to identify the payment transaction and, where appropriate, the payer and any information transferred with the payment transaction;

(b) the amount of the payment transaction in the currency in which the funds are at the payee's disposal;

(c) the amount of any charges for the payment transaction payable by the payee and, where applicable, a breakdown of the amount of such charges;

(d) where applicable, the exchange rate used in the payment transaction by the payee's payment service provider, and the amount of the payment transaction before that currency conversion; and

(e) the credit value date.

[2.667]
39 Avoidance of duplication of information

Where a payment order for a single payment transaction is transmitted by way of a payment instrument issued under a framework contract, the payment service provider in respect of that single payment transaction need not provide or make available under regulations 36 to 38 information which has been provided or made available, or will be provided or made available, under regulations 40 to 45 by another payment service provider in respect of the framework contract.

Framework contracts

[2.668]
40 Prior general information for framework contracts

(1) A payment service provider must provide to the payment service user the information specified in Schedule 4, either—

(a) in good time before the payment service user is bound by the framework contract; or

(b) where the contract is concluded at the payment service user's request using a means of distance communication which does not enable provision of such information in accordance with sub-paragraph (a), immediately after the conclusion of the contract.

(2) The payment service provider may discharge the duty under paragraph (1) by supplying a copy of the draft framework contract provided that such contract includes the information specified in Schedule 4.

[2.669]
41 Information during period of contract

If the payment service user so requests at any time during the contractual relationship, the payment service provider must provide the information specified in Schedule 4 and the terms of the framework contract.

[2.670]
42 Changes in contractual information

(1) Subject to paragraph (4), any proposed changes to—

(a) the existing terms of the framework contract; or

(b) the information specified in Schedule 4,

must be [provided] by the payment service provider to the payment service user no later than two months before the date on which they are to take effect.

(2) The framework contract may provide for any such proposed changes to be made unilaterally by the payment service provider where the payment service user does not, before the proposed date of entry into force of the changes, notify the payment service provider to the contrary.

(3) Where paragraph (2) applies, the payment service provider must inform the payment service user that—

(a) the payment service user will be deemed to have accepted the changes in the circumstances referred to in that paragraph; and

(b) the payment service user has the right to terminate the framework contract immediately and without charge before the proposed date of their entry into force.

(4)   Changes in the interest or exchange rates may be applied immediately and without notice where—
  (a)   such a right is agreed under the framework contract and the changes are based on the reference interest or exchange rates information on which has been provided to the payment service user in accordance with this Part; or
  (b)   the changes are more favourable to the payment service user.

(5)   The payment service provider must inform the payment service user of any change to the interest rate as soon as possible unless the parties have agreed on a specific frequency or manner in which the information is to be provided or made available.

(6)   Any change in the interest or exchange rate used in payment transactions must be implemented and calculated in a neutral manner that does not discriminate against payment service users.

NOTES
  Para (1): word in square brackets substituted by the Payment Services (Amendment) Regulations 2009, SI 2009/2475, regs 2, 4.
  Transitional provision: the Financial Services Act 2012 (Consequential Amendments and Transitional Provisions) Order 2013, SI 2013/472, art 3, Sch 2, para 156, provides as follows—

  "156   Transitional provision in connection with the Payment Services Regulations 2009
  (1)   Regulation 42 (changes in contractual information) of the Payment Services Regulations 2009 does not require a payment service provider to provide its payment service users with notice of the proposed change of the name or identity of its regulator resulting from section 6 of the Financial Services Act 2012 (the new Regulators).
  (2)   Each payment service provider must inform its relevant payment service users no later than 1st April 2014 of the name or identity of its regulator resulting from section 6 of that Act.
  (3)   In this paragraph—
    (a)   terms which are defined in the Payment Services Regulations 2009 have the meaning given in those Regulations;
    (b)   "relevant payment service users", in relation to a payment service provider, means those persons who were payment service users of that payment service provider immediately before 1st April 2013 and which are such payment service users on the date on which the information required under sub-paragraph (2) is given.".

[2.671]
43   Termination of framework contract

(1)   The payment service user may terminate the framework contract at any time unless the parties have agreed on a period of notice not exceeding one month.

(2)   Subject to paragraph (3), any charges for the termination of the contract must reasonably correspond to the actual costs to the payment service provider of termination.

(3)   The payment service provider may not charge the payment service user for the termination, after the expiry of 12 months, of a framework contract concluded for a fixed period of more than 12 months or for an indefinite period.

(4)   The payment service provider may terminate a framework contract concluded for an indefinite period by giving at least two months' notice, if the contract so provides.

(5)   Notice of termination given in accordance with paragraph (4) must be provided in the same way as information is required by regulation 47(1) to be provided or made available.

(6)   Where charges for the payment service are levied on a regular basis, such charges must be apportioned up until the time of the termination of the contract and any charges paid in advance must be reimbursed proportionally.

(7)   This regulation does not affect any right of a party to the framework contract to treat it[, in accordance with the general law of contract, as unenforceable, void or discharged].

NOTES
  Para (7): words in square brackets substituted by the Payment Services (Amendment) Regulations 2009, SI 2009/2475, regs 2, 5.

[2.672]
44   Information prior to execution of individual payment transaction
Where an individual payment transaction under a framework contract is initiated by the payer, at the payer's request the payer's payment service provider must inform the payer of—
  (a)   the maximum execution time;
  (b)   the charges payable by the payer in respect of the payment transaction; and
  (c)   where applicable, a breakdown of the amounts of such charges.

[2.673]
45   Information for the payer on individual payment transactions
(1)   The payer's payment service provider under a framework contract must provide to the payer the information specified in paragraph (2) as soon as reasonably practicable either—
  (a)   after the amount of an individual payment transaction is debited from the payer's payment account; or
  (b)   where the payer does not use a payment account, after receipt of the payment order.

(2)   The information referred to in paragraph (1) is—
(a)   a reference enabling the payer to identify each payment transaction and, where appropriate, information relating to the payee;
(b)   the amount of the payment transaction in the currency in which the payer's payment account is debited or in the currency used for the payment order;
(c)   the amount of any charges for the payment transaction and, where applicable, a breakdown of the amounts of such charges, or the interest payable by the payer;
(d)   where applicable, the exchange rate used in the payment transaction by the payer's payment service provider and the amount of the payment transaction after that currency conversion; and
(e)   the debit value date or the date of receipt of the payment order.

(3)   A framework contract may include a condition that the information specified in paragraph (2) be provided or made available periodically at least once a month and in an agreed manner which enables the payer to store and reproduce the information unchanged.

[2.674]
46   Information for the payee on individual payment transactions
(1)   As soon as reasonably practicable after the execution of an individual payment transaction under a framework contract, the payee's payment service provider must provide to the payee the information specified in paragraph (2).

(2)   The information referred to in paragraph (1) is—
(a)   a reference enabling the payee to identify the payment transaction and, where appropriate, the payer, and any information transferred with the payment transaction;
(b)   the amount of the payment transaction in the currency in which the payee's payment account is credited;
(c)   the amount of any charges for the payment transaction and, where applicable, a breakdown of the amounts of such charges, or the interest payable by the payee;
(d)   where applicable, the exchange rate used in the payment transaction by the payee's payment service provider, and the amount of the payment transaction before that currency conversion; and
(e)   the credit value date.

(3)   A framework contract may include a condition that the information specified in paragraph (2) is to be provided or made available periodically at least once a month and in an agreed manner which enables the payee to store and reproduce the information unchanged.

Common provisions

[2.675]
47   Communication of information
(1)   Subject to regulation 35(2)(c), any information provided or made available in accordance with this Part must be provided or made available—
(a)   [in the case of single payment service contracts,] in an easily accessible manner;
(b)   [subject to paragraph (2)], on paper or on another durable medium;
(c)   in easily understandable language and in a clear and comprehensible form; and
(d)   in English or in the language agreed by the parties.

[(2)   Paragraph (1)(b)—
(a)   in the case of single payment service contracts, only applies where the payment service user so requests; and
(b)   in the case of framework contracts, is subject to any agreement in accordance with regulation 45(3) or 46(3) as to the manner in which information is to be provided or made available.]

NOTES
Para (1): words in square brackets in sub-para (a) inserted, and words in square brackets in sub-para (b) substituted by the Payment Services (Amendment) Regulations 2009, SI 2009/2475, regs 2, 6(a), (b).
Para (2): substituted by SI 2009/2475, regs 2, 6(c).

[2.676]
48   Charges for information
(1)   A payment service provider may not charge for providing or making available information which is required to be provided or made available by this Part.

(2)   The payment service provider and the payment service user may agree on charges for any information which is provided at the request of the payment service user where such information is—
(a)   additional to the information required to be provided or made available by this Part;
(b)   provided more frequently than is specified in this Part; or
(c)   transmitted by means of communication other than those specified in the framework contract.

(3)   Any charges imposed under paragraph (2) must reasonably correspond to the payment service provider's actual costs.

[2.677]
49   Currency and currency conversion
(1)   Payment transactions must be executed in the currency agreed between the parties.

(2)   Where a currency conversion service is offered before the initiation of the payment transaction—
    (a)   at the point of sale; or
    (b)   by the payee,
the party offering the currency conversion service to the payer must disclose to the payer all charges as well as the exchange rate to be used for converting the payment transaction.

[2.678]
50   Information on additional charges or reductions
(1)   The payee must inform the payer of any charge requested or reduction offered by the payee for the use of a particular payment instrument before the initiation of the payment transaction.

(2)   The payment service provider, or any relevant third party, must inform the payment service user of any charge requested by the payment service provider or third party, as the case may be, for the use of a particular payment instrument before the initiation of the payment transaction.

PART 6
RIGHTS AND OBLIGATIONS IN RELATION TO THE PROVISION OF PAYMENT SERVICES

Application

[2.679]
51   Application of Part 6
(1)   This Part applies to a contract for payment services where—
    (a)   the services are provided from an establishment maintained by a payment service provider or its agent in the United Kingdom;
    (b)   subject to paragraph (2), the payment service providers of both the payer and the payee are located within the EEA; and
    (c)   where the payment services are carried out in euro or in the currency of an EEA State that has not adopted the euro as its currency.

(2)   Regulation 73 applies whether or not the payment service providers of both the payer and the payee are located within the EEA.

(3)   Except where the payment service user is a consumer, a micro-enterprise or a charity, the parties may agree that—
    (a)   any or all of regulations 54(1), [55(3) or (4)], 60, 62, 63, 64, 67, 75, 76 and 77 do not apply;
    (b)   a different time period applies for the purposes of regulation 59(1).

NOTES
Para (3): figure in square brackets substituted by the Payment Services (Amendment) Regulations 2009, SI 2009/2475, regs 2, 7.

[2.680]
52   Disapplication of certain regulations in the case of consumer credit agreements
The following provisions of the Consumer Credit Act 1974 shall apply in relation to contracts for the provision of payment services which are regulated agreements for the purposes of that Act in place of the following provisions of these Regulations—
    (a)   section 51 (prohibition of unsolicited credit tokens) [(which continues to have effect for the purposes of this regulation by virtue of article 13 of the Financial Services and Markets Act 2000 (Regulated Activities) (Amendment) Order 2014)] in place of regulation 58(1)(b);
    (b)   sections 66 (acceptance of credit tokens) and 84 (misuse of credit tokens) in place of regulations 59, 61 and 62;
    (c)   section 83 (liability for misuse of credit facilities) in place of regulations 59, 61 and 62;
    (d)   sections 76 (duty to give notice before taking certain action) and 87 (need for default notice) in relation to the grounds mentioned in regulation 56(2) in place of regulation 56(3) to (6)[; and]
    [(e)   section 98A(4) to (6) (termination of open-end consumer credit agreement) in place of regulation 56(2) to (6).]

NOTES
Words in square brackets in para (a) inserted by the Financial Services and Markets Act 2000 (Regulated Activities) (Amendment) Order 2014, SI 2014/366, art 12(1), (2) (note that the 2014 Order comes into force on 18 February 2014 for the purpose of the FCA making rules, giving guidance etc, and comes into force on 1 April 2014, immediately after SI 2013/1881 (and SI 2013/1882) come into force, in so far as not already in force (see art 1 of the 2014 Order)); for savings see art 13 of the

2014 Order at **[2.1119]**. Note that para (a) was due to be revoked by SI 2013/1881, Schedule, Pt 1, para 40(b), as from 1 April 2014, but that sub-paragraph was itself revoked by art 19(4) of the 2014 Order as from 31 March 2014.

Para (e): inserted, together with word immediately preceding it, by the Consumer Credit (EU Directive) Regulations 2010, SI 2010/1010, reg 97, with effect in relation to certain agreements entered into before 1 February 2011, as provided in regs 100–101A thereof at **[2.803]–[2.805]**.

[2.681]
53 Disapplication of certain regulations in the case of low value payment instruments

(1) This regulation applies in respect of payment instruments which, under the framework contract governing their use—

   (a)   can be used only to execute individual payment transactions of 30 euro or less, or in relation to payment transactions executed wholly within the United Kingdom, 60 euro or less;

   (b)   have a spending limit of 150 euro, or where payment transactions must be executed wholly within the United Kingdom, 300 euro; or

   (c)   store funds that do not exceed 500 euro at any time.

(2) Where this regulation applies the parties may agree that—

   (a)   regulations 57(1)(b), 58(1)(c), (d) and (e) and 62(3) do not apply where the payment instrument does not allow for the stopping or prevention of its use;

   (b)   regulations 60, 61 and 62(1) and (2) do not apply where the payment instrument is used anonymously or the payment service provider is not in a position, for other reasons concerning the payment instrument, to prove that a payment transaction was authorised;

   (c)   the payment service provider is not required under regulation 66(1) to notify the payment service user of the refusal of a payment order if the non-execution is apparent from the context;

   (d)   the payer may not revoke the payment order under regulation 67 after transmitting the payment order or giving their consent to execute the payment transaction to the payee;

   (e)   execution periods other than those provided by regulations 70 and 71 apply.

(3) Subject to paragraph (2)(b), regulations 61 and 62(1) and (2) apply to electronic money as defined in [Article 2(2)] of the electronic money directive unless the payer's payment service provider does not have the ability under the contract to—

   (a)   freeze the payment account; or

   (b)   stop the use of the payment instrument.

NOTES

Para (3): words in square brackets substituted by the Electronic Money Regulations 2011, SI 2011/99, reg 79, Sch 4, Pt 2, para 21(c).

Charges

[2.682]
54 Charges

(1) The payment service provider may only charge the payment service user for the fulfilment of any of its obligations under this Part—

   (a)   in accordance with regulation 66(3), 67(6) or 74(2)(b);

   (b)   where agreed between the parties; and

   (c)   where such charges reasonably correspond to the payment service provider's actual costs.

(2) Where a payment transaction does not involve any currency conversion, the respective payment service providers must ensure that—

   (a)   the payee pays any charges levied by the payee's payment service provider; and

   (b)   the payer pays any charges levied by the payer's payment service provider.

(3) The payee's payment service provider may not prevent the payee from—

   (a)   requiring payment of a charge by; or

   (b)   offering a reduction to,

the payer for the use of a particular payment instrument.

Authorisation of payment transactions

[2.683]
55 Consent and withdrawal of consent

(1) A payment transaction is to be regarded as having been authorised by the payer for the purposes of this Part only if the payer has given its consent to—

   (a)   the execution of the payment transaction; or

   (b)   the execution of a series of payment transactions of which that payment transaction forms part.

(2) Such consent—

   (a)   may be given before or, if agreed between the payer and its payment service provider, after the execution of the payment transaction; and

   (b)   must be given in the form, and in accordance with the procedure, agreed between the payer and its payment service provider.

(3) The payer may withdraw its consent to a payment transaction at any time before the point at which the payment order can no longer be revoked under regulation 67.

(4) Subject to regulation 67(3) to (5), the payer may withdraw its consent to the execution of a series of payment transactions at any time with the effect that any future payment transactions are not regarded as authorised for the purposes of this Part.

[2.684]
56   Limits on the use of payment instruments

(1) Where a specific payment instrument is used for the purpose of giving consent to the execution of a payment transaction, the payer and its payment service provider may agree on spending limits for any payment transactions executed through that payment instrument.

(2) A framework contract may provide for the payment service provider to have the right to stop the use of a payment instrument on reasonable grounds relating to—
  (a)   the security of the payment instrument;
  (b)   the suspected unauthorised or fraudulent use of the payment instrument; or
  (c)   in the case of a payment instrument with a credit line, a significantly increased risk that the payer may be unable to fulfil its liability to pay.

(3) The payment service provider must, in the manner agreed between the payment service provider and the payer and before carrying out any measures to stop the use of the payment instrument—
  (a)   inform the payer that it intends to stop the use of the payment instrument; and
  (b)   give its reasons for doing so.

(4) Where the payment service provider is unable to inform the payer in accordance with paragraph (3) before carrying out any measures to stop the use of the payment instrument, it must do so immediately after.

(5) Paragraphs (3) and (4) do not apply where provision of the information in accordance with paragraph (3) would compromise reasonable security measures or is otherwise unlawful.

(6) The payment service provider must allow the use of the payment instrument or replace it with a new payment instrument as soon as practicable after the reasons for stopping its use cease to exist.

[2.685]
57   Obligations of the payment service user in relation to payment instruments

(1) A payment service user to whom a payment instrument has been issued must—
  (a)   use the payment instrument in accordance with the terms and conditions governing its issue and use; and
  (b)   notify the payment service provider in the agreed manner and without undue delay on becoming aware of the loss, theft, misappropriation or unauthorised use of the payment instrument.

(2) The payment service user must on receiving a payment instrument take all reasonable steps to keep its personalised security features safe.

[2.686]
58   Obligations of the payment service provider in relation to payment instruments

(1) A payment service provider issuing a payment instrument must—
  (a)   subject to regulation 57, ensure that the personalised security features of the payment instrument are not accessible to persons other than the payment service user to whom the payment instrument has been issued;
  (b)   not send an unsolicited payment instrument, except where a payment instrument already issued to a payment service user is to be replaced;
  (c)   ensure that appropriate means are available at all times to enable the payment service user to notify the payment service provider in accordance with regulation 57(1)(b) or to request that the use of the payment instrument is no longer stopped in accordance with regulation 56(6);
  (d)   on request, provide the payment service user at any time during a period of 18 months after the alleged date of notification under regulation 57(1)(b) with the means to prove that such notification to the payment service provider was made;
  (e)   prevent any use of the payment instrument once notification has been made under regulation 57(1)(b).

(2) The payment service provider bears the risk of sending a payment instrument or any of its personalised security features to the payment service user.

[2.687]
59   Notification of unauthorised or incorrectly executed payment transactions

(1) A payment service user is entitled to redress under regulation 61, 75, 76 or 77 only if it notifies the payment service provider without undue delay, and in any event no later than 13 months after the debit date, on becoming aware of any unauthorised or incorrectly executed payment transaction.

Part 2   Statutory Instruments

(2)   Where the payment service provider has failed to provide or make available information concerning the payment transaction in accordance with Part 5 of these Regulations, the payment service user is entitled to redress under the regulations referred to in paragraph (1) notwithstanding that the payment service user has failed to notify the payment service provider as mentioned in that paragraph.

[2.688]
60   Evidence on authentication and execution of payment transactions

(1)   Where a payment service user—
   (a)   denies having authorised an executed payment transaction; or
   (b)   claims that a payment transaction has not been correctly executed,
it is for the payment service provider to prove that the payment transaction was authenticated, accurately recorded, entered in the payment service provider's accounts and not affected by a technical breakdown or some other deficiency.

(2)   In paragraph (1) "authenticated" means the use of any procedure by which a payment service provider is able to verify the use of a specific payment instrument, including its personalised security features.

(3)   Where a payment service user denies having authorised an executed payment transaction, the use of a payment instrument recorded by the payment service provider is not in itself necessarily sufficient to prove either that—
   (a)   the payment transaction was authorised by the payer; or
   (b)   the payer acted fraudulently or failed with intent or gross negligence to comply with regulation 57.

[2.689]
61   Payment service provider's liability for unauthorised payment transactions

Subject to regulations 59 and 60, where an executed payment transaction was not authorised in accordance with regulation 55, the payment service provider must immediately—
   (a)   refund the amount of the unauthorised payment transaction to the payer; and
   (b)   where applicable, restore the debited payment account to the state it would have been in had the unauthorised payment transaction not taken place.

[2.690]
62   Payer's liability for unauthorised payment transaction

(1)   Subject to paragraphs (2) and (3), the payer is liable up to a maximum of £50 for any losses incurred in respect of unauthorised payment transactions arising—
   (a)   from the use of a lost or stolen payment instrument; or
   (b)   where the payer has failed to keep the personalised security features of the payment instrument safe, from the misappropriation of the payment instrument.

(2)   The payer is liable for all losses incurred in respect of an unauthorised payment transaction where the payer—
   (a)   has acted fraudulently; or
   (b)   has with intent or gross negligence failed to comply with regulation 57.

(3)   Except where the payer has acted fraudulently, the payer is not liable for any losses incurred in respect of an unauthorised payment transaction—
   (a)   arising after notification under regulation 57(1)(b);
   (b)   where the payment service provider has failed at any time to provide, in accordance with regulation 58(1)(c), appropriate means for notification; or
   (c)   where the payment instrument has been used in connection with a distance contract (other than an excepted contract).

[(4)   In paragraph (3)(c)—
   "distance contract" means a distance contract as defined by regulation 5 of the Consumer Contracts (Information, Cancellation and Additional Charges) Regulations 2013;
   "excepted contract" means a contract that—
      (a)   falls to any extent within regulation 6(1) of those Regulations, or
      (b)   falls within regulation 6(2) of those Regulations.]

NOTES

Para (4): substituted by the Consumer Contracts (Information, Cancellation and Additional Charges) Regulations 2013, SI 2013/3134, reg 47, Sch 4, para 10, in relation to contracts entered into on or 13 June 2014; the original text read as follows—

"(4)   In paragraph (3)(c) "distance contract" and "excepted contract" have the meanings given in the Consumer Protection (Distance Selling) Regulations 2000.".

[2.691]
63   Refunds for payment transactions initiated by or through a payee

(1)   Where the conditions in paragraph (2) and the requirement in regulation 64(1) are satisfied, the payer is entitled to a refund from its payment service provider of the full amount of any authorised payment transaction initiated by or through the payee.

(2)   The conditions are that—

   (a)   the authorisation did not specify the exact amount of the payment transaction when the authorisation was given in accordance with regulation 55; and

   (b)   the amount of the payment transaction exceeded the amount that the payer could reasonably have expected taking into account the payer's previous spending pattern, the conditions of the framework contract and the circumstances of the case.

(3)   The payer and payment service provider may agree in the framework contract, in respect of direct debits, that the conditions in paragraph (2) need not be satisfied in order for the payer to be entitled to a refund.

(4)   For the purposes of paragraph (2)(b), the payer cannot rely on currency exchange fluctuations where the reference exchange rate provided under regulation 36(2)(d) or paragraph 3(b) of Schedule 4 was applied.

(5)   The payer and payment service provider may agree in the framework contract that the right to a refund does not apply where—

   (a)   the payer has given consent directly to the payment service provider for the payment transaction to be executed; and

   (b)   if applicable, information on the payment transaction was provided or made available in an agreed manner to the payer for at least four weeks before the due date by the payment service provider or by the payee.

[2.692]
64   Requests for refunds for payment transactions initiated by or through a payee

(1)   The payer must request a refund under regulation 63 from its payment service provider within 8 weeks from the date on which the funds were debited.

(2)   The payment service provider may require the payer to provide such information as is reasonably necessary to ascertain whether the conditions in regulation 63(2) are satisfied.

(3)   Subject to paragraph (4), the payment service provider must either—

   (a)   refund the full amount of the payment transaction; or

   (b)   provide justification for refusing to refund the payment transaction, indicating the bodies to which the payer may refer the matter if the payer does not accept the justification provided.

(4)   Where an agreement in accordance with regulation 63(3) applies, the payment service provider must, notwithstanding that a condition in regulation 63(2) is not satisfied, refund the full amount of the payment transaction.

(5)   Any refund or justification for refusing a refund must be provided within 10 business days of receiving a request for a refund or, where applicable, within 10 business days of receiving any further information requested under paragraph (2).

Execution of payment transactions

[2.693]
65   Receipt of payment orders

(1)   Subject to paragraphs (2) to (5), for the purposes of these Regulations the time of receipt of a payment order is the time at which the payment order, given directly by the payer or indirectly by or through a payee, is received by the payer's payment service provider.

(2)   If the time of receipt of a payment order does not fall on a business day for the payer's payment service provider, the payment order is deemed to have been received on the first business day thereafter.

(3)   The payment service provider may set a time towards the end of a business day after which any payment order received will be deemed to have been received on the following business day.

(4)   Where the payment service user initiating a payment order agrees with its payment service provider that execution of the payment order is to take place—

   (a)   on a specific day;

   (b)   on the last day of a certain period; or

   (c)   on the day on which the payer has put funds at the disposal of its payment service provider, the time of receipt is deemed to be the day so agreed.

(5)   If the day agreed under paragraph (4) is not a business day for the payer's payment service provider, the payment order is deemed to have been received on the first business day thereafter.

[2.694]
66   Refusal of payment orders

(1)   Subject to paragraph (4), where a payment service provider refuses to execute a payment order, it must notify the payment service user of—

Part 2   Statutory Instruments

(a)   the refusal;

(b)   if possible, the reasons for such refusal; and

(c)   [where it is possible to provide reasons for the refusal and those reasons relate to factual matters,] the procedure for rectifying any factual errors that led to the refusal.

(2)   Any notification under paragraph (1) must be given or made available in an agreed manner and at the earliest opportunity, and in any event within the periods specified in regulation 70.

(3)   The framework contract may provide for the payment service provider to charge the payment service user for such notification where the refusal is reasonably justified.

(4)   The payment service provider is not required to notify the payment service user under paragraph (1) where such notification would be otherwise unlawful.

(5)   Where all the conditions set out in the payer's framework contract have been satisfied, the payment service provider may not refuse to execute an authorised payment order irrespective of whether the payment order is initiated by the payer or by or through a payee, unless such execution is otherwise unlawful.

(6)   For the purposes of regulations 70, 75 and 76 a payment order of which execution has been refused is deemed not to have been received.

NOTES

Para (1): words in square brackets inserted by the Payment Services (Amendment) Regulations 2009, SI 2009/2475, regs 2, 8.

[2.695]
67   Revocation of a payment order

(1)   Subject to paragraphs (2) to (5), a payment service user may not revoke a payment order after it has been received by the payer's payment service provider.

(2)   In the case of a payment transaction initiated by or through the payee, the payer may not revoke the payment order after transmitting the payment order or giving consent to execute the payment transaction to the payee.

(3)   In the case of a direct debit, the payer may not revoke the payment order after the end of the business day preceding the day agreed for debiting the funds.

(4)   Where a day is agreed under regulation 65(4), the payment service user may not revoke a payment order after the end of the business day preceding the agreed day.

(5)   At any time after the time limits for revocation set out in paragraphs (1) to (4), the payment order may only be revoked if the revocation is—

(a)   agreed between the payment service user and its payment service provider; and

(b)   in the case of a payment transaction initiated by or through the payee, including in the case of a direct debit, also agreed with the payee.

(6)   A framework contract may provide for the payment service provider to charge for revocation under this regulation.

[2.696]
68   Amounts transferred and amounts received

(1)   Subject to paragraph (2), the payment service providers of the payer and payee must ensure that the full amount of the payment transaction is transferred and that no charges are deducted from the amount transferred.

(2)   The payee and its payment service provider may agree for the payment service provider to deduct its charges from the amount transferred before crediting it to the payee provided that the full amount of the payment transaction and the amount of the charges are clearly stated in the information provided to the payee.

(3)   If charges other than those provided for by paragraph (2) are deducted from the amount transferred—

(a)   in the case of a payment transaction initiated by the payer, the payer's payment service provider must ensure that the payee receives the full amount of the payment transaction;

(b)   in the case of a payment transaction initiated by the payee, the payee's payment service provider must ensure that the payee receives the full amount of the payment transaction.

Execution time and value date

[2.697]
69   Application of regulations 70 to 72

(1)   Regulations 70 to 72 apply to any [payment] transaction—

(a)   in euro;

[(b)   executed wholly within the United Kingdom in sterling; or]

(c)   involving only one currency conversion between the euro and sterling, provided that—

(i)   the currency conversion is carried out in the United Kingdom; and

(ii)   in the case of cross-border payment transactions, the cross-border transfer takes place in euro.

(2)   In respect of any other [payment] transaction, the payment service user may agree with the payment service provider that regulations 70 (other than regulation 70(4)) to 72 do not apply.

NOTES

   Para (1): word in first pair of square brackets inserted, and sub-para (b) substituted by the Payment Services (Amendment) Regulations 2009, SI 2009/2475, regs 2, 9(a), (b).

   Para (2): word in square brackets inserted by SI 2009/2475, regs 2, 9(a).

[2.698]
70   Payment transactions to a payment account

(1)   Subject to paragraphs (2), (3) and (4), the payer's payment service provider must ensure that the amount of the payment transaction is credited to the payee's payment service provider's account by the end of the business day following the time of receipt of the payment order.

(2)   Until 1st January 2012, the payer and their payment service provider may agree that the amount of the payment transaction is to be credited to the payee's payment service provider's account by the end of the third business day following the time of receipt of the payment order.

(3)   Where a payment transaction is initiated by way of a paper payment order—
   (a)   the reference in paragraph (1) to the end of the business day following the time of receipt of the payment order is to be treated as a reference to the end of the second business day following the time of receipt of the payment order; and
   (b)   the reference in paragraph (2) to the end of the third business day following the time of receipt of the payment order is to be treated as a reference to the end of the fourth business day following the time of receipt of the payment order.

(4)   Where a payment transaction—
   (a)   does not fall within paragraphs (a) to (c) of regulation 69(1); but
   (b)   is to be executed wholly within the EEA,
the payer's payment service provider must ensure that the amount of the payment transaction is credited to the payee's payment service provider's account by the end of the fourth business day following the time of receipt of the payment order.

(5)   The payee's payment service provider must value date and credit the amount of the payment transaction to the payee's payment account following its receipt of the funds.

(6)   The payee's payment service provider must transmit a payment order initiated by or through the payee to the payer's payment service provider within the time limits agreed between the payee and its payment service provider, enabling settlement in respect of a direct debit to occur on the agreed due date.

[2.699]
71   Absence of payee's payment account with the payment service provider

(1)   Paragraph (2) applies where a payment service provider accepts funds on behalf of a payee who does not have a payment account with that payment service provider.

(2)   The payment service provider must make the funds available to the payee immediately after the funds have been credited to that payment service provider's account.

[2.700]
72   Cash placed on a payment account

Where a payment service user places cash on its payment account with a payment service provider in the same currency as that payment account, the payment service provider must—
   (a)   if the user is a consumer, micro-enterprise or charity, ensure that the amount is made available and value dated immediately after the receipt of the funds;
   (b)   in any other case, ensure that the amount is made available and value dated no later than the end of the [next] business day after the receipt of the funds.

NOTES

   Para (b): word in square brackets inserted by the Payment Services (Amendment) Regulations 2009, SI 2009/2475, regs 2, 10.

[2.701]
73   Value date and availability of funds

(1)   The credit value date for the payee's payment account must be no later than the business day on which the amount of the payment transaction is credited to the account of the payee's payment service provider.

(2)   The payee's payment service provider must ensure that the amount of the payment transaction is at the payee's disposal immediately after that amount has been credited to that payment service provider's account.

(3)   The debit value date for the payer's payment account must be no earlier than the time at which the amount of the payment transaction is debited to that payment account.

Part 2   Statutory Instruments

Liability

[2.702]

74   Incorrect unique identifiers

(1)   Where a payment order is executed in accordance with the unique identifier, the payment order is deemed to have been correctly executed by each payment service provider involved in executing the payment order with respect to the payee specified by the unique identifier.

(2)   Where the unique identifier provided by the payment service user is incorrect, the payment service provider is not liable under regulation 75 or 76 for non-execution or defective execution of the payment transaction, but the payment service provider—

    (a)   must make reasonable efforts to recover the funds involved in the payment transaction; and

    (b)   may, if agreed in the framework contract, charge the payment service user for any such recovery.

(3)   Where the payment service user provides information additional to that specified in regulation 36(2)(a) or paragraph 2(b) of Schedule 4, the payment service provider is liable only for the execution of payment transactions in accordance with the unique identifier provided by the payment service user.

[2.703]

75   Non-execution or defective execution of payment transactions initiated by the payer

(1)   This regulation applies where a payment order is initiated by the payer.

(2)   The payer's payment service provider is liable to the payer for the correct execution of the payment transaction unless it can prove to the payer and, where relevant, to the payee's payment service provider, that the payee's payment service provider received the amount of the payment transaction in accordance with regulation 70.

(3)   The payer's payment service provider must, on request, make immediate efforts to trace the payment transaction and notify the payer of the outcome.

(4)   Where the payer's payment service provider is liable under paragraph (2), it must without undue delay refund to the payer the amount of the non-executed or defective payment transaction and, where applicable, restore the debited payment account to the state in which it would have been had the defective payment transaction not taken place.

(5)   Where the payer's payment service provider can prove (as set out in paragraph (2)) that the payee's payment service provider received the amount of the payment transaction in accordance with regulation 70, the payee's payment service provider is liable to the payee for the correct execution of the payment transaction and must—

    (a)   immediately make available the amount of the payment transaction to the payee; and

    (b)   where applicable, credit the corresponding amount to the payee's payment account.

[2.704]

76   Non-execution or defective execution of payment transactions initiated by the payee

(1)   This regulation applies where a payment order is initiated by the payee.

(2)   The payee's payment service provider is liable to the payee for the correct transmission of the payment order to the payer's payment service provider in accordance with regulation 70(6).

(3)   Where the payee's payment service provider is liable under paragraph (2), it must immediately re-transmit the payment order in question to the payer's payment service provider.

(4)   The payee's payment service provider must, on request, make immediate efforts to trace the payment transaction and notify the payee of the outcome.

(5)   Where the payee's payment service provider can prove to the payee and, where relevant, to the payer's payment service provider, that it is not liable under paragraph (2) in respect of a non-executed or defectively executed payment transaction, the payer's payment service provider is liable to the payer and must, as appropriate and without undue delay—

    (a)   refund to the payer the amount of the payment transaction; and

    (b)   restore the debited payment account to the state in which it would have been had the defective payment transaction not taken place.

[2.705]

77   Liability of payment service provider for charges and interest

A payment service provider is liable to its payment service user for—

    (a)   any charges for which the payment service user is responsible; and

    (b)   any interest which the payment service user must pay,

as a consequence of the non-execution or defective execution of the payment transaction.

[2.706]

78   Right of recourse

Where the liability of a payment service provider ("the first provider") under regulation 75 or 76 is attributable to another payment service provider or an intermediary, the other payment service provider or intermediary must compensate the first provider for any losses incurred or sums paid pursuant to those regulations.

[2.707]
79 Force majeure

(1)   A person is not liable for any contravention of a requirement imposed on it by or under this Part where the contravention is due to abnormal and unforeseeable circumstances beyond the person's control, the consequences of which would have been unavoidable despite all efforts to the contrary.

(2)   A payment service provider is not liable for any contravention of a requirement imposed on it by or under this Part where the contravention is due to the obligations of the payment service provider under other provisions of Community or national law.

NOTES

References to the European Community and related expressions: see the note "References to "the European Community", "Community", etc" in the introductory notes to these Regulations.

PART 7
THE AUTHORITY

The functions of the Authority

[2.708]
80 Functions of the Authority

(1)   The Authority is to have the functions conferred on it by these Regulations.

(2)   In discharging its function of determining the general policy and principles by reference to which it performs particular functions under these Regulations, the Authority must have regard to—
- (a)   the need to use its resources in the most efficient and economic way;
- (b)   the responsibilities of those who manage the affairs of payment service providers;
- (c)   the principle that a burden or restriction which is imposed on a person, or on the carrying on of an activity, should be proportionate to the benefits, considered in general terms, which are expected to result from the imposition of that burden or restriction;
- (d)   the desirability of facilitating innovation in connection with payment services;
- (e)   the international character of financial services and markets and the desirability of maintaining the competitive position of the United Kingdom;
- (f)   the need to minimise the adverse effects on competition that may arise from anything done in the discharge of those functions; and
- (g)   the desirability of facilitating competition in relation to payment services.

Supervision and enforcement

[2.709]
81 Monitoring and enforcement

(1)   The Authority must maintain arrangements designed to enable it to determine whether—
- (a)   persons on whom requirements are imposed by or under Part 2, 3 or 4 of these Regulations are complying with them;
- (b)   there has been any contravention of regulation 110(1), 111(1) or 114(1)(a) or (2).

(2)   The Authority may maintain arrangements designed to enable it to determine whether persons on whom requirements are imposed by or under Part 5 or 6 of these Regulations are complying with them.

(3)   The arrangements referred to in paragraphs (1) and (2) may provide for functions to be performed on behalf of the Authority by any body or person who is, in its opinion, competent to perform them.

(4)   The Authority must also maintain arrangements for enforcing the provisions of these Regulations.

(5)   Paragraph (3) does not affect the Authority's duty under paragraph (1).

[2.710]
82 Reporting requirements

(1)   A payment service provider must give the Authority such information in respect of its provision of payment services and its compliance with requirements imposed by or under Parts 2 to 6 of these Regulations as the Authority may direct.

(2)   Information required under this regulation must be given at such times and in such form, and verified in such manner, as the Authority may direct.

83   *(Revoked by the Protection of Freedoms Act 2012, ss 39(2), 115(2), Sch 2, Pt 3, para 15(1), Sch 10, Pt 2.)*

[2.711]
84 Public censure

If the Authority considers that a payment service provider has contravened a requirement imposed on them by or under these Regulations the Authority may publish a statement to that effect.

[2.712]
85 Financial penalties

(1)   The Authority may impose a penalty of such amount as it considers appropriate on—
  (a)   a payment service provider who has contravened a requirement imposed on them by or under these Regulations; or
  (b)   a person who has contravened regulation 110(1),111(1) or 114(1)(a) or (2).

(2)   The Authority may not in respect of any contravention both require a person to pay a penalty under this regulation and cancel their authorisation as a payment institution or their registration as a small payment institution (as the case may be).

(3)   A penalty under this regulation is a debt due from that person to the Authority, and is recoverable accordingly.

[2.713]
86 Proposal to take disciplinary measures

(1)   Where the Authority proposes to publish a statement under regulation 84 or to impose a penalty under regulation 85, it must give the person concerned a warning notice.

(2)   The warning notice must set out the terms of the proposed statement or state the amount of the proposed penalty.

(3)   If, having considered any representations made in response to the warning notice, the Authority decides to publish a statement under regulation 84 or to impose a penalty under regulation 85, it must without delay give the person concerned a decision notice.

(4)   The decision notice must set out the terms of the statement or state the amount of the penalty.

(5)   If the Authority decides to publish a statement under regulation 84 or impose a penalty on a person under regulation 85, the person concerned may refer the matter to the [Upper Tribunal].

(6)   Sections 210 (statements of policy) and 211 (statements of policy: procedure) of the 2000 Act apply in respect of the imposition of penalties under regulation 85 and the amount of such penalties as they apply in respect of the imposition of penalties under Part 14 of the 2000 Act (disciplinary measures) and the amount of penalties under that Part of that Act.

(7)   After a statement under regulation 84 is published, the Authority must send a copy of it to the person concerned and to any person to whom a copy of the decision notice was given under section 393(4) of the 2000 Act (third party rights) (as applied by paragraph 7 of Schedule 5 to these Regulations).

NOTES

Para (5): words in square brackets substituted by the Transfer of Tribunal Functions Order 2010, SI 2010/22, art 5(2), Sch 3, paras 177, 186, subject to transitional provisions and savings in Sch 5 thereto.

[2.714]
87 Injunctions

(1)   If, on the application of the Authority, the court is satisfied—
  (a)   that there is a reasonable likelihood that any person will contravene a requirement imposed by or under these Regulations; or
  (b)   that any person has contravened such a requirement and that there is a reasonable likelihood that the contravention will continue or be repeated,
the court may make an order restraining (or in Scotland an interdict prohibiting) the contravention.

(2)   If, on the application of the Authority, the court is satisfied—
  (a)   that any person has contravened a requirement imposed by or under these Regulations, and
  (b)   that there are steps which could be taken for remedying the contravention,
the court may make an order requiring that person, and any other person who appears to have been knowingly concerned in the contravention, to take such steps as the court may direct to remedy it.

(3)   If, on the application of the Authority, the court is satisfied that any person may have—
  (a)   contravened a requirement imposed by or under these Regulations, or
  (b)   been knowingly concerned in the contravention of such a requirement,
it may make an order restraining (or in Scotland an interdict prohibiting) them from disposing of, or otherwise dealing with, any assets of theirs which it is satisfied they are reasonably likely to dispose of or otherwise deal with.

(4)   The jurisdiction conferred by this regulation is exercisable by the High Court and the Court of Session.

(5)   In paragraph (2), references to remedying a contravention include references to mitigating its effect.

[2.715]
88 Power of Authority to require restitution

(1)   The Authority may exercise the power in paragraph (2) if it is satisfied that a payment service provider (referred to in this regulation and regulation 89 as "the person concerned") has contravened a requirement imposed by or under these Regulations, or been knowingly concerned in the contravention of such a requirement, and that—

  (a)   profits have accrued to the person concerned as a result of the contravention; or
  (b)   one or more persons have suffered loss or been otherwise adversely affected as a result of the contravention.

(2)   The power referred to in paragraph (1) is a power to require the person concerned, in accordance with such arrangements as the Authority considers appropriate, to pay to the appropriate person or distribute among the appropriate persons such amount as appears to the Authority to be just having regard—

  (a)   in a case within sub-paragraph (a) of paragraph (1), to the profits appearing to the Authority to have accrued;
  (b)   in a case within sub-paragraph (b) of that paragraph, to the extent of the loss or other adverse effect;
  (c)   in a case within both of those paragraphs, to the profits appearing to the Authority to have accrued and to the extent of the loss or other adverse effect.

(3)   In paragraph (2) "appropriate person" means a person appearing to the Authority to be someone—

  (a)   to whom the profits mentioned in paragraph (1)(a) are attributable; or
  (b)   who has suffered the loss or adverse effect mentioned in paragraph (1)(b).

[2.716]
89 Proposal to require restitution

(1)   If the Authority proposes to exercise the power under regulation 88(2), it must give the person concerned a warning notice.

(2)   The warning notice must state the amount which the Authority propose to require the person concerned to pay or distribute as mentioned in regulation 88(2).

(3)   If, having considered any representations made in response to the warning notice, the Authority decides to exercise the power under regulation 88(2), it must without delay give the person concerned a decision notice.

(4)   The decision notice must—

  (a)   state the amount that the person concerned is to pay or distribute;
  (b)   identify the person or persons to whom that amount is to be paid or among whom that amount is to be distributed; and
  (c)   state the arrangements in accordance with which the payment or distribution is to be made.

(5)   If the Authority decides to exercise the power under regulation 88(2), the person concerned may refer the matter to the [Upper Tribunal].

NOTES
Para (5): words in square brackets substituted by the Transfer of Tribunal Functions Order 2010, SI 2010/22, art 5(2), Sch 3, paras 177, 187, subject to transitional provisions and savings in Sch 5 thereto.

[2.717]
90 Restitution orders

(1)   The court may, on the application of the Authority, make an order under paragraph (2) if it is satisfied that a payment service provider has contravened a requirement imposed by or under these Regulations, or been knowingly concerned in the contravention of such a requirement, and that—

  (a)   profits have accrued to them as a result of the contravention; or
  (b)   one or more persons have suffered loss or been otherwise adversely affected as a result of the contravention.

(2)   The court may order the person concerned to pay to the Authority such sum as appears to the court to be just having regard—

  (a)   in a case within sub-paragraph (a) of paragraph (1), to the profits appearing to the court to have accrued;
  (b)   in a case within sub-paragraph (b) of that paragraph, to the extent of the loss or other adverse effect;
  (c)   in a case within both of those sub-paragraphs, to the profits appearing to the court to have accrued and to the extent of the loss or other adverse effect.

(3)   Any amount paid to the Authority in pursuance of an order under paragraph (2) must be paid by it to such qualifying person or distributed by it among such qualifying persons as the court may direct.

(4)   In paragraph (3), "qualifying person" means a person appearing to the court to be someone—

  (a)   to whom the profits mentioned in paragraph (1)(a) are attributable; or
  (b)   who has suffered the loss or adverse effect mentioned in paragraph (1)(b).

(5) On an application under paragraph (1) the court may require the person concerned to supply it with such accounts or other information as it may require for any one or more of the following purposes—

   (a) establishing whether any and, if so, what profits have accrued to them as mentioned in sub-paragraph (a) of that paragraph;

   (b) establishing whether any person or persons have suffered any loss or adverse effect as mentioned in sub-paragraph (b) of that paragraph; and

   (c) determining how any amounts are to be paid or distributed under paragraph (3).

(6) The court may require any accounts or other information supplied under paragraph (5) to be verified in such manner as it may direct.

(7) The jurisdiction conferred by this regulation is exercisable by the High Court and the Court of Session.

(8) Nothing in this regulation affects the right of any person other than the Authority to bring proceedings in respect of the matters to which this regulation applies.

[2.718]
91 Complaints

(1) The Authority must maintain arrangements designed to enable payment service users and other interested parties to submit complaints to it that a requirement imposed by or under Parts 2 to 6 of these Regulations has been breached by a payment service provider.

(2) Where it considers it appropriate, the Authority must include in any reply to a complaint under paragraph (1) details of the ombudsman scheme established under Part 16 of the 2000 Act (the ombudsman scheme).

Miscellaneous

[2.719]
92 Costs of supervision

(1) The functions of the Authority under these Regulations are to be treated for the purposes of [paragraph 23 of Schedule 1ZA (fees) to the 2000 Act] as functions conferred on the Authority under that Act with the following modifications—

   (a) section [1B(5)(a) of the 2000 Act (FCA's general duties)] does not apply to the making of rules under paragraph 17 by virtue of this regulation;

   (b) rules made under paragraph [23] by virtue of this regulation are not to be treated as regulating provisions for the purposes of section [140A(1)] of the 2000 Act (competition scrutiny);

   (c) [paragraph 23(7)] are omitted.

[(2) The Authority must in respect of each of its financial years pay to the Treasury any amounts received by it during the year by way of penalties imposed under regulation 85.

(3) The Treasury may give directions to the Authority as to how the Authority is to comply with its duty under paragraph (2).

(4) The directions may in particular—

   (a) specify the time when any payment is required to be made to the Treasury, and

   (b) require the Authority to provide the Treasury at specified times with information relating to penalties that the Authority has imposed under regulation 85.

(5) The Treasury must pay into the Consolidated Fund any sums received by them under this regulation.]

NOTES

Para (1): words and number in square brackets substituted by the Financial Services Act 2012 (Consequential Amendments and Transitional Provisions) Order 2013, SI 2013/472, art 3, Sch 2, para 155(1), (3).

Paras (2)–(5): substituted (for the original para (2)) by the Payment to Treasury of Penalties Regulations 2013, SI 2013/429, reg 2(4).

[2.720]
[92A Credit agreements

Schedule 4A, which contains provisions concerning credit agreements, has effect.]

NOTES

Commencement: 1 April 2014.

Inserted by the Financial Services and Markets Act 2000 (Regulated Activities) (Amendment) Order 2014, SI 2014/366, art 12(1), (3) (note that the 2014 Order comes into force on 18 February 2014 for the purpose of the FCA making rules, giving guidance etc, and comes into force on 1 April 2014, immediately after SI 2013/1881 (and SI 2013/1882) come into force, in so far as not already in force (see art 1 of the 2014 Order)).

[2.721]
93 Guidance

(1) The Authority may give guidance consisting of such information and advice as it considers appropriate with respect to—

(a)   the operation of these Regulations;
(b)   any matters relating to the functions of the Authority under these Regulations;
(c)   any other matters about which it appears to the Authority to be desirable to give information or advice in connection with these Regulations.

(2)   The Authority may—
(a)   publish its guidance;
(b)   offer copies of its published guidance for sale at a reasonable price;
(c)   if it gives guidance in response to a request made by any person, make a reasonable charge for that guidance.

[2.722]
94   Authority's exemption from liability in damages
The functions of the Authority under these Regulations are to be treated for the purposes of paragraph [25] (exemption from liability in damages) of Part 4 of [Schedule 1ZA] to the 2000 Act as functions conferred on the Authority under that Act.

NOTES
Number and words in square brackets substituted by the Financial Services Act 2012 (Consequential Amendments and Transitional Provisions) Order 2013, SI 2013/472, art 3, Sch 2, para 155(1), (4).

95   (*Introduces Sch 5 to the Regulations (outside the scope of this work).*)

PART 8
ACCESS TO PAYMENT SYSTEMS
General

[2.723]
96   Application of Part 8
(1)   This Part does not apply to the following kinds of payment systems—
(a)   a designated system;
(b)   a payment system consisting solely of payment service providers belonging to the same group where one of the payment service providers enjoys effective control over the others;
(c)   a payment system where the sole payment service provider (whether as a single entity or a group)—
(i)   acts or is able to act as the payment service provider for both the payer and the payee and is solely responsible for the management of the system; and
(ii)   licenses other payment service providers to participate in the system subject to their having no right to negotiate fees in respect of the system between or amongst themselves (although they may establish their own pricing in relation to payers and payees).

(2)   In paragraph (1)(a), "designated system" means a system which is declared by a designation order for the time being in force under regulation 4 of the Financial Markets and Insolvency (Settlement Finality) Regulations 1999 to be a designated system for the purposes of those Regulations.

[2.724]
97   Prohibition on restrictive rules on access to payment systems
(1)   Rules or conditions governing access to, or participation in, a payment system by [authorised or registered payment service providers] must—
(a)   be objective, proportionate and non-discriminatory; and
(b)   not prevent, restrict or inhibit access or participation more than is necessary to—
(i)   safeguard against specific risks such as settlement risk, operational risk or business risk; or
(ii)   protect the financial and operational stability of the payment system.

(2)   Paragraph (1) applies only to such [payment service providers] as are legal persons.

(3)   Rules or conditions governing access to, or participation in, a payment system which, in respect of payment service providers, payment service users or other payment systems—
(a)   restrict effective participation in other payment systems;
(b)   discriminate (whether directly or indirectly) between—
(i)   different authorised payment institutions, or
(ii)   different small payment institutions,
in relation to the rights, obligations or entitlements of participants in the payment system; or
(c)   impose any restrictions on the basis [of institutional status],
are prohibited.

NOTES
Words in square brackets substituted by the Payment Services (Amendment) Regulations 2015, SI 2015/422, reg 2(1), (3).

Supervision and enforcement

[2.725]
98   Power of [Payment Systems Regulator] to investigate

(1)   The [Payment Systems Regulator] may conduct an investigation where there are reasonable grounds for suspecting that any rule or condition governing access to, or participation in, a payment system contravenes regulation 97(1) or (3).

(2)   Where the investigation relates to a possible breach of regulation 97(1)(b)(ii), the [Payment Systems Regulator] must consult the Bank of England and the Authority.

NOTES
Words in square brackets substituted by the Payment Services (Amendment) Regulations 2015, SI 2015/422, reg 2(1), (4).

[2.726]
99   [Payment Systems Regulator] power to require information

(1)   For the purposes of an investigation under regulation 98 the [Payment Systems Regulator] may require any person—
   (a)   to produce to it or to a person appointed by it, at a specified time and place, any specified document, or
   (b)   to provide to it or to a person appointed by it, at a specified time and place, any specified information,
which the [Payment Systems Regulator] considers relates to any matter relevant to the investigation.

(2)   The power conferred by paragraph (1) is to be exercised by a notice indicating the subject matter and purpose of the investigation.

(3)   Information required to be provided under paragraph (1) must be provided in the specified manner and form, or, if that is not possible, in the nearest equivalent manner and form.

(4)   The power conferred by paragraph (1) to require a person to produce a document includes power—
   (a)   to require them to provide an explanation of the document, or
   (b)   if the document is not produced, to require them to state, to the best of their knowledge and belief, where it is.

(5)   In this regulation—
   "document" includes information recorded in any form;
   "information" includes estimates and forecasts;
   "specified" means—
      (a)   specified, or described, in the notice referred to in paragraph (2), or
      (b)   falling within a category which is specified, or described, in such notice.

NOTES
Words in square brackets substituted by the Payment Services (Amendment) Regulations 2015, SI 2015/422, reg 2(1), (4).

[2.727]
100   Failure to comply with information requirement

(1)   If, on an application made by the [Payment Systems Regulator], it appears to the court that a person (the "information defaulter") has failed to do something that they were required to do under regulation 99, the court may make an order under this regulation.

(2)   An order under this regulation may require the information defaulter—
   (a)   to do the thing that they failed to do within such period as may be specified in the order;
   (b)   otherwise to take such steps to remedy the consequence of the failure as may be so specified.

(3)   In this regulation, "the court" means—
   (a)   in England and Wales and Northern Ireland, the High Court or the county court;
   (b)   in Scotland, the Court of Session or the sheriff court.

NOTES
Words in square brackets substituted by the Payment Services (Amendment) Regulations 2015, SI 2015/422, reg 2(1), (4).

[2.728]
101   Privileged communications

(1)   A person is not required under regulation 99 to produce or disclose a privileged communication.

(2)   In paragraph (1) "privileged communication" means a communication—
   (a)   between a professional legal adviser and their client, or
   (b)   made in connection with, or in contemplation of, legal proceedings and for the purposes of those proceedings,
which in proceedings in the High Court would be protected from disclosure on grounds of legal professional privilege.

(3) In the application of this regulation to Scotland the reference in paragraph (2) to—

    (a) proceedings in the High Court is to be read as a reference to legal proceedings generally; and

    (b) an entitlement on grounds of legal professional privilege is to be read as a reference to an entitlement on the grounds of confidentiality of communications.

[2.729]
102 Notice of [Payment Systems Regulator] decision

Before the [Payment Systems Regulator], as the result of an investigation under regulation 98, makes a decision that any rules or conditions governing access to, or participation in, a payment system contravene regulation 97(1) or (3), the [Payment Systems Regulator] must—

    (a) give notice to the person (or persons) who the [Payment Systems Regulator] considers are responsible for the contravention, and

    (b) give that person (or those persons) an opportunity to make representations.

NOTES

Words in square brackets substituted by the Payment Services (Amendment) Regulations 2015, SI 2015/422, reg 2(1), (4).

[2.730]
103 Publication of [Payment Systems Regulator] decision

Where the [Payment Systems Regulator] makes a decision after an investigation under regulation 98, the [Payment Systems Regulator] must publish its decision, together with its reasons for making it.

NOTES

Words in square brackets substituted by the Payment Services (Amendment) Regulations 2015, SI 2015/422, reg 2(1), (4).

[2.731]
104 Enforcement of decisions

(1) If the [Payment Systems Regulator] makes a decision that any rules or conditions governing access to, or participation in, a payment system contravene regulation 97(1) or (3), the [Payment Systems Regulator] may give such directions as the [Payment Systems Regulator] considers appropriate to such person or persons as it considers appropriate.

(2) A direction under paragraph (1) may (in particular)—

    (a) require the person concerned to change any rule or condition so that it no longer contravenes regulation 97(1) or (3); and

    (b) relate to the conduct of the person in implementing any rule or condition.

(3) A direction under paragraph (1) must be given in writing.

(4) If a person fails, without reasonable excuse, to comply with a direction under paragraph (1), the [Payment Systems Regulator] may apply to the High Court (or, in Scotland, the Court of Session) for an order requiring that person to comply with the direction within a time specified in the order.

(5) An order under paragraph (4) may provide for all of the costs of, or incidental to, the application for the order to be borne by the person in default.

NOTES

Words in square brackets substituted by the Payment Services (Amendment) Regulations 2015, SI 2015/422, reg 2(1), (4).

[2.732]
105 Power of [Payment Systems Regulator] to impose financial penalties

(1) Where the [Payment Systems Regulator] is satisfied that any rules or conditions governing access to, or participation in, a payment system contravene regulation 97(1) or (3), the [Payment Systems Regulator] may impose a penalty of such amount as it considers appropriate on such persons as it considers appropriate.

(2) The [Payment Systems Regulator] may impose a penalty on a person under paragraph (1) only if the [Payment Systems Regulator] is satisfied that the infringement has been committed intentionally or negligently by that person.

(3) Notice of a penalty under this regulation must—

    (a) be in writing; and

    (b) specify the date before which the penalty is required to be paid.

(4) The date specified must not be earlier than the end of the period within which an appeal against the notice may be brought under regulation 106.

(5) Any sums received by the [Payment Systems Regulator] under this regulation are to be [regarded as penalty receipts of the Payment Systems Regulator for the purposes of paragraph 10 of Schedule 4 to the Financial Services (Banking Reform) Act 2013 (penalty receipts)].

NOTES

Words in square brackets substituted by the Payment Services (Amendment) Regulations 2015, SI 2015/422, reg 2(1), (4), (5).

Miscellaneous

[2.733]
106 Appeal to the Competition Appeal Tribunal

(1) A person may appeal to the Competition Appeal Tribunal from a decision by the [Payment Systems Regulator] to give a direction under regulation 104(1) to that person or to impose a penalty under regulation 105 on that person.

(2) In determining an appeal under paragraph (1) the Competition Appeal Tribunal shall apply the same principles as would be applied by a court on an application for judicial review.

(3) Sections 14 (constitution of tribunal) and 15 (tribunal rules) of the Enterprise Act 2002 apply in respect of appeals to the Competition Appeal Tribunal under paragraph (1) as they apply in respect of appeals to the Competition Appeal Tribunal under that Act.

NOTES

Para (1): words in square brackets substituted by the Payment Services (Amendment) Regulations 2015, SI 2015/422, reg 2(1), (4).

[2.734]
107 Disclosure of information by [Payment Systems Regulator]

Subject to regulation 119(2) and (3), Part 9 of the Enterprise Act 2002 (information) applies in respect of information which comes to the [Payment Systems Regulator] by virtue of these Regulations as it applies in respect of information which is specified information for the purposes of Part 9.

NOTES

Words in square brackets substituted by the Payment Services (Amendment) Regulations 2015, SI 2015/422, reg 2(1), (4).

[2.735]
108 Defamation

For the purposes of the law relating to defamation, absolute privilege attaches to any decision made or notice given by the [Payment Systems Regulator] in the exercise of any of its functions under this Part.

NOTES

Words in square brackets substituted by the Payment Services (Amendment) Regulations 2015, SI 2015/422, reg 2(1), (4).

[2.736]
109 Guidance

(1) The [Payment Systems Regulator] may give guidance consisting of such information and advice as it considers appropriate with respect to the exercise of its functions under this Part.

(2) The [Payment Systems Regulator] may—
   (a) publish its guidance;
   (b) if it gives guidance in response to a request made by any person, make a reasonable charge for that guidance.

NOTES

Words in square brackets substituted by the Payment Services (Amendment) Regulations 2015, SI 2015/422, reg 2(1), (4).

[2.737]
[109A Payment Systems Regulator's arrangements for discharging functions, funding and exemption from liability in damages

The functions of the Payment Systems Regulator under these Regulations are to be regarded for the purposes of paragraphs 5(1) (arrangements for discharging functions), 9 (funding) and 14 (exemption from liability in damages) of Schedule 4 to the Financial Services (Banking Reform) Act 2013 as functions conferred on the Payment Systems Regulator by or under Part 5 of that Act.]

NOTES

Commencement 1 April 2015.
Inserted by the Payment Services (Amendment) Regulations 2015, SI 2015/422, reg 2(1), (6).

PART 9
GENERAL

Criminal Offences

[2.738]
110 Prohibition on provision of payment services by persons other than payment service providers

(1) A person may not provide a payment service in the United Kingdom, or purport to do so, unless the person is—

  (a) an authorised payment institution;

  (b) a small payment institution;

  (c) an EEA authorised payment institution exercising its passport rights;

  [(d) a credit institution authorised in the UK or exercising an EEA right in accordance with Part 2 of Schedule 3 to the 2000 Act (exercise of passport rights by EEA firms);

  [(e) an electronic money institution which for the purposes of the Electronic Money Regulations 2011 is—

    (i) registered in the United Kingdom as an authorised electronic money institution or a small electronic money institution; or

    (ii) an EEA authorised electronic money institution exercising passport rights in the United Kingdom or treated as such by virtue of regulation 75 of those Regulations;]

  (f) the Post Office Limited;

  (g) the Bank of England, the European Central Bank or a national central bank of an EEA State other than the United Kingdom,

  (h) a government department or a local authority; or

  (i) exempt under regulation 3.]

(2) A person who contravenes paragraph (1) is guilty of an offence and is liable—

  (a) on summary conviction, to imprisonment for a term not exceeding three months or to a fine not exceeding the statutory maximum, or both;

  (b) on conviction on indictment, to imprisonment for a term not exceeding two years or to a fine, or both.

NOTES

Para (1): sub-paras (d)–(i) substituted for original sub-paras (d), (e) by the Payment Services (Amendment) Regulations 2009, SI 2009/2475, regs 2, 11; sub-para (e) substituted by the Electronic Money Regulations 2011, SI 2011/99, reg 79, Sch 4, Pt 2, para 21(d).

[2.739]
111 False claims to be a payment service provider or exempt

(1) A person who does not fall within any of sub-paragraphs (a) to (e) of regulation 110(1) may not—

  (a) describe themselves (in whatever terms) as a person falling within any of those sub-paragraphs; or

  (b) behave, or otherwise hold themselves out, in a manner which indicates (or which is reasonably likely to be understood as indicating) that they are such a person.

(2) A person who contravenes paragraph (1) is guilty of an offence and is liable on summary conviction to imprisonment for a term not exceeding three months or to a fine not exceeding level 5 on the standard scale, or both.

[2.740]
112 Defences

In proceedings for an offence under regulation 110 or 111 it is a defence for the accused to show that they took all reasonable precautions and exercised all due diligence to avoid committing the offence.

[2.741]
113 Contravention of regulations 49 and 50

(1) A person (not being a payment service provider) who contravenes regulation 49(2) or 50(2) is guilty of an offence and liable on summary conviction to a fine not exceeding level 5 on the standard scale.

(2) No offence is committed if the person took all reasonable steps and exercised all due diligence to ensure that the requirement imposed on the person by regulation 49(2) or 50(2), as the case may be, would be complied with.

[2.742]
114 Misleading the Authority or the [Payment Systems Regulator]

(1) A person may not, in purported compliance with any requirement imposed by or under these Regulations, knowingly or recklessly give—

  (a) the Authority; or

(b)   the [Payment Systems Regulator],

information which is false or misleading in a material particular.

(2)   A person may not—

    (a)   provide any information to another person, knowing the information to be false or misleading in a material particular, or

    (b)   recklessly provide to another person any information which is false or misleading in a material particular,

knowing that the information is to be used for the purpose of providing information to the Authority in connection with its functions under these Regulations.

(3)   A person may not—

    (a)   provide any information to another person, knowing the information to be false or misleading in a material particular, or

    (b)   recklessly provide to another person any information which is false or misleading in a material particular,

knowing that the information is to be used for the purpose of providing information to the [Payment Systems Regulator] in connection with their functions under these Regulations.

(4)   A person who knows or suspects that an investigation by the [Payment Systems Regulator] under regulation 98 is being or is likely to be conducted may not—

    (a)   intentionally or recklessly destroy or otherwise dispose of, falsify or conceal a document (as defined by regulation 99(5)) which may be relevant to such an investigation; or

    (b)   cause or permit its destruction, disposal, falsification or concealment.

(5)   A person who contravenes paragraph (1), (2), (3) or (4) is guilty of an offence and is liable—

    (a)   on summary conviction, to a fine not exceeding the statutory maximum;

    (b)   on conviction on indictment, to a fine.

NOTES

    Words in square brackets substituted by the Payment Services (Amendment) Regulations 2015, SI 2015/422, reg 2(1), (4).

[2.743]
115   Restriction on penalties

A person who is convicted of an offence under these Regulations is not liable to a penalty under regulation 85 or 105 in respect of the same contravention of a requirement imposed by or under these Regulations.

[2.744]
116   Liability of officers of bodies corporate etc

(1)   If an offence under these Regulations committed by a body corporate is shown—

    (a)   to have been committed with the consent or connivance of an officer, or

    (b)   to be attributable to any neglect on their part,

the officer as well as the body corporate is guilty of the offence and liable to be proceeded against and punished accordingly.

(2)   If the affairs of a body corporate are managed by its members, paragraph (1) applies in relation to the acts and defaults of a member in connection with such member's functions of management as if the member were a director of the body.

(3)   If an offence under these Regulations committed by a partnership is shown—

    (a)   to have been committed with the consent or connivance of a partner, or

    (b)   to be attributable to any neglect on their part,

the partner as well as the partnership is guilty of the offence and liable to be proceeded against and punished accordingly.

(4)   If an offence under these Regulations committed by an unincorporated association (other than a partnership) is shown—

    (a)   to have been committed with the consent or connivance of an officer, or

    (b)   to be attributable to any neglect of such officer,

the officer as well as the association is guilty of the offence and liable to be proceeded against and punished accordingly.

(5)   In this regulation—

"officer"—

    (a)   in relation to a body corporate, means a director, manager, secretary, chief executive, member of the committee of management, or a person purporting to act in such a capacity; and

    (b)   in relation to an unincorporated association, means any officer of the association or any member of its governing body, or a person purporting to act in such capacity; and

"partner" includes a person purporting to act as a partner.

[2.745]
117   Prosecution of offences

(1)   Proceedings for an offence under these Regulations may be instituted only—
 (a)   in respect of an offence under regulation 110, 111, 113, or 114(1)(a) or (2), by the Authority;
 (b)   in respect of an offence under regulation 114(1)(b), (3) or (4), by the [Payment Systems Regulator]; or
 (c)   by or with the consent of the Director of Public Prosecutions.

(2)   Paragraph (1) does not apply to proceedings in Scotland.

NOTES

Para (1): words in square brackets substituted by the Payment Services (Amendment) Regulations 2015, SI 2015/422, reg 2(1), (4).

[2.746]
118   Proceedings against unincorporated bodies

(1)   Proceedings for an offence alleged to have been committed by a partnership or an unincorporated association must be brought in the name of the partnership or association (and not in that of its members).

(2)   A fine imposed on the partnership or association on its conviction of an offence is to be paid out of the funds of the partnership or association.

(3)   Rules of court relating to the service of documents are to have effect as if the partnership or association were a body corporate.

(4)   In proceedings for an offence brought against the partnership or association—
 (a)   section 33 of the Criminal Justice Act 1925 (procedure on charge of offence against corporation) and section 46 of and Schedule 3 to the Magistrates' Courts Act 1980 (corporations) apply as they do in relation to a body corporate;
 (b)   section 70 of the Criminal Procedure (Scotland) Act 1995 (proceedings against bodies corporate) applies as it does in relation to a body corporate;
 (c)   section 18 of the Criminal Justice (Northern Ireland) Act 1945 (procedure on charge) and Schedule 4 to the Magistrates' Courts (Northern Ireland) Order 1981 (corporations) apply as they do in relation to a body corporate.

(5)   Summary proceedings for an offence under these Regulations may be taken—
 (a)   against a body corporate or unincorporated association at any place at which it has a place of business;
 (b)   against an individual at any place where they are for the time being.

(6)   Paragraph (5) does not affect any jurisdiction exercisable apart from this regulation.

Duties of the Authority, the Commissioners and the [Payment Systems Regulator] to cooperate

[2.747]
119   Duty to co-operate and exchange of information

(1)   The Authority, the Commissioners and the [Payment Systems Regulator] must take such steps as they consider appropriate to co-operate with each other and—
 (a)   the competent authorities designated under Article 20(1), or referred to in Article 82(1), of the payment services directive, of EEA States other than the United Kingdom;
 (b)   the European Central Bank, the Bank of England and the national central banks of EEA States other than the United Kingdom; and
 (c)   any other relevant competent authorities designated under Community law or the law of the United Kingdom or any other EEA State which is applicable to payment service providers,
for the purposes of the exercise by those bodies of their functions under the payment services directive and other relevant Community or national legislation.

(2)   Subject to the requirements of the Data Protection Act 1998, sections 348 and 349 of the 2000 Act (as applied with modifications by paragraph 5 of Schedule 5 to these Regulations), regulation 49A of the Money Laundering Regulations 2007 (as inserted by paragraph 6(g) of Schedule 6 to these Regulations) and any other applicable restrictions on the disclosure of information, the Authority, the Commissioners and the [Payment Systems Regulator] may provide information to each other and—
 (a)   the bodies mentioned in paragraph (1)(a) and (c);
 (b)   the European Central Bank, the Bank of England and the national central banks of EEA States other than the United Kingdom when acting in their capacity as monetary and oversight authorities;
 (c)   where relevant, other public authorities responsible for the oversight of payment and settlement systems;
for the purposes of the exercise by those bodies of their functions under the payment services directive and other relevant Community or national legislation.

Part 2 Statutory Instruments

(3) Part 9 of the Enterprise Act 2002 does not prohibit disclosure by the [Payment Systems Regulator] under paragraph (2) but the [Payment Systems Regulator] must have regard to the considerations mentioned in section 244 of that Act (specified information: considerations relevant to disclosure) before making any such disclosure.

NOTES

Words in square brackets (including in the heading preceding this regulation) substituted by the Payment Services (Amendment) Regulations 2015, SI 2015/422, reg 2(1), (4).

References to the European Community and related expressions: see the note "References to "the European Community", "Community", etc" in the introductory notes to these Regulations.

Actions for breach of requirements

[2.748]
120 Right to bring actions

(1) A contravention—
- (a) which is to be taken to have occurred by virtue of regulation 17;
- (b) of a requirement imposed by regulation 19; or
- (c) of a requirement imposed by or under Part 5 or 6,

is actionable at the suit of a private person who suffers loss as a result of the contravention, subject to the defences and other incidents applying to actions for breach of statutory duty.

(2) A person acting in a fiduciary or representative capacity may bring an action under paragraph (1) on behalf of a private person if any remedy—
- (a) will be exclusively for the benefit of the private person; and
- (b) cannot be obtained by way of an action brought otherwise than at the suit of the fiduciary or representative.

(3) In this regulation "private person" means—
- (a) any individual, except where the individual suffers the loss in question in the course of providing payment services; and
- (b) any person who is not an individual, except where that person suffers the loss in question in the course of carrying on business of any kind;

but does not include a government, a local authority (in the United Kingdom or elsewhere) or an international organisation.

Transitional provisions

[2.749]
121 Transitional provisions: deemed authorisation

(1) Any financial institution (within the meaning of the [Directive 2006/48/EC of the European Parliament and of the Council]) which—
- (a) is constituted under the law of a part of the United Kingdom and has its head office and, if it has a registered office, that office, in the United Kingdom; and
- (b) before 25th December 2007 had—
  - (i) lawfully provided payment services in the United Kingdom; and
  - (ii) met the condition in Article 24(1)(e) of the [Directive 2006/48/EC of the European Parliament and of the Council];

shall be deemed to have been granted authorisation by the Authority under regulation 9.

(2) An institution which is deemed to have been granted authorisation by virtue of paragraph (1) shall continue on or after 25th December 2009 to be deemed to have been granted authorisation only if it has by that date—
- (a) notified the Authority of the payment services referred to in sub-paragraph (b)(i); and
- (b) provided the Authority with the information specified in paragraph 1, 4, 7 to 9 and 12 of Schedule 2 ("the required information").

(3) Authorisation which continues on or after 25th December 2009 to be deemed to have been granted by virtue of paragraph (2) shall continue to be so deemed until such time as the Authority decides whether to include the institution in the register as an authorised payment institution.

(4) If the Authority decides to include the institution in the register as an authorised payment institution—
- (a) it must as soon as practicable update the register accordingly; and
- (b) the institution shall cease to be deemed to have been granted authorisation by virtue of paragraph (1) or (2).

(5) The Authority may decide that an institution is not to be included in the register as an authorised payment institution only if—
- (a) it has not received the required information; or
- (b) any of the conditions in regulation 6(4) to (6) (other than the condition that a person must be a body corporate) ("the required conditions") are not met in respect of that institution.

(6) If the Authority is satisfied that—
- (a) it has received the required information; and
- (b) the required conditions are met,

it must give the institution notice of its decision.

(7) If the Authority proposes to decide that—

    (a)   it has not received the required information; or

    (b)   any of the required conditions is not met,

it must give the institution a warning notice.

(8) The Authority must, having considered any representations in response to the warning notice—

    (a)   if it decides that it has not received the required information or that any of the required conditions is not met, give the institution a decision notice; or

    (b)   if it decides that it has received the required information and that the required conditions have been met, give the institution notice of its decision.

(9) If the Authority gives the institution a decision notice, the institution may refer the matter to the [Upper Tribunal].

(10) Where the period for a reference to the [Upper Tribunal] has expired without a reference being made, the institution shall cease to be deemed to have been granted authorisation by virtue of paragraph (1) or (2).

(11) Where an institution is deemed to have been granted authorisation by virtue of paragraph (1) or (2)—

    (a)   the duty to which the Authority is subject under regulation 4(1)(a) to maintain a register shall not apply in respect of it; and

    (b)   Parts 3 and 4 shall not apply to it.

NOTES

Para (1): words in square brackets substituted by the Capital Requirements Regulations 2013, SI 2013/3115, reg 46(1), Sch 2, Pt 3, para 70(1), (5).

Paras (9), (10): words in square brackets substituted by the Transfer of Tribunal Functions Order 2010, SI 2010/22, art 5(2), Sch 3, paras 177, 188, subject to transitional provisions and savings in Sch 5 thereto.

[2.750]

122　Transitional provisions: requirement to be authorised as a payment institution

(1) Any person which—

    (a)   is a body corporate constituted under the law of a part of the United Kingdom and has its head office and, if it has a registered office, that office, in the United Kingdom;

    (b)   is not a body—

        (i)   mentioned in any of paragraphs (d) to (h) of the definition in regulation 2(1) of a payment service provider; or

        (ii)   which is deemed to have been granted authorisation by virtue of regulation 121(1) or (2); and

    (c)   immediately before 25th December 2007, was lawfully providing payment services in the United Kingdom,

may continue until 1st May 2011 to provide payment services in the United Kingdom notwithstanding that the person has not been granted authorisation by the Authority under regulation 9.

(2) Parts 5 to 8 and regulation 110(1) apply to a person falling within paragraph (1) as if the person were an authorised payment institution.

[2.751]

123　Transitional provisions: requirement to be registered as a small payment institution

(1) Any person who—

    (a)   immediately before 25th December 2007, was lawfully providing payment services in the United Kingdom;

    (b)   is not a body—

        (i)   mentioned in any of paragraphs (d) to (h) of the definition in regulation 2(1) of a payment service provider; or

        (ii)   which is deemed to have been granted authorisation by virtue of regulation 121(1) or (2) or which falls within regulation 122(1); and

    (c)   meets the conditions set out in regulation 13(4) to (6) and complies with the financial limit referred to in regulation 8 (as applied by regulation 14(c)),

may continue until 25th December 2010 to provide payment services in the United Kingdom notwithstanding that the person has not been granted registration by the Authority under regulation 9 (as applied by regulation 14).

(2) Parts 5 to 8 and regulation 110(1) apply to a person falling within paragraph (1) as if the person were a small payment institution.

[2.752]

124　Transitional provisions: early applications

(1) Where an application is made under regulation 5(1) or (2) or 12(1) or (2) before 1st August 2009 and is a completed application, the Authority must determine it before 1st November 2009.

(2) The requirement under regulation 23(2) for information to be given to the host state competent authority within one month of receipt by the Authority of a notice of intention does not apply where the notice of intention is received by the Authority before 1st November 2009.

(3) Any requirement under these Regulations to update the register does not apply until 1st November 2009.

[2.753]
125 Transitional provisions: the ombudsman scheme

Part 16 of, and Schedule 17 to, the 2000 Act (the ombudsman scheme) shall apply as if persons who fall within regulation 122(1) or 123(1) were payment service providers within the meaning of these Regulations.

[2.754]
[125A Transitional provisions: small payment institutions registered before 1st October 2012 and applications pending on that date

(1) Where a person has applied for registration as a small payment institution before 1st October 2012 and its application has not been determined before that date, it must provide the Authority with the information referred to in paragraphs 1, 7, 8 and 9 of Schedule 2 to the extent relevant to that person.

(2) Where a small payment institution is included on the register maintained under regulation 4(1)(b) on 1st October 2012, it must provide the Authority before 1st October 2013 with the information referred to in paragraphs 1, 7, 8 and 9 of Schedule 2 to the extent relevant to that institution.

(3) Any information to be provided to the Authority under this regulation must be in such form or verified in such manner as it may direct.]

NOTES
Commencement: 1 October 2012.
Inserted by the Payment Services Regulations 2012, SI 2012/1791, reg 3(1), (5).

[2.755]
[125B Transitional provisions: references to the Authority

For the purposes of regulations 121 to 125A (transitional provisions), in the period up to the end of 31st March 2013, references to "the Authority" are to be read as references to the Financial Services Authority.]

NOTES
Commencement: 1 April 2013.
Inserted by the Financial Services Act 2012 (Consequential Amendments and Transitional Provisions) Order 2013, SI 2013/472, art 3, Sch 2, para 155(1), (5).

Amendments to primary and secondary legislation

[2.756]
126 Amendments to primary and secondary legislation

Schedule 6, which contains amendments to primary and secondary legislation, has effect.

[2.757]
[127 Application to Gibraltar

Schedule 7, which contains provisions concerning the application of these Regulations to Gibraltar, has effect.]

NOTES
Inserted by the Payment Services (Amendment) Regulations 2009, SI 2009/2475, regs 2, 12.

SCHEDULES
SCHEDULE 1
PAYMENT SERVICES

Regulation 2(1)

PART 1
PAYMENT SERVICES

[2.758]
1. Subject to Part 2, the following activities, when carried out as a regular occupation or business activity, are payment services—

   (a) services enabling cash to be placed on a payment account and all of the operations required for operating a payment account;

(b)   services enabling cash withdrawals from a payment account and all of the operations required for operating a payment account;

(c)   the execution of the following types of payment transaction—
     (i)   direct debits, including one-off direct debits;
     (ii)   payment transactions executed through a payment card or a similar device;
     (iii)   credit transfers, including standing orders;

(d)   the execution of the following types of payment transaction where the funds are covered by a credit line for the payment service user—
     (i)   direct debits, including one-off direct debits;
     (ii)   payment transactions executed through a payment card or a similar device;
     (iii)   credit transfers, including standing orders;

(e)   issuing payment instruments or acquiring payment transactions;

(f)   money remittance;

(g)   the execution of payment transactions where the consent of the payer to execute the payment transaction is given by means of any telecommunication, digital or IT device and the payment is made to the telecommunication, IT system or network operator acting only as an intermediary between the payment service user and the supplier of the goods or services.

PART 2
ACTIVITIES WHICH DO NOT CONSTITUTE PAYMENT SERVICES

[2.759]

2. The following activities do not constitute payment services—

(a)   payment transactions executed wholly in cash and directly between the payer and the payee, without any intermediary intervention;

(b)   payment transactions between the payer and the payee through a commercial agent authorised to negotiate or conclude the sale or purchase of goods or services on behalf of the payer or the payee;

(c)   the professional physical transport of banknotes and coins, including their collection, processing and delivery;

(d)   payment transactions consisting of non-professional cash collection and delivery as part of a not-for-profit or charitable activity;

(e)   services where cash is provided by the payee to the payer as part of a payment transaction for the purchase of goods or services following an explicit request by the payer immediately before the execution of the payment transaction;

(f)   money exchange business consisting of cash-to-cash operations where the funds are not held on a payment account;

(g)   payment transactions based on any of the following documents drawn on the payment service provider with a view to placing funds at the disposal of the payee—
     (i)   paper cheques of any kind, including traveller's cheques;
     (ii)   bankers' drafts;
     (iii)   paper-based vouchers;
     (iv)   paper postal orders;

(h)   payment transactions carried out within a payment or securities settlement system between payment service providers and settlement agents, central counterparties, clearing houses, central banks or other participants in the system;

(i)   payment transactions related to securities asset servicing, including dividends, income or other distributions, or redemption or sale, carried out by persons referred to in sub-paragraph (h) or by investment firms, credit institutions, collective investment undertakings or asset management companies providing investment services or by any other entities allowed to have the custody of financial instruments;

(j)   services provided by technical service providers, which support the provision of payment services, without the provider entering at any time into possession of the funds to be transferred, including—
     (i)   the processing and storage of data;
     (ii)   trust and privacy protection services;
     (iii)   data and entity authentication;
     (iv)   information technology;
     (v)   communication network provision; and
     (vi)   the provision and maintenance of terminals and devices used for payment services;

(k)   services based on instruments that can be used to acquire goods or services only—
     (i)   in or on the issuer's premises; or
     (ii)   under a commercial agreement with the issuer, either within a limited network of service providers or for a limited range of goods or services,
   and for these purposes the "issuer" is the person who issues the instrument in question;

(l)   payment transactions executed by means of any telecommunication, digital or IT device, where the goods or services purchased are delivered to and are to be used through a telecommunication, digital or IT device, provided that the telecommunication, digital or IT operator does not act only as an intermediary between the payment service user and the supplier of the goods and services;

(m)   payment transactions carried out between payment service providers, or their agents or branches, for their own account;

(n)   payment transactions between a parent undertaking and its subsidiary or between subsidiaries of the same parent undertaking, without any intermediary intervention by a payment service provider other than an undertaking belonging to the same group;

(o)   services by providers to withdraw cash by means of automated teller machines acting on behalf of one or more card issuers, which are not party to the framework contract with the customer withdrawing money from a payment account, where no other payment service is conducted by the provider.

SCHEDULE 2
INFORMATION TO BE INCLUDED IN OR WITH AN APPLICATION FOR AUTHORISATION

Regulation 5(1)

[2.760]

1. A programme of operations setting out, in particular, the type of payment services envisaged.

2. A business plan including a forecast budget calculation for the first three financial years which demonstrates that the applicant is able to employ appropriate and proportionate systems, resources and procedures to operate soundly.

3. Evidence that the applicant holds initial capital for the purposes of regulation 6(3).

4. Where regulation 19 applies, a description of the measures taken for safeguarding payment service users' funds in accordance with that regulation.

5. A description of the applicant's governance arrangements and internal control mechanisms, including administrative risk management and accounting procedures, which demonstrates that such arrangements, mechanisms and procedures are proportionate, appropriate, sound and adequate.

6. A description of the internal control mechanisms which the applicant has established in order to comply with the Money Laundering Regulations 2007 and Regulation (EC) No 1781/2006 of the European Parliament and of the Council of 15 November 2006 on information on the payer accompanying transfers of funds.

7. A description of the applicant's structural organisation, including, where applicable, a description of the intended use of agents and branches and a description of outsourcing arrangements, and of its participation in a national or international payment system.

8. (1)   In relation to each person holding, directly or indirectly, a qualifying holding in the applicant—

(a)   the size and nature of their qualifying holding; and

(b)   evidence of their suitability taking into account the need to ensure the sound and prudent management of a payment institution.

9. (1)   The identity of directors and persons who are or will be responsible for the management of the applicant and, where relevant, persons who are or will be responsible for the management of the payment services activities of the applicant.

(2)   Evidence that the persons described in sub-paragraph (1) are of good repute and that they possess appropriate knowledge and experience to perform payment services.

10. The identity of the auditors of the applicant, if any.

11. (1)   The legal status of the applicant and, where the applicant is a limited company, its articles.

(2)   In this paragraph "articles" has the meaning given in section 7 of the Companies Act 1985 (articles prescribing regulations for companies) until the coming into force of section 18 of the Companies Act 2006 (articles of association) when it will have the meaning given by that section.

12. The address of the head office of the applicant.

13. For the purposes of paragraphs 4, 5 and 7, a description of the audit arrangements of the applicant and of the organisational arrangements the applicant has set up with a view to taking all reasonable steps to protect the interests of its payment service users and to ensure continuity and reliability in the performance of payment services.

NOTES

Note: para 8 above is reproduced as it appears in the Queen's Printer's copy of these Regulations, ie, there is no sub-paragraph (2).

SCHEDULE 3
CAPITAL REQUIREMENTS

Regulations 6(3), 18

PART 1
INITIAL CAPITAL

[2.761]

1. For the purposes of this Part, "initial capital" comprises the items specified in paragraph 3(a), (b) and (c) of this Schedule.

2. (1) An applicant for authorisation as a payment institution must hold the amount of initial capital specified in the second column of the table, corresponding to the payment services provided or to be provided (as specified in the first column).

(2) Where more than one initial capital requirement applies, the applicant must hold initial capital of whichever is the greater amount.

Payment services	Initial capital requirement (euro)
Payment services specified in paragraph 127(f) of Schedule 1	20,000
Payment services specified in paragraph 127(g) of Schedule 1	50,000
Any of the payment services specified in paragraph 127(a) to (e) of Schedule 1	125,000

PART 2
OWN FUNDS

Qualifying items

[2.762]

3. For the purposes of this Part, "own funds" means the following items, subject to the deductions specified in paragraph 147 and to the limits specified in paragraph 149—

(a) paid up capital, including share premium accounts but excluding amounts arising in respect of cumulative preference shares;

(b) reserves other than—

(i) revaluation reserves;

(ii) fair value reserves related to gains or losses on cash flow hedges of financial instruments measured at amortised cost; and

(iii) that part of profit and loss reserves that arises from any gains on liabilities valued at fair value that are due to changes in the authorised payment institution's credit standing;

(c) profit or loss brought forward as a result of the application of the final profit or loss, provided that—

(i) interim profits may only be included if they are—

(aa) verified by persons responsible for the auditing of the authorised payment institution's accounts;

(bb) shown to the satisfaction of the Authority that the amount has been evaluated in accordance with the principles set out in directive 86/635/EEC of the Council of the 8th December 1986 on the annual accounts and consolidated accounts of banks and other financial institutions; and

(cc) net of any foreseeable charge or dividend;

(ii) in the case of an authorised payment institution which is the originator of a securitisation, net gains arising from the capitalisation of future income from the securitised assets and providing credit enhancement to positions in the securitisation are excluded;

(d) revaluation reserves;

(e) general or collective provisions if—

(i) they are freely available to the authorised payment institution to cover normal payment services risks where revenue or capital losses have not yet been identified;

(ii) their existence is disclosed in internal accounting records; and

(iii) their amount is determined by the management of the authorised payment institution, verified by a statutory auditor or audit firm (as defined by regulation 20(2)) and notified to the Authority;

(f) securities of indeterminate duration and other instruments that fulfil the following conditions—
   (i) they may not be reimbursed on the bearer's initiative or without the prior agreement of the Authority;
   (ii) the debt agreement provides for the authorised payment institution to have the option of deferring the payment of interest on the debt;
   (iii) the lender's claim on the authorised payment institution is wholly subordinated to those of all non-subordinated creditors;
   (iv) the documents governing the issue of the securities provide for debt and unpaid interest to be such as to absorb losses, whilst leaving the authorised payment institution in a position to continue trading;
  provided that only fully paid-up amounts are to be taken into account;

(g) cumulative preferential shares, other than fixed-term cumulative preference shares referred to in paragraph (j);

(h) the commitments of the members of an authorised payment institution set up as a cooperative, comprising—
   (i) that institution's uncalled capital; and
   (ii) the legal commitments of the members of that institution to make additional non-refundable payments should the institution incur a loss provided that such payments can be demanded without delay;

(i) the joint and several commitments of the borrower in the case of an authorised payment institution organised as a fund, comprising—
   (i) that institution's uncalled capital; and
   (ii) the legal commitments of the borrowers of that institution to make additional non-refundable payments should the institution incur a loss provided that such payments can be demanded without delay;

(j) fixed-term cumulative preferential shares and subordinated loan capital if—
   (i) binding agreements exist under which, in the event of the winding-up of the authorised payment institution, they rank after the claims of all other creditors and are not to be repaid until all other debts outstanding at the time have been settled; and
   (ii) in the case of subordinated loan capital—
     (aa) only fully paid-up funds are taken into account;
     (bb) the loans involved have an original maturity of at least five years, after which they may be repaid;
     (cc) the extent to which they may rank as own funds is gradually reduced during at least the last five years before the repayment date; and
     (dd) the loan agreement does not include any clause providing that in specified circumstances, other than the winding-up of the authorised payment institution, the debt will become repayable before the agreed repayment date.

4. The items specified in paragraph 144(a) to (d) must be—
(a) available to the authorised payment institution for unrestricted and immediate use to cover risks or losses as soon as these occur; and
(b) net of any foreseeable tax charge at the moment of their calculation or be suitably adjusted in so far as such tax charges reduce the amount up to which these items may be applied to cover risks or losses.

5. Own funds are not to include guarantees provided by the Crown or a local authority to a payment institution which is a public sector entity for the purposes of the [capital requirements regulation].

Deductions from own funds

6. The deductions from own funds are—
(a) own shares at book value held by the authorised payment institution;
(b) intangible assets;
(c) material losses of the current financial year;
(d) holdings of shares in credit institutions and financial institutions exceeding 10% of their capital;
(e) if sub-paragraph (d) applies, the items specified in paragraph 144(f), (g) and (j) held in the relevant credit institution or financial institution;
(f) holdings of shares or of the items specified in paragraph 3(f), (g) and (j) held in other credit institutions or financial institutions where—
   (i) the holding has not been deducted in accordance with sub-paragraph (d) or (e) of this paragraph; and
   (ii) the total amount of such holdings exceeds 10% of the authorised payment institution's own funds calculated before deduction of the items specified in this sub-paragraph and sub-paragraphs (d), (e), (g) and (h);
(g) participations which the authorised payment institution holds in an insurance undertaking, reinsurance undertaking or insurance holding company; and

(h)   the following instruments held in an insurance undertaking, reinsurance undertaking or insurance holding company in which the authorised payment institution holds a participation—
  (i)   instruments referred to in article 16(3) of directive 73/239/EEC of the Council on the coordination of laws, regulations and administrative provisions relating to the taking-up and pursuit of the business of direct insurance other than life assurance;
  (ii)   instruments referred to in article 27(3) of directive 2002/83/EC of the European Parliament and of the Council of 5th November 2002 concerning life assurance.

7. Where shares in another credit institution, financial institution, insurance undertaking, reinsurance undertaking or insurance holding company are held temporarily for the purposes of a financial assistance operation designed to reorganise and save that entity, the Authority may direct that any or all of the items specified in paragraph 147(d) to (h) are not to be deducted from own funds.

Limits on qualifying items

8. (1)   The limits referred to in paragraph 144 are—
  (a)   that A must not exceed B; and
  (b)   that C must not exceed 50% of B.
(2)   After applying such limits—
  (a)   50% of the total of the items specified in paragraph 6(d) to (h) must be deducted from A and the remaining 50% must be deducted from B; and
  (b)   the amount, if any, by which the amount to be deducted from A exceeds A must be deducted from B.
(3)   In this paragraph—
  (a)   "A" means the total of the items specified in paragraph 144(d) to (j);
  (b)   "B" means the total of the items specified in paragraph 144(a) to (c) less the total of the items specified in paragraph 147(a) to (c); and
  (c)   "C" means the total of the items specified in paragraph 144(h) to (j).

9. The Authority may in temporary and exceptional circumstances direct that an authorised payment institution may exceed one or more of the limits described in paragraph 8(1).

10. An authorised payment institution must not include in its own funds calculation any item—
  (a)   used in an equivalent calculation by an authorised payment institution, credit institution, investment firm, asset management company or insurance undertaking in the same group; or
  (b)   in the case of an authorised payment institution which carries out activities other than providing payment services, is used in carrying out those activities.

Own funds requirement

11. An authorised payment institution must hold own funds calculated in accordance with such of Method A, Method B or Method C as the Authority may direct.

Adjustment by the Authority

12. The Authority may direct that an authorised payment institution must hold own funds up to 20% higher, or up to 20% lower, than the amount which would result from paragraph 152.

13. A direction made under paragraph 153 must be on the basis of an evaluation of the relevant authorised payment institution including, if available and where the Authority considers it appropriate, any risk-management processes, risk loss database or internal control mechanisms of the authorised payment institution.

14. The Authority may make a reasonable charge for making an evaluation required under paragraph 154.

Provision for start-up payment institutions

15. If an authorised payment institution has not completed a full financial year's business, references to a figure for the preceding financial year are to be read as the equivalent figure projected in the business plan provided in the payment institution's application for authorisation, subject to any adjustment to that plan required by the Authority.

Method A

16. (1)   "Method A" means the calculation method set out in this paragraph.
(2)   The own funds requirement is 10% of the authorised payment institution's fixed overheads for the preceding financial year.

(3)   If a material change has occurred in an authorised payment institution's business since the preceding financial year, the Authority may direct that the own funds requirement is to be a higher or lower amount than that calculated in accordance with sub-paragraph (2).

Method B

17.   (1)   "Method B" means the calculation method set out in this paragraph.

(2)   The own funds requirement is the sum of the following elements multiplied by the scaling factor—

(a)   4% of the first 5,000,000 euro of payment volume;

(b)   2.5% of the next 5,000,000 euro of payment volume;

(c)   1% of the next 90,000,000 euro of payment volume;

(d)   0.5% of the next 150,000,000 euro of payment volume; and

(e)   0.25% of any remaining payment volume.

(3)   "Payment volume" means the total amount of payment transactions executed by the authorised payment institution in the preceding financial year divided by the number of months in that year.

(4)   The "scaling factor" is—

(a)   0.5 for a payment institution that is authorised to provide the payment service specified in paragraph 127(f) of Schedule 1;

(b)   0.8 for a payment institution that is authorised to provide the payment service specified in paragraph 127(g) of Schedule 1; and

(c)   1 for a payment institution that is authorised to provide any other payment service.

Method C

18.   (1)   "Method C" means the calculation method set out in this paragraph.

(2)   The own funds requirement is the relevant indicator multiplied by—

(a)   the multiplication factor; and

(b)   the scaling factor;

subject to the proviso in sub-paragraph (7).

(3)   The "relevant indicator" is the sum of the following elements—

(a)   interest income;

(b)   interest expenses;

(c)   gross commissions and fees received; and

(d)   gross other operating income.

(4)   For the purpose of calculating the relevant indicator—

(a)   each element must be included in the sum with its positive or negative sign;

(b)   income from extraordinary or irregular items may not be used;

(c)   expenditure on the outsourcing of services rendered by third parties may reduce the relevant indicator if the expenditure is incurred from a payment service provider;

(d)   the relevant indicator is calculated on the basis of the twelve-monthly observation at the end of the previous financial year;

(e)   the relevant indicator must be calculated over the previous financial year; and

(f)   audited figures must be used unless they are not available in which case business estimates may be used.

(5)   The "multiplication factor" is the sum of—

(a)   10% of the first 2,500,000 euro of the relevant indicator;

(b)   8% of the next 2,500,000 euro of the relevant indicator;

(c)   6% of the next 20,000,000 euro of the relevant indicator;

(d)   3% of the next 25,000,000 euro of the relevant indicator; and

(e)   1.5% of any remaining amount of the relevant indicator.

(6)   "Scaling factor" has the meaning given in paragraph 158(4).

(7)   The proviso is that the own funds requirement must not be less than 80 % of the average of the previous three financial years for the relevant indicator.

Application of accounting standards

19.   Except where this Schedule provides for a different method of recognition, measurement or valuation, whenever a provision in this Schedule refers to an asset, liability, equity or income statement item, an authorised payment institution must, for the purpose of that provision, recognise the asset, liability, equity or income statement item and measure its value in accordance with whichever of the following are applicable for the purpose of the institution's external financial reporting—

(a)   Financial Reporting Standards and Statements of Standard Accounting Practice issued or adopted by [the Financial Reporting Council Limited];

(b)   Statements of Recommended Practice, issued by industry or sectoral bodies recognised for this purpose by [the Financial Reporting Council Limited];

(c)   International Financial Reporting Standards and International Accounting Standards issued or adopted by the International Accounting Standards Board;

   (d)   International Standards on Auditing (United Kingdom and Ireland) issued by the [Financial Reporting Council Limited or a predecessor body]; and

   (e)   the Companies Act 2006.

NOTES

Para 5: words in square brackets substituted by the Capital Requirements Regulations 2013, SI 2013/3115, reg 46(1), Sch 2, Pt 3, para 70(1), (6).

Para 19: words in square brackets in sub-paras (a), (b) substituted by the Statutory Auditors (Amendment of Companies Act 2006 and Delegation of Functions etc) Order 2012, SI 2012/1741, art 3, Schedule, Pt 2, para 11; words in square brackets in sub-para (d) substituted by the Payment Services Regulations 2012, SI 2012/1791, reg 3(1), (6).

SCHEDULE 4
PRIOR GENERAL INFORMATION FOR FRAMEWORK CONTRACTS

Regulations 36(2), 40(1)

[2.763]

1. The following information about the payment service provider—
   (a)   the name of the payment service provider;
   (b)   the address and contact details of the payment service provider's head office;
   (c)   if different from the information under sub-paragraph (b), the address and contact details of the branch or agent from which the payment service is being provided;
   (d)   details of the payment service provider's regulators, including any reference or registration number of the payment service provider.

2. The following information about the payment service—
   (a)   a description of the main characteristics of the payment service to be provided;
   (b)   the information or unique identifier that must be provided by the payment service user in order for a payment order to be properly executed;
   (c)   the form and procedure for giving consent to the execution of a payment transaction and for the withdrawal of consent in accordance with regulation 55;
   (d)   a reference to the time of receipt of a payment order, as defined in regulation 65, and the cut-off time, if any, established by the payment service provider;
   (e)   the maximum execution time for the payment services to be provided;
   (f)   whether spending limits for the use of a payment instrument may be agreed in accordance with regulation 56(1).

3. The following information about charges, interest and exchange rates—
   (a)   details of all charges payable by the payment service user to the payment service provider and, where applicable, a breakdown of the amounts of any charges;
   (b)   where relevant, details of the interest and exchange rates to be applied or, if reference interest and exchange rates are to be used, the method of calculating the actual interest and the relevant date and index or base for determining such reference interest or exchange rates;
   (c)   if agreed, the immediate application of changes in reference interest or exchange rates and information requirements relating to the changes in accordance with regulation 42(4).

4. The following information about communication—
   (a)   the means of communication agreed between the parties for the transmission of information or notifications under these Regulations including, where relevant, any technical requirements for the payment service user's equipment for receipt of the information or notifications;
   (b)   the manner in which and frequency with which information under these Regulations is to be provided or made available;
   (c)   the language or languages in which the framework contract will be concluded and in which any information or notifications under these Regulations will be communicated;
   (d)   the payment service user's right to receive the terms of the framework contract and information in accordance with regulation 41.

5. The following information about safeguards and corrective measures—
   (a)   where relevant, a description of the steps that the payment service user is to take in order to keep safe a payment instrument and how to notify the payment service provider for the purposes of regulation 57(1)(b);
   (b)   where relevant, the conditions under which the payment service provider proposes to reserve the right to stop or prevent the use of a payment instrument in accordance with regulation 56;
   (c)   the payer's liability under regulation 62, including details of any limits on such liability;
   (d)   how and within what period of time the payment service user is to notify the payment service provider of any unauthorised or incorrectly executed payment transaction under regulation 59, and the payment service provider's liability for unauthorised payment transactions under regulation 61;

(e)   the payment service provider's liability for the execution of payment transactions under regulation 75 or 76;

(f)   the conditions for the payment of any refund under regulation 63.

6. The following information about changes to and termination of the framework contract—

(a)   where relevant, the proposed terms under which the payment service user will be deemed to have accepted changes to the framework contract in accordance with regulation 42(2), unless they notify the payment service provider that they do not accept such changes before the proposed date of their entry into force;

(b)   the duration of the framework contract;

(c)   the right of the payment service user to terminate the framework contract and any agreements relating to termination in accordance with regulation 43.

7. The following information about redress—

(a)   any contractual clause on—

(i)   the law applicable to the framework contract;

(ii)   the competent courts;

(b)   the availability of out-of-court complaint and redress procedures for the payment service user and the methods for having access to them.

[SCHEDULE 4A
CREDIT AGREEMENTS

Regulation 92A

PART 1
PROHIBITIONS AND RESTRICTIONS

[2.764]
1   Power to prohibit the entry into credit agreements

(1)   If it appears to the Authority that sub-paragraph (4) has been, or is likely to be, contravened as respects an EEA authorised payment institution exercising passport rights in the United Kingdom, it may by notice given to the institution in accordance with Part 2 of this Schedule impose on the institution a credit prohibition.

(2)   If it appears to the Authority that a restriction imposed under paragraph 2 on an EEA authorised payment institution exercising passport rights in the United Kingdom has not been complied with, it may by notice given to the institution in accordance with Part 2 of this Schedule impose on the institution a credit prohibition.

(3)   "A credit prohibition" means a prohibition on carrying on, or purporting to carry on, in the United Kingdom any business which consists of or includes carrying on an activity—

(a)   of the kind specified by article 36A, 36H, 39D, 39E, 39F, 39G, 60B, 60N, 89A or 89B of the Financial Services and Markets Act 2000 (Regulated Activities) Order 2001, and

(b)   listed in the Annex to the payment services directive or which the institution is entitled to carry on in accordance with Article 16 of that directive.

(4)   This sub-paragraph is contravened as respects an EEA authorised payment institution exercising passport rights in the United Kingdom if—

(a)   the institution or any of its employees, agents or associates (whether past or present), or

(b)   where the institution is a body corporate, any controller of the institution or an associate of any such controller,

does any of the things specified in sub-paragraph (5).

(5)   A person does a thing specified in this sub-paragraph if the person—

(a)   commits any offence involving fraud or other dishonesty or violence;

(b)   contravenes any provision made by or under—

(i)   the Consumer Credit Act 1974;

(ii)   the 2000 Act, to the extent that that Act relates to any activity of the kind specified by article 36A, 36H, 39D, 39E, 39F, 39G, 60B, 60N, 89A or 89B of the Financial Services and Markets Act 2000 (Regulated Activities) Order 2001;

(iii)   any other enactment regulating the provision of credit to individuals or other transactions with individuals;

(c)   contravenes any provision in force in an EEA State which corresponds to a provision of the kind mentioned in paragraph (b);

(d)   practices discrimination on grounds of sex, colour, race or ethnic or national origins in, or in connection with, the carrying on of any business;

(e)   engages in business practices appearing to the Authority to be deceitful or oppressive or otherwise unfair or improper (including practices that appear to the Authority to involve irresponsible lending).

(6)   A credit prohibition may be absolute or may be imposed—

(a)   for such period,

(b)   until the occurrence of such event, or

(c)   until such conditions are complied with,

as may be specified in the notice given under sub-paragraph (1) or (2).

(7)   Any period, event or condition so specified may be varied by the Authority on the application of the institution concerned (for which, see paragraph 5).

(8)   A credit prohibition may be withdrawn in whole or in part—
  (a)   on the initiative of the Authority, by notice served by the Authority on the institution concerned, and any such notice takes effect on such date as is specified in the notice;
  (b)   on an application submitted by the institution concerned (for which, see paragraph 5).

(9)   Where the Authority withdraws a credit prohibition and imposes a restriction under paragraph 2, the Authority may specify that the withdrawal of the credit prohibition only takes effect when the imposition of the restriction is no longer open to review.

(10)   For the purposes of sub-paragraph (9), whether the imposition of a restriction is open to review is to be determined in accordance with section 391(8) of the 2000 Act as if the imposition of the restriction were a matter to which a supervisory notice (within the meaning of that section) relates.

(11)   An institution contravening a prohibition imposed under this paragraph is guilty of an offence and liable—
  (a)   on summary conviction, to a fine not exceeding the statutory maximum;
  (b)   on conviction on indictment, to a fine.

(12)   In this paragraph—
    "associate" has the same meaning as in article 60L of the Financial Services and Markets Act 2000 (Regulated Activities) Order 2001;
    "controller" has the meaning given by section 422 of the 2000 Act.

(13)   If a credit prohibition is in effect in relation to an institution, article 60JA of the Financial Services and Markets Act 2000 (Regulated Activities) Order 2001 does not apply in relation to that institution.

2   Power to restrict the entry into credit agreements

(1)   In this paragraph, "restriction" means a direction that an EEA authorised payment institution exercising passport rights in the United Kingdom may not carry on in the United Kingdom, otherwise than in accordance with such conditions as may be specified in the direction, any business which consists of or includes carrying on an activity—
  (a)   of the kind specified in article 36A, 36H, 39D, 39E, 39F, 39G, 60B, 60N, 89A or 89B of the Financial Services and Markets Act 2000 (Regulated Activities) Order 2001;
  (b)   listed in the Annex to the payment services directive or which the institution is entitled to carry on in accordance with Article 16 of that directive; and
  (c)   specified in the direction.

(2)   If it appears to the Authority that the situation as respects an EEA authorised payment institution exercising passport rights in the United Kingdom is such that the powers conferred by paragraph 1 are exercisable, the Authority may, instead of imposing a credit prohibition—
  (a)   impose by notice given in accordance with Part 2 of this Schedule such restriction as appears to it desirable;
  (b)   where it has already imposed a restriction, vary the restriction on the Authority's own initiative by notice given in accordance with Part 2 of this Schedule.

(3)   The Authority may also impose a restriction by notice given in accordance with Part 2 of this Schedule if it withdraws a credit prohibition.

(4)   A restriction may be—
  (a)   withdrawn on the initiative of the Authority, by notice served by the Authority on the institution concerned, and any such notice takes effect on such date as is specified in the notice;
  (b)   withdrawn or varied on an application submitted by the institution concerned (for which, see paragraph 5).

(5)   An institution contravening a restriction is guilty of an offence and liable—
  (a)   on summary conviction, to a fine not exceeding the statutory maximum;
  (b)   on conviction on indictment, to a fine.]

NOTES

Commencement: see below.

Inserted by the Financial Services and Markets Act 2000 (Regulated Activities) (Amendment) Order 2014, SI 2014/366, art 12(1), (4) (note that the 2014 Order comes into force on 18 February 2014 for the purpose of the FCA making rules, giving guidance etc, and comes into force on 1 April 2014, immediately after SI 2013/1881 (and SI 2013/1882) come into force, in so far as not already in force (see art 1 of the 2014 Order)).

Part 2   Statutory Instruments

[PART 2
PROCEDURE AND APPEALS

[2.765]
3 Interpretation

In this Part—

"prohibition" means a credit prohibition imposed under paragraph 1(1) or (2) of Part 1 of this Schedule;

"restriction" means a restriction imposed under paragraph 2(2) or (3) of Part 1 of this Schedule;

"the Tribunal" means the Upper Tribunal.

4 Notice of prohibition or restriction

(1) A prohibition or restriction takes effect—
  (a) immediately, if the relevant notice states that that is the case,
  (b) on such date as may be specified in the notice, or
  (c) if no date is specified in the notice, when the matter to which the notice relates is no longer open to review.

(2) An institution which is aggrieved by the imposition of a prohibition or a restriction by a notice given under this paragraph may refer the matter to the Tribunal.

(3) A prohibition or restriction may be expressed to take effect immediately (or on a specified date) only if the Authority, having regard to the ground on which it is imposing the prohibition or restriction, reasonably considers that it is necessary for the prohibition or restriction to take effect immediately (or on that date).

(4) The notice must—
  (a) give details of the prohibition or restriction,
  (b) state the Authority's reasons for the prohibition or restriction,
  (c) inform the institution that it may make representations to the Authority within such period as is specified in the notice (whether or not the institution has referred the matter to the Tribunal),
  (d) inform the institution of when the prohibition or restriction takes effect, and
  (e) inform the institution of its right to refer the matter to the Tribunal.

(5) The Authority may extend the period allowed under the notice for making representations.

(6) If, having considered any representations made by the institution, the Authority decides—
  (a) to impose the proposed prohibition or restriction, or
  (b) if the prohibition or restriction has already taken effect, not to withdraw the prohibition or restriction,

it must give the institution a notice.

(6) If, having considered any representations made by the institution, the Authority decides—
  (a) not to impose the proposed prohibition or restriction,
  (b) to impose a different prohibition or restriction, or
  (c) if the prohibition or restriction has already taken effect, to withdraw the prohibition or restriction,

it must give the institution a notice.

(7) A notice under sub-paragraph (6) must inform the institution of its right to refer the matter to the Tribunal.

(8) A notice under sub-paragraph (7)(b) must comply with sub-paragraph (4).

(9) If a notice under this paragraph informs an institution of its right to refer a matter to the Tribunal, it must give an indication of the procedure on such a reference.

(10) For the purposes of sub-paragraph (1)(c)—
  (a) whether a matter is open to review is to be determined in accordance with section 391(8) of the 2000 Act;
  (b) the notice to which the matter relates is to be treated as a supervisory notice for the purposes of that section.

(11) References in this paragraph to the imposition of a restriction include references to the variation of a restriction on the initiative of the Authority.

5 Application to revoke or vary prohibition or restriction

(1) An application under Part 1 of this Schedule must—
  (a) be made in such manner as the Authority may direct, and
  (b) contain, or be accompanied by, such other information as the Authority may reasonably require.

(2) At any time after the application is received and before it is determined, the Authority may require the applicant to provide it with such further information as it reasonably considers necessary to enable it to determine the application.

(3) Different directions may be given, and different requirements imposed, in relation to different applications or categories of application.

(4) The Authority may require an applicant to provide information required under this paragraph in such form, or to verify it in such a way, as the Authority may direct.

(5) If the Authority decides to grant an application, it must give the applicant a notice.

(6) If the Authority proposes to refuse an application, or to take an action different from or in addition to the one applied for (including a proposal to impose a restriction when withdrawing a prohibition on an application under paragraph 1(8)(b)), it must give the applicant a warning notice.

(7) If the Authority decides to refuse an application, or to take an action different from or in addition to the one applied for (including a decision to impose a restriction when withdrawing a prohibition on an application under paragraph 1(8)(b)), it must give the applicant a decision notice.

(8) An applicant who is aggrieved by a decision notice given under this paragraph may refer the matter to the Tribunal.

6   Notice to the home state competent authority

If the Authority sends a notice to an institution under this Schedule which imposes, varies or withdraws a prohibition or restriction, it must send a copy of the notice to the institution's home state competent authority.]

NOTES

Commencement: see below.

Inserted by the Financial Services and Markets Act 2000 (Regulated Activities) (Amendment) Order 2014, SI 2014/366, art 12(1), (4) (note that the 2014 Order comes into force on 18 February 2014 for the purpose of the FCA making rules, giving guidance etc, and comes into force on 1 April 2014, immediately after SI 2013/1881 (and SI 2013/1882) come into force, in so far as not already in force (see art 1 of the 2014 Order)).

SCHEDULES 5 AND 6

(Sch 5 makes modifications to legislation outside the scope of this work; Sch 6 amends the Financial Services and Markets Act 2000, ss 226, 234, Sch 17, Pt III (see the 2000 Act at **[1.1395]** *et seq), the Financial Services (Distance Marketing) Regulations 2004, SI 2004/2095 at* **[2.330]**, *the Money Laundering Regulations 2007, SI 2007/2157 at* **[2.464]**, *revokes the Consumer Protection (Distance Selling) Regulations 2000, SI 2000/2334, reg 21, and amends other legislation outside the scope of this work.)*

[SCHEDULE 7

Regulation 127

[2.766]
1   Exercise of deemed passport rights by Gibraltar-based firms

(1) These Regulations apply in relation to a firm which—
   (a)   has its head office in Gibraltar; and
   (b)   is authorised in Gibraltar to provide payment services;
as follows.

(2) The firm is to be treated as having an entitlement, corresponding to its passport right deriving from the payment services directive, to establish a branch or provide services in the United Kingdom.

(3) References in these Regulations to—
   (a)   "an EEA authorised payment institution" are to be treated as references to the firm;
   (b)   "home state competent authority" are to be treated as references to the competent authority (within the meaning of the payment services directive) in Gibraltar in relation to the firm; and
   (c)   "passport rights" are to be treated as references to the entitlement mentioned in sub-paragraph (2).

2   Exercise by authorised payment institutions of deemed passport rights in Gibraltar

(1) For the purposes of these Regulations, an authorised payment institution is to be treated as having an entitlement, corresponding to its passport right, to establish a branch or provide services in Gibraltar.

(2) In relation to an authorised payment institution which establishes a branch, or provides services, in Gibraltar, references in these Regulations to—
   (a)   "EEA branch" are to be treated as including a reference to such a branch;
   (b)   "host state competent authority" are to be treated as including a reference to the competent authority (within the meaning of the payment services directive) in Gibraltar in relation to the institution;
   (c)   "passport rights" are to be treated as including references to the entitlement mentioned in sub-paragraph (1); and

(d) "EEA State" are to be treated as including references to Gibraltar.

3 Modification of legislation

(1) Section 155(7) of the 2000 Act (consultation) has effect for the purposes of these Regulations as if modified by adding at the end "or if it is making rules for the purpose of extending rules that apply to EEA authorised payment institutions to Gibraltar-based firms".

(2) Paragraph 14 of Schedule 17 to the 2000 Act (the ombudsman scheme) has effect for the purposes of these Regulations as if modified by adding at the end—

"(8) Sub-paragraphs (4), (5) and (6) above do not apply if the scheme operator is making rules for the purpose of extending rules that apply to EEA authorised payment institutions to Gibraltar-based firms.".]

NOTES

Inserted by the Payment Services (Amendment) Regulations 2009, SI 2009/2475, regs 2, 13.

COMPANIES (DISCLOSURE OF ADDRESS) REGULATIONS 2009

(SI 2009/214)

NOTES

Made: 1 February 2009.
Authority: Companies Act 2006, ss 243(2)–(6), 1088(1)–(3), (5), 1292(1), (4).
Commencement: 1 October 2009.
Application: these Regulations are applied, with modifications, in so far as they relates to LLPs, by the Limited Liability Partnerships (Application of Companies Act 2006) Regulations 2009, SI 2009/1804, reg 83, Sch 1, Pt 4, para 11.

ARRANGEMENT OF REGULATIONS

PART 1

[2.767]
1   Citation, commencement and interpretation

(1)   These Regulations may be cited as the Companies (Disclosure of Address) Regulations 2009 and come into force on 1st October 2009.

(2)   In these Regulations—

"the Act" means the Companies Act 2006 and, unless the context otherwise requires, any reference to a numbered section is to a section so numbered in that Act;

"the 1985 Act" means the Companies Act 1985;

"the 1986 Order" means the Companies (Northern Ireland) Order 1986;

"confidentiality order" means an order under section 723B of the 1985 Act (confidentiality orders);

"former name" means a name by which an individual was formerly known and which has been notified to the registrar under section 10 (documents to be sent to the registrar) or section 288 (register of directors and secretaries) of the 1985 Act, or Article 21 or 296 of the 1986 Order, [or regulation 80C of the SEs Regulations, or regulation 79 of the old SEs Regulations, or regulation 77 of the Northern Ireland SEs Regulations,] or section 12 (statement of proposed officers) or section 167 (duty to notify registrar of changes) of the Act;

"limited liability partnership" means a limited liability partnership incorporated under the Limited Liability Partnerships Act 2000 or Limited Liability Partnerships Act (Northern Ireland) 2002;

"name" means a person's Christian name (or other forename) and surname, except that in the case of—

    (a)   a peer; or

    (b)   an individual usually known by a title,

the title may be stated instead of his Christian name (or other forename) and surname or in addition to either or both of them;

["the Northern Ireland SEs Regulations" means the European Public Limited-Liability Company Regulations (Northern Ireland) 2004;]

["the old SEs Regulations" means the SEs Regulations, disregarding the amendments made by the European Public Limited-Liability Company (Amendment) Regulations 2009;]

"permanent representative" means an individual who was a permanent representative for the purposes of sections 723B and 723C (effect of confidentiality orders) of the 1985 Act;

"police force" means a police force within the meaning of section 101(1) of the Police Act 1996 (interpretation), section 50 of the Police (Scotland) Act 1967 (meaning of police area, etc) or section 1 of the Police (Northern Ireland) Act 2000 (name of the police in Northern Ireland);

"relevant body" means any police force and any other person whom the registrar considers may be able to assist in answering a question referred to that person by the registrar under these Regulations;

"relevant organisation" means the Government Communications Headquarters, the Secret Intelligence Service, the Security Service or a police force;

"section 243 applicant" means an individual by whom or in respect of whom a section 243 application has been made but in respect of which application the registrar either has not made a determination, or has made a determination, not being a section 243 decision, and any appeal to the court in respect of that application under regulation 14 has not been determined by the court;

"section 243 application" means an application under section 243(4) (permitted use or disclosure by the registrar) for the purpose of requiring the registrar to refrain from disclosing protected information relating to a director to a credit reference agency;

"section 243 beneficiary" means—

    (a)   an individual who has made a section 243 application in respect of which a section 243 decision has been made; or

    (b)   an individual on whose behalf a company or a subscriber to a memorandum of association has made a section 243 application in respect of which a section 243 decision has been made; or

    (c)   an individual in relation to whom a confidentiality order was in force immediately before 1st October 2009 and who, by paragraph 37 of Schedule 2 to the Companies Act 2006 (Commencement No 8, Transitional Provisions and Savings) Order 2008 is treated as having made a section 243 application in respect of which a section 243 decision has been made;

"section 243 decision" means a determination by the registrar on a section 243 application in favour of the applicant;

"section 1088 application" means an application under section 1088 (application to registrar to make address unavailable for public inspection) for the purpose of requiring the registrar to make an address on the register unavailable for public inspection;

"section 1088 beneficiary" means a person who has made a section 1088 application in respect of which a section 1088 decision has been made;

"section 1088 decision" means a determination by the registrar on a section 1088 application in favour of the applicant;

["the SEs Regulations" means the European Public Limited-Liability Company Regulations 2004;]

"specified public authority" means any public authority specified in Schedule 1 to these Regulations; and

"working day" means a day that is not a Saturday or Sunday, Christmas Day, Good Friday or any day that is a bank holiday under the Banking and Financial Dealings Act 1971 in England and Wales.

NOTES

Para (2): words in square brackets in definition "former name" inserted, and definitions "the Northern Ireland SEs Regulations", "the old SEs Regulations", "the SEs Regulations" inserted by the European Public Limited-Liability Company (Amendment) Regulations 2009, SI 2009/2400, reg 42(1), (2), subject to transitional provisions in reg 2 thereof.

PART 2
DISCLOSURE OF PROTECTED INFORMATION

[2.768]
2 Permitted disclosure by the registrar to specified public authorities

(1) The registrar may disclose protected information to a specified public authority where the conditions specified in paragraphs 2 and 3 of Schedule 2 are satisfied.

(2) A specified public authority shall deliver to the registrar such information or evidence as he may direct for the purpose of enabling him to determine in accordance with these Regulations whether to disclose protected information.

(3) The registrar may require such information or evidence to be verified in such manner as he may direct.

(4) The specified public authority must inform the registrar immediately of any change in respect of any statement delivered to the registrar pursuant to Schedule 2 or information or evidence provided for the purpose of enabling the registrar to determine whether to disclose protected information.

(5) The public authorities specified for the purposes of section 243(2) are set out in Schedule 1 to these Regulations.

[2.769]
3 Permitted disclosure by the registrar to credit reference agencies

(1) Subject to regulation 4, the registrar may disclose protected information to a credit reference agency where the conditions specified in paragraphs 6 to 10 of Schedule 2 are satisfied.

(2) The registrar may rely on a statement delivered to him by a credit reference agency under paragraph 10 of Schedule 2 as sufficient evidence of the matters stated in it.

(3) Notwithstanding paragraph (2), a credit reference agency shall deliver to the registrar such information or evidence in addition to the statement required by paragraph 10 of Schedule 2 as he may direct for the purpose of enabling him to determine in accordance with these Regulations whether to disclose protected information.

(4) The registrar may require such information or evidence to be verified in such manner as he may direct.

(5) The credit reference agency must inform the registrar immediately of any change in respect of any statement delivered to the registrar pursuant to Schedule 2 or information or evidence provided for the purpose of enabling the registrar to determine whether to disclose protected information.

[2.770]
4 Registrar to refrain from disclosure of protected information

The registrar shall refrain from disclosing protected information to a credit reference agency if such information relates to a section 243 beneficiary or a section 243 applicant.

[2.771]
5 Application under section 243 by an individual

(1) A section 243 application may be made to the registrar by an individual who is, or proposes to become, a director.

(2) The grounds on which an application under paragraph (1) may be made are that the individual making the application—
  (a) considers that there is a serious risk that he, or a person who lives with him, will be subjected to violence or intimidation as a result of the activities of at least one of—
    (i) the companies of which he is, or proposes to become, a director;
    (ii) the companies of which he was a director;

      (iii)   the overseas companies of which he is or has been a director, secretary or permanent representative; or,

      (iv)   the limited liability partnerships of which he is or has been a member; or

  (b)   is or has been employed by a relevant organisation.

(3)   The application shall—

  (a)   contain—

      (i)   a statement of the grounds on which the application is made;

      (ii)   the name and any former name of the applicant;

      (iii)   the date of birth of the applicant;

      (iv)   the usual residential address of the applicant;

      (v)   where the registrar has allocated a unique identifier to the applicant, that unique identifier;

      (vi)   the name and registered number of each company of which the applicant is, or proposes to become, a director;

      (vii)   where the grounds of the application are those described in paragraph (2)(a)(ii), (iii) or (iv), the name and registered number of the company, overseas company or limited liability partnership; and

  (b)   be accompanied by evidence which—

      (i)   where the grounds of the application are those described in paragraph (2)(a) supports the applicant's statement of the grounds of the application; or,

      (ii)   where the grounds of the application are those described in paragraph (2)(b), establishes that the applicant is or has been employed by a relevant organisation.

(4)   The registrar may refer to a relevant body any question relating to an assessment of—

  (a)   where the grounds of the application are those described in paragraph (2)(a), the nature and extent of any risk of violence or intimidation considered by the applicant to arise in relation to himself, or to a person who lives with him; or

  (b)   where the grounds of the application are those described in paragraph (2)(b), whether the applicant is or has been employed by a relevant organisation.

(5)   The registrar shall determine the application and send the applicant to his usual residential address, as stated in his application, notice of his determination on the section 243 application within five working days of that determination being made.

[2.772]

6   Application under section 243 by a company

(1)   A section 243 application may be made to the registrar by a company on behalf of any of its directors who are individuals.

(2)   The grounds on which an application under paragraph (1) may be made are that the company making the application considers that there is a serious risk that the director on behalf of whom the application is made, or a person who lives with that director, will be subjected to violence or intimidation as a result of the activities of the company making the application.

(3)   The application shall—

  (a)   contain—

      (i)   a statement of the grounds on which the application is made;

      (ii)   the name and registered number of the applicant;

      (iii)   the name and any former name of each director on behalf of whom the application is made;

      (iv)   the date of birth of each such director;

      (v)   the usual residential address of each such director;

      (vi)   where the registrar has allocated a unique identifier to any such director, that unique identifier;

      (vii)   the name and registered number of each company of which each such director is a director; and

  (b)   be accompanied by evidence which supports the applicant's statement of the grounds of the application.

(4)   The registrar may refer to a relevant body any question relating to an assessment of the nature and extent of any risk of violence or intimidation considered by the applicant to arise in relation to its directors on behalf of whom the application is made or to persons who live with those directors as a result of any of its activities.

(5)   The registrar shall determine the application and send—

  (a)   the applicant, to its registered office; and

  (b)   each director on behalf of whom the application was made, to his usual residential address as stated in the application,

notice of his determination on the section 243 application within five working days of that determination being made.

Part 2 Statutory Instruments

[2.773]
7   Application under section 243 by a subscriber to a memorandum of association

(1)   A section 243 application may be made to the registrar by a subscriber to a memorandum of association on behalf of any of the proposed directors of a proposed company who are individuals.

(2)   The grounds on which an application under paragraph (1) may be made are that the subscriber making the application considers that there is a serious risk that the proposed directors of the proposed company on behalf of whom the application is made, or persons who live with them, will be subjected to violence or intimidation as a result of the proposed activities of that proposed company.

(3)   The application shall—

  (a) contain—

    (i)   a statement of the grounds on which the application is made;
    (ii)   the name of the applicant;
    (iii) the address of the applicant;
    (iv) the name of the proposed company;
    (v)   the name and any former name of each of the proposed directors on behalf of whom the application is made;
    (vi) the date of birth of each such proposed director;
    (vii) the usual residential address of each such proposed director;
    (viii) the name and registered number of each company of which each such proposed director is a director; and

  (b) be accompanied by evidence which supports the applicant's statement of the grounds of the application.

(4)   The registrar may refer to a relevant body any question relating to an assessment of the nature and extent of any risk of violence or intimidation considered by the applicant to arise in relation to its proposed directors on behalf of whom the application is made or to persons who live with those proposed directors as a result of any of the proposed activities of the proposed company.

(5)   The registrar shall determine the application and send—

  (a) the applicant, to the address stated in the application, and
  (b) each of the proposed directors on behalf of whom the application was made, to their usual residential address as stated in the application,

notice of his determination on the section 243 application within five working days of that determination being made.

[2.774]
8   Matters relating to a section 243 application

(1)   For the purpose of regulations 5, 6 and 7 the registrar may direct that additional information or evidence should be delivered to him, what such information or evidence should be and how it should be verified.

(2)   The registrar shall not make available for public inspection—

  (a) any section 243 application; or
  (b) any documents provided in support of that application.

(3)   For the purpose of determining any section 243 application the registrar may accept any answer to a question referred in accordance with regulation 5(4), 6(4) or 7(4) as providing sufficient evidence of—

  (a) the nature and extent of any risk relevant to—

    (i)   where the grounds of the application are those described in regulation 5(2)(a), the applicant;
    (ii)   where the grounds of the application are those described in regulation 6(2), the directors on behalf of whom the application is made;
    (iii) where the grounds of the application are those described in regulation 7(2), the proposed directors on behalf of whom the application is made,

    or to persons who live with any of the above individuals, or

  (b) whether an applicant is or has been employed by a relevant organisation.

PART 3
APPLICATION TO MAKE AN ADDRESS UNAVAILABLE FOR PUBLIC INSPECTION UNDER SECTION 1088

[2.775]
9   Application under section 1088 to make an address unavailable for public inspection by an individual

(1)   A section 1088 application may be made to the registrar by an individual whose usual residential address was placed on the register either—

(a)	under section 10 (documents to be sent to registrar), 288 (register of directors and secretaries), 363 (duty to deliver annual returns), 691 (documents to be delivered to registrar) or 692 (registration of altered particulars) of or paragraph 2 of Schedule 21A to the 1985 Act;

(b)	under Article 21, 296, 371, 641 or 642 of the 1986 Order; . . .

[(ba)	as a service address under regulation 80C of the SEs Regulations (duty to notify registrar of changes of particulars of members of an SE's supervisory organ),

(bb)	under regulation 79 of the old SEs Regulations or regulation 77 of the Northern Ireland SEs Regulations, or]

(c)	as a service address under section 12 (statement of proposed officers), 167 (duty to notify registrar of changes of director's particulars) or 855 (contents of annual return) of the Act [or under regulations made under section 1046],

in respect of that usual residential address where it was placed on the register on or after 1st January 2003.

(2)	The grounds on which an application under paragraph (1) may be made are that the individual making the application—

(a)	considers that there is a serious risk that he, or a person who lives with him, will be subjected to violence or intimidation as a result of the activities of at least one of the companies of which—

(i)	he is, or proposes to become, a director; or

(ii)	he is not a director but of which he has been at any time a director, secretary or permanent representative;

(b)	he is or has been employed by a relevant organisation;

(c)	is a section 243 beneficiary.

(3)	The application shall—

(a)	contain—

(i)	a statement of the grounds on which the application is made;

(ii)	the name and any former name of the applicant;

(iii)	the usual residential address of the applicant that is to be made unavailable for public inspection;

(iv)	an address for correspondence in respect of the application;

(v)	the name and registered number of each company of which the applicant is or has been at any time since 1st January 2003 a director, secretary or permanent representative;

(vi)	the service address which is to replace that usual residential address on the register;

(vii)	subject to paragraph (4)—

(aa)	the date of birth of the applicant;

(bb)	the name of each company of which the applicant proposes to become a director; and

(cc)	where the registrar has allotted a unique identifier to the applicant, that unique identifier; and

(b)	be accompanied by evidence which—

(i)	where the grounds of the application are those described in paragraph (2)(a), supports the applicant's assertion that his application falls within the grounds stated in his application;

(ii)	where the grounds of the application are those described in paragraph (2)(b), establishes that the applicant is or has been employed by a relevant organisation;

(iii)	where the grounds of the application are those described in paragraph (2)(c), establishes that he is a section 243 beneficiary.

(4)	The application need not contain the information described at paragraph (3)(a)(vii) where the application is delivered to the registrar on the same day as the applicant delivers a section 243 application.

(5)	The registrar may refer to a relevant body any question relating to an assessment of—

(a)	the nature and extent of any risk of violence or intimidation considered by the applicant to arise in relation to himself, or a person who lives with him, as a result of the activities of any company of which he is or proposes to become a director or has been at any time a director, secretary or permanent representative; or

(b)	whether the applicant is or has been employed by a relevant organisation.

(6)	The registrar shall determine the application and send the applicant to the address for correspondence stated in his application, notice of his determination on the section 1088 application within five working days of that determination being made.

NOTES

Para (1): word omitted from sub-para (b) revoked and sub-paras (ba), (bb) inserted by the European Public Limited-Liability Company (Amendment) Regulations 2009, SI 2009/2400, reg 42(1), (3), subject to transitional provisions in reg 2 thereof; words in square brackets in sub-para (c) inserted by the Companies Act 2006 (Consequential Amendments, Transitional Provisions and Savings) Order 2009, SI 2009/1941, art 2(1), Sch 1, para 270(1), (2).

Part 2   Statutory Instruments

[2.776]
10 Application under section 1088 to make an address unavailable for public inspection by a company

(1) A section 1088 application may be made to the registrar by a company in respect of the addresses of—
- (a) all of its members and former members whose addresses were contained in—
  - (i) an annual return; or
  - (ii) a return of allotment of shares,

  delivered to the registrar on or after 1st January 2003; or
- (b) the subscribers to its memorandum of association where that memorandum was delivered to the registrar on or after 1st January 2003.

(2) The grounds on which an application under paragraph (1) may be made are that the company making the application considers that, as a result of its activities, the availability to members of the public of the addresses described in paragraph (1) creates a serious risk that its members or former members or subscribers, or persons who live at those addresses, will be subjected to violence or intimidation.

(3) The application shall—
- (a) contain—
  - (i) the name of the applicant and its registered number; and
  - (ii) a statement of the grounds on which the application is made; and
- (b) be accompanied by evidence—
  - (i) which supports the applicant's assertion that its application falls within the grounds stated in its application; or
  - (ii) where the court has made an order under section 117(3) (register of members: response to request for inspection or copy) directing the applicant not to comply with a request under section 116 (rights to inspect and require copies), a copy of that order.

(4) The registrar may refer to a relevant body any question relating to the assessment of the nature and extent of any risk of violence or intimidation considered by the applicant to arise in relation to any of its members or former members or subscribers, or persons who live at the addresses described in paragraph (1), as a result of its activities by virtue of the availability to members of the public of particulars of the addresses of such members or former members or subscribers.

(5) The registrar shall determine the application and send the applicant to its registered office notice of his determination on the section 1088 application within five working days of that determination being made.

[2.777]
11 Application under section 1088 to make an address unavailable for public inspection by a person who registers a charge

(1) A section 1088 application may be made to the registrar by a person who—
- (a)
  - (i) on or after 1st January 2003, registered a charge under Part 12 of the 1985 Act (registration of charges) or Part 13 of the 1986 Order; or
  - (ii) has registered a charge under Part 25 of the Act (company charges) [or under regulations made under section 1052]; and
- (b) is not the company which created the charge or acquired the property subject to a charge,

in respect of his address delivered to the registrar for the purposes of that registration.

(2) The grounds on which an application under paragraph (1) may be made are that the person making the application considers that there is a serious risk that he, or if applicable his employees, or persons who live with him or his employees, will be subjected to violence or intimidation as a result of the activities of the company which is, or was, subject to the charge.

(3) The application shall—
- (a) contain—
  - (i) a statement of the grounds on which the application is made;
  - (ii) the name of the applicant, and where the applicant is a company, its registered number;
  - (iii) the address of the applicant that is to be made unavailable for public inspection;
  - (iv) the name and registered number of the company which is or was subject to the charge;
  - (v) an address for correspondence with the registrar in respect of the application;
  - (vi) where the applicant is the chargee, the service address which is to replace the address of the applicant on the register; and
- (b) be accompanied by evidence which supports the applicant's assertion that there is a serious risk that he or, if applicable, his employees, or persons who live with him or his employees, will be subjected to violence or intimidation as a result of the activities of the company which is or was subject to the charge.

(4)   The registrar may refer to a relevant body any question relating to the assessment of the nature and extent of any risk of violence or intimidation considered by the applicant to arise in relation to himself or, if applicable, his employees, or persons who live with him or his employees, as a result of the activities of the company which is or was subject to the charge.

(5)   The registrar shall determine the application and send the applicant to the address stated in the application in accordance with paragraph (3)(a)(v) notice of his determination on the section 1088 application within five working days of that determination being made.

NOTES

Para (1): words in square brackets in sub-para (a) inserted by the Companies Act 2006 (Consequential Amendments, Transitional Provisions and Savings) Order 2009, SI 2009/1941, art 2(1), Sch 1, para 270(1), (3).

[2.778]
12   Matters relevant to section 1088 applications

(1)   For the purpose of regulations 9, 10 and 11 the registrar may direct that additional information or evidence should be delivered to him, what such information or evidence should be and how it should be verified.

(2)   For the purpose of determining any section 1088 application the registrar may accept any answer to a question referred in accordance with regulation 9(5), 10(4) or 11(4) as providing sufficient evidence of—

(a)   the nature and extent of any risk relevant to—
   (i)   where the grounds of the application are those described in regulation 9(2)(a), the applicant;
   (ii)   where the grounds of the application are those described in regulation 10(2), the subscribers or members or former members of an applicant; or
   (iii) where the grounds of the application are those described in regulation 11(2), where the applicant is an individual, the applicant, or any employees of an applicant,
   or to persons who live with any of the above individuals or, in the case of members, former members or subscribers, to persons who live at their addresses, or

(b)   whether an applicant is or has been employed by a relevant organisation.

[2.779]
13   Effect of a successful section 1088 application

(1)   Where a section 1088 application has been determined in favour of the applicant the registrar shall—

(a)   in the case of an application made under regulation 9(1) or 11(1) make the specified address unavailable for public inspection;

(b)   in the case of an application under regulation 10(1) make all of the members', former members' or subscribers' addresses unavailable for public inspection;

(c)   in the case of a person to whom paragraph 36 of Schedule 2 to the Companies Act 2006 (Commencement No 8, Transitional Provisions and Savings) Order 2008 applies, make unavailable for public inspection the address referred to in sub-paragraph (1)(a) of that paragraph.

(2)   In this regulation "specified address" means the address specified in the application as being the one to be made unavailable for public inspection.

PART 4
MATTERS RELATING TO APPLICATIONS UNDER SECTION 243 AND UNDER SECTION 1088

[2.780]
14   Appeals

(1)   An applicant who has received notice under regulation 5(5), 6(5), 7(5), 9(6), 10(5) or 11(5) that his application has been unsuccessful may appeal to the High Court or, in Scotland, the Court of Session on the grounds that the decision—

(a)   is unlawful;

(b)   is irrational or unreasonable;

(c)   has been made on the basis of a procedural impropriety or otherwise contravenes the rules of natural justice.

(2)   No appeal under this regulation may be brought unless the leave of the court has been obtained.

(3)   An applicant must bring an appeal within 21 days of the date of the notice or, with the court's permission, after the end of such period, but only if the court is satisfied—

(a)   where permission is sought before the end of that period, that there is good reason for the applicant being unable to bring the appeal in time; or

(b)   where permission is sought after that time, that there was a good reason for the applicant's failure to bring the appeal in time and for any delay in applying for permission.

Part 2   Statutory Instruments

(4)   The court determining an appeal may—
   (a)   dismiss the appeal; or
   (b)   quash the decision,
and where the court quashes a decision it may refer the matter to the registrar with a direction to reconsider it and make a determination in accordance with the findings of the court.

[2.781]
15   Duration of a section 243 decision or a section 1088 decision
(1)   A section 243 decision shall continue to have effect until—
   (a)   either—
      (i)   the section 243 beneficiary, or
      (ii)   his personal representative,
      has notified the registrar in writing that he wishes the section 243 decision to cease to apply; or
   (b)   the registrar has made a revocation decision in relation to that beneficiary,
whichever first occurs.
(2)   A section 1088 decision shall continue to have effect until the registrar has made a revocation decision in relation to the section 1088 beneficiary.
(3)   In this regulation—
"personal representative" means the executor, original or by representation, or administrator for the time being of a deceased person; and
"revocation decision" in relation to a section 243 decision or a section 1088 decision means a determination by the registrar to revoke that decision in accordance with regulation 16.

[2.782]
16   Revocation of a section 243 decision or a section 1088 decision
(1)   The registrar may revoke a section 243 decision or a section 1088 decision at any time if he is satisfied that the section 243 beneficiary or section 1088 beneficiary, as the case may be, or any other person, in purported compliance with any provision of these Regulations, is found guilty of an offence under section 1112 (general false statement offence) ("a revocation decision").
(2)   If the registrar proposes to make a revocation decision he shall send the beneficiary notice of his intention.
(3)   The notice must—
   (a)   inform the beneficiary that he may, within the period of 28 days beginning with the date of the notice, deliver representations in writing to the registrar; and
   (b)   state that if representations are not received by the registrar within that period, the revocation decision will be made at the expiry of that period.
(4)   If within the period specified in paragraph (3) the beneficiary delivers representations as to why the revocation decision should not be made, the registrar shall have regard to the representations in determining whether to make the revocation decision, and shall, within five working days of making his decision, send notice of it to the beneficiary.
(5)   Any communication by the registrar in respect of a revocation decision or proposed revocation decision shall be sent to the beneficiary—
   (a)   in the case of an individual, to his usual residential address;
   (b)   in the case of a company, to its registered office; or
   (c)   in the case of a partnership, to the address specified in its section 1088 application.
(6)   In this regulation—
"partnership" includes a limited liability partnership;
"section 243 beneficiary" includes where the section 243 decision was made following an application under regulation 6 or 7, the applicant.

SCHEDULES

SCHEDULE 1
SPECIFIED PUBLIC AUTHORITIES

Regulation 2

[2.783]
The Secretary of State;

[the Minister for the Cabinet Office;]

any Northern Ireland Department;

the Scottish Ministers;

the Welsh Ministers;

the Treasury;

the Commissioners for Her Majesty's Revenue and Customs;

the Bank of England;

the Director of Public Prosecutions;

the Director of Public Prosecutions for Northern Ireland;

the Serious Fraud Office;

the Secret Intelligence Service;

the Security Service;

the Government Communications Headquarters;

[the Financial Conduct Authority;

the Prudential Regulation Authority;]

[the Competition and Markets Authority;]

the Pensions Regulator;

the Panel on Takeovers and Mergers;

the Regulator of Community Interest Companies;

the Registrar of Credit Unions for Northern Ireland;

. . .

the Office of the Information Commissioner;

the Charity Commission;

the Charity Commission for Northern Ireland;

the Office of the Scottish Charity Regulator;

[the Office of Communications;]

the Gas and Electricity Markets Authority;

the Northern Ireland Authority for Utility Regulation;

the Gambling Commission;

[the National Crime Agency];

the Health and Safety Executive;

[the Office for Nuclear Regulation;]

the Health and Safety Executive for Northern Ireland;

the Food Standards Agency;

the Gangmasters Licensing Authority;

the Security Industry Authority;

a local authority within the meaning of section 54(2) of the Act;

an official receiver appointed under section 399 of the Insolvency Act 1986 (appointment, etc, of official receivers);

the Official Receiver for Northern Ireland;

the Crown Office and Procurator Fiscal Services;

[the Marine Management Organisation;]

a person acting as an insolvency practitioner within the meaning of section 388 of the Insolvency Act 1986 (meaning of "act as an insolvency practitioner") or Article 3 of the Insolvency (Northern Ireland) Order 1989 ("act as an insolvency practitioner");

an inspector appointed under Part 14 of the 1985 Act (investigation of companies and their affairs: requisition of documents) or Part 15 of the 1986 Order or a person appointed under regulation 30 of the Open-Ended Investment Companies Regulations 2001 (power to investigate) or regulation 22 of the Open-Ended Investment Companies Regulations (Northern Ireland) 2004;

any person authorised to exercise powers under section 447 of the 1985 Act (power to require documents and information), or section 84 of the Companies Act 1989 (exercise of powers by officers, etc) or Article 440 of the 1986 Order;

any person exercising functions conferred by Part 6 of the Financial Services and Markets Act 2000 (official listing) . . .;

a person appointed to make a report under section 166 [or 166A] (reports by skilled persons) of the Financial Services and Markets Act 2000;

a person appointed to conduct an investigation under section 167 (appointment of persons to carry out general investigations) or 168(3) or (5) (appointment of persons to carry out investigations in particular cases) of the Financial Services and Markets Act 2000;

an inspector appointed under section 284 (power to investigate) of the Financial Services and Markets Act 2000;

an overseas regulatory authority within the meaning of section 82 of the Companies Act 1989 (request for assistance by overseas regulatory authority);

a police force[;

the Scottish Housing Regulator][;

the lead enforcement authority (as defined in section 33(1) of the Estate Agents Act 1979) exercising functions under the Estate Agents Act 1979].

NOTES

This Schedule is amended as follows—

Entry "the Minister for the Cabinet Office" inserted by the Companies (Disclosure of Address) (Amendment) Regulations 2015, SI 2015/842, reg 2;

Entries the "Financial Conduct Authority" and "the Prudential Regulation Authority" substituted, for entry "the Financial Services Authority" as originally enacted, words omitted from entry beginning "any person exercising functions conferred by Part 6 of the Financial Services and Markets Act 2000" revoked, and in entry beginning "a person appointed to make a report under section 166" words in square brackets inserted, by the Financial Services Act 2012 (Consequential Amendments and Transitional Provisions) Order 2013, SI 2013/472, art 3, Sch 2, para 157(a).

Entry "the Competition and Markets Authority" substituted for entry "the Competition Commission", and entry "the Office of Fair Trading" (omitted) revoked, by the Enterprise and Regulatory Reform Act 2013 (Competition) (Consequential, Transitional and Saving Provisions) (No 2) Order 2014, SI 2014/549, art 2, Sch 1, Pt 2, para 37 (for transitional provisions in relation to the continuity of functions, etc, see art 3 of the 2014 Order).

Entry "the Office of Communications" substituted, for original entry "the Postal Services Commission", by the Postal Services Act 2011 (Consequential Modifications and Amendments) Order 2011, SI 2011/2085, art 5(1), Sch 1, para 79.

Entry "the National Crime Agency" substituted, for entry "the Serious Organised Crime Agency" as originally enacted, by virtue of the Crime and Courts Act 2013, s 15(3), Sch 8, Pt 4, para 190; for transitional provisions and savings see s 15(3), Sch 8, Pt 1 thereto.

Entry "the Office for Nuclear Regulation" inserted by the Energy Act 2013 (Office for Nuclear Regulation) (Consequential Amendments, Transitional Provisions and Savings) Order 2014, SI 2014/469, art 6(2), Sch 3, Pt 5, para 195.

Entry "the Marine Management Organisation" inserted by the Companies (Disclosure of Address) (Amendment) Regulations 2010, SI 2010/2156, reg 2.

Entry "the Scottish Housing Regulator" inserted by the Housing (Scotland) Act 2010 (Consequential Provisions and Modifications) Order 2012, SI 2012/700, art 4, Schedule, Pt 2, para 20.

Entry relating to "the lead enforcement authority (as defined in section 33(1) of the Estate Agents Act 1979)" added by the Public Bodies (Abolition of the National Consumer Council and Transfer of the Office of Fair Trading's Functions in relation to Estate Agents etc) Order 2014, SI 2014/631, art 5(3)(a), Sch 2, Pt 3, para 12.

SCHEDULE 2
CONDITIONS FOR PERMITTED DISCLOSURE
Regulations 2 and 3

PART 1
DISCLOSURE TO SPECIFIED PUBLIC AUTHORITIES

[2.784]

1. Paragraphs 2 and 3 set out the conditions specified for the disclosure of protected information by the registrar to a specified public authority.

2. The specified public authority has delivered to the registrar a statement that it intends to use the protected information only for the purpose of facilitating the carrying out by that specified public authority of a public function ("the permitted purpose").

3. Subject to paragraph 4, the specified public authority ("the authority") has delivered to the registrar a statement that it will, where it supplies a copy of the protected information to a processor for the purpose of processing the information for use in respect of the permitted purpose—
    (a)   ensure that the processor is one who carries on business in the European Economic Area;

(b)   require that the information is not transmitted outside the European Economic Area by the processor; and

(c)   require that the processor does not disclose the information except to the authority or an employee of the authority.

4. Paragraph 3 does not apply where the specified public authority is the Secret Intelligence Service, Security Service or Government Communications Headquarters.

PART 2
DISCLOSURE TO A CREDIT REFERENCE AGENCY

[2.785]
5. Paragraphs 6 to 10 set out the conditions specified for the disclosure of protected information by the registrar to a credit reference agency.

6. The credit reference agency—
(a)   is carrying on in the United Kingdom or in another EEA State a business comprising the furnishing of information relevant to the financial standing of individuals, being information collected by the agency for that purpose;
(b)   maintains appropriate procedures—
    (i)   to ensure that an independent person can investigate and audit the measures maintained by the agency for the purposes of ensuring the security of any protected information disclosed to that agency; and
    (ii)   for the purposes of ensuring that it complies with its obligations under the Data Protection Act 1998, or, where the agency carries on business in a EEA State other than the United Kingdom, with its obligations under legislation implementing Directive 95/46/EC of the European Parliament and of the Council of 24 October 1995 on the protection of individuals with regard to the processing of personal data and on the free movement of such data;
(c)   has not been found guilty of an offence under—
    (i)   section 1112 (general false statement offence) of the Act or section 2 of the Fraud Act 2006 (fraud by false representation); or
    (ii)   section 47 (failure to comply with enforcement notice) of the Data Protection Act 1998 in circumstances where it has used the protected information for purposes other than those described in sub-paragraphs (a) to (e) of paragraph 7 below.

7. The credit reference agency has delivered to the registrar a statement that it intends to use the protected information only for the purposes of—
(a)   providing an assessment of the financial standing of a person;
(b)   meeting any obligations contained in the Money Laundering Regulations 2007 or any [rules made pursuant to section 137A of the Financial Services and Markets Act 2000 which relate to the prevention and detection of money laundering in connection with the carrying on of regulated activities by authorised persons], or in any legislation of another EEA State implementing Directive 2005/60/EC of the European Parliament and of the Council of 26 October 2005 on the prevention of the use of the financial system for the purpose of money laundering and terrorist financing;
(c)   conducting conflict of interest checks required or made necessary by any enactment;
(d)   the provision of protected information to—
    (i)   a public authority specified in Schedule 1 which has satisfied the requirements of paragraphs 2 and 3 of this Schedule; or
    (ii)   a credit reference agency which has satisfied the requirements of this Part of this Schedule; or
(e)   conducting checks for the prevention and detection of crime and fraud.

8. The credit reference agency has delivered to the registrar a statement that it intends to take delivery of and to use the protected information only in the United Kingdom or in another EEA State.

9. The credit reference agency has delivered to the registrar a statement that it will, where it supplies a copy of the protected information to a processor for the purpose of processing the information for use in respect of the purposes referred to in paragraph 7—
(a)   ensure that the processor is one who carries on business in the European Economic Area;
(b)   require that the information is not transmitted outside the European Economic Area by the processor; and
(c)   require that the processor does not disclose the information except to the credit reference agency or an employee of the credit reference agency.

10. The credit reference agency has delivered to the registrar a statement that it meets the conditions in paragraph 6 above.

Part 2   Statutory Instruments

NOTES

Para 7: in sub-para (b) words in square brackets substituted by the Financial Services Act 2012 (Consequential Amendments and Transitional Provisions) Order 2013, SI 2013/472, art 3, Sch 2, para 157(b).

PART 3
INTERPRETATION OF THIS SCHEDULE

[2.786]

11. (1) In this Schedule—

"processor" means any person who provides a service which consists of putting information into data form or processing information in data form and any reference to a processor includes a reference to his employees; and

"public function" includes—

(a) any function conferred by or in accordance with any provision contained in any enactment;

(b) any function conferred by or in accordance with any provision contained in the [EU] Treaties or any [EU] instrument;

(c) any similar function conferred on persons by or under provisions having effect as part of the law of a country or territory outside the United Kingdom; and

(d) any function exercisable in relation to the investigation of any criminal offence or for the purpose of any criminal proceedings.

(2) In this Schedule any reference to—

(a) an employee of any person who has access to protected information shall be deemed to include any person working or providing services for the purposes of that person or employed by or on behalf of, or working for, any person who is so working or who is supplying such a service; and

(b) the disclosure for the purpose of facilitating the carrying out of a public function includes disclosure in relation to, and for the purpose of, any proceedings whether civil, criminal or disciplinary in which the specified public authority engages while carrying out its public functions.

NOTES

Para 11: references in square brackets in sub-para (1) substituted by the Treaty of Lisbon (Changes in Terminology) Order 2011, SI 2011/1043, art 6(1)(a), (d).

TRANSFER OF FUNCTIONS OF THE CONSUMER CREDIT APPEALS TRIBUNAL ORDER 2009

(SI 2009/1835)

NOTES

Made: 7 July 2009.

Authority: Tribunals, Courts and Enforcement Act 2007, ss 30(1), (4), 31(1), (2), (9), 38, Sch 5, para 30.

Commencement: 1 September 2009.

[2.787]

1 Citation and commencement

This Order may be cited as the Transfer of Functions of the Consumer Credit Appeals Tribunal Order 2009 and comes into force on 1st September 2009.

[2.788]

2 Transfer of functions and abolition of tribunal

(1) The functions of the Consumer Credit Appeals Tribunal are transferred to the First-tier Tribunal.

(2) The Consumer Credit Appeals Tribunal is abolished.

[2.789]

3 Transfer of persons into the First-tier Tribunal and the Upper Tribunal

A person who, immediately before this Order comes into force, holds an office listed in column (1) of the following table is to hold the office or offices listed in the corresponding entry in column (2) of the table.

(1) Office held	(2) Office to be held
President of the Consumer Credit Appeals Tribunal appointed under paragraph 2(1) of Schedule A1 to the Consumer Credit Act 1974	Transferred-in judge of the First-tier Tribunal and deputy judge of the Upper Tribunal
Deputy President of the Consumer Credit Appeals Tribunal appointed under paragraph 2(3) of Schedule A1 to the Consumer Credit Act 1974	Transferred-in judge of the First-tier Tribunal
Member of the panel of chairmen of the Consumer Credit Appeals Tribunal appointed under paragraph 3(1) of Schedule A1 to the Consumer Credit Tribunal 1974	Transferred-in judge of the First-tier Tribunal
Other member of the Consumer Credit Appeals Tribunal appointed under paragraph 3(3) of Schedule A1 to the Consumer Credit Act 1974	Transferred-in other member of the First-tier Tribunal

[2.790]
4   Consequential and transitional provisions

(1)   Schedule 1 contains amendments to primary legislation as a consequence of the transfer effected by this Order.

(2)   Schedule 2 contains amendments to secondary legislation as a consequence of the transfer effected by this Order.

(3)   Schedule 3 contains repeals and revocations as a consequence of the amendments in Schedules 1 and 2.

(4)   Schedule 4 contains transitional and saving provisions.

SCHEDULES

SCHEDULES 1–3

(*Sch 1: paras 1–9 amend the Consumer Credit Act 1974, ss 2, 41, 182, 189 (see the 1974 Act at* **[1.520]** *et seq), insert ss 41ZA, 41ZB, and repeal ss 40A, 41A of, and Sch A1 to, that Act; paras 10, 11 amend provisions outside the scope of this work. Sch 2: para 1 amends the Money Laundering Regulations 2007, SI 2007/2157, reg 44 at* **[2.513]**; *para 2 amends provisions outside the scope of this work. Sch 3 repeals the Consumer Credit Act 2006, ss 55, 56(2), 57, 58, Sch 1, the Tribunals, Courts and Enforcement Act 2007, Sch 10, para 11 and revokes the Consumer Credit Appeals Tribunal Rules 2008, SI 2008/668.*)

SCHEDULE 4
TRANSITIONAL AND SAVING PROVISIONS

Article 4(4)

[2.791]
1.   Transitional and saving provisions

Any proceedings before the Consumer Credit Appeals Tribunal which are pending immediately before 1st September 2009 shall continue on and after 1st September 2009 as proceedings before the First-tier Tribunal.

2. (1)   The following sub-paragraphs apply where proceedings are continued in the First-tier Tribunal by virtue of paragraph 1.

(2)   Where a hearing began before 1st September 2009 but was not completed by that date, the First-tier Tribunal must be comprised for the continuation of that hearing of the person or persons who began it.

(3)   The First-tier Tribunal may give any direction to ensure that proceedings are dealt with fairly and, in particular, may—
   (a)   apply any provision in procedural rules which applied to the proceedings before 1st September 2009; or
   (b)   disapply provisions of Tribunal Procedure Rules.

(4)   In sub-paragraph (3) "procedural rules" means provision (whether called rules or not) regulating practice or procedure before a tribunal.

(5)   Any direction or order given or made in proceedings which is in force immediately before 1st September 2009 remains in force on and after that date as if it were a direction or order of the First-tier Tribunal.

(6) A time period which has started to run before 1st September 2009 and which has not expired shall continue to apply.

(7) An order for costs may only be made if, and to the extent that, an order could have been made before 1st September 2009.

3. Where an appeal lies to a court from any decision made by the Consumer Credit Appeals Tribunal before 1st September 2009, that right of appeal has not been exercised, and the time to exercise that right of appeal has not expired prior to 1st September 2009, section 11 of the Tribunals, Courts and Enforcement Act 2007 (right to appeal to Upper Tribunal) shall apply as if the decision were a decision made on or after 1st September 2009 by the First-tier Tribunal, and any reference to the Consumer Credit Appeals Tribunal in an enactment relating to such an appeal, express or otherwise, is to be taken as a reference to the First-tier Tribunal.

4. Any case to be remitted by a court on or after 1st September 2009 and which, if it had been remitted before 1st September 2009, would have been remitted to the Consumer Credit Appeals Tribunal, shall be remitted to the First-tier Tribunal.

5. Staff appointed to the Consumer Credit Appeals Tribunal before 1st September 2009 are to be treated on and after that date, for the purpose of any enactment, as if they had been appointed by the Lord Chancellor under section 40(1) of the Tribunals, Courts and Enforcement Act 2007 (tribunal staff and services).

6. A decision made by the Consumer Credit Appeals Tribunal before 1st September 2009 is to be treated as a decision of the First-tier Tribunal on or after 1st September 2009.

CREDIT RATING AGENCIES REGULATIONS 2010

(SI 2010/906)

NOTES
Made: 22 March 2010.
Authority: European Communities Act 1972, s 2(2); Financial Services and Markets Act 2000, s 349(1)(b).
Commencement: 7 June 2010.

ARRANGEMENT OF REGULATIONS

PART 1
GENERAL

PART 2
THE FINANCIAL CONDUCT AUTHORITY

PART 10
ESMA: INVESTIGATORY POWERS

PART 1
GENERAL

[2.792]
1   Citation and commencement
These Regulations may be cited as the Credit Rating Agencies Regulations 2010 and shall come into force on 7th June 2010.

[2.793]
2   Interpretation
(1) In these Regulations—
   "the Act" means the Financial Services and Markets Act 2000;
   . . .

"the EC Regulation" means Regulation (EC) No 1060/2009 of the European Parliament and of the Council of 16 September 2009 on credit rating agencies[, as amended by Regulation (EU) No 513/2011 of the European Parliament and of the Council of 11 May 2011 amending Regulation (EC) No 1060/2009 on credit rating agencies];

["ESMA" means the European Securities and Markets Authority established by Regulation (EU) No 1095/2010 of the European Parliament and of the Council of 24 November 2010 establishing a European Supervisory Authority (European Securities and Markets Authority), amending Decision No 716/2009/EC and repealing Commission Decision 2009/77/EC;]

["the FCA" means the Financial Conduct Authority.]

. . . .

. . . .

NOTES

Para (1): definition "the Authority" (omitted) revoked, and definition "the FCA" inserted, by the Financial Services Act 2012 (Consequential Amendments and Transitional Provisions) Order 2013, SI 2013/472, art 3, Sch 2, para 188(a); words in square brackets in the definition "the EC Regulation" inserted, definition "ESMA" inserted, and definitions "overseas competent authority" and "protected item" (omitted) revoked, by the Credit Rating Agencies (Amendment) Regulations 2011, SI 2011/1435, reg 4(a).

PART 2
[THE FINANCIAL CONDUCT AUTHORITY]

NOTES

Words in square brackets in Part heading substituted by the Financial Services Act 2012 (Consequential Amendments and Transitional Provisions) Order 2013, SI 2013/472, art 3, Sch 2, para 188(b).

[2.794]
3 Designation of competent authority

[The FCA] is the competent authority for the purposes of the EC Regulation.

NOTES

Words in square brackets substituted by the Financial Services Act 2012 (Consequential Amendments and Transitional Provisions) Order 2013, SI 2013/472, art 3, Sch 2, para 188(c).

4 (*Revoked by the Credit Rating Agencies (Amendment) Regulations 2011, SI 2011/1435, regs 4(b), 5(1), except in relation to any registration or supervisory fee charged by the Authority before 1 July 2011.*.)

[2.795]
5 Disclosure of confidential information

Section 348(1) of the Act (restrictions on disclosure of confidential information by [FCA, PRA etc]) does not prevent the [FCA] from disclosing confidential information where the disclosure is permitted by the EC Regulation.

NOTES

Words in square brackets substituted by the Financial Services Act 2012 (Consequential Amendments and Transitional Provisions) Order 2013, SI 2013/472, art 3, Sch 2, para 188(d).

[2.796]
6 Guidance

[(1) The [FCA] may give guidance consisting of such information and advice as it considers appropriate with respect to any matter relating to the functions of the [FCA] under the EC Regulation.]

(2) The [FCA] may—
  (a) publish its guidance;
  (b) offer copies of its published guidance for sale at a reasonable price;
  (c) if it gives guidance in response to a request made by any person, make a reasonable charge for that guidance.

NOTES

Para (1): substituted by the Credit Rating Agencies (Amendment) Regulations 2011, SI 2011/1435, reg 4(c); words in square brackets substituted by the Financial Services Act 2012 (Consequential Amendments and Transitional Provisions) Order 2013, SI 2013/472, art 3, Sch 2, para 188(e).

Para (2): word in square brackets substituted by SI 2013/472, art 3, Sch 2, para 188(e).

[2.797]
7 Miscellaneous

The functions of the [FCA] under the EC Regulation are to be treated for the purposes of [Part 1 (general) and paragraphs 16 (status) and 33 (exemption from liability in damages) of Schedule

1ZA] to the Act as functions conferred on the [FCA] under the Act.

NOTES

Words in square brackets substituted by the Financial Services Act 2012 (Consequential Amendments and Transitional Provisions) Order 2013, SI 2013/472, art 3, Sch 2, para 188(f).

8–20 *(Regs 8–13 (Pts 3, 4) and reg 29 (Pt 7) revoked by the Credit Rating Agencies (Amendment) Regulations 2011, SI 2011/1435, regs 4(d), 5(2), except in relation to any application for registration received by the Authority on or before 7 September 2010; regs 14–18, regs 19, 20 (Pt 5), regs 21–23 (Pt 6) and reg 30 (Pt 8) revoked by SI 2011/1435, reg 4(d); regs 24–28 revoked by SI 2011/1435, regs 4(d), 5(2), except in relation to any application for registration received by the Authority on or before 7 September 2010; reg 31 (Pt 9) revoked by the Capital Requirements Regulations 2013, SI 2013/3115, reg 46(2), Sch 3.)*

[PART 10
ESMA: INVESTIGATORY POWERS

[2.798]
32   Records of telephone and data traffic: Article 23c(1)(e) of the EC Regulation

(1)   ESMA must obtain authorisation from the High Court before any official of, or person authorised by, ESMA requests any records of telephone or data traffic under Article 23c(1)(e) of the EC Regulation from a person domiciled or established in the United Kingdom.

(2)   The [FCA] must obtain authorisation from the High Court before requesting on behalf of ESMA any records of telephone or data traffic under Article 23c(1)(e) of the EC Regulation.

(3)   The High Court may grant authorisation under paragraph (1) or (2) if satisfied, on an application made to the High Court in accordance with rules of court by ESMA or the [FCA], that—

   (a)   ESMA has ordered an investigation under Article 23c(1) of the EC Regulation; and
   (b)   requiring the records of telephone or data traffic would be neither arbitrary nor excessive having regard to the subject matter of the investigation.

(4)   The High Court must conduct the assessment referred to in paragraph (3) in accordance with Article 23c(6) of the EC Regulation, and may exercise the powers conferred by that paragraph for the purposes of making its assessment.

(5)   In the application of this regulation to Scotland, references to the High Court are to be read as references to the Court of Session.]

NOTES

Pt 10 (regs 32–34) inserted by the Credit Rating Agencies (Amendment) Regulations 2011, SI 2011/1435, reg 4(e).

Paras (2), (3): words in square brackets substituted by the Financial Services Act 2012 (Consequential Amendments and Transitional Provisions) Order 2013, SI 2013/472, art 3, Sch 2, para 188(g).

[2.799]
[33   Inspections: Article 23d of the EC Regulation

(1)   ESMA must obtain authorisation from the High Court before any official of, or person authorised by, ESMA carries out an Article 23d inspection.

(2)   Where ESMA requires the [FCA] to carry out an Article 23d inspection on its behalf, the [FCA] must obtain authorisation from the High Court before carrying out that inspection.

(3)   The High Court may grant authorisation for the purposes of paragraph (1) or (2) if satisfied, on an application made to the High Court in accordance with rules of court by ESMA or the [FCA], that—

   (a)   ESMA has ordered an Article 23d inspection; and
   (b)   the Article 23d inspection is neither arbitrary nor excessive having regard to the subject matter of the inspection.

(4)   The High Court must conduct the assessment referred to in paragraph (3) in accordance with Article 23d(9) of the EC Regulation, and may exercise the powers conferred by that paragraph for the purposes of making its assessment.

(5)   The High Court may issue a warrant if satisfied on information on oath given by or on behalf of ESMA or the [FCA] that there are reasonable grounds for believing that—

   (a)   the premises specified in the warrant are the business premises of any legal person referred to in Article 23b(1) of the EC Regulation; and
   (b)   the person referred to in sub-paragraph (a) has failed to comply with an Article 23d inspection, or would fail to comply with such an inspection if a warrant were not issued under this paragraph.

(6)   A warrant issued under paragraph (5) shall authorise a constable, together with a named official of ESMA or the [FCA] and any other official or person authorised by ESMA or the [FCA] to accompany that official—

(a)   to enter any premises specified in the warrant using such force as is reasonably necessary for the purpose;

(b)   to search for such records, data, procedures and other material as may be examined under Article 23c(1) of the EC Regulation, or such records of telephone or data traffic as ESMA or the [FCA] has been authorised to request under regulation 32(3), using such force as is reasonably necessary for the purpose;

(c)   to take or obtain certified copies of or extracts from such records, data, procedures and other material; and

(d)   to seal any business premises and books or records in accordance with Article 23d(2) of the EC Regulation.

(7)   In England and Wales, sections 15(5) to (8) and 16 of the Police and Criminal Evidence Act 1984 (execution of search warrants and safeguards) apply to warrants issued under paragraph (5).

(8)   In Northern Ireland, Articles 17(5) to (8) and 18 of the Police and Criminal Evidence (Northern Ireland) Order 1989 apply to warrants issued under paragraph (5).

(9)   In the application of this regulation to Scotland—

(a)   references to the High Court are to be read as references to the Court of Session;

(b)   references to information on oath are to be read as references to evidence on oath.

(10)   In this regulation, an "Article 23d inspection" means an inspection ordered by decision of ESMA under Article 23d of the EC Regulation.]

NOTES
Inserted as noted to reg 32 at **[2.798]**.
Word "FCA" in square brackets (in each place it occurs) substituted by the Financial Services Act 2012 (Consequential Amendments and Transitional Provisions) Order 2013, SI 2013/472, art 3, Sch 2, para 188(h).

[2.800]
[34   Offences: Article 23d inspections
Any person who intentionally obstructs the exercise of any rights conferred by a warrant under regulation 33(5) is guilty of an offence and liable on summary conviction to imprisonment for a term not exceeding three months or a fine not exceeding level 5 on the standard scale, or both.]

NOTES
Inserted as noted to reg 32 at **[2.798]**.

CONSUMER CREDIT (EU DIRECTIVE) REGULATIONS 2010

(SI 2010/1010)

NOTES
Made: 28 March 2010.
Authority: European Communities Act 1972, s 2(2).
Commencement: see regs 99, 101, 101A at **[2.802]**, **[2.804]**, **[2.805]**.
These Regulations implement European Parliament and Council Directive 2008/48/EC at **[4.431]**.

ARRANGEMENT OF REGULATIONS

PART 1
GENERAL

[2.801]
1   Citation and commencement
These Regulations may be cited as the Consumer Credit (EU Directive) Regulations 2010 and shall come into force in accordance with [regulations 99, 101 and 101A].

NOTES
Words in square brackets substituted by the Consumer Credit (Amendment) Regulations 2010, SI 2010/1969, regs 4, 5.

2–98   ((Pts 2, 3) *Reg 2 introduces amendments to the Consumer Credit Act 1974 specified in regs 3–45; reg 3 inserts s 55A at* **[1.537]**; *reg 4 amends s 185 at* **[1.677]**; *reg 5 inserts s 55B at* **[1.538]**; *reg 6 inserts s 55C at* **[1.539]**; *reg 7 amends s 60 at* **[1.544]**; *reg 8 inserts s 61A at* **[1.546]**;

Part 2   Statutory Instruments

reg 9 inserts s 61B at **[1.547]**; *reg 10 amends s 62 at* **[1.548]**; *reg 11 amends s 63 at* **[1.549]**; *regs 12, 18 amend s 127 at* **[1.627]**; *reg 13 inserts s 66A at* **[1.553]**; *reg 14 amends s 67 at* **[1.554]**; *reg 15 amends s 82 at* **[1.575]**; *reg 16 amends s 55 at* **[1.536]**; *reg 17 amends s 74 at* **[1.561]**; *regs 19, 39, 42 amend s 189 at* **[1.682]**; *reg 20 amends Sch 2 at* **[1.691]**; *reg 21 inserts s 74A at* **[1.562]**; *reg 22 inserts s 74B at* **[1.563]**; *reg 23 amends s 77A at* **[1.568]**; *reg 24 amends s 75 at* **[1.564]**; *reg 25 inserts s 75A at* **[1.565]**; *reg 26 inserts s 77B at* **[1.569]**; *reg 27 inserts s 78A at* **[1.571]**; *regs 28, 29 amend s 82 at* **[1.575]**; *reg 30 amends s 94 at* **[1.594]**; *reg 31 amends s 95 at* **[1.595]**; *reg 32 inserts s 95A at [741A]*; *reg 33 amends s 97 at* **[1.599]**; *reg 34 inserts s 97A at* **[1.600]**; *reg 35 amends s 120 at* **[1.621]**; *reg 36 inserts s 82A at* **[1.576]**; *reg 37 amends s 87 at* **[1.587]**; *reg 38 inserts s 98A at* **[1.602]**; *reg 40 amends s 157 at* **[1.648]**; *reg 41 inserts s 160A (repealed); reg 43 amends Sch 1 at* **[1.689]**; *reg 44 amends s 10 at* **[1.522]**; *reg 45 amends s 17 at* **[1.528]**; *regs 46–49, 57–63, 68, 69, 90, 91, 93, 98 amend provisions outside the scope of this work; reg 50 inserts the Consumer Credit (Total Charge for Credit) Regulations 1980, SI 1980/51 at* **[2.2]**; *regs 51–56 amend the Consumer Credit (Agreements) Regulations 1983, SI 1983/1553, regs 1, 8 and Schs 1, 2, 8 at* **[2.23]**, **[2.30]–[2.32]**, **[2.41]**; *regs 64–67 amend the Consumer Credit (Exempt Agreements) Order 1989, SI 1989/869, arts 1, 3, 4 (revoked); regs 70–72 amend the Consumer Credit (Advertisements) Regulations 2004, SI 2004/1484, reg 1 and insert reg 1A thereof (revoked); regs 73–76 amend the Consumer Credit (Disclosure of Information) Regulations 2004, SI 2004/1481, regs 1, 3 at* **[2.315]**, **[2.317]** *and substitute reg 2 thereof at* **[2.316]**; *regs 77–84 amend the Consumer Credit (Early Settlement) Regulations 2004, SI 2004/1483, regs 1–5 at* **[2.319]–[2.324]**, *insert reg 4A thereof at* **[2.323]** *and revoke the Schedule thereto; regs 85–89 amend the Financial Services (Distance Marketing) Regulations 2004, SI 2004/2095, regs 2, 7, 8, 11 at* **[2.331]**, **[2.336]**, **[2.337]**, **[2.340]**; *reg 92 amends the Consumer Credit (Exempt Agreements) Order 2007, SI 2007/1168, art 2 (revoked); regs 94–96 amend the Cancellation of Contracts made in a Consumer's Home or Place of Work etc Regulations 2008, SI 2008/1816, regs 6, 11 at* **[2.607]**, **[2.612]**; *reg 97 amends the Payment Services Regulations 2009, SI 2009/209, reg 52 at* **[2.680]**.)

PART 4
COMMENCEMENT, TRANSITIONAL AND SAVING PROVISION

[2.802]
99 Commencement

(1)   Subject to paragraph (2) and [regulations 101 and 101A], these Regulations come into force on 1st February 2011.

(2)   The following provisions come into force on 30th April 2010—
   (a)   regulation 19 (definition of certain overdraft agreements);
   (b)   regulation 39 (definition of open-end);
   (c)   regulation 41 (credit intermediaries) for the purposes of the definition of credit intermediary;
   (d)   regulation 42 (definition of credit intermediary);
   (e)   the regulations in this Part.

NOTES
   Para (1): words in square brackets substituted by the Consumer Credit (Amendment) Regulations 2010, SI 2010/1969, regs 4, 28.

[2.803]
100 Application of regulations to agreements entered into before 1st February 2011

(1)   Subject to paragraphs (2) to (5) and [regulations 101 and 101A] these Regulations apply only to a regulated consumer credit agreement entered into on or after 1st February 2011.

(2)   The following regulations apply (from 1st February 2011) to a regulated consumer credit agreement which is an open-end agreement and is entered into before 11th June 2010—
   [(za) regulation 22 (information to be provided on significant overdrawing without prior arrangement);]
   (a)   regulations 27 and 28 (information on change of interest rate etc);
   (b)   regulation 36 (assignment);
   (c)   regulations 37 to 39 (open-end agreements);
   (d)   regulation 46(b) (amendments to Enterprise Act 2002);
   (e)   regulation 63 (amendments to Consumer Credit (Running-Account Credit Information) Regulations 1983);
   (f)   regulation 69(b) (amendments to Enterprise Act 2002 (Part 8 Community Infringements Specified UK Laws) Order 2003);
   (g)   regulation 97 (amendments to Payment Services Regulations 2009).

(3)   The following regulations apply (from 1st February 2011) to a regulated consumer credit agreement which is an open-end agreement and is entered into on or after 11th June 2010 and before 1st February 2011—
   [(za) regulation 22 (information to be provided on significant overdrawing without prior arrangement);]

(a)	regulation 25 (linked credit agreements);
(b)	regulations 27 and 28 (information on change of interest rate etc);
(c)	regulations 29 to 35 (early repayment);
(d)	regulation 36 (assignment);
(e)	regulations 37 to 39 (open-end agreements);
(f)	regulation 46 (amendments to Enterprise Act 2002);
(g)	regulations 59 to 62 (amendments to Consumer Credit (Settlement Information) Regulations 1983);
(h)	regulation 63 (amendments to Consumer Credit (Running-Account Credit Information) Regulations 1983);
(i)	regulation 69 (amendments to Enterprise Act 2002 (Part 8 Community Infringements Specified UK Laws) Order 2003);
(j)	regulations 77 to 84 (amendments to Consumer Credit (Early Settlement) Regulations 2004);
(k)	regulation 97 (amendments to Payment Services Regulations 2009).

(4)	The following regulations apply (from 1st February 2011) to a regulated consumer credit agreement which not an open-end agreement and is entered into on or after 11th June 2010 and before 1st February 2011—
(a)	regulation 25 (linked credit agreements);
(b)	regulation 26 (statement of account);
(c)	regulations 29 to 35 (early repayment);
(d)	regulation 36 (assignment);
(e)	regulation 46 (amendments to Enterprise Act 2002);
(f)	regulations 59 to 62 (amendments to Consumer Credit (Settlement Information) Regulations 1983);
(g)	regulation 69 (amendments to Enterprise Act 2002 (Part 8 Community Infringements Specified UK Laws) Order 2003);
(h)	regulations 77 to 84 (amendments to Consumer Credit (Early Settlement) Regulations 2004).

(5)	Section 95A of the Consumer Credit Act 1974 (compensation for early repayment) applies in relation to an agreement by virtue of sub-paragraph (3)(c) or (4)(c) only where the debtor's entitlement to discharge his indebtedness arises by virtue of a notice made on or after 1st February 2011.

NOTES

Para (1): words in square brackets substituted by the Consumer Credit (Amendment) Regulations 2010, SI 2010/1969, regs 4, 29(a).

Para (2): sub-para (za) inserted by SI 2010/1969, regs 4, 29(b).

Para (3): sub-para (za) inserted by SI 2010/1969, regs 4, 29(c).

[2.804]
**101	Early application of regulations to certain agreements before 1st February 2011**

(1)	Where one of the conditions A to E is satisfied in relation to a prospective regulated consumer credit agreement on a date on or after 30th April 2010 and before 1st February 2011, Parts 1 to 3 of these Regulations apply to that agreement (and to any subsequent regulated consumer credit agreement entered into before 1st February 2011), from the date and time that the condition is satisfied.

(2)	Condition A is that information relating to the agreement is disclosed by a creditor or a credit intermediary before the agreement is made in compliance or in purported compliance with the Information Regulations 2010.

(3)	Condition B is that—
(a)	the agreement would, if made, be an agreement entered into at the debtor's request using a means of distance communication (other than voice telephony) which does not enable the provision before the agreement is made of the information referred to in regulation 3(4) of the Information Regulations 2010, and
(b)	the debtor is informed by the creditor before the agreement is made that the information referred to in regulation 3(4) of the Information Regulations 2010 will be disclosed immediately after the agreement is made in accordance with regulation 5 of those Regulations.

(4)	Condition C is that—
(a)	the agreement would, if made, be a distance agreement entered into by the debtor wholly or predominantly for the purposes of a business carried on, or intended to be carried on, by him, and
(b)	the debtor is informed by the creditor before the agreement is made that information referred to in regulation 3(4) of the Information Regulations 2010 will be disclosed immediately after the agreement is made in accordance with regulation 6 of those Regulations.

(5)	Condition D is that—

   (a)   the agreement would, if made, be an authorised non-business overdraft agreement (other than a qualifying overdraft agreement referred to in paragraph (7)(b)),

   (b)   the agreement would, if made, be one made at the debtor's request using a means of distance communication which does not enable the provision before the agreement is made of the information referred to in regulation 10(2) of the Information Regulations 2010, and

   (c)   the creditor has informed the debtor before the agreement is made that a document containing the terms of the agreement will be provided immediately after the agreement is made as though the amendment made by regulation 9 of these Regulations (insertion of section 61B in the Consumer Credit Act 1974) applied.

(6)   Condition E is that the agreement would, if made, be a qualifying overdraft agreement and—

   (a)   the creditor has provided a document containing the terms of the agreement before the agreement is made as though the amendment made by regulation 9 (insertion of section 61B in the Consumer Credit Act 1974) applied, or

   (b)   the creditor has informed the debtor before the agreement is made that a document containing the terms of the agreement will be provided at, or immediately after, the time the agreement is made as though the amendment made by regulation 9 applied.

(7)   In paragraph (6) "qualifying overdraft agreement" means—

   (a)   an authorised business overdraft agreement, or

   (b)   an authorised non-business overdraft agreement under which the creditor provides the debtor with credit exceeding £60,260 or which is secured on land.

[2.805]
[101A

(1)   Where condition F is satisfied on a date on or after 26th August 2010 and before 1st February 2011 in relation to a prospective regulated consumer credit agreement falling within paragraph (2), Parts 1 to 3 of these Regulations apply to that agreement (and to any subsequent regulated consumer credit agreement entered into before 1st February 2011), from the date and time that the condition is satisfied.

(2)   An agreement falls within this paragraph if it is an agreement which would, if made, be—

   (a)   an agreement under which the creditor provides the debtor with credit exceeding £60,260 and is not an authorised non-business overdraft agreement, or

   (b)   an agreement entered into by the debtor wholly or predominantly for the purposes of a business carried on, or intended to be carried on, by him.

(3)   Condition F is that the Consumer Credit (Disclosure of Information) Regulations 2004 apply to the agreement, but the creditor—

   (a)   does what would be required by regulations 3(1)(a) and (c) of those Regulations (pre-contractual information requirement to disclose information and statements required by the Consumer Credit (Agreements) Regulations 1983) if the amendments to the Consumer Credit (Agreements) Regulations 1983 made by regulations 52 to 56 were in force; and

   (b)   also provides the debtor with a statement before the agreement is made that, if the creditor decides not to proceed with the agreement on the basis of information obtained from a credit reference agency, the creditor will, when informing the debtor of the decision—

      (i)   inform the debtor that this decision has been reached on the basis of information from a credit reference agency, and

      (ii)   provide the debtor with the particulars of the agency including its name, address and telephone number.]

NOTES

Inserted by the Consumer Credit (Amendment) Regulations 2010, SI 2010/1969, regs 4, 30.

[2.806]
102 Interpretation

In this Part—

   (a)   "authorised business overdraft agreement", "authorised non-business overdraft agreement", "consumer credit agreement", "creditor", "debtor", "open-end" and "regulated" have the meanings given by section 189(1) of the Consumer Credit Act 1974;

   (b)   "distance agreement" means any regulated consumer credit agreement made under an organised distance sales or service-provision scheme run by the creditor or on behalf of the creditor who, in any such case, for the purpose of that agreement makes exclusive use of one or more means of distance communication up to and including the time at which the agreement is made;

   (c)   "Information Regulations 2010" means the Consumer Credit (Disclosure of Information) Regulations 2010;

   (d)   "means of distance communication" means any means which, without the simultaneous physical presence of the creditor or a person acting on behalf of the creditor and of the debtor, may be used for the making of a regulated consumer credit agreement between the parties to that agreement.

CONSUMER CREDIT (TOTAL CHARGE FOR CREDIT) REGULATIONS 2010

(SI 2010/1011)

NOTES

Made: 28 March 2010.

Authority: Consumer Credit Act 1974, ss 20, 182(2).

Commencement: 1 February 2011 (see further reg 1(2)(b)).

These Regulations implement European Parliament and Council Directive 2008/48/EC, Art 19, Annex 1 at **[4.449]**, **[4.463]**.

These Regulations were revoked by the Financial Services and Markets Act 2000 (Regulated Activities) (Amendment) (No 2) Order 2013, SI 2013/1881, art 21(d), for transitional provisions see Pt 8 thereof at **[2.1007]** et seq, and are reproduced here for reference only.

ARRANGEMENT OF REGULATIONS

[2.807]

1   Citation and commencement

(1)   These Regulations may be cited as the Consumer Credit (Total Charge for Credit) Regulations 2010.

(2)   These Regulations shall come into force—

    (a)   on 1st February 2011, or

    (b)   in relation to a prospective or actual regulated consumer credit agreement, on the date and at the time Parts 1 to 3 of the Consumer Credit (EU Directive) Regulations 2010 apply to such an agreement, being a date before 1st February 2011,

    [(c)   a reference to an open-end consumer credit agreement is to a consumer credit agreement of no fixed duration and includes credits which must be repaid in full within or after a period but, once repaid, become available to be drawn down again.]

NOTES

Revoked as noted to the start of these Regulations.

Para (2): sub-para (c) added by the Consumer Credit (Total Charge for Credit) (Amendment) Regulations 2012, SI 2012/1745, regs 2, 3.

[2.808]

2   Interpretation

(1)   In these Regulations—

    "annual percentage rate of charge" means the rate of the total charge for credit (calculated in accordance with regulation 4), expressed as an annual percentage of the total amount of credit;

    "current account" means an account under which the customer may, by means of cheques or similar orders payable to the customer or to any other person or by any other means, obtain or have the use of money held or made available by the person with whom the account is kept and which records alterations in the financial relationship between the said person and the customer;

    "overdraft facility" means an explicit agreement whereby a creditor makes available to a debtor funds which exceed the current balance in the debtor's current account;

    "total amount of credit" means the credit limit or the total sums made available under a consumer credit agreement;

    "total cost of credit to the debtor" means all costs, including interest, commissions, taxes and any other kind of fees which are required to be paid by or on behalf of the debtor or a relative of the debtor in connection with the consumer credit agreement, whether payable to the creditor or to any other person, and which are known to the creditor, except for notarial costs.

(2)   In these Regulations—

    (a)   a reference to a rate of interest is a reference to the interest rate expressed as a fixed or variable percentage applied on an annual basis to the amount of credit drawn down;

    (b)   a reference to a consumer credit agreement is to a consumer credit agreement regulated by [the Consumer Credit Act 1974].

Part 2   Statutory Instruments

NOTES

Revoked as noted to the start of these Regulations.

Para (2): words in square brackets substituted by the Consumer Credit (Amendment) Regulations 2011, SI 2011/11, reg 7.

[2.809]

3   Application

These Regulations shall not apply to consumer credit agreements which are secured on land or to prospective consumer credit agreements which are to be secured on land except to the extent that the Consumer Credit (Disclosure of Information) Regulations 2010 apply to such agreements.

NOTES

Revoked as noted to the start of these Regulations.

[2.810]

4   Total charge for credit

(1)   The total charge for credit which may be provided under an actual or prospective consumer credit agreement shall be the total cost of credit to the debtor determined in accordance with the requirements in paragraphs (2) to (5) below.

(2)   Subject to paragraph (3), the following costs shall be included in the total cost of credit to the debtor—

> *(a)   the costs of maintaining an account recording both payment transactions and drawdowns;*
>
> *(b)   the costs of using a means of payment for both payment transactions and drawdowns;*
>
> *(c)   other costs relating to payment transactions.*

(3)   The costs at paragraph (2) shall not be included in the total cost of credit to the debtor where—

> *(a)   the opening of the account is optional and the costs of the account have been clearly and separately shown in the consumer credit agreement or in any other agreement made with the debtor;*
>
> *(b)   in the case of an overdraft facility the costs do not relate to that facility.*

(4)   Costs in respect of an ancillary service shall be included in the total cost of credit to the debtor if the conclusion of a service contract is compulsory in order to obtain the credit or to obtain it on the terms and conditions marketed.

(5)   The total cost of credit to the debtor shall not include—

> *(a)   any charges payable by or on behalf of the debtor or a relative of his for non-compliance with his commitments contained in the consumer credit agreement;*
>
> *(b)   charges which, for purchases of goods or services, he or a relative of his is obliged to pay whether the transaction is effected in cash or on credit.*

(6)   In paragraph (4), the reference to an ancillary service means a service that relates to the provision of credit under the consumer credit agreement and includes in particular an insurance or payment protection policy.

NOTES

Revoked as noted to the start of these Regulations.

[2.811]

5   Calculation of the annual percentage rate of charge

The annual percentage rate of charge shall be calculated in accordance with the mathematical formula set out in the Schedule to these Regulations.

NOTES

Revoked as noted to the start of these Regulations.

[2.812]

6   [Assumptions for calculation

For the purposes of calculating the total charge for credit and the annual percentage rate of charge—

> *(a)   it shall be assumed that the consumer credit agreement is to remain valid for the period agreed and that the creditor and the debtor will fulfil their obligations under the terms and by the dates specified in that agreement;*
>
> *(b)   in the case of a consumer credit agreement allowing variations in—*
>
>> *(i)   the rate of interest, or*
>>
>> *(ii)   where applicable, charges contained in the annual percentage rate of charge,*
>
> *where these cannot be quantified at the time of calculation, it shall be assumed that they will remain at the initial level and will be applicable for the duration of the agreement;*

(c)   *where not all rates of interest are determined in the consumer credit agreement, a rate of interest shall be assumed to be fixed only for the partial periods for which the rate of interest is determined exclusively by a fixed specific percentage agreed when the agreement is made;*

(d)   *where the duration of the consumer credit agreement cannot be determined at the date of calculation and where different rates of interest and charges are to be offered for limited periods during that agreement, the rate of interest and the charge shall be assumed to be at the highest level for the duration of the agreement;*

(e)   *where there is a fixed rate of interest agreed in relation to an initial period under a consumer credit agreement, at the end of which a new rate of interest is determined and subsequently periodically adjusted according to an agreed indicator, it shall be assumed that, at the end of the period of the fixed rate of interest, the rate of interest is the same as at the time of making the calculation, based on the value of the agreed indicator at that time;*

(f)   *where the consumer credit agreement gives the debtor freedom of drawdown, the total amount of credit shall be assumed to be drawn down immediately and in full;*

(fa)   *where the consumer credit agreement imposes, amongst the different ways of drawdown, a limitation with regard to the amount of credit and period of time, the amount of credit shall be assumed to be the maximum amount provided for in the agreement and to be drawn down on the earliest date provided for in the agreement;*

(g)   *where the consumer credit agreement provides different ways of drawdown with different charges or rates of interest, the total amount of credit shall be assumed to be drawn down at the highest charge and rate of interest applied to the most common drawdown mechanism for the credit product to which the agreement relates;*

(h)   *for the purposes of paragraph (g), the most common drawdown mechanism for a particular credit product shall be assessed on the basis of the volume of transactions for that product in the preceding 12 months, or expected volumes in the case of a new credit product;*

(i)   *in the case of an overdraft facility, the total amount of credit shall be assumed to be drawn down in full and for the entire duration of the consumer credit agreement;*

(j)   *for the purposes of paragraph (i) if the duration of the overdraft facility is not known it shall be assumed that the duration of the facility is three months;*

(k)   *in the case of an open-end consumer credit agreement, other than an overdraft facility, it shall be assumed that the credit is provided for a period of one year starting from the date of the initial drawdown, and that the final payment made by the debtor clears the balance of capital, interest and other charges, if any;*

(l)   *for the purposes of paragraph (k)—*

   (i)   *the capital is repaid by the debtor in equal monthly payments, commencing one month after the date of initial drawdown;*

   (ii)   *in cases where the capital must be repaid in full, in a single payment, within or after each payment period, successive drawdowns and repayments of the entire capital by the debtor shall be assumed to occur over the period of one year;*

   (iii) *interest and other charges shall be applied in accordance with those drawdowns and repayments of capital and as provided for in the consumer credit agreement;*

(m)   *in the case of a consumer credit agreement, other than an overdraft facility, or an open-end consumer credit agreement—*

   (i)   *where the date or amount of a repayment of capital to be made by the debtor cannot be ascertained, it shall be assumed that the repayment is made at the earliest date provided for under the consumer credit agreement and is for the lowest amount for which the consumer credit agreement provides;*

   (ii)   *where it is not known on which date the consumer credit agreement is made, the date of the initial drawdown shall be assumed to be the date which results in the shortest interval between that date and the date of the first payment to be made by the debtor;*

(n)   *where the date or amount of a payment to be made by the debtor cannot be ascertained on the basis of the consumer credit agreement or the assumptions set out in paragraphs (i) to (m), it shall be assumed that the payment is made in accordance with the dates and conditions required by the creditor and, when these are unknown—*

   (i)   *interest charges are paid together with repayments of capital;*

   (ii)   *a non-interest charge expressed as a single sum is paid on the date of the making of the consumer credit agreement;*

   (iii) *non-interest charges expressed as several payments are paid at regular intervals, commencing with the date of the first repayment of capital, and if the amount of such payments is not known they shall be assumed to be equal amounts;*

   (iv)   *the final payment clears the balance of capital, interest and other charges, if any;*

(o)   *in the case of an agreement for running-account credit, where the credit limit applicable to the credit is not yet known, that credit limit shall be assumed to be £1,200.]*

Part 2   Statutory Instruments

NOTES

Revoked as noted to the start of these Regulations.

Substituted by the Consumer Credit (Total Charge for Credit) (Amendment) Regulations 2012, SI 2012/1745, regs 2, 4, subject to transitional provisions in reg 6 thereof.

SCHEDULE
CALCULATION OF THE ANNUAL PERCENTAGE RATE OF CHARGE

Regulation 5

[2.813]
1. *The annual percentage rate of charge ("APR") is calculated by means of the equation in paragraph 2 which equates, on an annual basis, the total present value of drawdowns with the total present value of repayments and payments of charges.*

2. *The equation referred to in paragraph 1 is—*

$$\sum_{k=1}^{m} C_k(1+X)^{-t_k} = \sum_{l=1}^{m'} D_l(1+X)^{-S_l}$$

where
  X is the APR;
  m is the number of the last drawdown;
  k is the number of a drawdown, thus $l \le k \le m$;
  C_k is the amount of drawdown k;
  t_k is the interval, expressed in years and fractions of a year, between the date of the first drawdown and the date of each subsequent drawdown, thus $t_l = 0$;
  m' is the number of the last repayment or payment of charges;
  l is the number of a repayment or payment of charges;
  D_l is the amount of a repayment or payment of charges;
  S_l is the interval, expressed in years and fractions of a year, between the date of the first drawdown and the date of each repayment or payment of charges.

3. *For the purposes of paragraph 2—*
  (a) *the amounts paid by both parties at different times shall not necessarily be equal and shall not necessarily be paid at equal intervals;*
  (b) *the starting date shall be that of the first drawdown;*
  (c) *intervals between dates used in the calculations shall be expressed in years or in fractions of a year;*
  (d) *a year is assumed to have 365 days (366 days for leap years), 52 weeks or 12 equal months;*
  (e) *an equal month is assumed to have 30.41666 days (365/12) regardless of whether or not it is a leap year;*
  (f) *the result of the calculation shall be expressed with an accuracy of at least one decimal place; if the figure at the following decimal place is greater than or equal to 5, the figure at that particular decimal place shall be increased by one;*
  (g) *the equation can be rewritten as set out in sub-paragraph (h) using a single sum and the concept of flows (A_k), which will be positive or negative, either paid or received during periods [l to k], expressed in years;*
  (h) *the equation referred to in sub-paragraph (g) is—*

$$S = \sum_{k=1}^{n} A_k(1+X)^{-t_k}$$

S being the present balance of flows; if the aim is to maintain the equivalence of flows, the value will be zero.

NOTES
NOTES
  Revoked as noted to the start of these Regulations.
  Para 3: words in square brackets substituted by the Consumer Credit (Total Charge for Credit) (Amendment) Regulations 2012, SI 2012/1745, regs 2, 5.

CONSUMER CREDIT (DISCLOSURE OF INFORMATION) REGULATIONS 2010

(SI 2010/1013)

NOTES
  Made: 28 March 2010.
  Authority: European Communities Act 1972, s 2(2); Consumer Credit Act 1974, ss 55(1), 182(2), 189(1).

Commencement: 30 April 2010.

These Regulations implement European Parliament and Council Directive 2002/65/EC, Arts 3, 5 at **[4.328]**, **[4.330]** and European Parliament and Council Directive 2008/48/EC, Arts 5, 6 at **[4.435]**, **[4.436]**.

ARRANGEMENT OF REGULATIONS

[2.814]
1   Citation, commencement and interpretation

(1)   These Regulations may be cited as the Consumer Credit (Disclosure of Information) Regulations 2010 and shall come into force on 30th April 2010.

(2)   In these Regulations—

"the Act" means the Consumer Credit Act 1974;

"advance payment" includes any deposit and in relation to a regulated consumer credit agreement includes also any part-exchange allowance in respect of any goods agreed in antecedent negotiations . . . to be taken by the creditor in part exchange but does not include a repayment of credit or any insurance premium or any amount entering into the total charge for credit;

"ancillary service" means a service that relates to the provision of credit under the agreement and includes in particular an insurance or payment protection policy;

"the APR" means the annual percentage rate of charge for credit determined in accordance with Schedule 2 to these Regulations and the [total charge for credit rules];

"cash price" in relation to any goods, services, land or other things means the price or charge at which the goods, services, land or other things may be purchased by, or supplied to, the debtor for cash account being taken of any discount generally available from the dealer or supplier in question;

"credit intermediary" has the same meaning as in [section 61A] of the Act;

"distance contract" means any regulated agreement made under an organised distance sales or service-provision scheme run by or on behalf of the creditor who, in any such case, for the purpose of that agreement makes exclusive use of one or more means of distance communication up to and including the time at which the agreement is made. For this purpose, "means of distance communication" means any means which, without the simultaneous physical presence of the creditor or a person acting on behalf of the creditor and of the debtor, may be used for the making of a regulated agreement between the parties to that agreement;

"excluded pawn agreement" means a pawn agreement—

(a)   where the debtor is not a new customer of the creditor (see [paragraph (6)]), and

(b)   where, before the agreement is made, the creditor has not received a request from the debtor for the pre-contract credit information (see regulation 9);

"linked credit agreement" means a regulated consumer credit agreement which—

(a)   serves exclusively to finance an agreement for the supply of specific goods or the provision of a specific service or land, and

(b)

(i)   where the supplier or service provider himself finances the credit for the debtor, or if it is financed by a third party, where the creditor uses the services of the supplier or service provider in connection with the preparation or making of the credit agreement, or

      (ii)   where the specific goods or land or the provision of a specific service are explicitly specified in the credit agreement;

"pawn agreement" means a consumer credit agreement under which the creditor takes an article in pawn;

"pre-contract credit information" means the information specified in regulation 3(4);

"total amount of credit" means the credit limit or the total sums made available under a consumer credit agreement;

"total amount payable" means the sum of the total charge for credit and the total amount of credit payable under the agreement as well as any advance payment;

"total charge for credit" means the total charge for credit determined in accordance with the [total charge for credit rules] and the Schedule to these Regulations;

["the total charge for credit rules" means rules made by the Financial Conduct Authority under article 60M of the Financial Services and Markets Act 2000 (Regulated Activities) Order 2001 for the purposes of Chapter 14A of Part 2 of that Order;]

(3)   In these Regulations, a reference to a repayment is a reference to—
   (a)   a repayment of the whole or any part of the credit,
   (b)   a payment of the whole or any part of the total charge for credit, or
   (c)   a combination of such repayments and payments.

(4)   In these Regulations, a reference to rate of interest is a reference to the interest rate expressed as a fixed or variable percentage applied on an annual basis to the amount of credit drawn down.

(5)   In these Regulations, a reference to an agreement includes a reference to a prospective agreement.

(6)   For the purposes of the definition of "excluded pawn agreement" and regulation 8 the debtor is a new customer if the debtor has not entered into a pawn agreement with the creditor in the three years preceding the start of the negotiations antecedent to the agreement.

(7)   . . .

NOTES

Para (2): word omitted from definition "advance payment" revoked, and words in square brackets in definition "excluded pawn agreement" substituted, by the Consumer Credit (Amendment) Regulations 2010, SI 2010/1969, regs 31, 32; words in square brackets in definitions "the APR", "credit intermediary" and "total charge for credit" substituted, and definition "the total charge for credit rules" substituted for original definition "the Total Charge for Credit Regulations", by the Financial Services and Markets Act 2000 (Regulated Activities) (Amendment) (No 2) Order 2013, SI 2013/1881, art 26(1), (2), (3)(a), (b), for transitional provisions see Pt 8 thereof at **[2.1007]** et seq.

Para (7): revoked by SI 2013/1881, art 26(1), (3)(c), for transitional provisions see Pt 8 thereof at **[2.1007]** et seq.

[2.815]
2 Agreements to which these Regulations apply

(1)   These Regulations apply in respect of a regulated consumer credit agreement, except as provided for in paragraphs (2) to (4).

(2)   These regulations do not apply to an agreement to which section 58 of the Act (opportunity for withdrawal from prospective land mortgage) applies.

(3)   These Regulations do not apply to an authorised non-business overdraft agreement which is—
   (a)   for credit which exceeds £60,260 [unless it is a residential renovation agreement], or
   (b)   secured on land.

(4)   Except as provided for in paragraph (5) these Regulations do not apply to an agreement—
   (a)   under which the creditor provides the debtor with credit exceeding £60,260 [unless it is a residential renovation agreement],
   (b)   secured on land,
   (c)   entered into by the debtor wholly or predominantly for the purposes of a business also carried on, or intended to be carried on, by him, or
   (d)   made before 1st February 2011.

(5)   These Regulations apply to an agreement mentioned in paragraph (4) (which is not also an agreement mentioned in paragraph (2) or (3)) where a creditor or, where applicable a credit intermediary, discloses or purports to disclose the pre-contract credit information in accordance with these Regulations rather than in accordance with the Consumer Credit (Disclosure of Information) Regulations 2004 or the Financial Services (Distance Marketing) Regulations 2004 (as the case may be).

[(6)   Article 60C(5) and (6) of the Financial Services and Markets Act 2000 (Regulated Activities) Order 2001 applies for the purposes of paragraph (4)(c).]

NOTES

Paras (3), (4): words in square brackets added by the Mortgage Credit Directive Order 2015, SI 2015/910, Sch 1, Pt 2, para 13, as from 21 March 2016 (note that the 2015 Order also comes into force on 20 April 2015 and 21 December 2015 for limited other purposes, and for transitional provisions, see Part 4 of that Order at **[2.1194]** et seq).

Para (6): substituted by the Financial Services and Markets Act 2000 (Regulated Activities) (Amendment) (No 2) Order 2013, SI 2013/1881, art 26(1), (4), for transitional provisions see Pt 8 thereof at **[2.1007]** et seq.

[2.816]
3   Information to be disclosed: agreements other than telephone contracts, non-telephone distance contracts, excluded pawn agreements and overdraft agreements

(1)   This regulation applies to an agreement other than—

[(a)   an agreement made by voice telephone communication where it is a distance contract and the debtor consents to the disclosure of the information referred to in regulation 4(2);

(aa)   an agreement made by voice telephone communication where it is not a distance contract (see regulation 4(3));]

(b)   an agreement made using a means of distance communication other than a voice telephone communication, which does not enable the provision of the pre-contract credit information before the agreement is made (see regulation 5);

(c)   an excluded pawn agreement;

(d)   an authorised non-business overdraft agreement (see regulations 10 and 11).

(2)   In good time before the agreement is made, the creditor must disclose to the debtor, in the manner set out in regulation 8, the pre-contract credit information.

(3)   Paragraph (2) does not require a creditor to disclose the pre-contract credit information where it has already been disclosed to the debtor by a credit intermediary in a manner which complies with paragraph (2).

(4)   For the purposes of these Regulations, the pre-contract credit information comprises—

(a)   the type of credit,

(b)   the identity and geographical address of the creditor and, where applicable, of the credit intermediary,

(c)   the total amount of credit to be provided under the agreement and the conditions governing the draw down of credit. In the case of an agreement for running-account credit, the total amount of credit may be expressed as a statement indicating the manner in which the credit limit will be determined where it is not practicable to express the limit as a sum of money,

(d)   the duration or minimum duration of the agreement or a statement that the agreement has no fixed or minimum duration,

(e)   in the case of—

  (i)   credit in the form of deferred payment for specific goods, services or land, or

  (ii)   a linked credit agreement,

  a description of the goods, services or land and the cash price of each and the total cash price,

(f)   the rate of interest charged, any conditions applicable to that rate, where available, any reference rate on which that rate is based and any information on any changes to the rate of interest (including the periods that the rate applies, and any conditions or procedure applicable to changing the rate),

(g)   where different rates of interest are charged in different circumstances the creditor must provide the information in paragraph (f) in respect of each rate,

(h)   the APR and the total amount payable under the agreement illustrated (if not known) by way of a representative example mentioning all the assumptions used in order to calculate that rate and amount,

(i)   the amount (expressed as a sum of money), number (if applicable) and frequency of repayments to be made by the debtor and, where appropriate, the order in which repayments will be allocated to different outstanding balances charged at different rates of interest,

(j)   in the case of an agreement for running-account credit, the amount of each repayment is to be expressed as (a) a sum of money; (b) a specified proportion of a specified amount; (c) a combination of (a) or (b); or (d) in a case where the amount of any repayment cannot be expressed in accordance with (a), (b) or (c), a statement indicating the manner in which the amount will be determined,

(k)   if applicable, any charges for maintaining an account recording both payment transactions and draw downs, unless the opening of an account is optional, and any charge payable for using a method of payment in respect of payment transactions or draw downs,

(l)   any other charges payable deriving from the credit agreement and the conditions under which those charges may be changed,

(m)   if applicable, a statement that fees will be payable by the debtor to a notary on conclusion of the credit agreement,

(n)   the obligation, if any, to enter into a contract for ancillary services relating to the consumer credit agreement, in particular insurance services, where the conclusion of such a contract is compulsory in order to obtain the credit or to obtain it on the terms and conditions marketed,

(o)   the rate of interest applicable in the case of late payments and the arrangements for its adjustment, and, where applicable, any charges payable for default,

(p)   a warning regarding the consequences of missing payments (for example, the possibility of legal proceedings and the possibility that the debtor's home may be repossessed),

(q)   where applicable, any security to be provided by the debtor or on behalf of the debtor,

(r)   the existence or absence of a right of withdrawal,

Part 2   Statutory Instruments

(s)   the debtor's right of early repayment under section 94 of the Act, and where applicable, information concerning the creditor's right to compensation and the way in which that compensation will be determined,

(t)   the requirement for a creditor to inform a debtor in accordance with section 157(A1) of the Act that a decision not to proceed with a prospective regulated consumer credit agreement has been reached on the basis of information from a credit reference agency and of the particulars of that agency,

(u)   the debtor's right to be supplied under section 55C of the Act on request and free of charge, with a copy of the draft agreement except where—

    (i)   the creditor is at the time of the request unwilling to proceed to the making of the agreement, or

    (ii)   the agreement is an agreement referred to in regulation 2(4)(a) to (c) or a pawn agreement, and

(v)   if applicable, the period of time during which the creditor is bound by the pre-contract credit information.

(5)   For the purpose of the representative example referred to in paragraph (4)(h)—

  (a)

    (i)   where the debtor has informed the creditor or credit intermediary of one or more components of his preferred credit, such as the duration of the consumer credit agreement or the total amount of credit, and

    (ii)   where the creditor would in principle agree to offer credit on such terms,

    the creditor or credit intermediary must take those components into account when calculating the representative APR and the total amount payable;

  (b)   where the creditor uses the assumption set out in [the total charge for credit rules] the creditor must indicate that other draw down mechanisms for this type of consumer credit agreement may result in a higher APR;

  (c)   subject to paragraph (a), in the case of an agreement for running-account credit, where the credit limit is not known at the date on which the pre-contract credit information is disclosed, the total amount of credit is to be assumed to be £1,200 or in a case where credit is to be provided subject to a maximum credit limit of less than £1,200, an amount equal to that maximum limit.

(6)   In the case of a consumer credit agreement under which repayments do not give rise to an immediate reduction in the total amount of credit advanced but are used to constitute capital as provided for under the agreement or under an ancillary agreement, the creditor or credit intermediary must provide a clear and concise statement that such agreements do not provide for a guarantee of repayment of the total amount of credit drawn down under the credit agreement unless such a guarantee is given.

NOTES

Para (1): sub-paras (a), (aa) substituted for original sub-para (a) by the Consumer Credit (Amendment) Regulations 2010, SI 2010/1969, regs 31, 34.

Para (5): words in square brackets substituted by the Financial Services and Markets Act 2000 (Regulated Activities) (Amendment) (No 2) Order 2013, SI 2013/1881, art 26(1), (5), for transitional provisions see Pt 8 thereof at **[2.1007]** et seq.

[2.817]
4   Information to be disclosed: telephone contracts

(1)   This regulation applies to an agreement (other than an authorised non-business overdraft agreement) made by way of a voice telephone communication (whether or not it is a distance contract).

(2)   Where the agreement is a distance contract and where the debtor explicitly consents, the creditor must disclose the following information before the agreement is made—

  (a)   the identity of the person in contact with the debtor and that person's link with the creditor,

  (b)   a description of the main characteristics of the credit agreement which includes the information set out in regulation 3(4)(c), (d), (e), (f), (g), (h), (i) and (j),

  (c)   the total price to be paid by the debtor to the creditor for the credit including all taxes paid via the creditor or, if an exact price cannot be indicated, the basis for the calculation of the price enabling the debtor to verify it,

  (d)   notice of the possibility that other taxes or costs may exist that are not paid via the creditor or imposed by the creditor,

  (e)   whether or not there is—

    (i)   a right to withdraw under section 66A of the Act, or

    (ii)   a right to cancel under regulation 9 of the Financial Services (Distance Marketing) Regulations 2004 and, where there is such a right, its duration and the conditions for exercising it, including information on the amount which the consumer may be required to pay in accordance with regulation 13 of those Regulations, as well as the consequences of not exercising that right,

  (f)   that other information is available on request and the nature of that information.

(3) Where the agreement is not a distance contract the creditor must disclose the information in paragraph (2)(b) before the agreement is made.

(4) The creditor must disclose the pre-contract credit information in the manner set out in regulation 8 immediately after the agreement is made.

[2.818]
5 Information to be disclosed: non-telephone distance contracts

(1) This regulation applies to an agreement (other than an authorised non-business overdraft agreement) made—
(a) at the debtor's request, and
(b) using a means of distance communication other than a voice telephone communication which does not enable the provision before the agreement is made of the pre-contract credit information.

(2) The creditor must disclose the pre-contract credit information in the manner set out in regulation 8 immediately after the agreement is made.

[2.819]
6 Information to be disclosed: distance contracts for the purpose of a business

(1) This regulation applies to an agreement that is a distance contract entered into by the debtor wholly or predominantly for the purposes of a business carried on, or intended to be carried on by him.

(2) Where the agreement is an agreement to which [regulations 3, 4 or 5] would otherwise apply the creditor may comply with those regulations by disclosing the pre-contract credit information immediately after the agreement is entered into.

[(3) Article 60C(5) and (6) of the Financial Services and Markets Act 2000 (Regulated Activities) Order 2001 applies for the purposes of paragraph (1).]

NOTES
Para (2): words in square brackets substituted by the Consumer Credit (Amendment) Regulations 2010, SI 2010/1969, regs 31, 35.
Para (3): substituted by the Financial Services and Markets Act 2000 (Regulated Activities) (Amendment) (No 2) Order 2013, SI 2013/1881, art 26(1), (6), for transitional provisions see Pt 8 thereof at **[2.1007]** et seq.

[2.820]
7 Information about contractual terms and conditions: [regulations 3, 4 and 5]

(1) This regulation applies to an agreement which is—
(a) a distance contract to which [regulation 3, 4 or 5] applies, and
(b) which is not entered into by the debtor wholly or predominantly for the purposes of a business carried on, or intended to be carried on, by him.

(2) The creditor must ensure that—
(a) the information provided to the debtor pursuant to [regulation 3, 4 or 5] includes the contractual terms and conditions, and
(b) the information provided to the debtor in relation to the contractual obligations which would arise if the distance contract were made accurately reflects the contractual obligations which would arise under the law presumed to be applicable to that contract.

[(3) Article 60C(5) and (6) of the Financial Services and Markets Act 2000 (Regulated Activities) Order 2001 applies for the purposes of paragraph (1).]

NOTES
Heading: words in square brackets substituted by the Consumer Credit (Amendment) Regulations 2010, SI 2010/1969, regs 31, 36(a).
Paras (1), (2): words in square brackets substituted by SI 2010/1969, regs 31, 36(b), (c).
Para (3): substituted by the Financial Services and Markets Act 2000 (Regulated Activities) (Amendment) (No 2) Order 2013, SI 2013/1881, art 26(1), (7), for transitional provisions see Pt 8 thereof at **[2.1007]** et seq.

[2.821]
8 Manner of disclosure

(1) The pre-contract credit information must be disclosed by means of the form contained in Schedule 1.

(2) The form must be—
(a) in writing, and
(b) of a nature that enables the debtor to remove it from the place where it is disclosed to him.

(3) The form must be completed as specified in this paragraph—
(a) the relevant pre-contract credit information is to be provided in the appropriate row,
(b) the form is to be completed in accordance with the notes to that form,
(c) the asterisks and notes may be deleted,
(d) gridlines and boxes may be omitted, and
(e) any information contained in the form must be clear and easily legible.

(4) Any additional information relating to the credit which is provided in writing by the creditor to the debtor must be provided in a separate document to the form.

(5) Where a consumer credit agreement is a multiple agreement containing more than one part for the purposes of section 18 of the Act, the pre-contract credit information in respect of each part may be provided in the same form provided that—

(a) information that is not common to each part of the agreement is disclosed separately within the relevant section of the form, and

(b) it is clear which information relates to which part.

[2.822]
9   Information to be disclosed: pawn agreements

(1) This Regulation applies to a pawn agreement.

(2) In good time before a pawn agreement is made (unless the debtor is a new customer), the creditor must inform the debtor of his right to receive the pre-contract credit information in the form contained in Schedule 1, free of charge, on request.

[2.823]
10   Information to be disclosed: overdraft agreements

(1) This regulation applies to an agreement which is an authorised non-business overdraft agreement.

(2) In good time before an authorised non-business overdraft agreement is made, the creditor must disclose to the debtor, the information in paragraph (3) in the manner set out in regulation 11.

(3) The information referred to in paragraph (2) is as follows—

(a) the type of credit,

(b) the identity and geographical address of the creditor and, where applicable, of the credit intermediary,

(c) the total amount of credit,

(d) the duration of the agreement,

(e) the rate of interest charged, any conditions applicable to that rate, any reference rate on which that rate is based and any information on any changes to the rate of interest (including the periods that the rate applies, and any conditions or procedure applicable to changing the rate),

(f) where different rates of interest are charged in different circumstances the creditor must provide the information in paragraph (e) in respect of each rate,

(g) the conditions and procedure for terminating the agreement,

(h) where applicable, an indication that the debtor may be requested to repay the amount of credit in full on demand at any time,

(i) the rate of interest applicable in the case of late payments and the arrangements for its adjustment, and, where applicable, any charges payable for default,

(j) the requirement for a creditor to inform a debtor in accordance with section 157(A1) of the Act that a decision not to proceed with a prospective regulated consumer credit agreement has been reached on the basis of information from a credit reference agency and of the particulars of that agency,

(k) the charges, other than the rates of interest, payable by the debtor under the agreement (and the conditions under which those charges may be varied),

(l) if applicable, the period of time during which the creditor is bound by the information set out in this paragraph.

(4) Paragraph (2) does not apply to—

(a) an agreement made by a voice telephone communication (whether or not it is a distance contract),

(b) an agreement made at the debtor's request using a means of distance communication, other than a voice telephone communication, which does not enable the provision of the information required by paragraph (2) before the agreement is made, or

(c) an agreement that does not come within sub-paragraph (a) or (b) but where the debtor requests the overdraft be made available with immediate effect.

(5) In the case of an agreement that falls within paragraph (4)(a) that is also a distance contract, where the debtor explicitly consents the creditor must disclose the following information before the agreement is made—

(a) the identity of the person in contact with the debtor and that person's link with the creditor,

(b) a description of the main characteristics of the financial service including at least the information in paragraph (3)(c), (e), (f), (h) and (k),

(c) the total price to be paid by the debtor to the creditor for the credit including all taxes paid via the creditor or, if an exact price cannot be indicated, the basis for the calculation of the price enabling the debtor to verify it,

(d) notice of the possibility that other taxes or costs may exist that are not paid via the creditor or imposed by the creditor,

(e)   whether or not there is a right to cancel under regulation 9 of the Financial Services (Distance Marketing) Regulations 2004 and where there is such a right, its duration and the conditions for exercising it including information on the amount which the consumer may be required to pay in accordance with regulation 13 of those regulations, as well as the consequences of not exercising that right, and

(f)   that other information is available on request and the nature of that information.

[(5A)   In the case of an agreement that falls within paragraph (4)(a) that is also a distance contract, where the debtor does not explicitly consent to the disclosure of the information in paragraph (5), the creditor must disclose the information in paragraph (3) to the debtor before the [agreement] is made.]

(6)   In the case of an agreement that falls within paragraph (4)(a) that is not a distance contract the creditor must disclose the information in paragraph (5)(b) before the agreement is made.

(7)   In the case of an agreement that is a distance contract to which this regulation applies the creditor must ensure that the information he provides to the debtor pursuant to this regulation regarding the contractual obligations which would arise if the distance contract were concluded, accurately reflects the contractual obligations which would arise under the law presumed to be applicable to that contract.

(8)   In the case of an agreement that falls within paragraph (4)(c), the creditor must disclose the information in paragraph (3)(c), (e), (f), (h), and (k) to the debtor before the agreement is made in the manner set out in regulation 11.

(9)   Where a current account is an agreement for two or more debtors jointly the creditor may comply with paragraphs (5), [(5A),] (6) or (8) by disclosing the information to one debtor provided that each of the debtors have given the creditor their consent that the creditor may not comply in each debtor's case with the relevant paragraph.

NOTES

Para (5A): inserted by the Consumer Credit (Amendment) Regulations 2010, SI 2010/1969, regs 31, 37(a); word in square brackets substituted by the Consumer Credit (Amendment) Regulations 2011, SI 2011/11, reg 8.

Para (9): figure in square brackets inserted by SI 2010/1969, regs 31, 37(b).

[2.824]
11

(1)   Where regulation 10(2) applies, the creditor must comply with that regulation by—
(a)   disclosing the information by means of the European Consumer Credit Information form set out in Schedule 3 to these Regulations and as specified in paragraph (2), or
(b)   disclosing the information in writing so that all information is equally prominent.

(2)   The specifications referred to in paragraph (1)(a) are that—
(a)   the relevant information must be provided in the appropriate row,
(b)   the form must be completed in accordance with the notes to that form,
(c)   the asterisks and notes may be deleted,
(d)   gridlines and boxes may be omitted, and
(e)   any information contained in the form must be clear and easily legible.

(3)   Where regulation 10(8) applies, the creditor may provide the information orally.

[2.825]
12   Modifying agreements

(1)   Subject to paragraphs (2) to (4), these Regulations apply to a modifying agreement which varies or supplements an earlier agreement and which is, or is treated under section 82(3) of the Act as, a regulated agreement.

[(2)   Where a modifying agreement modifies an earlier consumer credit agreement, the requirements of regulations 3, 4 and 10 will be deemed to be satisfied if—
(a)   in good time before the modifying agreement is made—
(i)   the information specified by regulations 3(4) and 10(3) is disclosed to the debtor in respect of any provision of the earlier agreement which is varied or supplemented, and
(ii)   the creditor informs the debtor in writing that the other information in the earlier agreement remains unchanged, and
(b)   where the Financial Services (Distance Marketing) Regulations 2004 apply, the creditor complies with regulations 7 and 8 of those Regulations.]

(3)   Where a modifying agreement is made in a manner that does not allow the creditor to comply with the requirement in [paragraph (2)(a)(ii)], the creditor is deemed to have complied with that requirement if—
(a)   before the agreement is made the creditor informs the debtor orally that the other information in the earlier agreement remains unchanged, and
(b)   this is confirmed to the debtor in writing immediately after the agreement is made.

(4)   This regulation does not apply to an excluded pawn agreement.

NOTES

Para (2): substituted by the Consumer Credit (Amendment) Regulations 2010, SI 2010/1969, regs 31, 38(a).
Para (3): words in square brackets substituted by SI 2010/1969, regs 31, 38(b).

SCHEDULES

SCHEDULE 1
PRE-CONTRACT CREDIT INFORMATION

Regulation 8(1)

[2.826]
(Standard European Consumer Credit Information)

1 Contact details	
Creditor.	[Identity.]
Address.	[Geographical address of the creditor
Telephone number(s).*	to be used by the debtor.]
E-mail address.*	
Fax number.*	
Web address.*	
If applicable	
Credit intermediary.	[Identity.]
Address.	[Geographical address of the credit
Telephone number(s).*	intermediary to be used by the debtor.]
E-mail address.*	
Fax number.*	
Web address.*	

* This information is optional for the creditor. The row may be deleted if the information is not provided.

Wherever "if applicable" is indicated, the creditor must give the information relevant to the credit product or, if the information is not relevant for the type of credit considered, delete the respective information or the entire row, or indicate that the information is not applicable.

Indications between square brackets provide explanations for the creditor and must be replaced with the corresponding information.

2 Key features of the credit product	
[The type of credit].	
The total amount of credit. This means the amount of credit to be provided under the proposed credit agreement or the credit limit.	[The amount is to be expressed as a sum of money. In the case of running-account credit, the total amount may be expressed as a statement indicating the manner in which the credit limit will be determined where it is not practicable to express the limit as a sum of money.]
How and when credit would be provided.	[Details of how and when any credit being advanced is to be drawn down.]
The duration of the credit agreement.	[The duration or minimum duration of the agreement or a statement that the agreement has no fixed or minimum duration.]
Repayments. If applicable: Your repayments will pay off what you owe in the following order.	[The amount (expressed as a sum of money), number (if applicable) and frequency of repayments to be made by the debtor. In the case of an agreement for running-account credit, the amount may be expressed as a sum of money or a specified proportion of a specified amount or both, or in a case where the amount of any repayment cannot be expressed as a sum of money or a specified proportion, a statement indicating the manner in which the amount will be determined.

2 Key features of the credit product	
	[The order in which repayments will be allocated to different outstanding balances charged at different rates of interest.]
The total amount you will have to pay. This means the amount you have borrowed plus interest and other costs.	[The amount payable by the debtor under the agreement (where necessary, illustrated by means of a representative example). The total amount payable will be the sum of the total amount of credit and the total charge for credit payable under the agreement as well as any advance payment where required. In the case of running account credit, where it is not practicable to express the limit as a sum of money, a credit limit of £1200 should be assumed. In a case where credit is to be provided subject to a maximum credit limit of less than £1200, an amount equal to that maximum limit. The total charge for credit is to be calculated using the relevant APR assumptions set out in Schedule 2 to the Consumer Credit (Disclosure of Information) Regulations 2010 and the [total charge for credit rules], and where appropriate the relevant components of the debtor's preferred credit.]
If applicable [The proposed credit will be granted in the form of a deferred payment for goods or service.] or [The proposed credit will be linked to the supply of specific goods or the provision of a service.] Description of goods/services/land (as applicable). Cash price.	[A list or other description] [Cash price of goods or service.] [Total cash price.]
If applicable Security required. This is a description of the security to be provided by you in relation to the credit agreement.	[Description of any security to be provided by or on behalf of the debtor.]
If applicable Repayments will not immediately reduce the amount you owe.	[In the case of a credit agreement under which repayments do not give rise to an immediate reduction in the total amount of credit advanced but are used to constitute capital as provided by the agreement (or an ancillary agreement a clear and concise statement) where applicable, that the agreement does not provide for a guarantee of the repayment of the total amount of credit drawn down under the credit agreement.]

3 Costs of the credit	
The rates of interest which apply to the credit agreement	[Details of the rate of interest charged, any conditions applicable to that rate, where available, any reference rate on which that rate is based and any information on changes to the rate of interest (including the periods that the rate applies, and any conditions or procedure applicable to changing the rate). Where different rates of interest are charged in different circumstances, the creditor must provide the above information in respect of each rate.]
Annual Percentage Rate of Charge (APR).	[% if known. If the APR is not known a representative example (expressed as a %) mentioning all the necessary assumptions used for calculating the rate (as set out in Schedule 2 to the Consumer Credit (Disclosure of Information) Regulations 2010, the [total charge for credit rules] and, where appropriate, the relevant components of the debtor's preferred credit).
This is the total cost expressed as an annual percentage of the total amount of credit. The APR is there to help you compare different offers.	Where the creditor uses the assumption set out in . . . the [total charge for credit rules], the creditor shall indicate that other draw down mechanisms for this type of agreement may result in a higher APR.]
If applicable In order to obtain the credit or to obtain it on the terms and conditions marketed, you must take out: —an insurance policy securing the credit, or —another ancillary service contract. If we do not know the costs of these services they are not included in the APR.	[Nature and description of any insurance or other ancillary service contract required.]
Related costs	
If applicable You must have a separate account for recording both payment transactions and draw-downs.	[Details of any account or accounts that the creditor requires to be set up in order to obtain the credit together with the amount of any charge for this.]
If applicable Charge for using a specific payment method.	[Specify means of payment and the amount of charge.]
If applicable Any other costs deriving from the credit agreement.	[Description and amount of any other charges not otherwise referred to in this form.]
If applicable Conditions under which the above charges can be changed.	[Details of the conditions under which any of the charges mentioned above can be changed.]
If applicable You will be required to pay notarial fees.	[Description and amount of any fee.]
Costs in the case of late payments.	Either [A statement that there are no charges for late or missed payments.] Or

3 Costs of the credit	
	[Applicable rate of interest in the case of late payments and arrangements for its adjustment and, where applicable any charges payable for default.]
Consequences of missing payments.	[A statement warning about the consequences of missing payments, including: —a reference to possible legal proceedings and repossession of the debtor's home where this is a possibility, and —the possibility of missing payments making it more difficult to obtain credit in the future.]

4 Other important legal aspects	
Right of withdrawal.	Either: [A statement that the debtor has the right to withdraw from the credit agreement before the end of 14 days beginning with the day after the day on which the agreement is made, or if information is provided after the agreement is made, the day on which the debtor receives a copy of the executed agreement under sections 61A or 63 of the Consumer Credit Act 1974, the day on which the debtor receives the information required in section 61A(3) of that Act or the day on which the creditor notifies the debtor of the credit limit, the first time it is provided, whichever is the latest.] Or [There is no right to withdraw from this agreement—if there is a right to cancel the agreement this should be stated.] [If the right to cancel is under the Financial Services (Distance Marketing) Regulations 2004 refer to section 5 of the form.]
Early repayment. If applicable	[A statement that the debtor has the right to repay the credit early at any time in full or partially.].
Compensation payable in the case of early repayment.	[Determination of the compensation (calculation method) in accordance with section 95A [(and, where applicable, section 95B)] of the Consumer Credit Act 1974.]
Consultation with a Credit Reference Agency.	[A statement that if the creditor decides not to proceed with a prospective regulated consumer credit agreement on the basis of information from a credit reference agency the creditor must, when informing the debtor of the decision, inform the debtor that it has been reached on the basis of information from a credit reference agency and of the particulars of that agency.]
Right to a draft credit agreement.	[A statement that the debtor has the right, upon request, to obtain a copy of the draft credit agreement free of charge, unless the creditor is unwilling at the time of the request to proceed to the conclusion of the credit agreement.]
If applicable The period of time during which the creditor is bound by the pre-contractual information.	[This information is valid from [—] until [—].] or [Period of time during which the information on this form is valid.]

If applicable

5 Additional information in the case of distance marketing of financial services	
(a) concerning the creditor	
If applicable The creditor's representative in your Member State of residence. Address. Telephone number(s). E-mail address.* Fax number.* Web address.*	[ie where different from section 1.] [Identity.] [Geographical address to be used by the debtor.]
If applicable Registration number.	[The Firm Reference Number (FRN) (if any) or Interim Permission Number (if any), and any other relevant registration number of the creditor.]
If applicable The supervisory authority.	[The [Financial Conduct Authority] or any other relevant supervisory authority or both.]
(b) concerning the credit agreement	
If applicable Right to cancel the credit agreement.	[Practical instructions for exercising the right to cancel indicating, amongst other things, the period for exercising the right, the address to which notification of exercise of the right to cancel should be sent and the consequences of non- exercise of that right.]
If applicable The law taken by the creditor as a basis for the establishment of relations with you before the conclusion of the credit agreement.	[English/other law]
If applicable The law applicable to the credit agreement and/or the competent court.	[A statement concerning the law which governs the contract and the courts to which disputes may be referred.]
If applicable Language to be used in connection with the credit agreement.	[Details of the language that the information and contractual terms will be supplied in and used, with your consent, for communication during the duration of the credit agreement.]
(c) concerning redress	
Access to out-of-court complaint and redress mechanism.	[Whether or not there is an out-of-court complaint and redress mechanism for the debtor and, if so, the methods of access to it.]
* This information is optional for the creditor. The row may be deleted if the information is not provided.	

NOTES

Para 2: words "The type of credit" in square brackets substituted by the Consumer Credit (Amendment) Regulations 2010, SI 2010/1969, regs 31, 39; words "total charge for credit rules" in square brackets substituted by the Financial Services and Markets Act 2000 (Regulated Activities) (Amendment) (No 2) Order 2013, SI 2013/1881, art 26(1), (2), for transitional provisions see Pt 8 thereof at **[2.1007]** et seq.

Para 3: words omitted revoked and words "total charge for credit rules" in square brackets substituted by SI 2013/1881, art 26(1), (2), (8)(a), for transitional provisions see note above.

Para 4: words "(and, where applicable, section 95B)" in square brackets inserted by the Consumer Credit (Green Deal) Regulations 2012, SI 2012/2798, reg 5, Schedule, para 5.

Para 5: words from "The Firm Reference" to "of the creditor." in square brackets substituted by the Financial Services and Markets Act 2000 (Consumer Credit) (Miscellaneous Provisions) Order 2014, SI 2014/208, art 5(a), for transitional provisions see art 6 thereof at **[2.1113]**; words "Financial Conduct Authority" in square brackets substituted by SI 2013/1881, art 26(1), (2), (8)(b), for transitional provisions see note above.

Note: remaining words in square brackets are as set out in the original and do not represent amendments to the text.

SCHEDULE 2
PROVISIONS RELATING TO CALCULATION AND DISCLOSURE OF THE TOTAL CHARGE FOR CREDIT AND APR

Regulation 1(2)

Assumptions about running-account credit

[2.827]

1.
  (a) In the case of an agreement for running-account credit, the assumption in paragraph (b) shall have effect for the purpose of calculating the total charge for credit and any APR in place of any assumptions in [the total charge for credit rules] that might otherwise apply—
  (b) in a case where the credit limit applicable to the credit is not known at the time the pre-contract credit information is disclosed but it is known that it will be subject to a maximum limit of less than £1,200, the credit limit shall be assumed to be an amount equal to that maximum limit.

Permissible tolerances in disclosure of an APR

2. For the purposes of these Regulations, it shall be sufficient compliance with the requirement to show an APR if there is included in the pre-contract credit information—
  (a) a rate which exceeds the APR by not more than one,
  (b) a rate which falls short of the APR by not more than 0.1, or
  (c) in a case to which paragraph 3 or 4 of this Schedule applies, a rate determined in accordance with those paragraphs or whichever of them applies to that case.

Tolerance where repayments are nearly equal

3. In the case of an agreement under which all repayments but one are equal and that one repayment does not differ from any other repayment by more whole pence than there are repayments of credit, there may be included in the pre-contract credit information a rate found under [the total charge for credit rules] as if that one repayment were equal to the other repayments to be made under the agreement.

Tolerance where interval between relevant date and first repayment is greater than interval between repayments

4. In the case of an agreement under which—
  (a) three or more repayments are to be made at equal intervals, and
  (b) the interval between the relevant date and the first repayment is greater than the interval between the repayments,

there may be included in the pre-contract credit information a rate found under [the total charge for credit rules] as if the interval between the relevant date and the first repayment were shortened so as to be equal to the interval between repayments.

NOTES

Paras 1, 3, 4: words in square brackets substituted by the Financial Services and Markets Act 2000 (Regulated Activities) (Amendment) (No 2) Order 2013, SI 2013/1881, art 26(1), (9), for transitional provisions see Pt 8 thereof at **[2.1007]** et seq.

SCHEDULE 3
EUROPEAN CONSUMER CREDIT INFORMATION

Regulation 11(1)

[2.828]

1 Contact details	
Creditor.	[Identity.]
Address.	[Geographical address of the creditor to be used by the debtor.]
Telephone number(s).*	
E-mail address.*	
Fax number.*	
Web address.*	
If applicable	
Credit intermediary.	[Identity.]
Address.	[Geographical address of the credit intermediary to be used by the debtor.]
Telephone number(s).*	
E-mail address.*	
Fax number.*	

Part 2   Statutory Instruments

1 Contact details	
Web address.*	

* This information is optional for the creditor. The row may be deleted if the information is not provided.

Wherever "if applicable" is indicated, the creditor must give the information relevant to the credit product or, if the information is not relevant for the type of credit considered, delete the respective information or the entire row or indicate that the information is not applicable.

Indications between square brackets provide explanations for the creditor and must be replaced with the corresponding information.

2 Description of the main features of the credit product	
[The type of credit].	
The total amount of credit. This means the amount of credit to be provided under the agreement or the credit limit.	[The amount is to be expressed as a sum of money. In the case of running account credit, the total amount may be expressed as a statement indicating the manner in which the credit limit will be determined where it is not practicable to express the limit as a sum of money.]
The duration of the credit agreement.	[The duration or minimum duration of the agreement or a statement that the agreement has no fixed or minimum duration.]
If applicable Repayment of the credit.	[A statement informing the debtor that the debtor may be required to repay the amount of credit in full on demand at any time.]

3 Costs of the credit	
The rates of interest which apply to the credit agreement.	[Details of the rates of interest charged, any conditions applicable to that rate, where available any reference rate on which that rate is based and any information on changes to the rate of interest (including the periods that the rate applies and any conditions or procedure applicable to changing the rate). Where different rates of interest are charged in different circumstances, the creditor must provide the above information in respect of each rate.]
If applicable Costs. If applicable The conditions under which those costs may be changed.	[The costs applicable from the time the credit agreement is concluded.]
Costs in the case of late payments.	Either [A statement that there are no charges for late or missed payments.] Or [Applicable rate of interest, in the case of late payments and arrangements for its adjustment and, where applicable, any charges payable for default.]

4 Other important legal aspects	
Termination of the credit agreement.	[The conditions and procedure for termination of the credit agreement.]

4 Other important legal aspects

Consultation with a credit reference agency.	[A statement that if the creditor decides not to proceed with a prospective regulated consumer credit agreement on the basis of information from a credit reference agency the creditor must, when informing the debtor of that decision, inform the debtor that it has been reached on the basis of information from a credit reference agency and of the particulars of that agency.]
If applicable The period of time during which the creditor is bound by the pre-contractual information.	[This information is valid from [—] until [—] or [Period of time during which the information on this form is valid.]
If applicable	

5 Additional information to be given in the case of distance marketing of financial services

(a) concerning the creditor	
If applicable The creditor's representative in [the UK] [your Member State of residence.] Address. Telephone number.* E-mail address.* Fax number.* Web address.*	[ie where different from section 1.] [Identity.] [Geographical address to be used by the debtor.]
If applicable Registration number.	[The Firm Reference Number (FRN) (if any) or Interim Permission Number (if any), and any other relevant registration number of the creditor.]
If applicable The supervisory authority.	[The [Financial Conduct Authority] or any other relevant supervisory authority or both.]
(b) concerning the credit agreement	
If applicable The law taken by the creditor as a basis for the establishment of relations with you before the conclusion of the credit contract.	[English/other law.]
If applicable The law applicable to the credit agreement and/or the competent court.	[A statement concerning the law which governs the contract and the courts to which disputes may be referred.]
If applicable Language to be used in connection your agreement.	[Details of the language that the information and contractual terms will be supplied in and used, with the debtor's consent, for communication during the duration of the credit agreement.]
(c) concerning redress	
Access to out-of-court complaint and redress mechanism.	[Whether or not there is an out-of-court complaint and redress mechanism for the debtor who is party to the distance contract and, if so, the methods of access to it.]

5 Additional information to be given in the case of distance marketing of financial services
* This information is optional for the creditor. The row may be deleted if the information is not provided.

NOTES

Para 2: words "The type of credit" in square brackets substituted by the Consumer Credit (Amendment) Regulations 2010, SI 2010/1969, regs 31, 40.

Para 5: words from "The Firm Reference" to "of the creditor." in square brackets substituted by the Financial Services and Markets Act 2000 (Consumer Credit) (Miscellaneous Provisions) Order 2014, SI 2014/208, art 5(b), for transitional provisions see art 6 thereof at **[2.1113]**; words "Financial Conduct Authority" in square brackets substituted by the Financial Services and Markets Act 2000 (Regulated Activities) (Amendment) (No 2) Order 2013, SI 2013/1881, art 26(1), (10), for transitional provisions see Pt 8 thereof at **[2.1007]** et seq.

Note: remaining words in square brackets are as set out in the original and do not represent amendments to the text.

CONSUMER CREDIT (AGREEMENTS) REGULATIONS 2010

(SI 2010/1014)

NOTES

Made: 28 March 2010.

Authority: Consumer Credit Act 1974, ss 60, 61(1)(a), 105(9), 114(1), 182(2), 189(1).

Commencement: 1 February 2011, subject to reg 1(2)(b).

These Regulations implement European Parliament and Council Directive 2008/48/EC, Art 10 at **[4.440]**.

ARRANGEMENT OF REGULATIONS

[2.829]
1 Citation, commencement and interpretation

(1) These Regulations may be cited as the Consumer Credit (Agreements) Regulations 2010.

(2) [Except as provided for in paragraphs (2A) and (2B)] these Regulations shall come into force—
  (a) on 1st February 2011, or
  (b) in relation to a regulated consumer credit agreement, on the date and at the time Parts 1 to 3 of the Consumer Credit (EU Directive) Regulations 2010 apply to such an agreement, being a date before 1st February 2011.

[(2A) Where the condition in paragraph (2B) is satisfied on a date on or after 26th August 2010 and before 1st February 2011 in relation to a prospective regulated consumer credit agreement to which section 58 of the Act applies, these Regulations apply to that agreement (and to any subsequent regulated consumer credit agreement entered into before 1st February 2011) from the date and time the condition is satisfied.

(2B) The condition referred to in paragraph (2A) is that—
  (a) before the creditor gives the debtor the unexecuted agreement for his signature the creditor gives the debtor a copy of the unexecuted agreement in compliance or purported compliance with regulations 3 and 7 of, and Schedules 1 and 2 to, these Regulations and

(b)   the copy of the unexecuted agreement contains a heading and notice as set out in regulation 4(a)(ii) and (b)(ii) respectively of the Consumer Credit (Cancellation Notices and Copies of Documents) Regulations 1983.]

(3)   In these Regulations, unless the context otherwise requires—

"the Act" means the Consumer Credit Act 1974;

"advance payment" includes any deposit and in relation to a regulated consumer credit agreement includes also any part-exchange allowance in respect of any goods agreed in antecedent negotiations to be taken by the creditor in part-exchange but does not include a repayment of credit or any insurance premium or any amount entering into the total charge for credit;

"the APR" means the annual percentage rate of charge for credit determined in accordance with Schedule 4 and the [total charge for credit rules];

"cash price" in relation to any goods, services, land or other things means the price or charge at which the goods, services, land or other things may be purchased by, or supplied to, the debtor for cash;

"contract of shortfall insurance" means anything in writing which contains or purports to contain some promise or assurance (however worded or presented) that if a sum payable under a contract of insurance against loss of or damage to goods is less than the amount necessary to defray—

(a)   any amount of credit provided to finance the purchase of those goods, and

(b)   any other amount included in the total charge for that credit,

to the extent that these remain unpaid at the date of the loss or damage, a sum up to but not exceeding that shortfall will be paid;

"credit intermediary" has the same meaning as in [section 61A] of the Act;

"distance contract" means any regulated agreement made under an organised distance sales or service provision scheme run by or on behalf of the creditor who, in any such case, for the purpose of the agreement makes exclusive use of one or more means of distance communication up to and including the time at which the agreement is made. For this purpose, "means of distance communication" means any means which, without the simultaneous physical presence of the creditor or a person acting on behalf of the creditor, and of the debtor, may be used for the making of a regulated agreement between the parties to that agreement;

"earlier agreement" means an earlier consumer credit agreement for the provision of credit;

"exempted agreement" means an agreement of the description specified in the Schedule to the Consumer Credit (Notices of Cancellation Rights) (Exemptions) Regulations 1983 in relation to which there are no charges forming part of the total charge for credit;

"the Information Regulations 2010" means the Consumer Credit (Disclosure of Information) Regulations 2010;

"lettering" includes figures and symbols;

"modified agreement" means an earlier agreement as varied or supplemented by a modifying agreement, which is treated as—

(a)   revoking the earlier agreement, and

(b)   containing provisions reproducing the combined effect of the two agreements;

"pawn agreement" means a regulated consumer credit agreement under which the creditor takes an article in pawn;

"pre-contract credit information" means the information required to be disclosed by regulation 3(4) of the Information Regulations 2010;

"total amount of credit" means the credit limit or the total sums made available under a consumer credit agreement;

"total amount payable" means the sum of the total charge for credit and the total amount of credit payable under the consumer credit agreement as well as any advance payment;

"total charge for credit" means the total charge for credit determined in accordance with Schedule 4 and the [total charge for credit rules];

["the total charge for credit rules" means rules made by the Financial Conduct Authority under article 60M of the Financial Services and Markets Act 2000 (Regulated Activities) Order 2001 for the purposes of Chapter 14A of Part 2 of that Order;]

(4)   References in these Regulations to a contract of insurance shall be read with—

(a)   section 22 of the Financial Services and Markets Act 2000,

(b)   any relevant order under that section, and

(c)   Schedule 2 to that Act.

(5)   In these Regulations—

(a)   a reference to a repayment is a reference to—

(i)   a repayment of the whole or any part of the credit,

(ii)   a payment of the whole or any part of the total charge for credit, or

(iii) a combination of such repayments and payments.

(b)   a reference to rate of interest is a reference to the interest rate expressed as a fixed or variable percentage applied on an annual basis to the amount of credit drawn down.

(6)   . . .

NOTES

Para (2): words in square brackets inserted by the Consumer Credit (Amendment) Regulations 2010, SI 2010/1969, regs 41, 42(a).

Paras (2A), (2B): inserted by SI 2010/1969, regs 41, 42(b).

Para (3): words in square brackets in definitions "the APR", "credit intermediary" and "total charge for credit" substituted, and definition "the total charge for credit rules" substituted for original definition "the Total Charge for Credit Regulations", by the Financial Services and Markets Act 2000 (Regulated Activities) (Amendment) (No 2) Order 2013, SI 2013/1881, art 27(1), (2), (3)(a), (b), for transitional provisions see Pt 8 thereof at **[2.1007]** et seq.

Para (6): revoked by SI 2013/1881, art 26(1), (3)(c), for transitional provisions see note above.

[2.830]
2 Agreements to which these regulations apply

(1) These Regulations apply in respect of a regulated consumer credit agreement except as provided for in [paragraphs (1A) to (5)].

[(1A) These Regulations apply to an agreement to which section 58 of the Act applies where—
  (a) before the creditor gives the debtor the unexecuted agreement for his signature the creditor gives the debtor a copy of the unexecuted agreement in compliance or purported compliance with regulations 3 and 7 of, and Schedules 1 and 2 to, these Regulations, and
  (b) the copy of the unexecuted agreement contains a heading and notice as set out in regulation 4(a)(ii) and (b)(ii) respectively of the Consumer Credit (Cancellation Notices and Copies of Documents) Regulations 1983.]

(2) These Regulations do not apply to an agreement mentioned in paragraph (3) unless pre-contract credit information has been disclosed in compliance (or in purported compliance) with the Information Regulations 2010.

(3) The agreements referred to in paragraph (2) are—
  (a) an agreement secured on land [other than an agreement to which section 58 applies];
  (b) an agreement under which the creditor provides the debtor with credit which exceeds £60,260 [other than a residential renovation agreement];
  (c) an agreement entered into by the debtor wholly or predominantly for the purposes of a business carried on, or intended to be carried on, by him.

(4) Paragraph (2) and regulations 3 to 4 and 6 to 7 do not apply to an authorised non-business overdraft agreement or an authorised business overdraft agreement.

(5) Regulation 5 does not apply to a regulated consumer credit agreement which is also a distance contract unless the agreement is entered into by the debtor wholly or predominantly for the purposes of a business carried on, or intended to be carried on, by him.

[(6) Article 60C(5) and (6) of the Financial Services and Markets Act 2000 (Regulated Activities) Order 2001 applies for the purposes of paragraphs (3)(c) and (5).]

NOTES

Para (1): words in square brackets substituted by the Consumer Credit (Amendment) Regulations 2010, SI 2010/1969, regs 41, 43(a).

Para (1A): inserted by SI 2010/1969, regs 41, 43(b).

Para (3): in sub-para (a) words in square brackets inserted by SI 2010/1969, regs 41, 43(c); in sub-para (b) words in square brackets added by the Mortgage Credit Directive Order 2015, SI 2015/910, Sch 1, Pt 2, para 14(2), as from 21 March 2016 (note that the 2015 Order also comes into force on 20 April 2015 and 21 December 2015 for limited other purposes, and for transitional provisions, see Part 4 of that Order at **[2.1194]** et seq).

Para (6): substituted by the Financial Services and Markets Act 2000 (Regulated Activities) (Amendment) (No 2) Order 2013, SI 2013/1881, art 27(1), (4), for transitional provisions see Pt 8 thereof at **[2.1007]** et seq.

[2.831]
3 Form and content of regulated consumer credit agreements

(1) Documents embodying a regulated consumer credit agreement shall contain the information set out in column 2 of Schedule 1 to these Regulations in so far as that information relates to the type of agreement referred to in column 1.

(2) The information specified in Schedule 1 shall be presented in a clear and concise manner.

(3) For the purposes of this regulation, the requirement for the information to be "clear" includes a requirement that the wording, apart from any signature, is to be easily legible and of a colour which is readily distinguishable from the background medium upon which the information is displayed.

(4) Documents embodying a regulated consumer credit agreement, other than an exempted agreement, shall contain statements of the protection and remedies available to debtors under the Act, in the Form numbered in column 1 of Schedule 2 to these Regulations and set out in column 3, in so far as those statements relate to the type of agreement referred to in column 2.

(5) Documents embodying a regulated consumer credit agreement shall contain details of any security provided in relation to the regulated agreement by the debtor.

(6)   Paragraph (7) applies to documents embodying a debtor-creditor-supplier agreement falling within section 12(a) of the Act or a debtor-creditor agreement (in this paragraph and paragraph (7) referred to as "the principal agreement") and also embodying, or containing the option of, a debtor-creditor-supplier agreement falling within section 12(b) of the Act (in this paragraph referred to as "the subsidiary agreement") where the subsidiary agreement is to finance a premium under one or more of—

(a)   a contract of insurance to provide a sum payable in the event of the death of a debtor or a debtor suffering one or more of the following—

  (i)   accident;

  (ii)   sickness;

  (iii) unemployment,

at any time before the credit under the principal agreement and the subsidiary agreement has been repaid, where

  (i)   the sum payable does not exceed the amount sufficient to defray the sums payable to the creditor in respect of that credit and of the total charge for credit, and

  (ii)   the policy monies payable under the contract of insurance are to be used for a repayment under the principal agreement and the subsidiary agreement;

(b)   a contract of shortfall insurance;

(c)   a contract of insurance in so far as it relates to the guarantee of goods.

(7)   Documents to which this regulation applies may contain instead of the headings specified in paragraph 1 of Schedule 1 to these Regulations and any applicable statements of protection and remedies available to debtors under the Act that would otherwise apply—

(a)   a heading in so far as it relates to the principal agreement, and

(b)   if applicable, statements of the protection and remedies available to debtors under the Act in so far as they relate to the principal agreement.

[2.832]
4   Signing of agreement

(1)   The information specified in paragraphs 5, 6, 7, 11 and 14 of Schedule 1 to these Regulations in relation to the type of regulated consumer credit agreement referred to in column 1 shall be "the prescribed terms" for the purposes of section 61(1)(a) of the Act (the terms which must be contained in a document if a regulated consumer credit agreement is not to be improperly executed).

(2)   The document containing the prescribed terms of the regulated consumer credit agreement referred to in paragraph (1) shall contain a space indicated for the purpose of the debtor's signature.

(3)   The signature of the document shall be made in the following manner—

(a)   by the debtor, or by or on behalf of the debtor in the case of a partnership or an unincorporated body of persons, in the space in the document indicated for the purpose and, subject to sub-paragraph (c), the date of the signature shall be inserted in the space in the document indicated for the purpose,

(b)   by the creditor, or by a person on behalf of the creditor, and subject to sub-paragraph (c), the date of the signature shall be inserted in the document,

(c)   except where the agreement is cancellable, the date on which the unexecuted agreement becomes an executed agreement may be inserted in the document and in such a case any other date specified in paragraphs (a) and (b) need not be inserted, and

(d)   nothing in this regulation shall prohibit the inclusion in the said document, near to any such signature, of the signature by any witness.

(4)   *(Applies to Scotland only.)*

(5)   Where an agreement is intended to be concluded by the use of electronic communication nothing in this regulation shall prohibit the inclusion in the document of information about the process or means of providing, communicating or verifying the signature to be made by the debtor.

[2.833]
5   Modifying agreements

(1)   These Regulations shall apply to a modifying agreement which varies or supplements an earlier agreement and which is, or is treated under section 82(3) of the Act as, a regulated agreement.

(2)   Where an item of information required by regulation 3(1) or 8(1) is unchanged by the modifying agreement, the requirements of regulation 3(1) or 8(1) may be satisfied in relation to such item of information by a statement in the modifying agreement clearly indicating that the information in the earlier agreement remains unchanged.

(3)   [Except as provided for in paragraph (3A)] a statement referred to in paragraph (2) shall be contained in the document which is signed by the debtor.

[(3A)   Where a modifying agreement is an authorised business overdraft agreement or an authorised non-business overdraft agreement the document referred to in paragraph (3) does not have to be signed by the debtor.]

(4)   The information referred to in regulation 4(1) as prescribed terms for the purposes of section 61(1)(a) of the Act shall not be prescribed for the purposes of a modifying agreement if the information contained in the earlier agreement has not been varied or supplemented by the modifying agreement.

(5)   For the purposes of Schedule 1 to these Regulations, in calculating—

   (a)   the amount of repayments of credit or of any capital outstanding under an earlier agreement,

   (b)   the total charge for credit (or any items included in it) in relation to the credit to be provided under the modified agreement, or

   (c)   the APR in relation to the modified agreement,

the relevant date shall be determined by reference to the date of the modifying agreement.

NOTES

Para (3): words in square brackets inserted by the Consumer Credit (Amendment) Regulations 2010, SI 2010/1969, regs 41, 44(a).

Para (3A): inserted by SI 2010/1969, regs 41, 44(b).

[2.834]
6   Pawn agreements

Where a pawn-receipt is given under section 114(1) of the Act by a person who takes any article in pawn under a regulated consumer credit agreement (or a modifying agreement varying or supplementing an earlier credit agreement which is, or is treated under section 82(3) of the Act as, a regulated consumer credit agreement) and where the pawn-receipt is not separate from any document embodying such an agreement, it shall contain—

   (a)   the information set out in paragraphs 1, 2 and 22 of Schedule 1 to these Regulations, and

   (b)   a notice in the form contained in Schedule 3 to these Regulations.

[2.835]
7   Statutory Forms

(1)   The wording of any Form specified in Schedules 2 and 3 to these Regulations shall be reproduced in documents embodying regulated consumer credit agreements where applicable without any alteration, except that—

   (a)   the words "the creditor" may be replaced by the name of the creditor, by the expression by which the creditor is referred to in the agreement or by an appropriate pronoun, and any consequential changes to pronouns and verbs or other consequential grammatical changes may be made,

   (b)   the word "DEBTOR" may be replaced by "BORROWER" or "CUSTOMER" and the word "Debtor(s)" may be replaced by "Borrower(s)" or "Customer(s)", and

   (c)   every Form shall be completed in accordance with any note.

(2)   Any such note shall not be treated as part of any Form specified in the said Schedules and may be reproduced in addition to any such Form.

(3)   Where any such note requires any words to be omitted, those words shall be omitted or deleted.

(4)   Where words are shown in capital letters in any Form specified in Schedule 2 or 3 to these Regulations, and are reproduced in documents embodying regulated consumer credit agreements, they shall be afforded more prominence (whether by capital letters, underlining, larger or bold print or otherwise) than any other lettering in that Form except lettering inserted in accordance with paragraph 1(c) and no less prominence than that given to any other information in the document apart from the heading to the document, trade names, names of parties to the agreement or lettering in the document inserted in handwriting.

[2.836]
8   Form and content of an authorised overdraft agreement

(1)   Subject to paragraph (3), in the case of an authorised non-business overdraft agreement or an authorised business overdraft agreement, the following information shall be specified in writing in a clear and concise manner—

   (a)   the type of credit,

   (b)   the identities and geographical addresses of the creditor, debtor and, where relevant, of any credit intermediary involved,

   (c)   the duration of the agreement,

   (d)   the credit limit and the conditions governing its drawdown,

   (e)   the rate of interest charged, any conditions applicable to that rate, any reference rate on which that rate is based and any information on changes to the rate of interest (including the periods that the rate applies, and any conditions or procedure applicable to changing the rate),

   (f)   where different rates of interest are charged in different circumstances the creditor must provide the information in paragraph (e) in respect of each rate,

(g)   the total charge for credit, calculated at the time the agreement is made, mentioning all the assumptions used in order to calculate it,

(h)   an indication that the debtor may be requested to repay the amount of credit in full on demand at any time, and

(i)   the charges payable by the debtor under the agreement (and the conditions under which those charges may be varied).

(2)   For the purposes of paragraph (1), the requirement for the information to be "clear" includes a requirement that the wording is easily legible and of a colour which is readily distinguishable from the background medium upon which the information is displayed.

(3)   Paragraph (1)(g) shall not apply—

(a)   in the case of an authorised business overdraft agreement, or

(b)   in the case of an authorised non-business overdraft agreement that is also an agreement secured on land.

SCHEDULES

SCHEDULE 1
INFORMATION TO BE INCLUDED IN REGULATED CONSUMER CREDIT AGREEMENTS

Regulation 3

[2.837]

Paragraph	Type of agreement (1)	Information (2)
	Nature of the agreement	
1	All types.	(1) Subject to paragraph (2) below, a heading in one of the following forms of words—
		a) "Hire Purchase Agreement regulated by the Consumer Credit Act 1974"
		b) "Conditional Sale Agreement regulated by the Consumer Credit Act 1974
		c) "Fixed Sum Loan Agreement regulated by the Consumer Credit Act 1974"
		d) "Credit Card Agreement regulated by the Consumer Credit Act 1974"
		e) "Agreement modifying a Credit Agreement regulated by the Consumer Credit Act 1974."
		as the case may require.
		(2) If none of the headings in (1)(a) to (e) above are applicable—
		a) a heading in the following form of words—"Credit Agreement regulated by the Consumer Credit Act 1974" and
		b) a description of the type of credit.
		(3) Where the document and a pawn-receipt are combined, the words "and Pawn-Receipt" shall be inserted in the heading after the word "Agreement".
		(4) Where the document embodies an agreement of which at least one part is a consumer credit agreement not regulated by the Act, the word "partly" shall be inserted before "regulated" unless the regulated and unregulated parts of the agreement are clearly separate.
		(5) Where the credit is secured on land the words "and secured on" followed by the address of the land shall be inserted at the end of the heading.
	Parties to the agreement	

Paragraph	Type of agreement (1)	Information (2)
2	All types.	The identity and geographical address of the creditor, debtor and, where relevant, the identity and geographical address of any credit intermediary involved.
3	*Duration of the agreement* Agreement of fixed duration.	The duration of the agreement.
4	Open end agreements.	A statement indicating that the agreement has no fixed duration. The statement shall include details of the minimum duration of the agreement where such a period is provided for under the agreement.
5	*Amount of credit* Agreements falling within paragraph 9 except agreements under which both— a) the total amount payable by the debtor is not greater than the total cash price referred to in paragraph 10; and b) there is no advance payment.	The amount of the credit to be provided under the agreement, namely the difference between the total cash price to be referred to in paragraph 10 and the total of any advance payments.
6	Agreements for fixed-sum credit not falling within paragraph 9.	The amount of the credit to be provided under the agreement.
7	*Credit limit* Agreements for running-account credit.	The credit limit expressed as— a) a sum of money, b) a statement that the credit limit will be determined by the creditor from time to time under the agreement and that notice of it will be given by the creditor to the debtor, c) a sum of money together with a statement that the creditor may vary the credit limit to such sum as the creditor may from time to time determine under the agreement and that notice of it will be given by the creditor to the debtor, or d) in a case not falling within head (a), (b) or (c), either a statement indicating the manner in which the credit limit will be determined and that notice of it will be given by the creditor to the debtor, or a statement indicating that there is no credit limit.
8	How and when credit will be provided. All types.	A statement indicating how and when the credit to be advanced under the agreement is to be drawn down.
9	*Description of goods, services, land etc* Restricted use debtor-creditor-supplier agreements for fixed-sum credit to finance a transaction comprising the acquisition of goods, services, land or other things specified in the agreement or identified and agreed on at the time the agreement is made	A list or other description of the goods, services or other things and, in the case of land, a general description of the land, the acquisition of which is to be financed by credit under the agreement.
	Cash price	

Paragraph	*Type of agreement* (1)	*Information* (2)
10	Agreements falling within paragraph 9.	The cash price in relation to each item referred to in paragraph 9 and, where applicable, the total cash price.
11	*Rate of interest* All types.	The rate(s) of interest and, where available, any reference rate on which that rate is based. The following additional information shall be given in relation to each rate that applies: (1) the conditions governing the application of the rate; (2) the period during which the rate will apply; (3) the conditions and procedure for changing the rate.
12	*Total amount payable* All types.	(1) The total amount payable by the debtor being the sum of the total amount of credit and the total charge for credit payable under the agreement as well as any advance payment. (2) In the case of running-account credit, where the credit limit is not known at the time the credit agreement is made, the total amount of credit referred to in paragraph (1) shall be assumed to be £1,200 or in a case where credit is to be provided subject to a maximum credit limit of less than £1,200, an amount equal to that maximum limit.
13	*APR* All Types.	The APR in relation to the agreement calculated at the time the credit agreement is made. All the assumptions used in order to calculate that rate shall be specified. Alternatively, where applicable, a statement indicating that the total amount payable under the agreement is not greater than the total cash price of the goods, services, land or other things the acquisition of which is to be financed by credit under the agreement.
14	*[Repayments]* All types.	[The number (if applicable) and frequency of repayments to be made by the debtor]
14A	*Allocation of payments* All types where different rates of interest are or will be at any time during the term of the agreement payable in respect of— a) credit provided under the agreement for different purposes, or b) credit provided under each of the different parts of the agreement, whether or not the agreement is a multiple agreement.	A statement of the order or proportions in which any amount paid by the debtor which is not sufficient to discharge the total debt then due under the agreement will be applied or appropriated by the creditor towards the discharge of the sums due— a) in respect of the amounts of credit provided for different purposes, or b) different parts of the agreement as the case may be.
	Amounts of repayments	

Paragraph	Type of agreement (1)	Information (2)
15	All types.	The amount of each repayment to be made under the agreement expressed as— a) a sum of money; b) a specified proportion of a specified amount (including the amount outstanding from time to time); c) a combination of heads (a) and (b); or d) in a case where the amount of any repayment cannot be expressed in accordance with head (a), (b) or (c), a statement indicating the manner in which the amount will be determined.
	Statement of account	
16	Agreements of fixed duration where the debtor's repayments under the agreement result in an immediate reduction in the total amount of credit owed, other than— a) agreements referred to in regulation 2(2), or b) agreements where the total amount payable by the debtor does not exceed the total amount of credit.	The right to receive, on request, and free of charge, at any time throughout the duration of the agreement pursuant to section 77B of the Act, a statement in the form of a table showing— a) the details of each instalment owing under the agreement; b) the date on which each instalment is due, the amount and any conditions relating to the payment of the instalment; c) a breakdown of each instalment showing how much comprises— i) capital repayment, ii) interest payment, and iii) if applicable, any other charges. Where the interest rate is variable or the other charges may be varied the statement shall indicate clearly and concisely that the information contained in the statement is valid only until the rates of interest or charges are varied.
	Statement where no credit reduction	
17	Agreements under which payments of interest and charges made by the debtor are not accompanied by a reduction in the total amount of credit owed under the agreement.	A statement indicating the periods and conditions for the payment of the interest and of any associated recurrent or non-recurrent charges.
17A	Agreements under which repayments made by the debtor do not give rise to an immediate corresponding reduction in the total amount of credit owed but are used to constitute capital during periods and under conditions laid down in the credit agreement or in an ancillary agreement.	A statement indicating that— a) the debtor's regular repayments will not repay the capital advanced, and

Paragraph (1)	Type of agreement (1)	Information (2)
		b) at the termination of the agreement the debtor must repay the capital advanced unless the agreement provides a guarantee that any capital constituted by the debtor's repayments will repay the total amount of credit.
18	*Charges* All types where applicable.	(1) Where applicable, the charges for maintaining an account recording both payment transactions and draw downs, unless the opening of the account is optional. (2) Any charge payable as a result of using a method of payment in respect of repayment transactions or drawdown. (3) Any other charges deriving from the credit agreements (other than those referred to in paragraph 19(3)) and the conditions under which those charges may be changed.
19	*Interest for late payment* All types where applicable.	(1) The rate of interest which applies in the case of late payments applicable at the time of the making of the credit agreement, (2) the arrangements for its adjustment and, (3) where applicable, any charges payable for late payment.
20	*Missing payment warning* All types under which periodic repayments are to be made except pawn agreements.	A statement warning about the consequences of missing payments, including, for example, a reference to possible legal proceedings and the possibility that the debtor's home may be repossessed and the possibility of missing payments making it more difficult to obtain credit.
21	*Notarial fees* All types.	Where applicable, a statement that notarial fees will be payable.
22	*Security provided by the debtor* Pawn agreements, to which section 114 of the Act applies and where no separate pawn receipt is given.	A statement indicating that an article has been taken in pawn under the agreement and a description of the article sufficient to identify it.
23	All types except those referred to in paragraph 22 in relation to which any security or guarantee is to be provided by the debtor or on his behalf.	A description of the security or guarantee as applicable.
24	*Compulsory insurance* All types.	A description of any contract of insurance which the debtor is required to conclude under the terms of the agreement.
25	*Right of withdrawal* All types except where the agreement is— a) an agreement secured on land,	A statement providing details of the debtor's right under section 66A of the Act to withdraw from the regulated consumer credit agreement including— (1) the right to withdraw within 14 days without the debtor having to give any reason,

Part 2   Statutory Instruments

Paragraph	Type of agreement (1)	Information (2)
	b) restricted-use credit agreements to finance the purchase of land,	(2) when that period of withdrawal begins and ends;
	c) an agreement for a bridging loan in connection with the purchase of land,	(3) the requirement of the debtor to notify the creditor of his intention to withdraw, in writing or orally,
	d) for credit which exceeds £60,260 [other than a residential renovation agreement], or	(4) contact details of the person/creditor whom he must notify of his intention to withdraw from the agreement;
	e) a cancellable agreement.	(5) the requirement to repay the credit without delay and no later than 30 calendar days after giving notice of withdrawal,
		(6) the requirement to pay, without delay and no later than 30 calendar days after giving notice of withdrawal, the interest accrued from the date the credit was provided to the date of repaying it,
		(7) the amount of interest payable per day expressed as a sum of money, and
		(8) details of how and to whom he must pay the credit and interest.
		Paragraph (7) does not apply in respect of agreements for running-account credit where it is not practicable for the creditor to state the amount of interest payable per day. In such cases, the agreement shall state that where credit is drawn down during the withdrawal period, the creditor shall inform the debtor, on request, without delay, of the amount of interest payable per day.
25A	Agreements referred to in paragraph 25 (a) to (e).	(1) A statement that there is no right of withdrawal under section 66A of the Act.
		(2) An indication of any other right to cancel the credit agreement whether under the Act or otherwise, with details as appropriate.
26	*Linked credit agreements* [Linked credit agreements to which section 75A of the Act applies]	A statement explaining—
		(1) that the credit agreement finances the supply of specific goods or services,
		(2) that if the goods or services are not supplied, or are supplied only in part, or do not conform with the contract, the debtor has the right to seek redress from the creditor, if he is unable to obtain redress from the supplier of the goods or services.
27	Agreements falling within section 12(b) or (c) of the Act to which section 75 of the Act applies.	A statement explaining that the debtor may have a right to sue the supplier, the creditor or both if he has received unsatisfactory goods or services paid for under the agreement costing more than £100 and not more than £30,000.
28	*Early repayment* All types.	A statement providing details of the debtor's right of early repayment under section 94 of the Act including—
		(1) the fact that the debtor has a right to repay early in full or (except where the agreement is secured on land) in part,
		(2) the procedure for early repayment, and

Paragraph	Type of agreement (1)	Information (2)
		(3) where applicable, details of the creditor's right to compensation under [sections 95A and 95B] of the Act and the manner in which that compensation shall be determined.
	Termination by debtor	
29	Open-end agreements.	A statement explaining how and when the debtor can terminate the agreement.
30	Hire-purchase and conditional sale agreements.	A statement explaining—
		(1) how and when the debtor can terminate the agreement under section 99 of the Act, and
		(2) the debtor's maximum liability under section 100 of the Act.
	Ombudsman Scheme	
31	All types.	A statement explaining that the debtor who is not a business debtor has the right to complain to the Financial Ombudsman Service. A debtor who is a business debtor may have a right to complain to the Financial Ombudsman Service.
	Contractual terms and conditions	
32	All types.	Where applicable, the other contractual terms and conditions.
	Supervisory authority	
33	All types.	A statement specifying that the [Financial Conduct Authority], [geographical address] is the supervisory authority under the Act [or, in a case where the supplier is carrying on an activity which is exempt from the general prohibition in section 19 of the Financial Services and Markets Act 2000 by virtue of section 327 of that Act, a statement specifying (i) that the activity of the supplier is so exempt and (ii) the relevant designated professional body (within the meaning of section 326 of that Act) as the supervisory authority under that Act, and (iii) the geographical address of the relevant designated professional body].

Part 2 Statutory Instruments

NOTES

Para 14: words in square brackets in columns 2, 3 substituted by the Consumer Credit (Amendment) Regulations 2010, SI 2010/1969, regs 41, 45(a).

Para 25: words in square brackets inserted by the Mortgage Credit Directive Order 2015, SI 2015/910, Sch 1, Pt 2, para 14(3), as from 21 March 2016 (note that the 2015 Order also comes into force on 20 April 2015 and 21 December 2015 for limited other purposes, and for transitional provisions, see Part 4 of that Order at **[2.1194]** et seq).

Para 26: words in square brackets in column 2 substituted by SI 2010/1969, regs 41, 45(b).

Para 28: words in square brackets substituted by the Consumer Credit (Green Deal) Regulations 2012, SI 2012/2798, reg 5, Schedule, para 6.

Para 33: in column (2) words "Financial Conduct Authority" in square brackets substituted by the Financial Services and Markets Act 2000 (Regulated Activities) (Amendment) (No 2) Order 2013, SI 2013/1881, art 27(1), (5), for transitional provisions see Pt 8 thereof at **[2.1007]** et seq; words from "or, in a" to "designated professional body" in square brackets added by the Financial Services and Markets Act 2000 (Regulated Activities) (Amendment) Order 2014, SI 2014/366, art 16, for transitional provision see art 17 thereof at **[2.1121]**.

SCHEDULE 2
FORMS OF STATEMENT OF PROTECTION AND REMEDIES AVAILABLE UNDER THE CONSUMER CREDIT ACT 1974 TO DEBTORS UNDER REGULATED CONSUMER CREDIT AGREEMENTS

Regulations 3(4) and 7

[2.838]

FORM (1)	TYPE OF AGREEMENT (2)	FORM OF STATEMENT (3)
1	Agreement to which section 58(1) of the Act applies.	YOUR RIGHTS Under the Consumer Credit Act 1974, you should have been given a copy of this agreement at least seven days ago so you could consider whether you wanted to go ahead. If the creditor did not give you a copy of this agreement he can only enforce it with a court order.
2	All agreements which are secured on land.	YOUR HOME MAY BE REPOSSESSED. Your home may be repossessed if you do not keep up repayments on a mortgage or other debt secured on it.
3	Cancellable agreements to which section 68(b) of the Act applies.	YOUR RIGHT TO CANCEL You can cancel this agreement within FOURTEEN days (starting the day after you signed it) by giving WRITTEN notice to*. If you intend to cancel you should not use any goods you have under the agreement and you should keep them safe. You can wait for them to be collected and you do not need to hand them over until you receive a written request for them. *Creditor or agent to insert the name and address of the person to whom the notice may be given or an indication of the person to whom a notice may be given with clear reference to the place in the document embodying the agreement where his name and address appear.
4	Cancellable agreements not included in paragraphs 3 or 5.	YOUR RIGHT TO CANCEL Once you have signed this agreement you will have a short time in which you can cancel [it]* [that part of this agreement which is regulated by the Consumer Credit Act 1974]*. The creditor will send you exact details of how and when you can do this. *Creditor to omit passage in square brackets which does not apply to the agreement.
5	Modifying agreement treated under section 82(5) of the Act as cancellable arrangements.	YOUR RIGHT TO CANCEL This agreement modifies an earlier agreement. Once you have signed this agreement your right to cancel [that part of]* the earlier agreement [which was regulated by the Consumer Credit Act 1974]* will be widened to cover the [regulated]* agreement as modified. The cancellation period itself will be unchanged. Details of how to cancel are given in your copy of this agreement.

FORM (1)	TYPE OF AGREEMENT (2)	FORM OF STATEMENT (3)
		*Creditor to omit passages in square brackets except in the case of an agreement of which at least one part is credit agreement not regulated by the Act.
6	Pawn agreements to which section 114 of the Act applies.	IMPORTANT—READ THIS CAREFULLY TO FIND OUT ABOUT YOUR RIGHTS The Consumer Credit Act 1974 ("the Act") lays down certain requirements for your protection which should have been complied with when this agreement was made. If they were not, the creditor cannot enforce this agreement without getting a court order. The Act also gives you a number of rights. In particular, you should read the NOTICE TO DEBTOR [in this agreement]* [in your pawn-receipt].** If you would like to know more about your rights under the Act, contact Consumer Direct, your local Trading Standards Department or your nearest Citizens' Advice Bureau. *Phrase in square brackets to be included by creditor in agreements where any document embodying the agreement is not separate from the pawn-receipt. Creditor to omit "in your pawn-receipt". **Phrase in square brackets to be included by creditor in agreements where a separate pawn-receipt is given to the debtor. Creditor to omit "in this agreement".
7	Conditional sale agreements secured on land.	TERMINATION: YOUR RIGHTS Until the title to the land has passed to you, you have a right to end this agreement. To do so write to the person you make your payments to. They will then be entitled to the return of the land and to [half the total amount payable under this agreement, that is]* £x. ** If, at the time you end this agreement, you have already paid at least this amount plus any overdue instalments and you have taken reasonable care of the land, you will not have to pay any more. *Creditor to insert the passage in square brackets where the amount calculated in accordance with the provisions of section 100 of the Act applies. If the agreement provides for a sum below the minimum prescribed in the Act, the passage in square brackets is to be omitted **Creditor to insert the amount calculated in accordance with the provisions of section 100 of the Act or such lesser sum as the agreement may provide.
8	Agreements modifying conditional sale agreements relating to land.	TERMINATION: YOUR RIGHTS

FORM (1)	TYPE OF AGREEMENT (2)	FORM OF STATEMENT (3)
		Until the title to the land has passed to you, you have a right to end this agreement. To do so write to the person you make your payments to. They will then be entitled to the return of the land and to [half the total amount payable under this agreement, that is]* [£[—**] If at the time you end this agreement, you have already paid at least this amount plus any overdue instalments and you have taken reasonable care of the land, you will not have to pay any more.
		*Creditor to insert the passage in square brackets where the amount calculated in accordance with the provisions of section 100 of the Act applies. If the agreement provides for a sum below the minimum prescribed in the Act, the passage in square brackets is to be omitted.
		** Creditor to insert the amount calculated in accordance with the provisions of section 100 of the Act or such lesser sum as the agreement may provide.
9	Hire purchase and conditional sale agreements relating to goods, not included in paragraph 10.	**TERMINATION: YOUR RIGHTS** You have a right to end this agreement. To do so, you should write to the person you make your payments to. They will then be entitled to the return of the goods and to [the cost of installing the goods plus half the rest of the total amount payable under this agreement, that is][half the total amount payable under this agreement, that is]*£x**. If you have already paid at least this amount plus any overdue instalments and have taken reasonable care of the goods, you will not have to pay any more.
		*Creditor to insert the appropriate passage in square brackets where the amount calculated in accordance with the provisions of section 100 of the Act apply. If the agreement provides for a sum below the minimum prescribed in the Act, both passages in square brackets are to be omitted.
		**Creditor to insert the amount calculated in accordance with the provisions of section 100 of the Act or such lesser sum as the agreement may provide.
10	Agreements modifying hire-purchase and conditional sale agreements relating to goods.	**TERMINATION: YOUR RIGHTS**

FORM (1)	TYPE OF AGREEMENT (2)	FORM OF STATEMENT (3)
		You have the right to end this agreement. To do so, write to the person you make your payments to. They will then be entitled to the return of the goods and to [the cost of installing the goods plus half the total amount yet to be paid under the earlier agreement as modified by this agreement, that is][half the total amount payable under the earlier agreement as modified by this agreement, that is]*£x**. If you have already paid at least this amount, plus any overdue instalments and have taken reasonable care of the goods, you will not have to pay any more.
		*Creditor to insert the appropriate passage in square brackets where the amount calculated in accordance with the provisions of section 100 of the Act applies. If the modified agreement provides for a sum below the minimum prescribed in the Act, both passages in square brackets are to be omitted.
		**Creditor to insert the amount calculated in accordance with the provisions of section 100 of the Act or such lesser sum as the agreement may provide.
11	Hire-purchase and conditional sale agreements relating to goods, not included in paragraph 12.	REPOSSESSION: YOUR RIGHTS If you do not keep your side of the agreement but you have paid at least [the cost of installing the goods plus one third of the rest of the total amount payable under this agreement, that is][one third of the total amount payable under this agreement, that is] *£x **the creditor may not take back the goods against your wishes unless he gets a court order. (In Scotland he may need to get a court order at any time). If he does take the goods without your consent or a court order, you have the right to get back any money that you have paid under this agreement.
		*Creditor to insert the appropriate passage in square brackets.
		**Creditor to insert the amount calculated in accordance with the provision of section 90 of the Act.
12	Agreements modifying hire-purchase and conditional sale agreements relating to goods.	REPOSSESSION: YOUR RIGHTS If you do not keep your side of this agreement [but you have paid at least £x*]** the creditor may not take back the goods against your wishes unless he gets a court order. (In Scotland he may need to get a court order at any time). If he does take the goods back without your consent or a court order, you have the right to get back all the money you have paid under this agreement.
		*Creditor to insert the amount calculated in accordance with the provisions of section 90 of the Act.

FORM (1)	TYPE OF AGREEMENT (2)	FORM OF STATEMENT (3)
		** Creditor to omit both passages in square brackets in the case of a modifying agreement where the goods are protected at the time the modifying agreement is made.

SCHEDULE 3
NOTICE TO BE CONTAINED IN DOCUMENTS EMBODYING A COMBINED CONSUMER CREDIT AGREEMENT AND PAWN-RECEIPT

Regulation 6

[2.839]

NOTICE TO DEBTOR

IMPORTANT—YOU SHOULD READ THIS CAREFULLY

Right to Redeem Articles

If you hand in this agreement (which is also your pawn receipt) and pay the amount you owe, you may redeem the article(s) in pawn at any time within 6 months of the date of this agreement or any longer time agreed with the creditor ("the redemption period").

IF YOU DO NOT REDEEM THE ARTICLE(S) ON OR BEFORE[1] YOU MAY LOSE YOUR RIGHT TO REDEEM IT (THEM).

Loss of Receipt

If you lose your receipt you may provide either a statutory declaration or, if the credit (or credit limit) is not more than £x [2] and the creditor agrees, a signed statement instead. The creditor may provide the form to be used and may charge for doing so.

Unredeemed Articles

An article not redeemed within the redemption period becomes the creditor's property if the credit (or credit limit) is not more than £x [3] and the redemption period is 6 months. In any other case it may be sold by the creditor, but it continues to be redeemable until it is sold. Interest is payable until the actual date of redemption. Where the credit (or credit limit) is more than £x [4] the creditor must give you 14 days notice of his intention to sell. When an article has been sold you will receive information about the sale. If the proceeds (less expenses) are more that the amount that would have been payable to redeem the article on the date of the sale you will be entitled to receive the extra amount. If the proceeds are less than the amount you will owe the creditor the shortfall.

Your goods will not be insured by the creditor while they are in pawn. [5]

[1] Creditor to insert the date at the end of the redemption period.

[2] Creditor to insert the amount specified in section 118(1)(b) of the Act.

[3] Creditor to insert the amount specified in section 120(1)(a) of the Act.

[4] Creditor to insert the amount specified in the Consumer Credit (Realisation of Pawn) Regulations 1983 (SI 1983/1568).

[5] Creditor to omit this paragraph if inapplicable.

SCHEDULE 4
PROVISIONS RELATING TO CALCULATION AND DISCLOSURE OF THE TOTAL CHARGE FOR CREDIT AND APR

Regulation 1(2)

Assumptions about running-account credit

[2.840]

1.
- (a) In the case of an agreement for running-account credit, the assumption in paragraph (b) below shall have effect for the purpose of calculating the total charge for credit and any APR in place of the assumption in [the total charge for credit rules] that might otherwise apply.
- (b) In a case where credit is to be provided subject to a maximum credit limit of less than £1,200, the credit limit shall be assumed to be an amount equal to that maximum limit.

Permissible tolerances in disclosure of an APR

2. For the purposes of these Regulations, it shall be sufficient compliance with the requirement to show an APR if there is included in the consumer credit agreement—
- (a) a rate which exceeds the APR by not more than one, or
- (b) a rate which falls short of the APR by not more than 0.1, or

(c)   in a case to which either of paragraphs 3 or 4 of this Schedule applies, a rate determined in accordance with those paragraphs or whichever of them applies to that case.

Tolerance where repayments are nearly equal

3. In the case of an agreement under which all repayments of credit but one are equal and that one repayment does not differ from any other repayment by more whole pence than there are repayments of credit, there may be included in a consumer credit agreement a rate found under [the total charge for credit rules] as if that one repayment were equal to the other repayments to be made under the agreement.

Tolerance where interval between relevant date and first repayment is greater than interval between repayments

4.

(a)   In the case of a consumer credit agreement under which—
     (i)   three or more repayments are to be made at equal intervals, and
     (ii)   the interval between the relevant date and the first repayment is greater than the interval between the repayments,
     there may be included in the agreement a rate found under [the total charge for credit rules] as if the interval between the relevant date and the first repayment were shortened so as to be equal to the interval between repayments.

(b)   In this paragraph "relevant date" means—
     (i)   in a case where a date is specified in or determinable under the consumer credit agreement at the date of its making as that on which the debtor is entitled to require provision of anything the subject of the agreement, the earliest such date, and
     (ii)   in any other case, the date of the making of the agreement.

NOTES

Paras 1, 3, 4: words in square brackets substituted by the Financial Services and Markets Act 2000 (Regulated Activities) (Amendment) (No 2) Order 2013, SI 2013/1881, art 27(1), (6), for transitional provisions see Pt 8 thereof at **[2.1007]** et seq.

TIMESHARE, HOLIDAY PRODUCTS, RESALE AND EXCHANGE CONTRACTS REGULATIONS 2010

(SI 2010/2960)

NOTES

Made: 11 December 2010.
Authority: European Communities Act 1972, s 2(2).
Commencement: 23 February 2011.
These Regulations implement European Parliament and Council Directive 2008/122/EC at **[4.466]**.

ARRANGEMENT OF REGULATIONS

Part 2   Statutory Instruments

PART 1
GENERAL

[2.841]
1 Citation and Commencement

(1) These Regulations may be cited as the Timeshare, Holiday Products, Resale and Exchange Contracts Regulations 2010.

(2) They come into force on 23rd February 2011.

[2.842]
2 Interpretation

(1) In these Regulations—
   "ancillary contract", in relation to a timeshare contract or long-term holiday product contract, has the meaning given in regulation 22(6);
   "consumer" has the meaning given in regulation 11;
   "enforcement authority" has the meaning given in regulation 32(1);
   "exchange contract" has the meaning given in regulation 10(1);
   "holiday accommodation contract" has the meaning given in regulation 4;
   "key information", in relation to a regulated contract, has the meaning given in regulation 12(3);
   "long-term holiday product contract" has the meaning given in regulation 8;

"regulated contract" has the meaning given in regulation 3;

"related credit agreement", in relation to a regulated contract, has the meaning given in regulation 23(4);

"resale contract" has the meaning given in regulation 9;

"standard information form" has the meaning given in regulation 13(2);

"timeshare contract" has the meaning given in regulation 7(1);

"timeshare exchange system" has the meaning given in regulation 10(2);

"trader" has the meaning given in regulation 11.

PART 2
KEY DEFINITIONS

[2.843]
3   Regulated contract

A "regulated contract" means a contract which—

    (a)   is a holiday accommodation contract (see regulation 4) to which these Regulations apply (see regulation 5), but

    (b)   is not an excluded arrangement (see regulation 6).

[2.844]
4   Holiday accommodation contracts

(1)   A "holiday accommodation contract" means—

    (a)   a timeshare contract,

    (b)   a long-term holiday product contract,

    (c)   a resale contract, or

    (d)   an exchange contract.

(2)   See regulations 7 to 10 for definitions of these types of contract.

[2.845]
5   Holiday accommodation contracts to which these Regulations apply

(1)   These Regulations apply to a holiday accommodation contract which falls within any of paragraphs (2) to (4).

(2)   A holiday accommodation contract falls within this paragraph if it is to any extent governed by the law of—

    (a)   the United Kingdom, or

    (b)   a part of the United Kingdom.

(3)   A holiday accommodation contract falls within this paragraph if—

    (a)   it is to any extent governed by the law of a third country,

    (b)   the relevant accommodation is in immovable property situated in an EEA State, and

    (c)   the parties to the contract are to any extent subject to the jurisdiction of a court in the United Kingdom in relation to the contract.

(4)   A holiday accommodation contract falls within this paragraph if—

    (a)   it is to any extent governed by the law of a third country,

    (b)   it is not directly related to immovable property,

    (c)   the trader carries on commercial or professional activities in the United Kingdom or by any means directs such activities to the United Kingdom, and

    (d)   the contract falls within the scope of those activities.

(5)   In this regulation—

    (a)   "relevant accommodation" means—

       (i)   the accommodation which is the subject of the contract, or

       (ii)   in a case where a pool of accommodation is the subject of the contract, some or all of the accommodation in that pool;

    (b)   "third country" means a country other than an EEA state.

[2.846]
6   Excluded arrangements

(1)   An "excluded arrangement" is an arrangement to which any of the following paragraphs apply.

(2)   This paragraph applies to multiple reservations of accommodation to the extent that they do not imply rights and obligations beyond those arising from the separate reservations.

(3)   This paragraph applies to a lease agreement which provides for a single continuous period of occupation.

(4)   This paragraph applies to a loyalty scheme, operating within a group of hotels, which provides consumers with discounts on future stays at hotels within the group where—

    (a)   no consideration is payable in respect of membership of the scheme, and

(b)   consideration payable by consumers for accommodation at hotels within the group is not payable primarily for the purpose of obtaining discounts or other benefits in respect of accommodation.

(5)   This paragraph applies to a contract of insurance where the effecting or carrying out of such a contract constitutes a regulated activity for the purposes of the Financial Services and Markets Act 2000.

[2.847]
7   Timeshare contracts

(1)   A "timeshare contract" means a contract between a trader and a consumer—
(a)   under which the consumer, for consideration, acquires the right to use overnight accommodation for more than one period of occupation, and
(b)   which has a duration of more than one year, or contains provision allowing for the contract to be renewed or extended so that it has a duration of more than one year.

(2)   The reference to "accommodation" in paragraph (1) includes a reference to accommodation within a pool of accommodation.

[2.848]
8   Long-term holiday product contracts

A "long-term holiday product contract" means a contract between a trader and a consumer—
(a)   the main effect of which is that the consumer, for consideration, acquires the right to obtain discounts or other benefits in respect of accommodation, and
(b)   which has a duration of more than one year, or contains provision allowing for the contract to be renewed or extended so that it has a duration of more than one year,
irrespective of whether the contract makes provision for the consumer to acquire other services.

[2.849]
9   Resale contracts

A "resale contract" means a contract between a trader and a consumer under which the trader, for consideration, assists the consumer in buying or selling rights under a timeshare contract or under a long-term holiday product contract.

[2.850]
10   Exchange contracts

(1)   An "exchange contract" means a contract between—
(a)   a consumer who is also party to a timeshare contract, and
(b)   a trader,
under which the consumer, for consideration, joins a timeshare exchange system.

(2)   A "timeshare exchange system" is a system which allows a consumer access to overnight accommodation or other services in exchange for giving other persons temporary access to the benefits deriving from the consumer's timeshare contract.

[2.851]
11   "Consumer" and "trader"

(1)   In these Regulations—
"consumer" means an individual who is not acting for the purposes of a trade, business, craft or profession;
"trader" means—
(a)   a person acting for purposes relating to that person's trade, business, craft or profession, or
(b)   anyone acting in the name of, or on behalf of, a person falling within paragraph (a).

(2)   Any reference in these Regulations to a consumer or trader in relation to a regulated contract, means—
(a)   in the case of a contract which has been entered into, the consumer or trader who is party to the contract, or
(b)   in the case of a proposed contract, the consumer and trader who will be parties to the contract, once it is entered into.

PART 3
PRE-CONTRACTUAL MATTERS

[2.852]
12   Key information

(1)   Before entering into a regulated contract, the trader must—
(a)   give the consumer the key information in relation to the contract, and
(b)   ensure that the information meets the requirements of this regulation.

(2)   The trader must comply with paragraph (1) in good time before entering into the contract.

(3)   The "key information" in relation to a contract means—

    (a)   the information required by Part 1 of the standard information form (see regulation 13(2)),

    (b)   the information set out in Part 2 of that form, and

    (c)   any additional information required by Part 3 of that form.

(4)   The information must be—

    (a)   clear, comprehensible and accurate, and

    (b)   sufficient to enable the consumer to make an informed decision about whether or not to enter into the contract.

(5)   The information must be provided—

    (a)   in the standard information form, completed in accordance with regulation 13(1),

    (b)   in writing,

    (c)   free of charge, and

    (d)   in a manner which is easily accessible to the consumer.

(6)   If the consumer is resident in, or a national of, an EEA State, the information must be provided in a language which is an official language of an EEA State and which is—

    (a)   the language, or one of the languages, of the EEA State in which the consumer is resident, or

    (b)   the language, or one of the languages, of the EEA State of which the consumer is a national.

(7)   If there are two or more languages in which the information could be provided under paragraph (6), the trader must give the consumer the opportunity to nominate one of them and—

    (a)   where the consumer does make a nomination, the information must be provided in the nominated language;

    (b)   where the consumer does not make any nomination, the information may be provided in any one of those languages.

(8)   A trader who contravenes paragraph (5) of this regulation commits an offence.

[2.853]

13   Completing the standard information form

(1)   The standard information form must be completed as follows—

    (a)   the information required by Part 1 of the form must be inserted in the appropriate places (without deleting the existing text in that Part),

    (b)   Part 2 of the form must not be amended, and

    (c)   the information required by Part 3 of the form must be inserted in the appropriate places in accordance with any applicable notes (which may then be deleted).

(2)   The "standard information form" means the form set out in—

    (a)   Schedule 1, in the case of a timeshare contract;

    (b)   Schedule 2, in the case of a long-term holiday product contract;

    (c)   Schedule 3, in the case of a resale contract; and

    (d)   Schedule 4, in the case of an exchange contract.

[2.854]

14   Marketing and sales

(1)   Any advertising related to a regulated contract must indicate how the key information in relation to the contract can be obtained.

(2)   A trader must not offer an opportunity to enter into a regulated contract to a consumer at a promotion or sales event unless—

    (a)   the invitation to the event clearly indicates the commercial purpose and nature of the event, and

    (b)   the key information in relation to the proposed regulated contract is made available to the consumer for the duration of the event.

(3)   A trader must not market or sell a proposed timeshare contract or long-term holiday product contract as an investment if the proposed contract would be a regulated contract.

(4)   The references to key information in this regulation are references to key information which meets the requirements of regulations 12(4) to (7).

(5)   A trader who contravenes paragraph (3) commits an offence.

PART 4

REGULATED CONTRACT: FORMALITIES

[2.855]

15   Form of contract

(1)   A trader must not enter into a regulated contract unless the contract complies with the requirements of this regulation.

(2)   The contract must be in writing and include—

    (a)   the identity, place of residence and signature of each of the parties;

    (b)   the date and place of conclusion of the contract.

(3) The contract must set out the key information in relation to the contract which is required under regulation 12.

(4) That key information must be set out—
  (a) as terms of the contract, and
  (b) with no changes, other than permitted changes.

(5) "Permitted changes" means changes to the key information which were communicated to the consumer in writing before the conclusion of the contract and which—
  (a) were expressly agreed between the trader and the consumer, or
  (b) resulted from unusual and unforeseeable circumstances beyond the trader's control, the consequences of which could not have been avoided even if all due care had been exercised.

(6) Any permitted changes must be expressly mentioned in the contract.

(7) The contract must include the standard withdrawal form set out in Schedule 5.

(8) If a trader contravenes paragraph (1)—
  (a) the trader commits an offence, and
  (b) the contract is unenforceable against the consumer.

[2.856]
16 Obligations of trader

(1) Before entering into a regulated contract a trader must draw the attention of the consumer to the following matters—
  (a) the right of withdrawal under the contract (see regulation 20),
  (b) the length of the withdrawal period (see regulation 21), and
  (c) the prohibition on advance consideration during the withdrawal period (see regulation 25).

(2) Before entering into a regulated contract a trader must obtain the signature of the consumer in relation to each section of the contract dealing with those matters.

(3) When a trader and consumer enter into a regulated contract, the trader must provide the consumer with a copy of the contract at the time the contract is concluded.

(4) If a trader fails to comply with any of paragraphs (1) to (3)—
  (a) the trader commits an offence, and
  (b) the contract is unenforceable against the consumer.

[2.857]
17 Language of the contract

(1) A trader must not enter into a regulated contract unless it complies with the requirements of this regulation, so far as applicable.

(2) If the consumer is resident in, or a national of, an EEA State, the contract must be drawn up in a language which is an official language of an EEA State and which is—
  (a) the language, or one of the languages, of the EEA State in which the consumer is resident, or
  (b) the language, or one of the languages, of the EEA State of which the consumer is a national.

(3) If there are two or more languages in which the contract could be drawn up under paragraph (2), the trader must give the consumer the opportunity to nominate one of them and—
  (a) where the consumer does make a nomination, the contract must be drawn up in the nominated language;
  (b) where the consumer does not make any nomination, the contract may be drawn up in any one of those languages.

(4) The contract must be drawn up in English (in addition to any other language in which it is drawn up under paragraphs (2) or (3)) if—
  (a) the consumer is resident in the United Kingdom, or
  (b) the trader carries on sales activities in the United Kingdom.

(5) If a trader fails to comply with paragraph (4) the contract is unenforceable against the consumer.

[2.858]
18 Translation of contract

(1) This regulation applies to a regulated contract if—
  (a) it is a timeshare contract, and
  (b) the subject of the contract is a single item of specific immovable property situated in an EEA State.

(2) The trader must not enter into the contract unless the trader has provided the consumer with a certified translation of the contract in the language, or one of the languages, of that State.

(3) The language of the translation must be an official language of an EEA State.

(4)　Paragraphs (2) and (3) do not apply if the contract is drawn up in a language in which the translation is required or permitted to be made.

(5)　A trader who contravenes paragraphs (2) or (3) of this regulation commits an offence.

(6)　A "certified translation" means a translation which is certified to be accurate by a person authorised to make or verify translations for the purposes of court proceedings.

[2.859]
19　Conflict with contractual terms

A term contained in a regulated contract is void to the extent that it purports to allow the consumer to waive the rights conferred on them by these Regulations.

PART 5
TERMINATION OF REGULATED CONTRACTS

[2.860]
20　Rights of withdrawal

(1)　A consumer may withdraw from a regulated contract by giving the trader written notice of withdrawal during the withdrawal period.

(2)　For the purposes of paragraph (1), written notice is to be regarded as having been given by the consumer at the time it is sent.

(3)　The consumer does not have to give any reason for the withdrawal.

(4)　The consumer may use the standard withdrawal form included in the contract under regulation 15(7) as the notice of withdrawal.

[2.861]
21　The withdrawal period

(1)　The withdrawal period for a regulated contract—
  (a)　begins on the start date, and
  (b)　ends on the date which is 14 days after the start date, subject to the following provisions.

(2)　The start date is the later of—
  (a)　the date of conclusion of the contract;
  (b)　the date on which the consumer receives a copy of the contract.

(3)　Paragraph (4) applies if a standard withdrawal form is not included in the contract in accordance with regulation 15(7).

(4)　The withdrawal period ends—
  (a)　on the date which is one year and 14 days after the start date, or
  (b)　in a case where the standard withdrawal form is provided to the consumer within the period of one year beginning on the start date, on the date which is 14 days after the day on which the consumer receives the form.

(5)　Paragraph (6) applies if the key information in relation to the contract is not provided to the consumer in accordance with the requirements in regulation 12(4) to (7).

(6)　The withdrawal period ends—
  (a)　on the date which is three months and 14 days after the start date, or
  (b)　in a case where the key information in relation to the contract is provided to the consumer within the period of three months beginning on the start date in accordance with the requirements in regulation 12(4) to (7), on the date which is 14 days after the day on which the consumer receives the information.

(7)　In a case where both paragraphs (4) and (6) apply, the withdrawal period ends on the later of the dates determined by those paragraphs.

(8)　Paragraph (9) applies in a case where a timeshare contract and a related exchange contract are offered to the consumer at the same time.

(9)　The withdrawal period for both contracts is to be the one which would apply to the timeshare contract under this regulation.

(10)　For the purposes of paragraph (8), an exchange contract is related to a timeshare contract if the exchange contract allows the consumer to give other persons access to benefits under the timeshare contract under a timeshare exchange system (see regulation 10(2)).

[2.862]
22　Effect of exercising right of withdrawal

(1)　This regulation applies if a consumer withdraws from a regulated contract by giving written notice of withdrawal to the trader under regulation 20.

(2)　The following obligations of the parties are terminated with effect from the date the consumer sends the notice of withdrawal—
  (a)　their obligations under the regulated contract, and
  (b)　if the regulated contract is a timeshare contract or a long-term holiday product contract, their obligations under any ancillary contract.

(3)   The reference to obligations in paragraph (2) includes, in the case of a long term holiday product contract, an obligation to pay any penalty or further instalments of the payment schedule (see regulation 26).

(4)   The consumer is not liable for any costs or charges—
   (a)   in respect of the regulated contract, or
   (b)   if the regulated contract is a timeshare contract or a long-term holiday product contract, in respect of any ancillary contract.

(5)   The reference to costs and charges in paragraph (4) includes any costs or charges corresponding to services provided under a contract before withdrawal.

(6)   "Ancillary contract", in relation to a timeshare contract or long-term holiday product contract ("the main contract"), means a contract under which the consumer acquires services which are related to the main contract and which are provided by—
   (a)   the trader, or
   (b)   a third party on the basis of an arrangement between the third party and the trader.

(7)   An exchange contract which is related to a timeshare contract (see regulation 21(10)), is an ancillary contract in relation to the timeshare contract for the purposes of paragraph (6).

[2.863]
23   Automatic termination of credit agreement

(1)   This regulation applies if a consumer withdraws from a regulated contract by giving written notice of withdrawal to the trader under regulation 20.

(2)   Any related credit agreement is automatically terminated at no cost to the consumer.

(3)   If the trader is not also the creditor under the related credit agreement, the trader must, on receipt of the notice of withdrawal, without delay inform the creditor that the notice has been received.

(4)   A credit agreement is related to a regulated contract if it is an agreement under which credit which fully or partly covers any payment under the regulated contract is granted to the consumer by—
   (a)   the trader, or
   (b)   a third party on the basis of an arrangement between the third party and the trader.

[2.864]
24   Termination of long-term holiday product contracts

(1)   A consumer who is party to a regulated contract that is a long-term holiday product contract may terminate the contract in accordance with this regulation without incurring any penalty.

(2)   The consumer may terminate the contract by giving notice of termination to the trader no later than 14 days after any day on which the consumer receives a request for payment of an instalment under regulation 26(4).

(3)   The right to terminate the contract under this regulation does not affect any other right available to the consumer to terminate or withdraw from the contract.

(4)   The reference to "instalment" in paragraph (2) does not include the first instalment.

PART 6
PAYMENTS

[2.865]
25   Advance consideration

(1)   This regulation makes provision about when consideration may be accepted in relation to regulated contracts.

(2)   Paragraph (3) applies in relation to a timeshare contract, long-term holiday product contract or exchange contract.

(3)   No person may accept any consideration from the consumer before the end of the withdrawal period in relation to the contract (see regulation 21).

(4)   Paragraph (5) applies in relation to a resale contract, the subject of which is rights under a timeshare contract or long-term holiday product contract.

(5)   No person may accept any consideration from the consumer before—
   (a)   the sale of those rights takes place, or
   (b)   the contract is otherwise terminated.

(6)   For the purposes of this regulation "consideration" includes any of the following—
   (a)   payments,
   (b)   guarantees,
   (c)   reservations of money on account,
   (d)   acknowledgements of debt.

(7)   A person who contravenes paragraph (3) or (5) commits an offence.

[2.866]
26   Payment schedule: long-term holiday product contracts

(1)   A trader must not accept any payment in respect of a regulated contract that is a long-term holiday product contract unless the payment is made in accordance with a schedule which complies with the requirements of this regulation.

(2)   The schedule must provide for all payments under the contract (including any membership fee) to be divided into yearly instalments of equal value, taking into account the duration of the contract.

(3)   The schedule must be prepared by the trader and provided to the consumer.

(4)   The trader must send a request for payment in writing to the consumer at least 14 days before a payment of an instalment becomes due under the schedule.

(5)   A trader who contravenes paragraph (1) or (4) commits an offence.

PART 7
OFFENCES: PENALTIES ETC

[2.867]
27   Penalties for offences

A person guilty of an offence under the preceding provisions of these Regulations is liable—
  (a)   on summary conviction, to a fine not exceeding the statutory maximum, or
  (b)   on conviction on indictment, to a fine.

[2.868]
28   Offences committed by bodies of persons

(1)   Paragraph (2) applies where an offence under these Regulations committed by a body corporate is proved—
  (a)   to have been committed with the consent or connivance of an officer of the body, or
  (b)   to be attributable to any neglect on the officer's part.

(2)   The officer (as well as the body corporate) is guilty of the offence and liable to be proceeded against and punished accordingly.

(3)   In paragraphs (1) and (2) each reference to an officer of the body corporate includes a reference to—
  (a)   a director, manager, secretary or other similar officer;
  (b)   a person purporting to act as a director, manager, secretary of other similar officer;
  (c)   in a case where the affairs of the body are managed by its members, a member.

(4)   Paragraph (5) applies where an offence under these Regulations committed by a Scottish partnership is proved—
  (a)   to have been committed with the consent or connivance of a partner, or
  (b)   to be attributable to any neglect on that partner's part.

(5)   The partner as well as the partnership is guilty of the offence and liable to be proceeded against and punished accordingly.

(6)   In paragraphs (4) and (5) each reference to a partner includes a reference to a person purporting to act as a partner.

[2.869]
29   Offences due to the default of another person

(1)   This regulation applies where a person ("X")—
  (a)   commits an offence under the preceding provisions of these Regulations, or
  (b)   would have committed such an offence but for a defence under regulations 30 (due diligence) or 31 (innocent publication of advertisement),
and the commission of the offence, or what would have been an offence but for the defence under regulations 30 or 31, is due to the act or default of another person ("Y").

(2)   Y is guilty of the offence (subject to regulations 30 and 31), whether or not Y is a trader.

(3)   Y may be charged with and convicted of the offence by virtue of paragraph (2), whether or not proceedings are taken against X.

[2.870]
30   Due diligence defence

(1)   In proceedings against a person for an offence under the preceding provisions of these Regulations it is a defence for the person to show that all reasonable steps were taken and all due diligence exercised to avoid committing the offence.

(2)   This is subject to the following provisions of this regulation.

(3)   Paragraph (4) applies where, in proceedings against any person ("the defendant") for such an offence, the defence provided by paragraph (1) involves an allegation that the commission of the offence was due to—
  (a)   the act or default of another, or

(b)   reliance on information given by another.

(4)   The defendant is not, without the leave of the court, entitled to rely on the defence unless the defendant has served a notice under paragraph (5) on the person bringing the proceedings no later than the day which is 8 days before—
(a)   the hearing of the proceedings or,
(b)   in Scotland, the diet of the trial.

(5)   A notice under this paragraph must give such information identifying or assisting in the identification of the person who committed the act or default, or gave the information, as is in the possession of the defendant at the time the notice is served.

(6)   A person is not entitled to rely on the defence provided by paragraph (1) by reason of reliance on information supplied by another, unless the person shows that it was reasonable, in all the circumstances to have relied on the information having regard in particular to—
(a)   the steps which the person took, and those which might reasonably have been taken, for the purpose of verifying the information, and
(b)   whether the person had any reason not to believe the information.

[2.871]
31   Innocent publication of advertisement defence
(1)   In proceedings against a person for an offence under regulation 14(5) committed by the publication of an advertisement it shall be a defence for the person to show that—
(a)   it is the person's business to publish or to arrange for the publication of advertisements,
(b)   the person received the advertisement for publication in the ordinary course of business, and
(c)   the person did not know and had no reason to suspect that its publication would amount to an offence under regulation 14(5).

PART 8
ENFORCEMENT

[2.872]
32   Enforcement authorities
(1)   "Enforcement authority" means—
(a)   a local weights and measures authority in Great Britain (within the meaning of section 69 of the Weights and Measures Act 1985);
(b)   the Department of Enterprise Trade and Investment in Northern Ireland.

(2)   An enforcement authority in Great Britain must enforce these Regulations within its area.

(3)   The enforcement authority in Northern Ireland must enforce these Regulations within Northern Ireland.

(4)   Nothing in this regulation authorises any enforcement authority to bring proceedings in Scotland for an offence under these Regulations.

[2.873]
33   *Powers of officers*
(1)   Paragraph (2) applies if a duly authorised officer of an enforcement authority has reasonable cause to suspect that an offence under the preceding provisions of these Regulations has been committed.

(2)   The officer may, for the purpose of ascertaining whether the offence has been committed, require a trader to produce any document relating to the trader's business and take copies of it or of any entry in it.

(3)   If such an officer has reason to believe that any documents may be required as evidence in proceedings for such an offence, the officer may seize and detain them and must, if the officer does so, inform the person from whom they are seized.

(4)   The powers in paragraphs (2) and (3) may only be exercised by an officer at a reasonable hour.

(5)   In this regulation "document" includes information recorded in any form.

(6)   The reference in paragraph (2) to the production of documents is, in the case of a document which contains information recorded otherwise than in legible form, a reference to the production of a copy of the information in legible form.

(7)   Nothing in this regulation is to be construed as requiring a person to answer any question or give any information if to do so might incriminate that person.

(8)   Nothing in this regulation gives any power to an officer of an enforcement authority to require any person to produce, or to seize from another person, a document to which paragraph (9) applies.

(9)   This paragraph applies to any document which the other person would be entitled to refuse to produce—
(a)   in proceedings in the High Court on the grounds of legal professional privilege, or

     (b)   (in Scotland) in proceedings in the Court of Session on the grounds of confidentiality of communications.

(10)   In paragraph (9) "communications" means—

     (a)   communications between a professional legal adviser and his or her client, or

     (b)   communications made in connection with or in contemplation of legal proceedings and for the purposes of those proceedings.

NOTES

Revoked, together with reg 34, by the Consumer Rights Act 2015 (Commencement No 3, Transitional Provisions, Savings and Consequential Amendments) Order 2015, SI 2015/1630, art 5, Sch 2, para 120, as from 1 October 2015 (for transitional provisions see arts 6–8 thereof at **[2.1220]** et seq).

[2.874]

34   Obstruction of authorised officers

(1)   A person commits an offence if the person—

     (a)   intentionally obstructs an officer of an enforcement authority acting in pursuance of these Regulations,

     (b)   intentionally fails to comply with any requirement properly made of the person by such an officer under regulation 33,

     (c)   without reasonable cause fails to give such an officer any other assistance or information which the officer may reasonably require of the person for the purpose of the officer's functions under these Regulations.

(2)   A person guilty of an offence under paragraph (1) is liable on summary conviction to a fine not exceeding level 5 on the standard scale.

(3)   A person commits an offence if the person, in giving information to an officer of an enforcement authority who is acting in pursuance of these Regulations—

     (a)   makes a statement which the person knows to be false in a material particular, or

     (b)   recklessly makes a statement which is false in a material particular.

(4)   A person guilty of an office under paragraph (3) is liable—

     (a)   on summary conviction to a fine not exceeding level 5 on the standard scale, or

     (b)   on conviction on indictment, to a fine.

NOTES

Revoked as noted to reg 33 at **[2.873]**.

[2.875]

35   Civil proceedings

(1)   The obligation to comply with regulation 12(1) is a duty owed by the trader who proposes to enter into a regulated contract to any person with whom the trader is required to provide with information under that provision.

(2)   The obligation to comply with Regulations 15(1), 16(1), 17(1) and 18(2) is, in each case, a duty owed by the trader who enters into a regulated contract to the consumer.

(3)   The obligation to comply with regulation 23(3) is a duty owed by the trader who enters into a regulated contract to the creditor under a related credit agreement.

(4)   A contravention of any of the obligations mentioned in paragraphs (1) to (3) is to be actionable accordingly.

(5)   Liability by virtue of paragraphs (1) to (3) is not to be limited or excluded by any contractual term, by any notice or by any other provision.

PART 9
SUPPLEMENTARY

[2.876]

36   Repeals, revocations, amendments and transitional and savings provisions

(1)   The Timeshare Act 1992 is repealed.

(2)   The following are revoked—

   (a)   the Timeshare Regulations 1997,

   (b)   the Timeshare Act 1992 (Amendment) Regulations 2003.

(3)   Schedule 6 (which contains consequential amendments) has effect.

(4)   Schedule 7 (which contains savings provision) has effect.

(5)   Schedule 8 (which contains repeals and revocations) has effect.

[2.877]

37 Application of the Package Travel, Package Holidays and Package Tours Regulations 1992

Nothing in these Regulations affects the application of the Package Travel, Package Holidays and Package Tours Regulations 1992 to regulated contracts falling within the scope of those Regulations.

SCHEDULES

SCHEDULE 1
STANDARD INFORMATION FORM FOR TIMESHARE CONTRACTS

Regulation 13(2)(a)

[2.878]

PART 1

Identity, place of residence and legal status of the trader(s) which will be party to the contract:
Short description of the product (eg description of the immovable property):
Exact nature and content of the right(s):
Exact period within which the right which is the subject of the contract may be exercised and, if necessary, its duration:
Date on which the consumer may start to exercise the contractual right:
If the contract concerns a specific property under construction, date when the accommodation and services/facilities will be completed/available:
Price to be paid by the consumer for acquiring the right(s):
Outline of additional obligatory costs imposed under the contract; type of costs and indication of amounts (eg annual fees, other recurrent fees, special levies, local taxes):
A summary of key services available to the consumer (eg electricity, water, maintenance, refuse collection) and an indication of the amount to be paid by the consumer for such services:
A summary of facilities available to the consumer (eg swimming pool or sauna):
Are these facilities included in the costs indicated above?
If not, specify what is included and what has to be paid for:
Is it possible to join an exchange scheme?
If yes, specify the name of the exchange scheme:
Indication of costs for membership/exchange:
Has the trader signed a code/codes of conduct and, if yes, where can it/they be found?

PART 2

General information:
—The consumer has the right to withdraw from this contract without giving any reason within 14 days from the conclusion of the contract or receipt of the contract if that takes place later.
—During this withdrawal period, any advance payment by the consumer is prohibited. The prohibition concerns any consideration, including payment, provision of guarantees, reservation of money on accounts, explicit acknowledgement of debt etc It includes not only payment to the trader, but also to third parties.
—The consumer shall not bear any costs or obligations other than those specified in the contract.
—In accordance with international private law, the contract may be governed by a law other than the law of the Member State in which the consumer is resident or is habitually domiciled and possible disputes may be referred to courts other than those of the Member State in which the consumer is resident or is habitually domiciled.
Signature of the consumer:

PART 3

Additional information to which the consumer is entitled and where it can be obtained specifically (for instance, under which chapter of a general brochure) if not provided below:
1 INFORMATION ABOUT THE RIGHTS ACQUIRED

—conditions governing the exercise of the right which is the subject of the contract within the territory of the Member States(s) in which the property or properties concerned are situated and information on whether those conditions have been fulfilled or, if they have not, what conditions remain to be fulfilled,

—where the contract provides rights to occupy accommodation to be selected from a pool of accommodation, information on restrictions on the consumer's ability to use any accommodation in the pool at any time.

2 INFORMATION ON THE PROPERTIES

—where the contract concerns a specific immovable property, an accurate and detailed description of that property and its location; where the contract concerns a number of properties (multi-resorts), an appropriate description of the properties and their location; where the contract concerns accommodation other than immovable property, an appropriate description of the accommodation and the facilities,

—the services (eg electricity, water, maintenance, refuse collection) to which the consumer has or will have access to and under what conditions,

—where applicable, the common facilities, such as swimming pool, sauna, etc, to which the consumer has or may have access and under what conditions.

3 ADDITIONAL REQUIREMENTS FOR ACCOMMODATION UNDER CONSTRUCTION (where applicable)

—the state of completion of the accommodation and of the services rendering the accommodation fully operational (gas, electricity, water and telephone connections) and any facilities to which the consumer will have access,

—the deadline for completion of the accommodation and of the services rendering it fully operational (gas, electricity, water and telephone connections) and a reasonable estimate of the deadline for the completion of any facilities to which the consumer will have access,

—the number of the building permit and the name(s) and full address(es) of the competent authority or authorities,

—a guarantee regarding completion of the accommodation or a guarantee regarding reimbursement of any payment made if the accommodation is not completed and, where appropriate, the conditions governing the operation of such guarantees.

4 INFORMATION ON THE COSTS

—an accurate and appropriate description of all costs associated with the timeshare contract; how these costs will be allocated to the consumer and how and when such costs may be increased; the method for the calculation of the amount of charges relating to occupation of the property, the mandatory statutory charges (for example, taxes and fees) and the administrative overheads (for example, management, maintenance and repairs),

—where applicable, information on whether there are any charges, mortgages, encumbrances or any other liens recorded against title to the accommodation.

5 INFORMATION ON TERMINATION OF THE CONTRACT

—where appropriate, information on the arrangements for the termination of ancillary contracts and the consequences of such termination,

—conditions for terminating the contract, the consequences of termination, and information on any liability of the consumer for any costs which might result from such termination.

6 ADDITIONAL INFORMATION

—information on how maintenance and repairs of the property and its administration and management are arranged, including whether and how consumers may influence and participate in the decisions regarding these issues,

—information on whether or not it is possible to join a system for the resale of the contractual rights, information about the relevant system and an indication of costs related to resale through this system,

—indication of the language(s) available for communication with the trader in relation to the contract, for instance in relation to management decisions, increase of costs and the handling of queries and complaints,

—where applicable, the possibility for out-of-court dispute resolution.

Acknowledgement of receipt of information:

Signature of the consumer:

SCHEDULE 2
STANDARD INFORMATION FORM FOR LONG-TERM HOLIDAY PRODUCT CONTRACTS

Regulation 13(2)(b)

[2.879]

PART 1

Identity, place of residence and legal status of the trader(s) which will be party to the contract:
Short description of the product:
Exact nature and content of the right(s):
Exact period within which the right which is the subject of the contract may be exercised and, if necessary, its duration:
Date on which the consumer may start to exercise the contractual right:
Price to be paid by the consumer for acquiring the right(s), including any recurring costs the consumer can expect to incur resulting from the right to obtain access to the accommodation, travel and any related products or services as specified:
The staggered payment schedule setting out equal amounts of instalments of this price for each year of the length of the contract and the dates on which they are due to be paid:
After year 1, subsequent amounts may be adjusted to ensure that the real value of those instalments is maintained, for instance to take account of inflation.
Outline of additional obligatory costs imposed under the contract; type of costs and indication of amounts (eg annual membership fees):
A summary of key services available to the consumer (eg discounted hotel stays and flights): Are they included in the costs indicated above?
If not, specify what is included and what has to be paid for (eg three-night stay included in annual membership fee, all other accommodation must be paid for separately):
Has the trader signed a code/codes of conduct and, if yes, where can it/they be found?

PART 2

General information:
—The consumer has the right to withdraw from this contract without giving any reason within 14 days from the conclusion of the contract or receipt of the contract if that takes place later.
—During this withdrawal period, any advance payment by the consumer is prohibited. The prohibition concerns any consideration, including payment, provision of guarantees, reservation of money on accounts, explicit acknowledgement of debt etc It includes not only payment to the trader, but also to third parties.
—The consumer has the right to terminate the contact without incurring any penalty by giving notice to the trader within 14 days of receiving the request for payment for each annual instalment.
—The consumer shall not bear any costs or obligations other than those specified in the contract.
—In accordance with international private law, the contract may be governed by a law other than the law of the Member State in which the consumer is resident or is habitually domiciled and possible disputes may be referred to courts other than those of the Member State in which the consumer is resident or is habitually domiciled.
Signature of the consumer:

PART 3

Additional information to which the consumer is entitled and where it can be obtained specifically (for instance, under which chapter of a general brochure) if not provided below:
1 INFORMATION ABOUT THE RIGHTS ACQUIRED
—an appropriate and correct description of discounts available for future bookings, illustrated by a set of examples of recent offers,
—information on the restrictions on the consumer's ability to use the rights, such as limited availability or offers provided on a first-come-first-served basis, time limits on particular promotions and special discounts.

2 INFORMATION ON THE TERMINATION OF THE CONTRACT

where appropriate, information on the arrangements for the termination of ancillary contracts and the consequences of such termination;

—conditions for terminating the contract, the consequences of termination, and information on any liability of the consumer for any costs which might result from such termination.

3 ADDITIONAL INFORMATION

—indication of the language(s) available for communication with the trader in relation to the contract, for instance in relation to the handling of queries and complaints,

—where applicable, the possibility for out-of-court dispute resolution.

Acknowledgement of receipt of information:

Signature of the consumer:

SCHEDULE 3
STANDARD INFORMATION FORM FOR RESALE CONTRACTS

Regulation 13(2)(c)

[2.880]

PART 1

Identity, place of residence and legal status of the trader(s) which will be party to the contract:
Short description of the services (eg marketing):
Duration of the contract:
Price to be paid by the consumer for acquiring the services:
Outline of additional obligatory costs imposed under the contact; type of costs and indication of amounts (eg local taxes, notary fees, cost of advertising):
Has the trader signed a code/codes of conduct and, if yes, where can it/they be found?

PART 2

General information:
—The consumer has the right to withdraw from this contract without giving any reason within 14 days from the conclusion of the contract or receipt of the contract if that takes place later.
—Any advance payment by the consumer is prohibited until the actual sale has taken place or resale contract otherwise is terminated. The prohibition concerns any consideration, including payment, provision of guarantees, reservation of money on accounts, explicit acknowledgement of debt etc It includes not only payment to the trader, but also to third parties.
—The consumer shall not bear any costs or obligations other than those specified in the contract.
—In accordance with international private law, the contract may be governed by a law other than the law of the Member State in which the consumer is resident or is habitually domiciled and possible disputes may be referred to courts other than those of the Member State in which the consumer is resident or is habitually domiciled.
Signature of the consumer:

PART 3

Additional information to which the consumer is entitled and where it can be obtained specifically (for instance, under which chapter of a general brochure) if not provided below:
—conditions for terminating the contract, the consequences of termination, and information on any liability of the consumer for any costs which might result from such termination,
—indication of the language(s) available for communication with the trader in relation to the contract, for instance in relation to the handling of queries and complaints,
—where applicable, the possibility for out-of-court dispute resolution.

Acknowledgement of receipt of information:

Signature of the consumer:

SCHEDULE 4
STANDARD INFORMATION FORM FOR EXCHANGE CONTRACTS
Regulation 13(2)(d)

[2.881]

PART 1

Identity, place of residence and legal status of the trader(s) which will be party to the contract:
Short description of the product:
Exact nature and content of the right(s):
Exact period within which the right which is the subject of the contract may be exercised and, if necessary, its duration:
Date on which the consumer may start to exercise the contractual right:
Price to be paid by the consumer for the exchange membership fees:
Outline of additional obligatory costs imposed under the contract; type of costs and indication of amounts (eg renewal fees, other recurrent fees, special levies, local taxes):
A summary of key services available to the consumer:
Are they included in the costs indicated above?
If not, specify what is included and what has to be paid for (type of costs and indication of amounts; eg an estimate of the price to be paid for individual exchange transactions, including any additional charges):
Has the trader signed a code/codes of conduct and, if yes, where can it/they be found?

PART 2

General information:
—The consumer has the right to withdraw from this contract without giving any reason within 14 days from the conclusion of the contract or receipt of the contract if that takes place later. In cases where the exchange contract is offered together with and at the same time as the timeshare contract, only a single withdrawal period shall apply to both contracts.
—During this withdrawal period, any advance payment by the consumer is prohibited. The prohibition concerns any consideration, including payment, provision of guarantees, reservation of money on accounts, explicit acknowledgement of debt etc It includes not only payment to the trader, but also to third parties.
—The consumer shall not bear any costs or obligations other than those specified in the contract.
—In accordance with international private law, the contract may be governed by the law other than the law of the Member State in which the consumer is resident or is habitually domiciled and possible disputes may be referred to courts other than those of the Member State in which the consumer is resident or habitually domiciled.
Signature of the consumer:

PART 3

Additional information to which the consumer is entitled and where it can be obtained specifically (for instance, under which chapter of a general brochure) if not provided below:
1 INFORMATION ABOUT THE RIGHTS ACQUIRED
—explanation of how the exchange system works; the possibilities and modalities for exchange; an indication of the value allotted to the consumer's timeshare in the exchange system and a set of examples of concrete exchange possibilities,
—an indication of the number of resorts available and the number of members in the exchange system, including any limitations on the availability of particular accommodation selected by the consumer, for example, as a result of peak periods of demand, the potential need to book a long time in advance, and indications of any restrictions on the choice resulting from the timeshare rights deposited into the exchange system by the consumer.
2 INFORMATION ON THE PROPERTIES
—a brief and appropriate description of the properties and their location; where the contract concerns accommodation other than immovable property, an appropriate description of the accommodation and the facilities; description of where the consumer can obtain further information.

---

3 INFORMATION ON THE COSTS

—information on the obligation on the trader to provide details before an exchange is arranged, in respect of each proposed exchange, of any additional charges for which the consumer is liable in respect of the exchange.

4 INFORMATION ON THE TERMINATION OF THE CONTRACT

—where appropriate, information on the arrangements for the termination of ancillary contracts and the consequences of such termination;

—conditions for terminating the contract, the consequences of termination, and information on any liability of the consumer for any costs which might result from such termination.

5 ADDITIONAL INFORMATION

—indication of the language(s) available for communication with the trader in relation to the contract, for instance in relation to the handling of queries and complaints,

—where applicable, the possibility for out-of-court dispute resolution.

Acknowledgement of receipt of information: Signature of the consumer:

SCHEDULE 5
SEPARATE STANDARD WITHDRAWAL FORM TO FACILITATE THE RIGHT OF WITHDRAWAL

Regulation 15(7)

[2.882]

Right of withdrawal

The consumer has the right to withdraw from this contract within 14 days without giving any reason.

The right of withdrawal starts from. .(to be filled in by the trader before providing the form to the consumer).

Where the consumer has not received this form, the withdrawal period starts when the consumer has received this form, but expires in any case after one year and 14 days.

Where the consumer has not received all the required information, the withdrawal period starts when the consumer has received that information, but expires in any case after three months and 14 days.

To exercise the right of withdrawal, the consumer shall notify the trader using the name and address indicated below by using a durable medium (eg written letter sent by post, e-mail). The consumer may use this form, but it is not obligatory.

Where the consumer exercises the right of withdrawal, the consumer shall not be liable for any costs.

In addition to the right of withdrawal, national contract law rules may provide for consumer rights, eg to terminate the contract in case of omission of information.

Ban on advance payment

During the withdrawal period any advance payment by the consumer is prohibited. The prohibition concerns any consideration, including payment, provision of guarantees, reservation of money on accounts, explicit acknowledgement of debt, etc

It includes not only payment to the trader, but also to third parties.

Notice of withdrawal

—To (Name and address of the trader) (*):

—I/We (**) herby give notice that I/We (**) withdraw from the contract,

—Date of conclusion of contract (*):

—Name(s) of consumer(s) (***):

—Address(es) of consumer(s) (***):

—Signature(s) of consumer(s) (only if this form is notified on paper) (***):

—Date (***):

(*) To be filled in by the trader before providing the form to the consumer.

(**) Delete as appropriate.

(***) To be filled in by the consumer(s) where this form is used to withdraw from the contract.

Acknowledgement of receipt of information:

Signature of the consumer:

SCHEDULE 6   *(Sch 6 contains consequential amendments which, in so far as relevant to this work, have been incorporated at the appropriate place.)*

SCHEDULE 7
TRANSITIONAL AND SAVINGS PROVISIONS

Regulation 36(4)

[2.883]

1   Enterprise Act 2002 (Part 8 Community Infringements Specified UK Laws) Order 2003

(1)   Despite paragraph 9(a) of Schedule 6, an act or omission to which sub-paragraph (2) applies is to continue to be a Community infringement under section 212 of the Enterprise Act 2002.

(2)   This sub-paragraph applies to an act or omission which immediately before the date on which these Regulations come into force is a Community infringement under section 212 of the Enterprise Act 2002 by contravening the provisions of—

    (a)   Directive 94/47/EC of the European Parliament and of the Council of 26th October 1994 on the protection of purchasers in respect of certain contracts relating to the purchase of the right to use immovable properties on a timeshare basis; or

    (b)   the Timeshare Act 1992 (not including its application to timeshare accommodation in caravans).

2   Enterprise Act 2002 (Part 8 Notice to OFT of Intended Prosecution, Specified Enactments, Revocation and Transitional Provision) Order 2003

Despite paragraph 10(2) of Schedule 6, section 230 of the Enterprise Act 2002 is to continue to apply in relation to an intention by a local weights and measures authority in England and Wales to start proceedings for an offence under the provisions of the Timeshare Act 1992.

3   Enterprise Act 2002 (Part 8 Domestic Infringements) Order 2003

(1)   Sub-paragraph (2) applies in relation to an act or omission which, immediately before the date on which these Regulations come into force, is a domestic infringement under section 211 of the Enterprise Act 2002 in respect of the provisions of the Timeshare Act 1992.

(2)   Despite paragraph 11 of Schedule 6, the act or omission is to continue to be a domestic infringement under section 211 of the Enterprise Act 2002.

4   Disclosure of information

(1)   This paragraph applies in relation to information which, immediately before the date on which these Regulations come into force, was subject to the provisions of any enactment which permitted the disclosure of information for the purposes of any function under, or proceedings brought under or by virtue of the Timeshare Act 1992.

(2)   Despite the repeal of such provisions by these Regulations, such disclosure is to continue to be permitted.

SCHEDULE 8

(Sch 8 contains repeals and revocations which, in so far as relevant to this work, have been incorporated at the appropriate place.)

ELECTRONIC MONEY REGULATIONS 2011

(SI 2011/99)

NOTES

Made: 18 January 2011.

Authority: European Communities Act 1972, s 2(2).

Commencement: 9 February 2011 (certain purposes); 30 April 2011 (otherwise); see reg 1 at **[2.884]**.

ARRANGEMENT OF REGULATIONS

PART 1
INTRODUCTORY PROVISIONS

PART 2
REGISTRATION

The register

PART 3
PRUDENTIAL SUPERVISION AND PASSPORTING

PART 4
ADDITIONAL ACTIVITIES AND USE OF DISTRIBUTORS AND AGENTS

PART 5
ISSUANCE AND REDEEMABILITY OF ELECTRONIC MONEY

PART 6
THE AUTHORITY

Part 2   Statutory Instruments

PART 7
GENERAL

SCHEDULES

PART 1
INTRODUCTORY PROVISIONS

[2.884]
1   Citation and commencement

(1)   These Regulations may be cited as the Electronic Money Regulations 2011.

(2)   These Regulations come into force on—
   (a)   9th February 2011 for the purposes of—
      (i)   enabling applications to become an authorised electronic money institution and for the variation of an authorisation to be made under regulation 5 and the Authority to determine such applications in accordance with regulations 6 to 9;

(ii) enabling applications for registration as a small electronic money institution and the variation of a registration to be made under regulation 12 and the Authority to determine such applications in accordance with regulation 13 and regulations 7 to 9 (as applied by regulation 15);

(iii) enabling applications for an agent to be included on the register under regulation 34 and the Authority to determine such applications in accordance with that regulation;

(iv) enabling the Authority to give directions as to the manner in which an application under regulation 5(1) or (2), 12(1) or (2) or 34(3) is to be made and enabling the Authority to require the applicant to provide further information in accordance with regulation 5(4), 12(4) or 34(3)(a)(iv), as the case may be;

(v) enabling the Authority to cancel an authorisation or registration or vary an authorisation or registration on its own initiative in accordance with regulation 10 or 11 (as applied, in the case of registration, by regulation 15);

(vi) requiring a person who has made an application under regulation 5(1) or (2) or 12(1) or (2) to provide information to the Authority in accordance with regulation 17 and enabling the Authority to give directions under that regulation;

(vii) enabling a person to make a reference to the Upper Tribunal under regulation 9(8), 10(6), 11(5), 29(4) or 34(11);

(viii) enabling an applicant for authorisation as an electronic money institution to give the Authority a notice of intention under regulation 28(2) and the Authority to give directions as to the manner in which such a notice is to be given and to inform the host state competent authority in accordance with regulation 28(3);

(ix) enabling the Authority to decide whether to register an EEA branch or to cancel such a registration under regulation 29(1);

(x) enabling the Authority to give directions under regulation 49 to a person whose application under regulation 5(1) or 12(1) has been granted before 30th April 2011 in respect of—

    (aa) its provision as from that date of electronic money issuance or payment services; and

    (bb) its compliance as from that date with requirements imposed by or under Parts 2 to 5 of these Regulations;

(xi) enabling the Authority to give directions under paragraph 8, 10, 13(a), 15 or 16 of Schedule 2 to a person whose application under regulation 5(1) or 12(1) has been granted before 30th April 2011;

(xii) requiring a person whose application under regulation 5(1), 12(1) or 34(3) has been granted before 30th April 2011 to provide information to the Authority in accordance with regulation 37 and enabling the Authority to give directions under that regulation;

(xiii) regulations 30, 47, 59 to 61, 66 to 71, 74 and 78;

(xiv) regulation 62 in respect of paragraphs 2, 6 and 8 to 11 of Schedule 3;

(xv) regulation 79 in respect of paragraphs 2, 18 and 19(g) of Schedule 4; and

(b) 30th April 2011 for all other purposes.

[2.885]
2 Interpretation

(1) In these Regulations—

"the 2000 Act" means the Financial Services and Markets Act 2000;

"agent" means a person who provides payment services on behalf of an electronic money institution;

"authorised electronic money institution" means—

(a) a person included by the Authority in the register as an authorised electronic money institution pursuant to regulation 4(1)(a); or

(b) a person deemed to have been granted authorisation by the Authority by virtue of regulation 74;

"the Authority" means the [Financial Conduct Authority];

"average outstanding electronic money" means the average total amount of financial liabilities related to electronic money in issue at the end of each calendar day over the preceding six calendar months, calculated on the first calendar day of each calendar month and applied for that calendar month;

["the capital requirements directive" means Directive 2013/36/EU of the European Parliament and of the Council of 26 June 2013 relating to the activity of credit institutions and the prudential supervision of credit institutions and investment firms, amending Directive 2002/87/EC and repealing Directives 2006/48/EC and 2006/49/EC;

"the capital requirements regulation" means Regulation (EU) 575/2013 of the European Parliament and of the Council of 26 June 2013 on prudential requirements for credit institutions and investment firms and amending Regulation (EU) No 648/2012;]

"consumer" means an individual who is acting for purposes other than a trade, business or profession;

"credit institution" has the meaning given in [Article 4(1)(1) of the capital requirements regulation] and includes a branch of the credit institution within the meaning of [Article 4(1)(17) of that regulation] which is situated within the EEA and which has its head office in a territory that is outside the EEA in accordance with [Article 47 of the capital requirements directive];

"credit union" means a credit union within the meaning of—
    (a)   the Credit Unions Act 1979; or
    (b)   the Credit Unions (Northern Ireland) Order 1985;

"decision notice" and "warning notice" have the same meaning as in the 2000 Act;

"distributor" means a person who distributes or redeems electronic money on behalf of an electronic money institution but who does not provide payment services on its behalf;

"the EEA" means the European Economic Area;

"EEA agent" means an agent through which an authorised electronic money institution, in exercise of its passport rights, provides payment services in an EEA state other than the United Kingdom;

"EEA authorised electronic money institution" means a person authorised in an EEA state other than the United Kingdom to issue electronic money and provide payment services in accordance with the electronic money directive;

"EEA branch" means a branch established by an authorised electronic money institution, in the exercise of its passport rights, to issue electronic money, provide payment services, distribute or redeem electronic money or carry out other activities in accordance with these Regulations in an EEA state other than the United Kingdom;

"electronic money" means electronically (including magnetically) stored monetary value as represented by a claim on the electronic money issuer which—
    (a)   is issued on receipt of funds for the purpose of making payment transactions;
    (b)   is accepted by a person other than the electronic money issuer; and
    (c)   is not excluded by regulation 3;

"the electronic money directive" means Directive 2009/110/EC of the European Parliament and of the Council of 16th September 2009 on the taking up, pursuit and prudential supervision of the business of electronic money institutions amending Directives 2005/60/EC and 2006/48/EC and repealing Directive 2000/46/EC;

"electronic money institution" means an authorised electronic money institution or a small electronic money institution;

"electronic money issuer" means any of the following persons when they issue electronic money—
    (a)   authorised electronic money institutions;
    (b)   small electronic money institutions;
    (c)   EEA authorised electronic money institutions;
    (d)   credit institutions;
    (e)   the Post Office Limited;
    (f)   the Bank of England, the European Central Bank and the national central banks of EEA states other than the United Kingdom, when not acting in their capacity as a monetary authority or other public authority;
    (g)   government departments and local authorities when acting in their capacity as public authorities;
    (h)   credit unions;
    (i)   municipal banks;
    (j)   the National Savings Bank;

"home state competent authority" means the competent authority designated in accordance with Article 3 of the electronic money directive as being responsible for the authorisation and prudential supervision of an EEA authorised electronic money institution which is exercising (or intends to exercise) its passport rights in the United Kingdom;

"host state competent authority" means the competent authority designated in accordance with Article 3 of the electronic money directive in an EEA state in which an authorised electronic money institution exercises (or intends to exercise) its passport rights;

"initial capital" has the meaning given by paragraph 1 of Schedule 2;

"the money laundering directive" means Directive 2005/60/EC of the European Parliament and of the Council of 26th October 2005 on the prevention of the use of the financial system for the purpose of money laundering and terrorist financing;

"municipal bank" means a company which, immediately before 1st December 2001, fell within the definition in section 103 of the Banking Act 1987;

"own funds" has the meaning given by paragraph 4 of Schedule 2;

"parent undertaking" has the same meaning as in the Companies Acts (see section 1162 of, and Schedule 7 to, the Companies Act 2006);

"passport right" means the entitlement of a person to establish a branch or provide services in an EEA state other than that in which they are authorised to provide electronic money issuance services—

> (a)　in accordance with the Treaty on the Functioning of the European Union as applied in the EEA; and
>
> (b)　subject to the conditions of the electronic money directive;

"payment account" means an account held in the name of one or more payment service users which is used for the execution of payment transactions;

"payment instrument" means any—

> (a)　personalised device; or
>
> (b)　personalised set of procedures agreed between the payment service user and the payment service provider;

"payment services" has the same meaning as in the Payment Services Regulations 2009;

"payment service user" means a person when making use of a payment service in the capacity of a payer or payee, or both;

"the payment services directive" means Directive 2007/64/EC of the European Parliament and of the Council of 13th November 2007 on payment services in the internal market;

"payment system" means a funds transfer system with formal and standardised arrangements and common rules for processing, clearing and settlement of payment transactions;

"payment transaction" has the meaning given in Article 4(5) of the payment services directive;

"qualifying holding" has the meaning given in [Article 4(1)(36) of the capital requirements regulation];

"the register" means the register maintained by the Authority under regulation 4;

"small electronic money institution" means a person included by the Authority in the register pursuant to regulation 4(1)(b);

"subsidiary undertaking" has the same meaning as in the Companies Acts (see section 1162 of, and Schedule 7 to, the Companies Act 2006).

(2)　In these Regulations references to amounts in euro include references to equivalent amounts in another currency.

(3)　Unless otherwise defined, expressions used in these Regulations which are also used in the electronic money directive have the same meaning as in that directive.

(4)　Expressions used in a modification to a provision in primary or secondary legislation applied by these Regulations have the same meaning as in these Regulations.

NOTES

Para (1): words in square brackets in definition "the Authority" substituted by the Financial Services Act 2012 (Consequential Amendments and Transitional Provisions) Order 2013, SI 2013/472, art 3, Sch 2, para 196(1), (2); definition "the banking consolidation directive" (omitted) revoked, definitions "the capital requirements directive" and "the capital requirements regulation" inserted, and words in square brackets in definitions "credit institution" and "qualifying holding" substituted by the Capital Requirements Regulations 2013, SI 2013/3115, reg 46(1), Sch 2, Pt 3, para 75(1), (2).

[2.886]

3　Electronic money: exclusions

For the purposes of these Regulations electronic money does not include—

> (a)　monetary value stored on instruments that can be used to acquire goods or services only—
>
> > (i)　in or on the electronic money issuer's premises; or
> >
> > (ii)　under a commercial agreement with the electronic money issuer, either within a limited network of service providers or for a limited range of goods or services;
>
> (b)　monetary value that is used to make payment transactions executed by means of any telecommunication, digital or IT device, where the goods or services purchased are delivered to and are to be used through a telecommunication, digital or IT device, provided that the telecommunication, digital or IT operator does not act only as an intermediary between the payment service user and the supplier of the goods and services.

PART 2
REGISTRATION

The register

[2.887]

4　The register of certain electronic money issuers

(1)　The Authority must maintain a register of—

> (a)　authorised electronic money institutions and their EEA branches;
>
> (b)　small electronic money institutions;
>
> (c)　agents of electronic money institutions required to be registered under regulation 34; and
>
> (d)　the National Savings Bank where it issues electronic money.

(2)　The Authority may include on the register any of the persons mentioned in paragraphs (c), (e), (f) and (g) of the definition of electronic money issuer in regulation 2(1) where such persons issue electronic money.

(3)　Where a person mentioned in paragraph (e), (f), (g) or (j) of the definition of an electronic money issuer in regulation 2(1)—

> (a)　is not included on the register; and

(b) issues, or proposes to issue, electronic money,

the person must give notice to the Authority.

(4) A notice under paragraph (3) must be given in such manner as the Authority may direct.

(5) The Authority may—

(a) keep the register in any form it thinks fit;

(b) include on the register such information as the Authority considers appropriate, provided that the register identifies the electronic money issuance for which the institution is authorised or registered under this Part; and

(c) exploit commercially the information contained in the register, or any part of that information.

(6) The Authority must—

(a) publish the register online and make it available for public inspection;

(b) update the register on a regular basis; and

(c) provide a certified copy of the register, or any part of it, to any person who asks for it—

(i) on payment of the fee (if any) fixed by the Authority; and

(ii) in a form (either written or electronic) in which it is legible to the person asking for it.

Authorisation

[2.888]
5 Application to become an authorised electronic money institution or variation of an existing authorisation

(1) An application to become an authorised electronic money institution must contain or be accompanied by the information specified in Schedule 1.

(2) An application for the variation of an authorisation must—

(a) contain a statement of the proposed variation;

(b) contain a statement of the electronic money issuance and payment services business which the applicant proposes to carry on if the authorisation is varied; and

(c) contain, or be accompanied by, such other information as the Authority may reasonably require.

(3) An application under paragraph (1) or (2) must be made in such manner as the Authority may direct.

(4) At any time after receiving an application and before determining it, the Authority may require the applicant to provide it with such further information as it reasonably considers necessary to enable it to determine the application.

(5) Different directions may be given, and different requirements imposed, in relation to different applications or categories of application.

[2.889]
6 Conditions for authorisation

(1) The Authority may refuse to grant an application for authorisation only if any of the conditions set out in paragraphs (2) to (8) is not met.

(2) The application must comply with the requirements of, and any requirements imposed under, regulation 5.

(3) The applicant must immediately before the time of authorisation hold the amount of initial capital required in accordance with Part 1 of Schedule 2.

(4) The applicant must be either—

(a) a body corporate constituted under the law of a part of the United Kingdom having—

(i) its head office; and

(ii) if it has a registered office, that office,

in the United Kingdom; or

(b) a body corporate which has a branch that is located in the United Kingdom and whose head office is situated in a territory that is outside the EEA.

(5) The applicant must satisfy the Authority that, taking into account the need to ensure the sound and prudent conduct of the affairs of the institution, it has—

(a) robust governance arrangements for its electronic money issuance and payment service business, including a clear organisational structure with well-defined, transparent and consistent lines of responsibility;

(b) effective procedures to identify, manage, monitor and report any risks to which it might be exposed; and

(c) adequate internal control mechanisms, including sound administrative, risk management and accounting procedures,

which are comprehensive and proportionate to the nature, scale and complexity of electronic money to be issued and payment services to be provided by the institution.

(6) The applicant must satisfy the Authority that—

(a) having regard to the need to ensure the sound and prudent conduct of the affairs of an authorised electronic money institution, any persons having a qualifying holding in the institution are fit and proper persons;

(b) the directors and persons responsible for the management of its electronic money and payment services business are of good repute and possess appropriate knowledge and experience to issue electronic money and provide payment services;

(c) it has a business plan (including for the first three years, a forecast budget calculation) under which appropriate and proportionate systems, resources and procedures will be employed by the institution to operate soundly;

(d) it has taken adequate measures for the purpose of safeguarding electronic money holders' funds in accordance with regulation 20.

(7) The applicant must comply with a requirement of the Money Laundering Regulations 2007 to be included in a register maintained under those Regulations where such a requirement applies to the applicant.

(8) If the applicant has close links with another person ("CL") the applicant must satisfy the Authority—

(a) that those links are not likely to prevent the Authority's effective supervision of the applicant; and

(b) if it appears to the Authority that CL is subject to the laws, regulations or administrative provisions of a territory which is not an EEA state ("the foreign provisions"), that neither the foreign provisions, nor any deficiency in their enforcement, would prevent the Authority's effective supervision of the applicant.

(9) For the purposes of paragraph (8), an applicant has close links with CL if—

(a) CL is a parent undertaking of the applicant;

(b) CL is a subsidiary undertaking of the applicant;

(c) CL is a parent undertaking of a subsidiary undertaking of the applicant;

(d) CL is a subsidiary undertaking of a parent undertaking of the applicant;

(e) CL owns or controls 20% or more of the voting rights or capital of the applicant; or

(f) the applicant owns or controls 20% or more of the voting rights or capital of CL.

[2.890]

7 Imposition of requirements

(1) The Authority may include in an authorisation such requirements as it considers appropriate.

(2) A requirement may, in particular, be imposed so as to require the person concerned to—

(a) take a specified action;

(b) refrain from taking a specified action.

(3) A requirement may be imposed by reference to the person's relationship with its group or other members of its group.

(4) Where—

(a) an applicant intends to carry on business activities other than the issuance of electronic money and provision of payment services; and

(b) the Authority considers that the carrying on of such other business activities will impair, or is likely to impair—

(i) the financial soundness of the applicant; or

(ii) the Authority's effective supervision of the applicant,

the Authority may require the applicant to establish a separate body corporate to carry on the issuance of electronic money and provision of payment services.

(5) A requirement expires at the end of such period as the Authority may specify in the authorisation.

(6) Paragraph (5) does not affect the Authority's powers under regulation 8 or 11.

[2.891]

8 Variation etc at request of an authorised electronic money institution

The Authority may, on the application of an authorised electronic money institution, vary the person's authorisation by—

(a) imposing a requirement such as may, under regulation 7, be included in an authorisation;

(b) cancelling a requirement included in the authorisation or previously imposed under paragraph (a); or

(c) varying such a requirement,

provided that the conditions set out in regulation 6(4) to (8), and the requirement in regulation 19(1) to maintain own funds, will continue to be met.

[2.892]

9 Determination of application for authorisation or variation of authorisation

(1) The Authority must determine an application for authorisation or for variation of an authorisation within three months beginning with the date on which it received the completed application.

Part 2 Statutory Instruments

(2) The Authority may determine an incomplete application if it considers it appropriate to do so, and it must in any event determine any such application within 12 months beginning with the date on which it received the application.

(3) The applicant may withdraw its application, by giving the Authority notice, at any time before the Authority determines it.

(4) If the Authority decides to grant an application for authorisation, or for variation of an authorisation, it must give the applicant notice of its decision stating—
  (a) that authorisation has been granted to carry out electronic money issuance; or
  (b) that the variation has been granted,
described in such manner as the Authority considers appropriate.

(5) The notice must state the date on which the authorisation or variation takes effect.

(6) If the Authority proposes to refuse an application or to impose a requirement it must give the applicant a warning notice.

(7) The Authority must, having considered any representations made in response to the warning notice—
  (a) if it decides to refuse the application or to impose a requirement, give the applicant a decision notice; or
  (b) if it grants the application without imposing a requirement, give the applicant notice of its decision, stating the date on which the authorisation or variation takes effect.

(8) If the Authority decides to refuse the application or to impose a requirement the applicant may refer the matter to the Upper Tribunal.

(9) If the Authority decides to authorise the applicant, or vary its authorisation, it must update the register as soon as practicable.

[2.893]
10 Cancellation of authorisation

(1) The Authority may cancel a person's authorisation and remove the person from the register where—
  (a) the person does not issue electronic money within 12 months beginning with the date on which the authorisation took effect;
  (b) the person requests, or consents to, the cancellation of the authorisation;
  (c) the person ceases to engage in business activity for more than six months;
  (d) the person has obtained authorisation through false statements or any other irregular means;
  (e) the person no longer meets, or is unlikely to meet, any of the conditions set out in regulation 6(4) to (8) or the requirement in regulation 19(1) to maintain own funds;
  (f) the person has issued electronic money or provided payment services other than in accordance with the authorisation granted to it;
  (g) the person would constitute a threat to the stability of a payment system by continuing its electronic money or payment services business;
  (h) the cancellation is desirable in order to protect the interests of consumers; or
  (i) the person's issuance of electronic money or provision of payment services is otherwise unlawful.

(2) A request for cancellation of a person's authorisation under paragraph (1)(b) must be made in such manner as the Authority may direct.

(3) At any time after receiving a request under paragraph (1)(b) and before determining it, the Authority may require the person making the request to provide it with such further information as it reasonably considers necessary to enable it to determine the request.

(4) Where the Authority proposes to cancel a person's authorisation, other than at the person's request, it must give the person a warning notice.

(5) The Authority must, having considered any representations made in response to the warning notice—
  (a) if it decides to cancel the authorisation, give the person a decision notice; or
  (b) if it decides not to cancel the authorisation, give the person notice of its decision.

(6) If the Authority decides to cancel the authorisation, other than at the person's request, the person may refer the matter to the Upper Tribunal.

(7) Where the period for a reference to the Upper Tribunal has expired without a reference being made, the Authority must as soon as practicable update the register accordingly.

[2.894]
11 Variation of authorisation on Authority's own initiative

(1) The Authority may vary a person's authorisation in any of the ways mentioned in regulation 8 if it appears to the Authority that—
  (a) the person no longer meets, or is unlikely to continue to meet, any of the conditions set out in regulation 6(4) to (8) or the requirement in regulation 19(1) to maintain own funds;

    (b)   the person has issued electronic money or provided a payment service other than in accordance with the authorisation granted to it;

    (c)   the person would constitute a threat to the stability of a payment system by continuing to issue electronic money or provide payment services;

    (d)   the variation is desirable in order to protect the interests of consumers; or

    (e)   the person's issuance of electronic money or provision of payment services is otherwise unlawful.

(2)   A variation under this regulation takes effect—

    (a)   immediately, if the notice given under paragraph (6) states that this is the case;

    (b)   on such date as may be specified in the notice; or

    (c)   if no date is specified in the notice, when the matter to which the notice relates is no longer open to review (see paragraph 13).

(3)   A variation may be expressed to take effect immediately or on a specified date only if the Authority, having regard to the ground on which it is exercising the power under paragraph (1), reasonably considers that it is necessary for the variation to take effect immediately or, as the case may be, on that date.

(4)   The Authority must as soon as practicable after the variation takes effect update the register accordingly.

(5)   A person who is aggrieved by the variation of their authorisation under this regulation may refer the matter to the Upper Tribunal.

(6)   Where the Authority proposes to vary a person's authorisation under this regulation, it must give the person notice.

(7)   The notice must—

    (a)   give details of the variation;

    (b)   state the Authority's reasons for the variation and its determination as to when the variation takes effect;

    (c)   inform the person that they may make representations to the Authority within such period as may be specified in the notice (whether or not the person has referred the matter to the Upper Tribunal);

    (d)   inform the person of the date on which the variation takes effect; and

    (e)   inform the person of their right to refer the matter to the Upper Tribunal and the procedure for such a reference.

(8)   The Authority may extend the period allowed under the notice for making representations.

(9)   If, having considered any representations made by the person, the Authority decides—

    (a)   to vary the authorisation in the way proposed; or

    (b)   if the authorisation has been varied, not to rescind the variation,

it must give the person notice.

(10)   If, having considered any representations made by the person, the Authority decides—

    (a)   not to vary the authorisation in the way proposed;

    (b)   to vary the authorisation in a different way; or

    (c)   to rescind a variation which has taken effect,

it must give the person notice.

(11)   A notice given under paragraph (9) must inform the person of their right to refer the matter to the Upper Tribunal and the procedure for such a reference.

(12)   A notice under paragraph (10)(b) must comply with paragraph (7).

(13)   For the purposes of paragraph (2)(c), paragraphs (a) to (d) of section 391(8) of the 2000 Act (publication) apply to determine whether a matter is open to review.

Registration as a small electronic money institution

[2.895]
12   Application for registration as a small electronic money institution or variation of an existing registration

(1)   An application for registration as a small electronic money institution must contain, or be accompanied by, such information as the Authority may reasonably require.

(2)   An application for the variation of a registration must—

    (a)   contain a statement of the proposed variation;

    (b)   contain a statement of the electronic money issuance and payment services business which the applicant proposes to carry on if the registration is varied; and

    (c)   contain, or be accompanied by, such other information as the Authority may reasonably require.

(3)   An application under paragraph (1) or (2) must be made in such manner as the Authority may direct.

(4)   At any time after receiving an application and before determining it, the Authority may require the applicant to provide it with such further information as it reasonably considers necessary to enable it to determine the application.

(5)   Different directions may be given, and different requirements imposed, in relation to different applications or categories of application.

[2.896]
13   Conditions for registration

(1)   The Authority may refuse to register an applicant as a small electronic money institution only if any of the conditions set out in paragraphs (2) to (10) is not met.

(2)   The application must comply with the requirements of, and any requirements imposed under, regulation 12.

(3)   The total business activities of the applicant immediately before the time of registration must not generate average outstanding electronic money that exceeds 5,000,000 euro.

(4)   The monthly average over the period of 12 months preceding the application of the total amount of relevant payment transactions must not exceed 3,000,000 euro.

(5)   The applicant must immediately before the time of registration hold such amount, if any, of initial capital as is required in accordance with Part 1 of Schedule 2.

(6)   The applicant must satisfy the Authority that, taking into account the need to ensure the sound and prudent conduct of the affairs of the institution, it has—

  (a)   robust governance arrangements for its electronic money and payment services business, including a clear organisational structure with well-defined, transparent and consistent lines of responsibility; and
  (b)   effective procedures to identify, manage, monitor and report any risks to which it might be exposed,

which are comprehensive and proportionate to the nature, scale and complexity of electronic money to be issued and payment services to be provided by the institution.

(7)   The applicant must satisfy the Authority that—

  (a)   the directors and persons responsible for the management of its electronic money and payment services business are of good repute and possess appropriate knowledge and experience to issue electronic money and provide payment services;
  (b)   it has a business plan (including for the first three years, a forecast budget calculation) under which appropriate and proportionate systems, resources and procedures will be employed by the institution to operate soundly; and
  (c)   it has taken adequate measures for the purpose of safeguarding electronic money holders' funds in accordance with regulation 20.

(8)   None of the individuals responsible for the management or operation of the business has been convicted of—

  (a)   an offence under Part 7 of the Proceeds of Crime Act 2002 (money laundering) or under the Money Laundering Regulations 2007;
  (b)   an offence under section 15 (fund-raising), 16 (use and possession), 17 (funding arrangements), 18 (money laundering) or 63 (terrorist finance: jurisdiction) of the Terrorism Act 2000;
  (c)   an offence under the 2000 Act;
  (d)   an offence under the Terrorist Asset-Freezing etc Act 2010[, the Al-Qaida and Taliban (Asset-Freezing) Regulations 2010 or the Al-Qaida (Asset-Freezing) Regulations 2011];
  (e)   an offence under these Regulations or the Payment Services Regulations 2009; or
  (f)   any other financial crime.

(9)   The applicant must be a body corporate whose head office is situated in the United Kingdom.

(10)   The applicant must comply with a requirement of the Money Laundering Regulations 2007 to be included in a register maintained under those Regulations where such a requirement applies to the applicant.

(11)   For the purposes of paragraph (4), where the applicant has yet to commence the provision of payment services which are not related to the issuance of electronic money, or has been providing such payment services for less than 12 months, the monthly average may be based on the projected total amount of relevant payment transactions over a 12 month period.

(12)   In paragraph (4) "relevant payment transactions" in respect of a small electronic money institution means payment transactions which—

  (a)   are not related to the issuance of electronic money; and
  (b)   are executed by the institution, including any of its agents who are in the United Kingdom.

(13)   In paragraph (8) "financial crime" includes any offence involving fraud or dishonesty and, for this purpose, "offence" includes any act or omission which would be an offence if it had taken place in the United Kingdom.

NOTES

Para (8): words in square brackets in sub-para (d) substituted by the Al-Qaida (Asset-Freezing) Regulations 2011, SI 2011/2742, reg 21, Sch 2, para 5.

[2.897]
14   Average outstanding electronic money

(1)   Where—
- (a)   an applicant provides payment services that are not related to the issuance of electronic money or carries out any of the activities referred to in regulation 32(1)(b) to (d) and (2); and
- (b)   the amount of outstanding electronic money is unknown in advance,

the applicant may make an assessment for the purposes of regulation 13(3) on the basis of a representative portion assumed to be used for the issuance of electronic money, provided that the representative portion can be reasonably estimated on the basis of historical data and to the satisfaction of the Authority.

(2)   Where an applicant has not completed a sufficiently long period of business to compile historical data adequate to make the assessment under paragraph (1), the applicant must make the assessment on the basis of projected outstanding electronic money as evidenced by its business plan, subject to any adjustments to that plan which are, or have been, required by the Authority.

[2.898]
15   Supplementary provisions

Regulations 7 to 11 apply to registration as a small electronic money institution as they apply to authorisation as an authorised electronic money institution with the following modifications—
- (a)   references to authorisation are to be treated as references to registration;
- (b)   for regulation 8 substitute—

"**8**

(1)   The Authority may, on the application of a small electronic money institution, vary the person's registration by—
- (a)   imposing a requirement such as may, under regulation 7, be included in a registration;
- (b)   cancelling a requirement included in the registration or previously imposed under paragraph (a); or
- (c)   varying such a requirement,

provided that the conditions set out in paragraph (2) continue to be met.

(2)   The conditions that must continue to be met are—
- (a)   the conditions in regulation 13(6) to (10);
- (b)   where applicable, compliance with the requirement in regulation 19(2) to maintain own funds;
- (c)   the condition that the total business activities of the applicant generate average outstanding electronic money that does not exceed 5,000,000 euro; and
- (d)   the condition that the monthly average over any period of 12 months of the total amount of relevant payment transactions does not exceed 3,000,000 euro.

(3)   In paragraph (2)(d) "relevant payment transactions" has the same meaning as in regulation 13.";

- (c)   in regulation 10 for paragraph (1)(e) substitute—

"(e)   the person no longer complies with, or is unlikely to continue to comply with, any of the conditions mentioned in regulation 8(2)(a), (b), (c) and (d);"; and

- (d)   in regulation 11 for paragraph (1)(a) substitute—

"(a)   the person no longer complies with, or is unlikely to continue to comply with, any of the conditions mentioned in regulation 8(2)(a), (b), (c) and (d);".

[2.899]
16   Application to become an authorised electronic money institution where a financial limit is exceeded

Where a small electronic money institution ceases to comply with a condition referred to in regulation 8(2)(c) or (d) (as applied by regulation 15), the institution concerned must, within 30 days of becoming aware of the change in circumstances, apply to become an authorised electronic money institution under regulation 5 if it intends to continue issuing electronic money in the United Kingdom.

Common provisions

[2.900]
17   Duty to notify changes

(1)   If at any time after an applicant has provided the Authority with any information under regulation 5(1), (2) or (4) or 12(1), (2) or (4) and before the Authority has determined the application—
- (a)   there is, or is likely to be, a material change affecting any matter contained in that information; or

(b) it becomes apparent to the applicant that the information is incomplete or contains a material inaccuracy,

the applicant must provide the Authority with details of the change, the complete information or a correction of the inaccuracy (as the case may be) without undue delay, or, in the case of a material change which has not yet taken place, the applicant must provide details of the likely change as soon as the applicant is aware of such change.

(2) The obligation in paragraph (1) also applies to material changes or significant inaccuracies affecting any matter contained in any supplementary information provided pursuant to that paragraph.

(3) Any information to be provided to the Authority under this regulation must be in such form or verified in such manner as it may direct.

[2.901]
18 Electronic money institutions acting without permission

If an electronic money institution issues electronic money or carries on a payment service in the United Kingdom, or purports to do so, other than in accordance with an authorisation or registration granted to it by the Authority under these Regulations, or deemed to be so granted under regulation 74, it is to be taken to have contravened a requirement imposed on it under these Regulations.

PART 3
PRUDENTIAL SUPERVISION AND PASSPORTING

Capital requirements

[2.902]
19 Capital requirements

(1) An authorised electronic money institution must maintain at all times own funds equal to or in excess of—

(a) 350,000 euro; or

(b) the amount of the own funds requirement calculated in accordance with paragraph 13 of Schedule 2 subject to any adjustment directed by the Authority under paragraph 15 of that Schedule,

whichever is the greater.

(2) Where the business activities of a small electronic money institution generate average outstanding electronic money of 500,000 euro or more, it must maintain at all times own funds equal to or in excess of the amount of the own funds requirement calculated in accordance with paragraph 14 of Schedule 2, subject to any adjustment directed by the Authority under paragraph 16 of that Schedule.

(3) Where a small electronic money institution has not completed a sufficiently long period of business to calculate the amount of average outstanding electronic money for the purposes of paragraph (2), it must make an estimate on the basis of projected outstanding electronic money as evidenced by its business plan, subject to any adjustments to that plan which are, or have been, required by the Authority.

Safeguarding

[2.903]
20 Safeguarding requirements

(1) Electronic money institutions must safeguard funds that have been received in exchange for electronic money that has been issued (referred to in this regulation and regulations 21 and 22 as "relevant funds").

(2) Relevant funds must be safeguarded in accordance with either regulation 21 or regulation 22.

(3) Where—

(a) only a proportion of the funds that have been received are to be used for the execution of a payment transaction (with the remainder being used for non-payment services); and

(b) the precise portion attributable to the execution of the payment transaction is variable or unknown in advance,

the relevant funds are such amount as may be reasonably estimated, on the basis of historical data and to the satisfaction of the Authority, to be representative of the portion attributable to the execution of the payment transaction.

(4) Funds received in the form of payment by payment instrument need not be safeguarded until they—

(a) are credited to the electronic money institution's payment account; or

(b) are otherwise made available to the electronic money institution,

provided that such funds must be safeguarded by the end of five business days after the date on which the electronic money has been issued.

(5) In paragraphs (1) to (4) and in regulations 21 to 24 references to an electronic money institution include references to a credit union.

(6)   Regulation 19 of the Payment Services Regulations 2009 applies in relation to funds received by electronic money institutions and credit unions for the execution of payment transactions that are not related to the issuance of electronic money with the following modifications—
   (a)   references to an "authorised payment institution" are to be treated as references to an authorised electronic money institution;
   (b)   references to a "small payment institution" are to be treated as references to—
      (i)   a small electronic money institution; and
      (ii)   a credit union; and
   (c)   references to a "payment transaction" are to be treated as references to a payment transaction that is not related to the issuance of electronic money.

[2.904]
21   Safeguarding option 1

(1)   An electronic money institution must keep relevant funds segregated from any other funds that it holds.

(2)   Where the institution continues to hold the relevant funds at the end of the business day following the day on which they were received it must—
   (a)   place them in a separate account that it holds with an authorised credit institution; or
   (b)   invest the relevant funds in secure, liquid, low-risk assets ("relevant assets") and place those assets in a separate account with an authorised custodian.

(3)   An account in which relevant funds or relevant assets are placed under paragraph (2) must—
   (a)   be designated in such a way as to show that it is an account which is held for the purpose of safeguarding relevant funds or relevant assets in accordance with this regulation; and
   (b)   be used only for holding those funds or assets.

(4)   No person other than the electronic money institution may have any interest in or right over the relevant funds or the relevant assets placed in an account in accordance with paragraph (2)(a) or (b) except as provided by this regulation.

(5)   The institution must keep a record of—
   (a)   any relevant funds segregated in accordance with paragraph (1);
   (b)   any relevant funds placed in an account in accordance with paragraph (2)(a); and
   (c)   any relevant assets placed in an account in accordance with paragraph (2)(b).

(6)   For the purposes of this regulation—
   (a)   assets are both "secure" and "low risk" if they are—
      [(i)   asset items falling into one of the categories set out in Article 336(1) of the capital requirements regulation, for which the specific risk capital charge is no higher than 1.6% but excluding other qualifying items as defined in Article 336(4); or]
      (ii)   units in an undertaking for collective investment in transferable securities which invests solely in the assets mentioned in paragraph (i); and
   (b)   assets are "liquid" if they are approved as such by the Authority.

(7)   In this regulation—
   "authorised credit institution" means a person authorised for the purposes of the 2000 Act to accept deposits or otherwise authorised as a credit institution in accordance with [Article 8 of the capital requirements directive] other than a person in the same group as the electronic money institution;
   "authorised custodian" means a person authorised for the purposes of the 2000 Act to safeguard and administer investments or authorised as an investment firm under Article 5 of Directive 2004/39/EC of 12th April 2004 on markets in financial instruments which holds those investments under regulatory standards at least equivalent to those set out under Article 13 of that directive.

NOTES
   Para (6): sub-para (a)(i) substituted by the Capital Requirements Regulations 2013, SI 2013/3115, reg 46(1), Sch 2, Pt 3, para 75(1), (3)(a).
   Para (7): words in square brackets in definition "authorised credit institution" substituted by SI 2013/3115, reg 46(1), Sch 2, Pt 3, para 75(1), (3)(b).

[2.905]
22   Safeguarding option 2

(1)   An electronic money institution must ensure that—
   (a)   any relevant funds are covered by—
      (i)   an insurance policy with an authorised insurer;
      (ii)   a guarantee from an authorised insurer; or
      (iii)   a guarantee from an authorised credit institution; and
   (b)   the proceeds of any such insurance policy or guarantee are payable upon an insolvency event into a separate account held by the electronic money institution which must—
      (i)   be designated in such a way as to show that it is an account which is held for the purpose of safeguarding relevant funds in accordance with this regulation; and
      (ii)   be used only for holding such proceeds.

Part 2   Statutory Instruments

(2)   No person other than the electronic money institution may have any interest or right over the proceeds placed in an account in accordance with paragraph (1)(b) except as provided by this regulation.

(3)   In this regulation—

"authorised credit institution" has the same meaning as in regulation 21;

"authorised insurer" means a person authorised for the purposes of the 2000 Act to effect and carry out a contract of general insurance as principal or otherwise authorised in accordance with *Article 6 of the First Council Directive 73/239/EEC of 24th July 1973 on the business of direct insurance other than life insurance*, other than a person in the same group as the electronic money institution;

"insolvency event" means any of the following procedures in relation to an electronic money institution—

    (a)   the making of a winding-up order;

    (b)   the passing of a resolution for voluntary winding-up;

    (c)   the entry of the institution into administration;

    (d)   the appointment of a receiver or manager of the institution's property;

    (e)   the approval of a proposed voluntary arrangement (being a composition in satisfaction of debts or a scheme of arrangement);

    (f)   the making of a bankruptcy order;

    (g)   in Scotland, the award of sequestration;

    (h)   the making of any deed of arrangement for the benefit of creditors or, in Scotland, the execution of a trust deed for creditors;

    (i)   the conclusion of any composition contract with creditors;

    (j)   the making of an insolvency administration order or, in Scotland, the execution of a trust deed for creditors;

    (k)   the conclusion of any composition contract with creditors; or

    (l)   the making of an insolvency administration order or, in Scotland, sequestration, in respect of the estate of a deceased person.

NOTES

Para (3): for the words in italics in definition "authorised insurer" there are substituted the words "Article 14 of Directive 2009/138/EC of the European Parliament and of the Council of 25 November 2009 on the taking-up and pursuit of the business of Insurance and Reinsurance (Solvency II) to carry out non-life insurance activities within the meaning of Article 2(2) of that Directive" by the Solvency 2 Regulations 2015, SI 2015/575, reg 60, Sch 2, para 34, as from 1 January 2016.

[2.906]
23   Power of the Authority to exclude assets

In exceptional circumstances the Authority may determine that an asset that would otherwise be secure and low-risk for the purposes of paragraph (2) of regulation 21 by virtue of paragraph (6) of that regulation is not such an asset provided that—

    (a)   the determination is based on an evaluation of the risks associated with the asset, including any risk arising from the security, maturity or value of the asset; and

    (b)   there is adequate justification for the determination.

[2.907]
24   Insolvency events

(1)   Subject to paragraph (2), where there is an insolvency event—

    (a)   the claims of electronic money holders are to be paid from the asset pool in priority to all other creditors; and

    (b)   until all the claims of electronic money holders have been paid, no right of set-off or security right may be exercised in respect of the asset pool except to the extent that the right of set-off relates to fees and expenses in relation to operating an account held in accordance with regulation 21(2)(a) or (b) or 22(1)(b).

(2)   The claims referred to in paragraph (1)(a) shall not be subject to the priority of expenses of an insolvency proceeding except in respect of the costs of distributing the asset pool.

(3)   An electronic money institution must maintain organisational arrangements sufficient to minimise the risk of the loss or diminution of relevant funds or relevant assets through fraud, misuse, negligence or poor administration.

(4)   In this regulation—

"asset pool" means—

    (a)   any relevant funds segregated in accordance with regulation 21(1);

    (b)   any relevant funds held in an account accordance with regulation 21(2)(a);

    (c)   any relevant assets held in an account in accordance with regulation 21(2)(b);

    (d)   any proceeds of an insurance policy or guarantee held in an account in accordance with regulation 22(1)(b);

"insolvency event" has the same meaning as in regulation 22;

"insolvency proceeding" means—

    (a)   winding-up, administration, receivership, bankruptcy or, in Scotland, sequestration;

(b)   a voluntary arrangement, deed of arrangement or trust deed for the benefit of creditors; or

(c)   the administration of the insolvent estate of a deceased person;

"security right" means—

(a)   security for a debt owed by an electronic money institution and includes any charge, lien, mortgage or other security over the asset pool or any part of the asset pool; and

(b)   any charge arising in respect of the expenses of a voluntary arrangement.

[2.908]
25   Accounting and statutory audit

(1)   An electronic money institution which carries on activities other than the issuance of electronic money and the provision of payment services, must provide to the Authority separate accounting information in respect of its issuance of electronic money and provision of payment services.

(2)   Such accounting information must be subject, where relevant, to an auditor's report prepared by the institution's statutory auditors or an audit firm (within the meaning of Directive 2006/43/EC of the European Parliament and of the Council of 17th May 2006 on statutory audits of annual accounts and consolidated accounts).

(3)   A statutory auditor or audit firm ("the auditor") must, in any of the circumstances referred to in paragraph (4), communicate to the Authority information on, or its opinion on, matters—

(a)   of which it has become aware in its capacity as an auditor of an electronic money institution or of a person with close links to an electronic money institution; and

(b)   which relate to the electronic money issued and payment services provided by that institution.

(4)   The circumstances are that—

(a)   the auditor reasonably believes that—

     (i)   there is or has been, or may be or may have been, a contravention of any requirement imposed on the electronic money institution by or under these Regulations; and

     (ii)   the contravention may be of material significance to the Authority in determining whether to exercise, in relation to that institution, any functions conferred on the Authority by these Regulations;

(b)   the auditor reasonably believes that the information on, or the auditor's opinion on, those matters may be of material significance to the Authority in determining whether the institution meets or will continue to meet—

     (i)   in the case of an authorised electronic money institution, the conditions set out in regulation 6(4) to (8) or the requirement in regulation 19(1) to maintain own funds; or

     (ii)   in the case of a small electronic money institution, the conditions set out in regulation 13(6) to (10) or the requirement in regulation 19(2) to maintain own funds;

(c)   the auditor reasonably believes that the institution is not, may not be or may cease to be, a going concern;

(d)   the auditor is precluded from stating in the auditor's report that the annual accounts have been properly prepared in accordance with the Companies Act 2006;

(e)   the auditor is precluded from stating in the auditor's report, where applicable, that the annual accounts give a true and fair view of the matters referred to in section 495 of the Companies Act 2006 (auditor's report on company's annual accounts) including as that section is applied and modified by regulation 39 of the Limited Liability Partnerships (Accounts and Audit) (Application of Companies Act 2006) Regulations 2008 ("the LLP Regulations"); or

(f)   the auditor is required to state in the auditor's report in relation to the person concerned any of the facts referred to in subsection (2), (3) or (5) of section 498 of the Companies Act 2006 (duties of auditor) or, in the case of limited liability partnerships, subsection (2), (3) or (4) of section 498 as applied and modified by regulation 40 of the LLP Regulations.

(5)   In this regulation a person has close links with an authorised electronic money institution ("A") if that person is—

(a)   a parent undertaking of A;

(b)   a subsidiary undertaking of A;

(c)   a parent undertaking of a subsidiary undertaking of A; or

(d)   a subsidiary undertaking of a parent undertaking of A.

[2.909]
26   Outsourcing

(1)   An authorised electronic money institution must notify the Authority of its intention to enter into a contract with another person under which that person will carry out any operational function relating to the issuance, distribution or redemption of electronic money or the provision of payment services ("outsourcing").

Part 2   Statutory Instruments

(2)   Where the institution intends to outsource any important operational function, all of the following conditions must be met—

(a)   the outsourcing is not undertaken in such a way as to impair—
  (i)   the quality of the institution's internal control; or
  (ii)   the ability of the Authority to monitor the authorised electronic money institution's compliance with these Regulations or the Payment Services Regulations 2009;

(b)   the outsourcing does not result in any delegation by the senior management of the institution of responsibility for complying with the requirements imposed by or under these Regulations or the Payment Services Regulations 2009;

(c)   the relationship and obligations of the institution towards its electronic money holders under these Regulations or the Payment Services Regulations 2009 is not substantially altered;

(d)   compliance with the conditions which the institution must observe in order to become an authorised electronic money institution and remain so is not adversely affected; and

(e)   none of the conditions of the institution's authorisation requires removal or variation.

(3)   For the purposes of paragraph (2), an operational function is important if a defect or failure in its performance would materially impair—

(a)   compliance by the institution with these Regulations or the Payment Services Regulations 2009 and any requirement of its authorisation under these Regulations;

(b)   the financial performance of the institution; or

(c)   the soundness or continuity of the institution's electronic money issuance or provision of payment services.

[2.910]
27   Record keeping

(1)   Electronic money institutions must maintain relevant records and keep them for at least five years from the date on which the record was created.

(2)   For the purposes of paragraph (1), records are relevant where they relate to the institution's compliance with this Part and, in particular, would enable the Authority to supervise effectively such compliance.

Exercise of passport rights

[2.911]
28   Notice of intention

(1)   An authorised electronic money institution (other than an institution mentioned in regulation 6(4)(b)) may exercise passport rights.

(2)   Where an authorised electronic money institution intends to exercise its passport rights for the first time in a particular EEA state it must give the Authority, in such manner as the Authority may direct, notice of its intention to do so ("notice of intention") which—

(a)   identifies the electronic money issuance, redemption, distribution or payment services which it seeks to carry on in exercise of those rights in that State;

(b)   gives the names of those responsible for the management of a proposed EEA branch, if any;

(c)   provides details of the organisational structure of a proposed EEA branch, if any; and

(d)   identifies the distributors, if any, whom the institution intends to engage to distribute or redeem electronic money in exercise of its passport rights in that State.

(3)   The Authority must, within one month beginning with the date on which it receives a notice of intention, inform the host state competent authority of—

(a)   the name and address of the authorised electronic money institution; and

(b)   the information contained in the notice.

(4)   Regulation 34 applies where an authorised electronic money institution wishes to exercise its passport rights through an agent.

[2.912]
29   Registration of EEA branch

(1)   If the Authority, taking into account any information received from the host competent authority, has reasonable grounds to suspect that, in connection with the establishment of an EEA branch by an authorised electronic money institution—

(a)   money laundering or terrorist financing within the meaning of the money laundering directive is taking place, has taken place, or has been attempted; or

(b)   the risk of such activities taking place would be increased,

the Authority may refuse to register the EEA branch, or cancel any such registration already made and remove the branch from the register.

(2)   If the Authority proposes to refuse to register, or cancel the registration of, an EEA branch, it must give the relevant authorised electronic money institution a warning notice.

(3)   The Authority must, having considered any representations made in response to the warning notice—

(a)   if it decides not to register the branch, or to cancel its registration, give the authorised electronic money institution a decision notice; or

(b)   if it decides to register the branch, or not to cancel its registration, give the authorised electronic money institution notice of its decision.

(4)   If the Authority decides not to register the branch, or to cancel its registration, the authorised electronic money institution may refer the matter to the Upper Tribunal.

(5)   If the Authority decides to register, or cancel the registration of, an EEA branch, it must update the register as soon as practicable.

(6)   If the Authority decides to cancel the registration the Authority must, where the period for a reference to the Upper Tribunal has expired without a reference being made, update the register as soon as practicable.

[2.913]
30   Supervision of firms exercising passport rights

(1)   Without prejudice to regulation 71, the Authority must co-operate with the relevant host state competent authority or home state competent authority, as the case may be, in relation to the exercise of passport rights by any authorised electronic money institution or EEA authorised electronic money institution.

(2)   The Authority must, in particular—

(a)   notify the host state competent authority, whenever it intends to carry out an on-site inspection in the host state competent authority's territory; and

(b)   provide the host state competent authority or home state competent authority, as the case may be—

(i)   on request, with all relevant information; and

(ii)   on its own initiative with all essential information,

relating to the exercise of the passport rights by an authorised electronic money institution or EEA authorised electronic money institution, including where there is an infringement or suspected infringement of these Regulations, or of the provisions of the electronic money directive, by a distributor, agent, branch or any other entity carrying out activities on behalf of such an institution.

(3)   Where the Authority and the home state competent authority agree, the Authority may carry out on-site inspections on behalf of the home state competent authority in respect of electronic money issuance or payment services provided by an EEA authorised electronic money institution exercising passport rights.

(4)   If the Authority has reasonable grounds to suspect that, in connection with the proposed establishment of a branch or the proposed provision of services by an EEA authorised electronic money institution—

(a)   money laundering or terrorist financing within the meaning of the Money Laundering Regulations 2007 is taking place, has taken place, or has been attempted; or

(b)   the risk of such activities taking place would be increased,

it must inform the relevant home state competent authority of its grounds for suspicion.

[2.914]

31   (*Revoked by the Financial Services and Markets Act 2000 (Regulated Activities) (Amendment) (No 2) Order 2013, SI 2013/1881, art 28, Schedule, para 42, for transitional provisions see Pt 8 thereof at* **[2.1007]** *et seq.*)

PART 4
ADDITIONAL ACTIVITIES AND USE OF DISTRIBUTORS AND AGENTS

[2.915]
32   Additional activities

(1)   Subject to paragraphs (2), (3) and (4), electronic money institutions may, in addition to issuing electronic money, engage in the following activities—

(a)   the provision of payment services;

(b)   the provision of operational and closely related ancillary services, including—

(i)   ensuring the execution of payment transactions;

(ii)   foreign exchange services;

(iii)   safe-keeping activities; and

(iv)   the storage and processing of data;

(c)   the operation of payment systems; and

(d)   business activities other than the issuance of electronic money, subject to any relevant European Union or national law.

Part 2   Statutory Instruments

(2)   Electronic money institutions may grant credit subject to the same conditions as apply to authorised payment institutions by virtue of regulation 27(2) of the Payment Services Regulations 2009 provided that such credit is not granted from funds safeguarded in accordance with regulation 20.

(3)   Any payment account held by an electronic money institution which is used for payment transactions which are not related to the issuance of electronic money must be used only in relation to such payment transactions.

(4)   An authorised electronic money institution which has a branch which is located in the United Kingdom and whose head office is situated in a territory which is outside the EEA may only provide payment services if those services are related to the issuance of electronic money.

[2.916]
33   Use of distributors and agents

(1)   An electronic money institution may distribute or redeem electronic money through a distributor or agent.

(2)   An electronic money institution may not issue electronic money through a distributor, agent or any other entity acting on its behalf.

(3)   An authorised electronic money institution may engage a distributor or an agent to distribute or redeem electronic money in the exercise of its passport rights.

[2.917]
34   Requirement for agents to be registered

(1)   An electronic money institution may provide payment services in the United Kingdom through an agent only if the agent is included on the register.

(2)   An authorised electronic money institution may provide payment services in the exercise of its passport rights through an agent only if the agent is included on the register.

(3)   An application for an agent to be included on the register must—
  (a)   contain, or be accompanied by, the following information—
    (i)   the name and address of the agent;
    (ii)   where relevant, a description of the internal control mechanisms that will be used by the agent—
      (aa)   in the case of an agent in the United Kingdom, to comply with the Money Laundering Regulations 2007; and
      (bb)   in the case of an EEA agent, to comply with provisions of the money laundering directive; and
    (iii)   the identity of the directors and persons responsible for the management of the agent and evidence that they are fit and proper persons; and
    (iv)   such other information as the Authority may reasonably require; and
  (b)   be made in such manner as the Authority may direct.

(4)   Different directions may be given, and different requirements imposed, in relation to different applications or categories of application.

(5)   At any time after receiving an application and before determining it, the Authority may require the applicant to provide it with such further information as it reasonably considers necessary to enable it to determine the application.

(6)   The Authority may refuse to include the agent on the register only if—
  (a)   it has not received the information referred to in paragraph (3)(a), or is not satisfied that such information is correct;
  (b)   it is not satisfied that the directors and persons responsible for the management of the agent are fit and proper persons;
  (c)   it has reasonable grounds to suspect that, in connection with the provision of services through the agent—
    (i)   money laundering or terrorist financing within the meaning of the money laundering directive (or, in the United Kingdom, the Money Laundering Regulations 2007) is taking place, has taken place, or has been attempted; or
    (ii)   the risk of such activities taking place would be increased.

(7)   Where—
  (a)   an authorised electronic money institution intends to provide payment services through an EEA agent; and
  (b)   the Authority proposes to include the EEA agent on the register,
the Authority must inform the host state competent authority and take account of its opinion (if provided within such reasonable period as the Authority specifies) on any of the matters referred to in paragraph (6)(b) or (c).

(8)   The Authority must decide whether to include the agent on the register within a reasonable period of it having received a completed application.

(9)   If the Authority proposes to refuse to include the agent on the register, it must give the applicant a warning notice.

(10)   The Authority must, having considered any representations made in response to the warning notice—

  (a)   if it decides not to include the agent on the register, give the applicant a decision notice; or

  (b)   if it decides to include the agent on the register, give the applicant notice of its decision, stating the date on which the registration takes effect.

(11)   If the Authority decides not to include the agent on the register the applicant may refer the matter to the Upper Tribunal.

(12)   If the Authority decides to include the agent on the register, it must update the register as soon as practicable.

(13)   An application under paragraph (3) may be combined with an application under regulation 5 or 12, in which case the application must be determined in the manner set out in regulation 9 (if relevant, as applied by regulation 15).

(14)   An electronic money institution must ensure that an agent acting on its behalf informs payment service users of the agency arrangement.

[2.918]
35   Removal of agents from the register

(1)   The Authority may remove an agent of an electronic money institution from the register where—

  (a)   the institution requests, or consents to, the agent's removal from the register;

  (b)   the institution has obtained registration through false statements or any other irregular means;

  (c)   regulation 34(6)(b) or (c) applies;

  (d)   the removal is desirable in order to protect the interests of consumers; or

  (e)   the agent's provision of payment services is otherwise unlawful.

(2)   Where the Authority proposes to remove an agent from the register, other than at the request of the institution, it must give the institution a warning notice.

(3)   The Authority must, having considered any representations made in response to the warning notice—

  (a)   if it decides to remove the agent, give the institution a decision notice; or

  (b)   if it decides not to remove the agent, give the institution notice of its decision.

(4)   If the Authority decides to remove the agent, other than at the request of the institution, the institution may refer the matter to the Upper Tribunal.

(5)   Where the period for a reference to the Upper Tribunal has expired without a reference being made, the Authority must as soon as practicable update the register accordingly.

[2.919]
36   Reliance

(1)   Where an electronic money institution relies on a third party for the performance of operational functions it must take all reasonable steps to ensure that these Regulations and the Payment Services Regulations 2009 are complied with.

(2)   Without prejudice to paragraph (1), an electronic money institution is responsible, to the same extent as if it had expressly permitted it, for anything done or omitted by any of its employees or by a distributor, agent, branch or any other entity issuing, distributing or redeeming electronic money, or providing payment services, on its behalf or to which activities are outsourced.

[2.920]
37   Duty to notify change in circumstance

(1)   Where it becomes apparent to an electronic money institution that there is, or is likely to be, a significant change in circumstances which is relevant to—

  (a)   in the case of an authorised electronic money institution—

  (i)   its fulfilment of any of the conditions set out in regulation 6(4) to (8) or the requirement in regulation 19(1) to maintain own funds; or

  (ii)   the issuance, distribution or redemption of electronic money, or the payment services, which it seeks to carry on in exercise of its passport rights;

  (b)   in the case of a small electronic money institution, its fulfilment of any of the conditions set out in regulation 8(2) (as applied by regulation 15); or

  (c)   in the case of the use of an agent to provide payment services, the matters referred to in regulation 34(6)(b) and (c),

it must provide the Authority with details of the change without undue delay, or, in the case of a substantial change in circumstance which has not yet taken place, details of the likely change a reasonable period before it takes place.

(2)   An electronic money institution must inform the Authority of any material change in the measures that it has taken in accordance with regulation 21 or 22 to safeguard funds that have been received in exchange for electronic money.

(3) Any information to be provided to the Authority under this regulation must be in such form or verified in such manner as it may direct.

PART 5
ISSUANCE AND REDEEMABILITY OF ELECTRONIC MONEY

[2.921]
38 Application of Part 5

This Part applies to the issuance and redemption of electronic money where the issuance or redemption is carried on from an establishment maintained by an electronic money issuer or its agent in the United Kingdom.

[2.922]
39 Issuance and redeemability

An electronic money issuer must—
- (a)   on receipt of funds, issue without delay electronic money at par value; and
- (b)   at the request of the electronic money holder, redeem—
  - (i)   at any time; and
  - (ii)   at par value,
  the monetary value of the electronic money held.

[2.923]
40 Conditions of redemption

An electronic money issuer must ensure—
- (a)   that the contract between the electronic money issuer and the electronic money holder clearly and prominently states the conditions of redemption, including any fees relating to redemption; and
- (b)   that the electronic money holder is informed of those conditions before being bound by any contract.

[2.924]
41 Fees for redemption

(1)   Redemption may be subject to a fee only where the fee is stated in the contract in accordance with regulation 40(a), and—
- (a)   redemption is requested before the termination of the contract;
- (b)   the contract provides for a termination date and the electronic money holder terminates the contract before that date; or
- (c)   redemption is requested more than one year after the date of termination of the contract.

(2)   Any fees for redemption must be proportionate and commensurate with the costs actually incurred by the electronic money issuer.

[2.925]
42 Amount of redemption

(1)   Where before the termination of the contract an electronic money holder makes a request for redemption, the electronic money holder may request redemption of the monetary value of the electronic money in whole or in part, and the electronic money issuer must redeem the amount so requested subject to any fee imposed in accordance with regulation 41.

(2)   Where an electronic money holder makes a request for redemption on, or up to one year after, the date of the termination of the contract, the electronic money issuer must redeem—
- (a)   the total monetary value of the electronic money held; or
- (b)   if the electronic money issuer carries out any business activities other than the issuance of electronic money and it is not known in advance what proportion of funds received by it is to be used for electronic money, all the funds requested by the electronic money holder.

[2.926]
43 Requests for redemption

An electronic money issuer is not required under regulation 39(b) to redeem the monetary value of electronic money where the electronic money holder makes a request for redemption more than six years after the date of termination of the contract.

[2.927]
44 Redemption rights of persons other than consumers

Regulations 41 and 42 shall not apply in the case of a person, other than a consumer, who accepts electronic money and, in such a case, the redemption rights of that person shall be subject to the contract between that person and the electronic money issuer.

[2.928]
45   Prohibition of interest

An electronic money issuer must not award—
- (a)   interest in respect of the holding of electronic money; or
- (b)   any other benefit related to the length of time during which an electronic money holder holds electronic money.

[2.929]
46   Termination of a contract

For the purposes of this Part a contract between an electronic money issuer and an electronic money holder terminates when the right to use electronic money for the purpose of making payment transactions ceases.

PART 6
THE AUTHORITY

The functions of the Authority

[2.930]
47   Functions of the Authority

(1)   The Authority is to have the functions conferred on it by these Regulations.

(2)   In discharging its function of determining the general policy and principles by reference to which it performs particular functions under these Regulations, the Authority must have regard to—
- (a)   the need to use its resources in the most efficient and economic way;
- (b)   the responsibilities of those who manage the affairs of electronic money issuers;
- (c)   the principle that a burden or restriction which is imposed on a person, or on the carrying on of an activity, should be proportionate to the benefits, considered in general terms, which are expected to result from the imposition of that burden or restriction;
- (d)   the desirability of facilitating innovation in connection with the issuance of electronic money and the provision of payment services;
- (e)   the international character of financial services and markets and the desirability of maintaining the competitive position of the United Kingdom;
- (f)   the need to minimise the adverse effects on competition that may arise from anything done in the discharge of those functions;
- (g)   the desirability of facilitating competition in relation to the issuance of electronic money and the provision of payment services; and
- (h)   the desirability of enhancing the understanding and knowledge of members of the public of financial matters (including the United Kingdom financial system).

Supervision and enforcement

[2.931]
48   Monitoring and enforcement

(1)   The Authority must maintain arrangements designed to enable it to determine whether—
- (a)   persons on whom requirements are imposed by or under Part 2, 3 or 4 of these Regulations are complying with them;
- (b)   there has been any contravention of regulation 63(1), 64(1) or 66(1) or (2).

(2)   The Authority may maintain arrangements designed to enable it to determine whether persons on whom requirements are imposed by or under Part 5 of these Regulations are complying with them.

(3)   The arrangements referred to in paragraphs (1) and (2) may provide for functions to be performed on behalf of the Authority by any body or person who is, in its opinion, competent to perform them.

(4)   The Authority must also maintain arrangements for enforcing the provisions of these Regulations.

(5)   Paragraph (3) does not affect the Authority's duty under paragraph (1).

[2.932]
49   Reporting requirements

(1)   An electronic money issuer must give the Authority such information in respect of its issuance of electronic money and provision of payment services and its compliance with requirements imposed by or under Parts 2 to 5 of these Regulations as the Authority may direct.

(2)   Information required under this regulation must be given at such times and in such form, and verified in such manner, as the Authority may direct.

[2.933]
50   Public censure

If the Authority considers that an electronic money issuer has contravened a requirement imposed on it by or under these Regulations the Authority may publish a statement to that effect.

[2.934]
51   Financial penalties

(1)   The Authority may impose a penalty of such amount as it considers appropriate on—
  (a)   an electronic money issuer who has contravened a requirement imposed on it by or under these Regulations; or
  (b)   a person who has contravened regulation 63(1), 64(1) or 66(1) or (2).

(2)   A penalty under this regulation is a debt due from that person to the Authority, and is recoverable accordingly.

[2.935]
52   Suspending authorisation etc

(1)   If the Authority considers that an electronic money institution has contravened a requirement imposed on it by or under these Regulations, it may—
  (a)   suspend, for such period as it considers appropriate, the institution's authorisation or, as the case may be, registration; or
  (b)   impose, for such period as it considers appropriate, such limitations or other restrictions in relation to the carrying on of electronic money issuance or payment services business by the institution as it considers appropriate.

(2)   The period for which a suspension or restriction is to have effect may not exceed 12 months.

(3)   A suspension may relate only to the carrying on of an activity in specified circumstances.

(4)   A restriction may, in particular, be imposed so as to require the institution concerned to take, or refrain from taking, specified action.

(5)   The Authority may—
  (a)   withdraw a suspension or restriction; or
  (b)   vary a suspension or restriction so as to reduce the period for which it has effect or otherwise to limit its effect.

(6)   Any one or more of the powers in—
  (a)   paragraph (1)(a) and (b) of this regulation; and
  (b)   regulations 50 and 51,
may be exercised in relation to the same contravention.

[2.936]
53   Proposal to take disciplinary measures

(1)   Where the Authority proposes—
  (a)   to publish a statement under regulation 50;
  (b)   to impose a penalty under regulation 51; or
  (c)   to suspend an institution's authorisation or registration or impose a restriction under regulation 52,
it must give the person concerned a warning notice.

(2)   The warning notice must set out the terms of the statement, the amount of the penalty or the period for which the suspension or restriction is to have effect, as the case may be.

(3)   If, having considered any representations made in response to the warning notice, the Authority decides to take any of the steps mentioned in paragraph (1), it must without delay give the person concerned a decision notice.

(4)   The decision notice must set out the terms of any statement, the amount of any penalty or the period for which any suspension or restriction is to have effect, as the case may be.

(5)   If the Authority decides to take any of the steps mentioned in paragraph (1) the person concerned may refer the matter to the Upper Tribunal.

(6)   Sections 210 (statements of policy) and 211 (statements of policy: procedure) of the 2000 Act apply—
  (a)   in respect of the imposition of penalties under regulation 51 as they apply in respect of the imposition of penalties under Part 14 of the 2000 Act (disciplinary measures); and
  (b)   in respect of the imposition of a suspension or restriction under regulation 52 as they apply in respect of the imposition of a suspension or restriction under that Part of that Act.

(7)   After a statement under regulation 50 is published, the Authority must send a copy of it to the person concerned and to any person to whom a copy of the decision notice was given under section 393(4) of the 2000 Act (third party rights) (as applied by paragraph 8 of Schedule 3 to these Regulations).

[2.937]
54   Injunctions

(1)   If, on the application of the Authority, the court is satisfied—
  (a)   that there is a reasonable likelihood that any person will contravene a requirement imposed by or under these Regulations; or
  (b)   that any person has contravened such a requirement and that there is a reasonable likelihood that the contravention will continue or be repeated,

the court may make an order restraining (or, in Scotland, an interdict prohibiting) the contravention.

(2) If, on the application of the Authority, the court is satisfied—

    (a)   that any person has contravened a requirement imposed by or under these Regulations; and

    (b)   that there are steps which could be taken for remedying the contravention,

the court may make an order requiring that person, and any other person who appears to have been knowingly concerned in the contravention, to take such steps as the court may direct to remedy it.

(3) If, on the application of the Authority, the court is satisfied that any person may have—

    (a)   contravened a requirement imposed by or under these Regulations; or

    (b)   been knowingly concerned in the contravention of such a requirement,

it may make an order restraining (or, in Scotland, an interdict prohibiting) them from disposing of, or otherwise dealing with, any assets of theirs which it is satisfied that they are reasonably likely to dispose of or otherwise deal with.

(4) The jurisdiction conferred by this regulation is exercisable by the High Court and the Court of Session.

(5) In paragraph (2), references to remedying a contravention include references to mitigating its effect.

[2.938]
55 Power of Authority to require restitution

(1) The Authority may exercise the power in paragraph (2) if it is satisfied that an electronic money issuer (referred to in this regulation and regulation 56 as "the person concerned") has contravened a requirement imposed by or under these Regulations, or been knowingly concerned in the contravention of such a requirement, and that—

    (a)   profits have accrued to the person concerned as a result of the contravention; or

    (b)   one or more persons have suffered loss or been otherwise adversely affected as a result of the contravention.

(2) The power referred to in paragraph (1) is a power to require the person concerned, in accordance with such arrangements as the Authority considers appropriate, to pay to the appropriate person or distribute among the appropriate persons such amount as appears to the Authority to be just having regard—

    (a)   in a case within sub-paragraph (a) of paragraph (1), to the profits appearing to the Authority to have accrued;

    (b)   in a case within sub-paragraph (b) of that paragraph, to the extent of the loss or other adverse effect;

    (c)   in a case within both of those sub-paragraphs, to the profits appearing to the Authority to have accrued and to the extent of the loss or other adverse effect.

(3) In paragraph (2) "appropriate person" means a person appearing to the Authority to be someone—

    (a)   to whom the profits mentioned in paragraph (1)(a) are attributable; or

    (b)   who has suffered the loss or adverse effect mentioned in paragraph (1)(b).

[2.939]
56 Proposal to require restitution

(1) If the Authority proposes to exercise the power in regulation 55(2), it must give the person concerned a warning notice.

(2) The warning notice must state the amount which the Authority proposes to require the person concerned to pay or distribute as mentioned in regulation 55(2).

(3) If, having considered any representations made in response to the warning notice, the Authority decides to exercise the power in regulation 55(2), it must without delay give the person concerned a decision notice.

(4) The decision notice must—

    (a)   state the amount that the person concerned is to pay or distribute;

    (b)   identify the person or persons to whom that amount is to be paid or among whom that amount is to be distributed; and

    (c)   state the arrangements in accordance with which the payment or distribution is to be made.

(5) If the Authority decides to exercise the power in regulation 55(2), the person concerned may refer the matter to the Upper Tribunal.

[2.940]
57 Restitution orders

(1) The court may, on the application of the Authority, make an order under paragraph (2) if it is satisfied that an electronic money issuer has contravened a requirement imposed by or under these Regulations, or been knowingly concerned in the contravention of such a requirement, and that—

    (a)   profits have accrued to the electronic money issuer as a result of the contravention; or

    (b)   one or more persons have suffered loss or been otherwise adversely affected as a result of the contravention.

(2)   The court may order the electronic money issuer to pay to the Authority such sum as appears to the court to be just having regard—

(a)   in a case within sub-paragraph (a) of paragraph (1), to the profits appearing to the court to have accrued;

(b)   in a case within sub-paragraph (b) of that paragraph, to the extent of the loss or other adverse effect;

(c)   in a case within both those sub-paragraphs, to the profits appearing to the court to have accrued and to the extent of the loss or other adverse effect.

(3)   Any amount paid to the Authority in pursuance of an order under paragraph (2) must be paid by it to such qualifying person or distributed by it among such qualifying persons as the court may direct.

(4)   In paragraph (3), "qualifying person" means a person appearing to the court to be someone—

(a)   to whom the profits mentioned in paragraph (1)(a) are attributable; or

(b)   who has suffered the loss or adverse effect mentioned in paragraph (1)(b).

(5)   On an application under paragraph (1) the court may require the electronic money issuer to supply it with such accounts or other information as it may require for any one or more of the following purposes—

(a)   establishing whether any and, if so, what profits have accrued to them as mentioned in sub-paragraph (a) of that paragraph;

(b)   establishing whether any person or persons have suffered any loss or adverse effect as mentioned in sub-paragraph (b) of that paragraph; and

(c)   determining how any amounts are to be paid or distributed under paragraph (3).

(6)   The court may require any accounts or other information supplied under paragraph (5) to be verified in such manner as it may direct.

(7)   The jurisdiction conferred by this regulation is exercisable by the High Court and the Court of Session.

(8)   Nothing in this regulation affects the right of any person other than the Authority to bring proceedings in respect of the matters to which this regulation applies.

[2.941]
58   Complaints

(1)   The Authority must maintain arrangements designed to enable electronic money holders and other interested parties to submit complaints to it that a requirement imposed by or under Part 5 of these Regulations has been breached by an electronic money issuer.

(2)   Where it considers it appropriate, the Authority must include in any reply to a complaint under paragraph (1) details of the ombudsman scheme established under Part 16 of the 2000 Act (the ombudsman scheme).

Miscellaneous

[2.942]
59   Costs of supervision

[(1)   The functions of the Authority under these Regulations are to be treated for the purposes of paragraph 23 (fees) of Part 3 of Schedule 1ZA to the 2000 Act as functions conferred on the Authority under that Act with the following modifications—

(a)   section 1B(5)(a) of the 2000 Act (the FCA's general duties) does not apply to the making of rules under paragraph 23 of Part 3 of Schedule 1ZA by virtue of this regulation;

(b)   rules made under paragraph 23 of Part 3 of Schedule 1ZA by virtue of this regulation are not to be treated as regulating provisions for the purposes of section 140A(1) of the 2000 Act (competition scrutiny);

(c)   paragraph 23(7) does not apply.]

[(2)   The Authority must in respect of each of its financial years pay to the Treasury any amounts received by it during the year by way of penalties imposed under regulation 51.

(3)   The Treasury may give directions to the Authority as to how the Authority is to comply with its duty under paragraph (2).

(4)   The directions may in particular—

(a)   specify the time when any payment is required to be made to the Treasury, and

(b)   require the Authority to provide the Treasury at specified times with information relating to penalties that the Authority has imposed under regulation 51.

(5)   The Treasury must pay into the Consolidated Fund any sums received by them under this regulation.]

NOTES

Para (1): substituted by the Financial Services Act 2012 (Consequential Amendments and Transitional Provisions) Order 2013, SI 2013/472, art 3, Sch 2, para 196(1), (3).

Paras (2)–(5): substituted, for original para (2), by the Payment to Treasury of Penalties Regulations 2013, SI 2013/429, reg 2(5).

[2.943]
[59A Credit agreements

Schedule 2A, which contains provisions concerning credit agreements, has effect.]

NOTES

Commencement: 14 February 2014 (for certain purposes); 1 April 2014 (otherwise).

Inserted by the Financial Services and Markets Act 2000 (Regulated Activities) (Amendment) Order 2014, SI 2014/366, art 18(1), (2).

[2.944]
60   Guidance

(1)   The Authority may give guidance consisting of such information and advice as it considers appropriate with respect to—

(a)   the operation of these Regulations;

(b)   any matters relating to the functions of the Authority under these Regulations;

(c)   any other matters about which it appears to the Authority to be desirable to give information or advice in connection with these Regulations.

(2)   The Authority may—

(a)   publish its guidance;

(b)   offer copies of its published guidance for sale at a reasonable price;

(c)   if it gives guidance in response to a request made by any person, make a reasonable charge for that guidance.

[2.945]
61   Authority's exemption from liability in damages

The functions of the Authority under these Regulations are to be treated for the purposes of [paragraph 25 (exemption from liability in damages) of Part 4 of Schedule 1ZA to the 2000 Act] as functions conferred on the Authority under that Act.

NOTES

Words in square brackets substituted by the Financial Services Act 2012 (Consequential Amendments and Transitional Provisions) Order 2013, SI 2013/472, art 3, Sch 2, para 196(1), (4).

62   *(Introduces Sch 3 to these Regulations; outside the scope of this work.)*

PART 7
GENERAL

Offences

[2.946]
63   Prohibition on issuing electronic money by persons other than electronic money issuers

(1)   A person may not issue electronic money in the United Kingdom, or purport to do so, unless the person is—

(a)   an authorised electronic money institution;

(b)   a small electronic money institution;

(c)   an EEA authorised electronic money institution exercising its passport rights;

(d)   a credit institution authorised in the UK or exercising an EEA right in accordance with Part 2 of Schedule 3 to the 2000 Act (exercise of passport rights by EEA firms);

(e)   the Post Office Limited;

(f)   the Bank of England, the European Central Bank or a national central bank of an EEA state other than the United Kingdom;

(g)   a government department or local authority;

(h)   a credit union;

(i)   a municipal bank; or

(j)   the National Savings Bank.

(2)   A person who contravenes paragraph (1) is guilty of an offence and is liable—

(a)   on summary conviction, to imprisonment for a term not exceeding three months or to a fine not exceeding level 5 on the standard scale, or both;

(b)   on conviction on indictment, to imprisonment for a term not exceeding two years, or to a fine, or both.

[2.947]
64   False claims to be an electronic money issuer

(1)   A person who does not fall within any of sub-paragraphs (a) to (j) of regulation 63(1) may not—

(a)   describe themselves (in whatever terms) as a person falling within any of those sub-paragraphs; or

(b)   behave, or otherwise hold themselves out, in a manner which indicates (or which is reasonably likely to be understood as indicating) that they are such a person.

(2)   A person who contravenes paragraph (1) is guilty of an offence and is liable on summary conviction to a fine not exceeding level 5 on the standard scale.

[2.948]
65   Defences

In proceedings for an offence under regulation 63 or 64 it is a defence for the accused to show that they took all reasonable precautions and exercised all due diligence to avoid committing the offence.

[2.949]
66   Misleading the authority

(1)   A person may not, in purported compliance with any requirement imposed by or under these Regulations, knowingly or recklessly give the Authority information which is false or misleading in any material particular.

(2)   A person may not—
  (a)   provide any information to another person, knowing the information to be false or misleading in a material particular; or
  (b)   recklessly provide to another person any information which is false or misleading in a material particular,
knowing that the information is to be used for the purpose of providing information to the Authority in connection with its functions under these Regulations.

(3)   A person who contravenes paragraph (1) or (2) is guilty of an offence and is liable—
  (a)   on summary conviction, to a fine not exceeding level 5 on the standard scale;
  (b)   on conviction on indictment, to a fine.

[2.950]
67   Restriction on penalties

A person who is convicted of an offence under these Regulations is not liable to a penalty under regulation 51 in respect of the same contravention of a requirement imposed by or under these Regulations.

[2.951]
68   Liability of officers of bodies corporate etc

(1)   If an offence under these Regulations committed by a body corporate is shown—
  (a)   to have been committed with the consent or connivance of an officer; or
  (b)   to be attributable to any neglect on their part,
the officer as well as the body corporate is guilty of the offence and liable to be proceeded against and punished accordingly.

(2)   If the affairs of a body corporate are managed by its members, paragraph (1) applies in relation to the acts and defaults of a member in connection with such member's functions of management as if the member were a director of the body.

(3)   If an offence under these Regulations committed by a partnership is shown—
  (a)   to have been committed with the consent or connivance of a partner; or
  (b)   to be attributable to any neglect on their part,
the partner as well as the partnership is guilty of the offence and liable to be proceeded against and punished accordingly.

(4)   If an offence under these Regulations committed by an unincorporated association (other than a partnership) is shown—
  (a)   to have been committed with the consent or connivance of an officer; or
  (b)   to be attributable to any neglect of such officer,
the officer as well as the association is guilty of the offence and liable to be proceeded against and punished accordingly.

(5)   In this regulation—
  "officer"—
      (a)   in relation to a body corporate, means a director, manager, secretary, chief executive, member of the committee of management, or a person purporting to act in that capacity; and
      (b)   in relation to an unincorporated association, means any officer of the association or any member of its governing body, or a person purporting to act in such capacity;
  "partner" includes a person purporting to act as a partner.

[2.952]
69   Prosecution

(1)   Proceedings for an offence under these Regulations may be instituted only—
  (a)   by the Authority; or
  (b)   by or with the consent of the Director of Public Prosecutions.

(2)   Paragraph (1) does not apply to proceedings in Scotland.

[2.953]

70   Proceedings against unincorporated bodies

(1)   Proceedings for an offence alleged to have been committed by a partnership or an unincorporated association must be brought in the name of the partnership or association (and not in that of its members).

(2)   A fine imposed on the partnership or association on its conviction of an offence is to be paid out of the funds of the partnership or association.

(3)   Rules of court relating to the service of documents are to have effect as if the partnership or association were a body corporate.

(4)   In proceedings for an offence brought against the partnership or association—
  (a)   section 33 of the Criminal Justice Act 1925 (procedure on charge of offence against corporation) and section 46 of, and Schedule 3 to, the Magistrates' Courts Act 1980 (corporations) apply as they do in relation to a body corporate;
  (b)   section 70 (of the Criminal Procedure (Scotland) Act 1995 (proceedings against bodies corporate) applies as it does in relation to a body corporate;
  (c)   section 18 of the Criminal Justice (Northern Ireland) Act 1945 (procedure on charge) and Schedule 4 to the Magistrates' Courts (Northern Ireland) Order 1981 (corporations) apply as they do in relation to a body corporate.

(5)   Summary proceedings for an offence under these Regulations may be taken—
  (a)   against a body corporate or unincorporated association at any place at which it has a place of business;
  (b)   against an individual at any place where they are for the time being.

(6)   Paragraph (5) does not affect any jurisdiction exercisable apart from this regulation.

Duties of the Authority and the Commissioners to co-operate

[2.954]

71   Duty to co-operate and exchange information

(1)   The Authority and the Commissioners of Her Majesty's Revenue and Customs ("the Commissioners") must take such steps as they consider appropriate to co-operate with each other and—
  (a)   the competent authorities, designated under Article 3 of the electronic money directive, or referred to in Article 13 of that directive, of EEA states other than the United Kingdom;
  (b)   the European Central Bank, the Bank of England and the national central banks of EEA states other than the United Kingdom; and
  (c)   any other relevant competent authorities designated under European Union law or the law of the United Kingdom or any other EEA state which is applicable to electronic money issuers,
for the purposes of the exercise by those bodies of their functions under the electronic money directive and other relevant European Union or national legislation.

(2)   Subject to the requirements of the Data Protection Act 1998, sections 348 and 349 of the 2000 Act (as applied with modifications by paragraph 6 of Schedule 3 to these Regulations), regulation 49A of the Money Laundering Regulations 2007 and any other applicable restrictions on the disclosure of information, the Authority and the Commissioners may provide information to each other and—
  (a)   the bodies mentioned in paragraph (1)(a) and (c);
  (b)   the European Central Bank, the Bank of England and the national central banks of EEA states other than the United Kingdom when acting in their capacity as monetary and oversight authorities;
  (c)   where relevant, other public authorities responsible for the oversight of payment and settlement systems,
for the purposes of the exercise by those bodies of their functions under the electronic money directive and other relevant European Union or national legislation.

Actions for breach of requirements

[2.955]

72   Right to bring actions

(1)   A contravention—
  (a)   which is to be taken to have occurred by virtue of regulation 18;
  (b)   of a requirement imposed by regulation 20, 21, 22 or 24; or
  (c)   of a requirement imposed by or under Part 5,
is actionable at the suit of a private person who suffers loss as a result of the contravention, subject to the defences and other incidents applying to actions for breach of statutory duty.

(2)   A person acting in a fiduciary or representative capacity may bring an action under paragraph (1) on behalf of a private person if any remedy—
  (a)   will be exclusively for the benefit of the private person; and
  (b)   cannot be obtained by way of an action brought otherwise than at the suit of the fiduciary or representative.

(3) In this regulation "private person" means—
  (a) any individual, except where the individual suffers the loss in question in the course of issuing electronic money or providing payment services; and
  (b) any person who is not an individual, except where that person suffers the loss in question in the course of carrying on business of any kind,
but does not include a government, a local authority (in the United Kingdom or elsewhere) or an international organisation.

[2.956]
73 Prohibition on contracting-out
A term contained in an agreement between an electronic money issuer and an electronic money holder or a payment service user is void if, and to the extent that, it is inconsistent with a provision for the protection of an electronic money holder or a payment service user contained in these Regulations or the Payment Services Regulations 2009.

Transitional provisions

[2.957]
74 Persons with a Part 4 permission
(1) Any person who—
  (a) has a Part 4 permission in respect of the activity of issuing electronic money;
  (b) before 30th April 2011 has carried on that activity in accordance with that permission; and
  (c) is not a person mentioned in any of paragraphs (c) to (j) of the definition in regulation 2(1) of electronic money issuer,
shall be deemed to have been granted authorisation by the Authority under regulation 9.

(2) A person who is deemed to have been granted authorisation by virtue of paragraph (1) must before 1st July 2011—
  (a) notify the Authority whether it wishes to become an authorised electronic money institution or to be registered as a small electronic money institution; and
  (b) provide the Authority with such information as it may reasonably require ("the required information").

(3) Where a person notifies the Authority before 1st July 2011 that it wishes to become an authorised electronic money institution or that it wishes to be registered as a small electronic money institution, the Authority must decide whether to include the person on the register as an authorised electronic money institution or as a small electronic institution, and—
  (a) if the Authority decides to include the person on the register, the person's authorisation shall cease to be deemed to have been granted by virtue of paragraph (1) at the time of such inclusion;
  (b) if the Authority decides not to include the person on the register, the person's authorisation shall cease to be so deemed when the period for a reference to the Upper Tribunal has elapsed without a reference being made or, if the matter is referred, at such time as the Tribunal may direct.

(4) Where a person who is deemed to have been granted authorisation by virtue of paragraph (1)—
  (a) notifies the Authority before 1st July 2011 that it does not wish to be an electronic money institution; or
  (b) fails to make by that date a notification in accordance with paragraph (2)(a),
such authorisation shall cease to be so deemed on 30th October 2011 or, if the person's Part 4 permission is cancelled before that date, on the cancellation of the permission.

(5) If the Authority decides to include the person on the register as an authorised electronic money institution or a small electronic money institution it must—
  (a) give the person notice of its decision; and
  (b) update the register as soon as practicable.

(6) The Authority may decide that a person is not to be included on the register only if—
  (a) it has not received the required information before 1st July 2011;
  (b) any of the conditions in regulation 6(3) to (8) or, as the case may be, regulation 13(3) to (10) ("the required conditions") is not met in respect of that person; or
  (c) it appears to the Authority that the person is unlikely to issue electronic money within 12 months beginning with 1st July 2011.

(7) If the Authority proposes to decide not to include a person on the register it must give the person a warning notice.

(8) The Authority must, having considered any representations in response to the warning notice—
  (a) if it decides not to include the person on the register, give the person a decision notice; or
  (b) if it decides to include the person on the register, give the person notice of its decision.

(9) If the Authority gives the person a decision notice, the person may refer the matter to the Upper Tribunal.

(10) Where a person is deemed to have been granted authorisation by virtue of paragraph (1)—

(a)   the duty to which the Authority is subject under regulation 4(1) to maintain a register shall not apply in respect of it; and

(b)   Parts 3 and 4 shall not apply to it.

(11)   A Part 4 permission in respect of the activity of issuing electronic money, which has not been cancelled, shall cease—

(a)   in the case of a person falling within paragraph (3)(a), on 30th April 2011 or, if later, at the time of the person's inclusion on the register as an electronic money institution;

(b)   in the case of a person falling within paragraph (3)(b), at the time at which the person's authorisation ceases to be deemed to have been granted;

(c)   in the case of a person falling within paragraph (4), on 30th October 2011.

(12)   In this regulation, "Part 4 permission" has the same meaning as in the 2000 Act.

[2.958]
75   EEA firms

(1)   Any person who—

(a)   immediately before 30th April 2011 is an electronic money institution;

(b)   is an EEA firm qualifying for authorisation under Schedule 3 to the 2000 Act in respect of the activity of issuing electronic money; and

(c)   before 30th April 2011 has carried on that activity,

may continue until 30th October 2011 to carry on that activity and engage in any related activity.

(2)   Parts 5 and 6 shall apply to a person falling within paragraph (1) as if the person were an EEA authorised electronic money institution.

(3)   In this regulation "electronic money institution" has the meaning given in Article 1(3)(a) of Directive 2000/46/EC of the European Parliament and of the Council of 18th September 2000 on the taking up, pursuit of and prudential supervision of the business of electronic money institutions ("the first electronic money directive").

(4)   In this regulation and in regulation 76 "related activity" means an activity mentioned in Article 1(5) of the first electronic money directive.

[2.959]
76   Certified persons

(1)   Any person who—

(a)   has a certificate (which has not been revoked) given by the Authority under article 9C of the Financial Services and Markets 2000 (Regulated Activities) Order 2001 ("the Order"); and

(b)   before 30th April 2011 has carried on the activity of issuing electronic money in accordance with that certificate,

may continue to carry on that activity in accordance with that certificate and engage in any related activity until 30th April 2012 or, if the person is included on the register as an electronic money institution before that date, until the time of such inclusion.

(2)   Parts 5 and 6 of these Regulations, and Part 16 of, and Schedule 17 to, the 2000 Act (the ombudsman scheme), shall apply to a person falling within paragraph (1) as if the person were an electronic money institution.

[2.960]
77   Existing fixed term contracts

(1)   Part 5 shall not apply in respect of the redemption of electronic money that has been issued before 30th April 2011 where the contract—

(a)   provides for a termination date up to two years after the date on which the contract was entered into; and

(b)   does not provide that the means of storing electronic money can be recharged.

(2)   In paragraph (1) "termination date" has the same meaning as in Part 5.

[2.961]
78   Amendments to the banking consolidation directive

(1)   For the purposes of the application of the 2000 Act or any provision made under or by virtue of it in relation to any person during the transitional period, paragraph 2 of Schedule 3 to that Act (definition of "Banking Consolidation Directive") shall be read as if the amendments of the banking consolidation directive by the electronic money directive had not been made.

(2)   The "transitional period" means the period beginning when this regulation comes into force and ending with—

(a)   29th October 2011 in the case of a person falling within regulation 75(1);

(b)   29th April 2011 otherwise.

79   (*Introduces Sch 4 to these Regulations.*)

SCHEDULES

[2.962]

SCHEDULE 1
INFORMATION TO BE INCLUDED IN OR WITH AN APPLICATION FOR AUTHORISATION

Regulation 5(1)

1. A programme of operations, setting out, in particular, the type of electronic money issuance and payment services which are envisaged.

2. A business plan including a forecast budget calculation for the first three financial years which demonstrates that the applicant is able to employ appropriate and proportionate systems, resources and procedures to operate soundly.

3. Evidence that the applicant holds initial capital for the purposes of regulation 6(3).

4. A description of the measures taken for safeguarding the electronic money holders' and payment service users' funds in accordance with regulation 20.

5. A description of the applicant's governance arrangements and internal control mechanisms including administrative risk management and accounting procedures, which demonstrates that such arrangements, mechanisms and procedures are proportionate, appropriate, sound and adequate.

6. A description of the internal control mechanisms which the applicant has established in order to comply with the Money Laundering Regulations 2007 and Regulation (EC) No 1781/2006 of the European Parliament and of the Council of 15 November 2006 on information on the payer accompanying transfers of funds.

7. A description of the applicant's structural organisation, including, where applicable, a description of the intended use of agents and branches and a description of outsourcing arrangements, and of its participation in a national and international payment system.

8. In relation to each person holding, directly or indirectly, a qualifying holding in the applicant—
    (a)   the size and nature of their qualifying holding; and
    (b)   evidence of their suitability taking into account the need to ensure the sound and prudent management of an electronic money institution.

9. (1) The identity of directors and persons who are or will be responsible for the management of the applicant and, where relevant, persons who are or will be responsible for the management of the electronic money issuance and payment services activities of the applicant.

(2) Evidence that the persons described in sub-paragraph (1) are of good repute and that they possess appropriate knowledge and experience to issue electronic money and perform payment services.

10. The identity of the auditors of the applicant, if any.

11. (1) The legal status of the applicant and, where the applicant is a limited company, its articles.

(2) In this paragraph "articles" has the meaning given in section 18 of the Companies Act 2006 (articles of association).

12. The address of the head office of the applicant.

13. For the purposes of paragraphs 4, 5 and 7, a description of—
    (a)   the audit arrangements of the applicant; and
    (b)   the organisational arrangements that the applicant has set up,
with a view to the applicant taking all reasonable steps to protect the interests of its electronic money holders and payment service users and to ensuring continuity and reliability in the performance of the issuance of electronic money and payment services activities.

SCHEDULE 2
CAPITAL REQUIREMENTS

Regulations 6, 13 and 19

PART 1
INITIAL CAPITAL

[2.963]

1. For the purposes of these Regulations "initial capital" comprises the items specified in paragraph 4(a), (b) and (c) of this Schedule.

2. An applicant for authorisation as an electronic money institution must hold an amount of initial capital of at least 350,000 euro.

3. (1) Where the business activities of an applicant for registration as a small electronic money institution generate average outstanding electronic money of 500,000 euro or more it must hold an amount of initial capital at least equal to 2% of the average outstanding electronic money of the institution.

(2)   Where the applicant has not completed a sufficiently long period of business to calculate the amount of average outstanding electronic money for the purposes of sub-paragraph (1), the applicant must make an estimate on the basis of projected outstanding electronic money as evidenced by its business plan, subject to any adjustments to that plan which are, or have been, required by the Authority.

PART 2
OWN FUNDS

Qualifying items

[2.964]
4. For the purposes of these Regulations "own funds" means the following items, subject to the deductions specified in paragraph 7 and to the limits specified in paragraph 9—

  (a) paid up capital, including share premium accounts but excluding amounts arising in respect of cumulative preference shares;

  (b) reserves other than—

     (i)   revaluation reserves;

     (ii)   fair value reserves related to gains or losses on cash flow hedges of financial instruments measured at amortised cost; and

     (iii) that part of profit and loss reserves that arises from any gains on liabilities valued at fair value that are due to changes in the electronic money institution's credit standing;

  (c) profit or loss brought forward as a result of the application of the final profit or loss provided that—

     (i)   interim profits may only be included if they are—

        (aa) verified by persons responsible for the auditing of the institution's accounts;

        (bb) shown to the satisfaction of the Authority that the amount has been evaluated in accordance with the principles set out in Directive 86/635/EEC of the Council of the 8th December 1986 on the annual accounts and consolidated accounts of banks and other financial institutions; and

        (cc) net of any foreseeable charge or dividend;

     (ii)   in the case of an electronic money institution which is the originator of a securitisation, net gains arising from the capitalisation of future income from the securitised assets and providing credit enhancement to positions in the securitisation are excluded;

  (d) revaluation reserves;

  (e) general or collective provisions if—

     (i)   they are freely available to the electronic money institution to cover normal electronic money issuance and payment services risks where revenue or capital losses have not yet been identified;

     (ii)   their existence is disclosed in internal accounting records; and

     (iii) their amount is determined by the management of the electronic money institution, verified by a statutory auditor or audit firm (as defined by regulation 25(2)) and notified to the Authority;

  (f) securities of indeterminate duration and other instruments that fulfil the following conditions—

     (i)   they may not be reimbursed on the bearer's initiative or without the prior agreement of the Authority;

     (ii)   the debt agreement provides for the electronic money institution to have the option of deferring the payment of interest on the debt;

     (iii) the lender's claim on the electronic money institution is wholly subordinated to those of all non-subordinated creditors;

     (iv) the documents governing the issue of the securities provide for debt and unpaid interest to be such as to absorb losses, whilst leaving the electronic money institution in a position to continue trading,

  provided that only fully paid-up amounts are to be taken into account;

  (g) cumulative preferential shares, other than fixed-term cumulative preference shares referred to in paragraph (j);

  (h) the commitments of the members of an electronic money institution set up as a cooperative, comprising—

     (i)   that institution's uncalled capital; and

     (ii)   the legal commitments of the members of that institution to make additional non-refundable payments should the institution incur a loss provided that such payments can be demanded without delay;

  (i) the joint and several commitments of the borrower in the case of an electronic money institution organised as a fund, comprising—

     (i)   that institution's uncalled capital; and

    (ii)   the legal commitments of the borrowers of that institution to make additional non-refundable payments should the institution incur a loss provided that such payments can be demanded without delay;

(j)   fixed-term cumulative preferential shares and subordinated loan capital if—

    (i)   binding agreements exist under which, in the event of the winding-up of the electronic money institution, they rank after the claims of all other creditors and are not to be repaid until all other debts outstanding at the time have been settled; and

    (ii)   in the case of subordinated loan capital—

        (aa)   only fully paid-up funds are taken into account;

        (bb)   the loans involved have an original maturity of at least five years, after which they may be repaid;

        (cc)   the extent to which they may rank as own funds is gradually reduced during at least the last five years before the repayment date; and

        (dd)   the loan agreement does not include any clause providing that in specified circumstances, other than the winding-up of the electronic money institution, the debt will become repayable before the agreed repayment date.

5. The items specified in paragraph 4(a) to (d) must be—

(a)   available to the electronic money institution for unrestricted and immediate use to cover risks or losses as soon as these occur; and

(b)   net of any foreseeable tax charge at the moment of their calculation or be suitably adjusted in so far as such tax charges reduce the amount up to which these items may be applied to cover risks or losses.

6. Own funds are not to include guarantees provided by the Crown or a local authority to an electronic money institution which is a public sector entity for the purposes of the [capital requirements regulation].

Deductions from own funds

7. The deductions from own funds are—

(a)   own shares at book value held by the electronic money institution;

(b)   intangible assets;

(c)   material losses of the current financial year;

(d)   holdings of shares in credit institutions and financial institutions exceeding 10% of their capital;

(e)   if sub-paragraph (d) applies, the items specified in paragraph 4(f), (g) and (j) held in the relevant credit institution or financial institution;

(f)   holdings of shares or of the items specified in paragraph 4(f), (g) and (j) held in other credit institutions or financial institutions where—

    (i)   the holding has not been deducted in accordance with sub-paragraph (d) or (e) of this paragraph; and

    (ii)   the total amount of such holdings exceeds 10% of the electronic money institution's own funds calculated before deduction of the items specified in this sub-paragraph and sub-paragraphs (d), (e), (g) and (h);

(g)   participations which the electronic money institution holds in an insurance undertaking, reinsurance undertaking or insurance holding company; and

(h)   the following instruments held in an insurance undertaking, reinsurance undertaking or insurance holding company in which the electronic money institution holds a participation—

    (i)   instruments referred to in article 16(3) of Directive 73/239/EEC of the Council on the coordination of laws, regulations and administrative provisions relating to the taking-up and pursuit of the business of direct insurance other than life assurance;

    (ii)   instruments referred to in article 27(3) of Directive 2002/83/EC of the European Parliament and of the Council of 5th November 2002 concerning life assurance.

8. Where shares in another credit institution, financial institution, insurance undertaking, reinsurance undertaking or insurance holding company are held temporarily for the purposes of a financial assistance operation designed to reorganise and save that entity, the Authority may direct that any or all of the items specified in paragraph 7(d) to (h) are not to be deducted from own funds.

Limits on qualifying items

9. (1) The limits referred to in paragraph 4 are—

(a)   that A must not exceed B; and

(b)   that C must not exceed 50% of B.

(2)   After applying such limits—

(a)   50% of the total of the items specified in paragraph 7(d) to (h) must be deducted from A and the remaining 50% must be deducted from B; and

(b)   the amount, if any, by which the amount to be deducted from A exceeds A must be deducted from B.

(3)   In this paragraph—
- (a)   "A" means the total of the items specified in paragraph 4(d) to (j);
- (b)   "B" means the total of the items specified in paragraph 4(a) to (c) less the total of the items specified in paragraph 7(a) to (c); and
- (c)   "C" means the total of the items specified in paragraph 4(h) to (j).

10.   The Authority may in temporary and exceptional circumstances direct that an electronic money institution may exceed one or more of the limits described in paragraph 9(1).

11.   An electronic money institution must not include in its own funds calculation—
- (a)   any item used in an equivalent calculation of own funds by an electronic money institution, authorised payment institution, credit institution, investment firm, asset management company or insurance undertaking in the same group; or
- (b)   in the case of an electronic money institution which carries on activities other than electronic money issuance or the provision of payment services, any item included in an own funds calculation required by or under any other enactment.

12.   An authorised electronic money institution that carries on activities other than the issuance of electronic money and the provision of payment services related to the issuance of electronic money must not use—
- (a)   in its calculation of own funds in accordance with Method A, B or C, any qualifying item included in its calculation of own funds in accordance with Method D;
- (b)   in its calculation of own funds in accordance with Method D, any qualifying item included in its calculation of own funds in accordance with Method A, B or C.

Own funds requirement

13.   An authorised electronic money institution must calculate its own funds requirement—
- (a)   in accordance with such of Method A, Method B or Method C as the Authority may direct in respect of any activities carried on by the authorised electronic money institution consisting of payment services that are not related to the issuance of electronic money; and
- (b)   in accordance with Method D in respect of any activities carried on by the authorised electronic money institution that consist of the issuance of electronic money and payment services that are related to the issuance of electronic money.

14.   Where a small electronic money institution is required by regulation 19(2) to maintain own funds, it must calculate its own funds requirement as an amount equal to 2% of the average outstanding electronic money of the institution.

Adjustment by the Authority

15.   The Authority may direct in respect of an authorised electronic money institution that—
- (a)   an amount of own funds resulting from a calculation made in accordance with paragraph 13(a) is to be up to 20% higher or up to 20% lower;
- (b)   an amount of own funds resulting from a calculation made in accordance with paragraph 13(b) is to be up to 20% higher or up to 20% lower; or
- (c)   the sum of the amounts of own funds resulting from calculations made in accordance with paragraph 13(a) and (b) is to be up to 20% higher or up to 20% lower.

16.   The Authority may direct in respect of a small electronic money institution that an amount of own funds resulting from a calculation made in accordance with paragraph 14 is to be up to 20% higher or up to 20% lower.

17.   A direction made under paragraph 15 or 16 must be on the basis of an evaluation of the relevant electronic money institution including, if available, and where the Authority considers it appropriate, any risk-management processes, risk loss database or internal control mechanisms of the electronic money institution.

18.   The Authority may make a reasonable charge for making an evaluation required under paragraph 17.

Provision for start-up electronic money institutions

19.   If an electronic money institution has not completed a full financial year's business, references to a figure for the preceding financial year are to be read as the equivalent figure projected in the business plan provided in the electronic money institution's application for authorisation or registration, subject to any adjustment to that plan required by the Authority.

Method A

20.   (1)   "Method A" means the calculation method set out in this paragraph.

(2)   The own funds requirement is 10% of the authorised electronic money institution's fixed overheads for the preceding financial year.

(3) If a material change has occurred in an authorised electronic money institution's business since the preceding financial year, the Authority may direct that the own funds requirement is to be a higher or lower amount than that calculated in accordance with sub-paragraph (2).

Method B

21. (1) "Method B" means the calculation method set out in this paragraph.

(2) The own funds requirement is the sum of the following elements multiplied by the scaling factor—

- (a) 4% of the first 5,000,000 euro of payment volume;
- (b) 2.5% of the next 5,000,000 euro of payment volume;
- (c) 1% of the next 90,000,000 euro of payment volume;
- (d) 0.5% of the next 150,000,000 euro of payment volume; and
- (e) 0.25% of any remaining payment volume.

(3) "Payment volume" means the total amount of payment transactions that are not related to the issuance of electronic money executed by the authorised electronic money institution in the preceding financial year divided by the number of months in that year.

(4) The "scaling factor" is—

- (a) 0.5 for an authorised electronic money institution providing a payment service specified in paragraph 1(f) of Schedule 1 to the Payment Services Regulations 2009;
- (b) 0.8 for an authorised electronic money institution providing the payment service specified in paragraph 1(g) of Schedule 1 to those Regulations; and
- (c) 1 for an authorised electronic money institution providing any other payment service.

Method C

22. (1) "Method C" means the calculation method set out in this paragraph.

(2) The own funds requirement is the relevant indicator multiplied by—

- (a) the multiplication factor; and
- (b) the scaling factor;

subject to the proviso in sub-paragraph (7).

(3) The "relevant indicator" is the sum of the following elements—

- (a) interest income;
- (b) interest expenses;
- (c) gross commissions and fees received; and
- (d) gross other operating income.

(4) For the purpose of calculating the relevant indicator—

- (a) each element must be included in the sum with its positive or negative sign;
- (b) income from extraordinary or irregular items may not be used;
- (c) expenditure on the outsourcing of services rendered by third parties may reduce the relevant indicator if the expenditure is incurred from a payment service provider;
- (d) the relevant indicator is calculated on the basis of the twelve-monthly observation at the end of the previous financial year;
- (e) the relevant indicator must be calculated over the previous financial year; and
- (f) audited figures must be used unless they are not available in which case business estimates may be used.

(5) The "multiplication factor" is the sum of—

- (a) 10% of the first 2,500,000 euro of the relevant indicator;
- (b) 8% of the next 2,500,000 euro of the relevant indicator;
- (c) 6% of the next 20,000,000 euro of the relevant indicator;
- (d) 3% of the next 25,000,000 euro of the relevant indicator; and
- (e) 1.5% of any remaining amount of the relevant indicator.

(6) "Scaling factor" has the meaning given in paragraph 21(4).

(7) The proviso is that the own funds requirement must not be less than 80% of the average of the previous three financial years for the relevant indicator.

23. (1) "Method D" means the calculation method set out in this paragraph.

(2) The own funds requirement in respect of the activity of issuing electronic money and providing payment services that are related to the issuance of electronic money is an amount equal to 2% of the average outstanding electronic money of the authorised electronic money institution.

24. (1) Where—

- (a) an electronic money institution provides payment services that are not related to the issuance of electronic money or carries out any of the activities referred to in regulation 32(1)(b) to (d) and (2); and
- (b) the amount of outstanding electronic money is unknown in advance,

the institution may calculate its own funds requirement on the basis of a representative portion assumed to be used for the issuance of electronic money and payment services related to the issuance of electronic money, provided that such representative portion can be reasonably estimated on the basis of historical data and to the satisfaction of the Authority.

(2) Where an electronic money institution has not completed a sufficiently long period of business to compile historical data adequate to make the calculation under sub-paragraph (1), it must make an estimate on the basis of projected outstanding electronic money as evidenced by its business plan, subject to any adjustments to that plan which are, or have been, required by the Authority.

Application of accounting standards

25. Except where this Schedule provides for a different method of recognition, measurement or valuation, whenever a provision in this Schedule refers to an asset, liability, equity or income statement item, an electronic money institution must, for the purpose of that provision, recognise the asset, liability, equity or income statement item and measure its value in accordance with whichever of the following are applicable for the purpose of the institution's external financial reporting—

    (a)   Financial Reporting Standards and Statements of Standard Accounting Practice issued or adopted by [the Financial Reporting Council Limited];

    (b)   Statements of Recommended Practice, issued by industry or sectoral bodies recognised for this purpose by [the Financial Reporting Council Limited];

    (c)   International Financial Reporting Standards and International Accounting Standards issued or adopted by the International Accounting Standards Board;

    (d)   International Standards on Auditing (United Kingdom and Ireland) issued by the [Financial Reporting Council Limited or a predecessor body]; and

    (e)   the Companies Act 2006.

NOTES

Para 6: words in square brackets substituted by the Capital Requirements Regulations 2013, SI 2013/3115, reg 46(1), Sch 2, Pt 3, para 75(1), (4).

Para 25: words in square brackets in sub-paras (a), (b) substituted by the Statutory Auditors (Amendment of Companies Act 2006 and Delegation of Functions etc) Order 2012, SI 2012/1741, art 3, Schedule, Pt 2, para 12; words in square brackets in sub-para (d) substituted by the Payment Services Regulations 2012, SI 2012/1791, reg 4.

[SCHEDULE 2A
CREDIT AGREEMENTS

Regulation 59A

PART 1
PROHIBITIONS AND RESTRICTIONS

Power to prohibit the entry into credit agreements

[2.965]

1 (1) If it appears to the Authority that sub-paragraph (4) has been, or is likely to be, contravened as respects an EEA authorised electronic money institution exercising passport rights in the United Kingdom, it may by notice given to the institution in accordance with Part 2 of this Schedule impose on the institution a credit prohibition.

(2) If it appears to the Authority that a restriction imposed under paragraph 2 on an EEA authorised electronic money institution exercising passport rights in the United Kingdom has not been complied with, it may by notice given to the institution in accordance with Part 2 of this Schedule impose on the institution a credit prohibition.

(3) "A credit prohibition" means a prohibition on carrying on, or purporting to carry on, in the United Kingdom any business which consists of or includes carrying on an activity—

    (a)   of the kind specified by article 36A, 36H, 39D, 39E, 39F, 39G, 60B, 60N, 89A or 89B of the Financial Services and Markets Act 2000 (Regulated Activities) Order 2001, and

    (b)   listed in the Annex to the payment services directive or which the institution is entitled to carry on in accordance with Article 16 of that directive as applied by Article 6 of the electronic money directive.

(4) This sub-paragraph is contravened as respects an EEA authorised electronic money institution exercising passport rights in the United Kingdom if—

    (a)   the institution or any of its employees, agents or associates (whether past or present), or

    (b)   where the institution is a body corporate, any controller of the institution or an associate of any such controller,

does any of the things specified in sub-paragraph (5).

(5) A person does a thing specified in this sub-paragraph if the person—

    (a)   commits any offence involving fraud or other dishonesty or violence;

    (b)   contravenes any provision made by or under—

        (i)   the Consumer Credit Act 1974;

        (ii)   the 2000 Act, to the extent that that Act relates to any activity of the kind specified by article 36A, 36H, 39D, 39E, 39F, 39G, 60B, 60N, 89A or 89B of the Financial Services and Markets Act 2000 (Regulated Activities) Order 2001;

(iii) any other enactment regulating the provision of credit to individuals or other transactions with individuals;

(c) contravenes any provision in force in an EEA State which corresponds to a provision of the kind mentioned in paragraph (b);

(d) practices discrimination on grounds of sex, colour, race or ethnic or national origins in, or in connection with, the carrying on of any business;

(e) engages in business practices appearing to the Authority to be deceitful or oppressive or otherwise unfair or improper (including practices that appear to the Authority to involve irresponsible lending).

(6) A credit prohibition may be absolute or may be imposed—

(a) for such period,

(b) until the occurrence of such event, or

(c) until such conditions are complied with,

as may be specified in the notice given under sub-paragraph (1) or (2).

(7) Any period, event or condition so specified may be varied by the Authority on the application of the institution concerned (for which, see paragraph 5).

(8) A credit prohibition may be withdrawn in whole or in part—

(a) on the initiative of the Authority, by notice served by the Authority on the institution concerned, and any such notice takes effect on such date as is specified in the notice;

(b) on an application submitted by the institution concerned (for which, see paragraph 5).

(9) Where the Authority withdraws a credit prohibition and imposes a restriction under paragraph (2), the Authority may specify that the withdrawal of the credit prohibition only takes effect when the imposition of the restriction is no longer subject to review (within the meaning of section 391(8) of the 2000 Act).

(10) For the purposes of sub-paragraph (9), whether the imposition of a restriction is open to review is to be determined in accordance with section 391(8) of the 2000 Act as if the imposition of the restriction were a matter to which a supervisory notice (within the meaning of that section) relates.

(11) An institution contravening a prohibition imposed under this paragraph is guilty of an offence and liable—

(a) on summary conviction, to a fine not exceeding the statutory maximum;

(b) on conviction on indictment, to a fine.

(12) In this paragraph—

"associate" has the same meaning as in article 60L of the Financial Services and Markets Act 2000 (Regulated Activities) Order 2001;

"controller" has the meaning given by section 422 of the 2000 Act.

(13) If a credit prohibition is in effect in relation to an institution, article 60JB of the Financial Services and Markets Act 2000 (Regulated Activities) Order 2001 does not apply in relation to that institution.

Power to restrict the entry into credit agreements

2 (1) In this paragraph, "restriction" means a direction that an EEA authorised electronic money institution exercising passport rights in the United Kingdom may not carry on in the United Kingdom, otherwise than in accordance with such conditions as may be specified in the direction, any business which consists of or includes carrying on an activity—

(a) of the kind specified in article 36A, 36H, 39D, 39E, 39F, 39G, 60B, 60N, 89A or 89B of the Financial Services and Markets Act 2000 (Regulated Activities) Order 2001;

(b) listed in the Annex to the payment services directive or which the institution is entitle to carry on in accordance with Article 16 of that directive as applied by Article 6 of the electronic money directive; and

(c) specified in the direction.

(2) If it appears to the Authority that the situation as respects an EEA authorised electronic money institution exercising passport rights in the United Kingdom is such that the powers conferred by paragraph 1 are exercisable, the Authority may, instead of imposing a credit prohibition impose—

(a) by notice given in accordance with Part 2 of this Schedule such restriction as appears to it desirable;

(b) where it has already imposed a restriction, vary the restriction on the Authority's own initiative by notice given in accordance with Part 2 of this Schedule.

(3) The Authority may also impose a restriction by notice given in accordance with Part 2 of this Schedule if it withdraws a credit prohibition.

(4) A restriction may be—

(a) withdrawn on the initiative of the Authority, by notice served by the Authority on the institution concerned, and any such notice takes effect on such date as is specified in the notice;

(b) withdrawn or varied on an application submitted by the institution concerned (for which, see paragraph 5).

(5)   An institution contravening a restriction is guilty of an offence and liable—

    (a)   on summary conviction, to a fine not exceeding the statutory maximum;

    (b)   on conviction on indictment, to a fine.]

NOTES

Commencement: 14 February 2014 (for certain purposes); 1 April 2014 (otherwise).

Sch 2A inserted by the Financial Services and Markets Act 2000 (Regulated Activities) (Amendment) Order 2014, SI 2014/366, art 18(1), (3).

[PART 2
PROCEDURE AND APPEALS

Interpretation

[2.966]

3   In this Part—

    "prohibition" means a credit prohibition imposed under paragraph 1(1) or (2) of Part 1 of this Schedule;

    "restriction" means a restriction imposed under paragraph 2(2) or (3) of Part 1 of this Schedule;

    "the Tribunal" means the Upper Tribunal.

Notice of prohibition or restriction

4   (1)   A prohibition or restriction takes effect—

    (a)   immediately, if the relevant notice states that that is the case,

    (b)   on such date as may be specified in the notice, or

    (c)   if no date is specified in the notice, when the matter to which the notice relates is no longer open to review.

(2)   An institution which is aggrieved by the imposition of a prohibition or a restriction by a notice given under this paragraph may refer the matter to the Tribunal.

(3)   A prohibition or restriction may be expressed to take effect immediately (or on a specified date) only if the Authority, having regard to the ground on which it is imposing the prohibition or restriction, reasonably considers that it is necessary for the prohibition or restriction to take effect immediately (or on that date).

(4)   The notice must—

    (a)   give details of the prohibition or restriction,

    (b)   state the Authority's reasons for the prohibition or restriction,

    (c)   inform the institution that it may make representations to the Authority within such period as is specified in the notice (whether or not the institution has referred the matter to the Tribunal),

    (d)   inform the institution of when the prohibition or restriction takes effect, and

    (e)   inform the institution of its right to refer the matter to the Tribunal.

(5)   The Authority may extend the period allowed under the notice for making representations.

(6)   If, having considered any representations made by the institution, the Authority decides—

    (a)   to impose the proposed prohibition or restriction, or

    (b)   if the prohibition or restriction has taken effect, not to withdraw the prohibition or restriction,

it must give the institution a notice.

(7)   If, having considered any representations made by the institution, the Authority decides—

    (a)   not to impose the proposed prohibition or restriction,

    (b)   to impose a different prohibition or restriction, or

    (c)   if the prohibition or restriction has already taken effect, to withdraw the prohibition or restriction,

it must give the institution a notice.

(7)   A notice under sub-paragraph (6) must inform the institution of its right to refer the matter to the Tribunal.

(8)   A notice under sub-paragraph (7)(b) must comply with sub-paragraph (4).

(9)   If a notice under this paragraph informs an institution of its right to refer a matter to the Tribunal, it must give an indication of the procedure on such a reference.

(10)   For the purposes of sub-paragraph (1)(c)—

    (a)   whether a matter is open to review is to be determined in accordance with section 391(8) of the 2000 Act;

    (b)   the notice to which the matter relates is to be treated as a supervisory notice for the purposes of that section.

(11)   References in this paragraph to the imposition of a restriction include references to the variation of a restriction on the initiative of the Authority.

Application to revoke or vary prohibition or restriction

5 (1) An application under Part 1 of this Schedule must—

(a) be made in such manner as the Authority may direct, and

(b) contain, or be accompanied by, such other information as the Authority may reasonably require.

(2) At any time after the application is received and before it is determined, the Authority may require the applicant to provide it with such further information as it reasonably considers necessary to enable it to determine the application.

(3) Different directions may be given, and different requirements imposed, in relation to different applications or categories of application.

(4) The Authority may require an applicant to provide information required under this paragraph in such form, or to verify it in such a way, as the Authority may direct.

(5) If the Authority decides to grant an application, it must give the applicant a notice.

(6) If the Authority proposes to refuse an application, or to take an action different from or in addition to the one applied for (including a proposal to impose a restriction when withdrawing a prohibition on an application under paragraph 1(8)(b)), it must give the applicant a warning notice.

(7) If the Authority decides to refuse an application, or to take an action different from or in addition to the one applied for (including a decision to impose a restriction when withdrawing a prohibition on an application under paragraph 1(8)(b)), it must give the applicant a decision notice.

(8) An applicant who is aggrieved by a decision notice given under this paragraph may refer the matter to the Tribunal.

Notice to the home state competent authority

6 If the Authority sends a notice to an institution under this Schedule which imposes, varies or withdraws a prohibition or restriction, it must send a copy of the notice to the institution's home state competent authority.]

NOTES

Commencement: 14 February 2014 (for certain purposes); 1 April 2014 (otherwise).
Sch 2A inserted as noted to Part 1 at **[2.965]**.

SCHEDULES 3, 4

(Sch 3 contains modifications to legislation outside the scope of this work; Sch 4 contains amendments which, in so far as relevant to this work, have been noted at the appropriate place.)

CONSUMER CREDIT (GREEN DEAL) REGULATIONS 2012

(SI 2012/2798)

NOTES

Made: 7 November 2012.
Authority: Consumer Credit Act 1974, ss 55(1), 60(1), 77A(2), 95(1), 95B(1)(b), (3)(c), 97(1), 182(2), 189(1).
Commencement: 28 January 2013.

[2.967]
1 Citation, commencement and extent

These Regulations—

(a) may be cited as the Consumer Credit (Green Deal) Regulations 2012;

(b) come into force on 28th January 2013; and

(c) extend to England and Wales and Scotland only.

NOTES

Commencement: 28 January 2013.

[2.968]
2 Interpretation

In these Regulations—

"the 1974 Act" means the Consumer Credit Act 1974;

"actual plan interest" means the total amount of interest that falls due for payment under the green deal plan between the settlement date and the full discharge date if early settlement takes place;

"administration amount" means the amount by which the creditor expects its administration costs will be reduced in consequence of early settlement taking place;

"compensatory amount" means the amount that a creditor is entitled to claim under section 95B(2) of the 1974 Act, calculated in accordance with regulation 4;

"early settlement" means, as appropriate, full early settlement or partial early settlement;

"expected plan interest" means the total amount of interest that falls due for payment by the debtor under the green deal plan between the settlement date and the full discharge date if early settlement does not take place;

"full discharge date" means the date fixed by the green deal plan for the discharge in full of the indebtedness of the debtor;

"full early settlement" means the discharge in full, pursuant to section 94(1) of the 1974 Act, of the debtor's indebtedness under a green deal plan;

"green deal plan" has the meaning given in section 1 of the Energy Act 2011;

"notice date" means the date on which the creditor receives notice from the debtor under, as appropriate, section 94(1) or section 94(4)(a) of the 1974 Act, in connection with early settlement;

"partial early settlement" means the discharge in part, pursuant to section 94(3) of the 1974 Act, of the debtor's indebtedness under a green deal plan;

"replacement interest" means, further to the third paragraph of Article 16(4)(b) of Directive 2008/48/EC of the European Parliament and of the Council on credit agreements for consumers, the total amount of interest that the creditor could obtain by lending the settlement amount on the market on the notice date;

"settlement amount" means, in respect of—
    (a)   full early settlement, the amount payable by the debtor to the creditor under section 94(1) of the 1974 Act, excluding any amount which the creditor claims under section 95A(2) or 95B(2) of the 1974 Act; or
    (b)   partial early settlement, the amount paid or to be paid by the debtor to the creditor pursuant to the notice provided by the debtor under section 94(4)(a) of the 1974 Act; and

"settlement date" means—
    (a)   the date falling 28 days after the notice date; or
    (b)   any later date specified by the debtor in the notice under, as appropriate, section 94(1) or section 94(4)(a) of the 1974 Act as the date of early settlement,
if the debtor pays the amount payable not later than that date.

NOTES

Commencement: 28 January 2013.

[2.969]
3   Specified duration of green deal plan under section 95B(1)(b) of the 1974 Act

For the purposes of section 95B(1)(b) of the 1974 Act, the specified duration of a green deal plan is a plan of more than 15 years.

NOTES

Commencement: 28 January 2013.

[2.970]
4   Compensatory amount: method of calculation

(1)   Subject to paragraph (3), for the purposes of section 95B(3)(c) of the 1974 Act, the compensatory amount is the amount given by the following formula—

$A - B - C - D$

(2)   The following apply for the purposes of the formula in paragraph (1)—
    "A" means the expected plan interest;
    "B" means the replacement interest;
    "C" means the administration amount; and
    "D" means—
        (a)   where full early settlement takes place or is to take place, zero; or
        (b)   where partial early settlement takes place or is to take place, the actual plan interest.

(3)   If the amount given by the formula in paragraph (1) is zero or less, for the purposes of section 95B(3)(c) of the 1974 Act, the compensatory amount is zero.

NOTES

Commencement: 28 January 2013.

[2.971]
5   Amendment of consumer credit regulations

The Schedule to these Regulations has effect.

NOTES

Commencement: 28 January 2013.

SCHEDULE

(This Schedule amends the Consumer Credit (Agreements) Regulations 1983, SI 1983/1553, Sch 1, para 24A, and Sch 8, Pt I, para 24A, at [2.31] and [2.41]; the Consumer Credit (Settlement Information) Regulations 1983, SI 1983/1564, Schedule; the Consumer Credit (Early Settlement) Regulations 2004, SI 2004/1483, regs 1, 4, 6, at [2.319] et seq; the Consumer Credit (Information Requirements and Duration of Licences and Charges) Regulations 2007, SI 2007/1167, regs 2, 4, Sch 1, at [2.401] et seq; the Consumer Credit (Disclosure of Information) Regulations 2010, SI 2010/1013, Sch 1, para 4, at [2.826]; and the Consumer Credit (Agreements) Regulations 2010, SI 2010/1014, Sch 1, para 28, at [2.837].)

CONSUMER RIGHTS (PAYMENT SURCHARGES) REGULATIONS 2012

(SI 2012/3110)

NOTES
Made: 18 December 2012.
Authority: European Communities Act 1972, s 2(2).
Commencement: 6 April 2013.

ARRANGEMENT OF REGULATIONS

[2.972]
1 Citation and commencement
(1)   These Regulations may be cited as the Consumer Rights (Payment Surcharges) Regulations 2012 and come into force on 6th April 2013.
(2)   These Regulations apply in relation to contracts entered into on or after that date.

NOTES
Commencement: 6 April 2013.

[2.973]
2 "Consumer" and "trader"
In these Regulations—
"consumer" means an individual acting for purposes which are wholly or mainly outside that individual's trade, business, craft or profession;
["trader" means a person acting for purposes relating to that person's trade, business, craft or profession, whether acting personally or through another person acting in the trader's name or on the trader's behalf].

NOTES
Commencement: 6 April 2013.
Definition "trader" substituted by the Consumer Contracts (Information, Cancellation and Additional Charges) Regulations 2013, SI 2013/3134, reg 47, Sch 4, para 15(1), (2), in relation to contracts entered into on or after 13 June 2014.

[2.974]
3 Other definitions
In these Regulations—
["business" includes the activities of any government department or local or public authority;]

["CMA" means the Competition and Markets Authority;]

"court" in relation to England and Wales and Northern Ireland means a county court or the High Court, and in relation to Scotland means the sheriff or the Court of Session;

"digital content" means data which are produced and supplied in digital form;

"district heating" means the supply of heat (in the form of steam or hot water or otherwise) from a central source of production through a transmission and distribution system to heat more than one building;

"goods" means any tangible movable items, but that includes water, gas and electricity if and only if they are put up for sale in a limited volume or a set quantity;

. . .

"sales contract" means a contract under which a trader transfers or agrees to transfer the ownership of goods to a consumer and the consumer pays or agrees to pay the price[, including any contract that has both goods and services as its object];

"service contract" means a contract, other than a sales contract, under which a trader supplies or agrees to supply a service to a consumer and the consumer pays or agrees to pay the price.

NOTES

Commencement: 6 April 2013.

Definition "business" inserted by the Consumer Contracts (Information, Cancellation and Additional Charges) Regulations 2013, SI 2013/3134, reg 47, Sch 4, para 15(1), (3)(a), in relation to contracts entered into on or after 13 June 2014.

Definition "CMA" inserted by the Enterprise and Regulatory Reform Act 2013 (Competition) (Consequential, Transitional and Saving Provisions) (No 2) Order 2014, SI 2014/549, art 2, Sch 1, Pt 2, para 48(1), (2)(b).

[2.975]
4   Excessive charges prohibited

A trader must not charge consumers, in respect of the use of a given means of payment, fees that exceed the cost borne by the trader for the use of that means.

NOTES

Commencement: 6 April 2013.

[2.976]
5   Contracts where prohibition applies

(1)   Regulation 4 applies only if the use is as a means for the consumer to make payments for the purposes of a contract with the trader, and only to the extent that that contract—

   (a)   is a sales or service contract, or a contract (other than a sales or service contract) for the supply of water, gas, electricity, district heating or digital content, and

   (b)   is not an excluded contract.

(2)   An excluded contract is a contract—

   (a)   for social services, including social housing, childcare and support of families and persons permanently or temporarily in need, including long-term care;

   (b)   for health services provided, whether or not via healthcare facilities, by health professionals to patients to assess, maintain or restore their state of health, including the prescription, dispensation and provision of medicinal products and medical devices (and "health professionals" has the meaning given by Article 3(f) of Directive 2011/24/EU of the European Parliament and of the Council on the application of patients' rights in cross-border healthcare);

   (c)   for gambling within the meaning of the Gambling Act 2005 (which includes gaming, betting and participating in a lottery);

   (d)   for services of a banking, credit, insurance, personal pension, investment or payment nature;

   (e)   for the creation of immovable property or of rights in immovable property;

   (f)   for rental of accommodation for residential purposes;

   (g)   for the construction of new buildings, or the construction of substantially new buildings by the conversion of existing buildings;

   (h)   which falls within the scope of Directive 2008/122/EC of the European Parliament and of the Council on the protection of consumers in respect of certain aspects of timeshare, long—term holiday product, resale and exchange contracts;

   (i)   for the supply of foodstuffs, beverages or other goods intended for current consumption in the household, and which are supplied by a trader on frequent and regular rounds to the consumer's home, residence or workplace;

   (j)   concluded by means of automatic vending machines or automated commercial premises;

   (k)   concluded with a telecommunications operator through a public telephone for the use of the telephone;

   (l)   concluded for the use of one single connection, by telephone, internet or fax, established by a consumer;

   (m)   under which goods are sold by way of execution or otherwise by authority of law.

NOTES
Commencement: 6 April 2013.

[2.977]
6 Temporary exemption for micro-businesses and new businesses
(1)   During the exemption period, regulation 4 does not apply if the trader is acting for purposes relating to the trader's business, and the business is—
   (a)   an existing micro-business, or
   (b)   a new business.
(2)   The Schedule defines those kinds of business, and the exemption period.

NOTES
Commencement: 6 April 2013.

[2.978]
7 Complaints
(1)   It is the duty of an enforcement authority to consider any complaint made to it about a contravention of regulation 4, unless—
   (a)   the complaint appears to the authority to be frivolous or vexatious; or
   (b)   another enforcement authority has notified the [CMA] that it agrees to consider the complaint.
(2)   If an enforcement authority has notified the [CMA] as mentioned in paragraph (1)(b), that authority is under a duty to consider the complaint.
(3)   An enforcement authority which is under a duty to consider a complaint must—
   (a)   decide whether or not to make an application under regulation 8, and
   (b)   give reasons for its decision.
(4)   In deciding whether or not to make an application, an enforcement authority may, if it considers it appropriate to do so, have regard to any undertaking given to it or another enforcement authority by or on behalf of any person as to compliance with regulation 4 [and to any enforcement action taken under Part 8 of the Enterprise Act 2002].
(5)   The following are enforcement authorities for the purposes of these Regulations—
   (a)   every local weights and measures authority in Great Britain (within the meaning of section 69 of the Weights and Measures Act 1985);
   (b)   the Department of Enterprise, Trade and Investment in Northern Ireland.

NOTES
Commencement: 6 April 2013.
Para (1): in sub-para (b) reference to "CMA" in square brackets substituted by the Enterprise and Regulatory Reform Act 2013 (Competition) (Consequential, Transitional and Saving Provisions) (No 2) Order 2014, SI 2014/549, art 2, Sch 1, Pt 2, para 48(1), (3).
Para (2): reference to "CMA" in square brackets substituted by SI 2014/549, art 2, Sch 1, Pt 2, para 48(1), (3).
Para (4): words in square brackets inserted by SI 2013/761, art 3.

[2.979]
8 Orders to secure compliance
(1)   An enforcement authority may apply for an injunction, or in Scotland an interdict or any other appropriate relief or remedy, against any person who appears to the authority to be responsible for a contravention of regulation 4.
(2)   The court on an application under this regulation may grant an injunction, interdict or order on such terms as it thinks fit to secure compliance with regulation 4.

NOTES
Commencement: 6 April 2013.

[2.980]
9 Notification of undertakings and orders to the [CMA]
An enforcement authority must notify the [CMA]—
   (a)   of any undertaking given to it by or on behalf of any person who appears to it to be responsible for a contravention of regulation 4;
   (b)   of the outcome of any application made by it under regulation 8, and of the terms of any undertaking given to the court or of any order made by the court;
   (c)   of the outcome of any application made by it to enforce a previous order of the court.

NOTES
Commencement: 6 April 2013.

Provision heading: reference to "CMA" in square brackets substituted by the Enterprise and Regulatory Reform Act 2013 (Competition) (Consequential, Transitional and Saving Provisions) (No 2) Order 2014, SI 2014/549, art 2, Sch 1, Pt 2, para 48(1), (4).

Reference to "CMA" in square brackets substituted by SI 2014/549, art 2, Sch 1, Pt 2, para 48(1), (4).

[2.981]
10 Consumer's right of redress

Where a trader charges a fee in contravention of regulation 4—
- (a) any provision of a contract requiring the consumer to pay the fee is unenforceable to the extent of the excess charged, and
- (b) the contract for the purposes of which the payment is made is to be treated as providing for the excess to be repaid to the consumer.

NOTES
Commencement: 6 April 2013.

SCHEDULE
MICRO-BUSINESSES AND NEW BUSINESSES

Regulation 6

Micro-businesses

[2.982]
1. A micro-business is a business that has fewer than 10 employees (see paragraphs 7 to 9).

Existing micro-businesses

2. An existing micro-business is a business that was a micro-business immediately before 6th April 2013.

New businesses

3. (1) A new business is a business which a person, or a number of persons, ("P") begins to carry on during the period beginning with 6th April 2013 and ending with 12th June 2014.

(2) That is subject to sub-paragraphs (3), (4) and (6).

(3) A business ("Business 2") is not a new business if—
- (a) P has, at any time during the period of 6 months ending immediately before the date on which P begins to carry on Business 2, carried on another business ("Business 1"), and
- (b) Business 1 consisted of the activities of which Business 2 consists (or most of them),

unless Business 1 was itself a new business.

(4) A business is not a new business if—
- (a) P begins to carry on the business on another person ceasing to carry on the activities of which it consists (or most of them), and
- (b) P does so in consequence of arrangements involving P and the other person,

unless the activities, when carried on by that other person, were activities of a new business.

(5) For this purpose, P is to be taken to begin to carry on a business on another person ceasing to carry on such activities if—
- (a) P begins to carry on the business otherwise than in partnership on such activities ceasing to be carried on by persons in partnership, or
- (b) P is a number of persons in partnership who begin to carry on the business on such activities ceasing to be carried on—
  - (i) by a person, or a number of persons, otherwise than in partnership,
  - (ii) by persons in partnership who do not consist only of all the persons who constitute P, or
  - (iii) partly as mentioned in paragraph (i) and partly as mentioned in paragraph (ii).

(6) P is not to be regarded as beginning to carry on a business for the purposes of sub-paragraph (1) if—
- (a) before P begins to carry on the business, P is a party to arrangements under which P may (at any time during the period beginning with 6th April 2013 and ending with 12th June 2014) carry on, as part of the business, activities carried on by any other person, and
- (b) the business would have been prevented by sub-paragraph (3) from being a new business if—
  - (i) P had begun to carry on the activities when beginning to carry on the business, and
  - (ii) the other person had at that time ceased to carry them on.

(7) "Arrangements" includes an agreement, understanding, scheme, transaction or series of transactions (whether or not legally enforceable).

The exemption period: existing micro-businesses

4. (1) This paragraph defines the exemption period in relation to an existing micro-business.

(2) The exemption period starts with 6th April 2013 and ends with—

    (a)   the day after a grace period in relation to the business ends, if the grace period is one in which the business grows (see paragraph 6), or

    (b)   (if sooner) 12th June 2014.

(3)   The following are grace periods in relation to a business for the purposes of this paragraph—

    (a)   the 6-month period that starts with the first day after 6th April 2013 on which the business has 10 or more employees;

    (b)   the 6-month period that starts after the end of a grace period (the "earlier grace period") that is not one in which the business grows, in accordance with sub-paragraph (4) or (5).

(4)   If the business has 10 or more employees on the day after the end of the earlier grace period, the next grace period starts on that day.

(5)   If the business has fewer than 10 employees on that day, the next grace period starts on the next day on which the business has 10 or more employees.

The exemption period: new businesses

5. (1)   This paragraph defines the exemption period in relation to a new business.

(2)   The exemption period starts with the date on which P begins to carry on the business and ends with—

    (a)   the date on which P ceases to carry on the business, or

    (b)   (if sooner) 12th June 2014.

(3)   If P is the members of a partnership, or other unincorporated association, P is not to be taken for the purposes of sub-paragraph (2) to cease to carry on the business if—

    (a)   the members of the partnership or association change, or the partnership or association is dissolved, and

    (b)   after the change or dissolution, the business is carried on by at least one of the persons who constituted P.

Grace periods in which business grows

6. For the purposes of this Schedule, a grace period is one in which a business grows if A is greater than B, where—

    A is the number of days in the grace period when the business has 10 or more employees, and

    B is the number of days in the grace period when the business has fewer than 10 employees.

Number of employees of a business

7. For the purposes of this Schedule, the number of employees of a business is calculated as follows—

$$TH/37.5$$

where TH is the total number of hours per week for which all the employees of the business are contracted to work.

Employees of a business

8. For the purposes of this Schedule, the employees of a business are the persons who are employed for the purposes of the business.

Employees

9. (1)   In this Schedule, "employee" means an individual who has entered into or works under a contract of employment.

(2)   In sub-paragraph (1) "contract of employment" means a contract of service, whether express or implied, and (if it is express) whether oral or in writing.

Franchises

10. For the purposes of this Schedule, a business that is carried on pursuant to a franchise agreement is treated as part of the business of the franchisor (and not as a separate business carried on by the franchisee).

NOTES

Commencement: 6 April 2013.

PUBLIC BODIES (THE OFFICE OF FAIR TRADING TRANSFER OF CONSUMER ADVICE SCHEME FUNCTION AND MODIFICATION OF ENFORCEMENT FUNCTIONS) ORDER 2013

(SI 2013/783)

NOTES

Made: 27 March 2013.
Authority: Public Bodies Act 2011, ss 5(1), 6(1), (2), 35(2).
Commencement: 28 March 2013.

[2.983]
1 Citation, commencement and interpretation

(1) This Order may be cited as the Public Bodies (The Office of Fair Trading Transfer of Consumer Advice Scheme Function and Modification of Enforcement Functions) Order 2013.

(2) The Order comes into force on the day after the day on which it is made.

(3) In this Order "the 2002 Act" means the Enterprise Act 2002.

NOTES

Commencement: 28 March 2013.

[2.984]
2 Transfer of consumer advice scheme function

(1) Subject to paragraph (3), the OFT's power under Part 1 of the 2002 Act to support a public consumer advice scheme is, so far as regards support of a scheme that takes the form of providing, or securing the provision of, an arrangement for giving advice without charge to individual consumers on matters personal to them, transferred to Citizens Advice and Citizens Advice Scotland.

(2) The function transferred may be exercised by Citizens Advice or Citizens Advice Scotland or by them jointly.

(3) The OFT's power to support a public consumer advice scheme in that manner is abolished in relation to Northern Ireland, except so far as that function relates to the giving of advice relating to postal services.

(4) In this article—
"Citizens Advice" means the National Association of Citizens Advice Bureaux;
"Citizens Advice Scotland" means the Scottish Association of Citizens Advice Bureaux; and
"the OFT" means the Office of Fair Trading.

NOTES

Commencement: 28 March 2013.

3 (*Inserts the Enterprise Act 2002, s 8A at* **[1.1703]**.)

[2.985]
4

(1) The function transferred by article 2(1) is not to be regarded as a function under Part 1 of the 2002 Act for the purposes of section 238(1) of the 2002 Act.

(2) The function transferred by article 2(1) is to be regarded as conferred by this Order for the purposes of section 241(3)(c) of the 2002 Act.

NOTES

Commencement: 28 March 2013.

5–13 (*Reg 5 amends the Utilities Act 2000, s 8; reg 6 amends the Postal Services Act 2011, s 51; reg 7 amends the Freedom of Information Act 2000, Sch 1, Pt 6; reg 8 amends the Freedom of Information (Scotland) Act 2002, Sch 1, Pt 7; reg 9 amends the Enterprise Act 2002, s 214 at* **[1.1804]**; *reg 10 amends the Unfair Terms in Consumer Contracts Regulations 1999, SI 1999/2083, regs 3, 10 at* **[2.122]** *and* **[2.129]**; *reg 11 amends the Consumer Protection (Distance Selling) Regulations 2000, SI 2000/2334, regs 3, 26, 27, 28, 29 at* **[2.139]** *et seq; reg 12 amends the Business Protection from Misleading Marketing Regulations 2008, SI 2008/1276, regs 2, 13, 20 at* **[2.527]** *et seq; and reg 13 amends the Consumer Protection from Unfair Trading Regulations 2008, SI 2008/1277, regs 2, 19 at* **[2.556]** *and* **[2.573]**.)

CREDIT RATING AGENCIES (CIVIL LIABILITY) REGULATIONS 2013

(SI 2013/1637)

NOTES

Made: 3 July 2013.
Authority: European Communities Act 1972, s 2(2).
Commencement: 25 July 2013.

ARRANGEMENT OF REGULATIONS

[2.986]
1   Citation and commencement

These Regulations may be cited as the Credit Rating Agencies (Civil Liability) Regulations 2013 and shall come into force on 25th July 2013.

NOTES

Commencement: 25 July 2013.

[2.987]
2   Interpretation

In these Regulations—
"Article 35a" means Article 35a of the EC Regulation;
"credit rating" has the meaning given by Article 3(1)(a) of the EC Regulation;
"credit rating agency" has the meaning given by Article 3(1)(b) of the EC Regulation;
"the EC Regulation" means Regulation (EC) No 1060/2009 of the European Parliament and of the Council of 16 September 2009 on credit rating agencies;
"an infringement" means an infringement listed in Annex III to the EC Regulation;
"an investor" has the same meaning as in Article 35a;
"an issuer" has the meaning given by Article 3(1)(s) of the EC Regulation;
"rating category" has the meaning given by Article 3(1)(h) of the EC Regulation;
"related third party" has the meaning given by Article 3(1)(i) of the EC Regulation;
"senior management" has the meaning given by article 3(1)(n) of the EC Regulation.

NOTES

Commencement: 25 July 2013.

[2.988]
3   "Intention"

In Article 35a, an infringement shall be considered to have been committed intentionally by the credit rating agency if the senior management of the credit rating agency acted deliberately to commit the infringement.

NOTES

Commencement: 25 July 2013.

[2.989]
4 "Gross negligence"

(1) In Article 35a, an infringement shall be considered to have been committed with gross negligence if the senior management of the credit rating agency were reckless as to whether the infringement occurred.

(2) For the purposes of this regulation, the senior management of a credit rating agency are reckless if they act without caring whether an infringement occurs.

NOTES
Commencement: 25 July 2013.

[2.990]
5 "Impact"

In Article 35a, an infringement has an impact on a credit rating if it results in a different rating category being assigned to the issuer or the financial instrument of the issuer to which the credit rating relates.

NOTES
Commencement: 25 July 2013.

[2.991]
6 "Reasonably relied"

(1) In Article 35a, an investor reasonably relies upon a credit rating where—
  (a)   the investor relies upon a credit rating when making an investment decision, and
  (b)   that reliance is reasonable.

(2) The test for whether the reliance is reasonable is the same as for whether it is reasonable for a person to rely on a statement for the purposes of determining whether the statement gives rise to a duty of care in negligence.

NOTES
Commencement: 25 July 2013.

[2.992]
7 "Due care"

In Article 35a, an investor shall be considered to have exercised due care if the investor took the care a reasonably prudent investor would have exercised in the circumstances.

NOTES
Commencement: 25 July 2013.

[2.993]
8 "Caused"

In Article 35a, the test of causation in negligence applies for the purposes of determining whether an infringement caused damage.

NOTES
Commencement: 25 July 2013.

[2.994]
9 Reasonable and proportionate limitations on liability

For the purposes of Article 35a(3)—
  (a)   a limitation on liability is allowed by the law of the United Kingdom; and
  (b)   "reasonable and proportionate" means the limitation on liability is reasonable and proportionate in all the relevant circumstances of the case, having regard to such of the factors in regulations 10, 11 and 12 as the court considers relevant.

NOTES
Commencement: 25 July 2013.

[2.995]
10 Issuers: solicited credit ratings

(1) If the claimant is an issuer and it, or a related third party, has entered into a contract with a credit rating agency to assign a credit rating in respect of such issuer or a financial instrument issued by such issuer, the court may consider the following factors, amongst others, to be indications that a limitation on liability is reasonable and proportionate—
  (a)   the limitation resulted from contractual negotiations between the issuer, or a related third party, and the credit rating agency;

(b)   the price agreed between the issuer or a related third party and the credit rating agency reflects the extent of the limitation on liability;

(c)   the credit rating agency gave the issuer a reasonable opportunity to submit additional factual information not previously available to the credit rating agency, or to clarify any factual inaccuracies regarding the proposed credit rating, before the credit rating was issued, and took account of those submissions or comments when finalising the credit rating;

(d)   the limitation relates to losses which the credit rating agency could not reasonably have foreseen when it assigned the credit rating;

(e)   the limitation relates to losses which no credit rating agency could reasonably insure against on a prudent commercial basis;

(f)   the limitation relates to losses which no credit rating agency would reasonably be expected to have the resources to meet.

(2)   The absence of a factor or factors in paragraph (1) does not indicate that a limitation on liability is unreasonable or disproportionate.

NOTES
Commencement: 25 July 2013.

[2.996]
11   Issuers: unsolicited credit ratings

(1)   If the claimant is an issuer and a credit rating agency has assigned a credit rating in respect of such issuer or a financial instrument issued by such issuer, without the issuer, or a related third party, entering into a contract with that credit rating agency to assign a credit rating, the court may consider the following factors, amongst others, to be indications that a limitation on liability is reasonable and proportionate—

(a)   the credit rating agency gave the issuer a reasonable opportunity to submit additional factual information not previously available to the credit rating agency, or to clarify any factual inaccuracies regarding the proposed credit rating, before the credit rating was issued, and took account of those submissions or comments when finalising the credit rating;

(b)   the limitation relates to losses which the credit rating agency could not reasonably have foreseen when it assigned the credit rating;

(c)   the limitation relates to losses which no credit rating agency could reasonably insure against on a prudent commercial basis;

(d)   the limitation relates to losses which no credit rating agency would reasonably be expected to have the resources to meet.

(2)   The absence of a factor or factors in paragraph (1) does not indicate that a limitation on liability is unreasonable or disproportionate.

NOTES
Commencement: 25 July 2013.

[2.997]
12   Investors

(1)   If the claimant is an investor. the court may consider the following factors, amongst others, to be indications that a limitation on liability is reasonable and proportionate—

(a)   the limitation resulted from contractual negotiations between the investor and the credit rating agency;

(b)   the price agreed between the investor and the credit rating agency reflects the extent of the limitation on liability;

(c)   there is no relationship of proximity between the credit rating agency and the investor;

(d)   the limitation relates to losses resulting from unexpected or unusual uses of the credit rating;

(e)   the limitation relates to losses which the credit rating agency could not reasonably have foreseen when it assigned the credit rating;

(f)   the limitation relates to losses which no credit rating agency could reasonably insure against on a prudent commercial basis;

(g)   the limitation relates to losses which no credit rating agency would reasonably be expected to have the resources to meet.

(2)   The absence of a factor or factors in paragraph (1) does not indicate that a limitation on liability is unreasonable or disproportionate.

(3)   A limitation of liability is not likely to be reasonable and proportionate if the credit rating agency fails to take reasonable steps to bring the limitation to the attention of investors.

NOTES
Commencement: 25 July 2013.

[2.998]
13   Issuers: general approach to determining damages

(1)   The damages recoverable by an issuer in a claim under Article 35a are—
- (a)   where the issuer, or a related third party, has entered into a contract with a credit rating agency to assign a credit rating in respect of such issuer or a financial instrument issued by such issuer, the damages recoverable by the issuer in accordance with that contract; or
- (b)   where there is no such contract, the increase in the financing costs of the issuer resulting from the affected credit rating.

(2)   For the purpose of this regulation, "affected credit rating" means, where a credit rating agency has committed an infringement, the rating category that the credit rating agency assigned to the issuer or financial instrument, where such rating category is different to that which would have been assigned if the infringement had not occurred.

NOTES
Commencement: 25 July 2013.

[2.999]
14   Investors: general approach to determining damages

The damages recoverable by an investor in a claim under Article 35a are—
- (a)   where the investor enters into a contract with a credit rating agency to provide a credit rating, the damages recoverable by the investor in accordance with that contract; or
- (b)   where there is no such contract, the damages that would be recoverable by the investor if the investor had succeeded in a claim against the credit rating agency in the tort of negligence.

NOTES
Commencement: 25 July 2013.

[2.1000]
15   Issuers and investors: duty to mitigate loss and contributory negligence

(1)   The common law principle that a claimant's damages may be reduced if the claimant fails to mitigate their loss applies to any damages assessed under regulations 13 and 14.

(2)   The provisions of the Law Reform (Contributory Negligence) Act 1945 apply to any damages assessed under regulations 13 and 14.

NOTES
Commencement: 25 July 2013.

[2.1001]
16   Limitation Period

No claim may be brought under Article 35a after the expiry of the period of one year beginning with the date on which the claimant discovered the infringement, or could with reasonable diligence have discovered it.

NOTES
Commencement: 25 July 2013.

[2.1002]
17   Courts with jurisdiction to hear Article 35a claims

A claim under Article 35a must be brought in the High Court or, in Scotland, the Court of Session.

NOTES
Commencement: 25 July 2013.

[2.1003]
18   Review

(1)   The Treasury must from time to time—
- (a)   carry out a review of these Regulations,
- (b)   set out the conclusions of the review in a report, and
- (c)   publish the report.

(2)   In carrying out the review, the Treasury must, so far as is reasonable, have regard to how Article 35a is implemented in other member States.

(3)   The report must in particular—
- (a)   set out the objectives intended to be achieved by these Regulations,
- (b)   assess the extent to which those objectives are achieved, and
- (c)   assess whether those objectives remain appropriate and, if so, the extent to which they could be achieved with a system that imposes less regulation.

(4) The first report under this regulation must be published before the end of the period of five years beginning with the day on which these Regulations come into force.

(5) Reports under this regulation are afterwards to be published at intervals not exceeding five years.

NOTES
Commencement: 25 July 2013.

FINANCIAL SERVICES AND MARKETS ACT 2000 (REGULATED ACTIVITIES) (AMENDMENT) (NO 2) ORDER 2013
(SI 2013/1881)

NOTES
Made: 25 July 2013.
Authority: Financial Services and Markets Act 2000, ss 22(1), (1A), (5), 428(3), Sch 2, para 25; European Communities Act 1972, s 2(2).
Commencement: see art 1.

ARRANGEMENT OF ARTICLES

PART 1
INTRODUCTION

PART 1
INTRODUCTION

[2.1004]
1   Citation, commencement and interpretation

(1)   This Order may be cited as the Financial Services and Markets Act 2000 (Regulated Activities) (Amendment) (No 2) Order 2013.

(2)   This Order comes into force on the day after the day on which this Order is made for the purpose of—

(a)   the FCA, PRA and the scheme operator making rules,

(b)   the FCA designating relevant instruments under Part 8 of this Order,

(c)   the FCA giving guidance, and

(d)   the FCA and PRA imposing requirements or giving directions.

(3)   Article 28 (consequential amendments to other legislation etc) and paragraph 17 of the Schedule come into force on the day after the day on which this Order is made for the purpose of making orders.

(4)   Articles 61, 62 (rules etc) and 66 (information sharing) come into force on the day after the day on which this Order is made.

(5)   Chapter 4 of Part 8 (transitional provisions in relation to permission etc) comes into force on 2nd September 2013 to the extent it is not already in force.

(6)   This Order comes into force on 1st April 2014 to the extent it is not already in force.

(7)   In this Order—

"the Act" means the Financial Services and Markets Act 2000;

"the 1974 Act" means the Consumer Credit Act 1974;

"the OFT" means the Office of Fair Trading;

"the Regulated Activities Order" means the Financial Services and Markets Act 2000 (Regulated Activities) Order 2001.

NOTES

Commencement: 26 July 2013 (for the purpose of (a) the FCA, PRA and the scheme operator making rules, (b) the FCA designating relevant instruments under Part 8 of this Order, (c) the FCA giving guidance, and (d) the FCA and PRA imposing requirements or giving directions); 1 April 2014 (otherwise).

2–9   (*Part 2 (arts 2–9) amends the Financial Services and Markets Act 2000 (Regulated Activities) Order 2001, SI 2001/544 at* **[2.168]** *et seq.*)

PART 3
AMENDMENTS OF THE ACT ETC

10   (*Amends the Financial Services and Markets Act 2000 at* **[1.1395]** *et seq.*)

[2.1005]
11 Transitional and savings provisions related to article 10

(1)   This article makes provision in connection with the amendments to the Act made by article 10.

(2)   The amendments to sections 1H and 404E do not apply in so far as those provisions relate to, or apply for the purposes of, anything done under the Act concerning things done (or not done) before 1st April 2014.

(3)   The repeal of section 194(2) to (4) does not affect the continued validity of any requirement imposed under section 194(3).

(4)   The repeal of sections 203 and 204 and Schedule 16 does not affect the continued validity of any prohibition or restriction imposed; and in relation to such a prohibition or restriction, sections 203(6) and (7) and 204(3) and Schedule 16 continue to apply as if each reference to the OFT were a reference to the FCA.

(5)   A complaint made under the ombudsman scheme before 1st April 2014 and being dealt with under section 226A (consumer credit jurisdiction) is to be dealt with under section 226 (compulsory jurisdiction)

(6)   It is immaterial for the purposes of paragraph (5) that the conditions mentioned in section 226(2) are not satisfied.

(7)   A complaint made under the ombudsman scheme on or after 1st April 2014—
   (a)   which relates to an act or omission which took place before 1st April 2014,
   (b)   which could have been dealt with under the ombudsman scheme under section 226A (disregarding the effect of section 226A(2)(a) and (b)) but for the repeal of that section, and
   (c)   in relation to which the condition mentioned in section 226(2)(a) is satisfied,
is to be dealt with under the ombudsman scheme under section 226 (compulsory jurisdiction).

(8)   It is immaterial for the purposes of paragraph (7) that the conditions mentioned in section 226(2)(b) and (c) are not satisfied.

(9)   Contributions received by the scheme operator under section 234A (funding by consumer credit licensees etc) may be used by the scheme operator for the purpose of funding its operation in relation to complaints of the kind referred to in paragraph (5) or (7) and other complaints dealt with under the ombudsman scheme by virtue of section 226.

(10)   The repeal of paragraph 23 of Schedule 3 does not affect the continued validity of anything done under section 55L or 55M.

NOTES
   Commencement: 26 July 2013 (for the purpose of (a) the FCA, PRA and the scheme operator making rules, (b) the FCA designating relevant instruments under Part 8 of this Order, (c) the FCA giving guidance, and (d) the FCA and PRA imposing requirements or giving directions); 1 April 2014 (otherwise).

[2.1006]
12 Obligations of certain [persons who carry on credit broking]

[(1)   This article applies to a person ("P") who is within the description in paragraph (1A) or the description in paragraph (1B).

(1A)   A person is within the description in this paragraph if the person—
   (a)   is not an authorised person,
   (b)   carries on an activity of the kind specified by article 36A(1)(d) to (f) of the Regulated Activities Order (credit broking), and
   (c)   is not exempt from the general prohibition in relation to the carrying on of that activity by virtue of section 327(1) of the Act (exemption from the general prohibition for members of a designated professional body).

(1B)   A person is within the description in this paragraph if the person would be carrying on an activity of the kind specified by article 36A(1)(d) to (f) (credit broking) of the Regulated Activities Order but for article 36B(1)(a) (introducing by individuals in the course of canvassing off trade premises), 36F (activities carried on by members of the legal profession etc) or 72G (local authorities) of that Order.]

(2)   P must indicate in advertising and documentation intended for borrowers or those who may become a borrower the extent of P's powers, in particular whether P works exclusively for one or more lenders or does not work for any lender.

(3)   P must disclose to the borrower or any person who may become a borrower the fee, if any, payable by the borrower to P for P's services.

(4)   Any fee to be paid by the borrower to P must be agreed between the borrower and P and that agreement must be recorded in writing or other durable medium before the credit agreement is entered into.

(5)   P must disclose to the lender the fee, if any, payable by the borrower to P for P's services for the purpose of enabling the lender to calculate the annual percentage rate of charge in relation to the credit agreement.

(6)   In this article, "borrower" and "lender" have the meanings given by Article 60L of the Regulated Activities Order.

(7)   A contravention by P of a provision of this article is actionable at the suit of a private person who suffers loss as a result of the contravention, subject to the defences and other incidents applying to actions for breach of statutory duties.

(8)   "Private person" has the meaning prescribed for the purposes of section 138D of the Act (action for damages).

(9)   Sections 165 (regulator's power to require information: authorised persons etc) and 167 (appointment of persons to carry out general investigations) apply as if each reference to an authorised person (except in section 165(11) and 167(2)) included a reference to a person who falls within paragraph (1).

(10)   Part 14 of the Act (disciplinary measures) applies to the requirements imposed by this article as if each reference to an authorised person included a reference to a person who, at the time of the contravention of the requirement, fell within paragraph (1).

NOTES

Commencement: 26 July 2013 (for the purpose of (a) the FCA, PRA and the scheme operator making rules, (b) the FCA designating relevant instruments under Part 8 of this Order, (c) the FCA giving guidance, and (d) the FCA and PRA imposing requirements or giving directions); 1 April 2014 (otherwise).

The words in square brackets in the article heading were substituted, and paras (1)–(1B) were substituted (for the original para (1)), by the Financial Services and Markets Act 2000 (Consumer Credit) (Miscellaneous Provisions) (No 2) Order 2014, SI 2014/506, art 5(1)–(3).

13–28   (*Arts 13–19 (Part 4) amend the Financial Services and Markets Act 2000 (Carrying on Regulated Activities By Way of Business) Order 2001, SI 2001/1177, the Financial Services and Markets Act 2000 (Exemption) Order 2001, SI 2001/1201, the Financial Services and Markets Act 2000 (Appointed Representatives) Regulations 2001, SI 2001/1217, the Financial Services and Markets Act 2000 (Rights of Action) Regulations 2001, SI 2001/2256, the Financial Services and Markets Act 2000 (Financial Promotion) Order 2005, SI 2005/1529, the Financial Services and Markets Act 2000 (Controllers) (Exemption) Order 2009, SI 2009/774, and revoke the Financial Services and Markets Act 2000 (Ombudsman Scheme) (Consumer Credit Jurisdiction) Order 2007, SI 2007/383. Art 20 (Part 5) amends the Consumer Credit Act 1974 at* **[1.520]**. *Arts 21–27 (Part 6) revoke and amend, subject to certain transitional provisions, a variety of secondary legislation made under the Consumer Credit Act 1974. Art 28 (Part 7) introduces the Schedule to this Order which contains further consequential amendments and transitional provisions.*)

PART 8
TRANSITIONAL PROVISIONS

CHAPTER 1
INTERPRETATION

[2.1007]
29   Interpretation of Part 8

In this Part—
"appeal period", "debtor", "hirer", "licence", "licensee", "regulated agreement" and "standard licence" have the meanings given by the 1974 Act (disregarding any repeal of the 1974 Act by this Order);
"appropriate regulator" means—
(a)   in relation to a person who is, or is applying to become, a PRA-authorised person, the PRA;
(b)   in any other case, the FCA.

NOTES

Commencement: 26 July 2013 (for the purpose of (a) the FCA, PRA and the scheme operator making rules, (b) the FCA designating relevant instruments under Part 8 of this Order, (c) the FCA giving guidance, and (d) the FCA and PRA imposing requirements or giving directions); 1 April 2014 (otherwise).

CHAPTER 2
LICENSING ETC

[2.1008]
30   Meaning of "relevant person" in Chapter 2

[(1)]   Paragraphs (3) to (9) apply if, before 1st April 2014—In this Chapter, "relevant person" means a person who—
(a)   immediately before 1st April 2014 held a licence under the 1974 Act, and
(b)   on 1st April 2014 has a Part 4A permission to carry on a regulated activity by virtue of this Order (regardless of whether the person had permission via other means).

[(2)   Paragraph (3) applies where, before 1st April 2014, the OFT—

(a) had given a notice to a person ("A") under section 32A(2) of the 1974 Act (suspension of a standard licence) that it is suspending A's licence, but

(b) had not determined under section 34ZA of that Act (representations to OFT: suspension under section 32A) whether or not to confirm such a decision.

(3) For the purposes of article 39 (suspension of licence where determination made before 1st April 2014 but not confirmed), and of paragraph (1) in so far as it defines "relevant person" for the purposes of that article—

(a) A is to be treated as holding a licence under the 1974 Act immediately before 1st April 2014, and

(b) section 32A of that Act (power to suspend licence) is to be treated as if subsection (5) did not apply at that time.

(4) Paragraph (5) applies where, before 1st April 2014—

(a) the OFT had—

  (i) given a notice to a person ("B") under section 32A(2) of the 1974 Act that it is suspending B's licence, and

  (ii) confirmed under section 34ZA of that Act its determination under section 32A of that Act, and

(b) either—

  (i) B had submitted a notice of appeal to the First-tier Tribunal under section 41 of the 1974 Act (appeals to First-tier Tribunal under Part 3) with respect to that suspension, and the appeal had not been determined, or

  (ii) B had not submitted such a notice of appeal, but the specified period in respect of an appeal against the suspension had not expired.

(5) For the purposes of article 40 (suspension of licence where determination made before 1st April 2014 and confirmed), and of paragraph (1) in so far as it defines "relevant person" for the purposes of that article—

(a) B is to be treated as holding a licence under the 1974 Act immediately before 1st April 2014, and

(b) section 32A of that Act (power to suspend licence) is to be treated as if subsection (5) did not apply at that time.

(6) In this article, "specified period" has the meaning given in section 41 of the 1974 Act.]

NOTES

Commencement: 26 July 2013 (for the purpose of (a) the FCA, PRA and the scheme operator making rules, (b) the FCA designating relevant instruments under Part 8 of this Order, (c) the FCA giving guidance, and (d) the FCA and PRA imposing requirements or giving directions); 1 April 2014 (otherwise).

Para (1) numbered as such, and paras (2)–(6) added, by the Financial Services and Markets Act 2000 (Consumer Credit) (Transitional Provisions) Order 2014, SI 2014/376, arts 2, 3.

[2.1009]
31 Applications for a standard licence where no determination made before 1st April 2014

(1) Paragraphs (3) to (9) apply if, before 1st April 2014—

(a) the OFT received an application under section 24A of the 1974 Act (applications for standard licences) for a standard licence,

(b) the applicant ("A") had not withdrawn the application, and

(c) the OFT had not determined whether to issue a licence in accordance with the application.

(2) It is immaterial for the purposes of this article whether the OFT had, before 1st April 2014, given notice to A under section 27 of the 1974 Act (determination of applications) that the OFT was minded to refuse A's application.

(3) The application is to be treated as if it had been made to the appropriate regulator—

(a) if A is an authorised person, and the appropriate regulator is the PRA, under section 55I of the Act (variation by PRA at request of authorised person);

(b) if A is not an authorised person, under section 55A of the Act (application for permission);

(c) if A is an authorised person and the appropriate regulator is the FCA, under section 55H of the Act (variation by the FCA at request of authorised person).

(4) The application is to be treated as relating to the following regulated activities—

(a) if A's application related to the carrying on of an ancillary credit business in so far as it comprised or related to credit brokerage (within the meaning of the 1974 Act), the regulated activity of the kind specified by article 36A of the Regulated Activities Order (credit broking),

(b) if—

  (i) A's application related to the carrying on of an ancillary credit business in so far as it comprised or related to the activity of debt-administration (within the meaning of the 1974 Act), and

  (ii) A—

    (aa) indicated in A's application that A envisaged carrying on a business in a manner which would, if carried on after 1st April 2014, involve the carrying on of an activity of the kind specified by article 36H of the Regulated Activities Order (operating an electronic system in relation to lending), or

(bb)   had, before 1stApril 2014, given notice to the FCA of A's intention to carry on such a business,

a regulated activity of the kind specified by article 36H of the Regulated Activities Order,

(c)   to the extent that A's application related to any other activity, those regulated activities which are activities which were described in the application.

(5)   If—

(a)   A's application related to the carrying on of an ancillary credit business in so far as it comprised or related to the activity of debt-administration (within the meaning of the 1974 Act),

(b)   A's application is not, by virtue of paragraph (4), treated as relating to a regulated activity of the kind specified by article 36H of the Regulated Activities Order, and

(c)   A, before 1st June 2014, gives notice to the FCA of A's intention to carry on that activity,

the application is, from the date on which the FCA receives the notice, to be treated as relating to that activity, in addition to any activity to which the application is to be treated as relating to under paragraph (4).

(6)   Any description of business specified in A's application is to be treated for the purposes of Part 4A of the Act as forming part of A's application.

(7)   Section 55U(1) to (4) of the Act (applications under Part 4A) does not apply to A's application.

(8)   For the purposes of section 55V of the Act (determination of applications), the appropriate regulator is to be treated as having received the application on 1st April 2014.

(9)   For the purpose of paragraph (4), it is the nature of the activities in relation to which a licence is sought that matters, not how they are described in the application.

NOTES

Commencement: 26 July 2013 (for the purpose of (a) the FCA, PRA and the scheme operator making rules, (b) the FCA designating relevant instruments under Part 8 of this Order, (c) the FCA giving guidance, and (d) the FCA and PRA imposing requirements or giving directions); 1 April 2014 (otherwise).

[2.1010]
32   Applications for a standard licence where determination has been made but appeal period has not ended

(1)   Paragraphs (2) to (4) apply if, before 1st April 2014—

(a)   the OFT had given a notice to a person ("A") of its determination to refuse to issue a standard licence to A in accordance with A's application, and

(b)   the appeal period in relation to that decision had not ended.

(2)   The notice is to be treated as—

(a)   if A does not have a Part 4A permission, a decision notice given under section 55X(4) of the Act by the FCA to A of the decision to refuse A's application for Part 4A permission;

(b)   in any other case, a decision notice given under section 55X(4) of the Act of the decision of the appropriate regulator to refuse A's application to vary A's Part 4A permission.

(3)   But if A had, before 1st April 2014, submitted a notice of appeal to the First-tier Tribunal under section 41 of the 1974 Act (appeals to First-tier Tribunal under Part 3)—

(a)   section 55Z3 of the Act (right to refer matters to the Tribunal) does not apply, and

(b)   for the purposes of section 55V(4) of the Act, the appropriate regulator is not to be taken as having determined the application.

(4)   The notice has effect subject to any necessary modifications.

NOTES

Commencement: 26 July 2013 (for the purpose of (a) the FCA, PRA and the scheme operator making rules, (b) the FCA designating relevant instruments under Part 8 of this Order, (c) the FCA giving guidance, and (d) the FCA and PRA imposing requirements or giving directions); 1 April 2014 (otherwise).

[2.1011]
33   Variation of licence at request of licensee where no determination made before 1st April 2014

(1)   Paragraphs (3) to (6) apply if, before 1st April 2014—

(a)   the OFT received an application under section 30(1) of the 1974 Act (variation by request) for a variation of a standard licence,

(b)   the applicant ("A") had not withdrawn the application,

(c)   the OFT had not determined whether to vary the licence in accordance with the application, and

A is a relevant person.

(2) It is immaterial for the purposes of this article whether the OFT had, before 1st April 2014, given notice to A under section 30(4) of the 1974 Act (variation by request) that the OFT was minded to refuse A's application.

(3) The application is to be treated as if it had been made to the appropriate regulator under section 55I or 55H of the Act (as the case may be).

(4) The application has effect subject to any necessary modifications.

(5) Section 55U(1) to (4) of the Act (applications under Part 4A) does not apply to A's application.

(6) For the purposes of section 55V of the Act (determination of applications), the appropriate regulator is to be treated as having received the application on 1st April 2014.

NOTES

Commencement: 26 July 2013 (for the purpose of (a) the FCA, PRA and the scheme operator making rules, (b) the FCA designating relevant instruments under Part 8 of this Order, (c) the FCA giving guidance, and (d) the FCA and PRA imposing requirements or giving directions); 1 April 2014 (otherwise).

[2.1012]
34 Variation of licence at request of licensee where determination has been made but appeal period has not ended

(1) Paragraphs (2) to (4) apply if, before 1st April 2014—
   (a) the OFT had given notice to a person ("A") of its decision to refuse to vary a standard licence in accordance with an application made by A,
   (b) the appeal period in relation to that determination had not ended, and

A is a relevant person.

(2) The notice is to be treated as a decision notice under section 55X(4) of the Act of the decision of the appropriate regulator to refuse A's application to vary A's Part 4A permission.

(3) But if A had, before 1st April 2014, submitted a notice of appeal to the First-tier Tribunal under section 41 of the 1974 Act (appeals to First-tier Tribunal under Part 3), section 55Z3 of the Act (right to refer matters to the Tribunal) does not apply.

(4) The notice has effect subject to any necessary modifications.

NOTES

Commencement: 26 July 2013 (for the purpose of (a) the FCA, PRA and the scheme operator making rules, (b) the FCA designating relevant instruments under Part 8 of this Order, (c) the FCA giving guidance, and (d) the FCA and PRA imposing requirements or giving directions); 1 April 2014 (otherwise).

[2.1013]
35 Compulsory variation of a licence where no determination to vary made before 1st April 2014

(1) Paragraphs (2) to (4) apply if, before 1st April 2014—
   (a) the OFT had given notice to a person ("A") under section 31(2) of the 1974 Act (compulsory variation) that it is minded to vary the terms of A's licence,
   (b) the OFT had not determined to vary A's licence under that section, and

A is a relevant person.

(2) The notice is to be treated as a written notice given under section 55Y(4) of the Act by the FCA of a proposal to vary A's Part 4A permission (except for subsections (5) and (6) of section 55Y which do not apply).

(3) The notice has effect subject to any necessary modifications.

(4) If the period for making representations under section 34 of the 1974 Act in connection with that notice had not expired before 1st April 2014, subsections (1) and (2) of that section continue to apply as if—
   (a) in subsection (1), references to the OFT (apart from the first reference) were references to the FCA or, before 1st April 2014, the OFT;
   (b) in subsection (2), the reference to the OFT was to the FCA.

NOTES

Commencement: 26 July 2013 (for the purpose of (a) the FCA, PRA and the scheme operator making rules, (b) the FCA designating relevant instruments under Part 8 of this Order, (c) the FCA giving guidance, and (d) the FCA and PRA imposing requirements or giving directions); 1 April 2014 (otherwise).

[2.1014]
36 Compulsory variation of a licence where determination to vary made before 1st April 2014

(1) Paragraphs (2) to (4) apply if, before 1st April 2014—
   (a) the OFT had given notice of its determination under section 31 of the 1974 Act to vary the terms of the licence of a person ("A"),
   (b) the appeal period in relation to that determination had not ended, and

A is a relevant person.

(2)   The notice is to be treated as a written notice given under section 55Y(7) of the Act by the FCA of its decision to vary A's Part 4A permission (except for subsection (9) of section 55Y which does not apply).

(3)   But if A had, before 1st April 2014, submitted a notice of appeal to the First-tier Tribunal under section 41 of the 1974 Act (appeals to First-tier Tribunal under Part 3), section 55Z3 of the Act (right to refer matters to the Tribunal) does not apply.

(4)   The notice has effect subject to any necessary modifications.

NOTES

Commencement: 26 July 2013 (for the purpose of (a) the FCA, PRA and the scheme operator making rules, (b) the FCA designating relevant instruments under Part 8 of this Order, (c) the FCA giving guidance, and (d) the FCA and PRA imposing requirements or giving directions); 1 April 2014 (otherwise).

[2.1015]
37   Revocation etc of licence where no determination made before 1st April 2014

(1)   Paragraphs (3) to (5) apply if, before 1st April 2014—
  (a)   the OFT had given a notice under section 27 of the 1974 Act (determination of applications) to a person ("A") that it is minded to refuse A's application to renew A's standard licence,
  (b)   the OFT had not determined to refuse to renew A's licence, and
A is a relevant person.

(2)   Paragraphs (3) [to (5) also] apply if, before 1st April 2014—
  (a)   the OFT had given a notice under section 32(2) of the 1974 Act (revocation of a standard licence) to a person ("A"),
  (b)   the OFT had not determined to revoke A's licence under that section, and
A is a relevant person.

(3)   The notice is to be treated as—
  (a)   if A has Part 4A permission only by virtue of this Order, a warning notice given under section 55Z(1) of the Act by the FCA to A of the proposal by the FCA to cancel A's Part 4A permission (except for the purposes of [sections 387 (warning notices), 392(a) (application of sections 393 and 394), in so far as it applies to section 393 (third party rights), and 393 of the Act, which do not apply]);
  (b)   in any other case, a written notice under section 55Y(4) of the Act of the proposal by the FCA to vary A's Part 4A permission (except for subsections (5) and (6) of section 55Y which do not apply).

(4)   The notice has effect subject to any necessary modifications.

(5)   If the period for making representations under section 34 of the 1974 Act in connection with that notice had not expired before 1st April 2014, subsections (1) and (2) of that section continue to apply as if—
  (a)   in subsection (1), references to the OFT (apart from the first reference) were references to the FCA or, before 1st April 2014, the OFT;
  (b)   in subsection (2), the reference to the OFT was to the FCA.

NOTES

Commencement: 26 July 2013 (for the purpose of (a) the FCA, PRA and the scheme operator making rules, (b) the FCA designating relevant instruments under Part 8 of this Order, (c) the FCA giving guidance, and (d) the FCA and PRA imposing requirements or giving directions); 1 April 2014 (otherwise).

Paras (2), (3): words in square brackets substituted by the Financial Services and Markets Act 2000 (Consumer Credit) (Transitional Provisions) Order 2014, SI 2014/376, arts 2, 4.

[2.1016]
38   Revocation etc of licence where determination made before 1st April 2014

(1)   Paragraphs (3) to (5) apply if, before 1st April 2014—
  (a)   the OFT had given notice of its determination under section 27 of the 1974 Act not to renew the standard licence of a person ("A"),
  (b)   the appeal period in relation to that determination had not ended, and
A is a relevant person.

(2)   Paragraphs (3) to (5) apply if, before 1st April 2014—
  (a)   the OFT had given notice of its determination under section 32 of the 1974 Act to revoke the standard licence of a person ("A"),
  (b)   the appeal period in relation to that determination had not ended, and
A is a relevant person.

(3)   The notice is to be treated as—
  (a)   if A has Part 4A permission only by virtue of this Order, a decision notice given under section 55Z(2) of the Act by the FCA to A of the decision by the FCA to cancel A's Part 4A

permission [(except for the purposes of sections 392(b) (application of sections 393 and 394), in so far as it applies to section 393 (third party rights), and 393 of the Act, which do not apply)];

(b)　in any other case, a written notice under section 55Y(7) of the Act of the decision of the FCA to vary A's Part 4A permission (except for subsection (9) of section 55Y which does not apply).

(4)　But if A had, before 1st April 2014, submitted a notice of appeal to the First-tier Tribunal under section 41 of the 1974 Act (appeals to First-tier Tribunal under Part 3), section 55Z3 of the Act (right to refer matters to the Tribunal) does not apply.

(5)　The notice has effect subject to any necessary modifications.

NOTES

Commencement: 26 July 2013 (for the purpose of (a) the FCA, PRA and the scheme operator making rules, (b) the FCA designating relevant instruments under Part 8 of this Order, (c) the FCA giving guidance, and (d) the FCA and PRA imposing requirements or giving directions); 1 April 2014 (otherwise).

Para (3): words in square brackets substituted by the Financial Services and Markets Act 2000 (Consumer Credit) (Transitional Provisions) Order 2014, SI 2014/376, arts 2, 5.

[2.1017]
39　Suspension of licence where determination made before 1st April 2014 but not confirmed

(1)　Paragraphs (2) to (4) apply if, before 1st April 2014—
(a)　the OFT had given a notice to a person ("A") under section 32A(2) of the 1974 Act (suspension of a standard licence) that it is suspending A's licence,
(b)　the OFT had not, under section 34ZA of the 1974 Act (representations to OFT: suspension under section 32A) determined whether or not to confirm such a decision, [and]
(c)　. . .

A is a relevant person.

(2)　The notice is to be treated as—
(a)　if A has Part 4A permission only by virtue of this Order—
(i)　a written notice under section 55Y(4) of the Act of the decision of the FCA to vary A's Part 4A permission (except for subsections (5) and (6) of section 55Y which do not apply), and
(ii)　a warning notice given under section 55Z(1) of the Act by the FCA to A of the proposal by the FCA to cancel A's Part 4A permission (except for [the purposes of sections 387 (warning notices), 392(a) (application of sections 393 and 394), in so far as it applies to section 393 (third party rights), and 393 of the Act, which do not apply]);
(b)　in any other case, a written notice under section 55Y(4) of the Act of the decision of the FCA to vary A's Part 4A permission (except for subsections (5) and (6) of section 55Y which do not apply).

(3)　The notice has effect subject to any necessary modifications.

(4)　If the period for making representations under section 34ZA of the 1974 Act in connection with that notice had not expired before 1st April 2014, subsections (1) and (2) of that section continue to apply as if—
(a)　in subsection (1) each reference to the OFT (apart from the first reference) were a reference to the FCA or, before 1st April 2014, the OFT;
(b)　in subsection (2)—
(i)　the reference to the OFT was to the FCA;
(ii)　the words from "reconsider its determination" to "doing so must" were omitted.

NOTES

Commencement: 26 July 2013 (for the purpose of (a) the FCA, PRA and the scheme operator making rules, (b) the FCA designating relevant instruments under Part 8 of this Order, (c) the FCA giving guidance, and (d) the FCA and PRA imposing requirements or giving directions); 1 April 2014 (otherwise).

The word "and" in square brackets in para (1)(b) was inserted, para (1)(c) was revoked, and the words in square brackets in para (2)(a)(ii) were substituted, by the Financial Services and Markets Act 2000 (Consumer Credit) (Transitional Provisions) Order 2014, SI 2014/376, arts 2, 6.

[2.1018]
40　Suspension of licence where determination made before 1st April 2014 and confirmed

(1)　Paragraphs (2) to (4) apply if, before 1st April 2014—
(a)　the OFT had given a notice to a person ("A") under section 34ZA of the 1974 Act (representations to OFT: suspension under section 32A) of its determination to confirm a decision to suspend A's licence under section 32A of that Act, [and]
(b)　. . .

A is a relevant person.

(2)　The notice is to be treated as—
(a)　if A has Part 4A permission only by virtue of this Order—

    (i)   a written notice under section 55Y(7) of the Act of the decision of the FCA to vary A's Part 4A permission (except for subsection (9) of section 55Y which does not apply), and

    (ii)   a decision notice given under section 55Z(2) of the Act by the FCA of the decision by the FCA to cancel A's Part 4A permission [(except for the purposes of sections 392(b) (application of sections 393 and 394), in so far as it applies to section 393 (third party rights), and 393 of the Act, which do not apply)];

  (b)   in any other case, a written notice under section 55Y(7) of the Act of the decision of the FCA to vary A's Part 4A permission (except for subsection (9) of section 55Y which does not apply).

(3)   But if A had, before 1st April 2014, submitted a notice of appeal to the First-tier Tribunal under section 41 of the 1974 Act (appeals to First-tier Tribunal under Part 3), section 55Z3 of the Act (right to refer matters to the Tribunal) does not apply.

(4)   The notice has effect subject to any necessary modifications.

NOTES

Commencement: 26 July 2013 (for the purpose of (a) the FCA, PRA and the scheme operator making rules, (b) the FCA designating relevant instruments under Part 8 of this Order, (c) the FCA giving guidance, and (d) the FCA and PRA imposing requirements or giving directions); 1 April 2014 (otherwise).

The word "and" in square brackets in para (1)(a) was inserted, para (1)(b) was revoked, and the words in square brackets in para (2)(a)(ii) were inserted, by the Financial Services and Markets Act 2000 (Consumer Credit) (Transitional Provisions) Order 2014, SI 2014/376, arts 2, 7.

[2.1019]
41   Imposition of requirements etc where no determination made before 1st April 2014

(1)   Paragraphs (2) to (5) apply if, before 1st April 2014—

  (a)   the OFT had given a notice under section 33D(2) of the 1974 Act (notice of intention of OFT to impose requirements on licensee) to a person ("A") that the OFT is minded to make a determination to impose a requirement on A under section 33A of the 1974 Act or to vary or revoke a requirement imposed under section 33A of that Act,

  (b)   the OFT had not determined to impose a requirement on A or to vary or revoke a requirement imposed on A, and

A is a relevant person.

(2)   The notice is to be treated as written notice under section 55Y(4) of the Act of a proposal by the FCA to impose a requirement on A or to vary or to cancel a requirement (except for subsections (5) and (6) of section 55Y which do not apply).

(3)   The notice has effect subject to any necessary modifications.

(4)   In deciding whether to impose a requirement on A, the FCA must have regard to the guidance prepared by the OFT under section 33E of the 1974 Act in force immediately before 1st April 2014.

(5)   If the period for making representations under section 34 of the 1974 Act in connection with that notice had not expired before 1st April 2014, subsections (1) and (2) of that section continue to apply as if—

  (a)   in subsection (1), references to the OFT (apart from the first reference) were references to the FCA or, before 1st April 2014, the OFT;

  (b)   in subsection (2), the reference to the OFT was to the FCA.

NOTES

Commencement: 26 July 2013 (for the purpose of (a) the FCA, PRA and the scheme operator making rules, (b) the FCA designating relevant instruments under Part 8 of this Order, (c) the FCA giving guidance, and (d) the FCA and PRA imposing requirements or giving directions); 1 April 2014 (otherwise).

[2.1020]
42   Imposition of requirements etc where determination made but appeal period has not ended

(1)   Paragraphs (2) to (4) apply if, before 1st April 2014—

  (a)   the OFT had given notice to a person ("A") under section 33D of the 1974 Act of its determination to impose a requirement on A under section 33A of the 1974 Act or to vary or revoke a requirement imposed under section 33A of that Act,

  (b)   the appeal period in relation to that determination had not ended, and

A is a relevant person.

(2)   The notice is to be treated as written notice under section 55Y(7) of the Act of the decision by the FCA under section 55L of the Act to impose a requirement on A or to vary or to cancel a requirement (except for subsection (9) of section 55Y which does not apply).

(3)   But if A had, before 1st April 2014, submitted a notice of appeal to the First-tier Tribunal under section 41 of the 1974 Act (appeals to First-tier Tribunal under Part 3), section 55Z3 of the Act (right to refer matters to the Tribunal) does not apply.

(4)   The notice has effect subject to any necessary modifications.

NOTES

Commencement: 26 July 2013 (for the purpose of (a) the FCA, PRA and the scheme operator making rules, (b) the FCA designating relevant instruments under Part 8 of this Order, (c) the FCA giving guidance, and (d) the FCA and PRA imposing requirements or giving directions); 1 April 2014 (otherwise).

[2.1021]
43 Failure to comply with information requirement

(1) Paragraph (2) applies if, before 1st April 2014, a relevant person ("A") had failed to do something A was required to do by virtue of section 36B or 36C of the 1974 Act (power of OFT to require information or to require access to premises).

(2) Section 36E of the 1974 Act (failure to comply with information requirement) continues to apply in connection with A's failure as if the reference to the OFT were a reference to the FCA.

NOTES

Commencement: 26 July 2013 (for the purpose of (a) the FCA, PRA and the scheme operator making rules, (b) the FCA designating relevant instruments under Part 8 of this Order, (c) the FCA giving guidance, and (d) the FCA and PRA imposing requirements or giving directions); 1 April 2014 (otherwise).

[2.1022]
44 Civil penalties—where no determination made before 1st April 2014

(1) Paragraphs (2) to (7) apply if, before 1st April 2014—
   (a) the OFT had given a notice under section 39B(1) of the 1974 Act (notice that OFT is minded to impose a civil penalty) to a person ("A") that it is minded to impose a penalty on A under section 39A of the 1974 Act (power to impose civil penalties), and
   (b) the OFT had not before 1st April 2014—
      (i) given A a penalty notice under section 39A of the 1974 Act, or
      (ii) given notice to A under section 34 of the 1974 Act of its determination not to give such a penalty notice.

(2) The notice is to be treated as a warning notice given by the FCA to A under section 207(1)(b) of the Act (except for the purposes of sections 210 (statements of policy)[, 387 (warning notices), 392(a) (application of sections 393 and 394), in so far as it applies to section 393 (third party rights), and 393 of the Act] which do not apply).

(3) The notice has effect subject to any necessary modifications.

(4) For the purposes of this article, each reference in Part 14 of the Act and any provision made under Part 14 of the Act to an "authorised person" is to be treated as including a reference to A.

(5) If the period for making representations under section 34 of the 1974 Act in connection with that notice had not expired before 1st April 2014, subsections (1) and (2) of that section continue to apply as if—
   (a) in subsection (1), references to the OFT (apart from the first reference) were references to the FCA or, before 1st April 2014, the OFT;
   (b) in subsection (2), the reference to the OFT was to the FCA.

(6) In determining what if any financial penalty to impose on A, the FCA must have regard to—
   (a) any penalty or fine that has been imposed on A by another body in relation to the conduct giving rise to the possible imposition of the penalty;
   (b) other steps the OFT or FCA has taken, or the FCA might take, in relation to that conduct;
   (c) the statement of policy prepared by the OFT under section 39C of the 1974 Act as most recently published at the time the conduct occurred.

(7) The financial penalty imposed on A by the FCA in relation to each failure to comply with a requirement may not exceed £50,000.

(8) Section 210 of the Act (statement of policy) does not apply to a penalty imposed by the FCA by virtue of this article.

NOTES

Commencement: 26 July 2013 (for the purpose of (a) the FCA, PRA and the scheme operator making rules, (b) the FCA designating relevant instruments under Part 8 of this Order, (c) the FCA giving guidance, and (d) the FCA and PRA imposing requirements or giving directions); 1 April 2014 (otherwise).

Para (2): words in square brackets substituted by the Financial Services and Markets Act 2000 (Consumer Credit) (Transitional Provisions) Order 2014, SI 2014/376, arts 2, 8.

[2.1023]
45 Civil penalties—where determination made but appeal period has not ended

(1) Paragraphs (2) to (5) apply if, before 1st April 2014—
   (a) the OFT had given A a penalty notice under section 39A of the 1974 Act, and
   (b) the appeal period in relation to that notice had not expired.

(2)   The notice is to be treated as a decision notice given by the FCA to A under section 208(1)(b) of the Act (except for the purposes of [sections 210 (statement of policy), 392(b) (application of sections 393 and 394), in so far as it applies to section 393 (third party rights), and 393 of the Act, which do not apply]).

(3)   But if A has, before 1st April 2014, submitted a notice of appeal to the First-tier Tribunal under section 41 of the 1974 Act (appeals to First-tier Tribunal under Part 3), section 208(4) of the Act (right to refer matters to the Tribunal) does not apply.

(4)   The notice has effect subject to any necessary modifications.

(5)   For the purposes of this article, each reference in Part 14 of the Act (disciplinary measures) and any provision made under Part 14 of the Act to an "authorised person" is to be treated as including a reference to A.

NOTES

Commencement: 26 July 2013 (for the purpose of (a) the FCA, PRA and the scheme operator making rules, (b) the FCA designating relevant instruments under Part 8 of this Order, (c) the FCA giving guidance, and (d) the FCA and PRA imposing requirements or giving directions); 1 April 2014 (otherwise).

Para (2): words in square brackets substituted by the Financial Services and Markets Act 2000 (Consumer Credit) (Transitional Provisions) Order 2014, SI 2014/376, arts 2, 9.

[2.1024]
46   Civil penalties—where determination made before 1stApril 2014 and penalty due

(1)   Paragraphs (2) to (4) apply if, before 1st April 2014—
   (a)   the OFT had given A a penalty notice under section 39A of the 1974 Act, and
   (b)   the appeal period in relation to that notice had expired.

(2)   The penalty is payable to the FCA (rather than the OFT).

(3)   If a defaulter (within the meaning of section 39A of the 1974 Act) had not paid to the OFT before 1st April 2014 the penalty imposed under that section—
   (a)   the defaulter must pay the unpaid balance to the FCA;
   (b)   section 39A(5) of the 1974 Act continues to apply to the defaulter with the following modifications—
      (i)   omit "to the OFT";
      (ii)   the reference to the OFT in paragraph (b) is to be treated as a reference to the FCA.

(4)   For the purposes of Part 3 of Schedule 1ZA to the Act (penalties and fees)—
   (a)   any amounts received by the FCA by virtue of this article are to be treated as amounts received by way of penalties imposed under the Act;
   (b)   any expenses incurred by the FCA in connection with the recovery of penalties due to it by virtue of this article are to be treated as incurred in connection with the recovery of penalties imposed under the Act.

NOTES

Commencement: 26 July 2013 (for the purpose of (a) the FCA, PRA and the scheme operator making rules, (b) the FCA designating relevant instruments under Part 8 of this Order, (c) the FCA giving guidance, and (d) the FCA and PRA imposing requirements or giving directions); 1 April 2014 (otherwise).

[2.1025]
47   Civil penalties—where no formal action taken before 1st April 2014

(1)   Paragraphs (2) to (6) apply if—
   (a)   the FCA is satisfied that a person ("A") had, before 1st April 2014, failed to comply with a requirement imposed on A under section 33A, 33B or 36A of the 1974 Act, and
   (b)   the OFT had not, before 1st April 2014, given a notice under section 39B(1) of the 1974 Act to A that the OFT was minded to impose a penalty on A under section 39A of the 1974 Act.

(2)   The FCA may impose a penalty, in respect of the failure, on A under section 206 of the Act (financial penalties).

(3)   For the purposes of this article, each reference in Part 14 of the Act and any provision made under Part 14 of the Act to an "authorised person" is to be treated as including a reference to A.

(4)   In determining what if any financial penalty to impose on A, the FCA must have regard to—
   (a)   any penalty or fine that has been imposed on A by another body in relation to the conduct giving rise to the possible imposition of the penalty;
   (b)   other steps the OFT or FCA has taken, or the FCA might take, in relation to that conduct;
   (c)   the statement of policy prepared by the OFT under section 39C of the 1974 Act as most recently published at the time the conduct occurred.

(5)   The financial penalty imposed on A by the FCA in relation to each failure to comply with a requirement may not exceed £50,000.

(6)   Section 210 of the Act (statement of policy) does not apply to a penalty imposed by the FCA by virtue of this article.

NOTES

Commencement: 26 July 2013 (for the purpose of (a) the FCA, PRA and the scheme operator making rules, (b) the FCA designating relevant instruments under Part 8 of this Order, (c) the FCA giving guidance, and (d) the FCA and PRA imposing requirements or giving directions); 1 April 2014 (otherwise).

[2.1026]
48 Enforcement of agreements made by unlicensed trader

(1) This article applies to a regulated agreement entered into before 1st April 2014 ("a relevant agreement").

(2) A relevant agreement is not enforceable against the debtor or hirer by a person carrying on a regulated activity of the kind specified by article 60B(2) or 60N(2) of the Regulated Activities Order (as the case may be) if that person does not have permission to carry on that activity.

(3) Section 40(1A) and (2) of the 1974 [Act] continue to apply to a relevant agreement with the following modifications—

 (a) after "Unless the OFT has" insert "before 1st April 2014";
 (b) after "applies to the agreement" insert "or the FCA has given a notice under section 28A of the Financial Services and Markets Act 2000 by virtue of subsection (1B)";
 (c) after subsection (1A) there is inserted—

"(1B) Sections 28A and 28B of the Financial Services and Markets Act 2000 apply to a regulated agreement which is not enforceable by virtue of subsection (1A) with the following modifications—

 (a) [subsections (1) and (2)] and paragraph (b) of subsection (3) of section 28A do not apply;
 (b) for subsections (4) to (6) of section 28A substitute—

"(4) In considering whether to allow the agreement to be enforced the FCA must have regard to whether the relevant firm reasonably believed that a licence under the Consumer Credit Act 1974 was not required by the creditor or owner (as the case may be) to enter into the agreement.";

 (c) for subsection (8) of section 28A substitute—

"(8) "The relevant firm" means the person who (disregarding the effect of [section 40(1A) of the Consumer Credit Act 1974]), would be entitled to enforce the agreement.".

NOTES

Commencement: 26 July 2013 (for the purpose of (a) the FCA, PRA and the scheme operator making rules, (b) the FCA designating relevant instruments under Part 8 of this Order, (c) the FCA giving guidance, and (d) the FCA and PRA imposing requirements or giving directions); 1 April 2014 (otherwise).

Para (3): word in first pair of square brackets inserted, and words in second and third pairs of square brackets substituted, by the Financial Services and Markets Act 2000 (Consumer Credit) (Miscellaneous Provisions) Order 2014, SI 2014/208, art 7(1), (2).

[2.1027]
[48A Enforcement of agreements for ancillary credit services

(1) Section 148(1) (agreement for services of unlicensed trader) of the Consumer Credit Act 1974 and section 145 (types of ancillary credit business) of that Act, in so far as that section relates to section 148(1), continue to apply to a relevant agreement and for that purpose section 148 is to be treated as if—

 (a) in subsection (1)—
  (i) after "the OFT has", there were inserted "before 1st April 2014;
  (ii) after "applies to the agreement", there were inserted "or the FCA has given a notice under section 28A of the Financial Services and Markets Act 2000 by virtue of subsection (1A);
 (b) after subsection (1), there were inserted—

"(1A) Sections 28A and 28B of the Financial Services and Markets Act 2000 apply to an agreement which is not enforceable by virtue of subsection (1) with the following modifications—

  (a) in section 28A, subsections (1), (2) and (3)(b) do not apply;
  (b) for section 28A(4) to (6), substitute—
"(4) In considering whether to allow the agreement to be enforced the FCA must have regard to whether the relevant firm reasonably believed that a licence under the Consumer Credit Act 1974 was not required by the trader to enter into the agreement.";
  (c) for section 28A(8), substitute—
"(8) "The relevant firm" means the person who, disregarding the effect of section 148(1) of the Consumer Credit Act 1974, would be entitled to enforce the agreement."".

(2)   In paragraph (1), a "relevant agreement" means an agreement entered into before 1st April 2014 to which section 148(1) of the Consumer Credit Act 1974 applies on 31st March 2014.]

NOTES
Commencement: 1 April 2014.
Inserted, together with art 49B, by the Financial Services and Markets Act 2000 (Consumer Credit) (Miscellaneous Provisions) Order 2014, SI 2014/208, art 7(1), (3).

[2.1028]
[48B   Enforcement of agreements made on introductions by unlicensed credit-broker
(1)   Section 149(1) (regulated agreements made on introductions by unlicensed credit broker) of the Consumer Credit Act 1974 continues to apply to a relevant agreement and for that purpose section 149 is to be treated as if—
    (a)   in subsection (1)—
        (i)   after "the OFT has", in each place, there were inserted "before 1st April 2014;
        (ii)   after "applies to the agreement", there were inserted "or the FCA has given a notice under section 28A of the Financial Services and Markets Act 2000 by virtue of subsection (1A);
    (b)   after subsection (1), there were inserted—
    "(1A)   Sections 28A and 28B of the Financial Services and Markets Act 2000 apply to an agreement which is not enforceable by virtue of subsection (1) with the following modifications—
        (a)   in section 28A, subsections (1), (2) and (3)(b) do not apply;
        (b)   for section 28A(4) to (6), substitute—
    "(4)   In considering whether to allow the agreement to be enforced the FCA must have regard to whether the relevant firm reasonably believed that a licence under the Consumer Credit Act 1974 was not required by the credit-broker when introducing the debtor or hirer to the creditor or owner.";
        (c)   for section 28A(8), substitute—
    "(8)   "The relevant firm" means the person who, disregarding the effect of section 149(1) of the Consumer Credit Act 1974, would be entitled to enforce the agreement."".

(2)   In paragraph (1), a "relevant agreement" means an agreement entered into before 1st April 2014 to which section 149(1) of the Consumer Credit Act 1974 applies on 31st March 2014.]

NOTES
Commencement: 1 April 2014.
Inserted as noted to art 48A at **[2.1027]**.

[2.1029]
49   Offences committed under the 1974 Act before 1st April 2014
Section 402(1) of the Act (power of FCA to institute proceedings for certain offences) applies as if it included a reference to offences committed under the 1974 Act before 1st April 2014.

NOTES
Commencement: 26 July 2013 (for the purpose of (a) the FCA, PRA and the scheme operator making rules, (b) the FCA designating relevant instruments under Part 8 of this Order, (c) the FCA giving guidance, and (d) the FCA and PRA imposing requirements or giving directions); 1 April 2014 (otherwise).

[2.1030]
50   Information and investigation powers
(1)   Section 165 of the Act (regulators' power to require information) has effect as if each reference to "authorised person" (except in subsection (7)) included a reference to a person who at any time held a standard licence under the 1974 Act.
(2)   Section 168 of the Act (appointment of persons to carry out investigations in particular cases) applies as if—
    (a)   subsection (1) included a reference to an offence under the 1974 Act;
    (b)   subsection (4) included a reference to circumstances suggesting that a person may have, before 1st April 2014, failed to comply with a requirement imposed on that person under section 33A, 33B or 36A of the 1974 Act.
(3)   Part 27 of the Act (offences) applies as if references to an offence included references to an offence under Part 11 of the Act as modified by this Order.

NOTES
Commencement: 26 July 2013 (for the purpose of (a) the FCA, PRA and the scheme operator making rules, (b) the FCA designating relevant instruments under Part 8 of this Order, (c) the FCA giving guidance, and (d) the FCA and PRA imposing requirements or giving directions); 1 April 2014 (otherwise).

[2.1031]
51 Applications made to the OFT which have not been determined by 1st April 2014

(1) Any application which before 1st April 2014—
- (a) had been made to the OFT under the 1974 Act, and
- (b) had not been determined by the OFT,

is to be treated as having been made to the FCA, unless paragraph (2) applies.

(2) This paragraph applies if the application had been made under a provision of the 1974 Act which is repealed by this Order.

NOTES

Commencement: 26 July 2013 (for the purpose of (a) the FCA, PRA and the scheme operator making rules, (b) the FCA designating relevant instruments under Part 8 of this Order, (c) the FCA giving guidance, and (d) the FCA and PRA imposing requirements or giving directions); 1 April 2014 (otherwise).

[2.1032]
52 Decision notices

In relation to any notice which is, by virtue of this Chapter of this Part, to be treated as a decision notice given under the Act—
- (a) it is immaterial whether the notice complies with section 388(1)(b) to (e) of the Act (decision notices), and
- (b) that section applies as if, for subsections (3) and (4), there were substituted—

"(3) The regulator concerned may, before it takes the action to which a decision notice ("the original notice") relates, give the person concerned a further decision notice.
(4) A further decision notice given under subsection (3) may in particular—
- (a) relate to different action in respect of the same matter, or
- (b) vary the original notice.".

NOTES

Commencement: 26 July 2013 (for the purpose of (a) the FCA, PRA and the scheme operator making rules, (b) the FCA designating relevant instruments under Part 8 of this Order, (c) the FCA giving guidance, and (d) the FCA and PRA imposing requirements or giving directions); 1 April 2014 (otherwise).

[2.1033]
53 Waivers

Any of the following given or made by the OFT which are in effect immediately before 1st April 2014 are to have effect as if they had been given or made by the FCA—
- (a) a direction given under section 60(3) of the 1974 Act (form and content of agreements);
- (b) a determination made under regulations made under section 64(4) of the 1974 Act (duty to give notice of cancellation rights);
- (c) a direction given under section 101(8) or (8A) of the 1974 Act (right to terminate hire agreement);
- (d) a direction given under section 160(1) of the 1974 Act (alternative procedure for business consumers).

NOTES

Commencement: 26 July 2013 (for the purpose of (a) the FCA, PRA and the scheme operator making rules, (b) the FCA designating relevant instruments under Part 8 of this Order, (c) the FCA giving guidance, and (d) the FCA and PRA imposing requirements or giving directions); 1 April 2014 (otherwise).

CHAPTER 3
APPEALS

[2.1034]
54 Appeals—where steps taken before 1st April 2014

(1) Paragraphs (2) and (3) (in addition to provision made in Chapter 2) apply where a person ("A") had, before 1st April 2014, submitted a notice of appeal to the First-tier Tribunal under section 41 of the 1974 Act (appeals to First-tier Tribunal under Part 3) ("a relevant appeal").

(2) Sections 41 to 41ZB of the 1974 Act (appeals, Tribunal procedure rules and disposal of appeals) continue to apply to a relevant appeal (notwithstanding any repeal made by this Order) with the following modifications to section 41ZB—
- (a) for each reference to the "OFT" substitute "FCA";
- (b) omit subsections (5) and (6).

(3) In any relevant appeal—
- (a) anything done by the OFT before 1st April 2014 in relation to the appeal is to be treated as having been done by the FCA;
- (b) the FCA is substituted for the OFT as a party to the appeal.

NOTES

Commencement: 26 July 2013 (for the purpose of (a) the FCA, PRA and the scheme operator making rules, (b) the FCA designating relevant instruments under Part 8 of this Order, (c) the FCA giving guidance, and (d) the FCA and PRA imposing requirements or giving directions); 1 April 2014 (otherwise).

[2.1035]
55   Appeals—where no steps taken before 1st April 2014

(1)   Paragraphs (2) to (4) (in addition to provision made in Chapter 2) apply where a person ("A") had, before 1st April 2014, a right to submit a notice of appeal to the First-tier Tribunal under section 41 of the 1974 Act but had not exercised that right before that date.

(2)   A may refer the matter to the Tribunal within the specified period.

(3)   Section 133 of the Act (proceedings before Tribunal: general provision) applies to any such reference as if it were a disciplinary reference (within the meaning of that section).

(4)   In this article, "specified period" has the same meaning as in the 1974 Act.

NOTES

Commencement: 26 July 2013 (for the purpose of (a) the FCA, PRA and the scheme operator making rules, (b) the FCA designating relevant instruments under Part 8 of this Order, (c) the FCA giving guidance, and (d) the FCA and PRA imposing requirements or giving directions); 1 April 2014 (otherwise).

CHAPTER 4
PERMISSION ETC

[2.1036]
56   Interim permission

(1)   Unless paragraph (12) applies, on and after 1st April 2014, any relevant person ("P") who, immediately before that date, held a standard licence under the 1974 Act is to be treated as having an interim permission to carry on—

    (a)   if P's licence covered the carrying on of an ancillary credit business in so far as it comprised or related to credit brokerage (within the meaning of the 1974 Act), the regulated activity specified in article 36A of the Regulated Activities Order (credit broking) and article 64 of that Order in so far as relevant to that activity;

    (b)   if—

        (i)   P's licence covered the carrying on of an ancillary credit business in so far as it comprised or related to the activity of debt-administration (within the meaning of the 1974 Act),

        (ii)   immediately before 1st April 2014, P carried on an activity which, if carried on after that date would be an activity of the kind specified by article 36H of the Regulated Activities Order (operating an electronic system in relation to lending), and

        (iii)   immediately before 1st April 2014, P did not also carry on an activity which, if carried on after that date, would be an activity of the kind specified by article 39G of that Order (debt administration),

    the regulated activity specified in article 36H of the Regulated Activities Order and article 64 of that Order in so far as relevant to that activity;

    (c)   if—

        (i)   P's licence covered the carrying on of an ancillary credit business in so far as it comprised or related to the activity of debt-administration (within the meaning of the 1974 Act),

        (ii)   immediately before 1st April 2014, P carried on an activity which, if carried on after that date would be an activity of the kind specified by article 36H of the Regulated Activities Order (operating an electronic system in relation to lending), and

        (iii)   immediately before that date, P also carried on an activity which, if carried on after that date, would be an activity of the kind specified by article 39G of that Order (debt administration),

    the regulated activities specified in articles 36H and 39G of the Regulated Activities Order and article 64 of that Order in so far as relevant to those activities;

    (d)   to the extent that P's licence covers any other activities, those regulated activities which are activities which were described in the licence and article 64 of that Order in so far as relevant to those activities.

(2)   On and after 1stApril 2014, any relevant person ("P") who, immediately before that date—

    (a)   held a standard licence under the 1974 Act,

    (b)   was a credit intermediary (within the meaning given by section 160A of the 1974 Act), but

    (c)   did not carry on an activity which, if carried on after 1st April 2014, would be an activity of the kind specified by article 36H of the Regulated Activities Order,

is to be treated as having an interim permission to carry on regulated activities of the kind specified by articles 36A(1)(d) to (f) of the Regulated Activities Order to the extent that P was carrying on such activities immediately before 1st April 2014 and article 64 of that Order in so far as relevant to that activity; and such interim permission may be in addition to any interim permission the person obtains by virtue of paragraph (1).

(3) On and after [the relevant date], any relevant person ("P") who is a local authority is to be treated as having an interim permission to carry on regulated activities [of the kind specified by article 60B (regulated credit agreements)] which are activities which P was carrying on at any point in the period of one year ending on [1st April 2014].

[(3A) . . .

(4) For the purposes of paragraphs (1) [and (2)], P is a "relevant person" if P has, in the period beginning with 2nd September 2013 and ending on 31st March 2014 (including both days), notified the FCA of P's desire to obtain interim permission under this article and paid any fee which is provided for in rules made by the FCA for this purpose.

[(4A) For the purposes of paragraph (3)—
   (a) P is a "relevant person" if P has, in the period beginning with 2nd September 2013 and ending on 30th September 2014 (including both days), notified the FCA of P's desire to obtain interim permission under this article and paid any fee which is provided for in rules made by the FCA for this purpose;
   (b) "the relevant date" means the day after the later of—
      (i) the day on which the local authority becomes a relevant person, and
      (ii) 31st March 2014;
   (c) there is to be disregarded any activity carried on by P in the period of one year ending on 1st April 2014 in so far as it relates to an agreement secured on land.]

(5) On and after the notice date (see paragraph (7)), a relevant recent licensee ("P") is to be treated as having an interim permission to carry on—
   (a) if P's licence covered the carrying on of an ancillary credit business in so far as it comprised or related to credit brokerage (within the meaning of the 1974 Act), the regulated activity specified in article 36A of the Regulated Activities Order (credit broking) and article 64 of that Order in so far as relevant to that activity;
   (b) if—
      (i) P's licence covered the carrying on of an ancillary credit business in so far as it comprised or related to the activity of debt-administration (within the meaning of the 1974 Act),
      (ii) immediately before 1st April 2014 P carried on an activity which, if carried on after that date would be an activity of the kind specified by article 36H of the Regulated Activities Order (operating an electronic system in relation to lending), and
      (iii) immediately before that date, P did not also carry on an activity which, if carried on after that date, would be an activity of the kind specified by article 39G of that Order (debt administration),
      the regulated activity specified in article 36H of the Regulated Activities Order and article 64 of that Order in so far as relevant to that activity;
   (c) if—
      (i) P's licence covered the carrying on of an ancillary credit business in so far as it comprised or related to the activity of debt-administration (within the meaning of the 1974 Act),
      (ii) immediately before 1st April 2014, P carried on an activity which, if carried on after that date would be an activity of the kind specified by article 36H of the Regulated Activities Order (operating an electronic system in relation to lending), and
      (iii) immediately before that date, P also carries on an activity which, if carried on after that date, would be an activity of the kind specified by article 39G of that Order (debt administration),
      the regulated activities specified in articles 36H and 39G of the Regulated Activities Order and article 64 of that Order in so far as relevant to those activities;
   (d) to the extent that P's licence covers any other activities, those regulated activities which are activities which were described in the licence and article 64 of that Order in so far as relevant to those activities.

(6) Unless paragraph (12) applies, on and after the notice date, any relevant recent licensee ("P") who, immediately before 1st April 2014—
   (a) held a standard licence under the 1974 Act,
   (b) was a credit intermediary (within the meaning given by section 160A of the 1974 Act), but
   (c) did not carry on an activity which, if carried on after 1st April 2014, would be an activity of the kind specified by article 36H of the Regulated Activities Order,
is to be treated as having an interim permission to carry on regulated activities of the kind specified by articles 36A(1)(d) to (f) of the Regulated Activities Order and article 64 of that Order in so far as relevant to that activity, to the extent that P was carrying on such activities immediately before 1st April 2014; and such interim permission may be in addition to any interim permission the person obtains by virtue of paragraph (5).

(7) For the purposes of paragraphs (5) and (6), P is a "relevant recent licensee" if—

(a)   P had been given a standard licence under the 1974 Act in the period beginning 18th March 2014 and ending on 31st March 2014 (including both days), and

(b)   on a date in the period beginning on 1st April 2014 and ending on 14th April 2014 (including both days) ("the notice date") P notified the FCA of P's desire to obtain interim permission under this article and has in that period paid any fee which is provided for in rules made by the FCA for this purpose.

(8)   Interim permission which a person ("A") is treated as having under this article does not permit A to canvass off trade premises borrower-lender-supplier agreements (within the meaning given by article 60L of the Regulated Activities Order) or regulated consumer hire agreements (within the meaning of article 60N of that Order) except to the extent that A's licence under the 1974 Act, immediately before 1st April 2014, specifically provided that A's licence covered that activity; and the reference to canvassing off trade premises is to be read with article 36B of that Order.

(9)   Subject to article [59] (application of Act), an interim permission is to be treated as—
(a)   if P was an authorised person immediately before [1st April 2014], a variation of permission,
(b)   in any other case, a Part 4A permission.

(10)   If P was, immediately before 1st April 2014, subject to a requirement imposed by the OFT under section 33A of the 1974 Act (power of OFT to impose requirements on licensees) and P obtains interim permission under this article, that requirement is to be treated as a requirement imposed by the FCA under section 55L of the Act (subject to any necessary modifications).

(11)   For the purpose of paragraphs (1) and (5), it is the effect of the licence that matters, not how the activities for which a licence is given are described.

(12)   This paragraph applies if—
(a)   P has, before 1st April 2014, notified the FCA that P does not wish to obtain interim permission under this article, or
(b)   the FCA has, before 1st April 2014, notified P in writing, that in the FCA's opinion, P is not carrying on the activities which are described in P's licence.

[(13)   Paragraph (15) applies where, before 1st April 2014, the OFT—
(a)   had given a notice to P under section 32A(2) of the 1974 Act (suspension of a standard licence) that it is suspending P's licence, but
(b)   had not determined under section 34ZA of that Act (representations to OFT: suspension under section 32A) whether or not to confirm such a decision.

(14)   Paragraph (15) also applies where, before 1st April 2014—
(a)   the OFT had—
    (i)   given a notice to P under section 32A(2) of the 1974 Act that it is suspending P's licence, and
    (ii)   confirmed under section 34ZA of that Act its determination under section 32A of that Act, and
(b)   either—
    (i)   P had, submitted a notice of appeal to the First-tier Tribunal under section 41 of the 1974 Act (appeals to First-tier Tribunal under Part 3) with respect to that suspension and the appeal had not been determined, or
    (ii)   P had not submitted such a notice of appeal, but the specified period in respect of an appeal against the suspension had not expired.

(15)   For the purposes of this article—
(a)   P is to be treated as holding a licence under the 1974 Act immediately before 1st April 2014, and
(b)   section 32A of that Act (power to suspend licence) is to be treated as if subsection (5) did not apply at that time.

(16)   In this article, "specified period" has the meaning given in section 41 of the 1974 Act.]

NOTES

Commencement: 26 July 2013 (for the purpose of (a) the FCA, PRA and the scheme operator making rules, (b) the FCA designating relevant instruments under Part 8 of this Order, (c) the FCA giving guidance, and (d) the FCA and PRA imposing requirements or giving directions); 2 September 2013 (otherwise).

Words "of the kind specified by article 60B (regulated credit agreements)" in square brackets in para (3) inserted, para (3A) originally inserted, and figure and words in square brackets in para (9) substituted, by the Financial Services and Markets Act 2000 (Regulated Activities) (Amendment) Order 2014, SI 2014/366, art 19(1), (2).

Other words in square brackets in para (3) substituted, para (3A) revoked, words in square brackets in para (4) substituted, and para (4A) inserted, by the Financial Services and Markets Act 2000 (Consumer Credit) (Transitional Provisions) (No 3) Order 2014, SI 2014/1446, art 2.

Paras (13)–(16) are added by the Financial Services and Markets Act 2000 (Consumer Credit) (Transitional Provisions) Order 2014, SI 2014/376, arts 2, 10.

[2.1037]
57   Procedure for notifying FCA

(1)   Notices under article 56 must—
(a)   be made in such manner as the FCA may direct; and

(b) contain or be accompanied by such other information as the FCA may reasonably require.

(2) Different directions may be given and different requirements imposed, in relation to different applications or categories of application.

(3) At any time after receiving the notification, the FCA may require the person giving the notification to provide the FCA with such further information as it reasonably considers necessary to enable the FCA to discharge its functions.

(4) The FCA may require information to be provided in such form, or for it to be verified in such a way, as the FCA may direct.

NOTES

Commencement: 26 July 2013 (for the purpose of (a) the FCA, PRA and the scheme operator making rules, (b) the FCA designating relevant instruments under Part 8 of this Order, (c) the FCA giving guidance, and (d) the FCA and PRA imposing requirements or giving directions); 2 September 2013 (otherwise).

[2.1038]
58 Duration of interim permission

(1) P's interim permission, in so far as it relates to a particular regulated activity or class of activity [other than an activity to which paragraph (1A) applies] ceases to have effect—
    (a) if P applies to the appropriate regulator for Part 4A permission to carry on that activity or (as the case may be) to vary P's permission to add that activity to those to which the permission relates, before a date specified in a direction given by the FCA ("the application date"), the date on which that application is determined;
    (b) if P does not make such an application before the application date, the application date;
    (c) in any other case, 1st April 2016.

[(1A) Paragraphs (1B) and (1C) apply to an activity—
    (a) of a kind specified by article 36A or 60B of the Regulated Activities Order (regulated credit agreements) as that Order is in force before 21st March 2016; and
    (b) which, if carried on on or after 21st March 2016, would be of a kind specified by article 25A, 53A or 61 of the Regulated Activities Order by virtue of the amendments made to that Order by the Mortgage Credit Directive Order 2015.

(1B) P's interim permission ceases to have effect—
    (a) if P applies to the appropriate regulator before 21st March 2016 for Part 4A permission to carry on an activity of the kind specified by article 25A, 53A or 61 of the Regulated Activities Order or (as the case may be) to vary P's permission to add an activity of a kind specified by those articles to those to which the permission relates, on the date on which that application is determined; and
    (b) in any other case, on 21st March 2016;

(1C) P's interim permission is to be treated as an interim permission to carry on the activity from 21st March 2016 until the interim permission ceases to have effect, if—
    (a) P's interim permission continues to have effect on 21st March 2016 by virtue of paragraph (1B)(a), and
    (b) P had permission to carry on the activity immediately before 21st March 2016 by virtue of the interim permission.

(1D) If P's interim permission continues to have effect on 21st March 2016 by virtue of paragraph (1B)(a), from 21st March 2016 until the interim permission ceases to have effect the interim permission is to be treated as giving permission to carry on an activity which—
    (a) if carried on immediately before 21st March 2016, would not have been a regulated activity, and
    (b) becomes a regulated activity on 21st March 2016 by virtue of the amendments made to the Regulated Activities Order by the Mortgage Credit Directive Order 2015.]

(2) *Paragraph (1) does* not affect the ability of the FCA or the PRA to vary or to cancel an interim permission under the Act.

(3) For the purposes of *paragraph (1)(a)* the date on which an application is determined is—
    (a) if the applicant by notice withdraws the application under section 55V(4) of the Act, the date on which the notice of withdrawal takes effect;
    (b) if the application is granted by the appropriate regulator, the date on which the written notice given under section 55V(5) of the Act takes effect;
    (c) if the appropriate regulator gives a decision notice under section 388 of the Act in relation to the application, the date on which that notice [is given].

(4) Directions under this article may—
    (a) relate to [a particular person or class of person (including a class of person] identified by reference to whether they have, or have not, provided the FCA with a notification in a form specified in the direction by the FCA);
    (b) contain different dates;
    (c) relate to different descriptions of activities;
    [(ca) specify a date before which an application may not be made ("the opening date"), provided that the opening date is at least three months before the application date;]

(d)   be amended by the FCA by further direction.

[(5)   Subject to article 59(5) and (5A), an application made before the opening date is to be treated for the purposes of sections 55A (application for permission) and 55V (determination of applications) of the Act as if it had not been made.]

[(6)   Where P's interim permission ceases to have effect in accordance with paragraph (1) [or (1B)]—

    (a)   paragraph (7) applies in respect of an act or omission by P which occurred at a time when P had an interim permission;

    (b)   any requirement—

        (i)   imposed on P under section 55L, 55M or 404F(7) of the Act at a time when P had an interim permission, and

        (ii)   which is in effect immediately before that interim permission ceases to have effect, continues to have effect and paragraph (7) applies in respect of any contravention of that requirement.

(7)   If P is no longer an authorised person, P is to be treated as an authorised person for the purposes of the following provisions of the Act—

    (a)   Part 11 (information gathering and investigations) and Part 14 (disciplinary measures);

    (b)   section 384 of the Act (power of FCA or PRA to require restitution).]

NOTES

Commencement: 26 July 2013 (for the purpose of (a) the FCA, PRA and the scheme operator making rules, (b) the FCA designating relevant instruments under Part 8 of this Order, (c) the FCA giving guidance, and (d) the FCA and PRA imposing requirements or giving directions); 2 September 2013 (otherwise).

The words in square brackets in paras (1), (6), and paras (1A)–(1D) were inserted, for the words in italics in para (2) there are substituted the words "Paragraphs (1) and (1B) to (1D) do", and for the words in italics in para (3) there are substituted the words "paragraphs (1)(a) and (1B)(a)", by the Mortgage Credit Directive Order 2015, SI 2015/910, Sch 1, Pt 2, para 15, as from 21 March 2016 (note that the 2015 Order also comes into force on 20 April 2015 and 21 December 2015 for limited other purposes, and for transitional provisions, see Part 4 of that Order at **[2.1194]** et seq).

Words in square brackets in para (3)(c) substituted by the Financial Services and Markets Act 2000 (Consumer Credit) (Transitional Provisions) (No 4) Order 2014, SI 2014/2632, art 2.

The words in square brackets in para (4)(a) were substituted, and para (4)(ca) and para (5) were inserted, by the Financial Services and Markets Act 2000 (Consumer Credit) (Miscellaneous Provisions) Order 2014, SI 2014/208, art 7(1), (4).

Paras (6) and (7) were added by the Financial Services and Markets Act 2000 (Regulated Activities) (Amendment) Order 2014, SI 2014/366, art 19(1), (3).

[2.1039]
59   Application of the Act to persons with an interim permission

(1)   This article applies to each person ("A") who has an interim permission by virtue of this Order.

(2)   A's interim permission is to be disregarded for the purposes of—

    (a)   section 38(2) of the Act (exemption orders);

    (b)   section 55A(3) of the Act (application for permission);

    (c)   sections 55E and 55F of the Act (giving permission);

    [(d)   . . .].

(3)   For the purposes of section 21(2) of the Act (restrictions on financial promotions), if A does not have permission other than an interim permission, A may only approve the content of a communication if the communication invites or induces a person to—

    (a)   enter into (or offer to enter into) an agreement the making or performance of which constitutes a controlled activity which corresponds to a regulated activity for which A has interim permission; or

    (b)   exercise any rights conferred by a credit agreement (within the meaning of the Regulated Activities Order) to acquire, dispose of, underwrite or convert a controlled investment which is relevant to the regulated activity for which A has interim permission to carry on.

(4)   For the purposes of section 39 of the Act (appointed representatives), A—

    (a)   may not be a principal in relation to an activity for which A has interim permission;

    (b)   may be an appointed representative in relation to an activity which A does not have interim permission to carry on.

(5)   If A applies to the appropriate regulator—

    (a)   under section 55A of the Act for Part 4A permission to carry on a regulated activity [other than a regulated activity for which A has interim permission], or

    (b)   under section 55H or 55I of the Act to vary a Part 4A permission that A has otherwise than by virtue of this Order by adding a regulated activity to those which the permission relates,

the application may be treated by the appropriate regulator as relating also to some or all of the regulated activities for which A has interim permission.

[(5A)   If the appropriate regulator treats the application as relating also to some or all of the regulated activities for which A has interim permission, article 58(5) does not apply in relation to the application.]

(6)   When the FCA or PRA—

(a)   exercises its power under section 55J of the Act (variation or cancellation on initiative of regulator) in relation to A,

(b)   exercises its power under section 55H (in the case of the FCA) or section 55I of the Act (in the case of the PRA) (variation at request of authorised person) to remove a regulated activity from those for which A has interim permission, or

(c)   exercises its power under section 55L of the Act (in the case of the FCA) or section 55M of the Act (in the case of the PRA) (imposition of requirements by the regulator) in relation to A,

section 55B(3) of the Act (satisfaction of threshold conditions) does not require the regulator to ensure that A will satisfy, and continue to satisfy, in relation to the regulated activities for which A has an interim permission, the threshold conditions for which that regulator is responsible.

(7)   A is not to be regarded as an authorised person for the purposes of Part 12 of the Act (control over authorised person) unless A has permission otherwise than by virtue of an interim permission.

(8)   Subsection (3)(a) of section 213 (compensation scheme) does not apply to a person who is a relevant person (within the meaning of that section) only by virtue of having an interim permission.

NOTES

Commencement: 26 July 2013 (for the purpose of (a) the FCA, PRA and the scheme operator making rules, (b) the FCA designating relevant instruments under Part 8 of this Order, (c) the FCA giving guidance, and (d) the FCA and PRA imposing requirements or giving directions); 2 September 2013 (otherwise).

Paras (2)(d) and (5A) were inserted, and the words in square brackets in para (5)(a) were inserted, by the Financial Services and Markets Act 2000 (Consumer Credit) (Miscellaneous Provisions) Order 2014, SI 2014/208, art 7(1), (5).

Para (2)(d) was subsequently revoked, and paras (9)–(11) were added, by the Financial Services and Markets Act 2000 (Consumer Credit) (Transitional Provisions) (No 2) Order 2014, SI 2014/835, art 2.

[2.1040]
[59A   Application of article 72B of the Regulated Activities Order to persons with an interim permission

(1)   For the purposes of the definition of "provider" in article 72B (activities carried on by a provider of relevant goods or services) of the Regulated Activities Order, any regulated activity of the kind specified by a provision of the Regulated Activities Order listed in paragraph (2) for which a person has interim permission are to be ignored.

(2)   The provisions are—
   (a)   article 36A (credit broking);
   (b)   article 36H (operating an electronic system in relation to lending);
   (c)   article 39D (debt adjusting);
   (d)   article 39E (debt-counselling);
   (e)   article 39F (debt-collecting);
   (f)   article 39G (debt administration);
   (g)   article 60B (regulated credit agreements);
   (h)   article 60N (regulated consumer hire agreements);
   (i)   article 89A (providing credit information services);
   (j)   article 89B (providing credit references);
   (k)   article 64 (agreeing to carry on specified kinds of activity) in so far as it relates to an activity of the kind specified by a provision listed in sub-paragraphs (a) to (j).]

NOTES

Commencement: 1 April 2014.

Inserted by the Financial Services and Markets Act 2000 (Consumer Credit) (Miscellaneous Provisions) Order 2014, SI 2014/208, art 7(1), (6).

[2.1041]
60   Grandfathered permission for certain debt-counsellors

(1)   On and after 1st April 2014, a not-for-profit body which, immediately before 1st April 2014, was covered by a group licence under the 1974 Act to carry on the activity of debt-counselling (within the meaning of the 1974 Act) is to be treated for all purposes as having Part 4A permission to carry on regulated activities of the kind specified by 39D (debt adjusting), articles 39E (debt-counselling) and 89A (providing credit information services) of the Regulated Activities Order and article 64 of that Order in so far as relevant to those activities, to the extent that those regulated activities are activities which are described in the licence.

(2)   In this article, a "not-for-profit body" means a body which, by virtue of its constitution or any enactment—
   (a)   is required (after payment of outgoings) to apply the whole of its income and any capital it expends for charitable or public purposes, and
   (b)   is prohibited from directly or indirectly distributing amongst its members any part of its assets (otherwise than for charitable or public purposes).

(3)   For the purposes of this article, it is the effect of the group licence that matters, not how the activities for which a licence is given are described.

NOTES
Commencement: 26 July 2013 (for the purpose of (a) the FCA, PRA and the scheme operator making rules, (b) the FCA designating relevant instruments under Part 8 of this Order, (c) the FCA giving guidance, and (d) the FCA and PRA imposing requirements or giving directions); 2 September 2013 (otherwise).

CHAPTER 5
RULES AND GUIDANCE

[2.1042]
61   Credit-related rules and guidance made by the FCA

(1)   This article applies to rules made or guidance given by the FCA which relate or relates to a credit-related regulated activity or the carrying on of such an activity.

(2)   Section 1B(4) of the Act (competition duty) does not apply to the extent that—
   (a)   the rules are the same as, or substantially the same as, or have the same, or substantially the same, effect as any of the Consumer Credit Act provisions, or
   (b)   the guidance is the same as, or substantially the same as, or which has the same, or substantially the same, effect as any of the Consumer Credit Act provisions.

(3)   Section 138I(2)(a) of the Act (cost benefit analysis) does not apply in relation to a draft of rules to which this article applies which are the same as, or substantially the same as, any of the Consumer Credit Act provisions or which have the same, or substantially the same, effect as any such provisions.

(4)   For the purposes of this article, the "Consumer Credit Act provisions" are—
   (a)   the Consumer Credit Act 1974,
   (b)   any subordinate legislation made, or guidance issued, under that Act, and
   (c)   any notice issued by the OFT under section 86A of that Act (information sheets on arrears and defaults),
disregarding the effect of article 20 (amendments of the Consumer Credit Act 1974) and any order made before 1st April 2014 under section 107 of the Financial Services Act 2012.

(5)   Section 138I of the Act (consultation by the FCA) applies as if for subsections (7) and (8) there were substituted—

   "(7)   "Cost benefit analysis" means—
      (a)   an analysis of the difference between the costs and benefits of the Consumer Credit Act provisions and the costs and benefits that will arise—
         (i)   if the proposed rules are made, or
         (ii)   if subsection (5) applies, from the rules that have been made, and
      (b)   subject to subsection (8), an estimate of that difference.
   (7A)   For the purposes of subsection (7), the "Consumer Credit Act provisions" are—
      (a)   the Consumer Credit Act 1974,
      (b)   any subordinate legislation made, or guidance issued, under that Act, and
      (c)   any notice issued by the OFT under section 86A of that Act (information sheets on arrears and defaults),
   disregarding the effect of article 20 (amendments of the Consumer Credit Act 1974) of the Financial Services and Markets Act 2000 (Regulated Activities) (Amendment) (No2) Order 2013 and any order made before 1st April 2014 under section 107 of the Financial Services Act 2012.
   (8)   If, in the opinion of the FCA—
      (a)   the difference referred to in subsection (7) cannot reasonably be estimated; or
      (b)   it is not reasonably practicable to produce an estimate,
   the cost benefit analysis need not estimate the difference but must include a statement of the FCA's opinion and an explanation of it.".

(6)   The requirements of section 138I of the Act (as modified above) in so far as they apply to a proposal to make rules to which this article applies may be satisfied by things done (wholly or in part) before the date on which this article comes into force.

(7)   It is immaterial for the purposes of paragraph (5) if, when the things were done, they were not compatible with section 138I of the Act or, in the case of things done by the Financial Services Authority before 1st April 2013, section 155 of the Act.

(8)   In this article, "credit-related regulated activities" means the activities which will, from 1st April 2014, be regulated activities by virtue of Part 2 of this Order.

NOTES
Commencement: 26 July 2013.

[2.1043]
62   Credit-related rules made by the PRA

(1)   This article applies to rules made by the PRA which relate to credit-related regulated activities or the carrying on of those activities.

(2)   Section 138J(2)(a) of the Act (cost benefit analysis) does not apply in relation to a draft of rules to which this article applies which are the same as, or substantially the same as, any of the Consumer Credit Act provisions or which have the same, or substantially the same, effect as any such provisions.

(3)   For the purposes of this article, the "Consumer Credit Act provisions" are—
   (a)   the Consumer Credit Act 1974,
   (b)   any subordinate legislation made, or guidance issued, under that Act, and
   (c)   any notice issued by the OFT under section 86A of that Act (information sheets on arrears and defaults),
disregarding the effect of article 20 (amendments of the Consumer Credit Act 1974) and any order made before 1st April 2014 under section 107 of the Financial Services Act 2012.

(4)   Section 138J of the Act (consultation by the PRA) is to apply as if for subsections (7) and (8) there were substituted—

   "(7)   "Cost benefit analysis" means—
      (a)   an analysis of the difference between the costs and benefits of the Consumer Credit Act provisions and the costs and benefits that will arise—
         (i)   if the proposed rules are made, or
         (ii)   if subsection (5) applies, from the rules that have been made, and
      (b)   subject to subsection (8), an estimate of that difference.
   (7A)   For the purposes of subsection (7), the "Consumer Credit Act provisions" are—
      (a)   the Consumer Credit Act 1974,
      (b)   any subordinate legislation made, or guidance issued, under that Act, and
      (c)   any notice issued by the OFT under section 86A of that Act (information sheets on arrears and defaults),
   disregarding the effect of article 20 (amendments of the Consumer Credit Act 1974) of the Financial Services and Markets Act 2000 (Regulated Activities) (Amendment) (No2) Order 2013 and any order made before 1st April 2014 under section 107 of the Financial Services Act 2012.
   (8)   If, in the opinion of the PRA—
      (a)   the difference referred to in subsection (7) cannot reasonably be estimated; or
      (b)   it is not reasonably practicable to produce an estimate,
   the cost benefit analysis need not estimate the difference but must include a statement of the PRA's opinion and an explanation of it.".

(5)   The requirements of section 138J of the Act (as modified above) in so far as they apply to a proposal to make rules to which this article applies may be satisfied by things done (wholly or in part) before the date on which this article comes into force.

(6)   For the purposes of paragraph (4)—
   (a)   it is immaterial if, when the things were done, they were not compatible with section 138J of the Act or, in the case of things done by the Financial Services Authority before 1st April 2013, section 155 of the Act;
   (b)   the requirements may be satisfied by things done by the Financial Services Authority.

(7)   In this article, "credit-related regulated activities" means the activities which will, from 1st April 2014, be regulated activities by virtue of Part 2 of this Order.

NOTES
   Commencement: 26 July 2013.

[2.1044]
63   Designation of provisions made under the 1974 Act

(1)   The FCA may designate a relevant instrument, or part of a relevant instrument, if the FCA considers it necessary or expedient to do so in consequence of any provision made by or under this Order.

(2)   If the FCA designates a relevant instrument or part of such an instrument, in accordance with this article, the FCA must specify whether the instrument or part is to be treated as having been made by the FCA as a rule under section 137A of the Act or under a specified provision of the Regulated Activities Order ("the specified section or provision").

(3)   An instrument or part which is designated by the FCA in accordance with this article is to be treated for all purposes as having been made as a rule under the specified section or provision.

(4)   The FCA may make such modifications to a relevant instrument or part designated, or being designated, as it considers necessary or expedient in consequence of any provision made by this Order.

(5)   For the purposes of this article and article 64—

"relevant instrument" means any subordinate legislation or part of any subordinate legislation which is—

   (a)   made under Part 2 of the 1974 Act (irrespective of whether it is also made under section 182 of that Act), and

   (b)   revoked by this Order;

"specified" means specified by the FCA in a designating instrument.

NOTES

Commencement: 26 July 2013 (for the purpose of (a) the FCA, PRA and the scheme operator making rules, (b) the FCA designating relevant instruments under Part 8 of this Order, (c) the FCA giving guidance, and (d) the FCA and PRA imposing requirements or giving directions); 1 April 2014 (otherwise).

[2.1045]
64   Designating instruments

(1)   To designate or modify a relevant instrument or part of a relevant instrument, the FCA must make an instrument in writing which specifies, or more than one instrument in writing which between them specify—

   (a)   the relevant instrument or part,

   (b)   any modifications being made to the relevant instrument or part,

   (c)   the date on which the designation is to come into effect, and

   (d)   whether the instrument or part is to be treated as having been made by the FCA as a rule under section 137A of the Act or under a specified provision of the Regulated Activities Order.

(2)   The FCA must publish each designating instrument in the way appearing to it to be best calculated to bring it to the attention of the public.

(3)   A person is not to be taken to have contravened a relevant instrument designated by the FCA if the person shows that, at the time of the alleged contravention, the designating instrument concerned had not been published.

(4)   A designating instrument is to be treated as a rule-making instrument for the purposes of section 138H (verification of rules) of the Act.

(5)   A designating instrument may contain provision other than that required by paragraph (1).

(6)   The making of a designating instrument is a legislative function of the FCA for the purposes of paragraph 8(2) of Schedule 1ZA to the Act (arrangements for discharging functions).

NOTES

Commencement: 26 July 2013 (for the purpose of (a) the FCA, PRA and the scheme operator making rules, (b) the FCA designating relevant instruments under Part 8 of this Order, (c) the FCA giving guidance, and (d) the FCA and PRA imposing requirements or giving directions); 1 April 2014 (otherwise).

CHAPTER 6
MISCELLANEOUS

[2.1046]
65   Definition of "consumers"

(1)   For the purposes of the provisions listed in paragraph (3), "consumers" includes persons—

   (a)   who before 1st April 2014 used a relevant credit service,

   (b)   who have rights or interests which are derived from, or are otherwise attributable to, the use of any such services by other persons, or

   (c)   who have rights or interests which may be adversely affected by the use of any such services by persons acting on their behalf or in a fiduciary capacity in relation to them.

(2)   For the purposes of paragraph (1), "relevant credit services" are services provided—

   (i)   by a person who held or was covered by a licence under the 1974 Act, or

   (ii)   in carrying on a consumer credit business or an ancillary credit business (in each case, within the meaning of the 1974 Act).

(3)   The provisions are—

   (a)   section 1G of the Act (meaning of consumer);

   (b)   section 1Q of the Act (Consumer Panel);

   (c)   section 391(6)(b) of the Act (publication);

   (d)   section 68 of the Financial Services Act 2012 (cases in which Treasury may arrange independent inquiries).

(4)   For the purposes of this article—

   (a)   where a person provided a service mentioned in paragraph (1) as a trustee, the persons who are, have been or may be beneficiaries of the trust are to be treated as persons who use, have used or may use the service;

   (b)   a person who deals, or dealt, with another person ("A") in the course of A providing a service mentioned in paragraph (1) is to be treated as using, or having used, the service.

NOTES

Commencement: 26 July 2013 (for the purpose of (a) the FCA, PRA and the scheme operator making rules, (b) the FCA designating relevant instruments under Part 8 of this Order, (c) the FCA giving guidance, and (d) the FCA and PRA imposing requirements or giving directions); 1 April 2014 (otherwise).

[2.1047]
66   Information sharing

(1)   The OFT may disclose to the FCA any information which the OFT considers is necessary or expedient to disclose to the FCA in preparation for the commencement of any provision of this Order or any order made under section 107 of the Financial Services Act 2012 which confers functions on the FCA.

(2)   A local weights and measures authority in England, Wales or Scotland and the Department of Enterprise, Trade and Investment in Northern Ireland may disclose to the FCA any information which that person considers is necessary or expedient to disclose to the FCA in preparation for the commencement of any provision of this Order or any order made under section 107 of the Financial Services Act 2012 which confers functions on the FCA.

NOTES

Commencement: 26 July 2013.

SCHEDULE

(The Schedule contains various amendments to the Companies Act 2006, the Counter-Terrorism Act 2008, the Financial Services (Distance Marketing) Regulations 2004, SI 2004/2095, the Money Laundering Regulations 2007, SI 2007/2157, the Cancellation of Contracts made in a Consumer's Home or Place of Work etc Regulations 2008, SI 2008/1816, the Payment Services Regulations 2009, SI 2009/209, the Electronic Money Regulations 2011, SI 2011/99, and various other enactments that are outside the scope of this work)

FINANCIAL SERVICES ACT 2012 (CONSUMER CREDIT) ORDER 2013

(SI 2013/1882)

NOTES

Made: 25 July 2013.
Authority: Financial Services Act 2012, ss 107, 115(2).
Commencement: see art 1.

ARRANGEMENT OF ARTICLES

[2.1048]
1   Citation, commencement and interpretation

(1)   This Order may be cited as the Financial Services Act 2012 (Consumer Credit) Order 2013 and comes into force—
  (a)   on the day after the day on which it is made, for the purpose of the FCA—
      (i)   preparing and issuing statements of policy or altering or replacing a statement of policy;
      (ii)   making determinations under the 1974 Act;
      (iii) preparing and issuing information sheets under the 1974 Act;
      (iv)   giving notices, directions or certificates under the 1974 Act;
      (v)   imposing requirements under the 1974 Act;
  (b)   in so far as it is not already in force, on 1st April 2014.

(2)   In this Order, "the 1974 Act" means the Consumer Credit Act 1974.

NOTES

Commencement: 26 July 2013 (for the purpose of the FCA (i) preparing and issuing statements of policy or altering or replacing a statement of policy; (ii) making determinations under the 1974 Act; (iii) preparing and issuing information sheets under the 1974 Act; (iv) giving notices, directions or certificates under the 1974 Act; and (v) imposing requirements under the 1974 Act); 1 April 2014 (otherwise).

[2.1049]
2   Functions of the FCA under the 1974 Act

References in FSMA 2000 to the FCA's functions under FSMA 2000 are to be treated as including the FCA's functions under the 1974 Act resulting from this Order.

NOTES
Commencement: 26 July 2013 (for the purpose of the FCA (i) preparing and issuing statements of policy or altering or replacing a statement of policy; (ii) making determinations under the 1974 Act; (iii) preparing and issuing information sheets under the 1974 Act; (iv) giving notices, directions or certificates under the 1974 Act; and (v) imposing requirements under the 1974 Act); 1 April 2014 (otherwise).

[2.1050]
3   Application of provisions of FSMA 2000 in connection with failure to comply with the 1974 Act

(1) The following provisions of FSMA 2000 apply in relation to a requirement imposed by or under the provisions of Parts 2, 4, 5 and 6 to 12 of the 1974 Act ("a relevant requirement") with the modifications specified.

(2) Section 1L (supervision, monitoring and enforcement) applies as if—
    (a) in subsection (1) the reference to "supervising authorised persons" included a reference to determining whether authorised persons are complying with relevant requirements;
    (b) in subsection (2), the reference to requirements imposed by or under FSMA 2000 in a case where the FCA is the appropriate regulator for the purposes of Part 14 of FSMA 2000 (disciplinary measures) included a reference to relevant requirements.

(3) Section 66 (disciplinary powers) applies as if the reference in subsection (2)(b)(i) to a requirement imposed by or under FSMA 2000 included a reference to a relevant requirement, and sections 67 (disciplinary measures: procedure and right to refer to Tribunal) and 68 (publication) apply as if the references to section 66 were to that section as applied by this Order.

(4) Part 9 (hearings and appeals) applies as if in section 133 (proceedings before Tribunal: general provision)—
    (a) the references to decisions under sections 66 (disciplinary powers), 205 (public censure), 206 (financial penalties) and 206A (suspending permission to carry on regulated activities etc) of FSMA 2000 were references to decisions under those sections as applied by this Order;
    (b) the references to a reference or appeal to the Tribunal includes a reference to a reference or appeal to the Tribunal under FSMA 2000 as applied by this Order.

(5) Part 11 (information gathering and investigations) (with the exception of section 169 (investigations etc in support of overseas regulator)) applies as if—
    (a) the reference in section 165(4) (regulators' power to require information: authorised persons etc) to functions conferred on the FCA by or under FSMA 2000 included a reference to functions conferred on it by this Order;
    (b) the reference in section 167(1) (appointment of persons to carry out general investigations) to a good reason included a good reason by virtue of the functions conferred on the FCA by this Order;
    (c) in section 168 (appointment of persons to carry out investigations in particular cases)—
        (i) subsection (1) included a reference to an offence under the 1974 Act;
        (ii) subsection (4) included a reference to circumstances suggesting that a person may have failed to comply with a relevant requirement (excluding circumstances suggesting that an offence under the 1974 Act may have been committed).

(6) Part 13 (incoming firms: intervention by FCA or PRA) (with the exception of sections 195 (exercise of power in support of overseas regulator), 195A (contravention by relevant EEA firm or EEA UCITS of directive requirements), 198 (power to apply to court for injunction in respect of certain overseas insurance companies) and 199A (management companies: loss of authorisation)) applies as if—
    (a) in section 194(1) (general grounds on which power of intervention is exercisable) each reference to a requirement imposed by or under FSMA 2000 included a reference to a relevant requirement;
    (b) in section 199 (additional procedure for EEA firms in certain cases) the reference in subsection (2)(a)(i) to a requirement imposed by the regulator under FSMA 2000 included a reference to a relevant requirement.

(7) Part 14 (disciplinary measures) applies (with the exception of sections 210 (statements of policy) and 211 (statements of policy: procedure)) as if in section 204A (meaning of "relevant requirement" and "appropriate regulator")—
    (a) in subsection (2), the definition of "relevant requirement" included a relevant requirement;

(b)   in subsection (6), the reference to any other requirement imposed by or under the Act included a relevant requirement.

(8)   Section 380 (injunctions) applies as if the reference in subsection (6)(a)(i) to a requirement imposed by or under FSMA 2000 included a reference to a relevant requirement.

(9)   Section 382 (restitution orders) applies as if the reference in subsection (9)(a)(i) to a requirement imposed by or under FSMA 2000 included a reference to a relevant requirement.

(10)   Section 384 (power of FCA or PRA to require restitution) applies as if the reference in subsection (7)(a) to a relevant requirement imposed by or under FSMA 2000 included a reference to a relevant requirement; and accordingly sections 385 (warning notices) and 386 (decision notices) apply where there has been a contravention of a requirement under section 384 as applied by this Order.

(11)   Part 26 (notices) applies as if—
   (a)   in section 391 (publication), the references in subsection (1ZB) to warning notices given under sections 67 (disciplinary measures: procedure and right to refer to Tribunal) and 207 (proposal to take disciplinary measures) of FSMA 2000 were to warning notices given under those sections as applied by this Order;
   (b)   in section 392 (application of sections 393 and 394), the references to a warning notice and a decision notice given under any of the provisions specified in that section included a warning notice and a decision notice given under any of those provisions as applied by this Order.

(12)   Part 27 (offences) applies as if—
   (a)   references to an offence under FSMA 2000 included an offence under that Act as applied by this Order;
   (b)   in section 401 (proceedings for offences), in subsection (1), the definition of "offence" included an offence under the 1974 Act.

NOTES

Commencement: 26 July 2013 (for the purpose of the FCA (i) preparing and issuing statements of policy or altering or replacing a statement of policy; (ii) making determinations under the 1974 Act; (iii) preparing and issuing information sheets under the 1974 Act; (iv) giving notices, directions or certificates under the 1974 Act; and (v) imposing requirements under the 1974 Act); 1 April 2014 (otherwise).

[2.1051]
4   Statements of policy

(1)   The FCA must prepare and issue a statement of its policy with respect to—
   (a)   the imposition of penalties, suspensions or restrictions imposed under sections 66 (disciplinary powers), 205 (public censure), 206 (financial penalties) and 206A (suspending permission to carry on regulated activities etc) of FSMA 2000 as applied by article 3;
   (b)   the amount of penalties imposed under sections 66 and 206 of FSMA 2000 as so applied;
   (c)   the period for which suspensions or restrictions imposed under sections 66 and 206A of FSMA 2000 as so applied are to have effect.

(2)   The FCA's policy in determining what the amount of a penalty should be, or what the period for which a suspension or restriction is to have effect should be, must include having regard to—
   (a)   the seriousness of the failure in question in relation to the nature of the requirement concerned;
   (b)   the extent to which that failure was deliberate or reckless; and
   (c)   whether the person against whom the action is to be taken is an individual.

(3)   The FCA may at any time alter or replace a statement issued by it under this article.

(4)   If a statement issued under this article is altered or replaced by the FCA, the FCA must issue the altered or replacement statement.

(5)   The FCA must, without delay, give the Treasury a copy of any statement which it publishes under this article.

(6)   A statement by the FCA issued under this article must be published by the FCA in the way appearing to the FCA to be best calculated to bring it to the attention of the public.

(7)   In exercising, or deciding whether to exercise, its powers under section 66, 205, 206 or 206A of FSMA 2000 as applied by article 3 in the case of any particular contravention, the FCA must have regard to any statement published by it under this article and in force at the time when the contravention in question occurred.

NOTES

Commencement: 26 July 2013 (for the purpose of the FCA (i) preparing and issuing statements of policy or altering or replacing a statement of policy; (ii) making determinations under the 1974 Act; (iii) preparing and issuing information sheets under the 1974 Act; (iv) giving notices, directions or certificates under the 1974 Act; and (v) imposing requirements under the 1974 Act); 1 April 2014 (otherwise).

[2.1052]
5   Statements of policy: procedure

(1)   Before the FCA issues a statement under article 4, the FCA must publish a draft of the proposed statement in the way appearing to it to be best calculated to bring it to the attention of the public.

(2)   The draft must be accompanied by notice that representations about the proposal may be made to the FCA within a specified time.

(3)   Before issuing the proposed statement, the FCA must have regard to any representations made in accordance with paragraph (2).

(4)   If the FCA issues the proposed statement it must publish an account, in general terms, of—
   (a)   the representations made to it in accordance with paragraph (2); and
   (b)   its response to them.

(5)   If the statement differs from the draft published under paragraph (1) in a way which is, in the opinion of the FCA, significant, the FCA must (in addition to complying with paragraph (4)) publish details of the difference.

(6)   This article also applies to a proposal to alter or replace a statement.

NOTES
   Commencement: 26 July 2013 (for the purpose of the FCA (i) preparing and issuing statements of policy or altering or replacing a statement of policy; (ii) making determinations under the 1974 Act; (iii) preparing and issuing information sheets under the 1974 Act; (iv) giving notices, directions or certificates under the 1974 Act; and (v) imposing requirements under the 1974 Act); 1 April 2014 (otherwise).

[2.1053]
6   Disciplinary measures: criminal proceedings and conviction under the 1974 Act

A person may not be convicted of an offence under the 1974 Act in respect of an act or omission in a case where the FCA has exercised its powers under section 66, 205, 206 or 206A of FSMA 2000 in relation to that person in respect of that act or omission.

NOTES
   Commencement: 26 July 2013 (for the purpose of the FCA (i) preparing and issuing statements of policy or altering or replacing a statement of policy; (ii) making determinations under the 1974 Act; (iii) preparing and issuing information sheets under the 1974 Act; (iv) giving notices, directions or certificates under the 1974 Act; and (v) imposing requirements under the 1974 Act); 1 April 2014 (otherwise).

7–10   (*Art 7 (Amendments to the 1974 Act) amends the Consumer Credit Act 1974. Art 8 (Application of provisions of the 1974 Act in relation to failure to comply with FSMA 2000) applies certain provisions of the 1974 Act to contraventions of certain provisions of FSMA 2000; these provisions ensure that where a duly appointed officer of a local weights and measures authority or the Department of Enterprise, Trade and Investment in Northern Ireland (both an "enforcement authority" under the 1974 Act) considers that a relevant offence under FSMA 2000 (as defined by FSA 2012, s 107(4)(b)) may have been committed in relation to consumer credit, that officer may use certain 1974 Act powers to investigate. Art 9 provides for trading standards bodies to institute proceedings in England and Wales for a relevant offence, and for the Department of Enterprise, Trade and Investment in Northern Ireland to institute proceedings in Northern Ireland for such offences. Art 10 amends the Companies Act 2006, Sch 2, Pt 2, and Sch 11A, Pt 2 and contains various other amendments that are outside the scope of this work.*)

FINANCIAL SERVICES AND MARKETS ACT 2000 (CONSUMER CREDIT) (TRANSITIONAL PROVISIONS) ORDER 2013

(SI 2013/3128)

NOTES
   Made: 9 December 2013.
   Authority: Financial Services and Markets Act 2000, s 426(1).
   Commencement: 31 January 2014.

[2.1054]
1   Citation, commencement and interpretation

(1)   This Order may be cited as the Financial Services and Markets Act 2000 (Consumer Credit) (Transitional Provisions) Order 2013 and comes into force on 31st December 2013.

(2)   In this Order—
   "the 1974 Act" means the Consumer Credit Act 1974;
   "the 2000 Act" means the Financial Services and Markets Act 2000;
   "the OFT" means the Office of Fair Trading.

NOTES
Commencement: 31 January 2014.

[2.1055]
2 Payments to eligible licensees

(1) The FCA may make a payment to any eligible licensee who—
  (a) has paid to the OFT a charge under section 6A (charge on applicants for licences etc) or 28A (charges to be paid by licensees etc before end of payment periods) of the 1974 Act—
    (i) after 31st March 2009, or
    (ii) before 1st April 2009 in respect of a licence issued or renewed on or after that date; and
  (b) is not a person—
    (i) to whom the OFT sent a letter substantially in the form set out (without annexes) in the Schedule to this Order; and
    (ii) who, pursuant to such a letter, received a visit from an officer of the OFT or a person acting on behalf of the OFT.

(2) In paragraph (1), an "eligible licensee" means a person who—
  (a) holds a standard licence under the 1974 Act at the relevant time;
  (b) was the applicant for a group licence under the 1974 Act that is in issue at the relevant time; or
  (c) held a standard licence under the 1974 Act on 23rd April 2012 in respect of which the person—
    (i) gave notice to the OFT before this Order comes into force, or
    (ii) gives notice to the OFT before 1st April 2014,
    relinquishing the licence (irrespective of whether the relinquishing of the licence takes effect before 1st April 2014).

(3) In paragraph (2), "the relevant time" means—
  (a) in relation to a payment made before 1st April 2014 to a person who is not required to make an application pursuant to a condition specified by the FCA under article 3, the time at which the payment is made;
  (b) in relation to an application made before 1st April 2014 pursuant to a condition specified by the FCA under article 3, the time at which the application is made; or
  (c) in any other case, immediately before 1st April 2014.

NOTES
Commencement: 31 January 2014.

[2.1056]
3 Payments: supplementary provisions

(1) A payment under article 2(1) may be made—
  (a) for such amount as the FCA may determine;
  (b) in such manner as the FCA thinks fit;
  (c) subject to conditions specified by the FCA being satisfied.

(2) Conditions may, in particular, include—
  (a) a condition requiring an application to be made to the FCA;
  (b) a condition relating to a person whom the OFT has informed that it is—
    (i) minded to revoke
    (ii) minded to refuse an application for, or
    (iii) suspending,
    a licence issued under the 1974 Act.

(3) The FCA may specify different conditions in relation to different descriptions or categories of person.

(4) If the FCA specifies a condition for the purposes of this article, it must publish the condition by the means it considers most likely to bring the condition to the attention of persons to whom the condition applies.

(5) Where the FCA determines that a payment under article 2(1) would be for less than £10.00, it is not obliged to make the payment.

NOTES
Commencement: 31 January 2014.

[2.1057]

4   FCA power to require information

(1)   Subject to paragraph (2), Part 11 of the 2000 Act (information gathering and investigations) has effect until 1st April 2014 as if each reference in section 165 (regulators' power to require information: authorised persons etc) to an authorised person (except for the references in subsections 165(7)(b) and (8)) included a reference to a person of the description in paragraph (3).

(2)   Part 11 of the 2000 Act only applies as so modified in respect of a requirement imposed—

(a)   by the FCA; and

(b)   by a notice specifying that the requirement is made for the purpose of or in connection with the FCA making rules under section 137C of the 2000 Act (FCA general rules: cost of credit and duration of credit agreements).

(3)   A person is within the description of this paragraph if the person—

(a)   holds a licence issued under the 1974 Act; and

(b)   carries on activities which, if those activities were carried on on 1st April 2014, would be activities of a kind specified by any of the following provisions of the Financial Services and Markets Act 2000 (Regulated Activities) Order 2001—

(i)   article 60B (regulated credit agreements);

(ii)   article 89B (providing credit references).

(4)   In determining whether a person is connected with a person of the description in paragraph (3) under section 165(11) of the 2000 Act, Part 1 of Schedule 15 to the 2000 Act has effect as if each reference to an authorised person were a reference to a person of the description in paragraph (3).

(5)   On 1st April 2014—

(a)   any requirement imposed under section 165 or 175(1) of the 2000 Act ceases to have effect if it could not be imposed under that enactment on or after that date;

(b)   any requirement imposed under section 175(2) or (3) of the 2000 Act ceases to have effect if the requirement pursuant to which the supplementary requirement was imposed ceases to have effect on 1st April 2014 by virtue of sub-paragraph (a) (and no such supplementary requirement may be imposed thereafter); and

(c)   no action may be taken or continued under or pursuant to the 2000 Act in relation to any requirement which ceases to have effect by virtue of this paragraph.

NOTES

Commencement: 31 January 2014.

SCHEDULE
FORM OF LETTER SENT BY OFT

Article 2

[2.1058]

Dear

NOTICE OF REQUIREMENT TO GIVE ACCESS TO PREMISES UNDER SECTION 36C OF THE CONSUMER CREDIT ACT 1974 ("the Act").

On 24 February 2012 the Office of Fair Trading ("OFT") launched its Irresponsible Lending Guidance Compliance Review of the payday lending industry (further details of the review can be found at www.oft.gov.uk). The OFT is conduction this review due to increasing numbers of complaints about businesses in the sector, the apparent level of consumer detriment suggested by these complaints and concerns about the activities of some companies in the sector. The OFT considers that it is therefore appropriate that we should review both industry compliance with relevant legal requirements and the extent to which businesses operating in the market are meeting the standards we expect of them – as set out in our guidance.

As part of the preparatory work for the review, the OFT carried out an initial assessment of a number of payday lenders' websites. Please find attached a copy of the letter sent by the OFT to relevant trade associations (the Consumer Finance Association, Finance & Leasing Association, BCCA, Consumer Credit Association, Consumer Credit Trade Association, and the National Pawnbrokers Association) which sets out some of the practices we identified. I wish to draw your attention to these examples and the other issues of concern we raised.

As part of the review we will be undertaking compliance visits to a number of payday lending licensees.

The OFT therefore proposes to visit your premises as part of this review into compliance with the Irresponsible Lending Guidance and relevant legislation across the payday lending industry. The visit will be undertaking with a view to the OFT carrying out its functions under section 1 of the Act, which includes:

i)   to administer the licensing system set up by the Act;

ii) to monitor, as the OFT sees fit, businesses being carried on under licenses issued under the Act; and

iii) to generally superintend the working and enforcement of the Act, and regulations made under it.

In particular, the reason for this visit is to carry out our duties under section 1(1)(ba) and 1(2)(a) of the Act.

Please find attached a formal Notice under section 36C of the Act which states that the OFT requires (the licensee) to secure that access to the premises described in the Notice is given to officers of the OFT in order for the officers to observe the carrying on of (the licensee's) licensed business and to inspect such documents relating to that business as are specified or described in the Notice and situated on the premises.

The compliance visit will assess your business's compliance with the OFT's Irresponsible Lending Guidance (ILG). In addition, the visit will also cover compliance with the Consumer Credit At 1974 (the Act) and applicable regulations alongside wider consumer protection legislation where relevant.

A Trading Standards Officer working on behalf of the OFT will contact you shortly to arrange a date for carrying out a compliance visit to your business premises. The evidence obtained will be used, along with that obtained from other payday lenders selected for a compliance visit, to inform the outcome of the OFT's ILG compliance review. Furthermore, such evidence obtained during the visit will be used by the OFT to assess your business's continuing fitness to hold a consumer credit licence. Follow up enforcement action against your business could therefore follow on from that visit.

You are referred to sections 36C, 36F and 174A of the Act which set out the powers the OFT will be exercising. Enclosed with this notice is an Explanatory Note (Annexe B) that provides additional information about the powers of the visiting officers when entering premises under section 36C of the Act and related safeguards. Section 36E of the Act sets out the circumstances in which the OFT may apply to the Court for an order in the event that you do not comply with the requirements of this Notice.

I would highlight section 36C(6) and (7) of the Act which provide that (the business) must secure that, at the time of the visit, the officer conducting the visit on behalf of the OFT is provided with such assistance or information as he may reasonably require in connection with his observation or inspection of documents, including the giving to the officer of an explanation of a document being inspected.

I should also draw your attention to section 174A(2) of the Act which provides that the OFT has power to take copies of, or extracts from, any documents inspected. In this regard it would be helpful if you could confirm to the Trading Standards Officer who arranges the visit that (the business) would be willing to make available to the OFT copying facilities located at the premises to be visited.

Yours sincerely

NOTES
Commencement: 31 January 2014.

CONSUMER CONTRACTS (INFORMATION, CANCELLATION AND ADDITIONAL CHARGES) REGULATIONS 2013

(SI 2013/3134)

NOTES
Made: 11 December 2013.
Authority: European Communities Act 1972, s 2(2).
Commencement: 13 June 2014.

ARRANGEMENT OF REGULATIONS

PART 1
GENERAL

Part 2   Statutory Instruments

PART 1
GENERAL

[2.1059]
1 Citation and commencement

(1) These Regulations may be cited as the Consumer Contracts (Information, Cancellation and Additional Charges) Regulations 2013 and come into force on 13th June 2014.

(2) These Regulations apply in relation to contracts entered into on or after that date.

NOTES
Commencement: 13 June 2014.

[2.1060]
2 Regulations superseded

The following do not apply in relation to contracts entered into on or after 13th June 2014—
  (a) the Consumer Protection (Distance Selling) Regulations 2000;
  (b) the Cancellation of Contracts made in a Consumer's Home or Place of Work etc Regulations 2008.

NOTES
Commencement: 13 June 2014.

[2.1061]
3 Review

(1) The Secretary of State must before the end of each review period—
  (a) carry out a review of these Regulations,
  (b) set out the conclusions of the review in a report, and
  (c) publish the report.

(2) In carrying out the review, the Secretary of State must, so far as is reasonable, have regard to what is done in other member States to implement Directive 2011/83/EU of the European Parliament and of the Council of 25 October 2011 on consumer rights, amending Council Directive 93/13/EEC and Directive 1999/44/EC of the European Parliament and of the Council and repealing Council Directive 85/577/EC and Directive 97/7/EC of the European Parliament and of the Council.

(3) The report must in particular—
  (a) set out the objectives intended to be achieved by these Regulations,
  (b) assess the extent to which those objectives have been achieved, and
  (c) assess whether those objectives remain appropriate and, if so, the extent to which they could be achieved in a way that imposes less regulation.

(4) A review period is—
  (a) the period of 5 years beginning with the day on which these Regulations come into force, and
  (b) each successive period of 5 years.

NOTES
Commencement: 13 June 2014.

[2.1062]
4 "Consumer" and "trader"

In these Regulations—
  "consumer" means an individual acting for purposes which are wholly or mainly outside that individual's trade, business, craft or profession;
  "trader" means a person acting for purposes relating to that person's trade, business, craft or profession, whether acting personally or through another person acting in the trader's name or on the trader's behalf.

NOTES
Commencement: 13 June 2014.

[2.1063]
5 Other definitions

In these Regulations—
  "business" includes the activities of any government department or local or public authority;
  "business premises" in relation to a trader means—

    (a)   any immovable retail premises where the activity of the trader is carried out on a permanent basis, or

    (b)   any movable retail premises where the activity of the trader is carried out on a usual basis;

"CMA" means the Competition and Markets Authority;

"commercial guarantee", in relation to a contract, means any undertaking by the trader or producer to the consumer (in addition to the trader's duty to supply goods that are in conformity with the contract) to reimburse the price paid or to replace, repair or service goods in any way if they do not meet the specifications or any other requirements not related to conformity set out in the guarantee statement or in the relevant advertising available at the time of the contract or before it is entered into;

"court"—

    (a)   in relation to England and Wales, means the county court or the High Court,

    (b)   in relation to Northern Ireland, means a county court or the High Court, and

    (c)   in relation to Scotland means the sheriff court or the Court of Session;

"delivery" means voluntary transfer of possession from one person to another;

"digital content" means data which are produced and supplied in digital form;

"distance contract" means a contract concluded between a trader and a consumer under an organised distance sales or service-provision scheme without the simultaneous physical presence of the trader and the consumer, with the exclusive use of one or more means of distance communication up to and including the time at which the contract is concluded;

"district heating" means the supply of heat (in the form of steam or hot water or otherwise) from a central source of production through a transmission and distribution system to heat more than one building;

"durable medium" means paper or email, or any other medium that—

    (a)   allows information to be addressed personally to the recipient,

    (b)   enables the recipient to store the information in a way accessible for future reference for a period that is long enough for the purposes of the information, and

    (c)   allows the unchanged reproduction of the information stored;

"functionality" in relation to digital content includes region coding, restrictions incorporated for the purposes of digital rights management, and other technical restrictions;

"goods" means any tangible moveable items, but that includes water, gas and electricity if and only if they are put up for sale in a limited volume or a set quantity;

"off-premises contract" means a contract between a trader and a consumer which is any of these—

    (a)   a contract concluded in the simultaneous physical presence of the trader and the consumer, in a place which is not the business premises of the trader;

    (b)   a contract for which an offer was made by the consumer in the simultaneous physical presence of the trader and the consumer, in a place which is not the business premises of the trader;

    (c)   a contract concluded on the business premises of the trader or through any means of distance communication immediately after the consumer was personally and individually addressed in a place which is not the business premises of the trader in the simultaneous physical presence of the trader and the consumer;

    (d)   a contract concluded during an excursion organised by the trader with the aim or effect of promoting and selling goods or services to the consumer;

"on-premises contract" means a contract between a trader and a consumer which is neither a distance contract nor an off-premises contract;

"public auction" means a method of sale where—

    (a)   goods or services are offered by a trader to consumers through a transparent, competitive bidding procedure run by an auctioneer,

    (b)   the consumers attend or are given the possibility to attend in person, and

    (c)   the successful bidder is bound to purchase the goods or services;

"sales contract" means a contract under which a trader transfers or agrees to transfer the ownership of goods to a consumer and the consumer pays or agrees to pay the price, including any contract that has both goods and services as its object;

"service" includes—

    (a)   the supply of water, gas or electricity if they are not put up for sale in a limited volume or a set quantity, and

    (b)   the supply of district heating;

"service contract" means a contract, other than a sales contract, under which a trader supplies or agrees to supply a service to a consumer and the consumer pays or agrees to pay the price.

NOTES

Commencement: 13 June 2014.

[2.1064]
6 Limits of application: general

(1)   These Regulations do not apply to a contract, to the extent that it is—

Part 2   Statutory Instruments

(a) for—
    (i) gambling within the meaning of the Gambling Act 2005 (which includes gaming, betting and participating in a lottery); *or*
    (ii) in relation to Northern Ireland, for betting, gaming or participating lawfully in a lottery within the meaning of the Betting, Gaming, Lotteries and Amusements (Northern Ireland) Order 1985; [or
    (iii) participating in a lottery which forms part of the National Lottery within the meaning of the National Lottery etc. Act 1993.]
(b) for services of a banking, credit, insurance, personal pension, investment or payment nature;
(c) for the creation of immovable property or of rights in immovable property;
(d) for rental of accommodation for residential purposes;
(e) for the construction of new buildings, or the construction of substantially new buildings by the conversion of existing buildings;
(f) for the supply of foodstuffs, beverages or other goods intended for current consumption in the household and which are supplied by a trader on frequent and regular rounds to the consumer's home, residence or workplace;
(g) within the scope of Council Directive 90/314/EEC of 13 June 1990 on package travel, package holidays and package tours;
(h) within the scope of Directive 2008/122/EC of the European Parliament and of the Council on the protection of consumers in respect of certain aspects of timeshare, long-term holiday product, resale and exchange contracts.

(2) These Regulations do not apply to contracts—
(a) concluded by means of automatic vending machines or automated commercial premises;
(b) concluded with a telecommunications operator through a public telephone for the use of the telephone;
(c) concluded for the use of one single connection, by telephone, internet or fax, established by a consumer;
(d) under which goods are sold by way of execution or otherwise by authority of law.

(3) Paragraph (1)(b) is subject to regulations 38(4) (ancillary contracts) and 40(3) (additional payments).

NOTES

Commencement: 13 June 2014.

Para (1): in sub-para (a)(i) word in italics revoked, and sub-para (a)(iii) and word immediately preceding it added, by the Consumer Contracts (Amendment) Regulations 2015, SI 2015/1629, regs 2, 3, in relation to contracts entered into on or after 1 October 2015.

PART 2
INFORMATION REQUIREMENTS

CHAPTER 1
PROVISION OF INFORMATION

[2.1065]
7 Application of Part 2

(1) This Part applies to on-premises, off-premises and distance contracts, subject to paragraphs (2), (3) and (4) and regulation 6.

(2) This Part does not apply to contracts to the extent that they are—
(a) for the supply of a medicinal product by administration by a prescriber, or under a prescription or directions given by a prescriber;
(b) for the supply of a product by a health care professional or a person included in a relevant list, under arrangements for the supply of services as part of the health service, where the product is one that, at least in some circumstances is available under such arrangements free or on prescription.

(3) This Part, except for regulation 14(1) to (5), does not apply to contracts to the extent that they are for passenger transport services.

(4) This Part does not apply to off-premises contracts under which the payment to be made by the consumer is not more than £42.

(5) In paragraph (2)—
"health care professional" and "prescriber" have the meaning given by regulation 2(1) of the National Health Service (Pharmaceutical and Local Pharmaceutical Services) Regulations 2013;
"health service" means—
    (a) the health service as defined by section 275(1) of the National Health Service Act 2006 or section 206(1) of the National Health Service (Wales) Act 2006,
    (b) the health service as defined by section 108(1) of the National Health Service (Scotland) Act 1978, or

(c) any of the health services under section 2(1)(a) of the Health and Social Care (Reform) Act (Northern Ireland) 2009;

"medicinal product" has the meaning given by regulation 2(1) of the Human Medicines Regulations 2012;

"relevant list" means—

(d) a relevant list for the purposes of the National Health Service (Pharmaceutical and Local Pharmaceutical Services) Regulations 2013, or

(e) a list maintained under those Regulations.

NOTES

Commencement: 13 June 2014.

[2.1066]
8 Making information etc available to a consumer

For the purposes of this Part, something is made available to a consumer only if the consumer can reasonably be expected to know how to access it.

NOTES

Commencement: 13 June 2014.

[2.1067]
9 Information to be provided before making an on-premises contract

(1) Before the consumer is bound by an on-premises contract, the trader must give or make available to the consumer the information described in Schedule 1 in a clear and comprehensible manner, if that information is not already apparent from the context.

(2) Paragraph (1) does not apply to a contract which involves a day-to-day transaction and is performed immediately at the time when the contract is entered into.

(3) *Any information that the trader gives the consumer as required by this regulation is to be treated as included as a term of the contract.*

(4) *A change to any of that information, made before entering into the contract or later, is not effective unless expressly agreed between the consumer and the trader.*

NOTES

Commencement: 13 June 2014.

Para (3) substituted as follows, and para (4) revoked, by the Consumer Contracts (Amendment) Regulations 2015, SI 2015/1629, regs 2, 4, in relation to contracts entered into on or after 1 October 2015—

"(3) If the contract is for the supply of digital content other than for a price paid by the consumer—

(a) any information that the trader gives the consumer as required by this regulation is to be treated as included as a term of the contract, and

(b) a change to any of that information, made before entering into the contract or later, is not effective unless expressly agreed between the consumer and the trader.".

[2.1068]
10 Information to be provided before making an off-premises contract

(1) Before the consumer is bound by an off-premises contract, the trader—

(a) must give the consumer the information listed in Schedule 2 in a clear and comprehensible manner, and

(b) if a right to cancel exists, must give the consumer a cancellation form as set out in part B of Schedule 3.

(2) The information and any cancellation form must be given on paper or, if the consumer agrees, on another durable medium and must be legible.

(3) The information referred to in paragraphs (l), (m) and (n) of Schedule 2 may be provided by means of the model instructions on cancellation set out in part A of Schedule 3; and a trader who has supplied those instructions to the consumer, correctly filled in, is to be treated as having complied with paragraph (1) in respect of those paragraphs.

(4) If the trader has not complied with paragraph (1) in respect of paragraph (g), (h) or (m) of Schedule 2, the consumer is not to bear the charges or costs referred to in those paragraphs.

(5) *Any information that the trader gives the consumer as required by this regulation is to be treated as included as a term of the contract.*

(6) *A change to any of that information, made before entering into the contract or later, is not effective unless expressly agreed between the consumer and the trader.*

(7) This regulation is subject to regulation 11.

NOTES

Commencement: 13 June 2014.

Para (5) substituted as follows, and para (6) revoked, by the Consumer Contracts (Amendment) Regulations 2015, SI 2015/1629, regs 2, 5, in relation to contracts entered into on or after 1 October 2015:

Part 2   Statutory Instruments

"(5) If the contract is for the supply of digital content other than for a price paid by the consumer—

(a)   any information that the trader gives the consumer as required by this regulation is to be treated as included as a term of the contract, and

(b)   a change to any of that information, made before entering into the contract or later, is not effective unless expressly agreed between the consumer and the trader.".

[2.1069]
11 Provision of information in connection with repair or maintenance contracts

(1) If the conditions in paragraphs (2), (3) and (4) are met, regulation 10(1) does not apply to an off-premises contract where—

(a)   the contract is a service contract,

(b)   the consumer has explicitly requested the trader to supply the service for the purpose of carrying out repairs or maintenance,

(c)   the obligations of the trader and the consumer under the contract are to be performed immediately, and

(d)   the payment to be made by the consumer is not more than £170.

(2) The first condition is that, before the consumer is bound by the contract, the trader gives or makes available to the consumer on paper or, if the consumer expressly agrees, on another durable medium—

(a)   the information referred to in paragraphs (b) to (d), (f) and (g) of Schedule 2,

(b)   an estimate of the total price, where it cannot reasonably be calculated in advance, and

(c)   where a right to cancel exists, a cancellation form as set out in part B of Schedule 3.

(3) The second condition is that, before the consumer is bound by the contract, the trader gives or makes available to the consumer the information referred to in paragraphs (a), (l) and (o) of Schedule 2, either on paper or another durable medium or otherwise if the consumer expressly agrees.

(4) The third condition is that the confirmation of the contract provided in accordance with regulation 12 contains the information required by regulation 10(1).

(5) For the right to cancel where this regulation applies, see in particular—

(a)   regulation 28(1)(e) and (2) (cases where cancellation excluded: visit requested for urgent work);

(b)   regulation 36 (form of consumer's request, and consequences).

NOTES

Commencement: 13 June 2014.

[2.1070]
12 Provision of copy or confirmation of off-premises contracts

(1) In the case of an off-premises contract, the trader must give the consumer—

(a)   a copy of the signed contract, or

(b)   confirmation of the contract.

(2) The confirmation must include all the information referred to in Schedule 2 unless the trader has already provided that information to the consumer on a durable medium prior to the conclusion of the off-premises contract.

(3) The copy or confirmation must be provided on paper or, if the consumer agrees, on another durable medium.

(4) The copy or confirmation must be provided within a reasonable time after the conclusion of the contract, but in any event—

(a)   not later than the time of the delivery of any goods supplied under the contract, and

(b)   before performance begins of any service supplied under the contract.

(5) If the contract is for the supply of digital content not on a tangible medium and the consumer has given the consent and acknowledgement referred to in regulation 37(1)(a) and (b), the copy or confirmation must include confirmation of the consent and acknowledgement.

NOTES

Commencement: 13 June 2014.

[2.1071]
13 Information to be provided before making a distance contract

(1) Before the consumer is bound by a distance contract, the trader—

(a)   must give or make available to the consumer the information listed in Schedule 2 in a clear and comprehensible manner, and in a way appropriate to the means of distance communication used, and

(b)   if a right to cancel exists, must give or make available to the consumer a cancellation form as set out in part B of Schedule 3.

(2) In so far as the information is provided on a durable medium, it must be legible.

(3)   The information referred to in paragraphs (l), (m) and (n) of Schedule 2 may be provided by means of the model instructions on cancellation set out in part A of Schedule 3; and a trader who has supplied those instructions to the consumer, correctly filled in, is to be treated as having complied with paragraph (1) in respect of those paragraphs.

(4)   Where a distance contract is concluded through a means of distance communication which allows limited space or time to display the information—

    (a)   the information listed in paragraphs (a), (b), (f), (g), (h), (l) and (s) of Schedule 2 must be provided on that means of communication in accordance with paragraphs (1) and (2), but

    (b)   the other information required by paragraph (1) may be provided in another appropriate way.

(5)   If the trader has not complied with paragraph (1) in respect of paragraph (g), (h) or (m) of Schedule 2, the consumer is not to bear the charges or costs referred to in those paragraphs.

(6)   Any information that the trader gives the consumer as required by this regulation is to be treated as included as a term of the contract.

(7)   A change to any of that information, made before entering into the contract or later, is not effective unless expressly agreed between the consumer and the trader.

NOTES

Commencement: 13 June 2014.

Para (6) substituted as follows, and para (7) revoked, by the Consumer Contracts (Amendment) Regulations 2015, SI 2015/1629, regs 2, 6, in relation to contracts entered into on or after 1 October 2015:

    "(6)   If the contract is for the supply of digital content other than for a price paid by the consumer—

        (a)   any information that the trader gives the consumer as required by this regulation is to be treated as included as a term of the contract, and

        (b)   a change to any of that information, made before entering into the contract or later, is not effective unless expressly agreed between the consumer and the trader.".

[2.1072]

14   Requirements for distance contracts concluded by electronic means

(1)   This regulation applies where a distance contract is concluded by electronic means.

(2)   If the contract places the consumer under an obligation to pay, the trader must make the consumer aware in a clear and prominent manner, and directly before the consumer places the order, of the information listed in paragraphs (a), (f), (g), (h), (s) and (t) of Schedule 2.

(3)   The trader must ensure that the consumer, when placing the order, explicitly acknowledges that the order implies an obligation to pay.

(4)   If placing an order entails activating a button or a similar function, the trader must ensure that the button or similar function is labelled in an easily legible manner only with the words 'order with obligation to pay' or a corresponding unambiguous formulation indicating that placing the order entails an obligation to pay the trader.

(5)   If the trader has not complied with paragraphs (3) and (4), the consumer is not bound by the contract or order.

(6)   The trader must ensure that any trading website through which the contract is concluded indicates clearly and legibly, at the latest at the beginning of the ordering process, whether any delivery restrictions apply and which means of payment are accepted.

NOTES

Commencement: 13 June 2014.

[2.1073]

15   Telephone calls to conclude a distance contract

If the trader makes a telephone call to the consumer with a view to concluding a distance contract, the trader must, at the beginning of the conversation with the consumer, disclose—

    (a)   the trader's identity,

    (b)   where applicable, the identity of the person on whose behalf the trader makes the call, and

    (c)   the commercial purpose of the call.

NOTES

Commencement: 13 June 2014.

[2.1074]

16   Confirmation of distance contracts

(1)   In the case of a distance contract the trader must give the consumer confirmation of the contract on a durable medium.

(2)   The confirmation must include all the information referred to in Schedule 2 unless the trader has already provided that information to the consumer on a durable medium prior to the conclusion of the distance contract.

(3) If the contract is for the supply of digital content not on a tangible medium and the consumer has given the consent and acknowledgment referred to in regulation 37(1)(a) and (b), the confirmation must include confirmation of the consent and acknowledgement.

(4) The confirmation must be provided within a reasonable time after the conclusion of the contract, but in any event—
 (a) not later than the time of delivery of any goods supplied under the contract, and
 (b) before performance begins of any service supplied under the contract.

(5) For the purposes of paragraph (4), the confirmation is treated as provided as soon as the trader has sent it or done what is necessary to make it available to the consumer.

NOTES
 Commencement: 13 June 2014.

[2.1075]
17 Burden of proof in relation to off-premises and distance contracts
(1) In case of dispute about the trader's compliance with any provision of regulations 10 to 16, it is for the trader to show that the provision was complied with.

(2) That does not apply to proceedings—
 (a) for an offence under regulation 19, or
 (b) relating to compliance with an injunction, interdict or order under regulation 45.

NOTES
 Commencement: 13 June 2014.

[2.1076]
18 Effect on contract of failure to provide information
Every contract to which this Part applies is to be treated as including a term that the trader has complied with the provisions of—
 (a) regulations 9 to 14, and
 (b) regulation 16.

NOTES
 Commencement: 13 June 2014.

CHAPTER 2
OFFENCES

[2.1077]
19 Offence relating to the failure to give notice of the right to cancel
(1) A trader is guilty of an offence if the trader enters into an off-premises contract to which regulation 10 applies but fails to give the consumer the information listed in paragraph (l), (m) or (n) of Schedule 2 in accordance with that regulation.

(2) A person who is guilty of an offence under paragraph (1) is liable on summary conviction to a fine not exceeding level 5 on the standard scale.

NOTES
 Commencement: 13 June 2014.

[2.1078]
20 Defence of due diligence
(1) In any proceedings against a person (A) for an offence under regulation 19 it is a defence for A to prove—
 (a) that the commission of the offence was due to—
  (i) the act or default of another, or
  (ii) reliance on information given by another, and
 (b) that A took all reasonable precautions and exercised all due diligence to avoid the commission of such an offence by A or any person under A's control.

(2) A person is not entitled to rely on the defence provided by paragraph (1) without leave of the court unless—
 (a) that person has served on the prosecutor a notice in writing giving such information as was in that person's possession identifying or assisting in the identification of the other person; and
 (b) the notice is served on the prosecutor not less than 7 days before the hearing of the proceedings or, in Scotland, 7 days before the intermediate diet or 14 days before the trial diet, whichever is earlier.

NOTES
 Commencement: 13 June 2014.

[2.1079]
21 Liability of persons other than the principal offender

Where the commission by a person of an offence under regulation 19 is due to the act or default of another person, that other person is guilty of the offence and may be proceeded against and punished whether or not proceedings are taken against the first person.

NOTES
Commencement: 13 June 2014.

[2.1080]
22 Offences committed by bodies of persons

(1)   Where an offence under regulation 19 committed by a body corporate is proved—
   (a)   to have been committed with the consent or connivance of an officer of the body corporate or
   (b)   to be attributable to any neglect on the part of an officer of the body corporate,
the officer, as well as the body corporate, is guilty of the offence and liable to be proceeded against and punished accordingly.

(2)   In paragraph (1) a reference to an officer of a body corporate includes a reference to—
   (a)   a director, manager, secretary or other similar officer; and
   (b)   a person purporting to act as a director, manager, secretary or other similar officer.

(3)   Where an offence under regulation 19 committed in Scotland by a Scottish partnership is proved—
   (a)   to have been committed with the consent or connivance of a partner, or
   (b)   to be attributable to any neglect on the part of a partner,
that partner, as well as the partnership shall be guilty of the offence and liable to be proceeded against and punished accordingly.

(4)   In paragraph (3) a reference to a partner includes a person purporting to act as a partner.

NOTES
Commencement: 13 June 2014.

[2.1081]
23 Duty to enforce

(1)   Subject to paragraphs (2) and (3)—
   (a)   it is the duty of every weights and measures authority in Great Britain to enforce regulation 19 within its area; and
   (b)   it is the duty of the Department of Enterprise, Trade and Investment in Northern Ireland to enforce regulation 19 within Northern Ireland.

(2)   No proceedings for an offence under regulation 19 may be instituted in England and Wales except by or on behalf of an enforcement authority.

(3)   Nothing in paragraph (1) authorises any weights and measures authority to bring proceedings in Scotland for an offence.

NOTES
Commencement: 13 June 2014.

[2.1082]
24 *Powers of investigation*

(1)   If a duly authorised officer of an enforcement authority has reasonable grounds for suspecting that an offence has been committed under regulation 19, the officer may require a person carrying on or employed in a business to produce any document relating to the business, and take copies of it or any entry in it for the purposes of ascertaining whether such an offence has been committed.

(2)   If the officer has reasonable grounds for believing that any documents may be required as evidence in proceedings for such an offence, the officer may seize and detain them and shall, if the officer does so, inform the person from whom they are seized.

(3)   In this regulation "document" includes information recorded in any form.

(4)   The reference in paragraph (1) to production of documents is, in the case of a document which contains information recorded otherwise than in a legible form, a reference to the production of a copy of the information in a legible form.

(5)   An officer seeking to exercise a power under this regulation must do so only at a reasonable hour and on production of the officer's identification and authority.

(6)   Nothing in this regulation requires a person to produce or provide, or authorises a person to inspect or take possession of, anything in respect of which a claim to legal professional privilege (in Scotland, to confidentiality of communications) could be maintained in legal proceedings.

NOTES
Commencement: 13 June 2014.

Revoked, together with regs, 25, 26, by the Consumer Rights Act 2015 (Consequential Amendments) Order 2015, SI 2015/1726, art 2, Schedule, Pt 2. For transitional provisions, see the note below.

The Consumer Rights Act 2015 (Consequential Amendments) Order 2015, SI 2015/1726, art 4, provides as follows:

"4   Transitional provision
(1)   This article applies where—
  (a)   a provision ("the old provision") is revoked by Part 2 of the Schedule, and
  (b)   a provision of Schedule 5 to the Consumer Rights Act 2015 (investigatory powers etc) ("the new provision") re-enacts, with or without modification, the old provision.

(2)   Anything done, or having effect as if done, under (or for the purposes of or in reliance on) the old provision and in force or effective immediately before 1st October 2015 has effect on and after 1st October 2015 as if done under (or for the purposes of or in reliance on) the new provision.

(3)   A reference, express or implied, in an enactment, instrument or document to the new provision is, subject to its context, to be read as being or including a reference to the old provision, in relation to times, circumstances or purposes in relation to which the old provision had effect.".

[2.1083]
25   Obstruction of authorised officers

(1)   A person commits an offence if that person—
  (a)   intentionally obstructs an officer of an enforcement authority acting in pursuance of functions under regulation 24;
  (b)   fails without reasonable cause to comply with any requirement properly made by such an officer under regulation 24; or
  (c)   fails without reasonable cause to give such an officer any other assistance or information which the officer may reasonably require for the purpose of the performance of functions under regulation 24.

(2)   A person giving any information which is required from that person under paragraph (1)(c) is guilty of an offence if, in doing so, the person makes any statement knowing it to be false in a material particular.

(3)   A person guilty of an offence under paragraph (1) or (2) is liable on summary conviction to a fine not exceeding level 3 on the standard scale.

NOTES
Commencement: 13 June 2014.
Revoked, subject to transitional provisions, as noted to reg 24 at **[2.1082]**.

[2.1084]
26   Freedom from self-incrimination

Nothing in regulation 24 or 25 is to be construed as requiring a person to answer any question or give any information if to do so might incriminate that person.

NOTES
Commencement: 13 June 2014.

PART 3
RIGHT TO CANCEL

[2.1085]
27   Application of Part 3

(1)   This Part applies to distance and off-premises contracts between a trader and a consumer, subject to paragraphs (2) and (3) and regulations 6 and 28.

(2)   This Part does not apply to contracts to the extent that they are—
  (a)   for the supply of a medicinal product by administration by a prescriber, or under a prescription or directions given by a prescriber;
  (b)   for the supply of a product by a health care professional or a person included in a relevant list, under arrangements for the supply of services as part of the health service, where the product is one that, at least in some circumstances is available under such arrangements free or on prescription;
  (c)   for passenger transport services.

(3)   This Part does not apply to off-premises contracts under which the payment to be made by the consumer is not more than £42.

(4)   In paragraph (2)(a) and (b), expressions defined in regulation 7(5) have the meaning given there.

NOTES
Commencement: 13 June 2014.
Revoked, subject to transitional provisions, as noted to reg 24 at **[2.1082]**.

[2.1086]
28   Limits of application: circumstances excluding cancellation

(1)   This Part does not apply as regards the following—
-   (a)   the supply of—
    -   (i)   goods, or
    -   (ii)   services, other than supply of water, gas, electricity or district heating,
        for which the price is dependent on fluctuations in the financial market which cannot be controlled by the trader and which may occur within the cancellation period;
-   (b)   the supply of goods that are made to the consumer's specifications or are clearly personalised;
-   (c)   the supply of goods which are liable to deteriorate or expire rapidly;
-   (d)   the supply of alcoholic beverages, where—
    -   (i)   their price has been agreed at the time of the conclusion of the sales contract,
    -   (ii)   delivery of them can only take place after 30 days, and
    -   (iii)   their value is dependent on fluctuations in the market which cannot be controlled by the trader;
-   (e)   contracts where the consumer has specifically requested a visit from the trader for the purpose of carrying out urgent repairs or maintenance;
-   (f)   the supply of a newspaper, periodical or magazine with the exception of subscription contracts for the supply of such publications;
-   (g)   contracts concluded at a public auction;
-   (h)   the supply of accommodation, transport of goods, vehicle rental services, catering or services related to leisure activities, if the contract provides for a specific date or period of performance.

(2)   Sub-paragraph (e) of paragraph (1) does not prevent this Part applying to a contract for—
-   (a)   services in addition to the urgent repairs or maintenance requested, or
-   (b)   goods other than replacement parts necessarily used in making the repairs or carrying out the maintenance,

if the trader supplies them on the occasion of a visit such as is mentioned in that sub-paragraph.

(3)   The rights conferred by this Part cease to be available in the following circumstances—
-   (a)   in the case of a contract for the supply of sealed goods which are not suitable for return due to health protection or hygiene reasons, if they become unsealed after delivery;
-   (b)   in the case of a contract for the supply of sealed audio or sealed video recordings or sealed computer software, if the goods become unsealed after delivery;
-   (c)   in the case of any sales contract, if the goods become mixed inseparably (according to their nature) with other items after delivery.

NOTES

Commencement: 13 June 2014.

[2.1087]
29   Right to cancel

(1)   The consumer may cancel a distance or off-premises contract at any time in the cancellation period without giving any reason, and without incurring any liability except under these provisions—
-   (a)   regulation 34(3) (where enhanced delivery chosen by consumer);
-   (b)   regulation 34(9) (where value of goods diminished by consumer handling);
-   (c)   regulation 35(5) (where goods returned by consumer);
-   (d)   regulation 36(4) (where consumer requests early supply of service).

(2)   The cancellation period begins when the contract is entered into and ends in accordance with regulation 30 or 31.

(3)   Paragraph (1) does not affect the consumer's right to withdraw an offer made by the consumer to enter into a distance or off-premises contract, at any time before the contract is entered into, without giving any reason and without incurring any liability.

NOTES

Commencement: 13 June 2014.

[2.1088]
30   Normal cancellation period

(1)   The cancellation period ends as follows, unless regulation 31 applies.

(2)   If the contract is—
-   (a)   a service contract, or
-   (b)   a contract for the supply of digital content which is not supplied on a tangible medium,

the cancellation period ends at the end of 14 days after the day on which the contract is entered into.

(3)   If the contract is a sales contract and none of paragraphs (4) to (6) applies, the cancellation period ends at the end of 14 days after the day on which the goods come into the physical possession of—

(a)   the consumer, or

(b)   a person, other than the carrier, identified by the consumer to take possession of them.

(4)   If the contract is a sales contract under which multiple goods are ordered by the consumer in one order but some are delivered on different days, the cancellation period ends at the end of 14 days after the day on which the last of the goods come into the physical possession of—

(a)   the consumer, or

(b)   a person, other than the carrier, identified by the consumer to take possession of them.

(5)   If the contract is a sales contract under which goods consisting of multiple lots or pieces of something are delivered on different days, the cancellation period ends at the end of 14 days after the day on which the last of the lots or pieces come into the physical possession of—

(a)   the consumer, or

(b)   a person, other than the carrier, identified by the consumer to take possession of them.

(6)   If the contract is a sales contract for regular delivery of goods during a defined period of more than one day, the cancellation period ends at the end of 14 days after the day on which the first of the goods come into the physical possession of—

(a)   the consumer, or

(b)   a person, other than the carrier, identified by the consumer to take possession of them.

NOTES

Commencement: 13 June 2014.

[2.1089]

31   Cancellation period extended for breach of information requirement

(1)   This regulation applies if the trader does not provide the consumer with the information on the right to cancel required by paragraph (l) of Schedule 2, in accordance with Part 2.

(2)   If the trader provides the consumer with that information in the period of 12 months beginning with the first day of the 14 days mentioned in regulation 30(2) to (6), but otherwise in accordance with Part 2, the cancellation period ends at the end of 14 days after the consumer receives the information.

(3)   Otherwise the cancellation period ends at the end of 12 months after the day on which it would have ended under regulation 30.

NOTES

Commencement: 13 June 2014.

[2.1090]

32   Exercise of the right to withdraw or cancel

(1)   To withdraw an offer to enter into a distance or off-premises contract, the consumer must inform the trader of the decision to withdraw it.

(2)   To cancel a contract under regulation 29(1), the consumer must inform the trader of the decision to cancel it.

(3)   To inform the trader under paragraph (2) the consumer may either—

(a)   use a form following the model cancellation form in part B of Schedule 3, or

(b)   make any other clear statement setting out the decision to cancel the contract.

(4)   If the trader gives the consumer the option of filling in and submitting such a form or other statement on the trader's website—

(a)   the consumer need not use it, but

(b)   if the consumer does, the trader must communicate to the consumer an acknowledgement of receipt of the cancellation on a durable medium without delay.

(5)   Where the consumer informs the trader under paragraph (2) by sending a communication, the consumer is to be treated as having cancelled the contract in the cancellation period if the communication is sent before the end of the period.

(6)   In case of dispute it is for the consumer to show that the contract was cancelled in the cancellation period in accordance with this regulation.

NOTES

Commencement: 13 June 2014.

[2.1091]

33   Effect of withdrawal or cancellation

(1)   If a contract is cancelled under regulation 29(1)—

(a)   the cancellation ends the obligations of the parties to perform the contract, and

(b)   regulations 34 to 38 apply.

(2) Regulations 34 and 38 also apply if the consumer withdraws an offer to enter into a distance or off-premises contract.

NOTES
Commencement: 13 June 2014.

[2.1092]
34 Reimbursement by trader in the event of withdrawal or cancellation

(1) The trader must reimburse all payments, other than payments for delivery, received from the consumer, subject to paragraph (10).

(2) The trader must reimburse any payment for delivery received from the consumer, unless the consumer expressly chose a kind of delivery costing more than the least expensive common and generally acceptable kind of delivery offered by the trader.

(3) In that case, the trader must reimburse any payment for delivery received from the consumer up to the amount the consumer would have paid if the consumer had chosen the least expensive common and generally acceptable kind of delivery offered by the trader.

(4) Reimbursement must be without undue delay, and in any event not later than the time specified in paragraph (5) or (6).

(5) If the contract is a sales contract and the trader has not offered to collect the goods, the time is the end of 14 days after—
    (a) the day on which the trader receives the goods back, or
    (b) if earlier, the day on which the consumer supplies evidence of having sent the goods back.

(6) Otherwise, the time is the end of 14 days after the day on which the trader is informed of the consumer's decision to withdraw the offer or cancel the contract, in accordance with regulation *44*.

(7) The trader must make the reimbursement using the same means of payment as the consumer used for the initial transaction, unless the consumer has expressly agreed otherwise.

(8) The trader must not impose any fee on the consumer in respect of the reimbursement.

(9) If (in the case of a sales contract) the value of the goods is diminished by any amount as a result of handling of the goods by the consumer beyond what is necessary to establish the nature, characteristics and functioning of the goods, the trader may recover that amount from the consumer, up to the contract price.

(10) An amount that may be recovered under paragraph (9)—
    (a) may be deducted from the amount to be reimbursed under paragraph (1);
    (b) otherwise, must be paid by the consumer to the trader.

(11) Paragraph (9) does not apply if the trader has failed to provide the consumer with the information on the right to cancel required by paragraph (l) of Schedule 2, in accordance with Part 2.

(12) For the purposes of paragraph (9) handling is beyond what is necessary to establish the nature, characteristics and functioning of the goods if, in particular, it goes beyond the sort of handling that might reasonably be allowed in a shop.

(13) Where the provisions of this regulation apply to cancellation of a contract, the contract is to be treated as including those provisions as terms.

NOTES
Commencement: 13 June 2014.
Para (6): for the figure in italics there is substituted the figure "32", by the Consumer Contracts (Amendment) Regulations 2015, SI 2015/1629, regs 2, 7, in relation to contracts entered into on or after 1 October 2015.

[2.1093]
35 Return of goods in the event of cancellation

(1) Where a sales contract is cancelled under regulation 29(1), it is the trader's responsibility to collect the goods if—
    (a) the trader has offered to collect them, or
    (b) in the case of an off-premises contract, the goods were delivered to the consumer's home when the contract was entered into and could not, by their nature, normally be returned by post.

(2) If it is not the trader's responsibility under paragraph (1) to collect the goods, the consumer must—
    (a) send them back, or
    (b) hand them over to the trader or to a person authorised by the trader to receive them.

(3) The address to which goods must be sent under paragraph (2)(a) is—
    (a) any address specified by the trader for sending the goods back;
    (b) if no address is specified for that purpose, any address specified by the trader for the consumer to contact the trader;
    (c) if no address is specified for either of those purposes, any place of business of the trader.

(4)   The consumer must send off the goods under paragraph (2)(a), or hand them over under paragraph (2)(b), without undue delay and in any event not later than 14 days after the day on which the consumer informs the trader as required by regulation 32(2).

(5)   The consumer must bear the direct cost of returning goods under paragraph (2), unless—
    (a)   the trader has agreed to bear those costs, or
    (b)   the trader failed to provide the consumer with the information about the consumer bearing those costs, required by paragraph (m) of Schedule 2, in accordance with Part 2.

(6)   The contract is to be treated as including a term that the trader must bear the direct cost of the consumer returning goods under paragraph (2) where paragraph (5)(b) applies.

(7)   The consumer is not required to bear any other cost of returning goods under paragraph (2).

(8)   The consumer is not required to bear any cost of collecting goods under paragraph (1) [unless the trader has offered to collect the goods and the consumer has agreed to bear the costs of the trader doing so].

NOTES
    Commencement: 13 June 2014.
    Para (8): words in square brackets substituted by the Consumer Protection (Amendment) Regulations 2014, SI 2014/870, reg 9(1), (2).

[2.1094]
36   Supply of service in cancellation period

(1)   The trader must not begin the supply of a service before the end of the cancellation period provided for in regulation 30(1) unless the consumer—
    (a)   has made an express request, and
    (b)   in the case of an off-premises contract, has made the request on a durable medium.

(2)   In the case of a service other than supply of water, gas, electricity or district heating, the consumer ceases to have the right to cancel a service contract under regulation 29(1) if the service has been fully performed, and performance of the service began—
    (a)   after a request by the consumer in accordance with paragraph (1), and
    (b)   with the acknowledgement that the consumer would lose that right once the contract had been fully performed by the trader.

(3)   Paragraphs (4) to (6) apply where a contract is cancelled under regulation 29(1) and a service has been supplied in the cancellation period.

(4)   Where the service is supplied in response to a request in accordance with paragraph (1), the consumer must (subject to paragraph (6)) pay to the trader an amount—
    (a)   for the supply of the service for the period for which it is supplied, ending with the time when the trader is informed of the consumer's decision to cancel the contract, in accordance with regulation 32(2), and
    (b)   which is in proportion to what has been supplied, in comparison with the full coverage of the contract.

(5)   The amount is to be calculated—
    (a)   on the basis of the total price agreed in the contract, or
    (b)   if the total price is excessive, on the basis of the market value of the service that has been supplied, calculated by comparing prices for equivalent services supplied by other traders.

(6)   The consumer bears no cost for supply of the service, in full or in part, in the cancellation period, if—
    (a)   the trader has failed to provide the consumer with the information on the right to cancel required by paragraph (l) of Schedule 2, or the information on payment of that cost required by paragraph (n) of that Schedule, in accordance with Part 2, or
    (b)   the service is not supplied in response to a request in accordance with paragraph (1).

NOTES
    Commencement: 13 June 2014.

[2.1095]
37   Supply of digital content in cancellation period

(1)   Under a contract for the supply of digital content not on a tangible medium, the trader must not begin supply of the digital content before the end of the cancellation period provided for in regulation 30(1), unless—
    (a)   the consumer has given express consent, and
    (b)   the consumer has acknowledged that the right to cancel the contract under regulation 29(1) will be lost.

(2)   The consumer ceases to have the right to cancel such a contract under regulation 29(1) if, before the end of the cancellation period, supply of the digital content has begun after the consumer has given the consent and acknowledgement required by paragraph (1).

(3)   Paragraph (4) applies where a contract is cancelled under regulation 29(1) and digital content has been supplied, not on a tangible medium, in the cancellation period.

(4)   The consumer bears no cost for supply of the digital content, in full or in part, in the cancellation period, if—

(a)   the consumer has not given prior express consent to the beginning of the performance of the digital content before the end of the 14-day period referred to in regulation 30,

(b)   the consumer gave that consent but did not acknowledge when giving it that the right to cancel would be lost, or

(c)   the trader failed to provide confirmation required by regulation 12(5) or 16(3).

NOTES
Commencement: 13 June 2014.

[2.1096]
38   Effects of withdrawal or cancellation on ancillary contracts

(1)   If a consumer withdraws an offer to enter into a distance or off-premises contract, or cancels such a contract under regulation 29(1), any ancillary contracts are automatically terminated, without any costs for the consumer, other than any costs under these provisions—

(a)   regulation 34(3) (where enhanced delivery chosen by consumer);

(b)   regulation 34(9) (where value of goods diminished by consumer handling);

(c)   regulation 35(5) (where goods returned by consumer);

(d)   regulation 36(4) (where consumer requests early supply of service).

(2)   When a trader is informed by a consumer under regulation 32(1) or (2) of a decision to withdraw an offer or cancel a contract, the trader must inform any other trader with whom the consumer has an ancillary contract that is terminated by paragraph (1).

(3)   An "ancillary contract", in relation to a distance or off-premises contract (the "main contract"), means a contract by which the consumer acquires goods or services related to the main contract, where those goods or services are provided—

(a)   by the trader, or

(b)   by a third party on the basis of an arrangement between the third party and the trader.

(4)   Regulation 6(1)(b) (exclusion of financial services contracts) does not limit the contracts that are ancillary contracts for the purposes of this regulation.

NOTES
Commencement: 13 June 2014.

PART 4
PROTECTION FROM INERTIA SELLING AND ADDITIONAL CHARGES

39   (*Inserts the Consumer Protection from Unfair Trading Regulations 2008, SI 2008/1277, reg 27A at* **[2.580]**)

[2.1097]
40   Additional payments under a contract

(1)   Under a contract between a trader and a consumer, no payment is payable in addition to the remuneration agreed for the trader's main obligation unless, before the consumer became bound by the contract, the trader obtained the consumer's express consent.

(2)   There is no express consent (if there would otherwise be) for the purposes of this paragraph if consent is inferred from the consumer not changing a default option (such as a pre-ticked box on a website).

(3)   This regulation does not apply if the trader's main obligation is to supply services within regulation 6(1)(b), but in any other case it applies even if an additional payment is for such services.

(4)   Where a trader receives an additional payment which, under this regulation, is not payable under a contract, the contract is to be treated as providing for the trader to reimburse the payment to the consumer.

NOTES
Commencement: 13 June 2014.

[2.1098]
41   Help-line charges over basic rate

(1)   Where a trader operates a telephone line for the purpose of consumers contacting the trader by telephone in relation to contracts entered into with the trader, a consumer contacting the trader must not be bound to pay more than the basic rate.

(2)   If in those circumstances a consumer who contacts a trader in relation to a contract is bound to pay more than the basic rate, the contract is to be treated as providing for the trader to pay to the consumer any amount by which the charge paid by the consumer for the call is more than the basic rate.

NOTES
   Commencement: 13 June 2014.

PART 5
DELIVERY AND RISK

[2.1099]
42   Time for delivery of goods
(1)   This regulation applies to any sales contract.

(2)   Unless the trader and the consumer have agreed otherwise, the contract is to be treated as including a term that the trader must deliver the goods to the consumer.

(3)   Unless there is an agreed time or period, the contract is to be treated as including a term that the trader must deliver the goods—
   (a)   without undue delay, and
   (b)   in any event, not more than 30 days after the day on which the contract is entered into.

(4)   In this regulation—
   (a)   an "agreed" time or period means a time or period agreed by the trader and the consumer for delivery of the goods, but
   (b)   if there is an obligation to deliver the goods at the time the contract is entered into, that time counts as the "agreed" time.

(5)   Paragraphs (6) and (7) apply if the trader does not deliver the goods in accordance with paragraph (3) or at the agreed time or within the agreed period.

(6)   If the circumstances are that—
   (a)   the trader has refused to deliver the goods,
   (b)   delivery of the goods at the agreed time or within the agreed period is essential taking into account all the relevant circumstances at the time the contract was entered into, or
   (c)   the consumer told the trader before the contract was entered into that delivery in accordance with paragraph (3), or at the agreed time or within the agreed period, was essential,
then the consumer may treat the contract as at an end.

(7)   In any other circumstances, the consumer may specify a period that is appropriate in the circumstances and require the trader to deliver the goods before the end of that period.

(8)   If the consumer specifies a period under paragraph (7) but the goods are not delivered within that period, then the consumer may treat the contract as at an end.

(9)   If the consumer treats the contract as at an end under paragraph (6) or (8), the trader must without undue delay reimburse all payments made under the contract.

(10)   If paragraph (6) or (8) applies but the consumer does not treat the contract as at an end—
   (a)   that does not prevent the consumer from cancelling the order for any of the goods or rejecting goods that have been delivered, and
   (b)   the trader must without undue delay reimburse all payments made under the contract in respect of any goods for which the consumer cancels the order or which the consumer rejects.

(11)   If any of the goods form a commercial unit, then the consumer cannot reject or cancel the order for some of those goods without also rejecting or cancelling the order for the rest of them.

(12)   A unit is a "commercial unit" if division of the unit would materially impair the value of the goods or the character of the unit.

(13)   This regulation does not prevent the consumer seeking other remedies where it is open to the consumer to do so.

NOTES
   Commencement: 13 June 2014.
   Part 5 (regs 42, 43) revoked by the Consumer Contracts (Amendment) Regulations 2015, SI 2015/1629, regs 2, 8, in relation to contracts entered into on or after 1 October 2015.

[2.1100]
43   Passing of risk
(1)   A sales contract is to be treated as including the following provisions as terms.

(2)   The goods remain at the trader's risk until they come into the physical possession of—
   (a)   the consumer, or
   (b)   a person identified by the consumer to take possession of the goods.

(3)   Paragraph (2) does not apply if the goods are delivered to a carrier who—

(a)   is commissioned by the consumer to deliver the goods, and

(b)   is not a carrier the trader named as an option for the consumer.

(4)   In that case the goods are at the consumer's risk on and after delivery to the carrier.

(5)   Paragraph (4) does not affect any liability of the carrier to the consumer in respect of the goods.

NOTES

Commencement: 13 June 2014.

Revoked as noted to reg 42 at **[2.1099]**.

PART 6
ENFORCEMENT

[2.1101]
44   Complaints

(1)   It is the duty of an enforcement authority to consider any complaint made to it about a contravention of these Regulations, unless—

(a)   the complaint appears to the authority to be frivolous or vexatious, or

(b)   another enforcement authority has notified the CMA that it agrees to consider the complaint.

(2)   If an enforcement authority has notified the CMA as mentioned in paragraph (1)(b), that authority is under a duty to consider the complaint.

(3)   The following are enforcement authorities for the purposes of these Regulations—

(a)   every local weights and measures authority in Great Britain;

(b)   the Department of Enterprise, Trade and Investment in Northern Ireland.

NOTES

Commencement: 13 June 2014.

[2.1102]
45   Orders to secure compliance

(1)   An enforcement authority may apply for an injunction, or in Scotland an interdict or order of specific implement, against any person who appears to the authority to be responsible for a contravention of these Regulations.

(2)   The court on an application under this regulation may grant an injunction, interdict or order on such terms as it thinks fit to secure compliance with these Regulations.

NOTES

Commencement: 13 June 2014.

[2.1103]
46   Notification of undertakings and orders to the CMA

An enforcement authority must notify the CMA—

(a)   of any undertaking given to it by or on behalf of any person who appears to it to be responsible for a contravention of these Regulations;

(b)   of the outcome of any application made by it under regulation 45, and of the terms of any undertaking given to the court or of any order made by the court;

(c)   of the outcome of any application made by it to enforce a previous order of the court.

NOTES

Commencement: 13 June 2014.

PART 7
CONSEQUENTIAL AMENDMENTS

[2.1104]
47   Consequential amendments

Schedule 4 makes amendments that are consequential on these Regulations.

NOTES

Commencement: 13 June 2014.

SCHEDULES

SCHEDULE 1
INFORMATION RELATING TO ON-PREMISES CONTRACTS

Regulation 9(1)

[2.1105]

The information referred to in regulation 9(1) is—

(a)   the main characteristics of the [goods, services or digital content], to the extent appropriate to the medium of communication and to the [goods, services or digital content];

(b)   the identity of the trader (such as the trader's trading name), the geographical address at which the trader is established and the trader's telephone number;

(c)   the total price of the [goods, services or digital content] inclusive of taxes, or where the nature of the [goods, services or digital content] is such that the price cannot reasonably be calculated in advance, the manner in which the price is to be calculated;

(d)   where applicable, all additional delivery charges or, where those charges cannot reasonably be calculated in advance, the fact that such additional charges may be payable;

(e)   where applicable, the arrangements for payment, delivery, performance, and the time by which the trader undertakes to deliver the goods [, to perform the service or to supply the digital content];

(f)   where applicable, the trader's complaint handling policy;

(g)   in the case of a sales contract, a reminder that the trader is under a legal duty to supply goods that are in conformity with the contract;

(h)   where applicable, the existence and the conditions of after-sales services and commercial guarantees;

(i)   the duration of the contract, where applicable, or, if the contract is of indeterminate duration or is to be extended automatically, the conditions for terminating the contract;

(j)   where applicable, the functionality, including applicable technical protection measures, of digital content;

(k)   where applicable, any relevant compatibility of digital content with hardware and software that the trader is aware of or can reasonably be expected to have been aware of.

NOTES

Commencement: 13 June 2014.

Words in square brackets substituted by the Consumer Protection (Amendment) Regulations 2014, SI 2014/870, reg 9(1), (3).

SCHEDULE 2
INFORMATION RELATING TO DISTANCE AND OFF-PREMISES CONTRACTS

Regulations 10(1) and 13(1)

[2.1106]

The information referred to in regulations 10(1) and 13(1) is (subject to the note at the end of this Schedule)—

(a)   the main characteristics of the [goods, services or digital content], to the extent appropriate to the medium of communication and to the [goods, services or digital content];

(b)   the identity of the trader (such as the trader's trading name);

(c)   the geographical address at which the trader is established and, where available, the trader's telephone number, fax number and e-mail address, to enable the consumer to contact the trader quickly and communicate efficiently;

(d)   where the trader is acting on behalf of another trader, the geographical address and identity of that other trader;

(e)   if different from the address provided in accordance with paragraph (c), the geographical address of the place of business of the trader, and, where the trader acts on behalf of another trader, the geographical address of the place of business of that other trader, where the consumer can address any complaints;

(f)   the total price of the [goods, services or digital content] inclusive of taxes, or where the nature of the [goods, services or digital content] is such that the price cannot reasonably be calculated in advance, the manner in which the price is to be calculated,

(g)   where applicable, all additional delivery charges and any other costs or, where those charges cannot reasonably be calculated in advance, the fact that such additional charges may be payable;

(h)   in the case of a contract of indeterminate duration or a contract containing a subscription, the total costs per billing period or (where such contracts are charged at a fixed rate) the total monthly costs;

(i)   the cost of using the means of distance communication for the conclusion of the contract where that cost is calculated other than at the basic rate;

(j)   the arrangements for payment, delivery, performance, and the time by which the trader undertakes to deliver the goods[, to perform the services or to supply the digital content];

(k)   where applicable, the trader's complaint handling policy;

(l)   where a right to cancel exists, the conditions, time limit and procedures for exercising that right in accordance with regulations 27 to 38;

(m)   where applicable, that the consumer will have to bear the cost of returning the goods in case of cancellation and, for distance contracts, if the goods, by their nature, cannot normally be returned by post, the cost of returning the goods;

(n)   that, if the consumer exercises the right to cancel after having made a request in accordance with regulation 36(1), the consumer is to be liable to pay the trader reasonable costs in accordance with regulation 36(4);

(o)   where under regulation 28, 36 or 37 there is no right to cancel or the right to cancel may be lost, the information that the consumer will not benefit from a right to cancel, or the circumstances under which the consumer loses the right to cancel;

(p)   in the case of a sales contract, a reminder that the trader is under a legal duty to supply goods that are in conformity with the contract;

(q)   where applicable, the existence and the conditions of after-sale customer assistance, after-sales services and commercial guarantees;

(r)   the existence of relevant codes of conduct, as defined in regulation 5(3)(b) of the Consumer Protection from Unfair Trading Regulations 2008, and how copies of them can be obtained, where applicable;

(s)   the duration of the contract, where applicable, or, if the contract is of indeterminate duration or is to be extended automatically, the conditions for terminating the contract;

(t)   where applicable, the minimum duration of the consumer's obligations under the contract;

(u)   where applicable, the existence and the conditions of deposits or other financial guarantees to be paid or provided by the consumer at the request of the trader;

(v)   where applicable, the functionality, including applicable technical protection measures, of digital content;

(w)   where applicable, any relevant compatibility of digital content with hardware and software that the trader is aware of or can reasonably be expected to have been aware of;

(x)   where applicable, the possibility of having recourse to an out-of-court complaint and redress mechanism, to which the trader is subject, and the methods for having access to it.

Note: In the case of a public auction, the information listed in paragraphs (b) to (e) may be replaced with the equivalent details for the auctioneer.

NOTES

Commencement: 13 June 2014.

Words in square brackets substituted by the Consumer Protection (Amendment) Regulations 2014, SI 2014/870, reg 9(1), (4).

SCHEDULE 3
INFORMATION ABOUT THE EXERCISE OF THE RIGHT TO CANCEL
Regulations 10 and 13

A MODEL INSTRUCTIONS FOR CANCELLATION

[2.1107]
Right to cancel

You have the right to cancel this contract within 14 days without giving any reason.

The cancellation period will expire after 14 days from the day [See Note 1].

To exercise the right to cancel, you must inform us [See Note 2] of your decision to cancel this contract by a clear statement (eg a letter sent by post, fax or e-mail). You may use the attached model cancellation form, but it is not obligatory. [See Note 3]

To meet the cancellation deadline, it is sufficient for you to send your communication concerning your exercise of the right to cancel before the cancellation period has expired.

Effects of cancellation

If you cancel this contract, we will reimburse to you all payments received from you, including the costs of delivery (except for the supplementary costs arising if you chose a type of delivery other than the least expensive type of standard delivery offered by us).

We may make a deduction from the reimbursement for loss in value of any goods supplied, if the loss is the result of unnecessary handling by you.

We will make the reimbursement without undue delay, and not later than—

(a)   14 days after the day we receive back from you any goods supplied, or

(b)   (if earlier) 14 days after the day you provide evidence that you have returned the goods, or

(c)   if there were no goods supplied, 14 days after the day on which we are informed about your decision to cancel this contract.

Part 2 Statutory Instruments

We will make the reimbursement using the same means of payment as you used for the initial transaction, unless you have expressly agreed otherwise; in any event, you will not incur any fees as a result of the reimbursement. [See Note 4]

[See Note 5]

[See Note 6]

Notes on instructions for completion:

1   Insert one of the following texts between the inverted commas:
   (a)   in the case of a service contract or a contract for the supply of digital content which is not supplied on a tangible medium: "of the conclusion of the contract.";
   (b)   in the case of a sales contract: "on which you acquire, or a third party other than the carrier and indicated by you acquires, physical possession of the goods.";
   (c)   in the case of a contract relating to multiple goods ordered by the consumer in one order and delivered separately: "on which you acquire, or a third party other than the carrier and indicated by you acquires, physical possession of the last good.";
   (d)   in the case of a contract relating to delivery of a good consisting of multiple lots or pieces: "on which you acquire, or a third party other than the carrier and indicated by you acquires, physical possession of the last lot or piece.";
   (e)   in the case of a contract for the regular delivery of goods during a defined period of time: "on which you acquire, or a third party other than the carrier and indicated by you acquires, physical possession of the first good.".

2   Insert your name, geographical address and, where available, your telephone number, fax number and e-mail address.

3   If you give the option to the consumer to electronically fill in and submit information about the consumer's cancellation from the contract on your website, insert the following: "You can also electronically fill in and submit the model cancellation form or any other clear statement on our website [insert Internet address]. If you use this option, we will communicate to you an acknowledgement of receipt of such a cancellation on a durable medium (eg by e-mail) without delay.".

4   In the case of sales contracts in which you have not offered to collect the goods in the event of cancellation insert the following: "We may withhold reimbursement until we have received the goods back or you have supplied evidence of having sent back the goods, whichever is the earliest.".

5   If the consumer has received goods in connection with the contract
   (a)   insert:
         —"We will collect the goods."; or,
         —"You shall send back the goods or hand them over to us or . . . [insert the name and geographical address, where applicable, of the person authorised by you to receive the goods], without undue delay and in any event not later than 14 days from the day on which you communicate your cancellation from this contract to us. The deadline is met if you send back the goods before the period of 14 days has expired."
   (b)   insert:
         —"We will bear the cost of returning the goods.";
         —"You will have to bear the direct cost of returning the goods";
         —If, in a distance contract, you do not offer to bear the cost of returning the goods and the goods, by their nature, cannot normally be returned by post: "You will have to bear the direct cost of returning the goods, . . . EUR [insert the amount]."; or if the cost of returning the goods cannot reasonably be calculated in advance: "You will have to bear the direct cost of returning the goods. The cost is estimated at a maximum of approximately . . . EUR [insert the amount]."; or
         —If, in an off-premises contract, the goods, by their nature, cannot normally be returned by post and have been delivered to the consumer's home at the time of the conclusion of the contract: "We will collect the goods at our own expense."; and,
   (c)   insert
         "You are only liable for any diminished value of the goods resulting from the handling other than what is necessary to establish the nature, characteristics and functioning of the goods."

6   In the case of a service contract insert the following: "If you requested to begin the performance of services during the cancellation period, you shall pay us an amount which is in proportion to what has been performed until you have communicated us your cancellation from this contract, in comparison with the full coverage of the contract.".

B MODEL CANCELLATION FORM

To [here the trader's name, geographical address and, where available, fax number and e-mail address are to be inserted by the trader]:

I/We [*] hereby give notice that I/We [*] cancel my/our [*] contract for the sale of the following goods [*]/for the supply of the following service [*],

Ordered on [*]/received on [*],

Name of consumer(s),

Address of consumer(s),

Signature of consumer(s) (only if this form is notified on paper),

Date

[*] Delete as appropriate.

NOTES
Commencement: 13 June 2014.

SCHEDULE 4

(Sch 4 amends the Unsolicited Goods and Services Act 1971, s 6, at **[1.488]**; *the Consumer Credit Act 1974, s 74 at* **[1.561]**; *the Companies Act 1985, Sch 15D; the Financial Services (Distance Marketing) Regulations 2004, SI 2004/2095, reg 11 at* **[2.340]**; *the Supply of Extended Warranties on Domestic Electrical Goods Order 2005, SI 2005/37, art 2; the Companies Act 2006 , Sch 2, Pt 2 and Sch 11A; the Waste Electrical & Electronic Equipment Regulations 2006, SI 2006/3289, reg 2; the Legislative and Regulatory Reform (Regulatory Functions) Order 2007, SI 2007/3544, Sch, Pts 3 and 6; the Consumer Protection from Unfair Trading Regulations 2008, SI 2008/1277, Sch 1, at* **[2.596]**; *the Payment Services Regulations 2009, SI 2009/209, reg 62, at* **[2.690]**; *the Co-ordination of Regulatory Enforcement (Regulatory Functions in Scotland and Northern Ireland) Order 2009, Si 2009/669, Sch 1, Pt 2; the Waste Batteries and Accumulators Regulations 2009, Si 2009/890, reg 2; the Postal Services Act 2011 (Disclosure of Information) Order 2012, Si 2012/1128, reg 4; the Consumer Rights (Payment Surcharges) Regulations 2012, SI 2012/3110, regs 2, 3; and revokes the Enterprise Act 2002 (Part 8 Domestic Infringements) Order 2013, SI 2013/761.)*

FINANCIAL SERVICES AND MARKETS ACT 2000 (DESIGNATED CONSUMER BODIES) ORDER 2013

(SI 2013/3191)

NOTES
Made: 16 December 2013.
Authority: Financial Services and Markets Act 2000, s 234C(2).
Commencement: 14 January 2014.

[2.1108]
1 Citation and commencement

This Order may be cited as the Financial Services and Markets Act 2000 (Designated Consumer Bodies) Order 2013 and comes into force on the 14th January 2014.

NOTES
Commencement: 14 January 2014.

[2.1109]
2 Designation of bodies

Each body listed in the Schedule is designated under section 234C(2) of the Financial Services and Markets Act 2000 for the purpose of making complaints under section 234C(1) of that Act.

NOTES
Commencement: 14 January 2014.

SCHEDULE

Designated bodies

[2.1110]

1. The National Association of Citizens Advice Bureaux

2. The Consumers' Association

3. The General Consumer Council for Northern Ireland

4. The National Federation of Self Employed and Small Businesses

NOTES
Commencement: 14 January 2014.

FINANCIAL SERVICES AND MARKETS ACT 2000 (CONSUMER CREDIT) (MISCELLANEOUS PROVISIONS) ORDER 2014

(SI 2014/208)

NOTES
Made: 3 February 2014.
Authority: European Communities Act 1972, s 2(2); Financial Services and Markets Act 2000, s 426(1).
Commencement: see art 1.

[2.1111]
1   Citation and commencement

(1)   This Order may be cited as the Financial Services and Markets Act 2000 (Consumer Credit) (Miscellaneous Provisions) Order 2014.

(2)   This article and articles 6 and 8 come into force on 26th February 2014.

(3)   This Order comes into force on 26th February 2014 for the purposes of the FCA—
  (a)   making rules;
  (b)   giving guidance;
  (c)   imposing requirements or giving directions.

(4)   This Order comes into force on 1st April 2014, to the extent it is not already in force, immediately after—
  (a)   the Financial Services and Markets Act 2000 (Regulated Activities) (Amendment) (No 2) Order 2013 comes into force, to the extent that it is not already in force, in accordance with article 1(6) (citation, commencement and interpretation) of that Order, and
  (b)   the Financial Services Act 2012 (Consumer Credit) Order 2013 comes into force, to the extent that it is not already in force, in accordance with article 1(1)(b) (citation, commencement and interpretation) of that Order.

NOTES
Commencement: 26 February 2014.

[2.1112]
2   Applications under section 28A of the Financial Services and Markets Act 2000

(1)   Section 55U(4), (5), (7) and (8) of the Financial Services and Markets Act 2000 (applications under this Part) apply to an application made under section 28A of that Act (credit-related agreements made unenforceable by section 26, 26A or 27) as if the application were an application made to the FCA under Part 4A of that Act (permission to carry on regulated activities).

(2)   Where a person ("A") has the right to exercise rights under an agreement entered into by another person ("B"), section 28A of the Financial Services and Markets Act 2000 applies as if the references to the relevant firm in subsections (3) and (7) of that section include a reference to A.

NOTES
Commencement: 26 February 2014 (certain purposes); 1 April 2014 (otherwise).

3–5   (*Art 3 amends the Financial Services (Distance Marketing) Regulations 2004, SI 2004/2095 at* **[2.330]** *et seq; art 4 amends the Financial Services and Markets Act 2000 (Financial Promotion) Order 2005, SI 2005/1529; art 5 amends the Consumer Credit (Disclosure of Information) Regulations 2010, SI 2010/1013, Schs 1, 3 at* **[2.826]** *and* **[2.828]**.)

[2.1113]
6   Transitional provision relating to the Consumer Credit (Disclosure of Information) Regulations 2010

(1)   Pre-contract credit information (within the meaning given by regulation 1(2) of the Consumer Credit (Disclosure of Information) Regulations 2010) disclosed to a debtor in the period specified in paragraph (2) which contains the information specified in paragraph (3) is to be treated as if it contained the information required by—

(a)   the entry in the second column of table 5 in Schedule 1 to the Consumer Credit (Disclosure of Information) Regulations 2010 opposite the entry "If applicable Registration number";

(b)   the entry in the second column of table 5 in Schedule 3 to those Regulations opposite the entry "If applicable Registration number".

(2)   The period is the period of five months beginning on the day on which this article comes into force.

(3)   The information is—

(a)   the consumer credit licence number (if any) of the creditor, which is valid before 1st April 2014,

(b)   the Firm Reference Number (FRN) (if any) or Interim Permission Number (if any) of the creditor, which is valid on or after 1st April 2014, and

(c)   any other relevant registration number of the creditor.

NOTES
Commencement: 26 February 2014.

7   (*Amends the Financial Services and Markets Act 2000 (Regulated Activities) (Amendment) (No 2) Order 2013, SI 2013/1881 at* **[2.1004]** *et seq.*)

[2.1114]
8   Legal professional privilege

(1)   The FCA is entitled to claim legal professional privilege or, in Scotland, confidentiality of communications in respect of legally privileged information disclosed to the FCA by the Office of Fair Trading ("the OFT").

(2)   In this article, "legally privileged information" means information received or generated by the OFT, before 1st April 2014, in respect of which the OFT would have been able, before that date, to maintain a claim to legal professional privilege or, in Scotland, to confidentiality of communications in legal proceedings.

(3)   For the purposes of this article, legally privileged information is to be treated as disclosed to the FCA by the OFT if it is contained in a document transferred by the OFT to the FCA—

(a)   under a transfer scheme made under Part 2 of Schedule 21 to the Financial Services Act 2012 (property, rights and liabilities of Office of Fair Trading); or

(b)   otherwise in connection with functions of the FCA becoming exercisable in respect of an activity which—

(i)   ceases on 1st April 2014 to be an activity in respect of which a licence under section 21 of the Consumer Credit Act 1974 (businesses needing a licence) is required or would be required but for the exemption conferred by subsection (2), (3) or (4) of that section or paragraph 15(3) in Part 2 of Schedule 3 to the Financial Services and Markets Act 2000 (grant of permission), and

(ii)   becomes on that date a regulated activity for the purposes of the Financial Services and Markets Act 2000.

NOTES
Commencement: 26 February 2014.

FINANCIAL SERVICES AND MARKETS ACT 2000 (CONSUMER CREDIT) (DESIGNATED ACTIVITIES) ORDER 2014

(SI 2014/334)

NOTES
Made: 13 February 2014.
Authority: Financial Services and Markets Act 2000, ss 23(1B), 428(3).
Commencement: 1 April 2014.

[2.1115]
1   Citation and commencement

This Order may be cited as the Financial Services and Markets Act 2000 (Consumer Credit) (Designated Activities) Order 2014 and comes into force on 1st April 2014.

NOTES
    Commencement: 1 April 2014.

[2.1116]
2   Credit-related regulated activities for the purpose of section 23 of the Financial Services and Markets Act 2000

The following kinds of regulated activities are designated for the purposes of section 23(1B) of the Financial Services and Markets Act 2000 (contravention of the general prohibition)—

(a)   an activity of the kind specified by article 39F(1) of the Financial Services and Markets Act 2000 (Regulated Activities) Order 2001 (debt-collecting),

(b)   an activity of the kind specified by article 60B of that Order (regulated credit agreements), except in so far as the activity relates to an agreement under which the obligation of the borrower is secured on land.

NOTES
    Commencement: 1 April 2014.

FINANCIAL SERVICES AND MARKETS ACT 2000 (REGULATED ACTIVITIES) (AMENDMENT) ORDER 2014

(SI 2014/366)

NOTES
    Made: 13 February 2014.
    Authority: Financial Services and Markets Act 2000, ss 22(1), (5) , 428(3), Sch 2, para 25; Financial Services Act 2012, s 118.
    Commencement: see art 1.

ARRANGEMENT OF ARTICLES

PART 1
INTRODUCTION

[2.1117]
1   Citation and commencement

(1)   This Order may be cited as the Financial Services and Markets Act 2000 (Regulated Activities) (Amendment) Order 2014.

(2)   This article and articles 15 [and 17] come into force on the day after the day on which this Order is made.

(3)   This Order comes into force on the day after the day on which this Order is made for the purposes of the FCA—

(a)   making rules;

(b)   giving guidance;

(c)   issuing information sheets under the Consumer Credit Act 1974;

(d)   imposing requirements or giving directions.

[(3A)   Article 19(4) comes into force on 31st March 2014, to the extent it is not already in force.]

(4)   This Order comes into force on 1st April 2014, to the extent it is not already in force, immediately after—

(a)   the Financial Services and Markets Act 2000 (Regulated Activities) (Amendment) (No 2) Order 2013 (citation, commencement and interpretation) comes into force, to the extent that it is not already in force, in accordance with article 1(6) of that Order, and

(b)   the Financial Services Act 2012 (Consumer Credit) Order 2013 (citation, commencement and interpretation) comes into force, to the extent that it is not already in force, in accordance with article 1(1)(b) of that Order.

NOTES

Commencement: 14 February 2014.

Para (2): words in square brackets substituted by the Financial Services and Markets Act 2000 (Consumer Credit) (Miscellaneous Provisions) (No 2) Order 2014, SI 2014/506, art 6(1), (2)(a).

Para (3A): inserted by SI 2014/506, art 6(1), (2)(b).

2   *(Art 2 (Pt 2) amends the Financial Services and Markets Act 2000 (Regulated Activities) Order 2001, SI 2001/544 at* **[2.168]** *et seq.)*

PART 3
AMENDMENTS OF PRIMARY LEGISLATION

3   *(Art 3 amends the Consumer Credit Act 1974, s 86A at* **[1.581]**)

[2.1118]
4   Applications under the Consumer Credit Act 1974

(1)   Section 55U(4), (5), (7) and (8) of the Financial Services and Markets Act 2000 (applications under this Part) apply to an application made under a provision of the Consumer Credit Act 1974 specified in paragraph (2) as if the application were an application made to the FCA under Part 4A of the Financial Services and Markets Act 2000.

(2)   The specified provisions are—

(a)   section 60(3) (form and content of agreements);

(b)   section 64(4) (duty to give notice of cancellation rights);

(c)   section 101(8) (right to terminate hire agreement);

(d)   section 160 (alternative procedure for business consumers).

NOTES

Commencement: 14 February 2014 (certain purposes); 1 April 2014 (otherwise).

5   *(Art 5 amends the Financial Services and Markets Act 2000, Sch 6, Pt 1B.)*

PART 4
AMENDMENTS OF SECONDARY LEGISLATION

6–12   *(Arts 6–10 amend legislation that is outside the scope of this work; art 11 amends the Consumer Credit (Information Requirements and Duration of Licences and Charges) Regulations 2007, SI 2007/1167, reg 26, Sch 3, Pt 5, and Sch 5, at* **[2.426]**, **[2.458]**, *and* **[2.461]** *et seq; art 12 amends the Payment Services Regulations 2009, SI 2009/209, reg 52, at* **[2.680]**, *inserts a new reg 92A and a new Sch 4A at* **[2.720]** *and* **[2.764]** *and amends Sch 5.)*

[2.1119]
13   Saving of section 51 of the Consumer Credit Act 1974 for the purposes of the Payment Services Regulations 2009

(1)   Notwithstanding the repeal by regulation 20(15) and (64) of the Financial Services and Markets Act 2000 (Regulated Activities) (Amendment) (No 2) Order 2013 of the provisions specified in paragraph (2), those provisions continue to have effect for the purposes of regulation 52(a) of the Payment Services Regulations 2009 (disapplication of certain regulations in the case of consumer credit agreements).

(2)   The provisions are—

(a)   section 51 of the Consumer Credit Act 1974 (prohibition of unsolicited credit tokens);

(b)   the entry relating to section 51(1) in Schedule 1 to that Act (prosecution and punishment of offences).

NOTES

Commencement: 14 February 2014 (certain purposes); 1 April 2014 (otherwise).

14   *(Amends legislation that is outside the scope of this work.)*

[2.1120]

15 Transitional provision relating to the Consumer Credit (Disclosure of Information) Regulations 2010

(1) Pre-contract credit information (within the meaning given by regulation 1(2) of the Consumer Credit (Disclosure of Information) Regulations 2010) disclosed to a debtor in the period specified in paragraph (2) which contains the information specified in paragraph (3) is to be treated as if it contained the information required by—

- (a) the entry in the second column of table 5 in Schedule 1 to the Consumer Credit (Disclosure of Information) Regulations 2010 opposite the entry "If applicable The supervisory authority";
- (b) the entry in the second column of table 5 in Schedule 3 to those Regulations opposite the entry "If applicable The supervisory authority".

(2) The period is the period of five months beginning on the day on which this article comes into force.

(3) The information is a statement specifying—

- (a) in the case of a person who is carrying on an activity which is exempt from the general prohibition in section 19 of the Financial Services and Markets Act 2000 by virtue of by virtue of section 327 of that Act, the Office of Fair Trading as the supervisory authority before 1st April 2014 and the relevant designated professional body as the supervisory authority after 31st March 2014, or
- (b) in any other case, the Office of Fair Trading as the supervisory authority before 1st April 2014 and the Financial Conduct Authority as the supervisory authority after 31st March 2014.

NOTES

Commencement: 14 February 2014.

16 (*Amends the Consumer Credit (Agreements) Regulations 2010, SI 2010/1014, Sch 1 at* **[2.837]**)

[2.1121]

17 Transitional provision relating to the Consumer Credit (Agreements) Regulations 2010

(1) An agreement presented, sent, given or delivered to the debtor (whether for signature or otherwise) in the period specified in paragraph (2) which contains the information specified in paragraph (3) is to be treated as if it contained the information required by paragraph 33 of Schedule 1 to the Consumer Credit (Agreements) Regulations 2010.

(2) The period is the period of five months beginning on the day on which this article comes into force.

(3) The information is a statement specifying—

- (a) in the case of a person who is carrying on an activity which is exempt from the general prohibition in section 19 of the Financial Services and Markets Act 2000 by virtue of by virtue of section 327 of that Act, the Office of Fair Trading, Fleetbank House, 2-6 Salisbury Square, London EC4Y 8JX as the supervisory authority before 1st April 2014 and the relevant designated professional body as the supervisory authority after 31st March 2014, or
- (b) in any other case, the Office of Fair Trading, Fleetbank House, 2-6 Salisbury Square, London EC4Y 8JX as the supervisory authority before 1st April 2014 and the Financial Conduct Authority, 25 The North Colonnade, Canary Wharf, London, E14 5HS as the supervisory authority after 31st March 2014.

NOTES

Commencement: 14 February 2014.

18 (*Art 18 amends the Electronic Money Regulations 2011, SI 2011/99, Sch 3, Pt 1, and inserts reg 59A and Sch 2A (see the 2011 Regulations at* **[2.884]** *et seq; Art 19 amends the Financial Services and Markets Act 2000 (Regulated Activities) (Amendment) (No 2) Order 2013, SI 2013/1881, arts 56, 58 and Sch, Pt 2 at* **[2.1004]** *et seq.*)

PART 5
REVIEW OF RETAINED PROVISIONS OF THE CONSUMER CREDIT ACT 1974

[2.1122]

20 Review of retained provisions of the Consumer Credit Act 1974

(1) The FCA must arrange for—

- (a) a review of the matter specified in paragraph (2);
- (b) the review to result in a report.

(2) The matter is whether the repeal (in whole or in part) of provisions of the Consumer Credit Act 1974 would adversely affect the appropriate degree of protection for consumers.

(3)   The FCA may extend the review to other matters which are relevant to or connected with the matter specified in paragraph (2).

(4)   The FCA may appoint one or more persons to conduct the review or, where the FCA is conducting the review, to provide advice to the FCA in connection with the review.

(5)   The review must in particular consider—

(a)   which provisions of the Consumer Credit Act 1974 could be replaced by rules or guidance made by the FCA under the Financial Services and Markets Act 2000;

(b)   the principle that a burden or restriction which is imposed on a person in relation to the carrying on of an activity, should be proportionate to the benefits, considered in general terms, which are expected to result from the imposition of that burden or restriction.

(6)   The report may include recommendations to the Treasury, including in particular recommendations relating to the exercise of their power to make an order under section 107 of the Financial Services Act 2012.

(7)   The FCA must—

(a)   submit the report to the Treasury before 1st April 2019;

(b)   publish the report in the way appearing to the FCA most likely to bring it to the attention of the public.

(8)   The Treasury must lay a copy of the report submitted under this article before Parliament.

NOTES
Commencement: 14 February 2014 (certain purposes); 1 April 2014 (otherwise).

[2.1123]
21   Conduct of review

(1)   The person conducting the review ("R") must prepare an interim report of the initial views of R on the matter specified in paragraph (2) of article 20 and (where appropriate) setting out proposed recommendations to the Treasury.

(2)   R may prepare additional interim reports.

(3)   The FCA must—

(a)   provide a copy of any interim report to the Treasury;

(b)   publish an interim report in the way appearing to the FCA most likely to bring it to the attention of the public.

(4)   An interim report must, when published, be accompanied by notice that representations about the interim report and any proposed recommendations may be made to R within a specified time.

(5)   Before making the report under article 20, R must have regard to any representations made to it in accordance with paragraph (4).

(6)   The Treasury may make a recommendation to the FCA in relation to—

(a)   the scope of the review;

(b)   the period during which the review is to be carried out (subject to article 20(7)(a));

(c)   the conduct of the review;

(d)   the making of reports.

(7)   Recommendations under paragraph (6) may in particular recommend—

(a)   confining the review to particular matters (subject to article 20(2));

(b)   extending the review to matters additional to the matter in article 20(2);

(c)   making additional interim reports.

(8)   The FCA must have regard to any recommendation made to it under paragraph (6).

NOTES
Commencement: 14 February 2014 (certain purposes); 1 April 2014 (otherwise).

FINANCIAL SERVICES AND MARKETS ACT 2000 (CONSUMER CREDIT) (TRANSITIONAL PROVISIONS) ORDER 2014 (NOTE)

(SI 2014/376)

[2.1124]

NOTES
The Order was made under the powers conferred by the Financial Services and Markets Act 2000, s 426(1) and came into force on 1 April 2014. It amends the Financial Services and Markets Act 2000 (Regulated Activities) (Amendment) (No 2) Order 2013, SI 2013/1881 at **[2.1004]** et seq. The amendments enable a person whose Consumer Credit Act licence is subject to a suspension immediately before 1 April 2014 to obtain interim permission under the Financial Services and Markets Act 2000 where an appeal against the suspension is successful, and make transitional provision in relation to certain disciplinary and enforcement notices served by the Office of Fair Trading.

ENTERPRISE AND REGULATORY REFORM ACT 2013 (COMMENCEMENT NO 6, TRANSITIONAL PROVISIONS AND SAVINGS) ORDER 2014 (NOTE)

(SI 2014/416)

[2.1125]

NOTES

This Order was made on 3 March 2014 under the powers conferred by the Enterprise and Regulatory Reform Act 2013, ss 100, 103(3), (4).

Article 1 provides for citation.

Article 2 provides that the following provisions of the 2013 Act come into force on 1 April 2014 (in so far as not already in force):

- in Part 3 (the Competition and Markets Authority): s 25(3) (the Competition and Markets Authority – duty to promote competition); and s 26 (abolition of the Competition Commission and the OFT);
- in Part 4 (competition reform): ss 29–51 (mergers, markets, anti-trust, cartels, etc); and ss 54–58 (miscellaneous);
- Schedule 4 (the Competition and Markets Authority);
- Schedules 5–13 (amendments relating to Part 3, Part 4, etc);
- Schedule 14, paras 1–19 and 23–29 (regulators: use of powers under the 1998 Act); and
- Schedule 15 (minor and consequential amendments: Part 4).

Article 2 also introduces the Schedule to this Order which provides for the transitional provisions set out below. Article 3 commences various provisions of the 2013 Act relating to town and country planning and is outside the scope of this work.

SCHEDULE
TRANSITIONAL PROVISIONS AND SAVINGS: THE COMPETITION AND MARKETS AUTHORITY AND COMPETITION REFORM

Article 2(2)

Introductory

1 Interpretation

(1)   In this Schedule—

"the Act" means the Enterprise and Regulatory Reform Act 2013;

"amendments" includes repeals;

"the CMA" means the Competition and Markets Authority;

"the commencement date" means 1st April 2014;

"the Commission" means the Competition Commission;

"enactment" includes—

(a)   an enactment comprised in subordinate legislation (within the meaning of the Interpretation Act 1978), and

(b)   an enactment comprised in (or in an instrument made under) an Act of the Scottish Parliament, a Measure or Act of the National Assembly for Wales or Northern Ireland legislation;

"the OFT" means the Office of Fair Trading; and

"the 2002 Act" means the Enterprise Act 2002.

(2)   For the purposes of this Schedule, the OFT has publicly launched a market study before the commencement date if it has publicly begun before that date activity which, if proposed to be undertaken by the CMA on or after that date, would require the publication of a market study notice under section 130A of the 2002 Act.

(3)   References in this Schedule to amendments made by provisions of the Act include references to any other amendments made by virtue of the Act in consequence of, or for the purposes of, those amendments.

Abolition of OFT and Competition Commission

2 Abolition of OFT and Competition Commission

(1)   Anything which, immediately before the commencement date, is in the process of being done by or in relation to the transferor may, so far as it relates to a relevant function, be continued by or in relation to the transferee.

(2)   Anything done (or having effect as if done) by or in relation to the transferor for the purposes of or in connection with a relevant function is, if in force or effective immediately before the commencement date, to have effect as if done by or in relation to the transferee so far as that is required for continuing its effect on or after the commencement date.

(3)   In the application of sub-paragraph (1) or (2)—

(a)   any reference made before the commencement date under section 22, 33, 45, 62, 131 or 132 of the 2002 Act or section 59 of the Legal Services Act 2007 to the Commission is to be treated, so far as provided by those sub-paragraphs, as a reference under that section to the chair of the CMA for the constitution of a CMA group,

(b)   where any functions exercisable immediately before the commencement date by a Commission group are to be exercisable on or after that date by a CMA group—

(i)   any person who, immediately before the commencement date, is a member of the Commission group is to be treated, on or after that date, as a member of the CMA group concerned if the person is a member of the CMA panel,

(ii)   any person who, immediately before the commencement date, is the chairman of the Commission group is to be treated, on or after that date, as the chair of the CMA group if the person is a member of the CMA panel, and

(iii)   the persons treated as mentioned in sub-paragraph (i) or (ii) are to be treated, on or after the commencement date, as if they have been constituted in accordance with Part 3 of Schedule 4 to the Act as the chair and other members of the CMA group (and that Part applies accordingly in relation to the operation of the group), and

(c)   an authorisation given (whether by warrant or otherwise) before the commencement date, so far as it authorises a named member, or member of staff, of the OFT or the Commission, continues to authorise that individual (but no other) on or after the commencement date if, and only if, the individual is a member, or (as the case may be) a member of staff, of the CMA.

(4)   Any enactment, instrument or other document passed or made before the commencement date is to have effect, so far as necessary for the purposes of or in consequence of sub-paragraphs (1) to (3), as if any references (however expressed) to the transferor were references to the transferee.

(5)   Sub-paragraphs (1) to (4)—

(a)   do not apply in relation to any matter dealt with by a transfer scheme under section 27 of the Act or by any other transitional provision made by virtue of the Act; and

(b)   do not apply so as to convert an appointment as a member of the OFT or the Commission into an appointment as a member of the CMA.

(6)   Any enactment, instrument or other document passed or made before the commencement date is to have effect, so far as necessary for the purposes of or in consequence of its continued effect by virtue of sub-paragraph (8), (10) or (11) below or any of paragraphs 4 to 7, 9 to 12 and 16, as if any references (however expressed) to the transferor were references to the transferee.

(7)   The repeals of section 45(4) of the Competition Act 1998 and section 2(3) of the 2002 Act (general conversion of references to the Monopolies and Mergers Commission and the Director General of Fair Trading) by paragraphs 220 and 229 of Schedule 5 to the Act do not apply so far as those sections create references to the transferor to which sub-paragraph (4) or (6) above are capable of applying.

(8)   The repeal of paragraph 12(1) to (3) of Schedule 7 to the Competition Act 1998 (annual accounts) by paragraph 222 of Schedule 5 to the Act does not apply in relation to any accounts for the financial year ending with 31 March 2014; and those provisions of the Act of 1998 continue to apply as if the obligations of the Commission in relation to its accounts were obligations of the CMA in relation to the Commission's accounts.

(9)   The CMA must prepare accounts (and send them to the Comptroller and Auditor General) under section 5 of the Government Resources and Accounts Act 2000 for the financial year ending with 31st March 2014 in respect of the OFT.

(10)   The repeals of paragraph 12A of Schedule 7 to the Competition Act 1998 and section 4(1) to (3) of the 2002 Act (annual reports) by paragraphs 222 and 229 of Schedule 5 to the Act do not apply in relation to any report for the financial year ending with 31st March 2014; and those provisions of the Act of 1998 and the 2002 Act continue to apply as if the obligation to make (and, in the case of the OFT, lay) a report about the Commission or OFT were an obligation of the CMA to make (or lay) such a report.

(11)   The repeal of Part 2 of Schedule 3 to the 2002 Act (transfers between the Commission and the Competition Service) by paragraph 226 of Schedule 5 to the Act does not apply in relation to any transfer effected by virtue of that Part before the commencement date so far as that Part is capable of continuing to apply on or after the commencement date in relation to the transfer.

(12)   The abolition of the OFT or the Commission does not affect the validity of anything done (or having effect as if done) by or in relation to the transferor before the commencement date.

(13)   In this paragraph—

"CMA Board" has the same meaning as in Schedule 4 to the Act (see Part 2 of that Schedule);

"CMA group" means a group constituted in accordance with Part 3 of Schedule 4 to the Act;

"CMA panel" has the same meaning as in Schedule 4 to the Act (see Part 3 of that Schedule);

"Commission group" means a group constituted under any enactment to perform functions of the Commission;

"the Council" means the Competition Commission Council;

"relevant function" means any function of the transferor which is transferred to the transferee by virtue of Part 3 or 4 of the Act or sub-paragraph (6) above;

"transferee" means the CMA, the CMA Board, a CMA group, the chair of the CMA, another member of the CMA or (as the case may be) a member of staff of the CMA;

"transferor" means the OFT, the Commission, the Council, a Commission group, the chairman of the OFT or Commission, another member of the OFT or Commission or a member of staff of the OFT or Commission;

and references in this paragraph to things done include references to things omitted to be done.

Mergers

3   General: existing matters

(1)   The amendments made by Chapter 1 of Part 4 of the Act, section 49 or 50 of the Act and paragraphs 16 to 20, 21(3) to (5), (6)(a) and (8) to (10), 23, 24, 26, 28, 29 and 35 of Schedule 15 to the Act (mergers) apply in relation to—

(a)   any reference under section 22, 33, 45 or 62 of the 2002 Act made before the commencement date, or

(b)   any possible reference under section 22, 33, 45 or 62 of that Act which arose before that date,

as they apply in relation to any such reference made, or arising, on or after that date.

(2)   In particular—

(a)   the amendments mentioned in sub-paragraph (1) apply in relation to investigations begun, notices given, reports published, undertakings accepted or adopted and orders made or adopted before the commencement date as they apply in relation to investigations begun, notices given, reports published, undertakings accepted or adopted and orders made or adopted on or after that date, and

(b)   the amendments made by section 29(2) to (9) of the Act (investigation powers) apply in relation to a matter which, before the commencement date, was the subject of a reference or possible reference under section 22, 33, 45 or 62 of the 2002 Act as they apply in relation to—

(i)   a matter that is or has been the subject of a reference made on or after that date under section 22, 33, 45 or 62 of the 2002 Act, or

(ii)   a matter that is or has been the subject, on or after that date, of a possible reference under section 22, 33, 45 or 62 of that Act.

(3)   Sub-paragraph (2) is without prejudice to the generality of sub-paragraph (1).

(4)   This paragraph is subject to paragraphs 4 to 7 and 16.

4   Investigation powers

(1)   The amendments made by section 29 of the Act (investigation powers) do not apply in relation to any notice given before the commencement date under section 109 of the 2002 Act.

(2)   The amendments made by paragraphs 16 to 20, 21(3) to (5), (6)(a) and (8) to (10), 23, 24, 26, 28, 29 and 35 of Schedule 15 to the Act (other amendments in relation to investigation powers) do not apply in relation to any notice given before the commencement date under section 31, 34B, 46C or (as the case may be) 99(2) of the 2002 Act.

5   Undertakings and orders

(1)   The amendments made by section 30(1) of, and paragraphs 2(5) to (7) and 4(2) of Schedule 7 to, the Act (initial and interim undertakings) do not apply in relation to undertakings accepted under section 71 of, or paragraph 1 of Schedule 7 to, the 2002 Act before the commencement date.

(2)   In their continued application by virtue of sub-paragraph (1)—

(a)   section 71 of the 2002 Act has effect as if there were no power under that section for an undertaking under that section to be varied or superseded,

(b)   section 80(4) of that Act continues to permit the varying or superseding of an undertaking under section 71 which has been adopted under section 80(3), and

(c)   paragraph 1 of Schedule 7 to that Act has effect as if there were no power under that paragraph for an undertaking accepted or adopted under that paragraph to be varied or superseded.

(3)   The amendments made by paragraphs 3(5) to (7) and 4(5) of Schedule 7 to the Act (interim orders) do not apply in relation to orders adopted before the commencement date.

(4)   The amendments made by section 31 of the Act (financial penalties in relation to interim measures) do not apply in relation to a failure to comply which—

(a)   occurs before the commencement date, and

(b)   does not continue on or after it,

but otherwise do apply in relation to undertakings accepted, or orders made, before that date.

6   Time-limits: general

(1)   The amendments made by paragraphs 2 to 4 and 7 to 12 of Schedule 8 to the Act (time-limits) do not apply in relation to any possible reference under section 22 or 33 of the 2002 Act which is active before the commencement date.

(2)   For the purposes of this paragraph, a possible reference is active before the commencement date if (and only if) condition A, B, or C is met.

(3)   Condition A is that, before the commencement date, the OFT—

(a)   has not received a merger notice under section 96 of the 2002 Act in relation to the subject-matter of the reference,

(b)   either—

(i)   has notified any relevant person that it has received a satisfactory submission for the purpose of considering whether to make the reference, or

(ii)   has received the case from the European Commission as mentioned in section 34A(1) of that Act, and

(c)   has neither made the reference nor decided not to make it.

(4)   Condition B is that, before the commencement date—

(a)   the OFT has received a merger notice under section 96 of the 2002 Act in relation to the subject-matter of the reference,

(b)   the period under section 97 of that Act for considering the notice has not expired,

(c)   the notice has not been rejected under section 99(5) of that Act or withdrawn, and

(d)   the OFT has neither made the reference nor decided not to make it.

(5)   Condition C is that, before the commencement date—

(a)   the OFT has received a merger notice under section 96 of the 2002 Act in relation to the subject-matter of the reference,

(b)   the notice has been rejected under section 99(5) of that Act or withdrawn,

(c)   the OFT has subsequently notified any relevant person that it has received a satisfactory submission for the purpose of considering whether to make the reference, and

(d)   the OFT has neither made the reference nor decided not to make it.

(6)   In its application, on or after the commencement date, to any possible reference under section 22 or 33 of the 2002 Act which is active before that date, section 97 of that Act has effect as if, for subsections (5) and (6), there were substituted—

"(5)   The CMA may by notice to the person who gave the merger notice extend the period for considering a merger notice if it considers that the person has failed (with or without reasonable excuse) to comply with any requirement of a notice under section 109 or (before, on or after the commencement date) with a notice given before that date under section 99(2).

(6)   An extension under subsection (5) shall end—

(a)   when the person concerned provides the information or documents to the satisfaction of the CMA or (as the case may be) appears as a witness in accordance with the requirements of the CMA; or

(b)   if earlier, when the CMA cancels the extension."

(7)   In its application, on or after the commencement date, to any possible reference under section 22 or 33 of the 2002 Act which is active before that date, subsection (2) of section 98 of that Act has effect as if, for that subsection, there were substituted—

"(2)   A notice under section 97(5)—

(a)   shall also be given within 5 days of—

(i)   the end of the period within which the information is to be provided and which is stated in the notice under section 99(2); or

(ii)   the date for compliance with a notice served under section 109; and

(b)   shall also inform the person who gave the merger notice of—

(i)   the CMA's opinion as mentioned in section 97(5) (in the case of a notice under section 99(2)) or the permitted purpose included in the notice in accordance with section 109(4) (in the case of a notice under section 109); and

(ii)   the CMA's intention to extend the period for considering the merger notice."

(8)   In its application, on or after the commencement date, to any possible reference under section 22 or 33 of the 2002 Act which is active before that date, section 110B of that Act has effect as if—

(a)   for subsection (1)(d) there were substituted—

"(d)   the making of the reference is prevented by section 96(3);",

(b)   subsection (1)(f) and (2)(f) were omitted, and

(c)   in subsection (2)(d), for the words "the expiry of the initial period" there were substituted "the time when the reference becomes prevented".

(9)   The amendments made by paragraph 7 of Schedule 8 to the Act (time-limits for consideration of undertakings in lieu of references) do not apply in relation to any case received, on or after the commencement date, by the CMA from the European Commission as mentioned in section 34A(1) of the 2002 Act where the European Commission's decision or deemed decision (whenever made) relates to—

(a)   a notification, under Article 4(1) of the EU Merger Regulation, which is made before the commencement date, or

(b)   a request, under Article 4(4) of that Regulation, which is made before that date.

(10)   In this paragraph—

"EU Merger Regulation" means Council Regulation (EC) No 139/2004 of 20th January 2004 on the control of concentrations between undertakings;

"relevant person" means any person carrying on an enterprise to which the possible reference relates and which has or might have ceased, or (as the case may be) would or might cease, to be distinct (within the meaning of section 26 of the 2002 Act).

7   Time-limits for duty to remedy adverse effects

The amendments made by paragraph 6 of Schedule 8 to the Act (time-limits for remedying adverse effects) do not apply in relation to a report of the Commission—

(a)   of the kind mentioned in section 41(1) of the 2002 Act, and

(b)   published before the commencement date.

Markets

8   General: existing matters

(1)   The amendments made by Chapter 2 of Part 4 of the Act or section 49 or 50 of the Act (markets) apply in relation to—

(a)   any reference made under section 131 or 132 of the 2002 Act before the commencement date, or

(b)   any possible reference under section 131 or 132 of the 2002 Act which arose before that date,

as they apply in relation to any such reference made, or arising, on or after that date.

(2)   In particular, the amendments mentioned in sub-paragraph (1) apply in relation to investigations begun, notices given, reports published, undertakings accepted and orders made before the commencement date as they apply in relation to investigations begun, notices given, reports published, undertakings accepted and orders made on or after that date.

(3)   Sub-paragraph (2) is without prejudice to the generality of sub-paragraph (1).

(4)   This paragraph is subject to paragraphs 9 to 12 and 16.

9   Public interest interventions

(1)   The amendments made by section 35 of, and Schedule 10 to, the Act (public interest interventions in markets investigations) do not apply in relation to—

(a)   any reference made under section 131 or 132 of the 2002 Act before the commencement date, or

(b)   any case where the OFT has published a notice of a proposed undertaking in lieu under section 155(1) or (4) of the 2002 Act before the commencement date.

(2)   In their application to cases where the OFT has publicly launched a market study before the commencement date but sub-paragraph (1) does not apply, sections 139 to 140A of the 2002 Act have effect as if—

(a)   section 139(A1) provided for section 139 to apply where the OFT has publicly launched a market study in relation to a matter,

(b)   the permitted period for the purposes of section 139(1) were the period beginning with the public launch of the market study and ending with—

(i)   the acceptance by the CMA of an undertaking under section 154 instead of the making of a reference under section 131 in relation to the matter,

(ii)   the publication of notice of the fact that the CMA has otherwise decided not to make such a reference in relation to the matter, or

(iii)   the making of such a reference in relation to the matter,

(c)   section 140(1)(a) and (b) required an intervention notice under section 139(1) to state—

(i)   the matter to which the publicly launched market study relates, and

(ii)   the date of the public launch,

(d)   the references in section 140(4B)(b) and 140A(1) to preparing a market study report in relation to a matter within the period permitted by section 131B(4) were references to preparing a report on the market study concerned in relation to a matter,

(e)   sections 140(4C) and (5)(zc) and 140A(2), (3)(c) and (11) were omitted,

(f)   in section 140(6)(a) the word ""(zc)," were omitted,

(g)   the reference in section 140A(1)(b) to the CMA being required to publish the report were a reference to the CMA publishing the report on the market study concerned,

(h)   section 140A(3)(b) required the CMA not to publish the report but to give it to the Secretary of State, and

(i)   the reference in section 140A(10) to the market study report were a reference to the report.

10   Investigation powers

(1)   The amendments made by section 36 of, and Schedule 11 to, the Act (investigation powers) do not apply in relation to any notice given before the commencement date under section 174 of the 2002 Act or section 109 of that Act as applied by section 176 of that Act.

(2)   In their continued application by virtue of sub-paragraph (1), sections 109 to 116 of the 2002 Act and any related provisions have effect without the amendments made by section 29 of the Act.

(3)   In its application to cases where the OFT has publicly launched a market study before the commencement date—

(a)   section 174(1)(a) of the 2002 Act has effect as if the reference to the publication of a market study notice were a reference to the public launch of a market study,

    (b)   section 174C(1) has effect as if for paragraphs (a) and (b) there were substituted "the CMA publishes the report on the market study concerned or (as the case may be) gives it to the Secretary of State under section 140A(3)(b)", and

    (c)   section 174C(2) has effect as if for paragraphs (a) and (b) there were substituted "the publication of the report or (as the case may be) the giving of it to the Secretary of State".

11   Time-limits for market studies and market references

(1)   The amendments made by paragraphs 1, 2, and 10 of Schedule 12 to the Act (market studies and time-limits) do not apply in relation to any market study publicly launched by the OFT before the commencement date (or any reference made under section 131 or 132 of that Act before that date).

(2)   The amendments made by paragraphs 3 and 6 of Schedule 12 to the Act (time-limits for market investigations and reports) do not apply in relation to any reference made under section 131 or 132 of the 2002 Act before the commencement date.

12   Time-limits for duty to remedy adverse effects

The amendments made by paragraphs 4 and 5 of Schedule 12 to the Act (time-limits for remedying adverse effects) do not apply in relation to a report of the Commission—

    (a)   of the kind mentioned in section 138(1) of the 2002 Act, and

    (b)   published before the commencement date.

Anti-trust

13   General: existing anti-trust investigations

Subject to paragraph 14, the amendments made by Chapter 3 of Part 4 of the Act (anti-trust) apply in relation to any investigation begun before, and continuing on, the commencement date as they apply in relation to any investigation begun on or after that date.

14   Penalties

The amendments made by section 40 of the Act (civil enforcement of investigation powers) do not apply in relation to any requirement imposed on a person under the Competition Act 1998 before the commencement date.

Price control references

15   Recovery of CMA's costs in respect of price control references

(1)   The amendments made by section 54 of, and paragraphs 42 to 45 of Schedule 15 to, the Act (recovery of CMA's costs in respect of price control references) do not apply in relation to a determination on a price control reference if the notice of the appeal which gave rise to the price control reference was received by the Competition Appeal Tribunal before the commencement date.

(2)   For the purposes of this paragraph, "price control reference" means a price control matter referred to the Commission before the commencement date or to the CMA on or after that date by virtue of section 193 of the Communications Act 2003 and "price control matter" has the same meaning as in that section.

General

16   Enactments applied by other enactments

(1)   Subject as follows, this Schedule applies in relation to enactments as applied by other enactments as it applies in relation to the enactments themselves.

(2)   In its application to provisions applied by Part 4 of the 2002 Act, paragraph 3(1) has effect as if the references to sections 22, 33, 45 or 62 of the 2002 Act were references to sections 131 or 132 of that Act.

(3)   Paragraph 4(1) does not apply in relation to any notice given before the commencement date under section 109 of the 2002 Act as applied by section 176 of that Act (for which see paragraph 10).

(4)   In its application to provisions applied by the Enterprise Act 2002 (Protection of Legitimate Interests) Order 2003, paragraph 3 has effect as if the references to sections 22, 33, 45 or 62 of the 2002 Act were references to article 5 of that Order.

(5)   In its application to provisions applied by virtue of Schedule 4ZA to the Water Industry Act 1991, paragraph 3 has effect as if the references to sections 22, 33, 45 or 62 of the 2002 Act were references to section 32 of the Act of 1991.

(6)   In their application to functions exercisable under the 2002 Act concurrently with a sectoral regulator, paragraphs 8 to 12 (other than paragraphs 9(2), 10(3) and 11(1)) have effect as if any reference to the OFT includes a reference to the sectoral regulator concerned.

(7)   In their application to sectoral regulators (and without prejudice to paragraphs 8(1) and 9(1)), sections 139(A1)(b) and (1B) and 140A(2)(a) of the 2002 Act and any related provisions have effect as if the references to consultation under section 169 of that Act in respect of a decision of the kind mentioned in section 169(6)(a)(i) of that Act included references to consultation begun before the commencement date in respect of a decision of the kind mentioned in section 169(6)(a)(i) of that Act as it had effect before that date.

(8)   In this paragraph "sectoral regulator" means—

    (a)   the Office of Communications,

    (b)   the Gas and Electricity Markets Authority,

    (c)   the Water Services Regulation Authority,

    (d)   the Office of Rail Regulation,

    (e)   the Northern Ireland Authority for Utility Regulation,

    (f)   the Civil Aviation Authority, or

    (g)   Monitor.

(9)   This paragraph is subject to any provision made otherwise than by this Schedule and dealing specifically with the enactments as applied.

FINANCIAL SERVICES AND MARKETS ACT 2000 (CONSUMER CREDIT) (MISC PROVISIONS) (NO 2) ORDER 2014

(SI 2014/506)

NOTES

Made: 5 March 2014.
Authority: European Communities Act 1972, s 2(2); Financial Services and Markets Act 2000, ss 38, 426(1).
Commencement: see art 1.

[2.1127]
1   Citation and commencement

(1)   This Order may be cited as the Financial Services and Markets Act 2000 (Consumer Credit) (Miscellaneous Provisions) (No 2) Order 2014.

(2)   This article and articles 5 and 6 come into force on 30th March 2014.

(3)   Articles 3, 4, and 7 come into force on 1st April 2014.

(4)   Article 2 comes into force on 1st April 2014 immediately after article 14(4) of the Financial Services and Markets Act 2000 (Regulated Activities) (Amendment) (No 2) Order 2013 comes into force in accordance with article 1(6) of that Order, to the extent that it is not already in force.

NOTES

Commencement: 30 March 2014.

2–6   (*Arts 2 and 3 amend legislation that is outside the scope of this work; art 4 amends the Money Laundering Regulations 2007, SI 2007/2157, reg 4 at* **[2.467]**; *art 5 amends the Financial Services and Markets Act 2000 (Regulated Activities) (Amendment) (No 2) Order 2013, SI 2013/1881, art 12 at* **[2.1006]** *and art 20, art 6 amends the Financial Services and Markets Act 2000 (Regulated Activities) (Amendment) Order 2014, SI 2014/366 at* **[2.1117]** *et seq.*)

[2.1128]
7   Complaints against the Office of Fair Trading

(1)   Paragraph (3) applies to—
  (a)   a complaint arising in connection with the exercise of, or the failure to exercise, any of the functions of the Office of Fair Trading under the Consumer Credit Act 1974, other than its functions under any of the following provisions of that Act—
    (i)   section 4 (dissemination of information and advice);
    (ii)   section 25A (guidance on fitness test);
    (iii) section 33E (guidance on requirements)
    (iv)   section 39C (statement of policy);
    (v)   section 86A (OFT to prepare information sheets on arrears and default);
  (b)   an appeal against the response of the Office of Fair Trading to such a complaint.

(2)   But this article does not apply if the complaint or appeal was made to the Parliamentary Commissioner for Administration on or before 31st March 2014.

(3)   The complaint or appeal is to be treated for the purposes of Part 6 of the Financial Services Act 2012 (investigation of complaints against regulators) as if it were complaint about a relevant function of the FCA if the condition in paragraph (4) is satisfied.

(4)   The condition in this paragraph is that—
  (a)   in case of a complaint—
    (i)   the complaint was not made to the Office of Fair Trading on or before 31st March 2014; or
    (ii)   if the complaint was made to the Office of Fair Trading on or before 31st March 2014, the Office of Fair Trading had not responded to the complaint on or before that date (other than sending a written acknowledgement of the complaint);
  (b)   in case of an appeal—
    (i)   the appeal was not made to the Office of Fair Trading on or before 31st March 2014; or
    (ii)   if the appeal was made to the Office of Fair Trading on or before 31st March 2014, the Office of Fair Trading had not responded to the appeal on or before that date (other than sending a written acknowledgement of the appeal).

NOTES

Commencement: 1 April 2014.

PUBLIC BODIES (ABOLITION OF THE NATIONAL CONSUMER COUNCIL AND TRANSFER OF THE OFFICE OF FAIR TRADING'S FUNCTIONS IN RELATION TO ESTATE AGENTS ETC) ORDER 2014

(SI 2014/631)

NOTES
Made: 13 March 2014.
Authority: Public Bodies Act 2011, ss 1(1), (2), 5(1)(b), 6(1), (2), (5), 35(2).
Commencement: see art 1.

ARRANGEMENT OF ARTICLES

[2.1129]
1   Citation, commencement, interpretation and extent

(1)   This Order may be cited as the Public Bodies (Abolition of the National Consumer Council and Transfer of the Office of Fair Trading's Functions in relation to Estate Agents etc) Order 2014.

(2)   This article comes into force on the day after the day on which this Order is made.

(3)   Subject to paragraph (4), articles 2, 3 and 4 of this Order come into force on 1st April 2014.

(4)   Article 3(1)(g) and paragraph 14 of Schedule 1 (repeal of reference to the National Consumer Council in Schedule 1 to the Public Bodies Act 2011) come into force on 2nd April 2014.

(5)   Subject to paragraphs (6) and (7), article 5 of this Order comes into force on 31st March 2014.

(6)   Article 5(3)(a)(ii) and paragraph 6 of Schedule 2 (repeal of reference to the Office of Fair Trading in Schedule 5 to the Public Bodies Act 2011) come into force on 1st April 2014.

(7)   Paragraph 16 of Schedule 2 (provision of information to the lead enforcement authority by the OFT) comes into force on the day after the day on which this Order is made.

(8)   An amendment or repeal made by this Order has the same extent as the enactment to which it relates.

(9)   In this Order—
    "the 1979 Act" means the Estate Agents Act 1979;
    "the 2002 Act" means the Enterprise Act 2002;
    "the 2007 Act" means the Consumers, Estate Agents and Redress Act 2007;
    "the 2007 Regulations" means the Money Laundering Regulations 2007;
    "Citizens Advice" means the National Association of Citizens Advice Bureaux;
    "Citizens Advice Scotland" means the Scottish Association of Citizens Advice Bureaux;
    "CMA" means the Competition and Markets Authority;
    "the Commissioners" means the Commissioners for Her Majesty's Revenue and Customs;
    "the First-tier Tribunal" means the First-tier Tribunal constituted under section 3(1) of the Tribunal, Courts and Enforcement Act 2007"
    "the GCCNI" means the General Consumer Council for Northern Ireland;
    "the lead enforcement authority" means Powys County Council;
    "the National Consumer Council" means the National Consumer Council established by section 1 of the 2007 Act;
    "the OFT" means the Office of Fair Trading established by section 1 of the 2002 Act.

(10)   A reference in this Order to a consumer advocacy body is a reference to—
- (a)   Citizens Advice,
- (b)   Citizens Advice Scotland, or
- (c)   the GCCNI.

NOTES
Commencement: 14 March 2014.

[2.1130]
2   Abolition of the National Consumer Council
The National Consumer Council is abolished.

NOTES
Commencement: 1 April 2014.

[2.1131]
3   Transfer of functions of the National Consumer Council
(1)   Schedule 1 has effect—
- (a)   to transfer certain functions of the National Consumer Council under—
  - (i)   the Postal Services Act 2000,
  - (ii)   the 2007 Act, and
  - (iii)   the Postal Services Act 2011,
  - to the consumer advocacy bodies;
- (b)   to transfer certain functions of the National Consumer Council under—
  - (i)   the Gas Act 1986,
  - (ii)   the Electricity Act 1989,
  - (iii)   the Utilities Act 2000,
  - (iv)   the Communications Act 2003, and
  - (v)   the 2007 Act,
  - to Citizens Advice and to Citizens Advice Scotland;
- (c)   to transfer certain functions of the National Consumer Council under—
  - (i)   the Warm Homes and Energy Conservation Act 2000, and
  - (ii)   the 2007 Act,
  - to Citizens Advice;
- (d)   to transfer certain functions of the National Consumer Council under—
  - (i)   the Water Industry (Scotland) Act 2002,
  - (ii)   the Water Services etc (Scotland) Act 2005, and
  - (iii)   the Public Service Reform (Scotland) Act 2010,
  - to Citizens Advice Scotland;
- (e)   to transfer certain functions of the National Consumer Council under the 2007 Act to the GCCNI;
- (f)   to make consequential, supplementary incidental and transitional provision relating to the abolition of the National Consumer Council and the transfer of certain functions;
- (g)   to repeal the entry relating to the National Consumer Council in Schedule 1 to the Public Bodies Act 2011.

(2)   A function transferred under paragraph (1)(a) or (b) to Citizens Advice or Citizens Advice Scotland—
- (a)   may be exercised by each of them jointly with the other;
- (b)   may be exercised on behalf of the one to which the function is transferred by the other of them, if they so agree.

(3)   The conferring of functions on Citizens Advice or Citizens Advice Scotland by or under this Order is without prejudice to the functions of Citizens Advice and Citizens Advice Scotland not so conferred.

(4)   A function transferred to the GCCNI under paragraph (1)(a) or (e) may be exercised by that body only in relation to consumer matters that relate to postal services in Northern Ireland.

(5)   In paragraph (4) "consumer matters" has the meaning given by section 3 of the 2007 Act.

NOTES
Commencement: 1 April 2014 (except para (1)(g)); 2 April 2014, (para (1)(g)).

[2.1132]
4   Transfer of OFT functions in relation to a consumer advice scheme
Schedule 1 also has effect—
- (a)   to transfer certain functions of the OFT under the 2007 Act in relation to a consumer advice scheme to Citizens Advice and Citizens Advice Scotland;
- (b)   to make consequential, supplementary and incidental provision relating to the transfer of certain functions relating to a consumer advice scheme from the OFT to Citizens Advice and Citizens Advice Scotland.

NOTES
Commencement: 1 April 2014.

[2.1133]
5   Transfer of OFT functions in relation to estate agents

(1)   The functions conferred on the OFT by the 1979 Act are transferred to the lead enforcement authority.

(2)   The functions exercisable by the OFT under the 2007 Regulations by virtue of its role as the supervisory authority for estate agents pursuant to regulation 23(1)(b)(ii) of those Regulations are transferred to the Commissioners.

(3)   The following Schedules have effect—
   (a)   Schedule 2, which—
      (i)   makes consequential, supplementary, incidental and transitional provision and savings relating to the transfer of functions under the Estate Agents Act 1979; and
      (ii) repeals the entry relating to the OFT in Schedule 5 to the Public Bodies Act 2011;
   (b)   Schedule 3 (consequential, supplementary, incidental and transitional provision and savings relating to the transfer of functions under the 2007 Regulations).

NOTES
Commencement: 31 March 2014 (paras (1), (2), (3)(a)(i), (b)); 1 April 2014 (otherwise).

SCHEDULE 1
TRANSFER OF CERTAIN FUNCTIONS OF THE NATIONAL CONSUMER COUNCIL, TRANSFER OF CERTAIN CONSUMER ADVICE SCHEME FUNCTIONS OF THE OFT AND CONSEQUENTIAL, SUPPLEMENTARY, INCIDENTAL AND TRANSITIONAL PROVISION

Articles 3 and 4

(Part 1 (Amendments to Acts), Part 2 (Amendments to Acts of the Scottish Parliament), Part 3 (Amendments to Northern Ireland Legislation), and Part 4 (Statutory Instruments) contain various amendments which, in so far as relevant to this work, have been incorporated in the appropriate place.)

PART 5
TRANSITIONAL PROVISIONS

[2.1134]
28 (1)   Nothing in this Order affects the validity of anything done (or having effect as if done) by or in relation to the National Consumer Council before the coming into force of articles 2 and 3.

(2)   Anything done (or having effect as if done) by or in relation to the National Consumer Council, so far as it relates to any of the functions transferred by article 3, has effect, so far as is necessary for continuing its effect after the coming into force of articles 2 and 3, as if done by or in relation to the transferee or transferees.

(3)   Anything (including legal proceedings) which at the coming into force of articles 2 and 3 is in the process of being done by or in relation to the National Consumer Council, so far as it relates to any function transferred by article 3, may be continued by or in relation to the transferee or transferees to which that function is transferred

(4)   So far as is necessary or appropriate for the purposes of or in consequence of the transfer effected by article 3, after the coming into force of articles 2 and 3, a reference to the National Consumer Council in an instrument or other document is to be treated as a reference to the transferee or the transferees to which that function is transferred.

(5)   Money paid by a person to the Gas and Electricity Markets Authority or the Office of Communications because of the obligation to make payments with respect to the expenses of the National Consumer Council under—
   (a)   a condition imposed by the Gas and Electricity Markets Authority under section 8 of the Utilities Act 2000, or
   (b)   a condition imposed by the Office of Communications under section 51 of the Postal Services Act 2011,
is to be treated by the Gas and Electricity Markets Authority or, as the case may be, the Office of Communications, as money paid by that person because of an obligation to make payments under such a condition with respect to those expenses of one or more of the transferees, that relate to a function transferred by article 3.

(6)   In this article "transferee" means—
   (a)   Citizens Advice,
   (b)   Citizens Advice Scotland, or
   (c)   the GCCNI.

Part 2 Statutory Instruments

NOTES

Commencement: 1 April 2014.

SCHEDULE 2
CONSEQUENTIAL, SUPPLEMENTARY, INCIDENTAL AND TRANSITIONAL PROVISION AND SAVINGS RELATING TO THE TRANSFER OF FUNCTIONS UNDER THE ESTATE AGENTS ACT 1979

Article 5(3)

(Part 1 (Amendments to Acts), Part 2 (Amendments to Acts of the Scottish Parliament), and Part 3 (Amendments to Statutory Instruments), contain various amendments which, in so far as relevant to this work, have been incorporated in the appropriate place.)

PART 4
TRANSITIONAL PROVISIONS AND SAVINGS

General

[2.1134A]

13 (1)   Nothing in this Order affects the validity of anything done (or having effect as if done) by or in relation to the OFT before the coming into force of article 5(1).

(2)   Anything done (or having effect as if done) by or in relation to the OFT, so far as it relates to any of the functions transferred by article 5(1), has effect, so far as is necessary for continuing its effect after the coming into force of article 5(1), as if done by or in relation to the lead enforcement authority.

(3)   Anything (including legal proceedings) which at the coming into force of article 5(1) is in the process of being done by or in relation to the OFT, so far as it relates to any of the functions transferred by article 5(1), may be continued by or in relation to the lead enforcement authority.

(4)   So far as is necessary or appropriate for the purposes of or in consequence of the transfer effected by article 5(1), after the coming into force of article 5(1), a reference to the OFT in an instrument or other document is to be treated as a reference to the lead enforcement authority.

(5)   This paragraph is subject to paragraphs 14 and 15.

Costs orders

14 Where the OFT is the receiving or paying party under a costs order made in connection with legal proceedings that relate to the exercise of any function transferred by article 5(1), the CMA is to be treated as the receiving or paying party, as the case may be, instead.

General notices issued by the OFT

15 (1)   Any general notices issued by the OFT under the 1979 Act cease to have effect.

(2)   In this paragraph "general notice" has the meaning given by section 33(1) of the 1979 Act.

Information

16 The OFT may disclose to the lead enforcement authority any information which the OFT considers it necessary or expedient to disclose to the lead enforcement authority in connection with the transfer of functions by article 5(1).

NOTES

Commencement: 14 March 2014 (para 16); 31 March 2014 (otherwise).

SCHEDULE 3
CONSEQUENTIAL, SUPPLEMENTARY, INCIDENTAL AND TRANSITIONAL PROVISION AND SAVINGS RELATING TO THE TRANSFER OF FUNCTIONS UNDER THE MONEY LAUNDERING REGULATIONS 2007

Article 5(3)

(Part 1 (Amendments to Statutory Instruments) contains various amendments which, in so far as relevant to this work, have been incorporated in the appropriate place.)

PART 2
TRANSITIONAL PROVISIONS AND SAVINGS

General

[2.1134B]
3 (1)   This paragraph and paragraphs 4 to 7 have effect in place of the provisions of paragraph 32 of the Schedule to the Financial Services and Markets Act 2000 (Regulated Activities) (Amendment) (No 2) Order 2013 (transitional provision in relation to the Money Laundering Regulations 2007).

(2)   Nothing in this Order affects the validity of anything done (or having effect as if done) by or in relation to the OFT before the commencement of article 5(2).

(3)   Anything done (or having effect as if done) by or in relation to the OFT, so far as it relates to any of the functions transferred by article 5(2), has effect, so far as is necessary for continuing its effect after the commencement of article 5(2), as if done by or in relation to the Commissioners.

(4)   Anything (including legal proceedings) which at the coming into force of article 5(2) is in the process of being done by or in relation to the OFT, so far as it relates to any of the functions transferred by article 5(2), may be continued by or in relation to the Commissioners.

(5)   So far as is necessary or appropriate for the purposes of or in consequence of the transfer effected by article 5(2), after the coming into force of that article, a reference to the OFT in an instrument or other document is to be treated as a reference to the Commissioners.

(6)   This paragraph is subject to paragraphs 4 to 7.

Costs orders
4   Where the OFT is the receiving or paying party under a costs order made in connection with legal proceedings that relate to the exercise of any function transferred by article 5(2), the CMA is to be treated as the receiving or paying party, as the case may be, instead.

Change in appeal procedure
5   Where the OFT has issued a notice under regulation 34(4)(b), 34(8) or 42(6) of the 2007 Regulations in relation to any of the functions transferred by article 5(2) but have not before the commencement of article 5(2) issued a notice of its decision under regulation 34(5)(b), 34(9)(b) or 42(7)(b), as the case may be, the notice ceases to have effect.

6   Where the OFT has issued a notice of its decision under regulation 34(5)(b), 34(9)(b) or 42(7)(b) of the 2007 Regulations in relation to any of the functions transferred by article 5(2) and an appeal has not been started before the commencement of article 5(2)—
  (a)   a person who is the subject of such a decision may appeal to the First-tier Tribunal;
  (b)   any such appeal must be started in accordance with the Tribunal Procedure (First Tier Tribunal) (General Regulatory Chamber) Rules 2009;
  (c)   after such an appeal has been started it is to be treated as an appeal under regulation 43 of the 2007 Regulations;
  (d)   the Commissioners may offer a review of such a decision and where they do so regulations 43 to 43F of the 2007 Regulations apply with the following modifications—
     (i)   in regulation 43 (appeals against decisions of the Commissioners)—
        (aa)   omit paragraph (1);
        (bb)   in paragraph (2) for "a decision to which this regulation applies" substitute "a decision under regulation 34(5)(b), 34(9)(b) or 42(7)(b)";
     (ii)   in regulation 43A (offer of review)—
        (aa)   omit paragraph (1);
        (bb)   in paragraph (2) omit "at the same time as the decision is notified to P";
     (iii)   in the following provisions after "under regulation 43F" insert "or paragraph 6(a) of Schedule 3 to the Public Bodies (Abolition of the National Consumer Council and Transfer of the Office of Fair Trading's Functions in relation to Estate Agents etc) Order 2014"-
        (aa)   regulation 43B(2) and (3);
        (bb)   regulation 43D(3).
     (iv)   in regulation 43E (nature of review etc), in paragraph (3)(a) for "Commissioners" substitute "Office of Fair Trading".

7   Where an appeal has been started against a decision of the OFT in relation to any of the functions transferred by article 5(2) under regulation 44 of the 2007 Regulations, after the commencement of article 5(2) it is to be treated as an appeal under regulation 43 of the 2007 Regulations.

NOTES
Commencement: 31 March 2014.

ALTERNATIVE DISPUTE RESOLUTION FOR CONSUMER DISPUTES (COMPETENT AUTHORITIES AND INFORMATION) REGULATIONS 2015

(SI 2015/542)

NOTES

Made: 16 March 2015.

Authority: European Communities Act 1972, s 2(2).

Commencement: see art 1.

ARRANGEMENT OF REGULATIONS

PART 1
GENERAL

Part 2   Statutory Instruments

PART 1
GENERAL

[2.1135]
1   Citation and commencement

(1)   These Regulations may be cited as the Alternative Dispute Resolution for Consumer Disputes (Competent Authorities and Information) Regulations 2015.

(2)   Parts 1 to 3 come into force on 7th April 2015.

(3)   Parts 4 and 5 come into force on [1st October 2015].

NOTES
Commencement: 7 April 2015.
Para (3): words in square brackets substituted by the Alternative Dispute Resolution for Consumer Disputes (Amendment) Regulations 2015, SI 2015/1392, reg 2(1), (3).

[2.1136]
2   Review

(1)   The Secretary of State must from time to time—
   (a)   carry out a review of these Regulations [and the amendments to legislation made by Parts 3 and 4 of the Alternative Dispute Resolution for Consumer Disputes (Amendment) Regulations 2015],
   (b)   set out the conclusions of the review in a report, and
   (c)   publish the report.

(2)   In carrying out the review, the Secretary of State must, so far as is reasonable, have regard to how Directive 2013/11/EU of the European Parliament and of the Council of 21st May 2013 on alternative dispute resolution for consumer disputes and amending Regulation (EC) No 2006/2004 and Directive 2009/22/EC[, and Regulation (EU) No 524/2013 of the European Parliament and of the Council of 21 May 2013 on online dispute resolution for consumer disputes and amending Regulation (EC) No 2006/2004 and Directive 2009/22/EC are implemented] in other Member States.

(3)   The report must in particular—
   (a)   set out the objectives intended to be achieved by these Regulations [and the amendments to legislation made by Parts 3 and 4 of the Alternative Dispute Resolution for Consumer Disputes (Amendment) Regulations 2015],
   (b)   assess the extent to which those objectives have been achieved, and
   (c)   assess whether those objectives remain appropriate and, if so, the extent to which they could be achieved in a way that imposes less regulation.

(4)   The first report under this regulation must be published before the end of the period of five years beginning with the day on which Parts 1 to 3 of these Regulations come into force.

(5)   Reports under this regulation are afterwards to be published at intervals not exceeding five years.

NOTES
Commencement: 7 April 2015.
Words in square brackets in paras (1), (3) added, and words in square brackets in para (2) substituted, by the Alternative Dispute Resolution for Consumer Disputes (Amendment) Regulations 2015, SI 2015/1392, reg 2(1), (4).

[2.1137]
3   "Consumer" and "trader"

In these Regulations—
   "consumer" means an individual acting for purposes which are wholly or mainly outside that individual's trade, business, craft or profession;
   "trader" means a person acting for purposes relating to that person's trade, business, craft or profession, whether acting personally or through another person acting in the trader's name or on the trader's behalf.

NOTES
Commencement: 7 April 2015.

[2.1138]
4   "ADR entity"

In these Regulations "ADR entity" means a [person] whose name appears on a list maintained in accordance with regulation 10.

NOTES
Commencement: 7 April 2015.
Word in square brackets substituted by the Alternative Dispute Resolution for Consumer Disputes (Amendment) Regulations 2015, SI 2015/1392, reg 2(1), (2).

[2.1139]
5   Other definitions

In these Regulations—

"ADR applicant" means a [person] who wishes to become an ADR entity;

["ADR official" means an individual who (solely or with other persons) is involved in the provision of alternative dispute resolution procedures offered by an ADR entity, or ADR applicant, whether as a case handler or in a management capacity;]

"competent authority" means the Secretary of State or a [person] specified in the first column of Part 1 or Part 2 of Schedule 1;

["complete complaint file" means all the relevant information relating to a dispute;]

"cross-border dispute" means a dispute concerning contractual obligations arising from a sales contract or a service contract where, at the time the consumer orders the goods or services, the trader is established in the United Kingdom and the consumer is resident in another member State;

"domestic dispute" means a dispute concerning contractual obligations arising from a sales contract or a service contract where, at the time the consumer orders the goods or services, the consumer is resident, and the trader is established, in the United Kingdom;

"durable medium" means paper or email, or any other medium that—

    (a)   allows information to be addressed personally to the recipient,

    (b)   enables the recipient to store the information in a way accessible for future reference for a period that is long enough for the purposes of the information, and

    (c)   allows the unchanged reproduction of the information stored;

["EU listed body" means a person, other than an ADR entity, whose name appears on a list referred to in Article 20(2) of Directive 2013/11/EU of the European Parliament and of the Council of 21 May 2013 on alternative dispute resolution for consumer disputes and amending Regulation (EC) No 2006/2004 and Directive 2009/22/EC;]

["ODR platform" means a European online dispute resolution platform established under Article 5 of Regulation (EU) No 524/2013 of the European Parliament and of the Council of 21 May 2013 on online dispute resolution for consumer disputes;]

"sales contract" means a contract under which a trader transfers or agrees to transfer the ownership of goods to a consumer, and the consumer pays or agrees to pay the price, including any contract that has both goods and services as its object;

"service contract" means a contract, other than a sales contract, under which a trader supplies, or agrees to supply a service to a consumer and the consumer pays, or agrees to pay, the price;

"single point of contact" means the person designated in regulation 17.

NOTES

Commencement: 7 April 2015.

In definitions "ADR applicant" and "competent authority" words in square brackets substituted, definition "ADR official" substituted, and definitions "complete complaint file" and "EU listed body" inserted, by the Alternative Dispute Resolution for Consumer Disputes (Amendment) Regulations 2015, SI 2015/1392, reg 2(1), (2), (5)(a), (b); definition "ODR platform" inserted by reg 2(1), (5)(c) of the 2015 Regulations, as from 9 January 2016.

[2.1140]
6   Interpretation

In regulation 5 a trader is "established"—

    (a)   if the trader is an individual, where the trader has his or her place of business;

    (b)   if the trader is a company or other legal person or an association of persons, where it has its statutory seat, central administration or place of business, including a branch, agency or any other establishment.

NOTES

Commencement: 7 April 2015.

[2.1141]
7   Contracts to which these Regulations do not apply

These Regulations do not apply to a contract to the extent that it is for health services provided by health professionals to patients to assess, maintain or restore their state of health, including the prescription, dispensation and provision of medicinal products and medical devices (and "health professionals" has the meaning given by Article 3(f) of Directive 2011/24/EU of the European Parliament and of the Council on the application of patients' rights in cross-border healthcare).

NOTES

Commencement: 7 April 2015.

PART 2
COMPETENT AUTHORITIES AND ADR ENTITIES

[2.1142]
8 Functions and designation of competent authorities

(1) A competent authority must perform the functions set out in this Part.

(2) Each [person] specified in the first column of Part 1 of Schedule 1 is—
  (a) a competent authority for the purposes of these Regulations, and
  (b) the relevant competent authority in relation to alternative dispute resolution services offered by the [person] specified alongside it in the second column of Part 1 of Schedule 1.

(3) Subject to paragraph (2), each [person] specified in Part 2 of Schedule 1 is—
  (a) a competent authority for the purposes of these Regulations in relation to the area for which it has regulatory responsibility or any area for which it has oversight under any enactment, and
  (b) the relevant competent authority in relation to an ADR entity or ADR applicant which offers alternative dispute resolution services in that area.

(4) The Secretary of State is the relevant competent authority in relation to—
  (a) alternative dispute resolution services offered by the Pensions Ombudsman, and
  (b) an ADR entity or ADR applicant which offers alternative dispute resolution services in an area other than one referred to in paragraph (3).

NOTES
Commencement: 7 April 2015.
Paras (2), (3): words in square brackets substituted by the Alternative Dispute Resolution for Consumer Disputes (Amendment) Regulations 2015, SI 2015/1392, reg 2(1), (2).

[2.1143]
9 Assessment of application to become an ADR entity

(1) An ADR applicant may apply to the relevant competent authority to become an ADR entity.

(2) The ADR applicant must supply with an application—
  (a) the information in Schedule 2; and
  (b) such other information as the competent authority may require in order to assess whether the ADR applicant meets the requirements in Schedule 3.

(3) The information referred to in paragraph (2) must be provided in such form as the competent authority may require.

(4) The competent authority may only approve an application if it is satisfied that—
  (a) . . .
  (b) the requirements in Schedule 3—
    (i) have been met by the ADR applicant, or
    (ii) will be met by the ADR applicant within a reasonable period of time of the application being granted.

(5) Where—
  (a) an enactment contains the power for a competent authority to impose additional requirements which go beyond those set out in Schedule 3, and
  (b) such requirements, including issuing binding solutions on traders, are imposed for the purpose of ensuring a higher level of consumer protection,
such requirements shall be deemed to be included in Schedule 3 for the purposes of this regulation, regulations 12 and 13(1) and (2) and paragraph (i) of Schedule 2.

(6) Where an application is approved, the competent authority must as soon as is reasonably practicable give written notice to the ADR applicant.

(7) Where an application is rejected, the competent authority must as soon as is reasonably practicable give written notice of this fact to the ADR applicant, which must include the grounds on which it has rejected the application.

(8) . . .

NOTES
Commencement: 7 April 2015.
Paras (4)(a), (8) revoked by the Alternative Dispute Resolution for Consumer Disputes (Amendment) Regulations 2015, SI 2015/1392, reg 2(1), (6).

[2.1144]
10 Listing of ADR entities

(1) A competent authority must maintain a list of the ADR applicants which have been approved by it to become an ADR entity under regulation 9(4) and that list must include the information in Schedule 4 in respect of each ADR applicant.

(2) A competent authority must, without undue delay following compilation of a list, send the list to the single point of contact.

(3)   If under regulation 11(1) a competent authority receives notification from an ADR entity containing information which differs from the information included in relation to that ADR entity in the list maintained under paragraph (1), the competent authority must—
  (a)   amend the list to reflect the change in that information, and
  (b)   without undue delay, send the amended list to the single point of contact.

NOTES
  Commencement: 7 April 2015.

[2.1145]
11   Ongoing information obligations of an ADR entity

(1)   In the event of a change to the information which an ADR entity has supplied under regulation 9(1), the ADR entity must, without undue delay, provide written notification of the change to the competent authority.

(2)   An ADR entity must, within a month of the first anniversary of the approval date and within a month of each subsequent anniversary, publish on its website a report ("an annual activity report") relating to the preceding year which contains the information in Schedule 5.

(3)   The ADR entity must, within a month of the second anniversary of the approval date and within a month of the expiry of each successive period of two years, supply the relevant competent authority with the information in Schedule 6 relating to the preceding two year period.

(4)   The annual activity report and information to be provided under paragraph (3) must be in such form as the competent authority may require.

(5)   In this regulation "approval date" means the date of the written notice granting approval to the ADR entity under regulation 9(6).

NOTES
  Commencement: 7 April 2015.

[2.1146]
12   Ongoing assessment of an ADR entity

Following receipt of the information received under regulation 11(3) the competent authority must review the information and assess whether the ADR entity still meets the requirements in Schedule 3.

NOTES
  Commencement: 7 April 2015.

[2.1147]
13   Removal of approval

(1)   A competent authority must provide notice in writing to an ADR entity approved by it under regulation 9(4) if the competent authority has reason to believe that—
  (a)   the ADR entity no longer meets a requirement in Schedule 3; and
  (b)   the reason the ADR entity no longer meets the requirement is within its control.

(2)   The written notice must—
  (a)   identify the requirement in Schedule 3 which is no longer met; and
  (b)   require the ADR entity to meet the requirement promptly or in any event within 3 months of the date of the notice.

(3)   If the ADR entity fails to meet the requirement notified to it on or before the expiry of the period specified in paragraph (2), and the competent authority considers that the failure to meet the requirement is sufficiently serious, the competent authority must—
  (a)   send notice in writing to the ADR entity of the withdrawal of its approval, and
  (b)   without undue delay, remove the ADR entity from the list maintained by it under regulation 10(1).

(4)   If a competent authority removes an ADR entity from the list under paragraph (3) it must, without undue delay, send the revised list to the single point of contact.

NOTES
  Commencement: 7 April 2015.

[2.1148]
14   Notification of the consolidated ADR entity list

[(1)]   A competent authority must make the consolidated list of ADR entities published by the European Commission—
  (a)   publicly available on its website by means of a link to the relevant European Commission website; and
  (b)   available on request by a member of the public on a durable medium.

[(2) An ADR entity must make the consolidated list of ADR entities published by the European Commission publicly available—

(a)   on its website by means of a link to the relevant European Commission website; and

(b)   wherever possible, at the ADR entity's premises on a durable medium.]

NOTES

Commencement: 7 April 2015.

Para (1) numbered as such, and para (2) added, by the Alternative Dispute Resolution for Consumer Disputes (Amendment) Regulations 2015, SI 2015/1392, reg 2(1), (7).

[2.1149]
[14A   The ADR entity's duty to cooperate

(1)   The ADR entity must take reasonable steps to—

(a)   cooperate with other ADR entities in the resolution of cross-border disputes; and

(b)   conduct regular exchanges of best practices with other ADR entities regarding the settlement of both cross-border disputes and domestic disputes.

(2)   The ADR entity must take such steps as it considers appropriate to cooperate with bodies or persons designated by the Secretary of State under Article 4(1) and 4(2) of Regulation (EC) No 2006/2004 of the European Parliament and of the Council of 27 October 2004 on cooperation between national authorities responsible for the enforcement of consumer protection laws as amended by Directive 2005/29/EC of the European Parliament and of the Council of 11 May 2005 concerning unfair business-to-consumer commercial practices in the internal market.

(3)   Cooperation under paragraph (2) includes, in particular, exchange of information on practices in specific business sectors about which consumers have repeatedly lodged complaints.]

NOTES

Commencement: 9 July 2015.

Inserted, together with regs 14B, 14C, by the Alternative Dispute Resolution for Consumer Disputes (Amendment) Regulations 2015, SI 2015/1392, reg 2(1), (8).

[2.1150]
[14B   Agreement to submit disputes to an ADR entity

An agreement between a consumer and a trader to submit a cross-border dispute or domestic dispute to an ADR entity is not binding on the consumer to the extent that the agreement—

(a)   was concluded before the cross-border dispute or domestic dispute materialised; and

(b)   has the effect of depriving the consumer of the right to bring judicial proceedings in relation to the cross-border dispute or domestic dispute.]

NOTES

Commencement: 9 July 2015.

Inserted as noted to reg 14A at **[2.1149]**.

[2.1151]
[14C   Binding outcome requirements

(1)   Where an ADR entity aims at resolving a dispute by imposing a solution, the solution will not be binding on a party to the dispute unless—

(a)   the ADR entity notifies the party that the outcome will be binding; and

(b)   the party specifically accepts that the outcome will be binding.

(2)   The requirements under paragraph (1) must be met before the ADR entity notifies the party of the outcome of the alternative dispute resolution procedure.

(3)   Paragraph (1)(b) does not apply in relation to a trader where an enactment, the rules of a trade association, or term of a contract, provides that the solution will be binding on the trader.]

NOTES

Commencement: 9 July 2015.

Inserted as noted to reg 14A at **[2.1149]**.

[2.1152]
15   [Fees payable to the Secretary of State]

(1)   Where the competent authority is the Secretary of State, the competent authority may charge—

(a)   an ADR applicant a fee in respect of the costs incurred by or on behalf of the Secretary of State in evaluating an application made under regulation 9, and

(b)   an ADR entity a periodic fee, in respect of costs incurred by or on behalf of the Secretary of State in carrying out the functions of the Secretary of State under regulations 10 to 14.

(2)   The fees referred to above shall not exceed the amount of all reasonable costs and expenses incurred by or on behalf of the Secretary of State in evaluating an application and carrying out the other functions referred to above, which shall include a sum calculated at the rate of £750 for every day, (based upon an eight hour day) spent by each person in carrying out the relevant function (which shall be pro-rated in respect of any period less than a day spent by any person).

(3)   The fees are payable on invoice, to the Secretary of State, or such person as the Secretary of State may direct, and any unpaid fee may be recovered by the Secretary of State as a civil debt.

(4)   The Secretary of State is not required to approve an application under [regulation] 9(4) if there is a fee outstanding under this regulation in relation to that application.

NOTES

Commencement: 7 April 2015.

Regulation heading and word in square brackets in para (4) substituted by the Alternative Dispute Resolution for Consumer Disputes (Amendment) Regulations 2015, SI 2015/1392, reg 2(1), (9).

[2.1153]
[15A   Fees payable to the Financial Conduct Authority

(1)   The functions of the FCA under these Regulations are to be treated for the purposes of paragraph 23 of Schedule 1ZA to the 2000 Act (fees) as qualifying functions conferred on the FCA under that Act with the following modifications—
   (a)   rules made under paragraph 23 by virtue of this regulation may not provide for payment of fees by any person other than the scheme operator as defined in section 225(2) of the 2000 Act (the ombudsman scheme);
   (b)   rules made under paragraph 23 by virtue of this regulation are not to be treated as regulating provisions for the purposes of Chapter 4 of Part 9A of the 2000 Act (competition scrutiny);
   (c)   in relation to the first rules made under paragraph 23 by virtue of this regulation, section 138I of the 2000 Act (consultation by the FCA) does not apply.

(2)   In this regulation—
   "the 2000 Act" means the Financial Services and Markets Act 2000;
   "the FCA" means the Financial Conduct Authority as defined in section 1A of the 2000 Act (the regulators).]

NOTES

Commencement: 9 July 2015.

Inserted by the Alternative Dispute Resolution for Consumer Disputes (Amendment) Regulations 2015, SI 2015/1392, reg 2(1), (10).

[2.1154]
16   Consequential amendments

Schedule 7 makes amendments that are consequential on these Regulations.

NOTES

Commencement: 7 April 2015.

PART 3
SINGLE POINT OF CONTACT

[2.1155]
17   Designation of single point of contact

The Secretary of State is the single point of contact for the purposes of these Regulations.

NOTES

Commencement: 7 April 2015.

[2.1156]
18   Functions of single point of contact

(1)   The single point of contact must—
   (a)   compile a consolidated list of ADR entities from the lists which it receives from time to time from each competent authority under regulations 10 and 13(4), and
   (b)   without undue delay, send the consolidated list to the European Commission [on the standardised electronic form provided by the European Commission].

(2)   On or before 9th July 2018, and within each successive period of four years after that date, the single point of contact must—
   (a)   publish on its website a report on the development and functioning of ADR entities; and
   (b)   send a copy of that report to the European Commission.

(3)   The report must, in particular—
   (a)   identify best practices of ADR entities,

(b) identify the shortcomings (if any), supported by statistics or any other data, that hinder the functioning of ADR entities in relation to domestic or cross-border disputes, and

(c) where appropriate, make recommendations on how to improve the effective and efficient functioning of ADR entities.

(4) The single point of contact may, for the purpose of enabling it to prepare the report, require a competent authority to provide such information as it may require relating to the development and functioning of an ADR entity for which it is the relevant competent authority.

(5) A competent authority must, if requested by the single point of contact under paragraph (4), provide the requested information in such form and within such period as may be required by the single point of contact.

NOTES
Commencement: 7 April 2015.
Para (1): words in square brackets in sub-para (b) added by the Alternative Dispute Resolution for Consumer Disputes (Amendment) Regulations 2015, SI 2015/1392, reg 2(1), (11).

PART 4
TRADER INFORMATION REQUIREMENTS

[2.1157]
[19 Consumer information by traders

(1) Where, under an enactment, rules of a trade association, or term of a contract, a trader is obliged to use an alternative dispute resolution procedure provided by an ADR entity or EU listed body the trader must provide the name and website address of the ADR entity or EU listed body—

(a) on the trader's website, if the trader has a website; and

(b) in the general terms and conditions of sales contracts or service contracts of the trader, where such general terms and conditions exist.

(2) Where a trader has exhausted its internal complaint handling procedure when considering a complaint from a consumer relating to a sales contract or a service contract, the trader must inform the consumer, on a durable medium—

(a) that the trader cannot settle the complaint with the consumer;

(b) of the name and website address of an ADR entity or EU listed body that would be competent to deal with the complaint; and

(c) whether the trader is obliged, or prepared, to submit to an alternative dispute resolution procedure operated by an ADR entity or EU listed body.

(3) The trader information requirements set out in paragraphs (1) and (2) apply in addition to any information requirements applicable to traders regarding out-of-court redress procedures contained in any other enactment.]

NOTES
Commencement: 9 July 2015.
Substituted by the Alternative Dispute Resolution for Consumer Disputes (Amendment) Regulations 2015, SI 2015/1392, reg 2(1), (12).

[2.1158]
[19A Consumer information by online traders and online marketplaces regarding the ODR platform

(1) Where under an enactment, rules of a trade association, or term of a contract, an online trader is obliged to use an alternative dispute resolution procedure provided by an ADR entity or EU listed body, the trader must—

(a) provide a link to the ODR platform in any offer made to a consumer by email; and

(b) inform consumers of—

(i) the existence of the ODR platform; and

(ii) the possibility of using the ODR platform for resolving disputes.

(2) The information in (1)(b) must also be included in the general terms and conditions of online sales contracts and online service contracts of the trader, where such general terms and conditions exist.

(3) An online trader must on its website—

(i) provide a link to the ODR platform; and

(ii) state the online trader's email address.

(4) An online marketplace must provide a link to the ODR platform on its website.

(5) The online trader requirements set out in paragraphs (1) to (3) apply in addition to the trader information requirements set out in regulation 19.

(6) The online trader and online marketplace requirements in paragraphs (1) to (4) apply in addition to any information requirements regarding out-of-court redress procedures contained in any other enactment.

(7) In this regulation—

"online marketplace" has the meaning given in Article 4(f) of the Regulation (EU) No 524/2013 of the European Parliament and of the Council of 21 May 2013 on online dispute resolution for consumer disputes and amending Regulation (EC) No 2006/2004 and Directive 2009/22/EC;

"online sales contract" means a sales contract where the trader, or the trader's intermediary, has offered goods on a website or by other electronic means and the consumer has ordered such goods on that website or by other electronic means;

"online service contract" means a service contract where the trader, or the trader's intermediary, has offered services on a website or by other electronic means and the consumer has ordered such services on that website or by other electronic means;

"online trader" means a trader who intends to enter into online sales contracts or online service contracts with consumers.]

NOTES

Commencement: 9 January 2016.

Inserted by the Alternative Dispute Resolution for Consumer Disputes (Amendment) Regulations 2015, SI 2015/1392, reg 2(1), (13), as from 9 January 2016.

PART 5
ENTERPRISE ACT 2002

[2.1159]

20   Amendment to Schedule 13 to the Enterprise Act 2002

(1)   (*Para 1 amends the Enterprise Act 2002, Sch 13*).

(2)   *The law in the United Kingdom set out in Schedule 8 to these Regulations is specified for the purposes of section 212 of the Enterprise Act 2002 to the extent that it gives effect to the listed Directive set out in that Schedule.*

NOTES

Commencement: 9 July 2015.

Para (2): revoked by the Alternative Dispute Resolution for Consumer Disputes (Amendment) Regulations 2015, SI 2015/1392, reg 2(1), (14), as from 9 January 2016.

SCHEDULES

SCHEDULE 1
COMPETENT AUTHORITIES

Regulation 8

PART 1

[2.1160]

Column 1	Column 2
Financial Conduct Authority	Financial Ombudsman Service
Legal Services Board	Office for Legal Complaints

NOTES

Commencement: 7 April 2015.

PART 2

[2.1161]

Civil Aviation Authority

Gambling Commission

Gas and Electricity Markets Authority

Office of Communications

The lead enforcement authority for the purposes of the Estate Agents Act 1979

NOTES

Commencement: 7 April 2015.

SCHEDULE 2
INFORMATION THAT AN ADR APPLICANT MUST SUPPLY

Regulation 9(2)

[2.1162]

a)   the ADR applicant's name, contact details and website address;

b)   information regarding the structure and funding of the ADR applicant, including such information as the competent authority may require regarding its ADR officials, their remuneration, term of office and by whom they are employed;

c)   the rules of the alternative dispute resolution procedure to be operated by the ADR applicant;

d)   any fees to be charged by the ADR applicant;

e)   where the ADR applicant already operates an alternative dispute resolution procedure, the average length of the alternative dispute resolution procedure;

f)   the language in which the ADR applicant is prepared to receive initial complaint submissions and conduct the alternative dispute resolution procedure;

g)   a statement as to the types of disputes covered by the alternative dispute resolution procedure operated by the ADR applicant;

h)   the grounds, if any, on which the ADR applicant may refuse to deal with a dispute;

i)   a reasoned statement which sets out how the ADR applicant complies, or proposes to comply, with the requirements set out in Schedule 3.

NOTES

Commencement: 7 April 2015.

SCHEDULE 3
REQUIREMENTS THAT A COMPETENT AUTHORITY MUST BE SATISFIED THAT THE [PERSON] MEETS

Regulation 9(4)

[2.1163]

Alternative dispute resolution services offered by the [person]
1   The [person]—
   (a)   offers alternative dispute resolution services in relation to a domestic dispute or cross-border dispute brought by a consumer against a trader;
   (b)   is not formed for the purpose of dealing only with one particular domestic dispute or cross-border dispute;
   (c)   does not offer alternative dispute resolution services in relation to a domestic or cross-border dispute in circumstances where an ADR official responsible for the dispute is either employed or remunerated directly by a trader who is a party to the dispute.

Access to the ADR entity
2   The [person]—
   (a)   maintains an up-to-date website which provides the parties to a domestic dispute or cross-border dispute with information regarding the alternative dispute resolution procedure operated by the [person];
   (b)   provides the information referred to in sub-paragraph (a) to a party on a durable medium, if a party requests it;
   (c)   ensures that its website enables a consumer to file an initial complaint submission and any necessary supporting documents online;
   (d)   permits the consumer to file an initial complaint submission by post, if the consumer wishes;
   (e)   enables the exchange of information between the parties via electronic means or, if a party wishes, by post;
   (f)   accepts disputes covered by Regulation (EU) No 524/2013 of the European Parliament and of the Council of 21 May 2013 on online dispute resolution for consumer disputes.

Expertise, Independence and Impartiality
3   The [person]—
   (a)   ensures that an ADR official possesses a general understanding of the law and the necessary knowledge and skills relating to the out-of-court or judicial resolution of consumer disputes, to be able to carry out his or her functions competently;
   (b)   appoints each ADR official for a term of office of sufficient duration to ensure the independence of that person's actions and provides that no ADR official can be relieved of his or her duties without just cause;

(c)   ensures that no ADR official discharges his or her duties in a way that is biased as regards a party to a dispute, or the representative of a party;

(d)   remunerates an ADR official in a way that is not linked to the outcome of the alternative dispute resolution procedure;

(e)   where it appoints more than one ADR official, ensures that an ADR official, without undue delay, discloses to the [person] a circumstance that may, or may be seen to—
  (i)   affect the ADR official's independence or impartiality; or
  (ii)   give rise to a conflict of interest with a party to the dispute which the ADR official is asked to resolve;

(f)   ensures that the obligation to disclose a conflict of interest is a continuing obligation throughout the alternative dispute resolution procedure;

(g)   ensures that in circumstances where its ADR officials are employed or remunerated exclusively by a professional organisation or business association, the [person] has a ring-fenced budget at its disposal which is sufficient to enable it to carry out its functions as an ADR entity;

(h)   ensures that where the operating model of its alternative dispute resolution procedure is to have a collegial [person] of representatives of both professional organisations or business associations, and consumer organisations, its ADR officials comprise an equal number of representatives of consumer interests and trader interests.

Conflict of interests procedure

4   The [person] has in place the following procedure in the event that an ADR official declares or is discovered to have a conflict of interest in relation to a domestic dispute or cross-border dispute—

(a)   where possible, the ADR official is replaced by another ADR official to handle the particular dispute;

(b)   if the ADR official cannot be replaced by another ADR official—
  (i)   the ADR official must refrain from conducting the alternative dispute resolution procedure, and
  (ii)   the [person] must, where possible, propose to the parties that they submit the dispute to another ADR entity which is competent to deal with it;

(c)   if the dispute cannot be transferred to another ADR entity, the [person]—
  (i)   must inform the parties to the dispute of the circumstances of the conflict of interest,
  (ii)   must inform the parties to the dispute that they have the right to object to the conflicted person continuing to handle the dispute, and
  (iii)   can only continue to deal with the dispute if no party to the dispute objects.

Transparency

5   The [person] makes the following information publicly available on its website in a clear and easily understandable manner, and provides, on request, this information to any person on a durable medium—

(a)   its contact details, including postal address and e-mail address;

(b)   a statement that it has been approved as an ADR entity by the relevant competent authority once this approval has been granted;

(c)   its ADR officials, the method of their appointment and the duration of their appointment;

(d)   the name of any network of bodies which facilitates cross-border alternative dispute resolution of which it is a member;

(e)   the type of domestic disputes and cross-border disputes which it is competent to deal with, including any financial thresholds which apply;

(f)   the procedural rules of the alternative dispute resolution procedure operated by it and the grounds on which it can refuse to deal with a given dispute in accordance with paragraph 13;

(g)   the language in which it is prepared to receive an initial complaint submission;

(h)   the language in which its alternative dispute resolution procedure can be conducted;

(i)   the principles the [person] applies, and the main considerations the [person] takes into account, when seeking to resolve a dispute;

(j)   the preliminary requirements, if any, that a party to a dispute needs to have met before the alternative dispute resolution procedure can commence;

(k)   a statement as to whether or not a party to the dispute can withdraw from the alternative dispute resolution procedure once it has commenced;

(l)   the costs, if any, to be borne by a party, including the rules, if any, on costs awarded by the [person] at the end of the alternative dispute resolution procedure;

(m)   the average length of each alternative dispute resolution procedure handled by the [person];

(n)   the legal effect of the outcome of the dispute resolution process, including whether the outcome is enforceable and the penalties for non-compliance with the outcome, if any;

(o)   a statement as to whether or not alternative dispute resolution procedures operated by it can be conducted by oral or written means (or both);

(p)   the annual activity report required to be prepared under regulation 11(2).

Effectiveness

6 The [person]—

(a) ensures that its alternative dispute resolution procedure is available and easily accessible to both parties irrespective of where they are located including by electronic means and non-electronic means;

(b) ensures that—

(i) the parties to a dispute are not obliged to obtain independent advice or be represented or assisted by a third party although they may choose to do so;

(ii) the alternative dispute resolution is available free of charge or at a nominal fee for consumers;

[(c) notifies the parties to a dispute as soon as it has received the complete complaint file, unless the person has already notified the parties that it refuses to deal with the dispute in accordance with paragraph 15;]

(d) notifies the parties of the outcome of the alternative dispute resolution procedure within a period of 90 days from the date on which the [person] [issues the notice under sub-paragraph (c)] except that, in the case of a highly complex dispute, the [person] may extend this period but must inform the parties of this extension and the expected length of time that it will need to conclude the alternative dispute resolution procedure.

Fairness

7 The [person]—

(a) ensures that during the alternative dispute resolution procedure the parties may, within a reasonable period of time, express their points of view;

(b) provides a party to a dispute within a reasonable period of time, upon request, with the arguments, evidence, documents and facts put forward by the other party to the dispute, including a statement made, or opinion given, by an expert;

(c) ensures that the parties may, within a reasonable period of time, comment on the information and documents provided under paragraph (b);

(d) informs the parties that they are not obliged to retain a legal advisor, but that they may seek independent advice or be represented or assisted by a third party at any stage of the alternative dispute resolution procedure;

(e) notifies the parties of the outcome of the alternative dispute resolution procedure on a durable medium and gives the parties a statement of the grounds on which the outcome is based.

8 Subject to paragraphs 9 and 10, in relation to an alternative dispute resolution procedure which aims at resolving a dispute by proposing a solution, the [person] ensures that the parties—

(a) have the possibility of withdrawing from the alternative dispute resolution procedure at any stage if they are dissatisfied with the performance or operation of the alternative dispute resolution procedure;

(b) before the alternative dispute resolution procedure commences, are informed of their right to withdraw from the alternative dispute resolution procedure at any stage;

(c) are informed, before agreeing to or following the proposed solution—

(i) that they have a choice as to whether or not to agree to, or follow, the proposed solution;

(ii) that their participation in the alternative dispute resolution procedure does not preclude the possibility of them seeking redress through court proceedings;

(iii) that the proposed solution may be different from an outcome determined by a court applying legal rules; and

(iv) of the legal effect of agreeing to, or following the proposed solution;

(d) before expressing their consent to a proposed solution or amicable agreement, are allowed a reasonable period of time to reflect.

9 Paragraphs 8(a) and 8(b) do not apply to the [person] in respect of a party who is—

(a) a trader; and

[(b) obliged under an enactment, rules of a trade association, or term of a contract, to participate in an alternative dispute resolution procedure.]

10 Paragraph 8 does not apply to the [person] in respect of a party who is—

(a) a trader; and

[(b) obliged under an enactment, rules of a trade association, or term of a contract, to accept the solution proposed by the person if the consumer accepts the solution.]

Legality

11 In relation to an alternative dispute resolution procedure which aims at resolving a dispute by imposing a solution on the consumer, the [person] ensures that—

(a) in a situation where there is no conflict of laws, the solution imposed by the [person] does not result in the consumer being deprived of the protection afforded to the consumer by the provisions that cannot be derogated from by agreement by virtue of any enactment;

(b) in a situation involving a conflict of laws—

(i)   where the law applicable to the sales contract or service contract is determined in accordance with Article 6(1) and (2) of Regulation (EC) No 593/2008 on the law applicable to contractual obligations the solution imposed by the [person] does not result in the consumer being deprived of the protection afforded to the consumer by the provisions that cannot be derogated from by virtue of the law of the member State in which the consumer is habitually resident;

(ii)   where the law applicable to the sales contract or service contract is determined in accordance with Article 5(1) to (3) of the Rome Convention of 19 June 1980 on the law applicable to contractual obligations the solution imposed by the [person] does not result in the consumer being deprived of the protection afforded to the consumer by the provisions that cannot be derogated from by virtue of the mandatory rules of the law of the member State in which the consumer is habitually resident.

12 For the purposes of paragraph 11 "habitual residence" is be determined in accordance with Regulation (EC) No 593/2008.

Grounds to refuse to deal with a dispute
13 The [person] may only refuse to deal with a domestic dispute or a cross-border dispute which it is competent to deal with on one of the following grounds—
(a)   prior to submitting the complaint to the [person], the consumer has not attempted to contact the trader concerned in order to discuss the consumer's complaint and sought, as a first step, to resolve the matter directly with the trader;
(b)   the dispute is frivolous or vexatious;
(c)   the dispute is being, or has been previously, considered by another ADR entity or by a court;
(d)   the value of the claim falls below or above the monetary thresholds set by the [person];
[(e)   the consumer has not submitted the complaint to the person within the time period specified by the person, which shall not be less than the prescribed period.]
(f)   dealing with such a type of dispute would seriously impair the effective operation of the [person].

[**13A** (1)   Subject to sub-paragraph (2), the "prescribed period" is 12 months from the date on which the trader informs the consumer that the trader is unable to resolve the consumer's complaint (the "notice date").
(2)   Where the notice date occurred prior to the date on which the relevant competent authority approved the person as an ADR entity, under regulation 9(4), the "prescribed period" is the time period for submission of complaints as set out in the rules operated by that person on the notice date.]

14 The [person] ensures that its policy regarding when it will refuse to deal with a dispute, including in relation to the level of any monetary threshold it sets, does not significantly impair consumers' access to its alternative dispute resolution procedures.

[**14A**   The decision in paragraph 13 can be made at any time prior to the expiry of three weeks of the date upon which the person received the final submissions of the parties, but it cannot be made after the person has notified the parties under paragraph 6(c) that it has received the complete complaint file.]

[**15** Where a person decides to refuse to deal with a dispute, the person must as soon as reasonably practicable, provide the parties with a reasoned explanation of the grounds for not considering the dispute.]

[**16** Where, following the expiry of the period referred to in paragraph 14A, it appears to the person that one of the parties has sought to mislead the person as regards the existence or non-existence of one of the grounds for it to refuse to deal with a dispute, the person may immediately refuse to deal further with the dispute.]

[**Compliance with the Online Dispute Resolution Regulation**
17 The person ensures that on receipt of a complaint transmitted to it by the ODR platform it informs the parties, without delay, whether it agrees or refuses to deal with the dispute.

18 Where the person agrees to deal with a dispute transmitted to it by the ODR platform, it ensures that it—
(a)   informs the parties of the procedural rules of the alternative dispute resolution procedure operated by it;
(b)   informs the parties of the costs, if any, to be borne by a party, including the rules, if any, on costs awarded by the person at the end of the alternative dispute resolution procedure;
(c)   does not require the physical presence of the parties or their representatives, unless its procedural rules provide for the possibility and the parties agree;
(d)   transmits, without delay, the following information to the ODR platform—

    (i)   the date it received all the documents containing the relevant information relating to the dispute constituting the complete complaint file;

    (ii)   the subject-matter of the dispute;

    (iii) the date of conclusion of the alternative dispute resolution procedure;

    (iv) the result of the alternative dispute resolution procedure.

19 Where the person refuses to deal with a dispute transmitted to it by the ODR platform, it ensures that it transmits, without delay, the refusal to the ODR platform.]

NOTES

Commencement: 7 April 2015.

Words in square brackets substituted, and paras 13A, 14A inserted, by the Alternative Dispute Resolution for Consumer Disputes (Amendment) Regulations 2015, SI 2015/1392, reg 2(1), (2), (15)(a)–(i); paras 17–19 added by reg 2(1), (15)(j) of the 2015 Regulations, as from 9 January 2016.

SCHEDULE 4
INFORMATION TO BE INCLUDED IN THE LIST MAINTAINED BY A COMPETENT AUTHORITY

Regulation 10(1)

[2.1164]

a)   the name, contact details and website address of the ADR entity;

b)   the fees, if any, charged by the ADR entity;

c)   the language in which complaints can be submitted to the ADR entity and in which the ADR entity can conduct alternative dispute resolution procedures;

d)   the types of domestic dispute and cross-border dispute covered by the alternative dispute resolution services provided by the ADR entity;

e)   the sectors and categories of domestic disputes and cross-border disputes covered by the ADR entity;

f)   whether or not the alternative dispute resolution procedure is or can be conducted as an oral or a written procedure;

g)   whether the outcome of the alternative dispute resolution procedure is binding;

h)   the grounds on which the ADR entity may refuse to deal with a given dispute in accordance with paragraph 13 of Schedule 3.

NOTES

Commencement: 7 April 2015.

SCHEDULE 5
INFORMATION TO BE INCLUDED IN AN ADR ENTITY'S ANNUAL ACTIVITY REPORT

Regulation 11(2)

[2.1165]

a)   the number of domestic disputes and cross-border disputes the ADR entity has received;

b)   the types of complaints to which the domestic disputes and cross-border disputes relate;

c)   a description of any systematic or significant problems that occur frequently and lead to disputes between consumers and traders of which the ADR entity has become aware due to its operations as an ADR entity;

d)   any recommendations the ADR entity may have as to how the problems referred to in paragraph (c) could be avoided or resolved in future, in order to raise traders' standards and to facilitate the exchange of information and best practices;

e)   the number of disputes which the ADR entity has refused to deal with, and percentage share of the grounds set out in paragraph 13 of Schedule 3 on which the ADR entity has declined to consider such disputes;

f)   the percentage of alternative dispute resolution procedures which were discontinued for operational reasons and, if known, the reasons for the discontinuation;

g)   the average time taken to resolve domestic disputes and cross-border disputes;

h)   the rate of compliance, if known, with the outcomes of the alternative dispute resolution procedures;

i)   the co-operation, if any, of the ADR entity within any network of ADR entities which facilitates the resolution of cross-border disputes.

NOTES
Commencement: 7 April 2015.

SCHEDULE 6
INFORMATION WHICH AN ADR ENTITY MUST COMMUNICATE TO THE RELEVANT COMPETENT AUTHORITY EVERY TWO YEARS

Regulation 11(3)

[2.1166]

a)   the number of disputes received by the ADR entity and the types of complaints to which the disputes related;

b)   the percentage share of alternative dispute resolution procedures which were discontinued before an outcome was reached;

c)   the average time taken to resolve the disputes which the ADR entity has received;

d)   the rate of compliance, if known, with the outcomes of its alternative dispute resolution procedures;

e)   any recommendations the ADR entity may have as to how any systematic or significant problems that occur frequently and lead to disputes between consumers and traders could be avoided or resolved in future;

f)   where the ADR entity is a member of any network of ADR entities which facilitates the resolution of cross-border disputes, an assessment of the effectiveness of its co-operation in that network;

g)   where the ADR entity provides training to its ADR officials, details of the training it provides;

h)   an assessment of the effectiveness of an alternative dispute resolution procedure offered by the ADR entity and of possible ways of improving its performance.

NOTES
Commencement: 7 April 2015.

SCHEDULE 7

(Schedule 7 amends the Financial Services and Markets Act 2000 at **[1.1395]** *et seq.)*

SCHEDULE 8
LISTED DIRECTIVE

Regulation 20(2)

[2.1167]

Provisions of Directive	Specified UK Law
Article 13 of Directive 2013/11/EU of the European Parliament and of the Council of 21 May 2013 on alternative dispute resolution for consumer disputes and amending Regulation (EC) 2006/2004 and Directive 2009/22/EC	Regulation 19(1) and (2) of the Alternative Dispute Resolution for Consumer Disputes (Competent Authorities and Information) Regulations 2015

NOTES
Commencement: 9 July 2015.
Revoked by the Alternative Dispute Resolution for Consumer Disputes (Amendment) Regulations 2015, SI 2015/1392, reg 2(1), (14), as from 9 January 2016.

MORTGAGE CREDIT DIRECTIVE ORDER 2015

(SI 2015/910)

NOTES
Made: 25 March 2015.
Authority: European Communities Act 1972, s 2(2), Sch 2, para 1A; Financial Services and Markets Act 2000 ss 21(9), (15), 22(1), (5), 38, 409, 428(3).
Commencement: see art 1.

Part 2 Statutory Instruments

ARRANGEMENT OF ARTICLES

PART 1
INTRODUCTORY PROVISIONS

PART 2
AMENDMENTS TO LEGISLATION

PART 3
CONSUMER BUY-TO-LET MORTGAGES

PART 4
TRANSITIONAL PROVISIONS

PART 5
REVIEW

SCHEDULES

PART 1
INTRODUCTORY PROVISIONS

[2.1168]
1   Citation and commencement

(1)   This Order may be cited as the Mortgage Credit Directive Order 2015.

(2)   Articles 2 (interpretation) and 32 (FCA power to direct timing of applications for permission and registration) come into force on 6th April 2015.

(3) Article 3 (amendments to legislation) comes into force on 20th April 2015 in so far as it gives effect to paragraph 15 of Schedule 1 (amendments to the Financial Services and Markets Act 2000 (Regulated Activities) (Amendment) (No 2) Order 2013).

(4) The following provisions come into force on 21st September 2015—

    (a)   article 3 in so far as it gives effect to paragraph 1(4) of Schedule 1 (amendments to section 137R of the Act); and

    (b)   article 31 (transitional provision: person subject to the Consumer Credit Act 1974 who chooses to adopt new rules before 21st March 2016).

(5) The other provisions of this Order come into force—

    (a)   on 20th April 2015 for the purposes of enabling the making and determination of applications for—

        (i)   a Part 4A permission, or a variation of a Part 4A permission, in relation to an activity of the kind specified by article 36A (credit broking), 53A (advising on regulated mortgage contracts) or 60B (regulated credit agreements) of the Regulated Activities Order, article 25A (arranging regulated mortgage contracts) or 61 (entering into and administering regulated mortgage contracts) of the Regulated Activities Order as amended by this Order, or article 53DA (advising on regulated credit agreements for the acquisition of land) of the Regulated Activities Order as inserted by this Order; or

        (ii)   entry on the register of consumer buy-to-let mortgage firms under article 8 of this Order (register of consumer buy-to-let mortgage firms);

    (b)   on 21st December 2015 for the purposes of—

        (i)   enabling the appropriate regulator to treat a consent notice referred to in paragraph 13(1)(a) or a regulator's notice referred to in paragraph 14(1)(b) of Schedule 3 to the Act (as amended by this Order) given on or after that date by an EEA firm falling within paragraph 5(i) of Schedule 3 to the Act (as amended by this Order) as effective for the purposes of paragraph 13(1) or 14(1) (as the case may be); and

        (ii)   enabling the appropriate regulator to treat a notice of intention referred to in paragraph 19(2) or 20(1) of Schedule 3 to the Act (as amended by this Order) given on or after that date by a UK firm wishing to exercise an EEA right under the mortgages directive as effective for the purposes of paragraph 19(2) or 20(1) (as the case may be); and

    (c)   for all other purposes, on 21st March 2016.

(6) Nothing in paragraph (5)(b) gives a person an EEA right to carry on, before 21st March 2016, any of the activities set out in sub-paragraphs (a) to (c) of Article 4(5) of the mortgages directive or to provide advisory services (as defined in Article 4(21) of that directive).

NOTES

Commencement: 20 April 2015 (certain purposes); 21 December 2015 (certain purposes); 21 March 2016 (otherwise) (see above).

[2.1169]
2 Interpretation

(1) In this Order—

"the Act" means the Financial Services and Markets Act 2000;

"appropriate regulator" means—

    (a)   in relation to a firm which is a PRA-authorised person, the PRA;

    (b)   in any other case, the FCA;

"borrower" has the meaning given by article 61(3)(a)(i) of the Regulated Activities Order;

"consumer credit back book mortgage contract" means a contract which—

        (i)   is entered into before 21st March 2016,

        (ii)   immediately before 21st March 2016 is a regulated credit agreement within the meaning of article 60B(3) of the Regulated Activities Order, and

        (iii)   but for article 28(1), would be a regulated mortgage contract if it were entered into on or after 21st March 2016; or

        (i)   relates to the granting of credit in the circumstances described in article 28(1),

        (ii)   is entered into on or after 21st March 2016,

        (iii)   would be a regulated credit agreement within the meaning of article 60B(3) of the Regulated Activities Order if it had been entered into immediately before 21st March 2016, and

        (iv)   but for article 28(1), would be a regulated mortgage contract at the time that it is entered into;

"the mortgages directive" means Directive 2014/17/EU of the European Parliament and of the Council of 4th February 2014 on credit agreements for consumers relating to residential immovable property and amending Directives 2008/48/EC and 2013/36/EU and Regulation (EU) No 1093/2010;

"the Regulated Activities Order" means the Financial Services and Markets Act 2000 (Regulated Activities) Order 2001.

(2) Unless otherwise defined—

(a) any expression used in this Order which is used in the mortgages directive has the same meaning as in that directive; and

(b) any other expression used in this Order which is defined for the purposes of the Act has the meaning given by the Act.

NOTES
Commencement: 6 April 2015.

PART 2
AMENDMENTS TO LEGISLATION

[2.1170]
3 Amendments to legislation

Schedule 1, which contains amendments to primary and secondary legislation, has effect.

NOTES
Commencement: see art 1 above.

PART 3
CONSUMER BUY-TO-LET MORTGAGES

[2.1171]
4 Interpretation of this Part

(1) In this Part—

"advisory services" has the meaning given by article 6;

"annual percentage rate of charge" has the meaning given by paragraph 9(6) of Schedule 2;

"buy-to-let mortgage contract" means a contract that—

(a) at the time it is entered into—

(i) meets the conditions in paragraphs (i) to (iii) of article 61(3)(a) of the Regulated Activities Order (regulated mortgage contracts); and

(ii) provides that the land subject to the mortgage cannot at any time be occupied as a dwelling by the borrower or by a related person, and is to be occupied as a dwelling on the basis of a rental agreement; or

(b) is a regulated credit agreement within the meaning of article 60B of the Regulated Activities Order which—

(i) falls within Article 3(1)(b) of the mortgages directive; and

(ii) provides that the land, or existing or projected building, to which it relates cannot at any time be occupied as a dwelling by the borrower or by a related person, and is to be occupied as a dwelling on the basis of a rental agreement;

"consumer" means a person acting for purposes which are outside that person's trade, business or profession;

"consumer buy-to-let mortgage business" means one or more of the following activities—

(a) acting as a creditor;

(b) acting as a credit intermediary; or

(c) providing advisory services;

"consumer buy-to-let mortgage contract" means a buy-to-let mortgage contract which is not entered into by the borrower wholly or predominantly for the purposes of a business carried on, or intended to be carried on, by the borrower;

"consumer buy-to-let mortgage firm" means a person carrying on consumer buy-to-let mortgage business;

"credit intermediary" has the meaning given by article 5;

"creditor" means a person who, in the course of a trade, business or profession—

(a) enters into, or promises to enter into, a consumer buy-to-let mortgage contract under which the person is to provide credit, or

(b) administers a consumer buy-to-let mortgage contract,

and for the purposes of paragraph (b) a person administers a consumer buy-to-let mortgage contract if the person carries on the regulated activity specified by article 61(2) of the Regulated Activities Order (regulated mortgage contracts) in respect of the contract, or would carry on that regulated activity in respect of the contract but for the exclusion in article 72I of that Order (registered consumer buy-to-let mortgage firms);

"decision notice" means a notice that complies with the requirements of section 388 of the Act (decision notices);

"foreign currency loan" means a consumer buy-to-let mortgage contract where the credit is denominated in a currency other than that in which the borrower receives the income or holds the assets from which the credit is to be repaid;

"register" means the register kept by the FCA under article 8(1);

"registered consumer buy-to-let mortgage firm" means a person who is included in the register;

"related person" has the meaning set out in article 61A of the Regulated Activities Order (mortgage contracts which are not regulated mortgage contracts); and

"warning notice" means a notice that complies with the requirements of section 387 of the Act (warning notices).

(2) For the purposes of this Part, if an agreement includes a declaration which—

   (a) is made by the borrower, and

   (b) includes—

      (i) a statement that the agreement is entered into by the borrower wholly or predominantly for the purposes of a business carried on, or intended to be carried on, by the borrower;

      (ii) a statement that the borrower understands that the borrower will not have the benefit of the protection and remedies that would be available to the borrower under this Order if the agreement were a consumer buy-to-let mortgage contract under this Order; and

      (iii) a statement that the borrower is aware that if the borrower is in any doubt as to the consequences of the agreement not being regulated by this Order, then the borrower should seek independent legal advice,

the agreement is to be presumed to have been entered into by the borrower wholly or predominantly for the purposes specified in sub-paragraph (b)(i), unless paragraph (3) applies.

(3) This paragraph applies if, when the agreement is entered into—

   (a) the creditor (or, if there is more than one creditor, any of the creditors), or

   (b) any person who has acted on behalf of the creditor (or, if there is more than one creditor, any of the creditors) in connection with the entering into of the agreement,

knows or has reasonable cause to suspect that the agreement is not entered into by the borrower wholly or predominantly for the purposes of a business carried on, or intended to be carried on, by the borrower.

(4) For the purposes of this Part, a borrower is to be regarded as entering into an agreement for the purposes of a business carried on, or intended to be carried on, by the borrower if the agreement is a buy-to-let mortgage contract and—

   (a)

      (i) the borrower previously purchased, or is entering into the contract in order to finance the purchase by the borrower of, the land to which the agreement relates;

      (ii) at the time of the purchase the borrower intended that the land would be occupied as a dwelling on the basis of a rental agreement and would not at any time be occupied as a dwelling by the borrower or by a related person, or where the borrower has not yet purchased the land the borrower has such an intention at the time of entering into the contract; and

      (iii) where the borrower has purchased the land, since the time of the purchase the land has not at any time been occupied as a dwelling by the borrower or by a related person; or

   (b) the borrower is the owner of land, other than the land to which the agreement relates, which is—

      (i) occupied as a dwelling on the basis of a rental agreement and is not occupied as a dwelling by the borrower or by a related person; or

      (ii) subject to a mortgage under a buy-to-let mortgage contract.

NOTES

Commencement: 20 April 2015 (certain purposes); 21 December 2015 (certain purposes); 21 March 2016 (otherwise) (see art 1 above).

[2.1172]

5 Meaning of credit intermediary

(1) A person acts as a credit intermediary if the person—

   (a) is not a creditor;

   (b) is not merely introducing, either directly or indirectly, a consumer to a creditor or credit intermediary;

   (c) is acting in the course of the person's trade, business or profession, for remuneration, which may take a pecuniary form or any other agreed form of financial consideration; and

   (d) meets one or more of conditions A to C.

(2) Condition A is that the person presents or offers consumer buy-to-let mortgage contracts to consumers.

(3) Condition B is that the person assists consumers by undertaking preparatory work or other pre-contractual administration in respect of consumer buy-to-let mortgage contracts other than as referred to in Condition A.

(4) Condition C is that the person concludes consumer buy-to-let mortgage contracts with consumers on behalf of the creditor.

Part 2   Statutory Instruments

NOTES

Commencement: 20 April 2015 (certain purposes); 21 December 2015 (certain purposes); 21 March 2016 (otherwise) (see art 1 above).

[2.1173]
6 Meaning of advisory services

(1) A person provides advisory services if, in the course of that person's trade, business or profession, the person provides personal recommendations to a consumer in respect of one or more transactions relating to consumer buy-to-let mortgage contracts.

(2) A person who provides personal recommendations to a consumer in respect of one or more transactions relating to consumer buy-to-let mortgage contracts is not providing advisory services if the recommendations are provided—

(a) in an incidental manner in the course of a professional activity and that activity is regulated by legal or regulatory provisions or a code of ethics governing the profession which do not exclude the making of those recommendations; or

(b) in the context of managing existing debt as an insolvency practitioner where that activity is regulated by legal or regulatory provisions or as part of public or voluntary debt advisory services which do not operate on a commercial basis.

NOTES

Commencement: 20 April 2015 (certain purposes); 21 December 2015 (certain purposes); 21 March 2016 (otherwise) (see art 1 above)).

[2.1174]
7 Limitation on permission to carry on regulated activities

If a person has a Part 4A permission to carry on an activity of the kind specified by article 25A, 36A, 53A, 53DA, 60B or 61 of the Regulated Activities Order, that person's Part 4A permission is subject to a requirement that the person does not carry on any activity that would constitute consumer buy-to-let mortgage business unless the person is a registered consumer buy-to-let mortgage firm.

NOTES

Commencement: 20 April 2015 (certain purposes); 21 December 2015 (certain purposes); 21 March 2016 (otherwise) (see art 1 above).

[2.1175]
8 Register of consumer buy-to-let mortgage firms

(1) The FCA must keep a register of consumer buy-to-let mortgage firms and must enter a person on the register if the conditions in paragraph (2) or (3) are met.

(2) The conditions in this paragraph are that—

(a) the person carries on, or is seeking to carry on, consumer buy-to-let mortgage business;

(b) the person—

(i) has a Part 4A permission to carry on one or more regulated activities; or

(ii) is treated as having an interim permission to carry on one or more regulated activities under article 56 of the Financial Services and Markets Act 2000 (Regulated Activities) (Amendment) (No 2) Order 2013;

(c) the person applies to the FCA in a manner that complies with the requirements of, and any requirements imposed under, article 9 for entry on the register; and

(d) the FCA has not previously revoked the registration of the person under article 13.

(3) The conditions in this paragraph are that—

(a) the person carries on, or is seeking to carry on, consumer buy-to-let mortgage business;

(b) the person's head office, registered office or place of residence, as the case may be, is in the United Kingdom;

(c) none of the individuals responsible for the management or operation of the person's consumer buy-to-let mortgage business—

(i) has been convicted of any offence involving fraud or dishonesty, or any indictable offence, and for this purpose "offence" includes any act or omission which would have been an offence if it had taken place in the United Kingdom; or

(ii) is subject to a prohibition order;

(d) if the registration is to be of a partnership, an unincorporated association or a body corporate, the FCA is satisfied that any persons having a controlling interest over the partnership, unincorporated association or body corporate are fit and proper persons having regard to the need to ensure the sound and prudent conduct of the affairs of a consumer buy-to-let mortgage firm;

(e) the FCA is satisfied that—

(i) where the registration is to be of a body corporate, the directors;

(ii) the persons responsible for the management of the firm; and

      (iii)   the persons responsible for consumer buy-to-let mortgage business, are of good repute;

(f)   if the person is not a creditor but is a credit intermediary or provides advisory services for the purposes of this Part, the person holds professional indemnity insurance covering its consumer buy-to-let mortgage business in the United Kingdom, or some other comparable guarantee against liability arising from professional negligence, of at least the minimum monetary amount specified in Commission Delegated Regulation (EU) No 1125/2014 of 19th September 2014 of the European Parliament and of the Council with regard to regulatory technical standards on the minimum monetary amount of the professional indemnity insurance or comparable guarantee to be held by credit intermediaries, as such Regulation may be amended from time to time;

(g)   the individuals responsible for the management or operation of the person's consumer buy-to-let mortgage business possess an appropriate level of knowledge and competence in relation to consumer buy-to-let mortgage contracts; and

(h)   the person applies to the FCA in a manner that complies with the requirements of, and any requirements imposed under, article 9 for entry on the register.

(4)   For the purposes of sub-paragraph (3)(d), a person ("C") has a controlling interest over the firm ("F") if—

(a)   C holds 10% or more of the shares in F or in a parent undertaking of F ("P");

(b)   C holds 10% or more of the voting power in F or P; or

(c)   C holds shares or voting power in F or P as a result of which C is able to exercise significant influence over the management of F.

(5)   The FCA may—

(a)   keep the register in any form it thinks fit;

(b)   include on the register such information as the FCA considers appropriate;

(c)   publish the register, or any part of it; and

(d)   exploit commercially the information contained in the register, or any part of that information.

(6)   The FCA must—

(a)   make the register available for inspection by members of the public in a legible form at such times and in such place or places as the FCA may determine; and

(b)   provide a certified copy of the register, or any part of it, to any person who asks for it—

      (i)   on payment of the fee (if any) fixed by the FCA; and

      (ii)   in a form (either written or electronic) in which it is legible to the person asking for it.

(7)   If a partnership or unincorporated association is entered on the register, its registration—

(a)   has effect for activities carried on in the name of the partnership or unincorporated association;

(b)   is not affected by any change in the membership of the partnership or unincorporated association; and

(c)   if the partnership or unincorporated association is dissolved, continues to have effect in relation to any individual, partnership or unincorporated association which succeeds to the whole or substantially the whole of the business of the former partnership or unincorporated association.

(8)   In paragraph (7) "partnership" does not include a partnership which is constituted under the law of any place other than the United Kingdom and is a body corporate.

NOTES

Commencement: 20 April 2015 (certain purposes); 21 December 2015 (certain purposes); 21 March 2016 (otherwise) (see art 1 above).

[2.1176]

9   Applications for entry on the register or variation of an existing entry on the register

(1)   An application for entry on the register may be made by an individual, a body corporate, a partnership or an unincorporated association.

(2)   An application for entry on the register or variation of an existing entry on the register must—

(a)   be made in such manner as the FCA may direct; and

(b)   contain or be accompanied by such information as the FCA may reasonably require for the purpose of determining the application.

(3)   At any time after receiving an application and before determining it, the FCA may require the applicant to provide it with such further information as it considers necessary to enable it to determine the application.

(4)   Different directions may be given, and different requirements imposed, in relation to different applications or categories of applications.

(5)   The FCA may require an applicant to provide information which the applicant is required to give under this article in such form, or to verify it in such manner, as the FCA may specify.

Commencement: 20 April 2015 (certain purposes); 21 December 2015 (certain purposes); 21 March 2016 (otherwise) (see art 1 above).

[2.1177]
10 Determination of applications

(1) The FCA must determine an application for entry on the register before the end of the period of six months beginning with the date on which it receives the completed application.

(2) The FCA may determine an incomplete application, and it must in any event determine such an application within twelve months beginning with the date on which it first receives the application.

(3) If the FCA enters a person on the register, it must give written notice of its determination to that person.

NOTES

Commencement: 20 April 2015 (certain purposes); 21 December 2015 (certain purposes); 21 March 2016 (otherwise) (see art 1 above).

[2.1178]
11 Procedure when refusing an application

(1) If the FCA proposes to refuse an application made under article 9(1) it must give the applicant a warning notice.

(2) If the FCA refuses an application—
   (a) it must give the applicant a decision notice; and
   (b) the applicant may refer the matter to the Tribunal.

NOTES

Commencement: 20 April 2015 (certain purposes); 21 December 2015 (certain purposes); 21 March 2016 (otherwise) (see art 1 above).

[2.1179]
12 Registered consumer buy-to-let mortgage firm ceasing to meet the requirements for registration

If a registered consumer buy-to-let mortgage firm ceases to meet a condition in article 8(2) or (3) that applies to it, the firm must inform the FCA immediately.

NOTES

Commencement: 20 April 2015 (certain purposes); 21 December 2015 (certain purposes); 21 March 2016 (otherwise) (see art 1 above).

[2.1180]
13 Revocation of registration

The FCA may revoke the registration of a registered consumer buy-to-let mortgage firm if—
   (a) the firm does not meet a condition in article 8(2) or (3) that applies to it;
   (b) the firm has contravened a requirement in Schedule 2 that applies to it;
   (c) the firm applies for or consents to the revocation of the registration;
   (d) the firm has ceased to engage in consumer buy-to-let mortgage business for more than twelve months;
   (e) a fee due in respect of the registration has not been paid; or
   (f) the revocation is desirable in order to protect the interests of consumers.

NOTES

Commencement: 20 April 2015 (certain purposes); 21 December 2015 (certain purposes); 21 March 2016 (otherwise) (see art 1 above).

[2.1181]
14 Procedure on revocation

(1) If the FCA proposes to revoke the registration of a registered consumer buy-to-let mortgage firm other than at the firm's request or with the firm's consent, the FCA must give that firm a warning notice.

(2) If the FCA decides to revoke the registration of a registered consumer buy-to-let mortgage firm other than at the firm's request or with the firm's consent—
   (a) the FCA must give that firm a decision notice, and
   (b) that firm may refer the matter to the Tribunal.

NOTES
Commencement: 20 April 2015 (certain purposes); 21 December 2015 (certain purposes); 21 March 2016 (otherwise) (see art 1 above).

[2.1182]
15   Suspension of registration
(1)   If it appears to the FCA that a registered consumer buy-to-let mortgage firm does not meet a condition in article 8(2) or (3) that applies to it, the FCA may suspend the registration of that firm for a specified period, until the occurrence of a specified event, or until specified conditions are complied with.

(2)   In this article "specified" means specified by the FCA in a notice given under article 16.

NOTES
Commencement: 20 April 2015 (certain purposes); 21 December 2015 (certain purposes); 21 March 2016 (otherwise) (see art 1 above).

[2.1183]
16   Procedure on suspension
(1)   The suspension of the registration of a registered consumer buy-to-let mortgage firm takes effect—
   (a)   immediately, if the notice given under paragraph (4) states that that is the case;
   (b)   on such date as may be specified in the notice; or
   (c)   if no date is specified in the notice, when the matter to which it relates is no longer open to review.

(2)   A suspension may take effect immediately or on a specified date only if the FCA, having regard to the ground on which it is exercising its power under article 15, considers that it is necessary for the suspension to take effect immediately or on that date.

(3)   If the FCA proposes to suspend the registration of a registered consumer buy-to-let mortgage firm other than at the firm's request or with the firm's consent, the FCA must give that firm a warning notice.

(4)   If the FCA decides to suspend the registration of a registered consumer buy-to-let mortgage firm other than at the firm's request or with the firm's consent—
   (a)   the FCA must give that firm a decision notice, and
   (b)   that firm may refer the matter to the Tribunal.

NOTES
Commencement: 20 April 2015 (certain purposes); 21 December 2015 (certain purposes); 21 March 2016 (otherwise) (see art 1 above).

[2.1184]
17   Appointed representatives
Section 39 of the Act (exemption of appointed representatives) applies in respect of consumer buy-to-let mortgage business as if in subsection (4), the reference to provisions contained in the Act included reference to provisions contained in this Order.

NOTES
Commencement: 20 April 2015 (certain purposes); 21 December 2015 (certain purposes); 21 March 2016 (otherwise) (see art 1 above).

[2.1185]
18   Obligations of registered consumer buy-to-let mortgage firms
(1)   A registered consumer buy-to-let mortgage firm must, in respect of its consumer buy-to-let mortgage business—
   (a)   comply with the requirements set out in Schedule 2;
   (b)   retain information relevant to demonstrating the firm's compliance or non-compliance with the requirements of that Schedule—
      (i)   in retrievable and legible form; and
      (ii)   so long as any sum remains outstanding, or any mortgage or charge remains in place, under the consumer buy-to-let mortgage contract to which the information relates;
   (c)   provide the FCA with such information in relation to the firm's consumer buy-to-let mortgage business and its compliance with the requirements of that Schedule as the FCA may direct, in order to enable the FCA to discharge its functions under this Part; and
   (d)   deal with the FCA in an open and co-operative manner.

(2)   Information provided under paragraph (1)(c) must be given at such times and in such manner, and verified in such manner, as the FCA may direct.

(3)   Sections 348, 349 and 352 of the Act (confidential information) and regulations made under section 349 of the Act apply in relation to information provided to the FCA under paragraph (1)(c) as they apply in relation to information received by the FCA in the discharge of its functions under the Act.

NOTES

Commencement: 20 April 2015 (certain purposes); 21 December 2015 (certain purposes); 21 March 2016 (otherwise) (see art 1 above).

[2.1186]
19   Power to direct registered consumer buy-to-let mortgage firms to take appropriate action
(1)   The FCA may direct a registered consumer buy-to-let mortgage firm to take such steps as are necessary for the purposes of securing compliance with the requirements of Schedule 2 in respect of the firm's consumer buy-to-let mortgage business.
(2)   A direction under paragraph (1) may, in particular, require the firm to—
   (a)   take specified action,
   (b)   refrain from taking specified action,
   (c)   review or take remedial action in respect of past conduct.
(3)   A direction under paragraph (1) may also be given to or apply to a person who was a registered consumer buy-to-let mortgage firm, in relation to conduct that occurred while the person was registered.
(4)   The FCA may direct registered consumer buy-to-let mortgage firms as to the steps to be taken where the FCA requires such a firm to appoint a person to make a report pursuant to section 166 of the Act (as applied by article 23(2)).
(5)   A person to whom a direction under paragraph (1) or (4) is given or to whom such a direction applies must comply with the direction.
(6)   Section 55Y (exercise of own-initiative power: procedure) and 55Z3(2) (right to refer matters to the Tribunal) of the Act apply to a direction to a person under paragraph (1) as they apply to a requirement imposed on an authorised person under section 55L(3) of the Act (imposition of requirements by the FCA).

NOTES

Commencement: 20 April 2015 (certain purposes); 21 December 2015 (certain purposes); 21 March 2016 (otherwise) (see art 1 above).

[2.1187]
20   Functions of the FCA in relation to this Part
(1)   The FCA is to have the functions conferred on it by this Part.
(2)   In discharging its function of determining the general policy and principles by reference to which it performs particular functions under this Part, the FCA must have regard to—
   (a)   the need to use its resources in the most efficient and economic way;
   (b)   the responsibilities of those who manage the affairs of consumer buy-to-let mortgage firms;
   (c)   the principle that a burden or restriction which is imposed on a person, or on the carrying on of an activity, should be proportionate to the benefits, considered in general terms, which are expected to result from the imposition of that burden or restriction;
   (d)   the desirability of facilitating innovation in connection with consumer buy-to-let mortgage business;
   (e)   the need to minimise the adverse effects on competition that may arise from anything done in the discharging of those functions; and
   (f)   the desirability of facilitating competition in relation to consumer buy-to-let mortgage business.

NOTES

Commencement: 20 April 2015 (certain purposes); 21 December 2015 (certain purposes); 21 March 2016 (otherwise) (see art 1 above).

[2.1188]
21   Monitoring and enforcement
(1)   The FCA must maintain arrangements designed to enable it to determine whether persons on whom requirements are imposed by or under this Part are complying with them.
(2)   The arrangements referred to in paragraph (1) may provide for functions to be performed on behalf of the FCA by any body or person who is, in the FCA's opinion, competent to perform them.
(3)   The FCA must also maintain arrangements for enforcing the provisions of this Part.
(4)   Paragraph (2) does not affect the FCA's duty under paragraph (1).

NOTES

Commencement: 20 April 2015 (certain purposes); 21 December 2015 (certain purposes); 21 March 2016 (otherwise) (see art 1 above).

[2.1189]
22   Guidance

(1)   The FCA may give guidance consisting of such information and advice as it considers appropriate with respect to—
   (a)   the operation of this Part;
   (b)   any matters relating to the functions of the FCA under this Part;
   (c)   any other matters about which it appears to the FCA to be desirable to give information or advice in connection with this Part.

(2)   The FCA may—
   (a)   publish its guidance;
   (b)   offer copies of its published guidance for sale at a reasonable price;
   (c)   if it gives guidance in response to a request made by any person, make a reasonable charge for that guidance.

NOTES

Commencement: 20 April 2015 (certain purposes); 21 December 2015 (certain purposes); 21 March 2016 (otherwise) (see art 1 above).

[2.1190]
23   Application of provisions of the Act to registered consumer-buy-to-let mortgage firms

(1)   For the purposes of the following provisions of the Act, a requirement imposed by or under this Part on a consumer buy-to-let mortgage firm in respect of its consumer buy-to-let mortgage business is to be treated as if it were a requirement imposed on an authorised person by or under the Act—
   (a)   section 204A (meaning of "relevant requirements");
   (b)   section 380 (injunctions);
   (c)   section 382 (restitution orders);
   (d)   section 384 (power of FCA or PRA to require restitution); and
   (e)   section 398 (misleading FCA or PRA: residual cases).

(2)   The following provisions of the Act apply in respect of the exercise by the FCA of its functions under this Part in relation to a registered consumer buy-to-let mortgage firm as they apply in respect of the exercise by the FCA of its functions under the Act in relation to an authorised person—
   (a)   section 165 (regulators' power to require information: authorised persons etc);
   (b)   section 166 (reports by skilled persons);
   (c)   section 167 (appointment of persons to carry out general investigations);
   (d)   section 168(4) to (6) (appointment of persons to carry out investigations in particular cases);
   (e)   section 169 (investigations etc in support of overseas regulator);
   (f)   section 170 (investigations: general);
   (g)   section 171 (powers of persons appointed under section 167);
   (h)   section 172 (additional power of persons appointed as a result of section 168(1) or (4));
   (i)   section 173 (powers of persons appointed as a result of section 168(2));
   (j)   section 174 (admissibility of statements made to investigators);
   (k)   section 175 (information and documents: supplemental provisions);
   (l)   section 176 (entry of premises under warrant);
   (m)   section 176A (retention of documents taken under section 176);
   (n)   section 177 (offences);
   (o)   section 205 (public censure); and
   (p)   section 206 (financial penalties).

(3)   Section 168 of the Act is to be read as if subsection (4) included a reference to circumstances suggesting that a person may have failed to comply with the obligations imposed by this Part.

(4)   Sections 207 to 211 (disciplinary measures: procedure and policy) of, and paragraph 20 (penalties) of Schedule 1ZA to, the Act apply in relation to the exercise of the FCA's powers under section 205 or 206 of the Act as applied by paragraph (2)(o) and (p) as they apply in relation to the exercise of such powers under section 205 or 206 of the Act in respect of authorised persons.

(5)   Registered consumer buy-to-let mortgage firms are to be treated as regulated persons for the purposes of paragraph 21 of Schedule 1ZA to the Act (financial penalty scheme).

NOTES

Commencement: 20 April 2015 (certain purposes); 21 December 2015 (certain purposes); 21 March 2016 (otherwise) (see art 1 above).

[2.1191]
24 Application of procedural provisions of the Act

(1)   Part 9 of the Act (hearings and appeals) applies in the case of a matter referred to the Tribunal under this Part as it applies in the case of a matter referred to the Tribunal under the Act.

(2)   Part 26 of the Act (notices) applies to warning notices and decision notices given under this Part as it applies to such notices given under the Act.

NOTES
Commencement: 20 April 2015 (certain purposes); 21 December 2015 (certain purposes); 21 March 2016 (otherwise) (see art 1 above).

[2.1192]
25 Application of provisions of the Act to the FCA in respect of its supervision of consumer buy-to-let mortgage firms

The functions of the FCA under this Order are to be treated as functions conferred on the FCA under the Act for the purposes of—
   (a)   paragraph 23 (fees) of Schedule 1ZA to the Act, and
   (b)   paragraph 25 (exemption from liability in damages) of Schedule 1ZA to the Act.

NOTES
Commencement: 20 April 2015 (certain purposes); 21 December 2015 (certain purposes); 21 March 2016 (otherwise) (see art 1 above).

[2.1193]
26 Extension of the compulsory jurisdiction of the Financial Ombudsman Scheme to registered consumer buy-to-let mortgage firms

(1)   Part 16 (the Ombudsman Scheme) of the 2000 Act applies in respect of a complaint relating to the act or omission of a registered consumer buy-to-let mortgage firm as if—
   (a)   in section 226(2)(b) of that Act (compulsory jurisdiction), after "Payment Services Regulations 2009," there were inserted "a registered consumer buy-to-let mortgage firm within the meaning of Part 3 of the Mortgage Credit Directive Order 2015,";
   (b)   in section 232A of that Act (scheme operator's duty to provide information to FCA), after "FCA's operational objectives" there were inserted ", or which might otherwise be of assistance to the FCA for the purposes of discharging any of the FCA's functions under Part 3 of the Mortgage Credit Directive Order 2015,";
   (c)   in section 234 of that Act (industry funding), after "any electronic money issuer within the meaning of the Electronic Money Regulations 2011" there were inserted ", any registered consumer buy-to-let mortgage firm within the meaning of Part 3 of the Mortgage Credit Directive Order 2015";
   (d)   in paragraph 13(4) of Schedule 17 to that Act (FCA's procedural rules), after "an electronic money issuer within the meaning of the Electronic Money Regulations 2011," there were inserted "a registered consumer buy-to-let mortgage firm within the meaning of the Mortgage Credit Directive Order 2015,".

NOTES
Commencement: 20 April 2015 (certain purposes); 21 December 2015 (certain purposes); 21 March 2016 (otherwise) (see art 1 above).

PART 4
TRANSITIONAL PROVISIONS

[2.1194]
27 Transitional provision: person with Part 4A permission to carry on an activity in relation to a regulated mortgage contract before 21st March 2016

(1)   Any person who immediately before 21st March 2016 had permission under Part 4A of the Act to carry on an activity of the kind specified by article 25A, 36A, 60B or 61 of the Regulated Activities Order is, from 21st March 2016, to be treated as having a Part 4A permission to carry on an activity of the kind specified by that article of the Regulated Activities Order as amended by this Order.

(2)   Paragraph (1) does not affect the ability of the FCA or the PRA to vary or cancel a Part 4A permission under the Act.

NOTES
Commencement: 20 April 2015 (certain purposes); 21 December 2015 (certain purposes); 21 March 2016 (otherwise) (see art 1 above).

[2.1195]
28 Transitional provision: agreements before 21st March 2016

(1)   Subject to paragraph (2), this Order does not apply to the granting of credit pursuant to an agreement existing before 21st March 2016.

(2)   Paragraph (1) does not prevent this Order from applying to a consumer credit back book mortgage contract from the later of—

(a)   21st March 2016, if the consumer credit back book mortgage contract was entered into before that date; or

(b)   the time at which the consumer credit back book mortgage contract is entered into.

NOTES
Commencement: 20 April 2015 (certain purposes); 21 December 2015 (certain purposes); 21 March 2016 (otherwise) (see art 1 above).

[2.1196]
29 Transitional provision: consumer credit back book mortgage contracts

(1)   This article applies to a consumer credit back book mortgage contract.

(2)   If the contract would be enforceable against the borrower only on an order of the court as a result of the application of any provision of the Consumer Credit Act 1974 specified in paragraph (3), but for the amendments to legislation made by this Order, the contract is enforceable against the borrower only on an order of the court, and section 127 of the Consumer Credit Act 1974 (enforcement orders in cases of infringement) applies in respect of the contract.

(3)   The provisions of the Consumer Credit Act 1974 specified by this paragraph are—

(a)   section 55(2) (disclosure of information),

(b)   section 61B(3) (duty to supply copy of overdraft agreement),

(c)   section 65(1) (improperly executed agreements),

(d)   section 105(7)(a) or (b) (improperly executed security instruments),

(e)   section 111(2) (failure to serve copy of notice on surety).

(4)   If the contract would be void, or part of the contract would be void, as a result of the application of section 56(3) of the Consumer Credit Act 1974 (antecedent negotiations), but for the amendments to legislation made by this Order, the contract, or that part of the contract, is void.

(5)   If a creditor would not be entitled to enforce a contract as a result of a failure to comply with a provision of the Consumer Credit Act 1974 specified in paragraph (6) but for the amendments to legislation made by this Order, then for the purposes only of correcting the failure to comply with the relevant provision of the Consumer Credit Act 1974, the contract is treated as if it were a regulated agreement and the creditor may enforce the contract only if the creditor has corrected the failure to comply.

(6)   The provisions of the Consumer Credit Act 1974 specified in this paragraph are—

(a)   section 77(1) (duty to give information to debtor under fixed-sum credit agreement),

(b)   section 77A(1) (statements to be provided in relation to fixed-sum credit agreements),

(c)   section 78(1) (duty to give information to debtor under running-account credit agreement),

(d)   section 85(1) (duty on issue of new credit-tokens),

(e)   section 97(1) (duty to give information about early repayment).

(7)   If a creditor would not be entitled to enforce a contract because a period of non-compliance applies to the contract under section 86D of the Consumer Credit Act 1974 (failure to give notice of sums in arrears), but for the amendments to legislation made by this Order, then for the purposes only of bringing the period of non-compliance to an end, the contract is treated as if it were a regulated agreement and the creditor may enforce the contract only if the period of non-compliance has ended.

(8)   If a creditor would not be entitled to enforce a contract because section 86E(5) of the Consumer Credit Act 1974 (notice of default sums) applies, but for the amendments to legislation made by this Order, then the creditor may enforce the contract only if the creditor has given the notice required by section 86E to the borrower.

(9)   If a creditor would not be entitled to enforce the security provided in relation to a contract as a result of a failure to comply with a provision of the Consumer Credit Act 1974 specified in paragraph (10) but for the amendments to legislation made by this Order, then for the purposes only of correcting the failure to comply with the relevant provision of the Consumer Credit Act 1974, the contract is treated as if it were a regulated agreement and the creditor may enforce the security only if the creditor has corrected the failure to comply.

(10)   The provisions of the Consumer Credit Act 1974 specified in this paragraph are—

(a)   section 107(1) (duty to give information to surety under fixed-sum credit agreement),

(b)   section 108(1) (duty to give information to surety under running-account credit agreement),

(c)   section 110(1) (duty to give information to debtor or hirer).

(11)   The following provisions of the Consumer Credit Act 1974 and regulations made under those provisions apply in respect of the contract as if the contract were a regulated agreement—

    (a)   section 93 (interest not to be increased on default),

    (b)   section 94 (right to complete payments ahead of time),

    (c)   section 95 (rebate on early settlement).

(12)   Sections 140A to 140C of the Consumer Credit Act 1974 (unfair relationships) apply to the contract as if section 140A(5) were omitted.

(13)   In this article "regulated agreement" means a regulated agreement within the meaning of section 8(3) of the Consumer Credit Act 1974.

NOTES

Commencement: 20 April 2015 (certain purposes); 21 December 2015 (certain purposes); 21 March 2016 (otherwise) (see art 1 above).

[2.1197]
30   Transitional provision: person engaged in consumer buy-to-let mortgage business before 20th March 2014

(1)   A creditor or credit intermediary who is engaged in consumer buy-to-let mortgage business before 20th March 2014 is not required to comply with paragraph 3 of Schedule 2 (knowledge and competence requirements for staff) until 21st March 2017.

(2)   In this article, the terms "creditor", "credit intermediary" and "consumer buy-to-let mortgage business" have the meanings set out in article 4.

NOTES

Commencement: 20 April 2015 (certain purposes); 21 December 2015 (certain purposes); 21 March 2016 (otherwise) (see art 1 above).

[2.1198]
31   Transitional provision: person subject to the Consumer Credit Act 1974 who chooses to adopt new rules before 21st March 2016

(1)   Paragraph (2) applies in relation to an agreement or proposed agreement where—

    (a)   if made before 21st March 2016, the agreement would be a regulated consumer credit agreement;

    (b)   if made on or after 21st March 2016, the agreement would not be a regulated consumer credit agreement;

    (c)   the creditor has not acted in compliance or in purported compliance with any provision of Part 4 of the Consumer Credit Act 1974, or regulations made under that Part, in relation to the agreement or proposed agreement; and

    (d)   before 21st March 2016, the creditor acts in compliance or in purported compliance with rules made by the FCA that would apply in relation to the agreement or proposed agreement from 21st March 2016.

(2)   From the date on which the creditor first acts in compliance or purported compliance with such rules, the Consumer Credit Act 1974 applies in relation to the agreement or proposed agreement as if the amendments to legislation made by paragraphs 2 and 4 of Schedule 1 (amendments to the Consumer Credit Act 1974 and the Regulated Activities Order) had come into force.

(3)   In this article—

    "creditor" means a creditor within the meaning of section 8(1) of the Consumer Credit Act 1974; and

    "regulated consumer credit agreement" means a regulated agreement within the meaning of section 8(3) of the Consumer Credit Act 1974.

NOTES

Commencement: 21 September 2015.

[2.1199]
32   FCA power to direct timing of applications for permission and registration

(1)   This article applies to an application made before 21st September 2015 for—

    (a)   a Part 4A permission or a variation of a Part 4A permission in relation to an activity of the kind specified by—

        (i)   article 53A of the Regulated Activities Order (advising on regulated mortgage contracts),

        (ii)   article 25A (arranging regulated mortgage contracts) or 61 (entering into and administering regulated mortgage contracts) of the Regulated Activities Order as amended by this Order, or

        (iii)   article 53DA of the Regulated Activities Order (advising on regulated credit agreements for the acquisition of land) as inserted by this Order; or

    (b)   entry on the register of consumer buy-to-let mortgage firms under article 8 of this Order (register of consumer buy-to-let mortgage firms).

(2)   The application may not be made before such date ("the opening date") as the FCA may direct.

(3)   Directions given under paragraph (2) may—
  (a)   relate to different categories of applications;
  (b)   set different opening dates for different categories of applications;
  (c)   be amended by the FCA by further direction.

(4)   An application made before the opening date is to be treated as if it had not been made.

NOTES
Commencement: 6 April 2015.

PART 5
REVIEW

[2.1200]
33   Review

(1)   The Treasury must from time to time—
  (a)   carry out a review of this Order;
  (b)   set out the conclusions of the review in a report; and
  (c)   publish the report.

(2)   In carrying out the review the Treasury must, so far as is reasonable, have regard to how the mortgages directive (which is implemented by means of this Order) is implemented in other EEA States.

(3)   The report must in particular—
  (a)   set out the objectives intended to be achieved by the regulatory system established by this Order;
  (b)   assess the extent to which those objectives are achieved; and
  (c)   assess whether those objectives remain appropriate and, if so, the extent to which they could be achieved with a system that imposes less regulation.

(4)   The first report under this article must be published on or before 1st September 2018.

(5)   Reports under this article are afterwards to be published at intervals not exceeding five years.

NOTES
Commencement: 20 April 2015 (certain purposes); 21 December 2015 (certain purposes); 21 March 2016 (otherwise) (see art 1 above).

SCHEDULES

SCHEDULE 1

(This Schedule amends the Financial Services and Markets Act 2000, the Consumer Credit Act 1974, the Consumer Credit (Agreements) Regulations 1983, SI 1983/1553, the Financial Services and Markets (Regulated Activities) Order 2001, SI 2001/544, the Financial Services and Markets Act 2000 (Exemption) Order 2001, SI 2001/1201, the Financial Services and Markets Act 2000 (Compensation Scheme: Electing Participants) Regulations 2001, 2001/1783, the Financial Services and Markets Act 2000 (Appointed Representatives) Regulations 2001, SI 2001/1217, the Financial Services and Markets Act 2000 (Disclosure of Confidential Information) Regulations 2001, SI 2001/2188, the Financial Services and Markets Act 2000 (EEA Passport Rights) Regulations 2001, SI 2001/2511, the Financial Services and Markets Act 2000 (Gibraltar) Order 2001, SI 2001/3084, the Consumer Credit (Disclosure of Information) Regulations 2004, SI 2004/1481, the Financial Services and Markets Act 2000 (Financial Promotion) Order 2005, SI 2005/1529, the Consumer Credit (Disclosure of Information) Regulations 2010, SI 2010/1013, the Consumer Credit (Agreements) Regulations 2010, SI 2010/1014, the Financial Services and Markets Act 2000 (Regulated Activities) (Amendment) (No 2) Order 2013, SI 2013/1881.)

SCHEDULE 2
REQUIREMENTS FOR REGISTERED CONSUMER BUY-TO-LET MORTGAGE FIRMS

Article 18

Conditions applicable to creditors and credit intermediaries

[2.1201]
1   Conduct of business obligations when providing consumer buy-to-let mortgage products to consumers

(1)   When manufacturing consumer buy-to-let mortgage contracts or granting, intermediating or providing advisory services on consumer buy-to-let mortgage contracts and, where appropriate, ancillary services to consumers or when executing a consumer buy-to-let mortgage contract, the creditor or credit intermediary must act honestly, fairly, transparently and professionally, taking account of the rights and interests of the consumers.

(2)   The granting, intermediating or provision of advisory services on consumer buy-to-let mortgage contracts and, where appropriate, the provision of ancillary services must be based on—
(a)   information about the borrower's circumstances;
(b)   any specific requirement made known by the borrower;
(c)   reasonable assumptions about risks to the borrower's situation over the term of the contract;
(d)   where the activity is the provision of advisory services, the information set out in paragraph 13(4)(a) and (b); and
(e)   information on the typical rental levels and rental demands within the property's locality and the impact of future interest rate rises, rental voids, rental arrears and typical letting costs.

(3)   The manner in which creditors remunerate their staff and credit intermediaries and the manner in which credit intermediaries remunerate their staff must not impede compliance with the obligation set out in sub-paragraph (1).

(4)   When establishing and applying remuneration policies for their staff responsible for the assessment of creditworthiness, creditors must comply with the following principles in a way and to the extent that is appropriate to their size, internal organisation and the nature, scope and complexity of their activities—
(a)   the remuneration policy must be consistent with and promote sound and effective risk management and must not encourage risk-taking that exceeds the level of tolerated risk of the creditor;
(b)   the remuneration policy must be in line with the business strategy, objectives, values and long-term interests of the creditor, and must incorporate measures to avoid conflicts of interest, in particular by providing that remuneration is not contingent on the number or proportion of applications accepted.

(5)   Where a creditor or credit intermediary provides advisory services, the remuneration structure of the staff involved must not prejudice their ability to act in the consumer's best interest and in particular must not be contingent on sales targets.

2   Obligation to provide information free of charge to consumers

Any information provided to consumers in compliance with the requirements set out in this Schedule must be provided free of charge.

3   Knowledge and competence requirements for staff

(1)   Creditors and credit intermediaries must require their staff to possess and keep up-to-date an appropriate level of knowledge and competence in relation to—
(a)   the manufacturing, offering or granting of consumer buy-to-let mortgage contracts,
(b)   acting as a credit intermediary in relation to consumer buy-to-let mortgage contracts, or
(c)   the provision of advisory services in respect of consumer buy-to-let mortgage contracts.

(2)   The appropriate level of knowledge and competence referred to in sub-paragraph (1) must include at least—
(a)   appropriate knowledge of consumer buy-to-let mortgage contracts and the ancillary services typically offered with them;
(b)   appropriate knowledge of the laws relating to consumer buy-to-let mortgage contracts, in particular consumer protection;
(c)   appropriate knowledge and understanding of the process for purchasing land;
(d)   appropriate knowledge of security valuation;
(e)   appropriate knowledge of the organisation and functioning of land registers;
(f)   appropriate knowledge of the market in the United Kingdom for consumer buy-to-let mortgage business;
(g)   appropriate knowledge of business ethics standards;
(h)   appropriate knowledge of the consumer creditworthiness assessment process or, where applicable, competence in assessing consumers' creditworthiness; and
(i)   an appropriate level of financial and economic competency.

Information and practices preliminary to the conclusion of the consumer buy-to-let mortgage contract

4   Tying and bundling practices

(1)   Except in the circumstances described in sub-paragraphs (2) to (4), a creditor must not offer or sell a consumer buy-to-let mortgage contract in a package with other distinct financial products or services where that mortgage contract is not made available to the borrower separately.

(2)   A creditor may request the borrower or a related person to—
- (a)   open or maintain a payment or savings account where the only purpose of such an account is to accumulate capital to repay the credit, to service the credit, to pool resources to obtain the credit, or to provide additional security for the creditor in the event of default;
- (b)   purchase or keep an investment product or a private pension product, where such product which primarily offers the investor an income in retirement serves also to provide additional security for the creditor in the event of default or to accumulate capital to repay the credit, to service the credit or to pool resources to obtain the credit; or
- (c)   conclude a separate credit agreement in conjunction with a shared-equity credit agreement to obtain the credit.

(3)   Notwithstanding sub-paragraph (1), a creditor may offer or sell a consumer buy-to-let mortgage contract where the creditor can demonstrate to the FCA that the tied products or categories of product offered, on terms and conditions similar to each other, which are not made available separately, result in a clear benefit to a borrower taking due account of the availability and the prices of the relevant products offered on the market.

(4)   A creditor may require the borrower to hold an insurance policy related to the consumer buy-to-let mortgage contract, provided that the creditor must accept an insurance policy from a supplier different to the creditor's preferred supplier where the policy has a level of guarantee equivalent to the level of guarantee in the insurance policy proposed by the creditor.

5   General information

(1)   A creditor must make available clear and comprehensible general information about consumer buy-to-let mortgage contracts at all times on paper or on another durable medium or in electronic form.

(2)   The general information referred to in sub-paragraph (1) must include at least the following—
- (a)   the name and address of the creditor;
- (b)   the purposes for which the credit provided under the consumer buy-to-let mortgage contract may be used;
- (c)   the form of any security, including, where applicable, the possibility for it to be located in another EEA State;
- (d)   the possible duration of the consumer buy-to-let mortgage contract;
- (e)   the types of available borrowing rate, indicating whether fixed or variable or both, with a short description of the characteristics of a fixed and variable rate, including related implications for the borrower;
- (f)   where foreign currency loans are available, an indication of the foreign currency or currencies, including an explanation of the implications for the borrower where the consumer buy-to-let mortgage contract is denominated in a foreign currency;
- (g)   a representative example of the total amount of credit, the total cost of the credit to the borrower, the total amount payable by the borrower and the annual percentage rate of charge;
- (h)   an indication of possible further costs not included in the total cost of the credit to the borrower, to be paid in connection with a consumer buy-to-let mortgage contract;
- (i)   the range of different options available for reimbursing the credit to the creditor, including te number, frequency and amount of the regular repayment instalments;
- (j)   where applicable, a clear and concise statement that compliance with the terms and conditions of the consumer buy-to-let mortgage contract does not guarantee repayment of the total amount of credit under that contract;
- (k)   a description of the conditions directly relating to early repayment;
- (l)   whether a valuation of the property is necessary and, where applicable, who is responsible for ensuring that the valuation is carried out, and whether any related costs arise for the borrower;
- (m)   an indication of any ancillary services the borrower is obliged to acquire in order to obtain the consumer buy-to-let mortgage contract or to obtain it on the terms and conditions marketed and, where applicable, a clarification that the ancillary services may be purchased from a provider that is not the creditor; and
- (n)   a general warning concerning possible consequences of non-compliance with the commitments linked to the consumer buy-to-let mortgage contract.

6   Pre-contractual information

(1)   A creditor and, where applicable, a credit intermediary must provide a borrower with a lending illustration on paper or another durable medium—

(a)   without undue delay after the borrower has given the necessary information on the borrower's needs, financial situation and preferences in accordance with paragraph 12; and

(b)   in good time before the borrower is bound by any credit agreement or offer.

(2)   The lending illustration must include at least the following—

(a)   the name of the borrower;

(b)   the date of issue of the lending illustration;

(c)   the date until which the lending illustration remains valid;

(d)   the name, address and telephone number of the creditor;

(e)   where applicable, the name, address and telephone number of the credit intermediary;

(f)   the amount of the loan required, including any charges added to the amount of the loan;

(g)   the value of any property against which the loan is to be secured;

(h)   the term of the consumer buy-to-let mortgage contract;

(i)   a description of whether the consumer buy-to-let mortgage contract is to be provided on an interest-only basis, a repayment basis or a combination of the two;

(j)   the type of interest rate payable;

(k)   the interest rate payable including, if applicable, the initial interest rate and any reversionary rate;

(l)   the frequency and amount of each instalment and the number of instalments;

(m)   the overall cost of the consumer buy-to-let mortgage contract;

(n)   the annual percentage rate of charge;

(o)   where the credit agreement allows for variations in the interest rate, either—

      (i)   an illustration of how the annual percentage rate of charge might change in the event of an increase in the interest rate of 1%, and the resulting increase in the amount of each instalment; or

      (ii)   an additional annual percentage rate of charge which illustrates the possible risks for the borrower linked to a significant increase in the interest rate, including the possible increase in the amount of each instalment;

(p)   details of any early repayment charges;

(q)   a warning of the risk that interest rates may rise;

(r)   a warning of the risk that rental income may fall;

(s)   where applicable, a warning of the risk that the property may be repossessed if the borrower does not keep up with mortgage repayments;

(t)   where applicable, a warning of the risk of foreign currency loans; and

(u)   where it is an interest-only loan, a warning that the borrower will still owe the loan amount at the end of the term.

(3)   The creditor or, where applicable, the credit intermediary, must provide the borrower with a copy of the draft consumer buy-to-let mortgage contract at the time of the provision of an offer.

(4)   In this paragraph "lending illustration" means the personalised information needed by the borrower to compare the products available on the market, assess their implications and make an informed decision on whether to conclude a consumer buy-to-let mortgage contract.

7   Information requirements concerning credit intermediaries

(1)   In good time before the carrying on of any of the credit intermediation activities described in article 5(2) to (4), a credit intermediary must provide the borrower with at least the following information on paper or another durable medium—

(a)   the name and address of the credit intermediary;

(b)   details of the register, the credit intermediary's registration number, where applicable, and the means for verifying such registration;

(c)   whether the credit intermediary is tied to or works exclusively for one or more creditors;

(d)   if the credit intermediary is tied to or works exclusively for one or more creditors, the names of the creditors for which the credit intermediary is acting;

(e)   if the credit intermediary meets the criteria set out in paragraph 13(5), a statement that the credit intermediary is independent;

(f)   whether the credit intermediary offers advisory services;

(g)   the fee, where applicable, payable by the borrower to the credit intermediary for its services or, where this is not possible, the method for calculating the fee;

(h)   the procedures allowing borrowers or other interested parties to register complaints internally about credit intermediaries and, where appropriate, the means by which recourse to out-of-court complaint and redress procedures can be sought;

(i)   where applicable, the existence of commissions or other inducements payable by the creditor or third parties to the credit intermediary for their services in relation to the contract; and

(j)   either the amount of such commissions or other inducements or, where the amount is not known at the time of disclosure, a statement that the credit intermediary shall inform the borrower of the actual amount as part of the lending illustration referred to in paragraph 6.

(2)   Where the credit intermediary charges a fee to the borrower and additionally receives commission from the creditor or a third party, the credit intermediary must explain to the borrower whether or not the commission will be offset against the fee, either in part or in full.

(3)   The credit intermediary must inform the creditor of the fee, if any, payable by the borrower to the credit intermediary for its services.

8   Adequate explanations

(1)   Creditors and, where applicable, credit intermediaries, must provide an adequate explanation to the borrower on a proposed consumer buy-to-let mortgage contract and any ancillary services, in order to place the borrower in a position enabling the borrower to assess whether the proposed agreement and ancillary services are adapted to the borrower's needs and financial situation.

(2)   The adequate explanation must, where applicable, include—

  (a)   in the case of creditors, the information described in paragraph 6(2);

  (b)   in the case of credit intermediaries, the information described in paragraphs 6(2) and 7(1); and

  (c)   in all cases—

    (i)   the essential characteristics of the consumer buy-to-let mortgage contract proposed;

    (ii)   the specific effect the contract proposed may have on the borrower, including the consequences of default in payment by the borrower; and

    (iii)   where ancillary services are bundled with a consumer buy-to-let mortgage contract, whether each component of the bundle can be terminated separately and the implications for the borrower of doing so.

Annual percentage rate of charge

9   Calculation of the annual percentage rate of charge

(1)   The annual percentage rate of charge must be calculated in accordance with the mathematical formula set out in paragraph 20.

(2)   The costs of opening and maintaining a specific account, the costs of using a means of payment for both transactions and drawdowns on that account and other costs relating to payment transactions shall be included in the total cost of credit to the borrower whenever the opening or maintaining of an account is obligatory in order to obtain the credit or to obtain it on the terms and conditions marketed.

(3)   The calculation of the annual percentage rate of charge must be based on the assumption that the consumer buy-to-let mortgage contract is to remain valid for the period agreed and that the creditor and the borrower will fulfil their obligations under the terms and by the dates specified in that contract.

(4)   If the consumer buy-to-let mortgage contract allows variations in the borrowing rate and, where applicable, in the charges contained in the annual percentage rate of charge but unquantifiable at the time of calculation, the annual percentage rate of charge must be calculated on the assumption that the borrowing rate and other charges will remain fixed in relation to the level set at the conclusion of the contract.

(5)   Where applicable, the additional assumptions set out in paragraph 21 must be used in calculating the annual percentage rate of charge.

(6)   In this paragraph—

  "annual percentage rate of charge" means the total cost of the credit to the borrower, expressed as an annual percentage of the total amount of credit, where applicable, including the costs referred to in sub-paragraph (2) and equates, on an annual basis, to the present value of all future or existing commitments (drawdowns, repayments and charges) agreed by the creditor and the borrower;

  "total amount of credit" means the ceiling or total sums made available under the consumer buy-to-let mortgage contract;

  "total cost of credit to the borrower" means all the costs which the borrower is required to pay in connection with the credit agreement and which are known to the creditor, including the costs referred to in sub-paragraph (7) but excluding the costs referred to in sub-paragraph (8).

(7)   The costs referred to in this sub-paragraph are—

  (a)   interest;

  (b)   commissions;

  (c)   taxes;

  (d)   any other kind of fees;

  (e)   the cost of valuation of property where such valuation is necessary to obtain the consumer buy-to-let mortgage contract; and

  (f)   costs in respect of ancillary services, in particular insurance premiums, where the purchase of those ancillary services is compulsory in order to obtain the consumer buy-to-let mortgage contract or to obtain it on the terms and conditions marketed.

(8)   The costs referred to in this sub-paragraph are—

  (a)   notarial costs;

  (b)   registration fees for the transfer of ownership of the property; and

  (c)   any charges payable by the borrower for non-compliance with the commitments laid down in the consumer buy-to-let mortgage contract.

Creditworthiness assessment

10 Obligation to assess the creditworthiness of the borrower

(1) Before concluding a consumer buy-to-let mortgage contract, the creditor must make a thorough assessment of the borrower's creditworthiness, taking appropriate account of factors relevant to verifying the prospect of the borrower meeting the borrower's obligations under that contract.

(2) The creditor must establish, document and maintain procedures on which it bases a creditworthiness assessment in relation to a consumer buy-to-let mortgage contract.

(3) The assessment of creditworthiness must not rely predominantly on the value of the property exceeding the amount of the credit or on the assumption that the property will increase in value unless the purpose of the consumer buy-to-let mortgage contract is to construct or renovate the property.

(4) Where a creditor concludes a consumer buy-to-let mortgage contract with a borrower the creditor must not subsequently cancel or alter the contract to the detriment of the borrower on the grounds that the assessment of creditworthiness was incorrectly conducted, unless the borrower knowingly withheld or falsified information as described in paragraph 12.

(5) The creditor must only enter into the consumer buy-to-let mortgage contract with the borrower where the result of the creditworthiness assessment indicates that the borrower is likely to meet the obligations resulting from that contract in the manner required under that contract.

(6) Where the application is rejected, the creditor must inform the borrower without delay of the rejection and, where applicable, that the decision is based on automated processing of data.

(7) Where the creditor consults a database as part of the creditworthiness assessment, the creditor must—
   (a) inform the borrower in advance that a database is to be consulted; and
   (b) where the application is rejected, and the rejection is based on the result of the database consultation, inform the borrower of the result of such consultation and of the particulars of the database consulted.

(8) Before granting any significant increase in the total sums made available under the consumer buy-to-let mortgage contract after the conclusion of that contract, the creditor must re-assess the borrower's creditworthiness on the basis of updated information, unless such an increase was envisaged and included in the original creditworthiness assessment.

11 Property valuation

A creditor must use reliable standards when carrying out a property valuation or take reasonable steps to ensure that reliable standards are applied where a valuation is conducted by a third party.

12 Disclosure and verification of borrower information

(1) A creditor must carry out the assessment of creditworthiness referred to in paragraph 10 on the basis of information which is necessary, sufficient and proportionate, including—
   (a) any values provided to the creditor as part of its assessment of the property;
   (b) typical rental levels and rental demands within the property's locality;
   (c) the impact of future interest rate rises, rental voids and rental arrears and the ability of the borrower to meet payments should such pressures arise; and
   (d) typical letting costs.

(2) The information referred to in sub-paragraph (1) may include information obtained by the creditor from relevant internal or external sources, including one or more of the following—
   (a) the borrower;
   (b) any credit intermediary or appointed representative which obtained information during the credit application process; and
   (c) a calculation developed by the creditor to demonstrate that the estimated rental income from the property will exceed the interest payments due by an amount sufficient to cover the estimated other costs associated with the property and its rental.

(3) The information referred to in sub-paragraph (1) must be appropriately verified through reference to independently verifiable documentation when necessary.

(4) A credit intermediary must accurately submit the necessary information obtained from the borrower to the creditor to enable the creditworthiness assessment to be carried out.

(5) A creditor must specify in a clear and straightforward way at the pre-contractual phase the necessary information and independently verifiable evidence that the borrower needs to provide and the timeframe within which the borrower needs to provide the information.

(6) A request for information referred to in sub-paragraph (5) must be proportionate and limited to what is necessary to conduct a proper creditworthiness assessment.

(7) A creditor may seek clarification of the information received in response to a request for information referred to in sub-paragraph (5) where necessary to enable the assessment of creditworthiness.

(8) A creditor must not terminate a consumer buy-to-let mortgage contract on the grounds that the information provided by the borrower before the conclusion of the contract was incomplete, unless the borrower knowingly withheld or falsified the information.

(9) The creditor or credit intermediary must inform the borrower of the need to provide correct and complete information in response to a request referred to in sub-paragraph (5) and must warn the borrower that, where the creditor is unable to carry out an assessment of creditworthiness because the borrower chooses not to provide the information or verification necessary for an assessment of creditworthiness, the credit cannot be granted.

Advisory services

13 Standards for advisory services

(1) A creditor or credit intermediary must explicitly inform the borrower, in the context of a given transaction, whether advisory services are being or can be provided to the borrower.

(2) Before the provision of advisory services or, where applicable, the conclusion of a contract for the provision of advisory services, the creditor or credit intermediary must provide the borrower with the following information on paper or another durable medium—

(a) whether the recommendation will be based on a consideration of only the creditor's or the credit intermediary's own product range or a consideration of a wide range of products from across the market; and

(b) where applicable, the fee payable by the borrower for the advisory services or, where the amount cannot be ascertained at the time of disclosure, the method used for its calculation.

(3) The information referred to in sub-paragraph (2) may be provided to the borrower as part of the lending illustration under paragraph 6.

(4) Where a creditor or credit intermediary provides advisory services to a borrower, the creditor or credit intermediary must—

(a) obtain the necessary information regarding the borrower's personal and financial situation, preferences and objectives so as to enable the recommendation of suitable consumer buy-to-let mortgage contracts;

(b) base its recommendation on information that is up-to-date and takes into account reasonable assumptions as to risks to the borrower's situation over the term of the proposed agreement, including information on the typical rental levels and rental demands within the property's locality, the impact of future interest rate rises, rental voids, and rental arrears and typical letting costs;

(c) act in the best interests of the borrower by—

(i) informing itself about the borrower's needs and circumstances; and

(ii) recommending suitable mortgages in accordance with paragraphs (a) and (b); and

(d) give the borrower a record on paper or another durable medium of the recommendation provided.

(5) A creditor or credit intermediary must not use the term "independent advice" or "independent advisor" in the course of providing advisory services unless—

(a) the creditor or credit intermediary considers a sufficiently large number of credit agreements available on the market; and

(b) if the number of creditors considered is less than a majority of the market, the creditor or credit intermediary is not remunerated for those advisory services by one or more creditors.

Foreign currency loans and variable rate loans

14 Foreign currency loans

(1) Where a borrower enters into a buy-to-let mortgage contract that is a foreign currency loan—

(a) the borrower must have a right to convert the contract into an alternative currency if conditions specified by the creditor are met;

(b) the creditor must put in place arrangements to limit the exchange rate risk to which the borrower is exposed under the contract; and

(c) if sub-paragraph (4) applies, the creditor must give the borrower, on a regular basis, foreign currency risk warnings.

(2) The creditor may specify the alternative currency referred to in sub-paragraph (1)(a), but it must be either—

(a) the currency in which the borrower primarily receives income or holds assets from which the credit is to be repaid, as indicated at the time the most recent creditworthiness assessment in relation to the contract was made; or

(b) the currency of the EEA State in which the borrower either was resident at the time the contract was concluded or is currently resident.

(3) Where a borrower has a right to convert the contract into an alternative currency in accordance with sub-paragraph (1)(a), the exchange rate at which the conversion is carried out must be the market exchange rate applicable on the day of application for conversion, unless otherwise specified in the contract.

(4) This sub-paragraph applies if the value of—

(a)   the total amount payable by the borrower which remains outstanding; or

(b)   the regular instalments,

varies by more than 20% from what it would be if the exchange rate between the currency of the contract and sterling applicable at the time of the conclusion of the contract were applied.

(5)   In this paragraph "foreign currency risk warning" means a warning, on paper or on another durable medium—

(a)   informing the borrower of a rise in the total amount payable by the borrower;

(b)   setting out, where applicable, the borrower's right to convert to an alternative currency and the conditions for doing so; and

(c)   explaining any other applicable mechanism for limiting the exchange rate risk to which the borrower is exposed.

15   Variable rate credits

Where the contract provides for variable rate credit, the creditor must—

(a)   make any indexes or reference rates used to calculate the borrowing rate clear, accessible, objective and verifiable by the borrower and the FCA; and

(b)   maintain historical records of indexes used by the creditor for calculating the borrowing rates.

Sound execution of consumer buy-to-let mortgage contracts and related rights

16   Early repayment

(1)   Subject to sub-paragraph (3), the creditor must allow the borrower to discharge fully or partially the borrower's obligations under the consumer buy-to-let mortgage contract prior to the expiry of that contract.

(2)   Where the borrower discharges, fully or partially, the borrower's obligations prior to the expiry of the contract, the creditor must provide the borrower with a reduction in the total cost of credit to the borrower, consisting of the interest and costs for the remaining duration of the contract.

(3)   The creditor may provide that the exercise of the right referred to in sub-paragraph (1) is subject to one or more of the following conditions—

(a)   time limitations on the exercise of the right;

(b)   different treatment depending on the type of borrowing rate or on the moment the borrower exercises the right;

(c)   restrictions with regard to the circumstances in which the right may be exercised; or

(d)   if the exercise of the right falls within a period for which the borrowing rate is fixed, the existence of a legitimate interest on the part of the borrower.

(4)   The creditor is entitled to fair and objective compensation, where justified, for possible costs directly linked to the early repayment but the creditor must not impose a sanction on the borrower and the amount of compensation must not exceed the financial loss of the creditor.

(5)   Where a borrower seeks to exercise the right referred to in sub-paragraph (1), the creditor must provide the borrower without delay after receipt of the borrower's request, on paper or on another durable medium, with the information necessary to consider whether to proceed with the exercise of the right.

(6)   The information referred to in sub-paragraph (5) must include—

(a)   a quantification of the implications for the borrower of exercising the right; and

(b)   any assumptions used by the creditor in making that quantification.

(7)   The assumptions referred to in sub-paragraph (6)(b) must be reasonable and justifiable.

17   Flexible and reliable markets

The creditor must keep appropriate records concerning, where applicable, the types of property accepted by the creditor as security and the related mortgage underwriting policies used by the creditor in relation to its consumer buy-to-let mortgage business.

18   Information concerning changes in the borrowing rate

(1)   Unless sub-paragraph (3) applies, the creditor must inform the borrower of any change in the borrowing rate, on paper or another durable medium, before the change takes effect.

(2)   The information referred to in sub-paragraph (1) must include—

(a)   a statement of the amount of the payments to be made after the new borrowing rate takes effect; and

(b)   in cases where the number or frequency of the payments changes, particulars of those changes.

(3)   This sub-paragraph applies if—

(a)   the change in the borrowing rate is correlated with a change in a reference rate;

(b)   the new reference rate is made publicly available by appropriate means;

(c)   the creditor agrees with the borrower in the contract that information about any change in borrowing rate may be given to the borrower periodically; and

(d)   the information concerning the new reference rate is kept available in the premises of the creditor and communicated personally to the borrower together with the amount of new periodic instalments.

19   Arrears and possession

(1)   A creditor must exercise reasonable forbearance before initiating possession proceedings.

(2)   Any charges that the creditor imposes on the borrower arising from the borrower's default must be no greater than is necessary to compensate the creditor for costs incurred by the creditor as a result of the default.

(3)   Where the price obtained for the secured property affects the amount owed by the borrower under the contract, the creditor must take all reasonable steps to obtain the best possible price for the secured property.

(4)   Where, after possession proceedings, outstanding debt remains, the creditor must put in place measures to facilitate repayment by the borrower.

Calculation of the annual percentage rate of charge

20   Basic equation expressing the equivalence of drawdowns on the one hand and repayments and charges on the other

(1)   The basic equation, which establishes the annual percentage rate of charge, equates, on an annual basis, the total present value of drawdowns on the one hand and the total present value of repayments and payments of charges on the other hand, expressed by means of the following formula—

$$\sum_{k=1}^{m} C_k(1+X)^{-t_k} = \sum_{l=1}^{m'} D_l(1+X)^{-s_l}$$

where—

    X is the annual percentage rate of charge;

    m is the number of the last drawdown;

    k is the number of a drawdown thus,

$$1 \le k \ge m;$$

    C_k is the amount of drawdown k;

    t_k is the interval between the date of the first drawdown and the date of each subsequent drawdown, thus $t_1=0$;

    m' is the number of the last repayment or payment of charges;

    l is the number of a repayment or payment of charges;

    D_l is the amount of a repayment or payment of charges; and

    s_1 is the interval, expressed in years and fractions of a year, between the date of the first drawdown and the date of each repayment or payment of charges.

(2)   The following remarks apply to the equation set out in sub-paragraph (1)—

    (a)   the amounts paid by both parties at different times shall not necessarily be equal and shall not necessarily be paid at equal intervals;

    (b)   the starting date must be that of the first drawdown;

    (c)   intervals between dates used in the calculation must be expressed in years or in fractions of a year, where—

       (i)   a year is presumed to have 365 days (or 366 days for leap years), 52 weeks or 12 equal months; and

       (ii)   an equal month is presumed to have 30.41666 days regardless of whether or not it is a leap year;

    (d)   where intervals between dates used in the calculations cannot be expressed as a whole number of weeks, months or years, the intervals must be expressed as a whole number of one of those periods in combination with a number of days;

    (e)   for the purposes of paragraph (d), where using days—

       (i)   every day must be counted, including weekends and holidays;

       (ii)   equal periods and then days must be counted backwards to the date of the initial drawdown; and

       (iii)   the length of the period of days must be—

          (aa)   obtained excluding the first day and including the last day; and

          (bb)   expressed in years by dividing this period by the number of days (365 or 366 days) of the complete year counted backwards from the last day to the same day of the previous year;

    (f)   the result of the calculation must be expressed with an accuracy of at least one decimal place and if the figure at the following decimal place is greater than or equal to 5, the figure at the preceding decimal place must be increased by one;

(g)   the equation may be rewritten using a single sum and the concept of flows (A_k), which will be positive or negative, in other words either paid or received during periods 1 to n, expressed in years, using the following formula—

$$s = \sum_{k=1}^{n} A_k(1+X)^{-t_k}$$

where s is the present balance of flows;

(h)   for the purposes of paragraph (g), if the aim is to maintain the equivalence of flows, the value of s will be zero.

21   Additional assumptions for the calculation of the annual percentage rate of charge

(1)   The following additional assumptions apply for the purposes of calculating the annual percentage rate of charge.

(2)   If a consumer buy-to-let mortgage contract gives the borrower freedom of drawdown, the total amount of credit must be deemed to be drawn down immediately and in full.

(3)   If a consumer buy-to-let mortgage contract provides different ways of drawdown with different charges or borrowing rates, the total amount of credit must be deemed to be drawn down at the highest charge and borrowing rate applied to the most common drawdown mechanism for this type of contract.

(4)   If a consumer buy-to-let mortgage contract gives the borrower freedom of drawdown in general but imposes, amongst the different ways of drawdown, a limitation with regard to the amount of credit and period of time, the amount of credit must be deemed to be drawn down on the earliest date provided for in the contract and in accordance with those drawdown limits.

(5)   If different borrowing rates and charges are offered for a limited period or amount, the highest borrowing rate and charges must be deemed to be the borrowing rate and charges for the whole duration of the contract.

(6)   For consumer buy-to-let mortgage contracts for which a fixed rate borrowing rate is agreed in relation to the initial period, at the end of which a new borrowing rate is determined and subsequently periodically adjusted according to an agreed indicator or internal reference rate the calculation of the annual percentage rate of charge must be based on the assumption that, at the end of the fixed borrowing rate period, the borrowing rate is the same as at the time of calculation of the annual percentage rate of charge, based on the value of the agreed indicator or internal reference rate at that time, but is not less than the fixed borrowing rate.

(7)   If the ceiling applicable to the credit has not yet been agreed, that ceiling is assumed to be—

(a)   in the case of credit agreements, other than contingent liabilities or guarantees, the purpose of which is not to acquire or retain a right in immovable property or land, overdrafts, deferred debit cards or credit cards, EUR 1,500; and

(b)   in all other cases, EUR 170,000.

(8)   In the case of credit agreements other than overdrafts, bridging loans, shared equity credit agreements, contingent liabilities or guarantees and open-ended credit agreements as referred to in the assumptions set out in sub-paragraphs (10), (11), (12), (16) and (17)—

(a)   if the date or amount of a repayment of capital to be made by the borrower cannot be ascertained, it must be assumed that the repayment is made at the earliest date provided for in the credit agreement and is for the lowest amount for which the credit agreement provides; and

(b)   if the interval between the date of initial drawdown and the date of the first payment to be made by the borrower cannot be ascertained, it must be assumed to be the shortest interval.

(9)   Where the date or amount of a payment to be made by the borrower cannot be ascertained on the basis of the credit agreement or the assumptions set out in sub-paragraphs (8), (10), (11), (12), (16) and (17) it must be assumed that the payment is made in accordance with the dates and conditions required by the creditor and, when these are unknown—

(a)   interest charges are paid together with the repayment of the capital;

(b)   non-interest charges expressed as a single sum are paid at the date of the conclusion of the credit agreement;

(c)   non-interest charges expressed as several payments are paid at regular intervals, commencing with the date of the first repayment of capital, and if the amount of such payments is not known they shall be assumed to be equal amounts; and

(d)   the final payment clears the balance of capital, interest and other charges, if any.

(10)   In the case of an overdraft facility, the total amount of credit must be deemed to be drawn down in full and for the whole duration of the credit agreement and, if the duration of the overdraft facility is not known, the annual percentage rate of charge must be calculated on the assumption that the duration of the credit is three months.

(11)   In the case of a bridging loan, the total amount of credit must be deemed to be drawn down in full and for the whole duration of the credit agreement and, if the duration of the credit agreement is not known, the annual percentage rate of charge must be calculated on the assumption that the duration of the credit is 12 months.

(12)   In the case of an open-ended credit agreement, other than an overdraft facility and bridging loan, it must be assumed that—

(a)   for credit agreements the purpose of which is to acquire or retain rights in immovable property, the credit is provided for a period of 20 years starting from the date of the initial drawdown, and the final payment made by the borrower clears the balance of capital, interest and other charges, if any;

(b)   for credit agreements the purpose of which is not to acquire or retain rights in immovable property or which are drawn down by deferred debit cards or credit cards, the credit is provided for a period of 1 year starting from the date of the initial drawdown;

(c)   unless sub-paragraph (13) applies, the capital is repaid by the borrower in equal monthly payments, commencing one month after the date of the initial drawdown.

(13)   This sub-paragraph applies in cases where the capital must be repaid only in full, in a single payment, within each payment period.

(14)   If sub-paragraph (13) applies—

(a)   successive drawdowns and repayments of the entire capital by the borrower must be assumed to occur over the period of one year; and

(b)   interest and other charges must be applied in accordance with those drawdowns and repayments of capital and as provided for in the credit agreement.

(15)   For the purposes of sub-paragraph (12), an open-ended credit agreement is a credit agreement without fixed duration and includes credits which must be repaid in full within or after a period but, once repaid, become available to be drawn down again.

(16)   In the case of contingent liabilities or guarantees, the total amount of credit must be deemed to be drawn down in full as a single amount at the earlier of—

(a)   the latest draw down date permitted under the credit agreement being the potential source of the contingent liability or guarantee; or

(b)   in the case of a rolling credit agreement at the end of the initial period prior to the rollover of the agreement.

(17)   In the case of a shared equity credit agreement—

(a)   the payments by borrowers must be deemed to occur at the latest date or dates permitted under the credit agreement; and

(b)   percentage increases in value of the immovable property which secures the shared equity credit agreement, and the rate of any inflation index referred to in the agreement, shall be assumed to be a percentage equal to the higher of the current central bank target inflation rate or the level of inflation rate in the EEA State where the property is located at the time of conclusion of the credit agreement or 0% if those percentages are negative.

NOTES

Commencement: 20 April 2015 (certain purposes); 21 December 2015 (certain purposes); 21 March 2016 (otherwise) (see art 1 above).

CONSUMER RIGHTS ACT 2015 (COMMENCEMENT) (ENGLAND) ORDER 2015

(SI 2015/965)

NOTES

Made: 26 March 2015.
Authority: Consumer Rights Act 2015, s 100(3)(a), (5), (6).

[2.1202]
1   Citation and application

(1)   This Order may be cited as the Consumer Rights Act 2015 (Commencement) (England) Order 2015.

(2)   This Order applies in relation to England only.

[2.1203]
2   Provisions coming into force on 27th May 2015

The following provisions of the Consumer Rights Act 2015 come into force on 27th May 2015—

(a)   Chapter 3 of Part 3, insofar as it is not already in force;

(b)   section 77 and Schedule 5 insofar as they relate to Chapter 3 of Part 3; and

(c)   Schedule 9.

Part 2   Statutory Instruments

CONSUMER RIGHTS ACT 2015 (COMMENCEMENT NO 1) ORDER 2015

(SI 2015/1333)

NOTES

Made: 21 May 2015.

Authority: Consumer Rights Act 2015, s 100(5).

[2.1204]

1 Citation

This Order may be cited as the Consumer Rights Act 2015 (Commencement No 1) Order 2015.

[2.1205]

2 Provisions coming into force on 27th May 2015

The following provisions of the Consumer Rights Act 2015 come into force on 27th May 2015—

(a) section 77 and Schedule 5 insofar as they relate to Chapter 5 of Part 3 and to the extent that they are not already in force; and

(b) section 82.

CONSUMER RIGHTS ACT 2015 (COMMENCEMENT NO 2 AND TRANSITIONAL PROVISION) (ENGLAND) ORDER 2015

(SI 2015/1575)

NOTES

Made: 22 July 2015.

Authority: Consumer Rights Act 2015, ss 97(1),100(3)(a).

[2.1206]

1 Citation, application and interpretation

(1) This Order may be cited as the Consumer Rights Act 2015 (Commencement No 2 and Transitional Provision) (England) Order 2015.

(2) This Order applies in relation to England only.

(3) In this Order "the Act" means the Consumer Rights Act 2015.

[2.1207]

2 Provisions coming into force on 1st September 2015

Chapter 4 of Part 3 of the Act comes into force on 1st September 2015.

[2.1208]

3 Transitional provision

(1) A qualifying complaint about an act or omission of a qualifying institution falling within section 11(e) or (f) of the Higher Education Act 2004 can only be reviewed by the designated operator where the act or omission complained of—

(a) occurs on or after 1st September 2015; or

(b) begins before that date but continues on or after it.

(2) In this article the terms "qualifying complaint", "qualifying institution" and "designated operator" bear the same meanings as they bear in Part 2 of the Higher Education Act 2004.

CONSUMER RIGHTS ACT 2015 (COMMENCEMENT NO 2) ORDER 2015

(SI 2015/1584)

NOTES

Made: 2 August 2015.

Authority: Consumer Rights Act 2015, s 100(5), (6).

[2.1209]

1 Citation and interpretation

This Order may be cited as the Consumer Rights Act 2015 (Commencement No 2) Order 2015.

[2.1210]
2

In this Order, "the Act" means the Consumer Rights Act 2015.

[2.1211]
3　Provisions coming into force on 3rd August 2015

Section 81 (private actions in competition law) of the Act comes into force on 3rd August 2015, so far as it relates to the following provisions of Schedule 8 to the Act, for the purposes of making regulations or guidance—

  (a)　paragraph 12;
  (b)　paragraph 18;
  (c)　paragraphs 20 to 22; and
  (d)　paragraphs 28 to 35.

CONSUMER RIGHTS ACT 2015 (COMMENCEMENT NO 1 AND TRANSITIONAL PROVISION) (WALES) ORDER 2015

(SI 2015/1605)

NOTES
Made: 10 August 2015.
Authority: Consumer Rights Act 2015, ss 97(2), 100(3)(b).

[2.1212]
1　Title, application and interpretation

(1)　The title of this Order is the Consumer Rights Act 2015 (Commencement No 1 and Transitional Provision) (Wales) Order 2015.

(2)　This Order applies in relation to Wales only.

(3)　In this Order, "the Act" ("*y Ddeddf*") means the Consumer Rights Act 2015.

[2.1213]
2　Provisions coming into force on 1 September 2015

Section 89 of the Act comes into force on the 1 September 2015.

[2.1214]
3　Transitional arrangements

(1)　A qualifying complaint about an act or omission of a qualifying institution falling within section 11(e) or (f) of the Higher Education Act 2004 can only be reviewed by the designated operator where the act or omission complained of—

  (a)　occurs on or after 1 September 2015; or
  (b)　occurs before that date but continues on or after it.

(2)　In this article the terms "qualifying complaint" ("*cwyn gymhwysol*"), "qualifying institution" ("*sefydliad cymhwysol*") and "designated operator" ("*gweithredwr dynodedig*") bear the same meanings as they bear in Part 2 of the Higher Education Act 2004.

CONSUMER RIGHTS ACT 2015 (COMMENCEMENT NO 3, TRANSITIONAL PROVISIONS, SAVINGS AND CONSEQUENTIAL AMENDMENTS) ORDER 2015

(SI 2015/1630)

NOTES
Made: 27 August 2015.
Authority: Consumer Rights Act 2015, ss 96(1), (2), 97(1), 100(5), (6).
Commencement: 1 October 2015.

ARRANGEMENT OF ARTICLES

8   Transitional and saving provisions in respect of investigatory powers. . . . .[2.1222]

[2.1215]
1   Citation and commencement

This Order may be cited as the Consumer Rights Act 2015 (Commencement No 3, Transitional Provisions, Savings and Consequential Amendments) Order 2015 and comes into force on 1st October 2015.

NOTES

Commencement: 1 October 2015.

[2.1216]
2   Interpretation

In this Order—

"the 2004 Regulation" means Regulation (EC) No 261/2004 of the European Parliament and of the Council establishing common rules on compensation and assistance to passengers in the event of denied boarding and of cancellation or long delay of flights, and repealing Regulation (EEC) No 295/91;

"the 2010 Regulation" means Regulation (EU) No 1177/2010 of the European Parliament and of the Council concerning the rights of passengers when travelling by sea and inland waterway and amending Regulation (EC) No 2006/2004;

"the Act" means the Consumer Rights Act 2015;

"the Carriage by Air Conventions" are—

    (a)   the Warsaw Convention;

    (b)   the Warsaw Convention, as amended at the Hague, 1955;

    (c)   the Warsaw Convention, as amended by Additional Protocol No 1 of Montreal, 1975;

    (d)   the Warsaw Convention, as amended at the Hague, 1955, and by Additional Protocol No 2 of Montreal, 1975;

    (e)   the Warsaw Convention, as amended at the Hague, 1955, and by Protocol No 4 of Montreal, 1975;

    (f)   the Convention supplementary to the Warsaw Convention, for the Unification of Certain Rules Relating to International Carriage by Air Performed by a Person other than the Contracting Carrier, signed at Guadalajara, 18th September 1961; and

    (g)   the Convention for the Unification of Certain Rules for International Carriage by Air, signed at Montreal 28th May 1999;

"consumer transport service" means—

    (a)   a rail passenger service;

    (b)   carriage by air to which the 2004 Regulation or the Carriage by Air Conventions or enactments giving effect to the provisions of those Conventions apply; and

    (c)   sea and inland waterway transport to which the 2010 Regulation applies;

"rail passenger service" means any rail passenger service supplied by any undertaking other than those specified in paragraphs (a) and (b) of article 2(2) of Directive 2012/34/EU of the European Parliament and of the Council of 21st November 2012 establishing a single European railway area (recast);

"the Warsaw Convention" means the Convention for the Unification of Certain Rules Relating to the International Carriage by Air, signed at Warsaw 12th October 1929.

NOTES

Commencement: 1 October 2015.

[2.1217]
3   Provisions coming into force on 1st October 2015

The following provisions of the Act come into force on 1st October 2015, subject to article 4 and the transitional provisions and savings in articles 6 to 8—

    (a)   sections 1 to 47;

    (b)   section 48(1) to (4) (contracts covered by this Chapter);

    (c)   sections 49 to 76;

    (d)   section 77 (investigatory powers etc) to the extent not already in force;

    (e)   sections 78 to 80;

    (f)   section 81 (private actions in competition law) to the extent not already in force;

    (g)   Schedules 1 to 4;

    (h)   Schedule 5 (investigatory powers etc) to the extent not already in force;

    (i)   Schedules 6 and 7; and

    (j)   Schedule 8 (private actions in competition law) to the extent not already in force.

NOTES

Commencement: 1 October 2015.

[2.1218]
4 Provisions coming into force on 6th April 2016

For the purpose of a contract to supply a consumer transport service the following provisions of the Act come into force on 6th April 2016, subject to the transitional provisions and savings in article 6—

    (a)   section 48(1) to (4) (contracts covered by this Chapter);

    (b)   sections 49 to 59; and

    (c)   paragraphs 2 to 6, 10 to 17 and 21 to 27 of Schedule 4.

NOTES
Commencement: 1 October 2015.

[2.1219]
5 Consequential amendments

The consequential amendments in Schedules 1 and 2 have effect.

NOTES
Commencement: 1 October 2015.

[2.1220]
6 Transitional and saving provisions in respect of Parts 1 and 2 of the Act

(1) The provisions brought into force by sub-paragraphs (a) to (c) and (g) of article 3 of this Order do not apply to—

    (a)   any contract entered into before 1st October 2015 which would, apart from these provisions, be covered by Parts 1 or 2 of the Act; and

    (b)   any notice provided or communicated before 1st October 2015 which would, apart from these provisions, constitute a consumer notice and be covered by Part 2 of the Act;

(2) The provisions brought into force by article 4 of this Order do not apply to any contract to supply a consumer transport service entered into before 6th April 2016.

(3) The amendments to the law enacted by the Sale and Supply of Goods to Consumers Regulations 2002 continue to have effect in relation to any contract specified in paragraph (1)(a) despite the revocation of those Regulations by paragraph 53 of Schedule 1 to the Act.

(4) The Unfair Terms in Consumer Contracts Regulations 1999 continue to have effect in relation to any contract or notice relating to any contract specified in paragraph (1)(a) provided or communicated before 1st October 2015 despite the revocation of those Regulations by paragraph 34 of Schedule 4 to the Act.

(5) The amendments made to the enactments specified in Schedule 1 to this Order do not apply to any contract or notice to which the transitional provisions of this article apply.

NOTES
Commencement: 1 October 2015.

[2.1221]
7 Transitional provision in respect of premium rate services

The amendments made by section 80 of the Act do not apply in respect of a contravention of a code approved under section 121 of the Communications Act 2003, directions given in accordance with such a code or an order made under section 122 of the Communications Act 2003 where that contravention occurs or begins before the commencement of section 80.

NOTES
Commencement: 1 October 2015.

[2.1222]
8 Transitional and saving provisions in respect of investigatory powers

(1) This article applies where—

    (a)   a provision ("the old provision") is repealed by Schedule 6 to the Act or revoked by Schedule 2 to this Order, and

    (b)   a provision of Schedule 5 to the Act (investigatory powers etc) ("the new provision") re-enacts, with or without modification, the old provision.

(2) The repeal or revocation mentioned in paragraph (1)(a) and the re-enactment mentioned in paragraph (1)(b) do not affect the continuity of the law.

(3) Paragraph (2) does not apply to any change in the law made by Schedule 5 to the Act.

(4) A reference, express or implied, in an enactment, instrument or document to the new provision is, subject to its context, to be read as being or including a reference to the old provision, in relation to times, circumstances or purposes in relation to which the old provision had effect.

(5)   A reference, express or implied, in any enactment, instrument or document to the old provision is, subject to its context, to be read as being or including a reference to the new provision, in relation to times, circumstances or purposes in relation to which the new provision has effect.

(6)   Anything done, or having effect as if done, under (or for the purposes of or in reliance on) the old provision, and in force or effective immediately before 1st October 2015, has effect on and after 1st October 2015 as if done under (or for the purposes of or in reliance on) the new provision.

(7)   Paragraphs (2) to (6) have effect in place of section 17(2) of the Interpretation Act 1978; but nothing in this Order affects any other provision of that Act.

(8)   For the purposes of enforcing the Pyrotechnic Articles (Safety) Regulations 2015, the Consumer Protection Act 1987 continues to apply as if Schedule 6 to the Act were not in force.

NOTES

Commencement: 1 October 2015.

SCHEDULES

SCHEDULES 1, 2

(Sch 1 (Amendments Consequential to the Commencement of Parts 1 and 2 and Chapter 5 of Part 3 of the Consumer Rights Act 2015) and Sch 2 (Amendments Consequential to the Commencement of Schedule 5 to the Consumer Rights Act 2015) contain various amendments which, in so far as relevant, have been incorporated at the appropriate place.)

PART 3
FCA HANDBOOK MATERIALS

A. GLOSSARY

GLOSSARY
the meaning of defined terms used in the Handbook

GUIDANCE ON THE GLOSSARY OF DEFINITIONS

(1)   The *rules* and *guidance* for interpreting the *Handbook* are to be found in GEN 2 (Interpreting the Handbook)

(2)   The *guidance* in the following paragraphs reminds the reader of some practical points for interpreting *Handbook* text.

(3)   Each sourcebook or manual has a reference code of two or more letters, usually a contraction or abbreviation of its title (for example, *GEN* stands for the General Provisions and *COBS* for the Conduct of Business sourcebook). The meaning of each of these codes is given in the *Glossary*.

(4)   Expressions used in the *Handbook* which are defined in the *Glossary* appear in the text in italic type (GEN 2.2.7 R (1) (Use of defined expressions)). An expression which is not shown in the text in italics has its natural meaning unless the context otherwise requires (GEN 2.2.9 G).

(5)   An expression which appears in the text in italics, but is not itself defined in the *Glossary*, should be read in the same sense as the expression to which it relates (for example, *"advice on investments"* and *"advise on investments"* are related to *"advising on investments"*, so the reader should refer to the definition of *"advising on investments"* for their meaning). (GEN 2.2.7 R (2) and GEN 2.2.8 G).

(6)   The words *"in writing"*, unless the contrary intention appears, mean in legible form and capable of reproduction on paper; they include electronic communication (GEN 2.2.14 R (References to writing)).

(7)   The Interpretation Act 1978 applies to the *Handbook*, so (unless the contrary intention appears): (1) the singular includes the plural, and the plural the singular (GEN 2.2.12 G (3)); (2) the masculine includes the feminine (GEN 2.2.12 G (3)); (3) a reference to a statutory provision is a reference to it as amended from time to time (GEN 2.2.12 G (2)); under GENPRU 2.2.13 G (Cross-references in the Handbook) the same applies to a provision in the Handbook.

(8)   Many of the defined expressions in the *Glossary* are used or defined in the *Act* or in a statutory instrument made under it. In these cases, the *Glossary* refers to the statutory provision which is the source of the *Handbook* definition. Where there is a short statutory definition, the *Glossary* sets out the definition in full. Where the statutory definition is long, the *Glossary* gives a summary of it, and states that it is a summary.

1986 Act

(in *BSOCS*) the Building Societies Act 1986.

ABCP internal assessment approach

the method for calculating the *risk weighted exposure amount* for a *securitisation position* in relation to an *asset backed commercial paper programme* as set out in BIPRU 9.12.20 R.

ABCP programme

(for the purposes of BIPRU 9 (Securitisation)) an *asset backed commercial paper programme*.

above-threshold non-EEA AIFM

a *non-EEA AIFM* that is not a *small AIFM*.

accepted channel for dissemination of information

(in relation to any *prescribed market*) an approved channel of communication by which information concerning *investments* traded on the market is formally disseminated to other market users on a structured and equitable basis.

accepted market practice

(as defined in section 130A(3) of the *Act*) practices that are reasonably expected in the financial market or markets in question and are accepted by the *FCA* or, in the case of a market situated in another *EEA State*, the competent authority of that *EEA State* within the meaning of the *Market Abuse Directive*.

accepting deposits

the *regulated activity*, specified in article 5 of the *Regulated Activities Order* (Accepting deposits), which is in summary: accepting *deposits* if:

(a) money received by way of *deposit* is lent to others; or

(b) any other activity of the *person* accepting the *deposit* is financed, wholly or to a material extent, out of the capital of or interest on money received by way of *deposit*.

accident

(in relation to a *class* of *contract of insurance*) the *class* of *contract of insurance*, specified in paragraph 1 of Part I of Schedule 1 to the *Regulated Activities Order* (Contracts of general insurance), providing fixed pecuniary benefits or benefits in the nature of indemnity (or a combination of both) against risks of the *person* insured or, in the case of a contract made under section 140, 140A or 140B of the Local Government Act 1972 (or, in Scotland, section 86(1) of the Local Government (Scotland) Act 1973), a *person* for whose benefit the contract is made:

(a) sustaining injury as the result of an accident or of an accident of a specified class; or

(b) dying as a result of an accident or an accident of a specified class; or

(c) becoming incapacitated in consequence of disease or of disease of a specified class;

including contracts relating to industrial injury and occupational disease but excluding contracts within paragraph 2 of Part I of Schedule 1 to the *Regulated Activities Order* (Sickness) and contracts within paragraph IV of Part II of that Schedule (Permanent health).

account

(in relation to a *dormant account*) has the meaning given in section 9 of the Dormant Bank and Building Society Accounts Act 2008, which is in summary:

(a) an account which has at all times consisted only of *money* and is provided by a *bank* or *building society* as part of its activity of *accepting deposits*; and

(b) in relation to a *building society*, it includes an *account* representing *shares* in the *society*, other than:
(i) preferential *shares*; or
(ii) deferred *shares* within the meaning given in section 119(1) of the Building Societies Act 1986.

accountable functions

(1) (in the *FCA Handbook* and in relation to an *approved person*) the functions described in APER 1.1A.2 P, which are in summary:

(a) *FCA controlled functions*;

(b) *PRA controlled functions*; and

(c) any other functions in relation to the carrying on of a *regulated activity*;

in relation to the *authorised persons* in relation to which that *person* is an *approved person*.

(2) (in the *PRA Handbook* and in relation to an *approved person*) the functions described in APER 1.1B.2 P, which are in summary:

(a) *PRA controlled functions*;

(b) *FCA controlled functions* that are *significant-influence functions*; and

(c) any other *significant-influence functions*;

in relation to the *PRA-authorised persons* in relation to which that *person* is an *approved person*.

accountable significant-influence function

(in the *FCA Handbook*) any *accountable function* that is a *significant-influence function*.

Accounting Directive

Directive 2013/34/EU of the European Parliament and of the Council of 26 June 2013 on the annual financial statements, consolidated financial statements and related reports of certain types of undertakings, amending Directive 2006/43/EC of the European Parliament and of the Council and repealing Council Directive 78/660/EEC and 83/349/EEC.

accounting reference date

(1) (except in *COLL*):
(a) (in relation to a *company* incorporated in the *United Kingdom* under the Companies Acts) the accounting reference date of that *company* determined in accordance with section 391 of

the Companies Act 2006;

(b) (in relation to any other body) the last *day* of its financial year.

(2) (in *COLL*): the date stipulated in the *prospectus* on which the *annual accounting period* of an *authorised fund* ends.

accredited body

(A) In the PRA Handbook
any of the following bodies recognised by the *FCA* the purpose of providing the independent verification required under TC 2.1.27 R
(a) CFA Society of the UK;
(b) The Chartered Insurance Institute;
(c) The Institute of Financial Planning;
(d) The Chartered Institute for Securities and Investment;
(e) The Chartered Institute of Bankers in Scotland;
(f) The ifs School of Finance; [Note: The ifs School of Finance acts through its Institute of Financial Services]
(g) The Institute of Chartered Accountants in England and Wales;
(h) The Pensions Management Institute.

(B) In the FCA Handbook
any of the following bodies recognised by the *FCA* the purpose of providing the independent verification required under TC 2.1.27 R
(a) CFA Society of the UK;
(b) The Chartered Insurance Institute;
(c) The Institute of Financial Planning;
(d) The Chartered Institute for Securities and Investment;
(e) The Chartered Institute of Bankers in Scotland;
(f) The ifs University College; [Note: The ifs University College acts through its Institute of Financial Services]
(g) The Institute of Chartered Accountants in England and Wales;
(h) The Pensions Management Institute.

accrued rights charge

a charge used by an *operator* for a *qualifying scheme* which is calculated solely by reference to the value of a member's rights accrued under a *qualifying scheme*. 'Rights' has the same meaning as in article 82 of the *Regulated Activities Order*, that is, the *specified investment* of rights under a *personal pension scheme* or a *stakeholder pension scheme*.

accumulating with-profits policy

a *with-profits insurance contract* which has a readily identifiable current benefit, whether or not this benefit is currently realisable, which is adjusted by an amount explicitly related to the amount of any *premium* payment and to which additional benefits are added in respect of participation in profits by additions directly related to the current benefit or a policy with similar characteristics.

accumulation unit

a *unit* in respect of which income is credited periodically to *capital property* under COLL 6.8.3 R (Income allocation and distribution).

ACD

authorised corporate director.

acknowledgement letter

(in CASS 7) a *client bank account acknowledgement letter* (a letter in the form of the template in CASS 7 Annex 2 R), a *client transaction account acknowledgement letter* (s a letter in the form of the template in CASS 7 Annex 3 R) or an *authorised central counterparty acknowledgment letter* (a letter in the form of the template in CASS 7 Annex 4 R).

acknowledgement letter fixed text

(1) (in CASS 7) the text in the template *acknowledgement letters* in CASS 7 Annex 2 R, CASS 7 Annex 3 R and CASS 7 Annex 4 R that is not in square brackets.

(2) (in CASS 11) the text in the template *acknowledgement letters* in CASS 11 Annex 1R that is not in square brackets.

acknowledgement letter variable text

(1) (in CASS 7) the text in the template *acknowledgement letters* in CASS 7 Annex 2 R, CASS 7 Annex 3 R, and CASS 7 Annex 4 R that is in square brackets.

(2) (in CASS 11) the text in the template *acknowledgement letters* in CASS 11 Annex 1R that is in square brackets.

ACS

an *authorised contractual scheme*.

Act

the Financial Services and Markets Act 2000.

acting as the depositary of an authorised contractual scheme

[deleted]

acting as the depositary or sole director of an open-ended investment company

the *regulated activity*, specified in article 51(1)(c) of the *Regulated Activities Order* (Establishing etc a collective investment scheme), of acting as the depositary or sole director of an *open-ended investment company*.

acting as trustee of an authorised unit trust scheme

the *regulated activity*, specified in article 51(1)(b) of the *Regulated Activities Order* (Establishing etc a collective investment scheme), of acting as a *trustee* of an *authorised unit trust scheme*.

acting as trustee or depositary of an AIF

the *regulated activity*, specified in article 51ZD of the *Regulated Activities Order*, which is, in summary, acting as:

(a) a depositary of an *AIF* falling within article 51ZD(2) of the *Regulated Activities Order*;

(b) the *trustee* of an authorised unit trust which is an *AIF* that does not fall within article 51ZD(2) of the *Regulated Activities Order*;

(c) the depositary of an *open-ended investment company* or of an *authorised contractual scheme* which is an *AIF* that does not fall within article 51ZD(2) of the *Regulated Activities Order*.

acting as trustee or depositary of a UCITS

the *regulated activity*, specified in article 51ZB of the *Regulated Activities Order* which is, in summary, acting as:

(a) a trustee of an *authorised unit trust scheme*; or

(b) a depositary of an *open-ended investment company*; or

(c) a depositary of an *authorised contractual scheme*;

where that company or *scheme* is a *UCITS*.

actuarial body

the Institute and Faculty of Actuaries.

actuarial function

(in the *PRA Handbook*) *PRA controlled function* CF12 in the *table of PRA controlled functions*, described more fully in SUP 4.3.13 R and SUP 10B.8.1 R.

actuarial health insurance

(in the context of the *rules* in INSPRU 1.1 concerning the calculation of the *general insurance capital requirement*), health insurance which meets all the conditions set out in INSPRU 1.1.72 R.

actuarial investigation

an investigation to which IPRU-INS rule 9.4 applies.

actuarial valuation date

the date as at which the *mathematical reserves* are calculated.

actuary

a fellow of an *actuarial body* or (in connection with *general insurance business*) a Fellow of the Casualty Actuarial Society who is a member of an *actuarial body*.

actuating purpose

a purpose which motivates or incites a *person* to act.

additional tier 1 capital

as defined in article 61 of the *EU CRR*.

additional tier 1 instrument

a capital instrument that qualifies as an additional tier 1 capital instrument under article 52 of the *EU CRR*.

adequate public disclosure

(as defined in Article 2 of the *Buy-back and Stabilisation Regulation*) disclosure made in accordance with the procedure laid down in Articles 102(1) and 103 of the *Consolidated Admissions and Reporting Directive*.

administering a home finance transaction

any of the *regulated activities* of *administering a regulated mortgage contract*, *administering a home purchase plan*, *administering a home reversion plan* or *administering a regulated sale and rent back agreement*.

administering a home purchase plan

the *regulated activity*, specified in article 63F(2) of the *Regulated Activities Order*, which is in summary: administering a *home purchase plan* where the plan was entered into by way of business on or after 6 April 2007.

administering a home reversion plan

the *regulated activity*, specified in article 63B(2) of the *Regulated Activities Order*, which is in summary: administering a *home reversion plan* where the plan was entered into on or after 6 April 2007.

administering a regulated lifetime mortgage contract

the *regulated activity*, specified in article 61(2) of the *Regulated Activities Order*, which is in summary: administering a *regulated mortgage contract* (which is a *lifetime mortgage*) where the contract was entered into on or after 31 October 2004.

administering a regulated mortgage contract

the *regulated activity*, specified in article 61(2) of the *Regulated Activities Order*, which is in summary: administering a *regulated mortgage contract* where the contract was entered into on or after 31 October 2004.

administration charge

any charge made which:

(a) relates to the money purchase benefits accruing to a member of a *qualifying scheme* whose *workplace pension contributions* are invested by way of a *default arrangement*; and

(b) is levied on:

(i) any of that member's *workplace pension contributions*; or

(ii) any income or capital gain arising from the investment of such *workplace pension contributions*; or

(iii) the value of the member's rights, insofar as those rights involve money purchase benefits, under the scheme; and

(c) is levied to meet the administrative expenses of the scheme, to pay commission or to be deployed in any other way that does not result in the provision of pension benefits for or in respect of such a member;

but an *administration charge* does not include any charge made for costs:

(d) incurred directly as a result of buying, selling, lending or borrowing investments;

(e) incurred solely in providing benefits in respect of the death of such a member of a *qualifying scheme*;

(f) in complying with a court order, where that order has provided that the *operator* may recover those costs;

(g) arising from earmarking orders or pension sharing arrangements pursuant to regulations made under section 24 or 41 of the Welfare Reform and Pensions Act 1999.

administrative expenses

has the meaning set out in the *insurance accounts rules*.

administering a regulated sale and rent back agreement

the *regulated activity*, specified in article 63J(2) of the *Regulated Activities Order*, which is in summary any of the following:

(a) notifying the agreement seller of changes in payment due under a *regulated sale and rent back agreement* or of other matters of which that *agreement* requires him to be notified;

(b) taking any necessary steps for the purpose of making payments to the agreement seller under that *agreement*; and

(c) taking any necessary steps for the purposes of collecting or recovering payments due under that *agreement* from the agreement seller;

but a *person* is not to be treated as administering a *regulated sale and rent back agreement* because he has, or exercises, a right to take action for the purposes of enforcing that *agreement* (or to require that such action is or is not taken);and in relation to a *person* who acquires obligations or rights under a *regulated sale and rent back agreement*, an activity is a specified kind of activity for the purposes of this definition only if the *agreement* was entered into by the agreement provider (rather than the obligations or rights acquired) on or after 1 July 2009.

administering a specified benchmark

The *regulated activity*, specified in article 63O(1)(b) of the *Regulated Activities Order*, which means:

(1) administering the arrangements for determining a *specified benchmark*, or

(2) collecting, analysing or processing information or expressions of opinion for the purpose of determining a *specified benchmark*, or

(3) determining a *specified benchmark* through the application of a formula or other method of calculation to the information or expressions of opinion provided for that purpose.

administrative functions

(a) (in relation to managing *investments*):
(i) arranging settlement;
(ii) monitoring and processing corporate actions;
(iii) *client* account administration, liaison and reporting, including valuation and performance measurement;
(iv) *ISA* or *CTF* administration;
(v) *investment trust savings scheme* administration;

(b) (in relation to *effecting* or carrying out *life policies*):
(i) new business administration;
(ii) *policy* alterations including surrenders and *policy* loans;
(iii) preparing *projections*;
(iv) processing claims including pension payments;
(v) fund switching;

(c) (in relation to the operation of a *stakeholder pension scheme*):
(i) new business administration;
(ii) receipt of or alteration to contributions;
(iii) preparing *projections* and annual statements;
(iv) administration of transfers;
(v) handling claims, including pension payments;
(vi) fund allocation and switching.

admissible asset

(1) (for the purpose of the *rules* in *GENPRU* and *INSPRU* as they apply to *members* of the *Society* of Lloyd's, the *Society* and *managing agents*) an asset that, subject to paragraphs (2) and (3) of GENPRU 2 Annex 7, falls into one or more categories in paragraph (1) of GENPRU 2 Annex 7 as modified by GENPRU 2.3.34 R.

(2) otherwise:
(a) (in relation to an *insurer* which is not a *pure reinsurer*) an asset that, subject to paragraphs (2) and (3) of GENPRU 2 Annex 7, falls into one or more categories in paragraph (1) of GENPRU 2

Annex 7; or

(b) (in relation to a *pure reinsurer*) an asset the holding of which is consistent with compliance by the *firm* with INSPRU 3.1.61A R.

admission or admission to listing

(in *LR*) *admission* of *securities* to the *official list*.

admission to trading

(1) (in *LR*) admission of *securities* to trading on an *RIE's* market for *listed securities*.

(2) (in *PR* and *DTR*) admission to trading on a *regulated market*.

(3) (elsewhere in the *Handbook*)(in relation to an *investment* and an exchange) the process by which the exchange permits members of the exchange to enter into transactions in that *investment* under and subject to the rules of the exchange.

advanced IRB approach

one of the following:

(a) (in relation to the *sovereign, institutional and corporate IRB exposure class*) the approach under the *IRB approach* under which a *firm* supplies its own estimates of *LGD* and *conversion factors*;

(b) (where the approach in (a) is being applied on a consolidated basis) the method in (a) as applied on a consolidated basis in accordance with BIPRU 8 (Group risk – consolidation); or

(c) when the reference is to the rules of or administered by a *regulatory body* other than the *appropriate regulator*, whatever corresponds to the approach in (a) or (b), as the case may be, under those rules.

advanced measurement approach

one of the following:

(a) the adjusted method of calculating the *operational risk capital requirement* set out in BIPRU 6.5 (Operational risk: advanced measurement approaches);

(b) (where the approach in (a) is being applied on a consolidated basis) the method in (a) as applied on a consolidated basis in accordance with BIPRU 8 (Group risk – consolidation); or

(c) when the reference is to the rules of or administered by a *regulatory body* other than the *appropriate regulator*, whatever corresponds to the approach in (a) or (b), as the case may be, under those rules.

advance payment

includes any deposit but does not include a *repayment* of *credit* or any insurance premium or any amount entering in the *total charge for credit*.

advanced prudential calculation approach

one of the following:

(a) the *IRB approach*; or

(b) the *advanced measurement approach*; or

(c) the *VaR model approach*; or

(d) the *CAD 1 model approach*; or

(e) the *master netting agreement internal models approach*; or

(f) the *CCR internal model method*;

including, in each case, whatever corresponds to that approach under the rules of or administered by a *regulatory body* other than the *appropriate regulator*.

advanced prudential calculation approach permission

one of the following:

(a) an *IRB permission*; or

(b) an *AMA permission*; or

(c) a *VaR model permission*; or

(d) a *CAD 1 model waiver*; or

(e) a *master netting agreement internal models approach permission*; or

(f) a *CCR internal model method permission*.

advertisement

(in *PR* and LR 4) (as defined in the *PD Regulation*) announcements:

(a) relating to a specific offer to the public of securities or to an admission to trading on a regulated market; and

(b) aiming to specifically promote the potential subscription or acquisition of securities.

adviser

(1) (except in *IPRU(INV)* 13) an individual who is: a *representative*, an *appointed representative* or a *tied agent*

(2) (in *IPRU(INV)* 13) a *financial adviser*.

adviser charge

any form of charge payable by or on behalf of a *retail client* to a *firm* in relation to the provision of a *personal recommendation* by the *firm* in respect of a *retail investment product* (or any related service provided by the *firm*) which:

(a) is agreed between that *firm* and the *retail client* in accordance with the *rules* on adviser charging and remuneration (COBS 6.1A); and

(b) is not a *consultancy charge*.

advising on a home finance transaction

any of the *regulated activities* of *advising on regulated mortgage contracts*, *advising on a home purchase plan*, *advising on a home reversion plan* or *advising on a regulated sale and rent back agreement*.

advising on a home purchase plan

the *regulated activity*, specified in article 53C of the *Regulated Activities Order*, which is in summary: advising a *person* if the advice:

(a) is given to him in his capacity as a *home purchaser* or potential *home purchaser*; and

(b) is advice on the merits of his:
(i) entering into a particular *home purchase plan*; or
(ii) varying the terms of a *home purchase plan* entered into by him on or after 6 April 2007 in such a way as to vary his obligations under that plan.

advising on a home reversion plan

the *regulated activity*, specified in article 53B of the *Regulated Activities Order*, which is in summary: advising a *person* if the advice:

(a) is given to him in his capacity as *reversion occupier* or plan provider or potential *reversion occupier* or potential plan provider; and

(b) is advice on the merits of his:
(i) entering into a particular *home reversion plan*; or
(ii) varying the terms of a *home reversion plan* entered into by him on or after 6 April 2007 in such a way as to vary his obligations under that plan.

advising on conversion or transfer of pension benefits

the *regulated activity* specified in article 53E of the *Regulated Activities Order*, which is described in PERG 2.7.16F G.

advising on investments

(A) In the PRA Handbook:

(1) (except in SUP 10A (Approved Persons) and *APER*) the *regulated activity*, specified in article 53 of the *Regulated Activities Order* (Advising on investments), which is in summary: advising a *person* if the advice is:
(a) given to the *person* in his capacity as an investor or potential investor, or in his capacity as agent for an investor or a potential investor; and
(b) advice on the merits of his doing any of the following (whether as principal or agent):
(i) *buying*, *selling*, subscribing for or underwriting a particular *investment* which is a *security* or *relevant investment* (that is, any *designated investment*, *funeral plan contract*, *pure protection contract*, *general insurance contract* or right to or interests in a *funeral plan contract*); or
(ii) exercising any right conferred by such an *investment* to *buy*, *sell*, subscribe for or underwrite such an *investment*.

(2) (in SUP 10A (Approved Persons) and *APER*) the *regulated activity* specified in article 53 (Advising on investments) of the *Regulated Activities Order*. For these purposes, *advising on investments* includes any activities that would be included but for the exclusion in article 72AA (Managers of UCITS and AIFs) of the *Regulated Activities Order*.

(B) In the FCA Handbook:

(1) (except in SUP 10A (Approved Persons) and *APER*) the *regulated activity*, specified in article 53 of the *Regulated Activities Order* (Advising on investments), which is in summary: advising a *person* if the advice is:

(a) given to the *person* in his capacity as an investor or potential investor, or in his capacity as agent for an investor or a potential investor; and

(b) advice on the merits of his doing any of the following (whether as principal or agent):

(i) *buying*, *selling*, subscribing for or underwriting a particular *investment* which is a *security* or *relevant investment* (that is, any *designated investment* (other than a *P2P agreement*), *funeral plan contract*, *pure protection contract*, *general insurance contract* or right to or interests in a *funeral plan contract*); or

(ii) exercising any right conferred by such an *investment* to *buy*, *sell*, subscribe for or underwrite such an *investment*.

(2) (in SUP 10A (Approved Persons) and *APER*) the *regulated activity* specified in article 53 (Advising on investments) of the *Regulated Activities Order*. For these purposes, *advising on investments* includes any activities that would be included but for the exclusion in article 72AA (Managers of UCITS and AIFs) of the *Regulated Activities Order*.

advising on investments (except pension transfers and pension opt-outs)

advising on investments except in respect of *pension transfers* and *pension opt-outs*.

advising on pension transfers and pension opt-outs

any of the following *regulated activities*:

(a) advising on *investments* in respect of *pension transfers* and *pension opt-outs* (article 53);

(b) *advising on conversion or transfer of pension benefits* (article 53E).

advising on regulated credit agreements for the acquisition of land

the *regulated activity*, specified in article 53DA of the *Regulated Activities Order* which is, in summary, advising a *person* if the advice:

(a) is given to the *person* in his capacity as a recipient, or potential recipient, of *credit* under a *regulated credit agreement*;

(b) the *person* intends to use the *credit* to acquire or retain property rights in land or in an existing or projected building; and

(c) the advice consists of the provision of personal recommendations to the *person* in respect of one or more transactions relating to *regulated credit agreements*.

[Note: article 4(21) of the *MCD*]

advising on regulated mortgage contracts

the *regulated activity*, specified in article 53A of the *Regulated Activities Order*, which is in summary: advising a *person* if the advice:

(a) is given to the *person* in his capacity as a borrower or potential borrower; and

(b) is advice on the merits of his:
(i) entering into a particular *regulated mortgage contract*; or
(ii) varying the terms of a *regulated mortgage contract* entered into by him on or after 31 October 2004 in such a way as to vary his obligations under that contract.

advising on a regulated sale and rent back agreement

the *regulated activity*, specified in article 53D of the *Regulated Activities Order*, which is in summary advising a *person* if the advice:

(a) is given to a *person* in his capacity as:
(i) an agreement seller or potential agreement seller; or
(ii) an agreement provider or potential agreement provider; and

(b) is advice on the merits of his doing either of the following:
(i) entering into a particular *regulated sale and rent back agreement*; or
(ii) varying the terms of a *regulated sale and rent back agreement* entered into on or after 1 July 2009 by him as agreement seller or agreement provider, in such a way as to vary his obligations under that *agreement* and in relation to a *person* who acquires obligations or rights under a *regulated sale and*

rent back agreement, an activity is a specified kind of activity for the purposes of this part of the definition only if the *agreement* was entered into by the agreement provider (rather than the obligations or rights acquired) on or after 1 July 2009.

advising on syndicate participation at Lloyd's

the *regulated activity*, specified in article 56 of the *Regulated Activities Order* (Advice on syndicate participation at Lloyd's), of advising a *person* to become, or continue or cease to be, a member of a particular Lloyd's *syndicate*.

affected person

(in *COLL*):

(a) (in relation to an *ICVC*):
(i) the *ICVC*;
(ii) its *depositary*;
(iii) a *director* of the *ICVC*;
(iv) any *investment adviser* of the *ICVC*;
(v) any *associate* of any *person* in (a)(i), (ii), (iii) or (iv);
(vi) the auditor of the *scheme*;

(b) (in relation to an *AUT*):
(i) the *manager*;
(ii) the *trustee*;
(iii) any *investment adviser* of the *manager*;
(iv) any *associate* of any *person* in (b)(i), (ii) or (iii);
(v) the auditor of the *scheme*.

(c) (in relation to an *ACS*):
(i) the *authorised fund manager*;
(ii) the *depositary*;
(iii) any *investment adviser* of the *authorised fund manager*;
(iv) any *associate* of any *person* in (c)(i), (ii) or (iii);
(v) the auditor of the *scheme*;
(vi) the *nominated partner*.

affiliated company

(in relation to a *person*) an *undertaking* in the same *group* as that *person*.

AFM

authorised fund manager.

agent

(in relation to *payment services* or *electronic money*) a *person* who acts on behalf of a *payment institution* or an *electronic money institution* in providing *payment services*. [Note: article 4(22) of the *Payment Services Directive*]

aggregate safe custody asset record

a *firm's* internal record or account of all the *safe custody assets* that the *firm* holds for its *clients* (including those *safe custody assets* deposited by the *firm* with third parties under CASS 6.3 and any *physical safe custody asset* held by the *firm*).

agreeing to carry on a regulated activity

(A) In the PRA Handbook: the *regulated activity*, specified in article 64 of the *Regulated Activities Order* (Agreeing to carry on specified kinds of activity), of agreeing to carry on an activity specified in Part II or Part 3A of that Order other than:

(a) *accepting deposits*;

(aa) *issuing electronic money*;

(b) *effecting contracts of insurance*;

(c) *carrying out contracts of insurance*;

(d) *establishing, operating or winding up a collective investment scheme*;

(e) *acting as trustee of an authorised unit trust scheme*;

(f) *acting as the depositary or sole director of an open-ended investment company*;

(ff) *acting as the depositary of an authorised contractual scheme*;

(g) *establishing, operating or winding up a stakeholder pension scheme*

(h) *establishing, operating or winding up a personal pension scheme.*

(B) In the FCA Handbook: the *regulated activity*, specified in article 64 of the *Regulated Activities Order* (Agreeing to carry on specified kinds of activity), of agreeing to carry on an activity specified in Part II or Part 3A of that Order other than:

(a) *accepting deposits*;

(aa) *issuing electronic money*;

(b) *effecting contracts of insurance*;

(c) *carrying out contracts of insurance*;

(ca) *managing a UCITS*;

(cb) *acting as trustee or depositary of a UCITS*;

(cc) *managing an AIF*;

(cd) *acting as trustee or depositary of an AIF*;

(d) *establishing, operating or winding up a collective investment scheme*;

(e)[deleted]

(f)[deleted]

(ff)[deleted]

(g) *establishing, operating or winding up a stakeholder pension scheme*

(h) *establishing, operating or winding up a personal pension scheme.*

AIF

alternative investment fund.

AIF custodial assets

financial instruments of an *AIF* that can be:

(a) registered in a *financial instruments* account opened in the *depositary's* books; or

(b) physically delivered to the *depositary.*

[Note: recital 100 and articles 88 (Financial instruments to be held in custody) and 89(3) (Safekeeping duties with regard to assets held in custody) of the *AIFMD level 2 regulation*.]

AIFM

alternative investment fund manager.

AIFM investment firm

a *firm* which:

(a) is:
(i) a *full-scope UK AIFM*; or
(ii) an *incoming EEA AIFM branch*; and

(b) has a *Part 4A permission* (or an equivalent permission from its *Home State regulator*) for *managing investments* where:
(i) the *investments* managed include one or more *financial instruments*; and
(ii) the *permission* is limited to the activities permitted by article 6(4) of *AIFMD*.

AIFM investment management functions

investment management functions of an *AIFM* as set out in 1(a) (portfolio management) or (b) (risk management) of Annex I to *AIFMD*.

AIFM management functions

the management functions of an *AIFM* listed in Annex I to *AIFMD*.

AIFM qualifier

an *EEA AIFM* which is *marketing*, or has *marketed*, an *AIF* in the *UK* by:

(a) exercising its EEA right to *market* under Schedule 3 of the *Act* (EEA Passport Rights); and

(b) is not exercising a right to manage a *UK AIF* under Schedule 3 of the *Act*.

AIFM Remuneration Code

as set out in SYSC 19B (AIFM Remuneration Code).

AIFM Remuneration Code staff

(for an *AIFM*) has the meaning given in SYSC 19B.1.3 R.

AIFM remuneration principles

the principles set out in SYSC 19B.1.5 R to SYSC 19B.1.24 R.

AIFMD

Directive 2011/61/EU of the European Parliament and of the Council of 8 June 2011 on Alternative Investment Fund Managers and amending Directives 2003/41/EC and 2009/65/EC and Regulations (EC) No 1060/2009 and (EU) No 1095/2010 (eur-lex.europa.eu/LexUriServ/LexUriServ. do?uri=OJ:L:2011:174:0001:0073:EN:PDF).

AIFMD host state requirements

Handbook rules transposing articles 12 and 14 of *AIFMD* and which fall under the responsibility of the *Host State* to supervise where an *AIFM* manages or *markets* an *AIF* through a *branch* in that *EEA State*, namely:

(a) FUND 3.8;

(b) SYSC 4.1.2C R;

(c) SYSC 10.1.22 R to SYSC 10.1.26 R; and

(d) COBS 2.1.4 R.

AIFMD level 2 regulation

Commission delegated regulation (EU) No 231/2013 supplementing Directive 2011/16/EU of the European Parliament and of the Council with regard to exemptions, general operating conditions, depositaries, leverage, transparency and supervision (eur-lex.europa.eu/LexUriServ/LexUriServ. do?uri=OJ:L:2013:083:0001:0095:en:PDF).

AIFMD UK regulation

(A) In the PRA Handbook: the Alternative Investment Fund Managers Regulations 2013 (SI 2013/....)

(B) In the FCA Handbook: the Alternative Investment Fund Managers Regulations 2013 (SI 2013/1773)

aircraft

(in relation to a *class* of *contract of insurance*) the *class* of *contract of insurance*, specified in paragraph 5 of Part I of Schedule 1 to the *Regulated Activities Order* (Contracts of general insurance), upon aircraft or upon the machinery, tackle, furniture or equipment of aircraft.

aircraft liability

(in relation to a *class* of *contract of insurance*) the *class* of *contract of insurance*, specified in paragraph 11 of Part I of Schedule 1 to the *Regulated Activities Order* (Contracts of general insurance), against damage arising out of or in connection with the use of aircraft, including third-party risks and carrier's liability.

allocation period

a single 24-hour period or, with the agreement of each *professional client* concerned, a period spanning five consecutive *business days*, during which an aggregated *series of transactions* may be *executed*.

allotment

(as defined in Article 2 of the *Buy-back and Stabilisation Regulation*) the process or processes by which the number of *relevant securities* to be received by investors who have previously subscribed or applied for them is determined.

all price risk measure

(in BIPRU 7.10 (Use of a Value at Risk Model)) has the meaning in BIPRU 7.10.116A R (Capital calculations for VaR models), which is, in relation to a *business day*, the *all price risk measure* required under the provisions in BIPRU 7.10 about *specific risk* for the *correlation trading portfolio*.

alternative approach mandatory prudent segregation

the requirement under CASS 7.13.65 R on a *firm* using the alternative approach to segregate an amount of *money* as *client money*.

alternative approach mandatory prudent segregation record

the record created and maintained by a *firm* under CASS 7.13.66 R to CASS 7.13.68 R.

alternative debenture

the *investment* specified in article 77A of the *Regulated Activities Order* (Alternative finance investment bonds).

alternative investment fund

(in accordance with article 4(1)(a) of *AIFMD*) a collective investment undertaking, including investment compartments thereof, which:

(a) raises capital from a number of investors, with a view to investing it in accordance with a defined investment policy for the benefit of those investors; and

(b) does not require authorisation pursuant to article 5 of the *UCITS Directive*.

alternative investment fund manager

(1) (in GENPRU 3.1) a manager of alternative investment funds within the meaning of Article 4(1)(b), (l) and (ab) of Directive 2011/61/EU or an *undertaking* which is outside the *EEA* and which would require authorisation in accordance with Directive 2011/61/EU if it had its registered office within the *EEA*.

(2) (except in GENPRU 3.1 and in accordance with article 4(1)(b) of *AIFMD*) a legal person whose regular business is performing *AIFM investment management functions* for one or more *AIF*.

alternative projection

(in *COBS*) a *projection* calculated on the basis described in paragraph 1.5R of the projection *rules* (COBS 13 Annex 2), rather than in accordance with the remainder of those *rules*.

alternative standardised approach

one of the following:

(a) a version of the *standardised approach* to *operational risk* under which a *firm* uses different indicators for certain business lines as referred to in BIPRU 6.4.19 R (The alternative standardised approach);

(b) (where the approach in (a) is being applied on a consolidated basis) the method in (a) as applied on a consolidated basis in accordance with BIPRU 8 (Group risk – consolidation); or

(c) when the reference is to the rules of or administered by a *regulatory body* other than the *appropriate regulator*, whatever corresponds to the approach in (a) or (b), as the case may be, under those rules.

AMA

the *advanced measurement approach*.

AMA permission

an *Article 129 implementing measure*, a *requirement* or a *waiver* that requires a *BIPRU firm* or a *CAD investment firm* to use the *advanced measurement approach* to *operational risk* on a solo basis or, if the context requires, a consolidated basis.

ancillary activity

an activity which is not a *regulated activity* but which is:

(a) carried on in connection with a *regulated activity*; or

(b) held out as being for the purposes of a *regulated activity*.

ancillary insurance services undertaking

(in relation to any *undertaking* in a *consolidation group*, *sub-group* or other group of *persons*) an *undertaking* complying with the following conditions:

(a) its principal activity consists of:
(i) owning or managing property; or

(ii) managing data-processing services; or

(iii) any other similar activity;

(b) the activity in (a) is ancillary to the principal activity of one or more *insurance undertakings*; and

(c) those *insurance undertakings* are also members of that *consolidation group, sub-group* or other group of *persons*.

ancillary risk

(in relation to an *insurer* with *permission* under the *Act* to insure a principal risk belonging to one *class* (as defined for the purposes of*INSPRU* and *SUP*) of *general insurance business*) a risk included in another such class which is:

(a) connected with the principal risk,

(b) concerned with the object which is covered against the principal risk, and

(c) the subject of the same contract insuring the principal risk.

However, the risks included in *classes* 14, 15 and 17 may not be treated as risks ancillary to other classes, except that the risk included in *class* 17 (legal expenses insurance) may be regarded as an ancillary risk of *class* 18 where:

(d) the conditions laid down in (a) to (c) are fulfilled, and

(e) the principal risk relates solely to assistance provided for *persons* who fall into difficulties while travelling, while away from home or while away from their permanent residence or where it concerns disputes or risks arising out of, or in connection with, the use of sea-going vessels.

ancillary service

(A) In the PRA Handbook: any of the services listed in Section B of Annex I to *MiFID*, that is:

(a) safekeeping and administration of *financial instruments* for the account of *clients*, including custodianship and related services such as cash/collateral management;

(b) granting credits or loans to an investor to allow him to carry out a transaction in one or more *financial instruments*, where the firm granting the credit or loan is involved in the transaction;

(c) advice to undertakings on capital structure, industrial strategy and related matters and advice and services relating to mergers and the purchase of undertakings;

(d) foreign exchange services where these are connected to the provision of *investment services*;

(e) *investment research* and financial analysis or other forms of general recommendation relating to transactions in *financial instruments*;

(f) services related to underwriting; and

(g) *investment services and activities* as well as ancillary services within (a) to (f), above, related to the underlying of the *derivatives* included under Section C – 5, 6, 7 and 10, that is (in accordance with that Annex and Recital 21 to, and Article 39 of, the *MiFID Regulation*):

(i) commodities;

(ii) climatic variables;

(iii) freight rates;

(iv) emission allowances;

(v) inflation rates or other official economic statistics;

(vi) telecommunications bandwidth;

(vii) commodity storage capacity;

(viii) transmission or transportation capacity relating to commodities, where cable, pipeline or other means;

(ix) an allowance, credit, permit, right or similar asset which is directly linked to the supply, distribution or consumption of energy derived from renewable resources;

(x) a geological, environmental or other physical variable;

(xi) any other asset or right of a fungible nature, other than a right to receive a service, that is capable of being transferred;

(xii) an index or measure related to the price or value of, or volume of transactions in any asset, right, service or obligation;

where these are connected to the provision of *investment services* or ancillary services.

[Note: article 4(1)(3) of *MiFID*]

(B) In the FCA Handbook: (1) (except in *CONC*) any of the services listed in Section B of Annex I to *MiFID*, that is:

(a) safekeeping and administration of *financial instruments* for the account of *clients*, including custodianship and related services such as cash/collateral management;

(b) granting credits or loans to an investor to allow him to carry out a transaction in one or more *financial instruments*, where the firm granting the credit or loan is involved in the transaction;

(c) advice to undertakings on capital structure, industrial strategy and related matters and advice and services relating to mergers and the purchase of undertakings;

(d) foreign exchange services where these are connected to the provision of *investment services*;

(e) *investment research* and financial analysis or other forms of general recommendation relating to transactions in *financial instruments*;

(f) services related to underwriting; and

(g) *investment services and activities* as well as ancillary services within (a) to (f), above, related to the underlying of the *derivatives* included under Section C – 5, 6, 7 and 10, that is (in accordance with that Annex and Recital 21 to, and Article 39 of, the *MiFID Regulation*):
(i) commodities;
(ii) climatic variables;
(iii) freight rates;
(iv) emission allowances;
(v) inflation rates or other official economic statistics;
(vi) telecommunications bandwidth;
(vii) commodity storage capacity;
(viii) transmission or transportation capacity relating to commodities, where cable, pipeline or other means;
(ix) an allowance, credit, permit, right or similar asset which is directly linked to the supply, distribution or consumption of energy derived from renewable resources;
(x) a geological, environmental or other physical variable;
(xi) any other asset or right of a fungible nature, other than a right to receive a service, that is capable of being transferred;
(xii) an index or measure related to the price or value of, or volume of transactions in any asset, right, service or obligation;
where these are connected to the provision of *investment services* or ancillary services.

[Note: article 4(1)(3) of *MiFID*]

(2) (in *CONC*) a service that relates to *entering into a regulated credit agreement as lender* and includes, in particular, an insurance or payment protection policy.

ancillary services undertaking

(A) In the PRA Handbook (1) (in accordance with Article 4(21) of the *Banking Consolidation Directive* (Definitions) and subject to (2)) and in relation to an *undertaking* in a *consolidation group*, *sub-group* or another group of *persons*) an *undertaking* complying with the following conditions:
(a) its principal activity consists of:
(i) owning or managing property; or
(ii) managing data-processing services; or
(iii) any other similar activity;
(b) the activity in (a) is ancillary to the principal activity of one or more *credit institutions* or *investment firms*; and
(c) those *credit institutions* or *investment firms* are also members of that *consolidation group*, *sub-group* or *group*.

(2) (for the purpose of GENPRU 1.3 (Valuation) and INSPRU 6.1 (Group Risk: Insurance Groups) an *undertaking* in (1) and an.

(B) In the FCA Handbook (1) (in accordance with Article 4(21) of the *Banking Consolidation Directive* (Definitions) for the purpose of *GENPRU* (except in GENPRU 3) and *BIPRU* (except in BIPRU 12) and subject to (2)) and in relation to an *undertaking* in a *consolidation group*, *sub-group* or another group of *persons*) an *undertaking* complying with the following conditions:
(a) its principal activity consists of:
(i) owning or managing property; or
(ii) managing data-processing services; or
(iii) any other similar activity;
(b) the activity in (a) is ancillary to the principal activity of one or more *credit institutions* or *investment firms*; and
(c) those *credit institutions* or *investment firms* are also members of that *consolidation group*, *sub-group* or *group*.

2) (for the purpose of GENPRU 1.3 (Valuation) and INSPRU 6.1 (Group Risk: Insurance Groups) an *undertaking* in (1) and an .

(3) (except in (1)) has the meaning in article 4(1)(18) of the *EU CRR*.

ancillary stabilisation

(as defined in Article 2 of the *Buy-back and Stabilisation Regulation*) the exercise of an *overallotment facility* or of a *greenshoe option* by *investment firms* or *credit institutions*, in the context of a *significant distribution* of *relevant securities,* exclusively for facilitating *stabilisation* activity.

announceable information

information which is usually the subject of a public announcement, although not subject to any formal disclosure requirement.

annual accounting period

(1) [deleted]

(2) (in *COLL*): the period determined in accordance with COLL 6.8.2 R (3) to COLL 6.8.2 R (7)(Accounting periods).

Annual Accounts

(A) In the PRA Handbook:

(1) the Council Directive of 19 December 1991 concerning the annual accounts and consolidated accounts of *insurance undertakings* (No. 91/674/EEC).

(2) (in *UPRU*) accounts prepared to comply with:
(a) the Companies Acts 1985 to 1989, and their equivalent in Northern Ireland, where these provisions are applicable; or
(b) the Companies Act 2006; or
(c) other statutory obligations.

(B) In the FCA Handbook:

(1) the Council Directive of 19 December 1991 concerning the annual accounts and consolidated accounts of *insurance undertakings* (No. 91/674/EEC).

(2) [deleted]

annual audited fixed expenditure

(in *UPRU*) has the meaning given in UPRU 2.1.3 R (Annual audited fixed expenditure).

annual bonus

(in relation to a *with-profits insurance contract*) a discretionary addition to *policy* benefits under a *with-profits insurance contract* made by a *long-term insurer* as a result of the annual *actuarial investigation.*

annual budget

the annual budgeted costs of operating the *Financial Ombudsman Service.*

annual eligible income

(in *FEES*) (in relation to a *firm* and a *class*) the annual income (as described in FEES 6 Annex 3 R) for the *firm's* last financial year ended in the year to 31 December preceding the date for submission of the information under FEES 6.5.13 R attributable to that *class.* A *firm* must calculate *annual eligible income* from such annual income in one of the following ways:

(a) only include such annual income if it is attributable to business conducted with or for the benefit of *eligible claimants* and is otherwise attributable to compensatable business; or

(b) include all such annual income.

annual financial statements

the financial statements in respect of the year ending on the *firm's* annual accounting reference date, which is the date to which a corporate *firm's* accounts are prepared for the purposes of the Companies Acts, or, where the *firm* is not subject to the Companies Acts, the equivalent date chosen by the *firm* and notified to the *FCA* or *PRA* as the case may be.

annual income

(in MIPRU) the income referred to in MIPRU 4.3

annual income allocation date

the date in any year stated in the most recently published *prospectus* as the date on or before which, in respect of each *annual accounting period,* an allocation of income is to be made.

annual percentage rate

the annual percentage rate of charge for a contract as calculated in accordance with MCOB 10 (Annual percentage rate).

annual percentage rate of charge

(1) (in CONC App 1.1) the rate of the *total charge for credit* (calculated in accordance with CONC App 1.1.7 R).

(2) (in CONC App 1.2) the rate of the *total charge for credit* (calculated in accordance with CONC App 1.2.4 R), expressed as an annual percentage of the *total amount of credit*.

annual report and accounts

(a) (in relation to a *company* incorporated in the *United Kingdom*) an annual report and annual accounts as those terms are defined in:
(i) section 262(1) of the Companies Act 1985, together with an auditor's report prepared in relation to those accounts under section 235 of the same Act where these provisions are applicable; or
(ii) section 471 of the Companies Act 2006 together with an auditor's report prepared in relation to those accounts under sections 495 to 497 of the same Act;

(b) (in relation to any other body) any similar or analogous *documents* which it is required to prepare whether by its constitution or by the law under which it is established.

annual statement provisions

(in *MCOB*) in relation to a:

(a) *regulated mortgage contract*, MCOB 7.5;

(b) *home purchase plan*, MCOB 7.8.3 R to MCOB 7.8.6 R; and

(c) *instalment reversion plan*, MCOB 9.9.1 R to MCOB 9.9.3R (2)(c).

annualised net written premiums

(for the purposes of INSPRU 1.4) in relation to a *financial year*, the *net written premiums* received during that *financial year*, except that in relation to a *financial year* that has been validly extended beyond, or shortened from, a period of 12 months, the amount of *net written premiums* is the amount determined in accordance with the formula: NWP x 365/D where:

(1) NWP is the amount of *net written premiums* received in the financial year; and

(2) D is the number of days in that *financial year*.

APER

the part of the *Handbook* in High Level Standards which has the title Statements of Principle and Code of Practice for Approved Persons.

applicable asset

(a) in relation to *MiFID business*, a *financial instrument*; or

(b) in relation to *safeguarding and administering investments* that is not *MiFID business*, *acting as trustee or depositary of a UCITS*, and/or *acting as trustee or depositary of an AIF*, a *designated investment* (other than a *P2P agreement*).

applicable provisions

the *Host State* rules with which:

(a) an *incoming EEA firm* is required to comply when carrying on a *permitted activity* through a *branch* or by providing services (as applicable) in the *United Kingdom*, as defined in paragraphs 13(4) and 14(4) of Part II of Schedule 3 to the *Act* (Exercise of passport rights by EEA firms); or

(b) a *UK firm* is required to comply when conducting business through a *branch* (in accordance with paragraph 19(13) of Part III of Schedule 3 to the *Act* (Exercise of passport rights by UK firms)) or by providing services (as applicable) in another *EEA State*.

applicable sectoral consolidation rules

(in respect of a *financial sector* and in accordance with paragraph 6.9 of GENPRU 3 Annex 1 (Applicable sectoral consolidation rules)) the *appropriate regulator's sectoral rules* about capital adequacy and solvency on a consolidated basis applicable to that *financial sector* under the table in paragraph 6.10 of GENPRU 3 Annex 1.

applicable sectoral rules

(in respect of a *financial sector*) *applicable sectoral consolidation rules* for that *financial sector* and the *appropriate regulator's sectoral rules* about capital adequacy and solvency for:

(a) the *banking and investment services sector* as set out in paragraph 6.2 of GENPRU 3 Annex 1; or

(b) *insurance undertakings*;

which of those sets of *rules* apply for the purpose of a particular calculation depends on the nature of that calculation.

applicant

(1) (in *LR*) an *issuer* which is applying for *admission* of *securities*.

(2) (in *PR*) an applicant for approval of a *prospectus* or *supplementary prospectus* relating to *transferable securities*.

appointed representative

(A) In the PRA Handbook: (1) (in relation to cases apart from in (2) (in accordance with section 39 of the *Act* (other than an *authorised person*) a person who:

(a) is a party to a contract with an *authorised person* (his *principal*) which:
(i) permits or requires him to carry on business of a description prescribed in the *Appointed Representatives Regulations*; and
(ii) complies with such requirements as are prescribed in those Regulations; and

(b) is someone for whose activities in carrying on the whole or part of that business his *principal* has accepted responsibility in writing;

and who is therefore an *exempt person* in relation to any *regulated activity* comprised in the carrying on of that business for which his *principal* has accepted responsibility.

(2) (in relation to a *firm* with a *permission* only to carry on one or more *regulated activities* prescribed for the purposes of section 39(1E)(a) of the *Act*) in accordance with section 39 of the *Act*, a person ("A") who:

(a) is a party to a contract with another *authorised person* (A's *principal*) which:
(i) permits or requires A to carry on business of a description prescribed in the *Appointed Representatives Regulations* ("the relevant business"); and
(ii) complies with such requirements as are prescribed in those Regulations; and

(b) is someone for whose activities in carrying on the whole or part of the relevant business A's *principal* has accepted responsibility in writing;

and, therefore, to whom sections 20(1) and (1A) and 23(1A) of the *Act* do not apply in relation to the carrying on by A of a *regulated activity* which is not one to which A's *permission* relates, and is comprised in the carrying on of the business for which A's *principal* has accepted responsibility.

(B) In the FCA Handbook:

(1) (in relation to cases apart from in (2) (in accordance with section 39 of the *Act* (other than an *authorised person*) a *person* who:
(a) is a party to a contract with an *authorised person* (his *principal*) which:
(i) permits or requires him to carry on business of a description prescribed in the *Appointed Representatives Regulations*; and
(ii) complies with such requirements as are prescribed in those Regulations; and
(b) is someone for whose activities in carrying on the whole or part of that business his *principal* has accepted responsibility in writing;
and who is therefore an *exempt person* in relation to any *regulated activity* comprised in the carrying on of that business for which his *principal* has accepted responsibility.

(2) (in relation to a *firm* with a *permission* only to carry on one or more *regulated activities* prescribed for the purposes of section 39(1E)(a) of the *Act*) in accordance with section 39 of the *Act*, a person ("A") who:
(a) is a party to a contract with another *authorised person* (A's *principal*) which:
(i) permits or requires A to carry on business of a description prescribed in the *Appointed Representatives Regulations* ("the relevant business"); and
(ii) complies with such requirements as are prescribed in those Regulations; and
(b) is someone for whose activities in carrying on the whole or part of the relevant business A's *principal* has accepted responsibility in writing;
and, therefore, to whom sections 20(1) and (1A) and 23(1A) of the *Act* do not apply in relation to the carrying on by A of a *regulated activity* which is not one to which A's *permission* relates, and is comprised in the carrying on of the business for which A's *principal* has accepted responsibility.

Appointed Representatives Regulations

the Financial Services and Markets Act 2000 (Appointed Representatives) Regulations 2001 (SI 2001/1217).

apportionment and oversight function

FCA controlled function CF8 in Parts 1 and Part 2 of the *table of FCA controlled functions*, described more fully in SUP 10A.7.1 R.

appropriate actuary

an *actuary* appointed under SUP 4.4.1 R (Appointment of an appropriate actuary).

appropriate charges information

(in *COBS*) information about charges which is calculated and presented in accordance with the charges *rules* in COBS 13.4.1 R and COBS 13 Annexes 3 or 4.

appropriate position risk adjustment

(1) (in relation to a *position* treated under BIPRU 7.6 (Option PRR)) the percentage figure applicable to that *position* under the table in BIPRU 7.6.8 R (Appropriate Position Risk Adjustment);

(2) (for any other purpose and in relation to a *position*) the *position risk adjustment* applicable to that position under BIPRU 7 (Market risk).

appropriate regulator

(1) In the *FCA Handbook*, the *FCA*; and in the *PRA Handbook*, the *PRA*;

(2)
(a) in SUP 11 "*appropriate regulator*" has the meaning given in section 178 of the *Act*, and
(b) [deleted]

appropriate valuer

(in *COLL*) a *person* who complies with the *requirements* of COLL 5.6.18 R (7) (Investment in property) or COLL 8.4.11 R (4) (Investment in property).

appropriate UK regulator

(1) in relation to an *EEA firm* (in accordance with Schedule 3 paragraph 13(4) and 14(4) to the *Act*), whichever of the *FCA* or *PRA* is the *competent authority* for the purposes of the relevant *Single Market Directive*;

(2) in relation to a *UK firm* (in accordance with Schedule 3 paragraph 18A to the *Act*), (a) the *PRA*, where the *firm* is a *PRA-authorised person*; and (b) in any other case, the *FCA*.

(3) in relation to a *Treaty firm* (in accordance with section 35(2A) of the *Act*), (a) in the case of a *PRA-authorised person*, the *PRA*; and (b) in any other case, the *FCA*.

approve

(in relation to a *financial promotion*) approve the content of the *financial promotion* for the purposes of section 21 of the *Act* (Restrictions on financial promotion).

approved bank

(except in *COLL*) (in relation to a *bank* account opened by a firm):

(a) if the account is opened at a branch in the *United Kingdom*:
(i) the Bank of England; or
(ii) the central bank of a member state of the *OECD*; or
(iii) a *bank*; or
(iv) a *building society*; or
(v) a bank which is supervised by the central bank or other banking regulator of a member state of the *OECD*; or

(b) if the account is opened elsewhere:
(i) a bank in (a); or
(ii) a *credit institution* established in an *EEA State* other than the *United Kingdom* and duly authorised by the relevant *Home State regulator*; or
(iii) a bank which is regulated in the Isle of Man or the Channel Islands; or

(c) a bank supervised by the South African Reserve Bank; or

(d) any other bank that:
(i) is subject to regulation by a national banking regulator;
(ii) is required to provide audited accounts;
(iii) has minimum net assets of £5 million (or its equivalent in any other currency at the relevant time) and has a surplus revenue over expenditure for the last two financial years; and
(iv) has an annual audit report which is not materially qualified.

(in *COLL*) any person falling within (a–c).

approved collateral

any form of security for the discharge of any liability arising from a *contingent liability investment* (other than a guarantee) which:

(a) (in relation to an *on-exchange* transaction) is acceptable under the rules of the relevant exchange or *clearing house*; and

(b) (in relation to an *OTC* transaction) would be acceptable for a similar transaction to the relevant exchange or *clearing house*.

approved counterparty

any of the following:

(a) an *approved credit institution*; or

(b) a *firm* whose *permission* includes *dealing in investments as principal* with respect to *derivatives* which are not *listed*; or

(c) a *MiFID investment firm* whose authorisation (as referred to in article 5 of *MiFID*) authorises it to carry on activities of the kind referred to in (b); or

(d) in respect of a transaction involving a new issue of *securities* which are to be *listed*, the *issuer* or a *MiFID investment firm* acting on behalf of the *issuer*.

approved credit institution

(A) In the PRA Handbook: a *credit institution* recognised or permitted under the law of an *EEA State* to carry on any of the activities set out in Annex 1 to the *CRD*.

(B) In the FCA Handbook: a *credit institution* recognised or permitted under the law of an *EEA State* to carry on any of the activities set out in Annex 1 to the *CRD*.

approved depositary

any *depositary*:

(a) which is subject to regulation by a national *regulatory body* in connection with its custody services;

(b) which is required to prepare audited accounts;

(c) whose latest annual audit report is not materially qualified; and

(d) which
(i) has minimum net assets of £5 million (or its equivalent in any other currency at the relevant time) and has surplus revenue over expenditure for the last two financial years; or
(ii) if not, nevertheless has adequate financial resources for its business.

approved derivative

(1) (in *COLL*) a derivative which is traded or *dealt* in on an eligible derivatives market.

(2) (in *INSPRU*) a *derivative* in respect of which the conditions in INSPRU 3.2.5 R are met.

approved financial institution

any of the following:

(a) the European Central Bank;

(b) the central bank of an *EEA State*;

(c) the International Bank for Reconstruction and Development;

(d) the European Bank for Reconstruction and Development;

(e) the International Finance Corporation;

(f) the International Monetary Fund;

(g) the Inter-American Development Bank;

(h) the African Development Bank;

(i) the Asian Development Bank;

(j) the Caribbean Development Bank;

(k) the European Investment Bank;

(l) the *EU*; and

(m) the European Atomic Energy Community.

approved index

in relation to *permitted links*:

(a) an index that is:
(i) calculated independently;
(ii) published at least once every week;
(iii) based on constituents that are *permitted links*; and
(iv) calculated on a basis that is made available to the public, and that includes both the rules for including and excluding constituents and the rules for valuation which must use an arithmetic average of the value of the constituents; or

(b) a national index of retail prices published by or under the authority of a government, or by a body recognised under the national legislation, of a *Zone A country*; or

(c) an index that is:
(i) based on constituents that are *permitted links*; and
(ii) in respect of which a *derivative* contract is *listed*; or

(d) the average earnings index when used for the purposes of orders made under section 148 of the Social Security Administration Act 1992 by the Department for Work and Pensions.

approved money-market instrument

(in accordance with COLL 5.2.7F R) a money-market instrument which is normally dealt in on the money market, is liquid and has a value which can be accurately determined at any time.

approved person

a *person* in relation to whom the *FCA* or the *PRA* has given its approval under section 59 of the *Act* (Approval for particular arrangements) for the performance of a *controlled function*.

approved quasi-derivative

a *quasi-derivative* in respect of which the conditions in INSPRU 3.2.5 R are met.

approved reinsurance to close

(a) a *reinsurance to close* effected before 1 January 2005; or

(b) an agreement under which *members* of a *syndicate* in one *syndicate year* ("the reinsured *members*") agree with the *members* of that *syndicate* in a later *syndicate year* or the *members* of one other *syndicate* ("the reinsuring *members*") that the reinsuring *members* will discharge, or procure the discharge of, or indemnify the reinsured *members* against, all known and unknown *insurance business* liabilities of the reinsured *members* arising out of the *insurance business* carried on by the reinsured *members* in that *syndicate year* that is:
(i) effected after 1 January 2005; and
(ii) not a balance transfer between two *syndicate years* where the *syndicate* has only one *member* and the *member* is the same in each of those years; or

(c) an agreement under which *members* of a *syndicate* in one *syndicate year* ("the reinsured *members*") agree with a *subsidiary* of the *Society* that that *subsidiary* will discharge, or procure the discharge of, or indemnify the reinsured *members* against, all known and unknown *insurance business* liabilities of the reinsured *members* arising out of the *insurance business* carried on by the reinsured *members* in that *syndicate year* ("the reinsured liabilities") and where:
(i) that *subsidiary* is wholly owned by the *Society* and if from time to time the *subsidiary* has an *asset* or cash flow deficiency such that the *subsidiary* is unable to meet any of the liabilities which it has reinsured, the *Society* is legally obliged to pay to the *subsidiary* a sum equal to that deficiency; and
(ii) at the effective date of the agreement, the relevant *syndicate year* has been open for at least two years after the date at which it would normally have been closed in accordance with the policies and practices in relation to the *syndicate* concerned.

approved reporting mechanism

a trade-matching or reporting system approved by the *FCA* in accordance with Section 412A of the *Act*.

approved security

(1) (in *COLL*) a *transferable security* that is admitted to *official listing* in an *EEA State* or is traded on or under the rules of an *eligible securities* market (otherwise than by the specific permission of the market authority).

(2) (in *INSPRU*) any of the following:
(a) any *security* issued or guaranteed by, or the repayment of the principal of which, or the interest

on which, is guaranteed by, and any loans to or deposits with, any government, public or local authority or nationalised industry or undertaking, which belongs to a *Zone A country*;

(b) any loan to, or deposit with, an *approved financial institution*;

(c) any *debenture* issued before 31 December 1994 by the Agricultural Mortgage Corporation Limited or the Scottish Agricultural Securities Corporation Limited.

(3) (in *COBS*) any of the following:

(a) any *security* issued or guaranteed by, or the repayment of the principal of which, or the interest on which is guaranteed by, and any loan to or deposit with, any government, public or local authority or nationalised industry or undertaking that belongs to Zone A as defined in the *Banking Consolidation Directive*; or

(b) any loan to, or deposit with, an *approved financial institution*; or

(c) debentures issued before 31 December 1994 by the Agricultural Mortgage Corporation Ltd or the Scottish Agricultural Securities Corporation Ltd.

approved stock lending transaction

a *stock lending* transaction in respect of which the conditions in INSPRU 3.2.36 R have been met.

APR

(A) In the PRA Handbook: *annual percentage rate*.

(B) In the FCA Handbook:

(1) (except in *CONC*) *annual percentage rate*.

(2) (in *CONC* for a *credit agreement* secured on *land*) the *annual percentage rate of charge* for credit determined in accordance with the rules in CONC App 1.1 and CONC 3.6.9 R.

(3) (in *CONC* for all other *credit agreements*) the *annual percentage rate of charge* for credit determined in accordance with the rules in CONC App 1.2 and CONC 3.5.13 R.

APR rules

MCOB 10.

arrangement

(as defined in section 59(10) of the *Act* (Approval for particular arrangements)) any kind of arrangement for the performance of a function of an *authorised person* ("A") which is entered into by A or any contractor of his with another *person*, including, in particular, that other *person's* appointment to an office, his becoming a partner, or his employment (whether under a contract of service or otherwise).

arranging

(a) (except in relation to a *home finance transaction*) *arranging (bringing about) deals in investments, making arrangements with a view to transactions in investments* or *agreeing to carry on either of those regulated activities.*

(b) (in relation to a *regulated mortgage contract*) *arranging (bringing about) regulated mortgage contracts, making arrangements with a view to regulated mortgage contracts* or *agreeing to carry on either of those regulated activities;*

(c) (in relation to a *home purchase plan*) *arranging (bringing about) a home purchase plan, making arrangements with a view to a home purchase plan* or agreeing to carry on either of those regulated activities.

(d) (in relation to a *home reversion plan*) *arranging (bringing about) a home reversion plan, making arrangements with a view to a home reversion plan* or *agreeing to carry on either of those regulated activities.*

arranging (bringing about) a home finance transaction

any of the *regulated activities* of *arranging (bringing about) a regulated mortgage contract, arranging (bringing about) a home purchase plan, arranging (bringing about) a home reversion plan* or *arranging (bringing about) a regulated sale and rent back agreement.*

arranging (bringing about) a home purchase plan

the *regulated activity*, specified in article 25C(1) of the *Regulated Activities Order*, which is in summary: making arrangements for another person to:

(a) enter into a *home purchase plan* as *home purchaser*; or

(b) vary the terms of a *home purchase plan* entered into by him as *home purchaser* on or after 6 April 2007.

arranging (bringing about) a home reversion plan

the *regulated activity*, specified in article 25B(1) of the *Regulated Activities Order*, which is in summary: making arrangements for another *person* to:

(a) enter into a *home reversion plan* as *reversion occupier* or as plan provider; or

(b) vary the terms of a *home reversion plan* entered into by him as *reversion occupier* or as plan provider on or after 6 April 2007.

arranging (bringing about) deals in investments

(A) In the PRA Handbook: the *regulated activity*, specified in article 25(1) of the *Regulated Activities Order*, which is in summary: making arrangements for another *person* (whether as *principal* or agent) to *buy*, *sell*, subscribe for or underwrite a particular *investment* which is:

(a) a *designated investment*; or

(b) a *funeral plan contract*; or

(c) the *underwriting capacity of a Lloyd's syndicate*; or

(d) *membership of a Lloyd's syndicate*; or

(da) a *pure protection contract*; or

(db) a *general insurance contract*; or

(e) *rights to or interests in investments* in (b), (c) or (d).

(B) In the FCA Handbook: the *regulated activity*, specified in article 25(1) of the *Regulated Activities Order*, which is in summary: making arrangements for another *person* (whether as *principal* or agent) to *buy*, *sell*, subscribe for or underwrite a particular *investment* which is:

(a) a *designated investment* (other than a *P2P agreement*); or

(b) a *funeral plan contract*; or

(c) the *underwriting capacity of a Lloyd's syndicate*; or

(d) *membership of a Lloyd's syndicate*; or

(da) a *pure protection contract*; or

(db) a *general insurance contract*; or

(e) *rights to or interests in investments* in (b), (c) or (d).

arranging (bringing about) regulated mortgage contracts

the *regulated activity*, specified in article 25A(1) of the *Regulated Activities Order*, which is in summary: making arrangements for another *person* to:

(a) enter into a *regulated mortgage contract* as borrower; or

(b) vary the terms of a *regulated mortgage contract* entered into by him as borrower on or after 31 October 2004.

(see also *arranging* (in relation to *regulated mortgage contracts*) and *making arrangements with a view to regulated mortgage contracts*.)

arranging (bringing about) a regulated sale and rent back agreement

the *regulated activity*, specified in article 25E(1) of the *Regulated Activities Order*, which is in summary making arrangements:

(a) for another *person* to enter into a *regulated sale and rent back agreement* as an agreement seller or as an agreement provider; or

(b) for another *person* to vary the terms of a *regulated sale and rent back agreement*, entered into on or after 1 July 2009 by him as agreement seller or agreement provider, in such a way so as to vary his obligations under that *agreement* and in relation to a *person* who acquires obligations or rights under a *regulated sale and rent back agreement*, an activity is a specified kind of activity for the purposes of this part of the definition only if the *agreement* was entered into by the agreement provider (rather than the obligations or rights acquired) on or after 1 July 2009;

including making arrangements with a view to a *person* who participates in the arrangements *entering into a regulated sale and rent back agreement* as agreement seller or agreement provider.

arranging deals in contracts of insurance written at Lloyd's

the *regulated activity*, specified in article 58 of the *Regulated Activities Order* (Arranging deals in contracts of insurance written at Lloyd's), carried on by the *Society of Lloyd's* of arranging deals in *contracts of insurance* written at Lloyd's.

arranging qualifying credit

the *controlled activity*, specified in paragraph 10A of Schedule 1 to the *Financial Promotion Order*, of making arrangements:

(a) for another *person* to enter as borrower into an agreement for the provision of *qualifying credit*; or

(b) for a borrower under a *regulated mortgage contract*, entered into on or after 31 October 2004, to vary the terms of that contract.

arranging safeguarding and administration of assets

that part of *safeguarding and administering investments* which consists solely of arranging for one or more other *persons* to carry on both:

(a) the safeguarding of assets belonging to another; and

(b) the administration of those assets.

arrears

(in relation to a *regulated mortgage contract* or a *home purchase plan*) either:

(a) a shortfall (equivalent to two or more regular payments) in the accumulated total payments actually made by the *customer* measured against the accumulated total amount of payments due to be received from the *customer*; or

(b) remaining in breach, for more than one month, of an agreed borrowing limit or of an obligation to pay or repay where the loan or *home purchase plan* does not have a regular payment or repayment plan.

article 12(1) relationship

(A) (in the PRA Handbook):
means a relationship where *undertakings* are linked by a relationship within the meaning of article 12(1) of Directive 83/349 EEC.

article 18(5) relationship

(A) (in the PRA Handbook) the relationship where there are participations or capital ties other than those referred to in article 18(1) and (2) of the *EU CRR* (Methods for prudential consolidation).

(B) (in the FCA Handbook) the relationship where there are participations or capital ties other than those referred to in article 18(1) and (4) of the *EU CRR* (Methods for prudential consolidation).

article 18(6) relationship

(in accordance with article 18 of the *EU CRR* (Methods for prudential consolidation)) a relationship of one of the following kinds:

(a) where an *institution* exercises a significant influence over one or more *institutions* or *financial institutions*, but without holding a *participation* or other capital ties in these *institutions*; or

(b) where two or more *institutions* or *financial institutions* are placed under single management other than under a contract or clauses of their memoranda or articles of association.

article 9 default

(as defined in article 2(2) of the *compensation transitionals order*) any of the following:

(a) the passing of a resolution for the voluntary winding up of an authorised insurance company within the meaning of section 3 of the Policyholders Protection Act 1975 in circumstances falling within section 5(1)(a) of that Act;

(b) the making by the court of an order for the winding up of such a company in accordance with section 5(1)(b) of that Act;

(c) the appointment of a provisional liquidator in the circumstances falling within section 15 of that Act in respect of such a company;

(d) such a company becoming a company in financial difficulties within the meaning of section 16 of that Act;

(e) a *participating deposit-taker* becoming insolvent for the purposes of Part II of the Banking Act 1987;

(f) a *participating institution* becoming insolvent within the meaning of section 25A of the Building Societies Act 1986;

(g) the beginning of a dissolution or transfer of engagements of a *member society* in accordance with rule 9(2) of the Rules of the Friendly Societies Protection Scheme.

Article 129 implementing measure

any:

(a) measure taken by the *appropriate regulator* under regulations 7–9 of the *Capital Requirements Regulations 2006*; or

(b) corresponding measure taken by another *competent authority* to apply an *Article 129 permission* as referred to in the last paragraph of Article 129(2) of the *Banking Consolidation Directive*.

Article 129 permission

a permission of the type referred to in Article 129(2) of the *Banking Consolidation Directive* (permission to apply the *IRB approach*, the *AMA approach* or the *CCR internal model method* on a consolidated basis) or Article 37(2) of the *Capital Adequacy Directive* (permission to apply the *VaR model approach* on a consolidated basis) excluding an *Article 129 implementing measure*.

Article 129 procedure

the procedure described in Article 129(2) of the *Banking Consolidation Directive* (permission to apply the *IRB approach*, the *AMA approach* or the *CCR internal model method* on a consolidated basis) or that applies under Article 37(2) of the *Capital Adequacy Directive* (permission to apply the *VaR model approach* on a consolidated basis) for the purpose of applying for and granting or refusing an *Article 129 permission* or the procedure for varying of revoking an *Article 129 permission* in accordance with the *Banking Consolidation Directive* or the *Capital Adequacy Directive*.

Article 134 relationship

(in accordance with Article 134 of the *Banking Consolidation Directive*) a relationship of one of the following kinds:

(a) where a *person* exercises a significant influence over one or more *persons*, but without holding a *participation* or other capital ties in these *persons* and without being a *parent undertaking* of these *persons*; or

(b) where two or more *persons* are placed under single management other than pursuant to a contract or clauses of their memoranda or articles of association.

assessable mutual

(for the purposes of INSPRU 1.4) a *mutual* where the *insurance business* carried on by the *mutual* is limited to the provision of *insurance business* to its members and whose articles of association, rules or bye-laws provide for the calling of additional contributions from members to meet *claims*.

asset

(in *RCB*) (as defined in Regulation 1(2) of the *RCB Regulations*) any property, right, entitlement or interest.

asset backed commercial paper programme

(for the purposes of BIPRU 9 (Securitisation) and in accordance with Part 1 of Annex IX of the *Banking Consolidation Directive* (Securitisation definitions)) a programme of *securitisations* (within the meaning of paragraph (2) of the definition of securitisation) the securities issued by which predominantly take the form of commercial paper with an original maturity of one year or less.

asset backed security

(as defined in the *PD Regulation*) *securities* which:

(a) represent an interest in assets, including any rights intended to assure servicing, or the receipt or timeliness of receipts by holders of assets of amounts payable thereunder; or

(b) are secured by assets and the terms of which provide for payments which relate to payments or reasonable projections of payments calculated by reference to identified or identifiable assets.

asset identification rules

rules made by the *appropriate regulator* which require an *authorised person* who has *permission* to *effecting* or *carry out contracts of insurance* to identify assets which belong to him and which are maintained in respect of a particular aspect of his business.

asset management company

a management company within the meaning of Article 2(1)(b) of the *UCITS Directive*, as well as an *undertaking* the registered office of which is outside the *EEA* and which would require authorisation in accordance with Article 6(1) of the *UCITS Directive* if it had its registered office within the *EEA*.

asset pool

(in *RCB*) (as defined in Regulation 1(2) of the *RCB Regulations*) an asset pool within the meaning of Regulation 3 of the *RCB Regulations*.

asset-related capital requirement

a component of the calculation of the *ECR* for a *firm* carrying on *general insurance business* as set out in INSPRU 2.2.

asset pool monitor

a *person* appointed under regulation 17A of the *RCB Regulations*.

assignment

in accordance with article 60L of the *Regulated Activities Order*, in relation to Scotland, means assignation.

assistance

(in relation to a *class* of *contract of insurance*) the *class* of *contract of insurance*, specified in paragraph 18 of Part I of Schedule 1 to the *Regulated Activities Order* (Contracts of general insurance), providing either or both of the following benefits:

(a) assistance (whether in cash or in kind) for *persons* who get into difficulties while travelling, while away from home or while away from their permanent residence;

(b) assistance (whether in cash or in kind) for *persons* who get into difficulties otherwise than as in (a).

assisting in the administration and performance of a contract of insurance

the *regulated activity*, specified in article 39A of the *Regulated Activities Order* (Assisting in the administration and performance of a contract of insurance) of assisting in the administration and performance of a contract of insurance.

associate

(A) in the *PRA Handbook*:
(1) (in *LR*) (in relation to a *director, substantial shareholder*, or *person exercising significant influence*, who is an individual):
(a) that individual's spouse, civil partner or child (together the "individual's family");
(b) the trustees (acting as such) of any trust of which the individual or any of the individual's family is a beneficiary or discretionary object (other than a trust which is either an *occupational pension scheme* or an *employees' share scheme* which does not, in either case, have the effect of conferring benefits on persons all or most of whom are related parties;
(c) any *company* in whose *equity securities* the individual or any member or members (taken together) of the individual's family or the individual and any such member or members (taken together) are directly or indirectly interested (or have a conditional or contingent entitlement to become interested) so that they are (or would on the fulfilment of the condition or the occurrence of the contingency be) able:
(i) to exercise or control the exercise of 30% or more of the votes able to be cast at general meetings on all, or substantially all, matters; or
(ii) to appoint or remove *directors* holding a majority of voting rights at board meetings on all, or substantially all, matters;
(d) any partnership whether a limited partnership or *limited liability partnership* in which the individual or any member or members (taken together) of the individual's family are directly or indirectly interested (or have a conditional or contingent entitlement to become interested) so that they hold or control or would on the fulfilment of the condition or the occurrence of the contingency be able to hold or control:
(i) a voting interest greater than 30% in the partnership; or
(ii) at least 30% of the partnership.
For the purpose of paragraph (c), if more than one *director* of the *listed company*, its *parent undertaking* or any of is *subsidiary undertakings* is interested in the *equity securities* of another *company*, then the interests of those *directors* and their *associates* will be aggregated when determining whether that *company* is an associate of the *director*.
(2) (in *LR*) (in relation to a *substantial shareholder* or *person exercising significant influence*, which is a *company*):
(a) any other *company* which is its *subsidiary undertakings* or *parent undertaking* or fellow *subsidiary undertakings* of the *parent undertaking*;
(b) any *company* whose *directors* are accustomed to act in accordance with the *substantial shareholder's* or *person exercising significant influence's*, directions or instructions;

(c) any *company* in the capital of which the *substantial shareholder* or *person exercising significant influence* and any other *company* under paragraph (1) or (2) taken together, is (or would on the fulfilment of a condition or the occurrence of a contingency be) able to exercise power of the type described in paragraph (1)(c)(i) or (ii) of this definition.

(3) (except in *LR*) (in relation to a *person* ("A")):

(a) an *affiliated company* of A;

(b) an *appointed representative* of A, or a *tied agent* of A, or of any *affiliated company* of A;

(c) any other whose business or domestic relationship with A or his *associate* might reasonably be expected to give rise to a community of interest between them which may involve a conflict of interest in dealings with third parties.

(B) in the *FCA Handbook*:

(1) (in *LR*) (in relation to a *director*, *substantial shareholder*, or *person exercising significant influence*, who is an individual):

(a) that individual's spouse, civil partner or child (together the "individual's family");

(b) the trustees (acting as such) of any trust of which the individual or any of the individual's family is a beneficiary or discretionary object (other than a trust which is either an *occupational pension scheme* or an *employees' share scheme* which does not, in either case, have the effect of conferring benefits on persons, all or most of whom are related parties;

(c) any *company* in whose *equity securities* the individual or any member or members (taken together) of the individual's family or the individual and any such member or members (taken together) are directly or indirectly interested (or have a conditional or contingent entitlement to become interested) so that they are (or would on the fulfilment of the condition or the occurrence of the contingency be) able:

(i) to exercise or control the exercise of 30% or more of the votes able to be cast at general meetings on all, or substantially all, matters; or

(ii) to appoint or remove *directors* holding a majority of voting rights at board meetings on all, or substantially all, matters;

(d) any partnership whether a limited partnership or *limited liability partnership* in which the individual or any member or members (taken together) of the individual's family are directly or indirectly interested (or have a conditional or contingent entitlement to become interested) so that they hold or control or would on the fulfilment of the condition or the occurrence of the contingency be able to hold or control:

(i) a voting interest greater than 30% in the partnership; or

(ii) at least 30% of the partnership.

For the purpose of paragraph (c), if more than one *director* of the *listed company*, its *parent undertaking* or any of its *subsidiary undertakings* is interested in the *equity securities* of another *company*, then the interests of those *directors* and their *associates* will be aggregated when determining whether that *company* is an associate of the *director*.

(2) (in LR) (in relation to a *substantial shareholder* or *person exercising significant influence* which is a *company*):

(a) any other *company* which is its *subsidiary undertaking* or *parent undertaking* or fellow *subsidiary undertaking* of the *parent undertaking*;

(b) any *company* whose *directors* are accustomed to act in accordance with the *substantial shareholder's* or *person exercising significant influence's*, directions or instruction;

(c) any *company* in the capital of which the *substantial shareholder* or *person exercising significant influence* and any other company under paragraph (1) or (2) taken together, is (or would on the fulfilment of a condition or the occurrence of a contingency be) able to exercise power of the type described in paragraph (1)(c)(i) or (ii) of this definition.

(2A) (in *CONC* or in relation to a *credit-related regulated activity*), as defined in article 60L of the *Regulated Activities Order*, in relation to a person ("P"):

(a) where P is an individual any *person* who is or who has been:

(i) P's spouse or P's civil partner;

(ii) a *relative* of P, P's spouse or P's civil partner;

(iii) the spouse or civil partner of a *relative* of P or P's spouse or civil partner;

(iv) if P is a member of a *partnership*, any of P's *partners* and the spouse or civil partner of any such *person*;

(b) where P is a *body corporate*:

(i) any *person* who is a *controller* ("C") of P;

(ii) any other *person* for whom C is a *controller*.

(3) (except in *LR* or in relation to a *credit-related regulated activity*) (in relation to a *person* ("A")):

(a) an *affiliated company* of A;

(b) an *appointed representative* of A, or a *tied agent* of A, or of any *affiliated company* of A;

(c) any other *person* whose business or domestic relationship with A or his *associate* might reasonably be expected to give rise to a community of interest between them which may involve a conflict of interest in dealings with third parties.

(4) (in *LR*) (when used in the context of a *controlling shareholder* who is an individual):

(a) that individual's spouse, civil partner or child (together "the individual's family");

(b) the trustees (acting as such) of any trust of which the individual or any of the individual's family is a beneficiary or discretionary object (other than a trust which is either an *occupational pension scheme* or an *employees' share scheme* which does not, in either case, have the effect of conferring benefits on persons all or most of whom are *controlling shareholders*);

(c) any *company* in whose *equity securities* the individual or any member or members (taken together) of the individual's family or the individual and any such member or members (taken together) are directly or indirectly interested (or have a conditional or contingent entitlement to become interested) so that they are (or would on the fulfilment of the condition or the occurrence of the contingency be) able:

(i) to exercise or control the exercise of 30% or more of the votes able to be cast at general meetings on all, or substantially all, matters; or

(ii) to appoint or remove *directors* holding a majority of voting rights at board meetings on all, or substantially all, matters;

(d) any partnership whether a limited partnership or *limited liability partnership* in which the individual or any member or members (taken together) of the individual's family are directly or indirectly interested (or have a conditional or contingent entitlement to become interested) so that they hold or control or would on the fulfilment of the condition or the occurrence of the contingency be able to hold or control:

(i) a voting interest greater than 30% in the partnership; or

(ii) at least 30% of the partnership.

For the purpose of paragraph (c), if more than one *controlling shareholder* of the *listed company*, its *parent undertaking* or any of its *subsidiary undertakings* is interested in the *equity securities* of another *company*, then the interests of those *controlling shareholders* and their *associates* will be aggregated when determining whether that *company* is an associate of the *controlling shareholder*.

(5) (in *LR*) (when used in the context of a *controlling shareholder* which is a company):

(a) any other *company* which is its *subsidiary undertaking* or *parent undertaking* or fellow *subsidiary undertaking* of the *parent undertaking*;

(b) any *company* whose *directors* are accustomed to act in accordance with the *controlling shareholder's* directions or instructions;

(c) any *company* in the capital of which the *controlling shareholder* and any other *company* under paragraph (a) or (b) taken together, is (or would on the fulfilment of a condition or the occurrence of a contingency be) able to exercise power of the type described in paragraph (4)(c)(i) or (ii) of this definition;

associated call option

a right to acquire a particular amount of the *relevant security* or of any *associated security* at a future date at a particular *price*.

associated instrument

(as defined in Article 2 of the *Buy-back and Stabilisation Regulation*) any of the following *financial instruments* (including those which are not admitted to trading on a *regulated market*, or for which a request for admission to trading on such a market has not been made, provided that the relevant competent authorities have agreed to standards of transparency for transactions in such *financial instruments*):

(a) contracts or rights to subscribe for, acquire or dispose of *relevant securities*;

(b) financial derivatives on *relevant securities*;

(c) where the *relevant securities* are convertible or exchangeable debt instruments, the securities into which such convertible or exchangeable debt instruments may be converted or exchanged;

(d) instruments which are issued or guaranteed by the *issuer* or guarantor of the *relevant securities* and whose market price is likely to materially influence the price of the *relevant securities*, or vice versa; and

(e) where the *relevant securities* are *securities* equivalent to *shares*, the *shares* represented by those *securities* (and any other *securities* equivalent to those *shares*).

attached shares

(in *CREDS*) means any shares in the *credit union* (other than any *deferred shares*):

(a) (in relation to a *Great Britain credit union*) the withdrawal of which is not permitted by section 7(5) of the Credit Unions Act 1979 or (in relation to a *Northern Ireland credit union*) the withdrawal of which is not permitted by article 23(4) of the Credit Unions (Northern Ireland) Order 1985; or

(b) (in relation to a *Great Britain credit union*) the withdrawal of which is not permitted by the terms of a loan made to a member; or

(c) the withdrawal of which is not permitted without seeking and obtaining the permission of the committee of management of the *credit union*.

In relation to a *Great Britain credit union*, paragraph (c) is relevant only where the *credit union* made a loan to the holder of the shares before the Legislative Reform (Industrial and Provident Societies and Credit Unions) Order 2011 came into force.

at the money

(for the purposes of BIPRU 7 (Market risk) and in relation to an *option* or *warrant*) the strike price of that *option* or *warrant* being equal to the current market value of the underlying instrument.

auction platform

a platform on which auctions of *emissions allowances* are held in accordance with the *auction regulation*.

auction regulation

Commission Regulation (EU) No 1031/2010 of 12 November 2010 on the timing, administration and other aspects of auctioning of greenhouse gas emission allowances pursuant to Directive 2003/87/EC of the European Parliament and of the Council establishing a scheme for greenhouse gas emission allowances trading within the Community.

auction regulation bidding

the *regulated activity* of *bidding in emissions auctions* where it is carried on by:

(a) a *firm* that is exempt from *MiFID* under article 2(1)(i); or

(b) a *MiFID investment firm* (other than a *UCITS investment firm*) on behalf of its *clients* in relation to a *two-day emissions spot*.

Audit Directive

Directive 2006/43/EC of the European Parliament and of the Council of 17 May 2006 on statutory audits of annual accounts and consolidated accounts, amending Council Directives 78/660/EEC and 83/349/EEC and repealing Council Directive 84/253/EEC.

AUT

an *authorised unit trust scheme*.

authorisation

authorisation as an *authorised person* for the purposes of the *Act*.

authorisation order

an order made by the *FCA*:

(a) in relation to an *AUT* under section 243 of the *Act* (Authorisation orders);

(b) in relation to an *ICVC* under regulation 14 of the *OEIC Regulations* (Authorisation);

(c) in relation to an *ACS* under section 261D of the *Act* (Authorisation orders);

as a result of which the *AUT* or *ACS* becomes authorised or the body becomes incorporated as an *ICVC* under regulation 3 of the *OEIC Regulations* (Open-ended investment company).

authorised business overdraft agreement

a *borrower-lender agreement* which provides authorisation in advance for the *borrower* to overdraw on a current account, where the agreement is entered into by the *borrower* wholly or predominantly for the purposes of the *borrower's* business.

authorised central counterparty

a *CCP* authorised or recognised under *EMIR*.

authorised central counterparty acknowledgement letter

a letter in the form of the template in CASS 7 Annex 4 R.

authorised corporate director

the director of an *ICVC* who is the *authorised corporate director* of the *ICVC* in accordance with COLL 6.5.3 R (Appointment of an ACD) including, if relevant, an *EEA UCITS management company* or *incoming EEA AIFM*.

authorised contractual scheme

a *co-ownership scheme* or a *limited partnership scheme*.

authorised contractual scheme manager

a *firm*, including, if relevant, an *EEA UCITS management company* or *incoming EEA AIFM*, which is the *authorised fund manager* of the *ACS* in accordance with the *contractual scheme deed*.

authorised electronic money institution

(in accordance with regulation 2(1) of the *Electronic Money Regulations*):

(a) a *person* included by the *FCA* in the *Financial Services Register* as an *authorised electronic money institution* pursuant to regulation 4(1)(a) of the *Electronic Money Regulations*; or

(b) a *person* deemed to have been granted authorisation by virtue of regulation 74 of the *Electronic Money Regulations*.

authorised fund

an *ICVC*, *ACS* or an *AUT*.

authorised fund manager

an *ACD*, an *authorised contractual scheme manager* or an *authorised unit trust manager*.

authorised insurance company

(In *COMP*) (in accordance with the *compensation transitionals order*) a *person* who was, at any time before *commencement*, authorised under section 3 or 4 of the Insurance Companies Act 1982 to carry on insurance business of any class in the *United Kingdom*.

authorised non-business overdraft agreement

a *borrower-lender agreement* which provides authorisation in advance for the *borrower* to overdraw on a current account, where:

(a) the *credit* must be repaid on demand or within three months;

(b) the agreement is not entered into by the *borrower* wholly or predominantly for the purposes of the *borrower's* business.

authorised payment institution

(in accordance with regulation 2(1) of the *Payment Services Regulations*) a *person* included by the *FCA* in the *Financial Services Register* as an authorised payment institution pursuant to regulation 4(1)(a), or a *person* deemed to have been granted authorisation by virtue of regulation 121 of the *Payment Services Regulations*.

authorised AIF

an *AIF* which is an *authorised fund*.

authorised person

(in accordance with section 31 of the *Act* (Authorised persons)) one of the following:

(a) a *person* who has a *Part 4A permission* to carry on one or more *regulated activities*;

(b) an *incoming EEA firm*;

(c) an *incoming Treaty firm*;

(d) a *UCITS qualifier*;

(e) an *ICVC*;

(f) the *Society of Lloyd's*.

(see also GEN 2.2.18 R for the position of an *authorised partnership* or unincorporated association which is dissolved.)

authorised primary dealer

(as defined in article 2(1)(n) of the *short selling regulation*) a natural or legal person who has signed an agreement with a *sovereign issuer* or who has been formally recognised as a primary dealer by or on behalf of a *sovereign issuer* and who, in accordance with that agreement or recognition, has committed to dealing as principal in connection with primary and secondary market operations relating to debt issued by that *sovereign issuer*.

authorised primary dealer exemption

an exemption from articles 7, 13 and 14 of the *short selling regulation* for the activities of an *authorised primary dealer* pursuant to article 17 of the *short selling regulation*.

authorised professional firm

a *professional firm* which is an *authorised person*.

authorised UK representative

(in relation to a *firm*) a *person* resident in the *United Kingdom* who is authorised to act generally, and to accept service of any *document*, on behalf of the *firm*.

authorised unit trust manager

a *manager* of an *AUT*.

authorised unit trust scheme

(as defined in section 237(3) of the *Act* (Other definitions)) a *unit trust scheme* which is authorised for the purposes of the *Act* by an *authorisation order*.

authorised Voluntary Jurisdiction participant

a participant in the *Voluntary Jurisdiction* who is an *authorised person*.

automatic enrolment scheme

a scheme that meets the conditions in Part 1 of the Pensions Act 2008. In summary this is a qualifying *occupational pension scheme* or qualifying *personal pension scheme* that enables automatic enrolment arrangements to take place.

AVC

a voluntary contribution arrangement paid by a member of an *occupational pension scheme* under the terms of the scheme or of a separate contract.

average outstanding electronic money

(in accordance with regulation 2(1) of the *Electronic Money Regulations*) the average total amount of financial liabilities related to *electronic money* in issue at the end of each calendar day over the preceding six calendar months, calculated on the first calendar day of each calendar month and applied for that calendar month.

backtesting exception

(in BIPRU 7.10 (Use of a value at risk model)) an exception (excluding a *specific risk backtesting exception*) arising out of backtesting a *VaR model* as more fully defined in BIPRU 7.10.103 R.

backwardation

a situation in which *futures* prices are lower than cash prices.

balance

(in relation to a *person's account*) has the meaning given in section 8 of the Dormant Bank and Building Society Accounts Act 2008, which is in summary the amount owing to the *person* in respect of the *account* at any particular time, after the appropriate adjustments have been made for such things as interest due and fees and charges payable. In relation to a time after a transfer of the *balance* to a *dormant account fund operator*, the adjustments include those that would fall to be made but for the transfer or transfers.

balancing amount

in respect of a *syndicate*, any part of the *capital resources* that:

(a) the *managing agent* of the *syndicate* has assessed to be necessary to support the *insurance business* carried on by the *members* of the *syndicate* through the *syndicate*, including those *capital resources* required to support the risks arising at *syndicate* level that affect that business; but

(b) are not managed by or at the direction of the *managing agent* of the *syndicate*.

Balancing and Settlement Code

the document designated by the Secretary of State and adopted by the National Grid Company plc as the Balancing and Settlement Code as modified from time to time in accordance with the terms of the transmission licence granted under section 6(1)(b) of the Electricity Act 1989 in respect of England and Wales, or any subsequent similar instrument or arrangements.

bank

(a) a *firm* with a *Part 4A permission* which includes *accepting deposits*, and:
(i) which is a *credit institution*; or
(ii) whose *Part 4A permission* includes a *requirement* that it comply with the rules in *GENPRU* and *BIPRU* relating to *banks*;
but which is not a *building society*, a *friendly society* or a *credit union*;

(b) an *EEA bank* which is a *full credit institution*.

Bank Accounts Directive

Council Directive 86/635/EEC of 8 December 1986 on the annual accounts and consolidated accounts of banks and other financial institutions.

banking and investment group

a group of *persons* (at least one of which is an *EEA regulated entity* that is a *credit institution* or an *investment firm*) who:

(a) form a group in respect of which the consolidated capital adequacy requirements for the *banking sector* or the *investment services sector* under:
(i) the *appropriate regulator's sectoral rules*; or
(ii) the *sectoral rules* of another *competent authority*; apply; or

(b) would form such a group if the scope of those *sectoral rules* were amended as described in paragraph 3.1 ofGENPRU 3 Annex 2 (removing restrictions relating to place of incorporation or head office of members of those *financial sectors*).

banking and investment services conglomerate

a *financial conglomerate* that is identified in paragraph 4.3 of GENPRU 3 Annex 1 (Types of financial conglomerate) as a *banking and investment services conglomerate*.

banking and investment services sector

(in relation to a *financial sector* in a *consolidation group* or a *financial conglomerate* and in accordance with GENPRU 3.1 (Cross sector groups)), the *investment services sector* and the *banking sector* taken together.

Banking Consolidation Directive

the Directive of the European Parliament and the Council of 14 June 2006 relating to the taking up and pursuit of the business of credit institutions (No 2006/48/EC).

banking customer

(in *BCOBS*):

(a) a *consumer*;

(b) a *micro-enterprise*; or

(c) a *charity* which has an annual income of less than £1 million.

A natural person acting in a capacity as a trustee is a *banking customer* if he is acting for purposes outside his trade, business or profession.

Banking Ombudsman scheme

the *former scheme* set up, on a voluntary basis, to handle complaints against those banks which subscribed to it.

banking sector

a sector composed of one or more of the following entities:

(a) a *credit institution*;

(b) a *financial institution*; and

(c) an *ancillary services undertaking* that is not an *ancillary insurance services undertaking*.

base capital resources requirement

(A) In the PRA Handbook

(1) (except in IPRU(INV)) an amount of *capital resources* that an *insurer* must hold as set out in GENPRU 2.1.30 R (Table: Base capital resources requirement for an insurer) or a *BIPRU firm* must hold under GENPRU 2.1.41 R (Base capital resources requirement for a BIPRU firm) and GENPRU 2.1.48 R (Table: Base capital resources requirement for a BIPRU firm) or, as the case may be, GENPRU 2.1.60 R (Calculation of the base capital resources requirement for banks authorised before 1993).

(2) (in IPRU(INV)) an amount of *own funds* that a *collective portfolio management firm* must hold in line with IPRU(INV) 11.3.1R (Base capital resources requirement).

(B) In the FCA Handbook

(1) an amount of *capital resources* that an *insurer* must hold as set out in GENPRU 2.1.30 R (Table: Base capital resources requirement for an insurer) or a *BIPRU firm* must hold under GEN-PRU 2.1.41 R (Base capital resources requirement for a BIPRU firm) and GENPRU 2.1.48 R (Table: Base capital resources requirement for a BIPRU firm).

(2) [deleted]

base costs

management expenses which are not attributable to any particular *class*.

base costs levy

a levy, forming part of the *management expenses levy*, to meet the *base costs* in the financial year of the *compensation scheme* to which the levy relates, each *participant firm's* share being calculated in accordance with FEES 6.4.5 R.

base currency

(1) (in *COLL*) the currency specified:
(a) in the *instrument of incorporation* of an *ICVC* as the currency in which its accounts are to be prepared; or
(b) in the *trust deed* of an *AUT* as the base currency of the *AUT.*; or
(c) in the *contractual scheme deed* of an *ACS* as the base currency of the *ACS*.

(2) (in *GENPRU* and *BIPRU*) (in relation to a *firm*) the currency in which that *firm's* books of account are drawn up.

base own funds requirement

(1) (for the purpose of *IFPRU*) an amount of *own funds* that an *IFPRU investment firm* must hold as set out in IFPRU 3.1.6 R (Own funds: main requirement).

(2) (for the purposes of IPRU(INV) 11) an amount of *own funds* that a *collective portfolio management firm* or a *collective portfolio management investment firm* must hold as set out in IPRU(INV) 11.3.1R (Base own funds requirement).

base prospectus

(in *Part 6 rules*) a base prospectus referred to in PR 2.2.7 R.

basic advice

the *regulated activity*, specified in article 52B of the *Regulated Activities Order* (Providing basic advice on stakeholder products) which is, in summary, providing advice on *stakeholder products* using a process that involves putting pre-scripted questions to a *retail client*.

basic indicator approach

the approach to calculating the *ORCR* set out in BIPRU 6.3 (Operational risk: Basic indicator approach).

basis risk

the risk that the relationship between two financial variables will change, particularly between two sorts of interest rate or between a hedge and the position it ostensibly hedges.

BCD

Banking Consolidation Directive.

BCOBS

the Banking: Conduct of Business sourcebook.

bearer certificate

(A) In the PRA Handbook: (in *COLL*) a certificate or other documentary evidence of title, for which provision is made in the *instrument constituting the scheme*, which indicates that:

(a) the *holder* of the document is entitled to the *units* specified in it; and

(b) no entry will be made on the *register* identifying the *holder* of those *units*.

(B) In the FCA Handbook: (in *COLL*) a certificate or other documentary evidence of title, for which provision is made in the *instrument constituting the fund*, which indicates that:

(a) the *holder* of the document is entitled to the *units* specified in it; and

(b) no entry will be made on the *register* identifying the *holder* of those *units*.

bearer form

(in relation to a *client's* certificate, *share* transfer or other *document*) in a form signed by the *client* so that it enables a *designated investment* or *deposit* to which it relates to be sold, transferred, surrendered or dealt with in any other way without the need to obtain further written instructions and allows the *firm* access to the sale proceeds.

behaviour

any kind of conduct, including action or inaction.

BENCH

Guide for Benchmark Activities (BENCH)

benchmark administration function

FCA-controlled function CF50 in the *table of FCA-controlled functions* which is the function of acting in the capacity of a *person* who is responsible for oversight of a *firm's* compliance with MAR 8.3 (requirements for *benchmark administrators*).

benchmark administrator

A person carrying out the *regulated activity* of *administering a specified benchmark*.

benchmark submitter

A person carrying out the *regulated activity* of *providing information in relation to a specified benchmark*.

benchmark submission

(a) the information or expression of opinion provided to a *benchmark administrator* for the purpose of determining a *specified benchmark* as defined in article 63O(2)(a) of the *Regulated Activities Order*; and

(b) any data or information made available by a person other than a *benchmark submitter* that is processed, considered or used by a *benchmark administrator* to determine the *specified benchmark* it administers.

benchmark submission function

FCA-controlled function CF40 in the *table of FCA-controlled functions* which is the function of acting in the capacity of a *person* who is responsible for oversight of a *firm's* compliance with MAR 8.2 (benchmark manager).

bid price

the price at which a *person* could sell a *unit* in a *dual-priced authorised fund* or a *security*.

bidding in emissions auctions

the *regulated activity*, specified in article 24A of the *Regulated Activities Order* (Bidding in emissions auctions), which is in summary the reception, transmission or submission of a bid at an auction of an *emissions auction product* conducted on an *auction platform*.

bill of sale loan agreement

a *regulated credit agreement* secured by a bill of sale under the Bills of Sale Act 1878, the Bills of Sale Act (1878) Amendment Act 1882 or the Bills of Sale Ireland Act (1878).

biofuel

liquid or gaseous fuel produced from *biomass*.

biofuel collective investment scheme

a *collective investment scheme*, the property of which consists only of property which is *biofuel* or a *biofuel investment* or cash awaiting investment.

biofuel investment

any of the following:

(a) a *unit* in a *biofuel collective investment scheme*;

(b) an *option* to acquire or dispose of a *biofuel investment*;

(c) a *future* where the *commodity* in question is *biofuel*;

(d) a *contract for differences* where the property in question is *biofuel* or a *biofuel investment* or the index or other factor in question is linked to or otherwise dependent upon fluctuations in the value or price of *biofuel* or any *biofuel investments*;

(e) *rights to or interests in investments* in (a) to (d).

biomass

the biodegradable fraction of products, waste and residues from agricultural (including vegetal and animal substances), forestry and related industries, as well as the biodegradable fraction of industrial and municipal waste.

biomass investment

any of the following:

(a) a *unit* in a *biomass collective investment scheme*;

(b) an *option* to acquire or dispose of a *biomass investment*;

(c) a *future* where the *commodity* in question is *biomass*;

(d) a *contract for differences* where the property in question is *biomass* or a *biomass investment* or the index or other factor in question is linked to or otherwise dependent upon fluctuations in the value or price of *biomass* or any *biomass investments*;

(e) *rights to or interests in investments* in (a) to (d).

biomass collective investment scheme

a *collective investment scheme*, the property of which consists only of property which is *biomass* or a *biomass investment* or cash awaiting investment.

BIPRU

the Prudential sourcebook for Banks, Building Societies and Investment Firms.

BIPRU 50K firm

has the meaning in BIPRU 1.1.20 R (Types of investment firm: BIPRU 50K firm) which in summary is a *BIPRU investment firm* that satisfies the following conditions:

(a) it satisfies the conditions in BIPRU 1.1.19 R (1) (does not *deal on own account* or underwrite issues of *financial instruments* on a firm commitment basis) and BIPRU 1.1.19 R (3) (offers one or more of certain specified services);

(b) it does not hold clients' money or securities in relation to *investment services* it provides and it is not authorised to do so;

(c) it is not a *collective portfolio management investment firm*; and

(d) it does not operate a *multilateral trading facility*.

BIPRU 125K firm

has the meaning in BIPRU 1.1.19 R (Types of investment firm: BIPRU 125K firm) which in summary is a *BIPRU investment firm* that satisfies the following conditions:

(1) it does not *deal on own account* or underwrite issues of *financial instruments* on a firm commitment basis;

(2) it holds clients' money or securities in relation to *investment services* it provides or is authorised to do so;

(3) it offers one or more of certain specified services;

(4) it is not a *collective portfolio management investment firm*; and

(5) it does not operate a *multilateral trading facility*.

BIPRU 730K firm

has the meaning in BIPRU 1.1.21 R (Types of investment firm: BIPRU 730K firm) which in summary is a *BIPRU investment firm* that is not a *collective portfolio management investment firm*, a *BIPRU 50K firm* or a *BIPRU 125K firm*.

BIPRU firm

(A) In the PRA Handbook: has the meaning set out BIPRU 1.1.6 R (The definition of a BIPRU firm), which is in summary a *firm* that is:

(a) a *building society*; or

(b) a *bank*; or

(c) a *full scope BIPRU investment firm*; or

(d) a *BIPRU limited licence firm*; or

(e) a *BIPRU limited activity firm*;

but excluding *firms* of the type listed in BIPRU 1.1.7 R (Exclusion of certain types of *firm* from the definition of *BIPRU firm*).

(B) In the FCA Handbook: a *firm*, as defined in article 4(1)(2)(c) of the *EU CRR* that satisfies the following conditions:

(a) it is authorised to provide one or more the following *investment services*:
(i) execution of orders on behalf of *clients*;
(ii) portfolio management; and

(b) it may provide one or more of the following *investment services*:
(i) reception and transmission of orders in relation to one or more *financial instruments*;
(ii) investment advice;
but excluding *firms* of the type listed in BIPRU 1.1.7 R (Exclusion of certain types of *firm* from the definition of *BIPRU firm*).

BIPRU investment firm

has the meaning set out BIPRU 1.1.8 R (Definition of a BIPRU investment firm), which is in summary one of the following types of *BIPRU firm*:

(a) a *full scope BIPRU investment firm*; or

(b) a *BIPRU limited licence firm*; or

(c) a *BIPRU limited activity firm*;

including a *collective portfolio management investment firm* that is not excluded under BIPRU 1.1.7 R (Exclusion of certain types of *firm* from the definition of *BIPRU firm*).

BIPRU limited activity firm

has the meaning in BIPRU 1.1.17 R (Types of BIPRU investment firm), which is in summary a *limited activity firm* that meets the following conditions:

(a) it is a *firm*; and

(b) its head office is in the *United Kingdom* and it is not otherwise excluded from the definition of *BIPRU firm* under BIPRU 1.1.7 R (Exclusion of certain types of *firm* from the definition of *BIPRU firm*).

BIPRU limited licence firm

has the meaning in BIPRU 1.1.17 R (Types of BIPRU investment firm), which is in summary a *limited licence firm* that meets the following conditions:

(a) it is a *firm*; and

(b) its head office is in the *United Kingdom* and it is not otherwise excluded from the definition of *BIPRU firm* under BIPRU 1.1.7 R (Exclusion of certain types of *firm* from the definition of *BIPRU firm*).

BIPRU Remuneration Code

SYSC 19C (BIPRU Remuneration Code).

BIPRU Remuneration Code staff

for a *BIPRU firm* and a *third country BIPRU firm*, has the meaning given in SYSC 19C.3.4 R.

BIPRU remuneration principles proportionality rule

(in SYSC 19C) has the meaning given in SYSC 19C.3.3 R.

body corporate

(in accordance with section 417(1) of the *Act* (Definitions)) any body corporate, including a body corporate constituted under the law of a country or territory outside the *United Kingdom*.

bonded investment

a *designated investment* not held by a trustee when acting as a trustee:

(a) which, except in the case of a *unit*, is one of the following:
(i) a *readily realisable security* held for a *customer*, whether or not held under a discretionary arrangement; or
(ii) a *designated investment* in *bearer form*; or
(iii) a *designated investment* held by a *nominee company* under the control of the *firm* or a *person* whom the *firm* controls; or
(iv) a *designated investment* to which the title is recorded in electronic form;

(b) which the *firm* may *sell* or procure the sale of without the signature or other action of the *customer* or an independent third party; and

(c) where the proceeds of such a sale are or could be payable to the *firm* or its *associate*.

book value of property

(in *LR*) (in relation to a *property company*) the value of a *property* (which is not classified as a net current asset) before the deduction of mortgages or borrowings as shown in the *company's* latest annual report and accounts.

borrow back

a feature of a *regulated mortgage contract* under which the *customer* has the ability to re-borrow monies paid by him.

borrower

(1) in accordance with article 60L of the *Regulated Activities Order*, in relation to a *credit agreement* other than a *regulated mortgage contract*, a *person* who receives *credit* under a *credit agreement* or a *person* to whom the rights and duties of a *borrower* under a *credit agreement* have passed by *assignment* or operation of law.

(2) in relation to a *P2P agreement* other than a *credit agreement* or a *regulated mortgage contract*, an *individual* who receives *credit* under a *P2P agreement* and under which the *lender* provides *credit* to the *individual* of less than or equal to £25,000 or the agreement is not entered into by the *individual* for the purposes of a business carried on by the *individual*.

(3) (in relation to *debt collecting* and *debt administration* (and so far as relevant to those activities in relation to article 64 (agreeing to carry on a regulated activity) of the *Regulated Activities Order*)) "borrower" includes, in addition to the persons in (1), any *person* providing a guarantee or an indemnity under the *credit agreement* and a *person* to whom the rights and duties of a *person* providing a guarantee or an indemnity have passed by assignment or operation of law.

borrower-lender agreement

in accordance with article 60L of the *Regulated Activities Order*,

(a) a *credit agreement*:
(i) to *finance* a transaction between the *borrower* and a *person* ("the supplier") other than the *lender*; and
(ii) which is not made by the *lender* under *pre-existing arrangements*, or in contemplation of *future arrangements*, between the *lender* and the supplier,

(b) a *credit agreement* to *refinance* any existing indebtedness of the *borrower*, whether to the *lender* or another *person*, or

(c) a *credit agreement* which is:
(i) an *unrestricted-use credit agreement*; and
(ii) not made by the *lender*:
(aa) under *pre-existing arrangements* between the *lender* and a *person* ("the supplier") other than the

borrower, and

(bb) in the knowledge that the *credit* is to be used to *finance* a transaction between the *borrower* and the supplier.

borrower-lender-supplier agreement

in accordance with article 60L of the *Regulated Activities Order*,

(a) a *credit agreement* to *finance* a transaction between the *borrower* and the *lender*, whether forming part of that agreement or not;

(b) a *credit agreement*:

(i) to *finance* a transaction between the *borrower* and a *person* ("the supplier") other than the *lender*, and

(ii) which is made by the *lender* under *pre-existing arrangements*, or in contemplation of *future arrangements*, between the *lender* and the supplier; or

(c) a *credit agreement* which is:

(i) an *unrestricted-use credit agreement*, and

(ii) made by the *lender* under *pre-existing arrangements* between the *lender* and a *person* ("the supplier") other than the *borrower* in the knowledge that the *credit* is to be used to *finance* a *transaction* between the *borrower* and the supplier.

branch

(A) In the PRA Handbook:

(a) (in relation to a *credit institution*):

(i) a place of business which forms a legally dependent part of a *credit institution* and which carries out directly all or some of the transactions inherent in the business of *credit institutions*;

(ii) for the purposes of the *CRD* and in accordance with article 38 of the *CRD*, any number of places of business set up in the same *EEA State* by a *credit institution* with headquarters in another *EEA State* are to be regarded as a single *branch*;

(b) (in relation to an *investment firm*):

(i) a place of business other than the head office which is a part of an *investment firm*, which has no legal personality and which provides *investment services and/or activities* and which may also perform *ancillary services* for which the *firm* has been authorized;

(ii) all the places of business set up in the same *EEA State* by an *investment firm* with headquarters in another *EEA State* are regarded as a single branch;

[Note: article 4(1)(26) of *MiFID*]

(c) (in relation to an *insurance undertaking*) any permanent presence of the *insurance undertaking* in an *EEA State* other than that in which it has its head office is to be regarded as a single *branch*, whether that presence consists of a single office which, or two or more offices each of which:

(i) is managed by the *insurance undertaking's* own staff; or

(ii) is an agency of the *insurance undertaking*; or

(iii) is managed by a *person* who is independent of the *insurance undertaking*, but has permanent authority to act for the *insurance undertaking* as an agency would.

(d) (in relation to an IMD insurance intermediary):

(i) a place of business which is a part of an *IMD insurance intermediary*, not being the principal place of business, which has no separate legal personality and which provides insurance mediation for which the *IMD insurance intermediary* has been registered;

(ii) for the purposes of the *Insurance Mediation Directive*, all the places of business set up in the same *EEA State* by an *IMD insurance intermediary* with headquarters in another *EEA State* are to be regarded as a single *branch*.

(e) (in relation to an *IMD reinsurance intermediary*):

(i) a place of business which is a part of an *IMD reinsurance intermediary*, not being the principal place of business, which has no separate legal personality and which provides *reinsurance mediation* for which the *IMD reinsurance intermediary* has been registered;

(ii) for the purposes of the *Insurance Mediation Directive*, all the places of business set up in the same *EEA State* by an *IMD reinsurance intermediary* with headquarters in another *EEA State* are to be regarded as a single *branch*.

(f) (in relation to an *EEA UCITS management company*):

(i) a place of business which is a part of an *EEA UCITS management company*, which has no separate legal personality and which provides the services for which the *EEA UCITS management company* has been authorised;

(ii) for the purposes of the *UCITS Directive*, all the places of business set up in the same *EEA State* by an *EEA UCITS management company* with headquarters in another *EEA State* are to be regarded as a single *branch*.

(g) (in accordance with regulation 2(1) of the *Payment Services Regulations*) (in relation to a *payment institution*) a place of business of a *payment institution*, other than its head office, which forms a legally dependent part of the institution and which carries out directly all or some of the transactions inherent in its business. For the purposes of the *Payment Services Regulations*, all places of business set up in the same *EEA State* other than the *United Kingdom* by an *authorised payment institution* are to be regarded as a single *branch*. [Note: article 4(29) of the *Payment Services Directive*]

(h) (in relation to a person carrying on *auction regulation bidding*) a branch.

(i) (in relation to an *AIFM*)

(i) a place of business which is a part of an *AIFM* that has no legal personality and provides the services for which the *AIFM* has been authorised;

(ii) for the purpose of (i), all places of business established in the same *EEA State* by an *AIFM* with its registered office in another *EEA State* shall be regarded as a single *branch*.

[Note: article 4(1)(c) of *AIFMD*]

(B) In the FCA Handbook:

(a) (in relation to a *credit institution*):

(i) a place of business which forms a legally dependent part of a *credit institution* and which carries out directly all or some of the transactions inherent in the business of *credit institutions*;

(ii) for the purposes of the *CRD* and in accordance with article 38 of the *CRD*, any number of places of business set up in the same *EEA State* by a *credit institution* with headquarters in another *EEA State* are to be regarded as a single *branch*;

(b) (in relation to an *investment firm*):

(i) a place of business other than the head office which is a part of an *investment firm*, which has no legal personality and which provides *investment services and/or activities* and which may also perform *ancillary services* for which the *firm* has been authorized;

(ii) all the places of business set up in the same *EEA State* by an *investment firm* with headquarters in another *EEA State* are regarded as a single branch;

[Note: article 4(1)(26) of *MiFID*]

(c) (in relation to an *insurance undertaking*) any permanent presence of the *insurance undertaking* in an *EEA State* other than that in which it has its head office is to be regarded as a single *branch*, whether that presence consists of a single office which, or two or more offices each of which:

(i) is managed by the *insurance undertaking's* own staff; or

(ii) is an agency of the *insurance undertaking*; or

(iii) is managed by a *person* who is independent of the *insurance undertaking*, but has permanent authority to act for the *insurance undertaking* as an agency would.

(d) (in relation to an IMD insurance intermediary):

(i) a place of business which is a part of an *IMD insurance intermediary*, not being the principal place of business, which has no separate legal personality and which provides insurance mediation for which the *IMD insurance intermediary* has been registered;

(ii) for the purposes of the *Insurance Mediation Directive*, all the places of business set up in the same *EEA State* by an *IMD insurance intermediary* with headquarters in another *EEA State* are to be regarded as a single *branch*.

(e) (in relation to an *IMD reinsurance intermediary*):

(i) a place of business which is a part of an *IMD reinsurance intermediary*, not being the principal place of business, which has no separate legal personality and which provides *reinsurance mediation* for which the *IMD reinsurance intermediary* has been registered;

(ii) for the purposes of the *Insurance Mediation Directive*, all the places of business set up in the same *EEA State* by an *IMD reinsurance intermediary* with headquarters in another *EEA State* are to be regarded as a single *branch*.

(f) (in relation to an *EEA UCITS management company*):

(i) a place of business which is a part of an *EEA UCITS management company*, which has no separate legal personality and which provides the services for which the *EEA UCITS management company* has been authorised;

(ii) for the purposes of the *UCITS Directive*, all the places of business set up in the same *EEA State* by an *EEA UCITS management company* with headquarters in another *EEA State* are to be regarded as a single *branch*.

(g) (in accordance with regulation 2(1) of the *Payment Services Regulations*) (in relation to a *payment institution*) a place of business of a *payment institution*, other than its head office, which forms a legally dependent part of the institution and which carries out directly all or some of the transactions inherent in its business. For the purposes of the *Payment Services Regulations*, all places of business set up in the same *EEA State* other than the *United Kingdom* by an *authorised payment institution* are to be regarded as a single *branch*. [Note: article 4(29) of the *Payment Services Directive*]

(h) (in relation to a person carrying on *auction regulation bidding*) a branch.

(i) (in relation to an *AIFM*)

(i) a place of business which is a part of an *AIFM* that has no legal personality and provides the services for which the *AIFM* has been authorised;

(ii) for the purpose of (i), all places of business established in the same *EEA State* by an *AIFM* with its registered office in another *EEA State* shall be regarded as a single *branch*.

[Note: article 4(1)(c) of *AIFMD*]

breach

in *DEPP*:

(1) misconduct in respect of which the *FCA* is empowered to take action pursuant to section 66 (Disciplinary powers) of the *Act*; or

(2) a contravention in respect of which the *FCA* is empowered to impose a penalty pursuant to section 91 (Penalties for breach of listing rules) of the *Act*; or

(3) a contravention for the purposes of Part XIV (Disciplinary Measures); or

(4) behaviour amounting to *market abuse*, or to *requiring or encouraging market abuse*, in respect of which the *FCA* takes action pursuant to section 123 (Power to impose penalties in cases of market abuse) of the *Act*;

(5) a contravention of any directly applicable *EU* regulation made under *MiFID*;

(6) a contravention in respect of which the *FCA* is empowered to take action pursuant to section 131G (Breach of short selling regulation: Power to impose penalty or issue censure) of the *Act*;

(7) a contravention in respect of which the *FCA* is empowered to take action pursuant to section 88A (Disciplinary powers: contravention of s. 88(3)(c) or (e)) of the *Act*;

(8) a contravention in respect of which the *FCA* is empowered to take action pursuant to section 89Q (Disciplinary powers: contravention of s. 89P(4)(b) or (d)) of the *Act*;

(9) a contravention in respect of which the *FCA* is empowered to take action pursuant to section 192K (Power to impose penalty or issue censure) of the *Act*;

(10) a contravention in respect of which the *FCA* is empowered to take action pursuant to section 249 (Disciplinary measures) of the *Act*;

(11) a contravention in respect of which the *FCA* is empowered to take action pursuant to section 312E (Public censure) or section 312F (Financial penalties) of the *Act*; or

(12) a contravention in respect of which the *FCA* is empowered to take action pursuant to section 345 (Disciplinary measures: FCA) of the *Act*.

break fee arrangement

(in *LR*) an arrangement falling within the definition in LR 10.2.6A R.

bridging loan

a *regulated mortgage contract* which has a term of twelve *months* or less.

broker

(in *MAR*, *SYSC* and *INSPRU*) any person when dealing as agent.

broker fund

(in relation to a fund for which the *firm* is or will be a *broker fund adviser*):

(a) an actual or notional fund of a *long-term insurer* or *overseas long-term insurer*, which contains or will contain contributions made or to be made by a *client* or *clients* of a *firm* in connection with a *life policy* or *policies*;

(b) a fund of a *collective investment scheme*, which contains or will contain cash contributions made or to be made by a *client* or *clients* of a *firm* in connection with the purchase of *units* in the *scheme*.

broker fund adviser

a *firm* which has, or whose *associate* being an *authorised person* has, an arrangement with a *long-term insurer*, *overseas long-term insurer* or *operator* of a *regulated collective investment scheme*, under which it is to be expected that the *long-term insurer*, *overseas long-term insurer* or *operator* will take into account the advice of that *firm* or its *associate*:

(a) in the case of a *long-term insurer* or *overseas long-term insurer*, on any matter likely to influence the performance of any of the *long-term insurer's* or *overseas long-term insurer's* funds or of any *investment* issued by the *long-term insurer* or *overseas long-term insurer* into which cash contributions of that *firm's customers* have been made;

(b) in the case of an *operator*, on the composition of the property of the *collective investment scheme* into which cash contributions of that *firm's customers* have been made;

in this definition *associate* includes any *authorised person* in respect of whose services the first *firm* receives any benefit or reward, either directly or indirectly, in connection with advice of the kind described in (a) and (b) given to a *long-term insurer* or *overseas long-term insurer* or to a *collective investment scheme operator.*

brought forward amount

an amount, as defined in INSPRU 1.1.51 R, used in the calculation of the *general insurance capital requirement.*

BSOCS

the Building Societies sourcebook.

buffer securities restriction

BIPRU 12.6.16R.

building block

(in *PR* and *LR*) (as defined in the *PD Regulation*) a list of additional information requirements, not included in one of the schedules, to be added to one or more schedules, as the case may be, depending on the type of instrument and/or transaction for which a prospectus or base prospectus is drawn up.

building society

(as defined in section 119(1) of the Building Societies Act 1986) a building society incorporated (or deemed to be incorporated) under that Act.

Building Societies Ombudsman scheme

the *former scheme* set up and recognised under the Building Societies Act 1986 to handle complaints about *building societies.*

business day

(1) (in relation to anything done or to be done in (including to be submitted to a place in) any part of the *United Kingdom*):
(a) (except in *REC*) any *day* which is not a Saturday or Sunday, Christmas Day, Good Friday or a bank holiday in that part of the *United Kingdom*;
(b) (in *REC*) (as defined in section 167 of the Companies Act 1989) any *day* which is not a Saturday or Sunday, Christmas Day, Good Friday or a bank holiday in any part of the *United Kingdom*.

(2) (in relation to anything done or to be done by reference to a market outside the *United Kingdom*) any *day* on which that market is normally open for business.

business illustration

an *illustration* for a *regulated mortgage contract* that is for a business purpose.

business offer document

an *offer document* for a *regulated mortgage contract* that is for a business purpose.

Business Order

the Financial Services and Markets Act 2000 (Carrying on Regulated Activities by Way of Business Order) 2001 (SI 2001/1177).

business premises

(in CONC App 1.3) premises for occupation for the purposes of a business (including any activity carried on by a body of *persons*, whether corporate or unincorporate) or for those and other purposes.

Buy-back and Stabilisation Regulation

Commission Regulation (EC) of 22 December 2003 implementing the *Market Abuse Directive* as regards exemptions for buy-back programmes and stabilisation of financial instruments (No 2273/2003).

buy-back programme

(as defined in Article 2 of the *Buy-back and Stabilisation Regulation*) trading in own shares in accordance with Articles 19 to 24 of the *PLC Safeguards Directive.*

buying

(in accordance with article 3(1) of the *Regulated Activities Order* (Interpretation)) any form of buying, including acquiring for valuable consideration.

byelaw

any Byelaw, direction, regulation, or other instrument made using the powers of the *Council* under section 6 of Lloyd's Act 1982 (including any regulation ratified by the *Council* by special resolution) and any condition or requirement made under any such Byelaw, direction, regulation or other instrument.

CAD

Capital Adequacy Directive.

CAD 1 model

a risk management model of the type described in BIPRU 7.9 (Use of a CAD 1 model).

CAD 1 model approach

one of the following

(a) the approach to calculating part of the *market risk capital requirement* set out in BIPRU 7.9 (Use of a CAD 1 model);

(b) (where the approach in (a) is being applied on a consolidated basis) the method in (a) as applied on a consolidated basis in accordance with BIPRU 8 (Group risk – consolidation); or

(c) when the reference is to the rules of or administered by a *regulatory body* other than the *appropriate regulator*, whatever corresponds to the approach in (a) or (b), as the case may be, under those rules.

CAD 1 model waiver

a *waiver* that requires a *firm* to use the *CAD 1 model approach* on a solo basis or, if the context requires, a consolidated basis.

CAD Article 22 group

a *UK consolidation group* or *non-EEA sub-group* that meets the conditions in BIPRU 8.4.9 R (Definition of a CAD Article 22 group).

CAD full scope firm

has the meaning set out BIPRU 1.1.13 R (Types of investment firm: CAD full scope firm), which in summary is a *CAD investment firm* that is not a *limited activity firm* or a *limited licence firm*.

CAD investment firm

(A) In the PRA Handbook: has the meaning set out BIPRU 1.1.14 R (Types of investment firm: CAD investment firm), which in summary is an *investment firm* that is subject to the requirements imposed by *MiFID* (or which would be subject to that Directive if its head office were in an *EEA State*) but excluding a *bank*, a *building society*, a *credit institution*, a *local* and an *exempt CAD firm*.

(B) In the FCA Handbook a *firm* that is subject to the requirements imposed by *MiFID* (or which would be subject to that Directive if its head office were in an *EEA State*) but excluding a *bank*, a *building society*, a *credit institution*, a *local* and an *exempt CAD firm* that meets the following conditions:

(a) it is a *firm* as defined in article 4(1)(2)(c) of the *EU CRR*;

(b) it is authorised to provide one or more the following *investment services*:
(i) (execution of orders on behalf of *clients*;
(ii) portfolio management; and

(c) it may provide one or more of the following *investment services*:
(i) reception and transmission of orders in relation to one or more *financial instruments*;
(ii) investment advice.

callable contribution

amounts that *members* are liable to pay to the *Society* (or may by resolution of the *Society* be liable to pay) as contributions to the *Central Fund*.

cancellation

(in *COLL*) (in relation to *units*) a cancellation of a *unit* by:

(a) an *ICVC*; or

(b) the *trustee* of an *AUT*; or

(c) the *depositary* of an *ACS*.

cancellation price

(in *COLL*) (in relation to the *cancellation* of *units* in a *dual-priced authorised fund*) the *price* for each *unit* payable by the *depositary* to the *authorised fund manager* on that *cancellation*.

candidate

a *person* in respect of whom an application is made for approval under section 59 of the *Act* (Approval for particular arrangements) of the performance of an *FCA controlled function* or a *PRA controlled function*.

canvassing off trade premises

(a) an activity by an individual ("the canvasser") of soliciting the entry of another *individual* ("B") into an agreement by making oral representations to B during a visit by the canvasser to any place (other than a place in (b)) where B is, being a visit made by the canvasser for the purpose of making such oral representations.

(b) a place where a business is carried on (whether on a permanent or temporary basis) by:
(i) the *lender* or *owner*; or
(ii) a *supplier*; or
(iii) the canvasser; or
(iv) a *person* who employs the canvasser or has appointed the canvasser as an agent; or
(v) B;
is excluded from (a).

capacity transfer market

any method of transferring capacity in *syndicates*, including capacity auctions, bilateral arrangements, capacity offers, minority buy-outs and conversion schemes.

capital account

(in *COLL*) an account relating to the *capital property* of an *authorised fund*.

Capital Adequacy Directive

the Directive of the European Parliament and the Council of 14 June 2006 on capital adequacy of investment firms and credit institutions (No 2006/49/EC).

capital instrument

(in *GENPRU*, *BIPRU* and INSPRU 6 and in relation to an *undertaking*) any *security* issued by or loan made to that *undertaking* or any other investment in, or external contribution to the capital of, that *undertaking*.

capital market-driven transaction

(in accordance with point 2 of Part 1 of Annex VIII of the *Banking Consolidation Directive* (Eligible forms of credit risk mitigation)) any transaction giving rise to an *exposure* secured by collateral which includes a provision conferring upon the *person* with the *exposure* the right to receive margin frequently.

capital planning buffer

(A) In the PRA Handbook: (in BIPRU 2.2) the amount and quality of capital resources that a *firm* should hold at a given time in accordance with the *general stress and scenario testing rule*, so that the *firm* is able to continue to meet the *overall financial adequacy rule* throughout the relevant capital planning period in the face of adverse circumstances, after allowing for realistic management actions.

(B) In the FCA Handbook: (in BIPRU 2.2 or IFPRU 2) the amount and quality of capital resources that a *firm* should hold at a given time in accordance with the *general stress and scenario testing rule*, so that the *firm* is able to continue to meet the *overall financial adequacy rule* throughout the relevant capital planning period in the face of adverse circumstances, after allowing for realistic management actions.

capital property

(in *COLL*) the *scheme property*, other than *income property* and any amount for the time being standing to the credit of the *distribution account*.

capital redemption

(in relation to a *class* of *contract of insurance*) capital redemption contracts where effected or carried out by a *person* who does not carry on a banking business, and otherwise carries on the *regulated activity* of *effecting* or *carrying out contracts of insurance*, as specified in paragraph VI of Part II of Schedule 1 to the *Regulated Activities Order* (Contracts of long-term insurance).

Capital Requirements Regulations 2006

the Capital Requirements Regulations 2006 (SI 2006/3221).

capital resources

(A) In the PRA Handbook:

(1) in relation to a *BIPRU firm* or an *insurer*, the *firm's* capital resources as calculated in accordance with the *capital resources table*, including, in relation to a *BIPRU firm*, as that calculation is adjusted under BIPRU 10.5 for the purposes of BIPRU 10 (Large exposures requirements); or

(2) (in relation to an *institution* that is an *EEA firm* and not a *BIPRU firm* and which is required to meet the capital resources requirements of the *CRD implementation measures* for its *EEA State* on an individual basis) capital resources calculated under those *CRD implementation measures*; or

(3) (for the purposes of *GENPRU* and *BIPRU*, in relation to an undertaking not falling within (1) or (2) and subject to (4)), capital resources calculated in accordance with (1) on the assumption that:
(a) it is a *BIPRU firm* with a *Part 4A permission*; and
(b) it carries on all its business in the *United Kingdom* and has obtained whatever *permissions* for doing so are required under the *Act*; or

(4) (for the purposes of *GENPRU* and *BIPRU* and in relation to any *undertaking* not falling within (1) or (2) for which the methodology in (3) does not give an answer whose *capital resources* a *BIPRU firm* (the "relevant firm") is required to calculate under a *Handbook rule*) capital resources calculated under (1) on the assumption that it is a *BIPRU firm* of the same category as the relevant firm.

(B) In the FCA Handbook:

(1) in relation to a *BIPRU firm* or an *insurer*, the *firm's* capital resources as calculated in accordance with the *capital resources table*; or

(2) (in relation to a *CAD investment firm* that is an *EEA firm* and not a *BIPRU firm* and which is required to meet the capital resources requirements of the *CRD implementation measures* for its *EEA State* on an individual basis) capital resources calculated under those *CRD implementation measures*; or

(3) (for the purposes of *GENPRU* and *BIPRU* (except BIPRU 12), in relation to an undertaking not falling within (1) or (2) and subject to (4)), capital resources calculated in accordance with (1) on the assumption that:
(a) it is a *BIPRU firm* with a *Part 4A permission*; and
(b) it carries on all its business in the *United Kingdom* and has obtained whatever *permissions* for doing so are required under the *Act*; or

(4) (for the purposes of *GENPRU* and *BIPRU* (except BIPRU 12) and in relation to any *undertaking* not falling within (1) or (2) for which the methodology in (3) does not give an answer whose *capital resources* a *BIPRU firm* (the "relevant firm") is required to calculate under a *Handbook rule*) capital resources calculated under (1) on the assumption that it is a *BIPRU firm* of the same category as the relevant firm; or

(5) (for a *firm* carrying on any *home financing* connected to *regulated mortgage contracts* or *home financing* and *home financing administration* connected to *regulated mortgage contracts*) *capital resources* calculated under MIPRU 4.2.23 R.

capital resources gearing rules

(A) In the PRA Handbook:
(1) (in relation to an *insurer*) GENPRU 2.2.29 R, GENPRU 2.2.30 R and GENPRU 2.2.32 R to GENPRU 2.2.41 R.
(2) [deleted]
(3) [deleted]

(B) In the FCA Handbook:
(1) (in relation to an *insurer*) GENPRU 2.2.29 R, GENPRU 2.2.30 R and GENPRU 2.2.32 R to GENPRU 2.2.41 R.
(2) [deleted]
(3) (in relation to a *BIPRU firm*) GENPRU 2.2.30 R, GENPRU 2.2.46 R and GENPRU 2.2.49 R and GENPRU 2.2.50 R.

capital resources requirement

an amount of *capital resources* that:

(1) a *BIPRU firm* must hold as set out in the *main BIPRU firm Pillar 1 rules*; or

(2) an *insurer* must hold as set out in GENPRU 2.1.17 R to GENPRU 2.1.23 R; or

(3) a *firm* carrying on any *home financing* connected to *regulated mortgage contracts* or *home financing* and *home financing administration* connected to *regulated mortgage contracts*, must hold under MIPRU 4.2.23 R.

capital resources table

(A) In the PRA Handbook:
(1) (in the case of an *insurer*) GENPRU 2 Annex 1.
(2) [deleted]
(3) [deleted]
(4) [deleted]

(B) In the FCA Handbook:
(1) (in the case of an *insurer*) GENPRU 2 Annex 1; and
(2) [deleted]
(3) [deleted]
(4) (in relation to a *BIPRU firm*) whichever of the tables in GENPRU 2 Annex 4, GENPRU 2 Annex 5 or GENPRU 2 Annex 6 applies to the *firm* under GENPRU 2.2.19 R.

captive reinsurer

a *pure reinsurer* owned by:

(a) a financial *undertaking* other than an *insurance undertaking* or a *reinsurance undertaking*; or

(b) a *group* of *insurance undertakings* or *reinsurance undertakings* to which the *Insurance Groups Directive* applies; or

(c) a non-financial *undertaking*,

the purpose of which is to provide *reinsurance* cover exclusively for the risks of the *undertaking* or *undertakings* to which it belongs or of an *undertaking* or *undertakings* of the *group* of which that *pure reinsurer* is a member.

CARD

Consolidated Admissions and Reporting Directive.

carried interest

a share in the profits of the *AIF* accrued to the *AIFM* as compensation for the management of the *AIF*, and excluding any share in the profits of the *AIF* accrued to the *AIFM* as a return on any investment by the *AIFM* into the *AIF*.

carrying out contracts of insurance

the *regulated activity*, specified in article 10(2) of the *Regulated Activities Order* (Effecting and carrying out contracts of insurance), of carrying out a *contract of insurance* as principal.

cash

in accordance with section 189(1) of the *CCA*, includes money in any form.

cash assimilated instrument

(in accordance with Article 4(35) of the *Banking Consolidation Directive* (Definitions)) a certificate of deposit or other similar instrument issued by a *lending firm*.

cashback

(in *MCOB*) a cash amount paid by a *mortgage lender* to a *customer* (typically at the beginning of a contract) as an inducement to enter into a *regulated mortgage contract* with the *mortgage lender*.

cash component

a *qualifying investment* prescribed in paragraph 8 of the *ISA Regulations* (Qualifying investments for a cash component).

cash deposit CTF

a *deposit* account held within a *CTF*.

cash deposit ISA

a *cash component* of an *ISA* which does not include the *qualifying investments* prescribed in paragraphs 8(2)(c), (d), (e) or (f) of the *ISA Regulations*.

cash price

(in relation to any *goods*, services, *land* or other things) the price or charge at which the *goods*, services, *land* or any other things may be purchased by, or supplied to, the *borrower* for *cash*, account being taken of any discount generally available from the *dealer* or *supplier* in question.

CASS

the Client Assets sourcebook.

CASS 7 asset management firm

a *firm* subject to the *client money rules* and which falls within either (a) or (b), or both, but not (c):

(a) a *firm* that was a member of *IMRO* immediately before *commencement*;

(b) a *firm* for which the most substantial part of its gross income (including *commissions*) from its *MiFID business* or *designated investment business* that is not *MiFID business*, or both, is derived from one or more of the following activities:
(i) *managing investments* other than *derivatives*;
(ii) *OPS activity*;
(iii) acting as the *manager* or *trustee* of an *AUT*;
(iv) *managing an AIF*;
(v) acting as the *ACD* or *depositary* of an *ICVC*;
(vi) acting as the *authorised contractual scheme manager* or *depositary* of an *ACS*;
(vii) *acting as trustee or depositary of an AIF*;
(viii) *acting as trustee or depositary of a UCITS*;
(ix) *establishing, operating or winding up a collective investment scheme* (other than an *AUT*, *ICVC* or *ACS*);
(x) *establishing, operating or winding up a personal pension scheme*;
(xi) *safeguarding and administering investments*; and
(xii) the provision of *platform services*;

(c) a *firm* for which the most substantial part of its gross income is derived from its *safeguarding and administering investments* activities.

CASS 7 loan-based crowdfunding firm

a *firm*:

(a) that is subject to the *client money rules* in CASS 7; and

(b) whose *designated investment business* includes *operating an electronic system in relation to lending*.

CASS 11 resolution pack

those documents and records specified in CASS 11.12.4 R.

CASS debt management firm

a *firm* which:

(a) carries on the activities of *debt counselling* or *debt adjusting*, alone or together, with a view to an *individual* entering into a particular *debt solution*; or

(b) carries on the activity of *debt counselling* where an *associate* carries on *debt adjusting* with the aim in (a) in view; or

(c) carries on *debt adjusting* where an *associate* carries on *debt counselling* with the aim in (a) in view; or

(d) is a *not-for-profit debt advice body*.

CASS large debt management firm

a *CASS debt management firm* falling within the classification of *CASS large debt management firm* in CASS 11.2.3 R.

CASS large debt management firm external client money reconciliation

the external client money reconciliation that *CASS large debt management firms* are obliged to undertake pursuant to CASS 11.11.25 R to CASS 11.11.26 R.

CASS large debt management firm internal client money reconciliation

the internal client money reconciliation that *CASS large debt management firms* are obliged to undertake pursuant to CASS 11.11.13 R to CASS 11.11.21 R.

CASS large firm

has the meaning in CASS 1A.2.7 R (CASS firm types).

CASS medium firm

has the meaning in CASS 1A.2.7 R (CASS firm types).

CASS operational oversight function

(in the *FCA Handbook*) *FCA controlled function* CF10a in Parts 1 and 2 of the *table of FCA controlled functions*, described more fully in SUP 10A.7.9 R.

CASS resolution pack

those documents and records which are specified in CASS 10.2 and CASS 10.3.

CASS small debt management firm

a *CASS debt management firm* falling within the classification of *CASS small debt management firm* in CASS 11.2.3 R.

CASS small firm

has the meaning in CASS 1A.2.7 R (CASS firm types).

CAT standards

the CAT standards for *ISAs* prescribed by the Treasury on 22 December 1998.

category B firm

a *personal investment firm*, other than an *exempt CAD firm*.

category B1 firm

a *category B firm* whose *permission* includes *dealing in investments as principal*.

category B2 firm

a *category B firm* whose *permission* does not include *dealing* as *principal*; and is not subject to a *requirement* preventing the holding or controlling of *client money* or *custody assets*.

category B3 firm

a *category B firm*:

(a) whose *permission* includes only *insurance mediation activity* in relation to *non-investment insurance contracts*, *home finance mediation activity*, *assisting in the administration and performance of a contracts of insurances*, *arranging* transactions in *life policies* and other insurance contracts, *advising on investments* and receiving and transmitting, on behalf of investors, orders in relation to *securities* and *units* in *collective investment schemes*; and

(b) which is subject to a *requirement* not to hold or control *client money* or *custody assets*.

causing dematerialised instructions to be sent

the *regulated activity*, specified in article 45(2) of the *Regulated Activities Order*, which is in summary: causing dematerialised instructions relating to a *security* to be sent by means of a relevant system in respect of which an operator is approved under the 1995 Regulations where the *person* causing them to be sent is a system-participant; in this definition:

(a) "the 1995 Regulations" means the Uncertificated Securities Regulations 1995 (SI 1995/3272);

(b) "dematerialised instruction", "operator" and "system-participant" have the meaning given by regulation 3 of the 1995 Regulations.

CBG

the Office of Fair Trading's Credit Brokers and Intermediaries Guidance.

CCA

the Consumer Credit Act 1974.

CCA order

the Financial Services Act 2012 (Consumer Credit) Order 2013.

CCA requirement

a requirement imposed by or under Parts 2, 4, 5 and 6 to 12 of the *CCA*.

CCAR 2004

Consumer Credit (Advertisements) Regulations 2004, SI 2004/1484.

CCAR 2010

Consumer Credit (Advertisements) Regulations 2010, SI 2010/1970.

CCP

a legal person that interposes itself between the counterparties to the contracts traded on one or more financial markets, becoming the buyer to every seller and the seller to every buyer, as defined in article 2(1) of *EMIR*.

CCR

counterparty credit risk

CCR internal model method

one of the following:

(a) the method of calculating the amount of an *exposure* set out in BIPRU 13.6 (CCR internal model method);

(b) (where the approach in (a) is being applied on a consolidated basis) the method in (a) as applied on a consolidated basis in accordance with BIPRU 8 (Group risk – consolidation); or

(c) when the reference is to the rules of or administered by a *regulatory body* other than the *appropriate regulator*, whatever corresponds to the approach in (a) or (b), as the case may be, under those rules.

CCR internal model method permission

(A) In the PRA Handbook:
an *Article 129 implementing measure*, *Article 129 permission*, a *requirement* or a *waiver* that requires a *BIPRU firm* or a *CAD investment firm* to use the *CCR internal model method*

(B) In the FCA Handbook:
an *Article 129 implementing measure*, *Article 129 permission*, a *requirement* or a *waiver* that requires a *BIPRU firm* or a *CAD investment firm* to use the *CCR internal model method*

CCR mark to market method

the method of calculating the amount of an *exposure* set out in BIPRU 13.4 (CCR mark to market method).

CCR standardised method

the method of calculating the amount of an *exposure* set out in BIPRU 13.5 (CCR standardised method).

ceding insurer's waiver

(in *FEES*) a *waiver* granted on the application of an *insurer* that waives or modifies its obligations under any one or more of GENPRU 2 Annex 7, INSPRU 1.1.92A R and INSPRU 1.2.28 R in order to enable it to:

(a) treat amounts recoverable from an *ISPV* as:

(i) an *admissible asset*; or

(ii) *reinsurance* for the purposes of calculating its *mathematical reserves*; or

(iii) *reinsurance* reducing its *MCR*; or

(b) otherwise ascribe a value to such amounts.

central assets

the *Society's* own assets that are available at its discretion to meet a *member's* liabilities in respect of *insurance business*.

central bank

(A) In the PRA Handbook: (in accordance with Article 4(23) of the *Banking Consolidation Directive* (Definitions) and for the purposes of *GENPRU* and *BIPRU*) includes the European Central Bank unless otherwise indicated.

(B) In the FCA Handbook:

(1) (in accordance with Article 4(23) of the *Banking Consolidation Directive* (Definitions) and for the purposes of *GENPRU* (except GENPRU 3) and *BIPRU* (except BIPRU 12)) includes the European Central Bank unless otherwise indicated.

(2) (except in (1)) has the meaning in article 4(1)(46) of the *EU CRR*.

central counterparty

(in accordance with Part 1 of Annex III of the *Banking Consolidation Directive* (Definitions) and for the purpose of BIPRU 13 (The calculation of counterparty risk exposure values for financial derivatives, securities financing transactions and long settlement transactions)) an entity that legally interposes itself between counterparties to contracts traded within one or more financial markets, becoming the buyer to every seller and the seller to every buyer.

Central Fund

the Central Fund established under Lloyd's Central Fund Byelaw (No 4 of 1986) and the New Central Fund established under Lloyd's New Central Fund Byelaw (No 23 of 1996).

certificate representing certain securities

the *investment* specified in article 80 of the *Regulated Activities Order* (Certificates representing certain securities), which is in summary: a certificate or other instrument which confers contractual or property rights (other than rights consisting of *options*):

(a) in respect of any *share*, *debenture*, *alternative debenture*, *government and public security* or *warrant* held by a *person* other than the *person* on whom the rights are conferred by the certificate or instrument; and

(b) the transfer of which may be effected without requiring the consent of that *person*;

but excluding any certificate or other instrument which confers rights in respect of two or more *investments* issued by different *persons* or in respect of two or more different *government and public securities* issued by the same *person*.

certificate representing debt securities

(in *LR*) a *certificate representing certain securities* where the certificate or other instrument confers rights in respect of *debentures*, *alternative debentures*, or *government and public securities*.

certificate representing equity securities

(in *LR*) a *certificate representing certain securities* where the certificate or other instrument confers rights in respect of *equity securities*.

certificate representing shares

(in *LR*) a *certificate representing certain securities* where the certificate or other instrument confers rights in respect of *equity shares*.

certified high net worth investor

a *person* who meets the requirements set out in article 21 of the Promotion of Collective Investment Schemes Order, in article 48 of the Financial Promotions Order or in COBS 4.12.6 R.

certified sophisticated investor

a person who meets the requirements set out in article 23 of the Promotion of Collective Investment Schemes Order, in article 50 of the Financial Promotions Order or in COBS 4.12.7 R.

CESR's guidelines on a common definition of European money market funds

the Committee of European Securities Regulators' guidelines on a common definition of European money market funds: 19 May 2010 (CESR/10-049). These are available at www.esma.europa.eu

CESR's UCITS eligible assets guidelines

The Committee of European Securities Regulators' guidelines concerning eligible assets for investment by undertakings for collective investment in transferable securities (CESR/07-044). These are available at www.fsa.gov.uk/pages/Library/Other_publications/EU/eu_docs/index.shtml

CF Arch cru payment scheme

the requirements included in the *permissions* of Capita Financial Managers Limited, BNY Mellon Trust & Depository (UK) Limited and HSBC Bank plc at their request under section 44 of the *Act* on 31 August 2011.

CFD

contract for differences.

CFEB

the consumer financial education body originally established by the *FSA* under section 6A(1) of the *Act* (Enhancing public understanding of financial matters etc) (as it had effect before the passing of the Financial Services Act 2012) and having the name Money Advice Service.

CFEB levy

the levy payable to the *FCA* pursuant to FEES 7.2.1 R by the *persons* listed in FEES 1.1.2R(5).

CFPPFM

the consumer-friendly version of a *firm's PPFM*, which must be produced pursuant to COBS 20.4.5 R.

CFTC

the Commodity Futures Trading Commission.

charge

(1) (In *LR*) (in relation to *securitised derivatives*) means any payment identified under the terms and conditions of the *securitised derivatives*

(2) (except in *LR*) any *fee* or charge made to:
(a) a *client* in connection with *designated investment business*; or
(b) a *customer* in connection with any *insurance mediation activities* in respect of a *non-investment insurance contract*;

whether levied by the *firm* or any other *person*, including a *mark-up or mark-down*.

chargeable case

any *complaint* referred to the *Financial Ombudsman Service*, except where:

(a) the *Ombudsman* considers it apparent from the *complaint*, when it is received, and from any *final response* or *redress determination* which has been issued by the *firm* or *licensee*, that the *complaint* should not proceed because:
(i) the complainant is not an *eligible complainant* in accordance with DISP 2; or
(ii) the *complaint* does not fall within the jurisdiction of the *Financial Ombudsman Service* (as described in DISP 2); or
(iii) the *Ombudsman* considers that the *complaint* should be dismissed without consideration of its merits under DISP 3.3 (Dismissal of complaints without consideration of the merits and test cases); or

(b) the *Ombudsman* considers, at any stage, that the *complaint* should be dismissed under DISP 3.3.4R(2) on the grounds that it is frivolous or vexatious.

chargeable case (general)

a *chargeable case* that is not a *chargeable case (PPI)*.

chargeable case (PPI)

a *chargeable case* that, in the *Ombudsman's* opinion, falls wholly or partly within the scope of DISP App 3 (Handling Payment Protection Insurance Complaints).

charging group

as defined in FEES 5 Annex 3R Part 3.

charity

(in *BCOBS* and *BIPRU*) includes:

(a) in England and Wales, a charity as defined by section 1(1) of the Charities Act 2006;

(b) in Scotland, a charity as defined by section 106 of the Charities and Trustee Investment (Scotland) Act 2005; or

(c) in Northern Ireland, a charity as defined by section 1(1) of the Charities Act (Northern Ireland) 2008 or, until that section comes into force, a body which is recognised as a charity for tax purposes by Her Majesty's Revenue and Customs.

charity AIF

an *AIF* constituted under:

(a) the Church Funds Investment Measure 1958; or

(b) section 96 of the Charities Act 2011; or

(c) section 25 of the Charities Act (Northern Ireland) 1964; or

(d) section 100 of the Charities Act 2011.

chief executive

(1) (in relation to an undertaking whose principal place of business is within the *United Kingdom*) the *person* who, alone or jointly with one or more others, is responsible under the immediate authority of the *directors* for the conduct of the whole of its business.

(2) (in relation to an undertaking whose principal place of business is outside the *United Kingdom*) the *person* who, alone or jointly with one or more others, is responsible for the conduct of its business within the *United Kingdom*.

chief executive function

(1) (in the *FCA Handbook*) *FCA controlled function* CF3 in Part 1 of the *table of FCA controlled functions*, described more fully in SUP 10A.6.17 R. (2) (in the *PRA Handbook*) *PRA controlled function* CF3 in the *table of PRA controlled functions*, described more fully in SUP 10B.6.7 R.

Chinese wall

an arrangement that requires information held by a *person* in the course of carrying on one part of its business to be withheld from, or not to be used for, *persons* with or for whom it acts in the course of carrying on another part of its business.

circular

(in *LR*) any document issued to holders of *listed securities* including notices of meetings but excluding *prospectuses*, *listing particulars*, annual reports and accounts, interim reports, proxy cards and dividend or interest vouchers.

CIS stakeholder product

the *stakeholder product* specified by regulations 5 (units in certain collective investment schemes) and 7 of the *Stakeholder Regulations*.

CIU

(A) In the PRA Handbook: collective investment undertaking.

(B) In the FCA Handbook:

(1) (except in *IFPRU*) collective investment undertaking.

(2) (in *IFPRU*) has the meaning in article 4(1)(7) of the *EU CRR*.

CIU look through method

one of the *standard CIU look through method* or the *modified CIU look through method*.

CIU PRR

the *collective investment undertaking PRR*.

claim

(1) (in *COMP*) a valid claim made in respect of a civil liability owed by a *relevant person* to the claimant.

(2) (in *INSPRU* and *SUP*) a claim under a *contract of insurance*.

claims amount

an amount, as defined in INSPRU 1.1.47 R, used in the calculation of the *general insurance capital requirement*.

class

(A) In the FCA Handbook:

(1) (in *GENPRU*, *INSPRU* and *SUP*) (in relation to a *contract of insurance*) any class of *contract of insurance* listed in Schedule 1 to the *Regulated Activities Order* (Contracts of insurance) and

references to:

(a) *general insurance business class* 1, 2 3, etc. are references to *contracts of insurance* of the kind mentioned in the corresponding numbered paragraph in Part I of Schedule 1 to that Order or, as the context may require, to the *effecting* or *carrying out of contracts of insurance* of that kind; and
(b) *long-term insurance business class* I, II, III, etc. are references to *contracts of insurance* of the kind mentioned in the corresponding numbered paragraph in Part II of Schedule 1 to that Order, as the context may require, to the *effecting* or *carrying out of contracts of insurance* of that kind.

(2) (in *COLL*):
(a) a particular class of *units* of an *authorised fund*; or
(b) all of the *units* relating to a single *sub-fund*; or
(c) a particular class of *units* relating to a single *sub-fund*; or
(d) in relation to an *EEA UCITS scheme*, any arrangement equivalent to (a), (b) or (c).

(3) (in *COBS*) a particular category or type of *packaged product*.

(4) (in *LR*) *securities* the rights attaching to which are or will be identical and which form a single issue or issues.

(5) (in *FEES*) one of the broad classes to which *FSCS* allocates levies as described in FEES 6.4.7A R, FEES 6.5.6A R and FEES 6 Annex 3AR.

(B) In the PRA Handbook:

(1) (in *GENPRU, INSPRU* and *SUP*) (in relation to a *contract of insurance*) any class of *contract of insurance* listed in Schedule 1 to the *Regulated Activities Order* (Contracts of insurance) and references to:

(a) *general insurance business class* 1, 2, 3, etc. are references to *contracts of insurance* of the kind mentioned in the corresponding numbered paragraph in Part I of Schedule 1 to that Order or, as the context may require, to the *effecting* or *carrying out of contracts of insurance* of that kind; and
(b) *long-term insurance business class* I, II, III, etc. are references to *contracts of insurance* of the kind mentioned in the corresponding numbered paragraph in Part II of Schedule 1 to that Order or, as the context may require, to the *effecting* or *carrying out of contracts of insurance* of that kind.

(2) (in *COLL*):
(a) a particular class of *units* of an *authorised fund*; or
(b) all of the *units* relating to a single *sub-fund*; or
(c) a particular class of *units* relating to a single *sub-fund*; or
(d) in relation to an *EEA UCITS scheme*, any arrangement equivalent to (a), (b) or (c).

(3) (in *COBS*) a particular category or type of *packaged product*.

(4) (in *LR*) *securities* the rights attaching to which are or will be identical and which form a single issue or issues.

(5) (in *FEES*) one of the classes to which *FSCS* allocates levies in accordance with the rules of the *compensation scheme*.

class 1 acquisition

(in *LR*) a *class 1 transaction* that involves an acquisition by the relevant *listed company* or its *subsidiary undertaking*.

class 1 circular

(in *LR*) a *circular* relating to a *class 1 transaction* or a transaction which must comply with the requirements of a *class 1 transaction*.

class 1 disposal

(in *LR*) a *class 1 transaction* that consists of a disposal by the relevant *listed company* or its *subsidiary undertaking*.

class 1 transaction

(in *LR* and *FEES*) a transaction classified as a class 1 transaction under LR 10.

class 2 transaction

(in *LR*) a transaction classified as a class 2 transaction under LR 10.

class meeting

(in *COLL*) a separate meeting of *holders* of a *class* of *units*.

class tests

(in *LR*) the tests set out in LR 10 Annex 1 (and for certain specialist companies, those tests as modified by LR 10.7), which are used to determine how a transaction is to be classified for the purposes of the *listing rules*.

clean-up call option

(1) (for the purposes of BIPRU 9 (Securitisation), in relation to a securitisation (within the meaning of paragraph (2) of the definition of securitisation) and in accordance with Part 1 of Annex IX of the *Banking Consolidation Directive* (Securitisation definitions)) a contractual option for the *originator* to repurchase or extinguish the *securitisation positions* before all of the underlying *exposures* have been repaid, when the amount of outstanding *exposures* falls below a specified level.

(2) (for the purposes of *MIPRU* and for a *securitisation*) a contractual option for the *originator* to repurchase or extinguish the *securitisation positions* before all of the underlying *exposures* have been repaid, when the amount of outstanding *exposures* falls below a specified level.

clearing arrangement mandatory prudent segregation

the requirement under CASS 7.13.73 R on a *firm* using the normal approach to segregate an amount of *money* as *client money*.

clearing arrangement mandatory prudent segregation record

the record created and maintained by a *firm* under CASS 7.13.74 R and CASS 7.13.75 R.

clearing member

in relation to an *authorised central counterparty*, as defined in article 2(14) of *EMIR*.

clearing facilitation service

(in relation to a *RIE*) any *regulated activity* carried on by an *RIE* for the purposes of, or in connection with, the provision by the *RIE* of services designed to facilitate the provision of clearing services by another person.

clearing firm

a *firm* which assumes primary responsibility (including legal liability) for the execution and settlement of transactions for *clients*.

clearing house

a clearing house through which transactions may be cleared and for the purposes of CASS 7 and CASS 7A, includes an *authorised central counterparty* and a *CCP*

client

(A) in the *PRA Handbook*:

(1) (except in *PROF* and except in relation to a *home finance transaction*) has the meaning given in COBS 3.2, that is (in summary and without prejudice to the detailed effect of COBS 3.2) a *person* to whom a *firm* provides, intends to provide or has provided a service in the course of carrying on a *regulated activity*, or in the case of *MiFID or equivalent third country business*, an *ancillary service*;
(a) every client is a *customer* or an *eligible counterparty*;
(b) "client" includes:
(i) a potential client;
(ii) a client of an *appointed representative* of a *firm* with or for whom the *appointed representative* acts or intends to act in the course of business for which the *firm* has accepted responsibility under section 39 of the *Act* (Exemption of appointed representatives) or, where applicable, a client of a *tied agent* of a *firm*;
(iii) a *fund* even if it does not have separate legal personality;
(iiiA) any *person* to whom *collective portfolio management* services are provided, irrespective of whether or not it is *authorised*;
(iv) if a *person* ("C1"), with or for whom the *firm* is conducting or intends to conduct *designated investment business*, is acting as agent for another *person* ("C2"), either C1 or C2 in accordance with the *rule* on agent as client COBS 2.4.3 R;
(v) for a *firm* that is *establishing, operating or winding up a personal pension scheme*, a member or beneficiary of that scheme;
(c) "client" does not include:
(i) a trust beneficiary not in (b)(v);
(ii) a *corporate finance contact*;
(iii) a *venture capital contact*.

(2) [deleted]

(3) (in *PROF*) (as defined in section 328(8) of the *Act* (Directions in relation to the general prohibition)) (in relation to *members* of a profession providing financial services under Part XX of the *Act* (Provision of Financial Services by Members of the Professions)):

(a) a *person* who uses, has used or may be contemplating using, any of the services provided by the *member* of a profession in the course of carrying on *exempt regulated activities* (including, where the *member* of the profession is acting in his capacity as a trustee, a *person* who is, has been or may be a beneficiary of the trust); or

(b) a *person* who has rights or interests which are derived from, or otherwise attributable to, the use of any such services by other *persons*; or

(c) a *person* who has rights or interests which may be adversely affected by the use of any such services by *persons* acting on his behalf or in a fiduciary capacity in relation to him.

(4) (in relation to a *regulated mortgage contract*, except in *PROF*) the individual or trustee who is the borrower or potential borrower under that contract.

(5) (in relation to a *home purchase plan*, except in *PROF*) the *home purchaser* or potential *home purchaser*.

(6) (in relation to a *home reversion plan*, except in *PROF*):

(a) the *reversion occupier* or potential *reversion occupier*; or

(b) an individual who is an *unauthorised reversion provider* and who is not, or would not, be required to have *permission* to *enter into a home reversion plan*.

(7) (in relation to a *dormant account* transferred to a *dormant account fund operator*) a *person* entitled to the *balance* in the *dormant account* held with a *bank* or *building society* which was transferred to a *dormant account fund operator*.

(8) (in relation to a *regulated sale and rent back agreement*, except in *PROF*):

(a) the individual or trustee who is the *SRB agreement seller* or potential *SRB agreement seller*; or

(b) an individual who is an *unauthorised SRB agreement provider* or potential *unauthorised SRB agreement provider* and who does not have, or would not be required to have, *permission* to *enter into a regulated sale and rent back agreement*.

(B) in the *FCA Handbook*:

(1) (except in *PROF*, in relation to a *credit-related regulated activity* and in relation to a *home finance transaction*) has the meaning given in COBS 3.2, that is (in summary and without prejudice to the detailed effect of COBS 3.2) a *person* to whom a *firm* provides, intends to provide or has provided a service in the course of carrying on a *regulated activity*, or in the case of *MiFID or equivalent third country business*, an *ancillary service*:

(a) every client is a *customer* or an *eligible counterparty*;

(b) "client" includes:

(i) a potential client;

(ii) a client of an *appointed representative* of a *firm* with or for whom the *appointed representative* acts or intends to act in the course of business for which the *firm* has accepted responsibility under section 39 of the *Act* (Exemption of appointed representatives) or, where applicable, a client of a *tied agent* of a *firm*;

(iii) a *fund* even if it does not have separate legal personality;

(iv) any *person* to whom *collective portfolio management services* are provided, irrespective of whether or not it is *authorised*;

(v) if a *person* ("C1"), with or for whom the *firm* is conducting or intends to conduct *designated investment business*, is acting as agent for another *person* ("C2"), either C1 or C2 in accordance with the *rule* on agent as client COBS 2.4.3 R;

(vi) for a *firm* that is *establishing, operating or winding up a personal pension scheme*, a member or beneficiary of that scheme;

(c) "client" does not include:

(i) a trust beneficiary not in (b)(v);

(ii) a *corporate finance contact*;

(iii) a *venture capital contact*.

(2) (in *PROF*) (as defined in section 328(8) of the *Act* (Directions in relation to the general prohibition)) (in relation to *members* of a profession providing financial services under Part XX of the *Act* (Provision of Financial Services by Members of the Professions)):

(a) a *person* who uses, has used or may be contemplating using, any of the services provided by the *member* of a profession in the course of carrying on *exempt regulated activities* (including, where the *members* of the profession is acting in his capacity as a trustee, a *person* who is, has been or may be a beneficiary of the trust); or

(b) a *person* who has rights or interests which are derived from, or otherwise attributable to, the use of any such services by other *persons*; or

(c) a *person* who has rights or interests which may be adversely affected by the use of any such services by *persons* acting on his behalf or in a fiduciary capacity in relation to him; and

(d) in relation to a *person* ("A") carrying on a *regulated activity* of the kind specified by article 39F

(Debt-collecting) or 39G (Debt administration) of the *Regulated Activities Order*, includes:

(i) the *borrower* under the *credit agreement* or the *hirer* under the *consumer hire agreement*;

(ii) someone who has been the *borrower* or *hirer* under the agreement;

(iii) a *person* who is treated by A as a *person* falling within (i) or (ii);

(iv) any *person* providing a guarantee or indemnity under the agreement; and

(v) a *person* to whom the rights and duties of a *person* falling within (iv) have passed by assignment or operation of law; and

(e) in relation to a *person* ("A") carrying on a *regulated activity* of the kind specified by article 60B (regulated credit agreements) or article 60N (regulated consumer hire agreements) of the *Regulated Activities Order*, includes a *person* who is treated by A as a person who is or has been:

(i) the *borrower* under a *regulated credit agreement* or the *hirer* under a *regulated consumer hire agreement*;

(ii) a *person* providing a guarantee or indemnity under the agreement; or

(iii) a *person* to whom the rights and duties of a *person* within (ii) have passed by assignment or operation of law; and

(f) includes an *individual* who is, may be, has been or may have been the subject of the information referred to in article 89A (Providing credit information services) of the *Regulated Activities Order*; and

(g) includes an *individual* who is, may be, has been or may have been the subject of information furnished in the course of a *person* carrying on an activity of the kind specified by article 89B (Providing credit references) of the *Regulated Activities Order*.

(3) in relation to a *regulated mortgage contract*, except in *PROF*) the individual or trustee who is the borrower or potential borrower under that contract.

(4) in relation to a *home purchase plan*, except in *PROF*) the *home purchaser* or potential *home purchaser*.

(5) (in relation to a *home reversion plan*, except in *PROF*):

(a) the *reversion occupier* or potential *reversion occupier*; or

(b) an individual who is an *unauthorised reversion provider* and who is not, or would not, be required to have *permission* to *enter into a home reversion plan*.

(6) (in relation to a *dormant account* transferred to a *dormant account fund operator*) a *person* entitled to the *balance* in the *dormant account* held with a *bank* or *building society* which was transferred to a *dormant account fund operator*.

(7) (in relation to a *regulated sale and rent back agreement*, except in *PROF*):

(a) the individual or trustee who is the *SRB agreement seller* or potential *SRB agreement seller*; or

(b) an individual who is an *unauthorised SRB agreement provider* or potential *unauthorised SRB agreement provider* and who does not have, or would not be required to have, *permission* to *enter into a regulated sale and rent back agreement*.

(8) (in relation to a *credit-related regulated activity*) a *customer*.

client asset rules

CASS.

client bank account

(A) In the PRA Handbook:

(1) (other than in CASS 7 and CASS 7A and principally in CASS 5):

(a) an account at a bank which:

(i) holds the *money* of one or more *clients*;

(ii) is in the name of the *firm*;

(iii) includes in its title an appropriate description to distinguish the *money* in the account from the *firm's money*; and

(iv) is a current or a deposit account; or

(b) a money market deposit of *client money* which is identified as being *client money*.

(2) (in CASS 7 and CASS 7A)

(a) an account at a bank which:

(i) holds the money of one or more *clients*;

(ii) is in the name of the *firm*; and

(iii) is a current or a deposit account; or

(b) a money market deposit account of *client money* which is identified as being *client money*.

(B) In the FCA Handbook:

(1) (other than in CASS 7 and CASS 7A and principally in CASS 5):

(a) an account at a bank which:

(i) holds the *money* of one or more *clients*;

(ii) is in the name of the *firm*; and

(iii) includes in its title an appropriate description to distinguish the *money* in the account from the

firm's money; and
(iv) is a current or a deposit account; or
(b) a money market deposit account of *client money* which is identified as being *client money*.

(2) (in CASS 7 and CASS 7A)
(a) an account at a bank which:
(i)[deleted]
(ii) is expressly held in the name of the *firm* that is subject to the requirement in CASS 7.13.3 R; and
(iii) is a current or a deposit account; or
(b) a money market deposit account of *client money* which is identified as being *client money*; and
(c) in either case, which is a *general client bank account*, a *designated client bank account* or a *designated client fund account*.

(3) (in CASS 11):
(a) an account at an *approved bank* which:
(i) holds the *money* of one or more *clients*;
(ii) is held in the name of the *firm* to which CASS 11.9 (segregation and the operation of client money accounts) applies;
(iii) includes in its title the word "client" (or, if the system constraints of the *approved bank* or the *firm* that holds the account (or both) make this impracticable, an appropriate abbreviation of "client" that has the same meaning); and
(iv) is a current or a deposit account.

client bank account acknowledgement letter

(1) (in CASS 7) a letter in the form of the template in CASS 7 Annex 2 R.

(2) (in CASS 11) a letter in the form of the template in CASS 11 Annex 1 R.

client equity balance

(A) In the PRA Handbook: the amount which a *firm* would be liable (ignoring any non-cash *collateral* held) to pay to a *client* (or the *client* to the *firm*) in respect of his *margined transactions* if each of his open positions was liquidated at the closing or settlement prices published by the relevant exchange or other appropriate pricing source and his account closed. This refers to cash values and does not include non-cash *collateral* or other *designated investments* held in respect of a *margined transaction*.

(B) In the FCA Handbook: the sum of *money* as described in CASS 7.16.28 R.

client money

(A) In the PRA Handbook:

(1) [deleted]

(2) (in CASS 5) subject to the *client money rules*, *money* of any currency which, in the course of carrying on *insurance mediation activity*, a *firm* holds on behalf of a *client* or which a *firm* treats as *client money* in accordance with the *client money rules*.

(2A) in FEES CASS 6, CASS 7, CASS 7A and CASS 10 and, in so far as it relates to matters covered by CASS 6, CASS 7, *COBS*, *GENPRU* or IPRU (INV) 11) subject to the *client money rules*, *money* of any currency:
(a) that a *firm* receives or holds for, or on behalf of, a client in the course of, or in connection with, its *MiFID business*; and/or
(b) which, in the course of carrying on *designated investment business* that is not *MiFID business*, a *firm* holds in respect of any *investment agreement* entered into, or to be entered into, with or for a *client*, or which a *firm* treats as *client money* in accordance with the *client money rules*.

(3) (in *MIPRU*):
(a) in relation to an *insurance intermediary* when acting as such, *money* which is *client money* in (2);
(b) in relation to a *home finance intermediary* when acting as such, *money* of any currency which in the course of carrying on *home finance mediation activity*, the *firm* holds on behalf of a *client*, either in a bank account or in the form of cash.

(4) (in *COMP*) client money for the purposes of the relevant *client money rules*.

(B) In the FCA Handbook:

(1) [deleted]

(2) (in CASS 5) subject to the *client money rules*, *money* of any currency which, in the course of carrying on *insurance mediation activity*, a *firm* holds on behalf of a *client* or which a *firm* treats as *client money* in accordance with the *client money rules*.

(2A) (in *FEES*, CASS 6, CASS 7, CASS 7A and CASS 10 and, in so far as it relates to matters covered by CASS 6, CASS 7, *COBS* or *GENPRU* and *IPRU(INV)* 11) subject to the *client money rules, money* of any currency:

(a) that a *firm* receives or holds for, or on behalf of, a *client* in the course of, or in connection with, its *MiFID business*; or

(b) that, in the course of carrying on *designated investment business* that is not *MiFID business*, a *firm* holds for a *client*; or

(ba) that a *firm* receives or holds for, or on behalf of, a *client* in the course of, or in connection with, its *stocks and shares ISA business*; or

(c) that a *firm* treats as *client money* in accordance with the *client money rules*.

(2B) (in CASS 11 and CONC 10) *money* which a *CASS debt management firm* receives or holds on behalf of a *client* in the course of or in connection with *debt management activity*.

(3) (in *MIPRU*):

(a) in relation to an *insurance intermediary* when acting as such, *money* which is *client money* in (2);

(b) in relation to a *home finance intermediary* when acting as such, *money* of any currency which in the course of carrying on *home finance mediation activity*, the *firm* holds on behalf of a *client*, either in a bank account or in the form of cash.

(4) (in *COMP*) client money for the purposes of the relevant *client money rules*.

client money distribution rules

CASS 7A.

client money (insurance) distribution rules

the rules in CASS 5.6 (Client money distribution).

client money chapter

CASS 7.

client money requirement

the total amount of *client money* a *firm* is required to have segregated in *client bank accounts* under the *client money rules* (see CASS 7.16.10 R).

client money resource

the aggregate balance on the *firm's client bank accounts* (see CASS 7.16.8 R).

client money rules

(A) In the PRA Handbook:

(1) [deleted]

(2) (in CASS 5) CASS 5.1 to CASS 5.5.

(3) (in CASS 3, CASS 6, CASS 7, CASS 7A, *UPRU*, *COBS* and *FEES*) CASS 7.1 to 7.8.

(B) In the FCA Handbook:

(1) [deleted]

(2) (in CASS 5) CASS 5.1 to CASS 5.5.

(3) (in CASS 3, CASS 6, CASS 7, CASS 7A, *COBS* and *FEES*) and CASS 7.15.5R (3) to CASS 7.19.

client money segregation requirements

(A) In the PRA Handbook: CASS 7.4.1 R and CASS 7.4.11 R(B) In the FCA Handbook: CASS 7.13.3 R and CASS 7.13.12 R

client's best interests rule

COBS 2.1.1 R.

client-specific safe custody asset record

a *firm's* internal record or account identifying each of the particular *safe custody assets* that the *firm* holds for each particular *client* (including those *safe custody assets* deposited by the *firm* with third parties under CASS 6.3 and any *physical safe custody asset* held by the *firm*).

client transaction account

(A) In the PRA Handbook: (in relation to a *firm* and an exchange, *clearing house*, or intermediate broker) an account maintained by the exchange, *clearing house*, or intermediate broker, as the case may be, in respect of transactions in contingent liability investments undertaken by the *firm* with or for its *clients*.

(B) In the FCA Handbook: (in relation to a *firm* and another *person*) an account maintained by that other *person*, such as an exchange, *clearing house*, intermediate broker or *OTC* counterparty, who a *firm* allows to hold *client money* under CASS 7.14 (Client money held by a third party), which:

(a) is the name of the *firm*;

(b) includes in its title the word "client" (or, if the system constraints of the relevant *person* or the *firm* that holds the account (or both) make this impracticable, an appropriate abbreviation of "client" that has the same meaning); and

(c) is not a *client bank account*.

client transaction account acknowledgement letter

a letter in the form of the template in CASS 7 Annex 3 R.

close links

(A) In the PRA Handbook:

(1) (in relation to *MiFID business* or in *FUND*) a situation in which two or more persons are linked by:
(a) participation which means the ownership, direct or by way of control, of 20% or more of the voting rights or capital of an undertaking;
(b) control which means the relationship between a parent undertaking and a subsidiary, in all the cases referred to in Article 1(1) and (2) of Directive 83/349/EEC, or a similar relationship between any person and an undertaking, any subsidiary undertaking of a subsidiary undertaking also being considered a subsidiary of the parent undertaking which is at the head of those undertakings.

A situation in which two or more persons are permanently linked to one and the same person by a control relationship is also to be regarded as constituting a close link between such persons. [Note: article 4(1)(31) of *MIFID* and article 4(1)(e) of *AIFMD*]

(2) (except where (1) applies and except in SUP 4 (Actuaries)) (in accordance with paragraph 3(2) in Schedule 6 to the *Act* (Close links)) the relationship between a *person* ("A") and another *person* ("CL") which exists if:
(a) CL is a *parent undertaking* of A; or
(b) CL is a *subsidiary undertaking* of A; or
(c) CL is a *parent undertaking* of a *subsidiary undertaking* of A; or
(d) CL is a *subsidiary undertaking* of a *parent undertaking* of A; or
(e) CL owns or controls 20% or more of the voting rights or capital of A; or
(f) A owns or controls 20% or more of the voting rights or capital of CL.

(3) (in SUP 4 (Actuaries)) (in accordance with section 343(8) of the *Act* (Information given by auditor or actuary to a regulator: persons with close links)) the relationship in (2), disregarding (e) and (f).

(B) In the FCA Handbook:

(1) (in relation to *MiFID business* or in *FUND*) a situation in which two or more persons are linked by:
(a) participation which means the ownership, direct or by way of control, of 20% or more of the voting rights or capital of an undertaking;
(b) control which means the relationship between a parent undertaking and a subsidiary, in all the cases referred to in Article 1(1) and (2) of Directive 83/349/EEC, or a similar relationship between any person and an undertaking, any subsidiary undertaking of a subsidiary undertaking also being considered a subsidiary of the parent undertaking which is at the head of those undertakings.

A situation in which two or more persons are permanently linked to one and the same person by a control relationship is also to be regarded as constituting a close link between such persons. [Note: article 4(1)(31) of *MIFID* and article 4(1)(e) of *AIFMD*]

(2) (except where (1) applies and except in SUP 3 (Auditors) and SUP 4 (Actuaries)) (in accordance with paragraph 3(2) in Schedule 6 to the *Act* (Close links)) the relationship between a *person* ("A") and another *person* ("CL") which exists if:
(a) CL is a *parent undertaking* of A; or
(b) CL is a *subsidiary undertaking* of A; or
(c) CL is a *parent undertaking* of a *subsidiary undertaking* of A; or
(d) CL is a *subsidiary undertaking* of a *parent undertaking* of A; or
(e) CL owns or controls 20% or more of the voting rights or capital of A; or
(f) A owns or controls 20% or more of the voting rights or capital of CL.

(3) (in SUP 3 (Auditors) and SUP 4 (Actuaries)) (in accordance with section 343(8) of the *Act* (Information given by auditor or actuary to a regulator: persons with close links)) the relationship in (2), disregarding (e) and (f).

close matching rules

for the purposes of *permitted links*, the *rules* in INSPRU 1.1.34 R, INSPRU 3.1.57 R, IN-SPRU 3.1.58 R, and INSPRU 3.1.59 G.

close out

(in *COLL*) enter into a further transaction under which the obligation to deliver or receive which arises or may, at the option of the other party to the transaction, arise under the original transaction is offset by an equivalent and opposite obligation or right to receive or deliver.

close relative

(as defined in article 3(1) of the *Regulated Activities Order* and article 2(1) of the *Financial Promotion Order*) (in relation to any *person*):

(a) his spouse or civil partner

(b) his children and step-children, his parents and step-parents, his brothers and sisters and his step-brothers and step-sisters; and

(c) the spouse or civil partner of any *person* within (b).

closed

(in relation to a *syndicate year*) closed by *reinsurance to close* in accordance with *byelaws*, either into another *syndicate year* or into an *insurer* approved by the *Council* for the purpose.

closed-ended

(in *LR*) (in relation to investment entities) an *investment company* which is not an *open-ended investment company*.

closed-ended corporate AIF

an *AIF* which is a *body corporate* and not a *collective investment scheme*.

closed-ended investment fund

(in *LR*) an entity:

(a) which is an undertaking with limited liability, including a company, limited partnership, or *limited liability partnership*; and

(b) whose primary object is investing and managing its assets (including pooled funds contributed by holders of its *listed securities*):
(i) in property of any description; and
(ii) with a view to spreading investment risk.

closely related

(in *GENPRU* and *BIPRU*) describes a relationship between two or more *persons* under which one or more of the following applies:

(a) the insolvency or default of one of them is likely to be associated with the insolvency or default of the others;

(b) it would be prudent when assessing the financial condition or creditworthiness of one to consider that of the others; or

(c) there is, or there is likely to be, a close relationship between the financial performance of those *persons*.

close period

(in *LR*) as defined in paragraph 1(a) of the *Model Code*.

closing date

the date specified in the earliest relevant *public announcement* of the *offer* as the last date for acceptance of the *offer*, or, if no such date is specified, then the date on which the *issuer* (or seller) of the *securities* offered receives any of the proceeds of the *offer*.

CMAR

a Client Money and Asset Return, containing the information specified in SUP 16 Annex 29.

CNCOM

[deleted]

COB

the Conduct of Business sourcebook up to 1 November 2007.

COBS

the Conduct of Business sourcebook from 1 November 2007.

Code of Market Conduct

the provisions in MAR 1 indicated by an "E" or "C" in the margin or heading, issued by the *FCA* as required by section 119 of the *Act* (The Code).

Code of Practice for Approved Persons

(1) (in the *FCA Handbook*) the provisions in APER 3 and APER 4 indicated by an "E" in the margin or heading, the purpose of which is to help determine whether or not an *approved person's* conduct complies with the Statements of Principle and which are issued by the *FCA* under section 64(2) of the *Act* (Conduct: statements and codes).

(2) (in the *PRA Handbook*) the provisions in APER 3 and APER 4 indicated by an "E" in the margin or heading, the purpose of which is to help determine whether or not an *approved person's* conduct complies with the and which are issued by the *PRA* under section 64(2) of the *Act* (Conduct: statements and codes). The provisions of APER 1 marked with an "E" in the margin also form part of the *Code of Practice for Approved Persons*.

cold call

a *financial promotion* made in the course of a personal visit, telephone conversation or other interactive dialogue:

(a) which:
(i) was not initiated by the recipient of the *financial promotion*; and
(ii) does not take place in response to an express request from the recipient of the *financial promotion*; or

(b) in relation to which it was not clear from all the circumstances when the call, visit or dialogue was initiated or requested, that during the course of the call, visit or dialogue, communications would be made concerning the kind of *controlled activities* and *controlled investments* to which the communications in fact made relate.

In this definition:

(c) a *person* is not to be treated as expressly requesting a call, visit or dialogue:
(i) because he omits to indicate that he does not wish to receive any or any further visits or calls or to engage in any or any further dialogue; or
(ii) because he agrees to standard terms that state that such visits, calls or dialogue will take place, unless he has signified clearly that, in addition to agreeing to the terms, he is willing for them to take place;

(d) if a call, visit or dialogue is initiated or requested by a recipient (R), it is treated as also having been initiated or requested by any other *person* to whom it is made at the same time as it is made to R if that other recipient is a *close relative* of R or expected to *engage in any investment activity* jointly with R.

[Note: article 8 of the *Financial Promotion Order*]

COLL

the Collective Investment Schemes sourcebook.

collateral

(1) (in *COLL* and *FUND*) any form of security, guarantee or indemnity provided by way of security for the discharge of any liability arising from a transaction.

(2) (in *COBS* and *CASS*) any of the following:
(a) an *investment* specified in articles 76 to 81 of the *Regulated Activities Order*; that is:
(i) *shares* (article 76);
(ii) *debentures* (article 77);
(iia) an *alternative debenture* (article 77A);
(iii) *government and public securities* (article 78);
(iv) *warrants* (article 79);
(v) *certificates representing certain securities* (article 80);
(vi) *units* (article 81); or
(b) *money*; or

(c) a *commodity* warrant (however title is recorded or evidenced);

which belongs to a *client* and which is held or controlled by the *firm* under the terms of a deposit, pledge, charge or other security arrangement.

(3) (in *INSPRU* and *SYSC*):

(a) (in relation to any transaction) a mortgage, charge, pledge or other security interest or, as the context may require, an asset that is subject to a mortgage, charge, pledge or other security interest; and

(b) (in relation to a *stock lending*, *repo* or *derivative* transaction only):

(i) a transfer of assets (other than by way of sale) subject to a right of the transferor to have transferred back to it the same, or equivalent, assets or, as the context may require, the assets so transferred by the original transferor; or

(ii) a letter of credit;

where the assets are transferred, or the letter of credit is issued, to secure the performance of the obligations of one of the parties to that transaction.

collateral rules

CASS 3.

collective insurance

(in relation to a *class* of *contract of insurance*) the *class* of *contract of insurance*, specified in paragraph VIII of Part II of Schedule 1 to the *Regulated Activities Order* (Contracts of long-term insurance), of a kind referred to in article 2(2)(e) of the *Consolidated Life Directive* ("the operations carried out by insurance companies such as those referred to in Chapter 1, Title 4 of Book IV of the French "Code des assurances"").

collective investment scheme

a collective investment scheme, as defined in section 235 of the *Act* (Collective Investment Schemes), which is in summary:

(a) any arrangements with respect to property of any description, including money, the purpose or effect of which is to enable *persons* taking part in the arrangements (whether by becoming owners of the property or any part of it or otherwise) to participate in or receive profits or income arising from the acquisition, holding, management or disposal of the property or sums paid out of such profits or income; and

(c) which are not excluded by the Financial Services and Markets Act (Collective Investment Schemes) Order 2001 (SI 2001/1062).

collective investment undertaking other than the closed-end type

(in *PR*) (as defined in Article 2.1(o) of the *prospectus directive*) unit trusts and investment companies:

(a) the object of which is the collective investment of capital provided by the public, and which operate on the principle of risk-spreading;

(b) the units of which are, at the holder's request, repurchased or redeemed, directly or indirectly, out of the assets of these undertakings.

collective investment undertaking PRR

the part of the *market risk capital requirement* calculated in accordance with BIPRU 7.7.5 R (Calculation of the collective investment undertaking PRR).

collective portfolio management

in relation to a *management company*, the activity of management of *UCITS schemes*, *EEA UCITS schemes* or other collective investment undertakings not covered by the *UCITS Directive* that the *firm* is permitted to carry on in accordance with article 6(2) of the *UCITS Directive*. This includes the functions mentioned in Annex II to that directive.

collective portfolio management investment firm

a *firm* which has a *Part 4A permission* for *managing investments* and which is:

(a) an *AIFM investment firm*; or

(b) a UCITS investment firm.

collective portfolio management firm

a *firm* which:

(a)

(i) is a *full-scope UK AIFM*; and

(ii) does not have a *Part 4A permission* to carry on any *regulated activities* other than those in connection with, or for the purpose of, managing collective investment undertakings; or

(b) is a *UCITS firm* that has a *Part 4A permission* for *managing a UCITS*.

COLLG

the Collective Investment Scheme Information Guide.

combination charge structure

a charging structure used by an *operator* of a *qualifying scheme* which is solely a combination of:

(a) an *accrued rights charge* and a *flat-fee charge*; or

(b) an *accrued rights charge* and a *contribution percentage charge*.

Combined Code

(in *LR* and *DTR*) in relation to an *issuer* the Combined Code on Corporate Governance published in June 2008 by the Financial Reporting Council.

combined initial disclosure document

information about the breadth of advice, *scope of advice* or *scope of basic advice* and the nature and costs of the services offered by a *firm* in relation to either:

(a) two or more of the following:
(i) *packaged products* or, for basic advice, *stakeholder products* that are not a *group personal pension scheme* or a *group stakeholder pension scheme* (but only if a *consultancy charge* will be made);
(ii) *non-investment insurance contracts*;
(iii) *home finance transactions* (other than *regulated sale and rent back agreement*); or

(b) *home finance transactions* (other than *regulated sale and rent back agreements*) only;

which contains the keyfacts logo, headings and text in the order shown in, and in accordance with the notes in, COBS 6 Annex 2.

commencement

the beginning of the *commencement day*.

commencement day

the *day* on which section 19 of the *Act* (The general prohibition) comes into force, being 1 December 2001.

commercial customer

(in *ICOBS* and CASS 5) a *customer* who is not a *consumer*.

commercial settlement system

a system commercially available to *firms* that are members or participants, a purpose of which is to facilitate the settlement of transactions using *money* and/or assets held on one or more *settlement accounts*.

commitment

a commitment represented by *insurance business* of any of the *classes* (as defined for the purposes of *INSPRU* and *SUP*) of *long-term insurance business*.

commission

any form of commission or remuneration, including a benefit of any kind, offered or given in connection with:

(a) *designated investment business* (other than commission equivalent);

(b) *insurance mediation activity* in connection with a *non-investment insurance contract*; or

(c) the sale of a *packaged product*, that is offered or given by the *product provider*.

commission equivalent

the cash payments, benefits and services listed in COBS 6 Annex 6 which satisfy the criteria in COBS 6.4.3 R.

commodity

(1)(except for (2) and (3)) a physical asset (other than a financial instrument or cash) which is capable of delivery.

(2) (for the purpose of calculating *position risk requirements*) any of the following (but excluding gold):
(a) a commodity within the meaning of paragraph (1); and
(b) any:
(i) physical or energy product; or
(ii) of the items referred to in paragraph 10 of Section C of Annex I of the *MIFID* as an underlying with respect to the *derivatives* mentioned in that paragraph;
which is, or can be, traded on a secondary market.

(3) (in relation to the *MiFID Regulation*, including the definitions of a *financial instrument* and an *ancillary service*) any goods of a fungible nature that are capable of being delivered, including metals and their ores and alloys, agricultural products, and energy such as electricity, not including services or other items that are not goods, such as currencies or rights in real estate, or that are entirely intangible.

[Note: article 2(1) of the *MiFID Regulation*]

commodity extended maturity ladder approach

the method of calculating the *commodity PRR* in BIPRU 7.4.32 R (Extended maturity ladder approach).

commodity future

a *future* relating to a *commodity*.

commodity maturity ladder approach

the method of calculating the *commodity PRR* in BIPRU 7.4.25 R (Maturity ladder approach).

commodity option

an *option* relating to a *commodity*.

commodity PRR

the part of the *market risk capital requirement* calculated in accordance with BIPRU 7.4 (Commodity PRR) or, in relation to a particular *position*, the portion of the overall *commodity PRR* attributable to that *position*.

commodity simplified approach

the method of calculating the *commodity PRR* in BIPRU 7.4.24 R (Simplified approach).

common equity tier 1 capital

as defined in article 50 of the *EU CRR*.

common equity tier 1 instrument

a capital instrument that qualifies as a common equity tier 1 instrument under article 26 of the *EU CRR*.

common platform firm

(A) In the PRA Handbook (except SYSC 4–9):
(a) a *BIPRU firm*; or
(aa) a *bank*; or
(ab) a *building society*; or
(ac) a *designated investment firm*; or
(ad) an *IFPRU investment firm*; or
(b) an *exempt CAD firm*; or
(c) a UK *MiFID investment firm* which falls within the definition of 'local firm' in Article 3.1P of the *Capital Adequacy Directive*
(d) a *dormant account fund operator*.

(AB) In the *PRA* Handbook (in SYSC 4–9), has the same meaning as in (A) except that it excludes *CRR firms*.

(B) In the FCA Handbook:
(a) a *BIPRU firm*; or
(aa) a *bank*; or

(ab) a *building society*; or

(ac) a *designated investment firm*; or

(ad) an *IFPRU investment firm*; or

(b) an *exempt CAD firm*; or

(c) a UK *MiFID investment firm* which falls within the definition of 'local firm' in Article 3.1P of the *Capital Adequacy Directive*

(d) a *dormant account fund operator*.

common platform organisational requirements

SYSC 4 to SYSC 9.

common platform outsourcing rules

SYSC 8.1.1 R to SYSC 8.1.12 G.

common platform record-keeping requirements

the record-keeping requirements applicable to *common platform firms* set out in SYSC 9.

common platform requirements

SYSC 4 to SYSC 10.

common platform requirements on financial crime

the requirements on *financial crime* applicable to *common platform firms* set out in SYSC 6.3.

communicate

(in relation to a *financial promotion*) to communicate in any way, including causing a communication to be made or directed. [Note: section 21(13) of the *Act* (Restrictions on financial promotion) and article 6(d) of the *Financial Promotion Order* (Interpretation: communications)]

communicated to a person inside the United Kingdom

communicated other than *communicated to a person outside the United Kingdom*.

communicated to a person outside the United Kingdom

(a) *made to* a *person* who receives it outside the *United Kingdom*; or

(b) *directed only at persons* outside the *United Kingdom*.

In this definition:

(c) If the conditions set out in (f)(i), (ii), (iii) and (iv) are met, a *financial promotion* directed from a place inside the *United Kingdom* will be regarded as *directed only at persons* outside the *United Kingdom*.

(d) If the conditions set out in (f)(iii) and (iv) are met, a *financial promotion* directed from a place outside the *United Kingdom* will be regarded as *directed only at persons* outside the *United Kingdom*.

(e) In any other case in which one or more of the conditions in (f)(i) to (v) is met, that fact will be taken into account in determining whether a *financial promotion* is *directed only at persons* outside the *United Kingdom* (but a *financial promotion* may still be regarded as *directed only at persons* outside the *United Kingdom* even if none of these conditions is met).

(f) The conditions are that:

(i) the *financial promotion* is accompanied by an indication that it is *directed only at persons* outside the *United Kingdom*;

(ii) the *financial promotion* is accompanied by an indication that it must not be acted upon by *persons* in the United Kingdom;

(iii) the *financial promotion* is not referred to in, or directly accessible from, any other *financial promotion* which is *made to* a *person* or *directed at persons* in the *United Kingdom* by the same communicator;

(iv) there are in place proper systems and procedures to prevent recipients in the *United Kingdom* (other than those to whom the *financial promotion* might otherwise lawfully have been made) engaging in the investment activity to which the *financial promotion* relates with the *person* directing the *financial promotion*, a *close relative* of his or a member of the same *group*;

(v) the *financial promotion* is included in:

(A) a website, newspaper, journal, magazine or periodical publication which is principally accessed in or intended for a market outside the *United Kingdom*;

(B) a radio or television broadcast or teletext service transmitted principally for reception outside the *United Kingdom*.

community benefit society

a society registered (or deemed to be registered) under the Industrial and Provident Societies Act 1965 which fulfils the condition in section 1(2)(b) of that Act or a society registered (or deemed to be registered) under the Industrial and Provident Societies Act (Northern Ireland) 1969 which fulfils the condition in section 1(2) of that Act.

Community Co-Insurance Directive

the Council Directive of 30 May 1978 on the coordination of laws, regulations and administrative provisions relating to Community co-insurance (No 78/473/EEC).

community co-insurance operation

an operation to which the *Community Co-Insurance Directive* applies, as modified by article 26 of the *Second Non-Life Directive*.

community finance organisation

a *community benefit society*, a *registered charity* or a community interest company limited by guarantee (within the meaning of Part 2 of the Companies (Audit, Investigations and Community Enterprise) Act 2004).

COMP

the Compensation sourcebook.

company

any *body corporate*.

Company Announcements Office

the Company Announcements Office of the London Stock Exchange, the information dissemination provider approved by the *UKLA*.

compensation costs

the costs incurred:

(a) in paying compensation; or

(b) as a result of making the arrangements contemplated in COMP 3.3.1 R or taking the measures contemplated in COMP 3.3.3 R; or

(c) in making payments or giving indemnities under COMP 11.2.3 R; or

(d) under section 214B or section 214D of the *Act*; or

(e) by virtue of section 61 (Sources of compensation) of the Banking Act 2009;

(including the costs of paying interest, principal and other costs of borrowing to pay such costs).

compensation costs levy

a levy imposed by the *FSCS* on *participant firms* to meet *compensation costs*, each *participant firm's* share being calculated in accordance with FEES 6.5

compensation fund

any *policyholder* compensation scheme in any *EEA State*.

compensation scheme

the Financial Services Compensation Scheme established under section 213 of the *Act* (The compensation scheme) for compensating *persons* in cases where *authorised persons* and *appointed representatives*, or, where applicable, a *tied agent* of a firm, are unable, or are likely to be unable, to satisfy *claims* against them.

compensation transitionals order

the Financial Services and Markets Act 2000 (Transitional Provisions, Repeals and Savings) (Financial Services Compensation Scheme) Order 2001 (SI 2001/2967).

competent authority

(A) In the PRA Handbook:

(1) (in relation to the functions referred to in Part VI of the *Act*)

(a) the *FCA*, or the functions referred to in Part VI of the Act under the laws of

(b) an authority exercising functions corresponding to the functions referred to in Part VI of the Act under the laws of another *EEA State*.

(2) (in relation to the exercise of an *EEA right* and the exercise of the *overseas financial stability information power*) a competent authority for the purposes of the relevant *Single Market Directive* or the *auction regulation*.

(3) (in relation to a group, and for the purposes of SYSC 12 (Group risk systems and controls requirement), *GENPRU*, *BIPRU* and *INSPRU*, any national authority of an *EEA State* which is empowered by law or regulation to supervise *regulated entities*, whether on an individual or group-wide basis.

(4) the authority, designated by each *EEA State* in accordance with Article 48 of *MiFID*, unless otherwise specified in *MiFID*. [Note: article 4(1)(22) of *MiFID*]

(5) (in *REC*) in relation to an *investment firm* or *credit institution*, means the competent authority in relation to that firm or institution for the purposes of *MiFID*.

(6) (in COBS 13.4) the authority designated by each *EEA State* in accordance with Article 11 of the *Market Abuse Directive*. [Note: article 1(7) of the *Market Abuse Directive*]

(7) the authority designated by each *EEA State* in accordance with article 32 of the *short selling regulation*.

(8) (for an *AIF*) the national authorities of an *EEA State* which are empowered by law or regulation to supervise *AIFs*.

(9) (for an *AIFM*) a national authority in an *EEA State* which is empowered by law or regulation to supervise *AIFMs*. [Note: This definition is based on the definition contained in the CRD (Consequential Amendments) Instrument 2006 which was consulted on in the consultation paper Strengthening Capital Standards 2 (CP 06/3)]

(B) In the FCA Handbook:

(1) (in relation to the functions referred to in Part VI of the *Act*)
(a) the *FCA*, or the functions referred to in Part VI of the Act under the laws of
(b) an authority exercising functions corresponding to the functions referred to in Part VI of the Act under the laws of another *EEA State*.

(2) (in relation to the exercise of an *EEA right* and the exercise of the *overseas financial stability information power*) a competent authority for the purposes of the relevant *Single Market Directive* or the *auction regulation*.

(3) (in relation to a group, and for the purposes of SYSC 12 (Group risk systems and controls requirement), *GENPRU*, *BIPRU* and *INSPRU*, any national authority of an *EEA State* which is empowered by law or regulation to supervise *regulated entities*, whether on an individual or group-wide basis.

(4) the authority, designated by each *EEA State* in accordance with Article 48 of *MiFID*, unless otherwise specified in *MiFID*. [Note: article 4(1)(22) of *MiFID*]

(5) (in *REC*) in relation to an *investment firm* or *credit institution*, means the competent authority in relation to that firm or institution for the purposes of *MiFID*.

(6) (in COBS 13.4) the authority designated by each *EEA State* in accordance with Article 11 of the *Market Abuse Directive*. [Note: article 1(7) of the *Market Abuse Directive*]

(7) the authority designated by each *EEA State* in accordance with article 32 of the *short selling regulation*.

(8) (for an *AIF*) the national authorities of an *EEA State* which are empowered by law or regulation to supervise *AIFs*.

(9) (for an *AIFM*) a national authority in an *EEA State* which is empowered by law or regulation to supervise *AIFMs*.

(10) (for the purposes of *IFPRU*) has the meaning in article 4(1)(40) of the *EU CRR*.

[Note: This definition is based on the definition contained in the CRD (Consequential Amendments) Instrument 2006 which was consulted on in the consultation paper Strengthening Capital Standards 2 (CP 06/3)]

competent employees rule

(a) for a *firm* which is not a *common platform firm* or a *CRR firm*, SYSC 3.1.6 R.

(b) for a *common platform firm*, SYSC 5.1.1 R.

(c) for a *CRR firm*, Skills, Knowledge and Expertise 2.1 of the *PRA* Rulebook.

complaint

(A) In the PRA Handbook:

(1) [deleted]

(2) (in SUP 10 and *DISP*, except DISP 1.1 and the *complaints handling rules* and the *complaints record rule* in relation to *MiFID business*, and in CREDS 9) any oral or written expression of dissatisfaction, whether justified or not, from, or on behalf of, a *person* about the provision of, or failure to provide, a financial service or a *redress determination*, which:

(a) alleges that the complainant has suffered (or may suffer) financial loss, material distress or material inconvenience; and

(b) relates to an activity of that *respondent*, or of any other *respondent* with whom that *respondent* has some connection in marketing or providing financial services or products, which comes under the jurisdiction of the *Financial Ombudsman Service*.

(3) (in DISP 1.1, the complaints awareness rules only in relation to *collective portfolio management* and the *complaints handling rules* and the *complaints record rule* only in relation to *MiFID business* and *collective portfolio management*) any oral or written expression of dissatisfaction, whether justified or not, from, or on behalf of, a *person* about the provision of, or failure to provide, a financial service or a *redress determination*, which alleges that the complainant has suffered (or may suffer) financial loss, material distress or material inconvenience.

(4) (in *DISP*) reference to a *complaint* includes:
(a) under all jurisdictions, part of a *complaint*; and
(b) under the *Compulsory Jurisdiction*, all or part of a *relevant complaint*.

(B) In the FCA Handbook:

(1) [deleted]

(2) (in SUP 10 and *DISP*, except DISP 1.1 and the *complaints handling rules* and the *complaints record rule* in relation to *MiFID business*, and in CREDS 9) any oral or written expression of dissatisfaction, whether justified or not, from, or on behalf of, a *person* about the provision of, or failure to provide, a financial service or a *redress determination*, which:

(a) alleges that the complainant has suffered (or may suffer) financial loss, material distress or material inconvenience; and

(b) relates to an activity of that *respondent*, or of any other *respondent* with whom that *respondent* has some connection in marketing or providing financial services or products, which comes under the jurisdiction of the *Financial Ombudsman Service*.

(3) (in DISP 1.1, the complaints awareness rules only in relation to *collective portfolio management* and the *complaints handling rules* and the *complaints record rule* only in relation to *MiFID business* and *collective portfolio management*) any oral or written expression of dissatisfaction, whether justified or not, from, or on behalf of, a *person* about the provision of, or failure to provide, a financial service or a *redress determination*, which alleges that the complainant has suffered (or may suffer) financial loss, material distress or material inconvenience.

(4) (in *DISP*) reference to a *complaint* includes:
(a) under all jurisdictions, part of a *complaint*; and
(b) under the *Compulsory Jurisdiction*, all or part of a *relevant complaint* or a *relevant credit-related complaint*.

complaints data publication rules

DISP 1.10A.

complaints handling rules

DISP 1.3.

complaints record rule

DISP 1.9.

complaints investigator

(1) (in relation to a *UK RIE*) the independent *person* appointed under arrangements referred to in paragraph 9(3) of the Schedule to the *Recognition Requirements Regulations* to investigate a complaint and to report on the result of his investigation to that *RIE* and to the complainant.

(2) (in relation to a *UK RCH*) the independent *person* appointed under arrangements referred to in paragraph 23(3) of the Schedule to the *Recognition Requirements Regulations* to investigate a complaint and to report on the result of his investigation to that *RCH* and to the complainant.

(3) (in relation to an *RAP*) the independent *person* appointed under arrangements referred to in regulations 22 and 23 of the *RAP regulations* to investigate a complaint and to report on the result of his investigation to that *RAP* and to the complainant.

complaints reporting rules

DISP 1.10.

complaints resolution rules

DISP 1.4.

complaints time barring rule

DISP 1.8.

complaints time limits rules

DISP 1.6.

compliance oversight function

(in the *FCA Handbook*) *FCA controlled function* CF10 in Parts 1 and 2 of the *table of FCA controlled functions*, described more fully in SUP 10A.7.8 R.

composite firm

a *firm* that carries on both *long-term insurance business* and *general insurance business*.

composite insurer

(in relation to *firm type* in SUP 16.10 (Confirmation of *standing data*)) an *insurer* with permission to effect or carry out both *long-term insurance contracts* and general insurance.

Compulsory Jurisdiction

the jurisdiction of the *Financial Ombudsman Service* to which *firms*, *payment service providers* and *electronic money issuers* (and certain other *persons* as a result of the *Ombudsman Transitional Order* or section 226(2)(b) and (c) of the *Act*) are compulsorily subject.

CONC

the Consumer Credit sourcebook.

concentration risk capital component

[deleted]

COND

the part of the *Handbook* in High Level Standards which has the title Threshold Conditions.

conditional sale agreement

in accordance with article 60L of the *Regulated Activities Order*, an agreement for the sale of *goods* or *land* under which the purchase price or part of it is payable by instalments, and the property in the *goods* or *land* is to remain with the seller (notwithstanding that the buyer is to be in possession of the *goods* or *land*) until such conditions as to the payment of instalments or otherwise as may be specified in the agreement are fulfilled.

conflicts of interest policy

(1) the policy established and maintained in accordance with SYSC 10.1.10 R; and (2) (in MAR 8) the policy established and maintained in accordance with MAR 8.2.8 G which identifies circumstances that constitute, or may give rise to, a conflict of interest arising from *benchmark submissions* and the process of gathering information in order to make *benchmark submissions*, and sets out the process to manage such conflicts.

conglomerate capital resources

(in relation to a *financial conglomerate* with respect to which GENPRU 3.1.29 R (Application of method 1 or 2 from Annex I of the *Financial Groups Directive*) applies) capital resources as defined in whichever of paragraphs 1.1 or 2.1 of GENPRU 3 Annex 1 (Capital adequacy calculations for financial conglomerates) applies with respect to that *financial conglomerate*.

conglomerate capital resources requirement

(in relation to a *financial conglomerate* with respect to which GENPRU 3.1.29 RR (Application of method 1 or 2 from Annex I of the *Financial Groups Directive*) applies) the capital resources requirement defined in whichever of paragraphs 1.3 or 2.4 of GENPRU 3 Annex 1 (Capital adequacy calculations for financial conglomerates) applies with respect to that *financial conglomerate*.

connected client

(in *LR*) in relation to a *sponsor* or securities house, any client of the *sponsor* or securities house who is:

(a) a partner, *director*, employee or controller (as defined in section 422 of the *Act*) of the *sponsor* or securities house or of an undertaking described in paragraph (d); or

(b) the spouse, civil partner or child of any individual described in paragraph (a); or

(c) a *person* in his capacity as a trustee of a private trust (other than a pension scheme or an *employees' share scheme*) the beneficiaries of which include any *person* described in paragraph (a) or (b); or

(d) an undertaking which in relation to the *sponsor* or securities house is a group undertaking.

connected contract

(A) In the PRA Handbook: a *non-investment insurance contract* which:

(a) is not a contract of long-term insurance (as defined by article 3 of the *Regulated Activities Order*);

(b) has a total duration (including *renewals*) of five years or less;

(c) has an annual *premium* (or the equivalent of annual *premium*) of 500 or less;

(d) covers the risk of:
(i) breakdown, loss of, or damage to, non-motor goods supplied by the provider; or
(ii) damage to, or loss of, baggage and other risks linked to the travel booked with the provider ("travel risks") in circumstances where:
(A) the travel booked with the provider relates to attendance at an event organised or managed by that provider and the party seeking insurance is not an individual (acting in his private capacity) or a small business; or
(B) the travel booked with the provider is only the hire of an aircraft, vehicle or vessel which does not provide sleeping accommodation;

(e) does not cover any liability risks (except, in the case of a contract which covers travel risks, where the cover is ancillary to the main cover provided by the contract);

(f) is complementary to the non-motor goods being supplied or service being provided by the provider; and

(g) is of such a nature that the only information that a person requires in order to carry on one of the *insurance mediation activities* is the cover provided by the contract.

In this definition:

(h) the transfer of possession of an aircraft, vehicle or vessel under an agreement for hire which is not:
(i) a hire-purchase agreement within the meaning of section 189(1) of the Consumer Credit Act 1974; or
(ii) any other agreement which contemplates that the property in those goods will also pass at some time in the future;
is the provision of a service related to travel, not a supply of goods;

(i) "small business" means a sole trader, *body corporate*, *partnership* or an unincorporated association which had a turnover in the last financial year of less than £1,000,000 (but where the small business is a member of a group within the meaning of section 262(1) of the Companies Act 1985 (and after the repeal of that section, within the meaning of section 474(1) of the Companies Act 2006), reference to its turnover means the combined turnover of the group);

(j) "turnover" means the amounts derived from the provision of goods and services falling within the business's ordinary activities, after deduction of trade discounts, value added tax and any other taxes based on the amounts so derived.

(B) In the FCA Handbook: a *non-investment insurance contract* which:

(a) is not a contract of long-term insurance (as defined by article 3 of the *Regulated Activities Order*);

(b) has a total duration (including *renewals*) of five years or less;

(c) has an annual *premium* (or the equivalent of annual *premium*) of 500 or less;

(d) covers the risk of:
(i) breakdown, loss of, or damage to, non-motor goods supplied by the provider; or
(ii) damage to, or loss of, baggage and other risks linked to the travel booked with the provider ("travel risks") in circumstances where:
(A) the travel booked with the provider relates to attendance at an event organised or managed by that provider and the party seeking insurance is not an individual (acting in his private capacity) or a small business; or
(B) the travel booked with the provider is only the hire of an aircraft, vehicle or vessel which does not provide sleeping accommodation;

(e) does not cover any liability risks (except, in the case of a contract which covers travel risks, where the cover is ancillary to the main cover provided by the contract);

(f) is complementary to the non-motor goods being supplied or service being provided by the provider; and

(g) is of such a nature that the only information that a person requires in order to carry on one of the *insurance mediation activities* is the cover provided by the contract.

(h) the transfer of possession of an aircraft, vehicle or vessel under an agreement for hire which is not:
(i) a *hire-purchase agreement*; or
(ii) any other agreement which contemplates that the property in those goods will also pass at some time in the future;
is the provision of a service related to travel, not a supply of goods;

(i) "small business" means a sole trader, *body corporate*, *partnership* or an unincorporated association which had a turnover in the last financial year of less than £1,000,000 (but where the small business is a member of a group within the meaning of section 262(1) of the Companies Act 1985 (and after the repeal of that section, within the meaning of section 474(1) of the Companies Act 2006), reference to its turnover means the combined turnover of the group);

(j) "turnover" means the amounts derived from the provision of goods and services falling within the business's ordinary activities, after deduction of trade discounts, value added tax and any other taxes based on the amounts so derived.

connected lending of a capital nature

[deleted]

connected person

(1) (in relation to the *FCA* or *PRA's* consideration of an application for, or of whether to vary or cancel, a *Part 4A permission*) (in accordance with section 55R of the *Act* (Persons connected with an applicant) any *person* appearing to the regulator concerned to be, or likely to be, in a relationship with the applicant or *person* given *permission*, which is relevant.

(2) (in relation to the *FCA* or *PRA's* power to gather information under section 165 of the *Act* (Regulators' power to require information)) (in accordance with section 165(11) of the *Act*) a *person* who has, or has at any relevant time had, the following relationship with another person ("A"):
(a) he is a member of A's *group*;
(b) he is a *controller* of A;
(c) he is a member of a *partnership* of which A is a member;
(d) he is or has been an employee of A;
(e) if A is a *body corporate*, he is or has been an *officer*, or *manager* or agent of A or of a *parent undertaking* of A;
(f) if A is a *partnership*, he is or has been a member, *manager* or agent of A;
(g) if A is an unincorporated association of *persons* which is neither a *partnership* nor an unincorporated *friendly society*, he is or has been an *officer*, *manager*, or agent of A;
(h) if A is a *friendly society*, he is or has been an officer or manager of A ("officer" and "manager" having the same meaning as in section 119(1) of the Friendly Societies Act 1992);
(i) if A is a *building society*, he is or has been an officer of A ("officer" having the same meaning as in section 119(1) of the Building Societies Act 1986);
(j) if A is an individual, he is or has been an agent of A.

(3) (in relation to the *FCA* or *PRA's* powers of investigation under sections 171 and 172 of the *Act* (Powers of persons appointed under section 167; Additional power of persons appointed as a result of section 168(1) or (4))) (in accordance with section 171(4) of the *Act*) a *person* who has, or has at any relevant time had, the following relationship with a *person* under investigation ("P"):
(a) he has the relationship specified in any of paragraphs (2) (a), (b) or (d) to (j) to P (where references in those paragraphs to A are taken to be references to P);
(b) it is a *partnership* of which P is a member;
(c) he is the partner, *manager*, employee, agent, *appointed representative*, or, where applicable, *tied agent*, banker, auditor, actuary or solicitor of:
(i) P; or
(ii) a *parent undertaking* of P; or
(iii) a *subsidiary undertaking* of P; or
(iv) a *subsidiary undertaking* of a *parent undertaking* of P; or
(v) a *parent undertaking* of a *subsidiary undertaking* of P.

(4) to follow

(5) (in *DTR* and *LR* in relation to a *person discharging managerial responsibilities* within an *issuer*) has the same meaning as in section 96B(2) of the *Act*.
(a) [deleted]
(b) [deleted]
(c) [deleted]

connected travel insurance contract

a *non-investment insurance contract* which covers the risk of damage to, or loss of, baggage and other risks linked to the travel booked with the provider but does not otherwise meet the conditions in paragraph (d)(ii) of the definition of *connected contract*.

connected travel insurance intermediary

an *insurance intermediary* whose *permission* includes a *requirement* that it must not conduct any *regulated activity* other than *insurance mediation activity* in relation to a *connected travel insurance contract*.

contingent convertible instrument

a *financial instrument* which meets the requirements for either:

(a) Additional Tier 1 instruments under article 52; or

(b) Tier 2 instruments under article 63, if the provisions governing the instrument require that, upon the occurrence of a trigger event, the principal amount of the instrument be written down on a permanent or temporary basis or the instrument be converted to one or more common equity Tier 1 instruments;

in each case of Regulation (EU) No 575/2013 of the European Parliament and of the Council of 26 June 2013 on prudential requirements for credit institutions and investment firms and amending Regulation (EU) No 648/2012.

consent notice

a notice given by the *FCA* or *PRA* as the case may be to a *Host State regulator* under: (a) paragraph 19(4) (Establishment) of Part III of Schedule 3 to the *Act* (Exercise of Passport Rights by UK firms); or (b) paragraph 20(3A) (Services) of Part III of Schedule 3 to the *Act* (Exercise of Passport Rights by UK firms).

Consolidated Admissions and Reporting Directive

Directive of the European Parliament and of the Council on the admission of securities to official stock exchange listing and on information to be published on those securities (No 2001/34/EC).

consolidated basis

has the meaning in article 4(1)(48) of the *EU CRR*.

consolidated capital resources

(in relation to a *UK consolidation group* or a *non-EEA sub-group* and in *GENPRU* and *BIPRU*) that group's capital resources calculated in accordance with BIPRU 8.6 (Consolidated capital resources).

consolidated capital resources requirement

(in relation to a *UK consolidation group* or a *non-EEA sub-group* and in *GENPRU* and *BIPRU*) an amount of *consolidated capital resources* that that group must hold in accordance with BIPRU 8.7 (Consolidated capital resources requirement).

consolidated credit risk requirement

(in relation to a *UK consolidation group* or a *non-EEA sub-group* and in *GENPRU* and *BIPRU*) has the meaning in BIPRU 8.7 (Consolidated capital resources requirements) which is in summary the part of that group's *consolidated capital resources requirement* relating to credit risk calculated in accordance with BIPRU 8.7.11 R (Calculation of the consolidated requirement components) and as adjusted under BIPRU 8.7.

consolidated fixed overheads requirement

(in relation to a *UK consolidation group* or a *non-EEA sub-group* and in *GENPRU* and *BIPRU*) has the meaning in BIPRU 8.7 (Consolidated capital resources requirements) which is in summary the part of that group's *consolidated capital resources requirement* relating to the *fixed overheads requirement* (as referred to Article 21 of the *Capital Adequacy Directive* and the definition of *fixed overheads requirement*) calculated in accordance with BIPRU 8.7.11 R (Calculation of the consolidated requirement components) and as adjusted under BIPRU 8.7.

consolidated indirectly issued capital

has the meaning in BIPRU 8.6.12 R (Indirectly issued capital and group capital resources), which is in summary any *capital instrument* issued by a member of a *UK consolidation group* or *non-EEA sub-group* where the conditions in BIPRU 8.6.12 R are met.

Consolidated Life Directive

the Council Directive of 5 November 2002 on the taking-up and pursuit of the business of life assurance (No 2002/83/EC), which consolidates the provisions of the *First, Second* and *Third Life Directives*.

Consolidated Life Directive information

(in *COBS*) the Consolidated Life Directive information (COBS 13 Annex 1).

consolidated market risk requirement

(in relation to a *UK consolidation group* or a *non-EEA sub-group* and in *GENPRU* and *BIPRU*) has the meaning in BIPRU 8.7 (Consolidated capital resources requirement) which is in summary the part of that group's *consolidated capital resources requirement* relating to *market risk* calculated in accordance with BIPRU 8.7.11 R (Calculation of the consolidated requirement components) and as adjusted under BIPRU 8.7.

Consolidated Motor Insurance Directive

the European Parliament and Council Directive of 16 September 2009 relating to insurance against civil liability in respect of the use of motor vehicles, and the enforcement of the obligation to insure against such liability (No 2009/103/EC). This Directive codifies Council Directives 72/166/EEC, 84/5/EEC, 90/232/EEC, 2000/26/EC and 2005/14/EC.

consolidated operational risk requirement

[deleted]

consolidated requirement component

has the meaning in BIPRU 8.7.11 R (Calculation of the consolidated requirement components), which in summary is one of the following:

(a) the *consolidated credit risk requirement*; or

(b) the *consolidated fixed overheads requirement*; or

(c) the *consolidated market risk requirement*; or

(d) [deleted]

consolidated situation

(A) (in the *PRA Handbook*) the situation that results from applying the requirements of the *EU CRR* in accordance with Part One, Title II, Chapter 2 of the *EU CRR* to an *institution* as if that *institution* formed, together with one or more other *institutions*, a single *institution*. (B) (in the FCA Handbook) has the meaning in article 4(1)(47) of the *EU CRR*.

consolidating supervisor

has the meaning in article 4(1)(41) of the *EU CRR*.

consolidation Article 12(1) relationship

a relationship between one *undertaking* (the first undertaking) and one or more other *undertakings* satisfying the conditions set out in Article 12(1) of the *Seventh Company Law Directive*, which in summary are as follows:

(a) those *undertakings* are not connected, as described in article 1(1) or (2) of that Directive; and

(b) one of the following conditions is satisfied:
(i) they are managed on a unified basis pursuant to a contract concluded with the first undertaking or provisions in the memorandum or articles of association of those *undertakings*; or
(ii) the administrative, management or supervisory bodies of those *undertakings* consist, for the major part, of the same *persons* in office during the financial year in respect of which it is being decided whether such a relationship exists.

consolidation group

(A) In the PRA Handbook:
(1) the following:
(a) a *conventional group*; or
(b) *undertakings* linked by a *consolidation Article 12(1) relationship* or (for the purposes of *BIPRU*) an *Article 134 relationship*.
If a *parent undertaking* or *subsidiary undertaking* in a *conventional group* (the first person) has a *consolidation Article 12(1) relationship* or (for the purposes of *BIPRU*) an *Article 134 relationship*

with another *person* (the second person), the second person (and any *subsidiary undertaking* of the second person) is also a member of the same *consolidation group*.

(2) (in *SYSC*) the *undertakings* included in the scope of prudential consolidation to the extent and in the manner prescribed in Part One, Title II, Chapter 2, Sections 2 and 3 of the *EU CRR* and IFPRU 8.1.3 R to IFPRU 8.1.4 R (Prudential consolidation) for which the *FCA* is the *consolidating supervisor* under [article 111 of the *CRD*].

(3) For the purposes of SUP 16, the *group* of *undertakings* which are included in the *consolidated situation* of a *parent institution in a Member State*, an *EEA parent institution*, an *EEA parent financial holding company* or an *EEA parent mixed financial holding company* (including any *undertaking* which is included in that consolidation because of an *Article 12(1) relationship*, *Article 18(5) relationship* or Article 18 relationship).

(B) In the FCA Handbook:

(1) the following:

(a) a *conventional group*; or

(b) *undertakings* linked by a *consolidation Article 12(1) relationship* or (for the purposes of *BIPRU*) an *Article 134 relationship*.

If a *parent undertaking* or *subsidiary undertaking* in a *conventional group* (the first person) has a *consolidation Article 12(1) relationship* or (for the purposes of *BIPRU*) an *Article 134 relationship* with another *person* (the second person), the second person (and any *subsidiary undertaking* of the second person) is also a member of the same *consolidation group*.

(2) (for the purposes of SUP 16) the *undertakings* included in the scope of prudential consolidation to the extent and in the manner prescribed in Part One, Title II, Chapter 2, Sections 2 and 3 of the *EU CRR* and IFPRU 8.1.3 R to IFPRU 8.1.4 R (Prudential consolidation) for which the *FCA* is the *consolidating supervisor* under article 111 of the *CRD*.

consolidation UK integrated group

[deleted]

consolidation wider integrated group

[deleted]

constable

a police officer in the *United Kingdom* or a *person* commissioned by the Commissioners for HM Revenue and Customs.

constitution

(in *LR*) memorandum and articles of association or equivalent constitutional document.

consultancy charge

any charge payable by or on behalf of an employee to a *firm* or other intermediary (whether or not that intermediary is an *employee benefit consultant*) in respect of advice given, or services provided, by the *firm* or intermediary to the employer or employee in connection with a *group personal pension scheme* or *group stakeholder pension scheme*, where those charges have been agreed between the *firm* or intermediary and the employer in accordance with the *rules* on consultancy charging and remuneration (COBS 6.1C).

consumer

(A) In the PRA Handbook:

(1) (except as specified in this definition) any natural person acting for purposes outside his trade, business or profession. [Note: article 2 of the *Distance Marketing Directive*, article 2 of the Unfair Terms in Consumer Contracts Directive (93/13/EEC), article 2 of the *E-Commerce Directive*, and article 4(11) of the Payment Services Directive].

(2) (as further defined in section 1G of the *Act*) (in relation to the discharge of the *FCA's* general functions (sections 1B to 1E of the *Act*), the application of the regulatory principles by the regulators in section 3B of the *Act* and references by scheme operators or regulated persons (section 234D of the *Act*)) a *person*:

(a) who uses, has used, or may use:

(i) regulated financial services; or

(ii) services that are provided by other than *authorised persons* but are provided in carrying on *regulated activities*; or

(b) who has relevant rights or interests in relation to any of those services; or

(c) who has invested, or may invest, in financial instruments; or

(ca) who has relevant rights or interests in relation to financial instruments; or

(d) (in relation to the *FCA's* power to make general *rules* (section 137A of the *Act* (The FCA's general rules)) a *person* within the extended definition of consumer in article 7 of the Financial Services Act 2012 (Transitional Provisions) (Miscellaneous Provisions) Order 2013 (SI

442/2013 Definition of "consumer");
(e) [deleted]
(2A) (as further defined in section 425A of the *Act*) (in relation to the issue of statements or codes under section 64 of the *Act*), general exemptions to consultation by the *FCA* (section 138L of the *Act*) in the publication of notices (section 391 of the *Act*) and the exercise of *Treaty rights* (Schedule 4 to the *Act*) a *person* who uses, has used, may have used, or has relevant rights or interests in relation to any services provided by:
(a) *authorised persons* in carrying on regulated activities;
(b) *authorised persons* who are investment *firms*, or credit institutions, in providing relevant ancillary services; or
(c) *persons* acting as appointed representatives.
for the purposes of this definition:
(A) if a *person* is providing a service within (2)(a) or (2A) as a trustee, the *persons* who are, have been or may be beneficiaries of the trust are to be treated as *persons* who use, have used or may use the service;
(AA) a *person* has a "relevant right or interest" in relation to any services within (2)(a) or (2A) if that *person* has a right or interest:
(i) which is derived from, or is otherwise attributable to, the use of the services by others; or
(ii) which may be adversely affected by the use of the services by persons acting on that *person's* behalf or in a fiduciary capacity in relation to that *person*;
(B) a *person* who deals with another person ("A") in the course of A providing a service within (2)(a) or (2A) is to be treated as using the service;
(C) a *person* has a "relevant right or interest" in relation to any financial instrument within (2)(ca) if that person has a right or interest:
(i) which is derived from, or is otherwise attributable to, investment in the instrument by others; or
(ii) which may be adversely affected by the investment in the instrument by persons acting on that *person's* behalf or in a fiduciary capacity in relation to that *person*;
(D) (for the purposes of (2A)(b)):
(a) "credit institution" means:
(i) a credit institution authorised under the *CRD*; or
(ii) an institution which would satisfy the requirements for authorisation as a credit institution under that directive if it had its registered office (or if it does not have one, its head office) in an EEA State;
(b) "relevant ancillary service" means any service of a kind mentioned in Section B of Annex I to *MiFID* the provision of which does not involve the carrying on of a *regulated activity*.
(3) [deleted]
(4) (as further defined in section 425A and 425B of the *Act*) (in relation to the establishment and maintenance of the Consumer Panel (section 1Q of the *Act* (The Consumer Panel))) (as defined in section 1Q of the *Act*), complaints by consumer bodies (section 234C of the *Act*):
(a) a *person* within (2A), other than an *authorised person*; and
(b) (in relation to *regulated activities* carried on otherwise than by *authorised persons*) a *person*, other than an *authorised person*, who would have been a "consumer" within (2A) if the activities were carried on by an *authorised person*.
(5) [deleted]
(5A) (as further defined in sections 425A and 425B of the *Act*) until 31 March 2014, with respect to the publication of information in relation to activities carried on by *Northern Ireland credit unions* (section 391 of the *Act* and article 5 of the Financial Services and Markets Act 2000 (Permissions, Transitional Provisions and Consequential Amendments) (Northern Ireland Credit Unions) Order 2011 (SI 2832/2011) a *person* within (4)(b).
(6) [deleted]

(B) In the FCA Handbook:
(1) (except as specified in this definition) any natural person acting for purposes outside his trade, business or profession. [Note: article 2 of the *Distance Marketing Directive*, article 2 of the Unfair Terms in Consumer Contracts Directive (93/13/EEC), article 2 of the *E-Commerce Directive*, article 4(11) of the Payment Services Directive and article 3 of the *Consumer Credit Directive*.]
(2) (as further defined in section 1G of the *Act*) (in relation to the discharge of the *FCA's* general functions (sections 1B to 1E of the *Act*), the application of the regulatory principles by the regulators in section 3B of the *Act* and references by scheme operators or regulated persons (section 234D of the *Act*)) a *person*:
(a) who uses, has used, or may use:
(i) regulated financial services; or
(ii) services that are provided by other than *authorised persons* but are provided in carrying on *regulated activities*; or
(b) who has relevant rights or interests in relation to any of those services; or
(c) who has invested, or may invest, in financial instruments; or
(ca) who has relevant rights or interests in relation to financial instruments; or
(d) (in relation to the *FCA's* power to make general *rules* (section 137A of the *Act* (The FCA's general rules)) a *person* within the extended definition of consumer in article 7 of the Financial Services Act 2012 (Transitional Provisions) (Miscellaneous Provisions) Order 2013 (SI

442/2013 Definition of "consumer");

(e) [deleted]

(2A) (as further defined in section 425A of the *Act*) (in relation to the issue of statements or codes under section 64 of the *Act*), general exemptions to consultation by the *FCA* (section 138L of the *Act*) in the publication of notices (section 391 of the *Act*) and the exercise of *Treaty rights* (Schedule 4 to the *Act*) a *person* who uses, has used, may have used, or has relevant rights or interests in relation to any services provided by:

(a) *authorised persons* in carrying on regulated activities;

(b) *authorised persons* who are investment *firms*, or credit institutions, in providing relevant ancillary services; or

(c) *persons* acting as appointed representatives.

for the purposes of this definition:

(A) if a *person* is providing a service within (2)(a) or (2A) as a trustee, the *persons* who are, have been or may be beneficiaries of the trust are to be treated as *persons* who use, have used or may use the service;

(AA) a *person* has a "relevant right or interest" in relation to any services within (2)(a) or (2A) if that *person* has a right or interest:

(i) which is derived from, or is otherwise attributable to, the use of the services by others; or

(ii) which may be adversely affected by the use of the services by persons acting on that *person's* behalf or in a fiduciary capacity in relation to that *person*;

(B) a *person* who deals with another person ("A") in the course of A providing a service within (2)(a) or (2A) is to be treated as using the service;

(C) a *person* has a "relevant right or interest" in relation to any financial instrument within (2)(ca) if that person has a right or interest:

(i) which is derived from, or is otherwise attributable to, investment in the instrument by others; or

(ii) which may be adversely affected by the investment in the instrument by persons acting on that *person's* behalf or in a fiduciary capacity in relation to that *person*;

(D) (for the purposes of (2A)(b)):

(a) "credit institution" means:

(i) a credit institution authorised under the *CRD*; or

(ii) an institution which would satisfy the requirements for authorisation as a credit institution under that directive if it had its registered office (or if it does not have one, its head office) in an EEA State;

(b) "relevant ancillary service" means any service of a kind mentioned in Section B of Annex I to *MiFID* the provision of which does not involve the carrying on of a *regulated activity*.

(3) [deleted]

(4) (as further defined in section 425A and 425B of the *Act*) (in relation to the establishment and maintenance of the Consumer Panel (section 1Q of the *Act* (The Consumer Panel))) (as defined in section 1Q of the *Act*), complaints by consumer bodies (section 234C of the *Act*):

(a) a *person* within (2A), other than an *authorised person*; and

(b) (in relation to *regulated activities* carried on otherwise than by *authorised persons*) a *person*, other than an *authorised person*, who would have been a "consumer" within (2A) if the activities were carried on by an *authorised person*.

(5) [deleted]

(5A) (as further defined in sections 425A and 425B of the *Act*) until 31 March 2014, with respect to the publication of information in relation to activities carried on by *Northern Ireland credit unions* (section 391 of the *Act* and article 5 of the Financial Services and Markets Act 2000 (Permissions, Transitional Provisions and Consequential Amendments) (Northern Ireland Credit Unions) Order 2011 (SI 2832/2011) a *person* within (4)(b).

(6) [deleted]

consumer awareness rules

DISP 1.2

Consumer Credit Directive

Directive 2008/48/EC of the European Parliament and of the Council of 23 April 2008 on credit agreements for consumers and repealing Council Directive 87/102/EEC.

Consumer Credit Jurisdiction

the jurisdiction of the *Financial Ombudsman Service* which resulted from section 226A (repealed) of the *Act*.

consumer credit lending

in accordance with article 60B of the *Regulated Activities Order*, *entering into a regulated credit agreement as lender* or exercising, or having the right to exercise, the lender's rights and duties under a regulated credit agreement.

consumer hire agreement

in accordance with article 60N of the *Regulated Activities Order*, an agreement between a *person* ("the owner") and an *individual* ("the hirer") for the bailment or, in Scotland, the hiring of *goods* to the hirer which:

(a) is not a *hire-purchase agreement*; and

(b) is capable of subsisting for more than three months.

Consumer Panel

the panel of *persons* which section 1Qof the *Act* (The Consumer Panel) requires the *FCA* to establish and maintain, as part of its arrangements for consultation under section 1M, to represent the interests of *consumers*.

consumer hiring

in accordance with article 60N of the *Regulated Activities Order*, entering into a *regulated consumer hire agreement* as *owner* or exercising, or having the right to exercise, the *owner's* rights and duties under a *regulated consumer hire agreement*.

consumer redress scheme

a scheme imposed:

(a) by *rules* on *authorised persons*, *payment service providers* or *electronic money issuers* under section 404 (Consumer redress schemes) of the *Act*; or

(b) on a particular *firm* by a *requirement* imposed on its *permission*, or on a particular *payment service provider* or *electronic money issuer* by a *requirement* imposed on its *authorisation*, as envisaged by section 404F(7) of the *Act* but only to the extent that section 404B of the *Act* is engaged by the scheme.

contingency funding plan

(1) (in SYSC 11) a plan for taking action to ensure that a *firm* has adequately liquid financial resources to meet its liabilities as they fall due, prepared under SYSC 11.1.24 E.

(2) (in BIPRU 12) a plan for dealing with liquidity crises as required by BIPRU 12.4.10 R.

contingent liability investment

a *derivative* under the terms of which the *client* will or may be liable to make further payments (other than *charges*, and whether or not secured by *margin*) when the transaction falls to be completed or upon the earlier *closing out* of his position.

continuous payment authority

consent given by a *customer* for a *firm* to make one or more requests to a *payment service provider* for one or more payments from the *customer's* payment account, but excluding:

(a) a direct debit to which the Direct Debit guarantee applies; and

(b) separate consent given by a *customer* to a *firm*, following the making of the *credit agreement*, for the *firm* to make a single request to a *payment service provider* for one payment of a specified amount from the *customer's* payment account on the same day as the consent is given or on a specified day.

contract for differences

the *investment*, specified in article 85 of the *Regulated Activities Order* (Contracts for differences etc), which is in summary rights under:

(a) a contract for differences; or

(b) any other contract the purpose or pretended purpose of which is to secure a profit or avoid a loss by reference to fluctuations in:

(i) the value or price of property of any description; or

(ii) an index or other factor designated for that purpose in the contract; or

(c) a derivative instrument for the transfer of credit risk to which article 85(3) of the *Regulated Activities Order* applies. [Note: paragraph 8 of Section C of Annex 1 to *MiFID*]

contract of insurance

(1) (in relation to a *specified investment*) the *investment*, specified in article 75 of the *Regulated Activities Order* (Contracts of insurance), which is rights under a contract of insurance in (2).

(2) (in relation to a contract) (in accordance with article 3(1) of the *Regulated Activities Order* (Interpretation)) any contract of insurance which is a *long-term insurance contract* or a *general*

insurance contract, including:

(a) fidelity bonds, performance bonds, administration bonds, bail bonds, customs bonds or similar contracts of guarantee, where these are:

(i) effected or carried out by a *person* not carrying on a banking business;

(ii) not effected merely incidentally to some other business carried on by the *person* effecting them; and

(iii) effected in return for the payment of one or more premiums;

(b) *tontines*;

(c) *capital redemption* contracts or *pension fund management* contracts, where these are effected or carried out by a *person* who:

(i) does not carry on a banking business; and

(ii) otherwise carries on the *regulated activity* of *effecting* or *carrying out contracts of insurance*;

(d) contracts to pay annuities on human life;

(e) contracts of a kind referred to in article 2(2)(e) of the *Consolidated Life Directive* (Collective insurance etc); and

(f) contracts of a kind referred to in article 2(3) of the *Consolidated Life Directive* (Social insurance);

but not including a *funeral plan contract* (or a contract which would be a *funeral plan contract* but for the exclusion in article 60 of the *Regulated Activities Order* (Plans covered by insurance or trust arrangements)); in this definition, "annuities on human life" does not include superannuation allowances and annuities payable out of any fund applicable solely to the relief and maintenance of *persons* engaged, or who have been engaged, in any particular profession, trade or employment, or of the dependants of such *persons*.

contract of significance

(in *LR*) a contract which represents in amount or value (or annual amount or value) a sum equal to 1% or more, calculated on a *group* basis where relevant, of:

(a) in the case of a capital transaction or a transaction of which the principal purpose or effect is the granting of credit, the aggregate of the *group's* share capital and reserves; or

(b) in other cases, the total annual purchases, sales, payments or receipts, as the case may be, of the *group*.

contracts of large risks

(in *ICOB*) *contracts of insurance* covering risks within the following categories, in accordance with article 5(d) of the *First Non-Life Directive*:

(a) *railway rolling stock*, *aircraft*, *ships* (sea, lake, river and canal vessels), *goods in transit*, *aircraft liability* and *liability of ships* (sea, lake, river and canal vessels);

(b) *credit* and *suretyship*, where the policyholder is engaged professionally in an industrial or commercial activity or in one of the liberal professions, and the risks relate to such activity;

(c) *land vehicles* (other than *railway rolling stock*), *fire and natural forces*, other *damage to property*, *motor vehicle liability*, *general liability*, and *miscellaneous financial loss*, in so far as the *policyholder* exceeds the limits of at least two of the following three criteria:

(i) balance sheet total: 6.2 million;

(ii) net turnover: 12.8 million;

(iii) average number of *employees* during the financial year: 250.

contractual cross product netting agreement

(for the purpose of BIPRU 13.7 (Contractual netting)) has the meaning set out in BIPRU 13.7.2 R, which is in summary a written bilateral agreement between a *firm* and a *counterparty* which creates a single legal obligation covering all included bilateral master agreements and transactions belonging to different product categories.

contractually based investment

(in accordance with article 3(1) of the *Regulated Activities Order* (Interpretation)):

(a) a *life policy* (except a *long-term care insurance* contract which is not a qualifying *contract of insurance*);

(b) an *option*, *future*, *contract for differences* or *funeral plan contract*;

(c) *rights to or interests in an investment* falling within (a) or (b).

contractual scheme deed

(in *COLL*) the deed referred to in COLL 3.2.3A R (The contractual scheme deed for ACSs), together with any deed expressed to be supplemental to it, made between the *authorised fund manager* and:

(a) the *depositary*, in the case of a *co-ownership scheme*; or

(b) the *nominated partner*, in the case of a *limited partnership scheme*.

Contractual Scheme Regulations

the Collective Investment in Transferable Securities (Contractual Scheme) Regulations 2013 (SI 2013/1388).

contractual scheme rules

rules in *COLL* made by the *FCA* under section 261I of the *Act* (Contractual scheme rules) in relation to:

(a) the constitution, management and operation of *ACSs*;

(b) the powers, duties, rights, and liabilities of the *authorised fund manager* and *depositary* of any such *scheme*;

(c) the rights and duties of the *participants* in any such *scheme*; and

(d) the winding up of any such *scheme*.

contribution percentage charge

a charge used by an *operator* of a *qualifying scheme* which is calculated as a percentage of contributions made by, or on behalf of, a member of that *qualifying scheme* over a defined period of time.

control

(1) (except in (2) and (2A)) (in relation to the acquisition, increase or reduction of control of a *firm*) the relationship between a *person* and the *firm* or other *undertaking* of which the *person* is a controller.

(2) (in SYSC 8 and SYSC 10) control as defined in Article 1 of the Seventh Council Directive 83/349/EEC (The Seventh Company Law Directive).

[Note: article 4 (1)(30) of *MiFID*]

(2A) (in relation to a *management company* carrying on *collective portfolio management* or an *AIFM*) control as defined in articles 1 and 2 of the Seventh Council Directive 83/349/EEC (The Seventh Company Law Directive).

(3) (except in (2) and (2A)) (in accordance with section 182 of the *Act*) a *controller* (″A″) (whether acting alone or in concert) increases control over a *firm* (″B″) when:
(a) the percentage of *shares* A holds in B or a *parent undertaking* (″P″) of B increases by any of the following steps:
(i) from less than 20% to 20% or more;
(ii) from less than 30% to 30% or more;
(iii) from less than 50% to 50% or more;
(b) the percentage of *voting power* A holds in B or P increases by any of the steps mentioned above; or
(c) A becomes a *parent undertaking* of B.

(4) (except in (2) and (2A)) (in accordance with section 183 of the *Act*) a *controller* (″A″) (whether alone or acting in concert) reduces control over a *firm* (″B″) whenever:
(a) the percentage of *shares* which A holds in B or a *parent undertaking* (″P″) of B decreases by any of the following steps:
(i) from 50% or more to less than 50%;
(ii) from 30% or more to less than 30%;
(iii) from 20% or more to less than 20%;
(b) the percentage of *voting power* which A holds in B or P decreases by any of the steps mentioned above; or
(c) A ceases to be a *parent undertaking* of B.

(5) (except in (2) and (2A)) (in accordance with section 183 of the *Act*) a *controller* (″A″) (whether acting alone or in concert) ceases to have control over a *firm* (″B″) if A ceases to hold any of the following:
(a) 10% or more of the *shares* in B or a *parent undertaking* (″P″) of B;
(b) 10% or more of the *voting power* in B or P;
(c) shares or *voting power* in B or in P as a result of which A is able to exercise significant influence over the management of B.

(6) (for the purposes of the calculations in (3) to (5)) the holding of *shares* or *voting power* by a *person* (″A1″) includes any *shares* or *voting power* held by another (″A2″) if A1 and A2 are acting in concert.

controlled activity

(a) *accepting deposits* (paragraph 1)

(b) *effecting contracts of insurance* (paragraph 2(1)):

(c) *carrying out contracts of insurance* (paragraph 2(2));

(d) dealing in securities and contractually based investments as principal or agent (paragraph 3(1));

(e) *arranging (bringing about) deals in investments* (paragraph 4(1));

(f) *making arrangements with a view to transactions in investments* (paragraph 4(2));

(fa) operating a *multilateral trading facility* (paragraph 4A);

(fab) credit broking (paragraph 4B);

(fac) operating an electronic system in relation to lending (paragraph 4C);

(g) *managing investments* (paragraph 5);

(ga) debt adjusting (paragraph 5A);

(gb) debt-counselling (paragraph 5B);

(h) *safeguarding and administering investments* (paragraph 6);

(i) *advising on investments* (paragraph 7);

(j) *advising on syndicate participation at Lloyd's* (paragraph 8);

(k) providing funeral plan contracts (paragraph 9);

(l) providing qualifying credit (paragraph 10);

(m) arranging qualifying credit etc. (paragraph 10A);

(n) advising on qualifying credit etc. (paragraph 10B);

(na) providing relevant consumer credit (paragraph 10BA);

(nb) providing consumer hire (paragraph 10BB);

(o) *entering into a home purchase plan* (paragraph 10C);

(p) *making arrangements with a view to a home purchase plan* (paragraph 10D);

(q) *advising on a home purchase plan* (paragraph 10E);

(r) *entering into a home reversion plan* (paragraph 10F);

(s) *making arrangements with a view to a home reversion plan* (paragraph 10G);

(t) *advising on a home reversion plan* (paragraph 10H);

(u) agreeing to carry on specified kinds of activity (paragraph 11) which are specified in paragraphs 3 to 10H (other than paragraph 4A) of Part 1 of Schedule 1 to the *Financial Promotion Order*.

controlled agreement

(as defined in section 30 of the *Act* (Enforceability of agreements resulting from unlawful communications)) an agreement the making or performance of which by either party constitutes a *controlled activity*.

controlled function

a function, relating to the carrying on of a *regulated activity* by a *firm*, which is specified by either the *FCA* (in the *table of FCA controlled functions*) or the *PRA* (in the *table of PRA controlled functions*), under section 59 of the *Act* (Approval for particular arrangements).

controlled investment

(A) In the PRA Handbook: (in accordance with section 21(10) of the *Act* (Restrictions on financial promotion) and article 4 of the *Financial Promotion Order* (Definitions of controlled activities and controlled investments)) an *investment* specified in Part II of Schedule 1 to the *Financial Promotion Order* (Controlled investments).

(B) In the FCA Handbook: (in accordance with section 21(10) of the *Act* (Restrictions on financial promotion) and article 4 of the *Financial Promotion Order* (Definitions of controlled activities and controlled investments)) an *investment* specified in Part II of Schedule 1 to the *Financial Promotion Order* (Controlled investments) (having regard to the effect of paragraph 4C (10) of that Schedule).

controlled undertaking

any subsidiary undertaking within the meaning of the *Act* other than one falling within section 1162(4)(b) of the Companies Act 2006 or section 420(2)(b) of the *Act*.

controller

(A) In the PRA Handbook

(1) (in relation to a *firm* or other *undertaking* ("B"), other than a *non-directive firm*) a *person* ("A") who (whether acting alone or in concert):

(a) holds 10% or more of the *shares* in B or in a *parent undertaking* ("P") of B;

(b) holds 10% or more of the *voting power* in B or in P; or

(c) holds *shares* or *voting power* in B or P as a result of which A is able to exercise significant influence over the management of B.

(2) (in relation to a *non-directive firm* ("B")) a *person* ("A") who (whether acting alone or in concert):

(a) holds 20% or more of the *shares* in B or in a *parent undertaking* ("P") of B;

(b) holds 20% or more of the *voting power* in B or in P; or

(c) holds *shares* or *voting power* in B or P as a result of which A is able to exercise significant influence over the management of B.

(3) for the purposes of calculations relating to (1) and (2), the holding of *shares* or *voting power* by a *person* ("A1") includes any *shares* or *voting power* held by another ("A2") if A1 and A2 are acting in concert.

(4) *shares* and *voting power* that a *person* holds in a *firm* ("B") or in a *parent undertaking* of B ("P") are disregarded for the purposes of determining *control* in the following circumstances:

(a) *shares* held for the sole purposes of clearing and settling within a short settlement cycle;

(b) *shares* held by a *custodian* or its nominee in its custodian capacity are disregarded, provided that the *custodian* or nominee is only able to exercise *voting power* attached to the *shares* in accordance with instructions given in writing;

(c) *shares* representing no more than 5% of the total voting power in B or P held by an *investment firm*, provided that:

(i) it holds the *shares* in the capacity of a *market maker* (as defined in article 4.1(8) of MIFID);

(ii) it is authorised by its *Home State regulator* under MIFID; and

(iii) it does not intervene in the management of B or P nor exerts any influence on B or P to buy the *shares* or back the share price;

(d) *shares* held by a *credit institution* or *investment firm* in its *trading book* are disregarded, provided that:

(i) the *shares* represent no more than 5% of the total *voting power* in B or P; and

(ii) the *credit institution* or *investment firm* ensures that the *voting power* is not used to intervene in the management of B or P;

(e) *shares* held by a *credit institution* or an *investment firm* are disregarded, provided that:

(i) the *shares* are held as a result of performing the *investment services* and activities of:

(A) underwriting share issues; or

(B) placing shares on a firm commitment basis in accordance with Annex I, section A.6 of MIFID; and

(ii) the *credit institution* or *investment firm*:

(A) does not exercise *voting power* represented by the *shares* or otherwise intervene in the management of the issuer; and

(B) retains the holding for a period of less than one year;

(f) where a *management company* and its *parent undertaking* both hold *shares* or *voting power*, each may disregard holdings of the other, provided that each exercises its *voting power* independently of the other;

(g) but (f) does not apply if the *management company*:

(i) manages holdings for its *parent undertaking* or an *undertaking* in respect of which the *parent undertaking* is a *controller*;

(ii) has no discretion to exercise the *voting power* attached to such holdings; and

(iii) may only exercise the *voting power* in relation to such holdings under direct or indirect instruction from:

(A) its *parent undertaking*; or

(B) an *undertaking* in respect of which of the *parent undertaking* is a *controller*;

(h) where an *investment firm* and its *parent undertaking* both hold *shares* or *voting power*, the *parent undertaking* may disregard holdings managed by the *investment firm* on a client by client basis and the *investment firm* may disregard holdings of the *parent undertaking*, provided that the *investment firm*:

(i) has permission to provide *portfolio management*;

(ii) exercises its *voting power* independently from the *parent undertaking*; and

(iii) may only exercise the *voting power* under instructions given in writing, or has appropriate mechanisms in place for ensuring that individual portfolio management services are conducted independently of any other services.

(B) In the FCA Handbook

(1) (in relation to a *firm* or other *undertaking* ("B"), other than a *non-directive firm* or a firm within (2A)) a *person* ("A") who (whether acting alone or in concert):

(a) holds 10% or more of the *shares* in B or in a *parent undertaking* ("P") of B;

(b) holds 10% or more of the *voting power* in B or in P; or

(c) holds *shares* or *voting power* in B or P as a result of which A is able to exercise significant influence over the management of B.

(2) (in relation to a *non-directive firm* ("B"), other than a firm within (2A)), a *person* ("A") who (whether acting alone or in concert):

(a) holds 20% or more of the *shares* in B or in a *parent undertaking* ("P") of B;

(b) holds 20% or more of the *voting power* in B or in P; or

(c) holds *shares* or *voting power* in B or P as a result of which A is able to exercise significant influence over the management of B.

(2A) (in relation to a *firm* ("B") with *limited permission* where the only regulated activities (other than ones in relation to which sections 20(1) and (1A) and 23(1A) of the *Act* do not apply under section 39(1D) of the *Act*) that B carries on, or seeks to carry on, are relevant credit activities within article 6A of the Financial Services and Markets Act 2000 (Controllers) (Exemption) Order 2009) a *person* ("A") who (whether acting alone or in concert):

(a) holds 33% or more of the *shares* in B or in a *parent undertaking* ("P") of B;

(b) holds 33% or more of the *voting power* in B or P; or

(c) holds *shares* or *voting power* in B or P as a result of which A is able to exercise significant influence over the management of B.

(3) for the purposes of calculations relating to (1), (2) and (2A), the holding of *shares* or *voting power* by a *person* ("A1") includes any *shares* or *voting power* held by another ("A2") if A1 and A2 are acting in concert.

(4) *shares* and *voting power* that a *person* holds in a *firm* ("B") or in a *parent undertaking* of B ("P") are disregarded for the purposes of determining *control* in the following circumstances:

(a) *shares* held for the sole purposes of clearing and settling within a short settlement cycle;

(b) *shares* held by a *custodian* or its nominee in its custodian capacity are disregarded, provided that the *custodian* or nominee is only able to exercise *voting power* attached to the *shares* in accordance with instructions given in writing;

(c) *shares* representing no more than 5% of the total voting power in B or P held by an *investment firm*, provided that:

(i) it holds the *shares* in the capacity of a *market maker* (as defined in article 4.1(8) of MIFID);

(ii) it is authorised by its *Home State regulator* under MIFID; and

(iii) it does not intervene in the management of B or P nor exerts any influence on B or P to buy the *shares* or back the share price;

(d) *shares* held by a *credit institution* or *investment firm* in its *trading book* are disregarded, provided that:

(i) the *shares* represent no more than 5% of the total *voting power* in B or P; and

(ii) the *credit institution* or *investment firm* ensures that the *voting power* is not used to intervene in the management of B or P;

(e) *shares* held by a *credit institution* or an *investment firm* are disregarded, provided that:

(i) the *shares* are held as a result of performing the *investment services* and activities of:

(A) underwriting share issues; or

(B) placing shares on a firm commitment basis in accordance with Annex I, section A.6 of MIFID; and

(ii) the *credit institution* or *investment firm*:

(A) does not exercise *voting power* represented by the *shares* or otherwise intervene in the management of the issuer; and

(B) retains the holding for a period of less than one year;

(f) where a *management company* and its *parent undertaking* both hold *shares* or *voting power*, each may disregard holdings of the other, provided that each exercises its *voting power* independently of the other;

(g) but (f) does not apply if the *management company*:

(i) manages holdings for its *parent undertaking* or an *undertaking* in respect of which the *parent undertaking* is a *controller*;

(ii) has no discretion to exercise the *voting power* attached to such holdings; and

(iii) may only exercise the *voting power* in relation to such holdings under direct or indirect instruction from:

(A) its *parent undertaking*; or

(B) an *undertaking* in respect of which of the *parent undertaking* is a *controller*;

(h) where an *investment firm* and its *parent undertaking* both hold *shares* or *voting power*, the *parent undertaking* may disregard holdings managed by the *investment firm* on a client by client basis and the *investment firm* may disregard holdings of the *parent undertaking*, provided that the *investment firm*:

(i) has permission to provide *portfolio management*;

(ii) exercises its *voting power* independently from the *parent undertaking*; and

(iii) may only exercise the *voting power* under instructions given in writing, or has appropriate mechanisms in place for ensuring that individual portfolio management services are conducted independently of any other services.

controlling shareholder

as defined in LR 6.1.2A R.

conventional group

a group of *undertakings* that consists of a *parent undertaking* and the rest of its *sub-group*.

convertible securities

(in *LR* and *FEES*) a *security* which is:

(a) convertible into, or exchangeable for, other *securities*; or

(b) accompanied by a *warrant* or *option* to subscribe for or purchase other *securities*.

conversion factor

(A) In the PRA Handbook:
(in accordance with Article 4(28) of the *Banking Consolidation Directive* (Definitions)) the ratio of the currently undrawn amount of a commitment that will be drawn and outstanding at default to the currently undrawn amount of the commitment; the extent of the commitment is determined by the advised limit, unless the unadvised limit is higher.

(B) In the FCA Handbook:
(in accordance with Article 4(28) of the *Banking Consolidation Directive* (Definitions) and for the purposes of *BIPRU*) the ratio of the currently undrawn amount of a commitment that will be drawn and outstanding at default to the currently undrawn amount of the commitment; the extent of the commitment is determined by the advised limit, unless the unadvised limit is higher.

convertible

(A) In the PRA Handbook: (for the purposes of *BIPRU*) a *security* which gives the investor the right to convert the *security* into a *share* at an agreed price or on an agreed basis.

(B) In the FCA Handbook: (for the purposes of *BIPRU* and *IFPRU*) a *security* which gives the investor the right to convert the *security* into a *share* at an agreed price or on an agreed basis.

coordinator

(in relation to a *financial conglomerate*) the *competent authority* which has been appointed, in accordance with Article 10 of the *Financial Groups Directive* (Competent authority responsible for exercising supplementary supervision (the coordinator)), as the *competent authority* which is responsible for the co-ordination and exercise of supplementary supervision of that *financial conglomerate*.

co-ownership scheme

(as defined in section 235A(2) of the *Act* (Contractual schemes)) a *collective investment scheme* which satisfies the conditions in section 235A(3) and which is authorised for the purposes of the *Act* by an *authorisation order*.

core business lines

business lines and associated services which represent material sources of revenue, profit or franchise value for an *RRD institution* or an *RRD group*. [Note: article 2(1)(36) of *RRD*]

core concentration risk group counterparty

(in relation to a *firm*) a counterparty which is its *parent undertaking*, its *subsidiary undertaking* or a *subsidiary undertaking* of its *parent undertaking*, provided that (in each case) both the counterparty and the *firm* are:

(a) included within the scope of consolidation on a full basis with respect to the same *UK consolidation group*; and

(b) (where relevant) held by one or more intermediate *parent undertaking* or *financial holding company*, all of which are incorporated in the *United Kingdom*.

core market participant

an entity of a type listed in BIPRU 5.4.64 R (The financial collateral comprehensive method: Conditions for applying a 0% volatility adjustment).

core provision

(as defined in section 316(3) of the *Act* (Direction by a regulator)) a provision of the *Act* mentioned in section 317 of the *Act* (The core provisions) which applies to the carrying on of an insurance market activity by a *member*, or the *members* of the *Society* taken together, if the *appropriate regulator* so directs.

core tier one capital

an item of capital that is stated in stage A of the *capital resources table* (Core tier one capital) to be core tier one capital.

core UK group

(A) In the PRA Handbook: has the meaning given in the *PRA* Rulebook: Large Exposures rules.

(B) In the FCA Handbook:

(1) (in relation to a *BIPRU firm*) all *undertakings* which, in relation to the *firm*, satisfy the conditions set out in BIPRU 3.2.25 R (Zero risk-weighting for intra-group exposures: core UK group).

(2) (in relation to an *IFPRU investment firm*) all counterparties which:
(a) are listed in the *firm's* core UK group permission;
(b) satisfy the conditions in article 113(6) of the *EU CRR* (Calculation of risk-weighted exposure amounts: intra-group); and
(c) (unless it is an *IFPRU limited-activity firm* or *IFPRU limited-licence firm*, or an exempt IFPRU commodities firm to which article 493(1) of the *EU CRR* (Transitional provision for large exposures) apply) for which *exposures* are exempted, under article 400(1)(f) of the *EU CRR* (Large exposures: exemptions), from the application of article 395(1) of the *EU CRR* (Limits to large exposures).

core UK group eligible capital

(A) In the PRA Handbook has the meaning given in the PRA Rulebook: Large Exposure rules.

(B) In the FCA Handbook means the eligible capital in the *core UK group* calculated in line with IFPRU 8.2.7 R.

core UK group permission

(A) In the PRA Handbook has the meaning given in the *PRA* Rulebook: Large Exposures rules

(B) In the FCA HAndbook a permission given by the *FCA* under article 113(6) of the *EU CRR* (see IFPRU 8.1.14 G to IFPRU 8.1.21 G).

core UK group waiver

(A) In the PRA Handbook: a *waiver* that has the result of requiring a *firm* to apply:

(a) (in relation to the *credit risk capital requirement*) BIPRU 3.2.25 R (Zero risk-weighting for intra-group exposures: core UK group), which in summary allows a *firm* to assign a *risk weight* of 0% to *exposures* to members of its *core UK group* instead of complying with BIPRU 3.2.20 R (Calculation of risk-weighted exposure amounts under the standardised approach); or

(b) (in relation to *large exposures*) BIPRU 10.8A (Intra-group exposures: core UK group), which in summary exempts all *exposures* between members of a *core UK group* from the limits described in BIPRU 10.5 (Limits on exposures).

(B) In the FCA Handbook: (in *BIPRU*) a *waiver* that has the result of requiring a *firm* to apply:

(a) (in relation to the *credit risk capital requirement*) BIPRU 3.2.25 R (Zero risk-weighting for intra-group exposures: core UK group), which in summary allows a *firm* to assign a *risk weight* of 0% to *exposures* to members of its *core UK group* instead of complying with BIPRU 3.2.20 R (Calculation of risk-weighted exposure amounts under the standardised approach); or

(b) [deleted]

corporate

(in relation to the *IRB approach* or the *standardised approach* to credit risk) a *person* an *exposure* to whom is a *corporate exposure*.

corporate access service

a service of arranging or bringing about contact between an *investment manager* and an *issuer* or potential *issuer*.

corporate exposure

(1) (in relation to the *IRB approach*) an *exposure* falling into BIPRU 4.3.2 R (3) (IRB exposure classes).

(2) (in relation to the *standardised approach* to credit risk) an *exposure* falling into BIPRU 3.2.9 R (7) (Standardised approach to credit risk exposure classes).

corporate finance advisory firm

a *firm* whose permission includes a *requirement* that the *firm* must not conduct *designated investment business* other than *corporate finance business*.

corporate finance business

(a) *designated investment business* carried on by a *firm* with or for:

(i) any *issuer*, holder or owner of *designated investments*, if that business relates to the *offer*, issue, underwriting, repurchase, exchange or redemption of, or the variation of the terms of, those *investments*, or any related matter;

(ii) any *eligible counterparty* or *professional client*, or other *body corporate*, *partnership* or supranational organisation, if that business relates to the manner in which, or the terms on which, or the *persons* by whom, any business, activities or undertakings relating to it, or any *associate*, are to be financed, structured, managed, controlled, regulated or reported upon;

(iii) any *person* in connection with:

(A) a proposed or actual *takeover or related operation* by or on behalf of that *person*, or involving *investments* issued by that *person* (being a *body corporate*), its *holding company*, *subsidiary* or *associate*; or

(B) a merger, de-merger, reorganisation or reconstruction involving any *investments* issued by that *person* (being a *body corporate*), its holding company, subsidiary or *associate*;

(iv) any shareholder or prospective shareholder of a *body corporate* established or to be established for the purpose of effecting a *takeover or related operation*, where that business is in connection with that *takeover or related operation*;

(v) any *person* who, acting as a *principal* for his own account:

(A) is involved in negotiations or decisions relating to the commercial, financial or strategic intentions or requirements of a business or prospective business; or

(B) (provided he is acting otherwise than solely in his capacity as an investor) assists the interests of another *person* with or for whom the *firm*, or another *authorised person* or *overseas person*, is undertaking business as specified in (a)(i), (ii), (iii) or (iv), by himself undertaking all or part of any transactions involved in such business;

(vi) any *person* undertaking business with or for a *person* as specified in (a)(i), (ii), (iii), (iv) or (v) in respect of activities described in those sub-paragraphs;

(b) *designated investment business* carried on by a *firm* as a *principal* for its own account where such business:

(i) is in the course of, or arises out of, activities undertaken in accordance with (a); and

(ii) does not involve transactions with or for, or *advice on investments* to, any other *person* who is a *retail client* in respect of such business;

(c) *designated investment business* carried on by a *firm* as *principal* for its own account if such business:

(i) is in the course of, or arises out of:

(A) the *offer*, issue, underwriting, repurchase, exchange or redemption of, or the variation of the terms of, *shares*, share warrants, *debentures* or debenture warrants issued by the *firm*, or any related matter; or

(B) a proposed or actual *takeover or related operation* by or on behalf of the *firm*, or involving *shares*, share warrants, *debentures* or debenture warrants issued by the *firm*; or

(C) a merger, de-merger, reorganisation or reconstruction involving any *shares*, share warrants, *debentures* or debenture warrants issued by the *firm*; and

(ii) does not involve *advice on investments* to any *person* who is a *retail client*;

in this definition, "share warrants" and "debenture warrants" mean any *warrants* which relate to *shares* in the *firm* concerned or, as the case may be, *debentures* issued by the *firm*.

corporate finance contact

(when a *firm* carries on *regulated activities* with or for a *person* in the course of or as a result of either carrying on *corporate finance business* with or for a *client*, or carrying on *corporate finance business* for the *firm*'s own account) that *person* in connection with that *regulated activity* if:

(a) the *firm* does not behave in a way towards that *person* which might reasonably be expected to lead that *person* to believe that he is being treated as a *client*; and

(b) the *firm* clearly indicates to that *person* that it:

(i) is not acting for him; and

(ii) will not be responsible to him for providing protections afforded to *clients* of the *firm* or be advising him on the relevant transaction.

corporate governance rules

(in accordance with sections 73A(1) and 89O(1) of the *Act*) *rules* for the purpose of implementing, enabling the implementation of or dealing with matters arising out of or related to, any *EU law* obligation relating to the corporate governance of *issuers* who have requested or approved *admission to trading* of their securities and about corporate governance in relation to such *issuers* for the purpose of implementing, or dealing with matters arising out of or related to, any *EU* law obligation. The *corporate governance rules* are located in chapters 1B, 4 and 7 of *DTR*.

corporate member

a *member* that is a *body corporate* or a Scottish Limited partnership.

correlation trading portfolio

(in BIPRU 7) a portfolio consisting of *securitisation positions* and nth-to-default credit derivatives that meet the criteria set out at BIPRU 7.2.42A R, or other *positions* which may be included in accordance with BIPRU 7.2.42B R.

cost of credit

any costs, including interest, commission, taxes and any other kind of fees which are required to be paid by or on behalf of the *borrower* or a relative of the *borrower* in connection with the *credit agreement*, whether payable to the *lender* or to any other *person*, and which are known to the *lender*, except for notarial costs.

Council

the *governing body* of the *Society* constituted by section 3 of Lloyd's Act 1982.

countercyclical buffer rate

(in accordance with article 128(7) of the *CRD* (Definitions)) the rate:

(a) expressed as a percentage of *total risk exposure amount* set by the *UK countercyclical buffer authority* or an *EEA countercyclical buffer authority*; or

(b) expressed in terms equivalent to a percentage of total risk exposure amount set by a *third-country countercyclical buffer authority*,

that a *firm* must apply in order to calculate its *countercyclical capital buffer*.

countercyclical capital buffer

(in accordance with article 128(2) of *CRD* (Definitions)) the amount of *common equity tier 1 capital* a *firm* must calculate in line with IFPRU 10.3.

counterparty

(A) In the PRA Handbook:

(1) (in *UPRU*) any *person* with or for whom a firm carries on *designated investment business* or an *ancillary activity*.

(2) (for the purposes of the rules relating to insurers in *GENPRU* and *INSPRU*) (in relation to an insurer, the *Society*, a *syndicate* or *member* ('A')):
(a) any one individual; or
(b) any one unincorporated body of *persons*; or
(c) any *company* which is not a member of a *group*; or
(d) any *group* of *companies* excluding:
(i) (for the purposes of INSPRU 2.1) any *companies* within the *group* which are *subsidiary undertakings* of A and which fall within GENPRU 1.3.43 R; and
(ii) (for all other purposes) any *companies* within the *group* which are *subsidiary undertakings* of A; or
(e) any government of a State together with all the public bodies, local authorities or nationalised industries of that State, in which A, or any of its *subsidiary undertakings*, has made *investments* or against whom, or in respect of whom, it, or any of its *subsidiary undertakings*, has rights or obligations under a contract entered into by A or any of its *subsidiary undertakings*.

(3) (for the purposes of the *rules* relating to *BIPRU firms* in *GENPRU* and *BIPRU* and in relation to an *exposure* of a *person* ('A')) the counterparty with respect to that *exposure* or, if the context requires, another *person* in respect of whom, under that *exposure*, A is exposed to credit risk or the risk of loss if that *person* fails to meet its obligations, such as the issuer of the underlying *security* in relation to a *derivative* held by A.

(B) In the FCA Handbook:

(1) [deleted]

(2) (for the purposes of the rules relating to insurers in *GENPRU* and *INSPRU*) (in relation to an insurer, the *Society*, a *syndicate* or *member* ('A')):
(a) any one individual; or

(b) any one unincorporated body of *persons*; or

(c) any *company* which is not a member of a *group*; or

(d) any *group* of *companies* excluding:

(i) (for the purposes of INSPRU 2.1) any *companies* within the *group* which are *subsidiary undertakings* of A and which fall within GENPRU 1.3.43 R; and

(ii) (for all other purposes) any *companies* within the *group* which are *subsidiary undertakings* of A; or

(e) any government of a State together with all the public bodies, local authorities or nationalised industries of that State, in which A, or any of its *subsidiary undertakings*, has made *investments* or against whom, or in respect of whom, it, or any of its *subsidiary undertakings*, has rights or obligations under a contract entered into by A or any of its *subsidiary undertakings*.

(3) (for the purposes of the *rules* relating to *BIPRU firms* in *GENPRU* and *BIPRU* and in relation to an *exposure* of a *person* ('A')) the counterparty with respect to that *exposure* or, if the context requires, another *person* in respect of whom, under that *exposure*, A is exposed to credit risk or the risk of loss if that *person* fails to meet its obligations, such as the issuer of the underlying *security* in relation to a *derivative* held by A.

counterparty credit risk

(A) In the PRA Handbook:

(in accordance with Part 1 of Annex III of the *Banking Consolidation Directive* (Definitions) and for the purposes of *BIPRU*) the risk that the counterparty to a transaction could default before the final settlement of the transaction's cash flows.

(2) (other than in (1)) has the meaning as used in the *EU CRR*.

(B) In the FCA Handbook:

(1) (in accordance with Part 1 of Annex III of the *Banking Consolidation Directive* (Definitions) and for the purposes of *BIPRU*) the risk that the counterparty to a transaction could default before the final settlement of the transaction's cash flows.

(2) (other than in (1)) has the meaning as used in the *EU CRR*.

counterparty risk

(in *COLL* and *FUND*) the risk of loss for a *UCITS* or an *AIF* resulting from the fact that the counterparty to a transaction may default on its obligations prior to the final settlement of the transaction's cash flow.

counterparty risk capital component

the part of the *credit risk capital requirement* calculated in accordance with BIPRU 14.2.1 R (Calculation of the counterparty risk capital component).

country of origin

in relation to an *electronic commerce activity*, the *EEA State* in which the *establishment* from which the service in question is provided is situated.

coupon

a dividend, interest payment or any similar payment.

covered bond

(A) In the PRA Handbook:

(1) (in accordance with Article 52(4) of the *UCITS Directive* and except for the purposes of the *IRB approach* or the *standardised approach* to credit risk) a bond that is issued by a *credit institution* which has its registered office in an *EEA State* and is subject by law to special public supervision designed to protect bondholders and in particular protection under which sums deriving from the issue of the bond must be invested in conformity with the law in assets which, during the whole period of validity of the bond, are capable of covering claims attaching to the bond and which, in the event of failure of the issuer, would be used on a priority basis for the reimbursement of the principal and payment of the accrued interest.

(2) (in accordance with point 68 of Part 1 of Annex VI of the *Banking Consolidation Directive* (Exposures in the form of covered bonds) and for the purposes of the IRB approach or the *standardised approach* to credit risk in *BIPRU*) a covered bond as defined in (1) collateralised in accordance with BIPRU 3.4.107 R (Exposures in the form of covered bonds).

(3) (in *RCB*) (as defined in Regulation 1(2) of the *RCB Regulations*) a bond in relation to which the claims attaching to that bond are guaranteed to be paid by an *owner* from an *asset pool* it owns.

(4) (in accordance with Article 22(4) of the *Third Non-Life Directive* and Article 24(4) of the *Consolidated Life Directive* and for the purposes of INSPRU 2.1) a *debenture* that is issued by a *credit institution* which:

(a) has its head office in an *EEA State*; and

(b) is subject by law to special official supervision designed to protect the holders of the *debenture*; in particular, sums deriving from the issue of the *debenture* must be invested in accordance with the law in assets which, during the whole period of validity of the *debenture*, are capable of covering claims attaching to the *debenture* and which, in the event of failure of the *issuer*, would be used on a priority basis for the reimbursement of the principal and payment of the accrued interest.

(B) In the FCA Handbook:

(1) (in accordance with Article 52(4) of the *UCITS Directive* and except for the purposes of the *IRB approach* or the *standardised approach* to credit risk) a bond that is issued by a *credit institution* which has its registered office in an *EEA State* and is subject by law to special public supervision designed to protect bondholders and in particular protection under which sums deriving from the issue of the bond must be invested in conformity with the law in assets which, during the whole period of validity of the bond, are capable of covering claims attaching to the bond and which, in the event of failure of the issuer, would be used on a priority basis for the reimbursement of the principal and payment of the accrued interest.

(2) (in accordance with point 68 of Part 1 of Annex VI of the *Banking Consolidation Directive* (Exposures in the form of covered bonds) and for the purposes of the IRB approach or the *standardised approach* to credit risk in *BIPRU*) a covered bond as defined in (1) collateralised in accordance with BIPRU 3.4.107 R (Exposures in the form of covered bonds).

(3) (in *RCB*) (as defined in Regulation 1(2) of the *RCB Regulations*) a bond in relation to which the claims attaching to that bond are guaranteed to be paid by an *owner* from an *asset pool* it owns.

(4) (in accordance with Article 22(4) of the *Third Non-Life Directive* and Article 24(4) of the *Consolidated Life Directive* and for the purposes of INSPRU 2.1) a *debenture* that is issued by a *credit institution* which:

(a) has its head office in an *EEA State*; and

(b) is subject by law to special official supervision designed to protect the holders of the *debenture*; in particular, sums deriving from the issue of the *debenture* must be invested in accordance with the law in assets which, during the whole period of validity of the *debenture*, are capable of covering claims attaching to the *debenture* and which, in the event of failure of the *issuer*, would be used on a priority basis for the reimbursement of the principal and payment of the accrued interest.

CPI

the Consumer Prices Index.

CRD

(A) In the PRA Handbook: Directive 2013/36/EU of the European Parliament and the Council of 26 June 2013 on access to the activity of credit institutions and the prudential supervision of credit institutions and investment firms, amending Directive 2002/87/EC and repealing Directives 2006/48/EC and 2006/49/EC.

(B) In the FCA Handbook:

(1) (in *GENPRU* (except GENPRU 3) and *BIPRU* (except BIPRU 12)) the *Capital Adequacy Directive* and the *Banking Consolidation Directive*.

(2) (except in (1)) the Directive of the European Parliament and the Council of 26 June 2013 on access to the activity of credit institutions and the prudential supervision of credit institutions and investment firms (No 2013/36/EU) and amending Directive 2002/87/EC and repealing Directives 2006/48/EC and 2006/49/EC.

CRD bank

(A) In the PRA Handbook:

a *bank* which uses the *EU CRR* to measure the capital requirement on its trading book.

(B) In the FCA Handbook:

a *bank* which uses the *EU CRR* to measure the capital requirement on its trading book.

CRD credit institution

(A) In the PRA Handbook:

a *credit institution* that has its registered office (or, if it has no registered office, its head office) in an *EEA State*, excluding an *institution* to which the *CRD* does not apply under article 2 of the *CRD* (see also *full CRD credit institution*).

(B) In the FCA Handbook:

a *credit institution* that has its registered office (or, if it has no registered office, its head office) in an *EEA State*, excluding an *institution* to which the *CRD* does not apply under article 2 of the *CRD* (see also *full CRD credit institution*).

CRD financial instrument

has the meaning set out in BIPRU 1.2.7 R to BIPRU 1.2.8 R (CRD financial instruments), which is in summary any contract that gives rise to both a financial asset of one party and a financial liability or equity instrument of another party.

CRD full-scope firm

an investment firm as defined in article 4(1)(2) of the *EU CRR* that is subject to the requirements imposed by *MiFID* (or which would be subject to that Directive if its head office were in an *EEA State*) and that is not a *limited activity firm* or a *limited licence firm*.

CRD implementation measure

(A) In the PRA Handbook:

(in relation to an *person* and for the purposes of *GENPRU* and *BIPRU* (except in GENPRU 3)), a provision of the *Banking Consolidation Directive* or the *Capital Adequacy Directive* and an *EEA State* other than the *United Kingdom*) a measure implementing that provision of that Directive for that type of *person* in that *EEA State*.

(B) In the FCA Handbook:

(in relation to an *person* and for the purposes of *GENPRU* and *BIPRU* (except in GENPRU 3 and BIPRU 12), a provision of the *Banking Consolidation Directive* or the *Capital Adequacy Directive* and an *EEA State* other than the *United Kingdom*) a measure implementing that provision of that Directive for that type of *person* in that *EEA State*.

credit

(A) In the PRA Handbook:

(1) (except in relation to a *class* of *contract of insurance*) any kind of loan, deferment of repayment of any loan or of interest on any loan, guarantee or indemnity, and any other kind of accommodation or facility in the nature of credit.

(2) (in relation to a *class* of *contract of insurance*) the *class* of *contract of insurance*, specified in paragraph 14 of Part I of Schedule 1 to the *Regulated Activities Order* (Contracts of general insurance), against risks of loss to the *persons* insured arising from the insolvency of debtors of theirs or from the failure (otherwise than through insolvency) of debtors of theirs to pay their debts when due.

(B) In the FCA Handbook:

(1) (except in relation to a *class* of *contract of insurance* and a *credit-related regulated activity*) any kind of loan, deferment of repayment of any loan or of interest on any loan, guarantee or indemnity, and any other kind of accommodation or facility in the nature of credit.

(2) (in relation to a *class* of *contract of insurance*) the *class* of *contract of insurance*, specified in paragraph 14 of Part I of Schedule 1 to the *Regulated Activities Order* (Contracts of general insurance), against risks of loss to the *persons* insured arising from the insolvency of debtors of theirs or from the failure (otherwise than through insolvency) of debtors of theirs to pay their debts when due.

(3) (in relation to a *credit-related regulated activity* or *operating an electronic system in relation to lending*) includes a cash loan and any other form of financial accommodation, but an item entering into the *total charge for credit* is not treated as credit even though time is allowed for its payment.

credit agreement

in accordance with article 60B of the *Regulated Activities Order*, an agreement between an *individual* ("A") and any other *person* ("B") under which B provides A with *credit* of any amount.

credit broker

a *person* that carries on an activity, by way of business, of the kind specified in article 36A of the *Regulated Activities Order*.

credit broking

an activity of the kind specified in article 36A of the *Regulated Activities Order*.

credit card cheque

a cheque (whether or not drawn on a banker) which, whenever used, will result in the provision of *credit* under a *credit-token agreement*, which does not include a cheque to be used only in connection with a current account.

credit enhancement

(1) (in accordance with Article 4(43) of the *Banking Consolidation Directive* (Definitions) and for the purposes of *BIPRU*) a contractual arrangement whereby the credit quality of a *position* in a *securitisation* (within the meaning of paragraph (2) of the definition of securitisation) is improved in relation to what it would have been if the enhancement had not been provided, including the enhancement provided by more junior *tranches* in the *securitisation* and other types of credit protection.

(2) (in *MIPRU*) a contractual arrangement which improves the credit quality of a *securitisation position* in relation to what it would have been if the enhancement had not been provided, including the enhancement provided by more junior *tranches* in the *securitisation* and other types of credit protection.

credit equalisation provision

the provision required to be established by INSPRU 1.4.43R.

credit firm

a *firm* with *permission* to carry on a *credit-related regulated activity*.

credit-impaired customer

a *customer* who:

(a) within the last two years has owed overdue payments, in an amount equivalent to three *months'* payments, on a mortgage or other loan (whether secured or unsecured), except where the amount overdue reached that level because of late payment caused by errors by a bank or other third party; or

(b) has been the subject of one or more county court judgments, with a total value greater than £500, within the last three years; or

(c) has been subject to an individual voluntary arrangement or bankruptcy order which was in force at any time within the last three years.

credit information agency

a *person* who carries on by way of business one or more of the following activities specified in the *Regulated Activities Order*:

(a) *credit broking* (article 36A);

(b) *debt adjusting* (article 39D);

(c) *debt counselling* (article 39E);

(d) *debt collecting* (article 39F);

(e) *debt administration* (article 39G);

(f) *entering into a regulated credit agreement as lender* (article 60B(1) (disregarding the effect of article 60F));

(g) exercising, or having the right to exercise, the lender's rights and duties under a regulated credit agreement (article 60B(2) (disregarding the effect of article 60F));

(h) entering into a regulated consumer hire agreement as owner (article 60N(1) (disregarding the effect of article 60P));

(i) exercising, or having the right to exercise, the owner's rights and duties under a regulated consumer hire agreement (article 60N(2) (disregarding the effect of article 60P);

(j) *providing credit references* (article 89B).

credit institution

(A) In the PRA Handbook:

(1) has the meaning in article 4(1)(1) of the *EU CRR*;
(a) [deleted]
(b) [deleted]
(c) [deleted]
(d) [deleted]

(2) (in *SUP* 11 (Controllers and close links) and *SUP* 16 (Reporting requirements)):
(a) a credit institution authorised under the *CRD*; or
(b) an institution which would satisfy the requirements for authorisation as a credit institution under the *CRD* if it had its registered office (or if it does not have a registered office, its head office) in an *EEA State*.

(3) (in relation to the definition of *electronic money issuer*) a credit institution as defined by (1)(a) and includes a branch of the credit institution within the meaning of article 4(1)(17) of the *EU CRR* which is situated within the *EEA* and which has its head office in a territory outside the *EEA* in accordance with article 47 of the *CRD*.

(B) In the FCA Handbook:

(1) (except in *REC*):
(a) has the meaning in article 4(1)(1) of the *EU CRR*; or

(b) [deleted]

(c) [deleted]

(d) [deleted]

(2) (in *REC* and in *SUP* 11 (Controllers and close links) and *SUP* 16 (Reporting requirements)):

(a) a credit institution authorised under the *CRD*; or

(b) an institution which would satisfy the requirements for authorisation as a credit institution under the *CRD* if it had its registered office (or if it does not have a registered office, its head office) in an *EEA State*.

(3) (in relation to the definition of *electronic money issuer*) a credit institution as defined by (1)(a) and includes a branch of the credit institution within the meaning of article 4(1)(17) of the *EU CRR* which is situated within the *EEA* and which has its head office in a territory outside the *EEA* in accordance with article 47 of the *CRD*.

credit limit

in accordance with article 60L of the *Regulated Activities Order*, in relation to *running-account credit*, as respects any period, the maximum debit balance which, under a *credit agreement*, is allowed to stand on the account during that period, disregarding any term of the agreement allowing that maximum to be exceeded on a temporary basis.

credit quality assessment scale

the credit quality assessment scale:

(1) onto which the credit assessments of an export credit agency are mapped under the table in BIPRU 3.4.9 R (Exposure for which a credit assessment by an export credit agency is recognised); or

(2) published by the *appropriate regulator* in accordance with the *Capital Requirements Regulations 2006* which determine:

(a) (in relation to an *eligible ECAI* whose recognition is for *risk weighting* purposes other than those in (2)(b)) with which of the *credit quality steps* set out in BIPRU 3.4 (Risk weights under the standardised approach to credit risk) the relevant credit assessments of an *eligible ECAI* are to be associated; or

(b) (in relation to an *eligible ECAI* whose recognition is for *securitisation risk-weighting* purposes) with which of the *credit quality steps* set out in BIPRU 9 (Securitisation) the relevant credit assessments of the *eligible ECAI* are to be associated.

credit quality step

(1) (except in *MIPRU*) a credit quality step in a *credit quality assessment scale* as set out in BIPRU 3.4 (Risk weights under the standardised approach to credit risk) and BIPRU 9 (Securitisation).

(2) (in *MIPRU*) a credit quality step in a credit quality assessment scale, as set out in MIPRU 4.2E (Use of external credit assessments).

credit reference agency

a *person providing credit references*.

credit repair firm

a *firm* which carries on the activity of *providing credit information services* with a view to securing or advising on the correction of or omission of anything from, or making of any modification of, information relevant to financial standing of an *individual* held by a *credit information agency* or to securing that the agency stops holding the information or does not provide it to another *person*.

credit-related regulated activity

(1) (except in *FEES*)(in accordance with section 22 of the *Act* (the classes of activity and categories of investments)) any of the following activities specified in Part 2 or 3A of the *Regulated Activities Order* (Specified Activities):

(a) *entering into a regulated credit agreement as lender* (article 60B(1));

(b) exercising, or having the right to exercise, the lender's rights and duties under a regulated credit agreement (article 60B(2));

(c) *credit broking* (article 36A);

(d) *debt adjusting* (article 39D(1) and (2));

(e) *debt counselling* (article 39E(1) and (2));

(f) *debt collecting* (article 39F(1) and (2));

(g) *debt administration* (article 39G(1) and (2));

(h) entering into a regulated consumer hire agreement as owner (article 60N(1));

(i) exercising, or having the right to exercise, the owner's rights and duties under a regulated consumer hire agreement (article 60N(2));

(j) *providing credit information services* (article 89A);

(k) *providing credit references* (article 89B);

(l) *operating an electronic system in relation to lending* (article 36H), but (other than in *FEES* and *SUP*) only insofar as it relates to a borrower or prospective borrower under a *P2P agreement*;

(m) *agreeing to carry on a regulated activity* (article 64) so far as relevant to any of the activities in (a) to (l);

which is carried on by way of business and relates to a *specified investment* applicable to that activity or, in the case of (j) and (k), relates to information about a *person's* financial standing.

(2) (in *FEES*) (in accordance with section 22 of the *Act* (the classes of activity and categories of investments)) any of the following activities specified in Part 2 or 3A of the *Regulated Activities Order* (Specified Activities):

(a) the activities in (1)(a)–(m); and

(b) *advising on regulated credit agreements for the acquisition of land* (article 53DA);

which is carried on by way of business and relates to a *specified investment* applicable to that activity or, in the case of (j) and (k) listed in (1), relates to information about a *person's* financial standing.

credit risk capital component

the part of the *credit risk capital requirement* calculated in accordance with BIPRU 3.1.5 R (Calculation of the credit risk capital component).

credit risk capital requirement

(1) (for a *BIPRU firm*) the part of the *capital resources requirement* of a *BIPRU firm* in respect of credit risk, calculated in accordance with GENPRU 2.1.51 R (Calculation of the credit risk capital requirement).

(2) (for a *firm* carrying on any *home financing* connected to *regulated mortgage contracts* or *home financing* and *home financing administration* connected to *regulated mortgage contracts*) the part of the *capital resources requirement* in respect of credit risk, calculated in accordance with MIPRU 4.2A (Credit risk capital requirement).

credit risk mitigation

(A) In the PRA Handbook: (in accordance with Article 4(30) of the *Banking Consolidation Directive* (Definitions)) a technique used by an *undertaking* to reduce the credit risk associated with an *exposure* or *exposures* which the *undertaking* continues to hold.

(B) In the FCA Handbook:

(1) (in *GENPRU* (except in GENPRU 3) and *BIPRU* (except in BIPRU 12)) (in accordance with Article 4(30) of the *Banking Consolidation Directive* (Definitions)) a technique used by an *undertaking* to reduce the credit risk associated with an *exposure* or *exposures* which the *undertaking* continues to hold.

(2) (except in (1)) has the meaning in article 4(1)(58) of the *EU CRR*.

credit-sale agreement

an agreement for the sale of goods under which the purchase price, or part of it, is payable by instalments, but which is not a *conditional sale agreement* (see section 189 of the *CCA*).

credit token

a credit token is a card, check, voucher, coupon, stamp, form, booklet or other document or thing given to an *individual* by a *person* carrying on a *credit-related regulated activity* ("the provider"), who undertakes that:

(a) on production of it (whether or not some other action is also required) the provider will supply *cash*, *goods* or services (or any of them) on *credit*; or

(b) where, on the production of it to a third party (whether or not any other action is also required), the third party supplies *cash*, *goods* and services (or any of them), the provider will pay the third party for them (whether or not deducting any discount or commission), in return for *payment* to the provider by the *individual* and the provider shall, without prejudice to the definition of *credit*, be taken to provide *credit* drawn on whenever a third party supplies the *individual* with *cash*, *goods* or services; and the use of an object to operate a machine provided by the person giving the object or a third party shall be treated as the production of the object to that *person* or third party.

credit-token agreement

a *regulated credit agreement* for the provision of *credit* in connection with the use of a *credit token*.

credit valuation adjustment

(in accordance with Part 1 of Annex III of the *Banking Consolidation Directive* (Definitions) and for the purposes of *BIPRU*) an adjustment to the mid-market valuation of the portfolio of transactions with a counterparty; and so that this adjustment:

(a) reflects the market value of the credit risk due to any failure to perform on contractual agreements with a counterparty; and

(b) may reflect the market value of the credit risk of the counterparty or the market value of the credit risk of both the *firm* and the counterparty.

credit union

a body corporate registered under the Industrial and Provident Societies Act 1965 as a credit union in accordance with the Credit Unions Act which is an *authorised person* or a body corporate registered under the Credit Unions (Northern Ireland) Order 1985 which is an *authorised person* or a body corporate registered under the Industrial and Provident Societies Act (Northern Ireland) 1969 as a credit union which is an *authorised person*.

credit unions day

(in relation to a *Great Britain credit union*) 1 July 2002 or (in relation to a *Northern Ireland credit union*) 31 March 2012.

credit-worthiness assessment

the assessment, including as to the affordability of credit by the customer, required by CONC 5.2.1 R.

CREDS

the Credit Unions sourcebook.

CREST

(A) In the PRA Handbook: the computer-based system which enables securities to be held and transferred in uncertificated form and which is operated by CRESTCo Limited.

(B) In the FCA Handbook: the computer-based system which enables securities to be held and transferred in uncertificated form and which is operated by Euroclear UK & Ireland Limited.

critical functions

activities, services or operations the discontinuance of which is likely, in one or more *EEA States*, to lead to the disruption of essential services to the real economy or to disrupt financial stability due to the:

(a) size;

(b) market share;

(c) external and internal interconnectedness;

(d) complexity; or

(e) cross-border activities,

of an *RRD institution* or *RRD group*, particularly bearing in mind the substitutability of those activities, service or operations. [Note: article 2(1)(35) of *RRD*]

CRM eligibility conditions

(1) (in relation to the *standardised approach* to credit risk), BIPRU 5.3.1 R-BIPRU 5.3.2 R, BIPRU 5.4.1 R-BIPRU 5.4.8 R, BIPRU 5.5.1 R, BIPRU 5.5.4 R, BIPRU 5.5.8 R, BIPRU 5.6.1 R and BIPRU 5.7.1 R-BIPRU 5.7.4 R; or

(2) (in relation to the *IRB approach*), the provisions in (1) and BIPRU 4.4.83 R, BIPRU 4.10–BIPRU 4.10.7 R, BIPRU 4.10.9 R, BIPRU 4.10.10 R-BIPRU 4.10.12 R, BIPRU 4.10.14 R, BIPRU 4.10.16 R, BIPRU 4.10.19 R, and BIPRU 4.10.38 R-BIPRU 4.10.39 R; or

(3) (for the purpose of *MIPRU*), MIPRU 4.2C.16 R.

CRM minimum requirements

(1) in relation to the *standardised approach* to credit risk); BIPRU 5.2.9 R-BIPRU 5.2.10 R, BIPRU 5.3.3 R, BIPRU 5.4.9 R-BIPRU 5.4.13 R, BIPRU 5.5.2 R, BIPRU 5.5.5 R-BIPRU 5.5.6 R, BIPRU 5.6.2 R-BIPRU 5.6.3 R, BIPRU 5.7.6 R-BIPRU 5.7.14 R; or

(2) (in relation to the *IRB approach*), the provisions in (1) and BIPRU 4.4.85 R, BIPRU 4.10.13 R, BIPRU 4.10.15 R, and BIPRU 4.10.18 R-BIPRU 4.10.19 R.

cross border services

(1) (in relation to a *UK firm*) services provided within an *EEA State* other than the *United Kingdom* under the freedom to provide services.

(2) (in relation to an *incoming EEA firm* or an *incoming Treaty firm*) services provided within the *United Kingdom* under the freedom to provide services.

Cross-Border Payments in Euro Regulations

the Cross-Border Payments in Euro Regulations 2010 (SI 2010/89).

cross-border UCITS merger

(in *COLL* and in accordance with article 2(1)(q) of the *UCITS Directive*) a *UCITS merger* of two or more *UCITS*:

(a) at least two of which are established in different *EEA States*; or

(b) established in the same *EEA State* into a newly constituted *UCITS* established in another *EEA State*;

but at least one of which is established in the *United Kingdom*.

cross product netting

(in accordance with Part 1 of Annex III of the *Banking Consolidation Directive* (Definitions) and for the purpose of BIPRU 13 (The calculation of counterparty risk exposure values for financial derivatives, securities financing transactions and long settlement transactions)) the inclusion of transactions of different product categories within the same *netting set* pursuant to the *rules* about cross-product netting set out in BIPRU 13.

cross-transaction

(a) a transaction by which a *person* matches, at the same price and on the same terms, the *buy* and *sell* orders of two or more *persons* for whom he is acting as agent;

(b) a transaction to which only one *person* is a party, by which he purports to *sell* to and *buy* from himself.

CRR

capital resources requirement.

CRR firm

(A) (in the PRA Handbook): for the purposes of *SYSC* means *UK banks*, *buildings society* and *investment firms* that are subject to the *EU CRR*.

(B) (in the FCA Handbook) (for the purposes of *SYSC*) a *UK bank*, *building society* and an *investment firm* that is subject to the *EU CRR*.

CTF

(as defined in section 1(2) of the Child Trust Funds Act 2004) a child trust fund, that is, an account which:

(1) is held by a child who is or has been an eligible child (as defined in section 2 of that Act);

(2) satisfies the requirements imposed by or under the Child Trust Funds Act 2004; and

(3) has been opened in accordance with the Child Trust Funds Act 2004.

CTF bank account

a bank account which fulfils the requirements of Regulation 11(5) of the *CTF Regulations*.

CTF provider

(in accordance with section 3(1) of the Child Trust Funds Act 2004) a *person* approved by HM Revenue and Customs in accordance with the *CTF Regulations*.

CTF Regulations

the Child Trust Funds Regulations 2004 (SI 2004/1450).

CTF transfer

a transaction resulting from a decision by a *customer*, made with or without advice from a *firm*, to transfer the *investments* (or their value) held in an existing *CTF* into another CTF whether or not provided by the same *CTF provider*.

currency class unit

(in *COLL*) a class of *unit* denominated in a currency that is not the *base currency* of the *authorised fund*, or if permitted, by COLL 3.3.4 R (1) (Currency class units: requirements).

current account

(in *CONC* App 1) an account under which the customer may, by means of cheques or similar orders payable to the customer or to any other *person* or by any other means, obtain or have the use of money held or made available by the *person* with whom the account is kept and which records alterations in the financial relationship between the said *person* and the customer.

current approved person approval

(in relation to an *approved person* in relation to a particular *firm* and *controlled function* as at any particular time) an approval under section 59 of the *Act* (Approval for particular arrangements) given by the *FCA* or the *PRA* in relation to that *person* for the performance of that *controlled function* in relation to that *firm* that is in force at that time.

current FCA approved person approval

a *current approved person approval* given by the *FCA*.

current PRA approved person approval

a *current approved person approval* given by the *PRA*.

current customer order

(a) a *customer order* to be *executed* immediately;

(b) a *customer order* which is to be *executed* only on fulfilment of a condition, after the condition has been fulfilled.

current exposure

(in accordance with Part 1 of Annex III of the *Banking Consolidation Directive* (Definitions) and for the purpose of BIPRU 13 (The calculation of counterparty risk exposure values for financial derivatives, securities financing transactions and long settlement transactions)) the larger of zero, or the market value of a transaction or portfolio of transactions within a *netting set* with a counterparty that would be lost upon the default of the counterparty, assuming no recovery on the value of those transactions in bankruptcy.

current market value

(in accordance with Part 1 of Annex III of the *Banking Consolidation Directive* (Definitions) and for the purpose of BIPRU 13.5 (CCR standardised method)) the net market value of the portfolio of transactions within the *netting set* with the counterparty; both positive and negative market values are used in computing *current market value*.

custodian

(A) In the PRA Handbook:
(a) an *approved bank*;
(b) an *approved depositary*;
(c) a member of a *recognised investment exchange*;
(d) a *firm* whose *permitted activities* include *safeguarding and administering investments*;
(e) a regulated *clearing firm*;
(f) where it is not feasible to use a *custodian* in (a) to (e), and there are reasonable grounds to show that a *person* outside the *United Kingdom*, whose business includes the provision of custodial services, is able to provide such services which are appropriate to the *client* and in the *client's* best interest to use, that *person*.

(B) In the FCA Handbook:
(a) an *approved bank*;
(b) an *approved depositary*

(c) a *member* of a *recognised investment exchange*;
(d) a *firm* whose *permitted activities* include *safeguarding and administering investments*;
(e) a regulated *clearing firm*;
(f) where it is not feasible to use a *custodian* in (a) to (e), and there are reasonable grounds to show that a *person* outside the *United Kingdom*, whose business includes the provision of custodial services, is able to provide such services which are appropriate to the *client* and in the *client's* best interest to use, that *person*.

custody

(in relation to *clients'* assets) *safeguarding and administering investments*.

custody asset

(A) (in the *FCA Handbook*)
(1) other than when *acting as trustee or depositary of an AIF*:
(a) a *designated investment* held for or on behalf of a *client*;
(b) any other asset which is or may be held with a *designated investment* held for, or on behalf of, a *client*.
(2) in relation to *acting as trustee or depositary of an AIF* in CASS 6:
(a) an *AIF custodial asset* held by a *depositary* in line with FUND 3.11.21 R (Depositary functions: safekeeping of financial instruments); or
(b) any other asset of an *AIF* in respect of which a *depositary* exercises safe-keeping functions in line with FUND 3.11.23 R (Depositary functions: safekeeping of other assets).

(B) (in the *PRA Handbook*)
(a) a *designated investment* held for or on behalf of a *client*;
(b) any other asset which is or may be held with a *designated investment* held for, or on behalf of, a *client*.

custody chapter

CASS 6.

custody rules

CASS 6.

customer

(A) in the *PRA Handbook*:

(1) (except in relation to *ICOBS*, MCOB 3 and CASS 5) a *client* who is not an *eligible counterparty* for the relevant purposes.

(2) (in relation to MCOB 3) a *person* in (1) or a *person* who would be such a *person* if he were a *client*.

(3) (in relation to *ICOBS*) a *person* who is a *policyholder*, or a prospective *policyholder* but (except in ICOBS 2 (general matters), and (in respect of that chapter) ICOBS 1 (application)) excluding a *policyholder* or prospective *policyholder* who does not make the arrangements preparatory to him concluding the *contract of insurance*.

(4) (in relation to CASS 5) a *client*.

(B) in the *FCA Handbook*:

(1) (except in relation to *ICOBS*, a *credit-related regulated activity*, MCOB 3 and CASS 5) a *client* who is not an *eligible counterparty* for the relevant purposes.

(2) (in relation to MCOB 3) a *person* in (1) or a *person* who would be such a *person* if he were a *client*.

(3) (in relation to *ICOBS*) a *person* who is a *policyholder*, or a prospective *policyholder* but (except in ICOBS 2 (general matters) and (in respect of that chapter) ICOBS 1 (application)) excluding a *policyholder* or prospective *policyholder* who does not make the arrangements preparatory to him concluding the *contract of insurance*.

(4) (in relation to CASS 5) a *client*.

(5) (in relation to a *credit-related regulated activity*) an *individual* who enters, may enter or has entered into a *credit agreement* or a *consumer hire agreement*; and:
(-a) (in relation to *consumer credit lending*) includes an *individual* who the *firm* treats as a *person* who is, or has been, the *borrower* under a *regulated credit agreement*;
(-aa) (in relation to *consumer hiring*) includes an *individual* who the *firm* treats as a *person* who is, or has been, the *hirer* under a *regulated consumer hire agreement*;
(a) (in relation to *credit broking*) an *individual* who uses, may use or has used the services of a *firm* in carrying on that *regulated activity*;

(b) (in relation to *operating an electronic system in relation to lending*) an *individual* who is, may be, has been or may have been the *borrower* under a *P2P agreement*;

(c) (in relation to *debt adjusting*) an *individual* who uses, may use or has used the services of a *firm* in carrying on that *regulated activity*;

(d) (in relation to *debt counselling*) an *individual* who uses, may use or has used the services of a *firm* in carrying on that *regulated activity*;

(e) (in relation to *debt collecting*) a *person* within (i) to (iv) in relation to whom the *firm* takes steps to procure the payment of a debt due under a *credit agreement* or a *consumer hire agreement* or a *P2P agreement* (whether or not that *person* is a party to the *credit agreement* or *consumer hire agreement* or *P2P agreement*):

(i) an *individual* who is or has been the *borrower* under a *credit agreement*, or is or has been the *hirer* under a *consumer hire agreement*, or is or has been the *borrower* under a *P2P agreement*;

(ii) an *individual* who the *firm* treats as a *person* within (i);

(iii) a *person* providing a guarantee or indemnity under the agreement; and

(iv) a *person* to whom the rights and duties of a *person* within (iii) have passed by *assignment* or operation of law;

(f) (in relation to *debt administration*) a *person* within (i) to (iv) in relation to whom the *firm* takes steps to perform duties or exercise or enforce rights under a *credit agreement* on behalf of the *lender* or under a *consumer hire agreement* on behalf of the *owner* or under a *P2P agreement* on behalf of the *lender*:

(i) an *individual* who is or has been the *borrower* under a *credit agreement*, or is or has been the *hirer* under a *consumer hire agreement*, or is or has been the *borrower* under a *P2P agreement*;

(ii) an *individual* who the *firm* treats as a *person* within (i);

(iii) a *person* providing a guarantee or indemnity under the agreement; and

(iv) a *person* to whom the rights and duties of a *person* within (iii) have passed by *assignment* or operation of law;

(g) (in relation to *providing credit information services*) an *individual* who uses, may use or has used the services of a *firm* in carrying on that *regulated activity*; and

(h) (in relation to *providing credit references*) an *individual* about whom information relevant to the *individual's* financial standing is or was, may be or may have been held by the *credit reference agency*.

customer-dealing function

(in accordance with section 59(7A) of the *Act* (Approval for particular arrangements) in relation to the carrying on of a *regulated activity* by an *authorised person* ("A") a function that will involve the *person* performing it in dealing with:

(a) customers of A; or

(b) property of customers of A;

in a manner substantially connected with the carrying on of the activity.

customer function

(in the *FCA Handbook*) *FCA controlled function* CF30 in Parts 1 and 2 of the table of *FCA controlled functions*, described more fully in SUP 10A.10.7 R.

customer order

(a) an order to a *firm* from a *customer* to *execute* a transaction as agent;

(b) any other order to a *firm* from a *customer* to *execute* a transaction in circumstances giving rise to duties similar to those arising on an order to *execute* a transaction as agent;

(c) a decision by a *firm* in the exercise of discretion to *execute* a transaction with or for a *customer*.

damage to property

(in relation to a *class* of contract of insurance) the *class* of *contract of insurance*, specified in paragraph 9 of Part I of Schedule 1 to the *Regulated Activities Order* (Contracts of general insurance), against loss of or damage to property (other than property to which paragraphs 3 to 7 of that Schedule (L and vehicles, Railway rolling stock, Aircraft, Ships and Goods in transit) relate) due to hail or frost or any other event (such as theft) other than those mentioned in paragraph 8 of that Schedule (Fire and natural forces).

data element

A discrete fact or individual piece of information relating to a particular field within a *data item* required to be submitted to the *appropriate regulator* by a *firm* or other regulated entity.

data item

One or more related *data elements* that are grouped together into a prescribed format and required to be submitted by a *firm* or other regulated entity under SUP 16 or provisions referred to in SUP 16.

data set

One or more *data items* relating to the same *regulated activity*.

date of allotment

the date on which amounts of the *relevant security* are allotted to subscribers or purchasers and, where there is an initial or preliminary allotment subject to confirmation, the date of that initial or preliminary allotment.

day

a period of 24 hours beginning at midnight.

DCG

the Office of Fair Trading's Debt Collection Guidance.

deal

a *dealing* transaction.

dealer

in relation to a *hire-purchase agreement*, *credit-sale agreement* or *conditional sale agreement* under which this *person* is not the *lender*, a *person* who sells or proposes to sell *goods*, *land* or other things to the *lender* before they form the subject matter of any such agreements and, in relation to any other agreements, means a *supplier* or the *supplier*'s agent.

dealing

(1) (other than in MAR 1 (The Code of Market Conduct)) (in accordance with paragraph 2 of Schedule 2 to the *Act* (*Regulated activities*) buying, selling, subscribing for or underwriting *investments* or offering or agreeing to do so, either as a *principal* or as an agent, including, in the case of an *investment* which is a *contract of insurance*, carrying out the contract.

(2) (in MAR 1) (as defined as in section 130A(3) of the *Act*), in relation to an investment, means acquiring or disposing of the investment whether as principal or agent or directly or indirectly, and includes agreeing to acquire or dispose of the investment, and entering into and bringing to an end a contract creating it.

dealing day

(in *COLL*) the period in a *business day* (in accordance with provisions of the *prospectus*) during which the *ACD* or the *operator* is open for business.

dealing in investments as agent

(A) In the PRA Handbook: the *regulated activity*, specified in article 21 of the *Regulated Activities Order* (Dealing in investments as agent), which is in summary: *buying*, *selling*, subscribing for or underwriting *designated investments*, *pure protection contracts* or *general insurance contracts* as agent.

(B) In the FCA Handbook: the *regulated activity*, specified in article 21 of the *Regulated Activities Order* (Dealing in investments as agent), which is in summary: *buying*, *selling*, subscribing for or underwriting *designated investments* (other than *P2P agreements*), *pure protection contracts* or *general insurance contracts* as agent.

dealing in investments as principal

(A) In the PRA Handbook: the *regulated activity*, specified in article 14 of the *Regulated Activities Order* (Dealing in investments as principal), which is in summary: *buying*, *selling*, subscribing for or underwriting *designated investments* as principal.

(B) In the FCA Handbook: the *regulated activity*, specified in article 14 of the *Regulated Activities Order* (Dealing in investments as principal), which is in summary: *buying*, *selling*, subscribing for or underwriting *designated investments* (other than *P2P agreements*) as principal.

dealing period

(in *COLL*) the period between one *valuation point* and the next.

deal on own account

(A) In the PRA Handbook: (for the purposes of *GENPRU* and *BIPRU*) has the meaning in BIPRU 1.1.23 R (Meaning of dealing on own account) which is in summary the service referred to in point 3 of Section A Annex I to *MiFID*, subject to the adjustments in BIPRU 1.1.23 R (2) and BIPRU 1.1.23 R (3) (Implementation of Article 5(2) of the *Capital Adequacy Directive*).

(B) In the FCA Handbook:

(1) (for the purposes of *GENPRU* and *BIPRU*) has the meaning in BIPRU 1.1.23 R (Meaning of dealing on own account) which is in summary the service referred to in point 3 of Section A Annex I to *MiFID*, subject to the adjustments in BIPRU 1.1.23 R (2) and BIPRU 1.1.23 R (3) (Implementation of Article 5(2) of the *Capital Adequacy Directive*).

(2) (other than in *GENPRU* and *BIPRU*) has the meaning in IFPRU 1.1.12 R (Meaning of dealing on own account) which is, in summary, the service referred to in point 3 of Section A of Annex I to *MiFID*, subject to the adjustments in IFPRU 1.1.12 R (2) and IFPRU 1.1.12 R (3) (Implementation of article 29(2) of *CRD*).

dealing on own account

trading against proprietary capital resulting in the conclusion of transactions in one or more *financial instruments*. [Note: article 4(1)(6) of *MIFID*]

debenture

the *investment*, specified in article 77 of the *Regulated Activities Order* (Instruments creating or acknowledging indebtedness), which is in summary: any of the following which are not *government and public securities*:

(a) debentures;

(b) debenture stock;

(c) loan stock;

(d) bonds;

(e) certificates of deposit;

(f) any other instrument creating or acknowledging indebtedness.

debt adjuster

a *person* who has, or ought to have, a *Part 4A permission* to carry on the *regulated activity* of *debt adjusting* and who negotiates with a *lender* on behalf of a *customer* the terms of discharge of a debt due under a *credit agreement* or a *consumer hire agreement*, or takes over the *customer's* obligations to discharge such debts in return for payments by the *customer*, or carries on any similar activity concerned with the liquidation of such a debt.

debt adjusting

a *regulated activity* of the kind specified in article 39D of the *Regulated Activities Order*.

debt administration

a *regulated activity* of the kind specified in article 39G of the *Regulated Activities Order*.

debt capital

(in *IPRU(INV)* 13) a *security* of indeterminate duration or other instrument the debt agreement for which provides that:

(a) it may not be reimbursed on the holder's initiative;

(b) the borrower has the option of deferring the payment of interest on the debt;

(c) the lender's claims on the borrower must be wholly subordinated to those of all non-subordinated creditors;

(d) debt and unpaid interest should be such as to absorb losses, whilst leaving the borrower in a position to continue trading;

and which is fully paid-up.

debt collecting

a *regulated activity* of the kind specified in article 39F of the *Regulated Activities Order*.

debt collector

a *person* who has, or ought to have, a *Part 4A permission* to carry on the *regulated activity* of *debt adjusting* and who takes steps to procure payment of debts due under *credit agreements* or *consumer hire agreements*.

debt counselling

a *regulated activity* of the kind specified in article 39E of the *Regulated Activities Order*.

debt counsellor

a *person* who has, or ought to have, a *Part 4A permission* to carry on the *regulated activity* of *debt counselling* and who gives advice to *borrowers* or *hirers* about the liquidation of debts under *credit agreements* or *consumer hire agreements*.

debt management activity

the activities of *debt counselling* or *debt adjusting*, alone or together, carried on with a view to an *individual* entering into a particular *debt solution* or in relation to any such *debt solution*, and activities connected with those activities.

debt management client money chapter

CASS 11.

debt management client money distribution rules

the rules and guidance in CASS 11.13.

debt management client money rules

the rules and guidance in CASS 11.1 to CASS 11.12.

debt management firm

(a) a *firm* which carries on the activities of *debt counselling* or *debt adjusting*, alone or together, with a view to an *individual* entering into a particular *debt solution*; or

(b) a *firm* which carries on the activity of *debt counselling* where an *associate* carries on *debt adjusting* with the aim in (a) in view; or

(c) a *firm* which carries on the activity of *debt adjusting* where an *associate* carries on *debt counselling* with the aim in (a) in view; and

in each case, other than a *not-for-profit debt advice body*.

debt management plan

a non-statutory agreement between a *customer* and one or more of the *customer's lenders* the aim of which is to discharge or liquidate the *customer's* debts, by making regular payments to a third party which administers the plan and distributes the money to the *lenders*.

debt security

(1) (in DTR 2, DTR 3 and *LR*) *debentures*, *alternative debentures*, debenture stock, loan stock, bonds, certificates of deposit or any other instrument creating or acknowledging indebtedness.

(2) (in DTR 4, DTR 5 and DTR 6) (in accordance with article 2.1(b) of the *Transparency Directive*) bonds or other forms of transferable securitised debts, with the exception of securities which are equivalent to *shares* in companies or which, if converted or if the rights conferred by them are exercised, give rise to a right to acquire *shares* or securities equivalent to *shares*.

(3) (except in *DTR* and *LR*) any of the following:
(a) a *debenture*;
(aa) an *alternative debenture*;
(b) a *government and public security*;
(c) a *warrant* which confers a right in respect of an *investment* in (a) or (b).

debt solution

an arrangement, scheme or procedure, whether statutory or not, the aim of which is to discharge or liquidate a *customer's* debts.

decision notice

a notice issued by the *appropriate regulator* in accordance with section 388 of the *Act* (Decision notices).

dedicated

(in relation to *investments* of an *authorised fund*) intended that the holders should participate in or receive:

(a) profits or income arising from the acquisition, holding, management or disposal of *investments* of the relevant description; or

(b) sums paid out of profits or income in (a); or

(c) other benefits where expressly permitted by a provision in *COLL*.

deductions plan

(in *COBS*) a plan that describes the deductions from asset share that a *firm* expects to make for the cost of guarantees and the use of capital (COBS 20.2.8 R).

default

(1) (in relation to the *IRB approach* and for the purposes of *BIPRU*) has the meaning in BIPRU 4.3 (The IRB approach: Provisions common to different exposure classes).

(2) (in *MIPRU*) for any credit obligation a borrower has with a *firm*, an event where:
(a) the borrower is past the contractual payment due date by more than 90 days; and
(b) the *firm* reasonably considers that the borrower is unlikely to pay or otherwise fulfil its credit obligations to the *firm*.

default arrangement

(a) an arrangement expressly provided by an *operator* of a *qualifying scheme* for the purpose of investing the *workplace pension contributions* of employees who have expressed no choice in relation to the investment of such contributions;

(b) where no such arrangement is expressly provided, an arrangement whereby, in relation to members who are employees of the same employer, at least 80% of those members of the *qualifying scheme*, whether they had expressed a choice or not prior to the *qualifying scheme* coming into being, have their *workplace pensions contributions* invested, is deemed to be a *default arrangement*;

(c) but an arrangement will not be a *default arrangement* under (b) if, prior to a scheme becoming a *qualifying scheme*:
(i) all members within that arrangement have been told that their *workplace pension contributions* will be invested in a new arrangement once the scheme becomes a *qualifying scheme*, unless they give express agreement for their contributions to continue to be invested in the original arrangement;
(ii) any members who wish to remain in the original arrangement have given express agreement in writing, including an acknowledgement that continuing in the original arrangement might mean that charges are higher than the limits set out in COBS 19.6 (Restriction on charges in qualifying schemes); and
(iii) any members who did not agree to remain in the original arrangement have had their *workplace pension contributions* invested in the new arrangement;

(d) where an arrangement is a *default arrangement* by virtue of (a) and (b), it continues to be such an arrangement regardless of whether it continues to satisfy those paragraphs.

default rules

(1) (in relation to a *UK RIE*) the default rules which it is required to have under paragraph 10 of the Schedule to the *Recognition Requirements* Regulations.

(2) (in relation to a *UK RCH*) the default rules which it is required to have under paragraph 24 of the Schedule to the *Recognition Requirements* Regulations.

deferred acquisition costs

deferred acquisition costs as defined in the *insurance accounts rules*.

deferred bonus

(in *LR*) any arrangement pursuant to the terms of which an *employee* or *director* may receive a bonus (including cash or any security) in respect of service and/or performance in a period not exceeding the length of the relevant financial year notwithstanding that the bonus may, subject only to the *person* remaining a *director* or *employee* of the group, be receivable by the *person* after the end of the period to which the award relates.

deferred share

(A) In the *FCA Handbook*:

(1) (other than in *CREDS* and *COMP*) in relation to a *building society*, a deferred share as defined in the Building Societies (Deferred Shares) Order 1991.

(2) (in *CREDS* and COMP 5.3.1 R (2)(cA)) in relation to a *Great Britain credit union*, means any share of a class defined as a deferred share by section 31A of the Credit Unions Act 1979.

(B) In the PRA Handbook: in relation to a *building society*, a deferred share as defined in the Building Societies (Deferred Shares) Order 1991.

deficit reduction amount

in respect of a *defined benefit occupational pension scheme*, the sum, determined by a *firm* in conjunction with the *defined benefit occupational pension scheme's* actuaries or trustees (or both), of the additional funding (net of tax) that will be required to be paid into that scheme by the *firm* over the following five year period for the purpose of reducing the *firm's defined benefit liability*.

defined benefit asset

the excess of the value of the assets in a *defined benefit occupational pension scheme* over the present value of the scheme liabilities, to the extent that a *firm*, as employer, in accordance with the accounting principles applicable to it, should recognise that excess as an asset in its balance sheet.

defined benefit liability

the shortfall of the value of the assets in a *defined benefit occupational pension scheme* below the present value of the scheme liabilities, to the extent that a *firm*, as employer, in accordance with the accounting principles applicable to it, should recognise that shortfall as a liability in its balance sheet.

defined benefit occupational pension scheme

an *occupational pension scheme* which is not a *defined contribution occupational pension scheme*.

defined benefits pension scheme

a *pension policy* or *pension contract* under which the only *money-purchase benefits* are benefits ancillary to other benefits which are not *money-purchase benefits*.

defined benefit scheme

in relation to a *director*, means a pension scheme which is not a *money purchase scheme*.

defined contribution occupational pension scheme

an *occupational pension scheme* into which a *firm*, as employer, pays regular fixed contributions and will have no legal or constructive obligation to pay further contributions if the scheme does not have sufficient assets to pay all employee benefits relating to employee service in the current and prior periods.

defined liquidity group

a *DLG by default* or *DLG by modification*.

delivery by value

a transaction type, described as "delivery by value", used to deliver and receive *securities* within *CREST*.

deposit

(A) In the *FCA Handbook*:

(1) (except in *COMP*) the *investment*, specified in article 74 and defined in articles 5(2) and 5(3) of the *Regulated Activities Order*, which is in summary: a sum of money (other than one excluded by any of articles 6 to 9 AB of the *Regulated Activities Order*) paid on terms:

(a) under which it will be repaid, with or without interest or a premium, and either on demand or at a time or in circumstances agreed by or on behalf of the *person* making the payment and the *person* receiving it; and

(b) which are not referable to the provision of property (other than currency) or services or the giving of security; in this definition, money is paid on terms which are referable to the provision of property or services or the giving of security if, and only if:

(i) it is paid by way of advance or part payment under a contract for the sale, hire or other provision of property or services, and is repayable only in the event that the property or services is or are not in fact sold, hired or otherwise provided; or

(ii) it is paid by way of security for the performance of a contract or by way of security in respect of loss which may result from the non-performance of a contract; or

(iii) without prejudice to (ii), it is paid by way of security for the delivery up or return of any property, whether in a particular state of repair or otherwise.

(2) (in *COMP*) the *investment* within (1), but including a sum of money that would otherwise be excluded:

(a) by article 6(1)(a)(ii) of the *Regulated Activities Order*, where the *person* making the payment is a *credit union* (unless the *person* receiving the payment is also a *credit union*); or

(b) by article 6(1)(d) of the *Regulated Activities Order*, where the *person* receiving it is a *credit union*; or

(c) by article 6 of the *Regulated Activities Order*, where the *person* paying it is an *eligible claimant*.

(B) In the *PRA Handbook*: the *investment*, specified in article 74 and defined in articles 5(2) and 5(3) of the *Regulated Activities Order*, which is in summary: a sum of money (other than one excluded by any of articles 6 to 9 AB of the *Regulated Activities Order*) paid on terms:

(1) under which it will be repaid, with or without interest or a premium, and either on demand or at a time or in circumstances agreed by or on behalf of the *person* making the payment and the *person* receiving it; and

(2) which are not referable to the provision of property (other than currency) or services or the giving of security; in this definition, money is paid on terms which are referable to the provision of property or services or the giving of security if, and only if:

(a) it is paid by way of advance or part payment under a contract for the sale, hire or other provision of property or services, and is repayable only in the event that the property or services is or are not in fact sold, hired or otherwise provided; or

(b) it is paid by way of security for the performance of a contract or by way of security in respect of loss which may result from the non-performance of a contract; or

(c) without prejudice to (ii), it is paid by way of security for the delivery up or return of any property, whether in a particular state of repair or otherwise.

deposit back arrangement

(in relation to any contract of *reinsurance*) an arrangement whereby an amount is deposited by the *reinsurer* with the cedant.

deposit-based stakeholder product

the *stakeholder product* specified by regulation 4 (certain deposit accounts) of the *Stakeholder Regulations*;

Deposit Guarantee Directive

the Council Directive of 13 May 1994 on deposit-guarantee schemes (No 94/19/EC).

deposit-taking firm

a *firm* which is a *bank*, *building society* or *credit union*.

depositary

(1) (except in *LR*):

(a) (in relation to an *ICVC*) the *person* to whom is entrusted the safekeeping of all of the *scheme property* of the *ICVC* and who has been appointed for this purpose in accordance with regulation 5 (Safekeeping of scheme property by depositary) of and Schedule 1 (Depositaries) to the *OEIC Regulations*;

(b) (in relation to an *AUT*) the *trustee*;

(c) (in relation to any other *unit trust scheme* other than an *AIF* specified in (e)) the *person* holding the property of the *scheme* on trust for the *participants*;

(ca) (in relation to an *EEA UCITS scheme*) the *person* fulfilling the function of a depositary in accordance with article 2(1)(a) of the *UCITS Directive*;

(cb) (in relation to an *ACS* which is a *co-ownership scheme*) the *person* who holds the property subject to the *scheme* or to whose order that property is held, as required by section 235A(3)(d) of the *Act* (Contractual schemes);

(cc) (in relation to an *ACS* which is a *limited partnership scheme*) the *person* who holds the property subject to the *scheme* or to whose order that property is held, and who has been appointed to be the *person* to whom the *property* subject to the *scheme* is entrusted for safekeeping, as required by section 235A(6)(e)(i) of the *Act* (Contractual schemes);

(d) (in relation to any other *fund* other than an *AIF* specified in (e))) any *person* to whom the *fund* property is entrusted for safekeeping.

(e) (for an *AIF* managed by a *full-scope UK AIFM* or a *full-scope EEA AIFM* (other than an *AIF* which is an *ICVC*, an *AUT* or an *ACS*)) the *person* fulfilling:

(i) the function of a depositary in accordance with article 21(1) of *AIFMD*; or

(ii) one or more of the functions of cash monitoring, safekeeping or oversight for a *non-EEA AIF*, in line with FUND 3.11.33R (1)(a) (AIFM of a non-EEA AIF).

(2) (in *LR*) a *person* that issues *certificates representing certain securities* that have been *admitted to listing* or are the subject of an application for *admission to listing*.

DEPP

the Decision Procedure and Penalties manual.

derivative

a *contract for differences*, a *future* or an *option*. (see also *securitised derivative*.)

designated client bank account

(A) In the PRA Handbook: a *client bank account* with the following characteristics:

(a) the account holds the money of one or more *clients*;

(b) the account includes in its title the word "designated";

(c) the *clients* whose *money* is in the account have each consented in writing to the use of the bank with which the *client money* is to be held; and

(d) in the event of the *failure* of that bank, the account is not pooled with any other type of account unless a *primary pooling event* occurs.

(B) In the FCA Handbook: a *client bank account* with the following characteristics:

(a) the account holds the money of one or more *clients*;

(b) the account includes in its title the words "designated client" (or, if the systems constraints of the approved bank or the *firm* that holds the account (or both) make this impracticable, an appropriate abbreviation of those words that has the same meaning);

(c) the *clients* whose *money* is in the account have each consented in writing to the use of the bank with which the *client money* is to be held; and

(d) in the event of the *failure* of that bank, the account is not pooled with any other type of account unless a *primary pooling event* occurs.

designated client fund account

(A) In the PRA Handbook: a *client bank account* with the following characteristics:

(a) the account holds at least part of the *client money* of one or more *clients*, each of whom has consented to that *money* being held in the same *client bank* accounts at the same banks (the *client money* of such *clients* constituting a designated fund);

(b) the account includes in its title the words "designated fund"; and

(c) in the event of the *failure* of a bank with which part of a designated fund is held, each *designated client fund account* held with the failed bank will form a pool with any other *designated client fund account* containing part of that same designated fund unless a *primary pooling event* occurs.

(B) In the FCA Handbook: a *client bank account* with the following characteristics:

(a) the account holds at least part of the *client money* of one or more *clients*, each of whom has consented to that *money* being held in the same *client bank* accounts at the same banks (the *client money* of such *clients* constituting a designated fund);

(b) the account includes in its title the words "designated client fund" (or, if the systems constraints of the approved bank or the firm that holds the account (or both) make this impracticable, an appropriate abbreviation of those words that has the same meaning); and

(c) in the event of the *failure* of a bank with which part of a designated fund is held, each *designated client fund account* held with the failed bank will form a pool with any other *designated client fund account* containing part of that same designated fund unless a *primary pooling event* occurs.

designated clearing house

one of the following *clearing houses*:

(a) ASX Settlement and Transfer Corporation Pty Ltd (ASTC);

(b) Austrian Kontroll Bank (OKB);

(c) Board of Trade Clearing Corporation;

(d) Cassa di Compensazione e Garanzia S.p.A (CCG);

(e) Commodity Clearing Corporation;

(f) Emerging Markets Clearing Corporation;

(g) FUTOP Clearing Centre (FUTOP Clearing Centralen A/S);

(h) Hong Kong Futures Exchange Clearing Corporation Ltd;

(i) Hong Kong Securities Clearing Company Ltd;

(j) Kansas City Board of Trade Clearing Corporation;

(k) Norwegian Futures & Options Clearing House (Norsk Opsjonssentral A.S. (NOS));

(l) N.V. Nederlandse Liquidatiekas (NLKKAS);

(m) OM Stockholm Exchange;

(n) Options Clearing Corporation;

(o) Options Clearing House Pty Ltd (OCH);

(p) Sydney Futures Exchange Clearing House (SFECH Ltd); and

(q) TNS Clearing Pty Ltd (TNSC).

designated committee

(in relation to a firm) a management body of the *firm* with delegated authority from the *firm's governing body* for approving either:

(a) (in relation to a *firm* that uses the *IRB approach*) all material aspects of the *firm's rating systems* and material changes to the *firm's rating systems*; or

(b) (in relation to a *firm* that uses the *advanced measurement approach*) all material aspects of the *advanced measurement approach* as carried out by the *firm* and material changes to the *firm's advanced measurement approach*; and

(c) a policy statement defining the *firm's* overall approach to material aspects of rating and estimation processes for all *rating systems* including non-material *rating systems* in relation to the *IRB approach*, or its overall approach to the *advanced measurement approach*, as relevant;

at least one of whose members is a member of the *firm's governing body*.

designated investment

(A) In the PRA Handbook: a *security* or a contractually-based investment (other than a *funeral plan contract* and a right to or interest in a *funeral plan contract*), that is, any of the following *investments*, specified in Part III of the *Regulated Activities Order* (Specified Investments), and a *long-term care insurance contract* which is a *pure protection contract*:

(a) *life policy* (subset of article 75 (Contracts of insurance));

(b) *share* (article 76);

(c) *debenture* (article 77);

(ca) *alternative debenture* (article 77A);

(d) *government and public security* (article 78);

(e) *warrant* (article 79);

(f) *certificate representing certain securities* (article 80);

(g) *unit* (article 81);

(h) *stakeholder pension scheme* (article 82(1))

(ha) *personal pension scheme* (article 82(2));

(hb) *emissions auction product* (article 82A) where it is a *financial instrument*.

(i) *option* (article 83); for the purposes of the *permission* regime, this is sub-divided into:
(i) *option* (excluding a *commodity option* and an *option* on a *commodity future*);
(ii) *commodity option* and *option* on a *commodity future*;

(j) *future* (article 84); for the purposes of the *permission* regime, this is sub-divided into:
(i) *future* (excluding a *commodity future* and a *rolling spot forex contract*);
(ii) *commodity future*;
(iii) *rolling spot forex contract*;

(k) *contract for differences* (article 85); for the purposes of the *permission* regime, this is sub-divided into:
(i) *contract for differences* (excluding a *spread bet* and a *rolling spot forex contract*);
(ii) *spread bet*;
(iii) *rolling spot forex contract*;

(l) *rights to or interests in investments* in (a) to (k) (article 89) but not including rights to or interests in rights under a *long-term care insurance contract* which is a *pure protection contract*.

(B) In the FCA Handbook: a *security* or a contractually-based investment (other than a *funeral plan contract* and a right to or interest in a *funeral plan contract*), that is, any of the following *investments*, specified in Part III of the *Regulated Activities Order* (Specified Investments), a *P2P agreement*, and a *long-term care insurance contract* which is a *pure protection contract*:

(a) *life policy* (subset of article 75 (Contracts of insurance));

(b) *share* (article 76);

(c) *debenture* (article 77);

(ca) *alternative debenture* (article 77A);

(d) *government and public security* (article 78);

(e) *warrant* (article 79);

(f) *certificate representing certain securities* (article 80);

(g) *unit* (article 81);

(h) *stakeholder pension scheme* (article 82(1))

(ha) *personal pension scheme* (article 82(2));

(hb) *emissions auction product* (article 82A) where it is a *financial instrument*.

(i) *option* (article 83); for the purposes of the *permission* regime, this is sub-divided into:
(i) *option* (excluding a *commodity option* and an *option* on a *commodity future*);
(ii) *commodity option* and *option* on a *commodity future*;

(j) *future* (article 84); for the purposes of the *permission* regime, this is sub-divided into:
(i) *future* (excluding a *commodity future* and a *rolling spot forex contract*);
(ii) *commodity future*;
(iii) *rolling spot forex contract*;

(k) *contract for differences* (article 85); for the purposes of the *permission* regime, this is sub-divided into:
(i) *contract for differences* (excluding a *spread bet* and a *rolling spot forex contract*);
(ii) *spread bet*;
(iii) *rolling spot forex contract*;

(l) *rights to or interests in investments* in (a) to (k) (article 89) but not including rights to or interests in rights under a *long-term care insurance contract* which is a *pure protection contract*.

designated investment business

(A) In the PRA Handbook: any of the following activities, specified in Part II of the *Regulated Activities Order* (Specified Activities), which is carried on by way of business:

(a) *dealing in investments as principal* (article 14), but disregarding the exclusion in article 15 (Absence of holding out etc);

(b) *dealing in investments as agent* (article 21) but only in relation to *designated investments*;

(ba) *MiFID business bidding* (part of *bidding in emissions auctions*) (article 24A);

(c) *arranging (bringing about) deals in investments* (article 25(1)), but only in relation to *designated investments*;

(d) *making arrangements with a view to transactions in investments* (article 25(2)), but only in relation to *designated investments*;

(da) *operating a multilateral trading facility* (article 25D);

(e) *managing investments* (article 37), but only if the assets consist of or include (or may consist of or include) *designated investments*;

(ea) assisting in the administration and performance of a *contract of insurance*, but only if the *contract of insurance* is a *designated investment*.

(f) *safeguarding and administering investments* (article 40), but only if the assets consist of or include (or may consist of or include) *designated investments*; for the purposes of the *permission* regime, this is sub-divided into:
(i) *safeguarding and administration of assets (without arranging)*;
(ii) *arranging safeguarding and administration of assets*;

(g) *sending dematerialised instructions* (article 45(1));

(h) *causing dematerialised instructions to be sent* (article 45(2));

(l) *establishing, operating or winding up a stakeholder pension scheme* (article 52(a))

(la) *establishing, operating or winding up a personal pension scheme* (article 52(b));

(lb) providing *basic advice* on a *stakeholder product* (article 52B);

(m) *advising on investments* (article 53), but only in relation to *designated investments*; for the purposes of the *permission* regime, this is sub-divided into:
(i) *advising on investments* (except *pension transfers* and *pension opt-outs*);
(ii) *advising on pension transfers and pension opt-outs*;

(n) *agreeing to carry on a regulated activity* in (a) to (h) and (m) (article 64).

(o) [deleted]

(p) *managing a UCITS*;

(q) *acting as trustee or depositary of a UCITS*;

(r) *managing an AIF*;

(s) *acting as trustee or depositary of an AIF*;

(t) *establishing, operating or winding up a collective investment scheme.*

(B) In the FCA Handbook: any of the following activities, specified in Part II of the *Regulated Activities Order* (Specified Activities), which is carried on by way of business:

(a) *dealing in investments as principal* (article 14), but disregarding the exclusion in article 15 (Absence of holding out etc);

(b) *dealing in investments as agent* (article 21) but only in relation to *designated investments* (other than *P2P agreements*);

(ba) *MiFID business bidding* (part of *bidding in emissions auctions*) (article 24A);

(c) *arranging (bringing about) deals in investments* (article 25(1)), but only in relation to *designated investments* (other than *P2P agreements*);

(d) *making arrangements with a view to transactions in investments* (article 25(2)), but only in relation to *designated investments* (other than *P2P agreements*);

(da) *operating a multilateral trading facility* (article 25D);

(db) *operating an electronic system in relation to lending* (article 36H) but only insofar as it relates to a lender or prospective lender under a *P2P agreement*;

(e) *managing investments* (article 37), but only if the assets consist of or include (or may consist of or include) *designated investments* (other than *P2P agreements*);

(ea) assisting in the administration and performance of a *contract of insurance*, but only if the *contract of insurance* is a *designated investment.*

(f) *safeguarding and administering investments* (article 40), but only if the assets consist of or include (or may consist of or include) *designated investments* (other than P2P agreements); for the purposes of the *permission* regime, this is sub-divided into:
(i) *safeguarding and administration of assets (without arranging)*;
(ii) *arranging safeguarding and administration of assets*;

(g) *sending dematerialised instructions* (article 45(1));

(h) *causing dematerialised instructions to be sent* (article 45(2));

(l) *establishing, operating or winding up a stakeholder pension scheme* (article 52(a))

(la) *establishing, operating or winding up a personal pension scheme* (article 52(b));

(lb) providing *basic advice* on a *stakeholder product* (article 52B);

(m) *advising on investments* (article 53), but only in relation to *designated investments* (other than *P2P agreements*); for the purposes of the *permission* regime, this includes:
(i) *advising on investments* (except *pension transfers* and *pension opt-outs*);
(ii) *advising on investments* in respect of *pension transfers* and *pension opt-outs*;

(ma) *advising on conversion or transfer of pension benefits* (article 53E);

(n) *agreeing to carry on a regulated activity* in (a) to (h) and (m) (article 64).

(o) [deleted]

(p) *managing a UCITS*;

(q) *acting as trustee or depositary of a UCITS*;

(r) *managing an AIF*;

(s) *acting as trustee or depositary of an AIF*;

(t) *establishing, operating or winding up a collective investment scheme.*

designated investment exchange

Any of the following investment exchanges:

American Stock Exchange

Australian Stock Exchange

Bermuda Stock Exchange

Bolsa Mexicana de Valores

Bourse de Montreal Inc

Channel Islands Stock Exchange

Chicago Board of Trade

Chicago Board Options Exchange

Chicago Stock Exchange

Coffee, Sugar and Cocoa Exchange, Inc

Euronext Amsterdam Commodities Market

Hong Kong Exchanges and Clearing Limited

International Securities Market Association

Johannesburg Stock Exchange

Kansas City Board of Trade

Korea Stock Exchange

Mid-America Commodity Exchange

Minneapolis Grain Exchange

New York Cotton Exchange

New York Futures Exchange

New York Stock Exchange

New Zealand Stock Exchange

Osaka Securities Exchange

Pacific Exchange

Philadelphia Stock Exchange

Singapore Exchange

South African Futures Exchange

Tokyo International Financial Futures Exchange

Tokyo Stock Exchange

Toronto Stock Exchange

designated investment firm

(A) (In the *PRA Handbook*) an *authorised person* that has been designated by the *PRA* under article 3 of the *PRA-regulated Activities Order*.

(B) (In the FCA Handbook) an authorised person that has been designated by the *PRA* under article 3 of the *PRA-regulated Activities Order*.

designated money market fund

(in BIPRU 12) a *collective investment scheme* authorised under the *UCITS Directive* or which is subject to supervision and, if applicable, authorised by an authority under the national law of an *EEA State*, and which satisfies the following conditions:

(a) its primary investment objective must be to maintain the net asset value of the undertaking either constant at par (net of earnings), or at the value of the investors' initial capital plus earnings;

(b) it must, with a view to achieving that primary investment objective, invest exclusively in either or both assets (i) of the kind mentioned in BIPRU 12.7.2R(1) and (2), or (ii) sight deposits with *credit institutions* that are at all times fully secured against assets of the kind mentioned in BIPRU 12.7.2R(1) and (2);

(c) it must, for the purpose of condition (b), only count assets with a maturity or residual maturity of no more than 397 days, or regular yield adjustments consistent with such a maturity, and with a weighted average maturity of no more than 60 days;

(d) it must, for the purpose of condition (b), ensure that if it invests in sight deposits with *credit institutions* of the kind mentioned in (b)(ii), no more than 20% of those deposits are held with any one body; and

(e) it must provide liquidity through same day settlement in respect of any request for redemption made at or before 1200 hours GMT or, as the case may be, BST.

designated multilateral development bank

Any of the following:

(a) African Development Bank;

(b) Asian Development Bank;

(c) Council of Europe Development Bank;

(d) European Bank for Reconstruction and Development;

(e) European Investment Bank;

(f) Inter-American Development Bank;

(g) International Bank for Reconstruction and Development;

(h) International Finance Corporation;

(i) Islamic Development Bank; and

(j) Nordic Investment Bank.

designated non-member

(in *REC*) (in relation to a *UK RIE*) a *person* in respect of whom action may be taken under the *default rules* of the *RIE* but who is not a *member* of the *RIE*.

designated professional body

a professional body designated by the Treasury under section 326 of the *Act* (Designation of professional bodies) for the purposes of Part XX of the *Act* (Provision of Financial Services by Members of the Professions); the following professional bodies have been designated in the Financial Services and Markets Act 2000 (Designated Professional Bodies) Order 2001 (SI 2001/1226), the Financial Services and Markets Act 2000 (Designated Professional Bodies) (Amendment) Order 2004 (SI 2004/3352) and the Financial Services and Markets Act 2000 (Designated Professional Bodies) (Amendment) Order 2006 (SI 2006/58):

(a) The Law Society of England & Wales;

(b) The Law Society of Scotland;

(c) The Law Society of Northern Ireland;

(d) The Institute of Chartered Accountants in England and Wales;

(e) The Institute of Chartered Accountants of Scotland;

(f) The Institute of Chartered Accountants in Ireland;

(g) The Association of Chartered Certified Accountants;

(h) The Institute of Actuaries;

(i) The Council for Licensed Conveyancers; and

(j) The Royal Institution of Chartered Surveyors.

designated State or territory

any *EEA State* (other than the *United Kingdom*), Australia, Canada or a province of Canada, Hong Kong, Singapore, South Africa, Switzerland, a State in the United States of America, the District of Columbia or Puerto Rico.

DGD claim

(A) In the PRA Handbook:
a *claim*, in relation to a *protected deposit*, against a CRD credit institution, whether established in the *United Kingdom* or in another *EEA State*.

(B) In the FCA Handbook:
a *claim*, in relation to a *protected deposit*, against a *CRD credit institution*, whether established in the *United Kingdom* or in another *EEA State*.

dilution

(in *COLL*) the amount of *dealing* costs incurred, or expected to be incurred, by or for the account of a *single-priced authorised fund* to the extent that these costs may reasonably be expected to result, or have resulted, from the acquisition or disposal of *investments* by or for the account of the *single-priced authorised fund* as a consequence (whether or not immediate) of the increase or decrease in the cash resources of the *single-priced authorised fund* resulting from the *issue* or *cancellation* of *units* over a period; for the purposes of this definition, *dealing* costs include both the costs of *dealing* in an *investment*, professional fees incurred, or expected to be incurred, in relation to the acquisition or disposal of an immovable and, where there is a spread between the *buying* and selling prices of the *investment*, the indirect cost resulting from the differences between those prices.

dilution adjustment

an adjustment to the *price* of a *unit* determined by the *authorised fund manager* of a *single-priced authorised fund*, under COLL 6.3.8 R (Dilution) for the purpose of reducing *dilution*.

dilution levy

a charge of such amount or at such rate as is determined by the *authorised fund manager* of a *single-priced authorised fund*to be made for the purpose of reducing the effect of *dilution*.

dilution risk

(in accordance with Article 4(24) of the *Banking Consolidation Directive* (Definitions)) the risk that an amount receivable is reduced through cash or non-cash credits to the obligor.

Diploma Directives

the First and Second Diploma Directives, that is:

(a) the Council Directive of 21 December 1988 on a general system for the recognition of higher-education diplomas, awarded on completion of professional education and training of at least three years' duration (No 89/48/EEC);

(b) the Council Directive of 18 June 1992 on a second general system for the recognition of professional education and training to supplement Directive 89/48/EEC (No 92/51/EEC).

direct deal

a *home finance transaction* that can only be obtained direct from a *home finance provider*, and where that *home finance provider* is not the selling *firm*.

direct offer financial promotion

a *financial promotion* that contains:

(a) an offer by the *firm* or another *person* to enter into a *controlled agreement* with any *person* who responds to the communication; or

(b) an invitation to any *person* who responds to the communication to make an offer to the *firm* or another *person* to enter into a *controlled agreement*;

and which specifies the manner of response or includes a form by which any response may be made. In relation to *MiFID or equivalent third country business* "controlled agreement" includes an agreement to carry on an *ancillary service*.

directed at

a *financial promotion* is directed at *persons* if it is addressed to *persons* generally (for example where it is contained in a television broadcast or web site).

directed only at

(a) If all the conditions set out in (c) are met, a communication is to be regarded as "directed only at" a certain *group* of *persons*.

(b) In any other case in which one or more of those conditions are met, that fact is to be taken into account in determining whether the communication is "directed only at" a certain *group* of *persons* (but a communication may still be regarded as so directed even if none of the conditions in (c) are met).

(c) The conditions are that:
(i) the communication includes an indication of the description of *persons* to whom it is directed and an indication of the fact that the *investment* or service to which it relates is available only to such *persons*;
(ii) the communication includes an indication that *persons* of any other description should not rely upon it;
(iii) there are in place proper systems and procedures to prevent recipients other than *persons* to whom it is directed engaging in the investment activity, or participating in the *collective investment scheme*, to which the communication relates with the *person* directing the communication, a *close relative* of his or a member of the same *group*.

directive friendly society

a *friendly society* other than a *non-directive friendly society*.

director

(1) (except in *COLL, DTR, LR* and *PR*) (in relation to any of the following (whether constituted in the *United Kingdom* or under the law of a country or territory outside it)):
(a) an unincorporated association;
(b) a *body corporate*;
(c) (in *SYSC*, MIPRU 2 (Insurance mediation activity: responsibility, knowledge, ability and good

repute) and SUP 10 (Approved persons)) a *partnership*;

(d) (in *SYSC* and SUP 10 (Approved persons)) a *sole trader*;

any *person* appointed to direct its affairs, including a *person* who is a member of its *governing body* and (in accordance with section 417(1) of the *Act*):

(i) a *person* occupying in relation to it the position of a director (by whatever name called); and

(ii) a *person* in accordance with whose directions or instructions (not being advice given in a professional capacity) the directors of that body are accustomed to *act*.

(2) (in *COLL*) a director of an *ICVC*, including (in accordance with regulation 2(1) of the *OEIC Regulations*) a *person* occupying in relation to the *ICVC* the position of director, by whatever name called.

(3) (in *DTR*, *LR* and *PR*) (in accordance with section 417(1)(a) of the *Act*) a *person* occupying in relation to it the position of a director (by whatever name called) and, in relation to an *issuer* which is not a *body corporate*, a *person* with corresponding powers and duties.

director function

(1) (in the *FCA Handbook*) *FCA controlled functions* CF1 in Part 1 of the *table of FCA controlled functions*, described more fully in SUP 10A.6.7 R and SUP 10A.6.8 R.

(2) (in the *PRA Handbook*) *PRA controlled function* CF1 in the *table of PRA controlled functions*, described more fully in SUP 10B.6.1 R and SUP 10B.6.2 R.

director of unincorporated association function

(1) (in the *FCA Handbook*) *FCA controlled function* CF5 in Part 1 of the *table of FCA controlled functions*, described more fully in SUP 10A.6.29 R.

(2) (in the *PRA Handbook*) *PRA controlled function* CF5 in the *table of PRA controlled functions*, described more fully in SUP 10B.6.15 R.

Disciplinary Tribunal

a Tribunal appointed under Schedule 2 to Lloyd's Disciplinary Committees Byelaw (No 31 of 1996).

disclosable information

any information which has to be disclosed in the market in accordance with any legal or regulatory requirement.

disclosure obligations

(in *REC*) the initial, ongoing and ad hoc disclosure requirements contained in the *relevant articles* and given effect:

(1) in the *United Kingdom* by Part 6 of the *Act* and Part 6 rules (within the meaning of section 73A of the *Act*); or

(2) in another *EEA State* by legislation transposing the *relevant articles* in that State.

disclosure regulations

as the case may be, the Consumer Credit (Disclosure of Information) Regulations 2010, SI 2010/1013 or the Consumer Credit (Disclosure of Information) Regulations 2004, SI 2004/1481.

disclosure rules

(in accordance with sections 73A(1) and 73A(3) of the *Act*) *rules* relating to the disclosure of information in respect of *financial instruments* which have been admitted to trading on a *regulated market* or for which a request for *admission to trading* on such a market has been made.

discounting

discounting or deductions to take account of investment income as set out in paragraph 48 of the *insurance accounts rules*.

discretionary investment manager

(in *COBS* and (in relation to *firm type*) in SUP 16.10 (Confirmation of standing data)) a *person* who, acting only on behalf of a *client*, manages *designated investments* in an account or portfolio on a discretionary basis under the terms of a discretionary management agreement.

discretionary pension benefit

(A) In the PRA Handbook: (in SYSC 19A) enhanced pension benefits granted on a discretionary basis by a *firm* to an *employee* as part of that *employee's* variable *remuneration* package, but excluding accrued benefits granted to an *employee* under the terms of his company pension scheme. [Note: article 4(49) of the *Banking Consolidation Directive*]

(B) In the FCA Handbook:

(1) (in SYSC 19C) enhanced pension benefits granted on a discretionary basis by a *firm* to an *employee* as part of that *employee's* variable *remuneration* package, but excluding accrued benefits granted to an *employee* under the terms of his company pension scheme. [Note: article 4(49) of the *Banking Consolidation Directive*]

(2) (in *IFPRU* and SYSC 19A) has the meaning in article 4(1)(73) of the *EU CRR*.

DISP

Dispute Resolution: the Complaints sourcebook.

distance contract

any contract concerning financial services concluded between a supplier and a *consumer* under an organised distance sales or service provision scheme run by the supplier which, for the purpose of that contract, makes exclusive use (directly or through an intermediary) of one or more means of distance communication (that is, any means which, without the simultaneous physical presence of the supplier or intermediary and the *consumer*, may be used for the distance marketing of a service between those parties) up to and including the time at which the contract is concluded. A contract is not a distance contract if:

(a) making, performing or marketing it does not constitute or form part of a *regulated activity*; or

(b) it is entered into on a strictly occasional basis outside a commercial structure dedicated to the conclusion of distance contracts; or

(c) a *consumer*, and an intermediary acting for a product provider, are simultaneously physically present at some stage before the conclusion of the contract; or

(d) it is entered into to comply with the requirement in Part 1 of the Pensions Act 2008 to automatically enrol or re-enrol employees into an *automatic enrolment scheme*.

[Note: recitals 15 and 18 to, and articles 2(a) and (e) of, the *Distance Marketing Directive*]

distance home purchase mediation contract

a *distance contract*, the making or performance of which constitutes, or is part of:

(a) *advising on a home purchase plan*;

(b) *arranging (bringing about) a home purchase plan*;

(c) *making arrangements with a view to a home purchase plan*; or

(d) *agreeing to carry on a regulated activity* in (a) to (c).

Distance Marketing Directive

The Directive of the Council and Parliament of 23 September 2002 on distance marketing of consumer financial services (No 2002/65/EC).

Distance Marketing Regulations

The Financial Services (Distance Marketing) Regulations 2004 (SI 2004/2095).

distance mortgage mediation contract

a *distance contract*, the making or performance of which constitutes, or is part of:

(a) *advising on regulated mortgage contracts*; or

(b) *arranging (bringing about) regulated mortgage contracts*; or

(c) *making arrangements with a view to regulated mortgage contracts*; or

(d) agreeing to carry on a regulated mortgage activity in (a) to (c).

distance regulated sale and rent back mediation contract

a *distance contract*, the making or performance of which constitutes, or is part of:

(a) *advising on a regulated sale and rent back agreement*; or

(b) *arranging (bringing about) a regulated sale and rent back agreement*; or

(c) *making arrangements with a view to a regulated sale and rent back agreement*; or

(d) agreeing to carry on a *regulated sale and rent back mediation activity* in (a) to (c).

distance selling contract

(in *BCOBS*) has the same meaning as "distance contract" in the Consumer Protection (Distance Selling) Regulations 2000 (SI 2000/2334).

distribution account

(in *COLL*) the account to which the amount of income of an *authorised fund* allocated to *classes* of *units* that distribute income must be transferred as at the end of each *annual accounting period* under COLL 6.8.3 R (Income allocation and distribution) or COLL 8.5.15 R (Income).

distribution channels

a channel through which information is, or is likely to become, publicly available. Information which is "likely to become publicly available" means information to which a large number of *persons* have access. [Note: article 2(1) of the *MiFID implementing Directive*]

distribution in connection with common equity tier 1 capital

(in accordance with article 141(10) of CRD) includes:

(a) a payment of cash dividends;

(b) a distribution of fully or partly paid bonus *shares* or other capital instruments referred to in article 26(1)(a) of the *EU CRR* (Common equity tier 1 items);

(c) a redemption or purchase by a *firm* of its own *shares* or other capital instruments referred to in article 26(1)(a) of the *EU CRR* (Common equity tier 1 items);

(d) a repayment of amounts paid in connection with capital instruments referred to in article 26(1)(a) of the *EU CRR* (Common equity tier 1 items); and

(e) a distribution of items referred to in article 26(1)(b) to (e) of the *EU CRR* (Common equity tier 1 items).

distribution of exposures

(in accordance with Part 1 of Annex III of the *Banking Consolidation Directive* (Definitions) and for the purpose of BIPRU 13 (The calculation of counterparty risk exposure values for financial derivatives, securities financing transactions and long settlement transactions)) the forecast of the probability distribution of market values that is generated by setting forecast instances of negative net market values equal to zero.

distribution of market values

(in accordance with Part 1 of Annex III of the *Banking Consolidation Directive* (Definitions) and for the purpose of BIPRU 13 (The calculation of counterparty risk exposure values for financial derivatives, securities financing transactions and long settlement transactions)) the forecast of the probability distribution of net market values of transactions within a *netting set* for some future date (the forecasting horizon), given the realised market value of those transactions up to the present time.

DLG by default

(A) In the PRA Handbook:

(in relation to a *UK ILAS BIPRU firm* (a *group liquidity reporting firm*) and any reporting period under SUP 16 (Reporting requirements)) the *firm* and each *person* identified in accordance with the following:

(a) (in a case in which the *firm* is the only *UK ILAS BIPRU firm* in its *group*) that *person* meets any of the following conditions for any part of that period:

(i) that *person* provides material support to the *firm* against *liquidity risk*; or

(ii) that *person* is committed to provide such support or would be committed to do so if that *person* were able to provide it; or

(iii) the *firm* has reasonable grounds to believe that that *person* would supply such support if asked or would do so if it were able to provide it; or

(iv) the *firm* provides material support to that *person* against *liquidity risk*; or

(v) the *firm* is committed to provide such support to that *person* or would be committed to do so if the *firm* were able to provide it; or

(vi) the *firm* has reasonable grounds to believe that that *person* would expect the *firm* to supply such support if asked or that the *firm* would do so if it were able to provide it; or

(b) (in a case in which the *firm* is not the only UK ILAS BIPRU firm in its *group*):

(i) each of those other *UK ILAS BIPRU firms*; and

(ii) each *person* identified by applying the tests in (a) separately to the *firm* and to each of those other *UK ILAS BIPRU firms*, so that applying (b) to the *firm* and to each of those *UK ILAS BIPRU firms* results in their having the same *defined liquidity group*;

(iii) no *DLG by default* exists where the group consists only of *UK ILAS BIPRU firms*.

The following provisions also apply for the purpose of this definition.
(c) A *person* is not a member of a firm's DLG by default unless it also satisfies one of the following conditions:
(i) it is a member of the *firm's group*; or
(ii) it is a *securitisation special purpose entity* or a *special purpose vehicle*; or
(iii) it is an *undertaking* whose main purpose is to raise funds for the *firm* or for a *group* to which that *firm* belongs.
(ca) In the case of a *group liquidity reporting firm* that is within paragraph (a) of the definition of *UK lead regulated firm* (it is not part of a group that is subject to consolidated supervision by the *FCA* or the *PRA* or any other *regulatory body*), paragraph (c)(i) of the definition of *DLG by default* is amended so that it only includes a member of the *firm's group* that falls into one of the following categories:
(i) it is a *credit institution*; or
(ii) it is an *investment firm* or *third country investment firm* authorised to *deal on own account*.
For these purposes:
(iii) *credit institution* has the meaning used in SUP 16 (Reporting requirements), namely either of the following:
(A) a credit institution authorised under the *CRD*; or
(B) an institution which would satisfy the requirements for authorisation as a credit institution under the *CRD* if it had its registered office (or if it does not have a registered office, its head office) in an *EEA State*; and
(iv) a *person* is authorised to *deal on own account* if:
(A) it is a *firm* and its *permission* includes that activity; or
(B) it is an *EEA firm* and it is authorised by its *Home State regulator* to do that activity; or
(C) (if the carrying on of that activity is prohibited in a state or territory without an authorisation in that state or territory) that *person* has such an authorisation.
(d) *Group* has the meaning in paragraph (1) of the definition in the *Glossary* (the definition in section 421 of the *Act*).
(e) The conditions in (a) are satisfied even if the *firm* or *person* in question provides or is committed or expected to provide support for only part of the period. (f) In deciding for the purpose
(f) In deciding for the purpose of (a) or (b) whether the *firm* is the only *UK ILAS BIPRU firm* in its *group* and identifying which are the other *UK ILAS BIPRU firms* in its *group*, any *group* member that is a member of the group through no more than a *participation* is ignored.
(g) A *firm* has a *DLG by default* for a period even if it only has one during part of that period.
(h) Liquidity support may be supplied by or to the *firm* directly or indirectly.
(i) Support is material if it is material either by reference to the *person* giving it or by reference to the *person* receiving it.
(*Guidance* about this definition, and its inter-relation with other related definitions, is set out in SUP 16 Annex 26 (Guidance on designated liquidity groups in SUP 16.12).)

(B) In the FCA Handbook:
(in relation to a *UK ILAS BIPRU firm* (a *group liquidity reporting firm*) and any reporting period under SUP 16 (Reporting requirements)) the *firm* and each *person* identified in accordance with the following:
(a) (in a case in which the *firm* is the only *UK ILAS BIPRU firm* in its *group*) that *person* meets any of the following conditions for any part of that period:
(i) that *person* provides material support to the *firm* against *liquidity risk*; or
(ii) that *person* is committed to provide such support or would be committed to do so if that *person* were able to provide it; or
(iii) the *firm* has reasonable grounds to believe that that *person* would supply such support if asked or would do so if it were able to provide it; or
(iv) the *firm* provides material support to that *person* against *liquidity risk*; or
(v) the *firm* is committed to provide such support to that *person* or would be committed to do so if the *firm* were able to provide it; or
(vi) the *firm* has reasonable grounds to believe that that *person* would expect the *firm* to supply such support if asked or that the *firm* would do so if it were able to provide it; or
(b) (in a case in which the *firm* is not the only UK ILAS BIPRU firm in its *group*):
(i) each of those other *UK ILAS BIPRU firms*; and
(ii) each *person* identified by applying the tests in (a) separately to the *firm* and to each of those other *UK ILAS BIPRU firms*, so that applying (b) to the *firm* and to each of those *UK ILAS BIPRU firms* results in their having the same *defined liquidity group*;
(iii) no *DLG by default* exists where the group consists only of *UK ILAS BIPRU firms*.
The following provisions also apply for the purpose of this definition.
(c) A *person* is not a member of a firm's DLG by default unless it also satisfies one of the following conditions:
(i) it is a member of the *firm's group*; or
(ii) it is a *securitisation special purpose entity* or a *special purpose vehicle*; or
(iii) it is an *undertaking* whose main purpose is to raise funds for the *firm* or for a *group* to which that *firm* belongs.

(ca) In the case of a *group liquidity reporting firm* that is within paragraph (a) of the definition of *UK lead regulated firm* (it is not part of a group that is subject to consolidated supervision by the *FCA* or the *PRA* or any other *regulatory body*), paragraph (c)(i) of the definition of *DLG by default* is amended so that it only includes a member of the *firm's group* that falls into one of the following categories:

(i) it is a *credit institution*; or

(ii) it is an *investment firm* or *third country investment firm* authorised to *deal on own account*. For these purposes:

(iii) *credit institution* has the meaning used in SUP 16 (Reporting requirements), namely either of the following:

(A) a credit institution authorised under the *CRD* or

(B) an institution which would satisfy the requirements for authorisation as a credit institution under the *CRD* if it had its registered office (or if it does not have a registered office, its head office) in an *EEA State*; and

(iv) a *person* is authorised to *deal on own account* if:

(A) it is a *firm* and its *permission* includes that activity; or

(B) it is an *EEA firm* and it is authorised by its *Home State regulator* to do that activity; or

(C) (if the carrying on of that activity is prohibited in a state or territory without an authorisation in that state or territory) that *person* has such an authorisation.

(d) *Group* has the meaning in paragraph (1) of the definition in the *Glossary* (the definition in section 421 of the *Act*).

(e) The conditions in (a) are satisfied even if the *firm* or *person* in question provides or is committed or expected to provide support for only part of the period. (f) In deciding for the purpose

(f) In deciding for the purpose of (a) or (b) whether the *firm* is the only *UK ILAS BIPRU firm* in its *group* and identifying which are the other *UK ILAS BIPRU firms* in its *group*, any *group* member that is a member of the group through no more than a *participation* is ignored.

(g) A *firm* has a *DLG by default* for a period even if it only has one during part of that period.

(h) Liquidity support may be supplied by or to the *firm* directly or indirectly.

(i) Support is material if it is material either by reference to the *person* giving it or by reference to the *person* receiving it.

(*Guidance* about this definition, and its inter-relation with other related definitions, is set out in SUP 16 Annex 26 (Guidance on designated liquidity groups in SUP 16.12).)

DLG by modification

either of the following:

(a) a *DLG by modification (firm level)*; or

(b) a *non-UK DLG by modification (DLG level)*.

(*Guidance* about this definition, and its inter-relation with other related definitions, is set out in SUP 16 Annex 26 (Guidance on designated liquidity groups in SUP 16.12).)

DLG by modification (firm level)

(in relation to any reporting period under SUP 16 (Reporting requirements) and a *UK ILAS BIPRU firm* that has an *intra-group liquidity modification* during any part of that period (a *group liquidity reporting firm*)) the *firm* and each *person* on whose liquidity support the *firm* can rely, under that *intra-group liquidity modification*, for any part of that period for the purpose of the *overall liquidity adequacy rule* (as the *overall liquidity adequacy rule* applies to the *firm* on a solo basis). A *firm* has a 'DLG by modification (firm level)' for a period even if it only has one during part of that period. (*Guidance* about this definition, and its inter-relation with other related definitions, is set out in SUP 16 Annex 26 (Guidance on designated liquidity groups in SUP 16.12).)

DMG

the Office of Fair Trading's Debt Management (and credit repair services Guidance).

document

any piece of recorded information, including (in accordance with section 417(1) of the *Act* (Interpretation)) information recorded in any form; in relation to information recorded otherwise than in legible form, references to its production include references to producing a copy of the information in legible form.

document evidencing title

any means of evidencing title whether in documentary form or otherwise.

document viewing facility

(in *LR*) a location identified on the *FCA* website where the public can inspect documents referred to in the *listing rules* as being documents to be made available at the document viewing facility.

domestic UCITS merger

(in *COLL* and in accordance with article 2(1)(r) of the *UCITS Directive*) a *UCITS merger* between two or more *UCITS schemes* in relation to which a *UCITS marketing notification* has been made in respect of at least one of the relevant *schemes*.

dormant account

has the meaning given in section 10 of the Dormant Bank and Building Society Accounts Act 2008, which is in summary an *account* that at a particular point in time:

(a) has been open throughout the period of 15 years ending at that time; and

(b) during that period no transactions have been carried out in relation to the *account* by or on the instructions of the holder of the *account*.

dormant account funds

has the meaning given in section 5(6) of the Dormant Bank and Building Society Accounts Act 2008, which is *money* paid to a *dormant account fund operator* by a *bank* or *building society* in respect of a *dormant account*.

dormant account fund operator

a *firm* with *permission* for *operating a dormant account fund*.

DTR

(A) In the PRA Handbook:
the Disclosure Rules and Transparency Rules sourcebook containing the *disclosure rules*, *transparency rules*, *corporate governance rules* and the *rules* relating to *primary information providers*.

(B) In the FCA Handbook:
the Disclosure Rules and Transparency Rules sourcebook containing the *disclosure rules*, *transparency rules*, *corporate governance rules* and the *rules* relating to *primary information providers*.

drawdown mortgage

a *lifetime mortgage* contract where:

(a) the amount borrowed is paid by the *mortgage lender* to the *customer* in instalments during the life of the mortgage; and

(b) the size and frequency of the instalments are:
(1) agreed between the *mortgage lender* and the *customer*; or
(2) set by reference to an index or interest rate (such as the Official Bank Rate).

drawdown pension

(as defined in paragraph 4 of Schedule 28 to the Finance Act 2004):

(a) a *short-term annuity*; or

(b) an *income withdrawal*.

drawn down capital

(in SUP 16, in the case of an *investment management firm* carrying out *venture capital business*) the total current value of contributions committed by investors under contractual agreement which has been invested by the *firm*.

dual-priced authorised fund

an *authorised fund* or, in the case of an *umbrella*, a *sub-fund* (if it were a separate fund), that is not a *single-priced authorised fund*.

durable medium

(a) paper; or

(b) any instrument which enables the recipient to store information addressed personally to him in a way accessible for future reference for a period of time adequate for the purposes of the information and which allows the unchanged reproduction of the information stored. In particular, *durable medium* covers floppy disks, CD-ROMs, DVDs and hard drives of personal computers on which electronic mail is stored, but it excludes Internet sites, unless such sites meet the criteria specified in the first sentence of this paragraph. (in relation to *MiFID or equivalent third country business* or *collective portfolio management*, if the relevant *rule* implements the *MiFID implementing Directive*, the *UCITS Directive*, the *UCITS implementing Directive* or the *UCITS implementing*

Directive No 2) the instrument used must be:

(i) appropriate to the context in which the business is to be carried on; and

(ii) specifically chosen by the recipient when offered the choice between that instrument and paper. For the purposes of this definition, the provision of information by means of electronic communications shall be treated as appropriate to the context in which the business between the *firm* and the *client* is, or is to be, carried on if there is evidence that the *client* has regular access to the internet. The provision by the *client* of an e-mail address for the purposes of the carrying on of that business is sufficient. [Note: article 2(f) and Recital 20 of the *Distance Marketing Directive*, article 2(12) of the *Insurance Mediation Directive*, articles 2(2), 3(1) and 3(3) of the *MiFID implementing Directive*, articles 75(2) and 81(1) of the *UCITS Directive*, article 20(3) of the *UCITS implementing Directive* and article 7 of the *UCITS implementing Directive No 2*]

early amortisation provision

(A) In the PRA Handbook: (in accordance with Article 100 of the *Banking Consolidation Directive* (Securitisation of revolving exposures) and in relation to a *securitisation* within the meaning of paragraph (2) of the definition of securitisation) a contractual clause which requires, on the occurrence of defined events, investors' positions to be redeemed prior to the originally stated maturity of the securities issued.

(B) In the FCA Handbook:

(1) (in *BIPRU*) (in accordance with Article 100 of the *Banking Consolidation Directive* (Securitisation of revolving exposures) and in relation to a *securitisation* within the meaning of paragraph (2) of the definition of securitisation) a contractual clause which requires, on the occurrence of defined events, investors' positions to be redeemed prior to the originally stated maturity of the securities issued.

(2) (except in (1)) has the meaning in article 242(14) of the *EU CRR*.

early repayment charge

(in *MCOB* and *BSOCS*) a charge levied by the *mortgage lender* on the *customer* in the event that the amount of the loan is repaid in full or in part before a date or event specified in the contract.

ECAI

(A) In the PRA Handbook: an external credit assessment institution.

(B) In the FCA Handbook:

(1) (except in *MIPRU*) an external credit assessment institution, as defined in article 4(1)(98) of the *EU CRR*.

(2) (in *MIPRU*) an external credit assessment institution.

ECA recipient

a *person* who is a user of an *electronic commerce activity*.

ECD Regulations

the Electronic Commerce Directive (Financial Services and Markets) Regulations 2002 (SI 2002/1775).

E-Commerce Directive

the Council Directive of 8 June 2002 on legal aspects of *information society services*, in particular electronic commerce, in the Internal Market (No 2000/31/EC).

ECR

enhanced capital requirement.

EE

expected exposure.

EEA

the *European Economic Area* (see also *EEA State*.)

EEA AIF

an *AIF*, other than a *UK AIF*, which:

(a) is authorised or registered in an *EEA State* under the applicable national law; or

(b) is not authorised or registered in an *EEA State* but has its registered office or head office in an *EEA State*.

EEA AIFM

an *AIFM* which has its registered office in an *EEA State* other than the *UK*.

EEA approved incoming information society service

an incoming *information society service* that has its *establishment* in an *EEA State* other than the *United Kingdom* which has been approved in that state as meeting the standards set out in article 21 of the *TD* and article 12 of the *TD implementing Directive*.

EEA authorisation

(in accordance with paragraph 6 of Schedule 3 to the *Act* (EEA Passport Rights)):

(a) in relation to an *IMD insurance intermediary* or an *IMD reinsurance intermediary*, registration with its *Home State regulator* under article 3 of the *Insurance Mediation Directive*;

(b) in relation to any other *EEA firm*, authorisation granted to an *EEA firm* by its *Home State regulator* for the purpose of the relevant *Single Market Directive* or the *auction regulation*.

EEA authorised electronic money institution

(in accordance with regulation 2(1) of the *Electronic Money Regulations*) a *person* authorised in an *EEA State* other than the *United Kingdom* to issue *electronic money* and provide *payment services* in accordance with the *Electronic Money Directive*.

EEA authorised payment institution

(a) (in accordance with regulation 2(1) of the *Payment Services Regulations*) a *person* authorised in an *EEA State* other than the *United Kingdom* to provide *payment services* in accordance with the *Payment Services Directive*; and

(b) (in accordance with paragraph 1 of Schedule 7 to the *Payment Services Regulations*) a firm which has its head office in Gibraltar, is authorised in Gibraltar to provide *payment services*, and has an entitlement corresponding to its passport right deriving from the *Payment Services Directive*, to establish a *branch* or provide services in the *United Kingdom*.

EEA bank

(A) In the PRA Handbook:
an *incoming EEA firm* which is a *CRD credit institution*.
(B) In the FCA Handbook:
an *incoming EEA firm* which is a *CRD credit institution*.

EEA banking and investment group

a *banking* and *investment group* that satisfies one or more of the following conditions:

(a) it is headed by:
(i) an *investment firm* or *credit institution* that is authorised and incorporated in an *EEA State*; or
(ii) a *financial holding company* that has its head office in an *EEA State*; or

(b) it has as a member an *investment firm* or *credit institution* that:
(i) is authorised and incorporated in an *EEA State*; and
(ii) is linked with another member that is in the *banking sector* or the *investment services sector* by a *consolidation Article 12(1) relationship*; or

(c) it is otherwise required by *EEA prudential sectoral legislation* for the *banking sector* or the *investment services sector* (except Article 143 of the *Banking Consolidation Directive* (Third-country parent undertakings)) to be subject to consolidated supervision by a *competent authority*.

EEA branch of an authorised electronic money institution

(in accordance with regulation 2(1) of the *Electronic Money Regulations*) a branch established by an *authorised electronic money institution*, in the exercise of its *passport rights*, to issue *electronic money*, provide *payment services*, distribute or redeem *electronic money* or carry out other activities in accordance with the *Electronic Money Regulations* in an *EEA State* other than the *United Kingdom*.

EEA commodities market

a market that facilitates trading in *derivatives* relating to *commodities* (other than a market operated by an *RIE*) and which is operated by an entity that has its head office situated in the *EEA* and that is regulated as an exchange.

EEA countercyclical buffer authority

(1) the authority or body of a *EEA State*, other than the *UK*, designated for the purpose of article 136 of *CRD* with responsibility for setting the *countercyclical buffer rate* for that *EEA State*; or

(2) the European Central Bank when it carries out the task of setting a countercyclical buffer rate for an *EEA State* conferred on it by article 5(2) of Council Regulation (EU) No. 1024/2013, conferring specific tasks on the European Central Bank concerning policies relating to the prudential supervision of credit institutions.

EEA-deposit insurer

a *non-EEA insurer* that has made a deposit in an *EEA State* (other than the *United Kingdom*) under article 23 of the *First Non-Life Directive* (as amended) in accordance with article 26 of that Directive or under article 51 of the *Consolidated Life Directive* in accordance with article 56 of that Directive.

EEA financial conglomerate

a *financial conglomerate* that is of a type that falls under Article 5(2) of the *Financial Groups Directive* (Scope of supplementary supervision of *regulated entities* referred to in Article 1 of that Directive) which in summary means a *financial conglomerate*:

(a) that is headed by an *EEA regulated entity*; or

(b) in which the *parent undertaking* of an *EEA regulated entity* is a *mixed financial holding company* which has its head office in the *EEA*; or

(c) in which an *EEA regulated entity* is linked with a member of the *financial conglomerate* in the *overall financial sector* by a *consolidation Article 12(1) relationship*.

EEA firm

(A) In the PRA Handbook:
(in accordance with paragraph 5 of Schedule 3 to the *Act* (EEA Passport Rights)) any of the following, if it does not have its relevant office in the *United Kingdom*:
(a) an investment firm (as defined in article 4(1) of *MiFID*) which is authorised (within the meaning of article 5) by its *Home State regulator*;
(b) a *credit institution* (as defined in article 4(1)(1) of the *EU CRR*)
(c) a financial institution (as defined in article 4(1)(26) of the *EU CRR*) which is a subsidiary of the kind mentioned in article 34 of the *CRD* and which fulfils the conditions in articles 33 and 34;
(d) an undertaking pursuing the activity of direct insurance (within the meaning of article 2 of the Consolidated Life Directive (No. 2002/83/EC) or of Article 1 of the First Non-Life Directive (No. 73/239/EEC)) which has received authorisation under Article 4 of the Consolidated Life Directive or Article 6 of the First Non-Life Directive from its *Home State regulator*;
(e) an *IMD insurance intermediary* or *IMD reinsurance intermediary* (as defined in article 2 of the *IMD*) which has registered under article 3 of that directive with its *Home State regulator*;
(f) (from 1 July 2011) a *management company*;
(g) an *undertaking* pursuing the activity of reinsurance (within the meaning of article 1 of the *Reinsurance Directive*) which has received authorisation under article 3 of the *Reinsurance Directive* from its *Home State Regulator*;
(h) a *person* who has received authorisation under article 18 of the *auction regulation*;
(hh) an *AIFM* which is authorised (under article 6 of *AIFMD*) by its *Home State regulator*;
in this definition, relevant office means:
(i) in relation to a *firm* falling within sub-paragraph (e), which has a registered office, its registered office;
(ii) in relation to any other *firm* falling within any other paragraph, its head office.

(B) In the FCA Handbook:
(in accordance with paragraph 5 of Schedule 3 to the *Act* (EEA Passport Rights)) any of the following, if it does not have its relevant office in the *United Kingdom*:
(a) an investment firm (as defined in article 4(1) of *MiFID*) which is authorised (within the meaning of article 5) by its *Home State regulator*;
(b) a *credit institution* (as defined in article 4(1)(1) of the *EU CRR*)
(c) a financial institution (as defined in article 41(26) of the *EU CRR*) which is a subsidiary of the kind mentioned in article 34 of the *CRD* and which fulfils the conditions in articles 33 and 34;
(d) an undertaking pursuing the activity of direct insurance (within the meaning of article 2 of the Consolidated Life Directive (No. 2002/83/EC) or of Article 1 of the First Non-Life Directive (No. 73/239/EEC)) which has received authorisation under Article 4 of the Consolidated Life Directive or Article 6 of the First Non-Life Directive from its *Home State regulator*;
(e) an *IMD insurance intermediary* or *IMD reinsurance intermediary* (as defined in article 2 of the *IMD*) which has registered under article 3 of that directive with its *Home State regulator*;
(f) (from 1 July 2011) a *management company*;
(g) an *undertaking* pursuing the activity of reinsurance (within the meaning of article 1 of the *Reinsurance Directive*) which has received authorisation under article 3 of the *Reinsurance Directive*

from its *Home State Regulator*;

(h) a *person* who has received authorisation under article 18 of the *auction regulation*;

(hh) an *AIFM* which is authorised (under article 6 of *AIFMD*) by its *Home State regulator*;

in this definition, relevant office means:

(i) in relation to a *firm* falling within sub-paragraph (e), which has a registered office, its registered office;

(ii) in relation to any other *firm* falling within any other paragraph, its head office.

EEA insurance parent undertaking

an *insurance parent undertaking* that has its head office in the *United Kingdom* or another *EEA State*.

EEA insurer

an *insurer*, other than a *pure reinsurer* or a *non-directive insurer*, whose head office is in any *EEA State* except the *United Kingdom* and which has received *authorisation* under article 6 of the *First Life Directive* or article 4 of the *Consolidated Life Directive* or article 6 of the *First Non-Life Directive* from its *Home State Regulator*.

EEA ISPV

an *ISPV* (including a *UK ISPV*) whose head office is in any *EEA State* and which has received authorisation pursuant to article 46 of the *Reinsurance Directive* from its *Home State Regulator*.

EEA key investor information document

a *document* that:

(a) relates to an *EEA UCITS scheme*;

(b) complies with the requirements of the *KII Regulation*; and

(c) is provided in a language stipulated by article 94(1)(b) of the *UCITS Directive*.

EEA market operator

(in *REC*) a *person* who is a *market operator* whose *home state* is an *EEA State* other than the *United Kingdom*.

EEA MCR

the *MCR* in relation to business carried on in all *EEA States*, taken together, calculated by a *UK-deposit insurer* in accordance with INSPRU 1.5.46R.

EEA MiFID investment firm

a *MiFID investment firm* whose *Home State* is not the *United Kingdom*.

EEA parent financial holding company

(A) In the PRA Handbook: (in accordance with Article 4(17) of the *Banking Consolidation Directive* (Definitions) and Article 3 of the *Capital Adequacy Directive* (Definitions)) a *parent financial holding company in a Member State* which is not a *subsidiary undertaking* of an *institution* authorised in any *EEA State* or of another *financial holding company* or *mixed financial holding company* established in any *EEA State*.

(B) In the FCA Handbook:

(1) (in accordance with Article 4(17) of the *Banking Consolidation Directive* (Definitions) and Article 3 of the *Capital Adequacy Directive* (Definitions)) for the purpose of *GENPRU* (except GENPRU 3) and *BIPRU* (except in BIPRU 12) a *parent financial holding company in a Member State* which is not a *subsidiary undertaking* of an *institution* authorised in any *EEA State* or of another *financial holding company* or *mixed financial holding company* established in any *EEA State*.

(2) (except in (1)) has the meaning as given to EU parent financial holding company in article 4(1)(31) of the *EU CRR*.

EEA parent institution

(A) In the PRA Handbook: (in accordance with Article 4(16) of the *Banking Consolidation Directive* and Article 2 of the *Capital Adequacy Directive* (Definitions)) a *parent institution in a Member State* which is not a *subsidiary undertaking* of another *institution* authorised in any *EEA State*, or of a *financial holding company* or *mixed financial holding company* established in any *EEA State*.

(B) In the FCA Handbook:

(1) (in accordance with Article 4(16) of the *Banking Consolidation Directive* and Article 2 of the *Capital Adequacy Directive* (Definitions)) for the purpose of *BIPRU* (except BIPRU 12) a *parent institution in a Member State* which is not a *subsidiary undertaking* of another *institution* authorised in any *EEA State*, or of a *financial holding company* or *mixed financial holding company* established in any *EEA State*.

(2) (except in (1)) has the meaning as given to EU parent institution in article 4(1)(29) of the *EU CRR*.

EEA parent mixed financial holding company

(A) In the PRA Handbook: (in accordance with Article 4(17a) of the *Banking Consolidation Directive* (Definitions)) a *parent mixed financial holding company in a Member State* which is not a *subsidiary undertaking* of an *institution* authorised in any *EEA State* or of another *financial holding company* or *mixed financial holding company* established in any *EEA State*.

(B) In the FCA Handbook:

(1) (in accordance with Article 4(17a) of the *Banking Consolidation Directive* (Definitions)) for the purpose of *GENPRU* (except GENPRU 3) and *BIPRU* (except in BIPRU 12) a *parent mixed financial holding company in a Member State* which is not a *subsidiary undertaking* of an *institution* authorised in any *EEA State* or of another *financial holding company* or *mixed financial holding company* established in any *EEA State*.

(2) (except in (1)) has the meaning as given to EU parent mixed financial holding company in article 4(1)(33) of the *EU CRR*.

EEA parent undertaking

(a) an *EEA parent institution*; or

(b) an *EEA parent financial holding company*; or

(c) an *EEA parent mixed financial holding company*.

[Note: article 2(1)(85) of *RRD*]

EEA Passport Rights Regulations

the Financial Services and Markets Act 2000 (EEA Passport Rights) Regulations 2001 (SI 2001/2511).

EEA prudential sectoral legislation

(A) In the PRA Handbook: (in relation to a *financial sector*) requirements applicable to *persons* in that *financial sector* in accordance with EEA legislation about prudential supervision of *regulated entities* in that *financial sector* and so that:

(a) (in relation to the *banking sector* and the *investment services sector*) in particular this includes the requirements laid down in the *Banking Consolidation Directive* and the *Capital Adequacy Directive*; and

(b) (in relation to the *insurance sector*) in particular this includes requirements laid down in the *First Non-Life Directive*, the *Consolidated Life Directive* and the *Insurance Groups Directive*.

(B) In the FCA Handbook: (in relation to a *financial sector*) requirements applicable to *persons* in that *financial sector* in accordance with EEA legislation about prudential supervision of *regulated entities* in that *financial sector* and so that:

(a) (in relation to the *banking sector* and the *investment services sector*) in particular this includes the requirements laid down in the *EU CRR* and (in relation to a *CAD investment firm*) the *Banking Consolidation Directive* and the *Capital Adequacy Directive*; and

(b) (in relation to the *insurance sector*) in particular this includes requirements laid down in the *First Non-Life Directive*, the *Consolidated Life Directive* and the *Insurance Groups Directive*.

EEA pure reinsurer

a *reinsurance undertaking* (other than an *ISPV*) whose head office is in any *EEA State* except the *United Kingdom* and which has received (or is deemed to have received) authorisation under article 3 of the *Reinsurance Directive* from its *Home State Regulator*.

EEA registered tied agent

a *tied agent* of a *UK MiFID investment firm* that is not an *appointed representative* and would have been an *FCA registered tied agent* but for the fact that it does business in an *EEA State* that permits *investment firms* authorised by the *competent authority* of that state to appoint *tied agents*.

EEA regulated entity

a *regulated entity* that is an *EEA firm* or a *UK firm*.

EEA regulator

(1) a *competent authority* for the purposes of any of the *Single Market Directives* or the *auction regulation*.

(2) (in DEPP 7) (as defined in section 131FA of the *Act*) the *competent authority* of an *EEA State* other than the *United Kingdom* for the purposes of the *short selling regulation*.

EEA right

(in accordance with paragraph 7 of Schedule 3 to the *Act* (EEA Passport Rights)) the entitlement of a *person* to establish a *branch* or provide services in an *EEA State* other than that in which he has his relevant office:

(a) in accordance with the *Treaty* as applied in the *European Economic Area*; and

(b) subject to the conditions of the relevant *Single Market Directive* or the *auction regulation*.

in this definition, relevant office means:

(i) in relation to a *person* who has a registered office and whose entitlement is subject to the conditions of the *Insurance Mediation Directive*, his registered office; and

(ii) in relation to any other *person*, his head office.

EEA simplified prospectus

a marketing *document* which meets the requirements of Article 28 of the UCITS Directive (No 85/611/EEC) (as at 30 June 2011).

EEA simplified prospectus scheme

an *EEA UCITS scheme* which is a *recognised scheme* under section 264 of the *Act* (Schemes constituted in other EEA States) and which is permitted by the laws and regulations of its *Home State* to market its *units* on the basis of an *EEA simplified prospectus*.

EEA State

(in accordance with Schedule 1 to the Interpretation Act 1978), in relation to any time—

(a) a state which at that time is a member State; or

(b) any other state which is at that time a party to the EEA agreement.

[Note: Current non-member State parties to the EEA agreement are Norway, Iceland and Lichtenstein. Where the context requires, references to an *EEA State* include references to Gibraltar as appropriate].

EEA territorial scope rule

COBS 1 Annex 1, Part 2 paragraph 1(1) (which provides that the territorial scope of *COBS* is modified to the extent necessary to be compatible with European law).

EEA tied agent

a *tied agent* who is an *FCA registered tied agent* or an *EEA registered tied agent*.

EEA UCITS management company

any *incoming EEA firm* that is a *management company*.

EEA UCITS scheme

a *collective investment scheme* established in accordance with the *UCITS Directive* in an *EEA State* other than the *United Kingdom*.

effecting contracts of insurance

the *regulated activity*, specified in article 10(1) of the *Regulated Activities Order* (Effecting and carrying out contracts of insurance), of effecting a *contract of insurance* as principal.

effective EE

effective expected exposure.

effective EPE

effective expected positive exposure.

effective expected exposure

(in accordance with Part 1 of Annex III of the *Banking Consolidation Directive* (Definitions) and for the purpose of BIPRU 13 (The calculation of counterparty risk exposure values for financial derivatives, securities financing transactions and long settlement transactions) and as at a specific date) the maximum *expected exposure* that occurs at that date or any prior date; alternatively, it may be defined for a specific date as the greater of the *expected exposure* at that date, or the effective *exposure* at the previous date.

effective expected positive exposure

(in accordance with Part 1 of Annex III of the *Banking Consolidation Directive* (Definitions) and for the purpose of BIPRU 13) the weighted average over time of *effective expected exposure* over the first year, or, if all the contracts within the *netting set* mature before one year, over the time period of the longest maturity contract in the *netting set*, where the weights are the proportion that an individual *expected exposure* represents of the entire time interval.

effective maturity

(in accordance with Part 1 of Annex III of the *Banking Consolidation Directive* (Definitions), for the purpose of the *CCR internal model method* and with respect to a *netting set* with maturity greater than one year) the ratio of the sum of *expected exposure* over the life of the transactions in the *netting set* discounted at the risk-free rate of return divided by the sum of *expected exposure* over one year in a *netting set* discounted at the risk-free rate; this effective maturity may be adjusted to reflect *rollover risk* by replacing *expected exposure* with *effective expected exposure* for forecasting horizons under one year.

efficient portfolio management

(in *COLL* and in accordance with article 11 of the *UCITS eligible assets Directive*) techniques and instruments which relate to *transferable securities* and *approved money-market instruments* and which fulfil the following criteria:

(a) they are economically appropriate in that they are realised in a cost effective way;

(b) they are entered into for one or more of the following specific aims:
(i) reduction of risk;
(ii) reduction of cost;
(iii) generation of additional capital or income for the *scheme* with a risk level which is consistent with the risk profile of the *scheme* and the risk diversification rules laid down in *COLL*.

EG

the Enforcement Guide.

EIS

Enterprise Investment Scheme.

EIS fund

an arrangement, specified in paragraph 2 of the Schedule to the Financial Services and Markets Act 2000 (Collective Investment Schemes) Order 2001 (SI 2001/1062), which is in summary: an arrangement in relation to *EIS shares* that would have been a *collective investment scheme* if the scheme arrangements had not provided that:

(a) the *operator* will, so far as practicable, make investments which, subject to each partici-pant's individual circumstances, qualify for relief under Chapter III of Part VII of the Income and Corporation Taxes Act 1988; and

(b) the minimum subscription to the arrangements by each participant must be not less than £2,000.

EIS managed portfolio

a managed portfolio which is, or is to be, invested wholly or mainly in *EIS shares*.

EIS manager

(a) (in relation to an *EIS managed portfolio*) the investment manager;

(b) (in relation to an *EIS fund*) the manager of the fund.

EIS particulars

a *document* containing particulars of an *Enterprise Investment Scheme*.

EIS share

a *share* in respect of which the beneficial owner may, subject to his individual circumstances, be qualified, or has been qualified, for relief under Chapter III of Part VII of the Income and Corporation Taxes Act 1988.

EIS subscription

any *money* which is subscribed:

(a) in the case of an *EIS managed portfolio*, by the *client* of the *EIS manager* whose portfolio it is;

(b) in the case of an *EIS fund*, by the participants in the *EIS*.

EL

expected loss.

Electing Participants Order

the Financial Services and Markets Act 2000 (Compensation Scheme: Electing Participants) Regulations 2001 (SI 2001/1783).

Electing Participants Regulations

the Financial Services and Markets Act 2000 (Compensation Scheme: Electing Participants) Regulations 2001 (SI 2001/1783).

elective eligible counterparty

a *client* categorised as an elective eligible counterparty in accordance with COBS 3.6 (Eligible counterparties).

elective professional client

a *client* categorised as an elective professional client in accordance with COBS 3.5 (Professional clients).

electricity

(a) electricity in any form, including electricity as deliverable through the *Balancing and Settlement Code*;

(b) any right that relates to electricity, for example the right under a contract or otherwise to require a person to take any action in relation to electricity, including:
(i) supplying electricity to any person or accepting supply of electricity; or
(ii) providing any information or notice in relation to electricity; or
(iii) making any payment in relation to the supply or nonsupply, or acceptance or non-acceptance of supply, of electricity.

electronic communication

has the meaning given in section 15(1) of the Electronic Communications Act 2000.

electronic commerce activity

an activity which:

(a) consists of the provision of an *information society service* from an *establishment* in an *EEA State*; and

(b) is, or but for article 72A (Information society services) of the *Regulated Activities Order* (Information society services) (and irrespective of the effect of article 72 of that Order (Overseas persons)) would be, a *regulated activity*.

electronic commerce activity direction

a direction made, or proposed to be made, by the *FCA* under regulation 6 of the *ECD Regulations*.

electronic commerce communication

(in accordance with article 6 of the *Financial Promotion Order*) a communication, the making of which constitutes the provision of an *information society service*.

electronic means

are means of electronic equipment for the processing (including digital compression), storage and transmission of data, employing wires, radio optical technologies, or any other electromagnetic means.

electronic money

electronically (including magnetically) stored monetary value as represented by a claim on the *electronic money issuer* which is:

(a) issued on receipt of funds for the purpose of making payment transactions as defined in Article 4(5) of the *Payment Services Directive*; and

(b) accepted by a *person* other than the *electronic money issuer*;

but does not include:

(c) monetary value stored on instruments that can be used to acquire goods or services only:

(i) in or on the *electronic money issuer's* premises; or

(ii) under a commercial agreement with the *electronic money issuer*, either within a limited network of service providers or for a limited range of goods or services; or

(d) monetary value that is used to make payment transactions executed by means of any telecommunication, digital or IT device, where the goods or services purchased are delivered to and are to be used through a telecommunication, digital or IT device, provided that the telecommunication, digital or IT operator does not act only as an intermediary between the payment service user and the supplier of the goods and services.

Electronic Money Directive

Directive 2009/110/EC of the European Parliament and of the Council of 16th September 2009 on the taking up, pursuit and prudential supervision of the business of electronic money institutions, amending Directives 2005/60/EC and 2006/48/EC and repealing Directive 2000/46/EC.

electronic money institution

(in accordance with regulation 2(1) of the *Electronic Money Regulations*) an *authorised electronic money institution* or a *small electronic money institution*.

electronic money issuer

(1) (except in *DISP*) any of the following *persons* when they issue *electronic money*:

(a) *authorised electronic money institutions*;

(b) *small electronic money institutions*;

(c) *EEA authorised electronic money institutions*;

(d) *credit institutions*;

(e) the Post Office Limited;

(f) the Bank of England, the European Central Bank and the national central banks of *EEA States* other than the United Kingdom, when not acting in their capacity as a monetary authority or other public authority;

(g) government departments and local authorities when acting in their capacity as public authorities;

(h) *credit unions*;

(i) municipal banks;

(j) the National Savings Bank.

[Note: article 2(3) of the *Electronic Money Directive*]

(2) (in *DISP* and FEES 5.5A) as in (1) but:

(a) excluding *credit institutions*, *credit unions* and municipal banks; and

(b) including a *person* who meets the conditions set out in regulation 75(1) or regulation 76(1) of the *Electronic Money Regulations*.

Electronic Money Regulations

the Electronic Money Regulations 2011 (SI 2011/99).

electronic SCV rules

(in *COMP*) COMP 17.2.1 R(2), COMP 17.2.3 R(3) and COMP 17.2.5 R, the application of which is determined by COMP 17.1 and COMP 17.2.7 R.

eligible

(in *COLL*) (in relation to a *securities* or a *derivatives* market) a market that satisfies the requirements in COLL 5.2.10 R (Eligible markets: requirements) in relation to schemes falling under COLL 5.

eligible capital

has the meaning in article 4(1)(71) of the *EU CRR*.

eligible claimant

a *person* who is eligible to bring a *claim* for compensation under COMP 4.2.1 R.

eligible complainant

a *person* eligible to have a *complaint* considered under the *Financial Ombudsman Service*, as defined in DISP 2.7 (Is the complainant eligible?).

eligible counterparty

(A) In the PRA Handbook:

(1) (in accordance with COBS 3.6.1 R) a *client* is either a *per se eligible counterparty* or an *elective eligible counterparty*.

(2) [deleted]

(B) In the FCA Handbook:

(1) (for the purposes other than those set out in (2)) (in accordance with COBS 3.6.1 R) a *client* that is either a *per se eligible counterparty* or an *elective eligible counterparty*.

(2) (for the purposes of *PRIN*, in relation to activities other than *designated investment business*) a *client* categorised as an *eligible counterparty* in accordance with PRIN 1 Annex 1.

eligible counterparty business

the following services and activities carried on by a *firm*:

(a) *dealing on own account, execution of orders on behalf of clients* or reception and transmission of orders; or

(b) any *ancillary service* directly related to a service or activity referred to in (a); or

(c) *arranging* in relation to business which is not MiFID or equivalent third country firm business;

but only to the extent that the service or activity is carried on with or for an *eligible counterparty*.

eligible ECAI

(A) In the PRA Handbook: an *ECAI*:

(a) (for *exposure risk weighting* purposes other than those in (b)) recognised by the *appropriate regulator* under regulation 22 of the *Capital Requirements Regulations 2006* (Recognition for exposure risk-weighting purposes); or

(b) (for *securitisation risk weighting* purposes) recognised by the *appropriate regulator* under regulation 23 of the *Capital Requirements Regulations 2006* (Recognition for securitisation risk-weighting purposes).

(B) In the FCA Handbook: an *ECAI*:

(a) (for *exposure risk weighting* purposes other than those in (b) or (d)) recognised by the *appropriate regulator* under regulation 22 of the *Capital Requirements Regulations 2006* (Recognition for exposure risk-weighting purposes); or

(b) (for *securitisation risk weighting* purposes except under MIPRU 4.2BA) recognised by the *appropriate regulator* under regulation 23 of the *Capital Requirements Regulations 2006* (Recognition for securitisation risk-weighting purposes).

(c) (in BIPRU 12) that is listed in the first row in the table set out in BIPRU 12 Annex 1R; or

(d) (in *MIPRU*) an *ECAI* listed in the table in MIPRU 4.2E.14 R.

eligible institution

(in *COLL*):

(a) a *CRD credit institution* authorised by its *Home State regulator*;

(b) a *MiFID investment firm* authorised by its *Home State regulator*.

eligible LLP members' capital

members' capital of a *limited liability partnership* that meets the conditions in *IPRU(INV)* Annex A or, for a *BIPRU firm*, the requirements of GENPRU 2.2.94 R (Core tier one capital: Eligible LLP members' capital).

eligible partnership capital

(in relation to a *BIPRU firm*) has the meaning in GENPRU 2.2.93 R.

EMIR

Regulation (EU) No 648/2012 on OTC derivatives, central counterparties and trade repositories, sometimes referred to as the "European Markets Infrastructure Regulation".

EMIR L2 Regulation

Commission Delegated Regulation (EU) No 149/2013 of 19 December 2012 supplementing Regulation (EU) No 648/2012 of the European Parliament and of the Council with regard to regulatory technical standards on indirect clearing arrangements, the clearing obligation, the public register, access to a trading venue, non-financial counterparties, and risk mitigation techniques for OTC derivatives contracts not cleared by a CCP.

EMIR requirements

requirements imposed under *EMIR* and any regulation made under it.

EMIR technical standards on OTC derivatives

means "Commission Delegated Regulation (EU) 149/2013 of 19 December 2012 supplementing *EMIR* with regard to regulatory technical standards on indirect clearing arrangements, the clearing obligation, the public register, access to a trading venue, non-financial counterparties, and risk mitigation techniques for OTC derivatives contracts not cleared by a central counterparty".

emissions allowance

an 'allowance', within the meaning of article 3(a) of Directive 2003/87/EC of the European Parliament and of the Council of 13 October 2003 establishing a scheme for greenhouse gas emission allowance trading within the Community and amending Council Directive 96/61/EC.

emissions auction product

the *investment* specified in article 82A of the *Regulated Activities Order* (Greenhouse gas *emissions allowances*), which is in summary an *emissions allowance* offered for sale on an *auction platform* as a *financial instrument* or a *two-day emissions spot*.

employee

(1) (for all purposes except those in (2)) an individual:
(a) who is employed or appointed by a *person* in connection with that *person's* business, whether under a contract of service or for services or otherwise; or
(b) whose services, under an arrangement between that *person* and a third party, are placed at the disposal and under the control of that *person*;
but excluding an *appointed representative* or a *tied agent* of that *person*.

(2) (for the purposes of:
(a) COBS 11.7 (Personal account dealing);
(aa) GEN 4 (Statutory status disclosure);
(ab) GEN 6.1 (Payment of financial penalties);
(b) SUP 12 (Appointed representatives); and
(c) *TC*)
an individual:
(i) within (1); or
(ii) who is:
(A) an *appointed representative* or, where applicable, a *tied agent* of the *person* referred to in (1); or
(B) employed or appointed by an *appointed representative* or, where applicable, a *tied agent* of that *person*, whether under a contract of service or for services or otherwise, in connection with the business of the *appointed representative* or *tied agent* for which that *person* has accepted responsibility.

employee benefit consultant

a *person* that gives advice, or provides services to, an employer in connection with a *group personal pension scheme* or *group stakeholder pension scheme* provided, or to be provided, by the employer for the benefit of its employees.

employees' share scheme

has the same meaning as in section 1166 of the Companies Act 2006.

employers' liability insurance

a *contract of insurance* against risks of the *persons* insured incurring liabilities to their employees.

EMPS

the Handbook Guide for energy market participants.

endowment assurance

a *life policy* which pays a sum of *money* on the survival of the life assured to a specific date or on his earlier death.

energy

coal, *electricity*, *natural gas* (or any by-product or form of any of them), *oil* or *biofuel*.

energy collective investment scheme

a *collective investment scheme*, the property of which consists only of *energy*, energy investments, *emissions allowances*, *tradable renewable energy credits* or cash awaiting investment.

energy investment

any of the following:

(a) a *unit* in an *energy collective investment scheme*;

(b) an *option* to acquire or dispose of an *energy investment*;

(c) a *future* or a *contract for differences* where the commodity or property of any other description in question is:
(i) *energy*; or
(ii) an *energy investment*; or
(iii) an *emissions allowance*; or
(iv) a *tradable renewable energy credit*;

(d) a *contract for differences* where the index or other factor in question is linked to or otherwise dependent upon fluctuations in the value or price of any of (c)(i) to (iv) (including any prices or charges in respect of imbalances under the *Network Code* or the *Balancing and Settlement Code*);

(e) a *weather derivative*;

(f) an *emissions allowance*, if it is a *specified investment*;

(g) a *tradable renewable energy credit*, if it is a *specified investment*;

(h) *rights to or interests in investments* in (a)-(g).

energy market activity

(A) In the PRA Handbook:

(a) any *regulated activity* other than *bidding in emissions auctions* in relation to an *energy investment* or to *energy*, or in relation to a *biomass investment* or *biomass* that is ancillary to activities related to *energy investments* or *energy*, which:
(i) is the *executing* of *own account transactions* on any *recognised investment exchange* or *designated investment exchange*; or
(ii) if it is not the *executing* of *transactions* on such exchanges, is performed in connection with or for persons who are not *retail clients*;

(b) *establishing, operating or winding up a collective investment scheme* which is an *energy collective investment scheme* in which *retail clients* do not participate.

(B) In the FCA Handbook:

(a) any *regulated activity* other than *bidding in emissions auctions* in relation to an *energy investment* or to *energy*, or in relation to a *biomass investment* or *biomass* that is ancillary to activities related to *energy investments* or *energy*, which:
(i) is the *executing* of *own account transactions* on any *recognised investment exchange* or *designated investment exchange*; or
(ii) if it is not the *executing* of *transactions* on such exchanges, is performed in connection with or for persons who are not *retail clients*;

(b) [deleted]

energy market participant

(A) In the PRA Handbook:
a firm:
(a) whose permission:
(i) includes a *requirement* that the firm must not carry on any *designated investment business* other than *energy market activity*;
(ii) does not include a *requirement* that it comply with IPRU-INV – link – 5 (Investment

management firms) or 13 (Personal investment firms); and

(b) which is not an *authorised professional firm*, *bank*, *BIPRU firm* (unless it is an *exempt BIPRU commodities firm*), *IFPRU investment firm* (unless it is an *exempt IFPRU commodities firm*), *building society*, *credit union*, *friendly society*, *ICVC*, *insurer*, *MiFID investment firm* (unless it is an *exempt BIPRU commodities firm* or *exempt IFPRU commodities firm*), *media firm*, *oil market participant*, *service company*, *insurance intermediary*, *home finance administrator*, *home finance provider*, *incoming EEA firm* (without a *top-up permission*), or *incoming Treaty firm* (without a *top-up permission*).

(B) In the FCA Handbook:
a firm:

(a) whose permission:

(i) includes a *requirement* that the firm must not carry on any *designated investment business* other than *energy market activity*;

(ii) does not include a *requirement* that it comply with IPRU-INV – link – 5 (Investment management firms) or 13 (Personal investment firms); and

(b) which is not an *authorised professional firm*, *bank*, *BIPRU firm* (unless it is an *exempt BIPRU commodities firm*), *IFPRU investment firm* (unless it is an *exempt IFPRU commodities firm*), *building society*, *credit union*, *friendly society*, *ICVC*, *insurer*, *MiFID investment firm* (unless it is an *exempt BIPRU commodities firm* or *exempt IFPRU commodities firm*), *media firm*, *oil market participant*, *service company*, *insurance intermediary*, *home finance administrator*, *home finance provider*, *incoming EEA firm* (without a *top-up permission*), or *incoming Treaty firm* (without a *top-up permission*).

engage in investment activity

(as defined in section 21(8) of the *Act*) (Restrictions on financial promotion)):

(a) enter or offer to enter into an agreement the making or performance of which by either party constitutes a *controlled activity*; or

(b) exercise any rights conferred by a *controlled investment* to acquire, dispose of, underwrite or convert a *controlled investment*.

enhanced capital requirement

(1) (in relation to a *firm* carrying on *general insurance business*) the amount calculated in accordance with INSPRU 1.1.72CR.

(2) (in relation to a *firm* carrying on *long-term insurance business*) an amount of *capital resources* that a *firm* must hold as set out in GENPRU 2.1.38R.

entering as provider into a funeral plan contract

the *regulated activity*, specified in article 59 of the *Regulated Activities Order* (Funeral plan contracts) which comes into force on 1 January 2002, of entering as provider into a *funeral plan contract*.

entering into a home finance transaction

any of the *regulated activities* of *entering into a regulated mortgage contract*, *entering into a home purchase plan*, *entering into a home reversion plan* or *entering into a regulated sale and rent back agreement*.

entering into a home purchase plan

the *regulated activity*, specified in article 63F(1) of the *Regulated Activities Order*, which is in summary: entering into a *home purchase plan* as provider.

entering into a home reversion plan

the *regulated activity*, specified in article 63B(1) of the *Regulated Activities Order*, which is in summary: entering into a *home reversion plan* as provider, or acquiring any obligations or rights (including his interest in land) of the plan provider under a *home reversion plan* entered into by him on or after 6 April 2007.

entering into a regulated credit agreement as lender

the *regulated activity* specified in article 60B(1) of the *Regulated Activities Order*.

entering into a regulated consumer hire agreement as owner

the *regulated activity* specified in article 60N(1) of the *Regulated Activities Order*.

entering into a regulated mortgage contract

the *regulated activity*, specified in article 61(1) of the *Regulated Activities Order*, which is in summary: entering into a *regulated mortgage contract* as lender.

entering into a regulated sale and rent back agreement

the *regulated activity*, specified in article 63J(1) of the *Regulated Activities Order*, which is in summary entering into a *regulated sale and rent back agreement* as an agreement provider, including acquiring any obligations or rights of the agreement provider, including the agreement provider's interest in land or interests under one or more such *agreements*.

Enterprise Investment Scheme

an arrangement which is an *EIS managed portfolio* or an *EIS fund*.

Enterprise Zone Property Unit Trust

an *unregulated collective investment scheme* of which the underlying assets are industrial and commercial buildings in an Enterprise Zone in accordance with section 749(2) of the Finance Act 1980.

EPE

expected positive exposure.

equalisation provision

a provision required to be established under the *rules* in INSPRU 1.4.

equity

(A) In the PRA Handbook: (for the purposes of BIPRU 7) a *share*.

(B) In the FCA Handbook: (for the purposes of BIPRU 7 and IFPRU 6) a *share*.

equity exposure

(in relation to the *IRB approach*) an exposure falling into the *IRB exposure class* referred to in BIPRU 4.3.2 R (5) (equity exposures).

equity market adjustment ratio

(1) (in relation to the *resilience capital requirement*) has the meaning set out in INSPRU 3.1.19R.

(2) (in relation to the *market risk* scenario for the *risk capital margin* of a *with-profits fund*) has the meaning set out in INSPRU 1.3.71R.

equity PRR

the part of the *market risk capital requirement* calculated in accordance with BIPRU 7.3 (Equity PRR and basic interest rate PRR for equity derivatives) but so that:

(a) the *equity PRR* excludes the part of the *market risk capital requirement* calculated under BIPRU 7.3.45 R (Basic interest rate PRR for equity derivatives); and

(b) in relation to a particular *position*, it means the portion of the overall *equity PRR* attributable to that *position*.

equity release activity

any *regulated mortgage activity* carried on in relation to a *lifetime mortgage*, or a *reversion activity*.

equity release adviser

a *firm* with *permission* (or which ought to have *permission*) for:

(a) *advising on regulated mortgage contracts* (when carried on in relation to a *lifetime mortgage*); or

(b) *advising on a home reversion plan*.

equity release arranger

a *firm* with *permission* (or which ought to have permission) for *arranging* a:

(a) *regulated mortgage contract* (when carried on in relation to a *lifetime mortgage*); or

(b) *home reversion plan*.

equity release intermediary

a *firm* with *permission* (or which ought to have *permission*) to carry on *equity release mediation activity*.

equity release mediation activity

any of the *regulated activities* of:

(a) *arranging a regulated mortgage contract* (when carried on in relation to a *lifetime mortgage*) or a *home reversion plan*;

(b) *advising on a regulated mortgage contract* (when carried on in relation to a *lifetime mortgage*) or a *home reversion plan*; or

(c) *agreeing to carry on a regulated activity* in (a) or (b).

equity release provider

a *firm* with *permission* (or which ought to have *permission*) for:

(a) *entering into a regulated mortgage contract* (when carried on in relation to a *lifetime mortgage*); or

(b) *entering into a home reversion plan*.

equity release transaction

a *lifetime mortgage* or a *home reversion plan*.

equity security

(1) (in *LR*) *equity shares* and *securities* convertible into *equity shares*; and

(2) (in *PR*) (as defined in Article 2.1(b) of the *prospectus directive*) shares and other transferable securities equivalent to shares in companies, as well as any other type of transferable securities giving the right to acquire any of the aforementioned securities as a consequence of their being converted or the rights conferred by them being exercised, provided that securities of the latter type are issued by the issuer of the underlying shares or by an entity belonging to the group of the said issuer.

equity share

shares comprised in a *company's equity share capital*.

equity share capital

(for a *company*), its issued share capital excluding any part of that capital which, neither as respects dividends nor as respects capital, carries any right to participate beyond a specified amount in a distribution.

equity stake

(in relation to a *company*) any kind of equity stake in that *company*, including *shares* in it (including non-voting and non-equity *shares*, *debt securities* that are convertible or exchangeable into such *shares*, a call *option* on such *shares* or an in-the-money put *option* on such *shares*, but excluding a *contract for differences* or other *investment* that provides merely an economic exposure to movement in the price of the company's shares).

equivalent

see *commission equivalent*.

equivalent business of a third country investment firm

the business of a *third country investment firm* carried on from an establishment in the *United Kingdom* that would be *MiFID business* if that firm were a *MiFID investment firm*.

equivalent document

(in *LR* and *FEES*) a document containing information equivalent to a *prospectus* for the purposes of PR 1.2.2R (2) or (3) or PR 1.2.3R (3) or (4).

ESMA

European Securities and Markets Authority.

ESMA AIFMD key concepts guidelines

ESMA's guidelines on key concepts of the *AIFMD*. (www.esma.europa.eu/system/files/ 2013-611_guidelines_on_key_concepts_of_the_aifmd_-_en.pdf)

ESMA Prospectus Opinion

the opinion published by *ESMA* on the 'Format of the base prospectus and consistent application of Article 26(4) of the Prospectus Regulation' (ESMA/2013/1944).

ESMA Prospectus Questions and Answers

the Questions and Answers for prospectuses published by *ESMA* (ESMA/2014/1279).

ESMA Prospectus Recommendations

the *ESMA* update of the CESR recommendations: The consistent implementation of Commission Regulation (EC) No 809/2004 implementing the Prospectus Directive (ESMA/2013/319).

established surplus

has the meaning in IPRU-INS 3.3(4).

established

(in accordance with article 4(1)(j) *AIFMD*):

(a) for *AIFMs*, 'having its registered office in';

(b) for *AIFs*, 'being authorised or registered in' or, if the AIF is not authorised or registered, 'having its registered office in'; or

(c) for *depositaries*, 'having its registered office or branch in'.

establishing, operating or winding up a collective investment scheme

the *regulated activity*, specified in article or 51ZE of the *Regulated Activities Order* (Establishing etc a collective investment scheme), of establishing, operating or winding up a *collective investment scheme*.

establishing, operating or winding up a personal pension scheme

the *regulated activity*, specified in article 52(b) of the *Regulated Activities Order* (Establishing etc. a pension scheme), of establishing, operating or winding up a *personal pension scheme*.

establishing, operating or winding up a regulated collective investment scheme

establishing, operating or winding up a collective investment scheme if the *scheme* is a *regulated collective investment scheme*.

establishing, operating or winding up a stakeholder pension scheme

the *regulated activity*, specified in article 52 (a) of the *Regulated Activities Order* (Establishing etc. a pension scheme), of establishing, operating or winding up a *stakeholder pension scheme*.

establishing, operating or winding up an unregulated collective investment scheme

establishing, operating or winding up a collective investment scheme if the *scheme* is an *unregulated collective investment scheme*.

establishment

(in relation to an *information society service*) the place at which the provider of the service effectively pursues an economic activity for an indefinite period; in this definition:

(a) the presence or use in a particular place of equipment or other technical means of providing an *information society service* does not, of itself, constitute that place as an establishment; and

(b) where it is unclear from which of a number of establishments a particular *information society service* is provided, that service is to be regarded as provided from the establishment where the provider has the centre of his activities relating to the service.

establishment conditions

(in relation to the establishment of a *branch* in the *United Kingdom*) the conditions specified in paragraph 13 of Schedule 3 to the *Act* (EEA Passport Rights), which are that:

(a) if the *firm* falls within paragraph (a), (b), (c), (d) or (f) in the definition of *"EEA firm"*:
(i)...

(b) if the *firm* falls within paragraph (e) in the definition of *"EEA firm"*:

(i) the *EEA firm* has given its *Home State regulator* notice of its intention to establish a *branch* in the *United Kingdom*;

(ii) the *FCA* or *PRA* (as the case may be) has received notice (*"a regulator's notice"*) from the firm's Home State regulator that the firm intends to establish a *branch* in the *United Kingdom*;

(iii) the EEA firm's Home State regulator has informed it that the regulator's notice has been sent to the *FCA* or *PRA* (as the case may be); and

(iv) one *month* has elapsed beginning with the date on which the EEA firm's Home State regulator informed the *firm* that it had sent the regulator's notice to the *FCA* or *PRA* (as the case may be).

(c) the *EEA firm* has been informed of the *applicable provisions* or two *months* have elapsed beginning with the date when the *FCA* or *PRA* (as the case may be) received the consent notice.

establishment costs

(1) (in FEES 6) the costs of establishing the *compensation scheme.*

(2) (in FEES 5) the costs of establishing the *Financial Ombudsman Service.*

EU

the European Union, being the Union established by the Treaty on European Union signed at Maastricht on 7 February 1992 (as amended).

EU Cross-Border Regulation

Regulation (EC) No. 924/2009 of the European Parliament and of the Council on cross-border payments in the European Community.

EU CRR

(A) (In the PRA Handbook) Regulation of the European Parliament and the Council on prudential requirements for credit institutions and investment firms (Regulation (EU) No 575/2013) and amending Regulation (EU) No 648/2012.

(B) (In the FCA Handbook) Regulation of the European Parliament and the Council on prudential requirements for credit institutions and investment firms (Regulation (EU) No 575/2013) and amending Regulation (EU) No 648/2012.

European Economic Area

the area established by the agreement on the European Economic Area signed at Oporto on 2 May 1992, as it has effect for the time being and which consists of the *EEA States.*

EuSEF

a qualifying social entrepreneurship fund (as defined in the *EuSEF regulation*).

EuSEF manager

the manager of a qualifying social entrepreneurship fund (as defined in the *EuSEF Regulation*) that is registered in accordance with article 15 of the *EuSEF Regulation.*

EuSEF regulation

Regulation (EU) No 346/2013 of the European Parliament and the Council of 17 April 2013 on European social entrepreneurship funds.

EuVECA

a qualifying venture capital fund (as defined in the *EuVECA regulation*).

EuVECA manager

the manager of a qualifying venture capital fund (as defined in the *EuVECA Regulation*) that is registered in accordance with article 14 of the *EuVECA Regulation.*

EuVECA regulation

Regulation (EU) No 345/2013 of the European Parliament and the Council of 17 April 2013 on European venture capital funds.

evidential provision

a *rule*, contravention of which does not give rise to any of the consequences provided for by other provisions of the *Act*; and which provides, in accordance with section 138C of the *Act*, that:

(a) contravention may be relied on as tending to establish contravention of such other *rule* as may be specified; or

(b) compliance may be relied on as tending to establish compliance with such other *rule* as may be specified; or

(c) both (a) and (b).

excepted contract

(in *BCOBS*) has the same meaning as in the Consumer Protection (Distance Selling) Regulations 2000 (SI 2000/2334).

excess LLP members' drawings

the amount by which the aggregate of the amounts withdrawn by a *limited liability partnership's* members exceeds the profits of that *firm*, as calculated in accordance with *IPRU(INV)* Annex A 2.5R (Limited liability partnership excess drawings).

excess spread

(for the purposes of BIPRU 9 (Securitisation), in relation to a *securitisation* (within the meaning of paragraph (2) of the definition of securitisation) and in accordance with Part 1 of Annex IX of the *Banking Consolidation Directive* (Securitisation definitions)) finance charge collections and other fee income received in respect of the *securitised exposures* net of costs and expenses.

excess surplus

a *firm* will have an excess surplus in a *with-profits fund* if, and to the extent that:

(a) the *regulatory surplus* (or, in the case of a *realistic basis life firm*, the excess of *realistic value of assets* over *realistic value of liabilities*) in that *with-profits fund*; and

(b) any other financial resources applied to, or expected to be applied to, that *with-profits fund*;

exceed:

(c) the amount required to meet the higher of any regulatory capital requirement or the *firm's* *individual capital assessment* (at the *firm's* own risk appetite) for existing business; and

(d) any further amount necessary to support the new business plans of that *with-profits fund*.

excess trading book position

has the meaning in GENPRU 2.2.264 R (Deductions from total capital: Excess trading book position).

exchange traded

(in *IPRU(INV)* 13) listed or traded on a *recognised* or *designated investment exchange*.

exchange traded fund

[deleted]

exchange traded product

any of the following *investments*:

(a) a *unit* or *share* in an *open-ended investment company*, a *debt security* or a *contract for differences* which meets all of the following criteria:
(i) it is admitted to trading on a *regulated market* or a market operated by a *ROIE*;
(ii) it is created and redeemed in response to demand from investors or arbitrage opportunities arising from the difference in price from the *unit*, *share*, *debt security* or *contract for differences* and the price of the underlying asset(s) it seeks to track;
(iii) it aims to closely simulate the performance of a specified index or other benchmark (relating to any assets such as *shares*, *debentures*, *commodities* or currencies), whether or not the simulated performance is delta 1, inverse, leveraged, achieved by physical replication or synthetically through *derivatives*.

(b) a senior, unsubordinated *debt security* traded on a *regulated market* or a market operated by a *ROIE* featuring no periodic coupon payments and whose return tracks the performance of a specific index or other benchmark (relating to any assets such as *shares*, *debentures*, *commodities* or currencies), minus applicable fees, whether or not featuring delta 1, inverse or leveraged exposure to the index or other benchmark being tracked.

excluded communication

the following types of *financial promotion* (a *firm* may rely on more than one of the paragraphs in relation to the same *financial promotion*):

(a) a *financial promotion* that would benefit from an exemption in the *Financial Promotion Order* if it were *communicated* by an *unauthorised person*, or which originates outside the *United Kingdom* and is not capable of having an effect in the *United Kingdom* (within the meaning of s. 21(3) of the *Act*);

(b) a *financial promotion* from outside the *United Kingdom* that would be exempt under articles 30, 31, 32 or 33 of the *Financial Promotion Order* (Overseas communicators) if the office from which the *financial promotion* is *communicated* were a separate *unauthorised person*;

(c) a *financial promotion* that is subject to, or exempted from, the *Takeover Code* or to the requirements relating to takeovers or related operations in another *EEA State*;

(d) a personal quotation or illustration form;

(e) a "one-off" *financial promotion* that is not a *cold call*. If the conditions set out in (i) to (iii), below, are satisfied, a *financial promotion* is "one-off". If not, the fact that any one or more of these conditions is met is to be taken into account in determining if a *financial promotion* is "one-off". However, a *financial promotion* may be regarded as "one-off" even if none of the conditions are met. The conditions are that:
(i) the *financial promotion* is *communicated* only to one recipient or only to one group of recipients in the expectation that they would engage in any investment activity jointly;
(ii) the identity of the product or service to which the *financial promotion* relates has been determined having regard to the particular circumstances of the recipient;
(iii) the *financial promotion* is not part of an organised marketing campaign; or

(f) a communication that is exempted by the Financial Services and Markets Act 2000 (Promotion of Collective Investment Schemes) (Exemptions) Order 2001.

excluded custody activities

any activities of a *firm* which:

(a) are carried on in connection with, or for the purposes of, managing a *UCITS* or an *AIF* (as the case may be); and

(b) would amount to *safeguarding and administering investments* but for the exclusion in article 72AA of the *RAO*.

excluded material

(in relation to access to *appropriate regulator* material) (as defined in section 394(7) of the *Act* (Access to FCA or PRA material)) material which:

(a) has been intercepted in obedience to a warrant issued under any enactment relating to the interception of communications; or

(b) indicates that such a warrant has been issued or that material has been intercepted in obedience to such a warrant; or

(c) is a *protected item*.

excluded security

any of the following *investments*:

(a) a *security* whereby the issuer's ability to fulfil its payment obligations to the investor, or the *investment* returns received in connection with the *security*, are wholly or predominantly linked to, contingent on, highly sensitive to or dependent on, the performance of or changes in the value of *shares*, *debentures* or *government and public securities*, whether or not such performance or changes in value are measured directly or via a market index or indices, and provided the relevant *shares* and *debentures* are not themselves issued by *special purpose vehicles*;

(b) a *covered bond*;

(c) a *security* issued by an *investment trust*;

(d) a *share* in a *company* resident outside the *EEA*, where that *company* would qualify for approval as an *investment trust* by the Commissioners for HM Revenue and Customs under sections 1158 and 1159 of the Corporation Tax Act 2010 if resident in the *United Kingdom*;

(e) a *share* in a *venture capital trust*;

(f) a *share* in a *company* to which Part 12 of the Corporation Tax Act 2010 (Real Estate Investment Trusts) applies or a member of a group to which that Part applies;

(g) an *exchange traded product*;

(h) a *security* issued by a *regulated collective investment scheme* other than a *qualified investor scheme*.

execute

(in relation to a transaction) carry into effect or perform the transaction, whether as *principal* or as agent, including instructing another *person* to execute the transaction.

execution criteria

(A) In the PRA Handbook: the criteria set out in COBS 11.2.6 R, that is:

(a) the characteristics of the *client* including the categorisation of the *client* as retail or professional;

(b) the characteristics of the *client* order;

(c) the characteristics of *financial instruments* that are the subject of that order;

(d) the characteristics of the *execution venues* to which that order can be directed; and

(e) for a *management company*, the objectives, investment policy and risks specific to the *UCITS scheme* or *EEA UCITS scheme*, as indicated in its *prospectus* or *instrument constituting the scheme*.

(B) In the FCA Handbook: the criteria set out in COBS 11.2.6 R, that is:

(a) the characteristics of the *client* including the categorisation of the *client* as retail or professional;

(b) the characteristics of the *client* order;

(c) the characteristics of *financial instruments* that are the subject of that order;

(d) the characteristics of the *execution venues* to which that order can be directed; and

(e) for a *management company*, the objectives, investment policy and risks specific to the *UCITS scheme* or *EEA UCITS scheme*, as indicated in its *prospectus* or *instrument constituting the fund*.

execution factors

price, costs, speed, likelihood of execution and settlement, size, nature or any other consideration relevant to the execution of an order.

execution of orders on behalf of clients

acting to conclude agreements to buy or sell one or more *financial instruments* on behalf of *clients*. [Note: article 4 (1)(5) of *MiFID*]

execution-only sale

(a) a *home finance transaction* entered into by a *firm* with, or *arranged* by a *firm* for, a *customer*; or

(b) a variation of an existing *home finance transaction* entered into by a *firm* with, or *arranged* by a *firm* for, a *customer*;

where the *firm* does not give *advice on home finance transactions* to that particular *customer*, or where the *customer* has rejected such advice given by the *firm*.

execution-only transaction

a transaction *executed* by a *firm* upon the specific instructions of a *client* where the *firm* does not give *advice on investments* relating to the merits of the transaction and in relation to which the *rules* on assessment of appropriateness (COBS 10) do not apply.

execution venue

for the purposes of the provisions relating to best execution in COBS 11.2 and in *COLL*, execution venue means a *regulated market*, an *MTF*, a *systematic internaliser*, or a *market maker* or other liquidity provider or an entity that performs a similar function in a third country to the functions performed by any of the foregoing. [Note: article 44(1) of the *MiFID implementing Directive*]

executive procedures

(1) the procedures relating to the giving of warning notices, decision notices and *supervisory notices* that are described in DEPP 4 (Decisions by *FCA* staff under executive procedures).

(2) the procedures relating to the giving of written notices under the *AIFMD UK regulation* that are described in FUND App 1.

exempt activity

(in relation to a *recognised body*) any *regulated activity* in respect of which the body is exempt from the *general prohibition* as a result of section 285(2) or (3) of the *Act* (Exemption for recognised investment exchanges and clearing houses).

exempt BIPRU commodities firm

a *BIPRU firm* to which the exemption in BIPRU TP 15.6R (Exemption for a BIPRU firm whose main business relates to commodities) applies.

exempt CAD firm

(A) In the PRA Handbook:

(1) (except in *SYSC* and *IPRU(INV)*) has the meaning set out BIPRU 1.1.16 R (Types of investment firm: exempt CAD firm) which is in summary an *investment firm* that satisfies certain specified conditions.

(2) (in *SYSC* and *IPRU(INV)*) a *firm* in (1) whose head office (or, if it has a registered office, that office) is in the United Kingdom.

(B) In the FCA Handbook:

(1) (except in *SYSC* and *IPRU(INV)*) a firm as defined in article 4(1)(2)(c) of the *EU CRR* that is authorised to provide only one or more the following *investment services*:
(a) investment advice;
(b) receive and transmit orders from investors as referred to in Section A of Annex I of *MiFID*).

(2) (in *SYSC* and *IPRU(INV)*) a *firm* in (1) whose head office (or, if it has a registered office, that office) is in the United Kingdom.

exempt full scope BIPRU investment firm

a *full scope BIPRU investment firm* falling into BIPRU 12.1.4R.

exempt full scope IFPRU investment firm

a *full-scope IFPRU investment firm* falling into BIPRU 12.1.4R.

exempt IFPRU commodities firm

an *IFPRU investment firm* which falls within the meaning in articles 493(1) and 498(1) of the *EU CRR*.

exempt insurance intermediary

an *insurance intermediary*:

(a) whose *Part 4A permission* is limited to or includes *insurance mediation activity*;

(b) which, in relation to *insurance mediation activity* (but disregarding *money* or other assets held in relation to other activities) either:
(i) does not hold any *client money* or other *client* assets in any form; or
(ii) holds *client money* as trustee under a statutory trust imposed by CASS 5.3 (statutory trust) but does not otherwise hold *client money*; and

(c) which (when aggregating the amount calculated in accordance with CASS 5.5.65 R) does not in relation to *insurance mediation activity* hold *client money* in excess of £30,000 at any time during a *financial year*.

exempt person

(1) (as defined in section 417(1) of the *Act* (Definitions)) (in relation to a *regulated activity*) a *person* who is exempt from the *general prohibition* in respect of that activity as a result of:

(a) the *Exemption Order*; or

(b) being an *appointed representative*; or

(c) section 285(2) or (3) of the *Act* (Exemption for recognised investment exchanges and clearing houses); and

(2) a *person* who is exempt from the general prohibition as a result of section 312A(2) of the *Act*.

exempt professional firm

a *person* to whom, under section 327 of the *Act*, the *general prohibition* does not apply; guidance is given in PROF 2.1 (Exempt *regulated activities*).

exempt regulated activity

(as defined in section 325(2) of the *Act* (*FCA*'s general duty)) a *regulated activity* which may, as a result of Part XX of the *Act* (Provision of Financial Services by Members of the Professions), be carried on by *members* of a profession which is supervised and regulated by a *designated professional body* without breaching the *general prohibition*.

Exemption Order

the Financial Services and Markets Act 2000 (Exemption) Order 2001 (SI 2001/1201).

exercise notice

(in *LR*) (in relation to *securitised derivatives*), a document that notifies the *issuer* of a holder's intention to exercise its rights under the *securitised derivative*.

exercise price

(in *LR*) (in relation to *securitised derivatives*), the price stipulated by the *issuer* at which the holder can buy or sell the *underlying instrument* from or to the *issuer*.

exercise time

(in *LR*) (in relation to *securitised derivatives*), the time stipulated by the *issuer* by which the holder must exercise their rights.

exercising, or having the right to exercise, the lender's rights and duties under a regulated credit agreement

the *regulated activity* specified in article 60B(2) of the *Regulated Activities Order*.

exercising, or having the right to exercise, the owner's rights and duties under a regulated consumer hire agreement

the *regulated activity* specified in article 60N(2) of the *Regulated Activities Order*.

expected exposure

(in accordance with Part 1 of Annex III of the *Banking Consolidation Directive* (Definitions) and for the purpose of BIPRU 13 (The calculation of counterparty risk exposure values for financial derivatives, securities financing transactions and long settlement transactions)) the average of the distribution of *exposures* at any particular future date before the longest maturity transaction in the *netting set* matures.

expected loss

(in accordance with Article 4(29) of the *Banking Consolidation Directive* (Definitions) and for the purposes of the *IRB approach* and the *standardised approach* to credit risk) the ratio of the amount expected to be lost on an *exposure* from a potential *default* of a counterparty or dilution over a one year period to the amount outstanding at default.

expected positive exposure

(in accordance with Part 1 of Annex III of the *Banking Consolidation Directive* (Definitions) and for the purpose of BIPRU 13 (The calculation of counterparty risk exposure values for financial derivatives, securities financing transactions and long settlement transactions)) the weighted average over time of *expected exposures* where the weights are the proportion that an individual *expected exposures* represents of the entire time interval; when calculating the minimum capital requirement, the average is taken over the first year or, if all the contracts within the *netting set* mature before one year, over the time period of the longest-maturity contract in the *netting set*.

expiration date

(in *LR*) (in relation to *securitised derivatives*), the date stipulated by the *issuer* on which the holder's rights in respect of the *securitised derivative* ends.

exposure

(A) In the PRA Handbook:

(1) (in relation to a *firm* but subject to (2) and (3)) the maximum loss which the firm might suffer if:

(a) a counterparty or a group of connected counterparties fail to meet their obligations; or

(b) it realises assets or off-balance sheet positions

(2) (in accordance with Article 77 of the *Banking Consolidation Directive* and for the purposes of the calculation of the *credit risk capital component* and the *counterparty risk capital component* (including BIPRU 3 (Standardised credit risk), BIPRU 4 (The IRB approach), BIPRU 5 (Credit risk mitigation), BIPRU 9 (Securitisation) or for the purposes of the calculation of the credit risk capital requirement in MIPRU 4.2 (Capital resources requirement)) an asset or off-balance sheet item.

(3) (for the purposes of BIPRU 10 (Large exposures requirements)) has the meaning in BIPRU 10.2 (Identification of exposures and recognition of credit risk mitigation).

(B) In the FCA Handbook:

(1) (in relation to a *firm* but subject to (2) and (6)) the maximum loss which the firm might suffer if:

(a) a counterparty or a group of connected counterparties fail to meet their obligations; or

(b) it realises assets or off-balance sheet positions

(2) (in accordance with Article 77 of the *Banking Consolidation Directive* and for the purposes of the calculation of the *credit risk capital component* and the *counterparty risk capital component* (including BIPRU 3 (Standardised credit risk), BIPRU 4 (The IRB approach), BIPRU 5 (Credit risk mitigation), BIPRU 9 (Securitisation) an asset or off-balance sheet item.

(3) [delete]

(4) (in *IFPRU* and to calculate *own funds requirements* under Part Three Title II (credit risk and counterparty credit risk)) has the meaning in article 5(1) of the *EU CRR*.

(5) (in IFPRU 8.2 (Large exposures) for the purpose of Part Four ((Large exposures) of the *EU CRR*) has the meaning in article 389 of the *EU CRR* (Large exposures: definitions).

(6) (in *MIPRU*) an asset or liability.

ex-section 43 firm

a *firm* that was a listed institution, as defined in section 43 of the Financial Services Act 1986, immediately before *commencement*.

ex-section 43 lead regulated firm

an *ex-section 43 firm* for which the *FSA* (in its capacity as the regulatory body under section 43 of the Financial Services Act 1986) was lead regulator for financial supervision purposes, and that was subject to the *section 43 capital requirements*, immediately before *commencement*.

external AIFM

(in accordance with regulation 4(3)(a) of the *AIFMD UK regulation*) an *AIFM* appointed by, or on behalf of, an *AIF* and which, through that appointment, is responsible for managing the *AIF*.

external client money reconciliation

the *client money* reconciliation described in CASS 7.15.20 R.

external custody reconciliation

the *safe custody asset* reconciliation described in CASS 6.6.34 R.

external management company

(in *LR* and *PR*) has the meaning in PR 5.5.3A R.

external valuer

a person who performs the valuation function described in article 19 of the *AIFMD* in respect of an *AIF* managed by a *full-scope UK AIFM*, and is not the *AIFM* of that *AIF*.

extraction

(in relation to *mineral companies*), includes mining, production, quarrying or similar activities and the reworking of mine tailings or waste dumps.

extraordinary public financial support

State aid within article 107(1) of the *Treaty*, or any other public financial support at supra-national level, which, if given at national level, would constitute state aid that is given to preserve or restore the viability, liquidity or solvency of any member of an *RRD group*. [Note: article 2(1)(28) of *RRD*]

extraordinary resolution

(in *COLL*) a resolution passed by a majority of not less than three-quarters of the votes validly cast (whether on a show of hands or on a poll) for and against the resolution at a general meeting or (as the case may be) *class meeting* of holders, of which notice specifying the intention to propose the resolution as an extraordinary resolution has been duly given.

EZPUT

Enterprise Zone Property Unit Trust.

facilities

(in relation to a *recognised body*) the facilities and services which it provides in the course of carrying on *exempt activities*. References to the use of the facilities of an *RIE* or *RAP* are to be construed as follows:

(a) dealings or transactions on an *RIE* or *RAP* are references to dealings or transactions which are effected by means of the *RIE's* or *RAP's* facilities or which are governed by the rules of the *RIE* or *RAP*;

(b) references to the use of the facilities of an *RIE* or *RAP* include use which consists of any such dealings or entering into any such transactions.

facility grade

(in relation to the *advanced IRB approach* and the *sovereign, institutional and corporate IRB exposure class* and in accordance with BIPRU 4.4.49 R) a risk category within a *rating system's* facility scale to which *exposures* are assigned on the basis of a specified and distinct set of rating criteria from which own estimates of *LGDs* are derived.

FAIF

fund of alternative investment funds.

failure

the appointment of a liquidator, receiver or administrator, or trustee in bankruptcy, or any equivalent procedure in any relevant jurisdiction.

fair, clear and not misleading rule

COBS 4.2.1 R.

FC

Financial crime: a guide for firms

FCA

Financial Conduct Authority

FCA-approved person

an *approved person* in relation to whom the *FCA* has given its approval under section 59 of the *Act* (Approval for particular arrangements) for the performance of an *FCA controlled function*.

FCA-authorised person

an *authorised person* who is not a *PRA-authorised person*.

FCA candidate

a *person* in respect of whom an application is made for approval under section 59 of the *Act* (Approval for particular arrangements) of the performance of an *FCA controlled function*.

FCA consolidation group

the *undertakings* included in the scope of prudential consolidation to the extent and in the manner prescribed in Part One, Title II, Chapter 2, Sections 2 and 3 of the *EU CRR* and IFPRU 8.1.3 R to IFPRU 8.1.4 R (Prudential consolidation) for which the *FCA* is the *consolidating supervisor* under article 111 of the *CRD*.

FCA controlled function

a *controlled function* which is specified by the *FCA* under section 59 of the *Act* (Approval for particular arrangements) in the *table of FCA controlled functions*.

FCA governing functions

any of the *FCA controlled functions* 1 to 6 in Part 1 of the *table of FCA controlled functions*.

FCA Handbook

the *FCA's* Handbook of rules and guidance

FCA provider contribution class

a *class* to which the *FSCS* may only allocate a *compensation costs levy* or *specific costs levy* allocated to the *retail pool*, as described in FEES 6.5A, namely: the deposit acceptor's contribution class; the insurers – life contribution *class*; the insurers – general contribution *class*; or the home finance providers and administrators' contribution *class*.

FCA registered tied agent

a *tied agent* who is an *agent* for the purposes of section 39A of the *Act*.

FCA required functions

any of the *FCA controlled functions* 8 to 11 in Part 1 or Part 2 of the *table of FCA controlled functions*.

FCA short name

the abbreviated name allocated to an *issuer* or organisation by the *FCA*.

FCA significant-influence functions

any of the *FCA controlled functions* 1 to 29 in Part 1 or Part 2 of the *table of FCA controlled functions*.

fee

any payment or remuneration offered or made by a *client* to a *firm* in connection with *designated investment business* or with any other business of the *firm*, including (where applicable) any *mark-up* or *mark-down*.

fee year

(1) in relation to the *PRA*:
(a) before 1 March 2014: from and including 1 April 2013 to 28 February 2014 inclusive;
(b) from and including 1 March 2014: 1 March to 28 February inclusive;

(2) in relation to the *FCA*, 1 April to 31 March inclusive.

feeder AIF

(in accordance with article 4(1)(m) of *AIFMD*) an *AIF* which:

(a) invests at least 85% of its assets in *units* or *shares* of another *AIF* (the '*master AIF*'); or

(b) invests at least 85 % of its assets in two or more *AIFs* where those *AIFs* (the '*master AIFs*') have identical investment strategies; or

(c) otherwise has an exposure of at least 85% of its assets to such a *master AIF*.

feeder fund

an *AUT* or *ACS* that is a *relevant pension scheme* and *dedicated* to *units* in a single *regulated collective investment scheme*.

feeder NURS

a *non-UCITS retail scheme* which:

(a) does not operate as:
(i) a *FAIF*; or
(ii) a *feeder fund*; or
(iii) a *scheme dedicated* to *units* in a single *property authorised investment fund*; and

(b) is *dedicated* to *units* in either:
(i) a single *qualifying master scheme*; or
(ii) a single *sub-fund* of a *qualifying master scheme* that is an *umbrella*; and
which, in the case of either (i) or (ii), is:
(A) a *UCITS*; or
(B) a *non-UCITS retail scheme*; or
(C) a *recognised scheme*.

feeder UCITS

(in accordance with article 58(1) of the *UCITS Directive*):

(a) a *UCITS scheme* or a *sub-fund* of a *UCITS scheme* which has been approved by the *FCA*; or

(b) an *EEA UCITS scheme* or a *sub-fund* of an *EEA UCITS scheme* which has been approved by the *competent authority* of the *UCITS Home State*;

to invest at least 85% of its assets in the *units* of a single *master UCITS*.

fee-paying electronic money issuer

(A) In the PRA Handbook:
any of the following when they issue *electronic money*:
(a) an *authorised electronic money institution*;
(b) a *small electronic money institution*;
(c) an *EEA authorised electronic money institution*;
(d) a *full credit institution*, including a branch of the *full credit institution* within the meaning of article 4(17) of the *EU CRR* which is situated within the *EEA* and which has its head office in a territory outside the *EEA* in accordance with article 47 of the *EU CRR*;
(e) the Post Office Limited;
(f) the Bank of England, when not acting in its capacity as a monetary authority or carrying out functions of a public nature;
(g) government departments and local authorities, when carrying out functions of a public nature;
(h) a *credit union*;
(i) a municipal bank; and
(j) the National Savings Bank.
A *full credit institution* that is an *EEA firm* is only a *fee-paying electronic money issuer* if it is exercising an *EEA right* in accordance with Part II of Schedule 3 to the *Act* (Exercise of passport rights by EEA firms) to issue *electronic money* in the *United Kingdom*. An *EEA authorised electronic money institution* is only a *fee-paying electronic money issuer* if it is exercising a right under Article 3 of the *Electronic Money Directive* to issue *electronic money* in the *United Kingdom*.

(B) In the FCA Handbook:
any of the following when they issue *electronic money*:
(a) an *authorised electronic money institution*;
(b) a *small electronic money institution*;
(c) an *EEA authorised electronic money institution*;
(d) a *full credit institution*, including a branch of the *full credit institution* within the meaning of article 4(17) of the *EU CRR* which is situated within the *EEA* and which has its head office in a territory outside the *EEA* in accordance with article 47 of the *EU CRR*;
(e) the Post Office Limited;
(f) the Bank of England, when not acting in its capacity as a monetary authority or carrying out functions of a public nature;
(g) government departments and local authorities, when carrying out functions of a public nature;
(h) a *credit union*;
(i) a municipal bank; and
(j) the National Savings Bank.
A *full credit institution* that is an *EEA firm* is only a *fee-paying electronic money issuer* if it is exercising an *EEA right* in accordance with Part II of Schedule 3 to the *Act* (Exercise of passport rights by EEA firms) to issue *electronic money* in the *United Kingdom*. An *EEA authorised electronic money institution* is only a *fee-paying electronic money issuer* if it is exercising a right under Article 3 of the *Electronic Money Directive* to issue *electronic money* in the *United Kingdom*.

fee-paying payment service provider

any of the following when they provide *payment services*:

(a) a *payment institution*;

(b) a *full credit institution*;

(c) an *electronic money issuer* (except where it is an *electronic money issuer* whose only *payment service* activities are those relating to the issuance of *electronic money* by itself or if it is a *credit union*, a municipal bank or the National Savings Bank);

(d) the Post Office Limited;

(e) the Bank of England, other than when acting in its capacity as a monetary authority or carrying out functions of a public nature; and

(f) government departments and local authorities, other than when carrying out functions of a public nature.

A *full credit institution* that is an *EEA firm* is only a *fee-paying payment service provider* if it is exercising an *EEA right* in accordance with Part 2 of Schedule 3 to the *Act* (exercise of passport rights) to provide *payment services* in the *United Kingdom*. An *EEA authorised payment institution* or an *EEA authorised electronic money institution* is only a *fee-paying payment service provider* if it is exercising a right under Article 25 of the *Payment Services Directive* or Article 3 of the *Electronic Money Directive* to provide *payment services* in the *United Kingdom*.

FEES

the *FEES* manual.

field representative

an *appointed representative* or, where applicable, a *tied agent*, or an *employee* of the *firm* (or of its *appointed representative* or, where applicable, its *tied agent*), whose normal fixed place of business is not a business address of the *firm* which appears on the *firm's* stationery.

FICOD 1

the European Parliament and Council Directive amending Directives 98/78/EC, 2002/87/EC, 2006/48/EC and 2009/138/EC regarding the supplementary supervision of financial entities in a financial conglomerate (No 2011/89/EU).

final bonus

(in relation to a *with-profits insurance contract*) a discretionary payment which might be made by a *long-term insurer*, in addition to the guaranteed benefits, when the benefits under the *with-profits insurance contract* become payable.

final notice

a notice given by the *appropriate regulator* under section 390 of the *Act* (Final notices).

final response

(1) (in CREDS 9) a written response from the *firm* which:

(a) accepts the complaint, and, where appropriate, offers redress; or

(b) offers redress without accepting the complaint; or

(c) rejects the complaint and gives reasons for doing so;

and which informs the complainant that, if he remains dissatisfied with the *firm's* response, he may now refer his complaint to the *Financial Ombudsman Service* and must do so within six months.

(2) [deleted]

(3) (in *DISP*) has the meaning given in DISP 1.6.2R (1).

final terms

(in *LR*) the document containing the final terms of each issue which is intended to be *listed*.

finance

in accordance with article 60L of the *Regulated Activities Order*, includes financing in whole or in part and "refinance" is to be read accordingly.

Financial Action Task Force

the inter-governmental body responsible for developing and promoting policies, both nationally and internationally, to combat money laundering.

financial analyst

a *relevant person* who produces the substance of *investment research*. [Note: article 2(4) of the *MiFID implementing Directive*]

financial collateral comprehensive method

the method for calculating the effects of credit risk mitigation described in those parts of BIPRU 5.4 (Financial collateral) that are expressed to apply to that method.

Financial Collateral Directive

the Council Directive of 6 June 2002 relating to financial collateral arrangements (No. 2002/47/EC).

financial collateral simple method

the method for calculating the effects of credit risk mitigation described in those parts of BIPRU 5.4 (Financial collateral) that are expressed to apply to that method.

financial conglomerate

(in accordance with Article 2(14) of the *Financial Groups Directive* (Definitions)) a *consolidation group* that is identified as a *financial conglomerate* by the *financial conglomerate definition decision tree*.

financial conglomerate definition decision tree

the decision tree in GENPRU 3 Ann 4R.

financial crime

(in accordance with section 1H of the *Act*) any kind of criminal conduct relating to money or to financial services or markets, including any offence involving:

(a) fraud or dishonesty; or

(b) misconduct in, or misuse of information relating to, a financial market; or

(c) handling the proceeds of crime; or

(d) the financing of terrorism;

in this definition, "offence" includes an act or omission which would be an offence if it had taken place in the *United Kingdom*.

financial derivative instrument

(for the purposes of *BIPRU*) has the meaning in BIPRU 13.3.3 R (Definition of a financial derivative instrument); the definition is adjusted for the purposes of the definition of *counterparty risk capital component* in accordance with BIPRU 14.2.3 R (Credit derivatives).

Financial Groups Directive

Directive 2002/87/EC of the European Parliament and of the Council of 16 December 2002 on the supplementary supervision of credit institutions, insurance undertakings and investment firms in a financial conglomerate.

Financial Groups Directive Regulations

the Financial Conglomerates and Other Financial Groups Regulations 2004 (SI 2004/1862).

financial holding company

(A) In the PRA Handbook: a *financial institution* that fulfils the following conditions:

(a) its *subsidiary undertakings* are either exclusively or mainly *credit institutions*, *investment firms* or *financial institutions*;

(b) at least one of those *subsidiary undertakings* is a *credit institution* or an *investment firm*; and

(c) it is not a *mixed financial holding company*.

(B) In the FCA Handbook: a *financial institution* that fulfils the following conditions:

(1) (except in (2)) has the meaning in article 4(1)(20) of the *EU CRR*.

(2) (in *GENPRU* (except GENPRU 3) and *BIPRU* (except BIPRU 12) a *financial institution* that fulfils the following conditions:
(a) its *subsidiary undertakings* are exclusively or mainly *CAD investment firms* or *financial institutions*;
(b) at least one of those *subsidiary undertakings* is a *CAD investment firm*; and
(c) it is not a *mixed financial holding company*.

financial information table

(in *LR*) financial information presented in tabular form that covers the reporting period set out in LR 13.5.13 R in relation to the entities set out in LR 13.5.14 R, and to the extent relevant LR 13.5.17A R.

financial institution

(A) In the PRA Handbook:

(1) (in accordance with paragraph 5(c) of Schedule 3 to the Act (EEA Passport Rights: EEA firm) and article 4 (5) of the *Banking Consolidation Directive* (Definitions)), but not for the purposes of *GENPRU*, *BIPRU* and *INSPRU*), an undertaking, other than a *credit institution*, the principal activity of which is to acquire holdings or to carry on one or more of the listed activities listed in points 2 to 12 and 15 of Annex I to the *BCD*, which is a subsidiary of the kind mentioned in article 24 of the *BCD* and which fulfils the conditions in that article

(2) for the purposes of *GENPRU*, *BIPRU* and *INSPRU* and in accordance with Articles 1(3) (Scope) and 4(5) (Definitions) of the *Banking Consolidation Directive*) the following:
(a) an *undertaking*, other than a *credit institution*, the principal activity of which is to acquire holdings or to carry on one or more of the *listed activities* listed in points 2 to 12 and 15 of Annex I to the *Banking Consolidation Directive* including the services and activities provided for in Sections A and B of Annex I of the *MIFID* when referring to the financial instruments provided for in Section C of Annex I of that Directive
(b) (for the purposes of consolidated requirements) those institutions permanently excluded by Article 2 of the *Banking Consolidation Directive* (Scope), with the exception of the *central banks* of *EEA States*

(B) In the FCA Handbook:

(1) (in accordance with paragraph 5(c) of Schedule 3 to the Act (EEA Passport Rights: EEA firm) and article 3 (22) of the *CRD* (Definitions)), but not for the purposes of *GENPRU*, *BIPRU*, *IFPRU* and *INSPRU*), an undertaking, other than a *credit institution*, the principal activity of which is to acquire holdings or to carry on one or more of the listed activities listed in points 2 to 12 and 15 of Annex I to the *CRD*, which is a subsidiary of the kind mentioned in article 34 of the *CRD* and which fulfils the conditions in that article

(2) for the purposes of *GENPRU* (except GENPRU 3), *BIPRU* (except in BIPRU 12) and in accordance with Articles 1(3) (Scope) and 4(5) (Definitions) of the *Banking Consolidation Directive*):
(a) an *undertaking*, other than a *credit institution* or an *investment firm*, the principal activity of which is to acquire holdings or to carry on one or more of the *listed activities* listed in points 2 to 12 and 15 of Annex I to the *Banking Consolidation Directive* including the services and activities provided for in Sections A and B of Annex I of the *MIFID* when referring to the financial instruments provided for in Section C of Annex I of that Directive
(b) (for the purposes of consolidated requirements) those institutions permanently excluded by Article 2 of the *Banking Consolidation Directive* (Scope), with the exception of the *central banks* of *EEA States*

(3) (except in (1) and (2) and subject to (4)) has the meaning in article 4(1)(26) of the *EU CRR*.

(4) (for the purposes of consolidated requirements in *IFPRU* and in accordance with article 2(6) of *CRD*) the following:
(a) financial institutions within the meaning in article 4(1)(26) of the *EU CRR*; and
(b) those institutions permanently excluded by article 2(5) of *CRD* (Scope) with the exception of the ESCB central banks as defined in article 4(1)(45) of the *EU CRR*.

financial instrument

(A) In the PRA Handbook:

(1) (other than in (2)) instruments specified in Section C of Annex I of *MiFID*, that is:
(a) *transferable securities*;
(b) *money-market instruments*;
(c) units in collective investment undertakings;
(d) options, futures, swaps, forward rate agreements and any other derivative contracts relating to securities, currencies, interest rates or yields, or other derivative instruments, financial indices or financial measures which may be settled physically or in cash;
(e) options, futures, swaps, forward rate agreements and any other derivative contracts relating to commodities that must be settled in cash or may be settled in cash at the option of one of the parties (otherwise than by reason of a default or other termination event);
(f) options, futures, swaps, and any other derivative contract relating to commodities that can be physically settled provided that they are traded on a *regulated market* and/or an *MTF*;
(g) options, futures, swaps, forwards and any other derivative contracts relating to commodities, that can be physically settled not otherwise mentioned in (f) and not being for commercial purposes, which have the characteristics of other derivative financial instruments, having regard to whether, inter alia, they are cleared and settled through recognised clearing houses or are subject to regular margin calls (see articles 38(1), (2) and (4) of the *MiFID Regulation*);
(h) derivative instruments for the transfer of credit risk;
(i) financial contracts for differences; and
(j) options, futures, swaps, forward rate agreements and any other derivative contracts relating to
(i) climatic variables;
(ii) freight rates;
(iii) emission allowances;
(iv) inflation rates or other official economic statistics;
(v) telecommunications bandwidth;
(vi) commodity storage capacity;
(vii) transmission or transportation capacity relating to commodities, whether cable, pipeline or other means;
(viii) an allowance, credit, permit, right or similar asset which is directly linked to the supply,

distribution or consumption of energy derived from renewable resources;

(ix) a geological, environmental or other physical variable;

(x) any other asset or right of a fungible nature, other than a right to receive a service, that is capable of being transferred;

(xi) an index or measure related to the price or value of, or volume of transactions in any asset, right, service or obligation;

where the conditions in Articles 38(3) and (4) of the *MiFID Regulation* are met. [Note: article 4(1)(17) and section C of Annex I to *MiFID* and articles 38 and 39 of the *MiFID Regulation*]

(2) (in MAR 1 and MAR 2, DTR 1, 2 and 3 and otherwise where used in relation to the *Market Abuse Directive*) (as defined in Article 5 of the *Prescribed Markets and Qualifying Investments Order* and Article 1(3) of the *Market Abuse Directive*, and which consequently carries the same meaning in the *Buy-back and Stabilisation Regulation*):

(B) In the FCA Handbook:

(1) (other than in (2) and (3)) instruments specified in Section C of Annex I of *MiFID*, that is:
(a) *transferable securities*;
(b) *money-market instruments*;
(c) units in collective investment undertakings;
(d) options, futures, swaps, forward rate agreements and any other derivative contracts relating to securities, currencies, interest rates or yields, or other derivative instruments, financial indices or financial measures which may be settled physically or in cash;
(e) options, futures, swaps, forward rate agreements and any other derivative contracts relating to commodities that must be settled in cash or may be settled in cash at the option of one of the parties (otherwise than by reason of a default or other termination event);
(f) options, futures, swaps, and any other derivative contract relating to commodities that can be physically settled provided that they are traded on a *regulated market* and/or an *MTF*;
(g) options, futures, swaps, forwards and any other derivative contracts relating to commodities, that can be physically settled not otherwise mentioned in (f) and not being for commercial purposes, which have the characteristics of other derivative financial instruments, having regard to whether, inter alia, they are cleared and settled through recognised clearing houses or are subject to regular margin calls (see articles 38(1), (2) and (4) of the *MiFID Regulation*);
(i) financial contracts for differences; and
(j) options, futures, swaps, forward rate agreements and any other derivative contracts relating to
(i) climatic variables;
(ii) freight rates;
(iii) emission allowances;
(iv) inflation rates or other official economic statistics;
(v) telecommunications bandwidth;
(vi) commodity storage capacity;
(vii) transmission or transportation capacity relating to commodities, whether cable, pipeline or other means;
(viii) an allowance, credit, permit, right or similar asset which is directly linked to the supply, distribution or consumption of energy derived from renewable resources;
(ix) a geological, environmental or other physical variable;
(x) any other asset or right of a fungible nature, other than a right to receive a service, that is capable of being transferred;
(xi) an index or measure related to the price or value of, or volume of transactions in any asset, right, service or obligation;
where the conditions in Articles 38(3) and (4) of the *MiFID Regulation* are met. [Note: article 4(1)(17) and section C of Annex I to *MiFID* and articles 38 and 39 of the *MiFID Regulation*]

(2) (in MAR 1 and MAR 2, DTR 1, 2 and 3 and otherwise where used in relation to the *Market Abuse Directive*) (as defined in Article 5 of the *Prescribed Markets and Qualifying Investments Order* and Article 1(3) of the *Market Abuse Directive*, and which consequently carries the same meaning in the *Buy-back and Stabilisation Regulation*):

(3) (in *IFPRU*) has the meaning in article 4(50) of the *EU CRR*.

Financial Ombudsman Service

the scheme provided under Part XVI of the *Act* (The Ombudsman Scheme) under which certain disputes may be resolved quickly and with minimum formality by an independent *person*.

Financial Ombudsman Service Limited

the *body corporate* established by the *FSA* under paragraph 2(1) of Schedule 17 to the *Act* (The Scheme Operator) (as originally enacted) to administer the *Financial Ombudsman Service*.

Financial Policy Committee

The sub-committee of the court of directors of the Bank of England, established by Part 1A of the Bank of England Act 1998 to contribute to the Bank of England's Financial Stability Objective and, subject to that, to support the economic policy of the Government.

financial promotion

(1) an invitation or inducement to *engage in investment activity* that is communicated in the course of business; [Note: section 21 of the *Act* (Restrictions on financial promotion)]

(2) (in relation to COBS 3.2.1R (3), COBS 4.3.1 R, COBS 4.5.8 R and COBS 4.7.1 R) (in addition to (1)) a marketing communication within the meaning of *MiFID* made by a *firm* in connection with its *MiFID or equivalent third country business*.

Financial Promotion Order

the Financial Services and Markets Act 2000 (Financial Promotion) Order 2005 (SI 2005/1529).

financial promotion rules

(1) (in relation to *COBS*) any or all of the *rules* in COBS 4 that impose requirements in relation to a *financial promotion* but only to the extent that they apply to a *financial promotion*.

(2) (in relation to *ICOBS*) ICOBS 2.2.

(3) (in relation to *MCOB*) MCOB 3.

(4) (in relation to *BCOBS*) all or any of the *rules* in BCOBS 2 that impose requirements in relation to a *financial promotion* but only to the extent that they apply to a *financial promotion*.

(5) (in relation to *CONC*) any or all of the *rules* in CONC 3, that impose requirements in relation to a *financial promotion* but only to the extent that they apply to a *financial promotion*.

financial resources

(in *UPRU*) the financial resources calculated in accordance with UPRU 2.2.1 R (Financial resources) that a *UCITS firm* needs to meet its *financial resources requirement*.

financial resources requirement

(in *UPRU*) has the meaning given in UPRU 2.1.2 R.

financial return

(in *UPRU*) means *annual financial return*, *quarterly financial return* or *monthly financial return* as the case may be.

financial sector

(1) (subject to (2)) one of the *banking sector*, the *insurance sector* or the *investment services sector*.

(2) (for the purposes of the definition of *financial conglomerate* and for any other provision of GENPRU 3 that treats the *banking sector* and the *investment services sector* as one) one of the *banking and investment services sector* or the *insurance sector*.

financial sector entity

has the meaning in article 4(1)(27) of the *EU CRR*.

Financial Services Compensation Scheme Limited

the *body corporate* established by the *FSA* under section 212 of the *Act* (The scheme manager) (as originally enacted) to administer the *compensation scheme*.

Financial Services Register

the public record, as required by section 347 of the *Act* (The public record), regulation 4 of the *Payment Services Regulations* (The register of certain payment service providers) and regulation 4 of the *Electronic Money Regulations*, of every:

(a) *authorised person*

(aa) *authorised payment institution* and its EEA branches;

(ab) *small payment institution*;

(ac) *agent* of an *authorised payment institution* or *small payment institution*;

(aca) *authorised electronic money institution* and an *EEA branch of an authorised electronic money institution*;

(acb) *small electronic money institution*;

(acc) *agent* of an *authorised electronic money institution* or *small electronic money institution*;

(ad) *credit union*, municipal bank and the National Savings Bank where such *persons* provide a *payment service*; or issue *electronic money*;

(b) *AUT*;

(c) *ICVC*;

(ca) *ACS*;

(d) *recognised scheme*;

(e) *recognised investment exchange*;

(f) [deleted]

(g) individual to whom a *prohibition order* relates;

(h) *approved person*; and

(i) *person* within such other class (if any) as the *FCA* may determine; except as provided by any transitional provisions.

financial stability information power

the *PRA's* power under section 165A of the *Act* (PRA's power to require information: financial stability) which, in summary, is a power to require a *person* to provide information or documents relevant to the stability of one or more aspects of the *UK financial system*.

financial stability information requirement

a requirement imposed on a *person* by the *PRA* using the *financial stability information power* or the *overseas financial stability information power*.

financial year

(1) (in *DISP* and FEES 5) the 12 *months* ending with 31 March.

(3) (in *GENPRU* and *INSPRU*) the period at the end of which the balance of the accounts of the *insurer* is struck, or, if no balance is struck, the calendar year.

financial year in question

(for the purposes of INSPRU 1.1 and of the definition of *non-directive insurer*) the last *financial year* to end before the date on which the latest accounts of the *insurer* are required to be deposited with the *appropriate regulator*; the preceding *financial year* and previous *financial years* are construed accordingly.

financing cost amount

(in relation to a *share*, *debenture* or other investment in, or external contribution to the capital of, a *firm*) an amount that represents a reasonable estimate of the part of the *coupon* on that instrument that reflects the cost of financing generally but excludes costs reflecting factors relating to the issuer, guarantor or other person to whom the instrument creates an exposure.

FINMAR

the Financial Stability and Market Confidence sourcebook.

fire and natural forces

(in relation to a *class* of *contract of insurance*) the *class* of *contract of insurance*, specified in paragraph 8 of Part I of Schedule 1 to the *Regulated Activities Order* (Contracts of general insurance), against loss of or damage to property (other than property to which paragraphs 3 to 7 of Part I of Schedule 1 to the *Regulated Activities Order* (Land vehicles; railway rolling stock; aircraft; ships; goods in transit) relate) due to fire, explosion, storm, natural forces other than storm, nuclear energy or land subsidence.

FINREP firm

(A) (In the *PRA Handbook*)

a *credit institution* or *investment firm* subject to the *EU CRR* that is also subject to article 4 of Regulation (EC) No 1606/2002; or

a *credit institution* other than one referred to in Article 4 of Regulation (EC) No 1606/2002 that prepares its consolidated accounts in conformity with the international accounting standards adopted in accordance with the procedure laid down in article 6(2) of that Regulation.

[Note: article 99 of the *EU CRR*]

(B) in the FCA Handbook)

(a) a *credit institution* or *investment firm* subject to the *EU CRR* that is also subject to article 4 of Regulation (EC) No 1606/2002; or

(b) a *credit institution* other than one referred to in article 4 of Regulation (EC) No 1606/2002 that prepares its consolidated accounts in conformity with the international accounting standards adopted in accordance with the procedure laid down in article 6(2) of that Regulation.

[Note: article 99 of the *EU CRR*]

firm

(A) In the PRA Handbook:

(1) in the *FCA Handbook*, an *authorised person*, but not a *professional firm* unless it is an *authorised professional firm* (see also GEN 2.2.18 R for the position of an authorised partnership or unincorporated association which is dissolved).

(1A) in the *PRA Handbook*, a *PRA-authorised person*.

(2) (in DISP 2 and 3) includes, in accordance with the *Ombudsman Transitional Order*, *unauthorised persons* subject to the *Compulsory Jurisdiction* in relation to *relevant existing complaints* and *relevant new complaints*.

(3) (in DISP 2 and 3) includes, in accordance with the *Mortgage and General Insurance Complaints Transitional Order*, former *firms* subject to the *Compulsory Jurisdiction* in relation to *relevant transitional complaints*.

(4) (in DISP 2 and 3) includes, as a result of the *insurance market direction* given in DISP 2.1.7 D under section 316 of the *Act* (Direction by a regulator), *members* of the *Society* of Lloyd's.

(5) (in FEES 3, FEES 4, FEES 5 and FEES 7) includes a *fee-paying payment service provider* and a *fee-paying electronic money issuer* in accordance with FEES 3.1.1A R, FEES 4.1.1A R, FEES 5.1.1A R and FEES 7.1.1 R.

(6) (in *CONRED*):
(a) an *authorised person*; or
(b) a *person* who was an *authorised person* when the relevant activity took place but has since ceased to be one.

(B) In the FCA Handbook:

(1) in the *FCA Handbook*, an *authorised person*, but not a *professional firm* unless it is an *authorised professional firm* (see also GEN 2.2.18 R for the position of an authorised partnership or unincorporated association which is dissolved).

(1A) in the *PRA Handbook*, a *PRA-authorised person*.

(2) (in DISP 2 and 3) includes, in accordance with the *Ombudsman Transitional Order*, *unauthorised persons* subject to the *Compulsory Jurisdiction* in relation to *relevant existing complaints* and *relevant new complaints*.

(3) (in DISP 2 and 3) includes, in accordance with the *Mortgage and General Insurance Complaints Transitional Order*, former *firms* subject to the *Compulsory Jurisdiction* in relation to *relevant transitional complaints*.

(4) (in DISP 2 and 3) includes, as a result of the *insurance market direction* given in DISP 2.1.7 D under section 316 of the *Act* (Direction by a regulator), *members* of the *Society* of Lloyd's.

(5) (in FEES 3, FEES 4, FEES 5 and FEES 7) includes a *fee-paying payment service provider* and a *fee-paying electronic money issuer* in accordance with FEES 3.1.1A R, FEES 4.1.1A R, FEES 5.1.1A R and FEES 7.1.1 R.

(6) (in *CONRED*):
(a) an *authorised person*; or
(b) a *person* who was an *authorised person* when the relevant activity took place but has since ceased to be one.

(7) (in DISP 2 and 3) includes, in accordance with the transitional provisions in article 11 of the *Regulated Activities Amendment Order*, *unauthorised persons* subject to the *Compulsory Juris-diction* in relation to *relevant existing credit-related complaints* and *relevant new credit-related complaints*.

firm's equity balance

the sum of *money* described in CASS 7.16.29 R.

firm in run-off

a *firm* whose *Part 4A permission* has been varied so as to remove the *regulated activity* of *effecting contracts of insurance*.

firm-specific liquidity stress

(in relation to a *firm* and any reporting obligations under SUP 16 (Reporting requirements)):

(a) (in the case of reporting obligations on a solo basis (including on the basis of the *firm's UK branch*) the *firm* failing to meet, not complying with or being in breach of:
(i) the liquidity resources requirement calculated by that *firm* as adequate in its current *Individual Liquidity Adequacy Assessment* or *Individual Liquidity Systems Assessment*; or
(ii) the level of its liquid assets buffer advised in any current *individual liquidity guidance* that the *firm* has accepted; or
(iii) its funding profile advised in any current *individual liquidity guidance* that the *firm* has accepted; or
(iv) the *overall liquidity adequacy rule*; or
(v) BIPRU 12.2.8R (*ILAS BIPRU firm* adequate buffer of high quality, unencumbered assets) or BIPRU 12.2.11R (liquid assets buffer is at least equal to the *simplified buffer requirement*); or
(vi) the *simplified buffer requirement* (taking into account BIPRU TP 29 (Liquid assets buffer scalar: simplified ILAS BIPRU firms) unless this has been superseded by *individual liquidity guidance* that it has accepted; or
(vii) any requirement imposed by or under the *regulatory system* under which the *firm* must hold a specified level of liquidity resources;
or it being likely that the *firm* will do so;

(b) (in the case of reporting obligations with respect to the *firm* and a group of other *persons*) has the same meaning as in (a) except that references to any *rule* or other requirement, *Individual Liquidity Adequacy Assessment*, *Individual Liquidity Systems Assessment* or *individual liquidity guidance* are to any such thing so far as it applies to the *firm* and that group considered together.

firm type

one of a list of firm types set out in SUP 16 Annex 17 used for the purposes of checking and correcting *standing data* under SUP 16.10.4 R.

First Life Directive

the Council Directive of 5 March 1979 on the coordination of laws, regulations and administrative provisions relating to the taking up and pursuit of the business of direct life assurance (No 79/267/EEC).

First Non-Life Directive

the Council Directive of 24 July 1973 on the coordination of laws, regulations and administrative provisions relating to the taking up and pursuit of the business of direct insurance other than life insurance (No 73/239/EEC).

FIT

the part of the *Handbook* in High Level Standards which has the title the Fit and Proper test for Approved Persons.

fixed-sum credit

(1) (except in *CONC*) (in accordance with section 10(1)(b) of the Consumer Credit Act 1974) any facility under a contract, other than *running-account credit*, by which the *customer* is enabled to receive credit (whether in one amount or by instalments).

(2) (in *CONC*) a facility under a *credit agreement* whereby the *borrower* is enabled to receive *credit* (whether in one amount or by instalments) but which is not *running-account credit*.

fixed overheads requirement

(A) In the PRA Handbook:
(1) (except in IPRU(INV)) and for the purposes of *GENPRU* (except in GENPRU 3) and *BIPRU* (except in BIPRU 12)) the part of the *capital resources requirement* calculated in accordance with GENPRU 2.1.53 R (Calculation of the fixed overheads requirement).
(2) (in IPRU(INV)) the part of the *own funds* requirement calculated in accordance with IPRU(INV) 11.3.3R (Fixed overheads requirement).

(B) In the FCA Handbook:
(1) (except in IPRU(INV) and for the purposes of *GENPRU* (except GENPRU 3 and *BIPRU* (except BIPRU 12)) the part of the *capital resources requirement* calculated in accordance with GEN-

PRU 2.1.53 R (Calculation of the fixed overheads requirement).
(2) (in IPRU(INV)) the part of the *own funds* requirement calculated in accordance with IPRU(INV) 11.3.3R (Fixed overheads requirement).

flat-fee charge

a charge used by an *operator* of a *qualifying scheme* which is a specified charge for a period of time and which is not calculated by reference to member's contributions or accrued rights.

flat rate benefits business friendly society

a *friendly society* whose *insurance business* is restricted to the provision of benefits which vary according to the resources available and in which the contributions of members are determined on a flat rate basis.

flexible benefits

has the meaning given in section 74 of the Pension Schemes Act 2015 which in relation to a *member of a pension scheme* or a *survivor* of a *member of a pension scheme* is:

(a) a money purchase benefit (defined in section 181 of the Pension Schemes Act 1993 and section 176 of the Pension Schemes (Northern Ireland) Act 1993); or

(b) a cash balance benefit (defined in Section 75 of the Pension Schemes Act 2015); or

(c) a benefit, other than a money purchase benefit or cash balance benefit, calculated by reference to an amount available for the provision of benefits to or in respect of the member (whether the amount so available is calculated by reference to payments made by the member or any other person in respect of the member or any other factor).

foreign currency

(in *GENPRU* and *BIPRU*) (in relation to a *firm*) any currency other than the *base currency*.

foreign currency PRR

the part of the *market risk capital requirement* calculated in accordance with BIPRU 7.5 (Foreign currency PRR) or, in relation to a particular position, the portion of the overall *foreign currency PRR* attributable to that *position*.

foreign law contract

any contract other than a contract:

(a) governed by the laws of any part of the *United Kingdom*; and

(b) whose parties agree to the exclusive jurisdiction of the courts of any part of the *United Kingdom*.

former member

a *person* who has ceased to be a *member*, whether by resignation or otherwise, in accordance with Lloyd's Act 1982 and any *byelaw* made under it.

former Ombudsman

an ombudsman, arbitrator or independent investigator appointed under a *former scheme*.

former scheme

(1) (except in relation to a *relevant transitional complaint*) any of the following:
(a) the *Banking Ombudsman scheme*;
(b) the *Building Societies Ombudsman scheme*;
(c) the *FSA scheme*;
(d) the *IMRO scheme*;
(e) the *Insurance Ombudsman scheme*;
(f) the *Personal Insurance Arbitration Service*;
(g) the PIA Ombudsman scheme;
(h) the *SFA scheme*;

(2) (in relation to a *relevant transitional complaint*)
(a) the *GISC facility*; or
(b) the *MCAS scheme*.

former underwriting member

(as defined in section 324(1) of the *Act* (Interpretation of Part XIX: Lloyd's)) a *person* ceasing to be an *underwriting member* on, or at any time after, 24 December 1996.

forward

a contract to buy or sell where the date for settlement has been agreed as a particular date in the future but excluding a *future*.

forward price

(in relation to *units*) a *price* calculated by reference to the *valuation point* next following the *authorised fund manager's* agreement to *sell* or, as the case may be, to redeem the *units* in question.

forward rate agreement

an agreement under which one party agrees to pay another an amount of interest based on an agreed interest rate for a specified period from a specified settlement date applied to an agreed principal amount but under which no commitment is made by either party to lend or borrow the principal amount.

FOS Ltd

Financial Ombudsman Service Limited.

foundation IRB approach

one of the following:

(a) (in relation to the *sovereign, institutional and corporate IRB exposure class*) the approach under the *IRB approach*, described in BIPRU 4.4 (The IRB approach: Exposures to corporates, institutions and sovereigns) under which a *firm* uses the values for *LGD* and *conversion factors* set out in BIPRU 4.4 rather than supplying its own estimates;

(b) (where the approach in (a) is being applied on a consolidated basis) the method in (a) as applied on a consolidated basis in accordance with BIPRU 8 (Group risk – consolidation); or

(c) when the reference is to the rules of or administered by a *regulatory body* other than the *appropriate regulator*, whatever corresponds to the approach in (a) or (b), as the case may be, under those rules.

Fourth Company Law Directive

Council Directive 78/660/EEC on the annual accounts of certain types of companies as amended by, amongst other instruments, Directive 2006/46/EC of the European Parliament and of the Council of 14 June 2006.

FRA

forward rate agreement.

framework contract

(in accordance with regulation 2(1) of the *Payment Services Regulations*) a contract for *payment services* which governs the future execution of individual and successive payment transactions and which may contain the obligation and conditions for setting up a payment account. [Note: article 4(12) of the *Payment Services Directive*]

free delivery

(for the purposes of *BIPRU*) a transaction of the type set out in BIPRU 14.4.2 R (Requirement to hold capital resources with respect to free deliveries) which, in summary, is a transaction under which a *person*:

(a) has paid for *securities, foreign currencies* or *commodities* before receiving them or it has delivered *securities, foreign currencies* or *commodities* before receiving payment for them; and

(b) in the case of cross-border transactions, one day or more has elapsed since it made that payment or delivery.

friendly society

an *incorporated friendly society* or a *registered friendly society*.

front end loaded

(in relation to an *investment*) one where deductions for *charges* and expenses are loaded disproportionately on the early years.

FSA

the Financial Services Authority.

Part 3   FCA Handbook Materials

FSA scheme

the *former scheme* operated by the *FSA* under paragraph 4 of Schedule 7 to the Financial Services Act 1986 for the investigation of complaints arising out of the conduct of investment business.

FSAVC

an arrangement which allows a member of an *occupational pension scheme* to make *AVCs* to a private *pension policy* or *pension contract*, where the policy or contract is separate from, but associated with, an *occupational pension scheme* which is a registered pension scheme under Chapter 2 of Part 4 of the Finance Act 2004.

FSB Compensation Standards

the Implementation Standards for Principles for Sound Compensation Practices issued by the Financial Stability Board on 25 September 2009.

FSBRA

(in FEES 9) the Financial Services (Banking Reform) Act 2013.

FSCS

Financial Services Compensation Scheme Limited.

full CRD credit institution

(A) In the PRA Handbook a *CRD credit institution* that falls within paragraph (1)(a) of the definition of *credit institution*

(B) In the FCA Handbook an *undertaking* whose business is to receive deposits or other repayable funds from the public and to grant credits for its own account and that has its registered office (or, if it has no registered office, its head office) in an *EEA state*, excluding an institution to which *CRD* does not apply under article 2 of *CRD*.

full credit institution

a *credit institution* that falls within paragraph (1)(a) of the definition of *credit institution*.

full scope BIPRU investment firm

has the meaning in BIPRU 1.1.17 R (Types of BIPRU investment firm) which is in summary a *CAD full scope firm* that satisfies the following conditions:

(a) it is a *firm*; and

(b) its head office is in the *United Kingdom* and it is not otherwise excluded from the definition of *BIPRU firm* under BIPRU 1.1.17 R (Exclusion of certain types of firm from the definition of BIPRU firm).

full-scope EEA AIFM

an *EEA AIFM* which is authorised by its *Home State* in accordance with article 6(1) of *AIFMD*.

full-scope IFPRU investment firm

a *CRD full-scope firm* that is an *IFPRU investment firm*.

full-scope UK AIFM

a *UK AIFM* which:

(a) is not a *small AIFM*; or

(b) is a *small AIFM* but has opted in to *AIFMD* in accordance with article 3(4) of *AIFMD*.

fund

an *AIF* or a *collective investment scheme*.

Fundamental Rules

the Fundamental Rules set out in Fundamental Rules 2 in the *PRA* Rulebook.

funded credit protection

(in accordance with Article 4(31) of the *Banking Consolidation Directive* (Definitions) and for the purposes of *BIPRU*) a technique of *credit risk mitigation* where the reduction of the credit risk on the *exposure* of an undertaking derives from the right of the *undertaking*, in the event of the default of the counterparty or on the occurrence of other specified credit events relating to the counterparty, to liquidate, or to obtain transfer or appropriation of, or to retain certain assets or amounts, or to reduce the amount of the *exposure* to, or to replace it with, the amount of the difference between the amount of the *exposure* and the amount of a claim on the *undertaking*.

fund application rules

(in *COLL* and *SUP*) the rules set out in COLL 12.3.5 R (COLL fund rules under the management company passport: the fund application rules) that relate to the constitution and functioning of a *UCITS scheme* and that an *EEA UCITS management company* must comply with when acting as the *operator* of the *UCITS scheme*, whether from a *branch* in the *United Kingdom* or under the freedom to provide *cross border services*, as required by article 19(3) of the *UCITS Directive*.

fund of alternative investment funds

a *non-UCITS retail scheme*, or a *sub-fund* of a *non-UCITS retail scheme* which is an *umbrella* whose *authorised fund manager* operates, or proposes to operate, it in accordance with the investment and borrowing powers in COLL 5.7 (Investment powers and borrowing limits for *NURS* operating as *FAIFs*).

funds at Lloyd's

assets (not being *syndicate assets*) provided by or on behalf of a *member* to meet the liabilities arising from the *member*'s *insurance business* at Lloyd's which are held in a *Lloyd's trust fund* and managed by the *Society* as trustee.

funds under management

(1) (in *UPRU*)

(a) *collective investment schemes* other than *OEICs* managed by the *firm* including *schemes* where it has delegated the management function but excluding *schemes* that it is managing as delegate; and

(b) *OEICs* for which the *firm* is the designated management company.

(2) (in IPRU(INV)) *funds* managed by the *firm*, calculated as the sum of the absolute value of all assets of all *funds* managed by the *firm*, including assets acquired through the use of leverage and, for such purpose, derivative instruments shall be valued at their market value. This includes *funds* where the *firm* has delegated the management function but excludes *funds* that it is managing as a delegate.

funds under management requirement

(1) (in IPRU(INV) 11) an amount of *own funds* that a *collective portfolio management firm* must hold under IPRU(INV) 11.3.2R (Funds under management requirement).

[deleted]

funeral plan contract

the *investment*, specified in articles 59(2), 60 and 87 of the *Regulated Activities Order* which come into force on 1 January 2002, which is in summary: rights under a contract under which:

(a) a *person* ("the customer") makes one or more payments to another *person* ("the provider"); and

(b) the provider undertakes to provide, or secure that another *person* provides, a funeral in the *United Kingdom* for the customer (or some other *person* who is living at the date when the contract is entered into) on his death;

unless, at the time of entering into the contract, the customer and the provider intend or expect the funeral to occur within one month; but excluding certain contracts under which sums paid will be applied towards a *contract of insurance* or will be held on trust.

future

the *investment*, specified in article 84 of the *Regulated Activities Order* (Futures), which is in summary: rights under a contract for the sale of a commodity or property of any other description under which delivery is to be made at a future date and at a price agreed on when the contract is made.

future arrangements

in relation to a *borrower-lender agreement* or a *borrower-lender-supplier agreement*, a *credit agreement* is entered into in contemplation of future arrangements between a *lender* and a *supplier* if it is entered into in the expectation that arrangements will subsequently be made between the *lender* (or the *lender's associate*) and the *supplier* (or the *supplier's associate*) for the supply of *cash*, *goods* or services to be *financed* by the *credit agreement* unless the arrangements are:

(a) for the making, in circumstances specified in the *credit agreement*, of payments to the *supplier* by the *lender* ("L") and L indicates that L is willing to make, in such circumstances, payments of the kind to *suppliers* generally; or

(b) for the electronic transfer of funds from a current account held with an *authorised person* with *permission* to *accept deposits*.

future policy-related liabilities

(in relation to a *with-profits fund*) the future policy-related liabilities of the *with-profits fund* calculated in accordance with the *rules* in PRU 7.4.137 R to PRU 7.4.189 G.

GCR

group capital resources.

GCRR

group capital resources requirement.

GEN

the part of the *Handbook* in High Level Standards which has the title General Provisions.

general application rule

COBS 1.1.1 R (which in summary provides that *COBS* applies to a *firm* with respect to certain activities carried on from an establishment maintained by it in the *United Kingdom*).

general client bank account

(A) In the PRA Handbook: a *client bank account* that holds *client money* of one or more *clients* and which is not:

(a) a *designated client bank account*; or

(b) a *designated client fund account*.

(B) In the FCA Handbook: a *client bank account* that holds *client money* of one or more *clients*, which includes in its title the word "client" (or, if the systems constraints of the approved bank or the firm that holds the account (or both) make this impracticable, an appropriate abbreviation of the word "client" that has the same meaning), and which is not:

(a) a *designated client bank account*; or

(b) a *designated client fund account*.

general insurance business

the business of *effecting* or *carrying out general insurance contracts*.

general insurance capital requirement

the highest of the *premiums amount*, *claims amount* and *brought forward amount* as set out in INSPRU 1.1.

general insurance contract

(in accordance with article 3(1) of the *Regulated Activities Order* (Interpretation: general)) any *contract of insurance* within Part I of Schedule 1 to the *Regulated Activities Order* (Contracts of general insurance), namely:

(a) *accident* (paragraph 1);

(b) *sickness* (paragraph 2);

(c) *land vehicles* (paragraph 3);

(d) *railway rolling stock* (paragraph 4);

(e) *aircraft* (paragraph 5);

(f) *ships* (paragraph 6);

(g) *goods in transit* (paragraph 7);

(h) *fire and natural forces* (paragraph 8);

(i) *damage to property* (paragraph 9);

(j) *motor vehicle liability* (paragraph 10);

(k) *aircraft liability* (paragraph 11);

(l) *liability of ships* (paragraph 12);

(m) *general liability* (paragraph 13);

(n) *credit* (paragraph 14);

(o) *suretyship* (paragraph 15);

(p) *miscellaneous financial loss* (paragraph 16);

(q) *legal expenses* (paragraph 17);

(r) *assistance* (paragraph 18).

general insurance liabilities

liabilities arising from *general insurance business*.

general levy

(in *FEES*) the annual fee raised from a *firm* under the *rules* to fund a part agreed between the *Financial Ombudsman Service* and the *FCA* of the *Financial Ombudsman Service's* annual budget.

general liability

(in relation to a *class* of *contract of insurance*) the *class* of *contract of insurance*, specified in paragraph 13 of Part I of Schedule 1 to the *Regulated Activities Order* (Contracts of general insurance), against risks of the *persons* insured incurring liabilities to third parties, the risks in question not being risks to which paragraph 10 (Motor vehicle liability), 11 (Aircraft liability) or 12 (Liability of ships) of that Schedule relates.

general market risk

(in accordance with paragraph 12 of Annex I of the *Capital Adequacy Directive*) the risk of a price change in an *investment*:

(a) (in relation to items that may or must be treated under BIPRU 7.2 (Interest Rate PRR)) owing to a change in the level of interest rates; or

(b) (in relation to items that may or must be treated under BIPRU 7.3 (Equity PRR and basic interest rate PRR for equity derivatives) except insofar as BIPRU 7.3 relates to the calculation of the *interest rate PRR*) owing to a broad equity-market movement unrelated to any specific attributes of individual *securities*.

general market risk position risk adjustment

a *position risk adjustment* with respect to *general market risk*

general pool

the discrete pool of *client money* held for all *clients* of the *firm* for whom the *firm* receives or holds *client money* in accordance with CASS 7.10.1 Rother than *client money* received or held in accordance with CASS 7.10.1 Rin respect of a *sub-pool*.

general prohibition

the prohibition imposed by section 19 of the *Act* (The general prohibition) which states that no *person* may carry on a *regulated activity* in the *United Kingdom*, or purport to do so, unless he is:

(a) an *authorised person*; or

(b) an *exempt person*.

General Protocol

the "General Protocol relating to the collaboration of the insurance supervisory authorities of the Member States of the European Union" issued by the Committee of European Insurance and Occupational Pensions Supervisors.

general representative

a *person* resident in the *United Kingdom* who is authorised to act generally, and to accept service of any *document*, on behalf of the *firm*.

general rule-making powers

(1) In the *FCA Handbook* section 137A of the *Act*.

(2) In the *PRA Handbook* section 137G of the *Act*.

general stress and scenario testing rule

(A) In the PRA Handbook:
GENPRU 1.2.42 R (Stress and scenario tests).

(B) In the FCA Handbook:
(1) (in *GENPRU*, *BIPRU* and *INSPRU*) GENPRU 1.2.42 R (Stress and scenario tests).
(2) (for the purpose of *IFPRU*) IFPRU 2.2.37R (Stress and scenario tests).

general wrong-way risk

(in accordance with Part 1 of Annex III of the *Banking Consolidation Directive* (Definitions) and for the purpose of BIPRU 13 (The calculation of counterparty risk exposure values for financial derivatives, securities financing transactions and long settlement transactions)) the risk that arises when the probability of default of counterparties is positively correlated with general market risk factors.

generic key features illustration

(in *COBS*) a *key features illustration* which reflects the terms of a contract which is representative of the type of business normally undertaken by the *firm*, or the type of business it is promoting, rather than the terms of a particular contract with, or that will be offered to, a particular *client*.

generic projection

(in *COBS*) a projection which reflects the terms of a contract which is representative of the type of business normally undertaken by the *firm*, or the type of business it is promoting, rather than the terms of a particular contract with, or that will be offered to, a particular *client*.

GENPRU

the General Prudential sourcebook.

Gibraltar Order

the Financial Services and Markets Act 2000 (Gibraltar) Order 2001 (SI 2001/3084).

GICR

general insurance capital requirement.

GISC facility

The Dispute Resolution Facility established by the General Insurance Standards Council.

global account

the aggregate accounts produced by the *Council* in accordance with Regulation 8(1) of the Insurance Accounts Directive (Lloyd's Syndicate and Aggregate Accounts) Regulations 2004.

Glossary

the Glossary giving the meanings of the defined expressions used in the *Handbook*.

goods

has the meaning in section 61(1) of the Sale of Goods Act 1979.

goods in transit

(in relation to a *class* of *contract of insurance*) the *class* of *contract of insurance*, specified in paragraph 7 of Part I of Schedule 1 to the *Regulated Activities Order* (Contracts of general insurance), against loss of or damage to merchandise, baggage and all other goods in transit, irrespective of the form of transport.

governance advisory arrangement

(in COBS 19.5) an arrangement between a *firm* and a third party under which the third party establishes a committee to represent the interests of *relevant policyholder* in the *firm's relevant schemes*.

governing body

the board of *directors*, committee of management or other governing body of a *firm* or *recognised body*, including, in relation to a *sole trader*, the *sole trader*.

government and public security

the *investment*, specified in article 78 of the *Regulated Activities Order* (Government and public securities), which is in summary: a loan stock, bond or other instrument creating or acknowledging indebtedness, issued by or on behalf of:

(a) the government of the *United Kingdom*; or

(b) the Scottish Administration; or

(c) the Executive Committee of the Northern Ireland Assembly; or

(d) the National Assembly of Wales; or

(e) the government of any country or territory outside the *United Kingdom*; or

(f) a local authority in the *United Kingdom* or elsewhere; or

(g) a body the members of which comprise:
(i) States including the *United Kingdom* or another *EEA State*; or
(ii) bodies whose members comprise States including the *United Kingdom* or another *EEA State*; but excluding:
(A) the instruments specified in article 77(2)(a) to (d) of the *Regulated Activities Order*;
(B) any instrument creating or acknowledging indebtedness in respect of:
(I) money received by the Director of Savings as *deposits* or otherwise in connection with the business of the National Savings Bank; or
(II) money raised under the National Loans Act 1968 under the auspices of the Director of Savings or treated as so raised under section 11(3) of the National Debt Act 1972.

Great Britain credit union

a body corporate registered under the Industrial and Provident Societies Act 1965 as a *credit union* in accordance with the Credit Unions Act which is an *authorised person*.

green deal plan

an arrangement by the occupier or owner of a property for a person to make energy efficient improvements to the property wholly or partly paid for in instalments, as defined in section 1 of the Energy Act 2011.

greenshoe option

(as defined in Article 2 of the *Buy-back and Stabilisation Regulation*) an option granted by the *offeror* in favour of the *investment firm(s)* or *credit institution(s)* involved in the *offer* for the purpose of covering *over allotments*, under the terms of which such firm(s) or institution(s) may purchase up to a certain amount of *relevant securities* at the offer price for a certain period of time after the *offer* of the relevant securities.

gross-minus-net amount

at any given time, in respect of an *omnibus client account* maintained by a *clearing member firm* and the positions recorded therein, an amount equal to the difference between:

(a) the sum of the margin amounts received from each *client* regarding positions held for such *client* in that *omnibus client account* and

(b) the amount of margin calculated on a net basis for all of the *client* positions recorded in that *omnibus client account* and paid by that *firm* to the *authorised central counterparty*.

gross adjusted claims amount

(for the purposes of INSPRU 1.1) an amount, as defined in INSPRU 1.1.60R to INSPRU 1.1.65G, used in calculating the *claims amount*.

gross adjusted premiums amount

(for the purposes of INSPRU 1.1) an amount as defined in INSPRU 1.1.56R to INSPRU 1.1.59G, used in calculating the *premiums amount*.

gross earned premiums

(in relation to a *financial year*) such proportion of *gross written premiums* as is attributable to risk borne by the *insurer* during that *financial year*.

gross leverage

the ratio of total assets to total equity.

gross written premiums

the amounts required by the *insurance accounts rules* to be shown in the profit and loss account of an *insurer*:

(a) (for *general insurance business*) at general business technical account item I.1.(a); and

(b) (for *long-term insurance business*) at long term business technical account item II.1.(a).

group

(A) In the PRA Handbook:

(1) (except in relation to an *ICVC* and except for the purposes of SYSC 12 (Group risk systems and controls requirement) and *LR*) as defined in section 421 of the *Act* (Group) (in relation to a *person* ("A")) A and any *person* who is:

(a) a *parent undertaking* of A;

(b) a *subsidiary undertaking* of A;

(c) a *subsidiary undertaking* of a *parent undertaking* of A;

(d) a *parent undertaking* of a *subsidiary undertaking* of A;

(e) an *undertaking* in which A or an *undertaking* in (a) to (d) has a participating interest;

(f) if A or an *undertaking* in (a) or (d) is a *building society*, an associated undertaking of that *building society*;

(g) if A or an *undertaking* in (a) or (d) is an incorporated friendly society, a *body corporate* of which that *friendly society* has joint control (as defined in section 13(9)(c) or (cc) of the Friendly Societies Act 1992); in this definition:

(i) "participating interest" has the same meaning as in:

(A) Part VII of the Companies Act 1985 or Part VIII of the Companies (Northern Ireland) Order 1986, where these provisions are applicable; or

(B) paragraph 11(1) of Schedule 10 to the Large and Medium-sized Companies and Groups (Accounts and Reports) Regulations 2008 (SI 2008/410) where applicable; or

(C) paragraph 8 of Schedule 7 to the Small Companies and Groups (Accounts and Directors' Report) Regulations 2008 (SI 2008/409) where applicable; or

(D) paragraph 8 of Schedule 4 to the Large and Medium-sized Limited Liability Partnerships (Accounts) Regulations 2008 (SI 2008/1913) where applicable; or

(E) paragraph 8 of Schedule 5 to the Small Limited Liability Partnerships (Accounts) Regulations 2008 (SI 2008/1912) where applicable;

In (A) to (E), the meaning also includes an interest held by an individual which would be a participating interest for the purposes of those provisions if he were an *undertaking*.

(ii) "associated undertaking" has the meaning given in section 119(1) of the Building Societies Act 1986.

(2) (in relation to an *ICVC*) a group as in (1) but (in *SYSC*) including also the *ICVC's authorised corporate director* (if any). (see also *immediate group*)

(3) (for the purposes of SYSC 12 (Group risk systems and controls requirement), SYSC 20 (Reverse stress testing) and GENPRU 1.2 (Adequacy of financial resources) and in relation to a *person* "A")) A and any *person*:

(a) who falls into (1);

(b) who is a member of the same *financial conglomerate* as A;

(c) who has a *consolidation Article 12(1) relationship* with A;

(d) who has a *consolidation Article 12(1) relationship* with any *person* in (3)(a);

(e) who is a *subsidiary undertaking* of a person in (3)(c) or (3)(d); or

(f) whose omission from an assessment of the risks to A of A's connection to any *person* coming within (3)(a)-(3)(e) or an assessment of the financial resources available to such *persons* would be misleading.

(4) (in *LR*):

(a) (except in LR 6.1.19 R and LR 8.7.8R (10)) an *issuer* and its *subsidiary undertakings* (if any); and

(b) in LR 6.1.19 R and LR 8.7.8R (10), as defined in section 421 of the Act.

(5) (in relation to a *common platform firm*) means the group of which that *firm* forms a part, consisting of a parent undertaking, its subsidiaries and the entities in which the parent undertaking or its subsidiaries hold a participation, as well as undertakings linked to each other by a relationship within the meaning of Article 12(1) of Directive 83/349/EEC on consolidated accounts.

[Note: article 2(5) of the *MiFID implementing Directive*]

(B) In the FCA Handbook:

(1) (except in relation to an *ICVC* and except for the purposes of SYSC 12 (Group risk systems and controls requirement) and *LR*) as defined in section 421 of the *Act* (Group) (in relation to a *person* ("A")) A and any *person* who is:

(a) a *parent undertaking* of A;

(b) a *subsidiary undertaking* of A;

(c) a *subsidiary undertaking* of a *parent undertaking* of A;

(d) a *parent undertaking* of a *subsidiary undertaking* of A;

(e) an *undertaking* in which A or an *undertaking* in (a) to (d) has a participating interest;

(f) if A or an *undertaking* in (a) or (d) is a *building society*, an associated undertaking of that *building society*;

(g) if A or an *undertaking* in (a) or (d) is an incorporated friendly society, a *body corporate* of which that *friendly society* has joint control (as defined in section 13(9)(c) or (cc) of the Friendly Societies Act 1992); in this definition:

(i) "participating interest" has the same meaning as in:

(A) Part VII of the Companies Act 1985 or Part VIII of the Companies (Northern Ireland) Order 1986, where these provisions are applicable; or

(B) paragraph 11(1) of Schedule 10 to the Large and Medium-sized Companies and Groups (Accounts and Reports) Regulations 2008 (SI 2008/410) where applicable; or

(C) paragraph 8 of Schedule 7 to the Small Companies and Groups (Accounts and Directors' Report) Regulations 2008 (SI 2008/409) where applicable; or

(D) paragraph 8 of Schedule 4 to the Large and Medium-sized Limited Liability Partnerships (Accounts) Regulations 2008 (SI 2008/1913) where applicable; or

(E) paragraph 8 of Schedule 5 to the Small Limited Liability Partnerships (Accounts) Regulations 2008 (SI 2008/1912) where applicable;

In (A) to (E), the meaning also includes an interest held by an individual which would be a participating interest for the purposes of those provisions if he were an *undertaking*.

(ii) "associated undertaking" has the meaning given in section 119(1) of the Building Societies Act 1986.

(2) (in relation to an *ICVC*) a group as in (1) but (in *SYSC*) including also the *ICVC's authorised corporate director* (if any). (see also *immediate group*)

(3) (for the purposes of SYSC 12 (Group risk systems and controls requirement), SYSC 20 (Reverse stress testing) and GENPRU 1.2 (Adequacy of financial resources) as applicable to a *BIPRU firm* and in relation to a *person* "A")) A and any *person*:

(a) who falls into (1);

(b) who is a member of the same *financial conglomerate* as A;

(c) who has a *consolidation Article 12(1) relationship* with A;

(d) who has a *consolidation Article 12(1) relationship* with any *person* in (3)(a);

(e) who is a *subsidiary undertaking* of a person in (3)(c) or (3)(d); or

(f) whose omission from an assessment of the risks to A of A's connection to any *person* coming within (3)(a)-(3)(e) or an assessment of the financial resources available to such *persons* would be misleading.

(3A) (for the purposes of SYSC 12 (Group risk systems and controls requirement) and SYSC 20 (Reverse stress testing), as applicable to an *IFPRU investment firm* and *IFPRU*) and in relation to a *person* "A"), A and any *person*:

(a) who falls into (1);

(b) who is a member of the same *financial conglomerate* as A;

(c) who has a *consolidation Article 12(1) relationship* with A;

(d) who has a *consolidation Article 12(1) relationship* with any *person* in (a);

(e) who is a *subsidiary* of a *person* in (c) or (d);

(f) whose omission from an assessment of the risks to A of A's connection to any *person* coming within (a) to (e) or an assessment of the financial resources available to such *persons* would be misleading.

(4) (in *LR*):

(a) (except in LR 6.1.4A G, LR 6.1.19 R, LR 6.1.20B G, LR 8.7.8R (10), LR 14.2.2 R, LR 14.2.3A G, LR 18.2.8 R and LR 18.2.9A G) an *issuer* and its *subsidiary undertakings* (if any); and

(b) (in LR 6.1.4A G, LR 6.1.19 R, LR 6.1.20B G, LR 8.7.8R (10), LR 14.2.2 R, LR 14.2.3A G, LR 18.2.8 R and LR 18.2.9A G), as defined in section 421 of the Act.

(5) (in relation to a *common platform firm*) means the group of which that *firm* forms a part, consisting of a parent undertaking, its subsidiaries and the entities in which the parent undertaking or its subsidiaries hold a participation, as well as undertakings linked to each other by a relationship within the meaning of Article 12(1) of Directive 83/349/EEC on consolidated accounts.

[Note: article 2(5) of the *MiFID implementing Directive*]

group capital resources

in relation to an *undertaking* in INSPRU 6.1.17R, that *undertaking's* group capital resources as calculated in accordance with INSPRU 6.1.36R.

group capital resources requirement

in relation to an *undertaking* in INSPRU 6.1.17R, that *undertaking's* group capital resources requirement as calculated in accordance with INSPRU 6.1.33R.

group ISA

an *individual savings account* of which the *plan manager* is the *authorised fund manager*, or in the same *group* as the *authorised fund manager*, of the *authorised fund* by reference to *units* in which the *plan register* is being, or is proposed to be, maintained.

group of connected clients

[deleted]

group liquidity low frequency reporting conditions

(in relation to a *group liquidity reporting firm* and its *defined liquidity group*) the *defined liquidity group* meets the group liquidity low frequency reporting conditions if the *defined liquidity group* meets the following conditions:

(a) the *firm* or any other member is a *low frequency liquidity reporting firm*; and

(b) no member of that group is a *standard frequency liquidity reporting firm*.

For the purpose of deciding whether these conditions are met in relation to a *DLG by default*, any group member (other than the *group liquidity reporting firm* itself) that is a member of the group through no more than a *participation* is ignored.

group liquidity reporting firm

see the definitions of *DLG by default*, *DLG by modification (firm level)*, and *non-UK DLG by modification (DLG level)*. (*Guidance* about this definition, and its inter-relation with other related definitions, is set out in SUP 16 Annex 26 (Guidance on designated liquidity groups in SUP 16.12).)

group liquidity standard frequency reporting conditions

(in relation to a *group liquidity reporting firm* and its *defined liquidity group*) the *defined liquidity group* meets the group liquidity standard frequency reporting conditions if the group does not meet the *group liquidity low frequency reporting conditions*.

group personal pension scheme

a *personal pension scheme* (including a group *SIPP*) which is available to employees of the same employer or of employers within a *group*.

group plan

a *group ISA* or a *group savings plan*.

group policy

a *non-investment insurance contract* which a *person* enters into as legal holder of the *policy* on his own behalf and for other persons who are or will become *policyholders* and:

(a) those other *persons* are or become *policyholders* by virtue of a common employment, occupation or activity which has arisen independently of the *contract of insurance*;

(b) the common employment, occupation or activity is not brought about, in relation to the *contract of insurance*, by
(i) the *insurance undertaking* which *effects* it or carries it out; or
(ii) any activity which if carried on by a firm would be an *insurance mediation activity*; and

(c) the risks insured under the *policy* are related to the common employment, occupation or activity of the *policyholders*.

group recovery plan

a document which provides for measures to be taken in relation to an *RRD group*, or any *RRD institution* in the *group*, to achieve the stabilisation of the *group* as a whole, in cases of financial stress, to address or remove the causes of the stress and restore the financial position of the *group* or the *RRD institution*. [Note: articles 2(1)(33) and 7(4) of *RRD*]

group respondents

all *respondents* identified as part of the relevant *charging group* as defined in FEES 5 Annex 3R Part 3.

group savings plan

a savings plan:

(a) of which the *plan manager* is the *authorised fund manager*, or in the same *group* as the *authorised fund manager*, of the *authorised fund* by reference to *units* in which the *plan register* is being, or is proposed to be, maintained;

(b) under which *investments* are periodically acquired and held by a nominee for the absolute benefit of the respective subscribers to the savings plan; and

(c) under which all the *investments* are *units* in one or more *authorised funds* managed by (or, in the case of an *ICVC*, whose *ACD* is) the *plan manager*, or a *body corporate* in the same *group* as the *plan manager*.

group stakeholder pension scheme

a *stakeholder pension scheme* which is available to employees of the same employer or of employers within a *group*.

guarantee

(1) (in *LR*) (in relation to *securitised derivatives*), either:
(a) a guarantee given in accordance with LR 19.2.2 R (3) (if any); or
(b) any other guarantee of the issue of *securitised derivatives*.

(2) (in *PR*) (as defined in the *PD Regulation*) any arrangement intended to ensure that any obligation material to the issue will be duly serviced, whether in the form of guarantee, surety, keep well agreement, mono-line insurance policy or other equivalent commitment.

guarantee fund

(1)
(a) subject to (1)(b), in relation to a *firm* carrying on *general insurance business*, the higher of one third of the *general insurance capital requirement* and the *base capital resources requirement* applicable to that *firm*;
(b) where the *firm* is required to calculate a *UK MCR* or an *EEA MCR* under INSPRU 1.5, for the purposes of that section in (1)(a) the reference to the *general insurance capital requirement* is replaced by *UK MCR* or *EEA MCR*, as appropriate, and the reference to the *base capital resources requirement* is replaced by the amount which is one half of the *base capital resources requirement* applicable to the *firm* set out inGENPRU 2.1.30 R.

(2)
(a) subject to (2)(b), in relation to a *firm* carrying on *long-term insurance business*, the higher of one third of the *long-term insurance capital requirement* and the *base capital resources requirement* applicable to that *firm*;
(b) where the *firm* is required to calculate a *UK MCR* or an *EEA MCR* under INSPRU 1.5, for the purposes of that section in (2)(a) the reference to the *long-term insurance capital requirement* is replaced by *UK MCR* or *EEA MCR*, as appropriate, and the reference to the *base capital resources requirement* is replaced by the amount which is one half of the *base capital resources requirement* applicable to the *firm* set out in GENPRU 2.1.30 R.

guaranteed annuity rate

an arrangement in a pension scheme to provide benefits whereby, in defined circumstances and irrespective of the prevailing market rate for annuities when those benefits come into payment, a member is entitled to:

(a) an annuity at a minimum specified rate; or

(b) benefits equivalent to that annuity at that minimum specified rate.

guarantor

(in *PR*) a *person* that provides a *guarantee*.

guidance

guidance given:

(a) in the *FCA Handbook*, by the *FCA* under the *Act*; or

(b) in the *PRA Handbook*, by the *PRA*.

habitual residence

(a) if the *policyholder* is an individual, the address given by the *policyholder* as his residence if it reasonably appears to be a residential address and there is no evidence to the contrary;

(b) if the *policyholder* is not an individual or a *group* of individuals, the State in which the *policyholder* has its place of establishment, or, if it has more than one, its relevant place of establishment;

(c) in respect of the variation of a *life policy*, or the purchase of a *pension annuity* related to a *life policy*, unless there is evidence to the contrary, the habitual residence of the *policyholder* at the date on which the *policyholder* signed the proposal for the *life policy*.

half-yearly accounting period

(in *COLL*) a period determined in accordance with COLL 6.8.2 R (2) (Accounting periods).

Handbook

the *FCA Handbook* or the *PRA Handbook* as appropriate.

headline information

the headline codes and headline categories for use with the announcement of *regulated information* that are listed in DTR 8 Annex 2.

hedging set

(in accordance with Part 1 of Annex III of the *Banking Consolidation Directive* (Definitions) and for the purpose of BIPRU 13 (The calculation of counterparty risk exposure values for financial derivatives, securities financing transactions and long settlement transactions)) a group of *risk positions* from the transactions within a single *netting set* for which only their balance is relevant for determining the *exposure* value under the *CCR standardised method*.

higher lending charge

a fee charged by a *mortgage lender* (under a *regulated mortgage contract*) where the amount borrowed exceeds a given percentage of the value of the property.

higher rate of return

(in *COBS*) the higher rate of return described in paragraph 2.3 of the projection *rules* (COBS 13 Annex 2).

higher stage of capital

(with respect to a particular item of capital in the capital resources table) a stage in the *capital resources table* above that in which that item of capital appears.

higher volatility fund

(a) a *regulated collective investment scheme* which is:
(i) a *scheme* where the investment policies which the *operator* adopts, or proposes to adopt, mean that, as a result of making investments in *warrants* or *derivatives*, or through borrowing that is not temporary in nature, movements in the *price* of *units* are likely to be significantly amplified; or
(ii) an *umbrella* with a *sub-fund* that would fall within (i) if that sub-fund were a separate *scheme*; or

(b) an *authorised fund dedicated* to *units* in:
(i) a number of *regulated collective investment schemes*; or
(ii) *sub-funds* of one or more *umbrellas* that are *regulated collective investment schemes*;
any one of which falls within (a).

high-cost short-term credit

a *regulated credit agreement*:

(a) which is a *borrower-lender agreement* or a *P2P agreement*;

(b) in relation to which the *APR* is equal to or exceeds 100%;

(c) either:
(i) in relation to which a *financial promotion* indicates (by express words or otherwise) that the *credit* is to be provided for any period up to a maximum of 12 months or otherwise indicates (by express words or otherwise) that the *credit* is to be provided for a short term; or
(ii) under which the *credit* is due to be repaid or substantially repaid within a maximum of 12 months of the date on which the *credit* is advanced;

(d) which is not secured by a mortgage, charge or pledge; and

(e) which is not:
(i) a *credit agreement* in relation to which the lender is a *community finance organisation*; or
(ii) a *home credit loan agreement*, a *bill of sale loan agreement* or a *borrower-lender agreement* enabling a *borrower* to overdraw on a current account or arising where the holder of a current account overdraws on the account without a pre-arranged overdraft or exceeds a pre-arranged overdraft limit.

high earner

(in *SYSC* and *SUP*) an *employee* whose total annual *remuneration* is EUR 1 million or more per year or its equivalent in another currency determined by reference to the conversion rate applicable to the corresponding High Earners Report under SUP 16.

high net worth illustration

an *illustration* for a *regulated mortgage contract* to a *high net worth mortgage customer*.

high net worth mortgage customer

a *customer* with an annual net income of no less than £300,000 or net assets of no less than £3,000,000, or whose obligations are guaranteed by a person with an income or assets of such amount.

high net worth offer document

an *offer document* for a *regulated mortgage contract* to a *high net worth mortgage customer*.

hire-purchase agreement

in accordance with article 60L of the *Regulated Activities Order*, an agreement:

(a) which is not a *conditional sale agreement*;

(b) under which *goods* are bailed or, in Scotland, hired to a *person* ("P") in return for periodical payments by P; and

(c) the property in the *goods* will pass to P if the terms of the agreement are complied with and one or more of the following occurs:
(i) the exercise by P of an option to purchase the *goods*;
(ii) the doing by any party to the agreement of any other act specified in the agreement; or
(iii) the happening of any event specified in the agreement

hirer

a *person* to whom *goods* are bailed or, in Scotland, hired under a *consumer hire agreement*, or a *person* to whom the rights and duties of a *hirer* under a *consumer hire agreement* have passed by assignment or operation of law.

historic price

a *price* calculated by reference to the *valuation point* immediately preceding the *authorised fund manager's* agreement to *sell* or, as the case may be, to redeem the *units* in question.

holder

(a) (in relation to a *unit* in an *authorised fund*):
(i) the *shareholder*; or
(ii) the *unitholder*;

(b) (in relation to a *unit* in any other *collective investment scheme*):
(i) the *person* who is entered in the *register* of the *scheme* as the *holder* of that *unit*; or
(ii) the bearer of a *bearer certificate* representing that *unit*.

HMRC allocated CTF

a CTF opened in accordance with regulation 6 of the *CTF Regulations*.

holding company

(as defined in section 1159(1) of the Companies Act 2006 (Meaning of "subsidiary" etc) (in relation to another *body corporate* ("S")) a *body corporate* which:

(a) holds a majority of the voting rights in S; or

(b) is a member of S and has the right to appoint or remove a majority of its board of directors; or

(c) is a member of S and controls alone, under an agreement with other shareholders and members, a majority of the voting rights in S.

Holloway policy special application conditions

conditions that will be met by a *firm* where:

(a) in the case of a *firm* which underwrites *Holloway sickness policies*:
(i) all of the *Holloway sickness policies* of a particular type underwritten by the *firm* show a projected maturity value of not more than 20% of accumulated *premiums* at the mid-rate projection in the *key*

features illustrations prepared for the purposes of COBS 13.1.1 R (2); except that no more than 5% of the relevant *Holloway sickness policies* underwritten by the *firm* may show a projected maturity value of between 20% and 25% of accumulated *premiums* at the mid-rate projection in the *key features illustrations* prepared for the purposes of COBS 13.1.1 R (2);

(ii) the *firm* conducts a regular assessment to determine whether the relevant *Holloway sickness policies* meet the conditions in (i) and, if such an assessment indicates that the conditions in (i) may no longer be met, takes any steps necessary to ensure that the relevant *Holloway sickness policies* will meet the conditions in (i) within three months of the relevant assessment having been carried out; and

(iii) the assessment in (ii) is carried out at least annually and on a more frequent basis if a change is made to the projection rates or pricing of the relevant *Holloway sickness policies*;

(b) in the case of an intermediary who makes a *personal recommendation* to a *retail client* in relation to a *Holloway sickness policy*, the intermediary has received a written notification from the *firm* which underwrites the policy confirming that the conditions in (a) have been met.

Holloway sickness policy

a*long-term insurance contract* offered or effected by a *friendly society* under the Holloway system, providing *permanent health* benefits and, in addition, investment benefits, where the investment benefits:

(a) are derived from surpluses accrued by the *friendly society* and apportioned to *policyholders*; and

(b) are payable to *policyholders* at maturity, on retirement, on death, or as otherwise specified by contractual provisions or individual society rules.

home credit loan agreement

a *regulated credit agreement* which is a *borrower-lender agreement* and which either:

(a) provides that all or most of the sums payable by the *customer* are to be collected by, or on behalf of, the *lender* at the *customer's* home or at the home of a natural person who makes payment to the *lender* on the *customer's* behalf (or, in either case, to be so collected if the *customer* so wishes); or

(b) at the time the agreement is entered into, the *customer* could reasonably expect, from representations made by, or on behalf of, the *lender* at or before that time, that all or most of the sums payable would be so collected (or, in either case, would be collected as specified in (a) if the *customer* so wished).

home finance activity

any *home finance mediation activity*, *home finance providing activity* or *administering a home finance transaction*.

home finance administration

any of the *regulated activities* of:

(a) *administering a regulated mortgage contract*;

(b) *administering a home purchase plan*;

(c) *administering a home reversion plan*;

(cc) *administering a regulated sale and rent back agreement*; or

(d) *agreeing to carry on a regulated activity* in (a) to (cc).

home finance administrator

a *firm* with *permission* (or which ought to have *permission*) for *administering a home finance transaction*.

home finance adviser

a *firm* with *permission* (or which ought to have *permission*) for *advising on a home finance transaction*.

home finance arranger

a *firm* with *permission* (or which ought to have *permission*) for *arranging a home finance transaction*.

home finance intermediary

a *firm* with *permission* (or which ought to have *permission*) to carry on a *home finance mediation activity*.

home finance mediation activity

any *mortgage mediation activity*, *home purchase mediation activity*, *reversion mediation activity* or *regulated sale and rent back mediation activity*.

home finance provider

a *firm* with *permission* (or which ought to have *permission*) for *entering into a home finance transaction*.

home finance providing activity

any of the *regulated activities* of:

(a) *entering into a regulated mortgage contract*;

(aa) *entering into a regulated sale and rent back agreement*;

(b) *entering into a home purchase plan*;

(c) *entering into a home reversion plan*; or

(d) *agreeing to carry on a regulated activity* in (a) to (c).

home finance transaction

a *regulated mortgage contract*, *home purchase plan*, *home reversion plan* or *regulated sale and rent back agreement*.

Home Member State

(in *DTR*; *PR* and *LR*) *Home State*.

home financing

any *home finance providing activity*.

home purchase activity

any of the *regulated activities* of:

(a) *arranging (bringing about) a home purchase plan* (article 25C(1));

(b) *making arrangements with a view to a home purchase plan* (article 25C(2));

(c) *advising on a home purchase plan* (article 53C);

(d) *entering into a home purchase plan* (article 63F(1));

(e) *administering a home purchase plan* (article 63F(2)); or

(f) *agreeing to carry on a regulated activity* in (a) to (e) (article 64).

home purchase administrator

a *firm* with *permission* (or which ought to have *permission*) for *administering a home purchase plan*.

home purchase adviser

a *firm* with *permission* (or which ought to have *permission*) for *advising on a home purchase plan*.

home purchase arranger

a *firm* with *permission* (or which ought to have *permission*) for *arranging a home purchase plan*.

home purchase intermediary

a *firm* with *permission* (or which ought to have *permission*) to carry on a *home purchase mediation activity*.

home purchase mediation activity

any of the following *regulated activities*:

(a) *arranging (bringing about) a home purchase plan* (article 25C(1));

(b) *making arrangements with a view to a home purchase plan* (article 25C(2));

(c) *advising on a home purchase plan* (article 53C); or

(d) *agreeing to carry on a regulated activity* in (a) to (c) (article 64).

home purchase plan

(in accordance with article 63F(3) of the *Regulated Activities Order*) an arrangement comprised in one or more instruments or agreements which meets the following conditions at the time it is entered into:

(a) the arrangement is one under which a *person* (the 'home purchase provider') buys a *qualifying interest in land* or an undivided share of a *qualifying interest in land*;

(b) where an undivided share of a *qualifying interest in land* is bought, the interest is held on trust for the home purchase provider and the individual or trustees in (c) as beneficial tenants in common;

(c) the arrangement provides for the obligation of an individual or trustees (the *home purchaser*) to buy the interest bought by the home purchase provider during the course of or at the end of a specified period; and

(d) the *home purchaser* (if he is an individual) or an individual who is a beneficiary of the trust (if the *home purchaser* is a trustee), or a related person, is entitled under the arrangement to occupy at least 40% of the land in question as or in connection with a dwelling during that period and intends to do so;

in this definition "related person" means:

(A) that *person's* spouse or civil partner;

(B) a *person* (whether or not of the opposite sex) whose relationship with that *person* has the characteristics of the relationship between husband and wife; or

(C) that *person's* parent, brother, sister, child, grandparent or grandchild.

home purchase provider

a *firm* with *permission* (or which ought to have *permission*) for *entering into a home purchase plan*.

home purchaser

the individual (or trustees), specified in article 63F(3) of the *Regulated Activities Order*, who in summary:

(a) is (or are) obliged under a *home purchase plan* to buy the interest in land bought by the home purchase provider (as defined in article 63F(3) of the *Regulated Activities Order*) over the course of or at the end of a specified period; and

(b)
(i) in the case of an individual, is entitled under the arrangement to occupy at least 40% of the land in question as or in connection with a dwelling and intends to do so; or
(ii) in the case of trustees, are trustees of a trust a beneficiary of which is an individual described in (i).

home reversion plan

(in accordance with article 63B(3) of the *Regulated Activities Order*) an arrangement comprised in one or more instruments or agreements which meets the following conditions at the time it is entered into:

(a) the arrangement is one under which a *person* (the *reversion provider*) buys all or part of a *qualifying interest in land* from an individual or trustees (the *reversion occupier*);

(b) the *reversion occupier* (if he is an individual) or an individual who is a beneficiary of the trust (if the *reversion occupier* is a trustee), or a related person, is entitled under the arrangement to occupy at least 40% of the land in question as or in connection with a dwelling and intends to do so; and

(c) the arrangement specifies that the entitlement to occupy will end on the occurrence of one or more of:
(i) a *person* in (b) becoming a resident of a care home;
(ii) a *person* in (b) dying; or
(iii) the end of a specified period of at least twenty years from the date the *reversion occupier* entered into the arrangement;

in this definition "related person" means:

(A) that *person's* spouse or civil partner;

(B) a *person* (whether or not of the opposite sex) whose relationship with that *person* has the characteristics of the relationship between husband and wife; or

(C) that *person's* parent, brother, sister, child, grandparent or grandchild.

Home State

(A) In the PRA Handbook:

(1) (in relation to a *credit institution*) the *EEA State* in which the *credit institution* has been authorised in accordance with the *CRD*.

(2) (in relation to an *investment firm*):

(a) if the *investment firm* is a natural *person*, the *EEA State* in which his head office is situated;

(b) if the *investment firm* is a legal *person*, the *EEA State* in which its registered office is situated; or

(c) if the *investment firm* has, under its national law, no registered office, the *EEA State* in which its head office is situated.

[Note: article 4(1)(20) of *MiFID*]

(3) (in relation to a *UCITS management company*) the *EEA State* in which the management company's registered office is situated;

(4) (in relation to an insurance undertaking with an *EEA right*) the *EEA State* in which the registered office of the insurance undertaking is situated.

(5) (in relation to an *IMD insurance intermediary* or an *IMD reinsurance intermediary*):

(a) where the *insurance intermediary* is a natural person, the *EEA State* in which his residence is situated and in which he carries on business;

(b) where the *insurance intermediary* is a legal person, the *EEA State* in which its registered office is situated or, if under its national law it has no registered office, the *EEA State* in which its head office is situated.

(6) (except in *REC*) (in relation to a market) the *EEA State* in which the registered office of the body which provides training facilities is situated or, if under its national law it has no registered office, the *EEA State* in which that body's head office is situated.

(7) (in relation to a *Treaty firm*) the *EEA State* in which its head office is situated, in accordance with paragraph 1 of Schedule 4 to the *Act* (Treaty Rights).

(8) (in *LR* and *PR*) (as defined in section 102C of the Act) in relation to an issuer of *transferable securities*, the *EEA State* which is the "home Member State" for the purposes of the *prospectus directive* (which is to be determined in accordance with Article 2.1(m) of that directive).

(9) (in *DTR*)

(a) in the case of an *issuer* of debt *securities* the denomination per unit of which is less than EUR 1 000 or an *issuer* of *shares*:

(i) where the *issuer* is incorporated in the *EEA*, the *EEA State* in which it has its registered office;

(ii) where the *issuer* is incorporated in a third country, the *EEA State* referred to in point (iii) of article 2(1)(m) of Directive 2003/71/EC.

The definition of *Home State* shall be applicable to debt securities in a currency other than Euro, provided that the value of such denomination per unit is, at the date of the issue, less than EUR 1 000, unless it is nearly equivalent to EUR 1 000;

(b) for an *issuer* not covered by (a), the *EEA State* chosen by the *issuer* from among the EEA States in which the *issuer* has its registered office and those EEA States which have admitted its securities to trading on a *regulated market* on their territory. The issuer may choose only one *EEA State* as its Home Member State. Its choice shall remain valid for at least three years unless its securities are no longer admitted to trading on any *regulated market* in the *EEA*;

(10) (in relation to a *UCITS*) the *EEA State* in which the unit trust, common fund or investment company is established and authorised under article 5 of the *UCITS Directive*.

(11) (in *REC*) in relation to an EEA market operator, the *EEA State* in which it has its registered office, or if it has no registered office, its head office.

(12) (in relation to a *person* who has received authorisation under article 18 of the *auction regulation*) the *EEA state* in which the person is established and authorised under the *auction regulation*.

(13) (for an *AIF*) the *EEA State* in which:

(a) the *AIF* is authorised or registered under applicable national law; or

(b) if the *AIF* is neither authorised nor registered in an *EEA State*, the *EEA State* in which the *AIF* has its registered office and/or head office.

[Note: article 4(1)(p) of *AIFMD*]

(14) (for an *AIFM*) the *EEA State* in which the *AIFM* has its registered office. [Note: article 4(1)(q) of *AIFMD*]

(B) In the FCA Handbook:

(1) (in relation to a *credit institution*) the *EEA State* in which the *credit institution* has been authorised in accordance with the *CRD*.

(2) (in relation to an *investment firm*):

(a) if the *investment firm* is a natural *person*, the *EEA State* in which his head office is situated;

(b) if the *investment firm* is a legal *person*, the *EEA State* in which its registered office is situated; or

(c) if the *investment firm* has, under its national law, no registered office, the *EEA State* in which its head office is situated.

[Note: article 4(1)(20) of *MiFID*]

(3) (in relation to a *UCITS management company*) the *EEA State* in which the management

company's registered office is situated;

(4) (in relation to an insurance undertaking with an *EEA right*) the *EEA State* in which the registered office of the insurance undertaking is situated.

(5) (in relation to an *IMD insurance intermediary* or an *IMD reinsurance intermediary*):

(a) where the *insurance intermediary* is a natural person, the *EEA State* in which his residence is situated and in which he carries on business;

(b) where the *insurance intermediary* is a legal person, the *EEA State* in which its registered office is situated or, if under its national law it has no registered office, the *EEA State* in which its head office is situated.

(6) (except in *REC*) (in relation to a market) the *EEA State* in which the registered office of the body which provides training facilities is situated or, if under its national law it has no registered office, the *EEA State* in which that body's head office is situated.

(7) (in relation to a *Treaty firm*) the *EEA State* in which its head office is situated, in accordance with paragraph 1 of Schedule 4 to the *Act* (Treaty Rights).

(8) (in *LR* and *PR*) (as defined in section 102C of the Act) in relation to an issuer of *transferable securities*, the *EEA State* which is the "home Member State" for the purposes of the *prospectus directive* (which is to be determined in accordance with Article 2.1(m) of that directive).

(9) (in *DTR*)

(a) in the case of an *issuer* of debt *securities* the denomination per unit of which is less than EUR 1 000 or an *issuer* of *shares*:

(i) where the *issuer* is incorporated in the *EEA*, the *EEA State* in which it has its registered office;

(ii) where the *issuer* is incorporated in a third country, the *EEA State* referred to in point (iii) of article 2(1)(m) of Directive 2003/71/EC.

The definition of *Home State* shall be applicable to debt securities in a currency other than Euro, provided that the value of such denomination per unit is, at the date of the issue, less than EUR 1 000, unless it is nearly equivalent to EUR 1 000;

(b) for an *issuer* not covered by (a), the *EEA State* chosen by the *issuer* from among the EEA States in which the *issuer* has its registered office and those EEA States which have admitted its securities to trading on a *regulated market* on their territory. The issuer may choose only one *EEA State* as its Home Member State. Its choice shall remain valid for at least three years unless its securities are no longer admitted to trading on any *regulated market* in the *EEA*;

(10) (in relation to a *UCITS*) the *EEA State* in which the unit trust, common fund or investment company is established and authorised under article 5 of the *UCITS Directive*.

(11) (in *REC*) in relation to an EEA market operator, the *EEA State* in which it has its registered office, or if it has no registered office, its head office.

(12) (in relation to a person who has received authorisation under article 18 of the *auction regulation*) the *EEA state* in which the person is established and authorised under the *auction regulation*.

(13) (for an *AIF*) the *EEA State* in which:

(a) the *AIF* is authorised or registered under applicable national law; or

(b) if the *AIF* is neither authorised nor registered in an *EEA State*, the *EEA State* in which the *AIF* has its registered office and/or head office.

[Note: article 4(1)(p) of *AIFMD*]

(14) (for an *AIFM*) the *EEA State* in which the *AIFM* has its registered office. [Note: article 4(1)(q) of *AIFMD*]

Home State authorisation

(as defined in paragraph 3(1)(a) of Schedule 4 to the *Act* (Treaty Rights)) authorisation of a *firm* under the law of its *Home State* to carry on a *regulated activity*.

Home State regulator

(1) (in relation to an *EEA firm*) (as defined in paragraph 9 of Schedule 3 to the *Act* (EEA Passport Rights)) the *competent authority* (under the relevant *Single Market Directive* or the *auction regulation*) of an *EEA State* (other than the *United Kingdom*) in relation to the *EEA firm* concerned.

(2) (in relation to a *UK firm* or *UCITS scheme*) the *FCA* or *PRA* as the case may be.

(3) (in relation to a *Treaty firm*) (as defined in paragraph 1 of Schedule 4 to the *Act* (Treaty Rights)) the competent authority of the *firm's Home State* for the purpose of its *Home State authorisation*.

(4) (in *REC*) the competent authority (within the meaning of Article (4)(1)(22) of *MiFID*) of the *EEA State* which is the *Home State* in relation to the *EEA market operator* concerned.

(5) (in relation to an *EEA UCITS scheme*) the *competent authority* of the *EEA State* in which the *scheme* is authorised.

home territory

(in relation to an *overseas investment exchange*) the country or territory in which its head office is situated.

Host Member State

(in *PR* and *LR*) *Host State*.

Host State

(1) (in *LR* and *PR*) as defined in Article 2.1(n) of the *Prospectus Directive*) the *EEA State* where an offer to the public is made or *admission to trading* is sought, when different from the *Home State*.

(2) (except in *LR* and *PR* and except in relation to *MiFID*) the *EEA State* in which an *EEA firm*, a *UK firm*, or a *Treaty firm* is exercising an *EEA right* or *Treaty right* to establish a *branch* or provide *cross border services*.

(3) (in relation to *MiFID*) the *EEA State*, other than the *Home State*, in which an *investment firm* has a branch or performs *investment services and/or activities* or the *EEA State* in which a *regulated market* provides appropriate arrangements so as to facilitate access to trading on its system by remote members or participants established in that same *EEA State*.

(4) (in relation to the *UCITS Directive*) the *EEA State*, other than the *UCITS Home State*, in which *units* of a *UCITS* are marketed in accordance with a notification made under article 93 of that directive.

(5) (for an *AIFM*) means:
(a) an *EEA state*, other than the *Home State*, in which an *EEA AIFM* or *UK AIFM* manages *EEA AIFs* or *UK AIFs*; or
(b) an *EEA state*, other than the *Home State*, in which an *EEA AIFM* or *UK AIFM* markets *units* or *shares* of an *EEA AIF* or *UK AIF*;
[Note: article 4(1)(r) of *AIFMD*]

[Note: article 4(1)(21) of MiFID]

Host State regulator

(1) (in relation to an *EEA firm* or a *Treaty firm* exercising an *EEA right* or *Treaty right* in the *United Kingdom*) the *FCA* or *PRA* as the case may be.

(2) (in relation to a *UK firm*) (as defined in paragraph 11 of Schedule 3 to the *Act* (EEA Passport Rights)) the *competent authority* (under the relevant *Single Market Directive* or the *auction regulation*) of an *EEA State* (other than the *United Kingdom*) in relation to a *UK firm's* exercise of *EEA rights* there.

(3) (in *REC* in relation to a *UK RIE*) the competent authority (within the meaning of Article (4)(1)(22) of MiFID) of the *EEA State* in which the *UK RIE* intends to make, or has made, arrangements to facilitate access to, or use of, a *regulated market* or a *multilateral trading facility* operated by the *UK RIE*.

(4) (in relation to an *EEA UCITS scheme* which is a *recognised scheme*) the *FCA*.

(5) (in relation to a *UCITS* that is the subject of a notification in accordance with article 93 of the *UCITS Directive*) the *competent authority* of an *EEA State* (other than the *United Kingdom*) in which *units* of the *UCITS* may be marketed to the public.

hybrid capital

an item of capital that is stated in GENPRU 2.2 as eligible for inclusion at stage B1, B2 or C of the calculation in the *capital resources table*.

hypothetical profit and loss figure

(in BIPRU 7.10 (Use of a value at risk model) and in relation to a *business day*) the *profit and loss figure* that would have occurred for that *business day* if the portfolio on which the *VaR number* for that *business day* is based remained unchanged, as more fully defined in BIPRU 7.10.111 R (Back-testing: Hypothetical profit and loss).

IAS

(in *LR*) *International Accounting Standards*.

IBNR

(in relation to *claims* (as defined for the purposes of *INSPRU*, *SUP* and *TC*)) *claims* that have been incurred but not reported arising out of events that have occurred by the balance sheet date but have not been reported to the *insurance undertaking* at that date.

ICA

individual capital assessment.

ICAAP

the *internal capital adequacy assessment process.*

ICAAP rules

(A) In the PRA Handbook:
the *rules* in GENPRU 1.2.30 R to GENPRU 1.2.39 R (Systems, strategies, processes and reviews), GENPRU 1.2.42 R (Main Requirements: Stress and scenario tests) and GENPRU 1.2.60 R to GENPRU 1.2.61 R (Documentation of risk assessments) as they apply on a solo level and on a consolidated level.

(B) In the FCA Handbook:
(1) (in *GENPRU*) the *rules* in GENPRU 1.2.30 R to GENPRU 1.2.39 R (Systems, strategies, processes and reviews), GENPRU 1.2.42 R (Main Requirements: Stress and scenario tests) and GENPRU 1.2.60 R to GENPRU 1.2.61 R (Documentation of risk assessments) as they apply on a solo level and on a consolidated level.
(2) (for the purpose of *IFPRU*) the *rules* in IFPRU 2.2.2R to IFPRU 2.2.7R (Strategies, processes and systems) to IFPRU 2.2.16R, IFPRU 2.2.37G (Stress and scenario tests) in relation to a *significant IFPRU firm* and IFPRU 2.2.43R to IFPRU 2.2.44R (Documentation of risk assessments) as they apply on a individual basis and on a *consolidated basis.*

ICD claim

a *claim*:

(a) against a *MiFID investment firm* (including a *credit institution* which is a *MiFID investment firm*), whether established in the *United Kingdom* or in another *EEA State*; and

(b) in relation to:
(i) any *investment services and activities* other than the making of a *personal recommendation*;
(ii) the *ancillary service* of safekeeping and administration of *financial instruments* for the account of *clients*, including custodianship and related services such as cash/collateral management;
(iii) the firm's inability to repay money owed to or belonging to investors and held on their behalf or the firm's inability to return to investors any instruments belonging to them and held, administered or managed on their behalf, in each case, in connection with the *investment service* of the making of a *personal recommendation* relating to a *financial instrument* in accordance with the legal and contractual conditions applicable.

[Note: Article 2(2) of the *Investor Compensation Directive*]

ICG

individual capital guidance.

ICVC

investment company with variable capital.

ICOBS

the Insurance: New Conduct of Business sourcebook.

IFA pensions review claim

a claim arising from the sale of a personal pension scheme by a former member of *PIA* which was an independent financial adviser; in this definition:

(a) a "personal pension scheme" includes:
(i) a personal pension scheme that was approved under Chapter IV Part XIV of ICTA 88 (when that chapter was in force);
(ii) a 'section 32' buy-out policy that was approved under Section 32 of the Finance Act 1981 (when that Act was in force); and
(iii) in relation to opt-outs and non-joiners, a retirement annuity contract that was approved under Chapter III Part XIV of ICTA 88 (when sections 618 to 628 of that Chapter were in force); and

(b) "ICTA 88" means the Income and Corporation Taxes Act 1988.

IFPRU

the Prudential sourcebook for Investment Firms

IFPRU 125K firm

has the meaning in IFPRU 1.1.9 R (Types of investment firm: IFPRU 125K firm), which in summary is an *IFPRU investment firm* that satisfies the following conditions:

(a) it does not *deal on own account* or underwrite issues of *financial instruments* on a firm commitment basis;

(b) it holds clients' money or securities in relation to *investment services* it provides or is authorised to do so;

(c) it offers one or more of certain specified services;

(d) it is not a *collective portfolio management investment firm*; and

(e) it does not operate a *multilateral trading facility*.

IFPRU 50K firm

has the meaning in IFPRU 1.1.10 R (Types of investment firm: IFPRU 50K firm) which in summary is an *IFPRU investment firm* that satisfies the following conditions:

(a) it satisfies the conditions in IFPRU 1.1.9 R (1) (does not deal on own account or underwrite issues of *financial instruments* on a firm commitment basis) and IFPRU 1.1.9 R (3) (offers one or more of certain specified services);

(b) it does not hold clients' money or securities in relation to *investment services* it provides and it is not authorised to do so;

(c) it is not a *collective portfolio management investment firm*; and

(d) it does not operate a *multilateral trading facility*.

IFPRU 730K firm

has the meaning in IFPRU 1.1.11 R (Types of investment firm: IFPRU 730K firm) which in summary is an *IFPRU investment firm* that is not a *collective portfolio management investment firm*, a *BIPRU 50K firm* or a *BIPRU 125K firm*.

IFPRU investment firm

(A) (In the PRA Handbook): an *investment firm*, as defined in article 4(1)(2) of the *EU CRR* (including a *collective portfolio management investment firm*), that satisfies the following conditions:

(a) it is a *FCA*-authorised *firm*;

(b) its head office is in the *UK* and

(c) it is not:
(i) an *incoming EEA firm*;
(ii) an *incoming Treaty firm*;
(iii) any other *overseas firm*;
(iv) a *designated investment firm*;
(v) an *insurer*; or
(vi) an *ICVC*.

(B) (In the FCA Handbook): an *investment firm*, as defined in article 4(1)(2) of the *EU CRR* (including a *collective portfolio management investment firm*), that satisfies the following conditions:

(a) it is a *firm*;

(b) its head office is in the *UK* and it is not otherwise excluded under IFPRU 1.1.5 R; and

(c) it is not a *designated investment firm*;

that is not excluded under IFPRU 1.1.5 R (Exclusion of certain types of firms).

IFPRU limited-activity firm

(A) (In the the PRA Handbook): a *limited activity firm* that meets the following conditions:

(a) it is a *FCA*-authorised *firm*;

(b) its head office is in the *UK* and

(c) it is not:
(i) an *incoming EEA firm*;
(ii) an *incoming Treaty firm*;
(iii) any other *overseas firm*;
(iv) a *designated investment firm*;
(v) an *insurer*; or

(B) (In the FCA Handbook): a *limited activity firm* that meets the following conditions:

(a) it is a *firm*; and

(b) its head office is in the *UK* and it is not otherwise excluded under IFPRU 1.1.5 R.

IFPRU limited-licence firm

(A) (In the PRA Handbook): a *limited activity firm* that meets the following conditions:

(a) it is a *FCA*-authorised *firm*;

(b) its head office is in the *UK* and

(c) it is not:
(i) an *incoming EEA firm*;
(ii) an *incoming Treaty firm*;
(iii) any other *overseas firm*;
(iv) a *designated investment firm*;
(v) an *insurer*; or
(vi) an incoming *EEA firm*

(B) (In the FCA Handbook): a *limited licence firm* that meets the following conditions:

(a) it is a *firm*; and

(b) its head office is in the *UK* and it is not otherwise excluded under IFPRU 1.1.5 R.

IFRS

International Financial Reporting Standards.

IGC

(in COBS 19.5) an independent governance committee established by a *firm* with terms of reference which satisfy COBS 19.5.5R with the purpose, in summary, to represent the interests of *relevant policyholders* in the *firm's relevant schemes.*

ILAA

Individual Liquidity Adequacy Assessment.

ILAS

Individual Liquidity Adequacy Standards.

ILAS BIPRU firm

(A) In the PRA Handbook:
(a) an *exempt full scope BIPRU investment firm*; or
(b) a *BIPRU limited licence firm*; or
(c) a *BIPRU limited activity firm*; or
(d) an *exempt BIPRU commodities firm*.

(B) In the FCA Handbook: a *firm* falling into BIPRU 12.1.1A R, but excluding a *firm* that is:
(a) an *exempt full scope IFPRU investment firm*; or
(b) an *IFPRU limited-licence firm*; or
(c) an *IPFRU limited-activity firm*; or
(d) an *exempt BIPRU commodities firm*; or
(e) an *exempt IFPRU commodities firm*; or
(f) a *BIPRU firm*.

ILG

the Office of Fair Trading's Irresponsible Lending Guidance.

illiquid asset

has the meaning in GENPRU 2.2.260 R (Deductions from total capital: Illiquid assets).

illustration

(in *MCOB*) the illustration of the costs and features of a *regulated mortgage contract* or *home reversion plan* which is required to be provided by MCOB 5 (Pre-application disclosure), MCOB 6 (Disclosure at the offer stage), MCOB 7 (Disclosure at start of contract and after sale) and MCOB 9 (Equity release: product disclosure) and the template for which is set out:

(a) for a *regulated mortgage contract* other than a *lifetime mortgage*, at MCOB 5 Annex 1;

(b) for a *lifetime mortgage*, at MCOB 9 Annex 1; and

(c) for a *home reversion plan*, at MCOB 9 Annex 2.

ILSA

Individual Liquidity Systems Assessment.

IMA SORP

the Statement of Recommended Practice for financial statements of *authorised funds* issued by the Investment Management Association on 14 May 2014.

image advertising

a communication that consists only of one or more of the following:

(a) the name of the *firm*;

(b) a logo or other image associated with the *firm*;

(c) a contact point; and

(d) a reference to the types of *regulated activities* provided by the *firm*, or to its fees or commissions.

IMD insurance intermediary

(as defined in article 2(5) of the *IMD*) any natural or legal person who, for remuneration, takes up or pursues *insurance mediation*.

IMD insurance undertaking

(as defined in article 2(1) of the *Insurance Mediation Directive*) an undertaking which has received official authorisation in accordance with article 6 of the *Consolidated Life Directive* or article 6 of the *First Non-Life Directive*.

interim permission

in accordance with article 56 of the Financial Services and Markets Act 2000 (Regulated Activities) (Amendment) (No. 2) Order 2013, subject to article 59 of that Order, to be treated as:

(a) in relation to a person who is a *firm* immediately before 1 April 2014, a variation of permission;

(b) in any other case, a *Part 4A permission*.

IMD reinsurance intermediary

(as defined in article 2(6) of the *Insurance Mediation Directive*) any natural or legal person who, for remuneration, takes up or pursues *reinsurance mediation*.

IMD reinsurance undertaking

(as defined in article 2(2) of the *Insurance Mediation Directive*) an undertaking, other than an *IMD insurance undertaking* or a non-member-country *insurance undertaking*, the main business of which consists in accepting risks ceded by an *IMD insurance undertaking*, a non-member country *insurance undertaking* or other *IMD reinsurance undertaking*.

immediate group

(1) (in relation to a person ("A")) (as defined in section 421ZA of the *Act* (Immediate group)):

(a) A;

(b) a *parent undertaking* of A;

(c) a *subsidiary undertaking* of A;

(d) a *subsidiary undertaking* of a *parent undertaking* of A;

(e) a *parent undertaking* of a *subsidiary undertaking* of A.

(2) (in *BIPRU* and in relation to any *person*) has the same meaning as in paragraph (1), with the omission of (1)(e).

Immigration Regulations

the Immigration Act 2014 (Bank Account) Regulations 2014.

implicit items

(in relation to *long-term insurance business*) economic reserves arising in respect of future profits, *zillmerising* or hidden reserves as more fully described in GENPRU 2 Annex 8.

IMRO

the Investment Management Regulatory Organisation Limited.

IMRO scheme

the *former scheme* set up by *IMRO* under the Financial Services Act 1986 and the *Investment Ombudsman* Memorandum to handle complaints against members of *IMRO*.

in default

the status of being in default following a determination made under COMP 6.3.1 R.

in the money

(1) (in *LR*) (in relation to *securitised derivatives*):
(a) where the holder has the right to buy the *underlying instrument* or instruments from the *issuer*, when the *settlement price* is greater than the *exercise price*; or
(b) where the holder has the right to sell the *underlying instrument* or instruments to the *issuer*, when the *exercise price* is greater than the *settlement price*;

(2) (for the purposes of BIPRU 7 (Market risk) and in relation to an *option* or *warrant*) the strike price of that *option* or *warrant* being less than the current market value of the underlying instrument (in the case of a call *option* or *warrant*) or vice versa (for a put *option*).

inception

in relation to *permitted links*, refers to the time when the liability of the *insurer* under a *linked long-term* contract of insurance commenced.

income account

(in *COLL*) an account relating to the *income property* of an *authorised fund*.

income equalisation

(A) In the PRA Handbook: (in relation to a *scheme*) a capital sum which, in accordance with a power contained in the *instrument constituting the scheme*, is included in an allocation of income for a *unit* issued, sold or converted during the accounting period in respect of which that income allocation is made.

(B) In the FCA Handbook: (in relation to a *scheme*) a capital sum which, in accordance with a power contained in the *instrument constituting the fund*, is included in an allocation of income for a *unit* issued, sold or converted during the accounting period in respect of which that income allocation is made.

income property

the amount available for income allocations calculated in accordance with COLL 6.8.3 R (3A) and not including any amount for the time being standing to the credit of the *distribution account*.

income unit

a *unit* in an *AUT* which is not an *accumulation unit*.

income withdrawals

(a) (as defined in paragraph 7 of Schedule 28 to the Finance Act 2004) in relation to a member of a pension scheme, amounts (other than an annuity) which the member is entitled to be paid from the member's drawdown pension fund (as defined in paragraph 8 of that Schedule) in respect of an arrangement; or

(b) payments made under interim arrangements in accordance with section 28A of the Pension Schemes Act 1993;

in respect of an election to make income withdrawals, a reference to a *retail client*, an investor or a *policyholder* includes, after that *person's* death, his surviving spouse, his surviving civil partner or anyone who is, at that time, his dependant, or both.

incoming ECA provider

a *person*, other than an *exempt person*, who:

(a) provides an *electronic commerce activity*, from an *establishment* in an *EEA State* other than the United Kingdom, with or for an *ECA recipient* present in the *United Kingdom*; and

(b) is a national of an *EEA State* or a company or firm mentioned in article 54 of the *Treaty*.

incoming EEA AIFM

an *incoming EEA firm* which is an *AIFM* and exercising its rights under *AIFMD*.

incoming EEA AIFM branch

an *incoming EEA firm* which is an *AIFM* and exercising its right to establish a *branch* under *AIFMD*.

incoming EEA firm

(in accordance with section 193(1)(a) of the *Act* (Interpretation of this Part)) an *EEA firm* which is exercising, or has exercised, its right to carry on a *regulated activity* in the *United Kingdom* in accordance with Schedule 3 to the *Act* (EEA Passport Rights).

incoming electronic commerce activity

(in accordance with regulation 2(1) of the *ECD Regulations*) an activity:

(a) which consists of the provision of an *information society service* from an *establishment* in an *EEA State* other than the *United Kingdom* to a *person* or *persons* in the *United Kingdom*; and

(b) which would, but for article 72A of the *Regulated Activities Order* (Information society services) (and irrespective of the effect of article 72 of that Order (Overseas Persons)), be a *regulated activity*.

incoming firm

(in accordance with section 193(1) of the *Act* (Interpretation of this Part)) an *incoming EEA firm* or an *incoming Treaty firm*.

incoming Treaty firm

(in accordance with section 193(1)(b) of the *Act* (Interpretation of this Part)) a *Treaty firm* which is exercising, or has exercised, its right to carry on a *regulated activity* in the *United Kingdom* in accordance with Schedule 4 to the *Act* (Treaty rights).

incorporated friendly society

a society incorporated under the Friendly Societies Act 1992.

incremental risk charge

(in BIPRU 7.10 (Use of a value at risk model)) has the meaning in BIPRU 7.10.116 R (Capital calculations for VaR models), which is in summary, in relation to a *business day*, the incremental risk charge required under the provisions in BIPRU 7.10 about *specific risk*, in respect of the previous *business day's* close-of-business *positions* with respect to which those provisions apply.

independent advice

a *personal recommendation* to a *retail client* in relation to a *retail investment product* where the *personal recommendation* provided meets the requirements of the *rule* on independent advice (COBS 6.2A.3 R).

independent director

a *director* whom a *new applicant* or *listed company* has determined to be independent under the *UK Corporate Governance Code*.

independent expert

(in SUP 18) the person approved or nominated by the *appropriate regulator* to make the *scheme report* for an *insurance business transfer scheme*.

Independent Investigator

the *former Ombudsman* under the *FSA scheme*.

independent shareholder

any *person* entitled to vote on the election of *directors* of a *listed company* that is not a *controlling shareholder* of the *listed company*.

index-linked assets

in relation to *permitted links*, the assets held by an *insurer* for the purposes of matching *index-linked liabilities*.

index-linked contract

a *linked long-term* contract conferring *index-linked benefits*.

index-linked benefits

benefits:

(a) provided for under a *linked long-term contract of insurance*; and

(b) determined by reference to an index of the value of property of any description (whether specified in the contract or not).

index-linked liabilities

insurance liabilities in respect of *index-linked benefits*.

index-linked security

(in *COLL*) a *debt security* for which the cash flows are determined by reference to an index of consumer prices.

indicative adviser charge

a cash figure which is indicative of the cost to the *pure protection contract insurer* of the services associated with making a *personal recommendation* in relation to a *pure protection contract*.

individual

(a) a natural *person*; or

(b) a *partnership* consisting of two or three *persons* not all of whom are bodies corporate; or

(c) an unincorporated body of *persons* which does not consist entirely of bodies corporate and is not a *partnership*.

individual capital assessment

(in *INSPRU* and COBS 20.2) an assessment by a *firm* of the adequacy of its capital resources undertaken as part of an assessment of the adequacy of the *firm's* overall financial resources carried out in accordance with GENPRU 1.2.

individual capital guidance

guidance given to a *firm* about the amount and quality of capital resources that the *appropriate regulator* thinks the *firm* should hold at all times under the *overall financial adequacy rule* as it applies on a solo level or a consolidated level.

individual capital resources requirement

has the meaning in INSPRU 6.1.34 R.

indirect client

as defined in article (1)(a) of the *EMIR L2 Regulation*.

individual client account

as the context requires, either:

(a) an account maintained by a *firm* at an *authorised central counterparty* for a *client* of the *firm* in respect of which the *authorised central counterparty* has agreed with the *firm* to provide *individual client segregation*; or

(b) an *account* maintained by a *firm* for an *indirect client* at a *clearing member* of an *authorised central counterparty* in respect of which the *clearing member* has agreed with the *firm* to provide segregation arrangements that satisfy the requirements of article 4(2)(b) of the *EMIR L2 Regulation*.

individual client balance

for each *client*, the total amount of all *money* the *firm* holds, has received or is obliged to have received or be holding as *client money* in a *client bank account* for that *client* in respect of *non-margined transactions*, calculated in accordance with CASS 7.16.21 R.

individual client balance method

the method of calculating a *firm's client money requirement* described in CASS 7.16.16R.

individual client segregation

as defined in article 39(3) of *EMIR*.

individual CNCOM

[deleted]

individual counterparty CNCOM

Individual Liquidity Adequacy Assessment

a *standard ILAS BIPRU firm's* assessment of the adequacy of its liquidity resources and systems and controls as required by the *rules* in BIPRU 12.5.

Individual Liquidity Adequacy Standards

the regime of liquidity assessment set out in the *rules* and *guidance* in BIPRU 12.5.

individual liquidity guidance

guidance given to a *firm* about the amount, quality and funding profile of liquidity resources that the *appropriate regulator* has asked the *firm* to maintain.

Individual Liquidity Systems Assessment

a *simplified ILAS BIPRU firm's* assessment of the adequacy of its systems and controls as required by the *rules* in BIPRU 12.6.

individual member

a *member*, or *former member*, who is a natural *person*.

individual pension account

an account for the holding of *IPA eligible investments*, which satisfies the conditions described in regulation 2(2) of the Stamp Duty and Stamp Duty Reserve Tax (Definition of Unit Trust Scheme and Open-ended Investment Company) Regulations 2001 (SI 2001/964).

individual pension contract

a *pension policy* or *pension contract* under which contributions are paid to:

(a) a *personal pension scheme*; or

(b) a retirement benefits scheme for the provision of relevant benefits by means of an annuity contract made with an insurance company of the employee's choice where that contract:
(i) was approved under section 591(2)(g) of the Income and Corporation Taxes Act 1988 (when that section was in force); or
(ii) is a registered pension scheme under Chapter 2 of Part 4 of the Finance Act 2004.

individual savings account

an account which is a scheme of investment satisfying the conditions prescribed in the *ISA Regulations*.

industrial and provident society

a society registered or deemed to be registered under the Industrial and Provident Societies Act 1965 or the Industrial and Provident Societies Act (Northern Ireland) 1969.

industrial assurance policy

a *contract of insurance* on human life, premiums in respect of which are received by means of collectors, but excluding:

(a) a *contract of insurance*, the premiums in respect of which are payable at intervals of two *months* or more;

(b) a *contract of insurance*, effected whether before or after the passing of the Industrial Assurance Act 1923 by a society or company established before the date of the passing of that Act which at that date had no *contracts of insurance* outstanding the premiums on which were payable at intervals of less than one *month* so long as the society or company continues not to effect any such contracts;

(c) a *contract of insurance* effected before the passing of the Industrial Assurance Act 1923, premiums in respect of which are payable at intervals of one *month* or more, and which have up to the passing of that Act been treated as part of the business transacted by a branch other than the industrial branch of the society or company; and

(d) a *contract of insurance* for £25 or more effected after the passing of the Industrial Assurance Act 1923, premiums in respect of which are payable at intervals of one *month* or more, and which are treated as part of the business transacted by a branch other than the industrial branch of the society or company, in cases where the relevant authority certified prior to 1 December 2001 under section 1(2)(d) of that Act that the terms and conditions of the contract is on the whole not less favourable to the assured than those imposed by that Act;

in this definition:

(i) "collector" includes every *person*, however remunerated, who, by himself or by any deputy or substitute, makes house to house visits for the purpose of receiving premiums payable on policies of insurance on human life, or holds any interest in a collecting book, and includes such a deputy or substitute;
(ii) "collecting book" includes any book or document held by a collector in which payments of premiums are recorded.

industry block

(in *FEES*) a grouping of *firms* by common business activity for the purposes of calculating the *general levy*.

information centre

a centre established by an *EEA State* to meet its obligations under article 23 of the *Consolidated Motor Insurance Directive* (Information Centres).

information society service

an information society service, as defined by article 2(a) of the *E-Commerce Directive* and article 1(2) of the Technical Standards and Regulations Directive (98/34/EC), which is in summary any service normally provided for remuneration, at a distance, by means of electronic equipment for the processing (including the digital compression) and storage of data at the individual request of a service recipient.

inherited estate

an amount representing the fair market value of the *with-profits assets* less the *realistic value of liabilities* of a with-profits fund.

initial capital

(A) In the PRA Handbook:

(1) [deleted]

(2) [deleted]

(3) (in *UPRU*) capital calculated in accordance with UPRU Table 2.2.1 R (Method of calculation of financial resources) composed of the specified items set out in that Table.

(3A) (in IPRU(INV) 11) capital calculated in line with IPRU(INV) Table 11.4 (Method of calculating initial capital and own funds) composed of the specified items in that Table.

(4) (in the case of a *BIPRU firm*) *capital resources* included in stage A (Core tier one capital) of the *capital resources table* plus *capital resources* included in stage B of the *capital resources table* (Perpetual non-cumulative preference shares);

(5) (in the case of an *institution* that is an *EEA firm*) capital resources calculated in accordance with the *CRD implementation measures* of its *Home State* for Article 4 of the *Capital Adequacy Directive* (Definition of initial capital) or Article 9 of the *Banking Consolidation Directive* (Initial capital requirements);

(6) (for the purposes of the definition of *dealing on own account* and in the case of an *undertaking* not falling within (3) or (4)) *capital resources* calculated in accordance with (3) and paragraphs (3) and (4) of the definition of *capital resources*

(7) (in *IPRU(INV)* 13) the initial capital of a *firm* calculated in accordance with *IPRU(INV)* 13.1A.6R.

(B) In the FCA Handbook:

(1) [deleted]

(2) [deleted]

(3) [deleted]

(3A) (in IPRU(INV) 11 and in accordance with article 28(1) of the *CRD*) he amount of *own funds* referred to in article 26(1)(a) to (e) of the *EU CRR* and calculated in line with Part Two of those Regulations (Own funds)

(4) (in the case of a *BIPRU firm*) *capital resources* included in stage A (Core tier one capital) of the *capital resources table* plus *capital resources* included in stage B of the *capital resources table* (Perpetual non-cumulative preference shares);

(5) (in the case of an *institution* that is an *EEA firm*) capital resources calculated in accordance with the *CRD implementation measures* of its *Home State* for Article 4 of the *Capital Adequacy Directive* (Definition of initial capital) or Article 9 of the *Banking Consolidation Directive* (Initial capital requirements);

(6) (for the purposes of the definition of *dealing on own account* in *BIPRU* and in the case of an *undertaking* not falling within (3) or (4)) *capital resources* calculated in accordance with (3) and paragraphs (3) and (4) of the definition of *capital resources*

(7) (in *IPRU(INV)* 13) the initial capital of a *firm* calculated in accordance with *IPRU(INV)* 13.1A.6R.

(8) (for an *IFPRU investment firm* and in accordance with article 28(1) of *CRD*) the amount of *own funds* referred to in article 26(1)(a) to (e) of the *EU CRR* and calculated in accordance with Part Two of those Regulations (Own funds).

(9) (for the purpose of the definition of dealing on own account in *IFPRU*) the amount of *own funds* referred to in article 26(1)(a) to (e) of the *EU CRR* and calculated in accordance with Part Two of those Regulations (Own funds).

initial commitment

(for the purposes of *BIPRU* and in relation to *underwriting*) the date specified in BIPRU 7.8.13 R (Time of initial commitment).

initial contact

the first occasion when a *firm* is in contact with the *customer* and may perform any of the following in relation to a *home finance transaction*:

(a) *advising* on the transaction;

(b) *arranging (bringing about)* the transaction; or

(c) *entering into* the transaction, when there is no *firm arranging (bringing about)* the transaction.

initial coupon rate

(in relation to a *tier one instrument*) the *coupon* rate of the instrument at the time it is issued.

initial disclosure document

information about the *scope of advice* and the nature of the services offered by a *firm* in relation to a non-investment insurance contract in accordance with ICOBS 4.5.1 G and set out in ICOBS 4 Annex 1.

initial fund

the items of capital which are available to a *mutual* at *authorisation*.

initial offer

(in *COLL*) an offer for sale of *units* in an *authorised fund* or in a *sub-fund* (otherwise than in accordance with *arrangements* of the type described in COLL 5.5.9 R (3) (b) (iii) (Guarantees and indemnities), where all or part of the consideration paid for the account of the *authorised fund* for the *units* is to be used to acquire the initial *scheme property* of the *authorised fund* or the initial *scheme property* attributable to the *sub-fund*.

initial outlay

(in relation to an *authorised fund*) the amount which the *authorised fund* is required to provide in order to obtain rights under a transaction in *derivatives*, excluding any payment or transfer on exercise of rights.

initial price

(in *COLL*) in relation to a *unit* of any *class*:

(a) in a *single-priced authorised fund*, the *price* to be paid; or

(b) in a *dual-priced authorised fund*, the amount agreed by the *depositary* and *authorised fund manager* as being the maximum *price*, inclusive of any *preliminary charge*, that may be paid to the *authorised fund manager*; during the period of the *initial offer* under COLL 6.2.3 R (Initial offer).

injunction

a court order made by the High Court that prohibits a *person* from doing or continuing to do a certain act or requires a *person* to carry out a certain act.

injured party

(in *ICOBS*) a resident of the *EEA* entitled to compensation in respect of any loss or injury caused by *vehicles*. [Note: article 1(2) of Directive 72/166/EC (First Motor Insurance Directive)]

innovative tier one capital

an item of capital that is stated in GENPRU 2.2(Capital resources) to be innovative tier one capital.

innovative tier one capital resources

the amount of *capital resources* at stage C of the *capital resources table* (Innovation tier one capital).

innovative tier one instrument

a *potential tier one instrument* that is stated in GENPRU 2.2 (Capital resources) to be an innovative instrument.

inside information

(as defined in section 118C of the *Act*):

(a) in relation to *qualifying investments*, or *related investments*, which are not commodity derivatives, *inside information* is information of a precise nature which:
(i) is not generally available,
(ii) relates, directly or indirectly, to one or more issuers of the *qualifying investments* or to one or more of the *qualifying investments*, and
(iii) would, if generally available, be likely to have a significant effect on the price of the *qualifying investments* or on the price of *related investments*.

(b) in relation to *qualifying investments*, or *related investments*, which are commodity derivatives, *inside information* is information of a precise nature which:
(i) is not generally available,
(ii) relates, directly or indirectly, to one or more such derivatives, and
(iii) users of markets in which the derivatives are traded would expect to receive in accordance with *accepted market practices* on those markets.

(c) in relation to a person charged with the execution of orders concerning any *qualifying investments* or *related investments*, *inside information* includes information conveyed by a client and related to the client's pending orders which:
(i) is of a precise nature;
(ii) is not generally available;
(iii) relates, directly or indirectly, to one or more issuers of *qualifying investments* or to one or more *qualifying investments*; and
(iv) would, if generally available, be likely to have a significant effect on the price of those *qualifying investments* or the price of *related investments*;

(d) information is precise if it:
(i) indicates circumstances that exist or may reasonably be expected to come into existence or an event that has occurred or may reasonably be expected to occur; and
(ii) is specific enough to enable a conclusion to be drawn as to the possible effect of those circumstances or that event on the price of *qualifying investments* or *related investments*;

(e) information would be likely to have a significant effect on price if and only if it is information of that kind which a reasonable investor would be likely to use as part of the basis of his investment decisions;

(f) for the purposes of (b)(iii), users of markets on which investments in commodity derivatives are traded are to be treated as expecting to receive information relating directly or indirectly to one or more such derivatives in accordances with any *accepted market practices*, which is:
(i) routinely made available to the users of those markets; or
(ii) required to be disclosed in accordance with any statutory provision, market rules, or contracts or customs on the relevant underlying commodity market or commodity derivatives market;

(g) information which can be obtained by research or analysis conducted by, or on behalf of, users of a market is to be regarded, for the purposes of *market abuse*, as being generally available to them.

insider

(as defined in section 118B of the *Act*) a *person* who has *inside information*:

(a) as a result of his membership of the administrative, management or supervisory bodies of an *issuer* of *qualifying investments*;

(b) as a result of his holding in the capital of an *issuer* of *qualifying investments*;

(c) as a result of having access to the information through the exercise of his employment, profession or duties;

(d) as a result of his criminal activities; or

(e) which he has obtained by other means and which he knows, or could reasonably be expected to know, is *inside information*.

insider dealing

the activity described in section 52 of the Criminal Justice Act 1993, which is in summary:

(a) the offence of which an individual is guilty if he has information as an insider and:
(i) in the circumstances described in (b), he deals in securities that are price-affected securities in relation to the information;
(ii)
(A) he encourages another *person* to deal in securities that are (whether or not that other knows it) price-affected securities in relation to the information, knowing or having reasonable cause to believe that the dealing would take place in the circumstances mentioned in (b); or
(B) he discloses the information, otherwise than in the proper performance of the functions of his employment, office or profession, to another *person*;

(b) the circumstances referred to in (a) are that the acquisition or disposal in question occurs on a regulated market (identified in an Order made by the Treasury), or that the *person* dealing relies on a professional intermediary or is himself acting as a professional intermediary.

insider list

a list, as required by DTR 2.8.1 R, of *persons* with access to *inside information*.

insolvency order

an administration order, compulsory winding up order, bankruptcy order, or sequestration order.

INSPRU

the Prudential sourcebook for Insurers.

instalment reversion plan

a *home reversion plan* under which more than one payment is made to the *customer* during the life of the plan.

institution

(A) In the PRA Handbook:
(1) has the meaning in article 4(1)(3) of the *EU CRR*).
(2) (for the purposes of *GENPRU* and *BIPRU*) includes a *CAD investment firm*.

(B) In the FCA Handbook:
(1) has the meaning in article 4(1)(3) of the *EU CRR*).
(2) (for the purposes of *GENPRU* and *BIPRU*) includes a *CAD investment firm*.

institutional linked policyholders

in relation to *permitted links*, *linked policyholders* who are trustees of a *defined benefit occupational pension scheme*.

instrument constituting the fund

(a) (in relation to an *ICVC*) the *instrument of incorporation*;

(b) (in relation to an *AUT*) the *trust deed*;

(ba) (in relation to an *EEA UCITS scheme*) the fund rules or instrument of incorporation of such a *scheme*;

(bb) (in relation to an *ACS*) the *contractual scheme deed*;

(bc) (for an *AIF* other than an *ICVC*, an *AUT* or an *ACS*) the fund rules, instrument of incorporation or other constituting documents of such an *AIF*;

(c) (in relation to a *collective investment scheme* other than an *AIF* or a *UCITS*) any instrument to which the *operator* is a party setting out any arrangements with any other *person* relating to any aspect of the operation or management of the *scheme*.

instrument of incorporation

the instrument of incorporation of an *ICVC* (as from time to time amended) initially provided to the *FCA* in accordance with regulation 14(1)(c) of the *OEIC regulations*.

insurance accounts rules

Schedule 9A to the Companies Act 1985 (Form and content of accounts of insurance companies) and Schedule 9A to the Companies Act (Northern Ireland) Order 1986 where these provisions are applicable, otherwise Schedule 3 to the Large and Medium-sized Companies and Groups (Accounts and Reports) Regulations 2008 (SI 2008/410).

insurance business

the business of *effecting* or *carrying out contracts of insurance*.

insurance business grouping

a grouping comprising descriptions of *general insurance business* determined in accordance with INSPRU 1.4.12 R.

insurance business transfer

a transfer in accordance with an *insurance business transfer scheme*.

insurance business transfer scheme

(a) a scheme, defined in section 105 of the *Act*, which is in summary: a scheme to transfer the whole or part of the business of an *insurer* (other than a *friendly society*) to another body;

(b) a similar scheme to transfer the whole or part of the business carried on by one or more *members* of the *Society* or *former underwriting members* that meets the conditions of article 4 of the Financial Services and Markets Act 2000 (Control of Transfers of Business Done at Lloyd's) Order 2001 (SI 2001/3626).

insurance client money chapter

CASS 5.

insurance component

a *qualifying investment* prescribed in regulation 9 of the *ISA Regulations*.

insurance conglomerate

a *financial conglomerate* that is identified in paragraph 4.3 of GENPRU 3 Annex 1 (Types of financial conglomerate) as an insurance conglomerate.

insurance death risk capital component

one of the components of the *long-term insurance capital requirement* as set out in IN-SPRU 1.1.81 R to INSPRU 1.1.83 R.

Insurance Directives

the *Consolidated Life Directive* and the *First Non-Life Directive*, *Second Non-Life Directive* and *Third Non-Life Directive*.

insurance expense risk capital component

one of the components of the *long-term insurance capital requirement* as set out in IN-SPRU 1.1.88 R.

insurance group

(1) an *insurance parent undertaking* and its *related undertakings*; or

(2) a *participating insurance undertaking* (not within (1)) and its *related undertakings*.

Insurance Groups Directive

Directive of the European Parliament and of the Council of 27 October 1998 on the supplementary supervision of insurance undertakings in an insurance group (1998/78/EC).

insurance health risk and life protection reinsurance capital component

one of the components of the *long-term insurance capital requirement* as set out in IN-SPRU 1.1.85 R to INSPRU 1.1.86 R.

insurance holding company

(1) a *parent undertaking*, other than an *insurance undertaking*, the main business of which is to acquire and hold participations in *subsidiary undertakings* and which fulfils the following

conditions:

(a) its *subsidiary undertakings* are either exclusively or mainly *insurance undertakings*; and

(b) at least one of those *subsidiary undertakings* is an *insurer* or an *EEA firm* that is a *regulated insurance entity* or a *reinsurance undertaking*; a *parent undertaking*, other than an *insurance undertaking*, that fulfils the conditions in paragraphs (1) (a) and (b) of this definition is not an *insurance holding company* if:

(c) it is a *mixed financial holding company*; and

(d) notice has been given in accordance with Article 4(2) of the *Financial Groups Directive* that the *financial conglomerate* of which it is a *mixed financial holding company* is a *financial conglomerate*.

(2) For the purposes of:

(a) the definition of the *insurance sector*;

(b) [deleted]

(c) the definition of *material insurance holding*; paragraph (1)(b) of this definition does not apply.

Insurance Intermediaries Order

the Financial Services and Markets Act 2000 (Regulated Activities) (Amendment) (No. 2) (Insurance Intermediaries) Order 2003 (SI 2003/1476).

insurance intermediary

a *firm* carrying on *insurance mediation activity* other than an *insurer*.

Insurance market activity

means a *regulated activity* relating to *contracts of insurance* written at Lloyd's.

Insurance market direction

a direction made by the *appropriate regulator* under section 316(1) of the *Act* (Direction by a regulator).

insurance market risk capital component

one of the components of the *long-term insurance capital requirement* as set out in IN-SPRU 1.1.89 R.

insurance mediation

(as defined in article 2(3) of the *IMD*) the activities of introducing, proposing or carrying out other work preparatory to the conclusion of contracts of insurance, or of concluding such contracts, or of assisting in the administration and performance of such contracts, in particular in the event of a claim. These activities when undertaken by an *IMD insurance undertaking* or an employee of an *IMD insurance undertaking* who is acting under the responsibility of the *IMD insurance undertaking* shall not be considered as *insurance mediation*. The provision of information on an incidental basis in the context of another professional activity provided that the purpose of that activity is not to assist the customer in concluding or performing an insurance contract, the management of claims of an *IMD insurance undertaking* on a professional basis, and loss adjusting and expert appraisal of claims shall also not be considered as *insurance mediation*.

insurance mediation activity

any of the following *regulated activities* carried on in relation to a *contract of insurance* or rights to or interests in a life policy:

(a) *dealing in investments as agent* (article 21);

(b) *arranging (bringing about) deals in investments* (article 25(1));

(c) *making arrangements with a view to transactions in investments* (article 25(2));

(d) *assisting in the administration and performance of a contract of insurance* (article 39A);

(e) *advising on investments* (article 53);

(f) *agreeing to carry on a regulated activity* in (a) to (e) (article 64).

Insurance Mediation Directive

the European Parliament and Council Directive of 9 December 2002 on insurance mediation (No 2002/92/EC).

Insurance Ombudsman scheme

the former scheme set up, on a voluntary basis, to handle complaints against those insurance companies which subscribed to it.

insurance parent undertaking

a *parent undertaking* which is:

(a) a *participating insurance undertaking* which has a *subsidiary undertaking* that is an *insurance undertaking*; or

(b) an *insurance holding company* which has a *subsidiary undertaking* which is an *insurer*; or

(c) an *insurance undertaking* (not within (a)) which has a *subsidiary undertaking* which is an *insurer*.

insurance-related capital requirement

a component of the calculation of the *ECR* for a *firm* carrying on *general insurance business* as set out in INSPRU 1.1.76 R to INSPRU 1.1.79 R.

insurance sector

a sector composed of one or more of the following entities:

(a) an *insurance undertaking*;

(b) an *insurance holding company*; and

(c) (in the circumstances described in GENPRU 3.1.39 R (The financial sectors: Asset management companies and alternative investment fund managers)) an *asset management company* or an *alternative investment fund manager*.

insurance special purpose vehicle

an *undertaking*, other than an *insurance undertaking* or *reinsurance undertaking* which has received an official authorisation in accordance with article 6 of the *First Non-Life Directive*, article 4 of the *Consolidated Life Directive* or article 3 of the *Reinsurance Directive*:

(a) which assumes risks from such *insurance undertakings* or *reinsurance undertakings*; and

(b) which fully funds its exposures to such risks through the proceeds of a debt issuance or some other financing mechanism where the repayment rights of the providers of such debt or other financing mechanism are subordinated to the *undertaking's reinsurance* obligations.

insurance undertaking

(1) (except in *COBS*) an undertaking, or (in CASS 5 and *COMP*) a *member*, whether or not an *insurer*, which carries on *insurance business*.

(2) (in *COBS*) an undertaking or a *member* which carries on *insurance business*.

insurer

a *firm* with *permission* to *effect* or *carry out contracts of insurance* (other than a *UK ISPV*).

interest-only mortgage

a *regulated mortgage contract* other than a *repayment mortgage*.

interest rate duration method

the method of calculating the part of the *interest rate PRR* that relates to *general market risk* set out in BIPRU 7.2.63 R (General market risk calculation: Duration method).

interest-rate contract

interest-rate contracts listed in paragraph 1 of Annex II to the *EU CRR*.

interest rate maturity method

the method of calculating the part of the *interest rate PRR* that relates to *general market risk* set out in BIPRU 7.2.59 R (General market risk calculation: The maturity method).

interest rate PRR

the part of the *market risk capital requirement* calculated in accordance with BIPRU 7.2 (Interest rate PRR) or BIPRU 7.3.45 R (Basic interest rate PRR for equity derivatives) or, in relation to a particular *position*, the portion of the overall *interest rate PRR* attributable to that *position*.

interest rate simplified maturity method

the method of calculating the part of the *interest rate PRR* that relates to *general market risk* set out in BIPRU 7.2.56 R (General market risk calculation: Simplified maturity method).

interest roll-up mortgage

an *interest-only mortgage* under which neither capital repayments, nor payment of any of the interest accruing under its terms, are required or anticipated until it comes to an end, whether on expiry of the term (if any), discharge of the mortgage or the happening of some other event.

inter-professional business

(for the purposes only of COBS TP 1 (Transitional Provisions in relation to Client Categorisation)) business which comes within the meaning of 'inter-professional business' as defined in *COB* on 31 October 2007.

inter-professional investment

[deleted]

internal approaches

one or more of the following, as referred to in the *EU CRR*:

(a) the Internal Ratings Based Approach in article 143(1);

(b) the Internal Models Approach in article 221;

(c) the own estimates approach in article 225;

(d) the Advanced Measurement Approaches in article 312(2);

(e) the Internal Model Method and internal models in articles 283 and 363; and

(f) the internal assessment approach in article 259(3).

internal capital adequacy assessment process

a *firm's* assessment of the adequacy of its capital and financial resources, as required by the *ICAAP rules*.

internal client money reconciliation

the *client money* reconciliation described in CASS 7.15.12R.

internal custody reconciliation method

a method for performing an *internal custody record check*, described in CASS 6.6.17 R.

internal custody record check

the *safe custody assets* record check described in CASS 6.6.10G (2) performed using either the *internal custody reconciliation method* or the *internal system evaluation method*.

internal system evaluation method

a method for performing an *internal custody record check*, described in CASS 6.6.19 R.

internally managed AIF

(in accordance with regulation 4(3)(b) of the *AIFMD UK regulation*) an *AIF* where the legal form permits internal management and where the *AIF's* governing body chooses not to appoint an *external AIFM*.

internally managed corporate AIF

a *closed-ended corporate AIF* which is an *internally managed AIF*.

International Financial Reporting Standards

international financial accounting standards within the meaning of EC Regulation No 1606/2002 of the European Parliament and of the Council of 19 July 2002 as adopted from time to time by the European Commission in accordance with that Regulation.

international organisation

(for the purposes of *GENPRU* and *BIPRU*) an organisation referred to in BIPRU 3.4.30 R (Exposures to international organisations).

inter-syndicate reinsurance

reinsurance between one *syndicate year* and another, not being *reinsurance to close*.

interdict

a Scottish court order made by the Court of Session that prohibits a *person* from doing or continuing to do a certain act or requires a *person* to carry out a certain act.

interested party

(in relation to an application made under section 60 of the *Act* (Applications for approval)):

(a) the *firm* making the application;

(b) the *person* in respect of whom the application is being made ("A"); and

(c) the *person* by whom A's services are to be retained, if not the *firm* making the application.

interim accounting period

(in *COLL*) a period within an *annual accounting period* in respect of which an allocation of income is to be made.

interim income allocation date

any date specified in the *prospectus* of an *authorised fund* as the date on or before which an allocation of income will be made.

intermediaries offer

(1) (in *LR*) a marketing of *securities* already or not yet in issue, by means of an offer by, or on behalf of, the *issuer* to intermediaries for them to allocate to their own clients.

(2) (for the purposes of the *Code of Market Conduct* (MAR 1)) a marketing of *securities* not yet in issue, by means of an *offer* by, or on behalf of, the *issuer* to intermediaries for them to allocate to their own clients.

intermediate broker

(in relation to a transaction in a *contingent liability investment*) any *person* acting in the capacity of an intermediary through whom the *firm* undertakes that transaction.

intermediate customer

(for the purposes only of COBS TP 1 (Transitional Provisions in relation to Client Categorisation)) any *person* classified as an 'intermediate customer' under *COB* on 31 October 2007, in accordance with the applicable conditions in force at the time.

intermediate holding vehicle

a *company*, trust or partnership but not a *collective investment scheme*, whose purpose is to enable the holding of overseas immovables on behalf of a *non-UCITS retail scheme* or a *qualified investor scheme*.

intermediate rate of return

(in *COBS*) the intermediate rate of return described in paragraph 2.3 of the *projection rules* (COBS 13 Annex 2).

intermediate unitholder

a *firm* whose name is entered in the *register* of a *non-UCITS retail scheme* or a *UCITS scheme*, or which holds *units* in a *non-UCITS retail scheme* or a *UCITS scheme* indirectly through a third party acting as a nominee, and which is not the beneficial owner of the relevant *unit*, and:

(a) does not *manage investments* on behalf of the relevant beneficial owner of the *unit*; or

(b) does not act as a *depositary* of a *collective investment scheme* or on behalf of such a *depositary* in connection with its role in holding property subject to the *scheme*.

For the purposes of this definition, "register" has the meaning set out in paragraph (3) of the *Glossary* definition of "register".

intermediate unitholder in a qualified investor scheme

a *firm* whose name is entered in the *register* of a *qualified investor scheme*, or which holds *units* in a *qualified investor scheme* indirectly through a third party acting as a nominee, and is not the beneficial owner of the relevant *unit*, and:

(a) does not manage investments on behalf of the relevant beneficial owner of the *unit*; or

(b) does not act as a *depositary* of a *collective investment scheme* or on behalf of such a *depositary* in connection with its role in holding property subject to the *scheme*.

For the purposes of this definition, "register" has the meaning set out in paragraph (3) of the *Glossary* definition of "register".

internal controls

the whole system of controls, financial or otherwise, established by the management of a *firm* in order to:

(a) carry on the business of the *firm* in an orderly and efficient manner;

(b) ensure adherence to management policies;

(c) safeguard the assets of the *firm* and other assets for which the *firm* is responsible; and

(d) secure as far as possible the completeness and accuracy of the *firm's* records (including those necessary to ensure continuous compliance with the requirements or standards under the *regulatory system* relating to the adequacy of the *firm's* financial resources).

international accounting standards

means the international accounting standards, within the meaning of EC Regulation No. 1606/2002 of the European Parliament and of the Council of 19 July 2002 on the application of international accounting standards, adopted from time to time by the European Commission in accordance with that Regulation.

International Securities Identification Number (ISIN)

a 12-character, alphanumeric code which uniquely identifies a *financial instrument* and provides for the uniform identification of *securities* at trading and settlement.

in the money percentage

(for the purposes of BIPRU 7 (Market risk) and in relation to an *option* or *warrant*) the percentage calculated under BIPRU 7.6.6 R (The in the money percentage).

intra-group liquidity modification

a modification to the *overall liquidity adequacy rule* of the kind described in BIPRU 12.8.7G.

intra-group transactions

(in accordance with Article 2(18) of the *Financial Groups Directive* (Definitions)) all transactions by which *regulated entities* within a *financial conglomerate* rely either directly or indirectly upon other *undertakings* within the same *financial conglomerate* or upon any *person* linked to the *undertakings* within that *financial conglomerate* by *close links*, for the fulfilment of an obligation whether or not contractual, and whether or not for payment.

introducer

an individual appointed by a *firm*, an *appointed representative* or, where applicable, a *tied agent*, to carry out in the course of *designated investment business* either or both of the following activities:

(a) effecting introductions;

(b) distributing *non-real time financial promotions*.

introducer appointed representative

an *appointed representative* appointed by a *firm* whose scope of appointment is limited to:

(a) effecting introductions; and

(b) distributing *non-real time financial promotions*.

introducing broker

a *firm* which introduces transactions relating to *designated investments arranged* (brought about) for its *clients* to a *clearing firm*.

investment

(in accordance with sections 22(4) of the *Act* (Regulated activities) and section 93(2) of the Financial Services Act 2012) any investment, including any asset, right or interest.

investment adviser

(in relation to an *authorised fund*) a *person* who is retained by an *ICVC*, its *directors* or its *ACD* or by a *manager* of an *AUT* or by an *authorised contractual scheme manager* of an *ACS* under a commercial arrangement which is not a contract of service:

(a) to supply any of them with advice in relation to the *authorised fund* as to the merits of investment opportunities or information relevant to the making of judgements about the merits of investment opportunities; or

(b) to exercise for any of them any function concerning the management of the *scheme property*.

investment agreement

any agreement the making or performance of which by either party constitutes a *regulated activity*, but disregarding the exclusions in Part II of the *Regulated Activities Order*.

investment business compensation scheme

(as defined in article 2(2) of the *compensation transitionals order*) any of the following:

(a) the scheme established under section 54 of the Financial Services Act 1986 and known as the Investors Compensation Scheme;

(b) the scheme established under section 22j of the Grey Paper published by the *FSA* on 26 September 1998 and known as the Section 43 Compensation Scheme;

(c) the scheme established by chapter II of part L:VIII of the *PIA* rule book and known as the PIA Indemnity Scheme;

(d) the scheme resulting from an agreement dated 1 February 1999 between the Association of British Insurers and the Investors Compensation Scheme Limited for the making of payments by way of compensation to widows, widowers and dependants of persons (since deceased), in connection with advice given to such persons in relation to pensions, or the arranging of pensions for such persons, and known as the ABI/ICS scheme.

investment company with variable capital

a body incorporated under the *OEIC Regulations*.

investment entity

(in *LR*) an entity whose primary object is investing and managing its assets with a view to spreading or otherwise managing investment risk.

investment firm

(A) In the PRA Handbook:
(1) any person whose regular occupation or business is the provision of one or more *investment services* to third parties and/or the performance of one or more investment activities on a professional basis.
[Note: article 4(1)(1) of *MiFID*]
(2) (in *REC*) a *MiFID investment firm*, or a person who would be a *MiFID investment firm* if it had its head office in the *EEA*.
(5) (in SYSC 19A) a *firm* in (3) except for a *BIPRU firm*

(B) In the FCA Handbook:
(1) any person whose regular occupation or business is the provision of one or more *investment services* to third parties and/or the performance of one or more investment activities on a professional basis.
[Note: article 4(1)(1) of *MiFID*]
(2) (in *REC*) a *MiFID investment firm*, or a person who would be a *MiFID investment firm* if it had its head office in the *EEA*.
(3) (in *IFPRU*, GENPRU 3 and BIPRU 12) has the meaning in article 4(1)(2) of the *EU CRR*.
(4) (in *GENPRU* (except GENPRU 3) and *BIPRU* (except BIPRU 12) any of the following:
(a) a *firm* in (3); and
(b) a *BIPRU firm*.
(5) (in SYSC 19A) a *firm* in (3).

investment firm consolidation waiver

(A) In the PRA Handbook:
a *waiver* (described in BIPRU 8.4 (CAD Article 22 groups and investment firm consolidation waiver)) that disapplies certain requirements so far as they apply on a consolidated basis with respect to a *CAD Article 22 group*.

(B) In the FCA Handbook:
(in relation to a *BIPRU firm*) a *waiver* (described in BIPRU 8.4 (CAD Article 22 groups and

investment firm consolidation waiver)) that disapplies certain requirements so far as they apply on a consolidated basis with respect to a *CAD Article 22 group*.

investment management firm

(A) In the PRA Handbook:

(a *firm* whose *permitted activities* include *designated investment business*, which is not an *authorised professional firm*, *bank*, *IFPRU investment firm*, *BIPRU firm*, *building society*, *collective portfolio management firm*, *credit union*, *energy market participant*, *friendly society*, *ICVC*, *insurer*, *media firm*, *oil market participant*, *service company*, *incoming EEA firm* (without a *top-up permission*), *incoming Treaty firm* (without a *top-up permission*), or *UCITS qualifier* (without a *top-up permission*), whose *permission* does not include a *requirement* that it comply with IPRU-INV 3 or IPRU-INV 13 (Personal investment firms) and which is within (a), (b) or (c):

(a) a *firm*:

(i) which was a member of *IMRO* immediately before *commencement*; and

(ii) which was not, immediately before *commencement*, subject to the financial supervision requirements of the *FSA* (under section 43 of the Financial Services Act 1986), or *PIA* or *SFA* (under lead regulation arrangements);

(b) a *firm* whose *permission* includes a *requirement* that it comply with IPRU-INV 5 (Investment management firms);

(c) a *firm*:

(i) which was given a *Part 4A permission* on or after *commencement*, or which was authorised under section 25 of the Financial Services Act 1986 immediately before *commencement* and was not a member of *IMRO*, *PIA* or the *SFA*; and

(ii) for which the most substantial part of its gross income (including *commissions*) from the *designated investment business* included in its *Part 4A permission* is derived from one or more of the following activities (based, for a *firm* given a *Part 4A permission* after *commencement*, on the business plan submitted as part of the *firm's* application for *permission* or, for a *firm* authorised under section 25 of the Financial Services Act 1986, on the *firm's* financial year preceding its *authorisation* under the *Act*):

(A) *managing investments* other than for retail clients or where the assets managed are primarily *derivatives*;

(B) *OPS activity*;

(C) acting as the *manager* or *trustee* of an *AUT*;

(Ca) *managing an AIF*;

(D) acting as the *ACD* or *depositary* of an *ICVC*;

(Da) acting as the *authorised contractual scheme manager* or *depositary* of an *ACS*;

(Db) *acting as trustee or depositary of an AIF*;

(Dc) *acting as trustee or depositary of a UCITS*;

(E) *establishing, operating or winding up a collective investment scheme* (other than an *AUT*, *ICVC* or *ACS*);

(Ea) *establishing, operating or winding up a personal pension scheme*; and

(F) *safeguarding and administering investments*.

(B) In the FCA Handbook:

a *firm* whose *permitted activities* include *designated investment business*, which is not an *authorised professional firm*, *bank*, *IFPRU investment firm*, *BIPRU firm*, *collective portfolio management firm*, *credit union*, *energy market participant*, *friendly society*, *ICVC*, *insurer*, *media firm*, *oil market participant*, *service company*, *incoming EEA firm* (without a *top-up permission*), *incoming Treaty firm* (without a *top-up permission*), or *UCITS qualifier* (without a *top-up permission*), whose *permission* does not include a *requirement* that it comply with IPRU-INV 3 or IPRU-INV 13 (Personal investment firms) and which is within (a), (b) or (c):

(a) a *firm*:

(i) which was a member of *IMRO* immediately before *commencement*; and

(ii) which was not, immediately before *commencement*, subject to the financial supervision requirements of the *FSA* (under section 43 of the Financial Services Act 1986), or *PIA* or *SFA* (under lead regulation arrangements);

(b) a *firm* whose *permission* includes a *requirement* that it comply with IPRU-INV 5 (Investment management firms);

(c) a *firm*:

(i) which was given a *Part 4A permission* on or after *commencement*, or which was authorised under section 25 of the Financial Services Act 1986 immediately before *commencement* and was not a member of *IMRO*, *PIA* or the *SFA*; and

(ii) for which the most substantial part of its gross income (including *commissions*) from the *designated investment business* included in its *Part 4A permission* is derived from one or more of the following activities (based, for a *firm* given a *Part 4A permission* after *commencement*, on the business plan submitted as part of the *firm's* application for *permission* or, for a *firm* authorised under section 25 of the Financial Services Act 1986, on the *firm's* financial year preceding its *authorisation* under the *Act*):

(A) *managing investments* other than for retail clients or where the assets managed are primarily *derivatives*;

(B) *OPS activity*;

(C) [deleted]

(Ca) *managing an AIF*;

(D) [deleted]

(Da) [deleted]

(Db) *acting as trustee or depositary of an AIF*;

(Dc) *acting as trustee or depositary of a UCITS*;

(E) *establishing, operating or winding up a collective investment scheme*;

(Ea) *establishing, operating or winding up a personal pension scheme*; and

(F) *safeguarding and administering investments*.

investment manager

(1) (except in *LR*) a *person* who, acting only on behalf of a *client*:

(a) manages *designated investments* in an account or portfolio on a discretionary basis under the terms of a discretionary management agreement; or

(b) manages *designated investments* in an account or portfolio on a non-discretionary basis under the terms of a non-discretionary management agreement.

(2) (in *LR*) a *person* who, on behalf of a *client*, manages *investments* and is not a wholly-owned *subsidiary* of the *client*.

Investment Ombudsman

the *former Ombudsman* under the *IMRO* scheme.

investment professional

(in accordance with article 19(5) of the *Financial Promotion Order*) (in relation to a *financial promotion*):

(a) an *authorised person*;

(b) an *exempt person* when the *financial promotion* relates to a *controlled activity* which is a *regulated activity* in relation to which the *person* is exempt;

(c) any other *person*:
(i) whose ordinary activities involve him in carrying on the *controlled activity* to which the *financial promotion* relates for the purposes of a business carried on by him; or
(ii) who it is reasonable to expect will carry on that activity for the purposes of a business carried on by him;

(d) a government, a local authority (whether in the *United Kingdom* or elsewhere) or an international organisation;

(e) a *person* ("A") who is a *director*, *officer* or employee of a *person* ("B") falling within any of (a) to (d) where the *financial promotion* is made to A in that capacity and where A's responsibilities when acting in that capacity involve him in the carrying on by B of *controlled activities*.

investment research

research or other information recommending or suggesting an investment strategy, explicitly or implicitly, concerning one or several *financial instruments* or the issuers of *financial instruments*, including any opinion as to the present or future value or price of such instruments, intended for *distribution channels* or for the public, and in relation to which the following conditions are met:

(a) it is labelled or described as investment research or in similar terms, or is otherwise presented as an objective or independent explanation of the matters contained in the recommendation;

(b) if the recommendation in question were to be made by an *investment firm* to a *client*, it would not constitute the provision of a *personal recommendation*.

[Note: article 24(1) of the *MiFID implementing Directive*]

investment service

any of the following involving the provision of a service in relation to a *financial instrument*:

(a) reception and transmission of orders in relation to one or more *financial instruments*;

(b) execution of orders on behalf of *clients*;

(c) *dealing on own account*;

(d) *portfolio management*;

(e) the making of a *personal recommendation*;

(f) underwriting of *financial instruments* and/or placing of *financial instruments* on a firm commitment basis;

(g) placing of *financial instruments* without a firm commitment basis;

(h) operation of *multilateral trading facilities*.

[Note: article 4(1)(2) of, and section A of Annex 1 to, *MiFID* and article 6(5) of the *auction regulation*]

investment services and/or activities

any of the services and activities listed in Section A of Annex I to *MiFID* relating to any *financial instrument*, that is:

(a) reception and transmission of orders in relation to one or more *financial instruments*;

(b) execution of orders on behalf of *clients*;

(c) *dealing on own account*;

(d) *portfolio management*;

(e) the making of a *personal recommendation*;

(f) underwriting of *financial instruments* and/or placing of *financial instruments* on a firm commitment basis;

(g) placing of *financial instruments* without a firm commitment basis;

(h) operation of *multilateral trading facilities*.

[Note: article 4(1)(2) of, and section A of Annex 1 to, *MiFID* and article 6(5) of the *auction regulation*]

Investment Services Directive

the Council Directive of 10 May 1993 on investment services in the securities field (No 93/22/EEC).

investment services or activities

any of the services and activities listed in Section A of Annex I to *MiFID* relating to any *financial instrument*, that is:

(a) reception and transmission of orders in relation to one or more *financial instruments*;

(b) execution of orders on behalf of *clients*;

(c) *dealing on own account*;

(d) *portfolio management*;

(e) the making of a *personal recommendation*;

(f) underwriting of *financial instruments* and/or placing of *financial instruments* on a firm commitment basis;

(g) placing of *financial instruments* without a firm commitment basis;

(h) operation of *multilateral trading facilities*.

[Note: article 4(1)(2) of, and section A of Annex 1 to, *MiFID* and article 6(5) of the *auction regulation*]

investment services sector

(A) In the PRA Handbook:
a sector composed of one or more of the following entities:
(a) an *investment firm*;
(b) a *financial institution*; and
(c) (in the circumstances described in GENPRU 3.1.39 R (The financial sectors: Asset management companies and alternative investment fund managers)) an *asset management company* or an *alternative investment fund manager*.

(B) In the FCA Handbook:
(1) a sector composed of one or more of the following entities:
(a) an *investment firm*;
(b) a *financial institution*; and
(c) (in the circumstances described in GENPRU 3.1.39 R (The financial sectors: Asset management companies and alternative investment fund managers)) an *asset management company* or an *alternative investment fund manager*.
(2) (in *BIPRU* (except in BIPRU 12) a sector comprised of one or more of the following entities:
(a) the entities in (1); and
(b) a *CAD investment firm*.

investment transaction

a transaction to *buy*, *sell*, subscribe for or underwrite a *security* or *contractually based investment*.

investment trust

(A) In the PRA Handbook: a *company listed* in the *United Kingdom* or another *EEA State* which:

(a) is approved by the Commissioners for HM Revenue and Customs under sections 1158 and 1159 of the Corporation Tax Act 2010 (or, in the case of a newly formed *company*, has declared its intention to conduct its affairs so as to obtain such approval); or

(b) is resident in an *EEA State* other than the *United Kingdom* and would qualify for such approval if resident and *listed* in the *United Kingdom*.

(B) In the FCA Handbook: a *company* which:

(a) is approved by the Commissioners for HM Revenue and Customs under sections 1158 and 1159 of the Corporation Tax Act 2010 (or, in the case of a newly formed *company*, has declared its intention to conduct its affairs so as to obtain such approval); or

(b) is resident in an *EEA State* other than the *United Kingdom* and would qualify for such approval if resident in the *United Kingdom*.

investment trust savings scheme

(a) a *dealing* service (whether or not held within a *pension contract*) dedicated to the *securities* of one or more *investment trusts*;

(b) *securities* to be acquired through an investment trust savings scheme in (a).

Investor Compensation Directive

the Council Directive of 3 March 1997 on investor compensation schemes (No 97/9/EC).

IOSCO

the International Organisation of Securities Commissions.

IPA

individual pension account.

IPA eligible investment

a type of investment specified in regulation 2(2) (condition 5) of the Stamp Duty and Stamp Duty Reserve Tax (Definition of Unit Trust Scheme and Open-ended Investment Company) Regulations 2001 (SI 2001/964).

IPRU

the Interim Prudential sourcebook, comprising IPRU(BANK), IPRU(FSOC), IPRU(INS) and IPRU(INV), or according to the context one of these Interim Prudential sourcebooks.

IPRU(BANK)

the Interim Prudential sourcebook for Banks.

IPRU(BSOC)

the Interim Prudential sourcebook for Building Societies.

IPRU(FSOC)

the Interim Prudential sourcebook for Friendly Societies.

IPRU(INS)

the Interim Prudential Sourcebook for Insurers.

IPRU(INV)

the Interim Prudential sourcebook for Investment Businesses.

IRB approach

one of the following:

(a) the adjusted method of calculating the *credit risk capital component* set out in BIPRU 4 (IRB approach) and BIPRU 9.12 (Calculation of risk weighted exposure amounts under the internal ratings based approach), including that approach as applied under BIPRU 14 (Capital requirements for settlement and counterparty risk);

(b) (where the approach in (a) is being applied on a consolidated basis) the method in (a) as applied on a consolidated basis in accordance with BIPRU 8 (Group risk – consolidation); or

(c) when the reference is to the rules of or administered by a *regulatory body* other than the *appropriate regulator*, whatever corresponds to the approach in (a) or (b), as the case may be, under those rules.

IRB exposure class

(in relation to the *IRB approach*) one of the classes of *exposure* set out in BIPRU 4.3.2 R (exposure classes).

IRB permission

(A) In the PRA Handbook:
an *Article 129 implementing measure*, a *requirement* or a *waiver* that requires a *BIPRU firm* or an *institution* to use the *IRB approach*.

(B) In the FCA Handbook:
an *Article 129 implementing measure*, a *requirement* or a *waiver* that requires a *BIPRU firm* or a *CAD investment firm* to use the *IRB approach*.

ISA

an *individual savings account*.

ISA manager

a *person* who is approved by HM Revenue and Customs for the purposes of the *ISA Regulations* as an account manager.

ISA Regulations

the Individual Savings Account Regulations 1998 (SI 1998/1870).

ISA transfer

a transaction resulting from a decision, made with or without advice from a *firm*, by a *customer* who is an individual, to transfer the *investments* (or their value) held in his existing *ISA* in favour of another *ISA* which may or may not be managed by the same *ISA manager*.

ISD

Investment Services Directive.

ISPV

an *insurance special purpose vehicle*.

issue

(in relation to *units*):

(1) (except in EG 14) the issue of new *units* by the *trustee* of an *AUT*, the *depositary* of an *ACS* or by an *ICVC*;

(2) (in EG 14):
(a) an issue in accordance with (1); and
(b) the sale of *units*.

issue price

(in relation to the *issue* of *units* of a *dual-priced authorised fund*) the *price* for each *unit* payable by the *authorised fund manager* to the *depositary* on that *issue*.

issuer

(1) (except as otherwise provided for below):
(a) (in relation to any *security*) (other than a *unit* in a *collective investment scheme*) the *person* by whom it is or is to be issued;
(b) (in relation to a *unit* in a *collective investment scheme*) the *operator* of the *scheme*;
(c) (in relation to an interest in a limited *partnership* except for a *limited partnership scheme*) the *partnership*;
(d) (in relation to *certificates representing certain securities*) the *person* who issued or is to issue the *security* to which the certificate or other instrument relates; or
(e) an entity which issues *transferable securities* and, where appropriate, other *financial instruments*.

[Note: article 2(2) of the *MiFID Regulation*]

(2) (in chapters 1, 2 and 3 of *DTR* and *FEES* in relation to *DTR*) any *company* or other legal person or undertaking (including a *public sector issuer*), any class of whose *financial instruments*:
(a) have been *admitted to trading* on a *regulated market*; or
(b) are the subject of an application for *admission to trading* on a *regulated market*;
other than *issuers* who have not requested or approved admission of their *financial instruments* to trading on a *regulated market*.

(2A) (in chapters 1A, 1B, 4, 6 and 7 of *DTR*) a legal entity governed by private or public law, including a State, whose securities are admitted to trading on a *regulated market*, the issuer being, in the case of depository receipts representing securities, the issuer of the securities represented;

(2B) (in chapter 5 of *DTR*):
(a) a legal entity governed by private or public law, including a State whose *shares* are admitted to trading on a *regulated market*, the issuer being in the case of depositary receipts representing securities, the issuer of the *shares* represented; or
(b) a public company within the meaning of section 4(2) of the Companies Act 2006 and any other body corporate incorporated in and having a principal place of business in the *United Kingdom*, whose *shares* are admitted to trading on a market which (not being a *regulated market*) is a *prescribed market*.

(3) (in *LR* and *FEES* in relation to *LR*) any *company* or other legal person or undertaking (including a *public sector issuer*), any *class* of whose *securities* has been *admitted to listing* or is the subject of an application for *admission to listing*.

(4) (in *PR* and *FEES* in relation to *PR*) (as defined in section 102A of the *Act*) a legal person who issues or proposes to issue the *transferable securities* in question.

(5) (in *RCB* and FEES 1 to FEES 4, where applicable) (as defined in Regulation 1(2) of the *RCB Regulations*) a person which issues a *covered bond*.

(6) (in *FUND*) means an issuer within the meaning of article 2(1)(d) of the Transparency Directive where that issuer has its registered office in the *EEA* and where its shares are admitted to trading on a *regulated market*.

issuing electronic money

the activity specified in article 9B of the *Regulated Activities Order* (Issuing electronic money), which is the activity of issuing *electronic money* by:

(a) a *credit institution*, a *credit union* or a municipal bank; or

(b) a person who is deemed to have been granted authorisation under regulation 74 of the *Electronic Money Regulations* or who falls within regulation 76(1) of the *Electronic Money Regulations*.

JGPPI

the FSA/OFT Joint Guidance on Payment Protection Products.

joint enterprise

(as defined in article 3(1) of the *Regulated Activities Order* (Interpretation)) an enterprise into which two or more *persons* ("the participators") enter for commercial purposes related to a business or businesses (other than the business of engaging in a *regulated activity*) carried on by them; where a participator is a member of a *group*, each other member of the *group* is also to be regarded as a participator in the enterprise.

keyfacts logo provisions

GEN 5.1 and GEN 5 Annex 1 G.

key features document

a *document* prepared in accordance with the *rules* on preparing product information (COBS 13).

key features illustration

information describing projected performance and the effect of charges prepared in accordance with the *rules* on preparing product information (COBS 13).

key features scheme

a *scheme* that is not:

(a) a *UCITS scheme* or an *EEA UCITS scheme*;

(b) a *qualified investor scheme*; or

(c) a recognised scheme under section 264 of the *Act* (Schemes constituted in other EEA States).

key individual

(in relation to a *UK recognised body*):

(a) its chairman or president;

(b) its *chief executive*;

(c) a member of its *governing body*;

(d) a *person* who, alone or jointly with one or more others, is responsible under the immediate authority of a *person* in (a), (b) or (c) or a committee of the *governing body* for the conduct of any *relevant function*.

key information

(in *PR*) (as defined in section 87A(9) and (10) of the *Act*) the information which is essential to enable investors to understand the *transferable securities* to which the *prospectus* relates and decide whether to consider the *offer* further. The *key information* must include:

(a) the essential characteristics of, and risks associated with, the *issuer* and any *guarantor*, including their assets, liabilities and financial positions;

(b) the essential characteristics of, and risks associated with, investment in the *transferable securities*, including any rights attaching to the *securities*;

(c) the general terms of the *offer*, including an estimate of the expenses charged to an investor by the *issuer* and the person offering the *securities* to the public, if not the *issuer*;

(d) details of the *admission to trading*; and

(e) the reasons for the *offer* and proposed use of the proceeds.

key investor information

key information for investors on the essential elements of a *UCITS scheme* or *EEA UCITS scheme*, as detailed in article 78 of the *UCITS Directive* and in the *KII Regulation*.

key investor information document

a short *document* containing *key investor information* for investors on the essential elements of a *UCITS scheme*, as detailed in COLL 4.7.2 R (Key investor information).

KII Regulation

Commission Regulation (EU) No 583/2010, specifying the form and contents of *key investor information*, the text of which is reproduced in COLL Appendix 1EU.

kind of control

(in relation to a *firm*) (for the purposes of *SUP*)):

(a) *control* arising as a result of holding shares in the *firm*;

(b) *control* arising as a result of holding shares in a *parent undertaking* of the *firm*;

(c) *control* arising as a result of the entitlement to exercise or control the exercise of *voting power* in the *firm*;

(d) *control* arising as a result of the entitlement to exercise or *control* the exercise of *voting power* in a *parent undertaking* of the *firm*;

in this definition, "shares" has the meaning given in the definition of *"controller"*.

KIRB

(for the purposes of BIPRU 9 (Securitisation), in relation to a *securitisation* (within the meaning of paragraph (2) of the definition of securitisation) and in accordance with Part 1 of Annex IX of the *Banking Consolidation Directive* (Securitisation definitions)) 8% of the *risk weighted exposure amounts* that would be calculated under the *IRB approach* in respect of the *securitised exposures*, had they not been *securitised*, plus the amount of *expected losses* associated with those *exposures* calculated under the *IRB approach*.

land

in accordance with section 189(1) of the *CCA*, includes an interest in land, and, in Scotland, includes heritable subjects of whatever description.

land-related agreement

(in CONC App 1.1) a *credit agreement* which is

(a) intended primarily to *finance* the acquisition or retention of *land*; or

(b) intended to *finance* the renovation or improvement of a building,

or any other *credit agreement* secured by a *legal mortgage* on *land* or, in Scotland, by a standard security within the meaning of the Conveyancing and Feudal Reform (Scotland) Act 1970.

land vehicles

(in relation to a *class* of *contract of insurance*) the *class* of *contract of insurance*, specified in paragraph 3 of Part I of Schedule 1 to the *Regulated Activities Order* (Contracts of general insurance), against loss of or damage to vehicles used on land, including motor vehicles but excluding railway rolling stock.

large ACS investor

in relation to an *ACS*, a *person* who in exchange for *units* in the *scheme*:

(a) makes a payment of not less than £1,000,000; or

(b) contributes property with a value of not less than £1,000,000.

large business customer

(in relation to a *regulated mortgage contract* or *qualifying credit*, and in relation to an activity to be carried on by a *firm*) a *client*, if the credit is for the purposes of a business which has a group annual turnover of £1 million or more.

large company

a *body corporate* which does not qualify as a small company under section 247 of the Companies Act 1985, or section 382 of the Companies Act 2006 as applicable.

large deal

(in *COLL*) a transaction (or *series of transactions*) in one *dealing period*) by any *person* to *buy*, *sell* or exchange *units* in an *authorised fund*, of any value as set out in the *prospectus*, for the purposes of:

(a) an *SDRT provision*;

(b) a *dilution levy*;

(c) a *dilution adjustment*; or

(d) calculating the *prices*, for a *dual-priced authorised fund*, at which *units* may be *sold* or *redeemed*.

large exposure

(A) In the PRA Handbook:
has the meaning given in the *PRA* Rulebook: Large Exposures rules.

(B) In the FCA Handbook:
(1) (in *BIPRU*) the *exposure* of a *firm* to a *counterparty*, or a *group of connected clients*, whether in the *firm's non-trading book* or *trading book* or both, which in aggregate equals or exceeds 10% of the *firm's capital resources*.
(2) (except in (1)) has the meaning in article 392 of the *EU CRR* (Definition of a large exposure).

large mutual association

(A) (in the *PRA Handbook*):
A mutual association or unincorporated association with net assets of more than £1.4 million (or its equivalent in any other currency at the relevant time).

(B) (in the *FCA Handbook*):
(1) (in *COMP*) an unincorporated mutual association or unincorporated association (which is not a mutual association) with net assets of more than £1.4 million (or its equivalent in any other currency at the relevant time).
(2) (except in *COMP*), a mutual association or unincorporated association with net assets of more than £1.4 million (or its equivalent in any other currency at the relevant time).

large partnership

(A) (in the *PRA Handbook*):
A *partnership* or unincorporated association with net assets of more than £1.4 million (or its equivalent in any other currency at the relevant time).

(B) (in the *FCA Handbook*):
(1) (in *COMP*), a *partnership* with net assets of more than £1.4 million (or its equivalent in any other currency at the relevant time).
(2) (except in *COMP*), a *partnership* or unincorporated association with net assets of more than £1.4 million (or its equivalent in any other currency at the relevant time).

larger denomination share

any *share* that is not a *smaller denomination share*.

lead generator

a *person* that acquires the personal contact details of *customers* and passes the *customers'* details to a *firm* in return for a fee.

lead regulated firm

a *firm* which is the subject of the financial supervision requirements of an *overseas regulator* in accordance with an agreement between the *appropriate regulator* and that regulator relating to the financial supervision of *firms* whose head office is within the country of that regulator. This definition is not related to the defined terms *UK lead regulated firm* or *non UK lead regulated firm*.

leading insurer

(in relation to a *community co-insurance operation*) has the same meaning as in the *Community Co-Insurance Directive*.

legal expenses

(in relation to a *class* of *contract of insurance*) the *class* of *contract of insurance*, specified in paragraph 17 of Part I of Schedule 1 to the *Regulated Activities Order* (Contracts of general insurance), against risks of loss to the *persons* insured attributable to their incurring legal expenses (including costs of litigation).

legal or equitable mortgage

in accordance with article 60L of the *Regulated Activities Order*, includes a legal or equitable charge and, in Scotland, a heritable security.

lender

(A) in the *PRA Handbook*:
(a) the *person* providing *credit* under a *credit agreement*, or
(b) a *person* who exercises, or has the right to exercise, the rights and duties of a *person* who provided *credit* under such an agreement.

(B) in the *FCA Handbook*:
(a) the *person* providing *credit* under a *credit agreement*, or
(b) a *person* who exercises, or has the right to exercise, the rights and duties of a *person* who provided *credit* under such an agreement; or
(c) in relation to a *P2P agreement* other than a *credit agreement* or a *regulated mortgage contract*, the *person* providing *credit* under the *P2P agreement*.

lending firm

(in accordance with Article 90 of the *Banking Consolidation Directive* (Credit risk mitigation) and for the purposes of *rules* in *BIPRU* about *credit risk mitigation*) a *firm* that has an *exposure*, whether or not deriving from a loan.

leverage

(in accordance with article 4(1)(v) of *AIFMD*) any method by which an *AIFM* increases the exposure of an *AIF* it manages whether through borrowing of cash or *securities*, or leverage embedded in *derivative* positions or by any other means.

levy limit

(A) In the FCA Handbook: (in *FEES*) the maximum aggregate amount of *compensation costs* and *specific costs* that may be allocated to a particular *class* in one financial year as set out in FEES 6 Annex 2, whether directly or (where relevant to that *class*) through the *retail pool*. *FCA provider contribution classes* do not have a *levy limit*: they have a *retail pool* levy limit: see FEES 6 Annex 5R.

LGD

loss given default.

liability of ships

(in relation to a *class* of *contract of insurance*) the *class* of *contract of insurance*, specified in paragraph 12 of Part I of Schedule 1 to the *Regulated Activities Order* (Contracts of general insurance), against damage arising out of or in connection with the use of vessels on the sea or on inland water, including third party risks and carrier's liability.

liability subject to compulsory insurance

any liability required under any of the following enactments to be covered by insurance or (as the case may be) by insurance or by some other provisions for securing its discharge:

(a) section 1(4A)(d) of the Riding Establishments Act 1964 (or any corresponding enactment for the time being in force in Northern Ireland);

(b) section 1 of the Employers' Liability (Compulsory Insurance) Act 1969 or Article 5 of the Employers' Liability Order (Defective Equipment and Compulsory Insurance) (Northern Ireland) Order 1972;

(c) Part VI of the Road Traffic Act 1988 or Part VIII of the Road Traffic (Northern Ireland) Order 1981;

(d) section 19 of the Nuclear Installations Act 1965.

liability to a policyholder

(in relation to a firm carrying out contracts of insurance) any liability or obligation of that *firm* to, or in respect of, a *policyholder*, including any liability or obligation arising:

(a) from the requirement to treat *customers* fairly under *Principle* 6, including with respect to *policyholders'* reasonable expectations; or

(b) from a determination of liability by an *Ombudsman*; or

(c) from any requirement to pay compensation under the *regulatory system*.

life and annuity

(in relation to a *class* of *contract of insurance*) the *class* of *contract of insurance*, specified in paragraph I of Part II of Schedule 1 to the *Regulated Activities Order* (Contracts of long-term insurance), on human life or a contract to pay annuities on human life, but excluding (in each case) contracts within paragraph III of Part II of that Schedule (Linked long-term).

life policy

(1) (in accordance with the definition of 'qualifying contract of insurance' in article 3(1) of the *Regulated Activities Order*) a *long-term insurance contract* (other than a reinsurance contract and a *pure protection contract*); and
(a) a *long-term care insurance contract*; and
(b) (in *COBS*) a *pension policy*;
unless (2) or (3) apply.

(2) In *PERG* (other than in relation to a *firm's permission* – see Note 5B to Table 1 in Annex 2, PERG 2) and for the purposes of the *financial promotion rules* in COBS 4, life policy does not include a *long-term care insurance contract*.

(3) In relation to a *firm's permission*:
(a) (in accordance with the definition of 'qualifying contract of insurance' in article 3(1) of the *Regulated Activities Order*) a *long-term insurance contract* (other than a reinsurance contract and a *pure protection contract*);
(b) a *long-term care insurance contract* which is a *pure protection contract*; and
(c) a *pension term assurance policy*.

life protection reinsurance business

reinsurance acceptances which are *contracts of insurance*:

(a) falling within *long-term insurance business class* I; or

(b) falling within *long-term insurance business class* III and providing *index-linked benefits*;

that are not:

(c) *with-profits insurance contracts*; or

(d) *whole life assurances*; or

(e) contracts to pay annuities on human life; or

(f) contracts which pay a sum of money on the survival of the life assured to a specific date or on his earlier death.

lifetime mortgage

a *regulated mortgage contract* under which:

(a) entry into the mortgage is restricted to older *customers* above a specified age;

and

(b) the *mortgage lender* may or may not specify a mortgage term, but will not seek full repayment of the loan (including interest, if any, outstanding) until the occurrence of one or more of the following:
(i) the death of the *customer*; or
(ii) the *customer* leaves the mortgaged land to live elsewhere and has no reasonable prospect of returning (for example by moving into residential care); or
(iii) the *customer* acquires another dwelling for use as his main residence; or
(iv) the *customer* sells the mortgaged land; or
(v) the *mortgage lender* exercises its legal right to take possession of the mortgaged land under the terms of the contract.

and

(c) while the *customer* continues to occupy the mortgaged land as his main residence:
(i) no instalment repayments of the capital and no payment of interest on the capital (other than interest charged when all or part of the capital is repaid voluntarily by the *customer*), are due or capable of becoming due; or
(ii) although interest payments may become due, no full or partial repayment of the capital is due or capable of becoming due; or
(iii) although interest payments and partial repayment of the capital may become due, no full repayment of the capital is due or capable of becoming due.

LIFFE

the London International Financial Futures and Options Exchange.

limit of indemnity

(in MIPRU 3 (Professional indemnity insurance)) the sum available to indemnify a *firm* in respect of each claim made under its professional indemnity insurance.

limitation

a limitation incorporated in a *Part 4A permission* under section 55E(5) of the *Act* (Giving permission): the FCA), section 55F(4) of the Act (Giving permission: the PRA) or section 55J(10) of the *Act* (Variation or cancellation on initiative of regulator).

limit order

an order to buy or sell a *financial instrument* at its specified price limit or better and for a specified size. [Note: article 4(1)(16) of *MiFID*]

limited activity firm

(A) In the PRA Handbook:
has the meaning set out BIPRU 1.1.11 R (Types of investment firm: Limited activity firms).

(B) In the FCA Handbook:
has the meaning in article 96(1) of the *EU CRR*.

limited assurance engagement

(A) In the PRA Handbook: a 'limited assurance engagement' as described in the Glossary of terms in the Auditing Practices Board Standards and Guidance for Auditors issued in 2010.

(B) In the FCA Handbook: a 'limited assurance engagement' as described in the Glossary of terms in Financial Reporting Council: Audit and Assurance: Standards and Guidance 2014.

limited licence firm

(A) In the PRA Handbook:
has the meaning set out BIPRU 1.1.12 R (Types of investment firm: Limited licence firms).

(B) In the FCA Handbook:
has the meaning in article 95(1) of the *EU CRR*.

limited liability partnership

(a) a *body corporate* incorporated under the Limited Liability Partnerships Act 2000;

(b) a *body corporate* incorporated under legislation having the equivalent effect to the Limited Liability Partnerships Act 2000.

limited partner

in relation to a *limited partnership scheme*, a *participant* in the *scheme* (other than the *nominated partner*).

limited permission

a *Part 4A permission* for a relevant credit activity as defined in paragraph 2G of Schedule 6 to the *Act* (guidance on which is given in COND 1.1A.5A G).

limited price indexation

in relation to transfer value analysis, benefits which increase in line with a recognised index but subject to a minimum and/or maximum rate.

limited redemption arrangements

the arrangements operated by an *authorised fund manager* for the *redemption* of *units* in an *authorised fund* where the *authorised fund manager* holds himself out to redeem units in that *scheme* less frequently than twice in a calendar *month* in accordance with COLL 6.2.19 R (Limited redemption).

linked assets

index-linked assets or *property-linked assets*.

linked benefit

(1) (in COBS 21 (Permitted Links)) *property-linked benefits* or *index-linked benefits*.

(2) (other than in COBS 21) a benefit payable under a *life policy* or a *regulated collective investment scheme* the amount of which is determined by reference to:
(a) the value of the property of any description (whether specified or not); or
(b) fluctuations in the value of any such property; or
(c) income from such property; or
(d) fluctuations in an index of the value of such property.

linked borrowing

additional credit facilities (which may be secured, unsecured, or both) that are integral to a *regulated mortgage contract* but which may be the subject of a separate contract.

linked deposits

additional facilities (which may be a current account, a savings account, or both) that are linked to a *regulated mortgage contract* but which may be the subject of a separate contract.

linked fund

a real or notional account to which an *insurer* appropriates *linked assets* for the purposes of their being *permitted links*, and which may be subdivided into units, the value of each of which is determined by the *insurer* by reference to the value of those *linked assets*.

linked liabilities

property-linked liabilities or *index-linked liabilities*.

linked life stakeholder product

the *stakeholder product* specified by regulations 6 and 7 (rights under certain linked long-term contracts) of the *Stakeholder Regulations*;

linked long-term

(in relation to a *contract of insurance*) a *long-term insurance contract* where the benefits are wholly or partly to be determined by reference to the value of, or the income from, property of any description (whether or not specified in the contract) or by reference to fluctuations in, or in an index of, the value of property of any description (whether or not so specified).

linked policyholders

policyholders under a *linked long-term* contract.

linked transaction

has the meaning in article 60E of the *Regulated Activities Order*; in summary, a transaction is a linked transaction in relation to a *credit agreement* ("the principal agreement") if:

(1) it is (or will be) entered into by the *borrower* under the principal agreement or by a *relative* of the *borrower*;

(2) it does not relate to the provision of *security*;

(3) it does not form part of the principal agreement; and

(4) one of the following conditions is satisfied:
(a) the transaction is entered into in compliance with a term of the principal agreement;
(b) the principal agreement is a *borrower-lender-supplier agreement* and the transaction is *financed*, or to be *financed*, by the principal agreement;
(c) the following conditions are met:
(i) the other party is
(aa) the *lender*,
(bb) the *lender's associate*,
(cc) a *person* who, in the negotiation of the transaction, is represented by a *credit broker* who is or was also a negotiator in negotiations for the principal agreement, or
(dd) a *person* who, at the time the transaction is initiated, knows that the principal agreement has been made or contemplates that it might be made;
(ii) the other party initiated the transaction by suggesting it to the *borrower* or the *relative* of the *borrower*; and
(iii) the *borrower* or the *relative* of the *borrower* enters into the transaction to induce the *lender* to enter into the principal agreement or for another purpose related to the principal agreement or to a transaction *financed* or to be *financed* by the principal agreement.

but a transaction is not a linked transaction if it is:

(5) a *contract of insurance*;

(6) a contract which contains a guarantee of *goods*; or

(7) a transaction which comprises, or is effected under:
(a) an agreement for the operation of an account (including any savings account) for the deposit of money, or
(b) an agreement for the operation of a *current account*.

liquidity facility

(for the purposes of BIPRU 9 (Securitisation), in relation to a *securitisation* (within the meaning of paragraph (2) of the definition of securitisation) and in accordance with Part 1 of Annex IX of the *Banking Consolidation Directive* (Securitisation definitions)) the *securitisation position* arising from a contractual agreement to provide funding to ensure timeliness of cash-flows to investors.

liquidity risk

(1) (in *COLL* and in accordance with article 3(8) of the *UCITS implementing Directive*) the risk that a position in a *UCITS'* portfolio cannot be sold, liquidated or closed out at limited cost in an adequately short time frame and that the ability of the *scheme* to comply at any time with COLL 6.2.16 R (Sale and redemption) or, in the case of an *EEA UCITS scheme*, article 84(1) of the *UCITS Directive* is thereby compromised.

(2) (except in *COLL*) the risk that a *firm*, although solvent, either does not have available sufficient financial resources to enable it to meet its obligations as they fall due, or can secure such resources only at excessive cost.

list of primary information providers

the list of *primary information providers* maintained by the *FCA* in accordance with section 89P(4)(a) of the *Act*.

list of sponsors

(in *LR*) the list of sponsors maintained by the *FCA* in accordance with section 88(3)(a) of the *Act*.

listed

(A) In the PRA Handbook:
(1) (except in SUP 11, *INSPRU* and *IPRU(INS)*) included in an official list.
(2) (in SUP 11, *INSPRU* and *IPRU(INS)*):

(a) included in an official list; or

(b) in respect of which facilities for *dealing* on a *regulated market* have been granted.

(3) (in *LR*) admitted to the official list maintained by the *FCA* in accordance with section 74 of the *Act*.

(B) In the FCA Handbook:

(1) (except in *LR*, SUP 11, *INSPRU* and *IPRU(INS)*) included in an official list.

(2) (in SUP 11, *INSPRU* and *IPRU(INS)*):

(a) included in an official list; or

(b) in respect of which facilities for *dealing* on a *regulated market* have been granted.

(3) (in *LR*) admitted to the official list maintained by the *FCA* in accordance with section 74 of the *Act*.

listed activity

(A) In the PRA Handbook:

an activity listed in Annex 1 to the *CRD*.

(B) In the FCA Handbook:

an activity listed in Annex 1 to the *CRD*.

listed company

(in *LR* and *DEPP*) a *company* that has any *class* of its securities listed.

listed security

any *security* that is admitted to an *official list*.

listing particulars

(in *LR*) (in accordance with section 79(2) of the *Act*), a document in such form and containing such information as may be specified in *listing rules*.

listing rules

(in accordance with sections 73A(1) and 73A(2) of the *Act*) *rules* relating to admission to the *official list*.

Lloyd's actuary

the *actuary* appointed by the *Society* under SUP 4.6.1 R.

Lloyd's actuary function

(in the *PRA Handbook*) *PRA controlled functions* CF12B in the *table of PRA controlled functions*, described more fully in SUP 10B.8.3 R.

Lloyd's Arbitration Scheme

the Lloyd's Arbitration Scheme (Members and Underwriting Agents Arbitration Scheme) established under Lloyd's Arbitration Scheme (Members and Underwriting Agents Scheme) Byelaw (No 15 of 1992).

Lloyd's complaint procedures

the procedures maintained by the *Society* under DISP 1.11.1 R.

Lloyd's complaint rules

DISP 1.7.

Lloyd's market activities

(a) *advising on syndicate participation at Lloyd's*, including *advising* on a transaction in the *capacity transfer market*;

(b) *managing the underwriting capacity of a Lloyd's syndicate as a managing agent at Lloyd's*;

(c) agreeing to carry on the *regulated activities* in (a) and (b);

(d) carrying on *designated investment business* which is not *MiFID business* in relation to *funds at Lloyd's*; or

(e) *communicating* or *approving* a *financial promotion* in relation to:

(i) the *underwriting capacity of a Lloyd's syndicate*; or

(ii) *membership of a Lloyd's syndicate*; or

(iii) *life policies* written at Lloyd's; or

(iv) any of the activities specified in (a) or (d).

Lloyd's member's contribution

assets:

(a) provided to a *managing agent* in response to a cash call; or

(b) held by the *Society* as funds at Lloyds.

Lloyd's Members' Ombudsman

the office of Ombudsman established under Lloyd's Members' Ombudsman Scheme Byelaw (No 13 of 1987).

Lloyd's Return

the financial report that the *Society* is required to submit to the *PRA* under IPRU(INS) 9.48(1).

Lloyd's trust deed

a trust deed in the form prescribed by the *Society* and notified to the *PRA*, for execution by a *member* in respect of his *insurance business*.

Lloyd's trust fund

a fund held on the terms of a *Lloyd's trust deed*.

LME

the London Metal Exchange Limited.

LME bond arrangement

an arrangement for the segregation of money held by *firms* on behalf of US customers for transactions undertaken on the exchange operated by the *LME*, which is an alternative to complying with condition 2(g) of the *Part 30 exemption order*, and which has been established in accordance with certain no-action letters issued by the Commodity Futures Trading Commission.

loaned funds

(in *IPRU(INV)*) any funds that have been provided to borrowers under a *P2P agreement* through an *operator of an electronic system in relation to lending*.

local

(A) In the PRA Handbook:

(1) (except in BIPRU 1.1 (Application and purpose)) a *firm* which is a member of a *futures* and *options* exchange and whose *permission* includes a *requirement* that:

(a) the *firm* will not conduct *designated investment business* other than:

(i) *dealing* for its own account on that *futures* or *options* exchange; or

(ii) *dealing* for the accounts of other members of the same *futures* and *options* exchange; or

(iii) making a price to other members of the same *futures* and *options* exchange; and

(iv) *dealing* for its own account in financial *futures* and *options* or other *derivatives* in the capacity of a customer; and

(b) the performance of the *firm's* contracts must be guaranteed by and must be the responsibility of one or more of the clearing members of the same *futures* and *options* exchange.

(2) (in BIPRU 1.1 (Application and purpose) and in accordance with article 3(1)(p) of the *Capital Adequacy Directive* (Definitions)) an *undertaking* dealing for its own account on markets in financial-futures or options or other derivatives and on cash markets for the sole purpose of hedging *positions* on derivatives markets or which deals for the accounts of other members of those markets and which are guaranteed by clearing members of the same markets, where responsibility for ensuring the performance of contracts entered into by such an *undertaking* is assumed by clearing members of the same markets; for these purposes a clearing member means a member of the exchange or the clearing house which has a direct contractual relationship with the central counterparty (market guarantor).

(B) In the FCA Handbook:

(1) (except in IFPRU 1.1 (Application and purpose)) a *firm* which is a member of a *futures* and *options* exchange and whose *permission* includes a *requirement* that:

(a) the *firm* will not conduct *designated investment business* other than:

(i) *dealing* for its own account on that *futures* or *options* exchange; or

(ii) *dealing* for the accounts of other members of the same *futures* and *options* exchange; or

(iii) making a price to other members of the same *futures* and *options* exchange; and

(iv) *dealing* for its own account in financial *futures* and *options* or other *derivatives* in the capacity of a customer; and

(b) the performance of the *firm's* contracts must be guaranteed by and must be the responsibility of one or more of the clearing members of the same *futures* and *options* exchange.

(2) [deleted]

(3) (in IFPRU 1.1 (Application and purpose) has the meaning given to the definition of "local firm" in article 4(1)(4) of the *EU CRR*.

local authority

(a) in England and Wales, a local authority within the meaning of the Local Government Act 1972, the Greater London Authority, the Common Council of the City of London or the Council of the Isles of Scilly;

(b) in Scotland, a local authority within the meaning of the Local Government (Scotland) Act 1973;

(c) in Northern Ireland, a district council within the meaning of the Local Government Act (Northern Ireland) 1972.

local firm

a *firm* which falls within the definition of "local firm" in Article 3.1P of *CAD*, that is a firm dealing for its own account on markets in financial futures or options or other derivatives and on cash markets for the sole purpose of hedging positions on derivatives markets, or dealing for the accounts of other members of those markets and being guaranteed by clearing members of the same markets, where responsibility for ensuring the performance of contracts entered into by such a firm is assumed by clearing members of the same markets.

London Stock Exchange

(in *LR*) London Stock Exchange Plc.

long settlement transaction

(in accordance with Part 1 of Annex III of the *Banking Consolidation Directive* (Definitions)) a transaction where a counterparty undertakes to deliver a security, a *commodity*, or a *foreign currency* amount against cash, other *CRD financial instruments*, or *commodities*, or vice versa, at a settlement or delivery date that is contractually specified as more than the lower of the market standard for this particular transaction and five *business days* after the date on which the *person* enters into the transaction.

long-term admissible asset

a *long-term insurance asset* which is an *admissible asset*.

long-term incentive scheme

(in *LR*) any arrangement (other than a retirement benefit plan, a deferred bonus or any other arrangement that is an element of an executive *director's* remuneration package) which may involve the receipt of any asset (including cash or any security) by a *director* or *employee* of the *group*:

(a) which includes one or more conditions in respect of service and/or performance to be satisfied over more than one financial year; and

(b) pursuant to which the *group* may incur (other than in relation to the establishment and administration of the arrangement) either cost or a liability, whether actual or contingent.

long-term care insurance contract

a *long-term insurance contract*:

(a) which provides, would provide at the *policyholder*'s option, or is sold or held out as providing, benefits that are payable or provided if the *policyholder*'s health deteriorates to the extent that he cannot live independently without assistance and that is not expected to change; and

(b) under which the benefits are capable of being paid for periodically for all or part of the period that the *policyholder* cannot live without assistance;

where 'benefits' are services, accommodation or goods necessary or desirable for the continuing care of the *policyholder* because he cannot live independently without assistance.

long-term insurance asset

has the meaning set out in INSPRU 1.5.21R.

long-term insurance business

the business of *effecting* or *carrying out long-term insurance contracts*.

long-term insurance business syndicate

a *syndicate* in which *members* carry on *long-term insurance business*.

long-term insurance capital requirement

(in relation to a *firm* carrying on *long-term insurance business*) an amount of *capital resources* that the *firm* must hold calculated in accordance with GENPRU 2.1.36R.

long-term insurance contract

(in accordance with article 3(1) of the *Regulated Activities Order* (Interpretation: general)) any *contract of insurance* within Part II of Schedule 1 to the *Regulated Activities Order* (Contracts of long-term insurance), namely:

(a) *life and annuity* (paragraph I);

(b) *marriage or the formation of a civil partnership and birth* (paragraph II);

(c) *linked long-term* (paragraph III);

(d) *permanent health* (paragraph IV);

(e) *tontines* (paragraph V);

(f) *capital redemption* (paragraph VI);

(g) *pension fund management* (paragraph VII);

(g) *collective insurance* etc (paragraph VIII);

(h) *social insurance* (paragraph IX).

long-term insurance fund

has the meaning set out in INSPRU 1.5.22R.

long-term insurance liabilities

liabilities arising from *long-term insurance business*.

long-term insurer

an *insurer* with *permission* to effect or carry out long-term insurance contracts.

loss

(in accordance with Article 4(26) of the *Banking Consolidation Directive* (Definitions) and for the purposes of the *IRB approach*, the *standardised approach* to credit risk and BIPRU 5 (Credit risk mitigation)) economic loss, including material discount effects, and material direct and indirect costs associated with collecting on the instrument.

(A) In the PRA Handbook:
(in accordance with Article 4(26) of the *Banking Consolidation Directive* (Definitions) and for the purposes of the *IRB approach*, the *standardised approach* to credit risk and BIPRU 5 (Credit risk mitigation)) economic loss, including material discount effects, and material direct and indirect costs associated with collecting on the instrument.

(B) In the FCA Handbook:
(1) (in *BIPRU* and in accordance with Article 4(26) of the *Banking Consolidation Directive* (Definitions) and for the purposes of the *IRB approach*, the *standardised approach* to credit risk and BIPRU 5 (Credit risk mitigation)) economic loss, including material discount effects, and material direct and indirect costs associated with collecting on the instrument.
(2) (except in (2)) has the meaning in article 5(1) of the *EU CRR*.

loss given default

(in accordance with Article 4(27) of the *Banking Consolidation Directive* (Definitions) and in relation to the *IRB approach*) the ratio of the *loss* on an *exposure* due to the *default* of a counterparty to the amount outstanding at *default*.

lower rate of return

(in *COBS*) the lower rate of return described in paragraph 2.3 of the projection *rules* (COBS 13 Annex 2).

lower stage of capital

(with respect to a particular item of capital in the *capital resources table*) a stage in the *capital resources table* below that in which that item of capital appears.

lower tier three capital

an item of capital that is specified in stage P of the *capital resources table* (Lower tier three).

lower tier three capital resources

the sum calculated at stage P of the *capital resources table* (Lower tier three).

lower tier two capital

(1) [deleted]

(2) (in *BIPRU*, *GENPRU* and *INSPRU*) an item of capital that is specified in stage H of the *capital resources table* (Lower tier two capital).

lower tier two capital resources

the sum calculated at stage H of the calculation in the *capital resources table* (Lower tier two capital).

lower tier two instrument

an item of capital that meets the conditions in GENPRU 2.2.194R (Lower tier two capital) and is eligible to form part of a *firm's lower tier two capital resources*.

low frequency liquidity reporting firm

any of the following:

(a) a *simplified ILAS BIPRU firm*; or

(b) a *standard ILAS BIPRU firm* whose most recent *annual report and accounts* show balance sheet assets of less than £5 billion (or its equivalent in foreign currency translated into sterling at the balance sheet date); or

(c) a *standard ILAS BIPRU firm* that meets the following conditions:
(i) it does not have any *annual report and accounts* and it has been too recently established to be required to have produced any;
(ii) it has submitted a projected balance sheet to the *FCA* or *PRA* (as the case may be) as part of an application for a *Part 4A permission* or a variation of one; and
(iii) the most recent such balance sheet shows that the *firm* will meet the size condition set out in (b) in all periods covered by those projections.

In respect of an *incoming EEA firm* or *third country BIPRU firm* that is also a *standard ILAS BIPRU firm* and which reports on the basis of its branch operation in the *United Kingdom*, if the balance sheet assets attributable to the *UK branch* can be determined from the *firm's* most recent *annual report and accounts* (or, if applicable, the projected balance sheet) or any *data item* submitted by the *firm*, then paragraphs (b) and (c) apply at the level of the *branch* rather than of the *firm*.

LR

the Listing Rules sourcebook.

LTICR

long-term insurance capital requirement.

MAD

(in *LR*) the *Market Abuse Directive*.

MAD Investment Recommendations Directive

The Commission Directive of 22 December 2003 implementing the *Market Abuse Directive* as regards the fair presentation of investment recommendations and the disclosure of conflicts of interest (No. 2003/125/EC).

made to; made only to; to whom it is made

a *financial promotion* is made to a *person* if it is addressed, whether orally or in legible form, to a particular *person* or *persons* (for example where it is contained in a telephone call or letter).

main BIPRU firm Pillar 1 rules

(A) In the PRA Handbook:
GENPRU 2.1.40 R (Variable capital requirement for *BIPRU firms*), GENPRU 2.1.41 R (*Base capital resources requirement* for *BIPRU firms*), GENPRU 2.1.48 R (Table: Base capital resources requirement for a BIPRU firm).

(B) In the FCA Handbook:
GENPRU 2.1.40 R (Variable capital requirement for *BIPRU firms*), GENPRU 2.1.41 R (*Base capital resources requirement* for *BIPRU firms*), GENPRU 2.1.48 R (Table: Base capital resources requirement for a BIPRU firm).

major subsidiary undertaking

(in *LR*) a *subsidiary undertaking* that represents 25% or more of the aggregate of the gross assets or profits (after deducting all charges except taxation) of the *group*.

making arrangements with a view to a home finance transaction

any of the *regulated activities* of *making arrangements with a view to a regulated mortgage contract*, *making arrangements with a view to a home reversion plan*, *making arrangements with a view to a home purchase plan* or *making arrangements with a view to a regulated sale and rent back agreement*.

making arrangements with a view to a home purchase plan

the *regulated activity*, specified in article 25C(2) of the *Regulated Activities Order*, which is in summary: making arrangements with a view to a person who participates in the arrangements entering into a *home purchase plan* as *home purchaser*.

making arrangements with a view to a home reversion plan

the *regulated activity*, specified in article 25B(2) of the *Regulated Activities Order*, which is in summary: making arrangements with a view to a *person* who participates in the arrangements *entering into a home reversion plan* as *reversion occupier* or as plan provider.

making arrangements with a view to regulated mortgage contracts

the *regulated activity*, specified in article 25A(2) of the *Regulated Activities Order*, which is in summary: making arrangements with a view to a *person* who participates in the arrangements entering into a *regulated mortgage contract* as borrower. (see also *arranging* (in relation to *regulated mortgage contracts*) and *arranging (bringing about) regulated mortgage contracts*.)

making arrangements with a view to transactions in investments

(A) In the PRA Handbook: the *regulated activity*, specified in article 25(2) of the *Regulated Activities Order* (Arranging deals in investments), which is in summary: making arrangements with a view to a *person* who participates in the arrangements *buying, selling,* subscribing for or underwriting any of the following *investments* (whether as *principal* or agent):

(a) a *designated investment*; or

(b) a *funeral plan contract*; or

(c) the *underwriting capacity of a Lloyd's syndicate*; or

(d) *membership of a Lloyd's syndicate*; or

(e) *rights to or interests in investments* in (b), (c) or (d); or

(f) a *pure protection contract*; or

(g) a *general insurance contract*.

(B) In the FCA Handbook: the *regulated activity*, specified in article 25(2) of the *Regulated Activities Order* (Arranging deals in investments), which is in summary: making arrangements with a view to a *person* who participates in the arrangements *buying, selling,* subscribing for or underwriting any of the following *investments* (whether as *principal* or agent):

(a) a *designated investment* (other than a *P2P agreement*); or

(b) a *funeral plan contract*; or

(c) the *underwriting capacity of a Lloyd's syndicate*; or

(d) *membership of a Lloyd's syndicate*; or

(e) *rights to or interests in investments* in (b), (c) or (d); or

(f) a *pure protection contract*; or

(g) a *general insurance contract*.

making arrangements with a view to a regulated sale and rent back agreement

the *regulated activity*, specified in article 25E(2) of the *Regulated Activities Order*, which is in summary making arrangements with a view to a *person* who participates in the arrangements entering into a *regulated sale and rent back agreement* as agreement seller or agreement provider.

management accounts

(in relation to a *UK recognised body*) accounts showing the actual and budgeted income and expenditure of that body over any period.

management body

(A) (In the PRA Handbook): (in accordance with article 3(7) of *CRD*) the *governing body* and *senior personnel* of a *CRR firm* who are empowered to set the *firm's* strategy, objectives and overall direction, and which oversee and monitor management decision-making.

(B) (In the FCA Handbook): (in accordance with article 3(7) of *CRD*) the *governing body* and *senior personnel* of a *CRR firm* who are empowered to set the *firm's* strategy, objectives and overall direction, and which oversee and monitor management decision-making.

management body in its supervisory function

(A) (In the PRA Handbook): the *management body* acting in its role of overseeing and monitoring management decision-making.

(B) (In the FCA Handbook): the *management body* acting in its role of overseeing and monitoring management decision-making.

management company

(in accordance with article 2(1)(b) of the *UCITS Directive*) a company, the regular business of which is the management of *UCITS* in the form of unit trusts, common funds (including *authorised contractual schemes*) or investment companies (*collective portfolio management*), including, where permitted by its *Home State regulator*, the additional services referred to in article 6(3) of that directive.

management expenses

(A) In the *FCA Handbook*:

(1) (except in *INSPRU*) (in accordance with section 223 of the *Act* (Management expenses)) expenses incurred or expected to be incurred by the *FSCS* in connection with its function under the *Act*, other than *compensation costs* and costs incurred under Part 15A of the *Act*; for the purposes of FEES 6 these are subdivided into *base costs*, *specific costs* and *establishment costs*.

(2) (in *INSPRU*) in relation to *long-term insurance business*, means all expenses, other than *commission*, incurred in the administration of an *insurer* or its business.

(B) In the PRA Handbook: in relation to *long-term insurance business*, means all expenses, other than *commission*, incurred in the administration of an *insurer* or its business.

management expenses levy

a levy imposed by the *FSCS* on *participant firms* to meet the *management expenses* and which is made up of one or more of a *base cost levy* and a *specific costs levy*, each *participant firm's* share being calculated in accordance with FEES 6.4.

manager

(1) (in relation to an *AUT*) the *firm*, including, if relevant, an *EEA UCITS management company* or *incoming EEA AIFM*, which is the manager of the *AUT* in accordance with the *trust deed*.

(1A) (in relation to an *OEIC* which is an undertaking for collective investment in transferable securities within the meaning of the *UCITS Directive* or which is an *AIF*, and which has appointed a *person* to manage the scheme) the *person* appointed to manage the scheme.

(2) (as defined in section 423(1) and (2) of the *Act* (Manager)) (except in relation to a *unit trust scheme* or an undertaking for collective investment in transferable securities within the meaning of the *UCITS Directive* (other than a unit trust scheme) or a *registered friendly society*):
(a) an employee who:
(i) under the immediate authority of his employer, is responsible, either alone or jointly with one or more other individuals, for the conduct of his employer's business; or
(ii) under the immediate authority of his employer or of a *person* who is a manager in accordance with (i) exercises managerial functions or is responsible for maintaining accounts or other records of his employer;
(b) if the employer is not an individual, references in (a) to the authority of the employer are references to the authority:
(i) in the case of a *body corporate*, of the directors;
(ii) in the case of a *partnership*, of the partners; and
(iii) in the case of an unincorporated association, of its officers or the members of its governing body.

(3) (as defined in section 423(3) of the *Act* (Manager)) (in relation to a *body corporate* other than one covered at (1A) above):
(a) a *person* (other than an employee of the body) who is appointed by the body to manage any part of its business, including an employee of the *body corporate* (other than the *chief executive*) who under the immediate authority of a director or *chief executive* of the *body corporate* exercises

managerial functions or is responsible for maintaining accounts or other records of the *body corporate*;

(b) for the purposes of (a) and in relation to a *body corporate* whose principal place of business is within the *United Kingdom*, the *chief executive* includes only a *person* who is an employee of the *body corporate* in accordance with section 417(1) of the *Act* (Definitions).

managing agent

(as defined in article 3(1) of the *Regulated Activities Order*) a *person* who is permitted by the *Council* in the conduct of his business as an *underwriting agent* to perform for a *member* one or more of the following functions:

(a) underwriting *contracts of insurance* at Lloyd's;

(b) reinsuring such contracts in whole or in part;

(c) paying claims on such contracts.

managing agent's agreement

an agreement in the form prescribed by the *Society*, between a *managing agent* and a *member*, under which the *managing agent* manages the *insurance business* of that *member*.

managing a UCITS

the *regulated activity*, specified in article 51ZA of the *Regulated Activities Order* of carrying on collective portfolio management within the meaning of the *UCITS Directive*, in relation to a *UCITS*.

managing an AIF

the *regulated activity*, specified in article 51ZC of the *Regulated Activities Order*, which is, in summary, performing at least risk management or portfolio management for an *AIF*.

managing dormant account funds (including the investment of such funds)

the *regulated activity*, specified in article 63N(1)(b) of the *Regulated Activities Order*, which is the acceptance of a transfer by a *bank* or *building society* of the *balance* of a *dormant account*, or a proportion of such a balance, and the management of those funds (including the investment of such funds) in such a way as to enable the dormant account fund operator to meet whatever *repayment claims* it is prudent to anticipate.

managing investments

(A) In the PRA Handbook: the *regulated activity*, specified in article 37 of the *Regulated Activities Order* (Managing investments), which is in summary: managing assets belonging to another *person* in circumstances which involve the exercise of discretion, if:

(a) the assets consist of or include any *security* or *contractually based investment* (that is, any *designated investment*, *funeral plan contract* or right to or interest in a *funeral plan contract*); or

(b) the arrangements for their management are such that the assets may consist of or include such *investments*, and either the assets have at any time since 29 April 1988 done so, or the arrangements have at any time (whether before or after that date) been held out as arrangements under which the assets would do so.

(B) In the FCA Handbook: the *regulated activity*, specified in article 37 of the *Regulated Activities Order* (Managing investments), which is in summary: managing assets belonging to another *person* in circumstances which involve the exercise of discretion, if:

(a) the assets consist of or include any *security* or *contractually based investment* (that is, any *designated investment* (other than a *P2P agreement*), *funeral plan contract* or right to or interest in a *funeral plan contract*); or

(b) the arrangements for their management are such that the assets may consist of or include such *investments*, and either the assets have at any time since 29 April 1988 done so, or the arrangements have at any time (whether before or after that date) been held out as arrangements under which the assets would do so.

manager of the relevant scheme

the *person* (including a *person* outside the *United Kingdom*) who administers the *relevant scheme* or (if there is no such *person*) the *person* responsible for making payments under it.

managing the underwriting capacity of a Lloyd's syndicate as a managing agent at Lloyd's

the *regulated activity*, specified in article 57 of the *Regulated Activities Order* (Managing the underwriting capacity of a Lloyd's syndicate), of managing the *underwriting capacity of a Lloyd's syndicate* as a *managing agent* at Lloyd's.

mandate

any means that give a *firm* the ability to control a *client's* assets or liabilities, which meet the conditions in CASS 8.2.1 R.

mandate rules

CASS 8.

MAR

the Market Conduct sourcebook.

margin

(in *COLL*) cash or other property paid, transferred or deposited under the terms of a *derivative*; for these purposes cash or property will be treated as having been paid, transferred or deposited if it must be paid, transferred or deposited in order to comply with a requirement imposed by the market on which the contract is made or traded.

margin agreement

(in accordance with Part 1 of Annex III of the *Banking Consolidation Directive* (Definitions) and for the purpose of BIPRU 13 (The calculation of counterparty risk exposure values for financial derivatives, securities financing transactions and long settlement transactions)) a contractual agreement or provisions to an agreement under which one counterparty must supply collateral to a second counterparty when an *exposure* of that second counterparty to the first counterparty exceeds a specified level.

margin lending transaction

(in accordance with Part 1 of Annex III of the *Banking Consolidation Directive* (Definitions) and for the purpose of BIPRU 13 (The calculation of counterparty risk exposure values for financial derivatives, securities financing transactions and long settlement transactions)) transactions in which a *person* extends credit in connection with the purchase, sale, carrying or trading of securities; the definition does not include other loans that happen to be secured by securities collateral.

margin period of risk

(in accordance with Part 1 of Annex III of the *Banking Consolidation Directive* (Definitions) and for the purpose of BIPRU 13 (The calculation of counterparty risk exposure values for financial derivatives, securities financing transactions and long settlement transactions)) the time period from the last exchange of collateral covering a *netting set* of transactions with a defaulting counterpart until that counterpart is closed out and the resulting market risk is re-hedged.

margin threshold

(in accordance with Part 1 of Annex III of the *Banking Consolidation Directive* (Definitions) and for the purpose of BIPRU 13 (The calculation of counterparty risk exposure values for financial derivatives, securities financing transactions and long settlement transactions)) the largest amount of an *exposure* that remains outstanding until one party has the right to call for collateral.

margined contract

(in *COLL*, CASS 4 and CASS 7) any contract in *derivatives*.

margined transaction

(1) (except in CASS 4 and CASS 7) a transaction *executed* by a *firm* with or for a *client* relating to a *future*, *option* or *contract for differences* (or any right to or any interest in such an *investment*) under the terms of which the *client* will or may be liable to provide cash or *collateral* to secure performance of obligations which he may have to perform when the transaction falls to be completed or upon the earlier *closing out* of his position.

(2) (in CASS 4 and CASS 7):
(a) a transaction within (1); or
(b) an *option* purchased by a *client*, the terms of which provide that the maximum liability of the *client* in respect of the transaction will be limited to the amount payable as premium.

margined transaction requirement

the total amount of *client money* a *firm* is required to segregate in *client bank accounts* for *margined transactions* under the *client money rules*, in accordance with CASS 7.16.32 R.

mark-up or mark-down

(a) (when a *firm* receives a *customer order* and takes a *principal* position in the relevant *investment* in order to fulfil that *customer order* (that is, when the *firm* takes a principal position in the relevant *investment* which it would not otherwise take, except to fulfil that *customer order*)) the difference, if any, between:
(i) the price at which the *firm* takes a principal position in the relevant *investment* in order to fulfil that *customer order*; and
(ii) the *price* at which the firm executes the transaction with its *customer*;

(b) (when a firm executes a *customer order* against its own book and owes a duty of best execution) the difference between:
(i) the *price* at which best execution would be achieved; and
(ii) the *price* at which the firm executes the transaction with its *customer*.

market abuse

(1) (in accordance with section 118 of the *Act* (Market abuse)) *behaviour* (whether by one *person* alone or by two or more *persons* jointly or in concert) which:
(a) occurs in relation to *qualifying investments* traded or admitted to trading on a *prescribed market* or in respect of which a request for admission to trading on such a market has been made; and
(b) falls within any one or more of the types of *behaviour* set out in section 118(2) to (8) of the Act.

(2) (in accordance with section 118 of the *Act* (Market abuse) as modified by the *RAP Regulations*) *behaviour* (whether by one *person* alone or by two or more *persons* jointly or in concert) which:
(a) occurs in relation to *qualifying investments* which are offered for sale on a *prescribed auction platform*; and
(b) falls within any one or more of the types of *behaviour* set out in subsections 118(2) to (8A) of the *Act*.

market abuse (dissemination)

the *behaviour* described in section 118(7) of the *Act*, which is the dissemination of information by any means which gives, or is likely to give, a false or misleading impression as to a *qualifying investment* by a *person* who knew or could reasonably be expected to have known that the information was false or misleading.

market abuse (distortion)

(1) (in accordance with section 118(8) of the *Act* (Market abuse)) the *behaviour* described in section 118(8) of the *Act* which satisfies the condition in section 118(8)(b) and is *behaviour* (not falling within sections 118(5), (6) or (7)) which:
(a) would be, or would be likely to be, regarded by a *regular user* of the market as behaviour that would distort, or would be likely to distort, the market in a *qualifying investment*; and
(b) is likely to be regarded by a *regular user* of the market as a failure on the part of the *person* concerned to observe the standard of *behaviour* reasonably expected of a *person* in his position in relation to the market.

(2) (in accordance with section 118(8) of the *Act* (Market abuse) as modified by the *RAP Regulations*) the *behaviour* described in section 118(8) of the *Act* as modified by the *RAP Regulations* which satisfies the condition in section 118(8)(b) and is *behaviour* (not falling within sections 118(5), (6) or (7)) which:
(a) would be, or would be likely to be, regarded by a *regular user* of the auction platform as *behaviour* that would distort, or would be likely to distort, the auction of such an investment,
(b) and is likely to be regarded by a *regular user* of the auction platform as a failure on the part of the *person* concerned to observe the standard of *behaviour* reasonably expected of a *person* in his position in relation to the market.

market abuse (improper disclosure)

the *behaviour* described in section 118(3) of the *Act*, which is an *insider* disclosing *inside information* to another *person* otherwise than in the proper course of the exercise of employment, profession or duties.

market abuse (insider dealing)

the *behaviour* described in section 118(2) of the *Act*, which is an *insider dealing*, or attempting to *deal*, in a *qualifying investment* or *related investment* on the basis of *inside information* relating to the *investment* in question.

market abuse (manipulating devices)

(1) (in accordance with section 118(6) of the *Act* (Market abuse)) the *behaviour* described in section 118(6) of the *Act*, which is effecting transactions or orders to trade which employ fictitious devices or any other form of deception or contrivance.

(2) (in accordance with section 118(6) of the *Act* (Market abuse) as modified by the *RAP Regulations*)) the *behaviour* described in section 118(6) of the *Act*, which is effecting transactions, bids or orders to trade which employ fictitious devices or any other form of deception or contrivance.

market abuse (manipulating transactions)

(1) (in accordance with section 118(5) of the Act (Market abuse)) the *behaviour* described in section 118(5) of the *Act*, which is *behaviour* effecting transactions or orders to trade (otherwise than for legitimate reasons and in conformity with *accepted market practices* on the relevant market) which:
(a) give, or are likely to give a false or misleading impression as to the supply of, or demand for, or as to the price of, one or more *qualifying investments*; or
(b) secure the price of one or more such investments at an abnormal or artificial level.

(2) (in accordance with section 118(5) of the *Act* (Market abuse) as modified by the *RAP Regulations*) the *behaviour* described in section 118(5) of the *Act* as modified by the *RAP Regulations*, which is *behaviour* effecting transactions, bids or orders to trade (otherwise than for legitimate reasons and in conformity with accepted market practices on the relevant auction platform) which:
(a) give, or are likely to give a false or misleading impression as to the supply of, or demand for, or as to the price of, one or more *qualifying investments*; or
(b) secure the price of one or more such investments at an abnormal or artificial level.

market abuse (misleading behaviour)

(1) (in accordance with section 118(8) of the *Act* (Market abuse)) the *behaviour* described in section 118(8) of the *Act* which satisfies the condition in section 118(8)(a) and is *behaviour* (not falling within sections 118(5), (6) or (7)) which:
(a) is likely to give a *regular user* of the market a false or misleading impression as to the supply of, demand for or price or value of, *qualifying investments*, and
(b) is likely to be regarded by a *regular user* of the market as a failure on the part of the *person* concerned to observe the standard of *behaviour* reasonably expected of a *person* in his position in relation to the market.

(2) (in accordance with section 118(8) of the *Act* (Market abuse) as modified by the *RAP Regulations*) the *behaviour* described in section 118(8) of the *Act* which satisfies the condition in section 118(8)(a) and is *behaviour* (not falling within sections 118(5), (6) or (7)) which:
(a) is likely to give a *regular user* of the auction platform a false or misleading impression as to the supply of, demand for or price or value of, *qualifying investments*, or
(b) and is likely to be regarded by a *regular user* of the auction platform as a failure on the part of the *person* concerned to observe the standard of *behaviour* reasonably expected of a *person* in his position in relation to the market.

market abuse (misuse of information)

(1) (in accordance with section 118(4) of the *Act* (Market abuse)) the *behaviour* described in section 118(4) of the *Act*, which is *behaviour* (not falling within sections 118 (2) or (3) of the *Act*):
(a) based on information which is not generally available to those using the market but which, if available to a *regular user* of the market, would be, or would be likely to be, regarded by him as relevant when deciding the terms on which transactions in *qualifying investments* should be effected; and
(b) likely to be regarded by a *regular user* of the market as a failure on the part of the *person* concerned to observe the standard of *behaviour* reasonably expected of a *person* in his position in relation to the market

(2) (in accordance with section 118(4) of the *Act* (Market abuse) as modified by the *RAP Regulations*) the *behaviour* described in section 118(4) of the *Act* as modified by the *RAP Regulations*, which is *behaviour* (not falling within sections 118 (2) or (3) of the *Act*):
(a) based on information which is not generally available to those using the auction platform but which, if available to a *regular user* of the auction platform, would be, or would be likely to be, regarded by him as relevant when deciding the terms on which transactions in *qualifying investments* should be effected, and
(b) is likely to be regarded by a *regular user* of the auction platform as a failure on the part of the *person* concerned to observe the standard of *behaviour* reasonably expected of a *person* in his position in relation to the auction platform.

Market Abuse Directive

Directive of the European Parliament and of the Council of 28 January 2003 on insider dealing and market manipulation (market abuse) (No 2003/6/EC).

market abuse regime

the regime established under the provisions of Part VIII of the *Act* (Penalties for market abuse).

market contract

a market contract as described in section 155(2)(a) of the Companies Act 1989 or article 80(2)(a) of the Companies (No2) (Northern Ireland) Order 1990 which is in summary a contract entered into by a *member* or *designated non-member* of an *RIE* with a person other than the *RIE* which is either:

(a) a contract made on the exchange or an exchange to whose undertaking the exchange has succeeded; or

(b) a contract in the making of which the member or *designated non-member* was subject to the rules of the exchange or of an exchange to whose undertaking the exchange has succeeded.

market counterparty

(for the purposes only of COBS TP 1 (Transitional Provisions in relation to Client Categorisation)) any *person* classified as a 'market counterparty' under *COB* on 31 October 2007, in accordance with the applicable conditions in force at the time.

market liquidity stress

(in relation to a *firm* and any reporting obligations under SUP 16 (Reporting requirements)):

(a) (in the case of reporting obligations on a solo basis) any market that is of material significance to the *firm* being materially adversely affected by crystallised *liquidity risk* or a substantial number of participants in any such market being materially adversely affected by crystallised *liquidity risk*, whether or not the *firm* itself is so affected;

(b) (in the case of reporting obligations with respect to the *firm* and a group of other persons) has the same meaning as in (a) except that references to the *firm* are to the *firm* and that group considered together;

(c) (in the case of reporting obligations with respect to a *firm's UK branch*) has the same meaning as in (a) except that references to the *firm* are to that *branch*.

market maker

(1) (except in *COBS* and *DTR*) (in relation to an *investment*) a *person* who (otherwise than in his capacity as the *operator* of a *regulated collective investment scheme*) holds himself out as able and willing to enter into transactions of sale and purchase in *investments* of that description at prices determined by him generally and continuously rather than in respect of each particular transaction.

(2) (in *COBS* and *DTR*) a *person* who holds himself out on the financial markets on a continuous basis as being willing to deal on own account by buying and selling *financial instruments* against his proprietary capital at prices defined by him.

[Note: article 4 (1)(8) of *MiFID*]

(3) [deleted]

market maker exemption

an exemption from articles 5, 6, 7, 12, 13 and 14 of the *short selling regulation* for transactions performed due to *market making activities* pursuant to article 17 of the *short selling regulation*.

market making activities

(as defined in article 2(1)(k) of the *short selling regulation*) the activities of an *investment firm*, a *credit institution*, a third-country entity, or a firm as referred to in point (l) of article 2(1) of *MIFID*, which is a member of a *trading venue* or of a market in a third country, the legal and supervisory framework of which has been declared equivalent by the European Commission pursuant to article 17(2) of the *short selling regulation* where it deals as principal in a *financial instrument*, whether traded on or outside a *trading venue*, in any of the following capacities:

(a) by posting firm, simultaneous two-way quotes of comparable size and at competitive prices, with the result of providing liquidity on a regular and ongoing basis to the market; or

(b) as part of its usual business, by fulfilling orders initiated by clients or in response to clients' requests to trade; or

(c) by hedging positions arising from the fulfilment of tasks under points (a) and (b).

market operator

a *person* who manages and/or operates the business of a *regulated market*. The *market operator* may be the *regulated market* itself. [Note: article 4(1)(13) of *MiFID*]

market risk

(1) (in *COLL* and *FUND*) the risk of loss for a *UCITS* or *AIF* resulting from fluctuation in the market value of positions in the *fund's* portfolio attributable to changes in market variables, such as interest rates, foreign exchange rates, equity and commodity prices or an issuer's credit worthiness.

(2) (except in *COLL* and *FUND*) (in relation to a *firm*) the risks that arise from fluctuations in values of, or income from, assets or in interest or exchange rates.

market risk capital requirement

the part of the *capital resources requirement* of a *BIPRU firm* in respect of *market risk*, calculated in accordance with GENPRU 2.1.52R (Calculation of the market risk capital requirement).

market value

the market value as determined in accordance with generally accepted accounting practice.

marketable investment

(a) an *investment* which is traded on or under the rules of an exchange;

(b) a debt instrument which may be transferred without the consent of the *issuer* or any other *person* (including a collateralised mortgage obligation);

(c) a *commodity*;

(d) a *warrant, option, future* or other instrument which entitles the holder to subscribe for or acquire:
(i) an *investment* or *commodity* in (a) to (c); or
(ii) any currency; or
(iii) any combination of (i) and (ii);

(e) a *contract for differences* (including interest rate and currency swaps) relating to fluctuations in:
(i) the value or price of an *investment* or *commodity* in (a) to (d); or
(ii) any currency; or
(iii) the rate of interest in any currency or any index of such rates; or
(iv) the level of any index which is derived from the prices of an *investment* or *commodity* in (a) to (c); or
(v) any combination of (i) to (iv);

(f) *warrants, options, futures* or other instruments entitling the holder to obtain the rights of those contracts in (d) or (e);

(g) a *unit* in a *regulated collective investment scheme*.

marketing

(1) (in *COLL*) (in relation to marketing *units* in a *regulated collective investment scheme* in a particular country or territory):
(a) *communicating* to a *person* in that country or territory an invitation or inducement to become, or offer to become, a *holder* in that *regulated collective investment scheme*;
(b) giving *advice on investments* to, or arranging (bringing about) a deal in an investment for a *person* in that country or territory to become a *holder* in that *regulated collective investment scheme*

(2) (except in *COLL*) a direct or indirect offering or placement, at the initiative of the *AIFM* or on behalf of the *AIFM* of *units* or *shares* of an *AIF* it manages, to or with investors domiciled or with a registered office in the *EEA*. [Note: article 4(1)(x) of *AIFMD*]

marketing group

a group of *persons* who:

(a) are allied together (either formally or informally) for the purposes of marketing *packaged products* of the *marketing group*; and

(b) each of whom, if it holds itself out in the *United Kingdom* as marketing *packaged products* to *private customers*, does so only as an *investment manager* or in relation to *packaged products* of the *marketing group*.

marketing group associate

a *firm* other than a *product provider* which is a member of a *marketing group*.

marriage or the formation of a civil partnership and birth

(in relation to a *class* of *contract of insurance*) the *class* of *contract of insurance*, specified in paragraph II of Part II of Schedule 1 to the *Regulated Activities Order* (Contracts of long-term insurance), to provide a sum on marriage or the formation of a civil partnership or on the birth of a child, being contracts expressed to be in effect for a period of more than one year.

master AIF

(in accordance with article 4(1)(y) of *AIFMD*) an *AIF* in which another *AIF* (a *feeder AIF*) invests or has an exposure in accordance with the definition of '*feeder AIF*'.

master-feeder agreement

(in *COLL*) a written agreement between the *management company* of a *master UCITS* and the *management company* of a *feeder UCITS* in accordance with COLL 11.3.2 R (1) (Master-feeder agreement and internal conduct of business rules).

master netting agreement internal models approach

one of the following:

(a) the method of calculating the effect of *credit risk mitigation* described in BIPRU 5.6.16 R to BIPRU 5.6.28 G;

(b) (where the approach in (a) is being applied on a consolidated basis) the method in (a) as applied on a consolidated basis in accordance with BIPRU 8 (Group risk – consolidation); or

(c) when the reference is to the rules of or administered by a *regulatory body* other than the *appropriate regulator*, whatever corresponds to the approach in (a) or (b), as the case may be, under those rules.

master netting agreement internal models approach permission

(A) In the PRA Handbook:
requirement or a *waiver* that requires a *firm* to use the *master netting agreement internal models approach* on a solo basis or, if the context requires, a consolidated basis.

(B) In the FCA Handbook:
requirement or a *waiver* that requires a *BIPRU firm* to use the *master netting agreement internal models approach* on a solo basis or, if the context requires, a consolidated basis.

master UCITS

(in accordance with article 58(3) of the *UCITS Directive*) a *UCITS scheme*, an *EEA UCITS scheme* or a *sub-fund* of such a *scheme* where:

(a) at least one of its *unitholders* is a *feeder UCITS*;

(b) it is not itself a *feeder UCITS*; and

(c) it does not hold *units* of a *feeder UCITS*.

matched principal exemption conditions

(1) (for the purposes of *BIPRU*) the conditions set out in BIPRU 1.1.23 R (2) (Meaning of dealing on own account).

(2) (other than in *BIPRU*) the conditions set out in IFPRU 1.1.12 R (Meaning of dealing on own account).

material currency

(a) *Material currencies*, in respect of a *firm* at any time, are currencies determined in accordance with the following.

(b) First, the amount of its assets and the amount of its liabilities in each currency (ignoring the sign) are separately calculated. The figures are as shown in the most recent *data item* FSA054 submitted to the *appropriate regulator*.

(c) Then, each such amount is converted into the reporting currency for the *data item* referred to in (b).

(d) Each currency (which may include the reporting currency) that represents 20% or more of the total asset figure or 20% or more of the total liabilities figure is a *material currency*.

(e) A currency is also a *material currency* if it is identified by the *firm's* current:
(i) *Individual Liquidity Adequacy Assessment*; or
(ii) *Individual Liquidity Systems Assessment*; or

(iii) *ILG* that has been accepted by the *firm*;

as being significant in the context of cross-currency *liquidity risk* (as referred to in BIPRU 12.5 (Individual Liquidity Adequacy Standards)).

(f) The conversion rate for a currency into the reporting currency is the exchange rate on the date as of which the calculation is being made.

(g) The reporting currency means the currency in which the most recent *data item* FSA054 (as referred to in (b)) is reported.

(h) A currency is a *material currency* in relation to a *firm's branch* or a *defined liquidity group* of which it is a *group liquidity reporting firm* if it is identified as such in accordance with the procedures in the previous paragraphs of this definition except that the identification is carried out by reference to that *branch* or *defined liquidity group*. For these purposes, *data item* FSA054 for the *reporting level* concerned is used.

(i) If the *firm* has not delivered *data item* FSA054 to the *appropriate regulator* at the *reporting level* concerned or is currently not required to do so at the *reporting level* concerned, the calculation is carried out using the methods for drawing up *data item* FSA054.

material current year losses

(in *IPRU(INV)* 13) losses of an amount equal to 10 per cent or more of the amount by which the *own funds* of an *undertaking* exceed the *own funds* needed to meet financial resources test 1 as prescribed in chapter 13.

material holding

(1) [deleted]

(2) (for the purposes of *GENPRU* and *BIPRU*) has the meaning in GENPRU 2.2.209 R (Deductions from tiers one and two: Material holdings (BIPRU firm only)).

material insurance holding

has the meaning in GENPRU 2.2.212R (Material holdings) or, for an *exempt CAD firm* which is an *investment management firm*, in *IPRU(INV)* Table 5.2.2(1).

material interest

(in*COBS*) (in relation to a transaction) any interest of a material nature, other than:

(a) disclosable *commission* on the transaction;

(b) goods or services which can reasonably be expected to assist in carrying on *designated investment business* with or for *clients* and which are provided or to be provided in compliance with COBS 11.6.3 R.

material outsourcing

(A) In the PRA Handbook:

outsourcing services of such importance that weakness, or failure, of the services would cast serious doubt upon the *firm's* continuing satisfaction of the *threshold conditions* or compliance with the *Fundamental Rules*.

(B) In the FCA Handbook:

outsourcing services of such importance that weakness, or failure, of the services would cast serious doubt upon the *firm's* continuing satisfaction of the *threshold conditions* or compliance with the *Principles*.

mathematical reserves

the provision made by an *insurer* to cover liabilities (excluding liabilities which have fallen due and liabilities arising from *deposit back arrangements*) arising under or in connection with *long-term insurance contracts*.

maxi-ISA

an *ISA* which includes a *stocks and shares component* and may also include other *qualifying investments* such as:

(a) a *cash component*;

(b) an *insurance component*;

as prescribed in paragraphs 7, 8 and 9 respectively of the *ISA Regulations*.

MCAS scheme

Mortgage Code Arbitration Scheme.

MCG

the Office of Fair Trading's Mental Capacity Guidance.

MCOB

the Mortgages and Home Finance: Conduct of Business sourcebook.

MCR

minimum capital requirement.

MDA

the maximum distributable amount calculated in line with IFPRU 10.4.3 R.

media firm

a *firm* whose only *permitted activities* are *advising on investments* and *agreeing to carry on that regulated activity*, and whose *Part 4A permission* includes *requirements* to the effect that the *firm* must advise:

(a) only through the media; and

(b) without conveying the impression that the advice is particularly suitable for any *person*, except when it is given in response to a specific request for advice from that *person*;

in this definition, "media" means:

(i) newspapers, journals, magazines or other periodical publications;

(ii) services comprising regularly updated news or information;

(iii) services consisting of the broadcast or transmission of television or radio programmes.

media operator

a news vendor that receives *regulated information* from a *regulatory information service* and then disseminates that information to the public as soon as possible.

meeting of repayment claims

the *regulated activity*, specified in article 63N(1)(a) of the *Regulated Activities Order*, which is the meeting of *repayment claims* by a *dormant account fund operator*.

member

(1) (except in *PROF*, *LR*, EG 16 and *REC*) a *person* admitted to membership of the *Society* or any *person* by law entitled or bound to administer his affairs.

(2) (in *PROF*, *LR* and EG 16) (as defined in section 325(2) of the *Act* (FCA's general duty)) (in relation to a profession) a *person* who is entitled to practise that profession and, in practising it, is subject to the rules of the relevant *designated professional body*, whether or not he is a member of that body.

(3) (in *REC*) (in relation to a *recognised body*) a *person* who is entitled, under an arrangement or agreement between him and that body, to use that body's *facilities*.

member contribution

any paid up contribution by a member of a *mutual* where the members' accounts meet the following criteria:

(a) the memorandum and articles of association or other constitutional documents must stipulate that payments may be made from these accounts to members only in so far as this does not cause the *firm's capital resources* to fall below the required level, or, if after dissolution of the *firm*, all the *firm's* other debts have been settled;

(b) the memorandum and articles of association or other constitutional documents must stipulate, with respect to the payments referred to in (a) made for reasons other than the individual termination of membership, that the *appropriate regulator* must be notified at least one month in advance of the intended date of such payments; and

(c) the *appropriate regulator* must be notified of any amendment to the relevant provisions of the memorandum and articles of association or other constitutional documents.

member of a pension scheme

has the same meaning as it has in article 53E(2) of the *Regulated Activities Order*, which is, a member of a pension scheme within the meaning of section 1(5) of the Pension Schemes Act 1993 (and section 1(5) of the Pension Schemes (Northern Ireland) Act 1993).

member society

(as defined in article 2(2) of the *compensation transitionals order*) a person who at any time before *commencement* was a member society within the rules of the Friendly Societies Protection Scheme established in accordance with section 141 of the Financial Services Act 1986.

members' adviser

a *firm* whose *permission* includes *advising on syndicate participation at Lloyd's*, but which is not an *underwriting agent*.

members' agent

an *underwriting agent* who carries on the *regulated activity* of *advising on syndicate participation at Lloyd's*.

membership of a Lloyd's syndicate

the *investment*, specified in article 86(2) of the *Regulated Activities Order*, which is a *person*'s membership (or prospective membership) of a Lloyd's *syndicate*.

merging UCITS

(in *COLL*) in relation to a *UCITS merger*, the *UCITS scheme*, *EEA UCITS scheme* or *sub-fund* of such a *scheme*, that under the proposed arrangements will be transferring all its assets and liabilities to the *receiving UCITS*.

MERS levy

a levy (management expenses in respect of relevant schemes levy) imposed by the *FSCS* on *participant firms* to meet the management expenses incurred by the *FSCS* in connection with acting on behalf of the *manager of the relevant scheme* in accordance with Part 15A of the *Act*.

mezzanine securitisation positions

for the purposes of BIPRU 9.3.7 R, BIPRU 9.4.11 R and BIPRU 9.5.1 R (6), *securitisation positions* to which a *risk weight* lower than 1250% applies and which are more junior than the most senior position in the relevant *securitisation* and more junior than any *securitisation* position in the relevant *securitisation* to which:

(a) in the case of a *securitisation position* subject to the *standardised approach* to *securitisation* set out in BIPRU 9.11.1 R and BIPRU 9.11.2 R, a *credit quality step* 1 is assigned; or

(b) in the case of a *securitisation position* subject to the *IRB approach* to *securitisation* set out in BIPRU 9.12.10 R and BIPRU 9.12.11 R, a *credit quality step* 1 or 2 is assigned under BIPRU 9.7.2 R, BIPRU 9.8.2 R to BIPRU 9.8.7 R and regulation 23 of the *Capital Requirements Regulations 2006*.

[Note: *BCD*, Annex IX, Part 2, Point 1, paragraph 1b]

MFHC conglomerate

a *financial conglomerate* which is headed by a *mixed financial holding company*.

mesothelioma regulations

The Compensation Act 2006 (Contribution for Mesothelioma Claims) Regulations 2006 (SI 2006/3259).

mesothelioma victim

(in accordance with section 3 (1) of the Compensation Act 2006) a *person* who has contracted mesothelioma as a result of exposure to asbestos by a *responsible person*.

micro-enterprise

an enterprise which:

(a) employs fewer than 10 *persons*; and

(b) has a turnover or annual balance sheet that does not exceed 2 million.

In this definition, "enterprise" means any *person* engaged in an economic activity, irrespective of legal form and includes, in particular, self-employed *persons* and family businesses engaged in craft or other activities, and *partnerships* or associations regularly engaged in an economic activity. [Note: article 4(26) of the *Payment Services Directive* and the Annex to the *Micro-enterprise Recommendation*]

Micro-enterprise Recommendation

Recommendation 2003/361/EC of the Commission of 6th May 2003 concerning the definition of micro, small and medium-sized enterprises.

MiFID

The European Parliament and Council Directive on markets in financial instruments (No. 2004/39/EC). See also *MiFID Regulation* and *MiFID implementing Directive*.

MiFID II

Directive 2014/65/EU of the European Parliament and of the Council of 15 May 2014 on markets in financial instruments and amending the *insurance mediation directive* and *AIFMD* (eur-lex.europa.eu/legal-content/EN/TXT/PDF/?uri=OJ:JOL_2014_173_R_0009&from=EN).

MiFID business

investment services and activities and, where relevant, *ancillary services* carried on by a *MiFID investment firm*.

MiFID business bidding

the *regulated activity* of *bidding in emissions auctions* where it is carried on by a *MiFID investment firm* (other than a *UCITS investment firm*) in relation to a *financial instrument*.

MiFID client money (minimum implementing) rules

(A) In the PRA Handbook: CASS 7.3.1 R, CASS 7.3.2 R, CASS 7.4.1 R, CASS 7.4.5 R, CASS 7.4.7 R, CASS 7.4.8 R, CASS 7.4.11 R, CASS 7.6.1 R, CASS 7.6.2 R and CASS 7.6.9 R.

(B) In the FCA Handbook: CASS 7.12.1 R, CASS 7.12.2 R, CASS 7.13.3 R, CASS 7.13.8 R, CASS 7.13.10 R, CASS 7.13.12 R, CASS 7.13.28 R, CASS 7.15.2 R, CASS 7.15.3 R, CASS 7.15.20 R.

MiFID implementing Directive

Commission Directive No. 2006/73/EC implementing Directive 2004/39/EC of the European Parliament and of the Council as regards organisational requirements and operating conditions for investment firms and defined terms for the purposes of that Directive.

MiFID implementing requirement

(1) (in relation to a *UK RIE*) any of the requirements applicable to that body under the *MiFID Regulation*.

(2) (in relation to a body applying for recognition as a *UK RIE*) any of the requirements under the *MiFID Regulation* which, if its application were successful, would apply to it.

MiFID investment firm

(A) In the PRA Handbook:
(in summary) a *firm* to which *MiFID* applies including, for some purposes only, a *credit institution* and *collective portfolio management investment firm*. (in full) a *firm* which is:
(1) an *investment firm* with its head office in the *EEA* (or, if it has a registered office, that office);
(2) a *CRD credit institution* (only when providing an *investment service or activity* in relation to the *rules* implementing the Articles referred to in Article 1(2) of *MiFID*);
(3) a *collective portfolio management investment firm* (only when providing the services referred to in article 6(4) *AIFMD* or Article 6(3) of the *UCITS Directive* in relation to the *rules* implementing the articles of *MiFID* referred to in article 6(6) of *AIFMD* or Article 20 6(4) of the *UCITS Directive* and for a *full-scope UK AIFM* the *rules* implementing article 12(2)(b) of *AIFMD*);
unless, and to the extent that, *MiFID* does not apply to it as a result of Article 2 (Exemptions) or Article 3 (Optional exemptions) of *MiFID*.

(B) In the FCA Handbook:
(in summary) a *firm* to which *MiFID* applies including, for some purposes only, a *credit institution* and *collective portfolio management investment firm*. (in full) a *firm* which is:
(1) an *investment firm* with its head office in the *EEA* (or, if it has a registered office, that office);
(2) a *CRD credit institution* (only when providing an *investment service or activity* in relation to the

rules implementing the Articles referred to in Article 1(2) of *MiFID*);

(3) a *collective portfolio management investment firm* (only when providing the services referred to in article 6(4) *AIFMD* or Article 6(3) of the *UCITS Directive* in relation to the *rules* implementing the articles of *MiFID* referred to in article 6(6) of *AIFMD* or Article 20 6(4) of the *UCITS Directive* and for a *full-scope UK AIFM* the *rules* implementing article 12(2)(b) of *AIFMD*);

unless, and to the extent that, *MiFID* does not apply to it as a result of Article 2 (Exemptions) or Article 3 (Optional exemptions) of *MiFID*.

MiFID or equivalent third country business

MiFID business or the *equivalent business of a third country investment firm*.

MiFID outsourcing rules

SYSC 8.1.1 R to SYSC 8.1.11 R.

MiFID Regulation

Commission Regulation (EC) 1287/2006 implementing Directive 2004/39/EC of the European Parliament and of the Council as regards organisational requirements and operating conditions for investment firms and defined terms for the purposes of that Directive.

MiFIR

Regulation (EU) No. 600/2014 of the European Parliament and of the Council of 15 May 2014 on markets in financial instruments and amending *EMIR* (eur-lex.europa.eu/legal-content/EN/TXT/PDF/?uri=OJ:JOL_2014_173_R_0005&from=EN).

MIIC

the *Motor Insurers' Information Centre*.

mineral company

(in *LR*) a *company* or *group*, whose principal activity is, or is planned to be, the *extraction* of *mineral resources* (which may or may not include exploration for *mineral resources*).

mineral expert's report

(in *LR*) a competent person's report prepared in accordance with paragraph 133 of the *ESMA Prospectus Recommendations*.

mineral resources

(in *LR*) include metallic and non-metallic ores, mineral concentrates, industrial minerals, construction aggregates, mineral oils, natural gases, hydrocarbons and solid fuels including coal.

mini-ISA

an *ISA* which contains only one of the following *qualifying investments*:

(a) a *stocks and shares component*;

(b) a *cash component*;

(c) an *insurance component*;

as prescribed in paragraph 7, 8 or 9 respectively of the *ISA Regulations*.

minimum capital requirement

an amount of capital resources that a *firm* must hold as set out in GENPRU 2.1.24 R and GENPRU 2.1.25 R.

minimum IRB standards

(in relation to the IRB approach) BIPRU 4.3.9 R, BIPRU 4.3.11 R-BIPRU 4.3.29 R, BIPRU 4.3.33 R-BIPRU 4.3.40 R, BIPRU 4.3.43 R-BIPRU 4.3.44 R, BIPRU 4.3.46 R-BIPRU 4.3.48 R, BIPRU 4.3.50 R-BIPRU 4.3.51 R, BIPRU 4.3.54 R, BIPRU 4.3.56 R-BIPRU 4.3.57 R, BIPRU 4.3.63 R, BIPRU 4.3.70 R-BIPRU 4.3.71 R, BIPRU 4.3.73 R-BIPRU 4.3.74 R, BIPRU 4.3.83 R-BIPRU 4.3.85 R, BIPRU 4.3.88 R, BIPRU 4.3.90 R-BIPRU 4.3.92 R, BIPRU 4.3.94 R, BIPRU 4.3.99 R, BIPRU 4.3.103 R, BIPRU 4.3.116 R-BIPRU 4.3.123 R, BIPRU 4.3.125 R-BIPRU 4.3.131 RBIPRU 4.4.6 R-BIPRU 4.4.9 R, BIPRU 4.4.11 R-BIPRU 4.4.13 R, BIPRU 4.4.15 R-BIPRU 4.4.18 R, BIPRU 4.4.21 R-BIPRU 4.4.22 R, BIPRU 4.4.24 R-BIPRU 4.4.25 R, BIPRU 4.4.27 R-BIPRU 4.4.28 R, BIPRU 4.4.30 R-BIPRU 4.4.31 R, BIPRU 4.4.48 R-BIPRU 4.4.51 R, BIPRU 4.4.53 R, BIPRU 4.4.54 R, BIPRU 4.5.5 R, BIPRU 4.6.6 R-BIPRU 4.6.9 R, BIPRU 4.6.11 R-BIPRU 4.6.12 R, BIPRU 4.6.14 R, BIPRU 4.6.18 R, BIPRU 4.6.20 R-BIPRU 4.6.21 R,

BIPRU 4.6.24 R-BIPRU 4.6.34 R, BIPRU 4.6.37 R-BIPRU 4.6.39 R, BIPRU 4.7.19 R, BIPRU 4.7.27 R-BIPRU 4.7.35 R, BIPRU 4.8.5 R-BIPRU 4.8.9 R, BIPRU 4.8.11 R-BIPRU 4.8.15 R, BIPRU 4.10.40 R-BIPRU 4.10.48 R.

minimum levy

(in *FEES*) the fixed minimum *general levy* payable by a *firm*.

minimum multiplication factor

(in BIPRU 7.10 (Use of a value at risk model)) has the meaning in BIPRU 7.10.119 R (Capital calculations: Multiplication factors), which is in summary the number three or any higher amount the *VaR model permission* defines it as.

MIPRU

the Prudential sourcebook for Mortgage and Home Finance Firms, and Insurance Intermediaries

miscellaneous financial loss

(in relation to a *class* of *contract of insurance*) the *class* of *contract of insurance*, specified in paragraph 16 of Part I of Schedule 1 to the *Regulated Activities Order* (General *contracts of insurance*), against any of the following risks:

(a) risks of loss to the *persons* insured attributable to interruptions of the carrying on of business carried on by them or to reduction of the scope of business so carried on;

(b) risks of loss to the *persons* insured attributable to their incurring unforeseen expense (other than loss such as is covered by contracts within paragraph 18 of Part I of Schedule 1 to the *Regulated Activities Order* (Assistance));

(c) risks which do not fall within paragraphs (a) or (b) and which are not of such a kind that *contracts of insurance* against them fall within any other provision of Schedule 1 to the *Regulated Activities Order*.

miscellaneous securities

(in *LR*) *securities* which are not:

(a) *shares*; or

(b) *debt securities*; or

(c) *asset backed securities*; or

(d) *certificate representing debt securities*; or

(e) *convertible securities* which convert to *debt securities*; or

(f) *convertible securities* which convert to *equity securities*; or

(g) *convertible securities* which are exchangeable for *securities* of another *company*; or

(h) *certificate representing certain securities*; or

(i) *securitised derivatives*.

misleading statements and practices offence

[deleted]

mixed-activity holding company

(A) In the PRA Handbook:
has the meaning given to the definition of "mixed activity holding company" in article 4(1)(22) of the *EU CRR*.
(B) In the FCA Handbook:
has the meaning given to the definition of "mixed activity holding company" in article 4(1)(22) of the *EU CRR*.

mixed-activity insurance holding company

(in accordance with Article 1(j) of the *Insurance Groups Directive* (Definitions)) a *parent undertaking*, other than an *insurance undertaking*, an *insurance holding company* or a *mixed financial holding company*, the *subsidiary undertakings* of which include at least one *insurance undertaking*.

mixed financial holding company

(in accordance with Article 2(15) of the *Financial Groups Directive* (Definitions)) a *parent undertaking*, other than a *regulated entity*, which meets the following conditions:

(a) it, together with its *subsidiary undertakings*, at least one of which is an *EEA regulated entity*, and other entities, constitutes a *financial conglomerate;*

(b) it has been notified by its *coordinator* that its group is a *financial conglomerate* in accordance with Article 4(2) of the *Financial Groups Directive*; and

(c) it has not been notified that its *coordinator* and other *relevant competent authorities* have agreed not to treat the group as a *financial conglomerate* in accordance with Article 3(3) or Article 3(3a) of the *Financial Groups Directive*.

mixed insurer

an *insurer* (other than a *pure reinsurer*) which carries on *reinsurance* business and where one or more of the following conditions is met in respect of its *reinsurance* acceptances:

(a) the *premiums* collected in respect of those acceptances during the previous *financial year* exceeded 10% of its total *premiums* collected during that year;

(b) the *premiums* collected in respect of those acceptances during the previous *financial year* exceeded 50 million; and

(c) the *technical provisions* in respect of those acceptances at the end of the previous *financial year* exceeded 10% of its total *technical provisions* at the end of that year.

mixed remittance

a remittance that is part *client money* and part other *money*.

MLAR

(in *SUP*) a Mortgage Lending and Administration Return containing data specified in SUP 16 Annex 19A and relevant to the *firm's* type and *regulated activities*.

MLRO

money laundering reporting officer.

Model Code

The Model Code on directors' dealings in securities set out in LR 9 Annex 1.

model risk

the potential loss an *institution* may incur, as a consequence of decisions that could be principally based on the output of internal models used under any of the internal approaches, due to errors in the development, implementation or use of such models.

model PRR

the part of the *market risk capital requirement* calculated under a *VaR model permission* as more fully defined in BIPRU 7.10 (Use of a Value at Risk Model).

modified CIU look through method

the method for calculating *PRR* for a *CIU* set out in BIPRU 7.7.4 R, BIPRU 7.7.7 R to BIPRU 7.7.8 R and BIPRU 7.7.11 R to BIPRU 7.7.12 R

modified report

(in *LR*) an accountant's or auditor's report:

(a) in which the opinion is modified; or

(b) which contains an emphasis-of-matter paragraph.

money

any form of money, including cheques and other payable orders.

Money Advice Service

the consumer financial education body (*CFEB*) originally established by the *FSA* under section 6A(1) of the *Act* (Enhancing public understanding of financial matters etc) (as it had effect before the passing of the Financial Services Act 2012).

money laundering

any act which:

(a) constitutes an offence under section 18 (Money laundering) of the Terrorism Act 2000; or

(b) constitutes an offence under section 327 (Concealing etc), section 328 (Arrangements) or section 329 (Acquisition, use and possession) of the Proceeds of Crime Act 2002; or

(c) constitutes an attempt, conspiracy or incitement to commit an offence specified in paragraph (b); or

(d) constitutes aiding, abetting, counselling or procuring the commission of an offence specified in paragraph (b); or

(e) would constitute an offence specified in paragraph (b), (c), or (d) if done in the *United Kingdom*.

Money Laundering Directive

the Council Directive of 10 June 1991 on the prevention of the use of the financial system for the purpose of money laundering (91/308/EEC) as amended by the Council Directive of 4 December 2001 (2001/97/EEC).

Money Laundering Regulations

the Money Laundering Regulations 2007 (SI 2007/2157).

money laundering reporting function

(in the *FCA Handbook*) *FCA controlled function* CF11 in Parts 1 and 2 of the *table of FCA controlled functions*, described more fully in SUP 10A.7.10 R.

money laundering reporting officer

the individual appointed by a *firm* in accordance with SYSC 3.2.6I R or SYSC 6.3.9 R.

money market fund

an *authorised fund* or, in the case of an *umbrella*, a *sub-fund* (if it were a separate fund) which satisfies the conditions in COLL 5.9.5 R (Investment conditions: money market funds) and is not a *qualifying money market fund*.

money-market instrument

(1) any of the following *investments*:

(a) a *debenture* which is issued on terms requiring repayment not later than five years from the date of issue;

(b) any *government and public security* which is issued on terms requiring repayment not later than one year or, if issued by a local authority in the *United Kingdom*, five years from the date of issue;

(c) a *warrant* which entitles the holder to subscribe for an *investment* within (a) or (b);

(d) a *certificate representing certain securities* or *rights to or interests in investments* relating, in either case, to an *investment* within (a) or (b);

(e) an *option* relating to:
(i) an instrument in (a) or (b); or
(ii) currency of the *United Kingdom* or of any other country or territory; or
(iii) gold or silver;

(f) a *future* for the sale of:
(i) an instrument in (a) or (b); or
(ii) currency of the *United Kingdom* or of any other country or territory; or
(iii) gold or silver;

(g) a *contract for differences* by reference to fluctuations in:
(i) the value or price of any instrument within any of (a) to (f); or
(ii) currency of the *United Kingdom* or of any other country or territory; or
(iii) the rate of interest on loans in any such currency or any index of such rates;

(h) an *option* to acquire or dispose of an instrument within (e), (f) or (g).

(2) those classes of *financial instruments* which are normally dealt in on the money market, such as treasury bills, certificates of deposit and commercial papers and excluding instruments of payment. [Note: article 4(1)(19) of *MiFID*]

money market instrument activity

an activity in respect of a transaction:

(a) which involves any of the following *investments* and is not regulated by the rules of a *recognised investment exchange*:
(i) a *debenture* which is issued on terms requiring repayment not later than five years from the date of issue;

(ii) any *government and public security* which is issued on terms requiring repayment not later than one year or, if issued by a local authority in the *United Kingdom*, five years from the date of issue; or

(iii) a *warrant* which entitles the holder to subscribe for an *investment* within (a)(i) or (a)(ii);

(b) which involves any of the following *investments* and is not made on a *recognised investment exchange* or expressed to be so made:

(i) a *certificate representing certain securities* or rights to or interests in *investments* relating, in either case, to an *investment* within (a)(i) or (a)(ii);

(ii) an *option* relating to:

(A) an instrument in (a)(i) or (a)(ii); or

(B) currency of the *United Kingdom* or of any other country or territory; or

(C) gold or silver;

(iii) a *future* for the sale of:

(A) an instrument in (a)(i) or (a)(ii); or

(B) currency of the *United Kingdom* or of any other country or territory; or

(C) gold or silver;

(iv) a *contract for differences* by reference to fluctuations in:

(A) the value or price of any instrument within any of (a)(i) to (a)(iii) or (b)(i) to (b)(iii); or

(B) currency of the *United Kingdom* or of any other country or territory; or

(C) the rate of interest on loans in any such currency or any index of such rates; or

(v) an *option* to acquire or dispose of an instrument within (b)(ii), (b)(iii) or (b)(iv); or

(c) where one of the parties agrees to sell or transfer a *debenture* or *government and public security* and by the same or a collateral agreement that party agrees, or acquires an option, to buy back or re-acquire that *investment* or an equivalent amount of a similar *investment* within twelve *months* of the sale or transfer.

For the purposes of (c) *investments* are regarded as similar if they entitle their holders to the same rights against the same *persons* as to capital and interest and the same remedies for the enforcement of those rights.

money-market instruments

those classes of *financial instruments* which are normally dealt in on the money market, such as treasury bills, certificates of deposit and commercial papers and excluding instruments of payment. [Note: article 4(1)(19) of *MiFID*]

money-purchase benefits

(A) In the *FCA Handbook*:

(1) (except in *COMP*) (in relation to an *occupational pension scheme*) benefits the rate or amount of which are calculated by reference to a payment or payments made by a member of the scheme.

(2) (in *COMP*) in relation to a member of a *personal pension scheme* or an *occupational pension scheme* or the widow or widower or surviving civil partner of a member of such a scheme, means benefits the rate or amount of which is calculated by reference to a payment or payments made by the member or by any other *person* in respect of the member and which are not average salary benefits.

(B) In the *PRA Handbook*: (in relation to an *occupational pension scheme*) benefits the rate or amount of which are calculated by reference to a payment or payments made by a member of the scheme.

money-purchase occupational scheme

an *occupational pension scheme* which provides *money-purchase benefits*.

money purchase scheme

in relation to a *director*, means a pension scheme under which all of the benefits that may become payable to or in respect of the *director* are money purchase benefits.

money service business

carrying on by way of business the activity of:

(a) operating a bureau de change; or

(b) transmitting money, or any representation of monetary value, by any means; or

(c) cashing cheques which are made payable to customers.

money service operator

a *person* who carries on *money service business* other than a *firm*, a *BCD credit institution* or a *financial institution*.

money remittance

(in accordance with regulation 2(1) of the *Payment Service Regulations*) a service for the transmission of money (or any representation of monetary value), without any payment accounts being created in the name of the payer or the payee, where:

(a) funds are received from a payer for the sole purpose of transferring a corresponding amount to a payee or to another *payment service provider* acting on behalf of the payee; or

(b) funds are received on behalf of, and made available to, the payee.

[Note: article 4(13) of the *Payment Services Directive*]

month

(in accordance with the Interpretation Act 1978) a calendar month.

monthly financial return

(in *UPRU*) means the return referred to in *SUP*.

mortgage administrator

a *firm* with *permission* (or which ought to have *permission*) for *administering a regulated mortgage contract*.

mortgage adviser

a *firm* with *permission* (or which ought to have *permission*) for *advising on regulated mortgage contracts*.

Mortgage and General Insurance Complaints Transitional Order

The Financial Services and Markets Act 2000 (Transitional Provisions) (Complaints Relating to General Insurance and Mortgages) Order 2004 (SI 2004/454).

mortgage arranger

a *firm* with *permission* (or which ought to have *permission*) for *arranging* (see also *arranging (bringing about) regulated mortgage contracts* and *making arrangements with a view to regulated mortgage contracts*).

mortgage credit card

a *plastic card* which is a credit card issued under a *regulated mortgage contract* and not regulated by the Consumer Credit Act 1974.

mortgage intermediary

a *firm* with *permission* (or which ought to have *permission*) to carry on *mortgage mediation activity*.

mortgage lender

a *firm* with *permission* (or which ought to have *permission*) for *entering into a regulated mortgage contract*.

mortgage mediation activity

(as defined in article 26 of the Financial Services and Markets Act 2000 (Regulated Activities) (Amendment) (No. 1) Order 2003 (SI 2003/1475)) any of the following *regulated activities*:

(a) *arranging (bringing about) regulated mortgage contracts* (article 25A(1));

(b) *making arrangements with a view to regulated mortgage contracts* (article 25A(2));

(c) *advising on regulated mortgage contracts* (article 53A);

(d) *agreeing to carry on a regulated activity* in (a) to (c) (article 64).

most important financial sector

(in relation to a financial sector in a *consolidation group* or a *financial conglomerate* and in accordance with GENPRU 3.1 (Cross sector groups)) the *financial sector* with the largest average referred to in the box titled Threshold Test 2 in the *financial conglomerate definition decision tree* (10% ratio of balance sheet size and solvency requirements); and so that the investment services sector and the banking sector are treated as one for the purpose of the definition of *financial conglomerate* and for any other purpose that GENPRU 3.1 (Cross sector groups) says they are.

Motor Insurers' Information Centre

the information centre appointed to meet the *United Kingdom's* obligations under article 23 of the *Consolidated Motor Insurance Directive* (Information Centres).

motor vehicle liability

(in relation to a *class* of *contract of insurance*) the *class* of *contract of insurance*, specified in paragraph 10 of Part I of Schedule 1 to the *Regulated Activities Order* (Contracts of general insurance), against damage arising out of or in connection with the use of motor vehicles on land, including third-party risks and carrier's liability.

motor vehicle liability insurance business

general insurance business of *class* 10, other than:

(a) carrier's liability;

(b) pure reinsurance of that class.

motor vehicle liability insurer

(a) a *firm* with *permission* to carry on *motor vehicle liability insurance business*;

(b) any *person* carrying on the *regulated activity* of managing the *underwriting capacity of a Lloyd's syndicate* in respect of *members* whose insurance business at Lloyd's includes *motor vehicle liability insurance business*.

MTF

a *multilateral trading facility*.

MTF transaction

a transaction concluded by a *firm* under the rules governing an *MTF* with another member or participant of that *MTF*.

multilateral development bank

(A) In the PRA Handbook:
(a) any of the following:
(i) African Development Bank;
(ii) Asian Development Bank;
(iii) Caribbean Development Bank;
(iv) Council of Europe Development Bank;
(v) European Bank for Reconstruction & Development;
(vi) European Investment Bank;
(vii) European Investment Fund;
(viii) Inter-American Development Bank;
(ix) International Bank for Reconstruction 91 and 91 Development;
(x) International Finance Corporation;
(xa) International Finance Facility for Immunisation;
(xb) Islamic Development Bank;
(xi) Multilateral Investment Guarantee Agency; and
(xii) Nordic Investment Bank;
(b) [deleted]

(B) In the FCA Handbook:
(a) any of the following:
(i) African Development Bank;
(ii) Asian Development Bank;
(iii) Caribbean Development Bank;
(iv) Council of Europe Development Bank;
(v) European Bank for Reconstruction & Development;
(vi) European Investment Bank;
(vii) European Investment Fund;
(viii) Inter-American Development Bank;
(ix) International Bank for Reconstruction 91 and 91 Development;
(x) International Finance Corporation;
(xa) International Finance Facility for Immunisation;
(xb) Islamic Development Bank;
(xi) Multilateral Investment Guarantee Agency; and
(xii) Nordic Investment Bank;
(b) (in *BIPRU*) for the purposes of the *standardised approach* to credit risk the following are considered to be a multilateral development bank;

(i) the Inter-American Investment Corporation;
(ii) the Black Sea Trade and Development Bank; and
(iii) the Central American Bank for Economic Integration

multilateral trading facility

a multilateral system, operated by an *investment firm* or a *market operator*, which brings together multiple third-party buying and selling interests in *financial instruments* – in the system and in accordance with non-discretionary rules – in a way that results in a contract in accordance with the provisions of Title II of *MiFID*. [Note: article 4(1)(15) of *MiFID*]

multiplication factor

(in BIPRU 7.10 (Use of a value at risk model)) a multiplication factor applied to a *VaR measure* for the purpose of calculating the *model PRR* made up of the *minimum multiplication factor* as increased by the *plus factor*, all as more fully defined in BIPRU 7.10.118 R (Capital calculations: Multiplication factors).

mutual

an *insurer* which:

(a) if it is a *body corporate* has no *share* capital (except a wholly owned *subsidiary* with no *share* capital but limited by guarantee); or

(b) is a *registered friendly society* or *incorporated friendly society*; or

(c) is a society registered or deemed to be registered under the Industrial and Provident Societies Act 1965 or the Industrial and Provident Societies (Northern Ireland) Act 1969.

mutual society share

a *share* which:

(a) meets the requirements for common equity Tier 1 capital instruments under article 28 or 29; and

(b) is issued by an institution which is of a type listed in article 27;

in each case of the Regulation (EU) No 575/2013 of the European Parliament and of the Council of 26 June 2013 on prudential requirements for credit institutions and investment firms and amending Regulation (EU) No 648/2012.

name-passing broker

a *person* who arranges (brings about) *deals* between counterparties at mutually acceptable terms and passes their names to each of them to facilitate the conclusion of a transaction.

national bureau

(in relation to an *EEA State*) a professional organisation which:

(a) has been constituted in that State in accordance with Recommendation No 5 adopted on 25 January 1949 by the Road Transport Sub-committee of the Inland Transport Committee of the United Nations Economic Commission for Europe; and

(b) groups together *insurance undertakings* which in that State are authorised to conduct the business of motor vehicle liability insurance.

national guarantee fund

(in relation to an *EEA State*) a body which:

(a) has been set up or authorised in that State in accordance with article 1(4) of Council Directive (84/5/EEC); and

(b) provides compensation for damages to property or personal injuries caused by unidentified vehicles for which the insurance obligation provided for in article 1(1) of that Directive has not been satisfied.

natural gas

(a) natural gas in any form, including natural gas as deliverable through the *Network Code*; and

(b) any right that relates to natural gas, for example the right under a contract or otherwise to require a person to take any action in relation to natural gas, including:
(i) delivering natural gas to any person or taking delivery of natural gas; or
(ii) providing any information or notice in relation to natural gas; or
(iii) making any payment in relation to the delivery or non-delivery, or the taking or non-taking of delivery, of natural gas.

NCIS

National Criminal Intelligence Service.

near cash

money, *deposits* or *investments* which, in each case, fall within any of the following:

(a) *money* which is deposited with an *eligible institution* or an *approved bank* in:

(i) a current account; or

(ii) a *deposit* account, if the *money* can be withdrawn immediately and without payment of a penalty exceeding seven days' interest calculated at ordinary commercial rates;

(b) certificates of *deposit* issued by an *eligible institution* or an *approved bank* if immediately redeemable at the option of the holder;

(c) *government and public securities*, if redeemable at the option of the holder or bound to be redeemed within two years;

(d) bills of exchange which are *government and public securities*;

(e) *deposits* with a *local* authority of a kind which fall within paragraph 9 of Part II of the First Schedule to the Trustee *Investments* Act 1961, and equivalent *deposits* with any *local* authority in another *EEA State*, if the *money* can be withdrawn immediately and without payment of a penalty as described in (a).

NCLEG non-trading book permission

(A) (in the PRA Handbook): has the meaning given in the *PRA* Rulebook: Large Exposures rules.

NCLEG trading book permission

(A) (in the PRA Handbook): has the meaning given in the *PRA* Rulebook: Large Exposures rules.

net annual rent

(in *LR*) (in relation to a *property*) the current income or income estimated by the valuer:

(a) ignoring any special receipts or deductions arising from the *property*;

(b) excluding Value Added Tax and before taxation (including tax on profits and any allowances for interest on capital or loans); and

(c) after making deductions for superior rents (but not for amortisation) and any disbursements including, if appropriate, expenses of managing the *property* and allowances to maintain it in a condition to command its rent.

net earned premiums

gross earned premiums, less reinsurance premiums earned.

net leverage

the ratio of total assets, less those bought under reverse *repo* arrangements, to total equity.

net liability

(in *CREDS*) means the outstanding balance of any loan made to the borrower and any interest on that loan that is due but unpaid, less any *attached shares* held by the borrower.

net long position

the situation in which a *firm* holds or will hold more *units* in an *investment* than it has contracted to *sell* or, in respect of *options*, where it has bought rights which exceed rights sold.

net margined omnibus client account

an *omnibus client account* maintained by a *clearing member firm* in respect of which the margining arrangements give rise to a *gross-minus-net amount* which is held by the *clearing member firm* as *client money*.

net negative add-back method

the method of calculating a *firm's client money requirement* described in CASS 7.16.17 R.

net open foreign currency position

(in *IPRU(INV)* 13) a *firm's net long position* or *net short position*, whichever is the higher, in a currency other than that in which the *firm's* books of account are maintained.

net premium

the *premium* that is calculated to provide the basic sum assured under a *with-profits insurance contract* taking into consideration only the mortality and interest rate risks and using the same assumptions as used in the calculation of the *mathematical reserves.*

net short position

(1) (except in *IPRU(INV)* 13) a net short position which gives rise to an economic exposure to the issued *share* capital of a company. Any calculation of whether a *person* has a short position must take account of any form of economic interest in the *shares* of the company.

(2) (in *IPRU(INV)* 13) the situation in which a *firm* has contracted to *sell* more of an *investment* than it holds or will hold or, in respect of *options*, where it has sold rights which exceed the rights bought.

(3) [deleted]

net written premiums

gross written premiums, less *reinsurance* premiums payable under *reinsurance* ceded.

netting

a process by which the claims and obligations between two counterparties are offset against each other to leave a single net sum.

netting set

(in accordance with Part 1 of Annex III of the *Banking Consolidation Directive* (Definitions) and for the purpose of BIPRU 13 (The calculation of counterparty risk exposure values for financial derivatives, securities financing transactions and long settlement transactions)) a group of transactions with a single counterparty that are subject to a legally enforceable bilateral netting arrangement and for which netting is recognised under BIPRU 13.7 (Contractual netting), BIPRU 5 (Credit risk mitigation) and, if applicable, BIPRU 4.10 (The IRB approach: Credit risk mitigation); each transaction that is not subject to a legally enforceable bilateral netting arrangement, which is recognised under BIPRU 13.7 must be interpreted as its own *netting set* for the purpose of BIPRU 13. Under the method set out at BIPRU 13.6, all *netting sets* with a single counterparty may be treated as a single *netting set* if negative simulated market values of the individual sets are set to zero in the estimation of *expected exposure* (*EE*).

[Note: *BCD*, Annex III, Part 1, point 5]

net underwriting exposure

has the meaning in BIPRU 7.8.34R (Large exposure risk from underwriting securities: Calculating the net underwriting exposure) which is in summary the amount calculated by applying the reduction factors in the table in BIPRU 7.8.35R to the *net underwriting position*.

net underwriting position

the net underwriting position calculated under BIPRU 7.8.17R (Calculating the net underwriting position).

network

a *firm*:

(a) which has five or more *appointed representatives* (not counting *introducer appointed representatives*); or

(b) whose *appointed representatives*, not counting *introducer appointed representatives* (and being fewer than five) have, between them, 26 or more *representatives*;

but not:

(i) a *product provider*; or

(ii) a *firm* which markets the *packaged products* of a *product provider* which is in the same *group* as the *firm* and which does so other than by selecting products from the whole market; or

(iii) an *insurer* in relation to a *non-investment insurance contract*; or

(iv) a *mortgage lender*.

Network Code

the network code prepared by Transco plc in accordance with condition 7 of the public gas transporter licence granted or treated as granted to Transco plc under section 7(2) of the Gas Act 1986, as in force from time to time, or any subsequent similar instrument or arrangement.

new applicant

(in *LR*) an *applicant* that does not have any *class* of its *securities* already *listed*.

nominated ECAI

(a) (in the case of an eligible ECAI within paragraph (a) of the definition of that term (Recognition for exposure risk-weighting purposes)) an *eligible ECAI* nominated by a *firm* in accordance with BIPRU 3.6 (Use of rating agencies' credit assessments for the determination of risk weights under the standardised approach to credit risk) for the purpose of calculating its *risk weighted exposure amounts* under the *standardised approach* to credit risk except under (b);

(b) (in the case of an eligible ECAI within paragraph (b) of the definition of that term (Recognition *securitisation risk-weighting* purposes)) an *eligible ECAI* nominated by a *firm* in accordance with BIPRU 9.8 (Use of ECAI credit assessments for the determination of applicable risk weights) for the purpose of calculating its *securitisation risk weighted exposure amounts*.

(c) (for paragraph (d) of the definition of an *eligible ECAI* (in *MIPRU*)) an *eligible ECAI* nominated by a *firm* in accordance with MIPRU 4.2E for calculating its *risk weighted exposure amounts*.

nominated partner

the *person* nominated by the *operator* of a proposed *limited partnership scheme* to be the only limited partner (but not a *participant*) of the *scheme* on its formation.

nominee company

a *body corporate* whose business consists solely of acting as a nominee holder of *investments* or other property.

non-authorised counterparty

in *EG*, in relation to *EMIR*:

(a) a financial counterparty which is not an *authorised person*; or

(b) a non-financial counterparty; or

(c) a third country entity referred to in article 4(1)(a)(v) of *EMIR*.

non-commercial agreement

a *credit agreement* or a *consumer hire agreement* not made by the *lender* in the course of a business carried on by the *lender* or *owner*.

non-authorised Voluntary Jurisdiction participant

a participant in the *Voluntary Jurisdiction* who is not a *firm*.

non-core concentration risk group counterparty

(in accordance with Article 113(4)(c) of the *Banking Consolidation Directive*) has the meaning in BIPRU 10.9A.4 R (Definition of non-core concentration risk group counterparty), which is in summary (in relation to a *firm*) each counterparty which is its *parent undertaking*, its *subsidiary undertaking* or a *subsidiary undertaking* of its *parent undertaking*, provided that (in each case) both the counterparty and the *firm* satisfy the conditions in BIPRU 10.9A.4 R (Definition of non-core concentration risk group counterparty).

non-core large exposures group

(A) In the PRA Handbook:

has the meaning given in the *PRA* Rulebook: Large Exposures rules.

(B) In the FCA Handbook:
(in relation to a *firm*) all counterparties which:
(1) are listed in the *firm's non-core large exposures group permission*;
(2) satisfy the conditions in IFPRU 8.2.6 R (Intra-group exposures: non-core large exposures group); and
(3) for which *exposures* are exempted, under article 400(2)(c) of the *EU CRR* (Exemptions), from the application of article 395(1) of the *EU CRR* (Limits to large exposures).

non-core large exposures group exemption

the exemption in IFPRU 8.2.6 R (Intra-group exposures: non-core large exposures group).

non-core large exposures group permission

a permission referred to in IFPRU 8.2.6 R given by the *FCA* for the purpose of article 400(2)(c) of the *EU CRR* (Large exposures: exemptions).

non-core large exposures group waiver

a *waiver* that has the result of requiring a *firm* to apply BIPRU 10.9A (Intra-group exposures: non-core large exposures), which in summary exempts partially or fully exposures between members of the *core UK group* and members of the *non-core large exposures group* from the limits described in BIPRU 10.5 (Limits on exposures).

non-credit equalisation provision

the provision required to be established under INSPRU 1.4.17R.

non credit-obligation asset

(in relation to the *IRB approach*) an *exposure* in the form of a non credit-obligation asset or falling under BIPRU 4.9.5R (Non credit-obligation assets).

non-directive firm

(in *SUP* 11 (Controllers and close links) and *SUP* 16 (Reporting requirements)) (in accordance with the Financial Services and Markets Act 2000 (Controllers) (Exemption) Order 2009 (SI 2009/774)) a *UK domestic firm* other than:

(a) a *credit institution* authorised under the *Banking Consolidation Directive*;

(b) an *investment firm* authorised under *MIFID*;

(c) a *management company* as defined in article 2(1)(b) of the *UCITS Directive*, authorised under that directive;

(d) an *undertaking* pursuing the activity of direct insurance within the meaning of:
(i) article 2 of the *Consolidated Life Directive*, authorised under that directive; or
(ii) article 1 of the *First Non-Life Directive*, authorised under that directive;

(e) an *undertaking* pursuing the activity of *reinsurance* within the meaning of article 2.1 (a) of the *Reinsurance Directive*, authorised under that directive.

non-directive friendly society

(a) a *friendly society* whose *insurance business* is restricted to the provision of benefits which vary according to the resources available and in which the contributions of the members are determined on a flat-rate basis;

(b) a *friendly society* whose *long-term insurance business* is restricted to the provision of benefits for employed and self-employed *persons* belonging to an undertaking or group of undertakings, or a trade or group of trades, in the event of death or survival or of discontinuance or curtailment of activity (whether or not the commitments arising from such operations are fully covered at all times by mathematical reserves);

(c) a *friendly society* which undertakes to provide benefits solely in the event of death where the amount of such benefits does not exceed the average funeral costs for a single death or where the benefits are provided in kind;

(d) a *friendly society* (carrying on *long-term insurance business*):
(i) whose registered rules contain provisions for calling up additional contributions from members or reducing their benefits or claiming assistance from other *persons* who have undertaken to provide it; and
(ii) whose annual gross premium income (other than from contracts of reinsurance) has not exceeded 5 million Euro for each of the three preceding financial years;

(e) a *friendly society* (carrying on *general insurance business*):
(i) whose registered rules contain provisions for calling up additional contributions from members or reducing their benefits;
(ii) whose gross premium income (other than from contracts of reinsurance) for the preceding financial year did not exceed 5 million Euro; and
(iii) whose members provided at least half of that gross premium income;

(f)
(i) a *friendly society* whose liabilities in respect of *general insurance contracts* are fully reinsured with or guaranteed by other *mutuals* (including *friendly societies*); and
(ii) the *mutuals* providing the *reinsurance* or the *guarantee* are subject to the rules of the *First Non-Life Directive*;

and in each case whose *insurance business* is limited to that described in any of (a) to (f).

non-directive insurer

(a) an *insurer* which is a provident or mutual benefit institution whose *insurance business* is restricted to the provision of benefits which vary according to the resources available and in which the contributions are determined on a flat-rate basis; or

(b) an *insurer* whose *long-term insurance business* is restricted to the provision of benefits for employed and self-employed persons belonging to an *undertaking* or group of *undertakings*, or a trade or group of trades, in the event of death or survival or of discontinuance or curtailment of activity (whether or not the commitments arising from such operations are fully covered at all times by mathematical reserves); or

(c) an *insurer* which undertakes to provide benefits solely in the event of death where the amount of such benefits does not exceed the average funeral costs for a single death or where the benefits are provided in kind; or

(d) a *mutual* (carrying on *long-term insurance business*) whose:
(i) articles of association contain provisions for calling up additional contributions from members or reducing their benefits or claiming assistance from other persons who have undertaken to provide it; and
(ii) annual gross *premium* income (other than from contracts of *reinsurance*) has not exceeded 5 million Euro for each of the *financial year* in question and the two previous *financial years*; or

(e) a *mutual* (carrying on *general insurance business*) whose:
(i) articles of association contain provisions for calling up additional contributions from members or reducing their benefits;
(ii) business does not cover liability risks, other than *ancillary risks*, or credit or suretyship risks;
(iii) gross *premium* income (other than from contracts of *reinsurance*) for the *financial year in question* did not exceed 5 million Euro; and
(iv) members provided at least half of that gross *premium* income; or

(f) an *insurer* whose *insurance business* (other than *reinsurance*) is:
(i) restricted to the provision of assistance for persons who get into difficulties while travelling, while away from home or while away from their permanent residence;
(ii) carried out exclusively on a local basis and consists only of benefits in kind; and
(iii) such that the gross *premium* income from the provision of assistance in the *financial year in question* did not exceed 200,000 Euro; or

(g)
(i) a *mutual* whose liabilities in respect of *general insurance contracts* are fully reinsured with or guaranteed by other *mutuals* (including *friendly societies*); and
(ii) the *mutuals* providing the *reinsurance* or the guarantee are subject to the rules of the *First Non-Life Directive*.

non-directive mutual

a *mutual* that falls into (d), (e) or (g) of the definition of a *non-directive insurer*.

non-discretionary investment manager

(in relation to *firm type* in SUP 16.10 (Confirmation of standing data)) a *person* who, acting only on behalf of a *client*, manages *designated investments* in an account or portfolio on a non-discretionary basis under the terms of a non-discretionary management agreement.

non-discretionary management agreement

an agreement for the non-discretionary management of *investments*:

(a) under which the *firm* agrees to conduct a regular review of the suitability of the *client's* account or portfolio, based on an assessment of the *client's* requirements; and

(b) that sets out the *client's* investment objectives, investment strategy, and attitude to risk, the intervals at which the portfolio will be reviewed, and the arrangements for consulting the *client* about proposed investment decisions.

non-EEA AIF

an *AIF* which is not a *UK AIF* or an *EEA AIF*.

non-EEA AIFM

an *AIFM* which is not a *UK AIFM* or an *EEA AIFM*.

non-EEA bank

a *bank* which is a *body corporate* or *partnership* formed under the law of any country or territory outside the *EEA*.

non-EEA direct insurer

an *insurer*, other than a *pure reinsurer*, whose head office is not in an *EEA State*.

non-EEA feeder AIF

a *UK AIF* or an *EEA AIF* that is a *feeder AIF*, the *master AIF* of which is a *non-EEA AIF* or is managed by a *non-EEA AIFM*.

non-EEA firm

a *firm* that has its registered office (or, if it has no registered office, its head office) in a *non-EEA state*.

non-EEA insurer

an *insurer* whose head office is not in an *EEA State*.

non-EEA state

a country or state that is not an *EEA State*.

non-EEA sub-group

(A) In the PRA Handbook:
a group of *undertakings* identified as a *non-EEA sub-group* in BIPRU 8.3.1R (Main consolidation rule for non-EEA sub-groups); however where the provision in question refers to a *non-EEA sub-group* in another *EEA State* it means a group of *undertakings* identified in Article 73(2) of the *Banking Consolidation Directive* (Non-EEA sub-groups) required to be supervised on a consolidated basis under Article 73(2) of the *Banking Consolidation Directive* by a competent authority in that *EEA State*.

(B) In the FCA Handbook:
(1) (in *GENPRU* (except GENPRU 3) and *BIPRU* (except BIPRU 12)) a group of *undertakings* identified as a *non-EEA sub-group* in BIPRU 8.3.1R (Main consolidation rule for non-EEA sub-groups); however where the provision in question refers to a *non-EEA sub-group* in another *EEA State* it means a group of *undertakings* identified in Article 73(2) of the *Banking Consolidation Directive* (Non-EEA sub-groups) required to be supervised on a consolidated basis under Article 73(2) of the *Banking Consolidation Directive* by a competent authority in that *EEA State*.
(2) (except in (1)) a group of *undertakings* identified in article 22 of the *EU CRR* (Sub-consolidation in cases of entities in third countries).

non-equity transferable securities

(in *PR*) (as defined in section 102A of the *Act*) all *transferable securities* that are not equity securities.

non-executive director

a *director* who has no responsibility for implementing the decisions or the policies of the *governing body* of a *firm*.

non-executive director function

(1) (in the *FCA Handbook*) *FCA controlled function* CF2 in Part 1 of the *table of FCA controlled functions*, described more fully in SUP 10A.6.12 R and SUP 10A.6.13 R.

(2) (in the *PRA Handbook*) *PRA controlled function* CF2 in the *table of PRA controlled functions*, described more fully in SUP 10B.6.3 R to SUP 10B.6.5 R.

Non-Exempt Activities Order

the Financial Services and Markets Act 2000 (Professions) (Non-Exempt Activities) Order 2001 (SI 2001/1227).

non-ILAS BIPRU firm

a *firm* falling into BIPRU 12.1.1R which is not an *ILAS BIPRU firm*.

non-independent research

a *research recommendation* which:

(a) relates to *financial instruments* (as specified in Section C of Annex 1 of *MiFID*, whether or not they are admitted to trading on a *regulated market*); and

(b) does not constitute *investment research*.

[Note: article 24(2) of the *MiFID implementing Directive*]

non-investment insurance contract

a *contract of insurance* which is a *general insurance contract* or a *pure protection contract* but which is not a *long-term care insurance contract*.

Non-Life Directives

the *First Non-Life Directive*, the *Second Non-Life Directive* and the *Third Non-Life Directive*.

non-listed company

(in accordance with article 4(1)(ac) of *AIFMD*) a *company* which has its registered office in the *EEA* and the *shares* of which are not admitted to trading on a *regulated market*.

non-mainstream pooled investment

any of the following *investments*:

(a) a *unit* in an *unregulated collective investment scheme*;

(b) a *unit* in a *qualified investor scheme*;

(c) a *security* issued by a *special purpose vehicle*, other than an *excluded security*;

(d) a *traded life policy investment*;

(e) *rights to or interests in investments* that are any of (a) to (d).

non-mainstream regulated activity

a *regulated activity* of an *authorised professional firm* in relation to which the conditions in PROF 5.2.1 R are satisfied.

non-margined transaction

a transaction *executed* by a *firm*:

(a) for, or on behalf of, a *client* in relation to *MiFID business* and/or *designated investment business*; and

(b) which is not a *margined transaction*.

non-market-price transaction

a transaction where:

(a) the *dealing* rate or price paid by the *firm* or its *client* differs from the prevailing market rate or price to a material extent; or

(b) the *firm* or its *client* otherwise gives materially more or less in value than it receives in return.

non-profit fund

a *long-term insurance fund* which is not a *with-profits fund*.

non-profit insurance business

the business of *effecting* or carrying out non-profit insurance contracts.

non-profit insurance contract

a *long-term insurance contract* which is not a *with-profits insurance contract*.

non-proportional reinsurance treaty

see *proportional reinsurance treaty*.

non-readily realisable security

a *security* which is not any of the following:

(a) a *readily realisable security*;

(b) a *packaged product*;

(c) a *non-mainstream pooled investment*;

(d) a *mutual society share*.

non-real time financial promotion

(in accordance with article 7(2) of the *Financial Promotion Order*) a *financial promotion* that is not a *real time financial promotion*.

non-retail communication

a *financial promotion* and:

(a) is *made only to recipient* who the *firm* reasonably believes are *professional clients* or *eligible counterparties*; or

(b) may reasonably be regarded as *directed only at recipients* who are *professional clients* or *eligible counterparties*.

non-standard method of internal client money reconciliation

the method of *internal client money reconciliation* described in CASS 7.15.17 R.

non-stakeholder CTF

a *CTF* that is not a *stakeholder CTF*.

non-trading book

positions, exposures, assets and liabilities that are not in the *trading book*.

non-UCITS retail scheme

an *authorised fund* which is neither a *UCITS scheme* or a *qualified investor scheme*.

non-UCITS scheme

an *authorised fund* that is not a *UCITS scheme*.

normally based

(in *ICOBS*) (in relation to a *vehicle*):

(a) the territory of the *EEA State* of which the *vehicle* bears a registration plate; or

(b) in cases where no registration is required for the type of *vehicle*, but the *vehicle* bears an insurance plate or a distinguishing sign analogous to a registration plate, the territory of the *EEA State* in which the insurance plate or the sign is issued; or

(c) in cases where neither registration plate nor insurance plate nor distinguishing sign is required for the type of *vehicle*, the territory of the *EEA State* in which the keeper of the *vehicle* is permanently resident.

[Note: article 1(4) of Directive 72/166/EC (First Motor Insurance Directive)]

normally resident

(in *MCOB*) normally resident; for the purposes of this definition:

(a) an individual (whether or not acting as trustee) is to be treated as normally resident in the country which he indicates is his country of residence, unless the *firm* has reason to doubt this; and

(b) a *body corporate* acting as trustee is to be treated as resident in the country in which its registered office (or, if it has no registered office, its head office) is located.

non-UK DLG by modification

either of the following:

(a) a *non-UK DLG by modification (firm level)*; or

(b) a *non-UK DLG by modification (DLG level)*.

non-UK DLG by modification (firm level)

(in relation to a *group liquidity reporting firm*) a *DLG by modification (firm level)* that is not a *UK DLG by modification*. A *firm* with a *non-UK DLG by modification (firm level)* cannot also have a *UK DLG by modification*. (*Guidance* about this definition, and its inter-relation with other related definitions, is set out in SUP 16 Annex 26 (Guidance on designated liquidity groups in SUP 16.12).)

non-UK DLG by modification (DLG level)

(in relation to any reporting period under SUP 16 (Reporting requirements) and in relation to a *firm* that meets the following conditions (a group liquidity reporting firm):

(a) it is a *UK ILAS BIPRU firm* with an *intra-group liquidity modification*;

(b) it is a *group liquidity reporting firm* in a *UK DLG by modification* created by that *intra-group liquidity modification*;

(c) the *overall liquidity adequacy rule* applies under that *intra-group liquidity modification* to that *UK DLG by modification*; and

(d) that *UK DLG by modification* can rely, under that *intra-group liquidity modification*, for any part of that period, on a group of other *persons* for the purpose of the *overall liquidity adequacy rule* as applied to that *UK DLG by modification*);

means the group made up of the following:

(e) that *ILAS BIPRU firm*;

(f) the other members of that *UK DLG by modification*; and

(g) the group of other *persons* mentioned in (d).

A *firm* has a 'non-UK DLG by modification (DLG level)' for a period even if it only has one during part of that period. (*Guidance* about this definition, and its inter-relation with other new definitions, is set out in SUP 16 Annex 26 (Guidance on designated liquidity groups in SUP 16.12).)

non UK lead regulated firm

a *firm* that is not a *UK lead regulated firm*. This definition is not related to the defined term *lead regulated firm*.

normal trading hours

(in relation to a *trading venue* or an *investment firm*) those hours which the *trading venue* or *investment firm* establishes in advance and makes public as its trading hours. [Note: article 2(5) of the *MiFID Regulation*]

Northern Ireland credit union

a body corporate registered under the Credit Unions (Northern Ireland) Order 1985 which is an *authorised person* or a body corporate registered under the Industrial and Provident Societies Act (Northern Ireland) 1969 as a *credit union* which is an *authorised person*.

not-for-profit body

a body which by virtue of its constitution or any enactment:

(a) is required (after payment of outgoings) to apply the whole of its income, and any capital which it expends, for charitable or public purposes; and

(b) is prohibited from directly or indirectly distributing among its members any part of its assets (otherwise than for charitable or public purposes).

not-for-profit debt advice body

a body which is a *not-for-profit body* with a *limited permission* to carry on *debt counselling* alone or together with either or both *debt adjusting* and *providing credit information services*, and *agreeing to carry on a regulated activity* so far as relevant to those activities, where no *associate* (other than a *not-for-profit debt advice body*) of the body carries on *debt adjusting* or *debt counselling* or *providing credit information services*.

notice of discontinuance

a notice given by the *appropriate regulator* in accordance with section 389 of the *Act* (Notices of discontinuance) which states that the *appropriate regulator* has decided not to take the action proposed in a *warning notice* or the action to which a *decision notice* relates.

notice of intention

a notice of intention (as described in SUP 13.5) given by a *UK firm* to: (a) establish a *branch* in an *EEA State* under paragraph 19(2) of Part III of Schedule 3 to the *Act* (Exercise of passport rights by UK firms); or (b) provide services in an *EEA State* under paragraph 20(1) of Part III of Schedule 3 to the *Act* (Exercise of passport rights by UK firms) or (c) establish a *branch* or provide services in an *EEA state* in the exercise of its *EEA right* under the *auction regulation*.

notification rule

(1) (in relation to a *firm*) a *rule* requiring a *firm* to give the *appropriate regulator* notice of, or information regarding, an event, but excluding:
(a) a *rule* requiring periodic submission of a report; and
(b) a *rule* in the *listing rules*.

(2) (in relation to a *recognised body*) a *rule* made by the *FCA* under section 293 of the *Act* (Notification requirements) or section 295 of the *Act* (Notification: overseas investment exchanges and overseas clearing houses):

(a) requiring a *recognised body* to give the *FCA*:

(i) notice of, and specified information regarding, specified events relating to the body;

(ii) specified information relating to the body at specified times or in respect of specified periods; and

(iii) any other information required to be given by such a *rule*; or

(b)(in relation to an *RIE*):

(i) specifying descriptions of *regulatory provision* in relation to which, or circumstances in which, the duty to notify the *FCA* of such *regulatory provision* in section 300B(1) of the *Act* does not apply or providing that the duty to notify applies only to specified descriptions of *regulatory provision* or in specified circumstances; or

(ii) making provision as to the form and contents of the notice required under (2)(b)(i), and requiring *recognised bodies* to provide specified information in connection with that notification.

notional principal

(a) (in relation to a *contract for differences* which is an index *derivative*):

(i) the current mark to market valuation of a *contract for differences* which resembles a *futures* contract; or

(ii) the exercise value of a *contract for differences* which resembles an *option* contract;

(b) (in relation to any other *contract for differences*) the notional lot size of the contract.

nuclear risks

risks falling within any *class* of *general insurance business* and arising in connection with the construction and use of any nuclear reactor or nuclear installation or the carriage of any nuclear matter.

occupational pension fund management business

(in *COMP*) the business of carrying on:

(1) *pension fund management*; or

(2) (other than in connection with a *personal pension scheme*) *pension fund management*, written as linked long term business, for an *occupational pension scheme* or for an institution falling within article 2 of the Council Directive of 3 June 2003 on the activities and supervision of institutions for occupational retirement provision (No 2003/41/EC) but only to the extent that:

(a) there is no transfer to the *participant firm* of:

(i) investment, market, or credit risk;

(iii) mortality or expense risk prior to any annuity being effected; and

(b) any annuity options provide for the *participant firm* to change the annuity rates without prior notice.

obligor grade

(in relation to the *IRB approach* and the *sovereign, institutional and corporate IRB exposure class* and in accordance with BIPRU 4.4.8R) a risk category within a *rating system's* obligor rating scale, to which obligors are assigned on the basis of a specified and distinct set of rating criteria, from which estimates of *PD* are derived.

occupational pension scheme

(a) (a scheme specified in article 3(1) of the *Regulated Activities Order* (Interpretation)) which is, in summary, a pension scheme established for the purpose of providing benefits to people with service in employments of a prescribed description.

OECD

Organisation for Economic Co-operation and Development.

OECD state guaranteed issuer

an *issuer* of *debt securities* whose obligations in relation to those securities have been guaranteed by a member state of the *OECD*.

OEIC

open-ended investment company. (see also *ICVC*.)

OEIC Regulations

the Open-Ended Investment Companies Regulations 2001 (SI 2001/1228)

off-exchange

(in relation to a transaction in an *investment*) a transaction which is not *on-exchange*.

offer

(1) (in MAR 1 (Code of market conduct)) an offer as defined in the *Takeover Code*.

(2) (in MAR 2(Buy-backs and Stabilisation)) an offer or invitation to make an offer.

(3) (in *LR* and *PR*) an *offer of transferable securities to the public*.

offer document

(in *MCOB*) a document in which the *home finance provider* offers to enter into a *home finance transaction* with a *customer*.

offer for sale

(in *LR*) an invitation to the public by, or on behalf of, a third party to purchase *securities* of the *issuer* already in issue or allotted (and may be in the form of an invitation to tender at or above a stated minimum price).

offer for subscription

(in *LR*) an invitation to the public by, or on behalf of, an *issuer* to subscribe for *securities* of the *issuer* not yet in issue or allotted (and may be in the form of an invitation to tender at or above a stated minimum price).

offer of transferable securities to the public

(in *PR* and *LR*) (as defined in section 102B of the *Act*), in summary:

(a) a communication to any person which presents sufficient information on:
(i) the transferable securities to be offered, and
(ii) the terms on which they are offered;
to enable an investor to decide to buy or subscribe for the securities in question;

(b) which is made in any form or by any means;

(c) including the placing of securities through a financial intermediary;

(d) but not including a communication in connection with trading on:
(i) a regulated market;
(ii) a multilateral trading facility; or
(iii) any market prescribed by an order under section 130A of the *Act*.

Note: This is only a summary; to see the full text of the definition, readers should consult section 102B of the *Act*.

offeree

(in MAR 1) an offeree as defined in the *Takeover Code*.

offering programme

(in *PR*) (as defined in Article 2.1(k) of the *prospectus directive*) a plan which would permit the issuance of non-equity securities, including warrants in any form, having a similar type and/or class, in a continuous or repeated manner during a specified issuing period.

offering programme

(in *PR*) (as defined in Article 2.1(k) of the *prospectus directive*) a plan which would permit the issuance of non-equity securities, including warrants in any form, having a similar type and/or class, in a continuous or repeated manner during a specified issuing period.

offeror

(1) (in MAR 1 (The Code of Market Conduct) and LR 5.2.10 R to LR 5.2.11D R) an offeror as defined in the *Takeover Code*.

(2) (in MAR 2 (Buy-backs and Stabilisation)) (as defined in Article 2 of the *Buy-back and Stabilisation Regulation*) the prior holders of, or the entity issuing, the *relevant securities*.

(3) (in *LR* (except LR 5.2.10 R to LR 5.2.11D R), *PR* and *FEES* provisions in relation to *PR*) a *person* who makes an *offer of transferable securities to the public*.

offer price

the price at which a *person* could purchase a *unit* in a *dual-priced authorised fund* or a *security*.

officer

(1) (in connection with the exercise of the *appropriate regulator's* power to require information) an officer of the *appropriate regulator*, a member of the *appropriate regulator's* staff or an agent of the *appropriate regulator*.

(2) (otherwise) (in relation to a *body corporate*) (as defined in section 400(5) of the *Act* (Offences by *bodies corporate* etc)) a director, member of the committee of management, *chief executive*, *manager*, secretary, or other similar officer of the body, or a *person* purporting to *act* in that capacity or a *controller* of the body.

official list

(1) (in *LR*) the list maintained by the *FCA* in accordance with section 74(1) of the *Act* for the purposes of Part VI of the *Act*.

(2) (except in *LR*):
(a) the list maintained by the *FCA* in accordance with section 74(1) of the *Act* (The official list) for the purposes of Part VI of the *Act* (Official Listing);
(b) any corresponding list maintained by a *competent authority* for listing in another *EEA State*.

oil

mineral oil of any description and petroleum gases, whether in liquid or vapour form, including products and derivatives of oil.

oil collective investment scheme

a *collective investment scheme*, the property of which consists only of property which is *oil* or an *oil* investment or cash awaiting investment.

oil investment

any of the following:

(a) a *unit* in an *oil* collective investment scheme;

(b) an *option* to acquire or dispose of an *oil* investment;

(c) a future where the *commodity* in question is *oil*;

(d) a *contract for differences* where the property in question is *oil* or an *oil* investment or the index or other factor in question is linked to or otherwise dependent upon fluctuations in the value or price of *oil* or any *oil* investments;

(e) *rights to or interests in investments* in (a)–(d).

oil market activity

(A) In the PRA Handbook:

(a) any *regulated activity* in relation to an *oil investment* or to *oil*, or in relation to a *biofuel investment*, *biofuel*, a *biomass investment* or *biomass* that is ancillary to activities related to *oil investments* or *oil*, which:
(i) is the *executing* of *own account transactions* on any *recognised investment exchange* or *designated investment exchange*; or
(ii) if it is not the *executing* of transactions on such exchanges, is performed in connection with or for persons who are not individuals; and

(b) *establishing, operating or winding up a collective investment scheme* which is an *oil collective investment scheme* in which individuals do not participate.

(B) In the FCA Handbook:

(a) any *regulated activity* in relation to an *oil investment* or to *oil*, or in relation to a *biofuel investment*, *biofuel*, a *biomass investment* or *biomass* that is ancillary to activities related to *oil investments* or *oil*, which:
(i) is the *executing* of *own account transactions* on any *recognised investment exchange* or *designated investment exchange*; or
(ii) if it is not the *executing* of transactions on such exchanges, is performed in connection with or for persons who are not individuals;

(b) [deleted]

oil market participant

(A) In the PRA Handbook:
a *firm*:
(a) whose permission:

(i) includes a *requirement* that the *firm* must not carry on any *designated investment business* other than oil market activity; and
(ii) does not include a *requirement* that it comply with IPRU(INV) 5 (Investment management *firms*) or 13 (Personal *investment firms*); and
(b) which is not an *authorised professional firm*, *bank*, *BIPRU firm*, (unless it is an *exempt BIPRU commodities firm*), *IFPRU investment firm* (unless it is an *exempt IFPRU commodities firm*), building society, credit union, friendly society, ICVC, insurer, MiFID investment firm (unless it is an *exempt BIPRU commodities firm* or *exempt IFPRU commodities firm*), media firm, service company, insurance intermediary, home finance administrator, mortgage intermediary, home finance provider, incoming EEA firm (without a *top-up permission*), or *incoming Treaty firm* (without a *top-up permission*).

(B) In the FCA Handbook:
a *firm*:
(a) whose permission:
(i) includes a *requirement* that the *firm* must not carry on any *designated investment business* other than oil market activity; and
(ii) does not include a *requirement* that it comply with IPRU(INV) 5 (Investment management *firms*) or 13 (Personal *investment firms*); and
(b) which is not an *authorised professional firm*, *bank*, *BIPRU firm*, (unless it is an *exempt BIPRU commodities firm*), *IFPRU investment firm* (unless it is an *exempt IFPRU commodities firm*), building society, credit union, friendly society, ICVC, insurer, MiFID investment firm (unless it is an *exempt BIPRU commodities firm* or *exempt IFPRU commodities firm*), media firm, service company, insurance intermediary, home finance administrator, mortgage intermediary, home finance provider, incoming EEA firm (without a *top-up permission*), or *incoming Treaty firm* (without a *top-up permission*).

Ombudsman

a *person* appointed to the panel of *persons* maintained by the *FOS Ltd* to determine complaints, including the Chief Ombudsman.

Ombudsman Transitional Order

the Financial Services and Markets Act 2000 (Transitional Provisions) (Ombudsman Scheme and Complaints Scheme) Order 2001 (SI 2001/2326).

omnibus client account

as the context requires, either:

an account maintained by a *firm* at an *authorised central counterparty* for more than one *client* of the *firm* in respect of which the *authorised central counterparty* has agreed with the *firm* to provide *omnibus client segregation*; or

an *account* maintained by a *firm* for more than one *indirect client* at a *clearing member* in respect of which that clearing member has agreed with the *firm* to provide segregation arrangements that satisfy the requirements of article 4(2)(a) of the *EMIR L2 Regulation*.

omnibus client segregation

as defined in article 39(2) of *EMIR*.

OMPS

the Handbook Guide for oil market participants.

ONA

(A) In the PRA Handbook: the *appropriate regulator's* online notifications and applications system, by whatever name known.

(B) In the FCA Handbook: the *appropriate regulator's* online notifications and applications system, by whatever name known.

one-day VaR measure

(in BIPRU 7.10 (Use of a value at risk model)) has the meaning in BIPRU 7.10.98R (Backtesting: One day VaR measure), which is in summary and in relation to a particular *business day*, the *VaR number* for that *business day* calibrated to a one *business day* holding period and a 99% one-tailed confidence level.

one-off promotion

a communication meeting the requirements set out in articles 15 or 15A of the Promotion of Collective Investment Schemes Order or in articles 28 or 28A of the Financial Promotions Order.

on-exchange

(a) (in relation to a transaction in the *United Kingdom*) effected by means of the *facilities* of, or governed by the *rules* of, an *RIE* or a *regulated market*;

(b) (in relation to any other transaction) effected by means of the *facilities* of, or governed by the *rules* of, an exchange.

one-off transaction

any transaction other than a transaction carried out in the course of an established business relationship formed by a *person* acting in the course of relevant financial business.

one-sided credit valuation adjustment

(in accordance with Part 1 of Annex III of the *Banking Consolidation Directive* (Definitions) and for the purposes of *BIPRU*) a *credit valuation adjustment* that reflects the market value of the credit risk of the counterparty to a *firm*, but does not reflect the market value of the credit risk of the *firm* to the counterparty.

ongoing basis

in BIPRU 9.15, maintaining on an *ongoing basis* means that the retained positions, interest or exposures are not hedged or sold.

[Note: *BCD*, Article 122a, paragraph 1]

open

in relation to a *syndicate year*, one which has not been *closed*.

open currency position

the amount calculated under BIPRU 7.5.19R (Open currency position) as part of the calculation of the *foreign currency PRR*.

open-end agreement

a *credit agreement* with no fixed duration.

open offer

(in *LR* and in DTR 5) an invitation to existing *securities* holders to subscribe or purchase *securities* in proportion to their holdings, which is not made by means of a renounceable letter (or other negotiable document).

open-ended investment company

(as defined in section 236 of the *Act* (Open-ended investment companies)) a *collective investment scheme* which satisfies both the property condition and the investment condition:

(a) the property condition is that the property belongs beneficially to, and is managed by or on behalf of, a *body corporate* ("BC") having as its purpose the investment of its funds with the aim of:
(i) spreading investment risk; and
(ii) giving its members the benefit of the results of the management of those funds by or on behalf of that body;

(b) the investment condition is that, in relation to BC, a reasonable investor would, if he were to participate in the *scheme*:
(i) expect that he would be able to realise, within a period appearing to him to be reasonable, his investment in the *scheme* (represented, at any given time, by the value of shares in, or securities of, BC held by him as a *participant* in the *scheme*); and
(ii) be satisfied that his investment would be realised on a basis calculated wholly or mainly by reference to the value of property in respect of which the *scheme* makes arrangements.
(see also *investment company with variable capital*.)

operating a dormant account fund

any of the *regulated activities* of:

(a) *meeting of repayment claims*; or

(b) *managing dormant account funds (including the investment of such funds)*.

operating a multilateral trading facility

the *regulated activity* in article 25D of the *Regulated Activities Order*, which is, in summary, the operation of a multilateral trading facility on which MiFID instruments are traded. In this definition "MiFID instrument" means any investment:

(a) of the kind specified by articles 76, 77, 78, 79, 80, 81, 83, 84 or 85 of the *Regulated Activities Order*; or

(b) of the kind specified by article 89 of the *Regulated Activities Order*, so far as relevant to an investment falling within (a),

that is a *financial instrument*.

operating an electronic system in relation to lending

a *regulated activity* of the kind specified in article 36H of the *Regulated Activities Order*.

operational objectives

as defined in section 1B(3) of the *Act*.

operational risk

(A) In the PRA Handbook:
(1) (in *COLL* and *FUND*) the risk of loss for a *UCITS* or *AIF* resulting from inadequate internal processes and failures in relation to the people and systems of the *management company* or *AIFM* or from external events, and it includes legal and documentation risk and risk resulting from the trading, settlement and valuation procedures operated on behalf of the *fund*.
(2) (in *GENPRU* (except GENPRU 3 (Cross sector groups) and *BIPRU* (except BIPRU 12 (Liquidity Standards)) (in accordance with Article 4(22) of the *Banking Consolidation Directive*) the risk of loss resulting from inadequate or failed internal processes, people and systems or from external events, including legal risk.
(3) (in GENPRU 3, *IFPRU*, and BIPRU 12) has the meaning in Article 4(1)(52) of the *EU CRR*.

(B) In the FCA Handbook:
(1) (in *COLL* and *FUND*) the risk of loss for a *UCITS* or *AIF* resulting from inadequate internal processes and failures in relation to the people and systems of the *management company* or *AIFM* or from external events, and it includes legal and documentation risk and risk resulting from the trading, settlement and valuation procedures operated on behalf of the *fund*.
(2) (in *GENPRU* (except GENPRU 3 (Cross sector groups) and *BIPRU* (except BIPRU 12 (Liquidity Standards)) (in accordance with Article 4(22) of the *Banking Consolidation Directive*) the risk of loss resulting from inadequate or failed internal processes, people and systems or from external events, including legal risk.
(3) (except in (1) and (2)) has the meaning in article 4(1)(52) of the *EU CRR*.

operational risk capital requirement

the part of the *capital resources requirement* of a *BIPRU firm* falling within BIPRU 6.1.1R in respect of *operational risk*, calculated in accordance with BIPRU 6.2.

operator

(1) (except in *EG*):
(a) (in relation to an *AUT*) the *manager*;
(aa) (in relation to an *ACS*) the *authorised contractual scheme manager*;
(b) (in relation to an *ICVC*) that *company* or, if applicable, the *authorised corporate director*;
(ba) (in relation to any other *OEIC* which is an undertaking for *collective investment* in transferable securities within the meaning of the *UCITS Directive* and which has appointed a *person* to manage the *scheme*) the *manager*;
(c) (in relation to any other *collective investment scheme* that is a *unit trust scheme* with a separate *trustee*) any *person* who, under the *trust deed* establishing the *scheme*, is responsible for the management of the property held for or within the *scheme*;
(ca) (in relation to any other *collective investment scheme* that is a contractual scheme) any *person* who, under the constituent instrument, is responsible for the management of the property held for or within the *scheme*;
(d) (in relation to any other *collective investment scheme* that is an *open-ended investment company*) that *company* or, if applicable, any *person* who, under the constitution or founding arrangements of the *scheme*, is responsible for the management of the property held for or within the *scheme*;
(e) (in relation to any other *collective investment scheme*) any *person* who, under the constitution or founding arrangements of the *scheme*, is responsible for the management of the property held for or within the *scheme*;
(f) (in relation to an *investment trust* savings *scheme*) any *person* appointed, by those responsible for managing the property of the *investment trust*, to manage the *investment trust* savings *scheme*;

(g) (in relation to a *personal pension scheme* or *stakeholder pension scheme*) the *person* who carries on the *regulated activity* specified in article 52 of the *Regulated Activities Order* (Establishing etc. a pension scheme).

(2) (in *EG*) (in accordance with section 237(2) of the *Act* (Other definitions)):
(a) (in relation to a *unit trust scheme* with a separate *trustee*) the *manager*;
(b) (in relation to an *OEIC* which is an undertaking for collective investment in transferable securities within the meaning of the *UCITS Directive* and which has appointed a *person* to manage the *scheme*) the *manager*;
(c) (in relation to any other *OEIC*) the *company*.

(3) (in FEES 1 and FEES 9), any *person* with responsibility under a *payment system* for managing or operating it; and any reference to the operation of a *payment system* includes a reference to its management. [Note: section 42(3) of *FSBRA*]

operator of an electronic system in relation to lending

a *person* who has, or ought to have, *permission* for *operating an electronic system in relation to lending*.

OPS activity

(a) *managing investments* in a case where the assets managed are:
(i) held for the purposes of an *occupational pension scheme*; or
(ii) held for the purposes of a *welfare trust* established by a *person* who is, or has been at any time during the last 12 *months*, an *associate* of the *OPS firm*; or
(iii) assets of an *OPS collective investment scheme*;

(b) any one or more of the following activities undertaken in the course of, or incidental to, the operation of an *occupational pension scheme*, *welfare trust* or *OPS collective investment scheme*:
(i) *dealing in investments as principal*;
(ii) *dealing in investments as agent*;
(iii) arranging (bringing about) deals in investments;
(iv) *making arrangements with a view to transactions in investments*;
(v) *safeguarding and administering investments*;
(vi) *advising on investments*;
(vii) receiving or holding *client money*.

OPS collective investment scheme

a *collective investment scheme* the contributions to which consist entirely of assets held for an *occupational pension scheme*.

OPS firm

(a) (except in *IPRU(INV)*) a *firm* which:
(i) carries on *OPS activity*; and
(ii) is one or more of the following:
(A) a trustee of the *occupational pension scheme* in question;
(B) a *company* owned by the trustees of the *occupational pension scheme* in question;
(C) a *company* which is:
(I) an employer in relation to the *occupational pension scheme* in question in respect of its employees or former employees or their dependants; or
(II) a *company* within the *group* which includes an employer within (I); or
(III) an administering authority subject to the Local Government Pension Scheme (Administration) Regulations 2008; or

(b) a *firm* which:
(i) has satisfied the requirements set out in (a) at any time during the past 12 *months*; but
(ii) is no longer able to comply with those requirements because of a change in the control or ownership of the employer referred to in (a)(ii) during that period.

opted-in exempt CAD firm

an *exempt CAD firm* which complies with the requirements in regulation 4C (or any successor provision) of the Financial Services and Markets Act 2000 (Markets in Financial Instruments) Regulations 2007 (SI 2007/126).

option

(A) In the PRA Handbook:
the *investment*, specified in article 83 of the *Regulated Activities Order* (Options), which is an option to acquire or dispose of:
(a) a *designated investment* (other than an option or one to which (d) or (e) applies); or

(b) currency of the *United Kingdom* or of any other country or territory; or

(c) palladium, platinum, gold or silver; or

(d) a commodity to which article 83(2) of the *Regulated Activities Order* applies; or

(e) a *financial instrument* in paragraph 10 of Section C of Annex 1 to *MiFID* to which article 83(3) of the *Regulated Activities Order* applies; or

(f) an option to acquire or dispose of an option specified in (a), (b), (c), (d) or (e);

but so that for the purposes of calculating capital requirements for *BIPRU firms* it also includes any of the items listed in the table in BIPRU 7.6.18 R (Option PRR: methods for different types of option) and any cash settled option.

(B) In the FCA Handbook:

the *investment*, specified in article 83 of the *Regulated Activities Order* (Options), which is an option to acquire or dispose of:

(a) a *designated investment* (other than a *P2P agreement*, an option or one to which (d) or (e) applies); or

(b) currency of the *United Kingdom* or of any other country or territory; or

(c) palladium, platinum, gold or silver; or

(d) a commodity to which article 83(2) of the *Regulated Activities Order* applies; or

(e) a *financial instrument* in paragraph 10 of Section C of Annex 1 to *MiFID* to which article 83(3) of the *Regulated Activities Order* applies; or

(f) an option to acquire or dispose of an option specified in (a), (b), (c), (d) or (e);

but so that for the purposes of calculating capital requirements for *BIPRU firms* it also includes any of the items listed in the table in BIPRU 7.6.18 R (Option PRR: methods for different types of option) and any cash settled option.

option hedging method

the method of calculating the *option PRR* in BIPRU 7.6.24R (The hedging method).

option PRR

the part of the market risk capital requirement calculated in accordance with BIPRU 7.6 (Option PRR) or, in relation to a particular position, the portion of the overall option PRR attributable to that position.

option standard method

the method of calculating the option PRR in BIPRU 7.6.20R to BIPRU 7.6.22R (The standard method).

organisation

a *body corporate*, a *partnership*, a trust or an unincorporated association.

original financing costing amount

(in relation to a *share*, *debenture* or other investment in, or external contribution to the capital of, a *firm* that is subject to a *step-up*) the *financing cost amount* for the instrument for a period beginning on or near the date of issue of the instrument and ending on or near the date of the first *step-up*.

originator

(A) In the PRA Handbook:

(in accordance with Article 4(41) of the *Banking Consolidation Directive* (Definitions) and in relation to a *securitisation* within the meaning of paragraph (2) of the definition of securitisation) either of the following:

(a) an entity which, either itself or through related entities, directly or indirectly, was involved in the original agreement which created the obligations or potential obligations of the debtor or potential debtor giving rise to the *exposures* being *securitised*; or

(b) an entity which purchases a third party's *exposures* onto its balance sheet and then *securitises* them.

(B) In the FCA Handbook:

(1) (in *GENPRU* (except GENPRU 3), *MIPRU* and *BIPRU* (except BIPRU 12)) (in accordance with Article 4(41) of the *Banking Consolidation Directive* (Definitions) and in relation to a *securitisation* within the meaning of paragraph (2) of the definition of securitisation) either of the following:

(a) an entity which, either itself or through related entities, directly or indirectly, was involved in the original agreement which created the obligations or potential obligations of the debtor or potential debtor giving rise to the *exposures* being *securitised*; or

(b) an entity which purchases a third party's *exposures* onto its balance sheet and then *securitises* them.

(2) (except in (1)) has the meaning in article 4(1)(13) of the *EU CRR*.

ORCR

the *operational risk capital requirement*.

OTC

over the counter.

OTC derivative

a *derivative* traded solely *over the counter*.

OTC derivatives, CCPs and trade repositories regulation

the Financial Services and Markets Act 2000 (Over the Counter Derivatives, Central Counterparties and Trade Repositories) Regulations 2013

OTC derivative transaction

a derivative financial instrument of a type listed on Annex II to the *CRR* that is traded over the counter.

outgoing ECA provider

a *firm* which:

(a) provides an *electronic commerce activity*, from an *establishment* in the *United Kingdom*, with or for an *ECA recipient* present in an *EEA State* other than the *United Kingdom*; and

(b) is a national of an *EEA State* or a firm or company mentioned in article 54 of the *Treaty*.

out of the money

(for the purposes of BIPRU 7 (Market risk) and in relation to an *option* or *warrant*) that *option* or *warrant* being neither *at the money* nor *in the money*.

outsourcing

(1) (except in SYSC 8, COBS 11.7 and the definition of *relevant person*) the use of a *person* to provide customised services to a *firm* other than:
(a) a member of the *firm's* governing body acting in his capacity as such; or
(b) an individual employed by a *firm* under a contract of service.

(2) (in SYSC 8, COBS 11.7 and the definition of *relevant person*) an arrangement of any form between a *firm* and a service provider by which that service provider performs a process, a service or an activity which would otherwise be undertaken by the *firm* itself.

[Note: article 2(6) of the *MiFID implementing Directive*]

overall financial adequacy rule

(A) In the PRA Handbook:
GENPRU 1.2.26 R (Requirement for certain *firms* to have adequate financial resources).

(B) In the FCA Handbook:
(1) (in *GENPRU*, *BIPRU* and *INSPRU*) GENPRU 1.2.26A G (Requirement for certain *firms* to have adequate financial resources).
(2) (in *IFPRU*) IFPRU 2.2.1R (Adequacy of financial resources).

overall liquidity adequacy rule

BIPRU 12.2.1R.

overall Pillar 2 rule

(A) In the PRA Handbook:
GENPRU 1.2.30 R (Systems, strategies, processes and reviews for certain *firms*).

(B) In the FCA Handbook:
(1) (in *GENPRU*, *BIPRU* and *INSPRU*) GENPRU 1.2.30 R (Systems, strategies, processes and reviews for certain *firms*).
(2) (in *IFPRU*) IFPRU 2.2.7R (Strategy processes and systems).

over collateralisation

(in *RCB*) (as defined in Regulation 3(3) of the *RCB Regulations*) the provision of additional *assets* that assist the payment from the *relevant asset pool* of claims attaching to a *regulated covered bond* in the event of the failure of the *issuer*.

over the counter

(in relation to a transaction in an *investment*) not *on-exchange*.

overall financial sector

a sector composed of one or more the following types of entities:

(a) members of each of the *financial sectors*; and

(b) (except where GENPRU 3.1 (Cross sector groups) or GENPRU 3 Ann 1R (Capital adequacy calculations for financial conglomerates) provide otherwise) a *mixed financial holding company*.

overallotment facility

(as defined in Article 2 of the *Buy-back and Stabilisation Regulation*) a clause in the underwriting agreement or lead management agreement which permits acceptance of subscriptions or offers to purchase a greater number of *relevant securities* than originally offered.

overdraft facility

(in CONC App 1.2) an explicit agreement whereby a *lender* makes available to a *borrower* funds which exceed the current balance in the *borrower's current account*.

overseas

outside the *United Kingdom*.

overseas company

(in *LR* and *PR*) a *company* incorporated outside the *United Kingdom*.

overseas financial services institution

an institution authorised to carry on any *regulated activity* or other financial service by an *overseas regulator*.

overseas financial stability information power

the *PRA's* power under section 169A of the *Act* (Support of overseas regulator with respect to financial stability) which, in summary, is a power exercisable at the request of an *overseas regulator* to require a *person* to provide information or documents relevant to the stability of one or more aspects of the *relevant financial system* operating in the country or territory of that regulator.

overseas firm

(1) (in relation to MAR 5) a *firm* which has its registered office (or, if it has no registered office, its head office) outside the *United Kingdom* excluding an *incoming EEA firm*.

(2) (in any other case) a *firm* which has its registered office (or, if it has no registered office, its head office) outside the *United Kingdom*.

overseas introducing broker

a *person*, who is not an *authorised person*:

(a) who is resident outside the *United Kingdom*; and

(b) who introduces transactions relating to designated investments arranged (brought about) for its *clients* to a *clearing firm* in the *United Kingdom*.

overseas investment exchange

an investment exchange which has neither its head office nor its registered office in the *United Kingdom*.

overseas long-term insurer

an *insurance undertaking* which is not an *authorised person* and which:

(a) has its head office in an *EEA State* other than the *United Kingdom*, and is entitled to carry on *long-term insurance business* in that *EEA State*; or

(b) has a *branch* or agency in an *EEA State* other than the *United Kingdom* and is entitled to carry on *long-term insurance business* in that *EEA State*; or

(c) is authorised to effect or carry on *long-term insurance business* in the Bailiwick of Jersey, the Bailiwick of Guernsey, the Isle of Man, the Commonwealth of Pennsylvania or the State of Iowa;

for the purposes of (a) and (b), Gibraltar is to be regarded as if it were an *EEA State*.

overseas person

(A) In the PRA Handbook: (in accordance with article 3(1) of the *Regulated Activities Order* (Interpretation)) a *person* who:

(a) carries on any of the following *regulated activities*:
(i) *dealing in investments as principal*;
(ii) *dealing in investments as agent*;
(iii) *arranging (bringing about) deals in investments*;
(iv) *arranging (bringing about) regulated mortgage contracts*;
(v) *making arrangements with a view to regulated mortgage contracts*;
(vi) *making arrangements with a view to transactions in investments*;
(vii) *managing investments*;
(viii) safe custody and administering investments;
(ix) *sending dematerialised instructions*;
(x) *causing dematerialised instructions to be sent*;
(xi) *establishing, operating or winding up a collective investment scheme*;
(xii) *acting as trustee of an authorised unit trust scheme*;
(xiii) *acting as the depositary or sole director of an open-ended investment company*;
(xiiia) *acting as the depositary of an authorised contractual scheme*;
(xiv) *establishing, operating or winding up a stakeholder pension scheme*;
(xiva) *establishing, operating or winding up a personal pension scheme*;
(xv) *advising on investments*;
(xvi) *advising on regulated mortgage contracts*;
(xvii) *entering into a regulated mortgage contract*;
(xviii) *administering a regulated mortgage contract*;
(xix) *arranging (bringing about) a home reversion plan*;
(xx) *making arrangements with a view to a home reversion plan*;
(xxi) *advising on a home reversion plan*;
(xxii) *entering into a home reversion plan*;
(xxiii) *administering a home reversion plan*;
(xxiv) *arranging (bringing about) a home purchase plan*;
(xxv) *making arrangements with a view to a home purchase plan*;
(xxvi) *advising on a home purchase plan*;
(xxvii) *entering into a home purchase plan*;
(xxviii) *administering a home purchase plan*;
(xxix) agreeing to carry on those regulated activities, disregarding the exclusion in article 72 of the *Regulated Activities Order* (Overseas persons); but

(b) does not carry on any such activities, or offer to do so, from a permanent place of business maintained by him in the *United Kingdom*.

(B) In the FCA Handbook: (in accordance with article 3(1) of the *Regulated Activities Order* (Interpretation)) a *person* who:

(a) carries on any of the following *regulated activities*:
(i) *dealing in investments as principal*;
(ii) *dealing in investments as agent*;
(iii) *arranging (bringing about) deals in investments*;
(iv) *arranging (bringing about) regulated mortgage contracts*;
(v) *making arrangements with a view to regulated mortgage contracts*;
(vi) *making arrangements with a view to transactions in investments*;
(vii) *managing investments*;
(viii) safe custody and administering investments;
(ix) *sending dematerialised instructions*;
(x) *causing dematerialised instructions to be sent*;
(xa) *managing a UCITS*;
(xb) *acting as trustee or depositary of a UCITS*;
(xc) *managing an AIF*;
(xd) *acting as trustee or depositary of an AIF*;
(xi) *establishing, operating or winding up a collective investment scheme*;
(xii) [deleted]
(xiii) [deleted]
(xiiia) [deleted]
(xiv) *establishing, operating or winding up a stakeholder pension scheme*;
(xiva) *establishing, operating or winding up a personal pension scheme*;
(xv) *advising on investments*;
(xvi) *advising on regulated mortgage contracts*;
(xvii) *entering into a regulated mortgage contract*;
(xviii) *administering a regulated mortgage contract*;
(xix) *arranging (bringing about) a home reversion plan*;
(xx) *making arrangements with a view to a home reversion plan*;

(xxi) *advising on a home reversion plan*;

(xxii) *entering into a home reversion plan*;

(xxiii) *administering a home reversion plan*;

(xxiv) *arranging (bringing about) a home purchase plan*;

(xxv) *making arrangements with a view to a home purchase plan*;

(xxvi) *advising on a home purchase plan*;

(xxvii) *entering into a home purchase plan*;

(xxviii) *administering a home purchase plan*;

(xxix) agreeing to carry on those regulated activities, disregarding the exclusion in article 72 of the *Regulated Activities Order* (Overseas persons); but

(b) does not carry on any such activities, or offer to do so, from a permanent place of business maintained by him in the *United Kingdom*.

overseas regulator

(1) (except in relation to the *overseas financial stability information power*) (as defined in section 195(3) of the *Act* (Exercise of power in support of overseas regulator)) an authority in a country or territory outside the *United Kingdom*:

(a) which is a *Home State regulator*; or

(b) which exercises any of the following functions:

(i) a function corresponding to any function of the *FCA* or *PRA* under the *Act*;

(ii) a function corresponding to any function exercised by the *FCA* in its capacity as *competent authority* in relation to the listing of securities;

(iii) a function corresponding to any function exercised by the Secretary of State under the Companies Acts (as defined in section 2 of the Companies Act 2006);

(iv) a function in connection with the investigation of conduct of the kind prohibited by Part V of the Criminal Justice *Act* 1993 (Insider Dealing), or with the enforcement of rules (whether or not having the force of law) relating to such conduct;

(v) a function prescribed by regulations made for the purposes of section 195(4) of the *Act* (Exercise of powers) which, in the opinion of the Treasury, relates to companies or financial services.

(2) (in relation to the *overseas financial stability information power*) (as defined in section 169A(2) of the *Act* (Support of overseas regulator with respect to financial stability)) an authority in a country or territory outside the *United Kingdom* which exercises functions with respect to the stability of the *relevant financial system* operating in that country or territory.

own account order

an order which relates to an *own account transaction*.

own account trading firm

(in relation to *firm type* in SUP 16.10 (Confirmation of *standing data*)) a *firm* that only *deals* or arranges *deals* in *securities* or *contractually based investments* for its own benefit, or for the benefit of an *associate*.

own account transaction

a transaction *executed* by the *firm* for its own benefit or for the benefit of its *associate*.

own funds

(A) In the PRA Handbook:

(1) (in *GENPRU* (except GENPRU 3 (Cross sector groups) and *BIPRU* (except BIPRU 12 (Liquidity standards)) own funds as described in articles 56 to 67 of the *Banking Consolidation Directive*.

(2) [deleted]

(2A) (in IPRU(INV) 11) the own funds of a *firm* calculated in line with IPRU(INV) Table 11.4 (Method of calculating initial capital and own funds).

(3) (in *IPRU(INV)* 8) capital, as defined in CREDS 5.2.1 R.

(3A) (in *IPRU(INV)* 13) the own funds of a *firm* calculated in accordance with 13.1A.14R.

(4) (in *UPRU*) funds calculated in accordance with UPRU Table 2.2.1 R (Method of calculation of financial resources) composed of the specified items set out in that Table.

(5) (except in (1) to (4)) has the meaning in article 4(1)(118) of the *EU CRR*.

(B) In the FCA Handbook:

(1) (in *GENPRU* (except GENPRU 3 (Cross sector groups) and *BIPRU* (except BIPRU 12 (Liquidity standards)) own funds as described in articles 56 to 67 of the *Banking Consolidation Directive*.

(2) [deleted]

(2A) (in IPRU(INV) 11) has the meaning in article 4(1)(118) of the *EU CRR*.

(3) (in *IPRU(INV)* 8) capital, as defined in CREDS 5.2.1 R.

(3A) (in *IPRU(INV)* 13) the own funds of a *firm* calculated in accordance with 13.1A.14R.

(4) [deleted]

(5) (except in (1) to (4)) has the meaning in article 4(1)(118) of the *CRR*.

own funds instruments

has the meaning in article 4(1)(119) of the *EU CRR*.

own funds requirements

(A) (In the PRA Handbook): as defined in article 92 (Own funds requirements) of the *EU CRR*.

(B) (In the FCA Handbook): as defined in article 92 (Own funds requirements) of the *EU CRR*.

own estimates of volatility adjustments approach

the approach to calculating volatility adjustments under the *financial collateral comprehensive method* under which the *firm* uses its own estimates of such adjustments, as more fully described in BIPRU 5.4 (Financial collateral) and including that approach as applied to master netting agreements as described in BIPRU 5.6 (Master netting agreements).

owner

(A) In the PRA Handbook
(in *RCB*) (as defined in Regulation 4 of the *RCB Regulations*) an owner which owns an *asset pool* and issues a guarantee to pay from that *asset pool* claims attaching to a *regulated covered bond* in the event of a failure of the *issuer* of that bond.

(B) In the FCA Handbook
(1) (in *RCB*) (as defined in Regulation 4 of the *RCB Regulations*) an owner which owns an *asset pool* and issues a guarantee to pay from that *asset pool* claims attaching to a *regulated covered bond* in the event of a failure of the *issuer* of that bond.
(2) (in relation to a *credit-related regulated activity*), in accordance with article 60N(3) of the *Regulated Activities Order*:
(a) the *person* who bails or, in Scotland, hires *goods* under a *consumer hire agreement*; or
(b) a *person* who exercises, or has the right to exercise, the rights and duties of a *person* who bailed or, in Scotland, hired *goods* under a *consumer hire agreement*.

ownership share

in accordance with the definition of a "share" in section 422(6) of the *Act* (Controller):

(a) (in relation to an *undertaking* with a share capital) an allotted share;

(b) (in relation to an *undertaking* with capital but no share capital) a right to share in the capital of the *undertaking*;

(c) (in relation to an *undertaking* without capital) an interest:
(i) conferring any right to share in the profits, or liability to contribute to the losses, of the *undertaking*; or
(ii) giving rise to an obligation to contribute to the debts or expenses of the *undertaking* in the event of a winding up.

own-initiative powers

FCA's or the *PRA's own-initiative variation power* and *own-initiative requirement power*.

own-initiative requirement power

The *FCA's* power under section 55L(3) of the *Act* or the *PRA's* power under section 55M(3) of the *Act* to impose a new *requirement* on a *firm*, to vary a *requirement* that it has imposed on the *firm* or to cancel any such *requirement* otherwise than on the application of a *firm*.

own-initiative variation power

The *FCA's* or the *PRA's* power under section 55J (Variation or cancellation on initiative of regulator) to vary or cancel a *Part 4A permission* otherwise than on the application of a *firm*.

P2P agreement

(a) (in relation to a *borrower*) in accordance with article 36H of the *Regulated Activities Order*, an agreement between one *person* ("the borrower") and another *person* ("the lender") by which the lender provides the borrower with credit (within the meaning of article 60L of the *Regulated*

Activities Order) and in relation to which the borrower is an *individual* and either:
(i) the lender provides credit (within that meaning) of less than or equal to £25,000; or
(ii) the agreement is not entered into by the borrower wholly or predominantly for the purposes of a business carried on, or intended to be carried on, by the borrower.

(b) (in relation to a lender) in accordance with article 36H of the *Regulated Activities Order*, an agreement between one person ("the borrower") and another person ("the lender") by which the lender provides the borrower with credit (within the meaning of article 60L of the *Regulated Activities Order*) and in relation to which either the lender is an *individual*, or if the lender is not an *individual*, the borrower is an *individual* and either:
(i) the lender provides credit (within that meaning) of less than or equal to £25,000; or
(ii) the agreement is not entered into by the borrower wholly or predominantly for the purposes of a business carried on, or intended to be carried on, by the borrower.

packaged bank account

an arrangement under which a *firm* provides a *retail banking service* as part of a package which includes access to other goods or services, whether or not a fee is charged.

packaged product

(a) a *life policy*;

(b) a *unit* in a *regulated collective investment scheme*;

(c) an interest in an *investment trust savings scheme*;

(d) a *stakeholder pension scheme*;

(e) a *personal pension scheme*;

whether or not (in the case of (a), (b) or (c)) held within an *ISA* or a *CTF* and whether or not the *packaged product* is also a *stakeholder product*.

parent undertaking

(A) In the PRA Handbook:

(1) (in accordance with section 420 of the *Act* (Parent and subsidiary undertaking) and section 1162 of the Companies Act 2006 (Parent and subsidiary undertakings)):
(a) (in relation to whether an *undertaking*, other than an incorporated friendly society, is a *parent undertaking* and except for the purposes described in (c)) an *undertaking* which has the following relationship to another *undertaking* ("S"):
(i) it holds a majority of the voting rights in S; or
(ii) it is a member of S and has the right to appoint or remove a majority of its board of directors; or
(iii) it has the right to exercise a dominant influence over S through:
(A) provisions contained in S's memorandum or articles; or
(B) a control contract; or
(iv) it is a member of S and controls alone, under an agreement with other shareholders or members, a majority of the voting rights in S; or
(v)
(A) it has the power to exercise, or actually exercises, dominant influence or control over S; or
(B) it and S are managed on a unified basis; or
(vi) it is a parent undertaking of a parent undertaking of S; or
(vii) (except in *REC* or for the purposes of the *rules* in *GENPRU* and *INSPRU* as they apply to *members* of the *Society* of Lloyd's or to the *Society* or *managing agents* in respect of *members*) he is an individual and would be a *parent undertaking* if he were an *undertaking*; or
(viii) (except in *REC* or for the purposes of *rules* in *GENPRU* and *INSPRU* as they apply to *members* of the *Society* of Lloyd's or to the *Society* or *managing agents* in respect of *members*) it is incorporated in or formed under the law of another *EEA State* and is a parent undertaking within the meaning of any rule of law in that State for purposes connected with implementation of the Seventh Company Law Directive;
in relation to (ii) and (iv); the *undertaking* will be treated as a member of S if any of its *subsidiary undertakings* is a member of S, or if any shares in S are held by a *person* acting on behalf of the *undertaking* or any of its *subsidiary undertakings*; the provisions of Schedule 7 to the Companies Act 2006 (Parent and subsidiary undertakings: supplementary provisions) explain the expressions used in and supplement paragraphs (i) to (vi);
(b) (in relation to whether an incorporated friendly society is a parent undertaking and except for the purposes escribed in (c)) an incorporated friendly society which has the following relationship to a *body corporate* ("S"):
(i) it holds a majority of the voting rights in S; or
(ii) it is a member of S and has the right to appoint or remove a majority of S's board of directors; or

(iii) it is a member of S and controls alone, under an agreement with other shareholders or members, a majority of the voting rights in S; or

(iv) it is the *parent undertaking* of a *body corporate* which has the relationship in (i), (ii) or (iii) to S.

(c) (for the purposes of *BIPRU* (except BIPRU 12), *GENPRU* (except GENPRU 3) and *INSPRU* as they apply on a consolidated basis and for the purposes of SYSC 12 (Group risk systems and controls requirement) and SYSC 19C (Remuneration Code for BIPRU firms) and in relation to whether an *undertaking* is a *parent undertaking*) an *undertaking* which has the following relationship to another *undertaking* ("S"):

(i) a relationship described in (a) other than (a)(vii); or

(ii) it effectively exercises a dominant influence over S;

and so that (a)(v) does not apply for the purpose of *BIPRU* as it applies on a consolidated basis (including BIPRU 8 (Group risk – consolidation)) or BIPRU 10.

(2) a *parent undertaking* within the meaning of (1) of a .

(3) (for the purposes of GENPRU 3, BIPRU 12, *IFPRU* and SYSC 19A (Remuneration Code)) has the meaning in article 4(1)(15) of the *EU CRR* but so that (in accordance with article 2(9) of the *Financial Groups Directive*) article 4(1)(15)(b) applies for the purpose of GENPRU 3.

(B) In the FCA Handbook:

(1) (in accordance with section 420 of the *Act* (Parent and subsidiary undertaking) and section 1162 of the Companies Act 2006 (Parent and subsidiary undertakings)):

(a) (in relation to whether an *undertaking*, other than an incorporated friendly society, is a *parent undertaking* and except for the purposes described in (c)) an *undertaking* which has the following relationship to another *undertaking* ("S"):

(i) it holds a majority of the voting rights in S; or

(ii) it is a member of S and has the right to appoint or remove a majority of its board of directors; or

(iii) it has the right to exercise a dominant influence over S through:

(A) provisions contained in S's memorandum or articles; or

(B) a control contract; or

(iv) it is a member of S and controls alone, under an agreement with other shareholders or members, a majority of the voting rights in S; or

(v)

(A) it has the power to exercise, or actually exercises, dominant influence or control over S; or

(B) it and S are managed on a unified basis; or

(vi) it is a parent undertaking of a parent undertaking of S; or

(vii) (except in *REC* or for the purposes of the *rules* in *GENPRU* and *INSPRU* as they apply to *members* of the *Society* of Lloyd's or to the *Society* or *managing agents* in respect of *members*) he is an individual and would be a *parent undertaking* if he were an *undertaking*; or

(viii) (except in *REC* or for the purposes of *rules* in *GENPRU* and *INSPRU* as they apply to *members* of the *Society* of Lloyd's or to the *Society* or *managing agents* in respect of *members*) it is incorporated in or formed under the law of another *EEA State* and is a parent undertaking within the meaning of any rule of law in that State for purposes connected with implementation of the Seventh Company Law Directive;

in relation to (ii) and (iv); the *undertaking* will be treated as a member of S if any of its *subsidiary undertakings* is a member of S, or if any shares in S are held by a *person* acting on behalf of the *undertaking* or any of its *subsidiary undertakings*; the provisions of Schedule 7 to the Companies Act 2006 (Parent and subsidiary undertakings: supplementary provisions) explain the expressions used in and supplement paragraphs (i) to (vi);

(b) (in relation to whether an incorporated friendly society is a parent undertaking and except for the purposes described in (c)) an incorporated friendly society which has the following relationship to a *body corporate* ("S"):

(i) it holds a majority of the voting rights in S; or

(ii) it is a member of S and has the right to appoint or remove a majority of S's board of directors; or

(iii) it is a member of S and controls alone, under an agreement with other shareholders or members, a majority of the voting rights in S; or

(iv) it is the *parent undertaking* of a *body corporate* which has the relationship in (i), (ii) or (iii) to S.

(c) (for the purposes of *BIPRU* (except BIPRU 12), *GENPRU* (except GENPRU 3) and *INSPRU* as they apply on a consolidated basis and for the purposes of SYSC 12 (Group risk systems and controls requirement) and SYSC 19C (Remuneration Code for BIPRU firms) and in relation to whether an *undertaking* is a *parent undertaking*) an *undertaking* which has the following relationship to another *undertaking* ("S"):

(i) a relationship described in (a) other than (a)(vii); or

(ii) it effectively exercises a dominant influence over S;

and so that (a)(v) does not apply for the purpose of *BIPRU* as it applies on a consolidated basis (including BIPRU 8 (Group risk – consolidation)) or BIPRU 10.

(2) a *parent undertaking* within the meaning of (1) of a .

(3) (for the purposes of GENPRU 3, BIPRU 12, *IFPRU* and SYSC 19A (Remuneration Code)) has the meaning in article 4(1)(15) of the *EU CRR* but so that (in accordance with article 2(9) of the *Financial Groups Directive*) article 4(1)(15)(b) applies for the purpose of GENPRU 3.

parental responsibility

(as defined in section 3(9) of the Child Trust Fund Act 2004):

(a) parental responsibility within the meaning of the Children Act 1989 or the Children (Northern Ireland) Order 1995 (SI 1995/755 (N.I. 2)); or

(b) parental responsibilities within the meaning of the Children (Scotland) Act 1995.

parent financial holding company in a Member State

(A) In the PRA Handbook:
(1) (in *GENPRU* (except GENPRU 3 and *BIPRU* (except BIPRU 12)) (in accordance with Article 4(15) of the *Banking Consolidation Directive* (Definitions) and Article 3 of the *Capital Adequacy Directive* (Definitions)) a *financial holding company* which is not itself a *subsidiary undertaking* of an *institution* authorised in the same *EEA State*, or of a *financial holding company* or *mixed financial holding company* established in the same *EEA State*.
(2) (except in (1)) has the meaning in article 4(1)(30) of the *EU CRR*.

(B) In the FCA Handbook:
(1) (in *GENPRU* (except GENPRU 3 and *BIPRU* (except BIPRU 12)) (in accordance with Article 4(15) of the *Banking Consolidation Directive* (Definitions) and Article 3 of the *Capital Adequacy Directive* (Definitions)) a *financial holding company* which is not itself a *subsidiary undertaking* of an *institution* authorised in the same *EEA State*, or of a *financial holding company* or *mixed financial holding company* established in the same *EEA State*.
(2) (except in (1)) has the meaning in article 4(1)(30) of the *EU CRR*.

parent institution in a Member State

(A) In the PRA Handbook:
(1) (in *GENPRU* (except GENPRU 3 and *BIPRU* (except BIPRU 12)) (in accordance with Article 4(14) of the *Banking Consolidation Directive* and Article 3 of the *Capital Adequacy Directive* (Definitions)) an *institution* which has an *institution* or a *financial institution* as a *subsidiary undertaking* or which holds a *participation* in such an institution, and which is not itself a *subsidiary undertaking* of another *institution* authorised in the same *EEA State*, or of a *financial holding company* or *mixed financial holding company* established in the same *EEA State*.
(2) (except in (1)) has the meaning in article 4(1)(28) of the *EU CRR*.

(B) In the FCA Handbook:
(1) (in *GENPRU* (except GENPRU 3 and *BIPRU* (except BIPRU 12)) (in accordance with Article 4(14) of the *Banking Consolidation Directive* and Article 3 of the *Capital Adequacy Directive* (Definitions)) an *institution* which has an *institution* or a *financial institution* as a *subsidiary undertaking* or which holds a *participation* in such an institution, and which is not itself a *subsidiary undertaking* of another *institution* authorised in the same *EEA State*, or of a *financial holding company* or *mixed financial holding company* established in the same *EEA State*.
(2) (except in (1)) has the meaning in article 4(1)(28) of the *EU CRR*.

parent mixed financial holding company in a Member State

(A) In the PRA Handbook:
(1) (in *GENPRU* (except GENPRU 3 and *BIPRU* (except BIPRU 12)) in accordance with Article 4(15a) of the *Banking Consolidation Directive* (Definitions)) a *mixed financial holding company* which is not itself a *subsidiary undertaking* of an *institution* authorised in the same *EEA State*, or of a *financial holding company* or *mixed financial holding company* established in the same *EEA State*
(2) (except in (1)) has the meaning in article 4(1)(32) of the *EU CRR*.

(B) In the FCA Handbook:
(1) (in *GENPRU* (except GENPRU 3 and *BIPRU* (except BIPRU 12)) in accordance with Article 4(15a) of the *Banking Consolidation Directive* (Definitions)) a *mixed financial holding company* which is not itself a *subsidiary undertaking* of an *institution* authorised in the same *EEA State*, or of a *financial holding company* or *mixed financial holding company* established in the same *EEA State*
(2) (except in (1)) has the meaning in article 4(1)(32) of the *EU CRR*.

Part 4A permission

(as defined in section 55A of the *Act* (Application for *permission*)) a *permission* given by the *FCA* or *PRA* under Part 4A of the *Act* (Permission to carry on regulated activities), or having effect as if so given.

Part 6 rules

(as defined in section 73A of the *Act*) *rules* made for the purposes of Part VI of the *Act*.

Part 30 exemption order

(A) In the PRA Handbook: an order under regulation 30.10 of the General Regulations under the US Commodity Exchange Act, issued by the Commodity Futures Trading Commission on 15 May 1989, granting a *person* exemption from the registration requirement contained in Part 30 of those General Regulations.

(B) In the FCA Handbook: the order under regulation 30.10 of the General Regulations under the US Commodity Exchange Act issued by the Commodity Futures Trading Commission on 10 October 2003 (consolidating and updating relief granted to *firms* in prior orders), granting a *person* authorised under the Act exemption from certain requirements contained in Part 30 of those General Regulations.

Part XX exemption

the exemption from the *general prohibition* conferred on an *exempt professional firm* by section 327 of the *Act* (Exemption from the *general prohibition*).

participant

(in accordance with section 235(2) of the *Act* (*Collective investment* schemes)) a *person* who participates in a *collective investment scheme*.

participant firm

(A) In the PRA Handbook: (1) (except in FEES 1) a *firm* or a *member* other than:

(a) (in accordance with section 213(10) of the *Act* (The compensation scheme) and regulation 2 of the *Electing Participants Regulations* (Persons not to be regarded as relevant persons) an *incoming EEA firm* which is:
(i) a *credit institution*;
(ii) a *MiFID investment firm*; or
(iii) [deleted]
(iv) both (i) and (ii); or
(v) an *IMD insurance intermediary* or an *IMD reinsurance intermediary* which is neither (i) or (ii);
(vi) an *AIFM* managing an *unauthorised AIF* or providing the services in article 6(4) of *AIFMD*;
in relation to its *passported activities*, unless it has *top-up cover*

(aa) (in accordance with section 213(10) of the *Act* (The compensation scheme) and regulation 2 of the *Electing Participants Regulations* (Persons not to be regarded as relevant persons) an *incoming EEA firm* which is a *management company* other than to the extent that it carries on the following activities from a *branch* in the *United Kingdom* or under the freedom to provide *cross border services*:
(i) *collective portfolio management* for a *UCITS scheme*; or
(ii) *managing investments* (other than of a *collective investment scheme*), *advising on investments* or *safeguarding and administering investments* (the services referred to in article 6(3) of the *UCITS Directive*), but only if it has top-up cover;

(b) a service company;

(c) [deleted]

(d) [deleted]

(e) an *underwriting agent*, or *members' adviser*, in respect of *advising on syndicate participation at Lloyd's* or managing the underwriting capacity of a Lloyd's syndicate as a managing agent at Lloyd's;

(f) an *authorised professional firm* that is subject to the rules of the Law Society (England and Wales) or the Law Society of Scotland and with respect to its *regulated activities* participates in the relevant society's compensation scheme;

(g) an *ICVC*;

(h) a UCITS qualifier;

(i) [deleted]

(j) in respect of the carrying on of *bidding in emissions auctions*, a *firm* that is exempt from *MiFID* under article 2(1)(i).

(k) an *AIFM qualifier*.

(2) (in FEES 1) a *firm* specified in paragraph (1) above that is not a *member*.

(B) In the FCA Handbook: (1) (except in FEES 1 and FEES 6) a *firm* or a *member* other than:

(a) (in accordance with section 213(10) of the *Act* (The compensation scheme) and regulation 2 of the *Electing Participants Regulations* (Persons not to be regarded as relevant persons) an *incoming EEA firm* which is:

(i) a *credit institution*;

(ii) a *MiFID investment firm*; or

(iii) [deleted]

(iv) both (i) and (ii); or

(v) an *IMD insurance intermediary* or an *IMD reinsurance intermediary* which is neither (i) or (ii);

(vi) an *AIFM* managing an *unauthorised AIF* or providing the services in article 6(4) of *AIFMD*;

in relation to its *passported activities*, unless it has *top-up cover*

(aa) (in accordance with section 213(10) of the *Act* (The compensation scheme) and regulation 2 of the *Electing Participants Regulations* (Persons not to be regarded as relevant persons) an *incoming EEA firm* which is a *management company* other than to the extent that it carries on the following activities from a *branch* in the *United Kingdom* or under the freedom to provide *cross border services*:

(i) *collective portfolio management* for a *UCITS scheme*; or

(ii) *managing investments* (other than of a *collective investment scheme*), *advising on investments* or *safeguarding and administering investments* (the services referred to in article 6(3) of the *UCITS Directive*), but only if it has top-up cover;

(b) a service company;

(c) [deleted]

(d) [deleted]

(e) an *underwriting agent*, or *members' adviser*, in respect of *advising on syndicate participation at Lloyd's* or managing the underwriting capacity of a Lloyd's syndicate as a managing agent at Lloyd's;

(f) an *authorised professional firm* that is subject to the rules of the Law Society (England and Wales) or the Law Society of Scotland and with respect to its *regulated activities* participates in the relevant society's compensation scheme;

(g) an *ICVC*;

(h) a UCITS qualifier;

(i) [deleted]

(j) in respect of the carrying on of *bidding in emissions auctions*, a *firm* that is exempt from *MiFID* under article 2(1)(i);

(k) an *AIFM qualifier*;

(l) an *operator of an electronic system in relation to lending* in respect of operating the system.

(2) (in FEES 1 and FEES 6) a *firm* specified in paragraph (1) above that is not a *member*.

participating deposit-taker

(as defined in article 2(2) of the *compensation transitionals order*) a *person* who was at any time before *commencement*:

(a) a UK institution, participating institution, former UK institution or former participating institution as defined in section 52(6) of the Banking Act 1987; or

(b) a former authorised institution (as defined in section 106(1) of the Banking Act 1987 (other than a former UK institution or former participating institution as defined in section 52(6) of that Act), which was not a recognised bank or licensed institution excluded by an order under section 23(2) of the Banking Act 1979.

participating insurance undertaking

an insurer which:

(a) has a *subsidiary undertaking* that is an *insurance undertaking*; or

(b) holds a *participation* in an *insurance undertaking*; or

(c) is linked to an *insurance undertaking* by a *consolidation Article 12(1) relationship*.

participating institution

(as defined in article 2(2) of the *compensation transitionals order*) a *person* who was at any time before *commencement* a participating institution within the meaning of section 24(4) of the Building Societies Act 1986.

participating security

a participating security as defined in regulation 3 of the Uncertificated Securities Regulations 1995 (SI 1995/3272), which enable title to participating securities to be evidenced otherwise than by a certificate and transferred otherwise than by a written instrument.

participation

(A) In the PRA Handbook:
(for the purposes of *UPRU* and *GENPRU* (except GENPRU 3) and for the purposes of *BIPRU* (except BIPRU 12) and *INSPRU* as they apply on a consolidated basis):
(a) a participating interest may be defined according to:
(i) section 421A of the *Act* where applicable; or
(ii) paragraph 11(1) of Schedule 10 to the Large and Medium-sized Companies and Groups (Accounts and Reports) Regulations 2008 (SI 2008/410) where applicable; or
(iii) paragraph 8 of Schedule 7 to the Small Companies and Groups (Accounts and Directors' Report) Regulations 2008 (SI 2008/409) where applicable; or
(iv) paragraph 8 of Schedule 4 to the Large and Medium-sized Limited Liability Partnerships (Accounts) Regulations 2008 (SI 2008/1913) where applicable; or
(v) paragraph 8 of Schedule 5 to the Small Limited Liability Partnerships (Accounts) Regulations 2008 (SI 2008/1912) where applicable; or
(b) (otherwise) the direct or indirect ownership of 20% or more of the voting rights or capital of an *undertaking*;
but excluding the interest of a *parent undertaking* in its *subsidiary undertaking*.
(2) (except in (1) has the meaning in article 4(1)(35) of the *EU CRR*.

(B) In the FCA Handbook:
(1) (for the purposes of *GENPRU* (except GENPRU 3) and for the purposes of *BIPRU* (except BIPRU 12) and *INSPRU* as they apply on a consolidated basis):
(a) a participating interest may be defined according to:
(i) section 421A of the *Act* where applicable; or
(ii) paragraph 11(1) of Schedule 10 to the Large and Medium-sized Companies and Groups (Accounts and Reports) Regulations 2008 (SI 2008/410) where applicable; or
(iii) paragraph 8 of Schedule 7 to the Small Companies and Groups (Accounts and Directors' Report) Regulations 2008 (SI 2008/409) where applicable; or
(iv) paragraph 8 of Schedule 4 to the Large and Medium-sized Limited Liability Partnerships (Accounts) Regulations 2008 (SI 2008/1913) where applicable; or
(v) paragraph 8 of Schedule 5 to the Small Limited Liability Partnerships (Accounts) Regulations 2008 (SI 2008/1912) where applicable; or
(b) (otherwise) the direct or indirect ownership of 20% or more of the voting rights or capital of an *undertaking*;
but excluding the interest of a *parent undertaking* in its *subsidiary undertaking*.
(2) (except in (1) has the meaning in article 4(1)(35) of the *EU CRR*.

partner

(in relation to a *firm* which is a *partnership*) any *person* appointed to direct its affairs, including:

(a) a *person* occupying the position of a partner (by whatever name called); and

(b) a *person* in accordance with whose directions or instructions (not being advice given in a professional capacity) the partners are accustomed to act.

partner function

(1) (in the *FCA Handbook*) *FCA controlled function* CF4 in Part 1 of the *table of FCA controlled functions*, described more fully in SUP 10A.6.23 R to SUP 10A.6.27 R.

(2) (in the *PRA Handbook*) *PRA controlled function* CF4 in the *table of PRA controlled functions*, described more fully in SUP 10B.6.12 R to SUP 10B.6.14 R.

partnership

(in accordance with section 417(1) of the *Act* (Definitions)) any partnership, including a partnership constituted under the law of a country or territory outside the *United Kingdom*, but not including a *limited liability partnership*.

passport right

(in accordance with regulation 2(1) of the *Electronic Money Regulations*) the entitlement of a *person* to establish a branch or provide services in an *EEA State* other than that in which they are authorised to provide *electronic money* issuance services:

(a) in accordance with the Treaty on the Functioning of the European Union as applied in the *EEA*; and

(b) subject to the conditions of the *Electronic Money Directive*.

passported activity

an activity carried on by an *EEA firm*, or by a *UK firm*, under an *EEA right*.

pawn

any article subject to a *pledge*.

pawnee

a *person* who takes any article in *pawn* and includes any *person* to whom the rights and duties of the original pawnee have passed by assignment or operation of law.

pawnor

includes any *person* to whom the rights and duties of the original pawnor have passed by assignment or operation of law.

pawn-receipt

has the meaning given by section 114 of the *CCA*.

payment

includes tender.

payment holiday

a feature of a *regulated mortgage contract* under which the *mortgage lender* permits the customer to make no payments for a specified period without being in *arrears*.

payment information

the information described in COBS 7.3.4R, that is, the amount and nature of any payments that the *client* will have to make, directly or indirectly, for the *personal recommendation*.

payment institution

an *authorised payment institution*, an *EEA authorised payment institution* or a *small payment institution*. [Note: articles 4(4) and 26(3) of the *Payment Services Directive*]

payment instrument

(in *BCOBS*) any personalised device or personalised set of procedures agreed between the *banking customer* and the *firm* used by the *banking customer* to initiate an instruction or request by the *banking customer* to the *firm* to make a payment.

payment leg

(for the purposes of the *CCR standardised method* and as more fully defined in BIPRU 13.5.2 R (Derivation of risk position: payment legs) the contractually agreed gross payments under a *financial derivative instrument*, including the notional amount of the transaction.

payment protection contract

A *non-investment insurance contract* which has elements of a *general insurance contract* and the benefits of which are described as enabling a *policyholder* to protect his ability to continue to make payments due to third parties, or can reasonably be expected to be used in this way.

payment routing information

a combination of letters, numbers or symbols specified by a *firm* to be provided when instructing or requesting the *firm* to make a payment from an account of a *banking customer* for the purpose of routing the payment to the correct destination and intended recipient.

payment service

(in accordance with regulation 2(1) of, and Schedule 1 to, the *Payment Services Regulations*):

(a) Any of the following activities when carried out as a regular occupation or business activity:
(i) services enabling cash to be placed on a payment account and all of the operations required for operating a payment account;
(ii) services enabling cash withdrawals from a payment account and all of the operations required for operating a payment account;
(iii) execution of the following types of payment transaction:

(A) direct debits, including one-off direct debits;

(B) payment transactions executed through a payment card or a similar device;

(C) credit transfers, including standing orders;

(iv) execution of the following types of payment transaction where the funds are covered by a credit line for the *payment service user*:

(A) direct debits, including one-off direct debits;

(B) payment transactions executed through a payment card or a similar device;

(C) credit transfers, including standing orders;

(v) issuing payment instruments or acquiring payment transactions;

(vi) *money remittance*;

(vii) execution of payment transactions where the consent of the payer to execute the payment transaction is given by means of any telecommunication, digital or IT device and the payment is made to the telecommunication, IT system or network operator, acting only as an intermediary between the *payment service user* and the supplier of the goods or services.

(b) The following activities do not constitute payment services:

(i) payment transactions executed wholly in cash and directly between the payer and the payee, without any intermediary intervention;

(ii) payment transactions between the payer and the payee through a commercial agent authorised to negotiate or conclude the sale or purchase of goods or services on behalf of the payer or the payee;

(iii) the professional physical transport of banknotes and coins, including their collection, processing and delivery;

(iv) payment transactions consisting of non-professional cash collection and delivery as part of a not-for-profit or charitable activity;

(v) services where cash is provided by the payee to the payer as part of a payment transaction for the purchase of goods or services following an explicit request by the payer immediately before the execution of the payment transaction;

(vi) money exchange business consisting of cash-to-cash operations where the funds are not held on a payment account;

(vii) payment transactions based on any of the following documents drawn on the *payment service provider* with a view to placing funds at the disposal of the payee:

(A) paper cheques of any kind, including traveller's cheques;

(B) bankers' drafts;

(C) paper-based vouchers;

(D) paper postal orders;

(viii) payment transactions carried out within a payment or securities settlement system between *payment service providers* and settlement agents, central counterparties, clearing houses, central banks or other participants in the system;

(ix) payment transactions related to securities asset servicing, including dividends, income or other distributions, or redemption or sale, carried out by *persons* referred to in (h) or by investment firms, *full credit institutions*, collective investment undertakings, asset management companies providing investment services or by any other entities allowed to have the custody of financial instruments;

(x) services provided by technical service providers, which support the provision of *payment services*, without the provider entering at any time into possession of the funds to be transferred, including:

(A) the processing and storage of data;

(B) trust and privacy protection services;

(C) data and entity authentication;

(D) information technology;

(E) communication network provision; and

(F) the provision and maintenance of terminals and devices used for *payment services*;

(xi) services based on instruments that can be used to acquire goods or services only:

(A) in or on the issuer's premises; or

(B) under a commercial agreement with the issuer, either within a limited network of service providers or for a limited range of goods or services,

and for these purposes the "issuer" is the person who issues the instrument in question;

(xii) payment transactions executed by means of any telecommunication, digital or IT device, where the goods or services purchased are delivered to and are to be used through a telecommunication, digital or IT device, provided that the telecommunication, digital or IT operator does not act only as an intermediary between the *payment service user* and the supplier of the goods and services;

(A) payment transactions carried out between *payment service providers*, or their agents or *branches*, for their own account;

(B) payment transactions between a parent undertaking and its subsidiary or between subsidiaries of the same parent undertaking, without any intermediary intervention by a *payment service provider* other than an undertaking belonging to the same group;

(C) services by providers to withdraw cash by means of automated teller machines acting on behalf of one or more card issuers, which are not party to the *framework contract* with the customer withdrawing money from a payment account, where no other *payment service* is conducted by the provider.

[Note: articles 3 and 4(3) of, and the Annex to, the *Payment Services Directive*]

Payment Services Directive

Directive 2007/64/EC of the European Parliament and of the Council of 13th November 2007 on payment services in the internal market.

payment service provider

(1) (except in *DISP*) (in accordance with regulation 2(1) of the *Payment Service Regulations*) any of the following *persons* when they carry out a *payment service*:

(a) an *authorised payment institution*;

(b) a *small payment institution*;

(c) an *EEA authorised payment institution*;

(d) a *full credit institution*;

(e) an *electronic money issuer*;

(f) the Post Office Limited;

(g) the Bank of England, the European Central Bank and the national central banks of *EEA States* other than the *United Kingdom*, other than when acting in their capacity as a monetary authority or carrying out other functions of a public nature; and

(h) government departments and local authorities, other than when carrying out functions of a public nature.

[Note: article 1(1) of the *Payment Services Directive*]

(2) (in *DISP* and FEES 5.5) as in (1) but excluding a *full credit institution*.

payment service user

(in accordance with regulation 2(1) of the *Payment Services Regulations*) a *person* when making use of a *payment service* in the capacity of either payer or payee, or both. [Note: article 4(10) of the *Payment Services Directive*]

Payment Services Regulations

the Payment Services Regulations 2009 (SI 2009/209).

payment shortfall

the outstanding amount to be paid measured against the amount of payments which have become due during the term of a *regulated mortgage contract* or *home purchase plan*, including any *arrears* amount due.

payment system

(a) (in accordance with section 41 of *FSBRA*), a system which is operated by one or more *persons* in the course of business for the purpose of enabling *persons* to make transfers of funds, and includes a system which is designed to facilitate the transfer of funds using another payment system;

(b) but "payment system" does not include:

(i) any arrangements for the physical movement of cash;

(ii) a system which does not make any provision for the transfer of funds by payers, or to recipients, in the *United Kingdom*;

(iii) a securities settlement system operated by a *person* approved under regulations made under section 785 of the Companies Act 2006 (provisions enabling procedures for evidencing the transferring title);

(iv) a system operated by a *recognised clearing house*;

(v) any other system whose primary purpose is not that of enabling *persons* to transfer funds.

PD

(1) (except in *GENPRU* and *BIPRU*) Prospectus Directive.

(2) (in *GENPRU*) *probability of default*.

PD/LGD approach

the method for treating *equity exposures* under the *IRB approach* set out in BIPRU 4.7.14 R-BIPRU 4.7.22 R.

PD Regulation

the Prospectus Directive Regulation (No 2004/809/EC).

peak exposure

(in accordance with Part 1 of Annex III of the *Banking Consolidation Directive* (Definitions) and for the purpose of BIPRU 13 (The calculation of counterparty risk exposure values for financial derivatives, securities financing transactions and long settlement transactions)) a high percentile of the distribution of exposures at any particular future date before the maturity date of the longest transaction in the *netting set*.

pending application

(as defined in article 3(1) of the *compensation transitionals order*):

(a) an application for compensation made under an *investment business compensation scheme* before *commencement* in relation to which a *terminating event* did not occur before *commencement*; and

(b) an application made to the *FSCS* after *commencement* under an *investment business compensation scheme*, even if at the time of application that scheme had otherwise ceased to exist.

penny share

a *readily realisable security* in relation to which the bid-offer spread is 10 per cent or more of the offer price, but not:

(a) a *government and public security*; or

(b) a *share* in a *company* quoted on The Financial Times Stock Exchange 100 Index; or

(c) a *security* issued by a *company* which, at the time that the firm *deals* or recommends to the *client* to *deal* in the *investment*, has a market capitalisation of £100 million or more (or its equivalent in any other currency at the relevant time).

pension annuity

an *investment* purchased with the sums derived from the vesting (partial or full) of a *pension policy* or *pension contract*, for the purposes of securing the beneficiary's entitlement to immediate or future benefits.

pension buy-out contract

a *pension policy* bought from an *insurer* using funds from:

(a) a scheme that was approved under Chapter 1 of Part 14 of the Income and Corporation Taxes Act 1988 when that chapter was in force; or

(b) a scheme that is a registered pension scheme under Chapter 2 of Part 4 of the Finance Act 2004.

pension contract

a contract under which rights to benefits are obtained by the making of contributions to an *occupational pension scheme* or to a *personal pension scheme*, where the contributions are paid to a *regulated collective investment scheme*.

pension conversion

a transaction resulting from a decision of a *retail client* to require the trustees or managers of a pension scheme to:

(a) convert *safeguarded benefits* into different benefits that are *flexible benefits* under that pension scheme; or

(b) pay an *uncrystallised funds pension lump sum* in respect of any of the *safeguarded benefits*.

[Note: see article 53E(1)(c)(i) and (iii) of the *RAO*]

pension fund management

(in relation to a class of contract of insurance) the class of contract of insurance specified in paragraph VII of Part II of Schedule 1 to the *Regulated Activities Order* (Contracts of long-term insurance) namely:

(a) pension fund management contracts; and

(b) pension fund management contracts which are combined with *contracts of insurance* covering either conservation of capital or payment of a minimum interest;

where effected or carried out by a *person* who does not carry on a banking business, and otherwise carries on *insurance business*.

pension fund management contract

(as defined in article 3(1) of the *Regulated Activities Order* (Interpretation)) a contract to manage the *investments* of pension funds (other than funds solely for the benefit of the officers or employees of the *person* effecting or carrying out the contract and their dependants or, in the case of a *company*, partly for the benefit of officers and employees of its subsidiary or holding company or a subsidiary of its holding company and their dependants; in this definition "subsidiary" and "holding company" mean either *subsidiary* and *holding company*, or *subsidiary* and *holding company* defined in accordance with article 4 of the Companies (Northern Ireland) Order 1986 (SI 1986) No 1032 (NI 6)) as amended by article 62 of the Companies (No 2) (Northern Ireland) Order 1990 (SI 1990 No 1504 (NI 10)).

pension opt-out

a transaction, resulting from the decision of a *retail client* who is an individual, to:

(a) opt out of an *occupational pension scheme*, *group personal pension scheme* or *group stakeholder pension scheme* to which his employer contributes and of which he is a member; or

(b) decline to become a member of an *occupational pension scheme*, *group personal pension scheme* or *group stakeholder pension scheme* to which his employer contributes and of which he is eligible to join, or will be eligible to join at the end of a waiting period;

in favour of a *stakeholder pension scheme* or *personal pension scheme*.

pension policy

a contract under which a right to benefits results from contributions made to an *occupational pension scheme* or to a *personal pension scheme*, where the contributions are paid to a *long-term insurer*.

pension scheme

a scheme under which a right to benefits results from contributions made under a *pension contract* or *pension policy*.

pension term assurance policy

a *personal pension policy* which is a *pure protection contract* and in connection with which tax relief is available under Chapter 4 of Part 4 of the Finance Act 2004.

pension transfer

a transaction, resulting from the decision of a *retail client* who is an individual:

(a) to transfer deferred benefits (regardless of when the *retail client* intends to crystallise such benefits) from:
(i) an *occupational pension scheme*;
(ii) an individual pension contract providing fixed or guaranteed benefits that replaced similar benefits under a *defined benefits pension scheme*; or
(iii) (in the cancellation *rules* (COBS 15)) a *stakeholder pension scheme* or *personal pension scheme*,
to:
(iv) a *stakeholder pension scheme*;
(v) a *personal pension scheme*; or
(vi) a deferred annuity *policy*, where the eventual benefits depend on investment performance in the period up to the date when those benefits will come into payment; or
(vii) a *defined contribution occupational pension scheme*; or

(b) to require the trustees or manager of a pension scheme to make a transfer payment in respect of any *safeguarded benefits* with a view to obtaining a right or entitlement to *flexible benefits* under another pension scheme.

pension transfer specialist

an individual appointed by a *firm* to check the suitability of a *pension transfer*, *pension conversion* or *pension opt-out* who has passed the required examinations as specified in *TC*.

pension wrapper

(in the cancellation rules (COBS 15)) a *SIPP*, *pension contract* or *personal pension product*.

pensions guidance levy

the amount payable to the *FCA* by the *firms* to which FEES 10 (Pensions guidance levy) applies.

percentage ratio

(in *LR*) (in relation to a transaction) the figure, expressed as a percentage, that results from applying a calculation under a *class test* to the transaction.

PERG

the Perimeter Guidance manual.

period rate of charge

(in CONC App 1.1) means a percentage rate of charge for a period, comprising all charges included in the *total charge for credit* determined in accordance with CONC App 1.1.4 R to CONC App 1.1.6 R.

periodic information

the information identified in the table in COBS 16 Annex 2R, and if the *client* has not elected to receive *trade confirmation information* on a transaction by transaction basis under COBS 16.3.3 R, the information identified in column 2 of COBS 16 Annex 1R.

periodic statement

a report which a *firm* is required to provide to a *client* under COBS 16.3 (Periodic reporting).

permanent health

(in relation to a *class* of *contract of insurance*) the *class* of *contract of insurance*, specified in paragraph IV of Part II of Schedule 1 to the *Regulated Activities Order* (Contracts of long-term insurance), providing specified benefits against risks of persons becoming incapacitated in consequence of sustaining injury as a result of an accident or of an accident of a specified class or of sickness or infirmity, being contracts that:

(a) are expressed to be in effect for a period of not less than five years, or until the normal retirement age of the persons concerned, or without limit of time; and

(b) either are not expressed to be terminable by the insurer, or are expressed to be so terminable only in special circumstances mentioned in the contract.

permanent health reinsurance business

reinsurance acceptances which are *contracts of insurance* falling within *long-term insurance business class* IV.

permanent interest bearing shares

(A) In the PRA Handbook:
any shares of a class defined as deferred shares for the purposes of section 119 of the Building Societies Act 1986 which are issued as permanent interest-bearing shares and on terms which qualify them as own funds for the purposes of the *EU CRR*.

(B) In the FCA Handbook:
any shares of a class defined as deferred shares for the purposes of section 119 of the Building Societies Act 1986 which are issued as permanent interest-bearing shares and on terms which qualify them as own funds for the purposes of the *EU CRR*.

permanent share capital

an item of capital that is stated in GENPRU 2.2.83R (Core tier one capital: permanent share capital) to be permanent share capital.

permission

permission to carry on *regulated activities*; that is, any of the following:

(a) a *Part 4A permission*;

(b) the permission that an *incoming EEA firm* has, under paragraph 15(1) or paragraph 15A(1), (3) or (4) of Schedule 3 to the *Act* (EEA Passport Rights), on qualifying for *authorisation* under paragraph 12 of that Schedule;

(c) the permission that an *incoming Treaty firm* has, under paragraph 4(1) of Schedule 4 to the *Act* (Treaty Rights), on qualifying for *authorisation* under paragraph 2 of that Schedule;

(d) the permission that a *UCITS qualifier* has, under paragraph 2(1) of Schedule 5 to the *Act* (Persons concerned in Collective Investment Schemes);

(e) the permission that an *ICVC* has, under paragraph 2(2) of Schedule 5 to the *Act* (Persons concerned in Collective Investment Schemes);

(f) the permission that the Society of Lloyd's has, under section 315(2) of the *Act* (The Society: authorisation and permission), which is to be treated as a *Part IV permission* for the purposes of *Part 4A* of the *Act* (Permission to carry on regulated activities) in accordance with section 315(3) of the *Act*.

permitted activity

(1) (except in SUP 13A and SUP 14) a *regulated activity* which a *firm* has *permission* to carry on.

(2) (in SUP 13A and SUP 14) an activity identified in a consent notice, a regulator's notice or, where none is required, a notice of intention.

permitted business

(in *UPRU*) means *permitted activity*.

permitted deposits

in relation to *permitted links*, *deposits* with any of the following:

(a) an *approved credit institution*; or

(b) an *approved financial institution*; or

(c) an approved *investment firm*.

permitted derivatives contract

in relation to *permitted links*, a contract involving a *derivative* or *quasi-derivative* that satisfies INSPRU 3.2.5 R to INSPRU 3.2.35A G with the exception of INSPRU 3.2.18 R, as applied in relation to assets covering liabilities in respect of *linked long-term* contracts of insurance.

permitted immovable

any interest in land or buildings which falls within COLL 5.6.18 R (2) and COLL 5.6.18 R (6) (Investment in property) and which, being a leasehold interest or its equivalent, has an unexpired term of at least 20 years, but excluding, in relation to an *ICVC*, immovable property that is necessary for the direct pursuit of its business.

permitted land and property

in relation to *permitted links*, any interest in land (and any buildings situated on it) provided that:

(a) it is considered by the *firm* to be located in a territory with a properly functioning market, indicated by the following criteria:
(i) a lack of artificial barriers, including barriers to foreign ownership and repatriation of capital;
(ii) fair and accurate valuation;
(iii) suitably qualified and independent surveyors;
(iv) accurate financial information;
(v) enforceable contractual and other property rights;
(vi) clarity of taxation;
(vii) availability of reliable economic and property market data;
(viii) ethical transaction standards; and

(b) it is:
(i) owned directly by the *firm*; or
(ii) held in a structure, or a series of structures, that do not pose a materially greater risk to *linked policyholders* than a direct holding; and

(c) it is not geared in excess of 10% of the gross asset value of the *linked fund* excluding any amounts represented by holdings in property detailed in *permitted scheme interests* (b) (i) to (iv). But this percentage restriction does not apply if the relevant *policyholder* or trustee or operator acting on behalf of an individual beneficiary requests, directly or indirectly, the *firm* to hold those investments based on the risk profile and objectives, stipulated by and specific for that individual under an investment management agreement with that individual.

permitted links

the property in COBS 21.3.1 R that an insurer may use for the purposes of determining *property-linked benefits* or *index-linked benefits* under *linked long-term* contracts of insurance.

permitted loans

in relation to *permitted links*, a loan with any of the following:

(a) an *approved credit institution*; or

(b) an *approved financial institution*; or

(c) an approved *investment firm*; or

(d) any person, provided that the loan:
(i) is documented in a written agreement setting out the rate of interest and the amount of, and due dates for, repayments; and

(ii) is fully secured by a mortgage or charge on *permitted land and property* that, if made to someone other than a body corporate, is not used wholly or mainly for domestic purposes.

permitted scheme interests

(a) in respect of a firm's business with *institutional linked policyholders* only, any of the following:
(i) a *qualified investor scheme* or its *EEA* equivalent;
(ii) any *unregulated collective investment scheme* that invests only in *permitted links* and publishes its prices regularly;
(iii) any of the interests set out in (b)(i) to (b)(iv);

(b) in respect of a firm's business with *linked policyholders* other than those described in (a), any of the following:
(i) an *authorised fund*;
(ii) a *recognised scheme*;
(iii) a scheme falling within the *UCITS Directive*;
(iv) a *non-UCITS retail scheme*;
(v) a *qualified investor scheme* or its *EEA* equivalent or any *unregulated collective investment scheme* that invests only in *permitted links* and publishes its prices regularly, provided that no more than 20% of the gross assets of the *linked fund* are so invested.

permitted stock lending

in relation to *permitted links*, a *stock lending* transaction (including a *repo* transaction) that satisfies INSPRU 3.2.36A R to INSPRU 3.2.42 G (inclusive).

permitted third party

a third party who is:

(a) an *authorised person*; or

(b) an *exempt person* for whom an *authorised person* is accepting responsibility; or

(c) a *person* lawfully carrying on a *regulated activity* in another *EEA State*.

permitted units

in relation to *permitted links*, units or beneficial interests in any real or notional fund that invests only in *permitted links* and is managed either:

(a) wholly by the *insurer*; or

(b) wholly or partly by:
(i) an agent on behalf of the *insurer*; or
(ii) a *reinsurer* in relation to a *reinsurance contract* with the *insurer*;
for whom the *insurer* retains all responsibility towards its *linked policyholders*.

permitted unlisted securities

in relation to *permitted links*, means any investment (including a *share*, *debt security*, Treasury Bill, Tax Reserve Certificate or Certificate of Tax Deposit) that is not a *listed security*, but provided always that it is realisable in the short term.

per se eligible counterparty

a *client* categorised as a per se eligible counterparty in accordance with COBS 3.6.

per se professional client

a *client* categorised as a per se professional *client* in accordance with COBS 3.5.

person

(in accordance with the Interpretation Act 1978) any person, including a body of persons corporate or unincorporate (that is, a natural person, a legal person and, for example, a *partnership*).

person discharging managerial responsibilities

(in accordance with section 96B(1) of the *Act*):

(a) a *director* of an *issuer*:
(i) registered in the *United Kingdom* that has requested or approved admission of its *shares* to trading on a *regulated market*; or
(ii) not registered in the *United Kingdom* or any other *EEA State* but has requested or approved admission of its shares to trading on a *regulated market* and for whom the *United Kingdom* is its *Home Member State*; or

(b) a senior executive of such an *issuer* who:

(i) has regular access to *inside information* relating, directly or indirectly, to the *issuer*; and

(ii) has power to make managerial decisions affecting the future development and business prospects of the *issuer*.

person exercising significant influence

(in *LR*) in relation to a *listed company*, a *person* or entity which exercises significant influence over that *listed company*.

person with whom a relevant person has a family relationship

any of the following:

(a) the spouse of the *relevant person* or any partner of that person considered by national law as equivalent to a spouse;

(b) a child or stepchild of the *relevant person*;

(c) any other relative of the *relevant person* who has shared the same household as that person for at least one year on the date of the personal transaction concerned. [Note: article 2(7) of the *MiFID implementing Directive*]

Personal Insurance Arbitration Service

the *former scheme* set up on a voluntary basis and run by the Chartered Institute of Arbitrators to handle complaints against those insurance companies which subscribed to it.

personal investment firm

(A) In the PRA Handbook:

a *firm* whose *permitted activities* include *designated investment business*, which is not an *authorised professional firm*, *bank*, *IFPRU investment firm*, *BIPRU firm*, *building society*, *collective portfolio management firm*, *credit union*, *energy market participant*, *ICVC*, *insurer*, *media firm*, *oil market participant*, *service company*, *incoming EEA firm* (without a *top-up permission*), *incoming Treaty firm* (without a *top-up permission*) or *UCITS qualifier* (without a *top-up permission*), whose *permission* does not include a *requirement* that it comply with IPRU(INV) 3 (Securities and futures firms) or 5 (Investment management firms), and which is within (a), (b) or (c):

(a) a *firm*:

(i) which was a member of PIA immediately before *commencement*; and

(ii) which was not, immediately before *commencement*, subject to the financial supervision requirements of the *FSA* (under section 43 of the Financial Services Act 1986), or *IMRO* or *SFA* (under lead regulation arrangements);

(b) a *firm* whose *permission* includes a *requirement* that it comply with IPRU(INV) 13 (Personal investment firms);

(c) a *firm*:

(i) which was given a *Part 4A permission* after *commencement*, or which was authorised under section 25 of the Financial Services Act 1986 immediately before *commencement* and not a member of *IMRO*, *PIA* or *SFA*; and

(ii) for which the most substantial part of its gross income (including commissions) from the *designated investment business* included in its *Part 4A permission* is derived from one or more of the following activities (based, for a *firm* given a *Part 4A permission* after *commencement*, on the business plan submitted as part of the *firm's* application for *permission* or, for a *firm* authorised under section 25 of the Financial Services Act 1986, on the *firm's* financial year preceding its *authorisation* under the *Act*):

(A) *advising on investments*, *arranging (bringing about) deals in investments* or *making arrangements with a view to transactions in investments*, in relation to *packaged products*;

(B) *managing investments* for *retail clients*.

(B) In the FCA Handbook:

a *firm* whose *permitted activities* include *designated investment business*, which is not an *authorised professional firm*, *bank*, *IFPRU investment firm*, *BIPRU firm*, *building society*, *collective portfolio management firm*, *credit union*, *energy market participant*, *ICVC*, *insurer*, *media firm*, *oil market participant*, *service company*, *incoming EEA firm* (without a *top-up permission*), *incoming Treaty firm* (without a *top-up permission*) or *UCITS qualifier* (without a *top-up permission*), whose *permission* does not include a *requirement* that it comply with IPRU(INV) 3 (Securities and futures firms) or 5 (Investment management firms), and which is within (a), (b) or (c):

(a) a *firm*:

(i) which was a member of PIA immediately before *commencement*; and

(ii) which was not, immediately before *commencement*, subject to the financial supervision requirements of the *FSA* (under section 43 of the Financial Services Act 1986), or *IMRO* or *SFA* (under lead regulation arrangements);

(b) a *firm* whose *permission* includes a *requirement* that it comply with IPRU(INV) 13 (Personal investment firms);

(c) a *firm*:

(i) which was given a *Part 4A permission* after *commencement*, or which was authorised under section 25 of the Financial Services Act 1986 immediately before *commencement* and not a member of *IMRO*, *PIA* or *SFA*; and

(ii) for which the most substantial part of its gross income (including commissions) from the *designated investment business* included in its *Part 4A permission* is derived from one or more of the following activities (based, for a *firm* given a *Part 4A permission* after *commencement*, on the business plan submitted as part of the *firm's* application for *permission* or, for a *firm* authorised under section 25 of the Financial Services Act 1986, on the *firm's* financial year preceding its *authorisation* under the *Act*):

(A) *advising on investments*, *arranging (bringing about) deals in investments* or *making arrangements with a view to transactions in investments*, in relation to *packaged products*;

(B) *managing investments* for *retail clients*.

personal pension contract

a *pension contract* under which contributions (single or regular) are paid to a *personal pension scheme*.

personal pension deposit

a contract under which rights to benefits are obtained by making contributions to a *personal pension scheme* operated by a *deposit-taking firm*.

personal pension policy

a *pension policy* under which contributions (single or regular) are paid to a *personal pension scheme*.

personal pension product

a contract under which rights to benefits are obtained by making contributions to a *personal pension scheme* other than a *personal pension policy*, a *personal pension contract*, a *personal pension deposit* or a *SIPP*.

personal pension scheme

a scheme or arrangement which is not an *occupational pension scheme* or *stakeholder pension scheme* and which is comprised in one or more instruments or agreements having or capable of having effect so as to provide benefits to or in respect of people:

(a) on retirement; or

(b) on having reached a particular age; or

(c) on termination of service in an employment.

personal projection

a *projection* that reflects the terms of a particular contract with, or to be offered to, a particular *client*.

personal recommendation

(except in CONRED) a recommendation that is *advice on investments*, *advice on conversion or transfer of pension benefits*, or *advice on a home finance transaction* and is presented as suitable for the person to whom it is made, or is based on a consideration of the circumstances of that person. A recommendation is not a personal recommendation if it is issued exclusively through distribution channels or to the public. [Note: article 52 of the *MiFID implementing Directive*] (in CONRED) a recommendation which is *advice on investments* and:

(a) where given on or before 31 October 2007, was given to a specific *person*; or

(b) where given on or after 1 November 2007, was presented as suitable for the *person* to whom the recommendation was made, or was based on a consideration of the circumstances of that *person*, other than a recommendation issued exclusively through distribution channels or to the public.

personal transaction

a trade in a *designated investment* effected by or on behalf of a *relevant person*, where at least one of the following criteria are met:

(1) that *relevant person* is acting outside the scope of the activities he carried out in that capacity;

(2) the trade is carried out for the account of any of the following *persons*:

(a) the *relevant person*;

(b) the spouse or civil partner of the *relevant person* or any partner of that *person* considered by national law as equivalent to a spouse;

(c) a dependent child or stepchild of the *relevant person*;

(d) any other relative of the *relevant person* who has shared the same household as that *person* for at least one year on the date of the *personal transaction* concerned;

(e) any *person* with whom he has *close links*;

(f) a *person* whose relationship with the *relevant person* is such that the *relevant person* has a direct or indirect material interest in the outcome of the trade, other than a fee or commission for the execution of the trade.

[Note: article 2(7) and article 11 of the *MiFID implementing Directive*]

physical asset reconciliation

the *safe custody assets* reconciliation described in CASS 6.6.24 R, using either the *total count method* or the *rolling stock method*.

physical commodities

a physical holding of a *commodity*, or documents evidencing title to a *commodity*.

physical safe custody asset

a *safe custody asset* (or tangible evidence of one) that is in a *firm's* physical custody and which may also be registered with the relevant issuer or agent of the issuer.

PIA

the Personal Investment Authority Limited.

PIA Ombudsman scheme

the *former scheme* set up by *PIA* under the Financial Services Act 1986 and operated by the PIA Ombudsman Bureau Ltd to handle complaints against members of *PIA*.

PIBS

permanent interest bearing shares.

PII capital requirement

(1) (in IPRU(INV) 11) an amount of *own funds* that a *collective portfolio management firm* must hold in relation to its professional indemnity insurance policy to cover any defined excess (as set out in article 15 of the *AIFMD level 2 regulation* (professional indemnity insurance) (as replicated in IPRU(INV) 11.3.15EU)) and exclusions to that policy (see IPRU(INV) 11.3.16R (Professional negligence)).

[deleted]

placing

(in *LR*) a marketing of *securities* already in issue but not *listed* or not yet in issue, to specified *persons* or clients of the *sponsor* or any securities house assisting in the placing, which does not involve an offer to the public or to existing holders of the *issuer's securities* generally.

plan investor

a *person* entered in the *plan register* under COLL 6.4.9 R (Plan registers).

plan manager

in relation to:

(a) [deleted]

(b) a *group ISA*, the *ISA manager*;

(c) a *group savings plan*, the *person* primarily responsible for that *group savings plan*.

plan register

(1) (in relation to an *ICVC*) a record of *persons* who subscribe to a *group plan* and for whom *shares* in the *ICVC* are held for the purposes of the *group plan* by the *plan manager* or a nominee (other than a record for the establishment or maintenance of which no payments are to be made out of the *scheme property*).

(2) (in relation to an *AUT* or *ACS*) a sub-*register* to the *register*, which sub-*register* records *persons* who subscribe to a *group plan* and for whom *units* in the *AUT* or *ACS* are held for the purposes of the plan by the *plan manager* or a nominee (other than any sub-*register* that has not been established

and maintained in accordance with COLL 6.4.4 R (Register: general requirements and contents) or for the establishment of which no payments are to be made out of the *scheme property*).

plastic card

a card, or a token with an equivalent function, which a *customer* can use to pay for goods and services, or to obtain cash or both, such as a credit card, charge card, debit card, cash card or electronic purse.

platform charge

any form of charge payable by or on behalf of a *retail client* to a *firm* in relation to the provision of a *platform service* and which is agreed between the *platform service provider* and the *retail client*.

platform service

a service which:

(a) involves *arranging* and *safeguarding and administering investments*; and

(b) distributes *retail investment products* which are offered to *retail clients* by more than one product provider;

but is neither:

(c) solely paid for by *adviser charges*; nor

(d) ancillary to the activity of *managing investments* for the *retail client*.

[Note: This definition applies only within the *FCA Handbook*.]

platform service provider

a *firm* providing a *platform service*.

PLC Safeguards Directive

the Second Council Directive of 13 December 1976 on coordination of safeguards for the protection of the interests of members and others in respect of the formation of public limited liability companies and the maintenance and alteration of their capital, with a view to making such safeguards equivalent (No 77/91/EEC).

pledge

a *pawnee*'s rights over an article taken in *pawn*.

plus factor

(in BIPRU 7.10 (Use of a value at risk model)) an increase to the *minimum multiplication factor* based on *backtesting exceptions* as more fully defined in BIPRU 7.10.124 R (Capital calculations: Multiplication factors).

policy

(as defined in article 2 of the Financial Services and Markets Act 2000 (Meaning of "Policy" and "Policyholder") Order 2001 (SI 2001/2361)) as the context requires:

(a) a *contract of insurance*, including one under which an existing liability has already accrued; or

(b) any instrument evidencing such a contract.

policy summary

a summary of a *non-investment insurance contract* in the format and containing the information specified in ICOBS 6 Annex 2.

policyholder

(as defined in article 3 of the Financial Services and Markets Act 2000 (Meaning of "Policy" and "Policyholder") Order 2001 (SI 2001/2361)) the *person* who for the time being is the legal holder of the *policy*, including any *person* to whom, under the *policy*, a sum is due, a periodic payment is payable or any other benefit is to be provided or to whom such a sum, payment or benefit is contingently due, payable or to be provided.

policyholder advocate

the *person* appointed under COBS 20.2.42 R to negotiate with a *firm* on its proposals for making a *reattribution* of its *inherited estate*.

pool

either a *sub-pool* or a *general pool*, as the context requires.

port

(A) In the PRA Handbook: means, in respect of the assets and positions recorded in a *client transaction account* that is an *individual client account* or an *omnibus client account* at an *authorised central counterparty*, action taken by that *authorised central counterparty* to transfer those assets and positions in accordance with article 48 of *EMIR* to another clearing member designated by the individual *client* (in the case of an *individual client account*) or designated by all of the *clients* for whom the account is held (in the case of an *omnibus client account*).

(B) In FCA Handbook: in respect of the assets and positions recorded in a *client transaction account* that is an *individual client account* or an *omnibus client account* at an *authorised central counterparty*, action taken by that *authorised central counterparty* to transfer those assets and positions in accordance with article 48 of *EMIR* to another clearing member designated by the individual *client* (in the case of an *individual client account*) or designated by all of the *clients* for whom the account is held (in the case of an *omnibus client account*).

portfolio management

managing portfolios in accordance with mandates given by *clients* on a discretionary *client*-by-*client* basis where such portfolios include one or more *financial instruments*. [Note: article 4(1)(9) of *MiFID*]

portfolio trade

a transaction in more than one security where those securities are grouped and traded as a single lot against a specific reference price. [Note: article 2(6) of the *MiFID Regulation*]

position

(A) In the PRA Handbook:
(in accordance BIPRU 1.2.4 R (Definition of the trading book: Positions)) includes proprietary positions and positions arising from client servicing and market making.
(B) In the FCA Handbook:
(1) (in accordance BIPRU 1.2.4 R (Definition of the trading book: Positions)) includes proprietary positions and positions arising from client servicing and market making.
(2) (in *IFPRU*) has the meaning which it has, or is used, in the *EU CRR*.

position risk adjustment

a percentage applied to a *position* as part of the process of calculating the *PRR* in relation to that *position* as set out in the tables in BIPRU 7.2.44 R (Specific risk position risk adjustments), BIPRU 7.2.57 R (General market risk position risk adjustments), BIPRU 7.3.30 R (Simplified equity method position risk adjustments), BIPRU 7.3.34 R (Position risk adjustments for specific risk under the standard equity method) and BIPRU 7.6.8 R (The appropriate position risk adjustment) and also as set out in BIPRU 7.2.48A R to BIPRU 7.2.48L R.

position risk requirement

a capital requirement applied to a position treated under BIPRU 7 (Market risk) as part of the calculation of the *market risk capital requirement* or, if the relevant provision of the *Handbook* distinguishes between *general market risk* and *specific risk*, the portion of that capital requirement with respect to whichever of *general market risk* or *specific risk* is specified by that provision.

POS Regulations

the Public Offers of Securities Regulations 1995 (SI 1995/1537).

post

(in relation to sending a *document* by post) sending pre-paid by a postal service which seeks to deliver *documents* by post within the *United Kingdom* no later than the next working day in all or the majority of cases, and to deliver by post outside the *United Kingdom* within such a period as is reasonable in all the circumstances.

Post-BCCI Directive

the European Parliament and Council Directive of 29 June 1995 amending certain directives with a view to reinforcing prudential supervision (No 95/26/EC).

potential tier one instrument

an item of capital that falls into GENPRU 2.2.62R (Tier one capital: General).

power of intervention

the power conferred on the *FCA* or the *PRA* under section 196 of the *Act* (The Power of Intervention) to impose a requirement on an *incoming firm*.

PPFM

Principles and Practices of Financial Management.

PPFM guidance table

the table in COBS 20.3.8 G (Guidance on with-profits principles and practices).

PPFM issues table

The table in COBS 20.3.6 R (Issues to be covered in PPFM).

PR

the Prospectus Rules sourcebook.

PRA

Prudential Regulation Authority.

PRA-approved person

an *approved person* in relation to whom the *PRA* has given its approval under section 59 of the *Act* (Approval for particular arrangements) for the performance of a *PRA controlled function*.

PRA chief executive function

(in the *FCA Handbook*) *PRA controlled function* CF3 in the *table of PRA controlled functions*.

PRA controlled function

a *controlled function* which is specified by the *PRA* under section 59 of the *Act* (Approval for particular arrangements) in the *table of PRA controlled functions*.

PRA director function

(in the *FCA Handbook*) *PRA controlled function* CF1 in the *table of PRA controlled functions*.

PRA governing function

any of the *PRA controlled functions* CF1 to CF6 in the *table of PRA controlled functions*.

PRA Handbook

the *PRA's* Handbook of rules and guidance.

PRA-authorised person

as defined in section 2B(5) of the *Act*, an *authorised person* who has permission:

(a) given under Part 4A of the *Act*; or

(b) resulting from any other provision of the *Act*;

to carry on *regulated activities* that consist of or include one or more *PRA-regulated activities*.

PRA-regulated Activities Order

(A) (In the PRA Handbook): the Financial Services and Market Act 2000 (PRA-regulated Activities) Order 2013 (SI 2013/556).

(B) (In the FCA Handbook): the Financial Services and Market Act 2000 (PRA-regulated Activities) Order 2013 (SI 2013/556).

PRA-regulated activity

a *regulated activity* specified in an order made under section 22A of the *Act* or specified pursuant to a power granted in such an order.

PRA required functions

any of the *PRA controlled functions* CF12 to CF12B in the *table of PRA controlled functions*.

PRA's SCV requirements

(in *COMP*) the *PRA's* requirements with respect to *single customer view*.

pre-existing arrangements

in relation to a *borrower-lender agreement* or a *borrower-lender-supplier agreement*, a *credit agreement* is entered into under pre-existing arrangements between a *lender* and a *supplier* if it is entered into in accordance with, or in connection with, arrangements previously made between the *lender* (or the *lender's associate*) and the *supplier* (or the *supplier's associate*) unless the arrangements are:

(a) for the making, in circumstances specified in the *credit agreement*, of payments to the *supplier* by the *lender* ("L") and L indicates that L is willing to make, in such circumstances, payments of the kind to *suppliers* generally, or

(b) for the electronic transfer of funds from a current account held with an *authorised person* with *permission* to *accept deposits*,

but if a *lender* is an *associate* of the *supplier's*, the *credit agreement* is to be treated as entered into under pre-existing arrangements between the *lender* and the *supplier* unless the *lender* can show that this is not the case.

precious metals

(in *COLL*) gold, silver or platinum.

predecessor scheme

any of the following:

(a) The Office of the Banking Ombudsman;

(b) The Office of the Building Societies Ombudsman;

(c) The Insurance Ombudsman Bureau;

(d) The Office of the Investment Ombudsman;

(e) The Personal Investment Authority Ombudsman Bureau;

(f) The Personal Insurance Arbitration Service;

(g) The Securities and Futures Authority Complaints Bureau and Arbitration Service;

(h) The FSA Complaints Unit and Independent Investigator.

preference share

a *share* conferring preference as to income or return of capital which does not form part of the *equity share capital* of a *company*.

preliminary charge

a *charge* upon a *sale* of *units* by an *authorised fund manager* whether or not acting as *principal*.

premium

(1) (except in *ICOBS* and CASS 5) (in relation to a *general insurance contract*) the consideration payable under the contract by the *policyholder* to the *insurer*.

(2) (except in *ICOBS* and CASS 5) (in relation to a *long-term insurance contract*) the consideration payable under the contract by the *policyholder* to the *insurer*; (except in SUP 16.8 (Persistency reports from insurers)) a premium is a regular premium if it is one of a series of payments under the contract:

(a)

(i) which are payable on dates that are certain or ascertainable at the time the contract is made;

(ii) which are payable over a period that exceeds one year in length; and

(iii) assuming the *policy* evidencing the contract is not surrendered or otherwise terminated before the *premiums* fall due, will fall due on those dates without either party to the contract exercising any option under the contract; or

(b) of which the first payment is an obligation under the contract, and subsequent payments, calculated according to an agreed formula, are payable over a period which exceeds one year in length under a collateral written arrangement with the *insurer* or *friendly society*.

(2A) (in *ICOBS* and CASS 5) as in (1) and (2) except that '*insurance undertaking*' is substituted for '*insurer*' (except where '*insurer*' is used in the heading to SUP 16.8).

(3) (in relation to an *option*) the total amount which the purchaser of the *option* is, or may be, required to pay in consideration for the right to exercise the *option*.

premiums amount

(for the purposes of INSPRU 1.1), an amount, as defined in INSPRU 1.1.45R, used in the calculation of the *general insurance capital requirement*.

premium listing

(a) in relation to *equity shares* (other than those of a *closed-ended investment fund* or of an *open-ended investment company*), means a *listing* where the *issuer* is required to comply with those requirements in LR 6 (Additional requirements for premium listing (commercial company)) and the other requirements in the *listing rules* that are expressed to apply to such *securities* with a *premium listing*;

(b) in relation to *equity shares* of a *closed-ended investment fund*, means a *listing* where the *issuer* is required to comply with those requirements in LR 15 (Closed-Ended Investment Funds: Premium listing) and other requirements in the *listing rules* that are expressed to apply to such *securities* with a *premium listing*;

(c) in relation to *equity shares* of an *open-ended investment company*, means a *listing* where the *issuer* is required to comply with LR 16 (Open-ended investment companies: Premium listing) and other requirements in the *listing rules* that are expressed to apply to such *securities* with a *premium listing*.

premium listing (commercial company)

a *premium listing* of *equity shares* (other than those of a *closed-ended investment fund* or of an *open-ended investment company*).

premium listing (investment company)

a *premium listing* of *equity shares* of a *closed-ended investment fund* or of an *open-ended investment company*.

prescribed asset share methodology

the methodology described in COBS 20.2.5 R for assessing maturity payments by reference to unsmoothed asset shares.

prescribed auction platform

an auction platform which has been prescribed by the Treasury in the *Prescribed Markets and Qualifying Investments Order*.

prescribed market

a market which has been prescribed by the Treasury in the *Prescribed Markets and Qualifying Investments Order*

Prescribed Markets and Qualifying Investments Order

the Financial Services and Markets Act 2000 (Prescribed Markets and Qualifying Investments) Order 2001 (SI 2001/996).

prescribed pricing basis

(in relation to a *derivative* contract, or *quasi-derivative contract*), the pricing basis set out in IPRU(INS) 4.12R(8) (Derivative contracts) as that rule was in force on 30 December 2004.

previous regulator

(1) (in relation to a *firm* which was authorised under the Banking Act 1987 immediately before *commencement* or which was a European institution (as defined in the Banking Coordination (Second Council Directive) Regulations 1992) immediately before *commencement*) the *FSA*.

(2) (in relation to a *firm* which was a *building society* immediately before *commencement*) the *Building Societies* Commission.

(3) (in relation to a *firm* which was a *friendly society* immediately before *commencement*) the *Friendly Societies* Commission.

(4) (in relation to a *firm* authorised under the Insurance Companies Act 1982 immediately before *commencement*) the Treasury.

(5) (in relation to an *underwriting agent* which obtained the *permission* relevant to that category under the Financial Services and Markets Act 2000 (Repeals, Transitional Provisions and Savings) Order 2001 (SI 2001/2636)) the *Society* of Lloyd's.

(6) (in relation to a *firm* which was authorised, or which was an *appointed representative*, under the Financial Services Act 1986 immediately before *commencement* or which was a European investment firm (as defined in the Investment Services Regulations 1995 (SI 1995/3275)) immediately before *commencement*) any of:
(a) *IMRO*;
(b) PIA;

(c) *SFA*;

(d) a *recognised professional body*; and

(e) the *FSA*;

if the *firm* (or, if relevant, its principal for the purposes of section 44 of the Financial Services Act 1986) was subject in carrying on business to the rules, requirements, regulations or guidance of that body.

(7) (in relation to an *ex-section 43 firm*) the *FSA*.

(8) (in relation to a *firm* which was authorised under the *Act* immediately before 1 April 2013) the *FSA*.

price

(in *COLL*) (in relation to a *unit* in an *authorised fund*) the price of the *unit* calculated in accordance with COLL 6.3 (Valuation and pricing).

price information

(in *MCOB*) information, in a *financial promotion*, that relates to:

(a) any rate of charge; or

(b) the presence or absence of any payments, fees or charges (other than the fees for advising on or *arranging* a *regulated mortgage contract* as required by MCOB 3.6.27 R); or

(c) the amount, frequency or number of any payments, repayments, fees or charges; or

(d) any monetary amounts.

price stabilising rules

the *rules* made under section 137Q of the *Act*, and appearing in MAR 2.1 to MAR 2.4, together with any other provisions available for their interpretation.

primary information provider

a *person* approved by the *FCA* under section 89P of the *Act*.

primary pooling event

(1) [deleted]

(2) (in CASS 5) an event that occurs in the circumstances described in CASS 5.6.5 R (Failure of the authorised firm: primary pooling event).

(3) (in CASS 7 and CASS 7A) an event that occurs in the circumstances described in CASS 7A.2.2 R (Failure of the authorised firm: primary pooling event).

(4) (in CASS 11) an event that occurs in the circumstances described in CASS 11.13.3 R.

prime brokerage agreement

an agreement between a *prime brokerage firm* and a *client* for *prime brokerage services*.

prime brokerage firm

a *firm* that provides *prime brokerage services* to a *client* and which may do so acting as *principal*.

(1) (except in *FUND*) a *firm* that provides *prime brokerage services* to a *client* and which may do so acting as *principal*.

(2) (in *FUND*) a *credit institution*, regulated *investment firm* or another entity subject to prudential regulation and ongoing supervision, offering services to *professional clients* primarily to finance or execute transactions in *financial instruments* as counterparty and which may also provide other services, such as clearing and settlement of trades, custodial services, *stock lending*, customised technology and operational support facilities.

[Note: article 4(1)(af) of *AIFMD*]

prime brokerage services

a package of services provided under a *prime brokerage agreement* which gives a *prime brokerage firm* a right to use *safe custody assets* for its own account and which comprises each of the following:

(a) *custody* or *arranging safeguarding and administration of assets*;

(b) clearing services; and

(c) financing, the provision of which includes one or more of the following:
(i) capital introduction;

(ii) margin financing;
(iii) *stock lending*;
(iv) stock borrowing;
(v) entering into repurchase or reverse repurchase transactions;

and which, in addition, may comprise consolidated reporting and other operational support.

PRIN

(A) In the PRA Handbook: In relation to any *rules* in *PRIN*, the equivalent provision (if any) in the *Fundamental Rules* Part of the *PRA* Rulebook.

(B) In the FCA Handbook: the part of the *Handbook* in High Level Standards that has the title Principles for Businesses.

principal

(A) In the PRA Handbook:

(1) in relation to a *person*:
(a) a *person* acting on his own account;
(b) (if the *person* is an *appointed representative* or, where applicable, a *tied agent*) the *authorised person* who is party to a contract with the *appointed representative*, or who is responsible for the acts of the *tied agent*, resulting in him being exempt, or in him carrying on a *regulated activity* to which sections 20(1) and (1A) and 23(1A) of the *Act* do not apply, under section 39 of the *Act* (Exemption of appointed representatives).

(2) in relation to an *option*, *future* or forward contract:
(a) (except in the case of an *option* on a *future*) the amount of property or the value of the property which must be delivered in order to satisfy settlement of the *option*, *future* or forward contract;
(b) (in relation to an *option* on a *future*) the amount of property or the value of the property which must be delivered in order to satisfy settlement of the *future*.

(B) In the FCA Handbook:

(1) in relation to a *person*:
(a) a *person* acting on his own account;
(b) (if the *person* is an *appointed representative* or, where applicable, a *tied agent*) the *authorised person* who is party to a contract with the *appointed representative*, or who is responsible for the acts of the *tied agent*, resulting in him being exempt, or in him carrying on a *regulated activity* to which sections 20(1) and (1A) and 23(1A) of the *Act* do not apply, under section 39 of the *Act* (Exemption of appointed representatives).

(2) in relation to an *option*, *future* or forward contract:
(a) (except in the case of an *option* on a *future*) the amount of property or the value of the property which must be delivered in order to satisfy settlement of the *option*, *future* or forward contract;
(b) (in relation to an *option* on a *future*) the amount of property or the value of the property which must be delivered in order to satisfy settlement of the *future*.

Principle

(A) In the PRA Handbook: one of the Principles set out in PRIN 2.1.1 R (Principles for Businesses) or:

(a) in relation to *Principle* 1, *Fundamental Rule* 1;

(b) in relation to *Principle* 2, *Fundamental Rule* 2;

(c) in relation to *Principle* 3, *Fundamental Rule* 5 or *Fundamental Rule* 6 as appropriate;

(d) in relation to *Principle* 4, *Fundamental Rule* 4; and

(e) in relation to *Principle* 11, *Fundamental Rule* 7.

(B) In the FCA Handbook: one of the Principles set out in PRIN 2.1.1 R (Principles for Businesses).

Principles and Practices of Financial Management

the Principles and Practices of Financial Management, containing *with-profits principles* and *with-profits practices*, which a *firm* carrying on *with-profits business* must establish, maintain and record under COBS 20.3(Principles and Practices of Financial Management).

priority debt

(in *BCOBS*) an obligation on the part of a *consumer* to make a payment:

(a) where the remedies for a breach of that obligation potentially include seeking possession of, or seeking to exercise a power of sale in respect of:
(i) the sole or main residence of the *consumer* (for example, an obligation to pay secured by a

mortgage or charge in respect of land, an obligation to pay rent under a tenancy, or an obligation to make payment under a licence to occupy land); or

(ii) the *consumer's* essential goods or services (for example, an obligation to pay under a hire purchase, conditional sale or hire agreement that relates to, or an obligation to pay secured by a charge on, the *consumer's* cooker, refrigerator, or the means to travel to work); or

(b) where that obligation arises out of an order of the court, an Act or secondary legislation (for example, an obligation to pay council tax, child support maintenance, income tax or court fines); or

(c) where that obligation arises under a contract for the provision of utility supplies (for example, water, gas or electricity).

private customer

(for the purposes only of COBS TP 1 (Transitional Provisions in relation to Client Categorisation)):

(1) (except in COB 3, COB 4.2 and COB 6.4) subject to (h), a *client* who is not a market counterparty or an *intermediate customer*, including:
(a) an individual who is not a *firm*;
(b) an overseas individual who is not an *overseas financial services institution*;
(c) [deleted]
(d) (except for the purposes of *DISP*) a *client* when he is classified as a *private customer* in accordance with COB 4.1.14 R (Client classified as a private customer);
(e) a *person* to whom a *firm* gives *basic advice*;
(f) (in COB 6.1 to 6.5) where the *regulated activity* (except for a personal recommendation relating to a contribution to a *CTF*) relates to a *CTF* and there is no *registered contact*, the *person* to whom the statement must be sent in accordance with Regulation 10 of the *CTF* Regulations;
(g) (in COB 6.7) where the *regulated activity* (except for a personal recommendation relating to a contribution to a *CTF*) relates to a *CTF* and there is no *registered contact*, the child, via the person to whom the statement must be sent in accordance with Regulation 10 of the *CTF* Regulations;
(h) a *client* who would otherwise be excluded as a market counterparty or *intermediate customer* if the *client* is within (e), (f) or (g);
but excluding a *client*, who would otherwise be a *private customer*:
(i) when he is classified as an *intermediate customer* in accordance with COB 4.1.9 R (Expert private customer classified as an intermediate customer); or
(ii) when the *regulated activity* relates to a *CTF*, any *person* other than (e), (f), (g) or (h).

(2) (in COB 3) a *person* in (1) or a *person* excluded under (1)(h)(ii) or a *person* who would be such a *person* if he were a *client*. (in COB 4.2 and 6.1 to 6.5) a *person* in (1) and, in relation to the conclusion of a *distance contract*, a *consumer*.

(3) (in COB 4.2 and 6.1 to 6.5) a person in (1) and, in relation to the conclusion of a *distance contract*, a *consumer*.

private person

(as defined in article 3 of the Financial Services and Markets Act 2000 (Rights of Action) Regulations 2000 (SI 2001/2256)):

(a) any individual, unless he suffers the loss in question in the course of carrying on:
(i) any *regulated activity*; or
(ii) any activity which would be a *regulated activity* apart from any exclusion made by article 72 of the *Regulated Activities* Order (Overseas persons);

(b) any *person* who is not an individual, unless he suffers the loss in question in the course of carrying on business of any kind;

(c) a relevant recipient of *credit* (within the meaning of article 60L of the *Regulated Activities Order*) who is not an individual and who has suffered the loss in question in connection with an activity of the kind specified by article 36A, 39D, 39E, 39F, 39G, 60B, 60N, 89A or 89B of that Order or article 64 of that Order, so far as relevant to any of those activities; and

(d) a person who is, by virtue of article 36J of the *Regulated Activities Order*, to be regarded as a person who uses, may use, has or may have used or has or may have contemplated using, services provided by *authorised persons* in carrying on a *regulated activity* of the kind specified by article 36H of that Order or article 64 of that Order so far as relevant to that activity;

but not including a government, a local authority (in the *United Kingdom* or elsewhere) or an international organisation; for the purposes of (a), an individual who suffers loss in the course of *effecting or carrying out contracts of insurance* written at Lloyd's is not to be taken to suffer loss in the course of carrying on a *regulated activity*; in this definition:

(A) "government" means:
(I) the government of the *United Kingdom*; or
(II) the Scottish Administration; or
(III) the Executive Committee of the Northern Ireland Assembly; or

(IV) the National Assembly for Wales; or
(V) the government of any country or territory outside the *United Kingdom*;

(B) "international organisation" means any international organisation the members of which include the *United Kingdom* or any other State;

(C) "local authority", in relation to the *United Kingdom*, means:
(I) in England and Wales, a local authority as defined in the Local Government Act 1972, the Greater London Authority, the Common Council of the City of London or the Council of the Isles of Scilly;
(II) in Scotland, a local authority as defined in the Local Government (Scotland) Act 1973; and
(III) in Northern Ireland, a district council as defined in the Local Government Act (Northern Ireland) 1972.

probability of default

(in accordance with Article 4(25) of the *Banking Consolidation Directive* (Definitions) and for the purpose of *BIPRU*) the probability of default of a counterparty over a one year period; for the purposes of the *IRB approach*, default has the meaning in the definition of *default*.

probable reserves

(in *LR*):

(a) in respect of *mineral companies* primarily involved in the *extraction* of oil and gas resources, those reserves which are not yet *proven* but which, on the available evidence and taking into account technical and economic factors, have a better than 50% chance of being produced; and

(b) in respect of *mineral companies* other than those primarily involved in the *extraction* of oil and gas resources, those measured and/or indicated mineral resources, which are not yet *proven* but of which detailed technical and economic studies have demonstrated that *extraction* can be justified at the time of the determination and under specified economic conditions.

procuration fee

the total amount paid by a *home finance provider* to a *home finance intermediary*, whether directly or indirectly, in connection with providing applications from *customers* to enter into *home finance transactions* with that *home finance provider*.

product provider

a *firm* which is:
(i) a *long-term insurer*;
(ii) a *friendly society*;
(iii) the *operator* of a *regulated collective investment scheme* or an *investment trust savings scheme*; or
(iv) the *operator* of a *personal pension scheme* or *stakeholder pension scheme*.

PROF

the Professional Firms sourcebook.

professional ACS investor

in relation to an *ACS*, a *person* who falls within one of the categories (1) to (4) of Section I of Annex II (professional clients for the purpose of that directive) to *MiFID*.

professional client

a *client* that is either a *per se professional client* or an *elective professional client* (see COBS 3.5.1 R). [Note: article 4(1)(12) of *MiFID*].

professional customer

a *customer* who works or has recently worked in the home finance sector for at least one year in a professional position, which requires knowledge of the *home finance transactions* or home finance services envisaged, and who the *firm* reasonably believes to be capable of understanding the risks involved in the transaction or transactions contemplated.

professional firm

a *person* which is:

(a) an individual who is entitled to practise a profession regulated by a *designated professional body* and, in practising it, is subject to its rules, whether or not he is a member of that body; or

(b) a *person* (not being an individual) which is controlled or managed by one or more such individuals.

professional negligence capital requirement

(1) (in IPRU(INV) 11) an amount of *own funds* that a *collective portfolio management firm* must hold professional liability risks as set out in article 14 of the *AIFMD level 2 regulation* (additional own funds) (as replicated in IPRU(INV) 11.3.14EU) (Professional negligence).

[deleted]

profit and loss figure

(in BIPRU 7.10 (Use of a value at risk model) and in relation to a *business day*) a *firm's* actual profit or loss for that day in respect of the trading activities within the scope of the *firm's VaR model permission*, adjusted by stripping out specified items, as more fully defined in BIPRU 7.10.100 R (Backtesting: Calculating the profit and loss).

profit estimate

(in *PR* and *LR*) (as defined in the *PD Regulation*) a profit forecast for a financial period which has expired and for which results have not yet been published.

programme

(in *RCB*) (as defined in Regulation 1(2) of the *RCB Regulations*) issues, or series of issues, of *covered bonds* which have substantially similar terms and are subject to a framework contract or contracts.

profit forecast

(in *PR* and *LR*) (as defined in the *PD Regulation*) a form of words which expressly states or by implication indicates a figure or a minimum or maximum figure for the likely level of profits or losses for the current financial period and/or financial periods subsequent to that period, or contains data from which a calculation of such a figure for future profits or losses may be made, even if no particular figure is mentioned and the word "profit" is not used.

prohibited period

(in *LR*) as defined by paragraph 1(e) of the *Model Code*.

prohibition order

an order made under section 56 of the *Act* (Prohibition orders) which prohibits an individual from performing a specified function, any function falling within a specified description or any function.

projection

a projection of the amount of any future benefit payable under a contract or *policy*, being a benefit the amount of which is not ascertainable under the terms of the contract or *policy* when the calculation is made.

projection date

the date to which the *projection* is made.

projection period

(in *COBS*) the period covered by a *standardised deterministic projection*, which begins on the date the investment is reasonably expected to be made and ends on the *projection date* described in paragraph 2.1 of COBS 13 Annex 2.

Promotion of Collective Investment Schemes Order

the Financial Services and Markets Act 2000 (Promotion of Collective Investment Schemes) (Exemptions) Order 2001.

property

(in *LR*) freehold, heritable or leasehold property.

property authorised investment fund

an *open-ended investment company* to which Part 4A of the Authorised Investment Funds (Tax) Regulations 2006 (SI 2006/964) applies.

property collective investment undertaking

(in *PR*) (as defined in the *PD Regulation*) a collective investment undertaking whose investment objective is the participation in the holding of property in the long term.

property company

(in *LR*) a *company* primarily engaged in *property* activities including:

(a) the holding of *properties* (directly or indirectly) for letting and retention as investments;

(b) the development of *properties* for letting and retention as investments;

(c) the purchase and development of *properties* for subsequent sale;

(d) the purchase of land for development *properties* for retention as investments.

property enterprise trust

an *unregulated collective investment scheme* of which the underlying assets are land and buildings.

property fund

(a) a *regulated collective investment scheme* dedicated to land and interests in land;

(b) a fund of funds of which one or more of the funds to which it is dedicated falls within (a);

(c) a constituent part of an umbrella fund which, if it were a separate fund, would fall within (a).

property-linked assets

in relation to an *insurer*, *long-term insurance assets* that are, for the time being, identified in the records of the *insurer* as being assets by reference to the value of which *property-linked benefits* are to be determined.

property-linked benefits

benefits other than *index-linked benefits* provided for under a *linked long-term contract of insurance*.

property valuation report

(in *LR*) a *property* valuation report prepared by an independent expert in accordance with:

(1) for an *issuer* incorporated in the *United Kingdom*, the Channel Islands or the Isle of Man, the Appraisal and Valuation Standards (5th edition) issued by the Royal Institution of Chartered Surveyors; or

(2) for an *issuer* incorporated in any other place, either the standards referred to in paragraph (1) or the International Valuation Standards (7th edition) issued by the International Valuation Standards Committee.

property-linked liabilities

insurance liabilities in respect of *property-linked benefits*.

proportional reinsurance treaty

a reinsurance treaty under which a pre-determined proportion of each *claim* payment by the cedant under *policies* subject to the treaty is recoverable from the *reinsurer*; *non-proportional reinsurance treaty* is construed accordingly.

proprietary trader

(in SUP 10 (Approved Persons) and *APER*) a *person* (A) whose responsibilities include committing another *person* (B) as part of B's *proprietary trading*.

proprietary trading

(in SUP 10A (Approved Persons) and *APER*) *dealing in investments as principal* as part of a business of trading in *specified investments*. For these purposes *dealing in investments as principal* includes any activities that would be included but for the exclusion in Article 15 (Absence of holding out), Article 16 (Dealing in contractually based investments) or, for a *UK AIFM* or *UK UCITS management company*, article 72AA (Managers of UCITS and AIFs) of the *Regulated Activities Order*.

prospectus

(1) (in *LR* and *PR*, *FEES* and FUND 3 (Requirements for managers of alternative investment funds)) a *prospectus* required under the *prospectus directive*.

(2) (except in *LR* and *PR*) (in relation to a *collective investment scheme*) a document containing information about the *scheme* and complying with the *requirements* in COLL 4.2.5 R (Table: contents of the prospectus), COLL 8.3.4 R (Table: contents of qualified investor scheme prospectus) or COLL 9.3.2 R (Additional information required in the prospectus for an application under section 272) applicable to a *prospectus* of a *scheme* of the type concerned.

Prospectus Directive

the Directive of the European Parliament and of the Council of 4 November 2003 on the prospectus to be published when securities are offered to the public or admitted to trading (No 2003/71/EC).

Prospectus RTS Regulation

the Commission Delegated Regulation (EU) No 382/2014 supplementing Directive 2003/71/EC of the European Parliament and of the Council with regard to regulatory technical standards for publication of supplements to the prospectus.

Prospectus Rules

(as defined in section 73A(4) of the *Act*) *rules* expressed to relate to *transferable securities*.

protected claim

a *claim* which is covered by the *compensation scheme*, as defined in COMP 5.2.1 R.

protected contract of insurance

a *contract of insurance* which is covered by the *compensation scheme*, as defined in COMP 5.4.1 R.

protected deposit

a *deposit* which is covered by the *compensation scheme*, as defined in COMP 5.3.1 R.

protected dormant account

a *dormant account* which is covered by the *compensation scheme*, as defined in COMP 5.3.2R.

protected home finance mediation

activities in relation to *home finance transactions* which are covered by the *compensation scheme*, as defined in COMP 5.6.1 R.

protected investment business

designated investment business which is covered by the *compensation scheme*, as defined in COMP 5.5.1 R.

protected items

(as defined in section 413 of the *Act* (Protected items)) communications (and items which they enclose or refer to and which are in the possession of a *person* entitled to possession of them) between:

(a) a professional legal adviser and his client or any *person* representing his client; or

(b) a professional legal adviser, his client or any *person* representing his client and any other *person*;

where the communication or the item is made:

(i) in connection with the giving of legal advice to the client; or

(ii) in connection with, or in contemplation of, legal proceedings and for the purposes of those proceedings; and

is not held with the intention of furthering a criminal purpose.

protected non-investment insurance mediation

insurance mediation activities which are covered by the *compensation scheme*, as defined in COMP 5.7.1 R.

protection buyer

(in *BIPRU*) (in relation to a credit derivative and in accordance with paragraph 8 of Annex I of the *Capital Adequacy Directive* (Calculating capital requirements for position risk)) the *person* who transfers credit risk.

protection seller

(in *BIPRU*) (in relation to a credit derivative and in accordance with paragraph 8 of Annex I of the *Capital Adequacy Directive* (Calculating capital requirements for position risk)) the *person* who assumes the credit risk.

proven reserves

(in *LR*):

(a) in respect of *mineral companies* primarily involved in the *extraction* of oil and gas resources, those reserves which, on the available evidence and taking into account technical and economic factors, have a better than 90% chance of being produced; and

(b) in respect of *mineral companies* other than those primarily involved in the *extraction* of oil and gas resources, those measured mineral resources of which detailed technical and economic studies have demonstrated that *extraction* can be justified at the time of the determination, and under specified economic conditions.

provider of credit information services

a person *providing credit information services* who has, or ought to have, a *Part 4A permission* to carry on the *regulated activity* of *providing credit information services*.

provider of credit references

a *person providing credit references* who has, or ought to have, a *Part 4A permission* to carry on the *regulated activity* of *providing credit references*.

providing credit information services

a *regulated activity* of the kind specified in article 89A of the *Regulated Activities Order*.

providing credit references

the *regulated activity* specified in article 89B of the *Regulated Activities Order*.

providing information in relation to a specified benchmark

The *regulated activity*, specified in article 63O(1)(a) of the *Regulated Activities Order*, which in summary means making *benchmark submissions*.

providing qualifying credit

the *controlled activity*, specified in paragraph 10 of Schedule 1 to the *Financial Promotion Order*, of providing *qualifying credit*.

proxy capital resources requirement

the *minimum capital requirement* to which an *undertaking* would have been subject if it had *permission* for each activity it carries on anywhere in the world, so far as that activity is a *regulated activity*.

PRR

position risk requirement.

PRR charge

one of the following:

(a) the *interest rate PRR*;

(b) the *equity PRR*;

(c) the *commodity PRR*;

(d) the *foreign currency PRR*;

(e) the *option PRR*;

(f) the *collective investment undertaking PRR*; and

(g) (if the context requires) the *model PRR*.

PRR identical product netting rules

the following:

(a) BIPRU 7.2.37 R (Deriving the net position in each debt security: Netting positions in the same debt security);

(b) BIPRU 7.2.40 R (Deriving the net position in each debt security: Netting zero-specific-risk securities with different maturities);

(c) BIPRU 7.3.23 R (Deriving the net position in each equity);

(d) BIPRU 7.4.20 R and BIPRU 7.4.22 R (Calculating the PRR for each commodity: General);

(e) BIPRU 7.5.19 R (1) (Open currency position); and

(f) the obligation under BIPRU 7.5.20 R (Net gold position) to calculate a separate *foreign exchange PRR* charge for gold).

PRR item

(in *BIPRU*) a *commodity* or a *CRD financial instrument*.

PRU

the Integrated Prudential Sourcebook

prudent segregation

a *firm's* segregation of an amount of *money* as *client money* under CASS 7.13.41 R

prudent segregation record

the records created and maintained by a *firm* under CASS 7.13.50 R to CASS 7.13.53 R.

prudential context

(A) In the PRA Handbook:

(1) For the *FCA*, in relation to activities carried on by a *firm*, the context in which the activities have, or might reasonably be regarded as likely to have, a negative effect on:

(a) the integrity of the *UK financial system*; or

(b) the ability of the *firm* to meet either:

(i) the "fit and proper" test in *threshold condition* 2E and 3D (Suitability); or

(ii) the applicable requirements and standards under the *regulatory system* relating to the *firm's* financial resources.

(2) For the *PRA*, in relation to activities carried on by a firm, the context in which the activities have, or might reasonably be regarded as likely to have, a negative effect on:

(a) the safety and soundness of *PRA-authorised persons*; or

(b) the ability of the *firm* to meet either:

(i) the "fit and proper" test in *threshold condition* 4E and 5E (Suitability); or

(ii) the applicable requirements and standards under the *regulatory system* relating to the *firm's* financial resources.

(B) In the FCA Handbook:

(1) For the *FCA*, in relation to activities carried on by a *firm*, the context in which the activities have, or might reasonably be regarded as likely to have, a negative effect on:

(a) the integrity of the *UK financial system*; or

(b) the ability of the *firm* to meet either:

(i) the "fit and proper" test in *threshold condition* 2E and 3D (Suitability); or

(ii) the applicable requirements and standards under the *regulatory system* relating to the *firm's* financial resources.

(2) For the *PRA*, in relation to activities carried on by a firm, the context in which the activities have, or might reasonably be regarded as likely to have, a negative effect on:

(a) the safety and soundness of *PRA-authorised persons*; or

(b) the ability of the *firm* to meet either:

(i) the "fit and proper" test in *threshold condition* 5 (Suitability); or

(ii) the applicable requirements and standards under the *regulatory system* relating to the *firm's* financial resources.

PSE

a *public sector entity*.

PSR

Payment Systems Regulator, the *body corporate* established by the *FCA* under section 40(1) of *FSBRA*.

PSR fee

the fee payable to the *FCA* by an *operator* of a *regulated payment system* under FEES 9.2.1 R.

public announcement

any communication made by or on behalf of the *issuer* or the *stabilising manager* being a communication made in circumstances in which it is likely that members of the public will become aware of the communication.

public censure

(1) a statement published under section 205 (Public censure) of the *Act*;

(2) a statement of misconduct published under section 66 (Disciplinary powers) of the *Act*;

(3) a statement published under section 123 (Power to impose penalties in cases of market abuse) of the *Act*;

(4) a statement published under section 87M (Public censure of issuer) of the *Act*, under section 88A (Disciplinary powers: contravention of s 88(3)(c) or (e)) of the *Act* or under section 91 (Penalties for breach of Part 6 rules) of the *Act*.

public international body

(1) (in *PR*) (as defined in the *PD Regulation*) a legal entity of public nature established by an international treaty between sovereign States and of which one or more Member States are members.

(2) (in *LR* and *DTR*) the African Development Bank, the Asian Development Bank, the Caribbean Development Bank, the Council of Europe Development Bank, the European Atomic Energy Community, the European Bank for Reconstruction and Development, the European Company for the Financing of Railroad Stock, the *EU*, the European Investment Bank, the Inter-American Development Bank, the International Bank for Reconstruction and Development, the International Finance Corporation, the International Monetary Fund and the Nordic Investment Bank.

public offer

an offer of *securities* to the public and described in the *POS Regulations*.

public sector entity

(in accordance with Article 4(18) of the *Banking Consolidation Directive* (Definitions) and for the purposes of *BIPRU*) any of the following:

(a) non-commercial administrative bodies responsible to central governments, regional governments or local authorities; or

(b) authorities that exercise the same responsibilities as regional and local authorities; or

(c) non commercial *undertakings* owned by central governments that have explicit guarantee arrangements; or

(d) self administered bodies governed by law that are under public supervision.

public sector issuer

states and their regional and local authorities, *state monopolies*, *state finance organisations*, *public international bodies*, statutory bodies and *OECD state guaranteed issuers*.

published recommendation

any publication by or on behalf of a *firm* (including publication by sound broadcasting or television or other electronic means) which contains:

(a) the results of research into *investments*; or

(b) analysis of factors likely to influence the future performance of *investments*; or

(c) advice or recommendations based on those results or analysis, including any communication of which the content is common to a number of communications although worded as if it were a *personal recommendation*.

pure protection contract

(1) a *long-term insurance contract* in respect of which the following conditions are met:
(a) the benefits under the contract are payable only on death or in respect of incapacity due to injury, sickness or infirmity;
(b) [deleted]
(c) the contract has no surrender value, or the consideration consists of a single premium and the surrender value does not exceed that premium; and
(d) the contract makes no provision for its conversion or extension in a manner which would result in it ceasing to comply with (a) or (c); or
(e) [deleted]

(2) a *reinsurance contract* covering all or part of a risk to which a *person* is exposed under a *long-term insurance contract*.

pure protection service

(a) making a *personal recommendation* to a *consumer* in relation to a *pure protection contract*;

(b) arranging for a *consumer* to enter into a *pure protection contract*.

pure reinsurer

an *insurer* whose *insurance business* is restricted to reinsurance.

qualified investor

(in *PR*) (as defined in section 86(7) of the *Act*) in relation to an *offer* of *transferable securities*:

(a) a *person* or entity described in points (1) to (4) of Section I of Annex II to *MiFID*, other than a *person* who, before the making of the *offer*, has agreed in writing with the relevant firm (or each of the relevant firms) to be treated as a non-*professional client* in accordance with *MiFID*; or

(b) a *person* who has made a request to one or more relevant firms to be treated as a *professional client* in accordance with Section II of Annex II to *MiFID* and has not subsequently, but before the making of the *offer*, agreed in writing with that relevant firm (or each of those relevant firms) to be treated as a non-*professional client* in accordance with the final paragraph of Section I of Annex II to *MiFID*; or

(c) a *person* who is an *eligible counterparty* in accordance with article 24 of *MiFID* and has not, before the making of the *offer*, agreed in writing with the relevant firm (or each of the relevant firms) to be treated as a non-*professional client* in accordance with the final paragraph of Section I of Annex II of *MiFID*; or

(d) a *person* whom any relevant firm is authorised to continue to treat as a *professional client* in accordance with article 71(6) of *MiFID*.

qualified investor scheme

(A) In the PRA Handbook: an *authorised fund* whose *instrument constituting the scheme* contains the statement in COLL 8.2.6 R 1(2) (Table: contents of the instrument constituting the scheme) that it is a *qualified investor scheme*.

(B) In the FCA Handbook: an *authorised fund* whose *instrument constituting the fund* contains the statement in COLL 8.2.6 R 1(2) (Table: contents of the instrument constituting the fund) that it is a *qualified investor scheme*.

qualified valuer

(in relation to any particular type of land in any particular area) a fellow or professional associate of the Royal Institution of Chartered Surveyors, a fellow or associate of the Incorporated Society of Valuers and Auctioneers, or a fellow or associate of the Rating and Valuation Association, who:

(a) has knowledge of and experience in the valuation of that particular type of land in that particular area; or

(b) has knowledge of and experience in the valuation of land and has taken advice from a valuer who he is satisfied has knowledge of and experience in the valuation of that particular type of land in that particular area; or

(c) immediately before 15 June 1981 was recognised as a qualified valuer by approval by the Secretary of State under the Insurance Companies (Valuation of Assets) Regulations 1976.

qualifying capital instrument

[deleted]

qualifying capital item

[deleted]

qualifying credit

(as defined in Schedule 1 paragraph 10 (Providing qualifying credit) of the *Financial Promotion Order*) credit (including a cash loan and any other form of financial accommodation) provided in accordance with an agreement under which:

(a) the lender is a person who enters into or administers *regulated mortgage contracts*; and

(b) the obligation of the borrower to repay is secured (in whole or in part) on land.

qualifying debt security

(1) [deleted]

(2) (for the purposes of *BIPRU*) a debt *security* that satisfies the conditions in BIPRU 7.2.49 R (Definition of a qualifying debt security).

qualifying equity index

(in *BIPRU*) an *equity* index falling within BIPRU 7.3.38 R (Definition of a qualifying equity index).

qualifying holding

(1) (in *GENPRU* and *BIPRU*) has the meaning in GENPRU 2.2.203R (Qualifying holdings), which is in summary a direct or indirect holding of a *bank* or *building society* in a non-financial *undertaking*

which represents 10% or more of the capital or of the voting rights or which makes it possible to exercise a significant influence over the management of that *undertaking*.

(2) (otherwise) any direct or indirect holding in an *investment firm* which represents 10% or more of the capital or of the voting rights, as set out in Article 92 of the European Parliament and Council Directive on the admission of securities to official stock exchange listing and on information to be published on those securities (No. 2001/34/EC) or which makes it possible to exercise a significant influence over the management of the *investment firm* in which that holding subsists. [Note: article 4(1)(27) of *MiFID*]

qualifying interest in land

(in accordance with article 63B(4)(a) of the *Regulated Activities Order*) land (other than timeshare accommodation) in the UK which is:

(a) in relation to land in England and Wales, an estate in fee simple absolute or a term of years absolute whether subsisting at law or in equity; or

(b) in relation to land in Scotland, the interest of an owner in land or the tenant's right over or interest in a property subject to a lease; or

(c) in relation to land in Northern Ireland, any freehold estate or any leasehold estate whether subsisting at law or in equity.

qualifying investment

an *investment* which has been prescribed by the Treasury in the *Prescribed Markets and Qualifying Investments Order*

qualifying management company holding

(in *COLL*) a direct or indirect holding in a *management company* which represents 10% or more of the capital or of the voting rights or which makes it possible to exercise a significant influence over the management of the company in which that holding subsists; and for this purpose the voting rights referred to in articles 9 and 10 of the *Transparency Directive* must be taken into account.

qualifying master scheme

where a *feeder NURS* is *dedicated* to *units* in a single *collective investment scheme*, which meets the requirements in COLL 5.6.26R (1), that *collective investment scheme*.

qualifying money market fund

(1) (in *COLL*, CASS 7 and *BSOCS*) a *collective investment scheme* authorised under the *UCITS Directive* or which is subject to supervision and, if applicable, authorised by an authority under the national law of an *EEA State*, and which satisfies the following conditions:
(a) its primary investment objective must be to maintain the net asset value of the undertaking either constant at par (net of earnings), or at the value of the investors' initial capital plus earnings;
(b) it must, with a view to achieving that primary investment objective, invest exclusively in high quality money market instruments with a maturity or residual maturity of no more than 397 days, or regular yield adjustments consistent with such a maturity, and with a weighted average maturity of no more than 60 days. It may also achieve this objective by investing on an ancillary basis in deposits with credit institutions;
(c) it must provide liquidity through same day or next day settlement.

(2) For the purposes of (1)(b), a money market instrument is to be considered to be of high quality if it has been awarded the highest available credit rating by each competent rating agency which has rated that instrument. An instrument that is not rated by any competent rating agency is not to be considered to be of high quality.

(3) For the purposes of (2), a rating agency is to be considered to be competent if it issues credit ratings in respect of money market funds regularly and on a professional basis and is an eligible ECAI within the meaning of Article 81(1) of the *BCD*.

[Note: article 18(2) of the *MiFID implementing Directive*]

qualifying parent undertaking

has the meaning in section 192B (meaning of "qualifying parent undertaking") of the *Act* which, in summary, is a *parent undertaking* of:

(a) an *authorised person* that is a *body corporate* incorporated in the *UK* that is:
(i) a *PRA-authorised person*; or
(ii) an *investment firm*; or

(b) a *recognised investment exchange* that is not an *overseas investment exchange*;

where the *parent undertaking* is:

(c) a *body corporate* which:
(i) is incorporated in the *UK*; or
(ii) has a place of business in the *UK*;

(d) not an *authorised person*, a *recognised investment exchange* or a *recognised clearing house*; and

(e) any of the following:
(i) an *insurance holding company*;
(ii) a *financial holding company*;
(iii) a *mixed financial holding company*;
(iv) for certain purposes, a *mixed-activity holding company*.

qualifying revolving retail exposure

(in relation to the *IRB approach*) *retail exposures* falling into BIPRU 4.6.44 R (2) (Qualifying revolving retail exposures).

qualifying scheme

(a) a *personal pension scheme* or *stakeholder pension scheme*, which provides money purchase benefits, used by an employer(s) to comply with duties imposed in Part 1, Chapter 1 of the Pensions Act 2008. In summary, these duties are to take necessary steps for particular employees, by a particular time, to make those employees members of a pension scheme which meets the criteria in that Act and in regulations made under that Act;

(b) but such a scheme will not be a *qualifying scheme* if the only members of that scheme are directors or former directors of the same employer, including at least one third of the current directors of that employer.

qualifying social entrepreneurship fund

has the meaning given in article 3(b) of the *EuSEF regulation*.

qualifying subordinated loan

[deleted]

qualifying undertaking

(in *UPRU*) has the meaning given in IPRU(INV) 5.2.6(3) (Qualifying undertakings).

qualifying venture capital fund

has the meaning given in article 3(b) of the *EuVECA regulation*.

quantification date

the date as at which the liability of the relevant person in default is to be determined under COMP 12.3.

quarterly financial return

(in *UPRU*) means the return referred to in *SUP*.

quasi-derivative contract or quasi-derivative

a contract or asset having the effect of a *derivative* contract.

RAG

regulated activity group.

railway rolling stock

(in relation to a *class* of *contract of insurance*) the *class* of *contract of insurance*, specified in paragraph 5 of Part I of Schedule 1 to the *Regulated Activities Order* (Contracts of general insurance), against loss of or damage to railway rolling stock.

range

see *range of packaged products* and range of stakeholder products.

range of packaged products, range

(in relation to a *firm*) the range of packaged products on which the *firm* gives *advice on investments* to *retail clients* (see COBS 6.3) or if appropriate the list of packaged products in which the *firm* deals.

range of stakeholder products, range

(in relation to a *firm*) the range of *stakeholder products* on which the *firm* gives *advice* (see COBS 9.6);References to a *firm's* range (or ranges) of *stakeholder products* include, where the context requires, a reference to the range (or ranges) of the *firm's appointed representatives*.

RAP

a *recognised auction platform*.

RAP recognition requirements

(1) (in relation to an *RAP*) any of the requirements applicable to an *RAP* under the *RAP regulations*, the *auction regulation* or the *MiFID Regulation*.

(2) (in relation to a *UK RIE* applying for recognition as an *RAP*) any of the requirements under the *RAP regulations*, the *auction regulation* or the *MiFID Regulation* which, if its application were successful, would apply to it.

RAP regulations

the Recognised Auction Platforms Regulations 2011 (SI 2011/2699).

recognised auction platform

a *recognised investment exchange* which is declared by a *recognition order* for the time being in force to be a *recognised auction platform*.

recognised body requirements

(1) (in relation to an *RIE*) the *recognition requirements*;

(2) (in relation to a *UK RIE*) the *MiFID implementing requirements*;

(3) (in relation to an *RAP*) the *RAP recognition requirements*; and

(4) (in relation to any of the bodies specified in (1) to (3)) any other obligations imposed by or under the *Act*.

rated position

(for the purposes of *MIPRU* and BIPRU 9 (Securitisation), in accordance with Part 1 of Annex IX of the *Banking Consolidation Directive* (Securitisation definitions) and in relation to a *securitisation position*) describes a *securitisation position* which has an eligible credit assessment by an *eligible ECAI*.

ratings based method

(for the purposes of BIPRU 9 (Securitisation) and in accordance with Part 1 of Annex IX of the *Banking Consolidation Directive* (Securitisation definitions)) the method of calculating *risk weighted exposure amounts* for *securitisation positions* set out in BIPRU 9.12.10 R-BIPRU 9.12.19 R and BIPRU 9.14.2 R.

rating system

(in relation to the *IRB approach* and in accordance with BIPRU 4.3.25 R) comprises all of the methods, processes, controls, data collection and IT systems that support the assessment of credit risk, the assignment of *exposures* to grades or pools (rating), and the quantification of *default* and *loss* estimates for a certain type of *exposure*.

RCB

the Regulated Covered Bond sourcebook.

RCB Regulations

the Regulated Covered Bonds Regulations 2008 (SI 2008/346).

RCH

a *recognised clearing house*.

RDC

Regulatory Decisions Committee.

readily realisable investment

(1)
(a) a *packaged product*;
(b) a *readily realisable security*.
[deleted]

readily realisable security

(a) a *government or public security* denominated in the currency of the country of its *issuer*;

(b) any other *security* which is:
(i) admitted to official listing on an exchange in an *EEA State*; or
(ii) regularly traded on or under the rules of such an exchange; or
(iii) regularly traded on or under the rules of a *recognised investment exchange* or (except in relation to *unsolicited real time financial promotions*) *designated investment exchange*;

(c) a newly issued *security* which can reasonably be expected to fall within (b) when it begins to be traded.

real estate market adjustment ratio

has the meaning set out, in relation to the *resilience capital requirement*, in INSPRU 3.1.21R.

real time financial promotion

(in accordance with article 7(1) of the Financial Promotion Order) a *financial promotion* made in the course of a personal visit, telephone conversation or other interactive dialogue.

realistic basis life firm

a *firm* to which GENPRU 2.1.18 R applies (and which is therefore required to calculate a *with-profits insurance capital component* in accordance with INSPRU 1.3).

realistic current liabilities

(in relation to a *with-profits fund*) the realistic current liabilities of the *with-profits fund* calculated in accordance with INSPRU 1.3.190R.

realistic excess capital

(in relation to a *with-profits fund*) has the meaning set out inINSPRU 1.3.32R.

realistic value of assets

(in relation to a *with-profits fund*) has the meaning set out in INSPRU 1.3.33R.

realistic value of liabilities

(in relation to a *with-profits fund*) the sum of the *with-profits benefit reserve*, the *future policy related liabilities* and the *realistic current liabilities* for the *with-profits fund*.

reasonable assurance engagement

(A) In PRA Handbook: a 'reasonable assurance engagement' as described in the Glossary of terms in the Auditing Practices Board Standards and Guidance for Auditors issued in 2010.

(B) In FCA Handbook: a 'reasonable assurance engagement' as described in the Glossary of terms in Financial Reporting Council: Audit and Assurance: Standards and Guidance 2014.

reattribution

the process under which a *firm* which carries on *with-profits business* seeks to redefine the rights and interests that the *with-profits policyholders* have over the *inherited estate*.

reattribution expert

the expert appointed by a *firm* to satisfy its obligations under COBS 20.2.47 R (Reattribution expert).

rebalancing of the portfolio

(in *COLL* and in accordance with article 2(1) of the *UCITS implementing Directive* No 2) means a significant modification of the composition of the *scheme property* of a *UCITS scheme* or the portfolio of an *EEA UCITS scheme*.

REC

the Recognised Investment Exchange and Recognised Clearing House sourcebook.

receivable

(in relation to a *member*, a period and a *premium*) a *premium* due to the *member* in respect of *contracts of insurance* effected during the period, whether or not the *premium* is received during that period.

receiving UCITS

(in *COLL*) in relation to a *UCITS merger*, the *UCITS scheme* or *EEA UCITS scheme* or *sub-fund* of that *scheme*, whether it is an existing *scheme* (or a *sub-fund* of it) or one that is being formed for the purpose of that merger, which under the proposed arrangements will be receiving the assets and liabilities of one or more *merging UCITS*.

recipient

the *person* to whom a communication is made or, in the case of a *non-real time financial promotion* which is *directed at persons* generally, any *person* who reads or hears the communication.

reciprocal cross-holding

has the meaning in GENPRU 2.2.219R (Deductions from tiers one and two: Reciprocal cross holdings) which is in summary a holding of a *firm* of *shares*, any other interest in the capital, and subordinated debt, whether in the *trading book* or *non-trading book*, in:

(a) a *credit institution*; or

(b) a *financial institution*;

that satisfies the conditions in GENPRU 2.2.219R.

recognised body

an *RIE* or *RAP*

recognised clearing house

a *clearing house* which is declared by an order made by the Bank of England under section 290 or 292 of the *Act* and for the time being in force to be a recognised clearing house.

recognised investment exchange

an investment exchange which is declared by a *recognition order* for the time being in force to be a recognised investment exchange.

recognised overseas investment exchange

an *overseas investment exchange* which is declared by a *recognition order* for the time being in force to be a *recognised investment exchange*.

recognised professional body

any of the following professional bodies (which were the recognised professional bodies for the purposes of the Financial Services Act 1986):

(a) The Law Society (England and Wales);

(b) The Law Society of Scotland;

(c) The Law Society of Northern Ireland;

(d) The Institute of Chartered Accountants in England and Wales;

(e) The Institute of Chartered Accountants of Scotland;

(f) The Institute of Chartered Accountants in Ireland;

(g) The Association of Chartered Certified Accountants;

(h) The Institute of Actuaries.

(see also *designated professional body*.)

recognised scheme

(A) In the PRA Handbook: a *scheme* recognised under:

(a) section 264 of the *Act* (Schemes constituted in other EEA States); or

(b) section 270 of the *Act* (Schemes authorised in designated countries or territories); or

(c) section 272 of the *Act* (Individually recognised overseas schemes).

(B) In the FCA Handbook: a *scheme* recognised under:

(a) section 264 of the *Act* (Schemes constituted in other EEA States); or

(b) [deleted]

(c) section 272 of the *Act* (Individually recognised overseas schemes).

recognised third country credit institution

(A) In the PRA Handbook:
a *full BCD credit institution* that satisfies the following conditions:
(a) its head office is outside the *EEA*;
(b) it is authorised by a *third country competent authority* in the state or territory in which the credit institution's head office is located;
(c) that *third country competent authority* is named in Part 1 of BIPRU 8 Annex 6 (Non-EEA banking regulators' requirements deemed CRD-equivalent for individual risks); and
(d) there is a tick against that *third country competent authority* in each of the columns headed "Market risk", "Credit risk" and "Operational Risk" in the table referred to in (c).

(B) In the FCA Handbook:
a *full CRD credit institution* that satisfies the following conditions:
(a) its head office is outside the *EEA*;
(b) it is authorised by a *third country competent authority* in the state or territory in which the credit institution's head office is located; and
(c) that *third country competent authority* applies prudential and supervisory requirements to that credit institution that are at least equivalent to those applied in the *EEA*.

recognised third country investment firm

(A) In the PRA Handbook:
a *CAD investment firm* that satisfies the following conditions:
(a) its head office is outside the *EEA*;
(b) it is authorised by a *third country competent authority* in the state or territory in which the *CAD investment firm's* head office is located;
(c) that *third country competent authority* is named in Part 2 of BIPRU 8 Annex 6 (Non-EEA investment firm regulators' requirements deemed CRD-equivalent for individual risks); and
(d) that *firm* is subject to and complies with prudential rules of or administered by that *third country competent authority* that are at least as stringent as those laid down in the *Banking Consolidation Directive* and the *Capital Adequacy Directive* as applied under the third paragraph of article 95(2) of the *EU CRR*.

(B) In the FCA Handbook:
a *CAD investment firm* that satisfies the following conditions:
(a) its head office is outside the *EEA*;
(b) it is authorised by a *third country competent authority* in the state or territory in which the *CAD investment firm's* head office is located;
(c) that *third country competent authority* is named in Part 2 of BIPRU 8 Annex 6 (Non-EEA investment firm regulators' requirements deemed CRD-equivalent for individual risks); and
(d) that *investment firm* is subject to and complies with prudential rules of or administered by that *third country competent authority* that are at least as stringent as those laid down in the *Banking Consolidation Directive* and the *Capital Adequacy Directive* as applied under the third paragraph of article 95(2) of the *EU CRR*.

recognition order

(in accordance with section 313 of the *Act* (Interpretation of Part XVIII)) an order made under section 290 or 292 of the *Act* which declares an investment exchange to be an *RIE* or (for *RAPs*) an order made under regulation 2 of the *RAP regulations* which declares a *UK RIE* to be an *RAP*.

recognition requirement

(1) (in relation to a *UK RIE*) any of the requirements applicable to that body under the Recognition Requirements Regulations.

(2) (in relation to a body applying for recognition as a *UK RIE*) any of the requirements under the Recognition Requirements Regulations which, if its application were successful, would apply to it.

(3) (in relation to an *ROIE*, or to an applicant for recognition as an *ROIE*) any of the requirements in section 292(3) of the *Act* (Overseas investment exchanges and overseas clearing houses).

Recognition Requirements Regulations

the Financial Services and Markets Act 2000 (Recognition Requirements for Investment Exchanges and Clearing Houses) Regulations 2001 (SI 2001/995).

recovery capacity

the capability of an *RRD institution* to restore its financial position following a significant deterioration. [Note: article 2(1)(103) of *RRD*]

recovery plan

a document which provides for measures to be taken by an *RRD institution* which is not subject to supervision on a *consolidated basis* to restore its financial position following a significant deterioration of its financial situation. [Note: articles 2(1)(32) and 5 of *RRD*]

redemption

(1) (except in EG 14 (Collective investment schemes)) (in relation to *units* in an *authorised fund*) the purchase of them from their *holder* by the *authorised fund* manager acting as a *principal*.

(in EG 14 (Collective investment schemes)) redemption as in (1) but including their cancellation by:
the trustee of an *AUT*;
the *depositary* of an *ACS*; or
an *ICVC*.

redemption charge

an amount levied by the *operator* of a *scheme* upon the *redemption* of *units*, in the case of an *authorised fund* under COLL 6.7.7R (Charges on buying and selling units).

redemption price

(in *COLL*) the *price* payable by the *authorised fund manager* for each *unit* it *redeems* from a unitholder, calculated in accordance with COLL 6.3 (Valuation and pricing).

redress determination

a written communication from a *respondent* under a *consumer redress scheme* which:

(a) sets out the results of the *respondent's* determination under the scheme;

(b) encloses a copy of the *Financial Ombudsman Service's* standard explanatory leaflet; and

(c) informs the complainant that if he is dissatisfied, he may now make a *complaint* to the *Financial Ombudsman Service* and must do so within six *months*.

reduced net underwriting position

the *net underwriting position* as adjusted under BIPRU 7.8.27 R (Calculating the reduced net underwriting position).

Referral Fees Regulations

the Legal Aid, Sentencing and Punishment of Offenders Act 2012 (Referral Fees) Regulations 2013 (SI 2013/1635).

refinance

see the definition of *finance* (except in relation to CONC 6.7.18 R to CONC 6.7.23 R and CONC 7.6.12 R).

register

(1) [deleted]

(2) [deleted]

(3) (in *COLL*) the register of *unitholders* kept under Schedule 3 to the *OEIC Regulations* or COLL 6.4.4 R (Register: general requirements and contents), or COLL 8.5.8 R (The register of unitholders: AUTs or ACSs) as appropriate or, in relation to a *collective investment scheme* that is not an *authorised fund*, a record of the holders (other than of *bearer certificates*) of *units* in it.

registered branch

a branch of a *friendly society* which is separately registered under the Friendly Societies Act 1974.

registered charity

a charity:

(a) registered on the Charity Commission's Register of Charities;

(b) registered on the Scottish Charity Register;

(c) registered on the Charity Commission of Northern Ireland's Register of Charities; or

(d) that is or will be required to register on the register in (c) and which is recognised as a charity for tax purposes by Her Majesty's Revenue and Customs.

registered contact

(as defined in regulation 8(1)(d) of the *CTF Regulations*) the *person* who is capable of giving instructions to the *CTF provider* with respect to the management of the *CTF*.

registered friendly society

a *friendly society* registered under section 7(1)(a) of the *Friendly Societies* Act 1974 or any enactment which it replaced, including any registered branches.

registrar

the *person* who maintains a *register*.

registration date

(in *RCB*) the date of the *FCA* decision to register a *regulated covered bond*.

registration document

(in *Part 6 rules*) a registration document referred to in PR 2.2.2 R.

regular user

(1) (as defined in section 130A(3) of the *Act* (Market abuse)) a *person* who is, in relation to a particular market, a reasonable *person* who regularly deals on that market in *investments* of the kind in question.

(2) (in accordance with section 130A(3) of the *Act* (Market abuse) as modified by the *RAP Regulations*) a *person* who is, in relation to a particular auction platform, a reasonable *person* who regularly makes bids on that market for *investments* of the kind in question.

Regulated Activities Order

the Financial Services and Markets Act 2000 (Regulated Activities) Order 2001 (SI 2001/544).

Regulated Activities Amendment Order

the Financial Services and Markets Act 2000 (Regulated Activities) (Amendment) (No 2) Order 2013 (SI 2013/1881).

regulated activity

(A) in the *PRA* Handbook:

(in accordance with section 22 of the *Act* (Regulated activities)) any of the following activities specified in Part II of the *Regulated Activities Order* (Specified Activities):

(a) *accepting deposits* (article 5);

(aa) *issuing electronic money* (article 9B);

(b) *effecting contracts of insurance* (article 10(1));

(c) *carrying out contracts of insurance* (article 10(2));

(d) *dealing in investments as principal* (article 14);

(e) *dealing in investments as agent* (article 21);

(ea) *bidding in emissions auctions* (article 24A);

(f) *arranging (bringing about) deals in investments* (article 25(1));

(g) *making arrangements with a view to transactions in investments* (article 25(2));

(ga) *arranging (bringing about) regulated mortgage contracts* (article 25A(1));

(gb) *making arrangements with a view to regulated mortgage contracts* (article 25A(2));

(gc) *arranging (bringing about) a home reversion plan* (article 25B(1));

(gd) *making arrangements with a view to a home reversion plan* (article 25B(2));

(ge) *arranging (bringing about) a home purchase plan* (article 25C(1));

(gf) *making arrangements with a view to a home purchase plan* (article 25C(2));

(gg) *operating a multilateral trading facility* (article 25D);

(gh) *arranging (bringing about) a regulated sale and rent back agreement* (article 25E(1));

(gi) *making arrangements with a view to a regulated sale and rent back agreement* (article 25E(2));

(h) *managing investments* (article 37);

(ha) *assisting in the administration and performance of a contract of insurance* (article 39A);

(i) *safeguarding and administering investments* (article 40); for the purposes of the *permission* regime, this is sub-divided into:
(i) *safeguarding and administration of assets (without arranging)*;
(ii) *arranging safeguarding and administration of assets*;

(j) *sending dematerialised instructions* (article 45(1));

(k) *causing dematerialised instructions to be sent* (article 45(2));

(l) *establishing, operating or winding up a collective investment scheme* (article 51(1)(a)); for the purposes of the *permission* regime, this is sub-divided into:
(i) *establishing, operating or winding up a regulated collective investment scheme*;
(ii) *establishing, operating or winding up an unregulated collective investment scheme*;

(m) *acting as trustee of an authorised unit trust scheme* (article 51(1)(b));

(ma) *acting as the depositary of an authorised contractual scheme* (article 51(1)(bb));

(n) *acting as the depositary or sole director of an open-ended investment company* (article 51(1)(c));

(na) *managing a UCITS* (article 51ZA);

(nb) *acting as trustee or depositary of a UCITS* (article 51ZB);

(nc) *managing an AIF* (article 51ZC);

(nd) *acting as trustee or depositary of an AIF* (article 51ZD);

(ne) *establishing, operating or winding up a collective investment scheme* (51ZE).

(o) *establishing, operating or winding up a stakeholder pension scheme* (article 52(a));

(oa) providing *basic advice* on *stakeholder products* (article 52B);

(ob) *establishing, operating or winding up a personal pension scheme* (article 52(b));

(p) *advising on investments* (article 53); for the purposes of the *permission* regime, this is sub-divided into:
(i) *advising on investments* (except pension transfers and pension opt-outs);
(ii) *advising on pension transfers and pension opt-outs*;

(pa) *advising on regulated mortgage contracts* (article 53A);

(pb) *advising on a home reversion plan* (article 53B);

(pc) *advising on a home purchase plan* (article 53C);

(pd) *advising on a regulated sale and rent back agreement* (article 53D);

(q) *advising on syndicate participation at Lloyd's* (article 56);

(r) *managing the underwriting capacity of a Lloyd's syndicate as a managing agent at Lloyd's* (article 57);

(s) *arranging deals in contracts of insurance written at Lloyd's* (article 58);

(sa) *entering into a regulated mortgage contract* (article 61(1));

(sb) *administering a regulated mortgage contract* (article 61(2));

(sc) *entering into a home reversion plan* (article 63B(1));

(sd) *administering a home reversion plan* (article 63B(2));

(se) *entering into a home purchase plan* (article 63F(1));

(sf) *administering a home purchase plan* (article 63F(2));

(sg) *entering into a regulated sale and rent back agreement* (article 63J(1));

(sh) *administering a regulated sale and rent back agreement* (article 63J(2));

(si) *meeting of repayment claims* (article 63N(1)(a));

(sj) *managing dormant account funds (including the investment of such funds)* (article 63N(1)(b));

(t) *entering as provider into a funeral plan contract* (article 59);

(B) in the *FCA* Handbook: (in accordance with section 22 of the *Act* (Regulated activities) the activities specified in Part II of the *Regulated Activities Order* (Specified Activities) which are, in summary:

(a) *accepting deposits* (article 5);

(aa) *issuing electronic money* (article 9B);

(b) *effecting contracts of insurance* (article 10(1));

(c) *carrying out contracts of insurance* (article 10(2));

(d) *dealing in investments as principal* (article 14);

(e) *dealing in investments as agent* (article 21);

(ea) *bidding in emissions auctions* (article 24A);

(f) *arranging (bringing about) deals in investments* (article 25(1));

(g) *making arrangements with a view to transactions in investments* (article 25(2));

(ga) *arranging (bringing about) regulated mortgage contracts* (article 25A(1));

(gb) *making arrangements with a view to regulated mortgage contracts* (article 25A(2));

(gc) *arranging (bringing about) a home reversion plan* (article 25B(1));

(gd) *making arrangements with a view to a home reversion plan* (article 25B(2));

(ge) *arranging (bringing about) a home purchase plan* (article 25C(1));

(gf) *making arrangements with a view to a home purchase plan* (article 25C(2));

(gg) *operating a multilateral trading facility* (article 25D);

(gh) *arranging (bringing about) a regulated sale and rent back agreement* (article 25E(1));

(gi) *making arrangements with a view to a regulated sale and rent back agreement* (article 25E(2));

(h) *managing investments* (article 37);

(ha) *assisting in the administration and performance of a contract of insurance* (article 39A);

(i) *safeguarding and administering investments* (article 40); for the purposes of the *permission* regime, this is sub-divided into:
(i) *safeguarding and administration of assets (without arranging)*;
(ii) *arranging safeguarding and administration of assets*;

(j) *sending dematerialised instructions* (article 45(1));

(k) *causing dematerialised instructions to be sent* (article 45(2));

(l) [deleted]

(m) [deleted]

(ma) [deleted]

[deleted]

(na) *managing a UCITS* (article 51ZA);

(nb) *acting as trustee or depositary of a UCITS* (article 51ZB);

(nc) *managing an AIF* (article 51ZC);

(nd) *acting as trustee or depositary of an AIF* (article 51ZD);

(ne) *establishing, operating or winding up a collective investment scheme* (article 51ZE);

(o) *establishing, operating or winding up a stakeholder pension scheme* (article 52(a));

(oa) providing *basic advice* on *stakeholder products* (article 52B);

(ob) *establishing, operating or winding up a personal pension scheme* (article 52(b));

(p) *advising on investments* (article 53); for the purposes of the *permission* regime, this includes:
(i) *advising on investments* (except pension transfers and pension opt-outs);
(ii) *advising on investments* in respect of *pensions transfers* and *pension opt-outs*;

(pa) *advising on regulated mortgage contracts* (article 53A);

(pb) *advising on a home reversion plan* (article 53B);

(pc) *advising on a home purchase plan* (article 53C);

(pd) *advising on a regulated sale and rent back agreement* (article 53D);

(pf) *advising on conversion or transfer of pension benefits* (article 53E);

(q) *advising on syndicate participation at Lloyd's* (article 56);

(r) *managing the underwriting capacity of a Lloyd's syndicate as a managing agent at Lloyd's* (article 57);

(s) *arranging deals in contracts of insurance written at Lloyd's* (article 58);

(sa) *entering into a regulated mortgage contract* (article 61(1));

(sb) *administering a regulated mortgage contract* (article 61(2));

(sc) *entering into a home reversion plan* (article 63B(1));

(sd) *administering a home reversion plan* (article 63B(2));

(se) *entering into a home purchase plan* (article 63F(1));

(sf) *administering a home purchase plan* (article 63F(2));

(sg) *entering into a regulated sale and rent back agreement* (article 63J(1));

(sh) *administering a regulated sale and rent back agreement* (article 63J(2));

(si) *meeting of repayment claims* (article 63N(1)(a));

(sj) *managing dormant account funds (including the investment of such funds)* (article 63N(1)(b));

(t) *entering as provider into a funeral plan contract* (article 59);

(ta) *providing information in relation to a specified benchmark*;

(tb) *administering a specified benchmark*;

(tc) *credit broking* (article 36A);

(td) *operating an electronic system in relation to lending* (article 36H);

(te) *debt adjusting* (article 39D);

(tf) *debt counselling* (article 39E);

(tg) *debt collecting* (article 39F);

(th) *debt administration* (article 39G);

(ti) *entering into a regulated credit agreement as lender* (article 60B(1));

(tj) exercising, or having the right to exercise, the lender's rights and duties under a regulated credit agreement (article 60B(2));

(tk) entering into a regulated consumer hire agreement as owner (article 60N(1));

(tl) exercising, or having the right to exercise, the owner's rights and duties under a regulated consumer hire agreement (article 60N(2));

(tm) *providing credit information services* (article 89A);

(tn) *providing credit references* (article 89B);

which is carried on by way of business and, except for (ta) and (tb), relates to a *specified investment* applicable to that activity or, in the case of (l), (m), (n) and (o), is carried on in relation to property of any kind or, in the case of (tm) and (tn), is carried on in relation to information about a *person's* financial standing;

(u) *agreeing to carry on a regulated activity* (article 64);

which is carried on by way of business and relates to a *specified investment* applicable to that activity or, in the case of (na), (nb), (nc), (nd), (ne) and (o), is carried on in relation to property of any kind or, in the case of (tm) and (tn), is carried on in relation to information about a *person's* financial standing.

regulated activity debt

an obligation to pay a sum due and payable under an agreement, the making or performance of which constitutes or is part of a *regulated activity* carried on by an individual who:

(a) is, or has been, an *authorised person*; or

(b) is carrying on, or has carried on, a *regulated activity* in contravention of the *general prohibition*.

regulated activity group

A set of one or more *regulated activities* (with associated *investment* types and *customer* types) referred to in SUP 16 to determine a *firm's* or other regulated person's *data item submission* requirements.

regulated agreement

any *credit agreement* which is not an exempt agreement (see articles 60C to 60H of the *Regulated Activities Order*) or any *consumer hire agreement* which is not an exempt agreement (see articles 60O to 60Q of the *Regulated Activities Order*).

regulated clearing arrangement

as the context requires, either:

(a) an arrangement under which a *firm* directly places *client money* in a *client transaction account* that is an *individual client account* or an *omnibus client account* at an *authorised central counterparty*; or

(b) an arrangement under which a *firm*, acting for a *client* who is also an *indirect client*, directly places *client money* of that *indirect client* in a *client transaction account* that is an *individual client account* or an *omnibus client account* at a *clearing member* for the purposes of having that *clearing member* clear the positions of that *indirect client* through an *authorised central counterparty*.

regulated collective investment scheme

(a) an *ICVC*; or

(b) an *AUT*; or

(ba) an *ACS*; or

(c) a *recognised scheme*;

whether or not the *units* are held within an *ISA* or *personal pension scheme*.

regulated consumer credit agreement

in accordance with section 8 of the Consumer Credit Act 1974 (as amended) an agreement between an individual "the debtor" and any other person "the creditor" by which the creditor provides the debtor with credit of any amount and which is not an exempt agreement for the purposes of that Act; and expressions used in that Act have the same meaning in this definition.

regulated consumer hire agreement

in accordance with article 60N of the *Regulated Activities Order*, a *consumer hire agreement* which is not an exempt agreement under articles 60O to 60Q of the *Regulated Activities Order*.

regulated covered bond

(in *RCB*) (as defined in Regulation 1(2) of the *RCB Regulations*) a *covered bond* or *programme* of *covered bonds*, as the case may be, which is admitted to the register of *regulated covered bonds* maintained under Regulation 7(1)(b) of the *RCB Regulations*.

regulated credit agreement

in accordance with article 60B of the *Regulated Activities Order*, a *credit agreement* which is not an exempt agreement under articles 60C to 60H of the *Regulated Activities Order*.

regulated entity

one of the following:

(a) a *credit institution*; or

(b) a regulated insurance entity; or

(c) an *investment firm*;

whether or not it is incorporated in, or has its head office in, an *EEA State*. An *asset management company* is treated as a regulated entity for the purposes described in GENPRU 3.1.39R (The financial sectors: *asset management companies*). An *alternative investment fund manager* is treated as a regulated entity for the purposes described in GENPRU 3.1.39 R (The financial sectors: alternative investment fund managers).

regulated information

all information which an *issuer*, or any other *person* who has applied for the admission of *financial instruments* to trading on a *regulated market* without the *issuer's* consent, is required to disclose under:

(a) the *Transparency Directive*;

(b) article 6 of the *Market Abuse Directive*; or

(c) *LR*, and *DTR*.

Regulated Information Service

a Regulated Information Service that is approved by the *FCA* as meeting the Criteria for Regulated Information Services and that is on the list of Regulated Information Services maintained by the *FCA*.

regulated institution

any of the following:

(a) an *EEA insurer* or *UK insurer*; or

(b) an *approved credit institution*; or

(c) a *friendly society* (not within (a)) which is authorised to carry on *insurance business*; or

(d) a *firm* whose *permission* includes dealing in investments as *principal* with respect to *derivatives* which are not *listed*; or

(e) a *MiFID investment firm* whose authorisation (as referred to in article 5 of *MiFID*) authorises it to carry on activities of the kind referred to in (d).

regulated insurance entity

an insurance undertaking within the meaning of Article 4 of the *Consolidated Life Directive*, Article 6 of the *First Non-Life Directive* or Article 1(b) of the *Insurance Groups Directive*.

regulated lifetime mortgage contract

a *regulated mortgage contract* which is a *lifetime mortgage*.

regulated market

(1) a multilateral system operated and/or managed by a *market operator*, which brings together or facilitates the bringing together of multiple third-party buying and selling interests in *financial instruments* – in the system and in accordance with its non-discretionary rules – in a way that results in a contract, in respect of the *financial instruments* admitted to trading under its rules and/or systems, and which is authorised and functions regularly and in accordance with the provisions of Title III of *MiFID*.

[Note: article 4(1)(14) of *MiFID*]

(2) (in addition, in *INSPRU* and *IPRU(INS)* only) a market situated outside the *EEA States* which is characterised by the fact that:
(a) it meets comparable requirements to those set out in (1); and
(b) the *financial instruments* dealt in are of a quality comparable to those in a regulated market in the United Kingdom.

regulated market transaction

a transaction concluded by a *firm* on a *regulated market* with another member or participant of that *regulated market*.

regulated mortgage activity

any of the following activities specified in Part II of the *Regulated Activities Order* (Specified Activities):

(a) *arranging (bringing about) regulated mortgage contracts* (article 25A(1));

(b) *making arrangements with a view to regulated mortgage contracts* (article 25A(2));

(c) *advising on regulated mortgage contracts* (article 53A);

(d) *entering into a regulated mortgage contract* (article 61(1));

(e) administering a regulated mortgage contract (article 61(2));

(f) *agreeing to carry on a regulated activity* in (a) to (e) (article 64).

regulated mortgage contract

(a) (in relation to a contract) a contract which:
(i) (in accordance with article 61(3) of the *Regulated Activities Order*) at the time it is entered into, meets the following conditions:
(A) a lender provides credit to an individual or to trustees (the 'borrower'); and
(B) the obligation of the borrower to repay is secured by a first legal mortgage on land (other than timeshare accommodation) in the *United Kingdom*, at least 40% of which is used, or is intended to be used, as or in connection with a dwelling by the borrower or (in the case of credit provided to trustees) by an individual who is a beneficiary of the trust, or by a *person* who is in relation to the borrower or (in the case of credit provided to trustees) a beneficiary of the trust: or (in the case of credit provided to trustees) a beneficiary of the trust:
(I) that *person's* spouse or civil partner; or
(II) a *person* (whether or not of the opposite sex) whose relationship with that *person* has the

characteristics of the relationship between husband and wife; or

(III) that *person's* parent, brother, sister, child, grandparent or grandchild; and

(ii) is not a *home purchase plan*.

(b) (in relation to a *specified investment*) the *investment*, specified in article 88 of the *Regulated Activities Order*, which is rights under a *regulated mortgage contract* within (a).

regulated payment system

a *payment system* designated by HM Treasury under section 43 of *FSBRA*.

regulated related undertaking

a *related undertaking* that is any of the following:

(a) a *regulated entity*; or

(b) an *insurance undertaking* which is not a *regulated insurance entity*; or

(c) an *asset management company*; or

(d) a *financial institution* which is neither a *credit institution* nor an *investment firm*; or

(e) a *financial holding company*; or

(f) an *insurance holding company*; or

(g) a *mixed financial holding company*.

regulated sale and rent back activity

any of the following *regulated activities*:

(a) *arranging (bringing about) a regulated sale and rent back agreement* (article 25E(1));

(b) *making arrangements with a view to a regulated sale and rent back agreement* (article 25E(2));

(c) *advising on a regulated sale and rent back agreement* (article 53D);

(d) *entering into a regulated sale and rent back agreement* (article 63J(1));

(e) *administering a regulated sale and rent back agreement* (article 63J(2)); or

(f) *agreeing to carry on a regulated activity* in (a) to (e) (article 64).

regulated sale and rent back agreement

(in accordance with article 63J(3)(a) of the *Regulated Activities Order*) an arrangement comprised in one or more instruments or agreements, in relation to which the following conditions are met at the time it is entered into:

(a) the arrangement is one under which a *person* (an agreement provider), buys all or part of the *qualifying interest in land* in the *United Kingdom* from an individual or trustees (the "agreement seller"); and

(b) the agreement seller (if he is an individual) or an individual who is the beneficiary of the trust (if the agreement seller is a trustee), or a related person, is entitled under the arrangement to occupy at least 40% of the land in question as or in connection with a dwelling, and intends to do so;

but excluding any arrangement that is a regulated *home reversion plan*.

regulated sale and rent back firm

a *firm* that carries on any *regulated sale and rent back activity*.

regulated sale and rent back mediation activity

any of the following *regulated activities*:

(a) *arranging (bringing about) regulated sale and rent back agreements* (article 25E(1));

(b) *making arrangements with a view to regulated sale and rent back agreements* (article 25E(2));

(c) *advising on regulated sale and rent back agreements* (article 53D);

(d) *agreeing to carry on a regulated activity* in (a) to (c) (article 64).

regulated sale and rent back transaction

a transaction involving a *regulated sale and rent back agreement* under which a *SRB agreement seller*, in return for the sale of a *qualifying interest in land* in whole or in part to a *SRB agreement provider*, is granted, or any member of his family is granted, a right to occupy the land in question as, or in connection with, a dwelling, and intends so to occupy it.

regulatory basis only life firm

a *firm* carrying on *long-term insurance business* which is not a *realistic basis life firm*.

regulatory body

(A) In the PRA Handbook:

any authority, body or *person* having, or who has had, responsibility for the supervision or regulation of any *regulated activities* or other financial services, whether in the *United Kingdom* or overseas.

(B) In the FCA Handbook:

(1) (except in *DTR*) any authority, body or *person* having, or who has had, responsibility for the supervision or regulation of any *regulated activities* or other financial services, whether in the *United Kingdom* or overseas.

(2) (in *DTR*) an organisation listed in DTR 8 Annex 1.

regulatory costs

the periodic fees payable to the *appropriate regulator* by a *participant firm* in accordance with FEES 4 (Periodic fees).

regulatory current liabilities

(in relation to a *with-profits fund*) the regulatory current liabilities of the *with-profits fund* calculated in accordance with INSPRU 1.1.30R.

Regulatory Decisions Committee

a committee of the Board of the *FCA*, described in DEPP 3.1 (The nature and procedure of the RDC).

regulatory excess capital

(in relation to a *with-profits fund*) has the meaning set out in INSPRU 1.3.32R.

regulatory function

(as defined in section 291 of the *Act* (Liability in relation to *recognised body*'s regulatory functions)) any function of a *recognised body* so far as relating to, or to matters arising out of, the obligations to which the body is subject under or by virtue of the *Act* and (for an *RAP*) under the *RAP recognition requirements*.

regulatory high risk category

(for the purposes of the *standardised approach* to credit risk) an item that falls into BIPRU 3.4.104 R (Items belonging to regulatory high risk categories under the standardised approach to credit risk).

regulatory information service or RIS

(A) In the PRA Handbook:
either:
(a) a *Regulated Information Service*; or
(b) an incoming *information society service* that has its *establishment* in an *EEA State* other than the *United Kingdom* and that disseminates *regulated information* in accordance with the minimum standards set out in [article 12 of the *TD implementing Directive*].

(B) In the FCA Handbook:
(a) a *primary information provider*; or
(b) an incoming *information society service* that has its *establishment* in an *EEA State* other than the *United Kingdom* and that disseminates *regulated information* in accordance with the minimum standards set out in article 12 of the *TD implementing Directive*; or
(c) a *person* to whom DTR TP 1.22 applies, for as long as DTR TP 1.22 remains in force.

regulatory objectives

[deleted]

regulatory provisions

any rules, guidance, arrangements or policy issued by the investment exchange in connection with its business as an investment exchange or in connection with the provision by it of *clearing facilitation services*.

regulatory surplus

(in relation to a long-term business fund, or sub-fund) the excess, if any, of the *regulatory value of assets* for the *with-profits fund* over the *regulatory value of liabilities* for that fund.

regulatory surplus value

has the meaning set out in GENPRU 1.3.48R.

regulatory system

(A) In the PRA Handbook:

the arrangements for regulating a *firm* or other *person* in or under the *Act*, including the *threshold conditions*, the *Fundamental Rules* and other *rules*, the *Statements of Principle*, codes and *guidance* and including any relevant directly applicable provisions of a Directive or Regulation such as those contained in the *MiFID implementing Directive*, the *MiFID Regulation* and the *EU CRR*.

(B) In the FCA Handbook:

the arrangements for regulating a *firm* or other *person* in or under the *Act*, including the *threshold conditions*, the *Principles* and other *rules*, the *Statements of Principle*, codes and *guidance*, or in or under the *CCA*, and including any relevant directly applicable provisions of a Directive or Regulation such as those contained in the *MiFID implementing Directive*, the *MiFID Regulation* and the *EU CRR*.

regulatory value of assets

(in relation to a *with-profits fund*) has the meaning set out in INSPRU 1.3.24R.

regulatory value of liabilities

(in relation to a *with-profits fund*) has the meaning set out in INSPRU 1.3.29R.

rehabilitation exceptions orders

the Rehabilitation of Offenders Act 1974 (Exceptions) Order 1975, the Rehabilitation of Offenders Act 1974 (Exclusions and Exceptions) (Scotland) Order 2003 and the Rehabilitation of Offenders (Exceptions) Order (Northern Ireland) 1979.

reinsurance

includes retrocession.

reinsurance contract

(in COBS 21, *ICOBS*, CASS 5 and *COMP*) a *contract of insurance* covering all or part of a risk to which a *person* is exposed under a *contract of insurance*.

Reinsurance Directive

the Directive of 16 November 2005 of the European Parliament and of the Council (No 2005/68/EC) on reinsurance and amending the *First Non-Life Directive* and the *Third Non-Life Directive* as well as the *Insurance Groups Directive* and the *Consolidated Life Directive*.

reinsurance mediation

(as defined in article 2.4 of the *Insurance Mediation Directive*) the activities of introducing, proposing or carrying out other work preparatory to the conclusion of contracts of reinsurance, or of concluding such contracts, or of assisting in the administration and performance of such contracts, in particular in the event of a claim. These activities when undertaken by a *IMD reinsurance undertaking* or an employee of a *IMD reinsurance undertaking* who is acting under the responsibility of the *IMD reinsurance undertaking* shall not be considered as *reinsurance mediation*. The provision of information on an incidental basis in the context of another professional activity provided that the purpose of that activity is not to assist the customer in concluding or performing a reinsurance contract, the management of claims of a *IMD reinsurance undertaking* on a professional basis, and loss adjusting and expert appraisal of claims shall also not be considered as *reinsurance mediation*.

reinsurance to close

(a) an agreement under which members of a *syndicate* in one *syndicate year* ("the reinsured members") agree with the members of that *syndicate* in a later *syndicate year* or the members of another *syndicate* ("the reinsuring members") that the reinsuring members will discharge, or procure the discharge of, or indemnify the reinsured members against, all known and unknown *insurance business* liabilities of the reinsured members arising out of the *insurance business* carried on by the reinsured members in that *syndicate year*; or

(b) a similar reinsurance agreement or arrangement that has been approved by the *Council* as a reinsurance to close.

reinsurance undertaking

an *insurance undertaking* whose *insurance business* is restricted to *reinsurance*.

reinsurer

an *insurance undertaking* whose business includes *effecting* or *carrying out* contracts of *reinsurance*; includes a retrocessionaire.

related designated investment

(in relation to a *designated investment* (the "first investment")) a *designated investment* whose value might reasonably be expected to be directly affected by:

(a) any fluctuation in the value of the first investment; or

(b) any *published recommendation* that concerns the first investment.

related financial instrument

means a *financial instrument*, the price of which is closely affected by price movements in another *financial instrument* which is the subject of *investment research*, and includes a derivative on that other *financial instrument*. [Note: article 25(2) of the *MiFID implementing Directive*]

related investment

(as defined in section 130A(3) of the *Act*) in relation to a *qualifying investment*, means an investment whose price or value depends on the price or value of the *qualifying investment*.

related party

(1) (in *LR*) as defined in LR 11.1.4 R;

(2) (in relation to an agreement seller under a *regulated sale and rent back agreement* or, where the agreement seller is a trustee, a beneficiary of the trust):

(a) that *person's* spouse or civil partner; or

(b) a *person* (whether or not of the opposite sex) whose relationship with that *person* has the characteristic of the relationship between husband and wife; or

(c) that *person's* parent, brother, sister, child, grandparent or grandchild.

related party circular

(in *LR*) a *circular* relating to a *related party transaction*.

related party transaction

(in *LR*) as defined in LR 11.1.5 R.

related undertaking

in relation to an *undertaking* ("U"):

(a) any *subsidiary undertaking* of U; or

(b) any *undertaking* in which U or any of U's *subsidiary undertakings* holds a participation; or

(c) any *undertaking* linked to U by a *consolidation Article 12(1) relationship*; or

(d) any *undertaking* linked by a *consolidation Article 12(1) relationship* to an *undertaking* in (a), (b) or (c).

relative

brother, sister, uncle, aunt, nephew, niece, lineal ancestor or lineal descendent.

relevant articles

(in *REC*):

(1) Article 6.1 to 6.4 of the *Market Abuse Directive*;

(2) Articles 3, 5, 7, 8, 10, 14 and 16 of the *Prospectus Directive*;

(3) Articles 4 to 6, 14, 16 to 19 and 30 of the *Transparency Directive*; and

(4) *EU* legislation made under the provisions mentioned in (1) to (3).

relevant asset pool

(in *RCB*) (as defined in Regulation 1(2) of the *RCB Regulations*) in relation to a *regulated covered bond* the *asset pool* from which the claims attaching to that bond are guaranteed to be paid by the *owner* of that pool in the event of the failure of the *issuer*.

relevant business

(A) (In the PRA Handbook) (1) (in *DISP* and *FEES*) that part of a *firm's* business which it conducts with *consumers* and which is subject to the jurisdiction of the *Financial Ombudsman Service* as provided for in DISP 2.3 (To which activities does the Compulsory Jurisdiction apply) and DISP 2.5 (To which activities does the Voluntary Jurisdiction apply?), measured by reference to the appropriate tariff-base for each *industry block*. (2) (in relation to information communicated to a client other than a *financial promotion*) *designated investment business*. (3) (in relation to a *financial promotion*) a *controlled activity*.

(B) (In the FCA Handbook) (1) (in *DISP* and *FEES*) that part of a *firm's* business which it conducts with *consumers* and which is subject to the jurisdiction of the *Financial Ombudsman Service* as provided for in DISP 2.3 (To which activities does the Compulsory Jurisdiction apply?) and DISP 2.5 (To which activities does the Voluntary Jurisdiction apply?), measured by reference to the appropriate tariff-base for each *industry block*. (2) (in relation to information communicated to a client other than a *financial promotion*) *designated investment business*. (3) (in relation to a *financial promotion*) a *controlled activity*.

relevant capital sum

for the purposes of INSPRU 1.3.34R, the sum under a *contract of insurance* which is:

(a) unless (b) applies:
(i) for whole life assurances, the sum assured;
(ii) for *contracts of insurance* where a sum is payable on maturity (including contracts where a sum is also payable on earlier death), the sum payable on maturity;
(iii) for deferred annuities, the capitalised value of the annuity at the vesting date (or the cash option if it is greater);
(iv) for *capital redemption* contracts, the sum payable at the end of the contract period; and
(v) for linked long-term contracts of insurance, notwithstanding (i) to (iv), the lesser of:
(A) the amount for the time being payable on death; and
(B) the aggregate of the value for the time being of the units allocated to the contract (or, where entitlement is not denoted by means of units, the value for the time being of any other measure of entitlement under the contract equivalent to units) and the total amount of the *premiums* remaining to be paid during such of the term of the contract as is appropriate for *zillmerising* or, if such *premiums* are payable beyond the age of seventy-five, until that age;
but excluding in all cases any vested reversionary bonus; and

(b) for temporary assurances, the sum assured on the *actuarial valuation date*.

relevant charitable scheme

an *authorised fund* which is:

(a) a registered charity; or

(b) a charitable unit trust scheme under regulation 7(2)(d) of the Income Tax (Definition of Unit Trust Scheme) Regulations 1988.

relevant collateral

in relation to a transaction:

(a) cash;

(b) letters of credit and guarantees to the extent of their face value, issued by an *approved bank* which is neither a counterparty nor an *associate* of a counterparty;

(c) gold and silver bullion and coinage;

(d) marketable investments;

(e) the performance guarantees issued in support of the securities lending and borrowing programmes of Euroclear and Cedel, in respect only of *exposure* arising from participation in such programmes;

subject in each case to:

(i) the *firm* having an unconditional right to apply or realise the relevant collateral for the purpose of repaying a counterparty's obligations;
(ii) marketable investments:
(A) being marked to market daily using the valuation principles in IPRU(INV) 3.41(9)R;
(B) not being issued by a counterparty nor by an *associate* of a counterparty.

relevant commencement date

(as defined in article 1 of the *Mortgage and General Insurance Complaints Transitional Order*):

(a) in relation to a complaint which relates to an activity to which, immediately before 14 January 2005, the *GISC facility* applied, the beginning of 14 January 2005;

(b) in relation to a complaint which relates to an activity to which, immediately before 31 October 2004, the *MCAS scheme* applied, the beginning of 31 October 2004.

relevant competent authorities

(in relation to a *financial conglomerate*) those *competent* authorities which are, or which have been appointed as, relevant *competent* authorities in relation to that *financial conglomerate* under Article 2(17) of the *Financial Groups Directive* (Definitions).

relevant competent authority

(in relation to a *financial instrument*) means the *competent authority* of the most relevant market in terms of liquidity for that *financial instrument*. [Note: article 2(7) of *MiFID Regulation*]

relevant complaint

(1) (in *DISP*) a *relevant existing complaint*, a *relevant new complaint* or a *relevant transitional complaint*.

(2) (in *REC*) (as defined in section 299(2) of the *Act* (Complaints about *recognised bodies*)) a complaint which the *FCA* considers is relevant to the question of whether a *recognised body* should remain a *recognised body*.

relevant credit activity

an activity of a kind specified as a *relevant credit activity* in paragraph 2G of Schedule 6 to the *Act*.

relevant credit agreement

a *credit agreement* (within the meaning given by article 60B of the *Regulated Activities Order*) other than a *regulated mortgage contract* or a regulated *home purchase plan* (within the meaning of that Order) (see paragraph 28 of Schedule 1 to the *Financial Promotion Order*).

relevant credit agreement relating to the purchase of land

in accordance with article 60E (7) of the *Regulated Activities Order*:

(a) a *borrower-lender-supplier agreement financing*:
(i) the purchase of *land*; or
(ii) the provision of dwellings on *land*;
and secured by a *legal or equitable mortgage* on that *land*;

(b) a *borrower-lender agreement* secured by a *legal or equitable mortgage* on *land*; or

(c) a *borrower-lender-supplier agreement financing* a transaction which is a *linked transaction* in relation to:
(i) an agreement falling within (a), or
(ii) an agreement falling within (b) *financing*:
(aa) the purchase of *land*; or
(bb) the provision of dwellings on *land*,
and secured by a *legal or equitable mortgage* on the *land* referred to in (a) or the *land* referred to in (c)(ii).

relevant credit exposures

(in accordance with article 140(4) of *CRD*) exposures, other than those referred to in article 112(a) to (f) of the *EU CRR* (Exposure classes), that are subject to:

(a) the *own funds requirements* for credit risk under Part Three, Title II of the *EU CRR*;

(b) where the *exposure* is held in the *trading book*, *own funds requirements* for specific risk under Part Three, Title IV, Chapter 5 of the *EU CRR*; or

(c) where the *exposure* is a *securitisation*, the *own funds requirements* under Part Three, Title II, Chapter 5 of the *EU CRR*.

relevant credit-related complaint

a *relevant existing credit-related complaint* or a *relevant new credit-related complaint*.

relevant date

(A) In the PRA Handbook
(in MCOB 10 (Annual percentage rate)):
(a) (where a date is specified in or determinable under an agreement at the date of its making as the date on which the debtor is entitled to require provision of anything which is the subject of the agreement) the earliest such date;
(b) (in any other case) the date of making the agreement.

(B) In the FCA Handbook
(1) (in MCOB 10 (Annual percentage rate)):
(a) (where a date is specified in or determinable under an agreement at the date of its making as the date on which the debtor is entitled to require provision of anything which is the subject of the agreement) the earliest such date;
(b) (in any other case) the date of making the agreement.
(2) (in CONC App 1.1):
(a) where a date is specified in or determinable under a *credit agreement* at the date of its making as the date on which the *borrower* is entitled to require provision of anything which is the subject of the *credit agreement*) the earliest such date;
(b) in any other case, the date of making the *credit agreement*.

relevant debts under management

in relation to a *firm*, a debt due under a *credit agreement* or a *consumer hire agreement* in relation to which the *firm* is carrying on *debt adjusting* or an activity connected to that activity.

relevant EEA details

the details listed in regulation 14 of the *EEA Passport Rights Regulations* and set out in SUP 13 Annex 1 (Requisite details or relevant details: branches).

relevant existing credit-related complaint

a complaint made under the ombudsman scheme before 1 April 2014 which was being dealt with under the *Consumer Credit Jurisdiction*.

relevant existing complaint

(in accordance with the Ombudsman Transitional Order) a complaint which:

(a) was referred to a *former scheme* at any time before *commencement*, by a person who was at that time entitled, under the terms of the *former scheme*, to refer such a complaint (whether described in that scheme as the making of a complaint, the referral of a dispute, the submission of a claim, or otherwise); and

(b) has not, before *commencement*, been rejected, withdrawn, settled or determined by the former Ombudsman (whether by a substantive decision, or by closure of the case without a substantive decision).

relevant financial system

(in accordance with section 169A(5) of the *Act* (Support of overseas regulator with respect to financial stability)) a financial system including:

(a) financial markets and exchanges;

(b) activities that would be *regulated activities* if carried on in the *United Kingdom*; and

(c) other activities connected with financial markets and exchanges.

relevant former scheme

(as defined in article 2(2) of the *compensation transitionals order*):

(a) in relation to a *pending application*, the *investment business compensation scheme* under which the application was made;

(b) in relation to an *article 9 default*, one of the following that applied to the default before *commencement*:
(i) the Policyholders Protection Scheme established by the Policyholders Protection Act 1975;
(ii) the Deposit Protection Scheme established by Part II of the Banking Act 1987;
(iii) the Building Societies Investor Protection Scheme established by Part IV of the Building Societies Act 1986;
(iv) the Friendly Societies Protection Scheme established in accordance with section 141 of the Financial Services Act 1986.

relevant function

(in relation to a *UK recognised body*) an *exempt activity* or a *regulatory function*.

relevant general insurance contract

(in *COMP*) any *general insurance contract* other than:

(a) [deleted]

(b) [deleted]

(c) a contract falling within any of the following classes:
(i) *aircraft*;
(ii) *ships*;
(iii) *goods in transit*;
(iv) *aircraft liability*;
(v) *liability of ships*;
(vi) *credit*.

relevant information

(1) [deleted]

(2) (in *REC*) (in relation to an *investment*) information which is relevant to determining the current value of that *investment* or (in relation to *RAPs*) information on the terms of *emissions auction products* and the terms on which they will be auctioned on an *RAP*.

relevant insurer

in relation to a *community co-insurance operation*, an *insurer* which is concerned in the operation but is not the *leading insurer*.

relevant investment

(1) (in COBS 12.4, in relation to a *research recommendation* or a public appearance), a *designated investment* that is the subject of that *research recommendation* or public appearance,

(2) (other than in COBS 4 or COBS 12.4) (in accordance with article 3(1) of the *Regulated Activities Order* (Interpretation)):
(a) a *contractually based investment*;
(b) a *pure protection contract*;
(c) a *general insurance contract*;
(d) rights to or interests in an *investment* falling within (a).

(3) (in COBS 4) a *specified investment* or a *controlled investment*.

relevant issuer

(1) (in relation to a *designated investment* that is the subject of a *research recommendation* or a public appearance) the *issuer* of that *designated investment*; or

(2) (in relation to a *related designated investment* that is the subject of a public appearance) either the *issuer* of the *related designated investment* or the *issuer* of a *designated investment* that might reasonably be expected directly to affect the value of the *related designated investment*.

relevant liquid market

a market for a share determined in accordance with paragraph 2 and 8 of Article 9 of the *MiFID Regulation*, in many cases this will be the Member State where the share or the unit was first admitted to trading on a regulated market. [Note: article 9 of the *MiFID Regulation*]

relevant net premium income

(1) (in relation to business which is not *occupational pension fund management business*) the premium income in respect of *protected contracts of insurance* of a *firm*; or

(2) (in relation to *occupational pension fund management business*) the *remuneration* retained by a *firm* in relation to its carrying on *occupational pension fund management business*

in the year preceding that in which the date for submission of the information under FEES 6.5.13 R falls, net of any relevant rebates or refunds.

relevant new complaint

(in accordance with the *Ombudsman Transitional Order*) a complaint referred to the *Financial Ombudsman Service* after *commencement* which relates to an act or omission occurring before *commencement* if:

(a) the act or omission is that of a person who was, immediately before *commencement*, subject to a *former scheme*;

(b) the act or omission occurred in the carrying on by that person of an activity to which that *former scheme* applied; and

(c) the complainant is eligible and wishes to have the complaint dealt with under the new scheme;

for the purposes of (c), where the complainant is not eligible in accordance with DISP 2 (Jurisdiction of the Financial Ombudsman Service), an *Ombudsman* may, nonetheless, if he considers it appropriate, treat the complainant as eligible if he would have been entitled to refer an equivalent complaint to the *former scheme* in question immediately before *commencement*.

relevant new credit-related complaint

(in accordance with the *Regulated Activities Amendment Order*) a complaint made under the ombudsman scheme on or after 1 April 2014:

(a) which relates to an act or omission which took place before 1 April 2014;

(b) which could have been dealt with under the *Consumer Credit Jurisdiction* (disregarding the effect of section 226A(2)(a) and (b) of the *Act*) but for the repeal of section 226A of the *Act*; and

(c) in relation to which the complainant is eligible and wishes for the complaint to be dealt with under the *Financial Ombudsman Service*.

relevant office-holder

a relevant office-holder as defined in section 189 of the Companies Act 1989, which is in summary:

(a) the official receiver;

(b) (in relation to a company) any *person* acting as its liquidator, provisional liquidator, administrator or administrative receiver;

(c) (in relation to an individual or a debtor within the Bankruptcy (Scotland) Act 1985) a trustee in bankruptcy, interim receiver of property, or permanent or interim trustee in the sequestration of an estate;

(d) any *person* acting as administrator of an insolvent estate of a deceased *person*.

relevant overseas USRs

the following overseas uncertificated securities regulations:

(a) the Jersey Companies (Uncertificated Securities) (Jersey) Order 1999;

(b) the Guernsey Uncertified Securities (Guernsey) Regulations 2009;

(c) the Isle of Man Companies Act 2006 Uncertificated Securities Regulations 2006; and

(d) the Irish Companies Act 1990 (Uncertificated Securities) Regulations 1996.

relevant pension scheme

a *pension scheme* or an *additional voluntary contribution*.

relevant person

(A) In the *FCA Handbook*:

(1) (in *COMP*) a *person* for *claims* against whom the *compensation scheme* provides cover, as defined in COMP 6.2.1 R.

(2) any of the following:
(a) a *director, partner* or equivalent, manager or *appointed representative* (or where applicable, *tied agent*) of the *firm*;
(b) a *director, partner* or equivalent, or manager of any *appointed representative* (or where applicable, *tied agent*) of the *firm*;
(c) an *employee* of the *firm* or of an *appointed representative* (or where applicable, *tied agent*) of the *firm*; as well as any other natural person whose services are placed at the disposal and under the control of the *firm* or an *appointed representative* or a *tied agent* of the *firm* and who is involved in the provision by the *firm* of *regulated activities*;
(d) a natural person who is directly involved in the provision of services to the *firm* or its *appointed representative* (or where applicable, *tied agent*) under an *outsourcing* arrangement or (in the case of a *management company*) a delegation arrangement to third parties, for the purpose of the provision by the *firm* of *regulated activities* or (in the case of a *management company*) collective portfolio management.

[Note: article 2(3) of the *MiFID implementing Directive* and article 3(3) of the *UCITS implementing Directive*]

(B) In the *PRA Handbook*: Any of the following:

(1) a *director*, *partner* or equivalent, manager or *appointed representative* (or where applicable, *tied agent*) of the *firm*;

(2) a *director*, *partner* or equivalent, or manager of any *appointed representative* (or where applicable, *tied agent*) of the *firm*;

(3) an *employee* of the *firm* or of an *appointed representative* (or where applicable, *tied agent*) of the *firm*; as well as any other natural person whose services are placed at the disposal and under the control of the *firm* or an *appointed representative* or a *tied agent* of the *firm* and who is involved in the provision by the *firm* of *regulated activities*;

(4) a natural person who is directly involved in the provision of services to the *firm* or its *appointed representative* (or where applicable, *tied agent*) under an *outsourcing* arrangement or (in the case of a *management company*) a delegation arrangement to third parties, for the purpose of the provision by the *firm* of *regulated activities* or (in the case of a *management company*) *collective portfolio management*.

[Note: article 2(3) of the *MiFID implementing Directive* and article 3(3) of the *UCITS implementing Directive*]

relevant policyholder

(in COBS 19.5) a member of a *relevant scheme* who is or has been a worker entitled to have contributions paid by or on behalf of his employer in respect of that *relevant scheme*. 'Worker' has the same meaning as in section 88 of the Pensions Act 2008, that is, in summary, an individual who has entered into or works under (a) a contract of employment, or (b) any other contract by which the individual undertakes to do work or perform services personally for another party to the contract.

relevant provisions

in accordance with article 36A of the *Regulated Activities Order*, articles 60C (exempt agreements: exemptions relating to the nature of the agreement), 60D (exempt agreements: exemption relating to the purchase of land for non-residential purposes), 60E (exempt agreements: exemptions relating to the nature of the lender), 60G (exempt agreements: exemptions relating to the total charge for credit) and 60H (exempt agreements: exemptions relating to the nature of the borrower) of that Order.

relevant scheme

(1) (except in FEES 6) a *collective investment scheme* managed by an *EEA UCITS management company*.

(2) (in FEES 6) a scheme or arrangement (other than the *compensation scheme*) for the payment of compensation (in certain cases) to customers (including customers outside the *United Kingdom*) of *persons* (including *persons* outside the *United Kingdom*) who provide financial services (including financial services provided outside the *United Kingdom*) or carry on a business connected with the provision of such services.

(3) (in COBS 19.5) a *personal pension scheme* or *stakeholder pension scheme* for which direct payment arrangements are, or have been, in place, and under which contributions have been paid for two or more *employees* of the same employer. 'Direct payment arrangements' has the same meaning as in section 111A of the Pension Schemes Act 1993, that is, arrangements under which contributions fall to be paid by or on behalf of the employer towards the scheme (a) on the employer's own account (but in respect of the employee); or (b) on behalf of the employee out of deductions from the employee's earnings.

relevant security

(1) (in MAR 2, when used with reference to the *Buy-back and Stabilisation Regulation*) (in accordance with Article 2(6) of the *Buy-back and Stabilisation Regulation*) *transferable securities* which are admitted to trading on a *regulated market* or for which a request for admission to trading on a *regulated market* has been made, and which are the subject of a *significant distribution*.

(2) (otherwise in MAR 2) *transferable securities*

(3) [deleted]

relevant transitional complaint

(A) In the PRA Handbook: (in accordance with the *Mortgage and General Insurance Complaints Transitional Order*) a complaint referred to the *Financial Ombudsman Service* after the *relevant commencement date* which relates to an act or omission occurring before that date if:

(a) the act or omission is that of a *person* ("R") who, at the time of that act or omission, was subject to a *former scheme*;

(b) R was an *authorised person* on or after the *relevant commencement date*;

(c) the act or omission occurred in the carrying on by R of an activity to which that *former scheme* applied; and

(d) the complainant is eligible and wishes to have the complaint dealt with under the new *scheme*.

(B) In the FCA Handbook: (in accordance with the *Mortgage and General Insurance Complaints Transitional Order*) a complaint referred to the *Financial Ombudsman Service* after the *relevant commencement date* which relates to an act or omission occurring before that date if:

(a) the act or omission is that of a *person* ("R") who, at the time of that act or omission, was subject to a *former scheme*;

(b) R was an *authorised person* on or after the *relevant commencement date*;

(c) the act or omission occurred in the carrying on by R of an activity to which that *former scheme* applied; and

(d) the complainant is eligible and wishes to have the complaint dealt with under the new scheme.

relevant UK details

the details required in regulation 15 of the *EEA Passport Rights Regulations* and set out in SUP 13 Annex 2 (Relevant UK details: branches of insurance undertakings).

remedial direction

[deleted]

remuneration

(A) In the PRA Handbook:
any form of remuneration, including salaries, *discretionary pension benefits* and benefits of any kind.
[Note: article 92(2) of the *CRD*]

(B) In the FCA Handbook:
any form of remuneration, including salaries, *discretionary pension benefits* and benefits of any kind.
[Note: article 92(2) of the *CRD*]

Remuneration Code

SYSC 19A (Remuneration Code).

Remuneration Code general requirement

SYSC 19A.2.1 R.

Remuneration Code staff

(A) In the PRA Handbook:
(for a *CRR firm* and an *overseas firm* in SYSC 19A1.1.1R(1)(f)) has the meaning given in SYSC 19A.3.4 R

(B) In the FCA Handbook:
(for a *CRR firm* and an *overseas firm* in SYSC 19A1.1.1R(1)(f)) has the meaning given in SYSC 19A.3.4 R

remuneration principles proportionality rule

(in SYSC 19A) has the meaning given in SYSC 19A.3.3 R.

renewal

carrying forward a contract, at the point of expiry and as a successive or separate operation of the same nature as the preceding contract, between the same contractual parties.

repayment

includes repayment of *credit* with or without any other amount.

repayment claim

(in relation to a *dormant account*) a claim for repayment made by virtue of sections 1(2)(b) or 2(2)(b) of the Dormant Bank and Building Society Accounts Act 2008, that is, in summary, that the customer has against the *dormant account fund operator* whatever right to payment of the *balance* the customer would have against the *bank* or *building society* if the transfer (or in the case of section 2(2)(b), transfers) had not happened. In this definition, 'customer' is the *person* who held with a *bank* or *building society* the *balance* of a *dormant account* transferred to a *dormant account fund operator*.

repayment mortgage

a *regulated mortgage contract* under which the *customer* is obliged to make payments of interest and capital which are designed to repay the mortgage in full over the stated term.

repayment strategy

the means by which the *customer* intends to repay the outstanding capital and, where applicable, pay the interest accrued under the *regulated mortgage contract*, where all or part of that contract is an *interest-only mortgage*.

repo

(a) an agreement between a seller and buyer for the sale of *securities*, under which the seller agrees to repurchase the *securities*, or equivalent *securities*, at an agreed date and, usually, at a stated price;

(b) an agreement between a buyer and seller for the purchase of *securities*, under which the buyer agrees to resell the *securities*, or equivalent *securities*, at an agreed date and, usually, at a stated price.

reporting accountant

an accountant appointed:

(a) by the *appropriate regulator*; or

(b) by a *firm*, having been nominated or approved by the *appropriate regulator* under section 166 of the *Act* (Reports by skilled persons); or

(c) by an applicant for *Part 4A permission*;

to report on one or more aspects of the business of a *firm* or applicant, such as its financial position, including *internal controls* and reporting returns.

repossess

(in *MCOB*) take possession of the property that is the subject of a *regulated mortgage contract* or *home purchase plan*.

representative

(1) an individual who:

(a) is appointed by a *firm*, or by an *appointed representative* of a *firm*, to carry on any of the following activities:
(i) *advising on investments*;
(ii) providing *basic advice* on *stakeholder products*;
(iii) *arranging (bringing about) deals in investments*;
(iv) dealing in investments; or

(b) although not appointed to do so, carries on any of the activities in (i) to (iii) on behalf of a *firm* or its *appointed representative*.

(2) (in *IPRU(INV)* 13 in relation to *designated investment business*) an individual appointed by a provider firm or by an *appointed representative* or *tied agent* of that *firm* to carry out either or both of the following activities:
(a) giving *advice on investments* to *customers* on the merits of *packaged products* offered by that *firm* (or any other provider firm within the same *marketing group*); or
(b) *arranging (bringing about) deals in investments* in relation to those products.

(3) In (2), a provider firm is a *firm* that is:
(a) a *product provider*; or
(b) a *marketing group associate*.

reporting level

(in SUP 16 (Reporting requirements) and in relation to a *data item*) refers to whether that *data item* is prepared on a solo basis or on the basis of a group such as a *UK DLG by modification* and, if it is prepared on the basis of a group, refers to the type of group (such as a *UK DLG by modification* or a *non-UK DLG by modification (firm level)*).

representative APR

an *APR* at or below which the *firm communicating* or *approving* the *financial promotion* reasonably expects, at the date on which the promotion is *communicated* or *approved*, that *credit* would be provided under at least 51% of the *credit agreements* which will be entered into as a result of the promotion.

repurchase agreement

see *repurchase transaction*.

repurchase transaction

(A) In the PRA Handbook:

(in accordance with Article 3(1)(m) of the *Capital Adequacy Directive* and Article 4(33) of the *Banking Consolidation Directive* (Definitions) and for the purposes of *BIPRU*) any agreement in which an *undertaking* or its counterparty transfers securities or *commodities* or guaranteed rights relating to title to securities or *commodities* where that guarantee is issued by a *designated investment exchange* or *recognised investment exchange* which holds the rights to the securities or *commodities* and the agreement does not allow an *undertaking* to transfer or pledge a particular security or *commodity* to more than one counterparty at one time, subject to a commitment to repurchase them or substituted securities or *commodities* of the same description at a specified price on a future date specified, or to be specified, by the transferor, being a *repurchase agreement* for the *undertaking* selling the securities or *commodities* and a *reverse repurchase agreement* for the *undertaking* buying them.

(B) In the FCA Handbook:

(in accordance with Article 3(1)(m) of the *Capital Adequacy Directive* and Article 4(33) of the *Banking Consolidation Directive* (Definitions) and for the purposes of *BIPRU*) any agreement in which an *undertaking* or its counterparty transfers securities or *commodities* or guaranteed rights relating to title to securities or *commodities* where that guarantee is issued by a *designated investment exchange* or *recognised investment exchange* which holds the rights to the securities or *commodities* and the agreement does not allow an *undertaking* to transfer or pledge a particular security or *commodity* to more than one counterparty at one time, subject to a commitment to repurchase them or substituted securities or *commodities* of the same description at a specified price on a future date specified, or to be specified, by the transferor, being a *repurchase agreement* for the *undertaking* selling the securities or *commodities* and a *reverse repurchase agreement* for the *undertaking* buying them.

required percentage

the *required percentage* referred to in COBS 20.2.17 R is, for each *with-profits fund*:

(a) the percentage (if any) required in respect of that fund by:
(i) the *firm's* articles of association, registered rules or other equivalent instrument; or
(ii) a relevant order made by a court of competent jurisdiction;

(b) if (a) does not apply, the percentage that reflects the *firm's* established practice, if it has one;

(c) if (a) and (b) do not apply, not less than 90 per cent.

requirement

a requirement included in a firm's *Part 4A permission* under section 55L(3) of the *Act* (Imposition of requirements by the FCA), section 55M(3) of the *Act* (Imposition of Requirements by the PRA) or section 55O of the *Act* (Imposition of requirements on acquisition of control).

requiring or encouraging

taking or refraining from taking any action which requires or encourages another *person* to engage in *behaviour* which, if engaged in by the *person* requiring or encouraging, would amount to *market abuse*.

requisite details

(A) In the PRA Handbook: the details required in regulation 1 of the *EEA Passport Rights Regulations*.

(B) In the FCA Handbook: the details required in regulation 1 of the *EEA Passport Rights Regulations* and set out in SUP 13 Annex 1 (Requisite details: branches).

research recommendation

research or other information:

(a) concerning one or several *financial instruments* admitted to trading on *regulated markets*, or in relation to which an application for admission to trading has been made, or *issuers* of such *financial instruments*;

(b) intended for distribution so that it is, or is likely to become, accessible by a large number of *persons*, or for the public, but not including:
(i) an informal short-term investment personal recommendation expressed to *clients*, which originates from inside the sales or trading department, and which is not likely to become publicly

available or available to a large number of persons; or

(ii) advice given by a *firm* to a *body corporate* in the context of a *takeover bid* and disclosed only as a result of compliance with a legal or regulatory obligation, including rule 3 of the *Takeover Code* or its equivalents outside the *UK*; and

(c) which:

(i) explicitly or implicitly, recommends or suggests an investment strategy; or

(ii) directly or indirectly, expresses a particular investment recommendation; or

(iii) expresses an opinion as to the present or future value or price of such instruments.

In this definition, "financial instruments" means the following (as defined in Article 5 of the *Prescribed Markets and Qualifying Investments Order* and Article 1(3) of the *Market Abuse Directive*, and which consequently carries the same meaning in the *Buy-back and Stabilisation Regulation*):

(a) *transferable securities*;

(b) units in collective investment undertakings;

(c) *money-market instruments*;

(d) financial futures contracts, including equivalent cash-settled instruments;

(e) forward interest-rate agreements;

(f) interest-rate, currency and equity swaps;

(g) options to acquire or dispose of any instrument falling into these categories, including equivalent cash-settled instruments. This category includes in particular options on currency and on interest rates;

(h) derivatives on commodities; and

(i) any other instrument admitted to trading on a regulated market in an *EEA State* or for which a request for admission to trading on such a market has been made.

resecuritisation

in BIPRU 7 and 9, a *securitisation* where the risk associated with an underlying pool of *exposures* is *tranched* and at least one of the underlying *exposures* is a *securitisation position*. [Note: *BCD*, Article 4(40a)]

resecuritisation position

in BIPRU 7 and 9, an *exposure* to a *resecuritisation*. [Note: *BCD*, Article 4(40b)]

residual CIS operator

a *firm* with a *Part 4A permission* to carry on the activity specified in article 51ZE (Establishing etc. a collective investment scheme) of the *Regulated Activities Order*.

residual risk

(in *MIPRU*) the risk that credit risk mitigation techniques used by the *firm* prove less effective than expected.

resilience capital requirement

the capital component for *long-term insurance business* calculated in accordance with the *rules* in INSPRU 3.1.9G to INSPRU 3.1.26R.

resolution authority

(a) (in the *UK*) the Bank of England; or

(b) (in another *EEA State*) an authority designated as a resolution authority by that *EEA State* under article 3 of *RRD*. [Note: article 2(1)(18) of *RRD*]

respondent

(A) In the PRA Handbook:

(1) (in *DISP*, FEES 5 and CREDS 9) a *firm* (except a *UCITS qualifier*), *payment service provider*, *electronic money issuer* or *VJ participant* covered by the *Compulsory Jurisdiction*, or *Voluntary Jurisdiction* of the *Financial Ombudsman Service*.

(2) (in DISP 2 and 3 and FEES 5) includes, as a result of section 226of the *Act*:

(a) an *unauthorised person* who was formerly a *firm* in respect of a *complaint* about an act or omission which occurred at the time when the *firm* was *authorised*, provided that the compulsory jurisdiction rules were in force in relation to the activity in question;

(b) [deleted]

(c) a *person* who was formerly a *payment service provider* in respect of a *complaint* about an act or omission which occurred at the time when it was a *payment service provider*, provided that the compulsory jurisdiction rules were in force in relation to the activity in question; and

(d) a *person* who was formerly an *electronic money issuer* in respect of a *complaint* about an act or omission which occurred at the time when it was an *electronic money issuer*, provided that the compulsory jurisdiction rules were in force in relation to the activity in question.

(3) (in DISP 2 and 3 and FEES 5) includes, in accordance with the *Ombudsman Transitional Order*, an *unauthorised person* subject to the *Compulsory Jurisdiction* in relation to *relevant existing complaints* and *relevant new complaints*.

(4) (in DISP 2 and 3 and FEES 5) includes, in accordance with the *Mortgage and General Insurance Complaints Transitional Order*, a former *firm* subject to the *Compulsory Jurisdiction* in relation to *relevant transitional complaints*.

(5) (in DISP 2 and 3 and FEES 5) includes, in accordance with article 11 of the *Regulated Activities Amendment Order*, *unauthorised persons* subject to the *Compulsory Jurisdiction* in relation to *relevant existing credit-related complaints* and relevant new credit-related complaints.

(B) In the FCA Handbook:

(1) (in *DISP*, FEES 5 and CREDS 9) a *firm* (except an *AIFM qualifier* or a *UCITS qualifier*), *payment service provider*, *electronic money issuer*, or *VJ participant* covered by the *Compulsory Jurisdiction*, *Consumer Credit Jurisdiction* or *Voluntary Jurisdiction* of the *Financial Ombudsman Service*.

(2) (in DISP 2 and 3 and FEES 5) includes, as a result of section 226 of the *Act*:

(a) an *unauthorised person* who was formerly a *firm* in respect of a *complaint* about an act or omission which occurred at the time when the *firm* was *authorised*, provided that the compulsory jurisdiction rules were in force in relation to the activity in question;

[deleted]

(c) a *person* who was formerly a *payment service provider* in respect of a *complaint* about an act or omission which occurred at the time when it was a *payment service provider*, provided that the compulsory jurisdiction rules were in force in relation to the activity in question; and

(d) a *person* who was formerly an *electronic money issuer* in respect of a *complaint* about an act or omission which occurred at the time when it was an *electronic money issuer*, provided that the compulsory jurisdiction rules were in force in relation to the activity in question.

(3) (in DISP 2 and 3 and FEES 5) includes, in accordance with the *Ombudsman Transitional Order*, an *unauthorised person* subject to the *Compulsory Jurisdiction* in relation to *relevant existing complaints* and *relevant new complaints*.

(4) (in DISP 2 and 3 and FEES 5) includes, in accordance with the *Mortgage and General Insurance Complaints Transitional Order*, a former *firm* subject to the *Compulsory Jurisdiction* in relation to *relevant transitional complaints*.

(5) (in DISP 2 and 3 and FEES 5) includes, in accordance with article 11 of the *Regulated Activities Amendment Order*, *unauthorised persons* subject to the *Compulsory Jurisdiction* in relation to *relevant existing credit-related complaints* and *relevant new credit-related complaints*.

responsible person

(1) (except in *COMP*) (as defined in section 3(8) of the Child Trust Funds Act 2004) a *person* with *parental responsibility* in relation to a child under 16 who is not:

(a) a local authority or, in Northern Ireland, an authority within the meaning of the Children (Northern Ireland) Order 1995 (SI 1995/755 (NI 2)); or

(b) a *person* under 16.

(2) (in *COMP*) (in accordance with section 3 (1) of the Compensation Act 2006) a *person* who has negligently or in breach of statutory duty caused or permitted another *person* to be exposed to asbestos (including an *insurer* of such a *person*).

restricted advice

(a) a *personal recommendation* to a *retail client* in relation to a *retail investment product* which is not *independent advice*; or

(b) *basic advice*.

restricted credit

a loan for which, as a result of an existing arrangement between a supplier and a *firm*, the *customer*'s application to the *firm* is submitted through the supplier and the terms of the loan require that it be paid to the supplier for goods or services supplied to the *customer*, not including loans secured by a charge over land or loans or payments by *plastic card* (other than a *store card*).

restricted-use credit agreement

(1) (except in *CONC*) (in accordance with section 11 of the Consumer Credit Act 1974) an agreement:

(a) to finance a transaction between the *customer* and the *firm*, whether forming part of that agreement or not;

(b) to finance a transaction between the *customer* and a person (the 'supplier') other than the *firm*;

(c) to refinance any existing indebtedness of the *customer's*, whether to the *firm* or another *person*.

(2) (in *CONC*) a *credit agreement*:

(a) to *finance* a transaction between the *borrower* and the *lender*, whether forming part of that agreement or not;

(b) to *finance* a transaction between the *borrower* and a ("the supplier") other than the *lender*; or

(c) to *refinance* any existing indebtedness of the *borrower's*, whether to the *lender* or another *person*, and

(d) an agreement may fall within (b) even though the identity of the supplier is unknown at the time the agreement is made,

but

(e) a *credit agreement* is not a restricted-use *credit* agreement if the credit is in fact provided in such a way as to leave the *borrower* free to use it as the *borrower* chooses, even though certain uses would contravene that or any other agreement.

restriction notice

a notice served under sections 191B or 301J of the *Act*.

retail banking service

an arrangement with a *banking customer*, under which a *firm* agrees to accept a *deposit* from a *banking customer* on terms to be held in an account for that customer, and to provide services in relation to that *deposit* including but not limited to repayment to the customer.

retail client

(A) in the *PRA Handbook*:

(1) (other than in relation to the provision of basic advice on stakeholder products) in accordance with COBS 3.4.1 R, a *client* who is neither a *professional client* or an *eligible counterparty*; or [Note: article 4(1)(12) of *MiFID*]

(2) (in relation to the provision of *basic advice* on a *stakeholder product* and in accordance with article 52B of the *RAO*) any *person* who is advised by a *firm* on the merits of opening or buying a *stakeholder product* where the advice is given in the course of a business carried on by that *firm* and it is received by a *person* not acting in the course of a business carried on by him.

(B) in the *FCA Handbook*:

(1) (other than in relation to the provision of basic advice on stakeholder products or to *credit-related regulated activities*) in accordance with COBS 3.4.1 R, a *client* who is neither a *professional client* or an *eligible counterparty*; or [Note: article 4(1)(12) of *MiFID*]

(2) (in relation to the provision of *basic advice* on a *stakeholder product* and in accordance with article 52B of the *RAO*) any *person* who is advised by a *firm* on the merits of opening or buying a *stakeholder product* where the advice is given in the course of a business carried on by that *firm* and it is received by a *person* not acting in the course of a business carried on by him; or

(3) (in relation to *credit-related regulated activity*) a *customer*.

retail customer

(in accordance with the meaning of 'consumer' in article 2(d) of the *Distance Marketing Directive* an individual who is acting for purposes which are outside his trade, business or profession.

retail exposure

(1) (in relation to the *IRB approach* and with respect to an *exposure*) an *exposure* falling into the *IRB exposure class* listed in BIPRU 4.3.2 R (4) (Retail exposures).

(2) (in relation to the *standardised approach* to credit risk and with respect to an *exposure*) an *exposure* falling into the *standardised credit risk exposure class* listed in BIPRU 3.2.9 R (8) (Retail exposures).

retail investment

(a) a *life policy*; or

(b) a *unit*; or

(c) a *stakeholder pension scheme*; or

(ca) a *personal pension scheme*; or

(d) an interest in an *investment trust savings scheme*; or

(e) a *structured capital-at-risk product*.

retail investment activity

(a) *advising on investments*;

(b) *arranging (bringing about) deals in investments*;

(c) *making arrangements with a view to transactions in investments*; or

(d) *advising on conversion or transfer of pension benefits*;

in relation to *retail investments*, except when carried on by a *firm* exclusively with or for *professional client* or *eligible counterparties*.

retail investment adviser

an *employee* who carries on activities 2, 3, 4, 6, 12 and 13 in TC Appendix 1.1.1 R (other than in relation to a *Holloway sickness policy* where the *Holloway policy special application conditions* are met).

retail (investment) customer

(in relation to a *firm's permission* and the *Financial Services Register*) a *retail client*.

retail investment firm

a *firm* that has *permission* to carry on an activity which is a *retail investment activity*.

retail (non-investment insurance) customer

(in relation to a *firm's permission* and the *Financial Services Register*) a *consumer* or a *customer* acting in the capacity of both a *consumer* and a *commercial customer* (see ICOBS 2.1.3 G).

retail investment product

(a) a *life policy*; or

(b) a *unit*; or

(c) a *stakeholder pension scheme* (including a *group stakeholder pension scheme*); or

(d) a *personal pension scheme* (including a *group personal pension scheme*); or

(e) an interest in an *investment trust savings scheme*; or

(f) a *security* in an *investment trust*; or

(g) any other *designated investment* which offers exposure to underlying financial assets, in a packaged form which modifies that exposure when compared with a direct holding in the financial asset; or

(h) a *structured capital-at-risk product*;

whether or not any of (a) to (h) are held within an *ISA* or a *CTF*.

[Note: Section 238 of the *Act* and COBS 4.12.3 R set out restrictions on the promotion of non-mainstream pooled investments to retail clients. See also COBS 9.3.5 G (Non-mainstream pooled investments).]

retail pool

the pool of *classes* to which the *FSCS* allocates levies as described in FEES 6.5A [to follow].

retail securitised derivative

a *securitised derivative* which is not a specialist securitised derivative; in this definition, a "specialist securitised derivative" is a *securitised derivative* which, in accordance with the *listing rules*, is required to be admitted to listing with a clear statement on any disclosure document that the issue is intended for a purchase by only investors who are particularly knowledgeable in investment matters.

retail SME

(1) (in relation to the *IRB approach*) a small or medium sized entity, an *exposure* to which may be treated as a *retail exposure* under BIPRU 4.6.2 R (Definition of retail exposures).

(2) (in relation to the *standardised approach* to credit risk) a small or medium sized entity, an *exposure* to which may be treated as a retail exposure under BIPRU 3.2.10 R (Definition of retail exposures).

retail SME exposure

(in relation to the *IRB approach* or the *standardised approach* to credit risk) an *exposure* to a *retail SME*.

retirement annuity

an individual *pension policy* effected before 1 July 1988 by a self-employed *person* or a *person* in non-pensionable employment which was approved under Chapter III, Part XIV of the Income and Corporation Taxes Act 1988 (when sections 618 to 628 of that Chapter were in force).

retirement fund

the amount which will be available, at the date on which the investor retires, for the provision of benefits.

return

the documents required (taken together) to be deposited under *IPRU(INS) rule* 9.6(1).

reverse repurchase agreement

see *repurchase transaction*.

reverse takeover

(in *LR*) a transaction classified as a *reverse takeover* under LR 5.6.

reversion activity

any of the *regulated activities* of:

(a) *arranging (bringing about) a home reversion plan* (article 25B(1));

(b) *making arrangements with a view to a home reversion plan* (article 25B(2));

(c) *advising on a home reversion plan* (article 53B);

(d) *entering into a home reversion plan* (article 63B(1));

(e) *administering a home reversion plan* (article 63B(2)); or

(f) *agreeing to carry on a regulated activity* in (a) to (e) (article 64).

reversion administrator

a *firm* with *permission* (or which ought to have *permission*) for *administering a home reversion plan*.

reversion adviser

a *firm* with *permission* (or which ought to have *permission*) for *advising on a home reversion plan*.

reversion arranger

a *firm* with *permission* (or which ought to have *permission*) for *arranging* a *home reversion plan*.

reversion intermediary

a *firm* with *permission* (or which ought to have *permission*) to carry on a *reversion mediation activity*.

reversion mediation activity

any of the following *regulated activities*:

(a) *arranging (bringing about) a home reversion plan* (article 25B(1));

(b) *making arrangements with a view to a home reversion plan* (article 25B(2));

(c) *advising on a home reversion plan* (article 53B); or

(d) *agreeing to carry on a regulated activity* in (a) to (c) (article 64).

reversion occupier

the individual (or trustees), specified in article 63B(3) of the *Regulated Activities Order*, who in summary:

(a) is (or are) the *person* (or *persons*) from whom all or part of an interest in land is bought as part of an arrangement comprising a *home reversion plan*; and

(b)

(i) in the case of an individual, is entitled under the arrangement to occupy at least 40% of the land in question as or in connection with a dwelling and intends to do so; or

(ii) in the case of trustees, are trustees of a trust a beneficiary of which is an individual described in (i).

reversion provider

a *firm* with *permission* (or which ought to have *permission*) for *entering into a home reversion plan*.

revolving exposure

(for the purpose of BIPRU 9.13 (Securitisations of revolving exposures with early amortisation provisions) and in accordance with Article 100 of the Banking Consolidation Directive (Securitisations of revolving exposures)) an *exposure* whereby customers' outstanding balances are permitted to fluctuate based on their decisions to borrow and repay, up to an agreed limit.

RIE

recognised investment exchange.

right of set-off

(in *BCOBS*) any right of a *firm*, whether under a contract for a *retail banking service* or the general law, to set off or combine:

(a) any debt due from a *consumer*; or

(b) any debit balance on an account held by a *consumer*;

against or with:

(c) any sum payable by the *firm* to the *consumer*; or

(d) any credit balance on an account held by the *consumer*;

that has the effect of reducing, discharging or extinguishing the *firm's* liability to the *consumer* or the credit balance on the account held by the *consumer*.

rights issue

(in *LR* and DTR 5) an offer to existing *security* holders to subscribe or purchase further *securities* in proportion to their holdings made by means of the issue of a renounceable letter (or other negotiable document) which may be traded (as "nil paid" rights) for a period before payment for the *securities* is due.

rights to or interests in investments

the *investment*, specified in article 89 of the *Regulated Activities Order* (Rights to or interests in investments), which is in summary: any right to or interest in any other *specified investment*, but excluding:

(a) interests under the trusts of an *occupational pension scheme*;

(b) rights to or interests in a *contract of insurance* of the kind referred to in paragraph (1)(a) of article 60 of the *Regulated Activities Order* (Plans covered by insurance or trust arrangements), or interests under a trust of the kind referred to in paragraph 1(b) of article 60 of the *Regulated Activities Order* (Plans covered by insurance or trust arrangements);

(c) any other *specified investment*.

risk capital margin

the risk capital margin for a *with-profits fund* calculated in accordance with the *rules* in INSPRU 1.3.43R to INSPRU 1.3.103G.

risk capital requirement

(1) (in relation to the *FCA's rules*) one of the following:

(a) the *credit risk capital requirement*;

(b) the *fixed overheads requirement*;

(c) the *market risk capital requirement*; or

(2) (in relation to the rules of another *regulatory body*) whatever corresponds to the items in (1) under the rules of that *regulatory body*.

risk concentration

(in accordance with Article 2(19) of the *Financial Groups Directive* (Definitions)) all risk exposures with a loss potential which is large enough to threaten the solvency or the financial position in general of the *regulated entities* in the *financial conglomerate*, whether such exposures are caused by counterparty risk/credit risk, investment risk, insurance risk, market risk, other risks, or a combination or interaction of these risks.

risk control rules

IFPRU 2.2.58 R to IFPRU 2.2.60 R.

risk factors

(in *PR*) (as defined in the *PD Regulation*) a list of risks which are specific to the situation of the issuer and/or the securities and which are material for taking investment decisions.

risk limit system

(in *COLL* and in accordance with article 40(2)(d) of the *UCITS implementing Directive*) a documented system of internal limits concerning the measures used by a *management company* to manage and control the relevant risks for each *UCITS* it manages, taking into account all the risks which may be material to the *UCITS*, as referred to in the second paragraph of article 38(1) of the *UCITS implementing Directive* and ensuring consistency with the *UCITS* risk profile.

risk of excessive leverage

has the meaning in article 4(1)(94) of the *EU CRR*.

risk position

(in accordance with Part 1 of Annex III of the *Banking Consolidation Directive* (Definitions) and for the purpose of BIPRU 13 (The calculation of counterparty risk exposure values for financial derivatives, securities financing transactions and long settlement transactions)) a risk number that is assigned to a transaction under the *CCR standardised method* following a predetermined algorithm.

risk weight

(A) In the PRA Handbook:
(in relation to an *exposure* for the purposes of *BIPRU*) a degree of risk expressed as a percentage assigned to that *exposure* in accordance with:
(a) whichever is applicable of the *standardised approach* to credit risk and the *IRB approach*, including (in relation to a *securitisation position*) under BIPRU 9 (Securitisation); or
(b) (for a *firm* to which MIPRU 4 applies), MIPRU 4.2A.10 R to MIPRU 4.2A.13 R.

(B) In the FCA Handbook:
(1)(in relation to an *exposure* for the purposes of *BIPRU*) a degree of risk expressed as a percentage assigned to that *exposure* in accordance with whichever is applicable of the *standardised approach* to credit risk and the *IRB approach*, including (in relation to a *securitisation position*) under BIPRU 9 (Securitisation).
(2) (for an *exposure* under *MIPRU*) a degree of risk expressed as a percentage assigned to that *exposure* in accordance with MIPRU 4.2A.10 R to MIPRU 4.2A.12 R, and MIPRU 4.2A.17 R.

risk weighted exposure amount

(A) In the PRA Handbook:
(in relation to an *exposure* for the purposes of *BIPRU*) the value of an *exposure* for the purposes of the calculation of (in the case of a *BIPRU firm*) the *credit risk capital component* or (in the case of a *firm* to which MIPRU 4 applies) the credit risk capital requirement under MIPRU 4.2A.4 R, in both cases after application of a *risk weight*.

(B) In the FCA Handbook:
(1) (in relation to an *exposure* for the purposes of *BIPRU*) the value of an *exposure* for the purposes of the calculation of the *credit risk capital component* after application of a *risk weight*.
(2) (for an *exposure* under *MIPRU*) the *credit risk capital requirement* under MIPRU 4.2A.4 R after application of a *risk weight*.

RMAR

(in *SUP*) a Retail Mediation Activities Return, containing data specified in SUP 16 Annex 18A and relevant to the *firm's* type and *regulated activities*.

ROIE

recognised overseas investment exchange.

rolling spot forex contract

either of the following:

(a) a *future*, other than a *future* traded or expressed to be as traded on a *recognised investment exchange*, where the property which is to be sold under the contract is foreign exchange or sterling; or

(b) a *contract for differences* where the profit is to be secured or loss avoided by reference to fluctuations in foreign exchange; and

in either case where the contract is entered into for the purpose of speculation.

rolling stock method

a method for performing a *physical asset reconciliation*, as described in CASS 6.6.28 R.

rollover risk

(in accordance with Part 1 of Annex III of the *Banking Consolidation Directive* (Definitions) and for the purpose of BIPRU 13 (The calculation of counterparty risk exposure values for financial derivatives, securities financing transactions and long settlement transactions)) the amount by which *expected positive exposure* is understated when future transactions with a counterpart are expected to be conducted on an ongoing basis; the additional *exposure* generated by those future transactions is not included in calculation of *expected positive exposure*.

roll-up of interest mortgage

a *regulated mortgage contract* where no payment of interest on the amount borrowed (other than interest charged when all or part of the amount borrowed is repaid voluntarily by the *customer*), is due or capable of becoming due while the *customer* continues to occupy the mortgaged property as his main residence and fulfil his obligations under the *regulated mortgage contract*.

RPI

the Retail Prices Index.

RPPD

the Regulatory Guide which contains a statement of the responsibilities of providers and distributors for the fair treatment of *customers*.

RRD

Directive 2014/59/EU of the European Parliament and of the Council of 15 May 2014 establishing a framework for the recovery and resolution of credit institutions and investment firms and amending the directives and regulations set out in that directive (eur-lex.europa.eu/legal-content/EN/TXT/PDF/?uri=OJ:JOL_2014_173_R_0008&from=EN).

RRD early intervention condition

the requirements of:

(a) the *EU CRR*; or

(b) the laws, regulations and administrative provisions necessary to comply with *CRD*; or

(c) the laws, regulations and administrative provisions necessary to comply with title II of *MiFID II*; or

(d) articles 3 to 7, 14 to 17, 24, 25 and 26 of *MiFIR*.

[Note: article 27(1) of *RRD*]

RRD group

a *group* that:

(a) includes an *RRD institution*; and

(b) is headed by an *EEA parent undertaking*.

RRD group financial support agreement

an agreement to give financial support to an *RRD institution* which, at any time after the agreement has been concluded, has infringed an *RRD early intervention condition* or is likely to infringe one of those conditions in the near future.

RRD group member

a member of an *RRD group* that is:

(a) an *RRD institution*; or

(b) a *financial institution*; or

(c) a *financial holding company*; or

(d) a *mixed financial holding company*.

RRD institution

(a) a *credit institution*; or

(b) an *investment firm* that is subject to the *initial capital* requirement in article 28(2) of the *CRD* (a *730k investment firm*).

[Note: article 2(1)(23) of *RRD*]

RSRB permission

(in *FEES*) an *authorisation* to carry on one or more *regulated sale and rent back activities*.

rule

(A) In the PRA Handbook: (in accordance with section 417(1) of the *Act* (Definitions)) a rule made by the *FCA* or the *PRA* under the *Act*, includes an *evidential provision*.

(a) [deleted]

(b) [deleted]

(B) In the FCA Handbook: (in accordance with section 417(1) of the *Act* (Definitions)) a rule made by the *FCA* or the *PRA* under the *Act*, including:

(a) a *Principle*; and

(b) an *evidential provision*.

rule on use of dealing commission

COBS 11.6.3 R.

running-account credit

(1) (except in *CONC*) (in accordance with section 10(1)(a) of the Consumer Credit Act 1974) a facility under a contract by which the *customer* is enabled to receive from time to time (whether in his own person, or by another person) from the *firm* or a third party cash, goods and services (or any of them) to an amount or value such that, taking into account payments made by or to the credit of the customer, the credit limit (if any) is not at any time exceeded.

(2) (in *CONC*) a facility under a *credit agreement* under which the *borrower* or another *person* is enabled to receive from time to time from the *lender* or a third party *cash*, *goods* or services to an amount or value such that, taking into account *payments* made by or to the credit of the *borrower*, the *credit limit* (if any) is not at any time exceeded.

safe custody investment

a *designated investment*, which is not the property of the *firm*, but for which the *firm*, or any *nominee company* controlled by the *firm* or by its *associate*, is accountable; which has been paid for in full by the *client*; and which ceases to be a *safe custody investment* when the *firm* has disposed of it in accordance with a valid instruction.

safeguarded benefits

has the meaning given in section 48(8) of the Pension Schemes Act 2015 which is benefits other than money purchase benefits and cash balance benefits.

safeguarding and administering investments

(A) In the PRA Handbook: the *regulated activity*, specified in article 40 of the *Regulated Activities Order* (Safeguarding and administering investments), which is in summary: the safeguarding of assets belonging to another and the administration of those assets, or arranging for one or more other *persons* to carry on that activity, where:

(a) the assets consist of or include any *security* or *contractually based investment* (that is, any designated investment, *funeral plan contract* or right to or interest in a *funeral plan contract*); or

(b) the arrangements for their safeguarding and administration are such that the assets may consist of or include *designated investments*, and either the assets have at any time since 1 June 1997 done so, or the arrangements have at any time (whether before or after that date) been held out as ones under which *designated investments* would be safeguarded and administered.

(B) In the FCA Handbook: the *regulated activity*, specified in article 40 of the *Regulated Activities Order* (Safeguarding and administering investments), which is in summary: the safeguarding of assets belonging to another and the administration of those assets, or arranging for one or more other *persons* to carry on that activity, where:

(a) the assets consist of or include any *security* or *contractually based investment* (that is, any designated investment (other than a *P2P agreement*), *funeral plan contract* or right to or interest in a *funeral plan contract*); or

(b) the arrangements for their safeguarding and administration are such that the assets may consist of or include *designated investments* (other than *P2P agreements*), and either the assets have at any time since 1 June 1997 done so, or the arrangements have at any time (whether before or after that date) been held out as ones under which *designated investments* (other than *P2P agreements*) would be safeguarded and administered.

safeguarding and administration of assets (without arranging)

that part of *safeguarding and administering investments* which consists of both:

(a) the safeguarding of assets belonging to another; and

(b) the administration of those assets.

safe custody asset

(a) in relation to *MiFID business*, a *financial instrument*;

(b) in relation to *safeguarding and administering investments* that is not *MiFID business* and/or *acting as trustee or depositary of a UCITS*, a *safe custody investment*;

(c) when *acting as trustee or depositary of an AIF*, an *AIF custodial asset*; or

(d) in relation to *excluded custody activities* carried on by a *small AIFM*, a *safe custody investment*.

sale

(in *COLL*) (in relation to *units* in an *authorised fund*) the sale of *units* by the *authorised fund manager* as *principal*.

sale price

(in *COLL*) the *price* payable to the *authorised fund manager* for each *unit* it *sells* to a *unitholder*, calculated in accordance with COLL 6.3 (Valuation and pricing).

sale shortfall

the outstanding amount due to the *home finance provider*, under a *home finance transaction*, following the sale of the property that is its subject.

same stage of capital

(with respect to a particular item of capital in the *capital resources table*) the stage in the *capital resources table* in which that item of capital appears.

schedule

(in *Part 6 rules*) (as defined in the *PD Regulation*) a list of minimum information requirements adapted to the particular nature of the different types of *issuers* and/or the different *securities* involved.

scheme

(1) (except in *COBS*, *CASS* and *SUP*) a *collective investment scheme*.

(2) (in *COBS*, *CASS* and *SUP*)
(a) a *regulated collective investment scheme*;
(b) an *investment trust* where the relevant *shares* have been, or will be, acquired through an*investment trust savings scheme*;
(c) an *investment trust*, if:
(i) the relevant *shares* will be held in a *wrapper* or *personal pension scheme*; and
(ii) the trust and the *wrapper* or *personal pension scheme* will be promoted together;
(d) (in COBS 18.5) in addition to (a), (b) and (c), an *unregulated collective investment scheme*.

scheme holding

a holding of:

(a) *units* in a *collective investment scheme*; or

(b) *shares* in an *investment trust savings scheme*.

scheme management activity

the management by an *operator* of the property held for or within the *scheme* of which it is the *operator*, excluding the receiving and holding of *client money* and *safeguarding and administering investments*.

scheme of arrangement

(in *COLL*) an arrangement relating to an *authorised fund* ("transferor fund") or to a *sub-fund* of a *scheme* that is an *umbrella* ("transferor *sub-fund*") under which:

(a) either:
(i) all or part of the property of the transferor fund, or all or part of the property attributed to the transferor *sub-fund*, is to become the property of one or more *regulated collective investment schemes* ("transferee *schemes*"); or
(ii) all or part of the property attributed to the transferor *sub-fund* is to become part of the property attributed to one or more other *sub-funds* of the same *umbrella* ("transferee *sub-funds*"); and

(b) holders of *units* in the transferor fund or transferor *sub-fund*, the property of which is being transferred or reattributed under (a), are to receive, in exchange for their respective interests in that property, either:
(i) *units* in the transferee *scheme* or one or more of the transferee *schemes*, to which the property is transferred; or
(ii) *units* in the transferee *sub-fund* or one or more of the transferee *sub-funds*, to which the property is reattributed.
This arrangement includes an arrangement that constitutes a *domestic UCITS merger* or a *cross-border UCITS merger*.

scheme of operations

a scheme which:

(a) describes the nature of the risks which the *insurer* is underwriting, or intends to underwrite, and the guiding principles which it intends to follow in reinsuring or covering those risks; and

(b) contains the information required under SUP App 2.12.1 R (Content of a scheme of operations).

scheme particulars

a *document* containing information about a *regulated collective investment scheme*.

scheme pension

a scheme pension, as defined in paragraph 2 of Schedule 28 to the Finance Act 2004, which is in summary a pension payable until a pension scheme member's death, or until the later of the member's death and the end of a term not exceeding 10 years.

scheme property

(a) (in relation to an *ICVC*) the property subject to the *collective investment scheme* constituted by it;

(b) (in relation to an *AUT* or *ACS*) the *capital property* and the *income property*.

scheme report

(in SUP 18) the report on the terms of an *insurance business transfer scheme* required by section 109 of the *Act* (Scheme reports).

scientific research based company

(in *LR*) a *company* primarily involved in the laboratory research and development of chemical or biological products or processes or any other similar innovative science based company.

SCLG

the Office of Fair Trading's Second Charge Lending Guidance.

scope of basic advice

the basis on which a *firm* gives *basic advice* on *stakeholder products*, that is, with reference to the *stakeholder products* of one, or more than one, *stakeholder product* provider.

scope of advice, scope

the basis on which *personal recommendations* on *packaged products* is given by a *firm*, that is, one of the following:

(1) the whole market (or the whole of a named sector of the market); or

(2) a limited number of *product providers*; or

(3) a single *company* or single group of *companies*.

References to a *firm's* scope of *personal recommendations* of *packaged products* include, where the context requires, a reference to the scope of *personal recommendations* of the *firm's appointed representatives* or, where applicable, *tied agent*.

SCV implementation report

(in *COMP*) a report in accordance with COMP 17.3.6 R explaining how the relevant *firm* has satisfied the *PRA's SCV requirements*.

SCV report

(in *COMP*) a report in accordance with COMP 17.3.9 R from the relevant *firm's* board of directors confirming that the *firm's SCV system* satisfies the *PRA's SCV requirements*.

SCV system

(in *COMP*) a *firm's* system for satisfying the *PRA's SCV requirements*.

SDL

(in *BSOCS*) the total of share and deposit liabilities, excluding amounts that qualify as *own funds* but including accrued interest not yet payable.

SDRT provision

a *charge* of such amount or at such rate as is determined by the *authorised fund manager* to be made as a provision for stamp duty reserve tax for which the *ICVC* may become liable under the Stamp Duty and Stamp Duty Reserve Tax (Open-Ended Investment Companies) (Amendment No 2) Regulations 2000 or the *trustee* may become liable under Schedule 19 to the Finance Act 1999 in respect of a surrender of *units* to the *authorised fund manager*.

Second Life Directive

the Council Directive of 8 November 1990 on the coordination of laws, etc and laying down provisions relating to facilitate the effective exercise of freedom to provide services and amending Directive 79/267/EEC (No 90/619/EEC).

Second Non-Life Directive

the Council Directive of 22 June 1988 on the coordination of laws, etc and laying down provisions to facilitate the effective exercise of freedom to provide services and amending Directive 73/239/EEC (No 88/357/EEC).

secondary material

(as more fully described in section 394 of the *Act* (Access to FCA or PRA material)) material, other than that which the *appropriate regulator* relied on in reaching its decision, which:

(a) the *appropriate regulator* considered in reaching its decision; or

(b) the *appropriate regulator* obtained in connection with, that is, in the investigation of, the matter in question.

secondary pooling event

(1) [deleted]

(2) (in CASS 5) an event that occurs in the circumstances described in CASS 5.6.14 R (Failure of a bank, other broker or settlement agent: secondary pooling events).

(3) (in CASS 7 and CASS 7A) an event that occurs in the circumstances described in CASS 7A.3.1R (Failure of a bank, intermediate broker, settlement agent or OTC counterparty: secondary pooling events).

(4) (in CASS 11) an event that occurs in the circumstances described in CASS 11.13.10 R.

section 43 capital requirements

the financial supervision requirements of the *FSA* for the purposes of the listing arrangements made under section 43 of the Financial Services Act 1986.

section 178 notice

(in accordance with section 178(3) of the *Act*) a notice given to the *appropriate regulator* under section 178 of the *Act*.

sectoral rules

(A) In the PRA Handbook:

(in relation to a *financial sector*) rules and requirements relating to the prudential supervision of *regulated entities* applicable to *regulated entities* in that *financial sector* as follows:

(a) (for the purposes of GENPRU 3.1.12 R (Definition of financial conglomerate: Solvency requirement)) *EEA prudential sectoral legislation* for that *financial sector* together with as appropriate the rules and requirements in (c); or

(b) (for the purpose of calculating *solo capital resources* a *solo capital resources requirement* and *regulatory surplus value*):

(i) (to the extent provided for in paragraphs 6.4 to 6.6 of GENPRU 3 Annex 1R) rules and requirements that are referred to in hose paragraphs; and

(ii) the rules and requirements in (c); or

(c) (for all other purposes) rules and requirements of the *appropriate regulator*

and so that:

(d) (in relation to prudential rules about consolidated supervision for any *financial sector*) those requirements include ones relating to the form and extent of consolidation;

(e) (in relation to any *financial sector*) those requirements include ones relating to the eligibility of different types of capital;

(f) (in relation to any *financial sector*) those requirements include both ones applying on a solo basis and ones applying on a consolidated basis;

(g) (in relation to the *insurance sector*) references in this definition to consolidated supervision are to supplementary supervision, similar expressions being interpreted accordingly; and

(h) references to the appropriate regulator's *sectoral rules* are to *sectoral rules* in the form of *rules*.

(B) In the FCA Handbook:

(in relation to a *financial sector*) rules and requirements relating to the prudential supervision of *regulated entities* applicable to *regulated entities* in that *financial sector* as follows:

(a) (for the purposes of GENPRU 3.1.12 R (Definition of financial conglomerate: Solvency requirement)) *EEA prudential sectoral legislation* for that *financial sector* together with as appropriate the rules and requirements in (c); or

(b) (for the purpose of calculating *solo capital resources* a *solo capital resources requirement* and *regulatory surplus value*):

(i) (to the extent provided for in paragraphs 6.4 to 6.6 of GENPRU 3 Annex 1R) rules and requirements that are referred to in hose paragraphs; and

(ii) the rules and requirements in (c); or

(c) (for all other purposes) rules and requirements of the *appropriate regulator*

and so that:

(d) (in relation to consolidated supervision for any *financial sector*) those requirements include ones relating to the form and extent of consolidation;

(e) (in relation to any *financial sector*) those requirements include ones relating to the eligibility of different types of capital;

(f) (in relation to any *financial sector*) those requirements include both ones applying on a solo basis and ones applying on a consolidated basis;

(g) (in relation to the *insurance sector*) references in this definition to consolidated supervision are to supplementary supervision, similar expressions being interpreted accordingly; and

(h) references to the appropriate regulator's *sectoral rules* are to *sectoral rules* in the form of *rules* and, as applicable, the *EU CRR*.

secured debt

a debt fully secured on:

(a) assets whose value at least equals the amount of debt; or

(b) a letter of credit or guarantee from an *approved counterparty*.

secured lending

lending where the *mortgage lender* takes security on land for the loan provided to the *customer*.

secured lending transaction

(in accordance with point 2 of Part 1 of Annex VIII of the *Banking Consolidation Directive* (Eligibility of credit risk mitigation) and for the purposes of *BIPRU*) any transaction giving rise to an *exposure* secured by collateral which does not include a provision conferring upon the *person* with the *exposure* the right to receive margin frequently.

securities and futures firm

(A) In the PRA Handbook:

a *firm* whose *permitted activities* include *designated investment business* or *bidding in emissions auctions*, which is not an *authorised professional firm*, bank, *BIPRU firm* (unless it is an *exempt BIPRU commodities firm*), *IFPRU investment firm* (unless it is an exempt IFPRU investment firm), *building society*, *collective portfolio management firm*, *credit union*, *friendly society*, *ICVC*, *insurer*, *media firm*, *service company*, *incoming EEA firm* (without a *top-up permission*), *incoming Treaty firm* (without a *top-up permission*) or *UCITS qualifier* (without a *top-up permission*), whose permission does not include a *requirement* that it comply with IPRU(INV) 5 (Investment management firms) or 13 (Personal investment firms), and which is within (a), (b), (c), (d), (e), (f), (g), (ga) or (h):

(a) a *firm* (other than one falling within (d)):

(i) which was a member of *SFA* immediately before *commencement*; and

(ii) which was not, immediately before *commencement*, subject to the financial supervision requirements of the *FSA* (under section 43 of the Financial Services Act 1986), or *PIA* or *IMRO* (under lead regulation arrangements);

(b) a *firm* whose *permission* includes a *requirement* that it comply with IPRU(INV) 3 (Securities and futures firms);

(c) a *firm*:

(i) which was given a *Part 4A permission* after *commencement*, or which was authorised under section 25 of the Financial Services Act 1986 immediately before commencement and not a member of *IMRO*, *PIA* or *SFA*; and

(ii) for which the most substantial part of its gross income (including commissions) from the *designated investment business* included in its *Part 4A permission* is derived from one or more of the following activities (based, for a *firm* given a *Part 4A permission* after *commencement*, on the business plan submitted as part of the *firm's* application for *permission* or, for a *firm* authorised under section 25 of the Financial Services Act 1986, on the *firm's financial year* preceding its *authorisation* under the *Act*):

(A) an activity carried on as a member of an exchange;

(B) making a market in *securities* or *derivatives*;

(C) *corporate finance business*;

(D) *dealing* (excluding, in the case of a *home finance provider*, *dealing as principal* in *contractually based investments* where this activity is carried out for risk management purposes and would have been excluded under article 16 of the *Regulated Activities Order* if the *firm* were an *unauthorised person* or under article 19 of the *Regulated Activities Order*), *arranging (bringing about) deals in investments* or *making arrangements with a view to transactions in investments*, in *securities* or *derivatives*;

(E) the provision of clearing services as a *clearing firm*;

(F) *managing investments*, where those *investments* are primarily *derivatives*;

(G) activities relating to *spread bets*;

(d) a *firm* that is:

(i) an ex-section 43 firm which was not authorised under the Financial Services Act 1986 immediately before *commencement*; or

(ii) an ex-section 43 lead regulated firm;

(e) an *energy market participant*;

(f) an *oil market participant*;

(g) an *exempt BIPRU commodities firm*;

(ga) an *exempt IFPRU commodities firm*;

(h) a *firm* that is exempt from *MiFID* under article 2(1)(i) whose *permitted activities* include *bidding in emissions auctions*.

(B) In the FCA Handbook:

a *firm* whose *permitted activities* include *designated investment business* or *bidding in emissions auctions*, which is not an *authorised professional firm*, bank, *BIPRU firm* (unless it is an *exempt BIPRU commodities firm*), *IFPRU investment firm* (unless it is an exempt IFPRU investment firm), *building society*, *collective portfolio management firm*, *credit union*, *friendly society*, *ICVC*, *insurer*, *media firm*, *service company*, *incoming EEA firm* (without a *top-up permission*), *incoming Treaty firm* (without a *top-up permission*) or *UCITS qualifier* (without a *top-up permission*), whose permission does not include a *requirement* that it comply with IPRU(INV) 5 (Investment management firms) or 13 (Personal investment firms), and which is within (a), (b), (c), (d), (e), (f), (g), (ga) or (h):

(a) a *firm* (other than one falling within (d)):

(i) which was a member of *SFA* immediately before *commencement*; and

(ii) which was not, immediately before *commencement*, subject to the financial supervision requirements of the *FSA* (under section 43 of the Financial Services Act 1986), or *PIA* or *IMRO* (under lead regulation arrangements);

(b) a *firm* whose *permission* includes a *requirement* that it comply with IPRU(INV) 3 (Securities and futures firms);

(c) a *firm*:

(i) which was given a *Part 4A permission* after *commencement*, or which was authorised under section 25 of the Financial Services Act 1986 immediately before commencement and not a member of *IMRO*, *PIA* or *SFA*; and

(ii) for which the most substantial part of its gross income (including commissions) from the *designated investment business* included in its *Part 4A permission* is derived from one or more of the following activities (based, for a *firm* given a *Part 4A permission* after *commencement*, on the business plan submitted as part of the *firm's* application for *permission* or, for a *firm* authorised under section 25 of the Financial Services Act 1986, on the *firm's financial year* preceding its *authorisation* under the *Act*):

(A) an activity carried on as a member of an exchange;

(B) making a market in *securities* or *derivatives*;

(C) *corporate finance business*;

(D) *dealing* (excluding, in the case of a *home finance provider*, *dealing as principal* in *contractually based investments* where this activity is carried out for risk management purposes and would have been excluded under article 16 of the *Regulated Activities Order* if the *firm* were an *unauthorised person* or under article 19 of the *Regulated Activities Order*), *arranging (bringing about) deals in investments* or *making arrangements with a view to transactions in investments*, in *securities* or *derivatives*;

(E) the provision of clearing services as a *clearing firm*;

(F) *managing investments*, where those *investments* are primarily *derivatives*;

(G) activities relating to *spread bets*;

(d) a *firm* that is:

(i) an ex-section 43 firm which was not authorised under the Financial Services Act 1986 immediately before *commencement*; or

(ii) an ex-section 43 lead regulated firm;

(e) an *energy market participant*;

(f) an *oil market participant*;

(g) an *exempt BIPRU commodities firm*;

(ga) an *exempt IFPRU commodities firm*;

(h) a *firm* that is exempt from *MiFID* under article 2(1)(i) whose *permitted activities* include *bidding in emissions auctions*.

securities derivative

a *derivative* instrument *admitted to trading* on a *regulated market* or *prescribed market*, the value of which is dependent on an underlying equity or debt instrument or index/basket of equity or debt instruments.

securities financing transaction

(1) (in *COBS*, in *CASS*) an instance of stock lending or stock borrowing or the lending or borrowing of other *financial instruments*, a repurchase or reverse repurchase transaction, or a buy-sell back or sell-buy back transaction. [Note: article 2(10) of the *MiFID Regulation*]

(2) (in any other case) any of the following:

(a) a *repurchase transaction*; or

(b) a *securities or commodities lending or borrowing transaction*; or

(c) a *margin lending transaction*.

securities issued in a continuous and repeated manner

(in *PR*) (as defined in Article 2.1(l) of the *prospectus directive*) issues on tap or at least two separate issues of securities of a similar type and/or class over a period of 12 months.

securities note

(in *Part 6 rules*) a securities note referred to in PR 2.2.2 R.

securities or commodities borrowing

see *securities or commodities lending or borrowing transaction*.

securities or commodities lending

see *securities or commodities lending or borrowing transaction*.

securities or commodities lending or borrowing transaction

(A) In the PRA Handbook:

(in accordance with Article 4(34) of the *Banking Consolidation Directive* and Article 3(1)(n) of the *Capital Adequacy Directive* (Definitions) and for the purposes of *BIPRU*) any transaction in which an *undertaking* or its counterparty transfers securities or *commodities* against appropriate collateral subject to a commitment that the borrower will return equivalent securities or *commodities* at some future date or when requested to do so by the transferor, that transaction being *securities or commodities lending* for the *undertaking* transferring the securities or *commodities* and being *securities or commodities borrowing* for the *undertaking* to which they are transferred.

(B) In the FCA Handbook:

(in accordance with Article 4(34) of the *Banking Consolidation Directive* and Article 3(1)(n) of the *Capital Adequacy Directive* (Definitions) and for the purposes of *BIPRU*) any transaction in which an *undertaking* or its counterparty transfers securities or *commodities* against appropriate collateral subject to a commitment that the borrower will return equivalent securities or *commodities* at some future date or when requested to do so by the transferor, that transaction being *securities or commodities lending* for the *undertaking* transferring the securities or *commodities* and being *securities or commodities borrowing* for the *undertaking* to which they are transferred.

securities PRR

the *interest rate PRR*, the *equity PRR*, the *option PRR* (but only in relation to *positions* which under BIPRU 7.6.5 R (Table: Appropriate calculation for an option or warrant) may be subject to one of the other *PRR* charges listed in this definition or which would be subject to such a *PRR* charge if BIPRU 7.6.5 R did not require an *option PRR* to be calculated), the *CIU PRR* and the *PRR* calculated under BIPRU 7.11 (Credit derivatives in the trading book) and so that:

(a) the *securities PRR* includes any *PRR charge* calculated under a *CAD 1 permission*; and

(b) the *securities PRR* does not include any *PRR charge* calculated under a *VaR model permission* unless the provision in question provides otherwise.

securitisation

(1) (subject to (2)) a process by which assets are sold to a bankruptcy-remote *special purpose vehicle* in return for immediate cash payment and that vehicle raises the immediate cash payment through the issue of debt securities in the form of tradable notes or commercial paper.

(2) (in accordance with Article 4(36) of the *Banking Consolidation Directive* (Definitions), in *BIPRU* and MIPRU 4) a transaction or scheme whereby the credit risk associated with an *exposure* or pool of *exposures* is *tranched* having the following characteristics:
(a) payments in the transaction or scheme are dependent upon the performance of the *exposure* or pool of *exposures*; and
(b) the subordination of *tranches* determines the distribution of *losses* during the ongoing life of the transaction or scheme.

(A) In the PRA Handbook:
(1) (subject to (2)) a process by which assets are sold to a bankruptcy-remote special purpose vehicle in return for immediate cash payment and that vehicle raises the immediate cash payment through the issue of debt securities in the form of tradable notes or commercial paper.
(2) (in accordance with Article 4(36) of the Banking Consolidation Directive (Definitions) and in *BIPRU* and MIPRU 4) a transaction or scheme whereby the credit risk associated with an *exposure* or pool of *exposures* is tranched having the following characteristics:
(a) payments in the transaction or scheme are dependent upon the performance of the *exposure* or pool of *exposures*; and
(b) the subordination of *tranches* determines the distribution of *losses* during the ongoing life of the transaction or scheme.

(B) In the FCA Handbook:
(1) (subject to (2) and (3)) a process by which assets are sold to a bankruptcy-remote special purpose vehicle in return for immediate cash payment and that vehicle raises the immediate cash payment through the issue of debt securities in the form of tradable notes or commercial paper.
(2) (in accordance with Article 4(36) of the Banking Consolidation Directive (Definitions) and in *BIPRU* and MIPRU 4) a transaction or scheme whereby the credit risk associated with an *exposure* or pool of *exposures* is tranched having the following characteristics:
(a) payments in the transaction or scheme are dependent upon the performance of the *exposure* or pool of *exposures*; and
(b) the subordination of *tranches* determines the distribution of *losses* during the ongoing life of the transaction or scheme.
(3) (in *IFPRU*) has the meaning in article 4(1)(61) of the *EU CRR*.

securitised derivative

an *option* or *contract for differences* which, in either case, is *listed* under LR 19of the listing *rules* (including such an *option* or *contract for differences* which is also a *debenture*).

securitisation position

(A) In the PRA Handbook:
(in accordance with Article 4(40) (Definitions) and Article 96 (Securitisation) of the *Banking Consolidation Directive* and for the purposes of *BIPRU*) an *exposure* to a *securitisation* within the meaning of paragraph (2) of the definition of securitisation; and so that:
(a) where there is an *exposure* to different *tranches* in a *securitisation*, the *exposure* to each *tranche* must be considered as a separate *securitisation position*;
(b) the providers of credit protection to *securitisation positions* must be considered to hold positions in the *securitisation*; and
(c) *securitisation positions* include *exposures* to a *securitisation* arising from interest rate or currency derivative contracts.

(B) In the FCA Handbook:
(1) (in *GENPRU*, *MIPRU* and *BIPRU*) (in accordance with Article 4(40) (Definitions) and Article 96 (Securitisation) of the *Banking Consolidation Directive*) an *exposure* to a *securitisation* within the meaning of paragraph (2) of the definition of securitisation; and so that:
(a) where there is an *exposure* to different *tranches* in a *securitisation*, the *exposure* to each *tranche* must be considered as a separate *securitisation position*;
(b) the providers of credit protection to *securitisation positions* must be considered to hold positions in the *securitisation*; and
(c) *securitisation positions* include *exposures* to a *securitisation* arising from interest rate or currency derivative contracts.
(2) (in *IFPRU*) has the meaning in article 4(1)(62) of the *EU CRR*.

securitisation special purpose entity

(A) In the PRA Handbook:
(in accordance with Article 4(44) of the *Banking Consolidation Directive* (Definitions) and for the purposes of *BIPRU*) a corporation, trust or other entity, other than a *credit institution*, organised for carrying on a *securitisation* or *securitisations* (within the meaning of paragraph (2) of the definition of securitisation), the activities of which are limited to those appropriate to accomplishing that objective, the structure of which is intended to isolate the obligations of the *SSPE* from those of the *originator*, and the holders of the beneficial interests in which have the right to pledge or exchange those interests without restriction.

(B) In the FCA Handbook:
(1) (in accordance with Article 4(44) of the *Banking Consolidation Directive* (Definitions) and for the purposes of *BIPRU*) a corporation, trust or other entity, other than a *credit institution*, organised for carrying on a *securitisation* or *securitisations* (within the meaning of paragraph (2) of the definition of securitisation), the activities of which are limited to those appropriate to accomplishing that objective, the structure of which is intended to isolate the obligations of the *SSPE* from those of the *originator*, and the holders of the beneficial interests in which have the right to pledge or exchange those interests without restriction.
(2) (in *MIPRU*) a corporation, trust or other entity that has the following characteristics:
(a) it is organised for carrying on a *securitisation* or *securitisations* (within the meaning of paragraph (2) of the definition of securitisation);
(b) its activities are limited to those appropriate to accomplishing such *securitisation* or *securitisations*; and
(c) its structure is intended to isolate its obligations from those of the *originator*.

securitised exposure

(A) In the PRA Handbook:
(for the purposes of *BIPRU*) an *exposure* in the pool of *exposures* that has been securitised, either via a *traditional securitisation* or a *synthetic securitisation*. The cash-flows generated by the securitised exposures are used to make payments to the *securitisation positions*.

(B) In the FCA Handbook:
(for the purposes of *BIPRU* and *MIPRU*) an *exposure* in the pool of *exposures* that has been securitised, either via a *traditional securitisation* or a *synthetic securitisation*. The cash-flows generated by the securitised exposures are used to make payments to the *securitisation positions*.

security

(A) In the PRA Handbook:
(in accordance with article 3(1) of the Regulated Activities Order (Interpretation)) any of the following investments specified in that Order:

Part 3 FCA Handbook Materials

(a) *share* (article 76);

(b) *debenture* (article 77);

(ba) *alternative debenture* (article 77A);

(c) *government and public security* (article 78);

(d) *warrant* (article 79);

(e) *certificate representing certain securities* (article 80);

(f) *unit* (article 81);

(g) *stakeholder pension scheme* (article 82(1));

(ga) *personal pension scheme* (article 82(2));

(h) *rights to or interests in investments* in (a) to (g) (article 89).

(B) In the FCA Handbook

(1) (except in *LR* and *CONC*) (in accordance with article 3(1) of the *Regulated Activities Order* (Interpretation)) any of the following *investments* specified in that Order:

(a) *share* (article 76);

(b) *debenture* (article 77);

(ba) *alternative debenture* (article 77A);

(c) *government and public security* (article 78);

(d) *warrant* (article 79);

(e) *certificate representing certain securities* (article 80);

(f) *unit* (article 81);

(g) *stakeholder pension scheme* (article 82(1));

(ga) *personal pension scheme* (article 82(2));

(h) *rights to or interests in investments* in (a) to (g) (article 89).

(2) (in *LR*) (in accordance with section 102A of the *Act*) anything which has been, or may be admitted to the *official list*.

(3) (in *CONC*) in accordance with article 60L of the *Regulated Activities Order*, in relation to a *credit agreement* or a *consumer hire agreement*, a mortgage, charge, pledge, bond, debenture, indemnity, guarantee, bill, note or other right provided by the *borrower* or *hirer* or at the implied or express request of the *borrower* or *hirer* to secure the carrying out of the obligations of the *borrower* or *hirer* under the agreement.

security-based CTF

a *CTF*, other than a *stakeholder CTF*, which is not limited to *deposit* based investment.

segregated client

a *client* whose *money* must be segregated by the *firm* under CASS 4.3.3 R (Segregation).

self-certified sophisticated investor

a *person* who meets the requirements set out in article 23A of the Promotion of Collective Investment Schemes Order, in article 50A of the Financial Promotions Order or in COBS 4.12.8 R.

self-invested personal pension scheme

an arrangement which forms all or part of a *personal pension scheme*, which gives the member the power to direct how some or all of the member's contributions are invested.

sell

(in accordance with article 3(1) of the *Regulated Activities Order* (Interpretation)) (in relation to any *investment*) sell in any way, including disposing of the *investment* for valuable consideration; in this definition, "disposing" includes:

(a) (in relation to an *investment* consisting of rights under a contract):

(i) surrendering, assigning or converting those rights; or

(ii) assuming the corresponding liabilities under the contract;

(b) (in relation to an *investment* consisting of rights under other arrangements) assuming the corresponding liabilities under the arrangements; and

(c) (except in *COLL*) (in relation to any other *investment*) issuing or creating the *investment* or granting the rights or interests of which it consists.

sending dematerialised instructions

the *regulated activity*, specified in article 45(1) of the *Regulated Activities Order*, of sending, on behalf of another *person*, dematerialised instructions relating to a *security*, where those instructions are sent by means of a relevant system in respect of which an operator is approved under the 2001 Regulations; in this definition:

(a) "the 2001 Regulations" means the Uncertificated Securities Regulations 2001 (SI 2001/3755);

(b) "dematerialised instruction" and "operator" have the meaning given by regulation 3 of the 2001 Regulations.

senior management

(A) In the PRA Handbook:

(in BIPRU 7.10 (Use of a value at risk model) and in relation to a *firm*) the *firm's governing body* and those of the firm's *senior managers* and other senior management who have responsibilities relating to the measurement and control of the risks which the *firm's VaR model* is designed to measure or whose responsibilities require them to take into account those risks.

(B) In the FCA Handbook:

(1) (in BIPRU 7.10 (Use of a value at risk model) and in relation to a *firm*) the *firm's governing body* and those of the firm's *senior managers* and other senior management who have responsibilities relating to the measurement and control of the risks which the *firm's VaR model* is designed to measure or whose responsibilities require them to take into account those risks.

(2) (in *SYSC* and *IFPRU* and in accordance with article 3(9) of *CRD*) those *persons* who are a natural person and who exercise executive functions in an *institution* and who are responsible and accountable to the *management body* for the day-to-day management of the *institution*.

senior manager

an individual other than a *director*:

(a) who is employed by:

(i) a *firm*; or

(ii) a *body corporate* within a *group* of which the *firm* is a member;

(b) to whom the *governing body* of the *firm*, or a member of the *governing body* of the *firm*, has given responsibility, either alone or jointly with others, for management and supervision;

(c) who, if the individual is employed by the *firm*, reports directly to:

(i) the *governing body*; or

(ii) a member of the *governing body*; or

(iii) the *chief executive*; or

(iv) the head of a significant business unit; and

(d) who, if the individual is employed by a *body corporate* within the *group*, reports directly to a *person* who is the equivalent of a body or *person* referred to in (c).

senior personnel

(1) those *persons* who effectively direct the business of the *firm*, which could include a *firm's governing body* and other *persons* who effectively direct the business of the *firm*.

(2) (in relation to a *management company* and in accordance with article 3(4) of the *UCITS implementing Directive*) the *person* or *persons* who effectively conduct the business of the *management company*.

senior staff committee

(in *DEPP* and *EG*) a committee consisting of senior *FCA* staff members that is empowered to make *statutory notice decisions* and *statutory notice associated decisions* by *executive procedures*.

series of transactions

a series of transactions *executed* with a view to achieving one investment decision or objective.

SERV

the Handbook Guide for service companies.

service company

a *firm* whose only *permitted activities* are *making arrangements with a view to transactions in investments*, and *agreeing to carry on that regulated activity*, and whose *Part 4A permission*:

(a) incorporates a *limitation* substantially to the effect that the *firm* carry on *regulated activities* only with *market counterparties* or *intermediate customers*; and

(b) includes *requirements* substantially to the effect that the *firm* must not:

(i) guarantee, or otherwise accept responsibility for, the performance, by a participant in arrangements made by the *firm* in carrying on *regulated activities*, of obligations undertaken by that participant in connection with those arrangements; or

(ii) *approve* any *financial promotion* on behalf of any other *person* or any specified class of *persons*; or

(iii) in carrying on its *regulated activities*, provide services otherwise than in accordance with *documents* (of a kind specified in the *requirement*) provided by the *firm* to the *FCA*.

Part 3   FCA Handbook Materials

service conditions

(in accordance with paragraph 14 of Schedule 3 to the *Act* (EEA Passport Rights)) the conditions that:

(a) the *firm* has given its *Home State regulator* notice of its intent to provide services in the *United Kingdom*;

(b) if the *firm* falls within paragraph (a), (d), (e) or (f) in the definition of *"EEA firm"*, the *FCA* or the *PRA* (as the case may be) has received notice from the *firm's Home State regulator* containing such information as may be prescribed;

(c) if the *firm* falls within paragraph (d) of that definition, its *Home State regulator* has informed it that the regulator's notice has been sent to the *FCA* or the *PRA* (as the case may be); and

(d) if the *firm* falls within paragraph (e) of that definition, one *month* has elapsed beginning with the date on which the *firm's Home State regulator* informed the *firm* that it had sent the regulator's notice to the *FCA* or the *PRA* (as the case may be).

services and costs disclosure document

information about the breadth of advice or *scope of basic advice* and the nature and costs of the services offered by a *firm* as described in COBS 6.3.7 G, which contains the keyfacts logo, headings and text described in COBS 6 Annex 1.

SETS

the Stock Exchange Electronic Trading Service.

settlement account

an account containing *money* and/or assets that is held with a *central bank*, central securities depository, *central counterparty* or any other institution acting as a *settlement agent*, which is used to settle transactions between participants or members of a *commercial settlement system*.

settlement agent

a *person* with or through whom the *firm* effects settlement of *UK*-settled or foreign-settled transactions.

settlement decision makers

(in *DEPP* and *EG*) two members of the *FCA's* senior management, one of whom will be of at least director of division level (which may include an acting director) and the other of whom will be of at least head of department level, with responsibility for deciding whether to give *statutory notices* in the circumstances described in DEPP 5. At least one of the decision makers will not be from the Enforcement and Financial Crime Division.

settlement decision procedure

(in *DEPP*) the procedure for the making of *statutory notice decisions* in the circumstances described in DEPP 5.

settlement discount scheme

(in *DEPP* and *EG*) the scheme described in DEPP 6.7 by which the financial penalty that might otherwise be payable, or the length of the period of suspension or restriction that might otherwise be imposed, in respect of a *person's* misconduct or contravention may be reduced to reflect the timing of any settlement agreement.

Settlement Finality Directive

Directive 98/26/EC of the European Parliament and of the Council of 19 May 1998 on settlement finality in payment and securities settlement systems.

settlement price

(in *LR*) (in relation to *securitised derivatives*), the reference price or prices of the *underlying instrument* or instruments stipulated by the *issuer* for the purposes of calculating its obligations to the holder.

Seventh Company Law Directive

the Council Directive of 13 June 1983 on consolidated accounts (No 83/349/EEC).

SFA

the Securities and Futures Authority Limited.

SFA Complaints Bureau

the first stage of the *SFA scheme*, which aimed to resolve complaints by conciliation.

SFA Consumer Arbitration Scheme

the second stage of the *SFA scheme*, which determined complaints by means of arbitration.

SFA scheme

the *former scheme* (including the *SFA Complaints Bureau* and the *SFA Consumer Arbitration Scheme*) set up by the *SFA* to handle complaints against members of the *SFA* under the Financial Services Act 1986.

SFT

securities financing transaction.

shadow director

(in *LR*) as in sub-paragraph (b) of the definition of director in section 417(1) of the *Act*.

share

(1) (except in *COLL, LR, DTR, REC, SUP* 11 (Controllers and close links) and *SUP* 16 (Reporting requirements)) the *investment*, specified in article 76 of the *Regulated Activities Order* (Shares etc), which is in summary: a share or stock in the share capital of:
(a) any *body corporate* (wherever incorporated);
(b) any unincorporated body constituted under the law of a country or territory outside the *United Kingdom*.

(2) (in *COLL*):
(a) (in relation to an *ICVC*) a *share* in the *ICVC* (including both *smaller denomination shares* and *larger denomination shares*);
(b) (otherwise) an *investment* within (1).

(3) (in *DTR* and *LR*, and in *FEES* where relevant to *DTR* or *LR*) (in accordance with section 540(1) of the Companies Act 2006) a share in the share capital of a *company*, and includes:
(a) stock (except where a distinction between shares and stock is express or implied);
(b) *preference shares*; and
(c) in chapters 4, 5, 6 and 7 of *DTR* a convertible share.

(4) (in *REC*) shares admitted to trading on a *regulated market*.

(5) (in *SUP* 11 (Controllers and close links) and *SUP* 16 (Reporting requirements)) (in accordance with section 422 of the *Act*):
(a) in relation to an *undertaking* with share capital, allotted shares;
(b) in relation to an *undertaking* with capital but no share capital, rights to share in the capital of the *undertaking*;
(c) in relation to an *undertaking* without capital, interests:
(i) conferring any right to share in the profits, or liability to contribute to the losses, of the *undertaking*; or
(ii) giving rise to an obligation to contribute to the debts or expenses of the *undertaking* in the event of a winding up.

shared appreciation mortgage

a *regulated mortgage contract*, a condition of which is that the *mortgage lender* will receive a share in any increase in value in the mortgaged property when the *customer* either sells the property or terminates the contract including a contract where, if there is a reduction in value, the *customer* is required to pay the *mortgage lender* all or part of the shortfall.

shareholder

(1) (in relation to an *ICVC*):

(a) (in relation to a *share* that is represented by a *bearer certificate*) the *person* who holds the certificate;

(b) (in relation to a *share* that is not represented by a *bearer certificate*) the *person* whose name is entered on the *register* in relation to that *share*.

(2) (in relation to chapters 5 [ ] of *DTR*) any natural person or legal entity governed by private or public law, who holds directly or indirectly:

(a) *shares* of the *issuer* in its own name and on its own account;

(b) *shares* of the *issuer* in its own name, but on behalf of another natural person or legal entity;

(c) depository receipts, in which case the holder of the depository receipt shall be considered as the shareholder of the underlying *shares* represented by the depository receipts.

Shari'ah compliant firm

a *firm* whose entire operations are structured and conducted in accordance with Islamic commercial jurisprudence and its investment principles.

ships

(in relation to a *class* of *contract of insurance*) the *class* of *contract of insurance*, specified in paragraph 6 of Part I of Schedule 1 to the *Regulated Activities Order* (Contracts of general insurance), upon vessels used on the sea or on inland water, or upon the machinery, tackle, furniture or equipment of such vessels.

shortfall

(A) In the PRA Handbook:

(1) (in relation to cancellation of an *investment agreement*) the amount a *firm* is entitled to charge a *customer* for the market loss in accordance with COBS 15.4.3 R.

(2) (in relation to *client money*) the amount by which the *client money* in a *client bank account* is insufficient to satisfy the claims of *clients* in respect of that *money*, or not immediately available to satisfy such claims.

(B) In FCA Handbook:

(1) (in relation to cancellation of an *investment agreement*) the amount a *firm* is entitled to charge a *customer* for the market loss in accordance with COBS 15.4.3 R.

(2) (in relation to *client money*) the amount by which the *client money* in a *client bank account* is insufficient to satisfy the claims of *clients* in respect of that *money*, or not immediately available to satisfy such claims.

(3) (in relation to *safe custody assets*) any amount by which the *safe custody assets* held by a *firm* under the *custody rules* fall short of the *firm's* obligations to its *clients* to hold *safe custody assets*.

short selling regulation

regulation (EU) No 236/2012 of the European Parliament and of the Council of 14 March 2012 on short selling and certain aspects of credit default swaps.

short-term annuity

(as defined in paragraph 6 of Schedule 28 to the Finance Act 2004) in relation to a member of a pension scheme, an annuity payable to the member if:

(a) it is purchased by the application of sums or assets representing the whole or any part of the member's drawdown pension fund (as defined in paragraph 8 of that Schedule) in respect of an arrangement;

(b) it is payable by an insurance company;

(c) the member had an opportunity to select an insurance company;

(d) it is payable for a term which does not exceed five years; and

(e) it is either a level annuity, an increasing annuity or a relevant linked annuity.

short-term money market fund

an *authorised fund* or, in the case of an *umbrella*, a *sub-fund* (if it were a separate fund) which satisfies the conditions in COLL 5.9.3 R (Investment conditions: short-term money market funds) and is not a *qualifying money market fund*.

sickness

(in relation to a *class* of *contract of insurance*) the *class* of *contract of insurance*, specified in paragraph 2 of Part I of Schedule 1 to the *Regulated Activities Order* (Contracts of general insurance), providing fixed pecuniary benefits or benefits in the nature of indemnity (or a combination of both) against risks of loss to the *persons* insured attributable to sickness or infirmity, but excluding contracts within paragraph IV of Part II of Schedule 1 to the Regulated Activities Order (Permanent health).

sickness or distressed circumstances contract

any contract in accordance with which benefits are provided for the relief or maintenance of any *person* during sickness or when in distressed circumstances.

SIFA

[deleted]

significant branch

a *branch* that would be considered significant in a *Host State* under article 51(1) of *CRD*. [Note: article 2(1)(34) of *RRD*]

significant distribution

(as defined in Article 2 of the *Buy-back and Stabilisation Regulation*) an initial or secondary *offer* of *relevant securities*, publicly announced and distinct from ordinary trading both in terms of the amount in value of the *securities* offered and the selling methods employed.

significant IFPRU firm

has the meaning in IFPRU 1.2 (Significant IFPRU firm).

significant-influence function

(in accordance with section 59(7B) of the *Act* and in relation to the carrying on of a *regulated activity* by an *authorised person*) a function that is likely to enable the *person* responsible for its performance to exercise a significant influence on the conduct of the *authorised person's* affairs, so far as relating to the activity.

significant management function

(in the *FCA Handbook*) *FCA controlled functions* CF29 in Parts 1 and 2 of the *table of FCA controlled functions*, described more fully in SUP 10A.9.9 R.

simple capital issuer

a *BIPRU firm* that meets the following conditions:

(a) it does not raise capital through a special purpose vehicle;

(b) it only includes non-convertible and non-exchangeable *capital instruments* in its *capital resources*;

(c) (if it includes *capital instruments* in its *capital resources* on which *coupons* are payable) such *coupons* are not subject to a *step-up*;

(d) it only includes *capital instruments* in its *tier one capital resources* consisting of ordinary *shares*, perpetual non-cumulative preference *shares* or partnership or *limited liability partnership* capital accounts;

(e) it only includes non-redeemable *capital instruments* in its *tier one capital resources*; and

(f) (if it includes *capital instruments* in its *tier one capital resources* on which *coupons* are payable) such coupons are non-cumulative, non-mandatory and in cash.

simplified buffer requirement

BIPRU 12.6.9R.

simplified equity method

the method of calculating the *equity PRR* set out in BIPRU 7.3.29 R (Simplified equity method).

simplified ILAS

the approach to the calculation of the liquid assets buffer of a *simplified ILAS BIPRU firm* described in BIPRU 12.6.

simplified ILAS waiver

a waiver permitting an *ILAS BIPRU firm* to operate *simplified ILAS*.

simplified ILAS BIPRU firm

an *ILAS BIPRU firm* that, in accordance with the procedures in BIPRU 12 (Liquidity), is using the *simplified ILAS*.

simplified prospectus

a marketing *document* containing information about a *simplified prospectus scheme*, which complies with COLL 4.6.2R (Production and publication of simplified prospectus) and COLL 4.6.8R (Table: Contents of the simplified prospectus).

simplified prospectus scheme

a *key features scheme* in respect of which a *simplified prospectus* has been, or will be, produced instead of a *key features document* (see COBS 13.1.3R (2)).

single customer view

(in *COMP*) a single, consistent view of an *eligible claimant's* aggregate *protected deposits* with the relevant *firm* which contains the information required by COMP 17.2.4 R, but excluding from that view those accounts where the *eligible claimant* is a beneficiary rather than the account holder or if the account is not active as defined in COMP 17.2.3R (2).

Single Market Directives

(A) In the PRA Handbook:
(a) the *Banking Consolidation Directive* (to the extent it applies to *CAD investment firms*);
(aa) the *CRD*;
(b) the Insurance Directives (within the meaning of paragraph 1 of Schedule 3 to the *Act*);
(ba) the *Reinsurance Directive*;
(c) *MiFID*;
(d) the *Insurance Mediation Directive*;
(e) the *UCITS Directive*; and
(f) *AIFMD*.

(B) In the FCA Handbook:
(a) the *Banking Consolidation Directive* (to the extent it applies to *CAD investment firms*);
(aa) the *CRD*;
(b) the Insurance Directives (within the meaning of paragraph 1 of Schedule 3 to the *Act*);
(ba) the *Reinsurance Directive*;
(c) *MiFID*;
(d) the *Insurance Mediation Directive*;
(e) the *UCITS Directive*; and
(f) *AIFMD*.

single-priced AUT

single-priced authorised fund

an *authorised fund* or, in the case of an *umbrella*, a *sub-fund* (if it were a separate fund), for the *units* of which there is only one *price* applicable by reference to a *valuation point*.

SIPP

a *self-invested personal pension scheme*.

skilled person

a *person* appointed to make a report required by section 166 (Reports by skilled persons) or section 166A (Appointment of skilled person to collect and update information) of the Act for provision to the *appropriate regulator* and who must be a person:

(a) nominated, approved or appointed by the *appropriate regulator*; and

(b) appearing to the *appropriate regulator* to have the skills necessary to make a report on the matter concerned.

SLRP

the *Supervisory Liquidity Review Process*.

small AIFM

an *AIFM* which meets the conditions in regulation 9 (meaning of "small AIFM") of the *AIFMD UK regulation*.

small authorised UK AIFM

a *UK AIFM* which:

(a) is a *small AIFM*; and

(b) has not opted in to *AIFMD* in accordance with article 3(4) of *AIFMD* to become a *full-scope UK AIFM*.

small and medium-sized enterprise

(in *PR*) (as defined in Article 2.1(f) of the *prospectus directive*) companies, which, according to their last annual or consolidated accounts, meet at least two of the following three criteria: an average number of employees during the financial year of less than 250, a total balance sheet not exceeding 43,000,000 and an annual net turnover not exceeding 50,000,000.

small business

(in *COMP*) a *partnership*, *body corporate*, unincorporated association or mutual association with an annual turnover of less than £1 million (or its equivalent in any other currency at the relevant time).

small borrower-lender-supplier agreement

a *borrower-lender-supplier agreement* which is a small agreement within the meaning of section 17 of the *CCA*.

small electronic money institution

(in accordance with regulation 2(1) of the *Electronic Money Regulations*) a person included by the *FCA* in the *Financial Services Register* pursuant to regulation 4(1)(b) of the *Electronic Money Regulations*.

smallest financial sector

(in relation to a *financial sector* in a *consolidation group* or a *financial conglomerate* and in accordance with GENPRU 3.1 (Cross sector groups)) the *financial sector* with the smallest average referred to in the box titled Threshold Test 2 in the *financial conglomerate definition decision tree* (10% ratio of balance sheet size and solvency requirements), the *banking sector* and *investment services sector* being treated as one *financial sector* in the circumstances set out in GENPRU 3.1.

small friendly society function

(1) (in the *FCA Handbook*) *FCA controlled function* CF6 in Part 1 of the *table of FCA controlled functions*, described more fully in SUP 10A.6.31 R to SUP 10A.6.32 R.

(2) (in the *PRA Handbook*) *PRA controlled function* CF6 in the *table of PRA controlled functions*, described more fully in SUP 10B.6.16 R to SUP 10B.6.17 R.

small non-EEA AIFM

a *non-EEA AIFM* that is a *small AIFM*.

small payment institution

(in accordance with regulation 2(1) of the *Payment Services Regulations*) a *person* included by the *FCA* in the *Financial Services Register* pursuant to regulation 4(1)(b) of the *Payment Services Regulations*.

small personal investment firm

a *personal investment firm*:

(a) which is not a *MiFID investment firm*;

(b) whose *permission* does not include *establishing, operating or winding up a personal pension scheme*;

(c) which is not a *network*; and

(d) which has fewer than 26 *representatives*.

small registered UK AIFM

a *small AIFM* that is registered by the *FCA* in accordance with regulation 10 of the *AIFMD UK regulation*.

small self-administered scheme

an *occupational pension scheme* of a kind described in article 4(4) and 4(5) of the Financial Services and Markets Act 2000 (Carrying on Regulated Activities by Way of Business) Order 2001 (SI 2001/1177).

smaller denomination share

a *share* to which are attached rights in a smaller denomination as provided by regulation 45 of the *OEIC regulations*.

smoothed linked long term stakeholder product

the *stakeholder product* specified by regulations 6, 7 and 8 (smoothed linked long term contracts) of the *Stakeholder Regulations*;

specialist investor

(in *LR*) an investor who is particularly knowledgeable in investment matters.

social housing firm

(in MIPRU 4 (Capital resources)) a wholly-owned *subsidiary* of:

(a) a local authority; or

(b) a registered social landlord;

which carries on non-profit *regulated activities* in connection with housing.

social insurance

(in relation to a *class* of *contract of insurance*) the *class* of *contract of insurance*, specified in paragraph IX of Part II of Schedule 1 to the *Regulated Activities Order* (Contracts of long-term insurance), of a kind referred to in article 2(3) of the *Consolidated Life Directive* ("operations relating to the length of human life which are prescribed by or provided for in *social insurance* legislation, when they are effected or managed at their own risk by assurance undertakings in accordance with the laws of an *EEA State*").

Society

(1) The society incorporated by Lloyd's Act 1871 by the name of Lloyd's.

(2) [deleted]

Society GICR

the *general insurance capital requirement* calculated by the *Society* as if it were an *insurer* under GENPRU 2.3.13R.

Society's regulatory functions

the *Society's* powers, duties or functions in relation to *members* or *underwriting agents* which are or may be exercised for the purposes of supervising or regulating the market at Lloyd's.

sole trader

an individual who is a *firm*.

solicited real time financial promotion

(in accordance with article 8 of the *Financial Promotion Order*) a *real time financial promotion* which is solicited, that is, it is made in the course of a personal visit, telephone call or other interactive dialogue if that call, visit or dialogue:

(a) was initiated by the recipient of the *financial promotion*; or

(b) takes place in response to an express request from the recipient of the *financial promotion*.

solo capital resources

(A) In the PRA Handbook:

(1) (for the purposes of GENPRU 3 and INSPRU 6) capital resources that are or would be eligible as capital under the *sectoral rules* that apply for the purpose of calculating its *solo capital resources requirement*. Paragraph 6.8 of GENPRU 3 Ann 1R (Solo capital resources requirement: the insurance sector) applies for the purpose of this definition in the same way as it does for the definition of *solo capital resources requirement*.

(2) for the purpose of BIPRU 10 (Large exposures requirements) the definition in (1) is adjusted in accordance with BIPRU 10.8A.10 R (Calculation of capital resources for a core UK group) so that it means *capital resources* calculated in accordance with the *rules* applicable to the category of *BIPRU firm* identified by applying the procedure in BIPRU 8.6.6 R to BIPRU 8.6.9 R (Consolidated capital resources).

(B) In the FCA Handbook:

(1) (for the purposes of GENPRU 3 and INSPRU 6) capital resources that are or would be eligible as capital under the *sectoral rules* that apply for the purpose of calculating its *solo capital resources requirement*. Paragraph 6.8 of GENPRU 3 Ann 1R (Solo capital resources requirement: the insurance sector) applies for the purpose of this definition in the same way as it does for the definition of *solo capital resources requirement*.

[deleted]

solo capital resources requirement

(1) (for the purpose of GENPRU 3) a capital resources requirement calculated on a solo basis as defined in paragraph 6.2 to 6.7 of GENPRU 3 Ann 1R.

(2) (for the purposes of INSPRU 6) a capital resources requirement calculated on a solo basis as defined in paragraph 6.2 to 6.7 of GENPRU 3 Ann 1R as it would apply if references to *financial conglomerate* in those paragraphs were replaced with references to *insurance group*.

(3) (for the purposes of GENPRU 2.2.214R (Deductions from tiers one and two: Material holdings)) a capital resources requirement calculated on a solo basis as defined in paragraph 6.2 to 6.7 of GENPRU 3 Ann 1R as those paragraphs apply to the *insurance sector*.

solo consolidation waiver

a waiver of the type described in BIPRU 2.1 (Solo consolidation).

solvency deficit

(in GENPRU 3 Ann 1R (Capital adequacy calculations with respect to financial conglomerates) and in respect of a member of the *overall financial sector*) the amount (if any) by which its *solo capital resources* fall short of its *solo capital resources requirement*.

Solvency 1 Directive

the Directive of the European Parliament and of the Council of 5 March 2002 amending Council Directive 79/267/EEC as regards the solvency margin requirements for life assurance undertakings (No. 2002/12/EC).

Solvency II Directive

the Directive of the European Parliament and of the Council of 25 November 2009 on the taking-up and pursuit of the business of Insurance and Reinsurance (No. 2009/138/EC).

sovereign issuer

(as defined in article 2(1)(d) of the *short selling regulation*) any of the following that issues debt instruments:

(a) the *EU*; or

(b) a Member State including a government department, an agency, or a special purpose vehicle of the Member State; or

(c) in the case of a federal Member State, a member of the federation; or

(d) a special purpose vehicle for several Member States; or

(e) an international financial institution established by two or more Member States which has the purpose of mobilising funding and provide financial assistance to the benefit of its members that are experiencing or threatened by severe financing problems; or

(f) the European Investment Bank.

sovereign large exposure waiver

a *waiver* that has the result of requiring the *firm* to apply BIPRU 10.6.35 R, which in summary exempts partially or fully any of the *exposures* listed in BIPRU 10.6.36 R constituting claims on *central banks* or central governments from the limits in BIPRU 10.5 (Limits on exposures).

sovereign, institution and corporate IRB exposure class

(in relation to the *IRB approach*) an *exposure* falling into the *IRB exposure classes* referred to in BIPRU 4.3.2 R (1)-(3) (Sovereigns, institutions and corporates).

special adjustment

(in *IPRU(INV)* 13) a *position* risk adjustment, counterparty risk adjustment and foreign exchange adjustment.

special purpose vehicle

(1) (in *PR*) (as defined in the *PD Regulation*) an *issuer* whose objects and purposes are primarily the issue of *securities*.

(2) (except in *PR*) a *body corporate*, explicitly established for the purpose of securitising assets, whose sole purpose (either generally or when acting in a particular capacity) is to carry out one or more of the following functions:
(a) issuing *designated investments*, other than *life policies*;

(b) redeeming or terminating or repurchasing (whether with a view to re-issue or to cancellation) an issue (in whole or part) of *designated investments*, other than *life policies*;

(c) entering into transactions or terminating transactions involving *designated investments* in connection with the *issue*, redemption, termination or re-purchase of *designated investments*, other than *life policies*;

specialised lending exposure

(in relation to the *IRB approach*) an *exposure* falling into BIPRU 4.5.3 R (Definition of specialised lending).

specialist securities

(in *LR* and *FEES*) *securities* which, because of their nature, are normally bought and traded by a limited number of investors who are particularly knowledgeable in investment matters.

specialist securitised derivative

(in *LR*) a *securitised derivative* which because of its nature is normally bought and traded by a limited number of investors who are particularly knowledgeable in investment matters.

specific costs

management expenses other than *base costs* and *establishment costs*.

specific costs levy

a levy, forming part of the *management expenses levy*, to meet the *specific costs* in the financial year of the *compensation scheme* to which the levy relates, each *participant firm's* share being calculated in accordance with FEES 6.4.7 R.

specific non-real time financial promotion

a *non-real time financial promotion* which identifies and promotes a particular *investment* or service.

specific risk backtesting exception

(in BIPRU 7.10 (Use of a value at risk model) and in relation to a *firm*) an exception arising out of backtesting a *VaR model* with respect to *specific risk* as more fully defined in that *firm's VaR model permission*.

specific risk position risk adjustment

(in *BIPRU*) a *position risk adjustment* for specific risk including any such *position risk adjustment* as applied under BIPRU 7.6.8 R (Table: Appropriate position risk adjustment).

specific wrong-way risk

(in accordance with Part 1 of Annex III of the *Banking Consolidation Directive* (Definitions) and for the purpose of BIPRU 13 (The calculation of counterparty risk exposure values for financial derivatives, securities financing transactions and long settlement transactions)) the risk that arises when the exposure to a particular counterparty is positively correlated with the *probability of default* of the counterparty due to the nature of the transactions with the counterparty; a *firm* is exposed to *specific wrong-way risk* if the future exposure to a specific counterparty is expected to be high when the counterparty's *probability of default* is also high.

specified benchmark

a benchmark as defined in section 22(1A)(b) of the *Act* and specified in Schedule 5 to the *Regulated Activities Order* pursuant to article 63R of the *Regulated Activities Order*

specified investment

(A) In the PRA Handbook: any of the following *investments* specified in Part III of the *Regulated Activities Order* (Specified Investments):

(a) *deposit* (article 74);

(aa) *electronic money* (article 74A);

(b) *contract of insurance* (article 75); for the purposes of the *permission* regime, this is sub-divided into:

(i) *general insurance contract*;
(ii) *long-term insurance contract*;
and then further sub-divided into *classes* of *contract of insurance*;

(c) *share* (article 76);

(d) *debenture* (article 77);

(da) *alternative debenture* (article 77A);

(e) *government and public security* (article 78);

(f) *warrant* (article 79);

(g) *certificate representing certain securities* (article 80);

(h) *unit* (article 81);

(i) *stakeholder pension scheme* (article 82(1));

(ia) *personal pension scheme* (article 82(2));

(j) *option* (article 83); for the purposes of the *permission* regime, this is sub-divided into:
(i) *option* (excluding a *commodity option* and an *option* on a *commodity future*);
(ii) *commodity option* and an *option* on a *commodity future*;

(k) *future* (article 84); for the purposes of the *permission* regime, this is sub-divided into:
(i) *future* (excluding a *commodity future* and a *rolling spot forex contract*);
(ii) *commodity future*;
(iii) *rolling spot forex contract*;

(l) *contract for differences* (article 85); for the purposes of the *permission* regime, this is sub-divided into:
(i) *contract for differences* (excluding a *spread bet* and a *rolling spot forex contract*);
(ii) *spread bet*;
(iii) *rolling spot forex contract*;

(m) *underwriting capacity of a Lloyd's syndicate* (article 86(1));

(n) *membership of a Lloyd's syndicate* (article 86(2));

(o) *funeral plan contract* (article 87);

(oa) *regulated mortgage contract* (article 61(3));

(ob) *home reversion plan* (article 63B(3));

(oc) *home purchase plan* (article 63F(3));

(od) *regulated sale and rent back agreement* (article 63J(3));

(oe) *emissions auction products* (article 82A);

(p) *rights to or interests in investments* (article 89).

(B) In the FCA Handbook: any of the following *investments* specified in Part III of the *Regulated Activities Order* (Specified Investments):

(a) *deposit* (article 74);

(aa) *electronic money* (article 74A);

(b) *contract of insurance* (article 75); for the purposes of the *permission* regime, this is sub-divided into:
(i) *general insurance contract*;
(ii) *long-term insurance contract*;
and then further sub-divided into *classes* of *contract of insurance*;

(c) *share* (article 76);

(d) *debenture* (article 77);

(e) *government and public security* (article 78);

(f) *warrant* (article 79);

(g) *certificate representing certain securities* (article 80);

(h) *unit* (article 81);

(i) *stakeholder pension scheme* (article 82(1));

(ia) *personal pension scheme* (article 82(2));

(j) *option* (article 83); for the purposes of the *permission* regime, this is sub-divided into:
(i) *option* (excluding a *commodity option* and an *option* on a *commodity future*);
(ii) *commodity option* and an *option* on a *commodity future*;

(k) *future* (article 84); for the purposes of the *permission* regime, this is sub-divided into:
(i) *future* (excluding a *commodity future* and a *rolling spot forex contract*);
(ii) *commodity future*;
(iii) *rolling spot forex contract*;

(l) *contract for differences* (article 85); for the purposes of the *permission* regime, this is sub-divided into:

(i) *contract for differences* (excluding a *spread bet* and a *rolling spot forex contract*);

(ii) *spread bet*;

(iii) *rolling spot forex contract*;

(m) *underwriting capacity of a Lloyd's syndicate* (article 86(1));

(n) *membership of a Lloyd's syndicate* (article 86(2));

(o) *funeral plan contract* (article 87);

(oa) *regulated mortgage contract* (article 61(3);

(ob) *home reversion plan* (article 63B(3));

(oc) *home purchase plan* (article 63F(3));

(od) *regulated sale and rent back agreement* (article 63J(3));

(oe) *emissions auction products* (article 82A);

(of) *credit agreement* (article 88D) for the purposes of the *permission* regime with respect to the *regulated activities* of *entering into a regulated credit agreement as lender* and exercising, or having the right to exercise, the lender's rights and duties under a regulated credit agreement, this is sub-divided into:

(i) a *credit agreement* (excluding *high-cost short-term credit*, a *home credit loan agreement* and a *bill of sale loan agreement*);

(ii) *high-cost short-term credit*;

(iii) a *home credit loan agreement*;

(iv) *bill of sale loan agreement*;

and this has effect as if the reference to a *credit agreement* includes a reference to an article 36H agreement within the meaning of article 36H (4) of the *Regulated Activities Order*;

(og) *consumer hire agreement* (article 88E);

(p) *rights to or interests in investments* (article 89).

specific risk

(1) (in *SYSC*) unique risk that is due to the individual nature of an asset and can potentially be diversified.

(2) (in *GENPRU* and *BIPRU* and in accordance with paragraph 12 of Annex I of the *Capital Adequacy Directive*) the risk of a price change in an *investment* due to factors related to its issuer or, in the case of a *derivative*, the issuer of the underlying *investment*.

sponsor

(A) In the *PRA* Handbook: (in *BIPRU*), in accordance with Article 4(42) of the *Banking Consolidation Directive* (Definitions) and in relation to a *securitisation* within the meaning of paragraph (2) of the definition of securitisation) an *undertaking* other than an *originator* that establishes and manages an *asset backed commercial paper programme* or other *securitisation* scheme that purchases *exposures* from third party entities.

(B) In the *FCA Handbook*:

(1) (in *LR*) approved, under section 88 of the *Act* by the *FCA*, as a sponsor.

(2) (in *BIPRU*), in accordance with Article 4(42) of the *Banking Consolidation Directive* (Definitions) and in MIPRU 4 and in relation to a *securitisation* within the meaning of paragraph (2) of the definition of securitisation, an *undertaking* other than an *originator* that establishes and manages an *asset backed commercial paper programme* or other *securitisation* scheme that purchases *exposures* from third party entities.

(3) in *IFPRU* and *FUND*) has the meaning in article 4(1)(14) of the *EU CRR*.

sponsor declaration

a declaration submitted by a *sponsor* to the *FCA* as required under LR 8.4.3 R (Application for listing), LR 8.4.9 R (Further application for listing), LR 8.4.13 R (Production of circular) or LR 8.4.14 R (Transfer between listing category).

sponsor service

a service relating to a matter referred to in LR 8.2 that a *sponsor* provides or is requested or appointed to provide, including preparatory work that a *sponsor* may undertake before a decision is taken as to whether or not it will act as *sponsor* for a a *listed company* or *applicant* or in relation to a particular transaction, and including all the *sponsor's* communications with the *FSA* in connection with the service. But nothing in this definition is to be taken as requiring a *sponsor* when requested to agree to act as a *sponsor* for a *company* or in relation to a transaction.

spread bet

a *contract for differences* that is a gaming contract, whether or not section 412 of the *Act* (Gaming contracts) applies to the contract; in this definition, "gaming" has the meaning given in the Gaming Act 1968, which is in summary: the playing of a game of chance for winnings in money or money's worth, whether any *person* playing the game is at risk of losing any money or money's worth or not.

spread risk

the risk that a spread (that is, the difference in price or yield) between two variables will change.

SPV

(1) (in GENPRU 2.2 (Capital resources)) has the meaning in GENPRU 2.2.126R (Other tier one capital: innovative tier one capital: indirectly issued tier one capital).

(2) (in BIPRU 8 (Group risk – consolidation)) has the meaning in BIPRU 8.6.15 R (Indirectly issued capital and group capital resources).

SRB administrator

a *firm* which carries on the *regulated activity* of *administering a regulated sale and rent back agreement*.

SRB adviser

a *firm* which carries on the *regulated activity* of *advising on a regulated sale and rent back agreement*.

SRB agreement provider

(in accordance with article 63J(3)(a) of the *Regulated Activities Order*) a *firm* which buys all or part of the *qualifying interest in land* in the *United Kingdom* from a *SRB agreement seller* under a *regulated sale and rent back agreement*, including a *firm* which acquires obligations or rights under a *regulated sale and rent back agreement*.

SRB agreement seller

(in accordance with article 63J(3)(a) of the *Regulated Activities Order*) an individual or trustees, who sells all or part of the *qualifying interest in land* in the *United Kingdom* to an agreement provider under a *regulated sale and rent back agreement*.

SRB arranger

a *firm* which carries on the *regulated activity* of *arranging (bringing about) a regulated sale and rent back agreement* or *making arrangements with a view to a regulated sale and rent back agreement*.

SRB intermediary

a *firm* with *permission* (or which ought to have *permission*) to carry on a *regulated sale and rent back mediation activity*.

SREP

the *supervisory review and evaluation process*.

SSAS

small self-administered scheme.

SSPE

a *securitisation special purpose entity*.

stabilisation

(in MAR 2) (as defined in Article 2 of the *Buy-back and Stabilisation Regulation*) any purchase or offer to purchase *relevant securities*, or any transaction in *associated instruments* equivalent thereto, by *investment firms* or *credit institutions*, which is undertaken in the context of a *significant distribution* of such *relevant securities* exclusively for supporting the market price of these *relevant securities* for a predetermined period of time, due to a selling pressure in such securities.

staff mortgage

a *regulated mortgage contract* between an employer, or an *undertaking* in the same *group* as the employer, as lender and the employee (alone or with another *person*) as borrower to defray money applied for any of the following purposes:

(a) acquiring any residential land which was intended, at the time of the acquisition, for occupation by the employee as their home;

(b) carrying out repairs or improvements to any residential land which was intended, at the time of taking out the loan, for occupation by the employee as their home; or

(c) payments in respect of a loan (whether of interest or capital).

stakeholder CTF

a *CTF* that has the characteristics, and complies with the conditions, set out in paragraph 2 of the Schedule to the *CTF Regulations*.

stakeholder pension scheme

a scheme that meets the conditions in section 1 of the Welfare Reform and Pensions Act 1999 or article 3 of the Welfare Reform and Pensions (Northern Ireland) Order 1999.

stakeholder product

(as defined in article 52B(3) of the *Regulated Activities Order*):

(a) a *stakeholder CTF*; or

(b) a *stakeholder pension scheme*; or

(c) an investment of a kind specified in the *Stakeholder Regulations*.

Stakeholder Regulations

the Financial Services and Markets Act 2000 (Stakeholder Products) Regulations 2004 (SI 2004/2738).

standard CIU look through method

the method for calculating the *PRR* for a *position* in a *CIU* set out in BIPRU 7.7.4 R and BIPRU 7.7.7 R to BIPRU 7.7.10 R.

standard equity method

the method of calculating the *equity PRR* set out in BIPRU 7.3.32R (Standard equity method).

standardised approach

(A) In the PRA Handbook:
(for the purposes of *BIPRU*) one of the following:
(a) (where expressed to relate to credit risk) the method for calculating capital requirements for credit risk in BIPRU 3 (Credit risk) and BIPRU 9.2.1R(1) and BIPRU 9.11 (Standardised approach);
(b) (where expressed to relate to *operational risk*) the method for calculating capital requirements for *operational risk* in BIPRU 6.3 (Standardised approach);
(c) (where not expressed to relate to any risk and used in BIPRU 3, BIPRU 4 (IRB approach), BIPRU 5 (Credit risk mitigation), BIPRU 9 (Securitisation) or BIPRU 10 (Large exposures requirements)) it has the meaning in (a);
(d) (where not expressed to relate to any risk and used in BIPRU 6 (Operational risk)) it has the meaning in (b);
(e) (where the one of the approaches in (a) to (d) is being applied on a consolidated basis) that approach as applied on a consolidated basis in accordance with BIPRU 8 (Group risk – consolidation); or
(f) when the reference is to the rules of or administered by a *regulatory body* other than the *appropriate regulator*, whatever corresponds to the approach in (a) to (e), as the case may be, under those rules.

(B) In the FCA Handbook:
(for the purposes of *BIPRU*) one of the following:
(a) (where expressed to relate to credit risk) the method for calculating capital requirements for credit risk in BIPRU 3 (Credit risk) and BIPRU 9.2.1R(1) and BIPRU 9.11 (Standardised approach);
(b) (where expressed to relate to *operational risk*) the method for calculating capital requirements for *operational risk* in BIPRU 6.3 (Standardised approach);
(c) (where not expressed to relate to any risk and used in BIPRU 3, BIPRU 4 (IRB approach), BIPRU 5 (Credit risk mitigation), BIPRU 9 (Securitisation) or BIPRU 10 (Large exposures requirements)) it has the meaning in (a);

(d) (where not expressed to relate to any risk and used in BIPRU 6 (Operational risk)) it has the meaning in (b);

(e) (where the one of the approaches in (a) to (d) is being applied on a consolidated basis) that approach as applied on a consolidated basis in accordance with BIPRU 8 (Group risk – consolidation); or

(f) when the reference is to the rules of or administered by a *regulatory body* other than the *appropriate regulator*, whatever corresponds to the approach in (a) to (e), as the case may be, under those rules.

standardised credit risk exposure class

(in relation to the *standardised approach* to credit risk) one of the classes of exposure set out in BIPRU 3.2.9R (Exposure classes).

standardised deterministic projection

a *projection* which is either a *generic projection* or a *personal projection* produced in accordance with the assumptions contained in COBS 13 Annex 2.

standard frequency liquidity reporting firm

a *standard ILAS BIPRU firm* that is not a *low frequency liquidity reporting firm*.

standard ILAS BIPRU firm

an *ILAS BIPRU firm* that is not a *simplified ILAS BIPRU firm*.

standard listing

in relation to *securities*, means a *listing* that is not a *premium listing*.

standard listing (shares)

a *standard listing* of *shares* other than *preference shares* that are *specialist securities*.

standard market risk PRR rules

(in *BIPRU*) the rules relating to the calculation of the *market risk capital requirement* excluding the *VaR model approach* and any *rules* modified so as to provide for the *CAD 1 model approach*.

standard methods of internal client money reconciliation

(A) In the PRA Handbook:

CASS 7 Annex 1;

(B) In the FCA Handbook:

(a) [deleted]

(b) the methods of *internal client money reconciliation* described in CASS 7.16.

standard terms

(in *DISP*) the contractual terms made under paragraph 18 of Schedule 17 to the *Act* (The Ombudsman Scheme), under which *VJ participants* participate in the *Voluntary Jurisdiction*.

standing data

the information relating to a *firm* held by the *appropriate regulator* on the matters set out in SUP 16 Annex 16A.

standing independent valuer

the person appointed as such under COLL 5.6.20 R (Standing independent valuer and valuation) and COLL 8.4.13R (1) (Standing independent valuer and valuation).

state finance organisation

a legal person other than a *company*:

(a) which is a national of an *EEA state*;

(b) which is set up by or pursuant to a special law;

(c) whose activities are governed by that law and consist solely of raising funds under state control through the issue of *debt securities*;

(d) which is financed by means of the resources they have raised and resources provided by the *EEA state*; and

(e) the *debt securities* issued by it are considered by the law of the relevant *EEA state* as securities issued or guaranteed by that state.

state monopoly

a *company* or other legal person which is a national of an *EEA state* and which:

(a) in carrying on its business benefits from a monopoly right granted by an *EEA state*; and

(b) is set up by or pursuant to a special law or whose borrowings are unconditionally and irrevocably guaranteed by an *EEA state* or one of the federated states of an *EEA state*.

State of the commitment

(in accordance with paragraph 6(1) of Schedule 12 to the *Act* (Transfer schemes: certificates)) (in relation to a commitment entered into at any date):

(a) if the *policyholder* is an individual, the State in which he had his habitual residence at that date;

(b) if the *policyholder* is not an individual, the State in which the establishment of the *policyholder* to which the commitment relates was established at that date;

in this definition, "commitment" means (in accordance with article 2 of the Financial Services and Markets Act 2000 (Control of Business Transfers) (Requirements on Applicants) Regulations 2001 (SI 2001/3625)) any contract of insurance of a kind referred to in article 2 of the *Consolidated Life Directive*.

State of the risk

(in accordance with paragraph 6(3) of Schedule 12 to the *Act* (Transfer schemes: certificates)) (in relation to the *EEA State* in which a risk is situated):

(a) if the insurance relates to a building or to a building and its contents (so far as the contents are covered by the same policy), the *EEA State* in which the building is situated;

(b) if the insurance relates to a vehicle of any type, the *EEA State* of registration;

(ba) if the insurance relates to a *vehicle* dispatched from one *EEA State* to another, in respect of the period of 30 days beginning with the day on which the purchaser accepts delivery, the *EEA State* of destination (and not, as provided by sub-paragraph (b), the *EEA State* of registration); [Note: article 15(1) of the *Consolidated Motor Insurance Directive*]

(c) in the case of *policies* of a duration of four months or less covering travel or holiday risks (whatever the class concerned), the *EEA State* in which the *policyholder* took out the *policy*;

(d) in a case not covered by (a) to (c):
(i) if the *policyholder* is an individual, the *EEA State* in which he has his habitual residence at the date when the contract is entered into; and
(ii) otherwise, the *EEA State* in which the establishment of the *policyholder* to which the *policy* relates is situated at that date.

Statement of Principle

(1) (in the *FCA Handbook*) one of the Statements of Principle issued by the *FCA* under section 64(1) of the *Act* (Conduct: Statements and codes) with respect to the conduct of *approved persons* and set out in APER 2.1A. The provisions of APER 1.1A marked with a "P" in the margin also form part of the *Statements of Principle*.

(2) (in the *PRA Handbook*) one of the Statements of Principle issued by the *PRA* under section 64(1A) of the *Act* (Conduct: Statements and codes) with respect to the conduct of *approved persons* and set out in APER 2.1B. The provisions of APER 1.1B marked with a "P" in the margin also form part of the *Statements of Principle*.

statutory auditor

a statutory auditor as that term is defined in section 1210 of the Companies Act 2006.

statutory money purchase illustration

an annual illustration of the contributions made for the benefit of, and the potential benefits due to, a member of a *personal pension scheme*, which is prepared in accordance with the Personal Pension Schemes (Disclosure of Information) Regulations 1987 (SI 1987/1110).

statutory notice

a *warning notice, decision notice* or *supervisory notice*.

statutory notice decision

a decision by the *appropriate regulator* on whether or not to give a *statutory notice*.

statutory notice associated decision

a decision which is made by the *appropriate regulator* and which is associated with a decision to give a *statutory notice*, including a decision:

(a) to determine or extend the period for making representations;

(b) to determine whether a copy of the *statutory notice* needs to be given to any third party and the period for him to make representations;

(c) to refuse access to *appropriate regulator* material.

(d) [deleted]

statutory objectives

(1) for the *FCA* (as described in sections 1B, 1C, 1D and 1E of the Act):
(a) its strategic objective of ensuring that the relevant markets function well; and
(b) its operational objectives:
(i) the *consumer* protection objective (as defined in section 1C of the *Act*);
(ii) the integrity objective (as defined in section 1D of the *Act*); and
(iii) the competition objective (as defined in section 1E of the *Act*);

(2) for the *PRA* (as described in sections 2B, 2C and 314A of the *Act*):
(a) its general objective of promoting the safety and soundness of *PRA-authorised persons*; and
(b) its insurance objective of contributing to the securing of an appropriate degree of protection for those who are or may become *policyholders*.

step-up

(in relation to any item of capital) any change in the *coupon* rate on that item that results in an increase in the amount payable at any time, including a change already provided in the original terms governing those payments. A step-up:

(a) includes (in the case of a fixed rate) an increase in that *coupon* rate;

(b) includes (in the case of a floating rate calculated by adding a fixed amount to a fluctuating amount) an increase in that fixed amount;

(c) includes (in the case of a floating rate) a change in the benchmark by reference to which the fluctuating element of the *coupon* is calculated that results in an increase in the absolute amount of the *coupon*; and

(d) does not include (in the case of a floating rate) an increase in the absolute amount of the *coupon* caused by fluctuations in the fluctuating figure by reference to which the absolute amount of the *coupon* floats.

stochastic projection

a *projection* showing a summary of results from repeated simulations using an investment model, where the model uses key financial parameters which are subject to random variations and are projected into the future.

stock financing

a transaction where a *physical commodity* is sold forward and the cost of funding is locked in until the date of the forward sale.

stock lending

the disposal of a *designated investment* subject to an obligation or right to reacquire the same or a similar *designated investment* from the same counterparty.

stock lending activity

the activity of undertaking a *stock lending* transaction.

stocks and shares component

a *qualifying investment* as prescribed in paragraph 7 of the *ISA Regulations*.

stocks and shares ISA business

a *firm's* activities, in its capacity as an *ISA manager*, in connection with an *ISA* which contains only a *stocks and shares component* and is not either or both *MiFID business* and *designated investment business*.

store card

a card restricted to paying for goods or services from a particular supplier or group of suppliers and where the price of the goods or services is paid directly to the supplier or group of suppliers by the customer or the *firm*, but excluding a *plastic card* used to pay for goods or services through a network such as Visa or MasterCard.

strategic investment

an investment which:

(a) is made for a strategic purpose;

(b) is made for an expected duration consistent with that purpose and is, or has the potential to be, illiquid or hard to value; and

(c) is significant in value in proportion to the size of the *with-profits fund*.

stressed VaR

(in *BIPRU*) the stressed VaR measure in respect of *positions* coming within the scope of the *VaR model permission*, calculated in accordance with the *VaR model*, BIPRU 7.10 (Use of a Value at Risk Model) and any methodology set out in the *VaR model permission* based on a stressed historical period.

structured capital-at-risk product

a product, other than a *derivative*, which provides an agreed level of income or growth over a specified investment period and displays the following characteristics:

(a) the *customer* is exposed to a range of outcomes in respect of the return of initial capital invested;

(b) the return of initial capital invested at the end of the investment period is linked by a pre-set formula to the performance of an index, a combination of indices, a 'basket' of selected stocks (typically from an index or indices), or other factor or combination of factors; and

(c) if the performance in (b) is within specified limits, repayment of initial capital invested occurs but if not, the *customer* could lose some or all of the initial capital invested.

structured deposit

a *deposit* paid on terms under which any interest or premium will be paid, or is at risk, according to a formula which involves the performance of:

(a) an index (or combination of indices) (other than money market indices);

(b) a stock (or combination of stocks); or

(c) a commodity (or combination of commodities).

sub-consolidated basis

has the meaning in article 4(1)(49) of the *EU CRR*.

sub-fund

(a) (in relation to an *authorised fund* that is an *umbrella*) a separate part of the *scheme property* of that *scheme* that is pooled separately;

(aa) (in relation to an *EEA UCITS scheme*) any part of that *scheme* that constitutes an investment compartment for the purposes of the *UCITS Directive*;

(b) (in relation to a *fund* that is not an *authorised fund* or an *EEA UCITS scheme*) any part of that *scheme* that is equivalent to (a).

sub-group

(in relation to a *person*):

(a) that *person*; and

(b) any *person* that is either:
(i) a *subsidiary undertaking* of that *person*; or
(ii) an *undertaking* in which that *person* or a *subsidiary undertaking* of that *person* holds a *participation*.

sub-pool

a discrete *pool* of *client money* established under CASS 7.19.

sub-pool disclosure document

a document prepared by a *firm* containing the information required by CASS 7.19.9 R.

subsidiary

(A) In the PRA Handbook:

(1) (except in relation to *MiFID business*) (as defined in section 1159(1) of the Companies Act 2006 (Meaning of "subsidiary", etc)) (in relation to another *body corporate* ("H")) a *body corporate* of which H is a *holding company*.

(2) (in relation to *MiFID business*) a subsidiary undertaking as defined in Articles 1 and 2 of Seventh Council Directive on consolidated accounts (No. 83/349/EEC), including any subsidiary of a subsidiary undertaking of an ultimate *parent undertaking*.

[Note: article 4 (1)(29) of *MiFID*]

(B) In the FCA Handbook:

(1) (except in relation to *MiFID business*) (as defined in section 1159(1) of the Companies Act 2006 (Meaning of "subsidiary", etc)) (in relation to another *body corporate* ("H")) a *body corporate* of which H is a *holding company*.

(2) (in relation to *MiFID business*) a subsidiary undertaking as defined in Articles 1 and 2 of Seventh Council Directive on consolidated accounts (No. 83/349/EEC), including any subsidiary of a subsidiary undertaking of an ultimate *parent undertaking*.

(3) (for the purpose of *IFPRU*) has the meaning in article 4(1)(16) of the *EU CRR*.

[Note: article 4 (1)(29) of *MiFID*]

subsidiary undertaking

(1) (except for the purposes of determining whether a *person* has *close links* with another *person*) an *undertaking* of which another *undertaking* is its *parent undertaking*.

(2) (for the purposes of determining whether a *person* has *close links* with another *person*) (in accordance with section 343(8) of the *Act* (Information given by auditor or actuary to a regulator) and paragraph 3(3) of Schedule 6 to the *Act* (Threshold conditions)):

(a) an *undertaking* in (1);

(b) an *undertaking* ("S") if:

(i) another *undertaking* (its parent) is a member of S;

(ii) a majority of S's board of directors who have held office during the financial year and during the preceding financial year have been appointed solely as a result of the exercise of the parent's voting rights; and

(iii) no one else is the parent undertaking of S under any of (a) (i) to (iii) or b(i) or (ii) in the definition of *parent undertaking*.

(3) [deleted]

subsistence balance

(in *BCOBS*) any sum of money payable by a *firm* to a *consumer* or standing to the credit of the *consumer* in an account with the *firm* where that sum is needed by the *consumer* to meet essential living expenses or *priority debts* (whether owed to the *firm* or a third party).

subsisting rights

has the meaning given in section 76 of the Pension Schemes Act 2015 which is:

(a) for a *member of a pension scheme*:

(i) any right which has accrued to or in respect of the member to future benefits under the scheme; or

(ii) any entitlement to benefits under the scheme;

(b) for a *survivor* of a *member of a pension scheme*, any right to future benefits, or entitlement to benefits, which the *survivor* has under the scheme in respect of the member.

substantial shareholder

as defined in LR 11.1.4A R.

suitability report

a report which a *firm* must provide to its *client* under COBS 9.4 (Suitability reports) which, among other things, explains why the *firm* has concluded that a recommended transaction is suitable for the *client*.

sukuk

certificates of equal value representing an undivided interest in the ownership of specified assets or investments acquired or to be acquired and that comply with Islamic commercial jurisprudence and its investment principles, but excluding *shares*.

summary

(in relation to a *prospectus*) the summary included in the *prospectus*.

SUP

the Supervision manual.

supervisory authority

(1) (in accordance with article 4(1)(al) of *AIFMD*) (for a *non-EEA AIF*) the national authority or authorities of the *non-EEA State* empowered by law or regulation to supervise *AIFs* in that *non-EEA State*.

(2) (in accordance with article 4(1)(am) of *AIFMD*) (for a *non-EEA AIFM*) the national authority or authorities of the *non-EEA State* empowered by law or regulation to supervise *AIFMs* in that *non-EEA State*.

supervisory formula method

(for the purposes of BIPRU 9 (Securitisation), in relation to a *securitisation* within the meaning of paragraph (2) of the definition of securitisation and in accordance with Part 1 of Annex IX of the *Banking Consolidation Directive* (Securitisation definitions)) the method of calculating *risk weighted exposure amounts* for *securitisation positions* set out in BIPRU 9.12.21R–BIPRU 9.12.23R and BIPRU 9.14.3R.

supervisory function

(1) any function within a *common platform firm* that is responsible for the supervision of its *senior personnel*.

(2) (in relation to a *management company* and in accordance with article 3(6) of the *UCITS implementing Directive*) the *relevant persons* or body or bodies responsible for the supervision of its *senior personnel* and for the assessment and periodic review of the adequacy and effectiveness of the risk management process and of the policies, arrangements and procedures put in place to comply with its obligations under the *UCITS Directive*.

Supervisory Liquidity Review Process

the *appropriate regulator's* assessment of the adequacy of certain *firms'* liquidity resources as described in BIPRU 12.2 and BIPRU 12.5.

supervisory notice

(as defined in section 395(13) of the *Act* (The FCA's and PRA's procedures)) a notice given by the *appropriate regulator* in accordance with section 55Y(4), (7) or (8)(b); 78(2) or (5); 197(3), (6) or (7)(b); 259(3), (8) or (9)(b); 268(3), (7)(a) or (9)(a) (as a result of subsection (8)(b)); 282(3), (6) or (7)(b); or 321(2) or (5).

supervisory review and evaluation process

(A) In the PRA Handbook:
the *appropriate regulator's* assessment of the adequacy of certain *firms'* capital, as more fully described in BIPRU 2.2.9 G and INSPRU 7.1.91 G to INSPRU 7.1.99 G.

(B) In the FCA Handbook:
(1) the *appropriate regulator's* assessment of the adequacy of certain *firms'* capital, as more fully described in BIPRU 2.2.9 G (*BIPRU firms*) and INSPRU 7.1.91 G to INSPRU 7.1.99 G (*insurers*).
(2) the *FCA's* assessment of the adequacy of an *IFPRU investment firm's* capital, as more fully described in IFPRU 2.3 (Supervisory review and evaluation process).

supervisory volatility adjustments approach

the approach to calculating volatility adjustments under the *financial collateral comprehensive method* under which the *firm* uses the adjustments specified in BIPRU 5.4 (Financial collateral) rather than in its own estimates, as more fully described in BIPRU 5.4 and including that approach as applied to master netting agreements as described in BIPRU 5.6 (Master netting agreements).

supplementary prospectus

(in *Part 6 rules*) a supplementary prospectus containing details of a new factor, mistake or inaccuracy.

supplier

(a) the *person* referred to as the supplier in the definitions of *borrower-lender agreement*, *borrower-lender-supplier agreement* and *restricted-use credit agreement*; and

(b) in relation to a *credit agreement* falling within (2) (a) of the definition of *restricted-use credit agreement*, is the *lender*; and

(c) includes a *person* to whom the rights and duties of a *person* falling within (a) or (b) have passed by *assignment* or operation of law.

supplementary listing particulars

(in *LR*) (in accordance with section 81(1) of the *Act*), supplementary listing particulars containing details of the change or new matter.

suretyship

(in relation to a *class* of *contract of insurance*) the *class* of *contract of insurance*, specified in paragraph 15 of Part I of Schedule 1 to the *Regulated Activities Order* (Contracts of general insurance), namely:

(a) a *contract of insurance* against the risks of loss to the *person* insured arising from their having to perform contracts of guarantee entered into by them;

(b) fidelity bonds, performance bonds, administration bonds, bail bonds or customs bonds or similar contracts of guarantee where these are:
(i) effected or carried out by a *person* not carrying on a banking business;
(ii) not effected merely incidentally to some other business carried on by the *person* effecting them; and
(iii) effected in return for the payment of one or more premiums.

surrender value

(a) where the contract is a contract of life assurance or a contract for an annuity, the amount (including a nil amount) payable by the *firm* or other body issuing the contract on surrender of the *policy*;

(b) where the contract is a *personal pension scheme* or *stakeholder pension scheme*, the amount payable on the transfer of the investor's accrued rights under that contract to another *personal pension scheme* or *stakeholder pension scheme*;

(c) where the contract is a *Holloway sickness policy*, the amount payable by the *firm* on surrender on or before the *projection date* for the *policy*;

(d) where the contract is for any other matter, the amount payable by the *firm* on the surrender of the *policy*.

survivor

has the meaning given in section 76 of the Pension Schemes Act 2015 which, for a *member of a pension scheme*, means a *person* who has survived the member and has a right to future benefits, or is entitled to benefits, under the scheme in respect of the member.

sustainable

(in *CONC*) has the meaning given in CONC 5.3.1 G.

swap

a transaction in which two counterparties agree to exchange streams of payments over time according to a predetermined basis or a *contract for differences*.

Swiss general insurance company

(in accordance with article 1(2) of the Financial Services and Markets Act 2000 (Variation of Threshold Conditions) Order 2001 (SI 201/2507)) a *person*:

(a) whose head office is in Switzerland;

(b) who is authorised by the supervisory authority in Switzerland as mentioned in article 7.1 of the *Swiss Treaty Agreement*; and

(c) who is seeking to carry on, or is carrying on, from a branch in the *United Kingdom*, a *regulated activity* consisting of the *effecting* or *carrying out* of *contracts of insurance* of a kind which is subject to that agreement.

Swiss general insurer

a *Swiss general insurance company* which has *permission* to effect or *carry out contracts of insurance* of a kind which is subject to the *Swiss Treaty Agreement*.

Swiss Treaty Agreement

the agreement of 10 October 1989 between the European Economic Community and the Swiss Confederation on direct insurance other than life insurance, approved on behalf of the European Economic Community by the Council Decision of 20 June 1999 (No 91/370/EEC).

syndicate

one or more *persons*, to whom a particular syndicate number has been assigned by or under the authority of the *Council*, *carrying out* or *effecting contracts of insurance* written at Lloyd's.

syndicate actuary

an *actuary* appointed to a *syndicate* as required by SUP 4.6.9R (1).

syndicate assets

assets managed by or at the direction of a *managing agent* in respect of *insurance business* carried on through a *syndicate* and overseas business regulatory deposits funded from those assets.

syndicate ICA

the capital assessment performed by a *managing agent* under the *overall Pillar 2 rule*, GENPRU 1.5.1R(1), INSPRU 7.1 and INSPRU 1.1.57R(1) in respect of each *syndicate* managed by it.

syndicate year

a year of account of a *syndicate*.

synthetic cash

a position in a *derivative* that offsets an exposure in property to the point where that exposure has effectively been neutralised, and the effect of the combined holding of both property and the position in the *derivative* is the same as if the *authorised fund* had received or stood to receive the value of the property in cash.

synthetic future

(a) a synthetic bought future, that is, a bought call *option* coupled with a written put *option*; or

(b) a synthetic sold future, that is, a bought put *option* coupled with a written call *option*; provided that in either case the two *options*:
(i) are bought and written, whether simultaneously or not, on a single *eligible derivatives* market;
(ii) relate to the same underlying *security* or other asset;
(iii) give the purchasers of the *options* the same rights of exercise (whether at the same price or not); and
(iv) will expire together, if not exercised.

synthetic risk and reward indicator

(in *COLL* and in accordance with article 2(2) of the *UCITS implementing Directive No 2*) a synthetic indicator within the meaning of article 8 of the *KII Regulation*.

synthetic securitisation

(in accordance with Article 4(38) of the *Banking Consolidation Directive* (Definitions) and for the purpose of *BIPRU*) a *securitisation* (within the meaning of paragraph (2) of the definition of securitisation) where the *tranching* is achieved by the use of credit derivatives or guarantees, and the pool of *exposures* is not removed from the balance sheet of the *originator*.

SYSC

the part of the *Handbook* in High Level Standards which has the title Senior Management Arrangements, Systems and Controls.

systemically important institution

(in accordance with article 3(30) of *CRD*) an *EEA parent institution*, an *EEA parent financial holding company*, an *EEA parent mixed financial holding company* or an *institution* the failure or malfunction of which could lead to systemic risk.

systemic risk

a risk of disruption in the financial system with the potential to have serious negative consequences for the financial system and the real economy.

systematic internaliser

investment firm which, on an organised, frequent and systematic basis, *deals on own account* by executing *client* orders outside a *regulated market* or an *MTF*. [Note: article 4(1)(7) of *MiFID*]

systems and controls function

(1) (in the *FCA Handbook*) *FCA controlled function* CF28 in Part 1 of the *table of FCA controlled functions*, described more fully in SUP 10A.8.1 R.

(2) (in the *PRA Handbook*) *PRA controlled function* CF28 in the *table of PRA controlled functions*, described more fully in SUP 10B.9.1 R.

table of FCA controlled functions

the table of *controlled functions* in SUP 10A.4.4 RS.

table of PRA controlled functions

the table of *controlled functions* in SUP 10B.4.3 R.

takeover bid

an offer, as the term is used in the *Takeover Code*, or any other similar conduct governed by that code.

Takeover Code

the City Code on Takeovers and Mergers issued by the *Takeover Panel*.

takeover or related operation

(a) any transaction falling within paragraph 3(b) (Companies, Transactions and Persons subject to the Code) of the introduction to the *Takeover Code* and, for this purpose, an offer for non-voting, non-equity share capital is to be regarded as falling within the *Takeover Code* even if not required by rule 15 of that Code;

(b) any transaction which would have fallen within (a) were it not for the fact that the company which is the subject of the transaction does not satisfy the tests set out in paragraph 3(a) (Companies, Transactions and Persons subject to the Code) of the introduction to the *Takeover Code*;

(c) any offer, transaction or arrangement relating to the purchase of *securities* with a view to establishing or increasing a strategic holding of a *person*, or of a *person* together with his *associates*, in the *securities* concerned;

(d) any transaction or arrangement entered into in contemplation or furtherance of any offer, transaction or arrangement falling within (a) to (c); and

(e) any transaction or arrangement entered into by way of defence or protection against any offer, transaction or arrangement falling within (a) to (d) which has taken place or which is contemplated.

Takeover Panel

the Panel on Takeovers and Mergers.

target

(in *LR*) the subject of a *class 1 transaction* or *reverse takeover*.

tariff of charges

a list of all the charges (including amounts) that are payable on a *home finance transaction*, including the reason for, and amount of, each charge.

tax exempt policy

any contract of assurance, offered or issued by a *friendly society*, which is tax exempt life or endowment business as defined in section 466 (2) of the Income and Corporation Taxes Act 1988.

TC

the Training and Competence sourcebook.

TD

Transparency Directive.

TD implementing Directive

(except in DTR 4.4 and DTR 6.3.5 R) the European Parliament and Council Directive on the harmonisation of transparency requirements in relation to information about issuers whose securities are admitted to trading on a regulated market or through a comparable mechanism for the disclosure of information under national requirements of a Member State concerning the dissemination of information (No. 2004/109/EC).

technical provision

a technical provision established:

(a) for *general insurance business*, in accordance with INSPRU 1.1.12R; and

(b) for *long-term insurance business*, in accordance with INSPRU 1.1.16R.

tender offer

(in *LR*) an offer by a *company* to purchase all or some of a *class* of its *listed equity securities* at a maximum or fixed price (that may be established by means of a formula) that is:

(a) communicated to all holders of that *class* by means of a *circular* or advertisement in two national newspapers;

(b) open to all holders of that *class* on the same terms for at least seven days; and

(c) open for acceptance by all holders of that *class* pro rata to their existing holdings.

terminating event

(as defined in article 2(1) of the *compensation transitionals order*) in relation to applications made under an *investment business compensation scheme*, the withdrawal, discontinuance or rejection of the application, or its determination by a final payment of compensation to the applicant.

terms of business

a statement in a *durable medium* of the terms and conditions on which a *firm* will carry on a *regulated activity* with or for a *client* or *consumer*.

terms of reference

the terms of reference of a *firm's with-profits committee*, or the terms of appointment of the person or persons acting as the *with-profits advisory arrangement*, satisfying the requirements set out in COBS 20.5.3 R.

third country

a territory or country which is not an *EEA State*.

third-country banking and investment group

a *banking and investment group* that meets the following conditions:

(a) it is headed by:
(i) a *credit institution*; or
(ii) an *asset management company*; or
(iii) an *investment firm*; or
(iv) a *financial holding company*;
that has its head office outside the *EEA*; and

(b) it is not part of a wider *EEA banking and investment group*.

third country BIPRU firm

(A) In the PRA Handbook:
(1) (in *BIPRU* (except in BIPRU 12) and SYSC 19C) an *overseas firm* that:
(a) is not an *EEA firm*;
(b) has its head office outside the *EEA*; and
(c) would be a *BIPRU firm* if it had been a *UK domestic firm*, it had carried on all its business in the *United Kingdom* and had obtained whatever authorisations for doing so are required under the *Act*.
(2) (in BIPRU 12) an *overseas firm* that:
(a) is a *bank*;
(b) is not an *EEA firm*; and
(c) has its head office outside the *EEA*.

(B) In the FCA Handbook:
(1) (in *BIPRU* (except in BIPRU 12) and SYSC 19C) an *overseas firm* that:
(a) is not an *EEA firm*;
(b) has its head office outside the *EEA*; and
(c) would be a *BIPRU firm* if it had been a *UK domestic firm*, it had carried on all its business in the *United Kingdom* and had obtained whatever authorisations for doing so are required under the *Act*.
(2) (in BIPRU 12) an *overseas firm* that:
(a) is a *bank*;
(b) is not an *EEA firm*; and
(c) has its head office outside the *EEA*.

third country BIPRU 730k firm

an *overseas firm* that:

(a) is not an *EEA firm*;

(b) has its head office outside the *EEA*; and

(c) would be a *BIPRU 730k firm* if it had been a *UK domestic firm*, had carried on all its business in the *United Kingdom* and had obtained whatever authorisations for doing so as are required under the *Act*.

third-country countercyclical buffer authority

the authority of a *third country* empowered by law or regulation with responsibility for setting the *countercyclical buffer rate* for that *third country*.

third country competent authority

a *regulatory body* of a state or territory that is not an *EEA State*.

third-country competent authority

the authority of a country or territory which is not an *EEA State* that is empowered by law or regulation to supervise (whether on an individual or group-wide basis) *regulated entities*.

third-country financial conglomerate

a *financial conglomerate* that is of a type that falls under Article 5(3) of the *Financial Groups Directive*, which in summary is a *financial conglomerate* headed by a *regulated entity* or a *mixed financial holding company* that has its head office outside the *EEA*.

third-country group

a *third-country financial conglomerate* or a *third-country banking and investment group*.

third country IFPRU 730K firm

an overseas firm that:

(a) is not an *EEA firm*;

(b) has its head office outside the *EEA*; and

(c) would be an *IFPRU 730k firm* if it had been a *UK domestic firm*, had carried on all its business in the *United Kingdom* and had obtained whatever authorisations for doing so as are required under the *Act*.

third country investment firm

a *firm* which would be a *MiFID investment firm* if it had its head office in the *EEA*.

third country issuer

an issuer which does not have its registered office in the *EEA*. [Note: article 2(4) of the *MiFID Regulation*]

Third Life Directive

the Council Directive of 10 November 1992 on the coordination of laws, etc, and amending Directives 79/267/EEC and 90/619/EEC (No 92/96/EEC).

Third Non-Life Directive

the Council Directive of 18 June 1992 on the coordination of laws, etc, and amending Directives 73/239/EEC and 88/357/EEC (No 92/49/EEC).

third country investment services undertaking

(A) In the PRA Handbook:
(in *BIPRU*) an *institution*, a *financial institution* or an *asset management company* in a *non-EEA state*.

(B) In the FCA Handbook:
(in *BIPRU*) a *CAD investment firm*, a *financial institution* or an *asset management company* in a *non-EEA state*.

third party processor

(1) A *firm* ("Firm A") which carries on *home finance activities* or *insurance mediation activities* other than *advising* on *life policies*, or both, for another *firm* (or an *appointed representative*) ("Firm B") under a properly documented *outsourcing* agreement, the terms of which provide that when Firm A carries on any of these activities ("the outsourced activities") for Firm B:

(a) Firm A acts only on the instructions of Firm B;

(b) in any communication with a *customer*, Firm A represents itself as Firm B;

(c) Firm A undertakes to co-operate fully with Firm B in relation to any complaints arising from Firm A's performance of the outsourced activities, even if the complaint is made after Firm A has ceased to carry on the outsourced activities for Firm B; and

(d) Firm B accepts full responsibility for the acts and omissions of Firm A when carrying on the outsourced activities and must pay any redress due to the *customer*;

or an *appointed representative* ("Firm A") which carries on such activities for its *principal* ("Firm B") under such an agreement.

(2) A *firm* ("Firm C") which carries on *home finance activities* or *insurance mediation activities* other than *advising* on *life policies*, or both, for a *third party processor* within (1) ("Firm A"), where:

(a) the *outsourcing* agreement between Firm A and the *firm* for which Firm A is carrying on outsourced activities ("Firm B") authorises Firm A to outsource some or all of those activities to third parties which are *firms*, and identifies Firm C by name as one of those third parties;

(b) under the *outsourcing* agreement between Firm A and Firm B, Firm B accepts full responsibility for the acts and omissions of Firm C when carrying on the activities which are outsourced to it by Firm A; and

(c) there is a properly documented *outsourcing* agreement between Firm C and Firm A the terms of which provide that when Firm C carries on any of the outsourced activities:

(i) Firm C acts only on the instructions of Firm A;

(ii) in any communication with a customer, Firm C represents itself as Firm B; and

(iii) Firm C undertakes to co-operate fully with Firm A and Firm B in relation to any complaints arising from Firm C's performance of the outsourced activities, even if the complaint is made after Firm C has ceased to carry on the outsourced activities for Firm A.

third party prospectus

a communication made by a *firm* if the communication is a prospectus that has been drawn up and published in accordance with the *Prospectus Directive* and the *firm* is not responsible under that directive for the information given in the prospectus. [Note: recital 52 to the *MiFID implementing Directive*]

threshold condition

(in relation to a *regulated activity*) any of the conditions set out in or under Schedule 6 to the *Act* (Threshold conditions), including the additional conditions in the Financial Services and Markets Act 2000 (Variation of Threshold Conditions) Order 2001 (SI 2001/2507) (see *COND*).

tied agent

a *person* who, under the full and unconditional responsibility of only one *MiFID investment firm* or *third country investment firm* on whose behalf it acts, promotes *investment services* and/or *ancillary services* to *clients* or prospective *clients*, receives and transmits instructions or orders from the *client* in respect of *investment services* or *financial instruments*, places *financial instruments* and/or provides advice to *clients* or prospective *clients* in respect of those *financial instruments* or *investment services*. [Note: article 4(1)(25) of *MiFID*]

tied product

a product, other than *linked borrowing* or a *linked deposit*, that a *customer* is obliged to purchase through a *mortgage lender* or *reversion provider* as a condition of taking out a *regulated mortgage contract* or *home reversion plan* with that *firm*.

tier 2 capital

as defined in article 71 of the *EU CRR*.

tier 2 instruments

(A) (In the PRA Handbook): a capital instrument that qualify as tier 2 instruments under article 62 of the *EU CRR*.

(B) (In the FCA Handbook): a capital instrument that qualify as tier 2 instruments under article 62 of the *EU CRR*.

tier one capital

(1) [deleted]

(2) (in *BIPRU*, *GENPRU* and *INSPRU*) an item of capital that is specified in stages A (Core tier one capital), B (Perpetual non-cumulative preference shares) or C (Innovative tier one capital) of the *capital resources table*.

tier one capital resources

the sum calculated at stage F of the calculation in the *capital resources table* (Total tier one capital after deductions).

tier one instrument

an item of capital that falls into GENPRU 2.2.62R (Tier one capital: General) and is eligible to form part of a *firm's tier one capital resources*.

tier three capital

an item of capital that is *upper tier three capital* or *lower tier three capital*.

tier three capital resources

the sum calculated at stage Q of the *capital resources table* (Total tier three capital).

tier three instrument

an item of capital that falls into GENPRU 2.2.242R (Tier three capital: upper tier three capital resources) and is eligible to form part of a *firm's upper tier three capital resources*.

tier two capital

(1) [deleted]

(2) (in *BIPRU*, *GENPRU* and *INSPRU*) an item of capital that is specified in stages G (Upper tier two capital) or H (Lower tier two capital) of the *capital resources table*.

tier two capital resources

the sum calculated at stage I (Total tier two capital) of the calculation in the *capital resources table*.

tier two instrument

a *capital instrument* that meets the conditions in GENPRU 2.2.159R (General conditions for eligibility as tier two capital instruments) or GENPRU 2.2.177R (Upper tier two capital: General) and is eligible to form part of a *firm's tier two capital resources*.

time-scheduled buy-back programme

(as defined in Article 2 of the *Buy-back and Stabilisation Regulation*) a *buy-back programme* where the dates and quantities of *securities* to be traded during the time period of the programme are set out at the time of the public disclosure of the *buy-back programme*.

tontines

(in relation to a *class* of *contract of insurance*) tontines as specified in paragraph V of Part II of Schedule 1 to the *Regulated Activities Order* (Contracts of long-term insurance).

top-up cover

cover provided by the *compensation scheme* for *claims* against an *incoming EEA firm* (which is a *credit institution*, an *IMD insurance intermediary*, an *IMD reinsurance intermediary*, a *MiFID investment firm*, a *UCITS management company* or an *AIFM*) in relation to the *firm's passported activities* and in addition to, or due to the absence of, the cover provided by the *firm's Home State* compensation scheme (see COMP 14 (Participation by EEA firms)).

top-up permission

a *Part 4A permission* given to an *incoming EEA firm*, an *incoming Treaty firm* or a *UCITS qualifier*.

total amount of credit

(in *CONC*) the *credit limit* or the total sums made available under a *regulated credit agreement*.

total amount payable

(1) (except in *CONC*) the *total charge for credit* plus the total amount of credit advanced.

(2) (in *CONC*) the sum of the *total charge for credit* and the *total amount of credit* payable under the *credit agreement*, as well as any *advance payment*.

total charge for credit

(1) (except in *CONC*) the total of the charges (determined as at the date of making the contract) specified in MCOB 10.4.2 R as applying in relation to the *secured lending* but excluding the charges specified in MCOB 10.4.4 R.

(2) (in *CONC*) the true cost to the *borrower* of the *credit* provided, or to be provided, under an actual or prospective *credit agreement* calculated in accordance with CONC App 1.

(3) (in *CONC* in relation to a *financial promotion* about a *credit agreement* secured on *land*) the sum calculated in accordance with the *rules* in CONC App 1.1 and, in relation to *financial promotions*, the rules in CONC 3.6.9 R.

(in *CONC* in relation to a *financial promotion* about all other *credit agreements*) the sum calculated in accordance with the *rules* in CONC App 1.2 and, in relation to *financial promotions*, the *rules* in CONC 3.5.13 R.

total cost of credit to the borrower

(in CONC App 1.2) all costs, including interest, commissions, taxes and any other kind of fees which are required to be paid by, or on behalf of, the *borrower* or a *relative* of the *borrower* in connection with the *regulated credit agreement*, whether payable to the *lender* or to any other *person*, and which are known to the *lender*, except for notarial costs.

total count method

a method for performing a *physical asset reconciliation*, as described in CASS 6.6.27 R.

total exposure

[deleted]

total group tier one capital

the sum calculated at stage A of the calculation in INSPRU 6.1.43R.

total group tier two capital

the sum calculated at stage B of the calculation in INSPRU 6.1.43R.

total non-deferred shares

(in *CREDS*) means the total of members' share balances in a *credit union* shown in the most recent annual return to have been sent to the *appropriate regulator* under SUP 16.7.62 R or SUP 16.12.5 R (see CREDS 8.2.3 G), excluding any *deferred shares* in the *credit union*.

total relevant liabilities

(in *CREDS*) means the sum of:

(a) *unattached shares* in the *credit union*, and *deposits* by persons too young to be members of the *credit union*; and

(b) liabilities (other than liabilities for shares) with an original or remaining maturity of less than three *months* (including overdrafts and instalments of loans).

total risk exposure amount

the total risk exposure amount of a *firm* calculated in accordance with article 92(3) of the *EU CRR* (Own funds requirements).

TPF rules

the rules and guidance in COBS 20.2.1 G to COBS 20.2.39 R and COBS 20.2.51 R to COBS 20.2.57 G.

tradable renewable energy credit

an allowance, licence, permit, right, note, unit, credit, asset, certificate or instrument (the "credit") where:

(a) the credit confers or may result in a benefit or advantage to its holder or someone else; and

(b) the credit, or the benefit or advantage in (a), is linked to the supply, distribution or consumption of energy derived from renewable sources by the holder of the credit or someone else.

trade confirmation information

the information identified in column 1 of the table in COBS 16 Annex 1R.

traded life policy

a *life policy* which is to be or has been assigned for value by the *policyholder* to another *person*.

traded life policy investment

an *investment* in relation to which one of the following conditions applies:

(a) it is a *traded life policy* other than an endowment assurance policy;

(b) its underlying assets are wholly or predominately *traded life policies* other than endowment assurance policies;

(c) its investment returns, or the issuer's payment obligations, are linked to, contingent on, or highly sensitive to, the performance of *traded life policies* other than endowment assurance policies.

trading book

(A) In the PRA Handbook:

(1) (in *UPRU*) in relation to a *firm's* business or *exposures*, means:

(a) its proprietary positions in financial instruments:

(i) which are held for resale and/or are taken on by the firm with the intention of benefiting in the short term from actual and/or expected differences between their buying and selling prices or from other price or interest-rate variations;

(ii) arising from matched principal broking;

(iii) taken in order to hedge other elements of the trading book;

(b) *exposures* due to unsettled securities transactions, free deliveries, *OTC derivative* instruments, repurchase agreements and securities lending transactions based on securities included in (a)(i) to (iii) above, reverse repurchase agreements and securities borrowing transactions based on securities included in (a)(i) to (iii) above; and

(c) fees, commission, interest and dividends, and margin on exchange-traded derivatives which are directly related to the items included in (a) and (b) above.

(2) (in *BIPRU* and *GENPRU* in relation to a *BIPRU firm*) has the meaning in BIPRU 1.2 (Definition of the trading book) which is in summary, all that *firm's positions* in *CRD financial instruments* and *commodities* held either with trading intent or in order to hedge other elements of the *trading book*, and which are either free of any restrictive covenants on their tradability or able to be hedged.

(3) (in *BIPRU* and *GENPRU* and in relation to a *person* other than a *BIPRU firm*) has the meaning in (2) with references to a *firm* replaced by ones to a *person*.

(4) (in *IFPRU* and in relation to an *IFPRU investment firm*) has the meaning in article 4(1)(86) of the *EU CRR*.

(B) In the FCA Handbook:

(1) [deleted]

(2) (in *BIPRU* and *GENPRU* in relation to a *BIPRU firm*) has the meaning in BIPRU 1.2 (Definition of the trading book) which is in summary, all that *firm's positions* in *CRD financial instruments* and *commodities* held either with trading intent or in order to hedge other elements of the *trading book*, and which are either free of any restrictive covenants on their tradability or able to be hedged.

(3) (in *BIPRU* and *GENPRU* and in relation to a *person* other than a *BIPRU firm*) has the meaning in (2) with references to a *firm* replaced by ones to a *person*.

(4) (in *IFPRU* and in relation to an *IFPRU investment firm*) has the meaning in article 4(1)(86) of the *EU CRR*.

trading book concentration risk excess

[deleted]

trading book policy statement

(A) In the PRA Handbook:

has the meaning in BIPRU 1.2.29R (Trading book policy statements) which is in summary a single document of a *person* recording the policies and procedures referred to in BIPRU 1.2.26R and BIPRU 1.2.27R.

(B) In the FCA Handbook:

(1) (in *BIPRU*) has the meaning in BIPRU 1.2.29R (Trading book policy statements) which is in summary a single document of a *person* recording the policies and procedures referred to in BIPRU 1.2.26R and BIPRU 1.2.27R.

(2) (in *IFPRU*) the statement of policies and procedures relating to the *trading book*.

trading book systems and controls rules

GENPRU 1.3.13R(2) to (3) (General requirements: Methods of valuation and systems and controls), GENPRU 1.3.14R to GENPRU 1.3.16R (Marking to market), GENPRU 1.3.17R to GENPRU 1.3.25R (Marking to model), GENPRU 1.3.26R to GENPRU 1.3.28R (Independent price verification), GENPRU 1.3.30R to GENPRU 1.3.33R (Valuation adjustments or reserves), GENPRU 2.2.86R (Core tier one capital: profit and loss account and other reserves: Losses arising from valuation adjustments) and GENPRU 2.2.248R to GENPRU 2.2.249R (Tier three capital: lower tier three capital resources).

trading day

(1) (in MAR 7 (Disclosure of information on certain trades undertaken outside a regulated market or MTF) and SUP 17 (Transaction reporting)) in relation to post-trade information to be made public about a share under MAR 7.2.10 EU, any day of normal trading in a share on a *trading venue* in the *relevant liquid market* for this share. [Note: article 4(2) of the *MiFID Regulation*]

[deleted]

(3) (in *FINMAR*) as defined in article 2(1)(p) of the *short selling regulation*, a trading day as referred to in article 4 of Regulation (EC) No 1287/2006.

trading information

information of the following kinds:

(1) that *investments* of a particular kind have been or are to be acquired or disposed of, or that their acquisition or disposal is under consideration or the subject of negotiation; or

(2) that *investments* of a particular kind have not been or are not to be acquired or disposed of; or

(3) the quantity of *investments* acquired or disposed of or to be acquired or disposed of or whose acquisition or disposal is under consideration or the subject of negotiation; or

(4) the price (or range of prices) at which *investments* have been or are to be acquired or disposed of or the price (or range of prices) at which *investments* whose acquisition or disposal is under consideration or the subject of negotiation may be acquired or disposed of; or

(5) the identity of the *persons* involved or likely to be involved in any capacity in an acquisition or disposal.

trading plan

(in *LR*) a written plan between a restricted person and an independent third party which sets out a strategy for the acquisition and/or disposal of *securities* by a specified person and:

(a) specifies the amount of *securities* to be dealt in and the price at which and the date on which the *securities* are to be dealt in; or

(b) gives discretion to that independent third party to make trading decisions about the amount of *securities* to be dealt in and the price at which and the date on which the *securities* are to be dealt in; or

(c) includes a written formula or algorithm, or computer program, for determining the amount of *securities* to be dealt in and the price at which and the date on which the *securities* are to be dealt in.

trading venue

(1) (except in *FINMAR*) a *regulated market*, *MTF* or *systematic internaliser* acting in its capacity as such, and, where appropriate, a system outside the *EU* with similar functions to a *regulated market* or *MTF*. [Note: article 2(8) of the *MIFID Regulation*]

(2) (in *FINMAR*) (as defined in article 2(1)(l) of the *short selling regulation*) a *regulated market* or an *MTF*.

traditional securitisation

(in accordance with Article 4(37) of the *Banking Consolidation Directive* (Definitions) and for the purpose of *BIPRU* and *MIPRU*) a *securitisation* (within the meaning of paragraph (2) of the definition of securitisation) involving the economic transfer of the *exposures* being *securitised* to a *securitisation special purpose entity* which issues securities; and so that:

(a) this must be accomplished by the transfer of ownership of the *securitised exposures* from the *originator* or through sub-participation; and

(b) the securities issued do not represent payment obligations of the *originator*.

transaction

(A) In the PRA Handbook
only the purchase and sale of a *financial instrument*. For the purposes of the *MiFID Regulation*, excluding Chapter II, this does not include:

(a) *securities financing transactions*; or
(b) the exercise of options or covered warrants; or
(c) primary market transactions (such as issuance allotment or subscription) in *financial instruments* falling within Article 4(1)(18)(a) and (b) of *MiFID*.
[Note: article 5 of the *MiFID Regulation*]

(B) In the FCA Handbook
(1) (except in CONC App 1.1) only the purchase and sale of a *financial instrument*. For the purposes of the *MiFID Regulation*, excluding Chapter II, this does not include:
(a) *securities financing transactions*; or
(b) the exercise of options or covered warrants; or
(c) primary market transactions (such as issuance allotment or subscription) in *financial instruments* falling within Article 4(1)(18)(a) and (b) of *MiFID*.
(2) (in CONC App 1.3, except in CONC App 1.1.6R (1)(c)) a *credit agreement*, any transaction which is a *linked transaction*, any contract for the provision of *security* relating to the *credit agreement*, any *credit broking* contract relating to the *credit agreement* and any other contract to which the *borrower* or a *relative* of his is a party and which the *lender* requires to be made or maintained as a condition of the making of the *credit agreement*.

[Note: article 5 of the *MiFID Regulation*]

transaction report

a report of a transaction which meets the requirements of SUP 17.4.1 EU.1 R and SUP 17.4.2 R (Information to appear in transaction reports).

transaction-specific advice

advice on investments:

(a) given in connection with:
(i) *dealing in investments as principal*; or
(ii) *dealing in investments as agent*; or
(iii) acting as an arranger; or

(b) with a view to carrying on any such activities;

with or for the *eligible counterparty* to whom the advice is given.

tranche

(in accordance with Article 4(39) of the *Banking Consolidation Directive* (Definitions) and in relation to a *securitisation* within the meaning of paragraph (2) of the definition of securitisation and for the purposes of *BIPRU* and *MIPRU*) a contractually established segment of the credit risk associated with an *exposure* or number of *exposures*, where a position in the segment entails a risk of credit loss greater than or less than a position of the same amount in each other such segment, without taking account of credit protection provided by third parties directly to the holders of positions in the segment or in other segments.

transferable security

(1) (in *PR* and *LR*) (as defined in section 102A of the *Act*) anything which is a transferable security for the purposes of *MiFID*, other than money-market instruments for the purposes of that directive which have a maturity of less than 12 months.

(2) (in *COLL*) an *investment* within COLL 5.2.7 R (Transferable securities) in relation to *schemes* falling under COLL 5.

(3) those classes of securities which are negotiable on the capital market, with the exception of instruments of payment, such as:
(a) shares in companies and other securities equivalent to shares in companies, partnerships or other entities, and depositary receipts in respect of shares;
(b) bonds or other forms of securitised debt, including depositary receipts in respect of such securities; and
(c) any other securities giving the right to acquire or sell any such transferable securities or giving rise to a cash settlement determined by reference to transferable securities, currencies, interest rates or yields, *commodities* or other indices or measures.
[Note: article 4(1)(18) of *MiFID*]

Transparency Directive

(1) (except in DTR 4.3A, DTR 4.4 and DTR 6.3.5 R (3)(d)) the European Parliament and Council Directive on the harmonisation of transparency requirements in relation to information about issuers whose securities are admitted to trading on a regulated market or through a comparable mechanism for the disclosure of information under national requirements of a Member State concerning the dissemination of information (No. 2004/109/EC).

(2) (in DTR 4.3A, DTR 4.4 and DTR 6.3.5 R (3)(d)) the European Parliament and Council Directive on the harmonisation of transparency requirements in relation to information about issuers whose securities are admitted to trading on a regulated market or through a comparable mechanism for the disclosure of information under national requirements of a Member State concerning the dissemination of information (No. 2004/109/EC) as amended by the Directive of the European Parliament and of the Council of 22 October 2013 (No. 2013/50/EU).

transparency rules

(in accordance with sections 73A(1) and 89A of the *Act*) *rules* relating to the notification and dissemination of information in respect of *issuers* of *transferable securities* and relating to major shareholdings.

treasury shares

shares which meet the conditions set out in paragraphs (a) and (b) of subsection 724(5) of the Companies Act 2006.

Treaty

the Treaty on the Functioning of the European Union.

Treaty activity

(as defined in section 417(1) of the *Act* (Definitions)) an activity carried on under a *permission* obtained in accordance with Schedule 4 to the *Act* (Treaty Rights).

Treaty firm

(as defined in paragraph 1 of Schedule 4 to the *Act* (Treaty Rights)) a *person*:

(a) whose head office is situated in an *EEA State* (its *"Home State"*) other than the *United Kingdom*; and

(b) which is recognised under the law of that State as its national.

Treaty right

the entitlement of a *Treaty firm* to qualify for *authorisation* under Schedule 4 to the *Act* (Treaty Rights) 2001/7

Tribunal

the Upper Tribunal, namely the Tribunal established under section 3 of the Tribunals, Courts and Enforcement Act 2007, and to which the functions of the Financial Services and Markets Tribunal were transferred on 6 April 2010 by the Transfer of Tribunal Functions Order 2010.

trust deed

(A) In the PRA Handbook:

(1) (in *LR*) a trust deed or equivalent document securing or constituting *debt securities*.

(2) (in *COLL*) the deed referred to in COLL 3.2.3 R (The trust deed for AUTs), together with any deed expressed to be supplemental to it, made between the *manager* and the *trustee* (or, in the case of a *recognised scheme* that is a *unit trust scheme*, the *instrument constituting the scheme* as amended from time to time).

(B) In the FCA Handbook:

(1) (in *LR*) a trust deed or equivalent document securing or constituting *debt securities*.

(2) (in *COLL*) the deed referred to in COLL 3.2.3 R (The trust deed for AUTs), together with any deed expressed to be supplemental to it, made between the *manager* and the *trustee* (or, in the case of a *recognised scheme* that is a *unit trust scheme*, the *instrument constituting the fund* as amended from time to time).

trust scheme rules

rules in *COLL* made by the *FCA* under section 247(1) of the *Act* (Trust scheme rules) in relation to:

(a) the constitution, management and operation of *AUTs*;

(b) the powers, duties, rights and liabilities of the *manager* and *trustee* of any such *scheme*;

(c) the rights and duties of the *participants* in any such *scheme*; and

(d) the winding up of any such *scheme*.

trustee

(in accordance with section 237(2) of the *Act* (Other definitions)) (in relation to a *unit trust scheme*) the *person* holding the property in question on trust for the *participants*.

trustee firm

(A) In the PRA Handbook: a *firm* which is not an *OPS firm* and which is acting as a: (a) trustee; or (b) personal representative.

(B) In the FCA Handbook: a *firm* which is not an *OPS firm* and which is acting as a: (a) trustee (other than for a trust of *client money* arising only under CASS 5.3.2 R, CASS 5.4 (Non-statutory client money trust), CASS 7.17.2 R or CASS 11.6.1 R); or (b) personal representative.

turnover

(in relation to a *financial instrument*) means the sum of the results of multiplying the number of units of that instrument exchanged between buyers and sellers in a defined period of time, pursuant to *transactions* taking place on a *trading venue* or otherwise, by the unit price applicable to each such transaction. [Note: article 2(9) of the *MiFID Regulation*]

two-day emissions spot

an *emissions allowance* where delivery is to be made at an agreed date no later than the second trading day from the day of an auction on an *auction platform* (within the meaning of article 3(3) of the *auction regulation*).

Type P projection

(in relation to a *pension scheme* or a *stakeholder pension scheme*) a *projection* in real value terms based on prices where the period to the *projection date* is one year or more.

Type Q projection

(in relation to *pension scheme* or a *stakeholder pension scheme*) a *projection* in real value terms based on earnings where the period to the *projection date* is one year or more.

typical APR

an *APR* at or below which the *firm communicating* or *approving* the *financial promotion* reasonably expects, at the date on which the *financial promotion* is *communicated* or *approved*, that *credit* would be provided under at least 66% of the agreements which will be entered into as a result of the *financial promotion*.

UCITS

undertakings for collective investment in transferable securities that are established in accordance with the *UCITS Directive*.

UCITS Directive

the European Parliament and Council Directive of 13 July 2009 on the coordination of laws, regulations and administrative provisions relating to undertakings for collective investment in transferable securities (UCITS) (No 2009/65/EC), as amended.

UCITS eligible assets Directive

Commission Directive 2007/16/EC implementing Council Directive 85/611/EEC on the coordination of laws, regulations and administrative provisions relating to undertakings for collective investment in transferable securities (UCITS) as regards the clarification of certain definitions.

UCITS firm

(A) In the PRA Handbook: a *firm* which:

(a) is a *management company*, including where in addition the *firm* is also an *AIFM*; and

(b) does not have a *Part 4A permission* (or an equivalent permission from its *Home State regulator*) to carry on any *regulated activities* other than those which are in connection with, or for the purpose of, managing collective investment undertakings.

(B) In the FCA Handbook: a *firm* which:

(a) is a *management company* (whether or not it is also the manager of *AIFs* or the *operator* of other *collective investment schemes*); and

(b) does not have a *Part 4A permission* (or an equivalent permission from its *Home State regulator*) to carry on any *regulated activities* other than those which are in connection with, or for the purpose of, managing collective investment undertakings.

UCITS Home State

the *Home State* of a *UCITS scheme* or *EEA UCITS scheme*.

UCITS implementing Directive

Commission Directive (2010/43/EU) of the European Parliament and of the Council implementing Directive 2009/65/EC (UCITS IV) as regards certain provisions concerning organisational require-ments, conflicts of interest, conduct of business, risk management and content of the agreement between a *depositary* and a *management company*.

UCITS implementing Directive No 2

Commission Directive (2010/44/EU) of the European Parliament and of the Council implementing Directive 2009/65/EC (UCITS IV) as regards certain provisions concerning fund mergers, master-feeder structures and notification procedure.

UCITS investment firm

(A) In the PRA Handbook: a *firm* which:

(a) is a *management company* (whether or not it is also the operator of other *collective investment schemes*); and

(b) has a *Part 4A permission* (or an equivalent permission from its *Home State regulator*) to manage *investments* where:
(i) the *investments* managed include one or more of the instruments listed in Section C of Annex 1 to *MiFID*; and
(ii) the *permission* extends to activities permitted by article 6(3) of the *UCITS Directive* as well as those permitted by article 6(2).

(B) In the FCA Handbook: a *firm* which:

(a) is a *management company* (whether or not it is also the manager of *AIFs* or the *operator* of other *collective investment schemes*); and

(b) has a *Part 4A permission* (or an equivalent permission from its *Home State regulator*) to manage *investments* where:
(i) the *investments* managed include one or more of the instruments listed in Section C of Annex 1 to *MiFID*; and
(ii) the *permission* extends to activities permitted by article 6(3) of the *UCITS Directive* as well as those permitted by article 6(2).

UCITS management company

(1) (except in relation to *MiFID business*) a *firm* which is either:

(a) a *UCITS firm*; or

(b) a *UCITS investment firm*.

(2) (in relation to *MiFID business*) a *management company* as defined in the *UCITS Directive*. [Note: article 4 (1)(24) of *MiFID*]

UCITS marketing notification

(in *COLL*) a notification in respect of a *UCITS scheme*, for the purpose of *marketing units* in another *EEA State*, pursuant to:

(a) paragraph 20B(5) (Notice of intention to market) of Schedule 3 (EEA Passport Rights) to the *Act*; or

(b) article 46 of the Council Directive of 20 December 1985 on the co-ordination of laws, regulations and administrative provisions relating to undertakings for collective investment in transferable securities (UCITS) (No 85/611/EEC).

UCITS merger

(in *COLL* and in accordance with article 2(1)(p) of the *UCITS Directive*) a merger between one or more *UCITS schemes* or between one or more *UCITS schemes* and *EEA UCITS schemes* being an operation whereby:

(a) one or more *merging UCITS*, on being dissolved without going into liquidation, transfers all of its assets and liabilities to an existing *receiving UCITS*, in exchange for the issue to its *unitholders* of *units* of the *receiving UCITS* and, if applicable, a cash payment not exceeding 10% of the net asset value of those *units* (a "merger by absorption"); or

(b) two or more *merging UCITS*, on being dissolved without going into liquidation, transfer all of its assets and liabilities to a *receiving UCITS* which they form, in exchange for the issue to their *unitholders* of *units* of the *receiving UCITS* and, if applicable, a cash payment not exceeding 10% of the net asset value of those *units* (a "merger by formation of a new *UCITS*"); or

(c) one or more *merging UCITS*, which continue to exist until the liabilities have been discharged, transfer its net assets to another *receiving UCITS*, and for this purpose the *merging UCITS* and the *receiving UCITS* may be *sub-funds* of the same UCITS (a "merger by *scheme of arrangement*");

but at least one of which is established in the *United Kingdom*.

UCITS qualifier

a *firm* (other than an *EEA UCITS management company*) which:

(a) for the time being is an *operator*, *trustee* or *depositary* of a *scheme* which is a *recognised scheme* under section 264 of the *Act*; and

(b) is an *authorised person* as a result of paragraph 1(1) of Schedule 5 to the *Act* (Persons Concerned in Collective Investment Schemes);

a reference to a *firm* as a *UCITS qualifier* applies in relation to the carrying on by the *firm* of activities for which it has *permission* in that capacity.

UCITS Regulations 2011

the Undertaking for Collective Investment in Transferable Securities Regulations 2011 (SI 2011/1613).

UCITS scheme

(A) In the PRA Handbook:

(a) an *authorised fund* authorised by the *FCA* in accordance with the *UCITS Directive*:
(i) with the sole object of collective investment in *transferable securities* or in other liquid financial instruments permitted by COLL 5.2 (General investment powers and limits for UCITS schemes) of capital raised from the public and which operates on the principle of risk-spreading; and
(ii) with *units* which are, at the request of *unitholders*, repurchased or *redeemed*, directly or indirectly, out of the *scheme's* assets; and for this purpose action taken by or on behalf of a *scheme* to ensure that the stock exchange value of its *units* does not significantly vary from their net asset value is to be regarded as equivalent to that repurchase or *redemption*; or

(b) an umbrella, each of whose *sub-funds* would be a *UCITS scheme* if it had a separate *authorisation order*;

unless:

(c) [deleted]

(d) the *scheme's units* under its *instrument constituting the scheme*, may be sold only to the public in non-EEA States; or

(e) the *scheme* (other than a *master UCITS* which has at least two *feeder UCITS* as *unitholders*) raises capital without promoting the *sale* of its *units* to the public within the *EEA* or any part of it.

[Note: article 1 of the *UCITS Directive*]

(B) In the FCA Handbook:

(a) an *authorised fund* authorised by the *FCA* in accordance with the *UCITS Directive*:
(i) with the sole object of collective investment in *transferable securities* or in other liquid financial instruments permitted by COLL 5.2 (General investment powers and limits for UCITS schemes) of capital raised from the public and which operates on the principle of risk-spreading; and
(ii) with *units* which are, at the request of *unitholders*, repurchased or *redeemed*, directly or indirectly, out of the *scheme's* assets; and for this purpose action taken by or on behalf of a *scheme* to ensure that the stock exchange value of its *units* does not significantly vary from their net asset value is to be regarded as equivalent to that repurchase or *redemption*; or

(b) an umbrella, each of whose *sub-funds* would be a *UCITS scheme* if it had a separate *authorisation order*;

unless:

(c) [deleted]

(d) the *scheme's units* under its *instrument constituting the fund*, may be sold only to the public in non-EEA States; or

(e) the *scheme* (other than a *master UCITS* which has at least two *feeder UCITS* as *unitholders*) raises capital without promoting the *sale* of its *units* to the public within the *EEA* or any part of it.

[Note: article 1 of the *UCITS Directive*]

UK

United Kingdom.

UK AIF

an *AIF* that is:

(a) an *authorised fund*; or

(b) not an *authorised fund* but has its registered office or head office in the *UK*;

UK AIFM

an *AIFM established* in the *UK* and with a *Part 4A permission* to carry on the *regulated activity* of *managing an AIF*.

UK bank

a *bank* which is a *body corporate* or *partnership* formed under the law of any part of the *United Kingdom*.

UK consolidation group

(A) In the PRA Handbook:
The *group* of *undertakings* which are included in the *consolidated situation* of a *parent institution in a Member State*, an *EEA parent institution*, an *EEA parent financial holding company* or an *EEA parent mixed financial holding company* (including any *undertaking* which is included in that consolidation because of an *Article 12(1) relationship*, *Article 18(5) relationship* or Article 18 relationship).

(B) In the FCA Handbook:
(1) (for the purposes of *SYSC* as it applies to a *CRR firm*) the *group* of *undertakings* which are included in the *consolidated situation* of a *parent institution in a Member State*, an *EEA parent institution*, an *EEA parent financial holding company* or an *EEA parent mixed financial holding company* (including any *undertaking* which is included in that consolidation because of a *consolidation article 12(1) relationship*, *article 18(5) relationship* or *article 18(6) relationship*).
(2) (for the purposes of *BIPRU* and *SYSC* as it applies to a *BIPRU firm*) has the meaning in BIPRU 8.2.4 R (Definition of UK consolidation group), which is in summary the group that is identified as a *UK consolidation group* in accordance with the decision tree in BIPRU 8 Annex 1 R (Decision tree identifying a UK consolidation group); in each case only *persons* included under BIPRU 8.5 (Basis of consolidation) are included in the *UK consolidation group*.

UK Corporate Governance Code

(a) (except in *LR* and *DTR*) the UK Corporate Governance Code published in May 2010 by the Financial Reporting Council.

(b) (in *LR* and *DTR*) the UK Corporate Governance Code published in September 2012 by the Financial Reporting Council.

UK countercyclical buffer authority

the Bank of England, designated for the purpose of article 136(1) of the *CRD* in article 7 of The Capital Requirements (Capital Buffers and Macro-prudential Measures) Regulations 2014.

UK-deposit insurer

a *non-EEA insurer* that has made a deposit in the *United Kingdom* under article 23 of the *First Non-Life Directive* in accordance with article 26 of that Directive or under article 51 of the *Consolidated Life Directive* in accordance with article 56 of that Directive.

UK depositary

a *depositary established* in the *UK*.

UK designated investment firm

(A) (In the PRA Handbook): (in BIPRU 12 and SUP 16) a *designated investment firm* which is a *body corporate* or *partnership* formed under the law of any part of the *UK*.

(B) (In the FCA Handbook): (in BIPRU 12) a *designated investment firm* which is a *body corporate* or *partnership* formed under the law of any part of the *UK*.

UK DLG by modification

a *DLG by modification (firm level)* in which each member is a *UK ILAS BIPRU firm*. A *firm* with a *UK DLG by modification* cannot also have a *non-UK DLG by modification (firm level)*.

UK domestic firm

a *firm* that has its registered office (or, if it has no registered office, its head office) in the *United Kingdom*.

UK financial sector company

a company that is a:

(a) *UK bank*; or

(b) *UK insurer*; or

(c) *UK* incorporated *parent undertaking* of a company referred to in (a) or (b) where the main business of the *group* to which the *parent undertaking* and the company belong is financial services.

UK financial system

(as defined in section 1I of the *Act* (Meaning of "the UK financial system")) the financial system operating in the *United Kingdom* including:

(a) financial markets and exchanges;

(b) *regulated activities*; and

(c) other activities connected with financial markets and exchanges.

UK firm

(1) (except in *REC*) (as defined in paragraph 10 of Schedule 3 to the *Act* (EEA Passport Rights)) a *person* whose head office is in the *United Kingdom* and who has an *EEA right* to carry on activity in an *EEA State* other than the *United Kingdom*.

(2) (in *REC*) means an *investment firm* or *credit institution* which has a *Part 4A permission* to carry on one or more *regulated activities*.

UK ILAS BIPRU firm

an *ILAS BIPRU firm* which has its registered office (or, if it does not have a registered office, its head office) in the *United Kingdom*.

UK insurance intermediary

a *UK domestic firm* which has *Part 4A permission* to carry on *insurance mediation activity* but no other *regulated activity*.

UK insurer

an *insurer*, other than a *pure reinsurer* or a *non-directive insurer*, whose head office is in the *United Kingdom*.

UK ISPV

an *ISPV* with a *Part 4A permission* to *effect* or *carry out contracts of insurance*.

UK lead regulated firm

(A) In the PRA Handbook:
a *UK firm* that:
(a) is not part of a group that is subject to consolidated supervision by the *FCA* or the *PRA* or any other *regulatory body*; or
(b) is part of a group that is subject to consolidated supervision by the *FCA* or the *PRA* and that group is not part of a wider group that is subject to consolidated supervision by a *regulatory body* other than the *FCA* or the *PRA*.
For the purposes of this definition:
(c) Consolidated supervision of a group of *persons* means supervision of the adequacy of financial and other resources of that group on a *consolidated basis*. For example, this includes supervision under BIPRU 8 (Group risk consolidation).
(d) It is not relevant whether or not any supervision by another *regulatory body* has been assessed as equivalent under the *CRD* and *EU CRR* or the *Financial Groups Directive*.
(e) If the group is a *UK consolidation group* or *financial conglomerate* of which the *FCA* or the *PRA* is lead regulator that is headed by an *undertaking* that is not itself the *subsidiary undertaking* of

another *undertaking* the *firm* is a 'UK lead regulated firm'.
This definition is not related to the defined term *lead regulated firm*.

(B) In the FCA Handbook:
a *UK firm* that:
(a) is not part of a group that is subject to consolidated supervision by the *FCA* or the *PRA* or any other *regulatory body*; or
(b) is part of a group that is subject to consolidated supervision by the *FCA* or the *PRA* and that group is not part of a wider group that is subject to consolidated supervision by a *regulatory body* other than the *FCA* or the *PRA*.
For the purposes of this definition:
(c) Consolidated supervision of a group of persons means supervision of the adequacy of financial and other resources of that group on a *consolidated basis*.
(d) It is not relevant whether or not any supervision by another *regulatory body* has been assessed as equivalent under the *CRD* and *EU CRR* or the *Financial Groups Directive*.
(e) If the group is a *consolidation group* or *financial conglomerate* of which the *FCA* or the *PRA* is lead regulator that is headed by an *undertaking* that is not itself the *subsidiary undertaking* of another *undertaking* the *firm* is a 'UK lead regulated firm'.
This definition is not related to the defined term *lead regulated firm*.

UK MCR

the *MCR* calculated in accordance with INSPRU 1.5.44R by a *non-EEA direct insurer* (except a *UK-deposit insurer*, an *EEA-deposit insurer* or a *Swiss general insurer*) in relation to business carried on by the *firm* in the *United Kingdom*.

UK MiFID investment firm

a *MiFID investment firm* whose *Home State* is the *United Kingdom* (this may include a natural *person* provided the conditions set out in Article 4(1)(1) of *MiFID* are satisfied).

UK parent financial holding company in a Member State

a *parent financial holding company in a Member State* where the *EEA State* in question is the *United Kingdom*.

UK parent mixed financial holding company in a Member State

a *parent mixed financial holding company in a Member State* where the *EEA State* in question is the *UK*.

UK pure reinsurer

a *pure reinsurer* whose head office is in the *United Kingdom*.

UK RCH

a *clearing house* which is declared by an order made by the Bank of England under section 290 of the *Act* and for the time being in force to be a recognised clearing house.

UK recognised body

a *UK RIE* or*RAP*.

UK regulated EEA financial conglomerate

a *financial conglomerate* (other than a *third-country financial conglomerate*) that satisfies one of the following conditions:

(a) GENPRU 3.1.29 R (Capital adequacy calculations for *financial conglomerates*) applies with respect to it; or

(b) a *firm* that is a member of that *financial conglomerate* is subject to obligations imposed through its *Part 4A permission* to ensure that *financial conglomerate* meets levels of capital adequacy based or stated to be based on Annex I of the *Financial Groups Directive*.

UK RIE

an *RIE* that is not an *ROIE*.

UK UCITS management company

a *management company* that is established in the *United Kingdom* and is *authorised* and regulated by the *FCA*.

UKLA

the *FCA* acting in its capacity as the *competent authority* for the purposes of Part VI of the *Act* (Official Listing).

ultimate EEA insurance parent undertaking

(A) In the PRA Handbook:

an *EEA insurance parent undertaking* that is not itself the *subsidiary undertaking* of another *EEA insurance parent undertaking* or of a *mixed financial holding company* which has its head office in an *EEA State*.

(B) In the FCA Handbook:

an *EEA insurance parent undertaking* that is not itself the *subsidiary undertaking* of another *EEA insurance parent undertaking*.

ultimate EEA mixed financial holding company

a *mixed financial holding company* which has its head office in an *EEA State* and which is not itself the *subsidiary undertaking* of another *mixed financial holding company*, *insurance parent undertaking* or financial holding company which has its head office in an *EEA State*.

ultimate insurance parent undertaking

(A) In the PRA Handbook:

an *insurance parent undertaking* that is not itself the *subsidiary undertaking* of another *insurance parent undertaking* or of a *mixed financial holding company*.

(B) In the FCA Handbook:

an *insurance parent undertaking* that is not itself the *subsidiary undertaking* of another *insurance parent undertaking*.

ultimate mixed financial holding company

a *mixed financial holding company* which is not itself the *subsidiary undertaking* of another *mixed financial holding company*, *insurance parent undertaking*, or *financial holding company*.

ultimate parent undertaking

(in relation to an *insurer*) a *parent undertaking* of the *insurer* that is not itself the *subsidiary undertaking* of another *undertaking*.

umbrella

(A) In the PRA Handbook: (in *FEES*, *COLL* and *COBS*) a *collective investment scheme* whose *instrument constituting the scheme* provides for such pooling as is mentioned in section 235(3)(a) of the *Act* (Collective investment schemes) in relation to separate parts of the *scheme property* and whose are entitled to exchange rights in one part for rights in another.

(B) In the FCA Handbook: (in *FEES*, *COLL* and *COBS*) a *collective investment scheme* whose *instrument constituting the fund* provides for such pooling as is mentioned in section 235(3)(a) of the *Act* (Collective investment schemes) in relation to separate parts of the *scheme property* and whose are entitled to exchange rights in one part for rights in another.

umbrella collective investment scheme

(in *PR*) (as defined in the *PD Regulation*) a collective investment undertaking invested in one or more collective investment undertakings, the asset of which is composed of separate class(es) or designation(s) of securities.

unattached shares

(in *CREDS*) means the total shares in the *credit union* other than any *attached shares* or *deferred shares*.

unauthorised AIF

an *AIF* which is not an *authorised fund*.

unauthorised AIFM

a person who is not an *authorised person* but who is:

(a) a *small registered UK AIFM*; or

(b) a small registered EEA AIFM, i.e. an *EEA AIFM* that is a *small AIFM* that has not opted in to become a *full-scope EEA AIFM*; or

(c) a *full-scope EEA AIFM* that is entitled to *market* an *AIF* in the *United Kingdom* following a notification under regulation 57 of the *AIFMD UK regulation*; or

(d) an *small non-EEA AIFM* that is entitled to *market* an *AIF* in the *United Kingdom* following a notification under regulation 58 of the *AIFMD UK regulation*; or

(e) an *above-threshold non-EEA AIFM* to which the requirement at regulation 59(3) of the *AIFMD UK regulation* applies; or

(f) a *full-scope EEA AIFM* that is exercising a right to *market* an *AIF* in the *United Kingdom* arising out of the *EuSEF regulation* or the *EuVECA regulation*.

unauthorised fund

a *fund* which is not an *authorised fund*.

unauthorised person

a *person* who is not an *authorised person*.

unauthorised reversion provider

a *person* who carries on, or proposes to carry on, the activity specified in article 63B(1) of the *Regulated Activities Order* which is entering into a *home reversion plan* as plan provider, and who does not have *permission* for, and is not an *exempt person* in relation to, *entering into a home reversion plan*.

unauthorised SRB agreement provider

a *person* who carries on, or proposes to carry on, the activity specified in article 63J(1) of the *Regulated Activities Order* which is entering into a *regulated sale and rent back agreement* as agreement provider, and who does not have *permission* for, and is not an *exempt person* in relation to, *entering into a regulated sale and rent back agreement*; and in this definition references to an agreement provider include a *person* who acquires obligations or rights under a *regulated sale and rent back agreement*.

uncrystallised funds pension lump sum

has the meaning given by paragraph 4A of Schedule 29 to the Finance Act 2004 which, subject to the exceptions in the Finance Act 2004, includes a lump sum that:

(a) is paid on or after 6 April 2015 in respect of a money purchase arrangement;

(b) is paid when all or part of the member's lifetime allowance is available;

(c) is paid when the member has reached normal minimum pension age (or the ill-health condition is met);

(d) is not a lump sum that, for the purposes of Part 9 of ITEPA 2003 (pension income), is treated by regulations under section 164(1)(f) and (2) of the Finance Act 2004 as a trivial commutation lump sum paid to the member; and

(e) immediately before the member becomes entitled to it, the sums or assets that are to be used to provide it:
(i) represent rights of the member under the scheme that are uncrystallised rights as defined by section 212(1) and (2) of the Finance Act 2004; and
(ii) do not to any extent represent rights attributable to a disqualifying pension credit.

underlying instrument

(in *LR*) (in relation to *securitised derivatives*) means either:

(a) if the *securitised derivative* is an *option* or *debt security* with the characteristics of an *option*, any of the underlying investments listed in article 83 of the *Regulated Activities Order*; or

(b) if the *securitised derivative* is a *contract for differences* or *debt security* with the characteristics of a *contract for differences*, any factor by reference to which a profit or loss under article 85 of the *Regulated Activities Order* can be calculated.

undertaking

(as defined in section 1161(1) of the Companies Act 2006 (Meaning of "undertaking" and related expressions)):

(a) a *body corporate* or *partnership*; or

(b) an unincorporated association carrying on a trade or business, with or without a view to profit.

underwrite

(for the purposes of BIPRU 7 (Market risk)) to undertake a firm commitment to buy a specified quantity of new *securities* on a given date and at a given price if no other has purchased or acquired them; and so that:

(a) new is defined in BIPRU 7.8.12R (New securities);

(b) a *firm* still underwrites *securities* at a time before the exact quantity of *securities* being underwritten or their price has been determined if it is committed at that time to underwrite them when the quantity and price is fixed;

(c) (in the case of provisions of the *Handbook* that distinguish between *underwriting* and sub-*underwriting*) *underwriting* does not include sub-*underwriting*; and

(d) (in any other case) *underwriting* includes sub-*underwriting*.

underwriting agent

a *firm* permitted by the *Council* to act as an underwriting agent at Lloyd's.

underwriting capacity of a Lloyd's syndicate

the *investment*, specified in article 86(1) of the *Regulated Activities Order*, which is the underwriting capacity of a *syndicate*.

underwriting member

a *person* admitted to the *Society* as an underwriting member.

unearned premium

the amount set aside by a *firm* at the end of its *financial year* out of *premiums* in respect of risks to be borne by the *firm* after the end of the *financial year* under *contracts of insurance* entered into before the end of that year.

Unfair Terms Regulations

the Unfair Terms in Consumer Contracts Regulations 1999 (SI 1999/2083), as amended by SI 2001/1186 and SI 2001/3649.

UNFCOG

the Unfair Contract Terms Regulatory Guide.

unfunded credit protection

(1) (in *BIPRU* and in accordance with Article 4(32) of the *Banking Consolidation Directive* (Definitions)) a technique of *credit risk mitigation* where the reduction of the credit risk on the *exposure* of an undertaking derives from the *undertaking* of a third party to pay an amount in the event of the default of the borrower or on the occurrence of other specified events.

(2) (in *IFPRU*) has the meaning in article 4(1)(59) of the *EU CRR*.

(3) (in *MIPRU*) a way of mitigating credit risk where the reduction of credit risk on the *exposure* of an *undertaking* (the borrower) derives from the enforceable obligation of a third party to pay an amount in the event of the default of the borrower or on the occurrence of other specified events.

unit

(1) (in relation to a *collective investment scheme*) the investment, specified in article 81 of the *Regulated Activities Order* (Units in a collective investment scheme) and defined in section 237(2) of the *Act* (Other definitions)), which is the right or interest (however described) of the *participants* in a *collective investment scheme*; this includes:
(a) (in relation to an *AUT*) a unit representing the rights or interests of the *unitholders* in the *AUT*;
(aa) (in relation to an *ACS*) a unit representing the rights or interests of the *unitholders* in the *ACS*; and
(b) (in relation to an *ICVC*) a *share* in the *ICVC*.; and

(2) (in relation to an *alternative investment fund*) the right or interest (however described) of an investor in an *alternative investment fund*.

unit trust scheme

(as defined in section 237(1) of the *Act* (Other definitions)) a *collective investment scheme* under which the property in question is held on trust for the *participants*, except that it does not include an *authorised contractual scheme*.

United Kingdom

England and Wales, Scotland and Northern Ireland (but not the Channel Islands or the Isle of Man).

unitholder

(a) (in relation to an *ICVC*, *ACS* or an *AUT* as appropriate, and subject to COLL 4.4.4 R (Special meaning of unitholder in COLL 4.4)):

(i) (in relation a *unit* which is represented by a *bearer certificate*) the *person* who holds that certificate; or

(ii) (in relation to a *unit* that is not represented by a *bearer certificate*) the *person* whose name is entered on the *register* in relation to that *unit*; or

(b) (in relation to a *unit* in *collective investment scheme* not within (a)):

(i) the holder of the *bearer certificate* representing that *unit*; or

(ii) the *person* who entered on the *register* of the *scheme* as the holder of that *unit*.

unitisation

arrangements for a newly formed *AUT* or *ACS* under which:

(a) the whole or part of the property of a *body corporate* (or a *collective investment scheme*) becomes the first *scheme property* of the *AUT* or *ACS*; and

(b) the *holders* of:

(i) *shares* in the *body corporate* being wound up; or

(ii) *units* in the *collective investment scheme*, the property of which is being transferred;

become the first *participants* in the *AUT* or *ACS*.

units of a collective investment scheme

(in *PR*) (as defined in Article 2.1(p) of the *prospectus directive*) securities issued by a collective investment undertaking as representing the rights of the participants in such an undertaking over its assets.

unpaid initial fund

part of the *initial fund* of a *mutual* which the *mutual* is prevented from including in its *tier one capital resources* as *permanent share capital* by reason of GENPRU 2.2.64R because it is not fully paid.

unrated position

(for the purposes of BIPRU 9 (Securitisation), in accordance with Part 1 of Annex IX of the *Banking Consolidation Directive* (Securitisation definitions) and in relation to a *securitisation position*) describes a *securitisation position* which does not have an eligible credit assessment by an *eligible ECAI*.

unrecognised scheme

(in *LR*) a *collective investment scheme* which is neither a *recognised scheme* nor a scheme that is constituted as an *authorised unit trust scheme* or *authorised contractual scheme*.

unregulated activity

an activity which is not a *regulated activity*.

unregulated collective investment scheme

a *collective investment scheme* which is not a *regulated collective investment scheme*.

unrestricted-use credit agreement

a *credit agreement* which is not a *restricted-use credit agreement*.

unsecured debt

debt that does not fall within the definition of *secured debt*.

unsecured lending

lending where the *mortgage lender* does not take a mortgage or other form of security in respect of the credit provided to the *customer*.

unsolicited real time financial promotion

(in accordance with article 8 of the *Financial Promotion Order*) a *real time financial promotion* which is not a *solicited real time financial promotion*.

unsustainable

(in *CONC*) has the meaning given in CONC 5.3.1 G.

upper tier three capital

an item of capital that is specified in stage O of the *capital resources table* (Upper tier three).

upper tier three capital resources

the sum calculated at stage O of the *capital resources table* (Upper tier three).

upper tier three instrument

an item of capital that meets the conditions in GENPRU 2.2.242R (Tier three capital: upper tier three capital resources) and is eligible to form part of a *firm's upper tier three capital resources*.

upper tier two capital

(1) [deleted]

(2) (in *BIPRU*, *GENPRU* and *INSPRU*) an item of capital that is specified in stage G of the *capital resources table* (Upper tier two capital).

upper tier two capital resources

the sum calculated at stage G of the calculation in the *capital resources table* (Upper tier two capital).

upper tier two instrument

a *capital instrument* that meets the conditions in GENPRU 2.2.177 R (Upper tier two capital: General) and is eligible to form part of a *firm*'s *upper tier two capital resources*.

UPRU

the Prudential sourcebook for UCITS Firms.

valuation point

(in *COLL*) a *valuation point* fixed by the *authorised fund manager* for the purpose of COLL 6.3.4 R (Valuation points) or COLL 8.5.9 R (Valuation, pricing and dealing).

value at risk

(in relation to risk modelling or estimation for the purposes of *BIPRU*) the measure of risk described in BIPRU 7.10.146 R (Requirement to use value at risk methodology).

VaR

value at risk

VaR measure

(in *BIPRU*) an estimate by a *VaR model* of the worst expected loss on a portfolio resulting from market movements over a period of time with a given confidence level.

VaR model

a value at risk model as described in BIPRU 7.10 (Use of a Value at Risk Model).

VaR model approach

one of the following:

(a) the approach to calculating part of the *market risk capital requirement* set out in BIPRU 7.10 (Use of a value at risk model);

(b) (where the approach in (a) is being applied on a consolidated basis) the method in (a) as applied on a consolidated basis in accordance with BIPRU 8 (Group risk – consolidation); or

(c) when the reference is to the rules of or administered by a *regulatory body* other than the *appropriate regulator*, whatever corresponds to the approach in (a) or (b), as the case may be, under those rules.

Part 3 FCA Handbook Materials

VaR model permission

(A) In the PRA Handbook:

an *Article 129 implementing measure*, a *requirement* or a *waiver* that requires a *BIPRU firm* or an *institution* to use the *VaR model approach* on a solo basis or, if the context requires, a consolidated basis.

(B) In the FCA Handbook:

an *Article 129 implementing measure*, a *requirement* or a *waiver* that requires a *BIPRU firm* or a *CAD investment firm* to use the *VaR model approach* on a solo basis or, if the context requires, a consolidated basis.

VaR number

has the meaning in BIPRU 7.10.115R (Capital calculations: General) which in summary is (in relation to a *business day* and a *VaR model*) the *VaR measure*, in respect of the previous *business day*'s close-of-business *positions* in products coming within the scope of the *VaR model permission*, calculated by the *VaR model* and in accordance with BIPRU 7.10 (Use of a Value at Risk Model) and any methodology set out in the *VaR model permission*.

VaR specific risk minimum requirements

BIPRU 7.10.46R to BIPRU 7.10.52R (Model standards: Risk factors: Specific risk) and BIPRU 7.10.107R (Backtesting: Specific risk backtesting).

vehicle

any motor vehicle intended for travel on land and propelled by mechanical power, but not running on rails, and any trailer whether or not coupled. [Note: article 1(1) of Council Directive 72/166/EEC (First Motor Insurance Directive)]

vendor consideration placing

(in *LR*) a marketing, by or on behalf of vendors, of *securities* that have been allotted as consideration for an acquisition.

venture capital business

(A) In the PRA Handbook: the business of carrying on any of:

(a) investing in, *advising on investments* which are, *managing investments* which are, *arranging* (bringing about) *transactions* in, or *making arrangements with a view to transactions in venture capital investments*;

(b) *advising on investments* or *managing investments* in relation to portfolios, or *establishing, operating or winding up collective investment schemes*, where the portfolios or *collective investment schemes* (apart from funds awaiting investment) invest only in *venture capital investments*;

(c) any *custody* activities provided in connection with the activities in (a) and (b);

(d) any related *ancillary activities*.

(B) In the FCA Handbook: the business of carrying on any of:

(a) investing in, *advising on investments* which are, *managing investments* which are, *arranging* (bringing about) *transactions* in, or *making arrangements with a view to transactions in venture capital investments*;

(b) *advising on investments* or *managing investments* in relation to portfolios, or *establishing, operating or winding up collective investment schemes* or *managing AIFs*, where the portfolios or *funds* (apart from funds awaiting investment) invest only in *venture capital investments*;

(c) any *custody* activities provided in connection with the activities in (a) and (b);

(d) any related *ancillary activities*.

venture capital contact

(when a *firm* carries on *regulated activities* with or for a *person* in the course of or as a result of carrying on *venture capital business*) that *person* in connection with that *regulated activity* if:

(a) the *firm* does not behave in a way towards that *person* which might reasonably be expected to lead that *person* to believe that he is being treated as a *client*; and

(b) the *firm* clearly indicates to that *person* that the *firm*:
(i) is not acting for him; and
(ii) will not be responsible to him for providing protections afforded to *clients* of the *firm* or be advising him on the relevant transaction.

venture capital firm

a *firm* whose *permission* includes a *requirement* that it must not conduct *designated investment business* other than *venture capital business*.

venture capital investment

a *designated investment* which, at the time the investment is made, is:

(a) in a new or developing *company* or venture; or

(b) in a management buy-out or buy-in; or

(c) made as a means of financing the investee *company* or venture and accompanied by a right of consultation, or rights to information, or board representation, or management rights; or

(d) acquired with a view to, or in order to, facilitate a transaction falling within (a) to (c).

venture capital trust

(in *LR*) a *company* which is, or which is seeking to become, approved as a venture capital trust under section 842AA of the Income and Corporation Taxes Act 1988.

verified

(in *IPRU(INV)* 13) where interim net profits are to be included in a *firm's* capital resources, checked by an external auditor who has undertaken at least to:

(a) satisfy himself that the figures forming the basis of the interim profits have been properly extracted from the underlying accounting records;

(b) review the accounting policies used in calculating the interim profits so as to obtain comfort that they are consistent with those normally adopted by the *firm* in drawing up its *annual financial statements* and are in accordance with the accounting principles set out in *IPRU(INV)* 13;

(c) perform analytical procedures on the result to date, including comparisons of actual performance to date with budget and with the results of prior period(s);

(d) discuss with management the overall performance and financial *position* of the *firm*;

(e) obtain adequate comfort that the implications of current and prospective litigation, all known claims and commitments, changes in business activities and provisioning for bad and doubtful debts have been properly taken into account in arriving at the interim profits; and

(f) follow up problem areas of which he is already aware in the course of auditing the *firm's* financial statements, a copy of whose report asserting that the interim net profits are reasonably stated has been submitted to the *FCA* (although this does not apply to *exempt CAD firms*).

version 1 credit union

a *credit union* whose *Part 4A permission* includes a *requirement* (whether for all or for particular purposes) that it must not lend more than £15,000, or such lesser amount as may be specified, in excess of a member's shareholding; in this definition a "member's shareholding" means any shares held by a member of the *credit union* in accordance with sections 5 and 7 of the Credit Unions Act 1979 or articles 14 and 23 of the Credit Unions (Northern Ireland) Order 1985 (as appropriate).

version 2 credit union

a *credit union* which is not a *version 1 credit union*.

VJ participant

a *person* subject to the *Voluntary Jurisdiction* by contract.

volatility risk

the potential loss due to fluctuations in implied *option* volatilities.

Voluntary Jurisdiction

the jurisdiction of the *Financial Ombudsman Service* in which *persons* (whether *authorised* or unauthorised) participate by contract.

voting power

(in *SUP* 11 (Controllers and close links) and *SUP* 16 (Reporting requirements) (in accordance with section 422 of the *Act*):

(a) includes, in relation to a *person* ("H"):

(i) voting power held by a third party with whom H has concluded an agreement, which obliges H and the third party to adopt, by concerted exercise of the voting power they hold, a lasting common policy towards the management of the *undertaking* in question;

(ii) voting power held by a third party under an agreement concluded with H providing for the temporary transfer for consideration of the voting power in question;

(iii) voting power attaching to *shares* which are lodged as collateral with H, provided that H controls the voting power and declares an intention to exercise it;

(iv) voting power attaching to *shares* in which H has a life interest;

(v) voting power which is held, or may be exercised within the meaning of subparagraphs (i) to (iv), by a subsidiary *undertaking* of H;

(vi) voting power attaching to *shares* deposited with H which H has discretion to exercise in the absence of specific instructions from the shareholders;

(vii) voting power held in the name of a third party on behalf of H;

(viii) voting power which H may exercise as a proxy where H has discretion about the exercise of the voting power in the absence of specific instructions from the shareholders; and

(b) in relation to an *undertaking* which does not have general meetings at which matters are decided by the exercise of voting rights, the right under the constitution of the *undertaking* to direct the overall policy of the *undertaking* or alter the terms of its constitution.

waiver

(A) In the PRA Handbook: a direction waiving or modifying a *rule*, given by the *PRA* under section 138A of the *Act* (Modification or waiver of rules) or by the *FCA* under sections 250, 261L or 294 of the Act (Modification or waiver of rules) or regulation 7 of the *OEIC Regulations* (see REC 3.3)

(B) In the FCA Handbook: a direction waiving or modifying a *rule*, given by the *appropriate regulator* under section 138A of the *Act* (Modification or waiver of rules) or by the *FCA* under sections 250, 261L or 294 of the *Act* (Modification or waiver of rules) or regulation 7 of the *OEIC Regulations* (see SUP 8 and REC 3.3).

warning notice

a notice issued by the *appropriate regulator* in accordance with section 387 of the *Act* (Warning notices).

warrant

(1) (except in *COLL*) the *investment*, specified in article 79 of the *Regulated Activities Order* (Instruments giving entitlements to investments), which is in summary: a warrant or other instrument entitling the holder to subscribe for a *share*, *debenture*, *alternative debenture* or *government and public security*.

(2) (in *COLL*) an *investment* in (1) and any other *transferable security* (not being a nil paid or partly paid *security*) which is:

(i) *listed* on an *eligible securities* market; and

(ii) akin to an *investment* within (1) in that it involves a down payment by the then holder and a right later to surrender the instrument and to pay more *money* in return for a further *transferable security*.

weather derivative

a *contract for differences* where the index or other factor in question is a climatic variable.

website conditions

the following conditions:

(1) the provision of information by means of a website must be appropriate to the context in which the business between the *firm* and the *client* is, or is to be, carried on (that is, there is evidence that the *client* has regular access to the internet, such as the provision by the client of an e-mail address for the purposes of the carrying on of that business);

(2) the *client* must specifically consent to the provision of that information in that form;

(3) the *client* must be notified electronically of the address of the website, and the place on the website where the information may be accessed;

(4) the information must be up to date; and

(5) the information must be accessible continuously by means of that website for such period of time as the *client* may reasonably need to inspect it.

[Note: article 3 of the *MiFID implementing Directive* and article 38(2) of the *KII Regulation*]

weighted average life

(in accordance with the definitions section in *CESR's guidelines on a common definition of European money market funds*) the weighted average of the remaining life (maturity) of each *security* held in a fund, meaning the time until the principal is repaid in full (disregarding interest and not discounting).

weighted average maturity

(in accordance with the definitions section in *CESR's guidelines on a common definition of European money market funds*) a measure of the average length of time to maturity of all of the underlying *securities* in a fund weighted to reflect the relative holdings in each instrument, assuming that the maturity of a floating rate instrument is the time remaining until the next interest rate reset to the money market rate, rather than the time remaining before the principal value of the *security* must be repaid.

welfare trust

any scheme or arrangement, not being an *occupational pension scheme*, that is comprised in one or more instruments or agreements and operates as a benevolent fund so as to provide benefits, at the discretion of the trustees and to which the beneficiaries have no contractual rights.

whole-firm liquidity modification

a modification to the *overall liquidity adequacy rule* of the kind described in BIPRU 12.8.22G.

whole life assurance

a *contract of insurance* which, disregarding any benefit payable on surrender, secures a capital sum only on death or either on death or on disability, but does not include a term assurance.

wholesale depositor

a *person* who is:

(a) a *credit institution*; or

(b) a *large company*; or

(c) a *large mutual association* which is:
(i) a *firm*; or
(ii) an *overseas financial services institution*; or
(iii) a *collective investment scheme* or an operator or trustee of a *collective investment scheme*; or
(iv) a pension or retirement fund, or a trustee of such a fund (except a trustee of a small self-administered scheme or an occupational scheme of an employer which is not a *large company* or a *large partnership*); or

(d) a supranational institution, government or central administrative authority; or

(e) a provincial, regional, local or municipal authority; or

(f) a *body corporate* in the same *group* as the *person* with whom the *deposit* is made.

wholesale market broker

a *firm* when carrying out the activities of *name-passing broker*, or acting on a matched principal basis, with or for *market counterparties*.

with-profits actuary

an *actuary* appointed to perform the *with-profits actuary function*.

with-profits actuary function

(in the *PRA Handbook*) PRA *controlled function* CF12A in the *table of PRA controlled functions*, described more fully in SUP 4.3.16A R and SUP 10B.8.2 R.

with-profits advisory arrangement

(a) an independent person; or

(b) if appropriate, one or more *non-executive directors* appointed to provide independent judgment to the *governing body* of a *firm*; *FCA controlled functions*

which satisfies the requirements of its *terms of reference*.

with-profits assets

assets that match liabilities in respect of *with-profits insurance business* or represent a with-profits surplus.

with-profits benefits reserve

(in relation to a *with-profits fund*) the with-profits benefits reserve for the *with-profits fund* calculated in accordance with the *rules* in INSPRU 1.3.116 R to INSPRU 1.3.135 G.

with-profits business

any business of an *insurer* that may affect the amount or value of the assets comprising a *with-profits fund*.

with-profits committee

a committee:

(a) the majority of the members of which are independent of the *firm*, or, where there is an equal number of independent and non-independent members, which is chaired by a *person* who is one of the independent members; and

(b) which satisfies the requirements of its *terms of reference*.

with-profits fund

(1) (except in *INSPRU*):

(a) a *long-term insurance fund* (or that part of such a fund) in which *policyholders* are eligible to participate in any *established surplus*; and

(b) where it is an *insurer's* usual practice to restrict *policyholders'* participation in any *established surplus* to that arising from only a part of the fund (or part fund) falling within (a), that part (or that part of the part fund).

(2) for the purposes of *INSPRU*, a *long-term insurance fund* in which *policyholders* are eligible to participate in any *established surplus*.

with-profits insurance business

the business of *effecting* or carrying out *with-profits insurance contracts*.

with-profits insurance capital component

the capital component for *with-profits insurance business* of a *realistic basis life firm* calculated in accordance with INSPRU 1.3.

with-profits insurance contract

a *long-term insurance contract* which provides for the *policyholder* to be eligible to participate in any surplus arising on the whole of, or any part of, the *insurer's long-term insurance business*.

with-profits insurance liabilities

insurance liabilities arising from *with-profits insurance business*.

with-profits policy

a contract falling within a *class* of *long-term insurance business* which is eligible to participate in any part of any *established surplus*.

with-profits policyholder

a *policyholder* under a *with-profits policy*.

with-profits practices

the with-profits practices that a *firm* must establish, maintain and record under COBS 20.3 (Principles and Practices of Financial Management).

with-profits principles

the with-profits principles that a *firm* must establish, maintain and record under COBS 20.3 (Principles and Practices of Financial Management).

working day

(1) (in *PR* and *COMP*) (as defined in section 103 of the *Act*) any day other than a Saturday, a Sunday, Christmas Day, Good Friday or a day which is a bank holiday under the Banking and Financial Dealings Act 1971 in any part of the *United Kingdom*.

(2) (in relation to an underwriter and for the purpose of *BIPRU* but not for the purpose of the definition of *working day 0*) the number of *business days* after *working day 0* specified by the provision in question so that, for example, *working day* one means the *business day* following *working day 0*.

working day 0

has the meaning in BIPRU 7.8.23R (Working day 0), which is in summary (in relation to an underwriter) the *business day* on which a *firm* that is *underwriting* or sub-*underwriting* becomes unconditionally committed to accepting a known quantity of *securities* at a specified price.

work-related insurance

work-related insurance, including:

(a) life assurance;

(b) long term disability insurance (also known as *permanent health* insurance); and

(c) accidental death, injury, critical illness, medical, dental, income protection or travel insurance.

workplace pension contributions

contributions made to a *qualifying scheme* by, or on behalf of, an employee who has become a member of that scheme, including transfers in from other schemes.

WPICC

with-profits insurance capital component.

wrapper

a *PEP*, *ISA* or *CTF*.

write-down and conversion powers

the powers referred to in article 59(2) and in points (e) to (i) of article 63(1) of *RRD*. [Note: articles 2(1)(66) of *RRD*]

zero-specific-risk security

a notional debt *security* used, for the purpose of calculating *PRR*, to represent the interest rate *general market risk* arising from certain *derivative* and forward transactions as specified in BIPRU 7.2 (Interest rate PRR).

zillmerising

the method known by that name for modifying the *net premium* reserve method of valuing a *long-term insurance contract* by increasing the part of the future *premiums* for which credit is taken so as to allow for initial expenses.

Zone A country

(a) any *EEA State*;

(b) all other countries which are full members of the *OECD*; and

(c) those countries which have concluded special lending arrangements with the International Monetary Fund (IMF) associated with the Fund's general arrangements to borrow (GAB),

save that any country falling with (a), (b) or (c) which reschedules its external sovereign debt is precluded from Zone A for a period of five years.

working day

(1) (in FN and CONV) as defined in section 103 of the Act [any day other than a Saturday, a Sunday, Christmas Day, Good Friday or a day which is a bank holiday under the Banking and Financial Dealings Act 1971 in any part of the United Kingdom.

(2) (in relation to an underwriter and for the purpose of *BIPRU* but not for the purpose of the definition of *working day 0*) the number of *business days* after *working day 0* specified by the *firm* in its question so that, for example, *working day* one means the *business day* following *working day 0*.

working day 0

has the meaning in *BIPRU* 7.8 75K (Working day 0) which defines *working day* in relation to an *underwriter*: the *business day* on which a *firm* that is *underwriting* or *sub-underwriting* becomes unconditionally committed to accepting a known quantity of *securities* at a specified price.

work-related insurance

work-related insurance, including:

(a) life assurance;

(b) long term disability insurance (also known as permanent health insurance); and

(c) accidental death, injury, critical illness, medical, dental, income protection or travel insurance.

workplace pension contributions

a contribution made in a *qualifying scheme* by or on behalf of an *employee* who has become a member of that *scheme*, including transfers in from other *schemes*.

WPCF

the *wind insurance market company*.

wrapper

as in *PERG* 10.4 per *FF*.

write-down and conversion powers

the powers referred to in article 59(2) and in points (e) to (i) of article 63(1) of *RRD* (Article 2.1(66) *RRD*)

zero-specific-risk security

a notional debt security used, for the purpose of calculating a *VaR*, to represent the interest rate general market risk arising from certain derivatives and forward transactions as specified in *BIPRU* 7.2 (Interest rate PRR).

zilla-rating

a method of zakat by that name for modelling the zekat flow reserve a method of valuing a *firm's* insurance reserve by measuring the total of future premiums for which credit is taken so as to allow for initial expenses.

Zone A country

(1) (in GENPRU) a state:
(a) all of the countries which are full members of the OECD; and

(2) those countries which have concluded special lending arrangements with the International Monetary Fund (IMF) associated with the Fund's General Arrangements to Borrow (GAB),

save that any country falling with item 1(a) or item (2) which reschedules its external sovereign debt is precluded from *Zone A* for a period of five years.

B. PRINCIPLES FOR BUSINESS (PRIN)

PRINCIPLES FOR BUSINESSES
the fundamental obligations of all firms under the regulatory system

CHAPTER 1
INTRODUCTION

1.1 APPLICATION AND PURPOSE

Application

[3.2]
1.1.1 G   FCA

The *Principles* (see **PRIN 2**) apply in whole or in part to every *firm*. The application of the *Principles* is modified for *firms* conducting *MiFID business, incoming EEA firms, incoming Treaty firms, UCITS qualifiers* and *AIFM qualifiers*. **PRIN 3** (Rules about application) specifies to whom, to what and where the *Principles* apply.

Purpose

1.1.2 G   FCA

The *Principles* are a general statement of the fundamental obligations of *firms* under the *regulatory system*. This includes provisions which implement the *Single Market Directives*. They derive their authority from the *appropriate regulator's* rule-making powers as set out in the *Act* and reflect the *statutory objectives*.

1.1.3 G

[deleted]

Link to fit and proper standard in the threshold conditions

1.1.4 G   FCA

In substance, the *Principles* express the main dimensions of the "fit and proper" standard set for *firms* in *threshold condition* 5 (Suitability), although they do not derive their authority from that standard or exhaust its implications. Being ready, willing and organised to abide by the *Principles* is therefore a critical factor in applications for *Part 4A permission*, and breaching the *Principles* may call into question whether a *firm* with *Part 4A permission* is still fit and proper.

Taking group activities into account

1.1.5 G   FCA

Principles 3 (Management and control), 4 (Financial prudence) and (in so far as it relates to disclosing to the *appropriate regulator*) 11 (Relations with regulators) take into account the activities of members of a *firm's group*. This does not mean that, for example, inadequacy of a *group* member's risk management systems or resources will automatically lead to a *firm* contravening *Principle* 3 or 4. Rather, the potential impact of a *group* member's activities (and, for example, risk management systems operating on a *group* basis) will be relevant in determining the adequacy of the *firm's* risk management systems or resources respectively.

Standards in markets outside the United Kingdom

1.1.6 G   FCA

As set out in **PRIN 4.3** (Where?), *Principles* 1 (Integrity), 2 (Skill, care and diligence) and 3 (Management and control) apply to world-wide activities in a *prudential context*. *Principle* 5 (Market conduct) applies to world-wide activities which might have a negative effect on confidence in the *UK financial system*. In considering whether to take regulatory action under these *Principles* in relation to activities carried on outside the *United Kingdom*, the *appropriate regulator* will take into account the standards expected in the market in which the *firm* is operating. *Principle* 11 (Relations with regulators) applies to world-wide activities; in considering whether to take regulatory action under *Principle* 11 in relation to cooperation with an overseas regulator, the *appropriate regulator* will have regard to the extent of, and limits to, the duties owed by the *firm* to that regulator. (*Principle* 4 (Financial prudence) also applies to world-wide activities.)

1.1.6A G   FCA

PRIN 4 (Principles: MiFID Business) provides *guidance* on the application of the *Principles* to *MiFID business*.

Consequences of breaching the Principles

1.1.7 G   FCA

Breaching a Principle makes a firm liable to disciplinary sanctions. In determining whether a Principle has been breached it is necessary to look to the standard of conduct required by the Principle in question. Under each of the Principles the onus will be on the appropriate regulator to show that a firm has been at fault in some way. What constitutes "fault" varies between different Principles. Under Principle 1 (Integrity), for example, the appropriate regulator would need to demonstrate a lack of integrity in the conduct of a firm's business. Under Principle 2 (Skill, care and diligence) a firm would be in breach if it was shown to have failed to act with due skill, care and diligence in the conduct of its business. Similarly, under Principle 3 (Management and control) a firm would not be in breach simply because it failed to control or prevent unforeseeable risks; but a breach would occur if the firm had failed to take reasonable care to organise and control its affairs responsibly or effectively.

1.1.8 G   FCA

The *Principles* are also relevant to the *FCA's* powers of information-gathering, to vary a *firm's Part 4A permission*, and of investigation and intervention, and provide a basis on which the *FCA* may apply to a court for an *injunction* or restitution order or require a *firm* to make restitution. However, the *Principles* do not give rise to actions for damages by a *private person* (see **PRIN 3.4.4 R**).

1.1.9 G   FCA

Some of the other *rules* and *guidance* in the *Handbook* deal with the bearing of the *Principles* upon particular circumstances. However, since the *Principles* are also designed as a general statement of regulatory requirements applicable in new or unforeseen situations, and in situations in which there is no need for *guidance*, the *appropriate regulator's* other *rules* and *guidance* should not be viewed as exhausting the implications of the *Principles* themselves.

Responsibilities of providers and distributors under the Principles

1.1.10 G   FCA

RPPD contains *guidance* on the responsibilities of providers and distributors for the fair treatment of *customers* under the *Principles*.

1.2   CLIENTS AND THE PRINCIPLES

Characteristics of the client

1.2.1 G   FCA

Principles 6 (Customers' interests), 7 (Communications with clients), 8 (Conflicts of interest), 9 (Customers: relationships of trust) and 10 (Clients' assets) impose requirements on *firms* expressly in relation to their *clients* or *customers*. These requirements depend, in part, on the characteristics of the *client* or *customer* concerned. This is because what is "due regard" (in *Principles* 6 and 7), "fairly" (in *Principles* 6 and 8), "clear, fair and not misleading" (in *Principle* 7), "reasonable care" (in *Principle* 9) or "adequate" (in *Principle* 10) will, of course, depend on those characteristics. For example, the information needs of a general insurance broker will be different from those of a retail general insurance *policyholder*.

Approach to client categorisation

1.2.2 G   FCA

Principles 6, 8 and 9 and parts of *Principle* 7, as qualified by **PRIN 3.4.1 R**, apply only in relation to *customers* (that is, *clients* which are not *eligible counterparties*). The approach that a *firm* (other than for *credit-related regulated activities* in relation to which *client* categorisation does not apply) needs to take regarding categorisation of *clients* into *customers* and *eligible counterparties* will depend on whether the *firm* is carrying on *designated investment business* or other activities, as described in **PRIN 1.2.3 G**.

1.2.3 G   FCA

(1) In relation to the carrying on of *designated investment business*, a *firm's* categorisation of a *client* under the *COBS client* categorisation chapter (**COBS 3**) will be applicable for the purposes of *Principles* 6, 7, 8 and 9.

(1A) *Client* categorisation under **COBS 3** or **PRIN 1 ANNEX 1** is not relevant to *credit-related regulated activities* and therefore the guidance on *client* categorisation does not apply in relation to a *credit-related regulated activity*. The definitions of *client* and *customer* in relation to those *regulated activities* reflect the modified meaning of "consumer" in articles 36J, 39M, 60LA, 60S and 89E of the *Regulated Activities Order*, as well as the definitions of "individual" and of "relevant recipient of credit" in that Order.

(2) The *person* to whom a *firm* gives *basic advice* on a *stakeholder product* will be a *retail client* for all purposes, including the purposes of *Principles* 6, 7, 8 and 9.

(3) In relation to carrying on activities other than *designated investment business* (for example, *general insurance business* or *accepting deposits*) the *firm* may choose to comply with *Principles* 6, 7, 8 and 9 as if all its *clients* were *customers*. Alternatively, it may choose to distinguish between *eligible counterparties* and *customers* in complying with those *Principles*. If it chooses to make such a distinction, it must comply with **PRIN 1 ANNEX 1** in determining whether that *client* is an *eligible counterparty* (see **PRIN 3.4.2 R**). In doing so, the requirements in *SYSC* will apply, including the requirement to make and retain adequate records.

(4) In relation to carrying on activities that fall within both (1) and (3) (for example, mixed *designated investment business* and *accepting deposits*), a *firm's* categorisation of a *client* under the *COBS client* categorisation chapter (**COBS 3**) will be applicable for the purposes of *Principles* 6, 7, 8 and 9.

1.2.4 G

[deleted]

1.2.5 G

[deleted]

1.2.6 G   FCA

If the *person* with or for whom the *firm* is carrying on an activity is acting through an agent, the ability of the *firm* to treat the agent as its *client* under **COBS 2.4.3 R** (Agent as client) will not be available. For example, if a *general insurer* is effecting a *general insurance contract* through a general insurance broker who is acting as agent for a disclosed *policyholder*, the *policyholder* will be a *client* of the *firm* and the *firm* must comply with the *Principles* accordingly.

1 ANNEX 1 R   NON-DESIGNATED INVESTMENT BUSINESS – CLIENTS THAT A FIRM MAY TREAT AS AN ELIGIBLE COUNTERPARTY FOR THE PURPOSES OF PRIN

1Ann1   FCA

1.1	A *firm* may categorise the following types of *client* as an *eligible counterparty* for the purposes of *PRIN*:
	(1) a properly constituted government (including a quasi-governmental body or a government agency) of any country or territory;
	(2) a central bank or other national monetary authority of any country or territory;
	(3) a supranational whose members are either countries or central banks or national monetary authorities;
	(4) a State investment body, or a body charged with, or intervening in, the management of the public debt;
	(5) another *firm*, or an *overseas financial services institution*;
	(6) any *associate* of a *firm* (except an *OPS firm*), or of an *overseas financial services institution*, if the *firm* or institution consents;
	(7) a *client* when he is classified as an *eligible counterparty* in accordance with 1.2; or
	(8) a *recognised investment exchange*, *regulated market* or *clearing house*.
1.2	A *firm* may classify a *client* (other than another *firm*, *regulated collective investment scheme*, or an *overseas financial services institution*) as an *eligible counterparty* for the purposes of *PRIN* under 1.1(7) if:
	(1) the *client* at the time he is classified is one of the following:
	(a) a *body corporate* (including a *limited liability partnership*) which has (or any of whose *holding companies* or *subsidiaries* has) called up share capital of at least £10 million (or its equivalent in any other currency at the relevant time);
	(b) a *body corporate* that meets (or any of whose holding companies or subsidiaries meets) two of the following tests:
	(i) a balance sheet total of 12.5 million euros (or its equivalent in any other currency at the relevant time);
	(ii) a net turnover of 25 million euros (or its equivalent in any other currency at the relevant time);
	(iii) an average number of employees during the year of 250;
	(c) a local authority or public authority;

(d) a *partnership* or unincorporated association which has net assets of at least £10 million (or its equivalent in any other currency at the relevant time) (and calculated, in the case of a limited *partnership*, without deducting loans owing to any of the *partners*);

(e) a trustee of a trust (other than an *occupational pension scheme*, *SSAS*, *personal pension scheme* or *stakeholder pension scheme*) with assets of at least £10 million (or its equivalent in any other currency), calculated by aggregating the value of the cash and *designated investments* forming part of the trust's assets, but before deducting its liabilities;

(f) a trustee of an *occupational pension scheme* or *SSAS*, or a trustee or operator of a *personal pension scheme* or *stakeholder pension scheme* where the *scheme* has (or has had at any time during the previous two years):

(i) at least 50 members; and

(ii) assets under management of not less than £10 million (or its equivalent in any other currency at the relevant time); and

(2) the *firm* has, before commencing business with the *client* on an *eligible counterparty* basis:

(a) advised the *client* in writing that he is being categorised as an *eligible counterparty* for the purposes of *PRIN*;

(b) given a written warning to the *client* that he will lose protections under the *regulatory system*;

(c) for a *client* falling under (1)(a) or (b):

(i) taken reasonable steps to ensure that the written notices required by (a) and (b) have been delivered to a *person* authorised to take such a decision for the *client*; and

(ii) not been notified by the *client* that the *client* objects to being classified as an *eligible counterparty*;

(d) for a *client* falling under (1)(c), (d), (e) or (f):

(i) taken reasonable steps to ensure that the written notices required by (a) and (b) have been delivered to a *person* authorised to take such a decision for the *client*; and

(ii) obtained the *client's* written consent or is otherwise able to demonstrate that consent has been given.

CHAPTER 2
THE PRINCIPLES

2.1 THE PRINCIPLES

[3.3]
2.1.1 R

The Principles

1 Integrity	A *firm* must conduct its business with integrity.
2 Skill, care and diligence	A *firm* must conduct its business with due skill, care and diligence.
3 Management and control	A *firm* must take reasonable care to organise and control its affairs responsibly and effectively, with adequate risk management systems.
4 Financial prudence	A *firm* must maintain adequate financial resources.
5 Market conduct	A *firm* must observe proper standards of market conduct.
6 Customers' interests	A *firm* must pay due regard to the interests of its *customers* and treat them fairly.
7 Communications with clients	A *firm* must pay due regard to the information needs of its *clients*, and communicate information to them in a way which is clear, fair and not misleading.
8 Conflicts of interest	A *firm* must manage conflicts of interest fairly, both between itself and its *customers* and between a *customer* and another *client*.

9 Customers: relationships of trust	A *firm* must take reasonable care to ensure the suitability of its advice and discretionary decisions for any *customer* who is entitled to rely upon its judgment.
10 Clients' assets	A *firm* must arrange adequate protection for *clients'* assets when it is responsible for them.
11 Relations with regulators	A *firm* must deal with its regulators in an open and cooperative way, and must disclose to the *appropriate regulator* appropriately anything relating to the *firm* of which that regulator would reasonably expect notice.

CHAPTER 3
RULES ABOUT APPLICATION

3.1   WHO?

[3.4]
3.1.1 R   FCA

PRIN applies to every *firm*, except that:

(1)   for an *incoming EEA firm* or an *incoming Treaty firm*, the *Principles* apply only in so far as responsibility for the matter in question is not reserved by an *EU* instrument to the *firm's Home State regulator*;

(2)   for an *incoming EEA firm* which is a *CRD credit institution* without a *top-up permission*, *Principle* 4 applies only in relation to the liquidity of a *branch* established in the *United Kingdom*;

(3)   for an *incoming EEA firm* which has *permission* only for *cross border services* and which does not carry on *regulated activities* in the *United Kingdom*, the *Principles* do not apply;

(4)   for a *UCITS qualifier* and *AIFM qualifier*, only *Principles* 1, 2, 3, 7 and 9 apply, and only with respect to the activities in **PRIN 3.2.2 R** (Communication and approval of financial promotions);

(5)   *PRIN* does not apply to an *incoming ECA provider* acting as such; and

(6)   *PRIN* does not apply to a *firm* in relation to its carrying on of *auction regulation bidding*.

3.1.2 G   FCA

COBS 1 ANNEX 1 and the territorial *guidance* in **PERG 13.6** all contain *guidance* that is relevant to the reservation of responsibility to a *Home State regulator* referred to in **PRIN 3.1.1 R (1)**.

3.1.3 G   FCA

PRIN 3.1.1 R (2) reflects article 156 of the *CRD* which provides that the *Host State regulator* retains responsibility in cooperation with the *Home State regulator* for the supervision of the liquidity of a *branch* of a *CRD credit institution*.

3.1.4 G   FCA

PRIN 3.1.1 R (3) puts *incoming EEA firms* on an equal footing with unauthorised overseas persons who utilise the overseas persons exclusions in article 72 of the *Regulated Activities Order*.

3.1.5 G   FCA

PRIN 3.1.1 R (4) reflects section 266 of the *Act* (Disapplication of rules).

3.1.6 R   FCA

A *firm* will not be subject to a *Principle* to the extent that it would be contrary to the *UK's* obligations under an *EU* instrument.

3.1.7 G   FCA

PRIN 4 provides specific guidance on the application of the *Principles* for *MiFID business*.

3.1.8 G   FCA

The *Principles* will not apply to the extent that they purport to impose an obligation which is inconsistent with the *Payment Services Directive*, the *Consumer Credit Directive* or the *Electronic Money Directive*. For example, there may be circumstances in which *Principle* 6 may be limited by the harmonised conduct of business obligations applied by the *Payment Services Directive* and *Electronic Money Directive* to *credit institutions* (see Parts 5 and 6 of the *Payment Services Regulations* and Part 5 of the *Electronic Money Regulations*) or applied by the *Consumer Credit Directive* (see, for example, the information requirements in the Consumer Credit (Disclosure of Information) Regulations 2010 (SI 2010/1013)).

3.2   WHAT?

3.2.1A R   FCA

PRIN applies with respect to the carrying on of:

(1)   *regulated activities*;

(2)   activities that constitute *dealing in investments as principal*, disregarding the exclusion in article 15 of the *Regulated Activities Order* (Absence of holding out etc); and

(3)   *ancillary activities* in relation to *designated investment business, home finance activity, credit-related regulated activity, insurance mediation activity* and *accepting deposits*.

3.2.2 R   FCA

PRIN also applies with respect to the *communication* and *approval* of *financial promotions* which:

(1)   if *communicated* by an *unauthorised person* without *approval* would contravene section 21(1) of the *Act* (Restrictions on financial promotion); and

(2)   may be *communicated* by a *firm* without contravening section 238(1) of the *Act* (Restrictions on promotion of collective investment schemes).

3.2.2A R   FCA

PRIN 1 ANNEX 1, PRIN 3.4.1 R and **PRIN 3.4.2 R** do not apply with respect to the carrying on of *credit-related regulated activities*.

3.2.3 R   FCA   PRA

Principles 3, 4 and (in so far as it relates to disclosing to the *appropriate regulator*) 11 (and this chapter) also:

(1)   apply with respect to the carrying on of *unregulated activities* (for *Principle* 3 this is only in a *prudential context*); and

(2)   take into account any activity of other members of a *group* of which the *firm* is a member.

3.3   WHERE?

3.3.1 R

Territorial application of the Principles

Principle	Territorial application
Principles **1, 2 and 3**	in a *prudential context*, apply with respect to activities wherever they are carried on; otherwise, apply with respect to activities carried on from an establishment maintained by the *firm* (or its *appointed representative*) in the *United Kingdom* unless another applicable *rule* which is relevant to the activity has a wider territorial scope, in which case the *Principle* applies with that wider scope in relation to the activity described in that *rule*.
Principle **4**	applies with respect to activities wherever they are carried on.
Principle **5**	if the activities have, or might reasonably be regarded as likely to have, a negative effect on confidence in the *UK financial system*, applies with respect to activities wherever they are carried on; otherwise, applies with respect to activities carried on from an establishment maintained by the *firm* (or its *appointed representative*) in the *United Kingdom*.
Principles **6, 7, 8, 9 and 10**	Principle 8, in a prudential context, applies with respect to activities wherever they are carried on; otherwise apply with respect to activities carried on from an establishment maintained by the *firm* (or its *appointed representative*) in the *United Kingdom* unless another applicable *rule* which is relevant to the activity has a wider territorial scope, in which case the *Principle* applies with that wider scope in relation to the activity described in that *rule*.
Principle **11**	applies with respect to activities wherever they are carried on.

3.3.2 G

[deleted]

3.4   GENERAL

Clients and the Principles

3.4.1 R   FCA

Although *Principle* 7 refers to *clients*, the only requirement of *Principle* 7 relating to *eligible counterparties* is that a *firm* must communicate information to *eligible counterparties* in a way that is not misleading.

3.4.2 R FCA

For the purposes of *PRIN*, a *firm* intending to carry on, or carrying on, activities that do not involve *designated investment business*, may treat a *client* as an *eligible counterparty* in accordance with **PRIN 1 ANNEX 1 R**.

3.4.3 G FCA

(1) **COBS 3** (Client categorisation) applies to a *firm* intending to conduct, or conducting, *designated investment business* (other than giving *basic advice*) and *ancillary activities* relating to *designated investment business*. Any *client* categorisation established in relation to such business will be applicable for the purposes of *Principles* 6, 7, 8 and 9.

(2) The *person* to whom a *firm* gives *basic advice* will be a *retail client* for all purposes including the purposes of *Principles* 6, 7, 8 and 9.

(3) **PRIN 3.4.1 R** and **PRIN 3.4.2 R** do not apply with respect to the carrying on of *credit-related regulated activities*. Client categorisation does not apply in relation to carrying on a *credit-related regulated activity*. The definitions of *client* and *customer* in relation to those *regulated activities* reflect the modified meaning of "consumer" in articles 36J, 39M and 89E of the *Regulated Activities Order*, as well as the definitions of "individual" and of "relevant recipient of credit" in that Order.

Actions for damages

3.4.4 R FCA

A contravention of the *rules* in *PRIN* does not give rise to a right of action by a *private person* under section 138D of the *Act* (and each of those *rules* is specified under section 138D(3) of the *Act* as a provision giving rise to no such right of action).

Reference to "regulators" in Principle 11

3.4.5 R FCA

Where *Principle* 11 refers to regulators, this means, in addition to the *appropriate regulator*, other regulators with recognised jurisdiction in relation to *regulated activities*, whether in the *United Kingdom* or abroad.

CHAPTER 4
PRINCIPLES: MIFID BUSINESS

4.1 PRINCIPLES: MIFID BUSINESS

[3.5]
4.1.1 G FCA

PRIN 3.1.6 R ensures that the *Principles* do not impose obligations upon *firms* which are inconsistent with an *EU* instrument. If a *Principles* does purport to impose such an obligation **PRIN 3.1.6 R** disapplies that *Principle* but only to the extent necessary to ensure compliance with European law. This disapplication has practical effect only for certain matters covered by *MiFID*, which are explained in this section.

Where?

4.1.2 G FCA

Under **PRIN 3.3.1 R**, the territorial application of a number of *Principles* to a *UK MiFID investment firm* is extended to the extent that another applicable rule which is relevant to an activity has a wider territorial scope. Under **PRIN 3.1.1 R**, the territorial application of a number of *Principles* to an *EEA MiFID investment firm* is narrowed to the extent that responsibility for the matter in question is reserved to the *firm's Home State regulator*. These modifications are relevant to *Principles* 1, 2, 3, 6, 7, 8, 9 and 10. We have added further *guidance* in *PERG* on the ability of a *Host State* to impose conduct of business requirements (see Q67).

4.1.3 G FCA

Principles 4, 5 and 11 will have the same scope of territorial application for *MiFID business* as for other business.

What?

4.1.4 G FCA

(1) Certain requirements under *MiFID* are disapplied for:

    (a) *eligible counterparty business*;

    (b) transactions concluded under the rules governing a *multilateral trading facility* between its members or participants or between the *multilateral trading facility* and its members or participants in relation to the use of the *multilateral trading facility*;

(c)   transactions concluded on a *regulated market* between its members or participants.

(2)   Under **PRIN 3.1.6 R**, these disapplications may affect *Principles* 1, 2, 6 and 9. **PRIN 3.1.6 R** applies only to the extent that the application of a *Principle* would be contrary to the *UK's* obligations under a *Single Market Directive* in respect of a particular transaction or matter. In line with *MiFID*, these limitations relating to *eligible counterparty business* and transactions under the rules of a *multilateral trading facility* or on a *regulated market* only apply in relation to a *firm's* conduct of business obligations to its clients under *MiFID*. They do not limit the application of those *Principles* in relation to other matters, such as *client* asset protections, systems and controls, prudential requirements and market integrity. Further information about these limitations is contained in **COBS 1 ANNEX 1**.

(3)   *Principles* 3, 4, 5, 7, 8, 10 and 11 are not limited in this way.

4.1.5 G   FCA

Although *Principle* 8 does not apply to *eligible counterparty business*, a *firm* will owe obligations in respect of conflicts of interest set out in **SYSC 10** which are wider than those contained in *Principle* 8 in that they apply to *eligible counterparty business*.

TRANSITIONAL PROVISIONS AND SCHEDULES

1   TRANSITIONAL PROVISIONS

[3.6]
TP1.1

	Material to which the transitional provision applies		Transitional Provision	Transitional Provision: dates in force	Handbook provision: coming into force
1.	**PRIN 1 AN-NEX 1R** 1.2(2)	R	A *firm* need not comply with **PRIN ANN 1R 1.2(2)** in relation to an *eligible counter-party* if the *client* was correctly categorised as a *market counterparty* on 31 October 2007 and the *firm* complied with **COB 4.1.12 R (2)** (Large intermediate customer classified as market counterparty).	From 1 November 2007 indefinitely	1 November 2007

SCHEDULE 1   RECORD KEEPING REQUIREMENTS

Sch1.1 G   FCA

There are no record keeping requirements in *PRIN*.

SCHEDULE 2   NOTIFICATION REQUIREMENTS

Sch2.1 G   FCA

The aim of the *guidance* in the following table is to give the reader a quick over-all view of the relevant requirements for notification and reporting.

It is not a complete statement of those requirements and should not be relied on as if it were.

Sch2.2 G   FCA

Handbook reference	Matter to be notified	Contents of notification	Trigger event	Time allowed
Principle 11 **(PRIN 2.1.1R)**	Anything relating to the firm of which the *appropriate regulator* would reasonably expect notice	Appropriate disclosure	Anything relating to the firm of which the *appropriate regulator* would reasonably expect notice	Appropriate

SCHEDULE 3   FEES AND OTHER REQUIRED PAYMENTS

Sch3.1 G   FCA

There are no requirements for fees or other payments in *PRIN*.

SCHEDULE 4   POWERS EXERCISED

[deleted]

SCHEDULE 5   RIGHTS OF ACTION FOR DAMAGES

Sch5.1 G   FCA

The table below sets out the *rules* in *PRIN* contravention of which by an *authorised person* may be actionable under section 138D of the *Act* (Actions for damages) by a *person* who suffers loss as a result of the contravention.

Sch5.2 G   FCA

If a "Yes" appears in the column headed "For private person?", the rule may be actionable by a "*private person*" under section 138D (or, in certain circumstances, his fiduciary or representative; see article 6(2) and (3)(c) of the Financial Services and Markets Act 2000 (Rights of Action) Regulations 2001 (SI 2001 No 2256)). A "Yes" in the column headed "Removed" indicates that the *FCA* has removed the right of action under section 138D(3) of the Act. If so, a reference to the *rule* in which it is removed is also given.

Sch5.3 G   FCA

The column headed "For other person?" indicates whether the *rule* may be actionable by a person other than a *private person* (or his fiduciary or representative) under article 6(2) and (3) of those Regulations. If so, an indication of the type of *person* by whom the *rule* may be actionable is given.

Sch5.4 G   FCA

Chapter/ Appendix	Section/ Annex	Paragraph	Right of Action		
			For private person?	Removed?	For other person?
All *rules* in *PRIN*			No	Yes **PRIN 3.4.4 R**	No

SCHEDULE 6   RULES THAT CAN BE WAIVED

Sch6.1A G   FCA

As a result of section 138A of the Act (Modification or waiver of rules) the FCA has power to waive all its rules, other than rules made under section 137O (Threshold condition code), section 247 (Trust scheme rules), section 248 (Scheme particular rules), section 261I (Contractual scheme rules) or section 261J (Contractual scheme particulars rules) of the Act. However, if the rules incorporate requirements laid down in European directives, it will not be possible for the FCA to grant a waiver that would be incompatible with the United Kingdom's responsibilities under those directives.

Part 3   FCA Handbook Materials

C. SENIOR MANAGEMENT ARRANGEMENTS, SYSTEMS AND CONTROLS (SYSC)

SENIOR MANAGEMENT ARRANGEMENTS, SYSTEMS AND CONTROLS
the responsibilities of directors and senior management

CHAPTER 1
APPLICATION AND PURPOSE

1.1A   APPLICATION

[3.7]

[**Note**: ESMA has also issued guidelines under article 16(3) of the ESMA Regulation covering:
– various topics relating to automated trading and direct electronic access. See
www.esma.europa.eu/content/
Final-report-Guidelines-systems-and-controls-automated-trading-environment-trading-platforms;
and
– certain aspects of the MiFID suitability requirements which also deal with the system and control
aspects of suitability. See
www.esma.europa.eu/content/Guidelines-certain-aspects-MiFID-suitability-requirements.]

1.1A.1 G   FCA PRA

The application of this sourcebook is summarised at a high level in the following table. The detailed
application is cut back in **SYSC 1 ANNEX 1** and in the text of each chapter.

Type of firm	Applicable chapters
Insurer	Chapters 2, 3, 11 to 18, 21
Managing agent	Chapters 2, 3, 11, 12, 18, 21
Society	Chapters 2, 3, 12, 18, 21
Every other *firm*	Chapters 4 to 12, 18, 19D, 21

Firms that **SYSC 19D** applies to should also refer to the Remuneration part of the *PRA* Rulebook.

1.1A.1AA G   FCA

The application of this sourcebook to *firms* that are not *PRA-authorised persons* is summarised at
a high level in the following table. The detailed application is cut back in **SYSC 1 ANNEX 1** and in
the text of each chapter.

Type of firm	Applicable chapters
Full-scope UK AIFM	Chapter 19B, 21
BIPRU firm (including a *third-country BIPRU firm*)	Chapters 4 to 10, 12, 18, 19C, 21
IFPRU investment firm (including an *overseas firm* that would have been an *IFPRU investment firm* if it had been a *UK domestic firm*)	Chapters 4 to 10, 12, 18, 19A, 21

1.1A.1A G   PRA

Chapters 4 to 9 are not applicable to *CRR firms*. *CRR firms* are subject to the rules in the General
Organisational Requirements Part of the *PRA* Rulebook.

1.1A.2 G   FCA PRA

The provisions in *SYSC* should be read in conjunction with **GEN 2.2.23 R** to **GEN 2.2.25 G**. In
particular:
(1)   Provisions made by both the *FCA* and *PRA* may contain obligations for or references to
FCA-authorised persons. **GEN 2.2.23 R** limits the application of those provisions so that the
PRA will only apply them in respect of *PRA-authorised persons* and not to such
FCA-authorised persons as are included within the provision.
(2)   Provisions made by both the *FCA* and *PRA* may be applied by both regulators to
PRA-authorised persons. Such provisions are applied by each regulator to the extent of its
powers and regulatory responsibilities.

1.2   PURPOSE

1.2.1 G   FCA

The purposes of *SYSC* are:

(1)   to encourage *firms' directors* and *senior managers* to take appropriate practical responsibility for their *firms'* arrangements on matters likely to be of interest to the *appropriate regulator* because they impinge on the *appropriate regulator's* functions under the *Act*;

(2)   to increase certainty by amplifying *Principle* 3, under which a *firm* must take reasonable care to organise and control its affairs responsibly and effectively, with adequate risk management systems;

(3)   to encourage *firms* to vest responsibility for effective and responsible organisation in specific *directors* and *senior managers*; and

(4)   to create a common platform of organisational and systems and controls requirements for all *firms*.

(5)   [deleted]

1.2.1A G   PRA

The purposes of *SYSC* are:

(1)   to encourage *firms' directors* and *senior managers* to take appropriate practical responsibility for their *firms'* arrangements on matters likely to be of interest to the *PRA* because they impinge on the *PRA's* functions under the *Act*;

(2)   to encourage *firms* to vest responsibility for effective and responsible organisation in specific *directors* and *senior managers*; and

(3)   to create a common platform of organisational and systems and controls requirements for all *firms*.

1.4   APPLICATION OF SYSC 11 TO SYSC 21

What?

1.4.1 G   FCA PRA

The application of each of chapters **SYSC 11** to **SYSC 21** is set out in those chapters and in **SYSC 1.4.1A R**.

1.4.1A R   FCA PRA

SYSC 12, **SYSC 19A**, **SYSC 19D**, **SYSC 20** and **SYSC 21** do not apply to a *firm* in relation to its carrying on of *auction regulation bidding*.

1.4.1B G   FCA PRA

Apart from **SYSC 12**, **SYSC 19A**, **SYSC 19D**, **SYSC 20** and **SYSC 21** which are disapplied by **SYSC 1.4.1A R**, the other chapters of **SYSC 11** to **SYSC 17** do not apply in relation to a *firm's* carrying on of *auction regulation bidding* because they only apply to an *insurer*. **SYSC 18** provides guidance on the Public Interest Disclosure Act.

Actions for damages

1.4.2 R   FCA

A contravention of a rule in **SYSC 11** to **SYSC 21** does not give rise to a right of action by a *private person* under section 138D of the *Act* (and each of those *rules* is specified under section 138D(3) of the *Act* as a provision giving rise to no such right of action).

1 ANNEX 1 DETAILED APPLICATION OF SYSC

Part 1 | **Application of SYSC 2 and SYSC 3 to an insurer, a managing agent and the Society**

Who?

1.1
[FCA]
[PRA]

R   **SYSC 2** and **SYSC 3** only apply to an *insurer*, a *managing agent* and the *Society* except that:

(1)   for an *incoming EEA firm* or an *incoming Treaty firm*:

    (a)   **SYSC 2.1.1 R** and **SYSC 2.1.2 G** do not apply;

    (b)   **SYSC 2.1.3 R** to **SYSC 2.2.3 G** apply, but only in relation to allocation of the function in **SYSC 2.1.3 R (2)** and only in so far as responsibility for the matter in question is not reserved by an *EU instrument* to the *firm's Home State regulator*; and

    (c)   **SYSC 3** applies, but only in so far as responsibility for the matter in question is not reserved by an *EU instrument* to the *firm's Home State regulator*;

(2)   for an *incoming EEA firm* which has *permission* only for *cross border services* and which does not carry on *regulated activities* in the United Kingdom, **SYSC 2** and **SYSC 3** do not apply;

(3)   for an *incoming Treaty firm* which has *permission* only for *cross border services* and which does not carry on *regulated activities* in the United Kingdom, **SYSC 3.2.6A R** to **SYSC 3.2.6J G** do not apply;

(4)   for a *sole trader*:

    (a)   **SYSC 2** applies but only if he employs any *person* who is required to be approved under section 59 of the *Act* (Approval for particular arrangements);

    (b)   **SYSC 3.2.6I R** does not apply if he has no *employees*; and

(5)   **SYSC 2** and **SYSC 3** do not apply to an *incoming ECA provider* acting as such.

1.2
[FCA]
[PRA]

G   (1)   Question 12 in **SYSC 2.1.6 G** contains guidance on **SYSC 1 ANNEX 1.1.1R(1)(b)** and **SYSC 1 ANNEX 1.1.1R(1)(c)**.

    (2)   **SYSC 1 ANNEX 1.1.8 R** further restricts the territorial application of **SYSC 2** and **SYSC 3** for an *incoming EEA firm* or an *incoming Treaty firm*.

    (3)   **SYSC 1 ANNEX 1.1.1 R (3)** puts an *incoming EEA firm* on an equal footing with unauthorised *overseas persons* who utilise the *overseas persons* exclusions in article 72 of the *Regulated Activities Order*.

    (4)   Further *guidance* on which matters are reserved to a *firm's Home State regulator* can be found at **SUP 13A ANNEX 2**.

What?

1.3
[FCA]
[PRA]

R   **SYSC 2** and **SYSC 3** apply with respect to the carrying on of:

Part 1   Application of SYSC 2 and SYSC 3 to an insurer, a managing agent and the Society

(1)   *regulated activities;*

(2)   activities that constitute *dealing in investments as principal*, disregarding the exclusion in article 15 of the *Regulated Activities Order* (Absence of holding out etc); and

(3)   *ancillary activities* in relation to *designated investment business, home finance activity* and *insurance mediation activity;*

except that **SYSC 3.2.6A R** to **SYSC 3.2.6J G** do not apply as described in **SYSC 1 ANNEX 1.1.4R.**

1.4
[FCA]   R   **SYSC 3.2.6A R** to **SYSC 3.2.6J G** do not apply:

(1)   with respect to the activities described in **SYSC 1 ANNEX 1.1.3R(2)** and **SYSC 1 ANNEX 1.1.3R(3)**; or

(2)   in relation to the following *regulated activities:*

(a)   *general insurance business;*

(b)   *insurance mediation activity* in relation to a *general insurance contract* or *pure protection contract;*

(c)   *long-term insurance business* which is outside the *Consolidated Life Directive* (unless it is otherwise one of the *regulated activities* specified in this *rule*);

(d)   business relating to contracts which are within the *Regulated Activities Order* only because they fall within paragraph (e) of the definition of "*contract of insurance*" in article 3 of that Order;

(e)   (i)   *arranging*, by the *Society*, of deals in *general insurance contracts* written at Lloyd's; and

(ii)   *managing the underwriting capacity of a Lloyd's syndicate as a managing agent* at Lloyd's;

(f)   *home finance mediation activity* and *administering a home finance transaction;* and

(g)   *reversion activity.*

1.5
[FCA]   R   **SYSC 2** and **SYSC 3**, except **SYSC 3.2.6A R** to **SYSC 3.2.6J G**, also apply with respect to the *communication* and *approval of financial promotions* which:

(1)   if *communicated* by an *unauthorised person* without *approval* would contravene section 21(1) of the *Act* (Restrictions on financial promotion); and

(2)   may be *communicated* by a *firm* without contravening section 238(1) of the *Act* (Restrictions on promotion of collective investment schemes).

1.6
[FCA]
[PRA]   R   **SYSC 2** and **SYSC 3**, except **SYSC 3.2.6A R** to **SYSC 3.2.6J G**, also:

(1)   apply with respect to the carrying on of *unregulated activities* in a *prudential context;* and

(2)   take into account any activity of other members of a *group* of which the *firm* is a member.

Part 1		**Application of SYSC 2 and SYSC 3 to an insurer, a managing agent and the Society**
1.7 [FCA] [PRA]	G	**SYSC 1 ANNEX 1.1.6R(2)** does not mean that inadequacy of a *group* member's systems and controls will automatically lead to a *firm* contravening, for example, **SYSC 3.1.1 R**. Rather, the potential impact of a *group* member's activities, including its systems and controls, and any systems and controls that operate on a *group* basis, will be relevant in determining the appropriateness of the *firm's* own systems and controls.
		Where?
1.8 [FCA] [PRA]	R	**SYSC 2** and **SYSC 3** apply with respect to activities carried on from an establishment maintained by the *firm* (or its *appointed representative* or, where applicable, its *tied agent*) in the *United Kingdom* unless another applicable *rule* which is relevant to the activity has a wider territorial scope, in which case **SYSC 2** and **SYSC 3** apply with that wider scope in relation to the activity described in that *rule*.
1.9 [FCA] [PRA]	R	**SYSC 2** and **SYSC 3**, except **SYSC 3.2.6A R** to **SYSC 3.2.6J G**, also apply in a *prudential context* to a *UK domestic firm* with respect to activities wherever they are carried on.
1.10 [FCA] [PRA]	R	**SYSC 3**, except **SYSC 3.2.6A R** to **SYSC 3.2.6J G**, also applies in a *prudential context* to an *overseas firm* (other than an *incoming EEA firm* or an *incoming Treaty firm*) with respect to activities wherever they are carried on.
1.11 [FCA] [PRA]	G	(1) In considering whether to take regulatory action under **SYSC 2** or **SYSC 3** in relation to activities carried on outside the *United Kingdom*, the *appropriate regulator* will take into account the standards expected in the market in which the *firm* is operating.
		(2) Most of the *rules* in **SYSC 3** are linked to other requirements and standards under the *regulatory system* which have their own territorial limitations so that those *SYSC rules* are similarly limited in scope.
		Actions for damages
1.12 [FCA]	R	A contravention of the *rules* in **SYSC 2** and **SYSC 3** does not give rise to a right of action by a *private person* under section 138D of the *Act* (and each of those *rules* is specified under section 138D(3) of the *Act* as a provision giving rise to no such right of action).

Part 2		**Application of the common platform requirements (SYSC 4 to 10)**
		Who?
2.1 [FCA]	R	The *common platform requirements* apply to every *firm* apart from an *insurer*, a *managing agent* and *the Society* unless provided otherwise in a specific *rule*.
2.1A [PRA]	R	The *common platform organisational requirements* apply to every *firm* apart from a *CRR firm*, an *insurer*, a *managing agent* and the *Society* unless provided otherwise in a specific *rule*.
2.1B [PRA]	R	**SYSC 10** applies to every *firm* apart from an *insurer*, a *managing agent* and *the Society* unless provided otherwise in a specific *rule*.
2.2 [FCA] [PRA]	R	For an *incoming EEA firm* or an *incoming Treaty firm*:
		(1) the *rule* on responsibility of senior personnel (**SYSC 4.3**) does not apply;

Part 3   FCA Handbook Materials

Part 2   Application of the common platform requirements (SYSC 4 to 10)

	(2)	the *common platform requirements* apply only in so far as responsibility for the matter in question is not reserved by an *EU instrument* to the *firm's Home State regulator*;
	(3)	for an *incoming EEA firm* which has *permission* only for *cross-border services* and which does not carry on *regulated activities* in the United Kingdom, the *common platform requirements* do not apply;
	(4)	for an *incoming Treaty firm* which has *permission* only for *cross-border services* and which does not carry on *regulated activities* in the United Kingdom, the *common platform requirements* on financial crime do not apply.
2.3 [FCA]	R	For a *sole trader*:
	(1)	**SYSC 4.3** and **4.4** do not apply as long as he does not employ any *person* who is required to be approved under section 59 of the *Act* (Approval for particular arrangements);
	(2)	**SYSC 4.1.4 R** and **SYSC 6.3.9 R** do not apply if he has no *employees*.
2.4 [FCA]	R	For a *UCITS qualifier*:
	(1)	the *rule* on responsibility of senior personnel (**SYSC 4.3**) does not apply; and
	(2)	the *common platform requirements* apply in relation to the *communication* and *approval* of *financial promotions* only as set out in **SYSC 1 ANNEX 1.2.12R.**
		[**Note**: section 266 of the *Act*.]
2.4A [FCA]	R	For an *AIFM qualifier*:
	(1)	the *rule* on responsibility of senior personnel (**SYSC 4.3**) does not apply; and
	(2)	the *common platform requirements* apply in relation to the *communication* and *approval* of *financial promotions* only as set out in **SYSC 1 ANNEX 1, 2.12R.**
2.5 [FCA]	R	For an *authorised professional firm* when carrying on *non-mainstream regulated activities*, the *common platform requirements* on financial crime, conflicts of interest and Chinese walls do not apply.
2.5A [FCA]	R	The *common platform requirements* on *financial crime* do not apply to a *firm* for which a professional body listed in Schedule 3 to the *Money Laundering Regulations*, and not the *FCA*, acts as the supervisory authority for the purposes of those regulations.
2.6 [FCA] [PRA]	R	The *common platform requirements* do not apply to an *incoming ECA provider* acting as such.
2.6A [FCA] [PRA]	R	The *common platform requirements* do not apply to a *firm* (including an *incoming EEA firm*) in relation to its carrying on of *auction regulation bidding*, except for:

Part 2		**Application of the common platform requirements (SYSC 4 to 10)**
	(1)	SYSC 6.1.1 R which only applies to the extent that it relates to the obligation to establish, implement and maintain adequate policies and procedures for countering the risk that the *firm* (including its managers, employees and *appointed representatives*) might be used to further *financial crime*; and
	(2)	SYSC 6.3 (Financial crime).
2.6B[FCA]R		Subject to SYSC 1 ANNEX 1 2.6CR, the *common platform requirements* do not apply to a *full-scope UK AIFM* of an *unauthorised AIF* except for:
	(1)	SYSC 4.1.1 R to SYSC 4.1.2 R and SYSC 4.1.2B R to SYSC 4.1.2D R;
	(2)	SYSC 4.2.1 R, SYSC 4.2.1B R, SYSC 4.2.2 R to SYSC 4.2.5 G, SYSC 4.2.7 R and SYSC 4.2.8 G;
	(3)	SYSC 6.1.1 R, which only applies to the extent that it relates to the obligation to establish, implement and maintain adequate policies and procedures for countering the risk that the *firm* (including its managers and *employees*) might be used to further *financial crime*;
	(4)	SYSC 6.14-B G
	(5)	SYSC 6.3;
	(6)	SYSC 7.1.7BA G
	(7)	SYSC 10.1.1 R and SYSC 10.1.22 R to SYSC 10.1.26 R; and
	(8)	SYSC 10.2.
2.6C [FCA]	R	The *common platform requirements* apply to an *AIFM investment firm* which is a *full-scope UK AIFM* in respect of its *MiFID business* in line with Column A of Part 3.
2.6D [FCA]	R	The *common platform requirements* apply to a *full-scope UK AIFM* of an *authorised AIF* in line with column A++ of Part 3.
2.6E [FCA]	G	The *common platform requirements* apply to a *small authorised UK AIFM* in line with Column B of Part 3 (unless such a *firm* is also a *common platform firm*, in which case they must comply with Column A).
2.6F [FCA]	R	The *common platform requirements* do not apply to an *incoming EEA AIFM branch* in respect of its management of a *UK AIF*, except for:
	(1)	those *common platform requirements* which are *AIFMD host state requirements*;
	(2)	SYSC 6.1.1 R which only applies to the extent that it relates to the obligation to establish, implement and maintain adequate policies and procedures for countering the risk that the *firm* (including its managers and *employees*) might be used to further *financial crime*; and
	(3)	SYSC 6.3.
2.7 [FCA]	G	EEA *MiFID investment firms* are reminded in particular that they must comply with the *common platform record-keeping requirements* in relation to a branch in the *United Kingdom*.
2.7A [FCA]	G	EEA *UCITS management companies* are also reminded that they must comply with:
	(1)	the *common platform requirements* indicated in Column A+ (Application to a management company) in Part 3 of this Annex;

Part 3 FCA Handbook Materials

Part 2   Application of the common platform requirements (SYSC 4 to 10)

    (2)   the *common platform record-keeping requirements*; and

    (3)   the *common platform requirements on financial crime*;

in relation to activities carried on from a *branch* in the *United Kingdom*. Where the *common platform requirement* addresses matters within the scope of article 12 of the *UCITS Directive*, an *EEA UCITS management company* should note that those matters may also be subject to the rules of its *Home State regulator*.

[Note: articles 12(1)(b), 14(1)(c),14(1)(d), 17(4), 18(3) and 19(1) of the *UCITS Directive* and articles 4(1)(e), 10(1), 10(2) and 10(3) of the *UCITS implementing Directive*]

What?

2.8
[FCA]
[PRA]
R   The *common platform organisational requirements* apply with respect to the carrying on of the following (unless provided otherwise within a specific *rule*):

    (1)   *regulated activities*;

    (2)   activities that constitute *dealing in investments as principal*, disregarding the exclusion in article 15 of the *Regulated Activities Order* (Absence of holding out etc);

    (3)   *ancillary activities*;

    (4)   in relation to *MiFID business*, *ancillary services*; and

    (5)   *collective portfolio management*.

2.9
[FCA]
[PRA]
G   The application of the provisions on the conflicts of interest in **SYSC 10** is set out in **SYSC 1 ANNEX 1.2.8R** and **SYSC 10.2.1 R**

2.10
[FCA]
R   The provisions on record-keeping in **SYSC 9** apply as set out in **SYSC 1 ANNEX 1.2.8R**, except that they only apply to the carrying on of *ancillary activities* that are performed in relation to:

    (1)   designated investment business;

    (2)   home finance activity;

    (3)   insurance mediation activity;

    (4)   credit-related regulated activity.

2.11
[FCA]
R   The *common platform requirements on financial crime* apply as set out in **SYSC 1 ANNEX 1.2.8R**, except that they do not apply:

    (1)   with respect to:

        (a)   activities that constitute *dealing in investments as principal*, disregarding the exclusion in article 15 of the *Regulated Activities Order* (Absence of holding out etc); and

Part 2		**Application of the common platform requirements (SYSC 4 to 10)**
		(b) *ancillary activities*; or
	(2)	in relation to the following *regulated activities*:
		(a) *general insurance business*;
		(b) *insurance mediation activity* in relation to a *general insurance contract* or *pure protection contract*;
		(c) *long-term insurance business* which is outside the *Consolidated Life Directive* (unless it is otherwise one of the *regulated activities* specified in this *rule*);
		(d) business relating to contracts which are within the *Regulated Activities Order* only because they fall within paragraph (e) of the definition of "*contract of insurance*" in article 3 of that Order;
		(e) (i) arranging by the *Society* of deals in *general insurance contracts* written at Lloyd's; and
		(ii) managing the underwriting capacity of a Lloyd's syndicate as a managing agent at Lloyd's;
		(f) *home finance mediation activity* and *administering a home finance transaction*;
		(g) *reversion activity*; and
		(h) *meeting of repayment claims and managing dormant account funds (including the investment of such funds).*
2.12 [FCA]	R	The *common platform organisational requirements*, except the *common platform requirements on financial crime*, also apply with respect to the *communication and approval of financial promotions* which:
		(1) if *communicated* by an *unauthorised person* without *approval* would contravene section 21(1) of the *Act* (Restrictions on financial promotion); and
		(2) may be *communicated* by a *firm* without contravening section 238(1) of the *Act* (Restrictions on promotion of collective investment schemes).
2.13 [FCA] [PRA]	R	The *common platform organisational requirements*, except the *common platform requirements on financial crime*, also:
		(1) apply with respect to the carrying on of *unregulated activities* in a *prudential context*; and
		(2) take into account any activity of other members of a *group* of which the *firm* is a member.
2.13A [FCA]	R	**SYSC 6.3** only applies to a *firm* in relation to carrying on a *credit-related regulated activity*, or operating an electronic system in relation to lending, to which the *Money Laundering Regulations* also apply.
2.13B [FCA]	R	**SYSC 6.3.8 R** and **SYSC 6.3.9 R** do not apply to a *firm* with a *limited permission* for *entering into a regulated credit agreement as lender*.
2.13C [FCA]	G	The *persons* to whom the *Money Laundering Regulations* apply are set out in regulation 3 of the *Money Laundering Regulations*. The *persons* include credit institutions (for example, banks) and financial institutions (for example, *persons* who carry on *regulated activities* which consist of or include *entering into regulated credit agreements as lender*). These expressions are defined in regulation 3 of those Regulations.

Part 3   FCA Handbook Materials

Part 2		Application of the common platform requirements (SYSC 4 to 10)
2.14 [FCA] [PRA]	G	SYSC 1 ANNEX 1.2.13R(2) does not mean that inadequacy of a *group* member's systems and controls will automatically lead to a *firm* contravening any of the *common platform organisational requirements*. Rather, the potential impact of a *group* member's activities, including its systems and controls, and any systems and controls that operate on a *group* basis, will be relevant in determining the appropriateness of the *firm's* own systems and controls.
		Where?
2.15 [FCA] [PRA]	R	The *common platform requirements*, except the *common platform record-keeping requirements*, apply to a *firm* in relation to activities carried on by it from an establishment in the United Kingdom.
2.16 [FCA] [PRA]	R	The *common platform requirements*, except the *common platform requirements on financial crime* and the *common platform record-keeping requirements*, apply to a *firm* that is not a *UK UCITS management company* in relation to *passported activities* carried on by it from a *branch* in another *EEA State*.
2.16A [FCA]	R	(1) The *common platform requirements* referred to in Column A+ of Part 3 (below) apply to a *UK UCITS management company* in relation to *passported activities* carried on by it from a *branch* in another *EEA State*.
		(2) Any other *common platform requirement* applies to a *UK UCITS management company* in relation to *passported activities* carried on by it from a *branch* in another *EEA State* to the extent that the requirement addresses matters within the scope of article 12 of the *UCITS Directive*.
2.16B [FCA]	G	The matters referred to in paragraph 2.16AR of this Annex may also be subject to the rules of the *UK UCITS management company's Host State regulator*.
2.16C [FCA]	R	The *common platform requirements* apply to a *full-scope UK AIFM* in respect of its management of an *AIF* where carried on from an establishment in the UK.
2.16D [FCA]	R	The *common platform requirements*, except those which are AIFMD *host state requirements*, apply to a *full-scope UK AIFM* in respect of its management of an *EEA AIF* from a *branch* in another *EEA State*.
2.16E [FCA]	R	The *common platform requirements* apply to an *AIFM investment firm* which is a *full-scope UK AIFM* in respect of its *MiFID business* where carried on from an establishment in the UK.
2.16F [FCA]	R	The *common platform requirements*, except the *common platform requirements on financial crime* and the *common platform record-keeping requirements*, apply to an *AIFM investment firm* in respect of its *MiFID business* where carried on from a *branch* in another *EEA State*.
2.17 [FCA] [PRA]	R	The *common platform record-keeping requirements* apply to activities carried on by a *firm* from an establishment maintained in the United Kingdom, unless another applicable *rule* which is relevant to the activity has a wider territorial scope, in which case the *common platform record-keeping requirements* apply with that wider scope in relation to the activity described in that *rule*. [**Note**: article 13(9) of *MiFID*]
2.18 [FCA] [PRA]	R	The *common platform organisational requirements on financial crime*, except the *common platform requirements on financial crime*, also apply in a *prudential context* to a *UK domestic firm* and to an *overseas firm* (other than an *incoming EEA firm* or an *Incoming Treaty firm*) with respect to activities wherever they are carried on.

Part 2

Application of the common platform requirements (SYSC 4 to 10)

Actions for damages

2.19 [FCA]	R	A contravention of a *rule* in the *common platform requirements* does not give rise to a right of action by a *private person* under section 138D of the *Act* (and each of those *rules* is specified under section 138D(3) of the *Act* as a provision giving rise to no such right of action).

Part 3

Tables summarising the application of the common platform requirements to different types of firm

3.1 [FCA]	G	The *common platform requirements* apply in the following four ways (subject to the provisions in Part 2 of this Annex).
3.1A [PRA]	G	The *common platform requirements* apply in accordance with Part 2 of this Annex and the provisions in 3.2BR, 3.2CR, 3.2DG, 3.2ER, 3.3AG and 3.4R.
3.2 [FCA]	G	For a *common platform firm*, they apply in accordance with Column A in the table below.
3.2A [FCA]	G	For a *management company*, they apply in accordance with Column A+ in the table below.
3.2B [FCA][PRA]	R	For a *full-scope UK AIFM* of an *authorised AIF*, they apply in line with Column A++ in the table below.
3.2C [PRA]	R	For a *common platform firm* other than a *CRR firm*, Provision **SYSC 4** to Provision **SYSC 9** apply in accordance with Column A in the table below.
3.2D [PRA]	G	**SYSC 4** to **SYSC 9** are not applicable to *CRR firms*. *CRR firms* are subject to the rules in the General Organisational Requirements, Skills, Knowledge and Expertise, Compliance and Internal Audit, Risk Control, Outsourcing and Record Keeping Parts of the *PRA* Rulebook.
3.2E [PRA]	R	For a *common platform firm*, Provision **SYSC 10** applies in accordance with Column A in the table below.
3.3 [FCA]	G	For all other *firms* apart from *insurers*, *managing agents*, the *Society* and *full-scope UK AIFMs* of *unauthorised AIFs*, they apply in accordance with Column B in the table below. For these *firms*, where a *rule* is shown modified in Column B as 'Guidance', it should be read as *guidance* (as if "should" appeared in that rule instead of "must") and should be applied in a proportionate manner, taking into account the nature, scale and complexity of the firm's business.
3.3A [PRA]	G	For all other *firms* apart from *CRR firms*, *insurers*, *managing agents*, the *Society* and *full-scope UK AIFMs* of *unauthorised AIFs*, they apply in accordance with Column B in the table below. For these *firms*, where a *rule* is shown modified in Column B as 'Guidance', it should be read as *guidance* (as if "should" appeared in that rule instead of "must") and should be applied in a proportionate manner, taking into account the nature, scale and complexity of the firm's business.
3.4 [PRA]	R	For the purposes of Provision 4 to Provision 9 in the table below, the reference to: (1) "common platform firm" in Column A must be read as "a common platform firm apart from a CRR firm"; and (2) "all other firms" in Column B must be read as "all other firms apart from CRR firms".

Part 3   FCA Handbook Materials

Provision SYSC 4	COLUMN A Application to a common platform firm other than to a UCITS investment firm	COLUMN A+ Application to a UCITS management company	COLUMN A++ Application to a full-scope UK AIFM of an authorised AIF	COLUMN B Application to all other firms apart from insurers, managing agents the Society, and full-scope UK AIFMs of unauthorised AIFs
SYSC 4.1.1 R [FCA] [PRA]	Rule	Rule	Rule	Rule
SYSC 4.1.1A R [FCA] [PRA]	Not applicable	Not applicable	Rule	Not applicable
SYSC 4.1.1B R [FCA]	Not applicable	Not applicable	Rule	Not applicable
SYSC 4.1.1C R [FCA]	Rule for a *BIPRU firm*	Rule for a *BIPRU firm* that is a *UCITS investment firm*	Not applicable	Not applicable
SYSC 4.1.2 R [FCA] [PRA]	Rule	Rule for a *UCITS* investment firm; otherwise guidance	Rule	Guidance
SYSC 4.1.2A G [FCA] [PRA]	Not applicable	Guidance for a *UCITS firm*; not applicable to a UCITS investment firm	Not applicable	Guidance
SYSC 4.1.2AA R [FCA]	Rule for a *BIPRU firm*	Rule for a *BIPRU firm* that is a *UCITS* investment firm	Not applicable	Not applicable
SYSC 4.1.2B R [FCA]	Not applicable	Rule	Rule	Not applicable
SYSC 4.1.2C R [FCA]	Not applicable	Not applicable	Rule	Not applicable
SYSC 4.1.2D R [FCA] [PRA]	Not applicable	Not applicable	Rule	Not applicable
SYSC 4.1.3 R [FCA] [PRA]	[deleted]	[deleted]	[deleted]	[deleted]
SYSC 4.1.4 R [FCA][PRA]	Rule	Rule	Not applicable	(1) and (3) Guidance (2) Rule

Provision SYSC 4	COLUMN A Application to a common platform firm other than to a UCITS investment firm	COLUMN A+ Application to a UCITS management company	COLUMN A++ Application to a full-scope UK AIFM of an authorised AIF	COLUMN B Application to all other firms apart from insurers, managing agents the Society, and full-scope UK AIFMs of unauthorised AIFs
SYSC 4.1.4A G [FCA] [PRA]	Not applicable	Not applicable	Not applicable	Guidance
SYSC 4.1.5 R [FCA] [PRA]	Rule applies only to a *MiFID investment firm*	Rule	Not applicable	Not applicable
SYSC 4.1.6 R [FCA] [PRA]	Rule	Rule for a UCITS investment firm; otherwise guidance	Not applicable	Guidance
SYSC 4.1.7 R [FCA] [PRA]	Rule	Rule	Not applicable	Guidance
SYSC 4.1.7A G [FCA] [PRA]	Not applicable	Not applicable	Not applicable	Guidance
SYSC 4.1.8 G [FCA] [PRA]	Guidance	Guidance	Guidance	Guidance
SYSC 4.1.9 R [FCA] [PRA]	Rule	Rule	Not applicable	Not applicable
SYSC 4.1.10 R [FCA] [PRA]	Rule	Rule	Not applicable	Guidance – except reference to SYSC 4.1.9 R which does not apply to these *firms*
SYSC 4.1.10A G [FCA] [PRA]	Not applicable	Not applicable	Not applicable	Guidance
SYSC 4.1.11 G [FCA] [PRA]	Guidance	Guidance	Guidance	Guidance

Part 3   FCA Handbook Materials

Provision SYSC 4	COLUMN A Application to a common platform firm other than to a UCITS investment firm	COLUMN A+ Application to a UCITS management company	COLUMN A++ Application to a full-scope UK AIFM of an authorised AIF	COLUMN B Application to all other firms apart from insurers, managing agents the Society, and full-scope UK AIFMs of unauthorised AIFs
SYSC 4.1.13 G [FCA] [PRA]	Guidance	Guidance	Guidance	Guidance
SYSC 4.1.14 G [FCA] [PRA]	Guidance	Guidance	Guidance	Guidance
SYSC 4.2.1 R [FCA] [PRA]	Rule	Rule	Rule	—UK branch of non-EEA bank – rule applies. —Other *firms* – Guidance
SYSC 4.2.1A G [FCA] [PRA]	Not applicable	Not applicable	Not applicable	Guidance
SYSC 4.2.2 R [FCA] [PRA]	Rule	Rule	Rule	—UK branch of a non-EEA bank – Rule applies —Other *firms* – this provision does not apply
SYSC 4.2.3 G – 4.2.5 G [FCA] [PRA]	Guidance	Guidance	Guidance	—UK branch of a non-EEA bank – Guidance —Other *firms* – these provisions do not apply
SYSC 4.2.6 R [FCA] [PRA]	Rule	Rule for a UCITS investment firm; otherwise not applicable	Not applicable	—UK branch of a non-EEA bank – Rule applies —Other *firms* – this provision does not apply
SYSC 4.2.7 R [FCA] [PRA]	Not applicable	Not applicable	Rule	Not applicable
SYSC 4.2.8 G [FCA] [PRA]	Not applicable	Not applicable	Rule	Not applicable

Provision SYSC 4	COLUMN A Application to a common platform firm other than to a UCITS investment firm	COLUMN A+ Application to a UCITS management company	COLUMN A++ Application to a full-scope UK AIFM of an authorised AIF	COLUMN B Application to all other firms apart from insurers, managing agents the Society, and full-scope UK AIFMs of unauthorised AIFs
SYSC 4.2.9G [FCA] [PRA]	Not applicable	Not applicable	Guidance	Not applicable
SYSC 4.3.1 R [FCA] [PRA]	Rule	Rule	Not applicable	Rule (but not applicable to *incoming EEA firms, incoming Treaty firms or UCITS qualifiers*)
SYSC 4.3.2 R [FCA] [PRA]	Rule	Rule	Not applicable	Guidance (but not applicable to *incoming EEA firms, incoming Treaty firms or UCITS qualifiers*)
SYSC 4.3.2A G [FCA] [PRA]	Not applicable	Not applicable	Not applicable	Guidance (but not applicable to *incoming EEA firms, incoming Treaty firms or UCITS qualifiers*)
SYSC 4.3.3 G [FCA] [PRA]	Guidance	Guidance	Not applicable	Guidance (but not applicable to *incoming EEA firms, incoming Treaty firms or UCITS qualifiers*)
SYSC 4.3A.-1 R [FCA]	Rule applicable to *CRR firms*	Rule for a *CRR firm* that is a *UCITS investment firm*	Not applicable	Not applicable
SYSC 4.3A.1 R [FCA]	Rule applicable to *CRR firms*	Rule for a *CRR firm* that is a *UCITS investment firm*	Not applicable	Not applicable
SYSC 4.3A.2 R [FCA]	Rule applicable to *CRR firms*	Rule for a *CRR firm* that is a *UCITS investment firm*	Not applicable	Not applicable
SYSC 4.3A.3 R [FCA]	Rule applicable to *CRR firms*	Rule for a *CRR firm* that is a *UCITS investment firm*	Not applicable	Not applicable
SYSC 4.3A.4 R [FCA]	Rule applicable to *CRR firms*	Rule for a *CRR firm* that is a *UCITS investment firm*	Not applicable	Not applicable

Part 3   FCA Handbook Materials

Provision SYSC 4	COLUMN A Application to a common platform firm other than to a UCITS investment firm	COLUMN A+ Application to a UCITS management company	COLUMN A++ Application to a full-scope UK AIFM of an authorised AIF	COLUMN B Application to all other firms apart from insurers, managing agents the Society, and full-scope UK AIFMs of unauthorised AIFs
SYSC 4.3A.5 R [FCA] [PRA]	Rule applicable to *CRR firms*	Rule for a *CRR firm* that is a *UCITS investment firm*	Not applicable	Not applicable
SYSC 4.3A.6 R [FCA] [PRA]	Rule applicable for *CRR firms*	Rule for a *CRR firm* that is a *UCITS investment firm*	Not applicable	Not applicable
SYSC 4.3A.7 R [FCA] [PRA]	Rule applicable to *CRR firms*	Rule for a *CRR firm* that is a *UCITS investment firm*	Not applicable	Not applicable
SYSC 4.3A.8 R [FCA] [PRA]	Rule applicable to *CRR firms*	Rule for a *CRR firm* that is a *UCITS investment firm*	Not applicable	Not applicable
SYSC 4.3A.9 R [FCA] [PRA]	Rule applicable to *CRR firms*	Rule for a *CRR firm* that is a *UCITS investment firm*	Not applicable	Not applicable
SYSC 4.3A.10 R [FCA] [PRA]	Rule applicable to *CRR firms*	Rule for a *CRR firm* that is a *UCITS investment firm*	Not applicable	Not applicable
SYSC 4.3A.11 R [FCA] [PRA]	Rule applicable to *CRR firms*	Rule for a *CRR firm* that is a *UCITS investment firm*	Not applicable	Not applicable
SYSC 4.4.1 R [PRA]	Not applicable	Not applicable	Not applicable	Rule applies this section only to: (1) an *authorised professional firm* in respect of its *non-mainstream regulated activities* unless the *firm* is also conducting other *regulated activities* and has appointed *approved persons* to perform the *governing functions* with equivalent responsibilities for the *firm's non-mainstream regulated activities* and other *regulated activities;*

Provision SYSC 4	COLUMN A Application to a common platform firm other than to a UCITS investment firm	COLUMN A+ Application to a UCITS management company	COLUMN A++ Application to a full-scope UK AIFM of an authorised AIF	COLUMN B Application to all other firms apart from insurers, managing agents the Society, and full-scope UK AIFMs of unauthorised AIFs
				(2) activities carried on by a *firm* whose principal purpose is to carry on activities other than *regulated activities* and which is: (a) an *oil market participant*; (b) a *service company*; (c) an *energy market participant*; (d) a wholly-owned subsidiary of: (i) a local authority; (ii) a registered social landlord; (e) a *firm* with *permission* to carry on *insurance mediation activity* in relation to non-investment insurance contracts but no other *regulated activity*; (3) an *incoming Treaty firm*, an *incoming EEA firm* and a *UCITS qualifier*, (but only SYSC 4.4.5 R (2) applies for these firms); and (4) a *sole trader*, but only if he employs any *person* who is required to be approved under section 59 of the *Act* (Approval for particular arrangements).
SYSC 4.4.1A R [FCA]	Not applicable	Not applicable	Not applicable	Rule applies this section only to: (1) an *authorised professional firm* in respect of its *non-mainstream regulated activities* unless the *firm* is also conducting other *regulated activities* and has appointed *approved persons* to perform the *governing functions* with equivalent responsibilities for the *firm's non-mainstream regulated activities* and other *regulated activities*;

Provision SYSC 4	COLUMN A Application to a common platform firm other than to a UCITS investment firm	COLUMN A+ Application to a UCITS management company	COLUMN A++ Application to a full-scope UK AIFM of an authorised AIF	COLUMN B Application to all other firms apart from insurers, managing agents the Society, and full-scope UK AIFMs of unauthorised AIFs
				(2) activities carried on by a *firm* whose principal purpose is to carry on activities other than *regulated activities* and which is: (a) an *oil market participant*; (b) a *service company*; (c) an *energy market participant*; (d) a wholly-owned subsidiary of: (i) a local authority; (ii) a registered social landlord; (e) a *firm* with *permission* to carry on *insurance mediation activity* in relation to non-investment insurance contracts but no other *regulated activity*; (2A) a *credit firm* which holds a *limited permission* (other than a *not-for-profit debt advice body*) with respect to the relevant credit activity (as defined in paragraph 2G of Schedule 6 to the *Act*) for which it has *limited permission*; (3) an *incoming Treaty firm*, an *incoming EEA firm* and a *UCITS qualifier*, (but only **SYSC 4.4.5R (2)** applies for these firms); and (4) a *sole trader*, but only if he employs any *person* who is required to be approved under section 59 of the *Act* (Approval for particular arrangements).
SYSC 4.4.2 G [FCA] [PRA]	Not applicable	Not applicable	Not applicable	Guidance only applying to the *firms* specified in SYSC 4.4.1 R or **SYSC 4.4.1A R**

Provision SYSC 4	COLUMN A Application to a common platform firm other than to a UCITS investment firm	COLUMN A+ Application to a UCITS management company	COLUMN A++ Application to a full-scope UK AIFM of an authorised AIF	COLUMN B Application to all other firms apart from insurers, managing agents the Society, and full-scope UK AIFMs of unauthorised AIFs
SYSC 4.4.3 R [FCA] [PRA]	Not applicable	Not applicable	Not applicable	Rule only applying to the *firms* specified in SYSC 4.4.1 R or **SYSC 4.4.1A R**
SYSC 4.4.4 G [FCA] [PRA]	Not applicable	Not applicable	Not applicable	Guidance only applying to the *firms* specified in SYSC 4.4.1 R or **SYSC 4.4.1A R**
SYSC 4.4.5 R [FCA] [PRA]	Not applicable	Not applicable	Not applicable	Rule only applying to the *firms* specified in SYSC 4.4.1 R or **SYSC 4.4.1A R**
SYSC 4.4.6 G [FCA] [PRA]	Not applicable	Not applicable	Not applicable	Guidance only applying to the *firms* specified in SYSC 4.4.1 R or **SYSC 4.4.1A R**

Provision SYSC 5	COLUMN A Application to a common platform firm other than to a UCITS investment firm	COLUMN A+ Application to a UCITS management company	COLUMN A++ Application to a full-scope UK AIFM of an authorised AIF	COLUMN B Application to all other firms apart from insurers, managing agents the Society, and full-scope UK AIFMs of unauthorised AIFs
SYSC 5.1.1 R [FCA] [PRA]	Rule	Rule	Not applicable	Rule
SYSC 5.1.2 G [FCA] [PRA]	Guidance	Guidance	Guidance	Guidance
SYSC 5.1.3 G [FCA] [PRA]	Guidance	Guidance	Not applicable	Guidance
SYSC 5.1.4 G [FCA]	Guidance	Guidance	Guidance	Guidance

Provision SYSC 5	COLUMN A Application to a common platform firm other than to a UCITS investment firm	COLUMN A+ Application to a UCITS management company	COLUMN A++ Application to a full-scope UK AIFM of an authorised AIF	COLUMN B Application to all other firms apart from insurers, managing agents the Society, and full-scope UK AIFMs of unauthorised AIFs
SYSC 5.1.4A G [FCA] [PRA]	Guidance	Guidance	Guidance	Guidance
SYSC 5.1.5 G [FCA] [PRA]	Guidance	Guidance	Guidance	Guidance
SYSC 5.1.5A G [FCA] [PRA]	Guidance	Guidance	Guidance	Guidance
SYSC 5.1.6 R [FCA] [PRA]	Rule	Rule	Guidance	Guidance
SYSC 5.1.7 R [FCA] [PRA]	Rule	Rule for a *UCITS investment firm*; otherwise guidance	Guidance	Guidance
SYSC 5.1.7A G [FCA] [PRA]	Not applicable	Not applicable to a *UCITS investment firm*; otherwise guidance	Guidance	Guidance
SYSC 5.1.8 G [FCA] [PRA]	Guidance	Guidance	Guidance	Guidance
SYSC 5.1.9 G [FCA] [PRA]	Guidance	Guidance	Guidance	Guidance
SYSC 5.1.10 G [FCA] [PRA]	Guidance	Guidance	Guidance, but not applicable for the segregation of risk management functions	Guidance
SYSC 5.1.11 G [FCA] [PRA]	Guidance	Guidance	Guidance	Guidance

Provision SYSC 5	COLUMN A Application to a common platform firm other than to a UCITS investment firm	COLUMN A+ Application to a UCITS management company	COLUMN A++ Application to a full-scope UK AIFM of an authorised AIF	COLUMN B Application to all other firms apart from insurers, managing agents the Society, and full-scope UK AIFMs of unauthorised AIFs
SYSC 5.1.12 R [FCA] [PRA]	Rule	Rule	Not applicable	Guidance
SYSC 5.1.12A G [FCA] [PRA]	Not applicable	Not applicable	Not applicable	Guidance
SYSC 5.1.13 R [FCA] [PRA]	Rule	Rule	Not applicable	Rule
SYSC 5.1.14 R [FCA] [PRA]	Rule	Rule	Not applicable	Guidance
SYSC 5.1.15 G [FCA] [PRA]	Not applicable	Not applicable	Not applicable	Guidance

Provision SYSC 6	COLUMN A Application to a common platform firm other than to a UCITS investment firm	COLUMN A+ Application to a UCITS management company	COLUMN A++ Application to a full-scope UK AIFM of an authorised AIF	COLUMN B Application to all other firms apart from insurers, managing agents, the Society and full-scope UK AIFMs of unauthorised AIFs
SYSC 6.1.1 R [FCA] [PRA]	Rule	Rule	Rule but only regarding the obligation to establish, implement and maintain adequate policies and procedures for countering the risk that the *firm* (including its managers and *employees*) might be used to further *financial crime*	Rule

Provision SYSC 6	COLUMN A Application to a common platform firm other than to a UCITS investment firm	COLUMN A+ Application to a UCITS management company	COLUMN A++ Application to a full-scope UK AIFM of an authorised AIF	COLUMN B Application to all other firms apart from insurers, managing agents, the Society and full-scope UK AIFMs of unauthorised AIFs
SYSC 6.1.1A G [FCA][PRA]	Guidance	Guidance	Guidance	Guidance
SYSC 6.1.2 R [FCA][PRA]	Rule	Rule	Not applicable	Guidance
SYSC 6.1.2A G [FCA][PRA]	Not applicable	Not applicable	Not applicable	Guidance
SYSC 6.1.3 R [FCA][PRA]	Rule	Rule	Not applicable	– Guidance This provision shall be read with the following additional sentence at the start. "Depending on the nature, scale and complexity of its business, it may be appropriate for a firm to have a separate compliance function. Where a firm has a separate compliance function, the firm should also take into account 6.1.3 R and 6.1.4 R as guidance."
SYSC 6.1.3A G [FCA][PRA]	Not applicable	Not applicable	Not applicable	Guidance
SYSC 6.1.4 R [FCA][PRA]	Rule	Rule	Not applicable	(1) (3) and (4) Guidance (2) – Rule for firms which carry on designated investment business with or for retail clients or professional clients. – Guidance for all other firms.
SYSC 6.1.4-A G [FCA][PRA]	Not applicable	Not applicable	Rule	Guidance
SYSC 6.1.4-B G [FCA]	Not applicable	Not applicable	Guidance	Not applicable

Provision SYSC 6	COLUMN A Application to a common platform firm other than to a UCITS investment firm	COLUMN A+ Application to a UCITS management company	COLUMN A++ Application to a full-scope UK AIFM of an authorised AIF	COLUMN B Application to all other firms apart from insurers, managing agents, the Society and full-scope UK AIFMs of unauthorised AIFs
SYSC 6.1.4A R [FCA]	Not applicable	Not applicable	Not applicable	Rule for *firms* which carry on *designated investment business* with or for *retail clients* or *professional clients*.
SYSC 6.1.4C R [FCA]	Not applicable	Not applicable	Not applicable	Rule for *debt management firms* and *credit repair firms*.
SYSC 6.1.5 R [FCA] [PRA]	Not applicable	Not applicable	Not applicable	– Guidance – *"investment services and activities"* shall be read as "financial services and activities"
SYSC 6.1.6 R [FCA] [PRA]	Not applicable	Not applicable	Not applicable	Guidance
SYSC 6.1.7 R [FCA]	Rule	Rule for a *UCITS investment firm*; otherwise not applicable	Not applicable	Guidance
SYSC 6.2.1 R [FCA] [PRA]	Rule	Rule	Not applicable	Guidance
SYSC 6.2.1A G [FCA] [PRA]	Not applicable	Not applicable	Not applicable	Guidance
SYSC 6.2.2 G [FCA] [PRA]	Guidance	Guidance	Not applicable	Guidance

Provision SYSC 6	COLUMN A Application to a common platform firm other than to a UCITS investment firm	COLUMN A+ Application to a UCITS management company	COLUMN A++ Application to a full-scope UK AIFM of an authorised AIF	COLUMN B Application to all other firms apart from insurers, managing agents, the Society and full-scope UK AIFMs of unauthorised AIFs
SYSC 6.3.1 R [FCA]	Rule	Rule	Rule	Rule For *firms* carrying on a *credit-related regulated activity*, or operating an *electronic system in relation to lending*, applies only where the *Money Laundering Regulations* apply to the *firm*. Rule does not apply to a *firm* for which a professional body listed in Schedule 3 to the *Money Laundering Regulations*, and not the *FCA*, acts as the supervisory authority for the purposes of those regulations. (FCA Handbook only)
SYSC 6.3.2 G [FCA]	Guidance	Guidance	Guidance	Guidance For *firms* carrying on a *credit-related regulated activity*, or operating an *electronic system in relation to lending*, applies only where the *Money Laundering Regulations* apply to the *firm*. Guidance does not apply to a *firm* for which a professional body listed in Schedule 3 to the *Money Laundering Regulations*, and not the *FCA*, acts as the supervisory authority for the purposes of those regulations. (FCA Handbook only)
SYSC 6.3.3 R [FCA]	Rule	Rule	Rule	Rule For *firms* carrying on a *credit-related regulated activity*, or operating an *electronic system in relation to lending*, applies only where the *Money Laundering Regulations* apply to the *firm*. Rule does not apply to a *firm* for which a professional body listed in Schedule 3 to the *Money Laundering Regulations*, and not the *FCA*, acts as the supervisory authority for the purposes of those regulations. (FCA Handbook only)

Provision SYSC 6	COLUMN A Application to a common platform firm other than to a UCITS investment firm	COLUMN A+ Application to a UCITS management company	COLUMN A++ Application to a full-scope UK AIFM of an authorised AIF	COLUMN B Application to all other firms apart from insurers, managing agents, the Society and full-scope UK AIFMs of unauthorised AIFs
SYSC 6.3.4 G [FCA]	Guidance	Guidance	Guidance	Guidance For *firms* carrying on a *credit-related regulated activity*, or operating an electronic system in relation to lending, applies only where the *Money Laundering Regulations* apply to the *firm*. Guidance does not apply to a *firm* for which a professional body listed in Schedule 3 to the *Money Laundering Regulations*, and not the *FCA*, acts as the supervisory authority for the purposes of those regulations. (FCA Handbook only)
SYSC 6.3.5 G [FCA]	Guidance	Guidance	Guidance	Guidance For *firms* carrying on a *credit-related regulated activity*, or operating an electronic system in relation to lending, applies only where the *Money Laundering Regulations* apply to the *firm*. Guidance does not apply to a *firm* for which a professional body listed in Schedule 3 to the *Money Laundering Regulations*, and not the *FCA*, acts as the supervisory authority for the purposes of those regulations. (FCA Handbook only)
SYSC 6.3.6 G [FCA]	Guidance	Guidance	Guidance	Guidance For *firms* carrying on a *credit-related regulated activity*, or operating an electronic system in relation to lending, applies only where the *Money Laundering Regulations* apply to the *firm*. Guidance does not apply to a *firm* for which a professional body listed in Schedule 3 to the *Money Laundering Regulations*, and not the *FCA*, acts as the supervisory authority for the purposes of those regulations. (FCA Handbook only)

Provision SYSC 6	COLUMN A Application to a common platform firm other than to a UCITS investment firm	COLUMN A+ Application to a UCITS management company	COLUMN A++ Application to a full-scope UK AIFM of an authorised AIF	COLUMN B Application to all other firms apart from insurers, managing agents, the Society and full-scope UK AIFMs of unauthorised AIFs
SYSC 6.3.7 G [FCA]	Guidance	Guidance	Guidance	Guidance For *firms* carrying on a *credit-related regulated activity*, or *operating an electronic system in relation to lending*, applies only where the *Money Laundering Regulations* apply to the *firm*. Guidance does not apply to a *firm* for which a professional body listed in Schedule 3 to the *Money Laundering Regulations*, and not the *FCA*, acts as the supervisory authority for the purposes of those regulations. (FCA Handbook only)
SYSC 6.3.8 R [FCA]	Rule	Rule	Rule	Rule For *firms* carrying on a *credit-related regulated activity*, or *operating an electronic system in relation to lending*, applies only where the *Money Laundering Regulations* apply to the *firm*. Rule does not apply to a *firm* with a *limited permission* for entering into a *regulated credit agreement as lender*. Rule does not apply to a *firm* for which a professional body listed in Schedule 3 to the *Money Laundering Regulations*, and not the *FCA*, acts as the supervisory authority for the purposes of those regulations. (FCA Handbook only)

Provision SYSC 6	COLUMN A Application to a common platform firm other than to a UCITS investment firm	COLUMN A+ Application to a UCITS management company	COLUMN A++ Application to a full-scope UK AIFM of an authorised AIF	COLUMN B Application to all other firms apart from insurers, managing agents, the Society and full-scope UK AIFMs of unauthorised AIFs
SYSC 6.3.9 R [FCA]	Rule	Rule	Rule	Rule For *firms* carrying on a *credit-related regulated activity*, or operating an electronic system in relation to lending, applies only where the *Money Laundering Regulations* apply to the *firm*. Rule does not apply to a *firm* with a limited permission for entering into a regulated credit agreement as lender. Rule does not apply to a *firm* for which a professional body listed in Schedule 3 to the *Money Laundering Regulations*, and not the *FCA*, acts as the supervisory authority for the purposes of those regulations. (FCA Handbook only)
SYSC 6.3.10 G [FCA]	Guidance	Guidance	Guidance	Guidance For *firms* carrying on a *credit-related regulated activity*, or operating an electronic system in relation to lending, applies only where the *Money Laundering Regulations* apply to the *firm*. Guidance does not apply to a *firm* for which a professional body listed in Schedule 3 to the *Money Laundering Regulations*, and not the *FCA*, acts as the supervisory authority for the purposes of those regulations. (FCA Handbook only)

Provision SYSC 6	COLUMN A Application to a common platform firm other than to a UCITS investment firm	COLUMN A+ Application to a UCITS management company	COLUMN A++ Application to a full-scope UK AIFM of an authorised AIF	COLUMN B Application to all other firms apart from insurers, managing agents, the Society and full-scope UK AIFMs of unauthorised AIFs
SYSC 6.3.11 G [FCA]	Guidance	Guidance	Guidance	Guidance For *firms* carrying on a *credit-related regulated activity*, or *operating an electronic system in relation to lending*, applies only where the *Money Laundering Regulations* apply to the *firm*. Guidance does not apply to a *firm* for which a professional body listed in Schedule 3 to the *Money Laundering Regulations*, and not the *FCA*, acts as the supervisory authority for the purposes of those regulations. (FCA Handbook only)

Provision SYSC 7	COLUMN A Application to a common platform firm other than to a UCITS investment firm	COLUMN A+ Application to a UCITS management company	COLUMN A++ Application to a full-scope UK AIFM of an authorised AIF	COLUMN B Application to all other firms apart from insurers, managing agents, the Society, and full-scope UK AIFMs of unauthorised AIFs
SYSC 7.1.1 G [FCA] [PRA]	Guidance	Guidance	Not applicable	Guidance
SYSC 7.1.2 R [FCA] [PRA]	Rule	Rule for a *UCITS investment firm*; otherwise guidance	Not applicable	Guidance
SYSC 7.1.2A G [FCA] [PRA]	Not applicable	Not applicable to a *UCITS investment firm*; otherwise guidance	Not applicable	Guidance
SYSC 7.1.2B G [FCA] [PRA]	Not applicable	Guidance	Not applicable	Not applicable
SYSC 7.1.3 R [FCA] [PRA]	Rule	Rule for a *UCITS investment firm*; otherwise guidance	Not applicable	Guidance
SYSC 7.1.4 R [FCA] [PRA]	Rule	Rule for a *UCITS investment firm*; otherwise guidance	Not applicable	Guidance
SYSC 7.1.4A G [FCA] [PRA]	Not applicable	Rule for a *UCITS investment firm*; otherwise guidance	Not applicable	Guidance

Provision SYSC 7	COLUMN A Application to a common platform firm other than to a UCITS investment firm	COLUMN A+ Application to a UCITS management company	COLUMN A++ Application to a full-scope UK AIFM of an authorised AIF	COLUMN B Application to all other firms apart from insurers, managing agents, the Society, and full-scope UK AIFMs of unauthorised AIFs
SYSC 7.1.4B G [FCA] [PRA]	Not applicable	Rule for a *UCITS investment firm*; otherwise guidance	Not applicable	Guidance
SYSC 7.1.5 R [FCA] [PRA]	Rule	Rule for a *UCITS investment firm*; otherwise guidance	Not applicable	Guidance
SYSC 7.1.6 R [FCA] [PRA]	Rule	Rule for a *UCITS investment firm*; otherwise guidance	Not applicable	Guidance
SYSC 7.1.7 R [FCA] [PRA]	Rule	Rule for a *UCITS investment firm*; otherwise guidance	Not applicable	Guidance
SYSC 7.1.7A G [FCA] [PRA]	Not applicable	Rule for a *UCITS investment firm*; otherwise guidance	Not applicable	Guidance
SYSC 7.1.7B G [FCA] [PRA]	Guidance applies only to a *BIPRU firm*	Rule for a *UCITS investment firm*; otherwise guidance	Guidance	Guidance
SYSC 7.1.7BA G [FCA]	Not applicable	Not applicable	Guidance	Not applicable
SYSC 7.1.7BB G [FCA]	Guidance applies only to a *BIPRU firm*	Guidance applies only to a *BIPRU firm* that is a *UCITS investment firm*	Not applicable	Not applicable
SYSC 7.1.7C G [FCA] [PRA]	Guidance	Guidance	Guidance	Guidance
SYSC 7.1.8 G [FCA] [PRA]	[deleted]	[deleted]	[deleted]	[deleted]
SYSC 7.1.9 R [FCA] [PRA]	Rule applies to a *BIPRU firm*	Rule for a *UCITS investment firm*; otherwise not applicable	Not applicable	Not applicable
SYSC 7.1.10 R [FCA] [PRA]	Rule applies to a *BIPRU firm*	Rule for a *UCITS investment firm*; otherwise not applicable	Not applicable	Not applicable
SYSC 7.1.11 R [FCA] [PRA]	Rule applies to a *BIPRU firm*	Rule for a *UCITS investment firm*; otherwise not applicable	Not applicable	Not applicable
SYSC 7.1.12 G [FCA] [PRA]	Guidance applies to a *BIPRU firm*	Rule for a *UCITS investment firm*; otherwise not applicable	Not applicable	Not applicable

Part 3   FCA Handbook Materials

Provision SYSC 7	COLUMN A Application to a common platform firm other than to a UCITS investment firm	COLUMN A+ Application to a UCITS management company	COLUMN A++ Application to a full-scope UK AIFM of an authorised AIF	COLUMN B Application to all other firms apart from insurers, managing agents, the Society, and full-scope UK AIFMs of unauthorised AIFs
SYSC 7.1.13 R–7.1.16 R [FCA] [PRA]	Rule applies to a *BIPRU firm*	Rule for a *UCITS investment firm*; otherwise not applicable	Not applicable	Not applicable
SYSC 7.1.16A G [FCA]	Guidance applies to a *BIPRU firm*	Guidance for a *UCITS investment firm* otherwise not applicable	Not applicable	Not applicable
SYSC 7.1.16B G [FCA]	Guidance applies to a *BIPRU firm*	Guidance for a *UCITS investment firm* otherwise not applicable	Not applicable	Not applicable
SYSC 7.1.16C R [FCA]	Rule applies to a *CRR firm*	Not applicable	Not applicable	Not applicable
SYSC 7.1.17 R [FCA] [PRA]	Rule applies to a *CRR firm*	Rule for a *UCITS investment firm* that is a *CRR firm*, otherwise not applicable	Not applicable	Not applicable
SYSC 7.1.18 R [FCA] [PRA]	Rule applies to a *CRR firm*	Rule for a *UCITS investment firm* that is a *CRR firm*, otherwise not applicable	Not applicable	Not applicable
SYSC 7.1.18A G [FCA]	Guide applies to a *CRR firm*	Guidance for a *UCITS investment firm* that is a *CRR firm*, otherwise not applicable	Not applicable	Not applicable
SYSC 7.1.18B R [FCA]	Rule applies to a *CRR firm*	Rule for a *UCITS investment firm* that is a *CRR firm*, otherwise not applicable	Not applicable	Not applicable
SYSC 7.1.19 R [FCA] [PRA]	Rule applies to a *CRR firm*	Rule for a *UCITS investment firm* that is a *CRR firm*, otherwise not applicable	Not applicable	Not applicable
SYSC 7.1.20 R [FCA] [PRA]	Rule applies to a *CRR firm*	Rule for a *UCITS investment firm* that is a *CRR firm*, otherwise not applicable	Not applicable	Not applicable
SYSC 7.1.21 R [FCA] [PRA]	Rule applies to a *CRR firm*	Rule for a *UCITS investment firm* that is a *CRR firm*, otherwise not applicable	Not applicable	Not applicable

Provision SYSC 7	COLUMN A Application to a common platform firm other than to a UCITS investment firm	COLUMN A+ Application to a UCITS management company	COLUMN A++ Application to a full-scope UK AIFM of an authorised AIF	COLUMN B Application to all other firms apart from insurers, managing agents, the Society, and full-scope UK AIFMs of unauthorised AIFs
SYSC 7.1.22 R [FCA] [PRA]	Rule applies to a *CRR firm*	Rule for a *UCITS investment firm* that is a *CRR firm*, otherwise not applicable	Not applicable	Not applicable

Provision SYSC 8	COLUMN A Application to a common platform firm other than to a UCITS investment firm	COLUMN A+ Application to a UCITS management company	COLUMN A++ Application to a full-scope UK AIFM of an authorised AIF	COLUMN B Application to all other firms apart from insurers, managing agents, the Society, and full-scope UK AIFMs of unauthorised AIFs
SYSC 8.1.1 R [FCA] [PRA]	Rule	Rule for a *UCITS investment firm*; otherwise guidance	Not applicable	Guidance
SYSC 8.1.1A G [FCA] [PRA]	Not applicable	Not applicable to a *UCITS investment firm*; otherwise guidance	Not applicable	Guidance
SYSC 8.1.2 G [FCA] [PRA]	Guidance	Guidance	Not applicable	Guidance
SYSC 8.1.3 G [FCA] [PRA]	Guidance	Guidance	Not applicable	Guidance
SYSC 8.1.4 R [FCA] [PRA]	Rule	Rule for a *UCITS investment firm*; otherwise guidance	Not applicable	Guidance
SYSC 8.1.5 R [FCA] [PRA]	Rule	Rule for a *UCITS investment firm*; otherwise guidance	Not applicable	Guidance
SYSC 8.1.5A G [FCA] [PRA]	Not applicable	Rule for a *UCITS investment firm*; otherwise guidance	Not applicable	Guidance
SYSC 8.1.6 R [FCA] [PRA]	Rule	Rule	Not applicable	Rule
SYSC 8.1.7 R [FCA] [PRA]	Rule	Rule for a *UCITS investment firm*; otherwise guidance	Not applicable	Guidance
SYSC 8.1.8 R [FCA] [PRA]	Rule	Rule for a *UCITS investment firm*; otherwise guidance	Not applicable	Guidance

Provision SYSC 8	COLUMN A Application to a common platform firm other than to a UCITS investment firm	COLUMN A+ Application to a UCITS management company	COLUMN A++ Application to a full-scope UK AIFM of an authorised AIF	COLUMN B Application to all other firms apart from insurers, managing agents, the Society, and full-scope UK AIFMs of unauthorised AIFs
SYSC 8.1.9 R [FCA] [PRA]	Rule	Rule for a *UCITS investment firm*; otherwise guidance	Not applicable	Guidance
SYSC 8.1.10 R [FCA] [PRA]	Rule	Rule for a *UCITS investment firm*; otherwise guidance	Not applicable	Guidance
SYSC 8.1.11 R [FCA] [PRA]	Rule	Rule for a *UCITS investment firm*; otherwise guidance	Not applicable	Guidance
SYSC 8.1.11A G [FCA] [PRA]	Not applicable	Not applicable to a *UCITS investment firm*; otherwise guidance	Not applicable	Guidance
SYSC 8.1.12 G [FCA] [PRA]	Guidance	Guidance	Not applicable	Guidance
SYSC 8.1.13 R [FCA]	Not applicable	Rule	Not applicable	Not applicable
SYSC 8.1.14 G [FCA]	Not applicable	Guidance	Not applicable	Not applicable
SYSC 8.2 [FCA]	*MiFID investment firms* only	*UCITS investment firms* only	Not applicable	Not applicable
SYSC 8.3 [FCA]	*MiFID investment firms* only	*UCITS investment firms* only	Not applicable	Not applicable

Provision SYSC 9	COLUMN A Application to a common platform firm other than to a UCITS investment firm	COLUMN A+ Application to a UCITS management company	COLUMN A++ Application to a full-scope UK AIFM of an authorised AIF	COLUMN B Application to all other firms apart from insurers, managing agents, the Society, and full-scope UK AIFMs of unauthorised AIFs
SYSC 9.1.1 R [FCA] [PRA]	Rule	Rule	Rule but only for the requirement to arrange for orderly records to be kept of its business and internal organisation which do not relate to portfolio transactions and subscription and redemptions orders	Rule
SYSC 9.1.2 R [FCA] [PRA]	Rule applies only in relation to *MiFID business*	Rule applies only in relation to *MiFID business* of a *UCITS investment firm*	Rule but only for records specified by the modified application of **SYSC 9.1.1 R**	Not applicable
SYSC 9.1.3 R [FCA] [PRA]	Rule applies only in relation to *MiFID business*	Rule applies only in relation to *MiFID business* of a *UCITS investment firm*	Not applicable	Not applicable
SYSC 9.1.4 G [FCA] [PRA]	Guidance	Guidance	Guidance	Guidance
SYSC 9.1.5 G [FCA] [PRA]	Guidance	Guidance	Not applicable	Guidance
SYSC 9.1.6 G [FCA] [PRA]	Guidance	Guidance	Not applicable	Guidance
SYSC 9.1.7 G [FCA] [PRA]	Guidance applies only in relation to *MiFID business*	Guidance applies only in relation to *MiFID business* of a *UCITS investment firm*	Not applicable	Not applicable

Provision SYSC 10	Column A Application to a common platform firm other than to a UCITS investment firm	COLUMN A+ Application to a UCITS management company	COLUMN A++ Application to a full-scope UK AIFM of an authorised AIF	Column B Application to all other firms apart from insurers, managing agents, the Society, and full-scope UK AIFMs of unauthorised AIFs
SYSC 10.1.1 R [FCA] [PRA]	Rule	Rule	Not applicable	Rule
SYSC 10.1.1A R [FCA]	Not applicable	Not applicable	Rule	Not applicable
SYSC 10.1.2 G [FCA] [PRA]	Guidance	Guidance	Not applicable	Guidance
SYSC 10.1.3 R [FCA] [PRA]	Rule	Rule	Not applicable	Rule
SYSC 10.1.4 R [FCA] [PRA]	Rule	Rule	Not applicable	Guidance – but applies as a rule in relation to the production or arrangement of investment research in accordance with **COBS 12.2**, or the production or dissemination of non-independent research in accordance with **COBS 12.3**
SYSC 10.1.4A G [FCA] [PRA]	Not applicable	Not applicable	Not applicable	Guidance
SYSC 10.1.5 G [FCA] [PRA]	Guidance	Guidance	Not applicable	Guidance
SYSC 10.1.6 R [FCA] [PRA]	Rule	Rule	Not applicable	Guidance – but applies as a rule in relation to the production or arrangement of investment research in accordance with **COBS 12.2**, or the production or dissemination of non-independent research in accordance with **COBS 12.3**
SYSC 10.1.6A G [FCA] [PRA]	Not applicable	Not applicable	Not applicable	Guidance
SYSC 10.1.7 R [FCA] [PRA]	Rule	Rule	Not applicable	Rule
SYSC 10.1.8 R [FCA] [PRA]	Rule	Rule	Not applicable	Rule

Provision SYSC 10	Column A Application to a common platform firm other than to a UCITS investment firm	COLUMN A+ Application to a UCITS management company	COLUMN A++ Application to a full-scope UK AIFM of an authorised AIF	Column B Application to all other firms apart from insurers, managing agents, the Society, and full-scope UK AIFMs of unauthorised AIFs
SYSC 10.1.8A R [FCA] [PRA]	Rule	Rule	Not applicable	Rule
SYSC 10.1.9 G [FCA] [PRA]	Guidance	Guidance	Not applicable	Guidance
SYSC 10.1.10 R [FCA] [PRA]	Rule	Rule	Not applicable	Guidance – but applies as a rule in relation to the production or arrangement of investment research in accordance with **COBS 12.2**, or the production or dissemination of non-independent research in accordance with **COBS 12.3**
SYSC 10.1.11 R [FCA] [PRA]	Rule	Rule	Not applicable	Guidance – but applies as a rule in relation to the production or arrangement of investment research in accordance with **COBS 12.2**, or the production or dissemination of non-independent research in accordance with **COBS 12.3**
SYSC 10.1.11A G [FCA] [PRA]	Not applicable	Not applicable	Not applicable	Guidance
SYSC 10.1.12 G –SYSC 10.1.15 G [FCA] [PRA]	Guidance	Guidance for **SYSC 10.1.12 G**; not applicable for **SYSC 10.1.15 G**	Guidance for SYSC 10.1.12 G; not applicable for **SYSC 10.1.13 G to SYSC 10.1.15 G**	Guidance
SYSC 10.1.16 R [FCA]	Not applicable	Not applicable	Not applicable	Rule
SYSC 10.1.17 R [FCA]	Not applicable	Rule	Not applicable	Not applicable
SYSC 10.1.18 G [FCA]	Not applicable	Guidance	Not applicable	Not applicable

Provision SYSC 10	Column A Application to a common platform firm other than to a UCITS investment firm	COLUMN A+ Application to a UCITS management company	COLUMN A++ Application to a full-scope UK AIFM of an authorised AIF	Column B Application to all other firms apart from insurers, managing agents, the Society, and full-scope UK AIFMs of unauthorised AIFs
SYSC 10.1.19 R [FCA]	Not applicable	Rule	Not applicable	Not applicable
SYSC 10.1.20 R [FCA]	Not applicable	Rule	Not applicable	Not applicable
SYSC 10.1.21 R [FCA]	Not applicable	Rule	Not applicable	Not applicable
SYSC 10.1.22 R [FCA] [PRA]	Not applicable	Rule	Rule	Not applicable
SYSC 10.1.23 R to SYSC 10.1.26 R [FCA] [PRA]	Not applicable	Not applicable	Rule	Not applicable
SYSC 10.2.1 R [FCA]	Rule	Rule	Rule	Rule
SYSC 10.2.2 R [FCA]	Rule	Rule	Rule	Rule
SYSC 10.2.3 G [FCA]	Guidance	Guidance	Guidance	Guidance
SYSC 10.2.4 R [FCA]	Rule	Rule	Rule	Rule
SYSC 10.2.5 G [FCA]	Guidance	Guidance	Guidance	Guidance

CHAPTER 2
SENIOR MANAGEMENT ARRANGEMENTS

2.1   APPORTIONMENT OF RESPONSIBILITIES

[3.8]
2.1.1R   FCA PRA

A *firm* must take reasonable care to maintain a clear and appropriate apportionment of significant responsibilities among its *directors* and *senior managers* in such a way that:
(1)   it is clear who has which of those responsibilities; and
(2)   the business and affairs of the *firm* can be adequately monitored and controlled by the *directors*, relevant *senior managers* and *governing body* of the *firm*.

2.1.1A G   FCA PRA

Firms should also consider the additional *guidance* on risk-centric governance arrangements for effective risk management contained in **SYSC 21**.

2.1.2 G   FCA PRA

The role undertaken by a *non-executive director* will vary from one *firm* to another. For example, the role of a *non-executive director* in a *friendly society* may be more extensive than in other *firms*. Where a *non-executive director* is an *approved person*, for example where the *firm* is a *body corporate*, his responsibility and therefore liability will be limited by the role that he undertakes.

2.1.3 R   FCA PRA

A *firm* must appropriately allocate to one or more individuals, in accordance with **SYSC 2.1.4 R**, the functions of:
(1)   dealing with the apportionment of responsibilities under **SYSC 2.1.1 R**; and
(2)   overseeing the establishment and maintenance of systems and controls under **SYSC 3.1.1 R**.

2.1.4 R

Allocation of functions

This table belongs to **SYSC 2.1.3 R**

1: Firm type	2: Allocation of both functions must be to the following individual, if any (see Note):	3: Allocation to one or more individuals selected from this column is compulsory if there is no allocation to an individual in column 2, but is otherwise optional and additional:
(1) A *firm* which is a *body corporate* and is a member of a *group*, other than a *firm* in row (2)	(1) the *firm's* chief executive (and all of them jointly, if more than one); or (2) a *director* or *senior manager* responsible for the overall management of: (a) the *group*; or (b) a *group* division within which some or all of the *firm's regulated activities* fall	the *firm's* and its *group's*: (1) *directors*; and (2) *senior managers*
(2) An *incoming EEA firm* or *incoming Treaty firm* (note: only the function in **SYSC 2.1.3 R (2)** must be allocated)	(not applicable)	the *firm's* and its *group's*: (1) *directors*; and (2) *senior managers*
(3) Any other *firm*	the *firm's* chief executive (and all of them jointly, if more than one)	the *firm's* and its *group's*: (1) *directors*; and (2) *senior manager's*
Note: Column 2 does not require the involvement of the *chief executive* or other executive *director* or *senior manager* in an aspect of corporate governance if that would be contrary to generally accepted principles of good corporate governance.		

2.1.5 G   FCA PRA

SYSC 2.1.3 R and **SYSC 2.1.4 R** give a *firm* some flexibility in the individuals to whom the functions may be allocated. It will be common for both the functions to be allocated solely to the *firm's chief executive*. **SYSC 2.1.6 G** contains further *guidance* on the requirements of **SYSC 2.1.3 R** and **SYSC 2.1.4 R** in a question and answer form.

2.1.6 G

Frequently asked questions about allocation of functions in **SYSC 2.1.3 R**

This table belongs to **SYSC 2.1.5 G**

	Question	Answer
1	Does an individual to whom a function is allocated under **SYSC 2.1.3 R** need to be an *approved person*?	An individual to whom a function is allocated under **SYSC 2.1.3 R** will be performing the *apportionment and oversight function* (CF 8, see **SUP 10A.7.1 R**) and an application must be made under section 59 of the *Act* for approval of the individual before the function is performed. There are exceptions from this in **SUP 10A.1** (Approved persons – Application).
2	If the allocation is to more than one individual, can they perform the functions, or aspects of the functions, separately?	If the functions are allocated to joint *chief executives* under **SYSC 2.1.4 R**, column 2, they are expected to act jointly. If the functions are allocated to an individual under **SYSC 2.1.4 R**, column 2, in addition to individuals under **SYSC 2.1.4 R**, column 3, the former may normally be expected to perform a leading role in relation to the functions that reflects his position. Otherwise, yes.
3	What is meant by "appropriately allocate" in this context?	The allocation of functions should be compatible with delivering compliance with *Principle* 3, **SYSC 2.1.1 R** and **SYSC 3.1.1 R**. The *appropriate regulator* considers that allocation to one or two individuals is likely to be appropriate for most *firms*.
4	If a committee of management governs a *firm* or *group*, can the functions be allocated to every member of that committee?	Yes, as long as the allocation remains appropriate (see Question 3).If the *firm* also has an individual as *chief executive*, then the functions must be allocated to that individual as well under **SYSC 2.1.4 R**, column 2 (see Question 7).
5	Does the definition of *chief executive* include the possessor of equivalent responsibilities with another title, such as a managing *director* or managing *partner*?	Yes.
6	Is it possible for a *firm* to have more than one individual as its *chief executive*?	Although unusual, some *firm* may wish the responsibility of a *chief executive* to be held jointly by more than one individual. In that case, each of them will be a *chief executive* and the functions must be allocated to all of them under **SYSC 2.1.4 R**, column 2 (see also Questions 2 and 7).
7	If a *firm* has an individual as *chief executive*, must the functions be allocated to that individual?	Normally, yes, under **SYSC 2.1.4 R**, column 2. But if the *firm* is a *body corporate* and a member of a *group*, the functions may, instead of to the *firm's chief executive*, be allocated to a *director* or *senior manager* from the *group* responsible for the overall management of the *group* or of a relevant *group* division, so long as this is appropriate (see Question 3). Such individuals may nevertheless require approval under section 59 (see Question 1).

	Question	Answer
		If the *firm* chooses to allocate the functions to a *director* or *senior manager* responsible for the overall management of a relevant *group* division, the *appropriate regulator* would expect that individual to be of a seniority equivalent to or greater than a *chief executive* of the *firm* for the allocation to be appropriate. See also Question 14.
8	If a *firm* has a *chief executive*, can the functions be allocated to other individuals in addition to the *chief executive*?	Yes. **SYSC 2.1.4 R**, column 3, permits a *firm* to allocate the functions, additionally, to the *firm's* (or where applicable the *group's*) directors and *senior managers* as long as this is appropriate (see Question 3).
9	What if a *firm* does not have a *chief executive*?	Normally, the functions must be allocated to one or more individuals selected from the *firm's* (or where applicable the *group's*) directors and *senior managers* under **SYSC 2.1.4 R**, column 3. But if the *firm*: (1) is a *body corporate* and a member of a *group*; and (2) the *group* has a *director* or *senior manager* responsible for the overall management of the *group* or of a relevant *group* division; then the functions must be allocated to that individual (together, optionally, with individuals from column 3 if appropriate) under **SYSC 2.1.4 R**, column 2.
10	What do you mean by "*group* division within which some or all of the *firm's* *regulated activities* fall"?	A "division" in this context should be interpreted by reference to geographical operations, product lines or any other method by which the *group's* business is divided. If the *firm's* *regulated activities* fall within more than one division and the *firm* does not wish to allocate the functions to its *chief executive*, the allocation must, under **SYSC 2.1.4 R**, be to: (1) a *director* or *senior manager* responsible for the overall management of the *group*; or (2) a *director* or *senior manager* responsible for the overall management of one of those divisions; together, optionally, with individuals from column 3 if appropriate. (See also Questions 7 and 9.)
11	How does the requirement to allocate the functions in **SYSC 2.1.3 R** apply to an *overseas firm* which is not an *incoming EEA firm, incoming Treaty firm* or *UCITS qualifier*?	The *firm* must appropriately allocate those functions to one or more individuals, in accordance with **SYSC 2.1.4 R**, but: (1) The responsibilities that must be apportioned and the systems and controls that must be overseen are those relating to activities carried on from a *UK* establishment with certain exceptions (see **SYSC 1 ANNEX 1.1.7 R**). Note that **SYSC 1 ANNEX 1.1.10 R** does not extend the territorial scope of **SYSC 2** for an *overseas firm*.

	Question	Answer
		(2) The *chief executive* of an *overseas firm* is the *person* responsible for the conduct of the *firm's* business within the United Kingdom (see the definition of "*chief executive*"). This might, for example, be the manager of the *firm's* UK establishment, or it might be the *chief executive* of the *firm* as a whole, if he has that responsibility.
		The *apportionment and oversight function* applies to such a *firm*, unless it falls within a particular exception from the *approved persons* regime (see Question 1).
12	How does the requirement to allocate the functions in **SYSC 2.1.3 R** apply to an *incoming EEA firm* or *incoming Treaty firm*?	**SYSC 1 ANNEX 1.1.1R** and **SYSC 1 ANNEX 1.1.8 R** restrict the application of **SYSC 2.1.3 R** for such a *firm*. Accordingly:
		(1) Such a *firm* is not required to allocate the function of dealing with apportionment in **SYSC 2.1.3 R (1)**.
		(2) Such a *firm* is required to allocate the function of oversight in **SYSC 2.1.3 R (2)**. However, the systems and controls that must be overseen are those relating to matters which the *appropriate regulator*, as *Host State regulator*, is entitled to regulate (there is *guidance* on this in **SUP 13A ANNEX 2 G**). Those are primarily, but not exclusively, the systems and controls relating to the conduct of the *firm's* activities carried on from its *UK branch*.
		(3) Such a *firm* need not allocate the function of oversight to its *chief executive*; it must allocate it to one or more *directors* and *senior managers* of the *firm* or the *firm's group* under **SYSC 2.1.4 R**, row (2).
		(4) An *incoming EEA firm* which has provision only for *cross border services* is not required to allocate either function if it does not carry on *regulated activities* in the United Kingdom; for example if they fall within the overseas persons exclusions in article 72 of the *Regulated Activities Order*.
		See also Questions 1 and 15.
13	What about a *firm* that is a *partnership* or a *limited liability partnership*?	The *appropriate regulator* envisages that most if not all *partners* or members will be either *directors* or *senior managers*, but this will depend on the constitution of the *partnership* (particularly in the case of a limited *partnership*) or *limited liability partnership*. A *partnership* or *limited liability partnership* may also have a *chief executive* (see Question 5). A *limited liability partnership* is a *body corporate* and, if a member of a *group*, will fall within **SYSC 2.1.4 R**, row (1) or (2).

	Question	Answer
14	What if generally accepted principles of good corporate governance recommend that the *chief executive* should not be involved in an aspect of corporate governance?	The Note to **SYSC 2.1.4 R** provides that the *chief executive* or other executive director or *senior manager* need not be involved in such circumstances. For example, the *UK Corporate Governance Code* recommends that the board of a listed company should establish an audit committee of non-executive directors to be responsible for oversight of the audit. That aspect of the oversight function may therefore be allocated to the members of such a committee without involving the *chief executive*. Such individuals may require approval under section 59 in relation to that function (see Question 1).
15	What about *electronic commerce activities* carried on from an *establishment* in another *EEA State* with or for a *person* in the *United Kingdom*?	*SYSC* does not apply to an *incoming ECA provider* acting as such.

2.2   RECORDING THE APPORTIONMENT

2.2.1 R   FCA PRA

(1)   A *firm* must make a record of the arrangements it has made to satisfy **SYSC 2.1.1 R** (apportionment) and **SYSC 2.1.3 R** (allocation) and take reasonable care to keep this up to date.

(2)   This record must be retained for six years from the date on which it was superseded by a more up-to-date record.

2.2.2 G   FCA PRA

(1)   A *firm* will be able to comply with **SYSC 2.2.1 R** by means of records which it keeps for its own purposes provided these records satisfy the requirements of **SYSC 2.2.1 R** and provided the *firm* takes reasonable care to keep them up to date. Appropriate records might, for this purpose, include organisational charts and diagrams, project management *documents*, job descriptions, committee constitutions and terms of reference provided they show a clear description of the *firm's* major functions.

(2)   *Firms* should record any material change to the arrangements described in **SYSC 2.2.1 R** as soon as reasonably practicable after that change has been made.

2.2.3 G   FCA PRA

Where responsibilities have been allocated to more than one individual, the *firm's* record should show clearly how those responsibilities are shared or divided between the individuals concerned.

CHAPTER 3
SYSTEMS AND CONTROLS

3.1   SYSTEMS AND CONTROLS

[3.9]
3.1.1R   FCA PRA

A *firm* must take reasonable care to establish and maintain such systems and controls as are appropriate to its business.

3.1.1A R

[deleted]

3.1.2 G   FCA PRA

(1)   The nature and extent of the systems and controls which a *firm* will need to maintain under **SYSC 3.1.1 R** will depend upon a variety of factors including:

    (a)   the nature, scale and complexity of its business;

    (b)   the diversity of its operations, including geographical diversity;

    (c)   the volume and size of its transactions; and

    (d)   the degree of risk associated with each area of its operation.

(2)   To enable it to comply with its obligation to maintain appropriate systems and controls, a *firm* should carry out a regular review of them.

(3)   The areas typically covered by the systems and controls referred to in **SYSC 3.1.1 R** are those identified in **SYSC 3.2**. Detailed requirements regarding systems and controls relevant to particular business areas or particular types of *firm* are covered elsewhere in the *Handbook*.

3.1.2A G   FCA PRA

Firms should also consider the additional *guidance* on risk-centric governance arrangements for effective risk management contained in **SYSC 21**.

3.1.3 G   FCA PRA

Where the *UK Corporate Governance Code* is relevant to a *firm*, the *appropriate regulator*, in considering whether the *firm's* obligations under **SYSC 3.1.1 R** have been met, will give it due credit for following corresponding provisions in the code and related guidance.

3.1.4 G   FCA

A *firm* has specific responsibilities regarding its *appointed representatives* or, where applicable, its *tied agents* (see **SUP 12**).

3.1.5 G   FCA PRA

SYSC 2.1.3 R (2) prescribes how a *firm* must allocate the function of overseeing the establishment and maintenance of systems and controls described in **SYSC 3.1.1 R**.

3.1.6 R   FCA PRA

A *firm* which is not a *common platform firm* must employ personnel with the skills, knowledge and expertise necessary for the discharge of the responsibilities allocated to them.

3.1.7 R   FCA PRA

When complying with the *competent employees rules*, a *firm* must take into account the nature, scale and complexity of its business and the nature and range of financial services and activities undertaken in the course of that business.

3.1.8 G   FCA

The Training and Competence sourcebook (*TC*) contains additional *rules* and *guidance* relating to specified retail activities undertaken by a *firm*.

3.1.9 G   FCA

Firms which are carrying on activities that are not subject to *TC* may nevertheless wish to take *TC* into account in complying with the competence requirements in *SYSC*.

3.1.10 G   FCA PRA

If a *firm* requires *employees* who are not subject to a qualification requirement in *TC* to pass a relevant examination from the list of appropriate qualifications maintained by the *FCA*, the *appropriate regulator* will take that into account when assessing whether the *firm* has ensured that the *employee* satisfies the knowledge component of the *competent employees rule*.

3.2   AREAS COVERED BY SYSTEMS AND CONTROLS

Introduction

3.2.1 G   FCA PRA

This section covers some of the main issues which a *firm* is expected to consider in establishing and maintaining the systems and controls appropriate to its business, as required by **SYSC 3.1.1 R**.

Organisation

3.2.2 G   FCA PRA

A *firm's* reporting lines should be clear and appropriate having regard to the nature, scale and complexity of its business. These reporting lines, together with clear management responsibilities, should be communicated as appropriate within the *firm*.

3.2.3 G   FCA PRA

(1)   A *firm's governing body* is likely to delegate many functions and tasks for the purpose of carrying out its business. When functions or tasks are delegated, either to *employees* or to *appointed representatives* or, where applicable, its *tied agents*, appropriate safeguards should be put in place.

(2)   When there is delegation, a *firm* should assess whether the recipient is suitable to carry out the delegated function or task, taking into account the degree of responsibility involved.

(3)   The extent and limits of any delegation should be made clear to those concerned.

(4)   There should be arrangements to supervise delegation, and to monitor the discharge of delegates functions or tasks.

(5)   If cause for concern arises through supervision and monitoring or otherwise, there should be appropriate follow-up action at an appropriate level of seniority within the *firm*.

3.2.4 G   FCA PRA

(1)   The *guidance* relevant to delegation within the *firm* is also relevant to external delegation ('*outsourcing*'). A *firm* cannot contract out its regulatory obligations. So, for example, under *Principle* 3 a *firm* should take reasonable care to supervise the discharge of outsourced functions by its contractor.

(2)   A *firm* should take steps to obtain sufficient information from its contractor to enable it to assess the impact of outsourcing on its systems and controls.

3.2.5 G   FCA PRA

Where it is made possible and appropriate by the nature, scale and complexity of its business, a *firm* should segregate the duties of individuals and departments in such a way as to reduce opportunities for *financial crime* or contravention of requirements and standards under the *regulatory system*. For example, the duties of front-office and back-office staff should be segregated so as to prevent a single individual initiating, processing and controlling transactions.

3.2.5A R

[deleted]

3.2.5B G

[deleted]

Systems and controls in relation to compliance, financial crime and money laundering

3.2.6 R   FCA

A *firm* must take reasonable care to establish and maintain effective systems and controls for compliance with applicable requirements and standards under the *regulatory system* and for countering the risk that the *firm* might be used to further *financial crime*.

3.2.6A R   FCA

A *firm* must ensure that these systems and controls:

(1)   enable it to identify, assess, monitor and manage *money laundering* risk; and

(2)   are comprehensive and proportionate to the nature, scale and complexity of its activities.

3.2.6B G   FCA

"*Money laundering* risk" is the risk that a *firm* may be used to further *money laundering*. Failure by a *firm* to manage this risk effectively will increase the risk to society of crime and terrorism.

3.2.6C R   FCA

A *firm* must carry out regular assessments of the adequacy of these systems and controls to ensure that it continues to comply with **SYSC 3.2.6A R**.

3.2.6D G   FCA

A *firm* may also have separate obligations to comply with relevant legal requirements, including the Terrorism Act 2000, the Proceeds of Crime Act 2002 and the *Money Laundering Regulations*. **SYSC 3.2.6 R** to **SYSC 3.2.6J G** are not relevant for the purposes of regulation 42(3) or 45(2) of the *Money Laundering Regulations*, section 330(8) of the Proceeds of Crime Act 2002 or section 21A(6) of the Terrorism Act 2000.

3.2.6E G   FCA

The *FCA*, when considering whether a breach of its *rules* on systems and controls against *money laundering* has occurred, will have regard to whether a *firm* has followed relevant provisions in the guidance for the *UK* financial sector issued by the Joint Money Laundering Steering Group.

3.2.6F G   FCA

In identifying its *money laundering* risk and in establishing the nature of these systems and controls, a *firm* should consider a range of factors, including:

(1)   its customer, product and activity profiles;

(2)   its distribution channels;

(3)   the complexity and volume of its transactions;

(4)   its processes and systems; and

(5)   its operating environment.

3.2.6G G   FCA

A *firm* should ensure that the systems and controls include:

(1)   appropriate training for its employees in relation to *money laundering*;

(2)   appropriate provision of information to its *governing body* and senior management, including a report at least annually by that *firm's money laundering reporting officer* (*MLRO*) on the operation and effectiveness of those systems and controls;

Part 3   FCA Handbook Materials

(3)   appropriate documentation of its risk management policies and risk profile in relation to *money laundering*, including documentation of its application of those policies (see **SYSC 3.2.20 R** to **SYSC 3.2.22 G**);

(4)   appropriate measures to ensure that *money laundering* risk is taken into account in its day-to-day operation, including in relation to:
     (a)   the development of new products;
     (b)   the taking-on of new customers; and
     (c)   changes in its business profile; and

(5)   appropriate measures to ensure that procedures for identification of new customers do not unreasonably deny access to its services to potential customers who cannot reasonably be expected to produce detailed evidence of identity.

3.2.6H R   FCA

A *firm* must allocate to a *director* or *senior manager* (who may also be the *money laundering reporting officer*) overall responsibility within the *firm* for the establishment and maintenance of effective anti- *money laundering* systems and controls.

The money laundering reporting officer

3.2.6I R   FCA

A *firm* must:
(1)   appoint an individual as *MLRO*, with responsibility for oversight of its compliance with the *FCA's rules* on systems and controls against *money laundering*; and
(2)   ensure that its *MLRO* has a level of authority and independence within the *firm* and access to resources and information sufficient to enable him to carry out that responsibility.

3.2.6J G   FCA

The job of the *MLRO* within a *firm* is to act as the focal point for all activity within the *firm* relating to anti- *money laundering*. The *FCA* expects that a *firm's MLRO* will be based in the *United Kingdom*.

Financial crime guidance

3.2.6K G   FCA

The *FCA* provides *guidance* on steps that a *firm* can take to reduce the risk that it might be used to further *financial crime* in *FC* (Financial crime: a guide for firms).

The compliance function

3.2.7 G   FCA PRA

(1)   Depending on the nature, scale and complexity of its business, it may be appropriate for a *firm* to have a separate compliance function. The organisation and responsibilities of a compliance function should be documented. A compliance function should be staffed by an appropriate number of competent staff who are sufficiently independent to perform their duties objectively. It should be adequately resourced and should have unrestricted access to the *firm's* relevant records as well as ultimate recourse to its *governing body*.
(2)   [deleted]
(3)   [deleted]

3.2.8 R   FCA

(1)   A *firm* which carries on *designated investment business* with or for *retail clients* or *professional clients* must allocate to a *director* or *senior manager* the function of:
     (a)   having responsibility for oversight of the *firm's* compliance; and
     (b)   reporting to the *governing body* in respect of that responsibility.
(2)   In (1) "compliance" means compliance with the *rules* in:
     (a)   *COBS* (Conduct of Business);
     (b)   *COLL* (Collective Investment Schemes sourcebook); and
     (c)   *CASS* (Client Assets)

3.2.9 G   FCA

(1)   **SUP 10A.7.8 R** uses **SYSC 3.2.8 R** to describe the *controlled function*, known as the *compliance oversight function*, of acting in the capacity of a *director* or *senior manager* to whom this function is allocated.
(2)   The *rules* referred to in **SYSC 3.2.8 R (2)** are the minimum area of focus for the *firm's* *compliance oversight function*. A *firm* is free to give additional responsibilities to a person performing this function if it wishes.

Risk assessment

3.2.10 G   FCA PRA

(1)   Depending on the nature, scale and complexity of its business, it may be appropriate for a *firm* to have a separate risk assessment function responsible for assessing the risks that the *firm* faces and advising the *governing body* and *senior managers* on them.

(2)   The organisation and responsibilities of a risk assessment function should be documented. The function should be adequately resourced and staffed by an appropriate number of competent staff who are sufficiently independent to perform their duties objectively.

(3)   The term 'risk assessment function' refers to the generally understood concept of risk assessment within a *firm*, that is, the function of setting and controlling risk exposure. The risk assessment function is not a *controlled function* itself, but is part of the *systems and controls function* (CF28).

Management information

3.2.11 G
(1)   [deleted]
(2)   [deleted]

3.2.11A G   FCA
(1)   A *firm's* arrangements should be such as to furnish its *governing body* with the information it needs to play its part in identifying, measuring, managing and controlling risks of regulatory concern. Three factors will be the relevance, reliability and timeliness of that information.
(2)   Risks of regulatory concern are those risks which relate to the fair treatment of the *firm's customers*, to the protection of *consumers*, to effective competition and to the integrity of the *UK financial system*. Risks which are relevant to the integrity of the *UK financial system* include risks which relate to its soundness, stability and resilience and to the use of the system in connection with *financial crime*.

3.2.11B G   PRA
(1)   A *firm's* arrangements should be such as to furnish its *governing body* with the information it needs to play its part in identifying, measuring, managing and controlling risks of regulatory concern. Three factors will be the relevance, reliability and timeliness of that information.
(2)   Risks of regulatory concern are those risks which relate to the safety and soundness of *PRA-authorised persons*.

3.2.12 G   FCA PRA

It is the responsibility of the *firm* to decide what information is required, when, and for whom, so that it can organise and control its activities and can comply with its regulatory obligations. The detail and extent of information required will depend on the nature, scale and complexity of the business.

Employees and agents

3.2.13 G   FCA PRA

A *firm's* systems and controls should enable it to satisfy itself of the suitability of anyone who acts for it.

3.2.14 G   FCA PRA
(1)   SYSC 3.2.13 G includes assessing an individual's honesty, and competence. This assessment should normally be made at the point of recruitment. An individual's honesty need not normally be revisited unless something happens to make a fresh look appropriate.
(2)   Any assessment of an individual's suitability should take into account the level of responsibility that the individual will assume within the *firm*. The nature of this assessment will generally differ depending upon whether it takes place at the start of the individual's recruitment, at the end of the probationary period (if there is one) or subsequently.
(3)   [deleted]
(4)   The requirements on *firms* with respect to *approved persons* are in Part V of the *Act* (Performance of regulated activities) and **SUP 10**.

Audit committee

3.2.15 G   FCA PRA

Depending on the nature, scale and complexity of its business, it may be appropriate for a *firm* to form an audit committee. An audit committee could typically examine management's process for ensuring the appropriateness and effectiveness of systems and controls, examine the arrangements made by management to ensure compliance with requirements and standards under the *regulatory system*, oversee the functioning of the internal audit function (if applicable – see **SYSC 3.2.16 G**) and provide an interface between management and the external auditors. It should have an appropriate number of *non-executive directors* and it should have formal terms of reference.

Internal audit

3.2.16 G   FCA PRA

(1)   Depending on the nature, scale and complexity of its business, it may be appropriate for a *firm* to delegate much of the task of monitoring the appropriateness and effectiveness of its systems and controls to an internal audit function. An internal audit function should have clear responsibilities and reporting lines to an audit committee or appropriate *senior manager*, be adequately resourced and staffed by competent individuals, be independent of the day-to-day activities of the *firm* and have appropriate access to a *firm's* records.

(2)   The term 'internal audit function' refers to the generally understood concept of internal audit within a *firm*, that is, the function of assessing adherence to and the effectiveness of internal systems and controls, procedures and policies. The internal audit function is not a *controlled function* itself, but is part of the *systems and controls function* (CF28).

Business strategy

3.2.17 G   FCA PRA

A *firm* should plan its business appropriately so that it is able to identify, measure, manage and control risks of regulatory concern (see **SYSC 3.2.11 G (2)**). In some *firms*, depending on the nature, scale and complexity of their business, it may be appropriate to have business plans or strategy plans documented and updated on a regular basis to take account of changes in the business environment.

Remuneration policies

3.2.18 G   FCA PRA

It is possible that *firms'* remuneration policies will from time to time lead to tensions between the ability of the *firm* to meet the requirements and standards under the *regulatory system* and the personal advantage of those who act for it. Where tensions exist, these should be appropriately managed.

Business continuity

3.2.19 G   FCA PRA

A *firm* should have in place appropriate arrangements, having regard to the nature, scale and complexity of its business, to ensure that it can continue to function and meet its regulatory obligations in the event of an unforeseen interruption. These arrangements should be regularly updated and tested to ensure their effectiveness.

Records

3.2.20 R   FCA PRA

(1)   A *firm* must take reasonable care to make and retain adequate records of matters and dealings (including accounting records) which are the subject of requirements and standards under the *regulatory system*.

(2)   Subject to (3) and to any other record-keeping *rule* in the *Handbook*, the records required by (1) or by such other *rule* must be capable of being reproduced in the English language on paper.

(3)   If a *firm's* records relate to business carried on from an establishment in a country or territory outside the *United Kingdom*, an official language of that country or territory may be used instead of the English language as required by (2).

3.2.21 G   FCA PRA

A *firm* should have appropriate systems and controls in place to fulfil the *firm's* regulatory and statutory obligations with respect to adequacy, access, periods of retention and security of records. The general principle is that records should be retained for as long as is relevant for the purposes for which they are made.

3.2.22 G   FCA PRA

Detailed record-keeping requirements for different types of *firm* are to be found elsewhere in the *Handbook*. Schedule 1 to the Handbook is a consolidated schedule of these requirements.

3.2.23–3.2.36 R

[deleted]

CHAPTER 4
GENERAL ORGANISATIONAL REQUIREMENTS

4.1   GENERAL REQUIREMENTS

[3.10]

[**Note**: ESMA has also issued guidelines under article 16(3) of the ESMA Regulation covering certain aspects of the MiFID compliance function requirements. See www.esma.europa.eu/content/Guidelines-certain-aspects-MiFID-compliance-function-requirements.]

4.1.1 R   FCA PRA

(1)   A *firm* must have robust governance arrangements, which include a clear organisational structure with well defined, transparent and consistent lines of responsibility, effective processes to identify, manage, monitor and report the risks it is or might be exposed to, and internal control mechanisms, including sound administrative and accounting procedures and effective control and safeguard arrangements for information processing systems.

(2)   [deleted]

[**Note**: article 74 (1) of *CRD*, article 13(5) second paragraph of *MiFID*, article 12(1)(a) of the *UCITS Directive*, and article 18(1) of *AIFMD*]

4.1.1A R   FCA

A *full-scope UK AIFM* must comply with the *AIFM Remuneration Code*.

[**Note**: article 13(1) of *AIFMD*]

4.1.1B R   FCA

A *full-scope UK AIFM* must, in particular:

(1)   have rules for personal transactions by its *employees* or for the holding or management of investments it invests on its own account;

(2)   ensure that each transaction involving the *AIFs* may be reconstructed according to its origin, the parties to it, its nature, and the time and place at which it was effected; and

(3)   ensure that the assets of the *AIFs* managed by the *AIFM* are invested in accordance with the *instrument constituting the fund* and the legal provisions in force.

[**Note**: article 18(1) second paragraph of *AIFMD*]

4.1.1C R   FCA

A *BIPRU firm* and a *third country BIPRU firm* must comply with the *BIPRU Remuneration Code*.

4.1.2 R   FCA PRA

For a *common platform firm*, the arrangements, processes and mechanisms referred to in **SYSC 4.1.1 R** must be comprehensive and proportionate to the nature, scale and complexity of the risks inherent in the business model and of the *common platform firm's* activities and must take into account the specific technical criteria described in **SYSC 4.1.7 R**, **SYSC 5.1.7 R**, **SYSC 7** and (for a *firm* to which **SYSC 19A** applies) **SYSC 19A**, or (for a *full-scope UK AIFM*) **SYSC 19B**.

[**Note**: article 74 (2) of *CRD*]

4.1.2A G   FCA PRA

Other *firms* should take account of the comprehensiveness and proportionality *rule* (**SYSC 4.1.2 R**) as if it were *guidance* (and as if "should" appeared in that rule instead of "must") as explained in **SYSC 1 ANNEX 1.3.3 G**.

4.1.2AA R   FCA

Where **SYSC 4.1.2 R** applies to a *BIPRU firm*, it must take into account the specific technical criteria described in **SYSC 19C**.

4.1.2B R   FCA

For a *management company* or a *full-scope UK AIFM*, the arrangements, processes and mechanisms referred to in **SYSC 4.1.1 R** and **SYSC 4.1.1A R** must also take account of the *UCITS schemes* and *EEA UCITS schemes* managed by the *management company* or the *AIFs* managed by the *full-scope UK AIFM*.

[**Note**: article 12(1) second paragraph of the *UCITS Directive* and article 18(1) second paragraph of *AIFMD*]

Resources for management companies and AIFMs

4.1.2C R   FCA

A *management company*, a *full-scope UK AIFM* and an *incoming EEA AIFM branch* must have, and employ effectively, the resources and procedures that are necessary for the proper performance of its business activities.

[**Note**: articles 12(1)(a) and 14(1)(c) of the *UCITS Directive* and article 12(1)(c) of *AIFMD*]

4.1.2D R   FCA

A *full-scope UK AIFM* must use, at all times, adequate and appropriate human and technical resources that are necessary for the proper management of *AIFs*.

[**Note**: article 18(1) first paragraph of *AIFMD*]

Subordinate measures relating to provisions implementing article 12(1) of AIFMD

4.1.2E G   FCA

Part 3   FCA Handbook Materials

Articles 16 to 29 of the *AIFMD level 2 regulation* provide detailed rules supplementing the provisions of article 12(1) of *AIFMD*, articles 57 to 66 of the *AIFMD level 2 regulation* provide detailed rules supplementing articles 12 and 18 of *AIFMD*.

Mechanisms and procedures for a firm

4.1.3 R

[deleted]

4.1.4 R   FCA PRA

A *firm* (with the exception of a *sole trader* who does not employ any *person* who is required to be approved under section 59 of the *Act* (Approval for particular arrangements)) must, taking into account the nature, scale and complexity of the business of the *firm*, and the nature and range of the financial services and activities undertaken in the course of that business:

(1)   (if it is a *common platform firm* or a *management company*) establish, implement and maintain decision-making procedures and an organisational structure which clearly and in a documented manner specifies reporting lines and allocates functions and responsibilities;

(2)   establish, implement and maintain adequate internal control mechanisms designed to secure compliance with decisions and procedures at all levels of the *firm*;

(3)   (if it is a *common platform firm*) establish, implement and maintain effective internal reporting and communication of information at all relevant levels of the *firm*; and

(4)   (if it is a *management company*) establish, implement and maintain effective internal reporting and communication of information at all relevant levels of the *management company* as well as effective information flows with any third party involved.

[**Note**: articles 5(1) final paragraph, 5(1)(a), 5(1)(c) and 5(1)(e) of the *MiFID implementing Directive* and articles 4(1) final paragraph, 4(1)(a), 4(1)(c) and 4(1)(d) of the *UCITS implementing Directive*]

4.1.4A G   FCA PRA

A *firm* that is not a *common platform firm* or a *management company* should take into account the decision-making procedures and effective internal reporting *rules* (**SYSC 4.1.4R (1), (3)** and **(4)**) as if they were *guidance* (and as if "should" appeared in those rules instead of "must") as explained in **SYSC 1 ANNEX 1.3.3 G**.

4.1.5 R   FCA PRA

A *MiFID investment firm* and a *management company* must establish, implement and maintain systems and procedures that are adequate to safeguard the security, integrity and confidentiality of information, taking into account the nature of the information in question.
[**Note**: article 5(2) of the *MiFID implementing Directive* and article 4(2) of the *UCITS implementing Directive*]

Business continuity

4.1.6 R   FCA PRA

A *common platform firm* must take reasonable steps to ensure continuity and regularity in the performance of its *regulated activities*. To this end the *common platform firm* must employ appropriate and proportionate systems, resources and procedures.
[**Note**: article 13(4) of *MiFID*]

4.1.7 R   FCA PRA

A *common platform firm* and a *management company* must establish, implement and maintain an adequate business continuity policy aimed at ensuring, in the case of an interruption to its systems and procedures, that any losses are limited, the preservation of essential data and functions, and the maintenance of its *regulated activities*, or, in the case of a *management company*, its *collective portfolio management* activities, or, where that is not possible, the timely recovery of such data and functions and the timely resumption of those activities.
[**Note**: article 5(3) of the *MiFID implementing Directive*, annex V paragraph 13 of the *Banking Consolidation Directive*, article 4(3) of the *UCITS implementing Directive* and article 85(2) of the *CRD*]

4.1.7A G   FCA PRA

Other *firms* should take account of the business continuity *rules* (**SYSC 4.1.6 R** and **4.1.7 R**) as if they were *guidance* (and as if "should" appeared in those rules instead of "must") as explained in **SYSC 1 ANNEX 1.3.3 G**.

4.1.8 G   FCA PRA

The matters dealt with in a business continuity policy should include:
(1)   resource requirements such as people, systems and other assets, and arrangements for obtaining these resources;
(2)   the recovery priorities for the *firm's* operations;

(3)   communication arrangements for internal and external concerned parties (including the *appropriate regulator*, *clients* and the press);

(4)   escalation and invocation plans that outline the processes for implementing the business continuity plans, together with relevant contact information;

(5)   processes to validate the integrity of information affected by the disruption; and

(6)   regular testing of the business continuity policy in an appropriate and proportionate manner in accordance with **SYSC 4.1.10 R**.

Operators of electronic systems in relation to lending: arrangements to administer loans in the event of platform failure

4.1.8A R   FCA

An *operator of an electronic system in relation to lending* must take reasonable steps to ensure that arrangements are in place to ensure that *P2P agreements* facilitated by it will continue to be managed and administered, in accordance with the contract terms, if at any time it ceases to carry on the activity of *operating an electronic system in relation to lending*.

4.1.8B R   FCA

Any arrangements made under **SYSC 4.1.8A R** must be notified to lenders under *P2P agreements*:

(1)   when such arrangements are made; or

(2)   if later, when the lender first becomes a lender under a *P2P agreement* with that operator; or

(3)   if the arrangements are changed, when that change is made; and

(4)   if the arrangement involves another *firm* taking over the management and administration of *P2P agreements* if the operator ceases to *operate the electronic system in relation to lending*, the notification to lenders must inform lenders of the identity of the *firm* with which the arrangements have been made and how that *firm* will hold the lenders' *money*.

4.1.8C G   FCA

Arrangements to ensure *P2P agreements* facilitated by the *firm* continue to be managed and administered may include:

(1)   entering into an arrangement with another *firm* to take over the management and administration of *P2P agreements* if the operator ceases to *operate the electronic system in relation to lending*; or

(2)   holding sufficient collateral in a segregated account to cover the cost of management and administration while the loan book is wound down; or

(3)   entering into an arrangement for another *firm* to act as guarantor for the *P2P agreements* which includes a legally enforceable arrangement to meet the costs of the guarantee in full; or

(4)   managing the loan book in a way that ensures that income from *P2P agreements* facilitated by the *firm* is sufficient to cover the costs of managing and administering those agreements during the winding down process, taking into account the reduction of the loan pool and fee income from it.

4.1.8D G   FCA

When designing its arrangements, a *firm* should take into account insolvency law to ensure that the insolvency of the *firm* does not prejudice the operation of arrangements that the *firm* has put in place.

Operators of electronic systems in relation to lending: title transfer

4.1.8E R   FCA

An *operator of an electronic system in relation to lending* must not accept, take, or receive the transfer of full ownership of *money* relating to *P2P agreements*.

Accounting policies

4.1.9 R   FCA PRA

A *common platform firm* and a *management company* must establish, implement and maintain accounting policies and procedures that enable it, at the request of the *appropriate regulator*, to deliver in a timely manner to the *appropriate regulator* financial reports which reflect a true and fair view of its financial position and which comply with all applicable accounting standards and rules. [**Note**: article 5(4) of the *MiFID implementing Directive* and article 4(4) of the *UCITS implementing Directive*]

Regular monitoring

4.1.10 R   FCA PRA

A *common platform firm* and a *management company* must monitor and, on a regular basis, evaluate the adequacy and effectiveness of its systems, internal control mechanisms and arrangements established in accordance with **SYSC 4.1.4 R** to **SYSC 4.1.9 R** and take appropriate measures to address any deficiencies.

[**Note**: article 5(5) of the *MiFID implementing Directive* and article 4(5) of the *UCITS implementing Directive*]

4.1.10A G   FCA PRA

Other *firms* should take account of the regular monitoring *rule* (**SYSC 4.1.10 R**) as if it were *guidance* (and as if "should" appeared in that rule instead of "must") as explained in **SYSC 1 ANNEX 1.3.3 G**, but ignoring the cross-reference to **SYSC 4.1.5 R** and **4.1.9 R**.

Audit committee

4.1.11 G   FCA PRA

Depending on the nature, scale and complexity of its business, it may be appropriate for a *firm* to form an audit committee. An audit committee could typically examine management's process for ensuring the appropriateness and effectiveness of systems and controls, examine the arrangements made by management to ensure compliance with requirements and standards under the *regulatory system*, oversee the functioning of the internal audit function (if applicable) and provide an interface between management and external auditors. It should have an appropriate number of *non-executive directors* and it should have formal terms of reference.

4.1.12 G

[deleted]

Risk control: additional guidance

4.1.13 G   FCA PRA

Firms should also consider the additional *guidance* on risk-centric governance arrangements for effective risk management contained in **SYSC 21**.

Apportionment of responsibilities: the role of the non-executive director

4.1.14 G   FCA PRA

The role undertaken by a *non-executive director* will vary from one *firm* to another. Where a *non-executive director* is an *approved person*, for example where the *firm* is a *body corporate*, his responsibility and therefore liability will be limited by the role that he undertakes.

4.1.15 R   PRA

(1)   A firm must have in place appropriate procedures for its employees to report breaches internally through a specific, independent and autonomous channel.

(2)   The channel in (1) may be provided through arrangements provided for by social partners.

[**Note**: article 71 (3) of *CRD*]

4.2   PERSONS WHO EFFECTIVELY DIRECT THE BUSINESS

4.2.1 R   FCA PRA

The *senior personnel* of a *common platform firm*, a *management company* a *full-scope UK AIFM*, or of the *UK* branch of a *non-EEA bank* must be of sufficiently good repute and sufficiently experienced as to ensure the sound and prudent management of the *firm*.

[**Note**: article 9(1) of *MiFID*, article 7(1)(b) of the *UCITS Directive* article 8(1)(c) of *AIFMD*, article 11(1) second paragraph of the *Banking Consolidation Directive* and article 13(1) of the *CRD*]

4.2.1A G   FCA PRA

Other *firms* should take account of the senior personnel *rule* (**SYSC 4.2.1 R**) as if it were *guidance* (and as if "should" appeared in that rule instead of "must") as explained in **SYSC 1 ANNEX 1.3.3 G**.

Responsibility of senior personnel of an AIFM

4.2.1B R   FCA

For a *full-scope UK AIFM*, the *senior personnel* must, in complying with **SYSC 4.2.1 R**, be sufficiently experienced in relation to the investment strategies pursued by the *AIFs* it manages.

[**Note**: article 8(1)(c) of *AIFMD*]

4.2.2 R   FCA PRA

A *common platform firm*, a *management company*, a *full-scope UK AIFM* and the *UK* branch of a *non-EEA bank* must ensure that its management is undertaken by at least two persons meeting the requirements laid down in **SYSC 4.2.1 R** and, for a *full-scope UK AIFM*, **SYSC 4.2.7 R**.

[**Note**: article 9(4) first paragraph of *MiFID*, article 7(1)(b) of the *UCITS Directive*, article 8(1)(c) of *AIFMD* and article 13(1) of *CRD*]

4.2.3 G   FCA PRA

In the case of a *body corporate*, the persons referred to in SYSC 4.2.2 R should either be executive *directors* or persons granted executive powers by, and reporting immediately to, the *governing body*. In the case of a *partnership*, they should be active *partners*.

4.2.4 G   FCA PRA

At least two independent minds should be applied to the formulation and implementation of the policies of a *common platform firm*, a *management company*, a *full-scope UK AIFM* and the *UK* branch of a *non-EEA bank*. Where a *firm* nominates just two individuals to direct its business, the *appropriate regulator* will not regard them as both effectively directing the business where one of them makes some, albeit significant, decisions relating to only a few aspects of the business. Each should play a part in the decision-making process on all significant decisions. Both should demonstrate the qualities and application to influence strategy, day-to-day policy and its implementation. This does not require their day-to-day involvement in the execution and implementation of policy. It does, however, require involvement in strategy and general direction, as well as knowledge of, and influence on, the way in which strategy is being implemented through day-to-day policy.

4.2.5 G   FCA PRA

Where there are more than two individuals directing the business of a *common platform firm*, a *management company*, a *full-scope UK AIFM* or the *UK* branch of a *non-EEA bank*, the *appropriate regulator* does not regard it as necessary for all of these individuals to be involved in all decisions relating to the determination of strategy and general direction. However, at least two individuals should be involved in all such decisions. Both individuals' judgement should be engaged so that major errors leading to difficulties for the *firm* are less likely to occur. Similarly, each individual should have sufficient experience and knowledge of the business and the necessary personal qualities and skills to detect and resist any imprudence, dishonesty or other irregularities by the other individual. Where a single individual, whether a chief executive, managing *director* or otherwise, is particularly dominant in such a *firm* this will raise doubts about whether SYSC 4.2.2 R is met.

4.2.6 R   FCA PRA

If a *common platform firm*, (other than a *credit institution* or *AIFM investment firm*) or the *UK* branch of a *non-EEA bank*, is:
(1)   a natural person; or
(2)   a legal person managed by a single natural person;

it must have alternative arrangements in place which ensure sound and prudent management of the *firm*.
[**Note**: article 9(4) second paragraph of *MiFID*]

4.2.7 R   FCA

A *full-scope UK AIFM* must notify the *FCA* of the names of the *senior personnel* of the *firm* and of every person succeeding them in office.

[**Note**: article 8(1)(c) of *AIFMD*]

4.2.8 G   FCA

Where the *senior personnel* of a *full-scope UK AIFM* will carry out a *FCA governing function* and the *firm* has applied for the *FCA's* approval under section 59 of the *Act*, this will be considered sufficient to comply with **SYSC 4.2.7 R.**

4.3   RESPONSIBILITY OF SENIOR PERSONNEL

4.3.1 R   FCA PRA

A *firm* (with the exception of a *sole trader* who does not employ any *person* who is required to be approved under section 59 of the *Act* (Approval for particular arrangements)), when allocating functions internally, must ensure that *senior personnel* and, where appropriate, the *supervisory function*, are responsible for ensuring that the *firm* complies with its obligations under the *regulatory system*. In particular, *senior personnel* and, where appropriate, the *supervisory function* must assess and periodically review the effectiveness of the policies, arrangements and procedures put in place to comply with the *firm's* obligations under the *regulatory system* and take appropriate measures to address any deficiencies.
[**Note**: article 9(1) of the *MiFID implementing Directive* and articles 9(1) and 9(3) of the *UCITS implementing Directive*]

4.3.2 R   FCA PRA

A *common platform firm* (with the exception of a *sole trader* who does not employ any *person* who is required to be approved under section 59 of the *Act* (Approval for particular arrangements)) and a *management company*, must ensure that:
(1)   its *senior personnel* receive on a frequent basis, and at least annually, written reports on the matters covered by **SYSC 6.1.2 R** to **SYSC 6.1.5 R**, **SYSC 6.2.1 R** and **SYSC 7.1.2 R**, **SYSC 7.1.3 R** and **SYSC 7.1.5 R** to **SYSC 7.1.7 R**, indicating in particular whether the appropriate remedial measures have been taken in the event of any deficiencies; and

(2)   the *supervisory function*, if any, receives on a regular basis written reports on the same matters.
         [**Note**: article 9(2) and article 9(3) of the *MiFID implementing Directive* and articles 9(4) and 9(6) of the *UCITS implementing Directive*]

4.3.2A G   FCA PRA

Other *firms* should take account of the written reports *rule* (**SYSC 4.3.2 R**) as if it were *guidance* (and as if "should" appeared in that rule instead of "must") as explained in **SYSC 1 ANNEX 1.3.3 G**.

4.3.3 G   FCA PRA

The *supervisory function* does not include a general meeting of the shareholders of a *firm*, or equivalent bodies, but could involve, for example, a separate supervisory board within a two-tier board structure or the establishment of a non-executive committee of a single-tier board structure.

4.3.4 G

[deleted]

4.3A   CRR FIRMS

Management body

4.3A.-1 R   FCA

In **SYSC 4.3A.6 R** and **SYSC 4.3A.8 R** a '*CRR firm* that is *significant*' means a *significant IFPRU firm*.

4.3A.1 R   FCA PRA

A *CRR firm* must ensure that the *management body* defines, oversees and is accountable for the implementation of governance arrangements that ensure effective and prudent management of the *firm*, including the segregation of duties in the organisation and the prevention of conflicts of interest. The *firm* must ensure that the *management body*:
(1)   has overall responsibility for the *firm*;
(2)   approves and oversees implementation of the *firm's* strategic objectives, risk strategy and internal governance;
(3)   ensures the integrity of the *firm's* accounting and financial reporting systems, including financial and operational controls and compliance with the *regulatory system*.
(4)   oversees the process of disclosure and communications;
(5)   has responsibility for providing effective oversight of *senior management*.
(6)   monitors and periodically assesses the effectiveness of the *firm's* governance arrangements and takes appropriate steps to address any deficiencies.

[**Note**: article 88(1) of *CRD*]

4.3A.2 R   FCA PRA

A *CRR firm* must ensure that the chairman of the *firm's management body* does not exercise simultaneously the *chief executive function* within the same *firm*, unless justified by the *firm* and authorised by the *appropriate regulator*.
[**Note**: article 88(1)(e) of *CRD*]

4.3A.3 R   FCA PRA

A *CRR firm* must ensure that the members of the *management body* of the *firm*:
(1)   are of sufficiently good repute;
(2)   possess sufficient knowledge, skills and experience to perform their duties;
(3)   possess adequate collective knowledge, skills and experience to understand the *firm's* activities, including the main risks;
(4)   reflect an adequately broad range of experiences;
(5)   commit sufficient time to perform their functions in the *firm*; and
(6)   act with honesty, integrity and independence of mind to effectively assess and challenge the decisions of *senior management* where necessary and to effectively oversee and monitor management decision-making.

[**Note**: article 91(1)-(2) and (7)-(8) of the *CRD*]

4.3A.4 R   FCA PRA

A *CRR firm* must devote adequate human and financial resources to the induction and training of members of the *management body*.
[**Note**: article 91(3) of the *CRD*]

4.3A.5 R   FCA PRA

A *CRR firm* must ensure that the members of the *management body* of the *firm* do not hold more directorships than is appropriate taking into account individual circumstances and the nature, scale and complexity of the *firm's* activities.

[**Note**: article 91(3) of the *CRD*]

4.3A.6 R   FCA PRA

(1)   A *CRR firm* that is significant must ensure that the members of the *management body* of the *firm* do not hold more than one of the following combinations of directorship in any organisation at the same time:

    (a)   one executive directorship with two non-executive directorships; and

    (b)   four non-executive directorships.

(2)   Paragraph (1) does not apply to members of the *management body* that represent the *United Kingdom*.

[**Note**: article 91(3) of the *CRD*]

4.3A.6A G   PRA

In **SYSC 4.3A.6 R** a '*CRR firm* that is significant' means a deposit-taker or designated investment firm whose size, interconnectedness, complexity and business type gives it the capacity to cause some disruption to the UK financial system (and through that to economic activity more widely) by failing or by carrying on its business in an unsafe manner.

4.3A.6B G   PRA

The limits on directorships set out in **SYSC 4.3A.6 R** also apply to members of the management body of the *UK consolidation group* or *non-EEA sub group* in accordance with **SYSC 12.1.13 R**. Individuals in any of the entities belonging to the *UK consolidation group* or *non-EEA sub group* are capable of forming part of this management body. For example, members of the management body of a non- *CRR firm* that is a *parent financial holding company in a Member State* and is a member of a *UK consolidation group* could be caught by the limits in **SYSC 4.3A.6 R** (**SYSC 12.1.14 R**). In particular, a person who requires approval under **SUP 10B.6.2 R** or **SUP 10B.6.4 R** because of the influence they exercise over the *CRR firm* is a member of the management body of the *UK consolidation group* or *non-EEA sub group* and therefore subject to the limit on directorships in **SYSC 4.3A.6 R**.

[**Note:** article 91(3) and article 109(2) of the *CRD*]

4.3A.7 R   FCA PRA

For the purposes of **SYSC 4.3A.5 R** and **SYSC 4.3A.6 R**:

(1)   directorships in organisations which do not pursue predominantly commercial objectives shall not count; and

(2)   the following shall count as a single directorship:

    (a)   executive or non-executive directorships held within the same *group*; or

    (b)   executive or non-executive directorships held within:

        (i)   *firms* that are members of the same institutional protection scheme provided that the conditions set out in Article 113(7) of the CRR are fulfilled; or

        (ii)   *undertakings* (including non-financial entities) in which the *firm* holds a *qualifying holding*.

[**Note**: article 91(4) and (5) of the *CRD*]

Nomination Committee

4.3A.8 R   FCA PRA

A *CRR firm* that is significant must:

(1)   establish a nomination committee composed of members of the *management body* who do not perform any executive function in the *firm*;

(2)   ensure that the nomination committee is able to use any forms of resources the nomination committee deems appropriate, including external advice; and

(3)   ensure that the nomination committee receives appropriate funding.

[**Note**: article 88(2) of the *CRD*]

4.3A.8A G   PRA

In **SYSC 4.3A.8 R** a '*CRR firm* that is significant' means a deposit-taker or designated investment firm whose size, interconnectedness, complexity and business type gives it the capacity to cause some disruption to the UK financial system (and through that to economic activity more widely) by failing or by carrying on its business in an unsafe manner.

4.3A.9 R   FCA PRA

A *CRR firm* that has a nomination committee must ensure that the nomination committee:

(1)   engage a broad set of qualities and competences when recruiting members to the *management body* and for that purpose puts in place a policy promoting diversity on the *management body*;

(2)   identifies and recommends for approval, by the *management body* or by general meeting, candidates to fill *management body* vacancies, having evaluated the balance of knowledge, skills, diversity and experience of the *management body*;

(3)   prepares a description of the roles and capabilities for a particular appointment, and assesses the time commitment required;

(4)   decides on a target for the representation of the underrepresented gender in the *management body* and prepares a policy on how to increase the number of the underrepresented gender in the *management body* in order to meet that target;

(5)   periodically, and at least annually, assesses the structure, size, composition and performance of the *management body* and makes recommendations to the *management body* with regard to any changes;

(6)   periodically, and at least annually, assesses the knowledge, skills and experience of individual members of the *management body* and of the *management body* collectively, and reports this to the *management body*;

(7)   periodically reviews the policy of the *management body* for selection and appointment of *senior management* and makes recommendations to the *management body*; and

(8)   in performing its duties, and to the extent possible, on an ongoing basis, takes account of the need to ensure that the *management body's* decision making is not dominated by any one individual or small group of individuals in a manner that is detrimental to the interest of the *firm* as a whole;

[**Note**: article 88(2) and article 91(10) of the *CRD*]

4.3A.10 R   FCA PRA

A *CRR firm* that does not have a nomination committee must engage a broad set of qualities and competences when recruiting members to the *management body*. For that purpose a *CRR firm* that does not have a nomination committee must put in place a policy promoting diversity on the *management body*.
[**Note**: article 91(10) of the *CRD*]

Website

4.3A.11 R   FCA PRA

A *CRR firm* that maintains a website must explain on the website how it complies with the requirements of **SYSC 4.3A.1 R** to **SYSC 4.3A.3 R** and **SYSC 4.3A.4 R** to **SYSC 4.3A.11 R**.
[**Note**: article 96 of the *CRD*]

4.4   APPORTIONMENT OF RESPONSIBILITIES

Application

4.4.1 R   PRA

This section applies to:

(1)   an *authorised professional firm* in respect of its *non-mainstream regulated activities* unless the *firm* is also conducting other *regulated activities* and has appointed *approved persons* to perform the *governing functions* with equivalent responsibilities for the *firm's non-mainstream regulated activities* and other *regulated activities*;

(2)   activities carried on by a *firm* whose principal purpose is to carry on activities other than *regulated activities* and which is:
  (a)   an *oil market participant*; or
  (b)   a *service company*; or
  (c)   an *energy market participant*; or
  (d)   a wholly-owned subsidiary of:
    (i)   a local authority; or
    (ii)   a registered social landlord; or
  (e)   a *firm* with *permission* to carry on *insurance mediation activity* in relation to *non-investment insurance contracts* but no other *regulated activity*;

(3)   [deleted]

(4)   [deleted]

(5)   [deleted]
  (a)   [deleted]
  (b)   [deleted]

(6)   [deleted]

(7)   an *incoming Treaty firm*, an *incoming EEA firm* or a *UCITS qualifier* (but only **SYSC 4.4.5R** (2) applies for these *firms*); and

(8)   a *sole trader*, but only if he employs any *person* who is required to be approved under section 59 of the *Act* (Approval for particular arrangements).

4.4.1A R   FCA

This section applies to:

(1)   an *authorised professional firm* in respect of its *non-mainstream regulated activities* unless the *firm* is also conducting other *regulated activities* and has appointed *approved persons* to perform the *governing functions* with equivalent responsibilities for the *firm's non-mainstream regulated activities* and other *regulated activities*;

(2) activities carried on by a *firm* whose principal purpose is to carry on activities other than *regulated activities* and which is:
   (a) an *oil market participant*; or
   (b) a *service company*; or
   (c) an *energy market participant*; or
   (d) a wholly-owned subsidiary of:
      (i) a local authority; or
      (ii) a registered social landlord; or
   (e) a *firm* with *permission* to carry on *insurance mediation activity* in relation to *non-investment insurance contracts* but no other *regulated activity*;

(3) a *credit firm* which holds only a *limited permission* (other than a *not-for-profit debt advice body*) with respect to the relevant credit activity (as defined in paragraph 2G of Schedule 6 to the *Act*) for which it has *limited permission*;

(4) an *incoming Treaty firm*, an *incoming EEA firm* or a *UCITS qualifier* (but only **SYSC 4.4.5R (2)** applies for these *firms*); and

(5) a *sole trader*, but only if he employs any *person* who is required to be approved under section 59 of the *Act* (Approval for particular arrangements).

4.4.2 G   FCA PRA

This section does not apply to a *common platform firm*.

Maintaining a clear and appropriate apportionment

4.4.3 R   FCA PRA

A *firm* must take reasonable care to maintain a clear and appropriate apportionment of significant responsibilities among its *directors* and *senior managers* in such a way that:
(1) it is clear who has which of those responsibilities; and
(2) the business and affairs of the *firm* can be adequately monitored and controlled by the *directors*, relevant *senior managers* and *governing body* of the *firm*.

4.4.4 G

[deleted]

Allocating functions of apportionment and oversight

4.4.5 R   FCA PRA

A *firm* must appropriately allocate to one or more individuals, in accordance with the following table, the functions of:
(1) dealing with the apportionment of responsibilities under **SYSC 4.4.3 R**; and
(2) overseeing the establishment and maintenance of systems and controls under **SYSC 4.1.1 R**.

1: Firm type	2: Allocation of both functions must be to the following individual, if any (see Note):	3: Allocation to one or more individuals selected from this column is compulsory if there is no allocation to an individual in column 2, but is otherwise optional and additional:
(1) A *firm* which is a *body corporate* and is a member of a *group*, other than a *firm* in row (2)	(1) the *firm's chief executive* (and all of them jointly, if more than one); or (2) a *director* or *senior manager* responsible for the overall management of: (a) the *group*; or (b) a *group* division within which some or all of the *firm's regulated activities* fall	the *firm's* and its *group's*: (1) *directors*; and (2) *senior managers*
(2) An *incoming EEA firm* or *incoming Treaty firm* (note: only the functions in **SYSC 4.4.5R (2)** must be allocated)	(not applicable)	the *firm's* and its *group's*: (1) *directors*; and (2) *senior managers*
(3) Any other *firm*	the *firm's chief executive* (and all of them jointly, if more than one)	the *firm's* and its *group's*: (1) *directors*; and (2) *senior managers*
Note: Column 2 does not require the involvement of the *chief executive* or other executive *director* or *senior manager* in an aspect of corporate governance if that would be contrary to generally accepted principles of good corporate governance.		

4.4.6 G   **FCA PRA**

Frequently asked questions about allocation of functions in **SYSC 4.4.5 R**

Question		Answer
1	Does an individual to whom a function is allocated under **SYSC 4.4.5 R** need to be an *approved person*?	An individual to whom a function is allocated under **SYSC 4.4.5 R** will be performing the *apportionment and oversight function* (CF 8, see **SUP 10A.7.1 R**) and an application must be made under section 59 of the *Act* for approval of the individual before the function is performed. There are exceptions from this in **SUP 10A.1** (Approved persons – Application).
2	If the allocation is to more than one individual, can they perform the functions, or aspects of the functions, separately?	If the functions are allocated to joint *chief executives* under **SYSC 4.4.5 R**, column 2, they are expected to act jointly. If the functions are allocated to an individual under **SYSC 4.4.5 R**, column 2, in addition to individuals under **SYSC 4.4.5 R**, column 3, the former may normally be expected to perform a leading role in relation to the functions that reflects his position. Otherwise, yes.
3	What is meant by "appropriately allocate" in this context?	The allocation of functions should be compatible with delivering compliance with *Principle* 3, **SYSC 4.4.3 R** and **SYSC 4.1.1 R**. The *appropriate regulator* considers that allocation to one or two individuals is likely to be appropriate for most *firms*.
4	If a committee of management governs a *firm* or *group*, can the functions be allocated to every member of that committee?	Yes, as long as the allocation remains appropriate (see Question 3). If the *firm* also has an individual as *chief executive*, then the functions must be allocated to that individual as well under **SYSC 4.4.5 R**, column 2 (see Question 7).
5	Does the definition of *chief executive* include the possessor of equivalent responsibilities with another title, such as a managing *director* or managing *partner*?	Yes.
6	Is it possible for a *firm* to have more than one individual as its *chief executive*?	Although unusual, some *firms* may wish the responsibility of a *chief executive* to be held jointly by more than one individual. In that case, each of them will be a *chief executive* and the functions must be allocated to all of them under **SYSC 4.4.5 R**, column 2 (see also Questions 2 and 7).
7	If a *firm* has an individual as *chief executive*, must the functions be allocated to that individual?	Normally, yes, under **SYSC 4.4.5 R**, column 2. But if the *firm* is a *body corporate* and a member of a *group*, the functions may, instead of being allocated to the *firm's chief executive*, be allocated to a *director* or *senior manager* from the *group* responsible for the overall management of the *group* or of a relevant *group* division, so long as this is appropriate (see Question 3). Such individuals may nevertheless require approval under section 59 (see Question 1).

Question	Answer
	If the *firm* chooses to allocate the functions to a *director* or *senior manager* responsible for the overall management of a relevant *group* division, the *FSA* would expect that individual to be of a seniority equivalent to or greater than a *chief executive* of the *firm* for the allocation to be appropriate. See also Question 14.
8 If a *firm* has a *chief executive*, can the functions be allocated to other individuals in addition to the *chief executive*?	Yes. **SYSC 4.4.5 R**, column 3, permits a *firm* to allocate the functions, additionally, to the *firm's* (or where applicable the *group's*) *directors* and *senior managers* as long as this is appropriate (see Question 3).
9 What if a *firm* does not have a *chief executive*?	Normally, the functions must be allocated to one or more individuals selected from the *firm's* (or where applicable the *group's*) *directors* and *senior managers* under **SYSC 4.4.5 R**, column 3. But if the *firm*: (1) is a *body corporate* and a member of a *group*; and (2) the *group* has a *director* or *senior manager* responsible for the overall management of the *group* or of a relevant *group* division; then the functions must be allocated to that individual (together, optionally, with individuals from column 3 if appropriate) under **SYSC 4.4.5 R**, column 2.
10 What do you mean by *"group* division within which some or all of the *firm's* *regulated activities* fall"*?	A *"division"* in this context should be interpreted by reference to geographical operations, product lines or any other method by which the *group's* business is divided. If the *firm's* *regulated activities* fall within more than one division and the *firm* does not wish to allocate the functions to its *chief executive*, the allocation must, under **SYSC 4.4.5 R**, be to: (1) a *director* or *senior manager* responsible for the overall management of the *group*; or (2) a *director* or *senior manager* responsible for the overall management of one of those divisions; together, optionally, with individuals from column 3 if appropriate. (See also Questions 7 and 9.)
11 How does the requirement to allocate the functions in **SYSC 4.4.5 R** apply to an *overseas firm* which is not an *incoming EEA firm, incoming Treaty firm* or *UCITS qualifier*?	The *firm* must appropriately allocate those functions to one or more individuals, in accordance with **SYSC 4.4.5 R**, but: (1) The responsibilities that must be apportioned and the systems and controls that must be overseen are those relating to activities carried on from a *UK* establishment with certain exceptions (see **SYSC 1 ANNEX 1.1.8R**). Note that **SYSC 1 ANNEX 1.1.10R** does not extend the territorial scope of **SYSC 4.4** for an *overseas firm*.

Question	Answer
	(2) The *chief executive* of an *overseas firm* is the *person* responsible for the conduct of the *firm's* business within the *United Kingdom* (see the definition of "*chief executive*"). This might, for example, be the manager of the *firm's* UK establishment, or it might be the *chief executive* of the *firm* as a whole, if he has that responsibility. The *apportionment and oversight function* applies to such a *firm*, unless it falls within a particular exception from the *approved persons* regime (see Question 1).
12 How does the requirement to allocate the functions in **SYSC 4.4.5 R** apply to an *incoming EEA firm* or *incoming Treaty firm*?	**SYSC 1 ANNEX 1.1.1R(2)** and **SYSC 1 ANNEX 1.1.8R** restrict the application of **SYSC 4.4.5 R** for such a *firm*. Accordingly: (1) Such a *firm* is not required to allocate the function of dealing with apportionment in **SYSC 4.4.5R (1)**. (2) Such a *firm* is required to allocate the function of oversight in **SYSC 4.4.5R (2)**. However, the systems and controls that must be overseen are those relating to matters which the *appropriate regulator*, as *Host State regulator*, is entitled to regulate (there is *guidance* on this in **SUP 13A ANNEX 2**). Those are primarily, but not exclusively, the systems and controls relating to the conduct of the *firm's* activities carried on from its *UK branch*. (3) Such a *firm* need not allocate the function of oversight to its *chief executive*; it must allocate it to one or more *directors* and *senior managers* of the *firm* or the *firm's group* under **SYSC 4.4.5 R**, row (2). (4) An *incoming EEA firm* which has provision only for *cross border services* is not required to allocate either function if it does not carry on *regulated activities* in the *United Kingdom*; for example if they fall within the overseas persons exclusions in article 72 of the *Regulated Activities Order*. See also Questions 1 and 15.
13 What about a *firm* that is a *partnership* or a *limited liability partnership*?	The *appropriate regulator* envisages that most if not all *partners* or members will be either *directors* or *senior managers*, but this will depend on the constitution of the *partnership* (particularly in the case of a limited *partnership*) or *limited liability partnership*. A *partnership* or *limited liability partnership* may also have a *chief executive* (see Question 5). A *limited liability partnership* is a *body corporate* and, if a member of a *group*, will fall within **SYSC 4.4.5 R**, row (1) or (2).

Question	Answer
14 What if generally accepted principles of good corporate governance recommend that the *chief executive* should not be involved in an aspect of corporate governance?	The Note to **SYSC 4.4.5 R** provides that the *chief executive* or other executive director or *senior manager* need not be involved in such circumstances. For example, the *UK Corporate Governance Code* recommends that the board of a listed company should establish an audit committee of non-executive directors to be responsible for oversight of the audit. That aspect of the oversight function may therefore be allocated to the members of such a committee without involving the *chief executive*. Such individuals may require approval under section 59 in relation to that function (see Question 1).
15 What about *incoming electronic commerce activities* carried on from an *establishment* in another *EEA State* with or for a *person* in the *United Kingdom*?	*SYSC* does not apply to an *incoming ECA provider* acting as such.

CHAPTER 5
EMPLOYEES, AGENTS AND OTHER RELEVANT PERSONS

5.1   SKILLS, KNOWLEDGE AND EXPERTISE

[3.11]
[**Note**: ESMA has also issued guidelines under article 16(3) of the ESMA Regulation covering certain aspects of the MiFID compliance function requirements. See www.esma.europa.eu/content/Guidelines-certain-aspects-MiFID-compliance-function-requirements.]

5.1.1 R   FCA PRA

A *firm* must employ personnel with the skills, knowledge and expertise necessary for the discharge of the responsibilities allocated to them.
[**Note**: article 5(1)(d) of the *MiFID implementing Directive*, articles 12(1)(a) and 14(1)(c) of the *UCITS Directive* and article 5(1) of the *UCITS implementing Directive*]

5.1.2 G   FCA PRA

A *firm's* systems and controls should enable it to satisfy itself of the suitability of anyone who acts for it. This includes assessing an individual's honesty and competence. This assessment should normally be made at the point of recruitment. An individual's honesty need not normally be revisited unless something happens to make a fresh look appropriate.

5.1.3 G   FCA PRA

Any assessment of an individual's suitability should take into account the level of responsibility that the individual will assume within the *firm*. The nature of this assessment will generally differ depending upon whether it takes place at the start of the individual's recruitment, at the end of the probationary period (if there is one) or subsequently.

5.1.4 G   FCA

The Training and Competence sourcebook (*TC*) contains additional *rules* and *guidance* relating to specified retail activities undertaken by a *firm*.

5.1.4A G   FCA PRA

Firms which are carrying on activities that are not subject to *TC* may nevertheless wish to take *TC* into account in complying with the competence requirements in *SYSC*.

5.1.5 G   FCA PRA

The requirements on *firms* with respect to *approved persons* are in Part V of the *Act* (Performance of regulated activities) and **SUP 10A** and **SUP 10B**.

5.1.5A G   FCA PRA

If a *firm* requires *employees* who are not subject to a qualification requirement in *TC* to pass a relevant examination from the list of recommended examinations maintained by the Financial Skills Partnership, the *appropriate regulator* will take that into account when assessing whether the *firm* has ensured that the *employee* satisfies the knowledge component of the *competent employees rule*.

Segregation of functions

5.1.6 R   FCA PRA

A *common platform firm* and a *management company* must ensure that the performance of multiple functions by its *relevant persons* does not and is not likely to prevent those persons from discharging any particular functions soundly, honestly and professionally.
[**Note:** article 5(1)(g) of the *MiFID implementing Directive* and article 5(3) of the *UCITS implementing Directive*]

5.1.7 R   FCA PRA

The *senior personnel* of a *common platform firm* must define arrangements concerning the segregation of duties within the *firm* and the prevention of conflicts of interest.
[**Note:** article 88 of the *CRD* and annex V paragraph 1 of the *Banking Consolidation Directive*]

5.1.7A G   FCA PRA

Other *firms* should take account of the segregation of functions *rules* (**SYSC 5.1.6 R** and **SYSC 5.1.7 R**) as if they were *guidance* (and as if should appeared in those rules instead of must) as explained in **SYSC 1 ANNEX 1.3.3 G**.

5.1.8 G   FCA PRA

The effective segregation of duties is an important element in the *internal controls* of a *firm* in the *prudential context*. In particular, it helps to ensure that no one individual is completely free to commit a *firm's* assets or incur liabilities on its behalf. Segregation can also help to ensure that a *firm's governing body* receives objective and accurate information on financial performance, the risks faced by the *firm* and the adequacy of its systems.

5.1.9 G   FCA PRA

A *firm* should normally ensure that no single individual has unrestricted authority to do all of the following:
(1)   initiate a transaction;
(2)   bind the *firm*;
(3)   make payments; and
(4)   account for it.

5.1.10 G   FCA PRA

Where a *firm* is unable to ensure the complete segregation of duties (for example, because it has a limited number of staff), it should ensure that there are adequate compensating controls in place (for example, frequent review of an area by relevant *senior managers*).

5.1.11 G   FCA PRA

Where a *common platform firm* outsources its internal audit function, it should take reasonable steps to ensure that every individual involved in the performance of this service is independent from the individuals who perform its external audit. This should not prevent services from being undertaken by a *firm's* external auditors provided that:
(1)   the work is carried out under the supervision and management of the *firm's* own internal staff; and
(2)   potential conflicts of interest between the provision of external audit services and the provision of internal audit are properly managed.

Awareness of procedures

5.1.12 R   FCA PRA

A *common platform firm* and a *management company* must ensure that its *relevant persons* are aware of the procedures which must be followed for the proper discharge of their responsibilities.
[**Note:** article 5(1)(b) of the *MiFID implementing Directive* and article 4(1)(b) of the *UCITS implementing Directive*]

5.1.12A G   FCA PRA

Other *firms* should take account of the *rule* concerning awareness of procedures (**SYSC 5.1.12 R**) as if it were *guidance* (and as if should appeared in that rule instead of must) as explained in **SYSC 1 ANNEX 1.3.3 G**.

General

5.1.13 R   FCA PRA

The systems, internal control mechanisms and arrangements established by a *firm* in accordance with this chapter must take into account the nature, scale and complexity of its business and the nature and range of financial services and activities undertaken in the course of that business.
[**Note:** article 5(1) final paragraph of the *MiFID implementing Directive* and articles 4(1) final paragraph and 5(4) of the *UCITS implementing Directive*]

5.1.14 R   FCA PRA

A *common platform firm* and a *management company* must monitor and, on a regular basis, evaluate the adequacy and effectiveness of its systems, internal control mechanisms and arrangements

established in accordance with this chapter, and take appropriate measures to address any deficiencies.
[**Note:** article 5(5) of the *MiFID implementing Directive* and articles 4(5) of the *UCITS implementing Directive*]

5.1.15 G   FCA PRA

Other *firms* should take account of the *rule* requiring monitoring and evaluation of the adequacy and effectiveness of systems (**SYSC 5.1.14 R**) as if it were *guidance* (and as if should appeared in that rule instead of must) as explained in **SYSC 1 ANNEX 1.3.3 G**.

CHAPTER 6
COMPLIANCE, INTERNAL AUDIT AND FINANCIAL CRIME

6.1   COMPLIANCE

[3.12]
[**Note:** ESMA has also issued guidelines under article 16(3) of the ESMA Regulation covering certain aspects of the MiFID compliance function requirements. See www.esma.europa.eu/content/Guidelines-certain-aspects-MiFID-compliance-function-requirements.]

6.1.1 R   FCA PRA

A *firm* must establish, implement and maintain adequate policies and procedures sufficient to ensure compliance of the *firm* including its managers, employees and *appointed representatives* (or where applicable, *tied agents*) with its obligations under the *regulatory system* and for countering the risk that the *firm* might be used to further *financial crime*.
[**Note:** article 13(2) of *MiFID* and article 12(1)(a) of the *UCITS Directive*]

6.1.1A G   FCA

The *FCA* provides *guidance* on steps that a *firm* can take to reduce the risk that it might be used to further *financial crime* in *FC* (Financial crime: a guide for firms).

6.1.2 R   FCA PRA

A *common platform firm* and a *management company* must, taking into account the nature, scale and complexity of its business, and the nature and range of financial services and activities undertaken in the course of that business, establish, implement and maintain adequate policies and procedures designed to detect any risk of failure by the *firm* to comply with its obligations under the *regulatory system*, as well as associated risks, and put in place adequate measures and procedures designed to minimise such risks and to enable the *appropriate regulator* to exercise its powers effectively under the *regulatory system* and to enable any other *competent authority* to exercise its powers effectively under *MiFID* or the *UCITS Directive*.
[**Note:** article 6(1) of the *MiFID implementing Directive* and article 10(1) of the *UCITS implementing Directive*]

6.1.2A G   FCA PRA

Other *firms* should take account of the adequate policies and procedures *rule* (**SYSC 6.1.2 R**) as if it were *guidance* (and as if should appeared in that rule instead of must) as explained in **SYSC 1 ANNEX 1.3.3 G**.

6.1.3 R   FCA PRA

A *common platform firm* and a *management company* must maintain a permanent and effective compliance function which operates independently and which has the following responsibilities:
(1)   to monitor and, on a regular basis, to assess the adequacy and effectiveness of the measures and procedures put in place in accordance with **SYSC 6.1.2 R**, and the actions taken to address any deficiencies in the *firm's* compliance with its obligations; and
(2)   to advise and assist the *relevant persons* responsible for carrying out *regulated activities* to comply with the *firm's* obligations under the *regulatory system*.

[**Note:** article 6(2) of the *MiFID implementing Directive* and article 10(2) of the *UCITS implementing Directive*]

6.1.3A G   FCA PRA
(1)   Other *firms* should take account of the compliance function *rule* (**SYSC 6.1.3 R**) as if it were *guidance* (and as if should appeared in that rule instead of must) as explained in **SYSC 1 ANNEX 1.3.3 G**.
(2)   Notwithstanding **SYSC 6.1.3 R**, as it applies under (1), depending on the nature, scale and complexity of its business, it may be appropriate for a *firm* to have a separate compliance function. Where a *firm* has a separate compliance function the *firm* should also take into account **SYSC 6.1.3 R** and **SYSC 6.1.4 R** as guidance.

6.1.4 R   FCA PRA

In order to enable the compliance function to discharge its responsibilities properly and independently, a *common platform firm* and a *management company* must ensure that the following conditions are satisfied:

(1)   the compliance function must have the necessary authority, resources, expertise and access to all relevant information;

(2)   a compliance officer must be appointed and must be responsible for the compliance function and for any reporting as to compliance required by **SYSC 4.3.2 R**;

(3)   the *relevant persons* involved in the compliance functions must not be involved in the performance of services or activities they monitor;

(4)   the method of determining the remuneration of the *relevant persons* involved in the compliance function must not compromise their objectivity and must not be likely to do so.

[**Note:** article 6(3) first paragraph of the *MiFID implementing Directive* and article 10(3) of the *UCITS implementing Directive*]

6.1.4-A G   FCA PRA

In setting the method of determining the *remuneration* of *relevant persons* involved in the compliance function:

(1)   *firms* that **SYSC 19A** applies to will also need to comply with the *Remuneration Code*;

(2)   *BIPRU firms* will also need to comply with the *BIPRU Remuneration Code*;

(3)   *firms* that **SYSC 19D** applies to will also need to comply with the *dual-regulated firms Remuneration Code*; and

(4)   *firms* that the remuneration part of the *PRA* Rulebook applies to will also need to comply with it.

6.1.4A R   FCA

(1)   A *firm* which is not a *common platform firm* or *management company* and which carries on *designated investment business* with or for retail clients or professional clients must allocate to a *director* or *senior manager* the function of:

    (a)   having responsibility for oversight of the *firm's* compliance; and

    (b)   reporting to the *governing body* in respect of that responsibility.

(2)   In **SYSC 6.1.4AR (1)** compliance means compliance with the rules in:

    (a)   *COBS* (Conduct of Business sourcebook);

    (b)   *COLL* (Collective Investment Schemes sourcebook);

    (c)   *CASS* (Client Assets sourcebook); and

    (d)   *ICOBS* (Insurance: Conduct of Business sourcebook).

6.1.4-B G   FCA

In setting the method of determining the remuneration of *relevant persons* involved in the compliance function, *full-scope UK AIFMs* will need to comply with the *AIFM Remuneration Code*.

6.1.4C R   FCA

A *debt management firm* and a *credit repair firm* must appoint a compliance officer to be responsible for ensuring the *firm* meets its obligations under **SYSC 6.1.1 R** for any compliance function the *firm* has and for any reporting as to compliance which may be made under **SYSC 4.3.2 R**.

6.1.5 R   FCA PRA

A *common platform firm* and a *management company* need not comply with **SYSC 6.1.4R (3)** or **SYSC 6.1.4R (4)** if it is able to demonstrate that in view of the nature, scale and complexity of its business, and the nature and range of financial services and activities, the requirements under those *rules* are not proportionate and that its compliance function continues to be effective.

[**Note**: article 6(3) second paragraph of the *MiFID implementing Directive* and article 10(3) second paragraph of the *UCITS implementing Directive*]

6.1.6 R   FCA PRA

Other *firms* should take account of the proportionality *rule* (**SYSC 6.1.5 R**) as if it were *guidance* (and as if should appeared in that rule instead of must) as explained in **SYSC 1 ANNEX 1.3.3 G**.

6.1.7 R   FCA PRA

(1)   This *rule* applies to a *common platform firm* conducting *investment services and activities* from a *branch* in another *EEA State*.

(2)   References to the *regulatory system* in **SYSC 6.1.1R**, **SYSC 6.1.2 R** and **SYSC 6.1.3 R** apply in respect of a *firm's branch* as if *regulatory system* includes a *Host State's* requirements under *MiFID* and the *MiFID implementing Directive* which are applicable to the *investment services and activities* conducted from the *firm's branch*.

[**Note:** article 13(2) of *MiFID*]

6.2   INTERNAL AUDIT

6.2.1 R   FCA PRA

A *common platform firm* and a *management company* must, where appropriate and proportionate in view of the nature, scale and complexity of its business and the nature and range of its financial services and activities, undertaken in the course of that business, establish and maintain an internal audit function which is separate and independent from the other functions and activities of the *firm* and which has the following responsibilities:

(1)   to establish, implement and maintain an audit plan to examine and evaluate the adequacy and effectiveness of the *firm's* systems, internal control mechanisms and arrangements;
(2)   to issue recommendations based on the result of work carried out in accordance with (1);
(3)   to verify compliance with those recommendations;
(4)   to report in relation to internal audit matters in accordance with **SYSC 4.3.2 R**.

[**Note**: article 8 of the *MiFID implementing Directive* and article 11 of the *UCITS implementing Directive*]

6.2.1A G   FCA PRA

Other *firms* should take account of the internal audit *rule* (**SYSC 6.2.1 R**) as if it were *guidance* (and as if should appeared in that rule instead of must) as explained in **SYSC 1 ANNEX 1.3.3 G**.

6.2.2 G   FCA PRA

The term 'internal audit function' in **SYSC 6.2.1 R** (and **SYSC 4.1.11 G**) refers to the generally understood concept of internal audit within a *firm*, that is, the function of assessing adherence to and the effectiveness of internal systems and controls, procedures and policies. The internal audit function is not a *controlled function* itself, but is part of the *systems and controls function* (CF28).

6.3   FINANCIAL CRIME

6.3.1 R   FCA

A *firm* must ensure the policies and procedures established under **SYSC 6.1.1 R** include systems and controls that:

(1)   enable it to identify, assess, monitor and manage *money laundering* risk; and
(2)   are comprehensive and proportionate to the nature, scale and complexity of its activities.

6.3.2 G   FCA

"*Money laundering* risk" is the risk that a *firm* may be used to further *money laundering*. Failure by a *firm* to manage this risk effectively will increase the risk to society of crime and terrorism.

6.3.3 R   FCA

A *firm* must carry out a regular assessment of the adequacy of these systems and controls to ensure that they continue to comply with **SYSC 6.3.1 R**.

6.3.4 G   FCA

A *firm* may also have separate obligations to comply with relevant legal requirements, including the Terrorism Act 2000, the Proceeds of Crime Act 2002 and the *Money Laundering Regulations*. **SYSC 6.1.1 R** and **SYSC 6.3.1 R** to **SYSC 6.3.10 G** are not relevant for the purposes of regulation 42(3) or 45(2) of the *Money Laundering Regulations*, section 330(8) of the Proceeds of Crime Act 2002 or section 21A(6) of the Terrorism Act 2000.

6.3.5 G   FCA

The *FCA*, when considering whether a breach of its *rules* on systems and controls against *money laundering* has occurred, will have regard to whether a *firm* has followed relevant provisions in the guidance for the *United Kingdom* financial sector issued by the Joint Money Laundering Steering Group.

6.3.6 G   FCA

In identifying its *money laundering* risk and in establishing the nature of these systems and controls, a *firm* should consider a range of factors, including:

(1)   its customer, product and activity profiles;
(2)   its distribution channels;
(3)   the complexity and volume of its transactions;
(4)   its processes and systems; and
(5)   its operating environment.

6.3.7 G   FCA

A *firm* should ensure that the systems and controls include:

(1)   appropriate training for its employees in relation to *money laundering*;
(2)   appropriate provision of information to its *governing body* and senior management, including a report at least annually by that *firm's money laundering reporting officer* (*MLRO*) on the operation and effectiveness of those systems and controls;
(3)   appropriate documentation of its risk management policies and risk profile in relation to *money laundering*, including documentation of its application of those policies (see **SYSC 9**);

(4)   appropriate measures to ensure that *money laundering* risk is taken into account in its
        day-to-day operation, including in relation to:
        (a)   the development of new products;
        (b)   the taking-on of new customers; and
        (c)   changes in its business profile; and
(5)   appropriate measures to ensure that procedures for identification of new customers do not
        unreasonably deny access to its services to potential customers who cannot reasonably be
        expected to produce detailed evidence of identity.

6.3.8 R   FCA

A *firm* must allocate to a *director* or *senior manager* (who may also be the *money laundering
reporting officer*) overall responsibility within the *firm* for the establishment and maintenance of
effective anti- *money laundering* systems and controls.

The money laundering reporting officer

6.3.9 R   FCA

A *firm* (with the exception of a *sole trader* who has no employees) must:
(1)   appoint an individual as *MLRO*, with responsibility for oversight of its compliance with the
        FCA's rules on systems and controls against *money laundering*; and
(2)   ensure that its *MLRO* has a level of authority and independence within the *firm* and access
        to resources and information sufficient to enable him to carry out that responsibility.

6.3.10 G   FCA

The job of the *MLRO* within a *firm* is to act as the focal point for all activity within the *firm* relating
to anti- *money laundering*. The *FCA* expects that a *firm's MLRO* will be based in the *United
Kingdom*.

Financial crime guidance

6.3.11 G   FCA

The *FCA* provides *guidance* on steps that a *firm* can take to reduce the risk that it might be used to
further *financial crime* in *FC* (Financial crime: a guide for firms).

CHAPTER 7
RISK CONTROL

7.1   RISK CONTROL

[3.13]
[Note: ESMA has also issued guidelines under article 16(3) of the ESMA Regulation covering
certain aspects of the MiFID compliance function requirements. See www.esma.europa.eu/content/
Guidelines-certain-aspects-MiFID-compliance-function-requirements.]

7.1.1 G   FCA PRA

SYSC 4.1.1 R requires a *firm* to have effective processes to identify, manage, monitor and report the
risks it is or might be exposed to.

7.1.2 R   FCA PRA

A *common platform firm* must establish, implement and maintain adequate risk management policies
and procedures, including effective procedures for risk assessment, which identify the risks relating
to the *firm's* activities, processes and systems, and where appropriate, set the level of risk tolerated
by the *firm*.
[Note: article 7(1)(a) of the *MiFID implementing Directive*, article 13(5) second paragraph of
MiFID]

7.1.2A G   FCA PRA

Other *firms* should take account of the risk management policies and procedures *rule* (SYSC
7.1.2 R) as if it were *guidance* (and as if should appeared in that rule instead of must) as explained
in SYSC 1 ANNEX 1.3.3 G.

7.1.2B G   FCA

A *management company* should be aware that COLL 6.11 contains requirements implementing
article 12 of the *UCITS implementing Directive* in relation to risk control and internal reporting that
will apply to it.

7.1.2C G   FCA

Full-scope UK AIFMs should be aware that FUND 3.7 and articles 38 to 47 of the *AIFMD level 2
regulation* contain further requirements in relation to risk management.

7.1.3 R   FCA PRA

A *common platform firm* must adopt effective arrangements, processes and mechanisms to manage the risk relating to the *firm's* activities, processes and systems, in light of that level of risk tolerance.
[**Note**: article 7(1)(b) of the *MiFID implementing Directive*]

7.1.4 R   FCA PRA

The *management body* of a *common platform firm* must approve and periodically review the strategies and policies for taking up, managing, monitoring and mitigating the risks the *firm* is or might be exposed to, including those posed by the macroeconomic environment in which it operates in relation to the status of the business cycle.
[**Note**: article 76(1) of *CRD*]

7.1.4A G   FCA PRA

For a *common platform firm* included within the scope of **SYSC 20** (Reverse stress testing), the strategies, policies and procedures for identifying, taking up, managing, monitoring and mitigating the risks to which the *firm* is or might be exposed include conducting reverse stress testing in accordance with **SYSC 20**. A *common platform firm* which falls outside the scope of **SYSC 20** should consider conducting reverse stress tests on its business plan as well. This would further *senior personnels* understanding of the *firm's* vulnerabilities and would help them design measures to prevent or mitigate the risk of business failure.

7.1.4B G   FCA PRA

Other *firms* should take account of the risk management *rules* (**SYSC 7.1.3 R** and **SYSC 7.1.4 R**) as if they were *guidance* (and as if "should" appeared in those rules instead of "must") as explained in **SYSC 1 ANNEX 1.3.3** G.

7.1.5 R   FCA PRA

A *common platform firm* must monitor the following:
(1)   the adequacy and effectiveness of the *firm's* risk management policies and procedures;
(2)   the level of compliance by the *firm* and its *relevant persons* with the arrangements, processes and mechanisms adopted in accordance with **SYSC 7.1.3 R**;
(3)   the adequacy and effectiveness of measures taken to address any deficiencies in those policies, procedures, arrangements, processes and mechanisms, including failures by the *relevant persons* to comply with such arrangements or processes and mechanisms or follow such policies and procedures.
        [**Note**: article 7(1)(c) of the *MiFID implementing Directive*]

7.1.6 R   FCA PRA

A *common platform firm* must, where appropriate and proportionate in view of the nature, scale and complexity of its business and the nature and range of the *investment services and activities* undertaken in the course of that business, establish and maintain a risk management function that operates independently and carries out the following tasks:
(1)   implementation of the policies and procedures referred to in **SYSC 7.1.2 R** to **SYSC 7.1.5 R**; and
(2)   provision of reports and advice to *senior personnel* in accordance with **SYSC 4.3.2 R**.
        [**Note**: *MiFID implementing Directive* Article 7(2) first paragraph]

7.1.7 R   FCA PRA

Where a *common platform firm* is not required under **SYSC 7.1.6 R** to maintain a risk management function that functions independently, it must nevertheless be able to demonstrate that the policies and procedures which it has adopted in accordance with **SYSC 7.1.2 R** to **SYSC 7.1.5 R** satisfy the requirements of those *rules* and are consistently effective.
[**Note**: article 7(2) second paragraph of the *MiFID implementing Directive*]

7.1.7A G   FCA PRA

Other *firms* should take account of the risk management *rules* (**SYSC 7.1.5 R** to **SYSC 7.1.7 R**) as if they were *guidance* (and as if should appeared in those rules instead of must) as explained in **SYSC 1 ANNEX 1.3.3** G.

7.1.7B G   FCA PRA

In setting the method of determining the *remuneration* of *employees* involved in the risk management function:
(1)   *firms* that **SYSC 19D** applies to will also need to comply with the *dual-regulated firms Remuneration Code*; and
(2)   *firms* that the remuneration part of the *PRA* Rulebook applies to will also need to comply with it.

7.1.7BA G   FCA

In setting the method of determining the *remuneration* of *employees* involved in the risk management function *full-scope UK AIFMs* will need to comply with the *AIFM Remuneration Code*.

7.1.7BB G   FCA

In setting the method of determining the *remuneration* of *employees* involved in the risk management function, *BIPRU firms* will also need to comply with the *BIPRU Remuneration Code*.

7.1.7BC G   FCA

In setting the method of determining the *remuneration* of *employees* involved in the risk management function, *firms* that **SYSC 19A** applies to will also need to comply with the *Remuneration Code*.

7.1.7C G   FCA PRA

Firms should also consider the additional *guidance* on risk-centric governance arrangements for effective risk management contained in **SYSC 21**.

7.1.8 G   FCA PRA
(1)   [deleted]
(2)   The term 'risk management function' in **SYSC 7.1.6 R** and **SYSC 7.1.7 R** refers to the generally understood concept of risk assessment within a *firm*, that is, the function of setting and controlling risk exposure. The risk management function is not a *controlled function* itself, but is part of the *systems and controls function* (CF28).

7.1.9 R   FCA

A *firm* must base credit-granting on sound and well-defined criteria and clearly establish the process for approving, amending, renewing, and re-financing credits.

7.1.10 R   FCA

A *BIPRU firm* must operate through effective systems the ongoing administration and monitoring of its various credit risk-bearing portfolios and exposures, including for identifying and managing problem credits and for making adequate value adjustments and provisions.

7.1.11 R   FCA

A *BIPRU firm* must adequately diversify credit portfolios given its target market and overall credit strategy.

7.1.12 G   FCA

The documentation maintained by a *BIPRU firm* under **SYSC 4.1.3 R** should include its policy for credit risk, including its risk appetite and provisioning policy and should describe how it measures, monitors and controls that risk. This should include descriptions of the systems used to ensure that the policy is correctly implemented.

7.1.13 R   FCA

A *BIPRU firm* must address and control by means of written policies and procedures the risk that recognised credit risk mitigation techniques used by it prove less effective than expected.

7.1.14 R   FCA

A *BIPRU firm* must implement policies and processes for the measurement and management of all material sources and effects of market risks.

7.1.15 R   FCA

A *BIPRU* firm must implement systems to evaluate and manage the risk arising from potential changes in interest rates as they affect a *BIPRU firm's* non-trading activities.

7.1.16 R   FCA

A *BIPRU firm* must implement policies and processes to evaluate and manage the exposure to operational risk, including to low-frequency high severity events. Without prejudice to the definition of *operational risk*, *BIPRU firms* must articulate what constitutes operational risk for the purposes of those policies and procedures.

7.1.16A G

[deleted]

7.1.16B G

[deleted]

Additional rules for CRR firms

7.1.16C R   FCA

In **SYSC 7.1.18 R** a '*CRR firm* that is significant' means a significant *IFPRU firm*.

7.1.17 R   FCA PRA
(1)   The *management body* of a *CRR firm* has overall responsibility for risk management. It must devote sufficient time to the consideration of risk issues.

(2)   The *management body* of a *CRR firm* must be actively involved in and ensure that adequate resources are allocated to the management of all material risks addressed in the rules implementing the *CRD* and in the *EU CRR* as well as in the valuation of assets, the use of external ratings and internal models related to those risks.

(3)   A *CRR firm* must establish reporting lines to the *management body* that cover all material risks and risk management policies and changes thereof.

[**Note**: article 76(2) of *CRD*]

7.1.18 R   FCA PRA

(1)   A *CRR firm* that is significant must establish a risk committee composed of members of the *management body* who do not perform any executive function in the firm. Members of the risk committee must have appropriate knowledge, skills and expertise to fully understand and monitor the risk strategy and the risk appetite of the *firm*.

(2)   The risk committee must advise the *management body* on the institution's overall current and future risk appetite and assist the *management body* in overseeing the implementation of that strategy by *senior management*.

(3)   The risk committee must review whether prices of liabilities and assets offered to clients take fully into account the *firm's* business model and risk strategy. Where prices do not properly reflect risks in accordance with the business model and risk strategy, the risk committee must present a remedy plan to the *management body*.

[**Note**: article 76(3) of *CRD*]

7.1.18A G   PRA

In **SYSC 7.1.18 R** a '*CRR firm* that is significant' means a deposit-taker or designated investment firm whose size, interconnectedness, complexity and business type gives it the capacity to cause some disruption to the UK financial system (and through that to economic activity more widely) by failing or by carrying on its business in an unsafe manner.

7.1.18AA G   FCA

A *CRR firm* which is not a *significant IFPRU firm* may combine the risk committee with the audit committee.

[**Note**: article 76(3) of *CRD*]

7.1.18B R   FCA

Members of the combined risk and audit committee must have the knowledge, skills and expertise required for both committees.

[**Note**: article 76(3) of *CRD*]

7.1.19 R   FCA PRA

(1)   A *CRR firm* must ensure that the *management body* in its supervisory function and, where a risk committee has been established, the risk committee have adequate access to information on the risk profile of the *firm* and, if necessary and appropriate, to the risk management function and to external expert advice.

(2)   The *management body* in its supervisory function and, where one has been established, the risk committee must determine the nature, the amount, the format, and the frequency of the information on risk which it is to receive.

[**Note**: article 76(4) of *CRD*]

7.1.20 R   FCA PRA

In order to assist in the establishment of sound remuneration policies and practices, the risk committee must, without prejudice to the tasks of the remuneration committee, examine whether incentives provided by the remuneration system take into consideration risk, capital, liquidity and the likelihood and timing of earnings.

[**Note**: article 76(4) of *CRD*]

7.1.21 R   FCA PRA

(1)   A *CRR firm's* risk management function (**SYSC 7.1.6 R**) must be independent from the operational functions and have sufficient authority, stature, resources and access to the *management body*.

(2)   The risk management function must ensure that all material risks are identified, measured and properly reported. It must be actively involved in elaborating the *firm's* risk strategy and in all material risk management decisions and it must be able to deliver a complete view of the whole range of risks of the *firm*.

(3)   A *CRR firm* must ensure that the risk management function is able to report directly to the *management body* in its supervisory function, independent from *senior management* and that it can raise concerns and warn the *management body*, where appropriate, where specific risk developments affect or may affect the *firm*, without prejudice to the responsibilities of the *management body* in its supervisory and/or managerial functions pursuant to the *CRD* and the *CRR*.

Part 3   FCA Handbook Materials

[**Note**: article 76(5) of *CRD*]

7.1.22 R   **FCA PRA**

The head of the risk management function must be an independent senior manager with distinct responsibility for the risk management function. Where the nature, scale and complexity of the activities of the *CRR firm* do not justify a specially appointed person, another senior person within the *firm* may fulfil that function, provided there is no conflict of interest. The head of the risk management function must not be removed without prior approval of the *management body* and must be able to have direct access to the *management body* where necessary.
[**Note**: article 76(5) of *CRD*]

CHAPTER 8
OUTSOURCING

8.1   GENERAL OUTSOURCING REQUIREMENTS

[3.14]

[**Note**: ESMA has also issued guidelines under article 16(3) of the ESMA Regulation covering certain aspects of the MiFID compliance function requirements. See www.esma.europa.eu/content/Guidelines-certain-aspects-MiFID-compliance-function-requirements.]

8.1.1 R   **FCA PRA**

A *common platform firm* must:
(1)   when relying on a third party for the performance of operational functions which are critical for the performance of *regulated activities*, *listed activities* or *ancillary services* (in this chapter "relevant services and activities") on a continuous and satisfactory basis, ensure that it takes reasonable steps to avoid undue additional operational risk;
(2)   not undertake the *outsourcing* of important operational functions in such a way as to impair materially:
    (a)   the quality of its internal control; and
    (b)   the ability of the *appropriate regulator* to monitor the *firm's* compliance with all obligations under the *regulatory system* and, if different, of a *competent authority* to monitor the *firm's* compliance with all obligations under *MiFID*.
    [**Note:** article 13(5) first paragraph of *MiFID*]

8.1.1A G   **FCA PRA**

Other *firms* should take account of the outsourcing *rule* (**SYSC 8.1.1 R**) as if it were *guidance* (and as if should appeared in that rule instead of must) as explained in **SYSC 1 ANNEX 1.3.3 G**.

8.1.2 G   **FCA PRA**

The application of **SYSC 8.1** to relevant services and activities (see **SYSC 8.1.1 R (1)**) is limited by **SYSC 1 ANNEX 1 (PART 2)** (Application of the common platform requirements).

8.1.3 G   **FCA PRA**

SYSC 4.1.1 R requires a *firm* to have effective processes to identify, manage, monitor and report risks and internal control mechanisms. Except in relation to those functions described in **SYSC 8.1.5 R**, where a *firm* relies on a third party for the performance of operational functions which are not critical or important for the performance of relevant services and activities (see **SYSC 8.1.1 R (1)**) on a continuous and satisfactory basis, it should take into account, in a manner that is proportionate given the nature, scale and complexity of the *outsourcing*, the *rules* in this section in complying with that requirement.

8.1.4 R   **FCA PRA**

For the purposes of this chapter an operational function is regarded as critical or important if a defect or failure in its performance would materially impair the continuing compliance of a *common platform firm* with the conditions and obligations of its *authorisation* or its other obligations under the *regulatory system*, or its financial performance, or the soundness or the continuity of its relevant services and activities.
[**Note**: article 13(1) of the *MiFID implementing Directive*]

8.1.5 R   **FCA PRA**

Without prejudice to the status of any other function, the following functions will not be considered as critical or important for the purposes of this chapter:
(1)   the provision to the *firm* of advisory services, and other services which do not form part of the relevant services and activities of the *firm*, including the provision of legal advice to the *firm*, the training of personnel of the *firm*, billing services and the security of the *firm's* premises and personnel;
(2)   the purchase of standardised services, including market information services and the provision of price feeds;
    [**Note:** article 13(2) of the *MiFID implementing Directive*]

(3)   the recording and retention of relevant telephone conversations or electronic communications subject to **COBS 11.8**.

8.1.5A G   FCA PRA

Other *firms* should take account of the critical functions *rules* (**SYSC 8.1.4 R** and **SYSC 8.1.5 R**) as if they were *guidance* (and as if should appeared in those rules instead of must) as explained in **SYSC 1 ANNEX 1.3.3 G**.

8.1.6 R   FCA PRA

If a *firm* *outsources* critical or important operational functions or any relevant services and activities, it remains fully responsible for discharging all of its obligations under the *regulatory system* and must comply, in particular, with the following conditions:

(1)   the *outsourcing* must not result in the delegation by *senior personnel* of their responsibility;

(2)   the relationship and obligations of the *firm* towards its *clients* under the *regulatory system* must not be altered;

(3)   the conditions with which the *firm* must comply in order to be *authorised*, and to remain so, must not be undermined;

(4)   none of the other conditions subject to which the *firm's authorisation* was granted must be removed or modified.
       [**Note:** article 14(1) of the *MiFID implementing Directive*]

8.1.7 R   FCA PRA

A *common platform firm* must exercise due skill and care and diligence when entering into, managing or terminating any arrangement for the *outsourcing* to a service provider of critical or important operational functions or of any relevant services and activities.
[**Note:** article 14(2) first paragraph of the *MiFID implementing Directive*]

8.1.8 R   FCA PRA

A *common platform firm* must in particular take the necessary steps to ensure that the following conditions are satisfied:

(1)   the service provider must have the ability, capacity, and any *authorisation* required by law to perform the *outsourced* functions, services or activities reliably and professionally;

(2)   the service provider must carry out the *outsourced* services effectively, and to this end the *firm* must establish methods for assessing the standard of performance of the service provider;

(3)   the service provider must properly supervise the carrying out of the *outsourced* functions, and adequately manage the risks associated with the *outsourcing*;

(4)   appropriate action must be taken if it appears that the service provider may not be carrying out the functions effectively and in compliance with applicable laws and regulatory requirements;

(5)   the *firm* must retain the necessary expertise to supervise the *outsourced* functions effectively and to manage the risks associated with the *outsourcing*, and must supervise those functions and manage those risks;

(6)   the service provider must disclose to the *firm* any development that may have a material impact on its ability to carry out the *outsourced* functions effectively and in compliance with applicable laws and regulatory requirements;

(7)   the *firm* must be able to terminate the arrangement for the *outsourcing* where necessary without detriment to the continuity and quality of its provision of services to *clients*;

(8)   the service provider must co-operate with the *appropriate regulator* and any other relevant *competent authority* in connection with the *outsourced* activities;

(9)   the *firm*, its auditors, the *appropriate regulator* and any other relevant *competent authority* must have effective access to data related to the *outsourced* activities, as well as to the business premises of the service provider; and the *appropriate regulator* and any other relevant *competent authority* must be able to exercise those rights of access;

(10)   the service provider must protect any confidential information relating to the *firm* and its *clients*;

(11)   the *firm* and the service provider must establish, implement and maintain a contingency plan for disaster recovery and periodic testing of backup facilities where that is necessary having regard to the function, service or activity that has been *outsourced*.
       [**Note:** article 14(2) second paragraph of the *MiFID implementing Directive*]

8.1.9 R   FCA PRA

A *common platform firm* must ensure that the respective rights and obligations of the *firm* and of the service provider are clearly allocated and set out in a written agreement.
[**Note:** article 14(3) of the *MiFID implementing Directive*]

8.1.10 R   FCA PRA

If a *common platform firm* and the service provider are members of the same *group*, the *firm* may, for the purpose of complying with **SYSC 8.1.7 R** to **SYSC 8.1.11 R** and **SYSC 8.2** and **SYSC 8.3**, take into account the extent to which the *common platform firm controls* the service provider or has the ability to influence its actions.

[**Note:** article 14(4) of the *MiFID implementing Directive*]

8.1.11 R   FCA PRA

A *common platform firm* must make available on request to the *appropriate regulator* and any other relevant *competent authority* all information necessary to enable the *appropriate regulator* and any other relevant *competent authority* to supervise the compliance of the performance of the *outsourced* activities with the requirements of the *regulatory system*.

[**Note:** article 14(5) of the *MiFID implementing Directive*]

8.1.11A G   FCA PRA

Other *firms* should take account of the outsourcing of important operational functions *rules* (**SYSC 8.1.7 R** to **SYSC 8.1.11 R**) as if they were *guidance* (and as if should appeared in those rules instead of must) as explained in **SYSC 1 ANNEX 1.3.3 G**.

8.1.12 G   FCA PRA

As **SUP 15.3.8 G** explains, a *firm* should notify the *appropriate regulator* when it intends to rely on a third party for the performance of operational functions which are critical or important for the performance of relevant services and activities on a continuous and satisfactory basis.

[**Note:** recital 20 of the *MiFID implementing Directive*]

Additional requirements for a management company

8.1.13 R   FCA

A *management company* must retain the necessary resources and expertise so as to monitor effectively the activities carried out by third parties on the basis of an arrangement with the *firm*, especially with regard to the management of the risk associated with those arrangements.

[**Note:** article 5(2) of the *UCITS implementing Directive*]

8.1.14 G   FCA

A *management company* should be aware that **SUP 15.8.6 R** (Delegation by UCITS management companies) and **COLL 6.6.15A R** (Committees and delegations) contain requirements implementing article 13 of the *UCITS Directive* in relation to delegation that will apply to it.

8.2   OUTSOURCING OF PORTFOLIO MANAGEMENT FOR RETAIL CLIENTS TO A NON-EEA STATE

8.2.1 R   FCA

(1)   In addition to the requirements set out in the *MiFID outsourcing rules*, when a *MiFID investment firm outsources* the *investment service* of *portfolio management* to *retail clients* to a service provider located in a *non-EEA state*, it must ensure that the following conditions are satisfied:

    (a)   the service provider must be authorised or registered in its home country to provide that service and must be subject to prudential supervision;

    (b)   there must be an appropriate cooperation agreement between the *FCA* and the supervisor in the *non-EEA state*;

(in this chapter the "conditions").

[**Note:** article 15(1) of the *MiFID implementing Directive*]

(2)   In addition to complying with the *common platform outsourcing rules*, if one or both of the conditions are not satisfied, a *MiFID investment firm* may enter into such an *outsourcing* only if it gives prior notification in writing to the *FCA* containing adequate details of the proposed *outsourcing* and the *FCA* does not object to that arrangement within a reasonable time following receipt of that notification.

[**Note:** article 15(2) and (4) of the *MiFID implementing Directive*]

(3)   For the purposes of this *rule* a "reasonable time" is within one month of receipt of a notification. However, the *FCA* may seek further information from the *MiFID investment firm* in relation to the *outsourcing* proposal if this is necessary to enable the *FCA* to make a decision. Any effect this may have on the *FCA's* response time will be notified to the *MiFID investment firm* and that revised response time will constitute a reasonable time for the purposes of this *rule*.

8.2.2 G   FCA

[intentionally blank]

8.2.3 G   FCA

The conditions do not apply if the *outsourcing* only concerns ancillary activities connected with *portfolio management*, for example IT processes or execution only activities.

8.2.4 G   FCA

If a *firm* has received no notice of objection or no request for further information from the *FCA* within one month of the *FCA* receiving the notification, it may *outsource* the *portfolio management* on the basis set out in the notification.

8.2.5 G   FCA

The *FCA* would use its powers under section 55J of the *Act* to vary a *firm's permission* if it objected to such a notification.

Notification requirements: timing of notification

8.2.6 G   FCA

A *firm* should only make an *outsourcing* proposal notification to the *FCA* after it has carried out due diligence on the service provider and has had regard to the guidance set out in **SYSC 8.3**. The *FCA* will expect a firm to only submit an *outsourcing* proposal notification in respect of a service provider that the *firm* has determined is suitable to carry on the *outsourcing* activity.

Notification requirements: content

8.2.7 G   FCA

The *guidance* set out in **SYSC 8.3** includes information on what the *FCA* will expect a firm to check before the submission of a notification.

8.2.8 G   FCA

A notification under this section should include:

(1)   details on which of the conditions is not met;
(2)   if applicable, details and evidence of the service provider's authorisation or regulation including the regulator's contact details;
(3)   the *firm's* proposals for meeting its obligations under this chapter on an ongoing basis;
(4)   why the *firm* wishes to *outsource* to the service provider;
(5)   a draft of the *outsourcing* agreement between the service provider and the *firm*;
(6)   the proposed start date of the *outsourcing*; and
(7)   confirmation that the *firm* has had regard to the *guidance* in **SYSC 8.3**, or if it has not, why not.

Notification requirements additional guidance

8.2.9 G   FCA

Where the *FCA* has not objected to the *outsourcing* agreement, the *firm* should have regard to its obligations under **SUP 15** which include making the *FCA* aware of any matters which could affect the *firm's* ability to provide adequate services to its *customers* or could result in serious detriment to its *customers* or where there has been material change in the information previously provided to the *FCA* in relation to the *outsourcing*.

8.3   GUIDANCE ON OUTSOURCING PORTFOLIO MANAGEMENT FOR RETAIL CLIENTS TO A NON-EEA STATE

8.3.1 G   FCA

This *guidance* is relevant regardless of whether a *firm outsources portfolio management* directly or indirectly via a third party. However, *firms* should note that they may notify a secondary or indirect *outsourcing* in the same notification as the direct *outsourcing*.

8.3.2 G   FCA

This *guidance* sets out examples of the type of actions that a firm proposing to *outsource* should have undertaken when assessing the suitability of the service provider and its ability to carry on the outsourced activity.
[**Note:** article 15(3) of the *MiFID implementing Directive*]

8.3.3 G   FCA

If a *firm* can demonstrate that it has taken the following guidance into account and has satisfactorily concluded that it would be able to continue to satisfy the common platform *outsourcing* rules and provide adequate protection for consumers despite not satisfying the conditions, the *FCA* would not be likely to object to that *outsourcing*.

8.3.4 G   FCA

If the *outsourcing* allows the service provider to sub-contract any of the services to be provided under the *outsourcing*, any such sub-contracting shall not affect the service provider's responsibilities under the *outsourcing* agreement.

8.3.5 G   FCA

The *outsourcing* agreement should entitle the *firm* to terminate the *outsourcing* if the service provider undergoes a change of control or becomes insolvent, goes into liquidation or receivership (or equivalent in its home state) or is in persistent material default under the agreement.

8.3.6 G FCA

The following should be taken into account where the service provider is not authorised or registered in its home country and/or not subject to prudential supervision.

(1)   The *firm* should examine, and be able to demonstrate, to what extent the service provider may be subject to any form of voluntary regulation, including self-regulation in its home state.

(2)   The *firm* should be able to satisfy the *FCA* that the service provider is committed for the term of the *outsourcing* agreement to devoting sufficient, competent resources to providing the service.

(3)   In addition to the requirement to ensure that a service provider discloses any developments that may have a material impact on its ability to carry out the *outsourcing* (**SYSC 8.1.8 R (6)**), where the conditions are not met the developments to be disclosed should include, but are not limited to:

(a)   any adverse effect that any laws or regulations introduced in the service provider's home country may have on its carrying on the *outsourced* activity; and

(b)   any changes to its capital reserve levels or its prudential risks.

(4)   The *firm* should satisfy itself that the service provider is able to meet its liabilities as they fall due and that it has positive net assets.

(5)   The *firm* should require that the service provider prepares annual reports and accounts which:

(a)   are in accordance with the service provider's national law which, in all material respects, is the same as or equivalent to the *international accounting standards*;

(b)   have been independently audited and reported on in accordance with the service provider's national law which is the same as or equivalent to international auditing standards.

(6)   The *firm* should receive copies of each set of the audited annual report and accounts of the service provider. If the service provider expects or knows its auditor will qualify his report on the audited report and accounts, or add an explanatory paragraph, the service provider should be required to notify the *firm* without delay.

(7)   The *firm* should satisfy itself, and be able to demonstrate, that it has in place appropriate procedures to ensure that it is fully aware of the service provider's controls for protecting confidential information.

(8)   In addition to the requirement at **SYSC 8.1.8 R (10)** that the service provider must protect any confidential information relating to the *firm* or its *clients*, the *outsourcing* agreement should require the service provider to notify the *firm* immediately if there is a breach of confidentiality.

(9)   The *outsourcing* agreement should be governed by the law and subject to the jurisdiction of an *EEA state*.

8.3.7 G FCA

The following should be taken into account by a *firm* where there is no cooperation agreement between the *FCA* and the supervisory authority of the service provider or there is no supervisory authority of the service provider.

(1)   The *outsourcing* agreement should ensure the *firm* can provide the *FCA* with any information relating to the *outsourced* activity the *FCA* may require in order to carry out effective supervision. The *firm* should therefore assess the extent to which the service provider's regulator and/or local laws and regulations may restrict access to information about the *outsourced* activity. Any such restriction should be described in the notification to be sent to the *FCA*.

(2)   The *outsourcing* agreement should require the service provider to provide the *firm's* offices in the *United Kingdom* with all requested information required to meet the *firm's* regulatory obligations. The *FCA* should be given an enforceable right under the agreement to obtain such information from the *firm* and to require the service provider to provide the information directly.

CHAPTER 9
RECORD-KEEPING

9.1 GENERAL RULES ON RECORD-KEEPING

[3.15]
9.1.-1 R

[deleted]

9.1.-2 R

[deleted]

9.1.1 R FCA PRA

A *firm* must arrange for orderly records to be kept of its business and internal organisation, including all services and transactions undertaken by it, which must be sufficient to enable the *appropriate regulator* or any other relevant *competent authority* under *MiFID* or the *UCITS Directive* to monitor the *firm's* compliance with the requirements under the *regulatory system*, and in particular to ascertain that the *firm* has complied with all obligations with respect to *clients*.
[**Note**: article 13(6) of *MiFID*, article 5(1)(f) of the *MiFID implementing Directive*, article 12(1)(a) of the *UCITS Directive* and article 4(1)(e) of the *UCITS implementing Directive*]

9.1.2 R   FCA PRA

A *common platform firm* must retain all records kept by it under this chapter in relation to its *MiFID business* for a period of at least five years.
[**Note**: article 51 (1) of the *MiFID implementing Directive*]

9.1.3 R   FCA PRA

In relation to its *MiFID business*, a *common platform firm* must retain records in a medium that allows the storage of information in a way accessible for future reference by the *appropriate regulator* or any other relevant *competent authority* under *MiFID*, and so that the following conditions are met:
(1)   the *appropriate regulator* or any other relevant *competent authority* under *MiFID* must be able to access them readily and to reconstitute each key stage of the processing of each transaction;
(2)   it must be possible for any corrections or other amendments, and the contents of the records prior to such corrections and amendments, to be easily ascertained;
(3)   it must not be possible for the records otherwise to be manipulated or altered.

[**Note**: article 51(2) of the *MiFID implementing Directive*]

Guidance on record-keeping

9.1.4 G   FCA PRA

Subject to any other record-keeping *rule* in the *Handbook*, the records required under the *Handbook* should be capable of being reproduced in the English language on paper. Where a *firm* is required to retain a record of a communication that was not made in the English language, it may retain it in that language. However, it should be able to provide a translation on request. If a *firm's* records relate to business carried on from an establishment in a country or territory outside the *United Kingdom*, an official language of that country or territory may be used instead of the English language.

9.1.5 G   FCA PRA

In relation to the retention of records for non-*MiFID business*, a *firm* should have appropriate systems and controls in place with respect to the adequacy of, access to, and the security of its records so that the *firm* may fulfil its regulatory and statutory obligations. With respect to retention periods, the general principle is that records should be retained for as long as is relevant for the purposes for which they are made.

9.1.6 G   FCA PRA

Schedule 1 to each module of the *Handbook* sets out a list summarising the record-keeping requirements of that module.

[Note: article 51(3) of *MiFID implementing Directive*]

9.1.7 G   FCA PRA

The Committee of European Securities Regulators (CESR) has issued recommendations on the list of minimum records under Article 51(3) of the *MiFID implementing Directive*.

CHAPTER 10
CONFLICTS OF INTEREST

10.1   APPLICATION

[3.16]
10.1.1 R   FCA PRA
(1)   This section applies to a *firm* which provides services to its *clients* in the course of carrying on *regulated activities* or *ancillary activities* or providing *ancillary services* (but only where the *ancillary services* constitute *MiFID business*).
(2)   This section also applies to a *management company*.

10.1.1A R   FCA

This section also applies to:
(1)   a *full-scope UK AIFM* of:
        (a)   a *UK AIF*;
        (b)   an *EEA AIF* managed or *marketed* from an establishment in the *UK*; and
        (c)   a *non-EEA AIF*; and

(2)   an *incoming EEA AIFM* branch which manages or *markets* a *UKAIF.*

Requirements only apply if a service is provided

10.1.2 G   FCA PRA

The requirements in this section only apply where a service is provided by a *firm*. The status of the *client* to whom the service is provided (as a *retail client, professional client* or *eligible counterparty*) is irrelevant for this purpose.
[**Note:** recital 25 of *MiFID implementing Directive*]

Identifying conflicts

10.1.3 R   FCA PRA

A *firm* must take all reasonable steps to identify conflicts of interest between:
(1)   the *firm*, including its managers, employees and *appointed representatives* (or where applicable, *tied agents*), or any *person* directly or indirectly linked to them by *control*, and a *client* of the *firm*; or
(2)   one *client* of the *firm* and another *client*;

that arise or may arise in the course of the *firm* providing any service referred to in **SYSC 10.1.1 R**.
[**Note:** article 18(1) of *MiFID*]

Types of conflicts

10.1.4 R   FCA PRA

For the purposes of identifying the types of conflict of interest that arise, or may arise, in the course of providing a service and whose existence may entail a material risk of damage to the interests of a *client*, a *common platform firm* and a *management company* must take into account, as a minimum, whether the *firm* or a *relevant person*, or a *person* directly or indirectly linked by *control* to the *firm*:
(1)   is likely to make a financial gain, or avoid a financial loss, at the expense of the *client*;
(2)   has an interest in the outcome of a service provided to the *client* or of a transaction carried out on behalf of the *client*, which is distinct from the *client's* interest in that outcome;
(3)   in the case of a *management company* providing *collective portfolio management* services for a *UCITS scheme*, (2) also applies where the service is provided to, or the transaction is carried out on behalf of, a *client* other than the *UCITS scheme*;
(4)   has a financial or other incentive to favour the interest of another *client* or group of *clients* over the interests of the *client*;
(5)   carries on the same business as the *client*; or in the case of a *management company*, carries on the same activities for the *UCITS scheme* and for another *client* or *clients* which are not *UCITS schemes*; or
(6)   receives or will receive from a *person* other than the *client* an inducement in relation to a service provided to the *client*, in the form of monies, goods or services, other than the standard commission or fee for that service.

The conflict of interest may result from the *firm* or *person* providing a service referred to in **SYSC 10.1.1 R** or engaging in any other activity or, in the case of a *management company*, whether as a result of providing *collective portfolio management* services or otherwise.
[**Note:** article 21 of *MiFID implementing Directive* and article 17(1) of the *UCITS implementing Directive*]

10.1.4A G   FCA

Other *firms* should take account of the *rule* on the types of conflicts (see **SYSC 10.1.4 R**) as if it were *guidance* (and as if "should" appeared in that rule instead of "must") as explained in **SYSC 1 ANNEX 1.3.3 G**, except when they produce or arrange the production of *investment research* in accordance with **COBS 12.2**, or produce or disseminate *non-independent research* in accordance with **COBS 12.3** (see **SYSC 10.1.16 R**).

10.1.4B G   PRA

Other firms should take account of the rule on the types of conflicts (see **SYSC 10.1.4 R**) as if it were guidance (and as if "should" appeared in that rule instead of "must") as explained in **SYSC 1 ANNEX 1.3.3 G**.

10.1.5 G   FCA PRA

The circumstances which should be treated as giving rise to a conflict of interest cover cases where there is a conflict between the interests of the *firm* or certain *persons* connected to the *firm* or the *firm's group* and the duty the *firm* owes to a *client*; or between the differing interests of two or more of its *clients*, to whom the *firm* owes in each case a duty. It is not enough that the *firm* may gain a benefit if there is not also a possible disadvantage to a *client*, or that one *client* to whom the *firm* owes a duty may make a gain or avoid a loss without there being a concomitant possible loss to another such *client*.
[**Note:** recital 24 of *MiFID implementing Directive*]

Record of conflicts

10.1.6 R   FCA PRA

A *common platform firm* and a *management company* must keep and regularly update a record of the kinds of service or activity carried out by or on behalf of that *firm* in which a conflict of interest entailing a material risk of damage to the interests of one or more *clients* has arisen or, in the case of an ongoing service or activity, may arise.
[Note: article 23 of *MiFID implementing Directive* and article 20(1) of the *UCITS implementing Directive*]

10.1.6A G   FCA

Other *firms* should take account of the *rule* on records of conflicts (see **SYSC 10.1.6 R**) as if it were *guidance* (and as if "should" appeared in that rule instead of "must", as explained in **SYSC 1 ANNEX 1.3.3 G**), except when they produce or arrange the production of *investment research* in accordance with **COBS 12.2**, or produce or disseminate *non-independent research* in accordance with **COBS 12.3** (see **SYSC 10.1.16 R**).

10.1.6B G   PRA

Other firms should take account of the rule on records of conflicts (see **SYSC 10.1.6 R**) as if it were guidance (and as if "should" appeared in that rule instead of "must", as explained in **SYSC 1 ANNEX 1.3.3 G**).

Managing conflicts

10.1.7 R   FCA PRA

A *firm* must maintain and operate effective organisational and administrative arrangements with a view to taking all reasonable steps to prevent conflicts of interest as defined in **SYSC 10.1.3 R** from constituting or giving rise to a material risk of damage to the interests of its *clients*.
[Note: article 13(3) of *MiFID*]

Disclosure of conflicts

10.1.8 R   FCA PRA
(1)   If arrangements made by a *firm* under **SYSC 10.1.7 R** to manage conflicts of interest are not sufficient to ensure, with reasonable confidence, that risks of damage to the interests of a *client* will be prevented, the *firm* must clearly disclose the general nature and/or sources of conflicts of interest to the *client* before undertaking business for the *client*.
(2)   The disclosure must:
     (a)   be made in a *durable medium*; and
     (b)   include sufficient detail, taking into account the nature of the *client*, to enable that *client* to take an informed decision with respect to the service in the context of which the conflict of interest arises.
(3)   This *rule* does not apply to the extent that **SYSC 10.1.21 R** applies.

[Note: article 18(2) of *MiFID* and Article 22(4) of *MiFID implementing Directive*]

10.1.8A R   FCA PRA

The obligation in **SYSC 10.1.8R (2)(A)** does not apply to a *firm* when carrying on *insurance mediation activity*.

10.1.9 G   FCA PRA

Firms should aim to identify and manage the conflicts of interest arising in relation to their various business lines and their *group's* activities under a comprehensive *conflicts of interest policy*. In particular, the disclosure of conflicts of interest by a *firm* should not exempt it from the obligation to maintain and operate the effective organisational and administrative arrangements under **SYSC 10.1.7 R**. While disclosure of specific conflicts of interest is required by **SYSC 10.1.8 R**, an over-reliance on disclosure without adequate consideration as to how conflicts may appropriately be managed is not permitted.
[Note: recital 27 of *MiFID implementing Directive*]

Conflicts policy

10.1.10 R   FCA PRA
(1)   A *common platform firm* and a *management company* must establish, implement and maintain an effective conflicts of interest policy that is set out in writing and is appropriate to the size and organisation of the *firm* and the nature, scale and complexity of its business.
(2)   Where the *common platform firm* or the *management company* is a member of a *group*, the policy must also take into account any circumstances, of which the *firm* is or should be aware, which may give rise to a conflict of interest arising as a result of the structure and business activities of other members of the *group*.

[**Note:** article 22(1) of *MiFID implementing Directive* and article 18(1) of the *UCITS implementing Directive*]

Contents of policy

10.1.11 R   FCA PRA
(1)   The *conflicts of interest policy* must include the following content:
  (a)   it must identify in accordance with **SYSC 10.1.3 R** and **SYSC 10.1.4 R**, by reference to the specific services and activities carried out by or on behalf of the *common platform firm* or *management company*, the circumstances which constitute or may give rise to a conflict of interest entailing a material risk of damage to the interests of one or more *clients*; and
  (b)   it must specify procedures to be followed and measures to be adopted in order to manage such conflicts.
(2)   The procedures and measures provided for in paragraph (1)(b) must:
  (a)   be designed to ensure that *relevant persons* engaged in different business activities involving a conflict of interest of the kind specified in paragraph (1)(a) carry on those activities at a level of independence appropriate to the size and activities of the *common platform firm* or the *management company* and of the *group* to which either of them respectively belongs, and to the materiality of the risk of damage to the interests of *clients*; and
  (b)   include such of the following as are necessary and appropriate for the *common platform firm* or the *management company* to ensure the requisite degree of independence:
    (i)   effective procedures to prevent or control the exchange of information between *relevant persons* engaged in activities involving a risk of a conflict of interest where the exchange of that information may harm the interests of one or more *clients*;
    (ii)   the separate supervision of *relevant persons* whose principal functions involve carrying out activities on behalf of, or providing services to, *clients* whose interests may conflict, or who otherwise represent different interests that may conflict, including those of the *firm*;
    (iii)   the removal of any direct link between the remuneration of *relevant persons* principally engaged in one activity and the remuneration of, or revenues generated by, different *relevant persons* principally engaged in another activity, where a conflict of interest may arise in relation to those activities;
    (iv)   measures to prevent or limit any *person* from exercising inappropriate influence over the way in which a *relevant person* carries out services or activities; and
    (v)   measures to prevent or control the simultaneous or sequential involvement of a *relevant person* in separate services or activities where such involvement may impair the proper management of conflicts of interest.
(3)   If the adoption or the practice of one or more of those measures and procedures does not ensure the requisite level of independence, a *common platform firm* and a *management company* must adopt such alternative or additional measures and procedures as are necessary and appropriate for the purposes of paragraph (1)(b).

[**Note:** article 22(2) and (3) of *MiFID implementing Directive* and articles 18(2), 19(1) and 19(2) of the *UCITS implementing Directive*]

10.1.11A G   FCA

Other *firms* should take account of the *rules* relating to *conflicts of interest policies* (see **SYSC 10.1.10 R** and **SYSC 10.1.11 R**) as if they were *guidance* (and as if "should" appeared in those rules instead of "must", as explained in **SYSC 1 ANNEX 1.3.3 G**), except when they produce or arrange the production of *investment research* in accordance with **COBS 12.2**, or produce or disseminate *non-independent research* in accordance with **COBS 12.3** (see **SYSC 10.1.16 R**).

10.1.11B G   PRA

Other firms should take account of the rules relating to conflicts of interest policies (see **SYSC 10.1.10 R** and **SYSC 10.1.11 R**) as if they were guidance (and as if "should" appeared in those rules instead of "must", as explained in **SYSC 1 ANNEX 1.3.3 G**).

10.1.12 G   FCA PRA

In drawing up a *conflicts of interest policy* which identifies circumstances which constitute or may give rise to a conflict of interest, a *firm* should pay special attention to the activities of investment research and advice, proprietary trading, portfolio management and corporate finance business, including underwriting or selling in an offering of securities and advising on mergers and acquisitions. In particular, such special attention is appropriate where the *firm* or a *person* directly or indirectly linked by *control* to the *firm* performs a combination of two or more of those activities. [**Note:** recital 26 of *MiFID implementing Directive*]

Corporate finance

10.1.13 G   FCA

This section is relevant to the management of a *securities* offering by any *firm*.

10.1.14 G   FCA

A *firm* will wish to note that when carrying on a mandate to manage an offering of *securities*, the *firm's* duty for that business is to its corporate finance *client* (in many cases, the corporate issuer or seller of the relevant *securities*), but that its responsibilities to provide services to its investment *clients* are unchanged.

10.1.15 G   FCA

Measures that a *firm* might wish to consider in drawing up its *conflicts of interest policy* in relation to the management of an offering of *securities* include:

(1)   at an early stage agreeing with its corporate finance *client* relevant aspects of the offering process such as the process the *firm* proposes to follow in order to determine what recommendations it will make about allocations for the offering; how the target investor group will be identified; how recommendations on allocation and pricing will be prepared; and whether the *firm* might place *securities* with its investment *clients* or with its own proprietary book, or with an associate, and how conflicts arising might be managed; and

(2)   agreeing allocation and pricing objectives with the corporate finance *client*; inviting the corporate finance *client* to participate actively in the allocation process; making the initial recommendation for allocation to *retail clients* of the *firm* as a single block and not on a named basis; having internal arrangements under which senior personnel responsible for providing services to *retail clients* make the initial allocation recommendations for allocation to *retail clients* of the *firm*; and disclosing to the *issuer* details of the allocations actually made.

[**Note:** The provisions in **SYSC 10.1** also implement articles 74(1) and 88 of the *CRD* and as applied under the discretion in the third paragraph of article 95(2) of the *EU CRR*, *BCD* Article 22 and *BCD* Annex V paragraph 1]

Application of conflicts of interest rules to non-common platform firms when producing investment research or non-independent research

10.1.16 R   FCA

The *rules* relating to:

(1)   types of conflict (see **SYSC 10.1.4 R**);

(2)   records of conflicts (see **SYSC 10.1.6 R**); and

(3)   *conflicts of interest policies* (see **SYSC 10.1.10 R** and **SYSC 10.1.11 R**);

also apply to a *firm* which is not a *common platform firm* when it produces, or arranges for the production of, *investment research* that is intended or likely to be subsequently disseminated to *clients* of the *firm* or to the public in accordance with **COBS 12.2**, and when it produces or disseminates *non-independent research* in accordance with **COBS 12.3**.

Additional requirements for a management company

10.1.17 R   FCA

A *management company*, when identifying the types of conflict of interests for the purposes of **SYSC 10.1.4 R**, must take into account:

(1)   the interests of the *firm*, including those deriving from its belonging to a *group* or from the performance of services and activities, the interests of the *clients* and the duty of the *firm* towards the *UCITS scheme* or *EEA UCITS scheme* it manages; and

(2)   where it manages two or more *UCITS schemes* or *EEA UCITS schemes*, the interests of all of them.

[**Note:** article 17(2) of the *UCITS implementing Directive*]

10.1.18 G   FCA

For a *management company*, references to client in **SYSC 10.1.4 R** and in the other *rules* in this section should be construed as referring to any *UCITS scheme* or *EEA UCITS scheme* managed by that *firm* or which it intends to manage, and with or for the benefit of which the relevant activity is to be carried on.

Structure and organisation of a management company

10.1.19 R   FCA

A *management company* must be structured and organised in such a way as to minimise the risk of a *UCITS scheme's*, *EEA UCITS scheme's* or *client's* interests being prejudiced by conflicts of interest between the *management company* and its *clients*, between two of its *clients*, between one of its *clients* and a *UCITS scheme* or an *EEA UCITS scheme*, or between two such *schemes*.

[**Note:** articles 12(1)(b) and 14(1)(d) of the *UCITS Directive*]

Avoidance of conflicts of interest for a management company

10.1.20 R FCA

A *management company* must try to avoid conflicts of interest and, when they cannot be avoided, ensure that the *UCITS schemes* and *EEA UCITS schemes* it manages are fairly treated.

[**Note:** articles 12(1)(b) and 14(1)(d) of the *UCITS Directive*]

Disclosure of conflicts of interest for a management company

10.1.21 R FCA
(1)   Where the organisational or administrative arrangements made by a *management company* for the management of conflicts of interest are not sufficient to ensure, with reasonable confidence, that risks of damage to the interests of the *UCITS scheme* or *EEA UCITS scheme* it manages or of its *unitholders* will be prevented, the *senior personnel* or other competent internal body of the *firm* must be promptly informed in order for them to take any necessary decision to ensure that in all cases the *firm* acts in the best interests of the *scheme* and of its *unitholders*.
(2)   A *management company* must report situations referred to in (1) to the *unitholders* of the *UCITS scheme* or *EEA UCITS scheme* it manages by any appropriate *durable medium* and give reasons for its decision.

[**Note:** articles 20(2) and 20(3) of the *UCITS implementing Directive*]

Collective portfolio management investment firms

10.1.22 R FCA

A *collective portfolio management investment firm* which manages investments other than for an *AIF* or *UCITS* for which it has been appointed as manager, must obtain approval from its *client* before it invests all or part of the *client's* portfolio in *units* or *shares* of an *AIF* or *UCITS* it manages.

[**Note**: article 12(2)(a) of the *UCITS Directive* and article 12(2)(a) of *AIFMD*]

Additional requirements for an AIFM

10.1.23 R FCA

An *AIFM* must take all reasonable steps to identify conflicts of interest that arise, in the course of managing *AIFs*, between:
(1)   the *AIFM*, including its managers, *employees* or any person directly or indirectly linked to the *AIFM* by *control*, and an *AIF* managed by the *AIFM* or the investors in that *AIF*; or
(2)   an *AIF* or the investors in that *AIF*, and another *AIF* or the investors in that *AIF*; or
(3)   an *AIF* or the investors in that *AIF*, and another *client* of the *AIFM*; or
(4)   an *AIF* or the investors in that *AIF*, and a *UCITS* managed by the *AIFM* or the investors in that *UCITS*; or
(5)   two *clients* of the *AIFM*.

[**Note**: article 14(1) first paragraph of *AIFMD*]

10.1.24 R FCA

An *AIFM* must take all reasonable steps to avoid conflicts of interest and, when they cannot be avoided, manage, monitor and (where applicable) disclose those conflicts of interest in order to prevent them from adversely affecting the interests of the *AIFs* and their investors, and to ensure that the *AIFs* it manages are fairly treated.

[**Note**: article 12(1)d of *AIFMD*]

10.1.25 R FCA

An *AIFM* must:
(1)   maintain and operate effective organisational and administrative arrangements, with a view to taking all reasonable steps designed to identify, prevent, manage and monitor conflicts of interest in order to prevent them from adversely affecting the interests of the *AIFs* and their investors;
(2)   segregate, within its own operating environment, tasks and responsibilities which may be regarded as incompatible with each other or which may potentially generate systematic conflicts of interest; and
(3)   assess whether its operating conditions may involve any other material conflicts of interest and disclose them to the *AIF's* investors.

[**Note**: article 14(1) second and third paragraphs of *AIFMD*]

10.1.26 R   FCA

If the organisational arrangements made by the *AIFM* to identify, prevent, manage and monitor conflicts of interest are not sufficient to ensure, with reasonable confidence, that risks of damage to investors' interests will be prevented, the *AIFM* must:

(1)   clearly disclose the general nature or sources of conflicts of interest to the investors before undertaking business on their behalf; and

(2)   develop appropriate policies and procedures.

[**Note**: article 14(2) of *AIFMD*]

Subordinate measures for alternative investment fund managers

10.1.27 G   FCA

Articles 30 to 37 of the *AIFMD level 2 regulation* provide detailed rules supplementing the provisions of article 14 of *AIFMD*.

10.2   CHINESE WALLS

Application

10.2.1 R   FCA PRA

This section applies to any *firm*.

Control of information

10.2.2 R   FCA PRA

(1)   When a *firm* establishes and maintains a *Chinese wall* (that is, an arrangement that requires information held by a *person* in the course of carrying on one part of the business to be withheld from, or not to be used for, *persons* with or for whom it acts in the course of carrying on another part of its business) it may:

    (a)   withhold or not use the information held; and

    (b)   for that purpose, permit *persons* employed in the first part of its business to withhold the information held from those employed in that other part of the business;

but only to the extent that the business of one of those parts involves the carrying on of *regulated activities*, *ancillary activities* or, in the case of *MiFID business*, the provision of *ancillary services*.

(2)   Information may also be withheld or not used by a *firm* when this is required by an established arrangement maintained between different parts of the business (of any kind) in the same *group*. This provision does not affect any requirement to transmit or use information that may arise apart from the *rules* in COBS.

(3)   For the purpose of this *rule*, "maintains" includes taking reasonable steps to ensure that the arrangements remain effective and are adequately monitored, and must be interpreted accordingly.

(4)   For the purposes of section 118A(5)(a) of the *Act*, behaviour conforming with paragraph (1) does not amount to market abuse.

Effect of rules

10.2.3 G   FCA PRA

SYSC 10.2.2 R is made under section 137P of the *Act* (Control of information rules). It has the following effect:

(1)   acting in conformity with **SYSC 10.2.2R (1)** provides a defence against proceedings brought under sections 89(2), 90(1) and 91(1) of the Financial Services Act 2012 (Misleading statements, Misleading impressions and Misleading statements etc. in relation to benchmarks) – see sections 89(3)(b), 90(9)(c) and 91(3)(b).

(2)   behaviour in conformity with **SYSC 10.2.2R (1)** does not amount to *market abuse* (see **SYSC 10.2.2R (4)**); and

(3)   acting in conformity with **SYSC 10.2.2R (1)** provides a defence for a firm against *FCA* enforcement action, or an action for damages under section 138D of the *Act*, based on a breach of a relevant requirement to disclose or use this information.

Attribution of knowledge

10.2.4 R   FCA PRA

When any of the *rules* of COBS or CASS apply to a *firm* that acts with knowledge, the *firm* will not be taken to act with knowledge for the purposes of that *rule* if none of the relevant individuals involved on behalf of the *firm* acts with that knowledge as a result of arrangements established under **SYSC 10.2.2 R**.

10.2.5 G   FCA PRA

When a *firm* manages a conflict of interest using the arrangements in **SYSC 10.2.2 R** which take the form of a *Chinese wall*, individuals on the other side of the wall will not be regarded as being in possession of knowledge denied to them as a result of the *Chinese wall*.

CHAPTER 11
LIQUIDITY RISK SYSTEMS AND CONTROLS

11.1   APPLICATION

[3.17]
11.1.1 R   PRA

SYSC 11 applies to an *insurer*, unless it is:
(1)   a *non-directive friendly society*; or
(2)   a *Swiss general insurer*; or
(3)   an *EEA-deposit insurer*; or
(4)   an *incoming EEA firm*; or
(5)   an *incoming Treaty firm*.

11.1.2 R

[deleted]

11.1.3 R

[deleted]

11.1.4 R

[deleted]

11.1.5 G
(1)   [deleted]
(2)   [deleted]

11.1.6 R   PRA

If a *firm* carries on:
(1)   *long-term insurance business*; and
(2)   *general insurance business*;

SYSC 11 applies separately to each type of business.

Purpose

11.1.7 G   PRA

The purpose of **SYSC 11** is to amplify *GENPRU* and *SYSC* in their specific application to *liquidity risk* and, in so doing, to indicate minimum standards for systems and controls in respect of that risk.

11.1.8 G   PRA

Appropriate systems and controls for the management of *liquidity risk* will vary with the scale, nature and complexity of the *firm's* activities. Most of the material in **SYSC 11** is, therefore, *guidance*. **SYSC 11** lays out some of the main issues that the *PRA* expects a *firm* to consider in relation to *liquidity risk*. A *firm* should assess the appropriateness of any particular item of *guidance* in the light of the scale, nature and complexity of its activities as well as its obligations to organise and control its affairs responsibly and effectively.

11.1.9 G   PRA

SYSC 11 addresses the need to have appropriate systems and controls to deal both with liquidity management issues under normal market conditions, and with stressed or extreme situations resulting from either general market turbulence or *firm*-specific difficulties.

11.1.10 G

[deleted]

11.1.11 R

[deleted]

11.1.12 R

[deleted]

11.1.13 G   PRA

An *insurer* is also required to comply with the requirements in relation to *liquidity risk* set out in **INSPRU 4.1**.

11.1.14 G

[deleted]

11.1.15 G

[deleted]

11.1.16 G

[deleted]

11.1.17 G   PRA

High level requirements in relation to carrying out stress testing and scenario analysis are set out in GENPRU 1.2. In particular, GENPRU 1.2.42R requires a *firm* to carry out appropriate stress testing and scenario analysis. **SYSC 11** gives *guidance* in relation to these tests in the case of *liquidity risk*.

Stress testing and scenario analysis

11.1.18 G   PRA

The effect of GENPRU 1.2.30R, GENPRU 1.2.34R, GENPRU 1.2.37R(1) and GENPRU 1.2.42R is that, for the purposes of determining the adequacy of its overall financial resources, a *firm* must carry out appropriate stress testing and scenario analysis, including taking reasonable steps to identify an appropriate range of realistic adverse circumstances and events in which *liquidity risk* might occur or crystallise.

11.1.19 G   PRA

GENPRU 1.2.40G and GENPRU 1.2.62G to GENPRU 1.2.78G give *guidance* on stress testing and scenario analysis, including on how to choose appropriate scenarios, but the precise scenarios that a *firm* chooses to use will depend on the nature of its activities. For the purposes of testing *liquidity risk*, however, a *firm* should normally consider scenarios based on varying degrees of stress and both *firm*-specific and market-wide difficulties. In developing any scenario of extreme market-wide stress that may pose systemic risk, it may be appropriate for a *firm* to make assumptions about the likelihood and nature of central bank intervention.

11.1.20 G   PRA

A *firm* should review frequently the assumptions used in stress testing scenarios to gain assurance that they continue to be appropriate.

11.1.21E .PRA

(1)   A scenario analysis in relation to *liquidity risk* required under GENPRU 1.2.42R should include a cash-flow projection for each scenario tested, based on reasonable estimates of the impact (both on and off balance sheet) of that scenario on the *firm's* funding needs and sources.

(2)   Contravention of (1) may be relied on as tending to establish contravention of GENPRU 1.2.42R.

11.1.22 G   PRA

In identifying the possible on and off balance sheet impact referred to in **SYSC 11.1.21E (1)**, a *firm* may take into account:

(1)   possible changes in the market's perception of the *firm* and the effects that this might have on the *firm's* access to the markets, including:

     (a)   (where the *firm* funds its holdings of assets in one currency with liabilities in another) access to foreign exchange markets, particularly in less frequently traded currencies;

     (b)   access to secured funding, including by way of repo transactions; and

     (c)   the extent to which the *firm* may rely on committed facilities made available to it;

(2)   (if applicable) the possible effect of each scenario analysed on currencies whose exchange rates are currently pegged or fixed; and

(3)   that:

     (a)   general market turbulence may trigger a substantial increase in the extent to which *persons* exercise rights against the *firm* under off balance sheet instruments to which the *firm* is party;

     (b)   access to *OTC derivative* and foreign exchange markets are sensitive to credit-ratings;

     (c)   the scenario may involve the triggering of early amortisation in asset securitisation transactions with which the *firm* has a connection; and

     (d)   its ability to securitise assets may be reduced.

Contingency funding plans

11.1.23 G   PRA

GENPRU 1.2.26R states that a *firm* must at all times maintain overall financial resources adequate to ensure that there is no significant risk that its liabilities cannot be met as they fall due. GENPRU 1.2.42R(1)(b) provides that for the purposes of determining the adequacy of its overall financial resources, a *firm* must estimate the financial resources it would need in each of the circumstances and events considered in carrying out its stress testing and scenario analysis in order to, inter alia, meet its liabilities as they fall due.

11.1.24E .PRA

(1)   A *firm* should have an adequately documented *contingency funding plan* for taking action to ensure, so far as it can, that, in each of the scenarios analysed under GENPRU 1.2.42R(1)(b), it would still have sufficient liquid financial resources to meet liabilities as they fall due.

(2)   The *contingency funding plan* should cover what events or circumstances will lead the *firm* to put into action any part of the plan.

(3)   [deleted]

(4)   A *firm's contingency funding plan* should, where relevant, take account of the impact of stressed market conditions on:

(a)   the behaviour of any credit-sensitive liabilities it has; and

(b)   its ability to securitise assets.

(5)   A *firm's contingency funding plan* should contain administrative policies and procedures that will enable the *firm* to manage the plan's implementation effectively, including:

(a)   the responsibilities of senior management;

(b)   names and contact details of members of the team responsible for implementing the *contingency funding plan*;

(c)   where, geographically, team members will be assigned;

(d)   who within the team is responsible for contact with head office (if appropriate), analysts, investors, external auditors, press, significant *client's*, regulators, lawyers and others; and

(e)   mechanisms that enable senior management and the *governing body* to receive management information that is both relevant and timely.

(6)   Contravention of any of (1) to (5) may be relied upon as tending to establish contravention of GENPRU 1.2.30R(2)(c).

Documentation

11.1.25 G   PRA

GENPRU 1.2.60R requires a *firm* to document its assessment of the adequacy of its liquidity financial resources, how it intends to deal with those risks, and details of the stress tests and scenario analyses carried out and the resulting financial resources estimated to be required. Accordingly, a *firm* should document both its stress testing and scenario analysis (see **SYSC 11.1.18 G**) and its *contingency funding plan* (see **SYSC 11.1.23 G**).

11.1.26 G

[deleted]

11.1.27 G

[deleted]

11.1.28 G

[deleted

11.1.29 G

[deleted]

11.1.30 G

[deleted]

11.1.31 G

[deleted]

11.1.32 G

[deleted]

CHAPTER 12
GROUP RISK SYSTEMS AND CONTROLS REQUIREMENTS

12.1   APPLICATION

[3.18]

12.1.1 R   FCA PRA

Subject to **SYSC 12.1.2 R** to **SYSC 12.1.4 R**, this section applies to each of the following which is a member of a *group*:

(1)   a *firm* that falls into any one or more of the following categories:

(a)   a *regulated entity*;

    (b)   [deleted]
    (c)   an *insurer*;
    (d)   a *BIPRU firm*;
    (e)   a non-*BIPRU firm* that is a *parent financial holding company in a Member State* and is a member of a *UK consolidation group*; and
    (f)   a *firm* subject to the *rules* in *IPRU(INV)* Chapter 14.
(2)   a *UCITS firm*, but only if its *group* contains a *firm* falling into (1); and
(3)   the *Society*.

12.1.2 R   FCA PRA

Except as set out in **SYSC 12.1.4 R**, this section applies with respect to different types of *group* as follows:
(1)   **SYSC 12.1.8 R** and **SYSC 12.1.10 R** apply with respect to all *groups*, including UK-regulated *EEA financial conglomerates*, other *financial conglomerates* and *groups* dealt with in **SYSC 12.1.13 R** to **SYSC 12.1.16 R**;
(2)   the additional requirements set out in **SYSC 12.1.11 R** and **SYSC 12.1.12 R** only apply with respect to UK-regulated *EEA financial conglomerates*; and
(3)   the additional requirements set out in **SYSC 12.1.13 R** to **SYSC 12.1.16 R** only apply with respect to *groups* of the kind dealt with by whichever of those *rules* apply.

12.1.3 R   FCA PRA

This section does not apply to:
(1)   an *incoming EEA firm*; or
(2)   an *incoming Treaty firm*; or
(3)   a *UCITS qualifier*; or
(4)   an *ICVC*; or
(5)   an *incoming ECA provider* acting as such.

12.1.4 R   FCA PRA
(1)   This *rule* applies in respect of the following *rules*:
    (a)   **SYSC 12.1.8R (2)**;
    (b)   **SYSC 12.1.10R (1)**, so far as it relates to **SYSC 12.1.8R (2)**;
    (c)   **SYSC 12.1.10R (2)**; and
    (d)   **SYSC 12.1.11 R** to **SYSC 12.1.15 R**.
(2)   The *rules* referred to in (1):
    (a)   only apply with respect to a *financial conglomerate* if it is a UK-regulated *EEA financial conglomerate*;
    (b)   (so far as they apply with respect to a *group* that is not a *financial conglomerate*) do not apply with respect to a *group* for which a *competent authority* in another *EEA state* is lead regulator;
    (c)   (so far as they apply with respect to a *financial conglomerate*) do not apply to a *firm* with respect to a *financial conglomerate* of which it is a member if the interest of the *financial conglomerate* in that *firm* is no more than a *participation*;
    (d)   (so far as they apply with respect to other *groups*) do not apply to a *firm* with respect to a *group* of which it is a member if the only relationship of the kind set out in paragraph (3) of the definition of *group* between it and the other members of the *group* is nothing more than a *participation*; and
    (e)   do not apply with respect to a *third-country group*.

12.1.5 G   FCA PRA

For the purpose of this section, a *group* is defined in the *Glossary*, and includes the whole of a *firm's* group, including financial and non-financial undertakings. It also covers undertakings with other links to *group* members if their omission from the scope of *group* risk systems and controls would be misleading. The scope of the *group* systems and controls requirements may therefore differ from the scope of the quantitative requirements for *groups*.

Purpose

12.1.6 G   FCA PRA

The purpose of this chapter is to set out how the systems and control requirements imposed by *SYSC* (Senior Management Arrangements, Systems and Controls) apply where a *firm* is part of a *group*. If a *firm* is a member of a *group*, it should be able to assess the potential impact of risks arising from other parts of its *group* as well as from its own activities.

12.1.7 G   FCA PRA

This section implements Articles 73(3) (Supervision on a consolidated basis of credit institutions) and 138 (Intra-group transactions with mixed activity holding companies) of the *Banking Consolidation Directive*, Article 9 of the *Financial Groups Directive* (Internal control mechanisms and risk management processes) and Article 8 of the *Insurance Groups Directive* (Intra-group transactions).

General rules

12.1.8 R   FCA PRA

A *firm* must:
(1)   have adequate, sound and appropriate risk management processes and internal control mechanisms for the purpose of assessing and managing its own exposure to *group* risk, including sound administrative and accounting procedures; and
(2)   ensure that its *group* has adequate, sound and appropriate risk management processes and internal control mechanisms at the level of the *group*, including sound administrative and accounting procedures.

12.1.9 G   FCA PRA

For the purposes of **SYSC 12.1.8 R**, the question of whether the risk management processes and internal control mechanisms are adequate, sound and appropriate should be judged in the light of the nature, scale and complexity of the *group's* business and of the risks that the *group* bears. Risk management processes must include the stress testing and scenario analysis required by **GENPRU 1.2.42 R** and **GENPRU 1.2.49R (1)(B)**.

12.1.10 R   FCA PRA

The internal control mechanisms referred to in **SYSC 12.1.8 R** must include:
(1)   mechanisms that are adequate for the purpose of producing any data and information which would be relevant for the purpose of monitoring compliance with any prudential requirements (including any reporting requirements and any requirements relating to capital adequacy, solvency, systems and controls and large exposures):
        (a)   to which the *firm* is subject with respect to its membership of a *group*; or
        (b)   that apply to or with respect to that *group* or part of it; and
(2)   mechanisms that are adequate to monitor funding within the *group*.

Financial conglomerates

12.1.11 R   FCA PRA

Where this section applies with respect to a *financial conglomerate*, the risk management processes referred to in **SYSC 12.1.8R (2)** must include:
(1)   sound governance and management processes, which must include the approval and periodic review by the appropriate managing bodies within the *financial conglomerate* of the strategies and policies of the *financial conglomerate* in respect of all the risks assumed by the *financial conglomerate*, such review and approval being carried out at the level of the *financial conglomerate*;
(2)   adequate capital adequacy policies at the level of the *financial conglomerate*, one of the purposes of which must be to anticipate the impact of the business strategy of the *financial conglomerate* on its risk profile and on the capital adequacy requirements to which it and its members are subject;
(3)   adequate procedures for the purpose of ensuring that the risk monitoring systems of the *financial conglomerate* and its members are well integrated into their organisation;
(4)   adequate procedures for the purpose of ensuring that the systems and controls of the members of the *financial conglomerate* are consistent and that the risks can be measured, monitored and controlled at the level of the *financial conglomerate*; and
(5)   arrangements in place to contribute to and develop, if required, adequate recovery and resolution arrangements and plans; a *firm* must update these arrangements regularly.

[**Note**: article 9(2) of the *Financial Groups Directive*]

12.1.12 R   FCA PRA

Where this section applies with respect to a *financial conglomerate*, the internal control mechanisms referred to in **SYSC 12.1.8R (2)** must include:
(1)   mechanisms that are adequate to identify and measure all material risks incurred by members of the *financial conglomerate* and appropriately relate capital in the *financial conglomerate* to risks; and
(2)   sound reporting and accounting procedures for the purpose of identifying, measuring, monitoring and controlling *intra-group transactions* and *risk concentrations*.

CRR firms and non-CRR firms that are parent financial holding companies in a Member State

12.1.13 R   FCA PRA

If this *rule* applies under **SYSC 12.1.14 R** to a *firm*, the *firm* must:
(1)   comply with **SYSC 12.1.8R (2)** in relation to any *UK consolidation group* or non- *EEA sub-group* of which it is a member, as well as in relation to its *group*; and
(2)   ensure that the risk management processes and internal control mechanisms at the level of any *consolidation group* or non-*EEA sub-group* of which it is a member comply with the obligations set out in the following provisions on a consolidated (or sub-consolidated) basis:

(a) **SYSC 4.1.1 R** and **SYSC 4.1.2 R**;
(b) **SYSC 4.1.7 R**;
(c) **SYSC 4.3A**;
(d) **SYSC 5.1.7 R**;
(e) **SYSC 7**;
(f) the *Remuneration Code* or the *dual-regulated firms Remuneration Code*, whichever is applicable;
(g) **BIPRU 12.3.4 R, BIPRU 12.3.5 R, BIPRU 12.3.7A R, BIPRU 12.3.8 R, BIPRU 12.3.22A R, BIPRU 12.3.22B R, BIPRU 12.3.27 R, BIPRU 12.4.-2 R, BIPRU 12.4.-1 R, BIPRU 12.4.5A R, BIPRU 12.4.10 R, BIPRU 12.4.11 R** and **BIPRU 12.4.11A R**;
(h) [deleted];
(i) [deleted];
(j) [deleted];
[**Note**: article 109(2) of *CRD*]

(3)   ensure that compliance with the obligations in (2) enables the consolidation group or the *non-EEA sub-group* to have arrangements, processes and mechanisms that are consistent and well integrated and that any data relevant to the purpose of supervision can be produced.
[**Note**: article 109(2) of *CRD*]

12.1.13A R   PRA

When applying **SYSC 12.1.13 R**, *CRR firms* must read references to:
(1)   **SYSC 4.1.1 R** and **SYSC 4.1.2 R** as references to General Organisation Requirements 2.1 and 2.2 of the *PRA* Rulebook;
(2)   **SYSC 4.1.7 R** as a reference to General Organisation Requirement 2.6 of the *PRA* Rulebook;
(3)   **SYSC 4.3A** as a reference to chapters 5 and 6 of the General Organisation Requirements Part of the *PRA* Rulebook;
(4)   **SYSC 5.1.7 R** as a reference to Skills, Knowledge and Expertise 3.2 of the *PRA* Rulebook;
(5)   **SYSC 7** as a reference to Chapters 2 and 3 of the Risk Control Part of the *PRA* Rulebook;

12.1.14 R   FCA PRA

SYSC 12.1.13 R applies to a *firm* that is:
(1)   [deleted]
(2)   a *CRR firm*; or
(3)   a non-*CRR firm* that is a *parent financial holding company in a Member State* and is a member of a *UK consolidation group*.

12.1.15 R   FCA PRA

In the case of a *firm* that:
(1)   is a *CRR firm*; and
(2)   has a *mixed-activity holding company* as a *parent undertaking*;

the risk management processes and internal control mechanisms referred to in **SYSC 12.1.8 R** must include sound reporting and accounting procedures and other mechanisms that are adequate to identify, measure, monitor and control transactions between the *firm's parent undertaking mixed-activity holding company* and any of the *mixed-activity holding company's subsidiary undertakings*.

12.1.15A R   FCA

SYSC 12.1.13 R applies to a *BIPRU firm* as if it were a *CRR firm* but the reference to *Remuneration Code* is to the *BIPRU Remuneration Code*.

Insurance undertakings

12.1.16 R   PRA

In the case of an *insurer* that has a *mixed-activity insurance holding company* as a *parent undertaking*, the risk management processes and internal control mechanisms referred to in **SYSC 12.1.8 R** must include sound reporting and accounting procedures and other mechanisms that are adequate to identify, measure, monitor and control transactions between the *firm's parent undertaking mixed-activity insurance holding company* and any of the *mixed-activity insurance holding company's subsidiary undertakings*.

12.1.17 G   PRA

SYSC 12.1.16 R cannot apply to a *building society* as it cannot have a *mixed-activity holding company* as a *parent undertaking*. **SYSC 12.1.16 R** cannot apply to a *friendly society* as it cannot have a *mixed-activity insurance holding company* as a *parent undertaking*.

Nature and extent of requirements and allocation of responsibilities within the group

12.1.18 G   FCA PRA

Assessment of the adequacy of a *group's* systems and controls required by this section will form part of the *appropriate regulator's* risk management process.

12.1.19 G   FCA PRA

The nature and extent of the systems and controls necessary under **SYSC 12.1.8R (1)** to address *group* risk will vary according to the materiality of those risks to the *firm* and the position of the *firm* within the *group*.

12.1.20 G   FCA PRA

In some cases the management of the systems and controls used to address the risks described in **SYSC 12.1.8R (1)** may be organised on a *group*-wide basis. If the *firm* is not carrying out those functions itself, it should delegate them to the *group* members that are carrying them out. However, this does not relieve the *firm* of responsibility for complying with its obligations under **SYSC 12.1.8R (1)**. A *firm* cannot absolve itself of such a responsibility by claiming that any breach of that *rule* is caused by the actions of another member of the *group* to whom the *firm* has delegated tasks. The risk management arrangements are still those of the *firm*, even though personnel elsewhere in the *firm's group* are carrying out these functions on its behalf.

12.1.21 G   FCA PRA

SYSC 12.1.8R (1) deals with the systems and controls that a *firm* should have in respect of the exposure it has to the rest of the *group*. On the other hand, the purpose of **SYSC 12.1.8R (2)** and the *rules* in this section that amplify it is to require *groups* to have adequate systems and controls. However a *group* is not a single legal entity on which obligations can be imposed. Therefore the obligations have to be placed on individual *firms*. The purpose of imposing the obligations on each *firm* in the *group* is to make sure that the *appropriate regulator* can take supervisory action against any *firm* in a *group* whose systems and controls do not meet the standards in this section. Thus responsibility for compliance with the *rules* for *group* systems and controls is a joint one.

12.1.22 G   FCA PRA

If both a *firm* and its *parent undertaking* are subject to **SYSC 12.1.8R (2)**, the *appropriate regulator* would not expect systems and controls to be duplicated. In this case, the *firm* should assess whether and to what extent it can rely on its parent's *group* risk systems and controls.

CHAPTER 13
OPERATIONAL RISK: SYSTEMS AND CONTROLS FOR INSURERS

13.1   APPLICATION

[3.19]
13.1.1 G   FCA PRA

SYSC 13 applies to an *insurer* unless it is:
(1)   a *non-directive friendly society*; or
(2)   an *incoming EEA firm*; or
(3)   an *incoming Treaty firm*.

13.1.2 G   FCA PRA

SYSC 13 applies to:
(1)   an *EEA-deposit insurer*; and
(2)   a *Swiss general insurer*;

only in respect of the activities of the *firm* carried on from a *branch* in the *United Kingdom*.

13.1.3 G   FCA PRA

SYSC 13 applies to a *UK ISPV*.

13.1.4 G   FCA PRA

SYSC 13 does not apply to an *incoming ECA provider* acting as such.

13.2   PURPOSE

13.2.1 G   FCA PRA

SYSC 13 provides *guidance* on how to interpret **SYSC 3.1.1 R** and **SYSC 3.2.6 R**, which deal with the establishment and maintenance of systems and controls, in relation to the management of operational risk. Operational risk has been described by the Basel Committee on Banking Supervision as "the risk of loss, resulting from inadequate or failed internal processes, people and systems, or from external events". This chapter covers systems and controls for managing risks concerning any of a *firm's* operations, such as its IT systems and *outsourcing* arrangements. It does not cover systems and controls for managing credit, market, liquidity and insurance risk.

13.2.2 G   FCA PRA

Operational risk is a concept that can have a different application for different *firms*. A *firm* should assess the appropriateness of the *guidance* in this chapter in the light of the scale, nature and complexity of its activities as well as its obligations as set out in *Principle* 3, to organise and control its affairs responsibly and effectively.

13.2.3 G   FCA PRA

A *firm* should take steps to understand the types of operational risk that are relevant to its particular circumstances, and the operational losses to which they expose the *firm*. This should include considering the potential sources of operational risk addressed in this chapter: people; processes and systems; external events.

13.2.4 G

[deleted]

13.2.4A G   FCA

Operational risk can, amongst other things, lead to unfair treatment of consumers or lead to financial crime. A *firm* should consider all operational risk events that may affect these matters in establishing and maintaining its systems and controls.

13.2.4B G   PRA

Operational risk can affect, amongst other things, a *firm's* solvency. A *firm* should consider all operational risk events that may affect these matters in establishing and maintaining its systems and controls.

13.3   OTHER RELATED HANDBOOK SECTIONS

13.3.1 G

[deleted]

13.3.1A G   FCA

The following is a non-exhaustive list of *rules* and *guidance* in the *Handbook* that are relevant to a *firm's* management of operational risk:

(1)   *COBS* contains *rules* and *guidance* that can relate to the management of operational risk; for example, **COBS 2** (Conduct of business obligations), **COBS 4** (Communicating with clients, including financial promotions), **COBS 6** (Information about the firm, its services and remuneration), **COBS 7** (Insurance mediation), **COBS 9** (Suitability (including basic advice)), **COBS 11** (Dealing and managing), **COBS 12** (Investment research), **COBS 14** (Providing product information to clients) and **COBS 19** (Pensions: supplementary provisions).

13.3.1B G   PRA

The following is a non-exhaustive list of *rules* and *guidance* in the *Handbook* that are relevant to a *firm's* management of operational risk:

(1)   **SYSC 14** and **INSPRU 5.1** contain specific *rules* and *guidance* for the establishment and maintenance of operational risk systems and controls.

13.4   REQUIREMENTS TO NOTIFY THE APPROPRIATE REGULATOR

13.4.1 G   FCA PRA

Under *Principle* 11 and **SUP 15.3.1 R**, a *firm* must notify the *appropriate regulator* immediately of any operational risk matter of which the *appropriate regulator* would reasonably expect notice. **SUP 15.3.8 G** provides *guidance* on the occurrences that this requirement covers, which include a significant failure in systems and controls and a significant operational loss.

13.4.2 G   FCA PRA

Regarding operational risk, matters of which the *appropriate regulator* would expect notice under *Principle* 11 include:

(1)   any significant operational exposures that a *firm* has identified;

(2)   the *firm's* invocation of a business continuity plan; and

(3)   any other significant change to a *firm's* organisation, infrastructure or business operating environment.

13.5   RISK MANAGEMENT TERMS

13.5.1 G   FCA PRA

In this chapter, the following interpretations of risk management terms apply:

(1)   a *firm's* risk culture encompasses the general awareness, attitude and behaviour of its *employees* and *appointed representatives* or, where applicable, its *tied agents*, to risk and the management of risk within the organisation;

(2)   operational exposure means the degree of operational risk faced by a *firm* and is usually expressed in terms of the likelihood and impact of a particular type of operational loss occurring (for example, fraud, damage to physical assets);

(3)   a *firm's* operational risk profile describes the types of operational risks that it faces, including those operational risks within a *firm* that may have an adverse impact upon the quality of service afforded to its *clients*, and its exposure to these risks.

13.6   PEOPLE

13.6.1 G   FCA PRA

A *firm* should consult **SYSC 3.2.2 G** to **SYSC 3.2.5 G** for *guidance* on reporting lines and delegation of functions within a *firm* and **SYSC 3.2.13 G** to **SYSC 3.2.14 G** for *guidance* on the suitability of *employees* and *appointed representatives* or, where applicable, its *tied agents*. This section provides additional *guidance* on management of *employees* and other human resources in the context of operational risk.

13.6.2 G   FCA PRA

A *firm* should establish and maintain appropriate systems and controls for the management of operational risks that can arise from *employees*. In doing so, a *firm* should have regard to:

(1)   its operational risk culture, and any variations in this or its human resource management practices, across its operations (including, for example, the extent to which the compliance culture is extended to in-house IT staff);

(2)   whether the way *employees* are remunerated exposes the *firm* to the risk that it will not be able to meet its regulatory obligations (see **SYSC 3.2.18 G**). For example, a *firm* should consider how well remuneration and performance indicators reflect the *firm's* tolerance for operational risk, and the adequacy of these indicators for measuring performance;

(3)   whether inadequate or inappropriate training of *client*-facing services exposes *clients* to risk of loss or unfair treatment including by not enabling effective communication with the *firm*;

(4)   the extent of its compliance with applicable regulatory and other requirements that relate to the welfare and conduct of *employees*;

(5)   its arrangements for the continuity of operations in the event of *employee* unavailability or loss;

(6)   the relationship between indicators of 'people risk' (such as overtime, sickness, and *employee* turnover levels) and exposure to operational losses; and

(7)   the relevance of all the above to *employees* of a third party supplier who are involved in performing an *outsourcing* arrangement. As necessary, a *firm* should review and consider the adequacy of the staffing arrangements and policies of a service provider.

Employee responsibilities

13.6.3 G   FCA PRA

A *firm* should ensure that all *employees* are capable of performing, and aware of, their operational risk management responsibilities, including by establishing and maintaining:

(1)   appropriate segregation of *employees'* duties and appropriate supervision of *employees* in the performance of their responsibilities (see **SYSC 3.2.5 G**);

(2)   appropriate recruitment and subsequent processes to review the fitness and propriety of *employees* (see **SYSC 3.2.13 G** and **SYSC 3.2.14 G**);

(3)   clear policy statements and appropriate systems and procedures manuals that are effectively communicated to *employees* and available for *employees* to refer to as required. These should cover, for example, compliance, IT security and health and safety issues;

(4)   training processes that enable *employees* to attain and maintain appropriate competence; and

(5)   appropriate and properly enforced disciplinary and employment termination policies and procedures.

13.6.4 G   FCA PRA

A *firm* should have regard to **SYSC 13.6.3 G** in relation to *approved persons*, people occupying positions of high personal trust (for example, security administration, payment and settlement functions); and people occupying positions requiring significant technical competence (for example, *derivatives* trading and technical security administration). A *firm* should also consider the *rules* and *guidance* for *approved persons* in other parts of the *Handbook* (including *APER* and *SUP*) and the *rules* and *guidance* on *senior manager* responsibilities in **SYSC 2.1** (Apportionment of Responsibilities).

13.7   PROCESSES AND SYSTEMS

13.7.1 G   FCA PRA

A *firm* should establish and maintain appropriate systems and controls for managing operational risks that can arise from inadequacies or failures in its processes and systems (and, as appropriate, the systems and processes of third party suppliers, agents and others). In doing so a *firm* should have regard to:

(1)   the importance and complexity of processes and systems used in the end-to-end operating cycle for products and activities (for example, the level of integration of systems);

(2)   controls that will help it to prevent system and process failures or identify them to permit prompt rectification (including pre-approval or reconciliation processes);

(3)   whether the design and use of its processes and systems allow it to comply adequately with regulatory and other requirements;

(4)   its arrangements for the continuity of operations in the event that a significant process or system becomes unavailable or is destroyed; and

(5)   the importance of monitoring indicators of process or system risk (including reconciliation exceptions, compensation payments for *client* losses and documentation errors) and experience of operational losses and exposures.

Internal documentation

13.7.2 G   FCA PRA

Internal documentation may enhance understanding and aid continuity of operations, so a *firm* should ensure the adequacy of its internal documentation of processes and systems (including how documentation is developed, maintained and distributed) in managing operational risk.

External documentation

13.7.3 G   FCA PRA

A *firm* may use external documentation (including contracts, transaction statements or advertising brochures) to define or clarify terms and conditions for its products or activities, its business strategy (for example, including through press statements), or its brand. Inappropriate or inaccurate information in external documents can lead to significant operational exposure.

13.7.4 G   FCA PRA

A *firm* should ensure the adequacy of its processes and systems to review external documentation prior to issue (including review by its compliance, legal and marketing departments or by appropriately qualified external advisers). In doing so, a *firm* should have regard to:

(1)   compliance with applicable regulatory and other requirements;

(2)   the extent to which its documentation uses standard terms (that are widely recognised, and have been tested in the courts) or non-standard terms (whose meaning may not yet be settled or whose effectiveness may be uncertain);

(3)   the manner in which its documentation is issued; and

(4)   the extent to which confirmation of acceptance is required (including by *customer* signature or counterparty confirmation).

IT systems

13.7.5 G   FCA PRA

IT systems include the computer systems and infrastructure required for the automation of processes, such as application and operating system software; network infrastructure; and desktop, server, and mainframe hardware. Automation may reduce a *firm's* exposure to some 'people risks' (including by reducing human errors or controlling access rights to enable segregation of duties), but will increase its dependency on the reliability of its IT systems.

13.7.6 G   FCA PRA

A *firm* should establish and maintain appropriate systems and controls for the management of its IT system risks, having regard to:

(1)   its organisation and reporting structure for technology operations (including the adequacy of senior management oversight);

(2)   the extent to which technology requirements are addressed in its business strategy;

(3)   the appropriateness of its systems acquisition, development and maintenance activities (including the allocation of responsibilities between IT development and operational areas, processes for embedding security requirements into systems); and

(4)   the appropriateness of its activities supporting the operation of IT systems (including the allocation of responsibilities between business and technology areas).

Information security

13.7.7 G   FCA PRA

Failures in processing information (whether physical, electronic or known by *employees* but not recorded) or of the security of the systems that maintain it can lead to significant operational losses. A *firm* should establish and maintain appropriate systems and controls to manage its information security risks. In doing so, a *firm* should have regard to:

(1)   confidentiality: information should be accessible only to *persons* or systems with appropriate
       authority, which may require firewalls within a system, as well as entry restrictions;
(2)   integrity: safeguarding the accuracy and completeness of information and its processing;
(3)   availability and authentication: ensuring that appropriately authorised *persons* or systems
       have access to the information when required and that their identity is verified;
(4)   non-repudiation and accountability: ensuring that the *person* or system that processed the
       information cannot deny their actions.

13.7.8 G   FCA PRA

A *firm* should ensure the adequacy of the systems and controls used to protect the processing and
security of its information, and should have regard to established security standards such as
ISO17799 (Information Security Management).

Geographic location

13.7.9 G   FCA PRA

Operating processes and systems at separate geographic locations may alter a *firm's* operational risk
profile (including by allowing alternative sites for the continuity of operations). A *firm* should
understand the effect of any differences in processes and systems at each of its locations, particularly
if they are in different countries, having regard to:
(1)   the business operating environment of each country (for example, the likelihood and impact
       of political disruptions or cultural differences on the provision of services);
(2)   relevant local regulatory and other requirements regarding data protection and transfer;
(3)   the extent to which local regulatory and other requirements may restrict its ability to meet
       regulatory obligations in the *United Kingdom* (for example, access to information by the
       appropriate regulator and local restrictions on internal or external audit); and
(4)   the timeliness of information flows to and from its headquarters and whether the level of
       delegated authority and the risk management structures of the overseas operation are
       compatible with the *firm's* head office arrangements.

13.8   EXTERNAL EVENTS AND OTHER CHANGES

13.8.1 G   FCA PRA

The exposure of a *firm* to operational risk may increase during times of significant change to its
organisation, infrastructure and business operating environment (for example, following a corporate
restructure or changes in regulatory requirements). Before, during, and after expected changes, a *firm*
should assess and monitor their effect on its risk profile, including with regard to:
(1)   untrained or de-motivated *employees* or a significant loss of *employees* during the period of
       change, or subsequently;
(2)   inadequate human resources or inexperienced *employees* carrying out routine business
       activities owing to the prioritisation of resources to the programme or project;
(3)   process or system instability and poor management information due to failures in integration
       or increased demand; and
(4)   inadequate or inappropriate processes following business re-engineering.

13.8.2 G   FCA PRA

A *firm* should establish and maintain appropriate systems and controls for the management of the
risks involved in expected changes, such as by ensuring:
(1)   the adequacy of its organisation and reporting structure for managing the change (including
       the adequacy of senior management oversight);
(2)   the adequacy of the management processes and systems for managing the change (including
       planning, approval, implementation and review processes); and
(3)   the adequacy of its strategy for communicating changes in systems and controls to its
       employees.

Unexpected changes and business continuity management

13.8.3 G   FCA PRA

SYSC 3.2.19 G provides high level *guidance* on business continuity. This section provides
additional *guidance* on managing business continuity in the context of operational risk.

13.8.4 G   FCA

The high level requirement for appropriate systems and controls at **SYSC 3.1.1 R** applies at all
times, including when a business continuity plan is invoked. However, the *appropriate regulator*
recognises that, in an emergency, a *firm* may be unable to comply with a particular *rule* and the
conditions for relief are outlined in **GEN 1.3** (Emergency).

13.8.4A G   PRA

The high level requirement for appropriate systems and controls at **SYSC 3.1.1 R** applies at all
times, including when a business continuity plan is invoked. However, the *appropriate regulator*

recognises that, in an emergency, a *firm* may be unable to comply with a particular *rule* and the conditions for relief are outlined in Chapter 2 of the General Provisions Part of the *PRA* Rulebook.

13.8.5 G   FCA PRA

A *firm* should consider the likelihood and impact of a disruption to the continuity of its operations from unexpected events. This should include assessing the disruptions to which it is particularly susceptible (and the likely timescale of those disruptions) including through:
(1)   loss or failure of internal and external resources (such as people, systems and other assets);
(2)   the loss or corruption of its information; and
(3)   external events (such as vandalism, war and "acts of God").

13.8.6 G   FCA PRA

A *firm* should implement appropriate arrangements to maintain the continuity of its operations. A *firm* should act to reduce both the likelihood of a disruption (including by succession planning, systems resilience and dual processing); and the impact of a disruption (including by contingency arrangements and insurance).

13.8.7 G   FCA PRA

A *firm* should document its strategy for maintaining continuity of its operations, and its plans for communicating and regularly testing the adequacy and effectiveness of this strategy. A *firm* should establish:
(1)   formal business continuity plans that outline arrangements to reduce the impact of a short, medium or long-term disruption, including:
    (a)   resource requirements such as people, systems and other assets, and arrangements for obtaining these resources;
    (b)   the recovery priorities for the *firm's* operations; and
    (c)   communication arrangements for internal and external concerned parties (including the *appropriate regulator, clients* and the press);
(2)   escalation and invocation plans that outline the processes for implementing the business continuity plans, together with relevant contact information;
(3)   processes to validate the integrity of information affected by the disruption;
(4)   processes to review and update (1) to (3) following changes to the *firm's* operations or risk profile (including changes identified through testing).

13.8.8 G   FCA PRA

The use of an alternative site for recovery of operations is common practice in business continuity management. A *firm* that uses an alternative site should assess the appropriateness of the site, particularly for location, speed of recovery and adequacy of resources. Where a site is shared, a *firm* should evaluate the risk of multiple calls on shared resources and adjust its plans accordingly.

13.9   OUTSOURCING

13.9.1 G   FCA PRA

As **SYSC 3.2.4 G** explains, a *firm* cannot contract out its regulatory obligations and should take reasonable care to supervise the discharge of outsourced functions. This section provides additional *guidance* on managing *outsourcing* arrangements (and will be relevant, to some extent, to other forms of third party dependency) in relation to operational risk. *Outsourcing* may affect a *firm's* exposure to operational risk through significant changes to, and reduced control over, people, processes and systems used in outsourced activities.

13.9.2 G   FCA PRA

Firms should take particular care to manage *material outsourcing* arrangements and, as **SUP 15.3.8 G (1)(E)** explains, a *firm* should notify the *appropriate regulator* when it intends to enter into a *material outsourcing* arrangement.

13.9.3 G   FCA PRA

A *firm* should not assume that because a service provider is either a regulated *firm* or an intra-group entity an *outsourcing* arrangement with that provider will, in itself, necessarily imply a reduction in operational risk.

13.9.4 G   FCA PRA

Before entering into, or significantly changing, an *outsourcing* arrangement, a *firm* should:
(1)   analyse how the arrangement will fit with its organisation and reporting structure; business strategy; overall risk profile; and ability to meet its regulatory obligations;
(2)   consider whether the agreements establishing the arrangement will allow it to monitor and control its operational risk exposure relating to the *outsourcing*;
(3)   conduct appropriate due diligence of the service provider's financial stability and expertise;
(4)   consider how it will ensure a smooth transition of its operations from its current arrangements to a new or changed *outsourcing* arrangement (including what will happen on the termination of the contract); and

Part 3   FCA Handbook Materials

(5)   consider any concentration risk implications such as the business continuity implications that may arise if a single service provider is used by several *firms*.

13.9.5 G   FCA PRA

In negotiating its contract with a service provider, a *firm* should have regard to:

(1)   reporting or notification requirements it may wish to impose on the service provider;

(2)   whether sufficient access will be available to its internal auditors, external auditors or *actuaries* (see section 341 of the *Act*) and to the *appropriate regulator* (see **SUP 2.3.5 R** (Access to premises) and **SUP 2.3.7 R** (Suppliers under material outsourcing arrangements);

(3)   information ownership rights, confidentiality agreements and *Chinese walls* to protect *client* and other information (including arrangements at the termination of the contract);

(4)   the adequacy of any guarantees and indemnities;

(5)   the extent to which the service provider must comply with the *firm's* policies and procedures (covering, for example, information security);

(6)   the extent to which a service provider will provide business continuity for outsourced operations, and whether exclusive access to its resources is agreed;

(7)   the need for continued availability of software following difficulty at a third party supplier;

(8)   the processes for making changes to the *outsourcing* arrangement (for example, changes in processing volumes, activities and other contractual terms) and the conditions under which the *firm* or service provider can choose to change or terminate the *outsourcing* arrangement, such as where there is:

     (a)   a change of ownership or *control* (including insolvency or receivership) of the service provider or *firm*; or

     (b)   significant change in the business operations (including sub-contracting) of the service provider or *firm*; or

     (c)   inadequate provision of services that may lead to the *firm* being unable to meet its regulatory obligations.

13.9.6 G   FCA PRA

In implementing a relationship management framework, and drafting the service level agreement with the service provider, a *firm* should have regard to:

(1)   the identification of qualitative and quantitative performance targets to assess the adequacy of service provision, to both the *firm* and its *clients*, where appropriate;

(2)   the evaluation of performance through service delivery reports and periodic self certification or independent review by internal or external auditors; and

(3)   remedial action and escalation processes for dealing with inadequate performance.

13.9.7 G   FCA PRA

In some circumstances, a *firm* may find it beneficial to use externally validated reports commissioned by the service provider, to seek comfort as to the adequacy and effectiveness of its systems and controls. The use of such reports does not absolve the *firm* of responsibility to maintain other oversight. In addition, the *firm* should not normally have to forfeit its right to access, for itself or its agents, to the service provider's premises.

13.9.8 G   FCA PRA

A *firm* should ensure that it has appropriate contingency arrangements to allow business continuity in the event of a significant loss of services from the service provider. Particular issues to consider include a significant loss of resources at, or financial failure of, the service provider, and unexpected termination of the *outsourcing* arrangement.

13.10   INSURANCE

13.10.1 G   FCA PRA

Whilst a *firm* may take out insurance with the aim of reducing the monetary impact of operational risk events, non-monetary impacts may remain (including impact on the *firm's* reputation). A *firm* should not assume that insurance alone can replace robust systems and controls.

13.10.2 G   FCA PRA

When considering utilising insurance, a *firm* should consider:

(1)   the time taken for the *insurer* to pay claims (including the potential time taken in disputing cover) and the *firm's* funding of operations whilst awaiting payment of claims;

(2)   the financial strength of the *insurer*, which may determine its ability to pay claims, particularly where large or numerous small claims are made at the same time; and

(3)   the effect of any limiting conditions and exclusion clauses that may restrict cover to a small number of specific operational losses and may exclude larger or hard to quantify indirect losses (such as lost business or reputational costs).

CHAPTER 14
RISK MANAGEMENT AND ASSOCIATED SYSTEMS AND CONTROLS FOR INSURERS

14.1　APPLICATION

[3.20]
14.1.1 R　FCA PRA

This section applies to an *insurer* unless it is:
(1)　a *non-directive friendly society*; or
(2)　an *incoming EEA firm*; or
(3)　an *incoming Treaty firm*.

14.1.2 R　FCA PRA

This section applies to:
(1)　an *EEA-deposit insurer*; and
(2)　a *Swiss general insurer*;

only in respect of the activities of the *firm* carried on from a *branch* in the *United Kingdom*.

14.1.2A R　FCA PRA

This section does not apply to an *incoming ECA provider* acting as such.

Purpose

14.1.3 G　PRA

This section sets out some *rules* and *guidance* on the establishment and maintenance of systems and controls for the management of a *firm's* prudential risks. A *firm's* prudential risks are those that can reduce the adequacy of its financial resources, and as a result may adversely affect its safety and soundness or prejudice policyholders. Some key prudential risks are credit, market, liquidity, operational, insurance and group risk.

14.1.4 G　PRA

The purpose of this section is to serve the *PRA's statutory objectives* of promoting the safety and soundness of *PRA-authorised persons* and contributing to the securing of an appropriate degree of protection for those who are, or may become, policyholders. In particular, this section aims to reduce the risk that a *firm* may pose a threat to these *statutory objectives*, either because it is not prudently managed, or because it has inadequate systems to permit appropriate senior management oversight and control of its business.

14.1.5 G　PRA

Both adequate financial resources and adequate systems and controls are necessary for the effective management of prudential risks. A *firm* may hold financial resources to help alleviate the financial consequences of minor weaknesses in its systems and controls (to reflect possible impairments in the accuracy or timing of its identification, measurement, monitoring and control of certain risks, for example). However, financial resources cannot adequately compensate for significant weaknesses in a *firm's* systems and controls that could fundamentally undermine its ability to control its affairs effectively.

How to interpret this section

14.1.6 G　PRA

This section is designed to amplify the requirement that a *firm* must organise and control its affairs responsibly and effectively, and have effective risk strategies and adequate risk management systems. This section is also designed to be complementary to **SYSC 2**, **SYSC 3** and **SYSC 13** in that it contains some additional *rules* and *guidance* on senior management arrangements and associated systems and controls for *firms* that could have a significant impact on the *PRA's* objectives.

14.1.7 G　PRA

In addition to supporting **SYSC 2**, **SYSC 3** and **SYSC 13**, this section lays the foundations for the more specific *rules* and *guidance* on the management of credit, market, liquidity, operational, insurance and group risks that are in **SYSC 11**, **SYSC 12**, **SYSC 15**, **SYSC 16** and **INSPRU 5.1**. Many of the elements raised here in general terms are expanded upon in these sections.

14.1.8 G　PRA

Appropriate systems and controls for the management of prudential risk will vary from *firm* to *firm*. Therefore, most of the material in this section is *guidance*. In interpreting this *guidance*, a *firm* should have regard to its own particular circumstances. Following from **SYSC 3.1.2 G**, this should include considering the nature, scale and complexity of its business, which may be influenced by factors such as:

(1)   the diversity of its operations, including geographical diversity;
(2)   the volume and size of its transactions; and
(3)   the degree of risk associated with each area of its operation.

14.1.9 G   PRA

The *guidance* contained within this section is not designed to be exhaustive. When establishing and maintaining its systems and controls a *firm* should have regard not only to other parts of the *Handbook*, but also to material that is issued by other industry or regulatory bodies.

The role of systems and controls

14.1.10 G   PRA

A *firm's* systems and controls should provide its senior management with an adequate means of managing the *firm*. As such, they should be designed and maintained to ensure that senior management is able to make and implement integrated business planning and risk management decisions on the basis of accurate information about the risks that the *firm* faces and the financial resources that it has.

The prudential responsibilities of senior management and the apportionment of those responsibilities

14.1.11 G   PRA

Ultimate responsibility for the management of prudential risks rests with a *firm's governing body* and relevant *senior managers*, and in particular with those individuals that undertake the *firm's governing functions* and the *apportionment and oversight function*. In particular, these responsibilities should include:
(1)   overseeing the establishment of an appropriate business plan and risk management strategy;
(2)   overseeing the development of appropriate systems for the management of prudential risks;
(3)   establishing adequate *internal controls*; and
(4)   ensuring that the *firm* maintains adequate financial resources.

The delegation of responsibilities within the firm

14.1.12 G   PRA

Although authority for the management of a *firm's* prudential risks is likely to be delegated, to some degree, to individuals at all levels of the organisation, overall responsibility for this activity should not be delegated from its *governing body* and relevant *senior managers*.

14.1.13 G   PRA

Where delegation does occur, a *firm* should ensure that appropriate systems and controls are in place to allow its *governing body* and relevant *senior managers* to participate in and control its prudential risk management activities. The *governing body* and relevant *senior managers* should approve and periodically review these systems and controls to ensure that delegated duties are being performed correctly.

Firms subject to risk management on a group basis

14.1.14 G   PRA

Some *firms* organise the management of their prudential risks on a stand-alone basis. In some cases, however, the management of a *firm's* prudential risks may be entirely or largely subsumed within a whole *group* or *sub-group* basis.
(1)   The latter arrangement may still comply with the *PRA's* policy on systems and controls if the *firm's governing body* formally delegates the functions that are to be carried out in this way to the *persons* or bodies that are to carry them out. Before doing so, however, the *firm's governing body* should have explicitly considered the arrangement and decided that it is appropriate and that it enables the *firm* to meet the *PRA's* policy on systems and controls. The *firm* should notify the *PRA* if the management of its prudential risks is to be carried out in this way.
(2)   Where the management of a *firm's* prudential risks is largely, but not entirely, subsumed within a whole *group* or *sub-group* basis, the *firm* should ensure that any prudential issues that are specific to the *firm* are:
    (a)   identified and adequately covered by those to whom it has delegated certain prudential risk management tasks; or
    (b)   dealt with by the *firm* itself.

14.1.15 G   PRA

Any delegation of the management of prudential risks to another part of a *firm's group* does not relieve it of responsibility for complying with the *PRA's* policy on systems and controls. A *firm* cannot absolve itself of such a responsibility by claiming that any breach of the *PRA's* policy on systems and controls is effected by the actions of a third party *firm* to whom the *firm* has delegated tasks. The risk management arrangements are still those of the *firm*, even though personnel elsewhere in the *firm's group* are carrying out these functions on its behalf. Thus any references in *GENPRU*, *INSPRU* or *SYSC* to what a *firm*, its personnel and its management should and should not do still apply, and do not need any adjustment to cover the situation in which risk management functions are carried out on a *group*-wide basis.

14.1.16 G   PRA

Where it is stated in *GENPRU*, *INSPRU* or *SYSC* that a particular task in relation to a *firm's* systems and controls should be carried out by a *firm's governing body* this task should not be delegated to another part of its *group*. Furthermore, even where the management of a *firm's* prudential risks is delegated as described in **SYSC 14.1.14 G**, responsibility for its effectiveness and for ensuring that it remains appropriate remains with the *firm's governing body*. The *firm's governing body* should therefore keep any delegation under review to ensure that delegated duties are being performed correctly.

Business planning and risk management

14.1.17 G   PRA

Business planning and risk management are closely related activities. In particular, the forward-looking assessment of a *firm's* financial resources needs, and of how business plans may affect the risks that it faces, are important elements of prudential risk management. A *firm's* business planning should also involve the creation of specific risk policies which will normally outline a *firm's* strategy and objectives for, as appropriate, the management of its market, credit, liquidity, operational, insurance and group risks and the processes that it intends to adopt to achieve these objectives. **SYSC 14.1.18 R** to **SYSC 14.1.25 G** set out some *rules* and *guidance* relating to business planning and risk management (see also **SYSC 3.2.17 G**, which states that a *firm* should plan its business appropriately).

14.1.18 R   PRA

A *firm* must take reasonable steps to ensure the establishment and maintenance of a business plan and appropriate systems for the management of prudential risk.

14.1.19 R   PRA

When establishing and maintaining its business plan and prudential risk management systems, a *firm* must document:
(1)   an explanation of its overall business strategy, including its business objectives;
(2)   a description of, as applicable, its policies towards market, credit (including provisioning), liquidity, operational, insurance and group risk (that is, its risk policies), including its appetite or tolerance for these risks and how it identifies, measures or assesses, monitors and controls these risks;
(3)   the systems and controls that it intends to use in order to ensure that its business plan and risk policies are implemented correctly;
(4)   a description of how the *firm* accounts for assets and liabilities, including the circumstances under which items are netted, included or excluded from the *firm's* balance sheet and the methods and assumptions for valuation;
(5)   appropriate financial *projections* and the results of its stress testing and scenario analysis (see *GENPRU* 1.2 (Adequacy of financial resources)); and
(6)   details of, and the justification for, the methods and assumptions used in financial *projections* and stress testing and scenario analysis.

14.1.20 G   PRA

The prudential risk management systems referred to in **SYSC 14.1.18 R** and **SYSC 14.1.19 R** are the means by which a *firm* is able to:
(1)   identify the prudential risks that are inherent in its business plan, operating environment and objectives, and determine its appetite or tolerance for these risks;
(2)   measure or assess its prudential risks;
(3)   monitor its prudential risks; and
(4)   control or mitigate its prudential risks.

INSPRU 4.1.63 E is an *evidential provision* relating to **SYSC 14.1.18 R** concerning risk management systems in respect of *liquidity risk* arising from substantial exposures in foreign currencies.

14.1.21 G   PRA

A *firm* should consider the relationship between its business plan, risk policies and the financial resources that it has available (or can readily access), recognising that decisions made in respect of one element may have consequences for the other two.

14.1.22 G   PRA

A *firm's* business plan and risk management systems should be:

(1) effectively communicated so that all *employees* and contractors understand and adhere to the procedures related to their own responsibilities;

(2) regularly updated and revised, in particular when there is significant new information or when actual practice or performance differs materially from the documented strategy, policy or systems.

14.1.23 G   PRA

The level of detail in a *firm's* business plan and its approach to the design of its risk management systems should be appropriate to the scale and complexity of its operations, and the nature and degree of risk that it faces.

14.1.24 G   PRA

A *firm's* business plan and systems documentation should be accessible to the *firm's* management in line with their respective responsibilities and, upon request, to the *PRA*.

14.1.25 G   PRA

SYSC 14.1.19 R (5) requires a *firm* to *document* its financial projections and the results of its stress testing and scenario analysis. Such financial projections, stress tests and scenario analysis should be used by a *firm's governing body* and relevant *senior managers* when deciding upon how much risk the *firm* is willing to accept in pursuit of its business objectives and how risk limits should be set. Further *rules* and *guidance* on stress testing and scenario analysis are outlined in **GENPRU 1.2** (Adequacy of financial resources) and **SYSC 11** (Liquidity risk systems and controls).

Internal controls: introduction

14.1.26 G   PRA

Internal controls should provide a *firm* with reasonable assurance that it will not be hindered in achieving its objectives, or in the orderly and legitimate conduct of its business, by events that may reasonably be foreseen. More specifically, *internal controls* should be concerned with ensuring that a *firm's* business plan and risk management systems are operating as expected and are being implemented as intended. The following *rule* (**SYSC 14.1.27 R**) reflects the importance of *internal controls*.

14.1.27 R   FCA PRA

A *firm* must take reasonable steps to establish and maintain adequate *internal controls*.

14.1.28 G   FCA PRA

The precise role and organisation of *internal controls* can vary from *firm* to *firm*. However, a *firm's internal controls* should normally be concerned with assisting its *governing body* and relevant *senior managers* to participate in ensuring that it meets the following objectives:

(1) safeguarding both the assets of the *firm* and its *customers*, as well as identifying and managing liabilities;

(2) maintaining the efficiency and effectiveness of its operations;

(3) ensuring the reliability and completeness of all accounting, financial and management information; and

(4) ensuring compliance with its internal policies and procedures as well as all applicable laws and regulations.

14.1.29 G   PRA

When determining the adequacy of its *internal controls*, a *firm* should consider both the potential risks that might hinder the achievement of the objectives listed in **SYSC 14.1.28 G**, and the extent to which it needs to control these risks. More specifically, this should normally include consideration of:

(1) the appropriateness of its reporting and communication lines (see **SYSC 3.2.2 G**);

(2) how the delegation or contracting of functions or activities to *employees*, *appointed representatives* or, where applicable, its *tied agents* or other third parties (for example *outsourcing*) is to be monitored and controlled (see **SYSC 3.2.3 G** to **SYSC 3.2.4 G**, **SYSC 14.1.12 G** to **SYSC 14.1.16 G** and **SYSC 14.1.33 G**; additional guidance on the management of *outsourcing* arrangements is also provided in **SYSC 13.9**);

(3) the risk that a *firm's employees* or contractors might accidentally or deliberately breach a *firm's* policies and procedures (see **SYSC 13.6.3 G**);

(4) the need for adequate segregation of duties (see **SYSC 3.2.5 G** and **SYSC 14.1.30 G** to **SYSC 14.1.33 G**);

(5) the establishment and control of risk management committees (see **SYSC 14.1.34 G** to **SYSC 14.1.37 G**);

(6) the need for risk assessment and the establishment of a risk assessment function (see **SYSC 3.2.10 G** and **SYSC 14.1.38 G** to **SYSC 14.1.41 G**);

(7)   the need for internal audit and the establishment of an internal audit function and audit committee (see **SYSC 3.2.15 G** to **SYSC 3.2.16 G** and **SYSC 14.1.42 G** to **SYSC 14.1.45 G**).

14.1.29A G   FCA

When determining the adequacy of its *internal controls*, a *firm* should consider both the potential risks that might hinder the achievement of the objectives listed in **SYSC 14.1.28 G**, and the extent to which it needs to control these risks. More specifically, this should normally include consideration of:

(1)   the appropriateness of its reporting and communication lines (see **SYSC 3.2.2 G**);

(2)   how the delegation or contracting of functions or activities to *employees*, *appointed representatives* or, where applicable, its *tied agents* or other third parties (for example *outsourcing*) is to be monitored and controlled (see **SYSC 3.2.3 G** to **SYSC 3.2.4 G** and the additional guidance on the management of *outsourcing* arrangements is also provided in **SYSC 13.9**);

(3)   the risk that a *firm's employees* or contractors might accidentally or deliberately breach a *firm's* policies and procedures (see **SYSC 13.6.3 G**);

(4)   the need for adequate segregation of duties (see **SYSC 3.2.5 G**);

(5)   the establishment and control of risk management committees;

(6)   the need for risk assessment and the establishment of a risk assessment function (see **SYSC 3.2.10 G**);

(7)   the need for internal audit and the establishment of an internal audit function and audit committee (see **SYSC 3.2.15 G** to **SYSC 3.2.16 G**).

Internal controls: segregation of duties

14.1.30 G   PRA

The effective segregation of duties is an important internal control. In particular, it helps to ensure that no one individual is completely free to commit a *firm's* assets or incur liabilities on its behalf. Segregation can also help to ensure that a *firm's governing body* receives objective and accurate information on financial performance, the risks faced by the *firm* and the adequacy of its systems. In this regard, a *firm* should ensure that there is adequate segregation of duties between *employees* involved in:

(1)   taking on or controlling risk (which could involve risk mitigation);

(2)   risk assessment (which includes the identification and analysis of risk); and

(3)   internal audit.

14.1.31 G   PRA

In addition, a *firm* should normally ensure that no single individual has unrestricted authority to do all of the following:

(1)   initiate a transaction;

(2)   bind the *firm*;

(3)   make payments; and

(4)   account for it.

14.1.32 G   PRA

Where a *firm* is unable to ensure the complete segregation of duties (for example, because it has a limited number of staff), it should ensure that there are adequate compensating controls in place (for example, frequent review of an area by relevant *senior managers*).

14.1.33 G   PRA

Where a *firm* outsources a *controlled function*, such as internal audit, it should take reasonable steps to ensure that every individual involved in the performance of this service is independent from the individuals who perform its external audit. This should not prevent services from being undertaken by a *firm's* external auditors provided that:

(1)   the work is carried out under the supervision and management of the *firm's* own internal staff; and

(2)   potential conflicts of interest between the provision of external audit services and the provision of *controlled functions* are properly managed.

Internal controls: risk management committees

14.1.34 G   PRA

In many *firms*, especially if there are multiple business lines, it is common for the *governing body* to delegate some tasks related to risk control and management to committees such as asset and liability committees (ALCO), credit risk committees and market risk committees.

14.1.35 G   PRA

Part 3   FCA Handbook Materials

Where a *firm* decides to create one or more risk management committee(s), adequate *internal controls* should be put in place to ensure that these committees are effective and that their actions are consistent with the objectives outlined in **SYSC 14.1.28 G**. This should normally include consideration of the following:

(1)   setting clear terms of reference, including membership, reporting lines and responsibilities of each committee;

(2)   setting limits on their authority;

(3)   agreeing routine reporting and non-routine reporting escalation procedures;

(4)   agreeing the minimum frequency of committee meetings; and

(5)   reviewing the performance of these risk management committees.

14.1.36 G   PRA

The decision to delegate risk management tasks, along with the terms of reference of the committees and their performance, should be reviewed periodically by the *firm's governing body* and revised as appropriate.

14.1.37 G   PRA

The effective use of risk management committees can help to enhance a *firm's internal controls*. In establishing and maintaining its risk management committees, a *firm* should consider:

(1)   their membership, which should normally include relevant *senior managers* (such as the head of group risk, head of legal, and the heads of market, credit, liquidity and operational risk, etc.), business line managers, risk management personnel and other appropriately skilled people, for example, actuaries, lawyers, accountants, IT specialists, etc.;

(2)   using these committees to:

    (a)   inform the decisions made by a *firm's governing body* regarding its appetite or tolerance for risk taking;

    (b)   highlight risk management issues that may require attention by the *governing body*;

    (c)   consider risk at the firm-wide level and, within delegated limits, to determine the allocation of risk limits and financial resources across business lines; and

    (d)   consider how exposures may be unwound, hedged, or otherwise mitigated, as appropriate.

Internal controls: risk assessment

14.1.38 G   PRA

Risk assessment is the process through which a *firm* identifies and analyses (using both qualitative and quantitative methodologies) the risks that it faces. A *firm's* risk assessment activities should normally include consideration of:

(1)   its total exposure to risk at the *firm*-wide level (that is, its exposure across business lines and risk categories);

(2)   capital allocation and the need to calculate risk weighted returns for different business lines;

(3)   the potential correlations that can exist between the risks in different business lines; this should also include looking for risks to which a *firm's* business plan is particularly sensitive, such as interest rate risk, or multiple dealings with the same *counterparty*;

(4)   the use of stress tests and scenario analysis;

(5)   whether there are risks inherent in the *firm's* business that are not being addressed adequately;

(6)   the risk adjusted return that the *firm* is achieving; and

(7)   the adequacy and timeliness of management information on market, credit, insurance, liquidity, operational and group risks from the business lines, including risk limit utilisation.

14.1.39 G   PRA

(1)   In accordance with **SYSC 3.2.10 G** a *firm* should consider whether it needs to set up a separate risk assessment function (or functions) that is responsible for assessing the risks that the *firm* faces and advising its *governing body* and *senior managers* on them.

(2)   The term 'risk assessment function' refers to the generally understood concept of risk assessment within a *firm*, that is, the function of setting and controlling risk exposure. The risk assessment function is not a *controlled function* itself, but is part of the *systems and controls function* (CF28).

14.1.40 G   PRA

Where a *firm* does decide that it needs a separate risk assessment function, the *employees* or contractors that carry out this function should not normally be involved in risk taking activities such as business line management (see **SYSC 14.1.30 G** to **SYSC 14.1.33 G** on the segregation of duties).

14.1.41 G   PRA

A summary of the results of the analysis undertaken by a *firm's* risk assessment function in accordance with **SYSC 14.1.39 G** (including, where necessary, an explanation of any assumptions that were adopted) should normally be reported to relevant *senior managers* as well as to the *firm's governing body*.

Internal audit

14.1.42 G   PRA

A *firm* should ensure that it has appropriate mechanisms in place to assess and monitor the appropriateness and effectiveness of its systems and controls. This should normally include consideration of:

(1)   adherence to and effectiveness of, as appropriate, its market, credit, liquidity, operational, insurance, and group risk policies;

(2)   whether departures and variances from its documented systems and controls and risk policies have been adequately documented and appropriately reported, including whether appropriate pre-clearance authorisation has been sought for material departures and variances;

(3)   adherence to and effectiveness of its accounting policies, and whether accounting records are complete and accurate;

(4)   adherence to and effectiveness of its management reporting arrangements, including the timeliness of reporting, and whether information is comprehensive and accurate; and

(5)   adherence to *PRA rules* and regulatory prudential standards.

14.1.43 G   PRA

(1)   In accordance with **SYSC 3.2.15 G** and **SYSC 3.2.16 G**, a *firm* should consider whether it needs to set up a dedicated internal audit function.

(2)   The term 'internal audit function' refers to the generally understood concept of internal audit within a *firm*, that is, the function of assessing adherence to and the effectiveness of internal systems and controls, procedures and policies. The internal audit function is not a *controlled function* itself, but is part of the *systems and controls function* (CF28).

14.1.44 G   PRA

Where a *firm* decides to set up an internal audit function, this function should provide independent assurance to its *governing body*, audit committee or an appropriate *senior manager* of the integrity and effectiveness of its systems and controls.

14.1.45 G   PRA

In forming its judgements, the *person* performing the internal audit function should test the practical operation of a *firm's* systems and controls as well as its accounting and risk policies. This should include examining the adequacy of supporting records.

Management information

14.1.46 G   PRA

Many individuals, at various levels of a *firm*, need management information relating to their activities. However, **SYSC 14.1.47 G** to **SYSC 14.1.50 G** concentrates on the management information that should be available to those at the highest level of a *firm*, that is, the *firm's governing body* and relevant *senior managers*. In so doing **SYSC 14.1.47 G** to **SYSC 14.1.50 G** amplify **SYSC 3.2.11 G** and **SYSC 3.2.12 G** (which outline the *PRA's* high level policy on senior management information) by providing some additional *guidance* on the management information that should be available.

14.1.47 G   PRA

The role of management information should be to help a *firm's governing body* and *senior managers* to understand risk at a firm-wide level. In so doing, it should help them to:

(1)   determine whether a *firm* is prudently managed with adequate financial resources;

(2)   make the decisions that fall within their ambit (for example, the high level business plans, strategy and risk tolerances of the *firm*); and

(3)   oversee the execution of tasks for which they are responsible.

14.1.48 G   PRA

A *firm* should consider what information needs to be made available to its *governing body* and *senior managers*. Some possible examples include:

(1)   firm-wide information such as the overall profitability and value of a *firm* and its total exposure to risk;

(2)   reports from committees to which the *governing body* has delegated risk management tasks, if applicable;

(3)   reports from a *firm's* internal audit and risk assessment functions (see **SYSC 14.1.43 G** and **SYSC 14.1.39 G**), if applicable, including exception reports, where risk limits and policies have been breached or systems circumvented;

(4)   financial projections under expected and abnormal (that is, stressed) conditions;

(5)   reconciliation of actual profit and loss to previous financial projections and an analysis of any significant variances;

(6)   matters which require a decision from the *governing body* or *senior managers*, for example a significant variation to a business plan, amendments to risk limits, the creation of a new business line, etc;

(7)   compliance with *PRA rules* and regulatory prudential standards;

(8)   risk weighted returns; and

(9)   liquidity and funding requirements.

14.1.49 G   PRA

The management information that is provided to a *firm's governing body* and *senior managers* should have the following characteristics:

(1)   it should be timely, its frequency being determined by factors such as:

    (a)   the volatility of the business in which the *firm* is engaged (that is, the speed at which its risks can change);

    (b)   any time constraints on when action needs to be taken; and

    (c)   the level of risk that the *firm* is exposed to, compared to its available financial resources and tolerance for risk;

(2)   it should be reliable, having regard to the fact that it may be necessary to sacrifice a degree of accuracy for timeliness; and

(3)   it should be presented in a manner that highlights any relevant issues on which those undertaking *governing functions* should focus particular attention.

14.1.50 G   PRA

The production of management and other information may require the collation of data from a variety of separate manual and automated systems. In such cases, responsibility for the integrity of the information may be spread amongst a number of operational areas. A *firm* should ensure that it has appropriate processes to validate the integrity of its information.

Record keeping

14.1.51 G   PRA

SYSC 3.2.20 R requires a *firm* to take reasonable care to make and retain adequate records. The following policy on record keeping supplements **SYSC 3.2.20 R** by providing some additional *rules* and *guidance* on record keeping. The purpose of this policy is to:

(1)   facilitate the prudential supervision of a *firm* by ensuring that adequate information is available regarding its past/current financial situation and business activities (which includes the design and implementation of systems and controls); and

(2)   help the *PRA* to satisfy itself that a *firm* is operating in a prudent manner and is not prejudicing its safety and soundness or the interests of policyholders.

14.1.52 G   PRA

In addition to the record keeping requirements in *GENPRU*, *INSPRU* and *SYSC*, a *firm* should remember that it may be obliged, under other applicable laws or regulations, to keep similar or additional records.

14.1.53 R   PRA

(1)   A *firm* must make and regularly update accounting and other records that are sufficient to enable the *firm* to demonstrate to the *PRA*:

    (a)   that the *firm* is financially sound and has appropriate systems and controls;

    (b)   the *firm's* financial position and exposure to risk (to a reasonable degree of accuracy); and

    (c)   the *firm's* compliance with the *rules* in *GENPRU*, *INSPRU* and *SYSC*.

(2)   The records in (1) must be retained for a minimum of three years, or longer as appropriate.

14.1.54 G   PRA

A *firm* should be able to make available the records described in **SYSC 14.1.53 R** within a reasonable time frame when requested to do so by the *PRA*.

14.1.55 G   PRA

The *PRA* recognises that not all records are specific to a particular point in time. As such, while it may be appropriate to update some records on a daily or continuous basis, for example expenditure and details of certain transactions, it may not be appropriate to update other records as regularly as this, for example those relating to its business plan and risk policies. A *firm* should decide how regularly it should update particular records.

14.1.56 G   PRA

A *firm* should decide which records it needs to hold, noting that compliance with **SYSC 14.1.53 R** does not require it to hold records on every single aspect of its activities. Some specific *guidance* on the types of records that a *firm* should hold is set out in each of the risk specific sections on systems and controls (see **SYSC 11**, **SYSC 12**, **SYSC 14.1.65 G**, **SYSC 15** to **SYSC 17** and *INSPRU* 5.1).

14.1.57 G   PRA

In deciding which records to hold, a *firm* should also take into account that failure to keep adequate records could make it harder for it to satisfy the *PRA* that it is compliant with the *rules* in *GENPRU*, *INSPRU* or *SYSC*, and to defend any enforcement action taken against it.

14.1.58 G   PRA

A *firm* should keep the records required in *GENPRU*, *INSPRU* and *SYSC* in an appropriate format and language (in terms of format this could include holding them on paper or in electronic or some other form). However, whatever format or language a *firm* chooses, **SYSC 3.2.20 R** requires that records be capable of being reproduced on paper and in English (except where they relate to business carried on from an establishment situated in a country where English is not an official language).

14.1.59 G   PRA

In accordance with **SYSC 3.2.20 R**, a *firm* should retain the records that it needs to comply with **SYSC 14.1.53 R** for as long as they are relevant for the purposes for which they were made.

14.1.60 R   PRA

A *firm* must keep the records required in **SYSC 14.1.53 R** in the *United Kingdom*, except where:
(1)   they relate to business carried on from an establishment in a country or territory that is outside the *United Kingdom*; and
(2)   they are kept in that country or territory.

14.1.61 R   PRA

When a *firm* keeps the records required in **SYSC 14.1.53 R** outside the *United Kingdom*, it must periodically send an adequate summary of those records to the *United Kingdom*.

14.1.62 G   PRA

Where a *firm* outsources the storage of some or all of its records to a third party service provider, it should ensure that these records are readily accessible and can be reproduced within a reasonable time period. The *firm* should also ensure that these records are stored in compliance with the *rules* and *guidance* on record keeping in *GENPRU*, *INSPRU* or *SYSC*. Additional *guidance* on the management of *outsourcing* agreements is provided in **SYSC 13**.

14.1.63 G   PRA

A *firm* may rely on records that have been produced by a third party (for example, another *group* company or an external agent, such as an outsource service provider). However where the *firm* does so it should ensure that these records are readily accessible and can be reproduced within a reasonable time period. The *firm* should also ensure that these records comply with the *rules* and *guidance* on record keeping in *GENPRU*, *INSPRU* or *SYSC*.

14.1.64 G   PRA

In accordance with **SYSC 3.2.21 G**, a *firm* should have adequate systems and controls for maintaining the security of its records so that they are reasonably safeguarded against loss, unauthorised access, alteration or destruction.

Operational risk

14.1.65 G   PRA

As well as covering other types of risk, the *rules* and *guidance* set out in this chapter deal with a *firm's* approach to operational risk. In particular:
(1)   **SYSC 14.1.18 R** requires a *firm* to take reasonable steps to ensure that the risk management systems put in place to identify, assess, monitor and control operational risk are adequate for that purpose;
(2)   **SYSC 14.1.19R (2)** requires a *firm* to document its policy for operational risk, including its risk appetite and how it identifies, assesses, monitors and controls that risk; and
(3)   **SYSC 14.1.27 R** requires a *firm* to take reasonable steps to establish and maintain adequate *internal controls* to enable it to assess and monitor the effectiveness and implementation of its business plan and prudential risk management systems.

CHAPTER 15
CREDIT RISK MANAGEMENT SYSTEMS AND CONTROLS FOR INSURERS

15.1   APPLICATION

[3.21]
15.1.1 G   PRA

SYSC 15.1 applies to an *insurer* unless it is:
(1)   a *non-directive friendly society*; or
(2)   an *incoming EEA firm*; or
(3)   an *incoming Treaty firm*.

15.1.2 G   PRA

SYSC 15.1 applies to:

(1)   an *EEA-deposit insurer*; and

(2)   a *Swiss general insurer*;

only in respect of the activities of the *firm* carried on from a *branch* in the *United Kingdom*.

15.1.2A G   PRA

This section does not apply to an *incoming ECA provider* acting as such.

Purpose

15.1.3 G   PRA

This section provides *guidance* on how to interpret **SYSC 14** insofar as it relates to the management of credit risk.

15.1.4 G   PRA

Credit risk is incurred whenever a *firm* is exposed to loss if another party fails to perform its financial obligations to the *firm*, including failing to perform them in a timely manner. It arises from both on and off balance sheet items. For contracts for traded *financial instruments*, for example the purchase and sale of *securities* or *over the counter derivatives*, risks may arise if the *firm's counterparty* does not honour its side of the contract. This constitutes counterparty risk, which can be considered a subset of credit risk. Another risk is issuer risk, which could potentially result in a *firm* losing the full price of a market instrument since default by the issuer could result in the value of its bonds or stocks falling to nil. In insurance *firms*, credit risk can arise from *premium* debtors, where cover under *contracts of insurance* may either commence before premiums become due or continue after their non-payment. Credit risk can also arise if a *reinsurer* fails to fulfil its financial obligation to repay a *firm* upon submission of a *claim*.

15.1.5 G   PRA

Credit risk concerns the *PRA* because inadequate systems and controls for credit risk management can create a threat to the *statutory objectives* of promoting the safety and soundness of *PRA authorised persons* and contributing to the securing of an appropriate degree of protection for those who are or may become policyholders by:

(1)   the erosion of a *firm's* capital due to excessive credit losses thereby threatening its viability as a going concern;

(2)   an inability of a *firm* to meet its own obligations to depositors, *policyholders* or other market *counterparties* due to its capital erosion.

15.1.6 G   PRA

Appropriate systems and controls for the management of credit risk will vary with the scale, nature and complexity of the *firm's* activities. Therefore the material in this section is *guidance*. A *firm* should assess the appropriateness of any particular item of *guidance* in the light of the scale, nature and complexity of its activities as well as its obligation to organise and control its affairs responsibly and effectively.

Requirements

15.1.7 G   PRA

High level requirements for prudential systems and controls, including those for credit risk, are set out in **SYSC 14**. In particular:

(1)   **SYSC 14.1.19R (2)** requires a *firm* to document its policy for credit risk, including its risk appetite and how it identifies, measures, monitors and controls that risk;

(2)   **SYSC 14.1.19R (2)** requires a *firm* to document its provisioning policy. Documentation should describe the systems and controls that it intends to use to ensure that the policy is correctly implemented;

(3)   **SYSC 14.1.18 R** requires it to establish and maintain risk management systems to identify, measure, monitor and control credit risk (in accordance with its credit risk policy), and to take reasonable steps to ensure that its systems are adequate for that purpose; or

(4)   in line with **SYSC 14.1.11 G**, the ultimate responsibility for the management of credit risk should rest with a *firm's governing body*. Where delegation of authority occurs the *governing body* and relevant *senior managers* should approve and periodically review systems and controls to ensure that delegated duties are being performed correctly.

Credit risk policy

15.1.8 G   PRA

SYSC 14.1.18 R requires a *firm* to establish, maintain and document a business plan and risk policies. They should provide a clear indication of the amount and nature of credit risk that the *firm* wishes to incur. In particular, they should cover for credit risk:

(1)   how, with particular reference to its activities, the *firm* defines and measures credit risk;

(2)   the *firm's* business aims in incurring credit risk including:

    (a)   identifying the types and sources of credit risk to which the *firm* wishes to be exposed (and the limits on that exposure) and those to which the *firm* wishes not to be exposed (and how that is to be achieved, for example how exposure is to be avoided or mitigated);

    (b)   specifying the level of diversification required by the *firm* and the *firm's* tolerance for risk concentrations (and the limits on those exposures and concentrations); and

    (c)   drawing the distinction between activities where credit risk is taken in order to achieve a return (for example, lending) and activities where credit exposure arises as a consequence of pursuing some other objective (for example, the purchase of a *derivative* in order to mitigate *market risk*);

(3)   how credit risk is assessed both when credit is granted or incurred and subsequently, including how the adequacy of any security and other risk mitigation techniques is assessed;

(4)   the detailed limit structure for credit risk which should:

    (a)   address all key risk factors, including intra-*group* exposures and indirect exposures (for example, exposures held by *related* and *subsidiary undertakings*);

    (b)   be commensurate with the volume and complexity of activity; and

    (c)   be consistent with the *firm's* business aims, historical performance, and its risk appetite;

(5)   procedures for:

    (a)   approving new or additional exposures to *counterparties*;

    (b)   approving new products and activities that give rise to credit risk;

    (c)   regular risk position and performance reporting;

    (d)   limit exception reporting and approval; and

    (e)   identifying and dealing with the problem exposures caused by the failure or downgrading of a *counterparty*;

(6)   the methods and assumptions used for the stress testing and scenario analysis required by GENPRU 1.2 (Adequacy of financial resources), including how these methods and assumptions are selected and tested; and

(7)   the allocation of responsibilities for implementing the credit risk policy and for monitoring adherence to, and the effectiveness of, the policy.

Counterparty assessment

15.1.9 G   PRA

The *firm* should make a suitable assessment of the risk profile of the *counterparty*. The factors to be considered will vary according to both the type of credit and the *counterparty* being considered. This may include:

(1)   the purpose of the credit, the duration of the agreement and the source of repayment;

(2)   an assessment and continuous monitoring of the credit quality of the *counterparty*;

(3)   an assessment of the *claims* payment record where the *counterparty* is a *reinsurer*;

(4)   an assessment of the nature and amount of risk attached to the *counterparty* in the context of the industrial sector or geographical region or country in which it operates, as well as the potential impact on the *counterparty* of political, economic and market changes; and

(5)   the proposed terms and conditions attached to the granting of credit, including ongoing provision of information by the *counterparty*, covenants attached to the facility as well as the adequacy and enforceability of *collateral*, security and guarantees.

15.1.10 G   PRA

It is important that sound and legally enforceable documentation is in place for each agreement that gives rise to credit risk as this may be called upon in the event of a default or dispute. A *firm* should therefore consider whether it is appropriate for an independent legal opinion to be sought on documentation used by the *firm*. Documentation should normally be in place before the *firm* enters into a contractual obligation or releases funds.

15.1.11 G   PRA

Where *premium* payments are made via *brokers* or *intermediaries*, the *firm* should describe how it monitors and controls its exposure to those *brokers* and *intermediaries*. In particular, the policy should identify whether the risk of default by the *broker* or *intermediary* is borne by the *firm* or the *policyholder*.

15.1.12 G   PRA

Any variation from the usual credit policy should be documented.

15.1.13 G   PRA

A *firm* involved in loan syndications or consortia should not rely on other parties' assessment of the credit risks involved. It will remain responsible for forming its own judgement on the appropriateness of the credit risk thereby incurred with reference to its stated credit risk policy. Similarly a *firm* remains responsible for assessing the credit risk associated with any insurance or *reinsurance* placed on its behalf by other parties.

15.1.14 G   PRA

Where a credit scoring approach or other *counterparty* assessment process is used, the *firm* should periodically assess the particular approach taken in the light of past and expected future *counterparty* performance and ensure that any statistical process is adjusted accordingly to ensure that the business written complies with the *firm's* risk appetite.

15.1.15 G   PRA

In assessing its contingent exposure to a *counterparty*, the *firm* should identify the amount which would be due from the *counterparty* if the value, index or other factor upon which that amount depends were to change.

Credit risk measurement

15.1.16 G   PRA

A *firm* should measure its credit risk using a robust and consistent methodology which should be described in its credit risk policy; the appropriate method of measurement will depend upon the nature of the credit product provided. The *firm* should consider whether the measurement methodologies should be backtested and the frequency of such backtesting.

15.1.17 G   PRA

A *firm* should also be able to measure its credit exposure across its entire portfolio or within particular categories such as exposures to particular industries, economic sectors or geographical areas.

15.1.18 G   PRA

Where a *firm* is a member of a *group* that is subject to consolidated reporting, the *group* should be able to monitor credit exposures on a consolidated basis. See **SYSC 12**, INSPRU 6.1 and GENPRU 3.

15.1.19 G   PRA

A *firm* should have the capability to measure its credit exposure to individual *counterparties* on at least a daily basis.

Risk monitoring

15.1.20 G   PRA

A *firm* should implement an effective system for monitoring its credit risk which should be described in its credit risk policy.

15.1.21 G   PRA

A *firm* should have a system of management reporting which provides clear, concise, timely and accurate credit risk reports to relevant functions within the *firm*. The reports could cover exceptions to the *firm's* credit risk policy, non-performing exposures and changes to the level of credit risk within the *firm's* credit portfolio. A *firm* should have procedures for taking appropriate action according to the information within the management reports, such as a review of *counterparty* limits, or of the overall credit policy.

15.1.22 G   PRA

Individual credit facilities and overall limits should be periodically reviewed in order to check their appropriateness for both the current circumstances of the *counterparty* and the *firm's* current internal and external economic environment. The frequency of review should be appropriate to the nature of the facility.

15.1.23 G   PRA

A *firm* should utilise appropriate stress testing and scenario analysis of credit exposures to examine the potential effects of economic or industry downturns, market events, changes in interest rates, changes in foreign exchange rates, changes in liquidity conditions and changes in levels of insurance losses where relevant.

Problem exposures

15.1.24 G   PRA

A *firm* should have systematic processes for the timely identification, management and monitoring of problem exposures. These processes should be described in the credit risk policy.

15.1.25 G   PRA

A *firm* should have adequate procedures for recovering exposures in arrears or that have had provisions made against them. A *firm* should allocate responsibility, either internally or externally, for its arrears management and recovery.

Provisioning

15.1.26 G   PRA

SYSC 14.1.19 R (2) requires a *firm* to document its provisioning policy. A *firm's* provisioning policy can be maintained either as a separate document or as part of its credit risk policy.

15.1.27 G   PRA

At intervals that are appropriate to the nature, scale and complexity of its activities a *firm* should review and update its provisioning policy and associated systems.

15.1.28 G   PRA

In line with **SYSC 15.1.6 G**, the *PRA* recognises that the frequency with which a *firm* reviews its provisioning policy once it has been established will vary from *firm* to *firm*. However, the *PRA* expects a *firm* to review at least annually whether its policy remains appropriate for the business it undertakes and the economic environment in which it operates.

15.1.29 G   PRA

In line with **SYSC 14.1.12 G**, the provisioning policy referred to in **SYSC 15.1.26 G** must be approved by the *firm's governing body* or another appropriate body to which the *firm's governing body* has delegated this responsibility.

15.1.30 G   PRA

In line with **SYSC 14.1.24 G**, the *PRA* may request a *firm* to provide it with a copy of its current provisioning policy.

15.1.31 G   PRA

Provisions may be general (against the whole of a given portfolio), specific (against particular exposures identified as bad or doubtful) or both. The *PRA* expects contingent liabilities (for example guarantees) and anticipated losses to be recognised in accordance with accepted accounting standards at the relevant time, such as those embodied in the Financial Reporting Standards issued by the Accounting Standards Board.

Risk mitigation

15.1.32 G   PRA

A *firm* may choose to use various credit risk mitigation techniques including the taking of *collateral*, the use of letters of credit or guarantees, or *counterparty netting* agreements to manage and control their *counterparty* exposures. The use of such techniques does not obviate the need for thorough credit analysis and procedures. The reliance placed by a *firm* on risk mitigation should be described in the credit risk policy.

15.1.33 G   PRA

A *firm* should consider the legal and financial ability of a guarantor to fulfil the guarantee if called upon to do so.

15.1.34 G   PRA

A *firm* should monitor the validity and enforceability of its *collateral* arrangements.

15.1.35 G   PRA

The *firm* should analyse carefully the protection afforded by risk mitigants such as netting agreements or credit *derivatives*, to ensure that any residual risk is identified, measured, monitored and controlled.

Record keeping

15.1.36 G   PRA

Prudential records made under **SYSC 14.1.53 R** should include appropriate records of:
(1)   credit exposures, including aggregations of credit exposures, as appropriate, by:
    (a)   groups of connected *counterparties*; or
    (b)   types of *counterparty* as defined, for example, by the nature or geographical location of the *counterparty*;
(2)   credit decisions, including details of the decision and the facts or circumstances upon which it was made; and
(3)   information relevant to assessing current *counterparty* and risk quality.

15.1.37 G   PRA

Credit records should be retained as long as they are needed for the purpose described in **SYSC 15.1.36 G** (subject to the minimum three year retention period). In particular, a *firm* should consider whether it is appropriate to retain information regarding *counterparty* history such as a record of credit events as well as a record indicating how credit decisions were taken.

CHAPTER 16
MARKET RISK MANAGEMENT SYSTEMS AND CONTROLS FOR INSURERS

16.1   APPLICATION

[3.22]

16.1.1 G   PRA

SYSC 16.1 applies to an *insurer* unless it is:

(1)   a *non-directive friendly society*; or

(2)   an *incoming EEA firm*; or

(3)   an *incoming Treaty firm*.

16.1.2 G   PRA

SYSC 16.1 applies to:

(1)   an *EEA-deposit insurer*; and

(2)   a *Swiss general insurer*;

only in respect of the activities of the *firm* carried on from a *branch* in the *United Kingdom*.

16.1.2A G   PRA

This section does not apply to an *incoming ECA provider* acting as such.

16.1.3 G   PRA

Firms should also see **GENPRU 1.2** (GENPRU 1.2.64G to GENPRU 1.2.78G) and INSPRU 3.1.

Purpose

16.1.4 G   PRA

(1)   The purpose of this section is to amplify **SYSC 14** insofar as it relates to *market risk*.

(2)   *Market risk* includes equity, interest rate, foreign exchange (FX), commodity risk and interest rate risk on *long-term insurance contracts*. The price of *financial instruments* may also be influenced by other risks such as *spread risk*, *basis risk*, correlation, *specific risk* and *volatility risk*.

(3)   This section does not deal with the risk management of *market risk* in a *group* context. A *firm* that is a member of a *group* should also read **SYSC 12** (Group risk systems and controls) which outlines the *PRA's* requirements for the risk management of *market risk* within a *group*.

(4)   Appropriate systems and controls for the management of *market risk* will vary with the scale, nature and complexity of the *firm's* activities. Therefore the material in this section is *guidance*. A *firm* should assess the appropriateness of any particular item of *guidance* in the light of the scale, nature and complexity of its activities as well as its obligations to organise and control its affairs responsibly and effectively.

Requirements

16.1.5 G   PRA

High level requirements for prudential systems and controls, including those for *market risk*, are set out in **SYSC 14**. In particular:

(1)   **SYSC 14.1.19R (2)** requires a *firm* to document its policy for *market risk*, including its risk appetite and how it identifies, measures, monitors and controls that risk;

(2)   **SYSC 14.1.19R (4)** requires a *firm* to document its asset and liability recognition policy. Documentation should describe the systems and controls that it intends to use to comply with the policy;

(3)   **SYSC 14.1.19 R** requires a *firm* to establish and maintain risk management systems to identify, measure, monitor and control *market risk* (in accordance with its *market risk* policy), and to take reasonable steps to establish systems adequate for that purpose; and

(4)   In line with **SYSC 14.1.11 G**, the ultimate responsibility for the management of *market risk* should rest with a *firm's governing body*. Where delegation of authority occurs the *governing body* and relevant *senior managers* should approve and adequately review systems and controls to check that delegated duties are being performed correctly.

Market risk policy

16.1.6 G   PRA

SYSC 14 requires a *firm* to establish, maintain and document a business plan and risk policies. They should provide a clear indication of the amount and nature of *market risk* that the *firm* wishes to incur. In particular, they should cover for *market risk*:

(1)   how, with particular reference to its activities, the *firm* defines and measures *market risk*;

(2)   the *firm's* business aims in incurring *market risk* including:

(a)   identifying the types and sources of *market risk* to which the *firm* wishes to be exposed (and the limits on that exposure) and those to which the *firm* wishes not to be exposed (and how that is to be achieved, for example how exposure is to be avoided or mitigated); and

(b)   specifying the level of diversification required by the *firm* and the *firm's* tolerance for risk concentrations (and the limits on those exposures and concentrations).

16.1.7 G PRA

The *market risk* policy of a *firm* should be endorsed by the *firm's governing body* and implemented by its senior management, who should take adequate steps to disseminate the policy and train the relevant staff such that they can effectively implement the policy.

16.1.8 G PRA

The *market risk* policy of a *firm* should enforce the risk management and control principles and include detailed information on:

(1)   the *financial instruments*, commodities, assets and liabilities (and mismatches between assets and liabilities) that a *firm* is exposed to and the limits on those exposures;

(2)   the *firm's* investment strategy as applicable between each insurance fund;

(3)   activities that are intended to hedge or mitigate *market risk* including mismatches caused by for example differences in the assets and liabilities and maturity mismatches; and

(4)   the methods and assumptions used for measuring linear, non-linear and geared *market risk* including the rationale for selection, ongoing validation and testing. Methods might include stress testing and scenario analysis, asset/liability analysis, correlation analysis, Value-at-Risk (VaR) and *options* such as delta, gamma, vega, rho and theta. Exposure to non-linear or geared *market risk* is typically through the use of *derivatives*.

Risk identification

16.1.9 G PRA

A *firm* should have in place appropriate risk reporting systems that enable it to identify the types and amount of *market risk* to which it is, and potentially could be, exposed. The information that systems should capture may include but is not limited to:

(1)   position information which may include a description of individual *financial instruments* and their cash flows; and

(2)   market data which may consist of raw time series of market rates, index levels and prices and derived time series of benchmark yield curves, spreads, implied volatilities, historical volatilities and correlations.

Risk measurement

16.1.10 G PRA

Having identified the *market risk* that the *firm* is exposed to on at least a daily basis, a *firm* should be able to measure and manage that *market risk* on a consistent basis. This may be achieved by:

(1)   regularly stress testing all or parts of the *firm's* portfolio to estimate potential economic losses in a range of market conditions including abnormal markets. Corporate level stress test results should be discussed regularly by risk monitors, senior management and risk takers, and should guide the *firm's market risk* appetite (for example, stress tests may lead to discussions on how best to unwind or hedge a position), and influence the internal capital allocation process;

(2)   measuring the *firm's* exposure to particular categories of *market risk* (for example, equity, interest rate, foreign exchange and commodities) as well as across its entire portfolio of *market risks*;

(3)   analysing the impact that new transactions or businesses may have on its *market risk* position on an on-going basis; and

(4)   regularly backtesting realised results against internal model generated *market risk* measures in order to evaluate and assess its accuracy. For example, a *firm* should keep a database of daily risk measures such as VaR and *options* such as delta, gamma, vega, rho and theta, and use these to back test predicted profit and loss against actual profit and loss for all trading desks and business units, and monitor the number of exceptions from agreed confidence bands.

Valuation

16.1.11 G PRA

A *firm* should take reasonable steps to establish systems and control procedures such that the *firm* complies with the requirements of GENPRU 1.3 (Valuation).

16.1.12 G PRA

The systems and controls referred to in **SYSC 16.1.11 G** should include the following:

(1)   the department responsible for the validation of the value of assets and liabilities should be independent of the business trading area, and should be adequately resourced by suitably qualified staff. The department should report to a suitably qualified individual, independent from the business trading area, who has sufficient authority to enforce the systems and controls policies and any alterations to valuation treatments where necessary;

(2)   all valuations should be checked and validated at appropriate intervals. Where a *firm* has chosen not to validate all valuations on a daily basis this should be agreed by senior management;

(3)   a *firm* should establish a review procedure to check that the valuation procedures are followed and are producing valuations in compliance with the requirements in this section. The review should be undertaken by suitably qualified staff independent of the business trading area, on a regular and ad hoc basis. In particular, this review procedure should include:

    (a)   the quality and appropriateness of the price sources used;

    (b)   valuation reserves held; and

    (c)   the valuation methodology employed for each product and consistent adherence to that methodology;

(4)   where a valuation is disputed and the dispute cannot be resolved in a timely manner it should be reported to senior management. It should continue to be reported to senior management until agreement is reached;

(5)   where a *firm* is marking positions to market it should take reasonable steps to establish a price source that is reliable and appropriate to enable compliance with the provisions in this section on an ongoing basis;

(6)   a *firm* should document its policies and procedures relating to the entire valuation process. In particular, the following should be documented:

    (a)   the valuation methodologies employed for all product categories;

    (b)   details of the price sources used for each product;

    (c)   the procedures to be followed where a valuation is disputed;

    (d)   the valuation adjustment and reserving policies;

    (e)   the level at which a difference between a valuation assigned to an asset or liability and the valuation used for validation purposes will be reported on an exceptions basis and investigated;

    (f)   where a *firm* is using its own internal estimate to produce a valuation, it should document in detail the process followed in order to produce the valuation; and

    (g)   the review procedures established by a *firm* in relation to the requirements of this section should be adequately documented and include the rationale for the policy;

(7)   a *firm* should maintain records which demonstrate:

    (a)   senior management's approval of the policies and procedures established; and

    (b)   management sign-off of the reviews undertaken in accordance with **SYSC 16.1.11 G**.

Risk monitoring

16.1.13 G   PRA

Risk monitoring is the operational process by which a *firm* monitors compliance with defined policies and procedures of the *market risk* policy. The *firm's* risk monitoring system should be independent of the *employees* who are responsible for exposing the *firm* to *market risk*.

16.1.14 G   PRA

The *market risk* policy of a *firm* may require the production of *market risk* reports at various levels within the *firm*. These reports should provide sufficiently accurate *market risk* data to relevant functions within the *firm*, and should be timely enough to allow any appropriate remedial action to be proposed and taken, for example:

(1)   at a *firm* wide level, a *market risk* report may include information:

    (a)   summarising and commenting on the total *market risk* that a *firm* is exposed to and *market risk* concentrations by business unit, asset class and country;

    (b)   on VaR reports against risk limits by business unit, asset class and country;

    (c)   commenting on significant risk concentrations and market developments; and

    (d)   on *market risk* in particular legal entities and geographical regions;

(2)   at the business unit level, a *market risk* report may include information summarising *market risk* by currency, trading desk, maturity or duration band, or by instrument type;

(3)   at the trading desk level, a *market risk* report may include detailed information summarising *market risk* by individual trader, instrument, position, currency, or maturity or duration band; and

(4)   all risk data should be readily reconcilable back to the prime books of entry with a fully documented audit trail.

16.1.15 G   PRA

Risk monitoring may also include information on:

(1)   the procedures for taking appropriate action in response to the information within the *market risk* reports;

(2)   ensuring that there are controls and procedures for identifying and reporting trades and positions booked at off-market rates;

(3)   the process for new product approvals;

(4)   the process for dealing with situations (authorised and unauthorised) where particular *market risk* exposures exceed predetermined risk limits and criteria; and

(5)   the periodic review of the risk monitoring process in order to check its suitability for both current market conditions and the *firm's* overall risk appetite.

16.1.16 G   PRA

Risk monitoring should be subject to periodic independent review by suitably qualified staff.

Risk control

16.1.17 G   PRA

Risk control is the independent monitoring, assessment and supervision of business units within the defined policies and procedures of the *market risk* policy. This may be achieved by:

(1)   setting an appropriate *market risk* limit structure to control the *firm's* exposure to *market risk*; for example, by setting out a detailed *market risk* limit structure at the corporate level, the business unit level and the trading desk level which addresses all the key *market risk* factors and is commensurate with the volume and complexity of activity that the *firm* undertakes;

(2)   setting limits on risks such as price or rate risk, as well as those factors arising from *options* such as delta, gamma, vega, rho and theta;

(3)   setting limits on net and gross positions, *market risk* concentrations, the maximum allowable loss (also called "stop-loss"), VaR, potential risks arising from stress testing and scenario analysis, gap analysis, correlation, liquidity and volatility; and

(4)   considering whether it is appropriate to set intermediate (early warning) thresholds that alert management when limits are being approached, triggering review and action where appropriate.

Record keeping

16.1.18 G   PRA

High level requirements for record keeping are set out in **SYSC 14**.

16.1.19 G   PRA

In relation to *market risk*, a *firm* should retain appropriate prudential records of:

(1)   off and on market trades in *financial instruments*;

(2)   the nature and amounts of off and on balance sheet exposures, including the aggregation of exposures;

(3)   trades in *financial instruments* and other assets and liabilities; and

(4)   methods and assumptions used in stress testing and scenario analysis and in VaR models.

16.1.20 G   PRA

A *firm* should keep a data history to enable it to perform back testing of methods and assumptions used for stress testing and scenario analysis and for VaR models.

CHAPTER 17
INSURANCE RISK SYSTEMS AND CONTROLS

17.1   APPLICATION

[3.23]
17.1.1 G   PRA

SYSC 17.1 applies to an *insurer* unless it is:

(1)   a *non-directive friendly society*; or

(2)   an *incoming EEA firm*; or

(3)   an *incoming Treaty firm*.

17.1.2 G   PRA

SYSC 17.1 applies to:

(1)   an *EEA-deposit insurer*; and

(2)   a *Swiss general insurer*;

only in respect of the activities of the *firm* carried on from a *branch* in the *United Kingdom*.

17.1.2A G   PRA

This section does not apply to an *incoming ECA provider* acting as such.

Purpose

17.1.3 G   PRA

This section provides *guidance* on how to interpret **SYSC 14** (Risk management and associated systems and controls) in so far as it relates to the management of insurance risk. Insurance risk refers to fluctuations in the timing, frequency and severity of insured events, relative to the expectations of the *firm* at the time of underwriting. Insurance risk can also refer to fluctuations in the timing and amount of *claim* settlements. For *general insurance business* some specific examples of insurance risk include variations in the amount or frequency of *claims* or the unexpected occurrence of multiple *claims* arising from a single cause. For *long-term insurance business* examples include variations in the mortality and persistency rates of *policyholders*, or the possibility that guarantees could acquire a value that adversely affects the finances of a *firm* and its ability to treat its *policyholders* fairly consistent with the *firm's* obligations under the *FCA's Principle* 6. More generally, insurance risk includes the potential for expense overruns relative to pricing or provisioning assumptions.

17.1.4 G   PRA

Insurance risk concerns the *PRA* because inadequate systems and controls for its management can create a threat to the *statutory objectives* of promoting the safety and soundness of *PRA-authorised person* and contributing to the securing of an appropriate degree of protection for those who are or may become policyholders. Inadequately managed insurance risk may result in:

(1)   the inability of a *firm* to meet its contractual insurance liabilities as they fall due; and
(2)   the inability of a *firm* to treat its *policyholders* fairly consistent with the *firm's* obligations under the *FCA's Principle* 6 (for example, in relation to bonus payments).

17.1.5 G   PRA

Guidance on the application of this section to a *firm* that is a member of a *group* is provided in **SYSC 12** (Group risk systems and controls).

17.1.6 G   PRA

The *guidance* contained within this section should be read in conjunction with the rest of *SYSC*.

17.1.7 G   PRA

Appropriate systems and controls for the management of insurance risk will vary with the scale, nature and complexity of a *firm's* activities. Therefore, the material in this section is *guidance*. A *firm* should assess the appropriateness of any particular item of *guidance* in the light of the scale, nature and complexity of its activities as well as its obligations, to organise and control its affairs responsibly and effectively.

General requirements

17.1.8 G   PRA

High level *rules* and *guidance* for prudential systems and controls for insurance risk are set out in **SYSC 14**. In particular:

(1)   **SYSC 14.1.18 R** requires a *firm* to take reasonable steps to establish and maintain a business plan and appropriate risk management systems;
(2)   **SYSC 14.1.19R (2)** requires a *firm* to document its policy for insurance risk, including its risk appetite and how it identifies, measures, monitors and controls that risk; and
(3)   **SYSC 14.1.27 R** requires a *firm* to take reasonable steps to establish and maintain adequate *internal controls* to enable it to assess and monitor the effectiveness and implementation of its business plan and prudential risk management systems.

Insurance risk policy

17.1.9 G   PRA

A *firm's* insurance risk policy should outline its objectives in carrying out *insurance business*, its appetite for insurance risk and its policies for identifying, measuring, monitoring and controlling insurance risk. The insurance risk policy should cover any activities that are associated with the creation or management of insurance risk. For example, underwriting, *claims* management and settlement, assessing *technical provisions* in the balance sheet, risk mitigation and risk transfer, record keeping and management reporting. Specific matters that should normally be in a *firm's* insurance risk policy include:

(1)   a statement of the *firm's* willingness and capacity to accept insurance risk;
(2)   the classes and characteristics of *insurance business* that the *firm* is prepared to accept;
(3)   the underwriting criteria that the *firm* intends to adopt, including how these can influence its rating and pricing decisions;
(4)   its approach to limiting significant aggregations of insurance risk, for example, by setting limits on the amount of business that can be underwritten in one region or with one *policyholder*;
(5)   where relevant, the *firm's* approach to pricing *long-term insurance contracts*, including the determination of the appropriate level of any reviewable *premiums*;

(6)   the *firm's* policy for identifying, monitoring and managing risk when it has delegated underwriting authority to another party (additional *guidance* on the management of *outsourcing* arrangements is provided in **SYSC 13.9**);

(7)   the *firm's* approach to managing its expense levels, including acquisition costs, recurring costs, and one-off costs, taking account of the margins available in both the prices for products and in the *technical provisions* in the balance sheet;

(8)   the *firm's* approach to the exercise of any discretion (e.g. on charges or the level of benefits payable) that is available in its *long-term insurance contracts*, in the context also of the legal and regulatory constraints existing on the application of this discretion;

(9)   the *firm's* approach to the inclusion of options within new *long-term insurance contracts* and to the possible exercise by *policyholders* of options on existing contracts;

(10)   the *firm's* approach to managing persistency risk;

(11)   the *firm's* approach to managing risks arising from timing differences in taxation or from changes in tax laws;

(12)   the *firm's* approach to the use of *reinsurance* or the use of some other means of risk transfer;

(13)   how the *firm* intends to assess the effectiveness of its risk transfer arrangements and manage the residual or transformed risks (for example, how it intends to handle disputes over contract wordings, potential payout delays and *counterparty* performance risks);

(14)   a summary of the data and information to be collected and reported on underwriting, *claims* and risk control (including internal accounting records), management reporting requirements and external data for risk assessment purposes;

(15)   the risk measurement and analysis techniques to be used for setting underwriting *premiums*, *technical provisions* in the balance sheet, and assessing capital requirements; and

(16)   the *firm's* approach to stress testing and scenario analysis, as required by GENPRU 1.2 (Adequacy of financial resources), including the methods adopted, any assumptions made and the use that is to be made of the results.

17.1.10 G PRA

Further, more detailed, *guidance* is given in **SYSC 17.1.11 G** to **SYSC 17.1.37 G** on the identification, measurement, monitoring and control (including the use of *reinsurance* and other forms of risk transfer) of insurance risk. A *firm* should consider what additional material to that set out above should be included in its insurance risk policy on each of these for its various activities.

Risk identification

17.1.11 G PRA

A *firm* should seek to identify the causes of fluctuations in the occurrence, amount and timing of its insurance liabilities. A *firm* should also seek to identify aggregations of risk that may give rise to large single or multiple *claims*.

17.1.12 G PRA

The identification of insurance risk should normally include:

(1)   in connection with the *firm's* business plan:

    (a)   processes for identifying the types of insurance risks that may be associated with a new product and for comparing the risk types that are present in different classes of business (in order to identify possible aggregations in particular insurance risks); and

    (b)   processes for identifying business environment changes (for example landmark legal rulings) and for collecting internal and external data to test and modify business plans;

(2)   at the point of sale, processes for identifying the underwriting risks associated with a particular *policyholder* or a group of *policyholders* (for example, processes for collecting information on the *claims* histories of *policyholders*, including whether they have made any potentially false or inaccurate claims, to identify possible adverse selection or moral hazard problems);

(3)   after the point of sale, processes for identifying potential and emerging *claims* for the purposes of *claims* management and *claims* provisioning; this could include:

    (a)   identifying possible judicial rulings;

    (b)   keeping up to date with developments in market practice; and

    (c)   collecting information on industry wide initiatives and settlements.

17.1.13 G PRA

A *firm* should also identify potential pricing risks, where the liabilities or costs arising from the sale of a product may not be as expected.

Risk measurement

17.1.14 G PRA

A *firm* should have in place appropriate systems for collecting the data it needs to measure insurance risk. At a minimum this data should be capable of allowing a *firm* to evaluate the types of *claims* experienced, *claims* frequency and severity, expense levels, persistency levels and, where relevant, potential changes in the value of guarantees and options in *long-term insurance contracts*.

17.1.15 G   PRA

A *firm* should ensure that the data it collects and the measurement methodologies that it uses are sufficient to enable it to evaluate, as appropriate:

(1)   its exposure to insurance risk at all relevant levels, for example, by contract, *policyholder*, product line or insurance class;

(2)   its exposure to insurance risk across different geographical areas and time horizons;

(3)   its total, *firm*-wide, exposure to insurance risk and any other risks that may arise out of the *contracts of insurance* that it issues;

(4)   how changes in the volume of business (for example via changes in *premium* levels or the number of new contracts that are underwritten) may influence its exposure to insurance risk;

(5)   how changes in *policy* terms may influence its exposure to insurance risk; and

(6)   the effects of specific loss scenarios on the insurance liabilities of the *firm*.

17.1.16 G   PRA

A *firm* should hold data in a manner that allows for it to be used in a flexible way. For example, data should be sufficiently detailed and disaggregated so that contract details may be aggregated in different combinations to assess different risks.

17.1.17 G   PRA

A *firm* should be able to justify its choice of measurement methodologies. This justification should normally be documented.

17.1.18 G   PRA

A *firm* should periodically review the appropriateness of the measurement methodologies that it uses. This could, for example, include back testing (that is, by comparing actual versus expected results) and updating for changes in market practice.

17.1.19 G   PRA

A *firm* should ensure that it has access to the necessary skills and resources that it needs to measure insurance risk using its chosen methodology.

17.1.20 G   PRA

When measuring its insurance risks, a *firm* should consider how emerging experience could be used to update its underwriting process, in particular in relation to contract terms and pricing and also its assessment of the *technical provisions* in the balance sheet.

17.1.21 G   PRA

A *firm* should have the capability to measure its exposure to insurance risk on a regular basis. In deciding on the frequency of measurement, a *firm* should consider:

(1)   the time it takes to acquire and process all necessary data;

(2)   the speed at which exposures could change; and

(3)   that it may need to measure its exposure to certain types of insurance risk on a daily basis (for example, weather catastrophes).

Risk monitoring

17.1.22 G   PRA

A *firm* should provide regular and timely information on its insurance risks to the appropriate level of management. This could include providing reports on the following:

(1)   a statement of the *firm's* profits or losses for each class of business that it underwrites (with an associated analysis of how these have arisen for any *long-term insurance contracts*), including a variance analysis detailing any deviations from budget or changes in the key performance indicators that are used to assess the success of its business plan for insurance;

(2)   the *firm's* exposure to insurance risk at all relevant levels (see **SYSC 17.1.15 G (1)**), as well as across different geographical areas and time zones (see **SYSC 17.1.15 G (2)**), also senior management should be kept informed of the *firm's* total exposure to insurance risk (see **SYSC 17.1.15 G (3)**);

(3)   an analysis of any internal or external trends that could influence the *firm's* exposure to insurance risk in the future (e.g. new weather patterns, socio-demographic changes, expense overruns etc);

(4)   any new or emerging developments in *claims* experience (e.g. changes in the type of *claims*, average *claim* amounts or the number of similar *claims*);

(5)   the results of any stress testing or scenario analyses;

(6)   the amount and details of new business written and the amount of business that has lapsed or been cancelled;

(7)   identified fraudulent *claims*;

(8)   a watch list, detailing, for example, material/catastrophic events that could give rise to significant numbers of new *claims* or very large *claims*, contested *claims*, client complaints, legal and other developments;

(9)   the performance of any *reinsurance*/risk transfer arrangements; and

(10)   progress reports on matters that have previously been referred under escalation procedures (see **SYSC 17.1.23 G**).

17.1.23 G   PRA

A *firm* should establish and maintain procedures for the escalation of appropriate matters to the relevant level of management. Such matters may include:

(1)   any significant new exposures to insurance risk, including for example any landmark rulings in the courts;

(2)   a significant increase in the size or number of *claims*;

(3)   any breaches of the limits set out in **SYSC 17.1.27 G** and **SYSC 17.1.28 G**, in particular senior management should be informed where any maximum limits have been breached (see **SYSC 17.1.29 G**); and

(4)   any unauthorised deviations from its insurance risk policy (including those by a *broker*, *appointed representative* or other delegated authority).

17.1.24 G   PRA

A *firm* should regularly monitor the effectiveness of its analysis techniques for setting provisions for *claims* on *general insurance contracts*.

17.1.25 G   PRA

A *firm* should have appropriate procedures in place to allow managers to monitor the application (and hence the effect) of its *reinsurance* programme. This would include, for a general *insurer*, procedures for monitoring how its *reinsurance* programme affects the gross provisions that it makes for outstanding *claims* (including *claims* that are incurred but not reported).

Risk control

17.1.26 G   PRA

A *firm* should take appropriate action to ensure that it is not exposed to insurance risk in excess of its risk appetite. In so doing, the *firm* should be both reactive, responding to actual increases in exposure, and proactive, responding to potential future increases. Being proactive should involve close co-ordination between the processes of risk control, risk identification and risk measurement, as potential future exposures need to be identified and understood before effective action can be taken to control them.

17.1.27 G   PRA

A *firm* should consider setting limits for its exposure to insurance risk, which trigger action to be taken to control exposure. Periodically these limits should be amended in the light of new information (e.g. on the expected number or size of *claims*). For example, limits could be set for:

(1)   the *firm's* aggregate exposure to a single source of insurance risk or for events that may be the result of a number of different sources;

(2)   the *firm's* exposure to specific geographic areas or any other groupings of risks whose outcomes may be positively correlated;

(3)   the number of fraudulent *claims*;

(4)   the number of very large *claims* that could arise;

(5)   the number of unauthorised deviations from its insurance risk policy;

(6)   the amount of insurance risk than can be transferred to a particular *reinsurer*;

(7)   the level of expenses incurred in respect of each relevant business area; and

(8)   the level of persistency by product line or distribution channel.

17.1.28 G   PRA

A *firm* should also consider setting individual underwriting limits for all *employees* and agents that have the authority to underwrite insurance risk. This could include both monetary limits and limits on the types of risk that they can underwrite. Where individual underwriting limits are set, the *firm* should ensure that they are adhered to.

17.1.29 G   PRA

In addition to setting some 'normal' limits for insurance risk, a *firm* should consider setting some maximum limits, beyond which immediate, emergency action should be taken. These maximum limits could be determined through stress testing and scenario analysis.

17.1.30 G   PRA

A *firm* should pay close attention to the wording of its *policy* documentation to ensure that these wordings do not expose it to more, or higher, *claims* than it is expecting. In so doing, the *firm* should consider:

(1)   whether it has adequate in-house legal resources;

(2)   the need for periodic independent legal review of *policy* documentation;
(3)   the use of standardised documentation and referral procedures for variation of terms;
(4)   reviewing the documentation used by other insurance companies;
(5)   revising documentation for new *policies* in the light of past experience; and
(6)   the operation of law in the jurisdiction of the *policyholder*.

17.1.31 G   PRA

A *firm* should ensure that it has appropriate systems and controls for assessing the validity of *claims*. This could involve consideration of the evidence that will be required from *policyholders* and how this evidence is to be tested as well as procedures to determine when experts such as loss adjusters, lawyers or accountants should be used.

17.1.32 G   PRA

Particular care should be taken to ensure that a *firm* has appropriate systems and controls to deal with large *claims* or large groups of *claims* that could significantly deplete its financial resources. This should include systems to ensure that senior management (that is, the *governing body* and relevant *senior managers*) is involved in the processing of such *claims* from the outset.

17.1.33 G   PRA

A *firm* should consider how it intends to use *reinsurance* or some other form of insurance risk transfer agreement to help to control its exposure to insurance risk. Additional *guidance* on the use of *reinsurance*/risk transfer is provided below.

Reinsurance and other forms of risk transfer

17.1.34 G   PRA

Before entering into or significantly changing a *reinsurance* agreement, or any other form of insurance risk transfer agreement, a *firm* should:
(1)   analyse how the proposed *reinsurance*/risk transfer agreement will affect its exposure to insurance risk, its underwriting strategy and its ability to meet its regulatory obligations;
(2)   ensure there are adequate legal checking procedures in respect of the draft agreement;
(3)   conduct an appropriate due diligence of the *reinsurer's* financial stability (that is, solvency) and expertise; and
(4)   understand the nature and limits of the agreement (particular attention should be given to the wording of contracts to ensure that all of the required risks are covered, that the level of available cover is appropriate, and that all the terms, conditions and warranties are unambiguous and understood).

17.1.34A G   PRA

A *firm* should analyse regularly the full effect of all its *reinsurance* agreements and other risk transfer agreements (both current and proposed), including any related agreements or side-letters, on both its current and potential future financial position, and ensure that:
(1)   all significant risks related to these agreements, and the residual risks borne by the *firm*, have been identified; and
(2)   appropriate risk mitigation techniques have been applied to manage and control the risks.

17.1.35 G   PRA

In managing its *reinsurance* agreements, or any other form of insurance risk transfer agreement, a *firm* should have in place appropriate systems that allow it to maintain its desired level of cover. This could involve systems for:
(1)   monitoring the risks that are covered (that is, the scope of cover) by these agreements and the level of available cover;
(2)   keeping underwriting staff informed of any changes in the scope or level of cover;
(3)   properly co-ordinating all *reinsurance*/risk transfer activities so that, in aggregate, the desired level and scope of cover is maintained;
(4)   ensuring that the *firm* does not become overly reliant on any one *reinsurer* or other risk transfer provider; or
(5)   conducting regular stress testing and scenario analysis to assess the resilience of its *reinsurance* and risk transfer programmes to catastrophic events that may give rise to large and or numerous *claims*.

17.1.36 G   PRA

In making a claim on a *reinsurance* contract (that is, its *reinsurance* recoveries) or some other risk transfer contract a *firm* should ensure:
(1)   that it is able to identify and recover any money that it is due in a timely manner; and
(2)   that it makes adequate financial provision for the risk that it is unable to recover any money that it expected to be due, as a result of either a dispute with or a default by the *reinsurer* /risk transfer provider. Additional *guidance* on credit risk in *reinsurance*/risk transfer contracts is provided in INSPRU 2.1 (Credit risk in insurance).

17.1.37 G   PRA

Where the planned level or scope of cover from a *reinsurance*/risk transfer contract is not obtained, a *firm* should consider revising its underwriting strategy.

Record keeping

17.1.38 G   PRA

The *PRA's* high level *rules* and *guidance* for record keeping are outlined in **SYSC 3.2.20 R** (Records). Additional *rules* and *guidance* are set out in **SYSC 14.1.51 G** to **SYSC 14.1.64 G**. In complying with these *rules* and *guidance*, a *firm* should retain an appropriate record of its insurance risk management activities. This may, for example, include records of:

(1)   each new risk that is underwritten (noting that these records may be held by agents or cedants, rather than directly by the *firm* provided that the *firm* has adequate access to those records);

(2)   any material aggregation of exposure to risk from a single source, or of the same kind or to the same potential catastrophe or event;

(3)   each notified *claim* including the amounts notified and paid, precautionary notices and any re-opened *claims*;

(4)   *policy* and contractual documents and any relevant representations made to *policyholders*;

(5)   other events or circumstances relevant to determining the risks and commitments that arise out of *contracts of insurance* (including discretionary benefits and charges under any *long-term insurance contracts*);

(6)   the formal wordings of *reinsurance* contracts; and

(7)   any other relevant information on the *firm's reinsurance* or other risk-transfer arrangements, including the extent to which they:

(a)   have been exhausted by recoveries on paid *claims*; and

(b)   will be exhausted by recoveries on reported *claims* and, to the extent known, on incurred but not reported *claims*.

17.1.39 G   PRA

A *firm* should retain its underwriting and *claims* histories for as long as they may be needed to inform pricing or provisioning decisions.

CHAPTER 18
GUIDANCE ON PUBLIC INTEREST DISCLOSURE ACT: WHISTLEBLOWING

18.1   APPLICATION

[3.24]
18.1.1 G   FCA

This chapter is relevant to every *firm* to the extent that the Public Interest Disclosure Act 1998 ("PIDA") applies to it.

Purpose

18.1.2 G   FCA

(1)   The purposes of this chapter are:

(a)   to remind *firms* of the provisions of PIDA; and

(b)   to encourage *firms* to consider adopting and communicating to workers appropriate internal procedures for handling workers' concerns as part of an effective risk management system.

(2)   In this chapter "worker" includes, but is not limited to, an individual who has entered into a contract of employment.

18.1.3 G   FCA

The *guidance* in this chapter concerns the effect of PIDA in the context of the relationship between *firms* and the *FCA*. It is not comprehensive guidance on PIDA itself.

18.2   PRACTICAL MEASURES

Effect of Public Interest Disclosure Act 1998 (PIDA)

18.2.1 G   FCA

(1)   Under PIDA, any clause or term in an agreement between a worker and his employer is void in so far as it purports to preclude the worker from making a protected disclosure (that is, "blow the whistle").

(2)   In accordance with section 1 of PIDA:

(a)   a protected disclosure is a qualifying disclosure which meets the relevant requirements set out in part 4A of the Employment Rights Act 1996;

(b)   a qualifying disclosure is a disclosure, made in the public interest, of information which, in the reasonable belief of the worker making the disclosure, tends to show that one or more of the following (a "failure") has been, is being, or is likely to be, committed:

(i)   a criminal offence; or

(ii)   a failure to comply with any legal obligation; or

(iii)   a miscarriage of justice; or

(iv)   the putting of the health and safety of an individual in danger; or

(v)   damage to the environment; or

(vi)   deliberate concealment relating to any of (i) to (v);

it is immaterial whether the relevant failure occurred, occurs or would occur in the *United Kingdom* or elsewhere, and whether the law applying to it is that of the *United Kingdom* or of any other country or territory.

Internal procedures

18.2.2 G   FCA

(1)   *Firms* are encouraged to consider adopting (and encouraged to invite their *appointed representatives* or, where applicable, their *tied agents* to consider adopting) appropriate internal procedures which will encourage workers with concerns to blow the whistle internally about matters which are relevant to the functions of the *FCA* or *PRA*.

(2)   Smaller *firms* may choose not to have as extensive procedures in place as larger *firms*. For example, smaller *firms* may not need written procedures. The following is a list of things that larger and smaller *firms* may want to do.

(a)   For larger *firms*, appropriate internal procedures may include:

(i)   a clear statement that the *firm* takes failures seriously (see **SYSC 18.2.1G (2)(B)**);

(ii)   an indication of what is regarded as a failure;

(iii)   respect for the confidentiality of workers who raise concerns, if they wish this;

(iv)   an assurance that, where a protected disclosure has been made, the *firm* will take all reasonable steps to ensure that no *person* under its control engages in victimisation;

(v)   the opportunity to raise concerns outside the line management structure, such as with the Compliance Director, Internal Auditor or Company Secretary;

(vi)   penalties for making false and malicious allegations;

(vii) an indication of the proper way in which concerns may be raised outside the *firm* if necessary (see (3));

(viii) providing access to an external body such as an independent charity for advice;

(ix)   making whistleblowing procedures accessible to staff of key contractors; and

(x)   written procedures.

(b)   For smaller *firms*, appropriate internal procedures may include:

(i)   telling workers that the *firm* takes failures seriously (see **SYSC 18.2.1G (2)(B)**) and explaining how wrongdoing affects the organisation;

(ii)   telling workers what conduct is regarded as failure;

(iii)   telling workers who raise concerns that their confidentiality will be respected, if they wish this;

(iv)   making it clear that concerned workers will be supported and protected from reprisals;

(v)   nominating a senior officer as an alternative route to line management and telling workers how they can contact that individual in confidence;

(vi)   making it clear that false and malicious allegations will be penalised by the *firm*;

(vii) telling workers how they can properly blow the whistle outside the *firm* if necessary (see (3));

(viii) providing access to an external body such as an independent charity for advice; and

(ix)   encouraging managers to be open to concerns.

(3)

(a)   *Firms* should also consider telling workers (through the *firm's* internal procedures, or by means of an information sheet available from the *FCA's* website, or by some other means) that they can blow the whistle to the *FCA*, as the regulator prescribed in respect of financial services and markets matters under PIDA.

(b)   The *FCA* will give priority to live concerns or matters of recent history, and will emphasise that the worker's first port of call should ordinarily be the *firm* (see Frequently Asked Questions on www.fca.org.uk/site-info/contact/whistleblowing/faq).

(c)   For the *FCA's* treatment of confidential information, see **SUP 2.2.4 G**.

Link to fitness and propriety

18.2.3 G   FCA

The *FCA* would regard as a serious matter any evidence that a *firm* had acted to the detriment of a worker because he had made a protected disclosure (see **SYSC 18.2.1G (2)**) about matters which are relevant to the functions of the *FCA* or *PRA*. Such evidence could call into question the fitness and propriety of the *firm* or relevant members of its staff, and could therefore, if relevant, affect the *firm's* continuing satisfaction of *threshold condition* 5 (Suitability) or, for an *approved person*, his status as such.

CHAPTER 19A
IFPRU REMUNERATION CODE

19A GENERAL APPLICATION AND PURPOSE

Who? What? Where?

[3.25]
19A.1.1 R	FCA
(1)	The *Remuneration Code* applies to:
	(a)	[deleted]
	(b)	[deleted]
	(c)	an *IFPRU investment firm*;
	(d)	an *overseas firm* that;
		(i)	is not an *EEA firm*;
		(ii)	has its head office outside the *EEA*; and
		(iii)	would be a *firm* referred to in (a), (b) or (c) if it had been a *UK domestic firm*, had carried on all of its business in the *UK* and had obtained whatever authorisations for doing so as are required under the Act.
(2)	In relation to a *firm* that falls under (1)(d), the *Remuneration Code* applies only in relation to activities carried on from an establishment in the *United Kingdom*.
(3)	Otherwise, the *Remuneration Code* applies to a *firm* within (1) in the same way as **SYSC 4.1.1 R** (General Requirements).

19A.1.1A G

[deleted]

19A.1.2 G	FCA

Part 2 of **SYSC 1 ANNEX 1** provides for the application of **SYSC 4.1.1 R** (General Requirements). In particular, and subject to the provisions on group risk systems and controls requirements in **SYSC 12**, this means that:
(1)	in relation to what the *Remuneration Code* applies to, it:
	(a)	applies in relation to *regulated activities*, activities that constitute *dealing in investments as principal* (disregarding the exclusion in article 15 of the *Regulated Activities Order* (Absence of holding out etc)), *ancillary activities* and (in relation to *MiFID business*) *ancillary services*;
	(b)	applies with respect to the carrying on of *unregulated activities* in a *prudential context*; and
	(c)	takes into account activities of other *group* members; and
(2)	in relation to where the *Remuneration Code* applies, it applies in relation to:
	(a)	a *firm's UK* activities;
	(b)	a *firm's passported activities* carried on from a *branch* in another *EEA State*; and
	(c)	a *UK domestic firm's* activities wherever they are carried on, in a *prudential context*.

When?

19A.1.3 R	FCA
(1)	A *firm* must apply the *remuneration* requirements in **SYSC 19A.3** other than **SYSC 19A.3.44R (3)** and **SYSC 19A.3.44A R** in relation to:
	(a)	*remuneration* awarded, whether pursuant to a contract or otherwise, on or after 1 January 2011;
	(b)	*remuneration* due on the basis of contracts concluded before 1 January 2011 which is awarded or paid on or after 1 January 2011; and
	(c)	*remuneration* awarded, but not yet paid, before 1 January 2011, for services provided in 2010.

	[**Note:** article 3(2) of the Third Capital Requirements Directive (Directive 2010/76/EU)]
(2)	A *firm* must apply the remuneration requirements in **SYSC 19A.3.44R (3)** and **SYSC 19A.3.44A R** in relation to remuneration awarded for services provided or performance from the year 2014 onwards, whether due on the basis of contracts concluded before, on or after 31 December 2013.
	[**Note:** article 162(3) of *CRD*]

19A.1.4 G   FCA

Subject to the requirements of **SYSC 19A.1.5 R**, in the *appropriate regulator's* view **SYSC 19A.1.3 R** does not require a *firm* to breach requirements of applicable contract or employment law.

[**Note:** recital 14 of the Third Capital Requirements Directive (Directive 2010/76/EU)]

19A.1.5 R   FCA

(1)   This *rule* applies to a *firm* that is unable to comply with the *Remuneration Code* because of an obligation it owes to a *Remuneration Code staff member* under a provision of an agreement made on or before 29 July 2010 (the "*provision*").

(2)   A *firm* must take reasonable steps to amend or terminate the provision referred to in (1) in a way that enables it to comply with the *Remuneration Code* at the earliest opportunity.

(3)   Until the provision referred to in (1) ceases to prevent the *firm* from complying with the *Remuneration Code*, the *firm* must adopt specific and effective arrangements, processes and mechanisms to manage the risks raised by the provision.

Purpose

19A.1.6 G   FCA

(1)   The aim of the *Remuneration Code* is to ensure that *firms* have risk-focused *remuneration* policies, which are consistent with and promote effective risk management and do not expose them to excessive risk. It expands upon the general organisational requirements in **SYSC 4**.

(2)   The *Remuneration Code* implements the main provisions of the *CRD* which relate to *remuneration*. The Committee of European Banking Supervisors published Guidelines on Remuneration Policies and Practices on 10 December 2010. Provisions of the Capital Requirements Regulations 2013 (SI 2013/3115) together with the European Banking Authority's Guidelines to article 75(1) and (3) of the *CRD* relating to the collection of *remuneration* benchmarking information and *high earners* information have been implemented through SUP 16 Annex 33AR and SUP 16 Annex 34AR. The Guidelines can be found at

www.eba.europa.eu/regulation-and-policy/remuneration/
guidelines-on-the-remuneration-benchmarking-exercise and
www.eba.europa.eu/regulation-and-policy/remuneration/
guidelines-on-the-data-collection-exercise-regarding-high-earners.

(3)   [deleted]

Notifications to the appropriate regulator

19A.1.7 G   FCA

(1)   The *Remuneration Code* does not contain specific notification requirements. However, general circumstances in which the *appropriate regulator* expects to be notified by *firms* of matters relating to their compliance with requirements under the *regulatory system* are set out in **SUP 15.3** (General notification requirements).

(2)   In particular, in relation to *remuneration* matters such circumstances should take into account *unregulated activities* as well as *regulated activities* and the activities of other members of a *group* and would include each of the following:

(a)   significant breaches of the *Remuneration Code*, including any breach of a *rule* to which the detailed provisions on voiding and recovery in **SYSC 19A ANNEX 1** apply;

(b)   any proposed *remuneration* policies, procedures or practices which could:

(i)   have a significant adverse impact on the *firms* reputation; or

(ii)   affect the *firms* ability to continue to provide adequate services to its *customers* and which could result in serious detriment to a *customer* of the *firm*; or

(iii)   result in serious financial consequences to the *financial system* or to other *firms*;

(c)   any proposed changes to *remuneration* policies, practices or procedures which could have a significant impact on the *firms* risk profile or resources;

(d)   fraud, errors and other irregularities described in **SUP 15.3.17 R** which may suggest weaknesses in, or be motivated by, the *firms remuneration* policies, procedures or practices.

(3)   Such notifications should be made immediately the *firm* becomes aware, or has information which reasonably suggests such circumstances have occurred, may have occurred or may occur in the foreseeable future.

Individual guidance

19A.1.8 G   FCA

The *FCA's* policy on individual *guidance* is set out in **SUP 9**. *Firms* should in particular note the policy on what the *FCA* considers to be a reasonable request for *guidance* (see **SUP 9.2.5 G**). For example, where a *firm* is seeking *guidance* on a proposed *remuneration* structure the *FCA* will expect the *firm* to provide a detailed analysis of how the structure complies with the *Remuneration Code*, including the general requirement for *remuneration* policies, procedures and practices to be consistent with and promote sound and effective risk management.

19A   GENERAL REQUIREMENT

Remuneration policies must promote effective risk management

19A.2.1 R   FCA

A *firm* must establish, implement and maintain *remuneration* policies, procedures and practices that are consistent with and promote sound and effective risk management.

[**Note:**article 74(1) of *CRD*]

19A.2.2 G   FCA

(1)   If a *firm's remuneration* policy is not aligned with effective risk management it is likely that *employees* will have incentives to act in ways that might undermine effective risk management.

(2)   The *Remuneration Code* covers all aspects of *remuneration* that could have a bearing on effective risk management including salaries, bonuses, long-term incentive plans, options, hiring bonuses, severance packages and pension arrangements. In applying the *Remuneration Code*, a *firm* should have regard to applicable good practice on *remuneration* and corporate governance, such as guidelines on executive contracts and severance produced by the Association of British Insurers (ABI) and the National Association of Pension Funds (NAPF). In considering the risks arising from its *remuneration* policies, a *firm* will also need to take into account its statutory duties in relation to equal pay and non-discrimination.

(3)   As with other aspects of a *firm's* systems and controls, in accordance with **SYSC 4.1.2 R** *remuneration* policies, procedures and practices must be comprehensive and proportionate to the nature, scale and complexity of the *common platform firm's* activities. What a *firm* must do in order to comply with the *Remuneration Code* will therefore vary. For example, while the *Remuneration Code* refers to a *firm's remuneration* committee and risk management function, it may be appropriate for the *governing body* of a smaller *firm* to act as the *remuneration* committee, and for the *firm* not to have a separate risk management function.

(4)   The principles in the *Remuneration Code* are used by the *appropriate regulator* to assess the quality of a *firm's remuneration* policies and whether they encourage excessive risk-taking by a *firm's employees*.

(5)   The *appropriate regulator* may also ask *remuneration* committees to provide the *appropriate regulator* with evidence of how well the *firm's remuneration* policies meet the *Remuneration Code's* principles, together with plans for improvement where there is a shortfall. The *appropriate regulator* also expects relevant *firms* to use the principles in assessing their exposure to risks arising from their *remuneration* policies as part of the *internal capital adequacy assessment process (ICAAP)*.

(6)   The *Remuneration Code* is principally concerned with the risks created by the way *remuneration* arrangements are structured, not with the absolute amount of *remuneration*, which is generally a matter for *firms' remuneration* committees.

19A.2.3 G   FCA

(1)   The specific *remuneration* requirements in this chapter may apply only in relation to certain categories of *employee*. But the *appropriate regulator* would expect *firms*, in complying with the *Remuneration Code* general requirement, to apply certain principles on a *firm*-wide basis.

(2)   In particular, the *appropriate regulator* considers that *firms* should apply the principle relating to guaranteed variable *remuneration* on a *firm*-wide basis (Remuneration Principle 12(c); **SYSC 19A.3.40 R** to **SYSC 19A.3.43 G**).

(3)   The *appropriate regulator* would also expect *firms* to apply at least the principles relating to risk management and risk tolerance (Remuneration Principle 1); supporting business strategy, objectives, values and long-term interests of the firm (Remuneration Principle 2); conflicts of interest (Remuneration Principle 3); governance (Remuneration Principle 4); risk adjustment (Remuneration Principle 8); pension policy (Remuneration Principle 9); personal investment strategies (Remuneration Principle 10); payments related to early termination (Remuneration Principle 12(e)) and deferral (Remuneration Principle 12(g)) on a *firm*-wide basis.

Record-keeping

19A.2.4 G   FCA

In line with the record-keeping requirements in **SYSC 9**, a *firm* should ensure that its *remuneration* policies, practices and procedures are clear and documented. Such policies, practices and procedures would include performance appraisal processes and decisions.

Interpretation of references to remuneration

19A.2.5 R　FCA

(1)　In this chapter references to *remuneration* include *remuneration* paid, provided or awarded by any *person* to the extent that it is paid, provided or awarded in connection with *employment* by a *firm*.

(2)　Paragraph (1) is without prejudice to the meaning of *remuneration* elsewhere in the *Handbook*.

19A.2.6 G　FCA

Remuneration includes, for example, payments made by a seconding organisation which is not subject to the *Remuneration Code* to a secondee in respect of their *employment* by a *firm* which is subject to the *Remuneration Code*.

19A　REMUNERATION PRINCIPLES FOR IFPRU INVESTMENT FIRMS

Application: groups

19A.3.1 R　FCA

(1)　A *firm* must apply the requirements of this section at *group*, *parent undertaking* and *subsidiary undertaking* levels, including those *subsidiaries* established in a country or territory which is not an *EEA State*.

(2)　Paragraph (1) does not limit **SYSC 12.1.13R (2)(DA)** (which relates to the application of the *Remuneration Code* within *UK consolidation groups* and *non-EEA sub-groups*).

[**Note:** article 92(1) of *CRD*]

19A.3.2 G　FCA

SYSC 12.1.13R (2)(DA) requires the *firm* to ensure that the risk management processes and internal control mechanisms at the level of any *UK consolidation group* or *non-EEA sub-group* of which a *firm* is a member comply with the obligations set out in this section on a consolidated (or sub-consolidated) basis. In the *appropriate regulator's* view, the requirement to apply this section at *group*, *parent undertaking* and *subsidiary undertaking* levels (as provided for in **SYSC 19A.3.1R (1)**) is in line with the requirements in article 109(2) of *CRD* concerning the application of systems and controls requirements to *groups* (as implemented in **SYSC 12.1.13 R**).

Application: categories of staff and proportionality

19A.3.3 R　FCA

(1)　This section applies in relation to *Remuneration Code staff*, except as set out in (3).

(2)　When establishing and applying the total *remuneration* policies for *Remuneration Code staff*, a *firm* must comply with this section in a way and to the extent that is appropriate to its size, internal organisation and the nature, the scope and the complexity of its activities (the *remuneration principles proportionality rule*).

(3)　Paragraphs (1) and (2) do not apply to the requirement for significant *firms* to have a *remuneration* committee (**SYSC 19A.3.12 R**).

[**Note:** article 92(2) of *CRD*]

[**Note:** In addition to the *guidance* in this section which relates to the *remuneration principles proportionality rule*, the *FSA* gave guidance on the division of *firms* into categories for the purpose of providing a framework for the operation of the *remuneration principles proportionality rule*. This guidance has been adopted by the FCA and is available in the FCA website at www.fca.org.uk/your-fca/documents/finalised-guidance/remuneration-code]

19A.3.4 R　FCA

(1)　*Remuneration Code staff* comprises:

　(a)　an *employee* of an *IFPRU investment firm* whose professional activities have a material impact on the *firm's* risk profile, including any *employee* who is deemed to have a material impact on the *firm's* risk profile in accordance with Regulation (EU) 604/2014 of 4 March 2014 (Regulatory technical standards to identify staff who are material risk takers); or

　(b)　subject to (2) and (3), an *employee* of an *overseas firm* in **SYSC 19A.1.1R (1)(D)** (i.e., an *overseas firm* that would have been an *IFPRU investment firm* if it had been a *UK domestic firm*) whose professional activities have a material impact on the *firm's* risk profile, including any *employee* who would meet any of the criteria set out in articles 3 or 4(1) of Regulation (EU) 604/2014 of 4 March 2014 (Regulatory technical standards to identify staff who are material risk takers) if it had applied to him.

(2)　An *overseas firm* in **SYSC 19A.1.1R (1)(D)** (i.e., an *overseas firm* that would have been an *IFPRU investment firm* if it had been a *UK domestic firm*) may deem an *employee* not to be *Remuneration Code staff* where:

(a)   the *employee*:
  (i)   would meet the criteria in article 4(1) of Regulation (EU) No 604/2014 of 4 March 2014;
  (ii)   would not meet any of the criteria in article 3 of Regulation (EU) No 604/2014 of 4 March 2014; and
  (iii)   was awarded total remuneration of less than 750,000 in the previous year; and
(b)   the *overseas firm* determines that the professional activities of the *employee* do not have a material impact on its risk profile on the grounds described in article 4(2) of Regulation (EU) 604/2014 of 4 March 2014.
(3)   Where the *overseas firm* deems an *employee* not to be *Remuneration Code staff* as set out in (2), it must notify the *FCA*, applying the approach described in article 4(4) of Regulation (EU) 604/2014 of 4 March 2014.

[**Note:** article 92(2) of *CRD* and articles 3 and 4 of Regulation (EU) No 604/2014 of 4 March 2014.]]

19A.3.4A G   FCA

Where an *overseas firm* in **SYSC 19A.1.1 R (1)(D)** (i.e., an *overseas firm* that would have been a *IFPRU investment firm* if it had been a *UK domestic firm*) wishes to deem an *employee* who earns more than 750,000 not to be *Remuneration Code staff*, the *overseas firm* may apply for a *waiver* of the requirement in **SYSC 19A.3.4 R** in respect of that *employee*.

19A.3.5 R   FCA

A *firm* must:
(1)   maintain a record of its *Remuneration Code staff* in accordance with the general record-keeping requirements (**SYSC 9**); and
(2)   take reasonable steps to ensure that its *Remuneration Code staff* understand the implications of their status as such, including the potential for *remuneration* which does not comply with certain requirements of the *Remuneration Code* to be rendered void and recoverable by the *firm*.

19A.3.6 G   FCA

(1)   In the *appropriate regulator's* view:
  (a)   a *firm's* staff includes its *employees*;
  (b)   a *person* who performs a *significant influence function* for, or is a *senior manager* of, a *firm* would normally be expected to be part of the *firm's Remuneration Code staff*;
  (c)   the table in (2) provides a non-exhaustive list of examples of key positions that should, subject to (d), be within a *firm's* definition of staff who are risk takers;
  (d)   *firms* should consider how the examples in the table in (2) apply in relation to their own organisational structure (as the description of suggested business lines in the first row may be most appropriate to a *firm* which *deals on its own account* to a significant extent);
  (e)   *firms* may find it useful to set their own metrics to identify their risk takers based, for example, on trading limits; and
  (f)   a *firm* should treat a *person* as being *Remuneration Code staff* in relation to *remuneration* in respect of a given performance year if they were *Remuneration Code staff* for any part of that year.
  [**Note:** The *FSA* gave *guidance* on the application of particular rules on *remuneration* structures in relation to individuals who are *Remuneration Code staff* for only part of a given performance year. This guidance has been adopted by the FCA and is available in the FCA website at www.fca.org.uk/your-fca/documents/finalised-guidance/remuneration-code]

High-level category	Suggested business lines
Heads of significant business lines (including regional heads) and any individuals or groups within their control who have a material impact on the *firm's* risk profile	Fixed income Foreign exchange Commodities Securitisation Sales areas Investment banking (including mergers and acquisitions advisory) Commercial banking Equities Structured finance Lending quality Trading areas Research

High-level category	Suggested business lines
Heads of support and control functions and other individuals within their control who have a material impact on the *firm's* risk profile	Credit / market / operational risk Legal Treasury controls Human resources Compliance Internal audit

Remuneration Principle 1: Risk management and risk tolerance

19A.3.7 R   FCA

A *firm* must ensure that its *remuneration* policy is consistent with and promotes sound and effective risk management and does not encourage risk-taking that exceeds the level of tolerated risk of the *firm*.

[**Note:** article 92(2)(a) of *CRD*]

Remuneration Principle 2: Supporting business strategy, objectives, values and long-term interests of the firm

19A.3.8 R   FCA

A *firm* must ensure that its *remuneration* policy is in line with the business strategy, objectives, values and long-term interests of the *firm*.

[**Note:** article 92(2)(b) of *CRD*]

Remuneration Principle 3: Avoiding conflicts of interest

19A.3.9 R   FCA

A *firm* must ensure that its *remuneration* policy includes measures to avoid conflicts of interest.

[**Note:** article 92(2)(b) of *CRD*]

Remuneration Principle 4: Governance

19A.3.10 R   FCA

A *firm* must ensure that its *management body* in its *supervisory function* adopts and periodically reviews the general principles of the *remuneration* policy and is responsible for overseeing its implementation.

[**Note:** article 92(2)(c) of *CRD* and Standard 1 of the *FSB Compensation Standards*]

19A.3.11 R   FCA

A *firm* must ensure that the implementation of the *remuneration* policy is, at least annually, subject to central and independent internal review for compliance with policies and procedures for *remuneration* adopted by the *management body* in its *supervisory function*.

[**Note:** article 92(2)(d) of *CRD* and Standard 1 of the *FSB Compensation Standards*]

19A.3.12 R   FCA

(1)   A *CRR firm* that is significant in terms of its size, internal organisation and the nature, the scope and the complexity of its activities must establish a *remuneration* committee.

(2)   The *remuneration* committee must be constituted in a way that enables it to exercise competent and independent judgment on *remuneration* policies and practices and the incentives created for managing risk, capital and liquidity.

(3)   The chairman and the members of the *remuneration* committee must be members of the *management body* who do not perform any executive function in the *firm*.

(4)   The *remuneration* committee must be responsible for the preparation of decisions regarding *remuneration*, including those which have implications for the risk and risk management of the *firm* and which are to be taken by the *management body*.

(5)   When preparing such decisions, the *remuneration* committee must take into account the long-term interests of shareholders, investors and other stakeholders in the *firm* and the public interest.

[**Note:** article 95 of *CRD* and Standard 1 of the *FSB Compensation Standards*]

[**Note:** The *guidance* referred to in the Note to **SYSC 19A.3.3 R** also gives *guidance* on proportionality in relation to *remuneration* committees.]

19A.3.12A R   FCA

A *firm* that maintains a website must explain on the website how it complies with the *Remuneration Code*.

[**Note:** article 96 of *CRD*]

19A.3.12B R FCA

In **SYSC 19A.3.12 R** a '*CRR firm* that is significant' means a *significant IFPRU firm*.

19A.3.13 G FCA
(1)   A *firm* should be able to demonstrate that its decisions are consistent with an assessment of its financial condition and future prospects. In particular, practices by which *remuneration* is paid for potential future revenues whose timing and likelihood remain uncertain should be evaluated carefully and the *governing body* or *remuneration* committee (or both) should work closely with the *firm's* risk function in evaluating the incentives created by its *remuneration* system.
(2)   The *governing body* and any *remuneration* committee are responsible for ensuring that the *firm's remuneration* policy complies with the *Remuneration Code* and where relevant should take into account relevant guidance, such as that issued by the Basel Committee on Banking Supervision, the International Association of Insurance Supervisors (IAIS) and the International Organization of Securities Commissions (IOSCO).
(3)   The periodic review of the implementation of the *remuneration* policy should assess compliance with the *Remuneration Code*.
(4)   Guidance on what the *supervisory function* might involve is set out in **SYSC 4.3.3 G**.

Remuneration Principle 5: Control functions

19A.3.14 R FCA

A *firm* must ensure that *employees* engaged in control functions:
(1)   are independent from the business units they oversee;
(2)   have appropriate authority; and
(3)   are *remunerated*:
          (a)   adequately to attract qualified and experienced staff; and
          (b)   in accordance with the achievement of the objectives linked to their functions, independent of the performance of the business areas they control.

[Note: article 92(2)(e) of *CRD* and Standard 2 of the *FSB Compensation Standards*]

19A.3.15 E FCA
(1)   A *firm's* risk management and compliance functions should have appropriate input into setting the *remuneration* policy for other business areas. The procedures for setting *remuneration* should allow risk and compliance functions to have significant input into the setting of individual *remuneration* awards where those functions have concerns about the behaviour of the individuals concerned or the riskiness of the business undertaken.
(2)   Contravention of (1) may be relied on as tending to establish contravention of the *rule* on *employees* engaged in control functions having appropriate authority (**SYSC 19A.3.14R (2)**).

19A.3.16 R FCA

A *firm* must ensure that the *remuneration* of the senior officers in risk management and compliance functions is directly overseen by the *remuneration* committee referred to in **SYSC 19A.3.12 R**, or, if such a committee has not been established, by the *governing body* in its *supervisory function*.

[Note: article 92(2)(f) of *CRD*]

19A.3.17 G FCA
(1)   This Remuneration Principle is designed to manage the conflicts of interest which might arise if other business areas had undue influence over the *remuneration* of *employees* within control functions. Conflicts of interest can easily arise when *employees* are involved in the determination of *remuneration* for their own business area. Where these could arise they need to be managed by having in place independent roles for control functions (including, notably, risk management and compliance) and human resources. It is good practice to seek input from a *firm's* human resources function when setting *remuneration* for other business areas.
(2)   The need to avoid undue influence is particularly important where *employees* from the control functions are embedded in other business areas. This Remuneration Principle does not prevent the views of other business areas being sought as an appropriate part of the assessment process.
(3)   The *appropriate regulator* would generally expect the ratio of the potential variable component of *remuneration* to the fixed component of *remuneration* to be significantly lower for *employees* in risk management and compliance functions than for *employees* in other business areas whose potential bonus is a significant proportion of their *remuneration*. *Firms* should nevertheless ensure that the total *remuneration* package offered to those *employees* is sufficient to attract and retain staff with the skills, knowledge and expertise to discharge those functions. The requirement that the method of determining the *remuneration* of *relevant persons* involved in the compliance function must not compromise their objectivity or be likely to do so also applies (see **SYSC 6.1.4 R (4)**).

Remuneration Principle 6: Remuneration and capital

19A.3.18 R FCA

Part 3   FCA Handbook Materials

A *firm* must ensure that total variable *remuneration* does not limit the *firm's* ability to strengthen its capital base.

[**Note:** article 94(1)(c) of *CRD* and Standard 3 of the *FSB Compensation Standards*]

19A.3.19 G FCA

This Remuneration Principle underlines the link between a *firm's* variable *remuneration* costs and the need to manage its capital base, including forward-looking capital planning measures. Where a *firm* needs to strengthen its capital base, its variable *remuneration* arrangements should be sufficiently flexible to allow it to direct the necessary resources towards capital building.

Remuneration Principle 7: Exceptional government intervention

19A.3.20 R FCA

A *firm* that benefits from exceptional government intervention must ensure that:
(1)   variable *remuneration* is strictly limited as a percentage of net revenues when it is inconsistent with the maintenance of a sound capital base and timely exit from government support;
(2)   it restructures *remuneration* in a manner aligned with sound risk management and long-term growth, including when appropriate establishing limits to the *remuneration* of members of its *management body*; and
(3)   no variable *remuneration* is paid to members of its *management body* unless this is justified.

[**Note:** article 93 of *CRD* and Standard 10 of the *FSB Compensation Standards*]

19A.3.21 G FCA

The *appropriate regulator* would normally expect it to be appropriate for the ban on paying variable *remuneration* to members of the *management body* of a *firm* that benefits from exceptional government intervention to apply only in relation to members of the *management body* who were in office at the time that the intervention was required.

Remuneration Principle 8: Profit-based measurement and risk adjustment

19A.3.22 R FCA
(1)   A *firm* must ensure that any measurement of performance used to calculate variable *remuneration* components or pools of variable *remuneration* components:
        (a)   includes adjustments for all types of current and future risks and takes into account the cost and quantity of the capital and the liquidity required; and
        (b)   takes into account the need for consistency with the timing and likelihood of the firm receiving potential future revenues incorporated into current earnings.
(2)   A *firm* must ensure that the allocation of variable *remuneration* components within the *firm* also takes into account all types of current and future risks.

[**Note:** article 94(1)(j), (k) of *CRD* and Standard 4 of the *FSB Compensation Standards*]

19A.3.23 G FCA
(1)   This Remuneration Principle stresses the importance of risk adjustment in measuring performance, and the importance within that process of applying judgment and common sense. A *firm* should ask the risk management function to validate and assess risk-adjustment techniques, and to attend a meeting of the *governing body* or *remuneration* committee for this purpose.
(2)   A number of risk-adjustment techniques and measures are available, and a *firm* should choose those most appropriate to its circumstances. Common measures include those based on economic profit or economic capital. Whichever technique is chosen, the full range of future risks should be covered. The *appropriate regulator* expects a *firm* to be able to provide it with details of all adjustments that the *firm* has made under a formulaic approach.
(3)   The *appropriate regulator* expects that a *firm* will apply qualitative judgments and common sense in the final decision about the performance-related components of variable *remuneration* pools.
(4)   A *firm's governing body* (or *remuneration* committee where appropriate) should take the lead in determining the measures to be used. It should offer the appropriate checks and balances to prevent inappropriate manipulation of the measures used. It should consult closely and frequently with the *firm's* risk management functions, in particular those relating to operational, market, credit and liquidity risk.

19A.3.24 G FCA
(1)   Long-term incentive plans should be treated as pools of variable *remuneration*. Many common measures of performance for long-term incentive plans, such as earnings per *share* (EPS), are not adjusted for longer-term risk factors. Total shareholder return (TSR), another common measure, includes in its measurement dividend distributions, which can also be based on unadjusted earnings data. If incentive plans mature within a two to four year period and are based on EPS or TSR, strategies can be devised to boost EPS or TSR during the life

of the plan, to the detriment of the true longer-term health of a *firm*. For example, increasing leverage is a technique which can be used to boost EPS and TSR. *Firms* should take account of these factors when developing risk-adjustment methods.

(2)   *Firms* that have long-term incentive plans should structure them with vesting subject to appropriate performance conditions, and at least half of the award vesting after not less than five years and the remainder after not less than three years.

(3)   Long-term incentive plan awards may be included in the calculation of the deferred portion of variable *remuneration* only if upside incentives are adequately balanced by downside adjustments. The valuation of the award should be based on its value when the award is granted, and determined using an appropriate technique.

19A.3.25 R   FCA

Assessments of financial performance used to calculate variable *remuneration* components or pools of variable *remuneration* components must be based principally on profits.

19A.3.26 G   FCA

(1)   Performance measures based primarily on revenues or turnover are unlikely to pay sufficient regard to the quality of business undertaken or services provided. Profits are a better measure provided they are adjusted for risk, including future risks not adequately captured by accounting profits.

(2)   Management accounts should provide profit data at such levels within the *firm's* structure as to enable a *firm* to see as accurate a picture of contributions of relevant staff to a *firm's* performance as is reasonably practicable. If revenue or turnover is used as a component in performance assessment, processes should be in place to ensure that the quality of business undertaken or services provided and their appropriateness for *clients* are taken into account.

19A.3.27 R   FCA

A *firm* must ensure that its total variable *remuneration* is generally considerably contracted where subdued or negative financial performance of the *firm* occurs, taking into account both current *remuneration* and reductions in payouts of amounts previously earned, including through malus or clawback arrangements.

[**Note:** article 94(1)(n) of *CRD* and Standard 5 of the *FSB Compensation Standards*]

19A.3.28 G   FCA

Where a *firm* makes a loss the *appropriate regulator* would generally expect no variable *remuneration* to be awarded. Variable *remuneration* may nevertheless be justified, for example, to incentivise *employees* involved in new business ventures which could be loss-making in their early stages.

Remuneration Principle 9: Pension policy

19A.3.29 R   FCA

A *firm* must ensure that:

(1)   its pension policy is in line with its business strategy, objectives, values and long-term interests;

(2)   when an *employee* leaves the *firm* before retirement, any *discretionary pension benefits* are held by the *firm* for a period of five years in the form of instruments referred to in **SYSC 19A.3.47 R (1)**; and

(3)   when an *employee* reaches retirement, *discretionary pension benefits* are paid to the *employee* in the form of instruments referred to in **SYSC 19A.3.47 R (1)** and subject to a five-year retention period.

[**Note:** article 94(1)(o) of *CRD*]

Remuneration Principle 10: Personal investment strategies

19A.3.30 R   FCA

(1)   A *firm* must ensure that its *employees* undertake not to use personal hedging strategies or *remuneration* – or liability-related *contracts of insurance* to undermine the risk alignment effects embedded in their *remuneration* arrangements.

(2)   A *firm* must maintain effective arrangements designed to ensure that *employees* comply with their undertaking.

[**Note:** article 94(1)(p) of *CRD* and Standard 14 of the *FSB Compensation Standards*]

19A.3.31 G   FCA

In the *appropriate regulator's* view, circumstances in which a *person* will be using a personal hedging strategy include entering into an arrangement with a third party under which the third party will make payments, directly or indirectly, to that *person* that are linked to or commensurate with the amounts by which the *person's remuneration* is subject to reductions.

Remuneration Principle 11: Non-compliance with the Remuneration Code

19A.3.32 R   FCA

A *firm* must ensure that variable *remuneration* is not paid through vehicles or methods that facilitate non-compliance with the *Remuneration Code*.

[**Note**: article 94(1)(q) of *CRD*]

Remuneration Principle 12: Remuneration structures – introduction

19A.3.33 G   FCA

Remuneration Principle 12 consists of a series of *rules*, *evidential provisions* and *guidance* relating to *remuneration* structures.

19A.3.34 G   FCA

(1)   Taking account of the *remuneration principles proportionality rule*, the *appropriate regulator* does not generally consider it necessary for a *firm* to apply the *rules* referred to in (2) where, in relation to an individual ("X"), both the following conditions are satisfied:

    (a)   Condition 1 is that Xs variable *remuneration* is no more than 33% of total *remuneration*; and

    (b)   Condition 2 is that Xs total *remuneration* is no more than 500,000.

(2)   The *rules* referred to in (1) are those relating to:

    (a)   guaranteed variable *remuneration* (**SYSC 19A.3.40 R**);

    (b)   retained *shares* or other instruments (**SYSC 19A.3.47 R**);

    (c)   deferral (**SYSC 19A.3.49 R**); and

    (d)   performance adjustment (**SYSC 19A.3.51 R**).

[**Note**: The *FSA* also gave *guidance* on the application of certain *rules* on *remuneration* structures in relation to individuals who are *Remuneration Code staff* for only part of a given performance year. This guidance has been adopted by the FCA and is available in the FCA website at www.fca.org.uk/your-fca/documents/finalised-guidance/remuneration-code.]

Remuneration Principle 12(a): Remuneration structures – general requirement

19A.3.35 R   FCA

A *firm* must ensure that the structure of an *employee's remuneration* is consistent with and promotes effective risk management.

19A.3.35A R   FCA

A *firm* must ensure that the *remuneration* policy makes a clear distinction between criteria for setting:

(1)   basic fixed *remuneration* that primarily reflects an *employee's* professional experience and organisational responsibility as set out in the *employee's* job description and terms of employment; and

(2)   variable *remuneration* that reflects performance in excess of that required to fulfil the *employee's* job description and terms of employment and that is subject to performance adjustment in accordance with the *Remuneration Code*.

[**Note**: article 92(2)(g) of *CRD*]

19A.3.35B R   FCA

A *firm* must ensure that the *remuneration* policy makes a clear distinction between criteria for setting:

(1)   basic fixed *remuneration* that primarily reflects an *employee's* professional experience and organisational responsibility as set out in the *employee's* job description and terms of employment; and

(2)   variable *remuneration* that reflects performance in excess of that required to fulfil the *employee's* job description and terms of employment and that is subject to performance adjustment in accordance with the *Remuneration Code*.

[**Note**: article 92(2)(g) of *CRD*]

Remuneration Principle 12(b): Remuneration structures – assessment of performance

19A.3.36 R   FCA

A *firm* must ensure that where *remuneration* is performance-related:

(1)   the total amount of *remuneration* is based on a combination of the assessment of the performance of:

    (a)   the individual;

    (b)   the business unit concerned; and

    (c)   the overall results of the *firm*; and

(2)   when assessing individual performance, financial as well as non-financial criteria are taken into account.

[**Note:** article 94(1)(a) of *CRD* and Standard 6 of the *FSB Compensation Standards*]

19A.3.37 G   FCA

Non-financial performance metrics should form a significant part of the performance assessment process and should include adherence to effective risk management and compliance with the *regulatory system* and with relevant overseas regulatory requirements. Poor performance as assessed by non-financial metrics such as poor risk management or other behaviours contrary to *firm* values can pose significant risks for a *firm* and should, as appropriate, override metrics of financial performance. The performance assessment process and the importance of non-financial assessment factors in the process should be clearly explained to relevant *employees* and implemented. A balanced scorecard can be a good technique.

19A.3.38 R   FCA

A *firm* must ensure that the assessment of performance is set in a multi-year framework in order to ensure that the assessment process is based on longer-term performance and that the actual payment of performance-based components of *remuneration* is spread over a period which takes account of the underlying business cycle of the *firm* and its business risks.

[**Note:**article 94(1)(b) of *CRD*]

19A.3.39 G   FCA

The requirement for assessment of performance to be in a multi-year framework reflects the fact that profits from a *firm's* activities can be volatile and subject to cycles. The financial performance of *firms* and individual *employees* can be exaggerated as a result. Performance assessment on a moving average of results can be a good way of meeting this requirement. However, other techniques such as good quality risk adjustment and deferral of a sufficiently large proportion of *remuneration* may also be useful.

Remuneration Principle 12(c): Remuneration structures – guaranteed variable remuneration

19A.3.40 R   FCA

A *firm* must ensure that guaranteed variable *remuneration* is not part of prospective *remuneration* plans. A *firm* must not award, pay or provide guaranteed variable *remuneration* unless:

(1)   it is exceptional;
(2)   it occurs in the context of hiring new *Remuneration Code staff*;
(3)   the *firm* has a sound and strong capital base; and
(4)   it is limited to the first year of service.

[**Note:** article 94(1)(d) and (e) of *CRD* and Standard 11 of the *FSB Compensation Standards*]

19A.3.40A R   FCA

A *firm* must ensure that *remuneration* packages relating to compensation for, or buy out from, an *employee's* contracts in previous employment align with the long term interests of the *firm* and are subject to appropriate retention, deferral and performance and clawback arrangements.

[**Note:** article 94(1)(i) of *CRD*]

19A.3.41 E   FCA

(1)   A *firm* should not award, pay or provide guaranteed variable *remuneration* in the context of hiring new *Remuneration Code staff* (X) unless:
        (a)   it has taken reasonable steps to ensure that the *remuneration* is not more generous in either its amount or terms (including any deferral or retention periods) than the variable *remuneration* awarded or offered by Xs previous employer; and
        (b)   it is subject to appropriate performance adjustment requirements.
(2)   Contravention of (1) may be relied on as tending to establish contravention of the *rule* on guaranteed variable *remuneration* (**SYSC 19A.3.40 R**).

19A.3.42 G   FCA

Guaranteed variable *remuneration* should be subject to the same deferral criteria as other forms of variable *remuneration* awarded by the *firm*.

19A.3.43 G   FCA

In the *appropriate regulator's* view, variable *remuneration* can be awarded to *Remuneration Code staff* in the form of retention awards where it is compatible with the *Remuneration Code general requirement* to do so. The *appropriate regulator* considers this is likely to be the case only where a *firm* is undergoing a major restructuring and a good case can be made for retention of particular key staff members on prudential grounds. Proposals to give retention awards should form part of any notice of the restructuring proposals required in accordance with *Principle* 11 and the general notification requirements in **SUP 15.3**.

Remuneration Principle 12(d): Remuneration structures – ratios between fixed and variable components of total remuneration

19A.3.44 R   FCA

A *firm* must set an appropriate ratio between the fixed and variable components of total *remuneration* and ensure that:

(1)   fixed and variable components of total *remuneration* are appropriately balanced;

(2)   the level of the fixed component represents a sufficiently high proportion of the total *remuneration* to allow the operation of a fully flexible policy on variable *remuneration* components, including the possibility to pay no variable *remuneration* component; and

(3)   subject to **SYSC 19A.3.44A R**, the level of the variable component of total *remuneration* must not exceed 100% of the fixed component of total *remuneration* for each *Remuneration Code staff*.

[**Note:** article 94(1)(f) and 94(1)(g)(i) of the *CRD*]

19A.3.44A R   FCA

A *firm* may set a higher maximum level of the ratio between the fixed and variable components of total *remuneration* provided:

(1)   the overall level of the variable component does not exceed 200% of the fixed component of the total *remuneration* for each *Remuneration Code staff*; and

(2)   is approved by the shareholders or owners or members of the *firm* in accordance with **SYSC 19A.3.44B R**.

[**Note**: article 94(1)(g)(ii) of *CRD*]

19A.3.44B R   FCA

A *firm* must ensure that any approval by its shareholders or owners or members for the purposes of **SYSC 19A.3.44A R** is carried out in accordance with the following procedure:

(1)   the *firm* must give reasonable notice to all its shareholders or owners or members of its intention to seek approval of the proposed higher ratio;

(2)   the *firm* must make a detailed recommendation to all its shareholders or owners or members that includes:

    (a)   the reasons for, and the scope of, the approval sought;

    (b)   the number of staff affected and their functions; and

    (c)   the expected impact on the requirement to maintain a sound capital base;

(3)   the *firm* must:

    (a)   without delay, inform the *FCA* of the recommendation to its shareholders or owners or members, including the proposed higher ratio and the reasons therefor; and

    (b)   demonstrate to the *FCA* that the proposed higher ratio does not conflict with its obligations under the *CRD* and the *EU CRR*, having particular regard to the *firm's own funds* obligations;

(4)   the *firm* must ensure that *employees* who have an interest in the proposed higher ratio are not allowed to exercise, directly or indirectly, any voting rights they may have as shareholders or owners or members of the *firm* in respect of the approval sought; and

(5)   the higher ratio is approved by a majority of:

    (a)   at least 66% of the shares or equivalent ownership rights represented, if at least 50% of the shares or equivalent ownership rights in the *firm* are represented; or

    (b)   at least 75% of the shares or equivalent ownership rights represented, if less than 50% of the shares or equivalent ownership rights in the *firm* are represented.

[**Note**: article 94(1)(g)(ii) of *CRD*]

19A.3.44C R   FCA

A *firm* must notify without delay the *appropriate regulator* of the decisions taken by its shareholders or members or owners including any approved higher maximum ratio.

[**Note**: article 94(1)(g)(ii) of *CRD*]

19A.3.44D R   FCA

A *firm* may apply a discount rate to a maximum of 25% of an *employee's* total variable remuneration provided it is paid in instruments that are deferred for a period of not less than five years.

[**Note**: article 94(1)(g)(iii) of *CRD*]

19A.3.44E R   FCA

In applying the discount rate in **SYSC 19A.3.44D R**, a *firm* must apply the *EBA* Guidelines on the applicable notional discount rate for variable remuneration published on 27 March 2014.

[Note: the *EBA* Guidelines on the applicable notional discount rate for variable remuneration can be found   at: www.eba.europa.eu/documents/10180/643987/ EBA-GL-2014-01+%28Final+Guidelines+on+the+discount+rate+for+remuneration%29.pdf/ e8b3b3f6-6258-439d-a2d9-633e6e5de5e9]

Remuneration Principle 12(e): Remuneration structures – payments related to early termination

19A.3.45 R   FCA

A *firm* must ensure that payments relating to the early termination of a contract reflect performance achieved over time and are designed in a way that does not reward failure or misconduct.

[**Note:** article 94(1)(h) of *CRD* and Standard 12 of the *FSB Compensation Standards*]

19A.3.46 G   FCA

Firms should review existing contractual payments related to termination of employment with a view to ensuring that these are payable only where there is a clear basis for concluding that they are consistent with the *Remuneration Code general requirement*.

[**Note:** Standard 12 of the *FSB Compensation Standards*]

Remuneration Principle 12(f): Remuneration structures – retained shares or other instruments

19A.3.47 R   FCA
(1)   A *firm* must ensure that a substantial portion, which is at least 50%, of any variable *remuneration* consists of an appropriate balance of:
    (a)   *shares* or equivalent ownership interests, subject to the legal structure of the *firm* concerned, or *share*-linked instruments or equivalent non-cash instruments in the case of a non-listed *firm*; and
    (b)   where possible other instruments which are eligible as Additional Tier 1 instruments or are eligible as Tier 2 instruments or other instruments that can be fully converted to Common Equity Tier 1 instruments or written down, that in each case adequately reflect the credit quality of the *firm* as a going concern and are appropriate for use as variable remuneration.
(2)   The instruments in (1) must be subject to an appropriate retention policy designed to align incentives with the longer-term interests of the *firm*.
(3)   This *rule* applies to both the portion of the variable *remuneration* component deferred in accordance with **SYSC 19A.3.49 R** and the portion not deferred.

[**Note:** article 94(1)(l) of *CRD* and Standard 8 of the *FSB Compensation Standards*]

19A.3.48 G   FCA
(1)   The Committee of European Banking Supervisors has given guidance on the interpretation of the Directive provision transposed by **SYSC 19A.3.47R (3)**. Its Guidelines provide that this requirement means that the 50% minimum threshold for instruments must be applied equally to the non-deferred and the deferred components; in other words, *firms* must apply the same chosen ratio between instruments and cash for their total variable *remuneration* to both the upfront and deferred components. (Guidelines on Remuneration Policies and Practices, 10 December 2010, paragraph 133.)
(2)   This simplified example illustrates the operation of (1). The variable remuneration of a material risk taker (X) is 100, and by **SYSC 19A.3.49R (3)** X is required to defer 60%. Xs upfront component is 40 and Xs deferred component is 60. At least 20 of Xs upfront component, and at least 30 of Xs deferred component, must be in instruments referred to in **SYSC 19A.3.47R (1)**.

Remuneration Principle 12(g): Remuneration structures – deferral

19A.3.49 R   FCA
(1)   A *firm* must not award, pay or provide a variable *remuneration* component unless a substantial portion of it, which is at least 40%, is deferred over a period which is not less than three to five years.
(2)   *Remuneration* under (1) must vest no faster than on a pro-rata basis.
(3)   In the case of a variable *remuneration* component:
    (a)   of a particularly high amount, or
    (b)   payable to a *director* of a *firm* that is significant in terms of its size, internal organisation and the nature, scope and complexity of its activities;
    at least 60% of the amount must be deferred.
(4)   Paragraph (3)(b) does not apply to a *non-executive director*.
(5)   The length of the deferral period must be established in accordance with the business cycle, the nature of the business, its risks and the activities of the *employee* in question.

[**Note:** article 94(1)(m) of *CRD* and Standards 6 and 7 of the *FSB Compensation Standards*]
(6)   500,000 is a particularly high amount for the purpose of (3)(a).
(7)   Paragraph (6) is without prejudice to the possibility of lower sums being considered a particularly high amount.

19A.3.50 G   FCA
(1)   Deferred *remuneration* paid in *shares* or *share*-linked instruments should be made under a scheme which meets appropriate criteria, including risk adjustment of the performance measure used to determine the initial allocation of shares. Deferred *remuneration* paid in cash should also be subject to performance criteria.

(2)   The *appropriate regulator* would generally expect a *firm* to have a *firm*-wide policy (and *group*-wide policy, where appropriate) on deferral. The proportion deferred should generally rise with the ratio of variable *remuneration* to fixed *remuneration* and with the amount of variable *remuneration*. While any variable *remuneration* component of 500,000 or more paid to *Remuneration Code staff* must be subject to 60% deferral, *firms* should also consider whether lesser amounts should be considered to be 'particularly high' taking account, for example, of whether there are significant differences within *Remuneration Code staff* in the levels of variable *remuneration* paid.

Remuneration Principle 12(h): Remuneration structures – performance adjustment, etc.

19A.3.51 R   FCA

A *firm* must ensure that any variable *remuneration*, including a deferred portion, is paid or vests only if it is sustainable according to the financial situation of the *firm* as a whole, and justified on the basis of the performance of the *firm*, the business unit and the individual concerned.

[**Note:** article 94(1)(n) of *CRD* and Standards 6 and 9 of the *FSB Compensation Standards*]

19A.3.51A R   FCA

A *firm* must:
(1)   ensure that any of the total variable *remuneration* is subject to malus or clawback arrangements;
(2)   set specific criteria for the application of malus and clawback; and
(3)   ensure that the criteria for the application of malus and clawback in particular cover situations where the *employee*:
    (a)   participated in or was responsible for conduct which resulted in significant losses to the *firm*;
    (b)   failed to meet appropriate standards of fitness and propriety.

[**Note**: article 94(1)(n) of *CRD*]

19A.3.52 E   FCA
(1)   A *firm* should reduce unvested deferred variable *remuneration* when, as a minimum:
    (a)   there is reasonable evidence of *employee* misbehaviour or material error; or
    (b)   the *firm* or the relevant business unit suffers a material downturn in its financial performance; or
    (c)   the *firm* or the relevant business unit suffers a material failure of risk management.
(2)   For performance adjustment purposes, awards of deferred variable *remuneration* made in *shares* or other non-cash instruments should provide the ability for the *firm* to reduce the number of *shares* or other non-cash instruments.
(3)   Contravention of (1) or (2) may be relied on as tending to establish contravention of the *rule* on performance adjustment (**SYSC 19A.3.51 R**).

19A.3.53 G   FCA
(1)   Variable *remuneration* may be justified, for example, to incentivise *employees* involved in new business ventures which could be loss-making in their early stages.
(2)   The *governing body* (or, where appropriate, the *remuneration* committee) should approve performance adjustment policies, including the triggers under which adjustment would take place. The *appropriate regulator* may ask *firms* to provide a copy of their policies and expects *firms* to make adequate records of material decisions to operate the adjustments.

Effect of breaches of the Remuneration Principles

19A.3.53A R   FCA

SYSC 19A ANNEX 1 makes provision about voiding and recovery.

19A.3.54 R   FCA
(1)   Subject to (1A) to (3), the *rules* in **SYSC 19A ANNEX 1.1R TO 1.4R** apply in relation to the prohibitions on *Remuneration Code staff* being *remunerated* in the ways specified in:
    (a)   **SYSC 19A.3.40 R** (guaranteed variable *remuneration*);
    (b)   **SYSC 19A.3.49 R** (non-deferred variable *remuneration*); and
    (c)   **SYSC 19A ANNEX 1.7R** (replacing payments recovered or property transferred).
(2)   Paragraph (1) applies only to those prohibitions as they apply in relation to a *firm* that satisfies at least one of the conditions set out in (1B) and (1D).
(3)   Condition 1 is that the *firm* is a relevant *IFPRU 730k firm* that has relevant total assets exceeding £50 billion.
(4)   [deleted]
(5)   Condition 2 is that the *firm*:
    (a)   is a relevant *IFPRU 730k firm* or a relevant *third country IFPRU 730k firm*; and
    (b)   is part of a *group* containing a *firm* that has relevant total assets exceeding £50 billion and that is a
        relevant *IFPRU 730k firm*.

(6)   In this rule:

       (a)   a "relevant *IFPRU 730k firm*" is any *IFPRU 730k firm* that is not a *limited activity firm* or a *limited licence firm*;

       (b)   a "relevant *third country IFPRU 730k firm*" is any *third country IFPRU 730k firm* that is not a *limited activity firm* or a *limited licence firm*; and

       (c)   "relevant total assets" means the arithmetic mean of the *firm's* total assets as set out in its balance sheet on its last three *accounting reference dates*.

(7)   This *rule* does not apply in relation to the prohibition on *Remuneration Code staff* being *remunerated* in the way specified in **SYSC 19A.3.40 R** (guaranteed variable *remuneration*) if both the conditions in paragraphs (2) and (3) of that *rule* are met.

(8)   This *rule* does not apply in relation to *Remuneration Code staff* (X) in respect of whom both the following conditions are satisfied:

       (a)   Condition 1 is that Xs variable *remuneration* is no more than 33% of total *remuneration*; and

       (b)   Condition 2 is that Xs total *remuneration* is no more than 500,000.

(9)   In relation to (3):

       (a)   references to *remuneration* are to *remuneration* awarded or paid in respect of the relevant performance year;

       (b)   the amount of any *remuneration* is:

            (i)   if it is money, its amount when awarded;

            (ii)   otherwise, whichever of the following is greatest: its value to the recipient when awarded; its market value when awarded; and the cost of providing it;

       (c)   where *remuneration* is, when awarded, subject to any condition, restriction or other similar provision which causes the amount of the *remuneration* to be less than it otherwise would be, that condition, restriction or provision is to be ignored in arriving at its value; and

       (d)   it is to be assumed that the member of *Remuneration Code staff* will remain so for the duration of the relevant performance year.

19A.3.55 G   FCA

(1)   Sections 137H and 137I of the *Act* enables the *appropriate regulator* to make *rules* that render void any provision of an agreement that contravenes specified prohibitions in the *Remuneration Code*, and that provide for the recovery of any payment made, or other property transferred, in pursuance of such a provision. **SYSC 19A.3.53A R** and **SYSC 19A.3.54 R** (together with **SYSC 19A ANNEX 1**) are such *rules* and render void provisions of an agreement that contravene the specified prohibitions on guaranteed variable *remuneration*, non-deferred variable *remuneration* and replacing payments recovered or property transferred. This is an exception to the general position set out in section 138E(2) of the *Act* that a contravention of a *rule* does not make any transaction void or unenforceable.

(2)   [deleted]

19A ANNEX 1   DETAILED PROVISIONS ON VOIDING AND RECOVERY (SYSC 19A.3.53AR AND SYSC 19A.3.54R)

		Rendering contravening provisions of agreements void
1	R	Any provision of an agreement that contravenes a prohibition on *persons* being *remunerated* in a way specified in a *rule* to which this*rule* applies (a "contravening provision") is void.
1A	R	A contravening provision does not cease to be void because:
		(1) the *firm* concerned ceases to satisfy any of the conditions set out in **SYSC 19A.3.54 R (1B)** to **(1D)**; or
		(2) the member of *Remuneration Code staff* concerned starts to satisfy both of the conditions set out in **SYSC 19A.3.54 R (3)(A)** and **(B)**.
2	R	A contravening provision that, at the time a *rule* to which this *rule* applies was made, is contained in an agreement made before that time is not rendered void by 1R unless it is subsequently amended so as to contravene such a *rule*.
3	G	The effect of 2R, in accordance with sections 137H and 137I of the *Act*, is to prevent contravening provisions being rendered void retrospectively. Contravening provisions may however be rendered void if they are contained in an agreement made after the *rule* containing the prohibition is made by the *appropriate regulator* but before the *rule* comes into effect. For further relevant transitional provisions, see **SYSC TP 3.6A**.
3A	R	(1) A pre-existing provision is not rendered void by 1R.
		(2) In this Annex a pre-existing provision is any provision of an agreement that would (but for this *rule*) be rendered void by 1R that was agreed at a time when either:

(a) the *firm* concerned did not satisfy any of the conditions set out in **SYSC 19A.3.54 R (1B)** to **(1D)**; or

(b) the member of *Remuneration Code staff* concerned satisfied both of the conditions set out in **SYSC 19A.3.54 R (3)(A)** and **(B)**.

(3) But an amendment to, or in relation to, a pre-existing provision is not to be treated as a pre-existing provision where the amendment is agreed at a time when both:

(a) the *firm* concerned satisfies at least one of the conditions set out in **SYSC 19A.3.54 R (1B)** to **(1D)**; and

(b) the member of *Remuneration Code staff* concerned does not satisfy both of the conditions set out in **SYSC 19A.3.54 R (3)(A)** and **(B)**.

| 4 | R | For the purposes of this chapter it is immaterial whether the law which (apart from this annex) governs a contravening provision is the law of the *United Kingdom*, or of a part of the *United Kingdom*. |

Recovery of payments made or property transferred pursuant to a void contravening provision

| 5 | R | In relation to any payment made or other property transferred in pursuance of a contravening provision other than a pre-existing provision, a *firm* must take reasonable steps to: |

(1) recover any such payment made or other property transferred by the *firm*; and

(2) ensure that any other *person* ("P") recovers any such payment made or other property transferred by that *person*.

| 5A | R | Paragraph 5R continues to apply in one or both of the following cases: |

(1) the *firm* concerned ceases to satisfy any of the conditions set out in **SYSC 19A.3.54R (1B)** to **(1D)**;

(2) the member of *Remuneration Code staff* concerned starts to satisfy both of the conditions set out in **SYSC 19A.3.54R (3)(A)** and **(B)**.

| 6 | G | The *rule* in 5R(2) would, for example, apply in the context of a secondment. Where a *group* member seconds an individual to a *firm* and continues to be responsible for the individuals *remuneration* in respect of services provided to the *firm*, the *firm* would need to take reasonable steps to ensure that the *group* member recovers from the secondee any *remuneration* paid in pursuance of a contravening provision. |

Replacing payments recovered or property transferred

| 7 | R | (1) A *firm* must not award, pay or provide variable *remuneration* to a *person* who has received *remuneration* in pursuance of a contravening provision other than a pre-existing provision (the "contravening *remuneration*") unless the *firm* has obtained a legal opinion stating that the award, payment or provision of the *remuneration* complies with the *Remuneration Code*. |

(2) This *rule* applies only to variable *remuneration* relating to a performance year to which the contravening *remuneration* related.

(3) The legal opinion in (1) must be properly reasoned and be provided by an appropriately qualified independent individual.

(4) Paragraph (1) continues to apply in one or both of the following cases:

(a) the *firm* concerned ceases to satisfy any of the conditions set out in **SYSC 19A.3.54R (1B)** to **(1D)**;

(b) the member of *Remuneration Code staff* concerned starts to satisfy both of the conditions set out in **SYSC 19A.3.54R (3)(A)** and **(B)**.

Notification to the appropriate regulator

| 8 | G | The *appropriate regulator* considers any breach of a *rule* to which this annex applies to be a significant breach which should be notified to the *appropriate regulator* in accordance with **SUP 15.3.11 R** (Breaches of rules and other requirements in or under the Act). Such a notification should include information on the steps which a *firm* or other *person* has taken or intends to take to recover payments or property in accordance with 5R. |

CHAPTER 19B
AIFM REMUNERATION CODE

19B   APPLICATION

[3.26]

19B.1.1 R   FCA

The *AIFM Remuneration Code* applies to a *full-scope UK AIFM* of:
(1)   a *UK AIF*;
(2)   an *EEA AIF*; and
(3)   a *non-EEA AIF*.

19B.1.1A G   FCA
(1)   *Full-scope UK AIFMs* are advised that *ESMA* published Guidelines on sound remuneration
       policies under the *AIFMD* on 3 July 2013, which *full-scope UK AIFMs* should comply with
       in applying the *rules* in this section. The Guidelines can be found at: www.esma.europa.eu/
       system/files/2013-232_aifmd_guidelines_on_remuneration_-_en.pdf
(2)   The *FCA* has provided additional *guidance* on the application of principles of proportionality
       to remuneration policies of *AIFM*. The *guidance* also addresses several other aspects of the
       AIFM Remuneration Code and the Guidelines. The *guidance* can be found at: [www.fca.org.
       uk/your-fca/documents/finalised-guidance/fg14-02]

Remuneration policies and practices

19B.1.2 R   FCA

An *AIFM* must establish, implement and maintain *remuneration* policies and practices for *AIFM
Remuneration Code staff* that are consistent with, and promote, sound and effective risk management
and do not encourage risk-taking which is inconsistent with the risk profile of the *instrument
constituting the fund* of the *AIFs* it manages.

[**Note:** article 13(1) of *AIFMD*]

19B.1.3 R   FCA

AIFM Remuneration Code staff comprise those categories of staff whose professional activities have
a material impact on the risk profiles of the *AIFMs* or of the *AIFs* the *AIFM* manages. This includes
senior management, risk takers, control functions, and any *employees* receiving total *remuneration*
that takes them into the same *remuneration* bracket as senior management and risk takers.

[**Note:** article 13(1) of *AIFMD*]

19B.1.4 R   FCA
(1)   When establishing and applying the total *remuneration* policies for *AIFM Remunera-
       tion Code staff* (inclusive of salaries and discretionary pension benefits), an *AIFM* must
       comply with the *AIFM remuneration principles* in a way and to the extent that is appropriate
       to its size, internal organisation and the nature, scope and complexity of its activities.
(2)   Paragraph (1) does not apply to the requirement for significant *AIFMs* to have a *remuneration*
       committee (**SYSC 19B.1.9 R**).
(3)   The *AIFM remuneration principles* apply to remuneration of any type paid by the *AIFM*, to
       any amount paid directly by the *AIF* itself, including *carried interest*, and to any transfer of
       units or *shares* of the *AIF* made to the benefits of *AIFM Remuneration Code staff*.

[**Note:** paragraph 1 and 2 of Annex II of *AIFMD*]

AIFM Remuneration Principle 1: Risk management

19B.1.5 R   FCA

An *AIFM* must ensure that its *remuneration* policy is consistent with, and promotes, sound and
effective risk management and does not encourage risk-taking which is inconsistent with the risk
profiles of the *instrument constituting the fund* of the *AIFs* it manages.

[**Note:** paragraph 1(a) of Annex II of *AIFMD*]

*AIFM Remuneration Principle 2: Supporting business strategy, objectives, values and interests, and
avoiding conflicts of interest*

19B.1.6 R   FCA

An *AIFM* must ensure that its *remuneration* policy is in line with the business strategy, objectives,
values and interests of the *AIFM* and the *AIFs* it manages or the investors of such *AIFs*, and includes
measures to avoid conflicts of interest.

[**Note:** paragraph 1(b) of Annex II of *AIFMD*]

AIFM Remuneration Principle 3: Governance

19B.1.7 R   FCA

An *AIFM* must ensure that the *governing body* of the *AIFM*, in its supervisory function, adopts and periodically reviews the general principles of the *remuneration* policy and is responsible for its implementation.

[**Note:** paragraph 1(c) of Annex II of *AIFMD*]

19B.1.8 R   FCA

An *AIFM* must ensure the implementation of the *remuneration* policy is, at least annually, subject to central and independent internal review for compliance with policies and procedures for *remuneration* adopted by the *governing body* in its supervisory function.

[**Note:** paragraph 1(d) of Annex II of *AIFMD*]

19B.1.9 R   FCA
(1)   An *AIFM* that is significant in terms of its size, internal organisation and the nature, the scope and the complexity of its activities must establish a *remuneration* committee.
(2)   The *remuneration* committee must be constituted in a way that enables it to exercise competent and independent judgment on *remuneration* policies and practices, and the incentives created for managing risk.
(3)   The chairman and the members of the *remuneration* committee must be members of the *governing body* who do not perform any executive function in the *AIFM*.
(4)   The *remuneration* committee must be responsible for the preparation of decisions regarding *remuneration*, including those which have implications for the risk and risk management of the *AIFM* or the *AIF* concerned and which are taken by the *governing body* in its supervisory function.

[**Note:** paragraph 3 of Annex II of *AIFMD*]

AIFM Remuneration Principle 4: Control functions

19B.1.10 R   FCA

An *AIFM* must ensure that *employees* engaged in control functions are compensated according to the achievement of the objectives linked to their functions, independent of the performance of the business areas they control.

[**Note:** paragraph 1(e) of Annex II of *AIFMD*]

19B.1.11 R   FCA

An *AIFM* must ensure the *remuneration* of the senior officers in the risk management and compliance functions is directly overseen by the *remuneration* committee, or, if such a committee has not been established, by the *governing body* in its supervisory function.

[**Note:** paragraph 1(f) of Annex II of *AIFMD*]

AIFM Remuneration Principle 5(a): Remuneration structures – assessment of performance

19B.1.12 R   FCA

An *AIFM* must ensure that, where *remuneration* is performance related, the total amount of *remuneration* is based on a combination of the assessment of the performance of the individual and of the business unit or *AIF* concerned and of the overall results of the *AIFM*. When assessing individual performance, financial and non-financial criteria are taken into account.

[**Note:** paragraph 1(g) of Annex II of *AIFMD*]

19B.1.13 R   FCA

An *AIFM* must ensure that the assessment of performance is set in a multi-year framework appropriate to the life-cycle of the *AIFs* managed by the *AIFM* to ensure that:
(1)   the assessment process is based on longer term performance; and
(2)   the actual payment of performance-based components of *remuneration* is spread over a period which takes account of the redemption policy of the *AIFs* it manages and their investment risks.

[**Note:** paragraph 1(h) of Annex II of *AIFMD*]

19B.1.13A G   FCA
(1)   Taking account of the remuneration principles proportionality *rule* in **SYSC 19B.1.4 R**, the FCA does not generally consider it necessary for a *firm* to apply the *rules* referred to in (2) where, in relation to an individual ("X"), both of the following conditions are satisfied:
        (a)   Condition 1 is that X's variable *remuneration* is no more than 33% of total *remuneration*; and
        (b)   Condition 2 is that X's total *remuneration* is more than £500,000.
(2)   The *rules* referred to in (1) are those relating to:
        (a)   guaranteed variable *remuneration* (**SYSC 19B.1.14 R**);
        (b)   retained *units*, *shares* or other instruments (**SYSC 19B.1.17 R**);

(c)   deferral (**SYSC 19B.1.18 R**); and

(d)   performance adjustment (**SYSC 19B.1.19 R**).

AIFM Remuneration Principle 5(b): Remuneration structures – guaranteed variable remuneration

19B.1.14 R   FCA

An *AIFM* must not award, pay or provide guaranteed variable remuneration unless it;

(1)   is exceptional;

(2)   occurs only in the context of hiring new staff; and

(3)   is limited to the first year of service.

[**Note:** paragraph 1(i) of Annex II of *AIFMD*]

AIFM Remuneration Principle 5(c): Remuneration structures – fixed and variable components of total remuneration

19B.1.15 R   FCA

An *AIFM* must ensure that:

(1)   fixed and variable components of total *remuneration* are appropriately balanced; and

(2)   the fixed component represents a sufficiently high proportion of the total *remuneration* to allow the operation of a fully flexible policy on variable *remuneration* components, including the possibility to pay no variable *remuneration* component.

[**Note:** paragraph 1(j) of Annex II of *AIFMD*]

AIFM Remuneration Principle 5(d): Remuneration structures – payments related to early termination

19B.1.16 R   FCA

An *AIFM* must ensure that payments related to the early termination of a contract reflect performance achieved over time and are designed in a way that does not reward failure.

[**Note:** paragraph 1(k) of Annex II of *AIFMD*]

AIFM Remuneration Principle 5(e): Remuneration structures – retained units, shares or other instruments

19B.1.17 R   FCA

(1)   Subject to the legal structure of the *AIF* and the *instrument constituting the fund*, an *AIFM* must ensure that a substantial portion, and in any event at least 50% of any variable *remuneration*, consists of *units* or *shares* of the *AIF* concerned, or equivalent ownership interests, or share-linked instruments or equivalent non-cash instruments. However, if the management of *AIFs* accounts for less than 50% of the total portfolio managed by the *AIFM*, the minimum of 50 % does not apply.

(2)   The instruments in (1) must be subject to an appropriate retention policy designed to align incentives with the long-term interests of the *AIFM* and the *AIFs* it manages and the investors of such *AIFs*.

(3)   This *rule* applies to the portion of the variable *remuneration* component deferred in line with **SYSC 19B.1.18R (1)** and the portion not deferred.

[**Note:** paragraph 1(m) of Annex II of *AIFMD*]

AIFM Remuneration Principle 5(f): Remuneration structures – deferral

19B.1.18 R   FCA

(1)   An *AIFM* must not award, pay or provide a variable *remuneration* component unless a substantial portion, and in any event at least 40%, of the variable *remuneration* component, is deferred over a period which is appropriate in view of the life cycle and redemption policy of the *AIF* concerned and is correctly aligned with the nature of the risks of the *AIF* in question

(2)   The period referred to in (1) must be at least three to five years, unless the life cycle of the *AIF* concerned is shorter.

(3)   *Remuneration* payable under (1) must vest no faster than on a pro-rata basis.

(4)   In the case of a variable remuneration component of a particularly high amount, at least 60 % of the amount must be deferred.

[**Note:** paragraph 1(n) of Annex II of *AIFMD*]

19B.1.18A G   FCA

(1)   £500,000 is a particularly high amount for the purpose of **SYSC 19B.1.18R (4)**.

(2)   Paragraph (1) is without prejudice to the possibility of lower sums being considered a particularly high amount.

Part 3   FCA Handbook Materials

(3)   Whilst any variable *remuneration* component of £500,000 or more paid to *AIFM Remuneration Code staff* should be subject to 60% deferral, *firms* should also consider whether lesser amounts should be considered to be 'particularly high', taking account, for example, of whether there are significant differences within *AIFM Remuneration Code staff* in the levels of variable *remuneration* paid.

AIFM Remuneration Principle 5(g): Remuneration structures – performance adjustment, etc.

19B.1.19 R   FCA

An *AIFM* must ensure that any variable *remuneration*, including a deferred portion, is paid or vests only if it is sustainable according to the financial situation of the *AIFM* as a whole and justified according to the performance of the *AIF*, the business unit and the individual concerned.

[**Note:** paragraph 1(o) first sub-paragraph of Annex II of *AIFMD*]

19B.1.20 G   FCA

The total variable *remuneration* should generally be considerably contracted where subdued or negative financial performance of the *AIFM* or of the *AIF* concerned occurs, taking into account both current compensation and reductions in payouts of amounts previously earned, including through malus or clawback arrangements.

[**Note:** paragraph 1(o) second sub-paragraph of Annex II of *AIFMD*]

AIFM Remuneration Principle 6: Measurement of performance

19B.1.21 R   FCA

An *AIFM* must ensure the measurement of performance used to calculate variable *remuneration* components, or pools of variable *remuneration* components, includes a comprehensive adjustment mechanism to integrate all relevant types of current and future risks.

[**Note:** paragraph 1(l) of Annex II of *AIFMD*]

AIFM Remuneration Principle 7: Pension policy

19B.1.22 R   FCA

An *AIFM* must ensure that:
(1)   its pension policy is in line with its business strategy, objectives, values and long-term interests of the *AIFs* it manages;
(2)   when an *employee* leaves the *firm* before retirement, any *discretionary pension benefits* are held by the *firm* for a period of five years in the form of instruments in **SYSC 19B.1.17R (1)**; and
(3)   in the case of an *employee* reaching retirement, *discretionary pension benefits* are paid to the *employee* in the form of instruments referred to in **SYSC 19B.1.17R (1)** and subject to a five-year retention period.

[**Note:** paragraph 1(p) of Annex II of *AIFMD*]

AIFM Remuneration Principle 8: Personal investment strategies

19B.1.23 R   FCA

An *AIFM* must ensure that its *employees* undertake not to use personal hedging strategies or *remuneration* – and liability-related insurance to undermine the risk alignment effects embedded in their *remuneration* arrangements.

[**Note:** paragraph 1(q) of Annex II of *AIFMD*]

AIFM Remuneration Principle 9: Avoidance of the remuneration code

19B.1.24 R   FCA

An *AIFM* must ensure that variable remuneration is not paid through vehicles or methods that facilitate the avoidance of the requirements of the *AIFM Remuneration Code*.

[**Note:** paragraph 1(r) of Annex II of *AIFMD*]

CHAPTER 19C
BIPRU REMUNERATION CODE

19C   GENERAL APPLICATION AND PURPOSE

Who? What? Where?

[3.27]
19C.1.1 R   FCA
(1)   The *BIPRU Remuneration Code* applies to a *BIPRU firm* and a *third country BIPRU firm*.

(2)   In relation to a *third country BIPRU firm*, the *BIPRU Remuneration Code* applies only in relation to activities carried on from an establishment in the *United Kingdom*.

19C.1.1A G   FCA

The *AIFM Remuneration Code* (**SYSC 19B**) also applies to a *BIPRU firm* which is a *full-scope UK AIFM* (ie, a *full-scope UK AIFM* that is an *AIFM investment firm* subject to *BIPRU*). Such a *full-scope UK AIFM* that complies with **SYSC 19B** will also comply with **SYSC 19C**. In such cases, the *FCA* will not require the *full-scope UK AIFM* to demonstrate compliance with **SYSC 19C**.

19C.1.2 G   FCA

Part 2 of **SYSC 1 ANNEX 1** provides for the application of **SYSC 4.1.1 R** and **SYSC 4.1.1C R** (General Requirements). In particular, and subject to the provisions on group risk systems and controls requirements in **SYSC 12**, this means that:

(1)   the *BIPRU Remuneration Code*:
       (a)   applies to *regulated activities*, *ancillary activities* and applicable *ancillary services*;
       (b)   applies to the carrying on of *unregulated activities* in a *prudential context*; and
       (c)   takes into account activities of other *group* members; and
(2)   where the *BIPRU Remuneration Code* applies, it applies to:
       (a)   a *firm's UK* activities;
       (b)   a *firm's passported activities* carried on from a *branch* in another *EEA State*; and
       (c)   a *UK domestic firm's* activities wherever they are carried on, in a *prudential context*.

When?

19C.1.3 R   FCA

A *firm* must apply the *remuneration* requirements in **SYSC 19C.3** to:

(1)   *remuneration* awarded, whether under a contract or otherwise, on or after 1 January 2014;
(2)   *remuneration* due on the basis of contracts concluded before 1 January 2014 which is awarded or paid on or after 1 January 2014; and
(3)   *remuneration* awarded, but not yet paid, before 1 January 2014, for services provided in 2013.

19C.1.4 G   FCA

Subject to the requirements of **SYSC 19C.1.5 R**, in the *FCA's* view **SYSC 19C.1.3 R** does not require a *firm* to breach requirements of applicable contract or employment law.

19C.1.5 R   FCA

(1)   This *rule* applies to a *firm* that is unable to comply with the *BIPRU Remuneration Code* because of an obligation it owes to a *BIPRU Remuneration Code staff member* under a provision of an agreement made on or before 29 July 2010.
(2)   A *firm* must take reasonable steps to amend or terminate the provision in (1) in a way that enables it to comply with the *BIPRU Remuneration Code* at the earliest opportunity.
(3)   Until the provision in (1) ceases to prevent the *firm* from complying with the *BIPRU Remuneration Code*, the *firm* must adopt specific and effective arrangements, processes and mechanisms to manage the risks raised by the provision.

Purpose

19C.1.6 G   FCA

The aim of the *BIPRU Remuneration Code* is to ensure that *firms* have risk-focused *remuneration* policies, which are consistent with and promote effective risk management and do not expose them to excessive risk. It expands upon the general organisational requirements in **SYSC 4**.

Notifications to the FCA

19C.1.7 G   FCA

(1)   The *BIPRU Remuneration Code* does not contain specific notification requirements. However, general circumstances in which the *FCA* expects to be notified by *firms* of matters relating to their compliance with requirements under the *regulatory system* are set out in **SUP 15.3** (General notification requirements).
(2)   In particular, in relation to *remuneration* matters, such circumstances should take into account *unregulated activities* as well as *regulated activities* and the activities of other members of a *group* and would include each of the following:
       (a)   significant breaches of the *BIPRU Remuneration Code*;
       (b)   any proposed *remuneration* policies, procedures or practices which could:
           (i)   have a significant adverse impact on the *firm's* reputation; or
           (ii)   affect the *firm's* ability to continue to provide adequate services to its *customers* and which could result in serious detriment to a *customer* of the *firm*; or
           (iii)   result in serious financial consequences to the *financial system* or to other *firms*;

(c)   any proposed changes to *remuneration* policies, practices or procedures which could have a significant impact on the *firms* risk profile or resources; and

(d)   fraud, errors and other irregularities described in **SUP 15.3.17 R** which may suggest weaknesses in, or be motivated by, the *firm's remuneration* policies, procedures or practices.

(3)   Such notifications should be made immediately the *firm* becomes aware of those circumstances, or has information which reasonably suggests that those circumstances have, or may have, occurred or may occur in the foreseeable future.

Individual guidance

19C.1.8 G   FCA

The *FCA's* policy on individual *guidance* is set out in **SUP 9**. *Firms* should particularly note the policy on what the *FCA* considers to be a reasonable request for *guidance* (see **SUP 9.2.5 G**). For example, where a *firm* is seeking *guidance* on a proposed *remuneration* structure, the *FCA* will expect the *firm* to provide a detailed analysis of how the structure complies with the *BIPRU Remuneration Code*, including the general requirement for *remuneration* policies, procedures and practices to be consistent with and promote sound and effective risk management.

19C   GENERAL REQUIREMENT

Remuneration policies must promote effective risk management

19C.2.1 R   FCA

A *firm* must establish, implement and maintain *remuneration* policies, procedures and practices that are consistent with and promote sound and effective risk management.

19C.2.2 G   FCA

(1)   If a *firm's remuneration* policy is not aligned with effective risk management, it is likely that *employees* will have incentives to act in ways that might undermine effective risk management.

(2)   The *BIPRU Remuneration Code* covers all aspects of *remuneration* that could have a bearing on effective risk management including salaries, bonuses, long-term incentive plans, options, hiring bonuses, severance packages and pension arrangements. In applying the *BIPRU Remuneration Code*, a *firm* should have regard to applicable good practice on *remuneration* and corporate governance, such as guidelines on executive contracts and severance produced by the Association of British Insurers (ABI) and the National Association of Pension Funds (NAPF). In considering the risks arising from its *remuneration* policies, a *firm* will also need to take into account its statutory duties in relation to equal pay and non-discrimination.

(3)   As with other aspects of a *firm's* systems and controls, in line with **SYSC 4.1.2 R** and **SYSC 4.1.2AA R**, *remuneration* policies, procedures and practices must be comprehensive and proportionate to the nature, scale and complexity of the *firm's* activities. Therefore, what a *firm* must do to comply with the *BIPRU Remuneration Code* will vary. For example, while the *BIPRU Remuneration Code* refers to a *firm's remuneration* committee and risk management function, it may be appropriate for the *governing body* of a smaller *firm* to act as the *remuneration* committee, and for the *firm* not to have a separate risk management function.

(4)   The principles in the *BIPRU Remuneration Code* are used by the *FCA* to assess the quality of a *firm's remuneration* policies and whether they encourage excessive risk-taking by a *firm's employees*.

(5)   The *FCA* may also ask *remuneration* committees to provide the *FCA* with evidence of how well the *firm's remuneration* policies meet the *BIPRU Remuneration Code's* principles, together with plans for improvement where there is a shortfall. The *FCA* also expects relevant *firms* to use the principles in assessing their exposure to risks arising from their *remuneration* policies as part of the *internal capital adequacy assessment process (ICAAP)*.

(6)   The *BIPRU Remuneration Code* is principally concerned with the risks created by the way *remuneration* arrangements are structured, not with the absolute amount of *remuneration*, which is generally a matter for *firms' remuneration* committees.

19C.2.3 G   FCA

(1)   The specific *remuneration* requirements in this chapter may apply only to certain categories of *employee*. However, the *FCA* expects *firms*, in complying with the *BIPRU Remuneration Code* general requirement, to apply certain principles on a *firm*-wide basis.

(2)   In particular, the *FCA* considers that *firms* should apply the principle relating to guaranteed variable *remuneration* on a *firm*-wide basis (Remuneration Principle 12(c); **SYSC 19C.3.40 R to SYSC 19C.3.43 G**.

(3)   The *FCA* also expects *firms* to apply, as a minimum, the principles relating to risk management and risk tolerance (Remuneration Principle 1); supporting business strategy, objectives, values and long-term interests of the firm (Remuneration Principle 2); conflicts of

interest (Remuneration Principle 3); governance (Remuneration Principle 4); risk adjustment (Remuneration Principle 8); pension policy (Remuneration Principle 9); personal investment strategies (Remuneration Principle 10); payments related to early termination (Remuneration Principle 12(e)) and deferral (Remuneration Principle 12(g)) on a *firm*-wide basis.

Record-keeping

19C.2.4 G   FCA

In line with the record-keeping requirements in **SYSC 9**, a *firm* should ensure that its *remuneration* policies, practices and procedures are clear and documented. Such policies, practices and procedures would include performance appraisal processes and decisions.

Interpretation of references to remuneration

19C.2.5 R   FCA
(1)   In this chapter, references to *remuneration* include *remuneration* paid, provided or awarded by any *person* to the extent that it is paid, provided or awarded in connection with employment by a *firm*.
(2)   Paragraph (1) is without prejudice to the meaning of *remuneration* elsewhere in the *Handbook*.

19C.2.6 G   FCA

Remuneration includes, for example, payments made by a seconding organisation which is not subject to the *BIPRU Remuneration Code* to a secondee in respect of their employment by a *firm* which is subject to the *BIPRU Remuneration Code*.

19C   REMUNERATION PRINCIPLES

Application: groups

19C.3.1 R   FCA
(1)   A *firm* must apply the requirements of this section at *group*, *parent undertaking* and *subsidiary undertaking* levels, including those *subsidiaries* established in a country or territory which is not an *EEA State*.
(2)   Paragraph (1) does not limit **SYSC 12.1.13 R** and **SYSC 12.1.15 R** (which relate to the application of the *BIPRU Remuneration Code* within *UK consolidation groups* and *non-EEA sub-groups*).

19C.3.2 G   FCA

The effect of **SYSC 12.1.13 R (2)(DA)** and **SYSC 12.1.15 R** is that the *firm* is required to ensure that the risk management processes and internal control mechanisms at the level of any *consolidation group* or *non-EEA sub-group* of which a *firm* is a member comply with the obligations set out in this section on a consolidated (or sub-consolidated) basis.

Application: categories of staff and proportionality

19C.3.3 R   FCA
(1)   This section applies to *BIPRU Remuneration Code staff*, except as set out in (3).
(2)   When establishing and applying the total *remuneration* policies for *BIPRU Remuneration Code staff*, a *firm* must comply with this section in a way and to the extent that is appropriate to its size, internal organisation and the nature, scope and complexity of its activities (the *BIPRU remuneration principles proportionality rule*).
(3)   Paragraphs (1) and (2) do not apply to the requirement for significant *firms* to have a *remuneration* committee (**SYSC 19C.3.12 R**).

[**Note:** In addition to the *guidance* in this section which relates to the *BIPRU remuneration principles proportionality rule*, the *FCA* has published guidance on the operation of the *BIPRU remuneration principles proportionality rule*. This *guidance* is available at www.fca.org.uk/firms/markets/international-markets/remuneration-code.]

19C.3.4 R   FCA

BIPRU Remuneration Code staff comprises categories of staff including senior management, risk-takers, staff engaged in control functions and any *employee* receiving total remuneration that takes them into the same *remuneration* bracket as senior management and risk-takers, whose professional activities have a material impact on the *firm's* risk profile.

19C.3.5 R   FCA

A *firm* must:
(1)   maintain a record of its *BIPRU Remuneration Code staff* in line with the general record-keeping requirements (**SYSC 9**); and

(2)   take reasonable steps to ensure that its *BIPRU Remuneration Code staff* understand the implications of their status, including the potential for *remuneration* which does not comply with certain requirements of the *BIPRU Remuneration Code* to be rendered void and recoverable by the *firm*.

19C.3.6 G   FCA

(1)   In the *FCA's* view:

    (a)   a *firm's* staff includes its *employees*;

    (b)   a *person* who performs a *significant influence function* for, or is a *senior manager* of, a *firm* would normally be expected to be part of the *firm's BIPRU Remuneration Code staff*;

    (c)   the table in (2) provides a non-exhaustive list of examples of key positions that should, subject to (d), be within a *firm's* definition of staff who are risk takers;

    (d)   *firms* should consider how the examples in the table in (2) apply to their own organisational structure;

    (e)   *firms* may find it useful to set their own metrics to identify their risk takers based, for example, on trading limits; and

    (f)   a *firm* should treat a person as being *BIPRU Remuneration Code staff* in relation to *remuneration* in respect of a given performance year if they were *BIPRU Remuneration Code staff* for any part of that year.

[Note: The *FCA* has published *guidance* on the application of particular rules on *remuneration* structures in relation to individuals who are *BIPRU Remuneration Code staff* for only part of a given performance year. This *guidance* is available at www.fca.org.uk/firms/markets/international-markets/remuneration-code.]

High-level category	Suggested business lines
Heads of significant business lines (including regional heads) and any individuals or groups within their control who have a material impact on the *firm's* risk profile	Fixed income Foreign exchange Commodities Securitisation Sales areas Investment banking (including mergers and acquisitions advisory) Commercial banking Equities Structured finance Lending quality Trading areas Research
Heads of support and control functions and other individuals within their control who have a material impact on the *firm's* risk profile	Credit/market/operational risk Legal Treasury controls Human resources Compliance Internal audit

Remuneration Principle 1: Risk management and risk tolerance

19C.3.7 R   FCA

A *firm* must ensure that its *remuneration* policy is consistent with and promotes sound and effective risk management, and does not encourage risk-taking that exceeds the level of tolerated risk of the *firm*.

Remuneration Principle 2: Supporting business strategy, objectives, values and long-term interests of the firm

19C.3.8 R   FCA

A *firm* must ensure that its *remuneration* policy is in line with the business strategy, objectives, values and long-term interests of the *firm*.

Remuneration Principle 3: Avoiding conflicts of interest

19C.3.9 R   FCA

A *firm* must ensure that its *remuneration* policy includes measures to avoid conflicts of interest.

Remuneration Principle 4: Governance

19C.3.10 R   FCA

A *firm* must ensure that its *governing body*, in its *supervisory function*, adopts and periodically reviews the general principles of the *remuneration* policy and is responsible for its implementation.

19C.3.11 R   FCA

A *firm* must ensure that the implementation of the *remuneration* policy is, at least annually, subject to central and independent internal review for compliance with policies and procedures for *remuneration* adopted by the *governing body* in its *supervisory function*.

19C.3.12 R   FCA

(1)   A *firm* that is significant in terms of its size, internal organisation and the nature, scope and complexity of its activities must establish a *remuneration* committee.

(2)   The *remuneration* committee must be constituted in a way that enables it to exercise competent and independent judgment on *remuneration* policies and practices and the incentives created for managing risk, capital and liquidity.

(3)   The chairman and the members of the *remuneration* committee must be members of the *governing body* who do not perform any executive function in the *firm*.

(4)   The *remuneration* committee must be responsible for the preparation of decisions regarding *remuneration*, including those which have implications for the risk and risk management of the *firm* and which are to be taken by the *governing body* in its *supervisory function*.

(5)   When preparing such decisions, the *remuneration* committee must take into account the long-term interests of shareholders, investors and other stakeholders in the *firm*.

[Note: The *guidance* referred to in the note to **SYSC 19C.3.3 R** also gives *guidance* on proportionality in relation to *remuneration* committees]

19C.3.13 G   FCA

(1)   A *firm* should be able to demonstrate that its decisions are consistent with an assessment of its financial condition and future prospects. In particular, practices by which *remuneration* is paid for potential future revenues whose timing and likelihood remain uncertain should be evaluated carefully and the *governing body* or *remuneration* committee (or both) should work closely with the *firm's* risk function in evaluating the incentives created by its *remuneration* system.

(2)   The *governing body* and any *remuneration* committee are responsible for ensuring that the *firm's remuneration* policy complies with the *BIPRU Remuneration Code* and, where relevant, should take into account relevant guidance, such as that issued by the International Organization of Securities Commissions (IOSCO).

(3)   The periodic review of the implementation of the *remuneration* policy should assess compliance with the *BIPRU Remuneration Code*.

(4)   Guidance on what the *supervisory function* might involve is set out in **SYSC 4.3.3 G**.

Remuneration Principle 5: Control functions

19C.3.14 R   FCA

A *firm* must ensure that *employees* engaged in control functions:

(1)   are independent from the business units they oversee;

(2)   have appropriate authority; and

(3)   are *remunerated*:

    (a)   adequately to attract qualified and experienced staff; and

    (b)   in line with the achievement of the objectives linked to their functions, independent of the performance of the business areas they control.

19C.3.15 E   FCA

(1)   A *firm's* risk management and compliance functions should have appropriate input into setting the *remuneration* policy for other business areas. The procedures for setting *remuneration* should allow risk and compliance functions to have significant input into the setting of individual *remuneration* awards where those functions have concerns about the behaviour of the individuals concerned or the riskiness of the business undertaken.

(2)   Contravention of (1) may be relied on as tending to establish contravention of the *rule* on *employees* engaged in control functions having appropriate authority (**SYSC 19C.3.14R (2)**).

19C.3.16 R   FCA

A *firm* must ensure that the *remuneration* of the senior officers in risk management and compliance functions is directly overseen by the *remuneration* committee referred to in **SYSC 19C.3.12 R**, or, if such a committee has not been established, by the *governing body* in its *supervisory function*.

19C.3.17 G   FCA

(1)   This Remuneration Principle is designed to manage the conflicts of interest which might arise if other business areas had undue influence over the *remuneration* of *employees* within control functions. Conflicts of interest can easily arise when *employees* are involved in the determination of *remuneration* for their own business area. Where these do arise they need to be managed by having in place independent roles for control functions (including, notably, risk management and compliance) and human resources. It is good practice to seek input from a *firm's* human resources function when setting *remuneration* for other business areas.

(2)   The need to avoid undue influence is particularly important where *employees* from the control functions are embedded in other business areas. This Remuneration Principle does not prevent the views of other business areas being sought as an appropriate part of the assessment process.

(3)   The *FCA* generally expects the ratio of the potential variable component of *remuneration* to the fixed component of *remuneration* to be significantly lower for *employees* in risk management and compliance functions than for *employees* in other business areas whose potential bonus is a significant proportion of their *remuneration*. *Firms* should nevertheless ensure that the total *remuneration* package offered to those *employees* is sufficient to attract and retain staff with the skills, knowledge and expertise to discharge those functions. The requirement that the method of determining the *remuneration* of *relevant persons* involved in the compliance function must not compromise their objectivity or be likely to do so also applies (see **SYSC 6.1.4 R (4)**).

Remuneration Principle 6: Remuneration and capital

19C.3.18 R   FCA

A *firm* must ensure that total variable *remuneration* does not limit the *firm's* ability to strengthen its capital base.

19C.3.19 G   FCA

This Remuneration Principle underlines the link between a *firm's* variable *remuneration* costs and the need to manage its capital base, including forward-looking capital planning measures. Where a *firm* needs to strengthen its capital base, its variable *remuneration* arrangements should be sufficiently flexible to allow it to direct the necessary resources towards capital building.

Remuneration Principle 7: Exceptional government intervention

19C.3.20 R   FCA

A *firm* that benefits from exceptional government intervention must ensure that:
(1)   variable *remuneration* is strictly limited as a percentage of net revenues when it is inconsistent with the maintenance of a sound capital base and timely exit from government support;
(2)   it restructures *remuneration* in alignment with sound risk management and long-term growth, including when appropriate establishing limits to the *remuneration* of *senior personnel*; and
(3)   no variable *remuneration* is paid to its *senior personnel* unless justified.

19C.3.21 G   FCA

The *FCA* would normally expect it to be appropriate for the ban on paying variable *remuneration* to *senior personnel* of a *firm* that benefits from exceptional government intervention to apply only in relation to *senior personnel* who were in office at the time that the intervention was required.

Remuneration Principle 8: Profit-based measurement and risk adjustment

19C.3.22 R   FCA
(1)   A *firm* must ensure that any measurement of performance used to calculate variable *remuneration* components or pools of variable *remuneration* components:
  (a)   includes adjustments for all types of current and future risks, taking into account the cost and quantity of the capital and the liquidity required; and
  (b)   takes into account the need for consistency with the timing and likelihood of the firm receiving potential future revenues incorporated into current earnings.
(2)   A *firm* must ensure that the allocation of variable *remuneration* components within the *firm* also takes into account all types of current and future risks.

19C.3.23 G   FCA
(1)   This Remuneration Principle stresses the importance of risk adjustment in measuring performance, and the importance of applying judgment and common sense. A *firm* should ask the risk management function to validate and assess risk-adjustment techniques and to attend a meeting of the *governing body* or *remuneration* committee for this purpose.
(2)   A number of risk-adjustment techniques and measures are available, and a *firm* should choose those that are most appropriate to its circumstances. Common measures include those that are based on economic profit or economic capital. Whichever technique is chosen, the full range of future risks should be covered. The *FCA* expects a *firm* to be able to provide it with details of all adjustments that the *firm* has made under a formulaic approach.
(3)   The *FCA* expects a *firm* to apply qualitative judgments and common sense in the final decision about the performance-related components of variable *remuneration* pools.
(4)   A *firm's* governing body (or *remuneration* committee, where appropriate) should take the lead in determining the measures to be used. It should offer the appropriate checks and balances to prevent inappropriate manipulation of the measures used. It should consult closely and frequently with the *firm's* risk management functions, in particular those relating to operational, market, credit and liquidity risk.

19C.3.24 G   FCA
(1)   Long-term incentive plans should be treated as pools of variable *remuneration*. Many common measures of performance for long-term incentive plans, such as earnings per *share* (EPS), are not adjusted for longer-term risk factors. Total shareholder return (TSR) includes dividend distributions in its measurement, which can also be based on unadjusted earnings data. If incentive plans mature within a two- to four-year period and are based on EPS or TSR, strategies can be devised to boost EPS or TSR during the life of the plan, to the detriment of the longer-term health of a *firm*. For example, increasing leverage is a technique which can be used to boost EPS and TSR. *Firms* should take account of these factors when developing risk-adjustment methods.
(2)   *Firms* that have long-term incentive plans should structure them with vesting, subject to appropriate performance conditions, and at least half of the award vesting after not less than five years and the remainder after not less than three years.
(3)   Long-term incentive plan awards may be included in the calculation of the deferred portion of variable *remuneration* only if upside incentives are adequately balanced by downside adjustments. The valuation of the award should be based on its value when the award is granted, and determined using an appropriate technique.

19C.3.25 R   FCA

Assessments of financial performance used to calculate variable *remuneration* components or pools of variable *remuneration* components must be based principally on profits.

19C.3.26 G   FCA
(1)   Performance measures based primarily on revenues or turnover are unlikely to pay sufficient regard to the quality of business undertaken or services provided. Profits are a better measure provided they are adjusted for risk, including future risks not adequately captured by accounting profits.
(2)   Management accounts should provide profit data at such levels within the *firm's* structure as to enable a *firm* to see as accurate a picture of contributions of relevant staff to a *firm's* performance, as reasonably practicable. If revenue or turnover is used as a component in performance assessment, processes should be in place to ensure that the quality of business undertaken or services provided and their appropriateness for *clients* are taken into account.

19C.3.27 R   FCA

A *firm* must ensure that its total variable *remuneration* is generally considerably contracted where subdued or negative financial performance of the *firm* occurs, taking into account both current *remuneration* and reductions in payouts of amounts previously earned.

[**Note:** Standard 5 of the *FSB Compensation Standards*]

19C.3.28 G   FCA

Where a *firm* makes a loss, the *FCA* generally expects no variable *remuneration* to be awarded. Variable *remuneration* may nevertheless be justified, for example to incentivise *employees* involved in new business ventures which could be loss-making in their early stages.

Remuneration Principle 9: Pension policy

19C.3.29 R   FCA

A *firm* must ensure that:
(1)   its pension policy is in line with its business strategy, objectives, values and long-term interests;
(2)   when an *employee* leaves the *firm* before retirement, any *discretionary pension benefits* are held by the *firm* for a period of five years in the form of instruments referred to in **SYSC 19C.3.47R (1)**; and
(3)   when *employees* reach retirement, *discretionary pension benefits* are paid to the *employee* in the form of instruments in **SYSC 19C.3.47R (1)** and subject to a five-year retention period.

Remuneration Principle 10: Personal investment strategies

19C.3.30 R   FCA
(1)   A *firm* must ensure that its *employees* undertake not to use personal hedging strategies or *remuneration* – or liability-related *contracts of insurance* to undermine the risk-alignment effects embedded in their *remuneration* arrangements.
(2)   A *firm* must maintain effective arrangements designed to ensure that *employees* comply with their undertaking.

19C.3.31 G   FCA

Circumstances in which a *person* will be using a personal hedging strategy include entering into an arrangement with a third party under which the third party will make payments, directly or indirectly, to that *person* linked to, or commensurate with, the amounts by which the *person's remuneration* is subject to reductions.

Remuneration Principle 11: Avoidance of the Remuneration Code

19C.3.32 R   FCA

A *firm* must ensure that variable *remuneration* is not paid through vehicles or methods that facilitate the avoidance of the *BIPRU Remuneration Code*.

Remuneration Principle 12: Remuneration structures – introduction

19C.3.33 G   FCA

This Remuneration Principle consists of a series of *rules, evidential provisions* and *guidance* relating to *remuneration* structures.

19C.3.34 G   FCA
(1)   Taking account of the *BIPRU remuneration principles proportionality rule*, the *FCA* does not generally consider it necessary for a *firm* to apply the *rules* in (2) where, in relation to an individual ("X"), both the following conditions are satisfied:
    (a)   condition 1 requires that X's variable *remuneration* is no more than 33% of total *remuneration*; and
    (b)   condition 2 requires that X's total *remuneration* is no more than 500,000.
(2)   The *rules* referred to in (1) relate to:
    (a)   guaranteed variable *remuneration* (**SYSC 19C.3.40 R**);
    (b)   retained *shares* or other instruments (**SYSC 19C.3.47 R**);
    (c)   deferral (**SYSC 19C.3.49 R**); and
    (d)   performance adjustment (**SYSC 19C.3.51 R**).

[**Note:** The *FCA* has published *guidance* on the application of certain *rules* on *remuneration* structures in relation to individuals who are *BIPRU Remuneration Code staff* for only part of a given performance year. This guidance is available at www.fca.org.uk/firms/markets/international-markets/remuneration-code.]

Remuneration Principle 12(a): Remuneration structures – general requirement

19C.3.35 R   FCA

A *firm* must ensure that the structure of an *employee's remuneration* is consistent with, and promotes, effective risk management.

Remuneration Principle 12(b): Remuneration structures – assessment of performance

19C.3.36 R   FCA

A *firm* must ensure that where *remuneration* is performance-related:
(1)   the total amount of *remuneration* is based on a combination of the assessment of the performance of:
    (a)   the individual;
    (b)   the business unit concerned; and
    (c)   the overall results of the *firm*; and
(2)   when assessing individual performance, financial as well as non-financial criteria are taken into account.

19C.3.37 G   FCA

Non-financial performance metrics should form a significant part of the performance assessment process and should include adherence to effective risk management and compliance with the *regulatory system* and with relevant overseas regulatory requirements. Poor performance as assessed by non-financial metrics, such as poor risk management or other behaviours contrary to *firm* values, can pose significant risks for a *firm* and should, as appropriate, override metrics of financial performance. The performance assessment process and the importance of non-financial assessment factors in the process should be clearly explained to relevant *employees* and implemented. A balanced scorecard can be a good technique.

19C.3.38 R   FCA

A *firm* must ensure that the assessment of performance is set in a multi-year framework, to ensure that the assessment process is based on longer-term performance and that the actual payment of performance-based components of *remuneration* is spread over a period which takes account of the underlying business cycle of the *firm* and its business risks.

19C.3.39 G   FCA

The requirement for assessment of performance to be in a multi-year framework reflects the fact that profits from a *firm's* activities can be volatile and subject to cycles. The financial performance of *firms* and individual *employees* can be exaggerated as a result. Performance assessment on a moving average of results can be a good way of meeting this requirement. However, other techniques, such as good quality risk adjustment and deferral of a sufficiently large proportion of *remuneration*, may also be useful.

Remuneration Principle 12(c): Remuneration structures – guaranteed variable remuneration

19C.3.40 R   FCA

A *firm* must not award, pay or provide guaranteed variable *remuneration* unless it:
(1)   is exceptional;
(2)   occurs in the context of hiring new *BIPRU Remuneration Code staff*; and
(3)   is limited to the first year of service.

19C.3.41 E   FCA
(1)   A *firm* should not award, pay or provide guaranteed variable *remuneration* in hiring new *BIPRU Remuneration Code staff* (X) unless:
    (a)   it has taken reasonable steps to ensure that the *remuneration* is not more generous in its amount or terms (including any deferral or retention periods) than the variable *remuneration* awarded or offered by X's previous employer; and
    (b)   it is subject to appropriate performance adjustment requirements.
(2)   Contravention of (1) may be relied on as tending to establish contravention of the *rule* on guaranteed variable *remuneration* (**SYSC 19C.3.40 R**).

19C.3.42 G   FCA

Guaranteed variable *remuneration* should be subject to the same deferral criteria as other forms of variable *remuneration* awarded by the *firm*.

19C.3.43 G   FCA

Variable *remuneration* can be awarded to *BIPRU Remuneration Code staff* in the form of retention awards where it is compatible with the BIPRU Remuneration Code general requirement to do so. The *FCA* considers this is likely to be the case only where a *firm* is undergoing a major restructuring and a good case can be made for retention of particular key staff members on prudential grounds. Proposals to give retention awards should form part of any notice of the restructuring proposals required in accordance with *Principle* 11 and the general notification requirements in **SUP 15.3**.

Remuneration Principle 12(d): Remuneration structures – ratios between fixed and variable components of total remuneration

19C.3.44 R   FCA

A *firm* must set appropriate ratios between the fixed and variable components of total *remuneration* and ensure that:
(1)   fixed and variable components of total *remuneration* are appropriately balanced; and
(2)   the fixed component represents a sufficiently high proportion of the total *remuneration* to allow the operation of a fully flexible policy on variable *remuneration* components, including the possibility to pay no variable *remuneration* component.

Remuneration Principle 12(e): Remuneration structures – payments related to early termination

19C.3.45 R   FCA

A *firm* must ensure that payments related to the early termination of a contract reflect performance achieved over time and are designed in a way that does not reward failure.

19C.3.46 G   FCA

Firms should review existing contractual payments related to termination of employment with a view to ensuring that these are payable only where there is a clear basis for concluding that they are consistent with the *BIPRU Remuneration Code* general requirement.

[**Note:** Standard 12 of the *FSB Compensation Standards*]

Remuneration Principle 12(f): Remuneration structures – retained shares or other instruments

19C.3.47 R   FCA
(1)   A *firm* must ensure that a substantial portion, at least 50%, of any variable *remuneration* consists of an appropriate balance of:
    (a)   *shares* or equivalent ownership interests, subject to the legal structure of the *firm* concerned, or *share*-linked instruments or equivalent non-cash instruments for a non-listed *firm*; and
    (b)   where appropriate, *capital instruments* which are eligible for inclusion at stage B1 of the calculation in the *capital resources table*, where applicable, adequately reflect the credit quality of the *firm* as a going concern.
(2)   The instruments in (1) must be subject to an appropriate retention policy designed to align incentives with the longer-term interests of the *firm*.
(3)   This *rule* applies to the portion of the variable *remuneration* component deferred, and not deferred, in line with **SYSC 19C.3.49 R**.

[**Note:** Standard 8 of the *FSB Compensation Standards*]

19C.3.48 G   FCA

(1)   Regarding **SYSC 19C.3.47R (3)**, the 50% minimum threshold for instruments must be applied equally to the non-deferred and the deferred components; in other words, *firms* must apply the same chosen ratio between instruments and cash for their total variable *remuneration* to both the upfront and deferred components.

(2)   This simplified example illustrates the operation of (1). The variable remuneration of a material risk taker (X) is 100, and by **SYSC 19C.3.49R (3)** X is required to defer 60%. X's upfront component is 40 and X's deferred component is 60. At least 20 of X's upfront component, and at least 30 of X's deferred component, must be in instruments referred to in **SYSC 19C.3.47R (1)**.

Remuneration Principle 12(g): Remuneration structures – deferral

19C.3.49 R   FCA

(1)   A *firm* must not award, pay or provide a variable *remuneration* component unless a substantial portion of it, which is at least 40%, is deferred over a period of not less than three to five years.

(2)   *Remuneration* under (1) must vest no faster than on a pro-rata basis.

(3)   In the case of a variable *remuneration* component:
   (a)   of a particularly high amount; or
   (b)   payable to a *director* of a *firm* that is significant in its size, internal organisation and the nature, scope and complexity of its activities; at least 60% of the amount must be deferred.

(4)   Paragraph (3)(b) does not apply to a *non-executive director*.

(5)   The length of the deferral period must be established in line with the business cycle, the nature of the business, its risks and the activities of the *employee* in question.
   [**Note:** Standards 6 and 7 of the *FSB Compensation Standards*]

(6)   500,000 is a particularly high amount for the purpose of (3)(a).

(7)   Paragraph (6) is without prejudice to the possibility of lower sums being considered a particularly high amount.

19C.3.50 G   FCA

(1)   Deferred *remuneration* paid in *shares* or *share*-linked instruments should be made under a scheme which meets appropriate criteria, including risk adjustment of the performance measure used to determine the initial allocation of shares. Deferred *remuneration* paid in cash should also be subject to performance criteria.

(2)   The *FCA* generally expects a *firm* to have a *firm*-wide policy (and group-wide policy, where appropriate) on deferral. The proportion deferred should generally rise with the ratio of variable *remuneration* to fixed *remuneration* and with the amount of variable *remuneration*. While any variable *remuneration* component of 500,000 or more paid to *BIPRU Remuneration Code staff* must be subject to 60% deferral, *firms* should also consider whether lesser amounts should be considered to be 'particularly high' taking account, for example, of whether there are significant differences within *BIPRU Remuneration Code staff* in the levels of variable *remuneration* paid.

Remuneration Principle 12(h): Remuneration structures – performance adjustment, etc.

19C.3.51 R   FCA

A *firm* must ensure that any variable *remuneration*, including a deferred portion, is paid or vests only if it is sustainable according to the financial situation of the *firm* as a whole, and justified according to the performance of the *firm*, the business unit and the individual concerned.

[**Note:** Standards 6 and 9 of the *FSB Compensation Standards*]

19C.3.52 E   FCA

(1)   A *firm* should reduce unvested deferred variable *remuneration* when, as a minimum:
   (a)   there is reasonable evidence of *employee* misbehaviour or material error; or
   (b)   the *firm* or the relevant business unit suffers a material downturn in its financial performance; or
   (c)   the *firm* or the relevant business unit suffers a material failure of risk management.

(2)   For performance adjustment purposes, awards of deferred variable *remuneration* made in *shares* or other non-cash instruments should provide the ability for the *firm* to reduce the number of *shares* or other non-cash instruments.

(3)   Contravention of (1) or (2) may be relied on as tending to establish contravention of the *rule* on performance adjustment (**SYSC 19C.3.51 R**).

19C.3.53 G   FCA

(1)   Variable *remuneration* may be justified, for example, to incentivise *employees* involved in new business ventures which could be loss-making in their early stages.

(2)   The *governing body* (or, where appropriate, the *remuneration* committee) should approve performance adjustment policies, including the triggers under which adjustment would take place. The *FCA* may ask *firms* to provide a copy of their policies and expects *firms* to make adequate records of material decisions to operate the adjustments.

CHAPTER 19D
DUAL-REGULATED FIRMS REMUNERATION CODE

19D APPLICATION AND PURPOSE

Who? What? Where?

[3.28]

19D.1.1 R   FCA

(1)   The *dual-regulated firms Remuneration Code* applies to:
     (a)   a *building society*;
     (b)   a *bank*;
     (c)   a *UK designated investment firm*;
     (d)   an *overseas firm* that;
         (i)   is not an *EEA firm*;
         (ii)   has its head office outside the *EEA*; and
         (iii)   would be a *firm* in (a), (b) or (c) if it had been a *UK domestic firm*, had carried on all of its business in the *United Kingdom* and had obtained whatever authorisations for doing so as are required under the *Act*.

(2)   For a *firm* which falls under (1)(a), (1)(b) or (1)(c), the *dual-regulated firms Remuneration Code* applies, in a *prudential context*, in relation to:
     (a)   its *UK* activities;
     (b)   its *passported activities* carried on from a *branch* in another *EEA State*; and
     (c)   a *UK domestic firm's* activities wherever they are carried on.

(3)   For a *firm* that falls under (1)(d), the *dual-regulated firms Remuneration Code* applies only in relation to activities carried on from an establishment in the *United Kingdom*.

19D.1.2 R   FCA

Subject to the provisions on group risk systems and controls requirements in **SYSC 12** (Group risk systems and controls requirements), the *dual-regulated firms Remuneration Code*:

(1)   applies in relation to *regulated activities*, activities that constitute *dealing in investments as principal* (disregarding the exclusion in article 15 of the *Regulated Activities Order* (Absence of holding out etc)), *ancillary activities* and (in relation to *MiFID business*) *ancillary services*;

(2)   applies in relation to the carrying on of *unregulated activities* in a *prudential context*; and

(3)   takes into account activities of other *group* members.

When?

19D.1.3 R   FCA

(1)   Except as set out in (2) and (3), a *firm* must apply the *remuneration* requirements in **SYSC 19D.3** (Remuneration principles) in relation to:
     (a)   *remuneration* awarded, whether pursuant to a contract or otherwise, on or after 1 January 2011;
     (b)   *remuneration* due on the basis of contracts concluded before 1 January 2011 which is awarded or paid on or after 1 January 2011; and
     (c)   *remuneration* awarded, but not yet paid, before 1 January 2011, for services provided in 2010.
     [**Note:** article 3(2) of Directive 2010/76/EU]

(2)   A *firm* must apply the *remuneration* requirements in **SYSC 19D.3.48R (3)** (1:1 ratio of variable to fixed components) and **SYSC 19D.3.49 R** (1:2 ratio of fixed to variable components) in relation to *remuneration* awarded for services provided or performance from the year 2014 onwards, whether due on the basis of contracts concluded before, on or after 31 December 2013.
     [**Note:** article 162(3) of *CRD*]

(3)   A *firm* must apply the *remuneration* requirements in **SYSC 19D.3.59R (1)(B)**, **SYSC 19D.3.61R (2)**, **SYSC 19D.3.61R (3)**, **SYSC 19D.3.61R (4)**, **SYSC 19D.3.61R (5)**, **SYSC 19D.3.64 R** and **SYSC 19D.3.67R (1)(C)** in relation to variable *remuneration* awarded in relation to the performance year starting on or after 1 January 2016.

19D.1.4 G   FCA

Subject to **SYSC 19D.1.5 R**, **SYSC 19D.1.3 R** does not require a *firm* to breach requirements of applicable contract or employment law.

[**Note:** recital 14 of Directive 2010/76/EU]

Conflict with other obligations

19D.1.5 R   FCA

(1)   Where a *firm* is unable to comply with the *dual-regulated firms Remuneration Code* because
        to do so would breach a provision of a prior contract (including a provision in a contract with
        a *dual-regulated firms Remuneration Code staff member*), it must take reasonable steps to
        amend or to terminate the provision in question in a way which enables it to comply with the
        dual-regulated firms Remuneration Code at the earliest opportunity.

(2)   Until the provision in (1) ceases to prevent the *firm* from complying with the *dual-regulated
        firms Remuneration Code*, it must adopt specific and effective arrangements, processes and
        mechanisms to manage the risks raised by the provision.

Purpose

19D.1.6 G   FCA

(1)   The aim of the *dual-regulated firms Remuneration Code* is to ensure that firms have
        risk-focused *remuneration* policies, which are consistent with and promote effective risk
        management and do not expose them to excessive risk. It expands upon the general
        organisational requirements in **SYSC 4**.

(2)   The *dual-regulated firms Remuneration Code* implements the main provisions of the *CRD*
        which relate to *remuneration*. The Committee of European Banking Supervisors published
        Guidelines on Remuneration Policies and Practices on 10 December 2010. Provisions of the
        Capital Requirements Regulations 2013 (SI 2013/3115) together with the *EBA's* Guidelines
        to article 75 of the *CRD* relating to the collection of *remuneration* benchmarking information
        and high earners information have been implemented through **SUP 16 ANNEX 33A** and **SUP
        16 ANNEX 34A**. The Guidelines can be found at www.eba.europa.eu/documents/10180/
        757286/EBA-GL-2014-08+%28GLs+on+remuneration+benchmarking+%29.pdf/
        9d87c18b-ed79-4ceb-a3f6-64928cc26065   and   www.eba.europa.eu/documents/10180/
        757283/EBA-GL-2014-07+%28GLs+on+high+earners+data+collection%29.pdf/
        da42488f-09c1-4558-ae4e-6258e11b8345.

Notifications to the FCA

19D.1.7 G   FCA

(1)   The *dual-regulated firms Remuneration Code* does not contain specific notification require-
        ments. However, general circumstances in which the *FCA* expects to be notified by *firms* of
        matters relating to their compliance with requirements under the *regulatory system* are set out
        in **SUP 15.3** (General notification requirements).

(2)   For *remuneration* matters in particular, those circumstances should take into account
        unregulated activities, as well as *regulated activities* and the activities of other members of
        a *group*, and would include each of the following:

        (a)   significant breaches of the *dual-regulated firms Remuneration Code*, including any
                breach of a *rule* to which the provisions on voiding and recovery in **SYSC 19D
                ANNEX 1** apply;

        (b)   any proposed *remuneration* policies, procedures or practices which could:
                (i)   have a significant adverse impact on the *firm's* reputation; or
                (ii)   affect the *firm's* ability to continue to provide adequate services to its
                        customers and which could result in serious detriment to a *customer* of the
                        firm; or
                (iii)   result in serious financial consequences to the *financial system* or to other
                        firms;

        (c)   any proposed changes to *remuneration* policies, practices or procedures which could
                have a significant impact on the *firm's* risk profile or resources;

        (d)   fraud, errors and other irregularities described in **SUP 15.3.17 R** (notification of
                fraud, errors and other irregularities) which may suggest weaknesses in, or be
                motivated by, the *firm's remuneration* policies, procedures or practices.

(3)   Notifications should be made immediately as the *firm* becomes aware or has information
        which reasonably suggests that those circumstances have occurred, may have occurred or
        may occur in the foreseeable future.

Individual guidance

19D.1.8 G   FCA

The *FCA's* policy on individual *guidance* is set out in **SUP 9**. *Firms* should particularly note the
policy on what the *FCA* considers to be a reasonable request for *guidance* (see **SUP 9.2.5 G**). For
example, where a *firm* is seeking *guidance* on a proposed *remuneration* structure, the *FCA* will
expect the *firm* to provide a detailed analysis of how the structure complies with the *dual-regulated
firms Remuneration Code*, including the general requirement for *remuneration* policies, procedures
and practices to be consistent with, and promote, sound and effective risk management.

Interpretation

19D.1.9 G   FCA

Except as provided in the *Glossary*, any expression used in, or for the purpose of, this chapter which is defined or used in *EU CRR* has the meaning given by, or used in, those Regulations.

19D   GENERAL REQUIREMENT

Remuneration policies must promote effective risk management

19D.2.1 R   FCA

A *firm* must establish, implement and maintain *remuneration* policies, procedures and practices that are consistent with, and promote, sound and effective risk management.

[**Note:** article 74(1) of *CRD*]

19D.2.2 G   FCA

(1)   The *dual-regulated firms Remuneration Code* covers all aspects of *remuneration* that could have a bearing on effective risk management, including salaries, bonuses, long-term incentive plans, options, hiring bonuses, severance packages and pension arrangements.

(2)   As with other aspects of a *firm's* systems and controls, in accordance with **SYSC 4.1.2 R** (general organisational requirements) *remuneration* policies, procedures and practices must be comprehensive and proportionate to the nature, scale and complexity of the *common platform firm's* activities. What a *firm* must do in order to comply with the *dual-regulated firms Remuneration Code* will therefore vary. For example, while the *dual-regulated firms Remuneration Code* refers to a *firm's remuneration committee* and risk management function, it may be appropriate for the *governing body* of a smaller *firm* to act as the *remuneration committee* and for the *firm* not to have a separate risk management function.

(3)   The *FCA* may also ask *remuneration committees* to provide it with evidence of how well the *firm's* remuneration policies meet the *dual-regulated firms Remuneration Code's* principles, together with plans for improvement where there is a shortfall. The *FCA* also expects relevant *firms* to use the principles in assessing their exposure to risks arising from their *remuneration* policies as part of the *internal capital adequacy assessment process* (*ICAAP*).

(4)   The *FCA* would also expect *firms* to apply, on a *firm*-wide basis, at least the following principles relating to:

(a)   risk management and risk tolerance (Remuneration Principle 1);

(b)   supporting business strategy, objectives, values and long-term interests of the firm (Remuneration Principle 2);

(c)   avoiding conflicts of interest (Remuneration Principle 3);

(d)   governance (Remuneration Principle 4);

(e)   risk adjustment (Remuneration Principle 8);

(f)   pension policy (Remuneration Principle 9);

(g)   personal investment strategies (Remuneration Principle 10);

(h)   payments related to early termination (Remuneration Principle 12(e)); and

(i)   deferral (Remuneration Principle 12(g)).

Record keeping

19D.2.3 R   FCA

In line with the record-keeping requirements in **SYSC 9**, a *firm* must ensure that its *remuneration* policies, practices and procedures, including performance appraisals processes and decisions, are clear and documented.

Interpretation of references to remuneration

19D.2.4 R   FCA

(1)   In this chapter, references to *remuneration* include *remuneration* paid, provided or awarded by any *person* to the extent that it is paid, provided or awarded in connection with employment by a *firm*.

(2)   Paragraph (1) is without prejudice to the meaning of *remuneration* elsewhere in the *Handbook*.

19D.2.5 G   FCA

For example, *remuneration* includes payments made by a seconding organisation which is not subject to the *dual-regulated firms Remuneration Code* to a secondee in respect of their employment by a *firm* which is subject to the *dual-regulated firms Remuneration Code*.

19D   REMUNERATION PRINCIPLES

Application: groups

19D.3.1 R   FCA

(1)   A *firm* must apply the requirements of this section at *group*, *parent undertaking* and *subsidiary undertaking* levels, including those *subsidiaries* established in a country or territory which is not an *EEA State*.

(2)   Paragraph (1) does not limit **SYSC 12.1.13 R (2)(DA)** (which relates to the application of the *dual-regulated firms Remuneration Code* within *UK consolidation groups* and *non-EEA sub-groups*).

[**Note:** article 92(1) of *CRD*]

19D.3.2 G   FCA

SYSC 12.1.13 R (2)(DA) requires the *firm* to ensure that the risk management processes and internal control mechanisms at the level of any *UK consolidation group* or *non-EEA sub-group* of which a *firm* is a member, comply with the obligations in this section on a consolidated basis (or sub-consolidated basis).

Application: categories of staff and proportionality

19D.3.3 R   FCA
(1)   This section applies in relation to *dual-regulated firms Remuneration Code staff*, except as set out in (3).
(2)   When establishing and applying the total *remuneration* policies for *dual-regulated firms Remuneration Code staff*, a *firm* must comply with this section in a way, and to the extent, that is appropriate to its size, internal organisation and the nature, the scope and the complexity of its activities (the *dual-regulated firms remuneration principles proportionality rule*).
(3)   Paragraphs (1) and (2) do not apply to the requirement for significant *firms* to have a *remuneration committee* (**SYSC 19D.3.12 R**).

[Note: article 92(2) of *CRD*]

[Note: In addition to the *guidance* in this section about the *dual-regulated firms remuneration principles proportionality rule*, the *FSA* gave guidance on the division of *firms* into categories for the purpose of providing a framework for the operation of the *dual-regulated firms remuneration principles proportionality rule*. This *guidance* is available on the *FCA* website at www.fca.org.uk/firms/being-regulated/remuneration-codes.]

19D.3.4 R   FCA
(1)   *Dual-regulated firms Remuneration Code staff* comprises:
        (a)   an *employee* of a *dual-regulated firm* whose professional activities have a material impact on the *firm's* risk profile, including any *employee* who is deemed to have a material impact on the *firm's* risk profile in accordance with Regulation (EU) 604/2014 of 4 March 2014 (Regulatory technical standards to identify staff who are material risk takers); or
        (b)   subject to (2) and (3), an *employee* of an *overseas firm* in **SYSC 19D.1.1 R (1)(D)** (ie, an *overseas firm* that would have been a *bank*, *building society* or *UK designated investment firm* if it had been a *UK domestic firm*) whose professional activities have a material impact on the *firm's* risk profile, including any *employee* who would meet any of the criteria set out in articles 3 or 4(1) of Regulation (EU) 604/2014 of 4 March 2014 if it had applied to him.
(2)   An *overseas firm* in **SYSC 19D.1.1 R (1)(D)** (i.e., an *overseas firm* that would have been a *dual-regulated firm* if it had been a *UK domestic firm*) may deem an *employee* not to be a *dual-regulated firms Remuneration Code staff* where:
        (a)   the *employee*:
                (i)   would meet the criteria in article 4(1) of Regulation (EU) No 604/2014 of 4 March 2014;
                (ii)   would not meet any of the criteria in article 3 of Regulation (EU) No 604/2014 of 4 March 2014; and
                (iii)   was awarded total remuneration of less than 750,000 in the previous year; and
        (b)   the *overseas firm* determines that the professional activities of the *employee* do not have a material impact on its risk profile on the grounds described in article 4(2) of Regulation (EU) 604/2014 of 4 March 2014.
(3)   Where the *overseas firm* deems an *employee* not to be *dual-regulated firms Remuneration Code staff* as set out in (2), it must notify the *FCA*, applying the approach described in article 4(4) of Regulation (EU) 604/2014 of 4 March 2014.

[**Note:** article 92(2) of *CRD* and articles 3 and 4 of Regulation (EU) No 604/2014 of 4 March 2014.]

19D.3.5 G   FCA

Where an *overseas firm* in **SYSC 19D.1.1 R (1)(D)** (i.e., an *overseas firm* that would have been a *dual-regulated firm* if it had been a *UK domestic firm*) wishes to deem an *employee* who earns more than 750,000 not to be *dual-regulated firms Remuneration Code staff*, the *overseas firm* may apply for a *waiver* of the requirement in **SYSC 19D.3.4 R** in respect of that *employee*.

19D.3.6 R   FCA

A *firm* must:

(1) maintain a record of its *dual-regulated firms Remuneration Code staff* under the general record-keeping requirements (**SYSC 9**); and

(2) take reasonable steps to ensure that its *dual-regulated firms Remuneration Code staff* understand the implications of their status as such, including the potential for *remuneration* which does not comply with certain requirements of the *dual-regulated firms Remuneration Code* to be rendered void and recoverable by the *firm*.

Remuneration Principle 1: Risk management and risk tolerance

19D.3.7 R   FCA

A *firm* must ensure that its *remuneration* policy is consistent with, and promotes, sound and effective risk management and does not encourage risk-taking that exceeds the level of tolerated risk of the *firm*.

[**Note:** article 92(2)(a) of *CRD*]

Remuneration Principle 2: Supporting business strategy, objectives, values and long-term interests of the firm

19D.3.8 R   FCA

A *firm* must ensure that its *remuneration* policy is in line with the business strategy, objectives, values and long-term interests of the *firm*.

[**Note:** article 92(2)(b) of *CRD*]

Remuneration Principle 3: Avoiding conflicts of interest

19D.3.9 R   FCA

A *firm* must ensure that its *remuneration* policy includes measures to avoid conflicts of interest.

[**Note:** article 92(2)(b) of *CRD*]

Remuneration Principle 4: Governance

19D.3.10 R   FCA

A *firm* must ensure that its *management body* in its *supervisory function* adopts and periodically reviews the general principles of the *remuneration* policy and is responsible for overseeing its implementation.

[**Note:** article 92(2)(c) of *CRD* and Standard 1 of the *FSB Compensation Standards*]

19D.3.11 R   FCA

A *firm* must ensure that the implementation of the *remuneration* policy is, at least annually, subject to central and independent internal review for compliance with policies and procedures for *remuneration* adopted by the *management body* in its *supervisory function*.

[**Note:** article 92(2)(d) of *CRD* and Standard 1 of the *FSB Compensation Standards*]

19D.3.12 R   FCA

(1) A *firm* that is significant in terms of its size, internal organisation and the nature, the scope and the complexity of its activities must establish a *remuneration committee*.

(2) A *firm* in (1) must ensure that:

(a) the *remuneration committee* is constituted in a way that enables it to exercise competent and independent judgement on *remuneration* policies and practices and the incentives created for managing risk, capital and liquidity;

(b) the chairman and the members of the *remuneration committee* must be members of the *management body* who do not perform any executive function in the *firm*;

(c) the *remuneration committee* is responsible for the preparation of decisions regarding *remuneration*, including those which have implications for the risk and risk management of the *firm* and which are to be taken by the *management body*; and

(d) when preparing those decisions, the *remuneration committee* must take into account the long-term interests of shareholders, investors and other stakeholders in the *firm* and the public interest.

[**Note:** article 95 of *CRD* and Standard 1 of the *FSB Compensation Standards*]

19D.3.13 R   FCA

A *firm* that maintains a website must explain on the website how it complies with the *dual-regulated firms Remuneration Code*.

[**Note:** article 96 of the *CRD*]

19D.3.14 G   FCA

(1)   A *firm* should be able to demonstrate that its decisions are consistent with an assessment of its financial condition and future prospects. In particular, practices by which *remuneration* is paid for potential future revenues whose timing and likelihood remain uncertain should be evaluated carefully and the *governing body* or *remuneration committee* (or both) should work closely with the *firm's* risk function in evaluating the incentives created by its *remuneration* system.

(2)   The *governing body* and any *remuneration committee* are responsible for ensuring that the *firm's remuneration* policy complies with the *dual-regulated firms Remuneration Code* and, where relevant, should take into account relevant guidance, such as that issued by the Basel Committee on Banking Supervision, the International Association of Insurance Supervisors (IAIS) and the International Organization of Securities Commissions (IOSCO).

(3)   Guidance on what the *supervisory function* might involve is set out in **SYSC 4.3.3 G** (responsibility of senior personnel, in particular, the *supervisory function*).

Remuneration Principle 5: Control functions

19D.3.15 R   FCA

A *firm* must ensure that *employees* engaged in control functions:
(1)   are independent from the business units they oversee;
(2)   have appropriate authority; and
(3)   are *remunerated*:
    (a)   adequately to attract qualified and experienced *employees*; and
    (b)   in accordance with the achievement of the objectives linked to their functions, independent of the performance of the business areas they control.

[**Note:** article 92(2)(e) of *CRD* and Standard 2 of the *FSB Compensation Standards*]

19D.3.16 E   FCA

(1)   A *firm's* risk management and compliance functions should have appropriate input into setting the *remuneration* policy for other business areas. The procedures for setting *remuneration* should allow risk and compliance functions to have significant input into the setting of individual *remuneration* awards where those functions have concerns about the behaviour of the individuals concerned or the riskiness of the business undertaken.

(2)   Contravention of (1) may be relied on as tending to establish contravention of the *rule* on *employees* engaged in control functions having appropriate authority (**SYSC 19D.3.15 R (2)**).

19D.3.17 R   FCA

A *firm* must ensure that the *remuneration* of the senior officers in risk management and compliance functions is directly overseen by the *remuneration committee* referred to in **SYSC 19D.3.12 R** or, if such a committee has not been established, by the *governing body* in its *supervisory function*.

[**Note:** article 92(2)(f) of *CRD*]

19D.3.18 G   FCA

(1)   This Remuneration Principle is designed to manage the conflicts of interest which might arise if other business areas had undue influence over the *remuneration* of *employees* within control functions. Conflicts of interest can easily arise when *employees* are involved in the determination of *remuneration* for their own business area. Where these could arise, they need to be managed by having in place independent roles for control functions (including, notably, risk management and compliance) and human resources. It is good practice to seek input from a *firm's* human resources function when setting *remuneration* for other business areas.

(2)   The need to avoid undue influence is particularly important where *employees* from the control functions are embedded in other business areas. This Remuneration Principle does not prevent the views of other business areas being sought as an appropriate part of the assessment process.

(3)   The *FCA* would generally expect the ratio of the potential variable component of *remuneration* to the fixed component of *remuneration* to be significantly lower for *employees* in risk management and compliance functions than for *employees* in other business areas whose potential bonus is a significant proportion of their *remuneration*. Firms should nevertheless ensure that the total *remuneration* package offered to those *employees* is sufficient to attract and retain staff with the skills, knowledge and expertise to discharge those functions. The requirement that the method of determining the *remuneration* of *relevant persons* involved in the compliance function must not compromise their objectivity or be likely to do so also applies (see **SYSC 6.1.4 R (4)**).

Remuneration Principle 6: Remuneration and capital

19D.3.19 R   FCA

A *firm* must ensure that total variable *remuneration* does not limit the *firm's* ability to strengthen its capital base.

[Note: article 94(1)(c) of the *CRD* and Standard 3 of the *FSB Compensation Standards*]

19D.3.20 G   FCA

A *firm* should have variable *remuneration* arrangements that are sufficiently flexible to allow it to direct the necessary resources towards capital building.

Remuneration Principle 7: Exceptional government intervention

19D.3.21 R   FCA

A *firm* that benefits from exceptional government intervention must ensure that:

(1)   variable *remuneration* is strictly limited as a percentage of net revenues when it is inconsistent with the maintenance of a sound capital base and timely exit from government support;

(2)   it restructures *remuneration* in a manner aligned with sound risk management and long-term growth, including (when appropriate) establishing limits to the *remuneration* of members of its *management body*; and

(3)   no variable or discretionary *remuneration* of any kind is paid to members of its *management body* unless this is justified.

[Note: article 93 of the *CRD* and Standard 10 of the *FSB Compensation Standards*]

19D.3.22 G   FCA

The *FCA* would normally expect it to be appropriate for the ban on paying variable *remuneration* to members of the *management body* of a *firm* that benefits from exceptional government intervention to apply only to members of the *management body* who were in office at the time that the intervention was required.

Remuneration Principle 8: Profit-based measurement and risk adjustment

19D.3.23 R   FCA

(1)   A *firm* must ensure that any measurement of performance used to calculate variable *remuneration* components or pools of variable *remuneration* components:

    (a)   includes adjustments for all types of current and future risks and takes into account the cost and quantity of the capital and the liquidity required; and

    (b)   takes into account the need for consistency with the timing and likelihood of the *firm* receiving potential future revenues incorporated into current earnings.

(2)   A *firm* must ensure that the allocation of variable *remuneration* components within the *firm* also takes into account all types of current and future risks.

[Note: article 94(1)(j), (k) of the *CRD* and Standard 4 of the *FSB Compensation Standards*]

19D.3.24 G   FCA

(1)   This Remuneration Principle stresses the importance of risk adjustment in measuring performance, and the importance within that process of applying judgment and common sense. The *FCA* expects that a *firm* will apply qualitative judgements and common sense in the final decision about the performance-related components of variable *remuneration* pools.

(2)   A number of risk-adjustment techniques and measures are available, and a *firm* should choose those most appropriate to its circumstances.

(3)   We consider good practice in this area to be represented by those *firms* who provide a quantitative reference or starting point that explicitly includes risk-adjusted metrics, before the application of more discretionary factors. Common measures include those based on economic profit or economic capital. Whichever technique is chosen, the full range of future risks should be covered.

(4)   The *FCA* expects a *firm* to be able to provide it with details of all adjustments that the *firm* has made whether through application of formulae or the exercise of discretion. This will enable the *FCA* to ensure that the *firm's* risk adjustment framework is sufficiently robust. Where discretion has been applied, the *firm* should be able to provide a clear explanation for, and quantification of such adjustments.

(5)   A *firm* should ask the risk management function to validate and assess risk-adjustment techniques, and to attend a meeting of the *governing body* or *remuneration committee* for this purpose.

19D.3.25 R   FCA

A *firm* must have a clear and verifiable mechanism for measuring performance, with risk adjustment applied thereafter in a clear and transparent manner.

19D.3.26 G   FCA

A *firm* may apply discretionary factors to the extent that is appropriate and consistent with the overall aims of the risk adjustment exercise. Where such further adjustments have been made, *firms* should provide clear quantification and explanation to ensure their risk adjustment frameworks are sufficiently transparent.

19D.3.27 R   FCA

A *firm* must base assessments of financial performance used to calculate variable *remuneration* components or pools of variable *remuneration* components principally on profits.

19D.3.28 G FCA
(1) Performance measures based primarily on revenues or turnover are unlikely to pay sufficient regard to the quality of business undertaken or services provided. Profits are a better measure provided they are adjusted for risk, including future risks not adequately captured by accounting profits.
(2) Management accounts should provide profit data at such levels within the *firm's* structure to enable it to see as accurate a picture of contributions of relevant staff to a *firm's* performance as is reasonably practicable.

19D.3.29 R FCA
(1) A *firm's* risk-adjustment approach must reflect both ex-ante adjustment (which adjusts remuneration for intrinsic risks that are inherent in its business activities) and ex-post adjustment (which adjusts *remuneration* for crystallisation of specific risks events).
(2) A *firm* must ensure that its total variable *remuneration* is generally considerably contracted where subdued or negative financial performance of the firm occurs, taking into account both current *remuneration* and reductions in payouts of amounts previously earned, including through malus or clawback arrangements.

[**Note:** article 94(1)(n) of *CRD* and Standard 5 of the *FSB Compensation Standards*]

19D.3.30 G FCA
(1) Aligning variable awards to sustainable financial performance requires *firms* to make appropriate ex-ante adjustments to take account of the potential for future unexpected losses. Performance measures commonly used (such as earnings per *share* (EPS), total shareholder return (TSR) and return on equity (RoE)) are not suitably adjusted for longer-term risk factors and have a tendency to incentive highly leveraged activities.
(2) Long-term incentive plans should be treated as pools of variable *remuneration*. *Firms* that have long-term incentive plans should ensure that the structure of the award is compliant with the *dual-regulated firms Remuneration Code's* deferral and vesting requirements and that performance conditions required for vesting are appropriate. The valuation of the award should be based on its value when the award is granted, and determined using an appropriate technique.
(3) *Firms* should demonstrate that both the ex-ante intrinsic risks and the ex-post crystallisation of risk event have been considered as part of their risk-adjustment approach.

[**Note:** In addition to the *guidance* in this section on the Remuneration Principle 8 (Profit-based measurement and risk adjustment), the *FSA* gave guidance on the application of the requirements on risk adjustments. This *guidance* is available on the *FCA* website at www.fca.org.uk/firms/being-regulated/remuneration-codes.]

Remuneration Principle 9: Pension policy

19D.3.31 R FCA

A *firm* must ensure that:
(1) its pension policy is in line with its business strategy, objectives, values and long-term interests;
(2) when an *employee* leaves the *firm* before retirement, any *discretionary pension benefits* are held by the *firm* for a period of five years in the form of instruments referred to in **SYSC 19D.3.56 R (1)**; and
(3) when an *employee* reaches retirement, *discretionary pension benefits* are paid to the *employee* in the form of instruments referred to in **SYSC 19D.3.56 R (1)** and subject to a five-year retention period.

[**Note:** article 94(1)(o) of the *CRD*]

Remuneration Principle 10: Personal investment strategies

19D.3.32 R FCA
(1) A *firm* must ensure that its *employees* undertake not to use personal hedging strategies to undermine the risk alignment effects embedded in their *remuneration* arrangements.
(2) A *firm* must ensure that its *employees* do not use *remuneration* – or liability-related *contracts of insurance* to undermine the risk alignment effects embedded in their *remuneration* arrangements.
(3) A *firm* must maintain effective arrangements designed to ensure that *employees* comply with their undertaking.

[**Note:** article 94(1)(p) of the *CRD* and Standard 14 of the *FSB Compensation Standards*]

19D.3.33 G FCA

In the *FCA's* view, circumstances in which a *person* will be using a personal hedging strategy include (and are not limited to) entering into an arrangement with a third party under which the third party will make payments, directly or indirectly, to that *person* that are linked to or commensurate with the amounts by which the *person's remuneration* is subject to reductions.

Remuneration Principle 11: Non-compliance with the dual-regulated firms Remuneration Code

19D.3.34 R   FCA

A *firm* must ensure that variable *remuneration* is not paid through vehicles or methods that facilitate non-compliance with obligations arising from the *Remuneration Code*, the *EU CRR* or the *CRD*.

[**Note:** article 94(1)(q) of the *CRD*]

Remuneration Principle 12: Remuneration structures – introduction

19D.3.35 G   FCA
(1)   Taking account of the *dual-regulated firms remuneration principles proportionality rule*, the FCA does not generally consider it necessary for a *firm* to apply the *rules* in (2) where, in relation to an individual (X), both the following conditions are satisfied:
         (a)   Condition 1 is that X's variable *remuneration* is no more than 33% of total *remuneration*; and
         (b)   Condition 2 is that X's total *remuneration* is no more than £500,000.
(2)   The *rules* referred to in (1) are those relating to:
         (a)   guaranteed variable *remuneration* (**SYSC 19D.3.44 R**);
         (b)   retained *shares* or other instruments (**SYSC 19D.3.56 R**);
         (c)   deferral (**SYSC 19D.3.59 R**); and
         (d)   performance adjustment (**SYSC 19D.3.61 R**).

[**Note:** The *FSA* also gave *guidance* on the application of certain *rules* on *remuneration* structures about individuals who are *dual-regulated firms Remuneration Code staff* for only part of a given performance year. This guidance is available on the *FCA* website at www.fca.org.uk/firms/being-regulated/remuneration-codes.

Remuneration Principle 12(a): Remuneration structures – general requirement

19D.3.36 R   FCA

A *firm* must ensure that the structure of an *employee's remuneration* is consistent with, and promotes, effective risk management.

19D.3.37 R   FCA

A *firm* must ensure that the *remuneration* policy makes a clear distinction between criteria for setting:
(1)   basic fixed *remuneration* that primarily reflects an *employee's* professional experience and organisational responsibility, as set out in the *employee's* job description and terms of employment; and
(2)   variable *remuneration* that reflects performance in excess of that required to fulfil the *employee's* job description and terms of employment and that is subject to performance adjustment in accordance with the *dual-regulated firms Remuneration Code*.

[**Note:** article 92(2)(g) of the *CRD*]

19D.3.38 R   FCA

A *firm* must not award variable *remuneration* to a *non-executive director* acting as such.

Remuneration Principle 12(b): Remuneration structures – assessment of performance

19D.3.39 R   FCA
(1)   A *firm* must ensure that where *remuneration* is performance-related:
         (a)   the total amount of *remuneration* is based on a combination of the assessment of the performance of:
                 (i)   the individual;
                 (ii)   the business unit concerned; and
                 (iii)   the overall results of the *firm*; and
         (b)   when assessing individual performance, financial as well as non-financial criteria are taken into account.

[**Note:** article 94(1)(a) of the *CRD* and Standard 6 of the *FSB Compensation Standards*]

19D.3.40 G   FCA

The non-financial criteria in **SYSC 19D.3.39 R (1)(B)** should include the extent of the *employee's* adherence to effective risk management, and compliance with the *regulatory system* and with relevant overseas regulatory requirements.

19D.3.41 G   FCA

Poor performance assessed by non-financial metrics, such as poor risk management or other behaviours contrary to *firm* values, can pose significant risks for a *firm* and should, as appropriate, override metrics of financial performance.

19D.3.42 R FCA

A *firm* must clearly explain the performance assessment process in **SYSC 19D.3.39 R** to relevant *employees*.

19D.3.43 R FCA

A *firm* must ensure that the assessment of performance is set in a multi-year framework in order to ensure that:
(1) the assessment process is based on longer-term performance; and
(2) the actual payment of performance-based components of *remuneration* is spread over a period which takes account of the underlying business cycle of the *firm* and its business risks.

[**Note:** article 94(1)(b) of *CRD*]

Remuneration Principle 12(c): Remuneration structures – guaranteed variable remuneration, buy-outs

19D.3.44 R FCA

(1) A *firm* must ensure that guaranteed variable *remuneration* is not part of prospective *remuneration* plans.
(2) A *firm* must not award, pay or provide guaranteed variable *remuneration* unless:
  (a) it is exceptional;
  (b) it occurs in the context of hiring new *dual-regulated firms Remuneration Code staff*;
  (c) the *firm* has a sound and strong capital base; and
  (d) it is limited to the first year of service.

[**Note:** article 94(1)(d) and (e) of the *CRD* and Standard 11 of the *FSB Compensation Standards*]

19D.3.45 R FCA

A *firm* must ensure that *remuneration* packages relating to compensation for, or buy out from, an *employee's* contracts in previous employment align with its long-term interests including appropriate retention, deferral and performance and clawback arrangements.

[**Note:** article 94(1)(i) of *CRD*]

19D.3.46 G FCA

(1) Guaranteed variable *remuneration* should be subject to the same requirements applicable to variable *remuneration* awarded by the *firm* including deferral, malus and clawback.
(2) The *FCA* expects that guaranteed variable awards and retention awards should not be common practice for *dual-regulated firms Remuneration Code staff* and should be limited to rare, infrequent occurrences. The *FCA* expects a *firm* to provide prior notification to the *FCA* of any such proposed awards.

19D.3.47 G FCA

Retention awards should form part of variable *remuneration* for the purpose of **SYSC 19D.3.48 R**.

Remuneration Principle 12(d): Remuneration structures – ratios between fixed and variable components of total remuneration

19D.3.48 R FCA

A *firm* must set an appropriate ratio between the fixed and variable components of total *remuneration* and ensure that:
(1) fixed and variable components of total *remuneration* are appropriately balanced;
(2) the level of the fixed component represents a sufficiently high proportion of the total *remuneration* to allow the operation of a fully flexible policy on variable *remuneration* components, including the possibility to pay no variable *remuneration* component; and
(3) subject to **SYSC 19D.3.49 R**, the level of the variable component of total *remuneration* must not exceed 100% of the fixed component of total *remuneration* for each *dual-regulated firms Remuneration Code staff*.

[**Note:** article 94(1)(f) and 94(1)(g)(i) of the *CRD*]

19D.3.49 R FCA

A *firm* may set a higher maximum level of the ratio between the fixed and variable components of total *remuneration* provided:
(1) the overall level of the variable component does not exceed 200% of the fixed component of the total *remuneration* for each *dual-regulated firms Remuneration Code staff*; and
(2) is approved by the shareholders or owners or members of the *firm* in accordance with **SYSC 19D.3.50 R**.

[**Note:** article 94(1)(g)(ii) of *CRD*]

19D.3.50 R   FCA

A *firm* must ensure that any approval by its shareholders or owners or members, for the purposes of **SYSC 19D.3.49 R**, is carried out in accordance with the following procedure:

(1)   the *firm* must give reasonable notice to all its shareholders or owners or members of its intention to seek approval of the proposed higher ratio;

(2)   the *firm* must make a detailed recommendation to all its shareholders or owners or members that includes:

    (a)   the reasons for, and the scope of, the approval sought;

    (b)   the number of staff affected and their functions; and

    (c)   the expected impact on the requirement to maintain a sound capital base;

(3)   the *firm* must:

    (a)   without delay, inform the *FCA* of the recommendation to its shareholders or owners or members, including the proposed higher ratio and the reasons therefor; and

    (b)   demonstrate to the *FCA* that the proposed higher ratio does not conflict with its obligations under the *CRD* and the *EU CRR*, having particular regard to the *firm's own funds* obligations;

(4)   the *firm* must ensure that *employees* who have an interest in the proposed higher ratio are not allowed to exercise, directly or indirectly, any voting rights they may have as shareholders or owners or members of the *firm* in respect of the approval sought; and

(5)   the higher ratio is approved by a majority of:

    (a)   at least 66% of the shares or equivalent ownership rights represented, if at least 50% of the shares or equivalent ownership rights in the *firm* are represented; or

    (b)   at least 75% of the shares or equivalent ownership rights represented, if less than 50% of the shares or equivalent ownership rights in the *firm* are represented.

[**Note:** article 94(1)(g)(ii) of the *CRD*]

19D.3.51 R   FCA

A *firm* must notify the *FCA* without delay of the decisions taken by its shareholders or members or owners including any approved higher maximum ratio.

[**Note:** article 94(1)(g)(ii) of the *CRD*]

19D.3.52 R   FCA

A *firm* may apply a discount rate to a maximum of 25% of an *employee's* total variable *remuneration* provided it is paid in instruments that are deferred for a period of not less than five years.

[**Note:** article 94(1)(g)(iii) of the *CRD*]

19D.3.53 R   FCA

In applying the discount rate in **SYSC 19D.3.52 R**, a *firm* must apply the *EBA* Guidelines on the applicable notional discount rate for variable remuneration published on 27 March 2014.

[**Note:** the *EBA* Guidelines on the applicable notional discount rate for variable remuneration can be found at:
www.eba.europa.eu/documents/10180/643987/EBA-GL-2014-01+%28Final+Guidelines+on+the+discount+rate+for+remuneration%29.pdf/e8b3b3f6-6258-439d-a2d9-633e6e5de5e9]

Remuneration Principle 12(e): Remuneration structures – payments related to early termination

19D.3.54 R   FCA

A *firm* must ensure that payments relating to the early termination of a contract reflect performance achieved over time and are designed in a way that does not reward failure or misconduct.

[**Note:** article 94(1)(h) of the *CRD* and Standard 12 of the *FSB Compensation Standards*]

19D.3.55 G   FCA

A *firm* should review existing contractual payments related to termination of employment with a view to ensuring that these are payable only where there is a clear basis for concluding that they are consistent with **SYSC 19D.2.1 R**, which states that remuneration policies must be consistent with, and promote, sound and effective risk management.

[**Note:** Standard 12 of the *FSB Compensation Standards*]

Remuneration Principle 12(f): Remuneration structures – retained shares or other instruments

19D.3.56 R   FCA

(1)   A *firm* must ensure that a substantial portion, which is at least 50%, of any variable *remuneration* consists of an appropriate balance of:

    (a)   *shares* or equivalent ownership interests, subject to the legal structure of the *firm* concerned, or *share*-linked instruments or equivalent non-cash instruments in the case of a non-listed *firm*; and

(b)   where possible, other instruments that in each case adequately reflect the credit quality of the *firm* as a going concern and are appropriate for use as variable remuneration, such as:

(i)   those which are eligible as *additional tier 1 instruments* or *tier 2 instruments*; or

(ii)   those that can be fully converted to *common equity tier 1 instruments* or written down;

(where the expressions in italics are defined, with the conditions for eligibility, in the Definition of the Capital part of the *PRA* Rulebook).

(2)   The instruments in (1) must be subject to an appropriate retention policy designed to align incentives with the longer-term interests of the *firm*.

(3)   This *rule* applies to both the portion of the variable *remuneration* component deferred in accordance with **SYSC 19D.3.59 R** and the portion not deferred.

[**Note:** article 94(1)(l) of the *CRD* and Standard 8 of the *FSB Compensation Standards*]

19D.3.57 G   FCA

The *FCA* would normally consider a period of retention of six months to be sufficient, provided that other risk management techniques within the *firm* are operating to secure sound and effective risk management.

19D.3.58 G   FCA

(1)   The Committee of European Banking Supervisors has given guidance on the interpretation of the *CRD* provision transposed by **SYSC 19D.3.56 R (3)**. Its guidelines provide that this requirement means that the 50% minimum threshold for instruments must be applied equally to the non-deferred and the deferred components; i.e., *firms* must apply the same chosen ratio between instruments and cash for their total variable *remuneration* to both the upfront and deferred components. (Guidelines on Remuneration Policies and Practices, 10 December 2010, paragraph 133, www.eba.europa.eu/documents/10180/106961/Guidelines.pdf.)

(2)   This simplified example illustrates the operation of (1). The variable remuneration of a material risk taker (X) is 100 and, under **SYSC 19D.3.59 R (2)**, X is required to defer 60%. X's upfront component is 40 and X's deferred component is 60. At least 20 of X's upfront component, and at least 30 of X's deferred component, must be in instruments referred to in **SYSC 19D.3.56 R (1)**.

Remuneration Principle 12(g): Remuneration structures – deferral

19D.3.59 R   FCA

(1)   A *firm* must not award, pay or provide a variable *remuneration* component unless a substantial portion of it, which is at least 40%, is deferred over a period which is not less than:

(a)   for *dual-regulated firms Remuneration Code staff* who do not perform a PRA-designated senior management function, three to five years, with no vesting taking place until one year after the award, and vesting no faster than on a pro-rata basis.

(b)   for *dual-regulated firms Remuneration Code staff* who perform a PRA-designated senior management function, seven years, with no vesting taking place until three years after the award, and vesting no faster than on a pro-rata basis.

(2)   In the case of a variable *remuneration* component:

(a)   of £500,000 or more, or

(b)   payable to a *director* of a *firm* that is significant in terms of its size, internal organisation and the nature, scope and complexity of its activities;

at least 60% of the amount must be deferred on the basis set out in **SYSC 19D.3.59 R (1)**.

(3)   Subject to (1), the length of the deferral period must be established in accordance with the business cycle, the nature of the business, its risks and the activities of the *employee* in question.

[**Note:** article 94(1)(m) of the *CRD* and Standards 6 and 7 of the *FSB Compensation Standards*]

19D.3.60 G   FCA

(1)   Deferred *remuneration* paid in:

(a)   *shares* or *share*-linked instruments should be made under a scheme which meets appropriate criteria, including risk adjustment of the performance measure used to determine the initial allocation of *shares*;

(b)   cash should also be subject to performance criteria.

(2)   The *FCA* would generally expect a *firm* to have a *firm*-wide policy (and *group*-wide policy, where appropriate) on deferral. The proportion deferred should generally rise with the ratio of variable *remuneration* to fixed *remuneration* and with the amount of variable *remuneration*. While any variable *remuneration* component of £500,000 or more paid to *dual-regulated firms Remuneration Code staff* must be subject to 60% deferral, *firms* should also

consider whether lesser amounts should be considered to be 'particularly high' taking account, for example, of whether there are significant differences within *dual-regulated firms Remuneration Code staff* in the levels of variable *remuneration* paid.

Remuneration Principle 12(h): Remuneration structures – performance adjustment (affordability, malus, clawback)

19D.3.61 R   FCA

A *firm* must ensure that:

(1)   any variable *remuneration*, including a deferred portion, is paid or vests only if it is sustainable according to the financial situation of the *firm* as a whole, and justified on the basis of the performance of the *firm*, the business unit and the individual concerned;

(2)   any variable *remuneration* is subject to clawback, such that it is only awarded if an amount corresponding to it can be recovered from the individual by the *firm* if the recovery is justified on the basis of the circumstances described in **SYSC 19D.3.62 R (2)** and **SYSC 19D.3.64 R**;

(3)   any variable *remuneration* is subject to clawback for a period of at least seven years from the date on which the variable *remuneration* is awarded; and

(4)   for *dual-regulated firms Remuneration Code staff* who perform a PRA-designated senior management function, it can, by notice to the *employee* to be given no later than seven years after the variable *remuneration* was awarded, extend the period during which variable *remuneration* is subject to clawback to at least ten years from the date on which the variable *remuneration* is awarded, where:

    (a)   the *firm* has commenced an investigation into facts or events which it considers could potentially lead to the application of clawback were it not for the expiry of the clawback period; or

    (b)   the *firm* has been notified by a regulatory authority (including an overseas regulatory authority) that an investigation has been commenced into facts or events which the *firm* considers could potentially lead to the application of clawback by the *firm* were it not for the expiry of the clawback period; and

(5)   it considers on an ongoing basis whether to use the power in (4).

[**Note:** article 94(1)(n) of the *CRD* and Standards 6 and 9 of the *FSB Compensation Standards*]

19D.3.62 R   FCA

A *firm* must:

(1)   set specific criteria for the application of malus and clawback; and

(2)   ensure that the criteria for the application of malus and clawback in particular cover situations where the *employee*:

    (a)   participated in, or was responsible for, conduct which resulted in significant losses to the *firm*; or

    (b)   failed to meet appropriate standards of fitness and propriety.

[**Note:** article 94(1)(n) of the *CRD* and Standards 6 and 9 of the *FSB Compensation Standards*]

[**Note:** The *FSA* also gave *guidance* on the application of the requirements on risk adjustments. This *guidance* is available on the *FCA* website at www.fca.org.uk/firms/being-regulated/remuneration-codes.]

19D.3.63 E   FCA

(1)   A *firm* should reduce unvested deferred variable remuneration when, as a minimum:

    (a)   there is reasonable evidence of *employee* misbehaviour or material error; or

    (b)   the *firm* or the relevant business unit suffers a material downturn in its financial performance; or

    (c)   the *firm* or the relevant business unit suffers a material failure of risk management.

(2)   For performance adjustment purposes, awards of deferred variable *remuneration* made in shares or other non-cash instruments should provide the ability for the *firm* to reduce the number of shares or other non-cash instruments.

(3)   Contravention of any of (1) or (2) may be relied on as tending to establish contravention of **SYSC 19D.3.61 R (1)** on performance adjustment.

19D.3.64 R   FCA

(1)   A *firm* must make all reasonable efforts to recover an appropriate amount corresponding to some or all vested variable *remuneration* where either of the following circumstances arise during the period in which clawback applies (including any part of such period occurring after the relevant employment has ceased):

    (a)   there is reasonable evidence of *employee* misbehaviour or material error; or

    (b)   the *firm* or the relevant business unit suffers a material failure of risk management.

(2)   A *firm* must take into account all relevant factors (including, where the circumstances described in (1)(b) arise, the proximity of the *employee* to the failure of risk-management in question and the *employee's* level of responsibility) in deciding whether, and to what extent it is reasonable, to seek recovery of any or all of their vested variable *remuneration*.

19D.3.65 G   FCA

The *governing body* (or, where appropriate, the *remuneration committee*) should approve performance adjustment policies, including the triggers under which adjustment would take place. The *FCA* may ask *firms* to provide a copy of their policies and expects *firms* to make adequate records of material decisions to operate the adjustments.

Effect of breaches of the Remuneration Principles

19D.3.66 R   FCA

SYSC 19D ANNEX 1 makes provision about voiding and recovery.

19D.3.67 R   FCA
(1)   Subject to (2) to (7), the *rules* in **SYSC 19D ANNEX 1.1 R** to 1.6 R apply in relation to the prohibitions on *dual-regulated firms Remuneration Code staff* being *remunerated* in the ways specified in:
    (a)   **SYSC 19D.3.44 R** (guaranteed variable *remuneration*);
    (b)   **SYSC 19D.3.59 R** (non-deferred variable *remuneration*);
    (c)   **SYSC 19D.3.61 R (2)** (performance adjustment – clawback); and
    (d)   **SYSC 19D ANNEX 1.10R** (replacing payments recovered or property transferred).
(2)   Paragraph (1) applies only to those prohibitions as they apply in relation to a *firm* that satisfies either Condition 1 or Condition 2 as set out in (3) and (4).
(3)   Condition 1 is that the *firm* is a *UK bank*, a *building society*, or a *UK designated investment firm*, that has relevant total assets exceeding £50 billion.
(4)   Condition 2 is that the *firm*:
    (a)   is either a *full credit institution* or a *UK designated investment firm*; and
    (b)   is part of a *group* containing a *firm* that has relevant total assets exceeding £50 billion and that is a *bank*, a *building society* or a *UK designated investment firm*.
(5)   For the purposes of this *rule*, 'relevant total assets' means the arithmetic mean of the *firm's* total assets as set out in its balance sheet on its last three *accounting reference dates*.
(6)   This *rule* does not apply in relation to the prohibition on *dual-regulated firms Remuneration Code staff* being *remunerated* in the way specified in **SYSC 19D.3.44 R** (guaranteed variable *remuneration*) if both the conditions in paragraphs (2) and (3) of that *rule* are met.
(7)   This *rule* does not apply in relation to *dual-regulated firms Remuneration Code staff* (X) in respect of whom both the following conditions are satisfied:
    (a)   Condition 1 is that X's variable *remuneration* is no more than 33% of total *remuneration*; and
    (b)   Condition 2 is that X's total *remuneration* is no more than £500,000.
(8)   In relation to (7):
    (a)   references to *remuneration* are to *remuneration* awarded or paid in respect of the relevant performance year;
    (b)   the amount of any *remuneration* is:
        (i)   if it is money, its amount when awarded;
        (ii)   otherwise, whichever of the following is greatest:
            (1)   its value to the recipient when awarded;
            (2)   its market value when awarded; and
            (3)   the cost of providing it;
    (c)   where *remuneration* is, when awarded, subject to any condition, restriction or other similar provision which causes the amount of the *remuneration* to be less than it otherwise would be, that condition, restriction or provision is to be ignored in arriving at its value; and
    (d)   it is to be assumed that the member of *dual-regulated firms Remuneration Code staff* will remain so for the duration of the relevant performance year.

19D.3.68 G   FCA
(1)   Sections 137H and 137I of the *Act* enable the *FCA* to make *rules* that render void any provision of an agreement that contravenes specified prohibitions in the *dual-regulated firms Remuneration Code*, and that provide for the recovery of any payment made, or other property transferred, in pursuance of such a provision.
(2)   **SYSC 19D.3.66 R** and **SYSC 19D.3.67 R** (together with **SYSC 19D ANNEX 1** are:
    (a)   *rules* referred to in (1) that render void provisions of an agreement that contravene the specified prohibitions on guaranteed variable *remuneration*, non-deferred variable *remuneration* and replacing payments recovered or property transferred; and
    (b)   the exception to the general position set out in section 138E(2) of the *Act* that a contravention of a *rule* does not make any transaction void or unenforceable.

19D ANNEX 1   DETAILED PROVISIONS ON VOIDING AND RECOVERY (SYSC
19D.3.66R AND SYSC 19D.3.67R

Rendering contravening provisions of agreements void		
1	R	Any provision of an agreement that contravenes a prohibition on *persons* being *remunerated* in a way specified in a *rule* to which this *rule* applies (a 'contravening provision') is void.
2	R	A contravening provision does not cease to be void because:
		(1) the *firm* concerned ceases to satisfy any of the conditions set out in **SYSC 19D.3.67 R (3)** to **(4)**; or
		(2) the member of *dual-regulated firms Remuneration Code staff* concerned starts to satisfy both of the conditions set out in **SYSC 19D.3.67 R (7)(A)** and **(B)**.
3	R	A contravening provision that, at the time a *rule* to which this *rule* applies was first made (including any previous *rules* in the *FCA Handbook*), is contained in an agreement made before that time is not rendered void by **SYSC 19D ANNEX 1.1 R**, unless it is subsequently amended so as to contravene such a rule.
4	G	The effect of **SYSC 19D ANNEX 1.3 R**, in accordance with sections 137H and 137I of the *Act*, is to prevent contravening provisions being rendered void retrospectively. However, contravening provisions may be rendered void if they are contained in an agreement made after the *rule* containing the prohibition is made by the *FCA* but before the *rule* comes into effect.
5	R	(1) A pre-existing provision is not rendered void by **SYSC 19D ANNEX 1.1 R**.
		(2) In this Annex, a pre-existing provision is any provision of an agreement that would (but for this *rule*) be rendered void by **SYSC 19D ANNEX 1.1 R** that was agreed at a time when either:
		(a) the *firm* concerned did not satisfy any of the conditions set out in **SYSC 19D.3.67 R (3)** to **(4)**; or
		(b) the member of *dual-regulated firms Remuneration Code staff* concerned satisfied both of the conditions set out in **SYSC 19D.3.67 R (7)(A)** and **(B)**.
		(3) But an amendment to, or in relation to, a pre-existing provision is not to be treated as a pre-existing provision where the amendment is agreed at a time when both:
		(a) the *firm* concerned satisfies at least one of the conditions set out in **SYSC 19D.3.67 R (3)** to **(4)**; and
		(b) the member of *dual-regulated firms Remuneration Code staff* concerned does not satisfy both of the conditions set out in **SYSC 19D.3.67 R (7)(A)** and **(B)**.
6	R	For the purposes of this chapter, it is immaterial whether the law which (apart from this annex) governs a contravening provision is the law of the *United Kingdom*, or of a part of the *United Kingdom*.
Recovery of payments made or property transferred pursuant to a void contravening provision		
7	R	In relation to any payment made or other property transferred in pursuance of a contravening provision other than a pre-existing provision, a *firm* must take reasonable steps to:
		(1) recover any such payment made or other property transferred by the *firm*; and
		(2) ensure that any other *person* (P) recovers any such payment made or other property transferred by that *person*.
8	R	**SYSC 19D ANNEX 1.7R** continues to apply in one or both of the following cases:
		(1) the *firm* concerned ceases to satisfy any of the conditions set out in **SYSC 19D.3.67 R (3)** to **(4)**;
		(2) the member of *dual-regulated firms Remuneration Code staff* concerned starts to satisfy both of the conditions set out in **SYSC 19D.3.67 R (7)(A)** and **(B)**.

Part 3   FCA Handbook Materials

| 9 | G | The *rule* in **SYSC 19D ANNEX 1**.7R(2) would, for example, apply in the context of a secondment. Where a *group* member seconds an individual to a *firm* and continues to be responsible for the individual's *remuneration* in respect of services provided to the *firm*, the *firm* would need to take reasonable steps to ensure that the *group* member recovers from the secondee any *remuneration* paid in pursuance of a contravening provision. |

Replacing payments recovered or property transferred

10	R	(1)	A *firm* must not award, pay or provide variable *remuneration* to a *person* who has received *remuneration* in pursuance of a contravening provision other than a pre-existing provision (the 'contravening *remuneration* ') unless the *firm* has obtained a legal opinion stating that the award, payment or provision of the *remuneration* complies with the *dual-regulated firms Remuneration Code*.
		(2)	This *rule* applies only to variable *remuneration* relating to a performance year to which the contravening *remuneration* related.
		(3)	The legal opinion in (1) must be properly reasoned and be provided by an appropriately qualified independent individual.
		(4)	Paragraph (1) continues to apply in one or both of the following cases:
			(a) the *firm* concerned ceases to satisfy any of the conditions set out in **SYSC 19D.3.67 R (3)** to **(4)**;
			(b) the member of *dual-regulated firms Remuneration Code staff* concerned starts to satisfy both of the conditions set out in **SYSC 19D.3.67 R (7)(A)** and **(B)**.

Notification to the FCA

| 11 | G | The *FCA* considers any breach of a *rule* to which this annex applies to be a significant breach which should be notified to the *FCA* in accordance with **SUP 15.3.11 R** (Breaches of rules and other requirements in or under the Act). Such a notification should include information on the steps which a *firm* or other *person* has taken or intends to take to recover payments or property in accordance with **SYSC 19D ANNEX 1.7 R**. |

CHAPTER 20
REVERSE STRESS TESTING

20.1 APPLICATION AND PURPOSE

Application

[3.29]

20.1.1 R PRA

(1)   **SYSC 20** applies to:

    (a)   a *firm*
        which is:
        (i)   a *bank*; or
        (ii)   a *building society*; or
        (iii)   a *designated investment firm* which meets any of the criteria set out in (2) on an individual basis, or in (3) on a consolidated basis; and

    (b)   an *insurer* unless it is:
        (i)   a *non-directive friendly society*; or
        (ii)   a *Swiss general insurer*; or
        (iii)   an *EEA-deposit insurer*; or
        (iv)   an *incoming EEA firm*; or
        (v)   an *incoming Treaty firm*.

(2)   Subject to (4), **SYSC 20** applies to a *designated investment firm* if:

    (a)   it has assets under management or administration of at least £10 billion (or the equivalent amount in foreign currency); or

    (b)   the total annual *fee* and *commission* income arising from its *regulated activities* is at least £250 million (or the equivalent amount in foreign currency); or

    (c)   it has assets or liabilities of at least £2 billion (or the equivalent amount in foreign currency).

(3)   Subject to (4), where all of the *designated investment firms* within the same *consolidation group* or *non-EEA sub-group*, taken together as if they were one *firm*, meet any of the criteria in (2), **SYSC 20** applies to each of those *designated investment firms* as if it individually met the inclusion criteria in (2).

(4) Any *designated investment firm* which is included within the scope of **SYSC 20** in accordance with (2) or (3) in any given year will continue to be subject to **SYSC 20** for the following two years irrespective of whether or not it continues to meet the inclusion criteria in any of those subsequent years.

20.1.1A R FCA

(1) **SYSC 20** applies to:

 (a) an *IFPRU investment firm*; and

 (b) a *BIPRU firm* which meets any of the criteria in (2) on an individual basis, or in (3) on a consolidated basis.

(2) Subject to (4), **SYSC 20** applies to a *BIPRU firm* if:

 (a) it has assets under management or administration of at least £10 billion (or the equivalent amount in foreign currency); or

 (b) the total annual fee and commission arising from regulated activities is at least £250 million (or the equivalent amount in foreign currency); or

 (c) it has assets or liabilities of at least £2 billion (or the equivalent amount in foreign currency).

(3) Subject to (4), where all of the *BIPRU firms* within the same *UK consolidation group* or *non-EEA sub-group*, taken together, as if they were one *firm*, meet any of the criteria in (2), **SYSC 20** applies to each of those *BIPRU firms* as if it individually met the criteria in (2).

(4) Any *BIPRU firm* which is included within the scope of **SYSC 20** in accordance with (2) or (3) in any given year will continue to be subject to **SYSC 20** for the following two years, irrespective of whether or not it continues to meet the inclusion criteria in any of those subsequent years.

Purpose

20.1.2 G FCA

This chapter amplifies *Principle* 2, under which a *firm* must conduct its business with due skill, care and diligence, and *Principle* 3, under which a *firm* must take reasonable care to organise and control its affairs responsibly and effectively, with adequate risk management systems.

20.1.3 G FCA PRA

This chapter contains *rules* on reverse stress testing, which require a *firm* to identify and assess events and circumstances that would cause its business model to become unviable. This chapter also requires the *firm's* senior management or *governing body* to review and approve the results of the reverse stress testing exercise. This should help the *firm's* senior management to identify the *firm's* vulnerabilities and design a strategy to prevent or mitigate the risk of business failure.

20.1.4 G PRA

The reverse stress testing requirements are an integral component of a *firm's* business planning and risk management under *SYSC* and the Risk Control Part of the *PRA* Rulebook. For *firms* referred to in **SYSC 20.1.1 R (1)(A)**, this chapter amplifies Risk Control in the *PRA* Rulebook. For *insurers* as referred to in **SYSC 20.1.1R (1)(B)**, this chapter amplifies **SYSC 14.1.17 G** to **SYSC 14.1.25 G** on business planning and risk management.

20.1.4A G FCA

The reverse stress testing requirements are an integral component of a *firm's* business planning and risk management under *SYSC*. For *IFPRU investment firms* as referred to in **SYSC 20.1.1A R (1)(A)**, this chapter amplifies **SYSC 7.1.1 G** to **SYSC 7.1.8 G** on risk control.

20.2 REVERSE STRESS TESTING REQUIREMENTS

20.2.1 R FCA PRA

As part of its business planning and risk management obligations under *SYSC*, a *firm* must reverse stress test its business plan; that is, it must carry out stress tests and scenario analyses that test its business plan to failure. To that end, the *firm* must:

(1) identify a range of adverse circumstances which would cause its business plan to become unviable and assess the likelihood that such events could crystallise; and

(2) where those tests reveal a risk of business failure that is unacceptably high when considered against the *firm's* risk appetite or tolerance, adopt effective arrangements, processes, systems or other measures to prevent or mitigate that risk.

20.2.2 R FCA PRA

Where the *firm* is a member of:

(1) an *insurance group*, in respect of which it is required to maintain group capital;

(2) a *UK consolidation group*; or

(3) a *non-EEA sub-group*;

it must conduct the reverse stress test on a solo basis as well as on a consolidated basis in relation to the *insurance group*, the *UK consolidation group* or the *non-EEA sub-group*, as the case may be.

20.2.3 R   FCA PRA

The design and results of a *firm's* reverse stress test must be documented and reviewed and approved at least annually by the *firm's* senior management or *governing body*. A *firm* must update its reverse stress test more frequently if it is appropriate to do so in the light of substantial changes in the market or in macroeconomic conditions.

20.2.4 G   FCA PRA
(1)   Business plan failure in the context of reverse stress testing should be understood as the point at which the market loses confidence in a *firm* and this results in the *firm* no longer being able to carry out its business activities. Examples of this would be the point at which all or a substantial portion of the *firm's* counterparties are unwilling to continue transacting with it or seek to terminate their contracts, or the point at which the *firm's* existing shareholders are unwilling to provide new capital. Such a point may be reached well before the *firm's* financial resources are exhausted.
(2)   The *appropriate regulator* may request a *firm* to quantify the level of financial resources which, in the *firm's* view, would place it in a situation of business failure should the identified adverse circumstances crystallise.
(3)   In carrying out the stress tests and scenario analyses required by **SYSC 20.2.1 R**, a *firm* should at least take into account each of the sources of risk identified in accordance with **GENPRU 1.2.30 R (2)**.

20.2.5 G   FCA PRA

Reverse stress testing should be appropriate to the nature, size and complexity of the *firm's* business and of the risks it bears. Where reverse stress testing reveals that a *firm's* risk of business failure is unacceptably high, the *firm* should devise realistic measures to prevent or mitigate the risk of business failure, taking into account the time that the *firm* would have to react to these events and implement those measures. As part of these measures, a *firm* should consider if changes to its business plan are appropriate. These measures, including any changes to the *firm's* business plan, should be documented as part of the results referred to in **SYSC 20.2.3 R**.

20.2.6 G   FCA PRA

In carrying out its reverse stress testing, a *firm* should consider scenarios in which the failure of one or more of its major counterparties or a significant market disruption arising from the failure of a major market participant, whether or not combined, would cause the *firm's* business to fail.

20.2.7 G   FCA PRA
(1)   The *appropriate regulator* may request a *firm* to submit the design and results of its reverse stress tests and any subsequent updates as part of its risk assessment.
(2)   In the light of the results of a *firm's* reverse stress tests, the *appropriate regulator* may require the *firm* to implement specific measures to prevent or mitigate the risk of business failure where that risk is not sufficiently mitigated by the measures adopted by the *firm* in accordance with **SYSC 20.2.1 R**, and the *firm's* potential failure poses an unacceptable risk to the *appropriate regulator's* statutory objectives.
(3)   The *appropriate regulator* recognises that not every business failure is driven by lack of financial resources and will take this into account when reviewing a *firm's* reverse stress test design and results.

CHAPTER 21
RISK CONTROL: ADDITIONAL GUIDANCE

21.1   RISK CONTROL: GUIDANCE ON GOVERNANCE ARRANGEMENTS

Additional guidance on governance arrangements

[3.30]
21.1.1 G   FCA
(1)   This chapter provides additional guidance on risk-centric governance arrangements for effective risk management. It expands upon the general organisational requirements in **SYSC 2**, **SYSC 3**, **SYSC 4**, **SYSC 7** and **FUND 3.7**, and so applies to the same extent as **SYSC 3.1.1 R** (for *insurers*, *managing agents* and the *Society*), **SYSC 4.1.1 R** (for every other *firm*) and **FUND 3.7** (for a *full-scope UK AIFM* of an *authorised AIF*).
(2)   *Firms* should, taking account of their size, nature and complexity, consider whether in order to fulfil the general organisational requirements in **SYSC 2**, **SYSC 3**, **SYSC 4**, **SYSC 7** and (for a *full-scope UK AIFM* of an *authorised AIF*) **FUND 3.7** their risk control arrangements should include:
    (a)   appointing a Chief Risk Officer; and
    (b)   establishing a *governing body* risk committee.
The functions of a Chief Risk Officer and *governing body* risk committee are explained further in this section.

(3)   The *appropriate regulator* considers that *banks* and *insurers* that are included in the FTSE 100 Index are examples of the types of *firm* that should structure their risk control arrangements in this way. However, this *guidance* will also be relevant to some similar sized *firms* (whether or not *listed*) and some smaller *firms*, by virtue of their risk profile or complexity.

21.1.1A G   PRA

(1)   This chapter provides additional guidance on risk-centric governance arrangements for effective risk management. It expands upon the general organisational requirements in **SYSC 2**, **SYSC 3**, **SYSC 4**, **SYSC 7** and the General Organisational Requirements Part and the Risk Control Part of the *PRA* Rulebook, and so applies to the same extent as **SYSC 3.1.1 R** (for *insurers*, *managing agents* and *the Society*), **SYSC 4.1.1 R** and the General Organisational Requirements Part and the Risk Control Part of the *PRA* Rulebook (for *CRR firms*).

(2)   *Firms* should, taking account of their size, nature and complexity, consider whether in order to fulfil the general organisational requirements in **SYSC 2**, **SYSC 3**, **SYSC 4**, **SYSC 7** and the General Organisational Requirements Part and the Risk Control Part of the *PRA* Rulebook and their risk control arrangements should include:

(a)   appointing a Chief Risk Officer; and

(b)   establishing a *governing body* risk committee.

The functions of a Chief Risk Officer and *governing body* risk committee are explained further in this section.

(3)   The *appropriate regulator* considers that *banks* and *insurers* that are included in the FTSE 100 Index are examples of the types of *firm* that should structure their risk control arrangements in this way. However, this *guidance* will also be relevant to some similar sized *firms* (whether or not *listed*) and some smaller *firms*, by virtue of their risk profile or complexity.

Chief Risk Officer

21.1.2 G   FCA PRA

(1)   A Chief Risk Officer should:

(a)   be accountable to the *firm's governing body* for oversight of *firm*-wide risk management;

(b)   be fully independent of a *firm's* individual business units;

(c)   have sufficient authority, stature and resources for the effective execution of his responsibilities;

(d)   have unfettered access to any parts of the *firm's* business capable of having an impact on the *firm's* risk profile;

(e)   ensure that the data used by the *firm* to assess its risks are fit for purpose in terms of quality, quantity and breadth;

(f)   provide oversight and challenge of the *firm's* systems and controls in respect of risk management;

(g)   provide oversight and validation of the *firm's* external reporting of risk;

(h)   ensure the adequacy of risk information, risk analysis and risk training provided to members of the *firm's governing body*;

(i)   report to the *firm's governing body* on the *firm's* risk exposures relative to its risk appetite and tolerance, and the extent to which the risks inherent in any proposed business strategy and plans are consistent with the *governing body's* risk appetite and tolerance. The Chief Risk Officer should also alert the *firm's governing body* to and provide challenge on, any business strategy or plans that exceed the *firm's* risk appetite and tolerance;

(j)   provide risk-focused advice and information into the setting and individual application of the *firm's remuneration* policy (Where the *Remuneration Code* applies, see in particular **SYSC 19A.3.15 E**. Where the *BIPRU Remuneration Code* applies, see in particular **SYSC 19C.3.15 E**. Where the *dual-regulated firms Remuneration Code* applies, see in particular **SYSC 19D.3.16 E**. Where the remuneration part of the *PRA* Rulebook applies, see the *PRA's* Supervisory Statement on Remuneration).

[Note: The *PRA's* Supervisory Statement on remuneration is available on the *PRA* website at www. bankofengland.co.uk/pra/Pages/default.aspx.]

(2)   *Firms* will need to seek the *appropriate regulator's* approval for a Chief Risk Officer to perform the *systems and controls function* (see **SUP 10** (Approved persons)).

(3)   The *appropriate regulator* expects that where a *firm* is part of a *group* it will structure its arrangements so that a Chief Risk Officer at an appropriate level within the *group* will exercise functions in (1) taking into account *group*-wide risks.

Reporting lines of Chief Risk Officer

21.1.3 G   FCA PRA

(1)   The Chief Risk Officer should be accountable to a *firm's governing body*.

(2)   The *appropriate regulator* recognises that in addition to the Chief Risk Officers primary accountability to the *governing body*, an executive reporting line will be necessary for operational purposes. Accordingly, to the extent necessary for effective operational management, the Chief Risk Officer should report into a very senior executive level in the *firm*. In practice, the *appropriate regulator* expects this will be to the *chief executive*, the chief finance officer or to another executive *director*.

Appointment of Chief Risk Officer

21.1.4 G   FCA PRA

(1)   *Firms* should ensure that a Chief Risk Officers *remuneration* is subject to approval by the *firm's governing body*, or an appropriate sub-committee.

(2)   *Firms* should also ensure that the Chief Risk Officer may not be removed from that role without the approval of the *firm's governing body*.

Governing body risk committee

21.1.5 G   FCA PRA

(1)   The *appropriate regulator* considers that, while the *firm's governing body* is ultimately responsible for risk governance throughout the business, *firms* should consider establishing a *governing body* risk committee to provide focused support and advice on risk governance.

(2)   Where a *firm* has established a *governing body* risk committee, its responsibilities will typically include:

    (a)   providing advice to the *firm's governing body* on risk strategy, including the oversight of current risk exposures of the *firm*, with particular, but not exclusive, emphasis on prudential risks;

    (b)   development of proposals for consideration by the *governing body* in respect of overall risk appetite and tolerance, as well as the metrics to be used to monitor the *firm's* risk management performance;

    (c)   oversight and challenge of the design and execution of stress and scenario testing;

    (d)   oversight and challenge of the day-to-day risk management and oversight arrangements of the executive;

    (e)   oversight and challenge of due diligence on risk issues relating to material transactions and strategic proposals that are subject to approval by the *governing body*;

    (f)   provide advice to the *firm's remuneration committee* on risk weightings to be applied to performance objectives incorporated in the incentive structure for the executive;

    (g)   providing advice, oversight and challenge necessary to embed and maintain a supportive risk culture throughout the *firm*.

(3)   Where a *governing body* risk committee is established, its chairman should be a *non-executive director*, and while its membership should predominantly be non-executive it may be appropriate to include senior executives such as the chief finance officer.

21.1.6 G   FCA PRA

In carrying out their risk governance responsibilities, a *firm's governing body* and *governing body* risk committee should have regard to any relevant advice from its audit committee or internal audit function concerning the effectiveness of its current control framework. In addition, they should remain alert to the possible need for expert advice and support on any risk issue, taking action to ensure that they receive such advice and support as may be necessary to meet their responsibilities effectively.

TRANSITIONAL PROVISIONS AND SCHEDULES

2 FIRMS OTHER THAN COMMON PLATFORM FIRMS, INSURERS, MANAGING AGENTS AND THE SOCIETY

[3.31]

(1)	(2) Material to which the transitional provision applies	(3)	(4) Transitional provision	(5) Transitional provision: dates in force	(6) Handbook provisions: Coming into force
2.1 [FCA] [PRA]	**SYSC 8.1**	R	If a *firm* other than a *common platform firm*, *insurer*, *managing agent* or the *Society* has in force on 1 April 2009 *outsourcing* arrangements which would be covered by **SYSC 8.1** it need not amend those contracts to comply with these provisions but should comply with the new rules and guidance in respect of any *outsourcing* contracts which are entered into, or materially amended, on or after 1 April 2009.	1 April 2009 indefinitely	1 April 2009
2.2 [FCA]	The changes to *SYSC* set out in Annex D of the Alternative Investment Fund Managers Directive Instrument 2013	R	[expired]		
2.3 [FCA]	**SYSC 4.2.2 R** to **SYSC 4.2.5 G**, **SYSC 9.1.2 R** and **SYSC 9.1.3 R**	R	[expired]		
2.4 [FCA]	**SYSC 4.1.8A R** to **SYSC 4.1.8E R** and 4.1.9AR	R	[expired]		

3 REMUNERATION CODE

1–3	R	[deleted]
4, 5	G	[deleted]
6 [FCA] [PRA]	R	[expired]

6A [FCA] [PRA]	R	(1)	Paragraph (2) applies in relation to a *firm* that was not subject to the version of the *Remuneration Code* that applied before 1 January 2011 but satisfies at least one of the conditions set out in **SYSC 19A.3.54 R (1B)** to **SYSC 19A.3.54R (1D)**.
		(2)	Where this paragraph applies, a contravening provision that is contained in an agreement made before 3 November 2011 is not rendered void by **SYSC 19A ANNEX 1.1 R** unless it is subsequently amended so as to contravene a rule to which **SYSC 19A ANNEX 1.1 R** applies.

6B	G	The effect of 6R is to limit the provisions on voiding and recovery to *firms* which were subject to the version of the *Remuneration Code* which applied be-
[FCA]		
[PRA]		

| 6B [FCA] [PRA] | G | The effect of 6R is to limit the provisions on voiding and recovery to *firms* which were subject to the version of the *Remuneration Code* which applied before 1 January 2011. That transitional provision comes to an end on 1 January 2012. A new limit providing for voiding to apply only in relation to certain types of firm is provided in **SYSC 19A.3.54 R (1B)** to **SYSC 19A.3.54 R (1D)**. Paragraph 6AR applies to *firms* which become subject to the provisions on voiding after the transitional provision in 6R comes to an end. It prevents certain contravening provisions which predate the making of the new *rules* limiting the application of voiding from becoming void. |

TRANSITIONAL PROVISION 4 COMBINED CODE [EXPIRED]

(1)	(2) Material to which the transitional provision applies	(3)	(4) Transitional provision	(5) Transitional provision: dates in force	(6) Handbook provisions: coming into force
1.	**SYSC 2.1.6 G**, **SYSC 3.1.3 G** and **SYSC 4.4.6 G**	R	[expired]		

SCH 1   RECORD KEEPING REQUIREMENTS

1.1 G   FCA PRA

The aim of the guidance in the following table is to give the reader a quick over-all view of the relevant record keeping requirements.
It is not a complete statement of those requirements and should not be relied on as if it were.

1.2 G   FCA PRA

Handbook reference	Subject of record	Contents of record	When record must be made	Retention period
SYSC 2.2.1 R	Arrangements made to satisfy **SYSC 2.1.1 R** (apportionment) and **SYSC 2.1.3 R** (allocation)	Those arrangements	On making the arrangements and when they are updated	Six years from the date on which the record is superseded by a more up-to-date record
SYSC 3.2.20 R	Matters and dealings (including accounting records) which are the subject of requirements and standards under the *regulatory system*	Adequate	Adequate time	Adequate
SYSC 9.1.1R	Business and internal organisation	Details of the *firm's* orderly records of services and transactions undertaken	Within a reasonable time	Adequate

Handbook reference	Subject of record	Contents of record	When record must be made	Retention period
SYSC 10.1.6 R	Conflict of interest	Kinds of service or activity carried out by or on behalf of the *firm* in which a conflict of interest entailing a material risk of damage to the interests of one or more *clients* has arisen or, in the case of an ongoing service or activity, may arise.	Not specified	5 years
SYSC 14.1.53 R	Prudential risk management and systems and controls	Accounting and other records that are sufficient to enable the *firm* to demonstrate to the *PRA*: (1) that the *firm* is financially sound and has appropriate systems and controls; (2) the *firm's* financial position and exposure to risk (to a reasonable degree of accuracy); (3) the *firm's* compliance with the *rules* in GEN-PRU, INSPRU and *SYSC*.	Not specified	3 years, or longer as appropriate

SCH 2 NOTIFICATION REQUIREMENTS

2.1 G   FCA PRA

There are no notification or reporting requirements in *SYSC*.

SCH 3 FEES AND OTHER REQUIRED PAYMENTS

3.1 G   FCA PRA

There are no requirement for fees or other payments in *SYSC*.

SCH 4 POWERS EXERCISED

4.1 G

[deleted]

4.2 G

[deleted]

SCH 5 RIGHTS OF ACTION FOR DAMAGES

5.1 G   FCA

The table below sets out the *rules* in *SYSC* contravention of which by an authorised person may be actionable under section 138D of the Act (Actions for damages) by a person who suffers loss as a result of the contravention.

5.2 G   FCA

If a 'Yes' appears in the column headed 'For private person', the *rule* may be actionable by a 'private person' under section 138D (or, in certain circumstances, his fiduciary or representative; see article 6(2) and (3)(c) of the Financial Services and Markets Act 2000 (Rights of Action) Regulations

2001 (SI 2001 No 2256)). A 'Yes' in the column headed 'Removed' indicates that the *FCA* has removed the right of action under section 138D(3) of the *Act*. If so, a reference to the *rule* in which it is removed is also given.

5.3 G   FCA

The column headed 'For other person' indicates whether the rule may be actionable by a person other than a private person (or his fiduciary or representative) under article 6(2) and (3) of those Regulations. If so, an indication of the type of person by whom the *rule* may be actionable is given.

5.4 G   FCA

Chapter/ Appendix	Section/ Annex	Paragraph	Right of action under section 138D		
			For private person?	Removed?	For other person?
SYSC 2 and SYSC 3			No	Yes SYSC 1 ANNEX 1.1.12R	No
SYSC 4 to SYSC 10			No	Yes SYSC 1 ANNEX 1.2.19R	No
SYSC 11 to SYSC 19A			No	Yes SYSC 1.4.2 R	No

SCH 6   RULES THAT CAN BE WAIVED

6.1 G

[deleted]

6.1A G   FCA

As a result of section 138A of the *Act* (Modification or waiver of rules) the *FCA* has power to waive all its *rules*, other than *rules* made under section 137O (Threshold condition code), section 247 (Trust scheme rules), section 248 (Scheme particular rules), section 261I (Contractual scheme rules) or section 261J (Contractual scheme particulars rules) of the *Act*. However, if the *rules* incorporate requirements laid down in European directives, it will not be possible for the *FCA* to grant a waiver that would be incompatible with the *United Kingdom's* responsibilities under those directives.

6.1B G   PRA

As a result of section 138A of the *Act* (Modification or waiver of rules) the *PRA* has power to waive all its *rules*, other than *rules* made under section 137O (Threshold condition code). However, if the *rules* incorporate requirements laid down in European directives, it will not be possible for the *PRA* to grant a waiver that would be incompatible with the *United Kingdom's* responsibilities under those directives.

D. THRESHOLD CONDITIONS (COND)

THRESHOLD CONDITIONS
the minimum standards for becoming and remaining authorised

CHAPTER 1
INTRODUCTION

1.1A   APPLICATION

To which threshold conditions does COND apply?

[3.32]
1.1A.1   FCA

(1)   Section 55C of the Financial Services Act 2012 (Power to amend Schedule 6) gave HM Treasury the power to amend Schedule 6 of the *Act*. HM Treasury exercised this power by making The Financial Services and Markets Act 2000 (Threshold Conditions) Order 2013 which entered into force on 1 April 2013 (the "TC Order"). The TC Order's main result is the creation of four sets of *threshold conditions*, namely:

    (a)   conditions for *firms* authorised and regulated by the *FCA* only (paragraphs 2B to 2F of Schedule 6 to the *Act*)

    (b)   *FCA* specific conditions for *firms* authorised by the *PRA* and subject to dual regulation (paragraphs 3B to 3E of Schedule 6 to the *Act*);

    (c)   *PRA*-specific conditions for *insurers* (paragraphs 4A to 4F of Schedule 6 to the *Act*); and

    (d)   *PRA*-specific conditions for other *PRA-authorised persons* (paragraphs 5A to 5F of Schedule 6 to the *Act*).

(2)   The *guidance* in *COND* is only applicable to the *threshold conditions* listed in **COND 1.1A.1 G (1)(I) AND (II)**, above. These are the *threshold conditions* stated in paragraphs 2A and 3A of Schedule 6 to the *Act* as being relevant to the discharge by the *FCA* of its functions under the *Act*.

(3)   In respect of a *person* which does not carry on, or seek to carry on, any *PRA-regulated activities*, the *threshold conditions* that are relevant to the discharge by the *FCA* of its functions under the *Act* are those set out in paragraphs 2B to 2F of Schedule 6 to the *Act*, subject to **COND 1.1A.4 G (1)**, below.

(4)   In respect of a *firm* which does carry on, or seeks to carry on, a *PRA-regulated activity*, the *threshold conditions* that are relevant to the discharge by the *FCA* of its functions under the *Act* are those set out in paragraphs 3B to 3E of Schedule 6 to the *Act*, subject to **COND 1.1A.4 G (2)**, below.

(5)   A reference to "*FCA threshold conditions*" in *COND* means a reference to the *threshold conditions* referred to in (3) and (4) that apply to a particular *firm*.

To whom does COND apply?

1.1A.2 G   FCA

(1)   *COND* applies to all *firms*, except where stated otherwise in this *guidance*.

(2)   In *COND*, "*firm*" includes an applicant for *Part 4A permission* unless the context otherwise requires.

To what extent does COND apply to firms authorised by the PRA (PRA-authorised persons) and subject to dual regulation?

1.1A.3 G   FCA

(1)   As a result of the new legal framework for *threshold conditions* described in **COND 1.1A.1 G (1)**, *PRA-authorised persons* and *firms* seeking to become *PRA-authorised persons* are subject to two sets of *threshold conditions*:

    (a)   the *FCA*-specific conditions referred to in **COND 1.1A.1 G (1)(II)** and

    (b)   one of the two *PRA*-specific conditions referred to in **COND 1.1A.1 G (1)(III)** or **(IV)**, depending on the *PRA-regulated activities* which the *PRA-authorised person* or *firm* carries on, or is seeking to carry on.

    The *FCA threshold conditions* set out in paragraphs 3B to 3E of the *Act* seek to reflect this. In particular, these *threshold conditions* do not contain a condition relating to adequate financial resources. This is a matter that falls to be considered by the *PRA* under its *threshold conditions*.

(2)   The majority of the *guidance* in *COND* is intended to assist all *firms* to understand how the *FCA* will approach its assessment of the applicable *FCA threshold conditions*, regardless of whether or not a *firm* is, or is seeking to become, a *PRA-authorised person*. This is because the *FCA threshold conditions* which apply to *PRA-authorised persons* and those which apply to *firms* authorised by the *FCA* only are, for the most part, the same.

(3)   However, where *guidance* in *COND* refers to an assessment of a *firm's* financial position or its compliance with prudential regulatory requirements, it is not intended to assist *firms* which are, or are seeking to become, *PRA-authorised persons*. This is because these are matters that are not covered by the *FCA's threshold conditions*, but rather fall to be considered by the *PRA* under its *threshold conditions*.

(4)   Although some of the *PRA threshold conditions* and *FCA threshold conditions* that apply to *firms* which are, or are seeking to become, *PRA-authorised persons* may appear to address similar subject matter, the *FCA* will approach the assessment of its *threshold conditions* with its unique *statutory objectives* in mind and in the light of the functions which the *FCA* is required to discharge in relation to them.

(5)   For the avoidance of doubt, the *guidance* in *COND* is not intended to apply to the *PRA's* assessment of its own *threshold conditions* in respect of a *PRA-authorised person*. This is a matter for the *PRA* alone.

To what extent does COND apply to incoming EEA firms and incoming Treaty firms?

1.1A.4 G   FCA

COND applies to *incoming EEA firms* and *incoming Treaty firms* as set out below:

(1)   for an *incoming EEA firm* or an *incoming Treaty firm* which does not carry on any *PRA-regulated activities*, *FCA threshold conditions* 2C to 2F apply; and

(2)   for an *incoming EEA firm* or an *incoming Treaty firm* which carries on a *PRA-regulated activity*, *FCA threshold conditions* 3B to 3E apply.

FCA threshold conditions apply to *incoming EEA firms* and *incoming Treaty firms* only in as far as relevant to the discharge by the *FCA* of its relevant functions in relation to an application for, or the exercise of its *own-initiative powers* in relation to, a *top-up permission* or the functions relating to the *FCA's* consent or consultation rights relating to the exercise by the *PRA* of its powers in relation to an application for, or use of its *own-initiative powers* relating to, a *top-up permission*.

To what extent does COND apply to Swiss general insurance companies?

1.1A.5 G   FCA

FCA threshold conditions 3B, 3C and 3E apply to *Swiss General Insurance Companies*.

To what extent does COND apply to credit firms with limited permission?

1.1A.5A G   FCA

(1)   The *FCA threshold conditions* apply to a *person* that carries on, or seeks to carry on, only relevant credit activities (within paragraph 2G of Schedule 6 to the *Act*) and which therefore has, or is applying for, *limited permission* with a number of modifications (see article 10(19) of the *Regulated Activities Amendment Order*). *Regulated activities* a *person* carries on in relation to which sections 20(1) and (1A) and 23(1A) of the *Act* do not apply as a result of section 39(1D) of the *Act* are disregarded for this purpose.

(2)   For a *person* within (1), the *FCA threshold conditions* are modified as follows:

(a)   in relation to paragraph 2C of Schedule 6 to the *Act* (Effective supervision), paragraphs (a), (b) and (e) of sub-paragraph (1) do not apply (see **COND 2.3**);

(b)   in relation to paragraph 2D of Schedule 6 to the *Act* (Appropriate resources), the *person* has adequate financial resources if it is capable of meeting its debts as they fall due (see **COND 2.4**);

(c)   paragraph 2F of Schedule 6 to the *Act* (Business model) does not apply (see **COND 2.7**).

(3)   Paragraph 2G of Schedule 6 to the *Act* defines relevant credit activity for the purposes of the *FCA Threshold Conditions*. The interpretation of some of the key expressions used in this specific context is as follows:

(a)   "borrower" includes any *person* providing a guarantee or indemnity under an agreement, and a *person* to whom the rights and duties of the borrower have passed by assignment or operation of law;

(b)   "supplier" means a *person* whose main business is to sell goods or supply services and not to carry on a *regulated activity*, other than *entering into a regulated consumer hire agreement as owner* or exercising, or having the right to exercise, the owner's rights and duties under a regulated consumer hire agreement;

(c)   "customer" means a *person* to whom a supplier sells goods or supplies services or agrees to do so;

    (d)   "domestic premises supplier" means a supplier who sells goods or supplies services to customers who are individuals while physically present in the dwelling of the customer or in consequence of an agreement concluded whilst the supplier was physically present in the dwelling of the customer (though a supplier who does so on an occasional basis is not to be treated as a "domestic premises supplier").

(4)   In summary, the following *credit-related regulated activities* are relevant credit activities for the purposes of the *FCA Threshold Conditions*:

    (a)   *credit broking* when carried on:

        (i)   by a supplier (other than a domestic premises supplier) for the purposes of or in connection with the sale of goods or supply of services by the supplier to a customer (who need not be the borrower under the *credit agreement* or the hirer under the *consumer hire agreement*); or

        (ii)   in relation to a *green deal plan*; or

        (iii)   in relation to a *consumer hire agreement* where the goods being hired is a vehicle;

    although, other than where the *credit broking* is carried on by a *not-for-profit body*, the *credit broking* will not be a relevant credit activity where it relates to an agreement under which the obligation of the borrower to repay or the hirer to pay is secured, or is to be secured, by a legal mortgage on land;

    (b)   *consumer credit lending* if carried on by a *local authority* or if:

        (i)   it is carried on by a supplier;

        (ii)   no charge (by way of interest or otherwise) is payable by the borrower in connection with the provision of *credit*; and

        (iii)   the *regulated credit agreement* is not a *hire purchase agreement* or a *conditional sale agreement*;

    although, other than where the *consumer credit lending* is carried on by a *not-for-profit body*, the *consumer credit lending* will not be a relevant credit activity if it relates to an agreement under which the obligation of the borrower to repay is secured, or is to be secured, by a legal mortgage on land;

    (c)   entering into a regulated consumer hire agreement as owner or exercising, or having the right to exercise, the owner's rights and duties under a regulated consumer hire agreement although, other than where these activities are carried on by a *not-for-profit body*, entering into a regulated consumer hire agreement as owner or exercising, or having the right to exercise, the owner's rights and duties under a regulated consumer hire agreement will not be a relevant credit activity if the obligation of the hirer to pay under the agreement is secured, or is to be secured, by a legal mortgage on land;

    (d)   *debt adjusting* or *debt counselling* when carried on:

        (i)   by a supplier who also carries on *credit broking* within (a)(i);

        (ii)   by a *person* in connection with an activity within (b) or (c) which the *person* also carries on;

        (iii)   by a *not-for-profit body*;

    although, other than where the *debt adjusting* or *debt counselling* is carried on by a *not-for-profit body*, the *debt adjusting* or *debt counselling* will not be a relevant credit activity if it relates to an agreement under which the obligation of the borrower to repay or the hirer to pay is secured, or is to be secured, by a legal mortgage on land;

    (e)   *providing credit information services* where carried on by a person in connection with an activity within (a) to (d) which the *person* also carries on;

    (f)   agreeing to carry on an activity within (a) to (e).

To which regulated activities does COND apply?

1.1A.6 G   FCA

Subject to the limitations referred to above, *COND* applies in relation to all of the *regulated activities* for which a *firm* has, or will have, *permission*.

Where does COND apply?

1.1A.7 G   FCA

COND applies in relation to all of the *regulated activities* wherever they are carried on, except as stated in **COND 1.1A.4 G**.

1.2   PURPOSE

1.2.1 G   FCA

COND gives *guidance* on the *threshold conditions*. The *FCA threshold conditions* represent the minimum conditions for which the *FCA* is responsible, which a *firm* is required to satisfy, and continue to satisfy, in order to be given and to retain *Part 4A permission*. A *PRA-authorised person* or, as appropriate, a *firm* seeking to become a *PRA-authorised person* must also satisfy, and continue to satisfy, the *threshold conditions* for which the *PRA* is responsible in order to be given and to retain *Part 4A permission* (these *threshold conditions* are not the subject of the *guidance* in *COND*).

Applications for Part 4A permission or variation of Part 4A permission

1.2.2 G   FCA

(1)   Under section 55B(3) of the *Act*, in giving or varying a *Part 4A permission*, imposing or varying any *requirement* or giving consent, the *FCA* must ensure that the *firm* concerned will satisfy, and continue to satisfy, the *FCA threshold conditions* in relation to all of the *regulated activities* for which it has or will have *permission*.

(2)   If, however, the applicant for *permission* is an *incoming firm* seeking *top-up permission*, or variation of *top-up permission*, under Part 4A of the *Act* (Permission to carry on regulated activities), then under paragraphs 6A and 7A of Schedule 6 to the *Act* (Threshold conditions), the *FCA* will have regard only to satisfaction of the *FCA threshold conditions* specified as applicable in **COND 1.1A.4 G**, as relevant to the *regulated activities* for which the applicant has, or will have, *Part 4A permission*.

Exercise of the FCA's own-initiative powers

1.2.3 G   FCA

(1)   If, among other things, a *firm* is failing to satisfy any of the *FCA threshold conditions*, or is likely to fail to do so, the *FCA* may exercise its *own-initiative powers* under either section 55J (Variation or cancellation on initiative of regulator) or section 55L (Imposition of requirements by FCA) of the *Act*. Use of the *FCA's own-initiative powers* is explained in **SUP 7** (Individual requirements), and **EG 8** (Variation and cancellation of permission on the FCA's own initiative and intervention against incoming firms).

(2)   If, when exercising its *own-initiative powers* under section 55J or section 55L of the *Act*, the *FCA* varies a *firm's permission*, or imposes or varies a *requirement*, then, under section 55B(3) of the *Act*, the *FCA* must ensure that the *firm* concerned will satisfy, and continue to satisfy, the *FCA threshold conditions* in relation to all of the relevant *regulated activities* for which it has or will have *permission*. However, section 55B(4) of the *Act* states that the duty imposed by section 55B(3) of the *Act* does not prevent the *FCA* taking such steps as it considers necessary in relation to a particular *firm* in order to advance any of its operational objectives.

(3)   The *FCA* can also exercise its *own-initiative powers* under section 55J or section 55L of the *Act* in relation to the *top-up permission* of an *incoming firm*. But this is only on the grounds that the *incoming firm* is failing, or likely to fail, to satisfy the *FCA threshold conditions* specified as applying to *incoming firms* under **COND 1.1A.4 G**.

1.2.4 G

(1)   [deleted]

(2)   [deleted]

Approval of acquisitions or increases of control

1.2.5 G   FCA

(1)   Under section 185 of the *Act* (Assessment: general) the *FCA* may, subject to consultation with the *PRA* where the conditions in section 187B of the *Act* are satisfied, object to an acquisition of an *FCA-authorised person* if there are reasonable grounds to do so on the basis of the matters set out in section 186 of the *Act* (Assessment: criteria) or if the information provided by the section 178 notice giver is incomplete. Section 186(d) of the *Act* (Assessment: criteria) specifies one such criteria as whether an *FCA-authorised person* will be able to comply with its prudential requirements (including the *threshold conditions* in relation to all of the *regulated activities* for which it has, or will have, *permission*.)

(2)   Under section 191A of the *Act* (Objection to control), subject to consultation with the *PRA* in the circumstances specified in that provision, the *FCA* may object to a *person's* existing control of an *FCA-authorised person* on the grounds specified under section 186 of the *Act*.

1.3   GENERAL

1.3.1 G   FCA

The *guidance* in **COND 2** explains each *FCA threshold condition* in Schedule 6 (threshold conditions) to the *Act* and indicates how the *FCA* will interpret it in practice. This *guidance* is not, however, exhaustive and is written in very general terms. A *firm* will need to have regard to the obligation placed upon the *FCA* under section 55B (The threshold conditions) of the *Act*; that is, the *FCA* must ensure that the *firm* will satisfy, and continue to satisfy, the *FCA threshold conditions* in relation to each *regulated activity* for which it has, or will have, *permission*.

1.3.2 G   FCA

(1)   The *FCA* will consider whether a *firm* satisfies, and will continue to satisfy, the *FCA threshold conditions* in the context of the size, nature, scale and complexity of the business which the *firm* carries on or will carry on if the relevant application is granted.

(2)   In relation to *threshold conditions* set out in paragraphs 2D to 2F of Schedule 6 to the *Act* in respect of *firms* which are not *PRA-authorised persons* and paragraphs 3C to 3E of Schedule 6 to the *Act* in respect of *firms* which are *PRA-authorised persons*, the *FCA* will

consider whether a *firm* is ready, willing and organised to comply, on a continuing basis, with the requirements and standards under the *regulatory system* which apply to the *firm*, or will apply to the *firm*, and for which the *FCA* is responsible, if it is granted *Part 4A permission*, or a variation of its *permission*. These matters will also be considered if the *FCA* is exercising its *own-initiative powers* (see **COND 1.2.3 G**). Guidance to *firms* on the implications of this is given under each of those *threshold conditions*.

1.3.3 G   FCA

Although the *FCA* may consider that a matter is relevant to its assessment of a *firm*, the fact that a matter is disclosed to the *FCA*, for example in an application, does not necessarily mean that the *firm* will fail to satisfy the *FCA threshold conditions*. The *FCA* will consider each matter in relation to the *regulated activities* for which the *firm* has, or will have, *permission*, having regard to its *statutory objectives*. A *firm* should disclose each relevant matter but, if it is appropriate to do so, it is encouraged to discuss it with the *FCA*. This will enable the *FCA* to consider fully how material or significant the matter is and how it affects the ability of the *firm* to satisfy, and continue to satisfy, the *FCA threshold conditions*.

1.3.3A G   FCA

In determining the weight to be given to any relevant matter, the *FCA* will consider its significance in relation to the *regulated activities* for which the *firm* has, or will have, *permission*, in the context of its ability to supervise the *firm* adequately, having regard to the *FCA's statutory objectives*. In this context, a series of matters may be significant when taken together, even though each of them in isolation might not give serious cause for concern.

1.3.3B G   FCA

In determining whether the *firm* will satisfy, and continue to satisfy, the *FCA threshold conditions*, the *FCA* will have regard to all relevant matters, whether arising in the *United Kingdom* or elsewhere.

1.3.3C G   FCA

When assessing the *FCA threshold conditions*, the *FCA* may have regard to any *person* appearing to be, or likely to be, in a relevant relationship with the *firm*, in accordance with section 55R of the *Act* (Persons connected with an applicant). For example, a *firm's controllers*, its *directors* or *partners*, other *persons* with *close links* to the *firm* (see **COND 2.3**), and other *persons* that exert influence on the *firm* which might pose a risk to the *firm's* satisfaction of the *FCA threshold conditions*, would be in a relevant relationship with the *firm*.

1.3.3D G   FCA

In making its assessment, the *FCA* will consider the individual circumstances of each *firm* on a case-by-case basis.

1.3.3E G   FCA

Notes on the contents of a business plan are given in the business plan section of the application pack for *Part 4A permission* on the *FCA's* website.

Statutory quotations

1.3.4 G   FCA
(1)   For ease of reference, the *FCA threshold conditions* in or under Schedule 6 to the *Act* have been quoted in full in **COND 2**.
(2)   Paragraphs 2A and 3A of Schedule 6 of the *Act* have not been quoted. These set out the application of the *FCA threshold conditions* to *firms* which do not carry on, or are not seeking to carry on, a *PRA regulated activity* and *firms* which carry on, or are seeking to carry on, a *PRA regulated activity* respectively. This application is summarised in **COND 1.1A**.
(3)   As the *FCA threshold conditions* impose obligations, they are printed in bold type. The use of bold type is not intended to indicate that these quotations are *rules* made by the *FCA*.
(4)   [deleted]
(5)   Paragraph 1A of Schedule 6 of the *Act* sets out interpretative provisions that apply to the *threshold conditions*. These are repeated in **COND 1.3.5 G** below for ease of reference.

1.3.5U

Paragraph 1A of Schedule 6 to the Act
(1)   **"assets" includes contingent assets;**
       "consolidated supervision" has the same meaning as in section 3M(a);
       "consumer" has the meaning given by section 425A(b);
       "financial crime" is to be read with section 1H(3)(c);
       "functions", in relation to either the FCA or the PRA, means the functions conferred on that regulator by or under this Act;
       "liabilities" includes contingent liabilities;
       "relevant directives" has the same meaning as in section 3M;

"**Society**" **means the society incorporated by Lloyd's Act 1871(d) by the name of Lloyd's;**

"**subsidiary undertaking**" **includes all the instances mentioned in Article 1(1) and (2) of the Seventh Company Law Directive in which an entity may be a subsidiary of an undertaking.**

(2)   **For the purposes of this Schedule, the "non-financial resources" of a person include any systems, controls, plans or policies that the person maintains and the human resources that the person has available.**

(3)   **In this Schedule, references to "integrity of the UK financial system" are to be read with section 1D(2)(e).**

(4)   **The reference to the failure of a person is to be read in accordance with section 2J(3) and (4)(f).**

CHAPTER 2
THE THRESHOLD CONDITIONS

2.2   LOCATION OF OFFICES

[3.33]
2.2.1 UK

[deleted]

Paragraph 2B of Schedule 6 to the Act

2.2.1A UK   FCA
(1)   Unless sub-paragraph (3), (4)(a) or (7) applies, if A is a body incorporated in the United Kingdom—
         (a)   A's head office, and
         (b)   if A has a registered office, that office,
         must be in the United Kingdom.
(2)   If A is not a body corporate but A's head office is in the United Kingdom, A must carry on business in the United Kingdom.
(3)   If—
         (a)   A is seeking to carry on, or is carrying on, a regulated activity which is any of the investment services and activities,
         (b)   A is a body corporate with no registered office, and
         (c)   A's head office is in the United Kingdom,
         A must carry on business in the United Kingdom.
(4)   If A is seeking to carry on, or is carrying on, an insurance mediation activity—
         (a)   where A is a body corporate incorporated in the United Kingdom, A's registered office, or if A has no registered office, A's head office, must be in the United Kingdom;
         (b)   where A is an individual, A is to be treated for the purposes of sub-paragraph (2), as having a head office in the United Kingdom if A's residence is resident in the United Kingdom.
(5)   "Insurance mediation activity" means any of the following activities—
         (a)   dealing in rights under a contract of insurance as agent;
         (b)   arranging deals in rights under a contract of insurance;
         (c)   assisting in the administration and performance of a contract of insurance;
         (d)   advising on buying or selling rights under a contract of insurance;
         (e)   agreeing to do any of the activities specified in paragraph (a) to (d).
(6)   Sub-paragraph (5) must be read with—
         (a)   section 22
         (b)   any relevant order under that section; and
         (c)   Schedule 2.
(7)   If A is seeking to carry on, or is carrying on, the regulated activity of managing an AIF and is, or upon being granted Part 4A permission to carry on that regulated activity would be, a full-scope UK AIFM, A's head office and registered office must be in the United Kingdom.

2.2.1B G   FCA

Paragraph 2B of Schedule 6 to the *Act* sets out the location of offices *threshold condition* for *firms* carrying on, or seeking to carry on, *regulated activities* which do not include a *PRA-regulated activity*.

2.2.1C G   FCA

The *FCA* is not responsible for the location of offices *threshold condition* for *firms* carrying on, or seeking to carry on, *regulated activities* which include a *PRA-regulated activity*.

2.2.2 G   FCA

Paragraph 2B(1) of Schedule 6 to the *Act* implements article 7(1)(d) of the *UCITS Directive*, paragraphs 2B(1) to 2B(23) of Schedule 6 to the *Act* implement article 5(4) of *MiFID*, paragraph 2B(4) of Schedule 6 to the *Act* implements article 2.9 of the *Insurance Mediation Directive* and paragraph 2B(7) of Schedule 6 to the *Act* implements article 8(1)(e) of *AIFMD*, although the *Act* extends the *threshold condition* set out in paragraph 2B of Schedule 6 of the *Act* to *authorised persons* that are not *PRA-authorised persons* who are outside the scope of these *Single Market Directives*.

2.2.3 G   FCA

Neither the *UCITS Directive*, *MiFID*, the *Insurance Mediation Directive*, *AIFMD* nor the *Act* define what is meant by a *firm's* 'head office'. This is not necessarily the *firm's* place of incorporation or the place where its business is wholly or mainly carried on. Although the *FCA* will judge each application on a case-by-case basis, the key issue in identifying the head office of a *firm* is the location of its central management and control, that is, the location of:

(1)   the *directors* and other senior management, who make decisions relating to the *firm's* central direction, and the material management decisions of the *firm* on a day-to-day basis; and

(2)   the central administrative functions of the *firm* (for example, central compliance, internal audit).

2.3   EFFECTIVE SUPERVISION

2.3.1 UK

[deleted]

Paragraph 2C of Schedule 6 to the Act

2.3.1A UK   FCA

(1)   A must be capable of being effectively supervised by the FCA having regard to all the circumstances including—

       (a)   the nature (including the complexity) of the regulated activities that A carries on or seeks to carry on;

       (b)   the complexity of any products that A provides or will provide in carrying on those activities;

       (c)   the way in which A's business is organised;

       (d)   if A is a member of a group, whether membership of the group is likely to prevent the FCA's effective supervision of A;

       (e)   whether A is subject to consolidated supervision required under any of the relevant directives;

       (f)   if A has close links with another person ("CL")—

             (i)   the nature of the relationship between A and CL;

             (ii)   whether those links are or that relationship is likely to prevent the FCA's effective supervision of A; and

             (iii)   if CL is subject to the laws, regulations or administrative provisions of a territory which is not an EEA State ("the foreign provisions"), whether those foreign provisions, or any deficiency in their enforcement, would prevent the FCA's effective supervision of A.

(1A)   Paragraphs (a), (b) and (e) of sub-paragraph (1) do not apply where the only regulated activities that the person concerned carries on, or seeks to carry on, are—

       (a)   relevant credit activities, and

       (b)   if any, activities to which, by virtue of section 39(1D), sections 20(1) and (1A) and 23(1A) do not apply when carried on by the person.

(2)   A has close links with CL if—

       (a)   CL is a parent undertaking of A;

       (b)   CL is a subsidiary undertaking of A;

       (c)   CL is a parent undertaking of a subsidiary undertaking of A;

       (d)   CL is a subsidiary undertaking of a parent undertaking of A;

       (e)   CL owns or controls 20% or more of the voting rights or capital of A; or

       (f)   A owns or controls 20% or more of the voting rights or capital of CL.

2.3.1B G   FCA

Paragraph 2C of Schedule 6 to the *Act* sets out the effective supervision *threshold condition* for *firms* carrying on, or seeking to carry on, *regulated activities* which do not include a *PRA-regulated activity*.

2.3.1BA G   FCA

For the purposes of paragraph 2C (1A) of Schedule 6 to the *Act*, relevant credit activity is defined in paragraph 2G of Schedule 6 to the *Act*. Guidance on the meaning of relevant credit activity is given in **COND 1.1A.5A G**.

Paragraph 3B of Schedule 6 to the Act

2.3.1C G   FCA

(1)   B must be capable of being effectively supervised by the FCA having regard to all the circumstances including-
- (a)   the nature (including the complexity) of the regulated activities that B carries on or seeks to carry on;
- (b)   the complexity of any products that B provides or will provide in carrying on those activities;
- (c)   the way in which B's business is organised;
- (d)   if B is a member of a group, whether membership of the group is likely to prevent the FCA's effective supervision of B;
- (e)   whether B is subject to consolidated supervision required under any of the relevant directives;
- (f)   if B has close links with another person ("CL")—
  - (i)   the nature of the relationship between B and CL;
  - (ii)   whether those links are or that relationship is likely to prevent the FCA's effective supervision of B; and
  - (iii)   if CL is subject to the laws, regulations or administrative provisions of a territory which is not an EEA State ("the foreign provisions"), whether those foreign provisions, or any deficiency in their enforcement, would prevent the FCA's effective supervision of B.

(2)   B has close links with CL if—
- (a)   CL is a parent undertaking of B;
- (b)   CL is a subsidiary undertaking of B;
- (c)   CL is a parent undertaking of a subsidiary undertaking of B;
- (d)   CL is a subsidiary undertaking of a parent undertaking of B;
- (e)   CL owns or controls 20% or more of the voting rights or capital of B; or
- (f)   B owns or controls 20% or more of the voting rights or capital of CL.

2.3.1D G   FCA

Paragraph 3B of Schedule 6 to the *Act* sets out the effective supervision *threshold condition* which is relevant to the discharge by the *FCA* of its functions under the *Act* in relation to *firms* carrying on, or seeking to carry on, *regulated activities* which include a *PRA-regulated activity*.

2.3.1E G   FCA

The guidance in **COND 2.3** should be read as applying to both paragraph 2C of Schedule 6 of the *Act* and, as far as relevant to the discharge by the *FCA* of its functions under the *Act* in respect of *firms* carrying on, or seeking to carry on, a *PRA-regulated activity*, paragraph 3B of Schedule 6 of the *Act*.

2.3.1F G   FCA

Firms carrying on, or seeking to carry on, a *PRA-regulated activity*, should note that the *PRA* is also responsible for assessing effective supervision under its own *threshold conditions*. Paragraphs 4F and 5F of Schedule 6 to the *Act* set out the effective supervision *threshold conditions* which are relevant to the discharge by the *PRA* of its functions under the *Act* in relation to *firms* carrying on, or seeking to carry on, a *PRA-regulated activity*. For the avoidance of doubt, this *guidance* does not apply to the *threshold conditions* set out in paragraphs 4F and 5F of Schedule 6 to the *Act*.

2.3.2 G   FCA

Paragraphs 2C and 3B of Schedule 6 to the *Act* implements requirements of the *Single Market Directives*, but the *Act* extends this condition to *firms* from outside the *EEA* and other *firms* which are outside the scope of the *Single Market Directives*.

2.3.3 G   FCA

In assessing the *threshold conditions* set out in paragraphs 2C and 3B of Schedule 6 to the *Act*, factors which the *FCA* will take into consideration include, among other things, whether:

(1)   it is likely that the *FCA* will receive adequate information from the *firm*, and those *persons* with whom the *firm* has *close links*, to enable it to determine whether the *firm* is complying with the requirements and standards under the *regulatory system* for which the *FCA* is responsible and to identify and assess the impact on its *statutory objectives*; this will include consideration of whether the *firm* is ready, willing and organised to comply with *Principle* 11 (Relations with regulators and the *rules* in *SUP* on the provision of information to the *FCA*;

(2)   the structure and geographical spread of the *firm*, the *group* to which it belongs and other *persons* with whom the *firm* has *close links*, might hinder the provision of adequate and reliable flows of information to the *FCA*; factors which may hinder these flows include the fact there may be branches or connected *companies* in territories which supervise *companies* to a different standard or territories with laws which restrict the free flow of information, although the *FCA* will consider the totality of information available from all sources; and

(3)   [deleted]

(4)   in respect of a *firm* not carrying on, or seeking to carry on, a *PRA-regulated activity*, it is possible to assess with confidence the overall financial position of the *group* at any particular time; factors which may make this difficult include lack of audited consolidated accounts for a *group*, if companies in the same *group* as the *firm* have different financial years and accounting dates and if they do not share common auditors.

2.3.4

[deleted]

2.3.5

[deleted]

Meaning of "parent undertaking" and "subsidiary undertaking"

2.3.6 G   FCA
(1)   Section 420(1) of the *Act* (Parent and subsidiary undertaking) states that, except in relation to an *incorporated friendly society*, *'parent undertaking'* and *'subsidiary undertaking'* have the same meaning as in the Companies Acts (see section 1162 of, and schedule 7 to, the Companies Act 2006). These are the cases referred to in **COND 2.3.7 G (1)(A)** to **(F)**.
(2)   Section 420(2) of the Act supplements these definitions in two ways; these are the cases referred to in **COND 2.3.7 G (1)(G)** and **(H)**.
(3)   Paragraph 1A of Schedule 6 to the *Act* extends the meaning of *'subsidiary undertaking'* for the purposes of the *threshold conditions* to all the cases in articles 1(1) and (2) of the *Seventh Company Law Directive* in which one *undertaking* may be a *subsidiary* of another *undertaking* (see **COND 2.3.11 G**).

2.3.7 G   FCA
(1)   For the purposes of the *threshold conditions* set out in paragraphs 2C and 3B of Schedule 6 to the *Act*, and except in relation to an *incorporated friendly society*, an undertaking is a *parent undertaking* of another *undertaking* (a *subsidiary undertaking*) if any of the following apply to it:
      (a)   it holds a majority of the voting rights in the *subsidiary undertaking*; or
      (b)   it is a member of the *subsidiary undertaking* and has the right to appoint or remove a majority of its board of *directors*; or
      (c)   it has the right to exercise a dominant influence over the *subsidiary undertaking* through:
           (i)   provisions contained in the *subsidiary undertaking's* memorandum or articles; or
           (ii)   a control contract; or
      (d)   it is a member of the *subsidiary undertaking* and controls alone, under an agreement with other shareholders or members, a majority of the voting rights in the *subsidiary undertaking*; or
      (e)   it has the power to exercise, or actually exercises, dominant influence or control over it, or it and the *subsidiary undertaking* are managed on a unified basis; or
      (f)   it is a *parent undertaking* of a *parent undertaking* of the *subsidiary undertaking*; or
      (g)   it is an individual and would be a *parent undertaking* if it were an *undertaking*; or
      (h)   it is incorporated in or formed under the law of another *EEA State* and is a *parent undertaking* within the meaning of any rule of law in that State for purposes connected with implementation of the *Seventh Company Law Directive*.
(2)   [deleted]

2.3.8 G
(1)   In relation to **COND 2.3.7 G (1)(B)** and **(D)**, an *undertaking* is treated as a member of another *undertaking* if any of its *subsidiary undertaking* is a member of that *undertaking*, or if any shares in that other *undertaking* are held by a *person* acting on behalf of the *undertaking* or any of its *subsidiary undertakings*.
(2)   [deleted]
(3)   [deleted]

2.3.9 G

The provisions of Schedule 7 to the Companies Act 2006(Parent and subsidiary undertakings: supplementary provisions) explain and supplement the provisions of section 1162 of the Companies Act 2006(outlined in **COND 2.3.7 G (1)(A)** to **(F)**).

2.3.10 G   FCA

Section 420(3) of the *Act* (Parent and subsidiary undertaking) states that an *incorporated friendly society* is a *parent undertaking* of another *body corporate* (a *subsidiary undertaking*) if it has the following relationship to it:
(1)   it holds a majority of the voting rights in the *subsidiary undertaking*; or
(2)   it is a member of the *subsidiary undertaking* and has the right to appoint or remove a majority of the *subsidiary undertaking's* board of *directors*; or

(3)   it is a member of the *subsidiary undertaking* and controls alone, under an agreement with other shareholders or members, a majority of the voting rights in it.

2.3.11 G   FCA

For the purposes of the *threshold conditions* set out in paragraphs 2C and 3B of Schedule 6 to the *Act*, an *undertaking* is a *subsidiary undertaking* of another *undertaking* if:

(1)   the other undertaking (its parent) is a member of the *undertaking*;

(2)   a majority of the *undertaking's* board of *directors* who have held office during the financial year and during the preceding financial year have been appointed solely as a result of the exercise of the parent's voting rights; and

(3)   no one else is the *parent undertaking* of the *undertaking* under **COND 2.3.7 G (1)(A)** or **COND 2.3.10 G (1)**.

2.3.11A G   FCA

Paragraphs 2C(2)(e) and (f) and 3B(2)(e) and (f) of Schedule 6 to the *Act* reflect legislation initially introduced in the *Post-BCCI Directive*, which defines close links, in part, by reference to participation. Recital 5 of the *Post-BCCI Directive* gives further guidance on what is meant by 'participation' for the purposes of the directive. It states that the sole fact of having acquired a significant proportion of a company's capital does not constitute participation for the purposes of the directive if that holding has been acquired solely as a temporary investment which does not make it possible to exercise influence over the structure or financial policy of the undertaking.

2.3.12 G   FCA

The *guidance* in **COND 2.3** is not comprehensive and is not a substitute for consulting the relevant legislation, for example the Companies Act 2006, the Friendly Societies Act 1992 and the *Seventh Company Law Directive*, or obtaining appropriate professional advice.

2.4   APPROPRIATE RESOURCES

2.4.1 UK

[deleted]

Paragraph 2D of Schedule 6 to the Act

2.4.1A UK   FCA

(1)   The resources of A must be appropriate in relation to the regulated activities that A carries on or seeks to carry on.

(2)   The matters which are relevant in determining whether A has appropriate resources include—

    (a)   the nature and scale of the business carried on, or to be carried on, by A;

    (b)   the risks to the continuity of the services provided by, or to be provided by, A; and

    (c)   A's membership of a group and any effect which that membership may have.

(3)   Except in a case within sub-paragraph (3A), the matters which are relevant in determining whether A has appropriate financial resources include—

    (a)   the provision A makes and, if A is a member of a group, which other members of the group make, in respect of liabilities; and

    (b)   the means by which A manages and, if A is a member of a group, by which other members of the group manage, the incidence of risk in connection with A's business.

(3A)   Where the only regulated activities that A carries on, or seeks to carry on, are—

    (a)   relevant credit activities, and

    (b)   if any, activities to which, by virtue of section 39(1D), sections 20(1) and (1A) and 23(1A) do not apply when carried on by A,

    A has adequate financial resources if A is capable of meeting A's debts as they fall due.

(4)   The matters which are relevant in determining whether A has appropriate non-financial resources include—

    (a)   the skills and experience of those who manage A's affairs;

    (b)   whether A's non-financial resources are sufficient to enable A to comply with—

        (i)   requirements imposed or likely to be imposed on A by the FCA in the course of the exercise of its functions;

        (ii)   any other requirement in relation to whose contravention the FCA would be the appropriate regulator for the purposes of any provision of Part 14 of this Act.

2.4.1B G   FCA

Paragraph 2D of Schedule 6 to the *Act* sets out the appropriate resources *threshold condition* for *firms* carrying on, or seeking to carry on, *regulated activities* which do not include a *PRA-regulated activity*.

2.4.1BA G   FCA

For the purposes of paragraph 2D (3A) of Schedule 6 to the *Act*, relevant credit activity is defined in paragraph 2G of Schedule 6 to the *Act*. Guidance on the meaning of relevant credit activity is given in **COND 1.1A.5A G**.

Paragraph 3C of Schedule 6 to the Act

2.4.1C UK FCA
(1) The non-financial resources of B must be appropriate in relation to the regulated activities that B carries on or seeks to carry on, having regard to the operational objectives of the FCA.
(2) The matters which are relevant in determining whether the condition in sub-paragraph (1) is met include—
  (a) the nature and scale of the business carried on, or to be carried on, by B;
  (b) the risks to the continuity of the services provided by, or to be provided by, B;
  (c) B's a member of a group and any effect which that membership may have;
  (d) the skills and experience of those who manage B's affairs;
  (e) whether B's non-financial resources are sufficient to enable B to comply with—
    (i) requirements imposed or likely to be imposed on B by the FCA in the exercise of its functions; or
    (ii) any other requirement in relation to whose contravention the FCA would be the appropriate regulator for the purpose of any provision of Part 14 of this Act.

2.4.1D G FCA

Paragraph 3C of Schedule 6 to the *Act* sets out the appropriate non-financial resources *threshold condition* which is relevant to the discharge by the *FCA* of its functions under the *Act* in relation to *firms* carrying on, or seeking to carry on, *regulated activities* which include a *PRA-regulated activity*.

2.4.1E G FCA

The guidance in **COND 2.4** should be read as applying to both paragraph 2D of Schedule 6 of the *Act* and, as far as relevant to the discharge by the *FCA* of its functions in respect of *firms* carrying on, or seeking to carry on, a *PRA-regulated activity* under the *Act*, paragraph 3C of Schedule 6 of the *Act*.

2.4.1F G FCA

As the *threshold condition* set out in paragraph 3C of Schedule 6 to the *Act* does not relate to financial resources, the *guidance* in **COND 2.4** relating to appropriate financial resources only applies to the *FCA's* assessment of the *threshold condition* set out in paragraph 2D of Schedule 6 of the *Act*.

2.4.1G G FCA

Firms carrying on, or seeking to carry on, a *PRA-regulated activity*, should note that the *PRA* is responsible for assessing their financial resources. Paragraphs 4D and 5D of Schedule 6 to the *Act* contain the *threshold conditions* relating to financial resources which are relevant to the discharge by the *PRA* of its functions under the *Act* in relation to *firms* carrying on, or seeking to carry on, a *PRA-regulated activity* (in addition to additional non-financial resources *threshold conditions* which are also relevant to the discharge by the *PRA* of its functions). For the avoidance of doubt, this *guidance* does not apply to *threshold conditions* set out in paragraphs 4D and 5D of Schedule 6 to the *Act*.

2.4.2 G FCA
(1) [deleted]
(2) In this context, the *FCA* will interpret the term "appropriate" as meaning sufficient in terms of quantity, quality and availability, and "resources" as including all financial resources (though only in the case of *firms* not carrying on, or seeking to carry on, a *PRA-regulated activity*), non-financial resources and means of managing its resources; for example, capital, provisions against liabilities, holdings of or access to cash and other liquid assets, human resources and effective means by which to manage risks.
(3) Paragraph 1A(2) of Schedule 6 to the *Act* provides that "non-financial resources" of a *firm* for the purposes of the *threshold conditions* include any systems, controls, plans or policies that the *firm* maintains and the human resources that the *firm* has available.
(4) High level systems and control requirements are in *SYSC*. The *FCA* will consider whether the *firm* is ready, willing and organised to comply with these and other applicable systems and controls requirements when assessing if it has appropriate non-financial resources for the purpose of the *threshold conditions* set out in paragraphs 2D and 3C to Schedule 6 of the *Act*.
(5) Detailed financial resources requirements are in the relevant section of the Prudential Standards part of the *FCA Handbook*, including specific provisions for particular types of *regulated activity*. The *FCA* will consider whether *firms* (other than *firms* carrying on, or seeking to carry on, *PRA-regulated activities*) are ready, willing and organised to comply with these requirements when assessing if they have appropriate financial resources for the purposes of the *threshold condition* set out in paragraph 2D of Schedule 6 to the *Act*.

2.4.3 G   FCA
(1)   [deleted]
(2)   Although it is the *firm* that is being assessed, the *FCA* may take into consideration the impact of other members of the *firm's group* on the adequacy of its resources, where relevant to the discharge of the *FCA's* functions. For example, in relation to a *firm* other than a *firm* carrying on, or seeking to carry on, a *PRA-regulated activity*, the *FCA* may assess the consolidated solvency of the *group*. The *FCA's* approach to the consolidated supervision of such a *firm*, and its *group*, is in the relevant part of the Prudential Standards part of the *FCA Handbook*.

2.4.4 G   FCA
(1)   [deleted]
(2)   Relevant matters to which the *FCA* may have regard when assessing whether a *firm* will satisfy, and continue to satisfy, this *threshold condition* may include but are not limited to:
   (a)   (in relation to a *firm* other than a *firm* carrying on, or seeking to carry on, a *PRA-regulated activity*), whether there are any indications that the *firm* may have difficulties if the application is granted, at the time of the grant or in the future, in complying with any of the *FCA's* prudential *rules* (see the relevant part of the Prudential Standards part of the *FCA Handbook*);
   (b)   (in relation to a *firm* other than a *firm* carrying on, or seeking to carry on, a *PRA-regulated activity*, whether there are any indications that the *firm* will not be able to meet its debts as they fall due;
   (c)   whether there are any implications for the adequacy of the *firm's* resources arising from the history of the *firm*; for example, whether the *firm* has:
      (i)   been adjudged bankrupt; or
      (ii)   entered into liquidation; or
      (iii) been the subject of a receiving or administration order; or
      (iv)   had a bankruptcy or winding-up petition served on it; or
      (v)   had its estate sequestrated; or
      (vi)   entered into a deed of arrangement or an individual voluntary agreement (or in Scotland, a trust deed) or other composition in favour of its creditors, or is doing so; or
      (vii) within the last ten years, failed to satisfy a judgment debt under a court order, whether in the *United Kingdom* or elsewhere;
   (d)   whether the *firm* has taken reasonable steps to identify and measure any risks of regulatory concern that it may encounter in conducting its business and has installed appropriate systems and controls and appointed appropriate human resources to measure them prudently at all times:
   (e)   whether the *firm* has conducted enquiries into the financial services sector in which it intends to conduct business that are sufficient to satisfy itself that:
      (i)   it has access to adequate capital, by reference to the *FCA's* prudential requirements, to support the business including any losses which may be expected during its start-up period (in relation to a *firm* other than a *firm* carrying on, or seeking to carry on, a *PRA-regulated activity*); and
      (ii)   *Client money, deposits, custody assets* and *policyholders'* rights will not be placed at risk if the business fails; and
   (f)   whether the resources of the *firm* are commensurate with the likely risks it will face.
(3)   [deleted]
(4)   [deleted]

2.4.5 G

[deleted]

2.4.6 G   FCA
(1)   [deleted]
(2)   [deleted]
(3)   [deleted]

2.5   SUITABILITY

2.5.1 UK

[deleted]

Paragraph 2E to Schedule 6 of the Act

2.5.1A UK   FCA
(1)   A must be a fit and proper person having regard to all the circumstances, including—
   (a)   A's connection with any person;
   (b)   the nature (including the complexity) of any regulated activity that A carries on or seeks to carry on;
   (c)   the need to ensure that A's affairs are conducted in an appropriate manner, having regard in particular to the interests of consumers and the integrity of the UK financial system;

(d)   whether A has complied and is complying with requirements imposed by the FCA in the exercise of its functions, or requests made by the FCA, relating to the provision of information to the FCA and, where A has so complied or is so complying, the manner of that compliance;

(e)   whether those who manage A's affairs have adequate skills and experience and act with probity;

(f)   whether A's business is being, or is to be, managed in such a way as to ensure that its affairs will be conducted in a sound and prudent manner; and

(g)   the need to minimise the extent to which it is possible for the business carried on by A, or to be carried on by A, to be used for a purpose connected with financial crime.

2.5.1B G   FCA

Paragraph 2E of Schedule 6 to the *Act* sets out the suitability *threshold condition* for *firms* carrying on, or seeking to carry on, *regulated activities* which do not consist of or include a *PRA-regulated activity*.

Paragraph 3D to Schedule 6 of the Act

2.5.1CU   FCA

(1)   B must be a fit and proper person, having regard to the operational objectives of the FCA.

(2)   The matters which are relevant in determining whether B satisfies the condition in sub-paragraph (1) include—

(a)   B's connection with any person;

(b)   the nature (including the complexity) of any regulated activity that B carries on or seeks to carry on;

(c)   the need to ensure that B's affairs are conducted in an appropriate manner, having regard in particular to the interests of consumers and the integrity of the UK financial system;

(d)   whether B has complied and is complying with requirements imposed by the FCA in the exercise its functions, or requests made by the FCA, relating to the provision of information to the FCA and, where B has so complied or is so complying, the manner of that compliance;

(e)   whether those who manage B's affairs have adequate skills and experience and act with probity; and

(f)   the need to minimise the extent to which it is possible for the business carried on by B, or to be carried on by B, to be used for a purpose connected with financial crime.

2.5.1D G   FCA

Paragraph 3D of Schedule 6 to the *Act* sets out the suitability *threshold condition* which is relevant to the discharge by the *FCA* of its functions under the *Act* in relation to *firms* carrying on, or seeking to carry on, *regulated activities* which include a *PRA-regulated activity*.

2.5.1E G   FCA

The *guidance* in **COND 2.5** should be read as applying to both paragraph 2E of Schedule 6 to the *Act* and, as far as relevant to the discharge by the *FCA* of its functions under the *Act* in respect of *firms* carrying on, or seeking to carry on, a *PRA-regulated activity*, paragraph 3D of Schedule 6 of the *Act*.

2.5.1F G   FCA

Firms carrying on, or seeking to carry on, a *PRA-regulated activity*, should note that the *PRA* is also responsible for assessing suitability under its own *threshold conditions*. Paragraphs 4E and 5E of Schedule 6 to the *Act* set out the suitability *threshold conditions* which are relevant to the discharge by the *PRA* of its functions under the *Act* in relation to *firms* carrying on, or seeking to carry on, a *PRA-regulated activity*. For the avoidance of doubt, this *guidance* does not apply to the *threshold conditions* set out in paragraph 4E and 5E of Schedule 6 to the *Act*.

2.5.2 G   FCA

(1)   [deleted]

(2)   The *FCA* will also take into consideration anything that could influence a *firm's* continuing ability to satisfy the *threshold conditions* set out in paragraphs 2E and 3D of Schedule 6 to the *Act*. Examples include the *firm's* position within a *UK* or international *group*, information provided by *overseas regulators* about the *firm*, and the *firm's* plans to seek to vary its *Part 4A permission* to carry on additional *regulated activities* once it has been granted that *permission*.

2.5.3 G   FCA

(1)   The emphasis of the *threshold conditions* set out in paragraphs 2E and 3D of Schedule 6 of the *Act* is on the suitability of the *firm* itself. The suitability of each *person* who performs a *controlled function* will be assessed by the *FCA* and/or the *PRA*, as appropriate, under the *approved persons* regime (see **SUP 10** (Approved persons) and *FIT*). In certain circumstances, however, the *FCA* may consider that the *firm* is not suitable because of doubts over the individual or collective suitability of *persons* connected with the *firm*.

Part 3   FCA Handbook Materials

(2)   [deleted]
(3)   [deleted]

2.5.4 G   FCA

(1)   [deleted]
(2)   Examples of the kind of general considerations to which the *FCA* may have regard when
        assessing whether a *firm* will satisfy, and continue to satisfy, the *threshold conditions* set out
        in paragraphs 2E and 3D of Schedule 6 to the *Act* include, but are not limited to, whether the
        firm:
        (a)   conducts, or will conduct, its business with integrity and in compliance with proper
                standards;
        (b)   has, or will have, a competent and prudent management; and
        (c)   can demonstrate that it conducts, or will conduct, its affairs with the exercise of due
                skill, care and diligence.
(3)   [deleted]
(4)   [deleted]

2.5.5 G

[deleted]

2.5.6 G   FCA

Examples of the kind of particular considerations to which the *FCA* may have regard when assessing
whether a *firm* will satisfy, and continue to satisfy, this *threshold condition* include, but are not
limited to, whether:

(1)   the *firm* has been open and co-operative in all its dealings with the *FCA* and any other
        regulatory body (see *Principle* 11 (Relations with regulators)) and is ready, willing and
        organised to comply with the requirements and standards under the *regulatory system*
        (such as the detailed requirements of *SYSC* and, in relation to a *firm* not carrying on, or
        seeking to carry on, a *PRA-regulated activity* only, the Prudential Standards part of the
        FCA Handbook) in addition to other legal, regulatory and professional obligations; the
        relevant requirements and standards will depend on the circumstances of each case,
        including the *regulated activities* which the *firm* has *permission*, or is seeking *permission*,
        to carry on;
(1A)   the *firm* has made arrangements to put in place an adequate system of internal control to
        comply with the requirements and standards for which the *FCA* is responsible under the
        regulatory system;
(2)   the *firm* has been convicted, or is connected with a *person* who has been convicted, of any
        criminal offence; this must include, where provided for by the *Rehabilitation Exceptions
        Orders* to the Rehabilitation of Offenders Act 1974 or the Rehabilitation of Offenders
        (Northern Ireland) Order 1978 (as applicable), any spent convictions; particular consid-
        eration will be given to offences of dishonesty, fraud, financial crime or an offence under
        legislation relating to companies, building societies, industrial and provident societies,
        credit unions, friendly societies, banking, other financial services, insolvency, consumer
        credit companies, insurance, consumer protection, *money laundering*, market manipula-
        tion and *insider dealing*, whether or not in the *United Kingdom*;
(3)   the *firm* has been the subject of, or connected to the subject of, any existing or previous
        investigation or enforcement proceedings by the *FCA*, the *Society of Lloyd's* or by other
        regulatory authorities (including the *FCA's* predecessors), *clearing houses* or exchanges,
        professional bodies or government bodies or agencies; the *FCA* will, however, take both
        the nature of the *firm's* involvement in, and the outcome of, any investigation or
        enforcement proceedings into account in determining whether it is a relevant matter;
(4)   the *firm* has contravened, or is connected with a *person* who has contravened, any
        provisions of the *Act* or any preceding financial services legislation, the *regulatory system*
        or the rules, regulations, statements of principles or codes of practice (for example the
        Society of Lloyd's Codes) of other regulatory authorities (including the *FCA's*
        predecessors), *clearing houses* or exchanges, professional bodies, or government bodies
        or agencies or relevant industry standards (such as the Non-Investment Products Code);
        the *FCA* will, however, take into account both the status of codes of practice or relevant
        industry standards and the nature of the contravention (for example, whether a *firm* has
        flouted or ignored a particular code);
(5)   the *firm*, or a *person* connected with the *firm*, has been refused registration, authorisation,
        membership or licence to carry out a trade, business or profession or has had that
        registration, authorisation, membership or licence revoked, withdrawn or terminated, or
        has been expelled by a regulatory or government body; whether the *FCA* considers such
        a refusal relevant will depend on the circumstances;
(6)   [deleted]
(7)   the *firm* has put in place procedures which are reasonably designed to:

    (a)   ensure that it has made its *employees* aware of, and compliant with, those requirements and standards under the *regulatory system* that apply to the *firm* for which the *FCA* is responsible and the *regulated activities* for which it has, or will have *permission*;

    (b)   ensure that its *approved persons* (whether or not employed by the *firm*) are aware of those requirements and standards under the *regulatory system* applicable to them;

    (c)   determine that its *employees* are acting in a way compatible with the *firm* adhering to those requirements and standards; and

    (d)   determine that its *approved persons* are adhering to those requirements and standards;

(8)   the *firm* or a *person* connected with the *firm* has been dismissed from employment or a position of trust, fiduciary relationship or similar or has ever been asked to resign from employment in such a position; whether the *FCA* considers a resignation to be relevant will depend on the circumstances, for example if a *firm* is asked to resign in circumstance that cast doubt over its honesty or integrity;

(9)   the *firm* or a *person* connected with the *firm* has ever been disqualified from acting as a *director*;

(10)   the *governing body* of the *firm* is made up of individuals with an appropriate range of skills and experience to understand, operate and manage the *firm's regulated activities*;

(11)   where appropriate, the *governing body* of the *firm* includes non-executive representation, at a level which is appropriate for the control of the *regulated activities* proposed, for example, as members of an audit committee;

(12)   those *persons* who perform *controlled functions* under certain *arrangements* entered into by the *firm* or its contractors (including *appointed representatives* or, where applicable, *tied agents*) act with due skill, care and diligence in carrying out their *controlled function* (see **APER 4.2** (Statement of Principle 2) or managing the business for which they are responsible (see **APER 4.7** (Statement of Principle 7));

(13)   the *firm*, or a *person* connected with the *firm*, has been a *director*, *partner* or otherwise concerned in the management of a *company*, *partnership* or other organisation or business that has gone into insolvency, liquidation or administration while having been connected with that organisation or within one year of such a connection;

(14)   the *governing body* of the *firm* is organised in a way that enables it to address and control the *regulated activities* of the *firm*, including those carried on by *managers* to whom particular functions have been delegated;

(15)   the *firm* has developed human resources policies and procedures that are reasonably designed to ensure that it employs only individuals who are honest and committed to high standards of integrity in the conduct of their activities;

(16)   the *firm* has taken reasonable care to ensure that robust information and reporting systems have been developed, tested and properly installed;

(17)   the *firm* has in place appropriate systems and controls against financial crime, including, for example, money laundering;

(18)   in the case of a *firm* that carries on insurance mediation activity:

    (a)   a reasonable proportion of the *persons* within its management structure who are responsible for the *insurance mediation activity*; and

    (b)   all other *persons* directly involved in its *insurance mediation activity*; demonstrate the knowledge and ability necessary for the performance of their duties; and

    (c)   all the persons in the *firm's* management structure and any staff directly involved in *insurance mediation activity* are of good repute (see **MIPRU 2.3.1 R** (Knowledge, ability and good repute); and

(19)   where appropriate, the *firm* has appointed auditors and actuaries, who have sufficient experience in the areas of business to be conducted.

2.5.7 G

[deleted]

2.7   BUSINESS MODEL

Paragraph 2F to Schedule 6 of the Act

2.7.1 UK   FCA

(1)   A's business model (that is, A's strategy for doing business) must be suitable for a person carrying on the regulated activities that A carries on or seeks to carry on.

(2)   The matters which are relevant in determining whether A satisfies the condition in sub-paragraph (1) include—

    (a)   whether the business model is compatible with A's affairs being conducted, and continuing to be conducted, in a sound and prudent manner;

    (b)   the interests of consumers;

    (c)   the integrity of the UK financial system.

(3)   This paragraph does not apply where the only regulated activities that the person concerned
       carries on, or seeks to carry on, are—
       (a)   relevant credit activities, and
       (b)   if any, activities to which, by virtue of section 39(1D), sections 20(1) and (1A) and
              23(1A) do not apply when carried on by the person.

2.7.2 G   FCA

Paragraph 2F of Schedule 6 to the *Act* sets out the business model *threshold condition* for *firms*
carrying on, or seeking to carry on, *regulated activities* which do not include a *PRA-regulated
activity*.

2.7.2A G   FCA

For the purposes of paragraph 2F(3) of Schedule 6 to the *Act*, relevant credit activity is defined in
paragraph 2G of Schedule 6 to the *Act*. Guidance on the meaning of relevant credit activity is given
in **COND 1.1A.5A G**.

Paragraph 3E to Schedule 6 of the Act

2.7.3 UK   FCA

B's business model (that is, B's strategy for doing business) must be suitable for a person carrying
on the regulated activities that B carries on or seeks to carry on, having regard to the
FCA's operational objectives.

2.7.4 G   FCA

Paragraph 3E of Schedule 6 to the *Act* sets out the business model *threshold condition* which is
relevant to the discharge by the *FCA* of its functions under the *Act* in relation to *firms* carrying on,
or seeking to carry on, *regulated activities* which include a *PRA-regulated activity*.

2.7.5 G   FCA

The *guidance* in **COND 2.7** should be read as applying to both paragraph 2F of Schedule 6 to the
Act and, as far as relevant to the discharge by the *FCA* of its functions under the *Act* in respect of
firms carrying on, or seeking to carry on, a *PRA-regulated activity*, paragraph 3E of Schedule 6 of
the *Act*.

2.7.6 G   FCA

Firms carrying on, or seeking to carry on, a *PRA-regulated activity*, should note that the *PRA* states
in its Approach Documents that analysis of such *firms'* business models will form an important part
of the *PRA's* supervisory approach. For the avoidance of doubt, this guidance does not apply to the
PRA's own assessment of the *firms'* business models.

2.7.7 G   FCA

In assessing whether the *threshold conditions* set out in paragraphs 2F and 3E of Schedule 6 to the
Act are satisfied, the *FCA* may consider all matters that might affect the design and execution of a
firm's business model, taking into account the nature, scale and complexity of a *firm's* business.

2.7.8 G   FCA

In deciding how they will satisfy and continue to satisfy the *threshold conditions* set out in
paragraphs 2F and 3E of Schedule 6 to the *Act*, *firms* should consider matters including (but not
limited to) the following:
(1)   the assumptions underlying the *firm's* business model and justification for it;
(2)   the rationale for the business the *firm* proposes to do or continues to do, its competitive
       advantage, viability and the longer-term profitability of the business;
(3)   the needs of and risks to *consumers*;
(4)   the expectations of stakeholders, for example, shareholders and regulators;
(5)   the products and services being offered and product strategy;
(6)   the governance and controls of the *firm* and of any member of its *group* (if appropriate);
(7)   the growth strategy and any risks arising from it;
(8)   any diversification strategies; and
(9)   the impact of the external macroeconomic and business environment.

2.7.9 G   FCA

Firms should consider the manner in which they intend to bring their business model into operation.
This plan could, for example, include matters such as procurement, outsourcing, and recruitment.

2.7.10 G   FCA

Firms should consider scenarios which may negatively impact on the *firm's* business model with a
view to ensuring the sustainability of the *firm* and, further, to consider the vulnerability of the
business model to specific events and the risks and consequences that might arise. Where
appropriate, this might include reverse stress-testing (see SYSC 20 'Reverse stress testing'). A *firm*
should put in place a credible plan to minimise the risks that it identifies from, or in relation to, its
business model and a contingency plan for dealing with risks that have crystallised.

2.7.11 G   FCA

Firms should ensure that any adjustments to its business model:

(1)   are approved at an appropriate level in the business;

(2)   are considered in the light of any potential risks, impacts and consequences of the proposed changes; and

(3)   appropriately take into account the needs of and risks to *clients* and relevant *consumers*.

2.7.12 G   FCA

The *FCA's* assessment of a *firm's* satisfaction of this *threshold conditions* set out in paragraphs 2F and 3E of Schedule 6 to the *Act* will not necessarily be limited to a *firm's regulated activities* if the *FCA* believes the *firm's* other business activities, if any, may impact on a *firm's regulated activities*.

CHAPTER 3
BANKING ACT 2009

[deleted]

TRANSITIONAL PROVISIONS AND SCHEDULES

1   TRANSITIONAL PROVISIONS

[3.34]
TP1

Table:

There are no transitional provisions in *COND*.

SCHEDULE 1   RECORD KEEPING REQUIREMENTS

Sch1.1 G

There are no record keeping requirements in *COND*.

SCHEDULE 2   NOTIFICATION REQUIREMENTS

Sch2.1 G

There are no notification *rules* in *COND* but guidance is given in **COND 1.3.3 G** on disclosure to the *FSA* in connection with applications.

SCHEDULE 3   FEES AND OTHER REQUIRED PAYMENTS

Sch3.1 G

There are no requirements for fees or other payments in *COND*.

SCHEDULE 4   POWERS EXERCISED

Sch4.1 G

The following power in the *Act* has been exercised by the *FSA* to give the *guidance* in *COND*: Section 157(1) (Guidance).

SCHEDULE 5   RIGHTS OF ACTION FOR DAMAGES

Sch5.1 G

There are no rules in *COND*.

SCHEDULE 6   RULES THAT CAN BE WAIVED

Sch6.1 G

There are no *rules* in *COND*.

E. STATEMENTS OF PRINCIPLE AND CODE OF PRACTICE FOR APPROVED PERSONS (APER)

STATEMENTS OF PRINCIPLE AND CODE OF PRACTICE FOR APPROVED PERSONS
the fundamental obligations of approved persons

CHAPTER 1
APPLICATION AND PURPOSE

1.1A   APPLICATION

Who?

[3.35]
1.1A.1 P

APER applies to *FCA-approved persons* and *PRA-approved persons.*

What?

1.1A.2 P
(1)   *APER* applies to the performance by an *approved person* of:
     (a)   *FCA controlled functions* (whether or not approval has been sought and granted); and
     (b)   *PRA controlled functions* (whether or not approval has been sought and granted);
     in relation to the authorised persons in relation to which that *person* is an *approved person.*
(2)   *APER* also applies to the performance by an *approved person* of any other functions in relation to the carrying on of a *regulated activity* by the *authorised persons* referred to in (1).

1.1A.3 G   FCA

The functions described in **APER 1.1A.2 P** are called accountable functions.

1.1A.4 G   FCA

The relevance of *MiFID* to the *Statements of Principle* will depend on the extent to which the corresponding requirement imposed on *firms* under *MiFID* is reserved to a *Home State regulator* or has been disapplied under *MiFID* (see **APER 2.1A.2 P** and **FIT 1.2.4 G**. See also **COBS 1 ANNEX 1**, Part 2, 1.1R (EEA territorial scope rule: compatibility with European law)).

Where?

1.1A.5 G   FCA

The territorial scope of the *approved persons* regime and its application to *incoming EEA firms* is set out in SUP 10A.1 (see SUP 10A.1.11R and SUP 10A.1.13R).

Coverage of APER

1.1A.6 G   FCA

APER 1.1A.7 G gives examples of the effect of **APER 1.1A.1 P** and **APER 1.1A.2 P**. The first column says whether the example involves an *FCA-approved person* and the second column says whether the example involves a *PRA-approved person*. So for example if there is a "Yes" in both columns that means that the example concerns a *person* who has been approved both by the *FCA* and by the *PRA*. The third column explains what functions *APER* covers in the scenario set out in the first two columns. The table is divided between cases in which the *person* performs the *controlled function* for an *FCA-authorised person* and ones where the *person* does so for a *PRA-authorised person.*

1.1A.7 G   FCA

Table: Examples of what activities *APER* covers

FCA approved	PRA approved	Coverage of *APER*
FCA-authorised person		
(1) Yes, in relation to *firm* A	Not applicable	Applies to the *FCA controlled function*. Also applies to any other function performed for *firm* A in relation to the carrying on by *firm* A of a *regulated activity* even if it is not a *controlled function*.

FCA approved	PRA approved	Coverage of *APER*
(2) Yes, in relation to *firm* A. No, in relation to *firm* B,	Not applicable	In relation to *firm* A, the answer is the same as for scenario (1). However, *APER* does not apply to any function that the *approved person* carries on in relation to *firm* B even if that function relates to *regulated activities* carried out by *firm* B. However, if the function that he performs in relation to *firm* B is a *controlled function* the *approved person* and *firm* B may be subject to legal sanctions (see **SUP 10A.13.1 G** to **SUP 10A.13.2 G**).
PRA-authorised person		
(3) Yes, in relation to *firm* A	No	The answer is the same as for scenario (1).
(4) No	Yes, in relation to *firm* A	Applies to *PRA controlled function*. Also applies to any other function performed for *firm* A in relation to the carrying on by *firm* A of a *regulated activity* even if it is not a *controlled function*.
(5) Yes, in relation to *firm* A	Yes, in relation to *firm* A	Applies to *FCA controlled function* and *PRA controlled function*. Also applies to any other function performed for *firm* A in relation to the carrying on by *firm* A of a *regulated activity* even if it is not a *controlled function*.
(6) Yes, in relation to *firm* A. No, in relation to *firm* B,	Yes, in relation to *firm* A. No, in relation to *firm* B,	In relation to *firm* A, the answer is the same as for scenario (5). However, *APER* does not apply to any function that the *approved person* carries on in relation to firm B even if that function relates to *regulated activities* carried out by *firm* B. However, if the function that he performs in relation to *firm* B is a *controlled function* the *approved person* and *firm* B may be subject to legal sanctions (see **SUP 10A.13.1 G** to SUP 10A.13.21G).

1.1A.8 G FCA

A *person* may be an *approved person* in relation to more than one *firm*. When that is the case, *APER* applies in relation to all those *firms*.

1.1A.9 G FCA

(1) **APER 1.1A.2 P** refers to the *authorised person* in relation to which a *person* is an *approved person*.

(2) Under section 59 of the *Act* (Approval for particular arrangements) there are two kinds of *approved person*.

(3) Section 59(1) of the *Act* describes the first. It covers a *person* who performs a *controlled function* under an arrangement entered into by an *authorised person* ("A"). In this case, **APER 1.1A.2 P** refers to A.

(4) Section 59(2) of the *Act* describes the second. It covers a *person* who performs a *controlled function* under an arrangement entered into by a contractor ("B") of an *authorised person* ("A"). In this case, **APER 1.1A.2 P** refers to A (and not B).

Rule in GEN about provisions shared between the FCA and PRA

1.1A.10 E FCA

GEN 2.2.23 R (Cutover: Application of provisions made by both the *FCA* and the *PRA*) does not apply to any provision of *APER* marked with an "E" in the margin.

1.1A.11 G FCA

GEN 2.2.23 R does not apply to any of *APER*. It does not apply to any part of *APER* that is not shared as **GEN 2.2.23 R** only applies to *Handbook* provisions made by both the *FCA* and the *PRA*. Hence **GEN 2.2.23 R** does not apply to the *Statements of Principle*. **APER 1.1A.10 E** means that **GEN 2.2.23 R** does not apply to shared provisions marked with an "E" in the margin. **GEN 2.2.23 R** does not apply to shared *guidance* in *APER* because the *guidance* is about material to which **GEN 2.2.23 R** does not apply

1.1B   APPLICATION

Who?

1.1B.1 P

APER applies to:

(1)   *PRA-approved persons*; and

(2)   *FCA-approved persons* in relation to whom the *FCA* has given its approval under section 59 of the *Act* in respect of the performance by them of *significant-influence functions* in relation to the carrying on by *PRA-authorised persons* of *regulated activities*.

What?

1.1B.2 P

(1)   *APER* applies to the performance by an *approved person* of:

    (a)   *PRA controlled functions* (whether or not approval has been sought and granted); and

    (b)   *FCA controlled functions* that are *significant-influence functions* (whether or not approval has been sought and granted);

    in relation to the *PRA-authorised persons* in relation to which that *person* is an *approved person*.

(2)   *APER* also applies to the performance by an *approved person* of any other *significant-influence functions* in relation to the *PRA-authorised persons* referred to in (1).

1.1B.3 G   PRA

The functions described in **APER 1.1B.2 P** are called *accountable functions*.

1.1B.4 G   PRA

The relevance of *MiFID* to the *Statements of Principle* will depend on the extent to which the corresponding requirement imposed on *firms* under *MiFID* is reserved to a *Home State regulator* or has been disapplied under *MiFID* (see **APER 2.1B.2 P** and **FIT 1.2.4A G**).

Where?

1.1B.5 G   PRA

The territorial scope of the *approved persons* regime and its application to *incoming EEA firms* is set out in **SUP 10B.1** (see **SUP 10B.1.11 R** and **SUP 10B.1.12 R**).

Coverage of APER

1.1B.6 G   PRA

APER 1.1B.7 G gives examples of the effect of **APER 1.1B.1 P** and **APER 1.1B.2 P**. The first column says whether the example involves an *FCA-approved person* and the second column says whether the example involves a *PRA-approved person*. So, for example, if there is a "Yes" in both columns that means that the example concerns a *person* who has been approved both by the *FCA* and by the *PRA*. The third column explains what functions *APER* covers in the scenario set out in the first two columns. The table is divided between cases in which the *person* performs the *controlled function* for an *FCA-authorised person*, and ones where the *person* does so for a *PRA-authorised person*.

1.1B.7 G   PRA

Table: Examples of what activities *APER* covers

FCA approved	PRA approved	Coverage of *APER*
FCA-authorised person		
(1) Yes, in relation to *firm* A	Not applicable	Does not apply
PRA-authorised person		
(2) No	Yes, in relation to *firm* A	Applies to *PRA controlled function*. Also applies to any other *significant-influence functions* performed for *firm* A, even if they are not *controlled functions*.
(3) Yes, in relation to *firm* A (for a *significant-influence function*)	No	Applies to *FCA controlled function*. Also applies to any other *significant-influence functions* performed for *firm* A, even if they are not *controlled functions*.
(4) Yes, in relation to *firm* A (for a *customer-dealing function*)	No	Does not apply. If he is also performing a *significant-influence function* that is not a *controlled function*, *APER* does not apply to that function either.

FCA approved	PRA approved	Coverage of *APER*
(5) Yes, in relation to *firm A* (for a *customer-dealing function*)	Yes, in relation to *firm A*	Applies to *PRA controlled function*. Does not apply to *customer-dealing function*. Also applies to any other *significant-influence functions* performed for *firm A*, even if they are not *controlled functions*.
(6) Yes, in relation to *firm A* (for a *significant-influence function*)	Yes, in relation to *firm A*	Applies to *FCA controlled function* and *PRA controlled function*. Also applies to any other *significant-influence functions* performed for *firm A*, even if they are not *controlled functions*.
(7) Yes, in relation to *firm A* (for a *significant-influence function* and *customer-dealing function*)	Yes, in relation to *firm A*	The answer is the same as for scenario (6). Does not apply to *customer-dealing function*.
(8) Yes, in relation to *firm A* (for a *significant-influence function*). No, in relation to *firm B*,	Yes, in relation to *firm A*. No, in relation to *firm B*,	In relation to *firm A*, the answer is the same as for scenario (6). However, *APER* does not apply to any function that the *approved person* carries on in relation to *firm B*, even if that function is a *significant-influence function*. However, if the function that he performs in relation to *firm B* is a *controlled function*, the *approved person* and *firm B* may be subject to legal sanctions (see **SUP 10B.11.1 G** and **SUP 10B.11.3 G**).

1.1B.8 G   PRA

A *person* may be an *approved person* in relation to more than one *PRA-authorised person*. When that is the case, *APER* applies in relation to all those *firms*.

1.1B.9 G   PRA

(1)   **APER 1.1B.2 P** refers to the *PRA-authorised person* in relation to which a person is an *approved person*.

(2)   Under section 59 of the *Act* (Approval for particular arrangements) there are two kinds of *approved person*.

(3)   Section 59(1) of the *Act* describes the first. It covers a *person* who performs a *controlled function* under an *arrangement* entered into by an *authorised person* ("A"). In this case, **APER 1.1B.2 P** refers to A.

(4)   Section 59(2) of the *Act* describes the second. It covers a *person* who performs a *controlled function* under an *arrangement* entered into by a contractor ("B") of an *authorised person* ("A"). In this case, **APER 1.1B.2 P** refers to A (and not B).

Rule in GEN about provisions shared between the FCA and PRA

1.1B.10 E   PRA

GEN 2.2.23 R (Cutover: Application of provisions made by both the FCA and the PRA) does not apply to any provision of *APER* marked with an "E" in the margin.

1.1B.11 G   PRA

GEN 2.2.23 R does not apply to any of *APER*. It does not apply to any part of *APER* that is not shared, as **GEN 2.2.23 R** only applies to Handbook provisions made by both the *FCA* and the *PRA*. Hence **GEN 2.2.23 R** does not apply to the *Statements of Principle*. **APER 1.1A.10 E** means that **GEN 2.2.23 R** does not apply to shared provisions marked with an "E" in the margin. **GEN 2.2.23 R** does not apply to shared *guidance* in *APER* because the *guidance* is about material to which **GEN 2.2.23 R** does not apply.

1.2   PURPOSE

1.2.1 G

[deleted]

1.2.1A G   FCA

The *Statements of Principle* contained in **APER 2** are issued under section 64(1) of the *Act* (Conduct: statements and codes). The paragraphs of the application section in **APER 1.1A** labelled "P" also form part of the *Statements of Principle*.

1.2.1B G   PRA

The *Statements of Principle* contained in **APER 2** are issued under section 64(1A) of the *Act* (Conduct: statements and codes). The paragraphs of the application section in **APER 1.1B** labelled "P" also form part of the *Statements of Principle*.

1.2.2 G   FCA PRA

Section 64(2) of the *Act* states that if an *appropriate regulator* issues *Statements of Principle* it must also issue a code of practice for the purpose of helping to determine whether or not a *person's* conduct complies with the *Statements of Principle*. The *Code of Practice for Approved Persons* in **APER 3** and **APER 4** fulfils this requirement.

1.2.3 G   FCA

The *Code of Practice for Approved Persons* sets out descriptions of conduct which, in the opinion of the *FCA*, do not comply with a *Statement of Principle* and, in the case of *Statement of Principle* 3, conduct which tends to show compliance within that statement. The *Code of Practice for Approved Persons* also sets out, in certain cases, factors which, in the opinion of the *FCA*, are to be taken into account in determining whether or not an *approved person's* conduct complies with a *Statement of Principle*. The *guidance* set out in **APER 3** and **APER 4** does not form part of the *Code of Practice for Approved Persons*.

1.2.3A G   PRA

The *Code of Practice for Approved Persons* sets out descriptions of conduct which, in the opinion of the *PRA*, do not comply with a *Statement of Principle*. The *Code of Practice for Approved Persons* also sets out, in certain cases, factors which, in the opinion of the *PRA*, are to be taken into account in determining whether or not an *approved person's* conduct complies with a *Statement of Principle*. The guidance set out in **APER 3** and **APER 4** does not form part of the *Code of Practice for Approved Persons*.

1.2.4 G

[deleted]

1.2.5 G   FCA

As set out in **SUP 10A.3.1 R** (Provisions related to the Act), a function is a *controlled function* only to the extent that it is performed under an *arrangement* entered into by:

(1)   a *firm*; or

(2)   a contractor of the *firm*;

in relation to the carrying on by the *firm* of a *regulated activity*.

1.2.6–1.2.9 G

[deleted]

CHAPTER 2
THE STATEMENTS OF PRINCIPLE FOR APPROVED PERSONS

2.1A   THE STATEMENTS OF PRINCIPLE

[3.36]
2.1A.1 G   FCA

APER 2.1A.3 P sets out the *Statements of Principle* issued by the *FCA* to which **APER 1.2.1A G** refers and to which the provisions of the *Code of Practice for Approved Persons* and *guidance* in **APER 3** and **APER 4** apply. The paragraphs of **APER 1.1A** labelled "P" also form part of the *Statements of Principle*.

2.1A.2 P

An *approved person* will not be subject to a *Statement of Principle* to the extent that it would be contrary to the UK's obligations under a *Single Market Directive* or the *auction regulation*.

2.1A.3 P

Statements of Principle issued under section 64 of the Act

Statement of Principle 1
An *approved person* must act with integrity in carrying out his *accountable functions*.

Statement of Principle 2
An *approved person* must act with due skill, care and diligence in carrying out his *accountable functions*.

Statement of Principle 3
An *approved person* must observe proper standards of market conduct in carrying out his *accountable functions*.

Statement of Principle 4
An *approved person* must deal with the *FCA*, the *PRA* and other regulators in an open and cooperative way and must disclose appropriately any information of which the *FCA* or the *PRA* would reasonably expect notice.

Statement of Principle 5
An *approved person* performing an *accountable significant-influence function* must take reasonable steps to ensure that the business of the *firm* for which he is responsible in his *accountable function* is organised so that it can be controlled effectively.

Statement of Principle 6
An *approved person* performing an *accountable significant-influence function* must exercise due skill, care and diligence in managing the business of the *firm* for which he is responsible in his *accountable function*.

Statement of Principle 7
An *approved person* performing an *accountable significant-influence function* must take reasonable steps to ensure that the business of the *firm* for which he is responsible in his *accountable function* complies with the relevant requirements and standards of the *regulatory system*.

2.1B   THE STATEMENTS OF PRINCIPLE

2.1B.1 G   PRA

APER 2.1B.3 P sets out the *Statements of Principle* issued by the *PRA* to which **APER 1.2.1B G** refers and to which the provisions of the *Code of Practice for Approved Persons* and *guidance* in **APER 3** and **APER 4** apply. The paragraphs of **APER 1.1B** labelled "P" also form part of the *Statements of Principle*.

2.1B.2 P

An *approved person* will not be subject to a *Statement of Principle* to the extent that it would be contrary to the UK's obligations under a *Single Market Directive* or the *auction regulation*.

2.1B.3 P

Statements of Principle issued under section 64 of the Act

Statement of Principle 1
An *approved person* must act with integrity in carrying out his *accountable functions*.

Statement of Principle 2
An *approved person* must act with due skill, care and diligence in carrying out his *accountable functions*.

Statement of Principle 3
[Not used]

Statement of Principle 4
An *approved person* must deal with the *FCA*, the *PRA* and other regulators in an open and cooperative way and must disclose appropriately any information of which the *FCA* or the *PRA* would reasonably expect notice.

Statement of Principle 5
An *approved person* performing an *accountable function* must take reasonable steps to ensure that the business of the *firm* for which he is responsible in his *accountable function* is organised so that it can be controlled effectively.

Statement of Principle 6
An *approved person* performing an *accountable function* must exercise due skill, care and diligence in managing the business of the *firm* for which he is responsible in his *accountable function*.

> Statement of Principle 7
> An *approved person* performing an *accountable function* must take reasonable steps to ensure that the business of the *firm* for which he is responsible in his *accountable function* complies with the relevant requirements and standards of the *regulatory system*.

CHAPTER 3
CODE OF PRACTICE FOR APPROVED PERSONS: GENERAL

3.1   INTRODUCTION

[3.37]
3.1.1 G

[deleted]

3.1.1A G   FCA

This *Code of Practice for Approved Persons* is issued under section 64 of the *Act* (Conduct: statements and codes) for the purpose of helping to determine whether or not an *approved person's* conduct complies with a *Statement of Principle*. The code sets out descriptions of conduct which, in the *FCA's* opinion, do not comply with the relevant *Statements of Principle*. The code also sets out certain factors which, in the opinion of the *FCA*, are to be taken into account in determining whether an *approved person's* conduct complies with a particular *Statement of Principle*. The description of conduct, the factors and related provisions are identified in the text by the letter 'E' as explained in chapter 6 of the Reader's Guide.

3.1.1B G   PRA

This *Code of Practice for Approved Persons* is issued under section 64 of the *Act* (Conduct: statements and codes) for the purpose of helping to determine whether or not an *approved person's* conduct complies with a *Statement of Principle*. The code sets out descriptions of conduct which, in the *PRA's* opinion, do not comply with the relevant *Statements of Principle*. The code also sets out certain factors which, in the opinion of the *PRA*, are to be taken into account in determining whether an *approved person's* conduct complies with a particular *Statement of Principle*. The description of conduct, the factors and related provisions are identified in the text by the letter 'E' as explained in the Reader's Guide.

3.1.2 G   FCA PRA

The *Code of Practice for Approved Persons* in issue at the time when any particular conduct takes place may be relied on so far as it tends to establish whether or not that conduct complies with a *Statement of Principle*.

3.1.3 G   FCA PRA

The significance of conduct identified in the *Code of Practice for Approved Persons* as tending to establish compliance with or a breach of a *Statement of Principle* will be assessed only after all the circumstances of a particular case have been considered. Account will be taken of the context in which a course of conduct was undertaken, including the precise circumstances of the individual case, the characteristics of the particular *accountable function* and the behaviour to be expected in that function.

3.1.4 G   FCA
(1)   An *approved person* will only be in breach of a *Statement of Principle* where he is personally culpable. Personal culpability arises where an *approved person's* conduct was deliberate or where the *approved person's* standard of conduct was below that which would be reasonable in all the circumstances (see **DEPP 6.2.4 G** (Action against approved persons under section 66 of the Act)).
(2)   For the avoidance of doubt, the *Statements of Principle* do not extend the duties of *approved persons* beyond those which the *firm* owes in its dealings with *customers* or others.

3.1.4A G   PRA
(1)   An *approved person* will only be in breach of a *Statement of Principle* where he is personally culpable. Personal culpability arises where an *approved person's* conduct was deliberate or where the *approved person's* standard of conduct was below that which would be reasonable in all the circumstances.
(2)   For the avoidance of doubt, the *Statements of Principle* do not extend the duties of *approved persons* beyond those which the *firm* owes in its dealings with *customers* or others.

3.1.5 G   FCA PRA

In particular, in determining whether or not an *approved person's* conduct complies with a *Statement of Principle*, the *appropriate regulator* will take into account the extent to which an *approved person* has acted in a way that is stated to be in breach of a *Statement of Principle*.

3.1.6 G   FCA PRA

The *Code of Practice for Approved Persons* (and in particular the specific examples of behaviour which may be in breach of a generic description of conduct in the code) is not exhaustive of the kind of conduct that may contravene the *Statements of Principle*. The purpose of the code is to help determine whether or not a *person's* conduct complies with a *Statement of Principle*. The code may be supplemented from time to time. The *appropriate regulator* will amend the code if there is a risk that unacceptable practice may become prevalent, so as to make clear what conduct falls below the standards expected of *approved persons* by the *Statements of Principle*.

3.1.7 G

[deleted]

3.1.7A G   FCA

Statements of Principle 1 to 4 apply to all *approved persons*. A *person* performing an *accountable significant-influence function* is also subject to the additional requirements set out in *Statements of Principle* 5 to 7 in performing that *accountable function*. Those responsible under **SYSC 2.1.3 R** or **SYSC 4.4.5 R** (Apportionment of responsibilities) for the *firm's* apportionment obligation will be specifically subject to *Statement of Principle* 5 (and see, in particular, **APER 4.5.6 E**). In addition, it will be the responsibility of any such *approved person* to oversee that the *firm* has appropriate systems and controls under *Statement of Principle* 7 (and see, in particular, **APER 4.7.3 E**).

3.1.7B G   PRA

Those responsible under **SYSC 2.1.3 R** or **SYSC 4.4.5 R** (Apportionment of responsibilities) for the *firm's* apportionment obligation will be specifically subject to *Statement of Principle* 5 (and see, in particular, **APER 4.5.6 E**). In addition, it will be the responsibility of any such *approved person* to oversee that the *firm* has appropriate systems and controls under *Statement of Principle* 7 (and see, in particular, **APER 4.7.3 E**).

3.1.8 G

[deleted]

3.1.8A G   FCA

In applying *Statements of Principle* 5 to 7, the nature, scale and complexity of the business under management and the role and responsibility of the individual performing an *accountable significant-influence function* within the *firm* will be relevant in assessing whether an *approved person's* conduct was reasonable. For example, the smaller and less complex the business, the less detailed and extensive the systems of control need to be. The *FCA* will be of the opinion that an individual performing an *accountable significant-influence function* may have breached *Statements of Principle* 5 to 7 only if his conduct was below the standard which would be reasonable in all the circumstances. (See also **APER 3.3.1 E (3)** to **APER 3.3.1 E (5)**.)

3.1.8B G   PRA

In applying *Statements of Principle* 5 to 7, the nature, scale and complexity of the business under management and the role and responsibility of the individual performing an *accountable function* within the firm will be relevant in assessing whether an *approved person's* conduct was reasonable. For example, the smaller and less complex the business, the less detailed and extensive the systems of control need to be. The *PRA* will be of the opinion that an individual performing an *accountable function* may have breached *Statements of Principle* 5 to 7 only if his conduct was below the standard which would be reasonable in all the circumstances. (See also **APER 3.3.1 E (3)** to **APER 3.3.1 E (5)**.)

3.1.9 G   FCA PRA

UK domestic firms listed on the London Stock Exchange are subject to the *UK Corporate Governance Code*, whose *internal control* provisions are amplified in the publication entitled "Internal Control: Revised Guidance for Directors on the Combined Code (October 2005)" issued by the Financial Reporting Council. *Firms* regulated by the *appropriate regulator* in this category will thus be subject to that code as well as to the requirements and standards of the *regulatory system*. In forming an opinion whether *approved persons* have complied with its requirements, the *appropriate regulator* will give due credit for their following corresponding provisions in the *UK Corporate Governance Code* and related *guidance*.

3.2 FACTORS RELATING TO ALL STATEMENTS OF PRINCIPLE

3.2.1 E   FCA PRA

In determining whether or not the particular conduct of an *approved person* within his *accountable function* complies with the *Statements of Principle*, the following are factors which, in the opinion of the *appropriate regulator*, are to be taken into account:

(1)   whether that conduct relates to activities that are subject to other provisions of the *Handbook*;

(2)   whether that conduct is consistent with the requirements and standards of the *regulatory system* relevant to his *firm*.

3.3 FACTORS RELATING TO STATEMENTS OF PRINCIPLE 5 TO 7

3.3.1 E   FCA

In determining whether or not the conduct of an *approved person* performing an *accountable significant-influence function* complies with *Statements of Principle* 5 to 7, the following are factors which, in the opinion of the *FCA*, are to be taken into account:

(1)   whether he exercised reasonable care when considering the information available to him;
(2)   whether he reached a reasonable conclusion which he acted on;
(3)   the nature, scale and complexity of the *firm's* business;
(4)   his role and responsibility as an *approved person* performing an *accountable significant-influence function*;
(5)   the knowledge he had, or should have had, of regulatory concerns, if any, arising in the business under his control.

3.3.2 E   PRA

In determining whether or not the conduct of an *approved person* performing an *accountable function* complies with *Statements of Principle* 5 to 7, the following are factors which, in the opinion of the *PRA*, are to be taken into account:

(1)   whether he exercised reasonable care when considering the information available to him;
(2)   whether he reached a reasonable conclusion which he acted on;
(3)   the nature, scale and complexity of the *firm's* business;
(4)   his role and responsibility as an *approved person* performing an *accountable function*;
(5)   the knowledge he had, or should have had, of regulatory concerns, if any, arising in the business under his control.

CHAPTER 4
CODE OF PRACTICE FOR APPROVED PERSONS: SPECIFIC

4.1 STATEMENT OF PRINCIPLE 1

[3.38]
4.1.1 G

[deleted]

4.1.1A G   FCA

The *Statement of Principle* 1 (see **APER 2.1A.3 P**) is in the following terms: "An *approved person* must act with integrity in carrying out his *accountable functions*."

4.1.1B G   PRA

The *Statement of Principle* 1 (see **APER 2.1B.3 P**) is in the following terms: "An *approved person* must act with integrity in carrying out his *accountable functions*."

4.1.2 E   FCA PRA

In the opinion of the *appropriate regulator*, conduct of the type described in **APER 4.1.3 E, APER 4.1.5 E, APER 4.1.6 E, APER 4.1.8 E, APER 4.1.10 E, APER 4.1.12 E, APER 4.1.13 E, APER 4.1.14 E** or **APER 4.1.15 E** does not comply with *Statement of Principle* 1.

4.1.3 E   FCA PRA

Deliberately misleading (or attempting to mislead) by act or omission:

(1)   a *client*; or
(2)   his *firm* (or its auditors or an *actuary* appointed by his *firm* under **SUP 4** (Actuaries)); or
(3)   the *FCA* or the *PRA*;

falls within **APER 4.1.2 E**.

4.1.4 E   FCA PRA

Behaviour of the type referred to in **APER 4.1.3 E** includes, but is not limited to, deliberately:

(1)   falsifying *documents*;
(2)   misleading a *client* about the risks of an *investment*;
(3)   misleading a *client* about the charges or surrender penalties of *investment* products;
(4)   misleading a *client* about the likely performance of *investment* products by providing inappropriate *projections* of future *investment* returns;
(5)   misleading a *client* by informing him that products require only a single payment when that is not the case;
(6)   mismarking the value of *investments* or trading positions;
(7)   procuring the unjustified alteration of prices on illiquid or *off-exchange* contracts, or both;
(8)   misleading others within the *firm* about the credit worthiness of a borrower;
(9)   providing false or inaccurate documentation or information, including details of training, qualifications, past employment record or experience;

(10)   providing false or inaccurate information to the *firm* (or to the *firm's* auditors or an *actuary* appointed by the *firm* under **SUP 4** (Actuaries));

(11)   providing false or inaccurate information to the *FCA* or the *PRA*;

(12)   destroying, or causing the destruction of, *documents* (including false documentation), or tapes or their contents, relevant to misleading (or attempting to mislead) a *client*, his *firm*, or the *FCA* or the *PRA*;

(13)   failing to disclose dealings where disclosure is required by the *firm's* personal account *dealing rules*;

(14)   misleading others in the *firm* about the nature of risks being accepted.

4.1.5 E   FCA PRA

Deliberately recommending an *investment* to a *customer*, or carrying out a discretionary *transaction* for a *customer* where the *approved person* knows that he is unable to justify its suitability for that *customer*, falls within **APER 4.1.2 E**.

4.1.6 E   FCA PRA

Deliberately failing to inform, without reasonable cause:

(1)   a *customer*; or

(2)   his *firm* (or its auditors or an *actuary* appointed by his *firm* under **SUP 4** (Actuaries)); or

(3)   the *FCA* or the *PRA*;

of the fact that their understanding of a material issue is incorrect, despite being aware of their misunderstanding, falls within **APER 4.1.2 E**.

4.1.7 E   FCA PRA

Behaviour of the type referred to in **APER 4.1.6 E** includes, but is not limited to, deliberately:

(1)   failing to disclose the existence of falsified *documents*;

(2)   failing to rectify mismarked positions immediately.

4.1.8 E   FCA PRA

Deliberately preparing inaccurate or inappropriate records or returns in connection with an *accountable function*, falls within **APER 4.1.2 E**.

4.1.9 E   FCA PRA

Behaviour of the type referred to in **APER 4.1.8 E** includes, but is not limited to, deliberately:

(1)   preparing performance reports for transmission to *customers* which are inaccurate or inappropriate (for example, by relying on past performance without appropriate warnings);

(2)   preparing inaccurate training records or inaccurate details of qualifications, past employment record or experience;

(3)   preparing inaccurate trading confirmations, contract notes or other records of *transactions* or holdings of *securities* for a *customer*, whether or not the *customer* is aware of these inaccuracies or has requested such records.

4.1.10 E   FCA PRA

Deliberately misusing the assets or confidential information of a *client* or of his *firm* falls within **APER 4.1.2 E**.

4.1.11 E   FCA PRA

Behaviour of the type referred to in **APER 4.1.10 E** includes, but is not limited to, deliberately:

(1)   front running *client* orders;

(2)   carrying out unjustified trading on *client* accounts to generate a benefit (whether direct or indirect) to the *approved person* (that is, churning);

(3)   misappropriating a *client's* assets, including wrongly transferring to personal accounts cash or *securities* belonging to *clients*;

(4)   wrongly using one *client's* funds to settle margin calls or to cover trading losses on another *client's* account or on *firm* accounts;

(5)   using a *client's* funds for purposes other than those for which they were provided;

(6)   retaining a *client's* funds wrongly;

(7)   pledging the assets of a *client* as security or margin in circumstances where the *firm* is not permitted to do so.

4.1.12 E   FCA PRA

Deliberately designing *transactions* so as to disguise breaches of requirements and standards of the *regulatory system* falls within **APER 4.1.2 E**.

4.1.13 E   FCA PRA

Deliberately failing to disclose the existence of a conflict of interest in connection with dealings with a *client* falls within **APER 4.1.2 E**.

4.1.14 E   FCA PRA

Deliberately not paying due regard to the interests of a *customer* falls within **APER 4.1.2 E**.

4.1.15 E   FCA PRA

Deliberate acts, omissions or business practices that could be reasonably expected to cause consumer detriment fall within **APER 4.1.2 E**.

4.2   STATEMENT OF PRINCIPLE 2

4.2.1 G

[deleted]

4.2.1A G   FCA

The *Statement of Principle* 2 (see **APER 2.1A.3 P**) is in the following terms: "An *approved person* must act with due skill, care and diligence in carrying out his *accountable functions*."

4.2.1B G   PRA

The *Statement of Principle* 2 (see **APER 2.1B.3 P**) is in the following terms: "An *approved person* must act with due skill, care and diligence in carrying out his *accountable functions*."

4.2.2 E   FCA PRA

In the opinion of the *appropriate regulator*, conduct of the type described in **APER 4.2.3 E**, **APER 4.2.5 E**, **APER 4.2.6 E**, **APER 4.2.8 E**, **APER 4.2.10 E**, **APER 4.2.11 E** or **APER 4.2.14 E** does not comply with *Statement of Principle* 2.

4.2.2A E   FCA

In the opinion of the *FCA*, conduct of the type described in **APER 4.2.13 E** does not comply with *Statement of Principle* 2.

4.2.3 E   FCA PRA

Failing to inform:
(1)   a *customer*; or
(2)   his *firm* (or its auditors or an *actuary* appointed by his *firm* under **SUP 4** Actuaries));

of material information in circumstances where he was aware, or ought to have been aware, of such information, and of the fact that he should provide it, falls within **APER 4.2.2 E**.

4.2.4 E   FCA PRA

Behaviour of the type referred to in **APER 4.2.3 E** includes, but is not limited to:
(1)   failing to explain the risks of an *investment* to a *customer*;
(2)   failing to disclose to a *customer* details of the charges or surrender penalties of *investment* products;
(3)   mismarking trading positions;
(4)   providing inaccurate or inadequate information to a *firm*, its auditors or an *actuary* appointed by his *firm* under **SUP 4** (Actuaries);
(5)   failing to disclose dealings where disclosure is required by the *firm's* personal account *dealing rules*.

4.2.5 E   FCA PRA

Recommending an *investment* to a *customer*, or carrying out a discretionary *transaction* for a *customer*, where he does not have reasonable grounds to believe that it is suitable for that *customer*, falls within **APER 4.2.2 E**.

4.2.6 E   FCA PRA

Undertaking, recommending or providing advice on *transactions* without a reasonable understanding of the risk exposure of the *transaction* to a *customer* falls within **APER 4.2.2 E**.

4.2.7 E   FCA PRA

Behaviour of the type referred to in **APER 4.2.6 E** includes, but is not limited to, recommending *transactions* in *investments* to a *customer* without a reasonable understanding of the liability (either potential or actual) of that *transaction*.

4.2.8 E   FCA PRA

Undertaking *transactions* without a reasonable understanding of the risk exposure of the *transaction* to the *firm* falls within **APER 4.2.2 E**.

4.2.9 E   FCA PRA

Behaviour of the type referred to in **APER 4.2.8 E** includes, but is not limited to, trading on the *firm's* own account without a reasonable understanding of the liability (either potential or actual) of the *transaction*.

4.2.10 E   FCA PRA

Failing without good reason to disclose the existence of a conflict of interest in connection with dealings with a *client* falls within **APER 4.2.2 E**.

4.2.11 E   FCA PRA

Failing to provide adequate control over a *client's* assets falls within **APER 4.2.2 E**.

4.2.12 E   FCA PRA

Behaviour of the type referred to in **APER 4.2.11 E** includes, but is not limited to:
(1)   failing to segregate a *client's* assets;
(2)   failing to process a *client's* payments in a timely manner.

4.2.13 E   FCA

Continuing to perform a *controlled function* despite having failed to meet the standards of knowledge and skill set out in the Training and Competence sourcebook (*TC*) for that *controlled function* falls within **APER 4.2.2A E**.

4.2.14 E   FCA PRA

Failing to pay due regard to the interests of a *customer*, without good reason, falls within **APER 4.2.2 E**.

4.3   STATEMENT OF PRINCIPLE 3

4.3.1 G   FCA

The *Statement of Principle* 3 (see **APER 2.1A.3 P**) is in the following terms: "An *approved person* must observe proper standards of market conduct in carrying out his *accountable functions*."

4.3.2 G

[deleted]

4.3.3 E   FCA

A factor to be taken into account in determining whether or not an *approved person's* conduct complies with this *Statement of Principle* is whether he, or his *firm*, has complied with the *Code of Market Conduct* (**MAR 1**) or relevant market codes and exchange rules.

4.3.4 E   FCA

Compliance with the code or *rules* described in **APER 4.3.3 E** will tend to show compliance with this *Statement of Principle*.

4.4   STATEMENT OF PRINCIPLE 4

4.4.1 G

[deleted]

4.4.1A G   FCA

The *Statement of Principle* 4 (see **APER 2.1A.3 P**) is in the following terms: "An *approved person* must deal with the *FCA*, the *PRA* and other regulators in an open and cooperative way and must disclose appropriately any information of which the *FCA* or the *PRA* would reasonably expect notice."

4.4.1B G   PRA

The *Statement of Principle* 4 (see **APER 2.1B.3 P**) is in the following terms: "An *approved person* must deal with the *FCA*, the *PRA* and other regulators in an open and cooperative way and must disclose appropriately any information of which the *FCA* or the *PRA* would reasonably expect notice."

4.4.2 G

[deleted]

4.4.2A G   FCA

For the purpose of this *Statement of Principle*, regulators in addition to the *FCA* and the *PRA* are those which have recognised jurisdiction in relation to *regulated activities* and a power to call for information from the *approved person* in connection with his *accountable function* or (in the case of an individual performing an *accountable significant-influence function*) in connection with the business for which he is responsible. This may include an exchange or an *overseas regulator*.

4.4.2B G   PRA

For the purpose of this *Statement of Principle*, regulators in addition to the *FCA* and the *PRA* are those which have recognised jurisdiction in relation to *regulated activities* and a power to call for information from the *approved person* in connection with his *accountable function* or in connection with the business for which he is responsible. This may include an exchange or an *overseas regulator*.

4.4.3 E   FCA PRA

In the opinion of the *appropriate regulator*, conduct of the type described in **APER 4.4.4 E**, **APER 4.4.7 E**, or **APER 4.4.9 E** does not comply with *Statement of Principle* 4.

4.4.4 E   FCA PRA

Failing to report promptly in accordance with his *firm's* internal procedures (or if none exist direct to the regulator concerned), information which it would be reasonable to assume would be of material significance to the regulator concerned, whether in response to questions or otherwise, falls within **APER 4.4.3 E**. The regulator concerned is:

(1)   the *FCA* if it would be reasonable to assume that it would be of material significance to it;
(2)   the *PRA* if it would be reasonable to assume that it would be of material significance to it;
(3)   both the *FCA* and the *PRA* if it would be reasonable to assume that it would be of material significance to both of them.

4.4.5 G   FCA PRA

There is no duty on an *approved person* to report such information directly to the regulator concerned unless he is one of the *approved persons* responsible within the *firm* for reporting matters to the regulator concerned. However, if an *approved person* takes steps to influence the decision so as not to report to the regulator concerned or acts in a way that is intended to obstruct the reporting of the information to the regulator concerned, then the *appropriate regulator* will, in respect of that information, view him as being one of those within the *firm* who has taken on responsibility for deciding whether to report that matter to the regulator concerned.

4.4.6 E   FCA PRA

In determining whether or not an *approved person's* conduct under **APER 4.4.4 E** complies with *Statement of Principle* 4, the following are factors which, in the opinion of the *appropriate regulator*, are to be taken into account:

(1)   the likely significance to the regulator concerned (as defined in **APER 4.4.4 E**) of the information which it was reasonable for the individual to assume;
(2)   whether the information related to the individual himself or to his *firm*;
(3)   whether any decision not to report the matter internally was taken after reasonable enquiry and analysis of the situation.

4.4.7 E   FCA PRA

Where the *approved person* is, or is one of the *approved persons* who is, responsible within the *firm* for reporting matters to the regulator concerned (as defined in **APER 4.4.4 E**), failing promptly to inform the regulator concerned of information of which he is aware and which it would be reasonable to assume would be of material significance to the regulator concerned, whether in response to questions or otherwise, falls within **APER 4.4.3 E**.

4.4.8 E   FCA PRA

In determining whether or not an *approved person's* conduct under **APER 4.4.7 E** complies with *Statement of Principle* 4, the following are factors which, in the opinion of the *appropriate regulator*, are to be taken into account:

(1)   the likely significance of the information to the regulator concerned (as defined in **APER 4.4.4 E**) which it was reasonable for the *approved person* to assume;
(2)   whether any decision not to inform the regulator concerned (as defined in **APER 4.4.4 E**) was taken after reasonable enquiry and analysis of the situation.

4.4.9 E   FCA PRA

Failing without good reason to:
(1)   inform a regulator of information of which the *approved person* was aware in response to questions from that regulator;
(2)   attend an interview or answer questions put by a regulator, despite a request or demand having been made;
(3)   supply a regulator with appropriate *documents* or information when requested or required to do so and within the time limits attaching to that request or requirement;

falls within **APER 4.4.3 E**.

4.5   STATEMENT OF PRINCIPLE 5

4.5.1 G
[deleted]

4.5.1A G   FCA

The *Statement of Principle* 5 (see **APER 2.1A.3 P**) is in the following terms: "An *approved person* performing an *accountable significant-influence function* must take reasonable steps to ensure that the business of the *firm* for which he is responsible in his *accountable function* is organised so that it can be controlled effectively." References in **APER 4.5** to a *significant-influence function* are to an *accountable function* to which *Statement of Principle* 5 applies.

4.5.1B G   PRA

The *Statement of Principle* 5 (see **APER 2.1B.3 P**) is in the following terms: "An *approved person* performing an *accountable function* must take reasonable steps to ensure that the business of the *firm* for which he is responsible in his *accountable function* is organised so that it can be controlled effectively." References in **APER 4.5** to a *significant-influence function* are to an *accountable function* to which *Statement of Principle* 5 applies.

4.5.2 E   FCA PRA

In the opinion of the *appropriate regulator*, conduct of the type described in **APER 4.5.3 E**, **APER 4.5.4 E**, **APER 4.5.6 E** or **APER 4.5.8 E** does not comply with *Statement of Principle* 5.

4.5.3 E   FCA PRA

Failing to take reasonable steps to apportion responsibilities for all areas of the business under the *approved person's* control falls within **APER 4.5.2 E** (see **APER 4.5.11 G**).

4.5.4 E   FCA PRA

Failing to take reasonable steps to apportion responsibilities clearly amongst those to whom responsibilities have been delegated falls within **APER 4.5.2 E** (see **APER 4.5.11 G**).

4.5.5 E   FCA PRA

Behaviour of the type referred to in **APER 4.5.4 E** includes, but is not limited to:

(1)   implementing confusing or uncertain reporting lines (see **APER 4.5.12 G**);
(2)   implementing confusing or uncertain authorisation levels (see **APER 4.5.13 G**);
(3)   implementing confusing or uncertain job descriptions and responsibilities (see **APER 4.5.13 G**).

4.5.6 E   FCA PRA

In the case of an *approved person* who is responsible under **SYSC 2.1.3 R (1)** or **SYSC 4.4.5 R (1)** for dealing with the apportionment of responsibilities under **SYSC 2.1.1 R** or **SYSC 4.4.3 R**, failing to take reasonable care to maintain a clear and appropriate apportionment of significant responsibilities among the *firm's directors* and senior managers falls within **APER 4.5.2 E**.

4.5.7 E   FCA PRA

Behaviour of the type referred to in **APER 4.5.6 E** includes, but is not limited to:

(1)   failing to review regularly the significant responsibilities which the *firm* is required to apportion;
(2)   failing to act where that review shows that those significant responsibilities have not been clearly apportioned.

4.5.8 E   FCA PRA

Failing to take reasonable steps to ensure that suitable individuals are responsible for those aspects of the business under the control of the individual performing a *significant influence function* falls within **APER 4.5.2 E** (see **APER 4.5.14 G**).

4.5.9 E   FCA PRA

Behaviour of the type referred to in **APER 4.5.8 E** includes, but is not limited to:

(1)   failing to review the competence, knowledge, skills and performance of staff to assess their suitability to fulfil their duties, despite evidence that their performance is unacceptable (see **APER 4.5.14 G**);
(2)   giving undue weight to financial performance when considering the suitability or continuing suitability of an individual for a particular role (see **APER 4.5.14 G**);
(3)   allowing managerial vacancies which put at risk compliance with the requirements and standards of the *regulatory system* to remain, without arranging suitable cover for the responsibilities (see **APER 4.5.15 G**).

4.5.10 G   FCA PRA

Strategy and plans will often dictate the risk which the business is prepared to take on and high level controls will dictate how the business is to be run. If the strategy of the business is to enter high-risk areas, then the degree of control and strength of monitoring reasonably required within the business will be high. In organising the business for which he is responsible, the *approved person* performing a *significant influence function* should bear this in mind.

Apportionment of responsibilities

4.5.11 G   FCA PRA

In order to comply with the obligations of *Statement of Principle* 5 (having regard to **APER 4.5.3 E** and **APER 4.5.4 E**), the *approved person* performing a *significant influence function* may find it helpful to review whether each area of the business for which he is responsible has been clearly assigned to a particular individual or individuals.

Reporting lines

4.5.12 G   FCA PRA

The organisation of the business and the responsibilities of those within it should be clearly defined (see **APER 4.5.5 E (1)**). Reporting lines should be clear to staff. Where staff have dual reporting lines there is a greater need to ensure that the responsibility and accountability of each individual line manager is clearly set out and understood.

Authorisation levels and job descriptions

4.5.13 G   FCA PRA

Where members of staff have particular levels of authorisation (see **APER 4.5.5 E (2)** and **APER 4.5.5 E (3)**), these should be clearly set out and communicated to staff. It may be appropriate for each member of staff to have a job description of which he is aware.

Suitability of individuals

4.5.13A G   FCA PRA

The appropriate *approved person* performing a *significant influence function* should take reasonable steps to satisfy himself, on reasonable grounds, that each area of the business for which he is responsible has in place appropriate policies and procedures for reviewing the competence, knowledge, skills and performance of each individual member of staff.

4.5.14 G   FCA PRA

If an individual's performance is unsatisfactory, then the appropriate *approved person* (if any) performing a *significant influence function* should review carefully whether to allow that individual to continue in position. In particular, if he is aware of concerns relating to the compliance with requirements and standards of the *regulatory system* (or internal controls) of the individual concerned, or of staff reporting to that individual, the *approved person* performing a *significant influence function* should take care not to give undue weight to the financial performance of the individual or group concerned when considering whether any action should be taken. An adequate investigation of the concerns should be undertaken (including, where appropriate, adherence to internal controls). The *approved person* performing a *significant influence function* should satisfy himself, on reasonable grounds, that the investigation is appropriate, the results are accurate and that the concerns do not pose an unacceptable risk to compliance with the requirements and standards of the *regulatory system* (see in particular *Statement of Principle* 6 and **APER 4.5.8 E** and **APER 4.5.9 E (1)** and **APER 4.5.9 E (2)**).

Temporary vacancies

4.5.15 G   FCA PRA

In organising the business, the *approved person* performing a *significant influence function* should pay attention to any temporary vacancies which exist (see **APER 4.5.9 E (3)**). He should take reasonable steps to ensure that suitable cover for responsibilities is arranged. This could include taking on temporary staff or external consultants. The *approved person* performing a *significant influence function* should assess the risk that is posed to compliance with the requirements and standards of the *regulatory system* as a result of the vacancy, and the higher the risk the greater the steps he should take to fill the vacancy. It may be appropriate to limit or suspend the activity if appropriate cover for responsibilities cannot be arranged. To the extent that those vacancies are in respect of one of the *customer functions*, they may only be filled by *persons* approved for that function.

4.6   STATEMENT OF PRINCIPLE 6

4.6.1 G

[deleted]

4.6.1A G   FCA

The *Statement of Principle* 6 (see **APER 2.1A.3 P**) is in the following terms: "An *approved person* performing an *accountable significant-influence function* must exercise due skill, care and diligence in managing the business of the *firm* for which he is responsible in his *accountable function*." References in **APER 4.6** to a *significant-influence function* are to an *accountable significant-influence function* to which *Statement of Principle* 6 applies.

4.6.1B G PRA

The *Statement of Principle* 6 (see **APER 2.1B.3 P**) is in the following terms: "An *approved person* performing an *accountable function* must exercise due skill, care and diligence in managing the business of the *firm* for which he is responsible in his *accountable function*." References in **APER 4.6** to a *significant-influence function* are to an *accountable function* to which *Statement of Principle* 6 applies.

4.6.2 E FCA PRA

In the opinion of the *appropriate regulator*, conduct of the type described in **APER 4.6.3 E, APER 4.6.5 E, APER 4.6.6 E** or **APER 4.6.8 E** does not comply with *Statement of Principle* 6.

4.6.3 E FCA PRA

Failing to take reasonable steps to adequately inform himself about the affairs of the business for which he is responsible falls within **APER 4.6.2 E**.

4.6.4 E FCA PRA

Behaviour of the type referred to in **APER 4.6.3 E** includes, but is not limited to:
(1) permitting *transactions* without a sufficient understanding of the risks involved;
(2) permitting expansion of the business without reasonably assessing the potential risks of that expansion;
(3) inadequately monitoring highly profitable *transactions* or business practices or unusual *transactions* or business practices;
(4) accepting implausible or unsatisfactory explanations from subordinates without testing the veracity of those explanations;
(5) failing to obtain independent, expert opinion where appropriate; (see **APER 4.6.12 G**).

4.6.5 E FCA PRA

Delegating the authority for dealing with an issue or a part of the business to an individual or individuals (whether in-house or outside contractors) without reasonable grounds for believing that the delegate had the necessary capacity, competence, knowledge, seniority or skill to deal with the issue or to take authority for dealing with part of the business, falls within **APER 4.6.2 E** (see **APER 4.6.13 G**).

4.6.6 E FCA PRA

Failing to take reasonable steps to maintain an appropriate level of understanding about an issue or part of the business that he has delegated to an individual or individuals (whether in-house or outside contractors) falls within **APER 4.6.2 E** (see **APER 4.6.14 G**).

4.6.7 E FCA PRA

Behaviour of the type referred to in **APER 4.6.6 E** includes but is not limited to:
(1) disregarding an issue or part of the business once it has been delegated;
(2) failing to require adequate reports once the resolution of an issue or management of part of the business has been delegated;
(3) accepting implausible or unsatisfactory explanations from delegates without testing their veracity.

4.6.8 E FCA PRA

Failing to supervise and monitor adequately the individual or individuals (whether in-house or outside contractors) to whom responsibility for dealing with an issue or authority for dealing with a part of the business has been delegated falls within **APER 4.6.2 E**.

4.6.9 E FCA PRA

Behaviour of the type referred to in **APER 4.6.8 E** includes, but is not limited to:
(1) failing to take personal action where progress is unreasonably slow, or where implausible or unsatisfactory explanations are provided;
(2) failing to review the performance of an outside contractor in connection with the delegated issue or business.

4.6.10 E FCA PRA

In determining whether or not the conduct of an *approved person* performing a *significant influence function* under **APER 4.6.5 E, APER 4.6.6 E** and **APER 4.6.8 E** complies with *Statement of Principle* 6, the following are factors which, in the opinion of the *appropriate regulator*, are to be taken into account:
(1) the competence, knowledge or seniority of the delegate; and

(2)   the past performance and record of the delegate.

4.6.11 G   FCA PRA

An *approved person* performing a *significant influence function* will not always manage the business on a day-to-day basis himself. The extent to which he does so will depend on a number of factors, including the nature, scale and complexity of the business and his position within it. The larger and more complex the business, the greater the need for clear and effective delegation and reporting lines. The *appropriate regulator* will look to the *approved person* performing a *significant-influence function* to take reasonable steps to ensure that systems are in place which result in issues being addressed at the appropriate level. When issues come to his attention, he should deal with them in an appropriate way.

Knowledge about the business

4.6.12 G   FCA PRA

(1)   It is important for the *approved person* performing a *significant influence function* to understand the business for which he is responsible (**APER 4.6.4 E**). An *approved person* performing a *significant influence function* is unlikely to be an expert in all aspects of a complex financial services business. However, he should understand and inform himself about the business sufficiently to understand the risks of its trading, credit or other business activities.

(2)   It is important for an *approved person* performing a *significant influence function* to understand the risks of expanding the business into new areas and, before approving the expansion, he should investigate and satisfy himself, on reasonable grounds, about the risks, if any, to the business.

(3)   Where unusually profitable business is undertaken, or where the profits are particularly volatile or the business involves funding requirements on the *firm* beyond those reasonably anticipated, he should require explanations from those who report to him. Where those explanations are implausible or unsatisfactory, he should take steps to test the veracity of those explanations.

(4)   Where the *approved person* performing a *significant influence function* is not an expert in a business area, he should consider whether he or those with whom he works have the necessary expertise to provide him with an adequate explanation of issues within that business area. If not he should seek an independent opinion from elsewhere within or outside the *firm*.

Delegation

4.6.13 G   FCA PRA

(1)   An *approved person* performing a *significant influence function* may delegate the investigation, resolution or management of an issue or authority for dealing with a part of the business to individuals who report to him or to others.

(2)   The *approved person* performing a *significant influence function* should have reasonable grounds for believing that the delegate has the competence, knowledge, skill and time to deal with the issue. For instance, if the compliance department only has sufficient resources to deal with day-to-day issues, it would be unreasonable to delegate to it the resolution of a complex or unusual issue without ensuring it had sufficient capacity to deal with the matter adequately.

(3)   If an issue raises questions of law or interpretation, the *approved person* performing a *significant influence function* may need to take legal advice. If appropriate legal expertise is not available in-house, he may need to consider appointing an appropriate external adviser.

(4)   The *FCA* and *PRA* recognise that the *approved person* performing a *significant-influence function* will have to exercise his own judgment in deciding how issues are dealt with, and that in some cases that judgment will, with the benefit of hindsight, be shown to have been wrong. He will not be in breach of *Statement of Principle* 6 unless he fails to exercise due and reasonable consideration before he delegates the resolution of an issue or authority for dealing with a part of the business and fails to reach a reasonable conclusion. If he is in doubt about how to deal with an issue or the seriousness of a particular compliance problem, then, although he cannot delegate to the *appropriate regulator* the responsibility for dealing with the problem or issue, he can speak to the *appropriate regulator* to discuss his approach (see **APER 4.6.5 E**).

Continuing responsibilities where an issue has been delegated

4.6.14 G   FCA PRA

Although an *approved person* performing a *significant influence function* may delegate the resolution of an issue, or authority for dealing with a part of the business, he cannot delegate responsibility for it. It is his responsibility to ensure that he receives reports on progress and questions those reports where appropriate. For instance, if progress appears to be slow or if the issue is not being resolved satisfactorily, then the *approved person* performing a *significant influence function* may need to challenge the explanations he receives and take action himself to resolve the problem. This may include increasing the resource applied to it, reassigning the resolution internally or obtaining external advice or assistance. Where an issue raises significant concerns, an *approved person* performing a *significant influence function* should act clearly and decisively. If appropriate, this may be by suspending members of staff or relieving them of all or part of their responsibilities (see **APER 4.6.6 E**).

4.7   STATEMENT OF PRINCIPLE 7

4.7.1 G

[deleted]

4.7.1A G   FCA

The *Statement of Principle* 7 (see **APER 2.1A.3 P**) is in the following terms: "An *approved person* performing an *accountable significant-influence function* must take reasonable steps to ensure that the business of the *firm* for which he is responsible in his *accountable function* complies with the relevant requirements and standards of the *regulatory system*." References in **APER 4.7** to a *significant-influence function* are to an *accountable significant-influence function* to which *Statement of Principle* 7 applies.

4.7.1B G   PRA

The *Statement of Principle* 7 (see **APER 2.1B.3 P**) is in the following terms: "An *approved person* performing an *accountable function* must take reasonable steps to ensure that the business of the *firm* for which he is responsible in his *accountable function* complies with the relevant requirements and standards of the *regulatory system*." References in **APER 4.7** to a *significant-influence function* are to an *accountable function* to which *Statement of Principle* 7 applies.

4.7.2 E   FCA PRA

In the opinion of the *appropriate regulator*, conduct of the type described in **APER 4.7.3 E, APER 4.7.4 E, APER 4.7.5 E** or **APER 4.7.7 E** does not comply with *Statement of Principle* 7.

4.7.2A E   FCA

In the opinion of the *FCA*, conduct of the type described in **APER 4.7.9 E, APER 4.7.10 E** or **APER 4.7.11A E** does not comply with *Statement of Principle* 7.

4.7.3 E   FCA PRA

Failing to take reasonable steps to implement (either personally or through a compliance department or other departments) adequate and appropriate systems of control to comply with the relevant requirements and standards of the *regulatory system* in respect of the *regulated activities* of the *firm* in question (as referred to in *Statement of Principle* 7) falls within **APER 4.7.2 E**. In the case of an *approved person* who is responsible, under **SYSC 2.1.3 R (2)** or **SYSC 4.4.5 R (2)**, with overseeing the *firm's* obligation under **SYSC 3.1.1 R** or **SYSC 4.1.1 R**, failing to take reasonable care to oversee the establishment and maintenance of appropriate systems and controls falls within **APER 4.7.2 E**.

4.7.4 E   FCA PRA

Failing to take reasonable steps to monitor (either personally or through a compliance department or other departments) compliance with the relevant requirements and standards of the *regulatory system* in respect of the *regulated activities* of the *firm* in question (as referred to in *Statement of Principle* 7) falls within **APER 4.7.2 E** (see **APER 4.7.12 G**).

4.7.5 E   FCA PRA

Failing to take reasonable steps adequately to inform himself about the reason why significant breaches (whether suspected or actual) of the relevant requirements and standards of the *regulatory system* in respect of the *regulated activities* of the *firm* in question (as referred to in *Statement of Principle* 7) may have arisen (taking account of the systems and procedures in place) falls within **APER 4.7.2 E**.

4.7.6 E   FCA PRA

Behaviour of the type referred to in **APER 4.7.5 E** includes, but is not limited to, failing to investigate what systems or procedures may have failed including, where appropriate, failing to obtain expert opinion on the adequacy of the systems and procedures.

4.7.7 E   FCA PRA

Failing to take reasonable steps to ensure that procedures and systems of control are reviewed and, if appropriate, improved, following the identification of significant breaches (whether suspected or actual) of the relevant requirements and standards of the *regulatory system* relating to the *regulated activities* of the *firm* in question (as referred to in *Statement of Principle* 7), falls within **APER 4.7.2 E** (see **APER 4.7.13 G** and **APER 4.7.14 G**).

4.7.8 E   FCA PRA

Behaviour of the type referred to in **APER 4.7.7 E** includes, but is not limited to:
(1)   unreasonably failing to implement recommendations for improvements in systems and procedures;
(2)   unreasonably failing to implement recommendations for improvements to systems and procedures in a timely manner.

4.7.9 E   FCA

In the case of the *money laundering reporting officer*, failing to discharge the responsibilities imposed on him by the *firm* in accordance with **SYSC 3.2.6I R** or **SYSC 6.3.9 R** falls within **APER 4.7.2A E**.

4.7.10 E   FCA

In the case of an *approved person* performing a *significant influence function* responsible for compliance under **SYSC 3.2.8 R, SYSC 6.1.4 R** or **SYSC 6.1.4A R**, failing to take reasonable steps to ensure that appropriate compliance systems and procedures are in place falls within **APER 4.7.2A E** (see **APER 4.7.13 G** and **APER 4.7.14 G**).

4.7.11 G   FCA PRA

The *appropriate regulator* expects an *approved person* performing a *significant influence function* to take reasonable steps both to ensure his *firm's* compliance with the relevant requirements and standards of the *regulatory system* and to ensure that all staff are aware of the need for compliance.

4.7.11A E   FCA

Where the *approved person* is a *proprietary trader* under **SUP 10A.9.10 R**, failing to maintain and comply with appropriate systems and controls in relation to that activity falls within **APER 4.7.2A E**.

Systems of control

4.7.12 G   FCA PRA

An *approved person* performing a *significant influence function* need not himself put in place the systems of control in his business (**APER 4.7.4 E**). Whether he does this depends on his role and responsibilities. He should, however, take reasonable steps to ensure that the business for which he is responsible has operating procedures and systems which include well-defined steps for complying with the detail of relevant requirements and standards of the *regulatory system* and for ensuring that the business is run prudently. The nature and extent of the systems of control that are required will depend upon the relevant requirements and standards of the *regulatory system*, and the nature, scale and complexity of the business.

Possible breaches of regulatory requirements

4.7.13 G   FCA PRA

Where the *approved person* performing a *significant influence function* becomes aware of actual or suspected problems that involve possible breaches of relevant requirements and standards of the *regulatory system* falling within his area of responsibility, then he should take reasonable steps to ensure that they are dealt with in a timely and appropriate manner (**APER 4.7.7 E**). This may involve an adequate investigation to find out what systems or procedures may have failed and why. He may need to obtain expert opinion on the adequacy and efficacy of the systems and procedures.

Review and improvement of systems and procedures

4.7.14 G   FCA PRA

Where independent reviews of systems and procedures have been undertaken and result in recommendations for improvement, the *approved person* performing a *significant influence function* should ensure that, unless there are good reasons not to, any reasonable recommendations are implemented in a timely manner (**APER 4.7.10 E**). What is reasonable will depend on the nature of the inadequacy and the cost of the improvement. It will be reasonable for the *approved person* performing a *significant influence function* to carry out a cost benefit analysis when assessing whether the recommendations are reasonable.

TRANSITIONAL PROVISIONS AND SCHEDULES

1   TRANSITIONAL PROVISIONS

[3.39]
TP1

In addition to the transitional provision below, *GEN* contains some technical transitional provisions that apply throughout the *Handbook*.

Part 3   FCA Handbook Materials

(1)	(2) Material to which the transitional provision applies	(3)	(4) Transitional provision	(5) Transitional provision: dates in force	(6) Handbook provision coming into force
1.	**APER 3.1.9 G**	G	[expired]		

SCHEDULE 1   RECORD KEEPING REQUIREMENTS

Sch1.1 G   FCA PRA

There are no record keeping requirements in *APER*.

SCHEDULE 2   NOTIFICATION REQUIREMENTS

Sch2.1 G   FCA PRA

The aim of the guidance in the following table is to give the reader a quick overall view of the relevant requirements for notification and reporting.

Sch2.2 G   FCA PRA

It is not a complete statement of those requirements and should not be relied on as if it were.

Sch2.3 G   FCA PRA

Handbook reference	Matter to be notified	Contents of notification	Trigger event	Time allowed
Statement of Principle 4 (**APER 2.1A.3 P**)	Any information of which the *FCA* or the *PRA* would reasonably expect notice	Appropriate disclosure	Any information of which the *FCA* or the *PRA* would reasonably expect notice	Appropriate

Sch2.4 G   PRA

Handbook reference	Matter to be notified	Contents of notification	Trigger event	Time allowed
Statement of Principle 4 (**APER 2.1B.3 P**)	Any information of which the *FCA* or the *PRA* would reasonably expect notice	Appropriate disclosure	Any information of which the *FCA* or the *PRA* would reasonably expect notice	Appropriate

SCHEDULE 3   FEES AND REQUIRED PAYMENTS

Sch3.1 G   FCA PRA

There are no requirements for fees or other payments in *APER*.

SCHEDULE 5   RIGHTS OF ACTION FOR DAMAGES

Sch5.1 G   FCA

There are no *rules* in *APER*.

SCHEDULE 6   RULES THAT CAN BE WAIVED

Sch6.1 G   FCA PRA

There are no *rules* in *APER*.

F. FIT AND PROPER TEST FOR APPROVED PERSONS (FIT)

THE FIT AND PROPER TEST FOR APPROVED PERSONS
the minimum standards for becoming and remaining an approved person

CHAPTER 1
GENERAL

1.1   APPLICATION AND PURPOSE

[3.40]
1.1.1 G   FCA PRA

FIT applies to:
(1)   a *firm*;
(2)   an applicant for *Part 4A permission*;
(3)   and *EEA firm*, a *Treaty firm* or a *UCITS qualifier* that wishes to establish a *branch* into the United Kingdom using *EEA rights*, *Treaty rights* or *UCITS directive* rights (see **SUP 10A.1.10 G** and **SUP 10B.1.10 G** and **SUP 10A.1.11 R** and **SUP 10B.1.11 R**), or apply for a *top-up permission* (see **SUP 10A.1.13 R**, **SUP 10B.1.12 R**);
(4)   an *approved person*; and
(5)   a *candidate*.

1.1.2 G   FCA PRA

The purpose of *FIT* is to set out and describe the criteria that the *appropriate regulator* will consider when assessing the fitness and propriety of a *candidate* for a *controlled function* (see generally **SUP 10A** and **SUP 10B** on *approved persons*). The criteria are also relevant in assessing the continuing fitness and propriety of *approved persons*.

1.2   INTRODUCTION

1.2.1 G   FCA PRA

Under section 61(1) of the *Act* (Determination of applications), the *appropriate regulator* may grant an application for approval made under section 60 (Applications for approval) only if it is satisfied that the *candidate* is fit and proper to perform the *controlled function* to which the application relates.

1.2.2 G

[deleted]

1.2.3 G

[deleted]

1.2.3A G   FCA

Under section 63(1) of the *Act* (Withdrawal of approval), the *FCA* may withdraw an approval under section 59 given by the *FCA* or the *PRA* in relation to the performance by a person of a function if it considers that the *person* is not a fit and proper *person* to perform the function.

1.2.3B G   PRA

Under section 63(1A) of the *Act* (Withdrawal of approval), the *PRA* may withdraw an approval under section 59 in relation to the performance by a *person* ("A") of a function if: (a) the *PRA* gave the approval, or the *FCA* gave the approval and the function is a *significant influence function* performed in relation to the carrying on by a *PRA-authorised person* of a regulated activity; and (b) the *PRA* considers that A is not a fit and proper person to perform the function.

1.2.4 G   FCA PRA

The *Act* does not prescribe the matters which the *appropriate regulator* should take into account when determining fitness and propriety. However, section 61(2) states that the *appropriate regulator* may have regard (among other things) to whether the *candidate* or *approved person* is competent to carry out a *controlled function*.

1.2.4A G   FCA PRA

Under Article 5(1)(d) of the *MiFID Implementing Directive* and Article 31 and 32 of *MiFID*, the requirement to employ personnel with the knowledge, skills and expertise necessary for the discharge of the responsibilities allocated to them is reserved to the *firm's Home State*. Therefore, in assessing the fitness and propriety of a *person* to perform a *controlled function* solely in relation to the *MiFID business* of an *incoming EEA firm*, the *appropriate regulator* will not have regard to that *person's* competence and capability. Where the *controlled function* relates to matters outside the scope of *MiFID*, for example *money laundering* responsibilities (see CF11) or activities related to a *specified benchmark* (see CF 40 and CF 50), or to business outside the scope of the *MiFID* business of an *incoming EEA firm*, for example *insurance mediation activities* in relation to *life policies*, the *FCA* will have regard to a *candidate's* competence and capability as well as his honesty, integrity, reputation and financial soundness.

1.3   ASSESSING FITNESS AND PROPRIETY

1.3.1 G   FCA PRA

The *appropriate regulator* will have regard to a number of factors when assessing the fitness and propriety of a *person* to perform a particular *controlled function*. The most important considerations will be the *person's*:
(1)   honesty, integrity and reputation;
(2)   competence and capability; and
(3)   financial soundness.

1.3.2 G   FCA PRA

In assessing fitness and propriety, the *appropriate regulator* will also take account of the activities of the *firm* for which the *controlled function* is or is to be performed, the *permission* held by that *firm* and the markets within which it operates.

1.3.3 G   FCA PRA

The criteria listed in **FIT 2.1** to **FIT 2.3** are *guidance* and will be applied in general terms when the *appropriate regulator* is determining a *person's* fitness and propriety. It would be impossible to produce a definitive list of all the matters which would be relevant to a particular determination.

1.3.4 G   FCA PRA

If a matter comes to the *appropriate regulator's* attention which suggests that the *person* might not be fit and proper, the *appropriate regulator* will take into account how relevant and how important it is.

1.3.5 G   FCA PRA

During the application process, the *appropriate regulator* may discuss the assessment of the *candidate's* fitness and propriety informally with the *firm* making the application and may retain any notes of those discussions.

CHAPTER 2
MAIN ASSESSMENT CRITERIA

2.1   HONESTY, INTEGRITY AND REPUTATION

[3.41]
2.1.1 G   FCA PRA

In determining a *person's* honesty, integrity and reputation, the *appropriate regulator* will have regard to all relevant matters including, but not limited to, those set out in **FIT 2.1.3 G** which may have arisen either in the *United Kingdom* or elsewhere. The *appropriate regulator* should be informed of these matters (see **SUP 10A.14.17 R** and **SUP 10B.12.18**), but will consider the circumstances only where relevant to the requirements and standards of the *regulatory system*. For example, under **FIT 2.1.3 G** (1), conviction for a criminal offence will not automatically mean an application will be rejected. The *appropriate regulator* treats each candidate's application on a case-by-case basis, taking into account the seriousness of, and circumstances surrounding, the offence, the explanation offered by the convicted *person*, the relevance of the offence to the proposed role, the passage of time since the offence was committed and evidence of the individual's rehabilitation.

2.1.2 G   FCA PRA

In considering the matters in **FIT 2.1.1 G**, the *appropriate regulator* will look at whether the *person's* reputation might have an adverse impact upon the *firm* for which the *controlled function* is or is to be performed and at the *person's* responsibilities.

2.1.3 G   FCA PRA

The matters referred to in **FIT 2.1.1 G** to which the *appropriate regulator* will have regard include, but are not limited to:
(1)   whether the *person* has been convicted of any criminal offence; this must include, where provided for by the *Rehabilitation Exceptions Orders* to the Rehabilitation of Offenders Act 1974 or the Rehabilitation of Offenders (Northern Ireland) Order 1978 (as applicable), any spent convictions; particular consideration will be given to offences of dishonesty, fraud, financial crime or an offence under legislation relating to companies, building societies, industrial and provident societies, credit unions, friendly societies, banking, other financial services, insolvency, consumer credit companies, insurance, consumer protection, *money laundering*, market manipulation and *insider dealing*, whether or not in the *United Kingdom*;

(2)   whether the *person* has been the subject of any adverse finding or any settlement in civil proceedings, particularly in connection with investment or other financial business, misconduct, fraud or the formation or management of a *body corporate*;

(3)   whether the *person* has been the subject of, or interviewed in the course of, any existing or previous investigation or disciplinary proceedings, by the *appropriate regulator*, by other regulatory authorities (including a *previous regulator*), *clearing houses* and exchanges, professional bodies, or government bodies or agencies;

(4)   whether the *person* is or has been the subject of any proceedings of a disciplinary or criminal nature, or has been notified of any potential proceedings or of any investigation which might lead to those proceedings;

(5)   whether the *person* has contravened any of the requirements and standards of the *regulatory system* or the equivalent standards or requirements of other regulatory authorities (including a *previous regulator*), *clearing houses* and exchanges, professional bodies, or government bodies or agencies;

(6)   whether the *person* has been the subject of any justified complaint relating to *regulated activities*;

(7)   whether the *person* has been involved with a *company*, *partnership* or other organisation that has been refused registration, authorisation, membership or a licence to carry out a trade, business or profession, or has had that registration, authorisation, membership or licence revoked, withdrawn or terminated, or has been expelled by a regulatory or government body;

(8)   whether, as a result of the removal of the relevant licence, registration or other authority, the *person* has been refused the right to carry on a trade, business or profession requiring a licence, registration or other authority;

(9)   whether the *person* has been a *director*, *partner*, or concerned in the management, of a business that has gone into insolvency, liquidation or administration while the *person* has been connected with that organisation or within one year of that connection;

(10)   whether the *person*, or any business with which the *person* has been involved, has been investigated, disciplined, censured or suspended or criticised by a regulatory or professional body, a court or Tribunal, whether publicly or privately;

(11)   whether the *person* has been dismissed, or asked to resign and resigned, from employment or from a position of trust, fiduciary appointment or similar;

(12)   whether the *person* has ever been disqualified from acting as a *director* or disqualified from acting in any managerial capacity;

(13)   whether, in the past, the *person* has been candid and truthful in all his dealings with any *regulatory body* and whether the *person* demonstrates a readiness and willingness to comply with the requirements and standards of the *regulatory system* and with other legal, regulatory and professional requirements and standards.

2.2   COMPETENCE AND CAPABILITY

2.2.1 G   FCA

In determining a *person's* competence and capability, the *FCA* will have regard to all relevant matters including but not limited to:

(1)   whether the *person* satisfies the relevant *FCA* training and competence requirements in relation to the *controlled function* the *person* performs or is intended to perform;

(2)   whether the *person* has demonstrated by experience and training that the *person* is suitable, or will be suitable if approved, to perform the *controlled function*;

(3)   whether the *person* has adequate time to perform the *controlled function* and meet the responsibilities associated with that function.

2.2.1A G   PRA

In determining a *person's* competence and capability, the *PRA* will have regard to all relevant matters including but not limited to:

(1)   whether the *person* has demonstrated by experience and training that the *person* is suitable, or will be suitable if approved, to perform the *controlled function*;

(2)   whether the *person* has adequate time to perform the *controlled function* and meet the responsibilities associated with that function.

2.2.2 G   FCA PRA

A *person* may have been convicted of, or dismissed or suspended from employment for, drug or alcohol abuses or other abusive acts. This will be considered only in relation to a *person's* continuing ability to perform the particular *controlled function* for which the *person* is or is to be employed.

2.3   FINANCIAL SOUNDNESS

2.3.1 G   FCA PRA

In determining a *person's* financial soundness, the *appropriate regulator* will have regard to any factors including, but not limited to:

(1)   whether the *person* has been the subject of any judgment debt or award, in the *United Kingdom* or elsewhere, that remains outstanding or was not satisfied within a reasonable period;

(2)   whether, in the *United Kingdom* or elsewhere, the *person* has made any arrangements with his creditors, filed for bankruptcy, had a bankruptcy petition served on him, been adjudged bankrupt, been the subject of a bankruptcy restrictions order (including an interim bankruptcy restrictions order), offered a bankruptcy restrictions undertaking, had assets sequestrated, or been involved in proceedings relating to any of these.

2.3.2 G   FCA PRA

The *appropriate regulator* will not normally require the *candidate* to supply a statement of assets or liabilities. The fact that a *person* may be of limited financial means will not, in itself, affect his suitability to perform a controlled function.

TRANSITIONAL PROVISIONS AND SCHEDULES

TP 1   TRANSITIONAL PROVISIONS

[3.42]
TP1

There are no transitional provisions in *FIT*. However, *GEN* contains some technical transitional provisions that apply throughout the Handbook and which are designed to ensure a smooth transition at commencement.

SCHEDULE 1   RECORD KEEPING REQUIREMENTS

Sch1.1 G   FCA PRA

There are no record keeping requirements in *FIT*.

SCHEDULE 2   NOTIFICATION REQUIREMENTS

Sch2.1 G   FCA PRA

There are no notification requirements in *FIT*.

SCHEDULE 3   FEES AND OTHER REQUIRED PAYMENTS

Sch3.1 G   FCA PRA

There are no requirements for fees or other payments in *FIT*.

SCHEDULE 4   POWERS EXERCISED

Sch4.1 G

[deleted]

SCHEDULE 5   RIGHTS OF ACTION FOR DAMAGES

Sch5.1 G   FCA

There are no *rules* in *FIT*.

SCHEDULE 6   RULES THAT CAN BE WAIVED

Sch6.1 G   FCA PRA

There are no *rules* in *FIT*.

G. GENERAL PROVISIONS (GEN)

GENERAL PROVISIONS
interpreting the Handbook, fees, approval by the FCA and PRA, emergencies, status disclosure, the FSA logo and insurance against fines

CHAPTER 1
APPROPRIATE REGULATOR APPROVAL AND EMERGENCIES

1.1   APPLICATION

[3.43]
[**Note**: ESMA has also issued guidelines under article 16(3) of the ESMA Regulation covering various topics relating to automated trading and direct electronic access. See www.fca.org.uk]

1.1.1 R   FCA
(1)   This chapter applies to every *firm*. **GEN 1.3** (Emergency) also applies to an *unauthorised person* to whom a *rule* in the *Handbook* applies.
(2)   For a *UCITS qualifier*, this chapter applies only with respect to the *communication* and *approval* of *financial promotions* to which **COBS 4** (Communicating with clients, including financial promotion) applies and to the maintenance of facilities to which **COLL 9.4** (Facilities in the United Kingdom) applies.

1.1.2 G   FCA

GEN 1.1.1 R (2) reflects section 266 of the *Act* (Disapplication of rules).

1.2   REFERRING TO APPROVAL BY THE APPROPRIATE REGULATOR

1.2.1 G   FCA

The purpose of **GEN 1.2.2 R** is to prevent *clients* being misled about the extent to which the *appropriate regulator* has approved a *firm's* affairs.

1.2.2A R   FCA
(1)   Unless required to do so under the *regulatory system*, a *firm* must ensure that neither it nor anyone acting on its behalf claims, in a public statement or to a client, expressly or by implication, that its affairs, or any aspect of them, have the approval or endorsement of the *appropriate regulator* or another competent authority.
(2)   Paragraph (1) does not apply to statements that explain, in a way that is fair, clear and not misleading, that:
  (a)   the *firm* is an *authorised person*;
  (b)   [deleted]
  (c)   the *firm* has *permission* to carry on a specific activity;
  (d)   an *authorisation order* has been made in relation to an *AUT*, *ACS* or *ICVC*;
  (e)   a *recognised scheme* has that status;
  (f)   the *firm's approved persons* have been approved by the *appropriate regulator* for the purposes of section 59 of the *Act* (Approval for particular arrangements);
  (g)   the *firm* has been given express written approval by the *appropriate regulator* in respect of a specific aspect of the *firm's* affairs.
(3)   Paragraph (1) applies with respect to the carrying on of both *regulated activities* and *unregulated activities*.
(4)   [deleted]

1.2.3 G   FCA

GEN 1.2.2 R (2)(F) is confined to written approval because of the need for clarity as to the scope of any approval given by the *appropriate regulator*.

1.3   EMERGENCY

1.3.1 G   FCA

The *appropriate regulator* recognises that there may be occasions when, because of a particular emergency, a *person* (generally a *firm*, but in certain circumstances, for example in relation to *price stabilising rules*, an *unauthorised person*) may be unable to comply with a particular *rule* in the *Handbook*. The purpose of **GEN 1.3.2 R** is to provide appropriate relief from the consequences of contravention of such a *rule* in those circumstances.

1.3.2 R   FCA
(1)   If any emergency arises which:
  (a)   makes it impracticable for a *person* to comply with a particular *rule* in the *Handbook*;

(b)   could not have been avoided by the *person* taking all reasonable steps; and

(c)   is outside the control of the *person*, its *associates* and agents (and of its and their *employees*);

the *person* will not be in contravention of that *rule* to the extent that, in consequence of the emergency, compliance with that *rule* is impracticable.

(2)   Paragraph (1) applies only for so long as:

(a)   the consequences of the emergency continue; and

(b)   the *person* can demonstrate that it is taking all practicable steps to deal with those consequences, to comply with the *rule*, and to mitigate losses and potential losses to its *clients* (if any).

(3)   The *person* must notify the *appropriate regulator* as soon as practicable of the emergency and of the steps it is taking and proposes to take to deal with the consequences of the emergency.

(4)   A notification under (3) must be given to or addressed and delivered in accordance with **SUP 15.7** (Form and method of notification) (whether or not the *person* is a *firm*). If the *person* is not a *firm*, the notification must be given to or addressed for the attention of: Contact Centre, The Financial Conduct Authority, 25 The North Colonnade, Canary Wharf, London E14 5HS (tel: 0300 500 0597).

1.3.3 G   FCA

A *firm* should continue to keep the *appropriate regulator* informed of the steps it is taking under **GEN 1.3.2 R (3)**, in order to comply with its obligations under *Principle* 11 (Relations with regulators).

1.3.4 G   FCA

In the context of **GEN 1.3.2 R**, an action is not practicable if it involves a *person* going to unreasonable lengths.

1.3.5 G   FCA

GEN 1.3.2 R operates on the *appropriate regulator's rules*. It does not affect the *appropriate regulator's* powers to take action against a *firm* in an emergency, based on contravention of other requirements and standards under the *regulatory system*. For example, the *appropriate regulator* may exercise its *own-initiative power* in appropriate cases to vary a *firm's* Part 4A permission based on a failure or potential failure to satisfy the *threshold conditions* (see **SUP 7** (Individual requirements) and **EG 8** (Variation and cancellation of permission and imposition of requirements on the *FCA's* own initiative and intervention against incoming firms)).

CHAPTER 2
INTERPRETING THE HANDBOOK

2.1   INTRODUCTION

Application

[3.44]

2.1.1 G

[deleted]

This chapter applies to every *person* to whom any provision in the *Handbook* applies. In relation to a provision other than a *rule*, the *rules* in this chapter apply as if they were part of that provision.

2.1.3 P

[deleted]

2.1.4 E

[deleted]

2.1.5 D

[deleted]

2.1.6 G

[deleted]

2.1.7 R

[deleted]

2.1.8 R   FCA

This chapter applies to all rules made by *FOS Ltd*.

2.1.9 G   FCA

The effect of **GEN 2.1.8 R** is that this chapter applies with respect to those provisions in **DISP 2** (Jurisdiction of the Financial Ombudsman Service), **DISP 3** (Complaint handling procedures of the Financial Ombudsman Service), **DISP 4** (Standard terms) and **FEES 5** (Financial Ombudsman Service Funding) made by *FOS Ltd*.

The Reader's Guide

2.1.10 G   FCA PRA

The Reader's Guide supplements this chapter. It provides an introduction to the structure and contents of the *Handbook* and its related materials, explaining how the different modules fit together and how to interpret and use the *Handbook*.

2.2   INTERPRETING THE HANDBOOK

Purposive interpretation

2.2.1 R   FCA PRA

Every provision in the *Handbook* must be interpreted in the light of its purpose.

2.2.2 G   FCA PRA

The purpose of any provision in the *Handbook* is to be gathered first and foremost from the text of the provision in question and its context among other relevant provisions. The *guidance* given on the purpose of a provision is intended as an explanation to assist readers of the *Handbook*. As such, *guidance* may assist the reader in assessing the purpose of the provision, but it should not be taken as a complete or definitive explanation of a provision's purpose.

Evidential provisions

2.2.3 R   FCA PRA

Any *rule* in the *Handbook* which has the status letter "E" in the margin or heading:
(1)   is to be taken also to provide that contravention of the *rule* does not give rise to any of the consequences provided for by provisions of the *Act* other than section 138C (Evidential provisions); and
(2)   incorporates the status letter "E" in the margin or heading as part of the *rule*.

2.2.4 G   FCA PRA
(1)   The *rules* to which section 138C of the *Act* applies ("evidential provisions") are identified in the *Handbook* by the status letter "E" in the margin or heading.
(2)   Other provisions in the *Handbook*, although also identified by the status letter "E" in the margin or heading, are actually not *rules* but provisions in codes and **GEN 2.2.3 R** does not apply to them. These code provisions are those provisions in the *Code of Practice for Approved Persons* (**APER 3** and **APER 4**) and the *Code of Market Conduct* (**MAR 1**) with the status letter "E".

2.2.5 G   FCA PRA

Chapter 6 of the Reader's Guide contains an explanation of the significance of the status letters R, E, G, D, UK, EU, P and C, and includes further information on *Handbook* provisions, including *evidential provisions*.

Use of defined expressions

2.2.6 G   FCA PRA

Expressions with defined meanings appear in italics in the *Handbook*, unless otherwise stated in individual sourcebooks or manuals.

2.2.7 R   FCA PRA

In the *Handbook* (except *IPRU*, unless otherwise indicated):
(1)   an expression in italics which is defined in the *Glossary* has the meaning given there; and
(2)   an expression in italics which relates to an expression defined in the *Glossary* must be interpreted accordingly.

2.2.8 G   FCA PRA

Examples of related expressions are:
(1)   *"advice on investments"* and *"advise on investments"*, which should be interpreted by reference to *"advising on investments"*;
(2)   *"closely linked"*, which should be interpreted by reference to *"close links"*;
(3)   *"controls"* and *"controlled"*, which should be interpreted by reference to *"control"*; and
(4)   *"effect"*, as for example in *"effect a life policy"*, which should be interpreted by reference to *"effecting contracts of insurance"*.

2.2.9 G   FCA PRA

Part 3   FCA Handbook Materials

Unless the context otherwise requires or unless otherwise stated in a particular sourcebook or manual, where italics have not been used, an expression bears its natural meaning (subject to the Interpretation Act 1978; see **GEN 2.2.11 R** to **GEN 2.2.12 G**).

2.2.10 G   FCA PRA

The Interim Prudential sourcebooks (*IPRU*) have individual arrangements for defined terms and each contains *rules* or *guidance* on its own arrangements. In respect of those sourcebooks, reliance should not be placed on the definitions which appear in the *Glossary* unless otherwise indicated.

Application of the Interpretation Act 1978

2.2.11 R   FCA PRA

The Interpretation Act 1978 applies to the *Handbook*.

2.2.12 G   FCA PRA

The application of the Interpretation Act 1978 to the *Handbook* has the effect, in particular, that:
(1)   expressions in the *Handbook* used in the *Act* have the meanings which they bear in the *Act*, unless the contrary intention appears;
(2)   where reference is made in the *Handbook* to an enactment, it is a reference to that enactment as amended, and includes a reference to that provision as extended or applied by or under any other enactment, unless the contrary intention appears; and
(3)   unless the contrary intention appears:
    (a)   words in the *Handbook* importing the masculine gender include the feminine and words importing the feminine gender include the masculine;
    (b)   words in the *Handbook* in the singular include the plural and words in the plural include the singular.

Civil partnership – references to stepchildren etc

2.2.12A R   FCA PRA

Any reference in a provision of the *Handbook* made before 5 December 2005 to a stepchild, step-parent, stepdaughter, stepson, stepbrother or stepsister is to be interpreted in accordance with section 246 of the Civil Partnership Act 2004.

2.2.12B G   FCA PRA

GEN 2.2.12A R and sections 246 and 247 of the Civil Partnership Act 2004 amend each reference in the *Handbook* to a stepchild, step-parent and certain related expressions to take account of civil partnerships. As a result a reference (for example) to a stepchild of a person (A) includes a reference to the child of the civil partner of A where that child is not A's child.

Cross-references in the Handbook

2.2.13 R   FCA PRA

A reference in the *Handbook* to another provision in the *Handbook* is a reference to that provision as amended from time to time.

2.2.13A R   FCA PRA

Unless a contrary intention appears, to the extent that a provision made by the *appropriate regulator* ('the referring provision') contains a cross-reference to another provision that is not made by that regulator ('the referred provision'), the referred provision is to be taken to have been made by the *appropriate regulator* to the extent necessary to make the referring provision function with the full effect indicated by the reference.

References to writing

2.2.14 R   FCA PRA

If a provision in the *Handbook* refers to a communication, notice, agreement or other *document* "in writing" then, unless the contrary intention appears, it means in legible form and capable of being reproduced on paper, irrespective of the medium used. Expressions related to writing must be interpreted accordingly.

2.2.15 G   FCA PRA

GEN 2.2.14 R means that, for example, electronic media may be used to make communications which are required by a provision of the *Handbook* to be "in writing", unless a contrary intention appears, or the use of electronic media would contravene some other requirement. **GEN 2.2.14 R** does not, however, affect any other legal requirement which may apply in relation to the form or manner of executing a *document* or agreement.

2.2.15A G   FCA

An example of a requirement relevant to whether a communication required by a provision of the *Handbook* to be "in writing" may be made by use of electronic media is the requirement to treat *customers* fairly under *Principle* 6.

2.2.16 G   FCA PRA

"Document" is a defined term in the *Glossary*, the definition of which includes information recorded in any form, including electronic form.

Activities covered by general rules

2.2.17 R   FCA PRA

A general *rule* (that is a *rule* made by the *appropriate regulator* under the *general rule making powers*) is to be interpreted as:

(1)   applying to a *firm* with respect to the carrying on of all *regulated activities*, except to the extent that a contrary intention appears; and

(2)   not applying to a *firm* with respect to the carrying on of *unregulated activities*, unless and then only to the extent that a contrary intention appears.

Continuity of authorised partnerships and unincorporated associations

2.2.18 R   FCA PRA

(1)   If a *firm*, which is a partnership or unincorporated association, is dissolved, but its authorisation continues to have effect under section 32 of the *Act* (Partnerships and unincorporated associations) in relation to any partnership or unincorporated association which succeeds to the business of the dissolved *firm*, the successor partnership or unincorporated association is to be regarded as the same *firm* for the purposes of the *Handbook* unless the context otherwise requires.

(2)   [deleted]

(3)   [deleted]

2.2.19 G   FCA PRA

In principle, it is possible to view a change of partners in a partnership, or a change in the membership of the unincorporated association, as the formation of a new partnership or association. **GEN 2.2.18 R** reflects section 32 of the *Act* (Partnerships and unincorporated associations), which provides for the continuing *authorisation* of partnerships and unincorporated associations following a change in partners or members if certain conditions are satisfied. **GEN 2.2.18 R** ensures a similar effect to section 32 in relation to the status of the partnership or unincorporated associations as a *"firm"* or *"authorised person"* for the purposes of the *Handbook*.

Designated investment exchanges

2.2.20 G   FCA

In the *Glossary*, the definition of *designated investment exchange* lists certain investment exchanges. Further information on *designated investment exchanges*, including *guidance* on the addition of an investment exchange to the list, is set out in **GEN 2 ANNEX 1** and the obligation to pay the application fee is set out in **FEES 3.2**.

European Economic Area (EEA)

2.2.21 G   FCA PRA

The agreement on the *European Economic Area*, signed at Oporto on 2 May 1992, extends certain *EU* legislation to those *EEA States* which are not Member States of the *EU*, namely Norway, Iceland and Liechtenstein. References in the *Handbook* concerning the territorial scope of *EU* law should therefore be read as extending throughout the *EEA* where the context requires.

Treaty of Lisbon

2.2.22 G   FCA PRA

As a result of the Treaty of Lisbon, the European Union has replaced and succeeded the European Community. References in the *Handbook* to the European Community should therefore be interpreted as references to the European Union, where the context requires. In particular, references which are copied out directly from *EU* or *UK* legislation may contain references to the Community which should be read in conjunction with section 3 of the European Union (Amendment) Act 2008.

Application of provisions made by both the FCA and the PRA

2.2.23 R   FCA PRA

(1)   This *rule* applies to *Handbook* provisions made by both the *FCA* and the *PRA*. It may affect their application by the *FCA* to *PRA-authorised persons* and *PRA approved persons*, and may affect their application by the *PRA* to any *authorised person* or *approved person*.

(2)   Where a *Handbook* provision (or part of one) goes beyond the *FCA's* or *PRA's* powers or regulatory responsibilities, it is to be interpreted as applied by that regulator to the extent of that regulator's powers and regulatory responsibilities only.

(3)   The extent of a *Handbook* provision is to be interpreted as cut back under **GEN 2.2.23 R (2)** by the minimum degree necessary.

2.2.24 G   FCA PRA

The published Memorandum of Understanding between the *FCA* and the *PRA* describes their regulatory responsibilities.

2.2.25 G   FCA

Examples of rules being interpreted as cut back by **GEN 2.2.23 R** include the following:
(1)   [deleted]
(2)   **SYSC 6.1.1 R** requires a *firm* to maintain adequate policies and procedures to ensure compliance with its obligations under the *regulatory system*; **SYSC 6.1.1 R** should be interpreted:
    (a)   as applied by the *FCA* in respect of a *PRA-authorised person's* compliance with regulatory obligations that are the responsibility of the *FCA* (for example, in respect of a *bank* maintaining policies and procedures to ensure compliance with banking conduct requirements in *BCOBS*); and,
    (b)   as applied by the *PRA* in respect of a *PRA-authorised person's* compliance with those regulatory obligations that are the responsibility of the *PRA* (for example, in respect of a *bank* maintaining policies and procedures to ensure compliance with financial resources requirements in the *PRA* Rulebook and the *EU CRR*).
(3)   **COMP 5.2.1 R** sets out types of *protected claims* to be covered by the *FSCS*. The powers of the *FCA* and the *PRA* to make this type of *rule* are set out in the order made under section 213(1A) of the *Act*. The *rule* must be read as applying only to the extent of those powers. For example, the *PRA* has no power to make **COMP 5.2.1 R (3)** creating *protected claims* in connection with *protected investment business*, and the *FCA* has no power to make **COMP 5.2.1 R (1)** as creating *protected claims* for a *protected deposit*. As such, those provisions are to be interpreted as not applied by the *PRA* and *FCA*, respectively.

2.2.25A G   PRA

Examples of rules being interpreted as cut back by **GEN 2.2.23 R** include the following:
(1)   **SYSC 6.1.1 R** requires a *firm* to maintain adequate policies and procedures to ensure compliance with its obligations under the *regulatory system*; **SYSC 6.1.1 R** should be interpreted:
    (a)   as applied by the *FCA* in respect of a *PRA-authorised person's* compliance with regulatory obligations that are the responsibility of the *FCA* (for example, in respect of a *bank* maintaining policies and procedures to ensure compliance with banking conduct requirements in *BCOBS*); and,
    (b)   as applied by the *PRA* in respect of a *PRA-authorised person's* compliance with those regulatory obligations that are the responsibility of the *PRA* (for example, in respect of a *bank* maintaining policies and procedures to ensure compliance with financial resources requirements in the *PRA* Rulebook and the *EU CRR*).

2 ANNEX 1   DESIGNATED INVESTMENT EXCHANGES

G   FCA

Introduction
1.   A *designated investment exchange* is an exchange appearing in the list of such exchanges in the *Glossary*.
Benefits of designation
2.   Under certain *rules*, *firms* may treat transactions effected on a *designated investment exchange* in the same way as transactions on *RIEs* (for example, see **CASS 2**).
Criteria for inclusion in the list of designated investment exchanges
3.   Before adding an investment exchange to the list of *designated investment exchanges* in the *Handbook*, the *FCA* will comply with all the requirements imposed by the *Act* in relation to the exercise of its rule-making powers. This will include consulting on the proposed amendment to the list.
4.   In considering compatibility of the proposed addition with the *statutory objectives*, the *FCA* will determine whether the investment exchange provides an appropriate degree of protection for *consumers* having regard in particular to:

(1)	the relevant law and practice, including the regulatory framework in which the investment exchange operates, in the country or territory in which the investment exchange's head office is situated and any other relevant country or territory; and
(2)	the rules and practices of the investment exchange.

Introduction

5.   Only investment exchanges which do not carry on a *regulated activity* in the *United Kingdom* and are not *regulated markets* may be added to the list. This is because an investment exchange carrying on a *regulated activity* in the *United Kingdom* will need to apply for recognition as an *RIE*, or authorisation, and because a regulated market is usually treated in the same way as an *RIE* in the *rules*.

Applications to be added to the list of designated investment exchanges

6.   An application to be added to the list should be in writing and delivered to the *FCA* by:

         (1)   post to:
                                       The Financial Conduct Authority
                                       25 The North Colonnade
                                       Canary Wharf
                                       London
                                       E14 5HS; or

         (2)   leaving the application at that address.

7.   In support of the application, an investment exchange should provide information on the questions set out in the table below.

8.   An application will not be considered by the *FCA* until the application fee has been paid. See **FEES 3.2**

Designated investment exchange questionnaire

1   In what way are members subject to formal supervision by the exchange or another supervisory or regulatory body? Describe how capital resources of members are monitored on an ongoing basis and how this is related to business done.

2   What powers does the exchange or any other supervisory or regulatory body have to intervene in a member's business in the event of misconduct, financial difficulties or otherwise?

3   What are the clearing arrangements of the exchange? How does the exchange ensure performance of a contract between its members? If relevant, what type of contract guarantee is available?

4   How is price information in respect of contracts effected on the exchange disseminated to investors, particularly those investors in the *United Kingdom*?

5   What are the exchange's arrangements for reporting and recording of transactions effected on the exchange? Please describe.

6   Does the exchange, or any other supervisory or regulatory body, require members to segregate the money and assets of the member's *clients* from the money and assets of the member? If so, please describe in outline how this operates. If not, are investors protected in any other way in the event of the insolvency of a member or the exchange?

7   Does the exchange have procedures for the investigation of complaints? Please describe what they are.

8   Does the exchange classify the different contracts traded on it in terms of liquidity? Is it possible to identify certain contracts which are more liquid than others and in which a ready market might be considered to exist?

2 ANNEX 2   [DELETED]

CHAPTER 3
FSA FEES: GENERAL PROVISIONS

3.1   GEN 3 [DELETED: THE GENERAL PROVISIONS IN RELATION TO FEES ARE SET
OUT IN FEES 2 (GENERAL PROVISIONS)]

3.2   GEN 3 [DELETED: THE GENERAL PROVISIONS IN RELATION TO FEES ARE SET
OUT IN FEES 2 (GENERAL PROVISIONS)]

3.3   GEN 3 [DELETED: THE GENERAL PROVISIONS IN RELATION TO FEES ARE SET
OUT IN FEES 2 (GENERAL PROVISIONS)]

CHAPTER 4
STATUTORY STATUS DISCLOSURE

4.1   APPLICATION

Who? What?

[3.45]
4.1.1 R   FCA

This chapter applies to every *firm* and with respect to every *regulated activity*, except that:
(1)   for an *incoming ECA provider*, this chapter does not apply when the *firm* is acting as such;
(2)   for an *incoming EEA firm* which has *permission* only for *cross-border services* and which
does not carry on *regulated activities* in the *United Kingdom*, this chapter does not apply;
(3)   for an *incoming firm* not falling under (1) or (2), this chapter does not apply to the extent that
the *firm* is subject to equivalent rules imposed by its *Home State*;
(4)   for a *UCITS qualifier*, this chapter does not apply; and
(5)   only **GEN 4.5** (Statements about authorisation and regulation by the appropriate regulator)
applies in relation to *MiFID or equivalent third country business* and only where that *MiFID
or equivalent third country business* is not business falling within paragraph 2 (Transactions
between an MTF operator and its users), 3 (Transactions concluded on an MTF) or 4
(Transactions concluded on a regulated market) of Part 1 of **COBS 1 ANNEX 1**.

Where?

4.1.2 R   FCA

GEN 4.3 (Letter disclosure) applies in relation to activities carried on from an establishment
maintained by the *firm* (or by its *appointed representative*) in the *United Kingdom*, subject to **GEN
4.3.4 R** (Exception: insurers).

4.1.3 R   FCA

GEN 4.4 (Business for private customers from non-UK offices) applies in connection with a
regulated activity carried on from an establishment of the *firm* (or its *appointed representative*) that
is not in the *United Kingdom*.

4.1.4 R   FCA

GEN 4.5 (Statements about authorisation and regulation by the *appropriate regulator*) applies in
relation to activities carried on from an establishment maintained by the *firm* (or by its *appointed
representative*) in the *United Kingdom*, provided that, in the case of the *MiFID business* of an *EEA
MiFID investment firm* or the activities of an *EEA UCITS management company*, it only applies to
business conducted within the territory of the *United Kingdom*.

4.2   PURPOSE

4.2.1 G   FCA

This chapter requires the provision of appropriate minimum information about the identity of the
regulator that authorised a *firm*. It also governs the way in which a *firm* may describe its regulation
by the *appropriate regulator*.

4.2.1A G

[deleted]

4.2.1B G   FCA

This chapter builds upon *Principle* 7 (Communications with clients), which requires a *firm* to pay
due regard to the information needs of its *clients*. This assists in the achievement of the *statutory
objectives*, including the *FCA's* strategic objective of ensuring that relevant markets function well
and the consumer protection and integrity objectives.

4.2.2 G FCA

There are other pre-contract information requirements outside this chapter, including:

(1) for *financial promotions*, in the *financial promotion rules*;

(2) for *designated investment business*, in **COBS 8** (Client agreements), **COBS 5** (Distance Communications), **COBS 6** (Information about the firm, its services and remuneration), **COBS 13** and **14** (which relate to product information) and CASS (Client assets);

(3) for *non-investment insurance contracts*, distance communication requirements in **ICOBS 3**, initial disclosure requirements in **ICOBS 4**, disclosures relating to client needs and advice in **ICOBS 5** and product information requirements in **ICOBS 6**;

(4) for *electronic commerce activities* carried on from an *establishment* in the *United Kingdom*, in **COBS 5.2, ICOBS 3.2** and **MCOB 2.8**;

(5) for *regulated mortgage contracts* and *home purchase plans*, initial disclosure requirements in **MCOB 4**, pre-application disclosure requirements in **MCOB 5**, and disclosure at the offer stage in **MCOB 6**;

(6) for *equity release transactions*, initial disclosure requirements in **MCOB 8.4**, pre-application disclosure requirements in **MCOB 9.4** and disclosure at the offer stage in **MCOB 9.5**;

(7) for *regulated sale and rent back agreements*, initial disclosure requirements in MCOB 4.11, pre-sale disclosure requirements in **MCOB 5.9** and disclosure at the offer stage requirements in **MCOB 6.9**; and

(8) for *regulated credit agreements*, the pre-contract information requirements in the Consumer Credit (Disclosure of Information) Regulations 2010 (SI 2010/1013) and in the Consumer Credit (Disclosure of Information) Regulations 2004 (SI 2004/1481).

4.3   LETTER DISCLOSURE

Disclosure in letters to retail clients

4.3.1 R FCA

A *firm* must take reasonable care to ensure that every letter (or electronic equivalent) which it or its *employees* send to a *retail client*, with a view to or in connection with the *firm* carrying on a *regulated activity*, includes the disclosure in **GEN 4 ANNEX 1** (firms that are not PRA-authorised persons) or GEN 4 Annex 1AR (PRA-authorised persons) as applicable.

4.3.1A G FCA

Where a letter covers both activities to which this section applies and activities to which this section does not apply, the *firm* should comply with the *rules* in this chapter in relation to the business to which it applies.

4.3.1B G FCA

An example for **GEN 4.3.1A G** would be where a letter covers business for which the *FCA* is the *competent authority* under the *Insurance Mediation Directive* and under *MiFID*.

4.3.2 G

[deleted]

4.3.2A G FCA

For a *UK domestic firm* that is not a *PRA-authorised person*, the required disclosure in **GEN 4 ANNEX 1 R** is "Authorised and regulated by the Financial Conduct Authority".

4.3.2B G FCA

For a *UK domestic firm* that is a *PRA-authorised person*, the required disclosure in GEN 4 Annex 1AR is "Authorised by the Prudential Regulation Authority and regulated by the Financial Conduct Authority and the Prudential Regulation Authority".

4.3.3 G FCA

(1) **GEN 4.3.1 R** (Disclosure in letters to retail clients) covers letters delivered by hand, sent by *post* and sent by fax and also electronic mail, but not text messages, account statements, business cards or compliment slips (used as such).

(2) **GEN 4.3.1 R** (Disclosure in letters to retail clients) applies in relation to letters sent by any of the *firm's employees*, which includes its *appointed representatives* and their *employees*.

(3) *Firms* are likely to find it convenient to include the required disclosure in their letterhead.

Exception: insurers

4.3.4 R FCA

GEN 4.3.1 R (Disclosure in letters to retail clients) does not apply in relation to:

(1) *general insurance business* if:

(a)   the *State of the risk* is an *EEA State* other than the *United Kingdom*; or
(b)   the *State of the risk* is outside the *EEA* and the *client* is not in the *United Kingdom* when the *contract of insurance* is entered into; or
(2)   *long-term insurance business* if:
(a)   the *client* is *habitually resident* in an *EEA State* other than the *United Kingdom*; or
(b)   the *client* is *habitually resident* outside the *EEA* and is not present in the *United Kingdom* when the *contract of insurance* is entered into.

Exception: authorised professional firms

4.3.5 R   FCA

For an *authorised professional firm*, **GEN 4.3.1 R** (Disclosure in letters to retail clients) does not apply with respect to its *non-mainstream regulated activities*.

Exception: use of third party processors in home finance and insurance mediation activities

4.3.6 R   FCA
(1)   Where a *firm* has outsourced activities to a *third party processor* other than *advising* on *life policies*, **GEN 4.3.1 R** does not apply to that *third party processor* when acting as such, so long as the outsourcing *firm* ensures that the *third party processor* and its *employees* comply with that *rule* as if it was the *firm* and they were *employees* of the *firm*.
(2)   Where an *appointed representative* has outsourced *insurance mediation activities* other than *advising* on *life policies* or *home finance mediation activities* to a *third party processor*, **GEN 4.3.1 R** does not apply to that *third party processor* when acting as such, so long as the *appointed representative's principal* ensures that the *third party processor* and its *employees* comply with that *rule* as if it was the *appointed representative* and they were the *employees* of the *appointed representative*.
(3)   Where an *appointed representative* of a *firm* is carrying on:
(a)   *insurance mediation activities* other than *advising* on *life policies*; or
(b)   *home finance mediation activities*;
which have been outsourced to it by the *firm*, **GEN 4.3.1 R** does not apply to the *firm* when the *appointed representative* is carrying on the outsourced activities, so long as the *firm* ensures that the *appointed representative* and its *employees* comply with that *rule* as if it was the *firm* and they were *employees* of the *firm*.

Exception: credit firms

4.3.7 R   FCA

GEN 4.3.1 R (Disclosure in letters to retail clients) does not apply to a *credit firm* (other than a *firm* with a *limited permission*) with respect to the activity of *entering into a regulated credit agreement as lender* to which the *Consumer Credit Directive* applies, to the extent it would be contrary to the *United Kingdom's* obligations under an EU instrument.

4.3.8 G   FCA

A *credit firm* which carries on the activity of *entering into a regulated credit agreement as lender*, in respect of an agreement to which articles 5 and 6 of the *Consumer Credit Directive* apply is under an obligation to disclose pre-contract information in the form and to the extent required by the Consumer Credit (Disclosure of Information) Regulations 2010 (SI 2010/1013). *Firms* which carry on *credit broking* may take on the same obligation. A *credit firm* must also ensure specified information is included in *credit agreements* to which the *Consumer Credit Directive* applies in the form and to the extent required by the Consumer Credit (Agreements) Regulations 2010 (SI 2010/1014).

4.3.9 G   FCA

The effect of **GEN 4.3.7 R** is that a *credit firm* in relation to a *regulated credit agreement* covered by the *Consumer Credit Directive* does not need to comply with **GEN 4.3.1 R** in relation to those letters (or electronic equivalents) that accompany the information required under the Regulations referred to in **GEN 4.3.8 G**.

4.3.10 G   FCA

Regulated activities covered by a *limited permission* (see the "relevant credit activities" set out in paragraph 2G of Schedule 6 to the *Act*) do not fall within the scope of articles 5 and 6 of the *Consumer Credit Directive*, therefore **GEN 4.3.7 R** and the guidance related to it are not relevant to those activities.

4.4   BUSINESS FOR RETAIL CLIENTS FROM NON-UK OFFICES

4.4.1 R   FCA
(1)   If, in any communication:

    (a)   made to:

        (i)

            (in relation to a *non-investment insurance contract*) a *consumer*;

        (ii)

            (in relation to a *home finance transaction*) a *customer*; or

        (iii)

            (in all other cases) a *retail client*; and

    (b)   in connection with a *regulated activity* carried on from an establishment of the *firm* (or its *appointed representative*) that is not in the *United Kingdom*;

the *firm* indicates that it is an *authorised person*, it must also, where relevant, and with equal prominence, give the information in (2) in writing.

(2)   The information required is that in some or all respects the *regulatory system* applying will be different from that of the *United Kingdom*. The *firm* may also indicate the protections and complaints or compensation arrangements available under another relevant system of regulation.

(3)   A *firm* need not provide the information required by (1) if it has already provided it in writing to the *customer* to whom the communication is made.

4.4.2 G

[deleted]

4.5 STATEMENTS ABOUT AUTHORISATION AND REGULATION BY THE APPROPRIATE REGULATOR

Application

4.5.1 R FCA

This section applies to a *firm*:

(1)   communicating with a *customer*; or

(2)   *communicating* or *approving* a *financial promotion* other than:

    (a)   a *financial promotion* that would benefit from an exemption in the *Financial Promotion Order* if it were *communicated* by an *unauthorised person*;

    (b)   a promotion of an *unregulated collective investment scheme* that would breach section 238(1) of the *Act* if made by an *authorised person* (*firms* may not *communicate* or *approve* such promotions).

4.5.2 G FCA

GEN 4.5.1 R (1) does not apply to a *firm* when communicating with an *eligible counterparty*.

4.5.2A G FCA

However, misleading statements by a *firm* when communicated with an *eligible counterparty* may involve a breach of *Principle* 7 (Communications with clients) or Part 7 (Offences relating to financial services) of the Financial Services *Act* 2012, as well as giving rise to private law actions for misrepresentation.

The duty

4.5.3 R FCA

A *firm* must not indicate or imply that it is authorised by the *FCA* in respect of business for which it is not so authorised.

4.5.3A R FCA

A *firm* must not indicate or imply that it is authorised by the *PRA* in respect of business for which it is not so authorised.

4.5.4 R FCA

A *firm* must not indicate or imply that it is regulated or otherwise supervised by the *FCA* in respect of business for which it is not regulated by the *FCA*.

4.5.4A R FCA

A *firm* must not indicate or imply that it is regulated or otherwise supervised by the *PRA* in respect of business for which it is not regulated by the *PRA*.

4.5.5 G FCA

SUP 13A ANNEX 1 provides *guidance* on the application of the *Handbook* to an *incoming EEA firm*.

4.5.6 G FCA

(1)   Neither an incoming *EEA firm* nor an *incoming Treaty firm* is *authorised* by the *FCA* or *PRA* when acting as such.

(2)   It is likely to be misleading for a *firm* that is not *authorised* by the *FCA* or *PRA* to state or imply that it is so *authorised*. It is also likely to be misleading for a *firm* to state or imply that a *client* will have recourse to the *Financial Ombudsman Service* or the *FSCS* where this is not the case.

(3)   [deleted]

4.5.6A G   FCA

As well as potentially breaching the requirements in this section, misleading statements by a *firm* may involve a breach of *Principle* 7 (Communications with clients) or section Part 7 (Offences relating to financial services) of the Financial Services *Act* 2012, as well as giving rise to private law actions for misrepresentation.FCA

4 ANNEX 1   STATUTORY STATUS DISCLOSURE

This *rule* applies to *firms* that are not *PRA-authorised persons*:

	Type of firm	Required disclosure (Note 5)
(1)	*UK domestic firm;* **or** *overseas firm* (**which is not an** *incoming firm*)	"**Authorised and regulated by the Financial Conduct Authority**" (Note 1)
(2)	*Incoming firm* **without a** *top-up permission*	(a) "**Authorised by [name of** *Home State regulator*]" **or** (b) "**Authorised by [name of** *Home State regulator*] **and subject to limited regulation by the Financial Conduct Authority. Details about the extent of our regulation by the Financial Conduct Authority are available from us on request**" (Notes 1, 2, 2a and 3)
(3)	*Incoming firm* **with a** *top-up permission*	"**Authorised by [name of** *Home State regulator*] **and authorised and subject to limited regulation by the Financial Conduct Authority. Details about the extent of our authorisation and regulation by the Financial Conduct Authority are available from us on request**" (Notes 1, 2 and 3)
(4)	*Appointed representative* **of a** *firm*	"**[Name of** *appointed representative*] **is an appointed representative of [name of** *firm*] **which is [then continue with the required disclosure of the** *firm*]" (Note 4)

Note 1 = A *firm* **must use the formulation** "Financial Conduct Authority" **and not the abbreviated formulation** "FCA".
Note 2 = An *incoming firm* **is free to translate the name of its** *Home State regulator* **into English if it wishes. In doing so, it must ensure that the State in which the regulator is based is clear.**

Note 2a = An *incoming firm* **without a** *top-up permission* **may make either disclosure (a) or disclosure (b) unless it otherwise indicates or implies to the** *customer* **that it is regulated or supervised by the** *FCA*, **in which case it must make disclosure (b).**
Note 3 = If a *firm* **offers to make details about the extent of its authorisation or regulation by the** *FCA* **available on request and a** *customer* **requests such details, it must provide those details in a way that is clear, fair and not misleading.**

Note 4 = If the *appointed representative* **has more than one** *principal*, **the disclosure must relate to the** *principal* **or** *principals* **responsible for the** *regulated activity* **or activities concerned. The required disclosure of the** *firm* **is that which would apply were the** *firm* **to make the disclosure under the** *rules* **applicable to it.**

Note 5 = Any *firm* **listed in this table is permitted to add words to the relevant required disclosure statement but only if the** *firm* **has taken reasonable steps to satisfy itself that the presentation of its statutory status will, as a consequence, be fair, clear and not misleading and be likely to be understood by the average member of the group to whom it is directed or by whom it is likely to be received. For example, an** *authorised professional firm* **may wish to make it clear that it is also regulated by its professional body**. FCA

4 ANNEX 1A   STATUTORY STATUS DISCLOSURE (PRA-AUTHORISED PERSONS)

This *rule* applies to *firms* that are *PRA-authorised persons*:

	Type of firm	Required disclosure (Note 5)
(1)	UK domestic firm	"Authorised by the Prudential Regulation Authority and regulated by the Financial Conduct Authority and the Prudential Regulation Authority" (Note 1)
(2)	overseas firm (which is not an incoming firm)	"[Authorised and regulated by [name of the *overseas regulator* of the overseas firm in the jurisdiction of that overseas firm's registered office (or, if it has no registered office, its head office)]]. Authorised by the Prudential Regulation Authority. Subject to regulation by the Financial Conduct Authority and limited regulation by the Prudential Regulation Authority. Details about the extent of our regulation by the Prudential Regulation Authority are available from us on request." (Notes 1, 2, 3, and 3a)
(3)	Incoming firm without a top-up permission	(a) "Authorised by [name of *Home State regulator*]" or (b) "Authorised by [name of *Home State regulator*] and subject to limited regulation by the Financial Conduct Authority and Prudential Regulation Authority. Details about the extent of our regulation by the Financial Conduct Authority and Prudential Regulation Authority are available from us on request" (Notes 1, 2, 2a, 2b and 3)
(4)	Incoming firm with a top-up permission	"Authorised by [name of *Home State regulator*] and the Prudential Regulation Authority and subject to limited regulation by the Financial Conduct Authority and Prudential Regulation Authority. Details about the extent of our authorisation and regulation by the Prudential Regulation Authority, and regulation by the Financial Conduct Authority are available from us on request" (Notes 1, 2, 2b and 3)
(5)	*Appointed representative* of a *firm*	"[Name of *appointed representative*] is an *appointed representative* of [name of *firm*] which is [then continue with the required disclosure of the *firm*]" (Note 4)
(6)	Society of Lloyd's	"Authorised under the Financial Services and Markets Act 2000"

Note 1 = A *firm* must use the formulation "Financial Conduct Authority" or "Prudential Regulation Authority" and not the abbreviated formulation "FCA" or "PRA" respectively.

Note 2 = An incoming firm or overseas firm is free to translate the name of its *Home State regulator* or *overseas regulator* into English if it wishes. In doing so, it must ensure that the State in which the regulator is based is clear.

Note 2a = An incoming firm without a top-up permission may make either disclosure (a) or disclosure (b) unless it otherwise indicates or implies to the *customer* that it is regulated or supervised by the *FCA* or *PRA*, in which case it must make disclosure (b).

Note 2b = An *incoming EEA firm* exercising establishment rights in the *UK* under the *Banking Consolidation Directive*, which do not include the activity of acceptance of deposits and other repayable funds, will be subject to branch liquidity and other supervision by the *FCA*.

Note 3 = If a *firm* offers to make details about the extent of its authorisation by the *PRA* or regulation by the *FCA* or *PRA* available on request and a *customer* requests such details, it must provide those details in a way that is clear, fair and not misleading.

Part 3   FCA Handbook Materials

Type of firm	Required disclosure (Note 5)

Note 3a = An overseas firm that is not an incoming firm is only required to disclose its authorisation and/or regulated by an *overseas regulator* if it is so authorised and/or regulated.
Note 4 = If the *appointed representative* has more than one *principal*, the disclosure must relate to the *principal* or *principals* responsible for the *regulated activity* or activities concerned. The required disclosure of the *firm* is that which would apply were the *firm* to make the disclosure under the *rules* applicable to the *firm*.

Note 5 = Any *firm* listed in this table is permitted to add words to the relevant required disclosure statement but only if the *firm* has taken reasonable steps to satisfy itself that the presentation of its statutory status will, as a consequence, be fair, clear and not misleading and be likely to be understood by the average member of the group to whom it is directed or by whom it is likely to be received.

CHAPTER 5
REGULATORS' LOGOS AND THE KEYFACTS LOGO

5.1   APPLICATION AND PURPOSE

Application

[3.46]
5.1.1 G   FCA

This chapter contains:
(1)   guidance for *firms*, *authorised payment institutions* and *authorised electronic money institutions* and their *appointed representatives*, *agents* or *tied agents* on the circumstances in which the *FCA* permits them to reproduce the *FSA* and *FCA* logos;
(2)   *rules* on the use by *firms* of the key facts logo.

Purpose

5.1.2 G   FCA

The FSA logo is a registered UK service mark, with number 2150560. The *FCA* logo is a registered UK service mark, with number 2629534. The keyfacts logo is a registered Community trade mark, with the number EU3866688. All are the property of the *FCA*. They are also subject to copyright and may be used or reproduced with permission of the *FCA* only. If the *FSA*, *FCA*, or keyfacts logos are reproduced or otherwise used by any person without such permission the *FCA* may seek to enforce its rights over its property through the Courts.

5.1.3 G   FCA

GEN 5 ANNEX 1 G is a general licence, which sets out the circumstances in which the *FCA* permits a *person* to whom this chapter applies to reproduce the FSA and keyfacts logos. Such a *person* need not apply for an individual licence if it uses or reproduces the logos in accordance with the general licence.

5.1.3A G   FCA

No general licence is granted by the *FCA* in respect of the FCA logo.

5.1.4 G   FCA

The *FCA* has no policy to allow use of the FSA or keyfacts logos by a *person* to whom this chapter applies other than as set out in **GEN 5 ANNEX 1 G**. If, however, such a *person* wishes to use or reproduce either of the logos other than in accordance with the general licence, it may apply to the *FCA* for an individual licence, giving full reasons why it considers the *FCA* should grant the licence.

The keyfacts logo

5.1.5 R   FCA

A *firm* must not use the keyfacts logo other than as and when it is required or expressly permitted to be used by the *rules*, and in accordance with the general licence in **GEN 5 ANNEX 1 G**.

5.1.6 R   FCA

A *firm* must take all reasonable steps to ensure that its *representatives* do not use the keyfacts logo other than as and when the logo is required to be used by the *rules*.

5.1.7 R   FCA

A *firm* must take all reasonable steps to ensure that the keyfacts logo is not reproduced on any document that the *firm*, or any *person* acting on its behalf, provides to a *customer* unless the reproduction is required by the *rules*.

The FSA logo

5.1.8 R   FCA

A *firm* must not use the FSA logo (and must take all reasonable steps to ensure that its *representatives* do not use the FSA logo) in any communication with a *client* other than in accordance with the general licence in **GEN 5 ANNEX 1 G** or any individual licence granted by the *FCA* to the *firm* or its *representatives*.

5.1.9 G   FCA

The general licence in **GEN 5 ANNEX 1 G** to use the FSA logo will continue till 1 April 2014 whereupon the general licence is revoked by **GEN 5 ANNEX 1 G**, 7.1.

The FCA logo

5.1.10 R   FCA

A *firm* must not use the FCA logo (and must take all reasonable steps to ensure that its *representatives* do not use the FCA logo) in any communication with a *client* other than in accordance with any individual licence granted by the *FCA* to the *firm* or its *representatives*.

5 ANNEX 1 G   LICENCE FOR USE OF THE FSA AND KEYFACTS LOGOS

G   FCA

Application

1.1   The *FCA* grants this licence to *firms*, *authorised payment institutions*, *authorised electronic money institutions*, *appointed representatives*, *agents* and *tied agents*.

The FSA logo

2.1   The FSA logo is made up of two elements which together make up the registered UK service mark, with number 2150560:

     (1)   the symbol (the scroll and globe device); and

     (2)   the FSA letters.

2.2   The keyfacts logo is made up of two elements which together make up the registered Community trade mark, with number E3866688:

     (1)   the symbol (the rectangular speech bubble); and

     (2)   the word 'keyfacts'.

2.3   There are two versions of the FSA logo, version A and a smaller version B in which the scroll has been simplified. There are two versions of the keyfacts logo, a low resolution version and a high resolution version.

2.4   Copyright subsists in the FSA logo.

2.5   Copies of the FSA logo that are capable of being reproduced for printing can be found on the *FCA's* website at www.fca.org.uk

Permission to use the FSA logo

3.1   A *UK domestic firm*, its *appointed representatives* and *tied agents*, an *authorised payment institution* and its *agents* and an *authorised electronic money institution* and its *agents* are permitted to use the FSA logo:

     (1)   as part of a statement by that *person*, in a letter or electronic equivalent, that it or, in relation to an *appointed representative*, *agent* or *tied agent*, its principal, is authorised and regulated by the *FSA*; or

     (2)   if required to do so by the *FCA*.

3.1A   [deleted]

3.2   The disclosure required by **GEN 4.3.1 R** (Disclosure in letters to *retail clients*) as continued in **GEN TP 1**.3(3).13 is an example of a statement within paragraph 3.1 above.

3.3   Business cards, compliment slips, text messages, account statements and other similar documents are not letters (or electronic equivalents). Therefore, the licence does not extend to documents such as these.

Permission to use the keyfacts logo

3A.1   A *firm*, its *appointed representatives* and *tied agents* are permitted to use the keyfacts logo as and when it is required or permitted to be used by the *rules*.

3A.2   The following are examples of places where the *rules* require or permit the keyfacts logo to be used:

     (1)   In *COBS*, in a *services and costs disclosure document* or *combined initial disclosure document* (**COBS 6.3**)

(2)   In *ICOBS*:

  (a)   in an *initial disclosure document* or *combined initial disclosure document*;

  (b)   in a *policy summary*; and

  (c)   in a *key features* as an alternative to a *policy summary*.

(3)   In *MCOB*

  (a)   in an *initial disclosure document* or *combined initial disclosure document*;

  (b)   in an *illustration* (**MCOB 5.6.2 R** and **MCOB 9.4.2 R**); and

  (c)   in a risks and features statement (**MCOB 4.10.11 R**) and financial information statement (**MCOB 5.8.7 R**).

Conditions on appearance of the FSA logo

4.1   The permission in paragraph 3.1 is subject to the following conditions:

  (1)   the regulatory mark is attached to the FSA logo;

  (2)   the FSA logo and regulatory mark appear in black type, or reversed out white on a coloured background;

  (3)   the FSA letters appear in type which is not more than three times the size of the accompanying script;

  (4)   the two elements of the FSA logo appear together in the same way, and in the same proportion, as in the registered service mark;

  (5)   the FSA logo is not redrawn in any way, or matched by a typesetter;

  (6)   version B of the FSA logo is used only at sizes below 10 mm in overall height; and

  (7)   if the FSA logo is reproduced electronically, no hyperlink is incorporated.

Conditions on appearance of the keyfacts logo

4A.1   The permission in paragraph 3A.1 is subject to the following conditions:

  (1)   the regulatory mark (®) is attached to the keyfacts logo;

  (2)   the keyfacts logo and regulatory mark appear:

    (a)   in black type;

    (b)   reversed out white on a coloured background; or

    (c)   in colour provided that this does not diminish their prominence;

  (3)   the two elements of the keyfacts logo appear together in the same way, and in the same proportion, as in the Community trade mark;

  (4)   the keyfacts logo is not redrawn in any way, or matched by a typesetter;

  (5)   the low resolution version of the keyfacts logo is used only in documents intended to be read on a computer, television or other screen; and

  (6)   if the keyfacts logo is reproduced electronically, no hyperlink is incorporated.

Further conditions on the use of the FSA and keyfacts logos

5.1   The permissions in paragraphs 3.1 and 3A.1 are also subject to the conditions that any material, whether produced on paper or electronically, on which the FSA or keyfacts logos are displayed does not:

  (1)   in any way imply that the *FCA* is endorsing the licensee or its products, services or communications (see also **GEN 1.2.2 R (1)**); or

  (2)   misrepresent the licensee's relationship with the *FCA* or present false information about the *FCA*; or

  (3)   contain content that could be construed as distasteful, offensive or controversial; or

  (4)   infringe any intellectual property or other rights of any *person* or otherwise not comply with any relevant law or regulation.

6.1   [deleted]

Commencement and duration

7.1   This licence comes into effect on 1 May 2003 except that in relation to the keyfacts logo it comes into effect on 6 November 2006. In relation to the FSA logo, this licence ceases to have effect and is revoked on 1 April 2014.

7.2   The *FCA* may alter or revoke this licence at any time, by giving at least two months' notice on the *FCA's* website.

Interpretation

8.1   This licence is to be interpreted in accordance with chapter 2 of the General provisions (Interpreting the Handbook) of the *Handbook*. In particular, expressions in italics are defined in the Handbook Glossary.

Governing law and jurisdiction

9.1   This licence is governed by and interpreted in line with English law. The courts of any jurisdiction in the United Kingdom have the exclusive jurisdiction to settle any dispute in connection with this licence.

CHAPTER 6
INSURANCE AGAINST FINANCIAL PENALTIES

6.1   PAYMENT OF FINANCIAL PENALTIES

Application

[3.47]
6.1.1 R   FCA

This chapter applies to every *firm*, but only with respect to business that can be regulated under sections 137A (The FCA's general rules) and 137G (The PRA's general rules) of the *Act*.

6.1.2 G   FCA

For the purposes of **GEN 2.2.17 R** (Activities covered by general rules), the chapter applies to *regulated* and *unregulated activities* carried on in the *United Kingdom* or overseas.

Purpose

6.1.3 G   FCA

The purpose of this section is to ensure that financial penalties are paid by the *person* on whom they are imposed.

Interpretation

6.1.4 R   FCA

In this chapter 'financial penalty' means a financial penalty that the *appropriate regulator* has imposed, or may impose, under the *Act*. It does not include a financial penalty imposed by any other body.

Payment of a penalty imposed on an employee

6.1.4A R   FCA

No *firm*, except a *sole trader*, may pay a financial penalty imposed by the *appropriate regulator* on a present or former *employee*, *director* or *partner* of the *firm* or of an *affiliated company*.

Insurance against financial penalties

6.1.5 R   FCA

No *firm* may enter into, arrange, claim on or make a payment under a *contract of insurance* that is intended to have, or has or would have, the effect of indemnifying any *person* against all or part of a financial penalty

6.1.6 R   FCA

The *Society*, *managing agents* and *members' agents* must not cause or permit any *member*, in the conduct of his *insurance business* at Lloyd's, to enter into, arrange, claim on or make a payment under a *contract of insurance* that is intended to have, or has or would have, the effect of indemnifying any *person* against all or part of a financial penalty.

6.1.7 G   FCA

GEN 6.1.4A R, **GEN 6.1.5 R** and **GEN 6.1.6 R** do not prevent a *firm* or *member* from entering into, arranging, claiming on or making any payment under a *contract of insurance* which indemnifies any *person* against all or part of the costs of defending *appropriate regulator* enforcement action or any costs they may be ordered to pay to the *appropriate regulator*.

TRANSITIONAL PROVISIONS AND SCHEDULES

1   TRANSITIONAL PROVISIONS

[3.48]
T P

(3) Transitional Provisions applying to GEN only

(1)	(2) Material to which the transitional provision applies	(3)	(4) Transitional provision	(5) Transitional provision: dates in force	(6) Handbook provision: coming into force
1	**GEN 2.2.7 R**	**R**	Expired		
2	**GEN 4.3.1 R**	**R**	Expired		
3	**GEN 4.3.1 R**	**R**	Expired		
4	**GEN 4.4.1 R**	**R**	Expired		
5	**GEN 6.1**	**R**	**GEN 6.1** does not: **(1) apply to an unamended** *contract of insurance*, **first entered into on or before 24 July 2003; or** **(2) prohibit a** *firm* **from claiming on, or making a payment under, a** *contract of insurance*: **(a) in connection with a financial penalty imposed by the** *FSA* **pursuant to a** *warning notice* **issued before 25 July 2003; or** **(b) first entered into between 25 July 2003 and 31 December 2003 in respect of a financial penalty imposed by the** *FSA* **by a** *final notice* **issued on or before 31 December 2003.** **(For these purposes only, a** *contract of insurance* **will be regarded as unamended if:** **(i) it was amended on or before 24 July 2003; or** **(ii) it was amended after 24 July 2003, but the amendments did not affect the duration or scope of any indemnity against a financial penalty imposed by the** *FSA* **under the** *Act***.)**	From 1 January 2004	1 January 2004
6	**GEN 4.3.1 R**	**R**	Expired		
7	**GEN 4.3.1 R**	**G**	Expired		
9	**GEN 5 ANNEX 1 G**	**G**	[expired]		
10	**GEN 4.3.1 R**	**R**	[expired]		
11	**GEN 4.5**	**R**	[expired]		
12	**GEN 4 ANNEX 1**	**R**	[expired]		
13	**GEN 4.3.1 R, GEN 4 ANNEX 1 and GEN 4 ANNEX 1A**	**R**	[expired]		
14	**GEN 4.5.3 R and GEN 4.5.4 R**	**R**	[expired]		

GEN TP 1.3 (4) Transitional Provisions applying to GEN only

The references to "GEN 6.1" in the table above must be read as "GEN 6.1 and General Provisions 7 in the *PRA* Rulebook".

TRANSITIONAL PROVISIONS APPLYING ACROSS THE FCA AND PRA HANDBOOKS

Table: 1 Transitional Provisions applying across the FCA and PRA Handbooks

(1)	The purpose of these transitional provisions is to assist a smooth transition at cutover. They comprise various technical provisions that will apply across the whole *FCA* and *PRA Handbooks* and achieve results that most people would probably expect to apply in any event.
(2)	These transitional provisions consist of general transitional provisions, which apply at a high level of generality, and more specific transitional provisions in relation to record keeping and notification rules.
(3)	The more specific transitional provisions relating to record keeping and notification rules override the general transitional provisions. Both the general and the more specific transitional provisions do not apply if the context requires otherwise and are subject to any more specific transitional provision elsewhere in the FCA and PRA Handbooks relating to the matter.
(4)	Definitions for these transitional provisions, additional to those in the *Glossary*, are provided at paragraph 15 of the table.

Table 2: Transitional Provisions applying across the FCA and PRA Handbooks

(1)	(2) Material to which the transitional provision applies	(3)	(4) Transitional provision	(5) Transitional provision: dates in force	(6) Handbook provision: coming into force
1	Every provision in the *FCA* and *PRA Handbooks*, unless the context otherwise requires and subject to any more specific transitional provision relating to the matter	R	**Acts under pre-cutover provisions** Anything done, or having effect as done, under or for the purposes of any pre-cutover provision has effect as if done under or for the purposes of any substantially similar provision in the *FCA* and *PRA Handbooks*.	From cutover	Cutover
2	Paragraph 1	G	For example, a *firm* may rely on action to establish the best price, taken shortly before cutover for the purposes of the *FSA's* best execution rule, for the purposes of compliance with the *FCA's* best execution rule, even if the transaction is *executed* after cutover.	From cutover	Cutover
3	Every provision in the *FCA* and *PRA Handbooks*, unless the context otherwise requires and subject to any more specific transitional provision relating to the matter	R	**Series of events** If the application of any provision in the *FCA* or *PRA Handbooks* is dependent on the occurrence of a series of events, some of which occur before, and some of which occur after, cutover, the provision applies with respect to the events that occur after cutover.	From cutover	Cutover
4	Paragraph 3	G	For example, a *firm* which *executes* an aggregated order shortly before cutover must comply with **COBS 11.3.8 R** (Requirement for fair allocation) if the allocation occurs after cutover.	From cutover	Cutover

(1)	(2) Material to which the transitional provision applies	(3)	(4) Transitional provision	(5) Transitional provision: dates in force	(6) Handbook provision: coming into force
5	Every provision in the *FCA* and *PRA Handbooks*, unless the context otherwise requires and subject to any more specific transitional provision relating to the matter	R	**Deemed references to pre-cutover provisions** Any reference (express or implied) in a provision in the *FCA* or *PRA Handbooks* to a provision of or made under the *Act* is to be read (so far as the context permits and according to the context) as being or including, in relation to times, circumstances and purposes before cutover, a reference to any substantially similar pre-cutover provision.	From cutover	Cutover
6	Paragraph 5	G	For example, **SUP 11.6.4 R** requires a *firm* authorised by the *FCA* to notify the *FCA* when a change in *control*, previously notified under **SUP 11.4.2 R**, has taken place. Such a *firm* must notify a change in *control* that takes place after cutover, even if previously notified under **SUP 11.4.2 R** as made by the *FSA* (and **SUP 11.6.4 R** is to be read as referring to that pre-cutover provision).	From cutover	Cutover
7	Every provision in the *FCA* and *PRA Handbooks*, unless the context otherwise requires and subject to any more specific transitional provision relating to the matter	R	**Time starting before cutover** If, at cutover, time has begun to run for any purpose under any pre-cutover provision applicable to a *firm* or other person, then: (1) time will be regarded as having started to run, for the purposes of any substantially similar provision in the *FCA* or *PRA Handbooks*, when it started to run for that other purpose; and (2) the *firm* or other person will be relieved of its obligation to comply with the relevant pre-cutover provision if and to the extent that it complies with the substantially similar provision as extended by this transitional provision.	From cutover	Cutover
8	Paragraph 7	G	For example, certain *firms* were required to submit product sales data reports within 20 *business days* of the end of the quarter by **SUP 16.11.3 R** as made by the *FSA*. If the quarter end fell five days before cutover, the *firms* must still submit the report within 20 *business days*, but in accordance with **SUP 16.7.8 R** as made by the *FCA*.	From cutover	Cutover

(1)	(2) Material to which the transitional provision applies	(3)	(4) Transitional provision	(5) Transitional provision: dates in force	(6) Handbook provision: coming into force
9	Every *rule* in the *FCA* and *PRA Handbooks* requiring a record to be made or retained (see schedule 1), unless the context otherwise requires and subject to any more specific transitional provision relating to the matter	R	**Record keeping** A *firm* or other person will not contravene a *rule* in the *FCA* or *PRA Handbooks* requiring a record to be made or retained to the extent that the *firm* or other person: (1) made a record of the matter before cutover in accordance with the *rule* or with a substantially similar pre-cutover provision applicable to the *firm* or other person; and (2) retains that record as if the *rule* was in force when the record was made.	From cutover	Cutover
10	Every *rule* in the *FCA* and *PRA Handbooks* requiring a record to be made or retained (see schedule 1), unless the context otherwise requires and subject to any more specific transitional provision relating to the matter	G	This transitional provision makes specific provision, in relation to record keeping, for the matters covered by paragraph 1. It is included for clarity and overrides those general transitional provisions.	From cutover	Cutover
11	Every *rule* in the *FCA* and *PRA Handbooks* requiring a record to be made or retained (see schedule 1), unless the context otherwise requires and subject to any more specific transitional provision relating to the matter	R	A *firm* or other person must retain a record in accordance with a *rule* in the *FCA* or *PRA Handbooks* requiring a record of that sort to be retained, if the *firm* or other person was required to make and retain that record before cutover under a substantially similar pre-cutover provision applicable to the *firm* or other person.	From cutover	Cutover
12	Paragraph 9	G	This transitional provision makes specific provision, in relation to records, for the matters covered by paragraphs 5 and 7. It is included for clarity and overrides those general transitional provisions.	From cutover	Cutover
13	Every notification rule in the *FCA* and *PRA Handbooks* (see schedule 2), unless the context otherwise requires and subject to any more specific transitional provision relating to the matter	R	**Notification** A *firm* (or its auditor, *appointed actuary* or *appropriate actuary*) or other person will not contravene a notification rule in the *FCA* or *PRA Handbooks* to the extent that notice of the relevant matter was given to the *FSA* before cutover in accordance with: (1) the notification rule; or (2) a substantially similar pre-cutover provision applicable to the *firm* or other person.	From cutover	Cutover

Part 3   FCA Handbook Materials

(1)	(2) **Material to which the transitional provision applies**	(3)	(4) **Transitional provision**	(5) **Transitional provision: dates in force**	(6) **Handbook provision: coming into force**
14	Paragraph 13	G	This transitional provision makes specific provision, in relation to notifications, for the matters covered by paragraphs 1 and 3. It is included for clarity and overrides those general transitional provisions.	From cutover	Cutover
15	As paragraphs 1 to 14	R	**Definitions** In these transitional provisions: (1) "pre-cutover provision" means a provision repealed or revoked by, or under, the Financial Services Act 2012 or a rule or guidance of the *FSA*, including (where the context permits) any relevant provision which it replaced before cutover; (2) "substantially similar" means substantially similar in purpose and effect; and (3) a reference to a "provision" in the *FCA* or *PRA Handbooks* means every type of provision, including *rules*, *guidance*, provisions in codes, and so on.	From cutover	Cutover
16	Paragraph 17	G	**Application for provisions which are not rules** The purpose of paragraph 17 is to ensure that the transitional provisions in paragraphs 1 to 8 apply throughout the *FCA* and *PRA Handbooks*.	From cutover	Cutover
17	*Statements of Principle*, the Code of Practice for Approved Persons and Code of Market Conduct and directions and requirements and guidance and other provisions in the *FCA Handbook* and *PRA Handbook* (that is, provisions with the status letter "D" or "G" in the margin or heading) unless the context otherwise requires and subject to any more specific transitional provision relating to the matter	P	The provisions in paragraphs 1 to 10 apply to every *person* to whom the provisions referred to in column (2) apply as if the *rules* in those paragraphs were part of those provisions.	From cutover	Cutover

TRANSITIONAL PROVISION IN RELATION TO THE ALTERNATIVE INVESTMENT
FUND MANAGERS DIRECTIVE INSTRUMENT 2013

FCAH

Table: 1 Transitional Provisions applying across the FCA Handbook

(1)	On 22 July 2013, the Alternative Investment Fund Managers Directive Instrument 2013 came into force. This instrument transposed provisions contained in the AIFMD into *UK* national law through provisions in the *FCA Handbook*.

(2)   The entry into force of the Alternative Investment Fund Managers Directive Instrument 2013 requires a number of further consequential changes to be made to the *FCA Handbook*. These will be made in due course.

(3)   Until that time, all provisions in the *FCA Handbook* must be interpreted in the light of the amendments made to the *FCA Handbook* by the Alternative Investment Fund Managers Directive Instrument 2013, unless the context requires otherwise. This is necessary to comply with the *rule* in **GEN 2.2.1 R**. It should achieve the result that most people would probably expect to apply in any event.

PRAH

Table: 2 Transitional Provision applying across the FCA and PRA Handbooks

(1)	(2) Material to which the transitional provision applies	(3)	(4) Transitional provision	(5) Transitional provision: dates in force	(6) Handbook provision: coming into force
1	Every provision in the *FCA Handbook*, unless the context requires otherwise	R	[expired]		
2	Paragraph 1	G	[expired]		
3	Amendments made to the *FCA Handbook* by the Alternative Investment Fund Managers Directive Instrument 2013	R	References to the "*EEA*" must be read as references to the "*EU*".	From 22 July 2013 until such time as *AIFMD* is annexed to the EEA Agreement in accordance with article 102 of the EEA Agreement	22 July 2013

SCH 1   RECORD KEEPING REQUIREMENTS

1.1 G   FCA PRA

There are no record keeping requirements in *GEN*.

SCH 2   NOTIFICATION REQUIREMENTS

2.1 G   FCA PRA

The aim of the guidance in the following table is to give the reader a quick overall view of the relevant requirements for notification and reporting.

It is not a complete statement of those requirements and should not be relied on as if it were.

2.2 G   FCA PRA

Handbook reference	Matter to be notified	Contents of notification	Trigger event	Time allowed
GEN 1.3.2 R	An emergency which makes it impracticable for a *firm* to comply with a particular *rule*.	Notification of the emergency and of the steps the *firm* is taking and proposes to take to deal with its consequences	An emergency which makes it impracticable for a *firm* to comply with a particular *rule*.	Notification as soon as practicable

SCH 3   FEES AND OTHER REQUIRED PAYMENTS

3.1 G   FCA PRA

There are no requirements for fees or other payments in *GEN*. **FEES 2** (General Provisions) contains general provisions relating to the payment of fees.

SCH 4   POWERS EXERCISED

4.1 G   FCA

In this Schedule, references to *GEN* include the *Glossary*.

4.2 G   FCA

Powers to make rules

The following powers and related provisions in or under the *Act* have been exercised by the *FCA* to make the rules in *GEN*:

Section 59 (Approval for particular arrangements)

Section 73A (Part 6 Rules)

Section 74 (The official list)

Section 75 (Applications for listing)

Section 77 (Discontinuance and suspension of listing)

Section 79 (Listing particulars and other documents)

Section 80 (General duty of disclosure in listing particulars)

Section 81 (Supplementary listing particulars)

Section 84 (Matters which may be dealt with by prospectus rules)

Section 85 (Prohibition of dealing etc in transferable securities without approved prospectus)

Section 87 (Election to have prospectus)

Section 87A (Criteria for approval of prospectus by competent authority)

Section 87B (Exemptions from disclosure)

Section 87G (Supplementary prospectus)

Section 88 (Sponsors)

Section 89A (Transparency rules)

Section 89B (Provision of voteholder information)

Section 89C (Provision of information by issuers of transferable securities)

Section 89D (Notification of voting rights held by issuer)

Section 89E (Notification of proposed amendment of issuer's constitution)

Section 89F (Transparency rules: interpretation etc)

Section 89G (Transparency rules: other supplementary provisions)

Section 89O (Corporate governance rules)

Section 89P (Primary information providers)

Section 96 (Obligations of issuers of listed securities)

Section 96A (Disclosure of information requirements)

Section 96C (Suspension of trading)

Section 101(2) (Part 6 Rules: general provisions)

Section 118(8) (Market abuse)

Section 136(2) (Funding of the legal assistance scheme)

Section 137A (The FCA's general rules)

Section 137B (FCA general rules: clients' money, right to rescind etc)

Section 137C (FCA general rules: cost of credit and duration of credit agreements)

Section 137D (FCA general rules: product intervention)

Section 137F (Rules requiring participation in benchmark)

Section 137H (General rules about remuneration)

Section 137O (Threshold condition code)

Section 137P (Control of information rules)

Section 137Q (Price stabilising rules)

Section 137R (Financial promotion rules)

Section 137T (General supplementary powers)

Section 138C (Evidential provisions)

Section 138D (Actions for damages)

Section 138M (Temporary product intervention rules)

Section 192J (Rules requiring provision of information by parent undertakings)

Section 213 (The compensation scheme) (including as referred to in section 216(5) (Continuity of long-term insurance policies) and section 217(7) (Insurers in financial difficulties)

Section 214 (General)

Section 214A (Contingency funding)

Section 214D(13) (Contributions under section 214B: supplementary)

Section 215 (Rights of the scheme in insolvency)

Section 216 (Continuity of long-term insurance policies)

Section 217 (Insurers in financial difficulties)

Section 218(2)(b) (Annual report)

Section 218A (Regulators' power to require information)

Section 223 (Management expenses)

Section 223C (Payments in error)

Section 224F (Rules about relevant schemes)

Section 226 (Compulsory jurisdiction) (including as applied by regulation 125 of the *Payment Services Regulations*)

Section 229 (Awards)

Section 234 (Industry funding)

Section 238 (Restrictions on promotion)

Section 239 (Single property schemes)

Section 242 (Applications for authorisation of unit trust schemes)

Section 247 (Trust scheme rules)

Section 248 (Scheme particulars rules)

Section 261C (Applications for authorisation of contractual schemes)

Section 261I (Contractual scheme rules)

Section 261J (Contractual scheme particulars rules)

Section 278 (Rules etc as to scheme particulars)

Section 283(1) (Facilities and information in UK)

Section 286(4F) (Qualification of recognition)

Section 293 (Notification requirements)

Section 295 (Notification: overseas investment exchanges and overseas clearing houses)

Section 300B (Duty to notify proposal to make regulatory provision)

Section 332(1) (Rules in relation to persons to whom the general prohibition does not apply)

Section 340 (Appointment)

Part 3 (Penalties and Fees) of Schedule 1ZA (The Financial Conduct Authority)

Paragraph 12 (Funding of the relevant costs by authorised persons or payment service providers) of Part 2 (Funding) of Schedule 1A (Further provision about the Consumer Financial Education Body)

Paragraphs 19 (Establishment), 20 (Services) and 20C (Notice of intention to market an AIF) of Schedule 3 (EEA Passport Rights)

Paragraphs 7(3) (Annual reports), 13 (FCA's procedural rules), 16B (Procedure for complaints etc) and 16D (Enforcement of money awards) of Schedule 17 (The Ombudsman Scheme)

Article 60E(3) of the *Regulated Activities Order*

Regulation 6 (FCA rules) of the *OEIC Regulations*

Article 15 (Record-keeping and reporting requirements relating to relevant complaints) of the *Ombudsman Transitional Order*

Articles 4 (Pending applications), 6 (Post-commencement applications), 9 (Article 9 defaults occurring before commencement), 9A (Contributions in relation to mesothelioma claims), 10 (Applications in respect of compulsory liability insurance), 12 (Applications under the new scheme) and 23 (Record-keeping and reporting requirements relating to pre-commencement) of the compensation transitionals order

Regulation 3 (Consumer contract requirements: modification of rule-making powers) of the Electronic Commerce Directive (Financial Services and Markets) Regulations 2002 (SI 2002/1775)

Regulation 2 (Power of the Authority to make rules under section 138 of the Financial Services and Markets Act 2000) of the Financial Services and Markets Act 2000 (Fourth Motor Insurance Directive) Regulations 2002 (SI 2002/2706)

Article 9 (Record-keeping and reporting requirements relating to relevant transitional complaints) of the *Mortgage and General Insurance Complaints Transitional Order*

4.3 G   FCA

The following additional powers have been exercised by the *FCA* to make the *rules* in *GEN*:

Regulation 2(3) (Application for permission) of the Capital Requirements Regulations 2006 (SI 2006/3221)

Regulations 82 (Reporting requirements), 86 (Proposal to take disciplinary measures) and 92 (Costs of supervision) of and paragraph 1 of Schedule 5 (Disciplinary powers) to the *Payment Services Regulations*

Regulations 49 (Reporting requirements) and 59 (Costs of supervision) of the *Electronic Money Regulations*

Regulations 8 (Applications for registration), 9 (Applications for admission to the register of issuers), 18 (Notification requirements), 20 (Material changes to the regulated covered bond), 24 (Requirements relating to the asset pool), 25 (Change of owner), 36 (financial penalties policy statement), 46 (Modifications of primary and secondary legislation) of, and paragraph 5 (fees) to the Schedule (Modifications to primary and secondary legislation) to, the RCB Regulations

4.4 G   FCA

Powers to make codes

The following powers and related provisions in the *Act* have been exercised by the *FCA* to issue the parts of the codes in *GEN*:

Section 64(2) (Conduct: statements and codes)

Section 119 (The code)

Section 120 (Provisions included in the Authority's code by reference to the City Code)

Section 121 (Codes: procedure)

4.5 G   FCA

Powers to issue statements

The following powers and related provisions in the *Act* have been exercised by the *FCA* to issue the parts of the statements in *GEN*:

Section 63C(1) (Statement of policy)

Section 64 (Conduct: statements and codes)

Section 69 (Statement of policy) (including as applied by paragraph 1 of Schedule 5 to the *Payment Services Regulations*, paragraph 1 of Schedule 3 to the *Electronic Money Regulations*, regulation 29(1) of the Legal Aid, Sentencing and Punishment of Offender Act 2012 (Referral Fees) Regulations 2013 (SI 2013/1635) and regulation 28(1) of the *Immigration Regulations*

Section 88C (Action under section 88A: statement of policy)

Section 89S (Action under section 89Q: statement of policy)

Section 93 (Statement of policy)

Section 124 (Statement of policy)

Section 131J(1) (Statement of policy)

Section 138N (Temporary product intervention rules: statement of policy)

Section 169(9) (Investigations etc in support of overseas regulator) (including as applied by paragraph 3 of Schedule 5 to the *Payment Services Regulations* and paragraph 3 of Schedule 3 to the *Electronic Money Regulations* and by regulation 71(2) of the *AIFMD UK regulation*

Section 192H (Statement of policy: directions under section 192C)

Section 192N (Imposition of penalties under section 192K: statement of policy)

Section 210 (Statements of policy) (including as applied by regulation 86(6) of the *Payment Services Regulations*, regulation 53 (6) of the *Electronic Money Regulations*, regulation 71(3) of the *AIFMD UK regulation*, regulation 29(2) of the Legal Aid, Sentencing and Punishment of Offenders Act 2012 (Referral Fees) Regulations 2013 (SI 2013/1635) and regulation 28(2) of the *Immigration Regulations*

Section 312J (Statement of policy under section 312F)

Section 395 (The FCA's and PRA's procedures) (including as applied by paragraph 7 of Schedule 5 to the *Payment Services Regulations*, paragraph 8 of Schedule 3 to the *Electronic Money Regulations*, regulation 30(7) of the Legal Aid, Sentencing and Punishment of Offenders Act 2012 (Referral Fees) Regulations 2013 (SI 2013/1635), article 3(11) of the Financial Act 2012 (Consumer Credit) Order 2013 and regulation 29 of the *Immigration Regulations*

Section 404(3) (Consumer redress schemes)

Section 404A (Rules under s 404: supplementary)

4.6 G   FCA

The following additional powers and related provisions have been exercised by the *FCA* to issue the parts of the statements in *GEN*:

Regulation 42 (Guidance) of the RCB Regulations

Regulation 44 (Warning notices and decision notices) of the *RCB Regulations*

Regulation 93 (Guidance) of the *Payment Services Regulations*

Regulation 14 (Guidance) of the *Cross-Border Payments in Euro Regulations*

Regulation 60 (Guidance) of the *Electronic Money Regulations*

Section 80 (Statement of policy under sections 73 to 79) of the Financial Services Act 2012

Regulations 70 (Application of procedural provisions of the Act) and 71 (Application of provisions of the Act to unauthorised AIFMs) of the *AIFMD UK regulation*

Article 4 (Statements of policy) of the Financial Services Act 2012 (Consumer Credit) Order 2013

Regulations 28 (Statements of policy) and 29 (Application of Part 26 of the 2000 Act) of the *Immigration Regulations*

4.7 G   FCA

Powers to direct, require or specify

The following powers and related provisions in the *Act* have been exercised by the *FCA* in *GEN* to direct, require or specify:

Section 55U (Applications under this Part)

Section 60 (Applications for approval)

Section 137S (Financial promotion rules: directions given by FCA)

Section 138A (Modification or waiver of rules)

Section 179 (Requirements for section 178 notices)

Section 218A (Authority's power to require information)

Section 242 (Applications for authorisation of unit trust schemes)

Section 250 (Modification or waiver of rules)

Section 274 (Applications for recognition of individual schemes)

Section 279 (Revocation of recognition)

Section 287 (Application by an investment exchange)

Section 293A (Information: compliance with EU requirements)

Section 294 (Modification or waiver of rules)

Section 316 (Direction by Authority)

Section 317 (The core provisions)

Section 318 (Exercise of powers through Council)

Paragraph 5(4) (Notice to UK Regulator) of Schedule 4 (Treaty Rights)

Regulations 7(3) and (4) (Modification or waiver of FCA rules) and 12 (Application for authorisation) of the *OEIC Regulations*

4.8 G   FCA

The following additional powers and related provisions have been exercised by the *FCA* in *GEN* to direct, require or specify:

> Regulation 49 (Reporting requirements) of the *Electronic Money Regulations*
>
> Regulations 21 (Disclosure obligations of small registered UK AIFMs), 54 (FCA approval for marketing), 58 (Marketing of AIFs managed by small third country AIFMs) and 60 (Manner and content of notifications) of the *AIFMD UK regulation*
>
> Regulation 9(1) of the *Immigration Regulations*

4.9 G   FCA

Power to make the complaints scheme

The following power has been exercised by the *FCA* to make the complaints scheme in *GEN*:

> Part 6 of the Financial Services Act 2012

4.10 G   FCA

Powers to give guidance

The following powers in or under the *Act* have been exercised by the *FCA* to give the guidance in *GEN*:

> Section 139A (Power of the FCA to give guidance)
>
> Section 234G (Guidance)

4.11 G   FCA

The following additional powers have been exercised by the *FCA* to give the other *guidance* in *GEN*:

> Article 14 (Guidance on continued provisions) of the Financial Services and Markets Act 2000 (Consequential Amendments and Transitional Provisions) (Credit Unions) Order 2002 (SI 2002/1501)
>
> Articles 9D (Applications for certificates), 9F (Revocation of certificate on request), 9G (Obtaining information from certified persons etc) and 9H (Rules prohibiting the issue of electronic money at a discount) of the *Regulated Activities Order*
>
> Regulation 93 (Guidance) of the *Payment Services Regulations*
>
> Section 123 of the Banking Act 2009
>
> Regulation 14 (Guidance) of the *Cross-Border Payments in Euro Regulations*
>
> Regulation 60 (Guidance) of the *Electronic Money Regulations*
>
> Regulation 42 of the *RCB Regulations*
>
> Regulation 15 of the Payments in Euro (Credit Transfers and Direct Debits) Regulations 2012 (SI 2012/3122)
>
> Regulation 5 (Guidance) of the Legal Aid, Sentencing and Punishment of Offenders Act 2012

4.12 G   FCA

Powers exercised by the FOS Ltd

GEN 2.1.8 R is made by *FOS Ltd* in exercise of its powers referred to in Schedule 4 to *DISP*.

SCH 5   RIGHTS OF ACTION FOR DAMAGES

5.1 G   FCA

The table below sets out the *rules* in *GEN* contravention of which by an *authorised person* may be actionable under section 138D of the *Act* (Actions for damages) by a person who suffers loss as a result of the contravention.

5.2 G   FCA

If a 'Yes' appears in the column headed 'For *private person*?', the *rule* may be actionable by a 'private person' under section 138D (or, in certain circumstances, his fiduciary or representative; see article 6(2) and (3)(c) of the Financial Services and Markets Act 2000 (Rights of Action) Regulations 2001 (SI 2001/2256)). A 'Yes' in the column headed 'Removed' indicates that the *FCA* has removed the right of action under section 138D(3) of the *Act*. If so, a reference to the *rule* in which it is removed is also given.

5.3 G FCA

> The column headed 'For other person?' indicates whether the *rule* may be actionable by a person other than a *private person* (or his fiduciary or representative) under article 6(2) and (3) of those Regulations. If so, an indication of the type of *person* by whom the *rule* may be actionable is given.

5.4 G FCA

Chapter/ Appendix	Section/ Annex	Paragraph	Right of action under section 138D		
			For private person?	Removed	For other person?
All *rules* in *GEN* with the status letter "E"			No	No	No
GEN 2.1.8 R			No	No	No
All other rules in *GEN*			Yes	No	No

SCH 6   RULES THAT CAN BE WAIVED

6.1 G

> [deleted]

6.1A G FCA

> As a result of section 138A of the *Act* (Modification or waiver of rules) the *FCA* has power to waive all its *rules*, other than *rules* made under section 137O (Threshold condition code), section 247 (Trust scheme rules), section 248 (Scheme particular rules), section 261I (Contractual scheme rules) or section 261J (Contractual scheme particulars rules) of the *Act*. However, if the *rules* incorporate requirements laid down in European directives, it will not be possible for the *FCA* to grant a waiver that would be incompatible with the *United Kingdom's* responsibilities under those directives.

6.1B G PRA

> As a result of section 138A of the *Act* (Modification or waiver of rules) the *PRA* has power to waive all its *rules*, other than *rules* made under section 137O (Threshold condition code). However, if the *rules* incorporate requirements laid down in European directives, it will not be possible for the *PRA* to grant a waiver that would be incompatible with the *United Kingdom's* responsibilities under those directives.

6.2 G FCA PRA

> 1   GEN 2.1.8 R is made by FOS Ltd and not by the *appropriate regulator* and cannot be waived by the *appropriate regulator*.
>
> 2   Every other rule in *GEN* can be waived by the *appropriate regulator* if, and to the extent that, the rules elsewhere in its *Handbook* which it modifies or to which it otherwise relates can be waived by the *appropriate regulator*.

H. CONDUCT OF BUSINESS SOURCEBOOK (COBS)

CONDUCT OF BUSINESS SOURCEBOOK
the conduct of business requirements applying to firms with effect from 1 November 2007

CHAPTER 1
APPLICATION

1.1 THE GENERAL APPLICATION RULE

[3.49]
[**Note:** ESMA has issued guidelines under article 16(3) of the ESMA Regulation on certain aspects of the MiFID suitability requirements which also includes guidelines on conduct of business obligations.
See www.esma.europa.eu/content/Guidelines-certain-aspects-MiFID-suitability-requirements.]

1.1.1 R   FCA   PRA

This sourcebook applies to a *firm* with respect to the following activities carried on from an establishment maintained by it, or its *appointed representative*, in the *United Kingdom*:
(1)   [deleted]
(2)   *designated investment business*;
(3)   *long-term insurance business* in relation to *life policies*;

and activities connected with them.

1.1.1A R   FCA

This sourcebook does not apply to a *firm* with respect to the activity of *accepting deposits* carried on from an establishment maintained by it, or its *appointed representative*, in the *United Kingdom*, except for **COBS 4.6** (Past, simulated past and future performance), **COBS 4.7.1 R** (Direct offer financial promotions), **COBS 4.10** (Systems and controls and approving and communicating financial promotions), **COBS 13** (Preparing product information) and **COBS 14** (Providing product information to clients) which apply as set out in those provisions, **COBS 4.1** and the Banking: Conduct of Business sourcebook (*BCOBS*).

1.1.1B R   FCA

COBS 4.4.3 R, **COBS 5** (Distance communications), **COBS 15.2** (The right to cancel), **COBS 15.3** (Exercising a right to cancel), **COBS 15.4** (Effects of cancellation) and **COBS 15 ANNEX 1** (Exemptions from the right to cancel) apply to a *firm* with respect to the activity of *issuing electronic money* as set out in those provisions.

1.1.1C R   FCA

The following *rules* in *COBS* apply to a *firm* in relation to its carrying on of *auction regulation bidding*:
(1)   **COBS 5** (Distance communications);
(2)   (for a *firm* that has exercised an opt-in to *CASS* in accordance with **CASS 1.4.9 R** in relation only to those *clients* for which it holds *client money* or *safe custody assets* in accordance with *CASS*) **COBS 3** (Client categorisation), **COBS 6.1.7 R** (Information concerning safeguarding of designated investments belonging to clients and client money), **COBS 6.1.11 R** (Timing of disclosure) and **COBS 16.4** (Statements of client designated investments or client money).

Modifications to the general application rule

1.1.2 R   FCA PRA

The *general application rule* is modified in **COBS 1 ANNEX 1** according to the activities of a *firm* (Part 1) and its location (Part 2).

1.1.3 R   FCA PRA

The general *rule* is also modified in the chapters to this sourcebook for particular purposes, including those relating to the type of *firm*, its activities or location, and for purposes relating to connected activities.

Guidance

1.1.4 G   FCA PRA

Guidance on the application provisions is in **COBS 1 ANNEX 1** (Part 3).

1 ANNEX 1   APPLICATION (SEE COBS 1.1.2R)

Part 1: What?
Modifications to the general application rule according to activities

1.	**Eligible counterparty business**	
1.1 [FCA]	R	The *COBS* provisions shown below do not apply to *eligible counterparty business*.

COBS provision	Description
COBS 2 (other than **COBS 2.4**)	Conduct of business obligations
COBS 4 (other than **COBS 4.4.1 R** and **COBS 4.4.2 G**)	Communicating with clients including financial promotions
COBS 6.1	Information about the firm, its services and remuneration
COBS 8	Client agreements
COBS 10	Appropriateness (for non-advised services)
COBS 11.2, **COBS 11.3** and **COBS 11.6**	Best execution, client order handling and use of dealing commission
COBS 12.3.1 R to **COBS 12.3.3 R**	Labelling of non-independent research
COBS 14.3	Information about designated investments
COBS 16	Reporting information to clients

[**Note:** article 24(1) of *MiFID*]

2.	**Transactions between an MTF operator and its users**	
2.1 [FCA]	R	The *COBS* provisions in paragraph 1.1R and **COBS 11.4** (Client limit orders) do not apply to a transaction between an operator of an *MTF* and a member or participant in relation to the use of the *MTF*.

[**Note:** article 14(3) of *MiFID*]

3.	**Transactions concluded on an MTF**	
3.1 [FCA]	R	The *COBS* provisions in paragraph 1.1R and **COBS 11.4** (client limit orders) do not apply to transactions concluded under the rules governing an *MTF* between members or participants of the *MTF*. However, the member or participant must comply with those provisions in respect of its *clients* if, acting on its *clients* behalf, it is executing their orders on an *MTF*.

[**Note:** article 14(3) of *MiFID*]

4.	**Transactions concluded on a regulated market**	
4.1 [FCA]	R	In relation to transactions concluded on a *regulated market*, members and participants of the *regulated market* are not required to apply to each other the *COBS* provisions in paragraph 1.1R and **COBS 11.4** (client limit orders). However, the member or participant must comply with those provisions in respect of its *clients* if, acting on its *clients* behalf, it is executing their orders on a *regulated market*.

[**Note:** article 42(4) of *MiFID*]

5.	**Consumer credit products**	
5.1 [FCA]	R	If a *firm*, in relation to its *MiFID business*, offers an *investment service* as part of a financial product that is subject to other provisions of *EU* legislation or common European standards related to *credit institutions* and consumer credits with respect to risk assessments of clients and/or information requirements, that service is not subject to the *rules* in this sourcebook that implement Article 19 of *MiFID*.

[**Note:** article 19(9) of *MiFID*]

5.2 [FCA]	G	This exclusion for consumer credit products is intended to apply on a narrow basis in relation to cases in which the *investment service* is a part of another financial product. It does not apply where the *investment service* is the essential or leading part of the financial product. It also does not apply where the service provided is a combination of an *investment service* and an *ancillary service* (for example, granting a credit for the execution of an order where the credit is instrumental to the buying or the selling of a *financial instrument*.) The exclusion also does not apply in relation to the sale of a *financial instrument* for the purpose of enabling a *client* to invest money to repay his obligations under a loan, mortgage or home reversion.

6		**Use of third party processors in life insurance mediation activities**	
6.1 [FCA]	R	If a *firm* (or its *appointed representative* or, where applicable, its *tied agent*) outsources *insurance mediation activities* to a *third party processor*:	
		(1)	the *firm* must accept responsibility for the acts and omissions of that *third party processor* conducting those out-sourced activities; and
		(2)	any *COBS rule* requiring the *third party processor's* identity to be disclosed to *clients* must be applied as a requirement to disclose the *firm's* identity;
		unless the *third party processor* is *advising on investments*.	
7		**Modified meaning of regulated activities for UK AIFMs and UK UCITS management companies**	
7.1 [FCA]	R	In determining whether a provision in *COBS* applies to a UK AIFM or a *UK UCITS management company*, an activity carried on by the *firm* which would be a *regulated activity* but for article 72AA (Managers of UCITS and AIFs) of the *Regulated Activities Order*, must be treated as a *regulated activity* carried on by the *firm*.	

Part 2: Where?
Modifications to the general application rule according to location

1.			**EEA territorial scope rule: compatibility with European law**	
1.1 [FCA] [PRA]	R	(1)	The territorial scope of this sourcebook is modified to the extent necessary to be compatible with European law (see Part 3 for *guidance* on this).	
		(2)	This *rule* overrides every other *rule* in this sourcebook.	
1.2 [FCA] [PRA]	R		In addition to the *EEA territorial scope rule*, the effect of the *Electronic Commerce Directive* on territorial scope is applied in the fields covered by the 'derogations' in the Annex to that Directive other than the 'insurance derogation' in the fourth indent (see paragraph 7.3 of Part 3 for *guidance* on this).	
			[**Note:** article 3(3) of, and Annex to, the *Electronic Commerce Directive*]	
2.			**Business with UK clients from overseas establishments**	
2.1 [FCA] [PRA]	R	(1)	This sourcebook applies to a *firm* which carries on business with a *client* in the *United Kingdom* from an establishment overseas.	
		(2)	But the sourcebook does not apply to those activities if the office from which the activity is carried on were a separate *person* and the activity:	
			(a)	would fall within the overseas *persons* exclusions in article 72 of the *Regulated Activities Order*; or
			(b)	would not be regarded as carried on in the *United Kingdom*.
2.2 [FCA] [PRA]	G		One of the effects of the *EEA territorial scope rule* is to override the application of this sourcebook to the overseas establishments of *EEA firms* in a number of cases, including circumstances covered by *MiFID*, the *Distance Marketing Directive* or the *Electronic Commerce Directive*. See Part 3 for *guidance* on this.	

Part 3: Guidance

1.		**The main extensions and restrictions to the general application rule**
1.1 [FCA] [PRA]	G	The *general application rule* is modified in Parts 1 and 2 of Annex 1 and in certain chapters of the *Handbook*. The modification may be an extension of this *rule*. For example, **COBS 4** (Communicating with clients, including financial promotions) has extended the application of the rule.

| 1.2
[FCA]
[PRA] | G | The provisions of the *Single Market Directives* and other directives also extensively modify the *general application rule*, particularly in relation to territorial scope. However, for the majority of circumstances, the *general application rule* is likely to apply. |

2.   The Single Market Directives and other directives

| 2.1
[FCA]
[PRA] | G | This *guidance* provides a general overview only and is not comprehensive. |

| 2.2
[FCA]
[PRA] | G | When considering the impact of a directive on the territorial application of a *rule*, a *firm* will first need to consider whether the relevant situation involves a non-*UK* element. The *EEA territorial scope rule* is unlikely to apply if a *UK firm* is doing business in a *UK establishment* for a *client* located in the *United Kingdom* in relation to a *United Kingdom* product. However, if there is a non-*UK* element, the *firm* should consider whether: |

> (1)   it is subject to the directive (in general, directives only apply to *UK firms* and *EEA firms*, but the implementing provisions may not treat non-*EEA firms* more favourably than *EEA firms*);
>
> (2)   the business it is performing is subject to the directive; and
>
> (3)   the particular *rule* is within the scope of the directive.
>
> If the answer to all three questions is 'yes', the *EEA territorial scope rule* may change the effect of the *general application rule*.

| 2.3
[FCA]
[PRA] | G | When considering a particular situation, a *firm* should also consider whether two or more directives apply. |

3.   MiFID: effect on territorial scope

| 3.1
[FCA] | G | **PERG 13** contains general *guidance* on the *persons* and businesses to which *MiFID* applies. |

| 3.2
[FCA] | G | This *guidance* concerns the *rules* within the scope of *MiFID* including those *rules* which are in the same subject area as the implementing *rules*. A *rule* is within the scope of *MiFID* if it is followed by a 'Note:' indicating the article of *MiFID* or the *MiFID implementing Directive* which it implements. |

| 3.3
[FCA] | G | For a *UK MiFID investment firm*, *rules* in this sourcebook that are within the scope of *MiFID* generally apply to its *MiFID business* carried on from an establishment in the *United Kingdom*. They also generally apply to its *MiFID business* carried on from an establishment in another *EEA State*, but only where that business is not carried on within the territory of that State. (See articles 31(1) and 32(1) and (7) of *MiFID*) |

| 3.4
[FCA] | G | For an *EEA MiFID investment firm*, *rules* in this sourcebook that are within the scope of *MiFID* generally apply only to its *MiFID business* if that business is carried on from an establishment in, and within the territory of, the *United Kingdom*. (See article 32(1) and (7) of *MiFID*) |

| 3.5
[FCA] | G | However, the *rules* on *investment research* and *non-independent research* (**COBS 12.2** and **12.3**) and the *rules* on *personal transactions* (**COBS 11.7**) apply on a "home state" basis. This means that they apply to the establishments of a *UK MiFID investment firm* in the *United Kingdom* and another *EEA State* and do not apply to an *EEA MiFID investment firm*. |

4.   Insurance Mediation Directive: effect on territorial scope

| 4.1
[FCA] | G | The *Insurance Mediation Directive's* scope covers most *firms* carrying on most types of *insurance mediation*. The *rules* in this sourcebook within the Directive's scope are those relating to *life policies* that require the provision of pre-contract information or the provision of advice on the basis of a fair analysis. The *rules* implementing the minimum information and other requirements in articles 12 and 13 of the Directive are set out in **COBS 7** (Insurance mediation) and **COBS 9** (Suitability (including basic advice)). |

| 4.2
[FCA] | G | In the *FCA's* view, the responsibility for these minimum requirements rests with the *Home State*, but a *Host State* is entitled to impose additional requirements within the Directive's scope in the 'general good'. Accordingly, the general rules on territorial scope are modified so that: |

> (1)   for a *UK firm* providing *passported activities* through a *branch* in another *EEA State* under the Directive, the *rules* implementing the Directive's minimum requirements apply but the territorial scope of the additional *rules* within the Directive's scope is not modified;

    (2)   for an *EEA firm* providing *passported activities* under the Directive in the *United Kingdom*, the *rules* implementing the Directive's minimum requirements do not apply, but the additional *rules* within the Directive's scope have their unmodified territorial scope unless the *Home State* imposes measures of like effect. (See recital 19 and article 12(5) of the *Insurance Mediation Directive*)

5.   Consolidated Life Directive: effect on territorial scope

5.1   G
[FCA]
The *Consolidated Life Directive's* scope covers *long-term insurers* authorised under that Directive conducting *long-term insurance business*. The *rules* in this sourcebook within the Directive's scope are the cancellation *rules* (**COBS 15**) and those *rules* requiring the provision of pre-contract information or information during the term of the contract concerning the *insurer* or the *contract of insurance*. The Directive specifies minimum information and cancellation requirements and permits *EEA States* to adopt additional information requirements that are necessary for a proper understanding by the *policy holder* of the essential elements of the commitment.

5.2   G
[FCA]
If the *State of the commitment* is an *EEA State*, the Directive provides that the applicable information rules and cancellation rules shall be determined by that state. Accordingly, if the *State of the commitment* is the *United Kingdom*, the relevant *rules* in this sourcebook apply. Those *rules* do not apply if the *State of the commitment* is another *EEA State*. The territorial scope of other *rules*, in particular the *financial promotion rules*, is not affected since the Directive explicitly permits *EEA States* to apply rules, including advertising rules, in the 'general good'. (See articles 33, 35, 36 and 47 of the *Consolidated Life Directive*)

6.   Distance Marketing Directive: effect on territorial scope

6.1   G
[FCA]
In broad terms, a *firm* is within the *Distance Marketing Directive's* scope when conducting an activity relating to a *distance contract* with a *consumer*. The *rules* in this sourcebook within the Directive's scope are those requiring the provision of pre-contract information, the cancellation rules (**COBS 15**) and the other specific *rules* implementing the Directive contained in **COBS 5** (Distance communications).

6.2   G
[FCA]
In the *FCA's* view, the Directive places responsibility for requirements within the Directive's scope on the *Home State* except in relation to business conducted through a branch, in which case the responsibility rests with the *EEA State* in which the branch is located (this is sometimes referred to as a 'country of origin' or 'country of establishment' basis). (See article 16 of the *Distance Marketing Directive*)

6.3   G
[FCA]
This means that relevant *rules* in this sourcebook will, in general, apply to a *firm* conducting business within the Directive's scope from an establishment in the *United Kingdom* (whether the *firm* is a national of the *UK* or of any other *EEA* or non-*EEA* state).

6.4   G
[FCA]
Conversely, the territorial scope of the relevant *rules* in this sourcebook is modified as necessary so that they do not apply to a *firm* conducting business within the Directive's scope from an establishment in another *EEA state* if the *firm* is a national of the *United Kingdom* or of any other *EEA state*.

6.5   G
[FCA]
In the *FCA's* view:

    (1)   the 'country of origin' basis of the Directive is in line with that of the *Electronic Commerce Directive*; (See recital 6 of the *Distance Marketing Directive*)

    (2)   for business within the scope of both the *Distance Marketing Directive* and the *Consolidated Life Directive*, the territorial application of the *Distance Marketing Directive* takes precedence; in other words, the *rules* requiring pre-contract information and cancellation rules (**COBS 15**) derived from the *Consolidated Life Directive* apply on a 'country of origin' basis rather than being based on the *state of the commitment*; (See articles 4(1) and 16 of the *Distance Marketing Directive* noting that the *Distance Marketing Directive* was adopted after the *Consolidated Life Directive*)

(3)   for business within the scope of both the *Distance Marketing Directive* and the *Insurance Mediation Directive*, the minimum information and other requirements in the *Insurance Mediation Directive* continue to be those applied by the '*Home State*', but the minimum requirements in the *Distance Marketing Directive* and any additional pre-contract information requirements are applied on a 'country of origin' basis. (The basis for this is that the *Insurance Mediation Directive* was adopted after the *Distance Marketing Directive* and is not expressed to be subject to it.)

7.   Electronic Commerce Directive: effect on territorial scope

7.1 [FCA]	G	The *Electronic Commerce Directive's* scope covers every *firm* carrying on an *electronic commerce activity*. Every *rule* in this sourcebook is within the Directive's scope.

7.2   G   A key element of the Directive is the ability of a *person* from one *EEA state* to
[FCA]   carry on an *electronic commerce activity* freely into another *EEA state*. Accordingly, the territorial application of the *rules* in this sourcebook is modified so that they apply at least to a *firm* carrying on an *electronic commerce activity* from an *establishment* in the *United Kingdom* with or for a *person* in the *United Kingdom* or another *EEA state*. Conversely, a *firm* that is a national of the *UK* or another *EEA State*, carrying on an *electronic commerce activity* from an *establishment* in another *EEA State* with or for a *person* in the *United Kingdom* need not comply with the *rules* in this sourcebook. (See article 3(1) and (2) of the *Electronic Commerce Directive*)

7.3   G   The effect of the Directive on this sourcebook is subject to the 'insurance
[FCA]   derogation', which is the only 'derogation' in the Directive that the *FCA* has adopted for this sourcebook. The derogation applies to an *insurer* that is authorised and carrying on an *electronic commerce activity* within the scope of the *Consolidated Life Directive* and permits *EEA States* to continue to apply their advertising rules in the 'general good'. Where the derogation applies, the *financial promotion rules* continue to apply for incoming *electronic commerce activities* (unless the *firm's* 'country of origin' applies rules of like effect) but do not apply for outgoing *electronic commerce activities*. (See article 3(3) and Annex, fourth indent of the *Electronic Commerce Directive*; Annex to European Commission Discussion Paper MARKT/2541/03)

7.4   G   In the *FCA's* view, the Directive's effect on the territorial scope of this source-
[FCA]   book (including the use of the 'insurance derogation'):

(1)   is in line with the *Distance Marketing Directive*; and

(2)   overrides that of any other Directive discussed in this Annex to the extent that it is incompatible.

7.5   G   The 'derogations' in the Directive may enable other *EEA States* to adopt a dif-
[FCA]   ferent approach to the *United Kingdom* in certain fields. (See recital 19 of the *Insurance Mediation Directive*, recital 6 of the *Distance Marketing Directive*, article 3 and Annex of the *Electronic Commerce Directive*)

8.   Investor Compensation Directive

8.1   G   (1)   The *Investor Compensation Directive* generally requires *MiFID invest-
[FCA]   ment firms* to belong to a compensation scheme established in accordance with the Directive. The *rules* in this sourcebook that implement the Directive are those (i) requiring *MiFID investment firms*, including their branches, to make available specified information about the compensation scheme to which they belong and specifying the language in which such information must be provided (**COBS 6.1.16 R**) and (ii) restricting mention of the compensation scheme in advertising to factual references (**COBS 4.2.5 G**).

(2)   In the *FCA's* view, these matters are a *Home State* responsibility although a *Host State* may continue to apply its own rules in the 'general good'. Accordingly, these *rules* apply to the establishments of a *UK MiFID investment firm* in the *United Kingdom* and another *EEA State* but also apply in accordance with their standard territorial scope to an *EEA MiFID investment firm* providing services in the *UK* unless its *Home State* applies rules of like effect.

9.   UCITS Directive: effect on territorial scope

9.1 [FCA]	G	The *UCITS Directive* covers undertakings for collective investment in transferable securities (*UCITS*) meeting the requirements of the Directive, and their *management companies* and *depositaries*. The *rules* in this sourcebook within the Directive's scope (all of which will apply to a *management company*) are those in:
		(1) **COBS 2.1** (Acting honestly, fairly and professionally);
		(2) **COBS 2.3** (Inducements);
		(3) **COBS 4.2.1 R** (The fair, clear and not misleading rule);
		(4) **COBS 4.3.1 R** (Financial promotions to be identifiable as such);
		(5) COBS 4.13 (UCITS);
		(6) **COBS 11.2** (Best execution);
		(7) **COBS 11.3** (Client order handling);
		(8) **COBS 11.7** (Personal account dealing);
		(9) **COBS 14** (Providing product information to clients) relating to the provision of *key investor information* by the *management company* (in addition to applying to a *management company*, **COBS 14.2** also applies to an *ICVC* that is a *UCITS scheme*); and
		(10) **COBS 16.2** (Occasional reporting).
9.1A [FCA]	G	The majority of the *COBS rules* referred to in paragraph 9.1 are rules of conduct which each *EEA State* must draw up under article 14.1 of the *UCITS Directive* which *management companies* authorised in that State must observe at all times. The exceptions are **COBS 4** and **COBS 14** in so far as they relate to a *UCITS scheme*, which form part of the *FCA's fund application rules* and which are the responsibility of the *UCITS Home State* (for a *UCITS scheme*, the *FCA* – see **COLL 12.3.5 R** (COLL fund rules under the management company passport: the fund application rules) and article 19 of the *UCITS Directive*).
9.1B [FCA]	G	Where a *management company* is providing *collective portfolio management* services for a *UCITS* established in a different *EEA State*, responsibility for its compliance with the applicable rules of conduct drawn up under article 14 will generally be for the *management company's Home State*, but when a *branch* is established it will be the responsibility of the *Host Member State* (*UCITS Home State*) (see articles 17(4) and 17(5) of the *UCITS Directive*).
9.1C [FCA]	G	Under the *UCITS Directive* certain *Host State* marketing and *MiFID* – specific rules might also apply to a *management company* providing *collective portfolio management* services for a *UCITS* established in a different *EEA State*. Consequently, an *EEA UCITS management company* should note that, under *COBS*, certain of the *FCA's rules* apply to it, including the *financial promotion rules*. COBS 4.13 (UCITS) is concerned with marketing communications for *UCITS schemes* and *EEA UCITS schemes*.
9.1D [FCA]	G	*EEA UCITS management companies* should be aware that there is a special narrower application of *COBS* for *scheme management activity* provided for by **COBS 18.5** (Residual CIS operators, UCITS management companies and AIFMs).
9.2	G	[deleted]
9.3 [FCA]	G	The Directive does not affect the territorial scope of *rules* as they apply to an intermediary (that is not a *management company*) selling *units* of a *UCITS*. [**Note:** articles 12, 14, 17, 18, 19 and 94 of the *UCITS Directive*]
10. [FCA]		**AIFMD: effect on territorial scope**
10.1	G	PERG 16 contains general *guidance* on the businesses to which AIFMD applies. **FUND 1** contains *guidance* on the types of AIFM.
10.2	G	The only *rule* in this sourcebook which implements AIFMD is **COBS 2.1.4 R**, which applies to:
		(1) a full-scope UK AIFM operating from an establishment in the *UK* or a *branch* in another *EEA State*; and
		(2) an incoming EEA AIFM branch.
10.3	G	The other rules in *COBS* which apply to a full-scope UK AIFM or incoming EEA AIFM (including an AIFM qualifier) fall outside the scope of AIFMD and are, therefore, not affected by its territorial scope.

10.4	G	*Incoming EEA AIFM branches* should be aware that there is a special narrower application of *COBS* for *AIFM investment management functions* provided for by **COBS 18.5** (Residual CIS operators, UCITS management companies and AIFMs).

CHAPTER 2
CONDUCT OF BUSINESS OBLIGATIONS

2.1   ACTING HONESTLY, FAIRLY AND PROFESSIONALLY

The client's best interests rule

[3.50]
2.1.1 R   FCA
(1)   A *firm* must act honestly, fairly and professionally in accordance with the best interests of its *client* (the *client's best interests rule*).
(2)   This *rule* applies in relation to *designated investment business* carried on:
  (a)   for a *retail client*; and
  (b)   in relation to *MiFID or equivalent third country business*, for any other *client*.
(3)   For a *management company*, this *rule* applies in relation to any *UCITS scheme* or *EEA UCITS scheme* the *firm* manages.

[**Note:** article 19(1) of *MiFID*] and article 14(1)(a) and (b) of the *UCITS Directive*]

Exclusion of liability

2.1.2 R   FCA
A *firm* must not, in any communication relating to *designated investment business* seek to:
(1)   exclude or restrict; or
(2)   rely on any exclusion or restriction of;

any duty or liability it may have to a *client* under the *regulatory system*.

2.1.3 G   FCA
(1)   In order to comply with the *client's best interests rule*, a *firm* should not, in any communication to a *retail client* relating to *designated investment business*:
  (a)   seek to exclude or restrict; or
  (b)   rely on any exclusion or restriction of;
  any duty or liability it may have to a *client* other than under the *regulatory system*, unless it is honest, fair and professional for it to do so.
(2)   The general law, including the *Unfair Terms Regulations*, also limits the scope for a *firm* to exclude or restrict any duty or liability to a *consumer*.

AIFMs

2.1.4 R   FCA
A *full-scope UK AIFM* and an *incoming EEA AIFM branch* must, for all *AIFs* it manages:
(1)   act honestly, fairly and with due skill care and diligence in conducting their activities;
(2)   act in the best interests of the *AIF* it manages or the investors of the AIF it manages and the integrity of the market;
(3)   treat all investors fairly; and
(4)   not allow any investor in an *AIF* to obtain preferential treatment, unless such preferential treatment is disclosed in the relevant *AIF's instrument constituting the fund*.

[**Note:** article 12(1)(a), (b) and (f) and article 12(1) last paragraph of *AIFMD*]

Subordinate measures for alternative investment fund managers

2.1.5 G   FCA

Articles 16 to 29 of the *AIFMD level 2 regulation* provide detailed rules supplementing the relevant provisions of Article 12(1) of *AIFMD*.

2.2   INFORMATION DISCLOSURE BEFORE PROVIDING SERVICES

Application

2.2.-1 R   FCA
(1)   This section applies in relation to *MiFID or equivalent third country business*.
(2)   This section applies in relation to other *designated investment business* carried on for a *retail client*:
  (a)   in relation to a *derivative*, a *warrant*, a *non-readily realisable security*, a *P2P agreement*, or *stock lending activity*, but as regards the matters in **COBS 2.2.1 R (1)(B)** only; and

(b)   in relation to a *retail investment product*, but as regards the matters in **COBS 2.2.1 R (1)(A)** and **(D)** only.

[**Note:** article 19(3) of *MiFID*]

Information disclosure before providing services

2.2.1 R   FCA

(1)   A *firm* must provide appropriate information in a comprehensible form to a *client* about:
    (a)   the *firm* and its services;
    (b)   *designated investments* and proposed investment strategies; including appropriate guidance on and warnings of the risks associated with investments in those *designated investments* or in respect of particular investment strategies;
    (c)   execution venues; and
    (d)   costs and associated charges;
    so that the *client* is reasonably able to understand the nature and risks of the service and of the specific type of *designated investment* that is being offered and, consequently, to take investment decisions on an informed basis.
(2)   That information may be provided in a standardised format.
(3)   [deleted]
(4)   [deleted]

[**Note:** article 19(3) of *MiFID*]

2.2.2 G   FCA

A *firm* to which the rule on providing appropriate information (**COBS 2.2.1 R**) applies should also consider the *rules* on disclosing information about a *firm*, its services, costs and associated charges and *designated investments* in **COBS 6.1** and **COBS 14**.

Disclosure of commitment to the Financial Reporting Council's Stewardship Code

2.2.3 R   FCA

A *firm*, other than a *venture capital firm*, which is *managing investments* for a *professional client* that is not a natural person must disclose clearly on its website, or if it does not have a website in another accessible form:
(1)   the nature of its commitment to the Financial Reporting Council's Stewardship Code; or
(2)   where it does not commit to the Code, its alternative investment strategy.

2.3   INDUCEMENTS

Interpretation

2.3.-1 R   FCA

In this section 'giving advice, or providing services, to an employer in connection with a *group personal pension scheme* or *group stakeholder pension scheme*' includes:
(1)   giving advice or assistance to an employer on the operation of such a scheme;
(2)   taking, or helping the employer to take, the steps that must be taken to enable an employee to become a member of such a *scheme*; and
(3)   giving advice to an employee, pursuant to an agreement between the employer and the adviser, about the benefits that are, or might be, available to the employee as an actual or potential member of such a scheme.

Rule on inducements

2.3.1 R   FCA

A *firm* must not pay or accept any fee or commission, or provide or receive any non-monetary benefit, in relation to *designated investment business* or, in the case of its *MiFID or equivalent third country business*, another *ancillary service*, carried on for a *client* other than:
(1)   a fee, commission or non-monetary benefit paid or provided to or by the *client* or a *person* on behalf of the *client*; or
(2)   a fee, commission or non-monetary benefit paid or provided to or by a third party or a *person* acting on behalf of a third party, if:
    (a)   the payment of the fee or commission, or the provision of the non-monetary benefit does not impair compliance with the *firm's* duty to act in the best interests of the *client*; and
    (b)   the existence, nature and amount of the fee, commission or benefit, or, where the amount cannot be ascertained, the method of calculating that amount, is clearly disclosed to the *client*, in a manner that is comprehensive, accurate and understandable, before the provision of the service;

(i)   this requirement only applies to business other than *MiFID or equivalent third country business* if it includes giving a *personal recommendation* in relation to a *retail investment product*, or giving advice, or providing services, to an employer in connection with a *group personal pension scheme* or *group stakeholder pension scheme*;

(ii)   where this requirement applies to business other than *MiFID or equivalent third country business*, a *firm* is not required to make a disclosure to the client in relation to a non-monetary benefit permitted under (a) and which falls within the table of reasonable non-monetary benefits in **COBS 2.3.15 G** as though that table were part of this *rule* for this purpose only;

(iii)   this requirement does not apply to a *firm* giving *basic advice*; and

(c)   in relation to *MiFID or equivalent third country business* or when carrying on a *regulated activity* in relation to a *retail investment product*, the payment of the fee or commission, or the provision of the non-monetary benefit is designed to enhance the quality of the service to the *client*; or

(3)   proper fees which enable or are necessary for the provision of *designated investment business* or *ancillary services*, such as custody costs, settlement and exchange fees, regulatory levies or legal fees, and which, by their nature, cannot give rise to conflicts with the *firm's* duties to act honestly, fairly and professionally in accordance with the best interests of its *clients*.

[**Note:** article 26 of the *MiFID implementing Directive* and articles 29(1) and 29(2) of the *UCITS implementing Directive*]

[**Note:** The European Securities and Markets Authority has issued recommendations on inducements under MiFID]

2.3.1A R   FCA

COBS 2.3.1 R applies to a *UK UCITS management company* and *EEA UCITS management company* when providing *collective portfolio management* services, as if:
(1)   references to a *client*, were references to any *UCITS* it manages; and
(2)   in (2)(b) and (c) and (3) of that *rule*, references to *MiFID or equivalent third country business* were also references to the *collective portfolio management* activities of investment management and administration for the *scheme*.

[**Note:** article 29(1) of the *UCITS implementing Directive*]

2.3.2 R   FCA

A *firm* will satisfy the disclosure obligation under this section if it:
(1)   discloses the essential arrangements relating to the fee, commission or non-monetary benefit in summary form;
(2)   undertakes to the *client* that further details will be disclosed on request; and
(3)   honours the undertaking in (2).

[**Note:** article 26 of the *MiFID implementing Directive* and article 29(2) of the *UCITS implementing Directive*]

2.3.2A R   FCA

COBS 2.3.2 R applies to a *UK UCITS management company* and *EEA UCITS management company* when providing *collective portfolio management* services, as if references to a *client* were references to a *unitholder* of the *scheme*.

[**Note:** article 29(2) of the *UCITS implementing Directive*]

Guidance on inducements

2.3.3 G   FCA

The obligation of a *firm* to act honestly, fairly and professionally in accordance with the best interests of its *clients* includes both the *client's best interests rule* and the duties under *Principles* 1 (integrity), 2 (skill, care and diligence) and 6 (customers' interests).

2.3.4 G   FCA

COBS 11.6 (Use of dealing commission) deals with the acceptance of certain inducements by *investment managers* and builds upon the requirements in this section. *Investment managers* should ensure they comply with this section and **COBS 11.6**.

2.3.5 G   FCA

For the purposes of this section, a non-monetary benefit would include the direction or referral by a *firm* of an actual or potential item of *designated investment business* to another *person*, whether on its own initiative or on the instructions of an *associate*.

2.3.6 G   FCA

For the purposes of this section, the receipt by an *investment firm* of a commission in connection with a *personal recommendation* or a general recommendation, in circumstances where the advice or recommendation is not biased as a result of the receipt of commission, should be considered as designed to enhance the quality of the recommendation to the *client*.

[**Note:** recital 39 of *MiFID implementing Directive*]

2.3.6A G   FCA

COBS 6.1A (Adviser charging and remuneration), **COBS 6.1B** (Retail investment product provider requirements relating to adviser charging and remuneration), **COBS 6.1C** (Consultancy charging and remuneration) and **COBS 6.1D** (Product provider requirements relating to consultancy charging and remuneration) set out specific requirements as to when it is acceptable for a *firm* to pay or receive commissions, fees or other benefits:

(1)   relating to the provision of a *personal recommendation* on *retail investment products*; or

(2)   for giving advice, or providing services, to an employer in connection with a *group personal pension scheme* or *group stakeholder pension scheme*.

2.3.7 G   FCA

The fact that a fee, commission or non-monetary benefit is paid or provided to or by an *appointed representative* or, where applicable, by a *tied agent*, does not prevent the application of the *rule* on inducements.

2.3.8 G   FCA

The *rule* on inducements is applicable to a *firm* and those acting on behalf of a *firm* in relation to the provision of an *investment service* or *ancillary service* to a *client*. Small gifts and minor hospitality received by an individual in their personal capacity below a level specified in the *firm's* conflict's of interest policy, will not be relevant for the purpose of the *rule* on inducements.

Paying commission on non-advised sales of packaged products

2.3.9 G   FCA

The following *guidance* and *evidential provisions* provide examples of arrangements the *FCA* believes will breach the *client's best interests rule* if a *firm* sells or *arranges* the sale of a *packaged product* for a *retail client*.

2.3.10 E   FCA

(1)   If a *firm* is required to disclose *commission* (see **COBS 6.4**) to a *client* in relation to the sale of a *packaged product* (other than in relation to arrangements between firms that are in the same *immediate group*) the firm should not enter into any of the following:

    (a)   volume overrides, if *commission* paid in respect of several transactions is more than a simple multiple of the *commission* payable in respect of one transaction of the same kind; and

    (b)   an agreement to indemnify the payment of *commission* on terms that would or might confer an additional financial benefit on the recipient in the event of the *commission* becoming repayable.

(2)   Contravention of (1) may be relied upon as tending to establish contravention of the *rule* on inducements (**COBS 2.3.1 R**).

2.3.11 G   FCA

(1)   If a *firm* enters into an arrangement with another firm under which it makes or receives a payment of *commission* in relation to the sale of a *packaged product* that is increased in excess of the amount disclosed to the *client*, the *firm* is likely to have breached the *rules* on disclosure of charges, remuneration and commission (see **COBS 6.4**) and, where applicable, the *rule* on inducements in **COBS 2.3.1 R (2)(B)**, unless the increase is attributable to an increase in the *premiums* or contributions payable by that *client*.

Providing credit and other benefits to firms that advise on retail investment products

2.3.11A G   FCA

The following *guidance* and *evidential provisions* provide examples of arrangements the *FCA* believes will breach the *client's best interests rule* in relation to a *personal recommendation* of a *retail investment product* to a *retail client*.

2.3.12 E   FCA

(1)   This *evidential provision* applies in relation to a holding in, or the provision of *credit* to, a *firm* which holds itself out as making *personal recommendations* to *retail clients* on *retail investment products*, except where the relevant transaction is between *persons* who are in the same *immediate group*.

(2)   A *retail investment product* provider should not take any step which would result in it:

    (a)   having a direct or indirect holding of the capital or *voting power* of a firm in (1); or

    (b)   providing *credit* to a *firm* in (1) (other than continuing to facilitate the payment of an *adviser charge* or *consultancy charge* where it is no longer payable by the *retail client*, as described in **COBS 6.1A.5 G** or **COBS 6.1C.6 G**);

unless all the conditions in (4) are satisfied. A *retail investment product* provider should also take reasonable steps to ensure that its *associates* do not take any step which would result in it having a holding as in (a) or providing *credit* as in (b).

(3)   A *firm* in (1) should not take any step which would result in a *retail investment product* provider having a holding as in (2)(a) or providing *credit* as in (2)(b), unless all the conditions in (4) are satisfied.

(4)   The conditions referred to in (2) and (3) are that:
- (a)   the holding is acquired, or *credit* is provided, on commercial terms, that is terms objectively comparable to those on which an independent *person* unconnected to a *retail investment product* provider would, taking into account all relevant circumstances, be willing to acquire the holding or provide credit;
- (b)   the *firm* (or, if applicable, each of the *firms*) taking the step has reliable written evidence that (a) is satisfied;
- (c)   there are no arrangements, in connection with the holding or *credit*, relating to the channelling of business from the *firm* in (1) to the *retail investment product* provider; and
- (d)   the *retail investment product* provider is not able, and none of its *associates* is able, because of the holding or *credit*, to exercise any influence over the *personal recommendations* made in relation to *retail investment products* given by the *firm* or the advice given, or services provided to, an employer in connection with a *group personal pension scheme* or *group stakeholder pension scheme*.

(5)   In this *evidential provision*, in applying (2) and (3) any holding of, or *credit* provided by, a *retail investment product* provider's *associate* is to be regarded as held by, or provided by, that *retail investment product* provider.

(6)   [deleted]

(7)   Contravention of (2) or (3) may be relied upon as tending to establish contravention of the *rule* on inducements (**COBS 2.3.1 R**).

2.3.12A G   FCA

Where a *retail investment product* provider, or its *associate*, provides *credit* to a *retail client* of a *firm* making *personal recommendations* in relation to *retail investment products* or giving advice, or providing services, to an employer in connection with a *group personal pension scheme* or *group stakeholder pension scheme*, this may create an indirect benefit for the *firm* and, to the extent that this is relevant, the provider of *retail investment products* may need to consider the examples in **COBS 2.3.12E** as if it had provided the *credit* to the *firm*.

2.3.13 G   FCA

In considering the compliance of arrangements between members of the same *immediate group* with the *rule* on inducements (**COBS 2.3.1 R**), *firms* may wish to consider the *evidential provisions* in **COBS 2.3.10 E** and **COBS 2.3.12 E**, to the extent that these are relevant.

Reasonable non-monetary benefits

2.3.14 G   FCA

(1)   In relation to the sale of *retail investment products*, the table on reasonable non-monetary benefits (**COBS 2.3.15 G**) indicates the kind of benefits which are capable of enhancing the quality of the service provided to a *client* and, depending on the circumstances, are capable of being paid or received without breaching the *client's best interests rule*. However, in each case, it will be a question of fact whether these conditions are satisfied.

(2)   The *guidance* in the table on reasonable non-monetary benefits is not relevant to non-monetary benefits which may be given by a *retail investment product* provider or its *associate* to its own *representatives*. The *guidance* in this provision does not apply directly to non-monetary benefits provided by a *firm* to another *firm* that is in the same *immediate group*. In this situation, the *rules* on *commission equivalent* (**COBS 6.4.3 R**), the requirements on a *retail investment product* provider making a *personal recommendation* in respect of its own *retail investment products* (**COBS 6.1A.9 R**) or the requirements on a *firm* giving advice, or providing services, to an employer in connection with a *group personal pension scheme* or *group stakeholder pension scheme* produced by the *firm* (**COBS 6.1C.8 R**) will apply.

Reasonable non-monetary benefits

2.3.15 G   FCA

This table belongs to **COBS 2.3.14 G**.

Reasonable non-monetary benefits
Gifts, Hospitality and Promotional Competition Prizes
1 A *retail investment product* provider giving and a *firm* receiving gifts, hospitality and promotional competition prizes of a reasonable value.
Promotion

2   A *retail investment product* provider assisting another *firm* to promote its *retail investment products* so that the quality of its service to *clients* is enhanced. Such assistance should not be of a kind or value that is likely to impair the recipient *firm's* ability to pay due regard to the interests of its *clients*, and to give advice on, and recommend, *retail investment products* available from the recipient *firm's* whole *range* or *ranges*.

Joint marketing exercises

3   A *retail investment product* provider providing generic product literature (that is, letter heading, leaflets, forms and envelopes) that is suitable for use and distribution by or on behalf of another *firm* if:

     (a)   the literature enhances the quality of the service to the *client* and is not primarily of promotional benefit to the *retail investment product* provider; and

     (b)   the total costs (for example, packaging, posting, mailing lists) of distributing such literature to its *client* are borne by the recipient *firm*.

4   A *retail investment product* provider supplying another *firm* with 'freepost' envelopes, for forwarding such items as completed applications, medical reports or copy client agreements.

5   A *retail investment product* provider supplying product specific literature (for example, *key features documents*, minimum information) to another *firm* if:

     (a)   the literature does not contain the name of any other *firm*; or

     (b)   if the name of the recipient *firm* is included, the literature enhances the quality of the service to the *client* and is not primarily of promotional benefit to the recipient *firm*.

6   A *retail investment product* provider supplying draft articles, news items and *financial promotions* for publication in another *firm's* magazine, only if in each case any costs paid by the *product provider* for placing the articles and *financial promotions* are not more than market rate, and exclude distribution costs.

Seminars and conferences

7   A *retail investment product* provider taking part in a seminar organised by another *firm* or a third party and paying toward the cost of the seminar, if:

     (a)   its participation is for a genuine business purpose; and

     (b)   the contribution is reasonable and proportionate to its participation and by reference to the time and sessions at the seminar when its staff play an active role.

Technical services and information technology

8   A *retail investment product* provider supplying a 'freephone' link to which it is connected.

9   A *retail investment product* provider supplying another *firm* with any of the following:

     (a)   quotations and *projections* relating to its *retail investment products* and, in relation to specific *investment* transactions (or for the purpose of any scheme for review of past business), advice on the completion of forms or other *documents*;

     (b)   access to data processing facilities, or access to data, that is related to the *retail investment product* provider's business;

     (c)   access to third party electronic dealing or quotation systems that are related to the *retail investment product* provider's business; and

     (d)   software that gives information about the *retail investment product* provider's *retail investment products* or which is appropriate to its business (for example, for use in a scheme for review of past business or for producing *projections* or technical product information).

10   A *retail investment product* provider paying cash amounts or giving other assistance to a *firm* not in the same *immediate group* for the development of software or other computer facilities necessary to operate software supplied by the *retail investment product* provider, but only to the extent that by doing so it will generate equivalent cost savings to itself or *clients*.

11   A *retail investment product* provider supplying another *firm* with information about sources of mortgage finance.

12   A *retail investment product* provider supplying another *firm* with generic technical information in writing, not necessarily related to the *product provider's* business, when this information states clearly and prominently that it is produced by the *product provider* or (if different) supplying *firm*.

Training

13	A *retail investment product* provider providing another *firm* with training facilities of any kind (for example, lectures, venue, written material and software).
	Travel and accommodation expenses
14	A *retail investment product* provider reimbursing another *firm's* reasonable travel and accommodation expenses when the other *firm*:
	(a)	participates in market research conducted by or for the *retail investment product* provider;
	(b)	attends an annual national event of a *United Kingdom* trade association, hosted or co-hosted by the *retail investment product* provider;
	(c)	participates in the *retail investment product* provider's training facilities (see 13);
	(d)	visits the *retail investment product* provider's *United Kingdom* office in order to:
		(i)	receive information about the *retail investment product* provider's administrative systems; or
		(ii)	attend a meeting with the *retail investment product* provider and an existing or prospective *client* of the receiving *firm*.

2.3.16 G   FCA

In interpreting the table of reasonable non-monetary benefits, *retail investment product* providers should be aware that where a benefit is made available to one *firm* and not another, this is more likely to impair compliance with the *client's best interests rule* and that, where any benefits of substantial size or value (such as adviser training programmes or significant software) are made available to *firms* that are subject to the *rules* on adviser charging and remuneration (**COBS 6.1A**) or consultancy charging and remuneration (**COBS 6.1C**), these benefits should be made available equally across those *firms* if they are provided at all.

2.3.16A G   FCA

In interpreting the table of reasonable non-monetary benefits, a *firm* that provides a *personal recommendation* in relation to a *retail investment product* to a *retail client* or gives advice, or provides a service, to an employer in connection with a *group personal pension scheme* or a *group stakeholder pension scheme* should be aware that acceptance of benefits on which the *firm* will have to rely for a period of time is more likely to impair compliance with the *client's best interests rule*. For example, accepting services which provide access to another *firm's* systems or software on which the *firm* will need to rely to gain access to the *firm's client* data in the future, would be likely to conflict with the *rule* on inducements (**COBS 2.3.1 R**).

Record keeping: inducements

2.3.17 R   FCA
(1)   A *firm* must make a record of the information disclosed to the *client* in accordance with **COBS 2.3.1 R (2)(B)** and must keep that record for at least five years from the date on which it was given.
(2)   A *firm* must also make a record of each benefit given to another *firm* which does not have to be disclosed to the *client* in accordance with **COBS 2.3.1 R (2)(B)(II)**, and must keep that record for at least five years from the date on which it was given.

[**Note:** see article 51(3) of the *MiFID implementing Directive*]

2.4 AGENT AS CLIENT AND RELIANCE ON OTHERS

2.4.1 R   FCA

This section applies to a *firm* that is conducting *designated investment business* or *ancillary activities* or, in the case of *MiFID or equivalent third country business*, other *ancillary services*.

2.4.2 G   FCA

This section is not relevant to the question of who is the *firm's* counterparty for prudential purposes and it does not affect any obligation a *firm* may owe to any other *person* under the general law.

Agent as client

2.4.3 R   FCA
(1)   If a *firm* (F) is aware that a *person* (C1) with or for whom it is providing services is acting as agent for another person (C2) in relation to those services, C1, and not C2, is the *client* of F in respect of that business.
(2)   Paragraph (1) does not apply if:
    (a)   F has agreed with C1 in writing to treat C2 as its *client*; or

(b)   C1 is neither a *firm* nor an *overseas financial services institution* and the main purpose of the arrangements between the parties is the avoidance of duties that F would otherwise owe to C2.

If this is the case, C2 is the *client* of F in respect of that business and C1 is not.

(3)   If there is an agreement under (2)(a) in relation to more than one C2 represented by C1, F may discharge any requirement to notify, obtain consent from, or enter into an agreement with each C2 by sending to, or receiving from, C1 a single communication expressed to cover each C2, except that the following will be required for each C2:

     (a)   separate risk warnings required under this sourcebook;

     (b)   separate confirmations under the requirements on occasional reporting (**COBS 16.3**); and

     (c)   separate *periodic statements*.

Reliance on other investment firms: MiFID and equivalent business

2.4.4 R   FCA

(1)   This *rule* applies if a *firm* (F1), in the course of performing *MiFID or equivalent third country business*, receives an instruction to perform an *investment* or *ancillary service* on behalf of a *client* (C) through another *firm* (F2), if F2 is:

     (a)   a *MiFID investment firm* or a *third country investment firm*; or

     (b)   an *investment firm* that is:

         (i)   a *firm* or authorised in another *EEA State*; and

         (ii)   subject to equivalent relevant requirements.

(2)   F1 may rely upon:

     (a)   any information about C transmitted to it by F2; and

     (b)   any recommendations in respect of the service or transaction that have been provided to C by F2.

(3)   F2 will remain responsible for:

     (a)   the completeness and accuracy of any information about C transmitted by it to F1; and

     (b)   the appropriateness for C of any advice or recommendations provided to C.

(4)   F1 will remain responsible for concluding the services or transaction based on any such information or recommendations in accordance with the applicable requirements under the *regulatory system*.

[**Note:** article 20 of *MiFID*]

2.4.5 G   FCA

(1)   If F1 is required to perform a suitability assessment or an appropriateness assessment under **COBS 9** or **COBS 10**, it may rely upon a suitability assessment performed by F2, if F2 was subject to the requirements for assessing suitability in **COBS 9** (excluding the *basic advice rules*) or equivalent requirements in another *EEA State* in performing that assessment.

(2)   If F1 is required to perform an appropriateness assessment under **COBS 10**, it may rely upon an appropriateness assessment performed by F2, if F2 was subject to the requirements for assessing appropriateness in **COBS 10.2** or equivalent requirements in another *EEA State* in performing that assessment.

Reliance on others: other situations

2.4.6 R   FCA

(1)   This *rule* applies if the *rule* on reliance on other *investment firms* (**COBS 2.4.4 R**) does not apply.

(2)   A *firm* will be taken to be in compliance with any *rule* in this sourcebook that requires it to obtain information to the extent it can show it was reasonable for it to rely on information provided to it in writing by another *person*.

2.4.7 E   FCA

(1)   In relying on **COBS 2.4.6 R**, a *firm* should take reasonable steps to establish that the other *person* providing written information is not connected with the *firm* and is competent to provide the information.

(2)   Compliance with (1) may be relied upon as tending to establish compliance with **COBS 2.4.6 R**.

(3)   Contravention of (1) may be relied upon as tending to establish contravention of **COBS 2.4.6 R**.

2.4.8 G   FCA

It will generally be reasonable (in accordance with **COBS 2.4.6 R (2)**) for a *firm* to rely on information provided to it in writing by an unconnected *authorised person* or a *professional firm*, unless it is aware or ought reasonably to be aware of any fact that would give reasonable grounds to question the accuracy of that information.

2.4.9 R   FCA

Any information that a *rule* in *COBS* or *CASS* requires to be sent to a *client* may be sent to another *person* on the instruction of the *client* so long as the recipient is not connected to the *firm*.

2.4.10 R   FCA

In the case of business that is not *MiFID or equivalent third country business*, if a *rule* in *COBS* or *CASS* requires information to be sent to a *client*, a *firm* need not send that information so long as it takes reasonable steps to establish that it has been or will be supplied by another *person*.

CHAPTER 3
CLIENT CATEGORISATION

3.1   APPLICATION

Scope

[3.51]
3.1.1 R   FCA

The scope of this chapter is the same as that of the *rules* in the *Handbook* to which it relates.

3.1.2 G   FCA

This chapter relates to parts of the *Handbook* whose application depends on whether a *person* is a *client*, a *retail client*, a *professional client* or an *eligible counterparty*. However, it does not apply to the extent that another part of the *Handbook* provides for a different approach to *client* categorisation. For example, a separate approach to *client* categorisation is set out in the definition of a *retail client* for a *firm* that gives *basic advice*.

3.1.3 R   FCA

The sections in this chapter on general notifications (**COBS 3.3**) and policies, procedures and records (**COBS 3.8**) do not apply in relation to a *firm* that is neither:
(1)   conducting *designated investment business*; nor
(2)   in the case of *MiFID or equivalent third country business* providing an *ancillary service* that does not constitute *designated investment business*.

Mixed business

3.1.4 R   FCA

If a *firm* conducts business for a *client* involving both:
(1)   *MiFID or equivalent third country business*; and
(2)   other *regulated activities* subject to this chapter;

it must categorise that *client* for such business in accordance with the provisions in this chapter that apply to *MiFID or equivalent third country business*.

3.1.5 G   FCA
(1)   For example, the requirement concerning mixed business will apply if a *MiFID investment firm* advises a *client* on whether to invest in a *scheme* or a *life policy*. This is because the former is within the scope of *MiFID* and the latter is not. In such a case, the *MiFID client* categorisation requirements prevail.
(2)   The requirement does not apply where the *MiFID or equivalent third country business* is provided separately from the other *regulated activities*. Where this is the case, in accordance with *Principle* 7 (communications with clients) the basis on which the different activities will be performed, including any differences in the categorisations that apply, should be made clear to the *client*.

3.2   CLIENTS

General definition

3.2.1 R   FCA
(1)   A *person* to whom a *firm* provides, intends to provide or has provided:
(a)   a service in the course of carrying on a *regulated activity*; or
(b)   in the case of *MiFID or equivalent third country business*, an *ancillary service*,
is a "client" of that *firm*;
(2)   A "client" includes a potential client.
(3)   In relation to the *financial promotion rules*, a *person* to whom a *financial promotion* is or is likely to be *communicated* is a "client" of a *firm* that *communicates* or *approves* it.
(4)   A client of an *appointed representative* or, if applicable, a *tied agent* is a "client" of the *firm* for whom that *appointed* representative, or *tied agent*, acts or intends to act in the course of business for which that *firm* has accepted responsibility under the *Act* or *MiFID* (see sections 39 and 39A of the *Act* and **SUP 12.3.5 R**).

[**Note:** article 4(1)(10) of *MiFID*]

3.2.2 G   FCA

(1)   A *corporate finance contact* or a *venture capital contact* is not a *client* under the first limb of the general definition. This is because a *firm* does not provide a service to such a contact. However, it will be a *client* under the third limb of the general definition for the purposes of the *financial promotion rules* if the *firm communicates* or *approves* a *financial promotion* that is or is likely to be *communicated* to such a contact.

(2)   *Communicating* or *approving* a *financial promotion* that is or is likely to be *communicated* to such a contact is not *MiFID or equivalent third country business*. In such circumstances, the "non-MiFID" *client* categorisations are relevant and, in categorising *elective professional clients*, the "quantitative test" will not need to be satisfied.

Who is the client?

3.2.3 R   FCA

(1)   If a *firm* provides services to a *person* that is acting as an agent, the identity of its client will be determined in accordance with the *rule* on agents as clients (see **COBS 2.4.3 R**).

(2)   In relation to a *firm* establishing, operating or winding up a *personal pension scheme* or a *stakeholder pension scheme*, a member or beneficiary of that scheme is a *client* of the *firm*.

(3)   If a *firm* that does not fall within (2) provides services to a *person* that is acting as the trustee of a trust, that *person* will be the *firm's client* and the underlying beneficiaries of the trust will not.

(4)   In relation to business that is neither *MiFID or equivalent third country business*, if a *firm* provides services to a fund that does not have separate legal personality, that fund will be the *firm's client*.

(5)   If a *firm* provides services relating to a contribution to or interest in a *CTF* (except for a *personal recommendation* relating to a contribution to a *CTF* or in relation to the *communication* or *approval* of a *financial promotion*), the *firm's* only *client* is:

     (a)   the *registered contact*, if there is one;

     (b)   otherwise, the *person* to whom the statement must be sent in accordance with Regulation 10 of the *CTF Regulations*.

3.3   GENERAL NOTIFICATIONS

3.3.1 R   FCA

A *firm* must:

(1)   notify a new *client* of its categorisation as a *retail client, professional client,* or *eligible counterparty* in accordance with this chapter; and

(2)   prior to the provision of services, inform a *client* in a *durable medium* about:

     (a)   any right that *client* has to request a different categorisation; and

     (b)   any limitations to the level of *client* protection that such a different categorisation would entail.

[**Note:** paragraph 2 of section I of annex II to *MiFID* and articles 28(1) and (2) and the second paragraph of article 50(2) of the *MiFID implementing Directive*]

3.3.2 G   FCA

This chapter requires a *firm* to allow a *client* to request re-categorisation as a *client* that benefits from a higher degree of protection (see **COBS 3.7.1 R**). A *firm* must therefore notify a *client* that is categorised as a *professional client* or an *eligible counterparty* of its right to request a different categorisation whether or not the *firm* will agree to such requests. However, a *firm* need only notify a *client* of a right to request a different categorisation involving a lower level of protection if it is prepared to consider such requests.

3.4   RETAIL CLIENTS

3.4.1 R   FCA

A *retail client* is a *client* who is not a *professional client* or an *eligible counterparty*.

[**Note:** article 4(1)(12) of *MiFID*]

3.4.2 R   FCA

If a *firm* provides services relating to a *CTF* (except for a *personal recommendation* relating to a contribution to a *CTF*), the *firm's client* is a *retail client* even if it would otherwise be categorised as a *professional client* or an *eligible counterparty* under this chapter.

3.5   PROFESSIONAL CLIENTS

3.5.1 R   FCA

A *professional client* is a *client* that is either a *per se professional client* or an *elective professional client*.

[**Note:** article 4(1)(11) of *MiFID*]

Per se professional clients

3.5.2 R   FCA

Each of the following is a *per se professional client* unless and to the extent it is an *eligible counterparty* or is given a different categorisation under this chapter:

(1)   an entity required to be authorised or regulated to operate in the financial markets. The following list includes all authorised entities carrying out the characteristic activities of the entities mentioned, whether authorised by an *EEA State* or a third country and whether or not authorised by reference to a directive:
    (a)   a *credit institution*;
    (b)   an *investment firm*;
    (c)   any other authorised or regulated financial institution;
    (d)   an insurance company;
    (e)   a collective investment scheme or the management company of such a scheme;
    (f)   a pension fund or the management company of a pension fund;
    (g)   a commodity or commodity derivatives dealer;
    (h)   a local;
    (i)   any other institutional investor;

(2)   in relation to *MiFID or equivalent third country business* a large undertaking meeting two of the following size requirements on a company basis:
    (a)   balance sheet total of EUR 20,000,000;
    (b)   net turnover of EUR 40,000,000;
    (c)   own funds of EUR 2,000,000;

(3)   in relation to business that is not *MiFID or equivalent third country business* a large undertaking meeting any of the following conditions:
    (a)   a *body corporate* (including a *limited liability partnership*) which has (or any of whose *holding companies* or *subsidiaries* has) (or has had at any time during the previous two years) called up share capital or net assets of at least £5 million (or its equivalent in any other currency at the relevant time);
    (b)   an undertaking that meets (or any of whose *holding companies* or *subsidiaries* meets) two of the following tests:
      (i)   a balance sheet total of EUR 12,500,000;
      (ii)   a net turnover of EUR 25,000,000;
      (iii)   an average number of employees during the year of 250;
    (c)   a *partnership* or unincorporated association which has (or has had at any time during the previous two years) net assets of at least £5 million (or its equivalent in any other currency at the relevant time) and calculated in the case of a limited *partnership* without deducting loans owing to any of the *partners*;
    (d)   a trustee of a trust (other than an *occupational pension scheme, SSAS, personal pension scheme* or *stakeholder pension scheme*) which has (or has had at any time during the previous two years) assets of at least £10 million (or its equivalent in any other currency at the relevant time) calculated by aggregating the value of the cash and *designated investments* forming part of the trust's assets, but before deducting its liabilities;
    (e)   a trustee of an *occupational pension scheme* or *SSAS*, or a trustee or *operator* of a *personal pension scheme* or *stakeholder pension scheme* where the scheme has (or has had at any time during the previous two years):
      (i)   at least 50 members; and
      (ii)   assets under management of at least £10 million (or its equivalent in any other currency at the relevant time);
    (f)   a local authority or public authority.

(4)   a national or regional government, a public body that manages public debt, a central bank, an international or supranational institution (such as the World Bank, the IMF, the ECP, the EIB) or another similar international organisation;

(5)   another institutional investor whose main activity is to invest in *financial instruments* (in relation to the *firm's MiFID or equivalent third country business*) or *designated investments* (in relation to the *firm's* other business). This includes entities dedicated to the securitisation of assets or other financing transactions.

[**Note:** first paragraph of section I of annex II to *MiFID*]

3.5.2A R   FCA

In relation to *MiFID or equivalent third country business* a local authority or a public authority is not likely to be a regional government for the purposes of **COBS 3.5.2 R (4)**. In the *FCA's* opinion, a local authority may be a *per se professional client* for those purposes if it meets the test for large undertakings in **COBS 3.5.2 R (2)**.

Elective professional clients

3.5.3 R FCA

A *firm* may treat a *client* as an *elective professional client* if it complies with (1) and (3) and, where applicable, (2):
(1)	the *firm* undertakes an adequate assessment of the expertise, experience and knowledge of the *client* that gives reasonable assurance, in light of the nature of the transactions or services envisaged, that the *client* is capable of making his own investment decisions and understanding the risks involved (the "qualitative test");
(2)	in relation to *MiFID or equivalent third country business* in the course of that assessment, at least two of the following criteria are satisfied:
    (a)	the *client* has carried out transactions, in significant size, on the relevant market at an average frequency of 10 per quarter over the previous four quarters;
    (b)	the size of the *client's financial instrument* portfolio, defined as including cash deposits and *financial instruments*, exceeds EUR 500,000;
    (c)	the *client* works or has worked in the financial sector for at least one year in a professional position, which requires knowledge of the transactions or services envisaged;
    (the "quantitative test"); and
(3)	the following procedure is followed:
    (a)	the *client* must state in writing to the *firm* that it wishes to be treated as a *professional client* either generally or in respect of a particular service or transaction or type of transaction or product;
    (b)	the *firm* must give the *client* a clear written warning of the protections and investor compensation rights the *client* may lose; and
    (c)	the *client* must state in writing, in a separate document from the contract, that it is aware of the consequences of losing such protections.

[**Note:** first, second, third and fifth paragraphs of section II.1 and first paragraph of section II.2 of annex II to *MiFID*]

3.5.4 R FCA

If the *client* is an entity, the qualitative test should be performed in relation to the *person* authorised to carry out transactions on its behalf.

[**Note:** fourth paragraph of section II.1 of annex II to *MiFID*]

3.5.5 G FCA

The fitness test applied to managers and directors of entities licensed under directives in the financial field is an example of the assessment of expertise and knowledge involved in the qualitative test.

[**Note:** fourth paragraph of section II.1 of annex II to *MiFID*]

3.5.6 R FCA

Before deciding to accept a request for re-categorisation as an *elective professional client* a *firm* must take all reasonable steps to ensure that the *client* requesting to be treated as an *elective professional client* satisfies the qualitative test and, where applicable, the quantitative test.

[**Note:** second paragraph of section II.2 of annex II to *MiFID*]

3.5.7 G FCA

An *elective professional client* should not be presumed to possess market knowledge and experience comparable to a *per se professional client*

[**Note:** second paragraph of section II.1 of annex II to *MiFID*]

3.5.8 G FCA

Professional client are responsible for keeping the *firm* informed about any change that could affect their current categorisation.

[**Note:** fourth paragraph of section II.2 of annex II to *MiFID*]

3.5.9 R FCA
(1)	If a *firm* becomes aware that a *client* no longer fulfils the initial conditions that made it eligible for categorisation as an *elective professional client* , the *firm* must take the appropriate action.
(2)	Where the appropriate action involves re-categorising that client as a *retail client*, the *firm* must notify that *client* of its new categorisation.

[**Note:** fourth paragraph of section II.2 of annex II to *MiFID* and article 28(1) of the *MiFID implementing Directive*]

3.6 ELIGIBLE COUNTERPARTIES

3.6.1 R FCA

(1)   An *eligible counterparty* is a *client* that is either a *per se eligible counterparty* or an *elective eligible counterparty*.

(2)   A *client* can only be an *eligible counterparty* in relation to *eligible counterparty business* (**PRIN 1 ANNEX 1** is an exception to this).

[**Note:** article 24(1) of *MiFID*]

Per se eligible counterparties

3.6.2 R   FCA

Each of the following is a *per se eligible counterparty* (including an entity that is not from an *EEA state* that is equivalent to any of the following) unless and to the extent it is given a different categorisation under this chapter:

(1)   an *investment firm*;

(2)   a *credit institution*;

(3)   an insurance company;

(4)   a *collective investment scheme* authorised under the *UCITS Directive* or its management company;

(5)   a pension fund or its management company;

(6)   another financial institution authorised or regulated under *EU* legislation or the national law of an *EEA State*;

(7)   an undertaking exempted from the application of *MiFID* under either Article 2(1)(k) (certain own account dealers in commodities or commodity derivatives) or Article 2(1)(l) (locals) of that directive;

(8)   a national government or its corresponding office, including a public body that deals with the public debt;

(9)   a central bank;

(10)   a supranational organisation.

[**Note:** first paragraph of article 24(2) and first paragraph of article 24(4) of *MiFID*]

3.6.3 G   FCA

For the purpose of **COBS 3.6.2 R (6)**, a financial institution includes regulated institutions in the securities, banking and insurance sectors.

Elective eligible counterparties

3.6.4 R   FCA

A *firm* may treat a *client* as an *elective eligible counterparty* if:

(1)   the *client* is an undertaking and:

    (a)   is a *per se professional client* (except for a *client* that is only a *per se professional client* because it is an institutional investor under **COBS 3.5.2 R (5)**) and, in relation to business other than *MiFID or equivalent third country business*:

        (i)   is a *body corporate* (including a *limited liability partnership*) which has (or any of whose *holding companies* or *subsidiaries* has) called up share capital of at least £10 million (or its equivalent in any other currency at the relevant time); or

        (ii)   meets the criteria in the *rule* on meeting two quantitative tests (**COBS 3.5.2 R (3)(B)**); or

    (b)   requests such categorisation and is an *elective professional client*, but only in respect of the services or transactions for which it could be treated as a *professional client*; and

(2)   the *firm* has, in relation to *MiFID or equivalent third country business*, obtained express confirmation from the prospective counterparty that it agrees to be treated as an *eligible counterparty*.

[**Note:** article 24(3) and the second paragraph of article 24(4) of *MiFID* and article 50(1) of the *MiFID implementing Directive*]

3.6.5 G   FCA

The categories of *elective eligible counterparties* include an equivalent undertaking that is not from an *EEA State* provided the above conditions and requirements are satisfied.

3.6.6 R   FCA

A *firm* may obtain a prospective counterparty's confirmation that it agrees to be treated as an *eligible counterparty* either in the form of a general agreement or in respect of each individual transaction.

[**Note:** second paragraph of article 24(3) of *MiFID*]

Client and firm located in different jurisdictions

3.6.7 R   FCA

In the case of *MiFID or equivalent third country business*, in the event of a transaction where the prospective counterparties are located in different *EEA States*, the *firm* shall defer to the status of the other undertaking as determined by the law or measures of the *EEA State* in which that undertaking is established.

[**Note:** first paragraph of article 24(3) of *MiFID*]

3.7 PROVIDING CLIENTS WITH A HIGHER LEVEL OF PROTECTION

3.7.1 R   FCA

A *firm* must allow a *professional client* or an *eligible counterparty* to request re-categorisation as a *client* that benefits from a higher degree of protection.

[**Note:** second paragraph of article 24(2) of, and the second paragraph of section I of annex II to, *MiFID* and the second paragraph of article 50(2) of the *MiFID implementing Directive*]

3.7.2 G   FCA

It is the responsibility of a *professional client* or *eligible counterparty* to ask for a higher level of protection when it deems it is unable to properly assess or manage the risks involved.

[**Note:** third paragraph of section I and fourth paragraph of section II.2 of annex II to *MiFID* and second paragraph of article 50(2) of the *MiFID implementing Directive*]

3.7.3 R   FCA

A *firm* may, either on its own initiative or at the request of the *client* concerned:
(1)   treat as a *professional client* or a *retail client* a *client* that might otherwise be categorised as a *per se eligible counterparty*;
(2)   treat as a *retail client* a *client* that might otherwise be categorised as a *per se professional client*;

and if it does so, the *client* will be re-categorised accordingly. Where applicable, this re-categorisation is subject to the requirement for a written agreement in **COBS 3.7.5 R**.

[**Note:** second paragraph of article 24(2) of, and second paragraph of section I of annex II to, *MiFID* and article 28(3) and the second paragraph of article 50(2) of the *MiFID implementing Directive*]

3.7.4 R   FCA

If a *per se eligible counterparty* requests treatment as a *client* whose business with the *firm* is subject to conduct of business protections, but does not expressly request treatment as a *retail client* and the *firm* agrees to that request, the *firm* must treat that *eligible counterparty* as a *professional client*.

[**Note:** first paragraph of article 50(2) of the *MiFID implementing Directive*]

3.7.5 R   FCA
(1)   If, in relation to *MiFID or equivalent third country business* a *per se professional client* or a *per se eligible counterparty* requests treatment as a *retail client*, the *client* will be classified as a *retail client* if it enters into a written agreement with the *firm* to the effect that it will not be treated as a *professional client* or *eligible counterparty* for the purposes of the applicable conduct of business regime.
(2)   This agreement must specify the scope of the re-categorisation, such as whether it applies to one or more particular services or transactions, to one or more types of product or transaction or to one or more *rules*.

[**Note:** fourth paragraph of section I of annex II to *MiFID* and second paragraph of article 50(2) of the *MiFID implementing Directive*]

3.7.6 G   FCA
(1)   In accordance with *Principle* 7 (communications with *clients*) if a *firm* at its own initiative re-categorises a *client* in accordance with this section, it should notify that *client* of its new category under this section.
(2)   If the *firm* already has an agreement with the *client*, it should also consider any contractual requirements concerning the amendment of that agreement.

3.7.7 G   FCA

The ways in which a *client* may be provided with additional protections under this section include re-categorisation:
(1)   on a general basis; or
(2)   on a trade by trade basis; or
(3)   in respect of one or more specified *rules*; or
(4)   in respect of one or more particular services or transactions; or
(5)   in respect of one or more types of product or transaction.

[**Note:** second paragraph of article 24(2) of *MiFID*]

3.7.8 G   FCA

Re-categorising a *client* as a *retail client* under this section does not necessarily mean it will become an *eligible complainant* under *DISP*.

3.8   POLICIES, PROCEDURES AND RECORDS

Policies and procedures

3.8.1 R   FCA

A *firm* must implement appropriate written internal policies and procedures to categorise its *clients*.

[**Note:** fourth paragraph of section II.2 of annex II to *MiFID*]

Records

3.8.2 R   FCA
(1) A *firm* must make a record of the form of each notice provided and each agreement entered into under this chapter. This record must be made at the time that standard form is first used and retained for the relevant period after the *firm* ceases to carry on business with *clients* who were provided with that form.
(2) A *firm* must make a record in relation to each *client* of:
    (a) the categorisation established for the *client* under this chapter, including sufficient information to support that categorisation;
    (b) evidence of despatch to the *client* of any notice required under this chapter and if such notice differs from the relevant standard form, a copy of the actual notice provided; and
    (c) a copy of any agreement entered into with the *client* under this chapter.
    This record must be made at the time of categorisation and should be retained for the relevant period after the *firm* ceases to carry on business with or for that *client*.
(3) The relevant periods are:
    (a) indefinitely, in relation to a *pension transfer*, *pension conversion*, *pension opt-out* or *FSAVC*;
    (b) at least five years, in relation to a *life policy* or *pension contract*;
    (c) five years in relation to *MiFID or equivalent third country business*; and
    (d) three years in any other case.

[**Note:** article 51(3) of the *MiFID implementing Directive*]

3.8.3 G   FCA

If a *firm* provides the same form of notice to more than one *client*, it need not maintain a separate copy of it for each *client*, provided it keeps evidence of despatch of the notice to each *client*.

CHAPTER 4
COMMUNICATING WITH CLIENTS, INCLUDING FINANCIAL PROMOTIONS

4.1   APPLICATION

Who? What?

[3.52]
4.1.1 R   FCA

This chapter applies to a *firm*:
(1) communicating with a *client* in relation to its *designated investment business*;
(2) *communicating* or *approving* a *financial promotion* other than:
    (a) a *financial promotion* of *qualifying credit*, a *home purchase plan* or a *home reversion plan*; or
    (b) a *financial promotion* in respect of a *non-investment insurance contract*; or
    (c) a promotion of an *unregulated collective investment scheme* that would breach section 238(1) of the *Act* if made by an *authorised person* (*firms* may not *communicate* or *approve* such promotions); or
    (d) a *financial promotion* in relation to a *credit agreement*, a *consumer hire agreement* or a *credit-related regulated activity*.

4.1.1A R   FCA

COBS 4.4.3 R applies to a *firm* with respect to the activity of *issuing electronic money*.

4.1.2 G   FCA
(1) This chapter applies in relation to an *authorised professional firm* in accordance with **COBS 18** (Specialist regimes).
(2) This chapter applies, to a limited extent, in relation to *communicating* or *approving* a *financial promotion* that relates to a *deposit* if the *deposit* is a *structured deposit*, *cash deposit ISA* or *cash deposit CTF*.

4.1.3 G   FCA

A *firm* is required to comply with the *financial promotion rules* in relation to a *financial promotion* *communicated* by its *appointed representative* even where the *financial promotion* does not require *approval* because of the exemption in article 16 of the *Financial Promotion Order* (Exempt persons).

[**Note:** see section 39 of the *Act*]

4.1.4 G   FCA

(1)   In **COBS 4.3.1 R**, **COBS 4.5.8 R** and **COBS 4.7.1 R**, the defined terms *"financial promotion"* and *"direct offer financial promotion"* include, in relation to *MiFID or equivalent third country business*, all communications that are marketing communications within the meaning of *MiFID*.

(2)   In the case of *MiFID or equivalent third country business*, certain requirements in this chapter are subject to an exemption for the communication of a *third party prospectus* in certain circumstances. This has a similar effect to the exemption in article 70(1)(c) of the *Financial Promotion Order*, which is referred to in the definition of an *excluded communication*.

(3)   In this chapter *"financial promotion"* and *"direct offer financial promotion"* include communications that are marketing communications for the purposes of the *UCITS Directive*.

4.1.5 G   FCA

(1)   A *firm* communicating with an *eligible counterparty* should have regard to the application of *COBS* to *eligible counterparty business* (**COBS 1 ANNEX 1** Part 1).

(2)   This chapter does not apply in relation to communicating with an *eligible counterparty* other than the section on compensation information (see **COBS 4.4**) but elements of the requirements in *PRIN* may apply.

4.1.6 G   FCA

Approving a *financial promotion* without *communicating* it (which includes causing it to be communicated) is not *MiFID or equivalent third country business*. *Communicating* a *financial promotion* to a *person*, such as a *corporate finance contact* or a *venture capital contact*, who is not a *client* within the meaning of **COBS 3.2.1 R (1)**, **COBS 3.2.1 R (2)** or **COBS 3.2.1 R (4)** in respect of the *MiFID or equivalent third country business* to which the *financial promotion* relates, is also not *MiFID or equivalent third country business*. Further *guidance* on what amounts to *MiFID business* may be found in **PERG 13**.

4.1.7 G   FCA

A reference in this chapter to *MiFID or equivalent third country business* includes a reference to communications that occur before an agreement to perform services in relation to *MiFID or equivalent third country business*.

[**Note:** see recital 82 to the *MiFID implementing Directive*]

Where? General position

4.1.8 R   FCA

(1)   In relation to communications by a *firm* to a *client* in relation to its *designated investment business* this chapter applies in accordance with the *general application rule* and the *rule* on business with *UK clients* from an overseas establishment (**COBS 1 ANNEX 1** Part 2 paragraph 2.1R).

(2)   In addition, the *financial promotion rules* apply to a *firm* in relation to:

     (a)   the *communication* of a *financial promotion* to a *person* inside the *United Kingdom*;

     (b)   the *communication* of a *cold call* to a *person* outside the *United Kingdom*, unless:

         (i)   it is made from a place outside the *United Kingdom*; and

         (ii)   it is made for the purposes of a business which is carried on outside the *United Kingdom* and which is not carried on in the *United Kingdom*; and

     (c)   the *approval* of a *financial promotion* for *communication* to a *person* inside the *United Kingdom*.

Where? Modifications to comply with EU law

4.1.9 G   FCA

(1)   The *EEA territorial scope rule* modifies the general territorial scope of the *rules* in this chapter to the extent necessary to be compatible with European law. This means that in a number of cases, the *rules* in this chapter will apply to *communications* made by *UK firms* to *persons* located outside the *United Kingdom* and will not apply to *communications* made to *persons* inside the *United Kingdom* by *EEA firms*. Further *guidance* on this is located in **COBS 1 ANNEX 1**.

(2)   One effect of the *EEA territorial scope rule* is that the *rules* in this chapter will not generally apply to an *EEA key investor information document* but will, for example, apply to a *firm* (including an *EEA UCITS management company*) when *marketing* in the *United Kingdom* the *units* of an *EEA UCITS scheme* that is a *recognised scheme*.

(3)   The *financial promotion rules* do not apply to incoming communications in relation to the *MiFID business* of an *investment firm* from another *EEA State* that are, in its *home member state*, regulated under *MiFID* other than to the extent **COBS 4.12** (Restrictions on the promotion of *non-mainstream pooled investments*) applies.

4.1.10 G   FCA

Firms should note the territorial scope of this chapter is also affected by:

(1)　the disapplication for *financial promotions* originating outside the *United Kingdom* that are not capable of having an effect within the *United Kingdom* (section 21(3) of the *Act* (Restrictions on financial promotion)) (see the defined term *"excluded communication"*);

(2)　the exemptions for overseas communicators (see the defined term *"excluded communication"*); and

(3)　the *rules* on *financial promotions* with an overseas element (see **COBS 4.9**).

4.2   FAIR, CLEAR AND NOT MISLEADING COMMUNICATIONS

The fair, clear and not misleading rule

4.2.1 R   FCA

(1)　A *firm* must ensure that a communication or a *financial promotion* is fair, clear and not misleading.

(2)　This *rule* applies in relation to:

　　(a)　a communication by the *firm* to a *client* in relation to *designated investment business* other than a *third party prospectus*;

　　(b)　a *financial promotion communicated* by the *firm* that is not:

　　　　(i)　an *excluded communication*;

　　　　(ii)　a *non-retail communication*;

　　　　(iii)　a *third party prospectus*; and

　　(c)　a *financial promotion* approved by the *firm*.

[Note: article 19(2) of *MiFID*, recital 52 to the *MiFID implementing Directive* and article 77 of the *UCITS Directive*]

4.2.2 G   FCA

(1)　The *fair, clear and not misleading rule* applies in a way that is appropriate and proportionate taking into account the means of communication and the information the communication is intended to convey. So a communication addressed to a *professional client* may not need to include the same information, or be presented in the same way, as a communication addressed to a *retail client*.

(2)　**COBS 4.2.1 R(2)(B)** does not limit the application of the *fair, clear and not misleading rule* under **COBS 4.2.1 R (2) (A)**. So, for example, a communication in relation to *designated investment business* that is both a communication to a *professional client* and a *financial promotion*, will still be subject to the *fair, clear and not misleading rule*.

4.2.3 G   FCA

Part 7 (Offences relating to Financial Services) of the Financial Services Act 2012 creates criminal offences relating to certain misleading statements and practices.

Fair, clear and not misleading financial promotions

4.2.4 G   FCA

A *firm* should ensure that a *financial promotion*:

(1)　for a product or service that places a *client's* capital at risk makes this clear;

(2)　that quotes a yield figure gives a balanced impression of both the short and long term prospects for the *investment*;

(3)　that promotes an *investment* or service whose charging structure is complex, or in relation to which the *firm* will receive more than one element of remuneration, includes the information necessary to ensure that it is fair, clear and not misleading and contains sufficient information taking into account the needs of the recipients;

(4)　that names the *FCA*, *PRA* or both as its regulator and refers to matters not regulated by either the *FCA*, *PRA* or both makes clear that those matters are not regulated by the *FCA*, *PRA* or either;

(5)　that offers *packaged products* or *stakeholder products* not produced by the *firm*, gives a fair, clear and not misleading impression of the producer of the product or the manager of the underlying investments.

4.2.5 G   FCA

A communication or a *financial promotion* should not describe a feature of a product or service as "guaranteed", "protected" or "secure", or use a similar term unless:

(1)　that term is capable of being a fair, clear and not misleading description of it; and

(2)　the *firm* communicates all of the information necessary, and presents that information with sufficient clarity and prominence, to make the use of that term fair, clear and not misleading.

The reasonable steps defence to an action for damages

4.2.6 R   FCA

If, in relation to a particular communication or *financial promotion*, a *firm* takes reasonable steps to ensure it complies with the *fair, clear and not misleading rule*, a contravention of that *rule* does not give rise to a right of action under section 138D of the *Act*.

4.3   FINANCIAL PROMOTIONS TO BE IDENTIFIABLE AS SUCH

4.3.1 R FCA

(1)   A *firm* must ensure that a *financial promotion* addressed to a *client* is clearly identifiable as such.

         [**Note**: article 19(2) of *MiFID* and article 77 of the *UCITS Directive*]

(2)   If a *financial promotion* relates to a *firm's MiFID or equivalent third country business*, this *rule* does not apply to the extent that the *financial promotion* is a *third party prospectus*.

(3)   If a *financial promotion* relates to a *firm's* business that is not *MiFID or equivalent third country business*, this *rule* applies to *communicating* or *approving* the *financial promotion* but does not apply:

         (a)   to the extent that it is an *excluded communication*;

         (b)   to the extent that it is a prospectus advertisement to which **PR 3.3** applies;

         (c)   if it is *image advertising*;

         (d)   if it is a *non-retail communication*;

         (e)   to the extent that it relates to a *pure protection contract* that is a *long-term care insurance contract*.

(4)   In the case of a marketing communication that relates to a *UCITS scheme* or an *EEA UCITS scheme*, (2) and (3) do not limit the application of this *rule*.

4.4   COMPENSATION INFORMATION

4.4.1 R FCA

A *firm* must ensure that any reference in advertising to an investor compensation scheme established under the *Investor Compensation Directive* is limited to a factual reference to the scheme.

[**Note:** article 10(3) of the *Investor Compensation Directive*]

4.4.2 G

[deleted]

4.4.3 R FCA

To ensure that a *firm* pays due regard to the information needs of its *clients*, and communicates information to them in a way which is clear, fair and not misleading with respect to the activity of *issuing electronic money*, a *firm* must ensure that, in good time before the *firm* issues *electronic money* to a *person*, it has been communicated to that *person* on paper or in another *durable medium* that the *compensation scheme* does not cover claims made in connection with *issuing electronic money*.

4.5   COMMUNICATING WITH RETAIL CLIENTS

Application

4.5.1 R FCA

(1)   Subject to (2) and (3), this section applies to a *firm* in relation to:

         (a)   the provision of information in relation to its *designated investment business*; and

         (b)   the *communication* or *approval* of a *financial promotion*;

         where such information or *financial promotion* is addressed to, or disseminated in such a way that it is likely to be received by, a *retail client*.

(2)   If a communication relates to a *firm's MiFID or equivalent third country business*, this section does not apply:

         (a)   to the extent that it is a *third party prospectus*;

         (b)   if it is *image advertising*.

(3)   If a communication relates to a *firm's* business that is not *MiFID or equivalent third country business*, this section does not apply:

         (a)   to the extent that it is an *excluded communication*;

         (b)   to the extent that it is a prospectus advertisement to which **PR 3.3** applies;

         (c)   if it is *image advertising*.

General rule

4.5.2 R FCA

A *firm* must ensure that information:

(1)   includes the name of the *firm*;

(2)   is accurate and in particular does not emphasise any potential benefits of *relevant business* or a *relevant investment* without also giving a fair and prominent indication of any relevant risks;

(3)   is sufficient for, and presented in a way that is likely to be understood by, the average member of the group to whom it is directed, or by whom it is likely to be received; and

(4)   does not disguise, diminish or obscure important items, statements or warnings.

[**Note:** article 27(2) of the *MiFID implementing Directive*]

4.5.3 G   FCA

The name of the *firm* may be a trading name or shortened version of the legal name of the *firm*, provided the *retail client* can identify the *firm* communicating the information.

4.5.4 G   FCA

In deciding whether, and how, to communicate information to a particular target audience, a *firm* should take into account the nature of the product or business, the risks involved, the *client's* commitment, the likely information needs of the average recipient, and the role of the information in the sales process.

4.5.5 G   FCA

When communicating information, a *firm* should consider whether omission of any relevant fact will result in information being insufficient, unclear, unfair or misleading.

Comparative information

4.5.6 R   FCA

(1)   If information compares *relevant business, relevant investment* s, or *persons* who carry on *relevant business*, a *firm* must ensure that:

    (a)   the comparison is meaningful and presented in a fair and balanced way; and

    (b)   in relation to *MiFID or equivalent third country business*;

        (i)

            the sources of the information used for the comparison are specified; and

        (ii)

            the key facts and assumptions used to make the comparison are included.

(2)   In this *rule*, in relation to *MiFID or equivalent third country business, ancillary services* are to be regarded as *relevant business*.

[**Note:** article 27(3) of the *MiFID implementing Directive*]

Referring to tax

4.5.7 R   FCA

(1)   If any information refers to a particular tax treatment, a *firm* must ensure that it prominently states that the tax treatment depends on the individual circumstances of each *client* and may be subject to change in future.

    [**Note:** article 27(7) of the *MiFID implementing Directive*]

(2)   This *rule* applies in relation to *MiFID or equivalent third country business* or, otherwise, to a *financial promotion*. However, it does not apply to a *financial promotion* to the extent that it relates to:

    (a)   [deleted]

    (b)   a *pure protection contract* that is a *long-term care insurance contract*.

Consistent financial promotions

4.5.8 R   FCA

(1)   A *firm* must ensure that information contained in a *financial promotion* is consistent with any information the *firm* provides to a *retail client* in the course of carrying on *designated investment business* or, in the case of *MiFID or equivalent third country business, ancillary services*.

    [**Note:** article 29(7) of the *MiFID implementing Directive*]

(2)   This *rule* does not apply to a *financial promotion* to the extent that it relates to:

    (a)   [deleted]

    (b)   a *pure protection contract* that is a *long-term care insurance contract*.

4.6   PAST, SIMULATED PAST AND FUTURE PERFORMANCE

Application

4.6.1 R   FCA

(1)   Subject to (2) and (3), this section applies to a *firm* in relation to:

    (a)   the provision of information in relation to its *MiFID or equivalent third country business*;

    (b)   the *communication* or *approval* of a *financial promotion*;

where such information or *financial promotion* is addressed to, or disseminated in such a way that it is likely to be received by, a *retail client*.

(2)   If a communication relates to a *firm's MiFID or equivalent third country business*, this section does not apply:

(a)   to the extent that the communication is a *third party prospectus*;

(b)   if it is *image advertising*.

(3)   If a communication relates to a *firm's* business that is not *MiFID or equivalent third country business*, this section does not apply:

(a)   to the extent that it is an *excluded communication*;

(b)   to the extent that it is a prospectus advertisement to which **PR 3.3** applies;

(c)   if it is *image advertising*;

(d)   to the extent that it relates to a *deposit* that is not a *structured deposit*;

(e)   to the extent that it relates to a *pure protection contract* that is a *long-term care insurance contract*.

Past performance

4.6.2 R   FCA

A *firm* must ensure that information that contains an indication of past performance of *relevant business*, a *relevant investment* or a financial index, satisfies the following conditions:

(1)   that indication is not the most prominent feature of the communication;

(2)   the information includes appropriate performance information which covers at least the immediately preceding five years, or the whole period for which the investment has been offered, the financial index has been established, or the service has been provided if less than five years, or such longer period as the *firm* may decide, and in every case that performance information must be based on and show complete 12-month periods;

(3)   the reference period and the source of information are clearly stated;

(4)   the information contains a prominent warning that the figures refer to the past and that past performance is not a reliable indicator of future results;

(5)   if the indication relies on figures denominated in a currency other than that of the *EEA State* in which the *retail client* is resident, the currency is clearly stated, together with a warning that the return may increase or decrease as a result of currency fluctuations;

(6)   if the indication is based on gross performance, the effect of commissions, fees or other charges is disclosed.

[**Note:** article 27(4) of the *MiFID implementing Directive*]

4.6.3 G   FCA

The obligations relating to describing performance should be interpreted in the light of their purpose and in a way that is appropriate and proportionate taking into account the means of communication and the information the communication is intended to convey. For example, a periodic statement in relation to *managing investments* that is sent in accordance with the *rules* on reporting information to *clients* (see **COBS 16**) may include past performance as its most prominent feature.

4.6.4 G   FCA

If a *financial promotion* includes information referring to the past performance of a *packaged product* that is not a *financial instrument*, a *firm* will comply with the *rule* on appropriate performance information (**COBS 4.6.2 R (2)**) if the *financial promotion* includes, in the case of a *scheme*, unit-linked *life policy*, unit-linked *personal pension scheme* or unit-linked *stakeholder pension scheme* (other than a unitised with-profits *life policy* or *stakeholder pension scheme*) past performance information calculated and presented in accordance with the table in **COBS 4.6.4A G**.

4.6.4A G   FCA

This Table belongs to **COBS 4.6.4 G**

Percentage growth				
[Fund name]	Quarter/Year – Quarter/Year	Quarter/Year – Quarter/Year	Quarter/ Year – Quarter/Year	Quarter/ Year – Quarter/Year	Quarter/ Year – Quarter/ Year
	pgr%	pgr%	pgr%	pgr%	pgr%

Notes:
1. The table should show performance information for five (or if performance information for fewer than five is available, all) complete 12-month periods, the most recent of which ends with the last full quarter preceding the date on which the *firm* first *communicates* or *approves* the *financial promotion*.
2. For products with performance data for fewer than five 12-month periods, *firms* should clearly indicate that performance data does not exist for the relevant periods.
3. No allowance should be made for tax recoveries on income for *pension contracts*, *ISAs* or *PEPs*.
4. pgr is the percentage growth rate for the year, where: pgr = ((P1 – P0)/P0)*100 and rounded to the nearest 0.1%, with exact 0.05% rounded to the nearest even 0.1%; and where P0 is the price at the start of the 12-month period and P1 is the price on the same day in the following 12-month period.
5. The prices should allow for any net distributions to be reinvested.
6. The price at P1 must be adjusted for any charges since the date of P0 which are based on a proportion of the fund and are levied by the cancellation of units.
7. The *firm* should use single pricing, or (if this is not available) bid to bid prices, unless the *firm* has reasonable grounds to be satisfied that another basis would better reflect the past performance of the fund.

4.6.4B G   FCA
(1)   The *firm* should present the information referred to in **COBS 4.6.4 G** no less prominently than any other past performance information.
(2)   This *guidance* does not apply to a *prospectus, key investor information document* or *simplified prospectus* drawn up in accordance with *COLL*.

4.6.5 G   FCA
(1)   In relation to a *packaged product* (other than a *scheme*, a unit-linked *life policy*, unit-linked *personal pension scheme* or a unit-linked *stakeholder pension scheme* (that is not a unitised with-profits *life policy* or *stakeholder pension scheme*)), the information should be given on:
    (a)   an offer to bid basis (which should be stated) if there is an actual return or comparison of performance with other *investments*; or
    (b)   an offer to offer, bid to bid or offer to bid basis (which should be stated) if there is a comparison of performance with an index or with movements in the price of *units*; or
    (c)   a single pricing basis with allowance for charges.
(2)   If the pricing policy of the *investment* has changed, the prices used should include such adjustments as are necessary to remove any distortions resulting from the pricing method.

Simulated past performance

4.6.6 R   FCA

A *firm* must ensure that information that contains an indication of simulated past performance of *relevant business*, a *relevant investment* or a financial index, satisfies the following conditions:
(1)   it relates to an investment or a financial index;
(2)   the simulated past performance is based on the actual past performance of one or more investments or financial indices which are the same as, or underlie, the investment concerned;
(3)   in respect of the actual past performance, the conditions set out in paragraphs (1) to (3), (5) and (6) of the *rule* on past performance (**COBS 4.6.2 R**) are complied with; and
(4)   the information contains a prominent warning that the figures refer to simulated past performance and that past performance is not a reliable indicator of future performance.

[**Note:** article 27(5) of the *MiFID implementing Directive*]

Future performance

4.6.7 R   FCA
(1)   A *firm* must ensure that information that contains an indication of future performance of *relevant business*, a *relevant investment*, a *structured deposit* or a financial index, satisfies the following conditions:
    (a)   it is not based on and does not refer to simulated past performance;
    (b)   it is based on reasonable assumptions supported by objective data;
    (c)   it discloses the effect of commissions, fees or other charges if the indication is based on gross performance; and
    (d)   it contains a prominent warning that such forecasts are not a reliable indicator of future performance.
(2)   Other than in relation to *MiFID or equivalent third country business*, this *rule* only applies to *financial promotions* that relate to a *financial instrument* (or a financial index that relates exclusively to *financial instruments*) or a *structured deposit*.

[**Note:** article 27(6) of the *MiFID implementing Directive*]

4.6.8 G   FCA

A *firm* should not provide information on future performance if it is not able to obtain the objective data needed to comply with the *rule* on future performance. For example, objective data in relation to *EIS shares* may be difficult to obtain.

4.6.9 R   FCA

(1)   A *firm* that communicates to a *client* a *projection* for a *packaged product* which is not a *financial instrument* must ensure that the *projection* complies with the *projections rules* in **COBS 13.4**, **COBS 13.5** and **COBS 13 ANNEX 2**.

(2)   A *firm* must not communicate a *projection* for a highly volatile product to a *client* unless the product is a *financial instrument*.

4.7   DIRECT OFFER FINANCIAL PROMOTIONS

4.7.1 R   FCA

(1)   Subject to (3) and (4), a *firm* must ensure that a *direct offer financial promotion* that is addressed to, or disseminated in such a way that it is likely to be received by, a *retail client* contains:

       (a)   such of the information referred to in the *rules* on information disclosure (**COBS 6.1.4 R**, **COBS 6.1.6 R**, **COBS 6.1.7 R**, **COBS 6.1.9 R**, **COBS 14.3.2 R**, **COBS 14.3.3 R**, **COBS 14.3.4 R** and **COBS 14.3.5 R**) as is relevant to that offer or invitation; and

           [**Note:** article 29(8) of the *MiFID implementing Directive*, the *rules* listed implement Articles 30 to 33 of the *MiFID implementing Directive*]

       (b)   if it does not relate to *MiFID or equivalent third country business*, additional appropriate information about the *relevant business* and *relevant investments* so that the *client* is reasonably able to understand the nature and risks of the *relevant business* and *relevant investments* and consequently to take investment decisions on an informed basis.

(2)   This *rule* does not require the information in (1) to be included in a *direct offer financial promotion* if, in order to respond to an offer or invitation contained in it, the *retail client* must refer to another document or documents, which, alone or in combination, contain that information.

(3)   If a communication relates to a *firm's MiFID or equivalent third country business*, this section does not apply:

       (a)   to the extent that it is a *third party prospectus*;

       (b)   if it is *image advertising*.

(4)   If a communication relates to a *firm's* business that is not *MiFID or equivalent third country business*, this section does not apply:

       (a)   to the extent that it is an *excluded communication*;

       (b)   to the extent that it is a prospectus advertisement to which **PR 3.3** applies;

       (c)   if it is *image advertising*;

       (d)   to the extent that it relates to a *deposit* that is not a *cash deposit ISA* or *cash deposit CTF*;

       (e)   to the extent that it relates to a *pure protection contract* that is a *long-term care insurance contract*.

(5)   In this *rule*, in relation to *MiFID or equivalent third country business*, *ancillary services* are to be regarded as *relevant business*.

Guidance

4.7.2 G   FCA

Although **COBS 4.7.1 R (1)(B)** does not apply in relation to *MiFID or equivalent third country business*, similar requirements may apply under **COBS 2.2**.

4.7.3 G   FCA

(1)   **COBS 4.7.1 R (2)** allows a *firm* to *communicate* a *direct offer financial promotion* that does not contain all the information required by **COBS 4.7.1 R (1)**, if the *firm* can demonstrate that the *client* has referred to the required information before the *client* makes or accepts an offer in response to the *direct offer financial promotion*.

(2)   A *firm communicating* or *approving* a *direct offer financial promotion* may also be subject to the *rules* on providing product information in **COBS 14.2**, including the exceptions in **COBS 14.2.5 R** to **14.2.9 R**.

4.7.4 G   FCA

In order to enable a *client* to make an informed assessment of a *relevant investment* or *relevant business*, a *firm* may wish to include in a *direct offer financial promotion*:

(1)   a summary of the taxation of any *investment* to which it relates and the taxation consequences for the average member of the group to whom it is directed or by whom it is likely to be received;

(2)   a statement that the recipient should seek a *personal recommendation* if he has any doubt about the suitability of the *investments* or services being promoted; and

(3)   (in relation to a promotion for a *packaged product* that is not a *financial instrument*) a *key features illustration*, in which a *generic projection* may generally be used.

4.7.5 G

[deleted]

4.7.5A G   FCA

COBS 4.13.2 R (Marketing communications relating to UCITS schemes or EEA UCITS schemes) and **COBS 4.13.3 R** (Marketing communications relating to feeder UCITS) contain additional disclosure requirements for *firms* in relation to marketing communications (other than *key investor information*) that concern particular investment strategies of a *UCITS scheme* or *EEA UCITS scheme*.

Warrants and derivatives

4.7.6 R   FCA
(1)   A *firm* must not *communicate* or *approve* a *direct offer financial promotion*:
    (a)   relating to a *warrant* or *derivative*;
    (b)   to or for *communication* to a *retail client*; and
    (c)   where the *firm* will not itself be required to comply with the *rules* on appropriateness (see **COBS 10**);
    unless the *firm* has adequate evidence that the condition in (2) is satisfied.

(2)   The condition is that the *person* who will *arrange* or *deal* in relation to the *derivative* or *warrant* will comply with the *rules* on appropriateness or equivalent requirements for any application or order that the *person* is aware, or ought reasonably to be aware, is in response to the *direct offer financial promotion*.

Non-readily realisable securities

4.7.7 R   FCA
(1)   Unless permitted by **COBS 4.7.8 R**, a *firm* must not *communicate* or *approve* a *direct-offer financial promotion* relating to a *non-readily realisable security* to or for *communication* to a *retail client* without the conditions in (2) and (3) being satisfied.

(2)   The first condition is that the *retail client* recipient of the *direct-offer financial promotion* is one of the following:
    (a)   certified as a 'high net worth investor' in accordance with **COBS 4.7.9 R**;
    (b)   certified as a 'sophisticated investor' in accordance with **COBS 4.7.9 R**;
    (c)   self-certified as a 'sophisticated investor' in accordance with **COBS 4.7.9 R**;
    (d)   certified as a 'restricted investor' in accordance with **COBS 4.7.10 R**.

(3)   The second condition is that *firm* itself or the *person* who will *arrange* or *deal* in relation to the *non-readily realisable security* will comply with the *rules* on appropriateness (see **COBS 10**) or equivalent requirements for any application or order that the *person* is aware, or ought reasonably to be aware, is in response to the *direct offer financial promotion*.

4.7.8 R   FCA

A *firm* may *communicate* or *approve* a *direct-offer financial promotion* relating to a *non-readily realisable security* to or for *communication* to a *retail client* if:

(1)   the *firm* itself will comply with the suitability *rules* (**COBS 9**) in relation to the *investment* promoted; or

(2)   the *retail client* has confirmed before the promotion is made that they are a *retail client* of another *firm* that will comply with the suitability *rules* (**COBS 9**) in relation to the *investment* promoted; or

(3)   the *retail client* is a *corporate finance contact* or a *venture capital contact*.

4.7.9 R   FCA

A certified high net worth investor, a certified sophisticated investor or a self-certified sophisticated investor is an individual who has signed, within the period of twelve months ending with the day on which the communication is made, a statement in the terms set out in the applicable rule listed below, substituting "non-readily realisable securities" for "non-mainstream pooled investments":

(1)   certified high net worth investor: **COBS 4.12.6 R**;
(2)   certified sophisticated investor: **COBS 4.12.7 R**;
(3)   self-certified sophisticated investor: **COBS 4.12.8 R**.

4.7.10 R   FCA

A certified restricted investor is an individual who has signed, within the period of twelve months ending with the day on which the communication is made, a statement in the following terms:

> "RESTRICTED INVESTOR STATEMENT
> I make this statement so that I can receive promotional communications relating to non-readily realisable securities as a restricted investor. I declare that I qualify as a restricted investor because:
>
> (a)   in the twelve months preceding the date below, I have not invested more than 10% of my net assets in non-readily realisable securities; and
>
> (b)   I undertake that in the twelve months following the date below, I will not invest more than 10% of my net assets in non-readily realisable securities.
>
> Net assets for these purposes do not include:
>
> (a)   the property which is my primary residence or any money raised through a loan secured on that property;
>
> (b)   any rights of mine under a qualifying contract of insurance; or
>
> (c)   any benefits (in the form of pensions or otherwise) which are payable on the termination of my service or on my death or retirement and to which I am (or my dependants are), or may be entitled.
>
> I accept that the investments to which the promotions will relate may expose me to a significant risk of losing all of the money or other property invested. I am aware that it is open to me to seek advice from an authorised person who specialises in advising on non-readily realisable securities.
> Signature:
> Date:"

4.8   COLD CALLS AND OTHER PROMOTIONS THAT ARE NOT IN WRITING

Application

4.8.1 R   FCA

This section applies to a *firm* in relation to the communication of a *financial promotion* that is not in writing, but it does not apply:
(1)   to the extent that the *financial promotion* is an *excluded communication*;
(2)   if the *financial promotion* is *image advertising*;
(3)   if the financial promotion is a *non-retail communication*;
(4)   [deleted]
(5)   to the extent that the *financial promotion* relates to a *pure protection contract* that is a *long-term care insurance contract*.

Restriction on cold calling

4.8.2 R   FCA

A *firm* must not make a *cold call* unless:
(1)   the recipient has an established existing client relationship with the *firm* and the relationship is such that the recipient envisages receiving *cold calls*; or
(2)   the *cold call* relates to a generally marketable *packaged product* which is not:
      (a)   a *higher volatility fund*; or
      (b)   a *life policy* with a link (including a potential link) to a *higher volatility fund*; or
(3)   the *cold call* relates to a *controlled activity* to be carried on by an *authorised person* or *exempt person* and the only *controlled investments* involved or which reasonably could be involved are:
      (a)   *readily realisable securities* (other than warrants); and
      (b)   generally marketable non-geared *packaged products*.

Promotions that are not in writing

4.8.3 R   FCA

A *firm* must not *communicate* a solicited or unsolicited *financial promotion* that is not in writing, to a *client* outside the *firm's* premises, unless the *person communicating* it:
(1)   only does so at an appropriate time of the day;
(2)   identifies himself and the *firm* he represents at the outset and makes clear the purpose of the communication;
(3)   clarifies if the *client* would like to continue with or terminate the communication, and terminates the communication at any time that the *client* requests it; and
(4)   gives a contact point to any *client* with whom he arranges an appointment.

4.9   FINANCIAL PROMOTIONS WITH AN OVERSEAS ELEMENT

Application

4.9.1 R   FCA

(1)   Subject to (2) and (3), this section applies to a *firm* in relation to the *communication* or *approval* of a *financial promotion* that relates to the business of an *overseas person*.

(2)   This section does not apply to a *firm* in relation to its *MiFID or equivalent third country business*.

(3)   If a communication relates to a *firm's* business that is not *MiFID or equivalent third country business*, this section does not apply:

    (a)   to the extent that it is an *excluded communication*;

    (b)   to the extent that it is a prospectus advertisement to which **PR 3.3** applies;

    (c)   if it is *image advertising*;

    (d)   if it is a *non-retail communication*;

    (e)   [deleted]

    (f)   to the extent that it relates to a *pure protection contract* that is a *long-term care insurance contract*.

4.9.2 G   FCA

Approving a *financial promotion* for *communication* by an *unauthorised person* is not *MiFID or equivalent third country business*.

Financial promotions for the business of an overseas person

4.9.3 R   FCA

A *firm* must not *communicate* or *approve* a *financial promotion* which relates to a particular *relevant investment* or *relevant business* of an *overseas person*, unless:

(1)   the *financial promotion* makes clear which *firm* has *approved* or *communicated* it and, where relevant, explains:

    (a)   that the *rules* made under the *Act* for the protection of *retail clients* do not apply;

    (b)   the extent and level to which the *compensation scheme* will be available, or if the scheme will not be available, a statement to that effect; and

    (c)   if the communicator wishes, the protection or compensation available under another system of regulation; and

(2)   the *firm* has taken reasonable steps to satisfy itself that the *overseas person* will deal with *retail clients* in the *United Kingdom* in an honest and reliable way.

Financial promotions for an overseas long-term insurer

4.9.4 R   FCA

A *firm* may only *communicate* or *approve* a *financial promotion* to enter into a *life policy* with a *person* who is:

(1)   an *authorised person*; or

(2)   an *exempt person* who is exempt in relation to *effecting or carrying out contracts of insurance* of the *class* to which the *financial promotion* relates; or

(3)   an *overseas long-term insurer* that is entitled under the law of its home country or territory to carry on there *insurance business* of the *class* to which the *financial promotion* relates.

4.9.5 R   FCA

A *financial promotion* for an *overseas long-term insurer*, which has no establishment in the *United Kingdom*, must include:

(1)   the full name of the *overseas long-term insurer*, the country where it is registered, and, if different, the country where its head office is situated;

(2)   a prominent statement that 'holders of policies issued by the company will not be protected by the Financial Services Compensation Scheme if the company becomes unable to meet its liabilities to them'; and

(3)   if any trustee, investment manager or *United Kingdom* agent of the *overseas long-term insurer* is named which is not independent of the *overseas long-term insurer*, a prominent statement of that fact.

4.9.6 R   FCA

A *financial promotion* for an *overseas long-term insurer* which is authorised to carry on *long-term insurance business* in any country or territory listed in paragraph (c) of the Glossary definition of *overseas long-term insurer* must also include:

(1)   the full name of any trustee of property of any description which is retained by the *overseas long-term insurer* in respect of the promoted contracts;

(2)   an indication whether the investment of such property (or any part of it) is managed by the *overseas long-term insurer* or by another *person* and the full name of any *investment manager*;

(3)   the registered office of any such trustee and of any *investment manager* and of his principal office (if different); and

(4)   where any *person* in the *United Kingdom* takes, or may take, any steps on behalf of the *overseas long-term insurer* to enter into a promoted contract, the following details:

       (a)   the full name of the *overseas long-term insurer*;

       (b)   the registered office, head office or principal place of business of that *person* in the *United Kingdom*; and

       (c)   if there is more than one such *person*, the principal or main *person* in the *United Kingdom*.

4.9.7 R   FCA

If a *financial promotion* relates to a *life policy* with an *overseas long-term insurer* but does not name the *overseas long-term insurer* by giving its full name or its business name:

(1)   it must include the following prominent statement: "This financial promotion relates to an insurance company which does not, and is not authorised to, carry on in any part of the United Kingdom the class of insurance business to which this promotion relates. This means that the management and solvency of the company are not supervised by the *Financial Conduct Authority* or the *Prudential Regulation Authority*. Holders of policies issued by the company will not have the right to complain to the Financial Ombudsman Service if they have a complaint against the company and will not be protected by the Financial Services Compensation Scheme if the company should become unable to meet its liabilities to them"; and

(2)   if it also refers to other *investments*, it must make this clear.

4.10   SYSTEMS AND CONTROLS AND APPROVING AND COMMUNICATING FINANCIAL PROMOTIONS

Systems and controls

4.10.1 G   FCA

The *rules* in **SYSC 3** and **SYSC 4** require a *firm* that communicates with a *client* in relation to *designated investment business*, or *communicates* or *approves* a *financial promotion*, to put in place systems and controls or policies and procedures in order to comply with the *rules* in this chapter.

Approving financial promotions

4.10.2 R   FCA

(1)   Before a *firm approves* a *financial promotion* for *communication* by an *unauthorised person*, it must confirm that the *financial promotion* complies with the *financial promotion rules*.

(2)   If, at any time after a *firm* has complied with (1), a *firm* becomes aware that a *financial promotion* no longer complies with the *financial promotion rules*, it must withdraw its *approval* and notify any *person* that it knows to be relying on its *approval* as soon as reasonably practicable.

(3)   When *approving* a *financial promotion*, the *firm* must confirm compliance with the *financial promotion rules* that would have applied if the *financial promotion* had been communicated by a *firm* other than in relation to *MiFID or equivalent third country business*.

4.10.3 G   FCA

(1)   Section 21(1) of the *Act* (Restrictions on financial promotion) prohibits an *unauthorised person* from *communicating* a *financial promotion*, in the course of business, unless an exemption applies or the *financial promotion* is *approved* by a *firm*. Many of the *rules* in this chapter apply when a *firm approves* a *financial promotion* in the same way as when a *firm communicates* a *financial promotion* itself.

(2)   A *firm* may also wish to *approve* a *financial promotion* that it *communicates* itself. This would ensure that an *unauthorised person* who then also *communicates* the *financial promotion* to another *person* will not contravene the restriction on *financial promotion* in the *Act* (section 21).

(3)   *Approving* a *financial promotion* for *communication* by an *unauthorised person* is not *MiFID or equivalent third country business*.

(4)   A *firm* may not *approve* a *financial promotion* relating to an *unregulated collective investment scheme* unless the *firm* would be able to *communicate* the promotion without breaching section 238(1) of the *Act* (see section 240 of the *Act*). The exemptions from that section in the Financial Services and Markets Act 2000 (Promotion of Collective Investment Schemes) (Exemptions) Order 2001 (as amended from time to time) are relevant.

4.10.4 R   FCA

A *firm* must not *approve* a *financial promotion* to be made in the course of a personal visit, telephone conversation or other interactive dialogue.

4.10.5 R   FCA

If a *firm approves* a *financial promotion* in circumstances in which one or more of the *financial promotion rules*, or the prohibition on approval of promotions for *collective investment schemes* in section 240(1) of the *Act* (Restriction on approval), are expressly disapplied, the *approval* must be given on terms that it is limited to those circumstances.

4.10.6 G   FCA

For example, if a *firm approves* a *financial promotion* for *communication* to a *professional client* or an *eligible counterparty*, the *approval* must be limited to *communication* to such *persons*.

4.10.7 G   FCA

If an *approval* is limited, and an *unauthorised person communicates* the *financial promotion* to *persons* not covered by the *approval*, the *unauthorised person* may commit an offence under the restriction on financial promotion in the *Act* (section 21). A *firm* giving a limited *approval* may wish to notify the *unauthorised person* accordingly.

Communicating financial promotions

4.10.8 G   FCA

If a *firm* continues to *communicate* a *financial promotion* when the *financial promotion* no longer complies with the *rules* in this chapter, it will breach those *rules*.

4.10.9 G   FCA

A *financial promotion* which is clearly only relevant at a particular date will not cease to comply with the *financial promotion rules* merely because the passage of time has rendered it out-of-date; an example would be a dated analyst's report.

Relying on another firm's confirmation of compliance

4.10.10 R   FCA

(1)   A *firm* (A) will not contravene any of the *financial promotion rules* if it *communicates* a *financial promotion* which has been produced by another *person* and:

    (a)   A takes reasonable care to establish that another *firm* (B) has confirmed that the *financial promotion* complies with the *financial promotion rules*;

    (b)   A takes reasonable care to establish that it *communicates* the *financial promotion* only to recipients of the type for whom it was intended at the time B carried out the confirmation exercise; and

    (c)   so far as A is, or ought reasonably to be, aware:

        (i)   the *financial promotion* has not ceased to be fair, clear and not misleading since that time; and

        (ii)   B has not withdrawn the *financial promotion*.

(2)   This *rule* does not apply in relation to *MiFID or equivalent third country business*.

4.10.11 G   FCA

A *firm* should inform anyone relying on its confirmation of compliance if it becomes aware that the *financial promotion* no longer complies with the *rules* in this chapter.

4.11   RECORD KEEPING: FINANCIAL PROMOTION

4.11.1 R   FCA

(1)   A *firm* must make an adequate record of any *financial promotion* it *communicates* or *approves*, other than a *financial promotion* made in the course of a personal visit, telephone conversation or other interactive dialogue.

(2)   For a telemarketing campaign, a *firm* must make an adequate record of copies of any scripts used.

(3)   If a *firm communicates* or *approves* an invitation or inducement to participate in, acquire, or underwrite a *non-mainstream pooled investment* which is addressed to or disseminated in such a way that it is likely to be received by a *retail client*:

    (a)   the *person* allocated the *compliance oversight function* in the *firm* must make a record at or near the time of the communication or approval certifying that the invitation or inducement complies with the restrictions set out in section 238 of the *Act* and in **COBS 4.12.3 R**, as applicable;

    (b)   the making of the record required in (a) may be delegated to one or more *employees* of the *firm* who report to and are supervised by the *person* allocated the *compliance oversight function*, provided the process for certification of compliance has been reviewed and approved by the *person* allocated the *compliance oversight function* no more than 12 months before the date of the invitation or inducement;

    (c)   when making the record required in (a), the *firm* must make a record of which exemption was relied on for the purposes of the invitation or inducement, together with the reason why the *firm* is satisfied that that exemption applies;

    (d)   where the *firm* relies on an exemption that requires investor certification and warnings to investors, the record required in (a) must include a record of any certificate or investor statement (as signed by the investor) and of any warnings or indications required by the exemption;

(e)   if the exemption relied on is that for an *excluded communication* under **COBS 4.12.4 R (5)**, the *firm* must identify in the record required in (a) which type of *financial promotion* defined as an *excluded communication* corresponds to the invitation or inducementbeing made, including, where applicable, which article in the *Financial Promotion Order* or in the *Promotion of Collective Investment Schemes Order* was relied on for the purposes of the invitation or inducement, together with the reason why the *firm* is satisfied that the exemption applies;

(4)   A *firm* must retain the record in relation to a *financial promotion* relating to:
   (a)   a *pension transfer, pension conversion, pension opt-out* or *FSAVC*, indefinitely;
   (b)   a *life policy, occupational pension scheme, SSAS, personal pension scheme* or *stakeholder pension scheme*, for six years;
   (c)   *MiFID or equivalent third country business*, for five years; and
   (d)   any other case, for three years.

(5)   If a communication relates to a *firm's MiFID or equivalent third country business*, this section does not apply:
   (a)   to the extent that the communication is a *third party prospectus*;
   (b)   if it is *image advertising*;
   (c)   if it is a *non-retail communication*.

(6)   If a communication relates to a *firm's* business that is not *MiFID or equivalent third country business*, this section does not apply:
   (a)   to the extent that it is an *excluded communication*;
   (b)   to the extent that it is a prospectus advertisement to which **PR 3.3** applies;
   (c)   if it is *image advertising*;
   (d)   if it is a *non-retail communication*;
   (e)   [deleted]
   (f)   to the extent that it relates to a *pure protection contract* that is a *long-term care insurance contract*.

[**Note:** see article 51(3) of the *MiFID implementing Directive*]

4.11.2 G   FCA

A *firm* should consider maintaining a record of why it is satisfied that the *financial promotion* complies with the *financial promotion rules*.

4.11.3 G   FCA

If the *financial promotion* includes market information that is updated continuously in line with the relevant market, the record-keeping *rules* do not require a firm to record that information.

4.12   RESTRICTIONS ON THE PROMOTION OF NON-MAINSTREAM POOLED INVESTMENTS

Restrictions on the promotion of non-mainstream pooled investments

4.12.3 R   FCA
(1)   A *firm* must not *communicate* or *approve* an invitation or inducement to participate in, acquire, or underwrite a *non-mainstream pooled investment* where that invitation or inducement is addressed to or disseminated in such a way that it is likely to be received by a *retail client*.
(2)   The restriction in (1) is subject to **COBS 4.12.4 R** and does not apply to *units* in *unregulated collective investment schemes*, which are subject to a statutory restriction on promotion in section 238 of the *Act*.

Exemptions from the restrictions on the promotion of non-mainstream pooled investments

4.12.4 R   FCA
(1)   The restriction in **COBS 4.12.3 R** does not apply if the promotion falls within an exemption in the table in (5) below.
(2)   A firm may communicate an invitation or inducement to participate in an *unregulated collective investment scheme* without breaching the restriction on promotion in section 238 of the *Act* if the promotion falls within an exemption in the table in (5) below.
(3)   Where the middle column in the table in (5) refers to promotion to a category of *person*, this means that the invitation or inducement:
   (a)   is made only to recipients who the *firm* has taken reasonable steps to establish are *persons* in that category; or
   (b)   is directed at recipients in a way that may reasonably be regarded as designed to reduce, so far as possible, the risk of participation in, acquisition or underwriting of the *non-mainstream pooled investment* by *persons* who are not in that category.
(4)   A *firm* may rely on more than one exemption in relation to the same invitation or inducement.
(5)

Title of Exemption	Promotion to:	Promotion of a non-mainstream pooled investment which is:
1. Replacement products and rights issues	A *person* who already participates in, owns, holds rights to or interests in, a *non-mainstream pooled investment* that is being liquidated or wound down or which is undergoing a rights issue. [See Note 1.]	1. A *non-mainstream pooled investment* which is intended by the operator or manager to absorb or take over the assets of that *non-mainstream pooled investment*, or which is being offered by the operator or manager of that *non-mainstream pooled investment* as an alternative to cash on its liquidation; or 2. *Securities* offered by the existing *non-mainstream pooled investment* as part of a rights issue.
2. Certified high net worth investors	An individual who meets the requirements set out in **COBS 4.12.6 R**, or a person (or persons) legally empowered to make investment decisions on behalf of such individual.	Any *non-mainstream pooled investment* the firm considers is likely to be suitable for that individual, based on a preliminary assessment of the *client's* profile and objectives. [See **COBS 4.12.5 G (2)**.]
3. Enterprise and charitable funds	A *person* who is eligible to participate or invest in an arrangement constituted under: (1) the Church Funds Investment Measure 1958; (2) section 96 or 100 of the Charities Act 2011; (3) section 25 of the Charities Act (Northern Ireland) 1964; (4) the Regulation on European Venture Capital Funds ('EuVECAs'); or (5) the Regulation on European Social Entrepreneurship Funds ('EuSEFs').	Any *non-mainstream pooled investment* which is such an arrangement.
4. Eligible employees	An eligible *employee*, that is, a *person* who is: (1) an officer; (2) an *employee*; (3) a former officer or *employee*; or (4) a member of the immediate family of any of (1)–(3), of an employer which is (or is in the same *group* as) the *firm*, or which has accepted responsibility for the activities of the *firm* in carrying out the *designated investment business* in question.	1. A *non-mainstream pooled investment*, the instrument constituting which: A. restricts the property of the *non-mainstream pooled investment*, apart from cash and near cash, to: (1) (where the employer is a company) *shares* in and *debentures* of the *company* or any other connected *company*; [See Note 2.] (2) (in any case), any property, provided that the *non-mainstream pooled investment* takes the form of: (i) a limited *partnership*, under the terms of which the employer (or connected *company*) will be the unlimited partner and the eligible employees will be some or all of the limited partners; or

Title of Exemption	Promotion to:	Promotion of a non-mainstream pooled investment which is:
		(ii) a trust which the *firm* reasonably believes not to contain any risk that any eligible employee may be liable to make any further payments (other than *charges*) for *investment* transactions earlier entered into, which the eligible *employee* was not aware of at the time he entered into them; and
		B. (in a case falling within A(1) above) restricts participation in the *non-mainstream pooled investment* to eligible *employees*, the employer and any connected *company*.
		2. Any *non-mainstream pooled investment*, provided that the participation of eligible employees is to facilitate their co-investment: (i) with one or more *companies* in the same *group* as their employer (which may include the employer); or (ii) with one or more *clients* of such a *company*.
5. Members of the Society of Lloyd's	A *person* admitted to membership of the Society of Lloyd's or any *person* by law entitled or bound to administer his affairs.	A *scheme* in the form of a limited *partnership* which is established for the sole purpose of underwriting *insurance business* at Lloyd's.
6. Exempt persons	An exempt *person* (other than a *person* exempted only by section 39 of the *Act* (Exemption of appointed representatives)) if the *financial promotion* relates to a *regulated activity* in respect of which the *person* is exempt from the *general prohibition*.	Any *non-mainstream pooled investment*.
7. Non-retail clients	An *eligible counterparty* or a *professional client*.	Any *non-mainstream pooled investment* in relation to which the *client* is categorised as a *professional client* or *eligible counterparty*. [See Note 4.]
8. Certified sophisticated investors	An individual who meets the requirements set out in **COBS 4.12.7 R**, including an individual who is legally empowered (solely or jointly with others) to make investment decisions on behalf of another *person* who is the *firm's client*.	Any *non-mainstream pooled investment*.
9. Self-certified sophisticated investors	An individual who meets the requirements set out in **COBS 4.12.8 R**, including an individual who is legally empowered (solely or jointly with others) to make investment decisions on behalf of another *person* who is the *firm's client*.	Any *non-mainstream pooled investment* the *firm* considers is likely to be suitable for that *client*, based on a preliminary assessment of the *client's* profile and objectives. [See **COBS 4.12.5 G (2)**]

Title of Exemption	Promotion to:	Promotion of a non-mainstream pooled investment which is:
10. Solicited advice	Any *person*.	Any *non-mainstream pooled investment*, provided the communication meets all of the following requirements: (a) the communication only amounts to a *financial promotion* because it is a *personal recommendation* on a *non-mainstream pooled investment*; (b) the *personal recommendation* is made following a specific request by that *client* for advice on the merits of investing in the *non-mainstream pooled investment*; and (c) the *client* has not previously received a *financial promotion* or any other communication from the *firm* (or from a *person* connected to the *firm*) which is intended to influence the *client* in relation to that *non-mainstream pooled investment*. [See Note 3.]
11. Excluded communications	Any *person*.	Any *non-mainstream pooled investment*, provided the *financial promotion* is an *excluded communication*. [See **COBS 4.12.12 G** and **COBS 4.12.13 G**.]
12. Non-recognised UCITS	Any *person*.	Any *EEA UCITS scheme* which is not a *recognised scheme*, provided the following requirements are met: (1) the *firm* considers it is likely to be suitable for that *client* based on a preliminary assessment of the *client's* profile and objectives; and (2) the *firm* provides that *client* with the same product information as it would be required to provide by **COBS 14.2** if the scheme was a *recognised scheme*. [See **COBS 4.12.5 G (2)**.]
13. US persons	A *person* who is classified as a United States person for tax purposes under United States legislation or who owns a US qualified retirement plan.	Any investment *company* registered and operated in the United States under the Investment Company Act 1940.

The following Notes explain certain words and phrases used in the table above.	
Note 1	Promotion of *non-mainstream pooled investments* to a category of person includes any nominee company acting for such a person.
Note 2	A *company* is 'connected' with another *company* if: (a) they are both in the same *group*; or (b) one *company* is entitled, either alone or with another *company* in the same *group*, to exercise or control the exercise of a majority of the voting rights attributable to the *share* capital, which are exercisable in all circumstances at any general meeting of the other *company* or of its *holding company*.
Note 3	A *person* is connected with a *firm* if it acts as an *introducer* or *appointed representative* for that *firm* or if it is any other *person*, regardless of *authorisation* status, who has a relevant business relationship with the *firm*.

Note 4	In deciding whether a promotion is permitted under the rules of this section or under section 238 of the Act, *firms* may use the *client* categorisation regime that applies to business other than *MiFID or equivalent third country business*. (This is the case even if the *firm* will be carrying on a *MiFID* activity at the same time as or following the promotion.)

Advice and preliminary assessment of suitability

4.12.5 G   FCA

(1)   Where a *firm* communicates any promotion of a *non-mainstream pooled investment* in the context of advice, it should have regard to and comply with its obligations under **COBS 9**. *Firms* should also be mindful of the appropriateness requirements in **COBS 10** which apply to a wide range of non-advised services.

(2)

(a)   A *firm* which wishes to rely on exemptions 2 (certified high net worth investors), 9 (self-certified sophisticated investors) or 12 (non-recognised UCITS), as provided under **COBS 4.12.4 R (5)**, should note that these exemptions require a preliminary assessment of suitability before promotion of the *non-mainstream pooled investment* to clients (in addition to other requirements).

(b)   There is no duty to communicate the preliminary assessment of suitability to the *client*. If the *firm* does so, it must not do so in a way that amounts to making a *personal recommendation* unless it complies with the rules in **COBS 9** on suitability.

(c)   The requirement for a preliminary assessment of suitability does not extend to a full suitability assessment, unless advice is being offered in relation to the *non-mainstream pooled investment* being promoted, in which case the requirements in **COBS 9** apply. However, it requires that the *firm* take reasonable steps to acquaint itself with the *client's* profile and objectives in order to ascertain whether the *non-mainstream pooled investment* under contemplation is likely to be suitable for that *client*. The *firm* should not promote the *non-mainstream pooled investment* to the *client* if it does not consider it likely to be suitable for that *client* following such preliminary assessment.

Definition of sophisticated and high net worth investors

4.12.6 R   FCA

A *certified high net worth investor* is an individual who has signed, within the period of twelve months ending with the day on which the communication is made, a statement in the following terms:

"HIGH NET WORTH INVESTOR STATEMENT

I make this statement so that I can receive promotional communications which are exempt from the restriction on promotion of non-mainstream pooled investments. The exemption relates to certified high net worth investors and I declare that I qualify as such because at least one of the following applies to me:

– I had, throughout the financial year immediately preceding the date below, an annual **income** to the value of **£100,000 or more**;

– I held, throughout the financial year immediately preceding the date below, **net assets** to the value of **£250,000 or more**. Net assets for these purposes do **not** include:

(a) the property which is my primary residence or any money raised through a loan secured on that property;

(b) any rights of mine under a qualifying contract of insurance; or

(c) any benefits (in the form of pensions or otherwise) which are payable on the termination of my service or on my death or retirement and to which I am (or my dependants are), or may be, entitled.

I accept that the investments to which the promotions will relate may expose me to a significant risk of losing all of the money or other property invested. I am aware that it is open to me to seek advice from an authorised person who specialises in advising on non-mainstream pooled investments.

Signature:

Date: "

4.12.7 R   FCA

A *certified sophisticated investor* is an individual:

(1)   who has a written certificate signed within the last 36 months by a *firm* confirming he has been assessed by that *firm* as sufficiently knowledgeable to understand the risks associated with engaging in investment activity in *non-mainstream pooled investments*; and

(2)   who has signed, within the period of twelve months ending with the day on which the communication is made, a statement in the following terms:

"SOPHISTICATED INVESTOR STATEMENT

I make this statement so that I can receive promotional communications which are exempt from the restriction on promotion of non-mainstream pooled investments. The exemption relates to certified sophisticated investors and I declare that I qualify as such.

I accept that the investments to which the promotions will relate may expose me to a significant risk of losing all of the money or other property invested. I am aware that it is open to me to seek advice from an authorised person who specialises in advising on non-mainstream pooled investments.

Signature:

Date: "

4.12.8 R   FCA

A *self-certified sophisticated investor* is an individual who has signed, within the period of twelve months ending with the day on which the communication is made, a statement in the following terms:

"SELF-CERTIFIED SOPHISTICATED INVESTOR STATEMENT

I declare that I am a self-certified sophisticated investor for the purposes of the restriction on promotion of non-mainstream pooled investments. I understand that this means:

(i) I can receive promotional communications made by a person who is authorised by the Financial Conduct Authority which relate to investment activity in non-mainstream pooled investments;

(ii) the investments to which the promotions will relate may expose me to a significant risk of losing all of the property invested.

I am a self-certified sophisticated investor because at least one of the following applies:

(a) I am a member of a network or syndicate of business angels and have been so for at least the last six months prior to the date below;

(b) I have made more than one investment in an unlisted company in the two years prior to the date below;

(c) I am working, or have worked in the two years prior to the date below, in a professional capacity in the private equity sector, or in the provision of finance for small and medium enterprises;

(d) I am currently, or have been in the two years prior to the date below, a director of a company with an annual turnover of at least £1 million.

I accept that the investments to which the promotions will relate may expose me to a significant risk of losing all of the money or other property invested. I am aware that it is open to me seek advice from someone who specialises in advising on non-mainstream pooled investments.

Signature:

Date: "

Sophisticated and high net worth investors: guidance on certification by authorised person and reliance on self-certification

4.12.9 G   FCA

(1)   A *firm* which wishes to rely on any of the *certified high net worth investor* exemptions (see Part I of the Schedule to the *Promotion of Collective Investment Schemes Order*, Part I of Schedule 5 to the *Financial Promotions Order* and **COBS 4.12.6 R**) should have regard to its duties under the *Principles* and the *client's best interests rule*. In particular, the *firm* should take reasonable steps to ascertain that the *retail client* does, in fact, meet the income and net assets criteria set out in the relevant statement for *certified high net worth investors*.

(2)   In addition, the *firm* should consider whether the promotion of the *non-mainstream pooled investment* is in the interests of the *retail client* and whether it is fair to make the promotion to that *client* on the basis that the *client* is a *certified high net worth investor*, having regard to the generally complex nature of *non-mainstream pooled investments*. A *retail client* who meets the criteria for a *certified high net worth investor* but not for a *certified sophisticated investor* may be unable to properly understand and evaluate the risks of the *non-mainstream pooled investment* in question.

4.12.10 G   FCA

(1)   A *firm* which is asked to or proposes to assess and certify a *retail client* as a *certified sophisticated investor* (see article 23 of the *Promotion of Collective Investment Schemes Order*, article 50 of the *Financial Promotions Order* and **COBS 4.12.7 R**) should have regard to its duties under the *Principles* and the *client's best interests rule*. In particular, the *firm* should carry out that assessment with due skill, care and diligence, having regard to the generally complex nature of *non-mainstream pooled investments* and the level of experience, knowledge and expertise the *retail client* being assessed must possess in order to be fairly and reasonably assessed and certified as a sophisticated investor.

(2)

(a)   For example, a *retail client* whose *investment* experience is limited to mainstream *investments* such as *securities* issued by *listed companies*, *life policies* or *units* in *regulated collective investment schemes* (other than *qualified investor schemes*) is generally unlikely to possess the requisite knowledge to adequately understand the risks associated with investing in *non-mainstream pooled investments*.

(b)   In exceptional circumstances, however, the *retail client* may have acquired the requisite knowledge through means other than his own investment experience, for example, if the *retail client* is a professional of several years' experience with the design, operation or marketing of complex investments such as *options*, *futures*, *contracts for differences* or *non-mainstream pooled investments*.

4.12.11 G   FCA

(1)   A *firm* which wishes to rely on any of the *self-certified sophisticated investor* exemptions (see Part II of the Schedule to the *Promotion of Collective Investment Schemes Order*, Part II of Schedule 5 to the *Financial Promotions Order* and **COBS 4.12.8 R**) should have regard to its duties under the *Principles* and the *client's best interests rule*. In particular, the *firm* should consider whether the promotion of the *non-mainstream pooled investment* is in the interests of the *client* and whether it is fair to make the promotion to that *client* on the basis of self-certification.

(2)   For example, it is unlikely to be appropriate for a *firm* to make a promotion under any of the *self-certified sophisticated investor* exemption without first taking reasonable steps to satisfy itself that the investor does in fact have the requisite experience, knowledge or expertise to understand the risks of the *non-mainstream pooled investment* in question. A *retail client* who meets the criteria for a *self-certified sophisticated investor* but not for a *certified sophisticated investor* may be unable to properly understand and evaluate the risks of a *non-mainstream pooled investment* which invests wholly or predominantly in assets other than *shares* in or *debentures* of unlisted *companies*.

One-off promotions

4.12.12 G   FCA

(1)   A firm which wishes to rely on one of the *one-off promotion* exemptions provided by the *Promotion of Collective Investment Schemes* or the *Financial Promotion Order* to promote a *non-mainstream pooled investment* to a *retail client* should have regard to its duties under the *Principles* and the *client's best interests rule*. In particular, the *firm* should consider whether the promotion of the *non-mainstream pooled investment* is in the interests of the *client* and whether it is fair to make the promotion to that *client* on the basis of a *one-off promotion* exemption.

(2)   The *one-off promotion* exemptions permit the promotion of investments to clients under certain conditions (see **PERG 8.14.3 G** to **PERG 8.14.13 G** for guidance on the scope of the one-off exemptions in the *Financial Promotion Order*). *Firms* should note that, in the *FCA's* view, promotion of a *non-mainstream pooled investment* to a *retail client* who is not a *certified high net worth investor*, a *certified sophisticated investor* or a *self-certified sophisticated investor* is unlikely to be appropriate or in that *client's* best interests.

Qualified investor schemes

4.12.13 G   FCA

(1)   A *firm* which wishes to rely on the *excluded communications* exemption in **COBS 4.12.4 R (5)** to promote *units* in a *qualified investor scheme* to a *retail client* should have regard to its duties under the *Principles* and the *client's best interests rule*.

(2)   As explained in **COLL 8.1**, *qualified investor schemes* are intended only for *professional clients* and *retail clients* who are sophisticated investors. Firms should note that, in the *FCA's* view, promotion of *units* in a *qualified investor scheme* to a *retail client* who is not a *certified sophisticated investor* or a *self-certified sophisticated investor* is unlikely to be appropriate or in that client's best interests.

Electronic documents

4.12.14 G   FCA

In this section:

(1)   any requirement that a document is signed may be satisfied by an electronic signature or electronic evidence of assent; and

(2)   any references to writing should be construed in accordance with **GEN 2.2.14 R** and its related *guidance* provisions.

4.13   UCITS

Application

4.13.1 R   FCA

(1)   This section applies to a *firm* in relation to a communication to a *client*, including an *excluded communication*, that is a marketing communication within the meaning of the *UCITS Directive*.

(2)   This section does not apply to:
   (a)   *image advertising*; or
   (b)   the *instrument constituting the fund*, the *prospectus*, the *key investor information* (or alternatively the *simplified prospectus* or *EEA simplified prospectus*) or the periodic reports and accounts of either a *UCITS scheme* or an *EEA UCITS scheme*.

[**Note:** recital (58) of the *UCITS Directive*]

Marketing communications relating to UCITS schemes or EEA UCITS schemes

4.13.2 R   FCA
(1)   A *firm* must ensure that a marketing communication that comprises an invitation to purchase *units* in a *UCITS scheme* or *EEA UCITS scheme* and that contains specific information about the *scheme*:
   (a)   makes no statement that contradicts or diminishes the significance of the information contained in the *prospectus* and the *key investor information document* or *EEA key investor information document* for the scheme;
   (b)   indicates that a *prospectus* exists for the *scheme* and that the *key investor information document* or *EEA key investor information document* is available; and
   (c)   specifies where and in which language such information or *documents* may be obtained by investors or potential investors or how they may obtain access to them.

(2)   Where a *UCITS scheme* or an *EEA UCITS scheme* may invest more than 35% of its *scheme property* in *transferable securities* and money market instruments issued or guaranteed by an *EEA State*, one or more of its local authorities, a third country or a public international body to which one or more *EEA States* belong, the *firm* must ensure that a marketing communication relating to the *scheme* contains a prominent statement drawing attention to the investment policy and indicating the particular *EEA States*, local authorities, third countries or public international bodies in the *securities* of which the *scheme* intends to invest or has invested more than 35% of its *scheme property*.

(3)   Where a *UCITS scheme* or *EEA UCITS scheme* invests principally in *units* in *collective investment schemes*, *deposits* or *derivatives*, or replicates a stock or debt securities index in accordance with **COLL 5.2.31 R** (Schemes replicating an index) or equivalent national measures implementing article 53 of the *UCITS Directive*, the *firm* must ensure that a marketing communication relating to the *scheme* contains a prominent statement drawing attention to the investment policy.

(4)   Where the net asset value of a *UCITS scheme* or *EEA UCITS scheme* has, or is likely to have, high volatility owing to its portfolio composition or the portfolio management techniques that are or may be used, the *firm* must ensure that a marketing communication relating to the *scheme* contains a prominent statement drawing attention to that characteristic.

[**Note:** articles 54(3), 70(2), 70(3) and 77 of the *UCITS Directive*]

Marketing communications relating to a feeder UCITS

4.13.3 R   FCA

A *firm* must ensure that a marketing communication (other than a *key investor information document* or *EEA key investor information document*) relating to a *feeder UCITS* contains a statement that the *feeder UCITS* permanently invests at least 85% in value of its assets in *units* of its *master UCITS*.

[**Note:** article 63(4) of the *UCITS Directive*]

CHAPTER 5
DISTANCE COMMUNICATIONS

5.1   THE DISTANCE MARKETING DISCLOSURE RULES

Application

[3.53]
5.1.-1 R   FCA
(1)   This section applies to a *firm* that carries on any distance marketing activity from an establishment in the *United Kingdom*, with or for a *consumer* in the *United Kingdom* or another *EEA State*.
(2)   If a *firm* is an intermediary rather than the supplier under the *distance contract*, references to '*firm*' in **COBS 5 ANNEX 1 R** and **COBS 5 ANNEX 2 R** are to be interpreted as referring to the supplier except for references to '*firm*' in **COBS 5 ANNEX 1 R** (2), (4) and (18).

The distance marketing disclosure rules

5.1.1 R   FCA

A *firm* must provide a *consumer* with the distance marketing information (**COBS 5 ANNEX 1 R**) in good time before the *consumer* is bound by a *distance contract* or offer.

[**Note:** article 3(1) of the *Distance Marketing Directive*]

5.1.2 R   FCA

A *firm* must ensure that the distance marketing information, the commercial purpose of which must be made clear, is provided in a clear and comprehensible manner in any way appropriate to the means of distance communication used, with due regard, in particular, to the principles of good faith in commercial transactions, and the legal principles governing the protection of those who are unable to give their consent, such as minors.

[**Note:** article 3(2) of the *Distance Marketing Directive*]

5.1.3 R   FCA

When a *firm* makes a voice telephony communication to a *consumer*, it must make its identity and the purpose of its call explicitly clear at the beginning of the conversation.

[**Note:** article 3(3)(a) of the *Distance Marketing Directive*]

Exception: contracts for payment services

5.1.3A R   FCA

Where a *distance contract* is also a contract for payment services to which the Payment Services Regulations apply, a *firm* is required to provide to the *consumer* only the information specified in rows 7 to 12, 15, 16 and 20 of **COBS 5 ANNEX 1 R**. [**Note**: article 4(5) of the *Distance Marketing Directive*]

5.1.3B G   FCA

Where a *distance contract* covers both payment services and non-payment services, this exception applies only to the payment services aspects of the contract. A *firm* taking advantage of this exception will need to comply with the information requirements in Part 5 of the Payment Services Regulations.

5.1.4 R   FCA

A *firm* must ensure that information on contractual obligations to be communicated to a *consumer* during the pre-contractual phase is in conformity with the contractual obligations which would result from the law presumed to be applicable to the *distance contract* if that contract is concluded.

[**Note:** article 3(4) of the *Distance Marketing Directive*]

Terms and conditions, and form

5.1.5 R   FCA

A *firm* must communicate to the *consumer* all the contractual terms and conditions and the information referred to in the distance marketing disclosure *rules* (**COBS 5.1.1 R** to **COBS 5.1.4 R**) on a *durable medium* available and accessible to the *consumer* in good time before the *consumer* is bound by any *distance contract* or offer.

[**Note:** article 5(1) of the *Distance Marketing Directive*]

5.1.6 G   FCA

A *firm* will provide information, or communicate contractual terms and conditions, to a *consumer* if another *person* provides the information, or communicates the terms and conditions, to the *consumer* on its behalf.

Exception: distance contract as a stage in the provision of another service

5.1.7 R   FCA

This section does not apply to a *distance contract* to deal as agent, advise or arrange, if the *distance contract* is concluded merely as a stage in the provision of another service by the *firm* or another *person*.

[**Note:** recital 19 to the *Distance Marketing Directive*]

Exception: successive operations

5.1.8 R   FCA

In the case of a *distance contract* comprising an initial service agreement, followed by successive operations or a series of separate operations of the same nature performed over time, the *rules* in this section only apply to the initial agreement.

[**Note:** article 1(2) of the *Distance Marketing Directive*]

5.1.9 R   FCA

Part 3   FCA Handbook Materials

If there is no initial service agreement but the successive operations or separate operations of the same nature performed over time are performed between the same contractual parties, the distance marketing disclosure *rules* (**COBS 5.1.1 R** to **COBS 5.1.4 R**) will only apply:

(1)   when the first operation is performed; and

(2)   if no operation of the same nature is performed for more than a year, when the next operation is performed (the next operation being deemed the first in a new series of operations).

[**Note:** recital 16 and article 1(2) of the *Distance Marketing Directive*]

5.1.10 G   FCA

In this section:

(1)   'initial service agreement' includes the opening of a bank account and the concluding of a portfolio management contract;

(2)   'operations' includes transactions made within the framework of a portfolio management contract; and

(3)   adding new elements to an initial service agreement, such as the ability to use an electronic payment instrument together with one's existing bank account, does not constitute an 'operation' but an additional contract to which the *rules* in this section apply. The subscription to new *units* of the same *fund* is considered to be one of 'successive operations of the same nature'.

[**Note:** recital 17 of the *Distance Marketing Directive*]

5.1.11 G   FCA

In the *FCA's* view, other examples of:

(1)   'initial service agreement' include:

    (a)   subscribing to an *investment trust savings scheme*; or

    (b)   concluding a *life policy, personal pension scheme* or *stakeholder pension scheme* that includes a pre-selected option providing for future increases or decreases in regular *premiums* or payments; and

(2)   'operations' include:

    (a)   successive purchases or sales of *shares* under an *investment trust savings scheme*; and

    (b)   subsequent index-linked changes to premiums or increases or decreases to pension contributions following fluctuations in salary.

Exception: voice telephony communications

5.1.12 R   FCA

In the case of a voice telephony communication, and subject to the explicit consent of the *consumer*, only the abbreviated distance marketing information (**COBS 5 ANNEX 2 R**) needs to be provided during that communication. However, a *firm* must still provide the distance marketing information (**COBS 5 ANNEX 1 R**) on a *durable medium* available and accessible to the *consumer* in good time before the *consumer* is bound by any *distance contract* or offer, unless another exception applies.

[**Note:** articles 3(3)(b) and 5(1) of the *Distance Marketing Directive*]

Exception: means of distance communication not enabling disclosure

5.1.13 R   FCA

A *firm* may provide the distance marketing information (**COBS 5 ANNEX 1 R**) and the contractual terms and conditions in a *durable medium* immediately after the conclusion of a *distance contract*, if the contract has been concluded at a *consumer's* request using a means of distance communication that does not enable the provision of that information in that form in good time before the *consumer* is bound by any *distance contract* or offer.

[**Note:** article 5(2) of the *Distance Marketing Directive*]

Exception: contracts for payment services

5.1.13A R   FCA

Where a *distance contract* is also a contract for *payment services* to which the *Payment Services Regulations* apply, a *firm* is required to provide to the *consumer* only the information specified in rows 7 to 12, 15, 16 and 20 of **COBS 5 ANNEX 1 R**.

[**Note:** article 4(5) of the *Distance Marketing Directive*]

5.1.13B G   FCA

Where a *distance contract* covers both *payment services* and non-*payment services*, this exception applies only to the *payment services* aspects of the contract. A *firm* taking advantage of this exception will need to comply with the information requirements in Part 5 of the *Payment Services Regulations*.

Distance marketing: other provisions

5.1.14 R   FCA

If, at any time during the contractual relationship, a *consumer* that is a party to a *distance contract* asks a *firm*:

(1)   for a paper copy of the terms and conditions of that contract; or

(2)   to change the means of distance communication used;

the *firm* must provide that paper copy or change the means of distance communication used, unless (in the latter case) that would be incompatible with the contract or the nature of the service provided.

[Note: article 5(3) of the *Distance Marketing Directive*]

Unsolicited services

5.1.15 R   FCA

(1)   A *firm* must not enforce, or seek to enforce, any obligations under a *distance contract* against a *consumer*, in the event of an unsolicited supply of services, the absence of reply not constituting consent.

(2)   This *rule* does not apply to the tacit renewal of a *distance contract*.

[Note: article 9 of the *Distance Marketing Directive*]

Mandatory nature of consumer's rights

5.1.16 R   FCA

If a *consumer* purports to waive any of the *consumer's* rights created or implied by the *rules* in this section, a *firm* must not accept that waiver, nor seek to rely on or enforce it against the *consumer*.

[Note: article 12 of the *Distance Marketing Directive*]

5.1.17 R   FCA

If a *firm* proposes to enter into a *distance contract* with a *consumer* that will be governed by the law of a country outside the *EEA*, the *firm* must ensure that the *consumer* will not lose the protection created by the *rules* in this section if the *distance contract* has a close link with the territory of one or more *EEA States*.

[Note: articles 12 and 16 of the *Distance Marketing Directive*]

5.2   E-COMMERCE

Application

5.2.1 R   FCA

This section applies to a *firm* carrying on an *electronic commerce activity* from an *establishment* in the *United Kingdom*, with or for a *person* in the *United Kingdom* or another *EEA State*.

Information about the firm and its products or services

5.2.2 R   FCA

A *firm* must make at least the following information easily, directly and permanently accessible to the recipients of the *information society services* it provides:

(1)   its name;

(2)   the geographic address at which it is established;

(3)   the details of the *firm*, including its e-mail address, which allow it to be contacted rapidly and communicated with in a direct and effective manner;

(4)   an appropriate statutory status disclosure statement (**GEN 4 ANNEX 1 R** or **GEN 4 ANNEX 1A R** as appropriate), together with a statement which explains that it is on the *Financial Services Register* and includes its Firm Reference Number;

(5)   if it is a *professional firm*, or a *person* regulated by the equivalent of a *designated professional body* in another *EEA State*:

    (a)   the name of the professional body (including any *designated professional body*) or similar institution with which it is registered;

    (b)   the professional title and the *EEA State* where it was granted;

    (c)   a reference to the applicable professional rules in the *EEA State* of establishment and the means to access them; and

(6)   where the *firm* undertakes an activity that is subject to VAT, its VAT number.

[Note: article 5(1) of the *E-Commerce Directive*]

5.2.3 R   FCA

If a *firm* refers to price, it must do so clearly and unambiguously, indicating whether the price is inclusive of tax and delivery costs.

[Note: article 5(2) of the *E-Commerce Directive*]

5.2.4 R   FCA

A *firm* must ensure that commercial communications which are part of, or constitute, an *information society service*, comply with the following conditions:

(1)   the commercial communication must be clearly identifiable as such;

(2)   the *person* on whose behalf the commercial communication is made must be clearly identifiable;

(3)   promotional offers must be clearly identifiable as such, and the conditions that must be met to qualify for them must be easily accessible and presented clearly and unambiguously; and

(4)   promotional competitions or games must be clearly identifiable as such, and the conditions for participation must be easily accessible and presented clearly and unambiguously.

[**Note:** article 6 of the *E-Commerce Directive*]

5.2.5 R   FCA

An unsolicited commercial communication sent by e-mail by a *firm* established in the *United Kingdom* must be identifiable clearly and unambiguously as an unsolicited commercial communication as soon as it is received by the recipient.

[**Note:** article 7(1) of the *E-Commerce Directive*]

Requirements relating to the placing and receipt of orders

5.2.6 R   FCA

A *firm* must (except when otherwise agreed by parties who are not *consumers*):

(1)   give an *ECA recipient* at least the following information, clearly, comprehensibly and unambiguously, and prior to the order being placed by the recipient of the service:

    (a)   the different technical steps to follow to conclude the contract;

    (b)   whether or not the concluded contract will be filed by the *firm* and whether it will be accessible;

    (c)   the technical means for identifying and correcting input errors prior to the placing of the order; and

    (d)   the languages offered for the conclusion of the contract;

(2)   indicate any relevant codes of conduct to which it subscribes and information on how those codes can be consulted electronically;

(3)   (when an *ECA recipient* places an order through technological means), acknowledge the receipt of the recipient's order without undue delay and by electronic means; and

(4)   make available to an *ECA recipient*, appropriate, effective and accessible technical means allowing the recipient to identify and correct input errors prior to the placing of an order.

[**Note:** articles 10(1) and (2) and 11(1) and (2) of the *E-Commerce Directive*]

5.2.7 R   FCA

For the purposes of **COBS 5.2.6 R (3)**, an order and an acknowledgement of receipt are deemed to be received when the parties to whom they are addressed are able to access them.

[**Note:** article 11(1) of the *E-Commerce Directive*]

5.2.8 R   FCA

Contractual terms and conditions provided by a *firm* to an *ECA recipient* must be made available in a way that allows the recipient to store and reproduce them.

[**Note:** article 10(3) of the *E-Commerce Directive*]

Exception: contract concluded by e-mail

5.2.9 R   FCA

The requirements relating to the placing and receipt of orders (**COBS 5.2.6 R**) do not apply to contracts concluded exclusively by exchange of e-mail or by equivalent individual communications.

[**Note:** article 10(4) and 11(3) of the *E-Commerce Directive*]FCA

5 ANNEX 1 R   DISTANCE MARKETING INFORMATION

This Annex belongs to **COBS 5.1.1 R** (The distance marketing disclosure rules)

Information about the firm
(1)   The name and the main business of the *firm*, the geographical address at which it is established and any other geographical address relevant for the *consumer's* relations with the *firm*.
(2)   Where the *firm* has a representative established in the *consumer's* *EEA State* of residence, the name of that representative and the geographical address relevant for the *consumer's* relations with that representative.

(3)   Where the *consumer's* dealings are with any professional other than the *firm*, the identity of that professional, the capacity in which he is acting with respect to the *consumer*, and the geographical address relevant to the *consumer's* relations with that professional.

(4)   An appropriate statutory status disclosure statement (**GEN 4**), a statement that the *firm* is on the *Financial Services Register* and its *FCA* registration number.

Information about the financial service

(5)   A description of the main characteristics of the service the *firm* will provide.

(6)   The total price to be paid by the *consumer* to the *firm* for the financial service, including all related fees, charges and expenses, and all taxes paid through the *firm* or, where an exact price cannot be indicated, the basis for the calculation of the price enabling the *consumer* to verify it.

(7)   Where relevant, notice indicating that the service is related to instruments involving special risks related to their specific features or the operations to be executed or whose price depends on fluctuations in the financial markets outside the *firm's* control and that past performance is no indicator of future performance.

(8)   Notice of the possibility that other taxes or costs may exist that are not paid via the *firm* or imposed by it.

(9)   Any limitations on the period for which the information provided is valid, including a clear explanation as to how long a *firm's* offer applies as it stands.

(10)   The arrangements for payment and performance.

(11)   Details of any specific additional cost to the *consumer* for using a means of distance communication.

Information about the contract

(12)   The existence or absence of a right to cancel or withdraw under the cancellation rules (**COBS 15**) and, where there is such a right, its duration and the conditions for exercising it, including information on the amount which the *consumer* may be required to pay (or which may not be returned to the *consumer*) in accordance with those *rules*, as well as the consequences of not exercising the right to cancel or withdraw.

(13)   The minimum duration of the contract, in the case of services to be performed permanently or recurrently.

(14)   Information on any rights the parties may have to terminate the contract early or unilaterally under its terms, including any penalties imposed by the contract in such cases.

(15)   Practical instructions for exercising any right to cancel or withdraw, including the address to which any cancellation or withdrawal notice should be sent.

(16)   The *EEA State* or States whose laws are taken by the *firm* as a basis for the establishment of relations with the *consumer* prior to the conclusion of the contract.

(17)   Any contractual clause on the law applicable to the contract or on the competent court, or both.

(18)   In which language, or languages, the contractual terms and conditions and the other information in this Annex will be supplied, and in which language, or languages, the *firm*, with the agreement of the *consumer*, undertakes to communicate during the duration of the contract.

Information about redress

(19)   How to complain to the *firm*, whether complaints may subsequently be referred to the *Financial Ombudsman Service* and, if so, the methods for having access to it, together with equivalent information about any other applicable named complaints scheme.

(20)   Whether compensation may be available from the *compensation scheme*, or any other named compensation scheme, if the *firm* is unable to meet its liabilities.

[**Note:** Recitals 21 and 23 to, and article 3(1) of, the *Distance Marketing Directive*]FCA

Part 3   FCA Handbook Materials

5 ANNEX 2 R   ABBREVIATED DISTANCE MARKETING DISCLOSURE

This Annex belongs to **COBS 5.1.12 R**

(1)   The identity of the *person* in contact with the *consumer* and his link with the *firm*.

(2)   A description of the main characteristics of the financial service.

(3)   The total price to be paid by the *consumer* to the *firm* for the financial service including all taxes paid via the *firm* or, when an exact price cannot be indicated, the basis for the calculation of the price enabling the *consumer* to verify it.

(4)   Notice of the possibility that other taxes and/or costs may exist that are not paid via the *firm* or imposed by him.

(5)   The existence or absence of a right to cancel or withdraw in accordance with the cancellation rules (**COBS 15**) and, where the right to cancel or withdraw exists, its duration and the conditions for exercising it, including information on the amount the *consumer* may be required to pay on the basis of the cancellation rules.

(6)   That other information is available on request and what the nature of that information is.

[**Note:** article 3(3)(b) of the *Distance Marketing Directive*]

CHAPTER 6
INFORMATION ABOUT THE FIRM, ITS SERVICES AND REMUNERATION

6.1   INFORMATION ABOUT THE FIRM AND COMPENSATION INFORMATION

Application

[3.54]

6.1.1 R   FCA

(1)   This section applies to a *firm* that carries on *designated investment business* for:
    (a)   a *retail client*; and
    (b)   in the case of *MiFID or equivalent third country business*, a *client*.

(2)   If expressly provided, this section also applies to *ancillary services* not covered by (1), but only in the course of *MiFID or equivalent third country business* carried on with or for a *client*.

6.1.2 R   FCA

If a *firm* provides *basic advice on stakeholder products* in accordance with the *basic advice rules*, this section does not apply to that service.

6.1.3 G   FCA

This section imposes requirements relating to disclosure of information to *clients* that are additional to the general requirement in **COBS 2.2**.

Information about a firm and its services

6.1.4 R   FCA

A *firm* must provide a *retail client* with the following general information, if relevant:

(1)   the name and address of the *firm*, and the contact details necessary to enable a *client* to communicate effectively with the *firm*;

(2)   in the case of *MiFID or equivalent third country business*, the languages in which the *client* may communicate with the *firm*, and receive documents and other information from the *firm*;

(3)   the methods of communication to be used between the *firm* and the *client* including, where relevant, those for the sending and reception of orders;

(4)   a statement of the fact that the *firm* is authorised and the name of the *competent authority* that has authorised it;

(5)   in the case of *MiFID or equivalent third country business*, the contact address of the *competent authority* that has authorised the *firm*;

(6)   if the *firm* is acting through an *appointed representative* or, where applicable, a *tied agent*, a statement of this fact specifying the *EEA State* in which that *appointed representative* or *tied agent* is registered;

(7)   the nature, frequency and timing of the reports on the performance of the service to be provided by the *firm* to the *client* in accordance with the *rules* on reporting to *clients* on the provision of services (**COBS 16**);

(8)
    (a)   in the case of a *common platform firm*, a description, which may be provided in summary form, of the *conflicts of interest policy*;
    (b)   other than in the case of a *common platform firm*, when a *material interest* or conflict of interest may or does arise, the manner in which the *firm* will ensure fair treatment of the *client*;

(9)   in the case of a *common platform firm*, at any time that the *client* requests it, further details of the *conflicts of interest policy*.

[**Note:** article 30(1) of the *MiFID implementing Directive*]

6.1.5 G   FCA

A *firm* disclosing details of its authorisation should refer to the appropriate forms of words set out in **GEN 4 ANNEX 1 R** or **GEN 4 ANNEX 1A R** as appropriate.

6.1.6 R   FCA

(1)   A *firm* that *manages investments* for a *client* must establish an appropriate method of evaluation and comparison such as a meaningful benchmark, based on the investment objectives of the *client* and the types of *designated investments* included in the *client* portfolio, so as to enable the *client* to assess the *firm's* performance.

(2)   If a *firm* proposes to *manage investments* for a *retail client*, the *firm* must provide the *client* with such of the following information as is applicable:

    (a)   information on the method and frequency of valuation of the *designated investments* in the *client* portfolio;

    (b)   details of any delegation of the discretionary management of all or part of the *designated investments* or funds in the *client* portfolio;

    (c)   a specification of any benchmark against which the performance of the *client* portfolio will be compared;

    (d)   the types of *designated investments* that may be included in the *client* portfolio and types of transaction that may be carried out in those *designated investments*, including any limits; and

    (e)   the management objectives, the level of risk to be reflected in the manager's exercise of discretion, and any specific constraints on that discretion.

[**Note:** articles 30(2) and (3) of the *MiFID implementing Directive*]

Information concerning safeguarding of designated investments belonging to clients and client money

6.1.7 R   FCA

(1)   A *firm* that holds *designated investments* or *client money* for a *retail client* subject to the *custody chapter* or the *client money chapter* must provide that *client* with the following information:

    (a)   if applicable,

        (i)   that the *designated investments* or *client money* of that *client* may be held by a third party on behalf of the *firm*;

        (ii)   the responsibility of the *firm* under the applicable national law for any acts or omissions of the third party; and

        (iii)   the consequences for the *client* of the insolvency of the third party;

    (b)   if applicable, that the *designated investments* belonging to the *retail client* may be held in an omnibus account by a third party and a prominent warning of the resulting risks;

    (c)   if it is not possible under national law for *designated investments* belonging to a *client* held with a third party to be separately identifiable from the proprietary *designated investments* of that third party or of the *firm*, that fact and a prominent warning of the resulting risks;

    (d)   if applicable, that accounts that contain *designated investments* or *client money* belonging to that *client* are or will be subject to the law of a jurisdiction other than that of a *EEA State*, an indication that the rights of the *client* relating to those instruments or money may differ accordingly;

    (e)   a summary description of the steps which it takes to ensure the protection of any *designated investments* belonging to the *client* or *client money* it holds, including summary details of any relevant investor compensation or deposit guarantee scheme which applies to the *firm* by virtue of its activities in an *EEA State*.

(2)   A *firm* that holds *designated investments* or *client money* for a *retail client* must inform the client:

    (a)   if applicable, about the existence and the terms of any security interest or lien which the *firm* has or may have over the *client's designated investments* or *client money*, or any right of set-off it holds in relation to the *client's designated investments* or *client money*; and

    (b)   if applicable, that a depositary may have a security interest or lien over, or right of set-off in relation to those instruments or money.

(3)   A *firm* within (1) must also, before entering into *securities financing transactions* in relation to *designated investments* held by it on behalf of a *retail client*, or before otherwise using such *designated investments* for its own account or the account of another *client*, in good time before the use of those *designated investments* provide the *client*, in a *durable medium*, with clear, full and accurate information on the obligations and responsibilities of the *firm* with respect to the use of those *designated investments*, including the terms for their restitution, and on the risks involved.

(4)   A *firm* within (1) that holds *client designated investments* or *client money* for a *professional client* must provide that *client* with the information in paragraphs (1)(d) and (2)(a) and (b).

[**Note:** articles 29(3), 30(1)(g) and 32 of the *MiFID implementing Directive*]

6.1.7A G   FCA

Firms subject to either or both the *custody rules* and the *client money rules* are reminded of the information requirements concerning *custody assets* and *client money* in **CASS 9.3** (Prime brokerage agreement disclosure annex) and **CASS 9.4** (Information to clients concerning custody assets and client money).

6.1.8 G

[deleted]

Information about costs and associated charges

6.1.9 R   FCA

A *firm* must provide a *retail client* with information on costs and associated charges including, if applicable:
(1) the total price to be paid by the *client* in connection with the *designated investment* or the *designated investment business* or *ancillary services*, including all related fees, commissions, charges and expenses, and all taxes payable via the *firm* or, if an exact price cannot be indicated, the basis for the calculation of the total price so that the *client* can verify it. The commissions charged by the *firm* must be itemised separately in every case;
(2) if any part of the total price referred to (1) is to be paid in or represents an amount of foreign currency, an indication of the currency involved and the applicable currency conversion rates and costs;
(3) notice of the possibility that other costs, including taxes, related to transactions in connection with the *designated investment* or the *designated investment business* may arise for the *client* that are not paid via the *firm* or imposed by it; and
(4) the arrangements for payment or other performance.

[**Note:** article 33 of the *MiFID implementing Directive*]

6.1.10 G   FCA

The *rules* on inducements in **COBS 2.3** may also require a *firm* to disclose information to a *client* in relation to benefits provided to the *firm*.

Timing of disclosure

6.1.11 R   FCA

(1) A *firm* must provide a *client* with the information required by this section in good time before the provision of *designated investment business* or *ancillary services* unless otherwise provided by this *rule*.
(2) A *firm* may instead provide that information immediately after starting to provide *designated investment business* or *ancillary services* if:
   (a) the *firm* was unable to comply with (1) because, at the request of the *client*, the agreement was concluded using a means of distance communication which prevented the *firm* from doing so; and
   (b) in any case where the *rule* on voice telephony communications (**COBS 5.1.12 R**) does not otherwise apply, the *firm* complies with that *rule* in relation to the *retail client*, as if that *client* were a *consumer*.

[**Note:** article 29(2), 29(3) and 29(5) of the *MiFID implementing Directive*]

6.1.12 G   FCA

A *firm* should take into account **COBS 8.1.3 R (1)**, which requires earlier disclosure of some items of information covered in this section.

Medium of disclosure

6.1.13 R   FCA

Except where expressly provided, a *firm* must provide the information required by this section in a *durable medium* or via a website (where it does not constitute a *durable medium*) where the *website conditions* are satisfied.

[**Note:** article 29(4) of the *MiFID implementing Directive*]

Keeping the client up to date

6.1.14 R   FCA

(1) A *firm* must notify a *client* in good time about any material change to the information provided under this section which is relevant to a service that the *firm* is providing to that *client*.
(2) A *firm* must provide this notification in a *durable medium* if the information to which it relates was given in a *durable medium*.

[**Note:** article 29(6) of the *MiFID implementing Directive*]

Existing clients

6.1.15 G   FCA

(1)   A *firm* need not treat each of several transactions in respect of the same type of *financial instrument* as a new or different service and so does not need to comply with the disclosure *rules* in this chapter in relation to each transaction.

[**Note:** recital 50 to the *MiFID implementing Directive*]

(2)   But a *firm* should ensure that the *client* has received all relevant information in relation to a subsequent transaction, such as details of product charges that differ from those disclosed in respect of a previous transaction.

Compensation information

6.1.16 R   FCA

(1)   A *firm* carrying on *MiFID business* must make available to a *client*, who has used or intends to use those services, information necessary for the identification of the *compensation scheme* or any other investor-compensation scheme of which the *firm* is a member (including, if relevant, membership through a *branch*) or any alternative arrangement provided for in accordance with the *Investor Compensation Directive*.

(2)   The information under (1) must include the amount and scope of the cover offered by the compensation scheme and any rules laid down by the *EEA State* pursuant to article 2 (3) of the *Investor Compensation Directive*.

(3)   A *firm* must provide, on the *client's* request, information concerning the conditions governing compensation and the formalities which must be completed to obtain compensation.

(4)   The information provided for in this *rule* must be made available in a *durable medium* or via a website if the *website conditions* are satisfied in the official language or languages of the *EEA State*.

[**Note:** article 10(1) and (2) of the *Investor Compensation Directive*]

Record keeping: information about the firm and compensation information

6.1.17 G   FCA

Firms are reminded of the general record-keeping requirements in **SYSC 3.2** and **SYSC 9**.

6.1A   ADVISER CHARGING AND REMUNERATION

Application – Who? What?

6.1A.1 R   FCA

(1)   This section applies to a *firm* which makes *personal recommendations* to *retail clients* in relation to *retail investment products*.

(2)   This section does not apply to a *firm* giving advice, or providing services, to an employer in connection with a *group personal pension scheme* or *group stakeholder pension scheme*.

6.1A.1A G   FCA

Guidance on the regulated activity of advising in relation to a new or existing *investment* can be found in **PERG 8.24** to **PERG 8.29**. Although the *guidance* in **PERG 8.29.7 G** relates to *advising on investments* under article 53 of the *Regulated Activities Order*, exactly the same answers apply to a *personal recommendation* because the examples given relate to the relationship between a *firm* and a particular *client* and advice given to that specific *client*. A *firm* wishing to know when it will be giving advice but not making a *personal recommendation* should refer to **PERG 13.3**.

6.1A.2 R   FCA

This section does not apply to a *firm* when it gives *basic advice* in accordance with the *basic advice rules*.

6.1A.2A R   FCA

This section does not apply to a *firm* when it makes a *personal recommendation* to a *retail client* in relation to a *Holloway sickness policy*, provided that the *Holloway policy special application conditions* are met.

Application – Where?

6.1A.3 R   FCA

This section does not apply if the *retail client* is outside the *United Kingdom*.

Requirement to be paid through adviser charges

6.1A.4 R   FCA

Except as specified in **COBS 6.1A.4A R**, **COBS 6.1A.4AB R**, **COBS 6.1A.4AC G** and **COBS 6.1A.4B R**, a *firm* must:

(1)   only be remunerated for the *personal recommendation* (and any other related services provided by the *firm*) by *adviser charges*; and

(2)   not solicit or accept (and ensure that none of its *associates* solicits or accepts) any other commissions, remuneration or benefit of any kind in relation to the *personal recommendation* or any other related service, regardless of whether it intends to refund the payments or pass the benefits on to the *retail client*; and

(3)   not solicit or accept (and ensure that none of its *associates* solicits or accepts) *adviser charges* in relation to the *retail client's retail investment product* which are paid out or advanced by another party over a materially different time period, or on a materially different basis, from that in or on which the *adviser charges* are recovered from the *retail client*.

6.1A.4A R   FCA

A *firm* and its *associates* may:

(1)   solicit and accept a commission, remuneration or benefit of any kind in the circumstances set out in **COBS 6.1A.4 R** if:

    (a)   the *personal recommendation* was made on or before 30 December 2012;

    (b)   the solicitation and acceptance of the commission, remuneration or benefit of any kind was permitted by the *rules* in force on 30 December 2012;

    (c)   the contract under which the right to receive the commission, remuneration or benefit of any kind was entered into on or before 30 December 2012;

    (d)   the terms of that contract as at 30 December 2012 included the right to receive the commission, remuneration or benefit of any kind; and

    (e)   the *retail client* enters into the transaction in respect of which the *personal recommendation* was given within a reasonable time of the *personal recommendation* being given; and

(2)   enter into an arrangement under which the right to receive the commission, remuneration or benefit of any kind in (1) is transferred to that *firm* or its *associate*.

6.1A.4AA G   FCA

(1)   A *firm* may continue to accept a commission, remuneration or benefit of any kind after 30 December 2012 if there is a clear link between the payment and an investment in a *retail investment product* which was made by the *retail client* following a *personal recommendation* made, or a transaction executed, on or before 30 December 2012. This is the case even if the *firm* makes a *personal recommendation* to the same *retail client* after 30 December 2012 to the extent that the continued payment can properly be regarded as linked to the pre 31 December 2012 *personal recommendation* or transaction, rather than the new *personal recommendation*. Of course this is dependent upon the terms of the contract contemplating the continued receipt of such payments.

(2)   Examples of circumstances where a commission, remuneration or benefit is clearly linked to the retention of an investment in a *retail investment product* and can therefore continue to be accepted include (in each case where the terms of the contract contemplate a continued payment of the kind referred to in (1)):

    (a)   no change is made to the *retail client's* investment in the relevant *retail investment product*;

    (b)   the *retail client's* investment in, or regular contribution to, the relevant *retail investment product* is reduced; the *firm* may continue to accept the payment associated with the reduced investment amount;

    (c)   the *retail client's* investment in the relevant *retail investment product* is transferred from accumulation *units* to income *units* or vice versa;

    (d)   the *retail client* transfers all or part of his investment between funds within a *life policy*.

(3)   If a *firm* makes a *personal recommendation* to a *retail client* and wishes to:

    (a)   receive remuneration for that *personal recommendation* in addition to any commission, remuneration or benefit of any kind it receives in the circumstances contemplated by (1); or

    (b)   be paid additional amounts for any actions which are linked to a new amount invested by the *retail client* in the relevant *retail investment product*;

it should only be paid those additional amounts for that *personal recommendation* or for those actions by *adviser charges*.

(4)   A *firm* may offset against any *adviser charges* which are payable by the *retail client* any commission, remuneration or benefit of any kind it receives in the circumstances contemplated in (1).

6.1A.4AB R   FCA

A *firm* and its *associates* may solicit and accept a commission, remuneration or benefit of any kind from a *discretionary investment manager* in the circumstances in **COBS 6.1A.4 R** if:

(1)   the *firm* or its associates recommended the *discretionary investment manager* to a *retail client* on or before 30 December 2012;

(2)   the solicitation and acceptance of the commission, remuneration or benefit of any kind was permitted by the *rules* in force on 30 December 2012;

(3)   the contract under which the right to receive the commission, remuneration or benefit of any kind was entered into on or before 30 December 2012;

(4)   the terms of that contract as at 30 December 2012 included the right to receive the commission, remuneration or benefit of any kind; and

(5)   the *retail client* agreed an investment mandate with the *discretionary investment manager* within a reasonable time of the recommendation to use the *discretionary investment manager* being made.

6.1A.4AC G   FCA

(1)   If a *firm* makes a recommendation of a *discretionary investment manager* to a *retail client* and wishes to:

      (a)   receive remuneration for that recommendation in addition to any commission, remuneration or benefit of any kind it receives in the circumstances contemplated by **COBS 6.1A.4AB R**; or

      (b)   be paid additional amounts for any actions linked to a new amount invested by the retail client through the same *discretionary investment manager*;

      it should only be paid those additional amounts for that recommendation or for those actions by *adviser charges*.

(2)   A *firm* may offset against any *adviser charges* which are payable by the *retail client* any commission, remuneration or benefit of any kind it receives in the circumstances contemplated in **COBS 6.1A.4AB R**.

Re-registration of commission when a retail client moves to a new adviser

6.1A.4B R   FCA

If a *retail client* chooses to become a *client* of a *firm* and that *firm* or its *associate* enters into an arrangement in **COBS 6.1A.4AR (2)**, the *firm* must:

(1)   before the arrangement is entered into, disclose to the *retail client* that the transfer of the commission, remuneration or benefit of any kind will be requested by the *firm* or its *associate*;

(2)   throughout the period during which the *firm* or its *associate* receives the commission, remuneration or benefit of any kind, provide the *retail client* with an ongoing service; and

(3)   as soon as reasonably practicable after it makes the disclosure in (1):

      (a)   disclose to the *retail client*, as a cash amount or percentage of funds under management, the amount of the commission, remuneration or benefit of any kind it expects to receive and any it has received; and

      (b)   provide the *retail client* with a description of the ongoing service it will provide to the *retail client* in accordance with (2).

6.1A.5 G   FCA

A *firm* may receive an *adviser charge* that is no longer payable (for example, after the service it is received in payment for has been amended or terminated) provided the *firm* refunds any such payment to the *retail client*.

6.1A.6 R   FCA

'Related service(s)' for the purposes of **COBS 6.1A** includes:

(1)   *arranging* or *executing* a transaction which has been recommended to a *retail client* by the *firm*, an *associate* or another *firm* in the same *group* or conducting administrative tasks associated with that transaction; or

(2)   managing a relationship between a *retail client* (to whom the *firm* provides *personal recommendations* on *retail investment products*) and a *discretionary investment manager* or providing a service to such a client in relation to the investments managed by such a manager; or

(3)   recommending a *discretionary investment manager* to a *retail client* (to whom the *firm* provides *personal recommendations* or other services in relation to *retail investment products*).

6.1A.6A G   FCA

'Other services' in **COBS 6.1A.6 R (3)** includes:

(1)   providing information relating to *retail investment products* to the *retail client*, for example, general market research; or

(2)   passing on information from the *discretionary investment manager* to the *retail client*.

6.1A.7 G   FCA

The requirement to be paid through *adviser charges* does not prevent a *firm* from making use of any facility for the payment of *adviser charges* on behalf of the *retail client* offered by another *firm* or other third parties provided that the facility complies with the requirements of **COBS 6.1B.9 R**.

6.1A.8 G   FCA

Examples of payments and benefits that should not be accepted under the requirement to be paid through *adviser charges* include:

(1)   a share of the *retail investment product* charges or *platform service provider's* charges, or *retail investment product* provider's or *platform service provider's* revenues or profits; and

(2)   a commission set and payable by a *retail investment product* provider in any jurisdiction.

Requirements on a retail investment product provider making a personal recommendation in respect of its own retail investment products

6.1A.9 R   FCA

If the *firm* or its *associate* is the *retail investment product* provider, the *firm* must ensure that the level of its *adviser charges* is at least reasonably representative of the services associated with making the *personal recommendation* (and related services).

6.1A.10 G   FCA

An *adviser charge* is likely to be reasonably representative of the services associated with making the *personal recommendation* if:

(1)   the expected long term costs associated with making a *personal recommendation* and distributing the *retail investment product* do not include the costs associated with manufacturing and administering the *retail investment product*;

(2)   the allocation of costs and profit to *adviser charges* and product charges is such that any cross-subsidisation is not significant in the long term; and

(3)   were the *personal recommendation* and any related services to be provided by an unconnected *firm*, the level of *adviser charges* would be appropriate in the context of the service being provided by the *firm*.

Requirement to use a charging structure

6.1A.11 R   FCA

A *firm* must determine and use an appropriate charging structure for calculating its *adviser charge* for each *retail client*.

6.1A.12 G   FCA

A *firm* can use a standard charging structure.

6.1A.13 G   FCA

In determining its charging structure and *adviser charges* a *firm* should have regard to its duties under the *client's best interests rule*. Practices which may indicate that a *firm* is not in compliance with this duty include:

(1)   varying its *adviser charges* inappropriately according to provider or, for substitutable and competing *retail investment products*, the type of *retail investment product*; or

(2)   allowing the availability or limitations of services offered by third parties to facilitate the payment of *adviser charges* to influence inappropriately its charging structure or *adviser charges*.

6.1A.14 R   FCA

A *firm* must not use a charging structure which conceals the amount or purpose of any of its *adviser charges* from a *retail client*.

6.1A.14A R   FCA

A *firm* must not make a *personal recommendation* to a *retail client* in relation to a *retail investment product* if it knows, or ought to know, that:

(1)   the product's charges or the *platform service provider's* charges are presented in a way that offsets or may appear to offset any *adviser charges* or *platform charges* that are payable by that *retail client*; or

(2)   the product's charges or other payments are maintained by the *retail investment product* provider at a level such that a cash rebate, other than a cash rebate permitted by **COBS 6.1B.7A R** or **COBS 6.1E.10 R (2)**, is payable to the *retail client*.

6.1A.15 G   FCA

A *firm* is likely to be viewed as operating a charging structure that conceals the amount or purpose of its *adviser charges* if, for example:

(1)   it makes arrangements for amounts in excess of its *adviser charges* to be deducted from a *retail client's* investments from the outset, in order to be able to provide a cash refund to the *retail client* later; or

(2)   it provides other services to a *retail client* (for example, *advising on a home finance transaction* or *advising* on an *equity release transaction*), and its *adviser charges* do not represent a reasonable proportion of the costs associated with the *personal recommendation* for the *retail investment product* and its related services.

Calculation of the cost of adviser services to a client

6.1A.16 G   FCA

In order to meet its responsibilities under the *client's best interests rule* and *Principle* 6 (Customers' interests), a *firm* should consider whether the *personal recommendation* or any other related service is likely to be of value to the *retail client* when the total charges the *retail client* is likely to be required to pay are taken into account.

Initial information for clients on the cost of adviser services

6.1A.17 R   FCA

A *firm* must disclose its charging structure to a *retail client* in writing, in good time before making the *personal recommendation* (or providing related services).

6.1A.18 G   FCA

A *firm* may wish to consider disclosing as its charging structure a list of the advisory services it offers with the associated indicative charges which will be used for calculating the *adviser charge* for each service.

6.1A.19 G   FCA

In order to meet the requirement in the *rule* on information disclosure before providing services (**COBS 2.2.1 R**), a *firm* should ensure that the disclosure of its charging structure is in clear and plain language and, as far as is practicable, uses cash terms. If a *firm's* charging structure is in non-cash terms, examples in cash terms should be used to illustrate how the charging structure will be applied in practice.

6.1A.20 G   FCA

A *firm* is unlikely to meet its obligations under the *fair, clear and not misleading rule* and the *client's best interests rule* unless it ensures that:
(1)   the charging structure it discloses reflects, as closely as is practicable, the total *adviser charge* to be paid; for example, the *firm* should avoid using a wide range; and
(2)   if using hourly rates in its charging structure, it states whether the rates are indicative or actual hourly rates, provides the basis (if any) upon which the rates may vary and provides an approximate indication of the number of hours that the provision of each service is likely to require.

6.1A.21 G   FCA

A *firm* may meet the disclosure requirements in this section by using a *services and costs disclosure document* or a *combined initial disclosure document* (**COBS 6.3** and **COBS 6 ANNEX 1 G** or **COBS 6 ANNEX 2**).

Ongoing payment of adviser charges

6.1A.22 R   FCA

A *firm* must not use an *adviser charge* which is structured to be payable by the *retail client* over a period of time unless (1) or (2) applies:
(1)   the *adviser charge* is in respect of an ongoing service for the provision of *personal recommendations* or related services and:
        (a)   the *firm* has disclosed that service along with the *adviser charge*; and
        (b)   the *retail client* is provided with a right to cancel the ongoing service, which must be reasonable in all the circumstances, without penalty and without requiring the *retail client* to give any reason; or
(2)   the *adviser charge* relates to a *retail investment product* for which an instruction from the *retail client* for regular payments is in place and the *firm* has disclosed that no ongoing *personal recommendations* or service will be provided.

6.1A.22A G   FCA

To comply with the *rule* on providing a *retail client* with the right to cancel an ongoing service for the provision of *personal recommendations* or related services without penalty (**COBS 6.1A.22 R (1)(B)**) a *firm* should:
(1)   ensure that any notice period of the *retail client's* right of cancellation is reasonable;
(2)   not make any charge in respect of cancellation of the ongoing service except for an amount which is in proportion to the extent of the service already provided by the *firm* up to the date of cancellation of the ongoing service; and
(3)   not make cancellation conditional on, for example, requiring the *retail client* to sell any *retail investment products* to which the ongoing service relates.

6.1A.22B R   FCA

If a *retail client* exercises his right to cancel an ongoing service, the *firm* must clearly disclose to the *retail client* whether charges for other services provided by the *firm*, such as *custody* services, will continue to be payable by the *retail client*.

6.1A.23 R   FCA

If **COBS 6.1A.22 R(1)** or **(2)** do not apply, a *firm* may not offer *credit* to a *retail client* for the purpose of paying *adviser charges* unless this would be in the best interests of the *retail client*.

Disclosure of total adviser charges payable

6.1A.24 R FCA

(1)   A firm must agree with and disclose to a *retail client* the total *adviser charge* payable to it or any of its *associates* by a *retail client*.

(2)   A disclosure under (1) must:

    (a)   be in cash terms (or convert non-cash terms into illustrative cash equivalents);

    (b)   be as early as practicable;

    (c)   be in a *durable medium* or through a website (if it does not constitute a *durable medium*) if the *website conditions* are satisfied; and

    (d)   if there are payments over a period of time, include the amount and frequency of each payment due, the period over which the *adviser charge* is payable and the implications for the *retail client* if the *retail investment product* is cancelled before the *adviser charge* is paid and, if there is no ongoing service, the sum total of all payments.

6.1A.24A G FCA

If the price of the *retail investment product* may vary as a result of fluctuations in the financial markets and the *adviser charge* is expressed as a percentage of that price, a *firm* need not disclose to the *retail client* the total *adviser charge* payable to the *firm* or any of its *associates* by the *retail client* until after execution of the transaction, provided it then does so promptly.

6.1A.25 G FCA

A *firm* may include the information required by the *rule* on disclosure of total *adviser charges* (**COBS 6.1A.24 R**) in a *suitability report*.

6.1A.26 G FCA

To comply with the *rule* on disclosure of total *adviser charges* (**COBS 6.1A.24 R**) and the *fair, clear and not misleading rule*, a *firm's* disclosure of the total *adviser charge* should:

(1)   provide information to the *retail client* as to which particular service an *adviser charge* applied to;

(2)   include information as to when payment of the *adviser charge* is due;

(3)   inform the *retail client* if the total *adviser charge* varies materially from the charge indicated for that service in the *firm's* charging structure;

(4)   if an ongoing *adviser charge* is expressed as a percentage of funds under management, clearly reflect in the disclosure that the *adviser charge* may increase as the fund grows; and

(5)   if an ongoing *adviser charge* applies for an ongoing service, clearly confirm the details of the ongoing service, its associated charges, and how the *retail client* can cancel this service and cease payment of the associated charges.

Record keeping

6.1A.27 R FCA

A *firm* must keep a record of:

(1)   its charging structure;

(2)   the total *adviser charge* payable by each *retail client*; and

(3)   if the total *adviser charge* paid by a *retail client* has varied materially from the charge indicated for that service in the *firm's* charging structure, the reasons for that difference.

    6.1B   RETAIL INVESTMENT PRODUCT PROVIDER AND PLATFORM SERVICE PRO-VIDER REQUIREMENTS RELATING TO ADVISER CHARGING AND REMUNERATION

Application – Who? What?

6.1B.1 R FCA

(1)   This section applies to:

    (a)   a *firm* which is a *retail investment product* provider; and

    (b)   in relation to **COBS 6.1B.9 R**, **COBS 6.1B.10 G** and **COBS 6.1B.11 G**, a *platform service provider*;

    in circumstances where a *retail client* receives a *personal recommendation* in relation to a *retail investment product* and also where a *retail investment product* transaction is executed by a *platform service provider* and no *personal recommendation* has been made.

(2)   This section does not apply to a *retail investment product* provider in circumstances where a *firm* gives advice or provides services to an employer in connection with a *group personal pension scheme* or *group stakeholder pension scheme*.

6.1B.1A G FCA

Guidance on the regulated activity of advising in relation to a new or existing *investment* can be found in **PERG 8.24** to **PERG 8.29**. Although the *guidance* in **PERG 8.29.7 G** relates to *advising* *on investments* under article 53 of the *Regulated Activities Order*, exactly the same answers apply to a *personal recommendation* because the examples given relate to the relationship between a *firm* and a particular *client* and advice given to that specific *client*. A *firm* wishing to know when it will be giving advice but not making a *personal recommendation* should refer to **PERG 13.3**.

6.1B.2 R   FCA

This section does not apply to a *firm* when a *retail client* receives *basic advice* in accordance with the *basic advice rules*.

6.1B.2A R   FCA

This section does not apply to a *firm* in circumstances where a *retail client* receives a *personal recommendation* in relation to one of the *firm's Holloway sickness policies*, provided that the *Holloway policy special application conditions* are met.

6.1B.3 G   FCA

This section applies to a *firm* when it makes a *personal recommendation* on a *retail investment product* and where a *retail investment product* for which it is the *retail investment product* provider is the subject of a *personal recommendation* made by another *firm*.

Application – Where?

6.1B.4 R   FCA

This section does not apply if the *retail client* is outside the *United Kingdom*.

Requirement not to offer commissions

6.1B.5 R   FCA

Except as specified in **COBS 6.1B.5A R**, a *firm* must not offer or pay (and must ensure that none of its *associates* offers or pays) any commissions, remuneration or benefit of any kind to another *firm*, or to any other third party for the benefit of that *firm*, in relation to a *personal recommendation* (or any related services), except those that facilitate the payment of *adviser charges* from a *retail client's* investments in accordance with this section.

6.1B.5A R   FCA

A *firm* and its *associates* may:
(1)   offer and pay a commission, remuneration and benefit of any kind in the circumstances set out in **COBS 6.1B.5 R** if:
     (a)   the *personal recommendation* was made on or before 30 December 2012;
     (b)   the offer and payment was permitted by the *rules* in force on 30 December 2012;
     (c)   the contract under which the right to receive the commission, remuneration or benefit of any kind was entered into on or before 30 December 2012;
     (d)   the terms of that contract as at 30 December 2012 included the right to receive the commission, remuneration or benefit of any kind; and
     (e)   the *retail client* enters into the transaction in respect of which the *personal recommendation* was given within a reasonable time of the *personal recommendation* being given; and
(2)   enter into an arrangement under which the right to receive the commission, remuneration or benefit of any kind in (1) is transferred to another *firm* or its *associate*.

6.1B.5B G   FCA

A *firm* may continue paying commission, remuneration or benefits of any kind to another *firm* in relation to a *personal recommendation* made by that other *firm* in circumstances where that other *firm* may accept that commission, remuneration or benefit of any kind (see **COBS 6.1A.4A R** and **COBS 6.1A.4AA G**).

6.1B.6 G   FCA

[deleted]

Distinguishing product charges from adviser charges

6.1B.7 R   FCA

A *firm* must:
(1)   take reasonable steps to ensure that its *retail investment product* charges are not structured so that they could mislead or conceal from a *retail client* the distinction between those charges and any *adviser charges* payable in respect of its *retail investment products*;
(2)   not include in any marketing materials in respect of its *retail investment products* or facilities for collecting *adviser charges* any statements about the appropriateness of levels of *adviser charges* that a *firm* could charge in making *personal recommendations* or providing related services in relation to its *retail investment products*; and

(3)   not defer, discount or rebate *retail investment product* charges in a way that offsets or may appear to offset any *adviser charges* or *platform charges* that are payable, including by maintaining *retail investment product* charges at a level such that a cash rebate, other than a cash rebate permitted by **COBS 6.1B.7A R** or **COBS 6.1E.10 R (2)**, is payable to the *retail client*.

6.1B.7A R   FCA

A *retail investment product* provider may maintain *retail investment product* charges at a level such that a cash rebate is payable to the *retail client* if:
(1)   the *retail investment product* transaction was agreed on or before 5 April 2014 and executed within a reasonable time of that agreement; and
(2)   the *retail client's* right to receive the cash rebate arose on or before 5 April 2014; and
(3)   on or after 6 April 2014 no change is made to that product, or, where there is such a change on or after 6 April 2014, only in relation to the unchanged part of that product.

6.1B.7B G   FCA

In the *FCA's* view, if the *platform service provider* retained any part of a rebate on or before 5 April 2014, the *retail client* is unlikely to have had a right to receive that part of the rebate.

6.1B.7C G   FCA

The following examples do not entail changes to the *retail investment product*:
(1)   no change is made to the *retail client's* investment in the relevant product or to the level of the *retail client's* regular contributions into that product;
(2)   the *retail client's* investment in, or regular contribution to, the relevant product is reduced: the *retail investment product* provider may continue to pay the cash rebate associated with the reduced investment amount;
(3)   the *retail client's* investment in the relevant product is transferred from accumulation *units* to income *units* or vice versa;
(4)   part of the *retail client's* investment is switched between funds within a *retail investment product*, such as a *SIPP*, or a *retail investment product* wrapper, such as an *ISA*: the *retail investment product* provider may continue to pay the cash rebate associated with the part of the *retail client's* investment which has not been switched into another fund;
(5)   the level of cash rebate payable to the *retail client* is reduced;
(6)   the product is converted to a share class which does not pay a commission, remuneration or benefit of any kind to a *firm* and is otherwise unchanged.

6.1B.8 G   FCA

COBS 6.1B.7 R does not prevent a *firm* from offering a promotional discount to a *retail client* in the form of extra *units* or additional investment, but a *firm* should not offer to invest more than 100% of the *retail client's* investment.

Requirements on firms facilitating the payment of adviser charges

6.1B.9 R   FCA

COBS 6.1B.7 R does not prevent a *firm* from offering a promotional discount to a *retail client* in the form of extra *units* or additional investment, but a *firm* that offers to facilitate, directly or through a third party, the payment of *adviser charges*, including by means of a *platform service* must:
(1)   obtain and validate instructions from a *retail client* in relation to an *adviser charge*;
(2)   offer sufficient flexibility in terms of the *adviser charges* it facilitates; and
(3)   not pay out or advance *adviser charges* to the *firm* to which the *adviser charge* is owed over a materially different time period, or on a materially different basis to that in which it recovers the *adviser charge* from the *retail client* (including paying any *adviser charges* to the *firm* that it cannot recover from the *retail client*).

6.1B.9A G   FCA

A *firm* facilitates the payment of *adviser charges* for the purposes of **COBS 6.1B.9 R** if the *adviser charge* is not paid directly by the *retail client*, but is instead paid on behalf of the *retail client* via the *firm*.

6.1B.9B G   FCA

A *firm* may facilitate the payment of *adviser charges* for the purposes of **COBS 6.1B.9 R** by:
(1)   selling all or part of the *retail client's* retail investment product* to pay the *adviser charge*; or
(2)   disposing of or reducing all or part of the *retail client's* rights under the *retail investment product* (for example, by way of a part disposal which creates benefits under a *life policy*) to pay the *adviser charge*; or
(3)   separating out an amount or amounts for the payment of the *adviser charge* from the amount received from the *retail client* to be invested or from the *premium* in the case of a *life policy*; or
(4)   paying the *adviser charge* from the *retail client's* cash account.

6.1B.10 G   FCA

A *firm* should consider whether the flexibility in levels of *adviser charges* it offers to facilitate is sufficient so as not to unduly influence or restrict the charging structure and *adviser charges* that the *firm* providing the *personal recommendation* or related services can use.

6.1B.11 G   FCA

COBS 6.1B.9 R(3) does not prevent a *firm*, if this is in the *retail client's* best interests, from entering into an agreement with another *firm* which is providing a *personal recommendation* to a *retail client*, or with a *retail client* of such a *firm*, to provide it with *credit* separately in accordance with the *rules* on providing credit and other benefits to *firms* that advise on *retail investment products* (**COBS 2.3.12 E** and **COBS 2.3.12A G**).

6.1C   CONSULTANCY CHARGING AND REMUNERATION

Application – Who? What?

6.1C.1 R   FCA

(1)   This section applies to a *firm* that gives advice, or provides services, to an employer in connection with a *group personal pension scheme* or *group stakeholder pension scheme*.

(2)   Without prejudice to (1), this section does not apply to a *firm* that makes a *personal recommendation* to a *retail client* in relation to a *retail investment product*.

Application – Where?

6.1C.2 R   FCA

This section does not apply if the employer is outside the *United Kingdom*.

Interpretation

6.1C.3 R   FCA

In this section 'giving advice, or providing services, to an employer in connection with a *group personal pension scheme* or *group stakeholder pension scheme*' includes:

(1)   giving advice or assistance to an employer on the operation of such a scheme;

(2)   taking, or helping the employer to take, the steps that must be taken to enable an employee of the employer to become a member of such a *scheme*; and

(3)   giving advice to an employee, pursuant to an agreement between the employer and the adviser, about the benefits that are, or might be, available to the employee if he is, or if he becomes, a member of such a scheme.

Requirement to be paid through consultancy charges

6.1C.4 G   FCA

COBS 6.1C.1 (Application – Who? What?) and **COBS 6.1C.3** (Interpretation) mean (for example) that the cost of any advice given to an employee pursuant to an agreement between the employer and the adviser about the benefits that are, or might be, available to the employee if he is, or if he becomes, a member of a *group personal pension scheme* or *group stakeholder pension scheme* are subject to the *rules* in this section, not the *rules* on *adviser charging* (**COBS 6.1A**).

6.1C.5 R   FCA

Except as specified in **COBS 6.1C.5A R**, **COBS 6.1C.5B R** and **COBS 6.1C.5C R**, a *firm* must:

(1)   only be remunerated for giving advice, or providing services, to an employer in connection with a *group personal pension scheme* or *group stakeholder pension scheme* by *consultancy charges* or by a fee payable by the employer;

(2)   not solicit or accept (and ensure that none of its *associates* solicits or accepts) any other commissions, remuneration or benefit of any kind in relation to that advice, or those services, regardless of whether it intends to refund the payments or pass the benefits on to the *group personal pension scheme* or *group stakeholder pension scheme*; and

(3)   not solicit or accept (and ensure that none of its *associates* solicits or accepts) *consultancy charges* which are paid out or advanced by another party over a materially different time period, or on a materially different basis, from that in or on which the *consultancy charges* are recovered from the relevant *group personal pension scheme* or *group stakeholder pension scheme*.

6.1C.5A R   FCA

A *firm* and its *associates* may:

(1)   solicit and accept a commission, remuneration or benefit of any kind in the circumstances set out in **COBS 6.1C.5 R** if:

     (a)   the employer's part of the relevant scheme was established on or before 30 December 2012; and

(b)   the solicitation and acceptance of the commission, remuneration or benefit of any kind was permitted by the *rules* in force on 30 December 2012; and

(2)   enter into an arrangement under which the right to receive the commission, remuneration or benefit in (1) is transferred to that *firm* or its *associate*.

Re-registration of commission when an employer moves to a new adviser

6.1C.5B R FCA

If an employer chooses to appoint a *firm* to provide advice or services in connection with a *group personal pension scheme* or a *group stakeholder pension scheme* and that *firm* or its *associate* enters into an arrangement in **COBS 6.1C.5AR (2)**, the *firm* must:

(1)   before the arrangement is entered into, disclose to the employer that the transfer of the commission, remuneration or benefit of any kind will be requested by the *firm* or its *associate*;

(2)   throughout the period during which the *firm* or its *associate* receives the commission, remuneration or benefit of any kind, provide the employer with an ongoing service; and

(3)   as soon as reasonably practicable after it makes the disclosure in (1):

    (a)   disclose to the employer the basis and amount of the commission, remuneration or benefit of any kind it expects to receive and any it has received; and

    (b)   provide the employer with a description of the ongoing service it will provide to the employer in accordance with (2).

6.1C.5C R FCA

In connection with a *qualifying scheme*, a *firm* may only solicit or accept *consultancy charges* from an operator of a *qualifying scheme* if the *operator* has confirmed that express agreement has been given by members of that scheme under **COBS 19.6.4 R**.

6.1C.6 G FCA

A *firm* may receive a *consultancy charge* that is no longer payable (for example, after the service it is received in payment for has been amended or terminated) provided the *firm* passes any such payments to the relevant *group personal pension scheme* or *group stakeholder pension scheme*.

6.1C.7 G FCA

The requirement to be paid through *consultancy charges* does not prevent a *firm* from making use of any facility for the payment of *consultancy charges* provided by another *firm* or other third parties provided that the facility complies with the requirements of **COBS 6.1D.9 R**.

6.1C.8 G FCA

Examples of payments and benefits that should not be accepted under the requirement only to be paid through *consultancy charges* include:

(1)   a share of the charges applied to a *group personal pension scheme*, *group stakeholder pension scheme* or the scheme provider's revenues or profits (except if the *firm* providing the advice to an employer in relation to such a scheme is the scheme provider);

(2)   a commission set and payable by a *retail investment product* provider in any jurisdiction.

Requirements on a product provider giving advice to an employer in respect of the product provider's own group personal pension scheme or group stakeholder pension scheme products.

6.1C.9 R FCA

If the *firm* or its *associate* is the *group personal pension scheme* or *group stakeholder pension scheme* provider, the *firm* must ensure that the level of its *consultancy charges* is at least reasonably representative of the cost associated with giving the advice to the employer in relation to the relevant scheme.

6.1C.10 G FCA

A *consultancy charge* is likely to be reasonably representative of the services associated with giving advice, or providing services, to an employer in connection with a *group personal pension scheme* or *group stakeholder pension scheme* if:

(1)   the expected long term costs associated with advising the employer in relation to the *group personal pension scheme* or *group stakeholder pension scheme* do not include the costs associated with establishing and operating that scheme;

(2)   the allocation of costs and profits to *consultancy charges* and product charges is such that any cross-subsidisation between the different activities is not significant in the long term; and

(3)   (were the services to be provided by an unconnected *firm*), the level of *consultancy charges* would be appropriate in the context of the service being provided by the *firm*.

Requirement to use a charging structure

6.1C.11 R FCA

A *firm* must determine and use an appropriate charging structure for calculating its *consultancy charge* for each employer.

6.1C.12 G   FCA

A *firm* can use a standard charging structure.

6.1C.13 G   FCA

(1)   In determining its charging structure and *consultancy charges* a *firm* should have regard to the best interests of the employer and the employer's employees.

(2)   A *firm* may not be acting in the best interests of the employer and the employer's employees if it:

      (a)   varies its *consultancy charges* inappropriately according to product provider; or

      (b)   allows the availability or limitation of services offered by third parties to facilitate the payment of *consultancy charges* to influence inappropriately its charging structure or *consultancy charges*.

(3)   *Firms* are reminded that the *client's best interests rule* may also apply.

6.1C.14 R   FCA

A *firm* must not use a charging structure which conceals the amount or purpose of any of its *consultancy charges* from an employer or an employee.

6.1C.15 G   FCA

A *firm* is likely to be viewed as operating a charging structure that conceals the amount or purpose of its *consultancy charges* if, for example, it makes arrangements for amounts in excess of its *consultancy charges* to be deducted from an employee's investments from the outset, in order to be able to provide a cash payment to the employer or employee later.

Initial information for clients on the cost of consultancy services

6.1C.16 R   FCA

A *firm* must disclose its charging structure to an employer in writing, in good time before giving advice, or providing services, to the employer in connection with a *group personal pension scheme* or *group stakeholder pension scheme*.

6.1C.17 G   FCA

A *firm* should ensure that the disclosure of its charging structure is in clear and plain language and, as far as is practicable, uses cash terms. If a *firm's* charging structure is in non-cash terms, examples in cash terms should be used to illustrate how the charging structure will be applied in practice.

Disclosure of total consultancy charges payable

6.1C.18 R   FCA

(1)   A *firm* must agree with and disclose to an employer the total *consultancy charge* payable to it or any of its *associates*.

(2)   A disclosure under (1) must:

      (a)   be in cash terms (or convert non-cash terms into illustrative cash equivalents);

      (b)   be made as early as practicable and, in any event, before the employer:

          (i)   selects a particular *group personal pension scheme* or *group stakeholder pension scheme* for the benefit of its employees; or

          (ii)   if applicable, reviews its *group personal pension scheme* or *group stakeholder pension scheme* arrangements;

      (c)   be in a *durable medium* or through a website (if it does not constitute a *durable medium*) if the *website conditions* are satisfied;

      (d)   if there are payments over a period of time, include:

          (i)   the amount and frequency of each payment due; and

          (ii)   the period over which the *consultancy charge* is payable;

          (iii)   an explanation of the implications for the employer and its employees if an employee leaves the employer's service; and

          (iv)   an explanation of the implications for the employer and its employees if contributions to the *group personal pension scheme* or *group stakeholder pension scheme* are cancelled before the *consultancy charge* is fully paid.

6.1C.19 G   FCA

To comply with the *rule* on disclosure of total *consultancy charges* payable (**COBS 6.1C.18 R**) and the *fair, clear and not misleading rule*, a *firm's* disclosure of the total *consultancy charge* should:

(1)   provide information to the employer as to which particular service a *consultancy charge* applies;

(2)   include information as to when payment of the *consultancy charge* is due;

(3)   if an ongoing *consultancy charge* is expressed as a percentage of funds under management, clearly reflect in the disclosure how that *consultancy charge* may increase as the fund grows.

Requirement not to make a consultancy charge in certain circumstances

6.1C.20 R   FCA

When an employer asks a *firm* to provide advice to the employer's employees, the *firm*:
(1)   may make a *consultancy charge* for the cost of preparing and giving advice to each employee who chooses to accept his employer's offer of advice;
(2)   must not make a *consultancy charge* for the cost of preparing or giving advice to an employee who chooses not to accept the offer of advice;
(3)   (if the *firm* prepares generic advice to be given to more than one employee) must not make more than one *consultancy charge* for preparing that advice.

Record-keeping

6.1C.21 R   FCA

A *firm* must keep a record of:
(1)   its charging structure;
(2)   the *consultancy charges* payable by each employer and each of the employer's employees; and
(3)   if the *consultancy charge* for a particular service has varied materially from that indicated in the *firm's* charging structure, the reasons for that difference.

6.1D   PRODUCT PROVIDER REQUIREMENTS RELATING TO CONSULTANCY CHARGING AND REMUNERATION

Application – Who? What?

6.1D.1 R   FCA

This section applies to a *firm* that is a *group personal pension scheme* or *group stakeholder pension scheme* provider, but only if the *firm* providing the relevant scheme (or another *firm*) gives advice, or provides services, to an employer in connection with that scheme.

Application – Where?

6.1D.2 R   FCA

This section does not apply if the employer is outside the *United Kingdom*.

Interpretation

6.1D.3 R   FCA

In this section 'giving advice, or providing services, to an employer in connection with a *group personal pension scheme* or *group stakeholder pension scheme*' includes:
(1)   giving advice or assistance to an employer on the operation of such a scheme;
(2)   taking, or helping the employer to take, the steps that must be taken to enable an employee of the employer to become a member of such a *scheme*; and
(3)   giving advice to an employee, pursuant to an agreement between the employer and the advisor, about the benefits that are, or might be, available to the employee if he is, or if he becomes, a member of such a scheme.

Requirement not to offer commission, provide factoring or offer credit to a third party

6.1D.4 R   FCA
(1)   Except as specified in **COBS 6.1D.6A R**, a *firm* must not offer or pay (and must ensure that none of its *associates* offers or pays) any commissions, remuneration or benefit of any kind to another *firm*, an *employee benefit consultant* or to any other third party for the benefit of that *firm*, *employee benefit consultant* or third party in relation to the sale or purchase of:
       (a)   a *group personal pension scheme* or *group stakeholder pension scheme*, whether or not that sale or purchase is accompanied or facilitated by advice given to the purchasing employer or the employer's employees; or
       (b)   an *investment*, if that sale or purchase is, or was, for the benefit of an *occupational pension scheme* established as an alternative to a *group personal pension scheme* or *group stakeholder pension scheme*.
(2)   Paragraph (1)(a) does not prevent a *firm* from making a payment to a third party that has facilitated the payment of a *consultancy charge* from a *group personal pension scheme* or *group stakeholder pension scheme*, provided that that payment is only in respect of that facilitation.
(3)   For the purposes of (1)(b) only, an *occupational pension scheme* will be established as an alternative to a *group personal pension scheme* or *group stakeholder pension scheme* if, in order to meet the most material of its objectives, an employer could reasonably have chosen to establish an *occupational pension scheme* on the one hand, or a *group personal pension scheme* or *group stakeholder pension scheme* on the other, and it chose to establish an *occupational pension scheme*.

6.1D.5 G   FCA

The requirement not to offer or pay commission does not prevent a *firm* from making a payment to a third party in respect of administration or other charges incurred, for example a payment to a fund supermarket or a third party administrator.

6.1D.6 R   FCA

A *firm* that produces a *group personal pension scheme* or *group stakeholder pension scheme* must not offer or make any credit available out of its own funds, and to or for the benefit of another *firm*, an *employee benefit consultant* or another third party.

6.1D.6A R   FCA

A *firm* and its *associates* may:
(1)   offer and pay a commission, remuneration or benefit of any kind in the circumstances set out in **COBS 6.1D.4 R** if:
    (a)   the employer's part of the relevant scheme was established on or before 30 December 2012; and
    (b)   the offer or payment was permitted by the *rules* in force on 30 December 2012; and
(2)   enter into an arrangement under which the right to receive the commission, remuneration or benefit of any kind in (1) is transferred to another *firm* or its *associate*.

Distinguishing product charges from consultancy charges

6.1D.7 R   FCA

A *firm* must:
(1)   take reasonable steps to ensure that its *group personal pension scheme* and *group stakeholder pension scheme* charges are not structured so that they could mislead or conceal from an employer the distinction between those charges and any *consultancy charges* payable in respect of the scheme; and
(2)   not include in any marketing materials in respect of its *group personal pension schemes* or *group stakeholder pension schemes* any statements about the appropriateness of levels of *consultancy charges* that a *firm* could charge in giving advice to an employer in relation to a such a scheme.

6.1D.8 G   FCA

A *firm* should not offer to invest more than 100% of the *retail client's* contribution to a *group personal pension scheme* or *group stakeholder pension scheme*.

Requirements on firms facilitating the payment of consultancy charges

6.1D.9 R   FCA

A *firm* that offers to facilitate, directly or through a third party, the payment of *consultancy charges* must:
(1)   obtain and validate instructions from the relevant employer in relation to the *consultancy charge*;
(2)   offer sufficient flexibility in terms of the *consultancy charges* it facilitates;
(3)   not pay out or advance *consultancy charges* to the *firm* to which the *consultancy charge* is owed over a materially different time period, or on a materially different basis to that in which it recovers the *consultancy charges* from the employee (including paying any *consultancy charges* to the *firm* that it cannot recover from the employee); and
(4)   ensure that the *consultancy charges* levied do not exceed those agreed between the employee's employer and the relevant adviser (unless the prior written consent of the employee is obtained).

6.1D.9A G   FCA

A *firm* facilitates the payment of *consultancy charges* for the purposes of **COBS 6.1D.9 R** if the *consultancy charge* is not paid directly by the employee, but is instead paid on behalf of the employee via the *firm*.

6.1D.9B G   FCA

A *firm* facilitates the payment of *consultancy charges* for the purposes of **COBS 6.1D.9 R** by:
(1)   selling all or part of, or rights under, the employee's investment in a *group personal pension scheme* or *group stakeholder pension scheme* to pay the *consultancy charge*; or
(2)   disposing of or reducing all or part of the employee's rights under the *group personal pension scheme* or *group stakeholder pension scheme* (for example, by way of a part disposal which creates benefits under a *life policy*) to pay the *consultancy charge*; or
(3)   separating out an amount or amounts for the payment of the *consultancy charge* from the amount received from the employer on behalf of the employee or from the premium in the case of a *life policy*.

6.1D.10 G   FCA

A *firm* should consider whether the flexibility in levels of *consultancy charges* it offers to facilitate is sufficient so as not to unduly influence or restrict the charging structure and *consultancy charges* that the *firm* providing advice to an employer in relation to a *group personal pension scheme* or *group stakeholder pension scheme* can use.

Disclosure of total consultancy charges payable

6.1D.11 R FCA

A *firm* must, in good time, provide an employee with sufficient information on the total *consultancy charge* payable by the employee.

6.1D.12 G FCA

To comply with **COBS 6.1D.11 R**, a *firm's* disclosure should be in cash terms (or convert non-cash terms into illustrative cash equivalents) and should:
(1)   include information as to the period over which the *consultancy charge* is payable;
(2)   provide information on the implications for the employee if the employee leaves the employer's service or their contributions to the *group personal pension scheme* or *group stakeholder pension scheme* are cancelled before the *consultancy charge* is fully paid.

6.1D.13 G FCA

A *firm* may provide the disclosure in **COBS 6.1D.11 R** at the same time as it provides a *key features document*.

6.1E   PLATFORM SERVICES: PLATFORM CHARGES AND USING A PLATFORM SER-
VICE FOR ADVISING

Platform service providers: platform charges

6.1E.-1 R FCA

This section does not apply if the *retail client* is outside the *United Kingdom*.

6.1E.1 R FCA
(1)   A *platform service provider* must clearly disclose the total *platform charge* to the *retail client* in a *durable medium* in good time before the provision of *designated investment business*.
(2)   In the event that it is not possible to make the disclosure in (1) in good time before the provision of *designated investment business*, the disclosure must be made as soon as practicable thereafter.

6.1E.2 G FCA

A *platform service provider* should pay due regard to its obligations under *Principle* 6 (Customers' interests), *Principle* 7 (Communications with clients) and the *client's best interests rule*, and ensure that it presents *retail investment products* without bias.

6.1E.3 G FCA

A *platform service provider* should pay due regard to its obligations under *Principle* 6 (Customers' interests) and the *client's best interests rule* and not vary its *platform charges* inappropriately according to provider or, for substitutable and competing *retail investment products*, the type of *retail investment product*.

Requirement to be paid through platform charges

6.1E.4 R FCA

Except as specified in **COBS 6.1E.6 R** and **COBS 6.1E.7 R**, a *platform service provider* must:
(1)   only be remunerated for its *platform service* (and any other related services it provides), by *platform charges*; and
(2)   ensure that none of its *associates* accepts any remuneration in respect of those services.

6.1E.5 G FCA

Examples of remuneration that should not be accepted by a *platform service provider* or its *associates* include (but are not limited to):
(1)   a share of an annual management charge; and
(2)   any payment (other than a product charge or a *platform charge*) made to a *platform service provider* in its capacity as a *retail investment product* provider where the relevant *retail investment product* is distributed to *retail clients* by its *platform service*.

Exceptions

6.1E.6 R FCA

A *platform service provider* or its *associates* may solicit and accept payments from:
(1)   a *firm*, other than a *retail investment product* provider, which is in the business of making *personal recommendations* to *retail clients* in relation to *retail investment products*; and/or

(2)   a *firm*, other than a *retail investment product* provider, which is in the business of *arranging* or *dealing retail investment products* for *retail clients*.

6.1E.7 R   FCA

Other than in **COBS 6.1E.6 R**, a *platform service provider* or its *associates* may solicit and accept payments from any *firm*, including a *retail investment product* provider, which are only for:

(1)   pricing error corrections;
(2)   administering corporate actions;
(3)   research carried out by the *platform service provider* and management information; and
(4)   advertising;

provided that:
(5)   the services are available to *firms* at a price which does not vary inappropriately according to *firm*;
(6)   the payments are reasonable and proportionate for the service; and
(7)   the payments or service could not reasonably be expected to result in a channelling of business to the *firm* other than through the normal effect of general advertising.

Distinguishing platform charges from product charges and adviser charges

6.1E.8 R   FCA

A *platform service provider* must not *arrange* for a *retail client* to buy a *retail investment product* if:

(1)   the product's charges are presented in a way that offsets or may appear to offset any *adviser charges* or *platform charges* that are payable by that *retail client*; or
(2)   the *platform service provider's* charges are presented in a way that offsets or may appear to offset any product charges or *adviser charges* that are payable by the *retail client*; or
(3)   the product's charges or other payments are maintained by the *retail investment product* provider at a level such that a cash rebate, other than a cash rebate permitted by **COBS 6.1E.10 R (2)**, is payable to the *retail client*.

Using a platform service when advising

6.1E.9 R   FCA

A *firm* must not use a *platform service* as part of a *personal recommendation* to a *retail client* in relation to a *retail investment product* unless it has satisfied itself that the *platform service provider*, and its *associates*, only receive remuneration for business carried on in the *UK* which is permitted by the *rules* in this section.

Providing additional units or payment in cash to a retail client

6.1E.10 R   FCA

COBS 6.1E.4 R does not prevent a *platform service provider* receiving a share of an annual management charge from an *authorised fund manager* if the *platform service provider* passes that share on to the *retail client* in the form of:

(1)   additional *units*; or
(2)   cash, provided that it does not offset or appear to offset any *adviser charges* or *platform charges*.

6.1E.11 G   FCA

Examples of a cash share of an annual management charge that would not offset or appear to offset any *adviser charges* or *platform charges* are:

(1)   where the *retail client* has redeemed his *retail investment product*; or
(2)   where the value of the payment made to the *retail client* in each month does not exceed £1 for each fund.

6.1E.12 G   FCA

If a *platform service provider* passes a share of an annual management charge on to a *retail client* by way of additional *units* or cash, it should pay due regard to its obligations under *Principle* 7 (Communications with clients).

6.1F   USING A PLATFORM SERVICE FOR ARRANGING AND ADVISING

Client's best interests rule and using a platform service

6.1F.-1 R   FCA

This section does not apply if the *retail client* is outside the *United Kingdom*.

6.1F.1 R   FCA

A *firm* which:

(1)   *arranges* for *retail clients* to buy *retail investment products* or makes *personal recommendations* to *retail clients* in relation to *retail investment products*; and

(2)   uses a *platform service* for that purpose;

must take reasonable steps to ensure that it uses a *platform service* which presents its *retail investment products* without bias.

6.1F.2   G   FCA

When selecting and using a *platform service* for the purpose described in **COBS 6.1F.1 R**, a *firm* should be mindful of its duty to comply with the *client's best interests rule* and the *rule* on inducements (**COBS 2.3.1 R**).

6.1G   RE-REGISTRATION OF TITLE TO RETAIL INVESTMENT PRODUCTS

6.1G.1   R   FCA

If a *client* requests a *firm* (F) to transfer the title to a *retail investment product* which is held by F directly, or indirectly through a third party, on that *client's* behalf to another *person* (P), and F may lawfully transfer the title to that *retail investment product* to P, F must execute the *client's* request within a reasonable time and in an efficient manner.

6.1G.2   R   FCA

A *firm* acting as a *registrar* should carry out a request by F for the re-registration of ownership of a *retail investment product* to P within a reasonable time.

6.2A   DESCRIBING ADVICE SERVICES

Application – Who? What?

6.2A.1   R   FCA
(1)   This section applies to a *firm* that either:
    (a)   makes a *personal recommendation* to a *retail client* in relation to a *retail investment product*; or
    (b)   provides *basic advice* to a *retail client*.
(2)   This section does not apply to a *firm* when it makes a *personal recommendation* or provides *basic advice* to an employee, if that recommendation or advice is provided under the terms of an agreement between the *firm* and that employee's employer which is subject to the *rules* on *consultancy charges* (**COBS 6.1C**).

6.2A.1A   R   FCA

This section does not apply to a *firm* when it makes a *personal recommendation* to a *retail client* in relation to a *Holloway sickness policy*, provided that the *Holloway policy special application conditions* are met.

Application – Where?

6.2A.2   R   FCA

This section does not apply if the *retail client* is outside the *United Kingdom*.

Firms holding themselves out as independent

6.2A.3   R   FCA
(1)   A *firm* must not hold itself out to a *retail client* as acting independently unless the only *personal recommendations* in relation to *retail investment products* it offers to that *retail client* are:
    (a)   based on a comprehensive and fair analysis of the relevant market; and
    (b)   unbiased and unrestricted.
(2)   Paragraph (1) does not apply to *group personal pension schemes* if a *firm* discloses information to a *client* in accordance with the *rule* on *group personal pension schemes* (**COBS 6.3.21 R**).

6.2A.4   G   FCA
(1)   A *firm* that provides both *independent advice* and *restricted advice* should not hold itself out as acting independently for its business as a whole.
(2)   A *firm* that offers an unlimited range of *regulated mortgage contracts*, or gives *advice* in relation to *contracts of insurance* on the basis of a fair analysis, but offers *restricted advice* on *retail investment products* should not hold itself out as acting independently for its business as a whole, for example by holding itself out as an independent financial adviser. However, it may disclose that it offers an unlimited range for *regulated mortgage contracts* or gives *advice* in relation to *contracts of insurance* on the basis of a fair analysis provided it makes clear in accordance with the *fair, clear and not misleading rule* that it provides *restricted advice* for *retail investment products*.

(3)   A *firm* whose relevant market is relatively narrow should not hold itself out as acting independently in a broader sense. For example, a *firm* "Greenfield", which specialises in ethical and socially responsible investments could not hold itself out as "Greenfield Independent Financial Advisers". "Greenfield – providing independent advice on ethical products" may be acceptable.

(4)   A *firm* that provides *basic advice* on *stakeholder products* may still use the facilities and stationery it uses for other business in accordance with the *rule* on basic advice on stakeholder products: other issues (**COBS 9.6.17 R (2)**).

6.2A.4A R   FCA

In complying with **COBS 6.2A.3 R**, a *firm* which:

(1)   holds itself out to a *retail client* as acting independently; and

(2)   relies upon a single *platform service* to facilitate the majority of its *personal recommendations* in relation to *retail investment products*;

must take reasonable steps to ensure that, as appropriate, the *platform service provider* bases its selection of *retail investment products* on a comprehensive, fair and unbiased analysis of the relevant market.

6.2A.4B G   FCA

When a *firm* considers whether a *platform service provider's* selection of *retail investment products* is based on an unbiased analysis of the relevant market, a *firm* should take into account any fees, commission or non-monetary benefits the *platform service provider* receives in relation to those *retail investment products*.

Describing the breadth of a firm's advice service

6.2A.5 R   FCA

A *firm* must disclose in writing to a *retail client*, in good time before the provision of its services in respect of a *personal recommendation* or *basic advice* in relation a *retail investment product*, whether its advice will be:

(1)   *independent advice*; or

(2)   *restricted advice*.

Content and wording of disclosure

6.2A.6 R   FCA

(1)   A *firm* must include the term "independent advice" or "restricted advice" or both, as relevant, in the disclosure.

(2)   If a *firm* provides *independent advice* in respect of a relevant market that does not include all *retail investment products*, a *firm* must include in the disclosure an explanation of that market, including the types of *retail investment products* which constitute that market.

(3)   If a *firm* provides *restricted advice*, its disclosure must explain the nature of the restriction.

(4)   If a *firm* provides both *independent advice* and *restricted advice*, the disclosure must clearly explain the different nature of the *independent advice* and *restricted advice* services.

Medium of disclosure

6.2A.7 R   FCA

A *firm* must provide the disclosure information required by the *rule* on describing the breadth of a *firm's* advice service (**COBS 6.2A.5 R**) in a *durable medium* or through a website (if it does not constitute a *durable medium*) provided the *website conditions* are satisfied.

6.2A.8 G   FCA

A *firm* may meet the disclosure requirements in the *rule* on describing the breadth of a *firm's* advice service (**COBS 6.2A.5 R**) and the *rule* on content and wording of disclosure (**COBS 6.2A.6 R**) by using a *services and costs disclosure document* or a *combined initial disclosure document* (**COBS 6.3 and COBS 6 ANNEX 1 G or COBS 6 ANNEX 2**).

Additional oral disclosure for firms providing restricted advice

6.2A.9 R   FCA

If a *firm* provides *restricted advice* and engages in spoken interaction with the *retail client*, a *firm* must disclose orally in good time before the provision of its services in respect of a *personal recommendation* that it provides *restricted advice* and the nature of that restriction.

6.2A.10 G   FCA

Examples of statements which would comply with **COBS 6.2A.9 R** include:

(1)   "I am a [Firm X] adviser offering restricted advice, which means that my advice is restricted to advice on [Firm X] [products/stakeholder products] only" or

(2)   "I am a [Firm X] adviser offering restricted advice, which means that my advice is restricted
       to advice on [products/stakeholder products] from a limited number of companies that [Firm
       X] has selected".

Guidance on what constitutes a relevant market

6.2A.11 G   FCA

A relevant market should comprise all *retail investment products* which are capable of meeting the
investment needs and objectives of a *retail client*.

6.2A.12 G   FCA

A relevant market can be limited by the investment needs and objectives of the *retail client*. For
example, ethical and socially responsible investments or Islamic financial products could both be
relevant markets. However, a *firm* would be expected to consider all *retail investment products*
within those investment parameters.

6.2A.13 G   FCA

For a *firm* not specialising in a particular market, the relevant market will generally include all *retail
investment products*.

Guidance on providing unbiased and unrestricted advice

6.2A.14 G   FCA

A *personal recommendation* on a *retail investment product* that invests in a number of underlying
investments would not of itself meet the requirements for providing unbiased and unrestricted advice
even if the *retail investment product* invests in a wide range of underlying *investments*.

6.2A.15 G   FCA

In order to satisfy the *rule* on *firms* holding themselves out as independent (**COBS 6.2A.3 R**) a *firm*
should ensure that it is not bound by any form of agreement with a *retail investment product* provider
that restricts the *personal recommendation* the *firm* can provide or imposes any obligation that may
limit the *firm's* ability to provide a *personal recommendation* which is unbiased and unrestricted.

6.2A.16 G   FCA

A *firm* may be owned by, or own in whole or part, or be financed by or provide finance to, a *retail
investment product* provider without contravening the 'unbiased, unrestricted' requirement provided
the *firm* ensures that that ownership or finance does not prevent the *firm* from providing a *personal
recommendation* which is unbiased and unrestricted.

6.2A.17 G   FCA

In providing unrestricted advice a *firm* should consider relevant financial products other than *retail
investment products* which are capable of meeting the investment needs and objectives of a *retail
client*, examples of which could include national savings and investments products and *cash deposit
ISAs*.

*Guidance on using panels and/or third parties to provide a comprehensive and fair analysis of the
market*

6.2A.18 G   FCA

A *firm* may provide a *personal recommendation* on a comprehensive and fair analysis basis required
by the *rule* on *firms* holding themselves out as independent (**COBS 6.2A.3 R**) by using 'panels'. A
firm would need to ensure that any panel is sufficiently broad in its composition to enable the *firm*
to make *personal recommendations* based on a comprehensive and fair analysis, is reviewed
regularly, and that the use of the panel does not materially disadvantage any *retail client*.

6.2A.19 G   FCA

When using a panel a *firm* may exclude a certain type or class of *retail investment product* from the
panel if, after review, there is a valid reason consistent with the *client's best interests rule*, for doing
so.

6.2A.20 G   FCA

If a *firm* chooses to use a third party to conduct a fair and comprehensive analysis of its relevant
market, the *firm* is responsible for ensuring the criteria used by the third party are sufficient to meet
the requirement. For example, criteria which selected *retail investment product* providers on the
basis of payment of a fee (or facilitation of *adviser charges*), whilst excluding those not paying a fee
(or such a facilitation) would not meet the comprehensive and fair analysis requirement.

Record keeping

6.2A.21 G   FCA

Firms are reminded of the general record keeping requirements in **SYSC 3.2** and **SYSC 9**. A *firm* should keep appropriate records of the disclosures required by this section.

Systems and controls

6.2A.22 G   FCA

(1)   *Firms* are reminded of the systems and controls requirements in *SYSC*.

(2)   A *firm* providing *restricted advice* should take reasonable care to establish and maintain appropriate systems and controls to ensure that if there is no *retail investment product* in the *firm's* range of products which meets the investment needs and objectives of the *retail client*, no *personal recommendation* should be made.

(3)   A *firm* specialising in a relevant market should take reasonable care to establish and maintain appropriate systems and controls to ensure that it does not make a *personal recommendation* if there is a *retail investment product* outside the relevant market which would meet the investment needs and objectives of the *retail client*.

6.3   DISCLOSING INFORMATION ABOUT SERVICES, FEES AND COMMISSION

Application

6.3.1 R   FCA

This section applies to a *firm* which makes a *personal recommendation* to, *deals in investments as agent* for, or *arranges* for, a *retail client* in relation to a *packaged product*.

6.3.1A R   FCA

This section does not apply to a *firm* when it makes a *personal recommendation* to a *retail client* and that *retail client* is outside the *United Kingdom*.

6.3.1B G   FCA

If a *firm* makes a *personal recommendation* to a *retail client* in relation to a *packaged product* and uses the *services and costs disclosure document* or *combined initial disclosure document* to make the disclosures required under the *rule* on describing the breadth of a *firm's* advice service (**COBS 6.2A.5 R**) and the *rule* on content and wording of disclosure (**COBS 6.2A.6 R**), it may also use these documents for its disclosures in respect of any other *retail investment products*.

6.3.2 R   FCA

This section does not apply to a *firm* giving *basic advice* where the *firm* follows the *basic advice rules* in **COBS 9.6**.

Disclosure to retail clients in good time

6.3.3 G   FCA

(1)   In the *FCA's* opinion, a *firm* may comply with the *rules* referred to in (4) of which (a) to (g) are derived from the *Single Market Directives* and the *Distance Marketing Directive* by ensuring that in good time before:

    (a)   a *retail client* is bound by an agreement for the provision of a *personal recommendation* on *packaged products*; or

    (b)   the *firm* performs an act preparatory to the provision of a *personal recommendation*;

    (c)   (in relation to the amendment of a *life policy* for that *retail client*) it gives a *personal recommendation* in relation to *packaged products*;

    its *representative* provides the *client* with a *services and costs disclosure document* or *combined initial disclosure document*.

(2)   A *firm* should consider the extent to which it is appropriate to provide a *services and costs disclosure document* or a *combined initial disclosure document* if the appropriate information has been given to the *client* on a previous occasion and the information is still accurate and appropriate for the *client*.

(3)   A *firm* should provide the information required by this section in a *durable medium*.

(4)   For the purposes of (1), provision of a *services and costs disclosure document* or *combined initial disclosure document* will comply with:

    (a)   the elements of the *rule* on summary disclosure of fees, commissions and non-monetary benefits (**COBS 2.3.1 R (2)(B)**, as qualified by **COBS 2.3.2 R**) that relate to disclosure of fees and commissions and, where included, non-monetary benefits;

    (b)   the *rule* on information about costs and charges (**COBS 6.1.9 R**) but only if in the *services and costs disclosure document* or *combined initial disclosure document*:

        (i)   if a *firm* is providing a *personal recommendation* or related services and the total *adviser charge* can be determined, the total *adviser charge* is disclosed as part of the charging structure; or

        (ii)   if the total *adviser charge* cannot be determined or a *firm* is not providing a *personal recommendation*, if hourly rates are disclosed, the hourly rates are actual hourly rates rather than indicative hourly rates;

(c) the *rule* on information disclosure before providing services (**COBS 2.2.1 R (1)(A)** and **COBS 2.2.1 R (1)(D)**);

(d) the items of distance marketing information, set out in paragraphs (1), (2), (4), (5), (19) and (20) of **COBS 5 ANNEX 1 R**;

(e) paragraphs (1) (so far as it relates to the *firm's* name and address), (4) and (6) of the *rule* on disclosure of information about a *firm* and its services (**COBS 6.1.4 R**);

(f) the investor compensation scheme *rule* in **COBS 6.1.16 R (1)** and (2);

(g) the *rule* on information to be provided by an *insurance intermediary* (**COBS 7.2.1 R (1)** and **COBS 7.2.1 R (2)**); and

(h) the *rule* on describing the breadth of a *firm's* advice service (**COBS 6.2A.5 R**), the *rule* on content and wording of disclosure (**COBS 6.2A.6 R**) and the *rule* on initial information for *clients* on the cost of advice services (**COBS 6.1A.15 G**).

(5) [deleted]
   (a) [deleted]
   (b) [deleted]
   (c) [deleted]
   (d) [deleted]
   (e) [deleted]

6.3.4 R   FCA

For the purposes of **GEN 5**, a *firm* may not use the keyfacts logo in relation to any *document* that is designed to comply with *rules* in **COBS 5**, **6.1** or **COBS 7** unless it is a *services and costs disclosure document* or a *combined initial disclosure document* produced in accordance with the templates and Notes in the annexes to this chapter.

6.3.5 G   FCA

Each of the *services and costs disclosure document* and *combined initial disclosure document* that a *firm* provides to a *client* should be *documents* which the *firm* reasonably considers will be, or are likely to be, appropriate for the *client* having regard to the type of service which the *firm* may provide or business which the *firm* may conduct.

6.3.6 G   FCA

(1) A *firm* will satisfy the requirements as to timing in the *rules* referred to in **COBS 6.3.3 G (4)** if its *representative* provides information to the *client* on first making contact with the *client*.

(2) [deleted]

Services and costs disclosure document and combined initial disclosure document

6.3.7 G   FCA

(1) A *services and costs disclosure document* is a document that contains the keyfacts logo, headings and text in the order shown in **COBS 6 ANNEX 1** and in accordance with the Notes.

(2) A *combined initial disclosure document* is a document that contains the keyfacts logo, headings and text in the order shown in **COBS 6 ANNEX 2** and in accordance with the Notes.

6.3.8 G   FCA

A *firm* may include, in a *services and costs disclosure document* or a *combined initial disclosure document*, information required by *COBS* or by the *rule* on disclosing a *tied agent's* capacity (**SUP 12.6.13 R**) and which is not in the template for the *services and costs disclosure document* or *combined initial disclosure document*, if the information would be sufficiently prominent. For example, a *firm* may wish to use those documents to satisfy:

(1) the parts of the *rule* on information about the *firm* and its services (**COBS 6.1.4 R**);

(2) the *rule* on costs and associated charges (**COBS 6.1.9 R**);

(3) the items of distance marketing information described in paragraphs (6), (8), (10) and (11) of **COBS 5 ANNEX 1 R**;

that would not otherwise be satisfied by providing the *services and costs disclosure document* or *combined initial disclosure document*.

6.3.9 G   FCA

Firms can obtain from the *FCA* website www.fca.org.uk a specimen of the *services and costs disclosure document* and the *combined initial disclosure document*. A *firm* may produce its *services and costs disclosure document* or *combined initial disclosure document* by using its own house style and brand. Electronic tools to help *firms* to construct their own versions of these documents are available from the *FCA* website.

6.3.10 G
(1) [deleted]
(2) [deleted]

6.3.11 R

(1)   [deleted]
(2)   [deleted]

6.3.12 G

[deleted]
(1)   [deleted]
(2)   [deleted]
(3)   [deleted]

6.3.13 G

[deleted]

6.3.14 G   FCA

A *firm* would be unlikely to comply with the *client's best interests rule* and the *fair, clear and not misleading rule*, if:
(1)   the *services and costs disclosure document* or the *combined initial disclosure document* that it provided initially did not reflect the relevant *adviser charge* or expected *commission* arrangements; or
(2)   the *firm* arranged to retain any *commission* which exceeded the amount or rate disclosed without first providing further appropriate inducements information and obtaining the *client's* prior informed consent to the proposed alteration in a *durable medium*.

6.3.15 G

[deleted]

6.3.16 G

[deleted]

6.3.17 G

[deleted]

6.3.18 G
(1)   [deleted]
(2)   [deleted]

Telephone sales

6.3.19 G   FCA

In cases where *firms* make initial contact with a *client* on the telephone a *firm* may, in addition, have to take into account and comply with the requirements in this sourcebook applicable to the conclusion of *distance contracts* (see **COBS 5**).

6.3.20 G   FCA
(1)   In accordance with the *rule* on information disclosure before providing services (**COBS 2.2.1 R**), if a *firm's* initial contact with a *retail client* with a view to providing a *personal recommendation* on *packaged products* is by telephone then the following information should be provided before proceeding further:
     (a)   the name of the *firm* and, if the call is initiated by or on behalf of a *firm*, the commercial purpose of the call;
     (b)   whether the *firm* provides *independent advice* or *restricted advice* and, if a *firm* provides *restricted advice*, the oral disclosure required by the *rule* on additional oral disclosure for *firms* providing *restricted advice* (**COBS 6.2A.9 R**);
     (c)   the *firm's* charging structure; and
     (d)   that the information given under (a) to (c) will subsequently be confirmed in writing.
     (e)   [deleted]
     (f)   [deleted]
(2)   If a *firm's* initial contact with a *retail client* is by telephone in circumstances in which the *firm* would otherwise provide a *services and costs disclosure document*, or a *combined initial disclosure document*, it should consider sending the *client* the *document* as soon as is reasonably practicable following the conclusion of the call.

Group Personal Pensions

6.3.21 R   FCA

A *firm* must take reasonable steps to ensure that its *representatives*, when making contact with an employee with a view to giving a *personal recommendation* on his employer's *group personal pension scheme* or *group stakeholder pension scheme*, inform the employee:
(1)   that the *firm* will be providing a *personal recommendation* on a *group personal pension scheme* and/or a *group stakeholder pension scheme* provided by the employer;
(2)   whether the employee will be provided with a *personal recommendation* that is restricted to the *group personal pension scheme* or *group stakeholder pension scheme* provided by the employer or the recommendation will also cover other products;

(3)   [deleted]
(4)   that the employee will have to pay an *adviser charge* (if applicable) unless the *representative* is making contact pursuant to an agreement made between the *firm* and the employer which is subject to *consultancy charging* (**COBS 6.1C** (Consultancy charging and remuneration)).

6.3.22 G

[deleted]

6.4   DISCLOSURE OF CHARGES, REMUNERATION AND COMMISSION

Application

6.4.1 R   FCA

This section applies to a *firm* when it sells or *arranges* the sale of a *packaged product* to a *retail client* and the *firm's* services to sell or *arrange* are not in connection with the provision of a *personal recommendation*.

6.4.2 G   FCA

Under the territorial application *rules* in **COBS 1**, the *rules* in this section apply to:
(1)   a *UK firm's* business carried on from an establishment in an *EEA State* other than the *United Kingdom* for a *retail client* in the *United Kingdom* unless, if the office from which the activity is carried on were a separate *person*, the activity:
        (a)   would fall within the overseas *persons* exclusion in article 72 of the *Regulated Activities Order*; or
        (b)   would not be regarded as carried on in the *United Kingdom*.
(2)   a *firm's* business carried on from an establishment in the *United Kingdom* carried on for a *client* in an other *EEA state*.

Disclosure of commission (or equivalent) for packaged products

6.4.3 R   FCA
(1)   If a *firm* sells or *arranges* the sale of a *packaged product* to a *retail client*, and subsequently if the *retail client* requests it, the *firm* must disclose to the *client* in cash terms:
        (a)   any *commission* receivable by it or any of its *associates* in connection with the transaction;
        (b)   if the *firm* is also the *product provider*, any *commission* or *commission equivalent* payable in connection with the transaction; and
        (c)   if the *firm* or any of its *associates* is in the same *immediate group* as the *product provider*, any *commission equivalent* in connection with the transaction.
(2)   Disclosure "in cash terms" in relation to *commission* does not include the value of any indirect benefits listed in the table at **COBS 2.3.15 G**.
(3)   In determining the amount to be disclosed as *commission equivalent*, a *firm* must put a proper value on the cash payments, benefits and services provided to its *representatives* in connection with the transaction.
(4)   This *rule* does not apply if:
        (a)   the *firm* is acting as an *investment manager*; or
        (b)   the *retail client* is not present in the *EEA* at the time of the transaction; or
        (c)   the *firm* provides the *client* with a *key features document*, a *simplified prospectus*, a *key investor information document* or *EEA key investor information document*, in accordance with **COBS 14**, provided that the *firm* discloses to the *client* the actual amount or value of *commission* or *equivalent* within five *business days* of effecting the transaction.
(5)   If the terms of a *packaged product* are varied in a way that results in a material increase in *commission* or *commission equivalent*, a *firm* must disclose to a *retail client* in writing any consequent increase in *commission* or *equivalent* receivable by it in relation to that transaction.

6.4.4 G   FCA

Where a *firm* is required to disclose the value of *commission equivalent*, the value will be at least as high as the amount of any *commission*.

6.4.4A R   FCA

If the *firm* or its *associate* is the *pure protection contract insurer*, it may comply with **COBS 6.4.3 R (1)(B)** and **(C)** by disclosing to the *consumer* an *indicative adviser charge* as an alternative to a *commission equivalent*.

6.4.4B R   FCA

The *indicative adviser charge* must be at least reasonably representative of the services associated with making the *personal recommendation* in relation to the *pure protection contract*.

6.4.4C G   FCA

An *indicative adviser charge* is likely to be reasonably representative of the services associated with making the *personal recommendation* if:

(1)　　the expected long term costs associated with making a *personal recommendation* and distributing the *pure protection contract* do not include the costs associated with manufacturing and administering the *pure protection contract*;

(2)　　the allocation of costs and profit to the *indicative adviser charge* and product charges is such that any cross-subsidisation is not significant in the long term; and

(3)　　the *personal recommendation* and any related services were to be provided by an unconnected *firm*, the level of the *indicative adviser charge* would be appropriate in the context of the service being provided by an unconnected *firm*.

6.4.5 R　FCA

(1)　　A *firm* must make the disclosure required by the *rule* on disclosure of *commission* or *equivalent* (**COBS 6.4.3 R**) as close as practicable to the time that it sells or *arranges* the sale of a *packaged product*.

(2)　　The *firm* must make the disclosure:

　　(a)　　in a *durable medium*; or

　　(b)　　when a *retail client* does not make a written application to enter into a transaction, orally. In these circumstances, the *firm* must give written confirmation as soon as possible after the date of the transaction, and in any event within five *business days*.

6.4.6 E　FCA

(1)　　When determining the value of cash payments, benefits and services under the *rule* on disclosure of *commission equivalent* (**COBS 6.4.3 R**), a *firm* should follow the provisions of **COBS 6 ANNEX 6**.

(2)　　Compliance with this *evidential provision* may be relied on as tending to establish compliance with **COBS 6.4.3 R**; and

(3)　　Contravention of this *evidential provision* may be relied on as tending to establish contravention of **COBS 6.4.3 R**.

Guidance on disclosure requirements for packaged products.

6.4.7 R　FCA

A *firm* must not enter into an arrangement to pay *commission* other than to the *firm* responsible for a sale, unless:

(1)　　the *firm* responsible for the sale has passed on its right to receive the *commission* to the recipient; or

(2)　　[deleted]

(3)　　the *commission* is paid following the sale of a *packaged product* by the *firm* in response to a *financial promotion* communicated by that *firm* to a *client* of the recipient *firm*; or

(4)　　the arrangement is with a *firm* in the same *immediate group*.

6.4.8 G　FCA

A disclosure made under this section should indicate the timing of any payment. For example, if a *firm* exchanges its right to future *commission* payments for a lump sum, whether by way of a loan or other commercial arrangement, it should disclose the amount of *commission* receivable by it that has been exchanged for the lump sum.

6.4.9 G　FCA

The *rules* in this section build on the disclosure of fees, commissions and non-monetary benefits made under the *rule* on inducements (**COBS 2.3.1 R**).

6.4.10 G　FCA

If the precise rate or value of *commission* or *equivalent* is not known in advance, the *firm* should estimate the rate likely to apply to the *representative* in respect of the transaction.

6.4.11 G　FCA

Commission or equivalent disclosure statements: content and wording
A *firm* should consider including the following in its written statement of *commission*:
(1)　Amounts or values of *commission* rounded as appropriate to help the *client* understand the document (for example, large amounts might be rounded to three significant figures).
(2)　The names of the *firms* involved in paying and receiving *commission* or *commission equivalent*.
(3)　A plain language description of whether remuneration takes the form of *commission* or *commission equivalent*. *Commission* equivalent could, for example, be described as "remuneration and services received from XYZ Ltd".
(4)　The timing of payments and period over which they are paid.

Commission or equivalent disclosure statements: content and wording

(5)   For payments relating to the *client's* fund, examples of how much money might be taken, such as:

 (a)   where the *commission* or *equivalent* is on an increasing basis, the amount to be taken in the first and tenth year in which it is paid; or

 (b)   where the *commission* or *equivalent* is a percentage of the fund, the amount that would taken if the fund was worth a certain value and the amount that would be taken if the fund was worth twice that value.FCA

6 ANNEX 1   SERVICES AND COSTS DISCLOSURE DOCUMENT DESCRIBED IN COBS 6.3.7 G(1)

Firms should omit the notes and square brackets which appear in the following specimen.
Services and costs disclosure document described in COBS 6.3.7 G(1) – COBS 6 Annex 1

6 ANNEX 2   COMBINED INITIAL DISCLOSURE DOCUMENT DESCRIBED IN COBS 6.3, ICOBS 4.5 AND MCOB 4.4A.20 G

This specimen covers services in relation to *packaged products*, *non-investment insurance contracts* and *home finance transactions* (including *equity release transactions*).
If the *firm* is not providing services in relation to all products, the parts of the *combined initial disclosure document* that are not relevant should be omitted.
Firms should omit the notes and square brackets that appear in the following *combined initial disclosure document*. The completed *combined initial disclosure document* should contain the keyfacts logo, headings and text in the order shown and in accordance with the notes. Subject to this, a *firm* may use its own house style and brand.
COBS 6 Annex 2: Combined initial disclosure document described in COBS 6.3, ICOBS 4.5, MCOB 4.4.1R(1) and MCOB 4.10.2R(1) – COBS 6 Annex 2

6 ANNEX 3   [DELETED]

6 ANNEX 4   [DELETED]

6 ANNEX 5   [DELETED]

6 ANNEX 6   CALCULATING COMMISSION EQUIVALENT

This table forms part of **COBS 6.4.6 E**.

Calculating commission equivalent

This table sets out the basis on which the *firm* should determine the value of cash payments, benefits and services to be disclosed as *commission equivalent*. Benefits and services, as set out in parts B and C below, need be included only if their value is such that they could not be provided to a *firm* as a non-monetary benefit listed in the table in **COBS 2.3.15 G**. The result of the calculation should be that the amounts disclosed as *commission equivalent* are, as far as possible, the same as the amounts and value of *commission* which would be paid in a corresponding sale.

 Part A: Cash payments

1.   These cover all payments by a *firm* to a *representative*, *appointed representative* or, where applicable, a *tied agent*, or a *firm* in the same *immediate group* in relation to a transaction in a *packaged product*. This includes bonus payments, manager's overrides, extra earnings from other transactions and other payments conditional on amounts of new business.

2.   In determining the amounts to be included in the calculation, a *firm* should have regard to the following:

 (a)   when the precise rate of *commission equivalent* is not known in advance (for example, if retrospective volume overrides apply), the *firm* should estimate the rate likely to apply to the *representative* in question. When an identical *commission equivalent* scale applies to all *representatives* (although they might earn differing percentages of it), the same average amount of *commission equivalent* (and the value of other benefits and services) in respect of identical transactions may be disclosed, regardless of the percentage of the scale paid to each individual *representative*. Averaging should not be used for *appointed representatives*, or, where applicable, *tied agents*.

 (b)   all credits to an account from which periodic withdrawals may be made should be included.

Calculating commission equivalent

(c)   when a payment is made before the *firm* receives the *premium* or the investment monies to which it relates (for example, indemnity *commission equivalent*), it should be included as being received at the time of payment. *Firms* that wish to explain this arrangement to the *clients* are free to do so, provided this does not detract from the required disclosure.

(d)   when the *firm* arranges for a third party to make a payment to a *representative* in exchange for the income stream to which the *representative* is entitled, or to make a loan to the *representative* on the security or expectation of future payments from the *firm*, this should be treated as if it were a payment from the *firm* at the time of the transaction.

(e)   when a *firm* provides, or arranges for a third party to provide, a loan to a *representative*, on the security of, or in the expectation of, future payments from the firm, the amounts to be included are the payments to the *representative* on which the provision of the loan is based, as if they were received at the time the transaction was effected, irrespective of their actual timing.

(f)   when an agent is employed and remunerated by the *firm's appointed representative*, or, where applicable, *tied agent*, the payments to be included should be those made by the *firm* to the *appointed representative* or *tied agent*, not those made by the *appointed representative* or *tied agent* to its own agent.

Part B: Benefits

3.   Benefits include the cost to the *firm* of all non-monetary benefits provided by it to a *representative*. A benefit should be included whether or not the *representative* is liable to income tax on it and whether it is chargeable to tax. Examples of benefits include the use of a car, attendance at conferences, subsidised loans, contributions to *pension schemes*, national insurance contributions, and the value of *share option* (taking into account any discount on issue and assuming that the *shares* in question grow at a reasonable rate in line with other *investments*).

Part C: Services

4.   Services include benefits which are not indirect benefits within the table in **COBS 2.3.15 G**.

5.   The following services should be included:

(a)   office accommodation and equipment, including telephone, photocopying and fax;

(b)   loans where a commercial rate of interest is not charged, including *commission equivalent* advances overdue for repayment;

(c)   general stationery and mailing or distribution costs;

(d)   computer hardware and software (except software which specifically relates to the *firm's packaged product*, such as software used for producing illustrations, *projection* and product information);

(e)   clerical and administrative support;

(f)   business insurance cover, including professional indemnity and fidelity guarantee;

(g)   recruitment;

(h)   compliance monitoring;

(i)   *client* services;

(j)   business planning services;

(k)   line management.

6.   To put a value on these services, the following costs should be included:

(a)   all overheads attributable to a particular cost item (for example, the cost of a compliance official);

(b)   salary costs pro rata if individuals are only engaged part-time on relevant business;

(c)   rent and associated premises costs at an appropriately reduced rate if the premises are also used for other business activities;

(d)   only that proportion of the cost of lead generation promotions attributable to the generation of relevant business (but including the placing of any *financial promotion*, and its mailing or provision of access to third party *clients*);

(e)   only the marginal additional compliance costs of ensuring that *representatives* and their support and training material comply with relevant *rules*;

Calculating commission equivalent

    (f)   the commercial value of a service which is the use of an asset owned by the *firm* (for example in the case of a property, its full market rent);

    (g)   in respect of *appointed representative*, or, where applicable *tied agent*, the costs of any promotion in a newspaper or elsewhere and the provision of *representative* – specific literature in connection with a *financial promotion*;

    (h)   in respect of a *firm* in the same *immediate group* and connected *appointed representatives* or, where applicable, *tied agents*, where the name of the company is included in the *financial promotion*, the costs of any promotion in a newspaper or elsewhere and the provision of literature specific to the *representative* in connection with a *financial promotion*.

7.   The following costs should be excluded:

    (a)   the cost of corporate awareness advertising;

    (b)   training costs;

    (c)   costs of developing and maintaining computer systems for the provision of *projections* of benefits, *client* – specific *key features documents*, *simplified prospectuses* or other product information;

    (d)   costs of compensating *clients*;

    (e)   the costs of head office and branch level management and support, other than payments to *managers* falling under Part 1, for *representatives*, if these services could also be provided to a *firm* not in the same *immediate group*, for example, broker consultants and 'inspectors'.

Part D: Calculation methodology

8.   Estimating commission equivalent

The cost of benefits and services should normally be based on the most recent relevant experience of the *firm*, except if the *firm* has grounds to believe that the *commission equivalent* for the period concerned will be higher or lower than that implied by the experience or no such experience is available. In such a case, the estimate should be based on and evidenced by business plans which the *firm* is satisfied are achievable.

9.   *Firms* that receive or expect to receive:

    (a)   *commission* in respect of *packaged products* which are not its own products or the products of a *product provider* who is in the same *immediate group*; and

    (b)   *commission equivalent* in respect of its own products;

must ensure that the costs and benefits attributed to these products do not exceed the amounts that can be financed from that *commission*.

Construction of commission equivalent scales

10.   The total costs of cash payments, benefits and services should be assessed and the normal approach is to split them into new business costs and after sale servicing costs. The costs of each of these functions should be assessed directly in relation to the work carried out by the *representatives*.

11.   (a)   The total *commission equivalent* costs identified in 10 should be spread across the business using a new business *commission equivalent* scale and a servicing *commission equivalent* scale respectively.

    (b)   The *commission equivalent* scales should distinguish between products for which the *commission equivalent* of *representatives* is likely to be different.

12.   If the *representative's commission equivalent* includes a cash payment related to volume and/or value of the transactions sold (which payment must be in accordance with the *client's best interest rule*), the following method would be appropriate:

    (a)   The payment scales should be grossed up by new business uplift factors or servicing uplift factors as appropriate to reflect the cost of benefits and services. The grossed up scales represent the new business and servicing *commission equivalent* scales, and are applied to each contract to derive the *commission equivalent* to be disclosed.

    (b)   If servicing costs are expected to be incurred in any year in which no servicing payments are to be made on a contract, disclosure should still be made, for example by using a technique similar to that described in 14.

13.   (a)   When a *representative* receives a salary, or other payment unrelated to volume or sales:

    (i) this should be amalgamated with the cost of benefits and services; and

    (ii) the total costs should be apportioned over individual transactions in a way that reflects the value of a contract to a *firm* or the *firm's immediate group*.

Calculating commission equivalent

(b)   If a *firm* is a distributor for a *product provider* within the same *immediate group*, the *firm* must apportion total costs over individual transactions in a way that reflects the value of the contract to the *firm's immediate group*.

14.   If a *representative* agrees to forgo part of his or her normal payment to improve the terms of the contract, the disclosure may be reduced in such a way that fairly reflects the overall effect of the amount foregone.

15.   The *firm* should review the *commission equivalent* scales if at any time it becomes aware that the *commission equivalent* figures have become misleading. A review should take place at least annually.

Payments to associates

16.   If a *firm* pays *commission equivalent* to another *firm* in the same *immediate group*, or an *appointed representative* or, where applicable *tied agent*, which is an *associate* of the *firm*, it should ensure that the calculation of the sum to be disclosed is the higher of:

(a)   all payments, benefits and services provided to the *firm* or *appointed representative* or *tied agent*, from whatever source, plus an additional allowance for profit of 15% – unless the *firm* can demonstrate that another figure (higher or lower) is more appropriate; and

(b)   the cash payments actually paid by the *firm*, plus the value of services provided.

CHAPTER 7
INSURANCE MEDIATION

7.1 APPLICATION

[3.55]
7.1.1 R   FCA

This chapter applies to a *firm* carrying on *insurance mediation* in relation to a *life policy*, but only if the *State of the commitment* is an *EEA State*.

[**Note:** articles 1 and 12 (4) and (5) of the *Insurance Mediation Directive*]

7.2 INFORMATION TO BE PROVIDED BY THE INSURANCE INTERMEDIARY

7.2.1 R   FCA

(1)   Prior to the conclusion of any initial *life policy* and, if necessary, on amendment or renewal, a *firm* must provide a *client* with at least the following information:

(a)   its name and address;

(b)   the fact that it is registered on the *Financial Services Register* and its Firm Reference Number (or, if it is not on the *Financial Services Register*, the register in which it has been included and the means for verifying that it has been registered);

(c)   whether it has a direct or indirect holding representing more than 10% of the voting rights or capital in a given *insurance undertaking* (that is not a *pure reinsurer*);

(d)   whether a given *insurance undertaking* (other than a *pure reinsurer*) or its *parent undertaking* has a direct or indirect holding representing more than 10% of the voting rights or capital in the *firm*; and

(e)   the procedures which allow a *client* and other interested parties to register complaints about the *firm* with the *firm* and the *Financial Ombudsman Service* or, if the *Financial Ombudsman Service* does not apply, information about the out-of-court complaint and redress procedures available for the settlement of disputes between the *firm* and its *clients*.

(2)   In addition, a *firm* must inform a *client*, concerning the *life policy* that is provided, whether:

(a)   it gives advice on the basis of a fair analysis of the market; or

(b)   it is contractually obliged to conduct its *insurance mediation* business exclusively with one or more *insurance undertakings* and, if that is the case, that the *client* can request the names of those *insurance undertakings*; or

(c)   it is not contractually obliged to conduct its *insurance mediation* business exclusively with one or more *insurance undertakings* and does not give advice on the basis of a fair analysis of the market and, if that is the case, that the *client* can request the names of the *insurance undertakings* with which the *firm* may and does conduct business.

(3)   If a *client* asks a *firm* to provide the names of the *insurance undertakings* with which the *firm* conducts, or may conduct, business (**COBS 7.2.1 R (2)**), the *firm* must provide it.

[**Note:** article 12(1) of the *Insurance Mediation Directive*]

Interface with the services and costs disclosure document

7.2.2 G   FCA

A *firm* will satisfy elements of the requirement immediately above if it provides a *services and costs disclosure document* or a *combined initial disclosure document* to a *client* (see **COBS 6.3**).

7.2.2A R

[deleted]

7.2.2B G   FCA

A *firm* may provide a *services and costs disclosure document* or a *combined disclosure document* to a *client* who buys a non-advised *life policy*.

Fair analysis for advised sales

7.2.3 R   FCA

When a *firm* informs a *client* that it gives advice on the basis of a fair analysis of the market, it must give that advice on the basis of an analysis of a sufficiently large number of *life policies* available on the market to enable the *firm* to make a recommendation, in accordance with professional criteria, regarding which *life policy* would be adequate to meet the *client's* needs.

[**Note:** article 12(2) of the *Insurance Mediation Directive*]

Specifying demands and needs

7.2.4 R   FCA

(1)   Prior to the conclusion of any specific *life policy*, a *firm* must at least specify, in particular on the basis of the information provided by the *client*, the demands and needs of that *client*. Those demands and needs must be modulated according to the complexity of the relevant *policy*.

(2)   This *rule* does not apply when a *firm* makes a *personal recommendation* in relation to a *life policy*.

[**Note:** article 12(3) of the *Insurance Mediation Directive*]

7.2.5 G   FCA

Firms are reminded that they are obliged to take reasonable steps to ensure that a *personal recommendation* is suitable for the *client* and that, whenever a *personal recommendation* relates to a *life policy*, a *suitability report* is required (**COBS 9**).

Means of communication to clients

7.2.6 R   FCA

All information to be provided to a *client* in accordance with the *rules* in this chapter must be communicated:

(1)   in a *durable medium* available and accessible to the *client*;

(2)   in a clear and accurate manner, comprehensible to the *client*; and

(3)   in an official language of the *State of the commitment* or in any other language agreed by the parties.

[**Note:** article 13(1) of the *Insurance Mediation Directive*]

Additional requirement: telephone selling

7.2.7 R   FCA

In the case of telephone selling, the prior information given to a *client* must be in accordance with the distance marketing disclosure *rules* (**COBS 5.1**). Moreover, information must be provided to the *client* in accordance with the means of communication to clients *rule* (**COBS 7.2.6 R**) immediately after the conclusion of the *life policy*.

[**Note:** article 13(3) of the *Insurance Mediation Directive*]

Exceptions: client request or immediate cover

7.2.8 R   FCA

The information referred to in the means of communication to clients *rule* (**COBS 7.2.6 R**) may be provided orally where the *client* requests it, or where immediate cover is necessary. In those cases, the information must be provided to the *client* in accordance with that *rule* immediately after the conclusion of the *life policy*.

[**Note:** article 13(2) of the *Insurance Mediation Directive*]

CHAPTER 8
CLIENT AGREEMENTS

8.1   CLIENT AGREEMENTS: DESIGNATED INVESTMENT BUSINESS

Providing a client agreement

[3.56]
8.1.1 R   FCA
(1)   This chapter applies to a *firm* in relation to *designated investment business* carried on for:
     (a)   a *retail client*; and
     (b)   in relation to *MiFID or equivalent third country business*, a *professional client*.
(2)   If expressly provided, this chapter also applies to a *firm* in relation to other *ancillary services* carried on for a *client*, but only in relation to its *MiFID or equivalent third country business*.
(3)   But this chapter does not apply to a *firm* to the extent that it is *effecting contracts of insurance* in relation to a *life policy* issued or to be issued by the *firm* as principal.

8.1.2 R   FCA

If a *firm* carries on *designated investment business*, other than *advising on investments* or *advising on conversion or transfer of pension benefits*, with or for a new *retail client*, the *firm* must enter into a written basic agreement, on paper or other *durable medium*, with the *client* setting out the essential rights and obligations of the *firm* and the *client*.

[**Note:** article 39 of the *MiFID implementing Directive*]

8.1.3 R   FCA
(1)   A *firm* must, in good time before a *retail client* is bound by any agreement relating to *designated investment business* or *ancillary services* or before the provision of those services, whichever is the earlier, provide that *client* with:
     (a)   the terms of any such agreement; and
     (b)   the information about the *firm* and its services relating to that agreement or to those services required by **COBS 6.1.4 R**, including information on communications, conflicts of interest and authorised status.
(2)   A *firm* must provide the agreement and information in a *durable medium* or, where the *website conditions* are satisfied, otherwise via a website.
(3)   A *firm* may provide the agreement and the information immediately after the *client* is bound by any such agreement if:
     (a)   the *firm* was unable to comply with (1) because, at the request of the *client*, the agreement was concluded using a means of distance communication which prevented the *firm* from doing so; and
     (b)   if the *rule* on voice telephony communications (**COBS 5.1.12 R**) does not otherwise apply, the *firm* complies with that *rule* in relation to the *retail client*, as if he were a *consumer*.
(4)
     (a)   A *firm* must notify a *client* in good time about any material change to the information provided under this *rule* which is relevant to a service that the *firm* is providing to that *client*.
     (b)   A *firm* must provide the notification in a *durable medium* if the information to which it relates was given in a *durable medium*.

[**Note:** article 29(1), (4), (5) and (6) of the *MiFID implementing Directive*]

Record keeping: client agreements

8.1.4 R   FCA
(1)   A *firm* must establish a record that includes the document or documents agreed between it and a *client* which set out the rights and obligations of the parties, and the other terms on which it will provide services to the *client*.
(2)   The record must be maintained for at least whichever is the longer of:
     (a)   5 years; or
     (b)   the duration of the relationship with the *client*; or
     (c)   in the case of a record relating to a *pension transfer*, *pension conversion*, *pension opt-out* or *FSAVC*, indefinitely.

[**Note:** article 19(7) of *MiFID* and article 51(1) of the *MiFID implementing Directive*. See article 51(3) of the *MiFID implementing Directive*]

8.1.5 R   FCA

For the purposes of this chapter, a *firm* may incorporate the rights and duties of the parties into an agreement by referring to other documents or legal texts.

[**Note:** article 19(7) of *MiFID* and article 39 of the *MiFID implementing Directive*]

8.1.6 G   FCA

Part 3   FCA Handbook Materials

When considering its approach to client agreements, a *firm* should be aware of other obligations in the *Handbook* which may be relevant. These include the *fair, clear and not misleading rule* and the *rules* on disclosure of information to a *client* before providing services and the *rules* on distance communications (principally in **COBS 2.2, 5, 6** and **13**).

CHAPTER 9
SUITABILITY (INCLUDING BASIC ADVICE)

9.1   APPLICATION AND PURPOSE PROVISIONS

[3.57]

[**Note:** ESMA has also issued guidelines under article 16(3) of the ESMA Regulation on certain aspects of the MiFID suitability requirements. See www.esma.europa.eu/content/Guidelines-certain-aspects-MiFID-suitability-requirements.]

Making personal recommendations

9.1.1 R   FCA

This chapter applies to a *firm* which makes a *personal recommendation* in relation to a *designated investment* (other than a *P2P agreement*).

Providing basic advice on a stakeholder product

9.1.2 R   FCA

If a *firm* makes a *personal recommendation* in relation to a *stakeholder product*, other than in the course of *MiFID or equivalent third country business*, it may choose to give *basic advice* under the *rules* in section 9.6 of this chapter instead of the *rules* in the remainder of this chapter.

Managing investments

9.1.3 R   FCA

This chapter applies to a *firm* which *manages investments*.

Business which is not MiFID or equivalent third country business

9.1.4 R   FCA

In respect of the business of a *firm* which is not *MiFID or equivalent third country business*, this chapter applies only if:

(1)   the *client* is a *retail client*; or
(2)   the *firm* is managing the assets of an *occupational pension scheme*, *stakeholder pension scheme* or *personal pension scheme*.

Life policies for professional clients

9.1.5 R   FCA

If the *firm* makes a *personal recommendation* to a *professional client* to take out a *life policy*, this chapter applies only those *rules* which implement the requirements of the *Insurance Mediation Directive*.

9.1.6 G   FCA

If a *rule* implements a requirement of the *Insurance Mediation Directive*, a Note follows the *rule* indicating which provision is being implemented. **COBS 7** (Insurance mediation) contains further *rules* implementing the *Insurance Mediation Directive*.

9.1.7 G   FCA

The effect of these application *rules* and the fact that the *Insurance Mediation Directive* does not apply to an *insurer* (unless it is involved in mediation activities) is that this chapter does not apply to an *insurer* when it is making a *personal recommendation* to a *professional client* to take out a *life policy*.

Related rules

9.1.8 G   FCA

For a *firm* making *personal recommendations* in relation to pensions, **COBS 19** contains additional provisions relevant to assessing suitability and the contents of *suitability reports*.

9.1.9 G   FCA

COBS 7 (Insurance mediation) contains requirements relating to the basis on which certain recommendations may be made, including requirements relating to fair analysis and range and scope.

9.2 ASSESSING SUITABILITY

Assessing suitability: the obligations

9.2.1 R   FCA

(1)   A *firm* must take reasonable steps to ensure that a *personal recommendation*, or a decision to trade, is suitable for its *client*.

(2)   When making the *personal recommendation* or *managing* his *investments*, the *firm* must obtain the necessary information regarding the *client's*:

   (a)   knowledge and experience in the investment field relevant to the specific type of *designated investment* or service;

   (b)   financial situation; and

   (c)   investment objectives;

   so as to enable the *firm* to make the recommendation, or take the decision, which is suitable for him.

[**Note:** article 19(4) of *MiFID*, article 12(2) of the *Insurance Mediation Directive*]

9.2.2 R   FCA

(1)   A *firm* must obtain from the *client* such information as is necessary for the *firm* to understand the essential facts about him and have a reasonable basis for believing, giving due consideration to the nature and extent of the service provided, that the specific transaction to be recommended, or entered into in the course of managing:

   (a)   meets his investment objectives;

   (b)   is such that he is able financially to bear any related investment risks consistent with his investment objectives; and

   (c)   is such that he has the necessary experience and knowledge in order to understand the risks involved in the transaction or in the management of his portfolio.

(2)   The information regarding the investment objectives of a *client* must include, where relevant, information on the length of time for which he wishes to hold the investment, his preferences regarding risk taking, his risk profile, and the purposes of the investment.

(3)   The information regarding the financial situation of a *client* must include, where relevant, information on the source and extent of his regular income, his assets, including liquid assets, investments and real property, and his regular financial commitments.

[**Note:** articles 35(1), (3) and (4) of the *MiFID implementing Directive*]

9.2.3 R   FCA

The information regarding a *client's* knowledge and experience in the investment field includes, to the extent appropriate to the nature of the *client*, the nature and extent of the service to be provided and the type of product or transaction envisaged, including their complexity and the risks involved, information on:

(1)   the types of service, transaction and *designated investment* with which the *client* is familiar;

(2)   the nature, volume, frequency of the *client's* transactions in *designated investments* and the period over which they have been carried out;

(3)   the level of education, profession or relevant former profession of the *client*.

[**Note:** article 37(1) of the *MiFID implementing Directive*]

9.2.4 R   FCA

A *firm* must not encourage a *client* not to provide information for the purposes of its assessment of suitability.

[**Note:** article 37(2) of the *MiFID implementing Directive*]

Reliance on information

9.2.5 R   FCA

A *firm* is entitled to rely on the information provided by its *clients* unless it is aware that the information is manifestly out of date, inaccurate or incomplete.

[**Note:** article 37(3) of the *MiFID implementing Directive*]

Insufficient information

9.2.6 R   FCA

If a *firm* does not obtain the necessary information to assess suitability, it must not make a *personal recommendation* to the *client* or take a decision to trade for him.

[**Note:** article 35(5) of the *MiFID implementing Directive*]

9.2.7 G   FCA

Although a *firm* may not be permitted to make a *personal recommendation* or take a decision to trade because it does not have the necessary information, its *client* may still ask the *firm* to provide another service such as, for example, to arrange a deal or to deal as agent for the *client*. If this happens, the *firm* should ensure that it receives written confirmation of the instructions. The *firm* should also bear in mind the *client's best interests rule* and any obligation it may have under the *rules* relating to appropriateness when providing the different service (see **COBS 10**, Appropriateness (for non-advised services)).

Professional clients (MiFID and equivalent third country business)

9.2.8 R   FCA
(1)   If a *firm* makes a *personal recommendation* or *manages investments* for a *professional client* in the course of *MiFID or equivalent third country business*, it is entitled to assume that, in relation to the products, transactions and services for which the *professional client* is so classified, the *client* has the necessary level of experience and knowledge for the purposes of **COBS 9.2.2 R (1)(C)**.
(2)   If the service consists of making a *personal recommendation* to a *per se professional client*, the *firm* is entitled to assume that the *client* is able financially to bear any related investment risks consistent with his investment objectives for the purposes of **COBS 9.2.2 R (1)(B)**.

[**Note:** article 35(2) of the *MiFID implementing Directive*]

Friendly society life policies

9.2.9 R   FCA
(1)   When recommending a small *friendly society life policy*, a *firm*, for the purpose of assessing suitability, need only obtain details of the net income and expenditure of the *client* and his dependants.
(2)   A *friendly society life policy* is small if the *premium*:
    (a)   does not exceed £50 a year; or
    (b)   if payable weekly, £1 a week.
(3)   The *firm* must keep for five years a record of the reasons why the recommendation is considered suitable.

9.3   GUIDANCE ON ASSESSING SUITABILITY

9.3.1 G   FCA
(1)   A transaction may be unsuitable for a *client* because of the risks of the *designated investments* involved, the type of transaction, the characteristics of the order or the frequency of the trading.
(2)   In the case of *managing investments*, a transaction might also be unsuitable if it would result in an unsuitable portfolio.

[**Note:** recital 57 to the *MiFID implementing Directive*]

Churning and switching

9.3.2 G   FCA
(1)   A series of transactions that are each suitable when viewed in isolation may be unsuitable if the recommendation or the decisions to trade are made with a frequency that is not in the best interests of the *client*.
(2)   A *firm* should have regard to the *client's* agreed investment strategy in determining the frequency of transactions. This would include, for example, the need to switch a *client* within or between *packaged products*.

[**Note:** recital 57 to the *MiFID implementing Directive*]

Income withdrawals and short-term annuities

9.3.3 G   FCA

When a *firm* is making a *personal recommendation* to a *retail client* about *income withdrawals* or purchase of *short-term annuities*, it should consider all the relevant circumstances including:
(1)   the *client's investment* objectives, need for tax-free cash and state of health;
(2)   current and future income requirements, existing pension assets and the relative importance of the plan, given the *client's* financial circumstances;
(3)   the *client's* attitude to risk, ensuring that any discrepancy is clearly explained between his attitude to an *income withdrawal* or purchase of a *short-term annuity* and other *investments*.

Loans and mortgages

9.3.4 G   FCA

When considering the suitability of a particular *investment* product which is linked directly or indirectly to any form of loan, mortgage or *home reversion plan*, a *firm* should take account of the suitability of the overall transaction. The *firm* should also have regard to any applicable suitability *rules* in *MCOB*.

Non-mainstream pooled investments

9.3.5 G   FCA

(1)   *Firms* should note that section 238 of the *Act* and **COBS 4.12.3 R** set out restrictions on the promotion of *non-mainstream pooled investments* to *retail clients*.

(2)

    (a)   *Firms* should bear in mind that the provision of advice or information may involve the communication of a *financial promotion* (see **PERG 8**). In particular, making a *personal recommendation* that a client should enter into a *non-mainstream pooled investment* will generally amount to a *financial promotion* of that investment because a *personal recommendation* typically includes an invitation or inducement to engage in investment activity.

    (b)   Due to the restrictions in section 238 of the *Act* and **COBS 4.12.3 R**, the promotion of a *non-mainstream pooled investment* to a *retail client* is not permitted except where a valid exemption is available and relied on by the *firm* communicating the promotion. *Firms* should therefore first satisfy themselves that an exemption is available in relation to the promotion of the *non-mainstream pooled investment* before recommending the investment to a *retail client*.

(3)

    (a)   In addition to assessing whether the promotion is permitted, a *firm* giving advice on a *non-mainstream pooled investment* should comply with their obligations in **COBS 9** and ensure any *personal recommendation* is suitable for its client.

    (b)   In considering its obligations under **COBS 9**, a *firm* purchasing a *non-mainstream pooled investment* on behalf of a *client* as part of a discretionary management agreement should have regard to whether that *client* is a *person* to whom promotion of that *non-mainstream pooled investment* is permissible under **COBS 4.12.4 R (5)**. Whilst the restriction in **COBS 4.12.3 R** does not affect transactions where there is no prior communication with the *client* in connection with the transaction, a *discretionary investment manager* should exercise particular care to satisfy himself that the transaction is suitable for the *client* and that it is in that *client's* best interests, if promotion of the investment would not have been permitted.

9.4   SUITABILITY REPORTS

Providing a suitability report

9.4.1 R   FCA

A *firm* must provide a *suitability report* to a *retail client* if the *firm* makes a *personal recommendation* to the *client* and the *client*:

(1)   acquires a holding in, or *sells* all or part of a holding in:

    (a)   a *regulated collective investment scheme*;

    (b)   an *investment trust* where the relevant *shares* have been or are to be acquired through an *investment trust savings scheme*;

    (c)   an *investment trust* where the relevant *shares* are to be held within an *ISA* which has been promoted as the means for investing in one or more specific *investment trusts*; or

(2)   *buys*, *sells*, surrenders, converts or cancels rights under, or suspends contributions to, a *personal pension scheme* or a *stakeholder pension scheme*; or

(3)   elects to make *income withdrawals* or purchase a *short-term annuity*; or

(4)   enters into a *pension transfer*, *pension conversion* or *pension opt-out*.

[**Note:** article 19(8) of *MiFID*]

9.4.2 R   FCA

If a *firm* makes a *personal recommendation* in relation to a *life policy*, it must provide the *client* with a *suitability report*.

[**Note:** article 12(3) of the *Insurance Mediation Directive*]

9.4.3 R   FCA

The obligation to provide a *suitability report* does not apply:

(1)   if the *firm*, acting as an *investment manager* for a *retail client*, makes a *personal recommendation* relating to a *regulated collective investment scheme*;

(2)   if the *client* is habitually resident outside the *EEA* and the *client* is not present in the *United Kingdom* at the time of acknowledging consent to the proposal form to which the *personal recommendation* relates;

(3)   to any *personal recommendation* by a *friendly society* for a small *life policy* sold by it with a *premium* not exceeding £50 a year or, if payable weekly, £1 a week;

(4)   if the *personal recommendation* is to increase a regular *premium* to an existing contract;

(5)   if the *personal recommendation* is to invest additional single *premiums* or single contributions to an existing *packaged product* to which a single *premium* or single contribution has previously been paid.

Timing

9.4.4 R   FCA

A *firm* must provide the *suitability report* to the *client*:
(1)   in the case of a *life policy*, before the contract is concluded unless the necessary information is provided orally or immediate cover is necessary; or
(2)   in the case of a *personal pension scheme* or *stakeholder pension scheme*, where the *rules* on cancellation (**COBS 15**) require notification of the right to cancel, no later than the fourteenth day after the contract is concluded; or
(3)   in any other case, when or as soon as possible after the transaction is effected or executed.

[Note: article 12(3) of the *Insurance Mediation Directive*]

9.4.5 R   FCA

If, in respect of a *life policy*, the *firm* gives necessary information orally or gives immediate cover, it must provide a *suitability report* to the *client* in a *durable medium* immediately after the contract is concluded.

[Note: article 13(2) of the *Insurance Mediation Directive*]

9.4.6 R   FCA

In the case of telephone selling of a *life policy*, when the only contact between a *firm* and its *client* before conclusion of a contract is by telephone, the *suitability report* must:
(1)   comply with the distance marketing disclosure *rules* (**COBS 5.1**);
(2)   be provided immediately after the conclusion of the contract; and
(3)   be in a *durable medium*.

[Note: article 13(3) of the *Insurance Mediation Directive*]

Contents

9.4.7 R   FCA

The *suitability report* must, at least:
(1)   specify the *client's* demands and needs;
(2)   explain why the *firm* has concluded that the recommended transaction is suitable for the *client* having regard to the information provided by the *client*; and
(3)   explain any possible disadvantages of the transaction for the *client*.

[Note: article 12(3) of the *Insurance Mediation Directive*]

9.4.8 G   FCA

A *firm* should give the *client* such details as are appropriate according to the complexity of the transaction.

[Note: article 12(3) of the *Insurance Mediation Directive*]

9.4.9 R   FCA

If a *firm* is providing a *suitability report* in the course of *insurance mediation activity*, the information must be provided:
(1)   in a *durable medium* which is available and accessible to the *client*;
(2)   in a clear and accurate manner, comprehensible to the *client*; and
(3)   in an official language of the *State of the commitment* in which the *contract of insurance* is made or in any other language agreed by the parties.

[Note: article 13 of the *Insurance Mediation Directive*]

Additional content for income withdrawals

9.4.10 G   FCA

When a *firm* is making a *personal recommendation* to a *retail client* about *income withdrawals* or purchase of *short-term annuities*, explanation of possible disadvantages in the *suitability report* should include the risk factors involved in entering into an *income withdrawal* or purchase of a *short-term annuity*. These may include:
(1)   the capital value of the fund may be eroded;
(2)   the *investment* returns may be less than those shown in the illustrations;
(3)   annuity or *scheme pension* rates may be at a worse level in the future;
(4)   the levels of income provided may not be sustainable; and
(5)   there may be tax implications.

9.5   RECORD KEEPING AND RETENTION PERIODS FOR SUITABILITY RECORDS

9.5.1 G   FCA

A *firm* to which **SYSC 9** applies is required to keep orderly records of its business and internal organisation (see **SYSC 9**, General rules on record-keeping). Other *firms* are required to take reasonable care to establish and maintain such systems and controls as are appropriate to their business (see **SYSC 3**, Systems and controls). The records may be expected to reflect the different effect of the *rules* in this chapter depending on whether the *client* is a *retail client* or a *professional client*: for example, in respect of the information about the *client* which the *firm* must obtain and whether the *firm* is required to provide a *suitability report*.

9.5.2 R   FCA

A *firm* must retain its records relating to suitability for a minimum of the following periods:
(1)   if relating to a *pension transfer, pension conversion, pension opt-out* or *FSAVC,* indefinitely;
(2)   if relating to a *life policy, personal pension scheme* or *stakeholder pension scheme*, five years;
(3)   if relating to *MiFID or equivalent third country business*, five years; and
(4)   in any other case, three years.

9.5.3 R   FCA

A *firm* need not retain its records relating to suitability if:
(1)   the *client* does not proceed with the recommendation; and
(2)   they do not relate to *MiFID or equivalent third country business.*

9.6   SPECIAL RULES FOR GIVING BASIC ADVICE ON A STAKEHOLDER PRODUCT

9.6.1 G   FCA

This section applies to a *firm* giving *basic advice*, which has chosen to comply with the *rules* in this section instead of the other *rules* in this chapter (see **COBS 9.1.2 R**).

Range

9.6.2 R   FCA

A *firm* is permitted to maintain more than one *range of stakeholder products*.

9.6.3 R   FCA

A *range of stakeholder products*:
(1)   may include more than one *deposit-based stakeholder product*;
(2)   may include the *stakeholder products* of more than one *stakeholder product* provider;
(3)   must not include any more than one:
       (a)   *CIS stakeholder product* or *linked life stakeholder product*; or
       (b)   *stakeholder CTF*; or
       (c)   *stakeholder pension scheme.*

9.6.4 R   FCA

When a *firm* provides *basic advice* it must:
(1)   explain why it chose the *stakeholder products* and *stakeholder product* providers that appear in the relevant *range*; and
(2)   give the *client* a list of the *stakeholder products* and *stakeholder product* providers that appear in that *range*;

if the *client* asks it do so.

Requirements on first contact

9.6.5 R   FCA

When a *firm* first has contact with a retail client with a view to giving *basic advice* on a *stakeholder product*, it must give the *retail client*:
(1)   the *basic advice* initial disclosure information (**COBS 9 ANNEX 1**), in a *durable medium*, together with an explanation of that information, unless:
       (a)   it has already done so and the *basic advice* initial disclosure information is likely still to be accurate and appropriate; or
       (b)   the contact is not face to face and is using a means of communication which makes it not practicable to provide the *basic advice* initial disclosure information in a *durable medium*; and
(2)   an explanation of how the advice will be paid for and the fact that any commission will be disclosed.

9.6.6 G   FCA
(1)   A *firm* may give a *retail client* the *basic advice* initial disclosure information (**COBS 9 ANNEX 1**) as part of:

> (a)   a *services and costs disclosure document*; or
> (b)   a *combined initial disclosure document* if it has reasonable grounds to believe that it will provide services relating to a *stakeholder product* and a *non-investment insurance contract*, a *regulated mortgage contract*, an *equity release transaction* or a *home purchase plan*.

(2)   If a *firm* provides a *services and costs disclosure document* or *combined initial disclosure document* to a *retail client* it will comply with the requirements under:

> (a)   **COBS 2.2.1 R (1)(A)** and **COBS 2.2.1 R (1)(D)**;
> (b)   **COBS 9.6.5 R (1)** and **COBS 9 ANNEX 1**;
> (c)   the items of distance marketing information set out in paragraphs (1), (2), (4), (5) (19) and (20) of **COBS 5 ANNEX 1 R**; and
> (d)   any duties that apply to it under the *rule* on information to be provided by the insurance intermediary (**COBS 7.2.1 R (1)** and **(2)**).

9.6.6A G   FCA

A *firm* will meet the requirements in respect of its obligation to provide written disclosure in the *rules* on describing the breadth of advice (**COBS 6.2A.5 R**) and content and wording of disclosure (**COBS 6.2A.6 R**) by providing its *basic advice* initial disclosure information (in **COBS 9 ANNEX 1 R**).

9.6.7 R   FCA

For the purposes of **GEN 5**, a *firm* may not use the keyfacts logo in relation to any *document* that is designed to comply with *rules* in **COBS 9.6** or **COBS 7** unless it is a *services and costs disclosure document* or a *combined initial disclosure document* produced in accordance with the templates and notes in the annexes to **COBS 6**.

9.6.8 R   FCA

If a *firm's* first contact with a *retail client* is not face to face, it must:

(1)   inform the *client* at the outset:

> (a)   (if the communication is initiated by or on behalf of a *firm*), of the name of the *firm* and the commercial purpose of the communication;
> (b)   [deleted]
> (c)   that the *firm* will provide the *retail client* with *basic advice* without carrying out a full assessment of the *retail client's* needs and circumstances; and
> (d)   that such information will be confirmed in writing; and

(2)   (if not provided at first contact) send the *client* the *basic advice* initial disclosure information (**COBS 9 ANNEX 1**) in a *durable medium* as soon as reasonably practicable following the conclusion of the first contact;

(3)   (unless the relevant product is a *deposit-based stakeholder product*) if the contact is by spoken interaction, provide the *client* with the disclosure required by the *rules* on additional oral disclosure for firms providing restricted advice (**COBS 6.2A.9 R**).

Sales process

9.6.9 R   FCA

When a *firm* gives *basic advice*, it must do so using:

(1)   a single range of *stakeholder products*; and

(2)   a sales process that includes putting pre-scripted questions to the *client*.

9.6.10 R   FCA

When a *firm* gives *basic advice* it must not:

(1)   describe or recommend a *stakeholder product* outside the *firm's* range; or

(2)   describe or recommend a *smoothed linked long term stakeholder product*; or

(3)   describe fund choice, or recommend a particular fund, if a *stakeholder product* offers a choice of funds; or

(4)   recommend the level of contributions required to be made to a *stakeholder pension scheme* to achieve a specific income in retirement; or

(5)   recommend or agree that a *client* makes a contribution to an *ISA* which exceeds the HM Revenue & Customs *ISA* limits.

9.6.11 R   FCA

(1)   If a *firm* starts the sales process for a *stakeholder product* that is not a *deposit-based stakeholder product*, it must not depart from that process unless it has advised the *retail client* that it will not provide *basic advice* on *stakeholder products* during the period of departure. A *firm* that does that must not provide *basic advice* during the departure period.

(2)   Before a *firm* returns to the sales process for *stakeholder products*, it must tell the *retail client* that that process is about to recommence.

Suitability of recommendations

9.6.12 R   FCA

A *firm* must only recommend a *stakeholder product* to a *retail client* if:

(1)   it has taken reasonable steps to assess the client's answers to the scripted questions and any other facts, circumstances or information disclosed by the *client* during the sales process;

(2)   (unless the relevant product is a *deposit-based stakeholder product*) having done so, it has reasonable grounds for believing that the *stakeholder product* is suitable for the *client*; and

(3)   the *firm* reasonably believes that the client understands the *firm's* advice and the basis on which it was provided.

9.6.13 G   FCA

COBS 9 ANNEX 2 gives *guidance* on the steps a *firm* could take to help it meet these suitability obligations.

9.6.14 R   FCA

If a *firm* giving *basic advice* recommends to a *retail client* to acquire a *stakeholder product*, it must ensure that, before the conclusion of the contract, its *representative*:

(1)   (unless the relevant product is a *deposit-based stakeholder product*) explains to the *client*, if necessary in summary form, but always in a way that will allow the client to make an informed decision about the *firm's* recommendation:

    (a)   the nature of the *stakeholder product*; and

    (b)   the "aims", "commitment" and "risks" sections of the appropriate *key features document*;

(2)   provides the *client* with a summary sheet, which is in a *durable medium* and sets out, for each product it recommends:

    (a)   the specific amount the *client* wishes to pay into the product; and

    (b)   the reasons for the recommendation, including the *client's* attitude to risk and any information provided by the *client* on which the recommendation is based; and

(3)   informs the *client* that in determining any subsequent complaint, the *Ombudsman* may take into account the limited information on which the recommendation was based and the fact that it was not tailored to take account of those aspects of the *client's* financial needs and circumstances not covered by the *firm's* sales process.

9.6.15 R   FCA

Notwithstanding **COBS 9.6.14 R (2)** a *firm* may provide the summary sheet (**COBS 9.6.14 R (2)**) as soon as reasonably practicable after the conclusion of the contract if the *client* asks it to do so, or the contract will be concluded using a means of distance communication that does not enable the provision of the summary sheet in a *durable medium* before the conclusion of the contract, but only if the *firm*:

(1)   reads the summary sheet to the *client* before it concludes the contract; and

(2)   sends the summary sheet to the *client* as soon as practicable after the conclusion of the contract.

Concluding the contract

9.6.16 R   FCA

If a *firm* concludes a contract for a *stakeholder product* with or for a *retail client* it must provide a copy of the completed questions and answers to the *client* in a *durable medium* as soon as reasonably practicable afterwards.

Basic advice on stakeholder products: other issues

9.6.17 R   FCA

(1)   [deleted]

(2)   When a *firm* provides *basic advice* on a *stakeholder product*, it may use the facilities and stationery it uses for other business in respect of which it does hold itself out as acting or advising independently.

9.6.18 R   FCA

A *firm* must ensure that none of its *representatives*:

(1)   is likely to be influenced by the structure of his or her *remuneration* to give unsuitable *basic advice* on *stakeholder products* to a *retail client*; or

(2)   refers a *retail client* to another *firm* in circumstances which would amount to the provision of any fee, commission or non-monetary benefit.

Records

9.6.19 R   FCA

A *firm* must record that it has chosen to give *basic advice* to a *retail client* and make a record of the *range* used and the summary sheet (**COBS 9.6.14 R (2)**) prepared for each *retail client*. That record must be retained for at least five years from the date of the relevant *basic advice*.

9.6.20 R   FCA

(1)   A *firm* must make an up-to-date record of:

    (a)   its *scope of basic advice*, and the *scope of basic advice* used by its *appointed representatives* (if any); and

    (b)   its *range* (or *ranges*) of *stakeholder products*, and the *range* (or *ranges*) used by its *appointed representatives* (if any).

(2)   Those records must be retained for five years from the date on which they are replaced by a more up-to-date record.FCA

9 ANNEX 1 BASIC ADVICE INITIAL DISCLOSURE INFORMATION

This Annex belongs to **COBS 9.6.5 R (1)**

Information that comprises the following:

1.   the name and address (head office or principal place of business if more appropriate) of the *firm*;

2.   [deleted]

3.   a statement that the service being offered is *basic advice* on a limited range of *stakeholder products* by asking questions about income, savings and other circumstances but without carrying out a full assessment of the *retail client's* needs and without offering advice on whether a non-stakeholder product may be more suitable;

4.   a statement, in accordance with **GEN 4** that the *firm* is regulated by the *FCA* (or if an *appointed representative*, a statement of whom it is an *appointed representative* and that that *firm* is regulated by the *FCA*) to give basic advice, together with the registration number of the firm and the fact that the *firm's* status can be checked with the *FCA* on 0845 730 0104 or on the *FCA* website at www.fca.org.uk;

5.   a statement disclosing any product provider loans (where such credit exceeds 10% of share and loan capital) and direct or indirect ownership (where that ownership exceeds 10% of share capital or voting power) either by, or of, a single *product provider* or *operator*; (See also notes 32-35 in **COBS 6 ANNEX 1** and notes 45-50 of **COBS 6 ANNEX 2**)

6.   a description of the arrangements concerning complaints and the circumstances in which the *retail client* can refer the matter to the *Financial Ombudsman Service*; (See also notes 36-37 in **COBS 6 ANNEX 1** and notes 51-54 of **COBS 6 ANNEX 2**)

7.   a description of the circumstances and the extent to which the *firm* is covered by the *compensation scheme* and the *retail client* will be entitled to compensation from the *compensation scheme*; (See also notes 38-39 of **COBS 6 ANNEX 1** and notes 55-58 of **COBS 6 ANNEX 2**)

8.   any relevant disclosure required by the *rules* on describing the breadth of advice (**COBS 6.2A.5 R**) and content and wording of disclosure (**COBS 6.2A.6 R**).

[Note: in respect of 1, 2, 4, 5, and 6, Articles 12 and 13 of the *Insurance mediation directive* and in respect of 7, Article 10 of the *Investors compensation directive*]FCA

---

9 ANNEX 2 SALES PROCESSES FOR STAKEHOLDER PRODUCTS

This Annex gives *guidance* on the standards and requirements to which a *firm* may have regard in designing a sales process for *stakeholder products* and assumes that *firms* will provide *basic advice* to *retail clients* who have no practical knowledge of investing in *stakeholder products* or *investments*.

General Standards – all sales

1.   A sales process for *stakeholder products* may allow the *representative* administering it to depart from scripted questions where this is desirable to enable the *retail client* to better understand the points that need to be made provided this is compatible with the *representative's* competence and the degree of support offered by the *firm's* software and other systems. A software-based system is more likely to provide an adaptable means of providing prompts and support for *representatives* which may accordingly support a more flexible sales process.

2.   Questions, statements and warnings provided should be short, simple and in plain language. Questions should address one issue at a time.

3.   The sales process should enable the *retail client* to exit freely and without pressure at any stage. It should also allow the *representative* to terminate the process at any stage if it appears unlikely (for affordability, mis-match, risk or other reasons) that there is a suitable product for the *retail client*.

4.   Where necessary the sales process should incorporate procedures to allow uncertainties in the *retail client*'s answers to be addressed before proceeding and should generally reflect caution about proceeding if clarification or further information cannot be obtained during the process (for example if a *retail client* cannot confirm whether he or she is eligible for membership of an *occupational pension scheme*).

Preliminary – all sales

5.   The *retail client* should be given the following preliminary information:

         (a)   the *retail client* will only be given *basic advice* about *stakeholder products*;

         (b)   *stakeholder products* are intended to provide a relatively simple and low-cost way of investing and saving;

         (c)   the *range of stakeholder products* on which the *representative* will give advice to that *retail client*;

         (d)   the *retail client* will be asked a series of questions about his or her needs and circumstances and, at the end of the procedure, he or she may be recommended to acquire a *stakeholder product*;

         (e)   the assessment of whether a *stakeholder product* is suitable will be made without a detailed assessment of the *retail client*'s needs but will be based only on the information disclosed during the questioning process; and

         (f)   the *retail client's* answers will be noted and, at the end of the process, if a recommendation to acquire a *stakeholder product* is made, the *retail client* will be provided with a copy of the completed questionnaire.

6.   Following 5, the *retail client* should be asked if he or she wishes to proceed and, if not, the sales process should cease.

Affordability – all sales

7.   If it appears that the *retail client* is unlikely to be able to afford a *stakeholder product*, the sale should be terminated and the *retail client* given an explanation together with a copy of the questions and answers completed to that point.

Financial Priorities and Debt – all sales

8.   A *retail client* should be assessed to ascertain other possible financial priorities – for example, does the *retail client* need (a) insurance protection; (b) access to liquid cash to meet an emergency; or (c) to reduce existing debts? If appropriate, the *retail client* should be given an unambiguous warning about the desirability of meeting those priorities before acquiring a *stakeholder product*.

9.   A stronger warning about the desirability of addressing debt as a priority should be given if it appears that the *retail client* is significantly indebted, especially if there is a strong indication that the debt commitments may render any new commitment unaffordable in the short-term. For this purpose a *firm* should consider using a threshold or indicator to decide whether a *retail client* should be excluded on the basis of affordability. Examples may include where the *retail client* has (a) annual unsecured debt repayments in excess of 20% of gross annual income or (b) four or more active forms of unsecured debt or (c) has consistently reached his overdraft limit. A *firm* should review its chosen indicator or threshold regularly to ensure that it reflects prevailing economic conditions and takes account of industry best practice.

10.   A *firm* should clearly explain what it needs to know about a *retail client*'s debt and consider using a range of alternative words (eg 'loans', 'student loans', 'borrowing' and 'other forms of credit') to ensure all relevant information is obtained. A *firm* may use a simple reckoner to assess *retail client* debt, but should be conscious of the nature of, and not give the impression that it is providing more than, *basic advice*.

11.   If a *firm* gives a warning about the desirability of meeting other priorities before acquiring a *stakeholder product*, or about affordability, it should also invite the *retail client* to consider terminating the sales process.

Saving and investment objectives – all sales (except establishing a stakeholder CTF)

12.   A *retail client's* savings and investment objectives, including the period over which the *retail client* wishes to save or invest, should be ascertained including whether the *retail client*:

         (a)   may need early access to some or all of the amount saved or invested; or

         (b)   wishes to save or invest for retirement; or

         (c)   wants to accumulate a specific sum by a specific date.

13.   If that information indicates that the *retail client's* objective is:

         (a)   to accumulate a specific sum by a specific date; or

         (b)   to save or invest only for the short term; or

(c)   early access may be required to the whole of the sum saved or invested;

the *firm* should not normally recommend a *CIS stakeholder product*, a *linked life stakeholder product*, a *stakeholder pension scheme* or topping up of a *stakeholder CTF*.

Tolerance of risk – all sales

14.   If a *retail client* is not willing to accept any risk of the capital value of an investment being reduced then *CIS stakeholder products*, *linked life stakeholder products* and *stakeholder CTFs* should not usually be recommended. However, a *firm* may, if appropriate, explain the effect of inflation on long-term savings especially in relation to pensions and invite the *retail client* to consider his attitude to risk in the light of that explanation.

15.   If a *retail client* is willing to accept the risk of capital reduction in some circumstances but not others then, before any recommendation to acquire a *CIS stakeholder product* or *linked life stakeholder product* is made, the *retail client* should be reminded of the other circumstances in which he or she is unwilling to accept risk to capital.

Stakeholder pensions

16.   A *stakeholder pension scheme* should not be recommended, and the *retail client* should be advised to seek alternative or further advice, if it appears that the *retail client*:

(a)   has or will have access to an *occupational pension scheme*; or

(b)   is likely to view income in retirement from state benefits as sufficient; or

(c)   already has a pension to which he or she could make further contributions; or

(d)   wishes to retire within five years.

17.   It may also be appropriate to advise the *retail client* that other courses of action may be more beneficial than buying a *stakeholder pension scheme* (for example joining an *occupational pension scheme*).

18.   A *firm* designing a sales process for use in the workplace may take account of the benefits offered by the employer. If a *firm* recommends a *stakeholder pension scheme* on the basis of benefits provided by an employer, then it should explain the basis of the recommendation to the *retail client* and suggest that the *retail client* seek *advice* if he or she has any concerns.

19.   A *firm* should design its processes with a view to addressing the risk that *retail clients* will fail to appreciate the significance of questions about their pension provision and should accordingly incorporate a range of questions and information designed to foster the *retail client*'s understanding of the issues and to elicit appropriate information.

20.   *Retail client* should be told that a *stakeholder pension scheme* is life-styled and what this means.

21.   A *firm* may provide a copy of the table setting out initial monthly pension amounts, found within the "Stakeholder pension decision tree" factsheet, available on www-.moneyadviceservice.org.uk in accordance with COBS 13 Annex 2 1.8R, but in doing so should also provide and explain the caveats and assumptions behind the table. A *firm* should make it clear that the decision on how much to invest is the *retail client's* responsibility and that he should get further advice if has any concerns.

ISAs

22.   A *firm* should ascertain whether the *retail client* has already opened a mini or maxi *ISA* and, if so, whether it would be appropriate for the *retail client* to open a non-*ISA* version of the same product.

CHAPTER 10
APPROPRIATENESS (FOR NON-ADVISED SERVICES)

10.1   APPLICATION AND PURPOSE PROVISIONS

[3.58]
10.1.1 R   FCA

This chapter applies to a *firm* which provides *investment services* in the course of *MiFID or equivalent third country business* other than making a *personal recommendation* and *managing investments*.

10.1.2 R   FCA

This chapter applies to a *firm* which *arranges* or *deals* in relation to a *non-readily realisable security*, *derivative* or a *warrant* with or for a *retail client* and the *firm* is aware, or ought reasonably to be aware, that the application or order is in response to a *direct offer financial promotion*.

10.1.3 R   FCA

This chapter applies to a *firm* which assesses appropriateness on behalf of another *MiFID investment firm* so that the other *firm* may rely on the assessment under **COBS 2.4.4 R** (Reliance on other investment firms: MiFID and equivalent business).

Related rules

10.1.4 G   FCA

A *firm* that is carrying on a *regulated activity* on a non-advised basis, whether or not the *rules* in this chapter apply to its activities, should also consider whether other *rules* in *COBS* apply. For example, a *firm* carrying on *insurance mediation activity* in relation to a *life policy* that does not involve the provision of advice, should have regard to **COBS 7** (Insurance mediation).

10.2   ASSESSING APPROPRIATENESS: THE OBLIGATIONS

10.2.1 R   FCA
(1)   When providing a service to which this chapter applies, a *firm* must ask the *client* to provide information regarding his knowledge and experience in the investment field relevant to the specific type of product or service offered or demanded so as to enable the *firm* to assess whether the service or product envisaged is appropriate for the *client*.
(2)   When assessing appropriateness, a *firm*:
   (a)   must determine whether the *client* has the necessary experience and knowledge in order to understand the risks involved in relation to the product or service offered or demanded;
   (b)   may assume that a *professional client* has the necessary experience and knowledge in order to understand the risks involved in relation to those particular *investment services* or transactions, or types of transaction or product, for which the *client* is classified as a *professional client*.

[**Note:** article 19(5) of *MiFID* and article 36 of the *MiFID implementing Directive*]

10.2.2 R   FCA

The information regarding a *client's* knowledge and experience in the investment field includes, to the extent appropriate to the nature of the *client*, the nature and extent of the service to be provided and the type of product or transaction envisaged, including their complexity and the risks involved, information on:
(1)   the types of service, transaction and *designated investment* with which the *client* is familiar;
(2)   the nature, volume, frequency of the *client's* transactions in *designated investments* and the period over which they have been carried out;
(3)   the level of education, profession or relevant former profession of the *client*.

[**Note:** article 37(1) of the *MiFID implementing Directive*]

10.2.3 R   FCA

A *firm* must not encourage a *client* not to provide information required for the purposes of its assessment of appropriateness.

[**Note:** article 37(2) of the *MiFID implementing Directive*]

Reliance on information

10.2.4 R   FCA

A *firm* is entitled to rely on the information provided by a *client* unless it is aware that the information is manifestly out of date, inaccurate or incomplete.

[**Note:** article 37(3) of the *MiFID implementing Directive*]

Use of existing information

10.2.5 G   FCA

When assessing appropriateness, a *firm* may use information it already has in its possession.

Knowledge and experience

10.2.6 G   FCA

Depending on the circumstances, a *firm* may be satisfied that the *client's* knowledge alone is sufficient for him to understand the risks involved in a product or service. Where reasonable, a *firm* may infer knowledge from experience.

Increasing the client's understanding

10.2.7 G   FCA

If, before assessing appropriateness, a *firm* seeks to increase the *client's* level of understanding of a service or product by providing information to him, relevant considerations are likely to include the nature and complexity of the information and the *client's* existing level of understanding.

No duty to communicate firm's assessment of knowledge and experience

10.2.8 G   FCA

If a *firm* is satisfied that the *client* has the necessary experience and knowledge in order to understand the risks involved in relation to the product or service, there is no duty to communicate this to the *client*. If the *firm* does so, it must not do so in a way that amounts to making a *personal recommendation* unless it complies with the *rules* in **COBS 9** on suitability.

10.3   WARNING THE CLIENT

10.3.1 R   FCA

(1)   If a *firm* considers, on the basis of the information received to enable it to assess appropriateness, that the product or service is not appropriate to the *client*, the *firm* must warn the *client*.

(2)   This warning may be provided in a standardised format.

[**Note:** article 19(5) of *MiFID*]

10.3.2 R   FCA

(1)   If the *client* elects not to provide the information to enable the *firm* to assess appropriateness, or if he provides insufficient information regarding his knowledge and experience, the *firm* must warn the *client* that such a decision will not allow the *firm* to determine whether the service or product envisaged is appropriate for him.

(2)   This warning may be provided in a standardised format.

[**Note:** article 19(5) of *MiFID*]

10.3.3 G   FCA

If a *client* asks a *firm* to go ahead with a transaction, despite being given a warning by the *firm*, it is for the *firm* to consider whether to do so having regard to the circumstances.

10.4   ASSESSING APPROPRIATENESS: WHEN IT NEED NOT BE DONE

10.4.1 R   FCA

(1)   A *firm* is not required to ask its *client* to provide information or assess appropriateness if:

(a)   the service only consists of execution and/or the reception and transmission of *client* orders, with or without *ancillary services*, it relates to particular *financial instruments* and is provided at the initiative of the *client*;

(b)   the *client* has been clearly informed (whether the warning is given in a standardised format or not) that in the provision of this service the *firm* is not required to assess the suitability of the instrument or service provided or offered and that therefore he does not benefit from the protection of the *rules* on assessing suitability; and

(c)   the *firm* complies with its obligations in relation to conflicts of interest.

(2)   The *financial instruments* are:

(a)   shares admitted to trading on a *regulated market* or an equivalent third country market (that is, one which is included in the list which is published by the European Commission and updated periodically); or

(b)   money market instruments, bonds or other forms of securitised debt (excluding those bonds or securitised debt that embed a *derivative*); or

(c)   *units* in a *scheme* authorised under the *UCITS directive*; or

(d)   other non-complex *financial instruments*.

(3)   A *financial instrument* is non-complex if it satisfies the following criteria:

(a)   it is not a *derivative* or other security giving the right to acquire or sell a *transferable security* or giving rise to a cash settlement determined by reference to transferable securities, currencies, interest rates or yields, commodities or other indices or measures;

(b)   there are frequent opportunities to dispose of, redeem, or otherwise realise the instrument at prices that are publicly available to the market participants and that are either market prices or prices made available, or validated, by valuation systems independent of the issuer;

(c)   it does not involve any actual or potential liability for the *client* that exceeds the cost of acquiring the instrument; and

(d)   adequately comprehensive information on its characteristics is publicly available and is likely to be readily understood so as to enable the average *retail client* to make an informed judgment as to whether to enter into a transaction in that instrument.

[**Note:** article 19(6) of *MiFID* and article 38 of the *MiFID implementing Directive*]

10.4.2 R   FCA

If a *client* engages in a course of dealings involving a specific type of product or service through the services of a *firm*, the *firm* is not required to make a new assessment on the occasion of each separate transaction. A *firm* complies with the *rules* in this chapter provided that it makes the necessary appropriateness assessment before beginning that service.

[**Note:** recital 59 to the *MiFID implementing Directive*]

10.4.3 R   FCA

A *client* who has engaged in a course of dealings involving a specific type of product or service beginning before 1 November 2007 is presumed to have the necessary experience and knowledge in order to understand the risks involved in relation to that specific type of product or service.

[**Note:** recital 59 of the *MiFID implementing Directive*]

10.5   ASSESSING APPROPRIATENESS: GUIDANCE

The initiative of the client

10.5.1 G   FCA

A service should be considered to be provided at the initiative of a *client* (see **COBS 10.4.1 R (1)(A)**) unless the *client* demands it in response to a personalised communication from or on behalf of the *firm* to that particular *client* which contains an invitation or is intended to influence the *client* in respect of a specific *financial instrument* or specific transaction.

[**Note:** recital 30 to *MiFID*]

10.5.2 G   FCA

A service can be considered to be provided at the initiative of a *client* notwithstanding that the *client* demands it on the basis of any communication containing a promotion or offer of *financial instruments* made by any means that by its very nature is general and addressed to the public or a larger group or category of *clients*.

[**Note:** recital 30 to *MiFID*]

Personalised communications

10.5.3 G   FCA
(1)   Communications to the world at large, such as those in newspapers or on billboards, are likely to be by their very nature general and therefore not personalised communications.
(2)   Communications addressed to a *client* (such as, for example, an email, a telephone call or a letter), may or may not be personalised depending on the content.
(3)   A communication is not personalised solely because it contains the name and address of the *client* or because a mailing list has been filtered.
(4)   If a *firm* is satisfied that a communication does not contain any personalised content, it may wish to make clear that it does not intend the communication to be personalised and that the personal circumstances of the recipient have not been taken into account.

Equivalent third country markets

10.5.4 G   FCA

[to insert the reference or hypertext link to the list of equivalent third country markets when available]

[**Note:** article 19(6) of *MiFID*]

Independent valuation systems

10.5.5 G   FCA

The circumstances in which valuation systems will be independent of the issuer (see **COBS 10.4.1 R (3)(B)**) include where they are overseen by a depositary that is regulated as a provider of depositary services in a *EEA State*.

[**Note:** recital 61 to the *MiFID implementing Directive*]

10.6   WHEN A FIRM NEED NOT ASSESS APPROPRIATENESS

10.6.1 G   FCA

A *firm* need not assess appropriateness if it is receiving or transmitting an order in relation to which it has assessed suitability under **COBS 9** (Suitability (including basic advice)).

10.6.2 G   FCA

A *firm* may not need to assess appropriateness if it is able to rely on a recommendation made by an *investment firm* (see **COBS 2.4.5 G** (Reliance on other investment firms: MiFID and equivalent business).

10.7   RECORD KEEPING AND RETENTION PERIODS FOR APPROPRIATENESS RECORDS

10.7.1 G   FCA

A *firm* is required to keep orderly records of its business and internal organisation, including all services and transactions undertaken by it. The records may be expected to include the *client* information a *firm* obtains to assess appropriateness and should be adequate to indicate what the assessment was.

10.7.2 R   FCA

The *firm* must retain its records relating to appropriateness for a minimum of five years.

CHAPTER 11
DEALING AND MANAGING

11.1   APPLICATION

General application

[3.59]
11.1.1 R   FCA

This chapter applies to a firm.
(1)   [deleted]
(2)   [deleted]

11.1.2 R   FCA

In this chapter, provisions marked "EU" apply to a *firm* which is not a *MiFID investment firm* as if they were rules.

Application to section on the use of dealing commission

11.1.3 R   FCA

The section on the use of dealing commission applies to a *firm* that acts as an *investment manager*.

Application of section on personal account dealing

11.1.4 R   FCA

The section on personal account dealing applies to the *designated investment business* of a *firm* in relation to activities carried on from an *establishment* in the *United Kingdom*.

11.1.5 G   FCA

The *EEA territorial scope rule* modifies the default territorial scope of the section on personal account dealing (see **COBS 11.7**) to the extent necessary to be compatible with European law (see paragraph 1.1G of Part 3 of **COBS 1 ANNEX 1**). This means that the section on personal account dealing also applies to passported activities carried on by a *UK MiFID investment firm* or a *UK UCITS management company* from a *branch* in another *EEA state*, but does not apply to the *UK branch* of an *EEA MiFID investment firm* in relation to its *MiFID business* or of an *EEA UCITS management company* in relation to activities it is entitled to carry on in the *United Kingdom* under the *UCITS Directive*.

Disapplication of best execution for non-financial spreads

11.1.6 R   FCA

The section on best execution (**COBS 11.2**) does not apply to a *firm* when:
(1)   executing orders: or
(2)   placing orders with other entities for execution; or
(3)   transmitting orders to other entities for execution;

in relation to a *spread-bet* which is not a *financial instrument*, where the *firm* has not made a *personal recommendation* in relation to that *spread-bet*.

Disapplication of best execution to CIS operators purchasing or selling own units

11.1.7 R   FCA

The section on best execution (**COBS 11.2**) does not apply to a *firm* when, acting in the capacity of *operator* of a *regulated collective investment scheme*, it purchases or sells *units* in that *scheme*.

11.2   BEST EXECUTION

Obligation to execute orders on terms most favourable to the client

11.2.1 R   FCA

A *firm* must take all reasonable steps to obtain, when executing orders, the best possible result for its *clients* taking into account the *execution factors*.

[**Note:** article 21(1) of *MiFID* and article 25(2) first sentence of the *UCITS implementing Directive*]

[**Note:** The Committee of European Securities Regulators (CESR) has issued a Question and Answer paper on best execution under *MiFID*. This paper also incorporates the European Commission's response to CESR's questions regarding the scope of the best execution obligations under *MiFID*. The paper can be found at: www.esma.europa.eu/system/files/07_320.pdf]

Execution of decisions by UCITS management companies to deal on behalf of the schemes they manage

11.2.1A R   FCA

A *management company* must, in relation to each *UCITS scheme* or *EEA UCITS scheme* it manages, act in the best interests of the *scheme* when *executing* decisions to deal on its behalf in the context of the management of its portfolio, and **COBS 11.2.1 R** applies in relation to all such decisions.

[**Note:** article 25(1) of the *UCITS implementing Directive*]

Application of best execution obligation

11.2.2 G   FCA

The obligation to take all reasonable steps to obtain the best possible result for its *clients* (see **COBS 11.2.1 R**) should apply to a *firm* which owes contractual or agency obligations to the *client*.

[**Note:** recital 33 to *MiFID*]

11.2.3 G   FCA

Dealing on own account with *clients* by a *firm* should be considered as the execution of *client* orders, and therefore subject to the requirements under *MiFID*, in particular, those obligations in relation to best execution.

[**Note:** first sentence of recital 69 to the *MiFID implementing Directive*]

11.2.4 G   FCA

If a *firm* provides a quote to a *client* and that quote would meet the *firm's* obligations to take all reasonable steps to obtain the best possible result for its *clients* if the *firm* executed that quote at the time the quote was provided, the *firm* will meet those same obligations if it executes its quote after the *client* accepts it, provided that, taking into account the changing market conditions and the time elapsed between the offer and acceptance of the quote, the quote is not manifestly out of date.

[**Note:** second sentence of recital 69 to the *MiFID implementing Directive*]

11.2.5 G   FCA

The obligation to deliver the best possible result when executing *client* orders applies in relation to all types of *financial instruments*. However, given the differences in market structures or the structure of *financial instruments*, it may be difficult to identify and apply a uniform standard of and procedure for best execution that would be valid and effective for all classes of instrument. Best execution obligations should therefore be applied in a manner that takes into account the different circumstances associated with the execution of orders related to particular types of *financial instruments*. For example, transactions involving a customised OTC *financial instrument* that involve a unique contractual relationship tailored to the circumstances of the *client* and the *firm* may not be comparable for best execution purposes with transactions involving shares traded on centralised *execution venues*.

[**Note:** recital 70 to the *MiFID implementing Directive*]

Management companies: execution and transmission of orders

11.2.5A G   FCA
(1)   A *management company* should, for each *UCITS scheme* or *EEA UCITS scheme* it manages, act in the best interests of the *scheme* when directly executing orders to deal on its behalf or when transmitting those orders to third parties.
(2)   When executing orders on behalf of any such *scheme* it manages, a *management company* is expected to take all reasonable steps to obtain the best possible result for the *scheme* on a consistent basis, taking into account price, costs, speed, likelihood of execution and settlement, size and nature of the order or any other consideration relevant to the execution of the order.

[**Note:** recital (19) to the *UCITS implementing Directive*]

Best execution criteria

11.2.6 R   FCA

Part 3   FCA Handbook Materials

When executing a *client* order, a *firm* must take into account the following criteria for determining the relative importance of the *execution factors*:

(1)   the characteristics of the *client* including the categorisation of the *client* as retail or professional;

(2)   the characteristics of the *client* order;

(3)   the characteristics of *financial instruments* that are the subject of that order;

(4)   the characteristics of the *execution venues* to which that order can be directed; and

(5)   for a *management company*, the objectives, investment policy and risks specific to the *UCITS scheme* or *EEA UCITS scheme*, as indicated in its *prospectus* or *instrument constituting the fund*.

[**Note:** article 44(1) of the *MiFID implementing Directive* and article 25(2) second sentence of the *UCITS implementing Directive*]

Role of price

11.2.7 R   FCA

Where a *firm* executes an order on behalf of a *retail client*, the best possible result must be determined in terms of the total consideration, representing the price of the *financial instrument* and the costs related to execution, which must include all expenses incurred by the *client* which are directly related to the execution of the order, including *execution venue* fees, clearing and settlement fees and any other fees paid to third parties involved in the execution of the order.

[**Note:** paragraph 1 of article 44(3) of the *MiFID implementing Directive*]

11.2.8 G   FCA

For the purposes of ensuring that a *firm* obtains the best possible result for the *client* when executing a *retail client* order in the absence of specific *client* instructions, the *firm* should take into consideration all factors that will allow it to deliver the best possible result in terms of the total consideration, representing the price of the *financial instrument* and the costs related to execution. Speed, likelihood of execution and settlement, the size and nature of the order, market impact and any other implicit transaction costs may be given precedence over the immediate price and cost consideration only insofar as they are instrumental in delivering the best possible result in terms of the total consideration to the *retail client*.

[**Note:** recital 67 to the *MiFID implementing Directive*]

11.2.9 G   FCA

A *firm's* execution policy should determine the relative importance of each of the *execution factors* or establish a process by which the *firm* will determine the relative importance of the *execution factors*. The relative importance that the *firm* gives to those *execution factors* must be designed to obtain the best possible result for the execution of its *client* orders. Ordinarily, the *FCA* would expect that price will merit a high relative importance in obtaining the best possible result for *professional clients*. However, in some circumstances for some *clients*, orders, *financial instruments* or markets, the policy may appropriately determine that other *execution factors* are more important than price in obtaining the best possible execution result.

Delivering best execution where there are competing execution venues

11.2.10 R   FCA

For the purposes of delivering best execution for a *retail client* where there is more than one competing venue to execute an order for a *financial instrument*, in order to assess and compare the results for the *client* that would be achieved by executing the order on each of the *execution venues* listed in the *firm's* order execution policy that is capable of executing that order, the *firm's* own commissions and costs for executing the order on each of the eligible *execution venues* must be taken into account in that assessment.

[**Note:** article 44(3) of paragraph 2 of the *MiFID implementing Directive*]

11.2.11 G   FCA

The obligation to deliver best execution for a *retail client* where there are competing *execution venues* is not intended to require a *firm* to compare the results that would be achieved for its *client* on the basis of its own execution policy and its own commissions and fees, with results that might be achieved for the same *client* by any other *firm* on the basis of a different execution policy or a different structure of commissions or fees. Nor is it intended to require a *firm* to compare the differences in its own commissions which are attributable to differences in the nature of the services that the *firm* provides to *clients*.

[**Note:** recital 71 to the *MiFID implementing Directive*]

11.2.12 R   FCA

A *firm* must not structure or charge its commissions in such a way as to discriminate unfairly between *execution venues*.

Part 3   FCA Handbook Materials

[Note: article 44(4) of the *MiFID implementing Directive*]

11.2.13 G   FCA

A *firm* would be considered to structure or charge its commissions in a way which discriminates unfairly between *execution venues* if it charges a different commission or spread to *clients* for execution on different *execution venues* and that difference does not reflect actual differences in the cost to the *firm* of executing on those venues.

[Note: recital 73 to the *MiFID implementing Directive*]

Requirement for order execution arrangements including an order execution policy

11.2.14 R   FCA

A *firm* must establish and implement effective arrangements for complying with the obligation to take all reasonable steps to obtain the best possible result for its *clients*. In particular, the *firm* must establish and implement an order execution policy to allow it to obtain, for its *client* orders, the best possible result in accordance with that obligation.

[Note: article 21(2) of *MiFID* and article 25(3) first paragraph of the *UCITS implementing Directive*]

11.2.15 R   FCA

The order execution policy must include, in respect of each class of *financial instruments*, information on the different *execution venues* where the *firm* executes its *client* orders and the factors affecting the choice of *execution venue*. It must at least include those *execution venues* that enable the *firm* to obtain on a consistent basis the best possible result for the execution of *client* orders.

[Note: paragraph 1 of article 21(3) of *MiFID*]

11.2.16 G   FCA
(1)   When establishing its execution policy, a *firm* should determine the relative importance of the *execution factors*, or at least establish the process by which it determines the relative importance of these factors, so that it can deliver the best possible result to its *clients*.
(2)   In order to give effect to that policy, a *firm* should select the *execution venues* that enable it to obtain on a consistent basis the best possible result for the execution of *client* orders.
(3)   A *firm* should apply its execution policy to each *client* order that it executes with a view to obtaining the best possible result for the *client* in accordance with that policy.
(4)   The obligation to take all reasonable steps to obtain the best possible result for the *client* should not be treated as requiring a *firm* to include in its execution policy all available *execution venues*.

[Note: recital 66 to the *MiFID implementing Directive*]

11.2.17 G   FCA

The provisions of this section which provide that costs of execution include a *firm's* own commissions or fees charged to the *client* for the provision of an *investment service* should not apply for the purpose of determining what *execution venues* must be included in the *firm's* execution policy.

[Note: recital 72 to the *MiFID implementing Directive*]

11.2.18 G   FCA

The provisions of this section as to execution policy are without prejudice to the general obligation of a *firm* to monitor the effectiveness of its order execution arrangements and policy and assess the *execution venues* in its execution policy on a regular basis.

[Note: recital 74 to the *MiFID implementing Directive*]

Following specific instructions from a client

11.2.19 R   FCA
(1)   Whenever there is a specific instruction from the *client*, the *firm* must execute the order following the specific instruction.

[Note: article 21(1) of *MiFID*]
(2)   A *firm* satisfies its obligation under this section to take all reasonable steps to obtain the best possible result for a *client* to the extent that it executes an order, or a specific aspect of an order, following specific instructions from the *client* relating to the order or the specific aspect of the order.

[Note: article 44(2) of the *MiFID implementing Directive*]

11.2.20 G   FCA

When a *firm* executes an order following specific instructions from the *client*, it should be treated as having satisfied its best execution obligations only in respect of the part or aspect of the order to which the *client* instructions relate. The fact that the *client* has given specific instructions which cover one part or aspect of the order should not be treated as releasing the *firm* from its best execution obligations in respect of any other parts or aspects of the *client* order that are not covered by such instructions.

[**Note:** recital 68 to the *MiFID implementing Directive*]

11.2.21 G   FCA

A *firm* should not induce a *client* to instruct it to execute an order in a particular way, by expressly indicating or implicitly suggesting the content of the instruction to the *client*, when the *firm* ought reasonably to know that an instruction to that effect is likely to prevent it from obtaining the best possible result for that *client*. However, this should not prevent a *firm* inviting a *client* to choose between two or more specified trading venues, provided that those venues are consistent with the execution policy of the *firm*.

[**Note:** recital 68 to the *MiFID implementing Directive*]

Information about the order execution policy

11.2.22 R   FCA

A *firm* must provide appropriate information to its *clients* on its order execution policy.

[**Note:** paragraph 2 of article 21(3) of *MiFID*]

11.2.23 R   FCA

(1)   A *firm* must provide a *retail client* with the following details on its execution policy in good time prior to the provision of the service:
  (a)   an account of the relative importance the *firm* assigns, in accordance with the *execution criteria*, to the *execution factors*, or the process by which the *firm* determines the relative importance of those factors;
  (b)   a list of the *execution venues* on which the *firm* places significant reliance in meeting its obligation to take all reasonable steps to obtain on a consistent basis the best possible result for the execution of *client* orders;
  (c)   a clear and prominent warning that any specific instructions from a *client* may prevent the *firm* from taking the steps that it has designed and implemented in its execution policy to obtain the best possible result for the execution of those orders in respect of the elements covered by those instructions.
(2)   This information must be provided in a *durable medium*, or by means of a website (where that does not constitute a *durable medium*) provided that the *website conditions* are satisfied.

[**Note:** article 46(2) of the *MiFID implementing Directive*]

11.2.23A R   FCA

A *management company* must make available appropriate information on its execution policy and on any material changes to that policy to the *unitholders* of each *scheme* it manages.

[**Note:** article 25(3) second part of the second paragraph of the *UCITS implementing Directive*]

11.2.24 R   FCA

Where the order execution policy provides for the possibility that *client* orders may be executed outside a *regulated market* or an *MTF*, the *firm* must, in particular, inform its *clients* about this possibility.

[**Note:** paragraph 3 of article 21(3) of *MiFID*]

Client consent to execution policy and execution of orders outside a regulated market or MTF

11.2.25 R   FCA

(1)   A *firm* (other than a *management company* providing -R03M-14D0-00000-00" type="artwork" version="\\fntd5bappp002\Neptune\Repository\Graphics\UK\FSA\fca_logo.tif"/>ontent>UCITS *scheme* or an *EEA UCITS scheme*) must obtain the prior consent of its *clients* to the execution policy.
(2)   In the case of a *management company* providing *collective portfolio management* services for an *ICVC* that is a *UCITS scheme*, or for an *EEA UCITS scheme* that is structured as an investment company, the *management company* must obtain the prior consent of the *ICVC* or investment company to the execution policy.
(3)   In the case of a *management company* that is the *ACD* of an *ICVC* that is a *UCITS scheme*, (2) does not apply where the *ACD* is the sole *director* of the *ICVC*.

[**Note:** paragraph 2 of article 21(3) of *MiFID* and article 25(3) first part of the second paragraph of the *UCITS implementing Directive*]

11.2.26 R   FCA

A *firm* must obtain the prior express consent of its *clients* before proceeding to execute their orders outside a *regulated market* or an *MTF*. The *firm* may obtain this consent either in the form of a general agreement or in respect of individual transactions.

[**Note:** paragraph 3 of article 21(3) of *MiFID*]

Monitoring the effectiveness of execution arrangements and policy

11.2.27 R   FCA

A *firm* must monitor the effectiveness of its order execution arrangements and execution policy in order to identify and, where appropriate, correct any deficiencies. In particular, it must assess, on a regular basis, whether the *execution venues* included in the order execution policy provide for the best possible result for the *client* or whether it needs to make changes to its execution arrangements. The *firm* must notify *clients* of any material changes to their order execution arrangements or execution policy.

[**Note:** article 21(4) of *MiFID* and article 25(4) first paragraph of the *UCITS implementing Directive*]

Review of the order execution policy

11.2.28 R   FCA
(1)   A *firm* must review annually its execution policy, as well as its order execution arrangements.
(2)   This review must also be carried out whenever a material change occurs that affects the *firm's* ability to continue to obtain the best possible result for the execution of its *client* orders on a consistent basis using the venues included in its execution policy.

[**Note:** article 46(1) of the *MiFID implementing Directive* and article 25(4) second paragraph of the *UCITS implementing Directive*]

Demonstration of execution of orders in accordance with execution policy

11.2.29 R   FCA
(1)   A *firm* other than a *management company* must be able to demonstrate to its *clients*, at their request, that it has executed their orders in accordance with its execution policy.
(2)   A *management company* must be able to demonstrate that it has executed orders on behalf of any *UCITS scheme* or *EEA UCITS scheme* it manages in accordance with its execution policy.

[**Note:** article 21(5) of *MiFID* and article 25(5) of the *UCITS implementing Directive*]

Duty of portfolio managers, receivers and transmitters and management companies to act in clients' best interests

11.2.30 R   FCA

A *firm* must, when providing the service of *portfolio management* or, for a *management company*, *collective portfolio management*, comply with the obligation to act in accordance with the best interests of its *clients* when placing orders with other entities for execution that result from decisions by the *firm* to deal in *financial instruments* on behalf of its *client*.

[**Note:** article 45(1) of *MiFID implementing Directive* and article 26(1) of the *UCITS implementing Directive*]

11.2.31 R   FCA

A *firm* must, when providing the service of reception and transmission of orders, comply with the obligation to act in accordance with the best interests of its *clients* when transmitting *client* orders to other entities for execution.

[**Note:** article 45(2) of the *MiFID implementing Directive*]

11.2.32 R   FCA

In order to comply with the obligation to act in accordance with the best interests of its *clients* when it places an order with, or transmits an order to, another entity for execution, a *firm* must:
[**Note:** article 45(3) of the *MiFID implementing Directive* and article 26(1) of the *UCITS implementing Directive*]
(1)   take all reasonable steps to obtain the best possible result for its *clients* taking into account the *execution factors*. The relative importance of these factors must be determined by reference to the *execution criteria* and, for *retail clients*, to the requirement to determine the best possible result in terms of the total consideration (see **COBS 11.2.7 R**).
      A *firm* satisfies its obligation to act in accordance with the best interests of its *clients*, and is not required to take the steps mentioned above, to the extent that it follows specific instructions from its *client* when placing an order with, or transmitting an order to, another entity for execution;

[**Note:** paragraph 1 and 2 of article 45(4) of the *MiFID implementing Directive* and article 26(2) first paragraph of the *UCITS implementing Directive*]
(2)   establish and implement a policy to enable it to comply with the obligation to take all reasonable steps to obtain the best possible result for its *clients*. The policy must identify, in respect of each class of instruments, the entities with which the orders are placed or to which

the *firm* transmits orders for execution. The entities identified must have execution arrangements that enable the *firm* to comply with its obligations under this section or, for a *management company*, must only enter into arrangements for execution where those arrangements are consistent with the requirements of this section, when it places an order with, or transmits an order to, that entity for execution;

[**Note:** paragraph 1 of article 45(5) of the *MiFID implementing Directive* and article 26(2) second paragraph of the *UCITS implementing Directive*]

(3)   provide appropriate information to its *clients* on the policy established in accordance with **COBS 11.2.32 R (2)** or, for a *management company*, make available to *unitholders* appropriate information on that policy and on any material changes to it;

[**Note:** paragraph 2 of article 45(5) of the *MiFID implementing Directive* and article 26(2) second paragraph last sentence of the *UCITS implementing Directive*]

(4)   monitor on a regular basis the effectiveness of the policy and, in particular, the execution quality of the entities identified in that policy and, where appropriate, correct any deficiencies; and

[**Note:** first paragraph of article 45(6) of the *MiFID implementing Directive* and article 26(3) first paragraph of the *UCITS implementing Directive*]

(5)   review the policy annually. This review must also be carried out whenever a material change occurs that affects the *firm's* ability to continue to obtain the best possible result for its *clients*.

[**Note:** second paragraph of article 45(6) of the *MiFID implementing Directive* and article 26(3) second paragraph of the *UCITS implementing Directive*]

11.2.32A R   FCA

A *management company* must be able to demonstrate that it has placed orders on behalf of any *UCITS scheme* or *EEA UCITS scheme* it manages in accordance with the policy referred to in **COBS 11.2.32 R (2)**.

[**Note:** article 26(4) of the *UCITS implementing Directive*]

11.2.33 G   FCA

This section is not intended to require a duplication of effort as to best execution between a *firm* which provides the service of reception and transmission of orders or *portfolio management* and any *firm* to which that *firm* transmits its orders for execution.

[**Note:** recital 75 to the *MiFID implementing Directive*]

11.2.34 R   FCA

The provisions applying to a *firm* which places orders with, or transmits orders to, other entities for execution (see **COBS 11.2.30 R** to **COBS 11.2.33 G**) will not apply when the *firm* which provides the service of *portfolio management* or *collective portfolio management* and/or service of reception and transmission of orders also executes the orders received or the decisions to deal on behalf of its *client's* portfolio. In those cases the requirements of this section for *firms* who execute orders apply (see **COBS 11.2.1 R** to **COBS 11.2.29 R**).

[**Note:** article 45(7) of the *MiFID implementing Directive* and article 25 of the *UCITS implementing Directive*]

11.3   CLIENT ORDER HANDLING

General principles

11.3.1 R   FCA

(1)   A *firm* (other than a *management company* providing *collective portfolio management* services) which is authorised to execute orders on behalf of *clients* must implement procedures and arrangements which provide for the prompt, fair and expeditious execution of *client* orders, relative to other orders or the trading interests of the *firm*.

[**Note:** paragraph 1 of article 22(1) of *MiFID*]

(2)   These procedures or arrangements must allow for the execution of otherwise comparable orders in accordance with the time of their reception by the *firm*.

[**Note:** paragraph 2 of article 22(1) of *MiFID*]

(3)   A *management company* providing *collective portfolio management* services, must establish and implement procedures and arrangements in respect of all *client* orders it carries out which provide for the prompt, fair and expeditious execution of portfolio transactions on behalf of the *UCITS scheme* or *EEA UCITS scheme* it manages.

[**Note:** article 27(1) first paragraph of the *UCITS implementing Directive*]

11.3.2 R   FCA

A *firm* must satisfy the following conditions when carrying out *client* orders:

(1)   it must ensure that orders executed on behalf of *clients* are promptly and accurately recorded and allocated;

(2)   it must carry out otherwise comparable orders sequentially and promptly unless the characteristics of the order or prevailing market conditions make this impracticable, or the interests of the *client* require otherwise; and

(3)   it must inform a *retail client* about any material difficulty relevant to the proper carrying out of orders promptly upon becoming aware of the difficulty.

[**Note:** article 47(1) of the *MiFID implementing Directive*, article 19(1) of *MiFID* and article 27(1) second paragraph of the *UCITS implementing Directive*]

11.3.3 G   FCA

For the purposes of the provisions of this section, orders should not be treated as otherwise comparable if they are received by different media and it would not be practicable for them to be treated sequentially.

[**Note:** recital 78 to the *MiFID implementing Directive*]

11.3.4 R   FCA

Where a *firm* is responsible for overseeing or arranging the settlement of an executed order or executes the order itself in the course of providing *collective portfolio management* services, it must take all reasonable steps to ensure that any *client financial instruments* or *client* funds received in settlement of that executed order are promptly and correctly delivered to the account of the appropriate *client*.

[**Note:** article 47(2) of the *MiFID implementing Directive*, article 19(1) of *MiFID* and article 27(1) third paragraph of the *UCITS implementing Directive*]

11.3.5 R   FCA

A *firm* must not misuse information relating to pending *client* orders, and shall take all reasonable steps to prevent the misuse of such information by any of its *relevant persons*.

[**Note:** article 47(3) of the *MiFID implementing Directive*, article 19(1) of *MiFID* and article 27(2) of the *UCITS implementing Directive*]

11.3.6 G   FCA

Without prejudice to the *Market Abuse Directive*, for the purposes of the *rule* on the misuse of information (see **COBS 11.3.5 R**), any use by a *firm* of information relating to a pending *client* order in order to deal on own account in the *financial instruments* to which the *client* order relates, or in related *financial instruments*, should be considered a misuse of that information. However, the mere fact that *market makers* or bodies authorised to act as counterparties confine themselves to pursuing their legitimate business of buying and selling *financial instruments*, or that persons authorised to execute orders on behalf of third parties confine themselves to carrying out an order dutifully, should not in itself be deemed to constitute a misuse of information.

[**Note:** recital 78 to the *MiFID implementing Directive*]

Aggregation and allocation of orders

11.3.7 R   FCA

A *firm* is not permitted to carry out a *client* order or a transaction for own account in aggregation with another *client* order unless the following conditions are met:

(1)   it must be unlikely that the aggregation of orders and transactions will work overall to the disadvantage of any *client* whose order is to be aggregated;

(2)   it must be disclosed to each *client* whose order is to be aggregated that the effect of aggregation may work to its disadvantage in relation to a particular order;

(3)   an order allocation policy must be established and effectively implemented, providing in sufficiently precise terms for the fair allocation of aggregated orders and transactions, including how the volume and price of orders determines allocations and the treatment of partial executions.

[**Note:** article 48(1) of the *MiFID implementing Directive*, article 19(1) of *MiFID* and article 28(1) of the *UCITS implementing Directive*]

11.3.8 R   FCA

If a *firm* aggregates a *client* order with one or more other orders and the aggregated order is partially executed, it must allocate the related trades in accordance with its order allocation policy.

[**Note:** article 48(2) of the *MiFID implementing Directive*, article 19(1) of *MiFID* and article 28(2) of the *UCITS implementing Directive*]

Aggregation and allocation of transactions for own account

11.3.9 R   FCA

A *firm* which has aggregated transactions for own account with one or more *client* orders must not allocate the related trades in a way which is detrimental to a *client*.

[**Note:** article 49(1) of the *MiFID implementing Directive*, article 19(1) of *MiFID* and article 28(3) of the *UCITS implementing Directive*]

11.3.10 R   FCA

(1)   If a *firm* aggregates a *client* order with a transaction for own account and the aggregated order is partially executed, it must allocate the related trades to the *client* in priority to the *firm*.

(2)   However, if the *firm* is able to demonstrate on reasonable grounds that without the combination it would not have been able to carry out the order on such advantageous terms, or at all, it may allocate the transaction for own account proportionally, in accordance with its order allocation policy.

[**Note:** article 49(2) of the *MiFID implementing Directive*, article 19(1) of *MiFID* and article 28(4) of the *UCITS implementing Directive*]

11.3.11 R   FCA

A *firm* must, as part of its order allocation policy, put in place procedures to prevent the reallocation, in a way that is detrimental to the *client*, of transactions for own account which are executed in combination with *client* orders.

[**Note:** article 49(3) of the *MiFID implementing Directive* and article 19(1) of *MiFID*]

11.3.12 G   FCA

For the purposes of the provisions of this section, the reallocation of transactions should be considered as detrimental to a *client* if, as an effect of that reallocation, unfair precedence is given to the *firm* or to any particular person.

[**Note:** recital 77 to the *MiFID implementing Directive*]

11.3.13 G   FCA

In this section, carrying out *client* orders includes:

(1)   the *execution of orders on behalf of clients*;

(2)   the placing of orders with other entities for execution that result from decisions to deal in *financial instruments* on behalf of *clients* when providing the service of *portfolio management* or *collective portfolio management*;

(3)   the transmission of *client* orders to other entities for execution when providing the service of reception and transmission of orders.

11.4   CLIENT LIMIT ORDERS

Obligation to make unexecuted client limit orders public

11.4.1 R   FCA

Unless a *client* expressly instructs otherwise, a *firm* must, in the case of a *client limit order* in respect of shares admitted to trading on a *regulated market* which is not immediately executed under prevailing market conditions, take measures to facilitate the earliest possible execution of that order by making public immediately that *client limit order* in a manner which is easily accessible to other market participants.

[**Note:** article 22(2) of *MiFID*]

11.4.2 G   FCA

In respect of transactions executed between *eligible counterparties*, the obligation to disclose *client limit orders* should only apply where the counterparty is explicitly sending a *limit order* to a *firm* for its execution.

[**Note:** recital 42 to *MiFID*]

How client limit orders may be made public

11.4.3 E   FCA

An *investment firm* shall be considered to disclose *client limit orders* that are not immediately executable if it transmits the order to a *regulated market* or *MTF* that operates an order book trading system, or ensures that the order is made public and can be easily executed as soon as market conditions allow.

[**Note:** article 31 of *MiFID Regulation*]

11.4.4 G   FCA

MAR 5.8.2 EU sets out the conditions required for an arrangement to make *client limit orders* public under this section. **MAR 5.8.3 G** and **MAR 5.8.4 G** provide guidance on these conditions.

Orders that are large in scale

11.4.5 R   FCA

The obligation to make public a *limit order* will not apply to a *limit order* that is large in scale compared with normal market size.

[**Note:** article 22(2) of *MiFID*]

11.4.6 G   FCA

MAR 5.7.10 EU and **MAR 5.7.11 EU** set out when an order shall be considered large in scale compared with normal market size.

11.5   RECORD KEEPING: CLIENT ORDERS AND TRANSACTIONS

Record keeping of client orders and decisions to deal

11.5.1 E   FCA

An *investment firm* shall, in relation to every order received from a *client*, and in relation to every decision to deal taken in providing the service of *portfolio management*, immediately make a record of the following details, to the extent they are applicable to the order or decision to deal in question:

(1)   the name or other designation of the *client*;
(2)   the name or other designation of any relevant person acting on behalf of the *client*;
(3)   the details specified in point 4, 6, and in points 16 to 19, of Table 1 of Annex I;
(4)   the nature of the order if other than buy or sell;
(5)   the type of the order;
(6)   any other details, conditions and particular instructions from the *client* that specify how the order must be carried out;
(7)   the date and exact time of the receipt of the order, or of the decision to deal, by the *investment firm*.

[**Note:** article 7 of *MiFID Regulation*]

Record-keeping of transactions

11.5.2 E   FCA

Immediately after executing a *client* order, or, in the case of *investment firms* that transmit orders to another person for execution, immediately after receiving confirmation that an order has been executed, *investment firms* shall record the following details of the transaction in question:

(1)   the name or other designation of the *client*;
(2)   the details specified in points 2, 3, 4, 6, and in points 16 to 21, of Table 1 of Annex I;
(3)   the total price, being the product of the unit price and the quantity;
(4)   the nature of the transaction if other than buy or sell;
(5)   the natural person who executed the transaction or who is responsible for the execution.

[**Note:** article 8(1) of *MiFID Regulation*]

11.5.3 E   FCA

If an *investment firm* transmits an order to another person for execution, the *investment firm* shall immediately record the following details after making the transmission:

(1)   the name or other designation of the *client* whose order has been transmitted;
(2)   the name or other designation of the person to whom the order was transmitted;
(3)   the terms of the order transmitted;
(4)   the date and exact time of transmission.

[**Note:** article 8(2) of *MiFID Regulation*]

11.5.4 E   FCA

Points 2, 3, 4, 6, 16–21 of Table 1 of Annex 1 of the MiFID Regulation

2.	Trading day	The trading day on which the transaction was executed.
3.	Trading time	The time at which the transaction was executed, reported in the local time of the competent authority to which the transaction will be reported, and the basis in which the transaction is reported expressed as Co-ordinated Universal Time (UTC) +/- hours.
4.	Buy/sell indicator	Identifies whether the transaction was a buy or sell from the perspective of the reporting investment firm or, in the case of a report to a *client*, of the *client*.

6.	Instrument identification	This shall consist of: - a unique code to be decided by the competent authority (if any) to which the report is made identifying the *financial instrument* which is the subject of the transaction; - if the *financial instrument* in question does not have a unique identification code, the report must include the name of the instrument or, in the case of a derivative contract, the characteristics of the contract.
16.	Unit price	The price per security or derivative contract excluding commission and (where relevant) accrued interest. In the case of a debt instrument, the price may be expressed either in terms of currency or as a percentage.
17.	Price notation	The currency in which the price is expressed. If, in the case of a bond or other form of securitised debt, the price is expressed as a percentage, that percentage shall be included.
18.	Quantity	The number of units of the *financial instruments*, the nominal value of bonds, or the number of derivative contracts included in the transaction.
19.	Quantity notation	An indication as to whether the quantity is the number of units of financial instruments, the nominal value of bonds or the number of derivative contracts.
20.	Counterparty	Identification of the counterparty to the transaction. That identification shall consist of: - where the counterparty is an *investment firm*, a unique code for that firm, to be determined by the competent authority (if any) to which the report is made; - where the counterparty is a *regulated market* or *MTF* or an entity acting as its central counterparty, the unique harmonised identification code for that market, *MTF* or entity acting as central counterparty, as specified in the list published by the competent authority of the home Member State of that entity in accordance with Article 13(2); - where the counterparty is not an *investment firm*, a *regulated market*, an *MTF* or an entity acting as central counterparty, it should be identified as 'customer/client' of the *investment firm* which executed the transaction.
21.	Venue identification	Identification of the venue where the transaction was executed. That identification shall consist in: - where the venue is a trading venue: its unique harmonised identification code; - otherwise: the code 'OTC'.

11.6 USE OF DEALING COMMISSION

11.6.1 G FCA

This section deals with the acceptance of certain inducements by *investment manager*s and builds upon the *rule* on inducements (**COBS 2.3.1 R**). *Investment manager*s should ensure they comply with both this section and the *rule* on inducements.

Application

11.6.2 R   FCA

This section applies to a *firm* that acts as an *investment manager* when it *executes customer orders* that relate to:

(1)   *shares*; and

(2)

      (a)   *warrants*;

      (b)   *certificates representing certain securities*;

      (c)   *options*; and

      (d)   *rights to or interests in investments* of the nature referred to in (a) to (c);

(3)   to the extent that they relate to *shares*.

11.6.2A G   FCA

COBS 11.6.3 R applies to a *full-scope UK AIFM* that is an *internally managed AIF* in accordance with the modification in **COBS 18.5.4C R**.

Use of dealing commission to purchase goods or services

11.6.3 R   FCA

(1)   Subject to (3), an *investment manager* must not accept any good or service in addition to the *execution* of its *customer orders* if it:

      (a)   *executes* its *customer orders* through a broker or another *person*;

      (b)   passes on the broker's or other *person's charges* to its *customers*; and

      (c)   is offered that good or service in return for the *charges* referred to in (b).

(2)   [deleted]

(3)   The prohibition under (1) does not apply where:

      (a)   the *investment manager* has reasonable grounds to be satisfied that the good or service received in return for the *charges* in (1)(b) will reasonably assist the *investment manager* in the provision of its services to its *customers*, on whose behalf the relevant *customer orders* are being *executed*;

      (b)   the *investment manager's* receipt of that good or service in return for the *charges* in (1)(b) does not, and is not likely to, impair compliance with the duty of the *investment manager* to act in the best interests of its *customers*; and

      (c)   that good or service either:

          (i)   is directly related to the *execution* of trades on behalf of the *investment manager's customers*; or

          (ii)   amounts to the provision of substantive research.

11.6.4 E   FCA

(1)   Under **COBS 11.6.3 R (3)(C)(I)**, for a good or service to be directly related to the *execution* of trades on behalf of the *investment manager's customers* it must be:

      (a)   linked to the arranging and conclusion of a specific investment transaction (or series of related transactions); and

      (b)   provided between the point at which the *investment manager* makes an investment or trading decision and the point at which the investment transaction (or series of related transactions) is concluded.

(2)   Compliance with (1) may be relied upon as tending to establish compliance with **COBS 11.6.3 R (3)(C)(I)**

(3)   Contravention of (1) may be relied on as tending to establish a contravention of **COBS 11.6.3 R (3)(C)(I)**.

11.6.5 E   FCA

(1)   Under **COBS 11.6.3 R (3)(C)(II)**, for a good or service to amount to the provision of substantive research the relevant research must:

      (a)   be capable of adding value to the investment or trading decisions by providing new insights that inform the *investment manager* when making such decisions about its *customers'* portfolios;

      (b)   whatever form its output takes, represent original thought, in the critical and careful consideration and assessment of new and existing facts, and must not merely repeat or repackage what has been presented before;

      (c)   have intellectual rigour and must not merely state what is commonplace or self-evident; and

      (d)   present the *investment manager* with meaningful conclusions based on analysis or manipulation of data.

(2)   Compliance with (1) may be relied upon as tending to establish compliance with **COBS 11.6.3 R (3)(C)(II)**.

(3)   Contravention of (1) may be relied on as tending to establish a contravention of **COBS 11.6.3 R (3)(C)(II)**.

11.6.6 G   FCA

An example of a good or service relating to the *execution* of trades that the *FCA* does not regard as meeting the requirements of the *rule* on use of dealing commission (**COBS 11.6.3 R**) is post-trade analytics. These would not meet the evidential criteria for a good or service to be directly related to the *execution* of trades under **COBS 11.6.4E (1)**.

11.6.7 G   FCA

Examples of goods or services that relate to the provision of research that the *FCA* does not regard as meeting the requirements of the *rule* on use of dealing commission (**COBS 11.6.3 R**) include price feeds or historical price data that have not been analysed or manipulated in order to present the *investment manager* with meaningful conclusions. These would not meet the evidential criteria for a good or service to amount to the provision of substantive research under **COBS 11.6.5E (1)**.

11.6.8 G   FCA

Examples of goods or services that relate to the *execution* of trades or the provision of research that the *FCA* does not regard as meeting the requirements of either evidential provisions **COBS 11.6.4E (1)** or **COBS 11.6.5E (1)** include:

(1) services relating to the valuation or performance measurement of portfolios;
(2) computer hardware;
(3) connectivity services such as electronic networks and dedicated telephone lines;
(4) seminar fees;
(5) *corporate access services*;
(6) subscriptions for publications;
(7) travel, accommodation or entertainment costs;
(8) order and execution management systems;
(9) office administrative computer software, such as word processing or accounting programmes;
(10) membership fees to professional associations;
(11) purchase or rental of standard office equipment or ancillary facilities;
(12) employees' salaries;
(13) direct money payments;
(14) publicly available information; and
(15) *custody* services relating to *designated investments* belonging to, or managed for, *customers* other than those services that are incidental to the *execution* of trades.

11.6.8A G   FCA

(1) An *investment manager* intending to pass on to its *customers* any *charges* under the exemption at **COBS 11.6.3 R (3)** should have regard to its duties under the *client's best interests rule*. For example, this means that:

    (a) an *investment manager* should not pass on a *charge* to a *customer* under the exemption at **COBS 11.6.3 R (3)** that is greater than the cost charged by the broker or relevant person specifically for the relevant good or service falling under **COBS 11.6.3 R (3)**;

    (b) if an *investment manager* intends to pass on a *charge* to a *customer* under the exemption at **COBS 11.6.3 R (3)**, and the relevant good or service being offered in return for a *broker's* or other *person's charges* is not distinctly priced, the *investment manager* should make a fair assessment of the *charge* that it would be permitted to pass onto its *customer* under that *rule*. In making this determination, the *investment manager* may need to consider whether it can carry out a fact-based analysis of the unpriced good or service. For example, it may be appropriate to use other comparable priced goods or services (whether produced internally or procured from another *person*) or an estimate of the cost of providing a comparable good or service internally as an indication of a fair *charge* to pass onto a *customer* for the relevant good or service; and

    (c) where the *investment manager* is in a position to negotiate or itself dictate the price of a good or service it receives that is to be charged to a *customer* under the exemption at **COBS 11.6.3 R (3)**, it should act honestly, fairly and professionally in accordance with the best interests of its *customer*.

(2)

    (a) Where a good or service received by an *investment manager* comprises the provision of substantive research together with elements that are not substantive research (see **COBS 11.6.7 G** and **COBS 11.6.8 G**), **COBS 11.6.3 R (3)** only applies for those elements that amount to the provision of substantive research. This means that the *investment manager* should disaggregate any such good or service received, to ensure that it only passes on *charges* under the exemption at **COBS 11.6.3 R (3)** for the substantive research elements that it receives.

    (b) In disaggregating elements under (a), it may be useful for an *investment manager* to consider the amount that it would be would be willing, in good faith, to pay for those elements of a good or service that cannot be charged to a *customer* under **COBS**

11.6.3 R. Such an exercise can assist the *investment manager*, when determining the charges to be passed on to the *customer* under the exemption at **COBS 11.6.3 R (3)** for the substantive research elements, to ensure that the *customer* will not subsidise the other elements that benefit the *investment manager*.

(c)　　The guidance under (a) and (b) is equally relevant to situations where:

　　(i)　　the good or service to be disaggregated is priced as a whole but the elements to be disaggregated are not distinctly priced; and

　　(ii)　　the overall good or service that is to be disaggregated is not distinctly priced.

(d)　　The considerations in (1) are equally relevant for any disaggregated good or service.

11.6.9 G　FCA

The reference to substantive research in the *rule* on use of dealing commission (**COBS 11.6.3 R**) is not confined to *investment research* as defined in the *Glossary*. Substantive research can potentially be or include *investment research*, but this is not part of the criteria under **COBS 11.6.5 E**. In addition, any goods or services that relate to the provision of research that the *FCA* regards as not acceptable under **COBS 11.6.7 G** or **COBS 11.6.8 G** should be viewed as not meeting the requirements of **COBS 11.6.3 R (3)**, notwithstanding that their content might qualify as *investment research*.

11.6.10 G　FCA

This section applies only to arrangements under which an *investment manager* receives from brokers or other *persons* a good or service that directly relates to the *execution* of trades or amounts to the provision of substantive research. It has no application in relation to *execution* and research generated internally by an *investment manager* itself.

11.6.11 G　FCA

An *investment manager* should not enter into any arrangements that could compromise its ability to comply with its best execution obligations (**COBS 11.2**).

Rule on prior disclosure

11.6.12 R　FCA

An *investment manager* that enters into arrangements under this section must make adequate prior disclosure to *customers* concerning the receipt of goods or services that directly relate to the *execution* of trades or amount to the provision of substantive research. This prior disclosure should form part of the summary form disclosure under the *rule* on inducements (**COBS 2.3.1 R**).

Guidance on prior disclosure

11.6.13 G　FCA

The *rule* on prior disclosure of goods and services under this section complements the requirements on the disclosure of inducements (**COBS 2.3.1 R (2)(B)**). *Investment managers* should ensure they comply with both requirements where relevant.

11.6.14 G　FCA

(1)　　The prior disclosure required by this section should include an adequate disclosure of the *firm's* policy relating to the receipt of goods or services that directly relate to the execution of trades or amount to the provision of substantive research in accordance with the *rule* on use of dealing commission (**COBS 11.6.3 R**).

(2)　　The prior disclosure should explain generally why the *firm* might find it necessary or desirable to use dealing commission to purchase goods or services, bearing in mind the practices in the markets in which it does business on behalf of its *customers*. While the appropriate method of making such a disclosure is for the *firm* to decide, this could, for example, be achieved in a client agreement.

Rule on periodic disclosure

11.6.15 R　FCA

If an *investment manager* enters into arrangements in accordance with the *rule* on use of dealing commission (**COBS 11.6.3 R**), it must in a timely manner make adequate periodic disclosure to its *customers* of the arrangements entered into.

Adequate prior and periodic disclosure

11.6.16 R　FCA

Adequate prior and periodic disclosure under this section must include details of the goods or services that directly relate to the execution of trades and, wherever appropriate, separately identify the details of the goods or services that are attributable amount to the provision of substantive research.

11.6.17 G   FCA

In assessing the adequacy of prior and periodic disclosures made by an *investment manager* under this section, the *FCA* will have regard to the extent to which the *investment manager* adopts disclosure standards developed by industry associations such as the Investment Management Association, the National Association of Pension Funds and the Association for Financial Markets in Europe.

Making periodic disclosures in a timely manner

11.6.18 E   FCA

(1)   A *firm* will make periodic disclosure to its customers under this section in a timely manner if it is made at least once a year.

(2)   Compliance with (1) may be relied upon as tending to establish compliance with the *rule* on periodic disclosure (**COBS 11.6.16 R**).

Record keeping

11.6.19 R   FCA

An *investment manager* must make a record of each prior and periodic disclosure it makes to its *customers* in accordance with this section and must maintain each such record for at least five years from the date on which it is provided.

11.6.20 G   FCA

Firms are also reminded of the general record keeping requirements in **SYSC 3.2** and **SYSC 9** (as applicable). An *investment manager* should keep appropriate records of the basis on which it concludes that a particular good or service may be received under the exemption at **COBS 11.6.3 R (3)** in return for the *charges* in **COBS 11.6.3 R (1)(B)**.

11.7 PERSONAL ACCOUNT DEALING

Rule on personal account dealing

11.7.1 R   FCA

A *firm* that conducts *designated investment business* must establish, implement and maintain adequate arrangements aimed at preventing the following activities in the case of any *relevant person* who is involved in activities that may give rise to a conflict of interest, or who has access to inside information as defined in the *Market Abuse Directive* or to other confidential information relating to *clients* or transactions with or for *clients* by virtue of an activity carried out by him on behalf of the *firm*:

(1)   entering into a *personal transaction* which meets at least one of the following criteria:
    (a)   that *person* is prohibited from entering into it under the *Market Abuse Directive*;
    (b)   it involves the misuse or improper disclosure of that confidential information;
    (c)   it conflicts or is likely to conflict with an obligation of the *firm* to a *customer* under the *regulatory system* or any other obligation of the *firm* under *MiFID* or the *UCITS Directive*;

(2)   advising or procuring, other than in the proper course of his employment or contract for services, any other *person* to enter into a transaction in *designated investments* which, if a *personal transaction* of the *relevant person*, would be covered by (1) or a relevant provision;

(3)   disclosing, other than in the normal course of his employment or contract for services, any information or opinion to any other *person* if the *relevant person* knows, or reasonably ought to know, that as a result of that disclosure that other *person* will or would be likely to take either of the following steps:
    (a)   to enter into a transaction in designated investments which, if a personal transaction of the relevant person, would be covered by (1) or a relevant provision;
    (b)   to advise or procure another *person* to enter into such a transaction.

[**Note:** article 12(1) of *MiFID implementing Directive* and article 13(1) of the *UCITS implementing Directive*]

11.7.2 R   FCA

For the purposes of this section, the relevant provisions are:

(1)   the *rules* on *personal transactions* undertaken by *financial analysts* in **COBS 12.2.5 R (1)** and **(2)**;

(2)   the *rule* on the misuse of information relating to pending *client* orders in **COBS 11.3.5 R**.

11.7.2A G   FCA

The requirements of this section are without prejudice to article 3(a) of the *Market Abuse Directive* which prohibits any *person* who possesses inside information under article 2 of that directive from disclosing that information to any other *person* unless that disclosure is made in the normal course of the exercise of his employment, profession or duties.

11.7.3 G   FCA

For the purposes of **COBS 11.7.1 R (1)(C)**, any other obligation of the *firm* under *MiFID* refers to a *firm's* obligations under the *regulatory system* that are not owed to a *customer* and any of the *firm's* obligations under another *EEA States'* implementation of *MiFID* where it operates a *branch* in the *EEA*.

11.7.4 R   FCA

The arrangements required under this section must in particular be designed to ensure that:

(1)   each *relevant person* covered by this section is aware of the restrictions on *personal transactions*, and of the measures established by the *firm* in connection with *personal transactions* and disclosure, in accordance with this section;

(2)   the *firm*:

      (a)   is informed promptly of any *personal transaction* entered into by a *relevant person*, either by notification of that transaction or by other procedures enabling the *firm* to identify such transactions; or

      (b)   in the case of *outsourcing* arrangements, ensures that the service provider to which the activity is *outsourced* maintains a record of *personal transactions* entered into by any *relevant person* and provides that information to the *firm* promptly on request;

(3)   a record is kept of the *personal transaction* notified to the *firm* or identified by it, including any authorisation or prohibition in connection with such a transaction.

[**Note:** article 12(2) of *MiFID implementing Directive* and article 13(2) of the *UCITS implementing Directive*]

Disapplication of rule on personal account dealing

11.7.5 R   FCA

This section does not apply to the following kinds of *personal transaction*:

(1)   *personal transactions* effected under a discretionary portfolio management service where there is no prior communication in connection with the transaction between the portfolio manager and the *relevant person* or other *person* for whose account the transaction is executed;

(2)   *personal transactions* in *units* or *shares* in collective undertakings that comply with the conditions necessary to enjoy the rights conferred by the *UCITS Directive* or are subject to supervision under the law of an *EEA State* which requires an equivalent level of risk spreading in their assets, where the *relevant person* and any other *person* for whose account the transactions are effected, are not involved in the management of that undertaking;

(3)   *personal transactions* in *life policies*.

[**Note:** article 12(3) of *MiFID implementing Directive* and article 13(3) of the *UCITS implementing Directive*]

11.7.6 R   FCA

For the purposes of this section, a *person* who is not:

(1)   a director, partner or equivalent, manager or *appointed representative* (or, where applicable, a *tied agent*) of the *firm*; or

(2)   a director, partner or equivalent, or manager of any *appointed representative* (or where applicable, a *tied agent*) of the *firm*;

will only be a *relevant person* to the extent that they are involved in the provision of *designated investment business* or *collective portfolio management* services.

Successive personal transactions

11.7.7 R   FCA

Where successive *personal transactions* are carried out on behalf of a *person* in accordance with prior instructions given by that *person*, the obligations under this section do not apply:

(1)   separately to each successive transaction if those instructions remain in force and unchanged; or

(2)   to the termination or withdrawal of such instructions, provided that any *financial instruments* which had previously been acquired pursuant to the instructions are not disposed of at the same time as the instructions terminate or are withdrawn.

Obligations under this section do apply in relation to a *personal transaction*, or the commencement of successive *personal transactions*, that are carried out on behalf of the same *person* if those instructions are changed or if new instructions are issued.

[**Note:** recital 17 to *MiFID implementing Directive*]

11.8   RECORDING TELEPHONE CONVERSATIONS AND ELECTRONIC COMMUNICATIONS

Application – Who?

11.8.1 R   FCA

This section applies to a *firm*:
(1)   which carries out any of the following activities:
    (a)   receiving *client* orders;
    (b)   executing *client* orders;
    (c)   arranging for *client* orders to be executed;
    (d)   carrying out transactions on behalf of the *firm*, or another person in the *firm's* group, and which are part of the *firm's* trading activities or the trading activities of another person in the *firm's* group;
    (e)   executing orders that result from decisions by the *firm* to deal on behalf of its *client*;
    (f)   placing orders with other entities for execution that result from decisions by the *firm* to deal on behalf of its *client*;
(2)   to the extent that the activities referred to in (1) relate to:
    (a)   *qualifying investments* admitted to trading on a *prescribed market*;
    (b)   *qualifying investments* in respect of which a request for admission to trading on such a market has been made;
    (c)   investments which are *related investments* in relation to such *qualifying investments*.

11.8.2 R   FCA

This section does not apply to the carrying on of the following activities:
(1)   activities carried on between *operators*, or between *operators* and depositories, of the same *fund* (when acting in that capacity);
(2)   *corporate finance business*;
(3)   corporate treasury functions.

11.8.3 R   FCA

This section does not apply to the following *firms* or *persons*:
(1)   a *service company*;
(2)   a *non-directive friendly society*;
(3)   a *non-directive insurer*;
(4)   a *UCITS qualifier*.

Application – Where?

11.8.4 R   FCA

This section applies only with respect to a *firm's* activities carried on from an establishment maintained by the *firm* in the *United Kingdom*.

Recording telephone conversations, etc

11.8.5 R   FCA

A *firm* must take reasonable steps to record relevant telephone conversations, and keep a copy of relevant electronic communications, made with, sent from or received on equipment:
(1)   provided by the *firm* to an employee or contractor; or
(2)   the use of which by an employee or contractor has been sanctioned or permitted by the *firm*;
to enable that employee or contractor to carry out any of the activities referred to in **COBS 11.8.1 R**.

11.8.5A R   FCA

A *firm* must take reasonable steps to prevent an employee or contractor from making, sending or receiving relevant telephone conversations and electronic communications on privately-owned equipment which the *firm* is unable to record or copy.

11.8.6 R   FCA

The obligation in **COBS 11.8.5 R** and **COBS 11.8.5A R** does not apply to:
(1)   [deleted]
(2)   a *discretionary investment manager*, in respect of telephone conversations or electronic communications made with, sent to or received from a *firm* which the *discretionary investment manager* reasonably believes is subject to the recording obligation in **COBS 11.8.5 R** in respect of that conversation or communication; or
(3)   a *discretionary investment manager*, in respect of telephone conversations or electronic communications made with, sent to or received from a *person* who is not subject to the recording obligation in **COBS 11.8.5 R**, provided that such telephone conversations or

electronic communications are made with, sent to or received from such *persons* on an infrequent basis, and represent a small proportion of the total telephone conversations and electronic communications made, sent or received by the *discretionary investment manager* to which **COBS 11.8.5 R** apply.

11.8.7 G   FCA

Electronic communications includes communications made by way of facsimile, email and instant messaging devices.

11.8.8 R   FCA

For the purposes of **COBS 11.8.5 R** and **COBS 11.8.5A R** a relevant conversation or communication is any one of the following:

(1)   a conversation or communication between an employee or contractor of the *firm* with a *client*, or when acting on behalf of a *client*, with another *person*, which concludes an agreement by the *firm* to carry out the activities referred to in **COBS 11.8.1 R** as principal or as agent;

(2)   a conversation or communication between an employee or contractor of the *firm* with a *professional client* or an *eligible counterparty*, or when acting on behalf of a *professional client* or an *eligible counterparty*, with another *person*, which is carried on with a view to the conclusion of an agreement referred to in (1) above, and whether or not it is part of the same conversation or communication as in (1).

11.8.9 G   FCA

(1)   **COBS 11.8.8 R (2)** includes conversations and communications relating to specific transactions which are intended to lead to the conclusion of an agreement by the *firm* to deal with or on behalf of the *client* as principal or agent, even if those conversations or communications do not lead to the conclusion of such an agreement. It does not include conversations or communications which are not intended to lead to the conclusion of such an agreement, such as general conversations or communications about market conditions.

(2)   The *FCA* would not usually expect the obligation in **COBS 11.8.5 R** to include conversations or communications made by investment analysts, retail financial advisers, and persons carrying on back office functions, as such persons will not normally make relevant conversations or communications when acting in those capacities.

Retention of records

11.8.10 R   FCA

A *firm* must take reasonable steps to retain all records made by it under **COBS 11.8.5 R**:

(1)   for a period of at least 6 *months* from the date the record was created;

(2)   in a medium that allows the storage of the information in a way accessible for future reference by the *FCA*, and so that the following conditions are met:

     (a)   the *FCA* must be able to access the records readily;

     (b)   it must be possible for any corrections or other amendments, and the contents of the records prior to such corrections and amendments, to be easily ascertained;

     (c)   it must not be possible for the records to be otherwise manipulated or altered.

CHAPTER 12
INVESTMENT RESEARCH

12.1   PURPOSE AND APPLICATION

Purpose

[3.60]
12.1.1 G   FCA

The purpose of this chapter is to:

(1)   set out specific requirements relating to the production and dissemination of *investment research* and *non-independent research*; and

(2)   implementing the provisions of the *Market Abuse Directive* relating to the disclosures to be made in, and about, *research recommendations*.

Application: Who?

12.1.2 R   FCA

This chapter applies to a firm.

(1)   [deleted]

(2)   [deleted]

Application: Where?

12.1.3 G   FCA

The *EEA territorial scope rule* modifies the general *rule* of application to the extent necessary to be compatible with European law (see paragraph 1.1 of Part 2 of **COBS 1 ANNEX 1**). This means that **COBS 12.2** and **COBS 12.3.4 G** also apply to *passported activities* carried on by a *UK MiFID investment firm* from a *branch* in another *EEA state*, but do not apply to the *United Kingdom branch* of an *EEA MiFID investment firm* in relation to its *MiFID business*.

12.2   INVESTMENT RESEARCH

Application

12.2.1 R   FCA

This section applies to a *firm* which produces, or arranges for the production of, *investment research* that is intended or likely to be subsequently disseminated to *clients* of the *firm* or to the public, under its own responsibility or that of a member of its *group*.

[**Note:** article 25(1) of the *MiFID implementing Directive*]

12.2.2 G   FCA

The concept of dissemination of *investment research* to *clients* or to the public is not intended to include dissemination exclusively to *persons* within the *group* of the *firm*.

[**Note:** recital 33 of the *MiFID implementing Directive*]

Measures and arrangements required for investment research

12.2.3 R   FCA

A *firm* must ensure the implementation of all of the measures for managing conflicts of interest in **SYSC 10.1.11 R** in relation to the *financial analyst*s involved in the production of *investment research* and other *relevant persons* whose responsibilities or business interests may conflict with the interests of the *persons* to whom *investment research* is disseminated.

[**Note:** article 25 (1) of the *MiFID implementing Directive*]

12.2.4 G   FCA

Persons whose responsibilities or business interests may reasonably be considered to conflict with the interests of the *persons* to whom *investment research* is disseminated include corporate finance personnel and *persons* involved in sales and trading on behalf of *clients* or the *firm*.

[**Note:** recital 30 of the *MiFID implementing Directive*]

12.2.5 R   FCA

A *firm* must have in place arrangements designed to ensure that the following conditions are satisfied:

(1)   if a *financial analyst* or other *relevant person* has knowledge of the likely timing or content of *investment research* which is not publicly available or available to *clients* and cannot readily be inferred from information that is so available, that *financial analyst* or other *relevant person* must not undertake *personal transactions* or trade on behalf of any other *person*, including the *firm*, other than as *market maker* acting in good faith and in the ordinary course of market making or in the execution of an unsolicited *client* order, in *financial instruments* to which the *investment research* relates, or in any *related financial instruments*, until the recipients of the *investment research* have had a reasonable opportunity to act on it;
         [**Note:** article 25(2)(a) of the *MiFID implementing Directive*]

(2)   in circumstances not covered by (1), *financial analyst* and any other *relevant persons* involved in the production of *investment research* must not undertake *personal transactions* in *financial instruments* to which the *investment research* relates, or in any *related financial instrument*, contrary to current recommendations, except in exceptional circumstances and with the prior approval of a member of the *firm's* legal or compliance function;
         [**Note:** article 25(2)(b) of the *MiFID implementing Directive*]

(3)   the *firm* itself, *financial analysts*, and other *relevant persons* involved in the production of *investment research* must not accept inducements from those with a material interest in the subject matter of the *investment research*;
         [**Note:** article 25(2)(c) of the *MiFID implementing Directive*]

(4)   the *firm* itself, *financial analysts*, and other *relevant persons* involved in the production of *investment research* must not promise issuers favourable research coverage; and
         [**Note:** article 25(2)(d) of the *MiFID implementing Directive*]

(5)   issuers, *relevant persons* other than *financial analyst* s, and any other *persons* must not, before the dissemination of *investment research*, be permitted to review a draft of the *investment research* for the purpose of verifying the accuracy of factual statements made in that *investment research*, or for any other purpose other than verifying compliance with the *firm's* legal obligations, if the draft includes a recommendation or a target price.
         [**Note:** article 25(2)(e) of the *MiFID implementing Directive*]

12.2.5A G   FCA

Firms are reminded that they must also comply with **COBS 11.7** (Rule on personal account dealing).

12.2.6 G   FCA

Knowledge by a *financial analyst* or other *relevant person* that the *firm* intends to produce or disseminate *investment research* to its *clients* or to the public (including in circumstances where research material has not yet been written) could constitute knowledge of the likely timing and content of *investment research* under **COBS 12.2.5 R (1)**.

12.2.7 G   FCA

For the purposes of **COBS 12.2.5 R (2)**:
(1)   current recommendations should be considered to be those recommendations contained in *investment research* which have not been withdrawn and which have not lapsed; and
         [**Note:** recital 34 of the *MiFID implementing Directive*]
(2)   exceptional circumstances in which *financial analyst*s and other *relevant persons* may, with prior written approval, undertake *personal transactions* in *financial instruments* to which *investment research* relates should include those circumstances where, for personal reasons relating to financial hardship, the *financial analyst* or other *relevant person* is required to liquidate a position.
         [**Note:** recital 31 of the *MiFID implementing Directive*]

12.2.8 G   FCA

Small gifts or minor hospitality below a level specified in the *firm's conflicts of interest policy* and mentioned in the description of that policy that is made available to *clients* in accordance with **COBS 6.1.4 R (8)** should not be considered as inducements for the purposes of **COBS 12.2.5 R (3)**.

[**Note:** recital 32 of the *MiFID implementing Directive*]

12.2.9 G   FCA

A *financial analyst* should not become involved in activities other than the preparation of *investment research* where such involvement is inconsistent with the maintenance of the *financial analysts* objectivity. The following should ordinarily be considered as inconsistent with the maintenance of a *financial analyst's* objectivity:
(1)   participating in investment banking activities such as corporate finance business and underwriting; or
(2)   participating in 'pitches' for new business or 'road shows' for new issues of *financial instruments*; or
(3)   being otherwise involved in the preparation of issuer marketing.

[**Note:** recital 36 of the *MiFID implementing Directive*]

Exemption from investment research measures and arrangements

12.2.10 R   FCA

A *firm* which disseminates *investment research* produced by another *person* to the public or to *clients* is exempt from complying with the requirements in **COBS 12.2.3 R** and **COBS 12.2.5 R** if the following criteria are met:
(1)   the *person* that produces the *investment research* is not a member of the *group* to which the *firm* belongs;
(2)   the *firm* does not substantially alter the recommendations within the *investment research*;
(3)   the *firm* does not present the *investment research* as having been produced by it; and
(4)   the *firm* verifies that the producer of the *investment research* is subject to requirements equivalent to those in **COBS 12.2.3 R** and **COBS 12.2.5 R** in relation to the production of that *investment research*, or has established a policy setting such requirements.

[**Note:** article 25(3) of the *MiFID implementing Directive*]

Means and timing of publication of investment research

12.2.11 G   FCA

The *FCA* would expect a *firm's conflicts of interest policy* to provide for *investment research* to be published or distributed to its *clients* in an appropriate manner. For example, the *FCA* considers it will be:
(1)   appropriate for a *firm* to take reasonable steps to ensure that its *investment research* is published or distributed only through its usual *distribution channels*; and
(2)   inappropriate for an *employee* (whether or not a *financial analyst*) to communicate the substance of any *investment research*, except as set out in the *firm's conflicts of interest policy*.

12.2.12 G   FCA

The *FCA* would expect a *firm* to consider whether or not other business activities of the *firm* could create the reasonable perception that its *investment research* may not be an impartial analysis of the market in, or the value or prospects of, a *financial instrument*. A *firm* would therefore be expected to consider whether its *conflicts of interest policy* should contain any restrictions on the timing of the publication of *investment research*. For example, a *firm* might consider whether it should restrict publication of relevant *investment research* around the time of an investment offering.

Investment research for internal use

12.2.13 G   FCA

The *FCA* considers that the significant conflicts of interest which could arise are likely to mean it is inappropriate for a *financial analyst* or other *relevant person* to prepare *investment research* which is intended firstly for internal use for the *firm*'s own advantage, and then for later publication to its *clients* (in circumstances in which it might reasonably be expected to have a material influence on its *clients*' investment decisions).

12.3   NON-INDEPENDENT RESEARCH

Application

12.3.1 R   FCA

This section applies to a *firm* that produces or disseminates *non-independent research*.

[Note: article 24(2) of the *MiFID implementing Directive*]

Labelling of non-independent research

12.3.2 R   FCA

A *firm* which produces or disseminates *non-independent research* must ensure that it:
(1)   is clearly identified as a marketing communication; and
(2)   contains a clear and prominent statement that (or, in the case of an oral recommendation, to the effect that) it:
    (a)   has not been prepared in accordance with legal requirements designed to promote the independence of *investment research*; and
    (b)   is not subject to any prohibition on dealing ahead of the dissemination of *investment research*.

[Note: article 24(2) of the *MiFID implementing Directive*]

12.3.3 R   FCA

The *financial promotion rules* apply to *non-independent research* as though it were a marketing communication.

[Note: article 24(2) of the *MiFID implementing Directive*]

Management of conflicts of interest in area of non-independent research

12.3.4 G   FCA

In accordance with **SYSC 10**, a *firm* will be expected to take reasonable steps to identify and manage conflicts of interest which may arise in the production of *non-independent research*. Situations where conflicts of interest can arise include:
(1)   *relevant persons* trading in *financial instruments* that are the subject of *non-independent research* which they know the *firm* has published or intends to publish before *clients* have had a reasonable opportunity to act on it (other than when the *firm* is acting as *market maker* in good faith and in the ordinary course of market making, or in the execution of an unsolicited *client* order); and
(2)   preparation of *non-independent research* which is intended firstly for internal use by the *firm* and then for later publication to *clients*.

12.4   RESEARCH RECOMMENDATIONS: REQUIRED DISCLOSURES

Application

12.4.1 R   FCA
(1)   This section applies to a *firm* that prepares or disseminates *research recommendations*.
(2)   This section does not apply to the extent that the Investment Recommendation (Media) Regulations 2005 apply to a *firm*.
(3)   If a *firm* is a *media firm* subject to equivalent appropriate regulation, only **COBS 12.4.2 G**, **COBS 12.4.4 R**, **COBS 12.4.15 R** and **COBS 12.4.16 R** apply.

[Note: articles 2(4), 3(4), 5(5) of the *MAD Investment Recommendations Directive*]

12.4.2 G   FCA

Appropriate regulatory or self-regulatory arrangements are sufficient to meet the condition in **COBS 12.4.1 R (3)**. Examples include those listed in regulation 3(5) of the Investment Recommendation

(Media) Regulations 2005, that is the Code of Practice issued by the Press Complaints Commission, the Producers' Guidelines issued by the British Broadcasting Corporation, and any code published by the Office of Communications pursuant to section 324 of the Communications Act 2003.

Use of information barriers

12.4.3 G   FCA

Obligations to disclose information do not require those producing *research recommendations* to breach effective information barriers put in place to prevent and avoid conflicts of interest.

[**Note:** recital 7 of the *MAD Investment Recommendations Directive*]

Fair presentation and disclosure

12.4.4 R   FCA

A *firm* must take reasonable care:
(1)   to ensure that a *research recommendation* produced or disseminated by it is fairly presented; and
(2)   to disclose its interests or indicate conflicts of interest concerning *relevant investments*.

[**Note:** article 6(5) of the *Market Abuse Directive*]

Identity of producers of recommendations

12.4.5 R   FCA
(1)   A *firm* must, in a *research recommendation* produced by it:
     (a)   disclose clearly and prominently the identity of the *person* responsible for its production, and in particular:
         (i)   the name and job title of the individual who prepared the *research recommendation*; and
         (ii)   the name of the *firm*; and
     (b)   (where the *firm* is an *investment firm* or a *credit institution*) disclose the identity of the *competent authority* of the *firm*.
(2)   The requirements in (1) may be met for non-written *research recommendations* by referring to a place where the disclosures can be directly and easily accessed by the public, such as an appropriate internet site of the *firm*.

[**Note:** article 2 of the *MAD Investment Recommendations Directive*]

General standard for fair presentation of recommendations

12.4.6 R   FCA
(1)   A *firm* must take reasonable care to ensure that:
     (a)   facts in a *research recommendation* are clearly distinguished from interpretations, estimates, opinions and other types of non-factual information;
     (b)   its sources for a *research recommendation* are reliable or if there is any doubt as to whether a source is reliable, this is clearly indicated;
     (c)   all projections, forecasts and price targets in a *research recommendation* are clearly labelled as such and the material assumptions made in producing or using them are indicated; and
     (d)   the substance of its *research recommendations* can be substantiated as reasonable, upon request by the *FCA*.
(2)   The requirements in (1) do not apply, in the case of non-written *research recommendations*, to the extent that they would be disproportionate.
(3)   A *firm* must make and retain sufficient records to disclose the basis of the substantiation required in (1)(d).

[**Note:** article 3 of the *MAD Investment Recommendations Directive*]

Additional obligations in relation to fair presentation of recommendations

12.4.7 R   FCA
(1)   In addition a *firm* must take reasonable care to ensure that, in a *research recommendation*, at least:
     (a)   all substantially material sources are indicated, including, if appropriate, the *issuer*, and in particular the *research recommendation* indicates whether the *research recommendation* has been disclosed to that *issuer* and amended following this disclosure before its dissemination;
     (b)   any basis of valuation or methodology used to evaluate a *security*, a *derivative* or an *issuer*, or to set a price target for a *security* or a *derivative*, is adequately summarised;
     (c)   the meaning of any recommendation made, such as "buy", "sell" or "hold", which may include the time horizon of the *security* or *derivative* to which the *research recommendation* relates, is adequately explained and any appropriate risk warning, including a sensitivity analysis of the relevant assumptions, indicated;

(d)   reference is made to the planned frequency, if any, of updates of the *research recommendation* and to any major changes in the coverage policy previously announced;

(e)   the date at which the *research recommendation* was first released for distribution is indicated clearly and prominently, as well as the relevant date and time for any *security* or *derivative* price mentioned; and

(f)   if the substance of a *research recommendation* differs from the substance of an earlier *research recommendation*, concerning the same *security*, *derivative* or *issuer* issued during the 12-month period immediately preceding its release, this change and the date of the earlier *research recommendation* are indicated clearly and prominently.

(2)   If the requirements in (1)(a), (b) or (c) would be disproportionate in relation to the length of the *research recommendation*, a *firm* may, instead, make clear and prominent reference in the *research recommendation* to the place where the required information can be directly and easily accessed by the public (such as a hyperlink to that information on an appropriate internet site of the *firm*) provided that there has been no change in the methodology or basis of valuation used.

(3)   In the case of a non-written *research recommendation*, the requirements of (1) do not apply to the extent that they would be disproportionate.

[**Note:** article 4 of the *MAD Investment Recommendations Directive*]

12.4.8 G   FCA

The disclosures required under **COBS 12.4.7 R (1)(E)** and **COBS 12.4.7 R (1)(F)** may, if the *firm* so chooses, be made by graphical means (for example by use of a line graph).

General standard for disclosure of interests and conflicts of interest

12.4.9 R   FCA

(1)   A *firm* must disclose, in a *research recommendation*:

(a)   all of its relationships and circumstances that may reasonably be expected to impair the objectivity of the *research recommendation*, in particular a significant financial interest in any *relevant investment* which is the subject of the *research recommendation*, or a significant conflict of interest with respect to a *relevant issuer*; and

(b)   relationships and circumstances, of the sort referred to in (a), of each legal or natural person working for the *firm* who was involved in preparing the substance of the *research recommendation*, including, in particular, for a *firm* which is an *investment firm*, disclosure of whether his remuneration is tied to investment banking transactions performed by the *firm* or any *affiliated company*.

(2)   If the *firm* is a legal person, the information to be disclosed in accordance with (1) must at least include the following:

(a)   any interests or conflicts of interest of the *firm* or of an *affiliated company* that are accessible, or reasonably expected to be accessible, to the *persons* involved in the preparation of the substance of the *research recommendation*; and

(b)   any interests or conflicts of interest of the *firm* or of *affiliated companies* known to *persons* who, although not involved in the preparation of the substance of the *research recommendation*, had or could reasonably be expected to have access to the substance of the *research recommendation* prior to its dissemination, other than *persons* whose only access to the *research recommendation* is to ensure compliance with relevant regulatory or statutory obligations, including the disclosures required under this section.

(3)   If the disclosures required under (1) and (2) would be disproportionate in relation to the length of the *research recommendation* distributed, a *firm* may, instead, make clear and prominent reference in the *research recommendation* to the place where such disclosures can be directly and easily accessed by the public (such as a hyperlink to the disclosure on an appropriate internet site of the *firm*).

(4)   The requirements in (1) do not apply, in the case of non-written *research recommendations*, to the extent that they are disproportionate.

[**Note:** article 5 of the *MAD Investment Recommendations Directive*]

Additional obligations for producers of research recommendations in relation to disclosure of interests or conflicts of interest

12.4.10 R   FCA

(1)   A *research recommendation* produced by a *firm* must disclose clearly and prominently the following information on its interests and conflicts of interest:

(a)   major shareholdings that exist between it or any *affiliated company* on the one hand and the *relevant issuer* on the other hand, including at least:

(i)   shareholdings exceeding 5% of the total issued share capital in the *relevant issuer* held by the *firm* or any *affiliated company*; or

(ii)   shareholdings exceeding 5% of the total issued share capital of the *firm* or any *affiliated company* held by the *relevant issuer*;

(b)   any other financial interests held by the *firm* or any *affiliated company* in relation to the *relevant issuer* which are significant in relation to the *research recommendation*;

(c)   if applicable, a statement that the *firm* or any *affiliated company* is a *market maker* or liquidity provider in the securities of the *relevant issuer* or in any related *derivatives*;

(d)   if applicable, a statement that the *firm* or any *affiliated company* has been lead manager or co-lead manager over the previous 12 months of any publicly disclosed offer of securities of the *relevant issuer* or in any related *derivatives*;

(e)   if applicable, a statement that the *firm* or any *affiliated company* is party to any other agreement with the *relevant issuer* relating to the provision of investment banking services, provided that:

      (i)   this would not entail the disclosure of any confidential commercial information; and

      (ii)   the agreement has been in effect over the previous 12 months or has given rise during the same period to a payment or to the promise of payment; and

(f)   if applicable, a statement that the *firm* or any *affiliated company* is party to an agreement with the *relevant issuer* relating to the production of the *research recommendation*.

(2)   A *firm* must disclose, in general terms, in the *research recommendation* the effective organisational and administrative arrangements set up within the *firm* for the prevention and avoidance of conflicts of interest with respect to *research recommendations*, including information barriers.

(3)   In the case of an *investment firm* or a *credit institution*, if a legal or natural *person* working for the *firm* who is involved in the preparation of a *research recommendation*, receives or purchases *shares* of the *relevant issuer* prior to a public offering of those *shares*, the price at which the *shares* were acquired and the date of acquisition must also be disclosed in the *research recommendation*.

(4)   A *firm*, which is an *investment firm* or a *credit institution*, must publish the following information on a quarterly basis, and must disclose it in its *research recommendations*:

      (a)   the proportion of all *research recommendations* published during the relevant quarter that are "buy", "hold", "sell" or equivalent terms; and

      (b)   the proportion of *relevant investments* in each of these categories, issued by *issuers* to which the *firm* supplied material investment banking services during the previous 12 months.

(5)   If the requirements under (1) to (4) would be disproportionate in relation to the length of the *research recommendation*, a *firm* may, instead, make clear and prominent reference in the *research recommendation* to the place where such disclosure can be directly and easily accessed by the public (such as a hyperlink to the disclosure on an appropriate internet site of the *firm*, or, if relevant, to the *firm's conflicts of interest policy*).

(6)   In the case of non-written *research recommendations*, the requirements of (1) do not apply to the extent that they are disproportionate.

[**Note:** article 6 of the *MAD Investment Recommendations Directive*]

12.4.11 G   FCA

Nothing in **COBS 12.4.10 R (1)(A)** prevents a *firm* from choosing to disclose significant shareholdings above a lower threshold (for example, 1%) than is required by **COBS 12.4.10 R (1)(A)**.

12.4.12 G   FCA

COBS 12.4.10 R (1)(A) and **COBS 12.4.10 R (1)(B)** only require a *firm* to aggregate its shareholdings with those of *affiliated companies* if they act in concert in relation to those shareholdings.

12.4.13 G   FCA

In relation to companies limited by shares and incorporated in Great Britain, the most meaningful measure of "total issued share capital" is likely to be the concept of "paid up and issued share capital" under the Companies Act 1985 or Companies Act 2006 (as applicable).

12.4.14 G   FCA

The *FCA* considers that it is important for the proportions published in compliance with **COBS 12.4.10 R (4)** to be consistent and meaningful to the recipients of the *research recommendations*. Accordingly for non-equity material, the relevant categories should be meaningful to the recipients in terms of the course of action being recommended.

Identity of disseminators of recommendations

12.4.15 R   FCA

If a *firm* disseminates a *research recommendation* produced by a third party, the *research recommendation* must identify the *firm* clearly and prominently.

[**Note:** article 7 of the *MAD Investment Recommendations Directive*]

General standard for dissemination of third party recommendations

12.4.16 R   FCA

(1)   If a *research recommendation* produced by a third party is substantially altered before dissemination by a *firm*:
    (a)   the disseminated material must clearly describe that alteration in detail; and
    (b)   if the substantial alteration consists of a change of the direction of the recommendation (such as changing a "buy" recommendation into a "hold" or "sell" recommendation or vice versa), the requirements laid down in **COBS 12.4.5 R** to **COBS 12.4.11 G** on producers must be met by the *firm*, to the extent of the substantial alteration.

(2)   A *firm* which disseminates a substantially altered *research recommendation* must have a formal written policy so that the *persons* receiving the information may be directed to where they can have access to the identity of the producer of the *research recommendation*, the *research recommendation* itself and the disclosure of the producer's interests or conflicts of interest, provided that these elements are publicly available.

(3)   If a *firm* disseminates a summary of a *research recommendation* produced by a third party, it must:
    (a)   ensure that the summary is fair, clear and not misleading;
    (b)   identify the source *research recommendation*; and
    (c)   identify where (to the extent that they are publicly available) the third party's disclosures relating to the source *research recommendation* can be directly and easily accessed by the public.

(4)   Paragraphs (1) and (2) do not apply to news reporting on *research recommendations* produced by a third party where the substance of the *research recommendation* is not altered.

[**Note:** article 8 of the *MAD Investment Recommendations Directive*]

Additional obligations for investment firms and credit institutions disseminating third party recommendations

12.4.17 R   FCA

If a *firm*, which is an *investment firm* or a *credit institution*, disseminates a *research recommendation* produced by a third party:
(1)   the name of the *competent authority* of the *firm* must be clearly and prominently indicated on the disseminated material;
(2)   if the producer of the *research recommendation* has not already disseminated it, the requirements in **COBS 12.4.10 R** must be met by the *firm* as if it had produced the *research recommendation* itself; and
(3)   if the *firm* has substantially altered the *research recommendation*, the requirements laid down in **COBS 12.4.4 R** to **COBS 12.4.10 R** must be met by the *firm* as if it had produced the *research recommendation* itself.

[**Note:** article 9 of the *MAD Investment Recommendations Directive*]

CHAPTER 13
PREPARING PRODUCT INFORMATION

13.1   THE OBLIGATION TO PREPARE PRODUCT INFORMATION

[3.61]
13.1.1 R   FCA

A *firm* must prepare:
(1)   a *key features document* for each *packaged product*, *cash-deposit ISA* and *cash-deposit CTF* it produces; and
(2)   a *key features illustration* for each *packaged product* it produces;

in good time before those *documents* have to be provided.

Information on life policies

13.1.2 R   FCA

A *firm* must prepare the *Consolidated Life Directive information* for each *life policy* it effects, in good time before that information has to be provided.
in good time before that information has to be provided.

[**Note:** article 36(1) of, and Annex III to, the *Consolidated Life Directive*]

Exceptions

13.1.3 R   FCA

A *firm* is not required to prepare:

(1)   a *document*, if another *firm* has agreed to prepare it; or

(2)   a *key features document* for:

     (a)   a *unit* in a *UCITS scheme* or a *simplified prospectus scheme*; or

     (b)   a *unit* in an *EEA UCITS scheme* which is a *recognised scheme*; or

     (c)   a *unit* in a *key features scheme*, if it prepares a *simplified prospectus*, or the information appears with due prominence in another *document*, instead; or

     (d)   a *stakeholder pension scheme*, or *personal pension scheme* that is not a *personal pension policy*, if the information appears with due prominence in another *document*; or

(3)   a *key features illustration*:

     (a)   for a *unit* in a *UCITS scheme* or a *simplified prospectus scheme*; or

     (b)   for a *unit* in an *EEA UCITS scheme* which is a *recognised scheme*; or

     (c)   if it includes the information from the *key features illustration* in a *key features document*; or

     (d)   for a *packaged product* which, at the end of its fixed term, provides for the return of the initial capital invested and a specified level of growth linked by a pre-set formula to the performance of a specified asset or index or a combination of assets or indices; or

(4)   the *Consolidated Life Directive information*, if the *policy* is a *reinsurance contract* or a *pure protection contract*.

13.1.4 R   FCA

A single *document* prepared for more than one *key features scheme* or *simplified prospectus scheme* may combine more than one *key features document*, *simplified prospectus* or *EEA simplified prospectus* or any combination of them, if the *schemes* are offered through a *platform service* and the *document* clearly describes the difference between the *schemes*.

13.2   PRODUCT INFORMATION: PRODUCTION STANDARDS, FORM AND CONTENTS

13.2.1 G   FCA

When a *firm* prepares *documents* or information in accordance with this chapter, the *firm* should consider the *rules* on providing product information (**COBS 14**). Those *rules* require a *firm* to provide the product information in a *durable medium* or via a website that meets the *website conditions* (if the website is not a *durable medium*).

[**Note:** article 29(4) of the *MiFID implementing Directive*]

13.2.1A G   FCA

When a *firm* prepares *documents* or information for a *life policy*, *personal pension* or *stakeholder pension* in accordance with this chapter, the *firm* should:

(1)   consider the *rules* on communicating with clients (**COBS 4**). Those *rules* require a *firm* to ensure that a communication is fair, clear and not misleading. In particular, a *firm* should:

     (a)   take into account its target market's understanding of financial services when preparing *documents* and information;

     (b)   present information in a logical order;

     (c)   use clear and descriptive headings, and where appropriate, cross references and sub-headings to aid navigation;

     (d)   where possible, use plain language and avoid the use of jargon, unfamiliar or technical language;

     (e)   if it is necessary to use jargon, unfamiliar or technical language, provide accompanying explanations in plain language;

     (f)   use short sentences;

     (g)   (if the *key features illustration* is separate from the *key features document*) clearly cross-reference between the two and avoid duplication where possible;

     (h)   concentrate on key product information, cross reference to background information, detailed explanations and information about how to apply for the product; and

     (i)   avoid duplication and unnecessary disclaimers;

(2)   taking into account the means of printing or display, consider whether the following can be used to improve the *client's* understanding of the product, in particular:

     (a)   design devices such as side annotations, shading, colour, bulleted lists, tables and graphics; and

     (b)   the type size, line width, line spacing, and use of white space.

13.2.2 R   FCA

A *key features document* and a *key features illustration* must also:

(1)   (if it is a *key features document*) be produced and presented to at least the same quality and standard as the sales or marketing material used to promote the relevant product;

(2)   (if it is a *key features document*) display the *firm's* brand at least as prominently as any other;

(3)   (if it is a *key features document* or a *key features illustration* which does not form an integral part of the *key features document*) include the 'keyfacts' logo in a prominent position at the top of the *document*; and

(4)   (if it is a *key features document* or a *key features illustration* which does not form an integral part of the *key features document*) include the following statement in a prominent position: "The Financial Conduct Authority is a financial services regulator. It requires us, [provider name], to give you this important information to help you to decide whether our [product name] is right for you. You should read this document carefully so that you understand what you are buying, and then keep it safe for future reference".

13.2.3 G   FCA

The *Consolidated Life Directive information* can be included in a *key features document*, a *key features illustration* or any other *document*.

13.2.4 R   FCA

The *documents* and information prepared in accordance with the *rules* in this chapter must not include anything that might reasonably cause a *retail client* to be mistaken about the identity of the *firm* that produced, or will produce, the product.

13.3   CONTENTS OF A KEY FEATURES DOCUMENT

General requirements

13.3.1 R   FCA

A *key features document* must:

(1)   include enough information about the nature and complexity of the product, how it works, any limitations or minimum standards that apply and the material benefits and risks of buying or investing for a *retail client* to be able to make an informed decision about whether to proceed; and

(2)   explain:

    (a)   the arrangements for handling complaints about the product;

    (b)   that compensation might be available from the *FSCS* if the *firm* cannot meet its liabilities in respect of the product (if applicable);

    (c)   that a right to cancel or withdraw exists, or does not exist, and, if it does exist, its duration and the conditions for exercising it, including information about the amount a *client* may have to pay if the right is exercised, the consequences of not exercising it and practical instructions for exercising it, indicating the address to which any notice must be sent;

    (d)   (for a *CTF*) that *stakeholder CTFs*, *cash-deposit CTFs* and *security-based CTFs* are available and which type the *firm* is offering; and

    (e)   (for a *personal pension scheme* that is not an *automatic enrolment scheme*) clearly and prominently, that *stakeholder pension schemes* are generally available and might meet the *client's* needs as well as the scheme on offer.

Additional requirements for packaged products

13.3.2 R   FCA

Table

A *key features document* for a *packaged product* must:	
(1) Include the title: 'key features of the [name of product]';	
(2) describe the product in the order of the following headings, and by giving the following information under those headings:	
Heading	Information to be given
'Its aims'	A brief description of the product's aims
'Your commitment' or 'Your investment'	What a *retail client* is committing to or investing in and any consequences of failing to maintain the commitment or investment
'Risks'	The material risks associated with the product, including a description of the factors that may have an adverse effect on performance or are material to the decision to invest
'Questions and Answers'	(in the form of questions and answers) the principle terms of the product, what it will do for a *retail client* and any other information necessary to enable a *retail client* to make an informed decision.

Money market funds

13.3.3 R   FCA

A *key features document* for a *short-term money market fund*, a *money market fund* or a *qualifying money market fund* must include a statement identifying it as such a fund and a statement that the *authorised fund's* investment objectives and policies will meet the conditions of the definition of *short-term money market fund*, *money market fund* or *qualifying money market fund*, as appropriate.

Feeder NURS

13.3.4 R   FCA

A *key features document* for a *feeder NURS* must include:
(1)   a statement identifying it as such a *scheme*;
(2)   information specific to the *feeder NURS* and its *qualifying master scheme* which enables investors to understand the *qualifying master scheme's* key particulars; and
(3)   a description and explanation of any material differences between the risk profile of the *feeder NURS* and that of the *qualifying master scheme*.

13.3.5 G   FCA

When producing the *key features document*, the *authorised fund manager* of the *feeder NURS* should have due regard to the provisions in **COLL 4.6.8 R** (Contents of the simplified prospectus) in terms of additional information appropriate to a *feeder NURS* and its *qualifying master scheme*. In particular, the *appropriate charges information* required by **COBS 13.4.1 R** and **COBS 13 ANNEX 3** (Charges) should represent the aggregate of the charges of the *feeder NURS* and its *qualifying master scheme* as disclosed in the *feeder NURS'* most up-to-date *prospectus*.

13.4   CONTENTS OF A KEY FEATURES ILLUSTRATION

13.4.1 R   FCA

A *key features illustration* must include *appropriate charges information*, information about any interest that will be paid to *clients* on money held within a *personal pension scheme* bank account and, if it is a *packaged product* which is not a *financial instrument*:
(1)   must include a *standardised deterministic projection*;
(2)   the projection and charges information must be consistent with each other so that:
      (a)   the same intermediate growth rate and assumptions about regular contributions are used;
      (b)   a *projection* in nominal terms is accompanied by an effect of charges table and reduction in yield information in nominal terms; and
      (c)   a *projection* in real terms is accompanied by an effect of charges table and reduction in yield information in real terms;
(3)   it may also include *stochastic projections* if there are reasonable grounds for believing that a *retail client* will be able to understand the *stochastic projection* except that the most prominent *projection* must be a *standardised deterministic projection*.

Exceptions

13.4.2 R   FCA

When the *rules* in this chapter require a *key features illustration* to be prepared, it must not take the form of a *generic key features illustration*:
(1)   unless there are reasonable grounds for believing that it will be sufficient to enable a *retail client* to make an informed decision about whether to invest; or
(2)   if it is part of a *direct offer financial promotion* which contains a *personal recommendation*; or
(3)   if a *personal pension scheme* or a *stakeholder pension scheme* is facilitating the payment of an *adviser charge*; or
(4)   if a *group personal pension scheme* or a *group stakeholder pension scheme* is facilitating the payment of a *consultancy charge* and the combined effect of the *consultancy charges* facilitated by the product and the product charges is not consistent for all investors in the relevant group or sub-group; or
(5)   unless it is prepared for groups or sub-groups of employees in a *group personal pension scheme* or a *group stakeholder pension scheme* and it contains:
      (a)   a *generic projection* which is prepared in accordance with **COBS 13 ANNEX 2** paragraph 1.3 and based on a default fund or other commonly selected fund;
      (b)   an effect of charges table calculated in accordance with **COBS 13 ANNEX 4 R** paragraph 2 and contains additional rows that show a range of typical periods to retirement age; and

(c)   reduction in yield information which is calculated in accordance with **COBS 13 ANNEX 4 R** paragraph 3.3(2) and combines the product charge and, if applicable, the *consultancy charge*.

13.4.3 G   FCA

A *generic key features illustration* is unlikely to be sufficient to enable a *retail client* to make an informed decision about whether to invest if the *premium* or investment returns on the product will be materially affected by the personal characteristics of the investor.

13.4.4 R   FCA

There is no requirement under **COBS 13.4.1 R** to include a *projection* in a *key features illustration*:

(1)   for a single *premium life policy* bought as a pure investment product, a product with benefits that do not depend on future investment returns or any other product if it is reasonable to believe that a *retail client* will not need one to be able to make an informed decision about whether to invest; or

(2)   if the product is a *life policy* that will be held in a *CTF* or sold with *basic advice* (unless the policy is a *stakeholder pension scheme*).

13.4.5 G   FCA

Although there may be no obligation to include a *projection* in a *key features illustration*, where a *firm* chooses to include one, the *projection* must follow the appropriate requirements, as outlined in this section, or for *financial instruments* under **COBS 4.6.7 R**.

13.5   PREPARING PRODUCT INFORMATION: OTHER PROJECTIONS

Projections for in-force products

13.5.1 R   FCA

A *firm* that communicates a *projection* for an in-force *packaged product* which is not a *financial instrument*:

(1)   must include a *standardised deterministic projection*;

(2)   may also include a *stochastic projection* except that the most prominent *projection* must be a *standardised deterministic projection*; and

must follow the *projection rules* in **COBS 13 ANNEX 2**.

Projections: other situations

13.5.2 R   FCA

A *firm* that communicates a *projection* for a *packaged product* which is not a *financial instrument*:

(1)   for which a *key features illustration* is not required to be provided; and

(2)   which is not an in-force *packaged product*;

must ensure that such a *projection* is either a *standardised deterministic projection* or a *stochastic projection* in accordance with **COBS 13 ANNEX 2**.

Exceptions to the projection rules: projections for more than one product

13.5.3 R   FCA

A *firm* that communicates a *projection* of benefits for a *packaged product* which is not a *financial instrument*, as part of a combined *projection* where other benefits being projected include those for a *financial instrument* or *structured deposit*, is not required to comply with the projection rules in **COBS 13.4**, **COBS 13.5**and **COBS 13 ANNEX 2** to the extent that it complies with the future performance *rule* (**COBS 4.6.7 R**).

13.5.4 G   FCA

The general requirement that communications be fair, clear and not misleading will nevertheless mean that a *firm* that elects to comply with the future performance rule in **COBS 4.6.7 R** will need to explain how the combined *projection* differs from other information that has been or could be provided to the client, including a *projection* provided under the *projection rules* in **COBS 13.4**, **COBS 13.5** and **COBS 13 ANNEX 2**, and in particular, the *firm* should identify where a *projection* in real terms is required under **COBS 13**.

13.6   PREPARING PRODUCT INFORMATION: CHANGES TO ADVISER AND CONSULTANCY CHARGES

13.6.1 R   FCA

A *firm* that agrees to start facilitating the payment of an *adviser charge* or *consultancy charge*, or an increase in such a charge, from an in-force *packaged product*, must prepare sufficient information for the *retail client* to be able to understand the likely effect of that facilitation, in good time before it takes effect.FCA

13 ANNEX 1   THE CONSOLIDATED LIFE DIRECTIVE INFORMATION

This annex belongs to **COBS 13.1.2 R** (The Consolidated Life Directive Information)

Information about the firm	
(1)	The *firm's* name and its legal form;
(2)	The name of the *EEA State* in which the head office and, where appropriate, agency or branch concluding the contract is situated; and
(3)	The address of the head office and, where appropriate, agency or branch concluding the contract.
Information about the commitment	
(4)	Definition of each benefit and each option;
(5)	Term of the contract;
(6)	Means of terminating the contract;
(7)	Means of payment of *premiums* and duration of payments;
(8)	Means of calculation and distribution of bonuses;
(9)	Indication of surrender and paid-up values and the extent to which they are guaranteed;
(10)	Information on the *premiums* for each benefit, both main benefits and supplementary benefits, where appropriate;
(11)	For unit-linked *policies*, definition of the units to which the benefits are linked;
(12)	Indication of the nature of the underlying assets for unit-linked *policies*;
(13)	Arrangements for application of the cooling-off period;
(14)	General information on the tax arrangements applicable to the type of *policy*;
(15)	The arrangements for handling complaints concerning contracts by *policyholders*, lives assured or beneficiaries under contracts including, were appropriate, the existence of a complaints body, without prejudice to the right to take legal proceedings; and
(16)	Law applicable to the contract where the parties do not have a free choice or, where the parties are free to choose the law applicable, the law the *insurer* proposes to choose.
[Note: article 36(1) of, and Annex III to, the *Consolidated Life Directive*]	

13 ANNEX 2   PROJECTIONS

This annex belongs to **COBS 13.4.1 R** *(Contents of a key features illustration),* **COBS 13.5.1 R** *(Projections for in-force products) and* **COBS 13.5.2 R** *(Projections: other situations).*

R Projections	
1	Calculating standardised deterministic projections
1.1	A *standardised deterministic projection* must:
(1)	include a *projection* of benefits at the lower, intermediate and *higher rates of return*;
(2)	be rounded down; and
(3)	show no more than three significant figures.

R **1.2**	Calculating projections: additional requirements for a *personal pension scheme* and *stakeholder pension scheme*
(1)	A *standardised deterministic projection* must be in real terms and be accompanied by information explaining why price inflation has been taken into account and that price inflation reduces the worth of all savings and investments.
(2)	A *standardised deterministic projection* in real terms must be calculated using:
(a)	the appropriate *lower, intermediate* and *higher rates of return*;
(b)	the intermediate rate of price inflation, in accordance with **COBS 13 ANNEX 2** 2.5R; and
(c)	an annuity calculated in accordance with **COBS 13 ANNEX 2** 3.1R.
(3)	The *standardised deterministic projection* must show only the numeric value of the three real rates of return after the appropriate price inflation assumption has been taken into account, that is, the real rate of projected growth which has been applied to the real value of the contributions.

G 1.2A	A *firm* is not prevented from providing a *retail client* with a *projection* of the fund or pension commencement lump sum in nominal terms for planning purposes (for example for a pension mortgage) if it is prepared in a way which is consistent with the *standardised deterministic projection*.

R 1.3	(1)	If a *generic projection* is prepared for a *stakeholder pension scheme* or *personal pension scheme* in circumstances where a *generic key features illustration* is permitted under **COBS 13.4.2 R**, sufficient separate *projections*, covering a range of different contractual periods and contributions, must be included for a *retail client* to be able to make an informed decision about whether to invest.
	(2)	A *projection* prepared on that basis may omit projections at the *lower* and *higher rates of return* and only show a range of benefits in real terms at the *intermediate rate of return*.

G 1.4	A *firm* will provide sufficient separate *projections* if it prepares a table that shows *projections* in real terms for a variety of periods to maturity and a variety of contribution levels, taking into account the *charges* and other material terms that apply to the *stakeholder pension scheme* or *personal pension scheme*. Such a table could be laid out like a specimen benefits table (see **COBS 13 ANNEX 2** 1.8).

R

Providing a stochastic projection

1.5	A *stochastic projection* may only be provided if:
(1)	[deleted]
(2)	[deleted]
(3)	[deleted]
(4)	it is based on a reasonable number of simulations and assumptions which are reasonable and supported by objective data;
(5)	it is accompanied by enough information for the *retail client* to be able to understand the difference between the *stochastic projection* and the *standardised deterministic projection* being provided; and
(6)	it is presented in real terms where the accompanying *standardised deterministic projection* is required to be in real terms.

1.6	[deleted]

R

Exceptions

1.7

A *projection* for an in-force product that will mature in six *months* or less may be prepared and presented on any reasonable basis.

R 1.8	In the case of a *stakeholder pension scheme* in circumstances where a *generic key features illustration* is permitted under **COBS 13.4.2 R**, the specimen benefits table, contained within the "Stakeholder pension decision tree" factsheet available on www.moneyadviceservice.org.uk and headed "Pension Table ... How much should I save towards a pension?" which sets out initial monthly pension amounts, may be used instead of a *standardised deterministic projection* but only if it is accompanied by an explanation of the caveats and assumptions behind the table.

R 1.9	The *rules* in this Annex do not apply to a *projection* for an in force product which is consistent with the *statutory money purchase illustration* requirements.

R 1.10	A *standardised deterministic projection* for an in force product may omit the *intermediate rate of return* except for *personal pension scheme* and *stakeholder pension scheme* contracts taken out after 5 April 2014.

R 2 Assumptions to follow when calculating projections.

Assumptions: projection date

2.1   A *standardised deterministic projection* must be calculated to the *projection date* described below:

	Product	Projection date
(1)	A contract which is a *whole life assurance* the *premiums* under which are regular *premiums*	The anniversary of the commencement date: (a) which first falls after the seventy-fifth birthday of the life assured; or (b) (if there is more than one life assured) the anniversary of the commencement date which falls after the seventy fifth birthday of: (i) (if benefits are payable on the first death) the oldest life assured; or (ii) (in all other cases) the youngest life assured; subject to a minimum *projection date* of ten years.
(2)	A contract that is not in (1): (a) where the relevant marketing refers to a surrender value or an option to take benefits before they would otherwise be paid; or (b) that is open-ended, or linked to one or more lives, which is not a *personal pension scheme* or *stakeholder pension scheme*	An appropriate date which highlights the features of the product
(3)	A contract that is not in (1) or (2) and has a specified maturity date	The maturity date specified in the contract
(4)	A contract that is not in (1) or (2) or (3)	The tenth anniversary of the commencement date

R
Assumptions: contributions

2.2   A *standardised deterministic projection* must:

    (1)   take account of all contributions due during the *projection period*;

    (2)   be calculated on the basis that contributions are accumulated, net of *charges*, at the appropriate rate of return compounded on an annual basis;

    (3)   (if it includes assumptions about contribution increases in line with an index) be based on an assumption that contribution increases are consistent with any assumptions regarding that index in this annex; and

    (4)   deduct from contributions any rider benefits or extra *premium* which may be charged for an increased underwriting risk.

R
Assumptions: rates of return

2.3   A *standardised deterministic projection* must be calculated using rates that accurately reflect the investment potential of the product and do not exceed the following maximum rates of return with the lower and higher rates each maintaining a differential of 3% relative to the intermediate rate:

Nominal rates	Lower rate	Inter-mediate rate	Higher rate
tax-exempt business held in a *wrapper* or by a *friendly society* *personal pension schemes*, *stakeholder pension schemes* and investment-linked annuities	2%	5%	8%
all other products	1½%	4½%	7½%

R
Exception

2.4   A *standardised deterministic projection*:

(1)   [deleted]

(2)   may be calculated using a lower rate of return if a *retail client* requests it.

R
Assumptions: inflation

2.5   If inflation is taken into account, the *standardised deterministic projection* must be calculated using the following rates:

	Lower rate	Inter-mediate rate	Higher rate
Price infla-tion	0.50%	2.50%	4.50%
Earn-ings infla-tion	$\geq 2\%$	$\geq 4\%$	$\geq 6\%$

R
Assumptions: charges

2.6   The *charges* allowed for in a *standardised deterministic projection*:

(1)   must properly reflect:

    (a)   all of the charges, expenses and deductions a *client* will, or may expect to be taken after investment into the product;

    (b)   the tax relief available to the *firm* in respect of so much of the *firm's* gross expenses as can properly be attributed to the contract; and

    (c)   the fact that certain *charges* will be fully or partially off-set, but only to the extent that the *firm* can show that the off-set funds will be available when the relevant *charges* arise; and

(2)   must not include the *firm's* dealing costs incurred on the underlying portfolio.

G
2.7

(1)   Development and capital costs should normally be written off in the year in which they are incurred. However, some costs (for example, exceptional new business expenses) may be amortised and previous years' costs may then be brought into account.

(2)   If it is reasonable to assume that higher expenses will be incurred in the future, appropriate allowances should be made, and any inflation assumptions should be consistent with those prescribed in these rules.

(3)   Expenses should be apportioned appropriately between products so that scales of expenses can be calculated and applied.

(4)   Where appropriate, mortality and morbidity should be allowed for on a best estimate basis. The basis for annuities should allow for future improvements in mortality.

(5)   A projection should not assume that *charges* will fall over time to a rate that is lower than the rate currently being charged on the relevant product (or, if there is no such charge, on a similar product).

(6)   A projection of surrender value, cash-in value or transfer value should take into account any specific current surrender value basis and penalties which may be applied.

(7)   If a *personal pension scheme* is invested in assets that are volatile or difficult to value, the *standardised deterministic projection* should be prepared using the best available reasonable assumptions.

R
Additional requirements: with-profits policies

2.8   (1)   A *standardised deterministic projection* for a *with-profits policy* must properly reflect the deductions from asset share which a *firm* expects to make in accordance with its *deductions plan*.

> (2) A *standardised deterministic projection* for a *with-profits policy* where bonus rates apply must assume that the bonus rates supported by the relevant premium and rate of return apply throughout the term of the contract.

R

Additional requirements: drawdown pensions

2.9 (1) A *standardised deterministic projection* for a *drawdown pension* must be based on the requirements contained in (2) to the extent that they impose additional or conflicting requirements to the balance of the *rules* in this section.

(2) A *standardised deterministic projection* for a *drawdown pension* must be based on an assumption that the current gilt-index yield will continue to apply throughout the relevant term and include:

(a) where relevant the maximum initial income specified in the tables published by the Government Actuaries Department for a *drawdown pension*;

(b) the assumed level of income;

(c) for a *short-term annuity*, where subsequent *short-term annuities* are assumed, a statement reflecting that fact;

(d) (under 'What the benefits might be' or similar heading), the amount of income and the projected value of the fund at five yearly intervals to age 99 for the *lower, intermediate* and *higher rate of return* for as long as the fund is projected to exist (at the *higher rate of return*);

(e) the projected open market values and the amounts of annuity that might be purchased after 10 years; and

(f) the amount of annuity that could be secured using an immediate annuity rate available in the market.

R

Drawdown Pension: Exception

2.10 A *standardised deterministic projection* for a *drawdown pension* can be prepared in nominal terms, rather than real terms.

R How to calculate a projection for a future annuity
3

3.1 A *projection* for a future annuity must:

(1) be calculated by rounding all factors to three decimal places before applying them to the relevant retirement fund;

(2) use a mortality rate based on the year of birth rate derived from each of the Institute and Faculty of Actuaries' Continuous Mortality Investigation tables PCMA00 and PCFA00 and including mortality improvements derived from each of the male and female annual mortality projection models, in equal parts;

(3) [deleted]

(4) (for an annuity where two lives are concerned):

(a) reflect the age difference between the two lives; or

(b) be based on the assumption that the male life is three years older than the female (if the genders differ) or the two lives have the same age (if the genders are the same);

(5) include an expenses allowance of 4%;

(6) be based on the following rates of return as appropriate:

R	Lower rate	Intermediate rate	Higher rate
Level or fixed rate of increase annuities	Y+1.5%	Y+3.5%	Y+5.5%
RPI or LPI linked annuities	Y-1%	Y	Y+1%

R

where:

'Y' is 0.5* (ILG0 + ILG5)-0.5 rounded to the nearest 0.2%, with an exact 0.1% rounded down; and

'ILG0' and 'ILG5' are the real yield on the FTSE Actuaries Government Securities Index-linked Real Yields over 5 years, assuming 0% and 5% inflation respectively, updated every 6 April to use the ILG0 and ILG5 which applied on or, if necessary, the *business day* immediately before, the preceding 15 February; and

    (7)   (in the case of a future annuity with less than one year to maturity) be calculated using annuity rates that are no more favourable than the *firm's* relevant current immediate annuity rate or (if there is no such rate) the relevant immediate annuity rate available in the market; and

    (8)   be assumed to be payable monthly in advance with a guaranteed period of 5 years, unless it is unreasonable to do so.

E
3.1A For any year commencing 6 April, the use of the male and female annual CMI Mortality Projections Models in the series CMI(20YY-1)_M_[1.25%] and CMI(20YY-1)_F_[1.25%], where YY-1 is the year of the Model used, will tend to show compliance with **COBS 13 ANNEX 2 3.1 R (2)**.

R
3.2 A *projection* for a future annuity:

    (1)   must be calculated using lower rates of return, if the rates described in this section overstate the investment potential of the product;

    (2)   may be calculated using a lower rate of return if a *retail client* requests it.

---

4   [deleted]

R
5   Projections: accompanying statements and presentation

5.1   A *standardised deterministic projection* must be accompanied by:

    (1)   appropriate risk warnings, including warnings about volatility and the impact of inflation and that the product may pay back less than paid in (if that could be the case), and the degree to which any figures can be relied upon; and

    (2)   a statement:

        (a)   [deleted]

        (b)   that *charges* may vary;

        (c)   of the contributions that have been assumed;

        (d)   that increases in contributions have been assumed (if that is the case), together with sufficient information for a *retail client* to be able to understand the nature and magnitude of the assumed increases;

        (e)   of the sum of any actual *premiums* charged for any rider benefits or increased underwriting risks (where these have been charged); and

        (f)   (for *personal pension schemes* and *stakeholder pension schemes*) of the assumptions used to calculate the regular income and that the *client* may choose when to take this income (if that is the case).

R
5.1A   When presenting a *standardised deterministic projection* a *firm* must:

    (1)   include a short introductory explanation of what the *projection* seeks to illustrate;

    (2)   use a descriptive heading such as 'What your regular income might be worth in future' or 'What might I get back from my plan?';

    (2)   use a descriptive heading such as 'What your regular income might be worth in future' or 'What might I get back from my plan?';

    (3)   place the *projection* and the associated explanation adjacent to each other on the same page; and

    (4)   explain that the *client* will be sent annual statements (if that is the case) which will allow them to keep track of their benefits.

R		
Additional requirements: pension schemes and products linked to other products		
5.2		A *standardised deterministic projection* for a product where the benefits illustrated depend on a link to a separate product must include an appropriate description of the material factors that might influence the returns available overall and any restrictions assumed in providing an illustration of benefits in relation to that separate product.

13 ANNEX 3   CHARGES INFORMATION FOR A PACKAGED PRODUCT

(except for a personal pension scheme and a stakeholder pension scheme where adviser charges or consultancy charges are to be facilitated by the product)
This annex belongs to **COBS 13.4.1 R** *(Contents of a key features illustration)*

R			
Charges			
1	Appropriate charges information		
1.1	*Appropriate charges information* comprises:		
	(1)	(a)	a description of the nature and amount of the *charges* a *client* will or may be expected to bear in relation to the product and, if applicable, any investments within the product;
		(b)	if applicable, a description of the nature and amount of the *adviser charges* a *retail client* has agreed may be taken, including whether it is taken before or after investment into the product;
	(2)		an 'effect of charges' table;
	(3)		'reduction in yield' information; and
	(4)		in relation to a *personal pension scheme*, the amounts (or if the amounts cannot be given, the formula by which the amounts can be calculated), if any, which a *personal pension scheme operator* or *pension scheme* trustee will receive as retained interest in relation to money held within the *personal pension scheme*.
1.2	Where a *firm* does not include a *projection* within its *key features illustration* the charges information can be on a generic basis.		
1.2A	The information described in 1.1(4) must be disclosed alongside information about any other *charges* the *client* will be expected to bear, and information about any interest that will be paid to *clients* on money held within a *personal pension scheme* bank account.		
Exceptions			
1.3	An effect of charges table and reduction in yield information are not required for:		
	(1)		a *life policy* without a *surrender value*, but an appropriate warning must be included to make it clear that the *policy* has no cash-in value at any time;
	(2)		[deleted];
	(3)		[deleted]
	(4)		a *stakeholder product* or a product that will be held in a *CTF* where the relevant product and the *CTF* levy their *charges* annually, if the following is included instead: "There is an annual charge of y% of the value of the funds you accumulate. If your fund is valued at £250 throughout the year, this means we charge [£250 x y/100] that year. If your fund is valued at £500 throughout the year, this means we charge [£500 x y/100] that year. [After ten years these deductions reduce to [£250 x r/100] and [£500 x r/100] respectively.]" where 'y' is the annual charge and 'r' is the reduced annual charge (if any).
1.4	Reduction in yield information is not required for a without profits *life policy* with guaranteed benefits (except on surrender or variation), a *life policy* with a term not exceeding five years or a *life policy* that will be held in a *CTF*.		

R 2	Effect of charges table	
2.1	Each 'effect of charges' table must be accompanied by, or refer to:	
	(1)	a statement that all relevant guarantees have been taken into account (if there are any);
	(2)	[deleted]

> (3)   the rate of return (for *personal pension schemes* and *stakeholder pension schemes*, this must be net of price inflation, where appropriate) used to calculate the figures in the table; and
>
> (4)   an explanation of the purpose of the table and what the table shows.

2.2 The effect of charges table:

(1) for a *life policy* must be in the following form unless the firm chooses to adopt the form of the effect of charges table in **COBS 13 ANNEX 4**:

R Note 1A	Note 2	Note 3	Note 4	Note 5	Note 6
At end of year	Total paid in to date	Withdrawals	Total actual deductions to date	Effect of deductions to date	What you might get back
	£	£	£	£	£
1					
...					
5					
10					
...					

(2) for any other *packaged product* must be in the following form:

R Note 1B	Note 2	Note 3	Note 5	Note 6
At end of year	Investment to date	Income	Effect of deductions to date	What you might get back
	£	£	£	£
1				
5				
10				
...				

(3) must be completed in accordance with the following notes:

R Note 1A	(a)	This column must include the first five years, every subsequent fifth year and the final year of the *projection period*.
	(b)	Figures may be shown for every subsequent tenth year rather than subsequent fifth year where the *projection period* exceeds 25 years, or for whole of life policies.
	(c)	For whole of life policies, should the projected fund reach zero before the end of the *projection period* this must be highlighted.
	(d)	[deleted]
	(e)	If there is discontinuity in the trend of *surrender values*, the appropriate intervening years must also be included.
	(f)	Figures for a longer term may be shown.
Note 1B	(a)	This column must include the first year, the fifth year and every subsequent fifth year of the *projection period*.
	(b)	[deleted]
	(c)	Figures for a longer term may be shown.
Note 2		This column must show the cumulative contributions paid to the end of each relevant year.
Note 3		This column must show the cumulative withdrawals taken or income paid to the end of each relevant year (if any). The column may be omitted if withdrawals or income are not anticipated or allowed.
Note 4		This column is optional. If it is retained, it must show the total actual deductions to the end of each relevant year calculated using the following method:
	(a)	apply the *intermediate rate of return* for the relevant product to the figure in the 'effect of deductions to date' column for the previous year;
	(b)	subtract this figure from the figure in the 'effect of deductions to date' column for the year being shown; and

(c)   add the resulting figure to the figure in the 'total actual deductions to date' column for the previous year (if any).

Note 5   This column may be deleted if the product is a without profits *life policy* with benefits that are guaranteed except on surrender or variation, a *life policy* with a term not exceeding five years, or a *life policy* that will be held in a *CTF*.

If this column is not deleted, the 'effect of deductions to date' figure must be calculated by taking the accumulated value of the fund without reference to *charges* and then subtracting from this figure the figure in the 'what you might get back column' for the same year.

Note 6   This column must show the *standardised deterministic projection* of the surrender value, cash-in value or transfer value, calculated in accordance with the *rules* in **COBS 13 ANNEX 2** (Projections) at the appropriate *intermediate rate of return* to the end of each relevant year.

R
Exception

2.3   An effect of charges table and its title can be amended to the extent that it is necessary:

     (1)   to properly reflect the nature and effect of, for example, the *adviser charges*, *consultancy charges* or the charges inherent in a particular product; or

     (2)   to ensure that the column labels and any explanatory text reflect the product and whether inflation has been taken into account; or

     (3)   to ensure consistency with the terminology used in relation to a particular product.

2.4   [deleted]

R
3   Reduction in yield

3.1   Reduction in yield ('A') is 'B' less 'C' where:

     (1)   'B' is the *intermediate rate of return* (for *personal pension schemes* and *stakeholder pension schemes*, net of price inflation, where appropriate) for the relevant product; and

     (2)   'C' is determined by:

         (a)   carrying out a *standardised deterministic projection* to the *projection date*, using 'B'; and then

         (b)   calculating the annual rate of return ('C') (rounded to the nearest tenth of 1 %) required to achieve the same projection value if *charges* are left out of account.

3.2   A *firm* must present reduction in yield as 'A%', as part of statements which explain that:

     (1)   charges have the effect of reducing investment growth (after price inflation for personal pension schemes and stakeholder pension schemes) from 'B%' to 'C%', or in some other appropriate way; and

     (2)   the information about the reduction in investment growth can be used to compare the effect of charges with similar products.

3.3   If contributions will be invested in more than one fund in a single designated investment or made by an initial lump sum payment that is followed by regular contributions, the reduction in yield must be:

     (1)   calculated separately for each fund or for the single contribution and the regular contributions (as the case may be); and

     (2)   presented:

         (a)   on a fund by fund, or single contribution and regular contribution, basis, together with a statement which explains the nature and effect of a reduction in yield, the reason for the inclusion of more than one reduction in yield figure and the reason for the differences between them; or

(b)   (if the reduction in yield results are so similar that one figure could reasonably be regarded as representative of the others), as a single figure together with a statement which explains the nature and effect of a reduction in yield, and that the reduction in yield figure given is representative of the reduction in yield figures for each of the funds or for the single and regular contributions (as the case may be); or

(c)   through a single figure combining the separate figures for each fund or contribution in a proportionate manner, with an appropriate description.

3.4   Where a *firm* is calculating reduction in yield information, it must:

(1)   disregard charges related to mortality and morbidity risks; or

(2)   (where the requirement in (1) produces figures that are misleading) include a statement with the reduction in yield information that it has been calculated taking into account charges related to mortality and morbidity risk.

13 ANNEX 4   CHARGES INFORMATION FOR A PERSONAL PENSION SCHEME AND A STAKEHOLDER PENSION SCHEME

(where adviser charges or consultancy charges are facilitated by the product)
This annex belongs to **COBS 13.4.1 R** *(Contents of a key features illustration)*

R
Charges

1   Appropriate charges information

1.1   *Appropriate charges information* comprises:

(1)   (a)   a description of the nature and amount of the *charges* a *client* will or may be expected to bear in relation to the product and, if applicable, any investments within the product;

(b)   if applicable, a description of the nature and amount of the *adviser charges* and *consultancy charges* a *retail client* or employer has agreed may be taken before investment into the product;

(c)   if applicable, a description of the nature and amount of the *adviser charges* and *consultancy charges* a *retail client* or employer has agreed may be taken after investment into the product;

(2)   an 'effect of charges' table;

(3)   'reduction in yield' information; and

(4)   in relation to a *personal pension scheme*, the amounts (or if the amounts cannot be given, the formula by which the amounts can be calculated), if any, which a *personal pension scheme operator* or *pension scheme* trustee will receive as retained interest in relation to money held within the *personal pension scheme*.

Exception

1.2   An effect of charges table and reduction in yield information are not required for a *stakeholder pension scheme*, where *adviser charges* or *consultancy charges* are not being facilitated by the scheme, if the following is included instead:
"There is an annual charge of y% of the value of the funds you accumulate. If your fund is valued at £500 throughout the year, this means we charge [£500 x y/100] that year. If your fund is valued at £7500 throughout the year, we will charge [£7500 x y/100] that year."

1.2A   The information described in 1.1(4) must be disclosed alongside information about any other *charges* the *client* will be expected to bear, and information about any interest that will be paid to *clients* on money held within a *personal pension scheme* bank account.

R
2   Effect of charges table

2.1   Each effect of charges table must be accompanied by:

(1)   an explanation of what the table shows;

(2)   a statement that all relevant guarantees have been taken into account (if there are any); and

(3)   [deleted]

(4)   the rate of return (after price inflation, where appropriate) used to calculate the figures in the table.

2.2   An effect of charges table must be in the following form:

Note 1	Note 2	Note 3	Note 4	Note 5	Note 6
At end of year	The payments into your plan	Withdrawals	Before charges are taken	If only plan and invest-ment charges are taken	After all charges are taken from this plan
	£	£	£	£	£
1					
...					
5					
At age [xx]					

Note 1	This column must include at least the first, third and fifth year and the intended date of retirement.
	For a *drawdown pension*, figures must be included for each of the first ten years, or less if the value of the fund is projected at the higher rate of return to reach zero before then.
Note 2	This column must show the cumulative contributions paid to the end of each relevant year.
Note 3	This column must show the cumulative withdrawals intended to be taken to the end of each relevant year. The column may be omitted if withdrawals are not anticipated or allowed.
Note 4	This column must show a *standardised deterministic projection* of the benefits, calculated in accordance with the *rules* in **COBS 13 ANNEX 2** (Projections) at the appropriate *intermediate rate of return*, to the end of each relevant year, but without taking any *charges* into account.
Note 5	This column must show a *standardised deterministic projection* of the benefits, calculated in accordance with the *rules* in **COBS 13 ANNEX 2** (Projections) at the appropriate *intermediate rate of return* to the end of each relevant year, but taking into account only the *charges* described in **COBS 13 ANNEX 4 R** paragraph 1.1(1)(a).
Note 6	This column must show a *standardised deterministic projection* of the benefits, calculated in accordance with the *rules* in **COBS 13 ANNEX 2** (Projections) at the appropriate *intermediate rate of return* to the end of each relevant year taking into account all charges described in **COBS 13 ANNEX 4 R** paragraph 1.1(1)(a) and (c).
	Where both *adviser charges* and *consultancy charges* are being facilitated from a product this column should show the combined effect of those charges.
	This column may be omitted if there are no *adviser charges* or *consultancy charges*.

R

Exception

2.3   An effect of charges table and its title can be amended, to the extent that it is necessary:

      (1)   to properly reflect the nature and effect of, for example, the adviser charges, consultancy charges or the charges inherent in a particular product; or

      (2)   to ensure that the column labels and any explanatory text reflect the nature of the product and to make it clear whether price inflation has been taken into account; or

      (3)   to ensure consistency with the terminology used in relation to a particular product.

G

2.4   [deleted]

2.5   An effect of charges table must be appropriately titled, for example, 'How the charges reduce the value of your pension fund'.

R

3   Reduction in yield

3.1   Product reduction in yield ('A') is 'B' less 'C' where:

(1)   'B' is the *intermediate rate of return* (net of price inflation, where appropriate) for the relevant product; and

(2)   'C' is determined by:

    (a)   carrying out a *standardised deterministic projection* to the *projection date*, but without taking any *adviser charges* or *consultancy charges* into account, using 'B'; and then

    (b)   calculating the annual rate of return ('C') (rounded to the nearest tenth of 1 %) required to achieve the same projection value if *charges* are excluded.

3.2   Total reduction in yield ('D') is 'B' less 'E' where:

(1)   'B' is the *intermediate rate of return* (net of price inflation, where appropriate) for the relevant product; and

(2)   'E' is determined by:

    (a)   carrying out a *standardised deterministic projection* to the *projection date* taking all *charges* into account, using 'B'; and then

    (b)   calculating the annual rate of return ('E') (rounded to the nearest tenth of 1 %) required to achieve the same projection value if *charges* are excluded.

3.3   (1)   A *firm* must present the product reduction in yield as 'A%', as part of statements which explain that:

    (a)   'product charges reduce investment growth after price inflation from 'B%' to 'C%'', or in some other appropriate way; and

    (b)   the information about the reduction in investment growth can be used to compare the effect of charges with similar products.

    (2)   If *adviser charges* or *consultancy charges*, or both *adviser charges* and *consultancy charges* are to be facilitated by the product, a *firm* must also present the reduction in yield as 'D%', as part of a statement which explains that 'all charges reduce the investment growth (after price inflation, where appropriate) from 'B%' to 'E'%'', or in some other appropriate way and explain the difference between the two reduction in yield figures.

3.4   If contributions will be invested in more than one fund in a single designated investment or made by an initial lump sum payment that is followed by regular contributions, the reduction in yield must be:

(1)   calculated separately for each fund or for the single contribution and the regular contributions, as applicable; and

(2)   presented:

    (a)   on a fund-by-fund, or single contribution and regular contribution, basis, together with a statement which explains the nature and effect of a reduction in yield, the reason for the inclusion of more than one reduction in yield figure and the reason for the differences between them; or

    (b)   (if the reduction in yield results are so similar that one figure could reasonably be regarded as representative of the others) as a single figure together with a statement which explains the nature and effect of a reduction in yield, and that the reduction in yield figure given is representative of the reduction in yield figures for each of the funds or for the single and regular contributions, as applicable; or

    (c)   through a single figure combining the separate figures for each fund or contribution in a proportionate manner, with an appropriate description.

CHAPTER 14
PROVIDING PRODUCT INFORMATION TO CLIENTS

14.1   INTERPRETATION

[3.62]
14.1.1 R   FCA

In this chapter:

(1)   'retail client' includes the trustee or *operator* of a *stakeholder pension scheme* or *personal pension scheme* and the trustee of a *money-purchase occupational pension scheme*; and

(2)   'sell' includes 'sell, *personally recommend* or *arrange* the sale of' in relation to a *designated investment* and equivalent activities in relation to a *cash-deposit ISA* and *cash-deposit CTF*.

14.2   PROVIDING PRODUCT INFORMATION TO CLIENTS

The provision rules

14.2.1 R   FCA

A *firm* that sells:

(1)　a *packaged product* to a *retail client*, must provide a *key features document* and a *key features illustration* to that *client* (unless the *packaged product* is a *unit* in a *UCITS scheme, simplified prospectus scheme* or an *EEA UCITS scheme* which is a *recognised scheme*);

(2)　a *life policy* that is not a *reinsurance contract* to a *client*, must provide the *Consolidated Life Directive information* to that *client*;

(3)　the variation of a *life policy* or *personal pension scheme* to a *retail client*, must provide that *client* with sufficient information about the variation for the *client* to be able to understand the consequences of the variation;

(4)　[deleted]

(5)　the variation of a *personal pension scheme* to a *retail client*, which involves an election by the *client* to make *income withdrawals* or a purchase of a *short-term annuity*, must provide that *client* with such information as is necessary for the *client* to understand the consequences of the variation, including where relevant, the information required by **COBS 13 AN-NEX 2.2.9 R** (Additional requirements: drawdown pensions);

(6)　a *cash-deposit ISA* or *cash-deposit CTF* to a *retail client*, must provide a *key features document* to that *client*;

(7)　a *unit* in a *simplified prospectus scheme* to a *client*, must offer the *scheme's* current *simplified prospectus* to that *client*. In addition, if the *client* is a *retail client* present in the *EEA*, the *firm* must provide the *simplified prospectus* to the *client* together with:

　　(a)　enough information for the *client* to be able to make an informed decision about whether to hold the *units* in a *wrapper* (if the *units* will, or may, be held in that way); and

　　(b)　information about the three types of *CTF* that are generally available (*stakeholder CTFs, cash-deposit CTFs* and *security-based CTFs*), and the type of *CTF* the *firm* is offering (if the *units* will, or may, be held in a *CTF*);

(8)　[deleted]

(9)　a *unit* in a *UCITS scheme,* or in an *EEA UCITS scheme* which is a *recognised scheme,* to a *client,* must:

　　(a)　provide a copy of the *scheme's key investor information document* or, as the case may be, *EEA key investor information document* to that *client*; and

　　(b)　where the *client* is a *retail client*, provide separately (unless already provided) the information required by **COBS 13.3.1 R (2)** (General requirements) and, if that *client* is present in the *EEA*, the information required by (5)(a) and (b);

(10)　where the *operator* of a *non-UCITS retail scheme* has a dispensation from the *FCA* in the form of a general *waiver* by consent under which it may market *units* of the *scheme* on the basis of a *key investor information document* (as modified by the general waiver direction, a "NURS KII document"), rather than on the basis of a *key features document* or *simplified prospectus*, a *firm* that sells *units* in the *scheme* must comply with its obligations under this *rule* by:

　　(a)　providing the *retail client* with the relevant NURS KII document; and

　　(b)　offering any *client* that is not a *retail client* the relevant NURS KII document;

on condition that it complies with each of the other *rules* in this section in relation to the provision of the document, as if references in those *rules* to a "key features document" or "simplified prospectus" were a reference to the "NURS KII document".

[**Note**: in respect of (2) article 36(1) of, and Annex III to, the *Consolidated Life Directive*]

[**Note**: in respect of (7), articles 1 and 80 of the *UCITS Directive*]

Provision of key investor information document

14.2.1A R   FCA

(1)　This *rule* applies to an *authorised fund manager* of a *UCITS scheme* that is either an *authorised unit trust, authorised contractual scheme* or an *ICVC*, and an *ICVC* that is a *UCITS scheme*.

(2)　An *authorised fund manager* and an *ICVC* in (1) that sells *units* in a *UCITS scheme* directly, or through another natural or legal *person* who acts on its behalf and under its full and unconditional responsibility, must ensure that investors are provided with the *key investor information document* for the *scheme.*

(3)　An *authorised fund manager* and an *ICVC* in (1) that does not sell *units* in a *UCITS scheme* directly, or through another natural or legal *person* who acts on its behalf and under its full and unconditional responsibility, must ensure that the *key investor information document* for the *scheme* is provided on request to product manufacturers and intermediaries selling, or advising investors on, potential *investments* in those *UCITS schemes* or in products offering exposure to them.

(4)   The *key investor information document* must be provided to investors free of charge.

(5)   An *authorised fund manager* and an *ICVC* in (1) may, instead of providing the *key investor information document* to investors in paper copy in accordance with (2), provide it in a *durable medium* other than paper or by means of a website that meets the *website conditions*, in which case the *authorised fund manager* and *ICVC* must:

(a)   deliver a paper copy of the *key investor information document* to the investor on request and free of charge; and

(b)   make available an up-to-date version of the *key investor information document* to investors on the website of the *ICVC* or *authorised fund manager*.

[**Note:** articles 80 and 81 of the *UCITS Directive*]

14.2.1B R   FCA

When the *rules* in this chapter require the offer or provision of a *key features illustration*, a *firm* may provide a *generic key features illustration* if that *generic key features illustration* has been prepared in accordance with **COBS 13.4.2 R**.

14.2.1C R   FCA

A *firm* that arranges to start the facilitation of, or an increase in, an *adviser charge* or *consultancy charge* from an in-force *packaged product*, must provide to the *retail client* sufficient information for the *retail client* to be able to understand the likely effect of that facilitation.

14.2.2 R   FCA

The *documents* or information required to be provided or offered by **COBS 14.2.1 R** and **COBS 14.2.1C R** must be in a *durable medium* or made available on a website (where that does not constitute a *durable medium*) that meets the *website conditions*.

14.2.3 R   FCA

(1)   A *firm* that *personally recommends* that a *retail client* holds a particular asset in a *SIPP* must provide that *client* with sufficient information for the *client* to be able to make an informed decision about whether to buy or invest.

(2)   This *rule* does not apply if the asset is described in **COBS 14.2.1 R**.

Firm not to cause confusion about the identity of the producer of a product

14.2.4 R   FCA

When a *firm* provides a *document* or information in accordance with the *rules* in this section, it must not do anything that might reasonably cause a *retail client* to be mistaken about the identity of the *firm* that has produced, or will produce, the product.

Exception to the provision rules: key features documents, simplified prospectuses and key investor information documents

14.2.5 R   FCA

A *firm* is not required to provide:

(1)   a *document*, if the *firm* produces the product and the *rules* in this section require another *firm* to provide the document;

(2)   a *key features document* or *key features illustration*, if another *person* is required to provide the *distance marketing information* by the *rules* of another *EEA State*;

(3)   the *Consolidated Life Directive information*, if another *person* is required to provide that information by the *rules* of another *EEA State*;

(4)   a *simplified prospectus* if:

(a)   [deleted]

(b)

(i)   the *client* is buying or investing in response to a *direct offer financial promotion* without receiving a *personal recommendation* to buy or invest; and

(ii)   the *firm* offers an up-to-date copy of the *simplified prospectus* to the *client* and provides materially the same information to the *client* in some other way.

[**Note:** in respect of (3), article 36(4) of, and Annex III to, the *Consolidated Life Directive*]

Exception: key features illustrations

14.2.6 R   FCA

A *firm* is not required to provide a *key features illustration* for a product if the information that would have been included in that illustration is included in the *key features document* provided to the *client*.

Exception to the provision rules: key features documents and key features illustrations

14.2.7 R   FCA

A *firm* is not required to provide a *key features document* or a *key features illustration* for:

(1)   a *key features scheme* if it provides a *simplified prospectus* instead;
(2)   a *life policy* that is not a *reinsurance contract* if:
         (a)   the *firm* is operating from an establishment in another *EEA State* and the sale is by *distance contract*; or
         (b)   the *client* is habitually resident outside the *United Kingdom* and the sale is not by *distance contract*.
(3)   a *traded life policy*.

[**Note**: in respect of (2), articles 4(1) and 16 of the *Distance Marketing Directive* and article 36 of the *Consolidated Life Directive*]

Exception to the provision rules: key features documents and key features illustrations

14.2.8 R   FCA

A *firm* is not required to provide a *key features document* or a *key features illustration*, if:
(1)   the *client* is buying or investing in response to a *direct offer financial promotion* without receiving a *personal recommendation* to buy or invest; and
(2)   the *firm* provides materially the same information in some other way.

Exception to the provision rules: key features documents, key features illustrations, simplified prospectuses and key investor information documents

14.2.9 R   FCA

A *firm* is not required to provide a *key features document*, a *key features illustration* or a *simplified prospectus* for a *key features scheme* or *simplified prospectus scheme* if:
(1)   the *client* is habitually resident outside the *EEA* and not present in the *EEA* when the relevant application is signed; or
(2)   the purchase is by a *discretionary investment manager* on behalf of a *retail client*; or
(3)   the sale is *arranged* or *personally recommended* by an *investment manager* and the *client* has agreed that a *key features document* or *simplified prospectus* is not required; or
(4)   a *retail client* is purchasing a holding in a *scheme* in which the *client* already has a holding, or the *client* is switching from one class of *shares* or *units* to another in the same *scheme*, and the relevant *document* has already been provided to that *client*.

14.2.9A R   FCA

For the purposes of the provision rules in relation to a *key investor information document*, a *firm*:
(1)   may satisfy the requirement to provide the document to the investor by providing it to a *person* who has written authority to make investment decisions on that investor's behalf; and
(2)   is not required to consider as a new transaction:
         (a)   a subscription to *units* in a *UCITS scheme* or an *EEA UCITS scheme* in which the *client* already holds *units*; or
         (b)   a series of connected transactions undertaken as the consequence of a single investment decision; or
         (c)   a decision by the *client* to switch from one class of *units* to another in the same *scheme*;
                  if an up-to-date version of the *key investor information document* for the *scheme* or the relevant class of *units* has already been provided to that *client*.

[**Note**: article 80 of the *UCITS Directive*]

14.2.10 G   FCA
(1)   Although a *firm* is not always required to provide a *simplified prospectus* to a *client* (**COBS 14.2.9 R**), the obligation to offer the prospectus to the *client* (**COBS 14.2.1 R (5)**) remains.
(2)   The *FCA* would regard a decision to subscribe to a regular monthly savings plan as a single investment decision for the purpose of **COBS 14.2.9AR (2)(A)**. However, a subsequent decision by the *client* to increase the amount of the regular contributions to be invested in *units* of a particular *scheme* or to direct the contributions to a different *scheme*, would in each case constitute a new transaction.

Exception to the provision rules: aggregated scheme documents

14.2.11 R   FCA

A *firm* may provide a single *document*, which describes more than one *key features scheme* or *simplified prospectus scheme*, or any combination of those *schemes*, if:
(1)   the *schemes* are offered through a *platform service*;
(2)   the *document* clearly describes the difference between the relevant *schemes*; and
(3)   (in the case of a *simplified prospectus scheme*) the *firm* also offers a copy of the relevant *prospectus* to the *client*.

Exception: successive operations

14.2.12 R   FCA

In the case of a *distance contract* comprising an initial service agreement, followed by successive operations or a series of separate operations of the same nature performed over time, the *rules* in this section only apply to the initial agreement.

14.2.13 R   FCA

If there is no initial service agreement but the successive operations or separate operations of the same nature performed over time are performed between the same contractual parties, the *rules* in this section only apply:

(1)   when the first operation is performed; and

(2)   if no operation of the same nature is performed for more than a year, when the next operation is performed (the next operation being deemed to be the first in a new series of operations).

The timing rules

14.2.14 R   FCA

When the *rules* in this section require a *firm* to:

(1)   offer a *simplified prospectus* to a *client*, that prospectus must be offered free of charge before the conclusion of the contract; or

(2)   provide a *key features document*, a *simplified prospectus*, or any other *document* or information to a *client*, the *document* or information must be provided free of charge and in good time before the *firm* carries on the relevant business; or

(3)   provide a *key investor information document* or *EEA key investor information document* to a *client*, it must be provided in good time before the *client's* proposed subscription for *units* in the *scheme*.

[**Note**: article 80 of the *UCITS Directive*]

Exception to the timing rules: child trust funds

14.2.15 R   FCA

A *key features document* for an *HMRC allocated CTF* must be provided as soon as reasonably possible after the *CTF* has been opened.

Exception to the timing rules: distance contracts and voice telephony communications

14.2.16 R   FCA

(1)   A *firm* may provide a *document*, or the information required to be provided by the *rules* in this section, in a *durable medium* immediately after the conclusion of a *distance contract*, if the contract has been concluded at a *client's* request using a means of distance communication that does not enable the *document* or information to be provided in that form in good time before the *client* is bound by the contract.

(2)   The exception in (1) does not apply in relation to the provision of an *EEA key investor information document* or a *key investor information document* required to be provided under **COBS 14.2.1 R** and **COBS 14.2.1A R**.

14.2.17 R   FCA

(1)   Where the *rules* in this section require a *document* or information to be provided, in the case of a voice telephony communication, a *firm* must:

(a)   if the *client* gives explicit consent to receiving only limited information, provide the abbreviated distance marketing disclosure information () orally to the *client*;

(b)   if the *client* does not give explicit consent to only receiving limited information, and the parties wish to proceed by voice telephony communication, provide the distance marketing information () orally to the *client*;

(c)   in the case of (a) or (b), send the *documents* or information to the *client* in a *durable medium* immediately after the contract is concluded.

(2)   The exception in (1) does not apply in relation to the provision of an *EEA key investor information document* or a *key investor information document* required to be provided under **COBS 14.2.1 R** and **COBS 14.2.1A R**.

14.3   INFORMATION ABOUT DESIGNATED INVESTMENTS

Application

14.3.1 R   FCA

This section applies to a *firm* in relation to:

(1)   *MiFID or equivalent third country business*; and

(2)   the following *regulated activities* when carried on for a *retail client*:

(a)   making a *personal recommendation* about a *designated investment* (other than a *P2P agreement*); or

(b)   *managing investments* that are *designated investments* (other than a *P2P agreements*); or

(c)   *arranging, (bringing about) or executing* a *deal* in a *warrant, non-readily realisable security* or *derivative*; or

(d)   engaging in *stock lending activity*; or

(e)   *operating an electronic system in relation to lending*, but only in relation to facilitating a person becoming a lender under a *P2P agreement*.

Providing a description of the nature and risks of designated investments

14.3.2 R   FCA

A *firm* must provide a *client* with a general description of the nature and risks of *designated investments*, taking into account, in particular, the *client's* categorisation as a *retail client* or a *professional client*. That description must:

(1)   explain the nature of the specific type of *designated investment* concerned, as well as the risks particular to that specific type of *designated investment*, in sufficient detail to enable the *client* to take investment decisions on an informed basis; and

(2)   include, where relevant to the specific type of *designated investment* concerned and the status and level of knowledge of the *client*, the following elements:

     (a)   the risks associated with that type of *designated investment* including an explanation of leverage and its effects and the risk of losing the entire investment;

     (b)   the volatility of the price of *designated investments* and any limitations on the available market for such investments;

     (c)   the fact that an investor might assume, as a result of transactions in such *designated investments*, financial commitments and other additional obligations, including contingent liabilities, additional to the cost of acquiring the *designated investments*; and

     (d)   any margin requirements or similar obligations, applicable to *designated investments* of that type.

[**Note:** article 31(1) and (2) of the *MiFID implementing Directive*]

14.3.3 R   FCA

If a *firm* provides a *retail client* with information about a *designated investment* that is the subject of a current offer to the public and a prospectus has been published in connection with that offer in accordance with the *Prospectus Directive*, that *firm* must inform the *retail client* where that prospectus is made available to the public.

[**Note:** article 31(3) of the *MiFID implementing Directive*]

14.3.4 R   FCA

Where the risks associated with a *designated investment* composed of two or more different *designated investments* or services are likely to be greater than the risks associated with any of the components, a *firm* must provide an adequate description of the components of that *designated investment* and the way in which its interaction increases the risks.

[**Note:** article 31(4) of the *MiFID implementing Directive*]

14.3.5 R   FCA

In the case of a *designated investment* that incorporates a guarantee by a third party, the information about the guarantee must include sufficient detail about the guarantor and the guarantee to enable the *retail client* to make a fair assessment of the guarantee.

[**Note:** article 31(5) of the *MiFID implementing Directive*]

Satisfying the provision rules

14.3.6 G   FCA

(1)   A *firm* need not treat each of several transactions in respect of the same type of *financial instrument* as a new or different service and so does not need to comply with the provision rules (**COBS 14.3.2 R** to **COBS 14.3.5 R**) in relation to each transaction.

(2)   But a *firm* should ensure that the *client* has received all relevant information in relation to a transaction, such as details of product charges that differ from those already disclosed.

[**Note:** in respect of (1), recital 50 to the *MiFID implementing Directive*]

14.3.7 G   FCA

Providing a *key features document, key investor information document, EEA key investor information document* or *simplified prospectus* may satisfy the requirements of the *rules* in this section.

P2P agreements

14.3.7A G   FCA

Examples of information a *firm* should provide to explain the specific nature and risks of a *P2P agreement* include:

Part 3   FCA Handbook Materials

(1)   expected and actual default rates in line with the requirements in **COBS 4.6** on past and future performance;

(2)   a summary of the assumptions used in determining expected future default rates;

(3)   a description of how loan risk is assessed, including a description of the criteria that must be met by the borrower before the *firm* considers the borrower eligible for a *P2P agreement*;

(4)   where lenders have the choice to invest in specific *P2P agreements*, details of the creditworthiness assessment of the borrower carried out;

(5)   whether the *P2P agreement* benefits from any security and if so, what;

(6)   a fair description of the likely actual return, taking into account fees, default rates and taxation;

(7)   an explanation of how any tax liability for lenders arising from investment in *P2P agreements* would be calculated;

(8)   an explanation of the *firm's* procedure for dealing with a loan in late payment or default;

(9)   the procedure for a lender to access their money before the term of the *P2P agreement* has expired;

(10)   an explanation of what would happen if the *firm* fails, including confirmation that there is no recourse to the Financial Services Compensation Scheme.

Product information: form

14.3.8 R   FCA

The *documents* and information provided in accordance with the *rules* in this section must be in a *durable medium* or available on a website (where that does not constitute a *durable medium*) that meets the *website conditions*.

[**Note:** article 29(4) of the *MiFID implementing Directive*]

The timing rules

14.3.9 R   FCA

(1)   The information to be provided in accordance with the *rules* in this section must be provided in good time before a *firm* carries on *designated investment business* or *ancillary services* with or for a *retail client*.

(2)   A *firm* may provide that information immediately after it begins to carry on that business if:

(a)   the *firm* was unable to comply with (1) because, at the request of the *client*, the agreement was concluded using a means of distance communication which prevented the *firm* from complying with that *rule*; and

(b)   in any case where the *rule* on voice telephony communications (**COBS 5.1.12 R**) does not otherwise apply, the *firm* complies with that *rule* as if the *client* was a *consumer*.

[**Note:** article 29(2) and (5) of the *MiFID implementing Directive*]

Keeping the client up-to-date

14.3.10 R   FCA

A *firm* must notify a *client* in good time about any material change to the information provided under the *rules* in this section which is relevant to a service that the *firm* is providing to that *client*. That notification must be given in a *durable medium* if the information to which it relates is given in a *durable medium*.

[**Note:** article 29(6) of the *MiFID implementing Directive*]

Information about UCITS schemes

14.3.11 R   FCA

If a *firm* provides a *client* with a *key investor information document* or *EEA key investor information document* that meets the requirements of articles 78 and 79 of the *UCITS Directive* (see **COLL 4.7** (Key investor information and marketing communications)) and the *KII Regulation*, it will have provided appropriate information for the purpose of the requirement to disclose information on:

(1)   *designated investments* and investment strategies (**COBS 2.2.1 R (1)(B)**); and

(2)   costs and associated charges (**COBS 2.2.1 R (1)(D)** and **COBS 6.1.9 R**;

in relation to the costs and associated charges in respect of the *UCITS scheme* itself, including the exit and entry commissions.

[**Note:** article 34 of the *MiFID implementing Directive*]

14.3.12 G   FCA

A *key investor information document* and *EEA key investor information document* provide sufficient information in relation to the costs and associated charges in respect of the *UCITS* itself. However, a *firm* distributing *units* in a *UCITS* should also inform a *client* about all of the other costs and associated charges related to the provision of its services in relation to *units* in the *UCITS*.

[Note: recital 55 to the *MiFID implementing Directive*]

14.4 PROVISION OF INFORMATION BY AN INTERMEDIATE UNITHOLDER

Provision of information to the beneficial owner

Information requests by authorised fund managers for liquidity management purposes

14.4.10 R   FCA

If an *intermediate unitholder* receives a reasonable request from an *authorised fund manager* for information relating to the beneficial owners of the *units* of a *scheme* that it operates which the *authorised fund manager* reasonably needs for the purposes of liquidity management, the *intermediate unitholder* must provide that information to the *authorised fund manager* as soon as is reasonably practicable.

14.4.11 G   FCA

Examples of information which may be reasonably requested by an *authorised fund manager* include:

(1)   a breakdown of the total number of *units* held by the *intermediate unitholder* in each *scheme* to indicate the number of *units* attributable to individual beneficial owners; and

(2)   information about the types of distribution channel which have been used to sell the *units* to the relevant beneficial owners.

14.4.12 G   FCA

In determining whether a request from an *authorised fund manager* is reasonable, an *intermediate unitholder* may take into account the frequency with which such requests have been received from that *authorised fund manager*.

CHAPTER 15
CANCELLATION

15.1   APPLICATION

[3.63]
15.1.1 G   FCA

This chapter is relevant to a *firm* that enters into a contract cancellable under this chapter. In summary, this means it is relevant to:

(1)   most providers of retail financial products that are based on *designated investments*; and

(2)   *firms* that enter into *distance contracts* with *consumers* that relate to *designated investment business*; and

(3)   *firms* that enter into *distance contracts* the making or performance of which by the *firm* constitutes, or is part of, the activity of *issuing electronic money*.

15.2   THE RIGHT TO CANCEL

Cancellable contracts

15.2.1 R   FCA

A *consumer* has a right to cancel any of the following contracts with a *firm*:

Cancellable contract	Cancellation period	Supplementary provisions
Life and pensions:		
• a *life policy* (including a *pension annuity*, a *pension policy* or within a *wrapper*) • a contract to join a *personal pension scheme* or a stakeholder *pension scheme* • a *pension contract* • a contract for a *pension transfer* • a contract to vary an existing *personal pension scheme* or *stakeholder pension scheme* by exercising, for the first time, an option to make *income withdrawals*,	30 calendar days	For a *life policy* effected when opening or transferring a *wrapper*, the 30 calendar day right to cancel applies to the entire arrangement For a contract to buy a *unit* in a *regulated collective investment scheme* within a *pension wrapper*, the cancellation right for 'non-life/pensions (advised but not at a distance)' below may apply Exemptions may apply (see **COBS 15 ANNEX 1**)
Cash deposit ISAs:		
• a contract for a *cash deposit ISA*	14 calendar days	Exemptions may apply (see **COBS 15 ANNEX 1**)

Cancellable contract	Cancellation period	Supplementary provisions
Non-life/pensions (advised but not at a distance): a non-*distance contract* ...		
• to *buy* a *unit* in a *regulated collective investment scheme* (including within a *wrapper* or *pension wrapper*) • to open or transfer a child trust fund (*CTF*) • to open or transfer an *ISA* • for an *Enterprise Investment Scheme*	14 calendar days	These rights arise only following a *personal recommendation* of the contract (by the *firm* or any other *person*). For a *unit* bought when opening or transferring a *wrapper* or *pension wrapper*, the 14 calendar day right to cancel applies to the entire arrangement. Exemptions may apply (see **COBS 15 ANNEX 1**).
Non-life/pensions (at a distance): a *distance contract*, relating to...		
• *accepting deposits* • *designated investment business* • *issuing electronic money*	14 calendar days	Exemptions may apply (see **COBS 15 ANNEX 1**)

[**Note:** article 35 of the *Consolidated Life Directive*, article 6(1) of the *Distance Marketing Directive*]

15.2.2 G   FCA

(1) If the same transaction attracts more than one right to cancel, the *firm* should apply the longest cancellation period applicable.

(2) A *firm* may provide longer or additional cancellation rights voluntarily, but if it does these should be on terms at least as favourable to the *consumer* as those in this chapter, unless the differences are clearly explained.

(3) If the right to cancel applies to a *wrapper* or *pension wrapper* and underlying investments, the *firm* may give the *consumer* the option of cancelling individual components separately if it wishes.

Start of cancellation period

15.2.3 R   FCA

The cancellation period begins:

(1) either from the day of the conclusion of the contract, except in respect of contracts relating to *life policies* where the time limit will begin from the time when the *consumer* is informed that the contract has been concluded; or

(2) from the day on which the *consumer* receives the contractual terms and conditions and any other pre-contractual information required under this sourcebook, if that is later than the date referred to above.

[**Note:** article 35 of the *Consolidated Life Directive*, article 6(1) of the *Distance Marketing Directive*]

15.2.4 G   FCA

If a *firm* does not give a *consumer* the required information about the right to cancel and other matters, the contract remains cancellable and the *consumer* will not be liable for any *shortfall*.

Disclosing a right to cancel or withdraw

15.2.5 R   FCA

(1) The *firm* must disclose to the *consumer*:

    (a) in good time before or, if that is not possible, immediately after the *consumer* is bound by a contract that attracts a right to cancel or withdraw; and

    (b) in a *durable medium*;

the existence of the right to cancel or withdraw, its duration and the conditions for exercising it including information on the amount which the *consumer* may be required to pay, the consequences of not exercising it and practical instructions for exercising it indicating the address to which the notification of cancellation or withdrawal should be sent.

(2) If the *firm* offers to facilitate, directly or through a third party, the payment of *adviser charges* or *consultancy charges*, it must disclose to the *consumer* at the same time as it makes the disclosure in (1):

    (a) whether any refund will include an *adviser charge* or *consultancy charge*; and

    (b) that the *consumer* may be liable to pay any outstanding *adviser charges* or *consultancy charges*.

(3)   This *rule* applies only where a *consumer* would not otherwise receive similar information under a *rule* in this sourcebook from the *firm* or another *authorised person* (such as under the distance marketing disclosure rules (**COBS 5.1.1 R** to **5.1.4 R**) or **COBS 14** (Providing product information)).

15.3   EXERCISING A RIGHT TO CANCEL

Notice of exercise

15.3.1 R   FCA

If a *consumer* exercises his right to cancel he must, before the expiry of the relevant deadline, notify this following the practical instructions given to him. The deadline shall be deemed to have been observed if the notification, if in a durable medium available and accessible to the recipient, is dispatched before the deadline expires.

[**Note:** article 6 (6) of the *Distance Marketing Directive*]

15.3.2 R   FCA

A *consumer* need not give any reason for exercising his right to cancel.

[**Note:** article 6(1) of the *Distance Marketing Directive*]

15.3.3 G   FCA

The *firm* should accept any indication that the *consumer* wishes to cancel as long as it satisfies the conditions for notification. In the event of any dispute, unless there is clear written evidence to the contrary, the *firm* should treat the date cited by the *consumer* as the date when the notification was dispatched.

Record keeping

15.3.4 R   FCA

The *firm* must make adequate records concerning the exercise of a right to cancel or withdraw and retain them:
(1)   indefinitely in relation to a *pension transfer*, *pension opt-out* or *FSAVC*;
(2)   for at least five years in relation to a *life policy*, *pension contract*, *personal pension scheme* or *stakeholder pension scheme*; and
(3)   for at least three years in any other case.

15.4   EFFECTS OF CANCELLATION

Termination of contract

15.4.1 R   FCA

By exercising a right to cancel, the *consumer* withdraws from the contract and the contract is terminated.

Payment for the service provided before cancellation

15.4.2 R   FCA
(1)   This *rule* applies in relation to a *distance contract* that is not a *life policy*, *personal pension scheme*, *cash deposit ISA* or *CTF*.
(2)   When the *consumer* exercises his right to cancel he may be required to pay, without any undue delay, for the service actually provided by the *firm* in accordance with the contract. The performance of the contract may only begin after the *consumer* has given his approval. The amount payable must not:
        (a)   exceed an amount which is in proportion to the extent of the service already provided in comparison with the full coverage of the contract;
        (b)   in any case be such that it could be construed as a penalty.
(3)   The *firm* may not require the *consumer* to pay any amount on the basis of this *rule* unless it can prove that the *consumer* was duly informed about the amount payable, in conformity with the distance marketing disclosure rules. However, in no case may the *firm* require such payment if it has commenced the performance of the contract before the expiry of the cancellation period without the *consumer's* prior request.

[**Note:** article 7(1), (2) and (3) of the *Distance Marketing Directive*]

Shortfall

15.4.3 R   FCA
(1)   The *firm* may require the *consumer* to pay for any loss under a contract caused by market movements that the *firm* would reasonably incur in cancelling it. The period for calculating the loss shall end on the day on which the *firm* receives the notification of cancellation.
(2)   This *rule*:

(a) does not apply for a *distance contract* or for a contract established on a regular or recurring premium or payment basis; and

(b) only applies if the *firm* has complied with its obligations to disclose information concerning the right to cancel.

Obligations on cancellation

15.4.4 R   FCA

The *firm* must, without any undue delay and no later than within 30 calendar days, return to the *consumer* any sums it has received from him in accordance with the contract, except for any amount that the *consumer* may be required to pay under this section. This period shall begin from the day on which the *firm* receives the notification of cancellation.

[**Note:** article 7(4) of the *Distance Marketing Directive*]

15.4.5 R   FCA

The *firm* is entitled to receive from the *consumer* any sums and/or property he has received from the *firm* without any undue delay and no later than within 30 calendar days. This period shall begin from the day on which the *consumer* dispatches the notification of cancellation.

[**Note:** article 7(5) of the *Distance Marketing Directive*]

15.4.6 R   FCA

Any sums payable under this section on cancellation of a contract are owed as simple contract debts and may be set off against each other.

15.5   SPECIAL SITUATIONS

Contracts with trustees and operators of pension schemes

15.5.1 R   FCA

In this chapter:

(1) references to a *consumer* include the trustees of an *occupational pension scheme* and the trustees or *operator* of a *personal pension scheme* or *stakeholder pension scheme*; and

(2) any contract with such *persons* is to be treated as a non-*distance contract*.

Other legislation including for child trust funds and automatic enrolment into pensions

15.5.2 R   FCA

This chapter applies as modified to the extent necessary for it to be compatible with any enactment.

15.5.3 G   FCA

For example:

(1) the *Child Trust Fund Regulations* contain provisions relevant to cancellation rights; in particular they provide that any uninvested sums held in connection with a *CTF* should be held in a designated bank account; and the effect of conditions 4(a) and (b) in regulation 5 of the *Child Trust Fund Regulations* (applicable to non-*HMRC allocated CTF*) is that a *CTF* opened by way of *distance contract* has a cancellable management agreement in all cases and the *CTF* cannot be opened until the cancellation period has expired, therefore the price fluctuation exemption is not engaged;

(2) where legislation does not permit sums within a *personal pension scheme* or *CTF* to be returned to a *consumer*, the requirement to do so on cancellation is modified to permit payment to another provider on behalf of the *consumer*; the *firm* should notify him, where relevant, as soon as possible that it holds money awaiting re-investment instructions; if that money is held in a non-interest bearing account this should be drawn to his attention;

(3) the Occupational and Personal Pension Schemes (Automatic Enrolment) Regulations 2010 contain provisions relevant to cancellation rights; in particular they provide rights of opt-out from an *automatic enrolment scheme*; the cancellation rights in this chapter are modified to permit a provider to adopt the opt-out process in the Occupational and Personal Pension Schemes (Automatic Enrolment) Regulations 2010 in relation to all members of an *automatic enrolment scheme*; the cancellation rules will continue to apply for any single premium contributions or transfers where these would normally attract this right.

Automatic cancellation of an attached distance contract

15.5.4 G   FCA

When a *consumer* cancels a *distance contract* under this chapter, his notice may also operate to cancel any attached contract which is also a distance financial services contract unless the *consumer* gives notice that cancellation of the main contract is not to operate to cancel the attached contract (see regulation 12 of the *Distance Marketing Regulations*). Where relevant, this should be disclosed to the *consumer* along with other information on cancellation.

Appointed representatives

15.5.5 G   FCA

This chapter does not act to cancel *distance contracts* entered into by an *appointed representative* or where applicable, by a *tied agent*, as principal such as a *distance contract* to provide advisory services, but the *Distance Marketing Regulations* (regulations 9 to 13, see regulation 4(3)) may have this effect.

Maxi-ISAs

15.5.6 G   FCA

Where a *life policy* or *unit* bought on opening or transferring an *ISA* is cancellable, the right to cancel, or substitute right to withdraw, applies to the entire arrangement. For example, a maxi-ISA comprising a *life policy* in the stocks and shares component and a *cash component* would be cancellable as a whole with a cancellation period of 30 calendar days. However, a *firm* is free to give the *consumer* the option of cancelling individual components separately with the same cancellation period if it wishes.

15 ANNEX 1   EXEMPTIONS FROM THE RIGHT TO CANCEL

		Exemptions for life policies and pension contracts (non-distance)
1.1	R	There is no right to cancel a non-*distance contract* that is a *life policy* or a *pension contract*:
		(1) that is a *pension fund management* policy; or
		(2) that relates to or is associated with securing benefits under a *defined benefits pension scheme*; or
		(3) for a term of six months or less, unless it is a single *premium* contract where the designated retirement date is within six months of the date of the policy; or
		(4) that is effected by the trustees of an *occupational pension scheme* or the employer, trustees or *operator* of a *stakeholder pension scheme* and that represents a: (a) *pension buy-out contract*; or (b) purchase of a without-profits deferred *pension annuity*; or (c) *defined benefits pension scheme* or a single *premium* payment to any *occupational pension scheme* with a pooled fund (that is, underlying investments are not earmarked for individual scheme members); or (d) purchase made to insure and secure members' pension benefits under a *money-purchase occupational scheme* or *stakeholder pension scheme* (unless it is the master, first or only policy); or
		(5) if the *consumer*, at the time he signs the application, is *habitually resident*: (a) in an *EEA State* other than the *UK* (but that state's rules may apply); or (b) outside the *EEA* and is not present in the *UK*.
1.2	G	There is no right to cancel a non-*distance contract* for a *traded life policy*. This is because the 30-day right to cancel a *life policy* (in **COBS 15.2.1 R**) applies at the point of conclusion of the *life policy* not on its assignment. However, there may be a 14-day right to cancel a *distance contract* for a *traded life policy* unless an exemption applies, since that *distance contract* relates to *designated investment business*.
		Exemption for SIPPs
1.3	R	There is no right to cancel a contract to join a *SIPP* whose performance has been fully completed by both parties at the *consumer's* express request before the *consumer* exercises his right to cancel.
1.4	G	If a *consumer* requests that a *firm* complete a transaction to join a *SIPP* before the expiry of the cancellation period, the *firm* should, in having regard to the information needs of the *consumer*, make him aware that he will lose his right to cancel and satisfy itself on reasonable grounds that the customer understands the cost and other implications.
		Exemptions for certain pension arrangements (the 'cancellation substitute')
1.5	R	There is no right to cancel:
		(1) a contract for or funded (wholly or in part) from a *pension transfer*; or
		(2) a *pension annuity* due to commence within a year and a day of the contract or a variation of one with similar commencement; or
		(3) the exercise of an option to make *income withdrawals*;

to the extent that the right to cancel is replaced with a pre-contract right to withdraw the *consumer's* offer of at least 14 calendar days. The combined period of the right to withdraw and any residual right to cancel must be at least 30 calendar days.

Exemption for pension compensation

1.6 R There is no right to cancel a *pension annuity*, a *pension policy*, a *pension contract*, or a contract to join a *personal pension scheme* or *stakeholder pension scheme*, which in each case is funded (wholly or in part) from payments derived from compensation or redress following a review undertaken in relation to a complaint.

Exemption for annuities after death of the life assured

1.7 R A *firm* need not accept notification of cancellation of a *pension annuity* contract if the life (or any of the lives) assured under it has died before notice is given.

Exemptions for units (non-distance)

1.8 R There is no right to cancel a non-*distance contract* to *buy* a *unit* in a *regulated collective investment scheme*:

(1) if the *unit* is not purchased from the scheme's *operator*, from the *operator's associate* acting as provider of a *wrapper*; or

(2) if the *consumer* is not a *retail client*; or

(3) if the contract represents an exchange of *units* between *sub-funds* of the same *umbrella*; or

(4) if the contract relates to a change between *units* of one class and *units* of another class in the same *scheme*; or

(5) if the contract relates to a *recognised scheme* and is with an *operator* who is not an *authorised person* or carrying on business in the *UK*; or

(6) if the *consumer* is not *habitually resident* in the *UK* at the date of the offer of the contract; or

(7) if the *firm* has reasonable grounds for assuming that no *personal recommendation* of the contract was provided by anyone carrying on *designated investment business* in the *UK*; or

(8) for the second and subsequent purchases of *units* under recurring single payment *unit* savings plans, provided that:
(a) the intention or option to make a series of single payments is disclosed at the outset (for example in pre-contract disclosure documents); or (b) the intention is evidenced (for example, by the establishment of a direct debit mandate).

Exemptions for ISAs, CTFs and EISs (non-distance)

1.9 R There is no right to cancel a non-*distance contract*:

(1) to open or transfer an *ISA* (mini or maxi and including all components whatever the underlying investment, but not a *cash deposit ISA* or an *ISA* containing a *life policy*); or

(2) to open or transfer a *CTF*; or

(3) [deleted]

(4) for an *EIS*;

provided that:

(5) (for an *EIS* or *ISA*) the right to cancel is replaced with a seven calendar day, pre-contract right to withdraw the *consumer's* offer; or

(6) the contract relates to an *EIS* or a non-*packaged product ISA* or *CTF* and is entered into following an explanation that neither a right to cancel nor a right to withdraw will apply given in accordance with the relevant rules on pre-contractual disclosure; or

(7) (for an *ISA* or *EIS*) the contract entered into is a second or subsequent *ISA* or *EIS* on substantially the same terms (such as mini-to-mini *ISA* or maxi-to-maxi *ISA*) as an *ISA* or *EIS* purchased from the same *ISA manager* or *EIS manager* in the previous tax year.

Exemptions for distance contracts (all products and services)

1.10 R There is no right to cancel a *distance contract*:

(1) whose price depends on fluctuations in the financial market outside the *firm's* control, which may occur during the cancellation period, such as:

(a)   foreign exchange; or

(b)   money market instruments; or

(c)   transferable securities; or

(d)   units in collective investment undertakings; or

(e)   financial-futures contracts, including equivalent cash-settled instruments; or

(f)   forward interest-rate agreements; or

(g)   interest-rate, currency and equity swaps; or

(h)   options to acquire or dispose of any instruments referred to above including cash-settled instruments and options on currency and on interest rates; or

(2)   whose performance has been fully completed by both parties at the *consumer's* express request before the *consumer* exercises his right to cancel; or

(3)   to *deal as agent*, *advise* or *arrange* if the *distance contract* is concluded merely as a stage in the provision of another service by the *firm* or another *person*.

[**Note:** article 6(2) and recital 19 of the *Distance Marketing Directive*]

1.11   R   In the case of *distance contracts* for financial services comprising an initial service agreement followed by successive operations or a series of separate operations of the same nature performed over time, the right to cancel shall apply only to the initial agreement.

[**Note:** article 1(2) of the *Distance Marketing Directive*]

CHAPTER 16
REPORTING INFORMATION TO CLIENTS

16.1   GENERAL CLIENT REPORTING REQUIREMENT

[3.64]
16.1.1 R   FCA

A *firm* must ensure in relation to *MiFID or equivalent third country business* that a *client* receives adequate reports on the services provided to it by the *firm*. The reports must include, where applicable, the costs associated with the transactions and services undertaken by the *firm* on behalf of the *client*.

[**Note:** article 19(8) of *MiFID*]

16.2   OCCASIONAL REPORTING

Execution of orders other than when managing investments

16.2.1 R   FCA

(1)   If a *firm* has carried out an order in the course of its *designated investment business* on behalf of a *client*, it must:

     (a)   promptly provide the *client*, in a *durable medium*, with the essential information concerning the execution of the order;

     (b)   in the case of a *retail client*, send the *client* a notice in a *durable medium* confirming the execution of the order and such of the *trade confirmation information* (**COBS 16 ANNEX 1 R**) as is applicable:

        (i)   as soon as possible and no later than the first *business day* following that execution; or

        (ii)   if the confirmation is received by the *firm* from a third party, no later than the first *business day* following receipt of the confirmation from the third party; and

     (c)   supply a *client*, on request, with information about the status of his order.

(2)   Paragraph (1) does not apply to a *firm managing investments*.

(3)   Paragraph (1)(b) does not apply if the confirmation would contain the same information as a confirmation that is to be promptly dispatched to the *client* by another *person*.

(4)   Paragraphs (1)(a) and (b) do not apply to an order executed on behalf of a *client* that relates to a bond funding a mortgage loan agreement with the *client*. The report on the transaction must be made at the same time as the terms of the mortgage loan are communicated, but no later than one month after the execution of the order.

(5)   If a *firm* carries out an order for a *retail client* relating to *units* or *shares* in a collective investment undertaking that is part of a series of orders that are executed periodically, it must:

     (a)   comply with paragraph (1)(b) in relation to that order; or

(b) provide the *client* at least once every six months with such of the *trade confirmation information* (**COBS 16 ANNEX 1 R**) as is applicable in relation to each transaction in that series carried out in the relevant reporting period.

(6) In relation to subscription and *redemption* orders for *units* in a *UCITS scheme* or *EEA UCITS scheme* executed by an *authorised fund manager*, paragraphs (1), (3) and (5) of this *rule* apply as if references to:

(a) a *client* and to a *retail client* were references to a *unitholder* in the *scheme*; and

(b) *trade confirmation information* in paragraphs (1)(b) and (5)(b) were to the information in paragraph (7).

(7) The notice referred to in paragraph (1)(b) must, where applicable, for subscription and *redemption* orders for *units* in a *UCITS scheme* or *EEA UCITS scheme* executed by an *authorised fund manager*, include the following information:

(a) the identification of the *management company*;

(b) the name or other designation of the *unitholder*;

(c) the date and time of receipt of the order and method of payment;

(d) the date of execution;

(e) the identification of the *UCITS scheme* or *EEA UCITS scheme*;

(f) the nature of the order (subscription or *redemption*);

(g) the number of *units* involved;

(h) the *unit* price at which the *units* were subscribed or redeemed;

(i) the reference valuation date;

(j) the gross value of the order including charges for subscription or net amount after charges for *redemptions*; and

(k) the total sum of the commissions and expenses charged and where the investor so requests, an itemised breakdown.

[**Note:** article 40 paragraphs (1) to (4) of the *MiFID implementing Directive* and article 24 of the *UCITS implementing Directive*]

16.2.2 G   FCA

The requirement concerning orders relating to bonds funding a mortgage loan agreement is unlikely to be relevant to products in the *United Kingdom* market.

16.2.3 R   FCA

For the purposes of calculating the unit price in the *trade confirmation information*, where the order is executed in tranches, the *firm* may supply the *client* with information about the price of each tranche or the average price. If the average price is provided, the *firm* must supply the *retail client* with information about the price of each tranche upon request.

[**Note:** article 40(4) of the *MiFID implementing Directive*]

16.2.3A G   FCA

In determining what is essential information, a *firm* should consider including:

(1) for transactions in a *derivative*:

(a) the maturity, delivery or expiry date of the derivative;

(b) in the case of an *option*, a reference to the last exercise date, whether it can be exercised before maturity and the strike price;

(c) if the transaction *closes out* an open *futures* position, all essential details required in respect of each contract comprised in the open position and each contract by which it was *closed out* and the profit or loss to the *client* arising out of *closing out* that position (a difference account);

(2) for the exercise of an *option*:

(a) the date of exercise, and either the time of exercise or that the *client* will be notified of that time on request;

(b) whether the exercise creates a sale or purchase in the underlying asset; and

(c) the strike price of the *option* (for a currency *option*, the rate of exchange will be the same as the strike price) and, if applicable, the total consideration from or to the *client*; and

(3) the fact that the transaction involves any dividend or capitalisation or other right which has been declared, but which has not been paid, allotted or otherwise become effective in respect of the *investment*, and under the terms of the transaction the benefit of which will not pass to the purchaser.

Guidance on the requirements

16.2.4 G   FCA

Where a *firm* executes an order in tranches, the *firm* may, where appropriate, indicate the trading time and the execution venue in a way that is consistent with this, such as, "multiple". In accordance with the *client's best interests rule*, a *firm* should provide additional information at the *client's* request.

16.2.5 G   FCA

In accordance with **COBS 2.4.9 R**, a *firm* may dispatch a confirmation to an agent, other than the *firm* or an *associate* of the *firm*, nominated by the *client* in writing.

Special cases

16.2.6 R FCA

In relation to business that is not *MiFID or equivalent third country business*, a *firm* need not despatch a confirmation if:

(1)   the *firm* has agreed with the *client* (in the case of a *retail client*, in writing and with the *client's* informed consent) that confirmations need not be supplied, either generally or in specified circumstances; or

(2)   the *designated investment* is a *life policy*, *stakeholder pension scheme* or a *personal pension scheme* (other than a *SIPP*); or

(3)   the *designated investment* is held within a *CTF* and the statement provided under the *CTF Regulations* includes the information that would have been contained in a confirmation under this section (other than information that has since become irrelevant).

Record keeping: occasional reporting

16.2.7 R FCA

A *firm* must retain a copy of any confirmation despatched to a *client* under this section:

(1)   for *MiFID or equivalent third country business*, for a period of at least five years; or

(2)   for business that is not *MiFID or equivalent third country business*, for a period of at least three years;

from the date of despatch.

[**Note:** see article 51(3) of the *MiFID implementing Directive*]

16.3   PERIODIC REPORTING

Provision by the firm and contents

16.3.1 R FCA

(1)   If a *firm* is *managing investments* on behalf of a *client*, it must provide the *client* with a *periodic statement* in a *durable medium* unless such a statement is provided by another *person*.

(2)   If the *client* is a *retail client*, the *periodic statement* must include such of the *periodic information* (**COBS 16 ANNEX 2 R**) as is applicable.

[**Note:** article 41(1) and (2) of the *MiFID implementing Directive*]

16.3.2 R FCA

(1)   In the case of a *retail client*, the *periodic statement* must be provided once every six *months*, except in the following cases:

    (a)   if the *retail client* so requests, the *periodic statement* must be provided every three *months*;

    (b)   if the *retail client* elects to receive information about executed transactions on a transaction-by-transaction basis (**COBS 16.3.3 R**) and there are no transactions in *derivatives* or other securities giving the right to acquire or sell a *transferable security* or giving rise to a cash settlement determined by reference to transferable securities, currencies, interest rates or yields, commodities or other indices or measures, the *periodic statement* must be provided at least once every twelve *months*;

    (c)   if the agreement between a *firm* and a *retail client* for the *managing of investments* authorises a leveraged portfolio, the *periodic statement* must be provided at least once a *month*.

(2)   A *firm* must inform a *retail client* that he has the right to request the provision of a *periodic statement* every three *months*.

[**Note:** article 41(3) of the *MiFID implementing Directive*]

16.3.3 R FCA

(1)   If the *client* elects to receive information about executed transactions on a transaction-by-transaction basis, a *firm managing investments* must provide promptly to the *client*, on the execution of a transaction, the essential information concerning that transaction in a *durable medium*.

(2)   If the *client* is a *retail client*, the *firm* must send him a notice confirming the transaction and containing such of the information identified in column (1) of the table in **COBS 16 ANNEX 1 R** as is applicable:

    (a)   no later than the first *business day* following that execution; or

    (b)   if the confirmation is received by the *firm* from a third party, no later than the first *business day* following receipt of the confirmation from the third party;

unless the confirmation would contain the same information as a confirmation that is to be promptly dispatched to the *retail client* by another *person*.

[**Note:** article 41(4) of the *MiFID implementing Directive*]

16.3.4 G   FCA

In accordance with **COBS 2.4.9 R**, a *firm* may dispatch a periodic statement to an agent, other than the *firm* or an *associate* of the *firm*, nominated by the *client* in writing.

16.3.5 R   FCA

For the purposes of calculating the unit price in the *trade confirmation information* or *periodic information*, where the order is executed in tranches, the *firm* may supply the *client* with information about the price of each tranche or the average price. If the average price is provided, the *firm* must supply the *retail client* with information about the price of each tranche upon request.

[**Note:** article 40(4) of the *MiFID implementing Directive*]

16.3.6 R   FCA
(1)   If a *firm*:
    (a)   *manages investments* for a *retail client*; or
    (b)   operates a *retail client* account that includes an uncovered open position in a contingent liability transaction,
    it must report to the *retail client* any losses exceeding any predetermined threshold, agreed between it and the *retail client*.
(2)   The *firm* must report:
    (a)   no later than the end of the *business day* in which the threshold is exceeded; or
    (b)   if the threshold is exceeded on a non-*business day*, the close of the next *business day*.

[**Note:** article 42 of the *MiFID implementing Directive*]

16.3.7 R   FCA

For the purposes of this section, a contingent liability transaction is one that involves any actual or potential liability for the *client* that exceeds the cost of acquiring the instrument.

[**Note:** recital 63 of the *MiFID implementing Directive*]

16.3.8 R   FCA

[intentionally blank]

Guidance on contingent liability transaction

16.3.9 G   FCA

When providing a *periodic statement* to a *retail client*, a *firm* should consider whether to include:
(1)   the *collateral* value in respect of any contingent liability transaction in the *client*'s portfolio during the relevant period; and
(2)   *option* account valuations in respect of each open *option* written by the *client* in the *client*'s portfolio at the end of the relevant period; stating:
    (a)   the *share*, *future*, index or other *investment* involved;
    (b)   the trade price and date for the opening transaction, unless the valuation statement follows the statement for the period in which the option was opened;
    (c)   the market price of the contract; and
    (d)   the exercise price of the contract.
(3)   Option account valuations may show an average trade price and market price in respect of an *option* series if the *retail client* buys a number of contracts within the same series.

Periodic reporting: special situations

16.3.10 R   FCA

In relation to business that is not *MiFID or equivalent third country business*, a *firm* need not provide a *periodic statement*:
(1)   to a *client* habitually resident outside the *United Kingdom* if the *client* concerned has so requested or the *firm* has taken reasonable steps to establish that he does not wish to receive it;
(2)   in respect of a *CTF*, if the statement provided under the *CTF Regulations* contains the *periodic information*.

Record keeping: periodic reporting

16.3.11 R   FCA

A *firm* must make, and retain, a copy of any *periodic statement*:
(1)   for *MiFID or equivalent third country business*, for a period of at least five years; or
(2)   for business that is not *MiFID* or, for a period of at least three years;

from the date of despatch.

[**Note:** see article 51(3) of the *MiFID implementing Directive*]

16.4   STATEMENTS OF CLIENT DESIGNATED INVESTMENTS OR CLIENT MONEY

16.4.1 R   FCA
(1)   A *firm* that holds *client designated investments* or *client money* for a *client* must send that *client* at least once a year a statement in a *durable medium* of those *designated investments* or that *client money* unless such a statement has been provided in a *periodic statement*.
(2)   A *credit institution* need not send a statement in respect of *deposits* held by it.
(3)   This *rule* does not apply in relation to a *firm* holding *client designated investments* or *client money* under a *personal pension scheme* or a *stakeholder pension scheme* where doing so is not *MiFID or equivalent third country business*.
(4)   A *CTF* account provider holding *client designated investments* or *client money* under a *CTF* where doing so is not *MiFID or equivalent third country business* must provide a statement but need not do so more frequently than required by Regulation 10 of the *CTF Regulations*.

[**Note:** article 43(1) of the *MiFID implementing Directive*]

16.4.2 R   FCA

A *firm* must include in a statement of *client* assets referred to under this section the following information:
(1)   details of all the *designated investments* or *client money* held by the *firm* for the *client* at the end of the period covered by the statement;
(2)   the extent to which any *client designated investments* or *client money* have been the subject of *securities financing transactions*; and
(3)   the extent of any benefit that has accrued to the *client* by virtue of participation in any *securities financing transactions*, and the basis on which that benefit has accrued.

[**Note:** article 43(2) of the *MiFID implementing Directive*]

16.4.3 R   FCA

In cases where the portfolio of a *client* includes the proceeds of one or more unsettled transactions, the information in a statement provided under this section may be based either on the trade date or the settlement date, provided that the same basis is applied consistently to all such information in the statement.

[**Note:** article 43(2) of the *MiFID implementing Directive*]

16.4.4 R   FCA

A *firm* which holds *designated investments* or *client money* and is *managing investments* for a *client* may include the statement under this section in the *periodic statement* it provides to that *client*.

[**Note:** article 43(3) of the *MiFID implementing Directive*]

16.4.5 G   FCA

In reporting to a *client* in accordance with this section, a *firm* should consider whether to provide details of any assets loaned or charged including:
(1)   which *investments* (if any) were at the end of the relevant period loaned to any third party and which *investments* (if any) were at that date charged to secure borrowings made on behalf of the portfolio; and
(2)   the aggregate of any interest payments made and income received during the period in respect of loans or borrowings made during that period

16.4.6 G   FCA

Firms subject to either or both the *custody chapter* and the *client money chapter* are reminded of the reporting obligations to *clients* in **CASS 9.2** (Prime broker's daily report to clients) and **CASS 9.5** (Reporting to clients on request).

16.5   QUOTATIONS FOR SURRENDER VALUES

16.5.1 R   FCA

When a *long-term insurer* receives any indication that a *retail client* wishes to surrender a *life policy* which is of the type that may be traded on an existing secondary market for *life policies*, it must, before accepting a surrender, make the *policyholder* aware that he may be able to sell his *policy* instead, how he may do so and that there may be financial benefits in doing so.

16.6   COMMUNICATIONS TO CLIENTS – LIFE INSURANCE, LONG TERM CARE IN-SURANCE AND INCOME WITHDRAWALS

Disclosure for life insurance contracts: information to be provided during the term of the contract

16.6.1 R   FCA

(1)   This section applies to a *long-term insurer*, unless, at the time of application, the *client*, other than an *EEA ECA recipient*, was *habitually resident*:

    (a)   in an *EEA State* other than the *United Kingdom*; or

    (b)   outside the *EEA* and he was not present in the *United Kingdom*.

(2)   In addition, **COBS 16.6.8 R** applies to an *operator* of a *personal pension scheme* or *stakeholder pension scheme* in relation to a *retail client* who elects to make *income withdrawals*.

16.6.2 R   FCA

If during the term of a *life policy* entered into on or after 1 July 1994 there is any proposed change in the information referred to in paragraphs (1) to (12) of the Consolidated Life Directive information (**COBS 13 ANNEX 1**) the *long-term insurer* must inform the *policyholder* of the effect of the change before the change is made.

[**Note:** article 36(2) of the *Consolidated Life Directive*]

16.6.3 R   FCA

If a *life policy* entered into on or after 1 July 1994 provides for the payment of bonuses and the amounts of bonuses are unspecified, the *long-term insurer* must, in every calendar year except the first, either:

(1)   notify the *policyholder* in writing of the amount of any bonus which has become payable under the contract, and which has not previously been notified under this *rule*; or

(2)   give the *policyholder* in writing sufficient information to enable him to determine the amount of any such bonus.

16.6.4 R   FCA

(1)   When a *firm* provides information in accordance with this section, it must provide the information in a *durable medium*, unless (2) applies.

(2)   If the contract is being made by telephone, the *firm* may give the information orally to the *customer*. If the *customer* enters into the contract, a written version of the required information must be sent to the *customer* within five *business days* of the contract being entered into.

16.6.5 R   FCA

Where a *life policy* is effected jointly, the information required by this section may be sent to the first named *client*.

16.6.6 R   FCA

A *firm* must make an adequate record of information provided to a *customer* under this section and retain that record for a minimum period after the information is provided of five years.

Long term care insurance

16.6.7 R   FCA

At each anniversary of the date on which a *long-term care insurance contract* which is based on single premium investment bonds was entered into, the *insurer* must:

(1)   provide the *retail client* with a table based on the format of **COBS 13 ANNEX 3** 2.2R containing at least the current fund value and projected future *policy* values (as in column "What you might get back");

(2)   where it is the case, inform the *retail client* of the possibility that future policy values may be insufficient to fulfil the original purpose of the contract; and

(3)   inform the *retail client* how to obtain advice on *investments* in respect of *long-term care insurance contracts*, and that it is in his best interest to do so.

Income withdrawals

16.6.8 R   FCA

At intervals no longer than 12 *months* from the date of an election by a *retail client* to make *income withdrawals*, the relevant *operator* of a *personal pension scheme* or *stakeholder pension scheme* must:

(1)   provide the *retail client* with such information as is necessary for the *retail client* to review the election, including where relevant the information required by **COBS 13 ANNEX 2 2.9 R**; and

(2)   inform the *retail client* how to obtain *advice on investments* in respect of his income withdrawals, and that it would be in his best interests to do so.FCA

16 ANNEX 1R   TRADE CONFIRMATION AND PERIODIC INFORMATION

This annex forms part of **COBS 16.2.1 R**

The information below must be provided, where relevant for the purposes of reporting to a *retail client*, in accordance with SUP 17 ANNEX 1	(1) Trade confirmation information	(2) Periodic information (where trade confirmation information is not provided on a transaction by transaction basis, to be provided for each transaction carried out during the reporting period)
General		
1. the reporting *firm* identification;	Y	
2. the name or other designation of the *client*;	Y	
3. the trading day;	Y	Y
4. the trading time;	Y	Y
5. the type of the order (for example, a limit order or a market order);	Y	Y
6. the venue identification;	Y	Y
7. the instrument identification;	Y	Y
8. the buy/sell indicator;	Y	Y
9. the nature of the order if other than buy/sell;	Y	Y
10. the quantity;	Y	Y
11. the unit price;	Y	Y
12. the total consideration;	Y	Y
13. a total sum of the commissions and expenses charged (for a *collective investment scheme operator*, initial *charges* may be disclosed in cash or percentage terms) and, where the *retail client* so requests, an itemised breakdown, including, where relevant, the amount of any *mark-up or mark-down* imposed by the *firm* or its *associate* where the *firm* or *associate* acted as *principal* in *executing* the transaction, and the *firm* owes a duty of best execution to the *client*;	Y	Y
14. the rate of exchange obtained where the transaction involves a conversion of currency;	Y	Y
15. [intentionally blank]		
16. [intentionally blank]		
17. the *client*'s responsibilities in relation to the settlement of the transaction, including the time limit for payment or delivery as well as the appropriate account details where these details and responsibilities have not previously been notified to the *client*; and	Y	
18. if the *client's* counterparty was the *firm* itself or any person in the *firm's group* or another *client* of the *firm*, the fact that this was the case unless the order was *executed* through a trading system that facilitates anonymous trading.	Y	

[**Note:** article 40(4) and recital 64 to the *MiFID implementing Directive*]

The information below must be provided, where relevant for the purposes of reporting to a *retail client*, in accordance with SUP 17 ANNEX 1	(1) Trade confirmation information	(2) Periodic information (where trade confirmation information is not provided on a transaction by transaction basis, to be provided for each transaction carried out during the reporting period)
General		

A *firm* may provide the *client* with the information referred to in this Annex using standard codes if it also provides an explanation of the codes used.

[**Note:** article 40(5) of the *MiFID implementing Directive*]FCA

16 ANNEX 2R   INFORMATION TO BE INCLUDED IN A PERIODIC REPORT

This annex forms part of **COBS 16.3.1 R**.

	Periodic information (all cases)
1.	the name of the *firm;*
2.	the name or other designation of the *retail client*'s account;
3.	a statement of the contents and the valuation of the portfolio, including details of:
	(a) each *designated investment* held, its market value or fair value if market value is unavailable;
	(b) the cash balance at the beginning and at the end of the reporting period; and
	(c) the performance of the portfolio during the reporting period;
4.	the total amount of *fees* and charges incurred during the reporting period, itemising at least total management *fees* and total costs associated with execution, and including, where relevant, a statement that a more detailed breakdown will be provided on request;
5.	a comparison of performance during the period covered by the statement with the investment performance benchmark (if any) agreed between the *firm* and the *client*;
6.	the total amount of dividends, interest and other payments received during the reporting period in relation to the *client*'s portfolio; and
7.	information about other corporate actions giving rights in relation to *designated investments* held in the portfolio.

[**Note:** article 41(2) of *MiFID implementing Directive*]

CHAPTER 17
CLAIMS HANDLING FOR LONG-TERM CARE INSURANCE

17.1   PROVIDING INFORMATION TO CLAIMANTS AND DEALING WITH CLAIMS

[3.65]
17.1.1 R   FCA

When an *insurer* or *managing agent* receives a claim under a *long-term care insurance contract*, it must respond promptly by providing the *policyholder*, or the *person* acting on the *policyholder's* behalf, with:
(1)   a claim form (if it requires one to be completed);
(2)   a summary of its claims handling procedure; and
(3)   appropriate information about the medical criteria that must be met, and any waiting periods that apply, under the terms of the *policy*.

Responding to a claim

17.1.2 R   FCA

As soon as reasonably practicable after receipt of a claim, the *insurer* or *managing agent* must tell the *policyholder*, or the *person* acting on the *policyholder's* behalf:
(1)   (for each part of the claim it accepts), whether the claim will be settled by paying the *policyholder*, providing goods or services to the *policyholder* or paying another *person* to provide those goods or services; and

(2)   (for each part of the claim it rejects), why the claim has been rejected and whether any future rights to claim exist.

Rejecting a claim

17.1.3 R   FCA

An *insurer* and a *managing agent* must not:

(1)   unreasonably reject a claim; or

(2)   except where there is evidence of fraud, reject a claim for:

     (a)   non-disclosure of a fact material to the risk which the *policyholder* could not reasonably have been expected to disclose; or

     (b)   misrepresentation of a fact material to the risk, unless the misrepresentation is negligent; or

     (c)   breach of warranty, unless the circumstances of the claim are connected to the breach, the warranty is material to the risk and was drawn to the *policyholder's* attention before the conclusion of the contract.

CHAPTER 18
SPECIALIST REGIMES

18.1   TRUSTEE FIRMS

Application

[3.66]

18.1.1 R   FCA

(1)   This section applies to the *MiFID or equivalent third country business* carried on by a *trustee firm*.

(2)   It does not apply to a *trustee firm* when acting as:

     (a)   a *depositary*; or

     (b)   the trustee of a *personal pension scheme* or *stakeholder pension scheme*.

Application of COBS to trustee firms

18.1.2 R   FCA

The provisions of *COBS* in the table do not apply to a *trustee firm* to which this section applies:

COBS	Description
6.1A	Adviser charging and remuneration
6.1B	Retail investment product provider requirements relating to adviser charging and remuneration
6.2A	Describing advice services
6.3	Disclosing information about services, fees and commission – packaged products
6.4	Disclosure of charges, remuneration and commission
9.4	Suitability reports
9.6	Special rules for providing basic advice on a stakeholder product
16.3.9	Guidance on contingent liability transaction
16.5	Quotations for surrender values
16.6	Life insurance contracts – communications to clients
16 Annex 1 R (1) 14	Information to be provided in accordance with **COBS 16.2.1 R** and **16.3**

18.1.3 G   FCA

The provisions of *COBS* in the table are unlikely to be relevant in relation to a *trustee firm* to which this section applies:

COBS	Description
5	Distance communications
13	Preparing product information
14.2	Providing product information
15	Cancellation
17	Claims handling for long-term care insurance
18.2	Energy market activity and oil market activity

COBS	Description
18.3	Corporate finance business
18.4	Stock lending activity
19	Pensions – supplementary provisions
20	With-profits

Duties of trustee firms under the general law

18.1.4 G   FCA

To the extent a *rule* in *COBS* applies to a *trustee firm*, that *rule*:

(1)   applies in addition to any duties or powers imposed or conferred upon a trustee by the general law; and

(2)   does not qualify or restrict the duties or powers that the general law imposes or confers upon a trustee; *trustee firms* will be under a duty to observe the provisions of their trust instrument; if its provisions conflict with any applicable *rule*, *trustee firms* will need to take advice in resolving the conflict.

Considering and complying with applicable COBS rules

18.1.5 G   FCA

In considering and reaching decisions as to how applicable rules in *COBS* apply in the context of a particular trust arrangement, a *trustee firm* should consider the nature of that arrangement and the provisions of the relevant trust instrument.

References to "client" in applicable COBS rules

18.1.6 G   FCA

Where an applicable *rule* in *COBS* requires the doing of any thing in relation to a *client*, the *trustee firm* should consider who, in the context of that *rule* and having regard to the particular trust arrangement, is the most appropriate person to treat as its *client*. This might, for example, be the beneficiary, another trustee or the trust, depending on the particular circumstances.

18.2   ENERGY MARKET ACTIVITY AND OIL MARKET ACTIVITY

Energy market activity and oil market activity – MiFID business

18.2.1 R   FCA

The provisions of *COBS* in the table do not apply in relation to any *energy market activity* or *oil market activity* carried on by a *firm* which is *MiFID or equivalent third country business*:

COBS	Description
6.1A	Adviser charging and remuneration
6.1B	Retail investment product provider requirements relating to adviser charging and remuneration
6.2A	Describing advice services
6.3	Disclosing information about services, fees and commission – packaged products
6.4	Disclosure of charges, remuneration and commission
9.4	Suitability reports
9.6	Special rules for providing basic advice on a stakeholder product
11.6	Use of dealing commission
16.3.9	Guidance on contingent liability transaction
16.5	Quotations for surrender values
16.6	Life insurance contracts – communications to clients
16 Annex 1 R (1) 14	Information to be provided in accordance with **COBS 16.2.1 R** and **16.3**

18.2.2 G   FCA

The provisions of *COBS* in the table are unlikely to be relevant to any *energy market activity* or *oil market activity* carried on by a *firm* which is *MiFID or equivalent third country business*:

COBS	Description
5	Distance communications

COBS	Description
7	Insurance mediation
13	Preparing product information
14.2	Providing product information to clients
15	Cancellation
17	Claims handling for long-term care insurance
18.1	Trustee firms' regime
18.3	Corporate finance business
18.4	Stock lending activity
19	Pensions – supplementary provisions
20	With-profits

Energy market activity and oil market activity – non-MiFID business

18.2.3 R   FCA

Only the *COBS* provisions in the table apply to *energy market activity* or *oil market activity* carried on by a *firm* which is not:

(1)   *MiFID or equivalent third country business*; or

(2)   *energy market activity* or *oil market activity* set out in **COBS 18.2.4 R**.

COBS	Description
1	Application
2.1.1	Acting honestly, fairly and professionally
2.4	Agent as client and reliance on others
3	Client categorisation
4	Communication to clients including financial promotions, but only in relation to *communicating* or *approving* a *financial promotion*
5.2	E-commerce
11.8	Recording telephone conversations and electronic communications
12	Investment research
16.2	Occasional reporting

Energy market activity and oil market activity – dealings with or through authorised persons

18.2.4 R   FCA

Only the *COBS* provisions in the table apply to *energy market activity* or *oil market activity* carried on by a *firm* which is not *MiFID or equivalent third country business* but which, if the *firm* were not *authorised*, would not be a *regulated activity* because of article 16 of the *Regulated Activities Order* (Dealing in contractually based investments) or article 22 of the *Regulated Activities Order* (Deals with or through authorised persons etc.).

COBS	Description
1	Application
2.4	Agent as client and reliance on others
4.12	Unregulated collective investment schemes
5.2	E-commerce

Other non-MiFID business related to commodity or exotic derivative instruments

18.2.5 R   FCA

COBS applies as set out in the table to *firms* in respect of activities referred to in the *general application rule* related to:

(1)   *commodity futures*; or

(2)   *commodity options*; or

(3)   *contracts for differences* related to an underlying *commodity*; or

(4)   other *futures* or *contracts for differences* which are not related to *commodities*, financial instruments or cash;

which is not *MiFID or equivalent third country business* and *energy market activity* or *oil market activity*.

> **Application of COBS to other non-MiFID business related to commodity derivative instruments**
>
> All of *COBS* applies, except **COBS 18.2.6 R** to **COBS 18.2.9 E** applies instead of **COBS 11.2** (Best execution)

Best execution for other non-MIFID business related to commodity and exotic derivative instruments

18.2.6 R   FCA

A *firm* that *executes* a *customer order* in the course of carrying out activities referred to in **COBS 18.2.5 R** must provide best execution.

Exceptions to best execution

18.2.7 R   FCA

The duty to provide best execution does not apply where:
(1)   the *firm* has agreed with a *professional client* that it does not owe a duty of best execution to him; or
(2)   the *firm* relies on another *person* to whom it passes a *customer order* for *execution* to provide best execution, but only if it has taken reasonable care to ensure that he will do so.

Providing best execution

18.2.8 R   FCA

To provide best execution, a *firm* must:
(1)   take reasonable care to ascertain the price which is the best available for the *customer order* in the relevant market at the time for transactions of the kind and size concerned; and
(2)   *execute* the *customer order* at a price which is no less advantageous to the *customer*, unless the *firm* has taken reasonable steps to ensure that it would be in the *customer's* best interests not to do so.

18.2.9 E   FCA
(1)   In order to take reasonable care to ascertain the price which is the best available, a *firm*:
      (a)   should disregard any *charges* and *commission* made by it or its agents that are disclosed to the *customer* under **COBS 6.1.9 R** (Information about costs and associated charges);
      (b)   need not have access to competing exchanges, or to all, or a minimum number of, available price sources; but if a *firm* can access prices displayed by different exchanges and trading platforms and make a direct and immediate comparison, it should *execute* the *customer order* at the best price available to the firm on such exchanges or trading platforms, if this is in the best interests of the *customer*;
      (c)   should pass on to the *customer* the price at which it *executes* the transaction to meet the *customer order*; and
      (d)   should not take a *mark-up or mark-down* from the price at which it *executes* the *customer order*.
(2)   Compliance with (1) may be relied on as tending to establish compliance with the requirement to take reasonable care to ascertain the price which is the best available for the *customer order* (see **COBS 18.2.8 R (1)**)
(3)   Contravention of (1) may be relied on as tending to establish contravention of the requirement to take reasonable care to ascertain the price which is the best available for the *customer order* (see **COBS 18.2.8 R (1)**)

18.3   CORPORATE FINANCE BUSINESS

Corporate finance business – MiFID business

18.3.1 R   FCA

The provisions of *COBS* in the table do not apply in respect of any *corporate finance business* carried on by a *firm* which is *MiFID or equivalent third country business*:

COBS	Description
6.1A	Adviser charging and remuneration
6.1B	Retail investment product provider requirements relating to adviser charging and remuneration
6.2A	Describing advice services
6.3	Disclosing information about services, fees and commission – packaged products
6.4	Disclosure of charges, remuneration and commission

COBS	Description
9.4	Suitability reports
9.6	Special rules for providing basic advice on a stakeholder product
11.6	Use of dealing commission
11.8	Recording telephone conversations and electronic communications
16.3.9	Guidance on contingent liability transaction
16.5	Quotations for surrender values
16.6	Life insurance contracts – communications to clients
16 Annex 1 R (1) 14	Information to be provided in accordance with **COBS 16.2.1 R** and **16.3**

18.3.2 G   FCA

The provisions of *COBS* in the table are unlikely to be relevant to any *corporate finance business* carried on by a *firm* which is *MiFID or equivalent third country business*:

COBS	Description
5	Distance communications, except in relation to *distance contracts* concluded with *consumers*
7	Insurance mediation
13	Preparing product information
14.2	Providing product information
15	Cancellation, except cancellation and withdrawal rights in relation to *distance contracts* concluded with *consumers*
17	Claims handling for long-term care insurance
18.1	Trustee firms' regime
18.2	Energy market activity and oil market activity
18.4	Stock lending activity
19	Pensions – supplementary provisions
20	With-profits

Corporate finance business – non-MiFID business

18.3.3 R   FCA

Only the provisions of *COBS* in the table apply to *corporate finance business* carried on by a *firm* which is not *MiFID or equivalent third country business*.

COBS	Description
1	Application
2.1.1	Acting honestly, fairly and professionally
2.3	Inducements
2.4	Agent as client and reliance on others
3	Client categorisation
4	Communication to clients including financial promotions, except **COBS 4.5–COBS 4.11**
5.1	The information and other requirements of the Distance Marketing Directive, but only in relation to *distance contracts* concluded with *consumers*
5.2	E-commerce
11.7	Personal account dealing
12	Investment research
15	Cancellation, but only in relation to *distance contracts* concluded with *consumers*

18.3.4 G   FCA

COBS 15 (Cancellation) is likely to be of limited application to *corporate finance business*. *Distance contracts* concluded with *consumers* in the course of *corporate finance business* will be exempt from **COBS 15** if the price of the financial service is dependent on fluctuations in the financial market outside the *firm's* control.

18.4   STOCK LENDING ACTIVITY

18.4.1 R   FCA

The provisions of *COBS* in the table do not apply in relation to any *stock lending activity* carried on by a *firm* which is *MiFID or equivalent third country business*:

COBS	Subject
6.1A	Adviser charging and remuneration
6.1B	Retail investment product provider requirements relating to adviser charging and remuneration
6.2A	Describing advice services
6.3	Disclosing information about services, fees and commission – packaged products
6.4	Disclosure of charges, remuneration and commission
9.4	Suitability reports
9.6	Special rules for providing basic advice on a stakeholder product
11.6	Use of dealing commission
16.3.9	Guidance on contingent liability transaction
16.5	Quotations for surrender values
16.6	Life insurance contracts – communications to clients
16 Annex 1 R (1) 14	Information to be provided in accordance with **COBS 16.2.1 R** and **16.3**

18.4.2 G   FCA

The provisions of *COBS* in the table are unlikely to be relevant in relation to any *stock lending activity* carried on by a firm which is *MiFID or equivalent third country business*:

COBS	Description
5	Distance communications, except in relation to *distance contracts* concluded with *consumers*
7	Insurance mediation
13	Preparing product information
14.2	Providing product information
15	Cancellation, except cancellation and withdrawal rights in relation to *distance contracts* concluded with *consumers*
17	Claims handling for long-term care insurance
18.1	Trustee firms' regime
18.2	Energy market activity and oil market activity
18.3	Corporate finance business
19	Pensions – supplementary provisions
20	With-profits

18.5   RESIDUAL CIS OPERATORS, UCITS MANAGEMENT COMPANIES AND AIFMS

Application

18.5.1 R   FCA

Subject to **COBS 18.5.1A R**, this section applies to a *firm* which is:
(1)   a *UCITS management company*;
(2)   a *full-scope UK AIFM*;
(3)   a *small authorised UK AIFM*;
(4)   a *residual CIS operator*; or
(5)   an *incoming EEA AIFM branch*.

18.5.1A R   FCA

COBS 18.5.3 R (2) and **COBS 18.5.5 R** to **COBS 18.5.18 E** do not apply to a *small authorised UK AIFM* of an *unauthorised AIF* which is not a *collective investment scheme*.

18.5.1B R   FCA

Only **COBS 18.5.1 R** to **COBS 18.5.4A R**, **COBS 18.5.4C R** to **COBS 18.5.4D G** and **COBS 18.5.10A R** apply to a *full-scope UK AIFM*, with the exception that **COBS 18.5.10A R** does not apply to a *full-scope UK AIFM* of an *unauthorised AIF* which is not a *collective investment scheme*. **COBS 18.5.4C R** to **COBS 18.5.4D G** only apply to a *full-scope UK AIFM* that is an *internally managed AIF*.

Application or modification of general COBS rules

18.5.2 R   FCA

A *firm* when it is carrying on *scheme management activity* or, for an AIFM, AIFM investment management functions:

(1)   must comply with the *COBS rules* specified in the table, as modified by this section; and

(2)   need not comply with any other *rule* in *COBS*.

18.5.2-A G   FCA

For activities carried on by *firms* which are not *scheme management activities* or, for an AIFM, AIFM investment management functions, the *COBS rules* apply under the general application rule, as modified in **COBS 1 ANNEX 1**.

Table: Application of conduct of business rules

This table belongs to **COBS 18.5.2 R**

Chapter, section, rule	Full-scope UK AIFM	Small authorised UK AIFM and a residual CIS operator	Incoming EEA AIFM branch	UCITS management company
1	Applies	Applies	Applies	Applies
2.1.1	Does not apply	Applies	Does not apply	Applies
2.1.4	Applies	Does not apply	Applies	Does not apply
2.3	Does not apply	Applies	Does not apply	Applies
2.4	Does not apply	Applies	Does not apply	Applies
4.2.1-4.2.3	Applies	Applies	Applies	Applies
5.2	Applies	Applies	Applies	Applies
6.1G.2	Applies	Applies	Applies	Applies
11.2	Applies as modified by **COBS 18.5.4A R**	Applies to a small authorised UK AIFM of an authorised AIF. Applies (as modified by **COBS 18.5.4 R**) to a small authorised UK AIFM of an unauthorised AIF or residual CIS operator	Applies as modified by **COBS 18.5.4A R**	Applies
11.3	Does not apply	Applies	Does not apply	Applies
11.5	Does not apply	Applies as *rules*	Does not apply	Does not apply
11.6	Applies, but as modified by **COBS 18.5.4C R** for *internally managed AIFs*.	Applies	Applies	Applies
11.8	Applies	Applies	Applies	Applies

Chapter, section, rule	Full-scope UK AIFM	Small authorised UK AIFM and a residual CIS operator	Incoming EEA AIFM branch	UCITS management company
16.3	Does not apply	Applies to a small authorised UK AIFM of an unauthorised AIF which is not a *collective investment scheme*, as modified by **COBS 18.5.4B R**. Otherwise does not apply.	Does not apply	Does not apply
18.5	Applies as modified by **COBS 18.5.1B R**	Applies	Applies	Applies

Additional application of COBS rules for management companies

18.5.2A R   FCA

A *management company* must:
(1)   in addition to complying with the *COBS rules* specified in **COBS 18.5.2 R**, comply with **COBS 11.7** (Personal account dealing); and
(2)   comply with **COBS 2.3** (Inducements) as modified by **COBS 2.3.2A R**

[**Note:** article 13(1) to 13(4) of the *UCITS implementing Directive*]

General modifications

18.5.3 R   FCA

Where *COBS rules* specified in the table in **COBS 18.5.2 R** apply to a *firm* carrying on *scheme management activities* or, for an AIFM, AIFM investment management functions, the following modifications apply:
(1)   subject to (2), references to *customer* or *client* are to be construed as references to any fund in respect of which the *firm* is acting or intends to act, and with or for the benefit of which the relevant activity is to be carried on;
(2)   in the case of a small authorised UK AIFM of an unauthorised AIF or a residual CIS operator, when a *firm* is required by the rules in *COBS* to provide information to, or obtain consent from, a *customer* or *client*, the *firm* must ensure that the information is provided to, or consent obtained from, an investor or a potential investor in the fund as the case may be;
(3)   references to the service of *portfolio management* in **COBS 11.2** (Best execution), **11.3** (Client order handling) and **COBS 11.5** (Record keeping: client orders and transactions) are to be read as references to the management by a *firm* of *financial instruments* held for or within the fund; and
(4)   references to *investment firm* in **COBS 11.5** are to be read as references to small authorised UK AIFM or residual CIS operator.

Modification of best execution

18.5.4 R   FCA

The best execution provisions applying to a small authorised UK AIFM of an unauthorised AIF or a residual CIS operator do not apply in relation to a fund whose fund documents include a statement that best execution does not apply in relation to the fund and in which:
(1)   no investor is a *retail client*; or
(2)   no current investor in the fund was a *retail client* when it invested in the fund.

18.5.4A R   FCA

Only the following provisions in **COBS 11.2** apply to a full-scope UK AIFM:
(1)   **COBS 11.2.5 G**;
(2)   **COBS 11.2.17 G**;
(3)   **COBS 11.2.23A R**, but references to management company should be read as references to an AIFM and references to *unitholders* read as references to investors. This obligation only applies for the execution policy required under article 27(3) of the AIFMD level 2 regulation (Execution of decisions to deal on behalf of the managed AIF);

(4)   **COBS 11.2.24 R**;

(5)   **COBS 11.2.25 R (1)** and **COBS 11.2.26 R**, but only where an AIF itself has a governing body which can provide prior consent; and

(6)   **COBS 11.2.27 R**, but only regarding the obligation on an AIFM to notify the AIF of any material changes to their order execution arrangements or execution policy.

Modification of periodic reporting requirements

18.5.4B R   FCA

A small authorised UK AIFM of an unauthorised AIF which is not a *collective investment scheme* must comply with **COBS 16.3** (Periodic reporting) with references to *managing investments* to be construed as providing AIFM investment management functions.

Modification of dealing commission rules for internally managed AIFs

18.5.4C R   FCA

Only **COBS 11.6.1 G** to **COBS 11.6.11 G** apply to a *full-scope UK AIFM* that is an *internally managed AIF* and references to an *investment manager* in **COBS 11.6** are to be read as including an *internally managed AIF* which manages *designated investments* on its own account and references to a *customer order* as a decision by an *internally managed AIF* to execute a transaction for these purposes.

18.5.4D G   FCA

To be an *investment manager*, a *person* needs to manage *designated investments* on a discretionary or non-discretionary basis under the terms of a management agreement. The purpose of **COBS 18.5.4C R** is to modify **COBS 11.6.1 G** to **COBS 11.6.11 G** so that these provisions apply to a *full-scope UK AIFM* that is an *internally managed AIF* because such *firms* manage *designated investments* on their own account rather than under the terms of a management agreement.

Scheme documents for an unauthorised fund

18.5.5 R   FCA

A small authorised UK AIFM of an unauthorised AIF or a residual CIS operator must not accept a *retail client* as an investor in the fund unless it has taken reasonable steps to offer and, if requested, provide to the potential investor, fund documents which adequately describe how the fund is governed.

Distance marketing

18.5.5A G   FCA

Firms should also be aware that if they are carrying on distance marketing activity from an establishment in the *UK*, with or for a *consumer* in the *UK* or another *EEA State*, **COBS 5.1** applies specific requirements for that activity.

Format and content of fund documents

18.5.6 G   FCA

The fund documents required under **COBS 18.5.5 R** may consist of any number of *documents* provided that it is clear that collectively they constitute the fund documents and provided the use of several *documents* in no way diminishes the significance of any of the statements which are required to be given to the potential investor.

18.5.7 G   FCA

The fund documents of an unauthorised fund managed by a small authorised UK AIFM or a residual CIS operator (if those fund documents exist) should make it clear that if an investor is reclassified as a *retail client*, this reclassification will not affect certain activities of the firm. In particular, despite such a reclassification, the *firm* will not be required to comply with the best execution provisions. It should be noted that there is no requirement that fund documents must be produced by a small authorised UK AIFM of an unauthorised fund or a residual CIS operator.

18.5.8 R   FCA

Where the fund is an unauthorised fund managed by a small authorised UK AIFM or a residual CIS operator and no current investor in the fund was a *retail client* when it invested in the fund, the fund documents must include a statement that:

(1)   explains that if an investor is reclassified as a *retail client* subsequent to investing in the fund, then the *firm* may continue to treat all investors in the fund as though they were not *retail clients*;

(2)   explains that if an investor is reclassified as a *retail client* subsequent to investing in the fund, then the modification of best execution (see **COBS 18.5.4 R**) will continue to apply to that fund; and

(3)   explains that, in the event of such a reclassification, the *firm* will not be required to provide best execution in relation to the fund.

18.5.9 G   FCA

A small authorised UK AIFM of an unauthorised AIF or a residual CIS operator will still have to comply with other *COBS* provisions as a result of the reclassification of an investor as a *retail client*. For example, the *firm* must provide *periodic statements* to investors who are *retail clients* in an unauthorised fund (see the rule on periodic statements for an unauthorised fund (**COBS 18.5.11 R**)).

Adequate information

18.5.10 E   FCA

(1)   In order to provide adequate information to describe how the fund is governed, a small authorised UK AIFM of an unauthorised AIF or a residual CIS operator should include in the fund documents a provision about each of the items of relevant information set out in the following table (Content of fund documents).

(2)   Compliance with (1) may be relied on as tending to establish compliance with **COBS 18.5.5 R**.

(3)   Contravention of (1) may be relied on as tending to establish contravention of **COBS 18.5.5 R**.

Table: Content of fund documents
Content of fund documents

The fund documents should include provision about:
(1)   Regulator The *firm* statutory status in accordance with **GEN 4 ANNEX 1 R** (Statutory status disclosure);
(2)   Services the nature of the services that the *firm* will provide;

(3)   Payments for services
details of any payment for services payable by the fund or from the property of the fund or investors in the fund to the *firm*, including where appropriate:
    (a)   the basis of calculation;
    (b)   how it is to be paid and collected;
    (c)   how frequently it is to be paid; and
    (d)   whether or not any other payment is receivable by the *firm* (or to its knowledge by any of its *associates*) in connection with any transactions effected by the *firm* with or for the fund, in addition to or in lieu of any fees;

(4)   Commencement when and how the *firm* is appointed;
(5)   Accounting the arrangements for accounting to the fund or investors in the fund for any transaction effected;
(6)   Termination method how the appointment of the *firm* may be terminated;
(7)   Complaints procedure how to complain to the *firm* and a statement that the investors in the fund may subsequently complain direct to the *Financial Ombudsman Service*;
(8)   Compensation whether or not compensation may be available from the *compensation scheme* should the *firm* be unable to meet its liabilities, and information about any other applicable compensation scheme; and, for each applicable compensation scheme, the extent and level of cover and how further information can be obtained;
(9)   Investment objectives the investment objectives for the portfolio of the fund;

(10)   Restrictions
    (a)   any restrictions on:
        (i)   the types of *investments* or property which may be included in the portfolio of the fund;
        (ii)   the markets on which *investments* or property may be acquired for the portfolio of the fund;
        (iii)   the amount or value of any one *investment* or asset, or on the proportion of the portfolio of the fund which any one *investment* or asset or any particular kind of *investment* or asset may constitute; or

The fund documents should include provision about:

(b)   that there are no such restrictions;

(11)   Holding fund assets

     (a)   if it is the case, that the *firm* will:

         (i)   hold *money* on behalf of the fund or be the *custodian* of *investments* or other property of the fund; or

         (ii)   arrange for some other *person* to act in either capacity and, if so, whether that *person* is an associate of the *firm* identifying that *person* and describing the nature of any association; and

     (b)   in either case:

         (i)   how any *money* is to be deposited;

         (ii)   the arrangements for recording and separately identifying registrable *investments* of the fund and, where the registered holder is the *firm's* own nominee, that the *firm* will be responsible for the acts and omissions of that *person*;

         (iii)   the extent to which the *firm* accepts liability for any loss of the *investment* of the fund;

         (iv)   the extent to which the *firm* or any other *person* mentioned in (11)(a)(ii), may hold a lien or security interest over *investments* of the fund;

         (v)   where *investments* of the fund will be registered collectively in the same name, a statement that the entitlements of the fund may not be identifiable by separate certificates or other physical documents of title, and that, should *the firm* default, any shortfall in *investments* of the fund registered in that name may be shared proportionately among all funds and any other *customers* of *the firm* whose *investments* are so registered;

         (vi)   whether or not *investments* or other property of the fund can be lent to, or deposited by way of collateral with, a third party and whether or not *money* can be borrowed on behalf of the fund against the security of those *investments* or property and, if so, the terms upon which they may be lent or deposited;

         (vii)   the arrangements for accounting to the fund for *investments* of the fund, for income received (including any interest on *money* and any income earned by lending *investments* or other property) of the fund, and for rights conferred in respect of *investments* or other property of the fund;

         (viii)   the arrangements for determining the exercise of any voting rights conferred by *investments* of the fund; and

         (ix)   where *investments* of the fund may be held by an eligible *custodian* outside the *United Kingdom*, a general statement that different settlement, legal and regulatory requirements, and different practices relating to the segregation of those *investments*, may apply;

(12)   Clients' money outside the United Kingdom
if it is the case, that *the firm* may hold the *money* of the fund in a *client bank account* outside the *United Kingdom*;

(13)   Exchange rates
if a liability of the fund in one currency is to be matched by an asset in a different currency, or if the services to be provided to *the firm* for the fund may relate to an *investment* denominated in a currency other than the currency in which the *investments* of the fund are valued, a warning that a movement of exchange rates may have a separate effect, unfavourable or favourable, on the gain or loss otherwise made on the *investments* of the fund;

(14)   Stabilised investments
if it is the case, that *the firm* is to have the right under the fund *documents* to effect transactions in *investments* the prices of which may be the subject of stabilisation;

(15)   Conflict of interest and material interest
if it is the case, that the *firm* is to have the right under the agreement or instrument constituting the fund to effect transactions on behalf of the fund in which *the firm* has directly or indirectly a material interest (except for an interest arising solely from the investment of the *firm* as agent for the fund), or a relationship of any description with another party which may involve a conflict with *the firm* duty to the fund, together with a disclosure of the nature of the interest or relationship;

The fund documents should include provision about:

(16) Use of dealing commission
if *the firm* receives goods or services in addition to the *execution* of its *customer orders* in accordance with the section on the use of dealing commission, the prior disclosure required by the *rule* on prior disclosure (see **COBS 11.6.2 R**);

(17) Acting as principal
if it is the case, that *the firm* may act as *principal* in a transaction with the fund;

(18) Stock lending
if it is the case, that *the firm* may undertake *stock lending activity* with or for the fund specifying the type of assets of the fund to be lent, the type and value of *relevant collateral* from the borrower and the method and amount of payment due to the fund in respect of the lending;

(19) Transactions involving contingent liability investments

    (a) if it is the case, that the agreement or instrument constituting the fund allows *the firm* to effect transactions involving *contingent liability investments* for the account of the portfolio of the fund;

    (b) if applicable, whether there are any limits on the amount to be committed by way of margin and, if so, what those limits are; and

    (c) if applicable, that *the firm* has the authority to effect transactions involving *contingent liability investments* otherwise than under the rules of a *recognised investment exchange* and in a contract traded thereon;

(20) Periodic statements

    (a) the frequency of any *periodic statement* (this should not be less than once every 12 months) except where a *periodic statement* is not required (see **COBS 18.5.13 R**); and

    (b) whether those statements will include some measure of performance, and, if so, what the basis of that measurement will be;

(21) Valuation
the bases on which assets comprised in the portfolio of the fund are to be valued;

(22) Borrowings
if it is the case, that *the firm* may supplement the funds in the portfolio of the fund and, if it may do so:

    (a) the circumstances in which *the firm* may do so;

    (b) whether there are any limits on the extent to which *the firm* may do so and, if so, what those limits are; and

    (c) any circumstances in which such limits may be exceeded;

(23) Underwriting commitments
if it is the case, that *the firm* may for the account of the portfolio of the fund underwrite or sub-underwrite any issue or offer for sale of *securities*, and:

    (a) whether there are any restrictions on the categories of *securities* which may be underwritten and, if so, what these restrictions are; and

    (b) whether there are any financial limits on the extent of the underwriting and, if so, what these limits are;

(24) Investments in other funds
whether or not the portfolio may invest in funds either managed or advised by the *firm* or by an *associate* of *the firm* or in a fund which is not a *regulated collective investment scheme*;

(25) Investments in securities underwritten by the firm
whether or not the portfolio may contain *securities* of which any issue or offer for sale was underwritten, managed or arranged by *the firm* or by an *associate* of *the firm* during the preceding 12 months.

Application of COBS 18.5.10E to a full-scope UK AIFM

18.5.10A R   FCA

A full-scope UK AIFM which markets an unauthorised AIF to a *retail client* must, in addition to providing the information in **FUND 3.2**, take reasonable steps to offer and, if requested, provide to that potential investor information about the following items in the **COBS 18.5.10 E** table (content of fund documents):

(1)   (1) (Regulator);
(2)   (4) (Commencement);
(3)   (5) (Accounting);

(4)	(6) (Termination method);
(5)	(7) (Complaints procedure);
(6)	(8) (Compensation);
(7)	(13) (Exchange rates);
(8)	(14) (Stabilised investments);
(9)	(16) (Use of dealing commission);
(10)	(17) (Acting as principal);
(11)	(23) (Underwriting commitments);
(12)	(24) (Investments in other funds); and
(13)	(25) (Investments in securities underwritten by the firm).

Periodic statements for an unauthorised fund

18.5.11 R   FCA

A small authorised UK AIFM of an unauthorised AIF or a residual CIS operator must, subject to the exceptions from the requirement to provide a *periodic statement*, provide to investors in the fund, promptly and at suitable intervals, a statement in a *durable medium* which contains adequate information on the value and composition of the portfolio of the fund at the beginning and end of the period of the statement.

Promptness, suitable intervals and adequate information

18.5.12 E   FCA
(1)	A small authorised UK AIFM of an unauthorised AIF or a residual CIS operator should act in accordance with the provisions in the right hand column of the periodic statements table (see **COBS 18.5.15E**) to fulfil the requirement to prepare and issue *periodic statements* indicated in the left hand column against these provisions.
(2)	Compliance with (1) may be relied on as tending to establish compliance with the requirement to prepare and issue *periodic statements*.
(3)	Contravention of (1) may be relied on as tending to establish contravention of the requirement to prepare and issue *periodic statements*.

Exceptions from the requirement to provide a periodic statement

18.5.13 R   FCA
(1)	A small authorised UK AIFM of an unauthorised AIF or a residual CIS operator need not provide a *periodic statement*:	
	(a)	
	(i)	to an investor in the fund who is a *retail client* ordinarily resident outside the *United Kingdom*; or
	(ii)	to an investor in the fund who is a *professional client*; if the investor has so requested or *the firm* has taken reasonable steps to establish that the investor does not wish to receive it; or
	(b)	if it would duplicate a statement to be provided by someone else.
(2)	For a *firm* acting as an *outgoing ECA provider*, the exemption for *retail client* investors ordinarily resident outside the *United Kingdom* applies only to an investor in the fund who is a *retail client* ordinarily resident outside the *EEA*.	

Record keeping requirements

18.5.14 R   FCA

A small authorised UK AIFM of an unauthorised AIF or a residual CIS operator must make a copy of any *periodic statement* it has provided in accordance with the requirement to prepare and issue *periodic statements* to investors in the fund. The record must be retained for a minimum period of three years.

18.5.15 E   FCA

Table: Periodic statements
This table belongs to **COBS 18.5.12 E**.

Periodic statements			
Suitable intervals	(1)	A *periodic statement* should be provided at least:	
		(a)	six-monthly; or
		(b)	once in any other period, not exceeding 12 months, which has been mutually agreed between *the firm* and the investor in the fund.
Adequate information	(2)	(a)	A *periodic statement* should contain:

Periodic statements

	(i)	(A)	The information set out in the table of general contents of a *periodic statement*;
		(B)	where the portfolio of the fund includes uncovered open positions in *contingent liability investments*, the additional information in the table listing the contents of a *periodic statement* (see **COBS 18.5.18 E**) in respect of contingent liability investments; or
	(ii)		such information as an investor who is a *retail client* ordinarily resident outside the *United Kingdom*, or a *professional client*, has on his own initiative agreed with *the firm* as adequate.
(b)			For a *firm* acting as an *outgoing ECA provider*, the words 'United Kingdom' is replaced by 'EEA'

18.5.16 G   FCA

Examples of uncovered open positions include:

(1)   selling a call *option* on an *investment* not held in the portfolio;

(2)   unsettled sales of call *options* on currency in amounts greater than the portfolio's holding of that currency in cash or in *readily realisable investments* denominated in that currency; and

(3)   transactions having the effect of *selling* an index to an amount greater than the portfolio's holdings of *investments* included in that index.

18.5.17 E   FCA

Table: General contents of a periodic statement
This table belongs to **COBS 18.5.15 E**.

General contents of periodic statements			
1	Contents and value		
	(a)		As at the beginning of the account period, the total value of the portfolio of the fund, being either:
		(i)	the value of the assets comprised in the portfolio on the date as at which the statement provided for the immediately preceding period of account is made up; or
		(ii)	in the case of the first *periodic statement*, the value of the assets comprised in the portfolio on the date on which *the firm* assumed responsibility for the management of the portfolio.
	(b)		As at the end of the account period:
		(i)	the number, description and value of each *investment* held on behalf of the fund;
		(ii)	the amount of cash held on behalf of the fund; and
		(iii)	the total value of the portfolio of the fund.
2	Basis of valuation		
	A statement of the basis on which the value of each *investment* has been calculated and, if applicable, a statement that the basis for valuing a particular *investment* has changed since the previous *periodic statement*. Where any *investments* are shown in a currency other than the usual one used for valuation of the portfolio of the fund, the relevant currency exchange rates must be shown.		
3	Details of any assets loaned or charged		
	(a)		A summary of those *investments* (if any) which were, at the closing date, loaned to any third party and those *investments* (if any) that were at that date charged to secure borrowings made on behalf of the portfolio of the fund; and
	(b)		the aggregate of any interest payments made and income received during the account period in respect of loans or borrowings made during the period.
4	Transactions and changes in composition		
	Except in the case of a portfolio which aims to track the performance of an external index:		
	(a)		a statement that summarises the transactions entered into for the portfolio of the fund during the period; and
	(b)		the aggregate of *money* and a summary of all investments transferred into and out of the portfolio of the fund during the period; and

General contents of periodic statements

    (c)   the aggregate of any interest payments, dividends and other benefits received by *the firm* for the portfolio of the fund during that period.

5   Charges and remuneration
     If not previously advised in writing, a statement for the account period:

    (a)   of the aggregate charges of *the firm* and its *associates*; and

    (b)   of any *remuneration* received by *the firm* or its *associates* or both from a third party in respect of the transactions entered into, or any other services provided, for the portfolio of the fund.

6   Movement in value of portfolio
     A statement of the difference between the value of the portfolio at the closing date and its value at the starting date of the account period, having regard at least, during the account period, to the following:

    (a)   the aggregate of assets received from investors of the fund and added to the portfolio of the fund;

    (b)   the aggregate of the value of assets transferred, or of amounts paid, to the fund;

    (c)   the aggregate income received on behalf of the fund in respect of the portfolio; and

    (d)   the aggregate of realised and unrealised profits or gains and losses attributable to the assets comprised in the portfolio of the fund.

Notes:

For the purposes of Item 1, where the fund is a *property enterprise trust*, it will be sufficient for the *periodic statement* to disclose the number of properties held in successive valuation bands where this is appropriate to the size and composition of the fund, rather than the value of each asset in the portfolio. The valuation bands of over £10m, £5-£10m, £2.5-£5m, £1-£2.5m and under £1m would be appropriate, unless a *firm* could show that different bands were justifiable in the circumstances.

The statement to be provided under Item 6 is not intended to be an indicator of the performance of the portfolio of the fund.

A *firm* may wish to distinguish capital and income, and thereby provide more information than referred to in this table. If the statement includes some measure of performance, the basis of measurement should be stated.

18.5.18 E   FCA

Table: Contents of a periodic statement in respect of contingent liability investments
This table belongs to **COBS 18.5.15 E**.

Contents of a periodic statement in respect of contingent liability investments

(1)   Changes in value
     The aggregate of *money* transferred into and out of the portfolio of the fund during the account period.

(2)   Open positions
     In relation to each open position in the portfolio of the fund at the end of the account period, the unrealised profit or loss to the portfolio of the fund (before deducting or adding any *commission* which would be payable on closing out).

(3)   Closed positions
     In relation to each transaction effected during the account period to close out a position of the fund, the resulting profit or loss to the portfolio of the fund after deducting or adding any *commission*.
     (Instead of the specific detail required by Items 2 or 3, the statement may show the net profit or loss in respect of the overall position of the fund in each contract)

(4)   Aggregate of contents
     The aggregate of each of the following in, or relating to, the portfolio of the fund at the close of business on the valuation date:

    (a)   cash;

    (b)   *collateral* value;

    (c)   management fees; and

    (d)   *commissions* attributable to transactions during the period or a statement that this information has been separately disclosed in writing on earlier statements or confirmations to the investor.

Contents of a periodic statement in respect of contingent liability investments

(5)   Option account valuations
In respect of each open *option* comprising the portfolio of the fund on the valuation date:

(a)   the *share*, *future*, index or other *investment* or asset involved;

(b)   (unless the valuation statement follows the statement for the period in which the *option* was opened) the trade price and date for the opening transaction;

(c)   the market price of the contract; and

(d)   the exercise price of the contract.

Options account valuations may show an average trade price and market price in respect of an *option* series where a number of contracts within the same series have been purchased on behalf of the fund.

18.6   LLOYD'S

Application

18.6.1 R   FCA

This section applies to a *firm* when it carries on *Lloyd's market activities*.

COBS rules that apply to Lloyd's market activities

18.6.2 R   FCA

Only **COBS 3** (Client categorisation) and the *financial promotion rules* apply when a *firm* is carrying out *Lloyd's market activities*.

18.6.3 G   FCA

Firms are reminded that *syndicate* business plans may be used in ways that bring them within the definition of a *financial promotion*.

Definitions and modifications

18.6.4 R   FCA

When a *firm* is carrying on *Lloyd's market activities*, any reference in *COBS* to the term:

(1)   *designated investment* is to be taken to include the following specified investments:
(a)   the *underwriting capacity of a Lloyd's syndicate*;
(b)   *membership of a Lloyd's syndicate*; and
(c)   *rights to or interests in the specified investments* in (a) or (b);

(2)   *designated investment business* is to be taken to include the following *regulated activities*:
(a)   *advising on syndicate participation at Lloyd's*;
(b)   *managing the underwriting capacity of a Lloyd's syndicate as a managing agent at Lloyd's*; and
(c)   *agreeing to carry on the regulated activities* in (a) or (b).

The Principles and Lloyd's market activities

18.6.5 G   FCA

Whilst *COBS* has limited application to *Lloyd's market activities*, firms conducting *Lloyd's market activities* are reminded that they are required to comply with the *Principles*.

18.7   DEPOSITARIES

18.7.1 R   FCA

Only the *COBS* provisions in the table apply to a *depositary* when acting as such, when carrying on business which is not *MiFID or equivalent third country business*:

COBS	Description
2.1	Acting honestly, fairly and professionally
2.3	Inducements, except **COBS 2.3.1 R (2)(B)** and **COBS 2.3.2 R**
4	Communication to clients including financial promotions, but only in relation to *communicating* or *approving* a *financial promotion*
11.7	Personal account dealing

18.8   OPS FIRMS – NON SCOPE BUSINESS

18.8.1 R   FCA

COBS applies to an *OPS firm* when it carries on business which is not *MiFID or equivalent third country business*, with the following modifications:

(1)   references to *client* are to be taken to be references to the OPS or *welfare trust*, as the case may be, in respect of which the *OPS firm* is acting or intends to act, and with or for the benefit of whom the relevant business is to be carried on;

(2)   if an *OPS firm* is required by any *COBS rule* to provide information to, or obtain consent from, a *client*, that *firm* must ensure that the information is provided to, or consent obtained from, each of the trustees of the OPS or *welfare trust* for whom that *firm* is acting; and

(3)   *COBS* is modified by the addition of the *rules* in the table below:

Additional COBS rules applicable to an OPS firm	
COBS	**Description**
16.2.6R (4)	If an *OPS firm* carries on *OPS activity* for an OPS trustee who is a *professional client* and who is habitually resident in the *United Kingdom*, it may rely upon the exceptions in **COBS 16.2.1 R (2)** or **COBS 16.2.6 R (1)** only if it provides a *periodic statement* to the *professional client* containing the information required by **COBS 18.8.2 R**

18.8.2 R   FCA

Where an *OPS firm* conducts *OPS activity* and is obliged to provide a *periodic statement*, the *periodic statement* must contain the information in the table below.

Information to be included in a periodic statement provided by an OPS firm conducting OPS activity	
(1)	Investment objectives
	A statement of any investment objectives governing the mandate of the portfolio of the *occupational pension scheme* as at the closing and starting date of the *periodic statement*.
(2)	Details of any asset loaned or charged
	(a) a summary of any *investments* that were, at the closing date, lent to a third party and any *investments* that were at that date charged to secure borrowings made on behalf of the portfolio; and
	(b) the aggregate of any interest payments made and income received during the account period in respect of loans or borrowings made during that period and a comparison with the previous period.
(3)	*Transactions* and changes in composition
	(a) a summary of the *transactions* entered into for the portfolio during the period and a comparison with the previous period;
	(b) the aggregate of *money* and a summary of all *investments* transferred into and out of the portfolio during the period; and
	(c) the aggregate of any interest payments, dividends and other benefits received by the firm for the portfolio during that period and a comparison with the previous period.
(4)	*Charges* and *remuneration*
	If not previously advised in writing, a statement for the period of account:
	(a) of the aggregate *charges* of the *firm* and its *associates*; and
	(b) of any *remuneration* received by the *firm* or its *associates* or both from a third party in respect of the *transactions* entered into, or any other services provided, for the portfolio.
(5)	Movement in value of portfolio
	A statement of the difference between the value of the portfolio at the closing date of the period of account and its value at the starting date, having regard, during the period of account, to:
	(a) the aggregate of assets received from the *occupational pension scheme* and added to the portfolio;
	(b) the aggregate of the value of assets transferred, or of amounts paid, to the *client*;
	(c) the aggregate income received on behalf of the *client* in respect of the portfolio; and
	(d) the aggregate of realised and unrealised profits or gains and losses attributable to the assets comprised in the portfolio.

18.8.3 R   FCA

COBS 8 (Client agreements) does not apply to an *OPS firm*, where the *OPS firm* is carrying on *designated investment business* as part of its *OPS activity* in relation to an *occupational pension scheme* of which it is a *trustee*.

18.9   ICVCS

18.9.1 R   FCA

(1)   The *financial promotion rules* in *COBS* apply to an *ICVC*, except that COBS 4.13 (UCITS) applies only to an *ICVC* that is a *UCITS scheme*.

(2)   **COBS 14.2** (Providing product information to clients) applies to an *ICVC* that is a *UCITS scheme*.

18.9.2 G   FCA

Firms should note that the *operator* of an *ICVC* when it is undertaking *scheme management activity* will be subject to **COBS 18.5.2 R**.

18.10   UCITS QUALIFIERS, AIFM QUALIFIERS AND SERVICE COMPANIES

18.10.1 R   FCA

The *COBS* provisions in the table apply to a *UCITS qualifier* and a *service company*:

COBS	Description
4	Communications to clients, but only in relation to *communicating* or *approving* a *financial promotion*
5.2	E-Commerce
12.4	Investment Research recommendations: required disclosures

18.10.2 R   FCA

COBS 4 and **COBS 12.4** apply to an AIFM qualifier.

18.11   AUTHORISED PROFESSIONAL FIRMS

18.11.1 R   FCA

COBS applies to an *authorised professional firm*, except that its application in relation to *non-mainstream regulated activities* and *financial promotion* is modified as set out below.

18.11.2 R   FCA

COBS does not apply to an *authorised professional firm* with respect to its *non-mainstream regulated activities*, except that:

(1)   the *fair, clear and not misleading rule* applies;

(2)   the *financial promotion rules* apply as modified below;

(3)   **COBS 7** (Insurance mediation) applies but only if the *designated professional body* of the *firm* does not have rules approved by the *FCA* under section 332(5) of the *Act* that implement articles 12 and 13 of the *Insurance Mediation Directive* and that apply to the *firm*;

(4)   **COBS 8.1.3 R** (Client agreements) applies, except for the requirement to provide information on conflicts of interest; and

(5)   **COBS 5.2** (E-commerce) applies.

18.11.3 R   FCA

The *financial promotion rules* do not apply to an *authorised professional firm* in relation to the communication of a *financial promotion* if:

(1)   the *firm's* main business is the practice of its profession (see IPRU(INV) 2.1.2R(3));

(2)   the *financial promotion* is made for the purposes of and incidental to the promotion or provision by the *firm* of its professional services or its *non-mainstream regulated activities*; and

(3)   the *financial promotion* is not *communicated* on behalf of another *person* who would not be able lawfully to *communicate* the *financial promotion* if he were acting in the course of business;

however, a *firm* may use the exemptions for promoting *unregulated collective investment schemes* in **COBS 4** (Communicating with clients, including financial promotions) if it wishes.

18.11.4 G   FCA

The *rules* on *approving financial promotions* continue to apply.

CHAPTER 19
PENSIONS SUPPLEMENTARY PROVISIONS

19.1   PENSION TRANSFERS, CONVERSIONS, AND OPT-OUTS

Application

[3.67]

19.1.-1 R   FCA

(1)   This section applies to a *firm* that gives advice or a *personal recommendation* about a *pension transfer*, a *pension conversion* or a *pension opt-out*.

(2)   This section does not apply to a *firm* that gives advice or a *personal recommendation* in relation to:

      (a)   a *pension transfer*, *pension conversion* or *pension opt-out* in relation to which the only *safeguarded benefit* is a *guaranteed annuity rate*;

      (b)   a *pension transfer* in which the *retail client* proposes to transfer out of a *defined contribution occupational pension scheme* where that client has no *safeguarded benefits* under that scheme.

Preparing and providing a transfer analysis

19.1.1 R   FCA

If an individual who is not a *pension transfer specialist* gives advice or a *personal recommendation* about a *pension transfer*, a *pension conversion* or *pension opt-out* on a *firm's* behalf, the *firm* must ensure that the recommendation or advice is checked by a *pension transfer specialist*.

19.1.2 R   FCA

A *firm* must:

(1)   compare the benefits likely (on reasonable assumptions) to be paid under a *defined benefits pension scheme* or other pension scheme with *safeguarded benefits* with the benefits afforded by a *personal pension scheme*, *stakeholder pension scheme* or other pension scheme with *flexible benefits*, before it advises a *retail client* to transfer out of a *defined benefits pension scheme* or other pension scheme with *safeguarded benefits*;

(2)   ensure that that comparison includes enough information for the *client* to be able to make an informed decision;

(3)   give the *client* a copy of the comparison, drawing the *client's* attention to the factors that do and do not support the *firm's* advice, in good time, and in any case no later than when the *key features document* is provided; and

(4)   take reasonable steps to ensure that the *client* understands the *firm's* comparison and its advice.

19.1.2A R   FCA

A *firm* need not carry out the comparison described in **COBS 19.1.2 R** if:

(1)   the *retail client* wishes to crystallise benefits immediately after the *pension transfer* or *pension conversion*; and

(2)   the *retail client* is at normal retirement age under the rules of the ceding scheme.

19.1.3 G   FCA

In particular, the comparison should:

(1)   take into account all of the *retail client's* relevant circumstances;

(2)   have regard to the benefits and options available under the ceding scheme and the effect of replacing them with the benefits and options under the proposed scheme;

(3)   explain the assumptions on which it is based and the rates of return that would have to be achieved to replicate the benefits being given up;

(4)   be illustrated on rates of return which take into account the likely expected returns of the assets in which the *retail client's* funds will be invested; and

(5)   where an immediate crystallisation of benefits is sought by the *retail client* prior to the ceding scheme's normal retirement age, compare the benefits available from crystallisation at normal retirement age under that scheme.

19.1.4 R   FCA

When a *firm* compares the benefits likely to be paid under a *defined benefits pension scheme* or other pension scheme with *safeguarded benefits* with the benefits afforded by a *personal pension scheme*, *stakeholder pension scheme* or other pension scheme with *flexible benefits* (**COBS 19.1.2 R (1)**), it must:

(1)   assume that:

> (a) the annuity interest rate is the intermediate rate of return appropri-
> ate for a level or fixed rate of increase annuity in **COBS 13 ANNEX 2**
> 3.1R(6) unless **COBS 19.1.4B R** applies or the rate for annuities in
> payment (if less);

(b) the *RPI* is	2.5%
(c) the average earnings index and the rate for section 21 orders is	4.0%
(d) for benefits linked to the *RPI*, the pre-retirement limited price indexation revaluation is	2.5%

(e) the annuity interest rate for post-retirement *limited price indexation* based on the *RPI* with maximum pension increases less than or equal to 3.5% or with minimum pension increases more than or equal to 3.5% is the rate in (a) above allowing for increases at the maximum rate of pension increase; otherwise it is the rate in (f) below;

(f) the index linked annuity interest rate for pension benefits linked to the *RPI* is the intermediate rate of return in **COBS 13 ANNEX 2 3.1 R (6)** for annuities linked to the *RPI* unless **COBS 19.1.4B R** applies;

(g) the mortality rate used to determine the annuity is based on the year of birth rate derived from each of the Institute and Faculty of Actuaries' Continuous Mortality Investigation tables PCMA00 and PCFA00 and including mortality improvements derived from each of the male and female annual mortality projections models, in equal parts;

(h) for benefits linked to the *CPI*, the pre-retirement *limited price indexation* revaluation is	2.0%

(i) the index linked annuity interest rate for pension benefits linked to the *CPI* is the intermediate rate of return in **COBS 13 ANNEX 2 3.1 R(6)** for annuities linked to the *RPI* plus 0.5% unless **COBS 19.1.4B R** applies in which case it is the annuity rate in **COBS 19.1.4B R** plus 0.5%;

(j) the annuity interest rate for post-retirement *limited price indexation* based on the *CPI* with maximum pension increases less than or equal to 3.0% or with minimum pension increases more than or equal to 3.5% is the rate in (a) above allowing for increases at the maximum rate of pension increase; where minimum pension increases are more than or equal to 3% but less than 3.5% the annuity rate is the rate in (a) above allowing for increases at the minimum rate of pension increase otherwise it is the rate in (i) above;

or use more cautious assumptions;

(2)   calculate the interest rate in deferment; and

(3)   have regard to benefits which commence at difference times.

19.1.4A E   FCA

For any year commencing 6 April, the use of the male and female annual CMI Mortality Projections Models in the series CMI(20YY-1)_M_[1.25%] and CMI(20YY-1)_F_[1.25%], where YY-1 is the year of the Model used, will tend to show compliance with **COBS 19.1.4 R (1)(G)**.

19.1.4B R   FCA

Firms must apply the annual provisions at **COBS 13 ANNEX 2 3.1 R(6)** on a monthly basis in any month where the yields on the 15th of the relevant month would give a rolling 12 month average annuity rate that varies by at least 0.2% from the previous rate.

19.1.5 R   FCA

If a *firm* arranges a *pension transfer* or *pension opt-out* for a *retail client* as an *execution-only transaction*, the *firm* must make, and retain indefinitely, a clear record of the fact that no *personal recommendation* was given to that *client*.

Suitability

19.1.6 G   FCA

When advising a *retail client* who is, or is eligible to be, a member of a *defined benefits occupational pension scheme* or other scheme with *safeguarded benefits* whether to transfer, convert or opt-out, a *firm* should start by assuming that a transfer, conversion or opt-out will not be suitable. A *firm* should only then consider a transfer, conversion or opt-out to be suitable if it can clearly demonstrate, on contemporary evidence, that the transfer, conversion or opt-out is in the *client's* best interests.

19.1.7 G   FCA

When a *firm* advises a *retail client* on a *pension transfer*, *pension conversion* or *pension opt-out*, it should consider the *client's* attitude to risk including, where relevant, in relation to the rate of investment growth that would have to be achieved to replicate the benefits being given up.

19.1.7A G   FCA

When giving a *personal recommendation* about a *pension transfer* or *pension conversion*, a *firm* should clearly inform the *retail client* about the loss of the *safeguarded benefits* and the consequent transfer of risk from the *defined benefits pension scheme* or other scheme with *safeguarded benefits* to the *retail client*, including:

(1)   the extent to which benefits may fall short of replicating those in the *defined benefits pension scheme* or other scheme with *safeguarded benefits*;

(2)   the uncertainty of the level of benefit that can be obtained from the purchase of a future annuity and the prior investment risk to which the *retail client* is exposed until an annuity is purchased with the proceeds of the proposed *personal pension scheme* or *stakeholder pension scheme*; and

(3)   the potential lack of availability of annuity types (for instance, annuity increases linked to different indices) to replicate the benefits being given up in the *defined benefits pension scheme*.

19.1.7B G   FCA

In considering whether to make a *personal recommendation*, a *firm* should not regard a rate of return which may replicate the benefits being given up from the *defined benefits pension scheme* or other scheme with *safeguarded benefits* as sufficient in itself.

19.1.8 G   FCA

When a *firm* prepares a *suitability report* it should include:

(1)   a summary of the advantages and disadvantages of its *personal recommendation*;

(2)   an analysis of the financial implications (if the recommendation is to opt-out); and

(3)   a summary of any other material information.

19.1.9 G   FCA

If a *firm* proposes to advise a *retail client* not to proceed with a *pension transfer*, *pension conversion* or *pension opt-out*, it should give that advice in writing.

19.1.10 G   FCA

Where a *firm* has advised a *retail client* in relation to a *pension transfer*, *pension conversion* or *pension opt-out*, and the *firm* is asked to confirm this for the purposes of section 48 of the Pension Schemes Act 2015, then the *firm* should provide such confirmation as soon as reasonably practicable.

19.2   PERSONAL PENSIONS, FSAVCS AND AVCS

Financial promotions

19.2.1 G   FCA

A *financial promotion* for a *FSAVC* should contain a prominent warning that, as an alternative an *AVC* arrangement exists, and that details can be obtained from the scheme administrator (if that is the case).

Suitability

19.2.2 R   FCA

When a *firm* prepares a *suitability report* it must:

(1)   (in the case of a *personal pension scheme*), explain why it considers the *personal pension scheme* to be at least as suitable as a *stakeholder pension scheme*; and

(2)   (in the case of a *personal pension scheme*, *stakeholder pension scheme* or *FSAVC*) explain why it considers the *personal pension scheme*, *stakeholder pension scheme* or *FSAVC* to be at least as suitable as any facility to make additional contributions to an *occupational pension scheme*, *group personal pension scheme* or *group stakeholder pension scheme* which is available to the *retail client*.

19.2.3 R   FCA

When a *firm* promotes a *personal pension scheme*, including a *group personal pension scheme*, to a group of *employees* it must:

(1)   be satisfied on reasonable grounds that the scheme is likely to be at least as suitable for the majority of the *employees* as a *stakeholder pension scheme*; and

(2)   record why it thinks the promotion is justified.

19.3   PRODUCT DISCLOSURE TO MEMBERS OF OCCUPATIONAL PENSION SCHEMES

19.3.1 R   FCA

(1)   When a *firm* sells, *personally recommends* or arranges the payment of an *AVC* contribution by a member of an *occupational pension scheme* to be secured by a *packaged product* purchased by the scheme trustees, it must give the trustees sufficient information to pass to the relevant member for that member to be able to make informed comparisons between the *AVC* and any alternative *personal pension schemes* and *stakeholder pension schemes* available.

(2)   This *rule* applies to an *AVC* where members' benefits are linked to the earmarked segments of a *life policy* or *scheme*, but it does not apply to an *AVC* where the trustees make pooled investments and have their own arrangements for allocating investment returns to determine members' *AVC* benefits.

19.4   OPEN MARKET OPTIONS

Definitions

19.4.1 R   FCA

In this section:
(1)   'intended retirement date' means:
    (a)   the date (according to the most recent recorded information available to the provider) when the scheme member intends to retire, or to bring the benefits in the scheme into payment, whichever is the earlier; or
    (b)   if there is no such date, the scheme member's state pension age;
(2)   'open market options' means the options available to a scheme member to use the proceeds of a *personal pension scheme*, *stakeholder pension scheme*, *FSAVC*, *retirement annuity* contract or *pension buy-out contract* on the open market; and
(3)   'open market options statement' means the information specified in **COBS 19.4.1A R** which is provided in a *durable medium* to assist the *retail client* to make an informed decision about their open market options.

Contents of open market options statement

19.4.1A R   FCA

An open market options statement must include:
(1)   the fact sheet "Your pension: it's time to choose" available on www.moneyadviceservice-.org.uk or a statement that gives materially the same information;
(2)   a summary of the *retail client's* open market options, which is sufficient for the *client* to be able to make an informed decision about whether to exercise, or to decline to exercise, open market options;
(3)   information about the *retail client's personal pension scheme*, *stakeholder pension scheme*, *FSAVC*, *retirement annuity* contract or *pension buy-out contract* provided by the *firm*, including:
    (a)   the sum of money that will be available to exercise open market options;
    (b)   whether any guarantees apply and, if so, information about how the guarantees work;
    (c)   any other relevant special features, restrictions, or conditions that apply, such as (for *with-profits funds*) any market value reduction conditions in place; and
    (d)   any other information relevant to the exercise of the *retail client's* open market options; and
(4)   a clear and prominent statement about the availability of the pensions guidance including:
    (a)   how to access the pensions guidance and its contact details;
    (b)   that the pensions guidance can be accessed on the internet, telephone, or face to face;
    (c)   that the pensions guidance is a free impartial service to help *consumers* to understand their options at retirement; and
    (d)   a recommendation that the *client* seeks appropriate guidance or advice to understand their options at retirement.

When to send open market options statement and six-week reminder

19.4.2 R   FCA
(1)   If a *retail client* asks a *firm* for a retirement quotation more than four *months* before the *client's* intended retirement date, the *firm* must give the *client* an open market options statement with or as part of its reply, unless the *firm* has given the *client* such a statement in the last 12 *months*.
(2)   If a *firm* does not receive such a request, it must provide a *retail client* with an open market options statement between four and six *months* before the *client's* intended retirement date.

19.4.3 R   FCA

The *firm* must:
(1)   remind the *retail client* about the open market options statement;
(2)   tell the *client* what sum of money will be available to exercise open market options;
(3)   remind the *client* about the availability of the pensions guidance; and
(4)   make a recommendation that the *client* seeks appropriate guidance or advice to understand their options at retirement;

at least six weeks before the *client's* intended retirement date.

19.4.4 R   FCA

If a *retail client* with an open market options tells a *firm* that he is considering, or has decided:

(1)   to discontinue an *income withdrawal* arrangement; or

(2)   to take a further sum of money from his pension to exercise open market options;

the *firm* must give the *client* an open market options statement, unless the *firm* has given the *client* such a statement in the last 12 *months*.

Signposting pensions guidance

19.4.5 R   FCA

(1)   Where a *firm* communicates with a *retail client* about the *retail client's personal pension scheme*, *stakeholder pension scheme*, *FSAVC*, *retirement annuity* contract or *pension buy-out contract* which is provided by the *firm*, unless the circumstances in (2) apply, the *firm* must:

      (a)   refer to the availability of the pensions guidance;

      (b)   offer to provide the *client* with information about how to access the pensions guidance; and

      (c)   [deleted]

      (d)   include a recommendation that the *client* seeks appropriate guidance or advice to understand their options at retirement.

(2)   A *firm* is not required to provide the *client* with the statement required in (1) where:

      (a)   the *firm* communicates with the *client* for a purpose other than:

           (i)   encouraging the *client* to think about their open market options; or

           (ii)   facilitating access to the proceeds of the *client's personal pension scheme*, *stakeholder pension scheme*, *FSAVC*, *retirement annuity* contract or *pension buy-out contract*; or

      (b)   the *client* has already accessed the pensions guidance; or

      (c)   the *client* has already received advice from a *firm* on their open market options, for example from an independent financial adviser; or

      (d)   the *firm* is providing the *client* with an open market options statement or six-week reminder in accordance with **COBS 19.4.2 R**, **COBS 19.4.3 R** or **COBS 19.4.4 R**.

19.4.6 G   FCA

An example of behaviour that is likely to contravene the *client's best interests rule* or *Principle* 6 and may contravene other *Principles* is for a *firm* to actively discourage a *retail client* from using the pensions guidance, for example by:

(1)   leading the *client* to believe that using the pensions guidance is unnecessary or would not be beneficial; or

(2)   obscuring the statement about the availability of the pensions guidance or any other information relevant to the exercise of open market options.

Tax implications

19.4.7 R   FCA

If a *firm* receives an application from a *retail client* to access some or all of the proceeds of a *personal pension scheme*, *stakeholder pension scheme*, *FSAVC*, *retirement annuity* contract or *pension buy-out contract*, the *firm* must provide the *client* with a description of the tax implications before the *client* accesses those proceeds.

19.4.8 R   FCA

A *firm* is not required to provide the information specified in **COBS 19.4.7 R** where it is provided in accordance with **COBS 14.2.1 R**.

19.5   INDEPENDENT GOVERNANCE COMMITTEES (IGCS)

Application

19.5.1 R   FCA

This section applies to a *firm* which operates a *relevant scheme* in which there are at least two *relevant policyholders*.

Requirement to establish an IGC

19.5.2 R   FCA

(1)   Subject to **COBS 19.5.3 R**, a *firm* must establish an *IGC*.

(2)   This *rule* does not apply to a *firm* ('Firm A') if another *firm* in Firm A's *group* has made arrangements under this section for an *IGC* to cover *relevant schemes* operated by Firm A.

Governance advisory arrangements

19.5.3 R   FCA

(1)   If a *firm* considers it appropriate, having regard to the size, nature and complexity of the *relevant schemes* it operates, it may establish a *governance advisory arrangement* instead of an *IGC*.

(2)   If a *firm* has decided to establish a *governance advisory arrangement* rather than an *IGC*, this section (other than **COBS 19.5.9 R (2)**, **COBS 19.5.9 R (3)**, **COBS 19.5.10 G**, **COBS 19.5.11 R** and **COBS 19.5.12 G**) apply to the *firm* by reading references to the *IGC* as references to the *governance advisory arrangement*.

(3)   A *firm* must establish a *governance advisory arrangement* on terms that secure the independence of the *governance advisory arrangement* and its Chair from the *firm*.

19.5.4 G   FCA

(1)   *Firms* with large or complex *relevant schemes* should establish an *IGC*. For the purposes of this section, a *firm* may determine whether it has large *relevant schemes* by reference to:
         (a)   the number of *relevant policyholders* in *relevant schemes*;
         (b)   the funds under management in *relevant schemes*; and
         (c)   the number of employers contributing to *relevant schemes*.

(2)   Examples of features that might indicate complex schemes include:
         (a)   schemes that are operated on multiple information technology systems;
         (b)   schemes that have multiple charging structures;
         (c)   schemes that offer a *with-profits fund*; and
         (d)   the *firm* offers *relevant policyholders* access to investment funds it operates or which are operated by an entity with the same ownership.

Terms of reference for an IGC

19.5.5 R   FCA

A *firm* must include, as a minimum, the following requirements in its terms of reference for an *IGC*:
(1)   the *IGC* will act solely in the interests of *relevant policyholders*;
(2)   the *IGC* will assess the ongoing value for money for *relevant policyholders* delivered by *relevant schemes* particularly, though not exclusively, through assessing:
         (a)   whether default investment strategies within those schemes:
                 (i)   are designed and executed in the interests of *relevant policyholders*;
                 (ii)   have clear statements of aims and objectives;
         (b)   whether the characteristics and net performance of investment strategies are regularly reviewed by the *firm* to ensure alignment with the interests of *relevant policyholders* and that the *firm* takes action to make any necessary changes;
         (c)   whether core scheme financial transactions are processed promptly and accurately;
         (d)   the levels of charges borne by *relevant policyholders*; and
         (e)   the direct and indirect costs incurred as a result of managing and investing, and activities in connection with the managing and investing of, the pension savings of *relevant policyholders*, including transaction costs;
(3)   the *IGC* will raise with the *firm's governing body* any concerns it may have in relation to the value for money for *relevant policyholders* delivered by a *relevant scheme*;
(4)   the *IGC* will escalate concerns as appropriate where the *firm* has not, in the *IGC's* opinion, addressed those concerns satisfactorily or at all;
(5)   the *IGC* will meet, or otherwise make decisions to discharge its duties, using a quorum of at least three members, with the majority of the quorum being independent;
(6)   the Chair of the *IGC* will be responsible for the production of an annual report setting out:
         (a)   the *IGC's* opinion on the value for money delivered by *relevant schemes*, particularly against the matters listed under (2);
         (b)   how the *IGC* has considered *relevant policyholders'* interests;
         (c)   any concerns raised by the *IGC* with the *firm's governing body* and the response received to those concerns;
         (d)   how the *IGC* has sufficient expertise, experience and independence to act in *relevant policyholders'* interests;
         (e)   how each independent member of the *IGC*, together with confirmation that the *IGC* considers these members to be independent, has taken into account **COBS 19.5.12 G**;
         (f)   the arrangements put in place by the *firm* to ensure that the views of *relevant policyholders* are directly represented to the *IGC*.

19.5.6 G   FCA

(1)   An *IGC* is expected to act in the interests of *relevant policyholders* both individually and collectively. Where there is the potential for conflict between individual and collective interests, the *IGC* should manage this conflict effectively. An *IGC* is not expected to deal directly with complaints from individual policyholders.

(2)   The primary focus of an *IGC* should be the interests of *relevant policyholders*. Should a *firm* ask an *IGC* to consider the interests of other members, the *firm* should provide additional resources and support to the *IGC* such that the *IGC's* ability to act in the interests of relevant policyholders is not compromised.

(3)   An *IGC* should assess whether all the investment choices available to *relevant policyholders*, including default options, are regularly reviewed to ensure alignment with the interests of *relevant policyholders*.

(4)   Where an *IGC* is unable to obtain from a *firm*, and ultimately from any other person providing relevant services, the information it requires to assess the matters in **COBS 19.5.5 R (2)**, the *IGC* should explain in the annual report why it has been unable to obtain the information and how it will take steps to be granted access to that information in the future.

(5)   If, having raised concerns with the *firm's governing body* about the value for money offered to *relevant policyholders* by a *relevant scheme*, the *IGC* is not satisfied with the response of the *firm's governing body*, the *IGC* Chair may escalate concerns to the *FCA* if the *IGC* thinks that would be appropriate. The *IGC* may also alert *relevant policyholders* and employers and make its concerns public.

(6)   The *IGC* Chair should raise with the *firm's governing body* any concerns that the *IGC* has about the information or resources that the *firm* provides, or arrangements that the *firm* puts in place to ensure that the views of *relevant policyholders* are directly represented to the *IGC*. If the *IGC* is not satisfied with the response of the *firm's governing body*, the *IGC* Chair may escalate its concerns to the *FCA*, if appropriate. The *IGC* may also make its concerns public.

(7)   The *IGC* should make public the names of those members who are *employees* of the provider *firm*, unless there are compelling reasons not to do so. The *IGC* should consult *employee* members as to whether there are such reasons.

Duties of firms in relation to an IGC

19.5.7 R   FCA

A *firm* must:
(1)   take reasonable steps to ensure that the *IGC* acts and continues to act in accordance with its terms of reference;
(2)   take reasonable steps to provide the *IGC* with all information reasonably requested by the *IGC* for the purposes of carrying out its role;
(3)   provide the *IGC* with sufficient resources as are reasonably necessary to allow it to carry out its role independently;
(4)   have arrangements to ensure that the views of *relevant policyholders* can be directly represented to the *IGC*;
(5)   take reasonable steps to address any concerns raised by the *IGC* under its terms of reference;
(6)   provide written reasons to the *IGC* as to why it has decided to depart in any material way from any advice or recommendations made by the *IGC* to address any concerns it has raised;
(7)   take all necessary steps to facilitate the escalation of concerns by the *IGC* under **COBS 19.5.5 R (4)** and **COBS 19.5.6 G (5)**; and
(8)   make the terms of reference and the annual report of the *IGC* publicly available.

19.5.8 G   FCA
(1)   A *firm* should consider allocating responsibility for the management of the relationship between the *firm* and its *IGC* to a person at the *firm* holding an *FCA significant-influence function*.
(2)   A *firm* should fund independent advice for the *IGC* if this is necessary and proportionate.
(3)   A *firm* should not unreasonably withhold from the *IGC* information that would enable the *IGC* to carry out a comprehensive assessment of value for money.
(4)   A *firm* should have arrangements for sharing confidential and commercially sensitive information with the *IGC*.
(5)   A *firm* should use best endeavours to obtain, and should provide the *IGC* with, information on the costs incurred as a result of managing and investing, and activities in connection with the managing and investing of, the assets of *relevant schemes*, including transaction costs. Information about costs and charges more broadly should also be provided, so that the *IGC* can properly assess the value for money of *relevant schemes* and the funds held within these.
(6)   If a *firm* asks an *IGC* to take on responsibilities in addition to those in **COBS 19.5.5 R**, the *firm* should provide additional resources and support to the *IGC* such that its ability to act within its terms of reference in **COBS 19.5.5 R** is not compromised.
(7)   A *firm* should provide secretarial and other administrative support to the *IGC*. The nature of the support, including how it is provided and by whom, should not conflict with the *IGC's* ability to act independently of the *firm*.
(8)   A *firm* can make the terms of reference for the *IGC* and the annual report of the *IGC* publicly available by placing them on its website and by providing them on request to *relevant policyholders* and their employers.

Appointment of IGC members

19.5.9 R   FCA
(1)   A *firm* must take reasonable steps to ensure that the *IGC* has sufficient collective expertise and experience to be able to make judgements on the value for money of *relevant schemes*.
(2)   A *firm* must recruit independent *IGC* members through an open and transparent recruitment process.

(3)   A *firm* must recruit independent *IGC* members through an open and transparent recruitment process.

     (a)   the *IGC* consists of at least five members, including an independent Chair and a majority of independent members;

     (b)   *IGC* members are bound by appropriate contracts which reflect the terms of reference in **COBS 19.5.5 R**, and on such terms as to secure the independence of independent members;

     (c)   independent *IGC* members who are individuals are appointed for fixed terms of no longer than five years, with a cumulative maximum duration of ten years;

     (d)   individuals acting as the representative of an independent corporate member are appointed to the *IGC* for a maximum duration of ten years;

     (e)   independent *IGC* members who are individuals, including those representing independent corporate members, are not eligible for reappointment to the *IGC* until five years have elapsed, after having served on the *firm's IGC* for the maximum duration of ten years;

     (f)   appointments to the *IGC* are managed to maintain continuity in terms of expertise and experience of the *IGC*.

19.5.10 G   FCA

(1)   The effect of **COBS 19.5.9 R (3)(B)** is that *employees* of the *firm* who serve on an *IGC* should be subject to appropriate contractual terms so that, when acting in the capacity of an *IGC* member, they are free to act within the terms of reference of the *IGC* without conflict with other terms of their employment. In particular, when acting as an *IGC* member, an *employee* will be expected to act solely in the interests of *relevant policyholders* and should be able to do so without breaching any terms of his employment contract.

(2)   An individual may serve on more than one *IGC*.

(3)   A *firm* should replace any vacancies that arise within *IGCs* as soon as possible and, in any event, within six months.

(4)   A *firm* should involve the *IGC* Chair in the appointment and removal of other members, both independent members and *employees* of the *firm*.

(5)   A *firm* should consider indemnifying *IGC* members against any liabilities incurred while fulfilling their duties as *IGC* members.

IGC members who are independent

19.5.11 R   FCA

The *firm*, in appointing independent *IGC* members, must determine whether such a member is independent in character and judgement and whether there are relationships or circumstances which are likely to affect, or could appear to affect, that member's judgement.

19.5.12 G   FCA

(1)   An *IGC* member is unlikely to be considered independent if any of the following circumstances exist:

     (a)   the individual is an *employee* of the *firm* or of a company within the *firm's group* or paid by them for any role other than as an *IGC* member, including participating in the *firm's* share option or performance-related pay scheme;

     (b)   the individual has been an *employee* of the *firm* or of another company within the *firm's group* within the five years preceding his appointment to the *IGC*;

     (c)   the individual has, or had within the three years preceding his appointment, a material business relationship of any description with the *firm* or with another company within the *firm's group*, either directly or indirectly.

(2)   A *firm* may appoint a *body corporate* to an *IGC*, including as Chair. The corporate member should notify the *firm* of the individual who will act as the member's representative on the *IGC*. A *firm* should consider the circumstances of a corporate *IGC* member and any representative of the corporate member with the objective of ensuring that any potential conflicts of interest are managed effectively so that they do not affect the corporate *IGC* member's ability to represent the interests of *relevant policyholders*.

(3)   Should the *firm*, or another company within the *firm's group*, operate a mastertrust, there may be benefits in a trustee of such a mastertrust also being an *IGC* member. If such circumstances exist, an individual or a corporate trustee may be suitable to be an independent *IGC* member, notwithstanding the relationship with the *firm*.

(4)   A *firm* should review on a regular basis whether its independent *IGC* members continue to be independent and take appropriate action if it considers that they are not.

19.6   RESTRICTION ON CHARGES IN QUALIFYING SCHEMES

Application

19.6.1 R   FCA

This section applies to an *operator* of a *qualifying scheme*.

19.6.2 R   FCA

The restrictions on *administration charges* in **COBS 19.6.4 R** do not apply in relation to a *default arrangement* under which, at any time before benefits come into payment, those benefits accruing to the member involve, or involve an option to have, a promise by or to be obtained from a third party about the rate or amount of those benefits.

Express agreement

19.6.3 G   FCA
(1)   In this section, where express agreement is required by a *rule*, the *FCA* would expect *firms* to take active steps to obtain the informed, active consent of the affected member(s) of the *qualifying scheme*, and to have that consent in writing in a *durable medium*, capable of being produced or reproduced when requested by the *FCA*.
(2)   The *FCA* does not consider the following to amount to express agreement (this list is not exhaustive):
     (a)   a member receiving a communication stating that by becoming or continuing to be a member of the scheme, the member has agreed to a particular service;
     (b)   a member being invited to click on a box to opt-out through a website link.

Default arrangements: charging structures and restrictions

19.6.4 R   FCA

A *firm*, for a *default arrangement* within a *qualifying scheme*, may only make, impose or otherwise facilitate payment of an *administration charge* by way of an *accrued rights charge* or a *combination charge structure* where:
(1)   the limits in **COBS 19.6.6 R** are not exceeded; or
(2)   the *firm* has obtained appropriate express agreement to exceed the limits and the following conditions are satisfied:
     (a)   the express agreement contains an acknowledgement by the member that the *administration charge* for the service is likely to exceed the limits;
     (b)   giving such express agreement is not a condition of becoming or remaining a member of the *qualifying scheme*;
     (c)   express agreement has not been given for services which the *operator* must provide under the *regulatory system* or the general law, or which are core services.

19.6.5 G   FCA

The effect of **COBS 19.6.4 R (2)(C)** is that a *firm* may not seek express agreement from a member to charges in excess of the limits for services which are obligatory under law, or form part of the core operation of the scheme. Such core services include, for example, designing and implementing an investment strategy, investing contributions to the scheme (to the extent that this would incur *administration charges*), holding investments relating to scheme members and transferring a member's accrued rights into or out of a *default arrangement*.

19.6.6 R   FCA

The limits on *administration charges* are as follows:
(1)   for a *qualifying scheme* which uses only an *accrued rights charge*, 0.75% of the value of those accrued rights;
(2)   for a *qualifying scheme* which uses a combination charge scheme:
     (a)   for the *flat-fee charge* element, £25 annually;
     (b)   for the *contribution percentage charge* element, 2.5% of the contributions annually;
     (c)   for the associated *accrued rights charge*, the limits as set out in column 2 of the table in **COBS 19.6.7 R**.

19.6.7 R   FCA

This is the table referred to in **COBS 19.6.6 R**.

Contribution percentage charge rate (%)	Accrued rights charge rate (%)
1 or lower	0.6
Higher than 1 but no higher than 2	0.5
Higher than 2 but no higher than 2.5	0.4

Flat-fee charge (£)	Accrued rights charge rate (%)
10 or less	0.6
More than 10 but no more than 20	0.5
More than 20 but no more than 25	0.4

Compliance with the restrictions on charges

19.6.8 E   FCA

(1)   To ensure that *administration charges* are within the limits set out in **COBS 19.6.6 R**:

   (a)   a *firm* should calculate the value of accrued rights in an *accrued rights charge* as the arithmetic mean over a 12-month period of membership of the *qualifying scheme*, using at least four evenly-distributed reference points over that period;

   (b)   a *firm* should calculate the value of contributions in a *contribution percentage charge* over a 12-month period of membership of the *qualifying scheme* of a member's *workplace pension contributions*;

   (c)   for members who have been members of the *qualifying scheme* for a period of less than 12 months, a *firm* should calculate administrative charges on a pro rata basis;

   (d)   the total *administration charges* imposed should not exceed the relevant restriction when measured over a 12-month period. However, where the *qualifying scheme* has been in operation for less than 12 months, and the *firm's* internal processes would involve assessment of *administration charges* before 12 months has elapsed, then for its initial assessment, the *firm* may use a period of up to 18 months.

(2)   Contravention of (1) may be relied on as tending to establish contravention of **COBS 19.6.4 R (1)**.

Consultancy charges

19.6.9 R   FCA

(1)   A *firm* must not make or otherwise facilitate any payment to a third party for advice or services provided pursuant to any agreement made between that third party and an employer for whom the *firm* is operating a *qualifying scheme*, including *consultancy charges*, which would have the effect of reducing the value of the accrued rights of a member of that *qualifying scheme* to whom this section applies.

(2)   The restriction in (1) does not apply where the *firm* has obtained express agreement from the relevant member to such a payment.

19.6.10 G   FCA

COBS 19.6.9 R complements **COBS 6.1C.5C R** and **COBS 6.1D**, which prevent a *firm* which gives advice or provides services within the meaning of those sections to an employer in relation to a *qualifying scheme* from soliciting or accepting *consultancy charges* in relation to those services. **COBS 19.6.9 R** prevents the provider of the *qualifying scheme* from providing such payments and prevents such payments to other advisers who give advice or provide services to employers, such as solicitors and accountants.

19.7   RETIREMENT RISK WARNINGS

Definitions

19.7.1 R   FCA

(1)   "payment out of uncrystallised funds" is an uncrystallised funds pension lump sum within the meaning of paragraph 4A of Schedule 29 of the Finance Act 2004;

(2)   "pension decumulation product" is a product used to access pension savings and includes a facility to enable a *retail client* to make a payment out of uncrystallised funds, a *drawdown pension* or *pension annuity*;

(3)   "pension savings" is the proceeds of the *client's personal pension scheme, stakeholder pension scheme,* or *occupational pension scheme*;

(4)   "retirement risk warnings" are the warnings required to be given to a *retail client* at step 3 of the process specified in this section;

(5)   "risk factors" are the attributes, characteristics, external factors or other variables that increase the risk associated with a *retail client's* decision to access their pension savings using a pension decumulation product;

(6)   "signpost" is the written or oral statement encouraging a *retail client* to use pensions guidance or to take regulated advice to understand their options at retirement which is at step 1 of the process specified in this section.

Application

19.7.2 R   FCA

This section applies to a *firm* communicating with a *retail client* in relation to accessing their pension savings using a pension decumulation product.

19.7.3 R   FCA

This section does not apply:

(1)   to a *firm* giving regulated advice to a *retail client* on options to access their pension savings;

(2)   if the *firm* has already provided the retirement risk warnings to the *retail client* in relation to their decision to access their pension savings and the *firm* has reasonable grounds to believe that the retirement risk warnings are still appropriate for the *client*.

Purpose

19.7.4 G　FCA

(1)　　The purpose of this section is to ensure that a *firm*, which is communicating with a *retail client* about a pension decumulation product, gives appropriate retirement risk warnings at the point when the *retail client* has decided how to access their pension savings.

(2)　　If the *retail client* has not yet decided what to do the *firm* should consider whether it is required to signpost the pensions guidance under COBS 19.4.5R (signposting pensions guidance).

19.7.5 G　FCA

This section amplifies *Principles* 6 and 7, but does not exhaust or restrict what they require. A *firm* will, in any event, need to ensure that its sales processes are consistent with the *Principles* and other *rules*.

19.7.6 G　FCA

An illustration of the steps a *firm* is required to take is set out in **COBS 19 ANNEX 1 G**.

Trigger: when does a firm have to follow the steps?

19.7.7 R　FCA

A *firm* must follow the steps specified in this section at the point when the *retail client* has decided (in principle) to take one of the following actions (and before the action is concluded):

(1)　　buy a pension decumulation product; or

(2)　　vary their *personal pension scheme, stakeholder pension scheme, FSAVC, retirement annuity contract* or *pension buy-out contract* to enable the *client* to:

　　(a)　　access pension savings using a *drawdown pension*; or

　　(b)　　elect to make one-off, regular or ad-hoc payments out of uncrystallised funds; or

(3)　　receive a one-off, regular or ad-hoc payment out of uncrystallised funds; or

(4)　　access their pension savings using a *drawdown pension*.

Step 1: determine whether the client has received guidance or regulated advice

19.7.8 R　FCA

(1)　　The first step is to ask the *retail client* whether they have received pensions guidance or regulated advice:

　　(a)　　if the *client* says that they have, the *firm* must proceed to step 2; or

　　(b)　　if the *client* says that they have not or is unsure, the *firm* must explain that the decision to access pension savings is an important one and encourage the *retail client* to use pensions guidance or to take regulated advice to understand their options at retirement.

(2)　　If, after giving the explanation in **COBS 19.7.8 R (1)(B)**, the *retail client* does not want to access pensions guidance or take regulated advice, the *firm* must proceed to step 2.

Step 2: identify risk factors

19.7.9 R　FCA

Based on how the *retail client* wants to access their pension savings, at step 2 the *firm* must ask the *client* questions to identify whether any risk factors are present.

19.7.10 R　FCA

A *firm* must prepare the questions required by **COBS 19.7.9 R** before taking the steps for the first time, and must keep the questions up to date.

19.7.11 G　FCA

To prepare for step 2, the *firm* should:

(1)　　identify the main risk factors relevant to each pension decumulation product it offers to enable *retail clients* to access their pension savings; and

(2)　　prepare questions to enable it to identify the presence of those risk factors for different *retail clients*.

19.7.12 G　FCA

Examples of the sorts of risk factors which relate to pension decumulation products are:

(1)　　the *client's* state of health;

(2)　　loss of any guarantees;

(3)　　whether the *client* has a partner or dependants;

(4)　　inflation;

(5)　　whether the *client* has shopped around;

(6)　　sustainability of income in retirement;

(7)　　tax implications;

(8)　　charges (if a *client* intends to invest their pension savings);

(9)　　impact on means-tested benefits;

(10)　　debt; and

(11)　　investment scams.

Step 3: provide appropriate retirement risk warnings

19.7.13 R　　FCA

At step 3, a *firm* must give the *retail client* appropriate retirement risk warnings in response to the *client's* answers to the *firm's* questions.

19.7.14 R　　FCA

A *firm* must prepare the retirement risk warnings required by **COBS 19.7.13 R** in good time before taking the steps for the first time, and must keep them up to date.

19.7.15 G　　FCA

If after considering the *retail client's* answers it is unclear whether a risk factor is present, a *firm* should give the *client* the appropriate retirement risk warning.

Communicating the signpost and retirement risk warning

19.7.16 R　　FCA

When communicating the signpost and retirement risk warnings, the *firm* must do so clearly and prominently.

19.7.17 R　　FCA

Whatever the means of communication, the *firm* must ensure that the *retail client* cannot progress to the next stage of the sale unless the relevant signpost or retirement risk warning has been communicated to the *client*.

19.7.18 G　　FCA

For an internet sale, a *firm* should display the required information on a screen which the *retail client* must access and acknowledge as part of the sales process. It would not be sufficient for the information to be accessible only by giving the *client* the option to click on a link or download a document.

Record keeping

19.7.19 R　　FCA

Firms must record whether the *retail client* has received:

(1)　　the retirement risk warnings at step 3 of the process specified in this section;

(2)　　regulated advice; and

(3)　　pensions guidance.FCA

19 ANNEX 1   RETIREMENT RISK WARNINGS – STEPS TO TAKE

This annex belongs to COBS 19.7.

COBS 19 Annex 1G
Retirement risk warnings – steps to take

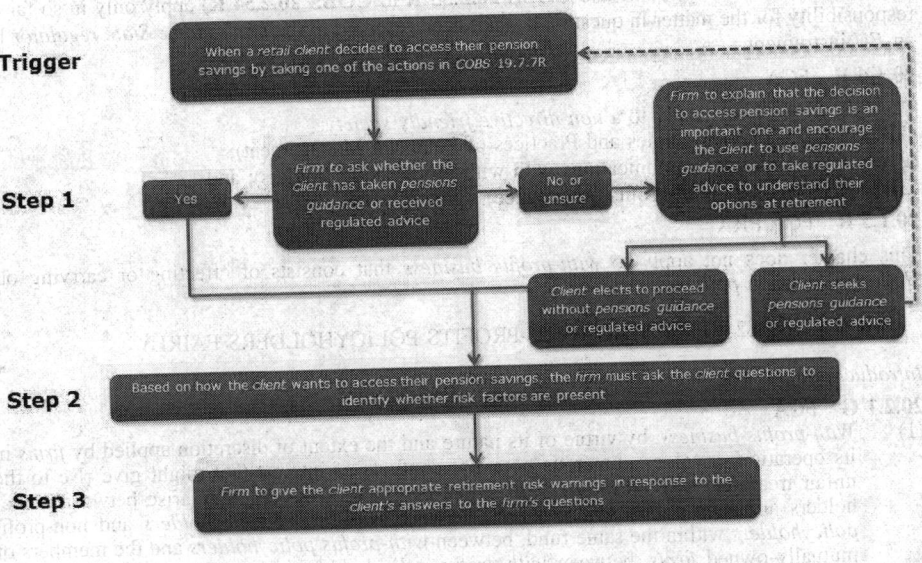

Trigger	When a *retail client* decides to access their pension savings by taking one of the actions in *COBS* 19.7.7R
Step 1	Yes — Firm to ask whether the *client* has taken *pensions guidance* or received regulated advice — No or unsure — Firm to explain that the decision to access pension savings is an important one and encourage the *client* to use *pensions guidance* or to take regulated advice to understand their options at retirement
	Client elects to proceed without *pensions guidance* or regulated advice *Client* seeks *pensions guidance* or regulated advice
Step 2	Based on how the *client* wants to access their pension savings, the *firm* must ask the *client* questions to identify whether risk factors are present
Step 3	Firm to give the *client* appropriate retirement risk warnings in response to the *client's* answers to the *firm's* questions

CHAPTER 20
WITH-PROFITS

20.1   APPLICATION

[3.68]
20.1.1 R   FCA PRA

This chapter applies to a *firm* carrying on *with-profits business*, except to the extent modified in the following *rules*.

20.1.2 R   FCA PRA
(1)   The section on the process for *reattribution* (**COBS 20.2.42 R to COBS 20.2.52 G**):
    (a)   applies to a *firm* that is proposing to make a *reattribution* of its *inherited estate*;
    (b)   but not if, and to the extent that, it would require the *firm* to breach, or would prevent the *firm* from complying with, an order made by a court of competent jurisdiction.
(2)   If a *firm* proposes to seek an order from a court of competent jurisdiction that would allow or require it to act in a way that is contrary to the *rules* on *reattribution* (**COBS 20.2.42 R to COBS 20.2.52 G**) (through, or because of, the exception in (1)(b)), the *firm* must:
    (a)   tell the *appropriate regulator* that that is what it proposes to do;
    (b)   seek the order at the earliest opportunity; and
    (c)   if it wishes to take a step that would be contrary to those *rules* in anticipation of such an order, secure a *waiver* before it does so.

20.1.3 R   FCA

For an *EEA insurer*:
(1)   the *rules* and *guidance* on treating *with-profits policyholders* fairly (**COBS 20.2.1 G to COBS 20.2.41 G** and **COBS 20.2.53 R to COBS 20.2.60 G**) apply only in so far as responsibility for the matter in question has not been reserved to the *firm's Home State regulator* by an *EU* instrument;
(2)   **COBS 20.3** (Principles and Practices of Financial Management) does not apply;
(3)   the *rule* on providing information to *with-profits policy holders* who are *habitually resident* in the *United Kingdom* (**COBS 20.4.4 R**) and the *rule* on production and provision of a *CFPPFM* (**COBS 20.4.5 R**) apply, but the rest of **COBS 20.4** (Communications with with-profits policyholders) does not; and

(4)   the *rule* on production and provision of a *CFPPFM* (**COBS 20.4.5 R**) applies as if a reference to a *firm* was a reference to an *EEA insurer* in relation to any of its *with-profits policy holders* who are *habitually resident* in the *United Kingdom*.

20.1.3A R   PRA

For an *EEA insurer* the *rules* and *guidance* on treating with-profits policyholders fairly (**COBS 20.2.33 G** to **COBS 20.2.35 G** and **COBS 20.2.53 R** to **COBS 20.2.54 R**) apply only in so far as responsibility for the matter in question has not been reserved to the *firm's Home State regulator* by an *EU* instrument.

20.1.4 R   FCA

The following do not apply to a *non-directive friendly society*:
(1)   **COBS 20.3** (Principles and Practices of Financial Management);
(2)   **COBS 20.4** (Communications with with-profits policyholders); and
(3)   **COBS 20.5** (With-profits governance).

20.1.5 R   FCA PRA

This chapter does not apply to *with-profits business* that consists of effecting or carrying out *Holloway sickness policies*.

20.2   TREATING WITH-PROFITS POLICYHOLDERS FAIRLY

Introduction

20.2.1 G   FCA
(1)   *With-profits business*, by virtue of its nature and the extent of discretion applied by *firms* in its operation, involves numerous potential conflicts of interest that might give rise to the unfair treatment of *policyholders*. Potential conflicts of interest may arise between shareholders and *with-profits policyholders*, between *with-profits policyholders* and non-profit *policyholders* within the same fund, between *with-profits policyholders* and the members of mutually-owned *firms*, between *with-profits policyholders* and management, and between different classes of with-profits policyholders, for example those with and without guarantees. The *rules* in this section address specific situations where the risk may be particularly acute.
(2)   *With-profits policyholders* have an interest in the whole and in every part of the *with-profits fund* into which their *policies* are written and from which the amounts payable in connection with their *policies* are to be paid. Those amounts include those required to satisfy their contractual rights and such other amounts as the *firm* is required to pay in order to treat them fairly (including but not limited to the amounts required to satisfy their reasonable expectations).
(3)   The fair treatment of *with-profits policyholders* requires the *firm's* pay-outs on individual *with-profits policies* to be fair (see **COBS 20.2.3 R** et seq.) and, if the *firm* makes a distribution from the *with-profits fund* into which their *policies* are written, the receipt by the *with-profits policyholders* of at least the *required percentage* (see **COBS 20.2.17 R**).

20.2.1A R   FCA

A *firm* must take reasonable care to ensure that all aspects of its operating practice are fair to the interests of its *with-profits policyholders* and do not lead to an undisclosed, or otherwise unfair, benefit to shareholders or to other *persons* with an interest in the *with-profits fund*.

20.2.1B G   FCA
(1)   Notwithstanding that there may not be a *rule* in the remainder of this section addressing a particular aspect of a *firm's* operating practices, *firms* will need to ensure that they take reasonable care to ensure that all aspects of their operating practice comply with **COBS 20.2.1A R**.
(2)   For the avoidance of doubt **COBS 20.2.1A R** does not exhaust or restrict the scope of *Principle* 6. *Firms* will in any event need to ensure that their operating practices are consistent with *Principle* 6.

20.2.1C G   FCA

When considering the provisions in this chapter a *firm* will need to ensure that, if applicable, it complies with the with-profits governance requirements in **COBS 20.5**.

20.2.1D G   FCA

For the purposes of **COBS 20.2.1A R** the *FCA* expects a *firm* to be able to demonstrate that it has taken reasonable care to ensure its operating practices are fair, including being able to produce appropriate evidence to show that it has followed relevant governance procedures.

20.2.2 R   FCA

Neither *Principle* 6 (Customers' interests) nor the *rules* on treating *with-profits policyholders* fairly (**COBS 20.2**) relieve a *firm* of its obligation to deliver each *policyholder's* contractual entitlement.

Amounts payable under with-profits policies

20.2.3 R   FCA

A *firm* must have good reason to believe that its pay-outs on individual *with-profits policies* are fair.

Amounts payable under with-profits policies: Maturity payments

20.2.4 G   FCA

In this section, maturity payments include payments made when a *with-profits policy* provides for a minimum guaranteed amount to be paid.

20.2.5 R   FCA

(1)   Unless a *firm* cannot reasonably compare a maturity payment with a calculated asset share, it must:
     (a)   set a target range for the maturity payments that it will make on:
        (i)   all of its *with-profits policies*; or
        (ii)   each group of its *with-profits policies*;
     (b)   ensure that each target range:
        (i)   is expressed as a percentage of unsmoothed asset share; and
        (ii)   includes 100% of unsmoothed asset share; and
     (c)   manage its *with-profits business*, and the business of each *with-profit fund*, with the aim of making on each *with-profit policy* a maturity payment that falls within the relevant target range.

(2)   Unsmoothed asset share means:
     (a)   the unsmoothed asset share of the relevant *with-profits policy*; or
     (b)   an estimate of the unsmoothed asset share of the relevant *with-profits policy* derived from the unsmoothed asset share of one or more specimen *with-profits policies*, which a *firm* has selected to represent a group, or all, of the *with-profits policies* effected in the same *with-profits fund*.

(3)   A *firm* must calculate unsmoothed asset share by:
     (a)   applying the methods in **INSPRU 1.3.119 R** to **INSPRU 1.3.123 R**;
     (b)   including any amounts that have been added to the *policy* as the result of a distribution from an *inherited estate*; and
     (c)   subject to (d), and where the terms of the *policy* so provide, adding or subtracting an amount that reflects the experience of the *insurance business* in the relevant *with-profits fund*; but
     (d)   if a *with-profits fund* has suffered adverse experience, which results from a *firm's* failure to comply with the *rules* and *guidance* on treating *with-profits policyholders* fairly (**COBS 20.2.1 G** to **COBS 20.2.41 G** and **COBS 20.2.53 R** to **COBS 20.2.60 G**), that adverse experience may only be taken into account if, and to the extent that, in the reasonable opinion of the *firm's governing body*, the amount referred to in (c) cannot be met from:
        (i)   the *firm's inherited estate* (if any); or
        (ii)   any assets attributable to shareholders, whether or not they are held in the relevant *with-profits fund*.

20.2.6 R   FCA

Notwithstanding that a *firm* must aim to make maturity payments that fall within the relevant target range, a *firm* may make a maturity payment that falls outside the target range if it has a good reason to believe that at least 90% of maturity payments on *with-profits policies* in that group have fallen, or will fall, within the relevant target range.

20.2.7 G   FCA

If it is not fair or reasonable to calculate or assess a maturity payment using the *prescribed asset share methodology*, a *firm* may use another methodology to set bonus rates, if that methodology properly reflects its representations to *with-profits policyholders* and it applies that methodology consistently.

20.2.8 R   FCA

A *firm* may make deductions from asset share to meet the cost of guarantees, or the cost of capital, only under a plan approved by its *governing body* and described in its *PPFM*. A *firm* must ensure that any deductions are proportionate to the costs they are intended to offset.

20.2.9 R   FCA

If a *firm* has approved a plan to make deductions from asset share, it must ensure that its planned deductions do not change unless justified by changes in the business or economic environment, or changes in the nature of the *firm's* liabilities as a result of *policyholders* exercising options in their *policies*.

20.2.10 R   FCA

If a *firm* calculates maturity payments using the *prescribed asset share methodology*, it must manage its *with-profits business*, and each *with-profits fund*, with the longer term aim that it will make aggregate maturity payments of 100% of unsmoothed asset share.

Amounts payable under with-profits policies: Surrender payments

20.2.11 G   FCA

A *firm* may use its own methodology to calculate surrender payments, but it should have good reason to believe that its methodology produces a result which, in aggregate across all similar policies, is not less than the result of the *prescribed asset share methodology*. A *firm* might, for example, test the surrender payments on a suitable range of specimen *with-profits policies*.

20.2.12 R   FCA

If a *firm* calculates surrender payments using the *prescribed asset share methodology*, it must first calculate what the surrender payment would be if it was a maturity payment calculated by that methodology.

20.2.13 R   FCA

A *firm* may then make a deduction from unsmoothed asset share if necessary, in the reasonable opinion of the *firm's governing body*, to protect the interests of the *firm's* remaining *with-profits policyholders*.

20.2.14 G   FCA

Amounts that might be deducted include:
(1)   the *firm's* unrecovered costs, including any financing costs incurred in effecting or carrying out the surrendered *with-profits policy* to the date of surrender, including the costs that might have been recovered if the *policy* had remained in force;
(2)   costs that would fall on the *with-profits fund*, if the surrender value is calculated by reference to an assumed *market value* of assets which exceeds the true *market value* of those assets;
(3)   the *firm's* costs incurred in administering the surrender; and
(4)   a fair contribution towards the cost of any contractual benefits due on the whole, or an appropriate part, of the continuing policies in the *with-profits fund* which would otherwise result in higher costs falling on the continuing *with-profits policies*.

20.2.15 G   FCA

The provisions dealing with the calculation of surrender payments (**COBS 20.2.11 G** to **COBS 20.2.12 R**) do not prevent a *firm* from setting a target range for surrender payments where the top-end of the range is lower than the top-end of the relevant range for maturity payments.

20.2.16 R   FCA

A *firm* must not, in so far as is reasonably practicable, make a market value reduction to the face value of the units of an accumulating *with-profits policy* unless:
(1)   the *market value* of the *with-profits assets* in the relevant *with-profits fund* is, or is expected to be, less than the assumed value of the assets on which the face value of the units of the *policy* has been based; and
(2)   the market value reduction is no greater than is necessary to reflect the impact of the difference in value referred to in (1) on the relevant payment out to the *policyholder*.

20.2.16A G   FCA

If a *firm* is able to satisfy **COBS 20.2.16 R (1)**, then the volume of surrenders, transfers, or other exits from the *with-profits fund* that there has been, or is expected to be, is a factor that a *firm* may take into account when it is considering whether to make a market value reduction, and if so, its amount, subject to the limit in **COBS 20.2.16 R (2)**.

Conditions relevant to distributions

20.2.17 R   FCA

A firm must ensure that the amount distributed to *policyholders* from a *with-profits fund*, taking into account any adjustments required by **COBS 20.2.17A R**, is not less than the *required percentage* of the total amount distributed.

20.2.17A R   FCA
(1)   Where a *firm* adjusts the amounts distributed to *policyholders*, either by market value reduction or otherwise, in a way that would result in a distribution to *policyholders* of less than the *required percentage*, taking both the relevant distributions and the adjustment into account, then the *firm* must apply a proportionate adjustment to amounts distributed to shareholders so that the distribution to *policyholders* will not be less than the *required percentage*.
(2)   The adjustments referred to in (1) include but are not limited to a situation where such an adjustment has the effect of retrospectively reducing past *policyholder* distributions.

20.2.17B G   FCA

An example of the application of **COBS 20.2.17A R**, without limitation to its scope generally, is where a *firm* reduces, for any reason, the amounts of a bonus or of bonus units added to *policies* in force. The *firm* should treat this as effectively a 'negative distribution', calculated by making the same assumptions regarding discount rates and other relevant factors as would be used for positive bonus additions. The amount so calculated should then be taken into account in ensuring that the amount distributed to *policyholders* from a *with-profits fund* is not less than the *required percentage* for the purposes of **COBS 20.2.17 R**.

20.2.17C R   FCA PRA

A *firm* must not make a distribution from a *with-profits fund*, unless the whole of the cost of that distribution can be met without eliminating the regulatory surplus in that *with-profits fund*.

20.2.18 R   FCA PRA

A *realistic basis life firm* must not make a distribution from a *with-profits fund* to any *person* who is not a *with-profits policyholder*, unless the whole of the cost of that distribution (including the cost of any obligations that will or may arise from the decision to make a distribution) can be met from the excess of the *realistic value of assets* over the *realistic value of liabilities* in that *with-profits fund*.

20.2.19 R   FCA PRA

A distribution to a *person* who is not a *with-profits policyholder* includes a transfer of assets out of a *with-profits fund* that is not made to satisfy a liability of that fund.

20.2.20 R   FCA

If, on a distribution, a *firm* incurs a tax liability on a transfer to shareholders, it must not attribute that tax liability to a *with-profits fund*, unless:
(1)   the *firm* can show that attributing the tax liability to that *with-profits fund* is consistent with its established practice;
(2)   that established practice is explained in the *firm's PPFM*; and
(3)   that liability is not charged to asset shares.

Requirement relating to distribution of an excess surplus

20.2.21 R   FCA

At least once a year (or, in the case of a *non-directive friendly society*, at least once in every three years) and whenever a *firm* is seeking to make a *reattribution* of its *inherited estate*, a *firm's governing body* must determine whether the *firm's with-profits fund*, or any of the *firm's with-profits fund*, has an *excess surplus*.

20.2.22 E   FCA
(1)   If a *with-profits fund* has an *excess surplus*, and to retain that surplus would be a breach of *Principle* 6 (Customers' interests), the *firm* should make a distribution from that *with-profits fund*.
(2)   Compliance with (1) may be relied on as tending to establish compliance with *Principle* 6 (Customers' interests).
(3)   Contravention of (1) may be relied on as tending to establish a contravention of *Principle* 6 (Customers' interests).

Charges to a with-profits fund

20.2.23 R   FCA

A *firm* must only charge costs to a *with-profits fund* which have been, or will be, incurred in operating the *with-profits fund*. This may include a fair proportion of overheads.

20.2.24 R   FCA

Subject to **COBS 20.2.25 R**, **COBS 20.2.25A R** and **COBS 20.2.25B R**, a *firm* must not pay compensation or redress from a *with-profits fund*.

20.2.25 R   FCA

A proprietary *firm* may pay compensation or redress due to a *policyholder*, or former *policyholder*, from assets attributable to shareholders, whether or not they are held within a *long-term insurance fund*.

20.2.25A R   FCA

A *mutual* may pay compensation or redress due to a *policyholder*, or *former policyholder*, from a *with-profits fund*, but may only pay from assets that would otherwise be attributable to asset shares if, in the reasonable opinion of the *firm's governing body*, the compensation or redress cannot be paid from any other assets in the *with-profits fund*.

20.2.25B R   FCA

A payment or transfer of liabilities made to correct an error and which has the effect of restoring a *policyholder*, or former *policyholder*, and the *with-profits fund* to the position they would have been in if the error had not occurred (a "rectification payment"), is not a payment of compensation or redress for the purposes of **COBS 20.2.24 R**.

20.2.25C G   FCA

Rectification payments may include, for example, a payment to a *policyholder* or former *policyholder* to correct an erroneous underpayment of policy proceeds, or a reimbursement of premiums overpaid. The effect of **COBS 20.2.25B R** is that a *firm* may make rectification payments using assets in a *with-profits fund*.

20.2.25D G   FCA

COBS TP 2.14 R has the effect that payments of compensation and redress arising out of events which took place before 31 July 2009 are subject to **COBS 20.2.23 R** to **COBS 20.2.25 R** as in force at 30 July 2009.

20.2.26 R   FCA

A proprietary *firm* must not charge to a *with-profits fund* any amounts paid or payable to a skilled person in connection with a report under section 166 of the *Act* (Reports by skilled persons) if the report indicates that the *firm* has, or may have, materially failed to satisfy its obligations under the *regulatory system*.

Tax charge to a with-profits fund

20.2.27 R   FCA

A *firm* must not charge a contribution to corporation tax to a *with-profits fund*, if that contribution exceeds the notional corporation tax liability that would be charged to that *with-profits fund* if it were assessed to tax as a separate *body corporate*.

New business

20.2.28 R   FCA

A *firm* must not effect new *contracts of insurance* in an existing *with-profits fund* unless:
(1)   the *firm's governing body* is satisfied, so far as it reasonably can be, and can demonstrate, having regard to the analysis in (2), that the terms on which each type of contract is to be effected are likely to have no adverse effect on the interests of the *with-profits policyholders* whose *policies* are written into that fund; and
(2)   the *firm* has:
        (a)   carried out or obtained appropriate analysis, based on relevant evidence and proportionate to the risks involved, as to the likely impact on *with-profits policyholders*, having regard to relevant factors including:
                (i)   the volumes of each type of contract that the *firm* expects to be effected; and
                (ii)   the periods over which the contracts are expected to remain in force; and
        (b)   provided the analysis referred to in (a) to its *with-profits committee* or, if applicable, its *with-profits advisory arrangement* and to its *governing body* for the purposes of (1).

20.2.28A G   FCA
(1)   Writing new *insurance business* into a *with-profits fund* is not, of itself, automatically adverse to the interests of *with-profits policyholders*. For example, new *insurance business* which defers the emergence or distribution of surplus to a limited extent for a number of *policyholders*, or which leads to a marginal change in the equity backing ratio, may, subject to satisfying the guidance in **COBS 20.2.60 G** and **COBS 20.2.29 G**, reasonably be considered not to have an adverse effect on the *with-profits policyholders* in a *with-profits fund*, if the *firm's governing body* is satisfied (and can demonstrate based on appropriate analysis) that each new line of *insurance business* is likely to be financially self-supporting over the periods during which the contracts are expected to remain in force and is likely to add sufficient value to the *with-profits fund* to offset the cost of acquiring the business.
(2)   Conversely, if the particular line of new *insurance business* is priced on loss-making terms or the terms are such that the new *insurance business* is not likely to generate sufficient value after covering all the costs associated with it (in either case when considered in aggregate over the periods over which the contracts are expected to remain in force), then in the *FCA's* view, the terms of that *insurance business* are likely to have an adverse impact on *with-profits policyholders* interests in the relevant fund.
(3)   *Firms* will need to ensure that they comply with **COBS 20.2.28 R** at all times, but in practice *firms* will be expected to pay particular attention when they are designing and pricing or re-pricing products, when they are preparing their financial plans that take into account their expected costs and levels of new business, and, in particular, when reviewing their financial performance, if that reveals that costs or levels of new business have varied significantly from those expected previously.

(4)   New business for the purposes of **COBS 20.2.28 R** will not, in general, include increments on existing *policies* or business written as a result of the exercise of options by an existing *policyholder*.

20.2.29 G   FCA

In some circumstances, it may be difficult or impossible for a *firm* to mitigate the risk of an adverse effect on its existing, or new, *with-profits policyholders*, unless it establishes a new bonus series or *with-profits fund*. Circumstances that might cause a *firm* to establish a new bonus series or *with-profits fund* include:
(1)   where the *firm* has a high level of guarantees or options in its existing *with-profits policies*, which might place an excessive burden on new *with-profits policies*, or vice versa; and
(2)   where the potential risks are likely to be so great that a single *with-profits fund* cannot provide adequately for the interests of new and existing *policyholders*, even after allowing for any beneficial effects of diversification. Such potential risks are likely to arise from significant differences in the terms and conditions of the new and existing *with-profits policies*, including the basis on which charges are levied and reviewed.

20.2.30 G   FCA
(1)   When a *firm* prices the new *insurance business* that it proposes to effect in an existing *with-profits fund*, it should estimate the volume of new *insurance business* that it is likely to effect and then build in adequate margins that will allow it to recover any acquisition costs to be charged to the *with-profits fund*.
(2)   **COBS 20.2.28 R** requires *firms* to obtain appropriate analysis and evidence and this should include at least a profitability analysis on a marginal cost basis.

20.2.31 G   FCA

When a *firm* sets a target volume for new *insurance business* in an existing *with-profits fund*, it should pay particular attention to the risk of disadvantage to existing *with-profits policyholders*. Those *policyholders* might be disadvantaged, for example, by the need to retain additional capital to support a rapid growth in new business, when that capital might have been distributed in the ordinary course of the *firm's* existing business.

Relationship of a with-profits fund with the firm and any connected persons

20.2.32 R   FCA

A *firm* carrying on *with-profits business* must not:
(1)   make a loan to a *connected person* using assets in a *with-profits fund*; or
(2)   give a guarantee to, or for the benefit of, a *connected person*, where the guarantee will be backed using assets in a *with-profits fund*;

unless that loan or guarantee:
(3)   will be on commercial terms;
(4)   will, in the reasonable opinion of the *firm's* senior management, be beneficial to the *with-profits policyholders* in the relevant *with-profits fund*; and
(5)   will not, in the reasonable opinion of the *firm's* senior management, expose those *policyholders* to undue *credit* or *group* risk.

Contingent loans and other forms of support for the with-profits fund

20.2.33 G   FCA PRA
(1)   If a *firm*, or a *connected person*, provides support to a *with-profits fund* (for example, by a contingent loan), no reliance should be placed on that support when the *firm* assesses the *with-profits fund's* financial position unless there are clear and unambiguous criteria governing any repayment obligations to the support provider.
(2)   The degree of reliance placed on that support should depend on the subordination of the support to the fair treatment of *with-profits policyholders* and clarification of what fair treatment means in various circumstances. For a *realistic basis life firm* this would normally be evidenced by the liability for such support being capable, under stress, of a progressively lower valuation in the *future policy-related liabilities*.

20.2.34 G   FCA PRA

Where assets from outside a *with-profits fund* are made available to support that fund (and there is no ambiguity in the criteria governing any repayment obligations to the support provider), a *firm* should manage the fund disregarding the liability to repay those assets, at least in so far as that is necessary for its *policyholders* to be treated fairly.

Other rules and guidance on the conduct of with-profits business

20.2.35 G   FCA

When a *firm* determines its investment strategy, and the acceptable level of risk within that strategy, it should take into account:

(1)   the extent of the guarantee in its *with-profits policies*;
(2)   any representation that it has made to its *with-profits policyholders*;
(3)   its established practice; and
(4)   the amount of capital support available.

20.2.35A G   PRA

When a *firm* determines its investment strategy, and the acceptable level of risk within that strategy, it should take into account:
(1)   the extent of the guarantee in its *with-profits policies*; and
(2)   the amount of capital support available.

20.2.36 R   FCA

A *firm* must not:
(1)   use *with-profits assets* to finance the purchase of a *strategic investment*, directly or by or through a *connected person*; or
(2)   retain an investment referred to in (1);

unless its *governing body* is satisfied, so far as it reasonably can be, and can demonstrate, that the purchase or retention is likely to have no adverse effect on the interests of its *with-profits policyholders* whose *policies* are written into the relevant fund.

20.2.36A R   FCA

A *firm* must keep adequate records setting out the strategic purpose for which a *strategic investment* has been purchased or retained.

20.2.36B G   FCA

(1)   In order for a *firm* to comply with **COBS 20.2.36 R**, a *firm's governing body* should consider:
    (a)   the size of the investment in relation to the *with-profits fund*;
    (b)   the expected rate of return on the investment;
    (c)   the risks associated with the investment, including, but not limited to, liquidity risk, the capital needs of the acquired business or investment and the difficulty of establishing fair value (if any);
    (d)   any costs that would result from divestment;
    (e)   whether the *with-profits actuary* would regard the investment as having no adverse effect on the interests of *with-profits policyholders* as a class;
    (f)   in the case of a proprietary *firm*, whether it would be more appropriate for the investment to be made using assets other than those in the *with-profits fund*; and
    (g)   any other relevant material factors.
(2)   A *firm* should also consider whether making or retaining the investment should be disclosed to *with-profits policyholders*.
(3)   Examples of *strategic investments* include, but are not limited to, a significant investment in another business or significant real estate assets used within the business of the *firm*.

20.2.37 G   FCA

If a *firm* carries out *non-profit insurance business* in a *with-profits fund*, it should review the profitability of the *non-profit insurance business* regularly.

20.2.38 G   FCA

If a *firm* has reinsured its *with-profits insurance business* into another *insurance undertaking*, it should take reasonable steps to discharge its responsibilities to its *with-profits policyholders*, in respect of the reinsured business. Those steps should include maintaining adequate controls.

Significant changes in with-profits funds

20.2.39 R   FCA

A *firm* must not enter into a material transaction relating to a *with-profits fund* unless, in the reasonable opinion of the *firm's governing body*, the transaction is unlikely to have a material adverse effect on the interests of that fund's existing *with-profits policyholders*.

20.2.40 R   FCA

A material transaction includes a series of related non-material transactions which, if taken together, are material.

20.2.41 G   FCA

Examples of material transactions include:
(1)   a significant bulk outwards *reinsurance* contract;
(2)   inwards *reinsurance* of *with-profits business* from another *insurance undertaking*;
(3)   a financial engineering transaction that would materially change the profile of any surplus expected to emerge on the *with-profits fund's* existing *insurance business*; and
(4)   a significant restructuring of the *with-profits fund*, especially if it involves the creation of new sub-funds.

20.2.41A R   FCA

A *firm* must contact the *FCA* as soon as is reasonably practicable to make arrangements to discuss what actions may be required to ensure the fair treatment of *with-profits policyholders* if, in relation to any *with-profits fund* it operates:

(1)   the *firm* reasonably expects, or if earlier, there has been, a sustained and substantial fall in either the volume of new *non-profit insurance contracts*, or in the volume of new *with-profits policies* (effected other than by *reinsurance*), or in both, effected into the *with-profits fund*; or

(2)   the *firm* cedes by way of *reinsurance* most or all of the new *with-profits policies* which it continues to effect.

20.2.41B G   FCA

(1)   The aim of the discussions in **COBS 20.2.41A R** is to:

    (a)   allow the *FCA* to comment on the adequacy of the *firm's* planning; and

    (b)   seek agreement with the *firm* on any other appropriate actions to ensure *with-profits policyholders* are treated fairly.

(2)   If the *firm* is no longer effecting a material volume of new *with-profits policies* (other than by *reinsurance*) into a *with-profits fund*; or if it is ceding by way of *reinsurance* most or all of the new *with-profits policies* which it continues to effect, then it may also be appropriate to consider whether, in the particular circumstances of the *firm*, it should be regarded as ceasing to effect new *contracts of insurance* for the purposes of **COBS 20.2.54 R (3)**.

(3)   In the discussions the *FCA* will have with regard to **COBS 20.2.28 R** (New business), if the volumes of new business are expected to be profitable and, in relation to *non-profit insurance business*, it is demonstrated that a fair distribution to *with-profits policyholders* out of the fund can be achieved and the economic value of any expected future profits is likely to be available for distribution during the lifetime of the *with-profits business* for the purposes of **COBS 20.2.60 G**, then, in the *FCA's* view, it is likely to be reasonable for a *firm* to be satisfied that there will be no adverse effect for *with-profits policyholders*, and accordingly that such business may continue to be written.

Process for reattribution of inherited estates: Policyholder advocate: appointment and role

20.2.42 R   FCA

A *firm* that is seeking to make a *reattribution* of its *inherited estate* must:

(1)   first discuss with the *FCA* (as part of its determination under **COBS 20.2.21 R**):

    (a)   its projections for capital required to support existing business, which must include an assessment of:

        (i)   the *firm's* future risk appetite for the *with-profits fund* and other relevant business; and

        (ii)   how much of the margin for prudence can be identified as excessive and removed from the projected capital requirements; and

    (b)   its projections for capital required to support future new business, which must include an assessment of:

        (i)   new business volumes;

        (ii)   product terms; and

        (iii)   pricing margins;

(2)   following the discussions referred to in (1), identify at the earliest appropriate point a *policyholder advocate*, who is free from any conflicts of interest that may be, or may appear to be, detrimental to the interests of *policyholders*, to negotiate with the *firm* on behalf of relevant *with-profits policyholders* and seek the approval of the *FCA* for the appointment of the *policyholder advocate* as soon as he is identified, or appoint a *policyholder advocate* nominated by the *FCA* if its approval is not granted; and

(3)   involve the policyholder advocate designate at the earliest possible opportunity to enable him to participate effectively in the negotiations about the proposals for the *reattribution*.

20.2.42A R   PRA

A *firm* that is seeking to make a *reattribution* of its inherited estate must first discuss with the *PRA*:

(1)   its projections for capital required to support existing business, which must include an assessment of:

    (a)   the *firm's* future risk appetite for the *with-profits fund* and other relevant business; and

    (b)   how much of the margin for prudence can be identified as excessive and removed from the projected capital requirements; and

(2)   its projections for capital required to support future new business, which must include an assessment of:

    (a)   new business volumes

    (b)   product terms; and

    (c)   pricing margins.

20.2.43 G   FCA

Part 3   FCA Handbook Materials

The *firm* should include an independent element in the *policyholder advocate* selection process, which may include consulting representative groups of *policyholders* or using the services of a recruitment consultant. When considering an application for approval of a nominee to perform the *policyholder advocate* role, the *FCA* will have regard to the extent to which the *firm* has involved others in the selection process.

20.2.44 G   FCA

The precise role of the *policyholder advocate* in any particular case will depend on the nature of the *firm* and the *reattribution* proposed. A *firm* will need to discuss, with a view to agreeing, with the *FCA* the precise role of the *policyholder advocate* in a particular case (**COBS 20.2.45 R**). However, the role of the *policyholder advocate* should include:

(1)   negotiating with the *firm*, on behalf of the relevant *with-profits policyholders*, the benefits to be offered to them in exchange for the rights or interests they will be asked to give up;

(2)   commenting to *with-profits policyholders*, on:

    (a)   the methodology used for the allocation of benefits amongst the relevant (or groups of) *with-profits policyholders* and the form of those benefits;

    (b)   the criteria used for determining the eligibility of the various *with-profits policyholders*;

    (c)   the terms and conditions of the proposals (to the extent that they materially affect the benefits to be offered, or the bonuses that may be added to *with-profits policies*); and

    (d)   the views expressed by the *independent expert* or the *reattribution expert* (as the case may be), and the *firm's with-profits actuary* on the allocation of any benefits amongst the relevant *with-profits policyholders*; and

(3)   telling *with-profits policyholders*, or each group of *with-profits policyholders*, with reasons, whether the *firm's* proposals are in their interests.

Process for reattribution of inherited estates: Policyholder advocate: terms of appointment

20.2.45 R   FCA

A *firm* must:

(1)   notify the *FCA* of the terms on which it proposes to appoint a *policyholder advocate* (whether or not the candidate was nominated by the *FCA*); and

(2)   ensure that the terms of appointment for the *policyholder advocate*:

    (a)   include a description of the role of the *policyholder advocate* as agreed with the *FCA* under **COBS 20.2.44 G**;

    (b)   stress the independent nature of the *policyholder advocate's* appointment and function, and are consistent with it;

    (c)   define the relationship of the *policyholder advocate* to the *firm* and its *policyholders*;

    (d)   set out arrangements for communications between the *policyholder advocate* and *policyholders*;

    (e)   make provision for the resolution of any disputes between the *firm* and the *policyholder advocate*;

    (f)   specify when and how the *policyholder advocate's* appointment may be terminated;

    (g)   allow the *policyholder advocate* to communicate freely and in confidence with the *FCA*;

    (h)   require the *policyholder advocate* to communicate with *policyholders*:

        (i)   as soon as is practicable after his appointment, having regard to (h)(i) and (iii); and

        (ii)   thereafter no less frequently than every six *months* for the duration of the *policyholder advocate's* appointment; and

    (i)   require the *policyholder advocate*:

        (i)   to make reasonable endeavours to agree with the *firm* the contents of any proposed *policyholder* communications;

        (ii)   to allow sufficient time for the process in (i) in order to meet any timescales in (g); and

        (iii)   to provide copies of the final draft of the intended *policyholder* communications, whether or not agreement has been reached in accordance with (i) above, both to the *firm* and to the *FCA* at least seven *days* in advance of the date on which the *policyholder advocate* intends to make the communications.

20.2.46 G   FCA

A *firm* may include, within the *policyholder advocate's* terms of appointment, arrangements for the *policyholder advocate* to be indemnified in respect of certain claims that may be made against him in connection with the performance of his functions. If such indemnity is included, it should not include protection against any liability arising from acts of bad faith.

Process for reattribution of inherited estates: Reattribution expert

20.2.47 R   FCA PRA

Where a *firm* is not otherwise required to appoint an *independent expert*, it must:
(1)   appoint a reattribution expert to undertake an objective assessment of its *reattribution* proposals, who must be:
    (a)   nominated or approved by the *appropriate regulator* before he is appointed; and
    (b)   free from any conflicts of interest that may, or may appear to, undermine his independence or the quality of his report;
(2)   ensure that the *reattribution expert's* terms of appointment allow him to communicate freely and in confidence with the *appropriate regulator*; and
(3)   require the *reattribution expert* to prepare a report which must be available to the *appropriate regulator*, the *policyholder advocate* and the court (if it is relevant to any court proceedings).

20.2.48 G   FCA

A *reattribution expert's* report should comply with the applicable rules on expert evidence. The scope and content of the report should be substantially similar to that of the report required of an *independent expert* under **SUP 18.2** (Insurance business transfers), as if (where appropriate) a reference to:
(1)   the 'scheme report' was a reference to the 'reattribution expert's report';
(2)   the 'independent expert' was a reference to the 'reattribution expert'; and
(3)   the 'scheme' was a reference to the proposal for a 'reattribution'.

20.2.48A G   PRA

A *reattribution expert's* report should comply with the applicable rules on expert evidence. The scope and content of the report should be substantially similar to that expected of the report of an independent expert as set out in the *PRA's* Statement of Policy: The Prudential Regulation Authority's approach to insurance business transfers, as if (where appropriate) a reference to:
(1)   the 'scheme report' was a reference to the 'reattribution expert's report';
(2)   the 'independent expert' was a reference to the 'reattribution expert'; and
(3)   the 'scheme' was a reference to the proposal for a 'reattribution'.

Process for reattribution of inherited estates: Information to policyholders

20.2.49 R   FCA

A *firm* must ensure that every *policyholder* that may be affected by the proposed *reattribution* is sent appropriate and timely information about:
(1)   the *reattribution* process, including the role of the *policyholder advocate*, the *independent expert* or *reattribution expert*, as the case may be, and other individuals appointed to perform particular functions;
(2)   the *reattribution* proposals and how they affect the relevant *policyholders*, including an explanation of any benefits they are likely to receive and the rights and interests that they are likely to be asked to give up;
(3)   the *policyholder advocate's* views on the *reattribution* proposals and any benefits the relevant *policyholders* are likely to receive and the rights and interests that they are likely to be asked to give up; and
(4)   the outcome of the negotiations between the *firm* and the *policyholder advocate* about the benefits that will be offered to relevant *with-profits policyholders*, in exchange for the rights and interests that they will be asked to give up.

20.2.50 R   FCA

An adequate summary of the report by the *reattribution expert* must be made available to every *policyholder* that may be affected by the proposed *reattribution*.

Process for reattribution of inherited estates: Consent of policyholders

20.2.51 R   FCA

A *firm* must give relevant *with-profits policyholders* the option to:
(1)   individually accept or reject the final proposals for the *reattribution*; or
(2)   (if the legal process to be followed allows the majority of *policyholders* to bind the minority) vote on whether the *firm* should go ahead with those proposals.

Process for reattribution of inherited estates: Costs

20.2.52 G   FCA

(1)   *Reattribution* and *insurance business transfer* costs (excluding *policyholder advocate* costs) should be met from shareholder funds. A *firm* may present alternative arrangements if it can show good reasons for doing so.
(2)   Shareholders should pay a reasonable proportion of the *policyholder advocate's* costs.
(3)   If a *reattribution* proposal is not successful, the *FCA* would expect the costs of the *policyholder advocate* to be met by the *person* initiating the proposal. That will usually be the shareholders of the *firm*.

Ceasing to effect new contracts of insurance in a with-profits fund

20.2.53 R   FCA PRA

A *firm* must:
(1)   inform the *appropriate regulator* and its *with-profits policyholders* within 28 days; and
(2)   submit a run-off plan to the *appropriate regulator* as soon as reasonably practicable and, in any event, within three months;

of first ceasing to effect new *contracts of insurance* in a *with-profits fund*.

20.2.54 R   FCA PRA

A *firm* will be taken to have ceased to effect new *contracts of insurance* in a *with-profits fund*:
(1)   when any decision by the *governing body* to cease to effect new *contracts of insurance* takes effect; or
(2)   where no such decision is made, when the *firm* is no longer:
   (a)   actively seeking to effect new *contracts of insurance* in that fund; or
   (b)   effecting new *contracts of insurance* in that fund, except by increment; or
(3)   if the *firm*:
   (a)
      (i)   is no longer effecting a material volume of *with-profits policies* (other than by *reinsurance*), into the *with-profits fund*; or
      (ii)   is ceding by way of *reinsurance* most or all of the new *with-profits policies* which it continues to effect; and
   (b)   cannot demonstrate that it will treat *with-profits policyholders* fairly if it does not cease to effect new *contracts of insurance*.

20.2.55 G   FCA

For the purposes of **COBS 20.2.54 R (3)** the *FCA* will have regard to, amongst other things, the factors set out in **COBS 20.2.41BG (3)**.

20.2.56 R   FCA

The run-off plan required by **COBS 20.2.53 R** must:
(1)   include an up-to-date plan to demonstrate how the *firm* will ensure a fair distribution of the closed *with-profits fund*, and its *inherited estate* (if any); and
(2)   be approved by the *firm's governing body*.

20.2.57 G   FCA
(1)   A *firm* should also include the information described in Appendix 2.15 (Run-off plans for closed with-profits funds) of the Supervision manual in its run-off plan.
(2)   A *firm* should periodically review and update its run-off plan and submit updated versions to the *FCA* when requested to do so.

20.2.58 G   FCA

When a *firm* tells its *with-profits policyholders* that it has ceased to effect new *contracts of insurance* in a *with-profits fund*, it should also explain:
(1)   why it has done so;
(2)   what changes it has made, or proposes to make, to the fund's investment strategy (if any);
(3)   how closure may affect *with-profits policyholders* (including any reasonably foreseeable effect on future bonus prospects);
(4)   the options available to *with-profits policyholders* and an indication of the potential costs associated with the exercise of each of those options; and
(5)   any other material factors that a *policyholder* may reasonably need to be aware of before deciding how to respond to this information.

20.2.59 G   FCA

A *firm* may not be able to provide its *with-profits policyholders* with all of the information described above until it has prepared the run-off plan. In those circumstances, the *firm* should:
(1)   tell its *with-profits policyholders* that that is the case;
(2)   explain what is missing and give a time estimate for its supply; and
(3)   provide the missing information as soon as possible, and within the time estimate given.

20.2.60 G   FCA
(1)   If *non-profit insurance business* is written in a *with-profits fund*, a *firm* should take reasonable steps to ensure that the economic value of any future profits expected to emerge on the *non-profit insurance business* is available for distribution during the lifetime of the *with-profits business*.
(2)   Where a *with-profits fund* contains assets which may not be readily realisable, the *firm* should take reasonable steps to ensure that the economic value of those assets is made available as part of a fair distribution to *with-profits policyholders*.
(3)   Where it is agreed by its *with-profits policyholders*, and subject to meeting the requirements for effecting new *contracts of insurance* in an existing *with-profits fund* (**COBS 20.2.28 R**), a *mutual* may make alternative arrangements for continuing to carry on *non-profit insurance*

business, and a *non-directive friendly society* may make alternative arrangements for continuing to carry on non-insurance related business. Where a *mutual* has been granted a *waiver* in accordance with **COBS 20.2.61 G**, the agreement of its *with-profits policyholders* to alternative arrangements for continuing to carry on *non-profit insurance business* may not be needed.

20.2.61 G   FCA

(1)   A *mutual* operating a common fund may seek to undertake an exercise to identify that part of the fund to which the *mutual* considers it would be fair for relevant provisions in **COBS 20** not to apply.

(2)   To give regulatory effect to the identification exercise, the *FCA* expects that a *mutual* will need to apply to the *FCA* to modify the relevant provisions in **COBS 20** and elsewhere which are dependent on the definition of the *with-profits fund*.

(3)   A *mutual* will need to demonstrate that the appropriate statutory tests in section 138A of the *Act* are met. The *FCA* expects that *mutuals* will need to do at least the following to allow the *FCA* to consider whether granting the modification would adversely affect the advancement of the *FCA's* consumer protection objective:

     (a)   demonstrate that the exercise does not amount to a *reattribution*;

     (b)   demonstrate that its proposals are fair to its *with-profits policyholders*, and other relevant *policyholders*, having regard to the *mutual's* own particular structure, origins and other relevant circumstances, and including reference to the items in (c) to (j) below;

     (c)   obtain the report of an independent expert approved by, and whose terms of reference are agreed with, the *FCA* on the terms of the *mutual's* proposals and the likely impact and effects on, and fairness to, the *mutual's with-profits policyholders* and other relevant *policyholders*. This report should consider whether the *firm* has sufficiently demonstrated the absence of a *reattribution* under (a). The *FCA* will consider using its powers in section 166 of the *Act* (Reports by skilled persons) in appropriate circumstances;

     (d)   demonstrate that the *mutual's with-profits policyholders* and other *policyholders* are appropriately engaged and informed about the proposals;

     (e)   demonstrate that it has complied with the relevant requirements in the *mutual's* constitutional documents, for example that members are appropriately involved in agreeing to any proposals;

     (f)   demonstrate that the *mutual* has a convincing and robust business case for continuing in business, as opposed to run-off;

     (g)   demonstrate how, and the extent to which, continuing membership rights will benefit *with-profits policyholders* and other *policyholders*;

     (h)   explain the nature and terms of any continuing support to be provided to the *with-profits fund* from outside the *with-profits fund*;

     (i)   demonstrate that *with-profits policyholders* under the *mutual's* proposals will not be at a disadvantage compared to equivalent *with-profits policyholders* in a proprietary *with-profits fund*; and

     (j)   explain how it proposes to pay any compensation or redress that is, or may become, due to a *policyholder*, or former *policyholder*.

(4)   For the purposes of (3)(a) and (c), where the issues to be considered by the independent expert include the extent or value (in the particular circumstances of the *mutual*) of the rights and interests of *with-profits policyholders* in the *with-profits fund*, the *FCA* expects the independent expert's terms of reference to require them to take into account other available analyses of such rights and interests which may be more favourable to *policyholders* than the *mutual's* own analysis. The *FCA* considers that any uncertainty in the extent or value of such rights and interests in the case of a particular *mutual* may mean that the independent expert will need to obtain their own independent legal advice on the issue. In the *FCA's* view the fact of any uncertainty as to the extent or value of the relevant rights and interests, following receipt of independent legal advice, may itself be taken into account by the independent expert when producing their report. The *FCA* will consider on a case by case basis what further information it may provide to the expert and/or independent legal adviser to ensure that the rights and interests of *policyholders* have been appropriately taken into account.

(5)   The *FCA* expects to consult and/or seek information or advice from the *PRA* in accordance with section 3D of the *Act* and the Memorandum of Understanding between the *FCA* and the *PRA* required by section 3E. As part of any such process the *FCA* expects that the *PRA* will wish to consider, among other things, that balance sheet safety and soundness issues have been identified and addressed appropriately.

20.3   PRINCIPLES AND PRACTICES OF FINANCIAL MANAGEMENT

Production of PPFM

20.3.1 R   FCA

(1)   A *firm* must:

(a)   establish and maintain the *PPFM* according to which its *with-profits business* is conducted (or, if appropriate, separate *PPFM* for each *with-profits fund*); and

(b)   retain a record of each version of its *PPFM* for five years.

(2)   A firm's *with-profits principles* must:

    (a)   be enduring statements of the standards it adopts in managing *with-profits funds*; and

    (b)   describe the business model it uses to meet its duties to *with-profits policyholders* and to respond to longer-term changes in the business and economic environment.

(3)   A firm's *with-profits practices* must:

    (a)   describe how a *firm* manages its *with-profits funds* and how it responds to shorter-term changes in the business and economic environment; and

    (b)   be sufficiently detailed for a knowledgeable observer to understand the material risks and rewards from effecting or maintaining a *with-profits policy* with it.

(4)   A *firm* must not change its *PPFM* unless, in the reasonable opinion of its *governing body*, that change is justified to:

    (a)   respond to changes in the business or economic environment; or

    (b)   protect the interests of *policyholders*; or

    (c)   change the *firm's with-profits practices* better to achieve its *with-profits principles*.

(5)   A *firm* may change its *PPFM* if that change:

    (a)   is necessary to correct an error or omission; or

    (b)   would improve clarity or presentation without materially affecting the *PPFM's* substance; or

    (c)   is immaterial.

20.3.2 G

[deleted]

20.3.3 G

[deleted]

Scope and content of PPFM

20.3.4 R   FCA

A *firm's PPFM* must cover the issues set out in the table in **COBS 20.3.6 R**.

20.3.5 R   FCA

A *firm's PPFM* must cover any matter that has, or it is reasonably foreseeable may have, a significant impact on the *firm's* management of *with-profits funds*, including but not limited to:

(1)   any requirements or constraints that apply as a result of previous dealings, including previous business transfer schemes; and

(2)   the nature and extent of any shareholder commitment to support the *with-profits fund*.

20.3.6 R   FCA

Table: Issues to be covered in PPFM

	Subject	Issues	
(1)	Amount payable under a with-profits policy	(a)	Methods used to guide determination of the amount that is appropriate to pay individual *with-profits policyholders*, including:
		(i)	the aims of the methods and approximations used;
		(ii)	how the current methods, including any relevant historical assumptions used and any systems maintained to deliver results of particular methods, are documented; and
		(iii)	the procedures for changing the current method or any assumptions or parameters relevant to a particular method.
		(b)	Approach to setting bonus rates.
		(c)	Approach to smoothing maturity payments and surrender payments, including:
		(i)	the smoothing policy applied to each type of *with-profits policy*;
		(ii)	the limits (if any) applied to the total cost of, or excess from, smoothing; and
		(iii)	any limits applied to any changes in the level of maturity payments between one period to another.
(2)	Investment strategy		Significant aspects of the *firm's* investment strategy for its *with-profits business* or, if different, any *with-profits fund*, including:

	Subject	Issues	
		(a)	the degree of matching to be maintained between assets relevant to *with-profits business* and liabilities to *with-profits policyholders* and other creditors;
		(b)	the *firm's* approach to assets of different credit or liquidity quality and different volatility of market values;
		(c)	the presence among the assets relevant to *with-profits business* of any assets that would not normally be traded because of their importance to the *firm*, and the justification for holding such assets; and
		(d)	the *firm's* controls on using new asset or liability instruments and the nature of any approval required before new instruments are used.
(3)	Business risk		The exposure of the *with-profits business* to business risks (new and existing), including the *firm's*:
		(a)	procedures for deciding if the *with-profits business* may undertake a particular business risk;
		(b)	arrangements for reviewing and setting a limit on the scale of such risks; and
		(c)	procedures for reflecting the profits or losses of such business risks in the amounts payable under *with-profits policies*.
(4)	Charges and expenses	(a)	The way in which the *firm* applies charges and apportions expenses to its *with-profits business*, including, if material, any interaction with connected firms.
		(b)	The cost apportionment principles that will determine which costs are, or may be, charged to a *with-profits fund* and which costs are, or may be, charged to the other parts of its business of its shareholders.
(5)	Management of inherited estate		Management of any *inherited estate* and the uses to which the *firm* may put that *inherited estate*.
(6)	Volumes of new business and arrangements on stopping taking new business		If a *firm's with-profits fund* is accepting new *with-profits business*, its practice for review of the limits on the quantity and type of new business and the actions that the *firm* would take if it ceased to take on new business of any significant amount.
(7)	Equity between the with-profits fund and any shareholders		The way in which the interests of *with-profits policyholders* are, or may be, affected by the interests of any shareholders of the *firm*.

20.3.7 G   FCA

The table in **COBS 20.3.8 G** sets out *guidance* on how various information relevant to some of the issues covered in a *firm's* PPFM (**COBS 20.3.6 R**) might be split between *with-profits principles* and *with-profits practices*. This is an example of the matters a *firm* should address in its *with-profits principles* and *with-profits practices* and is not exhaustive. A *firm* should consider carefully the scope and content of its *PPFM* as appropriate.

20.3.8 G   FCA

Table: Guidance on with-profits principles and practices

Reference to PPFM issues (COBS 20.3.6R)	With-profits principles	With-profits practices
(1) Amount payable under a with-profits policy	General (a) Circumstances under which any historical assumptions or parameters, relevant to methods used to determine the amount payable, may be changed;	General (e) For each major class of *with-profits policy*, methods establishing the main assumptions or parameters that decide the output of methods that determine the amount payable;

Part 3   FCA Handbook Materials

Reference to PPFM issues (COBS 20.3.6R)	With-profits principles	With-profits practices
		(f) Degree of approximation allowed when assumptions or parameters are applied across generations of *with-profits policyholders* or across different types or classes of *with-profits policies*;
		(g) Formality with which the methods, parameters or assumptions used are documented;
		(h) Target range, or target ranges, that have been set for maturity payments;
		(i) Factors likely to be regarded as relevant to address *policyholders'* interests or security when determining *excess surplus*; and Investment return, expenses or charges and tax
		(j) How investment return, expenses or charges and tax are brought into account and how the impact of those items is determined on the amount payable. In particular: .
		(i) any distinctions made in recognising the investment return from a subset of the total assets of a *with-profits fund*;
		(ii) whether expenses are apportioned between all the policies in a *with-profits fund* or apportioned in some other way;
		(iii) the relationship between the liability to tax attributed to a *with-profits fund* and the tax that the *firm* imputes to determine the amount payable;
		(iv) impact on the amount payable of any attributed liability to tax of a *with-profits fund* as a result of the *firm* making a transfer to shareholders; and
		(v) how any other items are brought into account.

Reference to PPFM issues (COBS 20.3.6R)	With-profits principles	With-profits practices
	Bonus rates (b) General aims in setting bonus rates and the constraints to which the *firm* may be subject in changing economic circumstances; (c) How the range of *with-profits policies* or generations of *with-profits policies* over which the *firm* believes a single bonus rate would be appropriate is determined and the circumstances under which it believes a new bonus series would be necessary; and	Bonus rates (k) Current approach to setting bonus rates, including the weight given to recent economic experience. For final bonus rates, the description should include any distinctions made between *with-profits policies* that remain in force until contractual dates, or dates on which no market value reduction applies (for example, maturity or retirement dates) and policies that are surrendered or transferred at other dates; (l) Frequency at which bonus rates are re-set or expected to be re-set and the circumstances under which changes in the economic environment would cause the time between re-setting to change; (m) Maximum amount by which annual bonuses would alter if annual bonus rates were reset; (n) Approach to setting any interim bonus rates before the next declaration of annual bonus rates; (o) Relationship or interaction between final bonus rates and any market value reductions, if both can apply at the same time; (p) How final bonus rates influence the value of *with-profits policies* that have formulaic surrender or transfer bases (for example, older conventional policies rather than unitised policies); and
	Smoothing (d) Statement as to whether smoothing is intended to be neutral over time.	Smoothing (q) Any differences in approach for: (i) the various types of *with-profits policy*; (ii) different categories of payout, such as between surrendered and maturing policies; and (iii) different generations of *with-profits policyholders*.
(2) Investment strategy	(a) How the types, classes or mix of assets are determined; and (b) Strategy in respect of derivatives and other instruments.	(c) Whether and to what extent there is hypothecation of assets; (d) Period between formal reviews of investment strategy;

Reference to PPFM issues (COBS 20.3.6R)	With-profits principles	With-profits practices
		(e) Approach to investment in different asset classes, and assets of different credit or liquidity quality, including assets not normally traded; and
		(f) Details of any external support available to the *with-profits fund* and how this affects the investment strategy.
(3) Business risk	(a) Where a *firm* explicitly excludes business risk from a class of *with-profits policies* but there are residual risks, clarification where these risks such as guarantee and smoothing costs are borne; and	(c) Current limits which apply to the taking on of business risk; and
	(b) Define where compensation costs from a business risk would be borne.	(d) Whether and to what extent particular generations of *with-profits policyholders* or classes of *with-profits policies* bear or might bear particular business risks, including for example, crystallised or contingent guarantees to other classes of *policyholders* or whether the out-turn from all business risk is pooled across all *with-profits policies*.
(4) Charges and expenses	(a) Factors that would drive any change to the basis on which the *firm* applies charges to or apportions its actual expenses amongst *with-profits policies*, or exercises any discretion to apply charges to particular *with-profits policies*.	(b) Charges currently applied and the expenses currently apportioned to major classes of *with-profits policies*;
		(c) Relationship between the *firm's* actual charges and expenses, as applied to determine the amounts payable under *with-profits policies*, and the charges and expenses borne by the *with-profits fund*;
		(d) Circumstances under which expenses will be charged to the *with-profits fund* at an amount other than cost, and the reasons why; and
		(e) Interval for reviewing any arrangements for out-sourced services, including those provided by connected parties, giving a broad indication of the terms for termination.
(5) Management of inherited estate	(a) Preferred size or scale of *inherited estate* and implications for the values of the *with profits policies*; and	(d) How the *inherited estate* is used, for example, in meeting costs;
	(b) Any existing division of the *inherited estate* between *with-profits funds*; and	(e) Whether the investment strategy for the *inherited estate* differs from the rest of the *with-profits fund*; and
	(c) Any constraints on the freedom to deal with the *inherited estate* as a result of previous dealings.	(f) Any current guidelines in place as to the size or scale of the *inherited estate* or as to how and over what time period the *inherited estate* would be managed, if it becomes too large or too small.

Reference to PPFM issues (COBS 20.3.6R)	With-profits principles	With-profits practices
(6) Equity between the with-profits fund and any shareholders	(a) Arrangements for, and any changes to, profit sharing between shareholders and *with-profits policyholders*.	(b) Current basis on which profit between *with-profits policyholders* and shareholders is divided; and (c) Whether the pricing of any policies being written, and particular policies open to new business, appear to be significantly and systematically reducing the *inherited estate* if the shareholder transfer is taken into account.

20.4   COMMUNICATIONS WITH WITH-PROFITS POLICYHOLDERS

Provision and publication of PPFM

20.4.1 R   FCA

A *firm* must:
(1)   on request, provide its *PPFM*, or the *PPFM* applicable to specified *with-profits funds*:
    (a)   free of charge to its *with-profits policyholders*; or
    (b)   for a reasonable charge to any person who is not its *with-profits policyholder*; and
(2)   if the *firm* publishes its *PPFM* on its website, prominently signpost its location there.

Notification of changes

20.4.2 R   FCA

A *firm* must send its *with-profits policyholders* who are affected by any change in its *PPFM*, written notice, setting out any:
(1)   proposed changes to the *with-profits principles*, three *months* in advance of the effective date; and
(2)   changes to the *with-profits practices*, within a reasonable time.

20.4.3 R   FCA

A *firm* need not give the notice required if the change to its *PPFM*:
(1)   is necessary to correct an error or omission; or
(2)   would improve clarity or presentation without materially affecting the *PPFM's* substance; or
(3)   is immaterial.

Requirements on EEA insurers

20.4.4 R   FCA

In relation to any *with-profits policyholder* who is *habitually resident* in the *United Kingdom*, an *EEA insurer* must:
(1)   on request, provide the information necessary to enable that *policyholder* properly to understand the *insurer's* commitment under the *policy*;
(2)   ensure that the information provided is not narrower in scope or less detailed in content than the equivalent *PPFM*; and
(3)   send the *policyholder* who is affected by any information being changed written notice, setting out:
    (a)   any proposed changes to information that is equivalent to the *with-profits principles*, three *months* in advance of the effective date; and
    (b)   any changes to information that is equivalent to the *with-profits practices*, within a reasonable time.

Consumer-friendly PPFM

20.4.5 R   FCA

A *firm* must:
(1)   produce a *CFPPFM* describing the most important information set out under each of the headings in its *PPFM* and keep it up to date as the *PPFM* changes over time;
(2)   express its *CFPPFM* in clear and plain language that can be easily understood by a *with-profits policyholder*, or potential *with-profits policyholder* who does not possess any specialist or technical knowledge;
(3)   provide its *CFPPFM* free of charge with any:

(a)   written notice sent to *with-profits policyholders* on proposed changes to its *with-profits principles* (where the *firm* must provide the version of the *CFPPFM* in use before the changes if this has not already been provided);

(b)   annual statements sent to its *with-profits policyholders* (unless there has been no material change in the *CFPPFM* since it was last supplied); and

(c)   *key features document* for a *with-profits policy*; and

(4)   make its *CFPPFM* publicly available and prominently signpost the availability on its website.

20.4.6 G   FCA

A *firm* may include the information set out in its *CFPPFM* in any other document it produces.

Annual report to with-profits policyholders

20.4.7 R   FCA

A *firm* must produce an annual report to its *with-profits policyholders*, which must:

(1)   state whether, throughout the *financial year* to which the report relates, the *firm* believes it has complied with its obligations relating to its *PPFM* and setting out its reasons for that belief;

(2)   address all significant relevant issues, including the way in which the *firm* has:

(a)   exercised, or failed to exercise, any discretion that it has in the conduct of its *with-profits business*; and

(b)   addressed any competing or conflicting rights, interests or expectations of its *policyholders* (or groups of *policyholders*) and, if applicable, *shareholders* (or groups of *shareholders*), including the competing interests of different classes and generations.

20.4.8 G   FCA

The following documents should be annexed to the annual report in this section:

(1)   the report to *with-profits policyholders* made by a *with-profits actuary* in respect of each financial year (see SUP 4.3.16AR(4)); and

(2)   any statement or report provided by the *person* or committee who provides the independent judgement under the *firm's* governance arrangements for its *with-profits business*.

20.4.9 G   FCA

In preparing the annual report to *with-profits policyholders*, a *firm* should take advice from a *with-profits actuary*.

20.4.10 G   FCA

A *firm* should make the annual report available to *with-profits policyholders* within six *months* of the end of the *financial year* to which it relates. A *firm* should notify its *with-profits policyholders* in any annual statements how copies of the report can be obtained.

20.5   WITH-PROFITS GOVERNANCE

Requirement to appoint a with-profits committee or advisory arrangement

20.5.1 R   FCA

A *firm* must, in relation to each *with-profits fund* it operates:

(1)   appoint:

(a)   a *with-profits committee*; or

(b)   a *with-profits advisory arrangement* (referred to in this section as an 'advisory arrangement'), but only if appropriate, in the opinion of the *firm's governing body*, having regard to the size, nature and complexity of the fund in question;

(2)   ensure that the *with-profits committee* or advisory arrangement operates in accordance with its *terms of reference*; and

(3)   make available a copy of any *terms of reference* on the *firm's* website, or if the *firm* does not have a website, at the request of *policyholders*.

20.5.2 G   FCA

(1)   Ultimate responsibility for managing a *with-profits fund* rests with the firm through its *governing body*. The role of the *with-profits committee* or advisory arrangement is, in part, to act in an advisory capacity to inform the decision-making of a *firm's governing body*. The *with-profits committee* or advisory arrangement also acts as a means by which the interests of *with-profits policyholders* are appropriately considered within a *firm's* governance structures. The *with-profits committee* or advisory arrangement should address issues affecting *policyholders* as a whole or as separately identifiable groups of *policyholders* generally rather than dealing with individual *policyholder* complaints or taking management decisions with respect to a *with-profits fund*.

(2)   If a *firm* considers that it is appropriate to appoint an advisory arrangement, a *firm's governing body* will need to decide whether it is appropriate to appoint an independent person or one or more *non-executive directors* to carry out the role. The *FCA* expects *firms*

to make this determination according to the nature, size and complexity of the fund in question. So the larger or more complex the fund is, the more likely it would be that it would be appropriate to appoint an independent person.

(3)   Where a *firm* has appointed a *with-profits committee* to one of its *with-profits funds* it may also decide to appoint that *with-profits committee* to some or all of its other *with-profits funds*, even if the *firm* would not have determined it appropriate to appoint a *with-profits committee* to those other funds when considered individually having regard to their size, nature or complexity.

Terms of reference of with-profits committee or advisory arrangement

20.5.3 R   FCA

A *firm* must ensure that the *terms of reference* contain, as a minimum, terms having the following effect:

(1)   the role of the *with-profits committee* or advisory arrangement is, as relevant, to assess, report on, and provide clear advice and, where appropriate, recommendations to the *firm's governing body* on:

     (a)   the way in which each *with-profits fund* is managed by the *firm* and, if a *PPFM* is required, whether this is properly reflected in the *PPFM*;

     (b)   if applicable, whether the *firm* is complying with the principles and practices set out in the *PPFM*;

     (c)   whether the *firm* has addressed effectively the conflicting rights and interests of *with-profits policyholders* and other *policyholders* or stakeholders including, if applicable, shareholders, in a way that is consistent with *Principle* 6 (treating customers fairly); and

     (d)   any other issues with which the *firm's governing body*, *with-profits committee* or advisory arrangement considers *with-profits policyholders* might reasonably expect the *with-profits committee* or advisory arrangements to be involved;

(2)   that the *with-profits committee* or advisory arrangement must:

     (a)   decide on the specific matters it will consider in order to enable it to carry out its role described in (1)(a) to (d) as appropriate to the particular circumstances of the *with-profits fund(s)*; and

     (b)   in any event give appropriate consideration to the following non-exhaustive list of specific matters:

         (i)   the identification of surplus and *excess surplus*, the merits of its distribution or retention and the proposed distribution policy;

         (ii)   how bonus rates, smoothing and, if relevant, market value reductions have been calculated and applied;

         (iii)   if relevant, the relative interests of *policyholders* with and without valuable guarantees;

         (iv)   the *firm's* with-profits customer communications such as annual policyholder statements and product literature and whether the *with-profits committee* or advisory arrangement wishes to make a statement or report to *with-profits policyholders* in addition to the annual report made by a *firm*;

         (v)   any significant changes to the risk or investment profile of the *with-profits fund* including the management of material illiquid investments and the *firm's* obligations in relation to *strategic investments*;

         (vi)   the *firm's* strategy for future sales supported by the assets of the *with-profits fund* and its impact on surplus;

         (vii)   the impact of any management actions planned or implemented;

         (viii)   relevant management information such as customer complaints data (but not necessarily information relating to individual customer complaints);

         (ix)   the drafting, review, updating of and compliance with run-off plans, court schemes and similar matters; and

         (x)   the costs incurred in operating the *with-profits fund*;

(3)   that any person appointed as a member of the *with-profits committee* or as a person carrying out the advisory arrangement must have the appropriate skills, knowledge and experience to perform, or contribute to, as appropriate, the role set out in (1) and (2);

(4)   if the firm appoints a *with-profits committee*:

     (a)   that there must be three or more members;

     (b)   that the quorum for any meeting (or decision by written procedure) must be at least half of the number of, and no less than two, members; and

(5)   that the *with-profits committee* or advisory arrangement must:

     (a)   advise the *governing body* on the suitability of candidates proposed for appointment as the *with-profits actuary*; and

     (b)   assess the performance of the *with-profits actuary* at least annually, and report its view to the *governing body* of the *firm*.

20.5.4 G   FCA

(1)   The *FCA* expects that a *with-profits committee* will meet at least quarterly and ad hoc if required.

(2)   The *FCA* expects that, in general, a *with-profits committee* or advisory arrangement will work closely with the *with-profits actuary*, and obtain his opinion and input as appropriate.

Role of with-profits committee or advisory arrangement in the firm's governance

20.5.5 R   FCA

A *firm* must:

(1)   ensure that its *governing body*, in the context of its consideration of issues referred to in **COBS 20.5.3 R (1)(A)** to **(D)** and **(2)(B)(I)** to **(X)**:

    (a)   obtains, as relevant, assessments, reports, advice and/or recommendations of the *with-profits committee* or advisory arrangement, if the *governing body*, the *with-profits committee* or advisory arrangement considers that significant issues concerning the interests of *with-profits policyholders* need to be considered by the *firm*;

    (b)   allows the *with-profits committee* or advisory arrangement sufficient time to enable it to provide fully considered input on the issues to be considered;

    (c)   considers fully and gives due regard to the input of the *with-profits committee* or advisory arrangement when determining issues concerning the management of the *with-profits funds* and the interests of *with-profits policyholders*;

    (d)   if the *governing body* decides to depart in any material way from the advice or recommendations of the *with-profits committee* or advisory arrangement, sets out fully its reasons and allows the *with-profits committee* or advisory arrangement a reasonable period to consider them and respond; and

    (e)   considers any further representations from the *with-profits committee* or advisory arrangement and, if appropriate, sets out fully any additional reasons if it continues to depart from the *with-profits committee* or advisory arrangement's advice or recommendation;

(2)   provide a *with-profits committee* or advisory arrangement with sufficient resources as it may reasonably require to enable it to perform its role effectively;

(3)   notify the *FCA* of the decision of the *governing body* to depart from the advice or recommendation of the *with-profits committee* or advisory arrangement if the *with-profits committee* or advisory arrangement considers that the issue is sufficiently significant and requests of the *governing body* that the *FCA* be informed; and

(4)   consult the *with-profits actuary* on the appointment of a new member of the *with-profits committee* or of the person or persons carrying out the advisory arrangement.

20.5.6 G   FCA

(1)   **COBS 20.5.5 R (2)** requires that a *firm* provides a *with-profits committee* or advisory arrangement with sufficient resources. A *with-profits committee* or advisory arrangement should be able to obtain external professional, including actuarial, advice, at the expense of the *firm*, if the *with-profits committee* or advisory arrangement considers the advice to be necessary to perform its role effectively. In a proprietary *firm* the *with-profits committee* or advisory arrangement should be able to request that the cost of the external professional advice either is not chargeable to the *with-profits fund* in question, or is shared with the *with-profits fund*, according to whether the issue under consideration is wholly or partly to the benefit of the *firm* rather than *policyholders*. A *with-profits committee* or advisory arrangement should also be adequately supported by the *firm's* own internal resources and support functions. This may include the *firm* ensuring that relevant employees, including the *with-profits actuary*, are made sufficiently available, and provide relevant information and input, to assist the *with-profits committee* in its role, as required.

(2)   If the *with-profits committee* or advisory arrangement wishes to make a statement or report to *with-profits policyholders* in addition to the annual report made by a *firm*, the effect of **COBS 20.5.5 R (2)** is that a *firm* will need to facilitate this.

(3)   In order to comply with **SYSC 3.2.20 R** the *FCA* expects *firms* to keep full records of all requests of, and material produced by, the *with-profits committee* or advisory arrangement, and of all decisions and reasons of the *governing body* as described in **COBS 20.5.5 R (1)(D)** and **(E)**.

(4)   For the purposes of **COBS 20.5.5 R (3)**, the *FCA* expects that it will only be in exceptional circumstances that a *with-profits committee* or alternative arrangement will consider a departure from a recommendation or advice to be sufficiently significant to warrant its making a request of the *governing body* that the *FCA* be informed.

Assessment of independence by governing body

20.5.7 G   FCA

(1)   The *FCA* expects the *governing body* of the *firm* to decide whether a member of the *with-profits committee* or a person (other than a *non-executive director*) carrying out the advisory arrangement is independent. The *FCA* expects a *firm's governing body* to adopt the following approach and have regard to the following factors when making this assessment:

    (a)   the *governing body* should determine whether the person is independent in character and judgment and whether there are relationships or circumstances which are likely to affect, or could appear to affect, the person's judgment; and

    (b)   the *governing body* should state its reasons if it determines that a person is independent notwithstanding the existence of relationships or circumstances which may appear relevant to its determination, including if the person:

        (i)   has been an employee of the *firm* or group within the last five years; or

        (ii)   has, or has had within the last three years, a material business relationship with the *firm* either directly, or as a partner, shareholder, director or senior employee of a body that has such a relationship with the *firm*; or

        (iii)   has received or receives additional remuneration from the *firm*, participates in the *firm's* share option or a performance-related pay scheme, or is a member of the *firm's* pension scheme; or

        (iv)   has close family ties with any of the *firm's* advisers, directors or senior employees; or

        (v)   has significant links with the *firm's* directors through involvement in other companies or bodies; or

        (vi)   represents a significant shareholder; or

        (vii)   has served on the *governing body* for more than nine years from the date of their first election.

(2)   If a *firm* appoints one or more *non-executive directors* to carry out the advisory arrangement, the *FCA* expects the *governing body* of the *firm* to be satisfied that that person or persons is or are adequately able to provide independent judgment.

Governance arrangements in relation to the PPFM

20.5.8 G   FCA

In complying with the *rule* on systems and controls in relation to compliance, financial crime and money laundering (**SYSC 3.2.6 R**), a *firm* should maintain governance arrangements designed to ensure that it complies with, maintains and records, any applicable *PPFM*. These arrangements should:

(1)   be appropriate to the scale, nature and complexity of the *firm's with-profits business*; and

(2)   include the approval of the *firm's PPFM* by its *governing body*.

CHAPTER 21
PERMITTED LINKS

21.1 APPLICATION

[3.69]

21.1.1 R   FCA PRA

The *rules* in this section apply on an ongoing basis to *linked long-term* contracts that are effected by:

(1)   *insurers* other than *EEA insurers*; and

(2)   *EEA insurers* in the *United Kingdom*.

21.1.2 R   FCA PRA

The *rules* in this section do not apply to:

(1)   contracts that were effected before 1 July 1994, and under which *linked benefits* were permitted to be determined before that date;

(2)   contracts effected by an *insurer* that are *linked long-term* contracts only because the *policyholder* is eligible to participate in any *established surplus*;

(3)   contracts effected by an *EEA insurer* that are *linked long-term* contracts only because the *policyholder* is eligible to participate in an excess of assets representing the whole or a particular part of the *long-term insurance fund* over the liabilities, or a particular part of the liabilities, of the *insurer* as determined by the law of the *EEA state* in which the head office of the *insurer* is situated;

(4)   [deleted]

(5)   contracts effected before 30 June 1995, to the extent that they provide for benefits to be determined by reference to a *collective investment scheme* that was a *listed security* immediately before 1 July 1994; and

(6)   contracts linked to *permitted units* that were effected before 1 February 1992, except to the extent that they relate to acts or omissions on or after that date.

PRINCIPLES FOR FIRMS ENGAGED IN LINKED LONG-TERM INSURANCE BUSINESS

21.2.1 R   FCA PRA

A *firm* must ensure that the values of its *permitted links* are determined fairly and accurately.

21.2.1B G

21.2.2 R   FCA PRA

A *firm* must ensure that its *linked assets*:
(1)   are capable of being realised in time for it to meet its obligations to *linked policyholders*; and
(2)   are matched with its *linked liabilities* as required by the *close matching rules*.

21.2.3 R   FCA PRA

A *firm* must ensure that there is no reasonably foreseeable risk that the aggregate value of any of its *linked funds* will become negative.

21.2.4 R   FCA

A *firm* must notify its *linked policyholders* of the risk profile and investment strategy for the *linked fund*:
(1)   at *inception*, and
(2)   before making any material changes.

21.2.5 R   FCA PRA

A *firm* must ensure that its systems and controls and other resources are appropriate for the risks associated with its *linked assets* and *linked liabilities*.

21.2.6 R   FCA PRA

(1)   A *firm* must ensure when selecting *linked assets* that there is no reasonably foreseeable risk of a conflict of interest with its *linked policyholders*.
(2)   If a conflict does arise, the *firm* must take reasonable steps to ensure that the interests of the *linked policyholders* are safeguarded.

21.2.7 R   FCA PRA

In applying the rules in this section, a *firm* must consider the economic effect of its *permitted links* and *linked assets* ahead of their legal form.

21.2.8 R   FCA PRA

A *firm* must notify the *appropriate regulator* in writing as soon as it becomes aware of any failure to meet the requirements of this section.

21.2.9 G   FCA

In considering what action to take in response to written notification of a failure to meet the requirements of this section, the *appropriate regulator* will have regard to the extent to which the relevant circumstances are exceptional and temporary and to any other reasons for the failure.

21.3   RULES FOR FIRMS ENGAGED IN LINKED LONG-TERM INSURANCE BUSINESS

21.3.1 R   FCA

An *insurer* must not contract to provide benefits under *linked long-term* contracts of insurance that are determined:
(1)   wholly or partly, or directly or indirectly, by reference to fluctuations in any index other than an *approved index*;
(2)   wholly or partly by reference to the value of, or the income from, or fluctuations in the value of, property other than any of the following:
    (a)   *approved securities*;
    (b)   *listed securities*;
    (c)   *permitted unlisted securities*;
    (d)   *permitted land and property*;
    (e)   *permitted loans*;
    (f)   *permitted deposits*;
    (g)   *permitted scheme interests*;
    (h)   [deleted]
    (i)   cash;
    (j)   *permitted units*;
    (k)   *permitted stock lending*; and
    (l)   *permitted derivatives contracts*.

21.3.2 G   FCA
(1)   Nothing in these rules prevents a *firm* making allowance in the value of any *permitted link* for any notional tax loss associated with the relevant *linked assets* for the purposes of fair pricing.

(2)   In the *appropriate regulator's* view the Consumer Prices Index, as well as the Retail Prices Index, is a national index of retail prices and so may be used as an *approved index* for the purposes of **COBS 21.3.1 R (1)**.

21.3.3 R   FCA

A *firm* that has entered into a *reinsurance contract* in respect of its *linked long-term insurance business* must nevertheless discharge its responsibilities under its *linked long-term* insurance contracts as if no *reinsurance contract* had been effected.

21.3.4 G   FCA

In order to comply with the requirements of **COBS 21.3.3 R** a *firm* should:
(1)   disclose to *policyholders* the implications of any credit risk exposure they may face in relation to the solvency of the reinsurer; and
(2)   suitably monitor the way the reinsurer manages the business in order to discharge its continuing responsibilities to *policyholders*.

21.3.5 R   FCA PRA
(1)   Except in the case specified in (2), a *firm* which proposes to undertake *linked long-term insurance business*, which is linked to the average earnings index and used for the purposes of orders made by the Department for Work and Pensions under section 148 of the Social Security Administration Act 1992, must notify the *appropriate regulator* in writing of its intention to do so in good time before effecting any such business for the first time, or if there is a material change in the volume of such business, and explain how the risks associated with this business will be safely managed.
(2)   These requirements do not apply in respect of liabilities for which a limited revaluation premium has been paid to the Department for Work and Pensions so that the liability for revaluation, while still linked to orders made under section 148 of the Social Security Administration Act 1992, is limited to 5%.

CHAPTER 22
RESTRICTIONS ON DISTRIBUTION OF CONTINGENT CONVERTIBLE INSTRUMENTS

22.1   TEMPORARY RESTRICTIONS ON CONTINGENT CONVERTIBLE INSTRUMENTS

[3.70]
22.1.1 R   FCA
(1)   A *firm* must not
     (a)   sell a *contingent convertible instrument* to a *retail client* in the *EEA*; or
     (b)   do anything that would or might result in the buying of a *contingent convertible instrument* or of a beneficial interest in a *contingent convertible instrument* by a *retail client* in the *EEA*.
(2)   The prohibition in (1) does not apply if the *firm* has taken reasonable steps to ensure that one or more of the exemptions in **COBS 22.1.2 R** applies.
(3)   In this section a *retail client* of the *firm* includes a *person* who would be a *retail client* if he were receiving services from the *firm* in the course of carrying on a *regulated activity*.
(4)   The rules in this section cease to have effect on 1 October 2015.

Exemptions

22.1.2 R   FCA

Title	Type of retail client	Additional conditions
Certified high net worth investors	An individual who meets the requirements set out in **COBS 4.12.6 R**, or a *person* (or *persons*) legally empowered to make investment decisions on behalf of such individual.	The *firm* must consider the *contingent convertible instrument* is likely to be suitable for that individual, based on a preliminary assessment of that individual's profile and objectives. (See **COBS 4.12.5 G (2)**.)
Exempt persons	An exempt *person* (other than a *person* exempted only by section 39 of the *Act* (Exemption of appointed representatives)) if the activity relates to a *regulated activity* in respect of which the *person* is exempt from the *general prohibition*.	Not applicable.

Title	Type of retail client	Additional conditions
Certified sophisticated investors	An individual who meets the requirements set out in **COBS 4.12.7 R**, including an individual who is legally empowered (solely or jointly with others) to make investment decisions on behalf of another *person* who is the *firm's client*.	Not applicable.
Self-certified sophisticated investors	An individual who meets the requirements set out in **COBS 4.12.8 R**, including an individual who is legally empowered (solely or jointly with others) to make investment decisions on behalf of another *person* who is the *firm's client*.	The *firm* must consider the *contingent convertible instrument* is likely to be suitable for that individual, based on a preliminary assessment of that individual's profile and objectives. (See **COBS 4.12.5 G (2)**.)
Solicited advice	Any *retail client*.	The prohibition does not apply provided all of the following requirements are met: (a) there is no *financial promotion* other than a *personal recommendation* on the *contingent convertible instrument*;
	(b) the *personal recommendation* is made following a specific request by that *client* for advice on the merits of investing in the *contingent convertible instrument*; and	
	(c) the *client* has not previously received a *financial promotion* or any other communication from the *firm* (or from a *person* connected to the *firm*) which is intended to influence the *client* in relation to investment in *contingent convertible instruments*. (See Note 1.)	
MiFID or equivalent third country business other than *financial promotions*	Any *retail client*.	If the prohibited activities amount to *MiFID or equivalent third country business*, that rule only applies to the extent that the prohibited activity is the *communication* or *approval* of a *financial promotion*.
Prospectus	Any *retail client*.	The prohibition does not apply to the distribution of a prospectus required under the *Prospectus Directive*.
Issuers	Any *retail client*	To the extent that the *firm* is acting as issuer of a *contingent convertible instrument*, the prohibition only applies to the original issuance of the *contingent convertible instrument* and not to subsequent trading in the secondary market.

Title	Type of retail client	Additional conditions
Clearing, custodial and processing services	Any *retail client*	The prohibition does not apply to the extent that the *firm's* activities relate to clearing, registration or settlement of transactions in *contingent convertible instruments* (or rights to or interests in such instruments), any back office processing or reporting of such transactions, or custody of *contingent convertible instruments*.
Indirect investment	Any *retail client*	The prohibition does not apply in relation to a beneficial interest in a *contingent convertible instrument* held from participation in a *regulated collective investment scheme*, investment in a *non-mainstream pooled investment*, or membership of an *occupational pension scheme*.
Note 1	A *person* is connected with a *firm* if it acts as an *introducer* or *appointed representative* for that *firm* or, if it is any other *person*, regardless of *authorisation* status, who has a relevant business relationship with the *firm*.	
Note 2	See **COBS 2.4** for rules and guidance on agent as *client* and reliance on others.	

22.1.3 R   FCA

(1) For the purposes of compliance with this section and with any assessments or certifications required by the exemptions set out in **COBS 22.1.2 R**, any references in **COBS 4.12** provisions to *non-mainstream pooled investments* must be read as though they are references to *contingent convertible instruments*.

(2) If the *firm* is relying on the high net worth investor exemption, the sophisticated investor exemption or the self-certified sophisticated investor exemption for the purposes of compliance with **COBS 22.1.1 R**, the statement the investor must sign should have references to *non-mainstream pooled investments* replaced with references to *contingent convertible instruments*.

(3) The *firm* must give the *retail client* a written copy of any statements that individual has been asked to sign as part of certification as a high net worth, sophisticated or self-certified sophisticated investor for the purposes of compliance with **COBS 22.1.1 R**.

22.1.4 R   FCA

If a *firm* communicates or approves an invitation or inducement to acquire or underwrite a *contingent convertible instrument* (or rights to interests in that instrument) which is addressed to, or disseminated in such a way that it is likely to be received by, a *retail client*, it must comply with the record-keeping requirements in **COBS 4.11.1 R**, adapted as follows:

(1) references to *non-mainstream pooled investments* should be read as references to *contingent convertible instruments*; and

(2) references to **COBS 4.12.3 R** should be read as references to **COBS 22.1.1 R**.

22.2 REQUIREMENTS ON THE RETAIL DISTRIBUTION OF MUTUAL SOCIETY SHARES

Application

22.2.1 R   FCA

(1) The requirements in this section apply to a *firm* when *dealing* in or *arranging* a *deal* in a *mutual society share* with or for a *retail client* in the *EEA* where the *retail client* is to enter into the *deal* as buyer.

(2) The requirements in this section do not apply if:

    (a) the *firm* has taken reasonable steps to ensure that one (or more) of the exemptions in **COBS 22.2.4 R** applies; or

    (b) the *deal* relates to the trading of a *mutual society share* in the secondary market.

(3) In this section, a *retail client* of the *firm* includes a *person* who would be a *retail client* if he were receiving services in the course of the *firm* carrying on a *regulated activity*.

Risk warning requirement

22.2.2 R   FCA

The *firm* must give the *retail client* the following risk warning on paper or another *durable medium* and obtain confirmation in writing from the *retail client* that he has read it, in good time before the *retail client* has committed to *buy* the *mutual society share*:

"The investment to which this communication relates is a share. Direct investment in shares can be high risk and is very different to investment in deposit accounts or other savings products. In particular, you should note that:

(a) the entire amount you invest is at risk;

(b) income, distribution or dividend payments are not guaranteed, are entirely discretionary, and may be suspended or cancelled at any time, for any reason;

(c) the share is a perpetual instrument with no maturity date, and there is no obligation on the issuer to buy the share back;

(d) the share may be difficult to sell on for the price you paid for it, or any price; and

(e) investing more than 10% of your savings or net investment portfolio in this type of instrument is unlikely to be in your best interests."

Further requirements for non-advised, non-MiFID sales

22.2.3 R   FCA

(1)   The requirements in (2) and (3) must be met if:

     (a)   the *firm* is not providing an *investment service* in the course of *MiFID or equivalent third country business*; and

     (b)   the *retail client* is not otherwise receiving advice on the *mutual society share* from the *firm* or another *person*.

(2)   The *firm* must give the *retail client* the following statement on paper or another *durable medium* and obtain confirmation in writing from the *retail client* that he has signed it, in good time before the *retail client* has committed to *buy* the *mutual society share*:

     "I make this statement in connection with proposed investment in mutual society shares. I have been made aware that investing more than 10% of my net assets in mutual society shares is unlikely to be in my best interests. I declare that the proposed investment would not result in more than 10% of my net assets being invested in mutual society shares. Net assets for these purposes mean my financial assets after deduction of any debts I have, and do not include:

     (a) the property which is my primary residence, any amount owed under a mortgage relating to the purchase of that property, or any money raised through a loan secured on that property;

     (b) any rights of mine under a qualifying contract of insurance (for example, a life assurance or critical illness policy); or

     (c) any benefits (in the form of pensions or otherwise) which are payable on the termination of my service or on my death or retirement and to which I am (or my dependants are) or may be entitled.

     I accept that the investment to which this statement relates will expose me to a significant risk of losing all the money invested.

     Signature:

     Date: "

(3)   The *firm* must assess whether investment in the *mutual society share* is appropriate for the *retail client*, complying with the requirements in **COBS 10** as though the *firm* was providing non-advised *investment services* in the course of *MiFID or equivalent third country business*.

Exemptions

22.2.4 R   FCA

Each of the exemptions listed below applies only if the *retail client* is of the type described for the exemption and provided any additional conditions for the exemption are met.

Title	Type of retail client	Additional conditions
Certified high net worth investor	(a) An individual who meets the requirements set out in **COBS 4.12.6 R**; or (b) an individual in an *EEA State* other than the *UK* who meets requirements which are broadly equivalent to those set out in **COBS 4.12.6 R**; or	The *firm* must consider that the *mutual society share* is likely to be suitable for that individual, based on a preliminary assessment of that individual' profile and objectives (see **COBS 4.12.5 G (2)**).

Title	Type of retail client	Additional conditions
	(c) a *person* (or *persons*) legally empowered to make investment decisions on behalf of an individual who meets the earnings or net asset requirements in (a) or (b) above.	
Certified sophisticated investor	(a) An individual who meets the requirements set out in **COBS 4.12.7 R**; or (b) an individual in an *EEA State* other than the *UK* who meets requirements which are broadly equivalent to those set out in **COBS 4.12.7 R**; or (c) an individual who meets the requirements for either (a) or (b) above and who is legally empowered (solely or jointly with others) to make investment decisions on behalf of another person who is the *firm's client*.	Not applicable.
Self-certified sophisticated investor	(a) An individual who meets the requirements set out in **COBS 4.12.8 R**; or (b) an individual in an *EEA State* other than the *UK* who meets requirements which are broadly equivalent to those set out in **COBS 4.12.8 R**; or (c) an individual who meets the requirements for either (a) or (b) above and who is legally empowered (solely or jointly with others) to make investment decisions on behalf of another *person* who is the *firm's client*.	Not applicable.

Adaptation of other rules and guidance to mutual society shares

22.2.5 R   FCA

(1)   For the purposes of any assessments or certifications required by the exemptions in **COBS 22.2.4 R**, any references in **COBS 4.12** provisions to *non-mainstream pooled investments* must be read as though they are references to *mutual society shares*.

(2)   If the *firm* is relying on the exemptions for *certified high net worth investors*, *certified sophisticated investors* or *self-certified sophisticated investors* to comply with this section, the statement the investor must sign should have references to *non-mainstream pooled investments* replaced with references to *mutual society shares*.

(3)   The *firm* must give the *retail client* a written copy of any risk warning or statement that that individual has been asked to sign for the purposes of compliance with this section.

Record keeping

22.2.6 R   FCA

A *firm* which carries on an activity which is subject to this section must comply with the following record-keeping requirements:

(1)   the *person* allocated the *compliance oversight function* in the *firm* must make a record at or near the time of the activity certifying it complies with the requirements set out in this section;

(2)   the making of the record required in (1) may be delegated to one or more *employees* of the *firm* who report to and are supervised by the *person* allocated the *compliance oversight function*, provided the process for certification of compliance has been reviewed and approved by the *person* allocated the *compliance oversight function* no more than 12 months before the date of the *deal*;

(3)   the record in (1) must include information and evidence demonstrating compliance with each of the requirements in this section, as applicable;

(4)   if the requirements in **COBS 22.2.2 R** and **COBS 22.2.3 R** did not apply because the *firm* relied on one of the exemptions, the record in (1) must include which exemption was relied on, together with the reason why the *firm* is satisfied that that exemption applies;

(5)   where the *firm* relies on the *certified high net worth investor*, the *certified sophisticated investor* or the *self-certified sophisticated investor* exemption, the record required in (1) must include a copy of the certificate or investor statement (as signed by the investor) and of the warnings or indications required by the exemption;

(6)   a *firm* must retain the record required in (1) for five years if it relates to *MiFID or equivalent third country business*, and otherwise for three years.

Electronic documents

22.2.7 G   FCA

In this section:

(1)   any requirement that a document is signed may be satisfied by an electronic signature or electronic evidence of assent; and

(2)   any references to writing should be construed in accordance with **GEN 2.2.14 R** and its related *guidance* provisions.

TRANSITIONAL PROVISIONS AND SCHEDULES

1   TRANSITIONAL PROVISIONS RELATING TO CLIENT CATEGORISATION

[3.70A]

(1)	(2) Material to which the transitional provision applies	(3)	(4) Transitional provision	(5) Transitional provision: dates in force	(6) Handbook provisions: coming into force
			Overview of transitional provisions for client categorisation		
1.1	**COBS 3**	G	(1) *COBS* TP 1.2 contains default transitional categorisation provisions in relation to the existing *clients* of a *firm* on 1 November 2007. In many cases, they allow a *client* to be automatically provided with the nearest equivalent categorisation under **COBS 3** to their previous categorisation..	From 1 November 2007 indefinitely	1 November 2007
			(2) *COBS* TP 1.3 explains how the transitional provisions for *client* categorisation relate to the requirement for a *firm* to act if it becomes aware that an *elective professional client* no longer satisfies the initial conditions for its categorisation.		
			(3) The default provisions do not prevent a *firm* categorising such a *client* differently in accordance with **COBS 3**. *COBS* TP 1.4 provides guidance on how some of the procedural requirements in **COBS 3** apply in some such cases.		
			(4) *COBS* TP 1.5 contains transitional notification obligations, which apply if the default provisions do not allow that *client* to be provided with the nearest equivalent categorisation or a *firm* chooses not to take advantage of those provisions in relation to a *client*.		

(1)	(2) Material to which the transitional provision applies	(3)	(4) Transitional provision	(5) Transitional provision: dates in force	(6) Handbook provisions: coming into force
			(5) *COBS* TP 1.6 contains a transitional notification obligation that applies to a *firm* that, in relation to *MiFID or equivalent third country business*, takes advantage of the default transitional categorisation provisions to classify a *client* as a *per se professional client*.		
			(6) *COBS* TP 1.9 contains transitional categorisation provisions in relation to *clients* of a *firm* that are taken on between 1 November 2007 and 30 June 2008 in relation to business that is not *MiFID or equivalent third country business*.		
			Categorisation of existing clients		
1.2	**COBS 3**	R	(1) An existing *client* that was correctly categorised as a *private customer* immediately before 1 November 2007 is a *retail client* unless and to the extent it is given a different categorisation by the *firm* under **COBS 3**. (2) An existing *client* that was correctly categorised as an *intermediate customer* immediately before 1 November 2007: (a) is an *elective professional client* if it was an expert *private customer* that had been re-classified as an *intermediate customer* on the basis of its experience and understanding; or (b) is otherwise a *per se professional client*; unless and to the extent it is given a different categorisation by the *firm* under **COBS 3**. (3) An existing *client* that was correctly categorised as a *market counterparty* immediately before 1 November 2007 is: (a) for *eligible counterparty business* that is not *MiFID or equivalent third country business*, an *eligible counterparty*; and (b) otherwise, a *per se professional client*; unless and to the extent it is given a different categorisation by the *firm* under **COBS 3**. [**Note:** Article 71(6) of, and third paragraph of section II.2 of Annex II to, *MiFID*]	From 1 November 2007 indefinitely	1 November 2007
1.3	**COBS 3**	G	Under **COBS 3.5.9 R**, if a *firm* becomes aware that a *client* no longer fulfils the initial conditions that made it eligible for categorisation as an *elective professional client*, the *investment firm* must take the appropriate action. In the case of a *client* that has been classified as an *elective professional client* under *COBS* TP 1.2R(2)(a), the initial conditions are those that applied to the *client's* initial categorisation as an *intermediate customer*. Former inter-professional business	From 1 November 2007 indefinitely	1 November 2007

(1)	(2) Material to which the transitional provision applies	(3)	(4) Transitional provision	(5) Transitional provision: dates in force	(6) Handbook provisions: coming into force
1.4	COBS 3	G	The requirement to provide notices under **COBS 3.3.1 R** only applies in relation to new *clients*. The requirement to obtain confirmation under **COBS 3.6.4 R (2)** only applies in relation to prospective counterparties. These obligations are therefore not relevant to the extent that an existing *client* with whom a *firm* conducted *inter-professional business* before 1 November 2007 is categorised as an *eligible counterparty* under **COBS 3** in relation to *eligible counterparty business*. Transitional notification obligations	From 1 November 2007 indefinitely	1 November 2007
1.5	COBS 3	R	(1) If a *firm* does not categorise a *client* that was a *private customer* immediately before 1 November 2007 as a *retail client*, it must notify that *client* of its categorisation as a *professional client* or *eligible counterparty*, as appropriate, on or before that date, or if later, before conducting any further business to which *COBS* applies for that *client*. (2) If a *firm* does not categorise a *client* that was an *intermediate customer* immediately before 1 November 2007 as a *professional client*, it must notify that *client* of its categorisation as a *retail client* or *eligible counterparty*, as appropriate, on or before that date, or if later, before conducting any further business to which *COBS* applies for that *client*. (3) If a *firm* does not categorise a *client* that was a *market counterparty* immediately before 1 November 2007 as an *eligible counterparty*, it must notify that *client* of its categorisation as a *retail client* or *professional client* on or before that date, or if later, before conducting any further business to which *COBS* applies for that *client*. [**Note:** article 28(1) of the *MiFID implementing Directive*]	From 1 November 2007 indefinitely	1 November 2007
1.6	COBS 3	R	If a *firm*, in relation to *MiFID or equivalent third country business*, categorises a *client* who would not otherwise have been a *professional client* as a *professional client* under *COBS* TP 1.2(2)(b) or (3)(b), it must inform that *client* about the relevant conditions for the categorisation of *clients*. This notification must be made on or before 1 November 2007, or if later, before conducting any further business to which *COBS* applies for that *client*. [**Note:** article 71(6) of *MiFID*]	From 1 November 2007 indefinitely	1 November 2007

(1)	(2) Material to which the transitional provision applies	(3)	(4) Transitional provision	(5) Transitional provision: dates in force	(6) Handbook provisions: coming into force
1.7		G	A notice to a *professional client* under *COBS* TP 1.6 should inform that *client*: (a) that they have been categorised as a *professional client*; and (b) of the main differences between the treatment of a *retail client* and a *professional client*.	From 1 November 2007 indefinitely	1 November 2007
1.8		R	The record-keeping requirements under **COBS 3.8.2 R** apply in relation to any *client* categorisations or re-categorisations made under the transitional provisions for **COBS 3**. Categorisation of new clients before 30 June (business that is not MiFID or equivalent third country business)	From 1 November 2007 indefinitely	1 November 2007
1.9	COBS 3	R	Expired		

2 OTHER TRANSITIONAL PROVISIONS

(1)	(2) Material to which the transitional provision applies	(3)	(4) Transitional provision	(5) Transitional provision: dates in force	(6) Handbook provisions: coming into force
2.-2	*COBS*, with the exception of **COBS 15**	R	Expired		
2.-1	COBS 4	R	Expired		
2.-1A	COBS 4.7.7 R to COBS 4.7.10 R	R	Expired		
2.1	COBS 6.1	G	(1) If a *firm* provides services of an ongoing nature to an existing *client* it need not provide information to that *client* that it would be required to provide under *COBS* to a new *client* but which it was not required to provide under *COB*. (2) Services of an ongoing nature include *safekeeping and administration investments* and *managing investments*,	From 1 November 2007 indefinitely	1 November 2007
2.2	COBS 6.1	G	(1) If a *firm* provides a service for an existing *client* that is not of an ongoing nature and which relates to the same particular type of *designated investment* as a previous service, the *firm* need not provide information to that *client* that it would be required to provide under **COBS 6.1** to a new *client* but which it was not required to provide under *COB*.	From 1 November 2007 indefinitely	1 November 2007

(1)	(2) Material to which the transitional provision applies	(3)	(4) Transitional provision	(5) Transitional provision: dates in force	(6) Handbook provisions: coming into force
			(2) But a *firm* should ensure that the *client* has received all relevant information in relation to a subsequent transaction, such as details of product charges that differ from those described in respect of a previous transaction.		
[deleted]					
2.2A	**COBS 6.1E**	R	A *platform service provider* may continue to accept remuneration in relation to a *retail investment product* transaction which was executed on or before 5 April 2014:	From 6 April 2014 to 5 April 2016	6 April 2014
			(1) if, after 5 April 2014, no change is made to that product or the investment held in that product; or		
			(2) where there is such a change on or after 6 April 2014, only in relation to the unchanged part of that product.		
2.2AA	**COBS 6.1E**	G	The *platform service provider* may be remunerated by way of a *platform charge* for the changed part of that product.	From 6 April 2014 to 5 April 2016	From 6 April 2014 to 5 April 2016
2.2AB	**COBS 6.1E**	G	The following examples do not entail changes to the *retail investment product*:	From 6 April 2014 to 5 April 2016	From 6 April 2014 to 5 April 2016
			(1) regular contributions to or a reinvestment of dividends from a *retail investment product* following instructions given on or before 5 April 2014;		
			(2) a rebalancing of the *retail investment product* following instructions given on or before 5 April 2014.		
2.2AC	**COBS 6.1E**	G	Examples of changes to the *retail investment product* are:	From 6 April 2014 to 5 April 2016	From 6 April 2014 to 5 April 2016
			(1) the *retail client's* investment in, or regular contribution to the relevant *retail investment product* is increased following instructions given on or after 6 April 2014. The *platform service provider* can continue to receive remuneration in relation to the amounts invested by the *retail client* following instructions given on or before 5 April 2014 but not in relation to any additional amounts invested by the *retail client* following instructions given on or after 6 April 2014.		

(1)	(2) Material to which the transitional provision applies	(3)	(4) Transitional provision	(5) Transitional provision: dates in force	(6) Handbook provisions: coming into force
			(2) the *retail client's* investment is switched between *retail investment products* held by the *platform service provider* following instructions given on or after 6 April 2014. This includes switching between funds within a *retail investment product* such as a *SIPP* or a *retail investment product* wrapper such as an *ISA*.		
			(3) the re-registration of the *retail client's* *retail investment product* to another *platform service provider* following instructions given on or after 6 April 2014.		
[deleted]					
2.2B	**COBS 6.3**	R	Expired		
2.2C	**COBS 6.3**	G	Expired		
2.2D	**COBS 6.3**	R	Expired		
2.2E	**COBS 6.3.7 G**	R	Expired		
2.3	**COBS 10.1.2 R**	R	Expired		
2.4	**COBS 10.1.2 R**	G	Expired		
2.4-A	**COBS 10.1.2 R**	R	Expired		
2.4A	**COBS 11.2**	R	Expired		
2.4B	**COBS 11.2**	G	Expired		
2.4C	**COBS 11.2**	R	Expired		
2.4D	**COBS 11.2**	R	Expired		
2.4E	**COBS 12.2 and COBS 12.3**	R	Expired		
2.4F	**COBS 12.2 and COBS 12.3**	G	Expired		
2.4G	**COBS 12.2 and COBS 12.3**	R	Expired		
2.5	**COBS 13**	R	Expired		
2.5-A	**COBS 13.4.1 R**	R	Expired		
2.5A	**COBS 13.4.2 R**	R	Expired		
2.5AA	**COBS 13.5.1 R**	R	Expired		

(1)	(2) Material to which the transitional provision applies	(3)	(4) Transitional provision	(5) Transitional provision: dates in force	(6) Handbook provisions: coming into force
2.5AB	**COBS 13.5.2 R**	R	Expired		
2.5-B	**COBS 13 ANNEX 2**	R	Expired		
2.5B	**COBS 13 ANNEX 2 2.3**	R	Expired		
2.5C	**COBS 13 ANNEX 2 2.4**	R	Expired		
2.5D	**COBS 13 ANNEX 3**	R	Expired		
2.5E	**COBS 13 ANNEX 4**	R	Expired		
2.6	**COBS 14.1** and **COBS 14.2**	R	Expired		
2.6A	**COBS 14.2** and **COBS 14.3** Expired		Expired		
2.7	**COBS 15**	R	Expired		
2.8	**COBS 16.3** (Periodic statements)	G	This transitional *rule* applies in relation to a periodic reporting period for a *periodic statement* that includes 1 November 2007. A *firm* may choose to comply with either **COBS 16.3** or **COB 8.2** in providing any *periodic statement* in relation to which this *rule* applies.	From 1 November 2007 indefinitely	1 November 2007
2.8A	**COBS 18**	R	Expired		
2.8B	**COBS 18**	G	Expired		
2.8C	**COBS 18**	R	Expired		
2.8D	**COBS 18**	G	[deleted]		
2.8E	**COBS 18**	R	Expired		
2.8F	**COBS 19.4.3 R**	R	(1) Where a *firm* has provided the *retail client* with an open market option statement in accordance with **COBS 19.4.2 R** but has not provided a six-week reminder before 6 April 2015, the rules in **COBS 19.4.3 R** do not apply. (2) Where (1) applies, the *firm* must: (a) tell the *client* what sum of money will be available to exercise open market options; and (b) provide the *client* with the fact sheet "Your pension: it's time to choose" available on www.moneyadviceservice.org.uk or a statement in a *durable medium* that gives materially the same information;	From 6 April 2015 to 5 August 2016	6 April 2015

(1)	(2)	(3)	(4)	(5)	(6)
	Material to which the transitional provision applies		**Transitional provision**	**Transitional provision: dates in force**	**Handbook provisions: coming into force**
			(c) provide the *client* with a clear and prominent statement about the availability of the pensions guidance including: (i) how to access the pensions guidance and its contact details; (ii) that the pensions guidance can be provided on the internet, telephone, or face to face; (iii) that the pensions guidance is a free impartial service to help *consumers* to understand their options at retirement; and (iv) a recommendation that the *client* seeks appropriate guidance or advice to understand their options at retirement; at least six weeks before the *client's* intended retirement date.		
			(3) If a *firm* has provided the *retail client* with a version of the fact sheet "Your pension: it's time to choose" available on www.moneyadviceservice.org.uk dated June 2014 or later, or a statement in a *durable medium* that gives materially the same information, the requirement in (2)(b) does not apply.		
2.9	**COBS 20.2.1 G** to **COBS 20.2.23 R**; **COBS 20.2.26 R** to **COBS 20.2.41 G**	R	The provisions listed in column (2) do not apply to a *firm* if, and to the extent that, they are inconsistent with an arrangement that was formally approved by the *appropriate regulator*, a *previous regulator* or a court of competent jurisdiction, on or before 20 January 2005.	From 1 November 2007 indefinitely	1 November 2007
2.9A	**COBS 20.2.24 R** to **COBS 20.2.25A R** (Charging payments of compensation and redress to a with-profits fund)	R	The provisions listed in column (2) do not apply to a *firm* if, and to the extent that, they are inconsistent with an arrangement that was formally approved by the *appropriate regulator*, a *previous regulator* or a court of competent jurisdiction, on or before 31 July 2009.	From 31 July 2009 indefinitely	31 July 2009
2.10	**COBS 20.2.42 R (3)** (Policyholder advocate: appointment and role)	R	Expired		

(1)	(2) Material to which the transitional provision applies	(3)	(4) Transitional provision	(5) Transitional provision: dates in force	(6) Handbook provisions: coming into force
2.11	*COBS* TP 2.9	G	The *rules* and *guidance* on treating with-profits policyholders fairly (**COBS 20.2.1 G –COBS 20.2.41 G;**) may be contrary to, or inconsistent with, some arrangements that were formally approved by the *appropriate regulator*, a *previous regulator* or a court of competent jurisdiction, on or before 20 January 2005. The effect of TP 2.9 is that these *rules* do not apply to such arrangements if, and to the extent that, it is inconsistent with them. A *firm* should be mindful, however, that, even if some or all of these *rules* are disapplied, the *firm* is still subject to the *rules* in the rest of the *Handbook*, including *Principle* 6.	From 1 November 2007 indefinitely	1 November 2007
2.12	*COBS*	R	[deleted]		
2.13	*COBS*	R	[deleted]		
2.14	**COBS 20.2.24 R** to **COBS 20.2.25A R**	R	(1) **COBS 20.2.24 R** to **COBS 20.2.25A R** have effect in relation to payments of compensation and redress arising out of events occurring on or after 31 July 2009. (2) For payments of compensation and redress arising out of events occurring before 31 July 2009, **COBS 20.2.23 R** to **COBS 20.2.25 R** apply as they were in force on 30 July 2009.	From 31 July 2009 indefinitely	31 July 2009
	[deleted]		[deleted]	[deleted]	
2.16	**COBS 9.4.10 G; COBS 13 ANNEX 2; COBS 13 ANNEX 3; COBS 14.2.1 R**	R	Expired		
2.17	**COBS 9.4.10 G; COBS 13 ANNEX 2; COBS 13 ANNEX 3; COBS 14.2.1 R**	G	Expired		
2.18	**COBS 20.2.53 R** to **COBS 20.2.60 G, SUP APP 2.15 G**	R	(1) Unless (2) applies, and subject to (3), a *firm* that has ceased to effect new *contracts of insurance* in a *with-profits fund* must submit to the *FCA* a run-off plan of the type described in **COBS 20.2.53 R (2); COBS 20.2.56 R,** and **COBS 20.2.57 G,** if it has not done so already, by 31 December 2012, regardless of when it closed to new business.	From 1 April 2012 indefinitely	1 November 2007 and 1 April 2012

(1)	(2) Material to which the transitional provision applies	(3)	(4) Transitional provision	(5) Transitional provision: dates in force	(6) Handbook provisions: coming into force
			(2) Paragraph (1) does not apply to a *firm* if, and to the extent that, to comply would be contrary to or inconsistent with an arrangement that was formally approved by a court of competent jurisdiction, on or before 1 April 2012.		
			(3) A *firm* required by (1) above to produce a run-off plan: (a) should consider the guidance in **SUP APP 2.15.6 G**, **2.15.7 G (11)**, **2.15.13 G**, **2.15.14 G** and **2.15.15 G** to continue to apply to it, as appropriate;		
			(b) may demonstrate compliance with the guidance in **SUP APP 2.15.2 G**, **2.15.3 G**, **2.15.4 G** and **2.15.5 G** by reference to existing documents created by or for the *firm*, provided that it submits copies of relevant extracts to the *FCA*;		
			(c) may disregard the remaining provisions in **SUP APP 2.15 G** if to do so would be consistent with meeting the requirements of **COBS 20.2.56 R (1)**; and (d) may otherwise tailor the run-off plan to reflect the fact that the fund in question has already been closed.		
2.19	**COBS 20.2.53 R to COBS 20.2.60 G**	G	The effect of *COBS* TP 2.18 is that *firms* which were not required to submit a run-off plan to the *FCA* because they ceased to effect new *contracts of insurance* before 1 November 2007 or because of previous transitional provisions in *COBS*, will need to submit a version of a run-off plan to the *FCA*, taking into account the fact that the fund has already closed, by 31 December 2012. However, this will not apply to the extent that it would be inconsistent with a formally approved court scheme.	From 1 April 2012 indefinitely	1 November 2007 and 1 April 2012
2.20	**COBS 20.2.28 R**	R	Expired		
2.21	**COBS 20.2.36 R to COBS 20.2.36A R**	R	Expired		
2.22	**COBS 20.5.1 R to COBS 20.5.5 R**	R	Expired		

(1)	(2) Material to which the transitional provision applies	(3)	(4) Transitional provision	(5) Transitional provision: dates in force	(6) Handbook provisions: coming into force
2.23	The changes to *COBS* set out in Annex K of the Alternative Investment Fund Managers Directive Instrument 2013	R	Expired		

SCH 1   RECORD KEEPING REQUIREMENTS

1.1 G   FCA

The aim of the *guidance* in the following table is to give the reader a quick overall view of the relevant record keeping requirements.

1.2 G   FCA

It is not a complete statement of those requirements and should not be relied on as if it were.

1.3 G   FCA

Handbook reference	Subject of record	Contents of record	When record must be made	Retention period
COBS 2.3.17 R (1)	Information disclosed to the *client* in accordance with **COBS 2.3.1 R (2)(B)**	The information disclosed	When information is disclosed	5 years from date information is given
COBS 2.3.17 R (2)	Each benefit given to another *firm* which does not have to be disclosed to the *client* in accordance with **COBS 2.3.1 R (2)(B)(II)**	Each benefit given	When benefit is given	5 years from date of benefit
COBS 3.8.2 R (1)	Standard form notice to *clients* and agreements under **COBS 3**	Each standard form notice and agreement	When standard form is first used	Relevant period from when the *firm* ceases to carry on business with clients under that standard form (see **COBS 3.8.2 R (3)**)

Handbook reference	Subject of record	Contents of record	When record must be made	Retention period
COBS 3.8.2 R (2)	*Client* categorisation	*Client* categorisation and supporting information, evidence of dispatch to client of any notice (the notice itself where this differs from standard form) and a copy of any agreement entered into	From time of categorisation	Relevant period from when the *firm* ceases to carry on business with or for that client (see **COBS 3.8.2 R (3)**)
COBS 4.11.1 R (1)	*Financial promotion*	A *financial promotion communicated* or *approved* (subject to exemptions)	When *communicated* or *approved*	See **COBS 4.11.1 R (3)**
COBS 4.11.1 R (2)	Telemarketing scripts	Copy of any script used	Date script used	See **COBS 4.11.1 R (3)**
COBS 4.11.1 R (2A)	*Non-mainstream pooled investments*: certification of compliance	(1) Certification by the *person* allocated the *compliance oversight function* or *employees* of the *firm* reporting to and supervised by that *person* confirming that the *financial promotion* is compliant with the restrictions in section 238 of the *Act* and **COBS 4.12.3 R**, as applicable. (2) Which exemption applies and the reason why that exemption applies. Where the exemption requires a certificate, investor statement, warning or indication, a copy of that certificate, investment statement, warning or indication.	(1) Date of certification (2) Date the invitation or inducement is communicated or approved	
COBS 4.11.2 G	Compliance of *financial promotions*	*Firms* encouraged to consider recording why a *financial promotion* is considered compliant.	Date of assessment of compliance	
COBS 6.1A.27 R	Adviser charging and remuneration	(1) the *firm's* charging structure; (2) the total adviser charge payable by each retail client;	(1) when the charging structure is first used; (2) from the date of disclosure; (3) from the date of disclosure;	See **COBS 6.1A.27 R (1)** to **(3)**

Handbook reference	Subject of record	Contents of record	When record must be made	Retention period
		(3) if the total *adviser charge* paid by a *retail client* has varied materially from the charge indicated for that service in the *firm's* charging structure, the reasons for that difference.		
COBS 6.1C.21 R	Consultancy charging and remuneration	(1) the *firm's* charging structure; (2) the total *consultancy charge* payable by each employer. (3) if the total *consultancy charge* for a particular service has varied materially from that indicated in the *firm's* charging structure, the reasons for that difference.	(1) when the charging structure is first used; (2) from the date of disclosure;	See COBS 6.1C.21 R
COBS 6.3.11 R	*Menu*	Copy of each *menu*	From date on which it was updated or replaced	5 years
COBS 8.1.4 R	*Client agreements*	Documents setting out rights and obligations of the *firm* and the *client*	From date of agreement	From whichever is the longer of 5 years or the duration of the relationship with the *client*. Records relating to a *pension transfer, pension conversion, pension opt-out* or *FSAVC* must be retained indefinitely
COBS 9.2.9 R	Recommendations on *friendly society life policies*.	Why the recommendation is considered suitable	Date of recommendation.	5 years.
COBS 9.5.1 G	Suitability	*Client* information for *suitability report* and *suitability report*	From date of *suitability report*	See COBS 9.5.2 R.
COBS 9.6.19 R	*Basic advice*	Decision to give *basic advice, range* used and *basic advice* summary prepared for *retail client*	Date on which *basic advice* given	5 years
COBS 9.6.20 R	*Scope* of *basic advice* (*stakeholder products*)	*Scope* of *basic advice* and its *range* (or *ranges*) of *stakeholder products*	Date on which the *scope* and *range* becomes relevant	5 years from the date replaced by more up-to-date record

Handbook reference	Subject of record	Contents of record	When record must be made	Retention period
COBS 10.7.1 G	Appropriateness	*Client* information obtained in making assessment of appropriateness and the appropriateness assessment	Date of assessment	5 years
COBS 11.3.2 R	Client orders	Orders executed for *clients*	See **COBS 11.5**	5 years
COBS 11.5.1 EU	*Client* orders and decisions to deal in *portfolio management*	Orders received from *clients* and decisions taken – details in **COBS 11.5.1 EU**	See **COBS 11.5.1 EU**	5 years
COBS 11.5.2 EU	*Client* orders	Execution of orders	See **COBS 11.5.1 EU**	5 years
COBS 11.5.3 EU	*Client* orders	Transmission details (see **COBS 11.5.3 EU**)	Date of transmission	5 years
COBS 11.6.19 R	Prior and periodic disclosure	Prior and periodic disclosure on use of dealing commission	From date of disclosure to *customers*	5 years
COBS 11.7.4 R	Personal account dealing	Notifications by outsourcing provider and authorisation or prohibition.	Date of notification or decision.	5 years
COBS 11.8.5 R	Telephone conversations and electronic communications subject to the taping obligation (see **COBS 11.8.5 R**)	Telephone conversations and electronic communications recorded under **COBS 11.8.5 R**	When the conversation or electronic communication is made, sent or received	6 months
COBS 12.4.6 R	*Research recommendations*	Basis of substantiation of *research recommendation*	Date of recommendation	5 years
COBS 15.3.4 R	Cancellation: exercise of right	Exercise of the right to cancel or withdraw	Date of exercise	As specified in **COBS 15.3.4 R** (1), (2) and (3)
COBS 16.2.7 R	Confirmation to *clients*	Copy of a confirmation	From date of despatch to *client*	*MiFID or equivalent third country business* – 5 years Other business – 3 years
COBS 16.3.11 R	*Periodic statements*	A copy of a *periodic statement* sent to a *client*	From date of despatch to *client*	*MiFID or equivalent third country business* – 5 years Other business – 3 years
COBS 16.6.6 R	Life insurance contracts	Information to be provided during the terms of the contract	When information is given	5 years after information given
COBS 18.5.14 R	*Residual CIS operators* and small authorised UK AIFMs of an unauthorised AIF	*Periodic statement* to be provided to *participants*	When provided	3 years

Handbook reference	Subject of record	Contents of record	When record must be made	Retention period
COBS 19.1.5 R	Execution only pension transfer or opt out	That no *personal recommendation* was given to the *client*	Date of transaction	5 years
COBS 19.2.3 R	Promotion of personal pension scheme	Why the promotion was justified	When promoted	5 years
COBS 20.2.36A R	*strategic investments*	A description of the strategic purpose for which a *strategic investment* has been purchased or retained	Before making a *strategic investment* or when reviewing whether to retain a *strategic investment*	Until the *firm* ceases to hold the *strategic investment* in question
COBS 20.3.1 R	*PPFMs*	Each version of the *PPFM*	Date on which the *PPFM* is relevant	5 years
COBS 22.2.6R	Retail distribution of mutual society shares	Information and evidence demonstrating compliance with the requirements of COBS 22.2	At or near the time of the sale to a *retail client*	5 years for *MiFID or equivalent third country business* and 3 years for other business
COBS TP 1	*Client* categorisation transitional	Categorisation or re-categorisation under TP1	Date of categorisation/ re-categorisation	See COBS 3.8.2 R (2)
COBS TP 2	*Investment research* transitional	Election to comply with COBS 12.2–COBS 12.3 sooner than 1 May 2008	Date of decision and date from which election is to be effective	5 years
COBS TP 2	Specialist regimes	Election to comply with COBS 18 sooner than 1 May 2008	Date of decision and date from which election is to be effective	5 years

SCH 2   NOTIFICATION REQUIREMENTS

2.1 G   FCA

Handbook reference	Matters to be notified	Contents of notification	Trigger event	Time allowed
COBS 20.2.45 R	Appointment of *policyholder advocate*.	The terms on which the *firm* proposes to appoint a *policyholder advocate*.	Proposal to appoint *policyholder advocate*.	As soon as reasonably practicable
COBS 21.2.8 R	Breach of COBS 21.3.5 R	Any failure to meet the requirements of COBS 21.3.5 R	Breach of COBS 21.3.5 R	As soon as the *firm* becomes aware of the failure
COBS 20.5.5 R (3)	The decision of a *firm's governing body* to depart from the advice or recommendation of the *with-profits committee* or advisory arrangement.	A description of: (1) the decision of, and reasons given by, the *firm's governing body*;	The *with-profits committee* or advisory arrangement considers that the issue is sufficiently significant and requests of the *governing body* that the *FSA* be informed.	As soon as reasonably practicable

Handbook reference	Matters to be notified	Contents of notification	Trigger event	Time allowed
		(2) the recommendation and advice of the *with-profits committee* or advisory arrangement; together with a copy of the *firm's* records of the decision, reasons, advice and recommendations.		

SCH 3   FEES AND OTHER REQUIRED PAYMENTS

3.1 G   FCA

There are no requirements for fees or other payments in *COBS*.

SCH 4   POWERS EXERCISED

4.1 G

[deleted]

4.2 G

[deleted]

SCH 5   RIGHTS OF ACTION FOR DAMAGES

5.1 G   FCA

The table below sets out the *rules* in *COBS* contravention of which by an *authorised person* may be actionable under section 138D of the *Act* (Actions for damages) by a *person* who suffers loss as a result of the contravention.

5.2 G   FCA

If a "Yes" appears in the column headed "For private person?", the *rule* may be actionable by a *"private person"* under section 138D (or, in certain circumstances, his fiduciary or representative; see article 6(2) and (3)(c) of the Financial Services and Markets Act 2000 (Rights of Action) Regulations 2001 (SI 2001/2256)). A "Yes" in the column headed "Removed" indicates that the *FCA* has removed the right of action under section 150(2) of the *Act*. If so, a reference to the *rule* in which it is removed is also given.

5.3 G   FCA

The column headed "For other person?" indicates whether the *rule* may be actionable by a *person* other than a *private person* (or his fiduciary or representative) under article 6(2) and (3) of those Regulations. If so, an indication of the type of *person* by whom the *rule* may be actionable is given.

5.4 G   FCA

Chapter/ Appendix Section/Annex Paragraph	Right of action under section 138D			
	For private person?	Removed?	For other person?	
All *rules* in *COBS* with the status letter "E"	No	No	No	
Any *rule* in *COBS* which prohibits an *authorised person* from seeking to make provision excluding or restricting any duty or liability	Yes	No	Yes	Any other person
Any *rule* in *COBS* which is directed at ensuring that transactions in *designated investments* are not effected with the benefit of unpublished information that, if made public, would be likely to affect the price of that designated investment	Yes	No	Yes	Any other person

The *fair, clear and not misleading rule*	Yes	In part (Note 1)	No
All other *rules* in *COBS*	Yes	No	No

Notes

1. *COBS* 4.2.6R provides that if, in relation to a particular communication or *financial promotion*, a *firm* takes reasonable steps to ensure it complies with the *fair, clear and not misleading rule*, a contravention of that *rule* does not give rise to a right of action under section 138D of the *Act*.

SCH 6   RULES THAT CAN BE WAIVED

6.1 G   FCA

As a result of section 138A of the *Act* (Modification or waiver of rules) the *FCA* has power to waive all its *rules*, other than *rules* made under section 137O (Threshold condition code), section 247 (Trust scheme rules), section 248 (Scheme particular rules), section 261I (Contractual scheme rules) or section 261J (Contractual scheme particulars rules) of the *Act*. However, if the *rules* incorporate requirements laid down in European directives, it will not be possible for the *FCA* to grant a waiver that would be incompatible with the *United Kingdom's* responsibilities under those directives.

I. DISPUTE RESOLUTION: COMPLAINTS (DISP)

DISPUTE RESOLUTION: COMPLAINTS
the detailed requirements for handling complaints and the Financial Ombudsman Service arrangements

DISP INTRO

1   INTRODUCTION

[3.71]

This part of the *FCA Handbook* sets out how *complaints* are to be dealt with by *respondents* (*firms, payment service providers, electronic money issuers*, and *VJ participants*) and the *Financial Ombudsman Service*.

It refers to relevant provisions in the *Act* and in transitional provisions made by the Treasury under the *Act*. It includes *rules* made by the *FCA* and rules made (and *standard terms* set) by *FOS Ltd* with the consent or approval of the *FCA*.

The powers to make rules (or set *standard terms*) relating to *firms, payment service providers, electronic money issuers*, and *VJ participants* derive from various legislative provisions; but the rules (and *standard terms*) have been co-ordinated to ensure that they are identical, wherever possible.

Chapter 1: Treating complainants fairly

DISP 1 contains rules and guidance on how *respondents* should deal with *complaints* promptly and fairly, including *complaints* that could be referred to the *FOS*. Some of these rules also apply to certain *branches* of *firms* elsewhere in the *EEA* and certain *EEA firms* carrying out activities in the *United Kingdom* under the freedom to provide *cross border services*.

Chapters 2–4: The Financial Ombudsman Service

Chapters 2, 3 and 4 set out how the *Financial Ombudsman Service* (operated by *FOS Ltd*) considers unresolved *complaints*.

Chapter 2 sets out the scope of the *Financial Ombudsman Service's* two jurisdictions:

     the *Compulsory Jurisdiction*; and
     the *Voluntary Jurisdiction*.

The scope of the two jurisdictions is defined by: the type of activity to which the *complaint* relates; the place where the activity took place; the eligibility of the complainant; and the time limits for referring a *complaint* to the *Financial Ombudsman Service*.

Chapter 3 sets out the procedures of the *Financial Ombudsman Service*, including consideration and determination of *complaints* and how the *Financial Ombudsman Service* deals with information received.

Chapter 4 sets out the terms under which *VJ participants* participate in the *Voluntary Jurisdiction*.

Appendix 1: FCA's guidance on handling mortgage-endowment complaints

This appendix contains the *FCA's guidance* to *firms* on handling *complaints* relating to mortgage endowments.

Appendix 3: FCA's rules and guidance on handling payment protection insurance complaints

This appendix sets out the approach which *firms* should use when handling *complaints* relating to the sale of *payment protection contracts*.

Financial Ombudsman Service fees

The rules on fees charged in respect of the *Financial Ombudsman Service* are in Chapter 5 of the Fees manual.

CHAPTER 1
TREATING COMPLAINANTS FAIRLY

1.1   PURPOSE AND APPLICATION

Purpose

[3.72]
1.1.1 G   FCA

This chapter contains *rules* and *guidance* on how *respondents* should deal promptly and fairly with *complaints* in respect of business carried on from establishments in the *United Kingdom*, by certain *branches* of *firms* in the *EEA* or by certain *EEA firms* carrying out activities in the *United Kingdom* under the freedom to provide *cross border services*. It is also relevant to those who may wish to make a *complaint* or refer it to the *Financial Ombudsman Service*.

Background

1.1.2 G   FCA

Details of how this chapter applies to each type of *respondent* are set out below. For this purpose, *respondents* include:

(1)   *persons* carrying on *regulated activities* (*firms*), providing *payment services* (*payment service providers*) or providing *electronic money* issuance services (*electronic money issuers*) and which are covered by the *Compulsory Jurisdiction*; and

(2)   [deleted]

(3)   *persons* who have opted in to the *Voluntary Jurisdiction* (*VJ participants*).

Application to firms

1.1.3 R   FCA

(1)   Subject to **DISP 1.1.5 R**, this chapter applies to a *firm* in respect of *complaints* from *eligible complainants* concerning activities carried on from an establishment maintained by it or its *appointed representative* in the *United Kingdom*.

(2)   For *complaints* relating to the *MiFID business* of a *firm*, the *complaints handling rules* and the *complaints record rule*:

    (a)   apply to *complaints* from *retail clients* and do not apply to *complaints* from *eligible complainants* who are not *retail clients*;

    (b)   also apply in respect of activities carried on from a *branch* of a *UK firm* in another *EEA State*; and

    (c)   do not apply in respect of activities carried on from a *branch* of an *EEA firm* in the *United Kingdom*.

(3)   The *complaints data publication rules* do not apply in respect of activities carried on from a *branch* of an *EEA firm* in the *United Kingdom* or activities carried on by an *EEA firm* in the *United Kingdom* under the freedom to provide *cross border services*.

(4)   This chapter, except the *complaints data publication rules*, also applies to an incoming EEA AIFM for *complaints* from *eligible complainants* concerning AIFM management functions carried on for an authorised AIF under the freedom to provide *cross-border services*.

1.1.4 R   FCA

Where a *firm* has outsourced activities to a *third party processor*, **DISP 1.1.3 R** does not apply to the *third party processor* when acting as such, but applies to the *firm* which is taking responsibility for the acts and omissions of the *third party processor* in respect of the outsourced activities.

1.1.5 R   FCA

This chapter does not apply to:

(1)   [deleted]

(2)   [deleted]

(3)   an *authorised professional firm* in respect of expressions of dissatisfaction about its *non-mainstream regulated activities*;

(4)   *complaints* in respect of *auction regulation bidding*;

(5)   a full-scope UK AIFM, small authorised UK AIFM or an incoming EEA AIFM, for *complaints* concerning AIFM management functions carried on for a closed-ended corporate AIF; and

(6)   a *depositary*, for *complaints* concerning activities carried on for:

    (a)   an unauthorised AIF which is not a charity AIF; or

    (b)   any closed-ended corporate AIF.

1.1.5-A G   FCA

References in **DISP 1.1.5 R** to a full-scope UK AIFM and small authorised UK AIFM carrying on AIFM management functions for a closed-ended corporate AIF include *firms* that are internally managed corporate AIFs.

1.1.5A R   FCA

The *complaints reporting rules* and the *complaints data publication rules* do not apply to a *credit union*.

1.1.6 G   FCA

CREDS 9 sets out *rules* for *credit unions* in relation to reporting *complaints*.

1.1.6A G   FCA

In relation to a *credit union*, the nature, scale and complexity of the *credit union's* business should be taken into account when deciding the appropriate procedures to put in place for dealing with *complaints*.

1.1.7 R   FCA

This chapter applies to the *Society*, *members* of the *Society* and *managing agents*, subject to the *Lloyd's complaint rules*.

1.1.8 R   FCA

An *insurance intermediary*, that is not also an *insurer*, must have in place and operate appropriate and effective procedures for registering and responding to *complaints* from a *person* who is not an *eligible complainant*.

[**Note**: article 10 of the *Insurance Mediation Directive*]

1.1.9 G

[deleted]

1.1.9A G   FCA

The scope of this sourcebook does not include:

(1)   a *complaint* about pre-*commencement* investment business which was regulated by a *recognised professional body* (those *complaints* will be handled under the arrangements of that professional body); or

(2)   a *complaint* about the administration of an *occupational pension scheme*, because this is not a *regulated activity* (*firms* should refer complainants to the Pensions Advisory Service rather than to the *Financial Ombudsman Service*).

1.1.10 R   FCA

In relation to a *firm's* obligations under this chapter, references to a *complaint* also include an expression of dissatisfaction which is capable of becoming a *relevant new complaint*, a *relevant transitional complaint* or a *relevant new credit-related complaint*.

Application to payment service providers

1.1.10A R   FCA

This chapter (except the *complaints record rule*, the *complaints reporting rules* and the *complaints data publication rules*) applies to *payment service providers* in respect of *complaints* from *eligible complainants* concerning activities carried on from an establishment maintained by it or its *agent* in the *United Kingdom*.

1.1.10B G   FCA

(1)   In this sourcebook, the term *payment service provider* does not include *full credit institutions* (which are covered by this sourcebook as *firms*), but it does include *small electronic money institutions*.

(2)   Although *payment service providers* are not required to comply with the *complaints record rule*, it is in their interest to retain records of *complaints* so that these can be used to assist the *Financial Ombudsman Service* should this be necessary.

Application to electronic money issuers

1.1.10C R   FCA

This chapter (except the *complaints record rule*, the *complaints reporting rules*, and the *complaints data publication rules*) applies to *electronic money issuers* in respect of *complaints* from *eligible complainants* concerning activities carried on from an establishment maintained by it or its *agent* in the *United Kingdom*.

1.1.10D G   FCA

(1)   In this sourcebook, the term *electronic money issuer* does not include *credit institutions*, *credit unions* or municipal banks (which will be carrying on a *regulated activity* if they issue *electronic money* and will be covered by this sourcebook as *firms* in those circumstances), but it does include *small electronic money institutions* and *persons* who meet the conditions set out in regulation 75(1) or regulation 76(1) of the *Electronic Money Regulations*.

(2)   Although *electronic money institutions* are not required to comply with the *complaints record rule*, it is in their interest to retain records of *complaints* so that these can be used to assist the *Financial Ombudsman Service* should this be necessary.

Application to UCITS management companies

1.1.10E R   FCA

For *complaints* related to *collective portfolio management* services of a *UK UCITS management company* for a *UCITS scheme* or an *EEA UCITS scheme*, **DISP 1.1.3 R (1)** applies, except where modified as follows:

(1)   the *consumer awareness rules*, *complaints handling rules* and *complaints record rule* apply in respect of *complaints* from *unitholders* rather than from *eligible complainants*; and

(2)   the *consumer awareness rules*, the *complaints handling rules* and the *complaints record rule*, as modified in (1), also apply where the services are provided from a *branch* in another *EEA State* (and any reference to *respondent* in the *consumer awareness rules* includes such a *branch*).

1.1.10F R   FCA

For *complaints* related to *collective portfolio management* services of an *EEA UCITS management company* for a *UCITS scheme*, **DISP 1.1.3 R (1)** applies, except where modified as follows:

(1)   where the services are provided from a *branch* in the *United Kingdom*, the *consumer awareness rules*, *complaints handling rules* and *complaints record rule* apply in respect of *complaints* from *unitholders* rather than from *eligible complainants*; and

(2)   this chapter, except the *consumer awareness rules*, *complaints handling rules*, *complaints record rule* and *complaints data publication rules*, also applies to an *EEA UCITS management company* providing services in the *United Kingdom* under the freedom to provide *cross border services*.

FSAVC Review

1.1.11 R   FCA

Where the subject matter of a *complaint* is subject to a review directly or indirectly under the terms of the policy statement for the review of specific categories of *FSAVC* business issued by the *FSA* on 28 February 2000, the *complaints resolution rules*, the *complaints time limit rules*, the *complaints record rule*, the *complaints reporting rules* and the *complaints data publication rules* will apply only if the *complaint* is about the outcome of the review.

Consumer redress schemes

1.1.11A R   FCA

Where the subject matter of a *complaint* falls to be dealt with (or has properly been dealt with) under a *consumer redress scheme*, the *complaints resolution rules*, the *complaints time limits rules*, the *complaints record rule* and the *complaints reporting rules* do not apply.

Exemptions for firms, payment service providers and electronic money issuers

1.1.12 R   FCA

(1)   A *firm*, *payment service provider* or *electronic money issuer* falling within the *Compulsory Jurisdiction* which does not conduct business with *eligible complainants* and has no reasonable likelihood of doing so, can, by written notification to the *FCA*, claim exemption from the *rules* relating to the funding of the *Financial Ombudsman Service*, and from the remainder of this chapter.

(2)   Notwithstanding (1):
  (a)   the *complaints handling rules* and *complaints record rule* will continue to apply in respect of *complaints* concerning *MiFID business*; and
  (b)   the *consumer awareness rules*, the *complaints handling rules* and the *complaints record rule* will continue to apply in respect of *complaints* concerning the provision of *collective portfolio management* services.

(3)   The exemption takes effect from the date on which the written notice is received by the *FCA* and will cease to apply when the conditions relating to the exemption no longer apply.

1.1.13 G   FCA

SUP 15.6 refers to and contains requirements regarding the steps that *firms* must take to ensure that information provided to the *FCA* is accurate and complete. Those requirements apply to information submitted to the *FCA* under this chapter.

Application to VJ participants

1.1.14 R

[deleted]

1.1.15 R   FCA

This chapter (except the *complaints record rule*, the *complaints reporting rules* and the *complaints data publication rules*) applies to *VJ participants* for *complaints* from *eligible complainants* as part of the *standard terms*.

1.1.16 G   FCA

Although *VJ participants* are not required to comply with the *complaints record rule*, it is in their interest to retain records of *complaints* so that these can be used to assist the *Financial Ombudsman Service* should it be necessary.

1.1.17 R

[deleted]

1.1.18 G

[deleted]

Outsourcing of complaint handling

1.1.19 G   FCA

(1)   This chapter does not prevent:
      (a)   the use by a *respondent* of a third party administrator to handle or resolve *complaints* (or both); or
      (b)   two or more *respondents* arranging a one-stop shop for handling or resolving *complaints* (or both) under a service level agreement.

(2)   These arrangements do not affect *respondents'* obligations as set out in *DISP* or the provisions relating to *outsourcing* by a *firm* set out in **SYSC 8** and **SYSC 13**.

1.1.20 G   FCA

Further *guidance* on the application of this chapter is set out in the table in **DISP 1 ANNEX 2**.

1.2   CONSUMER AWARENESS RULES

Publishing and providing summary details, and information about the Financial Ombudsman Service

1.2.1 R   FCA

To aid consumer awareness of the protections offered by the provisions in this chapter, *respondents* must:

(1)   publish appropriate information regarding their internal procedures for the reasonable and prompt handling of *complaints*;

(2)   refer *eligible complainants* to the availability of this information:
      (a)   in relation to a *payment service*, in the information on out-of-court complaint and redress procedures required to be provided or made available under regulations 36(2)(e) (Information required prior to the conclusion of a single payment service contract) or 40 (Prior general information for framework contracts) of the *Payment Services Regulations*; or
      (b)   otherwise, in writing at, or immediately after, the point of sale;

(3)   provide such information in writing and free of charge to *eligible complainants*:
      (a)   on request; and
      (b)   when acknowledging a *complaint*; and

(4)   provide information to *eligible complainants*, in a clear, comprehensible and easily accessible way, about the *Financial Ombudsman Service*, including the *Financial Ombudsman Service's* website address:
      (a)   on the *respondent's* website, where one exists; and
      (b)   if applicable, in the general terms and conditions of the *respondent's* contract with the *eligible complainant*.

[**Note:** article 15 of the *UCITS Directive*, article 13(2) of the *ADR Directive* and article 14(1) of the *ODR Regulation*]

1.2.2 R   FCA

Where the activity does not involve a sale, the obligation in **DISP 1.2.1 R (2)(B)** shall apply at, or immediately after, the point when contact is first made with an *eligible complainant*.

Content of summary details

1.2.3 G   FCA

The summary details concerning internal complaints handling procedures should cover at least:

(1)   how the *respondent* fulfils its obligation to handle and seek to resolve relevant *complaints*; and

(2)   (where the *complaint* falls within the jurisdiction of the *Financial Ombudsman Service*) that, if the *complaint* is not resolved, the complainant may be entitled to refer it to the *Financial Ombudsman Service*.

1.2.4 G   FCA

Those summary details may be set out in a leaflet, and their availability may be referred to in contractual documentation.

Financial Ombudsman Service logo

1.2.5 G   FCA

Respondents may also display or reproduce the *Financial Ombudsman Service* logo (under licence) in:

(1)   branches and sales offices to which *eligible complainants* have access; or

(2)   marketing literature or correspondence directed at *eligible complainants*;

provided it is done in a way which is not misleading.

1.2.5A G   FCA

DISP 1.2.5 G does not apply to a *branch* of a *UK UCITS management company* in another *EEA State*.

1.3   COMPLAINTS HANDLING RULES

1.3.1 R   FCA

Effective and transparent procedures for the reasonable and prompt handling of *complaints* must be established, implemented and maintained by:

(1)   a *respondent*; and

(2)   a *branch* of a *UK firm* in another *EEA State*.

[**Note:** article 10 of the *MiFID implementing Directive* and article 6(1) of the *UCITS implementing Directive*]

1.3.1A R   FCA

These procedures must ensure that a *complaint* may be made free of charge.

[**Note:** article 6(3) of the *UCITS implementing Directive*]

Procedures for UCITS management companies

1.3.1B R   FCA

A *UK UCITS management company* must ensure that the procedures it establishes under **DISP 1.3.1 R** for the reasonable and prompt handling of *complaints* require that:

(1)   there are no restrictions on *unitholders* exercising their rights in the event that the *UCITS* is authorised in an *EEA State* other than the *United Kingdom*; and

(2)   *unitholders* are allowed to file complaints in any of the official languages of the *Home State* of the *UCITS scheme* or *EEA UCITS scheme* or of any *EEA State* to which a notification has been transmitted by the *competent authority* of the *scheme's Home State* in accordance with article 93 of the *UCITS Directive*.

[**Note:** article 15 of the *UCITS Directive*]

1.3.2 G   FCA

These procedures should:

(1)   allow *complaints* to be made by any reasonable means; and

(2)   recognise *complaints* as requiring resolution.

1.3.2A G   FCA

These procedures should, taking into account the nature, scale and complexity of the *respondent's* business, ensure that lessons learned as a result of determinations by the *Ombudsman* are effectively applied in future *complaint* handling, for example by:

(1)   relaying a determination by the *Ombudsman* to the individuals in the *respondent* who handled the *complaint* and using it in their training and development;

(2)   analysing any patterns in determinations by the *Ombudsman* concerning *complaints* received by the *respondent* and using this in training and development of the individuals dealing with *complaints* in the *respondent*; and

(3)   analysing guidance produced by the *FCA*, other relevant regulators and the *Financial Ombudsman Service* and communicating it to the individuals dealing with *complaints* in the *respondent*.

1.3.3 R   FCA

In respect of *complaints* that do not relate to *MiFID business*, a *respondent* must put in place appropriate management controls and take reasonable steps to ensure that in handling *complaints* it identifies and remedies any recurring or systemic problems, for example, by:

(1)   analysing the causes of individual *complaints* so as to identify root causes common to types of *complaint*;

(2)   considering whether such root causes may also affect other processes or products, including those not directly complained of; and

(3)   correcting, where reasonable to do so, such root causes.

1.3.3B G   FCA

The processes that a *firm* should have in place in order to comply with **DISP 1.3.3 R** may include, taking into account the nature, scale and complexity of the *firm's* business including, in particular, the number of *complaints* the *firm* receives:

(1)   the collection of management information on the causes of *complaints* and the products and services *complaints* relate to, including information about *complaints* that are resolved by the *firm* by close of business on the *business day* following its receipt;

(2)   a process to identify the root causes of *complaints* (**DISP 1.3.3 R (1)**);

(3)   a process to prioritise dealing with the root causes of *complaints*;

(4)   a process to consider whether the root causes identified may affect other processes or products (**DISP 1.3.3 R (2)**);

(5)   a process for deciding whether root causes discovered should be corrected and how this should be done (**DISP 1.3.3 R (3)**);

(6)   regular reporting to the *senior personnel* where information on recurring or systemic problems may be needed for them to play their part in identifying, measuring, managing and controlling risks of regulatory concern; and

(7)   keeping records of analysis and decisions taken by *senior personnel* in response to management information on the root causes of *complaints*.

1.3.4 G   FCA

In respect of *complaints* that relate to *MiFID business*, a *firm* should put in place appropriate management controls and take reasonable steps, in the same way as for *complaints* that do not relate to *MiFID business* (see **DISP 1.3.3 R** and **DISP 1.3.3B G**), in order to detect and minimise any risk of compliance failures (**SYSC 6.1**) and to comply with *Principle* 6 (Customers' interests).

1.3.5 G

[deleted]

1.3.6 G   FCA

Where a *firm* identifies (from its *complaints* or otherwise) recurring or systemic problems in its provision of, or failure to provide, a financial service, it should (in accordance with *Principle* 6 (Customers' interests) and to the extent that it applies) consider whether it ought to act with regard to the position of *customers* who may have suffered detriment from, or been potentially disadvantaged by, such problems but who have not complained and, if so, take appropriate and proportionate measures to ensure that those *customers* are given appropriate redress or a proper opportunity to obtain it. In particular, the *firm* should:

(1)   ascertain the scope and severity of the consumer detriment that might have arisen; and

(2)   consider whether it is fair and reasonable for the *firm* to undertake proactively a redress or remediation exercise, which may include contacting *customers* who have not complained.

1.3.7 R   FCA

(1)   A *firm* must appoint an individual at the *firm*, or in the same *group* as the *firm*, to have responsibility for oversight of the *firm's* compliance with **DISP 1**.

(2)   The individual appointed must be carrying out a *FCA governing function* at the *firm* or in the same *group* as the *firm*.

1.3.8 G   FCA

Firms are not required to notify the name of the individual to the *FCA* or the *Financial Ombudsman Service* but would be expected to do so promptly on request. There is no bar on a *firm* appointing different individuals to have the responsibility at different times where this is to accommodate part-time or flexible working.

1.4   COMPLAINTS RESOLUTION RULES

1.4.1 R   FCA

Once a *complaint* has been received by a *respondent*, it must:

(1)   investigate the *complaint* competently, diligently and impartially, obtaining additional information as necessary;

(2)   assess fairly, consistently and promptly:

     (a)   the subject matter of the *complaint*;

     (b)   whether the *complaint* should be upheld;

     (c)   what remedial action or redress (or both) may be appropriate;

     (d)   if appropriate, whether it has reasonable grounds to be satisfied that another *respondent* may be solely or jointly responsible for the matter alleged in the *complaint*;

taking into account all relevant factors;

(3)   offer redress or remedial action when it decides this is appropriate;

(4)   explain to the complainant promptly and, in a way that is fair, clear and not misleading, its assessment of the *complaint*, its decision on it, and any offer of remedial action or redress; and

(5)   comply promptly with any offer of remedial action or redress accepted by the complainant.

1.4.2 G   FCA

Factors that may be relevant in the assessment of a *complaint* under **DISP 1.4.1 R (2)** include the following:

(1)   all the evidence available and the particular circumstances of the *complaint*;

(2)   similarities with other *complaints* received by the *respondent*;

(3)   relevant *guidance* published by the *FCA*, other relevant regulators, the *Financial Ombudsman Service* or *former schemes*; and

(4)   appropriate analysis of decisions by the *Financial Ombudsman Service* concerning similar *complaints* received by the *respondent* (procedures for which are described in **DISP 1.3.2A G**).

1.4.3 G FCA

The *respondent* should aim to resolve *complaints* at the earliest possible opportunity, minimising the number of unresolved *complaints* which need to be referred to the *Financial Ombudsman Service*.

1.4.4 R FCA

Where a *complaint* against a *respondent* is referred to the *Financial Ombudsman Service*, the *respondent* must cooperate fully with the *Financial Ombudsman Service* and comply promptly with any settlements or awards made by it.

1.4.5 G FCA

DISP App 1 contains *guidance* to *respondents* on the approach to assessing financial loss and appropriate redress where a *respondent* upholds a *complaint* concerning the sale of an endowment policy for the purposes of repaying a *mortgage*.

1.4.6 R FCA

DISP App 3 sets out the approach which *respondents* should use in assessing *complaints* relating to the sale of *payment protection contracts* and determining appropriate redress where a *complaint* is upheld.

1.5 COMPLAINTS RESOLVED BY CLOSE OF THE NEXT BUSINESS DAY

1.5.1 R FCA

The following *rules* do not apply to a *complaint* that is resolved by a *respondent* by close of business on the *business day* following its receipt:

(1)   the *complaints time limit rules*;
(2)   the complaints forwarding *rules*;
(3)   the *complaints reporting rules*;
(4)   the *complaints record rule*, if the *complaint* does not relate to *MiFID business* or *collective portfolio management* services for a *UCITS scheme* or an *EEA UCITS scheme*; and
(5)   the *complaints data publication rules*.

1.5.2 G FCA

Complaints falling within this section are still subject to the *complaint resolution rules*.

1.5.3 G FCA

For the purposes of this section:

(1)   a *complaint* received on any day other than a *business day*, or after close of business on a *business day*, may be treated as received on the next *business day*; and
(2)   a *complaint* is resolved where the complainant has indicated acceptance of a response from the *respondent*, with neither the response nor acceptance having to be in writing

1.6 COMPLAINTS TIME LIMIT RULES

Keeping the complainant informed

1.6.1 R FCA

On receipt of a *complaint*, a *respondent* must:

(1)   send the complainant a prompt written acknowledgement providing early reassurance that it has received the *complaint* and is dealing with it; and
(2)   ensure the complainant is kept informed thereafter of the progress of the measures being taken for the *complaint's* resolution.

Final or other response within eight weeks

1.6.2 R FCA

The *respondent* must, by the end of eight weeks after its receipt of the *complaint*, send the complainant:

(1)   a 'final response', being a written response from the *respondent* which:
  (a)   accepts the *complaint* and, where appropriate, offers redress or remedial action; or
  (b)   offers redress or remedial action without accepting the *complaint*; or
  (c)   rejects the *complaint* and gives reasons for doing so;
  and which:
  (d)   encloses a copy of the *Financial Ombudsman Service's* standard explanatory leaflet;
  (e)   provides the website address of the *Financial Ombudsman Service*;
  (f)   informs the complainant that if he remains dissatisfied with the *respondent's* response, he may now refer his *complaint* to the *Financial Ombudsman Service*; and
  (g)   indicates whether or not the *respondent* consents to waive the relevant time limits in **DISP 2.8.2 R** or **DISP 2.8.7 R** (Was the complaint referred to the Financial Ombudsman Service in time?) by including the appropriate wording set out in **DISP 1 ANNEX 3 R**; or

(2) a written response which:
  (a) explains why it is not in a position to make a *final response* and indicates when it expects to be able to provide one;
  (b) informs the complainant that he may now refer the *complaint* to the *Financial Ombudsman Service*;
  (c) indicates whether or not the *respondent* consents to waive the relevant time limits in **DISP 2.8.2 R** or **DISP 2.8.7 R** (Was the complaint referred to the Financial Ombudsman Service in time?) if it becomes apparent that the complaint has been made or is referred outside those time limits;
  (d) encloses a copy of the *Financial Ombudsman Service* standard explanatory leaflet; and
  (e) provides the website address of the *Financial Ombudsman Service*.

[**Note:** article 13 of the *ADR Directive*]

1.6.3 G

[deleted]

Complainant's written acceptance

1.6.4 R FCA

DISP 1.6.2 R does not apply if the complainant has already indicated in writing acceptance of a response by the *respondent*, provided that the response:
(1) informed the complainant how to pursue his *complaint* with the *respondent* if he remains dissatisfied;
(2) referred to the ultimate availability of the *Financial Ombudsman Service* if he remains dissatisfied with the *respondent's* response;
(3) enclosed a copy of the *Financial Ombudsman Service* standard explanatory leaflet;
(4) provided the website address of the *Financial Ombudsman Service*; and
(5) indicated whether or not the *respondent* consents to waive the relevant time limits in **DISP 2.8.2 R** or **DISP 2.8.7 R** (Was the complaint referred to the Financial Ombudsman Service in time?) by including the appropriate wording set out in **DISP 1 ANNEX 3 R**.

1.6.5 R

[deleted]

1.6.6 R

[deleted]

1.6.6A G FCA

The information regarding the *Financial Ombudsman Service* required to be provided in responses sent under the *complaints* time limit *rules* (**DISP 1.6.2 R** and **DISP 1.6.4 R**) should be set out clearly, comprehensibly, in an easily accessible way and prominently within the text of those responses.

[**Note:** article 13 of the *ADR Directive*]

Speed and quality of response

1.6.7 G FCA

It is expected that within eight weeks of their receipt, almost all *complaints* to a *respondent* will have been substantively addressed by it through a *final response* or response as described in **DISP 1.6.4 R**.

1.6.8 G FCA

When assessing a *respondent's* response to a *complaint*, the *FCA* may have regard to a number of factors, including, the quality of response, as against the *complaints resolution rules*, as well as the speed with which it was made.

1.7 COMPLAINTS FORWARDING RULES

1.7.1 R FCA

A *respondent* that has reasonable grounds to be satisfied that another *respondent* may be solely or jointly responsible for the matter alleged in a *complaint* may forward the *complaint*, or the relevant part of it, in writing to that other *respondent*, provided it:
(1) does so promptly;
(2) informs the complainant promptly in a *final response* of why the *complaint* has been forwarded by it to the other *respondent*, and of the other *respondent's* contact details; and
(3) where jointly responsible for the fault alleged in the *complaint*, it complies with its own obligations under this chapter in respect of that part of the *complaint* it has not forwarded.

Dealing with a forwarded complaint

1.7.2 R FCA

When a *respondent* receives a *complaint* that has been forwarded to it under **DISP 1.7.1 R**, the *complaint* is treated for the purposes of *DISP* as if made directly to that *respondent*, and as if received by it when the forwarded *complaint* was received.

1.7.3 G   FCA

On receiving a forwarded *complaint*, the standard time limits will apply from the date on which the *respondent* receives the forwarded *complaint*.

1.8 COMPLAINTS TIME BARRING RULE

1.8.1 R   FCA

If a *respondent* receives a *complaint* which is outside the time limits for referral to the *Financial Ombudsman Service* (see **DISP 2.8**) it may reject the complaint without considering the merits, but must explain this to the complainant in a *final response* in accordance with **DISP 1.6.2 R**.

1.9 COMPLAINTS RECORD RULE

1.9.1 R   FCA

A *firm*, including, in the case of *MiFID business* or *collective portfolio management* services for a *UCITS scheme* or an *EEA UCITS scheme*, a *branch* of a *UK firm* in another *EEA state*, must keep a record of each *complaint* received and the measures taken for its resolution, and retain that record for:

(1)   at least five years where the *complaint* relates to *MiFID business* or *collective portfolio management* services for a *UCITS scheme* or an *EEA UCITS scheme*; and
(2)   three years for all other *complaints*;

from the date the *complaint* was received.

[Note: article 10 of the *MiFID implementing Directive* and article 6(2) of the *UCITS implementing Directive*]

1.9.2 G   FCA

The records of the measures taken for resolution of *complaints* may be used to assist with the collection of management information pursuant to **DISP 1.3.3BG (1)** and regular reporting to the *senior personnel* pursuant to **DISP 1.3.3BG (6)**.

1.10 COMPLAINTS REPORTING RULES

1.10.1 R   FCA

(1)   Unless (2) applies, twice a year a *firm* must provide the *FCA* with a complete report concerning *complaints* received from *eligible complainants*.
(2)   If a *firm* has *permission* to carry on only *credit-related regulated activities* or *operating an electronic system in relation to lending* and has revenue arising from those activities that is less than or equal to £5,000,000 a year, the *firm* must provide the *FCA* with a complete report concerning *complaints* received from *eligible complainants* once a year.
(3)   The report required by (1) and (2) must be set out in the format in **DISP 1 ANNEX 1**.
(4)   Paragraphs (1) and (2) do not apply to a *firm* with only a *limited permission* unless that *firm* is a *not-for-profit debt advice body* that at any point in the last 12 *months* has held £1 million or more in *client money* or as the case may be, projects that it will hold £1million or more in *client money* in the next 12 *months*.

1.10.1-A G   FCA

A *firm* with only a *limited permission* to whom **DISP 1.10.1 R (1)** and **DISP 1.10.1 R (2)** do not apply is required to submit information to the *FCA* about the number of complaints it has received in relation to credit-related activities under the reporting requirements in **SUP 16.12** (see, in particular, *data item* CCR007 in SUP 16.12.29C R). A *firm* with *limited permission* to whom **DISP 1.10.1 R (1)** and **DISP 1.10.1 R (2)** do not apply is also subject to the complaints data publication rules in **DISP 1.10A**.

Forwarded complaints

1.10.1A R   FCA

A *firm* must not include in the report a *complaint* that has been forwarded in its entirety to another *respondent* under the complaints forwarding *rules*.

1.10.1B G   FCA

Where a *firm* has forwarded to another *respondent* only part of a *complaint* or where two *respondents* may be jointly responsible for a *complaint*, then the *complaint* should be reported by both *firms*.

Joint reports

1.10.1C R   FCA

Firms that are part of a *group* may submit a joint report to the *FCA*. The joint report must contain the information required from all *firms* concerned and clearly indicate the *firms* on whose behalf the report is submitted. The requirement to provide a report, and the responsibility for the report, remains with each *firm* in the *group*.

1.10.1D G   FCA

Not all the *firms* in the *group* need to submit the report jointly. *Firms* should only consider submitting a joint report if it is logical to do so, for example, where the *firms* have a common central *complaints* handling team and the same *accounting reference date* and are all subject to the same reporting frequencies and submission deadlines.

Information requirements

1.10.2 R   FCA

Part A of **DISP 1 ANNEX 1** requires (for the relevant reporting period) information about:

(1)   the total number of *complaints* received by the *firm*;
(2)   the total number of *complaints* closed by the *firm*:
  (a)   within four weeks or less of receipt;
  (b)   more than four weeks and up to eight weeks of receipt; and
  (c)   more than eight weeks after receipt;
(3)   the total number of *complaints*:
  (a)   upheld by the *firm* in the reporting period; and
  (b)   outstanding at the beginning of the reporting period; and
(4)   the total amount of redress paid in respect of *complaints* during the reporting period.

1.10.2-A R   FCA

Part B of **DISP 1 ANNEX 1** requires (for the relevant reporting period) information about:

(1)   the total number of *complaints* received by the *firm*;
(2)   the total number of *complaints* closed by the *firm*;
(3)   the total number of *complaints*:
  (a)   upheld by the *firm* in the reporting period; and
  (b)   outstanding at the beginning of the reporting period; and
(4)   the total amount of redress paid in respect of *complaints* during the reporting period.

1.10.2A R   FCA

(1)   Twice a year a *firm* must provide the *FCA* with a complete report concerning *complaints* received from *eligible complainants* about matters relating to activities carried out by its *employees* when acting as *retail investment advisers*. The report must be set out in the format in **DISP 1 ANNEX 1C R**.
(2)   **DISP 1 ANNEX 1C R** requires (for the relevant reporting period) information about:
  (a)   the total number of *complaints* received by the *firm* about matters relating to activities carried out by its *employees* when acting as *retail investment advisers*;
  (b)   the total number of *complaints* closed by the *firm* about matters relating to activities carried out by its *employees* when acting as *retail investment advisers*;
  (c)   the total number of *complaints* upheld by the *firm* about matters relating to activities carried out by its *employees* when acting as *retail investment advisers*; and
  (d)   the total amount of redress paid in respect of *complaints* upheld during the reporting period about matters relating to activities carried out by its *employees* when acting as *retail investment advisers*.
(3)   For the purpose of **DISP 1 ANNEX 1C R** *retail investment adviser* information must be reported by Individual Reference Number (IRN).

1.10.3 G   FCA

For the purpose of **DISP 1.10.2 R**, **DISP 1.10.2-A R** and **DISP 1.10.2A R**, when completing the return, the *firm* should take into account the following matters.

(1)   If a *complaint* could fall into more than one category, the *complaint* should be recorded in the category which the *firm* considers to form the main part of the *complaint*.
(2)   Under **DISP 1.10.2 R (3)(A)** or **DISP 1.10.2-A R**, a *firm* should report any *complaint* to which it has given a response which upholds the *complaint*, even if any redress offered is disputed by the complainant. For this purpose, 'response' includes a response under the complainant's written acceptance *rule* (**DISP 1.6.4 R**) and a *final response*. Where a *complaint* is upheld in part or where the *firm* does not have enough information to make a decision yet chooses to make a goodwill payment to the complainant, a *firm* should treat the *complaint* as upheld for reporting purposes. However, where a *firm* rejects a *complaint*, yet chooses to make a goodwill payment to the complainant, the *complaint* should be recorded as 'rejected'.
(3)   If a *firm* reports on the amount of redress paid under **DISP 1.10.2 R (4)**, **DISP 1.10.2-AR (4)** or **DISP 1.10.2A R**, redress should be interpreted to include an amount paid, or cost borne, by the *firm*, where a cash value can be readily identified, and should include:

(a)   amounts paid for distress and inconvenience;
(b)   a free transfer out to another provider which transfer would normally be paid for;
(c)   goodwill payments and goodwill gestures;
(d)   interest on delayed settlements;
(e)   waiver of an excess on an insurance policy; and
(f)   payments to put the consumer back into the position the consumer should have been in had the act or omission not occurred.

(4)   If a *firm* reports on the amount of redress paid under **DISP 1.10.2 R (4)**, **DISP 1.10.2-AR (4)** or **DISP 1.10.2A R**, the redress should not, however, include repayments or refunds of premiums which had been taken in error (for example where a *firm* had been taking, by direct debit, twice the actual premium amount due under a policy). The refund of the overcharge would not count as redress.

[Note: See **SUP 10A.14.24 R** for the ongoing duty to notify *complaints* about matters relating to activities carried out by any *employee* when acting as a *retail investment adviser*.]

1.10.4 R   FCA

Unless **DISP 1.10.4A R** applies, the relevant reporting periods are:
(1)   the six *months* immediately following a *firm's accounting reference date*; and
(2)   the six *months* immediately preceding a *firm's accounting reference date*.

1.10.4A R   FCA

If a *firm* has *permission* to carry on only *credit-related regulated activities* or *operating an electronic system in relation to lending* and has revenue arising from those activities that is less than or equal to £5,000,000 a year, the relevant reporting period is the year immediately following the *firm's accounting reference date*.

1.10.5 R   FCA

Reports are to be submitted to the *FCA* within 30 *business days* of the end of the relevant reporting periods through, and in the electronic format specified in, the *FCA* Complaints Reporting System or the appropriate section of the *FCA* website.

1.10.6 R   FCA

If a *firm* is unable to submit a report in electronic format because of a systems failure of any kind, the *firm* must notify the *FCA*, in writing and without delay, of that systems failure.

1.10.6A R   FCA

(1)   If a *firm* does not submit a complete report by the date on which it is due, in accordance with **DISP 1.10.5 R**, the *firm* must pay an administrative fee of £250.
(2)   The administrative fee in (1) does not apply if the *firm* has notified the *FCA* of a systems failure in accordance with **DISP 1.10.6 R**.

1.10.7 R   FCA

A closed *complaint* is a *complaint* where:
(1)   the *firm* has sent a *final response*; or
(2)   the complainant has indicated in writing acceptance of the *firm's* earlier response under **DISP 1.6.4 R**.

1.10.8 G

[deleted]

Notification of contact point for complainants

1.10.9 R   FCA

For the purpose of inclusion in the public record maintained by the *FCA*, a *firm* must:
(1)   provide the *FCA*, at the time of its *authorisation*, with details of a single contact point within the *firm* for complainants; and
(2)   notify the *FCA* of any subsequent change in those details when convenient and, at the latest, in the *firm's* next report under the *complaints reporting rules*.

Meaning of revenue

1.10.10 G   FCA

In **DISP 1.10**, references to revenue in relation to any *firm* do not include the amount of any repayment of any *credit* provided by that *firm* as *lender*.

1.10A   COMPLAINTS DATA PUBLICATION RULES

Obligation to publish summary of complaints data or total number of complaints

1.10A.1 R   FCA

(1) Unless (1A) applies to the *firm*, where, in accordance with **DISP 1.10.1 R**, a *firm* submits a report to the *FCA* reporting 500 or more *complaints*, it must publish a summary of the *complaints* data contained in that report (the *complaints* data summary).

(1A)

    (a)   This paragraph applies to a *firm* which:

        (i)   has *permission* to carry on only *credit-related regulated activities* or to *operate an electronic system in relation to lending*; and

        (ii)   has revenue arising from those activities that is less than or equal to £5,000,000 a year.

    (b)   Where a *firm* to which this paragraph applies submits a report to the *FCA* in accordance with **DISP 1.10.1 R** reporting 1000 or more *complaints*, it must publish a summary of the *complaints* data contained in that report (the *complaints* data summary).

(2) Where, in accordance with **DISP 1.10.1C R**, a *firm* submits a joint report on behalf of itself and other *firms* within a *group* and that report reports 500 or more *complaints*, it must publish a summary of the *complaints* data contained in the joint report (the *complaints* data summary), unless it is a *firm* to which (1A) applies.

(3) Where, in accordance with **DISP 1.10.1C R**, a *firm* to which (1A) applies submits a joint report on behalf of itself and other *firms* within a *group* and that report reports 1000 or more *complaints*, it must publish a summary of the *complaints* data contained in the joint report (the *complaints* data summary).

(4) Where, in accordance with **SUP 16.12.4 R** and **SUP 16.12.29C R**, a *firm* with a *limited permission* submits *data item* CCR007 to the *FCA* reporting 1000 or more *complaints*, it must publish the total number of *complaints* received.

Format of publication

1.10A.2 R   FCA

The *complaints* data summary required by **DISP 1.10A.1 R** must be published in the format set out in **DISP 1 ANNEX 1B R**.

Time limits for publication

1.10A.3 R   FCA

(1)   Where the *firm's* relevant reporting period (as defined in **DISP 1.10.4 R** or **DISP 1.10.4A R** as the case may be) ends between 1 January and 30 June, the *firm* must publish the *complaints* data summary no later than 31 August of the same year.

(2)   Where the *firm's* relevant reporting period (as defined in **DISP 1.10.4 R** or **DISP 1.10.4A R** as the case may be) ends between 1 July and 31 December, the *firm* must publish the *complaints* data summary no later than 28 February of the following year.

(3)   Where the *firm* is a *firm* with only a *limited permission* and its *accounting reference date* falls between 1 January and 30 June, the *firm* must publish the total number of *complaints* received no later than 31 August of the same year.

(4)   Where the *firm* is a *firm* with only a *limited permission* and its *accounting reference date* falls between 1 July and 31 December, the *firm* must publish the total number of *complaints* received no later than 28 February of the following year.

Confirmation of publication

1.10A.4 R   FCA

A *firm* must immediately confirm to the *FCA*, in an email submitted to complaintsdatasummary@fca.org.uk, that the *complaints* data summary or total number of *complaints* (as appropriate) accurately reflects the report submitted to the *FCA*, that the summary or total number of *complaints* (as appropriate) has been published and where it has been published.

Publication on behalf of the firm

1.10A.5 E   FCA

A *firm* will be taken to have complied with **DISP 1.10A.1 R (1)**, **DISP 1.10A.1 R (1A)(2)**, **DISP 1.10A.1 R (3)** or **DISP 1.10A.1 R (4)** if within the relevant time limit set out in **DISP 1.10A.3 R** the *firm*:

(1)   ensures that another *person* publishes the *complaints* data summary or total number of *complaints* (as appropriate) on its behalf; and

(2)   publishes details of where this summary or total number of *complaints* (as appropriate) is published.

Joint reports: provision of information to third party on request

1.10A.6 R   FCA

Any *firm* covered by a joint report, other than the *firm* that submitted the joint report, must provide details of where the *complaints* data summary or total number of *complaints* (as appropriate) is published to any *person* who requests them.

Mode and content of publication

1.10A.7 G   FCA

Firms may choose how they publish the *complaints* data summary or total number of *complaints* (as appropriate). However, the summary or total number of *complaints* (as appropriate) should be readily available. For this reason, the *FCA* recommends that *firms* should publish the summary or total number of *complaints* (as appropriate) on their websites.

1.10A.8 G   FCA

(1)   The *FCA* recommends that *firms* should publish additional information alongside their *complaints* data summaries or total number of *complaints* (as appropriate) in order to relate the number of complaints to the scale of the *firm's* relevant business. *Firms* are recommended to publish the relevant standard metrics set out in the table at **DISP 1 ANNEX 1A G** with the summaries. Where the *complaints* data summary or total number of *complaints* (as appropriate) relates to a joint report the metrics should cover all the *firms* included in the joint report.

(2)   If the recommended metrics do not accurately reflect the scale of the *firm's* relevant business, the *FCA* recommends that the *firm* should publish metrics which best reflect the scale of its business based on the number of its customers or accounts or policies. *Firms* may also publish other metrics where they consider that these would better reflect the scale of their business.

(3)   *Firms* may also publish other information to aid understanding, for example details of their internal processes for dealing with complaints.

Meaning of revenue

1.10A.9 G   FCA

In **DISP 1.10A**, references to revenue in relation to any *firm* do not include the amount of any repayment of any *credit* provided by that *firm* as *lender*.

1.11   THE SOCIETY OF LLOYD'S

Complaints handling procedures

1.11.1 R   FCA

The *Society* must establish and maintain appropriate and effective procedures for handling *complaints* by *policyholders* against *members* of the *Society* which comply with this chapter.

1.11.2 R   FCA

A *member* of the *Society* must, in complying with this chapter, ensure that the arrangements which the *member* maintains are compatible with the *Lloyd's complaint procedures*, so that, taken as a whole, the requirements of this sourcebook are met.

1.11.2A R   FCA

The *Society* must ensure that the arrangements which the *member* maintains include a requirement which corresponds to **DISP 1.2.1 R (4)** (Publishing and providing summary details, and information about the Financial Ombudsman Service).

[**Note:** article 13 of the *ADR Directive* and article 14 of the *ODR Regulation*]

1.11.3 R   FCA

The *Society* must take reasonable steps to ensure that *complaints* by *policyholders* against *members* of the *Society* are dealt with under the *Lloyd's complaint procedures* and that *members* comply with the requirements of those procedures.

Referral to the Financial Ombudsman Service

1.11.4 R   FCA

A *complaint* by a *policyholder* against a *member* of the *Society* may not be referred to the *Financial Ombudsman Service* until after the *Lloyd's complaint procedures* have been completed or until after the end of eight weeks from receipt of the *complaint*, whichever is the earlier.

Exemptions for members

1.11.5 R   FCA

(1)   A notification claiming exemption under **DISP 1.1.12 R** from the *complaints reporting rules* and the *rules* relating to the funding of the *Financial Ombudsman Service* must be given to the *FCA* by the *Society* on behalf of any *member* eligible for an exemption.

(2)   The *Society* must notify the *FCA* if the conditions relating to such an exemption no longer apply to a *member* who is exempt.

Complaints reporting rule

1.11.6 R   FCA

The report to be sent to the *FCA* under the *complaints reporting rules* must be provided by the *Society* and must cover all *complaints* by *policyholders* against *members* falling within the scope of the *complaints reporting rules*.

Obligation to publish summary of complaints data

1.11.6A R   FCA

Where, in accordance with **DISP 1.11.6 R**, the *Society* submits a report to the *FCA* reporting 500 or more *complaints*, it must publish a summary of the *complaints* data contained in that report (the *complaints* data summary).

Format of publication

1.11.6B R   FCA

The *Society* must publish the *complaints* data summary in the format set out in the *complaints* publication form in **DISP 1 ANNEX 1B R** omitting details as to the *firms* and brands/trading names covered by the summary.

Time limits for publication

1.11.6C R   FCA

The deadlines for publication of the *Society's complaints* data summaries are:
(1)   28 February for the summary of its report relating to the reporting period ending on 31 December of the previous year; and
(2)   31 August for the summary of its report relating to the reporting period ending on 30 June of the same year.

Confirmation of publication

1.11.6D R   FCA

The *Society* must immediately confirm to the *FCA*, in an email submitted to complaintsdatasummary@fca.org.uk, that the *complaints* data summary accurately reflects the report submitted to the *FCA*, that the summary has been published and where it has been published.

Mode and content of publication

1.11.6E G   FCA

The *Society* may choose how it publishes the *complaints* data summary. However, the *complaints* data summary should be readily available. For this reason, the *FCA* recommends that the *Society* publishes the summary on its website. The *Society* may publish further information with the *complaints* data summary to aid understanding.

Application to members

1.11.7 G   FCA

Each *member* of the *Society* is individually subject to the *rules* in this chapter as a result of the *insurance market direction* given in **DISP 2.1.7 D** under section 316 of the *Act* (Direction by a regulator).

1.11.8 G   FCA

However, the *Society* operates a two-tier internal complaints handling procedure, currently set out in the "Code for Underwriting agents: UK Personal Lines Claims and Complaints Handling". Under this procedure, *complaints* by *policyholders* against *members* of the *Society* are considered by the *managing agent* and then, if necessary, by the *Society's* in-house Complaints Department. This procedure (and any procedure that may replace it) will be subject to the requirements in this chapter.

1.11.9 G   FCA

Members will individually comply with this chapter if and only if all *complaints* by *policyholders* against *members* are dealt with under the *Lloyd's complaints procedures*. Accordingly, certain of the obligations under this chapter, for example the obligation to report on *complaints* received and the obligation to pay fees under the *rules* relating to the funding of the *Financial Ombudsman Service* (**FEES 5**), must be complied with by the *Society* on behalf of *members*. *Managing agents* will not have to make a separate report to the *FCA* on *complaints* reported under the *complaints reporting rules* sent by the *Society*.

Complaints about the activities of members' advisers

1.11.10 R   FCA

A *members' adviser* must establish and maintain effective arrangements for handling any *complaint* from a *member* of the *Society* regarding advice given to the *member* in connection with the acquiring or disposing of *syndicate* participation.

1.11.11 G   FCA

Complaints from *members* of the *Society* regarding the activities of *members' advisers*, which cannot be resolved by the *members' adviser*, cannot be referred to the *Financial Ombudsman Service*.

Complaints from members or former members

1.11.12 G   FCA

The *Financial Ombudsman Service* is not able to deal with the *complaints* listed in **DISP 1.11.13 R** and separate *rules* and *guidance* are therefore required.

1.11.13 R   FCA

The *Society* must establish and maintain appropriate and effective arrangements for handling any *complaint* from a *member* or a *former member* about:

(1)   *regulated activities* carried on by the *Society*;
(2)   the *Society's regulatory functions* carried on by the *Society*, the *Council* or those to whom the *Council* delegates authority to carry out such functions;
(3)   advice given by an *underwriting agent* to a *person* to become, continue or cease to be, a *member* of a particular *syndicate*; and
(4)   the management by a *managing agent* of the underwriting capacity of a *syndicate* on which the complainant participates or has participated.

1.11.14 R   FCA

The *Society* must maintain by *byelaw* one or more appropriate effective schemes for the resolution of disputes between an *individual member* or a *former member* who was an *individual member* and:

(1)   his *underwriting agent*; or
(2)   the *Society*.

1.11.15 R   FCA

For the purposes of **DISP 1.11.13 R** "*individual member*" includes a *member* which is a *limited liability partnership* or a *body corporate* whose *members* consist only of, or of the nominees for, a single natural person or a group of *connected persons*.

1.11.16 G   FCA

The schemes to which **DISP 1.11.13 R** currently refers are the *Lloyd's Arbitration Scheme* and the *Lloyd's Members' Ombudsman* respectively, but the *Society* may maintain other independent dispute resolution schemes in addition to, or instead of, either of these schemes.

1.11.17 G   FCA

The schemes referred to in **DISP 1.11.13 R** should be operationally independent of the *Society*.

1.11.18 G   FCA

An *individual member* or *former member* who was an *individual member* should not have access to the schemes referred to in **DISP 1.11.13 R** unless the *complaints* arrangements maintained by the *Society* have failed to resolve the *complaint* to his satisfaction within eight weeks of receiving it.

1.11.19 G   FCA

The *Society* should give the *FCA* adequate notice of all proposed changes to the *byelaws* relating to the schemes referred to in **DISP 1.11.13 R**.

1.11.20 G   FCA

When considering what is required to ensure the operational independence of the schemes referred to in **DISP 1.11.13 R**, or proposed changes in such schemes, the *Society* should take account of similar arrangements operated by the *Financial Ombudsman Service*.

1.11.21 R   FCA

A contravention of **DISP 1.11.13 R** or **DISP 1.11.14 R** does not give rise to a right of action by a *private person* under section 138D of the *Act* (Actions for damages) and each of those *rules* is specified under section 138D(3) of the *Act* as a provision giving rise to no such right of action.FCA

1 ANNEX 1   COMPLAINTS RETURN FORM

Complaints return form
This annex consists only of one or more forms. Forms are to be found through the following address:
Complaints return form – DISP 1 Annex 1 RFCA

1 ANNEX 1A   RECOMMENDED METRICS

This table belongs to **DISP 1.10A.8 G**

Type of business	Contextualised new complaint numbers	Recommended metrics
Banking and credit cards	*Complaints* per 1,000 accounts	The tariff base (number of accounts) at row 1, column 2 of the table in **FEES 5 ANNEX 1** as reported in the *firm's* most recent statement of total amount of *relevant business* or if this tariff base is not relevant, the applicable tariff base under **FEES 5 ANNEX 1 R**
General insurance and pure protection (provision)	*Complaints* per £1m of annual gross premium income	The tariff base (annual gross premium income) at row 2, column 2 of the table in **FEES 5 ANNEX 1** as reported in the *firm's* most recent statement of total amount of *relevant business*
General insurance and pure protection (intermediation)	*Complaints* per £1m of annual income	The tariff base (annual income) at row 17, column 2 of the table in **FEES 5 ANNEX 1** reported in the *firm's* most recent statement of total amount of *relevant business*
Home finance	*Complaints* per 1,000 loans outstanding	The total number of balances outstanding (all loans) at row E.45 or E.53 of E(2) in **SUP 16 ANNEX 19A** (Mortgage Lenders and Administrators Return) as reported in the *firm's* most recent return
Investment (provision)	*Complaints* per £1m of annual eligible income	The *firm's* annual eligible income as defined in class D1 of **FEES 6 ANNEX 3 R**
Investment (intermediation)	*Complaints* per £1m of annual eligible income	The *firm's* annual eligible income as defined in class D2 of **FEES 6 ANNEX 3 R**
Decumulation, life and pensions (provision)	*Complaints* per 1,000 policyholders	The number of the *firm's* policyholders at row 3 of Forms 51–54 (whichever are relevant) in **IPRU(INS)** Appendix 9.3R as reported in the *firm's* most recent form
Decumulation, life and pensions (intermediation)	*Complaints* per £1m of annual eligible income	The *firm's* annual eligible income as defined in class C2 of **FEES 6 ANNEX 3 R**
Credit-related activities	*Complaints* per £1m of annual eligible income	The applicable tariff base under **FEES 5 ANNEX 1 R**

Note 1: For the purposes of this annex the reference to *complaints* is a reference to *complaints* opened during the relevant reporting period.

Note 2: Where a *firm* undertakes both (a) general insurance and pure protection provision and (b) general insurance and pure protection intermediation, it can choose to use the metric which forms the greater part of its business.

Note 3: Where a *firm* undertakes both (a) fund management and (b) investment intermediation, it can choose to use the metric which forms the greater part of its business.

Note 4: Where a *firm* undertakes both (a) decumulation, life and pensions provision and (b) decumulation, life and pensions intermediation, it can choose to use the metric which forms the greater part of its business.

Note 5: Where a *firm* undertakes both (a) banking and credit cards and (b) other credit-related activities, it can chose to use the metric which forms the greater part of its business.

Note 6: Where a *firm* undertakes both (a) home finance and (b) credit-related activities, it can chose to use the metric which forms the greater part of its business. FCA

1 ANNEX 1B COMPLAINTS PUBLICATION REPORT

This table belongs to **DISP 1.10A.2 R** – DISP 1 Annex 1B RFCA

1 ANNEX 1C ILLUSTRATION OF THE ONLINE REPORTING REQUIREMENTS, REFERRED TO IN DISP 1.10.2AR

This annex belongs to **DISP 1.10.2A R** – DISP 1 Annex 1C R

1 ANNEX 2 APPLICATION OF DISP 1 TO TYPE OF RESPONDENT / COMPLAINT

2 G FCA

1.	The table below summarises the application of **DISP 1**. Where the table indicates that a particular section may apply, its application in relation to any particular activity or *complaint* is dependent on the detailed application provisions set out in **DISP 1**.

2.	In some cases the application of **DISP 1** to *firms* depends on whether responsibility for the matter is reserved under an *EU* instrument to an *incoming EEA firm's Home State regulator*. Reference should be made to the detailed application provisions set out in **DISP 1**.

Type of respondent/ complaint	DISP 1.2 Consumer awareness rules	DISP 1.3 Complaints handling rules	DISP 1.4–1.8 Complaints resolution rules etc.	DISP 1.9 Complaints record rule	DISP 1.10 Complaints reporting rules	DISP 1.10A Complaints data publication rules
firm (other than a *UCITS management company* when providing collective portfolio management services in respect of a *UCITS scheme* or an *EEA UCITS scheme*) in relation to *complaints* concerning non-*MiFID business*	Applies for *eligible complainants*	Applies for *eligible complainants* (**DISP 1.3.4 G** does not apply)	Applies for *eligible complainants*	Applies for *eligible complainants*	Applies for *eligible complainants*	Applies for *eligible complainants*
firm in relation to *complaints* concerning *MiFID business*	Applies for *eligible complainants*	Applies for *retail clients* (**DISP 1.3.3 R** does not apply)	Applies for *eligible complainants*	Applies for *retail clients*	Applies for *eligible complainants*	Applies for *eligible complainants*
UK UCITS management company in relation to *complaints* concerning collective portfolio management services in respect of a *UCITS scheme* or an *EEA UCITS scheme* provided under the freedom to provide *cross border services*	Applies for *unitholders*	Applies for *unitholders*	Applies for *eligible complainants*	Applies for *unitholders*	Applies for *eligible complainants*	Applies for *eligible complainants*
branch of a *UK UCITS management company* in another *EEA State* in relation to *complaints* concerning collective portfolio management services in respect of an *EEA UCITS scheme*	Applies for *unitholders*	Applies for *unitholders*	Does not apply	Applies for *unitholders*	Does not apply	Does not apply
branch of a *UK firm* (other than a *UK UCITS management company* when providing collective portfolio management services in respect of an *EEA UCITS scheme*) in another *EEA State* in relation to *complaints* concerning non-*MiFID business*	Does not apply	Does not apply	Does not apply	Does not apply	Does not apply	Does not apply

Type of respondent/ complaint	DISP 1.2 Consumer awareness rules	DISP 1.3 Complaints handling rules	DISP 1.4–1.8 Complaints resolution rules etc.	DISP 1.9 Complaints record rule	DISP 1.10 Complaints reporting rules	DISP 1.10A Complaints data publication rules
branch of a UK firm in another EEA State in relation to complaints concerning MiFID business	Does not apply	Applies for retail clients (DISP 1.3.3 R does not apply)	Does not apply	Applies for retail clients	Does not apply	Does not apply
incoming branch of an EEA firm (other than an EEA firm when providing collective portfolio management services in respect of an EEA UCITS scheme) in relation to complaints concerning non-MiFID business	Applies for eligible complainants	Applies for eligible complainants	Applies for eligible complainants	Applies for eligible complainants	Applies for eligible complainants	Does not apply
incoming branch of an EEA firm in relation to complaints concerning MiFID business	Applies for eligible complainants	Does not apply	Applies for eligible complainants	Does not apply	Applies for eligible complainants	Does not apply
incoming branch of an EEA UCITS management company in relation to complaints concerning collective portfolio management services in respect of a UCITS scheme	Applies for unitholders	Applies for unitholders	Applies for eligible complainants	Applies for unitholders	Applies for eligible complainants	Does not apply
incoming EEA UCITS management company in relation to complaints concerning collective portfolio management services in respect of a UCITS scheme provided under the freedom to provide cross border services	Does not apply	Does not apply	Applies for eligible complainants	Does not apply	Applies for eligible complainants	Does not apply
incoming EEA firm providing cross-border services from outside the UK	Does not apply	Does not apply	Does not apply	Does not apply	Does not apply	Does not apply
branch of an overseas firm (in relation to all complaints)	Applies for eligible complainants	Applies for eligible complainants	Applies for eligible complainants	Applies for eligible complainants	Applies for eligible complainants	Applies for eligible complainants

Type of respondent/ complaint	DISP 1.2 Consumer awareness rules	DISP 1.3 Complaints handling rules	DISP 1.4–1.8 Complaints resolution rules etc.	DISP 1.9 Complaints record rule	DISP 1.10 Complaints reporting rules	DISP 1.10A Complaints data publication rules
payment service provider in relation to *complaints* concerning *payment services*	Applies for *eligible complainants*	Applies for *eligible complainants*	Applies for *eligible complainants*	Does not apply	Does not apply	Does not apply
EEA branch of a *UK payment service provider* in relation to *complaints* concerning *payment services*	Does not apply	Does not apply	Does not apply	Does not apply	Does not apply	Does not apply
incoming branch of an *EEA authorised payment institution* in relation to *complaints* concerning *payment services*	Applies for *eligible complainants*	Applies for *eligible complainants*	Applies for *eligible complainants*	Does not apply	Does not apply	Does not apply
incoming *EEA authorised payment institution* providing cross border *payment services* from outside the *UK*	Does not apply	Does not apply	Does not apply	Does not apply	Does not apply	Does not apply
electronic money issuer in relation to *complaints* concerning issuance of *electronic money*	Applies for *eligible complainants*	Applies for *eligible complainants*	Applies for *eligible complainants*	Does not apply	Does not apply	Does not apply
EEA branch of an *authorised electronic money institution* or an *EEA branch* of any other *UK electronic money issuer* in relation to *complaints* concerning issuance of *electronic money*	Does not apply	Does not apply	Does not apply	Does not apply	Does not apply	Does not apply
incoming branch of an *EEA authorised electronic money institution* in relation to *complaints* concerning issuance of *electronic money*	Applies for *eligible complainants*	Applies for *eligible complainants*	Applies for *eligible complainants*	Does not apply	Does not apply	Does not apply
incoming *EEA authorised electronic money institution* providing cross border *electronic money* issuance services from outside the *UK*	Does not apply	Does not apply	Does not apply	Does not apply	Does not apply	Does not apply

Type of respondent/ complaint	DISP 1.2 Consumer awareness rules	DISP 1.3 Complaints handling rules	DISP 1.4–1.8 Complaints resolution rules etc.	DISP 1.9 Complaints record rule	DISP 1.10 Complaints reporting rules	DISP 1.10A Complaints data publication rules
VJ participant	Applies for eligible complainants	Applies for eligible complainants (DISP 1.3.4 G to DISP 1.3.5 G do not apply)	Applies for eligible complainants (DISP 1.6.8 G does not apply)	Does not apply	Does not apply	Does not apply
complaints relating to auction regulation bidding	Does not apply	Does not apply	Does not apply	Does not apply	Does not apply	Does not apply
a full-scope UK AIFM, small authorised UK AIFM or an incoming EEA AIFM, for complaints concerning AIFM management functions carried on for a closed-ended corporate AIF	Does not apply	Does not apply	Does not apply	Does not apply	Does not apply	Does not apply
a depositary, for complaints concerning activities carried on for an unauthorised AIF (where the AIF is not a charity AIF) or a closed-ended corporate AIF.	Does not apply	Does not apply	Does not apply	Does not apply	Does not apply	Does not apply
an incoming EEA AIFM, for complaints concerning AIFM management functions carried on for an authorised AIF under the freedom to provide cross-border services	Applies for eligible complainants	Applies for eligible complainants	Applies for eligible complainants	Applies for eligible complainants	Applies for eligible complainants	Does not apply-FCA

1 ANNEX 3   APPROPRIATE WORDING FOR INCLUSION IN A FINAL RESPONSE OR WRITTEN ACCEPTANCE

The respondent does not consent to waive the six-month time limit in **DISP 2.8.2 R (1)**

(1)   **"You have the right to refer your complaint to the Financial Ombudsman Service, free of charge? but you must do so within six months of the date of this letter.**
If you do not refer your complaint in time, the Ombudsman will not have our permission to consider your complaint and so will only be able to do so in very limited circumstances. For example, if the Ombudsman believes that the delay was as a result of exceptional circumstances."

The complaint was received outside the time limits in **DISP 2.8.2 R (2)** and the respondent does not consent to waive those time limits or the six-month time limit in **DISP 2.8.2 R (1)**

(2)   **"You have the right to refer your complaint to the Financial Ombudsman Service, free of charge.**
The Ombudsman might not be able to consider your complaint if:
what you're complaining about happened more than **six years** ago, **and**
you're complaining more than **three years** after you realised (or should have realised) that there was a problem.
We think that your complaint was made outside of these time limits but this is a matter for the Ombudsman to decide. If the Ombudsman agrees with us, they will not have our permission to consider your complaint and so will only be able to do so in very limited circumstances (see below).
If you do decide to refer your complaint to the Ombudsman you must do so within six months of the date of this letter.
If you do not refer your complaint to the Ombudsman within six months of the date of this letter, the Ombudsman will not have our permission to consider your complaint and so will only be able to do so in very limited circumstances.
The very limited circumstances referred to above include, where the Ombudsman believes that the delay was as a result of exceptional circumstances."

The complaint was received outside the time limits in **DISP 2.8.2 R (2)** and the respondent does not consent to waive those time limits but does consent to waive the six-month time limit in **DISP 2.8.2 R (1)**

(3)   **"You have the right to refer your complaint to the Financial Ombudsman Service, free of charge.**
The Ombudsman might not be able to consider your complaint if:
what you're complaining about happened more than **six years** ago, **and**
you're complaining more than **three years** after you realised (or should have realised) that there was a problem.
We think that your complaint was made outside of these time limits but this is a matter for the Ombudsman to decide. If the Ombudsman agrees with us, they will not have our permission to consider your complaint and so will only be able to do so in very limited circumstances. For example, if the Ombudsman believes that the delay was as a result of exceptional circumstances.
The time limit for referring complaints to the Ombudsman is usually six months but we will consent to the Ombudsman considering your complaint even if you refer the complaint later than this."

The respondent does not consent to waive the time limits in **DISP 2.8.7 R** relating to mortgage endowment complaints

(4)   **"You have the right to refer your complaint to the Financial Ombudsman Service, free of charge? but you must do so within six months of the date of this letter.**
The Ombudsman might not be able to consider your complaint if:
you received a letter warning you that there was a high risk that your mortgage endowment policy would not produce a sum large enough to repay the target amount at maturity; and
you're complaining more than **three years** after you received that letter, and
you're complaining more than **six months** after the date on which we sent you a further communication notifying you when the three-year period would expire.
We think that your complaint was made outside of these time limits but this is a matter for the Ombudsman to decide. If the Ombudsman agrees with us, they will not have our permission to consider your complaint and so will only be able to do so in limited circumstances."

<table>
<tr><td></td><td>The respondent consents to waive all applicable time limits</td></tr>
</table>

(5)   **"You have the right to refer your complaint to the Financial Ombudsman Service, free of charge.**
Although there are time limits for referring your complaint to the Ombudsman, we will consent to the Ombudsman considering your complaint even if you refer the complaint outside the time limits."

Other circumstances not dealt with above

(6)   Where the *respondent* proposes to waive the time limits in **DISP 2.8.2 R** or **DISP 2.8.7 R** and appropriate wording for the *respondent's* circumstances is not set out in (1) to (5), the *respondent* must adapt the appropriate wording as necessary.

CHAPTER 2
JURISDICTION OF THE FINANCIAL OMBUDSMAN SERVICE

2.1   PURPOSE, INTERPRETATION AND APPLICATION

Purpose

[3.73]
2.1.1 G   FCA

The purpose of this chapter is to set out *rules* and guidance on the scope of the *Compulsory Jurisdiction* and the *Voluntary Jurisdiction*, which are the *Financial Ombudsman Service's* two jurisdictions:
(1)   the *Compulsory Jurisdiction* is not restricted to *regulated activities*, *payment services* and issuance of *electronic money*, and covers:
    (a)   certain *complaints* against *firms* (and businesses which were *firms* at the time of the events complained about);
    (b)   *relevant complaints* against former members of *former schemes* under the *Ombudsman Transitional Order* and the *Mortgage and General Insurance Complaints Transitional Order*; and
    (c)   *relevant credit-related complaints* against businesses which were, at the time of the events complained about, covered by a standard licence under the Consumer Credit Act 1974, or formerly authorised to carry on an activity by virtue of section 34(A) of that Act, in accordance with article 11 of the *Regulated Activities Amendment Order*;
(2)   [deleted]
(3)   the *Voluntary Jurisdiction* covers certain *complaints* against *VJ participants*, including in relation to events before they joined the *Voluntary Jurisdiction*.

2.1.2 G   FCA

Relevant complaints covered by the *Compulsory Jurisdiction* comprise:
(1)   *relevant existing complaints* referred to a *former scheme* before *commencement* and inherited by the *Financial Ombudsman Service* under the *Ombudsman Transitional Order*;
(2)   *relevant new complaints* about events before *commencement* but referred to the *Financial Ombudsman Service* after *commencement* under the *Ombudsman Transitional Order*;
(3)   *relevant transitional complaints* referred to the *Financial Ombudsman Service* after the *relevant commencement date* under the *Mortgages and General Insurance Complaints Transitional Order*;
(4)   *relevant existing credit-related complaints* referred to the *Financial Ombudsman Service* before 1 April 2014 which were formerly being dealt with under the *Consumer Credit Jurisdiction* and which are to be dealt with under the *Compulsory Jurisdiction* in accordance with article 11 of the *Regulated Activities Amendment Order*; and
(5)   *relevant new credit-related complaints* about events which took place before 1 April 2014 but referred to the *Financial Ombudsman Service* on or after 1 April 2014 which are to be dealt with under the *Compulsory Jurisdiction* in accordance with article 11 of the *Regulated Activities Amendment Order*.

2.1.3 G   FCA

The *Ombudsman Transitional Order* requires the *Financial Ombudsman Service* to complete the handling of *relevant existing complaints*, in a significant number of respects, in accordance with the requirements of the relevant *former scheme* rather than in accordance with the requirements of this chapter.

Interpretation

2.1.4 G   FCA

In this chapter, carrying on an activity includes:

(1)   offering, providing or failing to provide a service in relation to an activity;
(2)   administering or failing to administer a service in relation to an activity; and
(3)   the manner in which a *respondent* has administered its business, provided that the business is an activity subject to the *Financial Ombudsman Service's* jurisdiction.

Purpose

2.1.5 G   FCA

In this chapter, ancillary banking services include, for example, the provision and operation of cash machines, foreign currency exchange, safe deposit boxes and account aggregation services (services where details of accounts held with different financial service providers can be accessed by a single password).

Application

2.1.6 R   FCA

This chapter applies to the *Ombudsman* and to *respondents*.

2.1.7 D

Part XVI of the *Act* (The Ombudsman Scheme), particularly section 226 (Compulsory jurisdiction), applies to *members* of the *Society* of Lloyd's in respect of the *regulated activities* of *effecting* or *carrying out contracts of insurance* written at Lloyd's.

2.2   WHICH COMPLAINTS CAN BE DEALT WITH UNDER THE *Financial Ombudsman Service*?

2.2.1 G   FCA

The scope of the *Financial Ombudsman Service's* two jurisdictions depends on:
(1)   the type of activity to which the *complaint* relates (see **DISP 2.3, DISP 2.4** and **DISP 2.5**);
(2)   the place where the activity to which the complaint relates was carried on (see **DISP 2.6**);
(3)   whether the complainant is eligible (see **DISP 2.7**); and
(4)   whether the *complaint* was referred to the *Financial Ombudsman Service* in time (see **DISP 2.8**).

2.3   TO WHICH ACTIVITIES DOES THE COMPULSORY JURISDICTION APPLY?

Activities by firms

2.3.1 R   FCA

The *Ombudsman* can consider a *complaint* under the *Compulsory Jurisdiction* if it relates to an act or omission by a *firm* in carrying on one or more of the following activities:
(1)   *regulated activities* (other than *auction regulation bidding*);
(2)   *payment services*;
(3)   [deleted]
(4)   [deleted]
(5)   lending *money* secured by a charge on land;
(6)   lending *money* (excluding *restricted credit* where that is not a *credit-related regulated activity*);
(7)   paying *money* by a *plastic card* (excluding a *store card* where that is not a *credit-related regulated activity*);
(8)   providing ancillary banking services;

or any ancillary activities, including advice, carried on by the *firm* in connection with them.

Activities by firms and unauthorised persons subject to a former scheme

2.3.2 G   FCA

The *Ombudsman* can also consider under the *Compulsory Jurisdiction*:
(1)   as a result of the *Ombudsman Transitional Order*, a *relevant existing complaint* or a *relevant new complaint* that relates to an act or omission by a *firm* or an *unauthorised person* which was subject to a *former scheme* immediately before *commencement*; or
(2)   as a result of the *Mortgages and General Insurance Complaints Transitional Order*, a *relevant transitional complaint* that relates to an act or omission by a *firm* (or an *unauthorised person* that ceased to be a *firm* after the *relevant commencement date*) which was subject to a *former scheme* at the time of the act or omission;

provided that:
(3)   the act or omission occurred in the carrying on by that *firm* or *unauthorised person* of an activity to which that *former scheme* applied; and
(4)   the complainant is eligible and wishes to have the *complaint* dealt with by the *Ombudsman*.

Activities by firms and unauthorised persons previously subject to the Consumer Credit Jurisdiction

2.3.2-A G   FCA

In accordance with article 11 of the *Regulated Activities Amendment Order*, the *Ombudsman* can also consider under the *Compulsory Jurisdiction*:

(1)   a *relevant existing credit-related complaint* referred to the *Financial Ombudsman Service* before 1 April 2014 which was formerly being dealt with under the *Consumer Credit Jurisdiction*; and

(2)   a *relevant new credit-related complaint* referred to the *Financial Ombudsman Service* on or after 1 April 2014 which relates to an act or omission which took place before 1 April 2014; provided that:

    (a)   the *complaint* could have been dealt with under the *Consumer Credit Jurisdiction* (disregarding whether the complainant would have been eligible under rules made for the purposes of the *Consumer Credit Jurisdiction* and whether the complaint would have fallen within a description specified in those rules) but for the repeal of section 226A of the *Act*; and

    (b)   the complainant is eligible and wishes to have the *complaint* dealt with under the *Financial Ombudsman Service*.

Activities by payment service providers

2.3.2A R   FCA

The *Ombudsman* can consider a *complaint* under the *Compulsory Jurisdiction* if it relates to an act or omission by a *payment service provider* in carrying on:

(1)   *payment services*; or

(2)   *credit-related regulated activities*;

or any ancillary activities, including advice, carried on by the *payment service provider* in connection with them.

Activities by electronic money issuers

2.3.2B R   FCA

The *Ombudsman* can consider a *complaint* under the *Compulsory Jurisdiction* if it relates to an act or omission by an *electronic money issuer* in carrying on:

(1)   issuance of *electronic money*; or

(2)   *credit-related regulated activities*;

or any ancillary activities, including advice, carried on by the *electronic money issuer* in connection with them.

Consumer redress schemes

2.3.2C G   FCA

As a result of section 404B(11) of the *Act*, the *Ombudsman* can also consider under the *Compulsory Jurisdiction* a *complaint* from a complainant who:

(1)   is not satisfied with a *redress determination* made by a *respondent* under a *consumer redress scheme*; or

(2)   considers that a *respondent* has failed to make a *redress determination* in accordance with a *consumer redress scheme*.

General

2.3.3 G   FCA

Complaints about acts or omissions include those in respect of activities for which the *firm*, *payment service provider* or *electronic money issuer* is responsible (including business of any *appointed representative* or *agent* for which the *firm*, *payment institution* or *electronic money institution* has accepted responsibility).

2.3.4 R   FCA

A *complaint* about an *authorised professional firm* cannot be handled under the *Compulsory Jurisdiction* of the *Financial Ombudsman Service* if it relates solely to a *non-mainstream regulated activity* and can be handled by a *designated professional body*.

2.3.5 G   FCA

The *Compulsory Jurisdiction* includes *complaints* about the *UK* end of 'one leg' *payment services* transactions, i.e. services provided from *UK* establishments that also involve a payment service provider located outside the *EEA*. The *Compulsory Jurisdiction* also includes *complaints* about *payment services* irrespective of the currency of the transaction.

2.5   TO WHICH ACTIVITIES DOES THE VOLUNTARY JURISDICTION APPLY?

2.5.1 R   FCA

The *Ombudsman* can consider a *complaint* under the *Voluntary Jurisdiction* if:

(1)   it is not covered by the *Compulsory Jurisdiction*; and

(2)   it relates to an act or omission by a *VJ participant* in carrying on one or more of the following activities:

     (a)   an activity carried on after 28 April 1988 which:

         (i)   was not a *regulated activity* at the time of the act or omission, but

         (ii)   was a *regulated activity* when the *VJ participant* joined the *Voluntary Jurisdiction* (or became an *authorised person*, if later);

     (b)   a financial services activity carried on after *commencement* by a *VJ participant* which was covered in respect of that activity by a *former scheme* immediately before the *commencement day*;

     (c)   activities which (at 24 April 2015) would be covered by the *Compulsory Jurisdiction*, if they were carried on from an establishment in the *United Kingdom* (these activities are listed in **DISP 2 ANNEX 1 G**);

     (d)   [deleted]

     (e)   lending *money* secured by a charge on land;

     (f)   lending *money* (excluding *restricted credit* where that is not a *credit-related regulated activity*);

     (g)   paying *money* by a *plastic card* (excluding a *store card* where that is not a *credit-related regulated activity*);

     (h)   providing ancillary banking services;

     (i)   acting as an intermediary for a loan secured by a charge over land;

     (j)   acting as an intermediary for *general insurance business* or *long-term insurance business*;

     (k)   National Savings and Investments' business;

     (l)   [deleted]

     (m)   [deleted]

or any ancillary activities, including advice, carried on by the *VJ participant* in connection with them.

2.5.2 G   FCA

The scope of the *Voluntary Jurisdiction* is wider than that of the *Compulsory Jurisdiction*, and so some activities are referred to in both jurisdictions.

2.5.3 G   FCA

DISP 2.5.1 R (2)(A) is for those that are subject to the *Compulsory Jurisdiction* for *regulated activities* but are not covered by the *Ombudsman Transitional Order* or the *Mortgage and General Insurance Complaints Transitional Order*. It enables the *Financial Ombudsman Scheme* to cover *complaints* about earlier events relating to those activities before they became *regulated activities*.

2.5.4 G   FCA

DISP 2.5.1 R (2)(B) is for those that were members of one of the *former schemes* replaced by the *Financial Ombudsman Service* immediately before *commencement*. It enables the *Financial Ombudsman Service* to cover *complaints* that arise out of acts or omissions occurring after *commencement* for any activities which are not covered by the *Compulsory Jurisdiction* but that would have been covered by the relevant *former scheme*.

2.5.4A G   FCA

DISP 2.5.1 R (2)(L) includes *complaints* about the *EEA* end of 'one leg' *payment services* transactions, i.e. services provided from *EEA* establishments that are subject to the territorial jurisdiction of the *Voluntary Jurisdiction* (see **DISP 2.6.4 R (2)**) that also involve a payment service provider located outside the *EEA*. It also includes *complaints* about *payment services* irrespective of the currency of the transaction.

2.5.5 R   FCA

The *Voluntary Jurisdiction* covers an act or omission that occurred before the *VJ participant* was participating in the *Voluntary Jurisdiction*, and whether the act or omission occurred before or after *commencement*, either:

(1)   if the *complaint* could have been dealt with under a *former scheme*; or

(2)   under the agreement by the *VJ participant* in the *Standard Terms*.

2.6   WHAT IS THE TERRITORIAL SCOPE OF THE RELEVANT JURISDICTION?

Compulsory Jurisdiction

2.6.1 R   FCA

(1)   The *Compulsory Jurisdiction* covers *complaints* about the activities of a *firm* (including its *appointed representatives*), of a *payment service provider* (including *agents* of a *payment institution*) or of an *electronic money issuer* (including agents of an *electronic money institution*) carried on from an establishment in the *United Kingdom*.

(2)   The *Compulsory Jurisdiction* also covers *complaints* about:

    (a)   *collective portfolio management* services provided by an *EEA UCITS management company* managing a *UCITS scheme*; and

    (b)   AIFM management functions provided by an incoming EEA AIFM managing an authorised AIF;

from an establishment in another *EEA State* under the freedom to provide *cross border services*.

(3)   [deleted]

(4)   [deleted]

(5)   [deleted]

(6)   [deleted]

2.6.2 G   FCA

This:

(1)   includes incoming *EEA firms*, incoming *EEA authorised payment institutions*, incoming *EEA authorised electronic money institutions* and *incoming Treaty firms*; but

(2)   excludes *complaints* about business conducted in the *United Kingdom* on a services basis from an establishment outside the *United Kingdom* (other than *complaints* about *collective portfolio management* services provided by an *EEA UCITS management company* in managing a *UCITS scheme*, and *complaints* about AIFM management functions provided by an incoming EEA AIFM managing an authorised AIF).

Consumer Credit Jurisdiction

2.6.3 R

[deleted]

Voluntary Jurisdiction

2.6.4 R   FCA

The *Voluntary Jurisdiction* covers only *complaints* about the activities of a *VJ participant* carried on from an establishment:

(1)   in the *United Kingdom*; or

(2)   elsewhere in the *EEA* if the following conditions are met:

    (a)   the activity is directed wholly or partly at the *United Kingdom* (or part of it);

    (b)   contracts governing the activity are (or, in the case of a potential customer, would have been) made under the law of England and Wales, Scotland or Northern Ireland; and

    (c)   the *VJ participant* has notified appropriate regulators in its *Home State* of its intention to participate in the *Voluntary Jurisdiction*.

Location of the complainant

2.6.5 G   FCA

A *complaint* can be dealt with under the *Financial Ombudsman Service* whether or not the complainant lives or is based in the *United Kingdom*.

2.7   IS THE COMPLAINANT ELIGIBLE?

2.7.1 R   FCA

A *complaint* may only be dealt with under the *Financial Ombudsman Service* if it is brought by or on behalf of an *eligible complainant*.

2.7.2 R   FCA

A *complaint* may be brought on behalf of an *eligible complainant* (or a deceased *person* who would have been an *eligible complainant*) by a *person* authorised by the *eligible complainant* or authorised by law. It is immaterial whether the *person* authorised to act on behalf of an *eligible complainant* is himself an *eligible complainant*.

Eligible complainants

2.7.3 R   FCA

An *eligible complainant* must be a *person* that is:

(1)   a *consumer*;

(2)   a *micro-enterprise*;

    (a)   in relation to a *complaint* relating wholly or partly to *payment services*, either at the time of the conclusion of the *payment service* contract or at the time the complainant refers the *complaint* to the *respondent*; or

(b)   otherwise, at the time the complainant refers the *complaint* to the *respondent*;

(3)   a charity which has an annual income of less than £1 million at the time the complainant refers the *complaint* to the *respondent*; or

(4)   a trustee of a trust which has a net asset value of less than £1 million at the time the complainant refers the *complaint* to the *respondent*.

2.7.4 G   FCA

In determining whether an enterprise meets the tests for being a *micro-enterprise*, account should be taken of the enterprise's 'partner enterprises' or 'linked enterprises' (as those terms are defined in the *Micro-enterprise Recommendation*). For example, where a parent company holds a majority shareholding in a *complainant*, if the parent company does not meet the tests for being a *micro-enterprise* then neither will the *complainant*. [**Note**: Articles 1 and 3 to 7 of the Annex to the *Micro-enterprise Recommendation*].

2.7.5 G   FCA

If a *respondent* is in doubt about the eligibility of a business, charity or trust, it should treat the complainant as if it were eligible. If the *complaint* is referred to the *Financial Ombudsman Service*, the *Ombudsman* will determine eligibility by reference to appropriate evidence, such as audited accounts or VAT returns.

2.7.6 R   FCA

To be an *eligible complainant* a *person* must also have a *complaint* which arises from matters relevant to one or more of the following relationships with the *respondent*:

(1)   the complainant is (or was) a customer, *payment service user* or electronic money holder of the *respondent*;

(2)   the complainant is (or was) a potential customer, *payment service user* or electronic money holder of the *respondent*;

(3)   the complainant is the holder, or the beneficial owner, of *units* in a *collective investment scheme* and the *respondent* is:

    (a)   the *operator* of a *scheme*;

    (b)   the *depositary* of an *authorised fund*; or

    (c)   the *depositary* of a charity AIF;

(4)   the complainant is the holder, or the beneficial owner, of *units* or *shares* in an AIF where the *respondent* is:

    (a)   the AIFM of an unauthorised AIF (apart from a closed-ended corporate AIF);

    (b)   the AIFM or *depositary* of an authorised AIF; or

    (c)   the AIFM or *depositary* of a charity AIF (apart from a charity AIF which is a closed-ended corporate AIF);

(5)   the complainant is a beneficiary of, or has a beneficial interest in, a *personal pension scheme* or *stakeholder pension scheme*;

(6)   the complainant is a *person* for whose benefit a *contract of insurance* was taken out or was intended to be taken out with or through the *respondent*;

(7)   the complainant is a *person* on whom the legal right to benefit from a claim against the *respondent* under a *contract of insurance* has been devolved by contract, assignment, subrogation or legislation (save the European Community (Rights against Insurers) Regulations 2002);

(8)   the complainant relied in the course of his business on a cheque guarantee card issued by the *respondent*;

(9)   the complainant is the true owner or the *person* entitled to immediate possession of a cheque or other bill of exchange, or of the funds it represents, collected by the *respondent* for someone else's account;

(10)   the complainant is the recipient of a banker's reference given by the *respondent*;

(11)   the complainant gave the *respondent* a guarantee or security for:

    (a)   a mortgage;

    (b)   a loan;

    (c)   an actual or prospective *regulated credit agreement*;

    (d)   an actual or prospective *regulated consumer hire agreement*; or

    (e)   any linked transaction as defined in the Consumer Credit Act 1974 (as amended);

(12)   the complainant is a *person* about whom information relevant to his financial standing is or was held by the *respondent* in *providing credit references*;

(13)   the complainant is a *person*:

    (a)   from whom the *respondent* has sought to recover payment under a *credit agreement* or *consumer hire agreement* (whether or not the *respondent* is a party to the agreement); or

    (b)   in relation to whom the *respondent* has sought to perform duties, or exercise or enforce rights, on behalf of the creditor or owner, under a *credit agreement* or *consumer hire agreement* in carrying on *debt administration*;

(14)   the complainant is a beneficiary under a trust or estate of which the *respondent* is trustee or personal representative;

(15)   (where the *respondent* is a *dormant account fund operator*) the complainant is (or was) a customer of a *bank* or *building society* which transferred any *balance* from a *dormant account* to the *respondent*;

(16)   the complainant is either a *borrower* or a lender under a *P2P agreement* and the *respondent* is the *operator of an electronic system in relation to lending*.

2.7.7 G   FCA

DISP 2.7.6 R (5) and **DISP 2.7.6 R (6)** include, for example, employees covered by a group permanent health policy taken out by an employer, which provides in the insurance contract that the policy was taken out for the benefit of the employee.

2.7.8 G   FCA

In the *Compulsory Jurisdiction*, under the *Ombudsman Transitional Order* and the *Mortgages and General Insurance Complaints Transitional Order*, where a complainant:

(1)   wishes to have a *relevant new complaint* or a *relevant transitional complaint* dealt with by the *Ombudsman*; and

(2)   is not otherwise eligible; but

(3)   would have been entitled to refer an equivalent *complaint* to the *former scheme* in question immediately before the relevant transitional order came into effect;

if the *Ombudsman* considers it appropriate, he may treat the complainant as an *eligible complainant*.

Exceptions

2.7.9 R   FCA

The following are not *eligible complainants*:

(1)   (in all jurisdictions) a *firm, payment service provider, electronic money issuer,* or *VJ participant* whose *complaint* relates in any way to an activity which:

    (a)   the *firm* itself has *permission* to carry on; or

    (b)   the *firm, payment service provider* or *electronic money issuer* itself is entitled to carry on under the *Payment Services Regulations* or the *Electronic Money Regulations*; or

    (c)   the *VJ participant* itself conducts;

and which is subject to the *Compulsory Jurisdiction* or the *Voluntary Jurisdiction*;

(2)   (in the *Compulsory Jurisdiction*) a complainant, other than a trustee of a *pension scheme trust*, who was:

    (a)   a *professional client*; or

    (b)   an *eligible counterparty*;

in relation to the *firm* and activity in question at the time of the act or omission which is the subject of the *complaint*; and

(3)   [deleted]

2.7.9A R   FCA

DISP 2.7.9 R (1) and **DISP 2.7.9 R (2)** do not apply to a complainant who is a *consumer* in relation to the activity to which the *complaint* relates.

2.7.10 G   FCA

In the *Compulsory Jurisdiction*, in relation to *relevant new complaints* under the *Ombudsman Transitional Order* and *relevant transitional complaints* under the *Mortgages and General Insurance Complaints Transitional Order*:

(1)   where the *former scheme* in question is the *Insurance Ombudsman Scheme*, a complainant is not to be treated as an *eligible complainant* unless:

    (a)   he is an individual; and

    (b)   the *relevant new complaint* does not concern aspects of a policy relating to a business or trade carried on by him;

(2)   where the *former scheme* in question is the *GISC facility*, a complainant is not to be treated as an *eligible complainant* unless:

    (a)   he is an individual; and

    (b)   he is acting otherwise than solely for the purposes of his business; and

(3)   where the *former scheme* in question is the *MCAS scheme*, a complainant is not to be treated as an *eligible complainant* if:

    (a)   the *relevant transitional complaint* does not relate to a breach of the Mortgage Code published by the Council of Mortgage Lenders;

    (b)   the *complaint* concerns physical injury, illness, nervous shock or their consequences; or

    (c)   the complainant is claiming a sum of money that exceeds £100,000.

2.8   WAS THE COMPLAINT REFERRED TO THE FINANCIAL OMBUDSMAN SERVICE IN TIME?

2.8.1 R   FCA

The *Ombudsman* can only consider a *complaint* if:

(1)   the *respondent* has already sent the complainant its *final response*; or
(2)   eight weeks have elapsed since the *respondent* received the *complaint*; or
(3)   in relation to a *complaint* the subject matter of which falls to be dealt with (or has properly been dealt with) under a *consumer redress scheme*:
    (a)   the *respondent* has already sent the complainant its *redress determination* under the scheme; or
    (b)   the *respondent* has failed to send a *redress determination* in accordance with the time limits specified under the scheme;

unless:
(4)   the *respondent* consents and:
    (a)   the *Ombudsman* has informed the complainant that the *respondent* must deal with the *complaint* within eight weeks and that it may resolve the complaint more quickly than the *Ombudsman*; and
    (b)   the complainant nevertheless wishes the *Ombudsman* to deal with the *complaint*.

2.8.2 R   FCA

The *Ombudsman* cannot consider a *complaint* if the complainant refers it to the *Financial Ombudsman Service*:
(1)   more than six *months* after the date on which the *respondent* sent the complainant its *final response* or *redress determination*; or
(2)   more than:
    (a)   six years after the event complained of; or (if later)
    (b)   three years from the date on which the complainant became aware (or ought reasonably to have become aware) that he had cause for complaint;
    unless the complainant referred the *complaint* to the *respondent* or to the *Ombudsman* within that period and has a written acknowledgement or some other record of the *complaint* having been received;

unless:
(3)   in the view of the *Ombudsman*, the failure to comply with the time limits in **DISP 2.8.2 R** or **DISP 2.8.7 R** was as a result of exceptional circumstances; or
(4)   the *Ombudsman* is required to do so by the *Ombudsman Transitional Order*; or
(5)   the *respondent* has consented to the *Ombudsman* considering the *complaint* where the time limits in **DISP 2.8.2 R** or **DISP 2.8.7 R** have expired (but this does not apply to a "relevant complaint" within the meaning of section 404B(3) of the *Act*).

2.8.2A R   FCA

If a *respondent* consents to the *Ombudsman* considering a *complaint* in accordance with **DISP 2.8.2 R (5)**, the *respondent* may not withdraw consent.

2.8.3 G   FCA

The six-month time limit is only triggered by a response which is a *final response* or *redress determination*. The response must tell the complainant about the six-month time limit that the complainant has to refer a *complaint* to the *Financial Ombudsman Service*.

2.8.4 G   FCA

An example of exceptional circumstances might be where the complainant has been or is incapacitated.

Reviews of past business

2.8.5 R   FCA

The six-year and the three-year time limits do not apply where:
(1)   [deleted]
(2)   the *complaint* concerns a contract or policy which is the subject of a review directly or indirectly under:
    (a)   the terms of the Statement of Policy on 'Pension transfers and Opt-outs' issued by the FSA on 25 October 1994; or
    (b)   the terms of the policy statement for the review of specific categories of *FSAVC* business issued by the FSA on 28 February 2000.

Mortgage endowment complaints

2.8.6 G   FCA

If a *complaint* relates to the sale of an endowment *policy* for the purpose of achieving capital repayment of a mortgage, the receipt by the complainant of a letter which states that there is a risk (rather than a high risk) that the *policy* would not, at maturity, produce a sum large enough to repay the target amount is not, itself, sufficient to cause the three year time period in **DISP 2.8.2 R (2)** to start to run.

2.8.7 R   FCA

(1)   If a *complaint* relates to the sale of an endowment *policy* for the purpose of achieving capital repayment of a mortgage and the complainant receives a letter from a *firm* or a *VJ participant* warning that there is a high risk that the *policy* will not, at maturity, produce a sum large enough to repay the target amount then, subject to (2), (3), (4) and (5):

    (a)   time for referring a *complaint* to the *Financial Ombudsman Service* starts to run from the date the complainant receives the letter; and

    (b)   ends three years from that date ("the final date").

(2)   Paragraph (1)(b) applies only if the complainant also receives within the three year period mentioned in (1)(b) and at least six months before the final date an explanation that the complainant's time to refer such a *complaint* would expire at the final date.

(3)   If an explanation is given but is sent outside the period referred to in (2), time for referring a *complaint* will run until a date specified in such an explanation which must not be less than six months after the date on which the notice is sent.

(4)   A complainant will be taken to have complied with the time limits in (1) to (3) above if in any case he refers the *complaint* to the *firm* or *VJ participant* within those limits and has a written acknowledgement or some other record of the *complaint* having been received.

(5)   Paragraph (1) does not apply if the *Ombudsman* is of the opinion that, in the circumstances of the case, it is appropriate for **DISP 2.8.2 R (2)** to apply.FCA

2 ANNEX 1   REGULATED ACTIVITIES FOR THE VOLUNTARY JURISDICTION AT
24 APRIL 2015

This table belongs to **DISP 2.5.1 R**

The activities which were covered by the *Compulsory Jurisdiction* (at 24 April 2015) were:

(1)   for *firms*:

    (a)   *regulated activities* (other than auction regulated bidding);

    (b)   *payment services*;

    (c)   [deleted]

    (d)   lending *money* secured by a charge on land;

    (e)   lending *money* (excluding *restricted credit* where that is not a *credit-related regulated activity*);

    (f)   paying *money* by a *plastic card* (excluding a *store card* where that is not a *credit-related regulated activity*);

    (g)   providing ancillary banking services;

    (h)   [deleted]

    or any ancillary activities, including advice, carried on by the *firm* in connection with them.

(2)   for *payment service providers*:

    (a)   *payment services*;

    (b)   (b) *credit-related regulated activities*;

    or any ancillary activities, including advice, carried on by the *payment service provider* in connection with them.

(3)   for *electronic money issuers*:

    (a)   issuance of electronic money;

    (b)   *credit-related regulated activities*;

    or any ancillary activities, including advice, carried on by the *electronic money issuer* in connection with them

The activities which (at 24 April 2015) were *regulated activities* were, in accordance with section 22 of the *Act* (The classes of activity and categories of investment), any of the following activities specified in Part II of the *Regulated Activities Order*:

(1) *accepting deposits* (article 5);

(2) *issuing electronic money* (article 9B);

(3) *effecting contracts of insurance* (article 10(1));

(4) *carrying out contracts of insurance* (article 10(2));

(5) *dealing in investments as principal* (article 14);

(6) *dealing in investments as agent* (article 21);

(7) *arranging (bringing about) deals in investments* (article 25(1));

(8) *making arrangements with a view to transactions in investments* (article 25(2));

(9) *arranging (bringing about) regulated mortgage contracts* (article 25A(1));

(10) *making arrangements with a view to regulated mortgage contracts* (article 25A(2));

(11) *arranging (bringing about) a home reversion plan* (article 25B(1));

(12) *making arrangements with a view to a home reversion plan* (article 25B(2));

(13) *arranging (bringing about) a home purchase plan* (article 25C(1));

(14) *making arrangements with a view to a home purchase plan* (article 25C(2));

(14A) *operating a multilateral trading facility* (article 25D);

(14B) *arranging (bringing about) a regulated sale and rent back agreement* (article 25E(1));

(14C) *making arrangements with a view to a regulated sale and rent back agreement* (article 25E(2));

(14D) *credit broking* (article 36A);

(14E) *operating an electronic system in relation to lending* (article 36H);

(15) *managing investments* (article 37);

(16) *assisting in the administration and performance of a contract of insurance* (article 39A);

(16A) *debt adjusting* (article 39D(1) and (2));

(16B) *debt counselling* (article 39E(1) and (2));

(16C) *debt collecting* (article 39F(1) and (2));

(16D) *debt administration* (article 39G(1) and (2));

(17) *safeguarding and administering investments* (article 40);

(18) *sending dematerialised instructions* (article 45(1));

(19) *causing dematerialised instructions to be sent* (article 45(2));

(22A) *managing a UCITS* (article 51ZA);

(22B) acting as a trustee or depositary of a UCITS (article 51ZB);

(22C) *managing an AIF* (article 51ZC);

(22D) acting as a trustee or depositary of an AIF (article 51ZD);

(22E) *establishing, operating or winding up a collective investment scheme* (article 51ZE);

(23) *establishing, operating or winding up a stakeholder pension scheme* (article 52(a));

(24) *providing basic advice on a stakeholder product* (article 52B);

(25) *establishing, operating or winding up a personal pension scheme* (article 52(b));

(26) *advising on investments* (article 53);

(27) *advising on regulated mortgage contracts* (article 53A);

(28) *advising on a home reversion plan* (article 53B);

(29) *advising on a home purchase plan* (article 53C);

(29A) *advising on a regulated sale and rent back agreement* (article 53D);

(29B) *advising on conversion or transfer of pension benefits* (article 53E);

(30) *advising on syndicate participation at Lloyd's* (article 56);

(31) *managing the underwriting capacity of a Lloyd's syndicate as a managing agent at Lloyd's* (article 57);(32) *arranging deals in contracts of insurance written at Lloyd's* (article 58);

(32A) entering into a regulated credit agreement (article 60B(1));

(32B) exercising, or having the right to exercise, rights and duties under a regulated credit agreement (article 60(B)(2);

(32C) entering into a regulated consumer hire agreement (article 60N(1));

(32D) exercising, or having the right to exercise rights and duties under a regulated consumer hire agreement (article 60N(2));

(33) *entering into a regulated mortgage contract* (article 61(1));

(34) *administering a regulated mortgage contract* (article 61(2));

(35) *entering into a home reversion plan* (article 63B(1));

(36) *administering a home reversion plan* (article 63B(2));

(37) *entering into a home purchase plan* (article 63F(1));

(38) *administering a home purchase plan* (article 63F(2));

(38A) *entering into a regulated sale and rent back agreement* (article 63J(1));

(38B) *administering a regulated sale and rent back agreement* (article 63J(2));

(38C) *meeting of repayment claims* (article 63N(1)(a));

(38D) *managing dormant account funds (including the investment of such funds)* (article 63N(1)(b));

(38E) *providing information in relation to a specified benchmark* (article 63O(1)(a));

(38F) *administering a specified benchmark* (article 63O(1)(b));

(39) *entering as provider into a funeral plan contract* (article 59);

(40) *agreeing to carry on a regulated activity* (article 64);

(40A) *providing credit information services* (article 89A);

(40B) *providing credit references* (article 89B);

which is carried on by way of business and relates to a *specified investment* applicable to that activity or, in the case of (22), (22A), (22B), (22C), (22D), (22E) and (23), is carried on in relation to property of any kind or, in the case of (40A) or (40B) relates to information about a *person's* financial standing.

CHAPTER 3
COMPLAINT HANDLING PROCEDURES OF THE FINANCIAL OMBUDSMAN SERVICE

3.1 PURPOSE, INTERPRETATION AND APPLICATION

Purpose

[3.74]
3.1.1 G FCA

The purpose of this chapter is to set out:
(1)   the procedures of the *Financial Ombudsman Service* for investigating and determining *complaints*;
(2)   the basis on which the *Ombudsman* makes decisions; and
(3)   the awards which the *Ombudsman* can make.

Interpretation

3.1.2 R FCA

In this chapter, 'out of jurisdiction' means outside the *Compulsory Jurisdiction* and the *Voluntary Jurisdiction* in accordance with **DISP 2**.

3.1.3 R FCA

Where the *respondent* is a *partnership* (or former *partnership*), it is sufficient for the *Ombudsman* to communicate with one partner (or former partner).

3.1.4 G FCA

The *Ombudsman Transitional Order* requires the *Financial Ombudsman Service* to complete the handling of *relevant existing complaints*, in a significant number of respects, in accordance with the requirements of the relevant *former scheme* rather than in accordance with the requirements of this chapter.

Application

3.1.5 R FCA

This chapter applies to the *Ombudsman* and to *respondents*.

3.2 JURISDICTION

3.2.1 R FCA

The *Ombudsman* will have regard to whether a *complaint* is out of jurisdiction.

3.2.2 R FCA

Unless the *respondent* has already had eight weeks to consider the *complaint* or issued a *final response*, the *Ombudsman* will refer the *complaint* to the *respondent*.

3.2.2A R FCA

If the subject matter of a *complaint* falls to be dealt with by the *respondent* under a *consumer redress scheme*, and the time limits specified under the scheme for doing so have not yet expired, the *Ombudsman* will refer it to the *respondent* to be dealt with under the scheme.

3.2.3 R FCA

Where the *respondent* alleges that the *complaint* is out of jurisdiction, the *Ombudsman* will give both parties an opportunity to make representations before he decides.

3.2.4 R FCA

Where the *Ombudsman* considers that the *complaint* may be out of jurisdiction, he will give the complainant an opportunity to make representations before he decides.

3.2.5 R   FCA

Where the *Ombudsman* then decides that the *complaint* is out of jurisdiction, he will give reasons for that decision to the complainant and inform the *respondent*.

3.2.6 R   FCA

Where the *Ombudsman* then decides that the *complaint* is not out of jurisdiction, he will inform the complainant and give reasons for that decision to the *respondent*.

3.3   DISMISSAL WITHOUT CONSIDERATION OF THE MERITS AND TEST CASES

3.3.1 R   FCA

Where the *Ombudsman* considers that the *complaint* may be one which should be dismissed without consideration of the merits, he will give the complainant an opportunity to make representations before he decides.

3.3.2 R   FCA

Where the *Ombudsman* then decides that the *complaint* should be dismissed without consideration of the merits, he will give reasons to the complainant for that decision and inform the *respondent*.

3.3.3 G   FCA

Under the *Ombudsman Transitional Order* and the *Mortgage and General Insurance Complaints Transitional Order*, where the *Ombudsman* is dealing with a *relevant complaint*, he must take into account whether an equivalent complaint would have been dismissed without consideration of its merits under the *former scheme* in question, as it had effect immediately before the relevant transitional order came into effect.

Grounds for dismissal

3.3.4 R   FCA

The *Ombudsman* may dismiss a *complaint* referred to the *Financial Ombudsman Service* before 9 July 2015 without considering its merits if the *Ombudsman* considers that:

(1)   the complainant has not suffered (or is unlikely to suffer) financial loss, material distress or material inconvenience; or

(2)   the *complaint* is frivolous or vexatious; or

(3)   the *complaint* clearly does not have any reasonable prospect of success; or

(4)   the *respondent* has already made an offer of compensation (or a goodwill payment) which is:
       (a)   fair and reasonable in relation to the circumstances alleged by the complainant; and
       (b)   still open for acceptance; or

(5)   the *respondent* has reviewed the subject matter of the *complaint* in accordance with:
       (a)   the regulatory standards for the review of such transactions prevailing at the time of the review; or
       (b)   [deleted]
       (c)   any formal regulatory requirement, standard or guidance published by the *FCA* or other regulator in respect of that type of *complaint*;
       (including, if appropriate, making an offer of redress to the complainant), unless he considers that they did not address the particular circumstances of the case; or

(6)   the *respondent* has reviewed the subject matter of the *complaint* and issued a *redress determination* in accordance with the terms of a *consumer redress scheme*; or

(7)   the subject matter of the *complaint* has previously been considered or excluded under the *Financial Ombudsman Service*, or a *former scheme* (unless material new evidence which the *Ombudsman* considers likely to affect the outcome has subsequently become available to the complainant); or

(8)   the subject matter of the *complaint* has been dealt with, or is being dealt with, by a comparable independent complaints scheme or dispute-resolution process; or

(9)   the subject matter of the *complaint* has been the subject of court proceedings where there has been a decision on the merits; or

(10)   the subject matter of the *complaint* is the subject of current court proceedings, unless proceedings are stayed or sisted (by agreement of all parties, or order of the court) so that the matter may be considered by the *Financial Ombudsman Service*; or

(11)   it would be more suitable for the subject matter of the *complaint* to be dealt with by a court, arbitration or another complaints scheme; or

(12)   it is a *complaint* about the legitimate exercise of a *respondent's* commercial judgment; or

(13)   it is a *complaint* about employment matters from an employee or employees of a *respondent*; or

(14)   it is a *complaint* about investment performance; or

(15)   it is a *complaint* about a *respondent's* decision when exercising a discretion under a will or private trust; or

(16)   it is a *complaint* about a *respondent's* failure to consult beneficiaries before exercising a discretion under a will or private trust, where there is no legal obligation to consult; or

(17)   it is a *complaint* which:
    (a)   involves (or might involve) more than one *eligible complainant*; and
    (b)   has been referred without the consent of the other complainant or complainants;
    and the *Ombudsman* considers that it would be inappropriate to deal with the *complaint* without that consent; or

(18)   it is a *complaint* about a pure landlord and tenant issue arising out of a *regulated sale and rent back agreement*; or

(19)   there are other compelling reasons why it is inappropriate for the *complaint* to be dealt with under the *Financial Ombudsman Service*.

3.3.4A R   FCA

The *Ombudsman* may dismiss a *complaint* referred to the *Financial Ombudsman Service* on or after 9 July 2015 without considering its merits if the *Ombudsman* considers that:

(1)   the *complaint* is frivolous or vexatious; or

(2)   the subject matter of the *complaint* has been dealt with, or is being dealt with, by a comparable *ADR entity*; or

(3)   the subject matter of the *complaint* has been the subject of court proceedings where there has been a decision on the merits; or

(4)   the subject matter of the *complaint* is the subject of current court proceedings, unless proceedings are stayed or sisted (by agreement of all parties, or order of the court) so that the matter may be considered by the *Financial Ombudsman Service*; or

(5)   dealing with such a type of *complaint* would otherwise seriously impair the effective operation of the *Financial Ombudsman Service*.

3.3.4B G   FCA

Examples of a type of *complaint* that would otherwise seriously impair the effective operation of the *Financial Ombudsman Service* may include:

(1)   where it would be more suitable for the *complaint* to be dealt with by a court or a comparable *ADR entity*; or

(2)   where the subject matter of the *complaint* has already been dealt with by a comparable dispute resolution scheme; or

(3)   where the subject matter of the *complaint* has previously been considered or excluded under the *Financial Ombudsman Service* (unless material new evidence which the *Ombudsman* considers likely to affect the outcome has subsequently become available to the complainant); or

(4)   it is a *complaint* which:
    (a)   involves (or might involve) more than one *eligible complainant*; and
    (b)   has been referred without the consent of the other *eligible complainant* or complainants,
    and the *Ombudsman* considers that it would be inappropriate to deal with the *complaint* without that consent.

3.4   REFERRING A COMPLAINT TO ANOTHER COMPLAINTS SCHEME

3.4.1 R   FCA

The *Ombudsman* may refer a *complaint* to another complaints scheme where:

(1)   he considers that it would be more suitable for the matter to be determined by that scheme; and

(2)   the complainant consents to the referral.

Test Cases

3.4.2 R   FCA

The *Ombudsman* may, with the complainant's consent, cease to consider the merits of a *complaint* so that it may be referred to a court to consider as a test case, if:

(1)   before the *Ombudsman* has made a determination, they have received in writing from the *respondent*:
    (a)   a detailed statement of how and why, in the *respondent's* opinion, the *complaint* raises an important or novel point of law with significant consequences; and
    (b)   an undertaking in favour of the complainant that, if the complainant or the *respondent* commences court proceedings against the other in respect of the *complaint* in any court in the *United Kingdom* within six *months* of the complaint being dismissed, the *respondent* will:
        (i)   pay the complainant's reasonable costs and disbursements (to be assessed, if not agreed, on an indemnity basis) in connection with the proceedings at first instance and any subsequent appeal proceedings brought by the *respondent*; and
        (ii)   make interim payments on account of such costs if and to the extent that it appears reasonable to do so; and

(2)   the *Ombudsman* considers that the *complaint*:

(a)   raises an important or novel point of law, which has important consequences; and

(b)   would more suitably be dealt with by a court as a test case.

3.4.3 G   FCA

Factors that the *Ombudsman* may take into account in considering whether to cease to consider the merits of a *complaint* so that it may be the subject of a test case in court include (but are not limited to):

(1)   whether the point of law is central to the outcome of the dispute;

(2)   how important or novel the point of law is in the context of the dispute;

(3)   the significance of the consequences of the dispute for the business of the *respondent* (or respondents in that sector) or for its (or their) customers;

(4)   the amount at stake in the dispute;

(5)   the remedies that a court could impose;

(6)   any representations made by the *respondent* or the complainant; and

(7)   the stage already reached in consideration of the dispute.

3.5   RESOLUTION OF COMPLAINTS BY THE OMBUDSMAN

3.5.1 R   FCA

The *Ombudsman* will attempt to resolve *complaints* at the earliest possible stage and by whatever means appear to him to be most appropriate, including mediation or investigation.

3.5.2 G   FCA

The *Ombudsman* may inform the complainant that it might be appropriate to complain against some other *respondent*.

3.5.3 G   FCA

Where two or more *complaints* from one complainant relate to connected circumstances, the *Ombudsman* may investigate them together, but will issue separate provisional assessments and determinations in respect of each *respondent*.

3.5.4 R   FCA

If the *Ombudsman* decides that an investigation is necessary, he will then:

(1)   ensure both parties have been given an opportunity of making representations;

(2)   send both parties a provisional assessment, setting out his reasons and a time limit within which either party must respond; and

(3)   if either party indicates disagreement with the provisional assessment within that time limit, proceed to determination.

Hearings

3.5.5 R   FCA

If the *Ombudsman* considers that the *complaint* can be fairly determined without convening a hearing, he will determine the *complaint*. If not, he will invite the parties to take part in a hearing. A hearing may be held by any means which the *Ombudsman* considers appropriate in the circumstances, including by telephone. No hearing will be held after the *Ombudsman* has determined the *complaint*.

3.5.6 R   FCA

A party who wishes to request a hearing must do so in writing, setting out:

(1)   the issues he wishes to raise; and

(2)   (if appropriate) any reasons why he considers the hearing should be in private;

so that the *Ombudsman* may consider whether:

(3)   the issues are material;

(4)   a hearing should take place; and

(5)   any hearing should be held in public or private.

3.5.7 G   FCA

In deciding whether there should be a hearing and, if so, whether it should be in public or private, the *Ombudsman* will have regard to the provisions of the European Convention on Human Rights.

Evidence

3.5.8 R   FCA

The *Ombudsman* may give directions as to:

(1)   the issues on which evidence is required;

(2)   the extent to which evidence should be oral or written; and

(3)   the way in which evidence should be presented.

3.5.9 R   FCA

The *Ombudsman* may:

(1)   exclude evidence that would otherwise be admissible in a court or include evidence that would not be admissible in a court;

(2)   accept information in confidence (so that only an edited version, summary or description is disclosed to the other party) where he considers it appropriate;

(3)   reach a decision on the basis of what has been supplied and take account of the failure by a party to provide information requested; and

(4)   treat the *complaint* as withdrawn and cease to consider the merits if a complainant fails to supply requested information.

3.5.10 G   FCA

Evidence which the *Ombudsman* may accept in confidence includes confidential evidence about third parties and security information.

3.5.11 G   FCA

The *Ombudsman* has the power to require a party to provide evidence. Failure to comply with the request can be dealt with by the court.

3.5.12 G   FCA

The *Ombudsman* may take into account evidence from third parties, including (but not limited to) the *FCA*, other regulators, experts in industry matters and experts in consumer matters.

Procedural time limits

3.5.13 R   FCA

The *Ombudsman* may fix (and extend) time limits for any aspect of the consideration of a *complaint* by the *Financial Ombudsman Service*.

3.5.14 R   FCA

If a *respondent* fails to comply with a time limit, the *Ombudsman* may:

(1)   proceed with consideration of the *complaint*; and

(2)   include provision for any material distress or material inconvenience caused by that failure in any award which he decides to make.

3.5.15 R   FCA

If a complainant fails to comply with a time limit, the *Ombudsman* may:

(1)   proceed with consideration of the *complaint*; or

(2)   treat the *complaint* as withdrawn and cease to consider the merits.

3.6   DETERMINATION BY THE OMBUDSMAN

Fair and reasonable

3.6.1 R   FCA

The *Ombudsman* will determine a *complaint* by reference to what is, in his opinion, fair and reasonable in all the circumstances of the case.

3.6.2 G   FCA

Section 228 of the *Act* sets the 'fair and reasonable' test for the *Compulsory Jurisdiction* (other than in relation to *consumer redress schemes*) and **DISP 3.6.1 R** extends it to the *Voluntary Jurisdiction*.

3.6.3 G   FCA

Where a complainant makes *complaints* against more than one *respondent* in respect of connected circumstances, the *Ombudsman* may determine that the *respondents* must contribute towards the overall award in the proportion that the *Ombudsman* considers appropriate.

3.6.4 R   FCA

In considering what is fair and reasonable in all the circumstances of the case, the *Ombudsman* will take into account:

(1)   relevant:

    (a)   law and regulations;

    (b)   regulators' rules, guidance and standards;

    (c)   codes of practice; and

(2)   (where appropriate) what he considers to have been good industry practice at the relevant time.

3.6.5 G   FCA

Where the *Ombudsman* is determining what is fair and reasonable in all the circumstances of a *relevant new complaint* or a *relevant transitional complaint*, the *Ombudsman Transitional Order* and the *Mortgage and General Insurance Complaints Transitional Order* require him to take into account what determination the *former Ombudsman* might have been expected to reach in relation to an equivalent complaint dealt with under the *former scheme* in question immediately before the relevant transitional order came into effect.

Consumer redress schemes

3.6.5A G   FCA

As a result of section 404B of the *Act*, if the subject matter of a *complaint* falls to be dealt with (or has properly been dealt with) under a *consumer redress scheme*, the *Ombudsman* will determine the *complaint* by reference to what, in the opinion of the *Ombudsman*, the *redress determination* under the *consumer redress scheme* should be or should have been, unless the complainant and the *respondent* agree that the *complaint* should not be dealt with in accordance with the *consumer redress scheme*.

The Ombudsman's determination

3.6.6 R   FCA

When the *Ombudsman* has determined a *complaint*:
(1)   the *Ombudsman* will give both parties a signed written statement of the determination, giving the reasons for it;
(2)   the statement will require the complainant to notify the *Ombudsman*, before the date specified in the statement, whether he accepts or rejects the determination;
(3)   if the complainant notifies the *Ombudsman* that he accepts the determination within that time limit, it is final and binding on both parties;
(4)   subject to paragraph (4A), if the complainant does not notify the *Ombudsman* that he accepts the determination within that time limit, the complainant will be treated as having rejected the determination, and neither party will be bound by it;
(5)   the complainant is not to be treated as having rejected the determination under paragraph (4) if all the following conditions are met:
     (a)   the complainant notifies the *Ombudsman* after the specified date of the complainant's acceptance of the determination;
     (b)   the complainant has not previously notified the *Ombudsman* of the complainant's rejection of the determination;
     (c)   in the view of the *Ombudsman*, the failure to comply with the time limit for acceptance was as a result of exceptional circumstances;
(6)   the *Ombudsman* will notify the *respondent* of the outcome and, if the complainant is treated as having rejected the determination under paragraph (4), the effect of paragraph (4A).

3.6.7 R   FCA
(1)   An *Ombudsman* may correct any clerical mistake in the written statement of an *Ombudsman's* determination, whether or not the determination has already been accepted or rejected.
(2)   Any failure to comply with any provisions of the procedural rules made by the *FOS Ltd* does not of itself render an *Ombudsman's* determination void.

Reports of determinations

3.6.8 G   FCA
(1)   The *FOS Ltd* will publish a report of any *Ombudsman's* determination, save that if the *Ombudsman* who made the determination informs the *FOS Ltd* that, in the *Ombudsman's* opinion, it is inappropriate to publish a report of that determination (or any part of it), the *FOS Ltd* will not publish a report of that determination (or that part, as appropriate).
(2)   Unless the complainant agrees, a report will not include the name of the complainant, or particulars which (in the opinion of the *FOS Ltd*) are likely to identify the complainant.
(3)   The *FOS Ltd* may charge a reasonable fee for providing a copy of a report.

3.7   AWARDS BY THE OMBUDSMAN

3.7.1 R   FCA

Where a *complaint* is determined in favour of the complainant, the *Ombudsman's* determination may include one or more of the following:
(1)   a money award against the *respondent*; or
(2)   an interest award against the *respondent*; or
(3)   a costs award against the *respondent*; or
(4)   a direction to the *respondent*.

Money awards

3.7.2 R   FCA

Except in relation to a *complaint* the subject matter of which falls to be dealt with (or has properly been dealt with) under a *consumer redress scheme*, a money award may be such amount as the *Ombudsman* considers to be fair compensation for one or more of the following:

(1)   financial loss (including consequential or prospective loss); or
(2)   pain and suffering; or
(3)   damage to reputation; or
(4)   distress or inconvenience;

whether or not a court would award compensation.

3.7.2A G   FCA

In relation to a *complaint* the subject matter of which falls to be dealt with (or has properly been dealt with) under a *consumer redress scheme*, a money award is a payment of such amount as the *Ombudsman* determines that a *respondent* should make (or should have made) to a complainant under the scheme.

3.7.2B G   FCA

A money award under **DISP 3.7.2A G** may specify the date by which the amount awarded is to be paid.

3.7.3 G   FCA

Where the *Ombudsman* is determining what amount (if any) constitutes fair compensation as a money award in relation to a *relevant new complaint* or a *relevant transitional complaint*, the *Ombudsman Transitional Order* and the *Mortgages and General Insurance Complaints Transitional Order* require him to take into account what amount (if any) might have been expected to be awarded by way of compensation in relation to an equivalent complaint dealt with under the *former scheme* in question immediately before the relevant transitional order came into effect.

3.7.4 R   FCA

The maximum money award which the *Ombudsman* may make is £150,000.

3.7.4A G   FCA

The effect of section 404B(5) of the *Act* is that the maximum award which the *Ombudsman* may make also applies in relation to a *complaint* the subject matter of which falls to be dealt with (or has properly been dealt with) under a *consumer redress scheme*.

3.7.5 G   FCA

For the purpose of calculating the maximum money award, the following are excluded:
(1)   any interest awarded on the amount payable under a money award;
(2)   any costs awarded; and
(3)   any interest awarded on costs.

3.7.6 G   FCA

If the *Ombudsman* considers that fair compensation requires payment of a larger amount, he may recommend that the *respondent* pays the complainant the balance. The effect of section 404B(6) of the *Act* is that this is also the case in relation to a *complaint* the subject matter of which falls to be dealt with (or has properly been dealt with) under a *consumer redress scheme*.

3.7.7 R   FCA

The *Ombudsman* will maintain a register of each money award.

Interest awards

3.7.8 R   FCA

Except in relation to a *complaint* the subject matter of which falls to be dealt with (or has properly been dealt with) under a *consumer redress scheme*, an interest award may provide for the amount payable under the money award to bear interest at a rate and as from a date specified in the award.

3.7.8A G   FCA

A money award under **DISP 3.7.2A G** may provide for interest to be payable, at a rate specified in the award, on any amount which is not paid by the date specified in the award.

Costs awards

3.7.9 R   FCA

A costs award may:
(1)   be such amount as the Ombudsman considers to be fair, to cover some or all of the costs which were reasonably incurred by the complainant in respect of the complaint; and
(2)   include interest on that amount at a rate and as from a date specified in the award.

3.7.10 G   FCA

In most cases complainants should not need to have professional advisers to bring *complaints* to the *Financial Ombudsman Service*, so awards of costs are unlikely to be common.

Directions

3.7.11 R   FCA

Except in relation to a *complaint* the subject matter of which falls to be dealt with (or has properly been dealt with) under a *consumer redress scheme*, a direction may require the *respondent* to take such steps in relation to the complainant as the *Ombudsman* considers just and appropriate (whether or not a court could order those steps to be taken).

3.7.11A G   FCA

In relation to a *complaint* the subject matter of which falls to be dealt with (or has properly been dealt with) under a *consumer redress scheme*, a direction may require the *respondent* to take such action as the *Ombudsman* determines the *respondent* should take (or should have taken) under the scheme.

Complying with awards and settlements

3.7.12 R   FCA

A *respondent* must comply promptly with:
(1)   any award or direction made by the *Ombudsman*; and
(2)   any settlement which it agrees at an earlier stage of the procedures.

3.7.13 G   FCA

Under the *Act*, a complainant can enforce through the courts a money award registered by the *Ombudsman* or a direction made by the *Ombudsman*.

3.8   DEALING WITH INFORMATION

3.8.1 R   FCA

In dealing with information received in relation to the consideration of a *complaint*, the *Financial Ombudsman Service* will have regard to the parties' rights of privacy.

3.8.2B R   FCA

This does not prevent the *Ombudsman* disclosing information:
(1)   to the extent that he is required or authorised to do so by law; or
(2)   to the parties to the *complaint*; or
(3)   in his determination; or
(4)   at a hearing in connection with the *complaint*.

3.8.3 R   FCA

So long as he has regard to the parties' rights of privacy, the *Ombudsman* may disclose information to the *FCA* or any other body exercising regulatory or statutory functions for the purpose of assisting that body or the *Financial Ombudsman Service* to discharge its functions.

3.9   DELEGATION OF THE OMBUDSMAN'S POWERS

3.9.1A R   FCA

The *Ombudsman* may designate members of the staff of *FOS Ltd* to exercise any of the powers of the *Ombudsman* relating to the consideration of a *complaint* apart from the powers to:
(1)   determine a *complaint*; or
(2)   authorise the disclosure of information to the *FCA* or any other body exercising regulatory or statutory functions.

3.9.2 G   FCA

In **DISP 2** to **DISP 4** any reference to "the *Ombudsman*" includes a reference to any member of the staff of *FOS Ltd* to whom the exercise of any of the powers of the *Ombudsman* has been delegated.

CHAPTER 4
STANDARD TERMS

4.1   PURPOSE AND APPLICATION

Purpose

[3.75]
4.1.1 G   FCA

The purpose of this chapter is to set out how *complaints* against *VJ participants* are dealt with under the *Voluntary Jurisdiction*.

Application

4.1.2 G   FCA

These *standard terms* apply to any business which has agreed to be a *VJ participant*.

4.2   STANDARD TERMS

4.2.1 R   FCA

A *VJ participant* is subject to these *standard terms*, which may be amended or supplemented by the *Financial Ombudsman Service* with the approval of the *FCA*.

4.2.2 R   FCA

By agreeing to participate, a *VJ participant* also agrees that the *Voluntary Jurisdiction* covers an act or omission that occurred before the *VJ participant* was participating in the *Voluntary Jurisdiction*, whether the act or omission occurred before or after *commencement*.

Application of DISP 1 to DISP 3

4.2.3 R   FCA

The following rules and guidance apply to *VJ participants* as part of the *standard terms*, except where the context requires otherwise:
(1)   **DISP 1** (Treating complainants fairly), except:
    (a)   **DISP 1.9** (Complaints record rule);
    (b)   **DISP 1.10** (Complaints reporting rules); and
    (c)   **DISP 1.11** (Lloyd's);
(2)   **DISP 2** (Jurisdiction of the Financial Ombudsman Service), except:
    (a)   **DISP 2.3** (Compulsory Jurisdiction); and
(3)   **DISP 3** (Complaint handling procedures of the Financial Ombudsman Service).

Determinations and awards

4.2.4 R   FCA

The *Ombudsman* has the same powers to make determinations and awards under the *Voluntary Jurisdiction* as he has under the *Compulsory Jurisdiction* (see **DISP 3.7** (Awards by the Ombudsman)).

4.2.5 R   FCA

If the complainant accepts the *Ombudsman's* determination within the time limit specified by the *Ombudsman*, the determination will be binding on the *VJ Participant* and may be enforced in court by the complainant.

4.2.6 R   FCA

The following *rules* in *FEES* apply to *VJ participants* as part of the *standard terms*, but substituting 'VJ participant' for 'firm':
(1)   **FEES 2.2.1 R** (late payment) but substituting 'FOS Ltd' for 'the FCA';
(2)   **FEES 2.3.1 R** and **2.3.2 R** (remission of fees);
(3)   **FEES 4.2.6 R (1)(B)** (periodic fees);
(4)   **FEES 5.3.6 R** (general levy) but substituting:
    (a)   'Voluntary Jurisdiction' for 'Compulsory Jurisdiction'; and
    (b)   'FOS Ltd' for 'the FCA';
(5)   **FEES 5.3.8 R** (calculation of general levy) but substituting '**FEES 5 ANNEX 2 R**' for '**FEES 5 ANNEX 1 R**';
(6)   **FEES 5.4.1 R** (information) but substituting:
    (a)   'FOS Ltd' for 'the FCA'; and
    (b)   '**FEES 5 ANNEX 2 R**' for '**FEES 5 ANNEX 1 R**';
(7)   **FEES 5.5B** (case fees);
(8)   [deleted]
(9)   [deleted]
(10)   **FEES 5.7.1 R** and **5.7.4 R** but substituting, in **FEES 5.7.1 R**, 'the FOS Ltd' for 'the FCA' and 'annual levy specified in **FEES 5 ANNEX 2 R**' for 'general levy';
(11)   **FEES 5.8.1 R** (joining the Financial Ombudsman Service); and
(12)   **FEES 5 ANNEX 2 R** and **FEES 5 ANNEX 3 R**.

Withdrawal from participation

4.2.7 R   FCA

A *VJ participant* may not withdraw from the *Voluntary Jurisdiction* unless:
(1)   the *VJ participant* has submitted to *FOS Ltd* a written plan for:
    (a)   notifying its existing customers of its intention to withdraw; and
    (b)   handling *complaints* against it before its withdrawal;
(2)   the *VJ participant* has paid the general levy for the year in which it withdraws and any other fees payable; and
(3)   *FOS Ltd* has approved in writing both the *VJ Participant's* plan and the date of withdrawal (which must be at least six months from the date of the approval of the plan).

Exemption from liability

4.2.8 R   FCA

None of the following is to be liable in damages for anything done or omitted to be done in the discharge (or purported discharge) of any functions in connection with the *Voluntary Jurisdiction*:

(1)   *FOS Ltd*;

(2)   any member of its governing body;

(3)   any member of its staff;

(4)   any person acting as an *Ombudsman* for the purposes of the *Financial Ombudsman Service*;

except where:

(5)   the act or omission is shown to have been in bad faith; or

(6)   it would prevent an award of damages being made in respect of an act or omission on the ground that the act or omission was unlawful as a result of section 6(1) of the Human Rights Act 1998.

CHAPTER 5
FUNDING RULES

5.1   [DELETED: PROVISIONS RELATING TO THE FUNDING RULES FOR THE FINAN-CIAL OMBUDSMAN SERVICE ARE SET OUT IN FEES 5 (FINANCIAL OMBUDSMAN SERVICE FUNDING).]

5.2   [DELETED: PROVISIONS RELATING TO THE FUNDING RULES FOR THE FINAN-CIAL OMBUDSMAN SERVICE ARE SET OUT IN FEES 5 (FINANCIAL OMBUDSMAN SERVICE FUNDING).]

5.3   [DELETED: PROVISIONS RELATING TO THE FUNDING RULES FOR THE FINAN-CIAL OMBUDSMAN SERVICE ARE SET OUT IN FEES 5 (FINANCIAL OMBUDSMAN SERVICE FUNDING).]

5.4   [DELETED: PROVISIONS RELATING TO THE FUNDING RULES FOR THE FINAN-CIAL OMBUDSMAN SERVICE ARE SET OUT IN FEES 5 (FINANCIAL OMBUDSMAN SERVICE FUNDING).]

5.5   [DELETED: PROVISIONS RELATING TO THE FUNDING RULES FOR THE FINAN-CIAL OMBUDSMAN SERVICE ARE SET OUT IN FEES 5 (FINANCIAL OMBUDSMAN SERVICE FUNDING).]

5.6   [DELETED: PROVISIONS RELATING TO THE FUNDING RULES FOR THE FINAN-CIAL OMBUDSMAN SERVICE ARE SET OUT IN FEES 5 (FINANCIAL OMBUDSMAN SERVICE FUNDING).]

5.7   [DELETED: PROVISIONS RELATING TO THE FUNDING RULES FOR THE FINAN-CIAL OMBUDSMAN SERVICE ARE SET OUT IN FEES 5 (FINANCIAL OMBUDSMAN SERVICE FUNDING).]

5.8   [DELETED: PROVISIONS RELATING TO THE FUNDING RULES FOR THE FINAN-CIAL OMBUDSMAN SERVICE ARE SET OUT IN FEES 5 (FINANCIAL OMBUDSMAN SERVICE FUNDING).]

5.9   [DELETED: PROVISIONS RELATING TO THE FUNDING RULES FOR THE FINAN-CIAL OMBUDSMAN SERVICE ARE SET OUT IN FEES 5 (FINANCIAL OMBUDSMAN SERVICE FUNDING).]

5.10   [DELETED: PROVISIONS RELATING TO THE FUNDING RULES FOR THE FINAN-CIAL OMBUDSMAN SERVICE ARE SET OUT IN FEES 5 (FINANCIAL OMBUDSMAN SERVICE FUNDING).]

5 ANNEX 1R R   [DELETED: PROVISIONS RELATING TO THE FUNDING RULES FOR THE FINANCIAL OMBUDSMAN SERVICE ARE SET OUT IN FEES 5 (FINANCIAL OM-BUDSMAN SERVICE FUNDING)]App 1

HANDLING MORTGAGE ENDOWMENT COMPLAINTS

1.1 INTRODUCTION

[3.76]
1.1.1 G   FCA

This appendix sets out the approach and standards which *firms* should use when investigating complaints relating to the sale of endowment *policies* for the purposes of achieving capital repayment of a mortgage. It is not intended to be comprehensive. It is primarily concerned with the assessment of whether the complainant may have suffered financial loss, and if so, how much that loss is, and therefore what amount a *firm* should consider offering by way of fair and appropriate compensation in circumstances where the *firm's* investigation of a complaint reveals:

(1)   the complainant has received negligent *advice on investments*; and

(2)   if this advice had not been negligent, either:

       (a)   the complainant would be unlikely to have acquired the endowment policy but instead would have taken out the same amount of loan on a repayment basis; or

       (b)   the complainant would have acquired an endowment mortgage for a shorter term.

1.1.2 G   FCA

There will also be cases where a *firm* will conclude after investigation that, notwithstanding its own failure to give compliant and proper advice, the complainant would nevertheless have proceeded with the endowment policy as sold, in which case no compensation will be due.

1.1.3 G   FCA

This appendix only addresses how *firms* should approach the assessment of loss and compensation where negligence on the part of the *firm* is established.

1.1.4 G   FCA

This appendix is relevant both to the obligations arising under the complaints handling *rules* contained in **DISP 1** and to the *FCA's* approach to the supervision of *firms*.

1.1.5 G   FCA

This appendix is also relevant to complaints which the *Ombudsman* may investigate under the Compulsory Jurisdiction or *Voluntary Jurisdiction* of the *Financial Ombudsman Service* established under Part XVI of the *Act* (The Ombudsman Scheme).

1.1.6 G   FCA

Before proceeding to assess the extent of a complainant's financial loss, a *firm* will usually have completed the following stages:

(1)   gathering all relevant facts and information;

(2)   making a fair and objective assessment whether it has failed to comply with a relevant duty owed to the complainant; and

(3)   assessing whether any failure of duty by it was in the circumstances a material failure in the sense that if it had not occurred the complainant would have been likely to have acted differently.

1.1.7 G   FCA

If it is concluded that the complainant would have acted differently, the *firm* should proceed to assess any direct or consequential loss.

1.1.8 G   FCA

Nothing in this appendix relieves *firms* of the obligation to consider the particular facts and circumstances of each complaint and to consider whether the assessment of loss and compensation should, in the light of those facts and circumstances, be carried out on a different basis. If, however, the facts and circumstances make it appropriate to do so, the *FCA's* expectation is that *firms* will apply the approach and standards set out in this appendix, and where they do not, the *FCA* is likely to require them to demonstrate the adequacy and completeness of their alternative approach.

1.2   THE STANDARD APPROACH TO REDRESS

1.2.1 G   FCA

If there has been a failure to give compliant and proper advice, or some other breach of the duty of care, the basic objective of redress is to put the complainant, so far as is possible, in the position he would have been in if the inappropriate advice had not been given, or the other breach had not occurred. In many cases, although it must be a matter for inquiry and assessment in each individual case, this position is likely to have resulted in the complainant taking a repayment mortgage with accompanying life cover, and this is the assumption which underpins the standard approach to redress.

1.2.2 G   FCA

Unless the contrary is demonstrated, it should be assumed that the complainant could have afforded the mortgage on a repayment basis.

1.2.3 G   FCA

The measure of any financial loss suffered by the complainant will be arrived at by:

(1)   comparing the complainant's current capital position with the position he would have been in had the loan been a standard repayment mortgage as at the date the *firm* decides to regard the complaint as justified; and

(2)　　comparing the cost of the complainant's actual monthly outgoings and those he would have made had his loan been on a standard repayment basis as at the date the *firm* decides to regard the complaint as justified.

1.2.4 G　FCA

In some cases other factors may be included in the overall calculation, for example, if mortgage arrangement fees were waived by agreement on the occasion of the endowment *policy* being taken out.

1.2.5 G　FCA

If, on comparing the complainant's current endowment position with the repayment alternative, the *surrender value* of the endowment *policy* exceeds the amount of the capital which the complainant would have repaid through the repayment method, then, at the point of the assessment, the complainant has suffered no capital loss (but the complainant may suffer some compensatable consequential loss associated with changing the mortgage arrangements to the repayment basis, see **DISP APP 1.3**). Conversely, if the capital which would have been repaid on the repayment basis exceeds the *surrender value*, there is a capital loss represented by the difference between the two amounts.

1.2.6 G　FCA

If the complainant's endowment mortgage outgoings exceed the equivalent cost for the repayment method, the complainant should be compensated for the higher payments in addition to any loss on the *surrender value* and capital repaid comparison. This means, for example, that if the endowment arrangement has been more expensive, this may result in compensatable loss even though the capital repayment against surrender comparison may be favourable to the endowment.

1.2.7 G　FCA

If the total cost of the outgoings for the endowment calculation is less than that for the repayment calculation, the "savings" should be brought into account in assessing any overall loss unless it is unreasonable to do so.

1.2.8 G　FCA

It is unlikely to be reasonable to bring "savings" into account in circumstances where, at the time of the sale of the *policy*:

(1)　　the complainant was advised or informed orally or in writing that he would have lower outgoings than would be the case under a repayment mortgage, whether or not the difference was quantified; and

(2)　　the complainant has dissipated those "savings" on the strength of this advice or information.

1.2.9 G　FCA

The circumstances in which it may be appropriate to take some or all of the "savings" into account are those where, subject to **DISP APP 1.2.7 G**, the complainant is of "sufficient means" so that it is reasonable for a *firm* to assume that the "savings" have contributed to those means.

1.2.10 G　FCA

Where it is otherwise reasonable for "savings" to be brought into account, determining whether or not a complainant is of sufficient means and, if so, to what extent the "savings" are to be brought into account, will have to be based on the facts of each individual case. It will be appropriate to require the complainant to provide adequate information to assist the *firm* in this task. Matters to be taken into account in this assessment may include:

(1)　　the length of the remaining mortgage term;

(2)　　the complainant's current and prospective resources;

(3)　　the amount of the capital shortfall in proportion to the endowment outgoings balance.

1.2.11 G　FCA

Firms may adopt streamlined processes to assist them in individual assessments of "sufficient means", but will have to satisfy themselves that the complainant's position is nevertheless protected. *Firms* will need to ensure that the complainant is given an opportunity to make an informed choice whether to accept the streamlined process, that the process itself is transparent, and that the *firm* is satisfied that the outcome would be fair to complainants.

1.2.12 G　FCA

If a *firm* intends to make a deduction for all or any part of the lower endowment outgoings, the *firm* should explain clearly to the complainant in writing both how the 'sufficient means' test has been satisfied, including details of the information taken into account in reaching the decision, and how the deduction has been arrived at. The letter should further inform the complainant that if he is unhappy with the proposal to make a deduction, either in principle or as to the amount, he should give his reasons to the *firm*.

1.2.13 G　FCA

If a complainant puts forward a case that it would be unreasonable for a deduction to be made, the *firm* should reach a fair and objective determination on the facts of all relevant matters including those set out at **DISP APP 1.2.8 G** and **DISP APP 1.2.9 G**.

1.2.14 G   FCA

In recognition that *firms* may not wish, for practical reasons, to make individual assessments of "sufficient means", *firms* may decide not to seek to bring into account any benefit to the complainant in assessing overall compensation.

1.2.15 G   FCA

It would not be unreasonable if a *firm* providing redress in these circumstances were to frame its offer of redress on the assumption that the complainant will agree to surrender the *policy*. However, *firms* should bear in mind that there may be circumstances where it is appropriate for the complainant to retain the *policy*, for example, where it is being retained as a savings vehicle.

1.2.16 G   FCA

If a complainant becomes aware that he has taken out the endowment *policy* on the basis of unsuitable advice and inadequate information, he should if necessary, after taking appropriate advice, take reasonable steps to limit his loss, and may in any subsequent *claim* be unable to recover for losses which are avoidable. The complainant may have to show that he has not delayed unreasonably since becoming aware of his loss. The reasonable costs and expenses the complainant may have incurred in limiting his loss are to be taken into account in assessing his compensation. These costs and expenses are likely to include the complainant taking advice on whether he should convert from an endowment to a repayment mortgage and incurring expenses in doing so, see **DISP APP 1.3**.

1.2.17 G   FCA

The standard approach to redress can be illustrated by the following examples, which show how redress would be calculated in certain hypothetical but typical scenarios. (Because the examples are illustrative, round numbers have been used for 'established facts' in each example. The payments should be taken as being made monthly: *firms* should not approximate by assuming that payments are made annually. If the complainant has benefited from MIRAS, the calculations should allow for the effect of MIRAS both on the endowment mortgage and the repayment comparison.)

1.2.18 G   FCA

Table of examples of typical redress calculations

Example 1	Capital shortfall and higher endowment outgoings
Example 2	Capital shortfall partially offset by lower endowment mortgage outgoings
Example 3	Capital shortfall more than offset by lower endowment mortgage outgoings
Example 4	Capital surplus more than offset by higher endowment mortgage outgoings
Example 5	Capital surplus partially offset by higher endowment mortgage outgoings
Example 6	Capital surplus and lower endowment mortgage outgoings
Example 7	Low start endowment mortgage

1.2.19 G   FCA

Example 1

Example 1	
Capital shortfall and higher endowment mortgage outgoings	
Background	
Capital sum of £50,000	
25 year endowment *policy*	
Duration to date: 5 years	
Endowment *premium* per *month*: £75	
Established facts	
Endowment *surrender value*:	£3,200
Capital repaid under equivalent repayment mortgage:	£4,200
Surrender value less capital repaid:	(£1,000)
Cost of converting from endowment mortgage to repayment mortgage:	(£200)
Total outgoings to date	
Equivalent repayment mortgage (capital + interest + DTA life cover):	£21,950
Endowment mortgage (endowment *premium* + interest):	£22,250

> **Example 1**
>
> Difference in outgoings (repayment – endowment): (£300)
>
> Basis of compensation
>
> In this example, the complainant has suffered loss because the *surrender value* of the endowment is less than the capital repaid and also because of the higher total outgoings to date of the endowment mortgage relative to the repayment mortgage. The two losses and the conversion cost are therefore added together in order to calculate the redress.
>
> Redress
>
> Loss from *surrender value* less capital repaid: (£1,000)
>
> Loss from total extra outgoings under endowment mortgage: (£300)
>
> Cost of converting to repayment mortgage: (£200)
>
> Total loss: (£1,500)
>
> **Therefore total redress is:** **£1,500**

1.2.20 G FCA

Example 2

> **Example 2**
>
> **Capital shortfall partially offset by lower endowment mortgage outgoings**
>
> Background
>
> Capital sum of £50,000
>
> 25 year endowment *policy*
>
> Duration to date: 5 years
>
> Endowment *premium* per *month*: £60
>
> Established facts
>
> Endowment *surrender value*: £2,500
>
> Capital repaid under equivalent repayment mortgage £4,200
>
> *Surrender value* less capital repaid under equivalent repayment mortgage: (£1,700)
>
> Cost of converting from endowment mortgage to repayment mortgage (£300)
>
> Total outgoings to date:
>
> Repayment mortgage (capital + interest + DTA life cover): £21,950
>
> Endowment mortgage (endowment *premium* + interest): £21,350
>
> Difference in outgoings (repayment – endowment): £600
>
> Basis of Compensation
>
> In this example, the complainant has suffered loss because the *surrender value* of the endowment is less than the capital repaid but has gained form the lower outgoings of the endowment mortgage to date. In calculating the redress the gain may be offset against the loss unless the complainant's particular circumstances are such that it would be unreasonable to take account of the gain.
>
> **Redress if it is not unreasonable to take account of the whole of the gain from lower outgoings**
>
> Loss from *surrender value* less capital repaid: (£1,700)
>
> Gain from total lower outgoings under endowment mortgage: £600
>
> Cost of converting to repayment mortgage: (£300)
>
> Net loss: (£1,400)
>
> **Therefore total redress is:** **£1,400**
>
> **Redress if it is unreasonable to take account of gain from lower outgoings**
>
> Loss from *surrender value* less capital repaid: (£1,700)
>
> Gain from total lower outgoings under endowment mortgage: Ignored*
>
> Cost of converting to repayment mortgage: (£300)
>
> Net loss taken into account: (£2,000)
>
> **Therefore total redress is:** **£2,000**
>
> * In this example, and also in Examples 3, 7, 8 and 9, the complainant's circumstances are assumed to be such as to make it unreasonable to take account of any of the gain from lower outgoings.

1.2.21 G FCA

Example 3

Example 3

Capital shortfall more than offset by lower endowment mortgage outgoings

Background

Capital sum of £50,000

25 year endowment *policy*

Duration to date: 8 years

Endowment *premium* per *month*: £65

Established facts

Endowment *surrender value*:	£7,300
Capital repaid under equivalent repayment mortgage:	£7,600
Surrender value less capital repaid:	(£300)
Cost of converting from endowment mortgage to repayment mortgage:	(£200)

Total outgoings to date:

Repayment mortgage (capital + interest + DTA life cover):	£34,510
Endowment mortgage (endowment *premium* + interest):	£33,990
Difference in outgoings (repayment – endowment):	£520

Basis of Compensation

In this example, the complainant has suffered loss because the surrender value of the endowment is less than the capital repaid but has gained from the lower total outgoings of the endowment mortgage. In calculating redress the gain may be offset against the loss unless the complainant's particular circumstances are such that it would be unreasonable to take account of the gain.

Redress if it is not unreasonable to take account of the whole of the gain from lower outgoings

Loss from *surrender value* less capital repaid:	(£300)
Gain from total lower outgoings under endowment mortgage:	£520
Cost of converting to repayment mortgage:	(£200)
Net gain:	£20

Therefore, there has been no loss and no redress is payable.

Redress if it is unreasonable to take account of gain from lower outgoings

Loss from *surrender value* less capital repaid:	(£300)
Gain from total lower outgoings under endowment mortgage:	Ignored
Cost of converting to repayment mortgage:	(£200)
Net loss taken into account:	(£500)
Therefore total redress is:	**£500**

1.2.22 G FCA

Example 4

Example 4

Capital surplus more than offset by higher endowment mortgage outgoings

Background

Capital sum of £50,000

25 year endowment *policy*

Duration to date: 8 years

Endowment *premium* per *month*: £75

Established facts

Endowment *surrender value*:	£7,800
Capital repaid under equivalent repayment mortgage:	£7,600
Surrender value less capital repaid:	£200
Cost of converting from endowment mortgage to repayment mortgage:	(£250)

Total outgoings to date:

Repayment mortgage (capital + interest + DTA life cover):	£34,510

Example 4

Endowment mortgage (endowment *premium* + interest):	£34,950
Difference in outgoings (repayment – endowment):	(£440)

Basis of Compensation

In this example, the complainant has suffered loss because of the higher total outgoings to date of the endowment mortgage but has gained because the *surrender value* of the endowment is greater than the capital repaid. Since the sum of the loss and the conversion cost is greater than the gain, the redress is calculated as the difference between the two.

Redress

Gain from *surrender value* less capital repaid:	£200
Loss from total extra outgoings under endowment mortgage:	(£440)
Cost of converting to repayment mortgage:	(£250)
Net loss:	(£490)
Therefore total redress is:	**£490**

1.2.23 G   FCA

Example 5

Example 5

Capital surplus partially offset by higher endowment mortgage outgoings

Background

Capital sum of £50,000

25 year endowment *policy*

Duration to date: 10 years

Endowment *premium* per *month*: £75

Established facts

Endowment *surrender value*:	£11,800
Capital repaid under equivalent repayment mortgage	£9,700
Surrender value less capital repaid:	£2,100
Cost of converting from endowment mortgage to repayment mortgage:	(£300)

Total outgoings to date:

Repayment mortgage (capital + interest + DTA life cover):	£46,800
Endowment mortgage (endowment *premium* + interest):	£47,500
Difference in outgoings (repayment – endowment):	(£700)

Basis of Compensation

In this example, the complainant has suffered loss because of the higher total outgoings to date of the endowment mortgage relative to the repayment mortgage. However the sum of this and the conversion cost is less than the complainant's gain from the difference between the *surrender value* of the endowment and the capital repaid. Thus no redress is payable.

Redress

Gain from *surrender value* less capital repaid:	£2,100
Loss from total extra outgoings under endowment mortgage:	(£700)
Cost of converting to repayment mortgage:	(£300)
Net gain:	£1,100
Therefore, there has been no loss and no redress is payable.	

1.2.24 G   FCA

Example 6

Example 6

Capital surplus and lower endowment mortgage outgoings

Background

Capital sum of £50,000

25 year endowment *policy*

Duration to date: 10 years

Endowment *premium* per *month*: £65

Example 6

Established facts

Endowment *surrender value*:	£10,100
Capital repaid under equivalent repayment mortgage	£9,700
Surrender value less capital repaid:	£400
Cost of converting from endowment mortgage to repayment mortgage:	(£200)
Total outgoings to date:	
Repayment mortgage (capital + interest + DTA life cover):	£46,800
Endowment mortgage (endowment *premium* + interest):	£46,300
Difference in outgoings (repayment – endowment):	£500

Basis of Compensation

In this example, the complainant has gained both because the *surrender value* of the endowment is greater than the capital repaid and because of the lower total outgoings of the endowment mortgage. These gains are larger than the cost of converting to a repayment mortgage. Thus no further action is necessary.

Redress

As there has been no loss, no redress is payable.

1.2.25 G   FCA

Example 7

Example 7
Low start endowment mortgage

Background

Capital sum of £50,000

25 year endowment *policy*

Duration to date: 10 years

Endowment *premium* per *month*: starting at £35 in first year, increasing by 20% simple on each *policy* anniversary, reaching £70 after five years and then remaining at that level.

Established facts:

Endowment *surrender value*:	£8,200
Capital repaid under equivalent repayment mortgage:	£9,700
Surrender value less capital repaid:	(£1,500)
Cost of converting from endowment mortgage to repayment mortgage:	(£250)
Total outgoings to date	
Repayment mortgage (capital + interest + DTA life cover):	£46,800
Endowment mortgage (endowment *premium* + interest):	£45,640
Difference in outgoings (repayment minus endowment):	£1,160

Of this difference in outgoings, £800 arose in the five year period when the complainant was paying a low endowment *premium*.

Basis of compensation

In this example, the complainant has suffered loss because the *surrender value* of the endowment is less than the capital repaid but has gained from the lower total outgoings of the endowment mortgage. As in Example 3, in calculating redress the whole of the gain should be offset against the loss unless the complainant's particular circumstances are such that it would be unreasonable to do so. However, unlike Example 3, in a low start endowment mortgage the complainant may have chosen to pay a lower than usual *premium* in the early years (this would need to be established on the facts of the case). Where it has been established that the complainant chose to make lower payments, even if it is unreasonable to take account of the whole of the gain from total outgoings, the gain from paying a lower *premium* during the low start period is normally taken into account. In such cases the redress is calculated as the capital loss plus the conversion cost minus the total amount by which repayment mortgage outgoings would have exceeded the actual low start endowment mortgage outgoings during the five year low start period.

Redress if it is not unreasonable to take account of the whole of the gain from lower outgoings

Loss from *surrender value* less capital repaid:	(£1,500)
Gain from total lower outgoings under endowment mortgage:	£1,160

Example 7	
Cost of converting to repayment mortgage:	(£250)
Net loss:	(£590)
Therefore total redress is:	**£590**
Redress if it is unreasonable to take account of gain from lower outgoings	
Loss from *surrender* value less capital repaid:	(£1,500)
Gain from total lower outgoings during low start period of endowment mortgage:	£800
Cost of converting to repayment mortgage:	(£250)
Net loss taken into account:	(£950)
Therefore total redress is:	**£950**

Interest rates

1.2.26 G   FCA

In fixing a repayment comparator, it would be appropriate to have regard to the repayment quotation actually provided at the time of sale. If more than one repayment quotation was obtained, the comparison should be with the quotation which approximates most closely to the terms of the endowment mortgage actually taken. If a repayment quotation was not provided, or is not now available, it should be assumed that the interest rate for the repayment comparison is the same as that of the mortgage endowment arrangements. *Firms* will then need to replicate interest rate changes throughout the lifetime of the comparator mortgage.

Life cover

1.2.27 G   FCA

Unless after due inquiry there is clear evidence that the complainant with a mortgage endowment had no foreseeable need for life cover at the time the endowment arrangements were concluded, in the overall comparison between a repayment mortgage and an endowment mortgage the monthly outgoings under the repayment will include the premium for the decreasing term assurance that would have been required. This adjustment for the cost of life cover is only to be made if the *firm* is undertaking a comparison of monthly outgoings. It is not appropriate to deduct the cost of life cover from the capital loss calculation, as this would constitute double counting.

1.2.28 G   FCA

If a deduction is to be attributed to the provision of life cover, the appropriate approach is to assume that the complainant took out the insurance quoted in the alternative repayment quotation provided at the time of the sale. If the quotation is not available, the deduction should be at the rates that would have been quoted at the time.

1.3   REMORTGAGING

1.3.1 G   FCA

As already noted, the basic objective of redress is to put the complainant, so far as is possible, in the position he would have been in if the inappropriate advice or other breach had not occurred: for their part, the complainants should take such reasonable steps as they can to limit loss once they are informed of the position they are in because of the failure of advice at the time of sale.

1.3.2 G   FCA

In practice, it is likely to be appropriate for a complainant whose complaint has been upheld to convert to a repayment mortgage, whether or not there is financial loss to date. It will normally be possible for complainants to do so without incurring unreasonable cost. Conversion will of course mean that the complainant no longer has a *policy*.

1.3.3 G   FCA

Firms should therefore in the case of upheld complaints inform complainants that it is likely to be appropriate and necessary for them to convert to a repayment arrangement.

1.3.4 G   FCA

Firms should make it clear that they will bear the costs of conversion if the rearrangement is made with the existing lender and to the equivalent repayment mortgage. If a complainant is not willing to rearrange with the existing lender, then the costs to be paid by the *firm* should normally be limited to those which would have been payable had the rearrangement been made with the existing lender and to the equivalent repayment mortgage. If it is not possible to rearrange with the existing lender, for example, if the lender has a closed book, the *firm* should pay all costs which are not unreasonable in completing the rearrangement with an alternative provider. Such costs might include an administration fee for changing the existing arrangement, redemption penalty, arrangement fee for the new mortgage and the reasonable cost of further advice if necessary.

1.3.5 G FCA

If the "new" mortgage is, in fact, arranged at a lower interest rate than the existing loan, the benefit to the complainant should usually be disregarded, as it is always open to complainants to change their underlying mortgage arrangements at any time.

1.3.6 G FCA

If the "new" mortgage is arranged at a higher interest rate than the existing loan, the increased payment should not normally be taken into account in calculating any payment to be made to the complainant.

1.3.7 G FCA

If the complainant takes the opportunity to increase his loan on the occasion of the remortgage, the expenses which a *firm* pays by way of compensation should be paid by reference to the capital sum due under the "old" loan.

1.3.8 G FCA

As stated, one aspect of the conversion process is the disposal of the endowment *policy*. The standard approach to assessing loss requires *firms* to calculate loss using the *surrender value*. However, once loss is established on this basis and *firms* move to deal with redress, they may wish to consider whether there is a role for the *policy's* 'market value' within the traded endowment *policy* (TEP) market.

1.3.9 G FCA

A *firm* may arrange the sale of the endowment *policy* on the traded endowment market, provided the full implications of such a course of action are explained to the complainant and his express consent is obtained for the firm to arrange the sale. This includes informing the investor that he will continue to be the life assured under the *policy*. The complainant should be informed that such an arrangement may reduce or eliminate the amount of redress actually borne by the *firm*, but not so as to affect the amount of redress he receives.

1.3.10 G FCA

In the event that a complainant is willing to pursue this option, a *firm* should first have assessed the complainant's loss using the approach set out in this appendix, and the minimum amount the complainant should receive under such a sale arrangement is the sum representing the position the complainant should have been in under this appendix together with the reimbursement of remortgaging costs. In order to ensure the process does not delay the provision of redress, the *firm* must pay this minimum sum immediately the complainant agrees to the sale arrangement. To the extent that the net amount realised by the sale of the *policy* on the traded endowment market exceeds the total redress due to the complainant, this greater sum is to be paid to the complainant on completion of the sale. If the amount realised by the sale of the *policy* on the traded endowment market is less than the total redress due to the complainant, the *firm* will be responsible for the amount of the shortfall.

1.3.11 G FCA

Example of assessment set out at 1.3.10

The following example illustrates the position:			
Surrender value	£10,000	TEP value	£16,000
Loss calculated by standard approach	£5,000		
Remortgaging costs	£300		
Total	£15,300		
Complainant receives £16,000 all ultimately funded from the TEP sale.			
Surrender value	£10,000	TEP value	£13,000
Redress calculated by standard approach	£5,000		
Remortgaging costs	£300		
Total	£15,300		
Complainant receives £15,300, £13,000 ultimately funded from the TEP sale and £2,300 ultimately funded from the *firm*.			

1.4 POLICY RECONSTRUCTION

1.4.1 G FCA

This section of this appendix is primarily concerned with circumstances where the term of the mortgage and associated endowment *policy* extend beyond the individual complainant's normal retirement age in circumstances where the *firm* regards a complaint as justified because the arrangement is not affordable in retirement; and this could have, and should have, been foreseen at the time of the advice.

1.4.2 G   FCA

Two sets of circumstances are examined at **DISP APP 1.4.3 G** to **DISP APP 1.4.13 G**. Although these are considered in isolation, *firms* should, as part of their investigation of all of the factors involved in the complaint, consider whether either set of circumstances should be considered in conjunction with those factors examined at **DISP APP 1.2**.

Case 1

1.4.3 G   FCA

If on enquiry it is found that no proper assessment of the complainant's post-retirement means had been undertaken at the time of *sale*, but if the likelihood had been that the complainant would have borrowed the same amount over a shorter term (up to retirement) using an endowment *policy* as a repayment vehicle, then an appropriate form of redress would be for the *policy* to be reconstructed with a shorter term.

1.4.4 G   FCA

Redress should in most cases be provided by meeting the cost of rearranging the *policy*, by way of a lump sum payment into the *policy* in respect of the higher rate of *premium* due from its inception. It may be appropriate in individual cases to take account of the lower *premiums* that the complainant will have paid to date. The *guidance* in **DISP APP 1.2**, as to the circumstances in which this will be appropriate, will be relevant here.

1.4.5 G   FCA

If the *policy* extends beyond retirement age and the complainant is already retired, the *policy* should be reconstructed to a maturity date as at the accepted retirement date, with the *policy* proceeds becoming immediately payable. The costs are to be borne by the *firm*, subject to any lower outgoings adjustment.

1.4.6 G   FCA

Firms should consider whether the reconstruction would have tax implications for complainants (see **DISP APP 1.5.8 G** and **DISP APP 1.5.9 G**).

1.4.7 G   FCA

The reconstruction process deals with the situation to the date the *policy* is reconstructed. The complainant will generally be responsible for paying the increased *premiums* for the remaining term.

1.4.8 G   FCA

At the time the complainant is advised of the revised *premium*, he should as a matter of good practice be provided with a reprojection based on the prevailing *projection* rates, which will allow him to address any projected shortfall.

1.4.9 G   FCA

If it is not possible for a *firm* to reconstruct a *policy*, then it should offer the investor equivalent redress, for example, by paying a cash lump sum equivalent to the amount that would have been credited to a reconstructed *policy*.

Case 2

1.4.10 G   FCA

If a loan extending into retirement was on any basis not affordable, whether or not it is reconstructed to the retirement date, *firms* will need to consider whether, if proper advice had been given, the loan would have been taken out at all and, if not, consider what arrangements might now need to be made in order to reduce the amount of the complainant's borrowings.

Mismatched loans and policy terms

1.4.11 G   FCA

If a complaint is regarded as justified by the *firm* on the basis that the endowment *policy* maturity date extends beyond the mortgage term expiry date and the *firm* is responsible for this situation, the *policy* should be reconstructed so that it matures at the expiry of the mortgage term.

1.4.12 G   FCA

In these circumstances the *guidance* given elsewhere in **DISP APP 1.4** will apply as appropriate.

Examples

1.4.13 G   FCA

The following examples illustrate the approach to redress as described in this section.

1.4.14 G   FCA

Example 8

Example 8

Term extends beyond retirement age and policy reconstruction

Background

45 year old male non-smoker, having taken out a £50,000 loan in 1998 for a term of 25 years. Unsuitable sale identified on the grounds of affordability and complaint raised on 12th *policy* anniversary.

It has always been the intention of the complainant to retire at State retirement age 65.

Term from date of sale to retirement is 20 years and the maturity date of the mortgage is 5 years after retirement.

Established facts

Established *premium* paid by investor on *policy* of original term (25 years):	£81.20
Premium that would have been payable on *policy* with term from *sale* to retirement (20 years):	£111.20
Actual *policy* value at time complaint assessed:	£12,500
Value of an equivalent 20-year *policy* at time complaint assessed:	£21,300
Difference in *policy* values at time complaint assessed:	£8,800
Difference in outgoings (20 year *policy* - 25 year *policy*):	£4,320

Basis of compensation

The *policy* is reconstructed as if it had been set up originally on a term to mature at retirement age, in this example, a term of 20 years. The difference in the current value of the *policy* actually sold to the complainant and the current value of the reconstructed *policy*, as if the *premium* on the reconstructed *policy* had been paid from outset, is calculated. The complainant has gained from lower outgoings (lower *premiums*) of the actual endowment *policy* to date. In calculating the redress, the gain may be offset against the loss unless the complainant's particular circumstances are such that it would be unreasonable to take account of the gain.

Redress generally if it is not unreasonable to take account of the whole of the gain from lower outgoings

Loss from current value of reconstructed *policy* less current value of actual *policy*:	(£8,800)
Gain from total lower outgoings under actual *policy*:	£4,320
Net loss:	(£4,480)
Therefore total redress is:	£4,480

Redress if it is unreasonable to take account of gain from lower outgoings

Loss from current value of reconstructed *policy* less current value of actual *policy*:	(£8,800)
Gain from total lower outgoings under actual *policy*:	Ignored
Therefore total redress is:	£8,800

Additional Information

If the *policy* is capable of reconstruction, the complainant must now fund the higher *premiums* himself for the remainder of the term of the shortened *policy* until maturity. In this example the higher *premium* could be £111.20. However the *firm* should provide the complainant with a reprojection letter based on the reconstructed *policy* such that the actual monthly payment required to achieve the target sum could be even higher, say £130. The reprojection letter should set out the range of options facing the complainant to deal with the projected shortfall, if any.

1.4.15 G   FCA

Example 9

Example 9

Term extends beyond retirement age: example of failure to explain investment risks

> **Example 9**
>
> Background
>
> 45 year old male non-smoker, having taken out a £50,000 loan in 1998 for a term of 25 years. Unsuitable sale identified on the grounds of affordability and complaint raised on 12th anniversary.
>
> It has always been the intention of the complainant to retire at state retirement age 65.
>
> Term from date of sale to retirement is 20 years and the maturity date of the mortgage is five years after retirement.
>
> In addition, an endowment does not meet the complainant's attitude to investment risk and a repayment mortgage would have been taken out if properly advised.
>
> Established facts
>
> | | |
> |---|---|
> | *Surrender value* (on the 25 year *policy*) at time complaint assessed: | £12,500 |
> | Capital repaid under repayment mortgage of term to retirement date (20 years): | £21,000 |
> | *Surrender value* less capital repaid: | (£8.500) |
> | Difference in outgoings (repayment – endowment): | £5,400 |
> | Cost of converting from endowment mortgage to repayment mortgage: | £200 |
>
> Basis of compensation:
>
> The *surrender value* of the (25 year term) endowment *policy* is compared to the capital that would have been repaid to date under a repayment mortgage arranged to repay the loan at retirement age, in this example, a repayment mortgage for a term of 20 years. The complainant has gained from lower outgoings of the endowment mortgage to date. In calculating the redress, the gain may be offset against the loss unless the complainant's particular circumstances are such that it would be unreasonable to take account of the gain. The conversion costs are also taken into account in calculating the redress.
>
> Redress generally
>
> | | |
> |---|---|
> | Loss from *surrender value* less capital repaid: | (£8,500) |
> | Gain from total lower outgoings under endowment mortgage: | £5,400 |
> | Cost of converting to a repayment mortgage: | (£200) |
> | Net loss: | (£3,300) |
> | **Therefore total redress is:** | **£3,300** |
>
> **Redress if it is unreasonable to take account of gain from lower outgoings**
>
> | | |
> |---|---|
> | Loss from *surrender value* less capital repaid: | (£8,500) |
> | Gain from total lower outgoings under endowment mortgage: | Ignored |
> | Cost of converting to a repayment mortgage: | (£8,700) |
> | **Therefore total redress is:** | **£8,700** |

1.5 ADDITIONAL CONSIDERATIONS

Introduction

1.5.1 G   FCA

This section addresses issues which may be relevant to the standard redress for unsuitability cases, as well as some post-retirement cases upheld on the grounds of affordability.

Continuing life cover and other policy benefits

1.5.2 G   FCA

Firms will need to consider the importance for many complainants of having life assurance in place to ensure a mortgage is paid off in the event of death.

1.5.3 G   FCA

If a complaint is upheld and the *policy* is to be surrendered as part of the settlement, the *firm* should remind the complainant in writing that the life cover within the endowment will be terminated and that it may therefore be appropriate to take advice about the merits or otherwise of taking out a stand-alone *life policy* in substitution.

1.5.4 G   FCA

If a need for life assurance at inception has been established so that a deduction representing its cost has been made from the redress payable under **DISP APP 1.2.4 G**, the *firm* should advise the complainant that the *firm* would be responsible for paying any *premium* for an appropriate replacement *policy* which exceeds that used for calculating the deduction or alternatively will, where possible, provide the cover itself at that cost. If it is not possible for the *firm* to provide the cover itself at the original cost, it may choose to discharge that obligation by the payment of an appropriate lump sum. Any such amount should enable the complainant to effect the cover at the original cost, with no additional cost in respect of increased age or deterioration in health. This option may be particularly relevant if the *firm* against which the complaint has been made is an independent intermediary which cannot itself provide the cover, although it may be possible for such a *firm* to arrange for the product provider to offer cover to the complainant at the original *premium* on payment by the independent intermediary of an appropriate lump sum to meet any increased cost.

1.5.5 G FCA

Firms will not be responsible for any increased costs resulting from the complainant choosing another *product provider* or for increased *premiums* charged by another provider chosen by the complainant in respect of the risk now presented, for example, higher *premiums* charged by the other provider due to deterioration in health, unless the original *product provider* no longer writes new business and is unable to offer revised life cover on a decreasing term assurance basis.

1.5.6 G FCA

There can be exceptional circumstances where, in order to retain suitable life cover, the endowment *policy* has to be retained and any additional costs will be the responsibility of the *firm* that sold the endowment *policy*.

1.5.7 G FCA

The same considerations will apply to the establishment of the need for other *policy* benefits including critical illness cover, disability cover and waiver of *premium*.

Taxation

1.5.8 G FCA

Firms will need to consider the likely taxation implications for complainants if *policies* are surrendered or reconstructed, or any form of underpinning or guarantee is given.

1.5.9 G FCA

If there is potential tax liability for the complainant, it will be appropriate for *firms* to undertake in writing to the complainant to reimburse any tax payable, or which becomes payable, and make payment on production of appropriate evidence of the liability and payment having been made.

"Underpinning"

1.5.10 G FCA

Firms proposing to offer arrangements involving some form of minimum underpinning or 'guarantee' should discuss their proposals with the *FCA* and HM Revenue and Customs at the earliest possible opportunity (see **DISP APP 1.5.8 G**). The *FCA* will need to be satisfied that these proposals provide complainants with redress which is at least commensurate with the standard approaches contained in this appendix.

Reference to the guidance in firms' complaints settlement letters

1.5.11 G FCA

One of the reasons for introducing the *guidance* in this appendix is to seek a reduction in the number of complaints which are referred to the *Financial Ombudsman Service*. If a *firm* writes to the complainant proposing terms for settlement which are in accordance with this appendix, the letter may include a statement that the calculation of loss and redress accords with the *FCA guidance*, but should not imply that this extends to the assessment of whether or not the complaint should be upheld. *Firms* should point out that if the complainant remains dissatisfied, he may refer the complaint to the *Financial Ombudsman Service*.

1.5.12 G FCA

A statement under **DISP APP 1.5.11 G** should not give the impression that the proposed terms of settlement have been expressly endorsed by either the *FCA* or the *Financial Ombudsman Service*.

Identification of windfall benefits

1.5.13 G FCA

Windfall benefits should be determined in accordance with the principle in Needler Financial Services and Taber ('Needler'). The basic legal principle in Needler is that a windfall benefit is not to be taken into account in determining the amount of an investor's recoverable loss. The following paragraphs explain our views as to how *firms* may act in accordance with that principle.

1.5.14 G FCA

A windfall benefit arises where:
(1)   there has been a demutualisation, distribution or reattribution of the inherited estate, or other extraordinary corporate event in a *long-term insurer*; and
(2)   the event gave rise to 'relevant benefits', as defined in **DISP APP 1.5.15 G** (below).

1.5.15 G   FCA

'Relevant benefits' are those benefits that fall outside what is required in order that *policyholders'* reasonable expectations at that point of sale can be fulfilled. (The phrase '*policyholders'* reasonable expectations' has technically been superseded. However, the concept now resides within the obligations imposed upon *firms* by *FCA* Principle 6 ('... a firm must pay due regard to the interests of its *customers* and treat them fairly ....') Additionally, most of these benefits would have been paid prior to *commencement*, when *policyholders'* reasonable expectations would have been a consideration for a *long-term insurer*.)

1.5.16 G   FCA

The issue of free *shares* or cash on a demutualisation, and additional bonuses and *policy* enhancements given by way of incentive to approve a reattribution or distribution of an inherited estate should, unless there is evidence to the contrary, be treated as relevant benefits for the purposes of **DISP APP 1.5.15 G**. Whether additional bonuses and *policy* enhancements on a demutualisation are relevant benefits should be determined by applying the test in **DISP APP 1.5.15 G** to each benefit.

1.5.17 G   FCA

Firms should review the terms on which proposals were put to *policyholders* and the reasons given for a corporate event when determining whether a benefit should be treated as a relevant benefit.

1.5.18 G   FCA

Firms should not normally bring windfall benefits which are relevant benefits (as defined in **DISP APP 1.5.14 G**) to account when assessing financial loss and redress. Where a windfall benefit is in the form of a *policy* augmentation the benefit should be deducted from the overall value of the *policy* when making this assessment.

1.5.19 G   FCA

A relevant benefit derived from a corporate event may only be brought to account if the *firm* is able to demonstrate, with written records created at the time of the advice, that:
(1)   The *firm* foresaw the prospect of the event and the benefit;
(2)   The *firm's* advice included a statement recommending the particular policy because of the possibility of the benefit in question; and
(3)   The statement was a material factor in the context of the advice and the decision to invest.

1.5.20 G   FCA

If a *firm* considers that it can meet this requirement, the *firm* should by letter explain clearly to the complainant the reasons why it proposes that the benefit should not be treated as a windfall and should be taken into account. The *firm* should provide the complainant with copies of the relevant documents.

1.5.21 G   FCA

The letter should also explain how the proposed value of the benefit has been calculated and should inform the complainant that if he does not accept the proposal to take the benefit into account he may tell the *firm*, with reasons. The letter should also say that, if he remains dissatisfied with the *firm's* response, he may refer the matter to the *Financial Ombudsman Service*.

1.6   VALUING RELEVANT BENEFITS

1.6.1 G   FCA

If, exceptionally under the *guidance* at **DISP APP 1.5.13 G** to **DISP APP 1.5.21 G**, cash or *shares* derived from a corporate event are to be taken into account when assessing loss and redress, cash should be valued at the amount actually received and *shares* should be valued at their issue price. In both cases there should be no addition for interest.

1.6.2 G   FCA

When valuing windfall augmentation benefits for the purposes of calculating loss and redress the objective is to exclude all changes arising from the windfall event. The amount of redress payable will then be equal to the amount that would have been payable if the windfall event had never occurred.

1.6.3 G   FCA

A *product provider* should ensure that the method it adopts for valuing augmentation benefits is consistent with the statements made in the documentation published about the windfall event. Relevant documentation for the purpose of valuing such benefits will include (but is not limited to):

Part 3   FCA Handbook Materials

(1)   Any description of increases in benefits in any circular to *policyholders* (and any other public information relating to the event);

(2)   Any principles of financial management established for the management of the fund after the event;

(3)   statements in any report produced by an *actuary* appointed under **SUP 4** (Actuaries) for the event;

(4)   statements in any independent *actuary* report produced for the event; and

(5)   subsequent statements relating to bonus practice, calculation *surrender values*, or both.

1.6.4 G   FCA

The method of valuation adopted should treat the complainant fairly overall.

1.6.5 G   FCA

Where an accurate calculation of the value of an augmentation benefit either cannot be made, or would result in disproportionate expense or delay, *product providers* may adopt a simplified approach or a proxy method for calculating its value.

1.6.6 G   FCA

A simplified approach should treat the complainants fairly overall.

1.6.7 G   FCA

An *actuary*, appointed by a *product provider* under **SUP 4** (Actuaries) should certify that the method adopted by the *product provider* for calculating the value of an augmentation benefit is in accordance with the *guidance* in **DISP APP 1.6.1 G** to **DISP APP 1.6.6 G**.

Implementation

1.6.8 G   FCA

The principles set out above (in **DISP APP 1.6.1 G** to **DISP APP 1.6.7 G**) should be applied directly to mortgage endowment complaints where the capital loss is calculated by comparing the *surrender value* of the endowment *policy* with the capital which would have been repaid using a repayment mortgage.

1.6.9 G   FCA

In most cases where there is a loss, the endowment *policy* will be surrendered and put towards the cost of setting up a suitable repayment mortgage. Where this is the case, that part of the *surrender value* relating to the windfall augmentation should be paid as a cash lump sum to the investor or to the investor's order as part of the redress package. Only that part of the *surrender value* which does not relate to the windfall augmentation should be put towards the cost of setting up a suitable repayment mortgage.

1.6.10 G   FCA

There may be some circumstances in which the *policy* will not be surrendered (see **DISP APP 1.2.15 G**). In these cases, there is no requirement to pay the value of the windfall augmentation as a cash lump sum since the value of the augmentation will become payable when the *policy* matures. However, any fund value used in the calculation of redress payable should exclude the value of the windfall augmentation.

1.6.11 G   FCA

Firms are entitled to mitigate losses by making use of the Traded Endowment Policy (TEP) market (see **DISP APP 1.3.8 G** to **DISP APP 1.3.10 G**). This allows *firms* to *sell* policies on the TEP market to meet the costs of redress, rather than using the *surrender value*. Where this method is adopted, *firms* should pay to the investor, as part of the redress package, a cash lump sum representing that proportion of the *policy* realised which would have related to the windfall augmentation.

1.6.12 G   FCA

As this windfall amount should be excluded from the fund value used in the calculation of loss and redress it would also be appropriate for this extra payment to be ignored when assessing whether, "the net amount realised by the sale of the *policy* on the traded endowment market exceeds the total redress due to the complainant ..." (**DISP APP 1.3.10 G**).

1.6.13 G   FCA

There may be circumstances in which a *policy* needs to be reconstructed (see **DISP APP 1.4**). In carrying out the required reconstruction, the windfall augmentation should be ignored in both the existing and the revised *policy*. However, the *policyholder's* revised *policy* should be credited with any windfall augmentation which would have applied if the *policy* had been set up with the revised terms from the original date of advice. This enhancement can be taken into account in assessing a suitable level for future premiums, in line with **DISP APP 1.4.8 G**.

1.6.14 G FCA

DISP App 1.5.10 G provides *firms* with the opinion of underpinning benefits. *Firms* should satisfy the *FCA* that their proposals provide complainants with a level of redress that is at least commensurate with the standard approaches and, to ensure consistency, windfall augmentations should be excluded when considering whether an underpin will apply. The *FCA* will take this into account when considering proposals put forward by *firms*.

1.6.15 G FCA

Product providers with windfall benefits in the form of *policy* augmentations should tell:
(1)   their own relevant *customers* (mortgage endowment complainants); and
(2)   other *firms* with such *customers* (and any other interested parties);

that they have excluded windfall augmentation benefits from values used or to be used for loss and redress. *Firms* should provide this information to the *Financial Services Compensation Scheme* when providing them with a value to be used for loss or redress. Should their own relevant *customers*, other *firms* with such *customers* (and any other interested parties) and the *Financial Services Compensation Scheme* request it, the *firm* should provide the value of these benefits and a description of the method used to exclude them.FCA

APP 3
HANDLING PAYMENT PROTECTION INSURANCE COMPLAINTS

3.1   INTRODUCTION

(1)   This appendix sets out how a *firm* should handle *complaints* relating to the sale of a *payment protection contract* by the *firm* which express dissatisfaction about the sale, or matters related to the sale, including where there is a rejection of claims on the grounds of ineligibility or exclusion (but not matters unrelated to the sale, such as delays in claims handling).
(2)   It relates to the sale of any *payment protection contract* whenever the sale took place and irrespective of whether it was on an advised or non-advised basis; conducted through any sales channel; in connection with any type of loan or credit product, or none; and for a regular premium or single premium payment. It applies whether the *policy* is currently in force, was cancelled during the *policy* term or ran its full term.

3.1.2 G FCA

The aspects of *complaint* handling dealt with in this appendix are how the *firm* should:
(1)   assess a *complaint* in order to establish whether the *firm's* conduct of the sale failed to comply with the *rules*, or was otherwise in breach of the duty of care or any other requirement of the general law (taking into account relevant materials published by the *FCA*, other relevant regulators, the *Financial Ombudsman Service* and *former schemes*). In this appendix this is referred to as a "breach or failing" by the *firm*;
(2)   determine the way the complainant would have acted if a breach or failing by the *firm* had not occurred; and
(3)   determine appropriate redress (if any) to offer to a complainant.

3.1.3 G FCA

Where the *firm* determines that there was a breach or failing, the *firm* should consider whether the complainant would have bought the *payment protection contract* in the absence of that breach or failing. This appendix establishes presumptions for the *firm* to apply about how the complainant would have acted if there had instead been no breach or failing by the *firm*. The presumptions are:
(1)   for some breaches or failings (see **DISP App 3.6.2 E**), the *firm* should presume that the complainant would not have bought the *payment protection contract* he bought; and
(2)   for certain of those breaches or failings (see **DISP App 3.7.7 E**), where the complainant bought a single premium *payment protection contract*, the *firm* may presume that the complainant would have bought a regular premium *payment protection contract* instead of the *payment protection contract* he bought.

3.1.4 G FCA

There may also be instances where a *firm* concludes after investigation that, notwithstanding breaches or failings by the *firm*, the complainant would nevertheless still have proceeded to buy the *payment protection contract* he bought.

3.1.5 G FCA

In this appendix:
(1)   "historic interest" means the interest the complainant paid to the *firm* because a single premium *payment protection contract* was added to a loan or credit product;
(2)   "simple interest" means a non-compound rate of 8% per annum; and
(3)   "claim" means a claim by a complainant seeking to rely upon the *policy* under the *payment protection contract* that is the subject of the *complaint*.

3.2   THE ASSESSMENT OF A COMPLAINT

3.2.1 G   FCA

The *firm* should consider, in the light of all the information provided by the complainant and otherwise already held by or available to the *firm*, whether there was a breach or failing by the *firm*.

3.2.2 G   FCA

The *firm* should seek to establish the true substance of the *complaint*, rather than taking a narrow interpretation of the issues raised, and should not focus solely on the specific expression of the *complaint*. This is likely to require an approach to *complaint* handling that seeks to clarify the nature of the *complaint*.

3.2.3 G   FCA

A *firm* may need to contact a complainant directly to understand fully the issues raised, even where the *firm* received the *complaint* from a third party acting on the complainant's behalf. The *firm* should not use this contact to delay the assessment of the *complaint*.

3.2.4 G   FCA

Where a *complaint* raises (expressly or otherwise) issues that may relate to the original sale or a subsequently rejected claim then, irrespective of the main focus of the *complaint*, the *firm* should pro-actively consider whether the issues relate to both the sale and the claim, and assess the *complaint* and determine redress accordingly.

3.2.5 G   FCA

If, during the assessment of the *complaint*, the *firm* uncovers evidence of a breach or failing not raised in the *complaint*, the *firm* should consider those other aspects as if they were part of the *complaint*.

3.2.6 G   FCA

The *firm* should take into account any information it already holds about the sale and consider other issues that may be relevant to the sale identified by the *firm* through other means, for example, the root cause analysis described in **DISP APP 3.4**.

3.2.7 G   FCA

The *firm* should consider all of its sales of *payment protection contracts* to the complainant in respect of re-financed loans that were rolled up into the loan covered by the *payment protection contract* that is the subject of the *complaint*. The *firm* should consider the cumulative financial impact on the complainant of any previous breaches or failings in those sales.

3.3   THE APPROACH TO CONSIDERING EVIDENCE

3.3.1 G   FCA

Where a *complaint* is made, the *firm* should assess the *complaint* fairly, giving appropriate weight and balanced consideration to all available evidence, including what the complainant says and other information about the sale that the *firm* identifies. The *firm* is not expected automatically to assume that there has been a breach or failing.

3.3.2 G   FCA

The *firm* should not rely solely on the detail within the wording of a *policy's* terms and conditions to reject what a complainant recalls was said during the sale.

3.3.3 G   FCA

The *firm* should recognise that oral evidence may be sufficient evidence and not dismiss evidence from the complainant solely because it is not supported by documentary proof. The *firm* should take account of a complainant's limited ability fully to articulate his *complaint* or to explain his actions or decisions made at the time of the sale.

3.3.4 G   FCA

Where the complainant's account of events conflicts with the *firm's* own records or leaves doubt, the *firm* should assess the reliability of the complainant's account fairly and in good faith. The *firm* should make all reasonable efforts (including by contact with the complainant where necessary) to clarify ambiguous issues or conflicts of evidence before making any finding against the complainant.

3.3.5 G   FCA

The *firm* should not reject a complainant's account of events solely on the basis that the complainant signed documentation relevant to the purchase of the *policy*.

3.3.6 G   FCA

The *firm* should not reject a *complaint* because the complainant failed to exercise the right to cancel the *policy*.

3.3.7 G FCA

The *firm* should not consider that a successful claim by the complainant is, in itself, sufficient evidence that the complainant had a need for the *policy* or had understood its terms or would have bought it regardless of any breach or failing by the *firm*.

3.3.8 G FCA

The *firm* should not draw a negative inference from a complainant not having kept documentation relating to the purchase of the *policy* for any particular period of time.

3.3.9 G FCA

In determining a particular *complaint*, the *firm* should (unless there are reasons not to because of the quality and plausibility of the respective evidence) give more weight to any specific evidence of what happened during the sale (including any relevant documentation and oral testimony) than to general evidence of selling practices at the time (such as training, instructions or sales scripts or relevant audit or compliance reports on those practices).

3.3.10 G FCA

The *firm* should not assume that because it was not authorised to give advice (or because it intended to sell without making a recommendation) it did not in fact give advice in a particular sale. The *firm* should consider the available evidence and assess whether or not it gave advice or made a recommendation (explicitly or implicitly) to the complainant.

3.3.11 G FCA

The *firm* should consider in all situations whether it communicated information to the complainant in a way that was fair, clear and not misleading and with due regard to the complainant's information needs.

3.3.12 G FCA

In considering the information communicated to the complainant and the complainant's information needs, the evidence to which a *firm* should have regard includes:
(1)   the complainant's individual circumstances at the time of the sale (for example, the *firm* should take into account any evidence of limited financial capability or understanding on the part of the complainant);
(2)   the complainant's objectives and intentions at the time of the sale;
(3)   whether, from a reasonable *customer's* perspective, the documentation provided to the complainant was sufficiently clear, concise and presented fairly (for example, was the documentation in plain and intelligible language?);
(4)   in a sale that was primarily conducted orally, whether sufficient information was communicated during the sale discussion for the *customer* to make an informed decision (for example, did the *firm* give an oral explanation of the main characteristics of the *policy* or specifically draw the complainant's attention to that information on a computer screen or in a document and give the complainant time to read and consider it?);
(5)   any evidence about the tone and pace of oral communication (for example, was documentation read out too quickly for the complainant to have understood it?); and
(6)   any extra explanation or information given by the *firm* in response to questions raised (or information disclosed) by the complainant.

3.3.13 G FCA

The *firm* should not reject a *complaint* solely because the complainant had held a *payment protection contract* previously.

3.4 ROOT CAUSE ANALYSIS

3.4.1 G FCA

DISP 1.3.3 R requires the *firm* to put in place appropriate management controls and take reasonable steps to ensure that in handling *complaints* it identifies and remedies any recurring or systemic problems. If a *firm* receives *complaints* about its sales of *payment protection contracts* it should analyse the root causes of those *complaints* including, but not limited to, the consideration of:
(1)   the concerns raised by complainants (both at the time of the sale and subsequently);
(2)   the reasons for both rejected claims and *complaints*;
(3)   the *firm's* stated sales practice(s) at the relevant time(s);
(4)   evidence available to the *firm* about the actual sales practice(s) at the relevant time(s) (this might include recollections of staff and complainants, compliance records, and other material produced at the time about specific transactions, for example call recordings and incentives given to *advisers*);
(5)   relevant regulatory findings; and
(6)   relevant decisions by the *Financial Ombudsman Service*.

3.4.2 G FCA

Where consideration of the root causes of *complaints* suggests recurring or systemic problems in the *firm's* sales practices for *payment protection contracts*, the *firm* should, in assessing an individual *complaint*, consider whether the problems were likely to have contributed to a breach or failing in the individual case, even if those problems were not referred to specifically by the complainant.

3.4.3 G FCA

Where a *firm* identifies (from its *complaints* or otherwise) recurring or systemic problems in its sales practices for a particular type of *payment protection contract*, either for its sales in general or for those from a particular location or sales channel, it should (in accordance with *Principle 6* (Customers' interests) and to the extent that it applies), consider whether it ought to act with regard to the position of *customers* who may have suffered detriment from, or been potentially disadvantaged by such problems but who have not complained and, if so, take appropriate and proportionate measures to ensure that those *customers* are given appropriate redress or a proper opportunity to obtain it. In particular, the *firm* should:

(1)   ascertain the scope and severity of the consumer detriment that might have arisen; and
(2)   consider whether it is fair and reasonable for the *firm* to undertake proactively a redress or remediation exercise, which may include contacting *customers* who have not complained.

3.5   RE-ASSESSING REJECTED CLAIMS

3.5.1 E   FCA

Where a *complaint* is about the sale of a *policy*, the *firm* should, as part of its investigation of the *complaint*, determine whether any claim on that *policy* was rejected, and if so, whether the complainant may have reasonably expected that the claim would have been paid.

3.5.2 G   FCA

For example, the complainant may have reasonably expected that the claim would have been paid where the *firm* failed to disclose appropriately an exclusion or limitation later relied on by the *insurer* to reject the claim and it should have been clear to the *firm* that that exclusion or limitation was relevant to the complainant.

3.6   DETERMINING THE EFFECT OF A BREACH OR FAILING

3.6.1 E   FCA

Where the *firm* determines that there was a breach or failing, the *firm* should consider whether the complainant would have bought the *payment protection contract* in the absence of that breach or failing.

3.6.2 E   FCA

In the absence of evidence to the contrary, the *firm* should presume that the complainant would not have bought the *payment protection contract* he bought if the sale was substantially flawed, for example where the *firm*:

(1)   pressured the complainant into purchasing the *payment protection contract*; or
(2)   did not disclose to the complainant, in good time before the sale was concluded, and in a way that was fair, clear and not misleading, that the *policy* was optional; or
(3)   made the sale without the complainant's explicit agreement to purchase the *policy*; or
(4)   did not disclose to the complainant, in good time before the sale was concluded, and in a way that was fair, clear and not misleading, the significant exclusions and limitations, i.e. those that would tend to affect the decisions of *customers* generally to buy the *policy*; or
(5)   did not, for an advised sale (including where the *firm* gave advice in a non-advised sales process) take reasonable care to ensure that the *policy* was suitable for the complainant's demands and needs taking into account all relevant factors, including level of cover, cost, and relevant exclusions, excesses, limitations and conditions; or
(6)   did not take reasonable steps to ensure the complainant only bought a *policy* for which he was eligible to claim benefits; or
(7)   found, while arranging the *policy*, that parts of the cover did not apply but did not disclose this to the *customer*, in good time before the sale was concluded, and in a way that was fair, clear and not misleading; or
(8)   did not disclose to the complainant, in good time before the sale was concluded, and in a way that was fair, clear and not misleading, the total (not just monthly) cost of the *policy* separately from any other prices (or the basis for calculating it so that the complainant could verify it); or
(9)   recommended a single premium *payment protection contract* without taking reasonable steps, where the *policy* did not have a pro-rata refund, to establish whether there was a prospect that the complainant would repay or refinance the loan before the end of the term; or
(10)   provided misleading or inaccurate information about the *policy* to the complainant; or
(11)   sold the complainant a *policy* where the total cost of the *policy* (including any interest paid on the premium) would exceed the benefits payable under the *policy* (other than benefits payable under life cover); or

(12) in a sale of a single premium *payment protection contract*, failed to disclose to the complainant, in good time before the sale was concluded, and in a way that was fair, clear and not misleading:
  (a) that the premium would be added to the amount provided under the credit agreement, that interest would be payable on the premium and the amount of that interest; or
  (b) (if applicable) that the term of the cover was shorter than the term of the credit agreement and the consequences of that mismatch; or
  (c) (if applicable) that the complainant would not receive a pro-rata refund if the complainant were to repay or refinance the loan or otherwise cancel the single premium *policy* after the cooling-off period.

3.6.3 E   FCA

Relevant evidence might include the complainant's demands, needs and intentions at the time of the sale and any other relevant evidence, including any testimony by the complainant about his reasons at the time of the sale for purchasing the *payment protection contract*.

3.7   APPROACH TO REDRESS

General approach to redress: all contract types

3.7.1 E   FCA

Where the *firm* concludes in accordance with **DISP App 3.6** that the complainant would still have bought the *payment protection contract* he bought, no redress will be due to the complainant in respect of the identified breach or failing, subject to **DISP App 3.7.6 E**.

3.7.2 E   FCA

Where the *firm* concludes that the complainant would not have bought the *payment protection contract* he bought, and the *firm* is not using the alternative approach to redress (set out in **DISP App 3.7.7 E** to **3.7.15 E**) or other appropriate redress (see **DISP App 3.8**), the *firm* should, as far as practicable, put the complainant in the position he would have been if he had not bought any *payment protection contract*.

3.7.3 E   FCA

In such cases the *firm* should pay to the complainant a sum equal to the total amount paid by the complainant in respect of the *payment protection contract* including historic interest where relevant (plus simple interest on that amount). If the complainant has received any rebate, for example if the *customer* cancelled a single premium *payment protection contract* before it ran full term and received a refund, the *firm* may deduct the value of this rebate from the amount otherwise payable to the complainant.

3.7.4 E   FCA

Additionally, where a single premium was added to a loan:
(1) for live *policies*:
  (a) subject to **DISP App 3.7.5 E**, where there remains an outstanding loan balance, the *firm* should, where possible, arrange for the loan to be restructured (without charge to the complainant but using any applicable cancellation value) with the effect of:
    (i) removing amounts relating to the *payment protection contract* (including any interest and charges); and
    (ii) ensuring the number and amounts of any future repayments (including any interest and charges) are the same as would have applied if the complainant had taken the loan without the *payment protection contract*; or
  (b) where the *firm* is not able to arrange for the loan to be restructured (e.g. because the loan is provided by a separate *firm*), it should pay the complainant an amount equal to the difference between the actual loan balance and what the loan balance would have been if the *payment protection contract* (including any interest and charges) had not been added, deducting the current cancellation value. The *firm* should offer to pay any charges incurred if the complainant uses this amount to reduce his loan balance; and
(2) for cancelled *policies*, the *firm* should pay the complainant the difference between the actual loan balance at the point of cancellation and what the loan balance would have been if no premium had been added (plus simple interest) minus any applicable cancellation value.

3.7.5 E   FCA

Where a claim was previously paid on the *policy*, the *firm* may deduct this from redress paid in accordance with **DISP App 3.7.3 E**. If the claim is higher than the amount to be paid under **DISP App 3.7.3 E** then the *firm* may also deduct the excess from the amount to be paid under **DISP App 3.7.4 E**.

3.7.6 E   FCA

Where the *firm* concludes that the complainant may have reasonably expected that a rejected claim would have been paid (see **DISP APP 3.5**) then:

(1) if the value of the claim exceeds the amount of the redress otherwise payable to the complainant for a breach or failing identified in accordance with this appendix, the *firm* should pay to the complainant only the value of the claim (and simple interest on it as appropriate); and

(2) if the value of the claim is less than the amount of the redress otherwise payable to the complainant for a breach or failing identified in accordance with this appendix, the *firm* should pay to the complainant the value of that redress.

Alternative approach to redress: single premium policies

3.7.7 E   FCA

Where the only breach or failing was within **DISP APP 3.6.2 E (9)** and/or **DISP APP 3.6.2 E (12)**, and in the absence of evidence to the contrary, the *firm* may presume that instead of buying the single premium *payment protection contract* he bought, the complainant would have bought a regular premium *payment protection contract*.

3.7.8 E   FCA

If a *firm* chooses to make this presumption, then it should do so fairly and for all relevant complainants in a relevant category of sale. It should not, for example, only use the approach for those complainants it views as being a lower underwriting risk or those complainants who have cancelled their *policies*.

3.7.9 E   FCA

Where the *firm* presumes that the complainant would have purchased a regular premium *payment protection contract*, the *firm* should offer redress that puts the complainant in the position he would have been if he had bought an alternative regular premium *payment protection contract*.

3.7.10 E   FCA

The *firm* should pay to the complainant a sum equal to the amount in **DISP APP 3.7.3 E** less the amount the complainant would have paid for the alternative regular premium *payment protection contract*.

3.7.11 E   FCA

The *firm* should consider whether it is appropriate to deduct the value of any paid claims from the redress.

3.7.12 E   FCA

Additionally, where a single premium was added to a loan, **DISP APP 3.7.4 E** applies except that in respect of **DISP APP 3.7.4 E (1)(A)** the cancellation value should only be used if the complainant expressly wishes to cancel the *policy*.

3.7.13 E   FCA

The *firm* should, for the purposes of redressing the *complaint*, use the value of £9 per £100 of benefits payable as the monthly price of the alternative regular premium *payment protection contract*. For example, if the monthly repayment amount in relation to the loan only is to be £200, the price of the alternative regular premium *payment protection contract* will be £18.

3.7.14 E   FCA

Where the *firm* presumes that the complainant would have purchased a regular premium *payment protection contract* and if the complainant expressly wishes it, the existing cover should continue until the end of the existing *policy* term. The complainant should pay the price of the alternative regular premium *payment protection contract* (at **DISP APP 3.7.13 E**) and should be able to cancel at any time. This pricing does not apply where **DISP APP 3.7.4 E (1)(B)** applies.

3.7.15 E   FCA

So that the complainant can make the decision on the continuation of cover from an informed position, the *firm* should:

(1) offer to provide details of the existing *payment protection contract*;

(2) inform the complainant that he may be able to find similar cover more cheaply from another provider in the event that he chooses to cancel the *policy* and take an alternative but remind the complainant that if his circumstances (for example, his health or employment prospects) have changed since the original sale, he may not be eligible for cover under any new *policy* he buys;

(3) make the complainant aware of the changes to the cancellation arrangements if cover continues;

(4) explain how the future premium will be collected and the cost of the future cover; and

(5) refer the complainant to www.moneyadviceservice.org.uk as a source of information about a range of alternative *payment protection contracts*.

3.8   OTHER APPROPRIATE REDRESS

3.8.1 E   FCA

The remedies in **DISP APP 3.7** are not exhaustive.

3.8.2 E   FCA

When applying a remedy other than those set out in **DISP APP 3.7**, the *firm* should satisfy itself that the remedy is appropriate to the matter complained of and is appropriate and fair in the individual circumstances.

3.9   OTHER MATTERS CONCERNING REDRESS

3.9.1 G   FCA

Where the complainant's loan or credit card is in arrears the *firm* may, if it has the contractual right to do so, make a payment to reduce the associated loan or credit card balance, if the complainant accepts the *firm's* offer of redress. The *firm* should act fairly and reasonably in deciding whether to make such a payment.

3.9.2 G   FCA

In assessing redress, the *firm* should consider whether there are any other further losses that flow from its breach or failing that were reasonably foreseeable as a consequence of the *firm's* breach or failing, for example, where the *payment protection contract's* cost or rejected claims contributed to affordability issues for the associated loan or credit which led to arrears charges, default interest, penal interest rates or other penalties levied by the lender.

3.9.3 G   FCA

Where, for single premium *policies*, there were previous breaches or failings (see **DISP APP 3.2.7 G**) the redress to the complainant should address the cumulative financial impact.

3.9.4 G   FCA

The *firm* should make any offer of redress to the complainant in a fair and balanced way. In particular, the *firm* should explain clearly to the complainant the basis for the redress offered including how any compensation is calculated and, where relevant, the rescheduling of the loan, and the consequences of accepting the offer of redress.

3.10   APPLICATION: EVIDENTIAL PROVISIONS

3.10.1 E   FCA

The *evidential provisions* in this appendix apply in relation to *complaints* about sales that took place on or after 14 January 2005.

3.10.2 G   FCA

For *complaints* about sales that took place prior to 14 January 2005, a *firm* should take account of the *evidential provisions* in this appendix as if they were *guidance*.

3.10.3 E   FCA

Contravention of an *evidential provision* in this appendix may be relied upon as tending to establish contravention of **DISP 1.4.1 R**.

[3.77] TP

TRANSITIONAL PROVISIONS AND SCHEDULES

1 TRANSITIONAL PROVISIONS

Transitional Provisions table

(1)	(2) Material provision to which transitional provision applies	(3)	(4) Transitional provision	(5) Transitional provision: dates in force	(6) Handbook provision: coming into force
1	DISP 1.2.15 G	R	Expired		
1A	DISP 1	R	A *complaint* received by a *respondent* on or before 31 October 2007 should be handled, resolved, recorded and reported in accordance with the requirements of *DISP* as they stood at the date the *complaint* was received.	From 1 November 2007	1 November 2007
1B	DISP 2.7.9 R		In relation to a *complaint* concerning an act or omission before 1 November 2007, in **DISP 2.7.9 R (2)** substitute "an intermediate customer or market counterparty" for "(a) a professional client or (b) eligible counterparty".	From 1 November 2007	1 November 2007
2	DISP 1.5.4 R–DISP 1.5.7 R	R	Expired		
3	DISP 1.5.4 R–DISP 1.5.7 R	G	Expired		
6	DISP 2, DISP 3 and FEES 5	R	In **DISP 2, DISP 3** and **FEES 5** references to a *"firm"* or *"firms"* include *unauthorised persons* subject to the *Compulsory Jurisdiction* in relation to *relevant complaints* in accordance with the *Ombudsman Transitional Order*.	From *commencement*	*Commencement*
7	DISP 2, DISP 3 and FEES 5	G	Under the *Ombudsman Transitional Order*, a *relevant complaint* is subject to the *Compulsory Jurisdiction* whether or not it is about a *firm* or an *unauthorised person*. *Unauthorised persons* are not subject to **DISP 1**, but references to *"firm"* in **DISP 2, DISP 3** and **FEES 5** include *unauthorised persons* subject to the *Compulsory Jurisdiction* in relation to *relevant complaints*, where applicable.	From *commencement*	*Commencement*
7A	DISP 2.8.7 R	R	Nothing in **DISP 2.8.7 R** affects the position of a *complaint* which, on 31 May 2004, could not have been considered by the *Ombudsman* under **DISP 2.8.2 R (2)**; or **DISP 2.8.7 R (1)(B)** as it then stood (as **DISP 2.3.6 R (1)(B)**).	From 1 June 2004	Amended with effect from 1 June 2004

(1)	(2) Material provision to which transitional provision applies	(3)	(4) Transitional provision	(5) Transitional provision: dates in force	(6) Handbook provision: coming into force
7B	**DISP 2.8.7 R**	R	In the case of a complainant falling within **DISP 2.8.7 R**, (and whose time for referring a *complaint* under the *rules* as they stood before 1 June 2004 has not expired), time will expire in accordance with **DISP 2.8.7 R** save that if the final date would otherwise be before 30 November 2004 an explanation of the final date will be in conformity with **DISP 2.8.7 R (2)**, provided it stipulates a final date which is not less than two months from the date on which the explanation is likely to be received by the complainant.	From 1 June 2004	Amended with effect from 1 June 2004
8	**DISP 1 DISP 2 DISP 3 DISP 4 and FEES 5**	R	In relation to *relevant complaints*, references in **DISP 1, DISP 2, DISP 3, DISP 4** and **FEES 5** to an *"eligible complainant"* include a person who is to be treated as an *eligible complainant* in accordance with the *Ombudsman Transitional Order* and references to a *complaint* shall be construed accordingly.	From *commencement*	*Commencement*
9	**DISP 5.5.1 R**	R	Expired		
10	**DISP 1.10.1 R** and **DISP 1.10.2 R**	R	Expired		
11	**DISP 1.10.1 R** and **DISP 1.10.2 R**	R	Expired		
12	**DISP 1.10.1 R** and **DISP 1.10.2 R**	R	Expired		
13	**DISP 1**	R	Deleted		
14		G	Expired		
15	**FEES 5.4.1 R**	R	Expired		
16	**FEES 5.4.1 R**	G	Expired		
17	**DISP 1.3.12 R–DISP 1.3.17 R**	R	Deleted		
18	**DISP 1.10.1 R** and **DISP 1.10.2 R, DISP 1.10.4 R** and **DISP 1 ANNEX 1**	R	Expired		
19	**DISP 1.10.1C R** and **DISP 1.10.1D G**	R	Expired		

(1)	(2) Material provision to which transitional provision applies	(3)	(4) Transitional provision	(5) Transitional provision: dates in force	(6) Handbook provision: coming into force
20	**DISP 1.6.4 R**	R	Expired		
21	**DISP 2.7.3 R**	R	A *person* is also an *eligible complainant* if: (a) it is a business with a group annual turnover of less than £1 million at the time it refers the *complaint* to the *respondent*; (b) the *complaint* relates to a contract or *policy* entered into by or for the benefit of the complainant before 1 November 2009; and (c) if the *complaint* had been made immediately before 1 November 2009 the *respondent* was subject to, or participated in, the *Ombudsman's* jurisdiction in respect of the activity to which the *complaint* relates.	From 1 November 2009	1 November 2009
22	**DISP 2.7.3 R**	G	Transitional provision 21R applies together with the other eligibility *rules* in **DISP 2.7**. So, for example, a *person* who is an *eligible complainant* under the transitional provision, will not be an *eligible complainant* if the *complaint* does not arise from matters relevant to one of the relationships set out in **DISP 2.7.6 R**.	From 1 November 2009	1 November 2009
23	**DISP 1.10A.1 R**	R	[deleted]		
24	**DISP 1.10A.1 R**	R	[deleted]		
25	**DISP 1.11.6A R**	R	[deleted]		
26	**DISP 2.8.2 R**	R	[deleted]		
27	**DISP 1.10.5 R**	R	[deleted]		
27A	Amendments to *DISP* made in the Consumer Redress Schemes Instrument 2011		The amendments do not apply in relation to any *consumer redress scheme* imposed before the instrument came into force on a particular *firm*, or on a particular *payment service provider* or *electronic money issuer*, as envisaged by section 404F(7) of the *Act*.	From 1 August 2011 indefinitely	1 August 2011
28	**DISP 3.7.4 R**	R	For a *complaint* referred to the *Financial Ombudsman Service* before 1 January 2012 the maximum money award which the *Ombudsman* may make is £100,000.	From 1 January 2012	1 January 2012
28A	The amendments to **DISP 2.7.6 R (12)** effected by the Dispute Resolution: Complaints (Amendment No 4) Instrument 2011	R	The amendments referred to in column (2) do not affect who is an *eligible complainant* for the purpose of **DISP 2.7.6 R (12)**(A) in respect of complaints that relate to acts or omissions that occurred before 1 January 2012.	From 1 January 2012	1 January 2012

(1)	(2) Material provision to which transitional provision applies	(3)	(4) Transitional provision	(5) Transitional provision: dates in force	(6) Handbook provision: coming into force
29	**DISP 1.10.2 R** and **DISP 1 ANNEX 1**	R	Where a *firm* reports information on any *complaints* closed under a two-stage procedure before 1 July 2012, the *rules* and *guidance* in **DISP 1.6.6 R**, **DISP 1.10.3 G (2)**, **DISP 1.10.7 R (3)**, and **DISP 1.10.8 G** and **DISP 1 ANNEX 1** apply as they stood on 30 June 2012.	1 July 2012 to 31 December 2012	1 August 2009
30	**DISP 1.10.2A R**	R	Where a *firm*, which has a reporting period ending on or before 30 June 2013 submits its report to the *FCA* in accordance with the *complaints reporting rule* at **DISP 1.10.2A R** the number of *complaints* must be calculated for the period from the 31 December 2012 to the end of the *firm's* relevant reporting period.	31 December 2012 to 30 June 2013.	31 December 2012
31	**DISP 1.10.6A R**	R	(1) A *firm* is not liable to pay the administrative fee in **DISP 1.10.6A R** in respect of a failure to submit a report in accordance with **DISP 1.10.5 R** for a relevant reporting period ending before 1 March 2012. (2) Relevant reporting period in (1) has the meaning in **DISP 1.10.4 R**.	From 1 March 2012	1 March 2012
32	The changes to **DISP 1.10** and **DISP 1.10A** set out in Annex K of the Consumer Credit (Consequential and Supplementary Amendments) Instrument 2014	R	The changes referred to in column (2) to **DISP 1.10** and **DISP 1.10A** do not apply until 1 October 2014.	1 April 2014 to 1 October 2014	1 April 2014
33	The changes to **DISP 1.10** and **DISP 1.10A** set out in Annex K of the Consumer Credit (Consequential and Supplementary Amendments) Instrument 2014	G	*Firms* are reminded that **CONC 12.1.4 R** provides that **DISP 1.10** and **DISP 1.10A** (a) do not apply to a *person* with only an *interim permission*; and (b) apply to a *firm* with an *interim permission* that is treated as a variation of *permission* with respect to *credit-related regulated activity* or *operating an electronic system in relation to lending* as if the changes to **DISP 1.10** and **DISP 1.10A** effected by the Consumer Credit (Consequential and Supplementary Amendments) Instrument 2014 had not been made.	1 April 2014 to the date on which *interim permission* ceases to have effect	1 April 2014

(1)	(2) Material provision to which transitional provision applies	(3)	(4) Transitional provision	(5) Transitional provision: dates in force	(6) Handbook provision: coming into force
			The effect of TP 32 and **CONC 12.1.4 R** is that:		
			(1) for a *firm* with only an *interim permission*:		
			(a) the reporting frequencies, submission deadlines and time limits for publication for the returns and complaints data summaries in **DISP 1.10** and **DISP 1.10A** are calculated by reference to the *firm's* next *accounting reference date* that follows 1 October 2014 or, if later, the date on which the *firm's* application for *permission* to carry on *credit-related regulated activity* or *operating an electronic system in relation to lending* is granted;		
			(b) the first complaints return in the form in **DISP 1 ANNEX 1** should cover *complaints* received in the period:		
			(i) starting on either 1 October 2014 or, if later, on the date on which the *firm's* application for *permission* to carry on *credit-related regulated activity* or *operating an electronic system in relation to lending* is granted; and		
			(ii) ending on either the *accounting reference date* or (if the frequency is twice a year and the start of the period under (i) is more than six months before the *accounting reference date*) the date that falls six months before the *firm's accounting reference date*.		
			(2) For a *firm* with an *interim permission* that is treated as a variation of *permission*, where the relevant reporting period includes a period after the date on which the *firm's* application for a variation of *permission* to add *credit-related regulated activity* or *operating an electronic system in relation to lending* is granted (or, if that date is before 1 October 2014, where the relevant reporting period includes a period after 1 October 2014):		
			(a) the complaints return form should be submitted in the form in **DISP 1 ANNEX 1** as amended by Annex K of the Consumer Credit (Consequential and Supplementary Amendments) Instrument 2014); and		
			(b) items 35 to 46 of the form should cover *complaints* received from 1 October 2014 or, if later, from the date on which the *firm's* application for *permission* to carry on *credit-related regulated activity* or *operating an electronic system in relation to lending* is granted.		
34	**DISP 1.10** and **DISP 1.10A**	R	**DISP 1.10** and **DISP 1.10A** do not apply to a *firm* with *permission* to carry on only one or more *credit-related regulated activities* or *operating an electronic system in relation to lending* (and no other *regulated activity*) until 1 October 2014.	1 April 2014 to 1 October 2014	1 April 2014

(1)	(2) Material provision to which transitional provision applies	(3)	(4) Transitional provision	(5) Transitional provision: dates in force	(6) Handbook provision: coming into force

35	**DISP 2.3.1 R, DISP 2.3.2A R and DISP 2.3.2B R**	R	(1) Except where indicated otherwise, expressions used in this *rule* have the same meaning as they had in the Consumer Credit Act 1974 on 31 March 2014, before the amendments made to that Act by the Financial Services and Markets Act 2000 (Regulated Activities) (Amendment) (No. 2) Order 2013, the Financial Services Act 2012 (Consumer Credit) Order 2013, the Financial Services and Markets Act 2000 (Consumer Credit) (Miscellaneous Provisions) Order 2014, the Financial Services and Markets Act 2000 (Regulated Activities) (Amendment) Order 2014, the Consumer Credit Act 1974 (Green Deal) (Amendment) Order 2014, and the Financial Services and Markets Act 2000 (Consumer Credit) (Miscellaneous Provisions) (No. 2) Order 2014 came into force.
			
			(2) In **DISP 2.3.1 R, DISP 2.3.2A R** and **DISP 2.3.2B R**, references to an act or omission by a *firm*, *payment service provider* or *electronic money issuer* in carrying on *regulated activities* or *credit-related regulated activities* include an act or omission which took place before 1 April 2014 in carrying on any one of the following activities:
			
			(a) providing credit or otherwise being a creditor under a regulated consumer credit agreement;
			
			(b) the bailment or (in Scotland) the hiring of goods or otherwise being an owner under a regulated consumer hire agreement;
			
			(c) credit brokerage in so far as it was the effecting of introductions of:
			
			  (i) individuals desiring to obtain credit to persons carrying on a consumer credit business; or
			
			  (ii) individuals desiring to obtain goods on hire to persons carrying on a consumer hire business;
			
			(d) in so far as they related to regulated consumer credit agreements or regulated consumer hire agreements:
			
			  (i) debt-adjusting;
			
			  (ii) debt-counselling;
			
			  (iii) debt-collecting; or
			
			  (iv) debt administration;
			
			(e) the provision of credit information services; or
				Indefinitely from 1 April 2014	1 April 2014

(1)	(2) Material provision to which transitional provision applies	(3)	(4) Transitional provision	(5) Transitional provision: dates in force	(6) Handbook provision: coming into force
			(f) the operation of a credit reference agency; where at the time of the act or omission complained of:		
			(g) the *firm, payment service provider or electronic money issuer* was:		
			(i) covered by a standard licence under the Consumer Credit Act 1974; or		
			(ii) authorised to carry on an activity by virtue of section 34A of that Act; or		
			(iii) in accordance with regulation 26(2) of the *Payment Services Regulations* or regulation 31 of the *Electronic Money Regulations* was not required to hold a licence for consumer credit business under section 21 of the Consumer Credit Act 1974; and		
			(h) the activity was carried on in the course of a business of a type which was specified in accordance with section 226A(2)(e) of the *Act* (now repealed).		
36	**DISP 2.3.1 R**	R	In **DISP 2.3.1 R (4)**, in relation to an act or omission by a *firm* in lending *money* that took place before 1 April 2014, the reference to "(excluding *restricted credit* where that is not a *credit-related regulated activity*)" is to be read as a reference to "(excluding *restricted credit* where that is not an activity described in TP 35(2))".	Indefinitely from 1 April 2014	1 April 2014
37	**DISP 2.3.1 R**	R	In **DISP 2.3.1 R (5)**, in relation to an act or omission by a *firm* in paying *money* by a *plastic card* that took place before 1 April 2014, the reference to "(excluding a *store card* where that is not a *credit-related regulated activity*)" is to be read as a reference to "(excluding a *store card* where that is not an activity described in TP 35(2))".	Indefinitely from 1 April 2014	1 April 2014
38	**DISP 1**	R	In respect of a *complaint* received by a *respondent* on or before 8 July 2015 the *respondent* must handle, resolve, record and report the *complaint* in accordance with the *rules* as they stood at the date on which the *complaint* was received by the *respondent*.	From 9 July 2015	From 9 July 2015.

Table Fee tariffs for industry blocks [deleted]

Payment Services Regulations 2009 transitioning payment institutions

1	R		This TP applies in relation to a *person* who falls within regulation 122(1) (Transitional provisions: requirement to be authorised as a payment institution) or regulation 123(1) (Transitional provisions: requirement to be registered as a small payment institution) of the *Payment Services Regulations* (a "transitioning payment institution").		

2	R	This TP applies from 1 November 2009 until 30 April 2011.
3	R	**DISP 1** (Treating complainants fairly) applies in relation to a transitioning payment institution as if the transitioning payment institution were a *payment institution*.
4	R	The *Ombudsman* can consider a *complaint* that relates to an act or omission by a transitioning payment institution under the *Compulsory Jurisdiction* if:
		(1) it could consider that *complaint* under the *Compulsory Jurisdiction* if it related to a *payment institution*; and
		(2) (where the transitioning payment institution is a *licensee*) the complaint relates to an act or omission in providing *payment services*.
5	G	The effect of this transitional provision is to:
		(1) apply to transitioning payment institutions the complaints-handling requirements in **DISP 1.1** to **DISP 1.8**; and
		(2) to bring them within the scope of the *Compulsory Jurisdiction* to the same extent as *payment institutions*.
6	G	*Complaints* relating to *payment services*, *consumer credit activities* or a combination of both can be considered under the *Compulsory Jurisdiction*. However, transitioning payment institutions that are *licensees* will remain subject to the *Consumer Credit Jurisdiction* for *complaints* that relate only to *consumer credit activities*.
7	R	The rules and guidance in **FEES 5.5.1 R**, **5.5.6 R**, **5.5.7 R**, **5.5.15 R**, **5.7.2 R**, **5.9.1 R** and **5.9.2 G** shall apply to transitioning payment institutions in the same way as they apply to *firms* and *persons* that cease to be authorised. The rules and guidance in **FEES 5.5.1 R**, **5.5.6 R**, **5.5.7 R**, **5.5.15 R**, **5.7.2 R**, **5.9.1 R** and **5.9.2 G** shall apply to transitioning payment institutions and *persons* that cease to be transitioning institutions in the same way as they apply to *firms* and *firms* that cease to be authorised.

SCH 1   RECORD KEEPING REQUIREMENTS

1.1 G   FCA

The aim of the *guidance* in the following table is to give the reader a quick overall view of the relevant record keeping requirements.

It is not a complete statement of those requirements and should not be relied on as if it were.

1.2 G   FCA

Handbook reference	Subject of record	When record must be made	Contents of record	Retention period
DISP 1.9.1 R	*Complaints* subject to **DISP 1.3–DISP 1.8** (other than **DISP 1.5**).	On receipt	Each *complaint* received and the measures taken for its resolution	5 years for *complaints* relating to *MiFID business or collective portfolio management services* and 3 years for all other *complaints*

Part 3   FCA Handbook Materials

SCH 2   NOTIFICATION REQUIREMENTS

2.1 G   FCA

The aim of the *guidance* in the following table is to give the reader a quick overall view of the relevant requirements for notification and reporting.
It is not a complete statement of those requirements and should not be relied on as if it were.

2.1 G   FCA

Handbook reference	Matter to be notified	Contents of notification	Trigger event	Time allowed
DISP 1.1.12 R	*Firm* qualifies for exemption	Confirmation that a *firm* does not do business with *eligible complainants* and has no reasonable likelihood of doing so	Conditions in **DISP 1.1.12 R** apply	N/A
DISP 1.10.1 R (1)	Complaints report	Details	- 6 months preceding the *accounting reference date* - *accounting reference date*	30 *business days*
DISP 1.10.1 R (2)	Complaints report	Details	A year immediately following the *firm's accounting reference date*	30 *business days*
DISP 1.10.8 G	Single contact point	Details	At the time of authorisation or on subsequent change	Not specified
DISP 1.10A.4 R	Publication of *complaints* data summary/ total number of *complaints* (as appropriate)	Email confirmation of publication, containing also a statement that the data summary or total number of *complaints* (as appropriate) accurately reflects the report submitted to the *FCA* and stating where the summary/total number of *complaints* has been published	Upon publication of *complaints* data summary/ total number of *complaints* (as appropriate)	Immediately
DISP 1.11.5 R (1)	*Member* of Lloyd's qualifies for exemption	Confirmation by the *Society* of Lloyd's that a specified *member* of Lloyd's does not do business with *eligible complainants* and has no reasonable likelihood of doing so	[As above]	N/A
DISP 1.11.5 R (2)	End of exemption for *member* of Lloyd's	Confirmation by the *Society* of Lloyd's that the condition in DISP 1.1.7 no longer apply to a specified *member* of Lloyd's	Conditions in DISP 1.1.7 no longer apply	Not specified
DISP 1.11.6 R	Complaints report by *Society* of Lloyd's	Details	- 30 September - 31 March each year	One *month*

Handbook reference	Matter to be notified	Contents of notification	Trigger event	Time allowed
DISP 1.11.6D R	Publication of *complaints* data summary	Email confirmation of publication, containing also a statement that the data summary accurately reflects the report submitted to the *FCA* and stating where the summary has been published	Upon publication of *complaints* data summary	Immediately

SCH 3   FEES AND OTHER REQUIRED PAYMENT

3.1 G   FCA

There are no requirements for fees or other payments in *DISP*.

3.2 G

[deleted]

SCH 4   POWERS EXERCISED

4.1G–4.5 G

[deleted]

[**Note:** certain rules in *FEES* are made exclusively by the *FOS Ltd*. A list of those rules is set out in **GEN SCH 4.12 G**.]

SCH 5   ACTIONS FOR DAMAGES FOR CONTRAVENTION UNDER SECTION 150 OF THE ACT

5.1 G   FCA

1   The table below sets out the *rules* in *DISP* contravention of which by an *authorised person* may be actionable under section 138D of the *Act* (Actions for damages) by a *person* who suffers loss as a result of the contravention.

2   If a "Yes" appears in the column headed "For private person?", the *rule* may be actionable by a *"private person"* under section 138D (or, in certain circumstances, his fiduciary or representative; see article 6(2) and (3)(c) of the Financial Services and Markets Act 2000 (Rights of Action) Regulations 2001 (SI 2001 No 2256)). A "Yes" in the column headed "Removed" indicates that the *FCA* has removed the right of action under section 138D(3) of the *Act*. If so, a reference to the *rule* in which it is removed is also given.

3   The column headed "For other person?" indicates whether the *rule* may be actionable by a *person* other than a *private person* (or his fiduciary or representative) under article 6(2) and (3) of those Regulations. If so, an indication of the type of *person* by whom the *rule* may be actionable is given.

5.2 G   FCA

Chapter/Appendix	Section/Annex	Paragraph	Right of Action under s138D		
			For private person?	**Removed?**	**For other person?**
1 Complaints handling arrangements for *firms*	All rules apart from **DISP 1.11.13 R** and **DISP 1.11.14 R**		Yes		-
1	7	14 and 15	No	Yes **DISP 1.11.21 R**	No
2 Jurisdiction rules			Yes	-	
3 Complaints handling procedures of the *Financial Ombudsman Service*			Yes		
4 The *standard terms*			N/A		

SCH 6   RULES THAT CAN BE WAIVED

6.1 G   FCA

As a result of section 138A of the *Act* (Modification or waiver of rules) the *FCA* has power to waive all its *rules*, other than *rules* made under section 137O (Threshold condition code), section 247 (Trust scheme rules), section 248 (Scheme particular rules), section 261I (Contractual scheme rules) or section 261J (Contractual scheme particulars rules) of the *Act*. However, if the *rules* incorporate requirements laid down in European directives or European Regulations, it will not be possible for the *FCA* to grant a waiver that would be incompatible with the *United Kingdom's* responsibilities under those directives or Regulations.

J. CONSUMER CREDIT SOURCEBOOK (CONC)

CONSUMER CREDIT SOURCEBOOK
The specialist sourcebook for credit-related regulated activities

CHAPTER 1
APPLICATION AND PURPOSE AND GUIDANCE ON FINANCIAL DIFFICULTIES

1.1   APPLICATION AND PURPOSE

Application

[3.78]
1.1.1 G   FCA
(1)   The Consumer Credit sourcebook (*CONC*) is the specialist sourcebook for *credit-related regulated activities*.
(2)   *CONC* applies as described in this chapter, unless the application of a chapter, section or a *rule* is described differently in the chapters, sections or *rules* in *CONC*.

Purpose

1.1.2 G   FCA

The purpose of *CONC* is to set out the detailed obligations that are specific to *credit-related regulated activities* and activities connected to those activities carried on by *firms*. These build on and add to the high-level obligations, for example, in *PRIN*, *GEN* and *SYSC*, and the requirements in or under the *CCA*.

1.1.3 G   FCA

Firms are reminded that other parts of the *FCA Handbook* and *PRA Handbook* also apply to *credit-related regulated activities*. For example, the arrangements for supervising *firms*, including applicable reporting obligations, are described in the Supervision manual (*SUP*) and the detailed requirements for handling complaints are set out in the Dispute Resolution: Complaints sourcebook (*DISP*). The Client Assets sourcebook (*CASS*) also contains *rules* about client money that apply in certain circumstances.

The Principles for Businesses: a reminder

1.1.4 G   FCA

The Principles for Businesses (*PRIN*) apply as a whole to *firms* with respect to *credit-related regulated activities* and *ancillary activities* in relation to *credit-related regulated activities* (see **PRIN 3**). In carrying on their activities, *firms* should pay particular attention to their obligations under:
(1)   *Principle* 1 (a *firm* must conduct its business with integrity);
(2)   *Principle* 2 (a *firm* must conduct its business with due skill, care and diligence);
(3)   *Principle* 3 (a *firm* must take reasonable care to organise and control its affairs responsibly and effectively, with adequate risk management systems);
(4)   *Principle* 6 (a *firm* must pay due regard to the interests of its *customers* and treat them fairly);
(5)   *Principle* 7 (a *firm* must pay due regard to the information needs of its *clients*, and communicate information to them in a way which is clear, fair and not misleading);
(6)   *Principle* 9 (a *firm* must take reasonable care to ensure the suitability of its advice and discretionary decisions for any *customer* who is entitled to rely upon its judgment);
(7)   *Principle* 10 (a *firm* must arrange adequate protection for clients' assets when it is responsible for them); and
(8)   *Principle* 11 (a *firm* must deal with its regulators in an open and cooperative way, and must disclose to the *appropriate regulator* appropriately anything relating to the *firm* of which that regulator would reasonably expect notice).

1.2   WHO? WHAT? WHERE?

1.2.1 R   FCA

CONC applies to a *firm* with respect to carrying on *credit-related regulated activities* and connected activities, unless otherwise stated in, or in relation to, a *rule*.

1.2.2 R   FCA

A *firm* must:
(1)   ensure that its employees and agents comply with *CONC*; and
(2)   take reasonable steps to ensure that other *persons* acting on its behalf comply with *CONC*.

Guidance on appointed representatives

1.2.3 G   FCA

(1)   Although *CONC* does not apply directly to a *firm's appointed representatives*, a *firm* will always be responsible for the acts and omissions of its *appointed representatives* in carrying on business for which the *firm* has accepted responsibility (section 39(3) of the *Act*). In determining whether a *firm* has complied with any provision of *CONC*, anything done or omitted by a *firm's appointed representative* (when acting as such) will be treated as having been done or omitted by the *firm* (section 39(4) of the *Act*).

(2)   *Firms* should refer to **SUP 12** (Appointed representatives), which sets out requirements which apply to *firms* using *appointed representatives*.

1.2.4 G   FCA

The *credit-related regulated activities* comprise *consumer credit lending, credit broking, debt counselling, debt adjusting, debt administration, debt collecting, providing credit information services, providing credit references, operating an electronic system in relation to lending* (but, other than in *FEES* and *SUP*, only insofar as it relates to a borrower or prospective borrower under a *P2P agreement*) and *consumer hiring*.

Where?

1.2.5 R   FCA

CONC, except in relation to **CONC 3**, applies with respect to activities carried on by a *firm*:

(1)   with a *customer* whose habitual residence is in the *UK* from an *establishment* maintained by the *firm* (or its *appointed representative*) in the *UK*; or

(2)   with a *customer* whose habitual residence is in the *UK* from an *establishment* of the *firm* (or its *appointed representative*) outside the *UK*.

EEA territorial scope rule: compatibility with European law

1.2.6 R   FCA

(1)   *CONC* does not apply to an *incoming ECA provider* where, in providing a service, the provider is acting as such.

(2)   *CONC* applies to an *outgoing ECA provider* where, in providing a service, the provider is acting as such.

(3)   The territorial scope of *CONC* is otherwise modified to the extent necessary to be compatible with European law.

(4)   This *rule* overrides every other *rule* in this sourcebook.

Note: article 3(3) of, and the Annex to, the E

1.3   GUIDANCE ON FINANCIAL DIFFICULTIES

1.3.1 G   FCA

In *CONC* (unless otherwise stated in or in relation to a *rule*), the following matters, among others, of which a *firm* is aware or ought reasonably to be aware, may indicate that a *customer* is in financial difficulties:

(1)   consecutively failing to meet minimum *repayments* in relation to a credit card or store card;

(2)   adverse accurate entries on a credit file, which are not in dispute;

(3)   outstanding county court judgments for non-payment of debt;

(4)   inability to meet *repayments* out of disposable income or at all, for example, where there is evidence of non-payment of essential bills (such as, utility bills), the *customer* having to borrow further to repay existing debts, or the *customer* only being able to meet *repayments* of debts by the disposal of assets or security;

(5)   consecutively failing to meet *repayments* when due;

(6)   agreement to a *debt management plan* or other *debt solution*;

(7)   evidence of discussions with a *firm* (including a *not-for-profit debt advice body*) with a view to entering into a *debt management plan* or other *debt solution* or to seeking *debt counselling*.

CHAPTER 2
CONDUCT OF BUSINESS STANDARDS: GENERAL

2.1   APPLICATION

[3.79]

2.1.1 G   FCA

This chapter applies as stated in the sections which follow.

2.2   GENERAL PRINCIPLES FOR CREDIT-RELATED REGULATED ACTIVITIES

2.2.1 R   FCA

This section applies to a *firm* with respect to *credit-related regulated activities*.

General principles

2.2.2 G   FCA

Principle 6 requires a *firm* to pay due regard to the interests of its *customers* and treat them fairly. Examples of behaviour by or on behalf of a *firm* which is likely to contravene *Principle* 6 include:

(1)   targeting *customers* with *regulated credit agreements* which are unsuitable for them, by virtue of their indebtedness, poor credit history, age, health, disability or any other reason;

(2)   subjecting *customers* to high-pressure selling, aggressive or oppressive behaviour, or unfair coercion;

(3)   not allowing *customers* who are unable to make payments a reasonable time and opportunity to meet *repayments*;

(4)   taking steps to repossess a *customer's* home, other than as a last resort.
[**Note** paragraph 7.14 of *ILG* and 6.3 of *SCLG*]

[**Note:** paragraphs 2.3 of *ILG*, 2.2 of *CBG* and 2.3 of *DMG*]

Duty not to use misleading names

2.2.3 R   FCA

A *firm* must not carry on a *credit-related regulated activity* under a name which is likely to mislead *customers* about the status of the *firm* or the nature of its business, or in any other way.

[**Note:** section 25(1AD) of *CCA*]

2.2.4 G   FCA

(1)   In relation to **CONC 2.2.3 R**, an example of where a name may mislead is if the average *customer* of the *firm* is likely to be misled by the name of the *firm*.

(2)   Examples of the matters concerning a *firm's* status or the nature of its business about which its name may mislead *customers* include:

       (a)   the identity or nature of the *firm*;

       (b)   its commercial or profit-seeking status;

       (c)   its role, including any relationship with any other *person*;

       (d)   the extent of its authority;

       (e)   stating or implying that the *firm* is a public body or that it is related or connected in some way to a charitable, not-for-profit or governmental or local governmental organisation or to the courts;

       (f)   the nature of the products or services supplied;

       (g)   the cost of those products or services; and

       (h)   the scale of the business including its geographical scope.

Effect on other rules and legislation

2.2.5 R   FCA

Any specific rule or piece of guidance in *CONC* is without prejudice to the application of *PRIN*, any other *rules* in the *Handbooks*, the *CCA* and secondary legislation made and things done under it, the Consumer Protection from Unfair Trading Regulations 2008, the Unfair Terms in Consumer Contracts Regulations 1999, Part 8 of the Enterprise Act 2002 and any other applicable consumer protection legislation.

     2.3   CONDUCT OF BUSINESS: LENDERS AND RESTRICTIONS ON PROVISION OF CREDIT CARD CHEQUES

Application

2.3.1 R   FCA

This section applies to a *firm* with respect to *consumer credit lending*.

General conduct

2.3.2 R   FCA

A *firm* must explain the key features of a *regulated credit agreement* to enable the *customer* to make an informed choice as required by **CONC 4.2.5 R** (adequate explanations).

[**Note:** paragraph 2.2 of *ILG*]

2.3.3 G   FCA

CONC 6.7.2 R requires a *firm* to monitor a *customer's* repayment record and take appropriate action where there are signs of actual or possible repayment difficulties.

2.3.4 R   FCA

A *firm* must take reasonable steps to satisfy itself that any *credit brokers* with whom the *firm* deals are *authorised persons* or *appointed representatives*.

[**Note:** paragraph 1.27 of *CBG*]

Provision of credit card cheques

2.3.5 R   FCA
(1)   A *firm* may provide *credit card cheques* only to a *customer* who has asked for them.
       [**Note:** section 51A(2) of *CCA*]
(2)   A *firm* may provide *credit card cheques* only on a single occasion in respect of each request
       that is made.
       [**Note:** section 51A(3) of *CCA*]
(3)   The number of *credit card cheques* provided in respect of a request must not exceed three (or,
       if less, the number requested).
       [**Note:** section 51A(4) of *CCA*]
(4)   Where a single request is made for the provision of *credit card cheques* in connection with
       more than one *credit-token agreement*, (2) and (3) apply as if a separate request had been
       made for each agreement.
       [**Note:** section 51A(5) of *CCA*]
(5)   Where more than one request for the provision of *credit card cheques* is made in the same
       document or at the same time:
       (a)   they may be provided in respect of only one of the requests, but
       (b)   if the requests relate to more than one *credit-token agreement*, in relation to each
              agreement they may be provided only in respect of one of the requests made in
              relation to that agreement.

       [**Note:** section 51A(6) of *CCA*]
(6)   This rule does not apply to *credit card cheques* provided in connection with a *credit-token
       agreement* that is entered into by the *customer* wholly or predominantly for the purposes of
       a business carried on, or intended to be carried on, by the *customer*.
       [**Note:** section 51B(1) of *CCA*]
(7)   If a *credit-token agreement* includes a declaration made by the *customer* to the effect that the
       agreement is entered into as mentioned in (6), the agreement is treated for the purposes of
       (6) as having been so entered into.
       [**Note:** section 51B(2) of *CCA*]
(8)   The declaration in (7) must be in the form and content set out in **CONC APP 1** for the
       exemption relating to business.
(9)   Paragraph (7) does not apply if, when the agreement is entered into
       (a)   the *lender*; or
       (b)   any *person* who has acted on behalf of the *lender* in connection with the entering into
              of the agreement;
       knows, or has reasonable cause to suspect, that the agreement is not entered into as
       mentioned in (6).
       [**Note:** section 51B(3) of *CCA*]
(10)   Where an agreement has two or more *lenders*, references in (9) to the *lender* are to any one
       or more of them.
       [**Note:** section 51B(5) of *CCA*]

2.4   CREDIT REFERENCES: CONDUCT OF BUSINESS: LENDERS AND OWNERS

Application

2.4.1 R   FCA

This section applies:
(1)   to a *firm* with respect to *consumer credit lending*; or
(2)   to a *firm* with respect to *consumer hiring*.

Disclosure of name and address of credit reference agencies consulted

2.4.2 R   FCA
(1)   Not later than the *lender* ("L") informs a *credit broker* that L is not willing to make a
       regulated credit agreement, L must, unless L informs the *customer* directly that L is not
       willing to make the agreement, inform the *credit broker* of the name and address (including
       an appropriate e-mail address) of any *credit reference agency* from which L has, during the
       negotiations relating to the proposed agreement, applied for information about the financial
       standing of the *customer*.
       [**Note:** regulation 2 of SI 1977/330]
(2)   Not later than the owner ("O") informs a *credit broker* that O is not willing to make a
       regulated consumer hire agreement, O must, unless O informs the *customer* directly that O
       is not willing to make the agreement, inform the *credit broker* of the name and address

(including an appropriate e-mail address) of any *credit reference agency* from which O has, during the negotiations relating to the proposed agreement, applied for information about the financial standing of the *customer*.

[**Note:** regulation 2 of SI 1977/330]

Searching credit files

2.4.3 G FCA

A *firm* undertaking a credit reference search should not leave evidence of an application on a credit file where a *customer* is not yet ready to apply. Where practicable, *firms* should facilitate *customers* shopping around for *credit* by offering a 'quotation search' facility.

[**Note:** paragraph 3.13 (box 2) of *ILG*]

2.5   CONDUCT OF BUSINESS: CREDIT BROKING

Conduct of business: credit broking

2.5.1 R   FCA

This section applies to a *firm* with respect to *credit broking*.

2.5.2 G   FCA

The scope of *credit broking* for the introducing activities (article 36A(a) to (c) of the *Regulated Activities Order*) covers *regulated credit agreements* and *regulated consumer hire agreements*. But additionally in relation to credit agreements it covers introductions concerning exempt agreements under articles 60C to 60H of that Order (other than agreements under article 60F of that Order (exempt agreements: exemptions relating to the number of repayments to be made)). Additionally in relation to *consumer hire agreements*, it covers exempt agreements articles 60O and 60Q of that Order.

Conduct of business

2.5.3 R   FCA

A *firm* must:

(1)   where it has responsibility for doing so, explain the key features of a *regulated credit agreement* to enable the *customer* to make an informed choice as required by **CONC 4.2.5 R**;
      [**Note:** paragraphs 4.27 to 4.30 of *CBG* and 2.2 of *ILG*]

(2)   take reasonable steps to satisfy itself that a product it wishes to recommend to a *customer* is not unsuitable for the *customer's* needs and circumstances;
      [**Note:** paragraph 4.22 of *CBG*]

(3)   advise a *customer* to read, and allow the *customer* sufficient opportunity to consider, the terms and conditions of a *credit agreement* or *consumer hire agreement* before entering into it;
      [**Note:** paragraph 3.9l of *CBG*]

(4)   before referring the *customer* to a third party which carries on *regulated activities* or to a claims management service (within the meaning of section 4 of the Compensation Act 2006) or other services, obtain the *customer's* consent, after having explained why the *customer's* details are to be disclosed to that third party;
      [**Note:** paragraph 3.9r of *CBG*]

(5)   before effecting an introduction of a *customer* to a *lender* or *owner* in relation to a *credit agreement* or *consumer hire agreement*, or before entering into such an agreement on behalf of the *lender* or *owner*, disclose (where applicable) the fact that the *lender* or *owner* is linked to the *firm* by being a member of the same *group* as the *firm*;
      [**Note:** paragraph 3.9y of *CBG*]

(6)   bring to the attention of a *customer* how the *firm* uses the *customer's* personal data it collects, in a manner appropriate to the means of communication used;
      [**Note:** paragraph 3.9q of *CBG*]

(7)   provide *customers* with a clear and simple method to cancel their consent for the processing of their personal data;
      [**Note:** paragraph 3.9u of *CBG*]

(8)   at the request of a *customer*, disclose from where the *customer's* personal data was obtained;
      [**Note:** paragraph 3.9w of *CBG*]

(9)   take reasonable steps not to pass a *customer's* personal data to a business which carries on a *credit-related regulated activity* for which the business has no *permission*.
      [**Note:** paragraph 3.9x of *CBG*]

2.5.4 G   FCA

A *firm* may comply with **CONC 2.5.3 R (6)** by presenting to the *customer* a privacy notice. The Information Commissioner's Office has prepared the Privacy Notices Code of Practice.

Conduct of business: credit references

2.5.5 R FCA

Where a *credit broker* ("B") is a negotiator (within the meaning of section 56(1) of the *CCA*), B must, at the same time as B gives notice to a *customer*, under section 157(1) of the *CCA* (which relates to the duty to disclose on request the name and address of any *credit reference agency* consulted by B) also give the *customer* notice of the name and address of any *credit reference agency* of which B has been informed under **CONC 2.4.2 R**.

[**Note:** regulation 3 of SI 1977/ 330]

2.5.6 R FCA

Where a *credit broker* ("B") is not a negotiator (within the meaning of section 56(1) of the *CCA*), B must, within seven *working days* after receiving a request in writing for any such information, which is made by a *customer* within 28 days after the termination of any negotiations relating to a *regulated credit agreement* or a *regulated consumer hire agreement* whether on the making of the agreement or otherwise, give to the *customer* notice of:

(1)   the name and address of any *credit reference agency* from which B has during those negotiations applied for information about the financial standing of the *customer*; and

(2)   the name and address of any *credit reference agency* of which B has been informed under **CONC 2.4.2 R**.

[**Note:** regulation 4 of SI 1977/ 330]

Searching credit files

2.5.7 G FCA

A *firm* undertaking a credit reference search should not leave evidence of an application on a credit file where a *customer* is not yet ready to apply. Where practicable, *firms* should facilitate *customers* shopping around for *credit* by offering a 'quotation search' facility".

[**Note:** paragraph 3.13 (box 2) of *ILG*]

Unfair business practices: credit brokers

2.5.8 R FCA

A *firm* must not:

(1)   make or cause to be made unsolicited calls to numbers entered on the register kept under regulation 25 or 26 of the Privacy and Electronic Communications (EC Directive) Regulations 2003 or to a *customer* who has notified the *firm* not to call the number being used to call;

      [**Note:** paragraph 3.9a of *CBG*]

(2)   other than where:

    (a)   the *firm* has obtained the contact details of a *customer* (C) in the course of the sale or negotiations for the sale of a product or service to C;

    (b)   the direct marketing is in respect of the *firm's* similar products and services only;

    (c)   C has been given a simple means of refusing (free of charge, except for the cost of the transmission of the refusal) the use of the contact details for the purposes of such direct marketing, at the time that the details were initially collected and, where C did not initially refuse the use of the details, at the time of each subsequent communication; and

    (d)   the *firm* has previously explained that the following calls or *electronic communications* would be sent or made or caused to be sent or made by the *firm* and following that explanation C consented for the time being to such calls or communications;

send or cause to be sent an *electronic communication*, for the purposes of marketing, to C, or make or cause to be made by means of an automated calling system (which is capable of automatically initiating a sequence of calls to more than one destination in accordance with instructions stored in that system, and transmitting sounds which are not live speech for reception by persons at some or all of the destinations so called) a call to C, for the purposes of marketing;

      [**Note** paragraph 3.9b of *CBG*]

(3)   make or cause to be made by means of an automated calling system (see paragraph (2)) a call to a *customer*, for the purposes of marketing, after the *firm* has received a request from the *customer* to stop doing so;

      [**Note:** paragraph 3.9c of *CBG*]

(4)   send, or cause to be sent, an *electronic communication* to a *customer*, for the purposes of marketing, after the *firm* has received a request from the *customer* to stop doing so;

      [**Note:** paragraph 3.9c of *CBG*]

(5)   visit a *customer* at a time that is known to be, or reasonably likely to be, inconvenient or particularly undesirable to the *customer*;

      [**Note:** paragraph 3.9f of *CBG*]

(6)   refuse to end a visit to a *customer* or to leave the *customer's* home, when requested to do so;
       [**Note:** paragraph 3.9g of *CBG*]

(7)   unfairly request, suggest or direct a *customer* to make contact on a premium rate telephone number;
       [**Note:** paragraph 3.9h of *CBG*]

(8)   conduct a telephone call with a *customer* who has called on a premium rate number for an unreasonable period;
       [**Note:** paragraph 3.9i of *CBG*]

(9)   inappropriately offer a financial or other incentive or inducement to a *customer* to enter, immediately or quickly, into a *credit agreement* or *consumer hire agreement* to which this section applies;
       [**Note:** paragraph 3.9j of *CBG*]

(10)   effect an introduction to a *lender* or an *owner* or to another *credit broker*, where the *firm* has considered whether the *customer* might meet the relevant lending or hiring criteria and it is or should be apparent to the *firm* that the *customer* does not meet those criteria;
       [**Note:** paragraph 3.9aa and 4.41i of *CBG*]

(11)   suggest to a *customer* that an application for credit will be met in full when a lower amount may be offered;
       [**Note:** paragraph 4.26d of *CBG*]

(12)   secure more *credit* for a *customer* than was requested where the object of doing so is for, or can reasonably be concluded as having been for, the personal gain of the *firm* or of a *person* acting on its behalf, rather than in the best interests of the *customer*;
       [**Note:** paragraph 4.26e of *CBG*]

(13)   secure *credit* for a *customer* at a higher rate of interest than was requested, where the object of doing so is for, or can reasonably be concluded as having been for, the personal gain of the *firm* or of a *person* acting on its behalf, rather than in the best interests of the *customer*;
       [**Note:** paragraph 4.26e of *CBG*]

(14)   give preference to the *credit* products of a particular *lender* where the object of doing so is for, or can reasonably be concluded as having been for, the personal gain of the *firm* or of a *person* acting on its behalf, rather than in the best interests of the *customer*;
       [**Note:** paragraph 4.41k of *CBG*]

(15)   in relation to a payment protection product (the meaning of which is set out in **CONC 2.5.10 R**) to the *credit agreement* or *consumer hire agreement* (whether the product is optional or required as a condition of the *credit agreement* or *consumer hire agreement*):
       (a)   pressurise the *customer* to buy the product; or
            [**Note:** paragraph 2.62, 2nd bullet of *JGPPI*]
       (b)   offer undue incentives to the *customer* to buy the product;
            [**Note:** paragraph 2.62, 2nd bullet of *JGPPI*]

(16)   in relation to an insurance product or service or other linked product or service to the *credit agreement* or *consumer hire agreement* (whether the service or product is optional or required as a condition of the *credit agreement* or *consumer hire agreement*) discourage or prevent the *customer* from seeking or obtaining the product or service from another source;
       [**Note:** paragraph 4.26f of *CBG*]

(17)   encourage a *customer* to enter into a *credit agreement* which is secured in any way, to which this section applies, to replace an unsecured *credit agreement* or to consolidate other debts where the *firm* knows, or ought reasonably to know, that it is not in the best interests of the *customer*;
       [**Note:** paragraph 4.26g of *CBG*]

(18)   unfairly encourage a *customer* to increase, consolidate or refinance (which expression has the same meaning as in **CONC 6.7.17 R**) an existing debt to the extent that *repayments* under an agreement would be *unsustainable* for the *customer*;
       [**Note:** paragraph 4.26h of *CBG*]

(19)   encourage a *customer* to take out additional *credit* or to extend the term of an existing *credit agreement* where to do so is, or is reasonably likely be, to the detriment of a *customer*;
       [**Note:** paragraph 4.41h of *CBG*]

(20)   charge a fee to a *customer* for effecting an introduction (directly or indirectly) to a *lender* or *owner* that provides a type of *credit* or hire of a different type to that:
       (a)   promised to the *customer*; or
       (b)   promoted by the *firm* to the *customer*; or
       (c)   which the *firm* is aware the *customer* is seeking;

       unless the *customer*, after the *firm* has explained the reason for the fee, consents to such an introduction;
       [**Note:** paragraph 4.17f of *CBG*]

(21)   take a fee from a *customer's* bank account without the *customer's* express authorisation to do so;
       [**Note:** paragraph 4.17c of *CBG*]

Part 3   FCA Handbook Materials

(22)   unfairly pass a *customer's* personal data to a third party without obtaining the *customer's* consent to do so after having explained the reason for disclosing the data;
       [**Note:** paragraph 3.9s of *CBG*]

(23)   unfairly pass a *customer's* personal data to a third party for a purpose other than that for which consent was sought and given.
       [**Note:** paragraph 3.9t of *CBG*]

Guidance on unfair business practices

2.5.9 G   FCA

(1)   It is likely to be an inappropriate offer of an inducement or incentive to enter into an *regulated credit agreement* or a *regulated consumer hire agreement* to state that the offer in relation to the agreement will be withdrawn or the terms and conditions of the offer will worsen if the agreement is not signed immediately or within a stated period after the communication, unless the *firm's* offer on those terms and conditions will in fact be withdrawn or worsen in the period indicated to the *customer*.
       [**Note:** paragraph 3.9j (box) of *CBG*]

(2)   An example of unfairly requesting, suggesting or directing a *customer* to a premium rate telephone number is likely to be to do so in relation to a *customer* wishing to complain about the *firm's* service or to request a refund, including, for example, under section 155 of the *CCA*.
       [**Note:** paragraph 6.19f of *CBG*]

(3)   It is unlikely to be reasonable for it to be necessary for a *customer* to make more than one telephone call exceeding 15 minutes to a *firm* to apply for *credit*. Where a longer call is required, the *firm* should ensure the call is not made on a premium rate telephone number.
       [**Note:** paragraph 3.9i (box) of *CBG*]

(4)   It is unlikely to be reasonable to request, suggest or direct a *customer* to call the *firm* repeatedly to check on the status of an application. A call to check on the status of an application should not last more than five minutes.
       [**Note:** paragraph 3.9i (box) of *CBG*]

(5)   A *firm* should disclose to a *customer* the amount, or likely amount, of any fee payable for its services as early as practicable in the *firm's* dealings with the *customer*. **CONC 4.4.2 R** requires a *credit broker* to disclose any such fee agreed with the *customer* in writing or in another *durable medium*.
       [**Note:** paragraphs 2.2, 7th bullet, 3.7l and 4.9 of *CBG*]

(6)   Where a *firm* makes an introduction of the type referred to in **CONC 2.5.8 R (19)** the *firm* should ensure that the *customer's* consent is preceded by a full explanation of the key features and key risks of the product to which the introduction applies.
       [**Note:** paragraph 4.17f of *CBG*]

(7)   A *customer's* personal data must be processed fairly and lawfully and only for specified purposes. While it may be possible to pass sensitive personal data in specified and limited circumstances to certain third parties without the *customer's* consent where a condition of the Data Protection Act 1998 is satisfied, a *firm* (other than where it is under a statutory obligation to pass personal data to a third party) should generally seek the *customer's* consent before passing such personal data to a third party.
       [**Note:** paragraph 3.9t (box) of *CBG*]

(8)   An example of where it is likely to be unfair for a *credit broker* in receipt of a *customer's* personal data to pass it to a third party, is where the personal data is passed on in return for a fee to a claims management firm, without the *customer's* consent.

2.5.10 R   FCA

In **CONC 2.5.8 R (14)**:

(1)   payment protection product means a product or feature of a product designed to offer *customers* short-term protection against potential loss of income, by providing the means for them to meet (or temporarily suspend) their financial obligations including *repayments* under a *credit agreement*. Payment protection products include, in particular, short term income protection, debt freeze or debt waiver;

(2)   short-term income protection means a contract of insurance which provides a pre-agreed amount paid directly to the policyholder or the policyholder's nominee in the event that the policyholder experiences involuntary unemployment or incapacity as a result of accident or sickness and may be combined with other forms of insurance cover or include other benefits and which:
       (a)   has a maximum time-limited benefit duration;
       (b)   is written for a term which is less than 5 years and not predetermined by the term of any *credit agreement*; and
       (c)   can be terminated by the *insurer*.

2.5.11 G   FCA

In **CONC 2.5.8 R (14)** and **CONC 2.5.10 R (1)**, the protection offered by a payment protection product will typically be triggered by life events such as accident, sickness and/or unemployment, although other events may be covered where they impact on the *consumer's* ability to meet certain financial commitments. The triggering events will usually be specified in the agreement but may be subject to some discretion (by the provider) at the time of claim.

2.6   CONDUCT OF BUSINESS: DEBT COUNSELLING, DEBT ADJUSTING AND PROVIDING CREDIT INFORMATION SERVICES

Application

2.6.1 R   FCA

This section applies to a *firm* with respect to:
(1)   *debt counselling*; or
(2)   *debt adjusting*; or
(3)   *providing credit information services*.

Conduct of business

2.6.2 R   FCA

A *firm* must bring to the attention of a *customer* how the *firm* uses the *customer's* personal data it collects in a manner appropriate to the means of communication used.

[**Note:** paragraph 2.5e of *DMG*]

Unfair business practices

2.6.3 R   FCA

A *firm* must not:
(1)   by any means, including during a visit to a *customer*, coerce or use pressure to sell its services;
     [**Note:** paragraph 3.12o of *DMG*]
(2)   take advantage of a *customer's* lack of knowledge or understanding of the law relating to consumer credit or to insolvency or to otherwise dealing with debts in order to sell its services;
     [**Note:** paragraph 3.12o of *DMG*]
(3)   in relation to a visit to a *customer*:
     (a)   make an appointment to visit or visit at a time which is unreasonable or inconvenient from the *customer's* point of view, unless the *consumer* expressly consents;
        [**Note:** paragraph 3.15a of *DMG*]
     (b)   refuse to end the visit, refuse to leave the *customer's* home or ignore the *customer's* request not to return there;
        [**Note:** paragraph 3.15b of *DMG*]
     (c)   make a visit which is unreasonably or unnecessarily long;
        [**Note:** paragraph 3.15c of *DMG*]
(4)   conduct a telephone call with a *customer* who has called on a premium rate number for an unreasonable period.
     [**Note:** paragraph 3.18x of *DMG*]

Guidance on unfair business practices

2.6.4 G   FCA

(1)   It is an offence for a *person* carrying on the business of *debt counselling*, *debt adjusting* or *providing credit information services* to canvass its services off trade premises under section 154 of the *CCA*. The definition of canvassing in section 153 of the *CCA* would include an unsolicited personal visit to a *customer's* home.
     [**Note:** paragraph 3.13 of *DMG*]
(2)   Where a long telephone call is required, the *firm* should ensure the call is not made on a premium rate number.
(3)   It is unlikely to be reasonable for it to be necessary for a *customer* to make a call exceeding one hour to a *firm* in relation to *debt counselling* or *debt adjusting*. Where a call longer than 15 minutes is required for the *firm* to provide its service to the *customer*, the *firm* should ensure the call is not made on a premium rate phone number.
(4)   It is unlikely to be reasonable for a call by the *customer* to check on the status of the *customer's* case to last more than five minutes.

2.7   DISTANCE MARKETING

Application

2.7.1 R   FCA

(1)   Subject to (2) and (3), this section applies to a *firm* that carries on any distance marketing activity from an establishment in the *UK*, with or for a *consumer* in the *UK* or another *EEA State*.
(2)   This section does not apply to an *authorised professional firm* with respect to its *non-mainstream regulated activities*.
(3)   This section does not apply to an activity in relation to a *consumer hire agreement*.

The distance marketing disclosure rules

2.7.2 R   FCA
(1)   Subject to (2), (3) and (4), a *firm* must provide a *consumer* with the distance marketing information (**CONC 2 ANNEX 1 R**) in good time before the *consumer* is bound by a *distance contract* or offer.
       [**Note:** regulation 7(1) of SI 2004/2095]

[**Note:** articles 3(1) and 4(5) of the *Distance Marketing Directive*]
(2)   Where a *distance contract* is also a contract for *payment services* to which the *Payment Services Regulations* apply, a *firm* is required to provide to the *consumer* only the information specified in rows 7 to 12, 15, 16 and 20 of **CONC 2 ANNEX 1 R**.
(3)   Paragraph (1) and the requirement to provide the abbreviated distance marketing information (**CONC 2 ANNEX 2R**) in **CONC 2.7.11 R** do not apply to a *distance contract* which is also a *credit agreement* (other than an *authorised non-business overdraft agreement*) in respect of which the *firm* has disclosed the pre-contract credit information required by regulations 3, 4 or 5, as the case may be, and 7, of the *disclosure regulations* (information to be disclosed to a debtor before a regulated consumer credit agreement is made) in accordance with the *disclosure regulations*.
       [**Note:** regulation 7(6) of SI 2004/2095]
(4)   Paragraph (1) and the requirement to provide the abbreviated distance marketing information (**CONC 2 ANNEX 2**) in **CONC 2.7.11 R** do not apply to a *distance contract* which is also an *authorised non-business overdraft agreement* in respect of which:
       (a)   the *firm* has disclosed the information required by regulation 10(2) of the *disclosure regulations* (authorised non-business overdraft agreements) by means of the European Consumer Credit Information form in accordance with the *disclosure regulations* and, unless **CONC 2.7.12 R** would otherwise apply, a copy of the contractual terms and conditions;
       (b)   in the case of a voice telephony communication, the *firm* has:
              (i)   disclosed the information required by regulation 10(5) of the *disclosure regulations* in accordance with the *disclosure regulations*; and
              (ii)   provided a copy of the written agreement in accordance with section 61B(2)(b) of the *CCA*; or
       (c)   in the case of an agreement made using a means of distance communication, other than voice telephony communication, where a *firm* is unable to provide the information required by regulation 10(2) of the *disclosure regulations*, the *firm* has:
              (i)   provided a copy of the written agreement in accordance with section 61B(2)(c) of the *CCA*, and
              (ii)   unless **CONC 2.7.12 R** would otherwise apply, in relation to the prospective *distance contract*, provided information which accurately reflects the contractual obligations which would arise under the law presumed to be applicable to that contract.
       [**Note:** regulation 7(6) of SI 2004/2095]

2.7.3 R   FCA

A *firm* must ensure that the distance marketing information, the commercial purpose of which must be made clear, is provided in a clear and comprehensible manner in a way appropriate to the means of distance communication used with due regard, in particular, to the principles of good faith in commercial transactions and the legal principles governing the protection of those who are unable to give their consent.

[**Note:** regulation 7(2) and (3) of SI 2004/2095]

[**Note:** article 3(2) of the *Distance Marketing Directive*]

2.7.4 R   FCA

When a *firm* makes a voice telephony communication to a *consumer*, it must make its identity and the purposes of its call explicitly clear at the beginning of the conversation.

[**Note:** regulation 7(4) of SI 2004/2095]

[**Note:** article 3(3)(a) of the *Distance Marketing Directive*]

2.7.5 R   FCA

A *firm* must ensure that information on contractual obligations to be communicated to a *consumer* during the pre-contractual phase accurately reflects the contractual obligations which would result from the law presumed to be applicable to the *distance contract* if that contract is concluded.

[**Note:** regulation 7(5) of SI 2004/2095]

[**Note:** article 3(4) of the *Distance Marketing Directive*]

Terms and conditions, and form

2.7.6 R   **FCA**

A *firm* must communicate to the *consumer* all the contractual terms and conditions and the information referred to in the distance marketing disclosure *rules* (**CONC 2.7.2 R** to **CONC 2.7.5 R**) in a *durable medium*. That information must be made available and accessible to the *consumer* in good time before the *consumer* is bound by any *distance contract* or offer.

[**Note:** regulation 8(1) of SI 2004/2095]

[**Note:** articles 4(5) and 5(1) of the *Distance Marketing Directive*]

2.7.7 G   **FCA**
(1)   Activities in relation to a *consumer hire agreement* are not financial services within the meaning of the *Distance Marketing Directive* and do not fall within **CONC 2.7**. Instead such agreements fall within the Consumer Protection (Distance Selling) Regulations 2000 (SI 2000/2334).
(2)   A *firm* will provide information, or communicate contractual terms and conditions, to a *consumer* if another *person* provides the information, or communicates the terms and conditions, to the *consumer* on its behalf.

Commencing performance of the distance contract

2.7.8 R   **FCA**

The performance of the *distance contract* may only begin after the *consumer* has given approval.

[**Note:** article 7(1) of the *Distance Marketing Directive*]

Exception: successive operations

2.7.9 R   **FCA**

In the case of a *distance contract* comprising an initial service agreement, followed by successive operations or a series of separate operations of the same nature performed over time, the *rules* in this chapter only apply to the initial agreement.

[**Note:** regulation 5(1) of SI 2004/2095]

[**Note:** article 1(2) of the *Distance Marketing Directive*]

2.7.10 R   **FCA**
(1)   If there is no initial service agreement but the successive or separate operations of the same nature performed over time are performed between the same contractual parties, the distance marketing disclosure *rules* (**CONC 2.7.2 R** to **CONC 2.7.5 R**) will only apply:
     (a)   when the first operation is performed; and
     (b)   if no operation of the same nature is performed for more than a year, when the next operation is performed (the next operation being deemed the first in a new series of operations).
         [**Note:** regulation 5(2) of SI 2004/2095]

     [**Note:** recital 16 and article 1(2) of the *Distance Marketing Directive*]
(2)   In this section:
     (a)   "initial service agreement" includes the opening of a bank account or the making of a *credit-token agreement*;
     (b)   "operations" includes the deposit or withdrawal of funds to or from a bank account and payments by a credit card or a store card; and
     (c)   adding new elements to an initial service agreement, such as the ability to use an electronic payment instrument together with an existing retail banking service, does not constitute an "operation" but an additional contract to which the *rules* in this chapter apply.
         [**Note:** regulation 5 of SI 2004/2095]

     [**Note:** recital 17 of the *Distance Marketing Directive*]

Exception: voice telephony communications

2.7.11 R   **FCA**

In the case of voice telephony communication, and subject to the explicit consent of the *consumer*, only the abbreviated distance marketing information (**CONC 2 ANNEX 2** R) needs to be provided during that communication. However, unless another exception applies (such as the exemption for means of distance communication not enabling disclosure), a *firm* must still provide the distance marketing information (**CONC 2 ANNEX 1 R**) in a *durable medium* that is available and accessible to the *consumer* in good time before the *consumer* is bound by any *distance contract* or offer.

[**Note:** regulation 7(4)(b) of SI 2004/2095]

[**Note:** articles 3(3)(b) and 5(1) of the *Distance Marketing Directive*]

Exception: means of distance communication not enabling disclosure

2.7.12 R   FCA

A *firm* may provide the distance marketing information (**CONC 2 ANNEX 1** R) and the contractual terms and conditions in a *durable medium* immediately after the conclusion of a *distance contract*, if the contract has been concluded at a *consumer's* request using a means of distance communication that does not enable the provision of that information in that form in good time before the *consumer* is bound by any *distance contract* or offer.

[**Note:** article 5(2) of the *Distance Marketing Directive*]

Exception: contracts for payment services

2.7.13 G   FCA

Where a *distance contract* covers both *payment services* and non-*payment services*, the exception in **CONC 2.7.2 R (2)** applies only to the *payment services* aspects of the contract. A *firm* taking advantage of this exception will need to comply with the information requirements in Part 5 of the *Payment Services Regulations*.

Consumer's right to request paper copies and change the means of communication

2.7.14 R   FCA

At any time during the contractual relationship, the *consumer* is entitled, at request, to receive the contractual terms and conditions on paper. The *consumer* is also entitled to change the means of distance communication used unless this is incompatible with the contract concluded or the nature of the service provided.

[**Note:** regulation 8(2) and (4) of SI 2004/2095]

[**Note:** article 5(3) of the *Distance Marketing Directive*]

Unsolicited services

2.7.15 R   FCA
(1)   A *firm* must not enforce, or seek to enforce, any obligations under a *distance contract* against a *consumer* in the event of an unsolicited supply of services. The absence of a reply does not constitute consent.
(2)   This *rule* does not apply to the tacit renewal of a *distance contract*.
        [**Note:** regulation 15 of SI 2004/2095]

[**Note:** article 9 of the *Distance Marketing Directive*]

Mandatory nature of consumer's right

2.7.16 R   FCA

If a *consumer* purports to waive any of the *consumer's* rights created or implied by the *rules* in this section, a *firm* must not accept that waiver, nor seek to rely on or enforce it against the *consumer*.

[**Note:** article 12 of the *Distance Marketing Directive*]

Contracts governed by law of a third party state

2.7.17 R   FCA

If a *firm* proposes to enter into a *distance contract* with a consumer that will be governed by the law of a country outside the *EEA*, the *firm* must ensure that the *consumer* will not lose the protection created by the *rules* in this section if the *distance contract* has a close link with the territory of one or more *EEA States*.

[**Note:** regulation 16(3) of SI 2004/2095]

[**Note:** articles 12 and 16 of the *Distance Marketing Directive*]

2.8   E-COMMERCE

Application

2.8.1 R   FCA

This section applies to a *firm* carrying on an *electronic commerce activity* from an *establishment* in the *UK* with or for a *person* in the *UK* or another *EEA State*.

Information about the firm and its products or services

2.8.2 R   FCA

A *firm* must make at least the following information easily, directly and permanently accessible to the recipients of the *information society services* it provides:

(1)   its name;

(2)   the geographic address at which it is established;

(3)   the details of the *firm*, including its e-mail address, which allow it to be contacted rapidly and communicated with in a direct and effective manner;

(4)   an appropriate statutory status disclosure statement (**GEN 4 ANNEX 1 R**), together with a statement which explains that it is on the *Financial Services Register* and includes its firm reference number;

(5)   if it is a professional firm, or a *person* regulated by the equivalent of a *designated professional body* in another *EEA State*:

    (a)   the name of the professional body (including any *designated professional body*) or similar institution with which it is registered;

    (b)   the professional title and the *EEA State* where it was granted;

    (c)   a reference to the applicable professional rules in the *EEA State* of establishment and the means to access them; and

    (d)   where the *firm* undertakes an activity that is subject to VAT, its VAT number.

[**Note:** article 5(1) of the E]

2.8.3 R   FCA

If a *firm* refers to price, it must do so clearly and unambiguously, indicating whether the price is inclusive of tax and delivery costs.

[**Note:** article 5(2) of the E]

2.8.4 R   FCA

A *firm* must ensure that commercial communications which are part of, or constitute, an *information society service*, comply with the following conditions:

(1)   the commercial communication must be clearly identifiable as such;

(2)   the *person* on whose behalf the commercial communication is made must be clearly identifiable;

(3)   promotional offers must be clearly identifiable as such, and the conditions that must be met to qualify for them must be easily accessible and presented clearly and unambiguously; and

(4)   promotional competitions or games must be clearly identifiable as such, and the conditions for participation must be easily accessible and presented clearly and unambiguously.

[**Note:** article 6 of the E]

2.8.5 R   FCA

An unsolicited commercial communication sent by e-mail by a *firm* established in the *UK* must be identifiable clearly and unambiguously as an unsolicited commercial communication as soon as it is received by the recipient.

[**Note:** article 7(1) of the E]

Requirements relating to the placing and receipt of orders

2.8.6 R   FCA

A *firm* must (except when otherwise agreed by parties who are not *consumers*):

(1)   give an *ECA recipient* at least the following information, clearly, comprehensibly and unambiguously, and prior to the order being placed by the recipient of the service:

    (a)   the different technical steps to follow to conclude the contract;

    (b)   whether or not the concluded contract will be filed by the *firm* and whether it will be accessible;

    (c)   the technical means for identifying and correcting input errors prior to the placing of the order; and

    (d)   the languages offered for the conclusion of the contract;

(2)   indicate any relevant codes of conduct to which it subscribes and information on how those codes can be consulted electronically;

(3)   (when an *ECA recipient* places an order through technological means) acknowledge the receipt of the recipient's order without undue delay and by electronic means; and

(4)   make available to the *ECA recipient* appropriate, effective and accessible technical means allowing the recipient to identify and correct input errors prior to the placing of an order.

[**Note:** articles 10(1) and 11(1) and (2) of the E]

2.8.7 R   FCA

For the purposes of **CONC 2.8.6 R (3)**, an order and an acknowledgement of receipt are deemed to be received when the parties to whom they are addressed are able to access them.

2.8.8 R   FCA

Contractual terms and conditions provided by a *firm* to an *ECA recipient* must be made available in a way that allows the recipient to store and reproduce them.

[**Note:** article 10(3) of the E]

Exception: contract concluded by e-mail

2.8.9 R   FCA

The requirements relating to the placing and receipt of orders (**CONC 2.8.6 R**) do not apply to contracts concluded exclusively by exchange of e-mail or by equivalent individual communications.

[**Note:** articles 10(4) and 11(3) of the E]

2.9   PROHIBITION OF UNSOLICITED CREDIT TOKENS

Application

2.9.1 R   FCA

This section applies to any *firm*.

Prohibition

2.9.2 R   FCA

(1)   A *firm* must not give a *person* a *credit token* if he has not asked for it.
        [**Note:** section 51 of *CCA*]

(2)   A request in (1) must be in a document signed by the *person* making the request, unless the *credit-token agreement* is a *small borrower-lender-supplier agreement*.

(3)   Paragraph (1) does not apply to the giving of a *credit token* to a *person*:
        (a)   for use under a *credit-token agreement* already made; or
        (b)   in renewal or replacement of a *credit token* previously accepted by that *person* under a *credit-token agreement* which continues in force, whether or not varied.

2.9.3 G   FCA

Section 51 of the *CCA* was repealed by article 20(15) of the Financial Services and Markets Act 2000 (Regulated Activities) (Amendment) (No 2) Order 2013 (SI 2013/1881). However, section 51 is saved for the purposes of regulation 52 of the *Payment Services Regulations*, the effect being that the section continues to apply in relation to a *regulated credit agreement* in place of regulation 58(1)(b) of the *Payment Services Regulations*.

2.10   MENTAL CAPACITY GUIDANCE

Application

2.10.1 G   FCA

This section applies:

(1)   to a *firm*;

(2)   in relation to the following decisions:
        (a)   granting *credit* under a *regulated credit agreement*;
        (b)   significantly increasing the amount of *credit* under a *regulated credit agreement*; and
        (c)   setting a *credit limit* for running account credit.

2.10.2 G   FCA

(1)   The Mental Capacity Act 2005 sets out the legal framework concerning mental capacity for England and Wales. The Ministry of Justice has issued the Mental Capacity Act Code of Practice which, among other things, includes information on indications of mental capacity limitations and on how to assist people with making decisions.

(2)   The Adults with Incapacity (Scotland) Act 2000 provides the framework in Scotland for safeguarding the welfare and managing the finances of adults who lack capacity due to mental disorder or inability to communicate.

(3)   References in this section to a *firm's* knowledge, understanding, observation, suspicion, assumption or belief include that of the *firm's* employees, *appointed representatives*, agents and any others who act on behalf of the *firm*.
        [**Note:** footnote 2 of *MCG*]

(4)   In making a decision within **CONC 2.10.1 G**, a *firm* should consider the *customer's* individual circumstances.

     [**Note:** paragraph 2.4 of *MCG*]

Mental capacity

2.10.3 G   FCA

Mental capacity is a person's ability to make a decision. Whether or not a *customer* has the ability to understand, remember, and weigh up relevant information will determine whether the *customer* is able to make a responsible borrowing decision based on that information.

[**Note:** paragraph 2.1 of *MCG*]

2.10.4 G   FCA

A *firm* should assume a *customer* has mental capacity at the time the decision has to be made, unless the *firm* knows, or is told by a *person* it reasonably believes should know, or reasonably suspects, that the *customer* lacks capacity.

[**Note:** paragraph 3.1 of *MCG*]

2.10.5 G   FCA

Where a *firm* reasonably suspects a *customer* has, or may have, some form of mental capacity limitation which would constrain the *customer's* ability to make a decision to borrow, the *firm* should not regard the *customer* as lacking capacity to make the decision unless the *firm* has taken reasonable steps without success to assist the *customer* to make a decision.

[**Note:** paragraph 3.2 of *MCG*]

2.10.6 G   FCA

Amongst the most common potential causes of mental capacity limitations are the following examples, a mental health condition, dementia, a learning disability, a developmental disorder, a neurological disability or brain injury and alcohol or drug (including prescribed drugs) induced intoxication.

[**Note:** paragraph 2.9 of *MCG*]

2.10.7 G   FCA

Where a *firm* understands or reasonably suspects a *customer* has a condition of a type in **CONC 2.10.6 G**, this does not necessarily mean that the *customer* does not have the mental capacity to make an informed borrowing decision. See also **CONC 2.10.15 G**.

[**Note:** paragraph 2.10 of *MCG*]

Indications that a person may have some form of mental capacity limitation

2.10.8 G   FCA

A *firm* is likely to have reasonable grounds to suspect a *customer* may have some form of mental capacity limitation if the *firm* observes a specific indication (behavioural or otherwise) that could be indicative of some form of limitation of the *customer's* mental capacity. Examples (amongst others) of indications might include:

(1)   where a *firm* has an existing relationship with a *customer*, the *customer* making a decision that appears to the *firm* to be unexpected or out of character;

(2)   a *person* who is likely to have an informed view of the matter, such as a relative, close friend, carer or clinician raising a concern with the *firm* as to the capacity of the *customer* to make a decision about borrowing;

(3)   the *firm* understands or has reason to believe the *customer* has been diagnosed as having an impairment which led to the *customer* not having had mental capacity for similar decisions in the past;

(4)   the *firm* understands or has reason to believe the customer does not understand what the customer is applying for;

(5)   the *firm* understands or has reason to believe the *customer* is unable to understand the information and explanations provided by the *firm*, in particular concerning the key risks of entering into the agreement;

(6)   the *firm* understands or has reason to believe the *customer* is unable to retain information and explanations provided by the *firm* to enable the *customer* to make the decision to borrow;

(7)   the *firm* understands or has reason to believe the *customer* is unable to weigh up the information and explanations provided by the *firm* to enable the *customer* to make the decision to borrow;

(8)   the *customer* is unable to communicate a decision to borrow by any reasonable means;

(9)   the *customer* being confused about the personal information that the *firm* requires, such as date of birth or address.

[**Note:** paragraphs 3.14 and 3.15 of *MCG*]

Practices and procedures

2.10.9 G   FCA

(1)   A *firm* should not unfairly discriminate against a *customer* who it understands, or reasonably suspects, has a mental capacity limitation, in particular, by inappropriately denying the *customer* access to *credit*. [**Note:** paragraph 4.8 of *MCG*]

(2)   It would not be inappropriate not to grant *credit* nor significantly increase the amount of *credit* under an agreement nor set a *credit* limit for running account credit where the *firm* reasonably believes the agreement or decision would be voidable at the instance of the *customer* or the agreement is void.

2.10.10 G   FCA

(1)   In accordance with *Principle 6*, *firms* should take reasonable steps to ensure they have suitable business practices and procedures in place for the fair treatment of *customers* who they understand, or reasonably suspect, have or may have a mental capacity limitation. [**Note:** paragraph 4.1 of *MCG*]

(2)   **CONC 7.2.1 R** requires *firms* to establish and implement arrears policies and procedures, which include policies and procedures for the fair and appropriate treatment of *customers* the *firm* understands or reasonably suspects of having mental capacity limitations.

2.10.11 G   FCA

A *firm* should document practices and procedures to set out the steps that it takes when it receives applications for *credit* from such *customers*.

[**Note:** paragraph 4.2 of *MCG*]

2.10.12 G   FCA

Where a *firm* understands, or reasonably suspects, a *customer* has or may have a mental capacity limitation the *firm* should use its business practices and procedures to:

(1)   assist the *customer*, where possible, to make an informed borrowing decision; and

(2)   ensure its lending decision is informed and responsible in the circumstances and mitigates the potential risks to the *customer*.

[**Note:** paragraphs 4.3 and 4.5 of *MCG*]

2.10.13 G   FCA

As stated in the Mental Capacity Act Code of Practice, it is important to balance a person's right to make a decision with that person's right to safety and protection when they are unable to make decisions to protect themselves.

[**Note:** paragraph 4.5 (box) of *MCG*]

2.10.14 G   FCA

Firms should present clear, jargon-free information in explaining *credit agreements* in a way that makes it as easy as possible for the *customer* to understand. *Firms* should consider ways to present information in alternative, more 'user-friendly' formats where it appears appropriate to do so, subject to compliance with the relevant statutory requirements.

[**Note:** paragraph 4.20 of *MCG*]

2.10.15 G   FCA

Where a *firm* knows, or reasonably suspects, that a *customer* has or may have one of the conditions in **CONC 2.10.6 G** this could justifiably act as a trigger for the *firm* to consider the potential specific steps in giving effect to the *firm's* practices and procedures for assessing:

(1)   whether or not the *customer* appears able to understand, remember, and weigh up the information and explanations provided and, when having done so, make an informed borrowing decision;

(2)   whether the *customer* appears able to afford to make *repayments* under the *credit agreement* in a *sustainable* manner without adverse consequences to the *customer's* financial circumstances; and

(3)   whether the *credit* the *customer* is seeking is clearly unsuitable (given the *customer's* individual circumstances and, to the extent that the *firm* is aware, the *customer's* intended use of the *credit*).

[**Note:** paragraphs 2.5 and 2.11 of *MCG*]

2.10.16 G   FCA

Firms' practices and procedures should be designed to assist *customers* that *firms* understand have, or reasonably suspect of having, mental capacity limitations to overcome, to the extent possible, the effect of the limitations and place them, to the extent possible, on an equivalent basis to *customers* who do not have such limitations, to increase the likelihood of *customers* being able to make informed borrowing decisions.

[**Note:** paragraph 4.4 of *MCG*]

Allowing sufficient time for decisions

2.10.17 G   FCA

Where a *firm* understands, or reasonably suspects, a *customer* has or may have a mental capacity limitation it should consider allowing the *customer*:

(1)   sufficient time in the circumstances to weigh up the information and explanations the *firm* has given;

(2)   sufficient time in the circumstances to make an informed borrowing decision;

(3)   to defer a decision to borrow to a later date.

[**Note:** paragraphs 4.26, 4.27 and 4.28 of *MCG*]

Sustainability of borrowing

2.10.18 G   FCA

Where a *firm* understands, or reasonably suspects, a *customer* has or may have a mental capacity limitation it should apply a high level of scrutiny to the *customer's* application for *credit*, in order to mitigate the risk of the *customer* entering into *unsustainable* borrowing (see **CONC 5.2** and **CONC 5.3**).

[**Note:** paragraphs 4.32 and 4.33 of *MCG*]

2.10.19 G   FCA

(1)   A *firm* should balance the risk of a *customer* taking on *unsustainable* borrowing against inappropriately or unnecessarily denying *credit* to a *customer*.

(2)   Where a *firm* understands or reasonably suspects a *customer* has or may have a mental capacity limitation, it should undertake an appropriate and effective *creditworthiness assessment* or assessment required by **CONC 5.2.2 R (1)** and it would be appropriate not to place over-reliance on information provided by the *customer* for the assessment.

[**Note:** paragraph 4.34 of *MCG*]

2.10.20 G   FCA

Where a *firm* understands, or reasonably suspects, a *customer* has or may have a mental capacity limitation the *firm* should take particular care that the *customer* is not provided with *credit* which the *firm* knows, or reasonably believes, to be unsuitable to the *customer's* needs, even where the *credit* would be affordable.

[**Note:** paragraph 4.43 of *MCG*] FCA

2 ANNEX 1   DISTANCE MARKETING INFORMATION

This Annex belongs to **CONC 2.7.2 R** (The distance marketing disclosure rules)

Information about the firm
(1)   The name and the main business of the *firm*, the geographical address at which it is established and any other geographical address relevant for the *consumer's* relations with the *firm*.
(2)   Where the *firm* has a representative established in the *consumer's EEA State* of residence, the name of that representative and the geographical address relevant for the *consumer's* relations with that representative.
(3)   Where the *consumer's* dealings are with any professional other than the *firm*, the identity of that professional, the capacity in which he is acting with respect to the *consumer*, and the geographical address relevant to the *consumer's* relations with that professional.
(4)   The particulars of the public register in which the *firm* is entered, its registration number in that register and the particulars of the relevant supervisory authority, including an appropriate statutory status disclosure statement (**GEN 4**), a statement that the *firm* is on the *Financial Services Register* and its firm reference number.
Information about the financial service
(5)   A description of the main characteristics of the service the *firm* will provide.
(6)   The total price to be paid by the *consumer* to the *firm* for the financial service, including all related fees, charges and expenses, and all taxes paid through the *firm* or, where an exact price cannot be indicated, the basis for the calculation of the price enabling the *consumer* to verify it.
(7)   Where relevant, notice indicating that the service is related to instruments involving special risks related to their specific features or the operations to be executed, or whose price depends on fluctuations in the financial markets outside the firm's control and that past performance is no indicator of future performance.
(8)   Notice of the possibility that other taxes or costs may exist that are not paid via the *firm* or imposed by it.

(9)   Any limitations on the period for which the information provided is valid, including a clear explanation as to how long the *firm's* offer applies as it stands.

(10)   The arrangements for payment and performance.

(11)   Details of any specific additional cost to the *consumer* for using a means of distance communication.

Information about the contract

(12)   The existence or absence of any right to cancel under section 66A or 67 of the *CCA* or the cancellation *rules* in **CONC 11.1** and, where there is such a right, its duration and the conditions for exercising it, including information on the amount which the *consumer* may be required to pay (or which may not be returned to the *consumer*) in accordance with those provisions or *rules*, as well as the consequences of not exercising the right to cancel.

(13)   The minimum duration of the contract, in the case of services to be performed permanently or recurrently.

(14)   Information on any rights the parties may have to terminate the contract early or unilaterally under its terms, including any penalties imposed by the contract in such cases.

(15)   Practical instructions for exercising any right to cancel, including the address to which any cancellation notice should be sent.

(16)   The *EEA State* or States whose laws are taken by the *firm* as a basis for the establishment of relations with the *consumer* prior to the conclusion of the contract.

(17)   Any contractual clause on the law applicable to the contract or on the competent court, or both.

(18)   In which language, or languages, the contractual terms and conditions and the other information in this Annex will be supplied and in which language, or languages, the *firm*, with the agreement of the *consumer*, undertakes to communicate during the duration of the contract.

Information about redress

(19)   How to complain to the *firm*, whether complaints may subsequently be referred to the *Financial Ombudsman Service* and, if so, the methods for having access to that body, together with equivalent information about any other applicable named complaints scheme

(20)   Whether compensation may be available from the *compensation scheme*, or any other named compensation scheme, if the *firm* is unable to meet its liabilities.

[**Note:** Recitals 21 and 23 to, and article 3(1) of, the *Distance Marketing Directive*]FCA

2 ANNEX 2   ABBREVIATED DISTANCE MARKETING INFORMATION

This Annex belongs to **CONC 2.7.11 R.**

(1)   The identity of the *person* in contact with the *consumer* and his link with the *firm*.

(2)   A description of the main characteristics of the financial service.

(3)   The total price to be paid by the *consumer* to the *firm* for the financial service, including all taxes paid via the *firm* or, where an exact price cannot be indicated, the basis for the calculation of the price enabling the *consumer* to verify it.

(4)   Notice of the possibility that other taxes and/or costs may exist that are not paid via the *firm* or imposed by the *firm*.

(5)   The existence or absence of any right to cancel in accordance with the cancellation provisions or *rules* (in sections 66A or 67 of the *CCA* or in **CONC 11.1**) and, where the right to cancel exists, its duration and the conditions for exercising it, including information on the amount the *consumer* may be required to pay on the basis of the cancellation provisions or *rules*.

(6)   That other information is available on request and the nature of that information

[**Note:** article 3(3)(b) of the *Distance Marketing Directive*]

CHAPTER 3
FINANCIAL PROMOTIONS AND COMMUNICATIONS WITH CUSTOMERS

3.1   APPLICATION

[**3.80**]
[**Note**: Until 31 March 2015, transitional provisions apply to **CONC 3**: see **CONC TP 6**.1]

Who? What?

3.1.1 R   FCA

This chapter, unless a *rule* in **CONC 3** specifies differently, applies to a *firm*.

3.1.2 G   FCA

Under section 39(3) of the *Act*, a *firm* is responsible for *financial promotions communicated* by its *appointed representatives* when acting as such.

3.1.3 R   FCA

This chapter, unless a *rule* in **CONC 3** specifies differently, applies to:
(1)   a communication with a *customer* in relation to a *credit agreement*;
(2)   the *communication* or *approval* for *communication* of a *financial promotion* in relation to a *credit agreement*;
(3)   a communication with a *customer* in relation to *credit broking*;
(4)   the *communication* or *approval* for *communication* of a *financial promotion* in relation to *credit broking*;
(5)   a communication with a *borrower* or a prospective *borrower* in relation to *operating an electronic system in relation to lending*; and
(6)   the *communication* or *approval* for *communication* of a *financial promotion* to a *borrower* or a prospective *borrower* in relation to *operating an electronic system in relation to lending*.

3.1.4 R   FCA

The clear fair and not misleading *rule* in **CONC 3.3.1 R** and the general requirements *rule* in **CONC 3.3.2 R** and the *guidance* in **CONC 3.3.5 G** to **CONC 3.3.11 G** also, unless a *rule* or *guidance* in those paragraphs specifies differently, apply to:
(1)   a communication with a *customer* in relation to *debt counselling* or *debt adjusting*; and
(2)   the *communication* or *approval* for *communication* of a *financial promotion* in relation to *debt counselling* or *debt adjusting*.

3.1.5 R   FCA

CONC 3.3.1 R also applies to:
(1)   a communication with a *customer* in relation to a *consumer hire agreement*;
(2)   the *communication* or *approval* for *communication* of a *financial promotion* in relation to a *consumer hire agreement*; and
(3)   a communication with a *customer* in relation to *providing credit information services*.

3.1.6 R   FCA

CONC 3 does not apply to:
(1)   a *financial promotion* or a communication which expressly or by implication indicates clearly that it is solely promoting *credit agreements* or *consumer hire agreements* or *P2P agreements* for the purposes in each case of a *customer's* business;
(2)   a *financial promotion* or a communication to the extent that it relates to *qualifying credit*; or
(3)   an *excluded communication*.

3.1.7 R   FCA

(1)   **CONC 3** does not apply (apart from the provisions in (2)) to a *financial promotion* or communication that consists of only one or more of the following:
      (a)   the name of the *firm* (or its *appointed representative*);
      (b)   a logo;
      (c)   a contact point (address (including e-mail address), telephone, facsimile number and website address);
      (d)   a brief, factual description of the type of product or service provided by the *firm*.
(2)   The provisions in **CONC 3** which apply to a *financial promotion* or communication which falls within (1) are:
      (a)   **CONC 3.1, CONC 3.5.1 R** and **CONC 3.6.1 R** (application);
      (b)   **CONC 3.3.1 R** (clear, fair and not misleading);
      (c)   **CONC 3.3.3 R** (credit regardless of status);
      (d)   **CONC 3.5.3 R, CONC 3.5.5 R, CONC 3.6.6 R** (requirement for representative example or typical APR etc);
      (e)   **CONC 3.5.7 R** (other financial promotions requiring a representative APR);
      (f)   **CONC 3.5.12 R** (restricted expressions) and **CONC 3.6.8 R** (restricted expressions); and
      (g)   any other *rules* in *CONC* which are necessary or expedient to apply the rules in (a) to (f).

3.1.8 G   FCA

CONC 3.1.7 R (1) does not enable detailed information to be given about *credit* available from the *firm*. *Firms* should note that the image advertising exclusion in **CONC 3.1.7 R (1)** is subject to compliance with the *rules* specified in (2), including the *rules* which require the inclusion of a *representative APR* in specified circumstances. A name or logo may trigger the requirement to include a *representative APR*. *Firms* should not include any information not referred to in **CONC 3.1.7 R (1)** and should avoid the use of names, logos or addresses, for example, which attempt to convey additional product or cost-related information.

Where?

3.1.9 R FCA

This chapter applies to a *firm* in relation to:
(1)   a communication with, or the *communication* or *approval* for *communication* of a *financial promotion* to, a *person* in the *UK*;
(2)   the *communication* of an *unsolicited real time financial promotion*, unless it is made from a place, and for the purposes of a business which is only carried on, outside the *UK*; and
(3)   the *communication* or *approval* for *communication* of a *financial promotion* that is an *electronic commerce communication* to a *person* in an *EEA State* other than the *UK*;

and for the purposes of the application of this chapter, it is immaterial whether the *credit agreement* or the *consumer hire agreement* to which the *financial promotion* or communication relates is subject to the law of a country outside the *UK*.

3.2   FINANCIAL PROMOTION GENERAL GUIDANCE

3.2.1 G FCA

The *rules* in this chapter adopt various concepts from the restriction on financial promotions by *unauthorised persons* in section 21(1) of the *Act* (Restrictions on financial promotion). *Guidance* on that restriction and the communications which are exempt from it is contained in **PERG 8** (Financial promotion and related activities) and that *guidance* will be relevant to interpreting these *rules*. In particular, *guidance* on the meaning of:
(1)   'communicate' is in **PERG 8.6** (Communicate); and
(2)   'invitation or inducement' and 'engage in investment activity' (two elements which, with 'communicate', make up the definition of 'financial promotion') is in **PERG 8.4** (Invitation or inducement).

3.2.2 G FCA

The Privacy and Electronic Communications (EC Directive) Regulations 2003 apply to unsolicited telephone calls, fax messages and electronic mail messages for direct marketing purposes. The Information Commissioner's Office has produced guidance on the Regulations.

3.3   THE CLEAR FAIR AND NOT MISLEADING RULE AND GENERAL REQUIREMENTS

3.3.1 R FCA
(1)   A *firm* must ensure that a communication or a *financial promotion* is clear, fair, and not misleading.
[**Note**: paragraphs 2.2 of *ILG*, 3.16 of *DMG* and 3.1 of *CBG*]
(2)   If, for a particular communication or *financial promotion*, a *firm* takes reasonable steps to ensure it complies with (1), a contravention does not give rise to a right of action under section 138D of the *Act*.

General requirements

3.3.2 R FCA

A *firm* must ensure that a communication or a *financial promotion*:
(1)   uses plain and intelligible language;
(2)   is easily legible (or, in the case of any information given orally, clearly audible);
(3)   specifies the name of the *person* making the communication or *communicating* the *financial promotion* or the *person* on whose behalf the *financial promotion* is made; and
(4)   in the case of a communication or *financial promotion* in relation to *credit broking*, indicates to the *customer* the identity of the *lender* (where it is known).
[**Note**: paragraph 4.8a of *CBG*]
[**Note**: regulation 3 of *CCAR 2004* and regulation 3 of *CCAR 2010*]

3.3.3 R FCA

A *firm* must not in a *financial promotion* or a communication to a *customer* suggest or state, expressly or by implication, that *credit* is available regardless of the *customer's* financial circumstances or status.
[**Note**: paragraphs 3.7o of *CBG* and 5.2 of *ILG*]

3.3.4 G FCA

(1)   A *firm's* trading name, internet address or logo, in particular, could fall within **CONC 3.3.3 R**.
       [**Note**: paragraph 5.2 (box) of *ILG*]

(2)   If *credit* is described as pre-approved, in accordance with **CONC 3.5.12 R** the provision of the *credit* should be free of any conditions regarding the *customer's* credit status, and the *lender* or, in relation to a *P2P agreement* the *operator of an electronic system in relation to lending*, should have carried out the required assessment under **CONC 5**.

Guidance on clear, fair and not misleading

3.3.5 G   FCA

A firm should ensure that each communication and each *financial promotion*:

(1)   is accurate and, in particular, should not emphasise any potential benefits of a product or service without also giving a fair and prominent indication of any relevant risks;

(2)   is sufficient for, and presented in a way that is likely to be understood by, the average member of the group to whom it is directed, or by whom it is likely to be received;

(3)   does not disguise, diminish or obscure important information, statements or warnings; and

(4)   is clearly identifiable as such.
       [**Note**: in relation to identifying marketing material as such, paragraphs 3.7p of *CBG* and 3.18q of *DMG*]

3.3.6 G   FCA

If a communication or a *financial promotion* names the *FCA*, *PRA* or both as the regulator of a *firm* and refers to matters not regulated by the *FCA*, *PRA* or both, the *firm* should ensure that the communication or *financial promotion* makes clear that those matters are not regulated by the *FCA*, *PRA* or both.

3.3.7 G   FCA

When *communicating* information, a *firm* should consider whether omission of any relevant fact will result in information given to the *customer* being insufficient, unclear, unfair or misleading.

3.3.8 G   FCA

If a communication or a *financial promotion* compares a product or service with one or more other products (whether or not provided by the *firm*), the *firm* should ensure that the comparison is meaningful and presented in a fair and balanced way.

3.3.9 G   FCA

A *firm* should in a *financial promotion* or other communication which includes a premium rate telephone number indicate in a prominent way the likely total cost of a premium rate call including the price per minute of a call, the likely duration of calls and the total cost a *customer* would incur if the *customer* calls for the full estimated duration.
[**Note**: paragraphs 3.9h of *CBG* and 3.18x (box) of *DMG*]

Unfair business practices: financial promotions and communications

3.3.10 G   FCA

Examples of practices that are likely to contravene the clear, fair and not misleading *rule* in **CONC 3.3.1 R** include:

(1)   stating or implying that a *firm* is a *lender* (where this is not the case);
       [**Note**: paragraph 3.7e (box) of *CBG*]

(2)   misleading a *customer* as to the availability of a particular *credit* product;
       [**Note**: paragraph 3.9p of *CBG*]

(3)   concealing or misrepresenting the identity or name of the *firm*;
       [**Note**: paragraph 3.7g (box) of *CBG*

(4)   using false testimonials, endorsements or case studies;
       [**Note**: paragraph 3.18s of *DMG*]

(5)   using false or unsubstantiated claims as to the *firm's* size or experience or pre-eminence;
       [**Note**: paragraph 3.18t of *DMG*]

(6)   in relation to *debt solutions*, claiming or implying that a *customer* will be free of debt in a specified period of time or making statements emphasising a debt-free life or that a *debt solution* is a stress free or immediate solution;
       [**Note**: paragraphs 3.18u and 3.18v of *DMG*]

(7)   providing online tools, which recommend a particular *debt solution* as suitable for a *customer*, such as, budget calculators or advice websites:

       (a)   which do not carry out a sufficiently full assessment of a *customer's* financial position; or

       (b)   which fail to provide clear warnings to a *customer* that financial data entered into a tool has to be accurate;

[**Note**: paragraph 3.20c of *DMG*]

(8)   emphasising any savings available to a *customer* by proposing to reschedule a *customer's* debts, without explaining that a *lender* is not obliged to accept less in settlement of the *customer's* debts than it is entitled to, nor to freeze interest and charges and that the result may be to increase the *total amount payable* or the period over which it is to be paid and to impair the *customer's* credit rating;
    [**Note**: paragraph 3.18l of *DMG*]

(9)   suggesting that a *customer's repayments* will be lower under a proposed agreement without also mentioning (where applicable) that the duration of the agreement will be longer or that the *total amount payable* will be higher.
    [**Note**: paragraph 5.13 of *ILG*]

Guidance on misleading introductions

3.3.11 G   FCA

Misleading a *customer* as to the availability of a particular *credit* product is likely to include stating or implying that the *firm* will introduce the *customer* to a provider of a standard personal loan based on repayment by instalments or of an overdraft facility on a current account (for example, a bank or building society) or of a credit card, but instead introducing the *customer* to a provider of *high-cost short-term credit*.
[**Note**: paragraph 3.9p (box) of *CBG*]

3.4   RISK WARNING FOR HIGH-COST SHORT-TERM CREDIT

[**Note**: Until the end of 30 June 2014, transitional provisions apply to **CONC 3.4**: see **CONC TP 3** 1]

Risk warnings

3.4.1 R   FCA

(1)   A *firm* must not *communicate* or *approve* for *communication* a *financial promotion* in relation to *high-cost short-term credit*, unless it contains the following risk warning:
    "Warning: Late repayment can cause you serious money problems. For help, go to moneyadviceservice.org.uk".

(2)   The risk warning in (1) must be included in a *financial promotion* contained in an *electronic communication* unless by reason of the limited space available on the medium in question it is not reasonably practicable to include the warning.

(3)   Instead of the website address in paragraph (1), a *firm* may include the Money Advice Service's logo registered community trade mark number EU009695909.

(4)   The risk warning must be included in a *financial promotion* in a prominent way.

3.4.2 G   FCA

The Money Advice Service has granted a licence to use the logo referred to in **CONC 3.4.1 R (3)** for the purposes of that *rule*. The terms of the licence are available from the Money Advice Service.

3.5   FINANCIAL PROMOTIONS ABOUT CREDIT AGREEMENTS NOT SECURED ON LAND

Application

3.5.1 R   FCA

This section applies:

(1)   to a *financial promotion* in relation to *consumer credit lending*;

(2)   to a *financial promotion* in relation to *credit broking* in relation to *regulated credit agreements*;

(3)   to a *financial promotion* in relation to activities specified in article 36A(1)(a) or (c) of the *Regulated Activities Order* in relation to what would be *regulated credit agreements* but for a relevant provision, but only where the *firm* also carries on such activities in relation to *regulated credit agreements*;

and in each case, other than to *financial promotions* to the extent that they relate to agreements secured on *land*.

Prohibition on financial promotion where goods etc. not sold for cash

3.5.2 R   FCA

A *financial promotion* must not be *communicated* where it indicates a *firm* is willing to provide *credit* under a regulated *restricted-use credit agreement* relating to *goods* or services to be supplied by any *person*, when at the time the *financial promotion* is *communicated*, the *firm* or any *supplier* under such an agreement does not hold itself out as prepared to sell the *goods* or provide the services (as the case may be) for cash.
[**Note**: section 45 of *CCA*]

Content of financial promotions

3.5.3 R   FCA

(1)   Where a *financial promotion* includes a rate of interest or an amount relating to the *cost of credit* whether expressed as a sum of money or a proportion of a specified amount, the *financial promotion* must also:

     (a)   include a representative example in accordance with **CONC 3.5.5 R**, and

     (b)   specify a postal address at which the *person* making the *financial promotion* may be contacted.

     [**Note**: regulation 4(1) of *CCAR 2010*]

(2)   Paragraph (1)(a) does not apply where the *financial promotion*:

     (a)   falls within **CONC 3.5.7 R**; and

     (b)   does not indicate a rate of interest or an amount relating to the *cost of credit* other than the *representative APR*.

     [**Note**: regulation 4(2) of *CCAR 2010*]

(3)   Paragraph (1)(b) does not apply to *financial promotions*:

     (a)   communicated by means of television or radio broadcast; or

     (b)   in any form on the premises of a *dealer* or *lender*, other than *financial promotions* in writing which *customers* are intended to take away; or

     (c)   which include the name and address of a *dealer*; or

     (d)   which include the name and postal address of a *credit broker*.

     [**Note**: regulation 4(1)b of *CCAR 2010*]

Guidance on showing interest rates and cost of credit

3.5.4 G   FCA

A rate of interest for the purpose of **CONC 3.5.3 R (1)** is not limited to an annual rate of interest but would include a *monthly* or daily rate or an *APR*. It would also include reference to 0% credit. An amount relating to the *cost of credit* would include the amount of any fee or charge, or any *repayment* of *credit* (where it includes interest or other charges).

[**Note**: paragraph 6.7 of BIS Guidance on regulations implementing the *Consumer Credit Directive*]

Representative example

3.5.5 R   FCA

(1)   The representative example in **CONC 3.5.3 R (1)** must comprise the following items of information:

     (a)   the rate of interest, and whether it is fixed or variable or both, expressed as a fixed or variable percentage applied on an annual basis to the amount of *credit* drawn down;

     (b)   the nature and amount of any other charge included in the *total charge for credit*;

     (c)   the *total amount of credit*;

     (d)   the *representative APR*;

     (e)   in the case of *credit* in the form of a deferred payment for specific *goods*, services, *land* or other things, the *cash price* and the amount of any *advance payment*;

     (f)   the duration of the agreement;

     (g)   the *total amount payable*; and

     (h)   the amount of each *repayment* of *credit*.

     [**Note**: regulation 5(1) of *CCAR 2010*]

     [**Note**: article 4 of the *Consumer Credit Directive*]

(2)   The items of information required by (1)(a), (b), (c), (e), (f) and (g) must be those which the *firm communicating* or *approving* the *financial promotion* reasonably expects at the date on which the *financial promotion* is made to be representative of *credit agreements* to which the *representative APR* applies and which are expected to be entered into as a result of the promotion.

     [**Note**: regulation 5(2) of *CCAR 2010*]

(3)   For (1)(e), the reference in (2) to "*credit agreements* to which the *representative APR* applies" is to agreements providing *credit* for the purchase of specific *goods*, services, *land* or other things, to which the *representative APR* applies.

     [**Note**: regulation 5(3) of *CCAR 2010*]

(4)   For the purposes of (1)(a), where the *credit agreement* provides for different ways of drawdown with different rates of interest, the rate of interest shall be assumed to be the highest rate applied to the most common drawdown mechanism for the product to which the agreement relates.

     [**Note**: regulation 5(4) of *CCAR 2010*]

(5)   The information required by (1) must be:

     (a)   specified in a clear and concise way;

     (b)   accompanied by the words "representative example";

     (c)   presented together with each item of information being given equal prominence; and

     (d)   given greater prominence than:

(i)   any other information relating to the *cost of credit* in the *financial promotion*, except for any statement relating to an obligation to enter into a contract for an *ancillary service* referred to in **CONC 3.5.10 R**; and

(ii)   any indication or incentive of a kind referred to in **CONC 3.5.7 R**.

[**Note**: regulation 5(6) of *CCAR 2010*]

(6)   A *financial promotion* for a *credit agreement* with no fixed duration is not required to include the duration of the agreement or the *total amount payable* or the amount of each *repayment* of *credit*.
[**Note**: regulation 5(1)f of *CCAR 2010*]

(7)   A *financial promotion* for an *authorised non-business overdraft agreement* is not required to include a *representative APR*.
[**Note**: regulation 5(5) of *CCAR 2010*]

Guidance on the representative example

3.5.6 G   FCA

(1)   The representative example in **CONC 3.5.5 R** should not be limited to being representative of agreements featured in the *financial promotion* if the *firm communicating* or *approving* the *financial promotion* expects other agreements to be entered into as a result of the *financial promotion*, whether with the *firm* or with a third party.
[**Note**: paragraph 6.8 of BIS Guidance on regulations implementing the *Consumer Credit Directive*]

(2)   Where the agreement provides for compounding, the rate of interest in **CONC 3.5.5 R (1)** should generally be the effective annual interest rate and *lenders* should use the same assumptions to calculate this interest rate as they do for the *APR*; the assumptions set out in **CONC APP 1.2**. If a *firm* uses a different rate to calculate the rate of interest in **CONC 3.5.5 R (1)** it must clearly explain this to the *customer*, so that the *customer* is clear whether and to what extent the rate used is comparable with rates shown by other *lenders*.
[**Note**: paragraph 6.13 of BIS Guidance on regulations implementing the *Consumer Credit Directive*]

(3)   If a rate of interest or a charge applies for only a limited period, the duration of the period and the rate or amount following that period, if known or ascertainable, should be shown.
[**Note**: paragraph 6.13 of BIS Guidance on regulations implementing the *Consumer Credit Directive*]

(4)   For charges other than interest which are included in the *total charge for credit*, the *financial promotion* should in each case make clear the nature of the charge and the amount of the charge if ascertainable or a reasonable estimate of the charge, making clear in that case it is an estimate.
[**Note**: paragraph 6.13 of BIS Guidance on regulations implementing the *Consumer Credit Directive*]

(5)   The *total amount of credit* equates to the sum available to the *customer* to use and does not include charges which are financed by the *credit agreement*; those are part of the *total charge for credit*.

(6)   For showing the *cash price*, the total *cash price* of all items should be shown, together with the price of each item individually.

Other financial promotions requiring a representative APR

3.5.7 R   FCA

(1)   A *financial promotion* must include the *representative APR* if it:

(a)   indicates in any way, whether expressly or by implication, including by means of the name given to the business or the product or of an address used by a business for the purposes of electronic communication, that:

(i)   *credit* is available to persons who might otherwise consider their access to *credit* restricted; or

(ii)   any of the terms on which *credit* is available is more favourable (either for a limited period or generally) than corresponding terms applied in any other case or by any other *lender*; or

(iii) the way in which the *credit* is offered is more favourable (either for a limited period or generally) than corresponding ways used in any other case or by any other *lender*; or

[**Note**: regulation 6 of *CCAR 2010*]

(b)   includes an incentive (including but not limited to gifts, special offers, discounts and rewards) to apply for *credit* or to enter into an agreement under which *credit* is provided;

(c)   includes an incentive (in the form of a statement about the speed or ease of processing, considering or granting an application, or of making funds available) to apply for *credit* or to enter into an agreement under which *credit* is provided.

(2)   The *representative APR* must be given greater prominence than any indication or incentive in (1).

(3)   This *rule* does not apply to a *financial promotion* for an *authorised non-business overdraft agreement*.

3.5.8 G   FCA

Whether or not a reference to speed or ease in **CONC 3.5.7 R (1)(C)** constitutes an incentive to apply for *credit* or enter into an agreement under which *credit* is provided would depend upon the circumstances, including whether it is likely to persuade or influence a *customer* to take those steps or is merely a factual statement about the product or service.

Annual percentage rate of charge

3.5.9 R   FCA

In a *financial promotion*:
(1)   an *APR* must be shown as "%APR";
(2)   where an *APR* is subject to change it must be accompanied by the word "variable"; and
(3)   the *representative APR* must be accompanied by the word "representative".

[**Note**: regulation 7 of *CCAR 2010*]

Ancillary services

3.5.10 R   FCA
(1)   A *financial promotion* must include a clear and concise statement in respect of any obligation to enter into a contract for an *ancillary service* where:
     (a)   the conclusion of that contract is compulsory in order to obtain the *credit* or to obtain it on the terms and conditions promoted; and
     (b)   the cost of that *ancillary service* cannot be determined in advance.

     [**Note**: regulation 8 of *CCAR 2010*]
(2)   The statement in (1) must:
     (a)   be no less prominent than any information in **CONC 3.5.5 R (1)** included in the *financial promotion*; and
     (b)   be presented together with any *representative APR* included in the *financial promotion*.
(3)   This *rule* does not apply to a *financial promotion* for an *authorised non-business overdraft agreement*.

Security

3.5.11 R   FCA

Where a *financial promotion* concerns a facility for which *security* is or may be required, the promotion must:
(1)   state that *security* is or may be required; and
(2)   specify the nature of the *security*.

[**Note**: regulation 9 of *CCAR 2010*]

Restricted expressions

3.5.12 R   FCA
(1)   A *financial promotion* must not include:
     (a)   the word "overdraft" or any similar expression as describing any agreement for *running-account credit*, except where an agreement enables a *customer* to overdraw on a current account;
     (b)   the expression "interest free" or any similar expression indicating that a *customer* is liable to pay no greater amount in respect of a transaction financed by *credit* than he would be liable to pay as a cash purchaser for the like transaction, except where the *total amount payable* does not exceed the *cash price*;
     (c)   the expression "no deposit" or any similar expression, except where no *advance payments* are to be made;
     (d)   the expression "loan guaranteed", "pre-approved" or "no credit checks" or any similar expression, except where the agreement is free of any conditions regarding the credit status of the *customer*; or
     (e)   the expression "gift", "present" or any similar expression, except where there are no conditions which would require the *customer* to repay the *credit* or to return the item that is the subject of the claim.

[Note: regulation 10 of *CCAR 2010*]

(2)   A *financial promotion* must not include for a *repayment* of *credit* the expression "weekly equivalent" or any expression to like effect or any expression of any other periodical equivalent, unless weekly *repayments* or the other periodical payments are provided for under the agreement.

(3)   In this *rule*, "cash purchaser" means a *person* who, for money consideration, acquires *goods*, *land* or other things or is provided with services under a transaction which is not financed by *credit*.

Total charge for credit and APR

3.5.13 R   FCA

(1)   Where a *financial promotion* is about *running-account credit* and the *credit limit* applicable is not yet known on the date the *financial promotion* is made, but it is known that it will be less than £1,200, the *credit limit* must be assumed to be an amount equal to that maximum limit.
        [Note: paragraph 1 of schedule to *CCAR 2010*]

(2)   The assumption in (1) applies in place of the assumption in **CONC APP 1.2.5 R** for the purpose of calculating the *total charge for credit*.

Total charge for credit and APR: tolerances for APR

(3)   For a *financial promotion*, it is sufficient to show an *APR* if there is included in the promotion:
        (a)   a rate which exceeds the *APR* by not more than one; or
        (b)   a rate which falls short of the *APR* by not more than 0.1; or
        (c)   where applicable, a rate determined in accordance with (4) or (5).

        [Note: paragraph 2 of schedule to *CCAR 2010*]

Total charge for credit and APR: tolerance where repayments are nearly equal

(4)   Where an agreement under which all *repayments* but one are equal and that one *repayment* does not differ from any other *repayment* by more whole pence than there are *repayments* of *credit*, there may be included in a *financial promotion* about the agreement a rate found under **CONC APP 1.2.4 R** as if that one *repayment* were equal to the other *repayments* to be made under the agreement.
        [Note: paragraph 3 of schedule to *CCAR 2010*]

Total charge for credit and APR: tolerance regarding interval between relevant date and first repayment

(5)   Where a *credit agreement* provides that:
        (a)   three or more *repayments* are to be made at equal intervals; and
        (b)   the interval between the relevant date and the first *repayment* is greater than the interval between the *repayments*;
        a *financial promotion* about the agreement may include a rate found under **CONC APP 1.2.4 R** as if the interval between the relevant date and the first *repayment* were shortened so as to be equal to the interval between the *repayments*.
        [Note: paragraph 4 of schedule to *CCAR 2010*]

(6)   The relevant date in (5) is:
        (a)   where a date on which the *customer* is entitled to require provision of the subject of a *credit agreement* is specified in or can be determined from the agreement, the earliest such date;
        (b)   in any other case, the date of making the agreement.

3.6   FINANCIAL PROMOTIONS ABOUT CREDIT AGREEMENTS SECURED ON LAND

Application

3.6.1 R   FCA

This section applies:

(1)   to a *financial promotion* in relation to *consumer credit lending* in relation to *regulated credit agreements* secured on *land*; and

(2)   to a *financial promotion* in relation to *credit broking* in relation to *regulated credit agreements* secured on *land*;

and in both cases other than *financial promotions* to the extent that they relate to *qualifying credit*.

Definitions

3.6.2 R   FCA

In this section, for a *financial promotion* relating to *credit* to be provided under a *credit agreement* "relevant date" means:

(1)   in a case where a date is specified in or determinable under the agreement at the date of its making as that on which the *customer* is entitled to require provision of anything the subject of the agreement, the earliest such date; and

(2)   in any other case, the date of the making of the agreement.

Prohibition on financial promotion where goods etc not sold for cash

3.6.3 R   FCA

A *financial promotion* must not be *communicated* where it indicates a *firm* is willing to provide *credit* under a regulated *restricted-use credit agreement* secured on *land* relating to *goods* or services to be supplied by any *person*, when at the time the *financial promotion* is *communicated*, the *firm* or any *supplier* under such an agreement does not hold itself out as prepared to sell the *goods* or provide the services (as the case may be) for cash.
[**Note:** section 45 of *CCA*]

Content of financial promotions

3.6.4 R   FCA

(1)   Where a *financial promotion* includes any of the amounts referred to in (5) to (7) of **CONC 3.6.10 R** the promotion must:

     (a)   include all the other items of information (other than any item inapplicable to the particular case) listed in **CONC 3.6.10 R**; and

     (b)   specify a postal address at which the *person* making the promotion may be contacted, except in the case of a *financial promotion*:

         (i)   *communicated* by means of television or radio broadcast;

         (ii)   in any form on the premises of a *lender* or *dealer* (other than a *financial promotion* in writing which *customers* are intended to take away);

         (iii)   which includes the name and address of a *dealer*; or

         (iv)   which includes the name and a postal address of a *credit broker*.
         [**Note:** regulation 4(1) of *CCAR 2004*]

(2)   The items of information listed in **CONC 3.6.10 R** must be given equal prominence and must be shown together as a whole.
     [**Note:** regulation 4(2) of *CCAR 2004*]

(3)   Any information in any book, catalogue, leaflet or other document which is likely to vary from time to time must be taken for the purpose of (2) to be shown together as a whole if:

     (a)   it is set out together as a whole in a separate document issued with the book, catalogue, leaflet or other document;

     (b)   the other information in the *financial promotion* is shown together as a whole in the book, catalogue, leaflet or other document; and

     (c)   the book, catalogue, leaflet or other document identifies the separate document in which the information likely to vary is set out.

     [**Note:** regulation 4(3) of *CCAR 2004*]

Statements in relation to security

3.6.5 R   FCA

(1)   Where a *financial promotion* concerns a facility for which *security* is or may be required, the promotion must:

     (a)   state that *security* is or may be required; and

     (b)   specify the nature of the *security*.
     [**Note:** regulation 7(1) of *CCAR 2004*]

(2)   Where, in the case of a *financial promotion*, the *security* comprises or may comprise a mortgage or charge on the *customer's* home:

     (a)   except where (c) applies, the *financial promotion* must contain a warning in the form: "YOUR HOME MAY BE REPOSSESSED IF YOU DO NOT KEEP UP REPAYMENTS ON A MORTGAGE OR ANY OTHER DEBT SECURED ON IT";

     (b)   where the *financial promotion* indicates that *credit* is available for the payment of debts due to other *lenders*, the warning in (a) must be preceded by the words: "THINK CAREFULLY BEFORE SECURING OTHER DEBTS AGAINST YOUR HOME."

     (c)   where the *credit agreement* is or would be an agreement of a kind described in (3), the *financial promotion* must contain a warning in the form: "CHECK THAT THIS MORTGAGE WILL MEET YOUR NEEDS IF YOU WANT TO MOVE OR SELL YOUR HOME OR YOU WANT YOUR FAMILY TO INHERIT IT. IF YOU ARE IN ANY DOUBT, SEEK INDEPENDENT ADVICE".
     [**Note:** regulation 7(2) of *CCAR 2004*]

(3)   The kinds of agreement in (2)(c) are:

(a) any *credit agreement* under which no instalment *repayments* secured by the mortgage on the *customer's* home, and no payment of interest on the *credit* (other than interest charged when all or part of the *credit* is repaid voluntarily by the *customer*), are due or capable of becoming due while the *customer* continues to occupy the mortgaged *land* as the *customer's* main residence; and

(b) any *credit agreement*:

    (i) which is secured by a mortgage which the *lender* cannot enforce by taking possession of or selling (or concurring with any other *person* in selling) the mortgaged *land* or any part of it while the *customer* continues to occupy it as the *customer's* main residence; and

    (ii) under which, although interest payments may become due, no full or partial repayment of the *credit* secured by the mortgage is due or capable of becoming due while the *customer* continues to occupy the mortgaged *land* as the *customer's* main residence.

      [**Note**: regulation 7(3) of *CCAR 2004*]

(4) Where a *financial promotion* is for a mortgage or other loan secured on property and *repayments* are to be made in a currency other than sterling, the *financial promotion* must contain a warning in the form:

"CHANGES IN THE EXCHANGE RATE MAY INCREASE THE STERLING EQUIVALENT OF YOUR DEBT".

[**Note**: regulation 7(4) of *CCAR 2004*]

(5) The warnings provided for in (2) and (4):

(a) must be given greater prominence in a *financial promotion* than is given to:

    (i) any rate of charge other than the *typical APR*; and

    (ii) any indication or incentive of a kind referred to in **CONC 3.6.6 R (1)**; and

(b) must be given no less prominence in a *financial promotion* than is given to any of the items listed in **CONC 3.6.10 R** that appear in the *financial promotion*.

    [**Note**: regulation 7(6) of *CCAR 2004*]

(6) Paragraphs (2), (3), (4) and (5) do not apply in the case of a *financial promotion* which:

(a) is communicated by means of television or radio broadcast in the course of programming the primary purpose of which is not financial promotion; or

(b) is communicated by exhibition of a film (other than exhibition by television broadcast); or

(c) contains only the name of the *firm communicating* the *financial promotion*.

    [**Note**: regulation 7(8) of *CCAR 2004*]

Annual percentage rate of charge

3.6.6 R FCA

(1) A *financial promotion* must specify the *typical APR* if the promotion:

(a) specifies any other rate of charge;

(b) includes any of the items of information listed in **CONC 3.6.10 R (5)** to (7);

(c) indicates in any way, whether expressly or by implication, including by means of the name given to a business or of an address used by a business for the purposes of *electronic communication*, that:

    (i) *credit* is available to *persons* who might otherwise consider their access to *credit* restricted; or

    (ii) any of the terms on which *credit* is available is more favourable (either for a limited period or generally) than corresponding terms applied in any other case or by any other *lender*; or

    (iii) the way in which the *credit* is offered is more favourable (either for a limited period or generally) than corresponding ways used in any other case or by any other *lender*; or

(d) includes any incentive (including but not limited to, gifts, special offers, discounts and rewards) to apply for *credit* or to enter into an agreement under which *credit* is provided;

    [**Note**: regulation 8(1) of *CCAR 2004*]

(e) includes an incentive (in the form of a statement about the speed or ease of, processing, considering or granting an application or of making funds available) to apply for *credit* or to enter into an agreement under which *credit* is provided.

(2) A *financial promotion* may not indicate the range of *APRs* charged where *credit* is provided otherwise than by specifying, with equal prominence, both:

(a) the *APR* which the *firm communicating* or *approving* the *financial promotion* reasonably expects, at the date on which the promotion is *communicated* or *approved*, would be the lowest *APR* at which *credit* would be provided under not less than 10% of the agreements which will be entered into as a result of that promotion; and

(b)   the *APR* which the *firm communicating* or *approving* the *financial promotion* reasonably expects, at that date, would be the highest *APR* at which *credit* would be provided under any of the agreements which will be entered into as a result of that promotion.
[**Note**: regulation 8(2) of *CCAR 2004*]

(3)   An *APR* must be shown as "%APR".
[**Note**: regulation 8(3) of *CCAR 2004*]

(4)   Where an *APR* is subject to change it must be accompanied by the word "variable".
[**Note**: regulation 8(4) of *CCAR 2004*]

(5)   The *typical APR* in a *financial promotion* must be:
    (a)   accompanied by the word "typical";
    (b)   presented together with any of the items listed in **CONC 3.6.10 R** that are included in the promotion;
    (c)   given greater prominence in the promotion than:
       (i)   any other rate of charge;
       (ii)   any items listed in **CONC 3.6.10 R**; and
       (iii)   any indication or incentive of a kind referred to in (1); and
    (d)   in the case of a promotion in printed or electronic form which includes any of the items listed in **CONC 3.6.10 R**, shown in characters at least one and a half times the size of the characters in which those items appear.
[**Note**: regulation 8(5) of *CCAR 2004*]

(6)   In the case of a *financial promotion* relating to a *borrower-lender agreement* enabling the *customer* to overdraw on a current account under which the *lender* is the Bank of England or an *authorised* person with permission to accept deposits, there may be substituted for the *typical APR* a reference to the statement of:
    (a)   a rate, expressed to be a rate of interest, being a rate determined as the rate of the *total charge for credit* calculated on the assumption that only interest is included in the *total charge for credit*, and
    (b)   the nature and amount of any other charge included in the *total charge for credit*.
[**Note**: regulation 8(6) of *CCAR 2004*]

3.6.7 G   FCA

Whether or not a reference to speed or ease in **CONC 3.6.6 R (1)(E)** constitutes an incentive to apply for *credit* or enter into an agreement under which *credit* is provided would depend upon the circumstances, including whether it is likely to persuade or influence a *customer* to take those steps or is merely a factual statement about the product or service.

Restricted expressions

3.6.8 R   FCA

(1)   A *financial promotion* must not include:
    (a)   the word "overdraft" or any similar expression as describing any agreement for *running-account credit*, except where the agreement enables a *customer* to overdraw on a current account;
    (b)   the expression "interest free" or any similar expression indicating that a *customer* is liable to pay no greater amount in respect of a transaction financed by *credit* than he would be liable to pay as a cash purchaser for the like transaction, except where the *total amount payable* by the *customer* does not exceed the *cash price*;
    (c)   the expression "no deposit" or any similar expression, except where no *advance payments* are to be made;
    (d)   the expression "loan guaranteed" or "pre-approved" or "no credit checks" or any similar expression, except where the agreement is free of any conditions regarding the credit status of the *customer*;
    (e)   the expression "gift", "present" or any similar expression, except where there are no conditions which would require the *customer* to repay the *credit* or return the item that is the subject of the claim.

[**Note**: regulation 9 of *CCAR 2004*]

(2)   A *financial promotion* must not include for a *repayment* of *credit* the expression "weekly equivalent" or any expression to like effect or any expression of any other periodical equivalent, unless weekly repayments or the other periodical payments are provided for under the agreement.

(3)   In this *rule* "cash purchaser" means a *person* who for money consideration acquires *goods*, *land* or other things or is provided with services, under a transaction which is not financed by *credit*.

Total charge for credit and any APR: assumptions about running account credit

3.6.9 R   FCA

(1)   In the case of a *financial promotion* about *running-account credit*, the following assumptions
      have effect for the purpose of calculating the *total charge for credit* and any *APR*,
      notwithstanding the terms of the transaction advertised and in place of any assumptions in
      CONC APP 1.1.11 R to **CONC APP 1.1.18 R** that might otherwise apply:

  (a)   the amount of the *credit* to be provided must be taken to be £1,500 or, in a case where
        credit is to be provided subject to a *credit limit* of less than £1,500, an amount equal
        to that limit;

  (b)   it must be assumed that the *credit* is provided for a period of one year beginning with
        the relevant date;

  (c)   it must be assumed that the *credit* is provided in full on the relevant date;

  (d)   where the rate of interest will change at a time provided in the transaction within a
        period of three years beginning with the relevant date, the rate must be taken to be
        the highest rate at any time obtaining under the transaction in that period;

  (e)   where the agreement provides *credit* to finance the purchase of *goods*, services, *land*
        or other things and also provides one or more of:

    (i)   cash loans;

    (ii)   *credit* to refinance existing indebtedness of the *customer*, whether to the
           lender or another *person*; and

    (iii) *credit* for any other purpose;

        and either or both different rates of interest and different charges are payable for the
        credit provided for all or some of these purposes, it must be assumed that the rate of
        interest and charges payable for the whole of the *credit* are those applicable to the
        provision of *credit* for the purchase of *goods*, services, *land* or other things; and

  (f)   it must be assumed that the *credit* is repaid:

    (i)   in twelve equal instalments; and

    (ii)   at *monthly* intervals, beginning one *month* after the relevant date.
           [**Note**: paragraph 1 of schedule 1 to *CCAR 2004*]

Total charge for credit and any APR: tolerances in disclosure of an APR

(2)   For the purposes of **CONC 3.6**, it is sufficient compliance with the requirement to show an
      APR if there is included in the *financial promotion*:

  (a)   a rate which exceeds the *APR* by not more than one; or

  (b)   a rate which falls short of the *APR* by not more than 0.1;

      or in a case to which (3) or (4) applies, a rate determined in accordance with those
      sub-paragraphs or whichever of them applies to that case.
      [**Note**: paragraph 2 of schedule 1 to *CCAR 2004*]

Total charge for credit and any APR: tolerance where repayments are nearly equal

(3)   In the case of an agreement under which all *repayments* but one are equal and that one
      repayment does not differ from any other *repayment* by more whole pence than there are
      repayments of *credit*, there may be included in a *financial promotion* about the agreement a
      rate found under **CONC APP 1.1.9 R** as if that one *repayment* were equal to the other
      repayments to be made under the agreement.
      [**Note**: paragraph 3 of schedule 1 to *CCAR 2004*]

Total charge for credit and any APR: tolerance of interval between relevant date and first repayment

(4)   In the case of an agreement under which:

  (a)   three or more *repayments* are to be made at equal intervals; and

  (b)   the interval between the relevant date and the first *repayment* is greater than the
        interval between the *repayments*;

      a *financial promotion* about the agreement may include a rate found under **CONC APP
      1.1.9 R** as if the interval between the relevant date and the first *repayment* were shortened
      so as to be equal to the interval between *repayments*.
      [**Note**: paragraph 4 of schedule 1 to *CCAR 2004*]

Information required in a financial promotion

3.6.10 R   FCA

(1)   The amount of *credit* which may be provided under a *credit agreement* or an indication of
      one or both of the maximum amount and the minimum amount of *credit* which may be
      provided.
      [**Note**: paragraph 1 of schedule 2 to *CCAR 2004*]

Deposit of money in an account

(2)   A statement of any requirement to place on deposit any sum of money in any account with
      any *person*.
      [**Note**: paragraph 2 of schedule 2 to *CCAR 2004*]

Cash price

(3)   In the case of a *financial promotion* about *credit* to be provided under a *borrower-lender-
      supplier agreement*, where the *financial promotion* specifies *goods*, services, *land* or other
      things having a particular *cash price*, the acquisition of which from an identified *dealer* may
      be financed by the *credit*, the *cash price* of such *goods*, services, *land* or other things.

[**Note**: paragraph 3 of schedule 2 to *CCAR 2004*]

Advance payment

(4)   A statement as to whether an *advance payment* is required and, if so, the amount or minimum amount of the payment expressed as a sum of money or a percentage.

[**Note**: paragraph 4 of schedule 2 to *CCAR 2004*]

Frequency, number and amount of repayments of credit

(5)

(a)   In the case of a *financial promotion* about *running-account credit*, a statement of the frequency of the *repayments* of *credit* under the transaction and of the amount of each *repayment* stating whether it is a fixed or minimum amount, or a statement indicating the manner in which the amount will be determined.

(b)   In the case of other *financial promotions*, a statement of the frequency, number and amounts of *repayments* of *credit*.

(c)   The amount of any *repayment* under this sub-paragraph may be expressed as a sum of money or as a specified proportion of a specified amount (including the amount outstanding from time to time).

[**Note**: paragraph 5 of schedule 2 to *CCAR 2004*]

Other payments and charges

(6)

(a)   Subject to (b) and (c), a statement indicating the description and amount of any other payments and charges which may be payable under the agreement promoted in the *financial promotion*.

(b)   Where the liability of the *customer* to make any payment cannot be ascertained at the date the *financial promotion* is *communicated*, a statement indicating the description of the payment in question and the circumstances in which the liability to make it will arise.

(c)   Paragraphs (a) and (b) do not apply to any charge payable under the transaction to the *lender* or any other *person* on behalf of the *lender* upon failure by the *customer* or a relative of the *customer* to do or refrain from doing anything which the *customer* is required to do or refrain from doing, as the case may be.

[**Note**: paragraph 6 of schedule 2 to *CCAR 2004*]

Total amount payable by the customer

(7)   In the case of a *financial promotion* about *fixed-sum credit* to be provided under a *credit agreement* which is repayable at specified intervals or in specified amounts and other than cases under which the sum of the payments within (a) to (c) is not greater than the *cash price* referred to in (3), the *total amount payable*, being the total of:

(a)   *advance payments*;

(b)   the amount of *credit* repayable by the *customer*, and

(c)   the amount of the *total charge for credit*.

[**Note**: paragraph 7 of schedule 2 to *CCAR 2004*]

3.7 FINANCIAL PROMOTIONS AND COMMUNICATIONS: CREDIT BROKERS

Application

3.7.1 R   FCA

This section applies to a *financial promotion* or a communication with a *customer* in relation to *credit broking* in relation to a *regulated credit agreement*.

3.7.2 R   FCA

CONC 3.7.4 G also applies to a *financial promotion* or a communication with a *customer* in relation to the activities specified in article 36A(1)(a) or (c) of the *Regulated Activities Order* in relation to a *credit agreement* that would be a *regulated credit agreement* but for the *relevant provisions*.

3.7.2A R   FCA

CONC 3.7.5 R to CONC 3.7.8 G:

(1)   apply to a *financial promotion* or a communication with a *customer* in relation to *credit broking* whether or not it is in relation to a *regulated credit agreement*; but

(2)   do not apply to a *financial promotion* or a communication with a *customer* which clearly indicates that it is made solely in respect of *credit broking* in relation to a *credit agreement* secured by a *legal or equitable mortgage* on land.

Credit brokers' registered name, and status

3.7.3 R   FCA

A *firm* must, in a *financial promotion* or a document which is intended for *individuals* which relates to its *credit broking*, indicate the extent of its powers and in particular whether it works exclusively with one or more *lenders* or works independently.

[**Note**: section 160A(3) of *CCA*]
[**Note**: article 21(a) of the *Consumer Credit Directive*]

3.7.4 G   FCA

A *firm* should in a *financial promotion* or in a communication with a *customer*:

(1)   make clear, to the extent an average *customer* of the *firm* would understand, the nature of the service that the *firm* provides;
       [**Note**: paragraphs 3.7e and 4.8b of *CBG*]

(2)   indicate to the *customer* in a prominent way the existence of any financial arrangements with a *lender* that might impact upon the *firm's* impartiality in promoting a *credit* product to a *customer*;
       [**Note**: paragraphs 2.2, 6th bullet and 4.6 of *CBG*]

(3)   only describe itself as independent if it is able to provide access to a representative range of *credit* products from the relevant product market on competitive terms and is not constrained in providing such access, for example, because of one or more agreements with *lenders*; and
       [**Note**: paragraph 4.5 of *CBG*]

(4)   ensure that any disclosure about the extent of its independence is prominent and in accordance with the clear, fair not misleading *rule* in **CONC 3.3.1 R**, clear and easily comprehensible.
       [**Note**: paragraph 4.6 of *CBG*]

3.7.5 R   FCA

A *firm* must ensure that a *financial promotion* or a communication with a *customer* specifies the legal name of the *firm* as it appears in the *Financial Services Register* and not merely a trading name.

3.7.6 G   FCA

CONC 3.7.5 R requires all *financial promotions* and communications with *customers* to specify the legal name of the *firm*: the *rule* does not prohibit the use of trading names, but does require the legal name to be given in addition to any trading name used. If the *firm* is a company registered under the Companies Act 2006, the *firm's* legal name will be the name by which it is registered.

3.7.7 R   FCA

(1)   A *firm* which is a *credit broker* and not a *lender* must ensure that any *financial promotion* states prominently that the *firm* is a *credit broker* and that it is not a *lender*.

(2)   A *firm* which is both a *credit broker* and a *lender* must ensure that any *financial promotion* that solely promotes its services as a *credit broker* states prominently that the *financial promotion* is promoting the *firm's* services as a *credit broker* and not its services as a *lender*.

3.7.8 G   FCA

For the purposes of **CONC 3.7.7 R**, a statement will not be treated as prominent unless it is presented, in relation to other content of the *financial promotion*, in such a way that it is likely that the attention of the average *person* to whom the *financial promotion* is directed would be drawn to it.

3.8 FINANCIAL PROMOTIONS AND COMMUNICATIONS: LENDERS

Application

3.8.1 R   FCA

This section applies to a *financial promotion* or a communication with a *customer* in relation to *consumer credit lending*.

Unfair business practices

3.8.2 R   FCA

A *firm* must not in a *financial promotion* or a communication with a *customer*:

(1)   provide an application for *credit* with a pre-completed amount of credit which is not based on having carried out a *creditworthiness assessment* or an assessment required by **CONC 5.2.2 R (1)**; or
       [**Note**: paragraph 5.3 of *ILG*]

(2)   suggest or state, expressly or by implication, that providing *credit* is dependent solely upon the value of the equity in property on which the agreement is to be secured; or
       [**Note**: paragraph 5.4 of *ILG*]

(3)   promote *credit* where the *firm* knows, or has reason to believe, that the agreement would be unsuitable for that *customer* in the light of the *customer's* financial circumstances or, if known, intended use of the *credit*.
       [**Note**: paragraph 5.5 of *ILG*]

3.8.3 G   FCA

An agreement is likely to be unsuitable for the purposes of **CONC 3.8.2 R (3)** including in the following situations where a *firm*:

(1)   promotes, suggests or advises taking out a secured loan or to take out a secured loan to replace or convert an unsecured loan when it is clearly not in that *person's* best interests to do so at that time; or

(2)   promotes, suggests or advises taking out *high-cost short-term credit* which would be expensive as a means of longer term borrowing, as being suitable for sustained borrowing over a longer period.

[**Note**: paragraph 5.5 (box) of *ILG*]

3.8.4 G   FCA

For the purposes of **CONC 3.8.2 R (3)** the unsuitability of an agreement does not apply to the question of whether a *customer* should enter into a *regulated credit agreement* at all.

[**Note**: paragraph 5.5 (box) of *ILG*]

3.9   FINANCIAL PROMOTIONS AND COMMUNICATIONS: DEBT COUNSELLORS AND DEBT ADJUSTERS

Application

3.9.1 R   FCA

This section applies to a *financial promotion* or a communication with a *customer* in relation to *debt counselling* and to *debt adjusting*.

Financial promotions and communications

3.9.2 G   FCA

(1)   The clear, fair and not misleading *rule* in **CONC 3.3.1 R** applies to a communication with a *customer* or the *communication* or *approval* for *communication* of a *financial promotion* in relation to *debt counselling* or *debt adjusting* and in relation to a communication with a *customer* in relation to *providing credit information services*.

(2)   In the light of the complexity of *debt counselling*, it is unlikely that media which provide restricted space for messages would be a suitable means of making *financial promotions* about *debt solutions*.

Contents of financial promotions and communications

3.9.3 R   FCA

A *firm* must ensure that a *financial promotion* or a communication with a *customer* (to the extent a previous communication to the same *customer* has not included the following information) includes:

(1)   a statement of the services the *firm* offers;

(2)   a statement of any relationship with a business associate which is relevant to the services offered in the promotion;

[**Note**: paragraph 2.5a of *DMG*]

(3)   a statement setting out the level of fees charged for the *firm's* services, how they are calculated, what service they cover and where it is not possible to state an exact amount, a reasonable estimate of the anticipated fees, or the average level of its fees, for the service in question;

[**Note**: paragraphs 2.5c and 3.18f of *DMG*]

(4)   a statement of whether any aspect of the services is provided by a third party or at extra cost;

[**Note**: paragraphs 2.5a and 3.18f of *DMG*]

(5)   a statement that a *customer* may be eligible under the *Financial Ombudsman Service* and referring by a link or otherwise to the information the *firm* is required to publish under **DISP 1.2.1 R (1)**;

[**Note**: paragraph 2.5b of *DMG*]

(6)   where this is the case, a statement that the *firm's* service is profit-seeking;

[**Note**: paragraphs 2.5c and 3.18a of *DMG*]

(7)   where this is the case, a statement that the *firm's* service is offered in return for payment from the *customer*;

[**Note**: paragraphs 2.5c and 3.18a of *DMG*]

(8)   other than for a *not-for-profit debt advice body*, a reference to impartial information and to sources of assistance from *not-for-profit debt advice bodies*;

[**Note**: paragraph 2.5d of *DMG*]

(9)   where the *financial promotion* or communication sets out detail of how a *customer* might resolve debt problems by explaining options, the most important actual or potential advantages, disadvantages and risk of each option, including those of the *debt solution* offered by the *firm*;

[**Note**: paragraphs 2.5d and 3.18h of *DMG*]

(10)   a statement setting out the likely adverse effect of entering into the *debt solution* in question on the *customer's* credit rating;

[**Note**: paragraph 3.18g of *DMG*]

(11)   a statement setting out that evidence of entering into an individual voluntary arrangement, a debt relief order or a protected trust deed will be entered on a public register;
       [**Note**: paragraph 3.18g of *DMG*]

(12)   where applicable, a statement setting out that a *debt solution* is only available in a particular country of the *UK*;
       [**Note**: paragraph 3.18i of *DMG*]

(13)   where entry into a *debt solution* with the *firm* will lead to a period when payments to a *customer's lenders* or *owners* (in whole or in part) are not made or are retained by the *firm*, a warning of the likelihood of falling into arrears or increasing arrears and an explanation of when distributions would be made to *lenders* or *owners*;
       [**Note**: paragraph 3.18n of *DMG*]

(14)   a statement of the risks of entering into an individual voluntary arrangement or a protected trust deed, as the case may be, including of the following risks:
       (a)   if the arrangement or deed fails, the risk of bankruptcy;
       (b)   homeowners may need to release equity from the value of their homes to pay off debts, and that a remortgage may attract higher interest rates or, if no remortgage is available, an individual voluntary arrangement may be extended for 12 *months*;
       (c)   there are restrictions on the expenditure of a person who enters into an individual voluntary arrangement or a protected trust deed;
       (d)   the *customer's lenders* or *owners* may not approve the individual voluntary arrangement or the protected trust deed; and
       (e)   only unsecured debts included within the individual voluntary arrangement or protected trust deed may be discharged at the end of the period and unsecured debts not included remain outstanding; and
       [**Note**: paragraph 3.18o of *DMG*]

(15)   a statement that where another option for dealing with a *customer's* debts is available, that another option is available and may be suitable for the *customer*.
       [**Note**: paragraph 3.18r of *DMG*]

3.9.4 G   FCA

In **CONC 3.9.3 R (8)** making reference to impartial sources of information should include making *customers* aware of publications concerning dealing with creditors published by the Insolvency Service (England and Wales), the Department of Enterprise, Trade and Investment (Northern Ireland) or debt advice published by the Scottish Government.

3.9.5 R   FCA

A *financial promotion* or a communication with a *customer* by a *firm* must not:
(1)   falsely claim or imply that the help and debt advice is provided on a free, impartial or independent basis, where the *firm* has a profit-seeking motive;
       [**Note**: paragraph 3.18b of *DMG*]
(2)   falsely claim in any way that the *firm* is, or represents, a charitable or *not-for-profit body* or government or local government organisation;
       [**Note**: paragraph 3.18c of *DMG*]
(3)   promote a claims management service (within the meaning of section 4 of the Compensation Act 2006) as a way of managing a *customer's* debts;
       [**Note**: paragraph 3.18k of *DMG*]
(4)   claim or imply that the *firm* can guarantee a favourable outcome in negotiations with a *lender* or *owner* concerning the *customer's* debts;
       [**Note**: paragraph 3.18m of *DMG*]
(5)   unfairly request, suggest or direct a *customer* to call the *firm* using a premium rate telephone number.
       [**Note**: paragraph 3.18w of *DMG*]

3.9.6 G   FCA

An example of unfairly directing a *customer* to a premium rate telephone number may be to direct a *person* wishing to complain to such a number.

On-line promotion of debt solutions

3.9.7 R   FCA

A *firm* must not:
(1)   unless it is a *not-for-profit debt advice body* or a person who will provide such services, operate a look alike website designed to attract *customers* seeking free, charitable, not-for-profit or governmental or local governmental debt advice; or
       [**Note**: paragraph 3.20a of *DMG*]
(2)   seek to use internet search tools or search engines so as to mislead a *customer* into visiting its website when the *customer* is seeking free, charitable, not-for-profit or governmental or local governmental debt advice.
       [**Note**: paragraph 3.20b of *DMG*]

3.10   FINANCIAL PROMOTIONS NOT IN WRITING

Application

3.10.1 R   FCA

This section applies:
(1)   to a *financial promotion* in relation to *consumer credit lending*, *credit broking*, *debt counselling*, *debt adjusting*, *operating an electronic system in relation to lending*in relation to prospective *borrowers* or *borrowers* under *P2P agreements*;
(2)   in relation to the communication of a *financial promotion* that is not in writing.

Promotions that are not in writing

3.10.2 R   FCA

A *firm* must not *communicate* a solicited or unsolicited *financial promotion* that is not in writing, to a *customer* outside the *firm's* premises, unless the *person communicating* it:
(1)   only does so at an appropriate time of the day; and
(2)   identifies that *person* and the *firm* represented at the outset and makes clear the purpose of the communication.
     [**Note**: paragraphs 3.9d of *CBG* and 3.12b of *DMG*]

3.11   NOT APPROVING CERTAIN FINANCIAL PROMOTIONS

3.11.1 R   FCA

This section applies to a *financial promotion* in relation to a *credit agreement*, *credit broking*, *debt counselling*, *debt adjusting* and *operating an electronic system in relation to lending* in relation to prospective *borrowers* or *borrowers* under *P2P agreements*.

Requirement not to approve certain financial promotions

3.11.2 R   FCA

A *firm* must not *approve* a *financial promotion* to be made in the course of a personal visit, telephone conversation or other interactive dialogue.

3.11.3 G   FCA

CONC 3.11.2 R does not prevent the communication by a *firm* itself (i.e. a firm with a permission) of a *financial promotion*. A *firm's* approval of a *financial promotion* concerns approval for the communication of the promotion by an *unauthorised person* which is prevented by **CONC 3.11.2 R**.

CHAPTER 4
PRE-CONTRACTUAL REQUIREMENTS

4.1   CONTENT OF QUOTATIONS

Application

4.1.1 R   FCA

This section, apart from **CONC 4.1.4 R**, applies to:
(1)   a *firm* with respect to *consumer credit lending*; or
(2)   a *firm* with respect to *consumer hiring*;
including where the *firm* provides a quotation acting on behalf of a *customer*.

4.1.2 R   FCA

CONC 4.1.4 R applies to a *firm* with respect to *credit broking*, including where the *firm* provides a quotation acting on behalf of a *customer*.

Lenders and owners: contents of quotation for certain agreements

4.1.3 R   FCA
(1)   When a *firm* provides a quotation to a *customer* in connection with a prospective *credit agreement* which would or might be secured on the *customer's* home, the *firm* must include (or cause to be included) in the quotation a statement that such *security* would or might be required.
     [**Note**: regulation 3a of SI 1999/2725]
(2)   When a *firm* provides a quotation to a *customer* (C) in connection with a prospective *credit agreement* which would or might be secured on C's home under which, while C continues to occupy the home as C's main residence and either:
     (a)   no instalment *repayments* of the *credit* secured by a mortgage on C's home and no payment of interest on the *credit* (other than interest charged when all or part of the *credit* is repaid voluntarily by C), are due or capable of becoming due; or

(b)   the *lender* cannot enforce the *credit agreement* by taking possession of or selling (or
         concurring with any other *person* in selling) the home or any part of it while C
         continues to occupy it as C's main residence; and

(c)   where (b) applies, although interest payments may become due, no full or partial
         repayment of the *credit* secured by a mortgage is due or capable of becoming due.
         [**Note**: regulation 3B of SI 1999/2725]

the *firm* must include (or cause to be included) in the quotation the following statement:
"CHECK THAT THIS MORTGAGE WILL MEET YOUR NEEDS IF YOU WANT TO
MOVE OR SELL YOUR HOME OR YOU WANT YOUR FAMILY TO INHERIT IT. IF
YOU ARE IN DOUBT, SEEK INDEPENDENT ADVICE."
[**Note**: regulation 3A of SI 1999/2725]

(3)   When a *firm* provides a quotation to a *customer* (C) in connection with a prospective *credit
      agreement* which would or might be secured on C's home, other than an agreement to which
      (2) applies, the *firm* must include (or cause to be included) in the quotation the following
      statement:
      "YOUR HOME IS AT RISK IF YOU DO NOT KEEP UP REPAYMENTS ON A
      MORTGAGE OR OTHER LOAN SECURED ON IT."
      [**Note**: regulation 3b of SI 1999/2725]

(4)   When a *firm* provides a quotation to a *customer* in connection with a prospective *credit
      agreement* which would or might be secured on *land* and under which *repayments* would be
      made in a currency other than sterling, the *firm* must include (or cause to be included) in the
      quotation the following statement:
      "THE STERLING EQUIVALENT OF YOUR LIABILITY UNDER A FOREIGN CUR-
      RENCY MORTGAGE MAY BE INCREASED BY EXCHANGE RATE MOVEMENT."
      [**Note**: regulation 4 of SI 1999/2725]

(5)   When a *firm* provides a quotation to a *customer* in connection with a prospective agreement
      for the bailment of *goods* which would or might be secured on the *customer's* home, the *firm*
      must include (or cause to be included) in the quotation a statement that such security would
      or might be required.
      [**Note**: regulation 5a of SI 1999/2725]

(6)   When a *firm* provides a quotation to a *customer* in connection with a prospective agreement
      for the bailment of *goods* which would or might be secured on the *customer's* home, the *firm*
      must include (or cause to be included) in the quotation the following statement:
      "YOUR HOME IS AT RISK IF YOU DO NOT KEEP UP PAYMENTS ON A HIRE
      AGREEMENT SECURED BY A MORTGAGE OR OTHER SECURITY ON YOUR
      HOME."
      [**Note**: regulation 5b of SI 1999/2725]

Credit brokers: contents of quotation for certain agreements

4.1.4 R   FCA

(1)   When a *firm* provides a quotation to a *customer* in connection with a prospective *credit
      agreement* which would or might be secured on the *customer's* home, the *firm* must include
      (or cause to be included) in the quotation a statement that such *security* would or might be
      required.
      [**Note**: regulation 6 of SI 1999/2725]

(2)   When a *firm* provides a quotation to a *customer* (C) in connection with a prospective *credit
      agreement* which would or might be secured on C's home under which, while C continues
      to occupy the home as C's main residence and either:

      (a)   no instalment *repayments* of the *credit* secured by a mortgage on C's home and no
               payment of interest on the *credit* (other than interest charged when all or part of the
               credit is repaid voluntarily by C), are due or capable of becoming due; or

      (b)   the *lender* cannot enforce the *credit agreement* by taking possession of or selling (or
               concurring with any other *person* in selling) the home or any part of it while C
               continues to occupy it as C's main residence; and

      (c)   where (b) applies, although interest payments may become due, no full or partial
               repayment of the *credit* secured by a mortgage is due or capable of becoming due;

      the *firm* must include (or cause to be included) in the quotation the following statement:
      "CHECK THAT THIS MORTGAGE WILL MEET YOUR NEEDS IF YOU WANT TO
      MOVE OR SELL YOUR HOME OR YOU WANT YOUR FAMILY TO INHERIT IT. IF
      YOU ARE IN DOUBT, SEEK INDEPENDENT ADVICE."

(3)   When a *firm* provides a quotation to a *customer* (C) in connection with a prospective *credit
      agreement* which would or might be secured on C's home, other than an agreement to which
      (2) applies, the *firm* must include (or cause to be included) in the quotation the following
      statement:
      "YOUR HOME IS AT RISK IF YOU DO NOT KEEP UP REPAYMENTS ON A
      MORTGAGE OR OTHER LOAN SECURED ON IT."

(4)   When a *firm* provides a quotation to a *customer* in connection with a prospective *credit agreement* which would be secured on *land* and under which *repayments* would be made in a currency other than sterling, the *firm* must include (or cause to be included) in the quotation the following statement:
"THE STERLING EQUIVALENT OF YOUR LIABILITY UNDER A FOREIGN CURRENCY MORTGAGE MAY BE INCREASED BY EXCHANGE RATE MOVEMENT."

(5)   When a *firm* provides a quotation to a *customer* in connection with a prospective agreement for the bailment of *goods* which would or might be secured on the *customer's* home, the *firm* must include (or cause to be included) in the quotation a statement that such *security* would or might be required.

(6)   When a *firm* provides a quotation to a *customer* in connection with a prospective agreement for the bailment of *goods* which would or might be secured on the *customer's* home, the *firm* must include (or cause to be included) in the quotation the following statement:
"YOUR HOME IS AT RISK IF YOU DO NOT KEEP UP PAYMENTS ON A HIRE AGREEMENT SECURED BY A MORTGAGE OR OTHER SECURITY ON YOUR HOME."

Interpretation: quotations

4.1.5 R   FCA

(1)   Paragraphs (2) to (5) apply to **CONC 4.1.3 R** and **CONC 4.1.4 R** (rules on content of quotations).

(2)   "Quotation" means any document by which a *person* gives a *customer* information about the terms on which the *person* or a *lender* or *owner* is prepared to do business, but it does not include:

    (a)   a communication which is also a *financial promotion*;

    (b)   any document given to a *customer* under section 58 of the *CCA* (opportunity for withdrawal from prospective land mortgage);

    (c)   any document sent to a *customer* for signature which embodies the terms or such of them as it is intended to reduce to writing of a *credit agreement* or a *consumer hire agreement*; or

    (d)   any copy of an unexecuted agreement delivered or sent to a *customer* under section 62 of the *CCA* (duty to supply copy of unexecuted agreement).

(3)   Where the words of a statement which must be included in a quotation are specified, the statement must be:

    (a)   in capital letters;

    (b)   clear and legible; and

    (c)   prominent.

(4)   Providing a quotation includes making a quotation available temporarily.

(5)   In these *rules* as they apply to Scotland:

    (a)   any reference to bailment is a reference to hiring; and

    (b)   any reference to a mortgage or a charge on *land* is a reference to a standard security over *land* within the meaning of the Conveyancing and Feudal Reform (Scotland) Act 1970.

4.2   PRE-CONTRACT DISCLOSURE AND ADEQUATE EXPLANATIONS

Application

4.2.1 R   FCA

This section, unless otherwise stated in or in relation to a *rule*:

(1)   applies to a *firm* with respect to *consumer credit lending*;

(2)   applies to a *firm* with respect to *credit broking* where the *firm* has or takes on responsibility for providing the disclosures and explanations to *customers* required by this section;

(3)   does not apply to an agreement under which the *lender* provides the *customer* with *credit* which exceeds £60,260;

(4)   does not apply to an agreement secured on *land*; and

(5)   does not apply to a *borrower-lender agreement* enabling the *customer* to overdraw on a current account other than such an agreement which would be an *authorised non-business overdraft agreement*, but for the fact that the *credit* is not repayable on demand or within three *months*.
[**Note**: section 74(1D) of *CCA*]

4.2.2 G   FCA

For the agreements referred to in **CONC 4.2.1 R (3)**, **(4)** and **(5)**, a *firm* within **CONC 4.2.1 R (1)** or **CONC 4.2.1 R (2)** should consider whether it is necessary or appropriate to provide explanations of the matters in **CONC 4.2.5 R (2)**; in particular, a *firm* should consider highlighting the principal consequences to the *customer* including the consequences of missing payments or under-paying, including, where applicable, the risk of repossession of the *customer's* property.
[**Note**: section 55A(6) of *CCA* and paragraphs 3.1(box) of *ILG* and 3.5 of *SCLG*]

Other disclosure requirements

4.2.3 G   FCA

(1)   The *disclosure regulations* made under section 55 of the *CCA* which require information to be disclosed before a *regulated credit agreement* is made remain in force.

(2)   Failure to comply with the *disclosure regulations* has the effect that agreements are enforceable against a borrower or hirer (as defined in the *CCA*) only with an order of court and enforcement for that purpose includes a retaking of goods or *land* to which the agreement relates.

(3)   Other relevant disclosure requirements are found in **CONC 2.7** (distance marketing) and **CONC 2.8** (electronic commerce), the Financial Services (Distance Marketing) Regulations 2004 (SI 2004/2095), the Electronic Commerce (EC Directive) Regulations 2002 (SI 2002/2013) and the Consumer Protection from Unfair Trading Regulations 2008 (SI 2008/1277) and the Cancellation of Contracts made in the Consumer's home etc Regulations 2008 (SI 2008/1816).

4.2.4 G   FCA

The pre-contractual information disclosed under the *disclosure regulations* and the pre-contractual explanations required under **CONC 4.2.5 R** should take into account any preferences expressed, or information provided by, the *customer* where the *firm* would in principle agree to offer *credit* on such terms

[**Note**: paragraph 3.13 (box) of *ILG*]

Pre-contractual adequate explanations

4.2.5 R   FCA

(1)   Before making a *regulated credit agreement* the *firm* must:

    (a)   provide the *customer* with an adequate explanation of the matters referred to in (2) in order to place the *customer* in a position to assess whether the agreement is adapted to the *customer's* needs and financial situation;

    (b)   advise the *customer*:

        (i)   to consider the information which is required to be disclosed under section 55 of the *CCA*; and

        (ii)   where the information is disclosed in person, that the *customer* is able to take it away;

    (c)   provide the *customer* with an opportunity to ask questions about the agreement; and

    (d)   advise the *customer* how to ask the *firm* for further information and explanation.

        [**Note**: section 55A(1) of *CCA*]

(2)   The matters referred to in (1)(a) are:

    (a)   the features of the agreement which may make the *credit* to be provided under the agreement unsuitable for particular types of use;

    (b)   how much the *customer* will have to pay periodically and, where the amount can be determined, in total under the agreement;

    (c)   the features of the agreement which may operate in a manner which would have a significant adverse effect on the *customer* in a way which the *customer* is unlikely to foresee;

    (d)   the principal consequences for the *customer* arising from a failure to make payments under the agreement at the times required by the agreement including, where applicable and depending upon the type and amount of *credit* and the circumstances of the *customer*:

        (i)   the total cost of the debt growing;

        (ii)   incurring any default charges or interest for late or missed payment or under-payment;

        (iii)   impaired credit rating and its effect on future access to or cost of *credit*;

        (iv)   legal proceedings, including reference to charging orders (or, in Scotland, inhibitions), and to the associated costs of such proceedings;

        (v)   repossession of the *customer's* home or other property; and

        (vi)   where an article is taken in *pawn*, that the article might be sold, if not redeemed; and

    (e)   the effect of the exercise of any right to withdraw from the agreement and how and when this right may be exercised.

        [**Note**: section 55A(2) of *CCA* and paragraph 3.13 *of ILG*]

(3)   The adequate explanation and advice in (1) may be given orally or in writing, except where (4) applies.

    [**Note**: section 55A(3) of *CCA*]

(4)   Where the matters in (2)(a), (b) or (e) are given orally or to the *customer* in person, the explanation of the matters in (2)(c) and (d) and the advice required in (1)(b) must be given orally to the *customer*.

    [**Note**: section 55A(4) of *CCA*]

(5)   Paragraphs (1) to (4) do not apply to a *lender* if a *credit broker* has complied with those sub-paragraphs in respect of the agreement.
        [**Note**: section 55A(5) of *CCA*]
(6)   Where the *regulated credit agreement* is an agreement under which a person takes an article in *pawn*:
        (a)   the requirement in (1)(a) only relates to the matters in (2)(d) and (e); and
        (b)   the requirements in (1)(b) and (d) do not apply.
        [**Note**: section 55A(7) of *CCA*]
(7)   This *rule* does not apply to:
        (a)   a *non-commercial agreement*;
        (b)   a *small borrower-lender-supplier agreement* for restricted-use credit
        [**Note**: section 74(1) of *CCA*]
(8)   Where this *rule* applies to a *borrower-lender agreement* to finance the making of payments arising on or connected with the death of a person, the payments in question are set out in (9).
        [**Note**: section 74(1F) of *CCA*]
(9)   The payments referred to in (8) are:
        (a)   inheritance tax chargeable in the *UK* on the death of any person;
        (b)   fees payable to a court:
                (i)   in England, Wales or Northern Ireland on an application for a grant of probate or of letters of administration;
                (ii)   in Scotland, in connection with a grant of confirmation; and
                (iii)   in the *UK*, on an application for resealing of a Commonwealth or colonial grant of probate or of letters of administration; and
        (c)   payments in England, Wales or Northern Ireland to a surety in connection with a guarantee required as a condition of a grant of letters of administration or payments in Scotland to a cautioner in connection with a bond of caution required as a condition of issuing a grant of confirmation.
                [**Note**: regulation 2 of SI 1983/1554]

        [**Note**: article 5(6) of the *Consumer Credit Directive*]

4.2.6 G   FCA

The explanation provided by a *lender* or a *credit broker* under **CONC 4.2.5 R** should enable the *customer* to make a reasonable assessment as to whether the *customer* can afford the *credit* and to understand the key associated risks.
[**Note**: paragraph 3.3 (box) of *ILG*]

4.2.7 G   FCA

In deciding on the level and extent of explanation required by **CONC 4.2.5 R**, the *lender* or *credit broker* should consider (and each of them should ensure that anyone acting on its behalf should consider), to the extent appropriate to do so, factors including:
(1)   the type of *credit* being sought;
(2)   the amount of *credit* to be provided and the associated cost and risk to the *customer* (the risk to the *customer* is likely to be greater the higher the total cost of the *credit* relative to the *customer's* financial situation);
(3)   to the extent it is evident and discernible, the *customer's* level of understanding of the explanation provided; and
(4)   the channel or medium through which the *credit* transaction takes place.
        [**Note**: paragraph 3.4 of *ILG*]

4.2.8 R   FCA

Where the *regulated credit agreement* is *high-cost short-term credit*, the *lender* or a *credit broker* must explain under **CONC 4.2.5 R (1)(A)** that entering into that agreement would be unsuitable to support sustained borrowing over long periods and would be expensive as a means of longer term borrowing.
[**Note**: paragraph 3.13 (box) of *ILG*]

4.2.9 R   FCA

Even where a *customer* states or implies that there is no need for an explanation of the *regulated credit agreement*, the *lender* or *credit broker* must continue to comply with **CONC 4.2.5 R**.
[**Note**: paragraph 3.10 of *ILG*]

4.2.10 R   FCA

A *lender* or a *credit broker* must not encourage or induce a *customer* to waive the rights in **CONC 4.2.5 R**.
[**Note**: paragraph 3.10 of *ILG*]

4.2.11 R   FCA

Before a *lender* concludes that **CONC 4.2.5 R (1)** to **CONC 4.2.5 R (4)** do not apply to it in relation to a *regulated credit agreement* by virtue of **CONC 4.2.5 R (5)**, the *lender* must take reasonable steps to satisfy itself that an explanation of that agreement complying with **CONC 4.2.5 R** has been provided to the *customer* by the *credit broker*.
[**Note**: paragraph 3.11 (box) of *ILG*]

4.2.12 R   FCA

The *lender* or the *credit broker* must enable a *customer* to request and obtain further information and explanation about a *regulated credit agreement* without incurring undue cost or delay.
[**Note**: paragraph 3.16 (box) of *ILG*]

4.2.13 R   FCA

Neither a *lender* nor a *credit broker* may require a *customer* to acknowledge that the information and explanations it has provided are adequate to satisfy the requirements of **CONC 4.2.5 R**.
[**Note**: paragraph 3.30 (box) of *ILG*]

4.2.14 G   FCA

A *lender* or *credit broker* may require an acknowledgement that it has provided an explanation, and of receipt of any written information that forms a part of the explanation, but not an acknowledgement as to its adequacy. **CONC 4.2.13 R** does not prevent the *lender* or *credit broker* asking if the *customer* has understood an explanation given.
[**Note**: paragraph 3.30 (box) of *ILG*]

Adequate explanations in relation to particular regulated credit agreements

4.2.15 R   FCA

The following information must be provided by the *lender* or a *credit broker* as part of, and in addition to that provided under, the adequate explanation required by **CONC 4.2.5 R**, where applicable, in the specified cases:
(1)   for *credit token agreements*:
    (a)   different rates of interest and different charges apply to different elements of the *credit* provided (for example, a higher cost of withdrawing cash);
    (b)   the implications of only making minimum *repayments*;
    (c)   interest rates or charges may be increased;
    (d)   where applicable, the interest rates may be increased based on the risks presented by the individual *customer*;
    (e)   the limitations on any zero percentage or low interest or other introductory offer; and
    (f)   conditions on any balance transfers, including any fees and charges which may apply;
(2)   for *credit card cheques*, the higher associated costs relative to payment by credit card;
(3)   for *home credit loan agreements* and *high-cost short-term credit*, the effect of refinancing (within the meaning in **CONC 6.7.17 R**) or otherwise extending the duration of the *credit* or of the *credit agreement*;
(4)   for *bill of sale loan agreements*:
    (a)   the risk of losing the asset which is the subject of the bill of sale and the loss this could entail;
    (b)   that repossession can take place without a court order;
    (c)   that repossession may not clear the debt owed; and
    (d)   unlike in the case of *hire-purchase agreements* and *conditional sale agreements*, the *customer* is not protected under this arrangement from repossession of the asset where one third or more of the *total amount payable* has been paid off;
(5)   for *hire purchase agreements* and *conditional sale agreements*:
    (a)   the *customer* does not own the *goods* until the sums required under the agreements have been paid, including any option to purchase fee and any other conditions have been satisfied;
    (b)   *goods* can be repossessed without a court order in the event of default, unless in relation to a *regulated credit agreement* the *customer* has paid a third or more of the *total amount payable*;
(6)   for a *credit agreement* which is used to consolidate existing debts of the *customer* (whether to the same *lender* or to another *person*) and where applicable in each case:
    (a)   the effect of consolidating the debts will involve payment of a higher rate of interest or charges or both (if the relevant information about existing debts is known to the *lender* or *credit broker*);
    (b)   the effect of consolidating the debts will involve increasing the period required for repayment (if the relevant information about existing debts is known to the *lender* or *credit broker*); and
    (c)   the *credit agreement* would be secured on the *customer's* property;
(7)   for a *credit agreement* which includes a condition requiring a guarantor, the requirement for the *customer* to provide *security* in the form of a guarantee.
[**Note**: paragraph 4.26c of *CBG*]

[**Note**: paragraph 3.13 of *ILG*]

4.2.16 G FCA

Where a *customer* does not have a good understanding of the English language, the *lender* or *credit broker* may need to consider alternative methods of providing relevant information concerning the explanation required by **CONC 4.2.5 R** in order for the *customer* to make an informed decision, such as, providing the information to a person with such understanding who can assist the *customer*, for example, a friend or relative.

[**Note**: paragraph 3.4 (box) of *ILG*]

Guidance for adequate explanations where agreements are marketed by distance or electronic means

4.2.17 G FCA

Since the use of distance means of communication (such as the internet) by their nature limit the *lender's* or *credit broker's* ability to ascertain the *customer's* level of understanding of explanations provided, a *lender* or *credit broker* using those means may, for example, wish to provide local rate telephone number for *customers* who wish to seek further explanation.

[**Note**: paragraph 3.6 (box) of *ILG*]

4.2.18 G FCA

Interaction is an important part of compliance with the requirement in **CONC 4.2.5 R (1)**, for example, where the agreement is marketed and concluded by *electronic means*. For an online application, the requirement in **CONC 4.2.5 R (1)(C)** (the right to ask questions) may be complied with by the *customer* being able to access an appropriately comprehensive set of answers to frequently asked questions about the agreement or by being able to speak to a representative of the online provider.

[**Note**: paragraph 3.8 (box) of *ILG*]

4.2.19 G FCA

For a *regulated credit agreement* marketed and concluded by *electronic means* to comply with **CONC 4.2.5 R** the *customer* should pass through screens containing the required information and explanations, giving the *customer* the opportunity to see and read the explanations provided. Merely providing a link to where such information can be found is unlikely to satisfy the requirements in **CONC 4.2.5 R**, where the agreement can be concluded without accessing the link.

[**Note**: paragraph 3.15 (box) of *ILG*]

4.2.20 G FCA

For telephone or face-to-face transactions, interaction between the *customer* and the *firm's* representative is also important. It should be made clear to the *customer* that the *customer* can ask questions or request further information or explanation and, for example, the representative solely providing the *customer* with a written explanation of an agreement, or relying solely on a written script in relation to an agreement, is unlikely to comply with the requirement in **CONC 4.2.5 R**.

[**Note**: paragraph 3.9 (box) of *ILG*]

4.2.21 G FCA

Where a *regulated credit agreement* is a modifying agreement under section 82(2) of the *CCA*, the requirements in **CONC 4.2** apply before the agreement is made.

[**Note**: paragraph 3.12 of *ILG*]

4.3 ADEQUATE EXPLANATIONS: P2P AGREEMENTS

Application

4.3.1 R FCA

This section applies to a *firm* with respect to *operating an electronic system in relation to lending* in relation to a *borrower* or a prospective *borrower* under a *P2P agreement*.

4.3.2 R FCA

This section (apart from **CONC 4.3.6 R**) does not apply to:

(1)   an agreement under which the *lender* provides the prospective *borrower* with *credit* which exceeds £60,260; or

(2)   an agreement secured on *land*.

4.3.3 G FCA

For the agreements referred to in **CONC 4.3.2 R**, a *firm* should consider whether it is necessary or appropriate to provide explanations of the matters in **CONC 4.5.3 R (2)**, in particular, a *firm* should consider highlighting key risks to the *borrower* including the consequences of missing payments or

under-paying, including, where applicable, the risk of repossession of the *borrower's* property.
[**Note**: section 55A(6) of *CCA* and paragraph 3.1 of *ILG*]

[**Note**: Until the end of 30 September 2014, transitional provisions apply to **CONC 4.3.3 G**: see **CONC TP 4.1**]

Adequate explanations

4.3.4 R   FCA

(1)   Before a *P2P agreement* is made, the *firm* must:

    (a)   provide the prospective *borrower* with an adequate explanation of the matters referred to in (2) in order to place the *borrower* in a position to assess whether the agreement is adapted to the *borrower's* needs and financial situation;

    (b)   where the *P2P agreement* is not a *non-commercial agreement*, advise the prospective *borrower*:

        (i)   to consider the information which is required to be disclosed under section 55(1) of the *CCA*; and

        (ii)   where the information is disclosed in person, that the *borrower* is able to take it away;

    (c)   provide the prospective *borrower* with an opportunity to ask questions about the agreement; and

    (d)   advise the prospective *borrower* how to ask the *firm* for further information and explanation.

(2)   The matters referred to in (1)(a) are:

    (a)   the features of the agreement which may make the *credit* to be provided under the agreement unsuitable for particular types of use;

    (b)   how much the *borrower* will have to pay periodically and, where the amount can be determined, in total under the agreement;

    (c)   the features of the agreement which may operate in a manner which would have a significant adverse effect on the *borrower* in a way which the prospective *borrower* is unlikely to foresee;

    (d)   the principal consequences for the *borrower* arising from a failure to make payments under the agreement at the times required by the agreement, including legal proceedings and, where this is a possibility, repossession of the *borrower's* home; and

    (e)   the effect of the exercise of any right to withdraw from the agreement and how and when this right may be exercised.

(3)   Except where (4) applies, the adequate explanation and advice in (1) may be given orally or in writing.

(4)   Where the matters in (2)(a), (b) or (e) are given orally or to the prospective *borrower* in person, the explanation of the matters in (2)(c) and (d) and the advice required in (1)(b) must be given orally to the *borrower*.

(5)   Where this *rule* applies to a *borrower-lender agreement* to finance the making of payments arising on or connected with the death of a person, this *rule* applies to the agreement to the extent the payments are:

    (a)   inheritance tax chargeable in the *UK* on the death of any person;

    (b)   fees payable to a court:

        (i)   in England, Wales or Northern Ireland on an application for a grant of probate or of letters of administration;

        (ii)   in Scotland, in connection with a grant of confirmation; and

        (iii)   in the *UK*, on an application for resealing of a Commonwealth or colonial grant of probate or of letters of administration; and

    (c)   payments in England, Wales or Northern Ireland to a surety in connection with a guarantee required as a condition of a grant of letters of administration or payments in Scotland to a cautioner in connection with a bond of caution required as a condition of issuing a grant of confirmation.

[**Note**: section 74(1F) of *CCA* and SI 1983/1554]

[**Note**: Until the end of 30 September 2014, transitional provisions apply to **CONC 4.3.4 R**: see **CONC TP 4.1**]

4.3.5 R   FCA

Where **CONC 4.3.4 R** applies to a *firm*, the *firm* must comply with the *rules*, and observe the *guidance*, in **CONC 4.2** to the same extent as if it were the *lender* under an agreement to which those *rules* apply.

[**Note**: Until the end of 30 September 2014, transitional provisions apply to **CONC 4.3.5 R**: see **CONC TP 4.1**]

4.3.6 R   FCA

Before a *P2P agreement* which is secured on the *borrower's* home is made, a *firm* must in a prominent way give the following warning:

"YOUR HOME MAY BE REPOSSESSED IF YOU DO NOT KEEP UP REPAYMENTS ON A MORTGAGE OR ANY OTHER DEBT SECURED ON IT"

4.4   PRE-CONTRACTUAL REQUIREMENTS: CREDIT BROKERS

Application

4.4.1 R   FCA

This section applies to a *firm* carrying on *credit broking* in relation to a *regulated credit agreement*.

4.4.1A R   FCA

CONC 4.4.3 R applies to a *firm* carrying on *credit broking* whether or not it is in relation to a *regulated credit agreement*.

Pre-contractual requirements

4.4.2 R   FCA

(1)   A *firm* must disclose to the *customer* the fee, if any, payable by a *customer* to the *firm* for its services.
     [**Note**: section 160A(4) of *CCA*]

(2)   Any fee to be paid by the *customer* to the *firm* must be agreed between the *customer* and the *firm*, and that agreement must be recorded in writing or other *durable medium* before a *regulated credit agreement* is entered into.
     [**Note**: section 160A(4) of *CCA*]

(3)   A *firm* must disclose to the *lender* the fee, if any, for its activity payable by the *customer* for the purpose of enabling the *lender* to calculate the *annual percentage rate of charge* for the *credit agreement*.
     [**Note**: section 160A(5) of *CCA*]

(4)   A *firm* must disclose to the *customer* how and when any fee for its service is payable and in what circumstances a refund may be payable, including how and when a refund is available under section 155 of the *CCA*.
     [**Note**: paragraphs 2.2 and 4.17b of *CBG*]

[**Note**: article 21(b) and (c) of the *Consumer Credit Directive*]

Credit broking information notice

4.4.3 R   FCA

(1)   A *firm* must not:
     (a)   request, claim, demand, initiate or take payment of a charge from a *customer*, or from the *customer's* payment account, in connection with services it has provided or is to provide; or
     (b)   if the purpose, or one of the purposes, is to collect such a charge from a *customer*, invite or induce a *customer* to provide information in relation to a payment card or instrument that would enable a payment from the *customer's* payment account to be initiated by or through the *firm* or a third party or facilitate the provision of that information by a *customer*;
     unless that *firm* has met the conditions in both (2) and (3) in respect of that charge.

(2)   The first condition referred to in (1) is that the *firm* has sent a notice on paper or in another *durable medium* to the *customer* setting out the following clearly, concisely and in plain language (in this *rule* and **CONC 4.4.5 G** referred to as the "information notice"):
     (a)   the legal name of the *firm* as it appears in the *Financial Services Register*;
     (b)   if the *firm* is not a *lender*, a statement that the *firm* is a *credit broker* and that it is not a *lender*;
     (c)   if the *firm* is also a *lender*, a statement that the *firm* is acting as a *credit broker* and that it is not acting as a *lender*;
     (d)   a statement that the *customer* will be required, or (where relevant) may be required, to pay a charge in connection with the *firm's* services;
     (e)   the amount of the charge, or, where that amount is not ascertainable at the time the notice is sent, the basis on which it will be calculated; and
     (f)   when and by what method the *firm* will initiate or take payment of the charge.

(3)   The second condition referred to in (1) is that the *firm* has received from the *customer* a reply to the information notice (in this *rule* and **CONC 4.4.5 G** referred to as the "customer confirmation") on paper or in another *durable medium* in which the *customer* acknowledges receipt of the information notice and confirms that he is aware of its contents.

(4)   The information notice may also contain the *firm's* trading name, address and other contact details but must not contain any other statements or information additional to those required by (2).

(5)   For the purposes of this *rule*:
     (a)   references to "charge" include any fee, charge or financial consideration however described;

(b)   it is immaterial whether the charge is payable to the *firm* or to a third party.

(6)   The *firm* must keep a record of:

(a)   each information notice; and

(b)   each customer confirmation.

4.4.4 R   FCA

CONC 4.4.3 R does not apply where:

(1)   the *customer* indicates to the *firm* that he wishes to enter into a *credit agreement* secured by a *legal or equitable mortgage* on *land*;

(2)   the *firm* makes it clear to the *customer* that it is willing to carry on *credit broking* for that *customer* only in relation to *credit agreements* secured by a *legal or equitable mortgage* on *land*; and

(3)   the *firm* does not indicate (by express words or otherwise) that it is willing to carry on *credit broking* for that *customer* in relation to *credit agreements* other than *credit agreements* secured by a *legal or equitable mortgage* on *land*.

4.4.5 G   FCA

(1)   **CONC 4.4.3 R** prohibits a *firm* from asking a *customer* for any payment details, including the card number and security code of a debit card or a credit card, or using those payment details, without first sending an information notice to the *customer* and receiving a customer confirmation.

(2)   **CONC 4.4.3 R** applies in respect of any sum due from a *customer*, however it is described and irrespective of whether it is payable to the *firm* or a third party (for example, a *firm* cannot avoid the application of this *rule* by describing a charge as a "membership fee" or a "web registration fee"). The fact that a fee or charge may be financed by *credit* does not take the fee or charge outside the *rule*.

(3)   The information notice must not contain anything other than the statements and information required by **CONC 4.4.3 R (2)**, except for the *firm's* trading name, address and other contact details. It should set out the required information clearly and concisely, in plain language. The information notice must be sent to the *customer* in a *durable medium*, for example on paper, as an email, or as an attachment to an email: it is insufficient to make the notice available on a website or to email a link to a webpage that contains the relevant information and statements.

(4)   The *firm* should not ask for or take the *customer's* payment details until it has received the customer confirmation. This means, for example, that *firms* should construct their websites so that *customers* cannot access any webpage that enables them to input their payment details before they have received the information notice and given the customer confirmation.

(5)   **CONC 4.4.3 R** applies to each *firm* in a chain of *credit brokers* separately. If *firm* A introduces the *customer* to *firm* B (where B is a *credit broker*), any information notice given by A cannot cover fees which B might charge: B will have to issue its own information notice to the *customer*, and the *customer* will have to provide a separate customer confirmation, before B can ask for or make use of the *customer's* payment details.

(6)   **CONC 4.4.3 R** does not apply to *credit broking* that relates only to *credit agreements* secured on *land*.

4.5   COMMISSIONS

Application

4.5.1 R   FCA

(1)   **CONC 4.5.2 G** applies to a *firm* with respect to *consumer credit lending*.

(2)   **CONC 4.5.3 R** and **CONC 4.5.4 R** apply to a *firm* with respect to *credit broking* in relation to:

(a)   *regulated credit agreements*; and

(b)   *regulated consumer hire agreements*.

(3)   **CONC 4.5.3 R** and **CONC 4.5.4 R** also apply to a *firm* carrying on the activities specified in article 36A(1)(a) or (c) of the *Regulated Activities Order* in relation to:

(a)   *credit agreements* that would be *regulated credit agreements* but for the *relevant provisions*; and

(b)   *consumer hire agreements* that would be *regulated consumer hire agreements* but for articles 60O and 60Q of the *Regulated Activities Order*.

Commissions lenders to credit brokers

4.5.2 G   FCA

A *lender* should only offer to, or enter into with, a *firm* a commission agreement providing for differential commission rates or providing for payments based on the volume and profitability of

business where such payments are justified based on the extra work of the *firm* involved in that business.
[**Note**: paragraph 5.5 (box) of *ILG*]

Commissions: credit brokers

4.5.3 R   FCA

A *credit broker* must disclose to a *customer* in good time before a *credit agreement* or a *consumer hire agreement* is entered into, the existence of any commission or fee or other remuneration payable to the *credit broker* by the *lender* or *owner* or a third party in relation to a *credit agreement* or a *consumer hire agreement*, where knowledge of the existence or amount of the commission could actually or potentially:
(1)   affect the impartiality of the *credit broker* in recommending a particular product; or
(2)   have a material impact on the *customer's* transactional decision.
[**Note**: paragraph 3.7i (box) and 3.7j of *CBG* and 5.5 (box) of *ILG*]

4.5.4 R   FCA

At the request of the *customer*, a *credit broker* must disclose to the *customer*, in good time before a *regulated credit agreement* or a *regulated consumer hire agreement* is entered into, the amount (or if the precise amount is not known, the likely amount) of any commission or fee or other remuneration payable to the *credit broker* by the *lender* or *owner* or a third party.
[**Note**: paragraph 3.7i (box) of *CBG*]

4.6   PRE-CONTRACT DISCLOSURE: CONTINUOUS PAYMENT AUTHORITIES

Application

4.6.1 R   FCA
(1)   This section applies to:
    (a)   a *firm* with respect to *consumer credit lending*; or
    (b)   a *firm* with respect to *consumer hiring*; or
    (c)   a *firm* with respect to *operating an electronic system in relation to lending* in relation to a prospective *borrower* under a *P2P agreement*.

Disclosure of continuous payment authorities

4.6.2 R   FCA
(1)   Before entering into a *regulated credit agreement* or *regulated consumer hire agreement*, or before a *P2P agreement* is entered into, under which the *customer* may grant a *continuous payment authority*, the firm must provide the *customer* with an adequate explanation of the matters in (2).
(2)   The matters referred to in (1) are:
    (a)   what a *continuous payment authority* is and how it works;
    (b)   how the *continuous payment authority* will be applied by the *firm*, including where the *firm* provides *high-cost short-term credit* that it may only be used twice to collect the whole sum due in relation to the agreement or where the agreement provides for repayment in instalments, in relation to an instalment;
    (c)   how the *customer* can cancel the *continuous payment authority*;
    (d)   whether alternative repayment options are available;
    (e)   the choice of an appropriate due date for payment;
    (f)   the choice of an alternative payment date (if applicable);
    (g)   the consequences if sufficient funds are not available on the due date (or an alternative payment date if agreed);
    (h)   whether further attempts may be made to collect payment and, if so, the basis on which further attempts would be made, the days or period over which the further attempts would be made and the frequency of the further attempts;
    (i)   other than in relation to *high-cost short-term credit*, whether part payment (a sum due which less than the full sum due at the time the *firm's* payment request is made) may be sought and, if so, the basis on which and frequency with which payment would be sought and whether part payments would be subject to a minimum amount or percentage;
    (j)   in relation to *high-cost short-term credit*, the *firm* will not seek part payment (a sum due which is less than the full sum due at the time the *firm's* payment request is made) unless the *firm* is willing to accept such less sum and, after being notified of that sum and when a payment request would be made, the *customer* has given express consent to the *firm* to make such a payment request; and
    (k)   whether default fees and other charges may be added and, if so, the circumstances in which these may be incurred and the amount of such fees and charges or the basis on which they will be calculated.
    [**Note**: paragraph 3.9miii of *DCG*]

4.6.3 R   FCA

A *firm* must include the terms of the *continuous payment authority* as part of the *credit agreement* or *consumer hire agreement* presented to the *customer* or *P2P agreement* presented to the *borrower*.
[**Note**: paragraph 3.9miii of *DCG*]

4.6.4 R   FCA

A *firm* must set out, in plain and intelligible language, the scope of the agreed *continuous payment authority* and how it will operate.
[**Note**: paragraph 3.9miii of *DCG*]

4.7   INFORMATION TO BE PROVIDED ON ENTERING A CURRENT ACCOUNT AGREEMENT

Application

4.7.1 R   FCA

This section applies to a *firm* with respect to *consumer credit lending*.

Information on entering into current account

4.7.2 R   FCA
(1)   When a *firm* enters into a current account agreement where:
    (a)   there is a possibility that the account-holder may be allowed to overdraw on the current account without a pre-arranged overdraft or exceed a pre-arranged overdraft limit; and
    (b)   if the account-holder did so, this would be a *regulated credit agreement*;
    the current account agreement must contain the information in (2) and (3).
    [**Note**: section 74A(1) of *CCA*]
(2)   The information required by (1) is:
    (a)   the rate of interest charged on the amount by which the account-holder overdraws on the current account or exceeds the pre-arranged overdraft limit;
    (b)   any conditions applicable to that rate;
    (c)   any reference rate on which that rate is based;
    (d)   information on any changes to that rate of interest (including the periods that the rate applies to and any conditions or procedure applicable to changing that rate); and
    (e)   any other charges payable by the account holder under the agreement (and the conditions under which those charges may be varied).
        [**Note**: section 74A(2) of *CCA*]
(3)   Where different rates of interest are charged in different circumstances, the *firm* must provide the information in (2)(a) to (d) in respect of each rate.
    [**Note**: section 74A(4) of *CCA*]

[**Note**: article 18 of the *Consumer Credit Directive*]

4.8   PRE-CONTRACT: UNFAIR BUSINESS PRACTICES: CONSUMER CREDIT LENDING

Application

4.8.1 R   FCA

This section applies to a *firm* carrying on *consumer credit lending*.

Unfair business practices

4.8.2 R   FCA

A *firm* must not unfairly encourage, incentivise or induce a *customer* to enter into a *regulated credit agreement* quickly without allowing the *customer* time to consider the pre-contract information under section 55 of the *CCA* and the explanations provided under **CONC 4.2.5 R**.
[**Note**: paragraph 5.10 of *ILG*]

4.8.3 G   FCA

Stating an end date for a promotion would not amount to the behaviour in **CONC 4.8.2 R**.
[**Note**: paragraph 5.10 (box) of *ILG*]

4.8.4 R   FCA

A *firm* must not unfairly encourage, incentivise or induce a *customer* to enter into a *regulated credit agreement* for an amount higher than the *customer* requests.
[**Note**: paragraph 5.11 of *ILG*]

4.8.5 G   FCA

Merely offering a *customer* more *credit* than the *customer* requested would not amount to the behaviour in **CONC 4.8.4 R** where:
(1)   the offer of the higher amount was based on a proper *creditworthiness assessment* or assessment required by **CONC 5.2.2 R (1)**; or

(2)   the *firm* offers more advantageous terms, conditions or prices to *customers* for larger loans, provided that such offers are sufficiently transparent and a proper *creditworthiness assessment* or assessment required by **CONC 5.2.2 R (1)** has been carried out;

and the *customer* was not pressurised or unfairly coerced into accepting the higher amount of *credit*.
[**Note**: paragraph 5.11 (box) of *ILG*]

4.8.6 R   FCA

A *firm* must not lead a *customer* to believe that the *customer's* current debt *repayments* can be reduced under a *regulated credit agreement* over the same term when this is not the case.
[**Note**: paragraph 5.13 of *ILG*]

CHAPTER 5
RESPONSIBLE LENDING

5.1   APPLICATION

[3.82]
5.1.1 R   FCA

This chapter applies to a *firm* with respect to *consumer credit lending*, unless otherwise stated in, or in relation to, a *rule*.

5.2   CREDITWORTHINESS ASSESSMENT: BEFORE AGREEMENT

5.2.1 R   FCA
(1)   Before making a *regulated credit agreement* the *firm* must undertake an assessment of the creditworthiness of the *customer*.
      [**Note**: section 55B(1) of *CCA*]
(2)   A *firm* carrying out the assessment required in (1) must consider:
     (a)   the potential for the commitments under the *regulated credit agreement* to adversely impact the *customer's* financial situation, taking into account the information of which the *firm* is aware at the time the *regulated credit agreement* is to be made; and
         [**Note**: paragraph 4.1 of *ILG*]
     (b)   the ability of the *customer* to make *repayments* as they fall due over the life of the *regulated credit agreement*, or for such an agreement which is an *open-end agreement*, to make *repayments* within a reasonable period.
         [**Note**: paragraph 4.3 of *ILG*]
(3)   A creditworthiness assessment must be based on sufficient information obtained from:
     (a)   the *customer*, where appropriate; and
     (b)   a *credit reference agency*, where necessary.
         [**Note**: section 55B(3) of *CCA*]
(4)   This *rule* does not apply to:
     (a)   an agreement secured on *land*; or
     (b)   an agreement under which a *person* takes an article in *pawn*.
         [**Note**: section 55B(4) of *CCA*]
(5)   This *rule* does not apply, except to the agreements in (6), to:
     (a)   a *non-commercial agreement*; or
     (b)   a *borrower-lender agreement* enabling the *borrower* to overdraw on a current account; or
     (c)   a *small borrower-lender-supplier agreement* for restricted-use credit.
         [**Note**: section 74 of *CCA*]
(6)   The agreements referred to in (5) and therefore to which this *rule* does apply are:
     (a)   a *borrower-lender agreement* enabling the *borrower* to overdraw on a current account which is an *authorised business overdraft agreement* or an *authorised non-business overdraft agreement*; and
         [**Note**: section 74(1B) and (1C) of *CCA*]
     (b)   a *borrower-lender agreement* enabling the *borrower* to overdraw on a current account which would be an *authorised non-business overdraft agreement* but for the fact that the *credit* is not repayable on demand or within three *months*.
         [**Note**: section 74(1D) of *CCA*]
(7)   Where the *borrower-lender agreement* in question is to finance the making of payments arising on or connected with the death of a person, this *rule* applies to the agreement to the extent the payments are:
     (a)   inheritance tax chargeable in the *UK* on the death of any person;
     (b)   fees payable to a court:
         (i)   in England, Wales or Northern Ireland on an application for a grant of probate or of letters of administration;
         (ii)   in Scotland, in connection with a grant of confirmation; and
         (iii)   in the *UK*, on an application for resealing of a Commonwealth or colonial grant of probate or of letters of administration; and

(c)   payments in England, Wales or Northern Ireland to a surety in connection with a guarantee required as a condition of a grant of letters of administration or payments in Scotland to a cautioner in connection with a bond of caution required as a condition of issuing a grant of confirmation.
[**Note**: section 74(1F) of *CCA* and SI 1983/1554]

[**Note**: article 8 of the *Consumer Credit Directive*]

Scope of the pre-contract assessments

5.2.2 R   **FCA**

(1)   Before entering into a *regulated credit agreement* which is excluded from **CONC 5.2.1 R** (see (4), (5) and (6)), a *firm* must carry out an assessment of the potential for the commitments under the agreement to adversely impact the *customer's* financial situation, taking into account the information of which the *firm* is aware at the time the agreement is to be made.
[**Note**: paragraphs 1.14 and 4.1 of *ILG*]

(2)   Paragraph (1) does not apply to an agreement to which **CONC 4.7.2 R (1)** applies (overrunning).

(3)   A *firm* must consider sufficient information to enable it to make a reasonable *creditworthiness assessment* or a reasonable assessment required by (1).
[**Note**: paragraph 4.21 of ILG]

5.2.3 G   **FCA**

The extent and scope of the *creditworthiness assessment* or the assessment required by **CONC 5.2.2 R (1)**, in a given case, should be dependent upon and proportionate to factors which may include one or more of the following:

(1)   the type of *credit*;
(2)   the amount of the *credit*;
(3)   the cost of the *credit*;
(4)   the financial position of the *customer* at the time of seeking the *credit*;
(5)   the *customer's* credit history, including any indications that the *customer* is experiencing or has experienced financial difficulties;
(6)   the *customer's* existing financial commitments including any repayments due in respect of other *credit agreements*, *consumer hire agreements*, *regulated mortgage contracts*, payments for rent, council tax, electricity, gas, telecommunications, water and other major outgoings known to the *firm*;
(7)   any future financial commitments of the *customer*;
(8)   any future changes in circumstances which could be reasonably expected to have a significant financial adverse impact on the *customer*;
(9)   the vulnerability of the *customer*, in particular where the *firm* understands the *customer* has some form of mental capacity limitation or reasonably suspects this to be so because the *customer* displays indications of some form of mental capacity limitation (see **CONC 2.10**).
[**Note**: paragraph 4.10 of *ILG*]

Proportionality of assessments

5.2.4 G   **FCA**

(1)   To consider all of the factors set out in **CONC 5.2.3 G** in all cases is likely to be disproportionate.
[**Note**: paragraph 4.11 of *ILG*]

(2)   A *firm* should consider what is appropriate in any particular circumstances dependent on, for example, the type and amount of the *credit* being sought and the potential risks to the *customer*. The risk of *credit* not being *sustainable* directly relates to the amount of *credit* granted and the *total charge for credit* relative to the *customer's* financial situation.
[**Note**: paragraph 4.11 and part of 4.16 of *ILG*]

(3)   A *firm* should consider the types and sources of information to use in its *creditworthiness assessment* and assessment required by **CONC 5.2.2 R (1)**, which may, depending on the circumstances, include some or all of the following:
(a)   its record of previous dealings;
(b)   evidence of income;
(c)   evidence of expenditure;
(d)   a credit score;
(e)   a *credit reference agency* report; and
(f)   information provided by the *customer*.
[**Note**: paragraph 4.12 of *ILG*]

(4)   A high level of scrutiny in the assessment required by **CONC 5.2.2 R (1)** would normally be expected before the *lender* enters into a *regulated credit agreement* secured by a second or subsequent charge on the *customer's* home.
        [**Note**: paragraph 4.17 of *ILG*]

5.3   CONDUCT OF BUSINESS IN RELATION TO CREDITWORTHINESS AND AFFORDABILITY

Creditworthiness and sustainability

5.3.1 G   FCA
(1)   In making the *creditworthiness assessment* or the assessment required by **CONC 5.2.2 R (1)**, a *firm* should take into account more than assessing the *customer's* ability to repay the *credit*.
        [**Note**: paragraph 4.2 of *ILG*]
(2)   The *creditworthiness assessment* and the assessment required by **CONC 5.2.2 R (1)** should include the *firm* taking reasonable steps to assess the *customer's* ability to meet *repayments* under a *regulated credit agreement* in a *sustainable* manner without the *customer* incurring financial difficulties or experiencing significant adverse consequences.
        [**Note**: paragraph 4.1 (box) and 4.2 of *ILG*]
(3)   A *firm* in making its *creditworthiness assessment* or the assessment required by **CONC 5.2.2 R (1)** may take into account future increases in income or future decreases in expenditure, where there is appropriate evidence of the change and the *repayments* are expected to be *sustainable* in the light of the change.
        [**Note**: paragraph 4.9 of *ILG*]
(4)   If a *firm* takes income or expenditure into account in its *creditworthiness assessment* or its assessment required under **CONC 5.2.2 R (1)**:
        (a)   the *firm* should take account of actual current income or expenditure and reasonably expected future income or expenditure (to the extent it is proportionate to do so) where it is reasonably foreseeable that it will differ from actual current income or expenditure over the anticipated repayment period of the agreement;
        (b)   it is not generally sufficient for a *firm* to rely solely for its assessment of the *customer's* income and expenditure, on a statement of those matters made by the *customer*;
        (c)   its assessment should be based on what the *firm* knows at the time of the assessment.
                [**Note**: paragraph 4.13, 4.14 and 4.15 of *ILG*]
(5)   An example of where it may be reasonable to take into account expected future income would be, in the case of loans to fund the provision of further or higher education, provided that an appropriate assessment required by this chapter is carried out and there is an appropriate exercise of forbearance in respect of initial repayments, for example, deferring or limiting the obligation to repay until the *customer's* income has reached a specified level. Any assumptions regarding future income should be reasonable and capable of substantiation in the individual case and the products should be designed in a way to minimise the risks to the *customer*.
        [**Note**: footnote 21 to paragraph 4.9 (box) of *ILG*
(6)   For the purposes of *CONC* "sustainable" means the *repayments* under the *regulated credit agreement* can be made by the *customer*:
        (a)   without undue difficulties, in particular:
                (i)   the *customer* should be able to make *repayments* on time, while meeting other reasonable commitments; and
                (ii)   without having to borrow to meet the *repayments*;
        (b)   over the life of the agreement, or for such an agreement which is an *open-end agreement*, within a reasonable period; and
        (c)   out of income and savings without having to realise security or assets; and

        "unsustainable" has the opposite meaning.
        [**Note**: paragraphs 4.3 and 4.4 of *ILG*]
(7)   For a *regulated credit agreement* which is an *open-end agreement* the *firm*, in making its *creditworthiness assessment* or the assessment required by **CONC 5.2.2 R (1)**, should:
        (a)   make a reasonable assessment of whether the *customer* is able to meet the *repayments* in a *sustainable* manner; and
        (b)   make the assessment based on reasonable assumptions about the likely duration of the *credit*.
                [**Note**: paragraph 4.5 of *ILG*]
(8)   For a *regulated credit agreement* for *running-account credit* the *firm*, in making its *creditworthiness assessment* or the assessment required by **CONC 5.2.2 R (1)**:
        (a)   should consider the *customer's* ability to repay the maximum amount of *credit* available (equivalent to the *credit limit*) under the agreement within a reasonable period;

(b)   may, in considering what is a reasonable period in which to repay the maximum amount of *credit* available, have regard to the typical time required for repayment that would apply to a fixed-sum unsecured personal loan for an amount equal to the *credit limit*; and

(c)   should not use the assumption of the amount necessary to make only the minimum *repayment* each *month*.
[**Note**: paragraph 4.6 of *ILG*]

(9)   For a *regulated credit agreement* for *running-account credit* the *firm* should set the *credit limit* based on the *creditworthiness assessment* or the assessment required by **CONC 5.2.2 R (1)** and taking into account the matters in **CONC 5.2.3 G**, and, in particular, the information it has on the *customer's* current disposable income taking into account any reasonably foreseeable future changes.
[**Note**: paragraph 4.6 (box) of *ILG*]

(10)   An example of a reasonably foreseeable future change in disposable income which a *firm* should take into account in setting a *credit limit* may include where a *customer* is known to be, or it is reasonably foreseeable that a *customer* is, close to retirement and faces a significant fall in disposable income.
[**Note**: paragraph 4.6 (box) of *ILG*]

(11)   Where a *firm* requests information from a *customer* for its *creditworthiness assessment* or its assessment required by **CONC 5.2.2 R (1)** and the information provided by the *customer* is false and the *firm* has no reason to know this is the case, the *firm* should not contravene **CONC 5.2.1 R** or **CONC 5.2.2 R**.
[**Note**: paragraph 4.10 of *ILG*]

(12)   Subject to the relevant legal constraints, *FCA* encourages the sharing between *lenders* of accurate data about the performance of a *customer's* account and the settlement of outstanding debts, as the process of making the assessments in this chapter is assisted by *lenders* registering such data with *credit reference agencies*, in a timely manner.

5.3.2 R   FCA

A *firm* must establish and implement clear and effective policies and procedures to make a reasonable *creditworthiness assessment* or a reasonable assessment required by **CONC 5.2.2 R (1)**.
[**Note**: paragraph 4.19 of *ILG*]

5.3.3 G   FCA

Under the procedures required by **CONC 5.3.2 R** a *firm* should take adequate steps, insofar as it is reasonable and practicable to do so, to ensure that information (including information supplied by the *customer*) on an application for *credit* relevant to a *creditworthiness assessment* or an assessment required by**CONC 5.2.2 R (1)** is complete and correct.
[**Note**: paragraph 4.29 of *ILG*]

Unfair business practices: lenders

5.3.4 R   FCA

A *firm* must not base its *creditworthiness assessment*, or its assessment required under **CONC 5.2.2 R (1)**, primarily or solely on the value of any *security* provided by the *customer*, but this *rule* does not apply in relation to a *regulated credit agreement* under which the *firm* takes an article in pawn and the *customer's*total financial liability (including capital, interest and all other charges) is limited under the agreement to the proceeds of sale which would represent the true market value (within the meaning of section 121 of the *CCA*) of the article or articles *pawned* by the *customer*.

5.3.5 R   FCA

A *firm* must not advise or encourage a *customer* to enter into a *regulated credit agreement* for an amount of *credit* higher than the *customer* initially requested if the *creditworthiness assessment* or the assessment required by **CONC 5.2.2 R (1)** indicates that repayment of the higher amount would not be *sustainable* or the *firm* ought reasonably to suspect that that is the case.
[**Note**: paragraph 4.28 of *ILG*]

5.3.6 R   FCA

A *firm* must not complete some or all of those parts of an application for *credit* under a *regulated credit agreement* intended to be completed by the *customer*, without the consent of the *customer*, unless the *customer* is permitted to check the application before signing the agreement.
[**Note**: paragraph 4.30 of *ILG*]

5.3.7 R   FCA

A *firm* must not accept an application for *credit* under a *regulated credit agreement* where the *firm* knows or ought reasonably to suspect that the *customer* has not been truthful in completing the application in relation to information supplied by the *customer* relevant to the *creditworthiness assessment* or the assessment required by **CONC 5.2.2 R (1)**.
[**Note**: paragraph 4.31 of *ILG*]

5.3.8 G   FCA

An example of where a *firm* ought reasonably to suspect that the *customer* has not been truthful may be that the information supplied by the *customer* concerning income or employment status is clearly inconsistent with other available information.

5.4   CONDUCT OF BUSINESS: CREDIT BROKERS

Application

5.4.1 R   FCA

This section applies to a *firm* with respect to *credit broking*.

Conduct of business

5.4.2 R   FCA
(1)   In giving explanations or advice, or in making recommendations, a *firm* must pay due regard to the *customer's* needs and circumstances.
(2)   In complying with (1) a *firm* must pay due regard to whether the *credit* product is affordable and whether there are any factors that the *firm* knows, or reasonably ought to know, that may make the product unsuitable for that *customer*.
[**Note**: paragraphs 4.32 to 4.36 of *CBG*]

5.4.3 R   FCA

A *firm* which undertakes to search the product market or a part of it before effecting an introduction must, before doing so, search the product market to the extent stated to the *customer*.
[**Note**: paragraph 4.41j of *CBG*]

5.5   CREDITWORTHINESS ASSESSMENT: P2P AGREEMENTS

[**Note**: Until the end of 30 September 2014, transitional provisions apply to **CONC 5.5**: see **CONC TP 4**.2]

Application

5.5.1 R   FCA

This section applies to a *firm* with respect to *operating an electronic system in relation to lending* in relation to a prospective *borrower* under a *P2P agreement*.

5.5.2 G   FCA
(1)   This section contains *rules* that apply to the *person* operating the electronic system that facilitates *persons* becoming *lenders* and borrowers under *P2P agreements*, in contrast to **CONC 5.2** which applies to the *lender*.
(2)   A *P2P agreement* may also be a *credit agreement* or a *regulated credit agreement* in which case applicable provisions of the *CCA* or *CONC* will apply to such agreements. The extent to which *CCA* provisions apply to a *lender* will depend largely on whether the *lender* makes the *credit agreement* in the course of carrying on a business.

Creditworthiness assessment

5.5.3 R   FCA
(1)   Before a *P2P agreement* is made, a *firm* must undertake an assessment of the creditworthiness of the prospective *borrower*.
(2)   A *firm* carrying out the assessment in (1) must consider:
  (a)   the potential for the commitments under the *P2P agreement* to adversely impact the prospective *borrower's* financial situation, taking into account the information of which the *firm* is aware at the time the *P2P agreement* is to be made; and
  (b)   the ability of the prospective *borrower* to make *repayments* as they fall due over the life of the *P2P agreement*, or for such an agreement which is an *open-end agreement*, to make *repayments* within a reasonable period.
(3)   A creditworthiness assessment must be based on sufficient information obtained from:
  (a)   a prospective *borrower*, where appropriate; and
  (b)   a *credit reference agency*, where necessary.
(4)   This *rule* does not apply to an agreement under which a *person* takes an article in *pawn*.

5.5.4 R   FCA

Where **CONC 5.5.3 R** applies to a *firm*, the *firm* must comply with **CONC 5.3.2 R**, **CONC 5.3.4 R**, **CONC 5.3.5 R**, **CONC 5.3.6 R** and **CONC 5.3.7 R** to the same extent as if it were the *lender* under an agreement to which those *rules* apply and should take into account the *guidance* in **CONC 5.3** to the same extent, and should also take into account **CONC 5.2.3 G** and **CONC 5.2.4 G** treating them as guidance on **CONC 5.5.3 R**.

5.5.5 R   FCA

Part 3   FCA Handbook Materials

A *firm* must consider sufficient information to enable it to make a reasonable assessment required by **CONC 5.5.3 R**.

[**Note**: paragraph 4.21 of *ILG*]

5.5.6 R   FCA

Before a *P2P agreement* is entered into under which a *person* takes an article in *pawn*, the *firm* must:
(1)   undertake the assessment referred to in **CONC 5.2.2 R (1)** of the prospective *borrower*; and
(2)   comply with **CONC 5.3.2 R**, **CONC 5.3.4 R**, **CONC 5.3.5 R**, **CONC 5.3.6 R** and **CONC 5.3.7 R** to the same extent as if it were the *lender* under an agreement to which those *rules* apply, and should also take into account the *guidance* in **CONC 5.2.3 G** and **CONC 5.2.4 G** and **CONC 5.3** to the same extent.

CHAPTER 5A
COST CAP FOR HIGH-COST SHORT-TERM CREDIT

5A.1   APPLICATION, PURPOSE AND GUIDANCE

Application

[3.83]
5A.1.1 R   FCA

This chapter applies to:
(1)   a *firm* with respect to an agreement for *high-cost short-term credit* entered into on or after 2 January 2015; or
(2)   a *firm* with respect to an agreement entered into on or after 2 January 2015 which varies or supplements an agreement for *high-cost short-term credit* which imposes one or more charges; or
(3)   a *firm* with respect to the exercise of a contractual power on or after 2 January 2015 to vary or supplement an agreement for *high-cost short-term credit* which imposes one or more charges.

5A.1.2 G   FCA
(1)   A variation or supplement of, or an exercise of a contractual power to vary or supplement, an agreement for *high-cost short-term credit* made before 2 January 2015 will be covered by this chapter if it has the result that a new charge, or an increase in an existing charge, is payable.
(2)   An example of where a charge results from a variation or supplement is where the duration of an agreement made before 2 January 2015 is extended and a further charge by way of interest or otherwise is calculated by reference to the period of the extension. A variation or supplement which alters the address of the borrower stated in the agreement or which is followed by the *firm* permanently waiving any right to interest or charges which would otherwise be imposed or result does not fall within **CONC 5A.1.1 R (2)** or **CONC 5A.1.1 R (3)**.
(3)   If this chapter applies to an agreement for *high-cost short-term credit* as a result of **CONC 5A.1.1 R (2)** or **CONC 5A.1.1 R (3)**, charges imposed under the agreement before 2 January 2015 are to be included in the calculation of the total cost cap, the initial cost cap and the default cap. If charges imposed before 2 January 2015 exceed the total cost cap, the initial cost cap or the default cap, a variation or supplement of that credit agreement on or after 2 January 2015 that results in any additional charge is not permitted.

5A.1.3 G   FCA

Firms are reminded that, as a result of **GEN 2.2.1 R**, the provisions of this chapter have to be interpreted in the light of their purpose.

Statutory context and purpose

5A.1.4 G   FCA

Section 137C of the *Act* (FCA general rules: cost of credit and duration of credit agreements) as amended by the Financial Services (Banking Reform) Act 2013, places a duty on the *FCA* to make general rules with a view to securing an appropriate degree of protection for borrowers against excessive charges.

5A.1.5 G   FCA

In accordance with that duty, the purpose of this chapter is:
(1)   to specify the descriptions of *regulated credit agreement* appearing to the *FCA* to involve the provision of high-cost short-term credit to which this chapter applies by using the definition of high-cost short-term credit set out in the *Glossary*;
(2)   to secure an appropriate degree of protection for borrowers against excessive charges; and
(3)   as a result, to restrict the charges for such high-cost short-term credit.

Guidance on application and interpretation

5A.1.6 G   FCA

Examples of the sorts of charge (which expression is defined in **CONC 5A.6**) applied in connection with the provision of *credit* covered by this chapter include, but are not limited to:

(1)   interest on the *credit* provided;

(2)   a charge related to late payment by, or default of, the borrower;

(3)   a charge related to the transmission of *credit* or for using a means of payment to or from the borrower;

(4)   a charge related to early repayment, or refinancing or changing the payment date or termination of the agreement;

(5)   a charge related to the application for, or drawing down of, *credit*;

(6)   a charge imposed by a *credit broker* in the same *group* or with whom the *lender* has arrangements to share the charge;

(7)   a charge for ancillary services related to the provision of *credit*; and

(8)   interest on any of the charges referred to in (1) to (7).

5A.1.7 G   FCA

Certain other terms used in this chapter are defined in **CONC 5A.6**.

5A.2   PROHIBITION FROM ENTERING INTO AGREEMENTS FOR HIGH-COST SHORT-TERM CREDIT

Application

5A.2.1 R   FCA

This section applies to:

(1)   a *firm* with respect to *consumer credit lending*; or

(2)   a *firm* with respect to *credit broking*.

Cost caps: entering into agreements: Total cost cap

5A.2.2 R   FCA

A *firm* must not enter into an agreement for *high-cost short-term credit* that provides for the payment by the borrower of one or more charges that, alone or in combination with any other charge under the agreement or a connected agreement, exceed or are capable of exceeding the amount of *credit* provided under the agreement.

Cost caps: entering into agreements: Initial cost cap

5A.2.3 R   FCA

A *firm* must not enter into an agreement for *high-cost short-term credit* that provides for the payment by the borrower of one or more charges that, alone or in combination with any other charge under the agreement or a connected agreement, exceed or are capable of exceeding 0.8% of the amount of *credit* provided under the agreement calculated per *day* from the date on which the borrower draws down the *credit* until the date on which repayment of the *credit* is due under the agreement, but if the date of repayment is postponed by an indulgence or waiver, the date to which it is postponed.

5A.2.4 R   FCA

A reference to a charge in **CONC 5A.2.3 R** (Initial cost cap) excludes a charge to which **CONC 5A.2.14 R** (Default cap) applies.

5A.2.5 G   FCA

(1)   The initial cost cap is calculated on a daily basis. However, a charge or charges that may be provided for in an agreement in compliance with this cap can amount to 0.8% of the credit provided (determined in accordance with **CONC 5A.2.7 R**) multiplied by the number of days from the date on which the borrower draws down the *credit* until the date indicated in **CONC 5A.2.3 R**.

(2)   Where *credit* is drawn down in tranches or is repaid in instalments, the calculation of the initial cost cap takes into account the different amounts of *credit* outstanding and the different durations for which the *credit* is provided.

Determining the amount of credit provided

5A.2.6 R   FCA

The amount of *credit* provided under an agreement for *high-cost short-term credit* for the purposes of **CONC 5A.2.2 R** (Total cost cap) is the lesser of:

(1)   the amount of credit that the lender actually advances under the agreement; or

(2)   the *credit limit*.

5A.2.7 R   FCA

The amount of *credit* provided under an agreement for *high-cost short-term credit* for the purposes of **CONC 5A.2.3 R** (Initial cost cap) is the amount of *credit* outstanding on the *day* in question under the agreement, disregarding for the purposes of that *rule* the effect of the borrower discharging all or part of the borrower's indebtedness in accordance with section 94 of the *CCA* (right to complete payments ahead of time) by repayment of *credit* before the date provided for in the agreement.

5A.2.8 G FCA

For the purpose of the calculation of the initial cost cap, if there is an early repayment by the borrower of an amount of *credit* repayable under an agreement for *high-cost short-term credit* (including where that early repayment is financed by a replacement agreement), the amount of *credit* outstanding on the *days* that follow the early repayment is not reduced to reflect the amount of the early repayment. There is no effect, however, on the right of a borrower to any rebate applicable under the Consumer Credit (Early Settlement) Regulations 2004 and, where applicable, a borrower therefore continues to be entitled to a rebate.

5A.2.9 G FCA

For the purposes of this chapter, where a *lender* allows a borrower to make a number of drawdowns of *credit* (which may be expressed to be possible up to a specified amount of *credit*) but only with the *lender's* consent to each respective drawdown, each drawdown is a separate agreement for *high-cost short-term credit* and each agreement needs to be documented as a separate *regulated credit agreement* in accordance with the *CCA* and with the rest of *CONC*. This chapter applies to each drawdown as a separate agreement accordingly.

Refinancing

5A.2.10 R FCA

A *firm* must not enter into an agreement for *high-cost short-term credit* that replaces an earlier agreement for *high-cost short-term credit* if the replacement agreement provides for the payment by the borrower of one or more charges that, taken together with the charges under the earlier agreement or a connected agreement to any of those agreements, exceed or are capable of exceeding the amount of *credit* provided (determined in accordance with **CONC 5A.2.6 R**) under the combined effect of the replacement agreement and the earlier agreement.

5A.2.11 R FCA

A *firm* must not enter into an agreement for *high-cost short-term credit* that replaces an earlier agreement for *high-cost short-term credit* if the replacement agreement provides for the payment by the borrower of one or more charges in connection with a breach of the agreement by the borrower that, taken together with such charges provided for by the earlier agreement or in a connected agreement to any of those agreements, exceed or are capable of exceeding £15.

5A.2.12 R FCA

If the effect of a replacement agreement is to repay an amount outstanding under an earlier agreement for *high-cost short-term credit* before the date on which the earlier agreement requires repayment, any charge imposed under the earlier agreement which never becomes payable as a result of the early settlement is disregarded for the purposes of **CONC 5A.2.10 R**.

5A.2.13 R FCA

A *firm* must not count any amount provided to the borrower to repay any amount of *credit* outstanding under an earlier agreement for *high-cost short-term credit* or any amount provided to pay any charge outstanding under the earlier agreement:

(1) in calculating the amount of *credit* provided for the purposes of **CONC 5A.2.10 R**; or

(2) where the *firm* replaces an earlier agreement for *high-cost short-term credit*, in calculating the amount of *credit* provided for the purposes of **CONC 5A.2.3 R** (Initial cost cap).

Default cap

5A.2.14 R FCA

A *firm* must not enter into an agreement for *high-cost short-term credit* if:

(1) it provides for one or more charges payable by the borrower in connection with a breach of the agreement by the borrower, which alone or in combination (and whether in relation to one breach or cumulatively in relation to multiple breaches of the agreement) exceed or are capable of exceeding £15; or

(2) it provides for the payment by the borrower of interest on a charge of a type in (1) that exceeds or is capable of exceeding 0.8% of the amount of the charge calculated per *day* from the date the charge is payable until the date the charge is paid; or

(3) it provides for the payment by the borrower of one or more charges (except for a charge to which (1) or (2) applies), on any amount of *credit* provided which in breach of the agreement has not been repaid, that alone or in combination exceed or are capable of exceeding 0.8% of that amount calculated per *day* from the date of the breach until the date that the amount has been repaid.

5A.2.15 G   FCA

Firms are also reminded of the provisions of section 93 of the *CCA* (Interest not to be increased on default).

Connected agreements

5A.2.16 R   FCA

Where a borrower or a prospective borrower pays a charge:

(1)   to a *firm*, that carries on or has carried on *credit broking* in relation to an agreement or prospective agreement for *high-cost short-term credit*, which is in the same *group* as the *firm* which is to provide, provides or has provided *credit* under the agreement for *high-cost short-term credit*; or

(2)   to a *firm*, that carries on or has carried on *credit broking* in relation to an agreement or prospective agreement for *high-cost short-term credit*, which shares some or all of that charge with the *firm* which is to provide, provides or has provided *credit* under the agreement for *high-cost short-term credit*;

the reference to a charge in **CONC 5A.2.2 R** (Total cost cap) and **CONC 5A.2.3 R** (Initial cost cap) includes this charge and the agreement providing for the charge is a connected agreement.

5A.2.17 R   FCA

Where a *person* imposes, on a borrower or a prospective borrower under an agreement for *high-cost short-term credit*, a charge for an ancillary service to the agreement, the reference to a charge in **CONC 5A.2.2 R** (Total cost cap), **CONC 5A.2.3 R** (Initial cost cap) and **CONC 5A.2.14 R** (Default cap) includes this charge and, if the charge is not provided for under the agreement for *high-cost short-term credit*, the agreement providing for the charge is a connected agreement.

5A.2.18 G   FCA

Examples of the types of ancillary service to an agreement for *high-cost short-term credit* referred to in **CONC 5A.2.17 R** include, but are not limited to, services related to processing the application and to the transmission of the money being lent, and insurance or insurance-like services ancillary to the agreement.

Prohibition on compound interest

5A.2.19 R   FCA

A *firm* must not enter into an agreement for *high-cost short-term credit*, which provides for a charge, by way of interest, other than a charge by way of simple interest.

5A.3   PROHIBITION FROM IMPOSING CHARGES UNDER AGREEMENTS FOR HIGH-COST SHORT-TERM CREDIT

Application

5A.3.1 R   FCA

This section applies to:

(1)   a *firm* with respect to *consumer credit lending*;

(2)   a *firm* with respect to *debt administration*;

(3)   a *firm* with respect to *debt collecting*; or

(4)   a *firm* with respect to *operating an electronic system in relation to lending*.

Cost caps: imposition of charges etc.: Total cost cap

5A.3.2 R   FCA

A *firm* must not:

(1)   impose one or more charges, on a borrower under an agreement for *high-cost short-term credit*, that, alone or in combination with any other charge under the agreement or a connected agreement, exceed or are capable of exceeding the amount of *credit* provided under the agreement;

(2)   arrange for or instruct another *person* to take the step described in (1).

Cost caps: imposition of charges etc.: Initial cost cap

5A.3.3 R   FCA

A *firm* must not impose one or more charges, on a borrower under an agreement for *high-cost short-term credit*, that, alone or in combination with any other charge under the agreement or a connected agreement, exceed or are capable of exceeding 0.8% of the amount of *credit* provided under the agreement calculated per *day* from the date on which the borrower draws down the *credit* until the date on which repayment of the *credit* is due under the agreement, but if the date of repayment is postponed by an indulgence or waiver, the date to which it is postponed.

5A.3.4 R   FCA

A reference to a charge in **CONC 5A.3.3 R** (Initial cost cap) excludes a charge to which **CONC 5A.3.18 R** (Default cap) applies.

5A.3.5 G   FCA
(1)   The initial cost cap is calculated on a daily basis. However, a charge or charges that may be imposed in compliance with this cap can amount to 0.8% of the *credit* provided (determined in accordance with **CONC 5A.3.7 R**) multiplied by the number of days from the date on which the borrower draws down the *credit* until the date indicated in **CONC 5A.3.3 R**.
(2)   Where *credit* is drawn down in tranches or is repaid in instalments, the calculation of the initial cost cap takes into account the different amounts of *credit* outstanding and the different durations for which the *credit* is provided.

Determining the amount of credit provided

5A.3.6 R   FCA

The amount of *credit* provided under an agreement for *high-cost short-term credit* for the purposes of **CONC 5A.3.2 R** (Total cost cap) is the lesser of:
(1)   the amount of *credit* that the *lender* actually advances under the agreement; or
(2)   the *credit limit*.

5A.3.7 R   FCA

The amount of *credit* provided under an agreement for *high-cost short-term credit* for the purposes of **CONC 5A.3.3 R** (Initial cost cap) is the amount of *credit* outstanding on the *day* in question under the agreement, disregarding for the purposes of that *rule* the effect of the borrower discharging all or part of the borrower's indebtedness in accordance with section 94 of the *CCA* (right to complete payments ahead of time) by repayment of *credit* before the date provided for in the agreement.

5A.3.8 G   FCA

For the purpose of the calculation of the initial cost cap, if there is an early repayment by the borrower of an amount of *credit* repayable under an agreement for *high-cost short-term credit* (including where that early repayment is financed by a replacement agreement), the amount of *credit* outstanding on the *days* that follow the early repayment is not reduced to reflect the amount of the early repayment. There is no effect, however, on the right of a borrower to any rebate applicable under the Consumer Credit (Early Settlement) Regulations 2004 and, where applicable, a borrower therefore continues to be entitled to a rebate.

5A.3.9 G   FCA

For the purposes of this chapter, where a *lender* allows a borrower to make a number of drawdowns of *credit* (which may be expressed to be possible up to a specified amount of *credit*) but only with the *lender's* consent to each respective drawdown, each drawdown is a separate agreement for *high-cost short-term credit* and each agreement needs to be documented as a separate *regulated credit agreement* in accordance with the *CCA* and with the rest of *CONC*. This chapter applies to each drawdown as a separate agreement accordingly.

Refinancing

5A.3.10 R   FCA

A *firm* must not impose one or more charges by way of an agreement that varies or supplements an earlier agreement for *high-cost short-term credit* if the amount of the charge or charges payable by the borrower taken together with such charges imposed under the earlier agreement or in a connected agreement to any of those agreements, exceed or are capable of exceeding the amount of *credit* provided (determined in accordance with **CONC 5A.3.6 R**) under the combined effect of the varying or supplemental agreement and the earlier agreement.

5A.3.11 R   FCA

A *firm* must not impose one or more charges by exercising a contractual power to vary or supplement an agreement for *high-cost short-term credit* if the amount of the charge or charges payable by the borrower taken together with such charges imposed under the agreement or in a connected agreement to that agreement, exceed or are capable of exceeding the amount of *credit* provided (determined in accordance with **CONC 5A.3.6 R**) under the agreement as varied or supplemented.

5A.3.12 R   FCA

A *firm* must not impose one or more charges in connection with a breach of the agreement by the borrower by way of an agreement that varies or supplements an earlier agreement for *high-cost short-term credit* if the amount of the charge or charges payable by the borrower, taken together with such charges imposed under the earlier agreement or in a connected agreement to any of those agreements, exceed or are capable of exceeding £15.

5A.3.13 R   FCA

A *firm* must not impose one or more charges in connection with a breach of the agreement by the borrower by exercising a contractual power to vary or supplement an agreement for *high-cost short-term credit* if the amount of the charge or charges payable by the borrower, taken together with such charges imposed under the agreement or in a connected agreement to any of those agreements, exceed or are capable of exceeding £15.

5A.3.14 R   FCA

A *firm* must not impose one or more charges under an agreement for *high-cost short-term credit* that replaces an earlier agreement for *high-cost short-term credit* if the charge or charges under the replacement agreement, taken together with the charges under the earlier agreement or a connected agreement to any of those agreements, exceed or are capable of exceeding the amount of *credit* provided (determined in accordance with **CONC 5A.3.6 R**) under the combined effect of the replacement agreement and the earlier agreement.

5A.3.15 R   FCA

A *firm* must not impose one or more charges in connection with a breach of the agreement by the borrower under an agreement for *high-cost short-term credit* that replaces an earlier agreement for *high-cost short-term credit* if the charge or charges under the replacement agreement payable by the borrower, taken together with such charges imposed under the earlier agreement or in a connected agreement to any of those agreements, exceed or are capable of exceeding £15.

5A.3.16 R   FCA

If the effect of a replacement agreement is to repay an amount outstanding under an earlier agreement for *high-cost short-term credit* before the date on which the earlier agreement requires repayment, any charge imposed under the earlier agreement which never becomes payable as a result of the early settlement is disregarded for the purposes of **CONC 5A.3.14 R**.

5A.3.17 R   FCA

A *firm* must not count any amount provided to the borrower to repay any amount of *credit* outstanding under an earlier agreement for *high-cost short-term credit* or any amount provided to pay any charge outstanding under the earlier agreement:

(1)   in calculating the amount of *credit* provided for the purposes of **CONC 5A.3.10 R**, **CONC 5A.3.11 R** or **CONC 5A.3.14 R**; or

(2)   where the *firm* replaces an earlier agreement for *high-cost short-term credit*, in calculating the amount of *credit* provided for the purposes of **CONC 5A.3.3 R** (Initial cost cap).

Default cap

5A.3.18 R   FCA

A *firm* must not impose, on a borrower under an agreement for *high-cost short-term credit*:

(1)   one or more charges payable by the borrower in connection with a breach of the agreement by the borrower, which charges alone or in combination (and whether in relation to one breach or in combination relate to multiple breaches of the agreement) exceed or are capable of exceeding £15;

(2)   a charge by way of interest on a charge of a type in (1) that exceeds or is capable of exceeding 0.8% of the amount of the charge calculated per *day* from the date the charge is payable until the date the charge is paid;

(3)   one or more charges (except for a charge to which (1) or (2) applies), on any amount of *credit* provided which in breach of the agreement has not been repaid, that alone or in combination, exceed or are capable of exceeding 0.8% of that amount calculated per *day* from the date of the breach until that amount has been repaid.

5A.3.19 G   FCA

Firms are also reminded of the provisions of section 93 of the *CCA* (Interest not to be increased on default).

Connected agreements and guidance on charges before assignment

5A.3.20 R   FCA

Where a borrower or a prospective borrower pays a charge:

(1)   to a *firm*, that carries on or has carried on *credit broking* in relation to an agreement or prospective agreement for *high-cost short-term credit*, which is in the same *group* as the *firm* which is to provide, provides or has provided *credit* under the agreement for *high-cost short-term credit*; or

(2)   to a *firm*, that carries on or has carried on *credit broking* in relation to an agreement or prospective agreement for *high-cost short-term credit*, which shares some or all of that charge with the *firm* which is to provide, provides or has provided *credit* under the agreement for *high-cost short-term credit*;

the reference to a charge in **CONC 5A.3.2 R** (Total cost cap) and **CONC 5A.3.3 R** (Initial cost cap) includes this charge and the agreement providing for the charge is a connected agreement.

Part 3   FCA Handbook Materials

5A.3.21 R   FCA

Where a *person* imposes on a borrower or a prospective borrower, under an agreement for *high-cost short-term credit*, a charge for an ancillary service to the agreement, the reference to a charge in **CONC 5A.3.2 R** (Total cost cap), **CONC 5A.3.3 R** (Initial cost cap) and **CONC 5A.3.18 R** (Default cap) includes this charge and, if the charge is not provided for under the agreement for *high-cost short-term credit*, the agreement providing for the charge is a connected agreement.

5A.3.22 G   FCA

Examples of the types of ancillary service to an agreement for *high-cost short-term credit* referred to in **CONC 5A.3.21 R** include, but are not limited to, services related to processing the application and to the transmission of the money being lent, and insurance or insurance-like services ancillary to the agreement.

5A.3.23 G   FCA

Where an agreement passes to another *firm* by assignment or by operation of law, any charges imposed in connection with the provision of *credit* under the agreement for *high-cost short-term credit* before the agreement passed to the *firm* are included within the charges referred to in **CONC 5A.3**.

Prohibition on compound interest

5A.3.24 R   FCA

A *firm* must not impose a charge under an agreement for *high-cost short-term credit*, which provides for a charge by way of interest, unless the *charge* is by way of simple interest.

5A.4   COST CAP FOR OPERATING AN ELECTRONIC SYSTEM IN RELATION TO LENDING

Application

5A.4.1 R   FCA

This section applies to a *firm* with respect to *operating an electronic system in relation to lending* in relation to a borrower or a prospective borrower under an agreement for *high-cost short-term credit*.

Cost cap rules for operating electronic systems in relation to lending: Total cost cap

5A.4.2 R   FCA

A *firm* must not facilitate an *individual* becoming a borrower under an agreement for *high-cost short-term credit* that provides for the payment by the borrower of one or more charges that, alone or in combination with any other charge under the agreement or a connected agreement, exceed or are capable of exceeding the amount of *credit* provided under the agreement.

Cost cap rules for operating electronic systems in relation to lending: Initial cost cap

5A.4.3 R   FCA

A *firm* must not facilitate an *individual* becoming a borrower under an agreement for *high-cost short-term credit* that provides for the payment by the borrower of one or more charges that, alone or in combination with any other charge under the agreement or a connected agreement, exceed or are capable of exceeding 0.8% of the amount of *credit* provided under the agreement calculated per *day* from the date on which the borrower draws down the *credit* until the date on which repayment of the *credit* is due under the agreement, but if the date of repayment is postponed by an indulgence or waiver, it is the date to which it is postponed.

5A.4.4 R   FCA

A reference to a charge in **CONC 5A.4.3 R** excludes a charge to which **CONC 5A.4.14 R** (Default cap) applies.

5A.4.5 G   FCA

(1)   The initial cost cap is calculated on a daily basis. However, a charge or charges that may be provided for in an agreement in compliance with this cap can amount to 0.8% of the credit provided (determined in accordance with **CONC 5A.4.7 R**) multiplied by the number of days from the date on which the borrower draws down the *credit* until the date indicated in **CONC 5A.4.3 R**.

(2)   Where *credit* is drawn down in tranches or is repaid in instalments, the calculation of the initial cost cap takes into account the different amounts of *credit* outstanding and the different durations for which the *credit* is provided.

Determining the amount of credit provided

5A.4.6 R   FCA

The amount of *credit* provided under an agreement for *high-cost short-term credit* for the purposes of **CONC 5A.4.2 R** (Total cost cap) is the lesser of:

(1)   the amount of *credit* that the *lender* actually advances under the agreement; or

(2)   the *credit limit*.

5A.4.7 R   FCA

The amount of *credit* provided under an agreement for *high-cost short-term credit* for the purposes of **CONC 5A.4.3 R** (Initial cost cap) is the amount of *credit* outstanding on the *day* in question under the agreement, disregarding for the purposes of that rule the effect of the borrower discharging all or part of the borrower's indebtedness in accordance with section 94 of the *CCA* (right to complete payments ahead of time) by repayment of *credit* before the date provided for in the agreement.

5A.4.8 G   FCA

For the purpose of the calculation of the initial cost cap, if there is an early repayment by the borrower of an amount of *credit* repayable under an agreement for *high-cost short-term credit* (including where that early repayment is financed by a replacement agreement), the amount of *credit* outstanding on the *days* that follow the early repayment is not reduced to reflect the amount of the early repayment. There is no effect, however, on the right of a borrower to any rebate applicable under the Consumer Credit (Early Settlement) Regulations 2004 and, where applicable, a borrower therefore continues to be entitled to a rebate.

5A.4.9 G   FCA

For the purposes of this chapter, where a *lender* allows a borrower to make a number of drawdowns of *credit* (which may be expressed to be possible up to a specified amount of *credit*) but only with the *lender's* consent to each respective drawdown, each drawdown is a separate agreement for *high-cost short-term credit* and, where applicable, each agreement needs to be documented as a separate *regulated credit agreement* in accordance with the *CCA* and with the rest of *CONC*. This chapter applies to each drawdown as a separate agreement accordingly.

Refinancing

5A.4.10 R   FCA

A *firm* must not facilitate an *individual* becoming a borrower under an agreement for *high-cost short-term credit* that replaces an earlier agreement for *high-cost short-term credit* if the replacement agreement provides for the payment by the borrower of one or more charges that, taken together with the charges under the earlier agreement or a connected agreement to any of those agreements, exceed or are capable of exceeding the amount of *credit* provided (determined in accordance with **CONC 5A.4.6 R**) under the combined effect of the replacement agreement and the earlier agreement.

5A.4.11 R   FCA

A *firm* must not facilitate an *individual* becoming a borrower under an agreement for *high-cost short-term credit* that replaces an earlier agreement for *high-cost short-term credit* if the replacement agreement provides for the payment by the borrower of one or more charges in connection with a breach of the agreement by the borrower that, taken together with such charges provided for by the earlier agreement or in a connected agreement to any of those agreements, exceed or are capable of exceeding £15.

5A.4.12 R   FCA

If the effect of a replacement agreement is to repay an amount outstanding under an earlier agreement for *high-cost short-term credit* before the date on which the earlier agreement requires repayment, any charge imposed under the earlier agreement which never becomes payable as a result of the early settlement is disregarded for the purposes of **CONC 5A.4.10 R**.

5A.4.13 R   FCA

No amount is to be counted which is provided to the borrower to repay any amount of *credit* outstanding under an earlier agreement for *high-cost short-term credit* or any amount provided to pay any charge outstanding under the earlier agreement:

(1)   in calculating the amount of *credit* provided for the purposes of **CONC 5A.4.10 R**; or

(2)   where an earlier agreement for *high-cost short-term credit* is replaced, in calculating the amount of *credit* provided for the purposes of **CONC 5A.4.3 R** (Initial cost cap).

Default cap

5A.4.14 R   FCA

A *firm* must not facilitate an *individual* becoming a borrower under an agreement for *high-cost short-term credit* if:

(1)   it provides for one or more charges payable by the borrower in connection with a breach of the agreement by the borrower, which alone or in combination (and whether in relation to one breach or cumulatively in relation to multiple breaches of the agreement) exceed or are capable of exceeding £15; or

(2)   it provides for the payment by the borrower of interest on a charge of a type in (1) that exceeds or is capable of exceeding 0.8% of the amount of the charge calculated per *day* from the date the charge is payable until the date the charge is paid; or

(3)   it provides for the payment by the borrower of one or more charges (except for a charge to which (1) or (2) applies), on any amount of *credit* provided which in breach of the agreement has not been repaid, that alone or in combination exceed or are capable of exceeding 0.8% of that amount calculated per *day* from the date of the breach until the date that the amount has been repaid.

5A.4.15 G   FCA

Firms are also reminded of the provisions of section 93 of the *CCA* (Interest not to be increased on default).

Connected agreements

5A.4.16 R   FCA

Where a borrower or a prospective borrower pays a charge:

(1)   to a *firm*, that carries on or has carried on *credit broking* in relation to an agreement or prospective agreement for *high-cost short-term credit*, which is in the same *group* as the *firm* which is to facilitate, facilitates or has facilitated the provision of *credit* under the agreement for *high-cost short-term credit*; or

(2)   to a *firm*, that carries on or has carried on *credit broking* in relation to an agreement or prospective agreement for *high-cost short-term credit*, which shares some or all of that charge with the *firm* which is to facilitate, facilitates or has facilitated the provision of *credit* under the agreement for *high-cost short-term credit*;

the reference to a charge in **CONC 5A.4.2 R** (Total cost cap) and **CONC 5A.4.3 R** (Initial cost cap) includes this charge and the agreement providing for the charge is a connected agreement.

5A.4.17 R   FCA

Where a *person* imposes, on a borrower or a prospective borrower under an agreement for *high-cost short-term credit*, a charge for an ancillary service to the agreement, the reference to a charge in **CONC 5A.4.2 R** (Total cost cap), **CONC 5A.4.3 R** (Initial cost cap) and **CONC 5A.4.14 R** (Default cap) includes this charge and, if the charge is not provided for under the agreement for *high-cost short-term credit*, the agreement providing for the charge is a connected agreement.

5A.4.18 G   FCA

Examples of the types of ancillary service to an agreement for *high-cost short-term credit* referred to in **CONC 5A.4.17 R** include, but are not limited to, services related to processing the application and to the transmission of the money being lent, and insurance or insurance-like services ancillary to the agreement.

Prohibition on compound interest

5A.4.19 R   FCA

A *firm* must not facilitate an *individual* becoming a borrower under an agreement for *high-cost short-term credit* which provides for a charge by way of interest, unless the charge is by way of simple interest.

5A.5   CONSEQUENCES OF CONTRAVENTION OF THE COST CAPS

Application

5A.5.1 R   FCA

This section applies to:

(1)   a *firm* with respect to *consumer credit lending*;

(2)   a *firm* with respect to *debt administration*;

(3)   a *firm* with respect to *debt collecting*; or

(4)   a *firm* with respect to *operating an electronic system in relation to lending*.

Contravention of cost caps and unenforceability of agreements and obligations

5A.5.2 R   FCA

Where:

(1)   a *firm* enters into an agreement for *high-cost short-term credit* in contravention of a rule in **CONC 5A.2**; or

(2)   a *firm* facilitates an *individual* becoming a borrower under an agreement for *high-cost short-term credit* in contravention of a *rule* in **CONC 5A.4**; or

(3)   a *firm* within **CONC 5A.5.1 R (1)** imposes a charge in contravention of a rule in **CONC 5A.3**; or

(4)   a *firm* within **CONC 5A.5.1 R (4)** imposes a charge on behalf of a lender in contravention of a *rule* in **CONC 5A.3**; or

(5)   a *firm* within **CONC 5A.5.1 R (2)** or **CONC 5A.5.1 R (3)** on behalf of a *firm* within **CONC 5A.5.1 R (1)** or **CONC 5A.5.1 R (4)** imposes a charge in contravention of a *rule* in **CONC 5A.3**:

     (a)   the agreement is unenforceable against the borrower; and

     (b)   the borrower may choose not to perform the agreement and if that is the case:

         (i)   at the written or oral request of the borrower, the *lender* must, as soon as reasonably practicable following the request and in any case within 7 *days* of the request, repay to the borrower any charges paid by the borrower under the agreement or confirm by notice in writing to the borrower that there are no charges to pay;

         (ii)   where the *lender* complies with (i), the borrower must repay any *credit* received by the borrower under the agreement to the *lender* within a reasonable period from the day on which the charges in (i) are received by the borrower or the day on which the notice of confirmation in (i) is received; and

         (iii)   in any case, the *lender* must not demand payment of the sum in (ii) in less than 30 days from the day in (ii).

5A.5.3 R   FCA

Where an agreement for *high-cost short-term credit* provides for or imposes one or more charges that alone or in combination exceed or are capable of exceeding an amount set out in **CONC 5A.2** or **CONC 5A.3**:

(1)   the agreement is unenforceable against the borrower to the extent that such a charge or such charges exceed or are capable of exceeding that amount; and

(2)   the borrower may choose not to perform the agreement to that extent and if that is the case at the written or oral request of the borrower, the *lender* must, as soon as reasonably practicable following the request and in any case within 7 *days* of the request, repay to the borrower any charges to the extent in (1) paid by the borrower under the agreement or confirm by notice in writing to the borrower that there are no charges to that extent to pay.

5A.5.4 G   FCA

Once the *lender* has repaid the charges to the borrower or has confirmed there are no charges to repay the borrower is then under a statutory obligation to repay any *credit* received under the agreement.

5A.5.5 G   FCA

What is a reasonable period for the borrower to repay the *credit* depends on the circumstances of the case, including the terms for repayment under the agreement. Where the agreement provided for repayment in instalments, the *firm* should consider issuing the borrower with a schedule for repayment under which the *firm* would collect the *credit* in instalments at the same periodic intervals as under the agreement.

5A.5.6 G   FCA

Firms are reminded that Principle 6 applies to how they deal with borrowers in relation to repayment of the *credit* required by **CONC 5A.5.2 R**. The *FCA* would expect firms to take into account the financial situation of the borrower in considering what is a reasonable period for repayment.

5A.5.7 G   FCA

CONC 5A.5.3 R is a residual provision that applies to a *firm* established in the *UK* which carries on *debt administration* or *debt collection*, but where the *rules* in **CONC 5A** do not apply to a *lender* because the *lender* is established outside the *UK* and provides *electronic commerce activities* into the *UK*. Where a borrower gives notice to the *lender* referred to in **CONC 5A.5.3 R**, only charges which exceed the amounts set out in **CONC 5A.2** or **CONC 5A.3** are void. The borrower remains under a contractual obligation to repay the *credit* received under the agreement and any charges under the agreement permitted by those provisions.

5A.6   INTERPRETATION

5A.6.1 R   FCA

In this chapter:

(1)   "ancillary service" is a service in connection with the provision of *credit* under the agreement for *high-cost short-term credit* and includes, but not limited to, an insurance or payment protection policy;

(2)   "borrower" is an *individual* and includes:

     (a)   any person providing a guarantee or indemnity under the *regulated credit agreement*; and

     (b)   a person to whom the rights and duties of the borrower under the *regulated credit agreement* or of a person falling within (a) have passed by assignment or operation of law;

(3)   "charge" is a charge payable, by way of interest or otherwise, in connection with the provision of *credit* under the *regulated credit agreement*, whether or not the agreement itself makes provision for it and whether or not the *person* to whom it is payable is a party to the *regulated credit agreement* or an *authorised person*;

(4)   "connected agreement" is an agreement which provides for a charge within **CONC 5A.2.16 R, CONC 5A.2.17 R, CONC 5A.3.20 R, CONC 5A.3.21 R, CONC 5A.4.16 R** and **CONC 5A.4.17 R**;

(5)   "impose one or more charges on a borrower under an agreement for *high-cost short-term credit*" includes taking the following actions under the agreement:

    (a)   taking steps to perform duties, or exercise or enforce rights, on behalf of a *lender* in relation to a charge; or in relation to a *firm* with respect to *operating an electronic system in relation to lending*, exercise or enforce rights, on behalf of a *lender* in relation to one or more charges;

    (b)   taking steps to procure the payment of a debt due in relation to one or more charges;

    (c)   undertaking to receive payments in respect of interest due under an agreement for *high-cost short-term credit* and make payments in respect of interest due under the agreement to the *lender*;

    (d)   arranging for or instructing another *person* to take any of the steps described in (a), (b) or (c); or

    (e)   exercising the rights of the *lender* in a way that enables the imposition on the borrower of one or more charges.

5A.6.2 G   FCA

The meaning of the expression "impose one or more charges on a borrower under an agreement for *high-cost short-term credit*" is set out in **CONC 5A.6.1 R (5)**. The meaning of "impose" in relation to a charge in this chapter is broad and includes, but is not limited to, situations including where a *firm*:

(1)   enters into an agreement containing a clause obliging the borrower to pay a charge;

(2)   varies or supplements an agreement and this has the result that there is:

    (a)   an increase in the amount of a charge; or

    (b)   where the amount of a charge is determined by reference to a period of time, an increase in the period of time to which a charge applies;

(3)   adds a charge to a borrower's account;

(4)   communicates with a borrower demanding payment of a charge or indicating that the borrower is, will be or may be obliged to pay the charge; and

(5)   is *operating an electronic system in relation to lending*, and it does any of activities in (1) to (4) for a *lender*.

CHAPTER 6
POST CONTRACTUAL REQUIREMENTS

6.1   APPLICATION

[3.84]
6.1.1 R   FCA

This chapter applies, unless otherwise stated in a *rule*, or in relation to a *rule*, to a *firm* with respect to *consumer credit lending*.

6.1.2 G   FCA

(1)   **CONC 6.2, CONC 6.5** and **CONC 6.7** apply to firms with respect to *consumer credit lending*.

(2)   **CONC 6.3** applies to current account agreements that would be *regulated credit agreements* if the *customer* overdraws on the account.

(3)   **CONC 6.4** and **CONC 6.6** apply to *firms* which carry on *consumer credit lending* in relation to *regulated credit agreements* and *firms* which carry on *consumer hiring* in relation to *regulated consumer hire agreements*.

(4)   **CONC 6.7.17 R** to **CONC 6.7.26 R** also apply to *firms* with respect to *operating an electronic system in relation to lending* in relation to a *borrower* in relation to a *P2P agreement*.

(5)   **CONC 6.8** applies to *credit broking*.

6.2   ASSESSMENT OF CREDITWORTHINESS: DURING AGREEMENT

6.2.1 R   FCA

(1)   Before significantly increasing:

    (a)   the amount of *credit* to be provided under a *regulated credit agreement*; or

    (b)   a *credit limit* for *running-account credit* under a *regulated credit agreement*;

the *lender* must undertake an assessment of the *customer's* creditworthiness.

[**Note**: section 55B(2) of *CCA*]

(2)   A *firm* carrying out the assessment in (1) must consider:
      (a)   the potential for the commitments under the *regulated credit agreement* to adversely impact the *customer's* financial situation, taking into account the information of which the *firm* is aware at the time that the increase in (1) is to be granted; and
      (b)   the ability of the *customer* to make *repayments* as they fall due over the life of the *regulated credit agreement*, or for such an agreement which is an *open-end agreement*, to make *repayments* within a reasonable period.
          [**Note**: paragraphs 4.1 and 4.3 of *ILG*]
(3)   A creditworthiness assessment must be based on sufficient information obtained from:
      (a)   the *customer*, where appropriate, and
      (b)   a *credit reference agency*, where necessary.
(4)   This *rule* does not apply to:
      (a)   an agreement secured on *land*; or
      (b)   an agreement under which a *person* takes an article in *pawn*.
(5)   This *rule* does not apply, except to the agreements in (6), to:
      (a)   a *non-commercial agreement*;
      (b)   a *borrower-lender agreement* enabling the *borrower* to overdraw on a current account;
      (c)   a *small borrower-lender-supplier agreement* for restricted-use credit.
(6)   The agreements referred to in (5) and therefore to which this *rule* does apply are:
      (a)   a *borrower-lender agreement* enabling the *borrower* to overdraw on a current account which is an *authorised business overdraft agreement* or an *authorised non-business overdraft agreement*; or
          [**Note**: section 74(1B)/(1C) of *CCA*]
      (b)   a *borrower-lender agreement* enabling the *borrower* to overdraw on a current account which would be an *authorised non-business overdraft agreement* but for the fact that the *credit* is not repayable on demand within three *months*.
          [**Note**: section 74(1D) of *CCA*].

6.2.2 R   FCA

Where **CONC 6.2.1 R** applies to a *firm*:
[**Note**: paragraph 4.2 of *ILG*]
(1)   the *firm* must comply with **CONC 5.3.2 R**, **CONC 5.3.4 R**, **CONC 5.3.5 R**, **CONC 5.3.6 R** and **CONC 5.3.7 R**
(2)   the *rules* in **CONC 5.3** referred to in (1) apply with the modifications necessary to take into account that **CONC 6.2.1 R** concerns increases in the amount of *credit* and in *credit limits* and when the increase is to take place; and
(3)   the *guidance* in **CONC 5.3** applies accordingly and **CONC 5.2.3 G** and **CONC 5.3.4 R** apply treating them as guidance on **CONC 6.2.1 R**.

6.2.3 R   FCA

A *firm* must consider sufficient information available to it at the time of the increase referred to in **CONC 6.2.1 R** to enable it to make a reasonable assessment required by that *rule*.
[Note: paragraph 4.21 of *ILG*]

6.3   INFORMATION TO BE PROVIDED ON A CURRENT ACCOUNT AGREEMENT AND ON SIGNIFICANT OVERDRAWING

Application

6.3.1 R   FCA

This section applies:
(1)   to a *firm* with respect to *consumer credit lending*; and
(2)   where a *firm* has entered into a current account agreement where:
      (a)   there is a possibility that the account-holder may be allowed to overdraw on the current account without a pre-arranged overdraft or exceed a pre-arranged overdraft limit; and
      (b)   if the account-holder did so, this would be a *regulated credit agreement*.

6.3.2 R   FCA

CONC 6.3.3 R does not apply where the overdraft or excess would be secured on *land*.

Current account information

6.3.3 R   FCA

A *firm* must provide to the account-holder, in writing, the information in **CONC 4.7.2 R (2)** at least annually.
[**Note**: section 74A of *CCA* (partial implementation of article 18 of the *Consumer Credit Directive*)]

Information to be provided on significant overdrawing without prior arrangement

6.3.4 R   FCA

(1)   A *firm* must inform the account-holder in writing of the matters in (2) without delay where:

    (a)   the account-holder overdraws on the current account without a pre-arranged overdraft, or exceeds a pre-arranged overdraft limit, for a period exceeding one *month*;

    (b)   the amount of that overdraft or excess is significant throughout that period;

    (c)   the overdraft or excess is a *regulated credit agreement*; and

    (d)   the account-holder has not been informed in writing of the matters in (2) within that period.

(2)   The matters in (1) are:

    (a)   the fact that the account is overdrawn or the overdraft limit has been exceeded;

    (b)   the amount of that overdraft or excess;

    (c)   the rate of interest charged on it; and

    (d)   any other charges payable by the *customer* in relation to it (including any penalties and any interest on those charges).

(3)   For the purposes of (1)(b) the amount of the overdraft or excess is significant if:

    (a)   the account-holder is liable to pay a charge for which he would not otherwise be liable; or

    (b)   the overdraft or excess is likely to have an adverse effect on the *customer's* ability to receive further *credit* (including any effect on the information about the *customer* held by a *credit reference agency*); or

    (c)   it otherwise appears significant, having regard to all the circumstances.

(4)   Where the overdraft or excess is secured on *land*, (1)(a) is to be read as if the reference to one *month* were a reference to three *months*.

[**Note**: section 74B of *CCA*]
[**Note**: article 18 of the *Consumer Credit Directive*]

6.4   APPROPRIATION OF PAYMENTS

Application

6.4.1 R   FCA

This section applies to

(1)   a *firm* with respect to *consumer credit lending*;

(2)   a *firm* with respect to *consumer hiring*.

Appropriation

6.4.2 R   FCA

(1)   Where a *firm* is entitled to payments from the same *customer* in respect of two or more *regulated agreements*, the *firm* must allow the *customer*, on making any payment in respect of those agreements which is not sufficient to discharge the total amount then due under all the agreements, to appropriate the sum paid by him:

    (a)   in or towards the satisfaction of the sum due under any one of the agreements; or

    (b)   in or towards the satisfaction of the sums due under any two or more of the agreements in such proportions as the *customer* thinks fit.

    [**Note**: section 81(1) of *CCA*]

(2)   If the *customer* fails to make any such appropriation where one or more of the agreements is:

    (a)   a *hire-purchase agreement* or *conditional sale agreement*; or

    (b)   a *consumer hire agreement*; or

    (c)   an agreement in relation to which any *security* is provided;

    the *firm* must appropriate the payment towards satisfaction of the sums due under the agreements in the proportions which those sums bear to one another.

    [**Note**: section 81(2) of *CCA*]

6.5   ASSIGNMENT OF RIGHTS

Application

6.5.1 R   FCA

This section applies to a *firm* with respect to *consumer credit lending*.

Notice of assignment

6.5.2 R   FCA

(1)   Where rights of a *lender* under a *regulated credit agreement* are assigned to a *firm*, that *firm* must arrange for notice of the assignment to be given to the *customer*:

    (a)   as soon as reasonably possible; or

(b)   if, after the assignment, the arrangements for servicing the *credit* under the agreement do not change as far as the *customer* is concerned, on or before the first occasion they do.

[**Note**: section 82A of *CCA*]

(2)   Paragraph (1) does not apply to an agreement secured on *land*.

(3)   A *firm* may assign the rights of a *lender* under a *regulated credit agreement* to a third party only if:

(a)   the third party is a *firm*; or

(b)   where the third party does not require *authorisation*, the *firm* has an agreement with the third party which requires the third party to arrange for a notice of assignment in accordance with (1).

[**Note**: article 17 of the *Consumer Credit Directive*]

6.6   PAWN BROKING: CONDUCT OF BUSINESS

Application

6.6.1 R   FCA

This section applies to:

(1)   a *firm* with respect to *consumer credit lending*;

(2)   a *firm* with respect to *consumer hiring*.

Failure to supply copies of pledge agreement etc

6.6.2 G   FCA

Sections 62 to 64 and 114(1) of the *CCA* continue to apply to a *regulated agreement* under which a *person* takes any article in *pawn*. A *firm* which fails to observe its obligations under those provisions may be subject to disciplinary action by the *FCA*.

[**Note**: section 115 of *CCA*]

Pawn records: relating to articles under a regulated credit agreement

6.6.3 R   FCA

A *firm* which takes any article in *pawn* under a *regulated credit agreement* must keep such books or other records as are sufficient to show and explain readily at any time all dealings with the article, including:

(1)   the taking of the article in *pawn*;

(2)   any redemption of the article; and

(3)   where the article has become realisable by the *firm*, any sale of the article under section 121(1) of the *CCA*.

[**Note**: regulation 2(1) of SI 1983/1565]

6.6.4 R   FCA

Without prejudice to the generality of **CONC 6.6.3 R**, the entries in the books or other records in respect of the dealings mentioned in **CONC 6.6.3 R (1)** to **CONC 6.6.3 R (3)** must contain the information in **CONC 6.6.7 R** to **CONC 6.6.9 R**.

[**Note**: regulation 2(2) of SI 1983/1565]

6.6.5 R   FCA

Where the entries in relation to any article taken in *pawn* in **CONC 6.6.4 R** are not shown together as a whole but are shown in separate places, then in each place where entries are made the record must show:

(1)   the date and the number or other reference of the agreement under which the article was taken in *pawn* and, where separate from any document embodying the agreement, the number or other reference of the pawn-receipt;

(2)   the date on which the article was taken in *pawn*; and

(3)   the name of the *customer*.

[**Note**: regulation 2(3) of SI 1983/1565]

6.6.6 R   FCA

A *firm* must retain the books or other records required by **CONC 6.6.3 R** at least until the expiration of whichever is the longer of the following periods:

(1)   five years from the date on which the article was taken in *pawn*; or

(2)   where an article has become realisable by the *firm*, three years from the date of sale under section 121(1) of the *CCA* or the redemption of the article, as the case may be.

[**Note**: regulation 2(4) of SI 1983/1565]

Information to be kept by a person who takes any article in pawn

6.6.7 R   FCA

The entries in the books or other records, in relation to the taking of the article in *pawn*, must contain the following information:

(1) the date and the number or other reference of the agreement under which the article was taken in *pawn*, and of the pawn-receipt if separate, sufficient to identify it or them;
(2) the date on which the article was taken in *pawn*;
(3) the name and a postal address and, where appropriate, other address of the *customer*;
(4) the description that appears in the pawn-receipt of the article taken in *pawn*;
(5) the amount of the *credit* secured by the *pledge*;
(6) the date of the end of the redemption period; and
(7) the rate of interest, and the amount or rate of any other charges for *credit*, as provided for in the agreement under which the article was take in *pawn*.
[**Note**: paragraph 1 of Schedule to SI 1983/1565]

6.6.8 R   FCA

The entries in the books or other records in relation to any redemption of the article must contain the date of the redemption.
[**Note**: paragraph 2 of Schedule to SI 1983/1565]

6.6.9 R   FCA

The entries in the books or other records, where the article has become realisable by the *firm*, in relation to any sale of the article under section 121(1) of the *CCA*, must contain the following information:

(1) the date of the sale;
(2) where the article was sold by auction, the name and a postal address of the auctioneer;
(3) where the article was not sold by auction, the postal address of the premises at which the sale took place;
(4) the gross amount realised;
(5) the itemised expenses, if any, of the sale;
(6) where (5) applies, the net proceeds of sale, being the difference between the gross amount in (4) and the total amount of the expenses in (5);
(7) the amount which would have been payable under the agreement under which the article was taken in *pawn* if the article had been redeemed on the date of the sale;
(8) where the net proceeds of sale are not less than the sum which, if the article taken in *pawn* had been redeemed on the date of the sale, would have been payable for its redemption, the amount of any surplus payable to the *customer*;
(9) where (8) does not apply, the amount by which the net proceeds of sale fall short of the sum which would have been payable for the redemption of the article taken in *pawn* on the date of the sale, being the amount for which the *customer* remains liable under section 121(4) of the *CCA*;
(10) the date on which any surplus in (8) was paid to the *customer*;
(11) the date on which any amount in (9) for which the *customer* remained liable under section 121(4) of the *CCA* was received from the *customer*.
[**Note**: paragraph 3 to Schedule to SI 1983/1565]

6.7   POST CONTRACT: BUSINESS PRACTICES

Application

6.7.1 R   FCA

(1) This section applies to a *firm* with respect to *consumer credit lending*.
(2) **CONC 6.7.17 R** to **CONC 6.7.26 R** also apply to a *firm* with respect to *operating an electronic system in relation to lending* in relation to lending to a *borrower* under a *P2P agreement* and references in those provisions to a *firm* refinancing an agreement refer to any action taken by an *operator of an electronic system in relation to lending* which has the result that a *P2P agreement* is refinanced.

Business practices

6.7.2 R   FCA

A *firm* must monitor a *customer's* repayment record and take appropriate action where there are signs of actual or possible repayment difficulties.
[**Note**: paragraph 6.2 of *ILG*]

6.7.3 G   FCA

The action referred to in **CONC 6.7.2 R** should generally include:

(1) notifying the *customer* of the risk of escalating debt, additional interest or charges and of potential financial difficulties; and
[**Note**: paragraph 6.16 of *ILG*]
(2) providing contact details for *not-for-profit debt advice bodies*.
[**Note**: paragraph 6.2 (box) of *ILG*]

Credit card and store card requirements

6.7.4 R   FCA

A *firm* must first allocate a *repayment* to the debt subject to the highest rate of interest (and then to the next highest rate of interest and so on) for:

(1)   the outstanding balance on a credit card; or

(2)   the outstanding balance on a store card; or

(3)   a credit card or a store card, in relation to which there is a *fixed-sum credit* element, to *repayments* beyond those required to satisfy the fixed instalments.

       [**Note**: paragraph 6.3 of *ILG*]

6.7.5 R   FCA

(1)   A *firm* must set the minimum required *repayment* under a *regulated credit agreement* for a credit card or a store card at an amount equal to at least that amount which repays the interest, fees and charges that have been applied to the *customer's* account, plus one percentage of the amount outstanding.

       [**Note**: paragraph 6.4 of *ILG*]

(2)   Where (1) applies and a *firm* applies interest to a period of more than one *month*, for the purpose of calculating the amount of the interest part of the minimum required *repayment* the *firm* may disregard any interest applied in respect of a period prior to the period of the statement in question.

       [**Note**: paragraph 6.4 (box) of *ILG*]

(3)   Paragraph (1) applies to agreements made on or after 1 April 2011.

6.7.6 R   FCA

A *firm* under a *regulated credit agreement* for a credit card or a store card must provide a *customer* with the option to pay any amount they choose (equal to or more than the minimum required repayment but less than the full outstanding balance) on a regular basis, when making automated *repayments*.

[**Note**: paragraph 6.5 of *ILG*]

6.7.7 R   FCA

A *firm* must not increase, nor offer to increase, the *customer's* credit limit on a credit card or store card where:

(1)   the *firm* has been advised that the *customer* does not wish to have any *credit limit* increases; or

(2)   a *customer* is at risk of financial difficulties.

       [**Note**: paragraphs 6.6 and 6.7 of *ILG*]

6.7.8 R   FCA

A *firm* under a *regulated credit agreement* for a credit card or a store card must:

(1)   permit a *customer* at any time to reduce or decline offers to increase the *credit limit*; and

(2)   permit a *customer* to decline to receive offers of *credit limit* increases.

       [**Note**: paragraphs 6.8 and 6.9 of *ILG*]

6.7.9 R   FCA

A *firm* under a *regulated credit agreement* for a credit card or store card must notify the *customer* of a proposed increase in the *credit limit* under the agreement at least 30 days before the increase comes into effect, except where:

[**Note**: paragraph 6.17 of *ILG*]

(1)   the increase is at the express request of the *customer*; or

(2)   the increase is proposed by the *firm*, but the *customer* agrees to it at that time and wishes it to come into effect in less than 30 days.

6.7.10 R   FCA

Where a *customer* is at risk of financial difficulties, a *firm* under a *regulated credit agreement* for a credit card or a store card must, other than where a promotional rate of interest ends, not increase the rate of interest under the agreement.

[**Note**: paragraph 6.10 of *ILG*]

6.7.11 G   FCA

For the purposes of **CONC 6.7.7 R** and **CONC 6.7.10 R** a *customer* is at risk of financial difficulties if the *customer*:

(1)   is two or more payments in arrears; or

(2)   has agreed a repayment plan with the *firm* in question; or

(3)   is in serious discussion with a *firm* which carries on *debt counselling* with a view to entering into a *debt management plan* and the *firm* has been notified of this fact.

       [**Note**: paragraph 6.10 (box) of *ILG*]

6.7.12 R   FCA

(1)   A *firm* under a *regulated credit agreement* for a credit card or store card must notify a *customer* at least 30 days before an increase in the rate of interest under the agreement comes into effect.
       [**Note**: paragraph 6.18) of *ILG*]

(2)   Paragraph (1) does not apply in the following cases where in relation to an agreement:
       (a)   the interest rate is set to directly track the movement in an external index (such as a base rate), which was adequately explained under **CONC 4.2.15 R** and was clearly stated in the agreement; or
       (b)   the period of a promotional interest rate has come to an end.

6.7.13 R   FCA

Where a *firm* proposes to exercise a power under a *regulated credit agreement* for a credit card or store card to increase the interest rate, the *firm* must:

(1)   permit the *customer* sixty days, from the date of the *firm's* notice of the proposed increase during which period the *customer* may give notice to the *firm* requiring it to close the account;

(2)   permit the *customer* to pay off the outstanding balance at the rate of interest before the proposed increase and over a reasonable period; and

(3)   give notice to the *customer* of the rights in (1) and (2).
       [**Note**: paragraphs 6.11 and 6.19 of *ILG*]

Interest rate variations

6.7.14 R   FCA

Where a *firm* has a right to increase the interest rate under a *regulated credit agreement*, the *firm* must not increase the interest rate unless there is a valid reason for doing so.
[**Note**: paragraph 6.20 of *ILG*]

6.7.15 G   FCA

Examples of valid reasons for increasing the rate of interest in **CONC 6.7.14 R** include:

(1)   recovering the genuine increased costs of funding the provision of *credit* under the agreement; and

(2)   a change in the risk presented by the *customer* which justifies the change in the interest rate, which would not generally include missing a single *repayment* or failing to repay in full on one or two occasions
       [**Note**: paragraph 6.20 (box) of *ILG*]

6.7.16 R   FCA

Where a *firm* increases a rate of interest based on a change in the risk presented by the *customer*, the *firm* must:

(1)   notify the *customer* that the rate of interest has been increased based on a change in risk presented by the *customer*; and

(2)   if requested by the *customer* provide a suitable explanation which may be a generic explanation for such increases.
       [**Note**: paragraph 6.20 (box) of *ILG*]

Rules on refinancing: general

6.7.17 R   FCA

(1)   In **CONC 6.7.18 R** to **CONC 6.7.23 R** "refinance" means to extend, or purport to extend, the period over which one or more *repayment* is to be made by a *customer* whether by:
       (a)   agreeing with the *customer* to replace, vary or supplement an existing *regulated credit agreement*;
       (b)   exercising a contractual power contained in an existing *regulated credit agreement*; or
       (c)   other means, for example, granting an indulgence or waiver to the *customer*.

(2)   "Exercise forbearance" means to refinance a *regulated credit agreement* where the result is that no interest accrues at any time in relation to that agreement or any which replaces, varies or supplements it from the date of the refinancing and either:
       (a)   there is no charge in connection with the refinancing; or
       (b)   the only additional charge is a reasonable estimate of the actual and necessary cost of the additional administration required in connection with the refinancing.

(3)   The term "refinance" within paragraph (1) does not include where under a *regulated credit agreement* repayable in instalments a *customer* requests a change in the regular payment date and as a result there is no charge or additional interest in connection with the change.

6.7.18 R   FCA

A *firm* must not encourage a *customer* to refinance a *regulated credit agreement* if the result would be the *customer's* commitments are not *sustainable*.
[**Note**: paragraph 4.27 of *ILG*]

6.7.19 R FCA

A *firm* must not refinance a *customer's* existing *credit* with the *firm* (other than by exercising forbearance), unless:
(1)   the *firm* does so at the *customer's* request or with the *customer's* consent; and
(2)   the *firm* reasonably believes that it is not against the *customer's* best interests to do so.
[**Note**: paragraph 6.24 of *ILG*]

Rules on refinancing: high-cost short-term credit

6.7.20 R FCA

Before a *firm* agrees to refinance *high-cost short-term credit*, it must:
(1)   give or send an information sheet to the *customer*; and
(2)   where reasonably practicable to do so, bring the sheet to the attention of the *customer* before the refinance;

in the form of the arrears information sheet issued by the *FCA* referred to in section 86A of the *CCA* with the following modifications:
(3)   for the title and first sentence of the information sheet substitute:
       "High-cost short-term loans
       Failing to repay on time
       Think carefully – rolling over or extending your loan may not be the best option and may make things worse."; and
(4)   for the bullet points substitute:
       "•**Think carefully before borrowing more**. Borrowing more money is likely to worsen your situation.
       •**Work out how much you owe**. To do this, you will need to make a list of all the organisations you owe money to. A debt adviser can help you
       •**Put priority debts first**. Some debts are more urgent than others because the consequences of not paying them can be more serious than for other debts, for example, mortgage, rent, council tax/ rates, or gas or electricity arrears. A debt adviser can help you to budget to keep your finances under control
       Discuss options with your lender
       •If you are having trouble paying back on time talk to your lender who can suggest ways to repay and make sure it is affordable for you.
       •If you don't, you may quickly face increased costs from interest or charges. Missed payments could affect your credit rating and make it more difficult to get credit in future.
       Get free help and advice
       •People that access advice resolve their issues more quickly than those that don't and hundreds of thousands get free debt advice every year.
       •Contact one of these organisations for free debt advice."
(5)   in relation to an arrears sheet to be used by an *operator of an electronic system in relation to lending*:
       (a)   for the bullet point headed "Work out how much money you owe" substitute:
              "**Work out how much money you owe**. To do this, you will need to make a list of all those you owe money to. A debt adviser can help you.";
       (b)   for the title "Discuss options with your lender" substitute
              "Discuss options with your peer to peer lending platform (P2P platform)";
       (c)   for the bullet point which begins "If you are having trouble?" substitute
              "If you are having trouble paying back on time talk to your P2P platform who can suggest ways to repay and make sure it is affordable for you.".
              [**Note**: Until the end of 30 June 2014, transitional provisions apply to **CONC 6.7.20 R**: see **CONC TP 3** 2]

6.7.21 G FCA

A *firm* should not refinance *high-cost short-term credit* where to do so is *unsustainable* or otherwise harmful.
[**Note**: paragraph 6.25 of *ILG*]

6.7.22 G FCA

A *firm* should not allow a *customer* to enter into consecutive agreements with the *firm* for *high-cost short-term credit* if the cumulative effect of the agreements would be that the *total amount payable* by the *customer* is *unsustainable*.
[**Note**: paragraph 6.25 (box) of *ILG*]

6.7.23 R FCA

A *firm* must not refinance *high-cost short-term credit* (other than by exercising forbearance) on more than two occasions.
[**Note**: Until the end of 30 June 2014, transitional provisions apply to **CONC 6.7.23 R**: see **CONC TP 3.**3]

Continuous payments authority: post agreement obligations

6.7.24 R FCA

A *firm* must not amend the terms of a *continuous payment authority* without first obtaining the *customer's* consent, after having fully explained to the *customer* the reason for the amendment.
[**Note**: paragraph 3.9miii of *DCG*]

6.7.25 R FCA

CONC 6.7.24 R does not preclude the *firm* from:
(1)　making amendments pursuant to a variation clause to which the *customer* has previously given consent, after it was fully explained to the *customer* the reason for the amendment; or
(2)　reducing or waiving payments unilaterally, for example, under a repayment plan, provided that this is explained to the *customer*.
[**Note**: paragraph 3.9miii of *DCG*]

6.7.26 R FCA

A *firm* must use the correct category code and identifier when presenting a payment request to the *payment service provider*.
[**Note**: paragraph 3.9miii of *DCG*]

6.8　POST CONTRACT BUSINESS PRACTICES CREDIT BROKERS

Application

6.8.1 R FCA

This section applies to a *firm* with respect to *credit broking*.

Business practices

6.8.2 G FCA

Where a *firm* takes on responsibility for giving information to a *customer* or receiving information from a *customer* in accordance with provisions of the *CCA* (for example, supplying a copy of an executed *regulated credit agreement* under section 61A of the *CCA*) the *firm* should ensure it is familiar with the relevant statutory requirements and has adequate system and procedures in place to comply with the provision in question.

Refunds of brokers' fees

6.8.3 G FCA
(1)　Under section 155 of the *CCA* an *individual* has a right to a refund of the *firm's* fee (less £5) (or for that fee not to be payable) where, following an introduction to a source of *credit* or of bailment (or in Scotland of hire), the *individual* has not entered into an agreement to which section 155 applies within six *months* of an introduction.
　　[**Note**: paragraph 6.1 of *CBG*]
(2)　It is immaterial for the purposes of section 155 of the *CCA* why no agreement has been entered into (for example, an *individual* should be entitled to a refund where the *individual* decides for any reason not to enter into an agreement within the relevant time period).
　　[**Note**: paragraph 6.2 of *CBG*]
(3)　Section 155 does not apply where the introduction is for a *regulated mortgage contract* or a *home purchase plan* and the *person* charging the fee is an *authorised person* or an *appointed representative*. Arranging and advising in relation to *regulated mortgages contracts* and *home purchase plans* are *regulated activities* under the *Regulated Activities Order* and carrying on those activities would require *permissions* covering those activities.
　　[**Note**: paragraph 6.4 of *CBG*]
(4)　In relation to a *credit agreement* the refund would apply to any sum which is an amount that is or would enter in to the *total charge for credit* paid or payable to or via the *credit broker* whether or not the *firm* describes it as a fee or commission.
　　[**Note**: paragraphs 6.11 and 6.13 of *CBG*]
(5)　Where an *individual* withdraws from a *regulated credit agreement* under section 66A of the *CCA* or cancels a cancellable agreement (see section 67 of the *CCA*) under section 69 of the *CCA* the agreement is treated as never have been entered into and hence the period referred to in section 155 continues to apply in these circumstances.
　　[**Note**: paragraph 6.10 of *CBG*]

6.8.4 R FCA

Where section 155 of the *CCA* applies, a *firm* must respond to a request for a refund.
[**Note**: paragraph 6.17 of *CBG*]

6.8.4A R FCA

If a *customer* has not entered into an agreement referred to in section 155(2) of the *CCA* within six months of the *customer* being introduced by the *firm* to a potential source of *credit*, as soon as reasonably practicable after the expiry of that six-month period a *firm* must by any method clearly bring to the *customer's* attention:
(1) the right to request a refund under section 155 of the *CCA*; and
(2) how to exercise the right to request the refund.

[**Note**: paragraph 6.19d of *CBG*]

6.8.4B G FCA

The *FCA* would consider it to be reasonably practicable to comply with **CONC 6.8.4A R** within five working days of the expiry of the six-month period.

6.8.5 G FCA
(1) An *individual* does not need to refer to the right under section 155 of the *CCA* in order to be entitled to a refund.
(2) A *firm* should respond promptly to a request for a refund.
(3) In circumstances where *individuals* request refunds and the *firm* knows, or ought to know, that agreements to which section 155 applies would not be entered into within six *months*, the *firm* should not make the *individuals* wait for the six *month* period to elapse before making the refund.
[**Note**: paragraphs 6.17 and 6.18 of *CBG*]

CHAPTER 7
ARREARS, DEFAULT AND RECOVERY (INCLUDING REPOSSESSIONS)

7.1 APPLICATION

[3.85]

Who? What?

7.1.1 R FCA

This chapter applies, unless otherwise stated in or in relation to a *rule*, to:
(1) a *firm* with respect to *consumer credit lending*;
(2) a *firm* with respect to *consumer hiring*;
(3) a *firm* with respect to *operating an electronic system in relation to lending*, in relation to a *borrower* under a *P2P agreement*;
(4) a *firm* with respect to *debt collecting*.

7.1.2 G FCA

The following sections provide otherwise for application:
(1) **CONC 7.12** (lenders' responsibilities in relation to debt) applies only to *firms* in respect of *consumer credit lending*;
(2) **CONC 7.17** to **CONC 7.19** apply only to *firms operating electronic systems in relation to lending* in relation to *borrowers* under *P2P agreements* as set out in those sections.

7.1.3 G FCA
(1) In accordance with **CONC 1.2.2 R** *firms* must ensure that their employees and agents comply with *CONC* and must take reasonable steps to ensure that other *persons* acting on the *firm's* behalf act in accordance with *CONC*.
(2) The *rule* in **CONC 1.2.2 R** is particularly important in relation to the requirements in **CONC 7**, for example, in dealing with an *individual* from whom the *person* referred to in the *rule* is seeking to collect a debt.
(3) In this chapter the expression "arrears" includes any shortfall in one or more payment due from a *customer* under an agreement to which the chapter applies.

7.2 CLEAR EFFECTIVE AND APPROPRIATE ARREARS POLICIES AND PROCEDURES

Arrears policies

7.2.1 R FCA

A *firm* must establish and implement clear, effective and appropriate policies and procedures for:
(1) dealing with *customers* whose accounts fall into arrears;
[**Note**: paragraph 7.2 of *ILG*]
(2) the fair and appropriate treatment of *customers*, who the *firm* understands or reasonably suspects to be particularly vulnerable.
[**Note**: paragraphs 7.2 and 7.2(box) of *ILG* and 2.2 (box) of *DCG*]

7.2.2 G FCA

Customers who have mental health difficulties or mental capacity limitations may fall into the category of particularly vulnerable *customers*.
[**Note**: paragraph 2.2 (box) of *DCG*]

7.2.3 G   FCA

In developing procedures and policies for dealing with *customers* who may not have the mental capacity to make financial decisions, *firms* may wish to have regard to the principles outlined in the Money Advice Liaison Group (MALG) Guidelines "Good Practice Awareness Guidelines for Consumers with Mental Health Problems and Debt".
[**Note**: paragraph 3.7r (box) of *DCG*]

7.3   TREATMENT OF CUSTOMERS IN DEFAULT OR ARREARS (INCLUDING REPOSSESSIONS): LENDERS, OWNERS AND DEBT COLLECTORS

7.3.1 G   FCA
(1) In relation to *debt collecting* and *debt administration*, the definition of *customer* refers to an *individual* from whom the payment of a debt is sought; this would include where a *firm* mistakenly treats an *individual* as the *borrower* under an agreement and mistakenly or wrongly pursues the *individual* for a debt.
[**Note**: paragraph 1.12 of *DCG*]
(2) In relation to *debt collecting* and *debt administration*, the definitions of *customer* and *borrower* are given extended meanings to include, as well as those other people they generally include, a *person* providing a guarantee or indemnity under a *credit agreement* and also a *person* to whom rights and duties under the agreement are passed by assignment or operation of law. This reflects article 39M of the *Regulated Activities Order*.

Dealing fairly with customers in arrears or default

7.3.2 G   FCA

When dealing with *customers* in default or in arrears difficulties a *firm* should pay due regard to its obligations under *Principle* 6 (Customers' interests) to treat its *customers* fairly.
[**Note**: paragraphs 7.12 of *ILG* and 2.2 of *DCG*]

Forbearance and due consideration

7.3.3 G   FCA

Where a *customer* under a *regulated credit agreement* fails to make an occasional payment when it becomes due, a *firm* should, in accordance with *Principle* 6, allow for such unmade payments to be made within the original term of the agreement unless:
(1) the *firm* reasonably believes that it is appropriate to allow a longer period for repayment and has no reason to believe that doing so will increase the *total amount payable* to be *unsustainable* or otherwise cause a *customer* to be in financial difficulties; or
[**Note**: paragraph 4.7 of *ILG*]
(2) the *firm* reasonably believes that terminating the agreement will mitigate such adverse consequences for the *customer* and before terminating the agreement it explains this to the *customer*.

7.3.4 R   FCA

A *firm* must treat *customers* in default or in arrears difficulties with forbearance and due consideration.
[**Note**: paragraphs 7.3 and 7.4 of *ILG* and 2.2 of *DCG*]

7.3.5 G   FCA

Examples of treating a *customer* with forbearance would include the *firm* doing one or more of the following, as may be relevant in the circumstances:
(1) considering suspending, reducing, waiving or cancelling any further interest or charges (for example, when a *customer* provides evidence of financial difficulties and is unable to meet *repayments* as they fall due or is only able to make token *repayments*, where in either case the level of debt would continue to rise if interest and charges continue to be applied);
[**Note**: paragraph 7.4 (box) of *ILG*]
(2) allowing deferment of payment of arrears:
    (a) where immediate payment of arrears may increase the *customer's repayments* to an *unsustainable* level; or
    (b) provided that doing so does not make the term for the *repayments* unreasonably excessive;
(3) accepting token payments for a reasonable period of time in order to allow a *customer* to recover from an unexpected income shock, from a *customer* who demonstrates that meeting the *customer's* existing debts would mean not being able to meet the *customer's* priority debts or other essential living expenses (such as in relation to a mortgage, rent, council tax, food bills and utility bills).

7.3.6 G   FCA

Where a *customer* is in default or in arrears difficulties, a *firm* should allow the *customer* reasonable time and opportunity to repay the debt.
[**Note**: paragraph 2.2 of *DCG*]

7.3.7 G FCA

Where appropriate, a *firm* should direct a *customer* in default or in arrears difficulties to sources of free and independent debt advice.
[**Note**: paragraph 2.2 of *DCG*]

7.3.8 G FCA

An example of where a *firm* is likely to contravene *Principle* 6 and **CONC 7.3.4 R** is where the *firm* does not allow for alternative, affordable payment amounts to repay the debt due in full, where the *customer* is in default or arrears difficulties and the *customer* makes a reasonable proposal for repaying the debt or a *debt counsellor* or another *person* acting on the *customer's* behalf makes such a proposal.
[**Note**: paragraphs 7.16 of *ILG* and 3.7j of *DCG*]

7.3.9 R FCA

A *firm* must not operate a policy of refusing to negotiate with a *customer* who is developing a repayment plan.
[**Note**: paragraph 3.9d (box) of *DCG*]

7.3.10 R FCA

A *firm* must not pressurise a *customer*:
(1)   to pay a debt in one single or very few *repayments* or in unreasonably large amounts, when to do so would have an adverse impact on the *customer's* financial circumstances;
        [**Note**: paragraph 7.18 of *ILG*]
(2)   to pay a debt within an unreasonably short period of time; or
        [**Note**: paragraphs 3.7i of *DCG* and 7.18 of *ILG*]
(3)   to raise funds to repay the debt by selling their property, borrowing money or increasing existing borrowing.
        [**Note**: paragraph 3.7b of *DCG*]

7.3.11 R FCA

A *firm* must suspend the active pursuit of recovery of a debt from a *customer* for a reasonable period where the *customer* informs the *firm* that a *debt counsellor* or another *person* acting on the *customer's* behalf or the *customer* is developing a repayment plan.
[**Note**: paragraphs 7.12 of *ILG* and 3.7m of *DCG*]

7.3.12 G FCA

A "reasonable period" in **CONC 7.3.11 R** should generally be for thirty days where there is evidence of a genuine intention to develop a plan and the *firm* should consider extending the period for a further thirty days where there is reasonable evidence demonstrating progress to agreeing a plan.
[**Note**: paragraphs 7.12 (box) *ILG* and 3.7m of *DCG*

7.3.13 G FCA

A *firm* seeking to recover debts should have regard, where appropriate, to the provisions in the Common Financial Statement or equivalent guidance.
[**Note**: paragraphs 7.16 (box) of *ILG* and 3.7k of *DCG*]

Proportionality

7.3.14 R FCA
(1)   A *firm* must not take disproportionate action against a customer in arrears or default.
        [**Note**: paragraphs 7.14 (box) of *ILG* and 3.7t of *DCG*]
(2)   In accordance with (1) a firm must not, in particular, apply to court for an order for sale or submit a bankruptcy petition, without first having fully explored any more proportionate options.
        [**Note**: paragraph 7.14 (box) of *ILG*]

7.3.15 G FCA

A *firm* should not make undue, excessive or otherwise unfair use of statutory demands (within the meaning of section 268 of the Insolvency Act 1986) when seeking to recover a debt from a *customer*.
[**Note**: paragraphs 7.10 of *ILG* and 3.7n of *DCG*]

Enforcement of debts

7.3.16 G FCA

A *firm* should not take steps to enforce a debt if it is aware that the *customer* is subject to a bankruptcy order (or in Scotland where sequestration is awarded in relation to the *customer*), a debt relief order or an individual voluntary arrangement (or, in Scotland, a protected trust deed or a Debt Arrangement Scheme).
[**Note**: paragraph 3.9h of *DCG*]

7.3.17 R FCA

A *firm* must not take steps to repossess a *customer's* home other than as a last resort, having explored all other possible options.
[**Note**: paragraphs 7.14 of *ILG*, 3.7t of *DCG* and 6.3 of *SCLG*]

7.3.18 R FCA

A *firm* must not threaten to commence court action, including an application for a charging order or (in Scotland) an inhibition or an order for sale, in order to pressurise a *customer* in default or arrears difficulties to pay more than they can reasonably afford.
[**Note**: paragraphs 7.14 of *ILG* and 3.7i (box) of *DCG*]

7.3.19 G FCA

Firms seeking to recover debts under *regulated credit agreements* secured by second or subsequent charges in England and Wales should have regard to the requirements of the relevant pre-action protocol (PAP) issued by the Civil Justice Council. The aims of the PAP are to ensure that a *firm* and a *customer* act fairly and reasonably with each other in resolving any matter concerning arrears, and to encourage more pre-action contact in an effort to seek agreement between the parties on alternatives to repossession. The Pre-action Protocol on Possession Proceedings applies to all mortgage repossession cases in Northern Ireland. The Home Owner and Debtor Protection (Scotland) Act 2010 provides for pre-action requirements to be placed on secured *lenders* in Scotland.
[**Note**: paragraphs 7.14 of *ILG* and 3.7s of *DCG*]

7.4 INFORMATION ON STATUS OF DEBTS

7.4.1 R FCA

A *firm* must provide the *customer* or another *person* acting on behalf of the *customer* with information on the amount of any arrears and the balance owing.
[**Note**: paragraph 3.3f of *DCG*]

7.4.2 R FCA

Where:
(1)   a *customer* offers a settlement payment lower than the total amount owing; or
(2)   a *lender* under a *regulated credit agreement* or an *owner* under a *regulated consumer hire agreement* decides to stop pursuing a *customer* in respect of a debt arising under the agreement;

and the debt (or part of it) continues to exist notwithstanding the acceptance of the *customer's* offer or the decision to cease to pursue the debt, the *lender* or *owner* must ensure that the continuing existence of the debt and the possibility of the *customer* being pursued by another *firm* who purchases the debt is explained in clear terms to the *customer*.
[**Note**: paragraph 3.3i of *DCG*]

7.5 PURSUING AND RECOVERING REPAYMENTS

7.5.1 G FCA

(1)   Failure to comply with **CONC 6.5.2 R**, which sets out when a *firm* must give notice to a *customer* where a *regulated credit agreement* has been assigned to a third party, will be taken into account by the *FCA* in taking decisions about a *firm's permission* or about taking other action.
[**Note**: paragraph 3.7g of *DCG*]

(2)   **CONC 6.5.2 R** makes it clear that where arrangements for servicing the *credit* change at the time of the assignment of a *regulated credit agreement*, notice must be given to the *customer* as soon as reasonably possible. A *firm* should give notice as required under that *rule* in order that any change should not adversely impact on a *customer's* existing repayment arrangements. In addition, if arrangements for servicing the debt otherwise change so far as the *customer* is concerned, the *firm* should notify the *customer* on or before that change.
[**Note**: paragraph 3.7h of *DCG*]

7.5.2 R FCA

A *firm* must not pursue an *individual* whom the *firm* knows or believes might not be the *borrower* or *hirer* under a *credit agreement* or a *consumer hire agreement*.
[**Note**: paragraph 3.5f of *DCG*]

7.5.3 R FCA

A *firm* must not ignore or disregard a *customer's* claim that a debt has been settled or is disputed and must not continue to make demands for payment without providing clear justification and/or evidence as to why the *customer's* claim is not valid.
[**Note**: paragraph 3.7o of *DCG*]

7.5.4 R   FCA

A *firm* acting on behalf of a *lender* or *owner* must, unless the *firm* has authority from the *lender* or *owner* to accept such an offer, refer a reasonable offer by the *customer* to pay by instalments to the *lender* or *owner*.
[**Note:** paragraph 3.9f of *DCG*]

7.5.5 R   FCA

A *firm* acting on behalf of a *lender* or *owner* must pass on payments received from a *customer* and/or details of a *customer's* outstanding balance to the *lender* or *owner* in a timely manner or, provided the effect of the agreement does not impact adversely on the *customer*, in accordance with an agreement between the *firm* and *lender* or *owner* in question
[**Note:** paragraph 3.9g of *DCG*]

7.5.6 G   FCA

A timely manner in **CONC 7.5.5 R** would normally be within five *working days* of receipt of payment by the *firm*.
[**Note:** paragraph 3.9g of *DCG*]

7.6   EXERCISE OF CONTINUOUS PAYMENT AUTHORITY

Recovery and continuous payment authorities etc.

7.6.1 R   FCA
(1)   A *firm* must not exercise its rights under a *continuous payment authority* (or purport to do so):
      (a)   unless it has been explained to the *customer* that the *continuous payment authority* would be used in the way in question; and
      (b)   other than in accordance with the terms specified in the *credit agreement* or the *P2P agreement*.
(2)   If a *firm* wishes a *customer* to change the terms of a *continuous payment authority* it must contact the *customer* and:
      (a)   provide the *customer* with an adequate explanation of the reason for and effect of the proposed change, including any effect it would have on the matters in **CONC 4.6.2 R (2)**; and
      (b)   once it has done so, obtain the consent of the *customer*.
[**Note:** paragraph 3.9mi of *DCG*]

7.6.2 G   FCA

A *firm* should not:
(1)   request a *payment service provider* to make a payment from the *customer's* payment account unless:
      (a)
           (i)   the amount of the payment (or the basis on which payments may be taken) is specified in or permitted by the *credit agreement* or *P2P agreement*; and
           (ii)   the amount of the payment (or the basis on which payments may be taken) was referred to in the adequate explanation required by **CONC 4.6.2 R**; or
      (b)   the *firm* has complied in relation to such a request with **CONC 7.6.1 R (2)**;
(2)   request a *payment service provider* to make a payment to recover default fees or other sums unless:
      (a)
           (i)   the amount (or the basis on which default fees or other sums may be taken) is specified in the *credit agreement* or *P2P agreement*; and
           (ii)   the amount (or the basis on which default fees or other sums may be taken) was referred to in the adequate explanation required by **CONC 4.6.2 R**; or
      (b)   the *firm* has complied in relation to such a request with **CONC 7.6.1 R (2)**;
(3)   other than where **CONC 7.6.14 R (2)** applies, request a *payment service provider* to make a payment from the *customer's* payment account of an amount that is less than the amount due at the time of the request, unless the *firm*:
      (a)
           (i)   is permitted to do so by the *credit agreement* or *P2P agreement*; and
           (ii)   the adequate explanation required by **CONC 4.6.2 R** indicated that part payment (a sum due which is less than the full sum due at the time the *firm's* payment request is made) could be requested if the full amount was not available and specified the basis on which and the frequency with which such requests for payment could be made and any minimum amount or percentage that would be requested; or
      (b)   the *firm* has complied in relation to such a request with **CONC 7.6.1 R (2)**.

(4)   request a *payment service provider* to make a payment from the *customer's* payment account
        before the due date of payment as specified in the *credit agreement* or *P2P agreement*, unless
        the *firm* has complied with **CONC 7.6.1 R (2)**;

(5)   request a *payment service provider* to make a payment from the *customer's* payment account
        after the due date on a date, or within a period, or with a frequency other than as specified
        in the *credit agreement* or *P2P agreement* and referred to in the adequate explanation, unless
        the *firm* has complied with **CONC 7.6.1 R (2)**;

(6)   request a *payment service provider* to make a payment from the payment account of a third
        party other than as specifically agreed with the third party or agreed with the *customer*
        following the third party's confirmation to the *firm* that the third party consents to the
        arrangement.

[**Note**: paragraph 3.9mi of *DCG*]

7.6.3 R   FCA

A *firm* must exercise its rights under a *continuous payment authority* in a manner which is
reasonable, proportionate and not excessive and must exercise appropriate forbearance if it becomes
aware that the *customer* is or may be experiencing financial difficulties.
[**Note**: paragraph 3.9mii of *DCG*]

7.6.4 G   FCA

Whether exercising rights under a *continuous payment authority* is reasonable, proportionate and not
excessive (as regards the frequency or period of collection attempts), will depend on the
circumstances, including:

(1)   whether the *firm* is aware or has reason to believe that the *customer* is in actual or potential
        financial difficulties which the exercise of rights under a *continuous payment authority* may
        exacerbate; and

(2)   whether the *customer* has been notified of the failure to collect the payment and has
        responded to contact from the *firm*.

[**Note**: paragraph 3.9mii of *DCG*]

7.6.5 G   FCA

A *firm* is likely to contravene **CONC 7.6.3 R** if it:

(1)   requests a *payment service provider* to make a payment from the *customer's* payment account
        before income or other funds may reasonably be expected to reach the account; for example,
        this is likely to be relevant where a *firm* is aware of the *customer's* salary payment date; or

(2)   requests a *payment service provider* to make a payment from the *customer's* payment account
        where it has reason to believe that there are insufficient funds in the account or that taking
        the payment would leave insufficient funds for priority debts or other essential living
        expenses (such as in relation to a mortgage, rent, council tax, food bills or utility bills); or

(3)   requests a *payment service provider* to make a part payment (a sum due which less than the
        full sum due at the time the *firm's* payment request is made) of the sum due from the
        customer's payment account before it has made reasonable attempts to collect the full
        payment of the sum due on the due date; or

(4)   continues to exercise its rights under the *continuous payment authority* for an unreasonable
        period after the payment due date without taking steps to establish the reason for the payment
        failure.
        [**Note**: paragraph 3.9mii of *DCG*]

7.6.6 G   FCA

Where permissible, a *firm* should only make a reasonable number of payment requests to a *payment
service provider* to collect a part payment (a sum due which is less than the full sum due at the time
the *firm's* payment request is made) from the *customer's* payment account, having regard to the
possibility that the *customer* may be in financial difficulties.
[**Note**: paragraph 3.9mii (box) of *DCG*]

7.6.7 R   FCA

A *firm* must not exercise its rights under a *continuous payment authority*:

(1)   if the *customer* provides reasonable evidence to the *firm* of being in financial difficulties and
        the *customer* cannot afford to repay the debt; or

(2)   where the *firm* otherwise becomes aware of the *customer* being in financial difficulties and
        that the *customer* cannot afford to repay the debt.
        [**Note**: paragraph 3.9mii (box) of *DCG*]

7.6.8 G   FCA

(1)   If a *firm* becomes aware that a *customer* is in financial difficulties, the *firm* should reassess
        the payment arrangement and should consider reasonable proposals to revise the payment
        schedule and alternative repayment arrangements.
        [**Note**: paragraph 3.9mii (box) of *DCG*]

(2)   Where a *customer* informs a *firm* of being in financial difficulties, pending receipt of evidence to that effect, a *firm* should consider suspending exercise of its rights under a *continuous payment authority*.

7.6.9 G   FCA

In the *FCA's* view, a *firm's* inability to recover the whole of the amount due by the end of the next *working day* after the date on which it was due would indicate that the *customer* may be experiencing financial difficulties. In such a case, a *firm* should suspend exercising its rights under the *continuous payment authority* until it has made reasonable efforts to contact the *customer* to establish the reason why payment was unsuccessful and whether the *customer* is in financial difficulties.
[**Note**: paragraph 3.9mii (box) of *DCG*]

7.6.10 G   FCA

If the *firm* and the *customer* have agreed an alternative payment date as a contingency option if payment is not available on the due date, the *firm* should suspend the exercise of its rights under the *continuous payment authority* after the due date, and again after the alternative payment date (if the *firm* is unable to recover the amount due at the end of that day) and make reasonable efforts (in accordance with **CONC 7.6.9 G**) to contact the *customer* to establish the reason why payment was unsuccessful and whether the *customer* is in financial difficulties.
[**Note**: paragraph 3.9mii (box) of *DCG*]

7.6.11 G   FCA

If reasonable efforts to contact the *customer* are unsuccessful or a *customer* refuses to engage with the *firm* and there is no further evidence of financial difficulties, any subsequent exercise of its rights under the *continuous payment authority* should be reasonable and not excessive, having regard to the possibility that an unresponsive *customer* may nevertheless be in financial difficulties and that a *customer* who was not in financial difficulties at the time of contact may subsequently be in financial difficulties.
[**Note**: paragraph 3.9mii (box) of *DCG*]

Continuous payment authorities and high-cost short-term credit

7.6.12 R   FCA

(1)   Subject to (3) to (5), a *firm* must not request a *payment service provider* to make a payment, under a *continuous payment authority*, to collect (in whole or in part) a sum due for *high-cost short-term credit* if it has done so in connection with the same agreement for *high-cost short-term credit* on two previous occasions and those previous payment requests have been refused.

(2)   For the purposes of (1) and (3):
      (a)   if *high-cost short-term credit* has been refinanced, except in exercise of forbearance, the agreement is to be regarded as the same agreement; and
      (b)   "refinance" and "exercise forbearance" have the same meaning as in **CONC 6.7.17 R**.

(3)   Where a *firm* exercises forbearance:
      (a)   paragraph (1) applies or continues to apply to the agreement; but
      (b)   any refusal of a payment request that took place before the time at which the forbearance was granted is to be disregarded for the purposes of (1).

(4)   Paragraph (5) applies following the refusal of two payment requests a *firm* has made to a *payment service provider* under a *continuous payment authority* to collect a sum due for *high-cost short-term credit*, where the *firm* proposes to refinance the *high-cost short term credit* in question in accordance with **CONC 6.7.17 R** to **CONC 6.7.23 R**.

(5)   If the *firm* contacts the *customer* and, in the course of an dialogue between the *firm* and the *customer*:
      (a)   the *firm* notifies the *customer* of the refusal of the payment requests;
      (b)   the *firm* reminds the *customer* of the matters in **CONC 4.6.2 R (2)**, taking account of any proposed changes to the terms of the *continuous payment authority* that will apply following the refinance if the *customer* consents; and
      (c)   the *customer* gives express consent to the *firm* further exercising its rights under the *continuous payment authority* following the refinance;
      the *firm* may then make further payment requests under the *continuous payment authority* following the refinance in accordance with **CONC 7.6**, and paragraph (1) applies as if the *firm* had not made a payment request under the *continuous payment authority* before the refinance.

(6)   This *rule* does not apply to an agreement which provides for repayment in instalments.
      [**Note**: Until the end of 30 June 2014, transitional provisions apply to **CONC 7.6.12 R**: see **CONC TP 3.4**]

Continuous payment authorities and high-cost short-term credit: instalment payments

7.6.13 R   FCA
(1)   Where:

(a)   *high-cost short-term credit* provides for *repayment* in instalments; and

(b)   a *firm* has on two previous occasions made a payment request, under a *continuous payment authority*, to collect (in whole or in part) the same instalment due under the agreement, which have been refused;

subject to (3) and (4), the *firm* must not make a further payment request under the *continuous payment authority* to collect that instalment.

(2)   The *firm* must not make a further payment request under the *continuous payment authority* to collect any other instalment that is or becomes due under the agreement, unless any request is in accordance with **CONC 7.6** and in the course of a dialogue between the *firm* and the *customer*:

(a)   the *firm* notifies the *customer* of the refusal of the payment requests;

(b)   repayment of the instalment referred to in (1)(b) has been made using a method other than a *continuous payment authority* and the *customer* is not in arrears; and

(c)   where (a) and (b) apply, the *firm* has reminded the *customer* of the date and amount of the next instalment.

(3)   If, where the prohibition in (1) applies, a *firm* exercises forbearance within the meaning of **CONC 6.7.17 R** the *firm* must not make a further payment request under the *continuous payment authority* to collect the instalment referred to in (1) or a payment request for any other instalment that is or becomes due under the agreement, unless:

(a)   a payment request is in accordance with **CONC 7.6**;

(b)   the *firm* notifies the *customer* of the refusal of the payment requests; and

(c)   in the course of a dialogue between the *firm* and the *customer*, the *firm* reminds the *customer* of the date and amount of the next instalment and following which the *customer* gives express consent to further payment requests being made under the *continuous payment authority*.

(4)   If, where the prohibition in (1) applies, a *firm* adds no charge or additional interest in connection with missing a payment on the due date, the *firm* must not make a further payment request under the *continuous payment authority* to collect the instalment referred to in (1) or a payment request for any other instalment that is or becomes due under the agreement, unless:

(a)   a payment request is in accordance with **CONC 7.6**;

(b)   the *customer* has missed making a payment on the due date; and

(c)   in the course of a dialogue between the *firm* and the *customer*, the *firm* reminds the *customer* of the date and amount of the next instalment and following which the *customer* gives express consent to further payment requests being made under the *continuous payment authority*.

[**Note:** Until the end of 30 June 2014, transitional provisions apply to **CONC 7.6.13 R**: see **CONC TP 3.5**]

7.6.14 R   FCA

(1)   Subject to (2), a *firm* must not request a *payment service provider* to make a payment under a *continuous payment authority* to collect a sum due for *high-cost short-term credit* if that sum is less than the full sum due at the time the request is made.

(2)   Where a *firm*:

(a)   following contact with a *customer*, refinances the agreement in accordance with **CONC 6.7.17 R** to **CONC 6.7.23 R** by granting an indulgence which allows for one or more *repayment* of a reduced amount under a repayment plan;

(b)   notifies the *customer* of the number and frequency of *repayments* and their amount under the repayment plan; and

(c)   the *customer* gives express consent to the *firm* to make payment requests to collect the *repayments* notified under the plan;

[**Note:** Until the end of 30 June 2014, transitional provisions apply to **CONC 7.6.14 R**: see **CONC TP 3.6**]

paragraph (1) does not prevent the *firm* from making a payment request in accordance with **CONC 7.6** under a *continuous payment authority* to collect *repayments* of those amounts in accordance with the plan.

7.6.15 G   FCA

(1)   **CONC 7.6.12 R**, **CONC 7.6.13 R** and **CONC 7.6.14 R** do not prevent a *firm* accepting payment (including a part payment) from a *customer* using a means of payment other than under a *continuous payment authority*. If, for example, a *customer* consents separately that a single payment of a specified amount may be taken on the same day or on another specified day using his or her debit card details, this is excluded from the definition of *continuous payment authority*.

(2)   **CONC 7.6.14 R** does not prevent a *firm* from making a payment request concerning a sum due where the *firm* has varied an agreement so that the sum due is less than it was before the variation.

(3)   *Firms* are reminded of their record-keeping obligations under **SYSC 9.1.1 R** (general rules on record-keeping) which in particular require sufficient records to be kept to ascertain that the *firm* has complied with all obligations with respect to *customers*. These should include, for example, arranging to keep records of payment requests (including refusals of payment requests) made under *continuous payment authorities* and to keep suitable written or other records of the consents referred to in **CONC 7.6.1 R**, **CONC 7.6.12 R**, **CONC 7.6.13 R** and **CONC 7.6.14 R**.

Cancelling a continuous payment authority

7.6.16 R   FCA

A *firm* must not by any means improperly or unfairly inhibit or discourage a *customer* from cancelling a *continuous payment authority* including by:
(1)   misleading the *customer*, expressly or by omission, regarding the right to cancel and how it may be exercised; or
(2)   failing to respond promptly to requests by or on behalf of the *customer* to amend or cancel the *continuous payment authority*; or
(3)   intimidating a *customer* who wishes to cancel the *continuous payment authority*; or
(4)   requiring *customers* who wish to cancel the *continuous payment authority* to go through an unduly complicated process.
     [**Note**: paragraph 3.9miv of *DCG*]

7.6.17 R   FCA

A *firm* must cease to exercise its rights under the *continuous payment authority* once it is notified that the *continuous payment authority* has been cancelled.
[**Note**: paragraph 3.9miv of *DCG*]

7.7   APPLICATION OF INTEREST AND CHARGES

7.7.1 G   FCA

When levying charges for debt recovery on *customers* in default or arrears difficulties *firms* should consider their obligation under *Principle* 6 to pay due regard to the interests of *customers* and treat them fairly.
[**Note**: paragraphs 3.1 and 3.10 of *DCG*]

7.7.2 R   FCA

A *firm* must not claim the costs of recovering a debt from a *customer* if it has no contractual right to claim such costs.
[**Note**: paragraph 3.11b of *DCG*]

7.7.3 R   FCA

A *firm* must not cause a *customer* to believe that the *customer* is legally liable to pay the costs of recovery where no such obligation exists.
[**Note**: paragraph 3.11a of *DCG*]

7.7.4 G   FCA

Where a *firm* has a contractual right to levy default charges, a *regulated credit agreement* must state the charges and the conditions for making the charge under, as the case may be, the Consumer Credit (Agreements) Regulations 2010 (SI 2010/1014) or the Consumer Credit (Agreements) Regulations 1983 (SI 1983/1553).
[**Note**: paragraphs 3.11c of *DCG* and 7.15 of *ILG*]

7.7.5 R   FCA

A *firm* must not impose charges on *customers* in default or arrears difficulties unless the charges are no higher than necessary to cover the reasonable costs of the *firm*.
[**Note**: paragraphs 3.11 of *DCG* and 7.15 of *ILG*]

7.8   JURISDICTIONAL REQUIREMENTS

7.8.1 R   FCA

A *firm* dealing with a *customer* who is resident in a different jurisdiction to the jurisdiction of the *firm's* place of business must ensure that it takes appropriate account of any differences in law and court procedure that may have a significant impact on the *customer's* rights.
[**Note**: paragraph 2.3 of *DCG*]

7.8.2 G   FCA

CONC 7.8.1 R will apply, for example, where a *firm's* place of business is in England and the *customer* resides in Scotland.
[**Note**: paragraph 2.3 of *DCG*]

7.8.3 R   FCA

A *firm* must not commence proceedings or threaten to commence proceedings in the wrong jurisdiction.
[**Note**: paragraph 3.5g of *DCG*]

7.9   CONTACT WITH CUSTOMERS

Contacting customers

7.9.1 R   FCA

A *firm* must ensure that a *person* contacting a *customer* on its behalf explains to the *customer* the following matters:
(1)   who the *person* contacting the *customer* works for;
(2)   the *person's* role in or relationship with the *firm*; and
(3)   the purpose of the contact.
          [**Note**: paragraph 3.3c of *DCG*]

7.9.2 R   FCA

A *firm* must not in a communication with the *customer* make a statement which may induce the *customer* to contact the *firm* misunderstanding the reason for making contact.
[**Note**: paragraph 3.3d of *DCG*]

7.9.3 G   FCA
(1)   An example of a misleading communication in **CONC 7.9.2 R** is a calling card left at the *customer's* address which states or implies that the *customer* has missed a delivery and encourages the *customer* to make contact.
          [**Note**: paragraph 3.3d (box) of *DCG*]
(2)   The clear fair and not misleading *rule* in **CONC 3.3.1 R** also applies to a *firm* in relation to a communication with a *customer* in relation to *credit agreement* or a *consumer hire agreement*.

7.9.4 R   FCA

A *firm* must not contact *customers* at unreasonable times and must pay due regard to the reasonable requests of *customers* (for example, *customers* who work in a shift pattern) in respect of when, where and how they may be contacted.
[**Note**: paragraphs 3.3j and k of *DCG*]

7.9.5 R   FCA

A *firm* must not require a *customer* to make contact on a premium rate or other special rate telephone number the charge for which is higher than to a standard geographic telephone number.
[**Note**: paragraph 3.3l of *DCG*]

Communication with third parties

7.9.6 R   FCA

A *firm* must not unfairly disclose or threaten to disclose information relating to the *customer's* debt to a third party.
[**Note**: paragraph 3.7p of *DCG*]

7.9.7 R   FCA

When contacting a *customer*:
(1)   a *firm* must ensure that it does not act in a way likely to be publicly embarrassing to the *customer*; and
(2)   a *firm* must take reasonable steps to ensure that third parties do not become aware that the *customer* is being pursued in respect of a debt
          [**Note**: paragraph 3.7q of *DCG*].

7.9.8 G   FCA

The reasonable steps required by **CONC 7.9.7 R** may, for example, require a *firm* to ensure that:
(1)   post sent by the *firm* is properly addressed to the *customer* and marked "private and confidential" or an expression to the same effect;
(2)   where the *firm* has a name which indicates its debt collection activities, its name is not shown so that third parties may see the name on the *firm's* communications.

7.9.9 G   FCA

CONC 7.9.7 R would not preclude a *firm* sending a statutory notice to a *customer's* last known address, where it takes reasonable steps including those referred to in **CONC 7.9.8 G**.

7.9.10 R   FCA

A *firm* must not disclose details of a debt to an *individual* without first establishing, by suitably appropriate means, that the *individual* is (or acts on behalf of) the *borrower* or *hirer* under the relevant agreement).
[**Note**: paragraph 3.9b of *DCG*]

7.9.11 G   FCA

A *firm* which:
(1)   threatens debt recovery action against the "occupier" of particular premises; or
(2)   sends a payment demand to all persons sharing the same name and date of birth or address as the *customer*;

is likely to contravene **CONC 7.9.10 R**.
[**Note**: paragraphs 3.9a (box) and 3.9b (box) of *DCG*]

Debt collection visits

7.9.12 R   FCA

Unless it is not practicable to do so, a *firm* must ensure that a *person* visiting a *customer* on its behalf:
(1)   clearly explains to the *customer* the purpose and intended outcome of the proposed visit; and
      [**Note**: paragraph 3.12 of *DCG*]
(2)   gives the *customer* adequate notice of the date and likely time (at a reasonable time of day) of the visit.
      [**Note**: paragraph 3.13g of *DCG*]

7.9.13 G   FCA

Failure to explain the purpose and intended outcome of a proposed initial visit to the *customer* or to give adequate notice prior to a proposed initial visit to the *customer* may not contravene **CONC 7.9.12 R**, provided that the *customer* is happy to speak to the *person* pursuing recovery of the debt at that time. However, where, at the initial visit the *customer* indicates a preference to use the first visit to agree a more convenient time for a future visit, the *person* pursuing recovery of the debt should respect the *customer's* wishes. It is important that the *customer* is given reasonable time to prepare for a visit and should not be coerced or pressurised into immediate discussions or decisions.
[**Note**: paragraph 3.13g (box) of *DCG*]

7.9.14 R   FCA

A *firm* must ensure that all *persons* visiting a *customer's* property on its behalf act at all times in accordance with the requirements of **CONC 7** and do not:
(1)   act in a threatening manner towards a *customer*;
(2)   visit a *customer* at a time when they know or suspect that the *customer* is, or may be, particularly vulnerable;
(3)   visit at an inappropriate location unless the *customer* has expressly consented to the visit;
(4)   enter a *customer's* property without the *customer's* consent or an appropriate court order;
(5)   refuse to leave a *customer's* property when it becomes apparent that the *customer* is unduly distressed or might not have the mental capacity to make an informed repayment decision or to engage in the debt recovery process;
(6)   refuse to leave a *customer's* property when reasonably asked to do so;
(7)   visit or threaten to visit a *customer* without the *customer's* prior agreement when a debt is deadlocked or reasonably queried or disputed (see **CONC 7.14** (Settlements, disputed and deadlocked debt)).
      [**Note**: paragraphs 3.12 and 3.13 of *DCG*]

7.9.15 G   FCA

It would normally be inappropriate to visit a *customer* at the *customer* place of work or at a hospital where the *customer* is a patient.

7.10   TREATMENT OF CUSTOMERS WITH MENTAL CAPACITY LIMITATIONS

7.10.1 R   FCA

A *firm* must suspend the pursuit of recovery of a debt from a *customer* when:
(1)   the *firm* has been notified that the *customer* might not have the mental capacity to make relevant financial decisions about the management of the *customer's* debt and/or to engage in the debt recovery process at the time; or
(2)   the *firm* understands or ought reasonably to be aware that the *customer* lacks mental capacity to make relevant financial decisions about the management of the *customer's* debt and/or to engage in the debt recovery process at the time.

[**Note**: paragraphs 3.7r of *DCG* and 7.13 of *ILG*]

7.10.2 G   FCA

A *firm* should allow a *customer* or a *person* acting on behalf of the *customer* a reasonable period of time to provide evidence as to the likely impact of any mental capacity limitation on the *customer's* ability to engage with the *firm*.
[**Note**: paragraph 3.7r (box) of *DCG*]

7.10.3 G   FCA

CONC 7.10.1 R does not prevent a *firm* from pursuing the debt through a responsible third party acting on behalf of the *customer*, where the *customer* has given prior consent, for example, pursuant to a registered lasting power of attorney.
[**Note**: paragraph 3.7r (box) of *DCG*]

7.10.4 G   FCA

Firms should note **CONC 7.2.1 R** (and its accompanying *guidance*) which requires *firms* to establish and implement policies and procedures for the fair and appropriate treatment of particularly vulnerable *customers*.

7.11   DISCLOSURES RELATING TO "AUTHORITY" OR "STATUS"

7.11.1 R   FCA

When contacting *customers*, a *firm* must not misrepresent its authority or its legal position with regards to the debt or debt recovery process.
[**Note**: paragraph 3.4 of *DCG*]

7.11.2 G   FCA

For example, a *person* misrepresents authority or the legal position if they claim to work on instructions from the courts as bailiffs or, in Scotland, sheriff officers or messengers-at-arms, or in Northern Ireland, to work on instructions from the Enforcement of Judgements Office when this is untrue.
[**Note**: paragraph 3.5a of *DCG*]

7.11.3 R   FCA

A *firm* must not use official looking documents which are designed to, or are likely to, mislead a *customer* as to the status of the *firm*.
[**Note**: paragraph 3.3a of *DCG*]

7.11.4 R   FCA

A *firm* must not falsely suggest or state that it is a member of a trade body or is accredited by a trade body.
[**Note**: paragraph 3.5c (box) of *DCG*]

7.11.5 G   FCA

It is an offence under section 17 of the Legal Services Act 2007 to falsely imply that a *person* is entitled to carry on a reserved legal activity, for example, to conduct litigation or to appear before and address a court, or to take or use any relevant name, title or description, for example, "solicitor".
[**Note**: paragraph 3.5c (box) of *DCG*]

7.11.6 R   FCA

A *firm* must not suggest or state that action can or will be taken when legally it cannot be taken.
[**Note**: paragraph 3.5b of *DCG*]

7.11.7 G   FCA

Examples of where a *firm* is likely to contravene **CONC 7.11.6 R** include where a *firm* or a *person* acting on its behalf:
(1)   states or implies that bankruptcy or sequestration proceedings may be initiated when the balance of the outstanding debt is too low to qualify for such proceedings;
(2)   states or implies that steps will be taken to enforce a debt where the *customer* is making payments under a Debt Payment Programme Arrangement agreed under the Debt Arrangement and Attachment (Scotland) Act 2002;
(3)   claims a right of entry will be exercised when no court order to this effect has been granted; or
(4)   states that *goods* will be repossessed when they are "protected goods" (as defined under section 90(7) of the *CCA*) and no specific authorisation to repossess the *goods* has been granted by a court.

[**Note**: paragraph 3.5b (box) of *DCG*]

7.11.8 R   FCA

A *firm* must not suggest or state that it will commence proceedings for a warrant of execution or an attachment of earnings order when a court judgment has not been obtained, or that it will take any other enforcement action before it is possible to know whether such action will be permissible.
[**Note**: paragraph 3.5c of *DCG*]

7.11.9 R   FCA

A *firm* must not suggest or state that an action has been taken when no such action has been taken.
[**Note**: paragraph 3.5d (box) of *DCG*]

7.12   LENDERS' RESPONSIBILITIES IN RELATION TO DEBT

Application

7.12.1 R   FCA

This section applies to a *firm* with respect to *consumer credit lending*.

Unfair business practices

7.12.2 R   FCA

A *firm* must not:
(1)   refuse to deal with a *not-for-profit debt advice body*, *debt counsellor*, *debt adjuster* or with another *person* acting on behalf of a *customer*, unless there is an objectively justifiable reason for doing so;
     [**Note**: paragraphs 3.9c of *DCG* and 3.48 of *DMG*]
(2)   unless the *credit agreement* requires payments to be made to a third party, refuse to accept a payment tendered to the *firm* by the *customer* or by a *person* acting on behalf of the *customer*;
     [**Note**: paragraphs 3.8 of *DCG* and 3.49a of *DMG*]
(3)   refuse to deal with a *customer* who is developing a repayment plan, a third party who is assisting a *customer* to develop a repayment plan or a third party who is developing a *debt management plan* for the *customer's* debts, unless there is an objectively justifiable reason for doing so;
     [**Note**: paragraphs 3.9c of *DCG* and 3.49b of *DMG*]
(4)   where a *person* is acting on behalf of a *customer*, directly contact the *customer* without the *customer's* consent, unless there is an objectively justifiable reason for doing so;
     [**Note**: paragraph 3.9d of *DCG*]
(5)   operate a policy:
     (a)   of only negotiating the freezing of interest and charges on a *customer's* debts where the *lender* has an existing arrangement with a *person* acting on behalf of the *customer*; or
         [**Note**: paragraph 3.49e of *DMG*]
     (b)   of refusing to negotiate with certain third parties or with a *customer* developing their own repayment plan; or
         [**Note**: paragraph 3.49c (box) of *DMG*]
(6)   return or refuse a *repayment* or refuse to credit a *repayment* to a *customer's* account merely because the *repayment* is tendered by a *debt management firm*.
     [**Note**: paragraph 3.49a of *DCG*]

7.12.3 G   FCA
(1)   **CONC 1.2.2 R** requires a *firm* to ensure its employees and agents comply with *CONC* and that it takes reasonable steps to ensure other *persons* who act on its behalf do so. This *rule* would apply where a *debt collector* acts as agent or on behalf of a *lender*.
(2)   Situations where it may be justified for a *firm* to refuse to deal with a *person* acting on behalf of a *customer* may include, for example, refusing to deal with that *person* where the *firm* is able to show that the *person* has failed to comply with consumer protection legislation or with *FCA rules*.
     [**Note**: paragraph 3.48 of *DMG*]
(3)   It may be justified for a *firm* to contact a *customer* directly where:
     (a)   repeated unsuccessful efforts have been made to contact a *person* acting on behalf of the *customer*; or
         [**Note**: paragraphs 3.9d of *DCG* and 3.49c (box) of *DMG*]
     (b)   the *firm* reasonably believes the *person* acting on behalf of the *customer* is acting against the best interests of the *customer*.
(4)   Situations where it would be justified for a *firm* to contact a *customer* directly include, for example:
     (a)   sending a statutory notice, taking the reasonable steps required by **CONC 7.9.7 R**; or
     (b)   where the sole purpose of the contact is to signpost the *customer* to *not-for-profit debt advice bodies*.
(5)   Where a *firm* is in dispute with a *person* acting on behalf of the *customer* it should make its position known to that *person* and to the *customer* as soon as practicable.
     [**Note**: paragraph 3.49d of *DMG*]
(6)   The *FCA* does not believe it is justified to bypass contacting a *person* acting on behalf of a *customer* merely because that *person* has not agreed to comply with the Insolvency Service's Debt Management Protocol.

7.13   DATA ACCURACY AND OUTSOURCED ACTIVITIES

Data accuracy

7.13.1 G   FCA

The obtaining, recording, holding and passing on of information about individuals for the purposes of tracing a *customer* and/or recovering a debt due under a *credit agreement* or a *consumer hire agreement* or a *P2P agreement* will involve the processing of personal data. Accordingly, *firms* processing such data are data controllers or data processors and are obliged to comply with the Data Protection Act 1998 and, in particular, to adhere to the eight data protection principles.
[**Note**: paragraph 3.16 of *DCG*]

7.13.2 R   FCA

A *firm* must take reasonable steps to ensure that it maintains accurate and adequate data (including in respect of debt and repayment history) so as to avoid the risk that:
(1)   an *individual* who is not the true *borrower* or *hirer* is pursued for the repayment of a debt; and
(2)   the *borrower* or *hirer* is pursued for an incorrect amount.
[**Note**: paragraphs 3.19 of *DCG* and 7.11 (box) of *ILG*]

7.13.3 R   FCA

A *firm* must endeavour to ensure that the information it passes on to its agent or to a *debt collector* or to a tracing agent (a person that carries on the activity in article 54 of the Exemption Order), whether for the *firm's* or another person's business, or to any other *person* involved in recovering the debt or, where appropriate, to a *credit reference agency* is accurate and adequate so as to facilitate the tracing and identification of the true *borrower* or *hirer*.
[**Note**: paragraphs 3.20 of *DCG* and 7.11 (box) *ILG*]

7.13.4 R   FCA

Before pursuing a *customer* for the repayment of a debt, a *firm* must take reasonable steps to verify the accuracy and adequacy of the available data so as to ensure that the true *customer* is pursued for the debt and that they are pursued for the correct amount.
[**Note**: paragraphs 3.7e and 3.23a of *DCG*]

7.13.5 G   FCA

A *firm* should ensure (subject to any legal requirements) that adequate and accurate information it holds about a *customer* in relation to a debt is made available to *persons* involved on its behalf in the debt recovery process. Information relating to the *customer* which should be made available to agents or employees includes, for example:
(1)   being in financial difficulties;
(2)   being particularly vulnerable;
(3)   disputing the debt;
(4)   a repayment plan or forbearance being in place;
(5)   having a representative acting on the *customer's* behalf.
[**Note**: paragraph 3.23b (box) of *DCG*]

7.13.6 G   FCA

A *firm* should not impose limitations on the number or the extent of reasonable applications that can be made to it for documents or other relevant information pertaining to a *customer* in respect of which it is, or has been, the *lender* or *owner*, by a *firm* seeking such information to facilitate its pursuance of the relevant debt.
[**Note**: paragraph 3.23i of *DCG*]

7.13.7 R   FCA

Where a *firm* has established that an *individual* being pursued for a debt is not the true *borrower* or *hirer* under the *credit agreement, regulated credit agreement, consumer hire agreement* or *regulated consumer hire agreement* or that the debt has been paid, the *firm* must update its records and the data supplied to the *credit reference agencies* (where applicable).
[**Note**: paragraph 3.23f of *DCG*]

Outsourcing

7.13.8 G   FCA

SYSC 8.1 includes *rules* and *guidance* on outsourcing with which *firms* must or should comply as appropriate.

7.13.9 G   FCA

A *firm* seeking to instruct a third party to pursue the recovery of debts or to trace *customers* on its behalf should exercise due care in selecting the third party.
[**Note**: paragraph 2.5 of *DCG*]

7.13.10 G   FCA

A *firm* should take reasonable steps to seek to ensure that, where it has engaged a third party to recover debts on its behalf, the *customer* is not subject to multiple approaches by different *persons*, resulting in repetitive or frequent contact with the *customer* by different parties.
[**Note**: paragraph 3.7c of *DCG*]

7.13.11 G   FCA

Where a *firm* has engaged a third party to recover debts or to trace *customers* on its behalf, it should properly investigate complaints about the third party.
[**Note**: paragraph 2.5 of *DCG*]

7.13.12 G   FCA

CONC 1.2.2 R requires a *firm* to ensure its employees and agents comply with *CONC* and that it takes reasonable steps to ensure other *persons* who act on its behalf do so.

7.13.13 R   FCA

A *firm* must ensure that a third party engaged by it, where required, has the appropriate *Part 4A permission* to engage in the *regulated activities* undertaken in the course of the third party's business.
[**Note**: paragraph 2.6 of *DCG*]

7.14   SETTLEMENTS, DISPUTED AND DEADLOCKED DEBT

Disputed debt

7.14.1 R   FCA
(1)   A *firm* must suspend any steps it takes or its agent takes in the recovery of a debt from a *customer* where the *customer* disputes the debt on valid grounds or what may be valid grounds.
      [**Note**: paragraph 3.9k of *DCG*]
(2)   Paragraph (1) does not apply where a *customer* under a green deal consumer credit agreement (within the meaning of section 189B of the *CCA*) alleges that the disclosure and acknowledgement provisions in Part 7 of the Green Deal Framework (Disclosure, Acknowledgement, Redress etc) Regulations 2012 (SI 2012/2079) have been breached, but the *lender* reasonably believes this not to be the case.

7.14.2 G   FCA

Valid grounds for disputing a debt include that:
(1)   the *individual* being pursued for the debt is not the true *borrower* or *hirer* under the agreement in question; or
(2)   the debt does not exist; or
(3)   the amount of the debt being pursued is incorrect.
      [**Note**: annex A3 of *DCG*]

7.14.3 R   FCA

Where a *customer* disputes a debt on valid grounds or what may be valid grounds, the *firm* must investigate the dispute and provide details of the debt to the *customer* in a timely manner.
[**Note**: paragraph 3.9i of *DCG*]

7.14.4 R   FCA

Where there is a dispute as to the identity of the *borrower* or *hirer* or as to the amount of the debt, it is for the *firm* (and not the *customer*) to establish, as the case may be, that the *customer* is the correct *person* in relation to the debt or that the amount is the correct amount owed under the agreement.
[**Note**: paragraphs 3.9j of *DCG* and 7.11 (box) of *ILG*]

7.14.5 R   FCA

A *firm* must provide a *customer* with information on the outcome of its investigations into a debt which the *customer* disputed on valid grounds.
[**Note**: paragraph 3.3g of *DCG*]

7.14.6 R   FCA

Where a *customer* disputes a debt and the *firm* seeking to recover the debt is not the *lender* or the *owner*, the *firm* must:
(1)   pass the information provided by the *customer* to the *lender* or the *owner*; or
      [**Note**: paragraph 3.23h of *DCG*]
(2)   if the *firm* has authority from the *lender* or *owner* to investigate a dispute, it must notify the *lender* or *owner* of the outcome of the investigation.

Settlements and deadlocked debt etc

7.14.7 G   FCA

A debt repayment is deadlocked where the *customer* (or the *customer's* representative) has acknowledged the *customer's* liability for a debt and has proposed a repayment plan, but the proposed repayment plan is not acceptable to the *firm* seeking to recover the debt.
[Note: annex A4 of *DCG*]

7.14.8 R   FCA

A *firm* must give due consideration to a reasonable offer of repayment made by the *customer* or the *customer's* representative.
[Note: annex A5 of *DCG*]

7.14.9 R   FCA

Where a *firm* rejects a proposal for repayment from a *customer* in default or in arrears difficulties or from the *customer's* representative, the *firm's* response must include a clear explanation of the reason for the rejection.
[Note: paragraph 7.16 (box) of *ILG*]

7.14.10 R   FCA

If a *firm* rejects a repayment offer because it is unacceptable, the *firm* must not engage in any conduct intended to, or likely to, have the effect of intimidating the customer into increasing the offer.
[**Note:** annex A5 of *DCG*]

7.14.11 G   FCA

Examples of conduct that may contravene **CONC 7.14.10 R** would, depending on the circumstances, include where following an unacceptable offer a *firm* immediately:
(1)   sends field agents to visit the *customer* or communicates to the *customer* that it will do so;
        [**Note:** annex A5 (box) to *DCG*]
(2)   substantially increases the rate of interest or imposes a substantial charge or communicates that is will do either of those things.

7.14.12 G   FCA

In considering the *customer's* repayment offer, a *firm* should have regard, where appropriate, to the provisions in the Common Financial Statement or equivalent guidance.
[**Note:** annex A6 of *DCG*]

7.14.13 G   FCA
(1)   Merely making a counter-offer to a *customer's* repayment offer or merely taking steps to enforce an agreement would not contravene **CONC 7.14.10 R**.
(2)   A *firm* which makes a counter offer to a proposal made by or on behalf of the *customer*, should allow the *customer* or the *customer's* representative, a reasonable period of time to consider and respond to the counter offer.
        [**Note:** paragraph 7.16 of *ILG*]

7.14.14 R   FCA

If a *firm* accepts a *customer's* offer to settle a debt, it must communicate formally and unequivocally that the offer accompanied by the relevant payment has been accepted as settlement of the *customer's* liability.
[**Note:** paragraph 3.3h of *DCG*]

7.15   STATUTE BARRED DEBTS

7.15.1 G   FCA

A debt is statute barred where the prescribed period within which a claim in relation to the debt may be brought expires. In England, Wales and Northern Ireland, the limitation period is generally six years in relation to debt. In Scotland, the prescriptive period is five years in relation to debt.
[**Note:** annex B1 of *DCG*]

7.15.2 G   FCA

In England, Wales and Northern Ireland, a statute barred debt still exists and is recoverable.
[**Note:** paragraph 3.15a and annex B3 of *DCG*]

7.15.3 G   FCA

In Scotland, a statute barred debt ceases to exist and is no longer recoverable if:
(1)   a relevant claim on behalf of the *lender* or *owner* has not been made during the relevant limitation period; and
(2)   the debt has not been acknowledged by, or on behalf of, the *customer* during the relevant limitation period.
        [**Note:** annex B3 of *DCG*]

7.15.4 R   FCA

Notwithstanding that a debt may be recoverable, a *firm* must not attempt to recover a statute barred debt in England, Wales or Northern Ireland if the *lender* or *owner* has not been in contact with the *customer* during the limitation period.
[**Note:** paragraph 3.15b of *DCG*]

7.15.5 G   FCA

If the *lender* or *owner* has been in regular contact with the *customer* during the limitation period, the *firm* may continue to attempt to recover the debt.
[**Note**: paragraph 3.15b of *DCG*]

7.15.6 R   FCA

A *firm* must endeavour to ensure that it does not mislead a *customer* as to the *customer's* rights and obligations.
[**Note**: paragraph 3.15b of *DCG*]

7.15.7 G   FCA

It is misleading for a *firm* to suggest or state that a *customer* may be the subject of court action for the sum of the statute barred debt when the *firm* knows, or reasonably ought to know, that the relevant limitation period has expired.
[**Note**: paragraph 3.15b of *DCG*]

7.15.8 R   FCA

A *firm* must not continue to demand payment from a *customer* after the *customer* has stated that he will not be paying the debt because it is statute barred.
[**Note**: paragraph 3.15b of *DCG*]

7.15.9 R   FCA

A *firm* must identify for prospective purchasers of debts arising under *credit agreements* or *consumer hire agreements* or *P2P agreements* those debts which it knows or ought reasonably to know are statute barred, so as to avoid a *firm* taking inappropriate action against *customers* in relation to such debts.
[**Note**: paragraph 3.23c of *DCG*]

Complaints to the Financial Ombudsman Service and initiating legal proceedings

7.15.10 R   FCA

A *lender* must not initiate legal proceedings in relation to a *regulated credit agreement* where the *lender* is aware that the *customer* has submitted a valid complaint or what appears to the *firm* may be a valid complaint relating to the agreement in question that is being considered by the *Financial Ombudsman Service*.
[**Note**: paragraph 7.9 (box) of *ILG*]

7.16   PASSING DATA TO LEAD GENERATORS ETC.

7.16.1 R   FCA

A *firm* must not pass on a *customer's* details to third parties, including *lead generators*, *debt management firms*, *lenders*, *owners*, *debt collectors* or *credit brokers*, unless it is appropriate to do so.
[**Note**: paragraph 3.9e of *DCG*]

7.16.2 G   FCA

[deleted]

7.17   NOTICE OF SUMS IN ARREARS UNDER P2P AGREEMENTS FOR FIXED-SUM CREDIT

Application

[**Note**: Until the end of 30 September 2014, transitional provisions apply to **CONC 7.17**: see **CONC TP 4**.3]

7.17.1 R   FCA

This section applies to a *firm* with respect to *operating an electronic system in relation to lending* in relation to a *borrower* under a *P2P agreement* for *fixed-sum credit*.

7.17.2 R   FCA
(1)   Subject to (2), this section does not apply where the *P2P agreement* provides for *credit* of less than £50.
(2)   Paragraph (1) does not apply where two or more *P2P agreements* in relation to the same *borrower* (whether or not with the same *lender*) are entered into at or about the same time.
(3)   Where (2) applies, the *firm's* obligations in **CONC 7.17** apply as if all of the *P2P agreements* made with a *borrower* at or about the same time were a single agreement.

Notice of sums in arrears for fixed-sum credit

7.17.3 R   FCA

A *firm* must comply with this section where the following conditions are satisfied:

(1) a *borrower* is required to have made at least two payments under the agreement before that time;

(2) the total sum paid under the agreement by the *borrower* is less than the total sum required to have been paid before that time;

(3) the amount of the shortfall is no less than the sum of the last two payments which the *borrower* is required to have made before that time;

(4) the *firm* is not already under a duty to give the *borrower* notices under **CONC 7.17.4 R** in relation to the agreement;

(5) the *lender* is not already under a duty to give the *borrower* notice under section 86B of the *CCA*; and

(6) if a judgment has been given in relation to the agreement before that time, there is no sum still to be paid under the judgment by the *borrower*.

7.17.4 R   FCA

(1) The *firm* must, within the period of 14 days beginning with the day on which the conditions in **CONC 7.17.3 R** are satisfied, give the *borrower* a notice including the information set out in **CONC 7.17.7 R** and **CONC 7.17.8 R**.

(2) After giving that notice, the *firm* must give the *borrower* further notices including the information in **CONC 7.17.7 R** and **CONC 7.17.8 R** at intervals of not more than six *months*.

7.17.5 R   FCA

(1) The duty of the *firm* to give the *borrower* notices under **CONC 7.17.4 R** will cease when either of the conditions mentioned in (2) is satisfied but, if either of those conditions is satisfied before the notice required by **CONC 7.17.4 R (1)** is given, the duty will not cease until that notice is given.

(2) The conditions referred to in (1) are:

(a) that the *borrower* ceases to be in arrears;

(b) that a judgment is given in relation to the agreement under which a sum is required to be paid by the *borrower*.

(3) For the purposes of (2)(a) the *borrower* ceases to be in arrears when:

(a) no payments, which the *borrower* has ever failed to make under the agreement when required, are still owing;

(b) no default sum, which has ever become payable under the agreement in connection with the *borrower's* failure to pay any sum under the agreement when required, is still owing;

(c) no sum of interest, which has ever become payable under the agreement in connection with such a default sum, is still owing; and

(d) no other sum of interest, which has ever become payable under the agreement in connection with the *borrower's* failure to pay any sum under the agreement when required, is still owing.

(4) A *firm* must accompany the notice required by **CONC 7.17.4 R** with a copy of the current arrears information sheet under section 86A of the *CCA* with the following modifications:

(a) for the bullet point headed "Work out how much money you owe" substitute: "Work out how much money you owe. To do this, you will need to make a list of all those you owe money to. A debt adviser can help you.";

(b) for the bullet point headed "Contact the organisations you owe money to" substitute: "Contact the peer-to-peer (P2P) platform which arranged your loan. Let them know you are having problems. They may be able to discuss options for paying back what you owe.";

(c) For the paragraph headed "Doing nothing could make things worse." substitute: "Doing nothing could make things worse.
You could end up paying more in interest and charges. Missed payments could affect your credit rating and make it more difficult to get credit in future. If you continue not to make payment this could lead to legal action against you for repayment or the return of goods on hire purchase.".

(5) The *firm* must not charge the *borrower* a fee in connection with preparation of or the giving of the notice required by **CONC 7.18.4 R**.

7.17.6 R   FCA

In this section "payments" means payments to be made at predetermined intervals provided for under the terms of the agreement.

Content of arrears notices: fixed-sum credit

7.17.7 R   FCA

The notice required by **CONC 7.17.4 R** must contain the following information:

(1) a form of wording to the effect that the notice is given in compliance with the *rules* because the *borrower* is behind with the sums payable under the agreement;

(2)   a form of wording encouraging the *borrower* to discuss the state of his account with the *firm*;

(3)   the date of the notice;

(4)

    (a)   the name, telephone number or numbers, the postal address, and, where appropriate, any other address of the *firm*; or

    (b)   where the *firm* and the *borrower* have entered into an arrangement under which the *borrower* has been given details of a particular employee or category of employee of the *firm* whom the *borrower* is entitled to contact for all the *borrower's* dealings with the *firm*, the *firm* may, instead of including the telephone number or numbers in (a), refer to that arrangement;

(5)   a description sufficient to identify any agreements and the opening balance under any agreements at the date on which the duty to give the notice arose;

(6)

    (a)   where default sums or interest (other than any set out in the notice) may be payable in connection with the amounts set out in the notice, a statement in the following form:

        "Default sums and interest
You may have to pay default sums and interest in relation to the missed or partly made payments referred to in this notice. Please contact us if you would like further details. This notice does not take account of any payments received after the date of the notice."; or

    (b)   in any other case, a statement in the following form:

        "Default sums and interest
You will not incur any default sums or extra interest in relation to the missed or partly made payments referred to in this notice. This notice does not take account of any payments received after the date of the notice.";

(7)   a statement in the following form:

    "Notices
For so long as you continue to be behind with your payments by any amount, you will be sent notices about this at least every six months. We are not required to send you notices more frequently than this, even if you get further behind with your payments in between notices."; and

(8)   a statement in the following form:

    "Financial Conduct Authority Information Sheet
This notice should include a copy of the current arrears information sheet prepared by the Financial Conduct Authority. This contains important information about your rights and where to go for support and advice, for example to think carefully before borrowing money to repay debts as well as our right to charge you interest. If it is not included you should contact us to get one. Please refer to the Financial Conduct Authority information sheet for more information about how to get advice on dealing with your debt.".

Content of first required arrears notices

7.17.8 R   FCA

Where the notice is given under **CONC 7.17.4 R (1)** the notice must also state the amount of the shortfall under the agreement which gave rise to the duty to give the notice and the *firm* must:

(1)   within 15 *working days* of receiving the *borrower's* request for further information about the shortfall which gave rise to the duty to give the notice, give the *borrower* in relation to each of the sums which comprise the shortfall, notice of:

    (a)   the amount of the sums due which comprise the shortfall;

    (b)   the date on which the sums became due; and

    (c)   the amounts the *borrower* has paid in respect of the sums due and the dates of those payments;

(2)   except where the original notice contained all the information specified in (1), include a statement in the following form

    "If you want more information about which payments you failed to make please get in touch with us. We are required to give you this information within fifteen working days of receiving your request for it."; and

(3)   where the *firm* and the *borrower* have entered into an agreement to aggregate, the references to sums due and to amounts paid in (1) may be construed as a reference to the aggregated sums due to the *firm* (on behalf of the *lender*) and the aggregated amounts paid by the *borrower* in accordance with the terms of that agreement.

Content of required arrears notices except first required notices

7.17.9 R   FCA

Where the notice is given under **CONC 7.17.4 R (2)** the notice must also contain the following information:

(1)   that part of the opening balance referred to in **CONC 7.17.7 R (5)** which comprises any sum which the *borrower* has failed to pay in full when it became due under the agreement, whether or not such sums have been included in a previous notice;

(2)   the amount and date of any sums paid into the account by, or to the credit of, the *borrower* during the period to which the notice relates;

(3)   the amount and date of any interest or other charges payable by the *borrower* which became due during the period to which the notice relates, whether or not the interest or other charges relate only to that period. But where the rate or rates of interest provided for under the agreement are not applicable on a per annum basis, this sub-paragraph does not require amounts and dates of interest which became due during the period to which the notice relates to be set out separately in the notice;

(4)   the amount and date of any movement in the account during the period to which the notice relates which is not required to be included in the notice under (2) and (3);

(5)   the balance under the agreement at the end of the period to which the notice relates;

(6)   that part of the balance referred to in (5) which comprises any sum which the *borrower* has failed to pay in full when it became due under the agreement and which remains unpaid at the end of the period to which the notice relates, whether or not such a sum has been included in a previous notice; and

(7)   add the following words to the end of the first sentence of the statement in **CONC 7.17.7 R (6)(A)**: "(in addition to any default sums and interest included in this notice)."

7.17.10 R   FCA

Where the notice includes a form of wording to the effect that it is not a demand for immediate payment, the *firm* must include wording explaining why it is not such a demand.

7.17.11 R   FCA

The reference to the account in **CONC 7.17.9 R (2)** and **CONC 7.17.9 R (4)** are to be construed as a reference to all accounts maintained by the *firm* (on behalf of a *lender*) which relate to the agreement with the *borrower*.

7.18   NOTICE OF SUMS IN ARREARS UNDER P2P AGREEMENTS FOR RUNNING-ACCOUNT CREDIT

[**Note**: Until the end of 30 September 2014, transitional provisions apply to **CONC 7.18**: see **CONC TP 4**.4]

Application

7.18.1 R   FCA

This section applies to a *firm* with respect to *operating an electronic system in relation to lending* in relation to a *borrower* under a *P2P agreement* for running account credit.

Notice of sums in arrears for running account credit

7.18.2 R   FCA

A *firm* must comply with this section where the following conditions are satisfied:

(1)   a *borrower* is required to have made at least two *repayments* under the agreement;

(2)   the last two *repayments* which the *borrower* is required to have made before that time have not been made;

(3)   the *firm* has not already been required to give a notice under **CONC 7.18.3 R** in relation to the agreement;

(4)   the *lender* is not already under a duty to give the *borrower* notice under section 86C of the *CCA*; and

(5)   if a judgment has been given in relation to the agreement before that time, that there is no sum still to be paid under the judgment by the *borrower*.

7.18.3 R   FCA

(1)   The *firm* must, when the *firm* next sends a statement to the *borrower*, give or send the *borrower* a notice including the information set out in **CONC 7.18.5 R**.

(2)   A *firm* must accompany the notice required by (1) with a copy of the current arrears information sheet under section 86A of the *CCA* with the following modifications:

(a)   for the bullet point headed "Work out how much money you owe" substitute: "Work out how much money you owe. To do this, you will need to make a list of all those you owe money to. A debt adviser can help you."

(b)   for the bullet point headed "Contact the organisations you owe money to" substitute: "Contact the peer-to-peer (P2P) platform which arranged your loan. Let them know you are having problems. They may be able to discuss options for paying back what you owe."

(c)   For the paragraph headed "Doing nothing could make things worse." substitute:
"Doing nothing could make things worse.

You could end up paying more in interest and charges. Missed payments could affect your credit rating and make it more difficult to get credit in future. If you continue not to make payment this could lead to legal action against you for repayment or the return of goods on hire purchase.".

(3)   The *firm* must not charge the *borrower* a fee in connection with the preparation of or the giving of the notice required by (1).

(4)   The notice required by (1) may be incorporated in a statement or other notice which the *firm* gives to the borrower in relation to the agreement by virtue of *FCA rules* or the *CCA*.

7.18.4 R   FCA

In this section "payments" means payments to be made at predetermined intervals provided for under the terms of the agreement.

Content of arrears notices: running account credit

7.18.5 R   FCA

The notice referred to in **CONC 7.18.3 R** must contain the following information:

(1)   a form of wording to the effect that it is given in compliance with the *rules* because the *borrower* is behind with his payments under the agreement;

(2)   a form of wording encouraging the *borrower* to discuss the state of his account with the *firm*;

(3)   the date of the notice;

(4)   a description of the agreement sufficient to identify it;

(5)

    (a)   the name, telephone number, postal address and, where appropriate, any other address of the *firm*; or

    (b)   where the *firm* and the *borrower* have entered into an arrangement under which the *firm* has given the *borrower* details of a particular employee or category of employee of the *firm* whom the *borrower* is entitled to contact for all his dealings with the *firm*, the *firm* may, instead of including the telephone number or numbers referred to in (a), refer to that arrangement;

(6)   in relation to each of the last two payments which the *borrower* is required under the agreement to have made and which have not been paid or not fully paid:

    (a)   the amount payable;

    (b)   the date on which that amount became due;

    (c)   in the event that the *borrower* has paid part of that amount, the amount the *borrower* has paid and the date on which that payment was made;

    (d)   the nature of the amount due; and

    (e)   the aggregate of the amounts payable as shown under (a), less the aggregate of the amounts paid as shown under (c);

(7)   a statement in the following form:
"Missed and partly made payments
This notice does not give details of missed or partly made payments previously notified whether or not they remain unpaid."

(8)

    (a)   where default sums or interest (other than any set out in the notice) may be payable in connection with the amounts set out in the notice, a statement in the following form:
"Default sums and Interest
You may have to pay default sums and interest in relation to the missed or partly made payments indicated above in addition to any default sums and interest already included in this notice. Please contact us if you would like further details. This notice does not take account of any payments received after the date of the notice."; or

    (b)   in any other case, a statement in the following form:
"Default sums and Interest
You will not incur any default sums or extra interest in relation to the missed or partly made payments indicated above. This notice does not take account of any payments received after the date of the notice."; and

(9)   a statement in the following form:
"Financial Conduct Authority Information Sheet
This notice should include a copy of the current arrears information sheet issued by the Financial Conduct Authority. This contains important information about your rights and where to go for support and advice, for example, to think carefully before borrowing money to repay debts, as well as our right to charge you interest. If it is not included you should contact us to get one. Please refer to the Financial Conduct Authority information sheet for more information about how to get advice on dealing with your debt."

7.18.6 R   FCA

Where the notice includes a form of wording to the effect that it is not a demand for immediate payment, the *firm* must include wording explaining why it is not such a demand.

7.18.7 R   FCA
(1)   Subject to (2), where the total amount which the *borrower* has failed to pay in relation to the last two payments due under the agreement prior to the date on which the *firm* came under a duty to give the *borrower* a notice under **CONC 7.18.3 R** is not more than £2, the notice:
    (a)   need not include any of the information or statements referred to in **CONC 7.18.4 R**;
    (b)   but, in that event, shall contain a statement in the following form:
        "You have failed to make two minimum payments
        Failing to make minimum payments can mean that you have broken the terms of this credit agreement. This could result in your having to pay additional costs. A copy of the Financial Conduct Authority Arrears information sheet is enclosed, which contains more information about what to do when you get behind with your payments.";
(2)   Paragraph (1) does not apply where at the date on which the duty to give notice arose a default sum or other charge has become payable as a result of the *borrower's* failure to pay sums as set out in (1).

7.19   NOTICE OF DEFAULT SUMS UNDER P2P AGREEMENTS

[**Note**: Until the end of 30 September 2014, transitional provisions apply to **CONC 7.19**: see **CONC TP 4.5**]

Application

7.19.1 R   FCA

This section applies to a *firm* with respect to *operating an electronic system in relation to lending* in relation to a *borrower* under a *P2P agreement*.

7.19.2 R   FCA
(1)   Subject to (2), this section does not apply where the *P2P agreement* provides for *credit* of less than £50.
(2)   Paragraph (1) does not apply where two or more *P2P agreements* in relation to the same *borrower* (but whether or not with the same *lender*) are entered into at or about the same time.
(3)   Where (2) applies, the *firm's* obligation in **CONC 7.19.4 R** applies as if all of the *P2P agreements* made with a *borrower* at or about the same time were a single agreement.

7.19.3 R   FCA
(1)   In this section "default sum" means in relation to the *borrower* under a *P2P agreement*, a sum (other than a sum of interest) which is payable by the *borrower* under the agreement in connection with a breach of the agreement by the *borrower*.
(2)   But a sum is not a default sum in relation to the *borrower* simply because as a consequence of the breach of the agreement the *borrower* is required to pay the sum earlier than would otherwise have been the case.

Notice of default sums

7.19.4 R   FCA

Where a default sum becomes payable under a *P2P agreement* by the *borrower*, the *firm* must give notice to the *borrower* within 35 days of a default sum becoming payable by the *borrower*.

7.19.5 R   FCA

The notice required by **CONC 7.19.4 R** must contain:
(1)   a form of wording to the effect that it relates to default sums and is given in compliance with *FCA rules*;
(2)   the date of the notice;
(3)   a description of the agreement sufficient to identify it;
(4)   the *firm's* name, telephone number, postal address and, where appropriate, any other address;
(5)   the amount and nature of each default sum payable under the agreement which has not been the subject of a previous notice of default sums;
(6)   the date upon which each default sum referred to in the notice became payable under the agreement;
(7)   the following statement:
    "This notice does not take account of default sums which we have already told you about in another default sum notice, whether or not those sums remain unpaid."; and
(8)   the total amount of all the default sums included in the notice.

CHAPTER 8
DEBT ADVICE

8.1 APPLICATION

[3.86]
8.1.1 R FCA

This chapter applies, unless otherwise stated in or in relation to a *rule* to every *firm* with respect to:
(1)   *debt counselling*;
(2)   *debt adjusting*; and
(3)   to the extent of giving the advice referred to in article 89A(2) of the *Regulated Activities Order*, *providing credit information services*.

8.1.2 G FCA

CONC 8.10 (Conduct of business: providing credit information services) sets out that that section applies to every *firm* with respect to *providing credit information services* and with respect to *operating an electronic system in relation to lending* in relation to activities specified in article 36H(3)(e) to (h) of the *Regulated Activities Order* which are similar to *providing credit information services*.

8.1.3 G FCA

CONC 8 covers all *firms* with respect to *debt counselling*, *debt adjusting* and *providing credit information services*, which includes profit-seeking as well as *not-for-profit bodies* which hold such *permissions* and in that case include those bodies with *permission* by virtue of article 62 of the *Regulated Activities Order*.

[**Note:** paragraph 1.10 of *DMG*]

8.1.4 G FCA

The activities of *debt counselling* and *debt adjusting* apply to *credit agreements* and *consumer hire agreements* whether they are regulated or not.

8.2 CONDUCT STANDARDS: DEBT ADVICE

Overarching principles

8.2.1 G FCA

The Principles for Businesses (*PRIN*) apply as a whole to *firms* with respect to *debt counselling*, *debt adjusting* and *providing credit information services*.

8.2.2 G FCA
(1)   One aspect of conducting a *firm's* business with due skill, care and diligence under *Principle* 2 is that a *firm* should ensure that it gives appropriate advice to *customers* residing in the different countries of the *UK*. Failure to pay proper regard to the differences in options for *debt solutions* available to those *customers* and to the differences in enforcement actions and procedures is likely to contravene *Principle* 2 and may contravene other *Principles*.
       [**Note:** paragraph 3.23d of *DMG*]
(2)   Recommending a *debt solution* which a *firm* knows, believes or ought to suspect is unaffordable for the *customer* is likely to contravene *Principle* 2, *Principle* 6 and *Principle* 9 and may contravene other *Principles*.
       [**Note:** paragraph 3.26j of *DMG*]
(3)   An example of behaviour that is likely to contravene *Principle* 6 and may contravene other *Principles* in this field is for a *firm* to actively discourage a *customer* from considering alternative sources of *debt counselling*.
       [**Note:** paragraph 3.23m of *DMG*]

8.2.3 G FCA

A *firm* covered by **CONC 8** has obligations under the *FCA's* Dispute Resolution: Complaints sourcebook (*DISP*) to treat complainants fairly; these are set out in **DISP 1**.

Signposting to sources of free debt counselling, etc

8.2.4 R FCA

A *debt management firm* must prominently include:
(1)   in its first written or oral communication with the *customer* a statement that free *debt counselling*, *debt adjusting* and *providing of credit information services* is available to *customers* and that the *customer* can find out more by contacting the Money Advice Service; and
(2)   on its web-site the following link to the Money Advice Service web-site (www. moneyadviceservice.org.uk/en/articles/where-to-go-to-get-free-debt-advice).
       [**Note:** paragraph 1.7 of Debt Management Protocol]

Dealing with lenders of customers

8.2.5 R   FCA

A *firm's* communications to *lenders* (or to *lenders'* representatives) on behalf of its *customers* must be transparent so as to ensure a *firm's customer's* interests are not adversely affected.

[**Note:** paragraph 2.5 of *DMG*]

8.2.6 R   FCA

Where entry into a *debt solution* will lead to a period when payments to *lenders* (in part or in whole) are not made or are retained by the *firm*, the *firm* must, as soon as possible after the *customer* enters into the *debt solution*, notify the *customer's lenders* of the reason payments are not to be made to the *lender* and the period during which that will be the case.

[**Note:** paragraph 3.18niv of *DMG*]

Vulnerable customers

8.2.7 R   FCA

A *firm* must establish and implement clear and effective policies and procedures to identify particularly vulnerable *customers* and to deal with such *customers* appropriately.

[**Note:** paragraph 2.4 of *DMG*]

8.2.8 G   FCA

Most *customers* seeking advice on their debts under *credit agreements* or *consumer hire agreements* may be regarded as vulnerable to some degree by virtue of their financial circumstances. Of these *customers* some may be particularly vulnerable because they are less able to deal with *lenders* or *debt collectors* pursuing them for debts owed. *Customers* with mental health and mental capacity issues may fall into this category.

[**Note:** paragraph 2.4 of *DMG*]

8.3   PRE CONTRACT INFORMATION AND ADVICE REQUIREMENTS

8.3.1 R   FCA

A *firm* must (except where the contract is a *credit agreement* to which the *disclosure regulations* apply) provide sufficient information, in a *durable medium*, when the *customer* first enquires about the *firm's* services, about the following matters to enable the *customer* to make a reasonable decision:

(1)   the nature of the *firm's* service offered in the contract to the *customer*;
        [**Note:** paragraph 3.38b of *DMG*]

(2)   the duration of the contract;
        [**Note:** paragraph 3.38c of *DMG*]

(3)   the total cost of the *firm's* service or, where it is not possible to state the total cost, the formula the *firm* uses for calculating its fees or charges or an estimate of the anticipated likely total cost may be given;
        [**Note:** paragraph 3.40c of *DMG*]

(4)   any fee or deposit, such as an arrangement fee, a periodic fee, a management fee, or an administrative fee;
        [**Note:** paragraph 3.38c of *DMG*]

(5)   any fee or charge which can be imposed on the *customer* in relation to cancellation of the contract;
        [**Note:** paragraph 3.38c of *DMG*]

(6)   any other costs likely to be incurred under the contract and the circumstances in which these would be payable;
        [**Note:** paragraph 3.38c of *DMG*]

(7)   where the *firm* bases its fees or charges on some percentage or an hourly rate or some other formula, an explanation of how the fees or charges are calculated;
        [**Note:** paragraph 3.9c of *DMG*]

(8)   the elements of the service that the fees cover;
        [**Note:** paragraph 3.38c of *DMG*]

(9)   the circumstances in which a *customer* may terminate the contract and receive a refund in accordance with relevant law and any fees or charges the *customer* may be required to pay in that case;
        [**Note:** paragraph 3.40d of *DMG*]

(10)   the consequences on the *customer's* credit rating, including how long the matter will show on the *customer's* credit file and that the *customer* may not be able to obtain *credit* or other financial services in the future;
        [**Note:** paragraph 3.38e of *DMG*]

(11)   whether a right to cancel applies and, if so, the period and any conditions for exercising the right to cancel the contract and any amount the *customer* may be required to pay;
        [**Note:** paragraph 3.38h of *DMG*]

(12)   how payments will be allocated to *lenders* and when payments will be made; and
        [**Note:** paragraph 3.38k of *DMG*]
(13)   the period of time between payments being received from the *customer* and payments being made to *lenders*, including the date when the first payment will be made to *lenders*.
        [**Note:** paragraph 3.38l of *DMG*]

[**Note:** paragraphs 3.33, 3.35 and 3.38 of *DMG*]

8.3.2 R   FCA

A *firm* must ensure that:
(1)   all advice given and action taken by the *firm* or its agent or its *appointed representative*:
      (a)   has regard to the best interests of the *customer*;
      (b)   is appropriate to the individual circumstances of the *customer*; and
      (c)   is based on a sufficiently full assessment of the financial circumstances of the *customer*;

      [**Note:** paragraph 2.6a of *DMG*]
(2)   *customers* receive sufficient information about the available options identified as suitable for the *customers'* needs; and
      [**Note:** paragraph 2.6b of *DMG*]
(3)   it explains the reasons why the *firm* considers the available options suitable and other options unsuitable.
      [**Note:** paragraph 2.6b of *DMG*]

8.3.3 G   FCA

The individual circumstances of the *customer* include, for example, the *customer's* financial position, the country in the *UK* to whose laws and procedures the *customer* and the *lender* in question are subject, and the level of understanding of the *customer*.

[**Note:** paragraph 2.6c of *DMG*]

8.3.4 R   FCA

A *firm* must ensure that advice provided to a *customer*, whether before the *firm* has entered into contract with the *customer* or after, is provided in a *durable medium* and:
(1)   makes clear which debts will be included in any *debt solution* and which debts will be excluded from any *debt solution*;
      [**Note:** paragraph 3.38j of *DMG*]
(2)   makes clear the actual or potential advantages, disadvantages, costs and risks of each option available to the *customer*, with any conditions that apply for entry into each option and which debts may be covered by each option;
      [**Note:** paragraphs 3.23a and 3.38b of *DMG*]
(3)   warns the *customer*:
      (a)   of the actual or potential consequences of failing to continue to pay taxes, fines, child support payments and debts which could result in loss of access to essential *goods* or services or repossession of, or eviction from, the *customer's* home;
          [**Note:** paragraph 3.38m of *DMG*]
      (b)   of the actual or potential consequences of not continuing to make *repayments* under *credit agreements* or *consumer hire agreements*;
          [**Note:** paragraph 3.26k of *DMG*]
      (c)   of the actual or potential consequences of ignoring correspondence or other contact from *lenders* and those acting on behalf of *lenders*;
          [**Note:** paragraph 3.38n of *DMG*]
      (d)   that action to recover debts may be commenced, which may involve further cost to the *customer*; and
          [**Note:** paragraph 3.38q of *DMG*]
      (e)   that by entering into a *debt management plan* or another non-statutory repayment plan there is no guarantee that any current recovery or legal action will be suspended or withdrawn;
          [**Note:** paragraph 3.38r of *DMG*]
(4)   where relevant to the *debt solution*, makes clear the risks, including the following risks:
      (a)   if the arrangement or deed fails, the risk of bankruptcy;
      (b)   homeowners may need to release equity from the value of their homes to pay off debts; and that a remortgage may attract higher interest rates or that if no remortgage is available, an individual voluntary arrangement may be extended for 12 *months*;
      (c)   there are restrictions on the expenditure of a *person* who enters into an individual voluntary arrangement or protected trust deed;
      (d)   the *customer's lenders* may not approve the individual voluntary arrangement or protected trust deed; and
      (e)   only unsecured debts included within the individual voluntary arrangement or protected trust deed may be discharged at the end of the period and unsecured debts not included remain outstanding;

[**Note:** paragraph 3.38s of *DMG*]
(5)   takes proper account of the individual needs of, and any requests made by, a *customer*; and
[**Note:** paragraph 3.23f of *DMG*]
(6)   where relevant, explains the nature of an insolvency procedure and the role of the *firm*.
[**Note:** paragraph 3.23o of *DMG*]

[**Note:** paragraphs 3.23 and 3.38 of *DMG*]

8.3.5 G   FCA

The information required by **CONC 8.3.4 R** should be provided leaving sufficient time for the *customer* (taking into account the complexity of the information and the *customer's* financial position) to consider it before having to make a decision on the appropriate course of action.

8.3.6 G   FCA

A *firm* should not unfairly incentivise debt advisers (whether employees, agents or *appointed representatives* of the *firm*) to the extent that an incentive might lead the *firm* not to comply with **CONC 8.3.2 R**.

[**Note:** paragraph 3.22 (box) of *DMG*]

8.3.7 R   FCA

A *firm* must:
(1)   provide the *customer* with a source of impartial information on the range of *debt solutions* available to the *customer* in the relevant country of the *UK*;
[**Note:** paragraph 3.23b of *DMG*]
(2)   before giving any advice or any recommendation on a particular course of action in relation to the *customer's debts*, carry out a reasonable and reliable assessment of:
    (a)   the *customer's* financial position (including the *customer's* income, capital and expenditure);
    (b)   the *customer's* personal circumstances (including the reasons for the financial difficulty, whether it is temporary or longer term and whether the *customer* has entered into a *debt solution* previously and, if it failed, the reason for its failure); and
    (c)   any other relevant factors (including any known or reasonably foreseeable changes in the *customer's* circumstances such as a change in employment status);
    [**Note:** paragraph 3.23c of *DMG*]
(3)   refer a *customer* to an appropriate *not-for-profit debt advice body* in circumstances where the *customer*:
    (a)   has problems related to debt requiring immediate attention with which the *firm* is unable or unwilling to assist the *customer*; or
    [**Note:** paragraph 3.23gi of *DMG*]
    (b)   does not have enough disposable income to pay the *firm's* fees;
    [**Note:** paragraph 3.23gii of *DMG*]
(4)   refer a *customer* to, or provide contact details for, another debt advice provider in circumstances where the *firm* is unable to provide appropriate advice or provide an appropriate *debt solution* for the *customer*; and
[**Note:** paragraph 3.23h of *DMG*]
(5)   seek to ensure that a *customer* understands the options available and the implications and consequences for the *customer* of the *firm's* recommended course of action.
[**Note:** paragraph 3.23i of *DMG*]

8.3.8 G   FCA
(1)   The information and advice referred to in **CONC 8.3** should be provided in a manner which is clear fair and not misleading to comply with *Principle* 7 and **CONC 3.3.1 R**, and should be in plain and intelligible language in accordance with **CONC 3.3.2 R**. A *firm* should encourage a *customer* to read the information and allow sufficient time between providing the information and entering into the contract to enable the *customer* to seek independent advice if so desired.
[**Note:** paragraphs 3.21, 3.35 and 3.36 of *DMG*]
(2)   The *firm's* services referred to in **CONC 8.3** include any *debt solution* the *firm* offers to a *customer*. Therefore, in setting out fees or charges for a *firm's* services, the fees and charges the *firm* charges in relation to a *debt solution* should be included.
(3)   The serious problems related to debt in **CONC 8.3.7 R** are likely to include, where non-payment of a debt may result in the loss of a *customer's* home or loss of access to essential *goods* or services and, in particular, where legal action is threatened or legal action is taken in relation to debts which may have that effect.
[**Note:** paragraph 3.23gi of *DMG*]
(4)   A *not-for-profit debt advice body* should refer a *customer* to another *not-for-profit debt advice body* under **CONC 8.3.7 R (3)** where, for example, it is unable to assist a *customer*.

(5)   An appropriate *not-for-profit debt advice body* would be one that provides the most appropriate *debt solution* given the *customer's* financial circumstances.

8.4   DEBT SOLUTION CONTRACTS

8.4.1 R   FCA

A *firm* must provide a *customer* with a written contract setting out its terms and conditions for the provision of its services.

[**Note:** paragraph 3.40a of *DMG*]

8.4.2 R   FCA

A *firm* must include in its written contract (other than a *credit agreement* to which the Consumer Credit (Agreements) Regulations 2010 apply) the following matters:

(1)   the nature of the service to be provided by the *firm*, including the specific *debt solution* to be offered to the *customer*;
         [**Note:** paragraph 3.40b of *DMG*]
(2)   the duration of the contract;
         [**Note:** paragraph 3.40c of *DMG*]
(3)   the total cost of the *firm's* service or, where it is not possible to state the total cost, the formula the *firm* uses for calculating its fees or charges or an estimate of the anticipated likely total cost may be given;
         [**Note:** paragraph 3.40c of *DMG*]
(4)   the circumstances in which a *customer* may terminate the contract and receive a refund in accordance with relevant law and any fees or charges the *customer* may be required to pay in that case; and
         [**Note:** paragraph 3.40d of *DMG*]
(5)   set out the duration and conditions for exercise of any right to cancel that may apply and any fees or charges the *customer* may be required to pay.
         [**Note:** paragraph 3.40e of *DMG*]

8.4.3 R   FCA

A *firm* must not include the following terms in a contract with a *customer*:

(1)   a term requiring the *customer* to sign a declaration stating in any way that the *customer* understands the requirements of the contract;
         [**Note:** paragraph 3.41a of *DMG*]
(2)   a term restricting or prohibiting the *customer* from corresponding with or responding to a *lender* or with any *person* acting on behalf of a *lender*;
         [**Note:** paragraph 3.41b of *DMG*]
(3)   a term which states or implies the *firm* has no liability to the *customer*; or
         [**Note:** paragraph 3.41c of *DMG*]
(4)   a term which states or implies that there are no circumstances in which a *customer* is entitled to a refund.
         [**Note:** paragraph 3.41d of *DMG*]

8.4.4 G   FCA

A *firm* may be required to make a refund of its fees and charges, in whole or in part, if a *firm* fails to deliver its service in whole or in part or it has carried out the service without reasonable care and skill.

8.5   FINANCIAL STATEMENTS AND DEBT REPAYMENT OFFERS

8.5.1 R   FCA

A *firm* must ensure that a financial statement sent to a *lender* on behalf of a *customer*:

(1)   is accurate and realistic and must present a sufficiently clear and complete account of the *customer's* income and expenditure, debts and the availability of surplus income;
         [**Note:** paragraph 3.24 of *DMG*]
(2)   state any fees or charges being made by the *firm*;
(3)   is sent only after having obtained the *customer's* consent to send the statement and the *customer's* confirmation as to the accuracy of the statement;
         [**Note:** paragraph 3.26f and g of *DMG*]
(4)   is provided to the *customer's lenders* as soon as practicable after the *customer* has confirmed its accuracy; and
         [**Note:** paragraph 3.26e of *DMG*]
(5)   is also sent to the *customer*, together with any accompanying correspondence.
         [**Note:** paragraph 3.26h of *DMG*]

8.5.2 G   FCA

The format of the financial statement sent to *lenders* on behalf of the *customer* should be uniform and logically structured in a way that encourages consistent responses from *lenders* and reduces queries and delays. *Firms* may wish to use the Common Financial Statement facilitated by the Money Advice Trust or an equivalent or similar statement.

[**Note:** paragraph 3.24 of *DMG*]

8.5.3 G   FCA

(1)   Where a *firm* makes an offer to a *lender* to repay a *customer's* debts on behalf of a *customer*, the offer should be realistic, sustainable and in accordance with **CONC 8.3.2 R** should, in particular, have regard to the best interests of the *customer*.

(2)   A sustainable offer should enable the *customer* to meet *repayments* in full when they are due out of the *customer's* disposable income for the whole duration of the repayment proposal.

(3)   Setting the offer should take full account of a *customer's* obligations to pay taxes, fines, child support payments and those debts which could result in loss of access to essential *goods* or services or repossession of, or eviction from, the *customer's* home.

(4)   In considering what are essential *goods* and services, the *firm* should consider the *customer's* personal circumstances, for example, for disabled persons debts for telecommunications services are likely to be essential.

[**Note:** paragraphs 3.25, 3.26c and 3.28d of *DMG*]

8.5.4 R   FCA

A *firm* must:

(1)   take reasonable steps to verify the *customer's* identity, income and outgoings;

[**Note:** paragraph 3.26a of *DMG*]

(2)   seek explanations if a *customer* indicates expenditure which is particularly high or low; and

[**Note:** paragraph 3.26b of *DMG*]

(3)   where applicable, notify a *customer* that a particular *lender* will not deal with the *firm* (for whatever reason), as soon as possible after the *firm* becomes aware that the *customer* owes a debt to that *lender*.

[**Note:** paragraph 3.26l of *DMG*]

8.5.5 G   FCA

What are reasonable steps for verification of the identity, income and outgoings of a *customer* depends on the circumstances of the case and the type of service offered by the *firm*. Estimates of expenditure would be reasonable where precise figures are not readily available. The Common Financial Statement includes expenditure guidelines, but where a *firm* uses the Common Financial Statement or an equivalent or similar statement which includes such guidelines, the use of expenditure guidelines needs to take into account the individual circumstances of the *customer*.

Note: paragraph 3.26a (box) of *DMG*]

8.6   CHANGES TO CONTRACTUAL PAYMENTS

8.6.1 R   FCA

(1)   Where a *firm* gives advice to a *customer* not to make a contractual *repayment* or to cancel any means of making such a *repayment* before any *debt solution* is agreed or entered into, the *firm* must be able to demonstrate the advice is in the *customer's* best interests.

(2)   Where a *firm* gives advice of the type in (1), the *firm* must advise the *customer* (C) that if C adopts the advice C should notify C's *lenders* without delay and explain that C is following the *firm's* advice to this effect.

[**Note:** paragraph 3.27 of *DMG*]

8.6.2 R   FCA

If the effect of advice the *firm* gives (if adopted by the *customer*) is that contractual *repayments* are not made or are not made in full (for one or more *repayments*), the *firm* must warn the *customer* of the actual or potential consequences of taking that course of action.

[**Note:** paragraph 3.28a of *DMG*]

8.6.3 R   FCA

A *firm* must only advise a *customer* to make *repayments* at a rate lower than the rate necessary to meet interest and charges accruing where it is in the *customer's* best interests.

[**Note:** paragraph 3.28b of *DMG*]

8.6.4 G   FCA

(1)   The *FCA* expects it will generally be in the *customer's* best interests to maintain regular payments to *lenders* (even if the repayment is less than the full sum due).

(2)   An example where it might be in the *customer's* best interests not to repay at the rate necessary to meet interest and charges accruing is where there is insufficient disposable income to meet essential expenditure of the type referred to in **CONC 8.5.3 G**. Where that is the case, the *firm* should explain clearly to the *customer* why this course of action is necessary and the consequences of the course of action.

8.6.5 R   FCA

Where a *firm* has advised a *customer* not to make contractual *repayments* (in full or in part) or to cancel the means of making such payments or not to make *repayments* necessary to meet interest and charges accruing, the *firm* must advise the *customer* if it becomes clear that that course of action is not producing effects in the *customer's* best interests to enable the *customer* to take action in the *customer's* best interests.

Note: paragraph 3.28c of *DMG*]

8.6.6 G   FCA

(1)   An example of an effect not in the *customer's* best interests would be if a *lender* does not agree to stop applying interest and charges to the *customer's* debt.
      [Note: paragraph 3.28c of *DMG*]

(2)   Where it becomes clear that the course of action in **CONC 8.6.5 R** is not producing effects in the *customer's* best interests the *firm* should, where withdrawing from the *debt management plan* may be in the *customer's* best interests, advise the *customer* of the possibility of withdrawing from the plan.

8.7   CHARGING FOR DEBT COUNSELLING, DEBT ADVICE AND RELATED SERVICES

8.7.1 G   FCA

(1)   The distance marketing *rules* in **CONC 2.6**, including the right to cancel in **CONC 11**, apply to *firms* with respect to *distance contracts* which are *credit agreements*, *consumer hire agreements* and agreements the subject matter of which comprises, or relates to, *debt counselling*, *debt adjusting*, *providing credit information services* and *providing credit references*. **CONC 11** excludes various *credit agreements* from the right to cancel.

(2)   Where a *consumer* uses the right to cancel under **CONC 11** or under the Financial Services (Distance Marketing) Regulations 2004 to cancel an agreement with a *firm* to set up or administer a *debt solution*, the *firm* should refund any sum paid, less a charge that the *firm* is entitled to make under **CONC 11.1.11 R** or regulation 13(6) to (9) of those Regulations.
      [Note: paragraphs 3.29 and 3.31 of *DMG*]

(3)   The firm may be entitled to impose a charge in (2) if the *customer* requested the *firm* to begin to carry out its service within the cancellation period (see **CONC 11.1.1 R** or regulation 10 of the Financial Services (Distance Marketing) Regulations 2004).

8.7.2 R   FCA

A *firm* must ensure that the obligations of the *customer* in relation to the amount, or the timing of payment, of its fees or charges:

(1)   do not have the effect that the *customer* pays all, or substantially all, of those fees in priority to making *repayments* to *lenders* in accordance with the *debt management plan*; and

(2)   do not undermine the *customer's* ability to make (through the *firm* acting on the *customer's* behalf) significant *repayments* to the *customer's* lenders throughout the duration of the *debt management plan*, starting with the first *month* of the plan; but

(3)   paragraphs (1) and (2) do not prevent, to the extent the *firm* complies with all applicable *rules*, a *firm* operating a full and final settlement model, in which the *firm* holds money on behalf of the *customer* and does not distribute that money promptly, pending negotiating a settlement with the *customer's* lenders.
      [Note: paragraphs 5.3 and 5.4 of the Debt Management Protocol]

8.7.3 G   FCA

(1)   For the purposes of **CONC 8.7.2 R (2)**, an obligation is likely to be viewed as undermining the *customer's* ability to make significant repayments to the *customer's* lenders if it has the effect that the *firm* may allocate more than half of the sums received from the *customer* in any one-*month* period from the start of the *debt management plan* to the discharge (in whole or in part) of its fees or charges.

(2)   Once the *customer* has paid any initial fee for the arrangement and preparation of the *debt management plan*, or, if earlier, once six *months* from the start of the plan have elapsed, the *FCA* would expect there usually to be a reduction in the proportion of the sums received from the *customer* that the *firm* allocates to the discharge of its fees and charges.

(3)   A *firm* should spread any charges or fees payable by the *customer* for the administration or operation of the *debt management plan* following its making evenly over the duration of the plan.

(4)   The proportion of the sums received from a *customer* in order to discharge the *firm's* fees or charges should take account of the level of *repayments* the *customer* in question makes.

8.7.4 R   FCA

A *firm* must:

(1)   in good time before entering into a contract with the *customer*, disclose the existence of any commission or incentive payments relevant to the service provided to the *customer* between the *firm* and any third party and at any time, if the *customer* requests, disclose the amount of any such commission or incentive payment;
[**Note:** paragraph 3.34b and c of *DMG*]

(2)   send a revised financial statement in the same format as that required under **CONC 8.5.1 R** to the *customer's lenders* where the *firm's* fees or charges alter during an arrangement and would affect the amount available for distribution to *lenders*;
[**Note:** paragraph 3.34f (box) of *DMG*]

(3)   at the earlier of, where the *firm* identifies or it is established that advice provided by the *firm* to the *customer* was incorrect or was not appropriate to the *customer*, refund or credit to the *customer's* account fees or charges imposed for that advice;
[**Note:** paragraph 3.34m of *DMG*]

(4)   make an appropriate refund of fees or charges paid where the whole or any part of the service as agreed with the *customer* has not been provided or not provided with a reasonable standard of skill and care.
[**Note:** paragraph 3.34o of *DMG*]

8.7.5 G   FCA

A *firm*, in presenting its fees, costs and charges, should distinguish the fees payable for the *firm's* services from any charges payable for court proceedings or other insolvency proceedings.

8.7.6 R   FCA

A *firm* must not:

(1)   without a reasonable justification, switch a *customer* from one *debt solution* to another while making a further charge for setting up or administering the new *debt solution* to the extent that some or all of that work has already been carried out by the *firm*;
[**Note:** paragraphs 3.32 and 34k of *DMG*]

(2)   switch a *customer* to a different *debt solution*, without obtaining the *customer's* consent after having fully explained to the *customer* the reason for the change;
[**Note:** paragraph 3.34l of *DMG*]

(3)   require or take any payment from a *customer* before the *firm* has entered into contract with the *customer* concerning a *debt solution*;
[**Note:** paragraph 3.34d of *DMG*]

(4)   request any payment from a *customer's* payment account, unless the *customer* has specifically authorised the *firm* to do so and has not cancelled that authorisation;
[**Note:** paragraph 3.34d (box) of *DMG*]

(5)   accept payment for fees or charges by credit card or another form of *credit* (excluding a payment where the *firm* does not know and cannot be expected to know that the *customer's* current account is in debit or would be taken into debit by the payment);
[**Note:** paragraph 3.34e of *DMG*]

(6)   impose cancellation charges that are unreasonable or disproportionate when compared to the actual costs necessarily incurred by the *firm* in reasonably providing its service;
[**Note:** paragraph 3.34h of *DMG*]

(7)   claim a fee or charge from a *customer* or take payment from a *customer's* account which is not provided for in the agreement with the *customer*, or where it is provided for but is, or is likely to be, unfair under the Unfair Terms in Consumer Contracts Regulations 1999;
[**Note:** paragraph 3.34i of *DMG*]

(8)   where the *firm* identifies that advice provided by the *firm* to the *customer* was incorrect or was not appropriate to the *customer*, charge an additional fee for further or revised advice; or
[**Note:** paragraph 3.34m of *DMG*]

(9)   request, suggest or instruct *customers* seeking to recover refunds of fees from the *firm* to make contact with the *firm* on a premium rate telephone number.
[**Note:** paragraph 3.34n of *DMG*]

8.8   DEBT MANAGEMENT PLANS

8.8.1 R   FCA

A *firm* in relation to a *customer* with whom it has entered into a *debt management plan* must:

(1)   maintain contact with the *customer*;
[**Note:** paragraph 3.44 of *DMG*]

(2)   regularly monitor and review the financial position and circumstances of the *customer*;
[**Note:** paragraph 3.44 of *DMG*]

(3)   adapt the *debt management plan* to take into account relevant changes in the financial position and circumstances of the *customer*;
[**Note:** paragraph 3.44 of *DMG*]

(4)   inform the *customer* without delay of the outcome of negotiations with *lenders*, in particular, where the *lender* has:

    (a)   refused to deal with the *firm*; or

    (b)   returned payments to the *firm*; or

    (c)   refused the debt repayment offer; or

    (d)   refused to freeze interest or charges accruing;

            [**Note:** paragraph 3.45a of *DMG*]

(5)   inform the *customer* of any material developments about the relationship between the *customer* and the *customer's lenders*;

      [**Note:** paragraph 3.45b of *DMG*]

(6)   provide the *customer* with copies of correspondence or documentation relating to material developments relevant to the relationship between the *customer* and the *customer's lenders*;

      [**Note:** paragraph 3.45b of *DMG*]

(7)   where the *firm* makes *repayments* on behalf of the *customer*:

    (a)   monitor the *customer's repayments* for evidence which suggests a change in the *customer's* financial circumstances;

    (b)   review, and amend or terminate, where appropriate, the *customer's debt management plan* at the earlier of:

        (i)   each anniversary of entering into the plan; or

        (ii)   as soon as the *firm* becomes aware of a material change in the *customer's* circumstances; and

    (c)   inform the *customer* of the outcome of any reassessment;

        [**Note:** paragraph 3.45c of *DMG*]

(8)   provide a statement to the *customer* at the start of the *debt management plan*, and at least annually or at the *customer's* reasonable request, setting out:

    (a)   a balance showing the amount owed by the *customer*, including any interest charges at the beginning of the statement period;

    (b)   fees, charges and other costs applied over the period of the statement, including any upfront fee or deposit, such as an initial arrangement fee, an arrangement fee, any periodic or management or administrative fee, any cancellation fee and any other costs incurred under the contract;

    (c)   a narrative explaining the type of fee applied, how the fee is calculated and to what it applies;

    (d)   the duration or estimated duration of the contract;

    (e)   the total cost of the *firm's* service over the duration or estimated duration of the contract; and

    (f)   *monthly* or other periodic payments made to *lenders*;

      [**Note:** paragraphs 3.45cde of *DMG*]

(9)   maintain adequate records relating to each *debt management plan* which the *firm* has administered for the *customer* until the contract between the *customer* and the *firm* is completed or terminated;

      [**Note:** paragraph 3.45i of *DMG*]

(10)   check the accuracy of the details of the *customer's* accounts; and

      [**Note:** paragraph 3.45j of *DMG*]

(11)   use reasonable endeavours not to send inaccurate information to *lenders*.

      [**Note:** paragraph 3.45j of *DMG*]

8.8.2 G FCA

(1)   Evidence that there may have been a material change in a *customer's* financial circumstances is likely to include where a *customer* who has not previously missed payments under a *debt management plan* misses such payments.

    [**Note:** paragraph 3.45ci of *DMG*]

(2)   Where the *firm* informs a *customer* of the outcome of a review of a *debt management plan*, it should seek to discuss with the *customer* any changes to the plan or to the *firm's* service at the earliest reasonably opportunity.

    [**Note:** paragraph 3.45ciii of *DMG*]

(3)   In **CONC 8.8.1 R (6)** correspondence or documentation relating to material developments would include, for example, the issue or threat of issue of default notices or legal proceedings.

    [**Note:** paragraph 3.45b of *DMG*]

8.9   LEAD GENERATORS: INCLUDING FIRM RESPONSIBILITY IN DEALING WITH LEAD GENERATORS

8.9.1 G FCA

The *Principles* (in particular *Principle* 6 and *Principle* 7) apply to actions of a *firm* dealing with a *customer* who has been referred to it through a *lead generator*. For example, where a *firm* acts on a sales lead and knows or ought to know that the *lead generator* is using misleading information, advice or actions to obtain a *customer's* personal data is likely to amount to a breach by the *firm* of *Principle* 6 and *Principle* 7.

8.9.2 R   FCA

A *firm* must take reasonable steps before entering into an agreement to accept sales leads from a *lead generator* for *debt counselling* or *debt adjusting* or *providing credit information services* to ensure:

(1)   that any of the *lead generator's* advice, any content of its website and advertising and any of its commercial practices comply with applicable legal requirements, including the Consumer Protection from Unfair Trading Regulations 2008;

(2)   that the *lead generator* is registered with the Information Commission's Office under the Data Protection Act 1998; and

(3)   that the *lead generator* has processes in place to ensure it complies with that Act and with the Privacy and Electronic Communications (EC Directive) Regulations 2003.

[**Note:** paragraph 3.9 of *DMG*]

8.9.3 G   FCA

The steps required to satisfy the requirement in **CONC 8.9.2 R** should depend upon the regularity with which the *firm* intends to accept sales leads from the *lead generator*. If sales leads provided by a *lead generator* are likely to be on a single or occasional basis, less rigorous checks should be required than for a specialist sales *lead generator*.

[**Note:** paragraph 3.9 (box) of *DMG*]

8.9.4 R   FCA

A *firm* must take reasonable steps, where it has agreed to accept sales leads from a *lead generator* for *debt counselling* or *debt adjusting* or *providing credit information services*, to ensure that the *lead generator*:

(1)   where it does not have a *Part 4A permission* for *debt counselling* and is not an *appointed representative* of a *firm* with such *permission*, does not carry on *debt counselling* in obtaining or passing on sales leads to the *firm*;

(2)   where it carries on *debt counselling*, has and continues to have a *Part 4A permission* for *debt counselling* or is an *appointed representative* of a *firm* with such *permission*;

(3)   where it does not have a *Part 4A permission* covering the relevant activity, does not claim to or imply that it provides *debt counselling* or *debt adjusting* or that it is *providing credit information services*;
       [**Note:** paragraph 3.12 of *DMG*]

(4)   complies with applicable legal requirements, including the Consumer Protection from Unfair Trading Regulations 2008 in relation to any of its advice, any content of its website, any of its advertising and any of its commercial practices;
       [**Note:** paragraph 3.9a *DMG*]

(5)   makes the true nature of its services clear to *customers*, through any means of communication or promotion it uses;
       [**Note:** paragraph 3.12 of *DMG*]

(6)   where it seeks a *customer's* personal data to pass on to a *firm* for a fee, it makes clear to the *customer* that the *customer's* personal data will be passed on to the *firm*;
       [**Note:** paragraph 3.12c of *DMG*]

(7)   makes clear to a *customer* any financial interest it has in passing on a sales lead to the *firm*;
       [**Note:** paragraph 3.12d of *DMG*]

(8)   makes clear, if asked by a *customer*, the nature of its relationship with the *firm*;
       [**Note:** paragraph 3.12e of *DMG*]

(9)   does not falsely claim or imply in any way that it is or represents a charitable or *not-for-profit body* or government or local government organisation;
       [**Note:** paragraph 3.12f of *DMG*]

(10)   communicates with customers consistent with, and promotes, services the *firm* is able to provide;
       [**Note:** paragraph 3.12h of *DMG*]

(11)   complies with the Privacy and Electronic Communications (EC Directive) Regulations 2003 and the Data Protection Act 1998;
       [**Note:** paragraph 3.11 of *DMG*]

(12)   does not send, or cause to be sent, an *electronic communication* to a *customer* (C) unless C has previously notified the *lead generator* that C consents for the time being to such communications being sent or caused to be sent by the *lead generator*;
       [**Note:** paragraph 3.12j of *DMG*]

(13)   does not make or cause to be made by means of an automated calling system (which is capable of automatically initiating a sequence of calls to more than one destination in accordance with instructions stored in that system, and transmitting sounds which are not live speech for reception by *persons* at some or all of the destinations so called) a call to a *customer* (C), unless C has previously notified the caller that for the time being C consents to such communications being made by or caused to be made by the caller on the line in question; and
       [**Note:** paragraph 3.12j of *DMG*]

(14)   enables *customers* to cancel using a clear and easy method their consent to be called or sent any communication.
[**Note:** paragraph 3.12m of *DMG*]

[**Note:** paragraphs 3.7 and 3.8 of *DMG*]

Guidance for firms

8.9.5 G   FCA

The *FCA* would expect *firms* that agree with *lead generators* to accept sales leads in relation to *debt counselling* or *debt adjusting* to be able to identify, upon request, all the *lead generators* from which they have received leads (with the *FCA* authorisation number, where applicable).

8.9.6 G   FCA

Claiming or implying a *person* is or represents, for example, a charitable organisation is likely to include operating a website which looks like, or is designed to look like, the website of such an organisation.

8.9.7 G   FCA

In complying with **CONC 8.9.4 R** a *firm* that agrees with a *lead generator* to accept sale leads should:
(1)   check with the Information Commissioner's Office that the *lead generator* is appropriately registered under the Data Protection Act 1998; and
(2)   check the *lead generator's* Privacy and Electronic Communications (EC Directive) Regulations 2003 process documentation.

8.10   CONDUCT OF BUSINESS: PROVIDING CREDIT INFORMATION SERVICES

Application

8.10.1 R   FCA

This section applies to:
(1)   a *firm* with respect to *providing credit information services* in relation to information relevant to the financial standing of an *individual*;
(2)   a *firm* with respect to the activities set out in article 36H(3)(e) to (h) of the *Regulated Activities Order* (Operating an electronic system in relation to lending) in relation to a *borrower* under a *P2P agreement*.

Conduct

8.10.2 G   FCA

The *Principles* apply to a *firm* with respect to *providing credit information services*. A *firm* providing such services should, for example, set out clearly in any communication to a *customer* the extent of the service it is able to offer.
[**Note:** paragraph 3.46 of *DMG*]

8.10.3 R   FCA

A *firm* must not:
(1)   claim to be able to remove negative but accurate information from a *customer's* credit file, including entries concerning adverse credit information and court judgments; or
[**Note:** paragraph 3.47ai of *DMG*]
(2)   mislead a *customer* about the length of time that negative information is held on the *customer's* credit file or any official register; or
[**Note:** paragraph 3.47aii of *DMG*]
(3)   claim that a new credit file can be created, such as by the *customer* changing address.
[**Note:** paragraph 3.47aiii of *DMG*]

8.10.4 G   FCA

It is likely to be a contravention of the *Principles*, for example *Principles* 6 and *Principle* 7, where a *firm*:
(1)   claims in a communication to a *customer* to be able to remove negative but accurate entries from a *customer's* credit file, but where the *customer* enquires about this service the *customer* is offered instead the *firm's* service as a *lender* or a *credit broker*; or
(2)   fails to inform a *customer* that a *credit reference agency* will not respond to the *firm* taking steps in relation to the *customer's* credit file and will only send the *customer's* credit file to the *customer*.
[**Note:** paragraphs 3.47cd of *DMG*]

CHAPTER 9
CREDIT REFERENCE AGENCIES

9.1   APPLICATION

[3.87]
9.1.1 R   FCA

This chapter applies to a *firm* with respect to *providing credit references*.

9.2   CONDUCT OF BUSINESS: CORRECTION OF ENTRIES IN CREDIT REFERENCE AGENCY FILES

9.2.1 R   FCA

Within 10 *working days* after any of the following events:
(1)   the *credit reference agency* giving notice under section 159(2) of the *CCA* that it has removed an entry from the file kept by it about an *individual* or has amended such an entry (including where it has amended an entry by removing information from it); or
(2)   the *credit reference agency* giving notice under section 159(4) of the *CCA* that it has received a notice under section 159(3) requiring it to add a notice of correction to the file and intends to comply with the notice; or
(3)   the expiry of the period specified in an order of the *FCA* or the Information Commissioner under section 159(5) of the *CCA* as the period within which the order is to be complied with;

the *credit reference agency* must give notice of the particulars specified in **CONC 9.2.2 R** to each *person* to whom at any time since the relevant date it has furnished information relevant to the financial standing of the *individual* concerned.
[Note: regulation 5 of SI 1977/330]

9.2.2 R   FCA

The particulars referred to in **CONC 9.2.1 R** are:
(1)   in relation to information included in any entry which has been removed or amended or which is referred to in a notice of correction:
   (a)   particulars of any entry which has been removed from the file and a statement that it has been removed;
   (b)   particulars of any entry which has been amended and of the amendment, or of the entry as amended; and
   (c)   particulars of the entry, together with a copy of the notice of correction; and
(2)   where the information did not include the entry which has been removed or amended or which is referred to in a notice of correction, but which (whether in the form of a rating or opinion or otherwise) was based in whole or in part on any such entry and has been, or falls to be, modified by reason of the removal, amendment or notice:
   (a)   particulars of the modified information; and
   (b)   a statement that the information has been modified by reason of the removal, amendment or notice, as the case may be.

9.2.3 R   FCA

In this section, "the relevant date" means the date one *month* immediately preceding the receipt by the *credit reference agency* from the *individual* of the request, particulars and fee referred to in section 158(1) of the *CCA*, or the request and fee (if a fee is payable) referred to in section 7(2) of the Data Protection Act 1998 and, if applicable, the receipt of any further information requested by the *credit reference agency* referred to in section 7(3) of that Act.

CHAPTER 10
PRUDENTIAL RULES FOR DEBT MANAGEMENT FIRMS

10.1   APPLICATION AND PURPOSE

Application

[3.88]
10.1.1 R   FCA

This chapter applies to:
(1)   a *debt management firm*; and
(2)   a *not-for-profit debt advice body* that, at any point in the last 12 *months*, has held £1 million or more in *client money* or as the case may be, projects that it will hold £1 million or more in *client money* at any point in the next 12 *months*.

Application: professional firms

10.1.2 R   FCA

(1)   This chapter does not apply to an *authorised professional firm*:

    (a)   whose main business is the practice of its profession; and

    (b)   whose *regulated activities* covered by this chapter are incidental to its main business.

(2)   A *firm's* main business is the practice of its profession if the proportion of income it derives from professional fees is, during its annual accounting period, at least 50% of the *firm's* total income (a temporary variation of not more than 5% may be disregarded for this purpose).

(3)   Professional fees are fees, commissions and other receipts receivable in respect of legal, accountancy, conveyancing and surveying services provided to clients but excluding any items receivable in respect of *regulated activities*.

Purpose

10.1.3 G   FCA

This chapter builds on the *threshold condition* referred to at **COND 2.4** (Appropriate resources) by providing that a *firm* must meet, on a continuing basis, a basic solvency requirement. This chapter also builds on *Principle* 4 which requires a *firm* to maintain adequate financial resources by setting out prudential requirements for a *firm* according to what type of *firm* it is.

10.1.4 G   FCA

Prudential standards have an important role in minimising the risk of harm to *customers* by ensuring that a *firm* behaves prudently in monitoring and managing business and financial risks.

10.1.5 G   FCA

More generally, having adequate prudential resources gives the *firm* a degree of resilience and some indication to *customers* of creditworthiness, substance and the commitment of its owners. Prudential standards aim to ensure that a *firm* has prudential resources which can provide cover for operational and compliance failures and pay redress, as well as reducing the possibility of a shortfall in funds and providing a cushion against disruption if the *firm* ceases to trade.

10.1.6 R   FCA

A contravention of the *rules* in this chapter does not give rise to a right of action by a *private person* under section 138D of the *Act* (and each of those *rules* is specified under section 138D(3) of the *Act* as a provision giving rise to no such right of action).

10.2   PRUDENTIAL RESOURCES REQUIREMENTS

General solvency requirement

10.2.1 R   FCA

A *firm* must, at all times, ensure that it is able to meet its liabilities as they fall due.

General prudential resource requirement

10.2.2 R   FCA

A *firm* must ensure that, at all times, its prudential resources are not less than its prudential resources requirement.

Prudential resources: relevant accounting principles

10.2.3 R   FCA

A *firm* must recognise an asset or liability, and measure its amount, in accordance with the relevant accounting principles applicable to it for the purpose of preparing its annual financial statements unless a *rule* requires otherwise.

Prudential resources requirement: firms carrying on other regulated activities

10.2.4 R   FCA

The prudential resources requirement for a *firm* carrying on a *regulated activity* or activities in addition to those covered by this chapter, is the higher of:

(1)   the requirement which is applied by this chapter; and

(2)   the prudential resources requirement which is applied by another *rule* or requirement to the *firm*.

Prudential resources requirement

10.2.5 R   FCA

On its *accounting reference date* in each year, a *firm* must calculate:

(1)   the total value of its *relevant debts under management* outstanding on that date; and

(2)   the sum of:

    (a)   0.25% of the first £5 million of that total value;

    (b)   0.15% of the next £95 million of that total value; and

(c)   0.05% of any remaining total value.

10.2.6 R   FCA

The total value of a *firm's relevant debts under management* outstanding referred to in **CONC 10.2.5 R (1)** is the sum of all the *firm's customers' relevant debts under management*.

10.2.7 G   FCA

The definition of *relevant debts under management* refers to a debt due under a *credit agreement* or a *consumer hire agreement* in relation to which the *firm* is carrying on *debt adjusting* or an activity connected to that activity. The reference to "debt due" covers not only amounts that are payable at the time the prudential resources requirement is calculated but also amounts the *borrower* or *hirer* is presently obliged to pay under the *credit agreement* or the *consumer hire agreement* in the future.

10.2.8 R   FCA

The prudential resources requirement for a *firm* to which this chapter applies is the higher of:
(1)   £5,000; or
(2)   the sum calculated in accordance with **CONC 10.2.5 R (2)**;

for the period until (subject to **CONC 10.2.13 R**) its next *accounting reference date*.

10.2.9 R   FCA

To determine a *firm's* prudential resources requirement for the period beginning on the date on which it obtains *Part 4A permission* and ending on the day before its next *accounting reference date*, the *firm* must carry out the calculation in **CONC 10.2.5 R (2)** on the basis of the total value of *relevant debts under management* the *firm* projects will be outstanding on the day before its next *accounting reference date*.

What is not included as relevant debts under management

10.2.10 G   FCA

Activities carried on by a *person* acting as an insolvency practitioner (within section 388 of the Insolvency Act 1986 or, as the case may be, article 3 of the Insolvency (Northern Ireland) Order 1989) or by a *person* acting in reasonable contemplation of that *person's* appointment as an insolvency practitioner are excluded from the *regulated activity* of *debt adjusting*. A debt in relation to which a *person* is acting in such a capacity is, therefore, excluded from the calculation of its *relevant debts under management* (but a debt in relation to which the same *person* is not acting in such capacity and is carrying on *debt-adjusting* is included in the calculation).

Determining the prudential resources requirement

10.2.11 G   FCA

If a *firm* has 1000 *relevant debts under management* and each of those debts is £10,000, the total value of the *firm's relevant debts under management* is £10,000,000. If the *firm* does not carry on any other *regulated activity* to which another higher prudential resources requirement applies, its prudential resources requirement is £20,000. This is calculated as follows:
(1)   0.25% x £5,000,000 = £12,500; and
(2)   0.15% x £5,000,000 = £7,500.

10.2.12 G   FCA

If during the following year 20% (£200) of each *relevant debt under management* is paid off by the *borrower* or *hirer* leaving an outstanding balance of £800 on each *relevant debt under management*, and during that year the *firm* does not carry on *debt adjusting* in relation to any further debts due under *credit agreements* or *consumer hire agreements*, the total value of the *firm's relevant debt under management* is £8,000,000. If the *firm* does not carry on any other *regulated activity* to which another higher prudential resources requirement applies, its prudential resources requirement is £17,000. This is calculated as follows:
(1)   0.25% x £5,000,000 = £12,500; and
(2)   0.15% x £3,000.000 = £4,500.

Recalculating the prudential resources requirement

10.2.13 R   FCA

If a *firm* experiences a greater than 15% increase in the total value of its *relevant debts under management* compared to the value used in its last prudential resources requirement calculation, it must recalculate its prudential resources requirement using the new total value of its *relevant debts under management*.

10.2.14 R   FCA

A *firm* must notify the *FCA* of any change in its prudential resources requirement within 14 *days* of that change.

10.3 CALCULATION OF PRUDENTIAL RESOURCES

10.3.1 R FCA

(1)   A *firm* must calculate its prudential resources only from the items which are eligible to contribute to a *firm's* prudential resources (see **CONC 10.3.2 R**).

(2)   In arriving at its calculation of its prudential resources a *firm* must deduct certain items (see **CONC 10.3.3 R**).

10.3.2 R FCA

Table: Items which are eligible to contribute to the prudential resources of a firm

	Item	Additional explanation
1	*Share* capital	This must be fully paid and may include:
		(1) ordinary *share* capital; or
		(2) preference *share* capital (excluding preference *shares* redeemable by shareholders within two years).
2	Capital other than *share* capital (for example, the capital of a *sole trader*, *partnership* or *limited liability partnership*)	The capital of a *sole trader* is the net balance on the *firm's* capital account and current account. The capital of a *partnership* is the capital made up of the *partners'*:
		(1) capital account, that is the account:
		(a) into which capital contributed by the *partners* is paid; and
		(b) from which, under the terms of the *partnership* agreement, an amount representing capital may be withdrawn by a *partner* only if:
		(i) he ceases to be a *partner* and an equal amount is transferred to another such account by his former *partners* or any *person* replacing him as their *partner*; or
		(ii) he ceases to be a partner and an equal amount is transferred to another such account by his former partners or any person replacing him as their partner; or
		(iii) the partnership is otherwise dissolved or wound up; and
		(2) current accounts according to the most recent financial statement.
		For the purpose of the calculation of capital resources in respect of a *defined benefit occupational pension scheme*:
		(1) a *firm* must derecognise any *defined benefit asset*;
		(2) a *firm* may substitute for a *defined benefit liability* the *firm's* *deficit reduction amount*, provided that the election is applied consistently in respect of any one financial year.
3	Reserves (Note 1)	These are, subject to Note 1, the audited accumulated profits retained by the *firm* (after deduction of tax, dividends and proprietors' or *partners'* drawings) and other reserves created by appropriations of share premiums and similar realised appropriations. Reserves also include gifts of capital, for example, from a *parent undertaking*.
		For the purposes of calculating capital resources, a *firm* must make the following adjustments to its reserves, where appropriate:
		(1) a *firm* must deduct any unrealised gains or, where applicable, add back in any unrealised losses on debt instruments held, or formerly held, in the available-for-sale financial assets category;
		(2) a *firm* must deduct any unrealised gains or, where applicable, add back in any unrealised losses on cash flow hedges of financial instruments measured at cost or amortised cost;
		(3) in respect of a *defined benefit occupational pension scheme*:
		(a) a *firm* must derecognise any *defined benefit asset*;
		(b) a *firm* may substitute for a *defined benefit liability* the *firm's deficit reduction amount*, provided that the election is applied consistently in respect of any one financial year.

	Item	Additional explanation
4	Interim net profits (Note 1)	If a *firm* seeks to include interim net profits in the calculation of its capital resources, the profits have, subject to Note 1, to be verified by the *firm's* external auditor, net of tax, anticipated dividends or proprietors' drawings and other appropriations.
5	Revaluation reserves	
6	Subordinated loans/debt	Subordinated loans/debts must be included in capital on the basis of the provisions in this chapter that apply to subordinated loans/debts.
Note:		
1		Reserves must be audited and interim net profits, general and collective provisions must be verified by the *firm's* external auditor unless the *firm* is exempt from the provisions of Part VII of the Companies Act 1985 (section 249A (Exemptions from audit)) or, where applicable, Part 16 of the Companies Act 2006 (section 477 (Small companies: Conditions for exemption from audit)) relating to the audit of accounts.

10.3.3 R   FCA

Table: Items which must be deducted in arriving at prudential resources

1	*Investments* in own *shares*
2	*Investments* in *subsidiaries* (Note 1)
3	Intangible assets (Note 2)
4	Interim net losses (Note 3)
5	Excess of drawings over profits for a *sole trader* or a *partnership* (Note 3)
Notes	1 *Investments* in *subsidiaries* are the full balance sheet value. 2 Intangible assets are the full balance sheet value of goodwill, capitalised development costs, brand names, trademarks and similar rights and licences. 3 The interim net losses in row 4, and the excess of drawings in row 5, are in relation to the period following the date as at which the capital resources are being computed.

[**Note:** Until 31 March 2017, transitional provisions apply to **CONC 10.3.3 R**: see **CONC TP 5**.1]

Subordinated loans/debt

10.3.4 R   FCA

A subordinated loan/debt must not form part of the prudential resources of the *firm* unless it meets the following conditions:

(1)   it has an original maturity of:
    (a)   at least five years; or
    (b)   it is subject to five years' notice of repayment;
(2)   the claims of the subordinated creditors must rank behind those of all unsubordinated creditors;
(3)   the only events of default must be non-payment of any interest or principal under the debt agreement or the winding up of the *firm*;
(4)   the remedies available to the subordinated creditor in the event of non-payment or other default in respect of the subordinated loan/debt must be limited to petitioning for the winding up of the *firm* or proving the debt and claiming in the liquidation of the *firm*;
(5)   the subordinated loan/debt must not become due and payable before its stated final maturity date, except on an event of default complying with (3);
(6)   the agreement and the debt are governed by the law of England and Wales, or of Scotland or of Northern Ireland;
(7)   to the fullest extent permitted under the rules of the relevant jurisdiction, creditors must waive their right to set off amounts they owe the *firm* against subordinated amounts owed to them by the *firm*;
(8)   the terms of the subordinated loan/debt must be set out in a written agreement that contains terms that provide for the conditions set out in this *rule*; and
(9)   the loan/debt must be unsecured and fully paid up.

10.3.5 R   FCA

When calculating its prudential resources, the *firm* must exclude any amount by which the aggregate amount of its subordinated loans/debts exceeds the amount calculated as follows:

a–b
where:

| a | = | Items 1–5 in the Table of items which are eligible to contribute to a *firm's* prudential resources (see **CONC 10.3.2 R**) |
| b | = | Items 1–5 in the Table of items which must be deducted in arriving at a *firm's* prudential resources (see **CONC 10.3.3 R**) |

[**Note:** Until 31 March 2017, transitional provisions apply to **CONC 10.3.5 R**: see **CONC TP 5**.2]

10.3.6 G   FCA

CONC 10.3.5 R can be illustrated by the examples set out below:

Share Capital	£20,000
Reserves	£30,000
Subordinated loans/debts	£10,000
Intangible assets	£10,000

As subordinated loans/debts (£10,000) are less than the total of share capital + reserves - intangible assets (£40,000) the *firm* need not exclude any of its subordinated loans/debts pursuant to **CONC 10.3.5 R**. Therefore total prudential resources will be £50,000.

Share Capital	£20,000
Reserves	£30,000
Subordinated loans/debts	£60,000
Intangible assets	£10,000

As subordinated loans/debts (£60,000) exceed the total of share capital + reserves - intangible assets (£40,000) by £20,000, the *firm* should exclude £20,000 of its subordinated loans/debts when calculating its prudential resources. Therefore total prudential resources will be £80,000.

[**Note:** Until 31 March 2017, transitional provisions apply to **CONC 10.3.6 G**: see **CONC TP 5**.3]

CHAPTER 11
CANCELLATION

11.1   THE RIGHT TO CANCEL

[3.89]
11.1.1 R   FCA

Except as provided for in **CONC 11.1.2 R** or where **PROF 5.4.1 R (1)** or **PROF 5.4.1 R (2)** applies, a *consumer* has a right to cancel a *distance contract* without penalty and without giving any reason, within 14 calendar days where that contract is:

(1)   a *credit agreement*;

(2)   an agreement between a *consumer* and a *firm* the subject matter of which comprises or relates to *credit broking, debt counselling, debt adjusting, providing credit information services* or *providing credit references*, other than an agreement that relates to any of those activities in relation to a *consumer hire agreement*.

[**Note**: article 6(1) of the *Distance Marketing Directive* in relation to distance contracts that are consumer credit agreements]

11.1.2 R   FCA

(1)   For a *credit agreement* there is no right to cancel under **CONC 11.1.1 R**, unless (2) or (3) applies, in respect of:

     (a)   a regulated consumer credit agreement (within the meaning of that section) to which section 66A (right to withdraw) of the *CCA* applies;

     (b)   a *credit agreement* under which a *lender* provides *credit* to a *consumer* and where the *consumer's* obligation to repay is secured by a legal mortgage on *land*;

     (c)   a *credit agreement* cancelled under regulation 15(1) of the Consumer Protection (Distance Selling) Regulations 2000 (automatic cancellation of a related credit agreement);

     (d)   a *credit agreement* cancelled under regulation 23 of the Timeshare, Holiday Products, Resale and Exchange Contracts Regulations 2010 (automatic termination of credit agreement); and

     (e)   a *restricted-use credit agreement* to finance the purchase of *land* or an existing building, or an agreement for a bridging loan in connection with the purchase of *land* or an existing building.

(2) There is a right to cancel under **CONC 11.1.1 R** where the *lender* has not complied with **CONC 2.7.6 R** (requirement to communicate terms and conditions etc), unless the *distance contract* falls with the exception in **CONC 2.7.12 R** and the *firm* has complied with the requirements of that *rule*.

(3) There is a right to cancel under **CONC 11.1.1 R** where the circumstances in **CONC 2.7.12 R** apply but the *lender* has not supplied all the contractual terms and conditions and information as required in **CONC 2.7.12 R**.

11.1.3 G   FCA

Section 66A of the *CCA* (right to withdraw) does not apply to an agreement for *credit* exceeding £60,260, an agreement secured on *land*, a *restricted-use credit agreement* to finance the purchase of *land* or an agreement for a bridging loan in connection with the purchase of *land*. Section 67 of the *CCA* (cancellable agreements) applies to *regulated credit agreements* (apart from agreements secured on *land*, *restricted-use credit agreements* to finance the purchase of *land* or agreements for a bridging loan in connection with the purchase of *land* and agreements covered by section 66A) and *consumer hire agreements* (to which this section does not apply) in the circumstances specified in the section. A *customer* with a right to cancel under section 67 of the *CCA* may choose to cancel the agreement under that section or under **CONC 11.1.1 R**.

11.1.4 G   FCA

A *firm* may provide longer or additional cancellation rights voluntarily but, if it does, these should be on terms at least as favourable to the *customer* as those in this chapter, unless the differences are clearly explained.

Beginning of cancellation period

11.1.5 R   FCA

The cancellation period begins:
(1) either from the day the *distance contract* is made; or
(2) from the day on which the *consumer* receives the contractual terms and conditions of the service and any other pre-contractual information required, as the case may be, under **CONC 2.7.6 R** or under **CONC 2.7.12 R**, if that is later than the date referred to in (1) above.
[**Note**: article 6(1) of the *Distance Marketing Directive* in relation to distance contracts]

Disclosing the right to cancel

11.1.6 R   FCA

(1) The *firm* must disclose to a *consumer* in good time before or, if that is not possible, immediately after the *consumer* is bound by a contract to which the right to cancel applies under **CONC 11.1.1 R**, and in a *durable medium*, the existence of the right to cancel, its duration and the conditions for exercising it including information on the amount which the *consumer* may be required to pay, the consequences of not exercising it and practical instructions for exercising it, indicating the address to which the notification of cancellation should be sent.

(2) This *rule* applies only where a *consumer* would not otherwise receive the information in (1) under a *rule* in this sourcebook from the *firm* (such as under **CONC 2.7.2 R** to **CONC 2.7.5 R** (the distance marketing disclosure rules)).

Exercising the right to cancel

11.1.7 R   FCA

If a *consumer* exercises the right to cancel the *consumer* must, before the expiry of the cancellation period, notify this following the practical instructions given to him. The deadline shall be deemed to have been observed if the notification, if in a *durable medium* available and accessible to the recipient, is dispatched before the cancellation period expires.
[**Note**: article 6(6) of the *Distance Marketing Directive* for distance contracts]

11.1.8 G   FCA

The *firm* should accept any indication that the *consumer* wishes to cancel as long as it satisfies the conditions for notification. In the event of any dispute, unless there is clear written evidence to the contrary, the *firm* should treat the date cited by the *consumer* as the date when the notification was dispatched.

Record keeping

11.1.9 R   FCA

The *firm* must make adequate records concerning the exercise of a right to cancel and retain them for at least three years.

Effects of cancellation

11.1.10 R FCA

By exercising a right to cancel, a *consumer* withdraws from the contract and the contract is terminated.

11.1.11 R FCA

(1) When a *consumer* exercises the right to cancel the *consumer* may only be required to pay, without any undue delay, for the service actually provided by the *firm* in accordance with the contract. The amount payable must not:
   (a) exceed an amount which is in proportion to the extent of the service already provided in comparison with the full coverage of the contract;
   (b) in any case be such that it could be construed as a penalty.
   [**Note**: article 7(1), (2) and (3) of the *Distance Marketing Directive* in relation to distance contracts]
(2) The *firm* may not require a *consumer* to pay any amount on the basis of this *rule* unless it can prove that the *consumer* was duly informed about the amount payable and, in conformity with the distance marketing disclosure *rules* (**CONC 2.7.2 R** to **CONC 2.7.5 R**). However, in no case may the *firm* require such payment if it has commenced the performance of the contract before expiry of the cancellation period without the *consumer's* prior request.
   [**Note**: article 7(1), (2) and (3) of the *Distance Marketing Directive* in relation to distance contracts]

Firm's obligations on cancellation

11.1.12 R FCA

The *firm* must, without undue delay and within 30 calendar days, return to the *consumer* any sums it has received from the *consumer* except for any amount that the *consumer* may be required to pay under **CONC 11.1.1 R**. This period begins from the day on which the *firm* receives the notification of cancellation.
[**Note**: article 7(1), (2) and (3) of the *Distance Marketing Directive* in relation to distance contracts]

Consumer's obligations on cancellation

11.1.13 R FCA

The *firm* is entitled to receive from the *consumer* any sums or property the *consumer* has received from the *firm* without any undue delay and no later than within 30 calendar days. This period begins from the day on which the *consumer* dispatches the notification of cancellation.
[**Note**: article 7(5) of the *Distance Marketing Directive* in relation to distance contracts]

11.1.14 R FCA

Any sums payable under this section on cancellation of a contract are owed as simple contract debts and may be set off against each other.

11.2   RIGHT OF WITHDRAWAL: P2P AGREEMENTS

[**Note:** Until the end of 30 September 2014, transitional provisions apply to **CONC 11.2**: see **CONC TP 4.6**]

Application

11.2.1 R FCA

This section applies to a *firm* with respect to *operating an electronic system in relation to lending* in relation to a *borrower* under a *P2P agreement*.

11.2.2 R FCA

This section does not apply to a *P2P agreement* under which *credit* exceeding £60,260 is, was or would be provided.

Right to cancel

11.2.3 R FCA

A *firm* must ensure that a *P2P agreement* that the *firm* makes available to a *borrower* and a *lender* provides for the following contractual rights and obligations and procedure for and effect of the exercise of those rights and obligations:
(1) a right for the *borrower*:
   (a) to withdraw from the agreement ("the right of withdrawal");
   (b) without giving any reason; and
   (c) by giving oral or written notice of the withdrawal to the *firm* (on behalf of the *lender*) before the end of the period of 14 days:

(i)   beginning with the day after the *P2P agreement* is made; or

(ii)   beginning with the day on which the *borrower* receives the contractual terms and conditions of the service and any other pre-contractual information required, as the case may be, under **CONC 4.3**, if that is later than the date in (1);

(2)   where written notice is given of the right of withdrawal by *electronic means*:

(a)   it may be sent to the number or electronic address specified for the purpose in the agreement; and

(b)   where it is so sent, it is to be regarded as having been received by the *firm* (on behalf of the *lender*) at the time it is sent;

(3)   where written notice is given of the right of withdrawal, other than by *electronic means*:

(a)   it may be sent by post to, or left at, the postal address specified for the purpose in the agreement; and

(b)   where it is sent by post to that address, it is to be regarded as having been received by the *firm* (on behalf of the *lender*) at the time of posting;

(4)   where the *borrower* exercises the right of withdrawal from a *P2P agreement*:

(a)   the *borrower* must repay to the *firm* (on behalf of the *lender*) or the *lender* any *credit* provided and the interest accrued on it (at the rate provided for under the agreement); but

(b)   the *borrower* is not liable to pay to the *firm* (on behalf of the *lender*) or the *lender* any compensation, fees or charges, except any non-returnable charges paid by the *lender* or by the *firm* (on behalf of the *lender*) to a public administrative body;

(5)   the effect of exercising the right to withdraw is that the obligations of the *borrower* under the agreement cease to have effect except for the obligation in (4); and

(6)   where an amount is payable where (4) applies, the agreement may provide that the amount must be paid without undue delay and no later than the end of the period of 30 days beginning with the day after the day on which the notice of withdrawal was given (and if not paid by the end of that period the agreement may provide that the sum may be recovered from the *borrower* as a debt).

11.2.4 R   FCA

A *firm* must ensure that a *P2P agreement* that it makes available to a *lender* and a *borrower* does not provide for any other obligations of the *borrower* in connection with the exercise of the rights in **CONC 11.2.3 R**.

CHAPTER 12
REQUIREMENTS FOR FIRMS WITH INTERIM PERMISSION FOR CREDIT-RELATED REGULATED ACTIVITIES

12.1   APPLICATION AND PURPOSE

[3.90]
12.1.1 R   FCA

This chapter applies to a *firm* with an *interim permission*.

12.1.2 G   FCA

The purpose of these *rules* is to provide that certain provisions of the *Handbook* or of a Regulatory Guide:

(1)   that would otherwise apply to *persons* with an *interim permission* are not to apply; or

(2)   are to apply to those *persons* with the modifications specified in the table in **CONC 12.1.4 R**.

Disapplication or modification of certain modules or provisions of the Handbook

12.1.3 R   FCA

The modules or parts of the modules of the *appropriate regulator's Handbook* of *rules* and guidance or of a Regulatory Guide listed in the table in **CONC 12.1.4 R** to this chapter:

(1)   do not apply, to the extent set out in the table, to a *person* with an *interim permission* with respect to the carrying on of a *credit-related regulated activity* or *operating an electronic system in relation to lending*; or

(2)   are to apply to such a *person* with respect to the carrying on of a *credit-related regulated activity* or *operating an electronic system in relation to lending* with the modifications specified in the table in **CONC 12.1.4 R**.

12.1.4 R   FCA

Table: Disapplied or modified modules or provisions of the Handbook

Module	Disapplication or modification
Senior Management Arrangements, Systems and Control sourcebook (*SYSC*) [FCA]	**SYSC 6.1.4C R** (requirement of debt management firm or credit repair firm to appoint a compliance officer) does not apply to a *firm* with an *interim permission*. **SYSC 6.3.8 R** (responsibility for anti-money laundering systems and controls) does not apply to a *firm* with only an *interim permission*. **SYSC 6.3.9 R** (requirement to appoint a money laundering reporting officer) does not apply to a *firm* with only an *interim permission*.
Fees manual (*FEES*) [FCA]	The Fees manual does not apply in respect of the fee provided for in **FEES 8.1.1 R (1)**, except for the rules and guidance in **FEES 2.3** and **FEES 8.1**.
Threshold Conditions (*COND*)	Guidance applies with necessary modifications to reflect Chapter 4 of Part 8 of the Financial Services and Markets Act 2000 (Regulated Activities) (Amendment) (No 2) Order 2013 (see Note 1).
	Note 1 A *firm* is treated as having an *interim permission* on and after 1 April 2014 to carry on *credit-related regulated activity* or *operating an electronic system in relation to lending* under the Financial Services and Markets Act 2000 (Regulated Activities) (Amendment) (No. 2) Order 2013 if it met the conditions set out in Chapter 4 of Part 8 of that Order. Section 55B(3) of the *Act* (satisfaction of threshold conditions) does not require the *FCA* or *PRA* to ensure that the *firm* will satisfy, and continue to satisfy, in relation to the *credit-related regulated activities* or *operating an electronic system in relation to lending* for which it has an *interim permission*, the *threshold conditions* for which that regulator is responsible. The *FCA* or *PRA* can, however, exercise its power under section 55J of the *Act* (variation or cancellation on initiative of regulator) or under section 55L of the *Act* (in the case of the *FCA*) or section 55M of the *Act* (in the case of the *PRA*) (imposition of requirements by the regulator) in relation to a *firm* if, among other things, it appears to the *FCA* or *PRA* that the *firm* is failing, or is likely to fail, to satisfy the *threshold conditions* in relation to the *credit-related regulated activities* or *operating an electronic system in relation to lending* for which it has an *interim permission* for which the regulator is responsible. The *guidance* in *COND* should be read accordingly.
Client Assets (*CASS*)	*CASS* does not apply with respect to *credit-related regulated activity* to a *firm* with: (1) only an *interim permission*; or (2) an *interim permission* that is treated as a variation of permission; if the *firm* acts in accordance with the provisions of paragraphs 3.42 and 3.43 of the Debt management (and credit repair services) guidance (OFT366rev) previously issued by the Office of Fair Trading, as they were in effect immediately before 1 April 2014.
Supervision manual (*SUP*)	**SUP 3** (Auditors), **SUP 10A** (FCA Approved persons) and **SUP 12** (Appointed representatives) (see Note 2) do not apply: (1) to a *firm* with only an *interim permission*; or (2) with respect to a *credit-related regulated activity* or *operating an electronic system in relation to lending* for which a *firm* has an *interim permission* that is treated as a variation of permission, except that **SUP 3.10** and **SUP 3.11** apply to a *firm* in relation to its *designated investment business* that comprises *operating an electronic system in relation to lending*.
	Note 2 A *firm* may not be a *principal* in relation to a *regulated activity* for which it has *interim permission*. A *firm* with *interim permission* may, however, be an *appointed representative* in relation to a *regulated activity* which it does not have *interim permission* to carry on (article 59 of the Financial Services and Markets Act 2000 (Regulated Activities) (Amendment) (No 2) Order 2013).
	SUP 6 (Applications to vary and cancel Part 4A permission and to impose, vary or cancel requirements) applies: (1) with necessary modifications to reflect Chapter 4 of Part 8 of the Financial Services and Markets Act 2000 (Regulated Activities) (Amendment) (No 2) Order 2013 (see Note 3); (2) with the modifications to SUP 6.3.15D and SUP 6.4.5D set out in paragraph 1.2 of this Schedule.

Module	Disapplication or modification
	Note 3 If a *firm* with *interim permission* applies to the appropriate regulator under section 55A of the *Act* for *Part 4A permission* to carry on a *regulated activity* or under section 55H or 55I of the *Act* to vary a *Part 4A permission* that the *firm* has otherwise than by virtue of the Financial Services and Markets Act 2000 (Regulated Activities) (Amendment) (No 2) Order 2013 by adding a *regulated activity* to those to which the *permission* relates, the application may be treated by the appropriate regulator as relating also to some or all of the *regulated activities* for which the *firm* has *interim permission*.
	SUP 11 (Controllers and close links) does not apply to a *firm* with only an *interim permission* (see Note 4).
	Note 4 A *firm* is not to be regarded as an *authorised person* for the purposes of Part 12 of the *Act* (control over authorised person) if it has only an *interim permission* (see article 59 of the Financial Services and Markets Act 2000 (Regulated Activities) (Amendment) (No 2) Order 2013).
	For a *firm* with only an *interim permission* (1) **SUP 15.5.1 R**, **SUP 15.5.2 G**, **SUP 15.5.4 R**, **SUP 15.5.5 R** are modified so that the words "reasonable advance", "and the date on which the *firm* intends to implement the change of name" and "and the date of the change" are omitted; and (2) **SUP 15.7.1 R**, **SUP 15.7.4 R** and **SUP 15.7.5A R** are modified so that a notification of a change in name, address or telephone number must be made using the online Consumer Credit Interim Permissions system available on the *FCA's* website. (3) If in a notification to the *FCA* the *firm* is required to enter its FRN number it must include it interim permission number.
	SUP 16 (Reporting requirements) does not apply to a *firm* with only an *interim permission* except: (1) for **SUP 16.14**; and (2) in relation to data item CCR008.
	SUP 16.11 and **SUP 16.12** apply to a *firm*, which was an *authorised person* immediately before 1 April 2014, with an *interim permission* that is treated as a variation of *permission* with respect to *credit-related regulated activity* or *operating an electronic system in relation to lending* as if the changes to **SUP 16.11** and **SUP 16.12** effected by the Consumer Credit (Consequential and Supplementary Amendments) Instrument 2014 had not been made, except in so far as those changes relate to *data item* CCR008.
Disputes Resolution: Complaints sourcebook (*DISP*)	**DISP 1.10** (Complaints reporting rules) and **DISP 1.10A** (Complaints data publication rules) do not apply to a *person* with only an *interim permission*.
	DISP 1.10 (Complaints reporting rules) and **DISP 1.10A** (Complaints data publication rules) apply to a *firm*, which was an *authorised person* immediately before 1 April 2014, with an *interim permission* that is treated as a variation of *permission* with respect to *credit-related regulated activity* or *operating an electronic system in relation to lending* as if the changes to **DISP 1.10** and **DISP 1.10A** effected by the Consumer Credit (Consequential and Supplementary Amendments) Instrument 2014 had not been made.
Consumer Credit sourcebook (*CONC*)	**CONC 10** (Prudential requirements for debt management firms) does not apply: (1) to a *firm* with only an *interim permission*; or (2) with respect to *credit-related regulated activity* or *operating an electronic system in relation to lending* for which a *firm* has an *interim permission* that is treated as a variation of permission.
	For a *firm* only with an *interim permission*, **PERG 5.11.13 G** is modified so that following the words "which does not otherwise consist of carrying on *regulated activities*" is added "(other than a *regulated activity* carried on by a *firm* only with an *interim permission* listed in article 59A of the Financial Services and Markets Act 2000 (Regulated Activities) (Amendment) (No.2) Order 2013 (SI 2013/1881) which is to be disregarded for this purpose)".

Module	Disapplication or modification
Perimeter Guidance manual (*PERG*)	Article 59A enables a *firm* with only an *interim permission* which would be able to benefit from article 72B of the *Regulated Activities Order*, but for carrying on the new consumer credit regulated activities to continue to do so.

Interpretation

12.1.5 R   FCA

In this section 12.1, the expression "interim permission" means a permission which a *person* is to be treated as having under article 56(9)(a) or (b) of the Financial Services and Markets Act 2000 (Regulated Activities) (Amendment) Order 2013.

CHAPTER 13

GUIDANCE ON THE DUTY TO GIVE INFORMATION UNDER SECTIONS 77, 78 AND 79 OF THE CONSUMER CREDIT ACT 1974

13.1   APPLICATION

[3.91]
13.1.1 G   FCA

This chapter:
(1)   applies to a *firm* with respect to *consumer credit lending* and a *firm* with respect to *consumer hiring*;
(2)   does not apply to the obligation in or under section 78(4), (4A) or (5) of the *CCA* on a *lender* to give regular statements where *running-account credit* is provided under a *regulated credit agreement*.

Guidance

13.1.2 G   FCA
(1)   The *FCA* takes the view that sections 77, 78 and 79 of the *CCA* should be read in a way that allows the *borrower* or *hirer* to obtain the information needed in order to be properly informed without imposing unnecessary burden on *firms*.
(2)   The statement referred to in the relevant section must be prepared according to the information to which it is 'practicable' for the *firm* to refer. In the *FCA's* view, this means practicable at the time of the request and includes information which can reasonably be obtained from third parties.
(3)   *Firms* should take steps to ensure that information is preserved and kept available to be used to give information to a *borrower* or *hirer*.

The request and the duty to give

13.1.3 G   FCA
(1)   A request must be from or on behalf of the *borrower* under sections 77 and 78 or from or on behalf of a *hirer* under section 79. This would include a friend or relative, a solicitor, a claims management company or other third party. Under the Data Protection Act 1998 and the Data Protection Principles, the *lender* or *owner* is not allowed to reveal such information to a third party without the authority of the *borrower* or *hirer*. It should therefore satisfy itself that the *person* making the request has proper authority to obtain the information. If a copy of such authority is not enclosed with the request, the *lender* or *owner* is entitled to reply by asking to see the authority.
(2)   Where there are two or more *borrowers* or *hirers* and the request comes from one only, it must be nevertheless complied with, and the response must be given to both (or all) *borrowers* or *hirers*.
(3)   If the recipient considers that another *person* is the *lender* or *owner*, the recipient should either inform the applicant of who it considers is the correct recipient or pass the request on to that *person*.
(4)   In accordance with the sections referred to in (1) the *firm* must 'give' a copy of the executed agreement and any other document referred to in it and the required statement. In the *FCA's* view, sending a copy of them by ordinary second class post will suffice. Guidance on what constitutes a copy is given below and found in the case of *Carey v HSBC Bank plc* [2009] EWHC 3417 (QB).
(5)   The duty under the relevant section does not apply if no sum is, or will or may become, payable by the *borrower* or *hirer* under the agreement. This is irrespective of whether the agreement may have been terminated.

The copy agreement

13.1.4 G   FCA

Part 3   FCA Handbook Materials

(1)   The copy of the executed agreement should be a 'true copy' of the original. However, as confirmed in the case of *Carey v HSBC Bank plc* [2009] EWHC 3417 (QB), in this context the term 'true copy' does not necessarily mean a carbon, photocopy, microfiche copy or other exact copy of the signed agreement. There is no obligation to provide a copy which includes a copy of the signature.

(2)   The *firm* can reconstitute a copy. It can do this by re-populating a template of the relevant agreement form with the details of the specific agreement taken from its records. If the *firm* does provide a reconstituted copy, it should explain that that is what it has done, to avoid misleading the *customer* that this is a contemporaneous copy.

(3)   The terms and conditions should be those applicable at the time the agreement was executed. The name and address at the time of execution must be included.

(4)   The reconstituted agreement should contain a heading prescribed by the *CCA* and any relevant cancellation notice.

(5)   If the reason why no copy is given in response to a request under these sections is that there never was an executed agreement, the *firm* should acknowledge this in its response.

(6)   If the agreement has been varied, the duty is to provide not only a copy of the agreement as originally executed but also either:

    (a)   a copy of the latest variation given in accordance with section 82(1) of the *CCA* relating to each discrete term of the agreement which has been varied; or,

    (b)   a clear statement of the terms of the agreement as varied.

(7)   Further, section 180(1)(b) of the *CCA* and regulation 3(2) of the Consumer Credit (Cancellation Notices and Copies of Documents) Regulations 1983 expressly allow certain matters to be omitted from the copy. There may be excluded from the copy of the executed agreement to be provided under these sections:

    (a)   any information relating to the *borrower*, *hirer* or surety, or information included for the use of the *lender* or *owner* only, which is not required to be included by the*CCA* or by any regulations made under the *CCA* as to the form and content of the agreement;

    (b)   any signature box, signature or date of signature;

    (c)   in the case of *pawn* agreements, any description of the article taken in *pawn*.

The statement of account

13.1.5 G   FCA

If the *firm* possesses insufficient information to enable it to ascertain the amount and date of any sum which is to become payable, it is sufficient to indicate the basis on which they would fall to be ascertained.

Failure to comply

13.1.6 G   FCA

(1)   Failure to comply with the provisions means that the agreement becomes unenforceable while the failure to comply persists, and the courts have no discretion to allow enforcement.

(2)   In such cases, a *firm* should in no way, either by act or omission, mislead a *customer* as to the enforceability of the agreement.

(3)   In particular, a *firm* should not in such cases either threaten court action or other enforcement of the debt or imply that the debt is enforceable when it is not.

(4)   The *firm* should, in any communication or request for payment in such cases, make clear to the *customer* that although the debt remains outstanding it is unenforceable.

(5)   In the judgment of *McGuffick -v- The Royal Bank of Scotland plc* [2009] EWHC 2386 (Comm) Flaux J held in a case under section 77 of the *CCA* that passing details of a debt to a *credit reference agency* and related activities do not constitute enforcement under the *CCA*. He also held that steps taken with a view to enforcement, including demanding payment from a claimant, issuing a default notice, threatening legal action and the actual bringing of proceedings, are not themselves 'enforcement' under the *CCA*. On the other hand he confirmed that the actions listed under sections 76(1) and 87(1) of the *CCA* did amount to enforcement notwithstanding that some of the actions 'less obviously' amounted to enforcement. These actions are demanding earlier payment, recovering possession of *goods* or *land*, treating any right conferred on the debtor by the agreement as terminated, restricted or deferred, enforcing any *security* and terminating the agreement.

(6)   While Flaux J agreed with the decision of HHJ Simon Brown QC (sitting as a Deputy High Court Judge) in *Tesco Personal Finance v Rankine* [2009] C.C.L.R. 3 that commencing proceedings was not enforcement, but a step taken with a view to enforcement, both he and HHJ Simon Brown appear to have been drawing a distinction between commencing proceedings and entering judgment in those proceedings.

(7)   This *guidance* deals only with the question of whether an agreement is unenforceable in relation to sections 77, 78 and 79 of the *CCA*. A *lender's* rights to enforce an agreement may be restricted for a variety of reasons, by the *Act*, by or under the *CCA* and by virtue of the general law.

(8) However, where a *firm* is aware that an agreement is unenforceable because of non-compliance with an information request under section 77, 78 or 79 of the *CCA*, a *firm* should make it clear when communicating to a *customer* about a debt that the debt is in fact unenforceable. Failure to do so, in that case, would in the *FCA's* view unfairly mislead the *customer* by omission. Any communication that implies expressly or otherwise that a debt is enforceable when it is known that it is not, would be misleading. One way to avoid this would be for the *firm* to explain to the *customer* the full meaning of 'unenforceable'.

CHAPTER 14
REQUIREMENT IN RELATION TO AGENTS

14.1   APPLICATION

[3.92]
14.1.1 R   FCA

This chapter applies to a *firm* with respect to a *credit-related regulated activity*.

Requirements

14.1.2 R   FCA

A *firm* must not appoint an individual, who is not an *authorised person* or an *exempt person*, to act as an agent of the *firm*, in carrying on *regulated activities* of the *firm* unless all of the following conditions are met at the date of the individual's appointment and while the individual continues to act as the *firm's* agent:
(1)   the *firm* appoints the individual as the *firm's* agent;
(2)   the individual works as agent only for the *firm* and not as agent for any other principal;
(3)   the *firm* has a written contract with the individual which:
   (a)   sets out effective measures for the *firm* to control the individual's activities when acting on its behalf in the course of its business; and
   (b)   requires the individual to make clear to *customers* that the individual is representing the firm as the individual's principal and the name of the *firm*;
(4)   (in the case of collecting debts) receipt of repayments by the individual is treated as receipt by the *firm*; and
(5)   the *firm* accepts full responsibility for the conduct of the individual when the individual is acting on the *firm's* behalf in the course of the *firm's* business.

14.1.3 G   FCA
(1)   A *firm* in **CONC 14.1.2 R** would need to have a *Part 4A permission* for every activity the individual carries on as its agent for which the *firm* would need permission if it were carrying on the activity itself.
(2)   **CONC 14** uses the expression "individual" in its natural meaning as referring to a single human being.

14.1.4 R   FCA

Where a *firm* appoints an agent in accordance with **CONC 14.1.2 R** to carry on the business of the *firm*:
(1)   the *firm* must establish, implement and maintain adequate policies and procedures sufficient to ensure compliance of the agent with the *firm's* obligations under the *regulatory system*; and
(2)   the *firm* must take all reasonable steps to identify conflicts of interest between the agent and a *client* of the *firm* that arise or may arise in the course of the *firm* carrying on *regulated activities* or *ancillary activities*.

CHAPTER 15
SECOND CHARGE LENDING

15.1   APPLICATION

[3.93]
15.1.1 R   FCA

This chapter applies to:
(1)   a *firm* with respect to *consumer credit lending* in relation to *regulated credit agreements* secured on *land*; and
(2)   a *firm* with respect to *credit broking* in relation to *credit agreements* secured on *land*.

15.1.2 G   FCA

Firms which carry on *consumer credit lending* or *credit broking* should comply with all *rules* which apply to that *regulated activity* in *CONC* and other parts of the Handbooks. For example, **CONC 7** applies to matters concerning arrears, default and recovery (including repossession) and applies generally to agreements to which this chapter applies. This chapter sets out specific requirements and *guidance* that apply in relation to agreements secured on *land*. *Regulated mortgage contracts* and *home purchase plans* are not *regulated credit agreements* and are excluded, to the extent specified in article 36E of the *Regulated Activities Order*, from *credit broking*.

Conduct

15.1.3 G   FCA

The financial promotion *rules* in **CONC 3** apply to *firms' financial promotions* concerning *credit agreements* secured on *land*, apart from the extent to which a *financial promotion* or communication concerns *qualifying credit*. **CONC 3.3.1 R** requires *financial promotions* to be clear fair and not misleading; *firms* should take particular care with respect to explaining the nature of the *credit* to be provided and the costs of borrowing.
[**Note**: paragraph 3.2 of *SCLG*]

15.1.4 R   FCA

A *firm* must make clear in advance the purpose of any visit off trade premises (which has the same meaning as in section 48 of the *CCA*) at which the *customer* may enter into a *regulated credit agreement*.
[**Note**: paragraph 3.8 of *SCLG*]

15.1.5 R   FCA

In good time before a *credit agreement* is made and, where section 58 applies, before an unexecuted agreement is sent to the *customer* for signature a *firm* must:
(1)   disclose key contract terms and conditions of the prospective *credit agreement*;
         [**Note**: paragraph 2.1 of *SCLG*]
(2)   disclose any features of the prospective *credit agreement* which carry a particular risk to the *customer*;
         [**Note**: paragraph 3.4 of *SCLG*]
(3)   inform the *customer* of the consequences of missing payments or of making underpayments, including the imposition of default charges, the risk of repossession of the *customer's* home, in relation to the *customer's* credit record and of inability to obtain *credit* in the future;
         [**Note**: paragraph 3.4 of *SCLG*]
(4)   inform the *customer* about the circumstances in which the rates or charges may change, in particular, if they may be varied at the discretion of the *firm* or can vary subject to a reference rate of interest; and
         [**Note**: paragraphs 3.6 and 4.4 of *SCLG*]
(5)   if the rate of interest can vary subject to a reference rate of interest, other than that of the Bank of England's base rate, inform the *customer* of the reference rate in question and the rate to be applied.
         [**Note**: paragraph 3.6 of *SCLG*]

15.1.6 G   FCA

Where appropriate, the disclosure required by **CONC 15.1.5 R** should be explained orally to the *customer*.
[**Note**: paragraph 3.4 of *SCLG*]

15.1.7 R   FCA

Where a *firm* has reasonable grounds to suspect that the *customer* does not understand material aspects of the obligations they will take on and the resulting risks, under a *regulated credit agreement*, the *firm*:
(1)   must not enter into a *regulated credit agreement*; and
(2)   must provide further explanation of any such obligations or risks.
         [**Note**: paragraph 3.5 of *SCLG*]

15.1.8 R   FCA

Before a *customer* enters into a *regulated credit agreement*, the firm must:
(1)   encourage the *customer* to read all contractual documentation carefully;
         [**Note**: paragraph 4.2 of *SCLG*]
(2)   take reasonable steps to ensure the *customer* has understood the nature of the obligations the *customer* will take on and the resulting risks;
         [**Note**: paragraph 3.5 of *SCLG*]
(3)   encourage the *customer* to obtain independent advice; and
         [**Note**: paragraphs 2.1 and 4.2 of *SCLG*]
(4)   permit the *customer* an adequate opportunity to seek and obtain such advice.
         [**Note**: paragraph 2.1 of *SCLG*]

15.1.9 G   FCA

Before a *regulated credit agreement* secured on *land* is entered into:
(1)   the *firm* should consider the adequate explanations it should give to the *customer* under **CONC 4.2**; and
         [**Note**: paragraph 3.1 (box) of *ILG*]

(2)   the *firm* is required under **CONC 5.2.2 R (1)** to assess the potential for commitments under the agreement to adversely impact the *customer's* financial situation.
[**Note:** paragraphs 1.14 and 4.1 of *ILG*]

15.1.10 G   FCA

In accordance with PRIN 9 (customer: relationships of trust):
(1)   a *firm* must take reasonable steps to ensure the suitability of its advice, which would include acting in the best interests of a *customer* where the *firm* makes a recommendation;
(2)   if it appears to the *firm* that entering into a *regulated credit agreement* secured on *land* is not in the best interests of the *customer*, that fact should be made clear to the *customer*; and
(3)   the *firm* should encourage the *customer* to consider whether the *credit* can be afforded, including in the event the *customer's* circumstances change, for example, through a change in employment or retirement.
[**Note:** paragraph 3.14 of *SCLG*]

15.1.11 R   FCA

A *firm* must set out the nature and purpose of the fees and charges payable by the *customer*, including any fees or charges payable on the *customer's* default:
(1)   in the *credit agreement*; and
(2)   in any booklet or leaflet relating to the agreement.
[**Note:** paragraph 4.3 of *SCLG*]

15.1.12 R   FCA

Where rates and charges under a *credit agreement* are variable, a *firm* must:
(1)   before entering into the agreement, explain to the *customer* the consequences of such variations on the amount of periodic instalments payable and on the *total amount payable*;
(2)   only increase rates or charges to recover genuine increases in costs of the *firm* which have an effect on the *credit* provided under the agreement; and
(3)   explain to the *customer* before changing any rate or charge under the agreement.
[**Note:** paragraph 4.4 of *SCLG*]

15.1.13 R   FCA

Where a *customer* wishes to make repayments ahead of time:
(1)   a *firm's* charges for early repayment must be fair and reasonable and must reflect the *firm's* necessary costs in relation to such repayment;
(2)   the *firm* must fully explain the process and costs involved in early repayment; and
(3)   the *firm* must allow the *customer* to make part early repayment of the capital.
[**Note:** paragraph 4.5 of *SCLG*]

15.1.14 G   FCA

Where a *firm* considers taking action to repossess a *customer's* home, it should, where permitted, establish contact with the holder of any charges in priority to the *firm's* charge to minimise adverse impacts on the *customer*.
[**Note:** paragraph 6.2 of *SCLG*]

15.1.15 R   FCA

If a shortfall remains following the sale of a property, the *firm* must notify the *customer* as soon as possible of the amount of the shortfall.
[**Note:** paragraph 6.5 of *SCLG*]

APP 1   TOTAL CHARGE FOR CREDIT RULES

1.1   TOTAL CHARGE FOR CREDIT RULES FOR CERTAIN AGREEMENTS SECURED ON LAND

Interpretation

App 1.1.1 R   FCA

(1)   For the purposes of this section, references to the period for which credit is provided:
    (a)   in the case of a *credit agreement* under which the period for which *credit* is to be provided is ascertainable at the date of the making of the *credit agreement*, are references to the period beginning with the *relevant date* and ending with the end of the period for which *credit* is to be provided;
    (b)   in the case of a *credit agreement* under which the period for which *credit* is to be provided can be ascertained at the *relevant date* if the assumption in **CONC App 1.1.12 R** is applied, are references to the period beginning with the *relevant date* and ending with the end of the period for which *credit* would be provided under the *credit agreement* if the amount given by that assumption were the amount of the *credit* so provided; and
    (c)   in any other case, are references to the period of one year referred to in **CONC App 1.1.13 R**.

(2)   References in this section to repayment of the *credit* under a *credit agreement* and of the *total charge for credit* include references to any repayment or payment, as the case may require, of any part of the *credit* and of the *total charge for credit*.

Application

App 1.1.2 R   FCA

This section applies to *regulated credit agreements* which are secured on *land* or to prospective *regulated credit agreements* which are to be secured on *land*, except to the extent that the Consumer Credit (Disclosure of Information) Regulations 2010 apply to such agreements.

General provisions about calculation

App 1.1.3 R   FCA

(1)   Any calculation under this section shall be made on the following assumptions
    (a)   the assumption that the *borrower* will not be entitled to any income tax relief relating to the *transaction* other than relief under section 19 of the Income and Corporation Taxes Act 1970 and Schedule 4 to the Finance Act 1976 (which afford relief in respect of premiums under certain policies of insurance) without any deduction under section 21 of the said Act of 1970;
    (b)   the assumption that no assistance is given under the Home Purchase Assistance and Housing Corporation Guarantee Act 1978;
    (c)
        (i)   in the case of a *transaction* which provides for repayment of the *credit* or of the *total charge for credit* at, or not later than, a specified time or times, the assumption that the *lender* will not exercise any right under the *transaction* to require repayment at any other time or times;
        (ii)   in any other case, the assumption that the *lender* will not exercise any right under the *transaction* to require repayment;
        the *borrower*, in any case, performing all his obligations under the *transaction*;
    (d)   subject to (e) below, in the case of a *transaction* which provides for variation of the rate or amount of any item included in the *total charge for credit* in consequence of the occurrence after the *relevant date* of any event, the assumption that the event will not occur; and, in this sub-paragraph, "event" means an act or omission of the *borrower* or of the *lender* or any other event (including where the *transaction* makes provision for variation upon the continuation of any circumstance, the continuation of that circumstance) but does not include an event which is certain to occur and of which the date of occurrence, or the earliest date of occurrence, can be ascertained at the date of the making of the *credit agreement*; and
    (e)   in the case of a *land-related agreement* which provides for the possibility of any variation of the rate of interest in consequence of the occurrence after the *relevant date* of any event (being an event which is certain to occur and of which the date of occurrence, or the earliest date of occurrence, can be ascertained at the date of the making of the *credit agreement*), the assumption that such a variation will, when the event occurs, take place.

(2)   For the purposes of this section
    (a)   subject to (b) below and **CONC APP 1.1.18 R**, in the case of any *credit agreement* each provision of *credit* and each repayment of the *credit* and of the *total charge for credit* shall be taken to be made:
        (i)   at the earliest time provided under the *transaction*, and
        (ii)   in a case where any such provision or repayment is to be made at or not later than a specified time, at that time
        and, where any such repayment is to be made before the *relevant date*, it shall be taken to be made on the *relevant date*;
    (b)   where under a *credit agreement* for *running-account credit* or a *credit agreement* for *fixed-sum credit* where the *credit* is not repayable at specified intervals or in specified amounts a constant *period rate of charge* in respect of periods of equal or of nearly equal length is charged, it shall be assumed for the purposes of calculations under this section, notwithstanding **CONC APP 1.1.17 R**, that
        (i)   the amount of *credit* outstanding at the beginning of a period is to remain outstanding throughout the period;
        (ii)   the amount of any *credit* provided during a period is provided immediately after the end of the period; and
        (iii)   any repayment of *credit* or of the *total charge for credit* made during a period is made immediately after the end of the period; and
    (c)   the assumption that the amount of any repayment of *credit* or of the *total charge for credit* will, at the time when the repayment is made, be the smallest for which the agreement provides.

(3)   In determining the amount of the total of the interest on the *credit* which may be provided under the *credit agreement*, any subsidy receivable by any *person* under Part II of the Housing Subsidies Act 1967 shall be deducted.

Total charge for credit

App 1.1.4 R   FCA

For the purposes of the *Regulated Activities Order*, the total charge for the *credit* which may be provided under an actual or prospective *credit agreement* shall be the total of the amounts determined as at the date of the making of the *credit agreement* of such of the charges specified in **CONC App 1.1.5 R** as apply in relation to the *credit agreement* but excluding the amount of the charges specified in **CONC App 1.1.6 R**.

Items included in total charge for credit

App 1.1.5 R   FCA

Except as provided in **CONC App 1.1.6 R**, the amounts of the following charges are included in the *total charge for credit* in relation to a *credit agreement*:

(1)   the total of the interest on the *credit* which may be provided under the *credit agreement*;

(2)   other charges at any time payable under the *transaction* by or on behalf of the *borrower* or a *relative* of his whether to the *lender* or any other *person*; and

(3)   a premium under a *contract of insurance*, payable under the *transaction* by the *borrower* or a *relative* of his, where the making or maintenance of the *contract of insurance* is required by the *lender*

      (a)   as a condition of making the *credit agreement*, and

      (b)   for the sole purpose of ensuring complete or partial repayment of the *credit*, and complete or partial payment to the *lender* of such of those charges included in the *total charge for credit* as are payable to him under the *transaction*, in the event of the death, invalidity, illness or unemployment of the *borrower*,

notwithstanding that the whole or part of the charge may be repayable at any time or that the consideration therefor may include matters not within the *transaction* or subsisting at a time not within the duration of the *credit agreement*.

Items excluded from total charge for credit

App 1.1.6 R   FCA

(1)   The amounts of the following items are not included in the *total charge for credit* in relation to a *credit agreement*:

      (a)   any charge payable under the *transaction* to the *lender* upon failure by the *borrower* or a *relative* of his to do or to refrain from doing anything which he is required to do or to refrain from doing, as the case may be;

      (b)   any charge

            (i)   which is payable by the *lender* to any *person* upon failure by the *borrower* or a *relative* of his to do or to refrain from doing anything which he is required under the *transaction* to do or to refrain from doing, as the case may be, and

            (ii)   which the *lender* may under the *transaction* require the *borrower* or a *relative* of his to pay to him or to another *person* on his behalf;

      (c)   any charge relating to a *credit agreement* which is a *credit agreement* to *finance* a transaction of a description referred to in (2)(a) or (b) of the definition of *restricted-use credit agreement*, being a charge which would be payable if the transaction were for *cash*;

      (d)   any charge (other than a fee or commission charged by a *credit broker*) not within (c) above

            (i)   of a description which relates to services or benefits incidental to the *credit agreement* and also to other services or benefits which may be supplied to the *borrower*, and

            (ii)   which is payable pursuant to an obligation incurred by the *borrower* under arrangements effected before he applies to enter into the *credit agreement*, not being arrangements under which the *borrower* is bound to enter into any *credit agreement*;

      (e)   subject to (2) below, any charge under arrangements for the care, maintenance or protection of any *land* or *goods*;

      (f)   charges for money transmission services relating to an arrangement for a *current account*, being charges which vary with the use made by the *borrower* of the arrangement;

      (g)   any charge for a guarantee other than a guarantee

            (i)   which is required by the *lender* as a condition of making the *credit agreement*, and

(ii) the purpose of which is to ensure complete or partial repayment of the *credit*, and complete or partial payment to the *lender* of such of those charges included in the *total charge for credit* as are payable to him under the *transaction*, in the event of the death, invalidity, illness or unemployment of the *borrower*;

(h) charges for the transfer of funds (other than charges within (f) above) and charges for keeping an account intended to receive payments towards the repayment of the *credit* and the payment of interest and other charges, except where the *borrower* does not have reasonable freedom of choice in the matter and where such charges are abnormally high; but this sub-paragraph does not exclude from the *total charge for credit* charges for collection of the payments to which it refers, whether such payments are made in *cash* or otherwise;

(i) a premium under a *contract of insurance* other than a *contract of insurance* referred to in **CONC APP 1.1.5 R (C)**.

(2) (1) above has effect only

(a) in the case of a charge within (e), where, in pursuance of the arrangements

(i) the services are to be performed if, after the date of the making of the *credit agreement*, the condition of the *land* or *goods* becomes, or is in immediate danger of becoming, such that the *land* or *goods* cannot reasonably be enjoyed or used, and

(ii) the charge will not accrue unless the services are performed; and

(b) in the case of any other charge within (e)

(i) where provision of substantially the same description as that to which the arrangements relate is available under comparable arrangements from a *person* who is not the *lender* or a *supplier* or a *credit broker* who introduced the *borrower* and the *lender*, and

(ii) where the arrangements are made with a *person* chosen by the *borrower*, and

(iii) if, in accordance with the *transaction*, the consent of the *lender* or of a *supplier* or of the *credit broker* who introduced the *borrower* and the *lender* is required to the making of the arrangements, where the *transaction* provides that such consent may not be unreasonably withheld whether because no incidental benefit will or may accrue to the *lender* or to the *supplier* or to the *credit broker* or on any other ground;

and references in this sub-paragraph to the *lender*, a *supplier* and a *credit broker* include references to his near relative, his partner and a member of a group of which he is a member, to any *person* nominated by him or any such person in relation to the arrangements, and to a near relative of his partner; and "near relative" means, in relation to any *person*, the husband, wife, father, mother, brother, sister, son or daughter of that person and "group" means the *person* (including a company) having control of a company together with all the companies directly or indirectly controlled by him.

Rate of total charge for credit

App 1.1.7 R   FCA

The rate of the *total charge for credit* in the case of an actual or prospective *credit agreement* shall be the *annual percentage rate of charge* determined in accordance with the following provisions of **CONC APP 1.1.8 R** to **CONC APP 1.1.10 R** and (where it has more than one decimal place) rounded to one decimal place in accordance with **CONC APP 1.1.8 R**.

App 1.1.8 R   FCA

The *annual percentage rate of charge* referred to in **CONC APP 1.1.7 R** shall be rounded to one decimal place as follows

(1) where the figure at the second decimal place is greater than or equal to 5, the figure at the first decimal place shall be increased by one and the decimal place (or places) following the first decimal place shall be disregarded; and

(2) where the figure at the second decimal place is less than 5, that decimal place and any decimal places following it shall be disregarded.

App 1.1.9 R   FCA

(1) Subject to (4) below, the *annual percentage rate of charge* is the rate for *i* which satisfies the equation set out in (2) below, expressed as a percentage.

(2) The equation referred to in (1) above is

$$\sum_{K=1}^{K=m} \frac{A_K}{(1+i)^{t_K}} = \sum_{K'=1}^{K'=m'} \frac{A'_{K'}}{(1+i)^{t_{K'}}}$$

where

K is the number identifying a particular advance of *credit*;

K' is the number identifying a particular instalment;

A_K is the amount of advance K;

$A'_{K'}$ is the amount of instalment K';

$\sum$ represents the sum of all the terms indicated;

m is the number of advances of *credit*;

m' is the total number of instalments;

t_K is the interval, expressed in years, between the *relevant date* and the date of the second advance and those of any subsequent advances number three to m; and

$t_{K'}$ is the interval, expressed in years, between the *relevant date* and the dates of instalments numbered one to m'.

(3)   In (2) above, references to instalments are references to any payment made by, or on behalf of, the *borrower* or a *relative* of his which comprises
   (a)   a repayment of all or part of the *credit* under the *credit agreement*;
   (b)   a payment of all or part of the *total charge for credit*; or
   (c)   both a repayment of all or part of the *credit* and a payment of all or part of the *total charge for credit*.

(4)   Where more than one rate is given under (1) above, the *annual percentage rate of charge* is the positive rate nearest to zero or, if no positive rate is so given, the negative rate nearest to zero.

Computation of time

App 1.1.10 R   FCA
(1)   This rule has effect for determining the length of any period for the purposes of calculations under **CONC APP 1.1.7 R** to **CONC APP 1.1.9 R**.

(2)   A period which is not a whole number of calendar months or a whole number of weeks shall be counted in years and days.

(3)   Subject to (4) below, a period which is a whole number of calendar months or a whole number of weeks shall be counted in calendar months or in weeks, as the case may be.

(4)   Where a period is both a whole number of calendar months and a whole number of weeks and
   (a)   one repayment only is to be made, the period shall be counted in calendar months, or
   (b)   more than one repayment is to be made
        (i)   if all such repayments are to be made at intervals from the *relevant date* of one or more weeks, the period shall be counted in weeks, and
        (ii)   in any other case, the period shall be counted in calendar months.

(5)   A period which is to be counted
   (a)   in calendar months shall be taken to be of a length equal to the relevant number of twelfth parts of a year, and
   (b)   in weeks, shall be taken to be of a length equal to the relevant number of fifty-second parts of a year.

(6)   A day may be taken to be either
   (a)   one three hundred and sixty-fifth part of a year or, if it is a leap year, one three hundred and sixty-sixth part of a year; or

$$\frac{1}{365.25}$$

(b)   of a year.

(7)   Every day shall be taken to be a working day.

Assumptions for calculations

App 1.1.11 R   FCA

(1)   The provisions of **CONC APP 1.1.11 R** to **CONC APP 1.1.18 R** shall have effect as the case may require for the purpose of the calculation of the *total charge for credit* under **CONC APP 1.1.4 R** to **CONC APP 1.1.6 R** above and of the rate of such charge under **CONC APP 1.1.7 R** to **CONC APP 1.1.10 R** above in relation to any actual or prospective *credit agreement* in respect of matters necessary for the calculation which cannot be ascertained by the *lender* at the date of the making of the *credit agreement*.

(2)   In a case where apart from this paragraph **CONC APP 1.1.12 R** and one or more other provisions of **CONC APP 1.1.11 R** to **CONC APP 1.1.18 R** would fall to be applied, the said **CONC APP 1.1.12 R** shall be applied first.

Assumption about the amount of credit

App 1.1.12 R   FCA

Where the amount of the *credit* to be provided under the *credit agreement* cannot be ascertained at the date of the making of the *credit agreement*,

(1)   in the case of a *credit agreement* for *running-account credit* under which there is a *credit limit*, that amount shall be taken to be such *credit limit*; and

(2)   in any other case, that amount shall be taken to be £100.

Assumption about period for which credit is provided

App 1.1.13 R   FCA

Where the period for which *credit* is to be provided is not ascertainable at the date of the making of the *credit agreement*, it shall be assumed that *credit* is provided for one year beginning with the *relevant date*.

Assumption about index-linked rates and amounts

App 1.1.14 R   FCA

Subject to **CONC APP 1.1.15 R**, where the rate or amount of any item included in the *total charge for credit* or the amount of any repayment of *credit* under a *transaction* falls to be ascertained thereunder by reference to the level of any index or other factor in accordance with any formula specified therein, the rate or amount, as the case may be, shall be taken to be the rate or amount so ascertained, the formula being applied as if the level of such index or other factor subsisting at the date of the making of the *credit agreement* were that subsisting at the date by reference to which the formula is to be applied.

Assumptions about variations of interest rates in land-related agreements

App 1.1.15 R   FCA

(1)   This rule applies to any *land-related agreement* which provides for the possibility of any variation of the rate of interest if it is to be assumed, by virtue of **CONC APP 1.1.3 R (1)(E)**, that the variation will take place but the amount of the variation cannot be ascertained at the date of the making of the *credit agreement*.

(2)   In this rule

"initial standard variable rate"	means	
	(a)	the standard variable rate of interest which would be applied by the *lender* to the *credit agreement* on the date of the making of the *credit agreement* if the *credit agreement* provided for interest to be paid at the *lender's* standard variable rate with effect from that date, or
	(b)	if there is no such rate, the standard variable rate of interest applied by the *lender* on the date of the making of the *credit agreement* in question to other *land-related agreements* or, where there is more than one such rate, the highest such rate,

	taking no account (for the avoidance of doubt) of any discount or other reduction to which the *borrower* would or might be entitled; and
"varied rate"	means any rate of interest charged when a variation of the rate of interest is to be assumed to take place by virtue of **CONC App 1.1.3 R (1)(E)**.

(3)   Where a *land-related agreement* provides a formula for calculating a varied rate by reference to a standard variable rate of interest applied by the *lender*, or any other fluctuating rate of interest, but does not enable the varied rate to be ascertained at the date of the making of the *credit agreement* because it is not known on that date what the standard variable rate will be or (as the case may be) at what level the fluctuating rate will be fixed when the varied rate falls to be calculated, it shall be assumed that that rate or level will be the same as the initial standard variable rate.

(4)   Where a *land-related agreement* provides for the possibility of any variation in the rate of interest (other than a variation referred to in (3) above) which it is to be assumed, by virtue of **CONC App 1.1.3 R (1)(E)** will take place but does not enable the amount of that variation to be ascertained at the date of the making of the *credit agreement*, it shall be assumed that the varied rate will be the same as the initial standard variable rate.

Assumption about changes in charges

App 1.1.16 R   FCA

Where
(1)   the period for which the *credit* or any part thereof is to be or may be provided cannot be ascertained at the date of the making of the *credit agreement*; and
(2)   the rate or amount of any item included in the *total charge for credit* will change at a time provided in the *transaction* within one year beginning with the *relevant date*,

the rate or amount shall be taken to be the highest rate or amount at any time obtaining under the *transaction* in that year.

Assumption about time of provision of credit

App 1.1.17 R   FCA

Where the earliest date on which *credit* is to be provided cannot be ascertained at the date of the making of the *credit agreement*, it shall be assumed that *credit* is provided on that date.

Assumptions about time of payment of charges

App 1.1.18 R   FCA

In the case of any *transaction* it shall be assumed
(1)   that a charge payable at a time which cannot be ascertained at the date of the making of the *credit agreement* shall be payable on the *relevant date* or, where it may reasonably be expected that a *borrower* will not make payment on that date, on the earliest date at which it may reasonably be expected that he will make payment; or
(2)   where more than one payment of a charge of the same description falls to be made at times which cannot be ascertained at the date of the making of the *credit agreement*, that the first such payment will be payable on the *relevant date* (or, where it may reasonably be expected that a *borrower* will not make payment on that date, at the earliest date on which it may reasonably be expected that he will make payment), that the last such payment will be payable at the end of the period for which *credit* is provided and that all other such payments (if any) will be payable at equal intervals between such times,

as the case may require.

     1.2   TOTAL CHARGE FOR CREDIT RULES FOR OTHER AGREEMENTS

Interpretation

App 1.2.1 R   FCA
(1)   In this section
     (a)   a reference to a rate of interest is a reference to the interest rate expressed as a fixed or variable percentage applied on an annual basis to the amount of *credit* drawn down;
     (b)   a reference to an open-end *regulated credit agreement* is to a *regulated credit agreement* of no fixed duration and includes credits which must be repaid in full within or after a period but, once repaid, become available to be drawn down again.

Application

App 1.2.2 R   FCA

This section shall not apply to *regulated credit agreements* which are secured on *land* or to prospective *regulated credit agreements* which are to be secured on *land* except to the extent that the Consumer Credit (Disclosure of Information) Regulations 2010 apply to such agreements.

Total charge for credit

App 1.2.3 R   FCA

(1)   The *total charge for credit* which may be provided under an actual or prospective *regulated credit agreement* shall be the *total cost of credit to the borrower* determined in accordance with the requirements in (2) to (5) below.

(2)   Subject to (3), the following costs shall be included in the *total cost of credit to the borrower*
    (a)   the costs of maintaining an account recording both payment transactions and drawdowns;
    (b)   the costs of using a means of payment for both payment transactions and drawdowns;
    (c)   other costs relating to payment transactions.

(3)   The costs at (2) shall not be included in the *total cost of credit to the borrower* where
    (a)   the opening of the account is optional and the costs of the account have been clearly and separately shown in the *regulated credit agreement* or in any other agreement made with the *borrower*;
    (b)   in the case of an *overdraft facility* the costs do not relate to that facility.

(4)   Costs in respect of an ancillary service shall be included in the *total cost of credit to the borrower* if the conclusion of a service contract is compulsory in order to obtain the *credit* or to obtain it on the terms and conditions marketed.

(5)   The *total cost of credit to the borrower* shall not include
    (a)   any charges payable by or on behalf of the *borrower* or a *relative* of his for non-compliance with his commitments contained in the *regulated credit agreement*;
    (b)   charges which, for purchases of *goods* or services, he or a *relative* of his is obliged to pay whether the transaction is effected in *cash* or on *credit*.

(6)   In (4), the reference to an ancillary service means a service that relates to the provision of *credit* under the *regulated credit agreement* and includes in particular an insurance or payment protection policy.

Calculation of the annual percentage rate of charge

App 1.2.4 R   FCA

The *annual percentage rate of charge* shall be calculated in accordance with the mathematical formula set out in **CONC APP 1.2.6 R**.

Assumptions for calculation

App 1.2.5 R   FCA

For the purposes of calculating the *total charge for credit* and the *annual percentage rate of charge*

(1)   it shall be assumed that the *regulated credit agreement* is to remain valid for the period agreed and that the *lender* and the *borrower* will fulfil their obligations under the terms and by the dates specified in that agreement;

(2)   in the case of a *regulated credit agreement* allowing variations in
    (a)   the rate of interest, or
    (b)   where applicable, charges contained in the *annual percentage rate of charge*,
    where these cannot be quantified at the time of calculation, it shall be assumed that they will remain at the initial level and will be applicable for the duration of the agreement;

(3)   where not all rates of interest are determined in the *regulated credit agreement*, a rate of interest shall be assumed to be fixed only for the partial periods for which the rate of interest is determined exclusively by a fixed specific percentage agreed when the agreement is made;

(4)   where the duration of the *regulated credit agreement* cannot be determined at the date of calculation and where different rates of interest and charges are to be offered for limited periods during that agreement, the rate of interest and the charge shall be assumed to be at the highest level for the duration of the agreement;

(5)   where there is a fixed rate of interest agreed in relation to an initial period under a *regulated credit agreement*, at the end of which a new rate of interest is determined and subsequently periodically adjusted according to an agreed indicator, it shall be assumed that, at the end of the period of the fixed rate of interest, the rate of interest is the same as at the time of making the calculation, based on the value of the agreed indicator at that time;

(6)   where the *regulated credit agreement* gives the *borrower* freedom of drawdown, the *total amount of credit* shall be assumed to be drawn down immediately and in full;

(7)   where the *regulated credit agreement* imposes, amongst the different ways of drawdown, a limitation with regard to the amount of *credit* and period of time, the amount of *credit* shall be assumed to be the maximum amount provided for in the agreement and to be drawn down on the earliest date provided for in the agreement;

(8)   where the *regulated credit agreement* provides different ways of drawdown with different charges or rates of interest, the *total amount of credit* shall be assumed to be drawn down at the highest charge and rate of interest applied to the most common drawdown mechanism for the *credit* product to which the agreement relates;

(9)   for the purposes of (g), the most common drawdown mechanism for a particular *credit* product shall be assessed on the basis of the volume of transactions for that product in the preceding 12 months, or expected volumes in the case of a new *credit* product;

(10)   in the case of an *overdraft facility*, the *total amount of credit* shall be assumed to be drawn down in full and for the entire duration of the *regulated credit agreement*;

(11)   for the purposes of (i) if the duration of the *overdraft facility* is not known it shall be assumed that the duration of the facility is three months;

(12)   in the case of an open-end *regulated credit agreement*, other than an *overdraft facility*, it shall be assumed that the *credit* is provided for a period of one year starting from the date of the initial drawdown, and that the final payment made by the *borrower* clears the balance of capital, interest and other charges, if any;

(13)   for the purposes of (k)

     (a)   the capital is repaid by the *borrower* in equal monthly payments, commencing one month after the date of initial drawdown;

     (b)   in cases where the capital must be repaid in full, in a single payment, within or after each payment period, successive drawdowns and repayments of the entire capital by the *borrower* shall be assumed to occur over the period of one year;

     (c)   interest and other charges shall be applied in accordance with those drawdowns and repayments of capital and as provided for in the *regulated credit agreement*;

(14)   in the case of a *regulated credit agreement*, other than an *overdraft facility*, or an open-end *regulated credit agreement*

     (a)   where the date or amount of a repayment of capital to be made by the *borrower* cannot be ascertained, it shall be assumed that the repayment is made at the earliest date provided for under the *regulated credit agreement* and is for the lowest amount for which the *regulated credit agreement* provides;

     (b)   where it is not known on which date the *regulated credit agreement* is made, the date of the initial drawdown shall be assumed to be the date which results in the shortest interval between that date and the date of the first payment to be made by the *borrower*;

(15)   where the date or amount of a payment to be made by the *borrower* cannot be ascertained on the basis of the *regulated credit agreement* or the assumptions set out in (i) to (m), it shall be assumed that the payment is made in accordance with the dates and conditions required by the *lender* and, when these are unknown

     (a)   interest charges are paid together with repayments of capital;

     (b)   a non-interest charge expressed as a single sum is paid on the date of the making of the *regulated credit agreement*;

     (c)   non-interest charges expressed as several payments are paid at regular intervals, commencing with the date of the first repayment of capital, and if the amount of such payments is not known they shall be assumed to be equal amounts;

     (d)   the final payment clears the balance of capital, interest and other charges, if any;

(16)   in the case of an agreement for *running-account credit*, where the *credit limit* applicable to the *credit* is not yet known, that *credit limit* shall be assumed to be £1,200.

Calculation of the Annual Percentage Rate of Charge

App 1.2.6 R   FCA

(1)   The *annual percentage rate of charge* ("APR") is calculated by means of the equation in (2) which equates, on an annual basis, the total present value of drawdowns with the total present value of repayments and payments of charges.

(2)   The equation referred to in (1) is

$$\sum_{k=1}^{m} C_k(1+X)^{-t_k} = \sum_{l=1}^{m''} D_l(1+X)^{-s_l}$$

where

X is the APR;

m is the number of the last drawdown;

k is the number of a drawdown, thus $l \leq k \leq m$;

C_k is the amount of drawdown k;

t_k is the interval, expressed in years and fractions of a year, between the date of the first drawdown and the date of each subsequent drawdown, thus $t_1 = 0$;

m' is the number of the last repayment or payment of charges;

l is the number of a repayment or payment of charges;

D_l is the amount of a repayment or payment of charges;

S_l is the interval, expressed in years and fractions of a year, between the date of the first drawdown and the date of each repayment or payment of charges

(3)   For the purposes of (2)

    (a)   the amounts paid by both parties at different times shall not necessarily be equal and shall not necessarily be paid at equal intervals;

    (b)   the starting date shall be that of the first drawdown;

    (c)   intervals between dates used in the calculations shall be expressed in years or in fractions of a year;

    (d)   a year is assumed to have 365 days (366 days for leap years), 52 weeks or 12 equal months;

    (e)   an equal month is assumed to have 30.41666 days (365/12) regardless of whether or not it is a leap year;

    (f)   the result of the calculation shall be expressed with an accuracy of at least one decimal place; if the figure at the following decimal place is greater than or equal to 5, the figure at that particular decimal place shall be increased by one;

    (g)   the equation can be rewritten as set out in (h) using a single sum and the concept of flows (A_k), which will be positive or negative, either paid or received during periods *l* to *k*, expressed in years;

    (h)   the equation referred to in (g) is

$$S = \sum_{k=1}^{n} A_k(1+X)^{-t_k}$$

S being the present balance of flows; if the aim is to maintain the equivalence of flows, the value will be zero.

1.3   EXEMPTION OF CERTAIN CREDIT AGREEMENTS SECURED ON LAND

Interpretation

App 1.3.1 R   FCA

(1)   This section specifies:

    (a)   the *persons* or classes of *persons* to whom the exemption in article 60E(2) of the *Regulated Activities Order* applies; and

    (b)   the agreements or classes of agreement to which the exemption in article 60E(2) of the *Regulated Activities Order* applies.

(2)   Where the *lender* is a body specified in **CONC App 1.3.2 R** or an *authorised person* with *permission* to *accept deposits*, article 60E(2) of the *Regulated Activities Order* applies only to

    (a)   a *borrower-lender-supplier agreement* falling within (a) or (c) of the definition of *relevant credit agreement relating to the purchase of land*;

    (b)   a *borrower-lender agreement* secured by any *legal or equitable mortgage* on *land* to finance

        (i)   the purchase of *land*; or

        (ii)   the provision of dwellings or *business premises* on any *land*; or

        (iii)   subject to (3) below, the alteration, enlarging, repair or improvement of a dwelling or *business premises* on any *land*;

    (c)   a *borrower-lender agreement* secured by any *legal or equitable mortgage* on *land* to refinance any existing indebtedness of the *borrower*, whether to the *lender* or another *person*, under any agreement by which the *borrower* was provided with *credit* for any of the purposes specified in (b)(i) to (iii) above.

(3)   (2)(b)(iii) above applies only

    (a)   where the *lender* is the *lender* under

        (i)   an agreement (whenever made) by which the *borrower* is provided with *credit* for any of the purposes specified in (2)(b)(i) and (2)(b)(ii); or

        (ii)   an agreement (whenever made) refinancing an agreement under which the *borrower* is provided with *credit* for any of the said purposes,

        being, in either case, an agreement relating to the *land* referred to in (2)(b)(iii) and secured by a *legal or equitable mortgage* on that *land*; or

    (b)   where a *borrower-lender agreement* to *finance* the alteration, enlarging, repair or improvement of a dwelling, secured by a *legal or equitable mortgage* on that dwelling, is made as a result of any such services as are described in section 4(3)(e) of the Housing Associations Act 1985 which are certified as having been provided by

        (i)   a *local authority*;

        (ii)   a housing association within the meaning of section 1 of the Housing Associations Act 1985 or article 3 of the Housing (Northern Ireland) Order 1992;

(iii)   a body established by such a housing association for the purpose of providing such services as are described in the said section 4(3)(e) of the Housing Associations Act 1985;

(iv)   a charity;

(v)   the National Home Improvement Council;

(vi)   the Northern Ireland Housing Executive; or

(vii)   a body, or a body of any description, that has been approved by the Secretary of State under section 169(4)(c) of the Local Government and Housing Act 1989 or the Department of the Environment for Northern Ireland under article 103(4)(c) of the Housing (Northern Ireland) Order 1992.

(4)   Where the *lender* is a body specified in **CONC App 1.3.3 R**, the exemption in article 60E(2) of the *Regulated Activities Order* applies only to an agreement of a description specified in that rule in relation to that body and made pursuant to an enactment or for a purpose so specified.

(5)   Where the *lender* is a body specified in **CONC App 1.3.4 R**, the exemption in article 60E (2) of the *Regulated Activities Order* applies only to an agreement of a description falling within **CONC App 1.3.1 R (2)(A)** to **CONC App 1.3.1 R (2)(C)**, being an agreement advancing money on the security of a dwelling-house.

App 1.3.2 R   FCA

Bodies whose agreements of the specified description are exempt agreements
INSURANCE COMPANIES
Abbey Life Assurance Company Limited
Abbey Life Pension and Annuities Limited
Albany Life Assurance Company Limited
Allchurches Life Assurance Limited
Alliance Assurance Company Limited
Allied Dunbar Assurance PLC
Ambassador Life Assurance Company Limited
American Life Insurance Company
Ansvar Insurance Company Limited
Atlas Assurance Company Limited
Australian Mutual Provident Society
Avon Insurance PLC
Black Horse Life Assurance Company Limited
Bradford Insurance Company Limited
Britannic Assurance Public Limited Company
The British & European Reinsurance Company Limited
British Equitable Assurance Company Limited
The British Life Office Limited
The British Oak Insurance Company Limited
British Reserve Insurance Company Limited
Caledonian Insurance Company
The Cambrian Insurance Company Limited
The Canada Life Assurance Company
Cannon Assurance Limited
Car and General Insurance Corporation Limited
City of Westminster Assurance Company Limited
City of Westminster Assurance Society Limited
Clerical, Medical and General Life Assurance Society
Colonial Life (UK) Limited
The Colonial Mutual Life Assurance Society Limited
Commercial Union Assurance Company plc
Commercial Union Pensions Management Limited
Commercial Union Life Assurance Company Limited
Confederation Life Insurance Company
The Contingency Insurance Company Limited

Bodies whose agreements of the specified description are exempt agreements

Co-operative Insurance Society Limited
Cornhill Insurance Public Limited Company
Criterion Insurance Company Limited
Crown Life Assurance Company Limited
Crown Life Insurance Company Limited
Crown Life Pensions Limited
Crusader Insurance PLC
The Dominion Insurance Company Limited
Eagle Star Insurance Company Limited
Ecclesiastical Insurance Office plc
Economic Insurance Company Limited
English & American Insurance Company Limited
The Equitable Life Assurance Society
Equico International Limited
Equity & Law Life Assurance Society plc
Essex and Suffolk Insurance Company Limited
Excess Insurance Company Limited
Federation Mutual Insurance Limited
Fine Art and General Insurance Company Limited
Friends' Provident Life Office
FS Assurance Limited
General Accident Fire and Life Assurance Corporation Public Limited Company
General Accident Life Assurance Limited
General Accident Linked Life Assurance Limited
General Portfolio Life Insurance Public Limited Company
Gisborne Life Assurance Company Limited
Gresham Life Assurance Society Limited
Guardian Assurance plc
Guardian Royal Exchange Assurance plc
Hill Samuel Life Assurance Limited
The Ideal Insurance Company Limited
The Imperial Life Assurance Company of Canada
Irish Life Assurance plc
The Iron Trades Employers Insurance Association Limited
Legal and General Assurance Society Limited
The Licenses and General Insurance Company Limited
The Life Association of Scotland Limited
London Aberdeen & Northern Mutual Assurance Society Limited
London and Manchester Assurance Company Limited
London and Manchester (Pensions) Limited
London & Scottish Assurance Corporation Limited
The London Assurance
The London Life Association Limited
The Manufacturers Life Insurance Company
Marine and General Mutual Life Assurance Society
Maritime Insurance Company Limited
Medical Sickness Annuity & Life Assurance Society Limited
The Mercantile and General Reinsurance Company plc
Midland Assurance Limited
The Motor Union Insurance Company Limited
Minister Insurance Company Limited

Bodies whose agreements of the specified description are exempt agreements

Municipal Life Assurance Limited
Municipal Mutual Insurance Limited
NALGO Insurance Association Limited
National Employers' Life Assurance Company Limited
National Employers' Mutual General Insurance Association Limited
The National Farmers Union Mutual Insurance Society Limited
National House-Building Council
The National Insurance and Guarantee Corporation PLC
The National Mutual Life Association of Australasia Limited
National Mutual Life Assurance Society
National Provident Institution
National Vulcan Engineering Insurance Group Limited
N.E.L. Pensions Limited
The New Zealand Insurance plc
North British & Mercantile Insurance Company Limited
The Northern Assurance Company Limited
Norwich Union Asset Management Limited
Norwich Union Fire Insurance Society Limited
Norwich Union Insurance Group (Pensions Management) Limited
Norwich Union Life Insurance Society
NRG London Reinsurance Company Limited
Oaklife Assurance Limited
The Ocean Accident & Guarantee Corporation Limited
The Orion Insurance Company P.L.C.
Pearl Assurance Public Limited Company
Pensions Management (SWF) Limited
Permanent Insurance Company Limited
Phoenix Assurance Public Limited Company
Pioneer Mutual Insurance Company Limited
Prolific Life and Pensions Limited
Property Growth Pensions & Annuities Limited
Provident Life Association Limited
Provident Mutual Life Assurance Association
Provincial Insurance Public Limited Company
The Prudential Assurance Company Limited
Railway Passengers Assurance Company
Refuge Assurance, public Limited company
Regency Life Assurance Company Limited
The Reliance Fire and Accident Insurance Corporation Limited
The Reliance Marine Insurance Company Limited
Reliance Mutual Insurance Society Limited
Royal Exchange Assurance
Royal Insurance Public Limited Company
Royal Insurance (Int.) Limited
Royal Insurance (U.K.) Limited
Royal Life Insurance Limited
Royal Life (Unit Linked Assurances) Limited
Royal Life (Unit Linked Pension Funds) Limited
The Royal London Mutual Insurance Society Limited
The Royal National Pension Fund for Nurses
Royal Reinsurance Company Limited

Bodies whose agreements of the specified description are exempt agreements

Schroder Life Assurance Limited

Scottish Amicable Life Assurance Society

Scottish Equitable Life Assurance Society

Scottish General Insurance Company Limited

Scottish Insurance Corporation Limited

The Scottish Life Assurance Company

The Scottish Mutual Assurance Society

The Scottish Provident Institution

Scottish Union and National Insurance Company

Scottish Widows' Fund and Life Assurance Society

Sentinel Life plc

Skandia Life Assurance Company Limited

Standard Life Assurance Company

Standard Life Pension Funds Limited

The State Assurance Company Limited

Suffolk Life Annuities Limited

Sun Alliance and London Assurance Company Limited

Sun Insurance Office Limited

Sun Life Assurance Company of Canada

Sun Life Assurance Society plc

Target Life Assurance Company Limited

Teachers Assurance Company Limited

Trident Investors Life Assurance Company Limited

Trident Life Assurance Company Limited

Trinity Insurance Company Limited

UK Life Assurance Company Limited

United British Insurance Company Limited

United Friendly Insurance plc

United Kingdom Temperance and General Provident Institution

United Standard Insurance Company Limited

The University Life Assurance Society

The Victory Reinsurance Company Limited

Wesleyan and General Assurance Society

The Western Australian Insurance Company Limited

The White Cross Insurance Company Limited

World-Wide Reassurance Company Limited

The Yorkshire Insurance Company Limited

Zurich Life Assurance Company Limited

FRIENDLY SOCIETIES

The Ancient Order of Foresters Friendly Society

Anglo-Saxons Friendly Society

Blackburn Philanthropic Mutual Assurance Society

British Benefit Society

British Order of Ancient Free Gardeners' Friendly Society

Brunel Assurance Society

Cirencester Benefit Society

Civil Servants' Annuities Assurance Society

Colmore Friendly Society

Coventry Assurance Society

Dentists' Provident Society

Devon and Exeter Women's Equitable Benefit Society

Bodies whose agreements of the specified description are exempt agreements

The Exeter Equitable Friendly Society

Grand United Order of Oddfellows Friendly Society

The Hampshire and General Friendly Society

Harvest Friendly Society

Hearts of Oak Benefit Society

The Ideal Benefit Society

Independent Order of Oddfellows Kingston Unity Friendly Society

The Independent Order of Odd Fellows Manchester Unity Friendly Society

The Independent Order of Rechabites, Salford Unity, Friendly Society

Leeds District of the Ancient Order of Foresters Investment Association

Leek Assurance Collecting Society

The Leicester District Foresters' Investment Society

Liverpool Victoria Friendly Society

The Manchester and Districts of the Ancient Order of Foresters Investment Association

National Deposit Friendly Society

National Equalized Druids Friendly Society

National United Order of Free Gardeners Friendly Society

New Tab Friendly Society

Northumberland and Durham Miners' Permanent Relief Fund Friendly Society

Nottingham Oddfellows Assurance Friendly Society

The Order of Druids Friendly Society

The Order of the Sons of Temperance Friendly Society

Original Holloway Society

Pioneer Benefit Society

Preston Catholic Collecting Society

Preston Shelley Assurance Collecting Society

Provident Reliance Friendly Society

Rational and County Assurance Society

Royal Liver Friendly Society

Scottish Friendly Assurance Society

The Scottish Legal Life Assurance Society

The Shepherds Friendly Society

Sons of Scotland Temperance Friendly Society

Stepney District Distressed Members' Pension Benevolent Fund

The Sussex Widow and Orphans Society

Teachers Provident Society

Time Assurance Society

Tunbridge Wells Equitable Friendly Society

Tunstall and District Assurance Collecting Society

United Ancient Order of Druids Friendly Society

United Kingdom Civil Service Benefit Society

United Patriots' National Benefit Society

West Surrey General Benefit Society

Widow and Orphan Fund of the Woolwich District of the Independent Order of Odd Fellows, Manchester Unity Friendly Society

Widow and Orphans' Fund, Stepney District of the Independent Order of Odd Fellows, Manchester Unity Friendly Society

Widow, Widowers and Orphans' Fund of the Godalming District of the Independent Order of Oddfellows, Manchester Unity, Friendly Society

Wiltshire Holloway Benefit Society

CHARITIES

The Central Board of Finance of the Church of England

Bodies whose agreements of the specified description are exempt agreements
Church Commissioners
The Church of England Pensions Board
The Church of Scotland
The Church of Scotland General Trustees
Church of Scotland Trust
The Representative Body of the Church in Wales
Timber Trades Benevolent Society
The Winchester Diocesan Board of Finance
York Diocesan Board of Finance Limited
AGRICULTURAL CORPORATIONS
The Agricultural Mortgage Corporation Public Limited Company
The Scottish Agricultural Securities Corporation Public Limited Company
OTHER BODIES
General Practice Finance Corporation Limited

App 1.3.3 R   FCA

Bodies Corporate	Description of Agreement and Enactments
	LAND IMPROVEMENT COMPANIES
The Lands Improvement Company:	*Relevant credit agreements relating to the purchase of land*, being agreements made pursuant to
	(a) the Lands Improvement Company's Acts 1853 to 1969; or
	(b) the Improvement of Land Acts 1864 and 1899.
	BODIES CORPORATE NAMED OR SPECIFICALLY REFERRED TO IN A PUBLIC GENERAL ACT – UNITED KINGDOM
The Greater London Authority	*Relevant credit agreements relating to the purchase of land*, being agreements made under the Authority's power to give financial assistance under section 30 of the Greater London Authority Act 1999.
Homes and Communities Agency	*Relevant credit agreements relating to the purchase of land*, being agreements made under the Agency's powers to give financial assistance under section 19 of the Housing and Regeneration Act 2008.
The Eastern Electricity Board:	Agreements of a description falling within **CONC APP 1.3.1 R (2)(A)** to **CONC APP 1.3.1 R (2)(C)**, being agreements made between the Board and employees or prospective employees of the Board pursuant to section 2(5) of the Electricity Act 1947.
The Electricity Council:	Agreements of a description falling within **CONC APP 1.3.1 R (2)(A)** to **CONC APP 1.3.1 R (2)(C)**, being agreements made between the Council and employees or prospective employees of the Council pursuant to section 2(5) of the Electricity Act 1947, as applied in relation to the Council by section 3(6) of the Electricity Act 1957.
The London Docklands Development Corporation:	Agreements of a description falling within **CONC APP 1.3.1 R (2)(A)** to **CONC APP 1.3.1 R (2)(C)**, being agreements made pursuant to section 136 of the Local Government, Planning and Land Act 1980.
The London Electricity Board:	Agreements of a description falling within **CONC APP 1.3.1 R (2)(A)** to **CONC APP 1.3.1 R (2)(C)**, being agreements made between the Board and employees or prospective employees of the Board pursuant to section 2(5) of the Electricity Act 1947.
The North Eastern Electricity Board:	Agreements of a description falling within **CONC APP 1.3.1 R (2)(A)** to **CONC APP 1.3.1 R (2)(C)**, being agreements made between the Board and employees or prospective employees of the Board pursuant to section 2(5) of the Electricity Act 1947.
Sea Fish Industry Authority:	*Relevant credit agreements relating to the purchase of land*, being agreements made pursuant to section 3(1)(e) and (f) of the Fisheries Act 1981.
The South Eastern Electricity Board:	Agreements of a description falling within **CONC APP 1.3.1 R (2)(A)** to **CONC APP 1.3.1 R (2)(C)**, being agreements made between the Board and employees or prospective employees of the Board pursuant to section 2(5) of the Electricity Act 1947.

The South Western Electricity Board:	Agreements of a description falling within **CONC App 1.3.1 R (2)(A)** to **CONC App 1.3.1 R (2)(C)**, being agreements made between the Board and employees or prospective employees of the Board pursuant to section 2(5) of the Electricity Act 1947.
The Southern Electricity Board:	Agreements of a description falling within **CONC App 1.3.1 R (2)(A)** to **CONC App 1.3.1 R (2)(C)**, being agreements made between the Board and employees or prospective employees of the Board pursuant to section 2(5) of the Electricity Act 1947.
The Yorkshire Electricity Board:	Agreements of a description falling within **CONC App 1.3.1 R (2)(A)** to **CONC App 1.3.1 R (2)(C)**, being agreements made between the Board and employees or prospective employees of the Board pursuant to section 2(5) of the Electricity Act 1947.

NORTHERN IRELAND

Eastern Health and Social Services Board:	*Relevant credit agreements relating to the purchase of land*, being agreements made pursuant to article 59 of and Schedule 9 to the Health and Personal Social Services (Northern Ireland) Order 1972.
Northern Health and Social Services Board:	*Relevant credit agreements relating to the purchase of land*, being agreements made pursuant to article 59 of and Schedule 9 to the Health and Personal Social Services (Northern Ireland) Order 1972
Southern Health and Social Services Board:	*Relevant credit agreements relating to the purchase of land*, being agreements made pursuant to article 59 of and Schedule 9 to the Health and Personal Social Services (Northern Ireland) Order 1972.
Welsh Ministers	*Relevant credit agreements relating to the purchase of land*, being agreements falling within **CONC App 1.3.1 R (2)(A)** to **CONC App 1.3.1 R (2)(C)** which are made pursuant to section 36 of the New Towns Act 1981 and which related to property of the Commission for the New Towns transferred to them under a scheme made under section 51(1) of the Housing and Regeneration Act 2008.
Western Health and Social Services Board:	*Relevant credit agreements relating to the purchase of land* being agreements made pursuant to article 59 of and Schedule 9 to the Health and Personal Social Services (Northern Ireland) Order 1972.

App 1.3.4 R   FCA

BODIES CORPORATE NAMED OR SPECIFICALLY REFERRED TO IN AN ORDER MADE UNDER SECTION 156(4), 444(1) OR 447(2)(a) OF THE HOUSING ACT 1985

Abbey Life Executive Mortgages Limited

Abbey Life Funding Limited

Abbey Life Home Loans Limited

Abbey Life Home Services Limited

Abbey Life Mortgage Finance Limited

Abbey Life Mortgage Loans Limited

Abbey Life Mortgage Securities Limited

Abbey Life Residential Loans Limited

Albion Home Loans Limited

Alliance & Leicester Mortgage Loans Limited

Alliance & Leicester Mortgage Loans (No. 2) Limited

Alliance & Leicester Mortgage Loans (No. 3) Limited

Alliance & Leicester Mortgage Loans (No. 4) Limited

Bradford & Bingley Homeloans Limited

Bradford & Bingley Homeloans Management Limited

Bradford & Bingley Loans Limited

Bradford & Bingley Management Limited

Bradford & Bingley Mortgages Limited

Bradford & Bingley Mortgage Management Limited

Bradford & Bingley Secured Loans Limited

Bradford & Bingley Secured Loans Management Limited

Britannia Mortgage Company Number One Limited

BODIES CORPORATE NAMED OR SPECIFICALLY REFERRED TO IN AN ORDER MADE UNDER SECTION 156(4), 444(1) OR 447(2)(a) OF THE HOUSING ACT 1985

Britannia Mortgage Company Number Two Limited

Chelsea Mortgage Services Limited

CIS Home Loans Limited

CIS Mortgage Finance Limited

CIS Mortgage Maker Limited

CIS Residential Mortgages Limited

CL Mortgages Limited

Darlington Mortgage Services Limited

Derbyshire Home Loans Limited

General Portfolio Finance Limited

Gracechurch Mortgage Finance (No. 2) PLC

Gracechurch Mortgage Finance (No. 3) PLC

Halifax Loans Limited

Halifax Loans (No. 2) Limited

Halifax Loans (No. 3) Limited

Halifax Loans (No. 4) Limited

HMC First Home National PLC

Home Loans Direct Limited

Home Loans Direct Funding PLC

Household Mortgage Corporation PLC

Ipswich Mortgage Services Limited

LBS Mortgages Limited

Leamington Mortgage Corporation Limited

Leeds & Holbeck Mortgage Corporation Limited

Leeds & Holbeck Mortgage Funding Limited

Legal and General Mortgage Services Limited

Lombard Home Loans Limited

London and Manchester (Mortgages) (No. 1) Limited

London and Manchester (Mortgages) (No. 2) Limited

London and Manchester (Mortgages) (No. 3) Limited

London and Manchester (Mortgages) (No. 4) Limited

London and Manchester (Mortgages) (No. 5) Limited

Market Harborough Mortgages Limited

The Mortgage Corporation Limited

The National Home Loans Corporation plc

National Mutual Home Loans plc

National Westminster Home Loans Limited

Newbury Mortgage Services Limited

Northern Rock Mortgage Services Limited

North Yorkshire Mortgages Limited

Norwich and Peterborough (LBS) Limited

Norwich Union Mortgage Finance Limited

Royal London Homebuy Limited

Saffron Walden Mortgage Services Limited

Secured Residential Funding PLC

Stroud and Swindon Mortgage Company Limited

Stroud and Swindon Mortgage Company (No. 2) Limited

Sun Life of Canada Home Loans Limited

Wesleyan Home Loans Limited

West Bromwich Mortgage Company Limited

1.4 EXEMPTION FOR HIGH NET WORTH BORROWERS AND HIRERS AND EXEMPTION RELATING TO BUSINESSES

Exemption for high net worth borrowers and hirers

App 1.4.1 R   FCA
(1) For the purposes of articles 60H(c) and 60Q(b) of the *Regulated Activities Order*, a declaration made by the *borrower* or *hirer* which provides that the *borrower* or *hirer* agrees to forgo the protection and remedies that would be available to the *borrower* or *hirer* if the agreement were a *regulated credit agreement* or a *regulated consumer hire agreement* must comply with **CONC APP 1.4.2 R** and **CONC APP 1.4.6 R**.
(2) For the purposes of articles 60H(d) and 60Q(c) of the *Regulated Activities Order*, a statement in relation to the income or assets of the *borrower* or *hirer* (referred to in this section as a statement of high net worth) must comply with **CONC APP 1.4.3 R**, **CONC APP 1.4.4 R** and **CONC APP 1.4.7 R**.
(3) For the purposes of articles 60H(e) and 60Q(d) of the *Regulated Activities Order*, the statement in (2) must be made during the period of one year ending with the day on which the agreement was made.

App 1.4.2 R   FCA
A declaration for the purposes of articles 60H(c) and 60Q(b) of the *Regulated Activities Order* shall
(1) be set out in the *credit agreement* or *consumer hire agreement* no less prominently than other information in the agreement and be readily distinguishable from the background medium; and
(2) be signed by the *borrower* or *hirer*, unless the agreement is so signed.

App 1.4.3 R   FCA
(1) Subject to **CONC APP 1.4.4 R**, a statement of high net worth shall be signed by
   (a) the *lender* or *owner*; or
   (b) an accountant who is a member of any of the bodies listed (2).
(2) The bodies referred to in (1)(b) are:
   (a) the Institute of Chartered Accountants in England and Wales;
   (b) the Institute of Chartered Accountants of Scotland;
   (c) the Institute of Chartered Accounts in Ireland;
   (d) the Association of Chartered Certified Accountants;
   (e) the Chartered Institute of Management Accountants;
   (f) the Chartered Institute of Public Finance and Accountancy;
   (g) a professional body for accountants established in a jurisdiction outside the United Kingdom.

App 1.4.4 R   FCA
A person who is
(1) the *lender* or *owner*;
(2) an employee or agent of the *lender* or *owner* or a *person* who otherwise acts on behalf of the *lender* or *owner* in relation to the *credit agreement* or *consumer hire agreement*; or
(3) an *associate* of the *lender* or *owner*,
may only make a statement of high net worth if the *lender* or *owner* is a *person* who has *Part 4A permission* to *accept deposits*.

Declaration for exemption relating to businesses

App 1.4.5 R   FCA
A declaration for the purposes of articles 60C or 60O of the *Regulated Activities Order* shall
(1) comply with **CONC APP 1.4.8 R**;
(2) be set out in the *credit agreement* or *consumer hire agreement* no less prominently than other information in the agreement and be readily distinguishable from the background medium; and
(3) be signed by the *borrower* or *hirer* or where the *borrower* or *hirer* is a *partnership* or unincorporated body of persons be signed by, or on behalf of, the *borrower* or *hirer*, unless the agreement is so signed.

Declaration by high net worth borrower or hirer

App 1.4.6 R   FCA
The declaration for the purposes of articles 60H(c) and 60Q(b) of the *Regulated Activities Order* must have the following form and content-
"**Declaration by high net worth borrower or hirer**
(articles 60H and 60Q of the Financial Services and Markets Act 2000 (Regulated Activities)

Order 2001)

I confirm that I have received a copy of the statement of high net worth made in relation to me for the purposes of article 60H(d) or article 60Q(c) of the Financial Services and Markets Act 2000 (Regulated Activities) Order 2001.

I understand that by making this declaration I will not have the benefit of the protection and remedies that would be available to me under the Financial Services and Markets Act 2000 or the Consumer Credit Act 1974 if this agreement were a regulated agreement under those Acts.

I understand that this declaration does not affect the powers of the court to make an order under section 140B of the Consumer Credit Act 1974 in relation to a credit agreement where it determines that the relationship between the lender and the borrower is unfair to the borrower.*

I am aware that if I am in any doubt as to the consequences of making this declaration then I should seek independent legal advice".

This section should be omitted in the case of a consumer hire agreement

Statement of high net worth

App 1.4.7 R   FCA

A statement of high net worth for the purposes of articles 60H(d) and 60Q(c) of the *Regulated Activities Order* must have the following form and content:

"Statement of High Net Worth
(articles 60H and 60Q of the Financial Services and Markets Act 2000 (Regulated Activities) Order 2001)

I/We* (insert full name).. of (insert address and postcode)... confirm that I am/we* are a person qualified to make a statement of high net worth under rules made by the Financial Conduct Authority, by virtue of the fact that..

In my/our* opinion (insert full name of borrower or hirer)
....

of (insert address and post code of borrower or hirer)
....
....

is an individual of high net worth because he/she*

(a) received during the previous financial year net income totalling an amount of not less than £150,000*; and/or

(b) had throughout that year net assets with a total value of not less than £500,000*.

(insert one of the following declarations as appropriate)

I/We* declare that I am/we are* not connected to [insert name of the lender(s)/owner(s)][any person who is a lender/owner offering credit agreements/consumer hire agreements*].

I/We* declare that I am/we are* [connected to] [insert name of lender(s)/owner(s)] as I am/we are* [the lender(s)/owner(s)/an employee of/an agent of the lender(s)//owner(s)/a person who otherwise acts on behalf of the lender(s)//owner(s) in relation to the credit agreement/consumer hire agreement/an associate of the lender(s)//owner(s)].*

I/We declare that I am/we are*/[a/an] lender(s)/owner(s) offering credit agreements/consumer hire agreements/ an employee of/an agent of/a person who otherwise acts on behalf of/ an associate of lender(s)/owner(s) offering credit agreements/consumer hire agreements.*

In this statement—

(a) "associate" shall be construed in accordance with article 60L of the Financial Services and Markets Act 2000 (Regulated Activities) Order 2001;

(b) "financial year" means a period of one year ending with 31st March;

(c) "net assets" shall not include—

(i) the value of the borrower's or hirer's primary residence or any loan secured on that residence;

(ii) any rights of the borrower or hirer under a qualifying contract of insurance within the meaning of the Financial Services and Markets Act 2000 (Regulated Activities) Order 2001; and

(iii) any benefits (in the form of pensions or otherwise) which are payable on the termination of the service of the borrower or hirer or on his retirement and to which he is (or his dependents are), or may be, entitled.

(d) "net income" means the total income of the borrower or hirer from all sources reduced by the amount of income tax and national insurance contributions payable in respect of it; and

(e) "previous financial year" means the financial year immediately preceding the financial year during which the statement is made".

Delete as appropriate.

Declaration for exemption relating to businesses

App 1.4.8 R   FCA

A declaration for the purposes of articles 60C or 60O of the *Regulated Activities Order* must have the following form and content

"Declaration for exemption relating to businesses
(articles 60C and 60O of the Financial Services and Markets Act 2000 (Regulated Activities)

Order 2001)

I am/We are* entering this agreement wholly or predominantly for the purposes of a business carried on by me/us or intended to be carried on by me/us.

I/We* understand that I/We* will not have the benefit of the protection and remedies that would be available to me/us* under the Financial Services and Markets Act 2000 or under the Consumer Credit Act 1974 if this agreement were a regulated agreement under those Acts.

I/We* understand that this declaration does not affect the powers of the court to make an order under section 140B of the Consumer Credit Act 1974 in relation to a credit agreement where it determines that the relationship between the lender and the borrower is unfair to the borrower.**

I am/We are aware that, if I am/we are in any doubts as to the consequences of the agreement not being regulated by the Financial Services and Markets Act 2000 or the Consumer Credit Act 1974, then I/we* should seek independent legal advice.".

**Delete as appropriate.*

***This section should be omitted in the case of a consumer hire agreement.*

TRANSITIONAL PROVISIONS AND SCHEDULES

TRANSITIONAL PROVISIONS FOR PRUDENTIAL PROVISIONS IN RELATION TO DEBT MANAGEMENT FIRMS

[3.94]

(1)	(2) Material to which the transitional provision applies	(3)	(4) Transitional provision	(5) Transitional provision: dates in force	(6) Handbook provision coming into force
5.1	CONC 10.3.3 R		A *firm* can calculate its prudential resources without deducting items 2 and 3 in CONC 10.3.3 R	From 1 April 2014 to 31 March 2017	1 April 2014
5.2	CONC 10.3.5 R		b = items 1, 4 and 5 in the Table of items which must be deducted from a *firm's* prudential resources (see CONC 10.3.3 R)	From 1 April 2014 to 31 March 2017	1 April 2014
5.3	CONC 10.3.6 G		The *guidance* at CONC 10.3.6 G should be read in the light of TP 5. 2	From 1 April 2014 to 31 March 2017	1 April 2014

TRANSITIONAL PROVISIONS FOR FINANCIAL PROMOTIONS AND COMMUNICATIONS IN RELATION TO CATALOGUES ETC.

(1)	(2) Material to which the transitional provision applies	(3)	(4) Transitional provision	(5) Transitional provision: dates in force	(6) Handbook provision coming into force
6.1	CONC 3	R	A *firm* will not contravene a rule in CONC 3 to the extent that a *financial promotion* or communication referred to in 6.2 would comply, as the case may be, with the Consumer Credit (Advertisements) Regulations 2010 or the Consumer Credit (Advertisements) Regulations 2004 (assuming they had not been repealed by Article 21 of the Financial Services and Markets Act 2000 (Regulated Activities) (Amendment) (No 2) Order 2013).	From 1 April 2014 to 31 March 2015	1 April 2014

| 6.2 | | R | A *financial promotion* or a communication first communicated to the public in a catalogue, diary or work of reference comprising at least fifty printed pages copies of which are first communicated before 1 October 2014 and which in a reasonably prominent position either contains the date of its first publication or specifies a period being a calendar or seasonal period throughout which it is intended to have effect. | From 1 April 2014 to 31 March 2015 | 1 April 2014 |

SCH 1   RECORD KEEPING REQUIREMENTS

| 1.1 | G | The aim of the *guidance* in the following table is to give the reader a quick overall view of the relevant record keeping requirements in *CONC*. |
| 1.2 | G | It is not a complete statement of those requirements and should not be relied on as if it were. |

Handbook reference	Subject of record	Contents of record	When record must be made	Retention period
4.4.3 R(6)(a)	Information notice	A copy of the notice, and details of the date on which and the manner by which it was sent	When the notice is sent	18 months from the date on which the notice is sent
4.4.3 R(6)(b)	Customer confirmation	A copy of the confirmation, and details of the date on which and the manner by which it was received	When the confirmation is received	18 months from the date on which the confirmation is received
6.6.3 R	Actions concerning articles taken in *pawn*.	Specified details concerning taking articles in *pawn*, redemption and sale of articles in *pawn*.	Date of event referred to in section.	At least the longer of 5 years from the date on which an article is taken in *pawn* or 3 years from date of sale under section 121(1) of the *CCA* or the redemption of the article as the case may be.
7.13.2 R	An *individual* who is, or is treated as, a *borrower* under a *credit agreement* or *consumer hire agreement*.	Accurate and adequate data (including in respect of debt and repayment history) in relation to *individuals* owing, or treated as owing, money under *credit agreements* or *consumer hire agreements*.	When a *firm* is notified in relation to an *individual* whom it is to pursue for recovery of a debt.	Not specified.
7.13.7 R	An *individual* not being the *borrower* under a *credit agreement* or *consumer hire agreement*.	Record that the *individual* is not the *borrower* and should not be pursued for debt.	Date on which the *firm* is aware of true state of affairs.	Not specified.

Handbook reference	Subject of record	Contents of record	When record must be made	Retention period
8.8.1 R(9)	Record of *debt management plans* entered into with *customers*.	An adequate record.	When the *firm* enters into *debt management plan*.	Until the contract between the *customer* and the *firm* is completed or terminated.
11.1.9 R	Exercise of right to cancel under **CONC 11.1.1 R**.	Adequate record of use of right to cancel by *consumer*.	Date of exercise.	3 years.

SCH 2   NOTIFICATION AND REPORTING REQUIREMENTS (IF ANY)

	Handbook reference	Matter to be notified	Contents of notification	Trigger event	Time allowed
G	**CONC 10.2.14 R**	Any change in a *firm's* prudential resources requirement	The changed prudential resources requirement	The change in the *firm's* prudential resources requirement	Within 14 *days* of the trigger event

SCH 3   FEES AND OTHER REQUIRED PAYMENT

Not used

SCH 4   NOT USED

Not used

SCH 5   RIGHTS OF ACTION FOR DAMAGES

Sch 5.1	G	The table below sets out the *rules* in *CONC* contravention of which by an *authorised person* may be actionable under section 138D of the *Act* (Actions for damages) by a *person* who suffers loss as a result of the contravention.
Sch 5.2	G	If a "Yes" appears in the column headed "For private person?", the *rule* may be actionable by a *"private person"* under section 138D (or, in certain circumstances, his fiduciary or representative; see article 6(2) and (3)(c) of the Financial Services and Markets Act 2000 (Rights of Action) Regulations 2001 (SI 2001/2256)). A "Yes" in the column headed "Removed" indicates that the *FCA* has removed the right of action under section 138D(2) of the *Act*. If so, a reference to the *rule* in which it is removed is also given.
Sch 5.3	G	The column headed "For other person?" indicates whether the *rule* may be actionable by a *person* other than a *private person* (or his fiduciary or representative) under article 6(2) and (3) of those Regulations. If so, an indication of the type of *person* by whom the rule may be actionable is given.

			Right of action under section 138D		
Chapter/ Appendix	Section/ Annex	Paragraph	For private person?	Removed?	For other person?
The clear, fair and not misleading *rule* in **CONC 3.3.1 R**			Yes (Notes 2 & 3)	In part (Note 1)	No
The prudential *rules* for *debt management firms* and *not-for-profit debt advice bodies* in **CONC 10**			No	Yes, **CONC 10.1.6 R**	No
All other *rules* in *CONC*			Yes (Notes 2 & 3)	No	No

Notes

(1)	**CONC 3.3.1 R (2)** provides that if, in relation to a particular communication or *financial promotion*, a *firm* takes reasonable steps to ensure it complies with the clear, fair and not misleading *rule*, a contravention of that rule does not give rise to a right of action under section 138D of the *Act*.

(2) The definition of private person includes a "relevant recipient of credit" which is defined on article 60L of the *Regulated Activities Order* as "a partnership consisting of two or three persons not all of whom are bodies corporate, or an unincorporated body of persons which does not consist entirely of bodies corporate and is not a partnership".

(3) The definition of private person includes a person who is, by virtue of article 36J of that Order, to be regarded as a person who uses, may use, has or may have used or has or may have contemplated using, services provided by authorised persons in carrying on a *regulated activity* of the kind specified by article 36H of that Order or article 64 of that Order so far as relevant to that activity.

SCH 6   RULES THAT CAN BE WAIVED

6.1 As a result of section 138A of the *Act* (Modification or waiver of rules) the *FCA* has power to waive all its *rules*, other than *rules* made under section 137O (Threshold condition code), section 247 (Trust scheme rules) or section 248 (Scheme particulars rules) of the *Act*. However, if the *rules* incorporate requirements laid down in European directives, it will not be possible for the *FCA* to grant a waiver that would be incompatible with the *UK's* responsibilities under those directives.

K. DECISION PROCEDURE AND PENALTIES MANUAL (DEPP)

DECISION PROCEDURE AND PENALTIES MANUAL

a description of the FCA's procedures for taking statutory notice decisions, the FCA's policy on the imposition and amount of penalties and the conduct of interviews to which a direction under section 169(7) of the Act has been given or the FSA is considering giving with effect from 28 August 2007

CHAPTER 1
APPLICATION AND PURPOSE

1.1   APPLICATION AND PURPOSE

Application

[3.95]
1.1.1 G   FCA

This manual (*DEPP*) is relevant to *firms*, *approved persons* and other *persons*, whether or not they are regulated by the *FCA*. It sets out:

(1)   the *FCA's* decision-making procedure for giving *statutory notices*. These are *warning notices*, *decision notices* and *supervisory notices* (**DEPP 1.2** to **DEPP 5**);

(2)   the *FCA's* decision-making procedure in cases where the *PRA* is required to seek the *FCA's* consent before approving an application (a) for *Part 4A permission*; (b) for the variation of a *Part 4A permission*; or (c) to perform a *controlled function* (see **DEPP 2.5.7A G**);

(3)   the *FCA's* decision-making procedure where it is deciding under section 391(1)(c) of the *Act* to publish information about the matter to which a *warning notice* relates (see **DEPP 3.2.14A G** to **DEPP 3.2.14H G**);

(4)   the *FCA's* policy with respect to the imposition and amount of penalties under the *Act* (see **DEPP 6**);

(5)   the *FCA's* policy with respect to the imposition of suspensions or restrictions, and the period for which those suspensions or restrictions are to have effect, under the *Act* (see **DEPP 6A**);

(6)   the *FCA's* policy with respect to the conduct of interviews by investigators appointed in response to a request from an overseas regulator or an *EEA regulator* (**DEPP 7**).

Purpose

1.1.2 G   FCA

The purpose of DEPP is to satisfy the requirements of sections 63C(1), 69(1), 88C(1), 89S(1), 93(1), 124(1), 131FA, 131J(1), 169(9), 192N(1), 210(1), 312J(1), 345D(1) and 395 of the *Act* that the *FCA* publish the statements of procedure or policy referred to in **DEPP 1.1.1 G**.

1.2   INTRODUCTION TO STATUTORY NOTICES

Statutory and related notices

1.2.1 G   FCA

Section 395 of the *Act* (The *FCA's* and *PRA's* procedures) requires the *FCA* to publish a statement of its procedure for the giving of *statutory notices*. The procedure must be designed to secure, among other things, that the decision which gives rise to the obligation to give a *statutory notice* is taken by a person not directly involved in establishing the evidence on which that decision is based or by two or more persons who include a person not directly involved in establishing that evidence. The types of *statutory notices* and related notices, and the principal references to them in the *Act* and DEPP are set out in **DEPP 1.2.2 G**.

1.2.2 G   FCA

Table: Summary of statutory and related notices

Notice	Description	Act reference	Further information
Warning notice	Gives the recipient details about action that the *FCA* proposes to take and about the right to make representations.	Section 387	**DEPP 2.2**

Notice	Description	Act reference	Further information
Decision notice	Gives the recipient details about action that the *FCA* has decided to take. The *FCA* may also give a further *decision notice* if the recipient of the original *decision notice* consents.	Section 388	**DEPP 2.3**
Notice of discontinuance	Identifies proceedings set out in a *warning notice* or *decision notice* and which are not being taken or are being discontinued.	Section 389	**DEPP 1.2.4 G** and **DEPP 3.2.26 G**
Final notice	Sets out the terms of the action that the *FCA* is taking.	Section 390	**DEPP 1.2.4 G**
Supervisory notice	Gives the recipient details about action that the *FCA* has taken or proposes to take, for example to vary a *Part 4A permission*.	Section 395(13)	**DEPP 2.2** and **DEPP 2.3**

1.2.3 G   FCA

In DEPP the *supervisory notice* about a matter first given to the recipient is referred to as the "first *supervisory notice*" and the *supervisory notice* given after consideration of any representations is referred to as the "second *supervisory notice*".

1.2.4 G   FCA

The requirement in section 395 of the *Act* to publish a procedure for the giving of notices does not extend to the giving of a *notice of discontinuance* or a *final notice*. Neither of these notices is a *statutory notice* for the purposes of *DEPP*; nor is the decision to give such a notice a *statutory notice associated decision*.

Decisions relating to applications for authorisation or approval made to the PRA

1.2.4A G   FCA

Section 395 of the *Act* also requires the *FCA* to publish a statement of its procedure for decisions which gives rise to an obligation for the *PRA* to include a statement under section 387(1A) in a *warning notice* or a statement under section 388(1A) in a *decision notice* as follows:

(1)   Section 387(1A) provides that where the *FCA* proposes to refuse consent for the purposes of section 55F, 55I or 59 of the *Act*, or to give conditional consent as mentioned in section 55F(5) or 55I(8), the *warning notice* given by the *PRA* must (a) state that fact, and (b) give the reasons for the *FCA's* proposal.

(2)   Section 388(1A) provides that where the *FCA* has decided to refuse consent for the purposes of section 55F, 55I or 59 of the *Act*, or to give conditional consent as mentioned in section 55F(5) or 55I(8), the *decision notice* given by the *PRA* must (a) state that fact, and (b) give the reasons for the *FCA's* decision.

1.2.4B G   FCA

Where an application for *Part 4A permission* is made to the *PRA* as the appropriate regulator (section 55A(2)(a) of the *Act*), the *PRA* may only give permission with the consent of the *FCA* (section 55F of the *Act*). *FCA* consent can be conditional on the *PRA* imposing limitations or specifying the permission is for certain regulated activities only.

1.2.4C G   FCA

Where an application to vary a *Part 4A permission* is made to the *PRA* as the appropriate regulator (section 55A(2)(a) of the *Act*), the *PRA* may only give permission with the consent of the *FCA* (section 55I of the *Act*). The *FCA* may withhold its consent to a proposed variation if it appears to it that it is desirable to do so in order to advance one or more of its operational objectives. *FCA* consent can be conditional on the *PRA* imposing limitations, or the *PRA* specifying the permission is for certain regulated activities only.

1.2.4D G   FCA

Where an application to perform a *controlled function* is made to the *PRA* as the appropriate regulator, the *PRA* can only approve a person to perform a *controlled function* with the consent of the *FCA* (section 59(4)(b)) of the *Act*.

1.2.4E G   FCA

The procedure must be designed to secure, among other things, that the decision is taken by a person not directly involved in establishing the evidence on which that decision is based, or by two or more persons who include a person not directly involved in establishing that evidence.

The decision makers

1.2.5 G FCA

Decisions on whether to give a *statutory notice* will be taken by a 'decision maker'. The *FCA's* assessment of who is the appropriate decision maker is subject to the requirements of section 395 of the *Act* and will depend upon the nature of the decision, including its complexity, importance and urgency. References to the 'decision maker' in DEPP are to:

(1) the *Regulatory Decisions Committee* (*RDC*); or

(2) *FCA* staff under *executive procedures*; or

(3) *FCA* staff under the *settlement decision procedure*.

1.2.6 G FCA

The decision maker will also take decisions associated with a *statutory notice* (a '*statutory notice associated decision*'). *Statutory notice associated decisions* include decisions:

(1) to set or extend the period for making representations;

(2) on whether the *FCA* is required to give a copy of the *statutory notice* to any third party and, if so, the period for the third party to make representations; and

(3) on whether to refuse access to *FCA* material, relevant to the relevant *statutory notice*, under section 394 of the *Act*.

1.2.6A G FCA

Statutory notice associated decisions do not include decisions relating to the publication of a *statutory notice*.

1.2.7 G FCA

In each case, the decision maker will make decisions by applying the relevant statutory tests, having regard to the context and nature of the matter, that is, the relevant facts, law, and *FCA* priorities and policies (including on matters of legal interpretation).

1.2.8 G FCA

The *FCA* will make and retain appropriate records of those decisions, including records of meetings and the representations (if any) and materials considered by the decision makers.

1.2.9 G FCA

DEPP 2 to **DEPP 5** set out:

(1) which decisions require the giving of statutory notices and who takes them (**DEPP 2**);

(2) the nature and procedures of the *RDC* (**DEPP 3**);

(3) the procedure for decision making by *FCA* staff under *executive procedures* (**DEPP 4**);

(4) the procedure for decision making by *FCA* staff under the *settlement decision procedure* (**DEPP 5**).

CHAPTER 2
STATUTORY NOTICES AND THE ALLOCATION OF DECISION MAKING

2.1 STATUTORY NOTICES

When statutory notices are required

[3.96]
2.1.1 G FCA

The circumstances in which the *warning notice* and *decision notice* procedure apply are set out in **DEPP 2 ANNEX 1**.

2.1.2 G FCA

The circumstances in which the *supervisory notice* procedure apply are set out in **DEPP 2 ANNEX 2**.

2.1.3 G FCA

DEPP 2 ANNEX 1 and **DEPP 2 ANNEX 2** identify the provisions of the *Act* or other enactment giving rise to the need for the relevant notice, and whether the decision maker is the *RDC* or *FCA* staff under *executive procedures* in each case.

Consistent decision making

2.1.4 G FCA

FCA staff responsible for the taking of a *statutory notice* decision under *executive procedures* may refer the matter to the *RDC* for the *RDC* to decide whether to give the statutory notice if:

(1) the *RDC* is already considering, or is shortly to consider, a closely related matter; and

(2) the relevant *FCA* staff believe, having regard to all the circumstances, that the *RDC* should have responsibility for the decision. The relevant considerations might include:

(a)   the desirability of consistency in *FCA* decision making;
(b)   potential savings in the time and cost of reaching a decision;
(c)   the factors identified in **DEPP 3.3.2 G** as relevant to an assessment of whether a
        decision should be regarded as straightforward.

2.2 WARNING NOTICES AND FIRST SUPERVISORY NOTICES

2.2.1 G   FCA

If *FCA* staff consider that action requiring a *warning notice* or first *supervisory notice* is appropriate,
they will recommend to the relevant decision maker that the notice be given.

2.2.2 G   FCA

For first *supervisory notices*, the *FCA* staff will recommend whether the action should take effect
immediately, on a specified date, or when the matter is no longer open to review (see **DEPP 2.2.5 G**).

2.2.3 G   FCA

The decision maker will:
(1)   consider whether the material on which the recommendation is based is adequate to support
        it; the decision maker may seek additional information about or clarification of the
        recommendation, which may necessitate additional work by the relevant *FCA* staff;
(2)   satisfy itself that the action recommended is appropriate in all the circumstances;
(3)   decide whether to give the notice and the terms of any notice given.

2.2.4 G   FCA

If the *FCA* decides to take no further action and the *FCA* had previously informed the *person*
concerned that it intended to recommend action, the *FCA* will communicate this decision promptly
to the *person* concerned.

2.2.5 G   FCA

A matter is open to review (as defined in section 391(8) (Publication) of the *Act*) (in relation to a
supervisory notice which does not take effect immediately or on a specified date) when:
(1)   the period during which any *person* may refer a matter to the *Tribunal* is still running; or
(2)   the matter has been referred to the *Tribunal* but has not been dealt with; or
(3)   the matter has been referred to the *Tribunal* and dealt with but the period during which an
        appeal may be brought against the *Tribunal*'s decision is still running; or
(4)   such an appeal has been brought but has not been determined.

2.3 DECISION NOTICES AND SECOND SUPERVISORY NOTICES

Approach of decision maker

2.3.1 G   FCA

If a decision maker is asked to decide whether to give a *decision notice* or second *supervisory notice*,
it will:
(1)   review the material before it;
(2)   consider any representations made (whether written, oral or both) and any comments by *FCA*
        staff or others in respect of those representations;
(3)   decide whether to give the notice and the terms of any notice given.

Default procedures

2.3.2 G   FCA

If the *FCA* receives no response or representations within the period specified in a *warning notice*,
the decision maker may regard as undisputed the allegations or matters in that notice and a *decision
notice* will be given accordingly. A *person* who has received a *decision notice* and has not previously
made any response or representations to the *FCA*, may nevertheless refer the *FCA*'s decision to the
Tribunal.

2.3.3 G   FCA

If the *FCA* receives no response or representations within the period specified in a first *supervisory
notice*, the *FCA* will not give a second *supervisory notice*. The outcome depends on when the
relevant action took or takes effect (as stated in the notice). If the action:
(1)   took effect immediately, or on a specified date which has already passed, it continues to have
        effect (subject to any decision on a referral to the *Tribunal*); or
(2)   was to take effect on a specified date which is still in the future, it takes effect on that date
        (subject to any decision on a referral to the *Tribunal*); or
(3)   was to take effect when the matter was no longer *open for review*, it takes effect when the
        period to make representations (or the period for referral to the *Tribunal*, if longer) expires,
        unless the matter has been referred to the *Tribunal*.

2.3.4 G   FCA

In exceptional cases, the decision maker may permit representations from a *person* who has received a *decision notice* (or a second *supervisory notice*) or against whom action, detailed in a first *supervisory notice*, has taken effect, and shows on reasonable grounds that he did not receive the *warning notice* (or first *supervisory notice*), or that he had reasonable grounds for not responding within the specified period. In these circumstances, the decision maker may decide to give a further *decision notice* (or a written notice or a *supervisory notice*).

Further decision notice

2.3.5 G   FCA

Under section 388(3) of the *Act*, following the giving of a *decision notice* but before the *FCA* takes action to which the *decision notice* relates, the *FCA* may give the *person* concerned a further *decision notice* relating to different action concerning the same matter. Under section 388(4) of the *Act*, the *FCA* can only do this if the *person* receiving the further *decision notice* gives its consent. In these circumstances the following procedure will apply:

(1)   *FCA* staff will recommend to the decision maker that a further *decision notice* be given, either before or after obtaining the *person's* consent;

(2)   the decision maker will consider whether the action proposed in the further *decision notice* is appropriate in the circumstances;

(3)   if the decision maker decides that the action proposed is inappropriate, he will decide not to give the further *decision notice*. In this case, the original *decision notice* will stand and the *person's* rights in relation to that notice will be unaffected. If the *person's* consent has already been obtained, the *FCA* will notify the *person* of the decision not to give the further *decision notice*;

(4)   if the decision maker decides that the action proposed is appropriate then, subject to the *person's* consent being (or having been) obtained, a further *decision notice* will be given;

(5)   a *person* who had the right to refer the matter to the *Tribunal* under the original *decision notice* will have that right under the further *decision notice*. The time period in which the reference to the *Tribunal* may be made will begin from the date on which the further *decision notice* is given.

2.3.6 G   FCA

For the purpose of establishing whether the *person* receiving the further *decision notice* gives its consent, the *FCA* will normally require consent in writing.

2.4   THIRD PARTY RIGHTS AND ACCESS TO FCA MATERIAL

2.4.1 G   FCA

Sections 393 (Third party rights) and 394 (Access to *FCA* material) of the *Act* confer additional procedural rights relating to third parties and to disclosure of *FCA* material. These rights apply in certain *warning notice* and *decision notice* cases referred to in section 392 of the *Act* (Application of sections 393 and 394). The cases in which these additional rights apply are identified in **DEPP 2 ANNEX 1** by asterisks; these are generally cases in which the *warning notice* or *decision notice* is given on the *FCA's* own initiative rather than in response to an application or notification made to the *FCA*.

2.5   PROVISION FOR CERTAIN CATEGORIES OF DECISION

Purpose

2.5.1 G   FCA

Some of the decisions referred to in **DEPP 2 ANNEX 1** and **DEPP 2 ANNEX 2** share similar characteristics. For convenience, **DEPP 2.5** sets out some of these and the particular features they have.

Different decision makers

2.5.2 G   FCA

The decision to give a *warning notice* and a *decision notice* in a particular matter will often not be taken by the same decision maker. Certain types of action require that the *warning notice* decision be taken by *FCA* staff under *executive procedures* and the *decision notice* decision be taken by the *RDC*. Similarly, in enforcement cases the *RDC* might take the decision to give a *warning notice*, but the decision to give a *decision notice* could be taken by the *settlement decision makers* on the basis that the *person* concerned does not contest the action proposed (see **DEPP 5**).

Decisions relating to applications for FCA authorisation or approval

2.5.3 G   FCA

FCA staff under *executive procedures* will take the decision to give a *warning notice* if the *FCA* proposes to:

(1)   refuse an application for a *Part 4A permission* or to refuse an application to cancel a *Part 4A permission*;

(2)   impose a limitation or a requirement which was not applied for, or specify a narrower description of regulated activity than that applied for, on the grant of a *Part 4A permission*;

(3)   refuse an application to vary a *Part 4A permission*, or to restrict a *Part 4A permission* on the grant of a variation (by imposing a limitation or a requirement which was not applied for or by specifying a narrower description of regulated activity than that applied for);

(4)   refuse an application to vary a *requirement* imposed under section 55L of the *Act*, or to impose a new *requirement*;

(5)   exercise its power under section 55L(1) of the *Act* in connection with an application to the *PRA* for a *Part 4A permission* or the variation of a *Part 4A permission*;

(6)   refuse *approved person* status;

(7)   refuse an application for a *small e-money issuer certificate* (see **ELM 8** (Small e-money issuers));

(8)   refuse an application for variation or rescission of a requirement imposed on an *incoming EEA firm*.

2.5.4 G   FCA

If no representations are made in response to a *warning notice* proposing the action set out at **DEPP 2.5.3 G** within the period specified, a *decision notice* will be given accordingly: see **DEPP 2.3.2 G** (Default procedures).

2.5.5 G   FCA

If representations are made in response to a *warning notice* proposing the action set out at **DEPP 2.5.3 G (1)**, **DEPP 2.5.3 G (4)** or **DEPP 2.5.3 G (5)**, then the *RDC* will take the decision to give a *decision notice*.

2.5.5A G   FCA

If representations are made in response to a *warning notice* proposing the action set out at **DEPP 2.5.3G (3B)**, *FCA* staff under *executive procedures* will take the decision to give a *decision notice*.

2.5.6 G   FCA

If representations are made in response to a *warning notice* proposing the action set out at **DEPP 2.5.3 G (2)**, **DEPP 2.5.3 G (3)**, **DEPP 2.5.3G (3A)**, or **DEPP 2.5.3 G (6)**, then the *RDC* will take the decision to give a *decision notice* if the action involves a fundamental variation or requirement (see **DEPP 2.5.8 G**). Otherwise, the decision to give the *decision notice* will be taken by *FCA* staff under *executive procedures*.

Decisions relating to applications for PRA authorisation or approval

2.5.6A G   FCA

FCA staff under *executive procedures* will take the decision where the *FCA* is proposing or deciding to:

(1)   refuse its consent to the granting by the *PRA* of an application for a *Part 4A permission*, or give its consent subject to conditions;

(2)   refuse its consent to the granting by the *PRA* of an application for the variation of a *Part 4A permission*, or give its consent subject to conditions; or

(3)   refuse its consent to the granting by the *PRA* of an application to perform a *controlled function*.

FCA's own-initiative powers

2.5.7 G   FCA

The *RDC* will take the decision to give a *supervisory notice* exercising the *FCA's own-initiative powers* (by removing a regulated activity, by imposing a limitation or requirement or by specifying a narrower description of regulated activity) if the action involves a fundamental variation or requirement (see **DEPP 2.5.8 G**). Otherwise, the decision to give the *supervisory notice* will be taken by *FCA* staff under *executive procedures*.

2.5.7A G   FCA

Notwithstanding **DEPP 2.5.7 G**, *FCA* staff under *executive procedures* will be the decision maker whenever a *firm* agrees not to contest the *FCA's* exercise of its *own-initiative powers*, including where the *FCA's* action involves a fundamental variation or requirement.

2.5.8 G   FCA

A fundamental variation or requirement means:

(1)   removing a type of activity or *investment* from the *firm's permission*; or

(2)   refusing an application to include a type of activity or *investment*; or

(3)   [deleted]

(4)   imposing or varying an assets requirement (as defined in section 55P of the *Act* (Prohibitions and restrictions)), or refusing an application to vary or cancel such a requirement.

Decisions relating to listing of securities

2.5.9 G   FCA

FCA staff under *executive procedures* will take the following *statutory notice* decisions:

(1)   the refusal of an application for listing of securities;

(2)   the suspension of *listing* on the *FCA's* own initiative or at the request of the issuer;

(3)   [deleted]

(4)   the discontinuance of *listing* of securities at the issuer's request;

(5)   the exercise of any of the powers in sections 87K or 87L of the *Act* in respect of a breach of any applicable provision; and

(6)   [deleted]

(7)   the refusal of an application by an issuer for cancellation of a suspension of *listing* made under section 77 of the *Act*.

2.5.10 G   FCA

The *RDC* will take *statutory notice decisions* relating to the discontinuance of listing of securities on the *FCA's* own initiative.

2.5.11 G   FCA

If securities have matured or otherwise ceased to exist the *FCA* will remove any reference to them from the official list. This is a purely administrative process, and not a discontinuance of listing in the sense used in Part 6 of the *Act*.

Decisions relating to imposition of limitations or other restrictions of sponsors and primary information providers

2.5.11A G   FCA

Under section 88(4)(aa) of the *Act*, if the *FCA* proposes to impose limitations or other restrictions on the services to which a *sponsor's* approval relates, it must give him a *warning notice*. If, after considering any representations made in response to the *warning notice*, the *FCA* decides to impose limitations or other restrictions on the services to which a *sponsor's* approval relates, it must give him a *decision notice*. Where the *sponsor* has requested or otherwise agrees to the limitation or other restriction, *FCA* staff under *executive procedures* will take the decision to give the *warning notice* and *decision notice*. Otherwise, the *RDC* will take the decision to give the *warning notice* and *decision notice*.

2.5.11B G   FCA

If the *FCA* is proposing or deciding to refuse a *sponsor's* application for the withdrawal or variation of a limitation or other restriction on the services to which a *sponsor's* approval relates under section 88(8)(d) of the *Act*, the decision maker will be *FCA* staff under executive procedures where *FCA* staff decided to impose the limitation or other restriction. Otherwise, the *RDC* will take the decision to give the *warning notice* and *decision notice*.

2.5.11C G   FCA

Under section 89P(5)(b) of the *Act*, if the *FCA* proposes to impose limitations or other restrictions on the dissemination of *regulated information* to which a *primary information provider's* approval relates, it must give him a *warning notice*. If, after considering any representations made in response to the *warning notice*, the *FCA* decides to impose limitations or other restrictions on the dissemination of *regulated information* to which a *primary information provider's* approval relates, it must give him a *decision notice*. Where the *primary information provider* has requested or otherwise agrees to the limitation or other restriction, *FCA* staff under *executive procedures* will take the decision to give the *warning notice* and *decision notice*. Otherwise, the *RDC* will take the decision to give the *warning notice* and *decision notice*.

2.5.11D G   FCA

Under section 89P(9)(d) of the *Act*, if the *FCA* is proposing or deciding to refuse a *primary information provider's* application for the withdrawal or variation of a limitation or other restriction on the dissemination of *regulated information* to which a *primary information provider's* approval relates, the decision maker will be *FCA* staff under *executive procedures* where *FCA* staff decided to impose the limitation or other restriction. Otherwise, the *RDC* will take the decision to give the *warning notice* and *decision notice*.

Modified procedures in collective investment scheme and certain other cases

2.5.12 G   FCA

FCA staff will usually inform or discuss with the *person* concerned any action they contemplate before they recommend to the *RDC* that the *FCA* takes formal action. The *FCA* may also be invited to exercise certain powers by the *persons* who would be affected by the exercise of those powers. In these circumstances if the *person* concerned has agreed to or accepted the action proposed then the decisions referred to in **DEPP 2.5.13 G** will be taken by *FCA* staff under *executive procedures* rather than by the *RDC*.

2.5.13 G   FCA

The decisions referred to in **DEPP 2.5.12 G** are:

(1)   the decision to give a *supervisory notice* pursuant to section 259(3), (8) or 9(b) (directions on authorised unit trust schemes); section 268(3), 7(a) or 9(a) (directions in respect of recognised overseas schemes); or section 282(3), (6) or (7)(b) (directions in respect of relevant recognised schemes) of the *Act*;

(2)   the decision to give a *supervisory notice* pursuant to section 261Z1(3), (8) or (9)(b) (Procedure on giving directions under section 261X or 261Z and varying them on FCA's own initiative) of the *Act*;

(3)   the decision to give a *warning notice* or *decision notice* pursuant to section 280(1) or (2)(a) (revocation of recognised investment scheme) of the *Act*;

(4)   the decision to give a *supervisory notice* in accordance with regulation 27(3), (8) or 9(b) of the *OEIC Regulations*; and

(5)   the decision to give a *warning notice* or *decision notice* pursuant to regulation 24 or regulation 28 of the *OEIC Regulations*.

(6)   the decision to give a *warning notice* or *decision notice* pursuant to section 255 or 260 of the *Act*;

(7)   the decision to give a *warning notice* or *decision notice* pursuant to section 261V or 261Z2 of the *Act*;

(8)   [deleted]

(9)   [deleted]

2.5.14 G   FCA

In determining whether there is agreement to or acceptance of the action proposed, an indication by the following *persons* will be regarded as conclusive:

(1)   in relation to an *authorised unit trust scheme*, the *manager* and *trustee*;

(2)   in relation to an *authorised contractual scheme*, the *authorised contractual scheme manager* and *depositary*;

(3)   in relation to an *ICVC*, the *directors* and the *depositary*;

(4)   in relation to a *recognised scheme*, the *operator* and, if any, the *trustee* or *depositary*.

2.5.15 G   FCA

A decision to give a *warning notice* or *decision notice* refusing an application for an *authorisation order* declaring a *scheme* to be an *AUT*, *ACS* or *ICVC* will be taken by the *RDC* only if the application is by an *authorised fund manager* who is not the *operator* of an existing *AUT*, *ACS* or *ICVC*. Otherwise, the decision to give the *warning notice* or *decision notice* will be taken by *FCA* staff under *executive procedures*.

2.5.16 G   FCA

A notice under paragraph 15A(4) of Schedule 3 to the *Act* relating to the application by an *EEA firm* for approval to manage a *UCITS scheme* is not a *warning notice*, but the *FCA* will operate a procedure for this notice which will be similar to the procedure for a *warning notice*.

Notices under other enactments

2.5.17 G   FCA

The *FCA* expects to adopt a procedure in respect of notices under enactments other than the *Act* which is similar to that for *statutory notices* under the *Act*, but which recognises any differences in the legislative framework and requirements. **DEPP 2 ANNEX 1 G** and **DEPP 2 ANNEX 2 G** therefore identify notices to be given pursuant to other enactments and the relevant *FCA* decision maker.

2.5.18 G   FCA

Some of the distinguishing features of notices given under enactments other than the *Act* are as follows:

(1)   [deleted]

(2)   [deleted]

(3)   Friendly Societies Act 1992, section 58A: The *warning notice* and *decision notice* must set out the terms of the direction which the *FCA* proposes or has decided to give and any specification of when the friendly society is to comply with it. A *decision notice* given under section 58A(3) must give an indication of the society's right, given by section 58A(5), to have the matter referred to the *Tribunal*. A *decision notice* under section 58A(3) may only relate to action under the same section of the Friendly Societies Act 1992 as the action proposed in the *warning notice*. A *final notice* under section 390 of the *Act* must set out the terms of the direction and state the date from which it takes effect. Section 392 of the *Act* is to be read as if it included references to a *warning notice* given under section 58A(1) and a *decision notice* given under section 58A(3).

2 ANNEX 1
WARNING NOTICES AND DECISION NOTICES UNDER THE ACT AND CERTAIN OTHER ENACTMENTS

2Ann1   FCA

Note: Third party rights and access to *FCA* material apply to the powers listed in this Annex where indicated by an asterisk * (see **DEPP 2.4**)

Section of the Act	Description	Handbook reference	Decision maker
55X(1)(a) and (b)	when the *FCA* is proposing to grant an application for a *Part 4A permission* with a *limitation* or a *requirement* which was not applied for, or with a narrower description of *regulated activity* than that applied for	SUP 6	*Executive procedures*
55X(1)(c) and (d)	when the *FCA* is proposing to grant an application to vary a *firm's Part 4A permission* but, other than as part of the application, to restrict the *Part 4A permission* (either by imposing a *limitation* or *requirement* which was not applied for or by specifying a narrower description of *regulated activity* than that applied for)		*Executive procedures*
55X(1)(e)	when the *FCA* is proposing to exercise its power under section 55L(1) in connection with an application to the *PRA* for a *Part 4A permission* or the variation of a *Part 4A permission*		*Executive procedures*
55X(2)	when the *FCA* is proposing to refuse an application for a *Part 4A permission*		*Executive procedures*
55X(2)	when the *FCA* is proposing to refuse an application to vary a *firm's Part 4A permission*	SUP 6	*Executive procedures*
55X(2)	when the *FCA* is proposing to refuse an application to cancel a *firm's Part 4A permission*	SUP 6	*Executive procedures*
55X(2)	when the *FCA* is proposing to refuse an application for the variation of a *requirement* imposed under section 55L or for the imposition of a new *requirement*		*RDC or executive procedures* See **DEPP 2.5.6 G**
55X(4)(a) 55X(4)(b)	when the *FCA* is deciding to grant an application for a *Part 4A permission* with a *limitation* or a *requirement* which was not applied for, or with a narrower description of *regulated activity* than that applied for		*RDC or executive procedures* See **DEPP 2.5.6 G**
55X(4)(c) 55X(4)(d)	when the *FCA* is deciding to grant an application to vary a *firm's Part 4A permission* but, other than as part of the application, to restrict the *Part 4A permission* (either by imposing a *limitation* or *requirement* which was not applied for or by specifying a narrower description of *regulated activity* than that applied for)	SUP 6	*RDC or executive procedures* See **DEPP 2.5.6 G**
55X(4)(e)	when the *FCA* is deciding to exercise its power under section 55L(1) in connection with an application to the *PRA* for a *Part 4A permission* or the variation of a *Part 4A permission*		*Executive procedures*

Section of the Act	Description	Handbook reference	Decision maker
55X(4)(f)	when the *FCA* is deciding to refuse an application for a *Part 4A permission*		*RDC* or *executive procedures* See **DEPP 2.5.5 G**
55X(4)(f)	when the *FCA* is deciding to refuse an application to vary a *firm*'s *Part 4A permission*	**SUP 6**	*RDC* or *executive procedures* See **DEPP 2.5.6 G**
55X(4)(f)	when the *FCA* is deciding to refuse an application to cancel a *firm*'s *Part 4A permission*	**SUP 6**	*RDC* or *executive procedures* See **DEPP 2.5.5 G**
55X(4)(f)	When the *FCA* is deciding to refuse an application for the variation of a *requirement* imposed under section 55L or for the imposition of a new *requirement*		*RDC* or *executive procedures* See **DEPP 2.5.6 G**
55Z(1) 55Z(2)	when the *FCA* is proposing or deciding to cancel a *firm*'s *Part 4A permission* otherwise than at its request*		*RDC*
57(1)/(3)	when the *FCA* is proposing or deciding to make a *prohibition order* against an individual*		*RDC*
58(3)/(4)	when the *FCA* is proposing or deciding to refuse an application for the variation or revocation of a *prohibition order*		*RDC*
62(2)	when the *FCA* is proposing to refuse an application for approval of a *person* performing a *controlled function*	**SUP 10**	*Executive procedures*
62(3)	when the *FCA* is deciding to refuse an application for approval of a *person* performing a *controlled function*	**SUP 10**	*RDC* or *executive procedures* See **DEPP 2.5.5 G**
63(3)/(4)	when the *FCA* is proposing or deciding to withdraw approval from an *approved person**		*RDC*
63B(1)/(3)	when the *FCA* is proposing or deciding to impose a penalty on a *person* under section 63A*		*RDC*
67(1)/(4)	when the *FCA* is proposing or deciding to take action against an *approved person* by exercising the disciplinary powers conferred by section 66*		*RDC*
76(4)/(5)	when the *FCA* is proposing or deciding to refuse an application for *listing* of securities	**LR 2** and **LR 3**	*Executive procedures*
78(10)/(11)(a)	when the *FCA* has suspended, on its own initiative, the *listing* of securities and is proposing or deciding to refuse an application by an issuer for cancellation of the suspension	**LR 5**	*Executive procedures*
78A(4)/(5)	When the *FCA* is proposing or deciding to refuse an application by the *issuer* of the *securities* for the discontinuance or suspension of the *listing* of the *securities*	**LR 5**	*Executive procedures*

Section of the Act	Description	Handbook reference	Decision maker
78A(7)/(8)(a)	When the *FCA* has suspended the *listing* of *securities* on the application of the *issuer* of the *securities* and is proposing or deciding to refuse an application by the *issuer* for the cancellation of the suspension	**LR 5**	*Executive procedures*
87M(2)/(3)	when the *FCA* is proposing or deciding to publish a statement censuring an issuer of *transferable securities*, a *person* offering *transferable securities* to the public or a *person* requesting the admission of *transferable securities* to trading on a *regulated market*		*RDC*
88(4)(a) 88(6)(a) 88(8)(a)	when the *FCA* is proposing or deciding to refuse a *person's* application for approval as a *sponsor*	**LR 8**	*RDC*
88(4)(a) 88(6)(a) 88(8)(b)	when the *FCA* is proposing or deciding to refuse a *sponsor's* application for the suspension of an approval as a *sponsor*		*Executive procedures*
88(4)(a) 88(6)(a) 88(8)(c)	when the *FCA* is proposing or deciding to refuse a *sponsor's* application for the withdrawal of the suspension of an approval as a *sponsor*		*Executive procedures*
88(4)(a) 88(6)(a) 88(8)(d)	when the *FCA* is proposing or deciding to refuse a *sponsor's* application for the withdrawal or variation of a limitation, or other restriction on the services to which a *sponsor's* approval relates		*RDC* or *executive procedures* See **DEPP 2.5.11B G**
88(4)(aa) 88(6)(aa)	when the *FCA* is proposing or deciding to impose limitations or restrictions on the services to which a *sponsor's* approval relates		*RDC* or *executive procedures* See **DEPP 2.5.11A G**
88(4)(b) 88(6)(b)	when the *FCA* is proposing or deciding to cancel a *sponsor's* approval as a *sponsor* otherwise than at the *sponsor's* request*		*RDC*
88B(1) 88B(5)	when the *FCA* is proposing or deciding to take action against a *sponsor* by exercising the disciplinary powers conferred by section 88A*		*RDC*
89K(2)/(3)	when the *FCA* is proposing or deciding to publish a statement that an *issuer* of *securities* admitted to trading on a *regulated market* is failing or has failed to comply with an applicable transparency obligation		*RDC*
89P(5)(a) 89P(7)(a) 89P(9)(a)	when the *FCA* is proposing or deciding to refuse a person's application for approval as a *primary information provider*		*RDC*
89P(5)(a) 89P(7)(a) 89P(9)(b	when the *FCA* is proposing or deciding to refuse a *primary information provider's* application for the suspension of an approval as a *primary information provider*		*Executive procedures*

Section of the Act	Description	Handbook reference	Decision maker
89P(5)(a) 89P(7)(a) 89P(9)(c)	when the *FCA* is proposing or deciding to refuse a *primary information provider's* application for the withdrawal of the suspension of an approval as a *primary information provider*		*Executive procedures*
89P(5)(a) 89P(7)(a) 89P(9)(d)	when the *FCA* is proposing or deciding to refuse a *primary information provider's* application for the withdrawal or variation of a limitation or other restriction on the dissemination of *regulated information* to which a *primary information provider's* approval relates		*RDC* or *executive procedures* See **DEPP 2.5.11D G**
89P(5)(b) 89P(7)(b)	when the *FCA* is proposing or deciding to impose *limitations* or other restrictions on the dissemination of *regulated information* to which a *primary information provider's* approval relates.		*RDC* or *executive procedures* See **DEPP 2.5.11A G**
89P(5)(c) 89P(7)(c)	when the *FCA* is proposing or deciding to cancel a *person's* approval as a *primary information provider* otherwise than at the *primary information provider's* request		*RDC*
89R(1) 89R(5)	when the *FCA* is proposing or deciding to take action against a *primary information provider* by exercising the disciplinary powers conferred by section 89Q		*RDC*
92(1)/(4)	when the *FCA* is proposing or deciding to take action against any person under section 91 for breach of Part 6 rules*		*RDC*
126(1)/127(1)	when the *FCA* is proposing or deciding to impose a sanction for *market abuse**		*RDC*
131H(1)/(4)	when the *FCA* is proposing or deciding to take action against a *person* under section 131G*		*RDC*
189(4)/(7)	when the *FCA* is proposing or deciding to object to a change in *control* following receipt of a *section 178 notice*	**SUP 11**	*Executive procedures*
189(4)/(7)	when the *FCA* is proposing or deciding to approve a change in *control* with conditions, following receipt of a *section 178 notice*	**SUP 11**	*Executive procedures*
187(1)/(3) and 188(1) 191A(4)/(6)	when the *FCA* is proposing or deciding to object to a *person* who has acquired or increased control without giving a *section 178 notice*	**SUP 11**	*Executive procedures*
191A(4)/(6)	when the *FCA* is proposing or deciding to object to a *person's control* on the basis of the matters in section 186	**SUP 11**	*Executive procedures*
191A(4)/(6)	when the *FCA* is proposing or deciding to object to a *person's control* on the grounds that he is in breach of a condition imposed under section 187	**SUP 11**	*Executive procedures*

Section of the Act	Description	Handbook reference	Decision maker
192L(1) 192L(4)	when the *FCA* is proposing or deciding to take action against a qualifying parent undertaking by exercising the disciplinary powers conferred by section 192K*		*RDC*
200(4)/(5)	when the is proposing or deciding to refuse an application for variation or rescission of a requirement imposed on an *EEA incoming firm*		*RDC* or *executive procedures* See **DEPP 2.5.6 G**
207(1) 208(1)	when the *FCA* is proposing or deciding to publish a statement (under section 205) or impose a financial penalty (under section 206) or suspend a *permission* or impose a restriction in relation to the carrying on of a *regulated activity* (under section 206A). This applies in respect of an *authorised person*, or an *unauthorised person* to whom section 404C applies.*		*RDC*
245(1)/(2)	when the *FCA* is proposing or deciding to refuse an application for an *authorisation* order declaring a *unit trust scheme* to be an *AUT*	**COLL 2**	*RDC* or *executive procedures* See **DEPP 2.5.15 G**
249 345B(1)/(4)	when the *FCA* is proposing or deciding to take action against an auditor by exercising the disciplinary powers conferred by section 249*		*RDC*
252(1)/(4)	when the *FCA* is proposing or deciding to refuse approval of a proposal to replace the *trustee* or *manager* of an *AUT*	**COLL 2**	*Executive procedures*
252A(4)(b) (6)(a)	when the *FCA* is proposing or deciding to refuse approval of a proposal by the *manager* of a *feeder UCITS* to make an alteration to the *trust deed* to enable the *feeder UCITS* to convert into a *UCITS scheme* which is not a *feeder UCITS*	**COLL 11**	*Executive procedures*
255(1)/(2)	when the *FCA* is proposing or deciding to make an order under section 254 revoking the *authorisation order* of an *AUT**	None, but see Chapter 14 of the Regulatory Guide *EG*.	*RDC*
256(4)/(5)	when the *FCA* is proposing or deciding to refuse a request for the revocation of the *authorisation order* of an *AUT*		*RDC*
260(1)/(2)	when the *FCA*, on an application to revoke or vary a direction under section 257, proposes or decides to refuse to revoke or vary the direction or proposes or decides to vary the direction otherwise than in accordance with the application		*RDC*
261G(1)/(2)	when the *FCA* is proposing or deciding to refuse an application for an *authorisation order* declaring a *scheme* to be an *ACS*	**COLL 2**	*RDC* or *executive procedures* See **DEPP 2.5.15 G**
261R(1)/(4)	when the *FCA* is proposing or deciding to refuse approval of a proposal to replace the *depositary* or *authorised contractual scheme manager* of an *ACS*	**COLL 2**	*Executive procedures*

Section of the Act	Description	Handbook reference	Decision maker
261S(4)(b) (6)(a)	when the *FCA* is proposing or deciding to refuse approval of a proposal by the *authorised contractual scheme manager* of an *ACS* which is a *feeder UCITS* to make an alteration to the *contractual scheme deed* to enable the *feeder UCITS* to convert into a *UCITS scheme* which is not a *feeder UCITS*	**COLL 11**	*Executive procedures*
261V(1)/(2)	when the *FCA* is proposing or deciding to make an order under section 261U revoking the *authorisation order* of an *ACS**	None, but see Chapter 14 of the Regulatory Guide EG.	*RDC*
261W(4)/(5)	when the *FCA* is proposing or deciding to refuse a request for the revocation of the *authorisation order* of an *ACS*		*RDC*
261Z2(1)/(2)	when the *FCA*, on an application to revoke or vary a direction under section 261X, proposes or decides to refuse to revoke or vary the direction or proposes or decides to vary the direction otherwise than in accordance with the application		*RDC*
264(2) 265(4)	[deleted]		
269(1)/(2)	when the *FCA*, on an application under section 267(4) or (5) by an *operator* of a section 264 *recognised scheme* to revoke or vary a direction that the promotion of the *scheme* be suspended, proposes or decides to refuse the application or to vary the direction otherwise than in accordance with the application		*RDC*
276(1)/(2)	when the *FCA* is proposing or deciding to refuse an application for an order declaring a *collective investment scheme* to be a *recognised scheme* under section 272	**COLL 9**	*Executive procedures*
280(1)/(2)	when the *FCA* is proposing or deciding to revoke a section 272 order in respect of a *recognised scheme**		*RDC*
301G(3)(b)/(5)	when the *FCA* is proposing or deciding to object to a proposed acquisition of a *UK RIE* following receipt of a section 301A notice.	**REC 4.2C**	*Executive procedures*
301I(3)/(4)	when the *FCA* is proposing or deciding to object to a *person* who has acquired or increased *control* in a *UK RIE* without giving a section 301 notice	**REC 4.2C**	*Executive procedures*
301I(3)/(4)	when the *FCA* is proposing or deciding to object to a *person's* control in a *UK RIE* on the basis of the approval requirement in section 301F(4)	**REC 4.2C**	*Executive procedures*
312G(1) 312H(1)	when the *FCA* is proposing or deciding to take action against a *recognised investment exchange* by exercising the disciplinary powers conferred by sections 312E and 312F*		*RDC*

Section of the Act	Description	Handbook reference	Decision maker
313B(9)	[deleted]		
313B(10)/(11)	[deleted]		
313BB(5) 313BC(5)	when, upon the application of an institution, the *FCA* is proposing or deciding not to revoke a requirement imposed on an institution under section 313A or is proposing or deciding that a requirement imposed on a class of institutions under section 313A will continue to apply to the applicant	**REC 4.2D**	*Executive procedures*
313BD(5) 313BE(4)	when, upon the application of an *issuer*, the *FCA* is proposing or deciding not to revoke a requirement imposed on an institution or a class of institutions under section 313A or to revoke a requirement imposed on a class of institutions under section 313A in relation to the class apart from one or more specified members of it, or one or more specified members of the class only	**REC 4.2D**	*Executive procedures*
331(1)/(3)	when the *FCA* is proposing or deciding to make an order disapplying the exemption from the *general prohibition* under section 327*		*RDC*
331(7)/(8)	when the *FCA* is proposing or deciding to refuse an application for the variation or revocation of an order made under section 329*		*RDC*
345B(1) 345B(4)	when the *FCA* is proposing or deciding to disqualify an auditor or actuary from being the auditor of, or acting as an actuary for, any *authorised person* or class of *authorised person* or from being the auditor of any *AUT*, *ACS* or *ICVC**		*RDC*
345B(1) 345B(4)	when the *FCA* is proposing or deciding to disqualify an auditor from being the auditor of any *recognised investment exchange* or any class of *recognised investment exchange**		*RDC*
345B(1) 345B(4)	when the *FCA* is proposing or deciding to take action against an auditor or *actuary* by exercising the disciplinary powers conferred by sections 345(2)(c) or (d)*		*RDC*
385(1) 386(1)	when the *FCA* is proposing or deciding to exercise the power under section 384(5) to require a *person* to pay restitution*		*RDC*
404A(8)(a)	In connection with a *consumer redress scheme*, when the *FCA* is proposing to make a determination of whether a failure by a relevant firm has caused (or may cause) loss or damage to a *consumer*, or what the redress should be in respect of the failure	*CONRED*	*Executive procedures*

Section of the Act	Description	Handbook reference	Decision maker
404A(8)(a)	In connection with a *consumer redress scheme*, when the *FCA* is deciding to make a determination of whether a failure by a relevant firm has caused (or may cause) loss or damage to a *consumer*, or what the redress should be in respect of the failure	*CONRED*	*Executive procedures*
412B(2)/(3)	when the *FCA* is proposing/deciding to refuse to approve a relevant system as defined in section 412A(9) of the *Act*		*Executive procedures*
412B(4)/(5)	when the *FCA* is proposing/deciding to suspend or withdraw its approval in relation to a relevant system as defined in section 412A(9) of the *Act**		*Executive procedures*
412B(8)/(9)	when the *FCA* is proposing/deciding to refuse an application to cancel the suspension of approval in relation to a relevant system as defined in section 412A(9) of the *Act**		*Executive procedures*
Paragraph 15A(4) of Schedule 3	when the *FCA* is notifying an *EEA firm* wishing to manage a *UCITS scheme* and its *Home State regulator* that the *EEA firm* does not comply with the *fund application rules*, or is not authorised by its *Home State regulator* to manage the type of *collective investment scheme* for which *authorisation* is required, or has not provided the documentation required under article 20(1) of the *UCITS Directive*	**SUP 13A** See **DEPP 2.5.16 G**	*Executive procedures*
Paragraph 15A(5) of Schedule 3	[deleted]		
Paragraph 15B(2)(a) of Schedule 3	when the *FCA* is deciding not to withdraw a notice issued to an *EEA firm* wishing to manage a *UCITS scheme* and to its *Home State regulator* that the *EEA firm* does not comply with the *fund application rules*, or is not authorised by its *Home State regulator* to manage the type of *collective investment scheme* for which *authorisation* is required, or has not provided the documentation required under article 20(1) of the *UCITS Directive*	**SUP 13A**	*Executive procedures*
Paragraph 19(8)/(12) of Schedule 3	when the *FCA* is proposing or deciding to refuse to give a *consent notice* to a *UK firm* wishing to establish a *branch* under an *EEA right*	**SUP 13**	*RDC*

Section of the Credit Unions Act 1979	Description	Handbook reference	Decision maker
20	where the *FCA* is proposing to cancel or suspend the registration of a *credit union* or to petition for the winding up of a *credit union*		*RDC*

Articles of the Credit Unions (Northern Ireland) Order 1985	Description	Handbook reference	Decision maker
60(1), 61(1) and 63	where the *FCA* is proposing to consent to the Registrar of Credit Unions for Northern Ireland cancelling or suspending the registration of a *Northern Ireland credit union*, or petitioning for the winding up of a *Northern Ireland credit union*		*RDC*

Section of the Friendly Societies Act 1992	Description	Handbook reference	Decision maker
58A(1)(a)/ (3)(a)	when the *FCA* is proposing or deciding to give a direction under section 54 or section 55 requiring a *friendly society* to take or refrain from taking steps where certain activities have become disproportionate to those of the *friendly society* group or, as the case may be, the society, or varying such a direction other than at the request of the society*	See **DEPP 2.5.18 G (3)**	*RDC*
58A(1)(b)/ (3)(b)	when the *FCA* is proposing or deciding to give a direction under section 90 providing for a transfer of the engagements of a *friendly society**		*RDC*
85(4A)	when the *FCA*, on an amalgamation between *friendly societies* each of which has a *Part 4A permission*, notifies the successor society of the terms of its *Part 4A permission*		*RDC* or *executive procedures* See **DEPP 2.5.12 G**

OEIC Regulations reference	Description	Handbook reference	Decision maker
Regulation 16(1)/(2)	when the *FCA* is proposing or deciding to refuse an application for an *authorisation order* in respect of a proposed *ICVC*	**COLL 2**	*RDC* or *executive procedures* See **DEPP 2.5.15 G**
Regulation 22(1)/(2)/ (4)/(5)	when the *FCA* is proposing to refuse approval of (or, having given a *warning notice*, deciding to refuse) a proposal to replace the *depositary* or director of an *ICVC*, or any other proposal or decision falling within regulation 21	**COLL 2**	*Executive procedures*
Regulation 22A(5)(b)/ (8)(a)	when the *FCA* is proposing or deciding to refuse approval of a proposal by an *ICVC* which is a *feeder UCITS* to make an alteration to its *instrument of incorporation* to enable it to convert into a *UCITS scheme* which is not a *feeder UCITS*	**COLL 11**	*Executive procedures*
Regulation 24(1)/(2)	when the *FCA* is proposing or deciding to revoke an *authorisation order* relating to an *ICVC* under regulation 23(1)*		*RDC*

OEIC Regulations reference	Description	Handbook reference	Decision maker
Regulation 28(1)/(2)	when the *FCA* is proposing or deciding to refuse an application to revoke or vary a direction in accordance with a request under regulation 25(7) or to vary the direction in accordance with the application		*RDC*
Paragraph 20 of Schedule 5	when the *FCA* is proposing or deciding to use the disqualification powers under section 249(1)*		*RDC*

Regulated Activities Order	Description	Handbook reference	Decision maker
Article 95(2)/(3)	when the *FCA* is proposing or deciding not to include, or to remove, an *appointed representative* from the *Register**	**SUP 12.4.10 G**	*RDC*
Article 95(7)/(8)	when the *FCA* is proposing or deciding to refuse an application to revoke a determination not to include, or to remove, an *appointed representative* from the *Register**	**SUP 12.4.10 G**	*RDC*

Payment Services Regulations	Description	Handbook reference	Decision maker
Regulations 9(7) and 14	when the *FCA* is proposing to refuse an application for authorisation as an *authorised payment institution*, or for registration as a *small payment institution*, or to impose a requirement, or to refuse an application to vary an authorisation		*Executive procedures*
Regulations 9(8)(a) and 14	when the *FCA* is deciding to refuse an application for authorisation as an *authorised payment institution*, or for registration of a *small payment institution*, or to impose a requirement, or to refuse an application to vary an authorisation		*Executive procedures* where no representations are made in response to a warning notice, otherwise by the *RDC*
Regulations 10(2) and 10(3)(a) and 14	when the *FCA* is proposing or deciding to either cancel an *authorised payment institution's* authorisation, or to cancel a *small payment institution's* registration, otherwise than at that institution's own request*		*RDC*
Regulation 24(2)	when the *FCA* is proposing to refuse to register an *EEA branch*		*Executive procedures*
Regulation 24(3)(a)	when the *FCA* is deciding to refuse to register an *EEA branch*		*Executive procedures* where no representations are made in response to a warning notice, otherwise by the *RDC*
Regulations 24(2) and 24(3)(a)	when the *FCA* is proposing or deciding to cancel the registration of an *EEA branch**		*RDC*
Regulation 29(9)	when the *FCA* is proposing to refuse an application for registration as an *agent*		*Executive procedures*

Payment Services Regulations	Description	Handbook reference	Decision maker
Regulation 29(10)(a)	when the *FCA* is deciding to refuse an application for registration as an *agent*		*Executive procedures* where no representations are made in response to a warning notice, otherwise by the *RDC*
Regulations 30(2) and 30(3)(a)	when the *FCA* is proposing or deciding to remove an *agent* from the *Financial Services Register* otherwise than at the request of a *payment institution**		*RDC*
Regulations 86(1) and 86(3)	when the *FCA* is proposing, or deciding, to impose a financial penalty*		*RDC*
Regulations 86(1) and 86(3)	when the *FCA* is proposing, or deciding, to publish a statement that a *payment service provider* has contravened the *Payment Services Regulations**		*RDC*
Regulations 89(1) and 89(3)	when the *FCA* is proposing or deciding to exercise its powers to require restitution*		*RDC*
Regulation 121(7)	when the *FCA* is proposing to decide that it has not received the required information or that the required conditions are not met as concerns deemed authorisation		*Executive Procedures*
Regulation 121(8)	when the *FCA* is deciding that it has not received the required information or that the required conditions are not met as concerns deemed authorisation		*Executive procedures* where no representations are made in response to a warning notice, otherwise by the *RDC*
Schedule 4A paragraph 5(6)	when the *FCA* is proposing to refuse an application to vary the period, event or condition of a prohibition, or to remove a prohibition, or to vary or remove a restriction		*Executive procedures*
Schedule 4A paragraph 5(7)	when the *FCA* is deciding to refuse an application to vary the period, event or condition of a prohibition, or to remove a prohibition, or to vary or remove a restriction		*Executive procedures*, where no representations are made in response to a warning notice, otherwise by the *RDC*
Schedule 5 paragraph 1	when the *FCA* is proposing or deciding to publish a statement that a relevant person has been knowingly concerned with a contravention of the *Payment Services Regulations* (Note 2)		*RDC*
Schedule 5 paragraph 1	when the *FCA* is proposing or deciding to impose a financial penalty against a relevant person (Note 3)		*RDC*

Payment Services Regulations	Description	Handbook reference	Decision maker
Notes: (2) The *Payment Services Regulations* do not require third party rights and access to *FCA* material when the *FCA* exercises this power. However, the *FCA* generally intends to allow for third party rights and access to material when exercising this power. (3) The *Payment Services Regulations* do not require third party rights and access to *FCA* material when the *FCA* exercises this power. However, the *FCA* generally intends to allow for third party rights and access to material when exercising this power.			

Regulated Covered Bonds Regulations 2008	Description	Handbook reference	Decision maker
Regulation 13(4)/(5)(a)	when the *FCA* is proposing or deciding to refuse an application under regulation 8	RCB 6	*Executive procedures*
Regulation 20(5)/(6)(a)	when the *FCA* is proposing or deciding not to approve a material change	RCB 6	*Executive procedures*
Regulation 25(5)/(6)(a)	when the *FCA* is proposing or deciding not to approve a change of ownership	RCB 6	*Executive procedures*
Regulation 32(1)(a)/ (2)(a)	before the *FCA* gives a direction under regulation 30 or when it decides to make the direction	RCB 6	*Executive procedures*
Regulation 32(1)(b)/(2)(b)	before the *FCA* removes an *issuer* from the register of *issuers* under regulation 31 or when it decides to remove the *issuer* from the register of *issuers**	RCB 6	*Executive procedures*
Regulation 35(1)/(3)	when the *FCA* is proposing or deciding to impose a penalty on a person under regulation 34*	RCB 6	*RDC*

Cross-Border Payments in Euro Regulations 2010	Description	Handbook reference	Decision maker
Regulations 7(1) and 7(3)	when the *FCA* is proposing or deciding to impose a financial penalty*		*RDC*
Regulations 7(1) and 7(3)	when the *FCA* is proposing or deciding to publish a statement that a *payment service provider* has contravened the *EU Cross-Border Regulation**		*RDC*
Regulations 10(1) and 10(3)	when the *FCA* is proposing or deciding to exercise its powers to require restitution*		*RDC*
Schedule paragraph 1	when the *FCA* is proposing or deciding to publish a statement that a relevant person has been knowingly concerned with a contravention of the *EU Cross-Border Regulation* (Note 1)		*RDC*
Schedule paragraph 1	when the *FCA* is proposing or deciding to impose a financial penalty against a relevant person (Note 1)		*RDC*
Note: (1) The *Cross-Border Payments in Euro Regulations* do not require third party rights and access to *FCA* material when the *FCA* exercises this power. However, the *FCA* generally intends to allow for third party rights and access to material when exercising this power.			

Electronic Money Regulations	Description	Handbook reference	Decision maker
Regulations 9(6) and 15	where the *FCA* is proposing to refuse an application for authorisation as an *authorised electronic money institution*, or for registration as a *small electronic money institution*, or impose a requirement, or refuse to vary an authorisation or registration		*Executive procedures*
Regulations 9(7)(a) and 15	when the *FCA* is deciding to refuse an application for authorisation as an *authorised electronic money institution*, or for registration as a *small electronic money institution*, or impose a requirement or refuse to vary an authorisation or registration		*Executive procedures* where no representations are made in response to a warning notice, otherwise by the *RDC*
Regulations 10(4), 10(5)(a) and 15	when the *FCA* is proposing or deciding to either cancel an *authorised electronic money institution's* authorisation, or to cancel a *small electronic money institution's* registration otherwise than at that institution's own request*		*RDC*
Regulations 11(6), 11(9), 11(10)(b) and 15	when the *FCA* is exercising its powers to vary an *electronic money institution's* authorisation or vary a *small electronic money institution's* registration on its own initiative		*RDC* or *Executive procedures* (Note 1)
Regulation 29(2)	when the *FCA* is proposing to refuse to register an *EEA branch of an authorised electronic money institution*		*Executive procedures*
Regulation 29(3)(a)	when the *FCA* is deciding to refuse to register an *EEA branch of an authorised electronic money institution*		*Executive procedures* where no representations are made in response to a warning notice, otherwise by the *RDC*
Regulation 29(2) and Regulation 29(3)(a)	when the *FCA* is proposing or deciding to cancel the registration of an *EEA branch of an authorised electronic money institution**		*RDC*
Regulation 34(9)	when the *FCA* is proposing to refuse an application for registration as an *agent*		*Executive procedures*
Regulation 34(10)(a)	when the *FCA* is deciding to refuse an application for registration as an *agent*		*Executive procedures* where no representations are made in response to a warning notice, otherwise by the *RDC*
Regulations 35(2) and 35(3)(a)	when the *FCA* is proposing or deciding to remove an *agent* from the *Financial Services Register* otherwise than at the request of the *electronic money institution**		*RDC*
Regulations 53(1) and 53(3)	when the *FCA* is proposing, or deciding, to publish a statement that an *electronic money issuer* has contravened the *Electronic Money Regulations**		*RDC*

Electronic Money Regulations	Description	Handbook reference	Decision maker
Regulations 53 (1) and 53 (3)	when the *FCA* is proposing or deciding, to impose a financial penalty*		*RDC*
Regulations 53(1) and 53(3)	When the *FCA* is proposing or deciding to suspend the authorisation of an *authorised electronic money institution* or registration of a *small electronic money institution*, or to limit or otherwise restrict the carrying on of *electronic money* issuance or *payment services* business by an *electronic money institution**		*RDC*
Regulations 56(1) and 56(3)	when the *FCA* is proposing or deciding to exercise its powers to require restitution*		*RDC*
Regulation 74(7)	when the *FCA* is proposing to decide not to include a person on the register		*Executive procedures*
Regulation 74(8) (a)	when the *FCA* is deciding not to include a person on the register		*Executive procedures* where no representations are made in response to a warning notice, otherwise by the *RDC*
Schedule 2A paragraph 5(6)	when the *FCA* is proposing to refuse an application to vary the period, event or condition of a prohibition, or to remove a prohibition, or to vary or remove a restriction		*Executive procedures*
Schedule 2A paragraph 5(7)	when the *FCA* is deciding to refuse an application to vary the period, event or condition of a prohibition, or to remove a prohibition, or to vary or remove a restriction		*Executive procedures*, where no representations are made in response to a warning notice, otherwise by the *RDC*
Schedule 3, paragraph 1	when the *FCA* is proposing or deciding to publish a statement that a relevant person has been knowingly concerned with a contravention of the *Electronic Money Regulations* (Note 2)		*RDC*
Schedule 3, paragraph 1	when the *FCA* is proposing or deciding to impose a financial penalty against a relevant person (Note 2)		*RDC*

Notes:

(1) The *RDC* will take the decision to give the notice exercising the *FCA's* own-initiative power if the action involves:

(a) removing a type of activity from an authorisation or registration; or

(b) refusing an application to include a type of activity in an authorisation or registration; or

(c) restricting a person from taking on new business, dealing with a particular category of customer or refusing an application to vary or cancel such a restriction; or

(d) imposing or varying a capital requirement, or refusing an application to vary or cancel such a requirement. (2) The *Electronic Money Regulations* do not require third party rights and access to *FCA* material when the *FCA* exercises this power. However, the *FCA* generally intends to allow for third party rights and access to material when exercising this power.

Recognised Auction Platforms Regulations 2011	Description	Handbook reference	Decision maker
Regulation 5A	where the *FCA* is proposing or deciding to publish a statement censuring an *RAP*, or to impose a financial penalty on an *RAP*	**REC 2A.4**	*RDC*

Alternative Investment Fund Managers Regulations 2013	Description	Handbook reference	Decision maker
Regulation 13(1)	where the *FCA* proposes to refuse an application for entry on the register of *small registered UK AIFMs*		*Executive procedures*
Regulation 13(2)(a)	where the *FCA* decides to refuse an application for entry on the register of *small registered UK AIFMs*		*Executive procedures* where no representations are made in response to a *warning notice* otherwise by the *RDC*
Regulation 18(1)	where the *FCA* proposes to revoke the registration of a *small registered UK AIFM* including, where applicable, its registration as a *EuSEF manager* or *EuVECA manager*		*RDC*
Regulation 18(2)(a)	where the *FCA* decides to revoke the registration of a *small registered UK AIFM* including where applicable its registration as a *EuSEF manager* or *EuVECA manager*		*RDC*
Regulation 25(2)	where the *FCA* proposes to disqualify an *external valuer*		*RDC*
Regulation 25(3)(a)	where the *FCA* decides to disqualify an *external valuer*		*RDC*
Regulation 27(2)	where the *FCA* proposes to revoke approval given to a *full-scope UK AIFM* for the delegation of functions of portfolio or risk management		*Executive procedures*
Regulation 27(3)(a)	where the *FCA* decides to revoke approval given to a *full-scope UK AIFM* for the delegation of functions of portfolio management or risk management		*Executive procedures*
Regulation 56	where the *FCA* is proposing to revoke a *full-scope UK AIFM's* approval to *market* an *AIF* under regulation 54		*RDC*
Regulation 56	where the *FCA* is deciding to revoke a *full-scope UK AIFM's* approval to market an *AIF* under regulation 54		*RDC*
Regulation 62(2)	where the *FCA* proposes to revoke an *AIFM's* entitlement to *market* an *AIF*		*RDC*
Regulation 62(3)	where the *FCA* decides to revoke the entitlement of an *AIFM* to market an *AIF*		*RDC*

Part 3   FCA Handbook Materials

Alternative Investment Fund Managers Regulations 2013	Description	Handbook reference	Decision maker
Regulation 71(1)(e)	where the *FCA* is proposing or deciding to publish a statement that an *unauthorised AIFM* has contravened the regulations or directly applicable *EuSEF regulation* or *EuVECA regulation*		*RDC*
Regulation 71(1)(f)	where the *FCA* is proposing or deciding to impose a financial penalty on an *unauthorised AIFM* that has contravened the regulations or directly applicable *EuSEF regulation* or *EuVECA regulation*		*RDC*

Legal Aid, Sentencing and Punishment of Offenders Act 2012 (Referral Fees) Regulations 2013	Description	Handbook reference	Decision maker
Regulation 24(1) and 24(6)	when the *FCA* is proposing or deciding to exercise its powers to require restitution*		*RDC*
Regulation 25(1) and 26(1)	when the *FCA* is proposing or deciding to publish a statement (under regulations 14 or 15) or impose a financial penalty (under regulation 16) or impose a restriction on permission (under regulation 17) or suspend or restrict an approval (under regulation 18)*		*RDC*

The Financial Services Act 2012 (Consumer Credit) Order 2013	Description	Handbook reference	Decision maker
Article 3(3)	when the *FCA* is proposing or deciding to take action against an *approved person* for being knowingly concerned in a contravention of a *CCA Requirement* by an *authorised person*, by exercising the disciplinary powers conferred by section 66*		*RDC*
Article 3(7)	when the *FCA* is proposing or deciding to publish a statement (under section 205) or impose a financial penalty (under section 206) or suspend a *permission* or impose a restriction in relation to the carrying on of a *regulated activity* (under section 206A) for the contravention of a *CCA Requirement*. This applies in respect of an *authorised person*, or an *unauthorised person* to whom section 404C applies*		*RDC*

The Financial Services Act 2012 (Consumer Credit) Order 2013	Description	Handbook reference	Decision maker
Article 3(10)	when the *FCA* is proposing or deciding to exercise the power under section 384(5) to require a *person* to pay restitution in relation to the contravention of a *CCA Requirement**		RDC

The Immigration Act 2014 (Bank Account) Regulations 2014	Description	Handbook reference	Decision maker
Regulation 24 and 25	where the *FCA* is proposing or deciding to publish a statement (under regulations 15 or 16) or impose a financial penalty (under regulation 17) or impose a restriction on permission (under regulation 18) or suspend or restrict an approval (under regulation 19)*		RDC

2 ANNEX 2
SUPERVISORY NOTICES

2Ann2   FCA

Section of the Act	Description	Handbook reference	Decision maker
55Y(4) 55Y(7) 55Y(8)(b)	when the *FCA* is exercising its *own-initiative variation power* to vary a firm's *Part 4A permission*	SUP 7	*RDC* or *executive procedures* See **DEPP 2.5.7 G**
55Y(4) 55Y(7) 55Y(8)(b)	when the *FCA* is exercising its *own-initiative requirement power*		*RDC* or *executive procedures* See **DEPP 2.5.7 G**
78(2)/(5)	when the *FCA* is proposing to discontinue or discontinues the *listing* of a security	LR 5	*RDC* or *executive procedures* See **DEPP 2.5.9 G (4)** and **DEPP 2.5.10 G**
78(2)/(5)	when the *FCA* is proposing to suspend or suspends the *listing* of a security	LR 5	*Executive procedures*
78A(2)/(8)(b)	when the *FCA* discontinues or suspends the *listing* of a *security* on the application of the *issuer* of the *security*	LR 5	*Executive procedures*
87O(2)/(5)	when the *FCA* is proposing or deciding to exercise or deciding to maintain, vary or revoke any of the powers in sections 87K or 87L in respect of an infringement of any applicable provision.	PR 5	*Executive procedures*
88F(2)/(5)/ (6)(b)	when the *FCA* is proposing or deciding to take action to suspend, limit or restrict a *sponsor's* approval under section 88E		*Executive procedures*

Section of the Act	Description	Handbook reference	Decision maker
89V(2) 89V(5) 89 V(6)(b)	when the *FCA* is proposing or deciding to take action to suspend, limit or restrict a *primary information provider's* approval under section 89U		*Executive procedures*
96C	when the *FCA* is proposing to suspend or suspends trading in a *financial instrument*	*DTR*	*Executive procedures*
137S(5) 137S(8)(a)	when the *FCA* gives a direction under section 137S		*Executive procedures*
191B(1)	when the *FCA* gives a *restriction notice* under section 191B		*Executive procedures*
197(3)/(6)/ (7)(b)	when the *FCA* is exercising its power of intervention in respect of an *incoming firm*	**SUP 14**	*RDC* or *executive procedures* See **DEPP 2.5.7 G** and **2.5.7A G**
259(3)/(8)/ (9)(b)	when the *FCA* is exercising its power to give or, on its own initiative, to vary a direction to the *manager* and *trustee* of an *AUT*	*COLL*	*RDC*
261Z1	when the *FCA* gives a direction under section 261X or section 261Z	*COLL*	*RDC*
268(3)/ (7)(a) or (9)(a) (as a result of (8)(b)/(13))	when the *FCA* is proposing or deciding to give or, on its own initiative, to vary a direction to the *operator* of a *recognised scheme*	*COLL*	*RDC*
282 (3)/(6)/ (7)(b)	when the *FCA* is exercising its power to give a direction to an *operator*, *trustee* or *depositary* of a *recognised scheme*	*COLL*	*RDC*
301J(1)	when the *FCA* gives a *restriction notice* under section 301J		*Executive procedures*
321(2)/(5)	when the *FCA* is exercising its power to impose a requirement on a former underwriting member of Lloyd's		*RDC*

OEIC Regulations reference	Description	Handbook reference	Decision maker
Regulation 27	when the *FCA* is exercising its power to give or, on its own initiative, to vary a direction to an *ICVC* and its *depositary*	*COLL*	*RDC*

Payment Services Regulations	Description	Handbook reference	Decision maker
11(6) 11(9) 11(10)(b) 14	When the *FCA* is exercising its powers to vary a person's authorisation on its own initiative		*RDC* or *Executive procedures* See also **DEPP 4.4** (Note 1)
Schedule 4A, paragraphs 1(1), 1(2), 2(2)(a), 2(2)(b), 2(3), 4(6) and 4(7)	when exercising its power to impose a prohibition or restriction, or to vary a restriction		*RDC* or *executive procedures* (Note 2) See also **DEPP 4.4**

Payment Services Regulations	Description	Handbook reference	Decision maker
Notes: (1) The *RDC* will take the decision to give a notice exercising the *FCA's* own initiative power if the action involves: (a) removing a type of activity from an authorisation or registration; or (b) refusing an application to include a type of activity in an authorisation or registration; or (c) restricting a person from taking on new business, dealing with a particular category of customer or refusing an application to vary or cancel such a restriction; or (d) imposing or varying a capital requirement, or refusing an application to vary or cancel such a requirement. For all other types of action the decision to give a notice will be taken by *FCA* staff under *executive procedures*. (2) The *RDC* will take the decision to give a notice imposing a prohibition or imposing or varying a restriction under Schedule 4A paragraphs 1(1), 1(2), 2(2)(a), 2(2)(b), 2(3), 4(6) and 4(7). However, *FCA* staff under *executive procedures* will be the decision maker whenever a *firm* agrees not to contest the imposition of a prohibition or imposition or variation of a restriction.			

Alternative Investment Fund Managers Regulations 2013	Description	Handbook reference	Decision maker
Regulation 22(4)	where the *FCA* is exercising its power on its own initiative to give or vary a direction under regulation 22(1) to a *small registered UK AIFM*, a *EuSEF manager* or *EuVECA manager*		*RDC* or *executive procedures* See **DEPP 2.5.7 G** to **DEPP 2.5.8 G**
Regulation 22(4)	where the *FCA* is exercising its power on its own initiative to give or vary a direction under regulation 22(2) to a *small registered UK AIFM* with its registered office in an *EEA State* other than the *UK* in accordance with article 19.3 of the *EuSEF regulation* or article 18.3 of the *EuVECA regulation*		*RDC* or *executive procedures* See **DEPP 2.5.7 G** to **DEPP 2.5.8 G**

Electronic Money Regulations	Description	Handbook reference	Decision maker
Schedule 2A, paragraphs 1(1), 1(2), 2(2)(a), 2(2)(b), 2(3), 4(6) and 4(7)	when exercising its power to impose a prohibition or restriction, or to vary a restriction		*RDC* or *executive procedures* (Note 1) See also **DEPP 4.4**
Notes: (1) The *RDC* will take the decision to give a notice imposing a prohibition or imposing or varying a restriction under Schedule 2A paragraphs 1(1), 1(2), 2(2)(a), 2(2)(b), 2(3), 4(6) and 4(7). However, *FCA* staff under *executive procedures* will be the decision maker whenever a *firm* agrees not to contest the imposition of a prohibition or imposition or variation of a restriction.			

The Financial Services Act 2012 (Consumer Credit) Order 2013	Description	Handbook reference	Decision maker
Article 3(6)	when the *FCA* is exercising its power of intervention in respect of an *incoming firm* by reference to the contravention or likely contravention of a *CCA Requirement*	**SUP 14**	*RDC* or *executive procedures* See **DEPP 2.5.7 G** and **DEPP 2.5.7A G**

The Immigration Act 2014 (Bank Account) Regulations 2014	Description	Handbook reference	Decision maker
Regulation 24 and 25	where the *FCA* is proposing or deciding to publish a statement (under regulations 15 or 16) or impose a financial penalty (under regulation 17) or impose a restriction on permission (under regulation 18) or suspend or restrict an approval (under regulation 19)*		*RDC*

CHAPTER 3
THE NATURE AND PROCEDURE OF THE RDC

3.1   THE REGULATORY DECISIONS COMMITTEE

[3.97]
3.1.1 G   FCA

The *Regulatory Decisions Committee* (*RDC*) is a committee of the *FCA* Board. It is part of the *FCA* It exercises certain regulatory powers on behalf of the *FCA* and is accountable to the *FCA* Board for its decisions generally.

3.1.2 G   FCA
(1)   The *RDC* is separate from the *FCA's* executive management structure. Apart from its Chairman, none of the members of the *RDC* is an *FCA* employee.
(2)   All members of the *RDC* are appointed for fixed periods by the *FCA* Board. The *FCA* Board may remove a member of the *RDC*, but only in the event of that member's misconduct or incapacity.

3.1.3 G   FCA

The *RDC* has its own legal advisers and support staff. The *RDC* staff are separate from the *FCA* staff involved in conducting investigations and making recommendations to the *RDC*.

3.2   THE OPERATION OF THE RDC

RDC meetings and composition of panels

3.2.1 G   FCA

The *RDC* meets as often as necessary to discharge its functions. It may do so, in appropriate cases, in writing or by telephone or email or other electronic means. The *RDC* meets in private.

3.2.2 G   FCA

The *RDC* may meet as a full committee, but will ordinarily meet in panels. Each meeting of the *RDC* will generally include:
(1)   its Chairman or a Deputy Chairman (who will chair the meeting); and
(2)   at least two other members.

3.2.3 G   FCA

The composition and size of panels of the *RDC* may vary depending on the nature of the particular matter under consideration. In cases in which representations are made, it will be usual for the panel that is to consider the representations and decide whether to give a *decision notice* to include additional members of the *RDC* who have not previously considered the matter.

Conflicts of interest

3.2.4 G FCA

The *RDC* will seek not to invite a member to join a panel to consider a matter in which he has a potential conflict of interest.

3.2.5 G FCA

(1)   If a member of the *RDC* has a potential conflict of interest in any matter in which he is asked to participate he will disclose the conflict to the *RDC* Office, and disclose it:

(a)   in the case of the Chairman of the *RDC*, to the Chairman or Deputy Chairman of the *FCA*; or

(b)   in the case of a Deputy Chairman of the *RDC*, to the Chairman of the *RDC*, or if he is unavailable to the Chairman or Deputy Chairman of the *FCA*; or

(c)   in the case of any other member, to the Chairman or a Deputy Chairman of the *RDC*.

(2)   If the *person* to whom a conflict has been disclosed in accordance with (1)(a) to (c) considers it reasonable and appropriate, he will require the member of the *RDC* to stand down from consideration of that matter. He may ask another member of the *RDC* to assist him in considering the potential conflict.

3.2.6 G FCA

The *RDC* Office will record and document all disclosures of potential conflicts of interest and the steps taken to manage them.

Procedure: general

3.2.7 G FCA

The *RDC* will follow the procedure described in this section, but subject to that it will conduct itself in the manner the *RDC* Chairman or a Deputy Chairman considers suitable in order to enable the *RDC* to determine fairly and expeditiously the matter which it is considering.

3.2.8 G FCA

Each member of the *RDC* present is entitled to vote on the matter under consideration. The chairman of the meeting will have a vote as a member of the *RDC* and will have the casting vote in a tie.

3.2.9 G FCA

The *RDC* Chairman or a Deputy Chairman may, acting alone, decide:

(1)   matters relating to the arrangements for an *RDC* meeting, including its timing; and

(2)   the composition of the panel to consider a particular matter.

3.2.10 G FCA

If the *RDC* considers it relevant to its consideration, it may ask *FCA* staff to explain or provide any or all of the following:

(1)   additional information about the matter (which *FCA* staff may seek by further investigation); or

(2)   further explanation of any aspect of the *FCA* staff recommendation or accompanying papers; or

(3)   information about *FCA* priorities and policies (including as to the *FCA's* view on the law or on the correct legal interpretation of provisions of the *Act*).

3.2.11 G FCA

The *RDC* has no power under the *Act* to require *persons* to attend before it or provide information. It is not a tribunal and will make a decision based on all the relevant information available to it, which may include views of *FCA* staff about the relative quality of witness and other evidence.

Procedure: warning notices and first supervisory notices

3.2.12 G FCA

If *FCA* staff consider that action is appropriate in a matter for which the *RDC* is the decision maker, they will make a recommendation to the *RDC* that a *warning notice* or a *supervisory notice* should be given.

3.2.13 G FCA

In accordance with **DEPP 2.2** the *RDC* will consider whether it is right in all the circumstances to give the statutory notice.

3.2.14 G FCA

If the *RDC* decides that the *FCA* should give a *warning notice* or a first *supervisory notice*:

(1)   the *RDC* will settle the wording of the *warning notice* or first *supervisory notice*, and will ensure that the notice complies with the relevant provisions of the *Act*;

(2)   the *RDC* will make any relevant *statutory notice associated decisions*;

(3)   the *RDC* staff will make appropriate arrangements for the notice to be given; and

(4)   the *RDC* staff will make appropriate arrangements for the disclosure of the substantive communications between the *RDC* and the *FCA* staff who made the recommendation on which the *RDC's* decision is based. This may include providing copies in electronic format.

3.2.14A G   FCA

If *FCA* staff consider that it is appropriate to publish information about the matter to which a *warning notice* falling within section 391(1ZB) of the *Act* relates, they will make a recommendation to the *RDC* that such information should be published.

3.2.14B G   FCA

The *RDC* will consider whether it is appropriate in all the circumstances to publish information about the matter to which a *warning notice* falling within section 391(1ZB) of the *Act* relates. The *FCA's* policy on publishing such information is set out in **EG 6**.

3.2.14C G   FCA

If the *RDC* proposes that the *FCA* should publish information about the matter to which a *warning notice* falling within section 391(1ZB) of the *Act* relates:

(1)   the *RDC* will settle the wording of the statement it proposes the *FCA* should publish (warning notice statement);

(2)   the *RDC* staff will make appropriate arrangements for the warning notice statement it proposes the *FCA* should publish to be given to the persons to whom the *warning notice* was given or copied;

(3)   the proposed warning notice statement will specify the time allowed for the recipient to respond in writing to the *RDC*. This will normally be 14 *days*;

(4)   the recipient of a proposed warning notice statement may request an extension of the time allowed for its response. Such a request must normally be made within seven days of the proposed warning notice statement being given; and

(5)   the *RDC* will not normally grant a request by a person to whom the warning notice statement was given to make his response in person.

3.2.14D G   FCA

If no response to the proposed warning notice statement is received, the *FCA* will make appropriate arrangements to publish the warning notice statement.

3.2.14E G   FCA

However, if the *RDC* receives a response from the person to whom the proposed warning notice statement was given, the *RDC* will consider their response and decide whether it is appropriate in all the circumstances to publish information about the matter to which the *warning notice* relates.

3.2.14F G   FCA

If the *RDC* decides that the *FCA* should publish a warning notice statement:

(1)   the *RDC* will notify the relevant parties (including the relevant *FCA* staff) in writing of that decision;

(2)   the *RDC* will settle the wording of the warning notice statement; and

(3)   the *FCA* will make appropriate arrangements for the warning notice statement to be published.

3.2.14G G   FCA

If the *RDC* decides that the *FCA* should not publish a warning notice statement the *RDC* staff will notify the relevant parties (including the relevant *FCA* staff) in writing of that decision.

3.2.14H G   FCA

References to the *RDC* in **DEPP 3.2.14A G** to **DEPP 3.2.14G G** are to the Chairman of the *RDC* panel which issued the *warning notice* or, if he is unavailable, either the Chairman of the *RDC* or a Deputy Chairman of the *RDC*.

Procedure: representations

3.2.15 G   FCA

(1)   A *warning notice* or a first *supervisory notice* will (as required by the *Act*) specify the time allowed for making representations. This will not be less than 14 days.

(2)   The *FCA* will also, when giving a *warning notice* or a first *supervisory notice*, specify a time within which the recipient is required to indicate whether he wishes to make oral representations.

3.2.16 G   FCA

(1)   The recipient of a *warning notice* or a first *supervisory notice* may request an extension of the time allowed for making representations. Such a request must normally be made within seven days of the notice being given.

(2)   If a request is made, the Chairman or a Deputy Chairman of the *RDC* will decide whether to allow an extension, and, if so, how much additional time is to be allowed for making representations. In reaching his decision he may take account of any relevant comments from the *FCA* staff responsible for the matter.

(3)   The *RDC* staff will notify the relevant party and the *FCA* staff responsible for the matter of the decision in writing.

3.2.17 G   FCA
(1)   If the recipient of a *warning notice* or a first *supervisory notice* indicates that he wishes to make oral representations, the *RDC* staff, in conjunction with the Chairman or a Deputy Chairman of the *RDC*, will fix a date or dates for a meeting at which the relevant *RDC* members will receive those representations.
(2)   In making those arrangements the *RDC* staff will draw the Chairman's or Deputy Chairman's attention to any particular issues about the timing of the meeting which have been raised by the recipient of the notice or the relevant *FCA* staff.

3.2.18 G   FCA
The chairman of the relevant meeting will ensure that the meeting is conducted so as to enable:
(1)   the recipient of the *warning notice* or first *supervisory notice* to make representations;
(2)   the relevant *FCA* staff to respond to those representations;
(3)   the *RDC* members to raise with those present any points or questions about the matter (whether in response to particular representations or more generally about the matter); and
(4)   the recipient of the notice to respond to points made by *FCA* staff or the *RDC*;

but the chairman may ask the recipient of the notice or *FCA* staff to limit their representations or response in length or to particular issues arising from the *warning notice* or first *supervisory notice*.

3.2.19 G   FCA
The recipient of the *warning notice* or *supervisory notice* may wish to be legally represented at the meeting, but this is not a requirement.

3.2.20 G   FCA
In appropriate cases, the chairman of a meeting for oral representations may ask those present to provide additional information in writing after the meeting. If he does so, he will specify the time within which that information is to be provided.

3.2.21 G   FCA
The *RDC* will not, after the *FCA* has given a *warning notice* or a first *supervisory notice*, meet with or discuss the matter whilst it is still ongoing with the *FCA* staff responsible for the case without other relevant parties being present or otherwise having the opportunity to respond.

Procedure: decision notices and second supervisory notices
3.2.22 G   FCA
If no representations are made in response to the *warning notice* or first *supervisory notice*, the *FCA* will regard as undisputed the allegations or matters set out in the notice and the default procedure will apply: see **DEPP 2.3.2 G** to **DEPP 2.3.4 G**.

3.2.23 G   FCA
However, if representations are made, in accordance with **DEPP 2.3.1 G** the *RDC* will consider whether it is right in all the circumstances to give the *decision notice* or a second *supervisory notice* (as appropriate).

3.2.24 G   FCA
If the *RDC* decides that the *FCA* should give a *decision notice* or a second *supervisory notice*:
(1)   the *RDC* will settle the wording of the notice which will include a brief summary of the key representations made and how they have been dealt with, and will ensure that the notice complies with the relevant provisions of the *Act*;
(2)   the *RDC* will make any relevant *statutory notice associated decisions*, including whether the *FCA* is required to give a copy of the notice to a third party; and
(3)   the *RDC* staff will make appropriate arrangements for the notice to be given.

3.2.25 G   FCA
If the *RDC* decides that the *FCA* should not give a *decision notice* or a second *supervisory notice* the *RDC* staff will notify the relevant parties (including the relevant *FCA* staff) in writing of that decision.

Discontinuance of FCA action
3.2.26 G   FCA
FCA staff responsible for recommending action to the *RDC* will continue to assess the appropriateness of the proposed action in the light of new information or representations they receive and any material change in the facts or circumstances relating to a particular matter. It may be therefore that they decide to give a *notice of discontinuance* to a *person* to whom a *warning notice* or *decision notice* has been given. The decision to give a *notice of discontinuance* does not require the agreement of the *RDC*, but *FCA* staff will inform the *RDC* of the discontinuance of the proceedings.

Tribunal proceedings

3.2.27 G   FCA

A decision by the *RDC* to give a *decision notice* or *supervisory notice* may lead to a reference to the *Tribunal* under the *Act*. The conduct of proceedings before the *Tribunal* is not however a matter for the *RDC*.

3.3   STRAIGHTFORWARD DECISIONS

3.3.1 G   FCA

In *statutory notice* cases for which the *RDC* is the decision-maker, the Chairman or a Deputy Chairman of the *RDC* may take a straightforward decision to give the *statutory notice*.

3.3.2 G   FCA

The Chairman or, if he is unavailable, a Deputy Chairman will decide whether a decision is straightforward. In doing so he will have regard to all the circumstances. These may include:
(1)   the significance of the decision to those who would be affected by it;
(2)   its novelty in the light of stated policy and established practice;
(3)   the complexity of the relevant considerations, including whether representations have been made;
(4)   the range of alternative options;
(5)   the extent to which the facts relating to the decision are or may be disputed.

3.3.3 G   FCA

The *RDC* Chairman or a Deputy Chairman may, notwithstanding the fact that a decision is straightforward, take the decision to give the *statutory notice* jointly with one or more other members of the *RDC* if he considers it appropriate to do so.

3.4   URGENT SUPERVISORY NOTICE CASES

3.4.1 G   FCA

In urgent *supervisory notice* cases for which the *RDC* is the decision maker, the decision to give the *supervisory notice* may be taken by the *RDC* Chairman or, if he is unavailable, a Deputy Chairman, and, if it is practicable, one or more other *RDC* members.

3.4.2 G   FCA

The *RDC* Chairman or Deputy Chairman will take such a decision only if satisfied that the action proposed should occur before it is practicable to convene an *RDC* panel.

3.4.3 G   FCA

In an exceptionally urgent case the decision to give a *supervisory notice* may be taken by a member of the *FCA's* executive of at least director of division level if:
(1)   *FCA* staff consider that the action should be taken before a recommendation to the Chairman or a Deputy Chairman of the *RDC* can be made; and
(2)   an urgent decision on the proposed action is necessary to protect the interests of consumers.

3.4.4 G   FCA

In the circumstances described in **DEPP 3.4.3 G**, the *FCA* considers that it may be necessary for an *FCA* director of division to take the decision to give the *supervisory notice* even if he has been involved in establishing the evidence on which the decision is based, as permitted by section 395(3) of the *Act*. Where practicable, however, *FCA* staff will seek to ensure that the *FCA* director has not been so involved.

CHAPTER 4
DECISIONS BY FCA STAFF UNDER EXECUTIVE PROCEDURES

4.1   EXECUTIVE DECISION MAKER

Who takes the decision
[3.98]
4.1.1 G   FCA

All *statutory notice decisions* under *executive procedures* and decisions referred to in **DEPP 2.5.6A G** will be taken either by a *senior staff committee* or by an individual *FCA* staff member.

4.1.2 G   FCA

In the case of a *senior staff committee*, the decision will be taken by *FCA* staff who have not been directly involved in establishing the evidence on which the decision is based or by two or more *FCA* staff who include a person not directly involved in establishing that evidence, except in accordance with section 395(3) of the *Act*.

4.1.2A G FCA

In the case of an individual *FCA* staff member, the decision will be taken by someone who has not been directly involved in establishing the evidence on which the decision is based, except in accordance with section 395(3) of the *Act*.

Decisions by senior staff committee

4.1.3 G FCA

The *FCA's* senior executive committee will from time to time determine that particular categories of *statutory notice decision* to be taken under *executive procedures* and decisions referred to in **DEPP 2.5.6A G** will be taken by a *senior staff committee*.

4.1.4 G FCA

A *senior staff committee* will consist of such *FCA* staff members as the *FCA's* senior executive committee may from time to time determine. The *FCA's* senior executive committee may authorise the chairman of a *senior staff committee* to select its other members. A *senior staff committee* is accountable for its decisions to the *FCA's* senior executive committee and, through it, to the *FCA* Board.

4.1.5 G FCA

A *senior staff committee* may operate through standing or specific sub-committees to consider particular decisions or classes of decision, for which accountability will lie through the committee. Each meeting of a *senior staff committee*, or sub-committee, will include:
(1)   an individual with authority to act as its chairman; and
(2)   at least two other members.

4.1.6 G FCA

A *senior staff committee* will operate on the basis of a recommendation from an *FCA* staff member of at least the level of associate, and with the benefit of legal advice from an *FCA* staff member of at least the level of associate.

Decisions by individual FCA staff members

4.1.7 G FCA

Statutory notice decisions to be taken under *executive procedures* and decisions referred to in **DEPP 2.5.6A G**, and not falling within the responsibility of a *senior staff committee*, will be taken by an individual *FCA* staff member. The decision will be:
(1)   made by an executive director of the *FCA* Board or his delegate (who will be of at least the level of associate);
(2)   on the recommendation of an *FCA* staff member of at least the level of associate; and
(3)   with the benefit of legal advice from an *FCA* staff member of at least the level of associate.

except for decisions made in relation to consumer redress schemes pursuant to provisions of the Consumer Redress Schemes sourcebook (*CONRED*), where (1) will apply, but not (2) or (3).

4.1.8 G FCA

The individual who takes a decision under *executive procedures* is accountable to the *FCA* Board directly (if an executive director) or otherwise through line management responsible for the decision concerned.

4.1.9 G FCA

An *FCA* staff member who considers that a *statutory notice decision* or a decision referred to in **DEPP 2.5.6A G** should be taken above his own level is free to refer that decision to a more senior level. If an *FCA* staff member consults another staff member about a decision, the decision remains the independent decision of the *FCA* staff member who consults his colleague, unless it is agreed that the decision should instead be taken by the colleague, and the colleague has the delegated authority to do so.

4.1.10 G FCA

If an individual responsible for a decision under *executive procedures* (or a more senior *FCA* staff member with responsibilities in relation to the decision concerned) considers that it warrants collective consideration, the individual may:
(1)   take the decision himself, following consultation with other *FCA* staff members, as above; or
(2)   refer it to a *senior staff committee*, which will take the decision itself.

Conflicts of interest

4.1.11 G FCA

Part 3 FCA Handbook Materials

(1)   *FCA* staff are required by their contract of employment to comply with a code of conduct
         which imposes strict rules to cover the handling of conflicts of interest which may arise from
         personal interests or associations. *FCA* staff subject to a conflict of interest must declare that
         interest to the *person* to whom they are immediately responsible for a decision.

(2)   If a member of a *senior staff committee* has a potential conflict of interest in any matter in
         which he is asked to participate he will disclose the conflict to the secretariat of the *senior
         staff committee*, and disclose it:

    (a)   in the case of the chairman of the senior staff committee, to a member of the *FCA's*
                  senior executive committee or, if the *person* with the conflict is the chairman of the
                  FCA's senior executive committee, to the Chairman of the *FCA*;

    (b)   in the case of the deputy chairman of the senior staff committee, to the chairman of
                  the committee, or if he is unavailable, to a member of the *FCA's* senior executive
                  committee;

    (c)   in the case of any other member to the chairman or deputy chairman of the *senior
                  staff committee*.

(3)   If the person to whom the conflict has been disclosed in accordance with **DEPP 4.1.11 G (2)**
         considers it reasonable and appropriate, he will require the member of the *senior staff
         committee* to stand down from consideration of the matter.

4.1.12 G   FCA

The secretariat to the *senior staff committee* will record and document all disclosures of potential
conflicts of interest and the steps taken to manage them.

Procedure

4.1.13 G   FCA

The procedure for taking decisions under *executive procedures* will generally be less formal and
structured than that for decisions by the *RDC*. Broadly, however, *FCA* staff responsible for taking
statutory notice decisions under *executive procedures* will follow a procedure similar to that
described at **DEPP 3.2.7 G** to **DEPP 3.2.27 G** for the *RDC* except that:

(1)   in a case where the decision will be taken by a *senior staff committee*:

    (a)   the chairman or deputy chairman of the *senior staff committee* will perform the role
                  of the Chairman of the *RDC*; and

    (b)   the secretariat to the *senior staff committee* will perform the role of the *RDC* staff;

(2)   in a case where the decision will be taken by individual members of *FCA* staff, the distinction
         between the role of the *RDC*, its Chairman and the *RDC* staff has no application;

(3)   the *FCA* staff responsible for taking the *statutory notice decision* may be advised by legal
         advisers who have also advised *FCA* staff recommending action by the *FCA*;

(4)   the *FCA* will not normally disclose the communications between the *FCA* staff recommend-
         ing that action be taken and those responsible for the decision to give the *statutory notice*
         unless the *FCA* has stated publicly that it will adopt a practice of disclosing such
         communications, or a class of communications, in respect of particular categories of decision
         taken by *FCA* staff under *executive procedures*; and

(5)   **DEPP 3.2.11 G** and **DEPP 3.2.21 G** will not apply.

4.1.14 G   FCA

Broadly, *FCA* staff responsible for taking decisions referred to in **DEPP 2.5.6A G** will follow a
procedure similar to that described at **DEPP 3.2.7 G** to **DEPP 3.2.27 G** for the *RDC* (subject to the
exceptions in **DEPP 4.1.13 G (1)** to **DEPP 4.1.13 G (5)** which also reflects that these decisions are
not *statutory notice* decisions.

4.2   URGENT STATUTORY NOTICE CASES

4.2.1 G   FCA

If *FCA* staff recommend that action be taken and they consider that the decision falls within the
responsibility of a *senior staff committee*:

(1)   in general the *FCA* staff's recommendation will go before the *senior staff committee*;

(2)   in urgent *statutory notice* cases for which a *senior staff committee* is responsible, the decision
         to give the *statutory notice* may be taken by the chairman or, if he is unavailable, a deputy
         chairman of the *senior staff committee*, and, if it is practicable, one or more other members
         of the committee;

(3)   the chairman or deputy chairman of the senior staff committee will take such a decision only
         if satisfied that the action proposed should occur before it is practicable to convene a meeting
         of the senior staff committee;

(4)   in an exceptionally urgent *statutory notice* case, if in the *FCA* staff's opinion:

    (a)   the action should be taken before a recommendation to the chairman or a deputy
                  chairman of the *senior staff committee* could be made; and

    (b)   an urgent decision on the proposed action is necessary to protect the interests of
                  consumers;

the decision may be taken by a member of the *FCA's* executive of at least director of division level (which may include an acting director) or, in the case of a *senior staff committee* which reports directly to the *FCA's* senior executive committee, by a member of that committee.

4.2.2 G   FCA

In the circumstances described in **DEPP 4.2.1 G (4)** the *FCA* considers that it may be necessary for an *FCA* director of division or member of a *senior staff committee* to take the decision to give a *supervisory notice* even if he has been involved in establishing the evidence on which the decision is based, as permitted by section 395(3) of the *Act*. Where practicable, however, *FCA* staff will seek to ensure that the *FCA* director or committee member has not been so involved.

CHAPTER 5
SETTLEMENT DECISION PROCEDURE

5.1   SETTLEMENT DECISION MAKERS

Introduction

[3.99]

5.1.1 G   FCA

(1)   A *person* subject to enforcement action may agree to a financial penalty or other outcome rather than contest formal action by the *FCA*.

(2)   The fact that he does so will not usually obviate the need for a statutory notice recording the *FCA's* decision to take that action. Where, however, the *person* subject to enforcement action agrees not to contest the content of a proposed *statutory notice*, the decision to give that statutory notice will be taken by senior *FCA* staff.

(3)   The decision will be taken jointly by two members of the *FCA's* senior management, one of whom will be of at least director of division level (which may include an acting director) and the other of whom will be of at least head of department level (the *"settlement decision makers"*).

(4)   At least one of the *settlement decision makers* will not be from the Enforcement and Financial Crime Division. The other *settlement decision maker* will usually be, but need not be, from the Enforcement and Financial Crime Division. A *settlement decision maker* will not have been directly involved in establishing the evidence on which the decision is based.

(5)   "Statutory notice" for these purposes:

(a)   means any *statutory notice* the giving of which would otherwise require a decision by the *RDC*;

(b)   includes a *statutory notice associated decision*.

Procedure: general

5.1.2 G   FCA

A *person* who is or may be subject to enforcement action may wish to discuss the proposed action with *FCA* staff through settlement discussions.

5.1.3 G   FCA

Settlement discussions may take place at any time during the enforcement process if both parties agree. This might be before the giving of a *warning notice*, before a *decision notice*, or even after referral of the matter to the *Tribunal*. But the *FCA* would not normally agree to detailed settlement discussions until it has a sufficient understanding of the nature and gravity of the suspected misconduct or issue to make a reasonable assessment of the appropriate outcome. Settlement after a *decision notice* will be rare.

5.1.4 G   FCA

FCA staff and the *person* concerned may agree that neither the *FCA* nor the *person* concerned would seek to rely against the other on any admissions or statements made in the course of their settlement discussions if the matter is considered subsequently by the *RDC* or the *Tribunal*.

Procedure: participation of decision makers in discussions

5.1.5 G   FCA

(1)   The *settlement decision makers* may, but need not, participate in the discussions exploring possible settlement.

(2)   If the *settlement decision makers* have not been involved in the discussions, but an agreement has been reached, they may ask to meet the relevant *FCA* staff or the *person* concerned in order to assist in the consideration of the proposed settlement.

5.1.6 G   FCA

The terms of any proposed settlement:

(1)   will be put in writing and be agreed by *FCA* staff and the *person* concerned;

(2)   may refer to a draft of the proposed *statutory notices* setting out the facts of the matter and the *FCA's* conclusions;

(3)   may, depending upon the stage in the enforcement process at which agreement is reached, include an agreement by the *person* concerned to:

    (a)   waive and not exercise any rights under sections 387 (Warning notices) and 394 (Access to Authority material) of the *Act* to notice of, or access to, material relied upon by the *FCA* and any secondary material which might undermine the *FCA* decision to give the *statutory* notice;

    (b)   waive and not exercise any rights under section 387 of the *Act* or otherwise to make representations to the *RDC* in respect of a *warning notice* or first *supervisory notice*;

    (c)   not object to the giving of a *decision notice* before the expiry of the 14 day period after the giving of a *warning notice* specified under section 387 of the *Act*;

    (d)   not dispute with the *FCA* the facts and matters set out in a *warning notice, decision notice, supervisory notice* or *final notice* and to waive and not exercise any right under section 208 (Decision notice) of the *Act* to refer the matter to the *Tribunal*.

5.1.7 G   FCA

The *settlement decision makers* may:

(1)   accept the proposed settlement by deciding to give a *statutory notice* based on the terms of the settlement; or

(2)   decline the proposed settlement;

whether or not the *settlement decision makers* have met with the relevant *FCA* staff or the *person* concerned.

5.1.8 G   FCA

(1)   Where the *settlement decision makers* decline to issue a *statutory notice* despite the proposed settlement, they may invite *FCA* staff and the *person* concerned to enter into further discussions to try to achieve an outcome the *settlement decision makers* would be prepared to endorse.

(2)   However, if the proposed action by the *FCA* has been submitted to the *RDC* for consideration, it will be for the *RDC* to decide:

    (a)   whether to extend the period for representations in response to a *warning notice or* first *supervisory notice*; or

    (b)   if representations have been made in response to a *warning notice or* first *supervisory notice*, whether to proceed to give a *decision notice or* second *supervisory notice*.

Settlement by mediation

5.1.9 G   FCA

The *FCA* and other parties may agree to mediation as a way of facilitating settlement in appropriate cases.

Third party rights

5.1.10 G   FCA

(1)   **DEPP 2.4** sets out the *FCA's* approach to giving third parties copies of *statutory notices* pursuant to section 393 (Third party rights) of the *Act*.

(2)   The decision to give a *warning notice* or a *decision notice* to a third party is a *statutory notice associated decision*.

(3)   In cases therefore where the decision to give a *warning notice* or *decision notice* is taken by *settlement decision makers*, those decision makers will decide whether a copy of the notice should be given to a third party in accordance with section 393 of the *Act*. Any representations made by the third party in response to a *warning notice* will be considered by the *settlement decision makers*

CHAPTER 6
PENALTIES

6.1   INTRODUCTION

[3.100]
6.1.1 G   FCA

DEPP 6 includes the *FCA's* statement of policy with respect to the imposition and amount of penalties under the *Act*, as required by sections 63C(1), 69(1), 88C, 89S, 93(1), 124(1), 131J(1), 192N, 210(1), 312J and 345D of the *Act*.

6.1.2 G   FCA

The principal purpose of imposing a financial penalty or issuing a *public censure* is to promote high standards of regulatory and/or market conduct by deterring *persons* who have committed *breaches* from committing further *breaches*, helping to deter other *persons* from committing similar *breaches*, and demonstrating generally the benefits of compliant behaviour. Financial penalties and *public censures* are therefore tools that the *FCA* may employ to help it to achieve its *statutory objectives*.

6.2 DECIDING WHETHER TO TAKE ACTION

6.2.1 G   FCA

The *FCA* will consider the full circumstances of each case when determining whether or not to take action for a financial penalty or *public censure*. Set out below is a list of factors that may be relevant for this purpose. The list is not exhaustive: not all of these factors may be applicable in a particular case, and there may be other factors, not listed, that are relevant.

(1)   The nature, seriousness and impact of the suspected *breach*, including:
     (a)   whether the *breach* was deliberate or reckless;
     (b)   the duration and frequency of the *breach*;
     (c)   the amount of any benefit gained or loss avoided as a result of the *breach*;
     (d)   whether the *breach* reveals serious or systemic weaknesses of the management systems or *internal controls* relating to all or part of a *person's* business;
     (e)   the impact or potential impact of the *breach* on the orderliness of markets including whether confidence in those markets has been damaged or put at risk;
     (f)   the loss or risk of loss caused to *consumers* or other market users;
     (g)   the nature and extent of any *financial crime* facilitated, occasioned or otherwise attributable to the *breach*; and
     (h)   whether there are a number of smaller issues, which individually may not justify disciplinary action, but which do so when taken collectively.

(2)   The conduct of the *person* after the *breach*, including the following:
     (a)   how quickly, effectively and completely the *person* brought the *breach* to the attention of the *FCA* or another relevant regulatory authority;
     (b)   the degree of co-operation the *person* showed during the investigation of the *breach*;
     (c)   any remedial steps the *person* has taken in respect of the *breach*;
     (d)   the likelihood that the same type of *breach* (whether on the part of the *person* under investigation or others) will recur if no action is taken;
     (e)   whether the *person* concerned has complied with any requirements or rulings of another regulatory authority relating to his *behaviour* (for example, where relevant, those of the *Takeover Panel* or an *RIE*); and
     (f)   the nature and extent of any false or inaccurate information given by the person and whether the information appears to have been given in an attempt to knowingly mislead the *FCA*.

(3)   The previous disciplinary record and compliance history of the *person* including:
     (a)   whether the *FCA* (or any *previous regulator*) has taken any previous disciplinary action resulting in adverse findings against the *person*;
     (b)   whether the *person* has previously undertaken not to do a particular act or engage in particular *behaviour*;
     (c)   whether the *FCA* (or any *previous regulator*) has previously taken protective action in respect of a *firm*, using its own initiative powers, by means of a variation of a *Part 4A permission* or otherwise, or has previously requested the *firm* to take remedial action, and the extent to which such action has been taken; and
     (d)   the general compliance history of the *person*, including whether the *FCA* (or any *previous regulator*) has previously issued the *person* with a private warning.

(4)   *FCA guidance* and other published materials:
     The *FCA* will not take action against a person for *behaviour* that it considers to be in line with *guidance*, other materials published by the *FCA* in support of the *Handbook* or *FCA*-confirmed Industry Guidance which were current at the time of the *behaviour* in question. (The manner in which *guidance* and other published materials may otherwise be relevant to an enforcement case is described in **EG 2**.)

(5)   Action taken by the *FSA* or *FCA* in previous similar cases.

(6)   Action taken by other domestic or international regulatory authorities:
     Where other regulatory authorities propose to take action in respect of the *breach* which is under consideration by the *FCA*, or one similar to it, the *FCA* will consider whether the other authority's action would be adequate to address the *FCA's* concerns, or whether it would be appropriate for the *FCA* to take its own action.

6.2.2 G   FCA

When deciding whether to take action for *market abuse* or *requiring or encouraging*, the *FCA* may consider the following additional factors:

(1)   The degree of sophistication of the users of the market in question, the size and liquidity of the market, and the susceptibility of the market to *market abuse*.

(2)   The impact, having regard to the nature of the *behaviour*, that any financial penalty or *public censure* may have on the financial markets or on the interests of *consumers*:
     (a)   a penalty may show that high standards of market conduct are being enforced in the financial markets, and may bolster market confidence;

(b)   a penalty may protect the interests of *consumers* by deterring future *market abuse* and improving standards of conduct in a market;

(c)   in the context of a *takeover bid*, the *FCA* may consider that the impact of the use of its powers is likely to have an adverse effect on the timing or outcome of that bid, and therefore it would not be in the interests of financial markets or *consumers* to take action for *market abuse* during the *takeover bid*. If the *FCA* considers that the proposed use of its powers may have that effect, it will consult the *Takeover Panel* and give due weight to its views.

6.2.2A G   FCA

The factors to which the *FCA* will have regard when deciding whether to impose a penalty under regulation 34 of the *RCB Regulations* are set out in **RCB 4.2.3 G**.

Discipline for breaches of FCA rules on systems and controls against money laundering

6.2.3 G   FCA

The *FCA's* rules on systems and controls against *money laundering* are set out in **SYSC 3.2** and **SYSC 6.3**. The *FCA*, when considering whether to take action for a financial penalty or censure in respect of a breach of those rules, will have regard to whether a *firm* has followed relevant provisions in the Guidance for the UK financial sector issued by the Joint Money Laundering Steering Group.

Action against approved persons under section 66 of the Act

6.2.4 G   FCA

The primary responsibility for ensuring compliance with a *firm's* regulatory obligations rests with the *firm* itself. However, the *FCA* may take disciplinary action against an *approved person* where there is evidence of personal culpability on the part of that *approved person*. Personal culpability arises where the *behaviour* was deliberate or where the *approved person's* standard of *behaviour* was below that which would be reasonable in all the circumstances at the time of the conduct concerned.

6.2.5 G   FCA

In some cases it may not be appropriate to take disciplinary measures against a *firm* for the actions of an *approved person* (an example might be where the *firm* can show that it took all reasonable steps to prevent the *breach*). In other cases, it may be appropriate for the *FCA* to take action against both the *firm* and the *approved person*. For example, a *firm* may have breached the *rule* requiring it to take reasonable care to establish and maintain such systems and controls as are appropriate to its business (**SYSC 3.1.1 R** or **SYSC 4.1.10 R**), and an *approved person* may have taken advantage of those deficiencies to front run orders or misappropriate assets.

6.2.6 G   FCA

In addition to the general factors outlined in **DEPP 6.2.1 G**, there are some additional considerations that may be relevant when deciding whether to take action against an *approved person* pursuant to section 66 of the *Act*. This list of those considerations is non-exhaustive. Not all considerations below may be relevant in every case, and there may be other considerations, not listed, that are relevant.

(1)   The *approved person's* position and responsibilities. The *FCA* may take into account the responsibility of those exercising *significant influence functions* in the *firm* for the conduct of the *firm*. The more senior the *approved person* responsible for the misconduct, the more seriously the *FCA* is likely to view the misconduct, and therefore the more likely it is to take action against the *approved person*.

(2)   Whether disciplinary action against the *firm* rather than the *approved person* would be a more appropriate regulatory response.

(3)   Whether disciplinary action would be a proportionate response to the nature and seriousness of the breach by the *approved person*.

6.2.7 G   FCA

The *FCA* will not discipline *approved persons* on the basis of vicarious liability (that is, holding them responsible for the acts of others), provided appropriate delegation and supervision has taken place (see **APER 4.6.13 G** and **APER 4.6.14 G**). In particular, disciplinary action will not be taken against an *approved person* performing a *significant influence function* simply because a regulatory failure has occurred in an area of business for which he is responsible. The *FCA* will consider that an *approved person* performing a *significant influence function* may have breached *Statements of Principle* 5 to 7 only if his conduct was below the standard which would be reasonable in all the circumstances at the time of the conduct concerned (see also **APER 3.1.8 G**).

6.2.8 G   FCA

An *approved person* will not be in breach if he has exercised due and reasonable care when assessing information, has reached a reasonable conclusion and has acted on it.

6.2.9 G   FCA

Where disciplinary action is taken against an *approved person* the onus will be on the *FCA* to show that the *approved person* has been guilty of misconduct.

Action under section 63A of the Act against persons that perform a controlled function without approval

6.2.9A G   FCA

In addition to the general factors outlined in **DEPP 6.2.1 G**, there are some additional considerations that the *FCA* will have regard to when deciding whether to take action against a *person* that performs a *controlled function* without approval contrary to section 63A of the *Act*.

(1)   The conduct of the *person*. The *FCA* will take into consideration whether, while performing *controlled functions* without approval, the *person* committed misconduct in respect of which, if he had been approved, the *FCA* could have taken action pursuant to section 66 of the *Act* and, if so, the seriousness of that misconduct.

(2)   The extent to which the *person* could reasonably be expected to have known that he was performing a *controlled function* without approval. The circumstances in which the *FCA* would expect to be satisfied that a *person* could reasonably be expected to have known that he was performing a *controlled function* without approval include:

     (a)   the *person* had previously performed a similar role at the same or another *firm* for which he had been approved;

     (b)   the *person's firm* or another *firm* had previously applied for approval for the *person* to perform the same or a similar *controlled function*;

     (c)   the *person's* seniority or experience was such that he could reasonably be expected to have known that he was performing a *controlled function* without approval; and

     (d)   the *person's firm* had clearly apportioned responsibilities so that the *person's* role, and the responsibilities associated with it, were clear.

(3)   The length of the period during which the *person* performed a *controlled function* without approval.

(4)   Whether the *person* is an individual.

(5)   The appropriateness of taking action against the *person* instead of, or in addition to, taking action against an *authorised person*. In assessing this, the *FCA* will take into consideration the extent of the culpability of an *authorised person* for the *person* performing a *controlled function* without approval. For example, a relevant factor may be that an *authorised person* decided that the *person* did not need to obtain approval and it was reasonable for the *person* to rely on the *authorised person's* judgment.

(6)   The *person's* position and responsibilities. The more senior the *person* that performs a *controlled function* without approval, the more seriously the *FCA* is likely to view his behaviour, and therefore the more likely it is to take action against the *person*.

Action against directors, former directors and persons discharging managerial responsibilities for breaches under Part VI of the Act

6.2.10 G   FCA

The primary responsibility for ensuring compliance with Part VI of the *Act*, the *Part 6 rules*, the *prospectus rules* or a provision otherwise made in accordance with the *Prospectus Directive* or a requirement imposed under such provision rests with the persons identified in section 91(1) and section 91(1A) (Penalties for breach of Part 6 rules) of the *Act* respectively. Normally therefore, any disciplinary action taken by the *FCA* for contraventions of these obligations will in the first instance be against those persons.

6.2.11 G   FCA

However, in the case of a contravention by a *person* referred to in section 91(1)(a) or section 91(1)(b) or section 91(1A) of the *Act* ("P"), where the *FCA* considers that another *person* who was at the material time a *director* of P was knowingly concerned in the contravention, the *FCA* may take disciplinary action against that *person*. In circumstances where the *FCA* does not consider it appropriate to seek a disciplinary sanction against P (notwithstanding a breach of relevant requirements by such person), the *FCA* may nonetheless seek a disciplinary sanction against any other person who was at the material time a *director* of P and was knowingly concerned in the contravention.

6.2.12 G   FCA

Persons discharging managerial responsibilities within an issuer and their *connected persons*, who have requested or approved the admission of a *financial instrument* to trading on a *regulated market*, and *connected persons* have their own responsibilities under the *disclosure rules*, as set out in **DTR 3**, for which they are primarily responsible. Accordingly, disciplinary action for a breach of the *disclosure rules* will not necessarily involve the issuer.

[**Note:** In paragraph 6.2.12, 'connected person' has the meaning in relation to a *person discharging managerial responsibilities* within an *issuer* attributed to it in subsection (5) of the definition of 'connected person' in the Handbook *Glossary*.]

6.2.13 G FCA

In deciding whether to take action, the *FCA* will consider the full circumstances of each case. Factors that may be relevant for this purpose include, but are not limited to, the factors at **DEPP 6.2.1 G**.

Discipline for breaches of the Principles for Businesses

6.2.14 G FCA

The *Principles* are set out in **PRIN 2.1.1 R**. The *Principles* are a general statement of the fundamental obligations of *firms* under the *regulatory system*. The *Principles* derive their authority from the *FCA's* rule-making powers set out in section 137A (General rule-making power) of the *Act*. A breach of a *Principle* will make a *firm* liable to disciplinary action. Where the *FCA* considers this is appropriate, it will discipline a *firm* on the basis of the *Principles* alone.

6.2.15 G FCA

In determining whether a *Principle* has been breached, it is necessary to look to the standard of conduct required by the *Principle* in question at the time. Under each of the *Principles*, the onus will be on the *FCA* to show that a *firm* has been at fault in some way.

Discipline for breaches of the Listing Principles and Premium Listing Principles

6.2.16 G FCA

The Listing Principles and Premium Listing Principles are set out in **LR 7**. The Listing Principles set out in **LR 7.2.1 R** are a general statement of the fundamental obligations of all *listed companies*. In addition to the Listing Principles, the Premium Listing Principles set out in **LR 7.2.1A R** are a general statement of the fundamental obligations of all *listed companies* with a *premium listing* of *equity shares*. The Listing Principles and Premium Listing Principles derive their authority from the *FCA's* rule making powers set out in section 73A(1) (Part 6 Rules) of the *Act*. A breach of a Listing Principle or, if applicable, a Premium Listing Principle, will make a *listed company* liable to disciplinary action by the *FCA*.

6.2.17 G FCA

In determining whether a Listing Principle or Premium Listing Principle has been broken, it is necessary to look to the standard of conduct required by the Listing Principle or Premium Listing Principle in question. Under each of the Listing Principles and Premium Listing Principles, the onus will be on the *FCA* to show that a *listed company* has been at fault in some way. This requirement will differ depending upon the relevant Listing Principle or Premium Listing Principle.

6.2.18 G FCA

In certain cases, it may be appropriate to discipline a *listed company* on the basis of the a Listing Principle or, if applicable, a Premium Listing Principle, alone. Examples include the following:
(1)   where there is no detailed *listing rule* which prohibits the *behaviour* in question, but the *behaviour* clearly contravenes a Listing Principle or, if applicable, a Premium Listing Principle;
(2)   where a *listed company* has committed a number of breaches of detailed *rules* which individually may not merit disciplinary action, but the cumulative effect of which indicates the breach of a Listing Principle or, if applicable, a Premium Listing Principle.

Action involving other regulatory authorities or enforcement agencies

6.2.19 G FCA

Some types of *breach* may potentially result not only in action by the *FCA*, but also action by other domestic or overseas regulatory authorities or enforcement agencies.

6.2.20 G FCA

When deciding how to proceed in such cases, the *FCA* will examine the circumstances of the case, and consider, in the light of the relevant investigation, disciplinary and enforcement powers, whether it is appropriate for the *FCA* or another authority to take action to address the *breach*. The *FCA* will have regard to all the circumstances of the case including whether the other authority has adequate powers to address the *breach* in question.

6.2.21 G FCA

In some cases, it may be appropriate for both the *FCA* and another authority to be involved, and for both to take action in a particular case arising from the same facts. For example, a breach of *RIE* rules may be so serious as to justify the *FCA* varying or cancelling the *firm's Part IV permission*, or withdrawing approval from *approved persons*, as well as action taken by the *RIE*. In such cases, the

FCA will work with the relevant authority to ensure that cases are dealt with efficiently and fairly, under operating arrangements in place (if any) between the *FCA* and the relevant authority.

6.2.22 G   FCA

In relation to *behaviour* which may have happened or be happening in the context of a *takeover bid*, the *FCA* will refer to the *Takeover Panel* and give due weight to its views. Where the *Takeover Code* has procedures for complaint about any behaviour, the *FCA* expects parties to exhaust those procedures. The *FCA* will not, save in exceptional circumstances, take action under any of section 123 (FCA's power to impose penalties), section 129 (Power of court to impose penalties), section 381 (Injunctions), sections 383 or 384 (Restitution) in respect of *behaviour* to which the *Takeover Code* is relevant before the conclusion of the procedures available under the *Takeover Code*.

6.2.23 G   FCA

The *FCA* will not take action against a *person* over *behaviour* which (a) conforms with the *Takeover Code* or rules of an *RIE* and (b) falls within the terms of any provision of the *Code of Market Conduct* which states that *behaviour* so conforming does not amount to *market abuse*. The *FCA* will seek the *Takeover Panel's* or relevant *RIE's* views on whether *behaviour* complies with the *Takeover Code* or *RIE* rules and will attach considerable weight to its views.

6.2.24 G   FCA

If any of the circumstances in **DEPP 6.2.26 G** apply, and the *FCA* considers that the use of its disciplinary powers under section 123 or section 129, or of its injunctive powers under section 381 or of its powers relating to restitution under section 383 or 384 is appropriate, it will not take action during an offer to which the *Takeover Code* applies except in the circumstances set out in **DEPP 6.2.27 G**.

6.2.25 G   FCA

In any case where the *FCA* considers that the use of its powers under any of sections 123, 129, 381, 383 or 384 of the *Act* may be appropriate, if that use may affect the timetable or outcome of a *takeover bid* or where it is appropriate in the context of any exercise by the *Takeover Panel* of its powers and authority, the *FCA* will consult the *Takeover Panel* before using any of those powers.

6.2.26 G   FCA

Where the *behaviour* of a *person* which amounts to *market abuse* is *behaviour* to which the *Takeover Code* is relevant, the use of the *Takeover Panel's* powers will often be sufficient to address the relevant concerns. In cases where this is not so, the *FCA* will need to consider whether it is appropriate to use any of its own powers under the *market abuse regime*. The principal circumstances in which the *FCA* is likely to consider such exercise are:

(1)   where the *behaviour* falls within sections 118(2), 118(3) or 118(4) of the *Act*;
(2)   where the *FCA's* approach in previous similar cases (which may have happened otherwise than in the context of a *takeover bid*) suggests that a financial penalty should be imposed;
(3)   where the *behaviour* extends to *securities* or a class of *securities* which may be outside the *Takeover Panel's* jurisdiction;
(4)   where the *behaviour* threatens or has threatened the stability of the *financial system*; and
(5)   where for any other reason the *Takeover Panel* asks the *FCA* to consider the use of any of its powers referred to in **DEPP 6.2.22 G**.

[Note: In this section, 'securities' has the same meaning given in subsection (1) of the definition of 'security' in the Handbook *Glossary*]

6.2.27 G   FCA

The exceptional circumstances in which the *FCA* will consider the use of powers during a *takeover bid* are listed in **DEPP 6.2.26 G (1)**, **DEPP 6.2.26 G (3)** and **DEPP 6.2.26 G (4)**, and, depending on the circumstances, **DEPP 6.2.26 G (5)**.

6.2.28 G

[deleted]

6.3   PENALTIES FOR MARKET ABUSE

6.3.1 G   FCA

Section 123(2) of the *Act* states that the *FCA* may not impose a penalty on a *person* if there are reasonable grounds to be satisfied that:

(1)   the *person* concerned believed, on reasonable grounds, that his *behaviour* did not amount to *market abuse* or *requiring or encouraging*; or
(2)   the *person* concerned took all reasonable precautions and exercised all due diligence to avoid engaging in *market abuse* or *requiring or encouraging*.

6.3.2 G   FCA

The factors which the *FCA* may take into account when deciding whether either of the two conditions in **DEPP 6.3.1 G** are met include, but are not limited to:

(1) whether, and if so to what extent, the *behaviour* in question was or was not analogous to *behaviour* described in the *Code of Market Conduct* (see **MAR 1**) as amounting or not amounting to *market abuse* or *requiring or encouraging*;

(2) whether the *FCA* has published any *guidance* or other materials on the *behaviour* in question and if so, the extent to which the *person* sought to follow that *guidance* or take account of those materials (see the Reader's Guide to the *Handbook* regarding the status of *guidance*.) The *FCA* will consider the nature and accessibility of any *guidance* or other published materials when deciding whether it is relevant in this context and, if so, what weight it should be given;

(3) whether, and if so to what extent, the *behaviour* complied with the rules of any relevant *prescribed market* or any other relevant market or other regulatory requirements (including the *Takeover Code*) or any relevant codes of conduct or best practice;

(4) the level of knowledge, skill and experience to be expected of the *person* concerned;

(5) whether, and if so to what extent, the *person* can demonstrate that the *behaviour* was engaged in for a legitimate purpose and in a proper way;

(6) whether, and if so to what extent, the *person* followed internal consultation and escalation procedures in relation to the *behaviour* (for example, did the *person* discuss the *behaviour* with internal line management and/or internal legal or compliance departments);

(7) whether, and if so the extent to which, the *person* sought any appropriate expert legal or other expert professional advice and followed that advice; and

(8) whether, and if so to what extent, the *person* sought advice from the market authorities of any relevant *prescribed market* or, where relevant, consulted the *Takeover Panel*, and followed the advice received.

6.4 FINANCIAL PENALTY OR PUBLIC CENSURE

6.4.1 G   FCA

The *FCA* will consider all the relevant circumstances of the case when deciding whether to impose a penalty or issue a *public censure*. As such, the factors set out in **DEPP 6.4.2 G** are not exhaustive. Not all of the factors may be relevant in a particular case and there may be other factors, not listed, that are relevant.

6.4.2 G   FCA

The criteria for determining whether it is appropriate to issue a *public censure* rather than impose a financial penalty include those factors that the *FCA* will consider in determining the amount of penalty set out in **DEPP 6.5 A** to **DEPP 6.5 D**. Some particular considerations that may be relevant when the *FCA* determines whether to issue a *public censure* rather than impose a financial penalty are:

(1) whether or not deterrence may be effectively achieved by issuing a *public censure*;

(2) if the *person* has made a profit or avoided a loss as a result of the *breach*, this may be a factor in favour of a financial penalty, on the basis that a *person* should not be permitted to benefit from its *breach*;

(3) if the *breach* is more serious in nature or degree, this may be a factor in favour of a financial penalty, on the basis that the sanction should reflect the seriousness of the *breach*; other things being equal, the more serious the *breach*, the more likely the *FCA* is to impose a financial penalty;

(4) if the *person* has brought the *breach* to the attention of the *FCA*, this may be a factor in favour of a *public censure*, depending upon the nature and seriousness of the *breach*;

(5) if the *person* has admitted the *breach* and provides full and immediate co-operation to the *FCA*, and takes steps to ensure that those who have suffered loss due to the *breach* are fully compensated for those losses, this may be a factor in favour of a *public censure*, rather than a financial penalty, depending upon the nature and seriousness of the *breach*;

(6) if the *person* has a poor disciplinary record or compliance history (for example, where the *FSA* or *FCA* has previously brought disciplinary action resulting in adverse findings in relation to the same or similar *behaviour*), this may be a factor in favour of a financial penalty, on the basis that it may be particularly important to deter future cases;

(7) the *FSA's* or *FCA's* approach in similar previous cases: the *FCA* will seek to achieve a consistent approach to its decisions on whether to impose a financial penalty or issue a *public censure*; and

(8) the impact on the *person* concerned. It would only be in an exceptional case that the *FCA* would be prepared to agree to issue a *public censure* rather than impose a financial penalty if a financial penalty would otherwise be the appropriate sanction. Examples of such exceptional cases could include:

    (a) where the application of the *FCA's* policy on serious financial hardship (set out in **DEPP 6.5D**) results in a financial penalty being reduced to zero;

(b)   where there is verifiable evidence that the *person* would be unable to meet other regulatory requirements, particularly financial resource requirements, if the *FCA* imposed a financial penalty at an appropriate level; or

(c)   in Part VI cases in which the *FCA* may impose a financial penalty, where there is the likelihood of a severe adverse impact on a *person's* shareholders or a consequential impact on market confidence or market stability if a financial penalty was imposed. However, this does not exclude the imposition of a financial penalty even though this may have an impact on a *person's* shareholders.

6.5   DETERMINING THE APPROPRIATE LEVEL OF FINANCIAL PENALTY

6.5.1 G   FCA

For the purpose of **DEPP 6.5** to **DEPP 6.5D** and **DEPP 6.6.2 G**, the term "firm" means *firms*, *sponsors*, *primary information providers*, *recognised investment exchanges*, qualifying parent undertakings, *actuaries*, auditors and those *unauthorised persons* who are not individuals.

6.5.2 G   FCA

The *FCA's* penalty-setting regime is based on the following principles:
(1)   Disgorgement – a firm or individual should not benefit from any *breach*;
(2)   Discipline – a firm or individual should be penalised for wrongdoing; and
(3)   Deterrence – any penalty imposed should deter the firm or individual who committed the *breach*, and others, from committing further or similar *breaches*.

6.5.3 G   FCA
(1)   The total amount payable by a person subject to enforcement action may be made up of two elements: (i) disgorgement of the benefit received as a result of the *breach*; and (ii) a financial penalty reflecting the seriousness of the *breach*. These elements are incorporated in a five-step framework, which can be summarised as follows:
(a)   Step 1: the removal of any financial benefit derived directly from the *breach*;
(b)   Step 2: the determination of a figure which reflects the seriousness of the *breach*;
(c)   Step 3: an adjustment made to the Step 2 figure to take account of any aggravating and mitigating circumstances;
(d)   Step 4: an upwards adjustment made to the amount arrived at after Steps 2 and 3, where appropriate, to ensure that the penalty has an appropriate deterrent effect; and
(e)   Step 5: if applicable, a settlement discount will be applied. This discount does not apply to disgorgement of any financial benefit derived directly from the *breach*.
(2)   These steps will apply in all cases, although the details of Steps 1 to 4 will differ for cases against firms (**DEPP 6.5A**), cases against individuals (**DEPP 6.5B**) and *market abuse* cases against individuals (**DEPP 6.5C**).
(3)   The *FCA* recognises that a penalty must be proportionate to the *breach*. The *FCA* may decrease the level of the penalty arrived at after applying Step 2 of the framework if it considers that the penalty is disproportionately high for the *breach* concerned. For cases against firms, the *FCA* will have regard to whether the *firm* is also an individual (for example, a sole trader) in determining whether the figure arrived at after applying Step 2 is disproportionate.
(4)   The lists of factors and circumstances in **DEPP 6.5A** to **DEPP 6.5D** are not exhaustive. Not all of the factors or circumstances listed will necessarily be relevant in a particular case and there may be other factors or circumstances not listed which are relevant.
(5)   The *FCA* may decide to impose a financial penalty on a mutual (such as a *building society*), even though this may have a direct impact on that mutual's *customers*. This reflects the fact that a significant proportion of a mutual's *customers* are shareholder-members; to that extent, their position involves an assumption of risk that is not assumed by *customers* of a firm that is not a mutual. Whether a firm is a mutual will not, by itself, increase or decrease the level of a financial penalty.
(6)   Part III (Penalties and Fees) of Schedule 1ZA to the *Act* specifically provides that the *FCA* may not, in determining its policy with respect to the amount of penalties, take account of expenses which it incurs, or expects to incur, in discharging its functions.

6.5A   THE FIVE STEPS FOR PENALTIES IMPOSED ON FIRMS

Step 1 – disgorgement

6.5A.1 G   FCA
(1)   The *FCA* will seek to deprive a firm of the financial benefit derived directly from the *breach* (which may include the profit made or loss avoided) where it is practicable to quantify this. The *FCA* will ordinarily also charge interest on the benefit.
(2)   Where the success of a firm's entire business model is dependent on breaching *FCA rules* or other requirements of the *regulatory system* and the *breach* is at the core of the firm's *regulated activities*, the *FCA* will seek to deprive the firm of all the financial benefit derived from such activities. Where a firm agrees to carry out a redress programme to

compensate those who have suffered loss as a result of the *breach*, or where the *FCA* decides to impose a redress programme, the *FCA* will take this into consideration. In such cases the final penalty might not include a disgorgement element, or the disgorgement element might be reduced.

[**Note:** For the purposes of **DEPP 6.5A**, "firm" has the special meaning given to it in **DEPP 6.5.1 G**]

Step 2 – the seriousness of the breach

6.5A.2 G   FCA

(1)   The *FCA* will determine a figure that reflects the seriousness of the *breach*. In many cases, the amount of revenue generated by a firm from a particular product line or business area is indicative of the harm or potential harm that its *breach* may cause, and in such cases the *FCA* will determine a figure which will be based on a percentage of the firm's revenue from the relevant products or business areas. The *FCA* also believes that the amount of revenue generated by a firm from a particular product or business area is relevant in terms of the size of the financial penalty necessary to act as a credible deterrent. However, the *FCA* recognises that there may be cases where revenue is not an appropriate indicator of the harm or potential harm that a firm's *breach* may cause, and in those cases the *FCA* will use an appropriate alternative.

(2)   In those cases where the *FCA* considers that revenue is an appropriate indicator of the harm or potential harm that a firm's *breach* may cause, the *FCA* will determine a figure which will be based on a percentage of the firm's "relevant revenue". "Relevant revenue" will be the revenue derived by the firm during the period of the *breach* from the products or business areas to which the *breach* relates. Where the *breach* lasted less than 12 *months*, or was a one-off event, the relevant revenue will be that derived by the firm in the 12 *months* preceding the end of the *breach*. Where the firm was in existence for less than 12 *months*, its relevant revenue will be calculated on a pro rata basis to the equivalent of 12 *months'* relevant revenue.

(3)   Having determined the relevant revenue, the *FCA* will then decide on the percentage of that revenue which will form the basis of the penalty. In making this determination the *FCA* will consider the seriousness of the *breach* and choose a percentage between 0% and 20%. This range is divided into five fixed levels which represent, on a sliding scale, the seriousness of the *breach*. The more serious the *breach*, the higher the level. For penalties imposed on firms there are the following five levels:
    (a)   level 1 - 0%;
    (b)   level 2 - 5%;
    (c)   level 3 - 10%;
    (d)   level 4 - 15%; and
    (e)   level 5 - 20%.

(4)   The *FCA* will assess the seriousness of a *breach* to determine which level is most appropriate to the case.

(5)   In deciding which level is most appropriate to a case involving a firm, the *FCA* will take into account various factors, which will usually fall into the following four categories:
    (a)   factors relating to the impact of the *breach*;
    (b)   factors relating to the nature of the *breach*;
    (c)   factors tending to show whether the *breach* was deliberate; and
    (d)   factors tending to show whether the *breach* was reckless.

(6)   Factors relating to the impact of a *breach* committed by a firm include:
    (a)   the level of benefit gained or loss avoided, or intended to be gained or avoided, by the firm from the *breach*, either directly or indirectly;
    (b)   the loss or risk of loss, as a whole, caused to *consumers*, investors or other market users in general;
    (c)   the loss or risk of loss caused to individual *consumers*, investors or other market users;
    (d)   whether the *breach* had an effect on particularly vulnerable people, whether intentionally or otherwise;
    (e)   the inconvenience or distress caused to *consumers*; and
    (f)   whether the *breach* had an adverse effect on markets and, if so, how serious that effect was. This may include having regard to whether the orderliness of, or confidence in, the markets in question has been damaged or put at risk.

(7)   Factors relating to the nature of a *breach* by a firm include:
    (a)   the nature of the *rules*, requirements or provisions breached;
    (b)   the frequency of the *breach*;
    (c)   whether the *breach* revealed serious or systemic weaknesses in the firm's procedures or in the management systems or internal controls relating to all or part of the firm's business;
    (d)   whether the firm's senior management were aware of the *breach*;
    (e)   the nature and extent of any *financial crime* facilitated, occasioned or otherwise attributable to the *breach*;

(f)   the scope for any potential *financial crime* to be facilitated, occasioned or otherwise occur as a result of the *breach*;

(g)   whether the firm failed to conduct its business with integrity;

(h)   whether the firm, in committing the *breach*, took any steps to comply with *FSA rules*, and the adequacy of those steps; and

(i)   in the context of contraventions of Part VI of the *Act*, the extent to which the *behaviour* which constitutes the contravention departs from current market practice.

(8)   Factors tending to show the *breach* was deliberate include:

(a)   the *breach* was intentional, in that the firm's senior management, or a responsible individual, intended or foresaw that the likely or actual consequences of their actions or inaction would result in a *breach*;

(b)   the firm's senior management, or a responsible individual, knew that their actions were not in accordance with the firm's internal procedures;

(c)   the firm's senior management, or a responsible individual, sought to conceal their misconduct;

(d)   the firm's senior management, or a responsible individual, committed the *breach* in such a way as to avoid or reduce the risk that the *breach* would be discovered;

(e)   the firm's senior management, or a responsible individual, were influenced to commit the *breach* by the belief that it would be difficult to detect;

(f)   the *breach* was repeated; and

(g)   in the context of a contravention of any *rule* or requirement imposed by or under Part VI of the *Act*, the firm obtained reasonable professional advice before the contravention occurred and failed to follow that advice. Obtaining professional advice does not remove a *person's* responsibility for compliance with applicable *rules* and requirements.

(9)   Factors tending to show the *breach* was reckless include:

(a)   the firm's senior management, or a responsible individual, appreciated there was a risk that their actions or inaction could result in a *breach* and failed adequately to mitigate that risk; and

(b)   the firm's senior management, or a responsible individual, were aware there was a risk that their actions or inaction could result in a *breach* but failed to check if they were acting in accordance with the firm's internal procedures.

(10)   Additional factors to which the *FCA* will have regard when determining the appropriate level of financial penalty to be imposed under regulation 34 of the *RCB Regulations* are set out in **RCB 4.2.5 G**.

(11)   In following this approach factors which are likely to be considered 'level 4 factors' or 'level 5 factors' include:

(a)   the *breach* caused a significant loss or risk of loss to individual *consumers*, investors or other market users;

(b)   the *breach* revealed serious or systemic weaknesses in the firm's procedures or in the management systems or internal controls relating to all or part of the firm's business;

(c)   *financial crime* was facilitated, occasioned or otherwise attributable to the *breach*;

(d)   the *breach* created a significant risk that *financial crime* would be facilitated, occasioned or otherwise occur;

(e)   the firm failed to conduct its business with integrity; and

(f)   the *breach* was committed deliberately or recklessly.

(12)   Factors which are likely to be considered 'level 1 factors', 'level 2 factors' or 'level 3 factors' include:

(a)   little, or no, profits were made or losses avoided as a result of the *breach*, either directly or indirectly;

(b)   there was no or little loss or risk of loss to *consumers*, investors or other market users individually and in general;

(c)   there was no, or limited, actual or potential effect on the orderliness of, or confidence in, markets as a result of the *breach*;

(d)   there is no evidence that the *breach* indicates a widespread problem or weakness at the firm; and

(e)   the *breach* was committed negligently or inadvertently.

(13)   In those cases where revenue is not an appropriate indicator of the harm or potential harm that a firm's *breach* may cause, the *FCA* will adopt a similar approach, and so will determine the appropriate Step 2 amount for a particular *breach* by taking into account relevant factors, including those listed above. In these cases the *FCA* may not use the percentage levels that are applied in those cases in which revenue is an appropriate indicator of the harm or potential harm that a firm's *breach* may cause.

Step 3 – mitigating and aggravating factors

6.5A.3 G   FCA

Part 3   FCA Handbook Materials

(1)   The *FCA* may increase or decrease the amount of the financial penalty arrived at after Step 2, but not including any amount to be disgorged as set out in Step 1, to take into account factors which aggravate or mitigate the *breach*. Any such adjustments will be made by way of a percentage adjustment to the figure determined at Step 2.

(2)   The following list of factors may have the effect of aggravating or mitigating the *breach*:

(a)   the conduct of the firm in bringing (or failing to bring) quickly, effectively and completely the *breach* to the *FCA's* attention (or the attention of other regulatory authorities, where relevant);

(b)   the degree of cooperation the firm showed during the investigation of the *breach* by the *FCA*, or any other regulatory authority allowed to share information with the *FCA*;

(c)   where the firm's senior management were aware of the *breach* or of the potential for a *breach*, whether they took any steps to stop the *breach*, and when these steps were taken;

(d)   any remedial steps taken since the *breach* was identified, including whether these were taken on the firm's own initiative or that of the *FCA* or another regulatory authority; for example, identifying whether *consumers* or investors or other market users suffered loss and compensating them where they have; correcting any misleading statement or impression; taking disciplinary action against staff involved (if appropriate); and taking steps to ensure that similar problems cannot arise in the future. The size and resources of the firm may be relevant to assessing the reasonableness of the steps taken;

(e)   whether the firm has arranged its resources in such a way as to allow or avoid disgorgement and/or payment of a financial penalty;

(f)   whether the firm had previously been told about the *FCA's* concerns in relation to the issue, either by means of a private warning or in supervisory correspondence;

(g)   whether the firm had previously undertaken not to perform a particular act or engage in particular behaviour;

(h)   whether the firm concerned has complied with any requirements or rulings of another regulatory authority relating to the *breach*;

(i)   the previous disciplinary record and general compliance history of the firm;

(j)   action taken against the firm by other domestic or international regulatory authorities that is relevant to the *breach* in question;

(k)   whether *FCA guidance* or other published materials had already raised relevant concerns, and the nature and accessibility of such materials; and

(l)   whether the *FCA* publicly called for an improvement in standards in relation to the behaviour constituting the *breach* or similar behaviour before or during the occurrence of the *breach*.

Step 4 – adjustment for deterrence

6.5A.4 G   FCA

(1)   If the *FCA* considers the figure arrived at after Step 3 is insufficient to deter the firm who committed the *breach*, or others, from committing further or similar breaches then the *FCA* may increase the penalty. Circumstances where the *FCA* may do this include:

(a)   where the *FCA* considers the absolute value of the penalty too small in relation to the *breach* to meet its objective of credible deterrence;

(b)   where previous *FCA* action in respect of similar *breaches* has failed to improve industry standards. This may include similar *breaches* relating to different products (for example, action for mis-selling or claims handling failures in respect of 'x' product may be relevant to a case for mis-selling or claims handling failures in respect of 'y' product);

(c)   where the *FCA* considers it is likely that similar *breaches* will be committed by the firm or by other firms in the future in the absence of such an increase to the penalty; and

(d)   where the *FCA* considers that the likelihood of the detection of such a *breach* is low.

Step 5 – settlement discount

6.5A.5 G   FCA

The *FCA* and the firm on whom a penalty is to be imposed may seek to agree the amount of any financial penalty and other terms. In recognition of the benefits of such agreements, **DEPP 6.7** provides that the amount of the financial penalty which might otherwise have been payable will be reduced to reflect the stage at which the *FCA* and the firm concerned reached an agreement. The settlement discount does not apply to the disgorgement of any benefit calculated at Step 1.

6.5B   THE FIVE STEPS FOR PENALTIES IMPOSED ON INDIVIDUALS IN NON-MARKET ABUSE CASES

Step 1 – disgorgement

6.5B.1 G   FCA

The *FCA* will seek to deprive an individual of the financial benefit derived directly from the *breach* (which may include the profit made or loss avoided) where it is practicable to quantify this. The *FCA* will ordinarily also charge interest on the benefit. Where the success of a firm's entire business model is dependent on breaching *FCA rules* or other requirements of the *regulatory system* and the individual's *breach* is at the core of the firm's *regulated activities*, the *FCA* will seek to deprive the individual of all the financial benefit he has derived from such activities.

[**Note:** For the purposes of **DEPP 6.5B**, "firm" has the special meaning given to it in **DEPP 6.5.1 G**.]

Step 2 – the seriousness of the breach

6.5B.2 G   FCA
(1)   The *FCA* will determine a figure which will be based on a percentage of an individual's "relevant income". "Relevant income" will be the gross amount of all benefits received by the individual from the employment in connection with which the *breach* occurred (the "relevant employment"), and for the period of the *breach*. In determining an individual's relevant income, "benefits" includes, but is not limited to, salary, bonus, pension contributions, *share* options and *share* schemes; and "employment" includes, but is not limited to, employment as an adviser, *director*, partner or contractor.
(2)   Where the *breach* lasted less than 12 *months*, or was a one-off event, the relevant income will be that earned by the individual in the 12 *months* preceding the end of the *breach*. Where the individual was in the relevant employment for less than 12 months, his relevant income will be calculated on a pro rata basis to the equivalent of 12 *months'* relevant income.
(3)   This approach reflects the *FCA's* view that an individual receives remuneration commensurate with his responsibilities, and so it is reasonable to base the amount of penalty for failure to discharge his duties properly on his remuneration. The *FCA* also believes that the extent of the financial benefit earned by an individual is relevant in terms of the size of the financial penalty necessary to act as a credible deterrent. The *FCA* recognises that in some cases an individual may be approved for only a small part of the work he carries out on a day-to-day basis. However, in these circumstances the *FCA* still considers it appropriate to base the relevant income figure on all of the benefit that an individual gains from the relevant employment, even if his employment is not totally related to a controlled function.
(4)   Having determined the relevant income the *FCA* will then decide on the percentage of that income which will form the basis of the penalty. In making this determination the *FCA* will consider the seriousness of the *breach* and choose a percentage between 0% and 40%.
(5)   This range is divided into five fixed levels which reflect, on a sliding scale, the seriousness of the *breach*. The more serious the *breach*, the higher the level. For penalties imposed on individuals there are the following five levels:
     (a)   level 1 - 0%;
     (b)   level 2 - 10%;
     (c)   level 3 - 20%;
     (d)   level 4 - 30%; and
     (e)   level 5 - 40%.
(6)   The *FCA* will assess the seriousness of a *breach* to determine which level is most appropriate to the case.
(7)   In deciding which level is most appropriate to a case against an individual, the *FCA* will take into account various factors which will usually fall into the following four categories:
     (a)   factors relating to the impact of the *breach*;
     (b)   factors relating to the nature of the *breach*;
     (c)   factors tending to show whether the *breach* was deliberate; and
     (d)   factors tending to show whether the *breach* was reckless.
(8)   Factors relating to the impact of a *breach* committed by an individual include:
     (a)   the level of benefit gained or loss avoided, or intended to be gained or avoided, by the individual from the *breach*, either directly or indirectly;
     (b)   the loss or risk of loss, as a whole, caused to *consumers*, investors or other market users in general;
     (c)   the loss or risk of loss caused to individual *consumers*, investors or other market users;
     (d)   whether the *breach* had an effect on particularly vulnerable people, whether intentionally or otherwise;
     (e)   the inconvenience or distress caused to *consumers*; and
     (f)   whether the *breach* had an adverse effect on markets and, if so, how serious that effect was. This may include having regard to whether the orderliness of, or confidence in, the markets in question has been damaged or put at risk.

Part 3   FCA Handbook Materials

(9)   Factors relating to the nature of a *breach* by an individual include:
  (a)   the nature of the *rules*, requirements or provisions breached;
  (b)   the frequency of the *breach*;
  (c)   the nature and extent of any *financial crime* facilitated, occasioned or otherwise attributable to the *breach*;
  (d)   the scope for any potential *financial crime* to be facilitated, occasioned or otherwise occur as a result of the *breach*;
  (e)   whether the individual failed to act with integrity;
  (f)   whether the individual abused a position of trust;
  (g)   whether the individual committed a breach of any professional code of conduct;
  (h)   whether the individual caused or encouraged other individuals to commit *breaches*;
  (i)   whether the individual held a prominent position within the industry;
  (j)   whether the individual is an experienced industry professional;
  (k)   whether the individual held a senior position with the firm;
  (l)   the extent of the responsibility of the individual for the product or business areas affected by the *breach*, and for the particular matter that was the subject of the *breach*;
  (m)   whether the individual acted under duress;
  (n)   whether the individual took any steps to comply with *FCA rules*, and the adequacy of those steps;
  (o)   in the context of contraventions of Part VI of the *Act*, the extent to which the *behaviour* which constitutes the contravention departs from current market practice;
  (p)   in relation to a contravention of section 63A of the *Act*, whether the individual's only misconduct was to perform a *controlled function* without approval;
  (q)   in relation to a contravention of section 63A of the *Act*, whether the individual performed *controlled functions* without approval and, while doing so, committed misconduct in respect of which, if the individual had been an *approved person*, the *FCA* would have been empowered to take action pursuant to section 66 of the *Act*; and
  (r)   in relation to a contravention of section 63A of the *Act*, the extent to which the individual could reasonably be expected to have known that he was performing a *controlled function* without approval. The circumstances in which the *FCA* would expect to be satisfied that a *person* could reasonably be expected to have known that he was performing a *controlled function* without approval include:
    (i)   the *person* had previously performed a similar role at the same or another *firm* for which he had been approved;
    (ii)   the *person's firm* or another *firm* had previously applied for approval for the *person* to perform the same or a similar *controlled function*;
    (iii)   the *person's* seniority or experience was such that he could reasonably be expected to have known that he was performing a *controlled function* without approval; and
    (iv)   the *person's* firm had clearly apportioned responsibilities so the *person's* role, and the responsibilities associated with it, were clear.
(10)   Factors tending to show the *breach* was deliberate include:
  (a)   the *breach* was intentional, in that the individual intended or foresaw that the likely or actual consequences of his actions or inaction would result in a *breach*;
  (b)   the individual intended to benefit financially from the *breach*, either directly or indirectly;
  (c)   the individual knew that his actions were not in accordance with his firm's internal procedures;
  (d)   the individual sought to conceal his misconduct;
  (e)   the individual committed the *breach* in such a way as to avoid or reduce the risk that the *breach* would be discovered;
  (f)   the individual was influenced to commit the *breach* by the belief that it would be difficult to detect;
  (g)   the individual knowingly took decisions relating to the *breach* beyond his field of competence; and
  (h)   the individual's actions were repeated.
(11)   Factors tending to show the *breach* was reckless include:
  (a)   the individual appreciated there was a risk that his actions or inaction could result in a *breach* and failed adequately to mitigate that risk; and
  (b)   the individual was aware there was a risk that his actions or inaction could result in a *breach* but failed to check if he was acting in accordance with internal procedures.
(12)   In following this approach factors which are likely to be considered 'level 4 factors' or 'level 5 factors' include:
  (a)   the *breach* caused a significant loss or risk of loss to individual *consumers*, investors or other market users;
  (b)   *financial crime* was facilitated, occasioned or otherwise attributable to the *breach*;
  (c)   the *breach* created a significant risk that *financial crime* would be facilitated, occasioned or otherwise occur;

      (d)   the individual failed to act with integrity;

      (e)   the individual abused a position of trust;

      (f)   the individual held a prominent position within the industry; and

      (g)   the *breach* was committed deliberately or recklessly.

(13)   Factors which are likely to be considered 'level 1 factors', 'level 2 factors' or 'level 3 factors' include:

      (a)   little, or no, profits were made or losses avoided as a result of the *breach*, either directly or indirectly;

      (b)   there was no or little loss or risk of loss to *consumers*, investors or other market users individually and in general;

      (c)   there was no, or limited, actual or potential effect on the orderliness of, or confidence in, markets as a result of the *breach*;

      (d)   the *breach* was committed negligently or inadvertently; and

      (e)   in relation to a contravention of section 63A of the *Act*, the individual's only misconduct was to perform a *controlled function* without approval.

Step 3 – mitigating and aggravating factors

6.5B.3 G   FCA

(1)   The *FCA* may increase or decrease the amount of the financial penalty arrived at after Step 2, but not including any amount to be disgorged as set out in Step 1, to take into account factors which aggravate or mitigate the *breach*. Any such adjustments will be made by way of a percentage adjustment to the figure determined at Step 2.

(2)   The following list of factors may have the effect of aggravating or mitigating the *breach*:

      (a)   the conduct of the individual in bringing (or failing to bring) quickly, effectively and completely the *breach* to the *FCA's* attention (or the attention of other regulatory authorities, where relevant);

      (b)   the degree of cooperation the individual showed during the investigation of the *breach* by the *FCA*, or any other regulatory authority allowed to share information with the *FCA*;

      (c)   whether the individual took any steps to stop the *breach*, and when these steps were taken;

      (d)   any remedial steps taken since the *breach* was identified, including whether these were taken on the individual's own initiative or that of the *FCA* or another regulatory authority;

      (e)   whether the individual has arranged his resources in such a way as to allow or avoid disgorgement and/or payment of a financial penalty;

      (f)   whether the individual had previously been told about the *FCA's* concerns in relation to the issue, either by means of a private warning or in supervisory correspondence;

      (g)   whether the individual had previously undertaken not to perform a particular act or engage in particular behaviour;

      (h)   whether the individual has complied with any requirements or rulings of another regulatory authority relating to the *breach*;

      (i)   the previous disciplinary record and general compliance history of the individual;

      (j)   action taken against the individual by other domestic or international regulatory authorities that is relevant to the *breach* in question;

      (k)   whether *FCA guidance* or other published materials had already raised relevant concerns, and the nature and accessibility of such materials;

      (l)   whether the *FCA* publicly called for an improvement in standards in relation to the behaviour constituting the *breach* or similar behaviour before or during the occurrence of the *breach*;

      (m)   whether the individual agreed to undertake training subsequent to the *breach*; and

      (n)   in relation to a contravention of section 63A of the *Act*, whether the *person's* firm or another firm has previously withdrawn an application for the *person* to perform the same or a similar *controlled function* or has had such an application rejected by the *FCA*.

Step 4 – adjustment for deterrence

6.5B.4 G   FCA

(1)   If the *FCA* considers the figure arrived at after Step 3 is insufficient to deter the individual who committed the *breach*, or others, from committing further or similar *breaches* then the *FCA* may increase the penalty. Circumstances where the *FCA* may do this include:

      (a)   where the *FCA* considers the absolute value of the penalty too small in relation to the *breach* to meet its objective of credible deterrence;

      (b)   where previous *FCA* action in respect of similar *breaches* has failed to improve industry standards. This may include similar *breaches* relating to different products (for example, action for mis-selling or claims handling failures in respect of 'x' product may be relevant to a case for mis-selling or claims handling failures in respect of 'y' product);

(c)   where the *FCA* considers it is likely that similar *breaches* will be committed by the individual or by other individuals in the future;

(d)   where the *FCA* considers that the likelihood of the detection of such a *breach* is low; and

(e)   where a penalty based on an individual's income may not act as a deterrent, for example, if an individual has a small or zero income but owns assets of high value.

Step 5 – settlement discount

6.5B.5 G   FCA

The *FCA* and the individual on whom a penalty is to be imposed may seek to agree the amount of any financial penalty and other terms. In recognition of the benefits of such agreements, **DEPP 6.7** provides that the amount of the financial penalty which might otherwise have been payable will be reduced to reflect the stage at which the *FCA* and the individual concerned reached an agreement. The settlement discount does not apply to the disgorgement of any benefit calculated at Step 1.

6.5C   THE FIVE STEPS FOR PENALTIES IMPOSED ON INDIVIDUALS IN MARKET ABUSE CASES

Step 1 – disgorgement

6.5C.1 G   FCA

The *FCA* will seek to deprive an individual of the financial benefit derived as a direct result of the *market abuse* (which may include the profit made or loss avoided) where it is practicable to quantify this. The *FCA* will ordinarily also charge interest on the benefit.

Step 2 – the seriousness of the market abuse

6.5C.2 G   FCA

(1)   The *FCA* will determine a figure dependent on the seriousness of the *market abuse* and whether or not it was referable to the individual's employment. This reflects the *FCA's* view that where an individual has been put into a position where he can commit *market abuse* because of his employment the fine imposed should reflect this by reference to the gross amount of all benefits derived from that employment.

(2)   In cases where the *market abuse* was referable to the individual's employment, the figure for the purpose of Step 2 will be the greater of:

    (a)   a figure based on a percentage of the individual's "relevant income". The percentage of relevant income which will apply is explained in paragraphs (6) and (8) to (16) below;

    (b)   a multiple of the profit made or loss avoided by the individual for his own benefit, or for the benefit of other individuals where the individual has been instrumental in achieving that benefit, as a direct result of the *market abuse* (the "profit multiple"). The profit multiple which will apply is explained in paragraphs (6) and (8) to (16) below; and

    (c)   for *market abuse* cases which the *FCA* assesses to be seriousness level 4 or 5, £100,000. How the *FCA* will assess the seriousness level of the *market abuse* is explained in paragraphs (9) to (16) below. The *FCA* usually expects to assess *market abuse* committed deliberately as seriousness level 4 or 5.

(3)   In cases where the *market abuse* was not referable to the individual's employment, the figure for the purpose of Step 2 will be the greater of:

    (a)   a multiple of the profit made or loss avoided by the individual for his own benefit, or for the benefit of other individuals where the individual has been instrumental in achieving that benefit, as a direct result of the *market abuse* (the "profit multiple"). The profit multiple which will apply is explained in paragraphs (7) to (16) below; and

    (b)   for *market abuse* cases which the *FCA* assesses to be seriousness level 4 or 5, £100,000. How the *FCA* will assess the seriousness level of the *market abuse* is explained in paragraphs (9) to (16) below. The *FCA* usually expects to assess *market abuse* committed deliberately as seriousness level 4 or 5.

(4)   An individual's "relevant income" will be the gross amount of all benefits received by the individual from the employment in connection with which the *market abuse* occurred (the "relevant employment") for the period of the *market abuse*. In determining an individual's relevant income, "benefits" includes, but is not limited to, salary, bonus, pension contributions, *share* options and *share* schemes; and "employment" includes, but is not limited to, employment as an adviser, *director*, partner or contractor.

(5)   Where the *market abuse* lasted less than 12 *months*, or was a one-off event, the relevant income will be that earned by the individual in the 12 *months* preceding the final *market abuse*. Where the individual was in the relevant employment for less than 12 *months*, his relevant income will be calculated on a pro rata basis to the equivalent of 12 *months'* relevant income.

(6)   In cases where the *market abuse* was referable to the individual's employment:

    (a)   the *FCA* will determine the percentage of relevant income which will apply by considering the seriousness of the *market abuse* and choosing a percentage between 0% and 40%; and

    (b)   the *FCA* will determine the profit multiple which will apply by considering the seriousness of the *market abuse* and choosing a multiple between 0 and 4.

(7)   In cases where the *market abuse* was not referable to the individual's employment the *FCA* will determine the profit multiple which will apply by considering the seriousness of the *market abuse* and choosing a multiple between 0 and 4.

(8)   The percentage range (where the *market abuse* was referable to the individual's employment) and profit multiple range (in all cases) are divided into five fixed levels which reflect, on a sliding scale, the seriousness of the *market abuse*. The more serious the *market abuse*, the higher the level. For penalties imposed on individuals for *market abuse* there are the following five levels (the percentage figures only apply where the *market abuse* was referable to the individual's employment):

    (a)   level 1 - 0%, profit multiple of 0;

    (b)   level 2 - 10%, profit multiple of 1;

    (c)   level 3 - 20%, profit multiple of 2;

    (d)   level 4 - 30%, profit multiple of 3; and

    (e)   level 5 - 40%, profit multiple of 4.

(9)   The *FCA* will assess the seriousness of the *market abuse* to determine which level is most appropriate to the case.

(10)   In deciding which level is most appropriate to a *market abuse* case, the *FCA* will take into account various factors which will usually fall into the following four categories:

    (a)   factors relating to the impact of the *market abuse*;

    (b)   factors relating to the nature of the *market abuse*;

    (c)   factors tending to show whether the *market abuse* was deliberate; and

    (d)   factors tending to show whether the *market abuse* was reckless.

(11)   Factors relating to the impact of the *market abuse* include:

    (a)   the level of benefit gained or loss avoided, or intended to be gained or avoided, by the individual from the *market abuse*, either directly or indirectly;

    (b)   whether the *market abuse* had an adverse effect on markets and, if so, how serious that effect was. This may include having regard to whether the orderliness of, or confidence in, the markets in question has been damaged or put at risk; and

    (c)   whether the *market abuse* had a significant impact on the price of *shares* or other *investments*.

(12)   Factors relating to the nature of the *market abuse* include:

    (a)   the frequency of the *market abuse*;

    (b)   whether the individual abused a position of trust;

    (c)   whether the individual caused or encouraged other individuals to commit *market abuse*;

    (d)   whether the individual has a prominent position in the market;

    (e)   whether the individual is an experienced industry professional;

    (f)   whether the individual held a senior position with the firm; and

    (g)   whether the individual acted under duress.

(13)   Factors tending to show the *market abuse* was deliberate include:

    (a)   the *market abuse* was intentional, in that the individual intended or foresaw that the likely or actual consequences of his actions would result in *market abuse*;

    (b)   the individual intended to benefit financially from the *market abuse*, either directly or indirectly;

    (c)   the individual knew that his actions were not in accordance with exchange rules, *share* dealing rules and/or the firm's internal procedures;

    (d)   the individual sought to conceal his misconduct;

    (e)   the individual committed the *market abuse* in such a way as to avoid or reduce the risk that the *market abuse* would be discovered;

    (f)   the individual was influenced to commit the *market abuse* by the belief that it would be difficult to detect;

    (g)   the individual's actions were repeated; and

    (h)   for *market abuse* falling within section 118(2) of the *Act*, the individual knew or recognised that the information on which the *dealing* was based was *inside information*.

(14)   Factors tending to show the *market abuse* was reckless include:

    (a)   the individual appreciated there was a risk that his actions could result in *market abuse* and failed adequately to mitigate that risk; and

    (b)   the individual was aware there was a risk that his actions could result in *market abuse* but failed to check if he was acting in accordance with internal procedures.

(15)   In following this approach factors which are likely to be considered 'level 4 factors' or 'level 5 factors' include:

    (a)   the level of benefit gained or loss avoided, or intended to be gained or avoided, directly by the individual from the *market abuse* was significant;

    (b)   the *market abuse* had a serious adverse effect on the orderliness of, or confidence in, markets;

    (c)   the *market abuse* was committed on multiple occasions;

    (d)   the individual breached a position of trust;

    (e)   the individual has a prominent position in the market; and

    (f)   the *market abuse* was committed deliberately or recklessly.

(16)   In following this approach factors which are likely to be considered 'level 1 factors', 'level 2 factors' or 'level 3 factors' include:

    (a)   little, or no, profits were made or losses avoided as a result of the *market abuse*, either directly or indirectly;

    (b)   there was no, or limited, actual or potential effect on the orderliness of, or confidence in, markets as a result of the *market abuse*; and

    (c)   the *market abuse* was committed negligently or inadvertently.

[Note: For the purposes of **DEPP 6.5C**, "firm" has the special meaning given to it in **DEPP 6.5.1 G**.]

Step 3 – mitigating and aggravating factors

6.5C.3 G   FCA

(1)   The *FCA* may increase or decrease the amount of the financial penalty arrived at after Step 2, but not including any amount to be disgorged as set out in Step 1, to take into account factors which aggravate or mitigate the *market abuse*. Any such adjustments will be made by way of a percentage adjustment to the figure determined at Step 2.

(2)   The following list of factors may have the effect of aggravating or mitigating the *market abuse*:

    (a)   the conduct of the individual in bringing (or failing to bring) quickly, effectively and completely the *market abuse* to the *FCA's* attention (or the attention of other regulatory authorities, where relevant);

    (b)   the degree of cooperation the individual showed during the investigation of the *market abuse* by the *FCA*, or any other regulatory authority allowed to share information with the *FCA*;

    (c)   whether the individual assists the *FCA* in action taken against other individuals for *market abuse* and/or in criminal proceedings;

    (d)   whether the individual has arranged his resources in such a way as to allow or avoid disgorgement and/or payment of a financial penalty;

    (e)   whether the individual had previously been told about the *FCA's* concerns in relation to the issue, either by means of a private warning or in supervisory correspondence;

    (f)   the previous disciplinary record and general compliance history of the individual;

    (g)   action taken against the individual by other domestic or international regulatory authorities that is relevant to the *market abuse* in question;

    (h)   whether *FCA guidance* or other published materials had already raised relevant concerns, and the nature and accessibility of such materials; and

    (i)   whether the individual agreed to undertake training subsequent to the *market abuse*.

Step 4 – adjustment for deterrence

6.5C.4 G   FCA

(1)   If the *FCA* considers the figure arrived at after Step 3 is insufficient to deter the individual who committed the *market abuse*, or others, from committing further or similar abuse then the *FCA* may increase the penalty. Circumstances where the *FCA* may do this include:

    (a)   where the *FCA* considers the absolute value of the penalty too small in relation to the *market abuse* to meet its objective of credible deterrence;

    (b)   where previous *FCA* action in respect of similar *market abuse* has failed to improve industry standards; and

    (c)   where the penalty may not act as a deterrent in light of the size of the individual's income or net assets.

Step 5 – settlement discount

6.5C.5 G   FCA

The *FCA* and the individual on whom a penalty is to be imposed may seek to agree the amount of any financial penalty and other terms. In recognition of the benefits of such agreements, **DEPP 6.7** provides that the amount of the financial penalty which might otherwise have been payable will be reduced to reflect the stage at which the *FCA* and the individual concerned reached an agreement. The settlement discount does not apply to the disgorgement of any benefit calculated at Step 1.

6.5D   SERIOUS FINANCIAL HARDSHIP

6.5D.1 G   FCA

(1) The *FCA's* approach to determining penalties described in **DEPP 6.5** to **DEPP 6.5C** is intended to ensure that financial penalties are proportionate to the *breach*. The *FCA* recognises that penalties may affect persons differently, and that the *FCA* should consider whether a reduction in the proposed penalty is appropriate if the penalty would cause the subject of enforcement action serious financial hardship.

(2) Where an individual or firm claims that payment of the penalty proposed by the *FCA* will cause them serious financial hardship, the *FCA* will consider whether to reduce the proposed penalty only if:

    (a) the individual or firm provides verifiable evidence that payment of the penalty will cause them serious financial hardship; and

    (b) the individual or firm provides full, frank and timely disclosure of the verifiable evidence, and cooperates fully in answering any questions asked by the *FCA* about their financial position.

(3) The onus is on the individual or firm to satisfy the *FCA* that payment of the penalty will cause them serious financial hardship.

[**Note:** For the purposes of **DEPP 6.5D**, "firm" has the special meaning given to it in **DEPP 6.5.1 G**.]

Individuals

6.5D.2 G FCA

(1) In assessing whether a penalty would cause an individual serious financial hardship, the *FCA* will consider the individual's ability to pay the penalty over a reasonable period (normally no greater than three years). The *FCA's* starting point is that an individual will suffer serious financial hardship only if during that period his net annual income will fall below £14,000 and his capital will fall below £16,000 as a result of payment of the penalty. Unless the *FCA* believes that both the individual's income and capital will fall below these respective thresholds as a result of payment of the penalty, the *FCA* is unlikely to be satisfied that the penalty will result in serious financial hardship.

(2) The *FCA* will consider all relevant circumstances in determining whether the income and capital threshold levels should be increased in a particular case.

(3) The *FCA* will consider agreeing to payment of the penalty by instalments where the individual requires time to realise his assets, for example by waiting for payment of a salary or by selling property.

(4) For the purposes of considering whether an individual will suffer serious financial hardship, the *FCA* will consider as capital anything that could provide the individual with a source of income, including savings, property (including personal possessions), *investments* and land. The *FCA* will normally consider as capital the equity that an individual has in the home in which he lives, but will consider any representations by the individual about this; for example, as to the exceptionally severe impact a sale of the property might have upon other occupants of the property or the impracticability of re-mortgaging or selling the property within a reasonable period.

(5) The *FCA* may also consider the extent to which the individual has access to other means of financial support in determining whether he is able to pay the penalty without being caused serious financial hardship.

(6) Where a penalty is reduced it will be reduced to an amount which the individual can pay without going below the threshold levels that apply in that case. If an individual has no income, any reduction in the penalty will be to an amount that the individual can pay without going below the capital threshold.

(7) There may be cases where, even though the individual has satisfied the *FCA* that payment of the financial penalty would cause him serious financial hardship, the *FCA* considers the *breach* to be so serious that it is not appropriate to reduce the penalty. The *FCA* will consider all the circumstances of the case in determining whether this course of action is appropriate, including whether:

    (a) the individual directly derived a financial benefit from the *breach* and, if so, the extent of that financial benefit;

    (b) the individual acted fraudulently or dishonestly with a view to personal gain;

    (c) previous *FCA* action in respect of similar *breaches* has failed to improve industry standards; or

    (d) the individual has spent money or dissipated assets in anticipation of *FCA* or other enforcement action with a view to frustrating or limiting the impact of action taken by the *FCA* or other authorities.

Prohibition orders and withdrawal of approval

6.5D.3 G FCA

In cases against individuals, including *market abuse* cases, the *FCA* may make a *prohibition order* under section 56 of the *Act* or withdraw an individual's approval under section 63 of the *Act*, as well as impose a financial penalty. Such action by the *FCA* reflects the *FCA's* assessment of the individual's fitness to perform *regulated activity* or suitability for a particular role, and does not affect the *FCA's* assessment of the appropriate financial penalty in relation to a *breach*. However, the fact that the *FCA* has made a *prohibition order* against an individual or withdrawn his approval, as a result of which the individual may have less earning potential, may be relevant in assessing whether the penalty will cause the individual serious financial hardship.

Firms

6.5D.4 G   FCA

(1)   The *FCA* will consider reducing the amount of a penalty if a firm will suffer serious financial hardship as a result of having to pay the entire penalty. In deciding whether it is appropriate to reduce the penalty, the *FCA* will take into consideration the firm's financial circumstances, including whether the penalty would render the firm insolvent or threaten the firm's solvency. The *FCA* will also take into account its statutory objectives, for example in situations where *consumers* would be harmed or market confidence would suffer, the *FCA* may consider it appropriate to reduce a penalty in order to allow a firm to continue in business and/or pay redress.

(2)   There may be cases where, even though the firm has satisfied the *FCA* that payment of the financial penalty would cause it serious financial hardship, the *FCA* considers the *breach* to be so serious that it is not appropriate to reduce the penalty. The *FCA* will consider all the circumstances of the case in determining whether this course of action is appropriate, including whether:

   (a)   the firm directly derived a financial benefit from the *breach* and, if so, the extent of that financial benefit;

   (b)   the firm acted fraudulently or dishonestly in order to benefit financially;

   (c)   previous *FCA* action in respect of similar *breaches* has failed to improve industry standards; or

   (d)   the firm has spent money or dissipated assets in anticipation of *FCA* or other enforcement action with a view to frustrating or limiting the impact of action taken by the *FCA* or other authorities.

Withdrawal of authorisation

6.5D.4A G   FCA

The *FCA* may withdraw a firm's *authorisation* under section 33 of the *Act*, as well as impose a financial penalty. Such action by the *FCA* does not affect the *FCA's* assessment of the appropriate financial penalty in relation to a *breach*. However, the fact that the *FCA* has withdrawn a firm's *authorisation*, as a result of which the firm may have less earning potential, may be relevant in assessing whether the penalty will cause the firm serious financial hardship.

Transfers of assets

6.5D.5 G   FCA

Where the *FCA* considers that, following commencement of an *FCA* investigation, an individual or firm has reduced their solvency in order to reduce the amount of any disgorgement or financial penalty payable, for example by transferring assets to third parties, the *FCA* will normally take account of those assets when determining whether the individual or firm would suffer serious financial hardship as a result of the disgorgement and financial penalty.

6.6   FINANCIAL PENALTIES FOR LATE AND INCOMPLETE SUBMISSION OF REPORTS

6.6.1 G   FCA

(1)   The *FCA* attaches considerable importance to the timely submission by *firms* of reports. This is because the information that they contain is essential to the *FCA's* assessment of whether a *firm* is complying with the requirements and standards of the *regulatory system* and to the *FCA* understanding of that *firm's* business.

(2)   **DEPP 6.6.1 G** to **DEPP 6.6.5 G** set out the *FCA's* policy in relation to financial penalties for late submission of reports and is in addition to the *FCA's* policy relating to financial penalties as set out in **DEPP 6.5** to **DEPP 6.5D**.

6.6.2 G   FCA

In addition to the factors considered in Step 2 for cases against firms (**DEPP 6.5A**) and cases against individuals (**DEPP 6.5B**), the following considerations are relevant.

(1)   In general, the *FCA's* approach to disciplinary action arising from the late submission of a report will depend upon the length of time after the due date that the report in question is submitted.

(2)   If the *person* concerned is an individual, it is open to him to make representations to the *FCA* as to why he should not be the subject of a financial penalty, or why a lower penalty should be imposed. If he does so, the matters to which the *FCA* will have regard will include the matters set out in **DEPP 6.5B**. It should be noted that an administrative difficulty such as pressure of work does not, in itself, constitute a relevant circumstance for this purpose.

(3)   The *FCA* will have regard to repeated failures to submit reports on time. In the majority of cases involving such repeated failure, the *FCA* considers that it will be appropriate to seek more serious disciplinary sanctions or other enforcement action, including seeking to apply for the cancellation of the firm's permission.

(4)   The *FCA* will also have regard to the submission frequency of the late report when assessing the seriousness of the contravention. For example, a short delay in submitting a weekly or monthly report can have serious implications for the supervision of the firm in question. Such a delay may therefore be subject to a higher penalty than might otherwise be the case.

[Note: For the purposes of **DEPP 6.6.2 G**, "firm" has the special meaning given to it in **DEPP 6.5.1**.]

6.6.3 G   FCA

In addition, in appropriate cases, the *FCA* may bring disciplinary action against the *approved persons* within the *firm's* management who are ultimately responsible for ensuring that the *firm's* reports are completed and returned to the *FCA*.

6.6.4 G   FCA

In applying the *guidance* in this section, the *FCA* may treat a report which is materially incomplete or inaccurate as not received until it has been submitted in a form which is materially complete and accurate. For the purposes of the *guidance*, the *FCA* may also treat a report as not received where the method by which it is submitted to the *FCA* does not comply with the prescribed method of submission.

6.6.5 G   FCA

In most late reporting cases, it will not be necessary for the *FCA* to appoint an investigator since the fact of the breach will be clear. It follows that the *FCA* will not usually send the *firm* concerned a preliminary findings letter for late-reporting disciplinary action.

6.7   DISCOUNT FOR EARLY SETTLEMENT

6.7.1 G   FCA

Persons subject to enforcement action may be prepared to agree the amount of any financial penalty, or the length of any period of suspension or restriction, and other conditions which the *FCA* seeks to impose by way of such action. Such conditions might include, for example, the amount or mechanism for the payment of compensation to consumers. The *FCA* recognises the benefits of such agreements, in that they offer the potential for securing earlier redress or protection for consumers and the saving of cost to the *person* concerned and the *FCA* itself in contesting the financial penalty, suspension or restriction. The penalty that might otherwise be payable, or the length of the period of suspension or restriction that might otherwise be imposed, in respect of a *breach* by the *person* concerned will therefore be reduced to reflect the timing of any settlement agreement.

The settlement discount scheme applied to financial penalties

6.7.2 G   FCA

In appropriate cases the *FCA's* approach will be to negotiate with the *person* concerned to agree in principle the amount of a financial penalty having regard to the *FCA's* statement of policy as set out in **DEPP 6.5** to **DEPP 6.5D** and **DEPP 6.6**. (This starting figure will take no account of the existence of the *settlement discount scheme* described in this section.) Such amount ("A") will then be reduced by a percentage of A according to the stage in the process at which agreement is reached. The resulting figure ("B") will be the amount actually payable by the *person* concerned in respect of the *breach*. However, where part of a proposed financial penalty specifically equates to the disgorgement of profit accrued or loss avoided then the percentage reduction will not apply to that part of the penalty.

6.7.3 G   FCA

(1)   The *FCA* has identified four stages of an action for these purposes:

     (a)   the period from commencement of an investigation until the *FCA* has:

         (i)   a sufficient understanding of the nature and gravity of the *breach* to make a reasonable assessment of the appropriate penalty; and

         (ii)   communicated that assessment to the *person* concerned and allowed a reasonable opportunity to reach agreement as to the amount of the penalty ("stage 1");

     (b)   the period from the end of stage 1 until the expiry of the period for making written representations or, if sooner, the date on which the written representations are sent in response to the giving of a *warning notice* ("stage 2");

     (c)   the period from the end of stage 2 until the giving of a *decision notice* ("stage 3");

     (d)   the period after the end of stage 3, including proceedings before the *Tribunal* and any subsequent appeals ("stage 4").

(2)   The communication of the *FCA's* assessment of the appropriate penalty for the purposes of **DEPP 6.7.3 G (1)(A)** need not be in a prescribed form but will include an indication of the *breaches* alleged by the *FCA*. It may include the provision of a draft *warning notice*.

(3)   The reductions in penalty will be as follows:

Stage at which agreement reached	Percentage reduction
Stage 1	30
Stage 2	20
Stage 3	10
Stage 4	0

6.7.4 G   FCA

(1)   Any settlement agreement between the *FCA* and the *person* concerned will therefore need to include a statement as to the appropriate penalty discount in accordance with this procedure.

(2)   In certain circumstances the *person* concerned may consider that it would have been possible to reach a settlement at an earlier stage in the action, and argue that it should be entitled to a greater percentage reduction in penalty than is suggested by the table at **DEPP 6.7.3 G (3)**. It may be, for example, that the *FCA* no longer wishes to pursue its action in respect of all of the acts or omissions previously alleged to give rise to the *breach*. In such cases, the *person* concerned might argue that it would have been prepared to agree an appropriate penalty at an earlier stage and should therefore benefit from the discount which would have been available at that time. Equally, *FCA* staff may consider that greater openness from the *person* concerned could have resulted in an earlier settlement.

(3)   Arguments of this nature risk compromising the goals of greater clarity and transparency in respect of the benefits of early settlement, and invite dispute in each case as to when an agreement might have been possible. It will not usually be appropriate therefore to argue for a greater reduction in the amount of penalty on the basis that settlement could have been achieved earlier.

(4)   However, in exceptional cases the *FCA* may accept that there has been a substantial change in the nature or seriousness of the action being taken against the *person* concerned, and that an agreement would have been possible at an earlier stage if the action had commenced on a different footing. In such cases the *FCA* and person concerned may agree that the amount of the reduction in penalty should reflect the stage at which a settlement might otherwise have been possible.

6.7.5 G   FCA

In cases in which the *settlement discount scheme* is applied, the fact of settlement and the level of the discount to the financial penalty imposed by the *FCA* will be set out in the *final notice*.

The settlement discount scheme applied to suspensions and restrictions

6.7.6 G   FCA

The *settlement discount scheme* which applies to the amount of a financial penalty, described in **DEPP 6.7.2 G** to **DEPP 6.7.5 G**, also applies to the length of the period of a suspension or restriction, having regard to the *FCA's* statement of policy as set out in **DEPP 6A.3**.

CHAPTER 6A
THE POWER TO IMPOSE A SUSPENSION OR RESTRICTION

6A.1   INTRODUCTION

[3.101]
6A.1.1 G   FCA

DEPP 6A sets out the *FCA's* statement of policy with respect to the imposition of suspensions or restrictions, and the period for which those suspensions or restrictions are to have effect, under the *Act*, as required by sections 69(1), 88C(1), 89S(1) and 210(1) of the *Act*.

6A.1.2 G   FCA

(1)   For the purposes of **DEPP 6A**, "suspension" refers to the suspension of:

(a)   any *permission* which an *authorised person* has to carry on a *regulated activity* (under section 206A of the *Act*),

(b)   any approval of the performance by an *approved person* of any function to which the approval relates (under section 66 of the *Act*),

(c)   a *sponsor's* approval (under section 88A(2)(b) of the *Act*),

(d)   and a *primary information provider's* approval (under section 89Q(2)(b) of the *Act*); and

(2)   "restriction" refers to limitations or other restrictions in relation to:

(a)   the carrying on of a *regulated activity* by an *authorised person* (under section 206A of the *Act*),

(b)   the performance by an *approved person* of any function to which any approval relates (under section 66 of the *Act*),

    (c)   the performance of services to which a *sponsor's* approval relates (under section 88A(2)(c) of the *Act*), and

    (d)   the dissemination of *regulated information* by a *primary information provider* (under section 89Q(2)(c) of the *Act*).

6A.1.3 G   FCA

The power to impose a suspension or a restriction is a disciplinary measure which the *FCA* may use in addition to, or instead of, imposing a financial penalty or issuing a *public censure*. The principal purpose of imposing a suspension or a restriction is to promote high standards of regulatory and/or market conduct by deterring *persons* who have committed *breaches* from committing further *breaches*, helping to deter other *persons* from committing similar *breaches*, and demonstrating generally the benefits of compliant behaviour. Suspensions and restrictions are therefore tools that the *FCA* may employ to help it to achieve its *statutory objectives*. Examples of restrictions that we may impose include:

(1)   we may limit an *authorised person's* carrying on of a *regulated activity* so that they can only sell certain products or provide certain services;

(2)   we may restrict an *approved person's* performance of their *controlled functions* so that they can only give advice to *consumers* or deal in certain products if they are appropriately supervised.

6A.1.4 G   FCA

The powers to impose a suspension or a restriction in relation to *authorised persons* and *approved persons* are disciplinary measures; where the *FCA* considers it necessary to take action, for example, to protect *consumers* from an *authorised person*, the *FCA* will seek to cancel or vary the *authorised person's permissions*. If the *FCA* has concerns with a *person's* fitness to be approved, and considers it necessary to take action, the *FCA* will seek to prohibit the *approved person* or withdraw its approval. While the powers to impose a suspension or a restriction in relation to *sponsors* and *primary information providers* under sections 88A(2)(b)/(c) and 89Q(2)(b)/(c) of the *Act* are disciplinary measures, the *FCA* can impose suspensions, limitations or other restrictions in relation to *sponsors* and *primary information providers* in other circumstances.

6A.2   DECIDING WHETHER TO TAKE ACTION

6A.2.1 G   FCA

The *FCA* will consider the full circumstances of each case and determine whether it is appropriate to impose a suspension or restriction. The *FCA* will usually make this decision at the same time as it determines whether or not to impose a financial penalty or a *public censure*.

6A.2.2 G   FCA

The *FCA* will take into account relevant factors in deciding whether it is appropriate to impose a suspension or restriction. These may include factors listed in **DEPP 6.2**. There may also be other factors, not listed in **DEPP 6.2**, that are relevant.

6A.2.3 G   FCA

The *FCA* will consider it appropriate to impose a suspension or restriction where it believes that such action will be a more effective and persuasive deterrent than the imposition of a financial penalty alone. This is likely to be the case where the *FCA* considers that direct and visible action in relation to a particular *breach* is necessary. Examples of circumstances where the *FCA* may consider it appropriate to impose a suspension or restriction include:

(1)   where the *FCA* (or any *previous regulator*) has taken any previous disciplinary action resulting in adverse findings against the *person*;

(2)   where the *FCA* has previously taken action in respect of similar *breaches* and has failed to improve industry standards;

(3)   where the *person* has failed properly to carry out an agreed redress package or other agreed remedial measures;

(4)   where the misconduct appears to be widespread across a number of individuals across a particular business area (suggesting a poor compliance culture);

(5)   where the *person's* competitive position in the market has improved as a result of the *breach*;

(6)   if, in accordance with **DEPP 6.5D**, the *FCA* considers that a proposed penalty would cause the subject of enforcement action serious financial hardship and that it is appropriate to reduce the proposed penalty.

6A.2.4 G   FCA

The *FCA* expects usually to suspend or restrict a *person* from carrying out activities directly linked to the *breach*. However, in certain circumstances the *FCA* may also suspend or restrict a *person* from carrying out activities that are not directly linked to the *breach*, for example, where an *authorised person's* relevant business area no longer exists or has been restructured.

6A.2.5 G   FCA

For the purposes of section 89S(1)(d) of the *Act*, the *FCA* expects usually to suspend the approval of a *primary information provider*.

6A.3   DETERMINING THE APPROPRIATE LENGTH OF THE PERIOD OF SUSPENSION OR RESTRICTION

6A.3.1 G   FCA

The *FCA* will consider all the relevant circumstances of a case when it determines the length of the period of suspension or restriction (if any) that is appropriate for the *breach* concerned, and is also a sufficient deterrent. Set out below is a list of factors that may be relevant for this purpose. The list is not exhaustive: not all of these factors may be applicable in a particular case, and there may be other factors, not listed, that are relevant.

6A.3.2 G   FCA

The following factors may be relevant to determining the appropriate length of the period of suspension or restriction to be imposed on a *person* under the *Act*:

(1)   Deterrence

When determining the appropriate length of the period of suspension or restriction, the *FCA* will have regard to the principal purpose for which it imposes sanctions, namely to promote high standards of regulatory and/or market conduct by deterring *persons* who have committed *breaches* from committing further *breaches* and helping to deter other *persons* from committing similar *breaches*, as well as demonstrating generally the benefits of compliant business.

(2)   The seriousness of the breach

The *FCA* will have regard to the seriousness of the *breach*. In assessing this, it will consider the impact and nature of the *breach*, and whether it was committed deliberately or recklessly. Where the *breach* was committed by an *authorised person*, relevant factors may include those listed in **DEPP 6.5A.2 G (6)** to **(9)**. Where the *breach* was committed by an *approved person*, relevant factors may include those listed in **DEPP 6.5B.2 G (8)** to **(11)**. There may also be other factors, not listed in these sections, that are relevant.

(3)   Aggravating and mitigating factors

The *FCA* will have regard to factors that may aggravate or mitigate a *breach*. Where the breach was committed by an *authorised person*, *sponsor* or *primary information provider*, relevant factors may include those listed in **DEPP 6.5A.3 G (2)**. Where the *breach* was committed by an *approved person*, relevant factors may include those listed in **DEPP 6.5B.3 G (2)**. There may also be other factors, not listed in these sections, that are relevant.

(4)   The impact of suspension or restriction on the person in breach

The following considerations may be relevant to the assessment of the impact of suspension or restriction on an *authorised person*, *sponsor* or *primary information provider*:

(a)   the *authorised person's*, *sponsor's* or *primary information provider's* expected lost revenue and profits from not being able to carry out the suspended or restricted activity;

(b)   the cost of any measures the *authorised person*, *sponsor* or *primary information provider* must undertake to comply with the suspension or restriction;

(c)   potential economic costs, for example, the payment of salaries to employees who will not work during the period of suspension or restriction or the payment of compensation to *consumers* who will suffer loss as a result of the suspension or restriction;

(d)   the effect on other areas of the *authorised person's*, *sponsor's* or *primary information provider's* business; and

(e)   whether the suspension or restriction would cause the *authorised person*, *sponsor* or *primary information provider* serious financial hardship.

The following considerations may be relevant to the assessment of the impact of suspension or restriction on an *approved person*:

(f)   the *approved person's* expected lost earnings from not being able to carry out the suspended or restricted activity; and

(g)   whether the suspension or restriction would cause the *approved person* serious financial hardship.

(5)   The impact of suspension or restriction on persons other than the person in breach

The following considerations may be relevant to the assessment of the impact of suspension or restriction on *persons* other than the *person in breach*:

(a)   the extent to which *consumers* may suffer loss or inconvenience as a result of the suspension or restriction. For example, if it is difficult for *consumers* to switch to a competitor, a longer period of suspension or restriction is likely to have more impact; and

(b)   the impact of the suspension or restriction on markets.

6A.3.3 G   FCA

The *FCA* may delay the commencement of the period of suspension or restriction. In deciding whether this is appropriate, the *FCA* will take into account all the circumstances of a case. Considerations that may be relevant in respect of an *authorised person, sponsor* or *primary information provider* include:

(1)   the impact of the suspension or restriction on consumers;

(2)   any practical measures the *authorised person, sponsor* or *primary information provider* needs to take before the period of suspension or restriction begins, for example, changes to its systems and controls to enable it to stop or limit the activity in question;

(3)   the impact of the suspension or restriction on other costs incurred by the *authorised person, sponsor* or *primary information provider*, for example, cancelling suppliers or suspending employees.

6A.3.4 G   FCA

The *FCA* and the *person* on whom a suspension or restriction is to be imposed may seek to agree the length of the period of suspension or restriction and other terms. In recognition of the benefits of such agreements, **DEPP 6.7** provides that the length of a period of suspension or restriction which might otherwise have been imposed will be reduced to reflect the stage at which the *FCA* and the *person* concerned reached an agreement.

6A.4   THE INTERACTION BETWEEN THE POWER TO IMPOSE SUSPENSIONS OR RESTRICTIONS AND THE POWER TO IMPOSE PENALTIES OR PUBLIC CENSURES

6A.4.1 G   FCA

The deterrent effect and impact on a *person* of a suspension or restriction, by itself or in combination with a financial penalty, may be greater than where only a financial penalty is imposed. The *FCA* will consider the overall impact and deterrent effect of the sanctions it imposes when determining the level of penalty and the length of suspension or restriction.

6A.4.2 G   FCA

The *FCA* expects usually to take the following approach in respect of the interaction between a suspension or restriction and a financial penalty or *public censure*:

(1)   The *FCA* will determine which sanction, or combination of sanctions, is appropriate for the *breach*.

(2)   If the *FCA*, following the approach set out in **DEPP 6.2**, considers it appropriate to impose a financial penalty, it will calculate the appropriate level of the financial penalty, following the approach set out in **DEPP 6.5** to **DEPP 6.5D**.

(3)   If the *FCA*, following the approach set out in **DEPP 6A.2**, considers it appropriate to impose a suspension or restriction, it will calculate the appropriate length of the period of suspension or restriction, following the approach set out in **DEPP 6A.3**.

(4)   Where the *FCA* considers it appropriate to impose both a financial penalty and a suspension or restriction, it will decide whether the combined impact on the *person* is likely to be disproportionate in respect to the *breach* and the deterrent effect of the sanctions.

(5)   If the *FCA* considers the combined impact on the *person* is likely to be disproportionate, it will decide whether to reduce the period of suspension or restriction, the amount of the financial penalty or both, so that the combined impact of the sanctions is proportionate in relation to the *breach* and the deterrent effect of the sanctions. The *FCA* will decide which sanction to reduce after considering all the circumstances of the case.

(6)   In deciding the final level of the financial penalty and the length of the period of suspension or restriction, the *FCA* will also take into account any representations by the *person* that the combined impact will cause them serious financial hardship. The *FCA* will take the approach set out in **DEPP 6.5D** in assessing this.

6A.4.3 G   FCA

The *FCA* may depart from the approach set out in **DEPP 6A.4.2 G**. For example, the *FCA* may at the outset consider that a financial penalty is the only appropriate sanction for a *breach* but, having determined the appropriate level of financial penalty, may consider it appropriate to reduce the amount of the financial penalty for serious financial hardship reasons. In such a situation, the *FCA* may consider it appropriate to impose a suspension or restriction even if the *FCA* at the outset did not consider such a sanction to be appropriate. The *FCA* will take into account whether the *person* would suffer serious financial hardship in deciding the length of the period of suspension or restriction, and may decide not to impose a suspension or restriction if it considers such action would result in serious financial hardship.

CHAPTER 7
STATEMENT OF POLICY ON INTERVIEWS CONDUCTED ON BEHALF OF OVERSEAS AND EEA REGULATORS

7.1   APPLICATION AND PURPOSE

Application

[3.102]

7.1.1 G   FCA

DEPP 7 applies when the *FCA*:

(1)   has appointed an investigator at the request of an *overseas regulator*, under section 169(1)(b) (Assistance to overseas regulators) or of an *EEA regulator* under section 131FA of the *Act*; and

(2)   has directed, or is considering directing, the investigator, under section 169(7) or section 131FA of the *Act*, to permit a representative of the *overseas regulator* or of the *EEA regulator* to attend, and take part in, any interview conducted for the purposes of the investigation.

7.1.2 G   FCA

In **DEPP 7**, a "requested interview" means any interview conducted for the purposes of an investigation under section 169(1)(b) or section 131FA of the *Act* in relation to which the *FCA* has given a direction under section 169(7) or section 131FA of the *Act*.

Purpose

7.1.3 G   FCA

The purpose of **DEPP 7** is to set out the *FCA*'s statement of policy on the conduct of interviews to which a direction under section 169(7) or section 131FA has been given or the *FCA* is considering giving. The *FCA* is required to prepare and publish this statement of policy by section 169(9) and (11) and section 131FA of the *Act*. As required by section 169(10) and section 131FA of the Act, the Treasury has approved the statement of policy.

7.1.4 G   FCA

The *FCA* is keen to promote co-operation with *overseas regulators* and *EEA regulators*. It views provision of assistance to *overseas regulators* and *EEA regulators* as an essential part of discharging its general functions.

7.2   INTERVIEWS

Appointment of investigator and confidentiality of information

7.2.1 G   FCA

Under section 169(1)(b) and section 131FA of the *Act*, the *FCA* may appoint an investigator to investigate any matter at the request of an *overseas regulator* or *EEA regulator*. The powers of the investigator appointed by the *FCA* (referred to here as the 'FCA's investigator') include the power to require *persons* to attend at a specified time and place and answer questions (the compulsory interview power).

7.2.2 G   FCA

Where the *FCA* appoints an investigator in response to a request from an *overseas regulator* or *EEA regulator* it may, under section 169(7) or section 131FA of the *Act*, direct him to permit a representative of that regulator to attend and take part in any interviews conducted for the purposes of the investigation. The *FCA* may only give a direction under section 169(7) or section 131FA if it is satisfied that any information obtained by an *overseas regulator* or *EEA regulator* as a result of the interview will be subject to the safeguards equivalent to those contained in Part XXIII (Public Record, Disclosure of Information and Cooperation) of the *Act*.

7.2.3 G   FCA

Part XXIII of the *Act* contains restrictions on the disclosure of confidential information. The restrictions are subject to exceptions contained in regulations made by the Treasury under section 349.

Policy on use of investigative powers

7.2.4 G   FCA

The *FCA's* policy on how it will use its investigative powers, including its power to appoint investigators, in support of *overseas regulators* and *EEA regulators*, is set out in the *FCA*'s Enforcement Guide (*EG*).

Use of direction powers

7.2.5 G   FCA

The *FCA* may need to consider whether to use its direction power at two stages of an investigation:
(1)   at the same time that it considers the request from the *overseas regulator* or *EEA regulator* to appoint investigators;
(2)   after it has appointed investigators, either at the request of the *overseas regulator* or *EEA regulator* or on the recommendation of the investigators.

7.2.6 G   FCA

Before making a direction under section 169(7) or section 131FA the *FCA* will discuss and determine with the *overseas regulator* or *EEA regulator* how this statement of policy will apply to the conduct of the interview, taking into account all the circumstances of the case. Amongst other matters, the *FCA* will at this stage determine the extent to which the representative of the *overseas regulator* or *EEA regulator* will be able to participate in the interview. The *overseas regulator* or *EEA regulator* will be notified of this determination on the issuing of the direction.

7.2.7 G   FCA

The direction will contain the identity of the representative of the *overseas regulator* or *EEA regulator* that is permitted to attend any interview and the role that he will play in the interview. If the *FCA* envisages that there will be more than one interview in the course of the investigation, the direction may also specify which interview(s) the representative is allowed to attend.

Conduct of interview

7.2.8 G   FCA

In circumstances where an interview is to be conducted as part of the investigation, the *FCA's* investigator will have conduct of the interview. In general, the *FCA's* investigators will be employees of the *FCA*, but in appropriate cases the *FCA* may appoint *persons* who are not its employees. In those cases, the *FCA* may choose to require that an *FCA* employee is present at the interview and may choose to appoint that *person* as an investigator.

7.2.9 G   FCA

The *FCA's* investigator will act on behalf of the *FCA* and under its control. He may be instructed to permit the representative of the *overseas regulator* or *EEA regulator* to assist in the preparation of the interview. Where the *FCA* considers it appropriate, it may permit the representative to attend and ask questions of the interviewee in the course of the interview. The interview will be conducted according to the terms of the direction and the notification referred to in **DEPP 7.2.6 G**.

7.2.10 G   FCA

If the direction does permit the representative of an *overseas regulator* or *EEA regulator* to attend the interview and ask the interviewee questions, the *FCA's* investigator will retain control of the interview throughout. Control of the interview means the following will apply:
(1)   The *FCA's* investigator instigates and concludes the interview, introduces everyone present and explains the procedure of the interview. He warns the interviewee of the possible consequences of refusing to answer questions and the uses to which any answers that are given can and cannot be put. The *FCA's* investigator will always ask preliminary questions, such as those establishing the identity of the interviewee.
(2)   The *FCA's* investigator determines the duration of the interview and when, if at all, there should be any breaks in the course of it.
(3)   The *FCA's* investigator has responsibility for making a record of the interview. The record should note the times and duration of any breaks in the interview and any periods when the representative of the *overseas regulator* or *EEA regulator* was either present or not present.
(4)   Where the *FCA's* investigator considers it appropriate, he may either suspend the interview, ask the overseas representative to leave the interview, or terminate the interview and reschedule it for another occasion. In making that decision he will bear in mind the terms of the direction, any agreement made with the *overseas regulator* or *EEA regulator* as to the conduct of the interview and the contents of this statement of policy.

7.2.11 G   FCA

The *FCA* will in general provide written notice of the appointment of an investigator to the *person* under investigation pursuant to the request of an *overseas regulator* or *EEA regulator*. Whether or not the interviewee is the *person* under investigation, the *FCA's* investigator will inform the interviewee of the provisions under which he has been appointed, the identity of the requesting authority and general nature of the matter under investigation. The interviewee will also normally be informed if a representative of the *overseas regulator* or *EEA regulator* is to attend and take part in the interview. Notification of any of these matters may not be provided in advance of the interview if the *FCA* believes that the circumstances are such that notification would be likely to result in the investigation being frustrated.

7.2.12 G   FCA

Part 3   FCA Handbook Materials

The interviewee will normally be given a copy of the direction issued under section 169(7) or section 131FA in advance of the interview unless to do so would be likely to result in the investigation being frustrated. The interviewee will also be provided with a copy of this statement of policy.

7.2.13 G   FCA

The *FCA's* investigator will determine the venue and timing of the interview. The interviewee will be notified of the venue and timing of the interview in advance and in writing.

7.2.14 G   FCA

When the *FCA's* investigator has exercised the compulsory interview power, at the outset of the interview the interviewee will be given an appropriate warning. The warning, amongst other things, must state that the interviewee is obliged to answer all questions put to them during the interview, including any put by the representative of the *overseas regulator* or *EEA regulator*. It will also state that in criminal proceedings or proceedings for *market abuse* the FCA will not use as evidence against the interviewee any information obtained under compulsion during the interview.

7.2.15 G   FCA

The *FCA's* investigator may decide which documents or other information may be put to the interviewee, and whether it is appropriate to give the interviewee sight of the *documents* before the interview takes place. Where the *overseas regulator* or *EEA regulator* wishes to ask questions about *documents* during the interview and the *FCA's* investigator wishes to inspect those *documents* before the interview, he will be given the opportunity to do so. If the *FCA's* investigator wishes to inspect them and has not been able to do so before the interview, he may suspend the interview until he has had an opportunity to inspect them.

7.2.16 G   FCA

When the *FCA's* investigator has exercised the compulsory interview power, the *FCA's* investigator will require the *person* attending the interview to answer questions. Where appropriate, questions may also be posed by the representative of the *overseas regulator* or *EEA regulator*. The interviewee will also be required to answer these questions. The *FCA's* investigator may intervene at any stage during questioning by the representative of the *overseas regulator* or *EEA regulator*.

Language

7.2.17 G   FCA

Interviews will, in general, be conducted in English. Where the interviewee's first language is not English, at the request of the interviewee arrangements will be made for the questions to be translated into the interviewee's first language and for his answers to be translated back into English. If a translator is employed at the request of the representative of the *overseas regulator* or *EEA regulator* then the translation costs will normally be met by the *overseas regulator* or *EEA regulator*. Where interviews are being conducted in pursuance of an *EU* law obligation these costs will be met by the *FCA*. In any event, the meeting of costs in relation to translators and, where applicable, the translation of *documents* will always be agreed in advance with the *overseas regulator* or *EEA regulator*.

Tape-recording

7.2.18 G   FCA

All compulsory interviews will be tape-recorded. The method of recording will be decided on and arranged by the *FCA's* investigator. Costs will be addressed similarly to that set out in the preceding paragraph. The *FCA* will not provide the *overseas regulator* or *EEA regulator* with transcripts of the tapes of interviews unless specifically agreed to, but copies of the tapes will normally be provided where requested. The interviewee will be provided with a copy of tapes of the interview but will only be provided with transcripts of the tapes or translations of any transcripts if he agrees to meet the cost of producing them.

Representation

7.2.19 G   FCA

The interviewee may be accompanied at the interview by a legal adviser or a non-legally qualified observer of his choice. The costs of any representation will not be met by the *FCA*. The presence at the interview of a representative of the *overseas regulator* or *EEA regulator* may mean that the interviewee wishes to be represented or accompanied by a *person* either from or familiar with that regulator's jurisdiction. As far as practical the arrangements for the interview should accommodate this wish. However, the *FCA* reserves the right to proceed with the interview if it is not possible to find such a *person* within a reasonable time or no such *person* is able to attend at a suitable venue.

7.2.20 G   FCA

In relation to the publication of investigations by *overseas regulators* or *EEA regulators*, the *FCA* will pursue a policy similar to the policy that relates to its own investigations.

TRANSITIONAL PROVISIONS AND SCHEDULES

1　TRANSITIONAL PROVISIONS APPLYING TO THE DECISION PROCEDURE AND PENALTIES MANUAL

1. Table DEPP TP 1

[3.102A]
TP1

(1)	(2) Material to which the transitional provision applies	(3)	(4) Transitional provision	(5) Transitional provision dates in force:	(6) Handbook provision coming into force
1	*DEPP*	G	Expired		
2	**DEPP 6.7** (Discount for early settlement),	G	Expired		
3	*DEPP*	G	Expired		
4	*DEPP*	G	Expired		

SCHEDULE 1　RECORD KEEPING REQUIREMENTS

Sch1.1 G　FCA

There are no record-keeping requirements in *DEPP*.

SCHEDULE 2　NOTIFICATION REQUIREMENTS

Sch2.1 G　FCA

There are no notification requirements in *DEPP*.

SCHEDULE 3　FEES AND OTHER REQUIRED PAYMENTS

Sch3.1　FCA

There are no requirements for fees in *DEPP*.

Sch3.2 G　FCA

The *FCA's* power to impose financial penalties is contained in:

Section 63A (Power to impose penalties) of the *Act*

Section 66 (Disciplinary powers) of the *Act*

Section 88A (Disciplinary powers: contravention of s 88(3)(c) or (e)) of the *Act*

Section 89Q (Disciplinary powers: contravention of s 89P(4)(b) or (d)) of the *Act*

Section 91 (Penalties for breach of Part 6 Rules) of the *Act*

Section 123 (Power to impose penalties in cases of market abuse) of the *Act*

section 131G (Power to impose penalty or issue censure) of the *Act*

Section 192K (Power to impose penalty or issue censure) of the *Act*

Section 206 (Financial penalties) of the *Act*

Section 249 (Disciplinary measures) of the *Act*

Section 312F (Financial penalties) of the *Act*

Section 345 (Disciplinary measures) of the *Act*

Part III of Schedule 1ZA (The Financial Conduct Authority) to the *Act*

the *Money Laundering Regulations*

the Transfer of Funds (Information on the Payer) Regulations 2007 (SI 2007/3298)

the *RCB Regulations*

the *Payment Services Regulations*

the *Cross-Border Payments in Euro Regulations*

the *OTC derivatives, CCPs and trade repositories regulation*

the *AIFMD UK regulation*

the *Referral Fees Regulations*

the *CCA Order*

the *Immigration Regulations*

SCHEDULE 4   POWERS EXERCISED

Sch4.1 G   FCA

The following powers and related provisions in or under the *Act* have been exercised by the *FCA* to make the statements of policy in *DEPP*:

Section 63C (Statement of policy)

Section 69 (Statement of policy) (including as applied by paragraph 1 of Schedule 5 to the *Payment Services Regulations* and by paragraph 1 of the Schedule to the *Cross-Border Payments in Euro Regulations*)

Section 88C (Action under s 88A: statement of policy)

Section 89S (Action under s 89Q: statement of policy)

Section 93(1) (Statement of policy)

Section 124(1) (Statement of policy)

Section 131J (Impositions of penalties under section 131G: statement of policy)

Section 139A (Power of the FCA to give guidance)

Section 169(9) (Investigations etc in support of overseas regulator) (including as applied by paragraph 3 of Schedule 5 to the *Payment Services Regulations*)

Section 192N (Imposition of penalties under section 192K: statement of policy)

Section 210(1) (Statements of policy) (including as applied by regulation 86(6) of the *Payment Services Regulations* and by paragraph 3 of the Schedule to the *Cross-Border Payments in Euro Regulations*)

Section 249 (Disciplinary measures)

Section 312J (Statement of policy)

Section 345D (Imposition of penalties on auditors or actuaries: statement of policy)

Section 395 (The Authority's procedures) (including as applied by paragraph 7 of Schedule 5 to the *Payment Services Regulations* and by paragraph 5 of the Schedule to the *Cross-Border Payments in Euro Regulations*)

Paragraph 16 (Penalties) of Schedule 1 (The Financial Services Authority)

Sch4.2 G   FCA

The following additional powers and related provisions have been exercised by the *FCA* to make the statements of policy in *DEPP*:

Regulation 42 (Guidance) of the *RCB Regulations*

Regulation 44 (Warning notices and decision notices) of the *RCB Regulations*

Regulation 86 (Proposal to take disciplinary measures) of the *Payment Services Regulations*

Regulation 93 (Guidance) of the *Payment Services Regulations*

Regulation 14 (Guidance) of the *Cross-Border Payments in Euro Regulations*

Regulation 70 (Warning Notices, Decision Notices and Supervisory Notices) of the *AIFMD UK regulation*

Regulation 71 (Application of Act to unauthorised AIFs) of the *AIFMD UK regulation*

Regulation 29 (Statements of policy) of the *Referral Fees Regulations*

Regulation 30 (Application of Part 26 of the 2000 Act) of the *Referral Fees Regulations*

Article 3(11) (Application of provisions of FSMA 2000 in connection with failure to comply with the 1974 Act) of the *CCA Order*

Article 4 (Statement of policy) of the *CCA Order*

Regulation 28 (Statements of policy) of the *Immigration Regulations*

Regulation 29 (Application of Part 26 of the 2000 Act) of the *Immigration Regulations*

SCHEDULE 5   RIGHTS OF ACTION FOR DAMAGES

Sch5.1 G   FCA

There are no rules in *DEPP*.

SCHEDULE 6   RULES THAT CAN BE WAIVED

Sch6.1 G   FCA

There are no rules in *DEPP*.

PART 4
OTHER MATERIALS

CONSOLIDATED VERSION OF THE TREATY ON THE FUNCTIONING OF THE EUROPEAN UNION

NOTES

Date of publication in OJ: OJ C326 , 26.10.2012, p 1.

Formerly titled the "Treaty Establishing the European Community" (Treaty of Rome). This is the Treaty currently in force which is the successor to the Treaty of Rome, as consolidated following the amendments to and the renaming of the Treaty, by the Treaty of Lisbon which came into force on 1 December 2009.

Cross-references to the equivalent article in the pre-Lisbon Treaty version of the Treaty are given at the beginning of each of the Articles reproduced; these cross-references are part of the official text. The abbreviation "TEC" refers to the Treaty Establishing the European Community.

PART THREE
UNION POLICIES AND INTERNAL ACTIONS

TITLE VII
COMMON RULES ON COMPETITION, TAXATION AND APPROXIMATION OF LAWS

CHAPTER 1
RULES ON COMPETITION

Section 1
Rules Applying to Undertakings

[4.1]
Article 101 (ex Article 81 TEC)

1. The following shall be prohibited as incompatible with the internal market: all agreements between undertakings, decisions by associations of undertakings and concerted practices which may affect trade between Member States and which have as their object or effect the prevention, restriction or distortion of competition within the internal market, and in particular those which

  (a)   directly or indirectly fix purchase or selling prices or any other trading conditions;

  (b)   limit or control production, markets, technical development, or investment;

  (c)   share markets or sources of supply;

  (d)   apply dissimilar conditions to equivalent transactions with other trading parties, thereby placing them at a competitive disadvantage;

  (e)   make the conclusion of contracts subject to acceptance by the other parties of supplementary obligations which, by their nature or according to commercial usage, have no connection with the subject of such contracts.

2. Any agreements or decisions prohibited pursuant to this Article shall be automatically void.

3. The provisions of paragraph 1 may, however, be declared inapplicable in the case of:

—   any agreement or category of agreements between undertakings,

—   any decision or category of decisions by associations of undertakings,

—   any concerted practice or category of concerted practices,

which contributes to improving the production or distribution of goods or to promoting technical or economic progress, while allowing consumers a fair share of the resulting benefit, and which does not:

  (a)   impose on the undertakings concerned restrictions which are not indispensable to the attainment of these objectives;

  (b)   afford such undertakings the possibility of eliminating competition in respect of a substantial part of the products in question.

[4.2]
Article 102 (ex Article 82 TEC)

Any abuse by one or more undertakings of a dominant position within the internal market or in a substantial part of it shall be prohibited as incompatible with the internal market in so far as it may affect trade between Member States.

Such abuse may, in particular, consist in:

  (a)   directly or indirectly imposing unfair purchase or selling prices or other unfair trading conditions;

  (b)   limiting production, markets or technical development to the prejudice of consumers;

  (c)   applying dissimilar conditions to equivalent transactions with other trading parties, thereby placing them at a competitive disadvantage;

  (d)   making the conclusion of contracts subject to acceptance by the other parties of supplementary obligations which, by their nature or according to commercial usage, have no connection with the subject of such contracts.

[4.3]
Article 103 (ex Article 83 TEC)
1.   The appropriate regulations or directives to give effect to the principles set out in Articles 101 and 102 shall be laid down by the Council, on a proposal from the Commission and after consulting the European Parliament.
2.   The regulations or directives referred to in paragraph 1 shall be designed in particular:
   (a)   to ensure compliance with the prohibitions laid down in Article 101(1) and in Article 102 by making provision for fines and periodic penalty payments;
   (b)   to lay down detailed rules for the application of Article 101(3), taking into account the need to ensure effective supervision on the one hand, and to simplify administration to the greatest possible extent on the other;
   (c)   to define, if need be, in the various branches of the economy, the scope of the provisions of Articles 101 and 102;
   (d)   to define the respective functions of the Commission and of the Court of Justice of the European Union in applying the provisions laid down in this paragraph;
   (e)   to determine the relationship between national laws and the provisions contained in this Section or adopted pursuant to this Article.

[4.4]
Article 104 (ex Article 84 TEC)
Until the entry into force of the provisions adopted in pursuance of Article 103, the authorities in Member States shall rule on the admissibility of agreements, decisions and concerted practices and on abuse of a dominant position in the internal market in accordance with the law of their country and with the provisions of Article 101, in particular paragraph 3, and of Article 102.

[4.5]
Article 105 (ex Article 85 TEC)
1.   Without prejudice to Article 104, the Commission shall ensure the application of the principles laid down in Articles 101 and 102. On application by a Member State or on its own initiative, and in cooperation with the competent authorities in the Member States, which shall give it their assistance, the Commission shall investigate cases of suspected infringement of these principles. If it finds that there has been an infringement, it shall propose appropriate measures to bring it to an end.
2.   If the infringement is not brought to an end, the Commission shall record such infringement of the principles in a reasoned decision. The Commission may publish its decision and authorise Member States to take the measures, the conditions and details of which it shall determine, needed to remedy the situation.
3.   The Commission may adopt regulations relating to the categories of agreement in respect of which the Council has adopted a regulation or a directive pursuant to Article 103(2)(b).

[4.6]
Article 106 (ex Article 86 TEC)
1.   In the case of public undertakings and undertakings to which Member States grant special or exclusive rights, Member States shall neither enact nor maintain in force any measure contrary to the rules contained in the Treaties, in particular to those rules provided for in Article 18 and Articles 101 to 109.
2.   Undertakings entrusted with the operation of services of general economic interest or having the character of a revenue-producing monopoly shall be subject to the rules contained in the Treaties, in particular to the rules on competition, in so far as the application of such rules does not obstruct the performance, in law or in fact, of the particular tasks assigned to them. The development of trade must not be affected to such an extent as would be contrary to the interests of the Union.
3.   The Commission shall ensure the application of the provisions of this Article and shall, where necessary, address appropriate directives or decisions to Member States.

Section 2
Aids Granted by States

[4.7]
Article 107 (ex Article 87 TEC)
1.   Save as otherwise provided in the Treaties, any aid granted by a Member State or through State resources in any form whatsoever which distorts or threatens to distort competition by favouring certain undertakings or the production of certain goods shall, in so far as it affects trade between Member States, be incompatible with the internal market.
2.   The following shall be compatible with the internal market:
   (a)   aid having a social character, granted to individual consumers, provided that such aid is granted without discrimination related to the origin of the products concerned;
   (b)   aid to make good the damage caused by natural disasters or exceptional occurrences;

(c) aid granted to the economy of certain areas of the Federal Republic of Germany affected by the division of Germany, in so far as such aid is required in order to compensate for the economic disadvantages caused by that division. Five years after the entry into force of the Treaty of Lisbon, the Council, acting on a proposal from the Commission, may adopt a decision repealing this point.
3. The following may be considered to be compatible with the internal market:
(a) aid to promote the economic development of areas where the standard of living is abnormally low or where there is serious underemployment, and of the regions referred to in Article 349, in view of their structural, economic and social situation;
(b) aid to promote the execution of an important project of common European interest or to remedy a serious disturbance in the economy of a Member State;
(c) aid to facilitate the development of certain economic activities or of certain economic areas, where such aid does not adversely affect trading conditions to an extent contrary to the common interest;
(d) aid to promote culture and heritage conservation where such aid does not affect trading conditions and competition in the Union to an extent that is contrary to the common interest;
(e) such other categories of aid as may be specified by decision of the Council on a proposal from the Commission.

[4.8]
Article 108 (ex Article 88 TEC)
1. The Commission shall, in cooperation with Member States, keep under constant review all systems of aid existing in those States. It shall propose to the latter any appropriate measures required by the progressive development or by the functioning of the internal market.
2. If, after giving notice to the parties concerned to submit their comments, the Commission finds that aid granted by a State or through State resources is not compatible with the internal market having regard to Article 107, or that such aid is being misused, it shall decide that the State concerned shall abolish or alter such aid within a period of time to be determined by the Commission.

If the State concerned does not comply with this decision within the prescribed time, the Commission or any other interested State may, in derogation from the provisions of Articles 258 and 259, refer the matter to the Court of Justice of the European Union direct.

On application by a Member State, the Council may, acting unanimously, decide that aid which that State is granting or intends to grant shall be considered to be compatible with the internal market, in derogation from the provisions of Article 107 or from the regulations provided for in Article 109, if such a decision is justified by exceptional circumstances. If, as regards the aid in question, the Commission has already initiated the procedure provided for in the first subparagraph of this paragraph, the fact that the State concerned has made its application to the Council shall have the effect of suspending that procedure until the Council has made its attitude known.

If, however, the Council has not made its attitude known within three months of the said application being made, the Commission shall give its decision on the case.
3. The Commission shall be informed, in sufficient time to enable it to submit its comments, of any plans to grant or alter aid. If it considers that any such plan is not compatible with the internal market having regard to Article 107, it shall without delay initiate the procedure provided for in paragraph 2. The Member State concerned shall not put its proposed measures into effect until this procedure has resulted in a final decision.
4. The Commission may adopt regulations relating to the categories of State aid that the Council has, pursuant to Article 109, determined may be exempted from the procedure provided for by paragraph 3 of this Article.

[4.9]
Article 109 (ex Article 89 TEC)
The Council, on a proposal from the Commission and after consulting the European Parliament, may make any appropriate regulations for the application of Articles 107 and 108 and may in particular determine the conditions in which Article 108(3) shall apply and the categories of aid exempted from this procedure.

COUNCIL OF EUROPE: EUROPEAN CONVENTION ON PRODUCTS LIABILITY IN REGARD TO PERSONAL INJURY AND DEATH

[Done at Strasbourg, 27 January 1977]

NOTES

On the occasion of the 59th Session of the Committee of Ministers of the Council of Europe, the Convention was opened to signature on 27 January 1977. It was signed by the plenipotentiaries of Belgium, France, and Luxembourg.

Part 4 Other Materials

The member States of the Council of Europe, signatory hereto,

Considering that the aim of the Council of Europe is to achieve a greater unity between its Members;

Considering the development of case law in the majority of member States extending liability of producers prompted by a desire to protect consumers taking into account the new production techniques and marketing and sales methods;

Desiring to ensure better protection of the public and, at the same time, to take producers' legitimate interests into account;

Considering that priority should be given to compensation for personal injury and death;

Aware of the importance of introducing special rules on the liability of producers at European level,

Have agreed as follows—

[4.10]
Article 1
1.   Each Contracting State shall make its national law conform with the provisions of this Convention not later than the date of the entry into force of the Convention in respect of that State.
2.   Each Contracting State shall communicate to the Secretary General of the Council of Europe, not later than the date of the entry into force of the Convention in respect of that State, any text adopted or a statement of the contents of the existing law which it relies on to implement the Convention.

[4.11]
Article 2
For the purpose of this Convention—
   (a)   the term 'product' indicates all movables, natural or industrial, whether raw or manufactured, even though incorporated into another movable or into an immovable;
   (b)   the term 'producer' indicates the manufacturers of finished products or of component parts and the producers of natural products;
   (c)   a product has a 'defect' when it does not provide the safety which a person is entitled to expect, having regard to all the circumstances including the presentation of the product;
   (d)   a product has been 'put into circulation' when the producer has delivered it to another person.

[4.12]
Article 3
1.   The producer shall be liable to pay compensation for death or personal injuries caused by a defect in his product.
2.   Any person who has imported a product for putting it into circulation in the course of a business and any person who has presented a product as his product by causing his name, trademark or other distinguishing feature to appear on the product, shall be deemed to be producers for the purpose of this Convention and shall be liable as such.
3.   When the product does not indicate the identity of any of the persons liable under paragraphs 1 and 2 of this article, each supplier shall be deemed to be a producer for the purpose of this Convention and liable as such, unless he discloses, within a reasonable time, at the request of the claimant, the identity of the producer or of the person who supplied him with the product. The same shall apply, in the case of an imported product, if this product does not indicate the identity of the importer referred to in paragraph 2, even if the name of the producer is indicated.
4.   In the case of damage caused by a defect in a product incorporated into another product, the producer of the incorporated product and the producer incorporating that product shall be liable.
5.   Where several persons are liable under this Convention for the same damage, each shall be liable in full (*in solidum*).

[4.13]
Article 4
1.   If the injured person or the person entitled to claim compensation has by his own fault contributed to the damage, the compensation may be reduced or disallowed having regard to all the circumstances.
2.   The same shall apply if a person, for whom the injured person or the person entitled to claim compensation is responsible under national law, has contributed to the damage by his fault.

[4.14]
Article 5
1.   A producer shall not be liable under this Convention if he proves—
   (a)   that the product has not been put into circulation by him; or
   (b)   that, having regard to the circumstances, it is probable that the defect which caused the damage did not exist at the time when the product was put into circulation by him or that this defect came into being afterwards; or

(c)   that the product was neither manufactured for sale, hire or any other form of distribution for the economic purposes of the producer nor manufactured or distributed in the course of his business.

2.   The liability of a producer shall not be reduced when the damage is caused both by a defect in the product and by the act or by omission of a third party.

[4.15]
Article 6
Proceedings for the recovery of the damages shall be subject to a limitation period of three years from the day the claimant became aware or should reasonably have been aware of the damage, the defect and the identity of the producer.

[4.16]
Article 7
The right to compensation under this Convention against a producer shall be extinguished if an action is not brought within ten years from the date on which the producer put into circulation the individual product which caused the damage.

[4.17]
Article 8
The liability of the producer under this Convention cannot be excluded or limited by any exemption or exoneration clause.

[4.18]
Article 9
This Convention shall not apply to—
     (a)   the liability of producers inter se and their rights of recourse against third parties;
     (b)   nuclear damage.

[4.19]
Article 10
Contracting States shall not adopt rules derogating from this Convention, even if these rules are more favourable to the victim.

[4.20]
Article 11
States may replace the liability of the producer, in a principal or subsidiary way, wholly or in part, in a general way, or for certain risks only, by the liability of a guarantee fund or other form of collective guarantee, provided that the victim shall receive protection at least equivalent to the protection he would have had under the liability scheme provided for by this Convention.

[4.21]
Article 12
This Convention shall not affect any rights which a person suffering damage may have according to the ordinary rules of the law of contractual and extra-contractual liability including any rules concerning the duties of a seller who sells goods in the course of his business.

[4.22]
Article 13
1.   This Convention shall be open to signature by the member States of the Council of Europe. It shall be subject to ratification, acceptance or approval. Instruments of ratification, acceptance or approval shall be deposited with the Secretary General of the Council of Europe.

2.   This Convention shall enter into force on the first day of the month following the expiration of a period of six months after the date of deposit of the third instrument of ratification, acceptance or approval.

3.   In respect of a signatory State ratifying, accepting or approving subsequently, the Convention shall come into force on the first day of the month following the expiration of a period of six months after the date of the deposit of its instrument of ratification, acceptance or approval.

[4.23]
Article 14
1.   After the entry into force of this Convention, the Committee of Ministers of the Council of Europe may invite any non-member State to accede thereto.

2.   Such accession shall be effected by depositing with the Secretary General of the Council of Europe an instrument of accession which shall take effect on the first day of the month following the expiration of a period of six months after the date of its deposit.

[4.24]
Article 15
1. Any State may, at the time of signature or when depositing its instrument of ratification, acceptance, approval or accession, specify the territory or territories to which this Convention shall apply.
2. Any State may, when depositing its instrument of ratification, acceptance, approval or accession or at any later date, by declaration addressed to the Secretary General of the Council of Europe, extend this Convention to any other territory or territories specified in the declaration and for whose international relations it is responsible or on whose behalf it is authorised to give undertakings.
3. Any declaration made in pursuance of the preceding paragraph may, in respect of any territory mentioned in such declaration, be withdrawn by means of a notification addressed to the Secretary General of the Council of Europe. Such withdrawal shall take effect on the first day of the month following the expiration of a period of six months after the date of receipt by the Secretary General of the Council of Europe of the declaration of withdrawal.

[4.25]
Article 16
1. Any State may, at the time of signature or when depositing its instrument of ratification, acceptance, approval or accession, or at any later date, by notification addressed to the Secretary General of the Council of Europe, declare that, in pursuance of an international agreement to which it is a Party, it will not consider imports from one or more specified States also Parties to that agreement as imports for the purpose of paragraphs 2 and 3 of Article 3; in this case the person importing the product into any of these States from another State shall be deemed to be an importer for all the States Parties to this agreement.
2. Any declaration made in pursuance of the preceding paragraph may be withdrawn by means of a notification addressed to the Secretary General of the Council of Europe. Such withdrawal shall take effect the first day of the month following the expiration of a period of one month after the date of receipt by the Secretary General of the Council of Europe of the declaration of withdrawal.

[4.26]
Article 17
1. No reservation shall be made to the provisions of this Convention except those mentioned in the Annex to this Convention.
2. The Contracting State which has made one of the reservations mentioned in the Annex to this Convention may withdraw it by means of a declaration addressed to the Secretary General of the Council of Europe which shall become effective the first day of the month following the expiration of a period of one month after the date of its receipt by the Secretary General.

[4.27]
Article 18
1. Any Contracting State may, in so far as it is concerned, denounce this Convention by means of a notification addressed to the Secretary General of the Council of Europe.
2. Such denunciation shall take effect on the first day of the month following the expiration of a period of six months after the date of receipt by the Secretary General of such notification.

[4.28]
Article 19
The Secretary General of the Council of Europe shall notify the member States of the Council and any State which has acceded to this Convention of—
  (a)   any signature;
  (b)   any deposit of an instrument of ratification, acceptance, approval or accession;
  (c)   any date of entry into force of this Convention in accordance with Article 13 thereof;
  (d)   any reservation made in pursuance of the provisions of Article 17, paragraph 1;
  (e)   withdrawal of any reservation carried out in pursuance of the provisions of Article 17, paragraph 2;
  (f)   any communication or notification received in pursuance of the provisions of Article 1, paragraph 2, Article 15, paragraphs 2 and 3 and Article 16, paragraphs 1 and 2;
  (g)   any notification received in pursuance of the provisions of Article 18 and the date on which denunciation takes effect.
  In witness whereof, the undersigned, being duly authorised thereto, have signed this Convention.
  Done at Strasbourg, this 27th day of January 1977, in English and in French, both texts being equally authoritative, in a single copy which shall remain deposited in the archives of the Council of Europe. The Secretary General of the Council of Europe shall transmit certified copies to each of the signatory and acceding Parties.

ANNEX

[4.29]
Each State may declare, at the moment of signature or at the moment of the deposit of its instrument of ratification, acceptance, approval or accession, that it reserves the right—

1. to apply its ordinary law, in place of the provisions of Article 4, in so far as such law provides that compensation may be reduced or disallowed only in case of gross negligence or intentional conduct by the injured person or the person entitled to claim compensation;

2. to limit, by provisions of its national law, the amount of compensation to be paid by a producer under this national law in compliance with the present Convention. However, this limit shall not be less than—

    (a) the sum in national currency corresponding to 70,000 Special Drawing Rights as defined by the International Monetary Fund at the time of the ratification, for each deceased person or person suffering personal injury;

    (b) the sum in national currency corresponding to 10 million Special Drawing Rights as defined by the International Monetary Fund at the time of ratification, for all damage caused by identical products having the same defect;

3. to exclude the retailer of primary agricultural products from liability under the terms of paragraph 3 of Article 3 providing he discloses to the claimant all information in his possession concerning the identity of the persons mentioned in Article 3.

UNITED NATIONS CONVENTION ON THE CARRIAGE OF GOODS BY SEA, 1978

(Hamburg, 31 March 1978)

NOTES

This Convention was adopted by the United Nations Conference on the Carriage of Goods by Sea convened in Hamburg, at the invitation of the Government of the Federal Republic of Germany, from 6 to 31 March 1978.

PREAMBLE

THE STATES PARTIES TO THIS CONVENTION,

HAVING RECOGNISED the desirability of determining by agreement certain rules relating to the carriage of goods by sea,

HAVE DECIDED to conclude a Convention for this purpose and have thereto agreed as follows—

PART I
GENERAL PROVISIONS

[4.30]
Article 1
Definitions
In this Convention—

1. 'Carrier' means any person by whom or in whose name a contract of carriage of goods by sea has been concluded with a shipper.

2. 'Actual carrier' means any person to whom the performance of the carriage of the goods, or of part of the carriage, has been entrusted by the carrier, and includes any other person to whom such performance has been entrusted.

3. 'Shipper' means any person by whom or in whose name or on whose behalf a contract of carriage of goods by sea has been concluded with a carrier, or any person by whom or in whose name or on whose behalf the goods are actually delivered to the carrier in relation to the contract of carriage by sea.

4. 'Consignee' means the person entitled to take delivery of the goods.

5. 'Goods' includes live animals; where the goods are consolidated in a container, pallet or similar article of transport or where they are packed, goods includes such article of transport or packaging if supplied by the shipper.

6. 'Contract of carriage by sea' means any contract whereby the carrier undertakes against payment of freight to carry goods by sea from one port to another; however, a contract which involves carriage by sea and also carriage by some other means is deemed to be a contract of carriage by sea for the purposes of this Convention only in so far as it relates to the carriage by sea.

7. 'Bill of lading' means a document which evidences a contract of carriage by sea and the taking over or loading of the goods by the carrier, and by which the carrier undertakes to deliver the goods against surrender of the document. A provision in the document that the goods are to be delivered to the order of a named person, or to order, or to bearer, constitutes such an undertaking.

8. 'Writing' includes, *inter alia*, telegram and telex.

[4.31]
Article 2
Scope of application

1.   The provisions of this Convention are applicable to all contracts of carriage by sea between two different States, if—

    (a) the port of loading as provided for in the contract of carriage by sea is located in a Contracting State, or

    (b) the port of discharge as provided for in the contract of carriage by sea is located in a Contracting State, or

    (c) one of the optional ports of discharge provided for in the contract of carriage by sea is the actual port of discharge and such port is located in a Contracting State, or

    (d) the bill of lading or other document evidencing the contract of carriage by sea is issued in a Contracting State, or

    (e) the bill of lading or other document evidencing the contract of carriage by sea provides that the provisions of this Convention or the legislation of any State giving effect to them are to govern the contract.

2.   The provisions of this Convention are applicable without regard to the nationality of the ship, the carrier, the actual carrier, the shipper, the consignee or any other interested person.

3.   The provisions of this Convention are not applicable to charter-parties. However, where a bill of lading is issued pursuant to a charter-party, the provisions of the Convention apply to such a bill of lading if it governs the relation between the carrier and the holder of the bill of lading, not being the charterer.

4.   If a contract provides for future carriage of goods in a series of shipments during an agreed period, the provisions of this Convention apply to each shipment. However, where a shipment is made under a charter-party, the provisions of paragraph 3 of this article apply.

[4.32]
Article 3
Interpretation of the Convention

In the interpretation and application of the provisions of this Convention regard shall be had to its international character and to the need to promote uniformity.

PART II
LIABILITY OF THE CARRIER

[4.33]
Article 4
Period of responsibility

1.   The responsibility of the carrier for the goods under this Convention covers the period during which the carrier is in charge of the goods at the port of loading, during the carriage and at the port of discharge.

2.   For the purpose of paragraph 1 of this article, the carrier is deemed to be in charge of the goods—

    (a) from the time he has taken over the goods from—

        (i)   the shipper, or a person acting on his behalf; or

        (ii) an authority or other third party to whom, pursuant to law or regulations applicable at the port of loading, the goods must be handed over for shipment;

    (b) until the time he has delivered the goods—

        (i)   by handing over the goods to the consignee; or

        (ii) in cases where the consignee does not receive the goods from the carrier, by placing them at the disposal of the consignee in accordance with the contract or with the law or with the usage of the particular trade, applicable at the port of discharge; or

        (iii) by handing over the goods to an authority or other third party to whom, pursuant to law or regulations applicable at the port of discharge, the goods must be handed over.

3.   In paragraphs 1 and 2 of this article, reference to the carrier or to the consignee means, in addition to the carrier or the consignee, the servants or agents, respectively of the carrier or the consignee.

[4.34]
Article 5
Basis of liability

1.   The carrier is liable for loss resulting from loss of or damage to the goods, as well as from delay in delivery, if the occurrence which caused the loss, damage or delay took place while the goods were in his charge as defined in article 4, unless the carrier proves that he, his servants or agents took all measures that could reasonably be required to avoid the occurrence and its consequences.

2.   Delay in delivery occurs when the goods have not been delivered at the port of discharge provided for in the contract of carriage by sea within the time expressly agreed upon or, in the absence of such agreement, within the time which it would be reasonable to require of a diligent carrier, having regard to the circumstances of the case.

3.   The person entitled to make a claim for the loss of goods may treat the goods as lost if they have not been delivered as required by article 4 within 60 consecutive days following the expiry of the time for delivery according to paragraph 2 of this article.

4.
   (a)   The carrier is liable
        (i)   for loss of or damage to the goods or delay in delivery caused by fire, if the claimant proves that the fire arose from fault or neglect on the part of the carrier, his servants or agents;
        (ii)   for such loss, damage or delay in delivery which is proved by the claimant to have resulted from the fault or neglect of the carrier, his servants or agents in taking all measures that could reasonably be required to put out the fire and avoid or mitigate its consequences.
   (b)   In case of fire on board the ship affecting the goods, if the claimant or the carrier so desires, a survey in accordance with shipping practices must be held into the cause and circumstances of the fire, and a copy of the surveyor's report shall be made available on demand to the carrier and the claimant.

5.   With respect to live animals, the carrier is not liable for loss, damage or delay in delivery resulting from any special risks inherent in that kind of carriage. If the carrier proves that he has complied with any special instructions given to him by the shipper respecting the animals and that, in the circumstances of the case, the loss, damage or delay in delivery could be attributed to such risks, it is presumed that the loss, damage or delay in delivery was so caused, unless there is proof that all or a part of the loss, damage or delay in delivery resulted from fault or neglect on the part of the carrier, his servants or agents.

6.   The carrier is not liable, except in general average, where loss, damage or delay in delivery resulted from measures to save life or from reasonable measures to save property at sea.

7.   Where fault or neglect on the part of the carrier, his servants or agents combines with another cause to produce loss, damage or delay in delivery, the carrier is liable only to the extent that the loss, damage or delay in delivery is attributable to such fault or neglect, provided that the carrier proves the amount of the loss, damage or delay in delivery not attributable thereto.

[4.35]
Article 6
Limits of liability
   1.
   (a)   The liability of the carrier for loss resulting from loss of or damage to goods according to the provisions of article 5 is limited to an amount equivalent to 835 units of account per package or other shipping unit or 2.5 units of account per kilogram of gross weight of the goods lost or damaged, whichever is the higher.
   (b)   The liability of the carrier for delay in delivery according to the provisions of article 5 is limited to an amount equivalent to two and a half times the freight payable for the goods delayed, but not exceeding the total freight payable under the contract of carriage of goods by sea.
   (c)   In no case shall the aggregate liability of the carrier, under both subparagraphs (a) and (b) of this paragraph, exceed the limitation which would be established under subparagraph (a) of this paragraph for total loss of the goods with respect to which such liability was incurred.

2.   For the purpose of calculating which amount is the higher in accordance with paragraph 1(a) of this article, the following rules apply—
   (a)   Where a container, pallet or similar article of transport is used to consolidate goods, the package or other shipping units enumerated in the bill of lading, if issued, or otherwise in any other document evidencing the contract of carriage by sea, as packed in such article of transport are deemed packages or shipping units. Except as aforesaid the goods in such article of transport are deemed one shipping unit.
   (b)   In cases where the article of transport itself has been lost or damaged, that article of transport, if not owned or otherwise supplied by the carrier, is considered one separate shipping unit.

3.   Unit of account means the unit of account mentioned in article 26.

4.   By agreement between the carrier and the shipper, limits of liability exceeding those provided for in paragraph 1 may be fixed.

[4.36]
Article 7
Application to non-contractual claims
1.   The defences and limits of liability provided for in this Convention apply in any action against the carrier in respect of loss or damage to the goods covered by the contract of carriage by sea, as well as of delay in delivery whether the action is founded in contract, in tort or otherwise.
2.   If such an action is brought against a servant or agent of the carrier, such servant or agent, if he proves that he acted within the scope of his employment, is entitled to avail himself of the defences and limits of liability which the carrier is entitled to invoke under this Convention.
3.   Except as provided in article 8, the aggregate of the amounts recoverable from the carrier and from any persons referred to in paragraph 2 of this article shall not exceed the limits of liability provided for in this Convention.

[4.37]
Article 8
Loss of right to limit responsibility
1.   The carrier is not entitled to the benefit of the limitation of liability provided for in article 6 if it is proved that the loss, damage or delay in delivery resulted from an act or omission of the carrier done with the intent to cause such loss, damage or delay, or recklessly and with knowledge that such loss, damage or delay would probably result.
2.   Notwithstanding the provisions of paragraph 2 of article 7, a servant or agent of the carrier is not entitled to the benefit of the limitation of liability provided for in article 6 if it is proved that the loss, damage or delay in delivery resulted from an act or omission of such servant or agent, done with the intent to cause such loss, damage or delay, or recklessly and with knowledge that such loss, damage or delay would probably result.

[4.38]
Article 9
Deck cargo
1.   The carrier is entitled to carry the goods on deck only if such carriage is in accordance with an agreement with the shipper or with the usage of the particular trade or is required by statutory rules or regulations.
2.   If the carrier and the shipper have agreed that the goods shall or may be carried on deck, the carrier must insert in the bill of lading or other document evidencing the contract of carriage by sea a statement to that effect. In the absence of such a statement the carrier has the burden of proving that an agreement for carriage on deck has been entered into; however, the carrier is not entitled to invoke such an agreement against a third party, including a consignee, who has acquired the bill of lading in good faith.
3.   Where the goods have been carried on deck contrary to the provisions of paragraph 1 of this article or where the carrier may not under paragraph 2 of this article invoke an agreement for carriage on deck, the carrier, notwithstanding the provisions of paragraph 1 of article 5, is liable for loss of or damage to the goods, as well as for delay in delivery, resulting solely from the carriage on deck, and the extent of his liability is to be determined in accordance with the provisions of article 6 or article 8 of this Convention, as the case may be.
4.   Carriage of goods on deck contrary to express agreement for carriage under deck is deemed to be an act or omission of the carrier within the meaning of article 8.

[4.39]
Article 10
Liability of the carrier and actual carrier
1.   Where the performance of the carriage or part thereof has been entrusted to an actual carrier, whether or not in pursuance of a liberty under the contract of carriage by sea to do so, the carrier nevertheless remains responsible for the entire carriage according to the provisions of this Convention. The carrier is responsible, in relation to the carriage performed by the actual carrier, for the acts and omissions of the actual carrier and of his servants and agents acting within the scope of their employment.
2.   All the provisions of this Convention governing the responsibility of the carrier also apply to the responsibility of the actual carrier for the carriage performed by him. The provisions of paragraphs 2 and 3 of article 7 and of paragraph 2 of article 8 apply if an action is brought against a servant or agent of the actual carrier.
3.   Any special agreement under which the carrier assumes obligations not imposed by this Convention or waives rights conferred by this Convention affects the actual carrier only if agreed to by him expressly and in writing. Whether or not the actual carrier has so agreed, the carrier nevertheless remains bound by the obligations or waivers resulting from such special agreement.
4.   Where and to the extent that both the carrier and the actual carrier are liable, their liability is joint and several.
5.   The aggregate of the amounts recoverable from the carrier, the actual carrier and their servants and agents shall not exceed the limits of liability provided for in this Convention.

6.   Nothing in this article shall prejudice any right of recourse as between the carrier and the actual carrier.

[4.40]
Article 11
Through carriage
1.   Notwithstanding the provisions of paragraph 1 of article 10, where a contract of carriage by sea provides explicitly that a specified part of the carriage covered by the said contract is to be performed by a named person other than the carrier, the contract may also provide that the carrier is not liable for loss, damage or delay in delivery caused by an occurrence which takes place while the goods are in the charge of the actual carrier during such part of the carriage. Nevertheless, any stipulation limiting or excluding such liability is without effect if no judicial proceedings can be instituted against the actual carrier in a court competent under paragraph 1 or 2 of article 21. The burden of proving that any loss, damage or delay in delivery has been caused by such an occurrence rests upon the carrier.
2.   The actual carrier is responsible in accordance with the provisions of paragraph 2 of article 10 for loss, damage or delay in delivery caused by an occurrence which takes place while the goods are in his charge.

PART III
LIABILITY OF THE SHIPPER

[4.41]
Article 12
General rule
The shipper is not liable for loss sustained by the carrier or the actual carrier, or for damage sustained by the ship, unless such loss or damage was caused by the fault or neglect of the shipper, his servants or agents. Nor is any servant or agent of the shipper liable for such loss or damage unless the loss or damage was caused by fault or neglect on his part.

[4.42]
Article 13
Special rules on dangerous goods
1.   The shipper must mark or label in a suitable manner dangerous goods as dangerous.
2.   Where the shipper hands over dangerous goods to the carrier or an actual carrier, as the case may be, the shipper must inform him of the dangerous character of the goods and, if necessary, of the precautions to be taken. If the shipper fails to do so and such carrier or actual carrier does not otherwise have knowledge of their dangerous character—
   (a)   the shipper is liable to the carrier and any actual carrier for the loss resulting from the shipment of such goods, and
   (b)   the goods may at any time be unloaded, destroyed or rendered innocuous, as the circumstances may require, without payment of compensation.
3.   The provisions of paragraph 2 of this article may not be invoked by any person if during the carriage he has taken the goods in his charge with knowledge of their dangerous character.
4.   If, in cases where the provisions of paragraph 2, subparagraph (b), of this article do not apply or may not be invoked, dangerous goods become an actual danger to life or property, they may be unloaded, destroyed or rendered innocuous, as the circumstances may require, without payment of compensation except where there is an obligation to contribute in general average or where the carrier is liable in accordance with the provisions of article 5.

PART IV
TRANSPORT DOCUMENTS

[4.43]
Article 14
Issue of bill of lading
1.   When the carrier or the actual carrier takes the goods in his charge, the carrier must, on demand of the shipper, issue to the shipper a bill of lading.
2.   The bill of lading may be signed by a person having authority from the carrier. A bill of lading signed by the master of the ship carrying the goods is deemed to have been signed on behalf of the carrier.
3.   The signature on the bill of lading may be in handwriting, printed in facsimile, perforated, stamped, in symbols, or made by any other mechanical or electronic means, if not inconsistent with the law of the country where the bill of lading is issued.

[4.44]
Article 15
Contents of bill of lading
1.   The bill of lading must include, *inter alia*, the following particulars—

(a) the general nature of the goods, the leading marks necessary for identification of the goods, an express statement, if applicable, as to the dangerous character of the goods, the number of packages or pieces, and the weight of the goods or their quantity otherwise expressed, all such particulars as furnished by the shipper;

(b) the apparent condition of the goods;

(c) the name and principal place of business of the carrier;

(d) the name of the shipper;

(e) the consignee if named by the shipper;

(f) the port of loading under the contract of carriage by sea and the date on which the goods were taken over by the carrier at the port of loading;

(g) the port of discharge under the contract of carriage by sea;

(h) the number of originals of the bill of lading, if more than one;

(i) the place of issuance of the bill of lading;

(j) the signature of the carrier or a person acting on his behalf;

(k) the freight to the extent payable by the consignee or other indication that freight is payable by him;

(l) the statement referred to in paragraph 3 of article 23;

(m) the statement, if applicable, that the goods shall or may be carried on deck;

(n) the date or the period of delivery of the goods at the port of discharge if expressly agreed upon between the parties; and

(o) any increased limit or limits of liability where agreed in accordance with paragraph 4 of article 6.

2.   After the goods have been loaded on board, if the shipper so demands, the carrier must issue to the shipper a "shipped" bill of lading which, in addition to the particulars required under paragraph 1 of this article, must state that the goods are on board a named ship or ships, and the date or dates of loading. If the carrier has previously issued to the shipper a bill of lading or other document of title with respect to any of such goods, on request of the carrier the shipper must surrender such document in exchange for a "shipped" bill of lading. The carrier may amend any previously issued document in order to meet the shipper's demand for a "shipped" bill of lading if, as amended, such document includes all the information required to be contained in a "shipped" bill of lading.

3.   The absence in the bill of lading of one or more particulars referred to in this article does not affect the legal character of the document as a bill of lading provided that it nevertheless meets the requirements set out in paragraph 7 of article 1.

[4.45]
Article 16
Bills of lading: reservations and evidentiary effect
1.   If the bill of lading contains particulars concerning the general nature, leading marks, number of packages or pieces, weight or quantity of the goods which the carrier or other person issuing the bill of lading on his behalf knows or has reasonable grounds to suspect do not accurately represent the goods actually taken over or, where a "shipped" bill of lading is issued, loaded, or if he had no reasonable means of checking such particulars, the carrier or such other person must insert in the bill of lading a reservation specifying these inaccuracies, grounds of suspicion or the absence of reasonable means of checking.

2.   If the carrier or other person issuing the bill of lading on his behalf fails to note on the bill of lading the apparent condition of the goods, he is deemed to have noted on the bill of lading that the goods were in apparent good condition.

3.   Except for particulars in respect of which and to the extent to which a reservation permitted under paragraph 1 of this article has been entered—

(a) the bill of lading is *prima facie* evidence of the taking over or, where a "shipped" bill of lading is issued, loading, by the carrier of the goods as described in the bill of lading; and

(b) proof to the contrary by the carrier is not admissible if the bill of lading has been transferred to a third party, including a consignee, who in good faith has acted in reliance on the description of the goods therein.

4.   A bill of lading which does not, as provided in paragraph 1, subparagraph (k), of article 15, set forth the freight or otherwise indicate that freight is payable by the consignee or does not set forth demurrage incurred at the port of loading payable by the consignee, is *prima facie* evidence that no freight or such demurrage is payable by him. However, proof to the contrary by the carrier is not admissible when the bill of lading has been transferred to a third party, including a consignee, who in good faith has acted in reliance on the absence in the bill of lading of any such indication.

[4.46]
Article 17
Guarantees by the shipper
1.   The shipper is deemed to have guaranteed to the carrier the accuracy of particulars relating to the general nature of the goods, their marks, number, weight and quantity as furnished by him for insertion in the bill of lading. The shipper must indemnify the carrier against the loss resulting from

inaccuracies in such particulars. The shipper remains liable even if the bill of lading has been transferred by him. The right of the carrier to such indemnity in no way limits his liability under the contract of carriage by sea to any person other than the shipper.

2. Any letter of guarantee or agreement by which the shipper undertakes to indemnify the carrier against loss resulting from the issuance of the bill of lading by the carrier, or by a person acting on his behalf, without entering a reservation relating to particulars furnished by the shipper for insertion in the bill of lading, or to the apparent condition of the goods, is void and of no effect as against any third party, including a consignee, to whom the bill of lading has been transferred.

3. Such a letter of guarantee or agreement is valid as against the shipper unless the carrier or the person acting on his behalf, by omitting the reservation referred to in paragraph 2 of this article, intends to defraud a third party, including a consignee, who acts in reliance on the description of the goods in the bill of lading. In the latter case, if the reservation omitted relates to particulars furnished by the shipper for insertion in the bill of lading, the carrier has no right of indemnity from the shipper pursuant to paragraph 1 of this article.

4. In the case of intended fraud referred to in paragraph 3 of this article, the carrier is liable, without the benefit of the limitation of liability provided for in this Convention, for the loss incurred by a third party, including a consignee, because he has acted in reliance on the description of the goods in the bill of lading.

[4.47]
Article 18
Documents other than bills of lading
Where a carrier issues a document other than a bill of lading to evidence the receipt of the goods to be carried, such a document is *prima facie* evidence of the conclusion of the contract of carriage by sea and the taking over by the carrier of the goods as therein described.

PART V
CLAIMS AND ACTIONS

[4.48]
Article 19
Notice of loss, damage or delay
1. Unless notice of loss or damage, specifying the general nature of such loss or damage, is given in writing by the consignee to the carrier not later than the working day after the day when the goods were handed over to the consignee, such handing over is *prima facie* evidence of the delivery by the carrier of the goods as described in the document of transport or, if no such document has been issued, in good condition.

2. Where the loss or damage is not apparent, the provisions of paragraph 1 of this article apply correspondingly if notice in writing is not given within 15 consecutive days after the day when the goods were handed over to the consignee.

3. If the state of the goods at the time they were handed over to the consignee has been the subject of a joint survey or inspection by the parties, notice in writing need not be given of loss or damage ascertained during such survey or inspection.

4. In the case of any actual or apprehended loss or damage, the carrier and the consignee must give all reasonable facilities to each other for inspecting and tallying the goods.

5. No compensation shall be payable for loss resulting from delay in delivery unless a notice has been given in writing to the carrier within 60 consecutive days after the day when the goods were handed over to the consignee.

6. If the goods have been delivered by an actual carrier, any notice given under this article to him shall have the same effect as if it had been given to the carrier; and any notice given to the carrier shall have effect as if given to such actual carrier.

7. Unless notice of loss or damage, specifying the general nature of the loss or damage, is given in writing by the carrier or actual carrier to the shipper not later than 90 consecutive days after the occurrence of such loss or damage or after the delivery of the goods in accordance with paragraph 2 of article 4, whichever is later, the failure to give such notice is *prima facie* evidence that the carrier or the actual carrier has sustained no loss or damage due to the fault or neglect of the shipper, his servants or agents.

8. For the purpose of this article, notice given to a person acting on the carrier's or the actual carrier's behalf, including the master or the officer in charge of the ship, or to a person acting on the shipper's behalf is deemed to have been given to the carrier, to the actual carrier or to the shipper, respectively.

[4.49]
Article 20
Limitation of actions
1. Any action relating to carriage of goods under this Convention is time-barred if judicial or arbitral proceedings have not been instituted within a period of two years.

2.   The limitation period commences on the day on which the carrier has delivered the goods or part thereof or, in cases where no goods have been delivered, on the last day on which the goods should have been delivered.

3.   The day on which the limitation period commences is not included in the period.

4.   The person against whom a claim is made may at any time during the running of the limitation period extend that period by a declaration in writing to the claimant. This period may be further extended by another declaration or declarations.

5.   An action for indemnity by a person held liable may be instituted even after the expiration of the limitation period provided for in the preceding paragraphs if instituted within the time allowed by the law of the State where proceedings are instituted. However, the time allowed shall not be less than 90 days commencing from the day when the person instituting such action for indemnity has settled the claim or has been served with process in the action against himself.

[4.50]
Article 21
Jurisdiction

1.   In judicial proceedings relating to carriage of goods under this Convention the plaintiff, at his option, may institute an action in a court which according to the law of the State where the court is situated, is competent and within the jurisdiction of which is situated one of the following places—
   (a)   the principal place of business or, in the absence thereof, the habitual residence of the defendant; or
   (b)   the place where the contract was made, provided that the defendant has there a place of business, branch or agency through which the contract was made; or
   (c)   the port of loading or the port of discharge; or
   (d)   any additional place designated for that purpose in the contract of carriage by sea.

2.
   (a)   Notwithstanding the preceding provisions of this article, an action may be instituted in the courts of any port or place in a Contracting State at which the carrying vessel or any other vessel of the same ownership may have been arrested in accordance with applicable rules of the law of that State and of international law. However, in such a case, at the petition of the defendant, the claimant must remove the action, at his choice, to one of the jurisdictions referred to in paragraph 1 of this article for the determination of the claim, but before such removal the defendant must furnish security sufficient to ensure payment of any judgment that may subsequently be awarded to the claimant in the action.
   (b)   All questions relating to the sufficiency or otherwise of the security shall be determined by the court of the port or place of the arrest.

3.   No judicial proceedings relating to carriage of goods under this Convention may be instituted in a place not specified in paragraph 1 or 2 of this article. The provisions of this paragraph do not constitute an obstacle to the jurisdiction of the Contracting States for provisional or protective measures.

4.
   (a)   Where an action has been instituted in a court competent under paragraphs 1 and 2 of this article or where judgment has been delivered by such a court, no new action may be started between the same parties on the same grounds unless the judgment of the court before which the first action was instituted is not enforceable in the country in which the new proceedings are instituted;
   (b)   for the purpose of this article, the institution of measures with a view to obtaining enforcement of a judgment is not to be considered as the starting of a new action;
   (c)   for the purpose of this article, the removal of an action to a different court within the same country, or to a court in another country, in accordance with paragraph 2(a) of this article, is not to be considered as the starting of a new action.

5.   Notwithstanding the provisions of the preceding paragraphs, an agreement made by the parties, after a claim under the contract of carriage by sea has arisen, which designates the place where the claimant may institute an action, is effective.

[4.51]
Article 22
Arbitration

1.   Subject to the provisions of this article, parties may provide by agreement evidenced in writing that any dispute that may arise relating to carriage of goods under this Convention shall be referred to arbitration.

2.   Where a charter-party contains a provision that disputes arising thereunder shall be referred to arbitration and a bill of lading issued pursuant to the charter-party does not contain a special annotation providing that such provision shall be binding upon the holder of the bill of lading, the carrier may not invoke such provision as against a holder having acquired the bill of lading in good faith.

3.   The arbitration proceedings shall, at the option of the claimant, be instituted at one of the following places—
   (a)   a place in a State within whose territory is situated—

      (i)   the principal place of business of the defendant or, in the absence thereof, the habitual residence of the defendant; or

      (ii)   the place where the contract was made, provided that the defendant has there a place of business, branch or agency through which the contract was made; or

      (iii) the port of loading or the port of discharge; or

  (b)   any place designated for that purpose in the arbitration clause or agreement.

4.   The arbitrator or arbitration tribunal shall apply the rules of this Convention.

5.   The provisions of paragraphs 3 and 4 of this article are deemed to be part of every arbitration clause or agreement, and any term of such clause or agreement which is inconsistent therewith is null and void.

6.   Nothing in this article affects the validity of an agreement relating to arbitration made by the parties after the claim under the contract of carriage by sea has arisen.

PART VI
SUPPLEMENTARY PROVISIONS

[4.52]
Article 23
Contractual stipulations

1.   Any stipulation in a contract of carriage by sea, in a bill of lading, or in any other document evidencing the contract of carriage by sea is null and void to the extent that it derogates, directly or indirectly, from the provisions of this Convention. The nullity of such a stipulation does not affect the validity of the other provisions of the contract or document of which it forms a part. A clause assigning benefit of insurance of goods in favour of the carrier, or any similar clause, is null and void.

2.   Notwithstanding the provisions of paragraph 1 of this article, a carrier may increase his responsibilities and obligations under this Convention.

3.   Where a bill of lading or any other document evidencing the contract of carriage by sea is issued, it must contain a statement that the carriage is subject to the provisions of this Convention which nullify any stipulation derogating therefrom to the detriment of the shipper or the consignee.

4.   Where the claimant in respect of the goods has incurred loss as a result of a stipulation which is null and void by virtue of the present article, or as a result of the omission of the statement referred to in paragraph 3 of this article, the carrier must pay compensation to the extent required in order to give the claimant compensation in accordance with the provisions of this Convention for any loss of or damage to the goods as well as for delay in delivery. The carrier must, in addition, pay compensation for costs incurred by the claimant for the purpose of exercising his right, provided that costs incurred in the action where the foregoing provision is invoked are to be determined in accordance with the law of the State where proceedings are instituted.

[4.53]
Article 24
General average

1.   Nothing in this Convention shall prevent the application of provisions in the contract of carriage by sea or national law regarding the adjustment of general average.

2.   With the exception of article 20, the provisions of this Convention relating to the liability of the carrier for loss of or damage to the goods also determine whether the consignee may refuse contribution in general average and the liability of the carrier to indemnify the consignee in respect of any such contribution made or any salvage paid.

[4.54]
Article 25
Other conventions

1.   This Convention does not modify the rights or duties of the carrier, the actual carrier and their servants and agents, provided for in international conventions or national law relating to the limitation of liability of owners of seagoing ships.

2.   The provisions of articles 21 and 22 of this Convention do not prevent the application of the mandatory provisions of any other multilateral convention already in force at the date of this Convention relating to matters dealt with in the said articles, provided that the dispute arises exclusively between parties having their principal place of business in States members of such other convention. However, this paragraph does not affect the application of paragraph 4 of article 22 of this Convention.

3.   No liability shall arise under the provisions of this Convention for damage caused by a nuclear incident if the operator of a nuclear installation is liable for such damage—

  (a)   under either the Paris Convention of 29 July 1960 on Third Party Liability in the Field of Nuclear Energy as amended by the Additional Protocol of 28 January 1964, or the Vienna Convention of 21 May 1963 on Civil Liability for Nuclear Damage, or

  (b)   by virtue of national law governing the liability for such damage, provided that such law is in all respects as favourable to persons who may suffer damage as either the Paris Convention or the Vienna Convention.

Part 4 Other Materials

4.   No liability shall arise under the provisions of this Convention for any loss of or damage to or delay in delivery of luggage for which the carrier is responsible under any international convention or national law relating to the carriage of passengers and their luggage by sea.

5.   Nothing contained in this Convention prevents a Contracting State from applying any other international convention which is already in force at the date of this Convention and which applies mandatorily to contracts of carriage of goods primarily by a mode of transport other than transport by sea. This provision also applies to any subsequent revision or amendment of such international convention.

[4.55]
Article 26
Unit of account

1.   The unit of account referred to in article 6 of this Convention is the special drawing right as defined by the International Monetary Fund. The amounts mentioned in article 6 are to be converted into the national currency of a State according to the value of such currency at the date of judgment or the date agreed upon by the parties. The value of a national currency, in terms of the special drawing right, of a Contracting State which is a member of the International Monetary Fund is to be calculated in accordance with the method of valuation applied by the International Monetary Fund in effect at the date in question for its operations and transactions. The value of a national currency, in terms of the special drawing right, of a Contracting State which is not a member of the International Monetary Fund is to be calculated in a manner determined by that State.

2.   Nevertheless, those States which are not members of the International Monetary Fund and whose law does not permit the application of the provisions of paragraph 1 of this article may, at the time of signature, or at the time of ratification, acceptance, approval or accession or at any time thereafter, declare that the limits of liability provided for in this Convention to be applied in their territories shall be fixed as 12,500 monetary units per package or other shipping unit or 37.5 monetary units per kilogram of gross weight of the goods.

3.   The monetary unit referred to in paragraph 2 of this article corresponds to sixty-five and a half milligrams of gold of millesimal fineness nine hundred. The conversion of the amounts referred to in paragraph 2 into the national currency is to be made according to the law of the State concerned.

4.   The calculation mentioned in the last sentence of paragraph 1 and the conversion mentioned in paragraph 3 of this article is to be made in such a manner as to express in the national currency of the Contracting State as far as possible the same real value for the amounts in article 6 as is expressed there in units of account. Contracting States must communicate to the depositary the manner of calculation pursuant to paragraph 1 of this article, or the result of the conversion mentioned in paragraph 3 of this article, as the case may be, at the time of signature or when depositing their instruments of ratification, acceptance, approval or accession, or when availing themselves of the option provided for in paragraph 2 of this article and whenever there is a change in the manner of such calculation or in the result of such conversion.

PART VII
FINAL CLAUSES

[4.56]
Article 27
Depository

The Secretary-General of the United Nations is hereby designated as the depositary of this Convention.

[4.57]
Article 28
Signature, Ratification, Acceptance, Approval, Accession

1.   This Convention is open for signature by all States until 30 April 1979 at the Headquarters of the United Nations, New York.

2.   This Convention is subject to ratification, acceptance or approval by the signatory States.

3.   After 30 April 1979, this Convention will be open for accession by all States which are not signatory States.

4.   Instruments of ratification, acceptance, approval and accession are to be deposited with the Secretary-General of the United Nations.

[4.58]
Article 29
Reservations

No reservations may be made to this Convention.

[4.59]
Article 30
Entry into force
1.   This Convention enters into force on the first day of the month following the expiration of one year from the date of deposit of the twentieth instrument of ratification, acceptance, approval or accession.
2.   For each State which becomes a Contracting State to this Convention after the date of the deposit of the twentieth instrument of ratification, acceptance, approval or accession, this Convention enters into force on the first day of the month following the expiration of one year after the deposit of the appropriate instrument on behalf of that State.
3.   Each Contracting State shall apply the provisions of this Convention to contracts of carriage by sea concluded on or after the date of the entry into force of this Convention in respect of that State.

[4.60]
Article 31
Denunciation of other conventions
1.   Upon becoming a Contracting State to this Convention, any State party to the International Convention for the Unification of certain Rules relating to Bills of Lading signed at Brussels on 25 August 1924 (1924 Convention) must notify the Government of Belgium as the depositary of the 1924 Convention of its denunciation of the said Convention with a declaration that the denunciation is to take effect as from the date when this Convention enters into force in respect of that State.
2.   Upon the entry into force of this Convention under paragraph 1 of article 30, the depositary of this Convention must notify the Government of Belgium as the depositary of the 1924 Convention of the date of such entry into force, and of the names of the Contracting States in respect of which the Convention has entered into force.
3.   The provisions of paragraphs 1 and 2 of this article apply correspondingly in respect of States parties to the Protocol signed on 23 February 1968 to amend the International Convention for the Unification of certain Rules relating to Bills of Lading signed at Brussels on 25 August 1924.
4.   Notwithstanding article 2 of this Convention, for the purposes of paragraph 1 of this article, a Contracting State may, if it deems it desirable, defer the denunciation of the 1924 Convention and of the 1924 Convention as modified by the 1968 Protocol for a maximum period of five years from the entry into force of this Convention. It will then notify the Government of Belgium of its intention. During this transitory period, it must apply to the Contracting States this Convention to the exclusion of any other one.

[4.61]
Article 32
Revision and amendment
1.   At the request of not less than one third of the Contracting States to this Convention, the depositary shall convene a conference of the Contracting States for revising or amending it.
2.   Any instrument of ratification, acceptance, approval or accession deposited after the entry into force of an amendment to this Convention is deemed to apply to the Convention as amended.

[4.62]
Article 33
Revision of the limitation amounts and unit of account or monetary unit
1.   Notwithstanding the provisions of article 32, a conference only for the purpose of altering the amount specified in article 6 and paragraph 2 of article 26, or of substituting either or both of the units defined in paragraphs 1 and 3 of article 26 by other units is to be convened by the depositary in accordance with paragraph 2 of this article. An alteration of the amounts shall be made only because of a significant change in their real value.
2.   A revision conference is to be convened by the depositary when not less than one fourth of the Contracting States so request.
3.   Any decision by the conference must be taken by a two thirds majority of the participating States. The amendment is communicated by the depositary to all the Contracting States for acceptance and to all the States signatories of the Convention for information.
4.   Any amendment adopted enters into force on the first day of the month following one year after its acceptance by two thirds of the Contracting States. Acceptance is to be effected by the deposit of a formal instrument to that effect with the depositary.
5.   After entry into force of an amendment a Contracting State which has accepted the amendment is entitled to apply the Convention as amended in its relations with Contracting States which have not within six months after the adoption of the amendment notified the depositary that they are not bound by the amendment.
6.   Any instrument of ratification, acceptance, approval or accession deposited after the entry into force of an amendment to this Convention is deemed to apply to the Convention as amended.

[4.63]
Article 34
Denunciation

1.   A Contracting State may denounce this Convention at any time by means of a notification in writing addressed to the depositary.

2.   The denunciation takes effect on the first day of the month following the expiration of one year after the notification is received by the depositary. Where a longer period is specified in the notification, the denunciation takes effect upon the expiration of such longer period after the notification is received by the depositary.

DONE at Hamburg, this thirty-first day of March, one thousand nine hundred and seventy-eight, in a single original, of which the Arabic, Chinese, English, French, Russian and Spanish texts are equally authentic.

IN WITNESS WHEREOF the undersigned plenipotentiaries, being duly authorised by their respective Governments, have signed the present Convention.

[4.64]

COMMON UNDERSTANDING ADOPTED BY THE UNITED NATIONS CONFERENCE ON THE CARRIAGE OF GOODS BY SEA

It is the common understanding that the liability of the carrier under this Convention is based on the principle of presumed fault or neglect. This means that, as a rule, the burden of proof rests on the carrier but, with respect to certain cases, the provisions of the Convention modify this rule.

RESOLUTION ADOPTED BY THE UNITED NATIONS CONFERENCE ON THE CARRIAGE OF GOODS BY SEA

The United Nations Conference on the Carriage of Goods by Sea,

Noting with appreciation the kind invitation of the Federal Republic of Germany to hold the Conference in Hamburg,

Being aware that the facilities placed at the disposal of the Conference and the generous hospitality bestowed on the participants by the Government of the Federal Republic of Germany and by the Free and Hanseatic City of Hamburg, have in no small measure contributed to the success of the Conference,

Expresses its gratitude to the Government and people of the Federal Republic of Germany, and

Having adopted the Convention on the Carriage of Goods by Sea on the basis of a draft Convention prepared by the United Nations Commission on International Trade Law at the request of the United Nations Conference on Trade and Development,

Expresses its gratitude to the United Nations Commission on International Trade Law and to the United Nations Conference on Trade and Development for their outstanding contribution to the simplification and harmonisation of the law of the carriage of goods by sea, and

Decides to designate the Convention adopted by the Conference as the—

'UNITED NATIONS CONVENTION ON THE CARRIAGE OF GOODS BY SEA', 1978, and

Recommends that the rues embodied therein be known as the 'HAMBURG RULES'.

NOTES

The text of this Convention was prepared by the United Nations Commission on International Trade Law.

UNITED NATIONS CONVENTION ON CONTRACTS FOR THE INTERNATIONAL SALE OF GOODS, 1980

The States Parties to this Convention,

Bearing in mind the broad objectives in the resolutions adopted by the sixth special session of the General Assembly of the United Nations on the establishment of a New International Economic Order,

Considering that the development of international trade on the basis of equality and mutual benefit is an important element in promoting friendly relations among States,

Being of the opinion that the adoption of uniform rules which govern contracts for the international sale of goods and take into account the different social, economic and legal systems would contribute to the removal of legal barriers in international trade and promote the development of international trade,

Have agreed as follows—

PART I
SPHERE OF APPLICATION AND GENERAL PROVISIONS

CHAPTER I
SPHERE OF APPLICATION

[4.65]
Article 1
(1) This Convention applies to contracts of sale of goods between parties whose places of business are in different States—
    (a)   when the States are Contracting States; or
    (b)   when the rules of private international law lead to the application of the law of a Contracting State.
(2) The fact that the parties have their places of business in different States is to be disregarded whenever this fact does not appear either from the contract or from any dealings between, or from information disclosed by, the parties at any time before or at the conclusion of the contract.
(3) Neither the nationality of the parties nor the civil or commercial character of the parties or of the contract is to be taken into consideration in determining the application of this Convention.

[4.66]
Article 2
This Convention does not apply to sales—
    (a)   of goods bought for personal, family or household use, unless the seller, at any time before or at the conclusion of the contract, neither knew nor ought to have known that the goods were bought for any such use;
    (b)   by auction;
    (c)   on execution or otherwise by authority of law;
    (d)   of stocks, shares, investment securities, negotiable instruments or money;
    (e)   of ships, vessels, hovercraft or aircraft;
    (f)   of electricity.

[4.67]
Article 3
(1) Contracts for the supply of goods to be manufactured or produced are to be considered sales unless the party who orders the goods undertakes to supply a substantial part of the materials necessary for such manufacture or production.
(2) This Convention does not apply to contracts in which the preponderant part of the obligations of the party who furnishes the goods consists in the supply of labour or other services.

[4.68]
Article 4
This Convention governs only the formation of the contract of sale and the rights and obligations of the seller and the buyer arising from such a contract. In particular, except as otherwise expressly provided in this Convention, it is not concerned with—
    (a)   the validity of the contract or of any of its provisions or of any usage;
    (b)   the effect which the contract may have on the property in the goods sold.

[4.69]
Article 5
This Convention does not apply to the liability of the seller for death or personal injury caused by the goods to any person.

[4.70]
Article 6
The parties may exclude the application of this Convention or, subject to article 12, derogate from or vary the effect of any of its provisions.

CHAPTER II
GENERAL PROVISIONS

[4.71]
Article 7
(1) In the interpretation of this Convention, regard is to be had to its international character and to the need to promote uniformity in its application and the observance of good faith in international trade.
(2) Questions concerning matters governed by this Convention which are not expressly settled in it are to be settled in conformity with the general principles on which it is based or, in the absence of such principles, in conformity with the law applicable by virtue of the rules of private international law.

[4.72]
Article 8

(1)   For the purposes of this Convention statements made by and other conduct of a party are to be interpreted according to his intent where the other party knew or could not have been unaware what that intent was.

(2)   If the preceding paragraph is not applicable, statements made by and other conduct of a party are to be interpreted according to the understanding that a reasonable person of the same kind as the other party would have had in the same circumstances.

(3)   In determining the intent of a party or the understanding a reasonable person would have had, due consideration is to be given to all relevant circumstances of the case including the negotiations, any practices which the parties have established between themselves, usages and any subsequent conduct of the parties.

[4.73]
Article 9

(1)   The parties are bound by any usage to which they have agreed and by any practices which they have established between themselves.

(2)   The parties are considered, unless otherwise agreed, to have impliedly made applicable to their contract or its formation a usage of which the parties knew or ought to have known and which in international trade is widely known to, and regularly observed by, parties to contracts of the type involved in the particular trade concerned.

[4.74]
Article 10

For the purposes of this Convention—

(a)   if a party has more than one place of business, the place of business is that which has the closest relationship to the contract and its performance, having regard to the circumstances known to or contemplated by the parties at any time before or at the conclusion of the contract;

(b)   if a party does not have a place of business, reference is to be made to his habitual residence.

[4.75]
Article 11

A contract of sale need not be concluded in or evidenced by writing and is not subject to any other requirement as to form. It may be proved by any means, including witnesses.

[4.76]
Article 12

Any provision of article 11, article 29 or Part II of this Convention that allows a contract of sale or its modification or termination by agreement or any offer, acceptance or other indication of intention to be made in any form other than in writing does not apply where any party has his place of business in a Contracting State which has made a declaration under article 96 of this Convention. The parties may not derogate from or vary the effect of this article.

[4.77]
Article 13

For the purposes of this Convention "writing" includes telegram and telex.

PART II
FORMATION OF THE CONTRACT

[4.78]
Article 14

(1)   A proposal for concluding a contract addressed to one or more specific persons constitutes an offer if it is sufficiently definite and indicates the intention of the offeror to be bound in case of acceptance. A proposal is sufficiently definite if it indicates the goods and expressly or implicitly fixes or makes provision for determining the quantity and the price.

(2)   A proposal other than one addressed to one or more specific persons is to be considered merely as an invitation to make offers, unless the contrary is clearly indicated by the person making the proposal.

[4.79]
Article 15

(1)   An offer becomes effective when it reaches the offeree.

(2)   An offer, even if it is irrevocable, may be withdrawn if the withdrawal reaches the offeree before or at the same time as the offer.

[4.80]
Article 16
(1)   Until a contract is concluded an offer may be revoked if the revocation reaches the offeree before he has dispatched an acceptance.
(2)   However, an offer cannot be revoked—
   (a)   if it indicates, whether by stating a fixed time for acceptance or otherwise, that it is irrevocable; or
   (b)   if it was reasonable for the offeree to rely on the offer as being irrevocable and the offeree has acted in reliance on the offer.

[4.81]
Article 17
An offer, even if it is irrevocable, is terminated when a rejection reaches the offeror.

[4.82]
Article 18
(1)   A statement made by or other conduct of the offeree indicating assent to an offer is an acceptance. Silence or inactivity does not in itself amount to acceptance.
(2)   An acceptance of an offer becomes effective at the moment the indication of assent reaches the offeror. An acceptance is not effective if the indication of assent does not reach the offeror within the time he has fixed or, if no time is fixed, within a reasonable time, due account being taken of the circumstances of the transaction, including the rapidity of the means of communication employed by the offeror. An oral offer must be accepted immediately unless the circumstances indicate otherwise.
(3)   However, if, by virtue of the offer or as a result of practices which the parties have established between themselves or of usage, the offeree may indicate assent by performing an act, such as one relating to the dispatch of the goods or payment of the price, without notice to the offeror, the acceptance is effective at the moment the act is performed, provided that the act is performed within the period of time laid down in the preceding paragraph.

[4.83]
Article 19
(1)   A reply to an offer which purports to be an acceptance but contains additions, limitations or other modifications is a rejection of the offer and constitutes a counter-offer.
(2)   However, a reply to an offer which purports to be an acceptance but contains additional or different terms which do not materially alter the terms of the offer constitutes an acceptance, unless the offeror, without undue delay, objects orally to the discrepancy or dispatches a notice to that effect. If he does not so object, the terms of the contract are the terms of the offer with the modifications contained in the acceptance.
(3)   Additional or different terms relating, among other things, to the price, payment, quality and quantity of the goods, place and time of delivery, extent of one party's liability to the other or the settlement of disputes are considered to alter the terms of the offer materially.

[4.84]
Article 20
(1)   A period of time for acceptance fixed by the offeror in a telegram or a letter begins to run from the moment the telegram is handed in for dispatch or from the date shown on the letter or, if no such date is shown, from the date shown on the envelope. A period of time for acceptance fixed by the offeror by telephone, telex or other means of instantaneous communication, begins to run from the moment that the offer reaches the offeree.
(2)   Official holidays or non-business days occurring during the period for acceptance are included in calculating the period. However, if a notice of acceptance cannot be delivered at the address of the offeror on the last day of the period because that day falls on an official holiday or a non-business day at the place of business of the offeror, the period is extended until the first business day which follows.

[4.85]
Article 21
(1)   A late acceptance is nevertheless effective as an acceptance if without delay the offeror orally so informs the offeree or dispatches a notice to that effect.
(2)   If a letter or other writing containing a late acceptance shows that it has been sent in such circumstances that if its transmission had been normal it would have reached the offeror in due time, the late acceptance is effective as an acceptance unless, without delay, the offeror orally informs the offeree that he considers his offer as having lapsed or dispatches a notice to that effect.

[4.86]
Article 22
An acceptance may be withdrawn if the withdrawal reaches the offeror before or at the same time as the acceptance would have become effective.

Part 4   Other Materials

[4.87]
Article 23
A contract is concluded at the moment when an acceptance of an offer becomes effective in accordance with the provisions of this Convention.

[4.88]
Article 24
For the purposes of this Part of the Convention, an offer, declaration of acceptance or any other indication of intention "reaches" the addressee when it is made orally to him or delivered by any other means to him personally, to his place of business or mailing address or, if he does not have a place of business or mailing address, to his habitual residence.

PART III
SALE OF GOODS

CHAPTER I
GENERAL PROVISIONS

[4.89]
Article 25
A breach of contract committed by one of the parties is fundamental if it results in such detriment to the other party as substantially to deprive him of what he is entitled to expect under the contract, unless the party in breach did not foresee and a reasonable person of the same kind in the same circumstances would not have foreseen such a result.

[4.90]
Article 26
A declaration of avoidance of the contract is effective only if made by notice to the other party.

[4.91]
Article 27
Unless otherwise expressly provided in this Part of the Convention, if any notice, request or other communication is given or made by a party in accordance with this Part and by means appropriate in the circumstances, a delay or error in the transmission of the communication or its failure to arrive does not deprive that party of the right to rely on the communication.

[4.92]
Article 28
If, in accordance with the provisions of this Convention, one party is entitled to require performance of any obligation by the other party, a court is not bound to enter a judgment for specific performance unless the court would do so under its own law in respect of similar contracts of sale not governed by this Convention.

[4.93]
Article 29
(1)   A contract may be modified or terminated by the mere agreement of the parties.
(2)   A contract in writing which contains a provision requiring any modification or termination by agreement to be in writing may not be otherwise modified or terminated by agreement. However, a party may be precluded by his conduct from asserting such a provision to the extent that the other party has relied on that conduct.

CHAPTER II
OBLIGATIONS OF THE SELLER

[4.94]
Article 30
The seller must deliver the goods, hand over any documents relating to them and transfer the property in the goods, as required by the contract and this Convention.

SECTION I
DELIVERY OF THE GOODS AND HANDING OVER OF DOCUMENTS

[4.95]
Article 31
If the seller is not bound to deliver the goods at any other particular place, his obligation to deliver consists—

    (a)   if the contract of sale involves carriage of the goods—in handing the goods over to the first carrier for transmission to the buyer;

    (b)   if, in cases not within the preceding subparagraph, the contract relates to specific goods, or unidentified goods to be drawn from a specific stock or to be manufactured or produced, and at the time of the conclusion of the contract the parties knew that the goods were at, or were to be manufactured or produced at, a particular place—in placing the goods at the buyer's disposal at that place;

(c)　in other cases—in placing the goods at the buyer's disposal at the place where the seller had his place of business at the time of the conclusion of the contract.

[4.96]
Article 32
(1)　If the seller, in accordance with the contract or this Convention, hands the goods over to a carrier and if the goods are not clearly identified to the contract by markings on the goods, by shipping documents or otherwise, the seller must give the buyer notice of the consignment specifying the goods.

(2)　If the seller is bound to arrange for carriage of the goods, he must make such contracts as are necessary for carriage to the place fixed by means of transportation appropriate in the circumstances and according to the usual terms for such transportation.

(3)　If the seller is not bound to effect insurance in respect of the carriage of the goods, he must, at the buyer's request, provide him with all available information necessary to enable him to effect such insurance.

[4.97]
Article 33
The seller must deliver the goods—
(a)　if a date is fixed by or determinable from the contract, on that date;
(b)　if a period of time is fixed by or determinable from the contract, at any time within that period unless circumstances indicate that the buyer is to choose a date; or
(c)　in any other case, within a reasonable time after the conclusion of the contract.

[4.98]
Article 34
If the seller is bound to hand over documents relating to the goods, he must hand them over at the time and place and in the form required by the contract. If the seller has handed over documents before that time, he may, up to that time, cure any lack of conformity in the documents, if the exercise of this right does not cause the buyer unreasonable inconvenience or unreasonable expense. However, the buyer retains any right to claim damages as provided for in this Convention.

SECTION II
CONFORMITY OF THE GOODS AND THIRD PARTY CLAIMS

[4.99]
Article 35
(1)　The seller must deliver goods which are of the quantity, quality and description required by the contract and which are contained or packaged in the manner required by the contract.

(2)　Except where the parties have agreed otherwise, the goods do not conform with the contract unless they—
(a)　are fit for the purposes for which goods of the same description would ordinarily be used;
(b)　are fit for any particular purpose expressly or impliedly made known to the seller at the time of the conclusion of the contract, except where the circumstances show that the buyer did not rely, or that it was unreasonable for him to rely, on the seller's skill and judgment;
(c)　possess the qualities of goods which the seller has held out to the buyer as a sample or model;
(d)　are contained or packaged in the manner usual for such goods or, where there is no such manner, in a manner adequate to preserve and protect the goods.

(3)　The seller is not liable under subparagraphs (a) to (d) of the preceding paragraph for any lack of conformity of the goods if at the time of the conclusion of the contract the buyer knew or could not have been unaware of such lack of conformity.

[4.100]
Article 36
(1)　The seller is liable in accordance with the contract and this Convention for any lack of conformity which exists at the time when the risk passes to the buyer, even though the lack of conformity becomes apparent only after that time.

(2)　The seller is also liable for any lack of conformity which occurs after the time indicated in the preceding paragraph and which is due to a breach of any of his obligations, including a breach of any guarantee that for a period of time the goods will remain fit for their ordinary purpose or for some particular purpose or will retain specified qualities or characteristics.

[4.101]
Article 37
If the seller has delivered goods before the date for delivery, he may, up to that date, deliver any missing part or make up any deficiency in the quantity of the goods delivered, or deliver goods in replacement of any non-conforming goods delivered or remedy any lack of conformity in the goods delivered, provided that the exercise of this right does not cause the buyer unreasonable inconvenience or unreasonable expense. However, the buyer retains any right to claim damages as provided for in this Convention.

[4.102]
Article 38
(1)   The buyer must examine the goods, or cause them to be examined, within as short a period as is practicable in the circumstances.
(2)   If the contract involves carriage of the goods, examination may be deferred until after the goods have arrived at their destination.
(3)   If the goods are redirected in transit or redispatched by the buyer without a reasonable opportunity for examination by him and at the time of the conclusion of the contract the seller knew or ought to have known of the possibility of such redirection or redispatch, examination may be deferred until after the goods have arrived at the new destination.

[4.103]
Article 39
(1)   The buyer loses the right to rely on a lack of conformity of the goods if he does not give notice to the seller specifying the nature of the lack of conformity within a reasonable time after he has discovered it or ought to have discovered it.
(2)   In any event, the buyer loses the right to rely on a lack of conformity of the goods if he does not give the seller notice thereof at the latest within a period of two years from the date on which the goods were actually handed over to the buyer, unless this time-limit is inconsistent with a contractual period of guarantee.

[4.104]
Article 40
The seller is not entitled to rely on the provisions of articles 38 and 39 if the lack of conformity relates to facts of which he knew or could not have been unaware and which he did not disclose to the buyer.

[4.105]
Article 41
The seller must deliver goods which are free from any right or claim of a third party, unless the buyer agreed to take the goods subject to that right or claim. However, if such right or claim is based on industrial property or other intellectual property, the seller's obligation is governed by article 42.

[4.106]
Article 42
(1)   The seller must deliver goods which are free from any right or claim of a third party based on industrial property or other intellectual property, of which at the time of the conclusion of the contract the seller knew or could not have been unaware, provided that the right or claim is based on industrial property or other intellectual property—
   (a)   under the law of the State where the goods will be resold or otherwise used, if it was contemplated by the parties at the time of the conclusion of the contract that the goods would be resold or otherwise used in that State; or
   (b)   in any other case, under the law of the State where the buyer has his place of business.
(2)   The obligation of the seller under the preceding paragraph does not extend to cases where—
   (a)   at the time of the conclusion of the contract the buyer knew or could not have been unaware of the right or claim; or
   (b)   the right or claim results from the seller's compliance with technical drawings, designs, formulae or other such specifications furnished by the buyer.

[4.107]
Article 43
(1)   The buyer loses the right to rely on the provisions of article 41 or article 42 if he does not give notice to the seller specifying the nature of the right or claim of the third party within a reasonable time after he has become aware or ought to have become aware of the right or claim.
(2)   The seller is not entitled to rely on the provisions of the preceding paragraph if he knew of the right or claim of the third party and the nature of it.

[4.108]
Article 44
Notwithstanding the provisions of paragraph (1) of article 39 and paragraph (1) of article 43, the buyer may reduce the price in accordance with article 50 or claim damages, except for loss of profit, if he has a reasonable excuse for his failure to give the required notice.

SECTION III
REMEDIES FOR BREACH OF CONTRACT BY THE SELLER

[4.109]
Article 45
(1)   If the seller fails to perform any of his obligations under the contract or this Convention, the buyer may—
    (a)   exercise the rights provided in articles 46 to 52;
    (b)   claim damages as provided in articles 74 to 77.
(2)   The buyer is not deprived of any right he may have to claim damages by exercising his right to other remedies.
(3)   No period of grace may be granted to the seller by a court or arbitral tribunal when the buyer resorts to a remedy for breach of contract.

[4.110]
Article 46
(1)   The buyer may require performance by the seller of his obligations unless the buyer has resorted to a remedy which is inconsistent with this requirement.
(2)   If the goods do not conform with the contract, the buyer may require delivery of substitute goods only if the lack of conformity constitutes a fundamental breach of contract and a request for substitute goods is made either in conjunction with notice given under article 39 or within a reasonable time thereafter.
(3)   If the goods do not conform with the contract, the buyer may require the seller to remedy the lack of conformity by repair, unless this is unreasonable having regard to all the circumstances. A request for repair must be made either in conjunction with notice given under article 39 or within a reasonable time thereafter.

[4.111]
Article 47
(1)   The buyer may fix an additional period of time of reasonable length for performance by the seller of his obligations.
(2)   Unless the buyer has received notice from the seller that he will not perform within the period so fixed, the buyer may not, during that period, resort to any remedy for breach of contract. However, the buyer is not deprived thereby of any right he may have to claim damages for delay in performance.

[4.112]
Article 48
(1)   Subject to article 49, the seller may, even after the date for delivery, remedy at his own expense any failure to perform his obligations, if he can do so without unreasonable delay and without causing the buyer unreasonable inconvenience or uncertainty of reimbursement by the seller of expenses advanced by the buyer. However, the buyer retains any right to claim damages as provided for in this Convention.
(2)   If the seller requests the buyer to make known whether he will accept performance and the buyer does not comply with the request within a reasonable time, the seller may perform within the time indicated in his request. The buyer may not, during that period of time, resort to any remedy which is inconsistent with performance by the seller.
(3)   A notice by the seller that he will perform within a specified period of time is assumed to include a request, under the preceding paragraph, that the buyer make known his decision.
(4)   A request or notice by the seller under paragraph (2) or (3) of this article is not effective unless received by the buyer.

[4.113]
Article 49
(1)   The buyer may declare the contract avoided—
    (a)   if the failure by the seller to perform any of his obligations under the contract or this Convention amounts to a fundamental breach of contract; or
    (b)   in case of non-delivery, if the seller does not deliver the goods within the additional period of time fixed by the buyer in accordance with paragraph (1) of article 47 or declares that he will not deliver within the period so fixed.
(2)   However, in cases where the seller has delivered the goods, the buyer loses the right to declare the contract avoided unless he does so—
    (a)   in respect of late delivery, within a reasonable time after he has become aware that delivery has been made;

(b) in respect of any breach other than late delivery, within a reasonable time—

    (i) after he knew or ought to have known of the breach;

    (ii) after the expiration of any additional period of time fixed by the buyer in accordance with paragraph (1) of article 47, or after the seller has declared that he will not perform his obligations within such an additional period; or

    (iii) after the expiration of any additional period of time indicated by the seller in accordance with paragraph (2) of article 48, or after the buyer has declared that he will not accept performance.

[4.114]
Article 50
If the goods do not conform with the contract and whether or not the price has already been paid, the buyer may reduce the price in the same proportion as the value that the goods actually delivered had at the time of the delivery bears to the value that conforming goods would have had at that time. However, if the seller remedies any failure to perform his obligations in accordance with article 37 or article 48 or if the buyer refuses to accept performance by the seller in accordance with those articles, the buyer may not reduce the price.

[4.115]
Article 51
(1) If the seller delivers only a part of the goods or if only a part of the goods delivered is in conformity with the contract, articles 46 to 50 apply in respect of the part which is missing or which does not conform.
(2) The buyer may declare the contract avoided in its entirety only if the failure to make delivery completely or in conformity with the contract amounts to a fundamental breach of the contract.

[4.116]
Article 52
(1) If the seller delivers the goods before the date fixed, the buyer may take delivery or refuse to take delivery.
(2) If the seller delivers a quantity of goods greater than that provided for in the contract, the buyer may take delivery or refuse to take delivery of the excess quantity. If the buyer takes delivery of all or part of the excess quantity, he must pay for it at the contract rate.

CHAPTER III
OBLIGATIONS OF THE BUYER

[4.117]
Article 53
The buyer must pay the price for the goods and take delivery of them as required by the contract and this Convention.

SECTION I
PAYMENT OF THE PRICE

[4.118]
Article 54
The buyer's obligation to pay the price includes taking such steps and complying with such formalities as may be required under the contract or any laws and regulations to enable payment to be made.

[4.119]
Article 55
Where a contract has been validly concluded but does not expressly or implicitly fix or make provision for determining the price, the parties are considered, in the absence of any indication to the contrary, to have impliedly made reference to the price generally charged at the time of the conclusion of the contract for such goods sold under comparable circumstances in the trade concerned.

[4.120]
Article 56
If the price is fixed according to the weight of goods, in case of doubt it is to be determined by the net weight.

[4.121]
Article 57
(1) If the buyer is not bound to pay the price at any other particular place, he must pay it to the seller—

    (a) at the seller's place of business; or

    (b) if the payment is to be made against the handing over of the goods or of documents, at the place where the handing over takes place.

(2)   The seller must bear any increase in the expenses incidental to payment which is caused by a change in his place of business subsequent to the conclusion of the contract.

[4.122]
Article 58
(1)   If the buyer is not bound to pay the price at any other specific time he must pay it when the seller places either the goods or documents controlling their disposition at the buyer's disposal in accordance with the contract and this Convention. The seller may make such payment a condition for handing over the goods or documents.
(2)   If the contract involves carriage of the goods, the seller may dispatch the goods on terms whereby the goods, or documents controlling their disposition, will not be handed over to the buyer except against payment of the price.
(3)   The buyer is not bound to pay the price until he has had an opportunity to examine the goods, unless the procedures for delivery or payment agreed upon by the parties are inconsistent with his having such an opportunity.

[4.123]
Article 59
The buyer must pay the price on the date fixed by or determinable from the contract and this Convention without the need for any request or compliance with any formality on the part of the seller.

SECTION II
TAKING DELIVERY

[4.124]
Article 60
The buyer's obligation to take delivery consists—
   (a)   in doing all the acts which could reasonably be expected of him in order to enable the seller to make delivery; and
   (b)   in taking over the goods.

SECTION III
REMEDIES FOR BREACH OF CONTRACT BY THE BUYER

[4.125]
Article 61
(1)   If the buyer fails to perform any of his obligations under the contract or this Convention, the seller may—
   (a)   exercise the rights provided in articles 62 to 65;
   (b)   claim damages as provided in articles 74 to 77.
(2)   The seller is not deprived of any right he may have to claim damages by exercising his right to other remedies.
(3)   No period of grace may be granted to the buyer by a court or arbitral tribunal when the seller resorts to a remedy for breach of contract.

[4.126]
Article 62
The seller may require the buyer to pay the price, take delivery or perform his other obligations, unless the seller has resorted to a remedy which is inconsistent with this requirement.

[4.127]
Article 63
(1)   The seller may fix an additional period of time of reasonable length for performance by the buyer of his obligations.
(2)   Unless the seller has received notice from the buyer that he will not perform within the period so fixed, the seller may not, during that period, resort to any remedy for breach of contract. However, the seller is not deprived thereby of any right he may have to claim damages for delay in performance.

[4.128]
Article 64
(1)   The seller may declare the contract avoided—
   (a)   if the failure by the buyer to perform any of his obligations under the contract or this Convention amounts to a fundamental breach of contract; or
   (b)   if the buyer does not, within the additional period of time fixed by the seller in accordance with paragraph (1) of article 63, perform his obligation to pay the price or take delivery of the goods, or if he declares that he will not do so within the period so fixed.
(2)   However, in cases where the buyer has paid the price, the seller loses the right to declare the contract avoided unless he does so—

(a)   in respect of late performance by the buyer, before the seller has become aware that performance has been rendered; or

(b)   in respect of any breach other than late performance by the buyer, within a reasonable time—

    (i)   after the seller knew or ought to have known of the breach; or

    (ii) after the expiration of any additional period of time fixed by the seller in accordance with paragraph (1) of article 63, or after the buyer has declared that he will not perform his obligations within such an additional period.

[4.129]
Article 65
(1)   If under the contract the buyer is to specify the form, measurement or other features of the goods and he fails to make such specification either on the date agreed upon or within a reasonable time after receipt of a request from the seller, the seller may, without prejudice to any other rights he may have, make the specification himself in accordance with the requirements of the buyer that may be known to him.

(2)   If the seller makes the specification himself, he must inform the buyer of the details thereof and must fix a reasonable time within which the buyer may make a different specification. If, after receipt of such a communication, the buyer fails to do so within the time so fixed, the specification made by the seller is binding.

CHAPTER IV
PASSING OF RISK

[4.130]
Article 66
Loss of or damage to the goods after the risk has passed to the buyer does not discharge him from his obligation to pay the price, unless the loss or damage is due to an act or omission of the seller.

[4.131]
Article 67
(1)   If the contract of sale involves carriage of the goods and the seller is not bound to hand them over at a particular place, the risk passes to the buyer when the goods are handed over to the first carrier for transmission to the buyer in accordance with the contract of sale. If the seller is bound to hand the goods over to a carrier at a particular place, the risk does not pass to the buyer until the goods are handed over to the carrier at that place. The fact that the seller is authorised to retain documents controlling the disposition of the goods does not affect the passage of the risk.

(2)   Nevertheless, the risk does not pass to the buyer until the goods are clearly identified to the contract, whether by markings on the goods, by shipping documents, by notice given to the buyer or otherwise.

[4.132]
Article 68
The risk in respect of goods sold in transit passes to the buyer from the time of the conclusion of the contract. However, if the circumstances so indicate, the risk is assumed by the buyer from the time the goods were handed over to the carrier who issued the documents embodying the contract of carriage. Nevertheless, if at the time of the conclusion of the contract of sale the seller knew or ought to have known that the goods had been lost or damaged and did not disclose this to the buyer, the loss or damage is at the risk of the seller.

[4.133]
Article 69
(1)   In cases not within articles 67 and 68, the risk passes to the buyer when he takes over the goods or, if he does not do so in due time, from the time when the goods are placed at his disposal and he commits a breach of contract by failing to take delivery.

(2)   However, if the buyer is bound to take over the goods at a place other than a place of business of the seller, the risk passes when delivery is due and the buyer is aware of the fact that the goods are placed at his disposal at that place.

(3)   If the contract relates to goods not then identified, the goods are considered not to be placed at the disposal of the buyer until they are clearly identified to the contract.

[4.134]
Article 70
If the seller has committed a fundamental breach of contract, articles 67, 68 and 69 do not impair the remedies available to the buyer on account of the breach.

CHAPTER V
PROVISIONS COMMON TO THE OBLIGATIONS OF THE SELLER AND OF THE BUYER

SECTION I
ANTICIPATORY BREACH AND INSTALMENT CONTRACTS

[4.135]
Article 71
(1)   A party may suspend the performance of his obligations if, after the conclusion of the contract, it becomes apparent that the other party will not perform a substantial part of his obligations as a result of—
    (a)   a serious deficiency in his ability to perform or in his creditworthiness; or
    (b)   his conduct in preparing to perform or in performing the contract.
(2)   If the seller has already dispatched the goods before the grounds described in the preceding paragraph become evident, he may prevent the handing over of the goods to the buyer even though the buyer holds a document which entitles him to obtain them. The present paragraph relates only to the rights in the goods as between the buyer and the seller.
(3)   A party suspending performance, whether before or after dispatch of the goods, must immediately give notice of the suspension to the other party and must continue with performance if the other party provides adequate assurance of his performance.

[4.136]
Article 72
(1)   If prior to the date for performance of the contract it is clear that one of the parties will commit a fundamental breach of contract, the other party may declare the contract avoided.
(2)   If time allows, the party intending to declare the contract avoided must give reasonable notice to the other party in order to permit him to provide adequate assurance of his performance.
(3)   The requirements of the preceding paragraph do not apply if the other party has declared that he will not perform his obligations.

[4.137]
Article 73
(1)   In the case of a contract for delivery of goods by instalments, if the failure of one party to perform any of his obligations in respect of any instalment constitutes a fundamental breach of contract with respect to that instalment, the other party may declare the contract avoided with respect to that instalment.
(2)   If one party's failure to perform any of his obligations in respect of any instalment gives the other party good grounds to conclude that a fundamental breach of contract will occur with respect to future instalments, he may declare the contract avoided for the future, provided that he does so within a reasonable time.
(3)   A buyer who declares the contract avoided in respect of any delivery may, at the same time, declare it avoided in respect of deliveries already made or of future deliveries if, by reason of their interdependence, those deliveries could not be used for the purpose contemplated by the parties at the time of the conclusion of the contract.

SECTION II
DAMAGES

[4.138]
Article 74
Damages for breach of contract by one party consist of a sum equal to the loss, including loss of profit, suffered by the other party as a consequence of the breach. Such damages may not exceed the loss which the party in breach foresaw or ought to have foreseen at the time of the conclusion of the contract, in the light of the facts and matters of which he then knew or ought to have known, as a possible consequence of the breach of contract.

[4.139]
Article 75
If the contract is avoided and if, in a reasonable manner and within a reasonable time after avoidance, the buyer has bought goods in replacement or the seller has resold the goods, the party claiming damages may recover the difference between the contract price and the price in the substitute transaction as well as any further damages recoverable under article 74.

[4.140]
Article 76
(1)   If the contract is avoided and there is a current price for the goods, the party claiming damages may, if he has not made a purchase or resale under article 75, recover the difference between the price fixed by the contract and the current price at the time of avoidance as well as any further

damages recoverable under article 74. If, however, the party claiming damages has avoided the contract after taking over the goods, the current price at the time of such taking over shall be applied instead of the current price at the time of avoidance.

(2)   For the purposes of the preceding paragraph, the current price is the price prevailing at the place where delivery of the goods should have been made or, if there is no current price at that place, the price at such other place as serves as a reasonable substitute, making due allowance for differences in the cost of transporting the goods.

[4.141]
Article 77

A party who relies on a breach of contract must take such measures as are reasonable in the circumstances to mitigate the loss, including loss of profit, resulting from the breach. If he fails to take such measures, the party in breach may claim a reduction in the damages in the amount by which the loss should have been mitigated.

SECTION III
INTEREST

[4.142]
Article 78

If a party fails to pay the price or any other sum that is in arrears, the other party is entitled to interest on it, without prejudice to any claim for damages recoverable under article 74.

SECTION IV
EXEMPTION

[4.143]
Article 79

(1)   A party is not liable for a failure to perform any of his obligations if he proves that the failure was due to an impediment beyond his control and that he could not reasonably be expected to have taken the impediment into account at the time of the conclusion of the contract or to have avoided or overcome it or its consequences.

(2)   If the party's failure is due to the failure by a third person whom he has engaged to perform the whole or a part of the contract, that party is exempt from liability only if—

  (a)   he is exempt under the preceding paragraph; and
  (b)   the person whom he has so engaged would be so exempt if the provisions of that paragraph were applied to him.

(3)   The exemption provided by this article has effect for the period during which the impediment exists.

(4)   The party who fails to perform must give notice to the other party of the impediment and its effect on his ability to perform. If the notice is not received by the other party within a reasonable time after the party who fails to perform knew or ought to have known of the impediment, he is liable for damages resulting from such non receipt.

(5)   Nothing in this article prevents either party from exercising any right other than to claim damages under this Convention.

[4.144]
Article 80

A party may not rely on a failure of the other party to perform, to the extent that such failure was caused by the first party's act or omission.

SECTION V
EFFECTS OF AVOIDANCE

[4.145]
Article 81

(1)   Avoidance of the contract releases both parties from their obligations under it, subject to any damages which may be due. Avoidance does not affect any provision of the contract for the settlement of disputes or any other provision of the contract governing the rights and obligations of the parties consequent upon the avoidance of the contract.

(2)   A party who has performed the contract either wholly or in part may claim restitution from the other party of whatever the first party has supplied or paid under the contract. If both parties are bound to make restitution, they must do so concurrently.

[4.146]
Article 82

(1)   The buyer loses the right to declare the contract avoided or to require the seller to deliver substitute goods if it is impossible for him to make restitution of the goods substantially in the condition in which he received them.

(2)   The preceding paragraph does not apply—

(a) if the impossibility of making restitution of the goods or of making restitution of the goods substantially in the condition in which the buyer received them is not due to his act or omission;

(b) if the goods or part of the goods have perished or deteriorated as a result of the examination provided for in article 38; or

(c) if the goods or part of the goods have been sold in the normal course of business or have been consumed or transformed by the buyer in the course of normal use before he discovered or ought to have discovered the lack of conformity.

[4.147]
Article 83
A buyer who has lost the right to declare the contract avoided or to require the seller to deliver substitute goods in accordance with article 82 retains all other remedies under the contract and this Convention.

[4.148]
Article 84
(1) If the seller is bound to refund the price, he must also pay interest on it, from the date on which the price was paid.
(2) The buyer must account to the seller for all benefits which he has derived from the goods or part of them—
    (a) if he must make restitution of the goods or part of them; or
    (b) if it is impossible for him to make restitution of all or part of the goods or to make restitution of all or part of the goods substantially in the condition in which he received them, but he has nevertheless declared the contract avoided or required the seller to deliver substitute goods.

SECTION VI
PRESERVATION OF THE GOODS

[4.149]
Article 85
If the buyer is in delay in taking delivery of the goods or, where payment of the price and delivery of the goods are to be made concurrently, if he fails to pay the price, and the seller is either in possession of the goods or otherwise able to control their disposition, the seller must take such steps as are reasonable in the circumstances to preserve them. He is entitled to retain them until he has been reimbursed his reasonable expenses by the buyer.

[4.150]
Article 86
(1) If the buyer has received the goods and intends to exercise any right under the contract or this Convention to reject them, he must take such steps to preserve them as are reasonable in the circumstances. He is entitled to retain them until he has been reimbursed his reasonable expenses by the seller.
(2) If goods dispatched to the buyer have been placed at his disposal at their destination and he exercises the right to reject them, he must take possession of them on behalf of the seller, provided that this can be done without payment of the price and without unreasonable inconvenience or unreasonable expense. This provision does not apply if the seller or a person authorised to take charge of the goods on his behalf is present at the destination. If the buyer takes possession of the goods under this paragraph, his rights and obligations are governed by the preceding paragraph.

[4.151]
Article 87
A party who is bound to take steps to preserve the goods may deposit them in a warehouse of a third person at the expense of the other party provided that the expense incurred is not unreasonable.

[4.152]
Article 88
(1) A party who is bound to preserve the goods in accordance with article 85 or 86 may sell them by any appropriate means if there has been an unreasonable delay by the other party in taking possession of the goods or in taking them back or in paying the price or the cost of preservation, provided that reasonable notice of the intention to sell has been given to the other party.
(2) If the goods are subject to rapid deterioration or their preservation would involve unreasonable expense, a party who is bound to preserve the goods in accordance with article 85 or 86 must take reasonable measures to sell them. To the extent possible he must give notice to the other party of his intention to sell.
(3) A party selling the goods has the right to retain out of the proceeds of sale an amount equal to the reasonable expenses of preserving the goods and of selling them. He must account to the other party for the balance.

PART IV
FINAL PROVISIONS

[4.153]
Article 89
The Secretary-General of the United Nations is hereby designated as the depositary for this Convention.

[4.154]
Article 90
This Convention does not prevail over any international agreement which has already been or may be entered into and which contains provisions concerning the matters governed by this Convention, provided that the parties have their places of business in States parties to such agreement.

[4.155]
Article 91
(1)   This Convention is open for signature at the concluding meeting of the United Nations Conference on Contracts for the International Sale of Goods and will remain open for signature by all States at the Headquarters of the United Nations, New York until 30 September 1981.
(2)   This Convention is subject to ratification, acceptance or approval by the signatory States.
(3)   This Convention is open for accession by all States which are not signatory States as from the date it is open for signature.
(4)   Instruments of ratification, acceptance, approval and accession are to be deposited with the Secretary-General of the United Nations.

[4.156]
Article 92
(1)   A Contracting State may declare at the time of signature, ratification, acceptance, approval or accession that it will not be bound by Part II of this Convention or that it will not be bound by Part III of this Convention.
(2)   A Contracting State which makes a declaration in accordance with the preceding paragraph in respect of Part II or Part III of this Convention is not to be considered a Contracting State within paragraph (1) of article 1 of this Convention in respect of matters governed by the Part to which the declaration applies.

[4.157]
Article 93
(1)   If a Contracting State has two or more territorial units in which, according to its constitution, different systems of law are applicable in relation to the matters dealt with in this Convention, it may, at the time of signature, ratification, acceptance, approval or accession, declare that this Convention is to extend to all its territorial units or only to one or more of them, and may amend its declaration by submitting another declaration at any time.
(2)   These declarations are to be notified to the depositary and are to state expressly the territorial units to which the Convention extends.
(3)   If, by virtue of a declaration under this article, this Convention extends to one or more but not all of the territorial units of a Contracting State, and if the place of business of a party is located in that State, this place of business, for the purposes of this Convention, is considered not to be in a Contracting State, unless it is in a territorial unit to which the Convention extends.
(4)   If a Contracting State makes no declaration under paragraph (1) of this article, the Convention is to extend to all territorial units of that State.

[4.158]
Article 94
(1)   Two or more Contracting States which have the same or closely related legal rules on matters governed by this Convention may at any time declare that the Convention is not to apply to contracts of sale or to their formation where the parties have their places of business in those States. Such declarations may be made jointly or by reciprocal unilateral declarations.
(2)   A Contracting State which has the same or closely related legal rules on matters governed by this Convention as one or more non-Contracting States may at any time declare that the Convention is not to apply to contracts of sale or to their formation where the parties have their places of business in those States.
(3)   If a State which is the object of a declaration under the preceding paragraph subsequently becomes a Contracting State, the declaration made will, as from the date on which the Convention enters into force in respect of the new Contracting State, have the effect of a declaration made under paragraph (1), provided that the new Contracting State joins in such declaration or makes a reciprocal unilateral declaration.

[4.159]
Article 95
Any State may declare at the time of the deposit of its instrument of ratification, acceptance, approval or accession that it will not be bound by subparagraph (1)(b) of article 1 of this Convention.

[4.160]
Article 96
A Contracting State whose legislation requires contracts of sale to be concluded in or evidenced by writing may at any time make a declaration in accordance with article 12 that any provision of article 11, article 29, or Part II of this Convention, that allows a contract of sale or its modification or termination by agreement or any offer, acceptance, or other indication of intention to be made in any form other than in writing, does not apply where any party has his place of business in that State.

[4.161]
Article 97
(1)   Declarations made under this Convention at the time of signature are subject to confirmation upon ratification, acceptance or approval.
(2)   Declarations and confirmations of declarations are to be in writing and be formally notified to the depositary.
(3)   A declaration takes effect simultaneously with the entry into force of this Convention in respect of the State concerned. However, a declaration of which the depositary receives formal notification after such entry into force takes effect on the first day of the month following the expiration of six months after the date of its receipt by the depositary. Reciprocal unilateral declarations under article 94 take effect on the first day of the month following the expiration of six months after the receipt of the latest declaration by the depositary.
(4)   Any State which makes a declaration under this Convention may withdraw it at any time by a formal notification in writing addressed to the depositary. Such withdrawal is to take effect on the first day of the month following the expiration of six months after the date of the receipt of the notification by the depositary.
(5)   A withdrawal of a declaration made under article 94 renders inoperative, as from the date on which the withdrawal takes effect, any reciprocal declaration made by another State under that article.

[4.162]
Article 98
No reservations are permitted except those expressly authorised in this Convention.

[4.163]
Article 99
(1)   This Convention enters into force, subject to the provisions of paragraph (6) of this article, on the first day of the month following the expiration of twelve months after the date of deposit of the tenth instrument of ratification, acceptance, approval or accession, including an instrument which contains a declaration made under article 92.
(2)   When a State ratifies, accepts, approves or accedes to this Convention after the deposit of the tenth instrument of ratification, acceptance, approval or accession, this Convention, with the exception of the Part excluded, enters into force in respect of that State, subject to the provisions of paragraph (6) of this article, on the first day of the month following the expiration of twelve months after the date of the deposit of its instrument of ratification, acceptance, approval or accession.
(3)   A State which ratifies, accepts, approves or accedes to this Convention and is a party to either or both the Convention relating to a Uniform Law on the Formation of Contracts for the International Sale of Goods done at The Hague on 1 July 1964 (1964 Hague Formation Convention) and the Convention relating to a Uniform Law on the International Sale of Goods done at The Hague on 1 July 1964 (1964 Hague Sales Convention) shall at the same time denounce, as the case may be, either or both the 1964 Hague Sales Convention and the 1964 Hague Formation Convention by notifying the Government of the Netherlands to that effect.
(4)   A State party to the 1964 Hague Sales Convention which ratifies, accepts, approves or accedes to the present Convention and declares or has declared under article 92 that it will not be bound by Part II of this Convention shall at the time of ratification, acceptance, approval or accession denounce the 1964 Hague Sales Convention by notifying the Government of the Netherlands to that effect.
(5)   A State party to the 1964 Hague Formation Convention which ratifies, accepts, approves or accedes to the present Convention and declares or has declared under article 92 that it will not be bound by Part III of this Convention shall at the time of ratification, acceptance, approval or accession denounce the 1964 Hague Formation Convention by notifying the Government of the Netherlands to that effect.
(6)   For the purpose of this article, ratifications, acceptances, approvals and accessions in respect of this Convention by States parties to the 1964 Hague Formation Convention or to the 1964 Hague Sales Convention shall not be effective until such denunciations as may be required on the part of

those States in respect of the latter two Conventions have themselves become effective. The depositary of this Convention shall consult with the Government of the Netherlands, as the depositary of the 1964 Conventions, so as to ensure necessary co-ordination in this respect.

[4.164]
Article 100
(1)   This Convention applies to the formation of a contract only when the proposal for concluding the contract is made on or after the date when the Convention enters into force in respect of the Contracting States referred to in subparagraph (1)(a) or the Contracting State referred to in subparagraph (1)(b) of article 1.
(2)   This Convention applies only to contracts concluded on or after the date when the Convention enters into force in respect of the Contracting States referred to in subparagraph (1)(a) or the Contracting State referred to in subparagraph (1)(b) of article 1.

[4.165]
Article 101
(1)   A Contracting State may denounce this Convention, or Part II or Part III of the Convention, by a formal notification in writing addressed to the depositary.
(2)   The denunciation takes effect on the first day of the month following the expiration of twelve months after the notification is received by the depositary. Where a longer period for the denunciation to take effect is specified in the notification, the denunciation takes effect upon the expiration of such longer period after the notification is received by the depositary.
DONE at Vienna, this day of eleventh day of April, one thousand nine hundred and eighty, in a single original, of which the Arabic, Chinese, English, French, Russian and Spanish texts are equally authentic.
IN WITNESS WHEREOF the undersigned plenipotentiaries, being duly authorised by their respective Governments, have signed this Convention.

NOTES
The text of this Convention was prepared by the United Nations Commission on International Trade Law.

COUNCIL DIRECTIVE

(85/374/EEC)

of 25 July 1985

on the approximation of the laws, regulations and administrative provisions of the Member States concerning liability for defective products

NOTE
Date of publication in OJ: OJ L210, 7.8.85, p 29.
This Directive has been implemented in the UK by the Consumer Protection Act 1987 at **[1.985]**.

THE COUNCIL OF THE EUROPEAN COMMUNITIES,
Having regard to the Treaty establishing the European Economic Community, and in particular Article 100 thereof,
Having regard to the proposal from the Commission,[1]
Having regard to the opinion of the European Parliament,[2]
Having regard to the opinion of the Economic and Social Committee,[3]
Whereas approximation of the laws of the Member States concerning the liability of the producer for damage caused by the defectiveness of his products is necessary because the existing divergences may distort competition and affect the movement of goods within the common market and entail a differing degree of protection of the consumer against damage caused by a defective product to his health or property;
Whereas liability without fault on the part of the producer is the sole means of adequately solving the problem, peculiar to our age of increasing technicality, of a fair apportionment of the risks inherent in modern technological production;
Whereas liability without fault should apply only to movables which have been industrially produced; whereas, as a result, it is appropriate to exclude liability for agricultural products and game, except where they have undergone a processing of an industrial nature which could cause a defect in these products; whereas the liability provided for in this Directive should also apply to movables which are used in the construction of immovables or are installed in immovables;
Whereas protection of the consumer requires that all producers involved in the production process should be made liable, in so far as their finished product, component part or any raw material supplied by them was defective; whereas, for the same reason, liability should extend to importers of products into the Community and to persons who present themselves as producers by affixing their name, trade mark or other distinguishing feature or who supply a product the producer of which cannot be identified;

Whereas, in situations where several persons are liable for the same damage, the protection of the consumer requires that the injured person should be able to claim full compensation for the damage from any one of them;

Whereas, to protect the physical well-being and property of the consumer, the defectiveness of the product should be determined by reference not to its fitness for use but to the lack of the safety which the public at large is entitled to expect; whereas the safety is assessed by excluding any misuse of the product not reasonable under the circumstances;

Whereas a fair apportionment of risk between the injured person and the producer implies that the producer should be able to free himself from liability if he furnishes proof as to the existence of certain exonerating circumstances;

Whereas the protection of the consumer requires that the liability of the producer remains unaffected by acts or omissions of other persons having contributed to cause the damage; whereas, however, the contributory negligence of the injured person may be taken into account to reduce or disallow such liability;

Whereas the protection of the consumer requires compensation for death and personal injury as well as compensation for damage to property; whereas the latter should nevertheless be limited to goods for private use or consumption and be subject to a deduction of a lower threshold of a fixed amount in order to avoid litigation in an excessive number of cases; whereas this Directive should not prejudice compensation for pain and suffering and other nonmaterial damages payable, where appropriate, under the law applicable to the case;

Whereas a uniform period of limitation for the bringing of action for compensation is in the interests both of the injured person and of the producer;

Whereas products age in the course of time, higher safety standards are developed and the state of science and technology progresses; whereas, therefore, it would not be reasonable to make the producer liable for an unlimited period for the defectiveness of his product; whereas, therefore, liability should expire after a reasonable length of time, without prejudice to claims pending at law;

Whereas, to achieve effective protection of consumers, no contractual derogation should be permitted as regards the liability of the producer in relation to the injured person;

Whereas under the legal systems of the Member States an injured party may have a claim for damages based on grounds of contractual liability or on grounds of non-contractual liability other than that provided for in this Directive; in so far as these provisions also serve to attain the objective of effective protection of consumers, they should remain unaffected by this Directive; whereas, in so far as effective protection of consumers in the sector of pharmaceutical products is already also attained in a Member State under a special liability system, claims based on this system should similarly remain possible;

Whereas, to the extent that liability for nuclear injury or damage is already covered in all Member States by adequate special rules, it has been possible to exclude damage of this type from the scope of this Directive;

Whereas, since the exclusion of primary agricultural products and game from the scope of this Directive may be felt, in certain Member States, in view of what is expected for the protection of consumers, to restrict unduly such protection, it should be possible for a Member State to extend liability to such products;

Whereas, for similar reasons, the possibility offered to a producer to free himself from liability if he proves that the state of scientific and technical knowledge at the time when he put the product into circulation was not such as to enable the existence of a defect to be discovered may be felt in certain Member States to restrict unduly the protection of the consumer; whereas it should therefore be possible for a Member State to maintain in its legislation or to provide by new legislation that this exonerating circumstance is not admitted; whereas, in the case of new legislation, making use of this derogation should, however, be subject to a Community stand-still procedure, in order to raise, if possible, the level of protection in a uniform manner throughout the Community;

Whereas, taking into account the legal traditions in most of the Member States, it is inappropriate to set any financial ceiling on the producer's liability without fault; whereas, in so far as there are, however, differing traditions, it seems possible to admit that a Member State may derogate from the principle of unlimited liability by providing a limit for the total liability of the producer for damage resulting from a death or personal injury and caused by identical items with the same defect, provided that this limit is established at a level sufficiently high to guarantee adequate protection of the consumer and the correct functioning of the common market;

Whereas the harmonisation resulting from this cannot be total at the present stage, but opens the way towards greater harmonisation; whereas it is therefore necessary that the Council receive at regular intervals, reports from the Commission on the application of this Directive, accompanied, as the case may be, by appropriate proposals;

Whereas it is particularly important in this respect that a re-examination be carried out of those parts of the Directive relating to the derogations open to the Member States, at the expiry of a period of sufficient length to gather practical experience on the effects of these derogations on the protection of consumers and on the functioning of the common market,

NOTES

¹   OJ C241, 14.10.76, p 9; OJ C271, 26.10.79, p 3.

²   OJ C127, 21.5.79, p 61.

³   OJ C114, 7.5.79, p 15.

HAS ADOPTED THIS DIRECTIVE:

[4.166]
Article 1

The producer shall be liable for damage caused by a defect in his product.

[4.167]
[Article 2

For the purpose of this Directive, "product" means all movables even if incorporated into another movable or into an immovable. "Product" includes electricity.]

NOTES

Substituted by European Parliament and Council Directive 1999/34/EC, Art 1(1).

[4.168]
Article 3

1.   "Producer" means the manufacturer of a finished product, the producer of any raw material or the manufacturer of a component part and any person who, by putting his name, trade mark or other distinguishing feature on the product presents himself as its producer.

2.   Without prejudice to the liability of the producer, any person who imports into the Community a product for sale, hire, leasing or any form of distribution in the course of his business shall be deemed to be a producer within the meaning of this Directive and shall be responsible as a producer.

3.   Where the producer of the product cannot be identified, each supplier of the product shall be treated as its producer unless he informs the injured person, within a reasonable time, of the identity of the producer or of the person who supplied him with the product. The same shall apply, in the case of an imported product, if this product does not indicate the identity of the importer referred to in paragraph 2, even if the name of the producer is indicated.

[4.169]
Article 4

The injured person shall be required to prove the damage, the defect and the causal relationship between defect and damage.

[4.170]
Article 5

Where, as a result of the provisions of this Directive, two or more persons are liable for the same damage, they shall be liable jointly and severally, without prejudice to the provisions of national law concerning the rights of contribution or recourse.

[4.171]
Article 6

1.   A product is defective when it does not provide the safety which a person is entitled to expect, taking all circumstances into account, including—
   (a)   the presentation of the product;
   (b)   the use to which it could reasonably be expected that the product would be put;
   (c)   the time when the product was put into circulation.
2.   A product shall not be considered defective for the sole reason that a better product is subsequently put into circulation.

[4.172]
Article 7

The producer shall not be liable as a result of this Directive if he proves—
   (a)   that he did not put the product into circulation; or
   (b)   that, having regard to the circumstances, it is probable that the defect which caused the damage did not exist at the time when the product was put into circulation by him or that this defect came into being afterwards; or
   (c)   that the product was neither manufactured by him for sale or any form of distribution for economic purpose nor manufactured or distributed by him in the course of his business; or
   (d)   that the defect is due to compliance of the product with mandatory regulations issued by the public authorities; or
   (e)   that the state of scientific and technical knowledge at the time when he put the product into circulation was not such as to enable the existence of the defect to be discovered; or

(f)   in the case of a manufacturer of a component, that the defect is attributable to the design of the product in which the component has been fitted or to the instructions given by the manufacturer of the product.

[4.173]
Article 8
1.   Without prejudice to the provisions of national law concerning the right of contribution or recourse, the liability of the producer shall not be reduced when the damage is caused both by a defect in product and by the act or omission of a third party.
2.   The liability of the producer may be reduced or disallowed when, having regard to all the circumstances, the damage is caused both by a defect in the product and by the fault of the injured person or any person for whom the injured person is responsible.

[4.174]
Article 9
For the purpose of Article 1, "damage" means—
    (a)   damage caused by death or by personal injuries;
    (b)   damage to, or destruction of, any item of property other than the defective product itself, with a lower threshold of 500 ECU, provided that the item of property—
        (i)   is of a type ordinarily intended for private use or consumption, and
        (ii)   was used by the injured person mainly for his own private use or consumption.
  This Article shall be without prejudice to national provisions relating to nonmaterial damage.

[4.175]
Article 10
1.   Member States shall provide in their legislation that a limitation period of three years shall apply to proceedings for the recovery of damages as provided for in this Directive. The limitation period shall begin to run from the day on which the plaintiff became aware, or should reasonably have become aware, of the damage, the defect and the identity of the producer.
2.   The laws of Member States regulating suspension or interruption of the limitation period shall not be affected by this Directive.

[4.176]
Article 11
Member States shall provide in their legislation that the rights conferred upon the injured person pursuant to this Directive shall be extinguished upon the expiry of a period of 10 years from the date on which the producer put into circulation the actual product which caused the damage, unless the injured person has in the meantime instituted proceedings against the producer.

[4.177]
Article 12
The liability of the producer arising from this Directive may not, in relation to the injured person, be limited or excluded by a provision limiting his liability or exempting him from liability.

[4.178]
Article 13
This Directive shall not affect any rights which an injured person may have according to the rules of the law of contractual or non-contractual liability or a special liability system existing at the moment when this Directive is notified.

[4.179]
Article 14
This Directive shall not apply to injury or damage arising from nuclear accidents and covered by international conventions ratified by the Member States.

[4.180]
Article 15
1.   Each Member State may—
    (a)   . . .
    (b)   by way of derogation from Article 7(e), maintain or, subject to the procedure set out in paragraph 2 of this Article, provide in this legislation that the producer shall be liable even if he proves that the state of scientific and technical knowledge at the time when he put the product into circulation was not such as to enable the existence of a defect to be discovered.
2.   A Member State wishing to introduce the measure specified in paragraph 1(b) shall communicate the text of the proposed measure to the Commission. The Commission shall inform the other Member States thereof.
  The Member State concerned shall hold the proposed measure in abeyance for nine months after the Commission is informed and provided that in the meantime the Commission has not submitted to the Council a proposal amending this Directive on the relevant matter. However, if within three

months of receiving the said information, the Commission does not advise the Member State concerned that it intends submitting such a proposal to the Council, the Member State may take the proposed measure immediately.

If the Commission does submit to the Council such a proposal amending this Directive within the aforementioned nine months, the Member State concerned shall hold the proposed measure in abeyance for a further period of 18 months from the date on which the proposal is submitted.
3.   Ten years after the date of notification of this Directive, the Commission shall submit to the Council a report on the effect that rulings by the courts as to the application of Article 7(e) and of paragraph 1(b) of this Article have on consumer protection and the functioning of the common market. In the light of this report the Council, acting on a proposal from the Commission and pursuant to the terms of Article 100 of the Treaty, shall decide whether to repeal Article 7(e).

NOTES

Para 1: sub-para (a) revoked by European Parliament and Council Directive 1999/34/EC, Art 1(2).

[4.181]
Article 16
1.   Any Member State may provide that a producer's total liability for damage resulting from a death or personal injury and caused by identical items with the same defect shall be limited to an amount which may not be less than 70 million ECU.
2.   Ten years after the date of notification of this Directive, the Commission shall submit to the Council a report on the effect on consumer protection and the functioning of the common market of the implementation of the financial limit on liability by those Member States which have used the option provided for in paragraph 1. In the light of this report the Council, acting on a proposal from the Commission and pursuant to the terms of Article 100 of the Treaty, shall decide whether to repeal paragraph 1.

[4.182]
Article 17
This Directive shall not apply to products put into circulation before the date on which the provisions referred to in Article 19 enter into force.

[4.183]
Article 18
1.   For the purposes of this Directive, the ECU shall be that defined by Regulation (EEC) No 3180/78,[1] as amended by Regulation (EEC) No 2626/84.[2] The equivalent in national currency shall initially be calculated at the rate obtaining on the date of adoption of this Directive.
2.   Every five years the Council, acting on a proposal from the Commission, shall examine and, if need be, revise the amounts in this Directive, in the light of economic and monetary trends in the Community.

NOTES

[1]   OJ L379, 30.12.78, p 1.
[2]   OJ L247, 16.9.84, p 1.

[4.184]
Article 19
1.   Member States shall bring into force, not later than three years from the date of notification of this Directive, the laws, regulations and administrative provisions necessary to comply with this Directive. They shall forthwith inform the Commission thereof.
2.   The procedure set out in Article 15(2) shall apply from the date of notification of this Directive.

NOTES

This Directive was notified to the Member States on 30 July 1985.

[4.185]
Article 20
Member States shall communicate to the Commission the texts of the main provisions of national law which they subsequently adopt in the field governed by this Directive.

[4.186]
Article 21
Every five years the Commission shall present a report to the Council on the application of this Directive and, if necessary, shall submit appropriate proposals to it.

[4.187]
Article 22
This Directive is addressed to the Member States.

COUNCIL DIRECTIVE

(86/653/EEC)

of 18 December 1986

on the coordination of the laws of the Member States relating to self-employed commercial agents

NOTES

Date of publication in OJ: OJ L382, 31.12.86, p 17.

This Directive has been implemented in the UK by the Commercial Agents (Council Directive) Regulations 1993, SI 1993/3053 at **[2.81]**.

THE COUNCIL OF THE EUROPEAN COMMUNITIES,

Having regard to the Treaty establishing the European Economic Community, and in particular Articles 57(2) and 100 thereof,

Having regard to the proposal from the Commission,[1]

Having regard to the opinion of the European Parliament,[2]

Having regard to the opinion of the Economic and Social Committee,[3]

Whereas the restrictions on the freedom of establishment and the freedom to provide services in respect of activities of intermediaries in commerce, industry and small craft industries were abolished by Directive 64/224/EEC;[4]

Whereas the differences in national laws concerning commercial representation substantially affect the conditions of competition and the carrying-on of that activity within the Community and are detrimental both to the protection available to commercial agents *vis-à-vis* their principals and to the security of commercial transactions; whereas moreover those differences are such as to inhibit substantially the conclusion and operation of commercial representation contracts where principal and commercial agent are established in different Member States;

Whereas trade in goods between Member States should be carried on under conditions which are similar to those of a single market, and this necessitates approximation of the legal systems of the Member States to the extent required for the proper functioning of the common market; whereas in this regard the rules concerning conflict of laws do not, in the matter of commercial representation, remove the inconsistencies referred to above, nor would they even if they were made uniform, and accordingly the proposed harmonisation is necessary notwithstanding the existence of those rules;

Whereas in this regard the legal relationship between commercial agent and principal must be given priority;

Whereas it is appropriate to be guided by the principles of Article 117 of the Treaty and to maintain improvements already made, when harmonising the laws of the Member States relating to commercial agents;

Whereas additional transitional periods should be allowed for certain Member States which have to make a particular effort to adapt their regulations, especially those concerning indemnity for termination of contract between the principal and the commercial agent, to the requirements of this Directive,

NOTES

[1]   OJ C13, 18.1.77, p 2 and OJ C56, 2.3.79, p 5.

[2]   OJ C239, 9.10.78, p 17.

[3]   OJ C59, 8.3.78, p 31.

[4]   OJ C56, 4.4.19, p 869/64.

HAS ADOPTED THIS DIRECTIVE—

CHAPTER I
SCOPE

[4.188]
Article 1

1.   The harmonisation measures prescribed by this Directive shall apply to the laws, regulations and administrative provisions of the Member States governing the relations between commercial agents and their principals.

2.   For the purposes of this Directive, "commercial agent" shall mean a self-employed intermediary who has continuing authority to negotiate the sale or the purchase of goods on behalf of another person, hereinafter called the "principal", or to negotiate and conclude such transactions on behalf of and in the name of that principal.

3.   A commercial agent shall be understood within the meaning of this Directive as not including in particular—

—   a person who, in his capacity as an officer, is empowered to enter into commitments binding on a company or association,

—   a partner who is lawfully authorised to enter into commitments binding on his partners,

—   a receiver, a receiver and manager, a liquidator or a trustee in bankruptcy.

[4.189]
Article 2
1.   This Directive shall not apply to—
—   commercial agents whose activities are unpaid,
—   commercial agents when they operate on commodity exchanges or in the commodity market, or
—   the body known as the Crown Agents for Overseas Governments and Administrations, as set up under the Crown Agents Act 1979 in the United Kingdom, or its subsidiaries.

2.   Each of the Member States shall have the right to provide that the Directive shall not apply to those persons whose activities as commercial agents are considered secondary by the law of that Member State.

CHAPTER II
RIGHTS AND OBLIGATIONS

[4.190]
Article 3
1.   In performing his activities a commercial agent must look after his principal's interests and act dutifully and in good faith.
2.   In particular, a commercial agent must—
(a)   make proper efforts to negotiate and, where appropriate, conclude the transactions he is instructed to take care of;
(b)   communicate to his principal all the necessary information available to him;
(c)   comply with reasonable instructions given by his principal.

[4.191]
Article 4
1.   In his relations with his commercial agent a principal must act dutifully and in good faith.
2.   A principal must in particular—
(a)   provide his commercial agent with the necessary documentation relating to the goods concerned;
(b)   obtain for his commercial agent the information necessary for the performance of the agency contract, and in particular notify the commercial agent within a reasonable period once he anticipates that the volume of commercial transactions will be significantly lower than that which the commercial agent could normally have expected.

3.   A principal must, in addition, inform the commercial agent within a reasonable period of his acceptance, refusal, and of any non-execution of a commercial transaction which the commercial agent has procured for the principal.

[4.192]
Article 5
The parties may not derogate from the provisions of Articles 3 and 4.

CHAPTER III
REMUNERATION

[4.193]
Article 6
1.   In the absence of any agreement on this matter between the parties, and without prejudice to the application of the compulsory provisions of the Member States concerning the level of remuneration, a commercial agent shall be entitled to the remuneration that commercial agents appointed for the goods forming the subject of his agency contract are customarily allowed in the place where he carries on his activities. If there is no such customary practice a commercial agent shall be entitled to reasonable remuneration taking into account all the aspects of the transaction.
2.   Any part of the remuneration which varies with the number or value of business transactions shall be deemed to be commission within the meaning of this Directive.
3.   Articles 7 to 12 shall not apply if the commercial agent is not remunerated wholly or in part by commission.

[4.194]
Article 7
1.   A commercial agent shall be entitled to commission on commercial transactions concluded during the period covered by the agency contract—
(a)   where the transaction has been concluded as a result of his action; or
(b)   where the transaction is concluded with a third party whom he has previously acquired as a customer for transactions of the same kind.

2. A commercial agent shall also be entitled to commission on transactions concluded during the period covered by the agency contract—

— either where he is entrusted with a specific geographical area or group of customers,

— or where he has an exclusive right to a specific geographical area or group of customers,

and where the transaction has been entered into with a customer belonging to that area or group.

Member States shall include in their legislation one of the possibilities referred to in the above two indents.

[4.195]
Article 8
A commercial agent shall be entitled to commission on commercial transactions concluded after the agency contract has terminated—

    (a)   if the transaction is mainly attributable to the commercial agent's efforts during the period covered by the agency contract and if the transaction was entered into within a reasonable period, after that contract terminated; or

    (b)   if, in accordance with the conditions mentioned in Article 7, the order of the third party reached the principal or the commercial agent before the agency contract terminated.

[4.196]
Article 9
A commercial agent shall not be entitled to the commission referred to in Article 7, if that commission is payable, pursuant to Article 8, to the previous commercial agent, unless it is equitable because of the circumstances for the commission to be shared between the commercial agents.

[4.197]
Article 10
1. The commission shall become due as soon as and to the extent that one of the following circumstances obtains—

    (a)   the principal has executed the transaction; or

    (b)   the principal should, according to his agreement with the third party, have executed the transaction; or

    (c)   the third party has executed the transaction.

2. The commission shall become due at the latest when the third party has executed his part of the transaction or should have done so if the principal had executed his part of the transaction, as he should have.

3. The commission shall be paid not later than on the last day of the month following the quarter in which it became due.

4. Agreements to derogate from paragraphs 2 and 3 to the detriment of the commercial agent shall not be permitted.

[4.198]
Article 11
1. The right to commission can be extinguished only if and to the extent that—

    —   it is established that the contract between the third party and the principal will not be executed, and

    —   that face is due to a reason for which the principal is not to blame.

2. Any commission which the commercial agent has already received shall be refunded if the right to it is extinguished.

3. Agreements to derogate from paragraph 1 to the detriment of the commercial agent shall not be permitted.

[4.199]
Article 12
1. The principal shall supply his commercial agent with a statement of the commission due, not later than the last day of the month following the quarter in which the commission has become due. This statement shall set out the main components used in calculating the amount of commission.

2. A commercial agent shall be entitled to demand that he be provided with all the information, and in particular an extract from the books, which is available to his principal and which he needs in order to check the amount of the commission due to him.

3. Agreements to derogate from paragraphs 1 and 2 to the detriment of the commercial agent shall not be permitted.

4. This Directive shall not conflict with the internal provisions of Member States which recognise the right of a commercial agent to inspect a principal's books.

CHAPTER IV
CONCLUSION AND TERMINATION OF THE AGENCY CONTRACT

[4.200]
Article 13
1.   Each party shall be entitled to receive from the other on request a signed written document setting out the terms of the agency contract including any terms subsequently agreed. Waiver of this right shall not be permitted.
2.   Notwithstanding paragraph 1 a Member State may provide that an agency contract shall not be valid unless evidenced in writing.

[4.201]
Article 14
An agency contract for a fixed period which continues to be performed by both parties after that period has expired shall be deemed to be converted into an agency contract for an indefinite period.

[4.202]
Article 15
1.   Where an agency contract is concluded for an indefinite period either party may terminate it by notice.
2.   The period of notice shall be one month for the first year of the contract, two months for the second year commenced, and three months for the third year commenced and subsequent years. The parties may not agree on shorter periods of notice.
3.   Member States may fix the period of notice at four months for the fourth year of the contract, five months for the fifth year and six months for the sixth and subsequent years. They may decide that the parties may not agree on shorter periods.
4.   If the parties agree on longer periods than those laid down in paragraphs 2 and 3, the period of notice to be observed by the principal must not be shorter than that to be observed by the commercial agent.
5.   Unless otherwise agreed by the parties, the end of the period of notice must coincide with the end of a calendar month.
6.   The provisions of this Article shall apply to an agency contract for a fixed period where it is converted under Article 14 into an agency contract for an indefinite period, subject to the proviso that the earlier fixed period must be taken into account in the calculation of the period of notice.

[4.203]
Article 16
Nothing in this Directive shall affect the application of the law of the Member States where the latter provides for the immediate termination of the agency contract—
   (a)   because of the failure of one party to carry out all or part of his obligations;
   (b)   where exceptional circumstances arise.

[4.204]
Article 17
1.   Member States shall take the measures necessary to ensure that the commercial agent is, after termination of the agency contract, indemnified in accordance with paragraph 2 or compensated for damage in accordance with paragraph 3.
2.
   (a)   The commercial agent shall be entitled to an indemnity if and to the extent that—
      —   he has brought the principal new customers or has significantly increased the volume of business with existing customers and the principal continues to derive substantial benefits from the business with such customers, and
      —   the payment of this indemnity is equitable having regard to all the circumstances and, in particular, the commission lost by the commercial agent on the business transacted with such customers. Member States may provide for such circumstances also to include the application or otherwise of a restraint of trade clause, within the meaning of Article 20;
   (b)   The amount of the indemnity may not exceed a figure equivalent to an indemnity for one year calculated from the commercial agent's average annual remuneration over the preceding five years and if the contract goes back less than five years the indemnity shall be calculated on the average for the period in question;
   (c)   The grant of such an indemnity shall not prevent the commercial agent from seeking damages.
3.   The commercial agent shall be entitled to compensation for the damage he suffers as a result of the termination, of his relations with the principal.
   Such damage shall be deemed to occur particularly when the termination takes place in circumstances—
      —   depriving the commercial agent of the commission which proper performance of the agency contract would have procured him whilst providing the principal with substantial benefits linked to the commercial agent's activities,

—   and/or which have not enabled the commercial agent to amortise the costs and expenses that he had incurred for the performance of the agency contract on the principal's advice.

4.   Entitlement to the indemnity as provided for in paragraph 2 or to compensation for damage as provided for under paragraph 3, shall also arise where the agency contract is terminated as a result of the commercial agent's death.

5.   The commercial agent shall lose his entitlement to the indemnity in the instances provided for in paragraph 2 or to compensation for damage in the instances provided for in paragraph 3, if within one year following termination of the contract he has not notified the principal that he intends pursuing his entitlement.

6.   The Commission shall submit to the Council, within eight years following the date of notification of this Directive, a report on the implementation of this Article, and shall if necessary submit to it proposals for amendments.

[4.205]
Article 18
The indemnity or compensation referred to in Article 17 shall not be payable—

  (a)   where the principal has terminated the agency contract because of default attributable to the commercial agent which would justify immediate termination of the agency contract under national law;

  (b)   where the commercial agent has terminated the agency contract, unless such termination is justified by circumstances attributable to the principal or on grounds of age, infirmity or illness of the commercial agent in consequence of which he cannot reasonably be required to continue his activities;

  (c)   where, with the agreement of the principal, the commercial agent assigns his rights and duties under the agency contract to another person.

[4.206]
Article 19
The parties may not derogate from Articles 17 and 18 to the detriment of the commercial agent before the agency contract expires.

[4.207]
Article 20
1.   For the purposes of this Directive, an agreement restricting the business activities of a commercial agent following termination of the agency contract is hereinafter referred to as a restraint of trade clause.

2.   A restraint of trade clause shall be valid only if and to the extent that—

  (a)   it is concluded in writing; and

  (b)   it relates to the geographical area or the group of customers and the geographical area entrusted to the commercial agent and to the kind of goods covered by his agency under the contract.

3.   A restraint of trade clause shall be valid for not more than two years after termination of the agency contract.

4.   This Article shall not affect provisions of national law which impose other restrictions on the validity or enforceability of restraint of trade clauses or which enable the courts to reduce the obligations on the parties resulting from such an agreement.

CHAPTER V
GENERAL AND FINAL PROVISIONS

[4.208]
Article 21
Nothing in this Directive shall require a Member State to provide for the disclosure of information where such disclosure would be contrary to public policy.

[4.209]
Article 22
1.   Member States shall bring into force the provisions necessary to comply with this Directive before 1 January 1990. They shall forthwith inform the Commission thereof. Such provisions shall apply at least to contracts concluded after their entry into force. They shall apply to contracts in operation by 1 January 1994 at the latest.

2.   As from the notification of this Directive, Member States shall communicate to the Commission the main laws, regulations and administrative provisions which they adopt in the field governed by this Directive.

3.   However, with regard to Ireland and the United Kingdom, 1 January 1990 referred to in paragraph 1 shall be replaced by 1 January 1994.

    With regard to Italy, 1 January 1990 shall be replaced by 1 January 1993 in the case of the obligations deriving from Article 17.

[4.210]
Article 23
This Directive is addressed to the Member States.

COUNCIL DIRECTIVE

(90/314/EEC)

of 13 June 1990

on package travel, package holidays and package tours

NOTES

Date of publication in OJ: OJ L158, 23.6.90, p 59.

This Directive has been implemented in the UK by the Package Travel, Package Holidays and Package Tours Regulations 1992, SI 1992/3288 at **[2.50]**.

THE COUNCIL OF THE EUROPEAN COMMUNITIES,

Having regard to the Treaty establishing the European Economic Community, and in particular Article 100a thereof,

Having regard to the proposal from the Commission,[1]

In cooperation with the European Parliament,[2]

Having regard to the opinion of the Economic and Social Committee,[3]

Whereas one of the main objectives of the Community is to complete the internal market, of which the tourist sector is an essential part;

Whereas the national laws of Member States concerning package travel, package holidays and package tours, hereinafter referred to as 'packages', show many disparities and national practices in this field are markedly different, which gives rise to obstacles to the freedom to provide services in respect of packages and distortions of competition amongst operators established in different Member States;

Whereas the establishment of common rules on packages will contribute to the elimination of these obstacles and thereby to the achievement of a common market in services, thus enabling operators established in one Member State to offer their services in other Member States and Community consumers to benefit from comparable conditions when buying a package in any Member State;

Whereas paragraph 36(b) of the Annex to the Council resolution of 19 May 1981 on a second programme of the European Economic Community for a consumer protection and information policy[4] invites the Commission to study, *inter alia*, tourism and, if appropriate, to put forward suitable proposals, with due regard for their significance for consumer protection and the effects of differences in Member States' legislation on the proper functioning of the common market;

Whereas in the resolution on a Community policy on tourism on 10 April 1984[5] the Council welcomed the Commission's initiative in drawing attention to the importance of tourism and took note of the Commission's initial guidelines for a Community policy on tourism;

Whereas the Commission communication to the Council entitled 'A New Impetus for Consumer Protection Policy', which was approved by resolution of the Council on 6 May 1986,[6] lists in paragraph 37, among the measures proposed by the Commission, the harmonization of legislation on packages;

Whereas tourism plays an increasingly important role in the economies of the Member States; whereas the package system is a fundamental part of tourism; whereas the package travel industry in Member States would be stimulated to greater growth and productivity if at least a minimum of common rules were adopted in order to give it a Community dimension; whereas this would not only produce benefits for Community citizens buying packages organized on the basis of those rules, but would attract tourists from outside the Community seeking the advantages of guaranteed standards in packages;

Whereas disparities in the rules protecting consumers in different Member States are a disincentive to consumers in one Member State from buying packages in another Member State;

Whereas this disincentive is particularly effective in deterring consumers from buying packages outside their own Member State, and more effective than it would be in relation to the acquisition of other services, having regard to the special nature of the services supplied in a package which generally involve the expenditure of substantial amounts of money in advance and the supply of the services in a State other than that in which the consumer is resident;

Whereas the consumer should have the benefit of the protection introduced by this Directive irrespective of whether he is a direct contracting party, a transferee or a member of a group on whose behalf another person has concluded a contract in respect of a package;

Whereas the organizer of the package and/or the retailer of it should be under obligation to ensure that in descriptive matter relating to packages which they respectively organize and sell, the information which is given is not misleading and brochures made available to consumers contain information which is comprehensible and accurate;

Whereas the consumer needs to have a record of the terms of contract applicable to the package; whereas this can conveniently be achieved by requiring that all the terms of the contract be stated in writing of such other documentary form as shall be comprehensible and accessible to him, and that he be given a copy thereof;

Whereas the consumer should be at liberty in certain circumstances to transfer to a willing third person a booking made by him for a package;

Whereas the price established under the contract should not in principle be subject to revision except where the possibility of upward or downward revision is expressly provided for in the contract; whereas that possibility should nonetheless be subject to certain conditions;

Whereas the consumer should in certain circumstances be free to withdraw before departure from a package travel contract;

Whereas there should be a clear definition of the rights available to the consumer in circumstances where the organizer of the package cancels it before the agreed date of departure;

Whereas if, after the consumer has departed, there occurs a significant failure of performance of the services for which he has contracted or the organizer perceives that he will be unable to procure a significant part of the services to be provided; the organizer should have certain obligations towards the consumer;

Whereas the organizer and/or retailer party to the contract should be liable to the consumer for the proper performance of the obligations arising from the contract; whereas, moreover, the organizer and/or retailer should be liable for the damage resulting for the consumer from failure to perform or improper performance of the contract unless the defects in the performance of the contract are attributable neither to any fault of theirs nor to that of another supplier of services;

Whereas in cases where the organizer and/or retailer is liable for failure to perform or improper performance of the services involved in the package, such liability should be limited in accordance with the international conventions governing such services, in particular the Warsaw Convention of 1929 in International Carriage by Air, the Berne Convention of 1961 on Carriage by Rail, the Athens Convention of 1974 on Carriage by Sea and the Paris Convention of 1962 on the Liability of Hotel-keepers; whereas, moreover, with regard to damage other than personal injury, it should be possible for liability also to be limited under the package contract provided, however, that such limits are not unreasonable;

Whereas certain arrangements should be made for the information of consumers and the handling of complaints;

Whereas both the consumer and the package travel industry would benefit if organizers and/or retailers were placed under an obligation to provide sufficient evidence of security in the event of insolvency;

Whereas Member States should be at liberty to adopt, or retain, more stringent provisions relating to package travel for the purpose of protecting the consumer,

---

NOTES

1   OJ C96, 12.4.88, p 5.

2   OJ C69, 20.3.89, p 102 and OJ C149, 18.6.90.

3   OJ C102, 24.4.89, p 27.

4   OJ C165, 23.6.81, p 24.

5   OJ C115, 30.4.84, p 1.

6   OJ C118, 7.3.86, p 28.

HAS ADOPTED THIS DIRECTIVE—

[4.211]
Article 1
The purpose of this Directive is to approximate the laws, regulations and administrative provisions of the Member States relating to packages sold or offered for sale in the territory of the Community.

[4.212]
Article 2
For the purposes of this Directive—

1.   'package' means the pre-arranged combination of not fewer than two of the following when sold or offered for sale at an inclusive price and when the service covers a period of more than twenty-four hours or includes overnight accommodation—
      (a)   transport;
      (b)   accommodation;
      (c)   other tourist services not ancillary to transport or accommodation and accounting for a significant proportion of the package.

      The separate billing of various components of the same package shall not absolve the organiser or retailer from the obligations under this Directive;

2.   'organiser' means the person who, other than occasionally, organises packages and sells or offers them for sale, whether directly or through a retailer;

3.   'retailer' means the person who sells or offers for sale the package put together by the organiser;

4.   'consumer' means the person who takes or agrees to take the package ('the principal contractor'), or any person on whose behalf the principal contractor agrees to purchase the package ('the other beneficiaries') or any person to whom the principal contractor or any of the other beneficiaries transfers the package ('the transferee');

5.   'contract' means the agreement linking the consumer to the organiser and/or the retailer.

[4.213]
Article 3
1.   Any descriptive matter concerning a package and supplied by the organiser or the retailer to the consumer, the price of the package and any other conditions applying to the contract must not contain any misleading information.
2.   When a brochure is made available to the consumer, it shall indicate in a legible, comprehensible and accurate manner both the price and adequate information concerning—
   (a)   the destination and the means, characteristics and categories of transport used;
   (b)   the type of accommodation, its location, category or degree of comfort and its main features, its approval and tourist classification under the rules of the host Member State concerned;
   (c)   the meal plan;
   (d)   the itinerary;
   (e)   general information on passport and visa requirements for nationals of the Member State or States concerned and health formalities required for the journey and the stay;
   (f)   either the monetary amount or the percentage of the price which is to be paid on account, and the timetable for payment of the balance;
   (g)   whether a minimum number of persons is required for the package to take place and, if so, the deadline for informing the consumer in the event of cancellation.
The particulars contained in the brochure are binding on the organiser or retailer, unless—
—   changes in such particulars have been clearly communicated to the consumer before conclusion of the contract, in which case the brochure shall expressly state so,
—   changes are made later following an agreement between the parties to the contract.

[4.214]
Article 4
1.
   (a)   The organiser and/or the retailer shall provide the consumer, in writing or any other appropriate form, before the contract is concluded, with general information on passport and visa requirements applicable to nationals of the Member State or States concerned and in particular on the periods for obtaining them, as well as with information on the health formalities required for the journey and the stay;
   (b)   The organiser and/or retailer shall also provide the consumer, in writing or any other appropriate form, with the following information in good time before the start of the journey—
      (i)   the times and places of intermediate stops and transport connections as well as details of the place to be occupied by the traveller, eg cabin or berth on ship, sleeper compartment on train;
      (ii)   the name, address and telephone number of the organiser's and/or retailer's local representative or, failing that, of local agencies on whose assistance a consumer in difficulty could call.
      Where no such representatives or agencies exist, the consumer must in any case be provided with an emergency telephone number or any other information that will enable him to contract the organiser and/or the retailer;
      (iii)   in the case of journeys or stays abroad by minors, information enabling direct contact to be established with the child or the person responsible at the child's place of stay;
      (iv)   information on the optional conclusion of an insurance policy to cover the cost of cancellation by the consumer or the cost of assistance, including repatriation, in the event of accident or illness.
2.   Member States shall ensure that in relation to the contract the following principles apply—
   (a)   depending on the particular package, the contract shall contain at least the elements listed in the Annex;
   (b)   all the terms of the contract are set out in writing or such other form as is comprehensible and accessible to the consumer and must be communicated to him before the conclusion of the contract; the consumer is given a copy of these terms;
   (c)   the provision under (b) shall not preclude the belated conclusion of last-minute reservations or contracts.
3.   Where the consumer is prevented from proceeding with the package, he may transfer his booking, having first given the organiser or the retailer reasonable notice of his intention before departure, to a person who satisfies all the conditions applicable to the package. The transferor of

the package and the transferee shall be jointly and severally liable to the organiser or retailer party to the contract for payment of the balance due and for any additional costs arising from such transfer.

4.

(a)   The prices laid down in the contract shall not be subject to revision unless the contract expressly provides for the possibility of upward or downward revision and states precisely how the revised price is to be calculated, and solely to allow for variations in—

— transportation costs, including the cost of fuel,
— dues, taxes or fees chargeable for certain services, such as landing taxes or embarkation or disembarkation fees at ports and airports,
— the exchange rates applied to the particular package.

(b)   During the twenty days prior to the departure date stipulated, the price stated in the contract shall not be increased.

5.   If the organiser finds that before the departure he is constrained to alter significantly any of the essential terms, such as the price, he shall notify the consumer as quickly as possible in order to enable him to take appropriate decisions and in particular—

— either to withdraw from the contract without penalty,
— or to accept a rider to the contract specifying the alterations made and their impact on the price.

The consumer shall inform the organiser or the retailer of his decision as soon as possible.

6.   If the consumer withdraws from the contract pursuant to paragraph 5, or if, for whatever cause, other than the fault of the consumer, the organiser cancels the package before the agreed date of departure, the consumer shall be entitled—

(a)   either to take a substitute package of equivalent or higher quality where the organiser and/or retailer is able to offer him such a substitute. If the replacement package offered is of lower quality, the organiser shall refund the difference in price to the consumer;

(b)   or to be repaid as soon as possible all sums paid by him under the contract.

In such a case, he shall be entitled, if appropriate, to be compensated by either the organiser or the retailer, whichever the relevant Member State's law requires, for non-performance of the contract, except where—

(i)   cancellation is on the grounds that the number of persons enrolled for the package is less than the minimum number required and the consumer is informed of the cancellation, in writing, within the period indicated in the package description; or

(ii)   cancellation, excluding overbooking, is for reasons of *force majeure*, ie unusual and unforeseeable circumstances beyond the control of the party by whom it is pleaded, the consequences of which could not have been avoided even if all due care had been exercised.

7.   Where, after departure, a significant proportion of the services contracted for is not provided or the organiser perceives that he will be unable to procure a significant proportion of the services to be provided, the organiser shall make suitable alternative arrangements, at no extra cost to the consumer, for the continuation of the package and where appropriate compensate the consumer for the difference between the services offered and those supplied.

If it is impossible to make such arrangements or these are not accepted by the consumer for good reasons, the organiser shall, where appropriate, provide the consumer, at no extra cost, with equivalent transport back to the place of departure, or to another return-point to which the consumer has agreed and shall, where appropriate, compensate the consumer.

[4.215]
Article 5

1.   Member States shall take the necessary steps to ensure that the organiser and/or retailer party to the contract is liable to the consumer for the proper performance of the obligations arising from the contract, irrespective of whether such obligations are to be performed by that organiser and/or retailer or by other suppliers of services without prejudice to the right of the organiser and/or retailer to pursue those other suppliers of services.

2.   With regard to the damage resulting for the consumer from the failure to perform or the improper performance of the contract, Member States shall take the necessary steps to ensure that the organiser and/or retailer is/are liable unless such failure to perform or improper performance is attributable neither to any fault of theirs nor to that of another supplier of services, because—

— the failures which occur in the performance of the contract are attributable to the consumer,
— such failures are attributable to a third party unconnected with the provision of the services contracted for, and are unforeseeable or unavoidable,
— such failures are due to a case of *force majeure* such as that defined in Article 4(6), second subparagraph (ii), or to an event which the organiser and/or retailer or the supplier of services, even with all due care, could not foresee or forestall.

In the cases referred to in the second and third indents, the organiser and/or retailer party to the contract shall be required to give prompt assistance to a consumer in difficulty.

In the matter of damages arising from the non-performance or improper performance of the services involved in the package, the Member States may allow compensation to be limited in accordance with the international conventions governing such services.

In the matter of damage other than personal injury resulting from the non-performance or improper performance of the services involved in the package, the Member States may allow compensation to be limited under the contract. Such limitation shall not be unreasonable.

3.   Without prejudice to the fourth subparagraph of paragraph 2, there may be no exclusion by means of a contractual clause from the provisions of paragraphs 1 and 2.

4.   The consumer must communicate any failure in the performance of a contract which he perceives on the spot to the supplier of the services concerned and to the organiser and/or retailer in writing or any other appropriate form at the earliest opportunity.

This obligation must be stated clearly and explicitly in the contract.

[4.216]
Article 6
In cases of complaint, the organiser and/or retailer or his local representative, if there is one, must make prompt efforts to find appropriate solutions.

[4.217]
Article 7
The organiser and/or retailer party to the contract shall provide sufficient evidence of security for the refund of money paid over and for the repatriation of the consumer in the event of insolvency.

[4.218]
Article 8
Member States may adopt or return more stringent provisions in the field covered by this Directive to protect the consumer.

[4.219]
Article 9
1.   Member States shall bring into force the measures necessary to comply with this Directive before 31 December 1992. They shall forthwith inform the Commission thereof.

2.   Member States shall communicate to the Commission the texts of the main provisions of national law which they adopt in the field governed by this Directive. The Commission shall inform the other Member States thereof.

[4.220]
Article 10
This Directive is addressed to the Member States.

ANNEX
[4.221]
Elements to be included in the contract if relevant to the particular package;

(a)   the travel destination(s) and, where periods of stay are involved, the relevant periods, with dates;

(b)   the means, characteristics and categories of transport to be used, the dates, times and points of departure and return;

(c)   where the package includes accommodation, its location, its tourist category or degree of comfort, its main features, its compliance with the rules of the host Member State concerned and the meal plan;

(d)   whether a minimum number of persons is required for the package to take place and, if so, the deadline for informing the consumer in the event of cancellation;

(e)   the itinerary;

(f)   visits, excursions or other services which are included in the total price agreed for the package;

(g)   the name and address of the organiser, the retailer and, where appropriate, the insurer;

(h)   the price of the package, an indication of the possibility of price revisions under Article 4(4) and an indication of any dues, taxes or fees chargeable for certain services (landing, embarkation or disembarkation fees at ports and airports, tourist taxes) where such costs are not included in the package;

(i)   the payment schedule and method of payment;

(j)   special requirements which the consumer has communicated to the organiser or retailer when making the booking, and which both have accepted;

(k)   periods within which the consumer must make any complaint concerning failure to perform or improper performance of the contract.

COUNCIL DIRECTIVE

(93/13/EEC)

of 5 April 1993

on unfair terms in consumer contracts

NOTES

Date of publication in OJ: OJ L95, 21.4.93, p 29.

This Directive has been implemented in the UK by the Unfair Terms in Consumer Contracts Regulations 1999, SI 1999/2083 at **[2.121]**.

THE COUNCIL OF THE EUROPEAN COMMUNITIES,

Having regard to the Treaty establishing the European Economic Community, and in particular Article 100A thereof,

Having regard to the proposal from the Commission,[1]

In co-operation with the European Parliament,[2]

Having regard to the opinion of the Economic and Social Committee,[3]

Whereas it is necessary to adopt measures with the aim of progressively establishing the internal market before 31 December 1992; whereas the internal market comprises an area without internal frontiers in which goods, persons, services and capital move freely;

Whereas the laws of Member States relating to the terms of contract between the seller of goods or supplier of services, on the one hand, and the consumer of them, on the other hand, show many disparities, with the result that the national markets for the sale of goods and services to consumers differ from each other and that distortions of competition may arise amongst the sellers and suppliers, notably when they sell and supply in other Member States;

Whereas, in particular, the laws of Member States relating to unfair terms in consumer contracts show marked divergences;

Whereas it is the responsibility of the Member States to ensure that contracts concluded with consumers do not contain unfair terms;

Whereas, generally speaking, consumers do not know the rules of law which, in Member States other than their own, govern contracts for the sale of goods or services; whereas this lack of awareness may deter them from direct transactions for the purchase of goods or services in another Member State;

Whereas, in order to facilitate the establishment of the internal market and to safeguard the citizen in his role as consumer when acquiring goods and services under contracts which are governed by the laws of Member States other than his own, it is essential to remove unfair terms from those contracts;

Whereas sellers of goods and suppliers of services will thereby be helped in their task of selling goods and supplying services, both at home and throughout the internal market; whereas competition will thus be stimulated, so contributing to increased choice for Community citizens as consumers;

Whereas the two Community programmes for a consumer protection and information policy[4] underlined the importance of safeguarding consumers in the matter of unfair terms of contract; whereas this protection ought to be provided by laws and regulations which are either harmonised at Community level or adopted directly at that level;

Whereas in accordance with the principle laid down under the heading "Protection of the economic interests of the consumers", as stated in those programmes: "acquirers of goods and services should be protected against the abuse of power by the seller or supplier, in particular against one-sided standard contracts and the unfair exclusion of essential rights in contracts";

Whereas more effective protection of the consumer can be achieved by adopting uniform rules of law in the matter of unfair terms; whereas those rules should apply to all contracts concluded between sellers or suppliers and consumers; whereas as a result inter alia contracts relating to employment, contracts relating to succession rights, contracts relating to rights under family law and contracts relating to the incorporation and organisation of companies or partnership agreements must be excluded from this Directive;

Whereas the consumer must receive equal protection under contracts concluded by word of mouth and written contracts regardless, in the latter case, of whether the terms of the contract are contained in one or more documents;

Whereas, however, as they now stand, national laws allow only partial harmonisation to be envisaged; whereas, in particular, only contractual terms which have not been individually negotiated are covered by this Directive; whereas Member States should have the option, with due regard for the Treaty, to afford consumers a higher level of protection through national provisions that are more stringent than those of this Directive;

Whereas the statutory or regulatory provisions of the Member States which directly or indirectly determine the terms of consumer contracts are presumed not to contain unfair terms; whereas, therefore, it does not appear to be necessary to subject the terms which reflect mandatory statutory or regulatory provisions and the principles or provisions of international conventions to which the

Member States or the Community are party; whereas in that respect the wording "mandatory statutory or regulatory provisions" in Article 1(2) also covers rules which, according to the law, shall apply between the contracting parties provided that no other arrangements have been established;

Whereas Member States must however ensure that unfair terms are not included, particularly because this Directive also applies to trades, business or professions of a public nature;

Whereas it is necessary to fix in a general way the criteria for assessing the unfair character of contract terms;

Whereas the assessment, according to the general criteria chosen, of the unfair character of terms, in particular in sale or supply activities of a public nature providing collective services which take account of solidarity among users, must be supplemented by a means of making an overall evaluation of the different interests involved; whereas this constitutes the requirement of good faith; whereas, in making an assessment of good faith, particular regard shall be had to the strength of the bargaining positions of the parties, whether the consumer had an inducement to agree to the term and whether the goods or services were sold or supplied to the special order of the consumer; whereas the requirement of good faith may be satisfied by the seller or supplier where he deals fairly and equitably with the other party whose legitimate interests he has to take into account;

Whereas, for the purposes of this Directive, the annexed list of terms can be of indicative value only and, because of the cause of the minimal character of the Directive, the scope of these terms may be the subject of amplification or more restrictive editing by the Member States in their national laws;

Whereas the nature of goods or services should have an influence on assessing the unfairness of contractual terms;

Whereas, for the purposes of this Directive, assessment of unfair character shall not be made of terms which describe the main subject matter of the contract nor the quality/price ratio of the goods or services supplied; whereas the main subject matter of the contract and the price/quality ratio may nevertheless be taken into account in assessing the fairness of other terms; whereas it follows, inter alia, that in insurance contracts, the terms which clearly define or circumscribe the insured risk and the insurer's liability shall not be subject to such assessment since these restrictions are taken into account in calculating the premium paid by the consumer;

Whereas contracts should be drafted in plain, intelligible language, the consumer should actually be given an opportunity to examine all the terms and, if in doubt, the interpretation most favourable to the consumer should prevail;

Whereas Member States should ensure that unfair terms are not used in contracts concluded with consumers by a seller or supplier and that if, nevertheless, such terms are so used, they will not bind the consumer, and the contract will continue to bind the parties upon those terms if it is capable of continuing in existence without the unfair provisions;

Whereas there is a risk that, in certain cases, the consumer may be deprived of protection under this Directive by designating the law of a non-Member country as the law applicable to the contract; whereas provisions should therefore be included in this Directive designed to avert this risk;

Whereas persons or organisations, if regarded under the law of a Member State as having a legitimate interest in the matter, must have facilities for initiating proceedings concerning terms of contract drawn up for general use in contracts concluded with consumers, and in particular unfair terms, either before a court or before an administrative authority competent to decide upon complaints or to initiate appropriate legal proceedings; whereas this possibility does not, however, entail prior verification of the general conditions obtaining in individual economic sectors;

Whereas the courts or administrative authorities of the Member States must have at their disposal adequate and effective means of preventing the continued application of unfair terms in consumer contracts,

NOTES

1   OJ C73, 24.3.92, p 7.
2   OJ C326, 16.12.91, p 108 and OJ C21, 25.1.93.
3   OJ C159, 17.6.91, p 34.
4   OJ C92, 25.4.75 and OJ C133, 3.6.81, p 1.

HAS ADOPTED THIS DIRECTIVE:

[4.222]
Article 1
1.   The purpose of this Directive is to approximate the laws, regulations and administrative provisions of the Member States relating to unfair terms in contracts concluded between a seller or supplier and a consumer.
2.   The contractual terms which reflect mandatory statutory or regulatory provisions and the provisions or principles of international conventions to which the Member States or the Community are party, particularly in the transport area, shall not be subject to the provisions of this Directive.

[4.223]
Article 2

For the purposes of this Directive—
  (a) "unfair terms" means the contractual terms defined in Article 3;
  (b) "consumer" means any natural person who, in contracts covered by this Directive, is acting for purposes which are outside his trade, business or profession;
  (c) "seller or supplier" means any natural or legal person who, in contracts covered by this Directive, is acting for purposes relating to his trade, business or profession, whether publicly owned or privately owned.

[4.224]
Article 3

1. A contractual term which has not been individually negotiated shall be regarded as unfair if, contrary to the requirement of good faith, it causes a significant imbalance in the parties' rights and obligations arising under the contract, to the detriment of the consumer.
2. A term shall always be regarded as not individually negotiated where it has been drafted in advance and the consumer has therefore not been able to influence the substance of the term, particularly in the context of a pre-formulated standard contract.

The fact that certain aspects of a term or one specific term have been individually negotiated shall not exclude the application of this Article to the rest of a contract if an overall assessment of the contract indicates that it is nevertheless a pre-formulated standard contract.

Where any seller or supplier claims that a standard term has been individually negotiated, the burden of proof in this respect shall be incumbent on him.
3. The Annex shall contain an indicative and non-exhaustive list of the terms which may be regarded as unfair.

[4.225]
Article 4

1. Without prejudice to Article 7, the unfairness of a contractual term shall be assessed, taking into account the nature of the goods or services for which the contract was concluded and by referring, at the time of conclusion of the contract, to all the circumstances attending the conclusion of the contract and to all the other terms of the contract or of another contract on which it is dependent.
2. Assessment of the unfair nature of the terms shall relate neither to the definition of the main subject matter of the contract nor to the adequacy of the price and remuneration, on the one hand, as against the services or goods supplies in exchange, on the other, in so far as these terms are in plain intelligible language.

[4.226]
Article 5

In the case of contracts where all or certain terms offered to the consumer are in writing, these terms must always be drafted in plain, intelligible language. Where there is doubt about the meaning of a term, the interpretation most favourable to the consumer shall prevail. This rule on interpretation shall not apply in the context of the procedures laid down in Article 7(2).

[4.227]
Article 6

1. Member States shall lay down that unfair terms used in a contract concluded with a consumer by a seller or supplier shall, as provided for under their national law, not be binding on the consumer and that the contract shall continue to bind the parties upon those terms if it is capable of continuing in existence without the unfair terms.
2. Member States shall take the necessary measures to ensure that the consumer does not lose the protection granted by this Directive by virtue of the choice of the law of a non-Member country as the law applicable to the contract if the latter has a close connection with the territory of the Member States.

[4.228]
Article 7

1. Member States shall ensure that, in the interests of consumers and of competitors, adequate and effective means exist to prevent the continued use of unfair terms in contracts concluded with consumers by sellers or suppliers.
2. The means referred to in paragraph 1 shall include provisions whereby persons or organisations, having a legitimate interest under national law in protecting consumers, may take action according to the national law concerned before the courts or before competent administrative bodies for a decision as to whether contractual terms drawn up for general use are unfair, so that they can apply appropriate and effective means to prevent the continued use of such terms.
3. With due regard for national laws, the legal remedies referred to in paragraph 2 may be directed separately or jointly against a number of sellers or suppliers from the same economic sector or their associations which use or recommend the use of the same general contractual terms or similar terms.

[4.229]
Article 8
Member States may adopt or retain the most stringent provisions compatible with the Treaty in the area covered by this Directive, to ensure a maximum degree of protection for the consumer.

[4.230]
[Article 8a
1.   Where a Member State adopts provisions in accordance with Article 8, it shall inform the Commission thereof, as well as of any subsequent changes, in particular where those provisions:
—   extend the unfairness assessment to individually negotiated contractual terms or to the adequacy of the price or remuneration; or,
—   contain lists of contractual terms which shall be considered as unfair,
2.   The Commission shall ensure that the information referred to in paragraph 1 is easily accessible to consumers and traders, inter alia, on a dedicated website.
3.   The Commission shall forward the information referred to in paragraph 1 to the other Member States and the European Parliament. The Commission shall consult stakeholders on that information.]

NOTES
Inserted by European Parliament and Council Directive 2011/83/EU, Art 32.

[4.231]
Article 9
The Commission shall present a report to the European Parliament and to the Council concerning the application of this Directive five years at the latest after the date in Article 10(1).

[4.232]
Article 10
1.   Member States shall bring into force the laws, regulations and administrative provisions necessary to comply with this Directive no later than 31 December 1994. They shall forthwith inform the Commission thereof.
    These provisions shall be applicable to all contracts concluded after 31 December 1994.
2.   When Member States adopt these measures, they shall contain a reference to this Directive or shall be accompanied by such reference on the occasion of their official publication. The methods of making such a reference shall be laid down by the Member States.
3.   Member States shall communicate the main provisions of national law which they adopt in the field covered by this Directive to the Commission.

[4.233]
Article 11
This Directive is addressed to the Member States.

ANNEX
TERMS REFERRED TO IN ARTICLE 3(3)

[4.234]
1.   Terms which have the object or effect of—
(a)   excluding or limiting the legal liability of a seller or supplier in the event of the death of a consumer or personal injury to the latter resulting from an act or omission of that seller or supplier;
(b)   inappropriately excluding or limiting the legal rights of the consumer *vis-à-vis* the seller or supplier or another party in the event of total or partial non-performance or inadequate performance by the seller or supplier of any of the contractual obligations, including the option of offsetting a debt owed to the seller or supplier against any claim which the consumer may have against him;
(c)   making an agreement binding on the consumer whereas provision of services by the seller or supplier is subject to a condition whose realisation depends on his own will alone;
(d)   permitting the seller or supplier to retain sums paid by the consumer where the latter decides not to conclude or perform the contract, without providing for the consumer to receive compensation of an equivalent amount from the seller or supplier where the latter is the party cancelling the contract;
(e)   requiring any consumer who fails to fulfil his obligation to pay a disproportionately high sum in compensation;
(f)   authorising the seller or supplier to dissolve the contract on a discretionary basis where the same facility is not granted to the consumer, or permitting the seller or supplier to retain the sums paid for services not yet supplied by him where it is the seller or supplier himself who dissolves the contract;
(g)   enabling the seller or supplier to terminate a contract of indeterminate duration without reasonable notice except where there are serious grounds for doing so;

(h)   automatically extending a contract of fixed duration where the consumer does not indicate otherwise, when the deadline fixed for the consumer to express this desire not to extend the contract is unreasonably early;

(i)   irrevocably binding the consumer to terms with which he had no real opportunity of becoming acquainted before the conclusion of the contract;

(j)   enabling the seller or supplier to alter the terms of the contract unilaterally without a valid reason which is specified in the contract;

(k)   enabling the seller or supplier to alter unilaterally without a valid reason any characteristics of the product or service to be provided;

(l)   providing for the price of goods to be determined at the time of delivery or allowing a seller of goods or supplier of services to increase their price without in both cases giving the consumer the corresponding right to cancel the contract if the final price is too high in relation to the price agreed when the contract was concluded;

(m)   giving the seller or supplier the right to determine whether the goods or services supplied are in conformity with the contract, or giving him the exclusive right to interpret any term of the contract;

(n)   limiting the seller's or supplier's obligation to respect commitments undertaken by his agents or making his commitments subject to compliance with a particular formality;

(o)   obliging the consumer to fulfil all his obligations where the seller or supplier does not perform his;

(p)   giving the seller or supplier the possibility of transferring his rights and obligations under the contract, where this may serve to reduce the guarantees for the consumer, without the latter's agreement;

(q)   excluding or hindering the consumer's right to take legal action or exercise any other legal remedy, particularly by requiring the consumer to take disputes exclusively to arbitration not covered by legal provisions, unduly restricting the evidence available to him or imposing on him a burden of proof which, according to the applicable law, should lie with another party to the contract.

2.   Scope of subparagraphs (g), (j) and (l)—

(a)   Subparagraph (g) is without hindrance to terms by which a supplier of financial services reserves the right to terminate unilaterally a contract of indeterminate duration without notice where there is a valid reason, provided that the supplier is required to inform the other contracting party or parties thereof immediately.

(b)   Subparagraph (j) is without hindrance to terms under which a supplier of financial services reserves the right to alter the rate of interest payable by the consumer or due to the latter, or the amount of other charges for financial services without notice where there is a valid reason, provided that the supplier is required to inform the other contracting party or parties thereof at the earliest opportunity and that the latter are free to dissolve the contract immediately.

Subparagraph (j) is also without hindrance to terms under which a seller or supplier reserves the right to alter unilaterally the conditions of a contract of indeterminate duration, provided that he is required to inform the consumer with reasonable notice and that the consumer is free to dissolve the contract.

(c)   Subparagraphs (g), (j) and (l) do not apply to—
    —   transactions in transferable securities, financial instruments and other products or services where the price is linked to fluctuations in a stock exchange quotation or index or a financial market rate that the seller or supplier does not control;
    —   contracts for the purchase or sale of foreign currency, traveller's cheques or international money orders denominated in foreign currency;

(d)   Subparagraph (l) is without hindrance to price-indexation clauses, where lawful, provided that the method by which prices vary is explicitly described.

DIRECTIVE OF THE EUROPEAN PARLIAMENT AND OF THE COUNCIL

(98/6/EC)

of 16 February 1998

on consumer protection in the indication of the prices of products offered to consumers

NOTES

Date of publication in OJ: OJ L80, 18.3.98, p 27.

This Directive has been implemented in the UK by the Price Marking Order 2004, SI 2004/102 at **[2.299]**.

THE EUROPEAN PARLIAMENT AND THE COUNCIL OF THE EUROPEAN UNION,

Having regard to the Treaty establishing the European Community, and in particular Article 129a(2) thereof,

Having regard to the proposal from the Commission,[1]

Having regard to the opinion of the Economic and Social Committee,[2]

Acting in accordance with the procedure laid down in Article 189b of the Treaty,[3] in the light of the joint text approved by the Conciliation Committee on 9 December 1997,

(1) Whereas transparent operation of the market and correct information is of benefit to consumer protection and healthy competition between enterprises and products;

(2) Whereas consumers must be guaranteed a high level of protection; whereas the Community should contribute thereto by specific action which supports and supplements the policy pursued by the Member States regarding precise, transparent and unambiguous information for consumers on the prices of products offered to them;

(3) Whereas the Council Resolution of 14 April 1975 on a preliminary programme of the European Economic Community for a consumer protection and information policy[4] and the Council Resolution of 19 May 1981 on a second programme of the European Economic Community for a consumer protection and information policy[5] provide for the establishment of common principles for indicating prices;

(4) Whereas these principles have been established by Directive 79/581/EEC concerning the indication of prices of certain foodstuffs[6] and Directive 88/314/EEC concerning the indication of prices of non-food products;[7]

(5) Whereas the link between indication of the unit price of products and their pre-packaging in pre-established quantities or capacities corresponding to the values of the ranges adopted at Community level has proved overly complex to apply; whereas it is thus necessary to abandon this link in favour of a new simplified mechanism and in the interest of the consumer, without prejudice to the rules governing packaging standardisation;

(6) Whereas the obligation to indicate the selling price and the unit price contributes substantially to improving consumer information, as this is the easiest way to enable consumers to evaluate and compare the price of products in an optimum manner and hence to make informed choices on the basis of simple comparisons;

(7) Whereas, therefore, there should be a general obligation to indicate both the selling price and the unit price for all products except for products sold in bulk, where the selling price cannot be determined until the consumer indicates how much of the product is required;

(8) Whereas it is necessary to take into account the fact that certain products are customarily sold in quantities different from one kilogramme, one litre, one metre, one square metre or one cubic metre; whereas it is thus appropriate to allow Member States to authorise that the unit price refer to a different single unit of quantity, taking into account the nature of the product and the quantities in which it is customarily sold in the Member State concerned;

(9) Whereas the obligation to indicate the unit price may entail an excessive burden for certain small retail businesses under certain circumstances; whereas Member States should therefore be allowed to refrain from applying this obligation during an appropriate transitional period;

(10) Whereas Member States should also remain free to waive the obligation to indicate the unit price in the case of products for which such price indication would not be useful or would be liable to cause confusion for instance when indication of the quantity is not relevant for price comparison purposes, or when different products are marketed in the same packaging;

(11) Whereas in the case of non-food products, Member States, with a view to facilitating application of the mechanism implemented, are free to draw up a list of products or categories of products for which the obligation to indicate the unit price remains applicable;

(12) Whereas Community-level rules can ensure homogenous and transparent information that will benefit all consumers in the context of the internal market; whereas the new, simplified approach is both necessary and sufficient to achieve this objective;

(13) Whereas Member States must make sure that the system is effective; whereas the transparency of the system should also be maintained when the euro is introduced; whereas, to that end, the maximum number of prices to be indicated should be limited;

(14) Whereas particular attention should be paid to small retail businesses; whereas, to this end, the Commission should, in its report on the application of this Directive to be presented no later than three years after the date referred to in Article 11(1), take particular account of the experience gleaned in the application of the Directive by small retail businesses, *inter alia*, regarding technological developments and the introduction of the single currency; whereas this report, having regard to the transitional period referred to in Article 6, should be accompanied by a proposal,

NOTES

[1]   OJ C260, 5.10.95, p 5 and OJ C249, 27.8.96, p 2.

[2]   OJ C82, 19.3.96, p 32.

[3]   Opinion of the European Parliament of 18 April 1996 (OJ C141, 13.5.96, p 191). Council Common Position of

27 September 1996 (OJ C333, 7.11.96, p 7) and Decision of the European Parliament of 18 February 1997 (OJ C85, 17.3.97, p 26). Decision of the European Parliament of 16 December 1997 and Decision of the Council of 18 December 1997.

⁴   OJ C92, 25.4.75, p 1.

⁵   OJ C133, 3.6.81, p 1.

⁶   OJ L158, 26.6.79, p 19. Directive as last amended by Directive 95/58/EC (OJ L299, 12.12.95, p 11).

⁷   OJ L142, 9.6.88, p 19. Directive as last amended by Directive 95/58/EC (OJ L299, 12.12.95, p 11).

HAVE ADOPTED THIS DIRECTIVE—

[4.235]
Article 1
The purpose of this Directive is to stipulate indication of the selling price and the price per unit of measurement of products offered by traders to consumers in order to improve consumer information and to facilitate comparison of prices.

[4.236]
Article 2
For the purposes of this Directive—
  (a) *selling price* shall mean the final price for a unit of the product, or a given quantity of the product, including VAT and all other taxes;
  (b) *unit price* shall mean the final price, including VAT and all other taxes, for one kilogramme, one litre, one metre, one square metre or one cubic metre of the product or a different single unit of quantity which is widely and customarily used in the Member State concerned in the marketing of specific products;
  (c) *products sold in bulk* shall mean products which are not pre-packaged and are measured in the presence of the consumer;
  (d) *trader* shall mean any natural or legal person who sells or offers for sale products which fall within his commercial or professional activity;
  (e) *consumer* shall mean any natural person who buys a product for purposes that do not fall within the sphere of his commercial or professional activity.

[4.237]
Article 3
1.   The selling price and the unit price shall be indicated for all products referred to in Article 1, the indication of the unit price being subject to the provisions of Article 5. The unit price need not be indicated if it is identical to the sales price.
2.   Member States may decide not to apply paragraph 1 to—
  —   products supplied in the course of the provision of a service,
  —   sales by auction and sales of works of art and antiques.
3.   For products sold in bulk, only the unit price must be indicated.
4.   Any advertisement which mentions the selling price of products referred to in Article 1 shall also indicate the unit price subject to Article 5.

[4.238]
Article 4
1.   The selling price and the unit price must be unambiguous, easily identifiable and clearly legible. Member States may provide that the maximum number of prices to be indicated be limited.
2.   The unit price shall refer to a quantity declared in accordance with national and Community provisions.
   Where national or Community provisions require the indication of the net weight and the net drained weight for certain pre-packed products, it shall be sufficient to indicate the unit price of the net drained weight.

[4.239]
Article 5
1.   Member States may waive the obligation to indicate the unit price of products for which such indication would not be useful because of the products' nature or purpose or would be liable to create confusion.
2.   With a view to implementing paragraph 1, Member States may, in the case of non-food products, establish a list of the products or product categories to which the obligation to indicate the unit price shall remain applicable.

[4.240]
Article 6
If the obligation to indicate the unit price were to constitute an excessive burden for certain small retail businesses because of the number of products on sale, the sales area, the nature of the place of sale, specific conditions of sale where the product is not directly accessible for the consumer or certain forms of business, such as certain types of itinerant trade, Member States may, for a transitional period following the date referred to in Article 11(1), provide that the obligation to

indicate the unit price of products other than those sold in bulk, which are sold in the said businesses, shall not apply, subject to Article 12.

[4.241]
Article 7
Member States shall provide appropriate measures to inform all persons concerned of the national law transposing this Directive.

[4.242]
Article 8
Member States shall lay down penalties for infringements of national provisions adopted in application of this Directive, and shall take all necessary measures to ensure that these are enforced. These penalties must be effective, proportionate and dissuasive.

[4.243]
Article 9
1.   The transition period of nine years referred to in Article 1 of Directive 95/58/EC of the European Parliament and of the Council of 29 November 1995 amending Directive 79/581/EEC on consumer protection in the indication of the prices of foodstuffs and Directive 88/314/EEC on consumer protection in the indication of the prices of non-food products[1] shall be extended until the date referred to in Article 11(1) of this Directive.
2.   Directives 79/581/EEC and 88/314/EEC shall be repealed with effect from the date referred to in Article 11(1) of this Directive.

NOTES
  [1]   OJ L299, 12.12.95, p 11.

[4.244]
Article 10
This Directive shall not prevent Member States from adopting or maintaining provisions which are more favourable as regards consumer information and comparison of prices, without prejudice to their obligations under the Treaty.

[4.245]
Article 11
1.   Member States shall bring into force the laws, regulations and administrative provisions necessary to comply with this Directive not later than 18 March 2000. They shall forthwith inform the Commission thereof. The provisions adopted shall be applicable as of that date.
    When Member States adopt these measures, they shall contain a reference to this Directive or shall be accompanied by such reference at the time of their official publication. The methods of making such reference shall be laid down by Member States.
2.   Member States shall communicate to the Commission the text of the provisions of national law which they adopt in the field governed by this Directive.
3.   Member States shall communicate the provisions governing the penalties provided for in Article 8, and any later amendments thereto.

[4.246]
Article 12
The Commission shall, not later than three years after the date referred to in Article 11(1), submit to the European Parliament and the Council a comprehensive report on the application of this Directive, in particular on the application of Article 6, accompanied by a proposal.
    The European Parliament and the Council shall, on this basis, re-examine the provisions of Article 6 and shall act, in accordance with the Treaty, within three years of the presentation by the Commission of the proposal referred to in the first paragraph.

[4.247]
Article 13
This Directive shall enter into force on the day of its publication in the *Official Journal of the European Communities*.

[4.248]
Article 14
This Directive is addressed to the Member States.

[4.249]
Commission Declaration
Article 2(b)—
The Commission takes the view that the expression 'for one kilogramme, one litre, one metre, one square metre or cubic metre of the product or a different single unit of quantity' in Article 2(b) also applies to products sold by individual item or singly.

[4.250]
Commission Declaration
Article 12, first paragraph—
The Commission considers that Article 12, first paragraph, of the Directive cannot be construed as calling into question its right of initiative.

DIRECTIVE OF THE EUROPEAN PARLIAMENT AND OF THE COUNCIL

(99/44/EC)
of 25 May 1999

on certain aspects of the sale of consumer goods and associated guarantees

NOTES
Date of publication in OJ: OJ L171, 7.7.99, p 12.
This Directive has been implemented in the UK by the Sale and Supply of Goods to Consumers Regulations 2002, SI 2002/3045 at **[2.253]**.

THE EUROPEAN PARLIAMENT AND THE COUNCIL OF THE EUROPEAN UNION,
Having regard to the Treaty establishing the European Community, and in particular Article 95 thereof,
Having regard to the proposal from the Commission,[1]
Having regard to the opinion of the Economic and Social Committee,[2]
Acting in accordance with the procedure laid down in Article 251 of the Treaty in the light of the joint text approved by the Conciliation Committee on 18 May 1999,[3]

(1) Whereas Article 153(1) and (3) of the Treaty provides that the Community should contribute to the achievement of a high level of consumer protection by the measures it adopts pursuant to Article 95 thereof;

(2) Whereas the internal market comprises an area without internal frontiers in which the free movement of goods, persons, services and capital is guaranteed; whereas free movement of goods concerns not only transactions by persons acting in the course of a business but also transactions by private individuals; whereas it implies that consumers resident in one Member State should be free to purchase goods in the territory of another Member State on the basis of a uniform minimum set of fair rules governing the sale of consumer goods;

(3) Whereas the laws of the Member States concerning the sale of consumer goods are somewhat disparate, with the result that national consumer goods markets differ from one another and that competition between sellers may be distorted;

(4) Whereas consumers who are keen to benefit from the large market by purchasing goods in Member States other than their State of residence play a fundamental role in the completion of the internal market; whereas the artificial reconstruction of frontiers and the compartmentalisation of markets should be prevented; whereas the opportunities available to consumers have been greatly broadened by new communication technologies which allow ready access to distribution systems in other Member States or in third countries; whereas, in the absence of minimum harmonisation of the rules governing the sale of consumer goods, the development of the sale of goods through the medium of new distance communication technologies risks being impeded;

(5) Whereas the creation of a common set of minimum rules of consumer law, valid no matter where goods are purchased within the Community, will strengthen consumer confidence and enable consumers to make the most of the internal market;

(6) Whereas the main difficulties encountered by consumers and the main source of disputes with sellers concern the non-conformity of goods with the contract; whereas it is therefore appropriate to approximate national legislation governing the sale of consumer goods in this respect, without however impinging on provisions and principles of national law relating to contractual and non-contractual liability;

(7) Whereas the goods must, above all, conform with the contractual specifications; whereas the principle of conformity with the contract may be considered as common to the different national legal traditions; whereas in certain national legal traditions it may not be possible to rely solely on this principle to ensure a minimum level of protection for the consumer; whereas under such legal traditions, in particular, additional national provisions may be useful to ensure that the consumer is protected in cases where the parties have agreed no specific contractual terms or where the parties have concluded contractual terms or agreements which directly or indirectly waive or restrict the rights of the consumer and which, to the extent that these rights result from this Directive, are not binding on the consumer;

(8) Whereas, in order to facilitate the application of the principle of conformity with the contract, it is useful to introduce a rebuttable presumption of conformity with the contract covering the most

common situations; whereas that presumption does not restrict the principle of freedom of contract; whereas, furthermore, in the absence of specific contractual terms, as well as where the minimum protection clause is applied, the elements mentioned in this presumption may be used to determine the lack of conformity of the goods with the contract; whereas the quality and performance which consumers can reasonably expect will depend *inter alia* on whether the goods are new or second-hand; whereas the elements mentioned in the presumption are cumulative; whereas, if the circumstances of the case render any particular element manifestly inappropriate, the remaining elements of the presumption nevertheless still apply;

(9)   Whereas the seller should be directly liable to the consumer for the conformity of the goods with the contract; whereas this is the traditional solution enshrined in the legal orders of the Member States; whereas nevertheless the seller should be free, as provided for by national law, to pursue remedies against the producer, a previous seller in the same chain of contracts or any other intermediary, unless he has renounced that entitlement; whereas this Directive does not affect the principle of freedom of contract between the seller, the producer, a previous seller or any other intermediary; whereas the rules governing against whom and how the seller may pursue such remedies are to be determined by national law;

(10)   Whereas, in the case of non-conformity of the goods with the contract, consumers should be entitled to have the goods restored to conformity with the contract free of charge, choosing either repair or replacement, or, failing this, to have the price reduced or the contract rescinded;

(11)   Whereas the consumer in the first place may require the seller to repair the goods or to replace them unless those remedies are impossible or disproportionate; whereas whether a remedy is disproportionate should be determined objectively; whereas a remedy would be disproportionate if it imposed, in comparison with the other remedy, unreasonable costs; whereas, in order to determine whether the costs are unreasonable, the costs of one remedy should be significantly higher than the costs of the other remedy;

(12)   Whereas in cases of a lack of conformity, the seller may always offer the consumer, by way of settlement, any available remedy; whereas it is for the consumer to decide whether to accept or reject this proposal;

(13)   Whereas, in order to enable consumers to take advantage of the internal market and to buy consumer goods in another Member State, it should be recommended that, in the interests of consumers, the producers of consumer goods that are marketed in several Member States attach to the product a list with at least one contact address in every Member State where the product is marketed;

(14)   Whereas the references to the time of delivery do not imply that Member States have to change their rules on the passing of the risk;

(15)   Whereas Member States may provide that any reimbursement to the consumer may be reduced to take account of the use the consumer has had of the goods since they were delivered to him; whereas the detailed arrangements whereby rescission of the contract is effected may be laid down in national law;

(16)   Whereas the specific nature of second-hand goods makes it generally impossible to replace them; whereas therefore the consumer's right of replacement is generally not available for these goods; whereas for such goods, Member States may enable the parties to agree a shortened period of liability;

(17)   Whereas it is appropriate to limit in time the period during which the seller is liable for any lack of conformity which exists at the time of delivery of the goods; whereas Member States may also provide for a limitation on the period during which consumers can exercise their rights, provided such a period does not expire within two years from the time of delivery; whereas where, under national legislation, the time when a limitation period starts is not the time of delivery of the goods, the total duration of the limitation period provided for by national law may not be shorter than two years from the time of delivery;

(18)   Whereas Member States may provide for suspension or interruption of the period during which any lack of conformity must become apparent and of the limitation period, where applicable and in accordance with their national law, in the event of repair, replacement or negotiations between seller and consumer with a view to an amicable settlement;

(19)   Whereas Member States should be allowed to set a period within which the consumer must inform the seller of any lack of conformity; whereas Member States may ensure a higher level of protection for the consumer by not introducing such an obligation; whereas in any case consumers throughout the Community should have at least two months in which to inform the seller that a lack of conformity exists;

(20)   Whereas Member States should guard against such a period placing at a disadvantage consumers shopping across borders; whereas all Member States should inform the Commission of their use of this provision; whereas the Commission should monitor the effect of the varied application of this provision on consumers and on the internal market; whereas information on the use made of this provision by a Member State should be available to the other Member States and to consumers and consumer organisations throughout the Community; whereas a summary of the

situation in all Member States should therefore be published in the *Official Journal of the European Communities*;

(21)   Whereas, for certain categories of goods, it is current practice for sellers and producers to offer guarantees on goods against any defect which becomes apparent within a certain period; whereas this practice can stimulate competition; whereas, while such guarantees are legitimate marketing tools, they should not mislead the consumer; whereas, to ensure that consumers are not misled, guarantees should contain certain information, including a statement that the guarantee does not affect the consumer's legal rights;

(22)   Whereas the parties may not, by common consent, restrict or waive the rights granted to consumers, since otherwise the legal protection afforded would be thwarted; whereas this principle should apply also to clauses which imply that the consumer was aware of any lack of conformity of the consumer goods existing at the time the contract was concluded; whereas the protection granted to consumers under this Directive should not be reduced on the grounds that the law of a non-member State has been chosen as being applicable to the contract;

(23)   Whereas legislation and case-law in this area in the various Member States show that there is growing concern to ensure a high level of consumer protection; whereas, in the light of this trend and the experience acquired in implementing this Directive, it may be necessary to envisage more far-reaching harmonisation, notably by providing for the producer's direct liability for defects for which he is responsible;

(24)   Whereas Member States should be allowed to adopt or maintain in force more stringent provisions in the field covered by this Directive to ensure an even higher level of consumer protection;

(25)   Whereas, according to the Commission recommendation of 30 March 1998 on the principles applicable to the bodies responsible for out-of-court settlement of consumer disputes,[4] Member States can create bodies that ensure impartial and efficient handling of complaints in a national and cross-border context and which consumers can use as mediators;

(26)   Whereas it is appropriate, in order to protect the collective interests of consumers, to add this Directive to the list of Directives contained in the Annex to Directive 98/27/EC of the European Parliament and of the Council of 19 May 1998 on injunctions for the protection of consumers' interests,[5]

NOTES

[1]   OJ C307, 16.10.1996, p 8 and OJ C148, 14.5.1998, p 12.

[2]   OJ C66, 3.3.1997, p 5.

[3]   Opinion of the European Parliament of 10 March 1998 (OJ C104, 6.4.1998, p 30), Council Common Position of 24 September 1998 (OJ C333, 30.10.1998, p 46) and Decision of the European Parliament of 17 December 1998 (OJ C98, 9.4.1999, p 226). Decision of the European Parliament of 5 May 1999. Council Decision of 17 May 1999.

[4]   OJ L115, 17.4.1998, p 31.

[5]   OJ L166, 11.6.1998, p 51.

HAVE ADOPTED THIS DIRECTIVE—

[4.251]
Article 1
Scope and definitions
1.   The purpose of this Directive is the approximation of the laws, regulations and administrative provisions of the Member States on certain aspects of the sale of consumer goods and associated guarantees in order to ensure a uniform minimum level of consumer protection in the context of the internal market.
2.   For the purposes of this Directive—
    (a)   *consumer:* shall mean any natural person who, in the contracts covered by this Directive, is acting for purposes which are not related to his trade, business or profession;
    (b)   *consumer goods:* shall mean any tangible movable item, with the exception of—
       —   goods sold by way of execution or otherwise by authority of law,
       —   water and gas where they are not put up for sale in a limited volume or set quantity,
       —   electricity;
    (c)   *seller:* shall mean any natural or legal person who, under a contract, sells consumer goods in the course of his trade, business or profession;
    (d)   *producer:* shall mean the manufacturer of consumer goods, the importer of consumer goods into the territory of the Community or any person purporting to be a producer by placing his name, trade mark or other distinctive sign on the consumer goods;
    (e)   *guarantee:* shall mean any undertaking by a seller or producer to the consumer, given without extra charge, to reimburse the price paid or to replace, repair or handle consumer goods in any way if they do not meet the specifications set out in the guarantee statement or in the relevant advertising;

(f)   *repair:* shall mean, in the event of lack of conformity, bringing consumer goods into conformity with the contract of sale.

3.   Member States may provide that the expression "consumer goods" does not cover second-hand goods sold at public auction where consumers have the opportunity of attending the sale in person.

4.   Contracts for the supply of consumer goods to be manufactured or produced shall also be deemed contracts of sale for the purpose of this Directive.

[4.252]
Article 2
Conformity with the contract

1.   The seller must deliver goods to the consumer which are in conformity with the contract of sale.

2.   Consumer goods are presumed to be in conformity with the contract if they—
   (a)   comply with the description given by the seller and possess the qualities of the goods which the seller has held out to the consumer as a sample or model;
   (b)   are fit for any particular purpose for which the consumer requires them and which he made known to the seller at the time of conclusion of the contract and which the seller has accepted;
   (c)   are fit for the purposes for which goods of the same type are normally used;
   (d)   show the quality and performance which are normal in goods of the same type and which the consumer can reasonably expect, given the nature of the goods and taking into account any public statements on the specific characteristics of the goods made about them by the seller, the producer or his representative, particularly in advertising or on labelling.

3.   There shall be deemed not to be a lack of conformity for the purposes of this Article if, at the time the contract was concluded, the consumer was aware, or could not reasonably be unaware of, the lack of conformity, or if the lack of conformity has its origin in materials supplied by the consumer.

4.   The seller shall not be bound by public statements, as referred to in paragraph 2(d) if he—
   —   shows that he was not, and could not reasonably have been, aware of the statement in question,
   —   shows that by the time of conclusion of the contract the statement had been corrected, or
   —   shows that the decision to buy the consumer goods could not have been influenced by the statement.

5.   Any lack of conformity resulting from incorrect installation of the consumer goods shall be deemed to be equivalent to lack of conformity of the goods if installation forms part of the contract of sale of the goods and the goods were installed by the seller or under his responsibility. This shall apply equally if the product, intended to be installed by the consumer, is installed by the consumer and the incorrect installation is due to a shortcoming in the installation instructions.

[4.253]
Article 3
Rights of the consumer

1.   The seller shall be liable to the consumer for any lack of conformity which exists at the time the goods were delivered.

2.   In the case of a lack of conformity, the consumer shall be entitled to have the goods brought into conformity free of charge by repair or replacement, in accordance with paragraph 3, or to have an appropriate reduction made in the price or the contract rescinded with regard to those goods, in accordance with paragraphs 5 and 6.

3.   In the first place, the consumer may require the seller to repair the goods or he may require the seller to replace them, in either case free of charge, unless this is impossible or disproportionate.

   A remedy shall be deemed to be disproportionate if it imposes costs on the seller which, in comparison with the alternative remedy, are unreasonable, taking into account—
   —   the value the goods would have if there were no lack of conformity,
   —   the significance of the lack of conformity, and
   —   whether the alternative remedy could be completed without significant inconvenience to the consumer.

   Any repair or replacement shall be completed within a reasonable time and without any significant inconvenience to the consumer, taking account of the nature of the goods and the purpose for which the consumer required the goods.

4.   The terms "free of charge" in paragraphs 2 and 3 refer to the necessary costs incurred to bring the goods into conformity, particularly the cost of postage, labour and materials.

5.   The consumer may require an appropriate reduction of the price or have the contract rescinded—
   —   if the consumer is entitled to neither repair nor replacement, or
   —   if the seller has not completed the remedy within a reasonable time, or
   —   if the seller has not completed the remedy without significant inconvenience to the consumer.

6.   The consumer is not entitled to have the contract rescinded if the lack of conformity is minor.

[4.254]
Article 4
Right of redress
Where the final seller is liable to the consumer because of a lack of conformity resulting from an act or omission by the producer, a previous seller in the same chain of contracts or any other intermediary, the final seller shall be entitled to pursue remedies against the person or persons liable in the contractual chain. The person or persons liable against whom the final seller may pursue remedies, together with the relevant actions and conditions of exercise, shall be determined by national law.

[4.255]
Article 5
Time limits
1. The seller shall be held liable under Article 3 where the lack of conformity becomes apparent within two years as from delivery of the goods. If, under national legislation, the rights laid down in Article 3(2) are subject to a limitation period, that period shall not expire within a period of two years from the time of delivery.
2. Member States may provide that, in order to benefit from his rights, the consumer must inform the seller of the lack of conformity within a period of two months from the date on which he detected such lack of conformity.
   Member States shall inform the Commission of their use of this paragraph. The Commission shall monitor the effect of the existence of this option for the Member States on consumers and on the internal market.
   Not later than 7 January 2003, the Commission shall prepare a report on the use made by Member States of this paragraph. This report shall be published in the *Official Journal of the European Communities*.
3. Unless proved otherwise, any lack of conformity which becomes apparent within six months of delivery of the goods shall be presumed to have existed at the time of delivery unless this presumption is incompatible with the nature of the goods or the nature of the lack of conformity.

[4.256]
Article 6
Guarantees
1. A guarantee shall be legally binding on the offerer under the conditions laid down in the guarantee statement and the associated advertising.
2. The guarantee shall—
   — state that the consumer has legal rights under applicable national legislation governing the sale of consumer goods and make clear that those rights are not affected by the guarantee,
   — set out in plain intelligible language the contents of the guarantee and the essential particulars necessary for making claims under the guarantee, notably the duration and territorial scope of the guarantee as well as the name and address of the guarantor.
3. On request by the consumer, the guarantee shall be made available in writing or feature in another durable medium available and accessible to him.
4. Within its own territory, the Member State in which the consumer goods are marketed may, in accordance with the rules of the Treaty, provide that the guarantee be drafted in one or more languages which it shall determine from among the official languages of the Community.
5. Should a guarantee infringe the requirements of paragraphs 2, 3 or 4, the validity of this guarantee shall in no way be affected, and the consumer can still rely on the guarantee and require that it be honoured.

[4.257]
Article 7
Binding nature
1. Any contractual terms or agreements concluded with the seller before the lack of conformity is brought to the seller's attention which directly or indirectly waive or restrict the rights resulting from this Directive shall, as provided for by national law, not be binding on the consumer.
   Member States may provide that, in the case of second-hand goods, the seller and consumer may agree contractual terms or agreements which have a shorter time period for the liability of the seller than that set down in Article 5(1). Such period may not be less than one year.
2. Member States shall take the necessary measures to ensure that consumers are not deprived of the protection afforded by this Directive as a result of opting for the law of a non-member State as the law applicable to the contract where the contract has a close connection with the territory of the Member States.

[4.258]
Article 8
National law and minimum protection
1. The rights resulting from this Directive shall be exercised without prejudice to other rights which the consumer may invoke under the national rules governing contractual or non-contractual liability.

2.   Member States may adopt or maintain in force more stringent provisions, compatible with the Treaty in the field covered by this Directive, to ensure a higher level of consumer protection.

[4.259]
[Article 8a
Reporting requirements
1.   Where, in accordance with Article 8(2), a Member State adopts more stringent consumer protection provisions than those provided for in Article 5(1) to (3) and in Article 7(1), it shall inform the Commission thereof, as well as of any subsequent changes.
2.   The Commission shall ensure that the information referred to in paragraph 1 is easily accessible to consumers and traders, inter alia, on a dedicated website.
3.   The Commission shall forward the information referred to in paragraph 1 to the other Member States and the European Parliament. The Commission shall consult stakeholders on that information.]

NOTES
   Inserted by European Parliament and Council Directive 2011/83/EU, Art 33.

[4.260]
Article 9
Member States shall take appropriate measures to inform the consumer of the national law transposing this Directive and shall encourage, where appropriate, professional organisations to inform consumers of their rights.

Article 10   *(Spent: amended Directive 98/27/EC, Annex (repealed).)*

[4.261]
Article 11
Transposition
1.   Member States shall bring into force the laws, regulations and administrative provisions necessary to comply with this Directive not later than 1 January 2002. They shall forthwith inform the Commission thereof.
   When Member States adopt these measures, they shall contain a reference to this Directive, or shall be accompanied by such reference at the time of their official publication. The procedure for such reference shall be adopted by Member States.
2.   Member States shall communicate to the Commission the provisions of national law which they adopt in the field covered by this Directive.

[4.262]
Article 12
Review
The Commission shall, not later than 7 July 2006, review the application of this Directive and submit to the European Parliament and the Council a report. The report shall examine, *inter alia*, the case for introducing the producer's direct liability and, if appropriate, shall be accompanied by proposals.

[4.263]
Article 13
Entry into force
This Directive shall enter into force on the day of its publication in the *Official Journal of the European Communities*.

[4.264]
Article 14
This Directive is addressed to the Member States.

DIRECTIVE OF THE EUROPEAN PARLIAMENT AND OF THE COUNCIL

(2000/31/EC)

of 8 June 2000

on certain legal aspects of information society services, in particular electronic commerce, in the Internal Market (Directive on electronic commerce)

NOTES
   Date of publication in OJ: OJ L178, 17.7.2000, p 1.
   This Directive has been implemented in the UK by the Electronic Commerce (Financial Services and Markets) Regulations 2002, SI 2002/1775 and by the Electronic Commerce (EC Directive) Regulations 2002, SI 2002/2013 at **[2.231]**.

THE EUROPEAN PARLIAMENT AND THE COUNCIL OF THE EUROPEAN UNION,

Having regard to the Treaty establishing the European Community, and in particular Articles 47(2), 55 and 95 thereof,

Having regard to the proposal from the Commission,[1]

Having regard to the opinion of the Economic and Social Committee,[2]

Acting in accordance with the procedure laid down in Article 251 of the Treaty,[3]

Whereas—

(1) The European Union is seeking to forge ever closer links between the States and peoples of Europe, to ensure economic and social progress; in accordance with Article 14(2) of the Treaty, the internal market comprises an area without internal frontiers in which the free movements of goods, services and the freedom of establishment are ensured; the development of information society services within the area without internal frontiers is vital to eliminating the barriers which divide the European peoples.

(2) The development of electronic commerce within the information society offers significant employment opportunities in the Community, particularly in small and medium-sized enterprises, and will stimulate economic growth and investment in innovation by European companies, and can also enhance the competitiveness of European industry, provided that everyone has access to the Internet.

(3) Community law and the characteristics of the Community legal order are a vital asset to enable European citizens and operators to take full advantage, without consideration of borders, of the opportunities afforded by electronic commerce; this Directive therefore has the purpose of ensuring a high level of Community legal integration in order to establish a real area without internal borders for information society services.

(4) It is important to ensure that electronic commerce could fully benefit from the internal market and therefore that, as with Council Directive 89/552/EEC of 3 October 1989 on the coordination of certain provisions laid down by law, regulation or administrative action in Member States concerning the pursuit of television broadcasting activities,[4] a high level of Community integration is achieved.

(5) The development of information society services within the Community is hampered by a number of legal obstacles to the proper functioning of the internal market which make less attractive the exercise of the freedom of establishment and the freedom to provide services; these obstacles arise from divergences in legislation and from the legal uncertainty as to which national rules apply to such services; in the absence of coordination and adjustment of legislation in the relevant areas, obstacles might be justified in the light of the case-law of the Court of Justice of the European Communities; legal uncertainty exists with regard to the extent to which Member States may control services originating from another Member State.

(6) In the light of Community objectives, of Articles 43 and 49 of the Treaty and of secondary Community law, these obstacles should be eliminated by coordinating certain national laws and by clarifying certain legal concepts at Community level to the extent necessary for the proper functioning of the internal market; by dealing only with certain specific matters which give rise to problems for the internal market, this Directive is fully consistent with the need to respect the principle of subsidiarity as set out in Article 5 of the Treaty.

(7) In order to ensure legal certainty and consumer confidence, this Directive must lay down a clear and general framework to cover certain legal aspects of electronic commerce in the internal market.

(8) The objective of this Directive is to create a legal framework to ensure the free movement of information society services between Member States and not to harmonise the field of criminal law as such.

(9) The free movement of information society services can in many cases be a specific reflection in Community law of a more general principle, namely freedom of expression as enshrined in Article 10(1) of the Convention for the Protection of Human Rights and Fundamental Freedoms, which has been ratified by all the Member States; for this reason, directives covering the supply of information society services must ensure that this activity may be engaged in freely in the light of that Article, subject only to the restrictions laid down in paragraph 2 of that Article and in Article 46(1) of the Treaty; this Directive is not intended to affect national fundamental rules and principles relating to freedom of expression.

(10) In accordance with the principle of proportionality, the measures provided for in this Directive are strictly limited to the minimum needed to achieve the objective of the proper functioning of the internal market; where action at Community level is necessary, and in order to guarantee an area which is truly without internal frontiers as far as electronic commerce is concerned, the Directive must ensure a high level of protection of objectives of general interest, in particular the protection of minors and human dignity, consumer protection and the protection of public health; according to Article 152 of the Treaty, the protection of public health is an essential component of other Community policies.

(11) This Directive is without prejudice to the level of protection for, in particular, public health

and consumer interests, as established by Community acts; amongst others, Council Directive 93/13/EEC of 5 April 1993 on unfair terms in consumer contracts[5] and Directive 97/7/EC of the European Parliament and of the Council of 20 May 1997 on the protection of consumers in respect of distance contracts[6] form a vital element for protecting consumers in contractual matters; those Directives also apply in their entirety to information society services; that same Community acquis, which is fully applicable to information society services, also embraces in particular Council Directive 84/450/EEC of 10 September 1984 concerning misleading and comparative advertising,[7] Council Directive 87/102/EEC of 22 December 1986 for the approximation of the laws, regulations and administrative provisions of the Member States concerning consumer credit,[8] Council Directive 93/22/EEC of 10 May 1993 on investment services in the securities field,[9] Council Directive 90/314/EEC of 13 June 1990 on package travel, package holidays and package tours,[10] Directive 98/6/EC of the European Parliament and of the Council of 16 February 1998 on consumer production in the indication of prices of products offered to consumers,[11] Council Directive 92/59/EEC of 29 June 1992 on general product safety,[12] Directive 94/47/EC of the European Parliament and of the Council of 26 October 1994 on the protection of purchasers in respect of certain aspects on contracts relating to the purchase of the right to use immovable properties on a timeshare basis,[13] Directive 98/27/EC of the European Parliament and of the Council of 19 May 1998 on injunctions for the protection of consumers' interests,[14] Council Directive 85/374/EEC of 25 July 1985 on the approximation of the laws, regulations and administrative provisions concerning liability for defective products,[15] Directive 1999/44/EC of the European Parliament and of the Council of 25 May 1999 on certain aspects of the sale of consumer goods and associated guarantees,[16] the future Directive of the European Parliament and of the Council concerning the distance marketing of consumer financial services and Council Directive 92/28/EEC of 31 March 1992 on the advertising of medicinal products;[17] this Directive should be without prejudice to Directive 98/43/EC of the European Parliament and of the Council of 6 July 1998 on the approximation of the laws, regulations and administrative provisions of the Member States relating to the advertising and sponsorship of tobacco products[18] adopted within the framework of the internal market, or to directives on the protection of public health; this Directive complements information requirements established by the abovementioned Directives and in particular Directive 97/7/EC.

(12) It is necessary to exclude certain activities from the scope of this Directive, on the grounds that the freedom to provide services in these fields cannot, at this stage, be guaranteed under the Treaty or existing secondary legislation; excluding these activities does not preclude any instruments which might prove necessary for the proper functioning of the internal market; taxation, particularly value added tax imposed on a large number of the services covered by this Directive, must be excluded from the scope of this Directive.

(13) This Directive does not aim to establish rules on fiscal obligations nor does it pre-empt the drawing up of Community instruments concerning fiscal aspects of electronic commerce.

(14) The protection of individuals with regard to the processing of personal data is solely governed by Directive 95/46/EC of the European Parliament and of the Council of 24 October 1995 on the protection of individuals with regard to the processing of personal data and on the free movement of such data[19] and Directive 97/66/EC of the European Parliament and of the Council of 15 December 1997 concerning the processing of personal data and the protection of privacy in the telecommunications sector[20] which are fully applicable to information society services; these Directives already establish a Community legal framework in the field of personal data and therefore it is not necessary to cover this issue in this Directive in order to ensure the smooth functioning of the internal market, in particular the free movement of personal data between Member States; the implementation and application of this Directive should be made in full compliance with the principles relating to the protection of personal data, in particular as regards unsolicited commercial communication and the liability of intermediaries; this Directive cannot prevent the anonymous use of open networks such as the Internet.

(15) The confidentiality of communications is guaranteed by Article 5 Directive 97/66/EC; in accordance with that Directive, Member States must prohibit any kind of interception or surveillance of such communications by others than the senders and receivers, except when legally authorised.

(16) The exclusion of gambling activities from the scope of application of this Directive covers only games of chance, lotteries and betting transactions, which involve wagering a stake with monetary value; this does not cover promotional competitions or games where the purpose is to encourage the sale of goods or services and where payments, if they arise, serve only to acquire the promoted goods or services.

(17) The definition of information society services already exists in Community law in Directive 98/34/EC of the European Parliament and of the Council of 22 June 1998 laying down a procedure for the provision of information in the field of technical standards and regulations and of rules on information society services[21] and in Directive 98/84/EC of the European Parliament and of the Council of 20 November 1998 on the legal protection of services based on, or consisting of, conditional access;[22] this definition covers any service normally provided for remuneration, at a distance, by means of electronic equipment for the processing (including digital compression) and storage of data, and at the individual request of a recipient of a service; those services referred to in

the indicative list in Annex V to Directive 98/34/EC which do not imply data processing and storage are not covered by this definition.

(18) Information society services span a wide range of economic activities which take place on-line; these activities can, in particular, consist of selling goods on-line; activities such as the delivery of goods as such or the provision of services off-line are not covered; information society services are not solely restricted to services giving rise to on-line contracting but also, in so far as they represent an economic activity, extend to services which are not remunerated by those who receive them, such as those offering on-line information or commercial communications, or those providing tools allowing for search, access and retrieval of data; information society services also include services consisting of the transmission of information via a communication network, in providing access to a communication network or in hosting information provided by a recipient of the service; television broadcasting within the meaning of Directive EEC/89/552 and radio broadcasting are not information society services because they are not provided at individual request; by contrast, services which are transmitted point to point, such as video-on-demand or the provision of commercial communications by electronic mail are information society services; the use of electronic mail or equivalent individual communications for instance by natural persons acting outside their trade, business or profession including their use for the conclusion of contracts between such persons is not an information society service; the contractual relationship between an employee and his employer is not an information society service; activities which by their very nature cannot be carried out at a distance and by electronic means, such as the statutory auditing of company accounts or medical advice requiring the physical examination of a patient are not information society services.

(19) The place at which a service provider is established should be determined in conformity with the case-law of the Court of Justice according to which the concept of establishment involves the actual pursuit of an economic activity through a fixed establishment for an indefinite period; this requirement is also fulfilled where a company is constituted for a given period; the place of establishment of a company providing services via an Internet website is not the place at which the technology supporting its website is located or the place at which its website is accessible but the place where it pursues its economic activity; in cases where a provider has several places of establishment it is important to determine from which place of establishment the service concerned is provided; in cases where it is difficult to determine from which of several places of establishment a given service is provided, this is the place where the provider has the centre of his activities relating to this particular service.

(20) The definition of "recipient of a service" covers all types of usage of information society services, both by persons who provide information on open networks such as the Internet and by persons who seek information on the Internet for private or professional reasons.

(21) The scope of the coordinated field is without prejudice to future Community harmonisation relating to information society services and to future legislation adopted at national level in accordance with Community law; the coordinated field covers only requirements relating to on-line activities such as on-line information, on-line advertising, online shopping, on-line contracting and does not concern Member States' legal requirements relating to goods such as safety standards, labelling obligations, or liability for goods, or Member States' requirements relating to the delivery or the transport of goods, including the distribution of medicinal products; the coordinated field does not cover the exercise of rights of pre-emption by public authorities concerning certain goods such as works of art.

(22) Information society services should be supervised at the source of the activity, in order to ensure an effective protection of public interest objectives; to that end, it is necessary to ensure that the competent authority provides such protection not only for the citizens of its own country but for all Community citizens; in order to improve mutual trust between Member States, it is essential to state clearly this responsibility on the part of the Member State where the services originate; moreover, in order to effectively guarantee freedom to provide services and legal certainty for suppliers and recipients of services, such information society services should in principle be subject to the law of the Member State in which the service provider is established.

(23) This Directive neither aims to establish additional rules on private international law relating to conflicts of law nor does it deal with the jurisdiction of Courts; provisions of the applicable law designated by rules of private international law must not restrict the freedom to provide information society services as established in this Directive.

(24) In the context of this Directive, notwithstanding the rule on the control at source of information society services, it is legitimate under the conditions established in this Directive for Member States to take measures to restrict the free movement of information society services.

(25) National courts, including civil courts, dealing with private law disputes can take measures to derogate from the freedom to provide information society services in conformity with conditions established in this Directive.

(26) Member States, in conformity with conditions established in this Directive, may apply their national rules on criminal law and criminal proceedings with a view to taking all investigative and other measures necessary for the detection and prosecution of criminal offences, without there being

a need to notify such measures to the Commission.

(27)   This Directive, together with the future Directive of the European Parliament and of the Council concerning the distance marketing of consumer financial services, contributes to the creating of a legal framework for the on-line provision of financial services; this Directive does not pre-empt future initiatives in the area of financial services in particular with regard to the harmonisation of rules of conduct in this field; the possibility for Member States, established in this Directive, under certain circumstances of restricting the freedom to provide information society services in order to protect consumers also covers measures in the area of financial services in particular measures aiming at protecting investors.

(28)   The Member States' obligation not to subject access to the activity of an information society service provider to prior authorisation does not concern postal services covered by Directive 97/67/EC of the European Parliament and of the Council of 15 December 1997 on common rules for the development of the internal market of Community postal services and the improvement of quality of service[23] consisting of the physical delivery of a printed electronic mail message and does not affect voluntary accreditation systems, in particular for providers of electronic signature certification service.

(29)   Commercial communications are essential for the financing of information society services and for developing a wide variety of new, charge-free services; in the interests of consumer protection and fair trading, commercial communications, including discounts, promotional offers and promotional competitions or games, must meet a number of transparency requirements; these requirements are without prejudice to Directive 97/7/EC; this Directive should not affect existing Directives on commercial communications, in particular Directive 98/43/EC.

(30)   The sending of unsolicited commercial communications by electronic mail may be undesirable for consumers and information society service providers and may disrupt the smooth functioning of interactive networks; the question of consent by recipient of certain forms of unsolicited commercial communications is not addressed by this Directive, but has already been addressed, in particular, by Directive 97/7/EC and by Directive 97/66/EC; in Member States which authorise unsolicited commercial communications by electronic mail, the setting up of appropriate industry filtering initiatives should be encouraged and facilitated; in addition it is necessary that in any event unsolicited commercial communities are clearly identifiable as such in order to improve transparency and to facilitate the functioning of such industry initiatives; unsolicited commercial communications by electronic mail should not result in additional communication costs for the recipient.

(31)   Member States which allow the sending of unsolicited commercial communications by electronic mail without prior consent of the recipient by service providers established in their territory have to ensure that the service providers consult regularly and respect the opt-out registers in which natural persons not wishing to receive such commercial communications can register themselves.

(32)   In order to remove barriers to the development of cross-border services within the Community which members of the regulated professions might offer on the Internet, it is necessary that compliance be guaranteed at Community level with professional rules aiming, in particular, to protect consumers or public health; codes of conduct at Community level would be the best means of determining the rules on professional ethics applicable to commercial communication; the drawing-up or, where appropriate, the adaptation of such rules should be encouraged without prejudice to the autonomy of professional bodies and associations.

(33)   This Directive complements Community law and national law relating to regulated professions maintaining a coherent set of applicable rules in this field.

(34)   Each Member State is to amend its legislation containing requirements, and in particular requirements as to form, which are likely to curb the use of contracts by electronic means; the examination of the legislation requiring such adjustment should be systematic and should cover all the necessary stages and acts of the contractual process, including the filing of the contract; the result of this amendment should be to make contracts concluded electronically workable; the legal effect of electronic signatures is dealt with by Directive 1999/93/EC of the European Parliament and of the Council of 13 December 1999 on a Community framework for electronic signatures;[24] the acknowledgement of receipt by a service provider may take the form of the on-line provision of the service paid for.

(35)   This Directive does not affect Member States' possibility of maintaining or establishing general or specific legal requirements for contracts which can be fulfilled by electronic means, in particular requirements concerning secure electronic signatures.

(36)   Member States may maintain restrictions for the use of electronic contracts with regard to contracts requiring by law the involvement of courts, public authorities, or professions exercising public authority; this possibility also covers contracts which require the involvement of courts, public authorities, or professions exercising public authority in order to have an effect with regard to third parties as well as contracts requiring by law certification or attestation by a notary.

(37)   Member States' obligation to remove obstacles to the use of electronic contracts concerns

only obstacles resulting from legal requirements and not practical obstacles resulting from the impossibility of using electronic means in certain cases.

(38) Member States' obligation to remove obstacles to the use of electronic contracts is to be implemented in conformity with legal requirements for contracts enshrined in Community law.

(39) The exceptions to the provisions concerning the contracts concluded exclusively by electronic mail or by equivalent individual communications provided for by this Directive, in relation to information to be provided and the placing of orders, should not enable, as a result, the by-passing of those provisions by providers of information society services.

(40) Both existing and emerging disparities in Member States' legislation and case-law concerning liability of service providers acting as intermediaries prevent the smooth functioning of the internal market, in particular by impairing the development of cross-border services and producing distortions of competition; service providers have a duty to act, under certain circumstances, with a view to preventing or stopping illegal activities; this Directive should constitute the appropriate basis for the development of rapid and reliable procedures for removing and disabling access to illegal information; such mechanisms could be developed on the basis of voluntary agreements between all parties concerned and should be encouraged by Member States; it is in the interest of all parties involved in the provision of information society services to adopt and implement such procedures; the provisions of this Directive relating to liability should not preclude the development and effective operation, by the different interested parties, of technical systems of protection and identification and of technical surveillance instruments made possible by digital technology within the limits laid down by Directives 95/46/EC and 97/66/EC.

(41) This Directive strikes a balance between the different interests at stake and establishes principles upon which industry agreements and standards can be based.

(42) The exemptions from liability established in this Directive cover only cases where the activity of the information society service provider is limited to the technical process of operating and giving access to a communication network over which information made available by third parties is transmitted or temporarily stored, for the sole purpose of making the transmission more efficient; this activity is of a mere technical, automatic and passive nature, which implies that the information society service provider has neither knowledge of nor control over the information which is transmitted or stored.

(43) A service provider can benefit from the exemptions for "mere conduit" and for "caching" when he is in no way involved with the information transmitted; this requires among other things that he does not modify the information that he transmits; this requirement does not cover manipulations of a technical nature which take place in the course of the transmission as they do not alter the integrity of the information contained in the transmission.

(44) A service provider who deliberately collaborates with one of the recipients of his service in order to undertake illegal acts goes beyond the activities of "mere conduit" or "caching" and as a result cannot benefit from the liability exemptions established for these activities.

(45) The limitations of the liability of intermediary service providers established in this Directive do not affect the possibility of injunctions of different kinds; such injunctions can in particular consist of orders by courts or administrative authorities requiring the termination or prevention of any infringement, including the removal of illegal information or the disabling of access to it.

(46) In order to benefit from a limitation of liability, the provider of an information society service, consisting of the storage of information, upon obtaining actual knowledge or awareness of illegal activities has to act expeditiously to remove or to disable access to the information concerned; the removal or disabling of access has to be undertaken in the observance of the principle of freedom of expression and of procedures established for this purpose at national level; this Directive does not affect Member States' possibility of establishing specific requirements which must be fulfilled expeditiously prior to the removal or disabling of information.

(47) Member States are prevented from imposing a monitoring obligation on service providers only with respect to obligations of a general nature; this does not concern monitoring obligations in a specific case and, in particular, does not affect orders by national authorities in accordance with national legislation.

(48) This Directive does not affect the possibility for Member States of requiring service providers, who host information provided by recipients of their service, to apply duties of care, which can reasonably be expected from them and which are specified by national law, in order to detect and prevent certain types of illegal activities.

(49) Member States and the Commission are to encourage the drawing-up of codes of conduct; this is not to impair the voluntary nature of such codes and the possibility for interested parties of deciding freely whether to adhere to such codes.

(50) It is important that the proposed directive on the harmonisation of certain aspects of copyright and related rights in the information society and this Directive come into force within a similar time scale with a view to establishing a clear framework of rules relevant to the issue of

liability of intermediaries for copyright and relating rights infringements at Community level.

(51)   Each Member State should be required, where necessary, to amend any legislation which is liable to hamper the use of schemes for the out-of-court settlement of disputes through electronic channels; the result of this amendment must be to make the functioning of such schemes genuinely and effectively possible in law and in practice, even across borders.

(52)   The effective exercise of the freedoms of the internal market makes it necessary to guarantee victims effective access to means of settling disputes; damage which may arise in connection with information society services is characterised both by its rapidity and by its geographical extent; in view of this specific character and the need to ensure that national authorities do not endanger the mutual confidence which they should have in one another, this Directive requests Member States to ensure that appropriate court actions are available; Member States should examine the need to provide access to judicial procedures by appropriate electronic means.

(53)   Directive 98/27/EC, which is applicable to information society services, provides a mechanism relating to actions for an injunction aimed at the protection of the collective interests of consumers; this mechanism will contribute to the free movement of information society services by ensuring a high level of consumer protection.

(54)   The sanctions provided for under this Directive are without prejudice to any other sanction or remedy provided under national law; Member States are not obliged to provide criminal sanctions for infringement of national provisions adopted pursuant to this Directive.

(55)   This Directive does not affect the law applicable to contractual obligations relating to consumer contracts; accordingly, this Directive cannot have the result of depriving the consumer of the protection afforded to him by the mandatory rules relating to contractual obligations of the law of the Member State in which he has his habitual residence.

(56)   As regards the derogation contained in this Directive regarding contractual obligations concerning contracts concluded by consumers, those obligations should be interpreted as including information on the essential elements of the content of the contract, including consumer rights, which have a determining influence on the decision to contract.

(57)   The Court of Justice has consistently held that a Member State retains the right to take measures against a service provider that is established in another Member State but directs all or most of his activity to the territory of the first Member State if the choice of establishment was made with a view to evading the legislation that would have applied to the provider had he been established on the territory of the first Member State.

(58)   This Directive should not apply to services supplied by service providers established in a third country; in view of the global dimension of electronic commerce, it is, however, appropriate to ensure that the Community rules are consistent with international rules; this Directive is without prejudice to the results of discussions within international organisations (amongst others WTO, OECD, Uncitral) on legal issues.

(59)   Despite the global nature of electronic communications, coordination of national regulatory measures at European Union level is necessary in order to avoid fragmentation of the internal market, and for the establishment of an appropriate European regulatory framework; such coordination should also contribute to the establishment of a common and strong negotiating position in international forums.

(60)   In order to allow the unhampered development of electronic commerce, the legal framework must be clear and simple, predictable and consistent with the rules applicable at international level so that it does not adversely affect the competitiveness of European industry or impede innovation in that sector.

(61)   If the market is actually to operate by electronic means in the context of globalisation, the European Union and the major non-European areas need to consult each other with a view to making laws and procedures compatible.

(62)   Cooperation with third countries should be strengthened in the area of electronic commerce, in particular with applicant countries, the developing countries and the European Union's other trading partners.

(63)   The adoption of this Directive will not prevent the Member States from taking into account the various social, societal and cultural implications which are inherent in the advent of the information society; in particular it should not hinder measures which Member States might adopt in conformity with Community law to achieve social, cultural and democratic goals taking into account their linguistic diversity, national and regional specificities as well as their cultural heritage, and to ensure and maintain public access to the widest possible range of information society services; in any case, the development of the information society is to ensure that Community citizens can have access to the cultural European heritage provided in the digital environment.

(64)   Electronic communication offers the Member States an excellent means of providing public services in the cultural, educational and linguistic fields.

(65)   The Council, in its resolution of 19 January 1999 on the consumer dimension of the information society,[25] stressed that the protection of consumers deserved special attention in this

field; the Commission will examine the degree to which existing consumer protection rules provide insufficient protection in the context of the information society and will identify, where necessary, the deficiencies of this legislation and those issues which could require additional measures; if need be, the Commission should make specific additional proposals to resolve such deficiencies that will thereby have been identified,

NOTES

1   OJ C30, 5.2.1999, p 4.

2   OJ C169, 16.6.1999, p 36.

3   Opinion of the European Parliament of 6 May 1999 (OJ C279, 1.10.1999, p 389), Council common position of 28 February 2000 (OJ C128, 8.5.2000, p 32) and Decision of the European Parliament of 4 May 2000 (not yet published in the Official Journal).

4   OJ L298, 17.10.1989, p 23. Directive as amended by Directive 97/36/EC of the European Parliament and of the Council (OJ L202, 30.7.1997, p 60).

5   OJ L95, 21.4.1993, p 29.

6   OJ L144, 4.6.1999, p 19.

7   OJ L250, 19.9.1984, p 17. Directive as amended by Directive 97/55/EC of the European Parliament and of the Council (OJ L290, 23.10.1997, p 18).

8   OJ L42, 12.2.1987, p 48. Directive as last amended by Directive 98/7/EC of the European Parliament and of the Council (OJ L101, 1.4.1998, p 17).

9   OJ L141, 11.6.1993, p 27. Directive as last amended by Directive 97/9/EC of the European Parliament and of the Council (OJ L84, 26.3.1997, p 22).

10   OJ L158, 23.6.1990, p 59.

11   OJ L80, 18.3.1998, p 27.

12   OJ L228, 11.8.1992, p 24.

13   OJ L280, 29.10.1994, p 83.

14   OJ L166, 11.6.1998, p 51. Directive as amended by Directive 1999/44/EC (OJ L171, 7.7.1999, p 12).

15   OJ L210, 7.8.1985, p 29. Directive as amended by Directive 1999/34/EC (OJ L141, 4.6.1999, p 20).

16   OJ L171, 7.7.1999, p 12.

17   OJ L113, 30.4.1992, p 13.

18   OJ L213, 30.7.1998, p 9.

19   OJ L281, 23.11.1995, p 31.

20   OJ L24, 30.1.1998, p 1.

21   OJ L204, 21.7.1998, p 37. Directive as amended by Directive 98/48/EC (OJ L217, 5.8.1998, p 18).

22   OJ L320, 28.11.1998, p 54.

23   OJ L15, 21.1.1998, p 14.

24   OJ L13, 19.1.2000, p 12.

25   OJ C23, 28.1.1999, p 1.

HAVE ADOPTED THIS DIRECTIVE—

CHAPTER I
GENERAL PROVISIONS

[4.265]
Article 1
Objective and scope
1.   This Directive seeks to contribute to the proper functioning of the internal market by ensuring the free movement of information society services between the Member States.
2.   This Directive approximates, to the extent necessary for the achievement of the objective set out in paragraph 1, certain national provisions on information society services relating to the internal market, the establishment of service providers, commercial communications, electronic contracts, the liability of intermediaries, codes of conduct, out-of-court dispute settlements, court actions and cooperation between Member States.
3.   This Directive complements Community law applicable to information society services without prejudice to the level of protection for, in particular, public health and consumer interests, as established by Community acts and national legislation implementing them in so far as this does not restrict the freedom to provide information society services.
4.   This Directive does not establish additional rules on private international law nor does it deal with the jurisdiction of Courts.
5.   This Directive shall not apply to—
   (a)   the field of taxation;
   (b)   questions relating to information society services covered by Directives 95/46/EC and 97/66/EC;
   (c)   questions relating to agreements or practices governed by cartel law;

Part 4   Other Materials

(d)   the following activities of information society services—
  — the activities of notaries or equivalent professions to the extent that they involve a direct and specific connection with the exercise of public authority,
  — the representation of a client and defence of his interests before the courts,
  — gambling activities which involve wagering a stake with monetary value in games of chance, including lotteries and betting transactions.

6.   This Directive does not affect measures taken at Community or national level, in the respect of Community law, in order to promote cultural and linguistic diversity and to ensure the defence of pluralism.

[4.266]
Article 2
Definitions
For the purpose of this Directive, the following terms shall bear the following meanings—
(a)   "information society services": services within the meaning of Article 1(2) of Directive 98/34/EC as amended by Directive 98/48/EC;
(b)   "service provider": any natural or legal person providing an information society service;
(c)   "established service provider": a service provider who effectively pursues an economic activity using a fixed establishment for an indefinite period. The presence and use of the technical means and technologies required to provide the service do not, in themselves, constitute an establishment of the provider;
(d)   "recipient of the service": any natural or legal person who, for professional ends or otherwise, uses an information society service, in particular for the purposes of seeking information or making it accessible;
(e)   "consumer": any natural person who is acting for purposes which are outside his or her trade, business or profession;
(f)   "commercial communication": any form of communication designed to promote, directly or indirectly, the goods, services or image of a company, organisation or person pursuing a commercial, industrial or craft activity or exercising a regulated profession. The following do not in themselves constitute commercial communications—
  — information allowing direct access to the activity of the company, organisation or person, in particular a domain name or an electronic-mail address,
  — communications relating to the goods, services or image of the company, organisation or person compiled in an independent manner, particularly when this is without financial consideration;
(g)   "regulated profession": any profession within the meaning of either Article 1(d) of Council Directive 89/48/EEC of 21 December 1988 on a general system for the recognition of higher-education diplomas awarded on completion of professional education and training of at least three-years duration[1] or of Article 1(f) of Council Directive 92/51/EEC of 18 June 1992 on a second general system for the recognition of professional education and training to supplement Directive 89/48/EEC;[2]
(h)   "coordinated field": requirements laid down in Member States' legal systems applicable to information society service providers or information society services, regardless of whether they are of a general nature or specifically designed for them.
  (i) The coordinated field concerns requirements with which the service provider has to comply in respect of—
    — the taking up of the activity of an information society service, such as requirements concerning qualifications, authorisation or notification,
    — the pursuit of the activity of an information society service, such as requirements concerning the behaviour of the service provider, requirements regarding the quality or content of the service including those applicable to advertising and contracts, or requirements concerning the liability of the service provider;
  (ii) The coordinated field does not cover requirements such as—
    — requirements applicable to goods as such,
    — requirements applicable to the delivery of goods,
    — requirements applicable to services not provided by electronic means.

NOTES
[1] OJ L19, 24.1.1989, p 16.
[2] OJ L209, 24.7.1992, p 25. Directive as last amended by Commission Directive 97/38/EC (OJ L184, 12.7.1997, p 31).

[4.267]
Article 3
Internal market
1.   Each Member State shall ensure that the information society services provided by a service provider established on its territory comply with the national provisions applicable in the Member State in question which fall within the coordinated field.

2. Member States may not, for reasons falling within the coordinated field, restrict the freedom to provide information society services from another Member State.

3. Paragraphs 1 and 2 shall not apply to the fields referred to in the Annex.

4. Member States may take measures to derogate from paragraph 2 in respect of a given information society service if the following conditions are fulfilled—

  (a) the measures shall be—

     (i) necessary for one of the following reasons—

       — public policy, in particular the prevention, investigation, detection and prosecution of criminal offences, including the protection of minors and the fight against any incitement to hatred on grounds of race, sex, religion or nationality, and violations of human dignity concerning individual persons,

       — the protection of public health,

       — public security, including the safeguarding of national security and defence,

       — the protection of consumers, including investors;

     (ii) taken against a given information society service which prejudices the objectives referred to in point (i) or which presents a serious and grave risk of prejudice to those objectives;

     (iii) proportionate to those objectives;

  (b) before taking the measures in question and without prejudice to court proceedings, including preliminary proceedings and acts carried out in the framework of a criminal investigation, the Member State has—

       — asked the Member State referred to in paragraph 1 to take measures and the latter did not take such measures, or they were inadequate,

       — notified the Commission and the Member State referred to in paragraph 1 of its intention to take such measures.

5. Member States may, in the case of urgency, derogate from the conditions stipulated in paragraph 4(b). Where this is the case, the measures shall be notified in the shortest possible time to the Commission and to the Member State referred to in paragraph 1, indicating the reasons for which the Member State considers that there is urgency.

6. Without prejudice to the Member State's possibility of proceeding with the measures in question, the Commission shall examine the compatibility of the notified measures with Community law in the shortest possible time; where it comes to the conclusion that the measure is incompatible with Community law, the Commission shall ask the Member State in question to refrain from taking any proposed measures or urgently to put an end to the measures in question.

CHAPTER II
PRINCIPLES

Section 1: Establishment and information requirements

[4.268]
Article 4
Principle excluding prior authorisation

1. Member States shall ensure that the taking up and pursuit of the activity of an information society service provider may not be made subject to prior authorisation or any other requirement having equivalent effect.

2. Paragraph 1 shall be without prejudice to authorisation schemes which are not specifically and exclusively targeted at information society services, or which are covered by Directive 97/13/EC of the European Parliament and of the Council of 10 April 1997 on a common framework for general authorisations and individual licences in the field of telecommunications services.[1]

NOTES

  [1] OJ L117, 7.5.1997, p 15.

[4.269]
Article 5
General information to be provided

1. In addition to other information requirements established by Community law, Member States shall ensure that the service provider shall render easily, directly and permanently accessible to the recipients of the service and competent authorities, at least the following information—

  (a) the name of the service provider;

  (b) the geographic address at which the service provider is established;

  (c) the details of the service provider, including his electronic mail address, which allow him to be contacted rapidly and communicated with in a direct and effective manner;

  (d) where the service provider is registered in a trade or similar public register, the trade register in which the service provider is entered and his registration number, or equivalent means of identification in that register;

(e)   where the activity is subject to an authorisation scheme, the particulars of the relevant supervisory authority;

(f)   as concerns the regulated professions—
— any professional body or similar institution with which the service provider is registered,
— the professional title and the Member State where it has been granted,
— a reference to the applicable professional rules in the Member State of establishment and the means to access them;

(g)   where the service provider undertakes an activity that is subject to VAT, the identification number referred to in Article 22(1) of the sixth Council Directive 77/388/EEC of 17 May 1977 on the harmonisation of the laws of the Member States relating to turnover taxes—Common system of value added tax: uniform basis of assessment.[1]

2.   In addition to other information requirements established by Community law, Member States shall at least ensure that, where information society services refer to prices, these are to be indicated clearly and unambiguously and, in particular, must indicate whether they are inclusive of tax and delivery costs.

NOTES

[1]   OJ L145, 13.6.1977, p 1. Directive as last amended by Directive 1999/85/EC (OJ L277, 28.10.1999, p 34).

Section 2: Commercial communications

[4.270]
Article 6
Information to be provided
In addition to other information requirements established by Community law, Member States shall ensure that commercial communications which are part of, or constitute, an information society service comply at least with the following conditions—
(a)   the commercial communication shall be clearly identifiable as such;
(b)   the natural or legal person on whose behalf the commercial communication is made shall be clearly identifiable;
(c)   promotional offers, such as discounts, premiums and gifts, where permitted in the Member State where the service provider is established, shall be clearly identifiable as such, and the conditions which are to be met to qualify for them shall be easily accessible and be presented clearly and unambiguously;
(d)   promotional competitions or games, where permitted in the Member State where the service provider is established, shall be clearly identifiable as such, and the conditions for participation shall be easily accessible and be presented clearly and unambiguously.

[4.271]
Article 7
Unsolicited commercial communication
1.   In addition to other requirements established by Community law, Member States which permit unsolicited commercial communication by electronic mail shall ensure that such commercial communication by a service provider established in their territory shall be identifiable clearly and unambiguously as such as soon as it is received by the recipient.
2.   Without prejudice to Directive 97/7/EC and Directive 97/66/EC, Member States shall take measures to ensure that service providers undertaking unsolicited commercial communications by electronic mail consult regularly and respect the opt-out registers in which natural persons not wishing to receive such commercial communications can register themselves.

[4.272]
Article 8
Regulated professions
1.   Member States shall ensure that the use of commercial communications which are part of, or constitute, an information society service provided by a member of a regulated profession is permitted subject to compliance with the professional rules regarding, in particular, the independence, dignity and honour of the profession, professional secrecy and fairness towards clients and other members of the profession.
2.   Without prejudice to the autonomy of professional bodies and associations, Member States and the Commission shall encourage professional associations and bodies to establish codes of conduct at Community level in order to determine the types of information that can be given for the purposes of commercial communication in conformity with the rules referred to in paragraph 1.
3.   When drawing up proposals for Community initiatives which may become necessary to ensure the proper functioning of the Internal Market with regard to the information referred to in paragraph 2, the Commission shall take due account of codes of conduct applicable at Community level and shall act in close cooperation with the relevant professional associations and bodies.
4.   This Directive shall apply in addition to Community Directives concerning access to, and the exercise of, activities of the regulated professions.

Section 3: Contracts concluded by electronic means

[4.273]
Article 9
Treatment of contracts
1. Member States shall ensure that their legal system allows contracts to be concluded by electronic means. Member States shall in particular ensure that the legal requirements applicable to the contractual process neither create obstacles for the use of electronic contracts nor result in such contracts being deprived of legal effectiveness and validity on account of their having been made by electronic means.
2. Member States may lay down that paragraph 1 shall not apply to all or certain contracts falling into one of the following categories—
    (a) contracts that create or transfer rights in real estate, except for rental rights;
    (b) contracts requiring by law the involvement of courts, public authorities or professions exercising public authority;
    (c) contracts of suretyship granted and on collateral securities furnished by persons acting for purposes outside their trade, business or profession;
    (d) contracts governed by family law or by the law of succession.
3. Member States shall indicate to the Commission the categories referred to in paragraph 2 to which they do not apply paragraph 1. Member States shall submit to the Commission every five years a report on the application of paragraph 2 explaining the reasons why they consider it necessary to maintain the category referred to in paragraph 2(b) to which they do not apply paragraph 1.

[4.274]
Article 10
Information to be provided
1. In addition to other information requirements established by Community law, Member States shall ensure, except when otherwise agreed by parties who are not consumers, that at least the following information is given by the service provider clearly, comprehensibly and unambiguously and prior to the order being placed by the recipient of the service—
    (a) the different technical steps to follow to conclude the contract;
    (b) whether or not the concluded contract will be filed by the service provider and whether it will be accessible;
    (c) the technical means for identifying and correcting input errors prior to the placing of the order;
    (d) the languages offered for the conclusion of the contract.
2. Member States shall ensure that, except when otherwise agreed by parties who are not consumers, the service provider indicates any relevant codes of conduct to which he subscribes and information on how those codes can be consulted electronically.
3. Contract terms and general conditions provided to the recipient must be made available in a way that allows him to store and reproduce them.
4. Paragraphs 1 and 2 shall not apply to contracts concluded exclusively by exchange of electronic mail or by equivalent individual communications.

[4.275]
Article 11
Placing of the order
1. Member States shall ensure, except when otherwise agreed by parties who are not consumers, that in cases where the recipient of the service places his order through technological means, the following principles apply—
    — the service provider has to acknowledge the receipt of the recipient's order without undue delay and by electronic means,
    — the order and the acknowledgement of receipt are deemed to be received when the parties to whom they are addressed are able to access them.
2. Member States shall ensure that, except when otherwise agreed by parties who are not consumers, the service provider makes available to the recipient of the service appropriate, effective and accessible technical means allowing him to identify and correct input errors, prior to the placing of the order.
3. Paragraph 1, first indent, and paragraph 2 shall not apply to contracts concluded exclusively by exchange of electronic mail or by equivalent individual communications.

Section 4: Liability of intermediary service providers

[4.276]
Article 12
"Mere conduit"
1. Where an information society service is provided that consists of the transmission in a communication network of information provided by a recipient of the service, or the provision of access to a communication network, Member States shall ensure that the service provider is not liable for the information transmitted, on condition that the provider—

(a)   does not initiate the transmission;

(b)   does not select the receiver of the transmission; and

(c)   does not select or modify the information contained in the transmission.

2.   The acts of transmission and of provision of access referred to in paragraph 1 include the automatic, intermediate and transient storage of the information transmitted in so far as this takes place for the sole purpose of carrying out the transmission in the communication network, and provided that the information is not stored for any period longer than is reasonably necessary for the transmission.

3.   This Article shall not affect the possibility for a court or administrative authority, in accordance with Member States' legal systems, of requiring the service provider to terminate or prevent an infringement.

[4.277]
Article 13
"Caching"

1.   Where an information society service is provided that consists of the transmission in a communication network of information provided by a recipient of the service, Member States shall ensure that the service provider is not liable for the automatic, intermediate and temporary storage of that information, performed for the sole purpose of making more efficient the information's onward transmission to other recipients of the service upon their request, on condition that—

(a)   the provider does not modify the information;

(b)   the provider complies with conditions on access to the information;

(c)   the provider complies with rules regarding the updating of the information, specified in a manner widely recognised and used by industry;

(d)   the provider does not interfere with the lawful use of technology, widely recognised and used by industry, to obtain data on the use of the information; and

(e)   the provider acts expeditiously to remove or to disable access to the information it has stored upon obtaining actual knowledge of the fact that the information at the initial source of the transmission has been removed from the network, or access to it has been disabled, or that a court or an administrative authority has ordered such removal or disablement.

2.   This Article shall not affect the possibility for a court or administrative authority, in accordance with Member States' legal systems, of requiring the service provider to terminate or prevent an infringement.

[4.278]
Article 14
Hosting

1.   Where an information society service is provided that consists of the storage of information provided by a recipient of the service, Member States shall ensure that the service provider is not liable for the information stored at the request of a recipient of the service, on condition that—

(a)   the provider does not have actual knowledge of illegal activity or information and, as regards claims for damages, is not aware of facts or circumstances from which the illegal activity or information is apparent; or

(b)   the provider, upon obtaining such knowledge or awareness, acts expeditiously to remove or to disable access to the information.

2.   Paragraph 1 shall not apply when the recipient of the service is acting under the authority or the control of the provider.

3.   This Article shall not affect the possibility for a court or administrative authority, in accordance with Member States' legal systems, of requiring the service provider to terminate or prevent an infringement, nor does it affect the possibility for Member States of establishing procedures governing the removal or disabling of access to information.

[4.279]
Article 15
No general obligation to monitor

1.   Member States shall not impose a general obligation on providers, when providing the services covered by Articles 12, 13 and 14, to monitor the information which they transmit or store, nor a general obligation actively to seek facts or circumstances indicating illegal activity.

2.   Member States may establish obligations for information society service providers promptly to inform the competent public authorities of alleged illegal activities undertaken or information provided by recipients of their service or obligations to communicate to the competent authorities, at their request, information enabling the identification of recipients of their service with whom they have storage agreements.

CHAPTER III
IMPLEMENTATION

[4.280]
Article 16
Codes of conduct
1.   Member States and the Commission shall encourage—
(a)   the drawing up of codes of conduct at Community level, by trade, professional and consumer associations or organisations, designed to contribute to the proper implementation of Articles 5 to 15;
(b)   the voluntary transmission of draft codes of conduct at national or Community level to the Commission;
(c)   the accessibility of these codes of conduct in the Community languages by electronic means;
(d)   the communication to the Member States and the Commission, by trade, professional and consumer associations or organisations, of their assessment of the application of their codes of conduct and their impact upon practices, habits or customs relating to electronic commerce;
(e)   the drawing up of codes of conduct regarding the protection of minors and human dignity.
2.   Member States and the Commission shall encourage the involvement of associations or organisations representing consumers in the drafting and implementation of codes of conduct affecting their interests and drawn up in accordance with paragraph 1(a). Where appropriate, to take account of their specific needs, associations representing the visually impaired and disabled should be consulted.

[4.281]
Article 17
Out-of-court dispute settlement
1.   Member States shall ensure that, in the event of disagreement between an information society service provider and the recipient of the service, their legislation does not hamper the use of out-of-court schemes, available under national law, for dispute settlement, including appropriate electronic means.
2.   Member States shall encourage bodies responsible for the out-of-court settlement of, in particular, consumer disputes to operate in a way which provides adequate procedural guarantees for the parties concerned.
3.   Member States shall encourage bodies responsible for out-of-court dispute settlement to inform the Commission of the significant decisions they take regarding information society services and to transmit any other information on the practices, usages or customs relating to electronic commerce.

[4.282]
Article 18
Court actions
1.   Member States shall ensure that court actions available under national law concerning information society services' activities allow for the rapid adoption of measures, including interim measures, designed to terminate any alleged infringement and to prevent any further impairment of the interests involved.
2.   . . .

NOTES
Para 2: spent (amended Directive 98/27/EC, Annex (repealed)).

[4.283]
Article 19
Cooperation
1.   Member States shall have adequate means of supervision and investigation necessary to implement this Directive effectively and shall ensure that service providers supply them with the requisite information.
2.   Member States shall cooperate with other Member States; they shall, to that end, appoint one or several contact points, whose details they shall communicate to the other Member States and to the Commission.
3.   Member States shall, as quickly as possible, and in conformity with national law, provide the assistance and information requested by other Member States or by the Commission, including by appropriate electronic means.
4.   Member States shall establish contact points which shall be accessible at least by electronic means and from which recipients and service providers may—
(a)   obtain general information on contractual rights and obligations as well as on the complaint and redress mechanisms available in the event of disputes, including practical aspects involved in the use of such mechanisms;
(b)   obtain the details of authorities, associations or organisations from which they may obtain further information or practical assistance.

5.   Member States shall encourage the communication to the Commission of any significant administrative or judicial decisions taken in their territory regarding disputes relating to information society services and practices, usages and customs relating to electronic commerce. The Commission shall communicate these decisions to the other Member States.

[4.284]
Article 20
Sanctions
Member States shall determine the sanctions applicable to infringements of national provisions adopted pursuant to this Directive and shall take all measures necessary to ensure that they are enforced. The sanctions they provide for shall be effective, proportionate and dissuasive.

CHAPTER IV
FINAL PROVISIONS

[4.285]
Article 21
Re-examination
1.   Before 17 July 2003, and thereafter every two years, the Commission shall submit to the European Parliament, the Council and the Economic and Social Committee a report on the application of this Directive, accompanied, where necessary, by proposals for adapting it to legal, technical and economic developments in the field of information society services, in particular with respect to crime prevention, the protection of minors, consumer protection and to the proper functioning of the internal market.
2.   In examining the need for an adaptation of this Directive, the report shall in particular analyse the need for proposals concerning the liability of providers of hyperlinks and location tool services, "notice and take down" procedures and the attribution of liability following the taking down of content. The report shall also analyse the need for additional conditions for the exemption from liability, provided for in Articles 12 and 13, in the light of technical developments, and the possibility of applying the internal market principles to unsolicited commercial communications by electronic mail.

[4.286]
Article 22
Transposition
1.   Member States shall bring into force the laws, regulations and administrative provisions necessary to comply with this Directive before 17 January 2002. They shall forthwith inform the Commission thereof.
2.   When Member States adopt the measures referred to in paragraph 1, these shall contain a reference to this Directive or shall be accompanied by such reference at the time of their official publication. The methods of making such reference shall be laid down by Member States.

[4.287]
Article 23
Entry into force
This Directive shall enter into force on the day of its publication in the *Official Journal of the European Communities.*

[4.288]
Article 24
Addressees
This Directive is addressed to the Member States.

ANNEX

DEROGATIONS FROM ARTICLE 3

[4.289]
As provided for in Article 3(3), Article 3(1) and (2) do not apply to—
— copyright, neighbouring rights, rights referred to in Directive 87/54/EEC[1] and Directive 96/9/EC[2] as well as industrial property rights,
— the emission of electronic money by institutions in respect of which Member States have applied one of the derogations provided for in Article 8(1) of Directive 2000/46/EC,[3]
— Article 44(2) of Directive 85/611/EEC,[4]
— Article 30 and Title IV of Directive 92/49/EEC,[5] Title IV of Directive 92/96/EEC,[6] Articles 7 and 8 of Directive 88/357/EEC[7] and Article 4 of Directive 90/619/EEC,[8]
— the freedom of the parties to choose the law applicable to their contract,
— contractual obligations concerning consumer contacts,

— formal validity of contracts creating or transferring rights in real estate where such contracts are subject to mandatory formal requirements of the law of the Member State where the real estate is situated,

— the permissibility of unsolicited commercial communications by electronic mail.

NOTES

[1]   OJ L24, 27.1.1987, p 36.

[2]   OJ L77, 27.3.1996, p 20.

[3]   Not yet published in the Official Journal.

[4]   OJ L375, 31.12.1985, p 3. Directive as last amended by Directive 95/26/EC (OJ L168, 18.7.1995, p 7).

[5]   OJ L228, 11.8.1992, p 1. Directive as last amended by Directive 95/26/EC.

[6]   OJ L360, 9.12.1992, p 2. Directive as last amended by Directive 95/26/EC.

[7]   OJ L172, 4.7.1988, p 1. Directive as last amended by Directive 92/49/EC.

[8]   OJ L330, 29.11.1990, p 50. Directive as last amended by Directive 92/96/EC.

DIRECTIVE OF THE EUROPEAN PARLIAMENT AND OF THE COUNCIL

(2000/35/EC)

of 29 June 2000

on combating late payment in commercial transactions

NOTES

Date of publication in OJ: OJ L200, 8.8.2000, p 35.

This Directive has been mainly implemented in the UK by the Late Payment of Commercial Debts Regulations 2002, SI 2002/1674 at **[2.228]**.

This Directive is repealed by European Parliament and Council Directive 2011/7/EU, except in its application to contracts concluded before 16 March 2013 to which that Directive does not apply pursuant to Art 12(4) thereof (see Art 13 thereof at **[4.519]**), and is reproduced for reference only.

THE EUROPEAN PARLIAMENT AND THE COUNCIL OF THE EUROPEAN UNION,

Having regard to the Treaty establishing the European Community, and in particular Article 95 thereof,

Having regard to the proposal from the Commission,[1]

Having regard to the opinion of the Economic and Social Committee,[2]

Acting in accordance with the procedure laid down in Article 251 of the Treaty,[3] in the light of the joint text approved by the Conciliation Committee on 4 May 2000,

Whereas:

(1)   In its resolution on the integrated programme in favour of SMEs and the craft sector,[4] the European Parliament urged the Commission to submit proposals to deal with the problem of late payment.

(2)   On 12 May 1995 the Commission adopted a recommendation on payment periods in commercial transactions.[5]

(3)   In its resolution on the Commission recommendation on payment periods in commercial transactions,[6] the European Parliament called on the Commission to consider transforming its recommendation into a proposal for a Council directive to be submitted as soon as possible.

(4)   On 29 May 1997 the Economic and Social Committee adopted an opinion on the Commission's Green Paper on Public procurement in the European Union: Exploring the way forward.[7]

(5)   On 4 June 1997 the Commission published an action plan for the single market, which underlined that late payment represents an increasingly serious obstacle for the success of the single market.

(6)   On 17 July 1997 the Commission published a report on late payments in commercial transactions,[8] summarising the results of an evaluation of the effects of the Commission's recommendation of 12 May 1995.

(7)   Heavy administrative and financial burdens are placed on businesses, particularly small and medium-sized ones, as a result of excessive payment periods and late payment. Moreover, these problems are a major cause of insolvencies threatening the survival of businesses and result in numerous job losses.

(8)   In some Member States contractual payment periods differ significantly from the Community average.

(9)   The differences between payment rules and practices in the Member States constitute an obstacle to the proper functioning of the internal market.

(10) This has the effect of considerably limiting commercial transactions between Member States. This is in contradiction with Article 14 of the Treaty as entrepreneurs should be able to trade throughout the internal market under conditions which ensure that transborder operations do not entail greater risks than domestic sales. Distortions of competition would ensue if substantially different rules applied to domestic and transborder operations.

(11) The most recent statistics indicate that there has been, at best, no improvement in late payments in many Member States since the adoption of the recommendation of 12 May 1995.

(12) The objective of combating late payments in the internal market cannot be sufficiently achieved by the Member States acting individually and can, therefore, be better achieved by the Community. This Directive does not go beyond what is necessary to achieve that objective. This Directive complies therefore, in its entirety, with the requirements of the principles of subsidiarity and proportionality as laid down in Article 5 of the Treaty.

(13) This Directive should be limited to payments made as remuneration for commercial transactions and does not regulate transactions with consumers, interest in connection with other payments, eg payments under the laws on cheques and bills of exchange, payments made as compensation for damages including payments from insurance companies.

(14) The fact that the liberal professions are covered by this Directive does not mean that Member States have to treat them as undertakings or merchants for purposes not covered by this Directive.

(15) This Directive only defines the term 'enforceable title' but does not regulate the various procedures of forced execution of such a title and the conditions under which forced execution of such a title can be stopped or suspended.

(16) Late payment constitutes a breach of contract which has been made financially attractive to debtors in most Member States by low interest rates on late payments and/or slow procedures for redress. A decisive shift, including compensation of creditors for the costs incurred, is necessary to reverse this trend and to ensure that the consequences of late payments are such as to discourage late payment.

(17) The reasonable compensation for the recovery costs has to be considered without prejudice to national provisions according to which a national judge can award to the creditor any additional damage caused by the debtor's late payment, taking also into account that such incurred costs may be already compensated for by the interest for late payment.

(18) This Directive takes into account the issue of long contractual payment periods and, in particular, the existence of certain categories of contracts where a longer payment period in combination with a restriction of freedom of contract or a higher interest rate can be justified.

(19) This Directive should prohibit abuse of freedom of contract to the disadvantage of the creditor. Where an agreement mainly serves the purpose of procuring the debtor additional liquidity at the expense of the creditor, or where the main contractor imposes on his suppliers and subcontractors terms of payment which are not justified on the grounds of the terms granted to himself, these may be considered to be factors constituting such an abuse. This Directive does not affect national provisions relating to the way contracts are concluded or regulating the. validity of contractual terms which are unfair to the debtor.

(20) The consequences of late payment can be dissuasive only if they are accompanied by procedures for redress which are rapid and effective for the creditor. In conformity with the principle of non-discrimination contained in Article 12 of the Treaty, those procedures should be available to all creditors who are established in the Community.

(21) It is desirable to ensure that creditors are in a position to exercise a retention of title on a non-discriminatory basis throughout the Community, if the retention of title clause is valid under the applicable national provisions designated by private international law.

(22) This Directive should regulate all commercial transactions irrespective of whether they are carried out between private or public undertakings or between undertakings and public authorities, having regard to the fact that the latter handle a considerable volume of payments to business. It should therefore also regulate all commercial transactions between main contractors and their suppliers and subcontractors.

(23) Article 5 of this Directive requires that the recovery procedure for unchallenged claims be completed within a short period of time in conformity with national legislation, but does not require Member States to adopt a specific procedure or to amend their existing legal procedures in a specific way,

NOTES

Repealed as noted at the beginning of this Directive.

[1]   OJ C168, 3.6.1998, p 13, and OJ C374, 3.12.1998, p 4.

[2]   OJ C407, 28.12.1998, p 50.

[3]   Opinion of the European Parliament of 17 September 1998 (OJ C313, 12.10.1998, p 142), Council Common Position of 29 July 1999 (OJ C284, 6.10.1999, p 1) and decision of the European Parliament of 16 December 1999. Decision of the

European Parliament of 15 June 2000 and Decision of the Council of 18 May 2000.

4　　OJ C323, 21.11.1994, p 19.

5　　OJ L127, 10.6.1995, p 19.

6　　OJ C211, 22.7.1996, p 43.

7　　OJ C287, 22.9.1997, p 92.

8　　OJ C216, 17.7.1997, p 10.

HAVE ADOPTED THIS DIRECTIVE:

[4.290]
Article 1
Scope
This Directive shall apply to all payments made as remuneration for commercial transactions.

NOTES
Repealed as noted at the beginning of this Directive.

[4.291]
Article 2
Definitions
For the purposes of this Directive—

1.　*'commercial transactions' means transactions between undertakings or between undertakings and public authorities which lead to the delivery of goods or the provision of services for remuneration,*
　　'public authority' means any contracting authority or entity, as defined by the Public Procurement Directives (92/50/EEC,[1] 93/36/EEC,[2] 93/37/EEC[3] and 93/38/EEC),[4]
　　'undertaking' means any organisation acting in the course of its independent economic or professional activity, even where it is carried on by a single person;
2.　*'late payment' means exceeding the contractual or statutory period of payment;*
3.　*'retention of title' means the contractual agreement according to which the seller retains title to the goods in question until the price has been paid in full;*
4.　*'interest rate applied by the European Central Bank to its main refinancing operations' means the interest rate applied to such operations in the rate of fixed-rate tenders. In the event that a main refinancing operation was conducted according to a variable-rate tender procedure, this interest rate refers to the marginal interest rate which resulted from that tender. This applies both in the case of single-rate and variable-rate auctions;*
5.　*'enforceable title' means any decision, judgment or order for payment issued by a court or other competent authority, whether for immediate payment or payment by instalments, which permits the creditor to have his claim against the debtor collected by means of forced execution; it shall include a decision, judgment or order for payment that is provisionally enforceable and remains so even if the debtor appeals against it.*

NOTES
Repealed as noted at the beginning of this Directive.

1　　OJ L209, 24.7.1992, p 1.

2　　OJ L199, 9.8.1993, p 1.

3　　OJ L199, 9.8.1993. p 54.

4　　OJ L199, 9.8.1993, p 84.

[4.292]
Article 3
Interest in case of late payment
Member States shall ensure that—
　(a)　*interest in accordance with point (d) shall become payable from the day following the date or the end of the period for payment fixed in the contract;*
　(b)　*if the date or period for payment is not fixed in the contract, interest shall become payable automatically without the necessity of a reminder—*
　　(i)　*30 days following the date of receipt by the debtor of the invoice or an equivalent request for payment; or*
　　(ii)　*if the date of the receipt of the invoice or the equivalent request for payment is uncertain, 30 days after the date of receipt of the goods or services; or*
　　(iii)　*if the debtor receives the invoice or the equivalent request for payment earlier than the goods or the services, 30 days after the receipt of the goods or services; or*
　　(iv)　*if a procedure of acceptance or verification, by which the conformity of the goods or services with the contract is to be ascertained, is provided for by statute or in the*

contract and if the debtor receives the invoice or the equivalent request for payment earlier or on the date on which such acceptance or verification takes place, 30 days after this latter date;

(c) the creditor shall be entitled to interest for late payment to the extent that—
  (i) he has fulfilled his contractual and legal obligations; and
  (ii) he has not received the amount due on time, unless the debtor is not responsible for the delay;

(d) the level of interest for late payment ('the statutory rate'), which the debtor is obliged to pay, shall be the sum of the interest rate applied by the European Central Bank to its most recent main refinancing operation carried out before the first calendar day of the half-year in question ('the reference rate'), plus at least seven percentage points ('the margin'), unless otherwise specified in the contract. For a Member State which is not participating in the third stage of economic and monetary union, the reference rate referred to above shall be the equivalent rate set by its national central bank. In both cases, the reference rate in force on the first calendar day of the half-year in question shall apply for the following six months;

(e) unless the debtor is not responsible for the delay, the creditor shall be entitled to claim reasonable compensation from the debtor for all relevant recovery costs incurred through the latter's late payment. Such recovery costs shall respect the principles of transparency and proportionality as regards the debt in question. Member States may, while respecting the principles referred to above, fix maximum amounts as regards the recovery costs for different levels of debt.

2.   For certain categories of contracts to be defined by national law, Member States may fix the period after which interest becomes payable to a maximum of 60 days provided that they either restrain the parties to the contract from exceeding this period or fix a mandatory interest rate that substantially exceeds the statutory rate.

3.   Member States shall provide that an agreement on the date for payment or on the consequences of late payment which is not in line with the provisions of paragraphs 1(b) to (d) and 2 either shall not be enforceable or shall give rise to a claim for damages if, when all circumstances of the case, including good commercial practice and the nature of the product, are considered, it is grossly unfair to the creditor. In determining whether an agreement is grossly unfair to the creditor, it will be taken, inter alia, into account whether the debtor has any objective reason to deviate from the provisions of paragraphs 1(b) to (d) and 2. If such an agreement is determined to be grossly unfair, the statutory terms will apply, unless the national courts determine different conditions which are fair.

4.   Member States shall ensure that, in the interests of creditors and of competitors, adequate and effective means exist to prevent the continued use of terms which are grossly unfair within the meaning of paragraph 3.

5.   The means referred to in paragraph 4 shall include provisions whereby organisations officially recognised as, or having a legitimate interest in, representing small and medium-sized enterprises may take action according to the national law concerned before the courts or before competent administrative bodies on the grounds that contractual terms drawn up for general use are grossly unfair within the meaning of paragraph 3, so that they can apply appropriate and effective means to prevent the continued use of such terms.

NOTES
  Repealed as noted at the beginning of this Directive.

[4.293]
Article 4
Retention of title

1.   Member States shall provide in conformity with the applicable national provisions designated by private international law that the seller retains title to goods until they are fully paid for if a retention of title clause has been expressly agreed between the buyer and the seller before the delivery of the goods.

2.   Member States may adopt or retain provisions dealing with down payments already made by the debtor.

NOTES
  Repealed as noted at the beginning of this Directive.

[4.294]
Article 5
Recovery procedures for unchallenged claims

1.   Member States shall ensure that an enforceable title can be obtained, irrespective of the amount of the debt, normally within 90 calendar days of the lodging of the creditor's action or application at the court or other competent authority, provided that the debt or aspects of the procedure are not disputed. This duty shall be carried out by Member States in conformity with their respective national legislation, regulations and administrative provisions.

2.   The respective national legislation, regulations and administrative provisions shall apply the same conditions for all creditors who are established in the European Community.

3.   The 90 calendar day period referred to in paragraph 1 shall not include the following:

    (a)   periods for service of documents;

    (b)   any delays caused by the creditor, such as periods devoted to correcting applications.

4.   This Article shall be without prejudice to the provisions of the Brussels Convention on jurisdiction and enforcement of judgments in civil and commercial matters.

NOTES

    Repealed as noted at the beginning of this Directive.

[4.295]
Article 6
Transposition

1.   Member States shall bring into force the laws, regulations and administrative provisions necessary to comply with this Directive before 8 August 2002. They shall forthwith inform the Commission thereof.

    When Member States adopt these measures, they shall contain a reference to this Directive or shall be accompanied by such reference on the occasion of their official publication. The methods of making such reference shall be laid down by Member States.

2.   Member States may maintain or bring into force provisions which are more favourable to the creditor than the provisions necessary to comply with this Directive.

3.   In transposing this Directive, Member States may exclude:

    (a)   debts that are subject to insolvency proceedings instituted against the debtor;

    (b)   contracts that have been concluded prior to 8 August 2002; and

    (c)   claims for interest of less than EUR 5.

4.   Member States shall communicate to the Commission the text of the main provisions of national law which they adopt in the field covered by this Directive.

5.   The Commission shall undertake two years after 8 August 2002 a review of, inter alia, the statutory rate, contractual payment periods and late payments, to assess the impact on commercial transactions and the operation of the legislation in practice. The results of this review and of other reviews will be made known to the European Parliament and the Council, accompanied where appropriate by proposals for improvement of this Directive.

NOTES

    Repealed as noted at the beginning of this Directive.

[4.296]
Article 7
Entry into force

This Directive shall enter into force on the day of its publication in the Official Journal of the European Communities.

NOTES

    Repealed as noted at the beginning of this Directive.

[4.297]
Article 8
Addressees

This Directive is addressed to the Member States.

NOTES

    Repealed as noted at the beginning of this Directive.

DIRECTIVE OF THE EUROPEAN PARLIAMENT AND OF THE COUNCIL

(2001/95/EC)

of 3 December 2001

on general product safety

(Text with EEA relevance)

NOTES

    Date of publication in OJ: OJ L11, 15.1.2002, p 4.

    This Directive has been implemented in the UK by the General Product Safety Regulations 2005, SI 2005/1803 at **[2.355]**.

THE EUROPEAN PARLIAMENT AND THE COUNCIL OF THE EUROPEAN UNION,
Having regard to the Treaty establishing the European Community, and in particular Article 95 thereof,
Having regard to the proposal from the Commission,[1]
Having regard to the opinion of the Economic and Social Committee,[2]
Acting in accordance with the procedure referred to in Article 251 of the Treaty,[3] in the light of the joint text approved by the Conciliation Committee on 2 August 2001,
Whereas:

(1)   Under Article 16 of Council Directive 92/59/EEC of 29 June 1992 on general product safety,[4] the Council was to decide, four years after the date set for the implementation of the said Directive, on the basis of a report of the Commission on the experience acquired, together with appropriate proposals, whether to adjust Directive 92/59/EEC. It is necessary to amend Directive 92/59/EEC in several respects, in order to complete, reinforce or clarify some of its provisions in the light of experience as well as new and relevant developments on consumer product safety, together with the changes made to the Treaty, especially in Articles 152 concerning public health and 153 concerning consumer protection, and in the light of the precautionary principle. Directive 92/59/EEC should therefore be recast in the interest of clarity. This recasting leaves the safety of services outside the scope of this Directive, since the Commission intends to identify the needs, possibilities and priorities for Community action on the safety of services and liability of service providers, with a view to presenting appropriate proposals.

(2)   It is important to adopt measures with the aim of improving the functioning of the internal market, comprising an area without internal frontiers in which the free movement of goods, persons, services and capital is assured.

(3)   In the absence of Community provisions, horizontal legislation of the Member States on product safety, imposing in particular a general obligation on economic operators to market only safe products, might differ in the level of protection afforded to consumers. Such disparities, and the absence of horizontal legislation in some Member States, would be liable to create barriers to trade and distortion of competition within the internal market.

(4)   In order to ensure a high level of consumer protection, the Community must contribute to protecting the health and safety of consumers. Horizontal Community legislation introducing a general product safety requirement, and containing provisions on the general obligations of producers and distributors, on the enforcement of Community product safety requirements and on rapid exchange of information and action at Community level in certain cases, should contribute to that aim.

(5)   It is very difficult to adopt Community legislation for every product which exists or which may be developed; there is a need for a broad-based, legislative framework of a horizontal nature to deal with such products, and also to cover lacunae, in particular pending revision of the existing specific legislation, and to complement provisions in existing or forthcoming specific legislation, in particular with a view to ensuring a high level of protection of safety and health of consumers, as required by Article 95 of the Treaty.

(6)   It is therefore necessary to establish at Community level a general safety requirement for any product placed on the market, or otherwise supplied or made available to consumers, intended for consumers, or likely to be used by consumers under reasonably foreseeable conditions even if not intended for them. In all these cases the products under consideration can pose risks for the health and safety of consumers which must be prevented. Certain second-hand goods should nevertheless be excluded by their very nature.

(7)   This Directive should apply to products irrespective of the selling techniques, including distance and electronic selling.

(8)   The safety of products should be assessed taking into account all the relevant aspects, in particular the categories of consumers which can be particularly vulnerable to the risks posed by the products under consideration, in particular children and the elderly.

(9)   This Directive does not cover services, but in order to secure the attainment of the protection objectives in question, its provisions should also apply to products that are supplied or made available to consumers in the context of service provision for use by them. The safety of the equipment used by service providers themselves to supply a service to consumers does not come within the scope of this Directive since it has to be dealt with in conjunction with the safety of the service provided. In particular, equipment on which consumers ride or travel which is operated by a service provider is excluded from the scope of this Directive.

(10)   Products which are designed exclusively for professional use but have subsequently migrated to the consumer market should be subject to the requirements of this Directive because they can pose risks to consumer health and safety when used under reasonably foreseeable conditions.

(11)   In the absence of more specific provisions, within the framework of Community legislation covering safety of the products concerned, all the provisions of this Directive should apply in order to ensure consumer health and safety.

(12)   If specific Community legislation sets out safety requirements covering only certain risks

or categories of risks, with regard to the products concerned the obligations of economic operators in respect of these risks are those determined by the provisions of the specific legislation, while the general safety requirement of this Directive should apply to the other risks.

(13)   The provisions of this Directive relating to the other obligations of producers and distributors, the obligations and powers of the Member States, the exchanges of information and rapid intervention situations and dissemination of information and confidentiality apply in the case of products covered by specific rules of Community law, if those rules do not already contain such obligations.

(14)   In order to facilitate the effective and consistent application of the general safety requirement of this Directive, it is important to establish European voluntary standards covering certain products and risks in such a way that a product which conforms to a national standard transposing a European standard is to be presumed to be in compliance with the said requirement.

(15)   With regard to the aims of this Directive, European standards should be established by European standardisation bodies, under mandates set by the Commission assisted by appropriate Committees. In order to ensure that products in compliance with the standards fulfil the general safety requirement, the Commission assisted by a committee composed of representatives of the Member States, should fix the requirements that the standards must meet. These requirements should be included in the mandates to the standardisation bodies.

(16)   In the absence of specific regulations and when the European standards established under mandates set by the Commission are not available or recourse is not made to such standards, the safety of products should be assessed taking into account in particular national standards transposing any other relevant European or international standards, Commission recommendations or national standards, international standards, codes of good practice, the state of the art and the safety which consumers may reasonably expect. In this context, the Commission's recommendations may facilitate the consistent and effective application of this Directive pending the introduction of European standards or as regards the risks and/or products for which such standards are deemed not to be possible or appropriate.

(17)   Appropriate independent certification recognised by the competent authorities may facilitate proof of compliance with the applicable product safety criteria.

(18)   It is appropriate to supplement the duty to observe the general safety requirement by other obligations on economic operators because action by such operators is necessary to prevent risks to consumers under certain circumstances.

(19)   The additional obligations on producers should include the duty to adopt measures commensurate with the characteristics of the products, enabling them to be informed of the risks that these products may present, to supply consumers with information enabling them to assess and prevent risks, to warn consumers of the risks posed by dangerous products already supplied to them, to withdraw those products from the market and, as a last resort, to recall them when necessary, which may involve, depending on the provisions applicable in the Member States, an appropriate form of compensation, for example exchange or reimbursement.

(20)   Distributors should help in ensuring compliance with the applicable safety requirements. The obligations placed on distributors apply in proportion to their respective responsibilities. In particular, it may prove impossible, in the context of charitable activities, to provide the competent authorities with information and documentation on possible risks and origin of the product in the case of isolated used objects provided by private individuals.

(21)   Both producers and distributors should cooperate with the competent authorities in action aimed at preventing risks and inform them when they conclude that certain products supplied are dangerous. The conditions regarding the provision of such information should be set in this Directive to facilitate its effective application, while avoiding an excessive burden for economic operators and the authorities.

(22)   In order to ensure the effective enforcement of the obligations incumbent on producers and distributors, the Member States should establish or designate authorities which are responsible for monitoring product safety and have powers to take appropriate measures, including the power to impose effective, proportionate and dissuasive penalties, and ensure appropriate coordination between the various designated authorities.

(23)   It is necessary in particular for the appropriate measures to include the power for Member States to order or organise, immediately and efficiently, the withdrawal of dangerous products already placed on the market and as a last resort to order, coordinate or organise the recall from consumers of dangerous products already supplied to them. Those powers should be applied when producers and distributors fail to prevent risks to consumers in accordance with their obligations. Where necessary, the appropriate powers and procedures should be available to the authorities to decide and apply any necessary measures rapidly.

(24)   The safety of consumers depends to a great extent on the active enforcement of Community product safety requirements. The Member States should, therefore, establish systematic approaches to ensure the effectiveness of market surveillance and other enforcement activities and should ensure their openness to the public and interested parties.

Part 4   Other Materials

(25) Collaboration between the enforcement authorities of the Member States is necessary in ensuring the attainment of the protection objectives of this Directive. It is, therefore, appropriate to promote the operation of a European network of the enforcement authorities of the Member States to facilitate, in a coordinated manner with other Community procedures, in particular the Community Rapid Information System (RAPEX), improved collaboration at operational level on market surveillance and other enforcement activities, in particular risk assessment, testing of products, exchange of expertise and scientific knowledge, execution of joint surveillance projects and tracing, withdrawing or recalling dangerous products.

(26) It is necessary, for the purpose of ensuring a consistent, high level of consumer health and safety protection and preserving the unity of the internal market, that the Commission be informed of any measure restricting the placing on the market of a product or requiring its withdrawal or recall from the market. Such measures should be taken in compliance with the provisions of the Treaty, and in particular Articles 28, 29 and 30 thereof.

(27) Effective supervision of product safety requires the setting-up at national and Community levels of a system of rapid exchange of information in situations of serious risk requiring rapid intervention in respect of the safety of a product. It is also appropriate in this Directive to set out detailed procedures for the operation of the system and to give the Commission, assisted by an advisory committee, power to adapt them.

(28) This Directive provides for the establishment of non-binding guidelines aimed at indicating simple and clear criteria and practical rules which may change, in particular for the purpose of allowing efficient notification of measures restricting the placing on the market of products in the cases referred to in this Directive, whilst taking into account the range of situations dealt with by Member States and economic operators. The guidelines should in particular include criteria for the application of the definition of serious risks in order to facilitate consistent implementation of the relevant provisions in case of such risks.

(29) It is primarily for Member States, in compliance with the Treaty and in particular with Articles 28, 29 and 30 thereof, to take appropriate measures with regard to dangerous products located within their territory.

(30) However, if the Member States differ as regards the approach to dealing with the risk posed by certain products, such differences could entail unacceptable disparities in consumer protection and constitute a barrier to intra-Community trade.

(31) It may be necessary to deal with serious product-safety problems requiring rapid intervention which affect or could affect, in the immediate future, all or a significant part of the Community and which, in view of the nature of the safety problem posed by the product, cannot be dealt with effectively in a manner commensurate with the degree of urgency, under the procedures laid down in the specific rules of Community law applicable to the products or category of products in question.

(32) It is therefore necessary to provide for an adequate mechanism allowing, as a last resort, for the adoption of measures applicable throughout the Community, in the form of a decision addressed to the Member States, to cope with situations created by products presenting a serious risk. Such a decision should entail a ban on the export of the product in question, unless in the case in point exceptional circumstances allow a partial ban or even no ban to be decided upon, particularly when a system of prior consent is established. In addition, the banning of exports should be examined with a view to preventing risks to the health and safety of consumers. Since such a decision is not directly applicable to economic operators, Member States should take all necessary measures for its implementation. Measures adopted under such a procedure are interim measures, save when they apply to individually identified products or batches of products. In order to ensure the appropriate assessment of the need for, and the best preparation of such measures, they should be taken by the Commission, assisted by a committee, in the light of consultations with the Member States, and, if scientific questions are involved falling within the competence of a Community scientific committee, with the scientific committee competent for the risk concerned.

(33) The measures necessary for the implementation of this Directive should be adopted in accordance with Council Decision 1999/468/EC of 28 June 1999 laying down the procedures for the exercise of implementing powers conferred on the Commission.[5]

(34) In order to facilitate effective and consistent application of this Directive, the various aspects of its application may need to be discussed within a committee.

(35) Public access to the information available to the authorities on product safety should be ensured. However, professional secrecy, as referred to in Article 287 of the Treaty, must be protected in a way which is compatible with the need to ensure the effectiveness of market surveillance activities and of protection measures.

(36) This Directive should not affect victims' rights within the meaning of Council Directive 85/374/EEC of 25 July 1985 on the approximation of the laws, regulations and administrative provisions of the Member States concerning liability for defective products.[6]

(37) It is necessary for Member States to provide for appropriate means of redress before the competent courts in respect of measures taken by the competent authorities which restrict the placing

on the market of a product or require its withdrawal or recall.

(38) In addition, the adoption of measures concerning imported products, like those concerning the banning of exports, with a view to preventing risks to the safety and health of consumers must comply with the Community's international obligations.

(39) The Commission should periodically examine the manner in which this Directive is applied and the results obtained, in particular in relation to the functioning of market surveillance systems, the rapid exchange of information and measures adopted at Community level, together with other issues relevant for consumer product safety in the Community, and submit regular reports to the European Parliament and the Council on the subject.

(40) This Directive should not affect the obligations of Member States concerning the deadline for transposition and application of Directive 92/59/EEC,

NOTES

[1] OJ C337E, 28.11.2000, p 109 and OJ C154E, 29.5.2000, p 265.

[2] OJ C367, 20.12.2000, p 34.

[3] Opinion of the European Parliament of 15.11.2000 (OJ C223, 8.8.2001, p 154), Council Common Position of 12.2.2001 (OJ C93, 23.3.2001, p 24) and Decision of the European Parliament of 16.5.2001 (not yet published in the Official Journal). Decision of the European Parliament of 4.10.2001 and Council Decision of 27.9.2001.

[4] OJ L228, 11.8.1992, p 24.

[5] OJ L184, 17.7.1999, p 23.

[6] OJ L210, 7.8.1985, p 29. Directive as amended by Directive 1999/34/EC of the European Parliament and of the Council (OJ L141, 4.6.1999, p 20).

HAVE ADOPTED THIS DIRECTIVE—

CHAPTER I
OBJECTIVE—SCOPE—DEFINITIONS

[4.298]
Article 1
1.   The purpose of this Directive is to ensure that products placed on the market are safe.
2.   This Directive shall apply to all the products defined in Article 2(a). Each of its provisions shall apply in so far as there are no specific provisions with the same objective in rules of Community law governing the safety of the products concerned.

Where products are subject to specific safety requirements imposed by Community legislation, this Directive shall apply only to the aspects and risks or categories of risks not covered by those requirements. This means that—
   (a)   Articles 2(b) and (c), 3 and 4 shall not apply to those products insofar as concerns the risks or categories of risks covered by the specific legislation;
   (b)   Articles 5 to 18 shall apply except where there are specific provisions governing the aspects covered by the said Articles with the same objective.

[4.299]
Article 2
For the purposes of this Directive—
   (a)   "product" shall mean any product—including in the context of providing a service—which is intended for consumers or likely, under reasonably foreseeable conditions, to be used by consumers even if not intended for them, and is supplied or made available, whether for consideration or not, in the course of a commercial activity, and whether new, used or reconditioned.
     This definition shall not apply to second-hand products supplied as antiques or as products to be repaired or reconditioned prior to being used, provided that the supplier clearly informs the person to whom he supplies the product to that effect;
   (b)   "safe product" shall mean any product which, under normal or reasonably foreseeable conditions of use including duration and, where applicable, putting into service, installation and maintenance requirements, does not present any risk or only the minimum risks compatible with the product's use, considered to be acceptable and consistent with a high level of protection for the safety and health of persons, taking into account the following points in particular—
     (i)   the characteristics of the product, including its composition, packaging, instructions for assembly and, where applicable, for installation and maintenance;
     (ii)   the effect on other products, where it is reasonably foreseeable that it will be used with other products;
     (iii)   the presentation of the product, the labelling, any warnings and instructions for its use and disposal and any other indication or information regarding the product;
     (iv)   the categories of consumers at risk when using the product, in particular children and the elderly.

The feasibility of obtaining higher levels of safety or the availability of other products presenting a lesser degree of risk shall not constitute grounds for considering a product to be "dangerous";

(c) "dangerous product" shall mean any product which does not meet the definition of "safe product" in (b);

(d) "serious risk" shall mean any serious risk, including those the effects of which are not immediate, requiring rapid intervention by the public authorities;

(e) "producer" shall mean—
   (i)   the manufacturer of the product, when he is established in the Community, and any other person presenting himself as the manufacturer by affixing to the product his name, trade mark or other distinctive mark, or the person who reconditions the product;
   (ii) the manufacturer's representative, when the manufacturer is not established in the Community or, if there is no representative established in the Community, the importer of the product;
   (iii) other professionals in the supply chain, insofar as their activities may affect the safety properties of a product;

(f) "distributor" shall mean any professional in the supply chain whose activity does not affect the safety properties of a product;

(g) "recall" shall mean any measure aimed at achieving the return of a dangerous product that has already been supplied or made available to consumers by the producer or distributor;

(h) "withdrawal" shall mean any measure aimed at preventing the distribution, display and offer of a product dangerous to the consumer.

CHAPTER II
GENERAL SAFETY REQUIREMENT, CONFORMITY ASSESSMENT CRITERIA AND EUROPEAN STANDARDS

[4.300]
Article 3
1. Producers shall be obliged to place only safe products on the market.
2. A product shall be deemed safe, as far as the aspects covered by the relevant national legislation are concerned, when, in the absence of specific Community provisions governing the safety of the product in question, it conforms to the specific rules of national law of the Member State in whose territory the product is marketed, such rules being drawn up in conformity with the Treaty, and in particular Articles 28 and 30 thereof, and laying down the health and safety requirements which the product must satisfy in order to be marketed.

A product shall be presumed safe as far as the risks and risk categories covered by relevant national standards are concerned when it conforms to voluntary national standards transposing European standards, the references of which have been published by the Commission in the *Official Journal of the European Communities* in accordance with Article 4. The Member States shall publish the references of such national standards.
3. In circumstances other than those referred to in paragraph 2, the conformity of a product to the general safety requirement shall be assessed by taking into account the following elements in particular, where they exist—
   (a) voluntary national standards transposing relevant European standards other than those referred to in paragraph 2;
   (b) the standards drawn up in the Member State in which the product is marketed;
   (c) Commission recommendations setting guidelines on product safety assessment;
   (d) product safety codes of good practice in force in the sector concerned;
   (e) the state of the art and technology;
   (f) reasonable consumer expectations concerning safety.
4. Conformity of a product with the criteria designed to ensure the general safety requirement, in particular the provisions mentioned in paragraphs 2 or 3, shall not bar the competent authorities of the Member States from taking appropriate measures to impose restrictions on its being placed on the market or to require its withdrawal from the market or recall where there is evidence that, despite such conformity, it is dangerous.

[4.301]
Article 4
1. For the purposes of this Directive, the European standards referred to in the second subparagraph of Article 3(2) shall be drawn up as follows—
   [(a) the requirements intended to ensure that products which conform to those standards satisfy the general safety requirement shall be determined by the Commission. Those measures, designed to amend non-essential elements of this Directive by supplementing it, shall be adopted in accordance with the regulatory procedure with scrutiny referred to in Article 15(4);]
   (b) on the basis of those requirements, the Commission shall, in accordance with Directive 98/34/EC of the European Parliament and of the Council of 22 June 1998 laying down a

procedure for the provision of information in the field of technical standards and regulations and of rules on information society services[1] call on the European standardisation bodies to draw up standards which satisfy these requirements;

(c)   on the basis of those mandates, the European standardisation bodies shall adopt the standards in accordance with the principles contained in the general guidelines for cooperation between the Commission and those bodies;

(d)   the Commission shall report every three years to the European Parliament and the Council, within the framework of the report referred to in Article 19(2), on its programmes for setting the requirements and the mandates for standardisation provided for in subparagraphs (a) and (b) above. This report will, in particular, include an analysis of the decisions taken regarding requirements and mandates for standardisation referred to in subparagraphs (a) and (b) and regarding the standards referred to in subparagraph (c). It will also include information on the products for which the Commission intends to set the requirements and the mandates in question, the product risks to be considered and the results of any preparatory work launched in this area.

2.   The Commission shall publish in the *Official Journal of the European Communities* the references of the European standards adopted in this way and drawn up in accordance with the requirements referred to in paragraph 1.

If a standard adopted by the European standardisation bodies before the entry into force of this Directive ensures compliance with the general safety requirement, the Commission shall decide to publish its references in the *Official Journal of the European Communities*.

If a standard does not ensure compliance with the general safety requirement, the Commission shall withdraw reference to the standard from publication in whole or in part.

In the cases referred to in the second and third subparagraphs, the Commission shall, on its own initiative or at the request of a Member State, decide in accordance with the procedure laid down in Article 15(2) whether the standard in question meets the general safety requirement. The Commission shall decide to publish or withdraw after consulting the Committee established by Article 5 of Directive 98/34/EC. The Commission shall notify the Member States of its decision.

NOTES

Para 1: sub-para (a) substituted by European Parliament and Council Regulation 596/2009/EC, Art 2, Annex, para 5.8(1).

[1]   OJ L204, 21.7.1998, p 37. Directive amended by Directive 98/48/EC (OJ L217, 5.8.1998, p 18).

CHAPTER III
OTHER OBLIGATIONS OF PRODUCERS AND OBLIGATIONS OF DISTRIBUTORS

[4.302]
Article 5

1.   Within the limits of their respective activities, producers shall provide consumers with the relevant information to enable them to assess the risks inherent in a product throughout the normal or reasonably foreseeable period of its use, where such risks are not immediately obvious without adequate warnings, and to take precautions against those risks.

The presence of warnings does not exempt any person from compliance with the other requirements laid down in this Directive.

Within the limits of their respective activities, producers shall adopt measures commensurate with the characteristics of the products which they supply, enabling them to—

(a)   be informed of risks which these products might pose;

(b)   choose to take appropriate action including, if necessary to avoid these risks, withdrawal from the market, adequately and effectively warning consumers or recall from consumers.

The measures referred to in the third subparagraph shall include, for example—

(a)   an indication, by means of the product or its packaging, of the identity and details of the producer and the product reference or, where applicable, the batch of products to which it belongs, except where not to give such indication is justified and

(b)   in all cases where appropriate, the carrying out of sample testing of marketed products, investigating and, if necessary, keeping a register of complaints and keeping distributors informed of such monitoring.

Action such as that referred to in (b) of the third subparagraph shall be undertaken on a voluntary basis or at the request of the competent authorities in accordance with Article 8(1)(f). Recall shall take place as a last resort, where other measures would not suffice to prevent the risks involved, in instances where the producers consider it necessary or where they are obliged to do so further to a measure taken by the competent authority. It may be effected within the framework of codes of good practice on the matter in the Member State concerned, where such codes exist.

2.   Distributors shall be required to act with due care to help to ensure compliance with the applicable safety requirements, in particular by not supplying products which they know or should have presumed, on the basis of the information in their possession and as professionals, do not comply with those requirements. Moreover, within the limits of their respective activities, they shall participate in monitoring the safety of products placed on the market, especially by passing on

information on product risks, keeping and providing the documentation necessary for tracing the origin of products, and cooperating in the action taken by producers and competent authorities to avoid the risks. Within the limits of their respective activities they shall take measures enabling them to cooperate efficiently.

3.   Where producers and distributors know or ought to know, on the basis of the information in their possession and as professionals, that a product that they have placed on the market poses risks to the consumer that are incompatible with the general safety requirement, they shall immediately inform the competent authorities of the Member States thereof under the conditions laid down in Annex I, giving details, in particular, of action taken to prevent risk to the consumer.

[The Commission shall adapt the specific requirements relating to the obligation to provide information laid down in Annex I. Those measures, designed to amend non-essential elements of this Directive by supplementing it, shall be adopted in accordance with the regulatory procedure with scrutiny referred to in Article 15(5).]

4.   Producers and distributors shall, within the limits of their respective activities, cooperate with the competent authorities, at the request of the latter, on action taken to avoid the risks posed by products which they supply or have supplied. The procedures for such cooperation, including procedures for dialogue with the producers and distributors concerned on issues related to product safety, shall be established by the competent authorities.

NOTES

Para 3: words in square brackets substituted by European Parliament and Council Regulation 596/2009/EC, Art 2, Annex, para 5.8(2).

CHAPTER IV
SPECIFIC OBLIGATIONS AND POWERS OF THE MEMBER STATES

[4.303]
Article 6
1.   Member States shall ensure that producers and distributors comply with their obligations under this Directive in such a way that products placed on the market are safe.

2.   Member States shall establish or nominate authorities competent to monitor the compliance of products with the general safety requirements and arrange for such authorities to have and use the necessary powers to take the appropriate measures incumbent upon them under this Directive.

3.   Member States shall define the tasks, powers, organisation and cooperation arrangements of the competent authorities. They shall keep the Commission informed, and the Commission shall pass on such information to the other Member States.

[4.304]
Article 7
Member States shall lay down the rules on penalties applicable to infringements of the national provisions adopted pursuant to this Directive and shall take all measures necessary to ensure that they are implemented. The penalties provided for shall be effective, proportionate and dissuasive. Member States shall notify those provisions to the Commission by 15 January 2004 and shall also notify it, without delay, of any amendment affecting them.

[4.305]
Article 8
1.   For the purposes of this Directive, and in particular of Article 6 thereof, the competent authorities of the Member States shall be entitled to take, *inter alia*, the measures in (a) and in (b) to (f) below, where appropriate—
   (a)   for any product—
      (i)   to organise, even after its being placed on the market as being safe, appropriate checks on its safety properties, on an adequate scale, up to the final stage of use or consumption;
      (ii)   to require all necessary information from the parties concerned;
      (iii)   to take samples of products and subject them to safety checks;
   (b)   for any product that could pose risks in certain conditions—
      (i)   to require that it be marked with suitable, clearly worded and easily comprehensible warnings, in the official languages of the Member State in which the product is marketed, on the risks it may present;
      (ii)   to make its marketing subject to prior conditions so as to make it safe;
   (c)   for any product that could pose risks for certain persons—
            to order that they be given warning of the risk in good time and in an appropriate form, including the publication of special warnings;
   (d)   for any product that could be dangerous—
            for the period needed for the various safety evaluations, checks and controls, temporarily to ban its supply, the offer to supply it or its display;
   (e)   for any dangerous product—

> to ban its marketing and introduce the accompanying measures required to ensure the ban is complied with;

(f) for any dangerous product already on the market—

    (i) to order or organise its actual and immediate withdrawal, and alert consumers to the risks it presents;

    (ii) to order or coordinate or, if appropriate, to organise together with producers and distributors its recall from consumers and its destruction in suitable conditions.

2. When the competent authorities of the Member States take measures such as those provided for in paragraph 1, in particular those referred to in (d) to (f), they shall act in accordance with the Treaty, and in particular Articles 28 and 30 thereof, in such a way as to implement the measures in a manner proportional to the seriousness of the risk, and taking due account of the precautionary principle.

In this context, they shall encourage and promote voluntary action by producers and distributors, in accordance with the obligations incumbent on them under this Directive, and in particular Chapter III thereof, including where applicable by the development of codes of good practice.

If necessary, they shall organise or order the measures provided for in paragraph 1(f) if the action undertaken by the producers and distributors in fulfilment of their obligations is unsatisfactory or insufficient. Recall shall take place as a last resort. It may be effected within the framework of codes of good practice on the matter in the Member State concerned, where such codes exist.

[3. In the case of products posing a serious risk, the competent authorities shall with due dispatch take the appropriate measures referred to in paragraph 1(b) to (f). The existence of a serious risk shall be determined by the Member States, assessing each individual case on its merits and taking into account the guidelines referred to in point 8 of Annex II.]

4. The measures to be taken by the competent authorities under this Article shall be addressed, as appropriate, to—

    (a) the producer;

    (b) within the limits of their respective activities, distributors and in particular the party responsible for the first stage of distribution on the national market;

    (c) any other person, where necessary, with a view to cooperation in action taken to avoid risks arising from a product.

NOTES

Para 3: substituted by European Parliament and Council Regulation 765/2008/EC, Art 42.

[4.306]
Article 9

1. In order to ensure effective market surveillance, aimed at guaranteeing a high level of consumer health and safety protection, which entails cooperation between their competent authorities, Member States shall ensure that approaches employing appropriate means and procedures are put in place, which may include in particular—

    (a) establishment, periodical updating and implementation of sectoral surveillance programmes by categories of products or risks and the monitoring of surveillance activities, findings and results;

    (b) follow-up and updating of scientific and technical knowledge concerning the safety of products;

    (c) periodical review and assessment of the functioning of the control activities and their effectiveness and, if necessary, revision of the surveillance approach and organisation put in place.

2. Member States shall ensure that consumers and other interested parties are given an opportunity to submit complaints to the competent authorities on product safety and on surveillance and control activities and that these complaints are followed up as appropriate. Member States shall actively inform consumers and other interested parties of the procedures established to that end.

[4.307]
Article 10

1. The Commission shall promote and take part in the operation in a European network of the authorities of the Member States competent for product safety, in particular in the form of administrative cooperation.

2. This network operation shall develop in a coordinated manner with the other existing Community procedures, particularly RAPEX. Its objective shall be, in particular, to facilitate—

    (a) the exchange of information on risk assessment, dangerous products, test methods and results, recent scientific developments as well as other aspects relevant for control activities;

    (b) the establishment and execution of joint surveillance and testing projects;

    (c) the exchange of expertise and best practices and cooperation in training activities;

    (d) improved cooperation at Community level with regard to the tracing, withdrawal and recall of dangerous products.

CHAPTER V
EXCHANGES OF INFORMATION AND RAPID INTERVENTION SITUATIONS

[4.308]
Article 11
1.   Where a Member State takes measures which restrict the placing on the market of products—or require their withdrawal or recall—such as those provided for in Article 8(1)(b) to (f), the Member State shall, to the extent that such notification is not required under Article 12 or any specific Community legislation, inform the Commission of the measures, specifying its reasons for adopting them. It shall also inform the Commission of any modification or lifting of such measures.

If the notifying Member State considers that the effects of the risk do not or cannot go beyond its territory, it shall notify the measures concerned insofar as they involve information likely to be of interest to Member States from the product safety standpoint, and in particular if they are in response to a new risk which has not yet been reported in other notifications.

In accordance with the procedure laid down in Article 15(3) of this Directive, the Commission shall, while ensuring the effectiveness and proper functioning of the system, adopt the guidelines referred to in point 8 of Annex II. These shall propose the content and standard form for the notifications provided for in this Article, and, in particular, shall provide precise criteria for determining the conditions for which notification is relevant for the purposes of the second subparagraph.
2.   The Commission shall forward the notification to the other Member States, unless it concludes, after examination on the basis of the information contained in the notification, that the measure does not comply with Community law. In such a case, it shall immediately inform the Member State which initiated the action.

[4.309]
Article 12
1.   Where a Member State adopts or decides to adopt, recommend or agree with producers and distributors, whether on a compulsory or voluntary basis, measures or actions to prevent, restrict or impose specific conditions on the possible marketing or use, within its own territory, of products by reason of a serious risk, it shall immediately notify the Commission thereof through RAPEX. It shall also inform the Commission without delay of modification or withdrawal of any such measure or action.

If the notifying Member State considers that the effects of the risk do not or cannot go beyond its territory, it shall follow the procedure laid down in Article 11, taking into account the relevant criteria proposed in the guidelines referred to in point 8 of Annex II.

Without prejudice to the first subparagraph, before deciding to adopt such measures or to take such action, Member States may pass on to the Commission any information in their possession regarding the existence of a serious risk.

In the case of a serious risk, they shall notify the Commission of the voluntary measures laid down in Article 5 of this Directive taken by producers and distributors.
2.   On receiving such notifications, the Commission shall check whether they comply with this Article and with the requirements applicable to the functioning of RAPEX, and shall forward them to the other Member States, which, in turn, shall immediately inform the Commission of any measures adopted.
[3.   Detailed procedures for RAPEX are set out in Annex II. They shall be adapted by the Commission. Those measures, designed to amend non-essential elements of this Directive by supplementing it, shall be adopted in accordance with the regulatory procedure with scrutiny referred to in Article 15(5).]
4.   Access to RAPEX shall be open to applicant countries, third countries or international organisations, within the framework of agreements between the Community and those countries or international organisations, according to arrangements defined in these agreements. Any such agreements shall be based on reciprocity and include provisions on confidentiality corresponding to those applicable in the Community.

NOTES
Para 3: substituted by European Parliament and Council Regulation 596/2009/EC, Art 2, Annex, para 5.8(3).

[4.310]
Article 13
1.   If the Commission becomes aware of a serious risk from certain products to the health and safety of consumers in various Member States, it may, after consulting the Member States, and, if scientific questions arise which fall within the competence of a Community Scientific Committee, the Scientific Committee competent to deal with the risk concerned, adopt a decision in the light of the result of those consultations, in accordance with the procedure laid down in Article 15(2), requiring Member States to take measures from among those listed in Article 8(1)(b) to (f) if, at one and the same time—
   (a)   it emerges from prior consultations with the Member States that they differ significantly on the approach adopted or to be adopted to deal with the risk; and

(b)   the risk cannot be dealt with, in view of the nature of the safety issue posed by the product, in a manner compatible with the degree of urgency of the case, under other procedures laid down by the specific Community legislation applicable to the products concerned; and

(c)   the risk can be eliminated effectively only by adopting appropriate measures applicable at Community level, in order to ensure a consistent and high level of protection of the health and safety of consumers and the proper functioning of the internal market.

2.   The decisions referred to in paragraph 1 shall be valid for a period not exceeding one year and may be confirmed, under the same procedure, for additional periods none of which shall exceed one year.

However, decisions concerning specific, individually identified products or batches of products shall be valid without a time limit.

3.   Export from the Community of dangerous products which have been the subject of a decision referred to in paragraph 1 shall be prohibited unless the decision provides otherwise.

4.   Member States shall take all necessary measures to implement the decisions referred to in paragraph 1 within less than 20 days, unless a different period is specified in those decisions.

5.   The competent authorities responsible for carrying out the measures referred to in paragraph 1 shall, within one month, give the parties concerned an opportunity to submit their views and shall inform the Commission accordingly.

CHAPTER VI
COMMITTEE PROCEDURES

[4.311]
Article 14
1.   The measures necessary for the implementation of this Directive relating to the matters referred to below shall be adopted in accordance with the regulatory procedure provided for in Article 15(2)—

(a)   the measures referred to in Article 4 concerning standards adopted by the European standardisation bodies;

(b)   the decisions referred to in Article 13 requiring Member States to take measures as listed in Article 8(1)(b) to (f).

2.   The measures necessary for the implementation of this Directive in respect of all other matters shall be adopted in accordance with the advisory procedure provided for in Article 15(3).

[4.312]
[Article 15
1.   The Commission shall be assisted by a Committee.
2.   Where reference is made to this paragraph, Articles 5 and 7 of Decision 1999/468/EC shall apply, having regard to the provisions of Article 8 thereof.

The period laid down in Article 5(6) of Decision 1999/468/EC shall be set at 15 days.

3.   Where reference is made to this paragraph, Articles 3 and 7 of Decision 1999/468/EC shall apply, having regard to the provisions of Article 8 thereof.

4.   Where reference is made to this paragraph, Article 5a(1) to (4) and Article 7 of Decision 1999/468/EC shall apply, having regard to the provisions of Article 8 thereof.

5.   Where reference is made to this paragraph, Article 5a(1) to (4) and (5)(b) and Article 7 of Decision 1999/468/EC shall apply, having regard to the provisions of Article 8 thereof.

The time-limits laid down in Article 5a(3)(c) and (4)(b) and (e) of Decision 1999/468/EC shall be set at two months, one month and two months respectively.]

NOTES
Substituted by European Parliament and Council Regulation 596/2009/EC, Art 2, Annex, para 5.8(4).

CHAPTER VII
FINAL PROVISIONS

[4.313]
Article 16
1.   Information available to the authorities of the Member States or the Commission relating to risks to consumer health and safety posed by products shall in general be available to the public, in accordance with the requirements of transparency and without prejudice to the restrictions required for monitoring and investigation activities. In particular the public shall have access to information on product identification, the nature of the risk and the measures taken.

However, Member States and the Commission shall take the steps necessary to ensure that their officials and agents are required not to disclose information obtained for the purposes of this Directive which, by its nature, is covered by professional secrecy in duly justified cases, except for information relating to the safety properties of products which must be made public if circumstances so require, in order to protect the health and safety of consumers.

2.   Protection of professional secrecy shall not prevent the dissemination to the competent authorities of information relevant for ensuring the effectiveness of market monitoring and surveillance activities. The authorities receiving information covered by professional secrecy shall ensure its protection.

[4.314]
Article 17
This Directive shall be without prejudice to the application of Directive 85/374/EEC.

[4.315]
Article 18
1.   Any measure adopted under this Directive and involving restrictions on the placing of a product on the market or requiring its withdrawal or recall must state the appropriate reasons on which it is based. It shall be notified as soon as possible to the party concerned and shall indicate the remedies available under the provisions in force in the Member State in question and the time limits applying to such remedies.

The parties concerned shall, whenever feasible, be given an opportunity to submit their views before the adoption of the measure. If this has not been done in advance because of the urgency of the measures to be taken, they shall be given such opportunity in due course after the measure has been implemented.

Measures requiring the withdrawal of a product or its recall shall take into consideration the need to encourage distributors, users and consumers to contribute to the implementation of such measures.
2.   Member States shall ensure that any measure taken by the competent authorities involving restrictions on the placing of a product on the market or requiring its withdrawal or recall can be challenged before the competent courts.
3.   Any decision taken by virtue of this Directive and involving restrictions on the placing of a product on the market or requiring its withdrawal or its recall shall be without prejudice to assessment of the liability of the party concerned, in the light of the national criminal law applying in the case in question.

[4.316]
Article 19
1.   The Commission may bring before the Committee referred to in Article 15 any matter concerning the application of this Directive and particularly those relating to market monitoring and surveillance activities.
2.   Every three years, following 15 January 2004, the Commission shall submit a report on the implementation of this Directive to the European Parliament and the Council.

The report shall in particular include information on the safety of consumer products, in particular on improved traceability of products, the functioning of market surveillance, standardisation work, the functioning of RAPEX and Community measures taken on the basis of Article 13. To this end the Commission shall conduct assessments of the relevant issues, in particular the approaches, systems and practices put in place in the Member States, in the light of the requirements of this Directive and the other Community legislation relating to product safety. The Member States shall provide the Commission with all the necessary assistance and information for carrying out the assessments and preparing the reports.

[4.317]
Article 20
The Commission shall identify the needs, possibilities and priorities for Community action on the safety of services and submit to the European Parliament and the Council, before 1 January 2003, a report, accompanied by proposals on the subject as appropriate.

[4.318]
Article 21
1.   Member States shall bring into force the laws, regulations and administrative provisions necessary in order to comply with this Directive with effect from 15 January 2004. They shall forthwith inform the Commission thereof.

When Member States adopt those measures, they shall contain a reference to this Directive or be accompanied by such reference on the occasion of their official publication. The methods of making such reference shall be laid down by Member States.
2.   Member States shall communicate to the Commission the provisions of national law which they adopt in the field covered by this Directive.

[4.319]
Article 22
Directive 92/59/EEC is hereby repealed from 15 January 2004, without prejudice to the obligations of Member States concerning the deadlines for transposition and application of the said Directive as indicated in Annex III.

References to Directive 92/59/EEC shall be construed as references to this Directive and shall be read in accordance with the correlation table in Annex IV.

[4.320]
Article 23
This Directive shall enter into force on the day of its publication in the *Official Journal of the European Communities.*

[4.321]
Article 24
This Directive is addressed to the Member States.

ANNEX I

REQUIREMENTS CONCERNING INFORMATION ON PRODUCTS THAT DO NOT COMPLY WITH THE GENERAL SAFETY REQUIREMENT TO BE PROVIDED TO THE COMPETENT AUTHORITIES BY PRODUCERS AND DISTRIBUTORS

[4.322]
1.   The information specified in Article 5(3), or where applicable by specific requirements of Community rules on the product concerned, shall be passed to the competent authorities appointed for the purpose in the Member States where the products in question are or have been marketed or otherwise supplied to consumers.

2.   The Commission, assisted by the Committee referred to in Article 15, shall define the content and draw up the standard form of the notifications provided for in this Annex, while ensuring the effectiveness and proper functioning of the system. In particular, it shall put forward, possibly in the form of a guide, simple and clear criteria for determining the special conditions, particularly those concerning isolated circumstances or products, for which notification is not relevant in relation to this Annex.

3.   In the event of serious risks, this information shall include at least the following—
   (a)   information enabling a precise identification of the product or batch of products in question;
   (b)   a full description of the risk that the products in question present;
   (c)   all available information relevant for tracing the product;
   (d)   a description of the action undertaken to prevent risks to consumers.

ANNEX II

PROCEDURES FOR THE APPLICATION OF RAPEX AND GUIDELINES FOR NOTIFICATIONS

[4.323]
1.   RAPEX covers products as defined in Article 2(a) that pose a serious risk to the health and safety of consumers.
   Pharmaceuticals, which come under Directives 75/319/EEC[1] and 81/851/EEC,[2] are excluded from the scope of RAPEX.

2.   RAPEX is essentially aimed at a rapid exchange of information in the event of a serious risk. The guidelines referred to in point 8 define specific criteria for identifying serious risks.

3.   Member States notifying under Article 12 shall provide all available details. In particular, the notification shall contain the information stipulated in the guidelines referred to in point 8 and at least—
   (a)   information enabling the product to be identified;
   (b)   a description of the risk involved, including a summary of the results of any tests/analyses and of their conclusions which are relevant to assessing the level of risk;
   (c)   the nature and the duration of the measures or action taken or decided on, if applicable;
   (d)   information on supply chains and distribution of the product, in particular on destination countries.
   Such information must be transmitted using the special standard notification form and by the means stipulated in the guidelines referred to in point 8.
   When the measure notified pursuant to Article 11 or Article 12 seeks to limit the marketing or use of a chemical substance or preparation, the Member States shall provide as soon as possible either a summary or the references of the relevant data relating to the substance or preparation considered and to known and available substitutes, where such information is available. They will also communicate the anticipated effects of the measure on consumer health and safety together with the assessment of the risk carried out in accordance with the general principles for the risk evaluation of chemical substances as referred to in Article 10(4) of Regulation (EEC) No 793/93[3] in the case

of an existing substance or in Article 3(2) of Directive 67/548/EEC[4] in the case of a new substance. The guidelines referred to in point 8 shall define the details and procedures for the information requested in that respect.

4.   When a Member State has informed the Commission, in accordance with Article 12(1), third subparagraph, of a serious risk before deciding to adopt measures, it must inform the Commission within 45 days whether it confirms or modifies this information.

5.   The Commission shall, in the shortest time possible, verify the conformity with the provisions of the Directive of the information received under RAPEX and, may, when it considers it to be necessary and in order to assess product safety, carry out an investigation on its own initiative. In the case of such an investigation, Member States shall supply the Commission with the requested information to the best of their ability.

6.   Upon receipt of a notification referred to in Article 12, the Member States are requested to inform the Commission, at the latest within the set period of time stipulated in the guidelines referred to in point 8, of the following—
   (a)   whether the product has been marketed in their territory;
   (b)   what measures concerning the product in question they may be adopting in the light of their own circumstances, stating the reasons, including any differing assessment of risk or any other special circumstance justifying their decision, in particular lack of action or of follow-up;
   (c)   any relevant supplementary information they have obtained on the risk involved, including the results of any tests or analyses carried out.
The guidelines referred to in point 8 shall provide precise criteria for notifying measures limited to national territory and shall specify how to deal with notifications concerning risks which are considered by the Member State not to go beyond its territory.

7.   Member States shall immediately inform the Commission of any modification or lifting of the measure(s) or action(s) in question.

8.   The Commission shall prepare and regularly update, in accordance with the procedure laid down in Article 15(3), guidelines concerning the management of RAPEX by the Commission and the Member States.

9.   The Commission may inform the national contact points regarding products posing serious risks, imported into or exported from the Community and the European Economic Area.

10.   Responsibility for the information provided lies with the notifying Member State.

11.   The Commission shall ensure the proper functioning of the system, in particular classifying and indexing notifications according to the degree of urgency. Detailed procedures shall be laid down by the guidelines referred to in point 8.

NOTES

[1]   OJ L147, 9.6.1975, p 13. Directive as last amended by Commission Directive 2000/38/EC (OJ L139, 10.6.2000, p 28).
[2]   OJ L317, 6.11.1981, p 1. Directive as last amended by Commission Directive 2000/37/EC (OJ L139, 10.6.2000, p 25).
[3]   OJ L84, 5.4.1993, p 1.
[4]   OJ 196, 16.8.1967, p 1/67. Directive as last amended by Commission Directive 2000/33/EC (OJ L136, 8.6.2000, p 90).

ANNEX III

PERIOD FOR THE TRANSPOSITION AND APPLICATION OF THE REPEALED DIRECTIVE

(REFERRED TO IN THE FIRST SUBPARAGRAPH OF ARTICLE 22)

[4.324]

Directive	Period for transposition	Period for bringing into application
Directive 92/59/EEC	29 June 1994	29 June 1994

ANNEX IV

CORRELATION TABLE

(REFERRED TO IN THE SECOND SUBPARAGRAPH OF ARTICLE 22)

[4.325]

This Directive	*Directive 92/59/EEC*
Article 1	Article 1
Article 2	Article 2
Article 3	Article 4
Article 4	—
Article 5	Article 3
Article 6	Article 5
Article 7	Article 5(2)
Article 8	Article 6
Article 9	—
Article 10	—
Article 11	Article 7
Article 12	Article 8
Article 13	Article 9
Articles 14 and 15	Article 10
Article 16	Article 12
Article 17	Article 13
Article 18	Article 14
Article 19	Article 15
Article 20	—
Article 21	Article 17
Article 22	Article 18
Article 23	Article 19
Annex I	—
Annex II	Annex
Annex III	—
Annex IV	—

DIRECTIVE OF THE EUROPEAN PARLIAMENT AND OF THE COUNCIL

(2002/65/EC)

of 23 September 2002

concerning the distance marketing of consumer financial services and amending Council Directive 90/619/EEC and Directives 97/7/EC and 98/27/EC

NOTES

Date of publication in OJ: OJ L271, 9.10.02, p 16.

This Directive has been implemented in the UK by the Financial Services (Distance Marketing) Regulations 2004, SI 2004/2095 at **[2.330]** and the Consumer Credit (Disclosure of Information) Regulations 2010, SI 2010/1013 at **[2.814]**.

Directive 90/619/EEC: repealed by European Parliament and Council Directive 2002/83/EC.

Directive 97/7/EC: repealed by European Parliament and Council Directive 2011/83/EU.

Directive 98/27/EC: repealed by European Parliament and Council Directive 2009/22/EC.

THE EUROPEAN PARLIAMENT AND THE COUNCIL OF THE EUROPEAN UNION,

Having regard to the Treaty establishing the European Community, and in particular Article 47(2), Article 55 and

Article 95 thereof,

Having regard to the proposal from the Commission,[1]

Having regard to the opinion of the Economic and Social Committee,[2]

Acting in accordance with the procedure laid down in Article 251 of the Treaty,[3]

Whereas:

(1)   It is important, in the context of achieving the aims of the single market, to adopt measures designed to consolidate progressively this market and those measures must contribute to attaining a high level of consumer protection, in accordance with Articles 95 and 153 of the Treaty.

(2)   Both for consumers and suppliers of financial services, the distance marketing of financial services will constitute one of the main tangible results of the completion of the internal market.

(3)   Within the framework of the internal market, it is in the interest of consumers to have access without discrimination to the widest possible range of financial services available in the Community so that they can choose those that are best suited to their needs. In order to safeguard freedom of choice, which is an essential consumer right, a high degree of consumer protection is required in order to enhance consumer confidence in distance selling.

(4)   It is essential to the smooth operation of the internal market for consumers to be able to negotiate and conclude contracts with a supplier established in other Member States, regardless of whether the supplier is also established in the Member State in which the consumer resides.

(5)   Because of their intangible nature, financial services are particularly suited to distance selling and the establishment of a legal framework governing the distance marketing of financial services should increase consumer confidence in the use of new techniques for the distance marketing of financial services, such as electronic commerce.

(6)   This Directive should be applied in conformity with the Treaty and with secondary law, including Directive 2000/31/EC[4] on electronic commerce, the latter being applicable solely to the transactions which it covers.

(7)   This Directive aims to achieve the objectives set forth above without prejudice to Community or national law governing freedom to provide services or, where applicable, host Member State control and/or authorisation or supervision systems in the Member States where this is compatible with Community legislation.

(8)   Moreover, this Directive, and in particular its provisions relating to information about any contractual clause on law applicable to the contract and/or on the competent court does not affect the applicability to the distance marketing of consumer financial services of Council Regulation (EC) No 44/2001 of 22 December 2000 on jurisdiction and the recognition and enforcement of judgements in civil and commercial matters[5] or of the 1980 Rome Convention on the law applicable to contractual obligations.

(9)   The achievement of the objectives of the Financial Services Action Plan requires a higher level of consumer protection in certain areas. This implies a greater convergence, in particular, in non harmonised collective investment funds, rules of conduct applicable to investment services and consumer credits. Pending the achievement of the above convergence, a high level of consumer protection should be maintained.

(10)   Directive 97/7/EC of the European Parliament and of the Council of 20 May 1997 on the protection of consumers in respect of distance contracts,[6] lays down the main rules applicable to distance contracts for goods or services concluded between a supplier and a consumer. However, that Directive does not cover financial services.

(11)   In the context of the analysis conducted by the Commission with a view to ascertaining the need for specific measures in the field of financial services, the Commission invited all the interested parties to transmit their comments, notably in connection with the preparation of its Green Paper entitled "Financial Services – Meeting Consumers' Expectations". The consultations in this context showed that there is a need to strengthen consumer protection in this area. The Commission therefore decided to present a specific proposal concerning the distance marketing of financial services.

(12)   The adoption by the Member States of conflicting or different consumer protection rules governing the distance marketing of consumer financial services could impede the functioning of the internal market and competition between firms in the market. It is therefore necessary to enact common rules at Community level in this area, consistent with no reduction in overall consumer protection in the Member States.

(13)   A high level of consumer protection should be guaranteed by this Directive, with a view to ensuring the free movement of financial services. Member States should not be able to adopt provisions other than those laid down in this Directive in the fields it harmonises, unless otherwise specifically indicated in it.

(14)   This Directive covers all financial services liable to be provided at a distance. However, certain financial services are governed by specific provisions of Community legislation which continue to apply to those financial services. However, principles governing the distance marketing of such services should be laid down.

(15)   Contracts negotiated at a distance involve the use of means of distance communication which are used as part of a distance sales or service-provision scheme not involving the simultaneous presence of the supplier and the consumer. The constant development of those means of communication requires principles to be defined that are valid even for those means which are not yet in widespread use. Therefore, distance contracts are those the offer, negotiation and conclusion of which are carried out at a distance.

(16) A single contract involving successive operations or separate operations of the same nature performed over time may be subject to different legal treatment in the different Member States, but it is important that this Directive be applied in the same way in all the Member States. To that end, it is appropriate that this Directive should be considered to apply to the first of a series of successive operations or separate operations of the same nature performed over time which may be considered as forming a whole, irrespective of whether that operation or series of operations is the subject of a single contract or several successive contracts.

(17) An "initial service agreement" may be considered to be for example the opening of a bank account, acquiring a credit card, concluding a portfolio management contract, and "operations" may be considered to be for example the deposit or withdrawal of funds to or from the bank account, payment by credit card, transactions made within the framework of a portfolio management contract. Adding new elements to an initial service agreement, such as a possibility to use an electronic payment instrument together with one's existing bank account, does not constitute an "operation" but an additional contract to which this Directive applies. The subscription to new units of the same collective investment fund is considered to be one of "successive operations of the same nature".

(18) By covering a service-provision scheme organised by the financial services provider, this Directive aims to exclude from its scope services provided on a strictly occasional basis and outside a commercial structure dedicated to the conclusion of distance contracts.

(19) The supplier is the person providing services at a distance. This Directive should however also apply when one of the marketing stages involves an intermediary. Having regard to the nature and degree of that involvement, the pertinent provisions of this Directive should apply to such an intermediary, irrespective of his or her legal status.

(20) Durable mediums include in particular floppy discs, CD-ROMs, DVDs and the hard drive of the consumer's computer on which the electronic mail is stored, but they do not include Internet websites unless they fulfil the criteria contained in the definition of a durable medium.

(21) The use of means of distance communications should not lead to an unwarranted restriction on the information provided to the client. In the interests of transparency this Directive lays down the requirements needed to ensure that an appropriate level of information is provided to the consumer both before and after conclusion of the contract. The consumer should receive, before conclusion of the contract, the prior information needed so as to properly appraise the financial service offered to him and hence make a well-informed choice. The supplier should specify how long his offer applies as it stands.

(22) Information items listed in this Directive cover information of a general nature applicable to all kinds of financial services. Other information requirements concerning a given financial service, such as the coverage of an insurance policy, are not solely specified in this Directive. This kind of information should be provided in accordance, where applicable, with relevant Community legislation or national legislation in conformity with Community law.

(23) With a view to optimum protection of the consumer, it is important that the consumer is adequately informed of the provisions of this Directive and of any codes of conduct existing in this area and that he has a right of withdrawal.

(24) When the right of withdrawal does not apply because the consumer has expressly requested the performance of a contract, the supplier should inform the consumer of this fact.

(25) Consumers should be protected against unsolicited services. Consumers should be exempt from any obligation in the case of unsolicited services, the absence of a reply not being construed as signifying consent on their part. However, this rule should be without prejudice to the tacit renewal of contracts validly concluded between the parties whenever the law of the Member States permits such tacit renewal.

(26) Member States should take appropriate measures to protect effectively consumers who do not wish to be contacted through certain means of communication or at certain times. This Directive should be without prejudice to the particular safeguards available to consumers under Community legislation concerning the protection of personal data and privacy.

(27) With a view to protecting consumers, there is a need for suitable and effective complaint and redress procedures in the Member States with a view to settling potential disputes between suppliers and consumers, by using, where appropriate, existing procedures.

(28) Member States should encourage public or private bodies established with a view to settling disputes out of court to cooperate in resolving cross-border disputes. Such cooperation could in particular entail allowing consumers to submit to extra-judicial bodies in the Member State of their residence complaints concerning suppliers established in other Member States. The establishment of FIN-NET offers increased assistance to consumers when using cross-border services.

(29) This Directive is without prejudice to extension by Member States, in accordance with Community law, of the protection provided by this Directive to non-profit organisations and persons making use of financial services in order to become entrepreneurs.

(30) This Directive should also cover cases where the national legislation includes the concept of a consumer making a binding contractual statement.

(31)   The provisions in this Directive on the supplier's choice of language should be without prejudice to provisions of national legislation, adopted in conformity with Community law governing the choice of language.

(32)   The Community and the Member States have entered into commitments in the context of the General Agreement on Trade in Services (GATS) concerning the possibility for consumers to purchase banking and investment services abroad. The GATS entitles Member States to adopt measures for prudential reasons, including measures to protect investors, depositors, policy-holders and persons to whom a financial service is owed by the supplier of the financial service. Such measures should not impose restrictions going beyond what is required to ensure the protection of consumers.

(33)   In view of the adoption of this Directive, the scope of Directive 97/7/EC and Directive 98/27/EC of the European Parliament and of the Council of 19 May 1998 on injunctions for the protection of consumers' interests[7] and the scope of the cancellation period in Council Directive 90/619/EEC of 8 November 1990 on the coordination of laws, regulations and administrative provisions relating to direct life assurance, laying down provisions to facilitate the effective exercise of freedom to provide services[8] should be adapted.

(34)   Since the objectives of this Directive, namely the establishment of common rules on the distance marketing of consumer financial services cannot be sufficiently achieved by the Member States and can therefore be better achieved at Community level, the Community may adopt measures, in accordance with the principles of subsidiarity as set out in Article 5 of the Treaty. In accordance with the principle of proportionality, as set out in that Article, this Directive does not go beyond what is necessary to achieve that objective,

NOTES

[1]   OJ C385, 11.12.1998, p 10 and OJ C177 E, 27.6.2000, p 21.

[2]   OJ C169, 16.6.1999, p 43.

[3]   Opinion of the European Parliament of 5 May 1999 (OJ C279, 1.10.1999, p 207), Council Common Position of 19 December 2001 (OJ C58 E, 5.3.2002, p 32) and Decision of the European Parliament of 14 May 2002 (not yet published in the Official Journal). Council Decision of 26 June 2002 (not yet published in the Official Journal).

[4]   OJ L178, 17.7.2000, p 1.

[5]   OJ L12, 16.1.2001, p 1.

[6]   OJ L144, 4.6.1997, p 19.

[7]   OJ L166, 11.6.1998, p 51. Directive as last amended by Directive 2000/31/EC (OJ L178, 17.7.2001, p 1).

[8]   OJ L330, 29.11.1990, p 50. Directive as last amended by Directive 92/96/EEC (OJ L360, 9.12.1992, p 1).

HAVE ADOPTED THIS DIRECTIVE—

[4.326]
Article 1
Object and scope
1.   The object of this Directive is to approximate the laws, regulations and administrative provisions of the Member States concerning the distance marketing of consumer financial services.
2.   In the case of contracts for financial services comprising an initial service agreement followed by successive operations or a series of separate operations of the same nature performed over time, the provisions of this Directive shall apply only to the initial agreement.
   In case there is no initial service agreement but the successive operations or the separate operations of the same nature performed over time are performed between the same contractual parties, Articles 3 and 4 apply only when the first operation is performed. Where, however, no operation of the same nature is performed for more than one year, the next operation will be deemed to be the first in a new series of operations and, accordingly, Articles 3 and 4 shall apply.

[4.327]
Article 2
Definitions
For the purposes of this Directive—
   (a)   'distance contract' means any contract concerning financial services concluded between a supplier and a consumer under an organised distance sales or service-provision scheme run by the supplier, who, for the purpose of that contract, makes exclusive use of one or more means of distance communication up to and including the time at which the contract is concluded;
   (b)   'financial service' means any service of a banking, credit, insurance, personal pension, investment or payment nature;
   (c)   'supplier' means any natural or legal person, public or private, who, acting in his commercial or professional capacity, is the contractual provider of services subject to distance contracts;
   (d)   'consumer' means any natural person who, in distance contracts covered by this Directive, is acting for purposes which are outside his trade, business or profession;

(e)   'means of distance communication' refers to any means which, without the simultaneous physical presence of the supplier and the consumer, may be used for the distance marketing of a service between those parties;

(f)   'durable medium' means any instrument which enables the consumer to store information addressed personally to him in a way accessible for future reference for a period of time adequate for the purposes of the information and which allows the unchanged reproduction of the information stored;

(g)   'operator or supplier of a means of distance communication' means any public or private, natural or legal person whose trade, business or profession involves making one or more means of distance communication available to suppliers.

[4.328]
Article 3
Information to the consumer prior to the conclusion of the distance contract
1.   In good time before the consumer is bound by any distance contract or offer, he shall be provided with the following information concerning—

(1)   the supplier
   (a)   the identity and the main business of the supplier, the geographical address at which the supplier is established and any other geographical address relevant for the customer's relations with the supplier;
   (b)   the identity of the representative of the supplier established in the consumer's Member State of residence and the geographical address relevant for the customer's relations with the representative, if such a representative exists;
   (c)   when the consumer's dealings are with any professional other than the supplier, the identity of this professional, the capacity in which he is acting vis-à-vis the consumer, and the geographical address relevant for the customer's relations with this professional;
   (d)   where the supplier is registered in a trade or similar public register, the trade register in which the supplier is entered and his registration number or an equivalent means of identification in that register;
   (e)   where the supplier's activity is subject to an authorisation scheme, the particulars of the relevant supervisory authority;

(2)   the financial service
   (a)   a description of the main characteristics of the financial service;
   (b)   the total price to be paid by the consumer to the supplier for the financial service, including all related fees, charges and expenses, and all taxes paid via the supplier or, when an exact price cannot be indicated, the basis for the calculation of the price enabling the consumer to verify it;
   (c)   where relevant notice indicating that the financial service is related to instruments involving special risks related to their specific features or the operations to be executed or whose price depends on fluctuations in the financial markets outside the supplier's control and that historical performances are no indicators for future performances;
   (d)   notice of the possibility that other taxes and/or costs may exist that are not paid via the supplier or imposed by him;
   (e)   any limitations of the period for which the information provided is valid;
   (f)   the arrangements for payment and for performance;
   (g)   any specific additional cost for the consumer of using the means of distance communication, if such additional cost is charged;

(3)   the distance contract
   (a)   the existence or absence of a right of withdrawal in accordance with Article 6 and, where the right of withdrawal exists, its duration and the conditions for exercising it, including information on the amount which the consumer may be required to pay on the basis of Article 7(1), as well as the consequences of non-exercise of that right;
   (b)   the minimum duration of the distance contract in the case of financial services to be performed permanently or recurrently;
   (c)   information on any rights the parties may have to terminate the contract early or unilaterally by virtue of the terms of the distance contract, including any penalties imposed by the contract in such cases;
   (d)   practical instructions for exercising the right of withdrawal indicating, inter alia, the address to which the notification of a withdrawal should be sent;
   (e)   the Member State or States whose laws are taken by the supplier as a basis for the establishment of relations with the consumer prior to the conclusion of the distance contract;
   (f)   any contractual clause on law applicable to the distance contract and/or on competent court;
   (g)   in which language, or languages, the contractual terms and conditions, and the prior information referred to in this Article are supplied, and furthermore in which

language, or languages, the supplier, with the agreement of the consumer, undertakes to communicate during the duration of this distance contract;

(4)   redress

(a)   whether or not there is an out-of-court complaint and redress mechanism for the consumer that is party to the distance contract and, if so, the methods for having access to it;

(b)   the existence of guarantee funds or other compensation arrangements, not covered by Directive 94/19/EC of the European Parliament and of the Council of 30 May 1994 on deposit guarantee schemes[1] and Directive 97/9/EC of the European Parliament and of the Council of 3 March 1997 on investor compensation schemes.[2]

2.   The information referred to in paragraph 1, the commercial purpose of which must be made clear, shall be provided in a clear and comprehensible manner in any way appropriate to the means of distance communication used, with due regard, in particular, to the principles of good faith in commercial transactions, and the principles governing the protection of those who are unable, pursuant to the legislation of the Member States, to give their consent, such as minors.

3.   In the case of voice telephony communications

(a)   the identity of the supplier and the commercial purpose of the call initiated by the supplier shall be made explicitly clear at the beginning of any conversation with the consumer;

(b)   subject to the explicit consent of the consumer only the following information needs to be given—

—   the identity of the person in contact with the consumer and his link with the supplier,

—   a description of the main characteristics of the financial service,

—   the total price to be paid by the consumer to the supplier for the financial service including all taxes paid via the supplier or, when an exact price cannot be indicated, the basis for the calculation of the price enabling the consumer to verify it,

—   notice of the possibility that other taxes and/or costs may exist that are not paid via the supplier or imposed by him,

—   the existence or absence of a right of withdrawal in accordance with Article 6 and, where the right of withdrawal exists, its duration and the conditions for exercising it, including information on the amount which the consumer may be required to pay on the basis of Article 7(1).

The supplier shall inform the consumer that other information is available on request and of what nature this information is. In any case the supplier shall provide the full information when he fulfils his obligations under Article 5.

4.   Information on contractual obligations, to be communicated to the consumer during the pre-contractual phase, shall be in conformity with the contractual obligations which would result from the law presumed to be applicable to the distance contract if the latter were concluded.

NOTES

[1]   OJ L135, 31.5.1994, p 5.

[2]   OJ L84, 26.3.1997, p 22.

[4.329]
Article 4
Additional information requirements

1.   Where there are provisions in the Community legislation governing financial services which contain prior information requirements additional to those listed in Article 3(1), these requirements shall continue to apply.

2.   Pending further harmonisation, Member States may maintain or introduce more stringent provisions on prior information requirements when the provisions are in conformity with Community law.

3.   Member States shall communicate to the Commission national provisions on prior information requirements under paragraphs 1 and 2 of this Article when these requirements are additional to those listed in Article 3(1). The Commission shall take account of the communicated national provisions when drawing up the report referred to in Article 20(2).

4.   The Commission shall, with a view to creating a high level of transparency by all appropriate means, ensure that information, on the national provisions communicated to it, is made available to consumers and suppliers.

[5.   Where Directive 2007/64/EC of the European Parliament and of the Council of 13 November 2007 on payment services in the internal market[1] is also applicable, the information provisions under Article 3(1) of this Directive, with the exception of paragraphs (2)(c) to (g), (3)(a), (d) and (e), and (4)(b), shall be replaced with Articles 36, 37, 41 and 42 of that Directive.]

NOTES

Para 5: added by European Parliament and Council Directive 2007/64/EC, Art 90(1).

[1]   OJ L319, 5.12.2007, p 1.

[4.330]
Article 5
Communication of the contractual terms and conditions and of the prior information
1. The supplier shall communicate to the consumer all the contractual terms and conditions and the information referred to in Article 3(1) and Article 4 on paper or on another durable medium available and accessible to the consumer in good time before the consumer is bound by any distance contract or offer.
2. The supplier shall fulfil his obligation under paragraph 1 immediately after the conclusion of the contract, if the contract has been concluded at the consumer's request using a means of distance communication which does not enable providing the contractual terms and conditions and the information in conformity with paragraph 1.
3. At any time during the contractual relationship the consumer is entitled, at his request, to receive the contractual terms and conditions on paper. In addition, the consumer is entitled to change the means of distance communication used, unless this is incompatible with the contract concluded or the nature of the financial service provided.

[4.331]
Article 6
Right of withdrawal
1. The Member States shall ensure that the consumer shall have a period of 14 calendar days to withdraw from the contract without penalty and without giving any reason. However, this period shall be extended to 30 calendar days in distance contracts relating to life insurance covered by Directive 90/619/EEC and personal pension operations.
    The period for withdrawal shall begin—
—   either from the day of the conclusion of the distance contract, except in respect of the said life assurance, where the time limit will begin from the time when the consumer is informed that the distance contract has been concluded, or
—   from the day on which the consumer receives the contractual terms and conditions and the information in accordance with Article 5(1) or (2), if that is later than the date referred to in the first indent.
    Member States, in addition to the right of withdrawal, may provide that the enforceability of contracts relating to investment services is suspended for the same period provided for in this paragraph.
2. The right of withdrawal shall not apply to—
  (a)   financial services whose price depends on fluctuations in the financial market outside the suppliers control, which may occur during the withdrawal period, such as services related to—
      —   foreign exchange,
      —   money market instruments,
      —   transferable securities,
      —   units in collective investment undertakings,
      —   financial-futures contracts, including equivalent cash-settled instruments,
      —   forward interest-rate agreements (FRAs),
      —   interest-rate, currency and equity swaps,
      —   options to acquire or dispose of any instruments referred to in this point including equivalent cash-settled instruments.
      This category includes in particular options on currency and on interest rates;
  (b)   travel and baggage insurance policies or similar short-term insurance policies of less than one month's duration;
  (c)   contracts whose performance has been fully completed by both parties at the consumer's express request before the consumer exercises his right of withdrawal.
3. Member States may provide that the right of withdrawal shall not apply to:
  (a)   any credit intended primarily for the purpose of acquiring or retaining property rights in land or in an existing or projected building, or for the purpose of renovating or improving a building, or
  (b)   any credit secured either by mortgage on immovable property or by a right related to immovable property, or
  (c)   declarations by consumers using the services of an official, provided that the official confirms that the consumer is guaranteed the rights under Article 5(1).
    This paragraph shall be without prejudice to the right to a reflection time to the benefit of the consumers that are resident in those Member States where it exists, at the time of the adoption of this Directive.
4. Member States making use of the possibility set out in paragraph 3 shall communicate it to the Commission.
5. The Commission shall make available the information communicated by Member States to the European Parliament and the Council and shall ensure that it is also available to consumers and suppliers who request it.

6.   If the consumer exercises his right of withdrawal he shall, before the expiry of the relevant deadline, notify this following the practical instructions given to him in accordance with Article 3(1)(3)(d) by means which can be proved in accordance with national law. The deadline shall be deemed to have been observed if the notification, if it is on paper or on another durable medium available and accessible to the recipient, is dispatched before the deadline expires.

7.   This Article does not apply to credit agreements cancelled under the conditions of Article 6(4) of Directive 97/7/EC or Article 7 of Directive 94/47/EC of the European Parliament and of the Council of 26 October 1994 on the protection of purchasers in respect of certain aspects of contracts relating to the purchase of the right to use immovable properties on a timeshare basis.[1]

If to a distance contract of a given financial service another distance contract has been attached concerning services provided by the supplier or by a third party on the basis of an agreement between the third party and the supplier, this additional distance contract shall be cancelled, without any penalty, if the consumer exercises his right of withdrawal as provided for in Article 6(1).

8.   The provisions of this Article are without prejudice to the Member States' laws and regulations governing the cancellation or termination or non-enforceability of a distance contract or the right of a consumer to fulfil his contractual obligations before the time fixed in the distance contract. This applies irrespective of the conditions for and the legal effects of the winding-up of the contract.

NOTES
[1]   OJ L280, 29.10.1994, p 83.

[4.332]
Article 7
Payment of the service provided before withdrawal
1.   When the consumer exercises his right of withdrawal under Article 6(1) he may only be required to pay, without any undue delay, for the service actually provided by the supplier in accordance with the contract. The performance of the contract may only begin after the consumer has given his approval. The amount payable shall not—
   —   exceed an amount which is in proportion to the extent of the service already provided in comparison with the full coverage of the contract,
   —   in any case be such that it could be construed as a penalty.
2.   Member States may provide that the consumer cannot be required to pay any amount when withdrawing from an insurance contract.
3.   The supplier may not require the consumer to pay any amount on the basis of paragraph 1 unless he can prove that the consumer was duly informed about the amount payable, in conformity with Article 3(1)(3)(a). However, in no case may he require such payment if he has commenced the performance of the contract before the expiry of the withdrawal period provided for in Article 6(1) without the consumer's prior request.
4.   The supplier shall, without any undue delay and no later than within 30 calendar days, return to the consumer any sums he has received from him in accordance with the distance contract, except for the amount referred to in paragraph 1. This period shall begin from the day on which the supplier receives the notification of withdrawal.
5.   The consumer shall return to the supplier any sums and/or property he has received from the supplier without any undue delay and no later than within 30 calendar days. This period shall begin from the day on which the consumer dispatches the notification of withdrawal.

Article 8   *(Repealed by European Parliament and Council Directive 2007/64/EC, Art 90(2).)*

[4.333]
[Article 9
Given the prohibition of inertia selling practices laid down in Directive 2005/29/EC of 11 May 2005 of the European Parliament and of the Council concerning unfair business-to-consumer commercial practices in the internal market[1] and without prejudice to the provisions of Member States' legislation on the tacit renewal of distance contracts, when such rules permit tacit renewal, Member States shall take measures to exempt the consumer from any obligation in the event of unsolicited supplies, the absence of a reply not constituting consent.]

NOTES
Substituted by European Parliament and Council Directive 2005/29/EC, Art 15(2).
[1]   OJ L149, 11.6.2005, p 22.

[4.334]
Article 10
Unsolicited communications
1.   The use by a supplier of the following distance communication techniques shall require the consumer's prior consent—
   (a)   automated calling systems without human intervention (automatic calling machines);
   (b)   fax machines.

2.   Member States shall ensure that means of distance communication other than those referred to in paragraph 1, when they allow individual communications:

   (a)   shall not be authorised unless the consent of the consumers concerned has been obtained, or

   (b)   may only be used if the consumer has not expressed his manifest objection.

3.   The measures referred to in paragraphs 1 and 2 shall not entail costs for consumers.

[4.335]
Article 11
Sanctions
Member States shall provide for appropriate sanctions in the event of the supplier's failure to comply with national provisions adopted pursuant to this Directive.

   They may provide for this purpose in particular that the consumer may cancel the contract at any time, free of charge and without penalty.

   These sanctions must be effective, proportional and dissuasive.

[4.336]
Article 12
Imperative nature of this Directive's provisions
1.   Consumers may not waive the rights conferred on them by this Directive.

2.   Member States shall take the measures needed to ensure that the consumer does not lose the protection granted by this Directive by virtue of the choice of the law of a non-member country as the law applicable to the contract, if this contract has a close link with the territory of one or more Member States.

[4.337]
Article 13
Judicial and administrative redress
1.   Member States shall ensure that adequate and effective means exist to ensure compliance with this Directive in the interests of consumers.

2.   The means referred to in paragraph 1 shall include provisions whereby one or more of the following bodies, as determined by national law, may take action in accordance with national law before the courts or competent administrative bodies to ensure that the national provisions for the implementation of this Directive are applied—

   (a)   public bodies or their representatives;

   (b)   consumer organisations having a legitimate interest in protecting consumers;

   (c)   professional organisations having a legitimate interest in acting.

3.   Member States shall take the measures necessary to ensure that operators and suppliers of means of distance communication put an end to practices that have been declared to be contrary to this Directive, on the basis of a judicial decision, an administrative decision or a decision issued by a supervisory authority notified to them, where those operators or suppliers are in a position to do so.

[4.338]
Article 14
Out-of-court redress
1.   Member States shall promote the setting up or development of adequate and effective out-of-court complaints and redress procedures for the settlement of consumer disputes concerning financial services provided at distance.

2.   Member States shall, in particular, encourage the bodies responsible for out-of-court settlement of disputes to cooperate in the resolution of cross-border disputes concerning financial services provided at distance.

[4.339]
Article 15
Burden of proof
Without prejudice to Article 7(3), Member States may stipulate that the burden of proof in respect of the supplier's obligations to inform the consumer and the consumer's consent to conclusion of the contract and, where appropriate, its performance, can be placed on the supplier.

   Any contractual term or condition providing that the burden of proof of the respect by the supplier of all or part of the obligations incumbent on him pursuant to this Directive should lie with the consumer shall be an unfair term within the meaning of Council Directive 93/13/EEC of 5 April 1993 on unfair terms in consumer contracts.[1]

NOTES
   [1]   OJ L95, 21.4.1993, p 29.

Part 4   Other Materials

[4.340]
Article 16
Transitional measures
Member States may impose national rules which are in conformity with this Directive on suppliers established in a Member State which has not yet transposed this Directive and whose law has no obligations corresponding to those provided for in this Directive.

Articles 17–19 *(Art 17 amends Directive 90/619/EEC, Art 15(1); Art 18 amended Directive 97/7/EC (repealed); Art 19 amended Directive 98/27/EC (repealed)).*

[4.341]
Article 20
Review
1. Following the implementation of this Directive, the Commission shall examine the functioning of the internal market in financial services in respect of the marketing of those services. It should seek to analyse and detail the difficulties that are, or might be faced by both consumers and suppliers, in particular arising from differences between national provisions regarding information and right of withdrawal.
2. Not later than 9 April 2006 the Commission shall report to the European Parliament and the Council on the problems facing both consumers and suppliers seeking to buy and sell financial services, and shall submit, where appropriate, proposals to amend and/or further harmonise the information and right of withdrawal provisions in Community legislation concerning financial services and/or those covered in Article 3.

[4.342]
Article 21
Transposition
1. Member States shall bring into force the laws, regulations and administrative provisions necessary to comply with this Directive not later than 9 October 2004. They shall forthwith inform the Commission thereof.
   When Member States adopt these measures, they shall contain a reference to this Directive or shall be accompanied by such a reference on the occasion of their official publication. The methods of making such reference shall be laid down by Member States.
2. Member States shall communicate to the Commission the text of the main provisions of national law which they adopt in the field governed by this Directive together with a table showing how the provisions of this Directive correspond to the national provisions adopted.

[4.343]
Article 22
Entry into force
This Directive shall enter into force on the day of its publication in the *Official Journal of the European Communities*.

[4.344]
Article 23
Addressees
This Directive is addressed to the Member States.

DIRECTIVE OF THE EUROPEAN PARLIAMENT AND OF THE COUNCIL

(2005/29/EC)

of 11 May 2005

concerning unfair business-to-consumer commercial practices in the internal market and amending Council Directive 84/450/EEC, Directives 97/7/EC, 98/27/EC and 2002/65/EC of the European Parliament and of the Council and Regulation (EC) No 2006/2004 of the European Parliament and of the Council

("Unfair Commercial Practices Directive")

(Text with EEA relevance)

NOTE
Date of publication in OJ: OJ L149, 11.6.2005, p 22.
This Directive has been implemented in the UK by the Consumer Protection from Unfair Trading Regulations 2008, SI 2008/1277 at **[2.555]**.
Council Directive 84/450/EEC: repealed by European Parliament and Council Directive 2006/114/EC
Directive 97/7/EC: repealed by European Parliament and Council Directive 2011/83/EU.

Directive 98/27/EC: repealed by European Parliament and Council Directive 2009/22/EC.

THE EUROPEAN PARLIAMENT AND THE COUNCIL OF THE EUROPEAN UNION,

Having regard to the Treaty establishing the European Community, and in particular Article 95 thereof,

Having regard to the proposal from the Commission,

Having regard to the opinion of the European Economic and Social Committee,[1]

Acting in accordance with the procedure laid down in Article 251 of the Treaty,[2]

Whereas:

(1)   Article 153(1) and (3)(a) of the Treaty provides that the Community is to contribute to the attainment of a high level of consumer protection by the measures it adopts pursuant to Article 95 thereof.

(2)   In accordance with Article 14(2) of the Treaty, the internal market comprises an area without internal frontiers in which the free movement of goods and services and freedom of establishment are ensured. The development of fair commercial practices within the area without internal frontiers is vital for the promotion of the development of cross-border activities.

(3)   The laws of the Member States relating to unfair commercial practices show marked differences which can generate appreciable distortions of competition and obstacles to the smooth functioning of the internal market. In the field of advertising, Council Directive 84/450/EEC of 10 September 1984 concerning misleading and comparative advertising[3] establishes minimum criteria for harmonising legislation on misleading advertising, but does not prevent the Member States from retaining or adopting measures which provide more extensive protection for consumers. As a result, Member States' provisions on misleading advertising diverge significantly.

(4)   These disparities cause uncertainty as to which national rules apply to unfair commercial practices harming consumers' economic interests and create many barriers affecting business and consumers. These barriers increase the cost to business of exercising internal market freedoms, in particular when businesses wish to engage in cross border marketing, advertising campaigns and sales promotions. Such barriers also make consumers uncertain of their rights and undermine their confidence in the internal market.

(5)   In the absence of uniform rules at Community level, obstacles to the free movement of services and goods across borders or the freedom of establishment could be justified in the light of the case-law of the Court of Justice of the European Communities as long as they seek to protect recognised public interest objectives and are proportionate to those objectives. In view of the Community's objectives, as set out in the provisions of the Treaty and in secondary Community law relating to freedom of movement, and in accordance with the Commission's policy on commercial communications as indicated in the Communication from the Commission entitled "The follow-up to the Green Paper on Commercial Communications in the Internal Market", such obstacles should be eliminated. These obstacles can only be eliminated by establishing uniform rules at Community level which establish a high level of consumer protection and by clarifying certain legal concepts at Community level to the extent necessary for the proper functioning of the internal market and to meet the requirement of legal certainty.

(6)   This Directive therefore approximates the laws of the Member States on unfair commercial practices, including unfair advertising, which directly harm consumers' economic interests and thereby indirectly harm the economic interests of legitimate competitors. In line with the principle of proportionality, this Directive protects consumers from the consequences of such unfair commercial practices where they are material but recognises that in some cases the impact on consumers may be negligible. It neither covers nor affects the national laws on unfair commercial practices which harm only competitors' economic interests or which relate to a transaction between traders; taking full account of the principle of subsidiarity, Member States will continue to be able to regulate such practices, in conformity with Community law, if they choose to do so. Nor does this Directive cover or affect the provisions of Directive 84/450/EEC on advertising which misleads business but which is not misleading for consumers and on comparative advertising. Further, this Directive does not affect accepted advertising and marketing practices, such as legitimate product placement, brand differentiation or the offering of incentives which may legitimately affect consumers' perceptions of products and influence their behaviour without impairing the consumer's ability to make an informed decision.

(7)   This Directive addresses commercial practices directly related to influencing consumers' transactional decisions in relation to products. It does not address commercial practices carried out primarily for other purposes, including for example commercial communication aimed at investors, such as annual reports and corporate promotional literature. It does not address legal requirements related to taste and decency which vary widely among the Member States. Commercial practices such as, for example, commercial solicitation in the streets, may be undesirable in Member States for cultural reasons. Member States should accordingly be able to continue to ban commercial practices in their territory, in conformity with Community law, for reasons of taste and decency even where such practices do not limit consumers' freedom of choice. Full account should be taken of the

context of the individual case concerned in applying this Directive, in particular the general clauses thereof.

(8) This Directive directly protects consumer economic interests from unfair business-to-consumer commercial practices. Thereby, it also indirectly protects legitimate businesses from their competitors who do not play by the rules in this Directive and thus guarantees fair competition in fields coordinated by it. It is understood that there are other commercial practices which, although not harming consumers, may hurt competitors and business customers. The Commission should carefully examine the need for Community action in the field of unfair competition beyond the remit of this Directive and, if necessary, make a legislative proposal to cover these other aspects of unfair competition.

(9) This Directive is without prejudice to individual actions brought by those who have been harmed by an unfair commercial practice. It is also without prejudice to Community and national rules on contract law, on intellectual property rights, on the health and safety aspects of products, on conditions of establishment and authorisation regimes, including those rules which, in conformity with Community law, relate to gambling activities, and to Community competition rules and the national provisions implementing them. The Member States will thus be able to retain or introduce restrictions and prohibitions of commercial practices on grounds of the protection of the health and safety of consumers in their territory wherever the trader is based, for example in relation to alcohol, tobacco or pharmaceuticals. Financial services and immovable property, by reason of their complexity and inherent serious risks, necessitate detailed requirements, including positive obligations on traders. For this reason, in the field of financial services and immovable property, this Directive is without prejudice to the right of Member States to go beyond its provisions to protect the economic interests of consumers. It is not appropriate to regulate here the certification and indication of the standard of fineness of articles of precious metal.

(10) It is necessary to ensure that the relationship between this Directive and existing Community law is coherent, particularly where detailed provisions on unfair commercial practices apply to specific sectors. This Directive therefore amends Directive 84/450/EEC, Directive 97/7/EC of the European Parliament and of the Council of 20 May 1997 on the protection of consumers in respect of distance contracts[4] Directive 98/27/EC of the European Parliament and of the Council of 19 May 1998 on injunctions for the protection of consumers' interests[5] and Directive 2002/65/EC of the European Parliament and of the Council of 23 September 2002 concerning the distance marketing of consumer financial services.[6] This Directive accordingly applies only in so far as there are no specific Community law provisions regulating specific aspects of unfair commercial practices, such as information requirements and rules on the way the information is presented to the consumer. It provides protection for consumers where there is no specific sectoral legislation at Community level and prohibits traders from creating a false impression of the nature of products. This is particularly important for complex products with high levels of risk to consumers, such as certain financial services products. This Directive consequently complements the Community acquis, which is applicable to commercial practices harming consumers' economic interests.

(11) The high level of convergence achieved by the approximation of national provisions through this Directive creates a high common level of consumer protection. This Directive establishes a single general prohibition of those unfair commercial practices distorting consumers' economic behaviour. It also sets rules on aggressive commercial practices, which are currently not regulated at Community level.

(12) Harmonisation will considerably increase legal certainty for both consumers and business. Both consumers and business will be able to rely on a single regulatory framework based on clearly defined legal concepts regulating all aspects of unfair commercial practices across the EU. The effect will be to eliminate the barriers stemming from the fragmentation of the rules on unfair commercial practices harming consumer economic interests and to enable the internal market to be achieved in this area.

(13) In order to achieve the Community's objectives through the removal of internal market barriers, it is necessary to replace Member States' existing, divergent general clauses and legal principles. The single, common general prohibition established by this Directive therefore covers unfair commercial practices distorting consumers' economic behaviour. In order to support consumer confidence the general prohibition should apply equally to unfair commercial practices which occur outside any contractual relationship between a trader and a consumer or following the conclusion of a contract and during its execution. The general prohibition is elaborated by rules on the two types of commercial practices which are by far the most common, namely misleading commercial practices and aggressive commercial practices.

(14) It is desirable that misleading commercial practices cover those practices, including misleading advertising, which by deceiving the consumer prevent him from making an informed and thus efficient choice. In conformity with the laws and practices of Member States on misleading advertising, this Directive classifies misleading practices into misleading actions and misleading omissions. In respect of omissions, this Directive sets out a limited number of key items of information which the consumer needs to make an informed transactional decision. Such information will not have to be disclosed in all advertisements, but only where the trader makes an

invitation to purchase, which is a concept clearly defined in this Directive. The full harmonisation approach adopted in this Directive does not preclude the Member States from specifying in national law the main characteristics of particular products such as, for example, collectors' items or electrical goods, the omission of which would be material when an invitation to purchase is made. It is not the intention of this Directive to reduce consumer choice by prohibiting the promotion of products which look similar to other products unless this similarity confuses consumers as to the commercial origin of the product and is therefore misleading. This Directive should be without prejudice to existing Community law which expressly affords Member States the choice between several regulatory options for the protection of consumers in the field of commercial practices. In particular, this Directive should be without prejudice to Article 13(3) of Directive 2002/58/EC of the European Parliament and of the Council of 12 July 2002 concerning the processing of personal data and the protection of privacy in the electronic communications sector.[7]

(15) Where Community law sets out information requirements in relation to commercial communication, advertising and marketing that information is considered as material under this Directive. Member States will be able to retain or add information requirements relating to contract law and having contract law consequences where this is allowed by the minimum clauses in the existing Community law instruments. A non-exhaustive list of such information requirements in the acquis is contained in Annex II. Given the full harmonisation introduced by this Directive only the information required in Community law is considered as material for the purpose of Article 7(5) thereof. Where Member States have introduced information requirements over and above what is specified in Community law, on the basis of minimum clauses, the omission of that extra information will not constitute a misleading omission under this Directive. By contrast Member States will be able, when allowed by the minimum clauses in Community law, to maintain or introduce more stringent provisions in conformity with Community law so as to ensure a higher level of protection of consumers' individual contractual rights.

(16) The provisions on aggressive commercial practices should cover those practices which significantly impair the consumer's freedom of choice. Those are practices using harassment, coercion, including the use of physical force, and undue influence.

(17) It is desirable that those commercial practices which are in all circumstances unfair be identified to provide greater legal certainty. Annex I therefore contains the full list of all such practices. These are the only commercial practices which can be deemed to be unfair without a case-by-case assessment against the provisions of Articles 5 to 9. The list may only be modified by revision of the Directive.

(18) It is appropriate to protect all consumers from unfair commercial practices; however the Court of Justice has found it necessary in adjudicating on advertising cases since the enactment of Directive 84/450/EEC to examine the effect on a notional, typical consumer. In line with the principle of proportionality, and to permit the effective application of the protections contained in it, this Directive takes as a benchmark the average consumer, who is reasonably well-informed and reasonably observant and circumspect, taking into account social, cultural and linguistic factors, as interpreted by the Court of Justice, but also contains provisions aimed at preventing the exploitation of consumers whose characteristics make them particularly vulnerable to unfair commercial practices. Where a commercial practice is specifically aimed at a particular group of consumers, such as children, it is desirable that the impact of the commercial practice be assessed from the perspective of the average member of that group. It is therefore appropriate to include in the list of practices which are in all circumstances unfair a provision which, without imposing an outright ban on advertising directed at children, protects them from direct exhortations to purchase. The average consumer test is not a statistical test. National courts and authorities will have to exercise their own faculty of judgement, having regard to the case-law of the Court of Justice, to determine the typical reaction of the average consumer in a given case.

(19) Where certain characteristics such as age, physical or mental infirmity or credulity make consumers particularly susceptible to a commercial practice or to the underlying product and the economic behaviour only of such consumers is likely to be distorted by the practice in a way that the trader can reasonably foresee, it is appropriate to ensure that they are adequately protected by assessing the practice from the perspective of the average member of that group.

(20) It is appropriate to provide a role for codes of conduct, which enable traders to apply the principles of this Directive effectively in specific economic fields. In sectors where there are specific mandatory requirements regulating the behaviour of traders, it is appropriate that these will also provide evidence as to the requirements of professional diligence in that sector. The control exercised by code owners at national or Community level to eliminate unfair commercial practices may avoid the need for recourse to administrative or judicial action and should therefore be encouraged. With the aim of pursuing a high level of consumer protection, consumers' organisations could be informed and involved in the drafting of codes of conduct.

(21) Persons or organisations regarded under national law as having a legitimate interest in the matter must have legal remedies for initiating proceedings against unfair commercial practices, either before a court or before an administrative authority which is competent to decide upon complaints or to initiate appropriate legal proceedings. While it is for national law to determine the

burden of proof, it is appropriate to enable courts and administrative authorities to require traders to produce evidence as to the accuracy of factual claims they have made.

(22)   It is necessary that Member States lay down penalties for infringements of the provisions of this Directive and they must ensure that these are enforced. The penalties must be effective, proportionate and dissuasive.

(23)   Since the objectives of this Directive, namely to eliminate the barriers to the functioning of the internal market represented by national laws on unfair commercial practices and to provide a high common level of consumer protection, by approximating the laws, regulations and adminis-trative provisions of the Member States on unfair commercial practices, cannot be sufficiently achieved by the Member States and can therefore be better achieved at Community level, the Community may adopt measures, in accordance with the principle of subsidiarity as set out in Article 5 of the Treaty. In accordance with the principle of proportionality, as set out in that Article, this Directive does not go beyond what is necessary in order to eliminate the internal market barriers and achieve a high common level of consumer protection.

(24)   It is appropriate to review this Directive to ensure that barriers to the internal market have been addressed and a high level of consumer protection achieved. The review could lead to a Commission proposal to amend this Directive, which may include a limited extension to the derogation in Article 3(5), and/or amendments to other consumer protection legislation reflecting the Commission's Consumer Policy Strategy commitment to review the existing acquis in order to achieve a high, common level of consumer protection.

(25)   This Directive respects the fundamental rights and observes the principles recognised in particular by the Charter of Fundamental Rights of the European Union,

HAVE ADOPTED THIS DIRECTIVE:

NOTES

[1]   OJ C108, 30.4.2004, p 81.

[2]   Opinion of the European Parliament of 20 April 2004 (OJ C104 E, 30.4.2004, p 260), Council Common Position of 15 November 2004 (OJ C38 E, 15.2.2005, p 1), Position of the European Parliament of 24 February 2005 (not yet published in the Official Journal) and Council Decision of 12 April 2005.

[3]   OJ L250, 19.9.1984, p 17. Directive as amended by Directive 97/55/EC of the European Parliament and of the Council (OJ L290, 23.10.1997, p 18).

[4]   OJ L144, 4.6.1997, p 19. Directive as amended by Directive 2002/65/EC (OJ L271, 9.10.2002, p 16).

[5]   OJ L166, 11.6.1998, p 51. Directive as last amended by Directive 2002/65/EC.

[6]   OJ L271, 9.10.2002, p 16.

[7]   OJ L201, 31.7.2002, p 37.

CHAPTER 1
GENERAL PROVISIONS

[4.345]
Article 1
Purpose

The purpose of this Directive is to contribute to the proper functioning of the internal market and achieve a high level of consumer protection by approximating the laws, regulations and administrative provisions of the Member States on unfair commercial practices harming consumers' economic interests.

[4.346]
Article 2
Definitions

For the purposes of this Directive:

(a)   'consumer' means any natural person who, in commercial practices covered by this Directive, is acting for purposes which are outside his trade, business, craft or profession;

(b)   'trader' means any natural or legal person who, in commercial practices covered by this Directive, is acting for purposes relating to his trade, business, craft or profession and anyone acting in the name of or on behalf of a trader;

(c)   'product' means any goods or service including immovable property, rights and obligations;

(d)   'business-to-consumer commercial practices' (hereinafter also referred to as commercial practices) means any act, omission, course of conduct or representation, commercial communication including advertising and marketing, by a trader, directly connected with the promotion, sale or supply of a product to consumers;

(e)   'to materially distort the economic behaviour of consumers' means using a commercial practice to appreciably impair the consumer's ability to make an informed decision, thereby causing the consumer to take a transactional decision that he would not have taken otherwise;

(f)   'code of conduct' means an agreement or set of rules not imposed by law, regulation or administrative provision of a Member State which defines the behaviour of traders who undertake to be bound by the code in relation to one or more particular commercial practices or business sectors;

(g)   'code owner' means any entity, including a trader or group of traders, which is responsible for the formulation and revision of a code of conduct and/or for monitoring compliance with the code by those who have undertaken to be bound by it;

(h)   'professional diligence' means the standard of special skill and care which a trader may reasonably be expected to exercise towards consumers, commensurate with honest market practice and/or the general principle of good faith in the trader's field of activity;

(i)   'invitation to purchase' means a commercial communication which indicates characteristics of the product and the price in a way appropriate to the means of the commercial communication used and thereby enables the consumer to make a purchase;

(j)   'undue influence' means exploiting a position of power in relation to the consumer so as to apply pressure, even without using or threatening to use physical force, in a way which significantly limits the consumer's ability to make an informed decision;

(k)   'transactional decision' means any decision taken by a consumer concerning whether, how and on what terms to purchase, make payment in whole or in part for, retain or dispose of a product or to exercise a contractual right in relation to the product, whether the consumer decides to act or to refrain from acting;

(l)   'regulated profession' means a professional activity or a group of professional activities, access to which or the pursuit of which, or one of the modes of pursuing which, is conditional, directly or indirectly, upon possession of specific professional qualifications, pursuant to laws, regulations or administrative provisions.

[4.347]
Article 3
Scope
1.   This Directive shall apply to unfair business-to-consumer commercial practices, as laid down in Article 5, before, during and after a commercial transaction in relation to a product.
2.   This Directive is without prejudice to contract law and, in particular, to the rules on the validity, formation or effect of a contract.
3.   This Directive is without prejudice to Community or national rules relating to the health and safety aspects of products.
4.   In the case of conflict between the provisions of this Directive and other Community rules regulating specific aspects of unfair commercial practices, the latter shall prevail and apply to those specific aspects.
5.   For a period of six years from 12 June 2007, Member States shall be able to continue to apply national provisions within the field approximated by this Directive which are more restrictive or prescriptive than this Directive and which implement directives containing minimum harmonisation clauses. These measures must be essential to ensure that consumers are adequately protected against unfair commercial practices and must be proportionate to the attainment of this objective. The review referred to in Article 18 may, if considered appropriate, include a proposal to prolong this derogation for a further limited period.
6.   Member States shall notify the Commission without delay of any national provisions applied on the basis of paragraph 5.
7.   This Directive is without prejudice to the rules determining the jurisdiction of the courts.
8.   This Directive is without prejudice to any conditions of establishment or of authorisation regimes, or to the deontological codes of conduct or other specific rules governing regulated professions in order to uphold high standards of integrity on the part of the professional, which Member States may, in conformity with Community law, impose on professionals.
9.   In relation to "financial services", as defined in Directive 2002/65/EC, and immovable property, Member States may impose requirements which are more restrictive or prescriptive than this Directive in the field which it approximates.
10.   This Directive shall not apply to the application of the laws, regulations and administrative provisions of Member States relating to the certification and indication of the standard of fineness of articles of precious metal.

[4.348]
Article 4
Internal market
Member States shall neither restrict the freedom to provide services nor restrict the free movement of goods for reasons falling within the field approximated by this Directive.

CHAPTER 2
UNFAIR COMMERCIAL PRACTICES

[4.349]
Article 5
Prohibition of unfair commercial practices
1. Unfair commercial practices shall be prohibited.
2. A commercial practice shall be unfair if:
   (a) it is contrary to the requirements of professional diligence, and
   (b) it materially distorts or is likely to materially distort the economic behaviour with regard to the product of the average consumer whom it reaches or to whom it is addressed, or of the average member of the group when a commercial practice is directed to a particular group of consumers.
3. Commercial practices which are likely to materially distort the economic behaviour only of a clearly identifiable group of consumers who are particularly vulnerable to the practice or the underlying product because of their mental or physical infirmity, age or credulity in a way which the trader could reasonably be expected to foresee, shall be assessed from the perspective of the average member of that group. This is without prejudice to the common and legitimate advertising practice of making exaggerated statements or statements which are not meant to be taken literally.
4. In particular, commercial practices shall be unfair which:
   (a) are misleading as set out in Articles 6 and 7, or
   (b) are aggressive as set out in Articles 8 and 9.
5. Annex I contains the list of those commercial practices which shall in all circumstances be regarded as unfair. The same single list shall apply in all Member States and may only be modified by revision of this Directive.

SECTION 1
MISLEADING COMMERCIAL PRACTICES

[4.350]
Article 6
Misleading actions
1. A commercial practice shall be regarded as misleading if it contains false information and is therefore untruthful or in any way, including overall presentation, deceives or is likely to deceive the average consumer, even if the information is factually correct, in relation to one or more of the following elements, and in either case causes or is likely to cause him to take a transactional decision that he would not have taken otherwise:
   (a) the existence or nature of the product;
   (b) the main characteristics of the product, such as its availability, benefits, risks, execution, composition, accessories, after-sale customer assistance and complaint handling, method and date of manufacture or provision, delivery, fitness for purpose, usage, quantity, specification, geographical or commercial origin or the results to be expected from its use, or the results and material features of tests or checks carried out on the product;
   (c) the extent of the trader's commitments, the motives for the commercial practice and the nature of the sales process, any statement or symbol in relation to direct or indirect sponsorship or approval of the trader or the product;
   (d) the price or the manner in which the price is calculated, or the existence of a specific price advantage;
   (e) the need for a service, part, replacement or repair;
   (f) the nature, attributes and rights of the trader or his agent, such as his identity and assets, his qualifications, status, approval, affiliation or connection and ownership of industrial, commercial or intellectual property rights or his awards and distinctions;
   (g) the consumer's rights, including the right to replacement or reimbursement under Directive 1999/44/EC of the European Parliament and of the Council of 25 May 1999 on certain aspects of the sale of consumer goods and associated guarantees,[1] or the risks he may face.
2. A commercial practice shall also be regarded as misleading if, in its factual context, taking account of all its features and circumstances, it causes or is likely to cause the average consumer to take a transactional decision that he would not have taken otherwise, and it involves:
   (a) any marketing of a product, including comparative advertising, which creates confusion with any products, trade marks, trade names or other distinguishing marks of a competitor;
   (b) non-compliance by the trader with commitments contained in codes of conduct by which the trader has undertaken to be bound, where:
      (i) the commitment is not aspirational but is firm and is capable of being verified, and
      (ii) the trader indicates in a commercial practice that he is bound by the code.

NOTES
[1]   OJ L171, 7.7.1999, p 12.

[4.351]
Article 7
Misleading omissions

1. A commercial practice shall be regarded as misleading if, in its factual context, taking account of all its features and circumstances and the limitations of the communication medium, it omits material information that the average consumer needs, according to the context, to take an informed transactional decision and thereby causes or is likely to cause the average consumer to take a transactional decision that he would not have taken otherwise.

2. It shall also be regarded as a misleading omission when, taking account of the matters described in paragraph 1, a trader hides or provides in an unclear, unintelligible, ambiguous or untimely manner such material information as referred to in that paragraph or fails to identify the commercial intent of the commercial practice if not already apparent from the context, and where, in either case, this causes or is likely to cause the average consumer to take a transactional decision that he would not have taken otherwise.

3. Where the medium used to communicate the commercial practice imposes limitations of space or time, these limitations and any measures taken by the trader to make the information available to consumers by other means shall be taken into account in deciding whether information has been omitted.

4. In the case of an invitation to purchase, the following information shall be regarded as material, if not already apparent from the context:

   (a) the main characteristics of the product, to an extent appropriate to the medium and the product;

   (b) the geographical address and the identity of the trader, such as his trading name and, where applicable, the geographical address and the identity of the trader on whose behalf he is acting;

   (c) the price inclusive of taxes, or where the nature of the product means that the price cannot reasonably be calculated in advance, the manner in which the price is calculated, as well as, where appropriate, all additional freight, delivery or postal charges or, where these charges cannot reasonably be calculated in advance, the fact that such additional charges may be payable;

   (d) the arrangements for payment, delivery, performance and the complaint handling policy, if they depart from the requirements of professional diligence;

   (e) for products and transactions involving a right of withdrawal or cancellation, the existence of such a right.

5. Information requirements established by Community law in relation to commercial communication including advertising or marketing, a non-exhaustive list of which is contained in Annex II, shall be regarded as material.

SECTION 2
AGGRESSIVE COMMERCIAL PRACTICES

[4.352]
Article 8
Aggressive commercial practices

A commercial practice shall be regarded as aggressive if, in its factual context, taking account of all its features and circumstances, by harassment, coercion, including the use of physical force, or undue influence, it significantly impairs or is likely to significantly impair the average consumer's freedom of choice or conduct with regard to the product and thereby causes him or is likely to cause him to take a transactional decision that he would not have taken otherwise.

[4.353]
Article 9
Use of harassment, coercion and undue influence

In determining whether a commercial practice uses harassment, coercion, including the use of physical force, or undue influence, account shall be taken of:

   (a) its timing, location, nature or persistence;

   (b) the use of threatening or abusive language or behaviour;

   (c) the exploitation by the trader of any specific misfortune or circumstance of such gravity as to impair the consumer's judgement, of which the trader is aware, to influence the consumer's decision with regard to the product;

   (d) any onerous or disproportionate non-contractual barriers imposed by the trader where a consumer wishes to exercise rights under the contract, including rights to terminate a contract or to switch to another product or another trader;

   (e) any threat to take any action that cannot legally be taken.

CHAPTER 3
CODES OF CONDUCT

[4.354]
Article 10
Codes of conduct
This Directive does not exclude the control, which Member States may encourage, of unfair commercial practices by code owners and recourse to such bodies by the persons or organisations referred to in Article 11 if proceedings before such bodies are in addition to the court or administrative proceedings referred to in that Article.

Recourse to such control bodies shall never be deemed the equivalent of foregoing a means of judicial or administrative recourse as provided for in Article 11.

CHAPTER 4
FINAL PROVISIONS

[4.355]
Article 11
Enforcement
1.   Member States shall ensure that adequate and effective means exist to combat unfair commercial practices in order to enforce compliance with the provisions of this Directive in the interest of consumers.

Such means shall include legal provisions under which persons or organisations regarded under national law as having a legitimate interest in combating unfair commercial practices, including competitors, may:
   (a)   take legal action against such unfair commercial practices; and/or
   (b)   bring such unfair commercial practices before an administrative authority competent either to decide on complaints or to initiate appropriate legal proceedings.
It shall be for each Member State to decide which of these facilities shall be available and whether to enable the courts or administrative authorities to require prior recourse to other established means of dealing with complaints, including those referred to in Article 10. These facilities shall be available regardless of whether the consumers affected are in the territory of the Member State where the trader is located or in another Member State.

It shall be for each Member State to decide:
   (a)   whether these legal facilities may be directed separately or jointly against a number of traders from the same economic sector; and
   (b)   whether these legal facilities may be directed against a code owner where the relevant code promotes non-compliance with legal requirements.
2.   Under the legal provisions referred to in paragraph 1, Member States shall confer upon the courts or administrative authorities powers enabling them, in cases where they deem such measures to be necessary taking into account all the interests involved and in particular the public interest:
   (a)   to order the cessation of, or to institute appropriate legal proceedings for an order for the cessation of, unfair commercial practices; or
   (b)   if the unfair commercial practice has not yet been carried out but is imminent, to order the prohibition of the practice, or to institute appropriate legal proceedings for an order for the prohibition of the practice,
even without proof of actual loss or damage or of intention or negligence on the part of the trader.

Member States shall also make provision for the measures referred to in the first subparagraph to be taken under an accelerated procedure:
   —   either with interim effect, or
   —   with definitive effect,
on the understanding that it is for each Member State to decide which of the two options to select.

Furthermore, Member States may confer upon the courts or administrative authorities powers enabling them, with a view to eliminating the continuing effects of unfair commercial practices the cessation of which has been ordered by a final decision:
   (a)   to require publication of that decision in full or in part and in such form as they deem adequate;
   (b)   to require in addition the publication of a corrective statement.
3.   The administrative authorities referred to in paragraph 1 must:
   (a)   be composed so as not to cast doubt on their impartiality;
   (b)   have adequate powers, where they decide on complaints, to monitor and enforce the observance of their decisions effectively;
   (c)   normally give reasons for their decisions.
Where the powers referred to in paragraph 2 are exercised exclusively by an administrative authority, reasons for its decisions shall always be given. Furthermore, in this case, provision must be made for procedures whereby improper or unreasonable exercise of its powers by the administrative authority or improper or unreasonable failure to exercise the said powers can be the subject of judicial review.

[4.356]
Article 12
Courts and administrative authorities: substantiation of claims
Member States shall confer upon the courts or administrative authorities powers enabling them in the civil or administrative proceedings provided for in Article 11:

   (a)   to require the trader to furnish evidence as to the accuracy of factual claims in relation to a commercial practice if, taking into account the legitimate interest of the trader and any other party to the proceedings, such a requirement appears appropriate on the basis of the circumstances of the particular case; and

   (b)   to consider factual claims as inaccurate if the evidence demanded in accordance with (a) is not furnished or is deemed insufficient by the court or administrative authority.

[4.357]
Article 13
Penalties
Member States shall lay down penalties for infringements of national provisions adopted in application of this Directive and shall take all necessary measures to ensure that these are enforced. These penalties must be effective, proportionate and dissuasive.

Articles 14–16   *(Art 14 amended Directive 84/450/EEC (repealed); Art 15 amended Directive 97/7/EC (repealed) and amends Directive 2002/65/EC, Art 9 at* **[4.333]***; Art 16 amended Directive 98/27/EC (repealed) and amends Regulation 2006/2004/EC.)*

[4.358]
Article 17
Information
Member States shall take appropriate measures to inform consumers of the national law transposing this Directive and shall, where appropriate, encourage traders and code owners to inform consumers of their codes of conduct.

[4.359]
Article 18
Review
1.   By 12 June 2011 the Commission shall submit to the European Parliament and the Council a comprehensive report on the application of this Directive, in particular of Articles 3(9) and 4 and Annex I, on the scope for further harmonisation and simplification of Community law relating to consumer protection, and, having regard to Article 3(5), on any measures that need to be taken at Community level to ensure that appropriate levels of consumer protection are maintained. The report shall be accompanied, if necessary, by a proposal to revise this Directive or other relevant parts of Community law.

2.   The European Parliament and the Council shall endeavour to act, in accordance with the Treaty, within two years of the presentation by the Commission of any proposal submitted under paragraph 1.

[4.360]
Article 19
Transposition
Member States shall adopt and publish the laws, regulations and administrative provisions necessary to comply with this Directive by 12 June 2007. They shall forthwith inform the Commission thereof and inform the Commission of any subsequent amendments without delay.

    They shall apply those measures by 12 December 2007. When Member States adopt those measures, they shall contain a reference to this Directive or be accompanied by such a reference on the occasion of their official publication. Member States shall determine how such reference is to be made.

[4.361]
Article 20
Entry into force
This Directive shall enter into force on the day following its publication in the *Official Journal of the European Union.*

[4.362]
Article 21
Addressees
This Directive is addressed to the Member States.

ANNEX I

COMMERCIAL PRACTICES WHICH ARE IN ALL CIRCUMSTANCES CONSIDERED UNFAIR

Misleading commercial practices

[4.363]

1.   Claiming to be a signatory to a code of conduct when the trader is not.

2.   Displaying a trust mark, quality mark or equivalent without having obtained the necessary authorisation.

3.   Claiming that a code of conduct has an endorsement from a public or other body which it does not have.

4.   Claiming that a trader (including his commercial practices) or a product has been approved, endorsed or authorised by a public or private body when he/it has not or making such a claim without complying with the terms of the approval, endorsement or authorisation.

5.   Making an invitation to purchase products at a specified price without disclosing the existence of any reasonable grounds the trader may have for believing that he will not be able to offer for supply or to procure another trader to supply, those products or equivalent products at that price for a period that is, and in quantities that are, reasonable having regard to the product, the scale of advertising of the product and the price offered (bait advertising).

6.   Making an invitation to purchase products at a specified price and then:
   (a)   refusing to show the advertised item to consumers;
      or
   (b)   refusing to take orders for it or deliver it within a reasonable time;
      or
   (c)   demonstrating a defective sample of it,
with the intention of promoting a different product (bait and switch)

7.   Falsely stating that a product will only be available for a very limited time, or that it will only be available on particular terms for a very limited time, in order to elicit an immediate decision and deprive consumers of sufficient opportunity or time to make an informed choice.

8.   Undertaking to provide after-sales service to consumers with whom the trader has communicated prior to a transaction in a language which is not an official language of the Member State where the trader is located and then making such service available only in another language without clearly disclosing this to the consumer before the consumer is committed to the transaction.

9.   Stating or otherwise creating the impression that a product can legally be sold when it cannot.

10.   Presenting rights given to consumers in law as a distinctive feature of the trader's offer.

11.   Using editorial content in the media to promote a product where a trader has paid for the promotion without making that clear in the content or by images or sounds clearly identifiable by the consumer (advertorial). This is without prejudice to Council Directive 89/552/EEC.[1]

12.   Making a materially inaccurate claim concerning the nature and extent of the risk to the personal security of the consumer or his family if the consumer does not purchase the product.

13.   Promoting a product similar to a product made by a particular manufacturer in such a manner as deliberately to mislead the consumer into believing that the product is made by that same manufacturer when it is not.

14.   Establishing, operating or promoting a pyramid promotional scheme where a consumer gives consideration for the opportunity to receive compensation that is derived primarily from the introduction of other consumers into the scheme rather than from the sale or consumption of products.

15.   Claiming that the trader is about to cease trading or move premises when he is not.

16.   Claiming that products are able to facilitate winning in games of chance.

17.   Falsely claiming that a product is able to cure illnesses, dysfunction or malformations.

18.   Passing on materially inaccurate information on market conditions or on the possibility of finding the product with the intention of inducing the consumer to acquire the product at conditions less favourable than normal market conditions.

19.   Claiming in a commercial practice to offer a competition or prize promotion without awarding the prizes described or a reasonable equivalent.

20.   Describing a product as "gratis", "free", "without charge" or similar if the consumer has to pay anything other than the unavoidable cost of responding to the commercial practice and collecting or paying for delivery of the item.

21.   Including in marketing material an invoice or similar document seeking payment which gives the consumer the impression that he has already ordered the marketed product when he has not.

22.   Falsely claiming or creating the impression that the trader is not acting for purposes relating to his trade, business, craft or profession, or falsely representing oneself as a consumer.

23. Creating the false impression that after-sales service in relation to a product is available in a Member State other than the one in which the product is sold.

Aggressive commercial practices

24. Creating the impression that the consumer cannot leave the premises until a contract is formed.

25. Conducting personal visits to the consumer's home ignoring the consumer's request to leave or not to return except in circumstances and to the extent justified, under national law, to enforce a contractual obligation.

26. Making persistent and unwanted solicitations by telephone, fax, e-mail or other remote media except in circumstances and to the extent justified under national law to enforce a contractual obligation. This is without prejudice to Article 10 of Directive 97/7/EC and Directives 95/46/EC[2] and 2002/58/EC.

27. Requiring a consumer who wishes to claim on an insurance policy to produce documents which could not reasonably be considered relevant as to whether the claim was valid, or failing systematically to respond to pertinent correspondence, in order to dissuade a consumer from exercising his contractual rights.

28. Including in an advertisement a direct exhortation to children to buy advertised products or persuade their parents or other adults to buy advertised products for them. This provision is without prejudice to Article 16 of Directive 89/552/EEC on television broadcasting.

29. Demanding immediate or deferred payment for or the return or safekeeping of products supplied by the trader, but not solicited by the consumer except where the product is a substitute supplied in conformity with Article 7(3) of Directive 97/7/EC (inertia selling).

30. Explicitly informing a consumer that if he does not buy the product or service, the trader's job or livelihood will be in jeopardy.

31. Creating the false impression that the consumer has already won, will win, or will on doing a particular act win, a prize or other equivalent benefit, when in fact either:

— there is no prize or other equivalent benefit, or
— taking any action in relation to claiming the prize or other equivalent benefit is subject to the consumer paying money or incurring a cost.

NOTES

1 Council Directive 89/552/EEC of 3 October 1989 on the coordination of certain provisions laid down by Law, Regulation or Administrative Action in Member States concerning the pursuit of television broadcasting activities (OJ L298, 17.10.1989, p 23). Directive as amended by Directive 97/36/EC of the European Parliament and of the Council (OJ L202, 30.7.1997, p 60).

2 Directive 95/46/EC of the European Parliament and of the Council of 24 October 1995 on the protection of individuals with regard to the processing of personal data and on the free movement of such data (OJ L281, 23.11.1995, p 31). Directive as amended by Regulation (EC) No 1882/2003 (OJ L284, 31.10.2003, p 1).

ANNEX II

COMMUNITY LAW PROVISIONS SETTING OUT RULES FOR ADVERTISING AND COMMERCIAL COMMUNICATION

[4.364]
Articles 4 and 5 of Directive 97/7/EC

Article 3 of Council Directive 90/314/EEC of 13 June 1990 on package travel, package holidays and package tours[1]

Article 3(3) of Directive 94/47/EC of the European Parliament and of the Council of 26 October 1994 on the protection of purchasers in respect of certain aspects of contracts relating to the purchase of a right to use immovable properties on a timeshare basis[2]

Article 3(4) of Directive 98/6/EC of the European Parliament and of the Council of 16 February 1998 on consumer protection in the indication of the prices of products offered to consumers[3]

Articles 86 to 100 of Directive 2001/83/EC of the European Parliament and of the Council of 6 November 2001 on the Community code relating to medicinal products for human use[4]

Articles 5 and 6 of Directive 2000/31/EC of the European Parliament and of the Council of 8 June 2000 on certain legal aspects of information society services, in particular electronic commerce, in the Internal Market (Directive on electronic commerce)[5]

Article 1(d) of Directive 98/7/EC of the European Parliament and of the Council of 16 February 1998 amending Council Directive 87/102/EEC for the approximation of the laws, regulations and administrative provisions of the Member States concerning consumer credit[6]

Articles 3 and 4 of Directive 2002/65/EC

Article 1(9) of Directive 2001/107/EC of the European Parliament and of the Council of 21 January 2002 amending Council Directive 85/611/EEC on the coordination of laws, regulations and administrative provisions relating to undertakings for collective investment in transferable securities (UCITS) with a view to regulating management companies and simplified prospectuses[7]

Articles 12 and 13 of Directive 2002/92/EC of the European Parliament and of the Council of 9 December 2002 on insurance mediation[8]

Article 36 of Directive 2002/83/EC of the European Parliament and of the Council of 5 November 2002 concerning life assurance[9]

Article 19 of Directive 2004/39/EC of the European Parliament and of the Council of 21 April 2004 on markets in financial instruments[10]

Articles 31 and 43 of Council Directive 92/49/EEC of 18 June 1992 on the coordination of laws, regulations and administrative provisions relating to direct insurance other than life assurance[11] (third non-life insurance Directive)

Articles 5, 7 and 8 of Directive 2003/71/EC of the European Parliament and of the Council of 4 November 2003 on the prospectus to be published when securities are offered to the public or admitted to trading[12]

NOTES

[1]   OJ L158, 23.6.1990, p 59.

[2]   OJ L280, 29.10.1994, p 83.

[3]   OJ L80, 18.3.1998, p 27.

[4]   OJ L311, 28.11.2001, p 67. Directive as last amended by Directive 2004/27/EC (OJ L136, 30.4.2004, p 34).

[5]   OJ L178, 17.7.2000, p 1.

[6]   OJ L101, 1.4.1998, p 17.

[7]   OJ L41, 13.2.2002, p 20.

[8]   OJ L9, 15.1.2003, p 3.

[9]   OJ L345, 19.12.2002, p 1. Directive as amended by Council Directive 2004/66/EC. (OJ L168, 1.5.2004, p 35).

[10]   OJ L145, 30.4.2004, p 1.

[11]   OJ L228, 11.8.1992, p 1. Directive as last amended by Directive 2002/87/EC of the European Parliament and of the Council (OJ L35, 11.2.2003, p 1).

[12]   OJ L345, 31.12.2003, p 64.

DIRECTIVE OF THE EUROPEAN PARLIAMENT AND OF THE COUNCIL

(2005/60/EC)

of 26 October 2005

on the prevention of the use of the financial system for the purpose of money laundering and terrorist financing

(Text with EEA relevance)

NOTES

Date of publication in OJ: OJ L309, 25.11.2005, p 15.

This Directive has been implemented in the UK by the Money Laundering Regulations 2007, SI 2007/2157 at **[2.464]**, the Terrorism Act 2000, and by the Proceeds of Crime Act 2002 at **[1.1625]**.

This Directive is repealed by European Parliament and Council Directive 2015/849/EU, art 66, as from 26 June 2017.

THE EUROPEAN PARLIAMENT AND THE COUNCIL OF THE EUROPEAN UNION,
  Having regard to the Treaty establishing the European Community, and in particular Article 47(2), first and third sentences, and Article 95 thereof,
  Having regard to the proposal from the Commission,
  Having regard to the opinion of the European Economic and Social Committee,[1]
  Having regard to the opinion of the European Central Bank,[2]
  Acting in accordance with the procedure laid down in Article 251 of the Treaty,[3]
  Whereas:

  (1)   Massive flows of dirty money can damage the stability and reputation of the financial sector and threaten the single market, and terrorism shakes the very foundations of our society. In addition to the criminal law approach, a preventive effort via the financial system can produce results.

  (2)   The soundness, integrity and stability of credit and financial institutions and confidence in

the financial system as a whole could be seriously jeopardised by the efforts of criminals and their associates either to disguise the origin of criminal proceeds or to channel lawful or unlawful money for terrorist purposes. In order to avoid Member States' adopting measures to protect their financial systems which could be inconsistent with the functioning of the internal market and with the prescriptions of the rule of law and Community public policy, Community action in this area is necessary.

(3) In order to facilitate their criminal activities, money launderers and terrorist financers could try to take advantage of the freedom of capital movements and the freedom to supply financial services which the integrated financial area entails, if certain coordinating measures are not adopted at Community level.

(4) In order to respond to these concerns in the field of money laundering, Council Directive 91/308/EEC of 10 June 1991 on prevention of the use of the financial system for the purpose of money laundering[4] was adopted. It required Member States to prohibit money laundering and to oblige the financial sector, comprising credit institutions and a wide range of other financial institutions, to identify their customers, keep appropriate records, establish internal procedures to train staff and guard against money laundering and to report any indications of money laundering to the competent authorities.

(5) Money laundering and terrorist financing are frequently carried out in an international context. Measures adopted solely at national or even Community level, without taking account of international coordination and cooperation, would have very limited effects. The measures adopted by the Community in this field should therefore be consistent with other action undertaken in other international fora. The Community action should continue to take particular account of the Recommendations of the Financial Action Task Force (hereinafter referred to as the FATF), which constitutes the foremost international body active in the fight against money laundering and terrorist financing. Since the FATF Recommendations were substantially revised and expanded in 2003, this Directive should be in line with that new international standard.

(6) The General Agreement on Trade in Services (GATS) allows Members to adopt measures necessary to protect public morals and prevent fraud and adopt measures for prudential reasons, including for ensuring the stability and integrity of the financial system.

(7) Although initially limited to drugs offences, there has been a trend in recent years towards a much wider definition of money laundering based on a broader range of predicate offences. A wider range of predicate offences facilitates the reporting of suspicious transactions and international cooperation in this area. Therefore, the definition of serious crime should be brought into line with the definition of serious crime in Council Framework Decision 2001/500/JHA of 26 June 2001 on money laundering, the identification, tracing, freezing, seizing and confiscation of instrumentalities and the proceeds of crime.[5]

(8) Furthermore, the misuse of the financial system to channel criminal or even clean money to terrorist purposes poses a clear risk to the integrity, proper functioning, reputation and stability of the financial system. Accordingly, the preventive measures of this Directive should cover not only the manipulation of money derived from crime but also the collection of money or property for terrorist purposes.

(9) Directive 91/308/EEC, though imposing a customer identification obligation, contained relatively little detail on the relevant procedures. In view of the crucial importance of this aspect of the prevention of money laundering and terrorist financing, it is appropriate, in accordance with the new international standards, to introduce more specific and detailed provisions relating to the identification of the customer and of any beneficial owner and the verification of their identity. To that end a precise definition of "beneficial owner" is essential. Where the individual beneficiaries of a legal entity or arrangement such as a foundation or trust are yet to be determined, and it is therefore impossible to identify an individual as the beneficial owner, it would suffice to identify the class of persons intended to be the beneficiaries of the foundation or trust. This requirement should not include the identification of the individuals within that class of persons.

(10) The institutions and persons covered by this Directive should, in conformity with this Directive, identify and verify the identity of the beneficial owner. To fulfil this requirement, it should be left to those institutions and persons whether they make use of public records of beneficial owners, ask their clients for relevant data or obtain the information otherwise, taking into account the fact that the extent of such customer due diligence measures relates to the risk of money laundering and terrorist financing, which depends on the type of customer, business relationship, product or transaction.

(11) Credit agreements in which the credit account serves exclusively to settle the loan and the repayment of the loan is effected from an account which was opened in the name of the customer with a credit institution covered by this Directive pursuant to Article 8(1)(a) to (c) should generally be considered as an example of types of less risky transactions.

(12) To the extent that the providers of the property of a legal entity or arrangement have significant control over the use of the property they should be identified as a beneficial owner.

(13) Trust relationships are widely used in commercial products as an internationally recognised

feature of the comprehensively supervised wholesale financial markets. An obligation to identify the beneficial owner does not arise from the fact alone that there is a trust relationship in this particular case.

(14)   This Directive should also apply to those activities of the institutions and persons covered hereunder which are performed on the Internet.

(15)   As the tightening of controls in the financial sector has prompted money launderers and terrorist financers to seek alternative methods for concealing the origin of the proceeds of crime and as such channels can be used for terrorist financing, the anti-money laundering and anti-terrorist financing obligations should cover life insurance intermediaries and trust and company service providers.

(16)   Entities already falling under the legal responsibility of an insurance undertaking, and therefore falling within the scope of this Directive, should not be included within the category of insurance intermediary.

(17)   Acting as a company director or secretary does not of itself make someone a trust and company service provider. For that reason, the definition covers only those persons that act as a company director or secretary for a third party and by way of business.

(18)   The use of large cash payments has repeatedly proven to be very vulnerable to money laundering and terrorist financing. Therefore, in those Member States that allow cash payments above the established threshold, all natural or legal persons trading in goods by way of business should be covered by this Directive when accepting such cash payments. Dealers in high-value goods, such as precious stones or metals, or works of art, and auctioneers are in any event covered by this Directive to the extent that payments to them are made in cash in an amount of EUR 15000 or more. To ensure effective monitoring of compliance with this Directive by that potentially wide group of institutions and persons, Member States may focus their monitoring activities in particular on those natural and legal persons trading in goods that are exposed to a relatively high risk of money laundering or terrorist financing, in accordance with the principle of risk-based supervision. In view of the different situations in the various Member States, Member States may decide to adopt stricter provisions, in order to properly address the risk involved with large cash payments.

(19)   Directive 91/308/EEC brought notaries and other independent legal professionals within the scope of the Community anti-money laundering regime; this coverage should be maintained unchanged in this Directive; these legal professionals, as defined by the Member States, are subject to the provisions of this Directive when participating in financial or corporate transactions, including providing tax advice, where there is the greatest risk of the services of those legal professionals being misused for the purpose of laundering the proceeds of criminal activity or for the purpose of terrorist financing.

(20)   Where independent members of professions providing legal advice which are legally recognised and controlled, such as lawyers, are ascertaining the legal position of a client or representing a client in legal proceedings, it would not be appropriate under this Directive to put those legal professionals in respect of these activities under an obligation to report suspicions of money laundering or terrorist financing. There must be exemptions from any obligation to report information obtained either before, during or after judicial proceedings, or in the course of ascertaining the legal position for a client. Thus, legal advice shall remain subject to the obligation of professional secrecy unless the legal counsellor is taking part in money laundering or terrorist financing, the legal advice is provided for money laundering or terrorist financing purposes or the lawyer knows that the client is seeking legal advice for money laundering or terrorist financing purposes.

(21)   Directly comparable services need to be treated in the same manner when provided by any of the professionals covered by this Directive. In order to ensure the respect of the rights laid down in the European Convention for the Protection of Human Rights and Fundamental Freedoms and the Treaty on European Union, in the case of auditors, external accountants and tax advisors, who, in some Member States, may defend or represent a client in the context of judicial proceedings or ascertain a client's legal position, the information they obtain in the performance of those tasks should not be subject to the reporting obligations in accordance with this Directive.

(22)   It should be recognised that the risk of money laundering and terrorist financing is not the same in every case. In line with a risk-based approach, the principle should be introduced into Community legislation that simplified customer due diligence is allowed in appropriate cases.

(23)   The derogation concerning the identification of beneficial owners of pooled accounts held by notaries or other independent legal professionals should be without prejudice to the obligations that those notaries or other independent legal professionals have pursuant to this Directive. Those obligations include the need for such notaries or other independent legal professionals themselves to identify the beneficial owners of the pooled accounts held by them.

(24)   Equally, Community legislation should recognise that certain situations present a greater risk of money laundering or terrorist financing. Although the identity and business profile of all customers should be established, there are cases where particularly rigorous customer identification and verification procedures are required.

(25) This is particularly true of business relationships with individuals holding, or having held, important public positions, particularly those from countries where corruption is widespread. Such relationships may expose the financial sector in particular to significant reputational and/or legal risks. The international effort to combat corruption also justifies the need to pay special attention to such cases and to apply the complete normal customer due diligence measures in respect of domestic politically exposed persons or enhanced customer due diligence measures in respect of politically exposed persons residing in another Member State or in a third country.

(26) Obtaining approval from senior management for establishing business relationships should not imply obtaining approval from the board of directors but from the immediate higher level of the hierarchy of the person seeking such approval.

(27) In order to avoid repeated customer identification procedures, leading to delays and inefficiency in business, it is appropriate, subject to suitable safeguards, to allow customers to be introduced whose identification has been carried out elsewhere. Where an institution or person covered by this Directive relies on a third party, the ultimate responsibility for the customer due diligence procedure remains with the institution or person to whom the customer is introduced. The third party, or introducer, also retains his own responsibility for all the requirements in this Directive, including the requirement to report suspicious transactions and maintain records, to the extent that he has a relationship with the customer that is covered by this Directive.

(28) In the case of agency or outsourcing relationships on a contractual basis between institutions or persons covered by this Directive and external natural or legal persons not covered hereby, any anti-money laundering and anti-terrorist financing obligations for those agents or outsourcing service providers as part of the institutions or persons covered by this Directive, may only arise from contract and not from this Directive. The responsibility for complying with this Directive should remain with the institution or person covered hereby.

(29) Suspicious transactions should be reported to the financial intelligence unit (FIU), which serves as a national centre for receiving, analysing and disseminating to the competent authorities suspicious transaction reports and other information regarding potential money laundering or terrorist financing. This should not compel Member States to change their existing reporting systems where the reporting is done through a public prosecutor or other law enforcement authorities, as long as the information is forwarded promptly and unfiltered to FIUs, allowing them to conduct their business properly, including international cooperation with other FIUs.

(30) By way of derogation from the general prohibition on executing suspicious transactions, the institutions and persons covered by this Directive may execute suspicious transactions before informing the competent authorities, where refraining from the execution thereof is impossible or likely to frustrate efforts to pursue the beneficiaries of a suspected money laundering or terrorist financing operation. This, however, should be without prejudice to the international obligations accepted by the Member States to freeze without delay funds or other assets of terrorists, terrorist organisations or those who finance terrorism, in accordance with the relevant United Nations Security Council resolutions.

(31) Where a Member State decides to make use of the exemptions provided for in Article 23(2), it may allow or require the self-regulatory body representing the persons referred to therein not to transmit to the FIU any information obtained from those persons in the circumstances referred to in that Article.

(32) There has been a number of cases of employees who report their suspicions of money laundering being subjected to threats or hostile action. Although this Directive cannot interfere with Member States' judicial procedures, this is a crucial issue for the effectiveness of the anti-money laundering and anti-terrorist financing system. Member States should be aware of this problem and should do whatever they can to protect employees from such threats or hostile action.

(33) Disclosure of information as referred to in Article 28 should be in accordance with the rules on transfer of personal data to third countries as laid down in Directive 95/46/EC of the European Parliament and of the Council of 24 October 1995 on the protection of individuals with regard to the processing of personal data and on the free movement of such data.[6] Moreover, Article 28 cannot interfere with national data protection and professional secrecy legislation.

(34) Persons who merely convert paper documents into electronic data and are acting under a contract with a credit institution or a financial institution do not fall within the scope of this Directive, nor does any natural or legal person that provides credit or financial institutions solely with a message or other support systems for transmitting funds or with clearing and settlement systems.

(35) Money laundering and terrorist financing are international problems and the effort to combat them should be global. Where Community credit and financial institutions have branches and subsidiaries located in third countries where the legislation in this area is deficient, they should, in order to avoid the application of very different standards within an institution or group of institutions, apply the Community standard or notify the competent authorities of the home Member State if this application is impossible.

(36) It is important that credit and financial institutions should be able to respond rapidly to

requests for information on whether they maintain business relationships with named persons. For the purpose of identifying such business relationships in order to be able to provide that information quickly, credit and financial institutions should have effective systems in place which are commensurate with the size and nature of their business. In particular it would be appropriate for credit institutions and larger financial institutions to have electronic systems at their disposal. This provision is of particular importance in the context of procedures leading to measures such as the freezing or seizing of assets (including terrorist assets), pursuant to applicable national or Community legislation with a view to combating terrorism.

(37)   This Directive establishes detailed rules for customer due diligence, including enhanced customer due diligence for high-risk customers or business relationships, such as appropriate procedures to determine whether a person is a politically exposed person, and certain additional, more detailed requirements, such as the existence of compliance management procedures and policies. All these requirements are to be met by each of the institutions and persons covered by this Directive, while Member States are expected to tailor the detailed implementation of those provisions to the particularities of the various professions and to the differences in scale and size of the institutions and persons covered by this Directive.

(38)   In order to ensure that the institutions and others subject to Community legislation in this field remain committed, feedback should, where practicable, be made available to them on the usefulness and follow-up of the reports they present. To make this possible, and to be able to review the effectiveness of their systems to combat money laundering and terrorist financing Member States should keep and improve the relevant statistics.

(39)   When registering or licensing a currency exchange office, a trust and company service provider or a casino nationally, competent authorities should ensure that the persons who effectively direct or will direct the business of such entities and the beneficial owners of such entities are fit and proper persons. The criteria for determining whether or not a person is fit and proper should be established in conformity with national law. As a minimum, such criteria should reflect the need to protect such entities from being misused by their managers or beneficial owners for criminal purposes.

(40)   Taking into account the international character of money laundering and terrorist financing, coordination and cooperation between FIUs as referred to in Council Decision 2000/642/JHA of 17 October 2000 concerning arrangements for cooperation between financial intelligence units of the Member States in respect of exchanging information,[7] including the establishment of an EU FIU-net, should be encouraged to the greatest possible extent. To that end, the Commission should lend such assistance as may be needed to facilitate such coordination, including financial assistance.

(41)   The importance of combating money laundering and terrorist financing should lead Member States to lay down effective, proportionate and dissuasive penalties in national law for failure to respect the national provisions adopted pursuant to this Directive. Provision should be made for penalties in respect of natural and legal persons. Since legal persons are often involved in complex money laundering or terrorist financing operations, sanctions should also be adjusted in line with the activity carried on by legal persons.

(42)   Natural persons exercising any of the activities referred to in Article 2(1)(3)(a) and (b) within the structure of a legal person, but on an independent basis, should be independently responsible for compliance with the provisions of this Directive, with the exception of Article 35.

(43)   Clarification of the technical aspects of the rules laid down in this Directive may be necessary to ensure an effective and sufficiently consistent implementation of this Directive, taking into account the different financial instruments, professions and risks in the different Member States and the technical developments in the fight against money laundering and terrorist financing. The Commission should accordingly be empowered to adopt implementing measures, such as certain criteria for identifying low and high risk situations in which simplified due diligence could suffice or enhanced due diligence would be appropriate, provided that they do not modify the essential elements of this Directive and provided that the Commission acts in accordance with the principles set out herein, after consulting the Committee on the Prevention of Money Laundering and Terrorist Financing.

(44)   The measures necessary for the implementation of this Directive should be adopted in accordance with Council Decision 1999/468/EC of 28 June 1999 laying down the procedures for the exercise of implementing powers conferred on the Commission.[8] To that end a new Committee on the Prevention of Money Laundering and Terrorist Financing, replacing the Money Laundering Contact Committee set up by Directive 91/308/EEC, should be established.

(45)   In view of the very substantial amendments that would need to be made to Directive 91/308/EEC, it should be repealed for reasons of clarity.

(46)   Since the objective of this Directive, namely the prevention of the use of the financial system for the purpose of money laundering and terrorist financing, cannot be sufficiently achieved by the Member States and can therefore, by reason of the scale and effects of the action, be better achieved at Community level, the Community may adopt measures, in accordance with the principle of

subsidiarity as set out in Article 5 of the Treaty. In accordance with the principle of proportionality, as set out in that Article, this Directive does not go beyond what is necessary in order to achieve that objective.

(47) In exercising its implementing powers in accordance with this Directive, the Commission should respect the following principles: the need for high levels of transparency and consultation with institutions and persons covered by this Directive and with the European Parliament and the Council; the need to ensure that competent authorities will be able to ensure compliance with the rules consistently; the balance of costs and benefits to institutions and persons covered by this Directive on a long-term basis in any implementing measures; the need to respect the necessary flexibility in the application of the implementing measures in accordance with a risk-sensitive approach; the need to ensure coherence with other Community legislation in this area; the need to protect the Community, its Member States and their citizens from the consequences of money laundering and terrorist financing.

(48) This Directive respects the fundamental rights and observes the principles recognised in particular by the Charter of Fundamental Rights of the European Union. Nothing in this Directive should be interpreted or implemented in a manner that is inconsistent with the European Convention on Human Rights,

HAVE ADOPTED THIS DIRECTIVE:

NOTES

1   Opinion delivered on 11 May 2005 (not yet published in the Official Journal).

2   OJ C40, 17.2.2005, p 9.

3   Opinion of the European Parliament of 26 May 2005 (not yet published in the Official Journal) and Council Decision of 19 September 2005.

4   OJ L166, 28.6.1991, p 77. Directive as amended by Directive 2001/97/EC of the European Parliament and of the Council (OJ L344, 28.12.2001, p 76).

5   OJ L182, 5.7.2001, p 1.

6   OJ L281, 23.11.1995, p 31. Directive as amended by Regulation (EC) No 1882/2003 (OJ L284, 31.10.2003, p 1).

7   OJ L271, 24.10.2000, p 4.

8   OJ L184, 17.7.1999, p 23.

CHAPTER I
SUBJECT MATTER, SCOPE AND DEFINITIONS

[4.365]
Article 1
1. Member States shall ensure that money laundering and terrorist financing are prohibited.
2. For the purposes of this Directive, the following conduct, when committed intentionally, shall be regarded as money laundering:
> (a) the conversion or transfer of property, knowing that such property is derived from criminal activity or from an act of participation in such activity, for the purpose of concealing or disguising the illicit origin of the property or of assisting any person who is involved in the commission of such activity to evade the legal consequences of his action;
> (b) the concealment or disguise of the true nature, source, location, disposition, movement, rights with respect to, or ownership of property, knowing that such property is derived from criminal activity or from an act of participation in such activity;
> (c) the acquisition, possession or use of property, knowing, at the time of receipt, that such property was derived from criminal activity or from an act of participation in such activity;
> (d) participation in, association to commit, attempts to commit and aiding, abetting, facilitating and counselling the commission of any of the actions mentioned in the foregoing points.

3. Money laundering shall be regarded as such even where the activities which generated the property to be laundered were carried out in the territory of another Member State or in that of a third country.
4. For the purposes of this Directive, "terrorist financing" means the provision or collection of funds, by any means, directly or indirectly, with the intention that they should be used or in the knowledge that they are to be used, in full or in part, in order to carry out any of the offences within the meaning of Articles 1 to 4 of Council Framework Decision 2002/475/JHA of 13 June 2002 on combating terrorism.[1]
5. Knowledge, intent or purpose required as an element of the activities mentioned in paragraphs 2 and 4 may be inferred from objective factual circumstances.

NOTES

Repealed as noted at the beginning of this Directive.

1   OJ L164, 22.6.2002, p 3.

[4.366]
Article 2

1. This Directive shall apply to:
    (1) credit institutions;
    (2) financial institutions;
    (3) the following legal or natural persons acting in the exercise of their professional activities:
        (a) auditors, external accountants and tax advisors;
        (b) notaries and other independent legal professionals, when they participate, whether by acting on behalf of and for their client in any financial or real estate transaction, or by assisting in the planning or execution of transactions for their client concerning the:
            (i) buying and selling of real property or business entities;
            (ii) managing of client money, securities or other assets;
            (iii) opening or management of bank, savings or securities accounts;
            (iv) organisation of contributions necessary for the creation, operation or management of companies;
            (v) creation, operation or management of trusts, companies or similar structures;
        (c) trust or company service providers not already covered under points (a) or (b);
        (d) real estate agents;
        (e) other natural or legal persons trading in goods, only to the extent that payments are made in cash in an amount of EUR 15000 or more, whether the transaction is executed in a single operation or in several operations which appear to be linked;
        (f) casinos.

2. Member States may decide that legal and natural persons who engage in a financial activity on an occasional or very limited basis and where there is little risk of money laundering or terrorist financing occurring do not fall within the scope of Article 3(1) or (2).

NOTES

Repealed as noted at the beginning of this Directive.

[4.367]
Article 3

For the purposes of this Directive the following definitions shall apply:
(1) 'credit institution' means a credit institution, as defined in the first subparagraph of Article 1(1) of Directive 2000/12/EC of the European Parliament and of the Council of 20 March 2000 relating to the taking up and pursuit of the business of credit institutions,[1] including branches within the meaning of Article 1(3) of that Directive located in the Community of credit institutions having their head offices inside or outside the Community;
(2) 'financial institution' means:
    [(a) an undertaking, other than a credit institution, which carries out one or more of the operations included in points 2 to 12 and points 14 and 15 of Annex I to Directive 2006/48/EC, including the activities of currency exchange offices (bureaux de change);]
    (b) an insurance company duly authorised in accordance with Directive 2002/83/EC of the European Parliament and of the Council of 5 November 2002 concerning life assurance,[2] insofar as it carries out activities covered by that Directive;
    (c) an investment firm as defined in point 1 of Article 4(1) of Directive 2004/39/EC of the European Parliament and of the Council of 21 April 2004 on markets in financial instruments;[3]
    (d) a collective investment undertaking marketing its units or shares;
    (e) an insurance intermediary as defined in Article 2(5) of Directive 2002/92/EC of the European Parliament and of the Council of 9 December 2002 on insurance mediation,[4] with the exception of intermediaries as mentioned in Article 2(7) of that Directive, when they act in respect of life insurance and other investment related services;
    (f) branches, when located in the Community, of financial institutions as referred to in points (a) to (e), whose head offices are inside or outside the Community;
(3) 'property' means assets of every kind, whether corporeal or incorporeal, movable or immovable, tangible or intangible, and legal documents or instruments in any form including electronic or digital, evidencing title to or an interest in such assets;
(4) 'criminal activity' means any kind of criminal involvement in the commission of a serious crime;
(5) 'serious crimes' means, at least:
    (a) acts as defined in Articles 1 to 4 of Framework Decision 2002/475/JHA;
    (b) any of the offences defined in Article 3(1)(a) of the 1988 United Nations Convention against Illicit Traffic in Narcotic Drugs and Psychotropic Substances;

  (c) the activities of criminal organisations as defined in Article 1 of Council Joint Action 98/733/JHA of 21 December 1998 on making it a criminal offence to participate in a criminal organisation in the Member States of the European Union;[5]

  (d) fraud, at least serious, as defined in Article 1(1) and Article 2 of the Convention on the Protection of the European Communities' Financial Interests;[6]

  (e) corruption;

  (f) all offences which are punishable by deprivation of liberty or a detention order for a maximum of more than one year or, as regards those States which have a minimum threshold for offences in their legal system, all offences punishable by deprivation of liberty or a detention order for a minimum of more than six months;

(6) 'beneficial owner' means the natural person(s) who ultimately owns or controls the customer and/or the natural person on whose behalf a transaction or activity is being conducted. The beneficial owner shall at least include:

  (a) in the case of corporate entities:

    (i) the natural person(s) who ultimately owns or controls a legal entity through direct or indirect ownership or control over a sufficient percentage of the shares or voting rights in that legal entity, including through bearer share holdings, other than a company listed on a regulated market that is subject to disclosure requirements consistent with Community legislation or subject to equivalent international standards; a percentage of 25% plus one share shall be deemed sufficient to meet this criterion;

    (ii) the natural person(s) who otherwise exercises control over the management of a legal entity:

  (b) in the case of legal entities, such as foundations, and legal arrangements, such as trusts, which administer and distribute funds:

    (i) where the future beneficiaries have already been determined, the natural person(s) who is the beneficiary of 25% or more of the property of a legal arrangement or entity;

    (ii) where the individuals that benefit from the legal arrangement or entity have yet to be determined, the class of persons in whose main interest the legal arrangement or entity is set up or operates;

    (iii) the natural person(s) who exercises control over 25% or more of the property of a legal arrangement or entity;

(7) 'trust and company service providers' means any natural or legal person which by way of business provides any of the following services to third parties:

  (a) forming companies or other legal persons;

  (b) acting as or arranging for another person to act as a director or secretary of a company, a partner of a partnership, or a similar position in relation to other legal persons;

  (c) providing a registered office, business address, correspondence or administrative address and other related services for a company, a partnership or any other legal person or arrangement;

  (d) acting as or arranging for another person to act as a trustee of an express trust or a similar legal arrangement;

  (e) acting as or arranging for another person to act as a nominee shareholder for another person other than a company listed on a regulated market that is subject to disclosure requirements in conformity with Community legislation or subject to equivalent international standards;

(8) 'politically exposed persons' means natural persons who are or have been entrusted with prominent public functions and immediate family members, or persons known to be close associates, of such persons;

(9) 'business relationship' means a business, professional or commercial relationship which is connected with the professional activities of the institutions and persons covered by this Directive and which is expected, at the time when the contact is established, to have an element of duration;

(10) 'shell bank' means a credit institution, or an institution engaged in equivalent activities, incorporated in a jurisdiction in which it has no physical presence, involving meaningful mind and management, and which is unaffiliated with a regulated financial group.

NOTES

Repealed as noted at the beginning of this Directive.

Para 2: sub-para (a) substituted by European Parliament and Council Directive 2009/110/EC, Art 19(1).

[1] OJ L126, 26.5.2000, p 1. Directive as last amended by Directive 2005/1/EC (OJ L79, 24.3.2005, p 9).

[2] OJ L345, 19.12.2002, p 1. Directive as last amended by Directive 2005/1/EC.

[3] OJ L145, 30.4.2004, p 1.

[4] OJ L9, 15.1.2003, p 3.

[5] OJ L351, 29.12.1998, p 1.

⁶   OJ C316, 27.11.1995, p 49.

[4.368]
Article 4
1.   *Member States shall ensure that the provisions of this Directive are extended in whole or in part to professions and to categories of undertakings, other than the institutions and persons referred to in Article 2(1), which engage in activities which are particularly likely to be used for money laundering or terrorist financing purposes.*
2.   *Where a Member State decides to extend the provisions of this Directive to professions and to categories of undertakings other than those referred to in Article 2(1), it shall inform the Commission thereof.*

NOTES
Repealed as noted at the beginning of this Directive.

[4.369]
Article 5
The Member States may adopt or retain in force stricter provisions in the field covered by this Directive to prevent money laundering and terrorist financing.

NOTES
Repealed as noted at the beginning of this Directive.

CHAPTER II
CUSTOMER DUE DILIGENCE

SECTION 1
GENERAL PROVISIONS

[4.370]
Article 6
Member States shall prohibit their credit and financial institutions from keeping anonymous accounts or anonymous passbooks. By way of derogation from Article 9(6), Member States shall in all cases require that the owners and beneficiaries of existing anonymous accounts or anonymous passbooks be made the subject of customer due diligence measures as soon as possible and in any event before such accounts or passbooks are used in any way.

NOTES
Repealed as noted at the beginning of this Directive.

[4.371]
Article 7
The institutions and persons covered by this Directive shall apply customer due diligence measures in the following cases:
  (a)   *when establishing a business relationship;*
  (b)   *when carrying out occasional transactions amounting to EUR 15000 or more, whether the transaction is carried out in a single operation or in several operations which appear to be linked;*
  (c)   *when there is a suspicion of money laundering or terrorist financing, regardless of any derogation, exemption or threshold;*
  (d)   *when there are doubts about the veracity or adequacy of previously obtained customer identification data.*

NOTES
Repealed as noted at the beginning of this Directive.

[4.372]
Article 8
1.   *Customer due diligence measures shall comprise:*
  (a)   *identifying the customer and verifying the customer's identity on the basis of documents, data or information obtained from a reliable and independent source;*
  (b)   *identifying, where applicable, the beneficial owner and taking risk-based and adequate measures to verify his identity so that the institution or person covered by this Directive is satisfied that it knows who the beneficial owner is, including, as regards legal persons, trusts and similar legal arrangements, taking risk-based and adequate measures to understand the ownership and control structure of the customer;*
  (c)   *obtaining information on the purpose and intended nature of the business relationship;*
  (d)   *conducting ongoing monitoring of the business relationship including scrutiny of transactions undertaken throughout the course of that relationship to ensure that the*

transactions being conducted are consistent with the institution's or person's knowledge of the customer, the business and risk profile, including, where necessary, the source of funds and ensuring that the documents, data or information held are kept up-to-date.

2.   *The institutions and persons covered by this Directive shall apply each of the customer due diligence requirements set out in paragraph 1, but may determine the extent of such measures on a risk-sensitive basis depending on the type of customer, business relationship, product or transaction. The institutions and persons covered by this Directive shall be able to demonstrate to the competent authorities mentioned in Article 37, including self-regulatory bodies, that the extent of the measures is appropriate in view of the risks of money laundering and terrorist financing.*

NOTES
Repealed as noted at the beginning of this Directive.

[4.373]
Article 9

1.   *Member States shall require that the verification of the identity of the customer and the beneficial owner takes place before the establishment of a business relationship or the carrying-out of the transaction.*

2.   *By way of derogation from paragraph 1, Member States may allow the verification of the identity of the customer and the beneficial owner to be completed during the establishment of a business relationship if this is necessary not to interrupt the normal conduct of business and where there is little risk of money laundering or terrorist financing occurring. In such situations these procedures shall be completed as soon as practicable after the initial contact.*

3.   *By way of derogation from paragraphs 1 and 2, Member States may, in relation to life insurance business, allow the verification of the identity of the beneficiary under the policy to take place after the business relationship has been established. In that case, verification shall take place at or before the time of payout or at or before the time the beneficiary intends to exercise rights vested under the policy.*

4.   *By way of derogation from paragraphs 1 and 2, Member States may allow the opening of a bank account provided that there are adequate safeguards in place to ensure that transactions are not carried out by the customer or on its behalf until full compliance with the aforementioned provisions is obtained.*

5.   *Member States shall require that, where the institution or person concerned is unable to comply with points (a), (b) and (c) of Article 8(1), it may not carry out a transaction through a bank account, establish a business relationship or carry out the transaction, or shall terminate the business relationship, and shall consider making a report to the financial intelligence unit (FIU) in accordance with Article 22 in relation to the customer.*

Member States shall not be obliged to apply the previous subparagraph in situations when notaries, independent legal professionals, auditors, external accountants and tax advisors are in the course of ascertaining the legal position for their client or performing their task of defending or representing that client in, or concerning judicial proceedings, including advice on instituting or avoiding proceedings.

6.   *Member States shall require that institutions and persons covered by this Directive apply the customer due diligence procedures not only to all new customers but also at appropriate times to existing customers on a risk-sensitive basis.*

NOTES
Repealed as noted at the beginning of this Directive.

[4.374]
Article 10

1.   *Member States shall require that all casino customers be identified and their identity verified if they purchase or exchange gambling chips with a value of EUR 2000 or more.*

2.   *Casinos subject to State supervision shall be deemed in any event to have satisfied the customer due diligence requirements if they register, identify and verify the identity of their customers immediately on or before entry, regardless of the amount of gambling chips purchased.*

NOTES
Repealed as noted at the beginning of this Directive.

SECTION 2
SIMPLIFIED CUSTOMER DUE DILIGENCE

[4.375]
Article 11

1.   By way of derogation from Articles 7(a), (b) and (d), 8 and 9(1), the institutions and persons covered by this Directive shall not be subject to the requirements provided for in those Articles where the customer is a credit or financial institution covered by this Directive, or a credit or financial institution situated in a third country which imposes requirements equivalent to those laid down in this Directive and supervised for compliance with those requirements.

2.   By way of derogation from Articles 7(a), (b) and (d), 8 and 9(1) Member States may allow the institutions and persons covered by this Directive not to apply customer due diligence in respect of:

(a)   listed companies whose securities are admitted to trading on a regulated market within the meaning of Directive 2004/39/EC in one or more Member States and listed companies from third countries which are subject to disclosure requirements consistent with Community legislation;

(b)   beneficial owners of pooled accounts held by notaries and other independent legal professionals from the Member States, or from third countries provided that they are subject to requirements to combat money laundering or terrorist financing consistent with international standards and are supervised for compliance with those requirements and provided that the information on the identity of the beneficial owner is available, on request, to the institutions that act as depository institutions for the pooled accounts;

(c)   domestic public authorities,

or in respect of any other customer representing a low risk of money laundering or terrorist financing which meets the technical criteria established in accordance with Article 40(1)(b).

3.   In the cases mentioned in paragraphs 1 and 2, institutions and persons covered by this Directive shall in any case gather sufficient information to establish if the customer qualifies for an exemption as mentioned in these paragraphs.

[4.   The Member States shall inform each other, the European Supervisory Authority (European Banking Authority) (hereinafter "EBA"), established by Regulation (EU) No 1093/2010 of the European Parliament and of the Council,* the European Supervisory Authority (European Insurance and Occupational Pensions Authority) (hereinafter "EIOPA"), established by Regulation (EU) No 1094/2010 of the European Parliament and of the Council,** and the European Supervisory Authority (European Securities and Markets Authority) (hereinafter "ESMA"),*** established by Regulation (EU) No 1095/2010 of the European Parliament and of the Council*** (collectively, the "ESA") to the extent relevant for the purposes of this Directive and in accordance with the relevant provisions of Regulation (EU) No 1093/2010, of Regulation (EU) No 1094/2010 and of Regulation (EU) No 1095/2010, and the Commission of cases where they consider that a third country meets the conditions laid down in paragraphs 1 or 2 or in other situations which meet the technical criteria established in accordance with Article 40(1)(b).]

5.   By way of derogation from Articles 7(a), (b) and (d), 8 and 9(1), Member States may allow the institutions and persons covered by this Directive not to apply customer due diligence in respect of:

(a)   life insurance policies where the annual premium is no more than EUR 1000 or the single premium is no more than EUR 2500;

(b)   insurance policies for pension schemes if there is no surrender clause and the policy cannot be used as collateral;

(c)   a pension, superannuation or similar scheme that provides retirement benefits to employees, where contributions are made by way of deduction from wages and the scheme rules do not permit the assignment of a member's interest under the scheme;

[(d)   electronic money, as defined in point 2 of Article 2 of Directive 2009/110/EC of the European Parliament and of the Council of 16 September 2009 on the taking up, pursuit and prudential supervision of the business of electronic money institutions[1] where, if it is not possible to recharge, the maximum amount stored electronically in the device is no more than EUR 250, or where, if it is possible to recharge, a limit of EUR 2 500 is imposed on the total amount transacted in a calendar year, except when an amount of EUR 1 000 or more is redeemed in that same calendar year upon the electronic money holder's request in accordance with Article 11 of Directive 2009/110/EC. As regards national payment transactions, Member States or their competent authorities may increase the amount of EUR 250 referred to in this point to a ceiling of EUR 500.]

or in respect of any other product or transaction representing a low risk of money laundering or terrorist financing which meets the technical criteria established in accordance with Article 40(1)(b).

NOTES

Repealed as noted at the beginning of this Directive.

Para 4: substituted, together with footnotes in square brackets below, by European Parliament and Council Directive 2010/78/EU, Art 8(1).

Para 5: sub-para (d) substituted by European Parliament and Council Directive 2009/110/EC, Art 19(2).

*   [OJ L331, 15.12.2010, p 12.

**   OJ L331, 15.12.2010, p 48.

***   OJ L331, 15.12.2010, p 84.]

¹   OJ L267, 10.10.2009, p 7.

[4.376]
Article 12

Where the Commission adopts a decision pursuant to Article 40(4), the Member States shall prohibit the institutions and persons covered by this Directive from applying simplified due diligence to credit and financial institutions or listed companies from the third country concerned or other entities following from situations which meet the technical criteria established in accordance with Article 40(1)(b).

NOTES

Repealed as noted at the beginning of this Directive.

SECTION 3
ENHANCED CUSTOMER DUE DILIGENCE

[4.377]
Article 13

1.   Member States shall require the institutions and persons covered by this Directive to apply, on a risk-sensitive basis, enhanced customer due diligence measures, in addition to the measures referred to in Articles 7, 8 and 9(6), in situations which by their nature can present a higher risk of money laundering or terrorist financing, and at least in the situations set out in paragraphs 2, 3, 4 and in other situations representing a high risk of money laundering or terrorist financing which meet the technical criteria established in accordance with Article 40(1)(c).

2.   Where the customer has not been physically present for identification purposes, Member States shall require those institutions and persons to take specific and adequate measures to compensate for the higher risk, for example by applying one or more of the following measures:

- *(a)   ensuring that the customer's identity is established by additional documents, data or information;*
- *(b)   supplementary measures to verify or certify the documents supplied, or requiring confirmatory certification by a credit or financial institution covered by this Directive;*
- *(c)   ensuring that the first payment of the operations is carried out through an account opened in the customer's name with a credit institution.*

3.   In respect of cross-frontier correspondent banking relationships with respondent institutions from third countries, Member States shall require their credit institutions to:

- *(a)   gather sufficient information about a respondent institution to understand fully the nature of the respondent's business and to determine from publicly available information the reputation of the institution and the quality of supervision;*
- *(b)   assess the respondent institution's anti-money laundering and anti-terrorist financing controls;*
- *(c)   obtain approval from senior management before establishing new correspondent banking relationships;*
- *(d)   document the respective responsibilities of each institution;*
- *(e)   with respect to payable-through accounts, be satisfied that the respondent credit institution has verified the identity of and performed ongoing due diligence on the customers having direct access to accounts of the correspondent and that it is able to provide relevant customer due diligence data to the correspondent institution, upon request.*

4.   In respect of transactions or business relationships with politically exposed persons residing in another Member State or in a third country, Member States shall require those institutions and persons covered by this Directive to:

- *(a)   have appropriate risk-based procedures to determine whether the customer is a politically exposed person;*
- *(b)   have senior management approval for establishing business relationships with such customers;*
- *(c)   take adequate measures to establish the source of wealth and source of funds that are involved in the business relationship or transaction;*
- *(d)   conduct enhanced ongoing monitoring of the business relationship.*

5.   Member States shall prohibit credit institutions from entering into or continuing a correspondent banking relationship with a shell bank and shall require that credit institutions take appropriate measures to ensure that they do not engage in or continue correspondent banking relationships with a bank that is known to permit its accounts to be used by a shell bank.

6.   Member States shall ensure that the institutions and persons covered by this Directive pay special attention to any money laundering or terrorist financing threat that may arise from products or transactions that might favour anonymity, and take measures, if needed, to prevent their use for money laundering or terrorist financing purposes.

SECTION 4
PERFORMANCE BY THIRD PARTIES

[4.378]
Article 14
Member States may permit the institutions and persons covered by this Directive to rely on third parties to meet the requirements laid down in Article 8(1)(a) to (c). However, the ultimate responsibility for meeting those requirements shall remain with the institution or person covered by this Directive which relies on the third party.

[4.379]
Article 15
[1.   Where a Member State permits credit and financial institutions referred to in Article 2(1)(1) or (2) situated in its territory to be relied on as a third party domestically, that Member State shall in any case permit institutions and persons referred to in Article 2(1) situated in its territory to recognise and accept, in accordance with Article 14, the outcome of the customer due diligence requirements laid down in Article 8(1)(a) to (c), carried out in accordance with this Directive by an institution referred to in Article 2 (1)(1) or (2) in another Member State, with the exception of currency exchange offices and payment institutions as defined in Article 4(4) of Directive 2007/64/EC of the European Parliament and of the Council of 13 November 2007 on payment services in the internal market,[1] which mainly provide the payment service listed in point 6 of the Annex to that Directive, including natural and legal persons benefiting from a waiver under Article 26 of that Directive, and meeting the requirements laid down in Articles 16 and 18 of this Directive, even if the documents or data on which these requirements have been based are different to those required in the Member State to which the customer is being referred.
2.   Where a Member State permits currency exchange offices referred to in Article 3(2)(a) and payment institutions as defined in Article 4(4) of Directive 2007/64/EC, which mainly provide the payment service listed in point 6 of the Annex to that Directive, situated in its territory to be relied on as a third party domestically, that Member State shall in any case permit them to recognise and accept, in accordance with Article 14 of this Directive, the outcome of the customer due diligence requirements laid down in Article 8(1)(a) to (c), carried out in accordance with this Directive by the same category of institution in another Member State and meeting the requirements laid down in Articles 16 and 18 of this Directive, even if the documents or data on which these requirements have been based are different to those required in the Member State to which the customer is being referred.]
3.   Where a Member State permits persons referred to in Article 2(1)(3)(a) to (c) situated in its territory to be relied on as a third party domestically, that Member State shall in any case permit them to recognise and accept, in accordance with Article 14, the outcome of the customer due diligence requirements laid down in Article 8(1)(a) to (c), carried out in accordance with this Directive by a person referred to in Article 2(1)(3)(a) to (c) in another Member State and meeting the requirements laid down in Articles 16 and 18, even if the documents or data on which these requirements have been based are different to those required in the Member State to which the customer is being referred.

[4.380]
Article 16
1.   For the purposes of this Section, 'third parties' shall mean institutions and persons who are listed in Article 2, or equivalent institutions and persons situated in a third country, who meet the following requirements:
   (a)   they are subject to mandatory professional registration, recognised by law;
   (b)   they apply customer due diligence requirements and record keeping requirements as laid down or equivalent to those laid down in this Directive and their compliance with the requirements of this Directive is supervised in accordance with Section 2 of Chapter V, or they are situated in a third country which imposes equivalent requirements to those laid down in this Directive.

[2. The Member States shall inform each other, the ESA to the extent relevant for the purposes of this Directive and in accordance with the relevant provisions of Regulation (EU) No 1093/2010, of Regulation (EU) No 1094/2010, and of Regulation (EU) No 1095/2010, and the Commission of cases where they consider that a third country meets the conditions laid down in paragraph 1(b).]

NOTES

Repealed as noted at the beginning of this Directive.
Para 2: substituted by European Parliament and Council Directive 2010/78/EU, Art 8(2).

[4.381]
Article 17
Where the Commission adopts a decision pursuant to Article 40(4), Member States shall prohibit the institutions and persons covered by this Directive from relying on third parties from the third country concerned to meet the requirements laid down in Article 8(1)(a) to (c).

NOTES

Repealed as noted at the beginning of this Directive.

[4.382]
Article 18
1. Third parties shall make information requested in accordance with the requirements laid down in Article 8(1)(a) to (c) immediately available to the institution or person covered by this Directive to which the customer is being referred.
2. Relevant copies of identification and verification data and other relevant documentation on the identity of the customer or the beneficial owner shall immediately be forwarded, on request, by the third party to the institution or person covered by this Directive to which the customer is being referred.

NOTES

Repealed as noted at the beginning of this Directive.

[4.383]
Article 19
This Section shall not apply to outsourcing or agency relationships where, on the basis of a contractual arrangement, the outsourcing service provider or agent is to be regarded as part of the institution or person covered by this Directive.

NOTES

Repealed as noted at the beginning of this Directive.

CHAPTER III
REPORTING OBLIGATIONS

SECTION 1
GENERAL PROVISIONS

[4.384]
Article 20
Member States shall require that the institutions and persons covered by this Directive pay special attention to any activity which they regard as particularly likely, by its nature, to be related to money laundering or terrorist financing and in particular complex or unusually large transactions and all unusual patterns of transactions which have no apparent economic or visible lawful purpose.

NOTES

Repealed as noted at the beginning of this Directive.

[4.385]
Article 21
1. Each Member State shall establish a FIU in order effectively to combat money laundering and terrorist financing.
2. That FIU shall be established as a central national unit. It shall be responsible for receiving (and to the extent permitted, requesting), analysing and disseminating to the competent authorities, disclosures of information which concern potential money laundering, potential terrorist financing or are required by national legislation or regulation. It shall be provided with adequate resources in order to fulfil its tasks.
3. Member States shall ensure that the FIU has access, directly or indirectly, on a timely basis, to the financial, administrative and law enforcement information that it requires to properly fulfil its tasks.

NOTES

Repealed as noted at the beginning of this Directive.

[4.386]
Article 22

1.   Member States shall require the institutions and persons covered by this Directive, and where applicable their directors and employees, to cooperate fully:
 (a)   by promptly informing the FIU, on their own initiative, where the institution or person covered by this Directive knows, suspects or has reasonable grounds to suspect that money laundering or terrorist financing is being or has been committed or attempted;
 (b)   by promptly furnishing the FIU, at its request, with all necessary information, in accordance with the procedures established by the applicable legislation.
2.   The information referred to in paragraph 1 shall be forwarded to the FIU of the Member State in whose territory the institution or person forwarding the information is situated. The person or persons designated in accordance with the procedures provided for in Article 34 shall normally forward the information.

NOTES

Repealed as noted at the beginning of this Directive.

[4.387]
Article 23

1.   By way of derogation from Article 22(1), Member States may, in the case of the persons referred to in Article 2(1)(3)(a) and (b), designate an appropriate self-regulatory body of the profession concerned as the authority to be informed in the first instance in place of the FIU. Without prejudice to paragraph 2, the designated self-regulatory body shall in such cases forward the information to the FIU promptly and unfiltered.
2.   Member States shall not be obliged to apply the obligations laid down in Article 22(1) to notaries, independent legal professionals, auditors, external accountants and tax advisors with regard to information they receive from or obtain on one of their clients, in the course of ascertaining the legal position for their client or performing their task of defending or representing that client in, or concerning judicial proceedings, including advice on instituting or avoiding proceedings, whether such information is received or obtained before, during or after such proceedings.

NOTES

Repealed as noted at the beginning of this Directive.

[4.388]
Article 24

1.   Member States shall require the institutions and persons covered by this Directive to refrain from carrying out transactions which they know or suspect to be related to money laundering or terrorist financing until they have completed the necessary action in accordance with Article 22(1)(a). In conformity with the legislation of the Member States, instructions may be given not to carry out the transaction.
2.   Where such a transaction is suspected of giving rise to money laundering or terrorist financing and where to refrain in such manner is impossible or is likely to frustrate efforts to pursue the beneficiaries of a suspected money laundering or terrorist financing operation, the institutions and persons concerned shall inform the FIU immediately afterwards.

NOTES

Repealed as noted at the beginning of this Directive.

[4.389]
Article 25

1.   Member States shall ensure that if, in the course of inspections carried out in the institutions and persons covered by this Directive by the competent authorities referred to in Article 37, or in any other way, those authorities discover facts that could be related to money laundering or terrorist financing, they shall promptly inform the FIU.
2.   Member States shall ensure that supervisory bodies empowered by law or regulation to oversee the stock, foreign exchange and financial derivatives markets inform the FIU if they discover facts that could be related to money laundering or terrorist financing.

NOTES

Repealed as noted at the beginning of this Directive.

[4.390]
Article 26
The disclosure in good faith as foreseen in Articles 22(1) and 23 by an institution or person covered by this Directive or by an employee or director of such an institution or person of the information referred to in Articles 22 and 23 shall not constitute a breach of any restriction on disclosure of information imposed by contract or by any legislative, regulatory or administrative provision, and shall not involve the institution or person or its directors or employees in liability of any kind.

NOTES
    Repealed as noted at the beginning of this Directive.

[4.391]
Article 27
Member States shall take all appropriate measures in order to protect employees of the institutions or persons covered by this Directive who report suspicions of money laundering or terrorist financing either internally or to the FIU from being exposed to threats or hostile action.

NOTES
    Repealed as noted at the beginning of this Directive.

SECTION 2
PROHIBITION OF DISCLOSURE

[4.392]
Article 28
1. The institutions and persons covered by this Directive and their directors and employees shall not disclose to the customer concerned or to other third persons the fact that information has been transmitted in accordance with Articles 22 and 23 or that a money laundering or terrorist financing investigation is being or may be carried out.
2. The prohibition laid down in paragraph 1 shall not include disclosure to the competent authorities referred to in Article 37, including the self-regulatory bodies, or disclosure for law enforcement purposes.
3. The prohibition laid down in paragraph 1 shall not prevent disclosure between institutions from Member States, or from third countries provided that they meet the conditions laid down in Article 11(1), belonging to the same group as defined by Article 2(12) of Directive 2002/87/EC of the European Parliament and of the Council of 16 December 2002 on the supplementary supervision of credit institutions, insurance undertakings and investment firms in a financial conglomerate.[1]
4. The prohibition laid down in paragraph 1 shall not prevent disclosure between persons referred to in Article 2(1)(3)(a) and (b) from Member States, or from third countries which impose requirements equivalent to those laid down in this Directive, who perform their professional activities, whether as employees or not, within the same legal person or a network. For the purposes of this Article, a 'network' means the larger structure to which the person belongs and which shares common ownership, management or compliance control.
5. For institutions or persons referred to in Article 2(1)(1), (2) and (3)(a) and (b) in cases related to the same customer and the same transaction involving two or more institutions or persons, the prohibition laid down in paragraph 1 shall not prevent disclosure between the relevant institutions or persons provided that they are situated in a Member State, or in a third country which imposes requirements equivalent to those laid down in this Directive, and that they are from the same professional category and are subject to equivalent obligations as regards professional secrecy and personal data protection. The information exchanged shall be used exclusively for the purposes of the prevention of money laundering and terrorist financing.
6. Where the persons referred to in Article 2(1)(3)(a) and (b) seek to dissuade a client from engaging in illegal activity, this shall not constitute a disclosure within the meaning of the paragraph 1.
[7. The Member States shall inform each other, the ESA to the extent relevant for the purposes of this Directive and in accordance with the relevant provisions of Regulation (EU) No 1093/2010, of Regulation (EU) No 1094/2010, and of Regulation (EU) No 1095/2010 and the Commission of cases where they consider that a third country meets the conditions laid down in paragraphs 3, 4 or 5.]

NOTES
    Repealed as noted at the beginning of this Directive.
    Para 7: substituted by European Parliament and Council Directive 2010/78/EU, Art 8(3).
    [1]   OJ L35, 11.2.2003, p 1.

[4.393]
Article 29
Where the Commission adopts a decision pursuant to Article 40(4), the Member States shall prohibit the disclosure between institutions and persons covered by this Directive and institutions and persons from the third country concerned.

NOTES
Repealed as noted at the beginning of this Directive.

CHAPTER IV
RECORD KEEPING AND STATISTICAL DATA

[4.394]
Article 30
Member States shall require the institutions and persons covered by this Directive to keep the following documents and information for use in any investigation into, or analysis of, possible money laundering or terrorist financing by the FIU or by other competent authorities in accordance with national law:

   (a)   in the case of the customer due diligence, a copy or the references of the evidence required, for a period of at least five years after the business relationship with their customer has ended;

   (b)   in the case of business relationships and transactions, the supporting evidence and records, consisting of the original documents or copies admissible in court proceedings under the applicable national legislation for a period of at least five years following the carrying-out of the transactions or the end of the business relationship.

NOTES
Repealed as noted at the beginning of this Directive.

[4.395]
Article 31
1.   Member States shall require the credit and financial institutions covered by this Directive to apply, where applicable, in their branches and majority-owned subsidiaries located in third countries measures at least equivalent to those laid down in this Directive with regard to customer due diligence and record keeping.

Where the legislation of the third country does not permit application of such equivalent measures, the Member States shall require the credit and financial institutions concerned to inform the competent authorities of the relevant home Member State accordingly.

[2.   The Member States, the ESA to the extent relevant for the purposes of this Directive and in accordance with the relevant provisions of Regulation (EU) No 1093/2010, of Regulation (EU) No 1094/2010, and of Regulation (EU) No 1095/2010 and the Commission shall inform each other of cases where the legislation of the third country does not permit application of the measures required under the first subparagraph of paragraph 1 and coordinated action could be taken to pursue a solution.]

3.   Member States shall require that, where the legislation of the third country does not permit application of the measures required under the first subparagraph of paragraph 1, credit or financial institutions take additional measures to effectively handle the risk of money laundering or terrorist financing.

[4.   In order to ensure consistent harmonisation of this Article and to take account of technical developments in the fight against money laundering and terrorist financing, the ESA taking into account the existing framework and cooperating, as appropriate, with other relevant Union bodies in that field, may develop draft regulatory technical standards in accordance with Article 56 of Regulation (EU) No 1093/2010, of Regulation (EU) No 1094/2010, and of Regulation (EU) No 1095/2010 respectively to specify the type of additional measures referred to in paragraph 3 of this Article and the minimum action to be taken by credit and financial institutions where the legislation of the third country does not permit application of the measures required under the first subparagraph of paragraph 1 of this Article.

Power is delegated to the Commission to adopt the regulatory technical standards referred to in the first subparagraph in accordance with Articles 10 to 14 of Regulation (EU) No 1093/2010.]

NOTES
Repealed as noted at the beginning of this Directive.
Para 2: substituted by European Parliament and Council Directive 2010/78/EU, Art 8(4)(a).
Para 4: added by European Parliament and Council Directive 2010/78/EU, Art 8(4)(b).

[4.396]
Article 32
Member States shall require that their credit and financial institutions have systems in place that enable them to respond fully and rapidly to enquiries from the FIU, or from other authorities, in accordance with their national law, as to whether they maintain or have maintained during the

previous five years a business relationship with specified natural or legal persons and on the nature of that relationship.

NOTES
Repealed as noted at the beginning of this Directive.

[4.397]
Article 33
1. Member States shall ensure that they are able to review the effectiveness of their systems to combat money laundering or terrorist financing by maintaining comprehensive statistics on matters relevant to the effectiveness of such systems.
2. Such statistics shall as a minimum cover the number of suspicious transaction reports made to the FIU, the follow-up given to these reports and indicate on an annual basis the number of cases investigated, the number of persons prosecuted, the number of persons convicted for money laundering or terrorist financing offences and how much property has been frozen, seized or confiscated.
3. Member States shall ensure that a consolidated review of these statistical reports is published.

NOTES
Repealed as noted at the beginning of this Directive.

CHAPTER V
ENFORCEMENT MEASURES

SECTION 1
INTERNAL PROCEDURES, TRAINING AND FEEDBACK

[4.398]
Article 34
1. Member States shall require that the institutions and persons covered by this Directive establish adequate and appropriate policies and procedures of customer due diligence, reporting, record keeping, internal control, risk assessment, risk management, compliance management and communication in order to forestall and prevent operations related to money laundering or terrorist financing.
2. Member States shall require that credit and financial institutions covered by this Directive communicate relevant policies and procedures where applicable to branches and majority-owned subsidiaries in third countries.
[3.   In order to ensure consistent harmonisation and to take account of technical developments in the fight against money laundering and terrorist financing, the ESA, taking into account the existing framework and cooperating, as appropriate, with other relevant Union bodies in that field, may develop draft regulatory technical standards in accordance with Article 56 of Regulation (EU) No 1093/2010, of Regulation (EU) No 1094/2010 and of Regulation (EU) No 1095/2010 respectively, to specify the minimum content of the communication referred to in paragraph 2.
   Power is delegated to the Commission to adopt the regulatory technical standards referred to in the first subparagraph in accordance with Articles 10 to 14 of Regulation (EU) No 1093/2010.]

NOTES
Repealed as noted at the beginning of this Directive.
Para 3: added by European Parliament and Council Directive 2010/78/EU, Art 8(5).

[4.399]
Article 35
1. Member States shall require that the institutions and persons covered by this Directive take appropriate measures so that their relevant employees are aware of the provisions in force on the basis of this Directive.
   These measures shall include participation of their relevant employees in special ongoing training programmes to help them recognise operations which may be related to money laundering or terrorist financing and to instruct them as to how to proceed in such cases.
   Where a natural person falling within any of the categories listed in Article 2(1)(3) performs his professional activities as an employee of a legal person, the obligations in this Section shall apply to that legal person rather than to the natural person.
2. Member States shall ensure that the institutions and persons covered by this Directive have access to up-to-date information on the practices of money launderers and terrorist financers and on indications leading to the recognition of suspicious transactions.
3. Member States shall ensure that, wherever practicable, timely feedback on the effectiveness of and follow-up to reports of suspected money laundering or terrorist financing is provided.

NOTES
Repealed as noted at the beginning of this Directive.

SECTION 2
SUPERVISION

[4.400]
Article 36

1. Member States shall provide that currency exchange offices and trust and company service providers shall be licensed or registered and casinos be licensed in order to operate their business legally. . . .

2. Member States shall require competent authorities to refuse licensing or registration of the entities referred to in paragraph 1 if they are not satisfied that the persons who effectively direct or will direct the business of such entities or the beneficial owners of such entities are fit and proper persons.

NOTES
Repealed as noted at the beginning of this Directive.
Para 1: words omitted repealed by European Parliament and Council Directive 2007/64/EC, Art 91(3).

[4.401]
Article 37

1. Member States shall require the competent authorities at least to effectively monitor and to take the necessary measures with a view to ensuring compliance with the requirements of this Directive by all the institutions and persons covered by this Directive.

2. Member States shall ensure that the competent authorities have adequate powers, including the power to compel the production of any information that is relevant to monitoring compliance and perform checks, and have adequate resources to perform their functions.

3. In the case of credit and financial institutions and casinos, competent authorities shall have enhanced supervisory powers, notably the possibility to conduct on-site inspections.

4. In the case of the natural and legal persons referred to in Article 2(1)(3)(a) to (e), Member States may allow the functions referred to in paragraph 1 to be performed on a risk-sensitive basis.

5. In the case of the persons referred to in Article 2(1)(3)(a) and (b), Member States may allow the functions referred to in paragraph 1 to be performed by self-regulatory bodies, provided that they comply with paragraph 2.

NOTES
Repealed as noted at the beginning of this Directive.

[4.402]
[Article 37a

1. The competent authorities shall cooperate with the ESA for the purposes of this Directive, in accordance with Regulation (EU) No 1093/2010, Regulation (EU) No 1094/2010, and Regulation (EU) No 1095/2010, respectively.

2. The competent authorities shall provide the ESA with all information necessary to carry out their duties under this Directive and under Regulation (EU) No 1093/2010, Regulation (EU) No 1094/2010 and Regulation (EU) No 1095/2010, respectively.]

NOTES
Inserted by European Parliament and Council Directive 2010/78/EU, Art 8(6).
Repealed as noted at the beginning of this Directive.

SECTION 3
COOPERATION

[4.403]
Article 38

The Commission shall lend such assistance as may be needed to facilitate coordination, including the exchange of information between FIUs within the Community.

NOTES
Repealed as noted at the beginning of this Directive.

SECTION 4
PENALTIES

[4.404]
Article 39

1. Member States shall ensure that natural and legal persons covered by this Directive can be held liable for infringements of the national provisions adopted pursuant to this Directive. The penalties must be effective, proportionate and dissuasive.

2.   *Without prejudice to the right of Member States to impose criminal penalties, Member States shall ensure, in conformity with their national law, that the appropriate administrative measures can be taken or administrative sanctions can be imposed against credit and financial institutions for infringements of the national provisions adopted pursuant to this Directive. Member States shall ensure that these measures or sanctions are effective, proportionate and dissuasive.*

3.   *In the case of legal persons, Member States shall ensure that at least they can be held liable for infringements referred to in paragraph 1 which are committed for their benefit by any person, acting either individually or as part of an organ of the legal person, who has a leading position within the legal person, based on:*

    (a)   *a power of representation of the legal person;*
    (b)   *an authority to take decisions on behalf of the legal person, or*
    (c)   *an authority to exercise control within the legal person.*

4.   *In addition to the cases already provided for in paragraph 3, Member States shall ensure that legal persons can be held liable where the lack of supervision or control by a person referred to in paragraph 3 has made possible the commission of the infringements referred to in paragraph 1 for the benefit of a legal person by a person under its authority.*

NOTES

Repealed as noted at the beginning of this Directive.

CHAPTER VI
[DELEGATED ACTS AND IMPLEMENTING MEASURES]

NOTES

Words in square brackets in Chapter heading substituted by European Parliament and Council Directive 2010/78/EU, Art 8(7).

[4.405]
Article 40

[1.   *In order to take account of technical developments in the fight against money laundering and terrorist financing and to specify the requirements laid down in this Directive, the Commission may, adopt the following measures:*]

    (a)   *clarification of the technical aspects of the definitions in Article 3(2)(a) and (d), (6), (7), (8), (9) and (10);*
    (b)   *establishment of technical criteria for assessing whether situations represent a low risk of money laundering or terrorist financing as referred to in Article 11(2) and (5);*
    (c)   *establishment of technical criteria for assessing whether situations represent a high risk of money laundering or terrorist financing as referred to in Article 13;*
    (d)   *establishment of technical criteria for assessing whether, in accordance with Article 2(2), it is justified not to apply this Directive to certain legal or natural persons carrying out a financial activity on an occasional or very limited basis.*

[The measures shall be adopted by means of delegated acts in accordance with Article 41(2a), (2b) and (2c), and subject to the conditions of Articles 41a and 41b.]

2.   *In any event, the Commission shall adopt the first implementing measures to give effect to paragraphs 1(b) and 1(d) by 15 June 2006.*

3.   *The Commission shall . . . adapt the amounts referred to in Articles 2(1)(3)(e), 7(b), 10(1) and 11(5)(a) and (d) taking into account Community legislation, economic developments and changes in international standards.*

[The measures shall be adopted by means of delegated acts in accordance with Article 41(2a), (2b) and (2c), and subject to the conditions of Articles 41a and 41b.]

4.   *Where the Commission finds that a third country does not meet the conditions laid down in Article 11(1) or (2), Article 28(3), (4) or (5), or in the measures established in accordance with paragraph 1(b) of this Article or in Article 16(1)(b), or that the legislation of that third country does not permit application of the measures required under the first subparagraph of Article 31(1), it shall adopt a decision so stating in accordance with the procedure referred to in Article 41(2).*

NOTES

Repealed as noted at the beginning of this Directive.

Para 1: words in square brackets substituted by European Parliament and Council Directive 2010/78/EU, Art 8(8)(a).

Para 3: words omitted repealed by European Parliament and Council Directive 2008/20/EC, Art 1(1), (2)(a); words in square brackets (originally inserted by Directive 2008/20/EC, Art 1(1), (2)(b)) substituted by European Parliament and Council Directive 2010/78/EU, Art 8(8)(b).

[4.406]
Article 41

1.   *The Commission shall be assisted by a Committee on the Prevention of Money Laundering and Terrorist Financing, hereinafter 'the Committee'.*

[2.   *Where reference is made to this paragraph, Articles 5 and 7 of Decision 1999/468/EC shall apply, having regard to Article 8 thereof and provided that the measures adopted in accordance with that procedure do not modify the essential provisions of this Directive.]*

The period laid down in Article 5(6) of Decision 1999/468/EC shall be set at three months.
[2a.   The power to adopt delegated acts referred to in Article 40 shall be conferred on the Commission for a period of 4 years from 4 January 2011. The Commission shall draw up a report in respect of the delegated power at the latest 6 months before the end of the four-year period. The delegation of power shall be automatically extended for periods of an identical duration, unless the European Parliament or the Council revokes it in accordance with Article 41a.]
[2b.   As soon as it adopts a delegated act, the Commission shall notify it simultaneously to the European Parliament and to the Council.
2c.   The power to adopt delegated acts is conferred on the Commission subject to the conditions laid down in Articles 41a and 41b.]
[3.   . . . .]

NOTES

Repealed as noted at the beginning of this Directive.
Para 2: words in square brackets substituted by European Parliament and Council Directive 2010/78/EU, Art 8(9)(a).
Para 2a: inserted by European Parliament and Council Directive 2008/20/EC, Art 1(3)(a) and substituted by European Parliament and Council Directive 2010/78/EU, Art 8(9)(b).
Paras 2b, 2c: inserted by European Parliament and Council Directive 2010/78/EU, Art 8(9)(c).
Para 3: substituted, for original paras 3, 4, by Directive 2008/20/EC, Art 1(3)(b), and repealed by European Parliament and Council Directive 2010/78/EU, Art 8(9)(d).

[4.407]
[Article 41a
Revocation of the delegation
1.   The delegation of power referred to in Article 40 maybe revoked at any time by the European Parliament or by the Council.
2.   The institution which has commenced an internal procedure for deciding whether to revoke a delegation of power shall endeavour to inform the other institution and the Commission within a reasonable time before the final decision is taken, indicating the delegated power which could be subject to revocation.
3.   The decision of revocation shall put an end to the delegation of the power specified in that decision. It shall take effect immediately or on a later date specified therein. It shall not affect the validity of the delegated acts already in force. It shall be published in the Official Journal of the European Union.]

NOTES

Repealed as noted at the beginning of this Directive.
Inserted, together with Art 41b, by European Parliament and Council Directive 2010/78/EU, Art 8(10).

[4.408]
[Article 41b
Objections to delegated acts
1.   The European Parliament or the Council may object to a delegated act within a period of 3 months from the date of notification. At the initiative of the European Parliament or the Council that period shall be extended by 3 months.
2.   If, on the expiry of the period referred to in paragraph 1, neither the European Parliament nor the Council has objected to the delegated act, it shall be published in the Official Journal of the European Union and shall enter into force on the date stated therein.
   The delegated act may be published in the Official Journal of the European Union and enter into force before the expiry of that period if the European Parliament and the Council have both informed the Commission of their intention not to raise objections.
3.   If either the European Parliament or the Council objects to a delegated act within the period referred to in paragraph 1, it shall not enter into force. In accordance with Article 296 TFEU, the institution which objects shall state the reasons for objecting to the delegated act.]

NOTES

Inserted as noted to Art 41a at **[4.407]**.
Repealed as noted at the beginning of this Directive.

CHAPTER VII
FINAL PROVISIONS

[4.409]
Article 42
By 15 December 2009, and at least at three-yearly intervals thereafter, the Commission shall draw up a report on the implementation of this Directive and submit it to the European Parliament and the Council. For the first such report, the Commission shall include a specific examination of the treatment of lawyers and other independent legal professionals.

NOTES
Repealed as noted at the beginning of this Directive.

[4.410]
Article 43
By 15 December 2010, the Commission shall present a report to the European Parliament and to the Council on the threshold percentages in Article 3(6), paying particular attention to the possible expediency and consequences of a reduction of the percentage in points (a)(i), (b)(i) and (b)(iii) of Article 3(6) from 25% to 20%. On the basis of the report the Commission may submit a proposal for amendments to this Directive.

NOTES
Repealed as noted at the beginning of this Directive.

[4.411]
Article 44
Directive 91/308/EEC is hereby repealed.
    References made to the repealed Directive shall be construed as being made to this Directive and should be read in accordance with the correlation table set out in the Annex.

NOTES
Repealed as noted at the beginning of this Directive.

[4.412]
Article 45
1.   Member States shall bring into force the laws, regulations and administrative provisions necessary to comply with this Directive by 15 December 2007. They shall forthwith communicate to the Commission the text of those provisions together with a table showing how the provisions of this Directive correspond to the national provisions adopted.
    When Member States adopt those measures, they shall contain a reference to this Directive or be accompanied by such a reference on the occasion of their official publication. The methods of making such reference shall be laid down by Member States.
2.   Member States shall communicate to the Commission the text of the main provisions of national law which they adopt in the field covered by this Directive.

NOTES
Repealed as noted at the beginning of this Directive.

[4.413]
Article 46
This Directive shall enter into force on the 20th day after its publication in the Official Journal of the European Union.

NOTES
Repealed as noted at the beginning of this Directive.

[4.414]
Article 47
This Directive is addressed to the Member States.

NOTES
Repealed as noted at the beginning of this Directive.

ANNEX
CORRELATION TABLE

[4.415]

This Directive	*Directive 91/308/EEC*
Article 1(1)	*Article 2*
Article 1(2)	*Article 1(C)*
Article 1(2)(a)	*Article 1(C) first point*
Article 1(2)(b)	*Article 1(C) second point*
Article 1(2)(c)	*Article 1(C) third point*
Article 1(2)(d)	*Article 1(C) fourth point*
Article 1(3)	*Article 1(C), third paragraph*
Article 1(4)	

This Directive	Directive 91/308/EEC
Article 1(5)	Article 1(C), second paragraph
Article 2(1)(1)	Article 2a(1)
Article 2(1)(2)	Article 2a(2)
Article 2(1)(3)(a), (b) and (d) to (f)	Article 2a(3) to (7)
Article 2(1)(3)(c)	
Article 2(2)	
Article 3(1)	Article 1(A)
Article 3(2)(a)	Article 1(B)(1)
Article 3(2)(b)	Article 1(B)(2)
Article 3(2)(c)	Article 1(B)(3)
Article 3(2)(d)	Article 1(B)(4)
Article 3(2)(e)	
Article 3(2)(f)	Article 1(B), second paragraph
Article 3(3)	Article 1(D)
Article 3(4)	Article 1(E), first paragraph
Article 3(5)	Article 1(E), second paragraph
Article 3(5)(a)	
Article 3(5)(b)	Article 1(E), first indent
Article 3(5)(c)	Article 1(E), second indent
Article 3(5)(d)	Article 1(E), third indent
Article 3(5)(e)	Article 1(E), fourth indent
Article 3(5)(f)	Article 1(E), fifth indent, and third paragraph
Article 3(6)	
Article 3(7)	
Article 3(8)	
Article 3(9)	
Article 3(10)	
Article 4	Article 12
Article 5	Article 15
Article 6	
Article 7(a)	Article 3(1)
Article 7(b)	Article 3(2)
Article 7(c)	Article 3(8)
Article 7(d)	Article 3(7)
Article 8(1)(a)	Article 3(1)
Article 8(1)(b) to (d)	
Article 8(2)	
Article 9(1)	Article 3(1)
Article 9(2) to (6)	
Article 10	Article 3(5) and (6)
Article 11(1)	Article 3(9)
Article 11(2)	
Article 11(3) and (4)	
Article 11(5)(a)	Article 3(3)
Article 11(5)(b)	Article 3(4)
Article 11(5)(c)	Article 3(4)
Article 11(5)(d)	
Article 12	
Article 13(1) and (2)	Article 3(10) and (11)
Article 13(3) to (5)	
Article 13(6)	Article 5

This Directive	Directive 91/308/EEC
Article 14	
Article 15	
Article 16	
Article 17	
Article 18	
Article 19	
Article 20	Article 5
Article 21	
Article 22	Article 6(1) and (2)
Article 23	Article 6(3)
Article 24	Article 7
Article 25	Article 10
Article 26	Article 9
Article 27	
Article 28(1)	Article 8(1)
Article 28(2) to (7)	
Article 29	
Article 30(a)	Article 4, first indent
Article 30(b)	Article 4, second indent
Article 31	
Article 32	
Article 33	
Article 34(1)	Article 11(1) (a)
Article 34(2)	
Article 35(1), first paragraph	Article 11(1)(b), first sentence
Article 35(1), second paragraph	Article 11(1)(b) second sentence
Article 35(1), third paragraph	Article 11(1), second paragraph
Article 35(2)	
Article 35(3)	
Article 36	
Article 37	
Article 38	
Article 39(1)	Article 14
Article 39(2) to (4)	
Article 40	
Article 41	
Article 42	Article 17
Article 43	
Article 44	
Article 45	Article 16
Article 46	Article 16

NOTES

Repealed as noted at the beginning of this Directive.

DIRECTIVE OF THE EUROPEAN PARLIAMENT AND OF THE COUNCIL

(2006/114/EC)

of 12 December 2006

concerning misleading and comparative advertising

(codified version)

(Text with EEA relevance)

NOTES

Date of publication in OJ: OJ L376, 27/12/2006, p 21.

This Directive has been implemented in the UK by the Business Protection from Misleading Marketing Regulations 2008, SI 2008/1276 at **[2.526]**.

THE EUROPEAN PARLIAMENT AND THE COUNCIL OF THE EUROPEAN UNION,

Having regard to the Treaty establishing the European Community, and in particular Article 95 thereof,

Having regard to the proposal from the Commission,

Having regard to the opinion of the European Economic and Social Committee,[1]

Acting in accordance with the procedure laid down in Article 251 of the Treaty,[2]

Whereas:

(1)   Council Directive 84/450/EEC of 10 September 1984 concerning misleading and comparative advertising[3] has been substantially amended several times.[4] In the interests of clarity and rationality the said Directive should be codified.

(2)   The laws against misleading advertising in force in the Member States differ widely. Since advertising reaches beyond the frontiers of individual Member States, it has a direct effect on the smooth functioning of the internal market.

(3)   Misleading and unlawful comparative advertising can lead to distortion of competition within the internal market.

(4)   Advertising, whether or not it induces a contract, affects the economic welfare of consumers and traders.

(5)   The differences between the laws of the Member States on advertising which misleads business hinder the execution of advertising campaigns beyond national boundaries and thus affect the free circulation of goods and provision of services.

(6)   The completion of the internal market means a wide range of choice. Given that consumers and traders can and must make the best possible use of the internal market, and that advertising is a very important means of creating genuine outlets for all goods and services throughout the Community, the basic provisions governing the form and content of comparative advertising should be uniform and the conditions of the use of comparative advertising in the Member States should be harmonised. If these conditions are met, this will help demonstrate objectively the merits of the various comparable products. Comparative advertising can also stimulate competition between suppliers of goods and services to the consumer's advantage.

(7)   Minimum and objective criteria for determining whether advertising is misleading should be established.

(8)   Comparative advertising, when it compares material, relevant, verifiable and representative features and is not misleading, may be a legitimate means of informing consumers of their advantage. It is desirable to provide a broad concept of comparative advertising to cover all modes of comparative advertising.

(9)   Conditions of permitted comparative advertising, as far as the comparison is concerned, should be established in order to determine which practices relating to comparative advertising may distort competition, be detrimental to competitors and have an adverse effect on consumer choice. Such conditions of permitted advertising should include criteria of objective comparison of the features of goods and services.

(10)   The international conventions on copyright as well as the national provisions on contractual and non-contractual liability should apply when the results of comparative tests carried out by third parties are referred to or reproduced in comparative advertising.

(11)   The conditions of comparative advertising should be cumulative and respected in their entirety. In accordance with the Treaty, the choice of forms and methods for the implementation of these conditions should be left to the Member States, insofar as those forms and methods are not already determined by this Directive.

(12)   These conditions should include, in particular, consideration of the provisions resulting

from Council Regulation (EC) No 510/2006 of 20 March 2006 on the protection of geographical indications and designations of origin for agricultural products and foodstuffs,[5] and in particular Article 13 thereof, and of the other Community provisions adopted in the agricultural sphere.

(13) Article 5 of First Council Directive 89/104/EEC of 21 December 1988 to approximate the laws of the Member States relating to trade marks[6] confers exclusive rights on the proprietor of a registered trade mark, including the right to prevent all third parties from using, in the course of trade, any sign which is identical to, or similar to, the trade mark in relation to identical goods or services or even, where appropriate, other goods.

(14) It may, however, be indispensable, in order to make comparative advertising effective, to identify the goods or services of a competitor, making reference to a trade mark or trade name of which the latter is the proprietor.

(15) Such use of another's trade mark, trade name or other distinguishing marks does not breach this exclusive right in cases where it complies with the conditions laid down by this Directive, the intended target being solely to distinguish between them and thus to highlight differences objectively.

(16) Persons or organisations regarded under national law as having a legitimate interest in the matter should have facilities for initiating proceedings against misleading and unlawful comparative advertising, either before a court or before an administrative authority which is competent to decide upon complaints or to initiate appropriate legal proceedings.

(17) The courts or administrative authorities should have powers enabling them to order or obtain the cessation of misleading and unlawful comparative advertising. In certain cases it may be desirable to prohibit misleading and unlawful comparative advertising even before it is published. However, this in no way implies that Member States are under an obligation to introduce rules requiring the systematic prior vetting of advertising.

(18) The voluntary control exercised by self-regulatory bodies to eliminate misleading or unlawful comparative advertising may avoid recourse to administrative or judicial action and ought therefore to be encouraged.

(19) While it is for national law to determine the burden of proof, it is appropriate to enable courts and administrative authorities to require traders to produce evidence as to the accuracy of factual claims they have made.

(20) Regulating comparative advertising is necessary for the smooth functioning of the internal market. Action at Community level is therefore required. The adoption of a Directive is the appropriate instrument because it lays down uniform general principles while allowing the Member States to choose the form and appropriate method by which to attain these objectives. It is in accordance with the principle of subsidiarity.

(21) This Directive should be without prejudice to the obligations of the Member States relating to the time-limits for transposition into national law and application of the Directives as set out in Part B of Annex I,

HAVE ADOPTED THIS DIRECTIVE:

NOTES

[1]   Opinion of 26 October 2006 (not yet published in the Official Journal).

[2]   Opinion of the European Parliament of 12 October 2006 (not yet published in the Official Journal) and Council Decision of 30 November 2006.

[3]   OJ L250, 19.9.1984, p 17. Directive as last amended by Directive 2005/29/EC of the European Parliament and of the Council (OJ L149, 11.6.2005, p 22).

[4]   See Annex I, Part A.

[5]   OJ L93, 31.3.2006, p 12.

[6]   OJ L40, 11.2.1989, p 1. Directive as amended by Decision 92/10/EEC (OJ L6, 11.1.1992, p 35).

[4.416]
Article 1
The purpose of this Directive is to protect traders against misleading advertising and the unfair consequences thereof and to lay down the conditions under which comparative advertising is permitted.

[4.417]
Article 2
For the purposes of this Directive:
    (a) 'advertising' means the making of a representation in any form in connection with a trade, business, craft or profession in order to promote the supply of goods or services, including immovable property, rights and obligations;

(b)   'misleading advertising' means any advertising which in any way, including its presentation, deceives or is likely to deceive the persons to whom it is addressed or whom it reaches and which, by reason of its deceptive nature, is likely to affect their economic behaviour or which, for those reasons, injures or is likely to injure a competitor;

(c)   'comparative advertising' means any advertising which explicitly or by implication identifies a competitor or goods or services offered by a competitor;

(d)   'trader' means any natural or legal person who is acting for purposes relating to his trade, craft, business or profession and anyone acting in the name of or on behalf of a trader;

(e)   'code owner' means any entity, including a trader or group of traders, which is responsible for the formulation and revision of a code of conduct and/or for monitoring compliance with the code by those who have undertaken to be bound by it.

[4.418]
Article 3
In determining whether advertising is misleading, account shall be taken of all its features, and in particular of any information it contains concerning:

(a)   the characteristics of goods or services, such as their availability, nature, execution, composition, method and date of manufacture or provision, fitness for purpose, uses, quantity, specification, geographical or commercial origin or the results to be expected from their use, or the results and material features of tests or checks carried out on the goods or services;

(b)   the price or the manner in which the price is calculated, and the conditions on which the goods are supplied or the services provided;

(c)   the nature, attributes and rights of the advertiser, such as his identity and assets, his qualifications and ownership of industrial, commercial or intellectual property rights or his awards and distinctions.

[4.419]
Article 4
Comparative advertising shall, as far as the comparison is concerned, be permitted when the following conditions are met:

(a)   it is not misleading within the meaning of Articles 2(b), 3 and 8(1) of this Directive or Articles 6 and 7 of Directive 2005/29/EC of the European Parliament and of the Council of 11 May 2005 concerning unfair business-to-consumer commercial practices in the internal market ("Unfair Commercial Practices Directive");[1]

(b)   it compares goods or services meeting the same needs or intended for the same purpose;

(c)   it objectively compares one or more material, relevant, verifiable and representative features of those goods and services, which may include price;

(d)   it does not discredit or denigrate the trade marks, trade names, other distinguishing marks, goods, services, activities or circumstances of a competitor;

(e)   for products with designation of origin, it relates in each case to products with the same designation;

(f)   it does not take unfair advantage of the reputation of a trade mark, trade name or other distinguishing marks of a competitor or of the designation of origin of competing products;

(g)   it does not present goods or services as imitations or replicas of goods or services bearing a protected trade mark or trade name;

(h)   it does not create confusion among traders, between the advertiser and a competitor or between the advertiser's trade marks, trade names, other distinguishing marks, goods or services and those of a competitor.

NOTES

[1]   OJ L149, 11.6.2005, p 22.

[4.420]
Article 5
1.   Member States shall ensure that adequate and effective means exist to combat misleading advertising and enforce compliance with the provisions on comparative advertising in the interests of traders and competitors.

Such means shall include legal provisions under which persons or organisations regarded under national law as having a legitimate interest in combating misleading advertising or regulating comparative advertising may:

(a)   take legal action against such advertising; or

(b)   bring such advertising before an administrative authority competent either to decide on complaints or to initiate appropriate legal proceedings.

2.   It shall be for each Member State to decide which of the facilities referred to in the second subparagraph of paragraph 1 shall be available and whether to enable the courts or administrative authorities to require prior recourse to other established means of dealing with complaints, including those referred to in Article 6.

It shall be for each Member State to decide:

(a)   whether these legal facilities may be directed separately or jointly against a number of traders from the same economic sector; and

(b)   whether these legal facilities may be directed against a code owner where the relevant code promotes non-compliance with legal requirements.

3.   Under the provisions referred to in paragraphs 1 and 2, Member States shall confer upon the courts or administrative authorities powers enabling them, in cases where they deem such measures to be necessary taking into account all the interests involved and in particular the public interest:

(a)   to order the cessation of, or to institute appropriate legal proceedings for an order for the cessation of, misleading advertising or unlawful comparative advertising; or

(b)   if the misleading advertising or unlawful comparative advertising has not yet been published but publication is imminent, to order the prohibition of, or to institute appropriate legal proceedings for an order for the prohibition of, such publication.

The first subparagraph shall apply even where there is no proof of actual loss or damage or of intention or negligence on the part of the advertiser.

Member States shall make provision for the measures referred to in the first subparagraph to be taken under an accelerated procedure either with interim effect or with definitive effect, at the Member States' discretion.

4.   Member States may confer upon the courts or administrative authorities powers enabling them, with a view to eliminating the continuing effects of misleading advertising or unlawful comparative advertising, the cessation of which has been ordered by a final decision:

(a)   to require publication of that decision in full or in part and in such form as they deem adequate;

(b)   to require in addition the publication of a corrective statement.

5.   The administrative authorities referred to in point (b) of the second subparagraph of paragraph 1 must:

(a)   be composed so as not to cast doubt on their impartiality;

(b)   have adequate powers, where they decide on complaints, to monitor and enforce the observance of their decisions effectively;

(c)   normally give reasons for their decisions.

6.   Where the powers referred to in paragraphs 3 and 4 are exercised exclusively by an administrative authority, reasons for its decisions shall always be given. In this case, provision must be made for procedures whereby improper or unreasonable exercise of its powers by the administrative authority or improper or unreasonable failure to exercise the said powers can be the subject of judicial review.

[4.421]
Article 6
This Directive does not exclude the voluntary control, which Member States may encourage, of misleading or comparative advertising by self-regulatory bodies and recourse to such bodies by the persons or organisations referred to in the second subparagraph of Article 5(1) on condition that proceedings before such bodies are additional to the court or administrative proceedings referred to in that Article.

[4.422]
Article 7
Member States shall confer upon the courts or administrative authorities powers enabling them in the civil or administrative proceedings referred to in Article 5:

(a)   to require the advertiser to furnish evidence as to the accuracy of factual claims in advertising if, taking into account the legitimate interest of the advertiser and any other party to the proceedings, such a requirement appears appropriate on the basis of the circumstances of the particular case and in the case of comparative advertising to require the advertiser to furnish such evidence in a short period of time; and

(b)   to consider factual claims as inaccurate if the evidence demanded in accordance with point (a) is not furnished or is deemed insufficient by the court or administrative authority.

[4.423]
Article 8
1.   This Directive shall not preclude Member States from retaining or adopting provisions with a view to ensuring more extensive protection, with regard to misleading advertising, for traders and competitors.

The first subparagraph shall not apply to comparative advertising as far as the comparison is concerned.

2.   The provisions of this Directive shall apply without prejudice to Community provisions on advertising for specific products and/or services or to restrictions or prohibitions on advertising in particular media.

3.   The provisions of this Directive concerning comparative advertising shall not oblige Member States which, in compliance with the provisions of the Treaty, maintain or introduce advertising bans regarding certain goods or services, whether imposed directly or by a body or

organisation responsible, under the law of the Member States, for regulating the exercise of a commercial, industrial, craft or professional activity, to permit comparative advertising regarding those goods or services. Where these bans are limited to particular media, this Directive shall apply to the media not covered by these bans.

4.   Nothing in this Directive shall prevent Member States, in compliance with the provisions of the Treaty, from maintaining or introducing bans or limitations on the use of comparisons in the advertising of professional services, whether imposed directly or by a body or organisation responsible, under the law of the Member States, for regulating the exercise of a professional activity.

[4.424]
Article 9
Member States shall communicate to the Commission the text of the main provisions of national law which they adopt in the field covered by this Directive.

[4.425]
Article 10
Directive 84/450/EEC is hereby repealed, without prejudice to the obligations of the Member States relating to the time-limits for transposition into national law and application of the Directives, as set out in Part B of Annex I.

References made to the repealed Directive shall be construed as being made to this Directive and should be read in accordance with the correlation table set out in Annex II.

[4.426]
Article 11
This Directive shall enter into force on 12 December 2007.

[4.427]
Article 12
This Directive is addressed to the Member States.

ANNEX I

PART A
REPEALED DIRECTIVE WITH ITS SUCCESSIVE AMENDMENTS

[4.428]

Council Directive 84/450/EEC	
(OJ L250, 19.9.1984, p 17)	
Directive 97/55/EC of the European Parliament and of the Council	
(OJ L290, 23.10.1997, p 18)	
Directive 2005/29/EC of the European Parliament and of the Council	only Article 14
(OJ L149, 11.6.2005, p 22)	

PART B
**LIST OF TIME-LIMITS FOR TRANSPOSITION INTO NATIONAL LAW
AND APPLICATION**

(referred to in Article 10)
[4.429]

Directive	*Time-limit for transposition*	*Date of application*
84/450/EEC	1 October 1986	—
97/55/EC	23 April 2000	—
2005/29/EC	12 June 2007	12 December 2007

ANNEX II
CORRELATION TABLE

[4.430]

Directive 84/450/EEC	*This Directive*
Article 1	Article 1
Article 2, introductory words	Article 2, introductory words
Article 2, point 1	Article 2(a)

DIRECTIVE OF THE EUROPEAN PARLIAMENT AND OF THE COUNCIL

(2008/48/EC)

of 23 April 2008

on credit agreements for consumers and repealing Council Directive 87/102/EEC

NOTES

    Date of publication in OJ: OJ L133, 22.5.2008, p 66.

    This Directive is reproduced as corrected by the corrigenda published in OJ L207, 11.8.2009, p 14, OJ L199, 31.7.2010, p 40 and OJ L234, 10.9.2011, p 46.

This Directive has been implemented in the UK by the Consumer Credit (EU Directive) Regulations 2010, SI 2010/1010 at **[2.801]**, the Consumer Credit (Total Charge for Credit) Regulations 2010, SI 2010/1011 (revoked and kept for reference at **[2.807]**), the Consumer Credit (Disclosure of Information) Regulations 2010, SI 2010/1013 at **[2.814]**, and the Consumer Credit (Agreements) Regulations 2010, SI 2010/1014 at **[2.829]**.

THE EUROPEAN PARLIAMENT AND THE COUNCIL OF THE EUROPEAN UNION,
     Having regard to the Treaty establishing the European Economic Community, and in particular Article 100 thereof,
     Having regard to the Treaty establishing the European Community, and in particular Article 95 thereof,
     Having regard to the proposal from the Commission,
     Having regard to the opinion of the European Economic and Social Committee,[1]
     Acting in accordance with the procedure laid down in Article 251 of the Treaty,[2]
     Whereas:

(1)   Council Directive 87/102/EEC of 22 December 1986 for the approximation of the laws, regulations and administrative provisions of the Member States concerning consumer credit[3] lays down rules at Community level concerning consumer credit agreements.

(2)   In 1995, the Commission presented a report on the operation of Directive 87/102/EEC and undertook a broad consultation of the interested parties. In 1997, the Commission presented a summary report of reactions to the 1995 report. A second report was produced in 1996 on the operation of Directive 87/102/EEC.

(3)   Those reports and consultations revealed substantial differences between the laws of the various Member States in the field of credit for natural persons in general and consumer credit in particular. An analysis of the national laws transposing Directive 87/102/EEC shows that Member States use a variety of consumer protection mechanisms, in addition to Directive 87/102/EEC, on account of differences in the legal or economic situation at national level.

(4)   The *de facto* and *de jure* situation resulting from those national differences in some cases leads to distortions of competition among creditors in the Community and creates obstacles to the internal market where Member States have adopted different mandatory provisions more stringent than those provided for in Directive 87/102/EEC. It restricts consumers' ability to make direct use of the gradually increasing availability of cross-border credit. Those distortions and restrictions may in turn have consequences in terms of the demand for goods and services.

(5)   In recent years the types of credit offered to and used by consumers have evolved considerably. New credit instruments have appeared, and their use continues to develop. It is therefore necessary to amend existing provisions and to extend their scope, where appropriate.

(6)   In accordance with the Treaty, the internal market comprises an area without internal frontiers in which the free movement of goods and services and freedom of establishment are ensured. The development of a more transparent and efficient credit market within the area without internal frontiers is vital in order to promote the development of cross-border activities.

(7)   In order to facilitate the emergence of a well-functioning internal market in consumer credit, it is necessary to make provision for a harmonised Community framework in a number of core areas. In view of the continuously developing market in consumer credit and the increasing mobility of European citizens, forward-looking Community legislation which is able to adapt to future forms of credit and which allows Member States the appropriate degree of flexibility in their implementation should help to establish a modern body of law on consumer credit.

(8)   It is important that the market should offer a sufficient degree of consumer protection to ensure consumer confidence. Thus, it should be possible for the free movement of credit offers to take place under optimum conditions for both those who offer credit and those who require it, with due regard to specific situations in the individual Member States.

(9) Full harmonisation is necessary in order to ensure that all consumers in the Community enjoy a high and equivalent level of protection of their interests and to create a genuine internal market. Member States should therefore not be allowed to maintain or introduce national provisions other than those laid down in this Directive. However, such restriction should only apply where there are provisions harmonised in this Directive. Where no such harmonised provisions exist, Member States should remain free to maintain or introduce national legislation. Accordingly, Member States may, for instance, maintain or introduce national provisions on joint and several liability of the seller or the service provider and the creditor. Another example of this possibility for Member States could be the maintenance or introduction of national provisions on the cancellation of a contract for the sale of goods or supply of services if the consumer exercises his right of withdrawal from the credit agreement. In this respect Member States, in the case of open-end credit agreements, should be allowed to fix a minimum period needing to elapse between the time when the creditor asks for reimbursement and the day on which the credit has to be reimbursed.

(10)   The definitions contained in this Directive determine the scope of harmonisation. The obligation on Member States to implement the provisions of this Directive should therefore be limited to its scope as determined by those definitions. However, this Directive should be without

prejudice to the application by Member States, in accordance with Community law, of the provisions of this Directive to areas not covered by its scope. A Member State could thereby maintain or introduce national legislation corresponding to the provisions of this Directive or certain of its provisions on credit agreements outside the scope of this Directive, for instance on credit agreements involving amounts less than EUR 200 or more than EUR 75 000. Furthermore, Member States could also apply the provisions of this Directive to linked credit which does not fall within the definition of a linked credit agreement as contained in this Directive. Thus, the provisions on linked credit agreements could be applied to credit agreements that serve only partially to finance a contract for the supply of goods or provision of a service.

(11)   In the case of specific credit agreements to which only some provisions of this Directive are applicable, Member States should not be allowed to adopt national legislation implementing other provisions of this Directive. However, Member States should remain free to regulate, in their national legislation, such types of credit agreements as regards other aspects not harmonised by this Directive.

(12)   Agreements for the provision on a continuing basis of services or for the supply of goods of the same kind, where the consumer pays for them for the duration of their provision by means of instalments, may differ considerably, in terms of the interests of the contractual parties involved, and the modalities and performance of the transactions, from credit agreements covered by this Directive. Therefore, it should be clarified that such agreements are not regarded as credit agreements for the purposes of this Directive. Such types of agreement include, for example, an insurance contract where the insurance is paid for in monthly instalments.

(13)   This Directive should not apply to certain types of credit agreement, such as deferred debit cards, under the terms of which the credit has to be repaid within three months and only insignificant charges are payable.

(14)   Credit agreements covering the granting of credit secured by real estate should be excluded from the scope of this Directive. That type of credit is of a very specific nature. Also, credit agreements the purpose of which is to finance the acquisition or retention of property rights in land or in an existing or projected building should be excluded from the scope of this Directive. However, credit agreements should not be excluded from the scope of this Directive only because their purpose is the renovation or increase of value of an existing building.

(15)   The provisions of this Directive apply irrespective of whether the creditor is a legal person or a natural person. However, this Directive does not affect the right of Member States to limit, in conformity with Community law, the provision of credit for consumers to legal persons only or to certain legal persons.

(16)   Certain provisions of this Directive should apply to natural and legal persons (credit intermediaries) who, in the course of their trade, business or profession, for a fee, present or offer credit agreements to consumers, assist consumers by undertaking preparatory work in respect of credit agreements or conclude credit agreements with consumers on behalf of the creditor. Organisations which allow their identity to be used in promoting credit products, such as credit cards, and which may also recommend those products to their members should not be regarded as credit intermediaries for the purposes of this Directive.

(17)   This Directive regulates only certain obligations of credit intermediaries in relation to consumers. Member States should therefore remain free to maintain or introduce additional obligations incumbent on credit intermediaries, including the conditions under which a credit intermediary may receive fees from a consumer who has requested his service.

(18)   Consumers should be protected against unfair or misleading practices, in particular with respect to the disclosure of information by the creditor, in line with Directive 2005/29/ EC of the European Parliament and of the Council of 11 May 2005 concerning unfair business-to-consumer commercial practices in the internal market ('Unfair Commercial Practices' Directive).[4] However, this Directive should contain specific provisions on advertising concerning credit agreements as well as certain items of standard information to be provided to consumers in order to enable them, in particular, to compare different offers. Such information should be given in a clear, concise and prominent way by means of a representative example. A ceiling should be provided where it is not possible to indicate the total amount of credit as the total sums made available, in particular where a credit agreement gives the consumer freedom of drawdown with a limitation with regard to the amount. The ceiling should indicate the upper limit of credit which can be made available to the consumer. In addition, Member States should remain free to regulate information requirements in their national law regarding advertising which does not contain information on the cost of the credit.

(19)   In order to enable consumers to make their decisions in full knowledge of the facts, they should receive adequate information, which the consumer may take away and consider, prior to the conclusion of the credit agreement, on the conditions and cost of the credit and on their obligations. To ensure the fullest possible transparency and comparability of offers, such information should, in particular, include the annual percentage rate of charge applicable to the credit, determined in the same way throughout the Community. As the annual percentage rate of charge can at this stage be indicated only through an example, such example should be representative. Therefore, it should correspond, for instance, to the average duration and total amount of credit granted for the type of

credit agreement under consideration and, if applicable, to the goods purchased. When determining the representative example, the frequency of certain types of credit agreement in a specific market should also be taken into account. As regards the borrowing rate, the frequency of instalments and the capitalisation of interest, creditors should use their conventional method of calculation for the consumer credit concerned.

(20)   The total cost of the credit to the consumer should comprise all the costs, including interest, commissions, taxes, fees for credit intermediaries and any other fees which the consumer has to pay in connection with the credit agreement, except for notarial costs. Creditors' actual knowledge of the costs should be assessed objectively, taking into account the requirements of professional diligence.

(21)   Credit agreements in which a borrowing rate is periodically revised in line with changes occurring in a reference rate referred to in the credit agreement should not be regarded as credit agreements with a fixed borrowing rate.

(22)   Member States should remain free to maintain or introduce national provisions prohibiting the creditor from requiring the consumer, in connection with the credit agreement, to open a bank account or conclude an agreement in respect of another ancillary service, or to pay the expenses or fees for such bank accounts or other ancillary services. In those Member States where such combined offers are allowed, consumers should be informed before the conclusion of the credit agreement about any ancillary services which are compulsory in order for the credit to be obtained in the first place or on the terms and conditions marketed. The costs payable in respect of those ancillary services should be included in the total cost of the credit; alternatively, if the amount of such costs cannot be determined in advance, consumers should receive adequate information about the existence of costs at a pre-contractual stage. The creditor must be presumed to have knowledge of the costs of the ancillary services which he offers to the consumer himself, or on behalf of a third party, unless the price thereof depends on the specific characteristics or situation of the consumer.

(23)   For specific types of credit agreements, however, it is appropriate, in order to ensure an adequate level of consumer protection without placing an excessive burden on creditors or, where applicable, credit intermediaries, to restrict the pre-contractual information requirements of this Directive, taking into account the specific character of such types of agreements.

(24)   The consumer needs to be given comprehensive information before he concludes the credit agreement, regardless of whether or not a credit intermediary is involved in the marketing of the credit. Therefore, in general, the pre-contractual information requirements should also apply to credit intermediaries. However, where suppliers of goods and services act as credit intermediaries in an ancillary capacity, it is not appropriate to burden them with the legal obligation to provide the pre-contractual information in accordance with this Directive. Suppliers of goods and services may be deemed, for example, to be acting as credit intermediaries in an ancillary capacity if their activity as credit intermediaries is not the main purpose of their trade, business or profession. In those cases, a sufficient level of consumer protection is still achieved since the creditor is responsible for ensuring that the consumer receives the full pre-contractual information, either from the intermediary, if the creditor and the intermediary so agree, or in some other appropriate manner.

(25)   The potentially binding character of the information to be provided to the consumer prior to the conclusion of the credit agreement and the period of time during which the creditor is to be bound by it may be regulated by the Member States.

(26)   Member States should take appropriate measures to promote responsible practices during all phases of the credit relationship, taking into account the specific features of their credit market. Those measures may include, for instance, the provision of information to, and the education of, consumers, including warnings about the risks attaching to default on payment and to over-indebtedness. In the expanding credit market, in particular, it is important that creditors should not engage in irresponsible lending or give out credit without prior assessment of creditworthiness, and the Member States should carry out the necessary supervision to avoid such behaviour and should determine the necessary means to sanction creditors in the event of their doing so. Without prejudice to the credit risk provisions of Directive 2006/48/EC of the European Parliament and of the Council of 14 June 2006 relating to the taking up and pursuit of the business of credit institutions,[5] creditors should bear the responsibility of checking individually the creditworthiness of the consumer. To that end, they should be allowed to use information provided by the consumer not only during the preparation of the credit agreement in question, but also during a longstanding commercial relationship. The Member States' authorities could also give appropriate instructions and guidelines to creditors. Consumers should also act with prudence and respect their contractual obligations.

(27)   Despite the pre-contractual information to be provided, the consumer may still need additional assistance in order to decide which credit agreement, within the range of products proposed, is the most appropriate for his needs and financial situation. Therefore, Member States should ensure that creditors provide such assistance in relation to the credit products which they offer to the consumer. Where appropriate, the relevant pre-contractual information, as well as the essential characteristics of the products proposed, should be explained to the consumer in a personalised manner so that the consumer can understand the effects which they may have on his economic situation. Where applicable, this duty to assist the consumer should also apply to credit intermediaries. Member States could determine when and to what extent such explanations are to be

given to the consumer, taking into account the particular circumstances in which the credit is offered, the consumer's need for assistance and the nature of individual credit products.

(28) To assess the credit status of a consumer, the creditor should also consult relevant databases; the legal and actual circumstances may require that such consultations vary in scope. To prevent any distortion of competition among creditors, it should be ensured that creditors have access to private or public databases concerning consumers in a Member State where they are not established under non-discriminatory conditions compared with creditors in that Member State.

(29) Where a decision to reject an application for credit is based on the consultation of a database, the creditor should inform the consumer of this fact and of the particulars of the database consulted. However, the creditor should not be obliged to give such information when this is prohibited by other Community legislation, for example legislation on money laundering or the financing of terrorism. Furthermore, such information should not be given if this would be contrary to objectives of public policy or public security, such as the prevention, investigation, detection or prosecution of criminal offences.

(30) This Directive does not regulate contract law issues related to the validity of credit agreements. Therefore, in that area, the Member States may maintain or introduce national provisions which are in conformity with Community law. Member States may regulate the legal regime governing the offer to conclude the credit agreement, in particular when it is to be given and the period during which it is to be binding on the creditor. If such an offer is made at the same time as the pre-contractual information provided for by this Directive is given, it should, like any additional information the creditor may wish to give to the consumer, be provided in a separate document which may be annexed to the Standard European Consumer Credit Information.

(31) In order to enable the consumer to know his rights and obligations under the credit agreement, it should contain all necessary information in a clear and concise manner.

(32) In order to ensure full transparency, the consumer should be provided with information concerning the borrowing rate, both at a pre-contractual stage and when the credit agreement is concluded. During the contractual relationship, the consumer should further be informed of changes to the variable borrowing rate and changes to the payments caused thereby. This is without prejudice to provisions of national law not related to consumer information which lay down conditions for, or prescribe the consequences of, changes, other than changes concerning payments, in borrowing rates and other economic conditions governing the credit, for instance rules providing that the creditor may change the borrowing rate only where there is a valid reason for such change or that the consumer may terminate the contract should there be a change in the borrowing rate or in some other economic condition concerning the credit.

(33) The contracting parties should have the right to effect a standard termination of an open-end credit agreement. In addition, if agreed in the credit agreement, the creditor should have the right to suspend the consumer's right to draw down on an open-end credit agreement for objectively justified reasons. Such reasons may include, for instance, suspicion of an unauthorised or fraudulent use of the credit or a significantly increased risk of the consumer being unable to fulfil his obligation to repay the credit. This Directive does not affect national law in the area of contract law regulating the rights of the contracting parties to terminate the credit agreement on the basis of a breach of contract.

(34) In order to approximate the procedures for exercising the right of withdrawal in similar areas, it is necessary to make provision for a right of withdrawal without penalty and with no obligation to provide justification, under conditions similar to those provided for by Directive 2002/65/EC of the European Parliament and of the Council of 23 September 2002 concerning the distance marketing of consumer financial services.[6]

(35) Where a consumer withdraws from a credit agreement in connection with which he has received goods, in particular from a purchase in instalments or from a hiring or leasing agreement providing for an obligation to purchase, this Directive should be without prejudice to any regulation by Member States of questions concerning the return of the goods or any related questions.

(36) In some cases, national legislation already provides that funds cannot be made available to the consumer before the expiry of a specific deadline. In these cases, consumers may wish to ensure that they receive the goods or services purchased early. Therefore, in the case of linked credit agreements, Member States may exceptionally provide that, if the consumer explicitly wishes early receipt, the deadline for the exercise of the right of withdrawal could be reduced to the same deadline before which funds cannot be made available.

(37) In the case of linked credit agreements, a relationship of interdependence exists between the purchase of goods or services and the credit agreement concluded for that purpose. Therefore, where the consumer exercises his right of withdrawal in respect of the purchase agreement, based on Community law, he should no longer be bound by the linked credit agreement. This should not affect national law applicable to linked credit agreements in cases where a purchase agreement has been voided or where the consumer has exercised his right of withdrawal based on national law. Nor should this affect the rights of consumers granted by national provisions according to which no commitment may be entered into between the consumer and a supplier of goods or services, nor any

payment made between those persons, as long as the consumer has not signed the credit agreement to finance the purchase of the goods or services.

(38) Under certain conditions, the consumer should be allowed to pursue remedies against the creditor in the event of problems related to the purchase agreement. However, Member States should determine to what extent and under what conditions the consumer is required to pursue his remedies against the supplier, in particular by bringing an action against the latter, before being in a position to pursue them against the creditor. This Directive should not deprive consumers of their rights under national provisions attaching joint and several liability to the seller or supplier of services and to the creditor.

(39) The consumer should have the right to discharge his obligations before the date agreed in the credit agreement. In the case of early repayment, either in part or in full, the creditor should be entitled to compensation for the costs directly linked to the early repayment, taking into account also any savings thereby made by the creditor. However, in order to determine the method of calculating the compensation, it is important to respect several principles. The calculation of the compensation due to the creditor should be transparent and comprehensible to consumers already at the pre-contractual stage and in any case during the performance of the credit agreement. In addition, the calculation method should be easy for creditors to apply, and supervisory control of the compensation by the responsible authorities should be facilitated. Therefore, and due to the fact that consumer credit is, given its duration and volume, not financed by long-term funding mechanisms, the ceiling for the compensation should be fixed in terms of a flat-rate amount. This approach reflects the special nature of credits for consumers and should not prejudice the possibly different approach in respect of other products which are financed by long-term funding mechanisms, such as fixed-rate mortgage loans.

(40) Member States should have the right to provide that compensation for early repayment may be claimed by the creditor only on condition that the amount repaid over a 12-month period exceeds a threshold defined by Member States. When fixing that threshold, which should not exceed EUR 10 000, Member States should for instance take into account the average amount of consumer credits in their market.

(41) Assignment of the creditor's rights under a credit agreement should not have the effect of placing the consumer in a less favourable position. The consumer should also be properly informed when the credit agreement is assigned to a third party. However, where the initial creditor, in agreement with the assignee, continues to service the credit vis-à-vis the consumer, the consumer has no significant interest in being informed of the assignment. Therefore, a requirement at EU level that the consumer be informed of the assignment in such cases would be excessive.

(42) Member States should remain free to maintain or introduce national rules providing for collective forms of communication when this is necessary for purposes relating to the effectiveness of complex transactions such as securitisations or liquidation of assets that take place in the compulsory administrative liquidation of banks.

(43) In order to promote the establishment and functioning of the internal market and to ensure a high degree of protection for consumers throughout the Community, it is necessary to ensure the comparability of information relating to annual percentage rates of charge throughout the Community. Despite the uniform mathematical formula for its calculation, the annual percentage rate of charge provided for in Directive 87/102/EEC is not yet fully comparable throughout the Community. In individual Member States different cost factors are taken into account in the calculation thereof. This Directive should therefore clearly and comprehensively define the total cost of a credit to the consumer.

(44) In order to ensure market transparency and stability, and pending further harmonisation, Member States should ensure that appropriate measures for the regulation or supervision of creditors are in place.

(45) This Directive respects fundamental rights and observes the principles recognised in particular by the Charter of Fundamental Rights of the European Union. In particular, this Directive seeks to ensure full respect for the rules on protection of personal data, the right to property, non-discrimination, protection of family and professional life, and consumer protection pursuant to the Charter of Fundamental Rights of the European Union.

(46) Since the objective of this Directive, namely the establishment of common rules for certain aspects of the laws, regulations and administrative provisions of the Member States concerning consumer credit, cannot be sufficiently achieved by the Member States and can therefore be better achieved at Community level, the Community may adopt measures, in accordance with the principle of subsidiarity as set out in Article 5 of the Treaty. In accordance with the principle of proportionality, as set out in that Article, this Directive does not go beyond what is necessary in order to achieve that objective.

(47) Member States should lay down rules on penalties applicable to infringements of the national provisions adopted pursuant to this Directive and ensure that they are implemented. While the choice of penalties remains within the discretion of the Member States, the penalties provided for should be effective, proportionate and dissuasive.

(48)   The measures necessary for the implementation of this Directive should be adopted in accordance with Council Decision 1999/468/EC of 28 June 1999 laying down the procedures for the exercise of implementing powers conferred on the Commission.[7]

(49)   In particular, the Commission should be empowered to adopt additional assumptions for the calculation of the annual percentage rate of charge. Since those measures are of general scope and are designed to amend non-essential elements of this Directive, they must be adopted in accordance with the regulatory procedure with scrutiny provided for in Article 5a of Decision 1999/468/EC.

(50)   In accordance with point 34 of the Interinstitutional Agreement on better law-making,[8] Member States are encouraged to draw up, for themselves and in the interests of the Community, their own tables illustrating, as far as possible, the correlation between this Directive and the transposition measures, and to make them public.

(51)   Accordingly, taking account of the number of amendments that need to be made to Directive 87/102/EEC due to the evolution of the consumer credit sector and in the interests of the clarity of Community legislation, that Directive should be repealed and replaced by this Directive,

NOTES

[1]   OJ C234, 30.9.2003, p 1.

[2]   Opinion of the European Parliament of 20 April 2004 (OJ C104 E, 30.4.2004, p 233), Council common position of 20 September 2007 (OJ C270 E, 13.11.2007, p 1) and Position of the European Parliament of 16 January 2008 (not yet published in the Official Journal). Council Decision of 7 April 2008.

[3]   OJ L42, 12.2.1987, p 48. Directive as last amended by Directive 98/7/EC of the European Parliament and of the Council (OJ L101, 1.4.1998, p 17).

[4]   OJ L149, 11.6.2005, p 22.

[5]   OJ L177, 30.6.2006, p 1. Directive as last amended by Directive 2008/24/EC (OJ L81, 20.3.2008, p 38).

[6]   OJ L271, 9.10.2002, p 16. Directive as last amended by Directive 2007/64/EC (OJ L319, 5.12.2007, p 1).

[7]   OJ L184, 17.7.1999, p 23. Decision as amended by Decision 2006/512/EC (OJ L200, 22.7.2006, p 11).

[8]   OJ C321, 31.12.2003, p 1.

HAVE ADOPTED THIS DIRECTIVE—

CHAPTER I
SUBJECT MATTER, SCOPE AND DEFINITIONS

[4.431]
Article 1
Subject matter
The purpose of this Directive is to harmonise certain aspects of the laws, regulations and administrative provisions of the Member States concerning agreements covering credit for consumers.

[4.432]
Article 2
Scope
1.   This Directive shall apply to credit agreements.
2.   This Directive shall not apply to the following—
    (a)   credit agreements which are secured either by a mortgage or by another comparable security commonly used in a Member State on immovable property or secured by a right related to immovable property;
    (b)   credit agreements the purpose of which is to acquire or retain property rights in land or in an existing or projected building;
    (c)   credit agreements involving a total amount of credit less than EUR 200 or more than EUR 75 000;
    (d)   hiring or leasing agreements where an obligation to purchase the object of the agreement is not laid down either by the agreement itself or by any separate agreement; such an obligation shall be deemed to exist if it is so decided unilaterally by the creditor;
    (e)   credit agreements in the form of an overdraft facility and where the credit has to be repaid within one month;
    (f)   credit agreements where the credit is granted free of interest and without any other charges and credit agreements under the terms of which the credit has to be repaid within three months and only insignificant charges are payable;
    (g)   credit agreements where the credit is granted by an employer to his employees as a secondary activity free of interest or at annual percentage rates of charge lower than those prevailing on the market and which are not offered to the public generally;
    (h)   credit agreements which are concluded with investment firms as defined in Article 4(1) of Directive 2004/39/EC of the European Parliament and of the Council of 21 April 2004 on markets in financial instruments[1] or with credit institutions as defined in Article 4 of

Directive 2006/48/EC for the purposes of allowing an investor to carry out a transaction relating to one or more of the instruments listed in Section C of Annex I to Directive 2004/39/EC, where the investment firm or credit institution granting the credit is involved in such transaction;

(i) credit agreements which are the outcome of a settlement reached in court or before another statutory authority;

(j) credit agreements which relate to the deferred payment, free of charge, of an existing debt;

(k) credit agreements upon the conclusion of which the consumer is requested to deposit an item as security in the creditor's safe-keeping and where the liability of the consumer is strictly limited to that pledged item;

(l) credit agreements which relate to loans granted to a restricted public under a statutory provision with a general interest purpose, and at lower interest rates than those prevailing on the market or free of interest or on other terms which are more favourable to the consumer than those prevailing on the market and at interest rates not higher than those prevailing on the market.

[2a. Notwithstanding point (c) of paragraph 2, this Directive shall apply to unsecured credit agreements the purpose of which is the renovation of a residential immovable property involving a total amount of credit above EUR 75 000.]

3. In the case of credit agreements in the form of an overdraft facility and where the credit has to be repaid on demand or within three months, only Articles 1 to 3, Article 4(1), Article 4(2)(a) to (c), Article 4(4), Articles 6 to 9, Article 10(1), Article 10(4), Article 10(5), Articles 12, 15, 17 and Articles 19 to 32 shall apply.

4. In the case of credit agreements in the form of overrunning, only Articles 1 to 3, 18, 20 and 22 to 32 shall apply.

5. Member States may determine that only Articles 1 to 4, 6, 7 and 9, Article 10(1), points (a) to (h) and (l) of Article 10(2), Article 10(4) and Articles 11, 13 and 16 to 32 shall apply to credit agreements which are concluded by an organisation which—

(a) is established for the mutual benefit of its members;

(b) does not make profits for any other person than its members;

(c) fulfils a social purpose required by domestic legislation;

(d) receives and manages the savings of, and provides sources of credit to, its members only; and

(e) provides credit on the basis of an annual percentage rate of charge which is lower than that prevailing on the market or subject to a ceiling laid down by national law,

and whose membership is restricted to persons residing or employed in a particular location or employees and retired employees of a particular employer, or to persons meeting other qualifications laid down under national law as the basis for the existence of a common bond between the members.

Member States may exempt from the application of this Directive credit agreements concluded by such an organisation where the total value of all existing credit agreements entered into by the organisation is insignificant in relation to the total value of all existing credit agreements in the Member State in which the organisation is based and the total value of all existing credit agreements entered into by all such organisations in the Member State is less than 1% of the total value of all existing credit agreements entered into in that Member State.

Member States shall each year review whether the conditions for the application of any such exemption continue to exist and shall take action to withdraw the exemption where they consider that the conditions are no longer met.

6. Member States may determine that only Articles 1 to 4, 6, 7, 9, Article 10(1), points (a) to (i), (l) and (r) of Article 10(2), Article 10(4), Articles 11, 13, 16 and Articles 18 to 32 shall apply to credit agreements which provide for arrangements to be agreed by the creditor and the consumer in respect of deferred payment or repayment methods, where the consumer is already in default on the initial credit agreement and where—

(a) such arrangements would be likely to avert the possibility of legal proceedings concerning such default; and

(b) the consumer would not thereby be subject to terms less favourable than those laid down in the initial credit agreement.

However, if the credit agreement falls within the scope of paragraph 3, only the provisions of that paragraph shall apply.

NOTES

Para 2a: inserted by European Parliament and Council Directive 2014/17/EU, art 46.

[1] OJ L145, 30.4.2004, p 1. Directive as last amended by Directive 2008/10/EC (OJ L76, 19.3.2008, p 33).

[4.433]
Article 3
Definitions

For the purposes of this Directive, the following definitions shall apply—

(a) 'consumer' means a natural person who, in transactions covered by this Directive, is acting for purposes which are outside his trade, business or profession;

(b)   'creditor' means a natural or legal person who grants or promises to grant credit in the course of his trade, business or profession;

(c)   'credit agreement' means an agreement whereby a creditor grants or promises to grant to a consumer credit in the form of a deferred payment, loan or other similar financial accommodation, except for agreements for the provision on a continuing basis of services or for the supply of goods of the same kind, where the consumer pays for such services or goods for the duration of their provision by means of instalments;

(d)   'overdraft facility' means an explicit credit agreement whereby a creditor makes available to a consumer funds which exceed the current balance in the consumer's current account;

(e)   'overrunning' means a tacitly accepted overdraft whereby a creditor makes available to a consumer funds which exceed the current balance in the consumer's current account or the agreed overdraft facility;

(f)   'credit intermediary' means a natural or legal person who is not acting as a creditor and who, in the course of his trade, business or profession, for a fee, which may take a pecuniary form or any other agreed form of financial consideration—

    (i)   presents or offers credit agreements to consumers;

    (ii)   assists consumers by undertaking preparatory work in respect of credit agreements other than as referred to in (i); or

    (iii)   concludes credit agreements with consumers on behalf of the creditor;

(g)   'total cost of the credit to the consumer' means all the costs, including interest, commissions, taxes and any other kind of fees which the consumer is required to pay in connection with the credit agreement and which are known to the creditor, except for notarial costs; costs in respect of ancillary services relating to the credit agreement, in particular insurance premiums, are also included if, in addition, the conclusion of a service contract is compulsory in order to obtain the credit or to obtain it on the terms and conditions marketed;

(h)   'total amount payable by the consumer' means the sum of the total amount of the credit and the total cost of the credit to the consumer;

(i)   'annual percentage rate of charge' means the total cost of the credit to the consumer, expressed as an annual percentage of the total amount of credit, where applicable including the costs referred to in Article 19(2);

(j)   'borrowing rate' means the interest rate expressed as a fixed or variable percentage applied on an annual basis to the amount of credit drawn down;

(k)   'fixed borrowing rate' means that the creditor and the consumer agree in the credit agreement on one borrowing rate for the entire duration of the credit agreement or on several borrowing rates for partial periods using exclusively a fixed specific percentage. If not all borrowing rates are determined in the credit agreement, the borrowing rate shall be deemed to be fixed only for the partial periods for which the borrowing rates are determined exclusively by a fixed specific percentage agreed on the conclusion of the credit agreement;

(l)   'total amount of credit' means the ceiling or the total sums made available under a credit agreement;

(m)   'durable medium' means any instrument which enables the consumer to store information addressed personally to him in a way accessible for future reference for a period of time adequate for the purposes of the information and which allows the unchanged reproduction of the information stored;

(n)   'linked credit agreement' means a credit agreement where

    (i)   the credit in question serves exclusively to finance an agreement for the supply of specific goods or the provision of a specific service, and

    (ii)   those two agreements form, from an objective point of view, a commercial unit; a commercial unit shall be deemed to exist where the supplier or service provider himself finances the credit for the consumer or, if it is financed by a third party, where the creditor uses the services of the supplier or service provider in connection with the conclusion or preparation of the credit agreement, or where the specific goods or the provision of a specific service are explicitly specified in the credit agreement.

CHAPTER II
INFORMATION AND PRACTICES PRELIMINARY TO THE CONCLUSION OF THE CREDIT AGREEMENT

[4.434]
Article 4
Standard information to be included in advertising
1. Any advertising concerning credit agreements which indicates an interest rate or any figures relating to the cost of the credit to the consumer shall include standard information in accordance with this Article.

This obligation shall not apply where national legislation requires the indication of the annual percentage rate of charge in advertising concerning credit agreements which does not indicate an interest rate or any figures relating to any cost of credit to the consumer within the meaning of the first subparagraph.

2.   The standard information shall specify in a clear, concise and prominent way by means of a representative example—

(a)   the borrowing rate, fixed or variable or both, together with particulars of any charges included in the total cost of the credit to the consumer;

(b)   the total amount of credit;

(c)   the annual percentage rate of charge; in the case of a credit agreement of the kind referred to in Article 2(3), Member States may decide that the annual percentage rate of charge need not be provided;

(d)   if applicable, the duration of the credit agreement;

(e)   in the case of a credit in the form of deferred payment for a specific good or service, the cash price and the amount of any advance payment; and

(f)   if applicable, the total amount payable by the consumer and the amount of the instalments.

3.   Where the conclusion of a contract regarding an ancillary service relating to the credit agreement, in particular insurance, is compulsory in order to obtain the credit or to obtain it on the terms and conditions marketed, and the cost of that service cannot be determined in advance, the obligation to enter into that contract shall also be stated in a clear, concise and prominent way, together with the annual percentage rate of charge.

4.   This Article shall be without prejudice to Directive 2005/29/EC.

[4.435]
Article 5
Pre-contractual information

1.   In good time before the consumer is bound by any credit agreement or offer, the creditor and, where applicable, the credit intermediary shall, on the basis of the credit terms and conditions offered by the creditor and, if applicable, the preferences expressed and information supplied by the consumer, provide the consumer with the information needed to compare different offers in order to take an informed decision on whether to conclude a credit agreement. Such information, on paper or on another durable medium, shall be provided by means of the Standard European Consumer Credit Information form set out in Annex II. The creditor shall be deemed to have fulfilled the information requirements in this paragraph and in Article 3, paragraphs (1) and (2) of Directive 2002/65/EC if he has supplied the Standard European Consumer Credit Information.

The information in question shall specify—

(a)   the type of credit;

(b)   the identity and the geographical address of the creditor as well as, if applicable, the identity and geographical address of the credit intermediary involved;

(c)   the total amount of credit and the conditions governing the drawdown;

(d)   the duration of the credit agreement;

(e)   in the case of a credit in the form of deferred payment for a specific good or service and linked credit agreements, that good or service and its cash price;

(f)   the borrowing rate, the conditions governing the application of the borrowing rate and, where available, any index or reference rate applicable to the initial borrowing rate, as well as the periods, conditions and procedure for changing the borrowing rate; if different borrowing rates apply in different circumstances, the abovementioned information on all the applicable rates;

(g)   the annual percentage rate of charge and the total amount payable by the consumer, illustrated by means of a representative example mentioning all the assumptions used in order to calculate that rate; where the consumer has informed the creditor of one or more components of his preferred credit, such as the duration of the credit agreement and the total amount of credit, the creditor shall take those components into account; if a credit agreement provides different ways of drawdown with different charges or borrowing rates and the creditor uses the assumption set out in point (b) of Part II of Annex I, he shall indicate that other drawdown mechanisms for this type of credit agreement may result in higher annual percentage rates of charge;

(h)   the amount, number and frequency of payments to be made by the consumer and, where appropriate, the order in which payments will be allocated to different outstanding balances charged at different borrowing rates for the purposes of reimbursement;

(i)   where applicable, the charges for maintaining one or several accounts recording both payment transactions and drawdowns, unless the opening of an account is optional, together with the charges for using a means of payment for both payment transactions and drawdowns, any other charges deriving from the credit agreement and the conditions under which those charges may be changed;

(j)   where applicable, the existence of costs payable by the consumer to a notary on conclusion of the credit agreement;

(k)   the obligation, if any, to enter into an ancillary service contract relating to the credit agreement, in particular an insurance policy, where the conclusion of such a contract is compulsory in order to obtain the credit or to obtain it on the terms and conditions marketed;

(l)   the interest rate applicable in the case of late payments and the arrangements for its adjustment, and, where applicable, any charges payable for default;

(m)   a warning regarding the consequences of missing payments;

(n)   where applicable, the sureties required;

(o)   the existence or absence of a right of withdrawal;

(p)   the right of early repayment, and, where applicable, information concerning the creditor's right to compensation and the way in which that compensation will be determined in accordance with Article 16;

(q)   the consumer's right to be informed immediately and free of charge, pursuant to Article 9(2), of the result of a database consultation carried out for the purposes of assessing his creditworthiness;

(r)   the consumer's right to be supplied, on request and free of charge, with a copy of the draft credit agreement. This provision shall not apply if the creditor is at the time of the request unwilling to proceed to the conclusion of the credit agreement with the consumer; and

(s)   if applicable, the period of time during which the creditor is bound by the pre-contractual information.

Any additional information which the creditor may provide to the consumer shall be given in a separate document which may be annexed to the Standard European Consumer Credit Information form.

2.   However, in the case of voice telephony communications, as referred to in Article 3(3) of Directive 2002/65/EC, the description of the main characteristics of the financial service to be provided pursuant to the second indent of Article 3(3)(b) of that Directive shall include at least the items referred to in points (c), (d), (e), (f) and (h) of paragraph (1) of this Article, together with the annual percentage rate of charge illustrated by means of a representative example and the total amount payable by the consumer.

3.   If the agreement has been concluded at the consumer's request using a means of distance communication which does not enable the information to be provided in accordance with paragraph 1, in particular in the case referred to in paragraph 2, the creditor shall provide the consumer with the full pre-contractual information using the Standard European Consumer Credit Information form immediately after the conclusion of the credit agreement.

4.   Upon request, the consumer shall, in addition to receiving the Standard European Consumer Credit Information, be supplied free of charge with a copy of the draft credit agreement. This provision shall not apply if the creditor is at the time of the request unwilling to proceed to the conclusion of the credit agreement with the consumer.

5.   In the case of a credit agreement under which payments made by the consumer do not give rise to an immediate corresponding amortisation of the total amount of credit, but are used to constitute capital during periods and under conditions laid down in the credit agreement or in an ancillary agreement, the pre-contractual information required under paragraph 1 shall include a clear and concise statement that such credit agreements do not provide for a guarantee of repayment of the total amount of credit drawn down under the credit agreement, unless such a guarantee is given.

6.   Member States shall ensure that creditors and, where applicable, credit intermediaries provide adequate explanations to the consumer, in order to place the consumer in a position enabling him to assess whether the proposed credit agreement is adapted to his needs and to his financial situation, where appropriate by explaining the pre-contractual information to be provided in accordance with paragraph 1, the essential characteristics of the products proposed and the specific effects they may have on the consumer, including the consequences of default in payment by the consumer. Member States may adapt the manner by which and the extent to which such assistance is given, as well as by whom it is given, to the particular circumstances of the situation in which the credit agreement is offered, the person to whom it is offered and the type of credit offered.

[4.436]
Article 6
Pre-contractual information requirements for certain credit agreements in the form of an overdraft facility and for certain specific credit agreements

1.   In good time before the consumer becomes bound by any credit agreement or offer concerning a credit agreement as referred to in Article 2(3), (5) or (6), the creditor and, where applicable, the credit intermediary shall, on the basis of the credit terms and conditions offered by the creditor and, if applicable, the preferences expressed and information supplied by the consumer, provide the consumer with the information needed to compare different offers in order to take an informed decision on whether to conclude a credit agreement.

The information in question shall specify—

(a)   the type of credit;

(b)   the identity and geographical address of the creditor as well as, if applicable, the identity and geographical address of the credit intermediary involved;

(c)   the total amount of credit;

(d)   the duration of the credit agreement;

(e)   the borrowing rate; the conditions governing the application of that rate, any index or reference rate applicable to the initial borrowing rate, the charges applicable from the time the credit agreement is concluded, and, where applicable, the conditions under which those charges may be changed;

(f)   the annual percentage rate of charge, illustrated by means of representative examples mentioning all the assumptions used in order to calculate that rate;

(g)   the conditions and procedure for terminating the credit agreement;

(h)   in the case of credit agreements as referred to in Article 2(3), where applicable, an indication that the consumer may be requested to repay the amount of credit in full at any time;

(i)   the interest rate applicable in the case of late payments and the arrangements for its adjustment, and, where applicable, any charges payable for default;

(j)   the consumer's right to be informed immediately and free of charge, pursuant to Article 9(2), of the result of a database consultation carried out for the purposes of assessing his creditworthiness;

(k)   in the case of credit agreements as referred to in Article 2(3), information about the charges applicable from the time such agreements are concluded and, if applicable, the conditions under which those charges may be changed;

(l)   if applicable, the period of time during which the creditor is bound by the pre-contractual information.

Such information shall be provided on paper or on another durable medium and all information shall be equally prominent. It may be provided by means of the European Consumer Credit Information form set out in Annex III. The creditor shall be deemed to have fulfilled the information requirements in this paragraph and in Article 3(1) and (2) of Directive 2002/65/EC if he has supplied the European Consumer Credit Information.

2.   In the case of a credit agreement of the kind referred to in Article 2(3), Member States may decide that the annual percentage rate of charge need not be provided.

3.   In the case of a credit agreement as referred to in Article 2(5) and (6), the information provided to the consumer in accordance with paragraph 1 of this Article shall also include—

(a)   the amount, number and frequency of payments to be made by the consumer and, where appropriate, the order in which payments will be allocated to different outstanding balances charged at different borrowing rates for the purposes of reimbursement; and

(b)   the right of early repayment, and, where applicable, information concerning the creditor's right to compensation and the way in which that compensation will be determined.

However, if the credit agreement falls within the scope of Article 2(3), only the provisions of paragraph 1 of this Article shall apply.

4.   However, in the case of voice telephony communications and where the consumer requests that the overdraft facility be made available with immediate effect, the description of the main characteristics of the financial service shall include at least the items referred to in points (c), (e), (f) and (h) of paragraph 1. In addition, in credit agreements of the kind referred to in paragraph 3, the description of the main characteristics shall include a specification of the duration of the credit agreement.

5.   Notwithstanding the exclusion provided for in Article 2(2)(e), the Member States shall apply at least the requirements of the first sentence of paragraph 4 of this Article to credit agreements in the form of an overdraft facility and where the credit has to be repaid within one month.

6.   Upon request, the consumer shall, in addition to receiving the information referred to in paragraphs 1 to 4, be supplied free of charge with a copy of the draft credit agreement containing the contractual information provided for by Article 10 insofar as that Article is applicable. This provision shall not apply if the creditor is at the time of the request unwilling to proceed to the conclusion of the credit agreement with the consumer.

7.   If the agreement has been concluded at the consumer's request using a means of distance communication which does not enable the information to be provided in accordance with paragraphs 1 and 3, including in the cases referred to in paragraph 4, the creditor shall immediately after the conclusion of the credit agreement fulfil his obligations under paragraphs 1 and 3 by providing the contractual information pursuant to Article 10 insofar as that Article is applicable.

[4.437]
Article 7
Exemptions from the pre-contractual information requirements
Articles 5 and 6 shall not apply to suppliers of goods or services acting as credit intermediaries in an ancillary capacity. This is without prejudice to the creditor's obligation to ensure that the consumer receives the pre-contractual information referred to in those Articles.

[4.438]
Article 8
Obligation to assess the creditworthiness of the consumer
1.   Member States shall ensure that, before the conclusion of the credit agreement, the creditor assesses the consumer's creditworthiness on the basis of sufficient information, where appropriate obtained from the consumer and, where necessary, on the basis of a consultation of the relevant database. Member States whose legislation requires creditors to assess the creditworthiness of consumers on the basis of a consultation of the relevant database may retain this requirement.
2.   Member States shall ensure that, if the parties agree to change the total amount of credit after the conclusion of the credit agreement, the creditor updates the financial information at his disposal concerning the consumer and assesses the consumer's creditworthiness before any significant increase in the total amount of credit.

CHAPTER III
DATABASE ACCESS

[4.439]
Article 9
Database access
1.   Each Member State shall in the case of cross-border credit ensure access for creditors from other Member States to databases used in that Member State for assessing the creditworthiness of consumers. The conditions for access shall be non-discriminatory.
2.   If the credit application is rejected on the basis of consultation of a database, the creditor shall inform the consumer immediately and without charge of the result of such consultation and of the particulars of the database consulted.
3.   The information shall be provided unless the provision of such information is prohibited by other Community legislation or is contrary to objectives of public policy or public security.
4.   This Article shall be without prejudice to the application of Directive 95/46/EC of the European Parliament and of the Council of 24 October 1995 on the protection of individuals with regard to the processing of personal data and on the free movement of such data.[1]

NOTES
[1]   OJ L281, 23.11.1995, p 31. Directive as amended by Regulation (EC) No 1882/2003 (OJ L284, 31.10.2003, p 1).

CHAPTER IV
INFORMATION AND RIGHTS CONCERNING CREDIT AGREEMENTS

[4.440]
Article 10
Information to be included in credit agreements
1.   Credit agreements shall be drawn up on paper or on another durable medium. All the contracting parties shall receive a copy of the credit agreement.
    This Article shall be without prejudice to any national rules regarding the validity of the conclusion of credit agreements which are in conformity with Community law.
2.   The credit agreement shall specify in a clear and concise manner—
   (a) the type of credit;
   (b) the identities and geographical addresses of the contracting parties as well as, if applicable, the identity and geographical address of the credit intermediary involved;
   (c) the duration of the credit agreement;
   (d) the total amount of credit and the conditions governing the drawdown;
   (e) in case of a credit in the form of deferred payment for a specific good or service or in the case of linked credit agreements, that good or service and its cash price;
   (f) the borrowing rate, the conditions governing the application of that rate and, where available, any index or reference rate applicable to the initial borrowing rate, as well as the periods, conditions and procedures for changing the borrowing rate and, if different borrowing rates apply in different circumstances, the abovementioned information in respect of all the applicable rates;
   (g) the annual percentage rate of charge and the total amount payable by the consumer, calculated at the time the credit agreement is concluded; all the assumptions used in order to calculate that rate shall be mentioned;
   (h) the amount, number and frequency of payments to be made by the consumer and, where appropriate, the order in which payments will be allocated to different outstanding balances charged at different borrowing rates for the purposes of reimbursement;
   (i) where capital amortisation of a credit agreement with a fixed duration is involved, the right of the consumer to receive, on request and free of charge, at any time throughout the duration of the credit agreement, a statement of account in the form of an amortisation table.
    The amortisation table shall indicate the payments owing and the periods and conditions relating to the payment of such amounts; the table shall contain a breakdown of each

repayment showing capital amortisation, the interest calculated on the basis of the borrowing rate and, where applicable, any additional costs; where the interest rate is not fixed or the additional costs may be changed under the credit agreement, the amortisation table shall indicate, clearly and concisely, that the data contained in the table will remain valid only until such time as the borrowing rate or the additional costs are changed in accordance with the credit agreement;

(j) if charges and interest are to be paid without capital amortisation, a statement showing the periods and conditions for the payment of the interest and of any associated recurrent and non-recurrent charges;

(k) where applicable, the charges for maintaining one or several accounts recording both payment transactions and drawdowns, unless the opening of an account is optional, together with the charges for using a means of payment for both payment transactions and drawdowns, and any other charges deriving from the credit agreement and the conditions under which those charges may be changed;

(l) the interest rate applicable in the case of late payments as applicable at the time of the conclusion of the credit agreement and the arrangements for its adjustment and, where applicable, any charges payable for default;

(m) a warning regarding the consequences of missing payments;

(n) where applicable, a statement, that notarial fees will be payable;

(o) the sureties and insurance required, if any;

(p) the existence or absence of a right of withdrawal, the period during which that right may be exercised and other conditions governing the exercise thereof, including information concerning the obligation of the consumer to pay the capital drawn down and the interest in accordance with Article 14(3)(b) and the amount of interest payable per day;

(q) information concerning the rights resulting from Article 15 as well as the conditions for the exercise of those rights;

(r) the right of early repayment, the procedure for early repayment, as well as, where applicable, information concerning the creditor's right to compensation and the way in which that compensation will be determined;

(s) the procedure to be followed in exercising the right of termination of the credit agreement;

(t) whether or not there is an out-of-court complaint and redress mechanism for the consumer and, if so, the methods for having access to it;

(u) where applicable, other contractual terms and conditions;

(v) where applicable, the name and address of the competent supervisory authority.

3.   Where paragraph 2(i) applies, the creditor shall make available to the consumer, free of charge and at any time throughout the duration of the credit agreement, a statement of account in the form of an amortisation table.

4.   In the case of a credit agreement under which payments made by the consumer do not give rise to an immediate corresponding amortisation of the total amount of credit, but are used to constitute capital during periods and under conditions laid down in the credit agreement or in an ancillary agreement, the information required under paragraph 2 shall include a clear and concise statement that such credit agreements do not provide for a guarantee of repayment of the total amount of credit drawn down under the credit agreement, unless such a guarantee is given.

5.   In the case of credit agreements in the form of overdraft facilities as referred to in Article 2(3), the following shall be specified in a clear and concise manner—

(a) the type of credit;

(b) the identities and geographical addresses of the contracting parties as well as, if applicable, the identity and geographical address of the credit intermediary involved;

(c) the duration of the credit agreement;

(d) the total amount of the credit and the conditions governing the drawdown;

(e) the borrowing rate, the conditions governing the application of the borrowing rate and, where available, any index or reference rate applicable to the initial borrowing rate, as well as the periods, conditions and procedure for changing the borrowing rate and, if different borrowing rates apply in different circumstances, the abovementioned information in respect of all the applicable rates;

(f) the annual percentage rate of charge and the total cost of the credit to the consumer, calculated at the time the credit agreement is concluded; all the assumptions used in order to calculate that rate as referred to in Article 19(2) in conjunction with Article 3(g) and (i) shall be mentioned; Member States may decide that the annual percentage rate of charge need not be provided;

(g) an indication that the consumer may be requested to repay the amount of credit in full on demand at any time;

(h) conditions governing the exercise of the right of withdrawal from the credit agreement; and

(i) information concerning the charges applicable from the time such agreements are concluded and, if applicable, the conditions under which those charges may be changed.

[4.441]
Article 11
Information concerning the borrowing rate
1.   Where applicable, the consumer shall be informed of any change in the borrowing rate, on paper or another durable medium, before the change enters into force. The information shall state the amount of the payments to be made after the entry into force of the new borrowing rate and, if the number or frequency of the payments changes, particulars thereof.
2.   However, the parties may agree in the credit agreement that the information referred to in paragraph 1 is to be given to the consumer periodically in cases where the change in the borrowing rate is caused by a change in a reference rate, the new reference rate is made publicly available by appropriate means and the information concerning the new reference rate is also kept available in the premises of the creditor.

[4.442]
Article 12
Obligations in connection with credit agreement in the form of an overdraft facility
1.   Where a credit agreement covers credit in the form of an overdraft facility, the consumer shall be kept regularly informed by means of a statement of account, on paper or on another durable medium, containing the following particulars—
   (a)   the precise period to which the statement of account relates;
   (b)   the amounts and dates of drawdowns;
   (c)   the balance from the previous statement, and the date thereof;
   (d)   the new balance;
   (e)   the dates and amounts of payments made by the consumer;
   (f)   the borrowing rate applied;
   (g)   any charges that have been applied;
   (h)   where applicable, the minimum amount to be paid.
2.   In addition, the consumer shall be informed on paper or another durable medium of increases in the borrowing rate, or in any charges payable, before the change in question enters into force.
   However, the parties may agree in the credit agreement that information concerning changes in the borrowing rate is to be given in the manner provided for in paragraph 1 in cases where the change in the borrowing rate is caused by a change in a reference rate, the new reference rate is made publicly available by appropriate means and the information concerning the new reference rate is also kept available in the premises of the creditor.

[4.443]
Article 13
Open-end credit agreements
1.   The consumer may effect standard termination of an open-end credit agreement free of charge at any time unless the parties have agreed on a period of notice. Such a period may not exceed one month.
   If agreed in the credit agreement, the creditor may effect standard termination of an open-end credit agreement by giving the consumer at least two months' notice drawn up on paper or on another durable medium.
2.   If agreed in the credit agreement, the creditor may, for objectively justified reasons, terminate the consumer's right to draw down on an open-end credit agreement. The creditor shall inform the consumer of the termination and the reasons for it on paper or on another durable medium, where possible before the termination and at the latest immediately thereafter, unless the provision of such information is prohibited by other Community legislation or is contrary to objectives of public policy or public security.

[4.444]
Article 14
Right of withdrawal
1.   The consumer shall have a period of 14 calendar days in which to withdraw from the credit agreement without giving any reason.
That period of withdrawal shall begin—
   (a)   either from the day of the conclusion of the credit agreement, or
   (b)   from the day on which the consumer receives the contractual terms and conditions and information in accordance with Article 10, if that day is later than the date referred to in point (a) of this subparagraph.
2.   Where in the case of a linked credit agreement, as defined in Article 3(n), national legislation at the time of the entry into force of this Directive already provides that funds cannot be made available to the consumer before the expiry of a specific period, Member States may exceptionally provide that the period referred to in paragraph 1 of this Article may be reduced to this specific period at the explicit request of the consumer.
3.   If the consumer exercises his right of withdrawal, he shall—
   (a)   in order to give effect to the withdrawal before the expiry of the deadline referred to in paragraph 1, notify this to the creditor in line with the information given by the creditor

pursuant to Article 10(2)(p) by means which can be proven in accordance with national law. The deadline shall be deemed to have been met if that notification, if it is on paper or on another durable medium that is available and accessible to the creditor, is dispatched before the deadline expires; and

(b) pay to the creditor the capital and the interest accrued thereon from the date the credit was drawn down until the date the capital is repaid, without any undue delay and no later than 30 calendar days after the despatch by him to the creditor of notification of the withdrawal. The interest shall be calculated on the basis of the agreed borrowing rate. The creditor shall not be entitled to any other compensation from the consumer in the event of withdrawal, except compensation for any non-returnable charges paid by the creditor to any public administrative body.

4.   If an ancillary service relating to the credit agreement is provided by the creditor or by a third party on the basis of an agreement between the third party and the creditor, the consumer shall no longer be bound by the ancillary service contract if the consumer exercises his right of withdrawal from the credit agreement in accordance with this Article.

5.   If the consumer has a right of withdrawal under paragraphs 1, 3 and 4, Articles 6 and 7 of Directive 2002/65/EC and Article 5 of Council Directive 85/577/EEC of 20 December 1985 to protect the consumer in respect of contracts negotiated away from business premises[1] shall not apply.

6.   Member States may provide that paragraphs 1 to 4 of this Article shall not apply to credit agreements which by law are required to be concluded through the services of a notary, provided that the notary confirms that the consumer is guaranteed the rights provided for under Articles 5 and 10.

7.   This Article shall be without prejudice to any rule of national law establishing a period of time during which the performance of the contract may not begin.

NOTES
[1]   OJ L372, 31.12.1985, p 31.

[4.445]
Article 15
Linked credit agreements

1.   Where the consumer has exercised a right of withdrawal, based on Community law, concerning a contract for the supply of goods or services, he shall no longer be bound by a linked credit agreement.

2.   Where the goods or services covered by a linked credit agreement are not supplied, or are supplied only in part, or are not in conformity with the contract for the supply thereof, the consumer shall have the right to pursue remedies against the creditor if the consumer has pursued his remedies against the supplier but has failed to obtain the satisfaction to which he is entitled according to the law or the contract for the supply of goods or services. Member States shall determine to what extent and under what conditions those remedies shall be exercisable.

3.   This Article shall be without prejudice to any national rules rendering the creditor jointly and severally liable in respect of any claim which the consumer may have against the supplier where the purchase of goods or services from the supplier has been financed by a credit agreement.

[4.446]
Article 16
Early repayment

1.   The consumer shall be entitled at any time to discharge fully or partially his obligations under a credit agreement. In such cases, he shall be entitled to a reduction in the total cost of the credit, such reduction consisting of the interest and the costs for the remaining duration of the contract.

2.   In the event of early repayment of credit the creditor shall be entitled to fair and objectively justified compensation for possible costs directly linked to early repayment of credit provided that the early repayment falls within a period for which the borrowing rate is fixed.

Such compensation may not exceed 1% of the amount of credit repaid early, if the period of time between the early repayment and the agreed termination of the credit agreement exceeds one year. If the period does not exceed one year, the compensation may not exceed 0,5% of the amount of credit repaid early.

3.   Compensation for early repayment shall not be claimed—
(a)   if the repayment has been made under an insurance contract intended to provide a credit repayment guarantee;
(b)   in the case of overdraft facilities; or
(c)   if the repayment falls within a period for which the borrowing rate is not fixed.

4.   Member States may provide that—
(a)   such compensation may be claimed by the creditor only on condition that the amount of the early repayment exceeds the threshold defined by national law. That threshold shall not exceed EUR 10 000 within any period of 12 months;
(b)   the creditor may exceptionally claim higher compensation if he can prove that the loss he suffered from early repayment exceeds the amount determined under paragraph 2.

If the compensation claimed by the creditor exceeds the loss actually suffered, the consumer may claim a corresponding reduction.

In this case, the loss shall consist of the difference between the initially agreed interest rate and the interest rate at which the creditor can lend out the amount repaid early on the market at the time of early repayment, and shall take into account the impact of early repayment on administrative costs.

5.   Any compensation shall not exceed the amount of interest the consumer would have paid during the period between the early repayment and the agreed date of termination of the credit agreement.

[4.447]
Article 17
Assignment of rights

1.   In the event of assignment to a third party of the creditor's rights under a credit agreement or the agreement itself, the consumer shall be entitled to plead against the assignee any defence which was available to him against the original creditor, including set-off where the latter is permitted in the Member State concerned.

2.   The consumer shall be informed of the assignment referred to in paragraph 1 except where the original creditor, by agreement with the assignee, continues to service the credit vis-à-vis the consumer.

[4.448]
Article 18
Overrunning

1.   In the case of an agreement to open a current account, where there is a possibility that the consumer is allowed an overrun, the agreement shall contain in addition the information referred to in Article 6(1)(e). The creditor shall in any case provide that information on paper or another durable medium on a regular basis.

2.   In the event of a significant overrunning exceeding a period of one month, the creditor shall inform the consumer without delay, on paper or on another durable medium,

    (a)   of the overrunning;
    (b)   of the amount involved;
    (c)   of the borrowing rate;
    (d)   of any penalties, charges or interest on arrears applicable.

3.   This Article shall be without prejudice to any rule of national law requiring the creditor to offer another kind of credit product when the duration of the overrunning is significant.

CHAPTER V
ANNUAL PERCENTAGE RATE OF CHARGE

[4.449]
Article 19
Calculation of the annual percentage rate of charge

1.   The annual percentage rate of charge, equating, on an annual basis, to the present value of all commitments (drawdowns, repayments and charges), future or existing, agreed by the creditor and the consumer, shall be calculated in accordance with the mathematical formula set out in Part I of Annex I.

2.   For the purpose of calculating the annual percentage rate of charge, the total cost of the credit to the consumer shall be determined, with the exception of any charges payable by the consumer for non-compliance with any of his commitments laid down in the credit agreement and charges other than the purchase price which, for purchases of goods or services, he is obliged to pay whether the transaction is effected in cash or on credit.

The costs of maintaining an account recording both payment transactions and drawdowns, the costs of using a means of payment for both payment transactions and drawdowns, and other costs relating to payment transactions shall be included in the total cost of credit to the consumer unless the opening of the account is optional and the costs of the account have been clearly and separately shown in the credit agreement or in any other agreement concluded with the consumer.

3.   The calculation of the annual percentage rate of charge shall be based on the assumption that the credit agreement is to remain valid for the period agreed and that the creditor and the consumer will fulfil their obligations under the terms and by the dates specified in the credit agreement.

4.   In the case of credit agreements containing clauses allowing variations in the borrowing rate and, where applicable, charges contained in the annual percentage rate of charge but unquantifiable at the time of calculation, the annual percentage rate of charge shall be calculated on the assumption that the borrowing rate and other charges will remain fixed in relation to the initial level and will remain applicable until the end of the credit agreement.

5.   Where necessary, the additional assumptions set out in Annex I may be used in calculating the annual percentage rate of charge.

If the assumptions set out in this Article and in Part II of Annex I do not suffice to calculate the annual percentage rate of charge in a uniform manner or are not adapted any more to the commercial situation at the market, the Commission may determine the necessary additional assumptions for the calculation of the annual percentage rate of charge, or modify existing ones. These measures, designed to amend non-essential elements of this Directive, shall be adopted in accordance with the regulatory procedure with scrutiny referred to in Article 25(2).

CHAPTER VI
CREDITORS AND CREDIT INTERMEDIARIES

[4.450]
Article 20
Regulation of creditors

Member States shall ensure that creditors are supervised by a body or authority independent from financial institutions, or regulated. This shall be without prejudice to Directive 2006/ 48/EC.

[4.451]
Article 21
Certain obligations of credit intermediaries vis-à-vis consumers

Member States shall ensure that—

- (a) a credit intermediary indicates in advertising and documentation intended for consumers the extent of his powers, in particular whether he works exclusively with one or more creditors or as an independent broker;
- (b) the fee, if any, payable by the consumer to the credit intermediary for his services is disclosed to the consumer, and agreed between the consumer and the credit intermediary on paper or another durable medium before the conclusion of the credit agreement;
- (c) the fee, if any, payable by the consumer to the credit intermediary for his services is communicated to the creditor by the credit intermediary, for the purpose of calculation of the annual percentage rate of charge.

CHAPTER VII
IMPLEMENTING MEASURES

[4.452]
Article 22
Harmonisation and imperative nature of this Directive

1. Insofar as this Directive contains harmonised provisions, Member States may not maintain or introduce in their national law provisions diverging from those laid down in this Directive.
2. Member States shall ensure that consumers may not waive the rights conferred on them by the provisions of national law implementing or corresponding to this Directive.
3. Member States shall further ensure that the provisions they adopt in implementation of this Directive cannot be circumvented as a result of the way in which agreements are formulated, in particular by integrating drawdowns or credit agreements falling within the scope of this Directive into credit agreements the character or purpose of which would make it possible to avoid its application.
4. Member States shall take the necessary measures to ensure that consumers do not lose the protection granted by this Directive by virtue of the choice of the law of a third country as the law applicable to the credit agreement, if the credit agreement has a close link with the territory of one or more Member States.

[4.453]
Article 23
Penalties

Member States shall lay down the rules on penalties applicable to infringements of the national provisions adopted pursuant to this Directive and shall take all measures necessary to ensure that they are implemented. The penalties provided for must be effective, proportionate and dissuasive.

[4.454]
Article 24
Out-of-court dispute resolution

1. Member States shall ensure that adequate and effective out-of-court dispute resolution procedures for the settlement of consumer disputes concerning credit agreements are put in place, using existing bodies where appropriate.
2. Member States shall encourage those bodies to cooperate in order to also resolve cross-border disputes concerning credit agreements.

[4.455]
Article 25
Committee procedure

1. The Commission shall be assisted by a Committee.
2. Where reference is made to this paragraph, Article 5a(1) to (4) and Article 7 of Decision 1999/468/EC shall apply, having regard to the provisions of Article 8 thereof.

[4.456]
Article 26
Information to be supplied to the Commission
Where a Member State makes use of any of the regulatory choices referred to in Article 2(5) and 2(6), Article 4(1), Article 4(2)(c), Article 6(2), Article 10(1), Article 10(5)(f), Article 14(2) and Article 16(4), it shall inform the Commission thereof as well as of any subsequent changes. The Commission shall make that information public on a website or in another easily accessible way. Member States shall take the appropriate measures to diffuse that information amongst national creditors and consumers.

[4.457]
Article 27
Transposition
1.   Before 11 June 2010 Member States shall adopt and publish the provisions necessary to comply with this Directive. They shall forthwith inform the Commission thereof.
   They shall apply those provisions from 11 June 2010.
   When Member States adopt these provisions, they shall contain a reference to this Directive or be accompanied by such reference on the occasion of their official publication. The methods of making such reference shall be laid down by Member States.
2.   The Commission shall undertake, every five years and for the first time 11 June 2013, a review of the thresholds laid down in this Directive and its annexes and the percentages used to calculate the compensation payable in the event of early repayment, assessing them in the light of economic trends in the Community and the situation of the market concerned. The Commission shall also monitor the effect of the existence of the regulatory choices referred to in Article 2(5) and 2(6), Article 4(1), Article 4(2)(c), Article 6(2), Article 10(1), Article 10(5)(f), Article 14(2) and Article 16(4) on the internal market and consumers. The results shall be made known to the European Parliament and the Council, accompanied where appropriate by a proposal to modify the thresholds and percentages as well as the abovementioned regulatory choices accordingly.

[4.458]
Article 28
Conversion of amounts expressed in euro into national currency
1.   For the purposes of this Directive, those Member States who convert the amounts expressed in euro into their national currency shall initially use in the conversion the exchange rate prevailing on the date of adoption of this Directive.
2.   Member States may round off the amounts resulting from the conversion provided that such rounding off does not exceed EUR 10.

CHAPTER VIII
TRANSITIONAL AND FINAL PROVISIONS

[4.459]
Article 29
Repeal
Directive 87/102/EEC shall be repealed with effect from 11 June 2010.

[4.460]
Article 30
Transitional measures
1.   This Directive shall not apply to credit agreements existing on the date when the national implementing measures enter into force.
2.   However, Member States shall ensure that Articles 11, 12, 13 and 17, the second sentence of Article 18(1), and Article 18(2) are applied also to open-end credit agreements existing on the date when the national implementing measures enter into force.

[4.461]
Article 31
Entry into force
This Directive shall enter into force on the 20th day following its publication in the Official Journal of the European Union.

[4.462]
Article 32
Addressees
This Directive is addressed to the Member States.

ANNEX I

[4.463]
I. The basic equation expressing the equivalence of drawdowns on the one hand and repayments and charges on the other.

The basic equation, which establishes the annual percentage rate of charge (APR), equates, on an annual basis, the total present value of drawdowns on the one hand and the total present value of repayments and payments of charges on the other hand, ie:

$$\sum_{k=1}^{m} C_k(1+X)^{-t_k} = \sum_{l=1}^{m'} D_l(1+X)^{-S_l}$$

where:
- X is the APR,
- m is the number of the last drawdown,
- k is the number of a drawdown, thus $1 \le k \le m$,
- C_k is the amount of drawdown k,
- t_k is the interval, expressed in years and fractions of a year, between the date of the first drawdown and the date of each subsequent drawdown, thus $t_1 = 0$,
- m' is the number of the last repayment or payment of charges,
- l is the number of a repayment or payment of charges,
- D_l is the amount of a repayment or payment of charges,
- s_l is the interval, expressed in years and fractions of a year, between the date of the first drawdown and the date of each repayment or payment of charges.

Remarks:
(a) The amounts paid by both parties at different times shall not necessarily be equal and shall not necessarily be paid at equal intervals.
(b) The starting date shall be that of the first drawdown.
(c) Intervals between dates used in the calculations shall be expressed in years or in fractions of a year. A year is presumed to have 365 days (or 366 days for leap years), 52 weeks or 12 equal months. An equal month is presumed to have 30,41666 days (ie 365/12) regardless of whether or not it is a leap year.
(d) The result of the calculation shall be expressed with an accuracy of at least one decimal place. If the figure at the following decimal place is greater than or equal to 5, the figure at that particular decimal place shall be increased by one.
(e) The equation can be rewritten using a single sum and the concept of flows (Ak), which will be positive or negative, in other words either paid or received during periods 1 to k, expressed in years, ie:

$$S = \sum_{k=1}^{n} A_k(1+X)^{-t_k},$$

S being the present balance of flows. If the aim is to maintain the equivalence of flows, the value will be zero.

[II.   The additional assumptions for the calculation of the annual percentage rate of charge shall be as follows:
(a) If a credit agreement gives the consumer freedom of drawdown, the total amount of credit shall be deemed to be drawn down immediately and in full.
(b) If a credit agreement gives the consumer freedom of drawdown in general but imposes, amongst the different ways of drawdown, a limitation with regard to the amount of credit and period of time, the amount of credit shall be deemed to be drawn down on the earliest date provided for in the credit agreement and in accordance with those drawdown limits.
(c) If a credit agreement provides different ways of drawdown with different charges or borrowing rates, the total amount of credit shall be deemed to be drawn down at the highest charge and borrowing rate applied to the most common drawdown mechanism for this type of credit agreement.
(d) In the case of an overdraft facility, the total amount of credit shall be deemed to be drawn down in full and for the whole duration of the credit agreement. If the duration of the overdraft facility is not known, the annual percentage rate of charge shall be calculated on the assumption that the duration of the credit is 3 months.
(e) In the case of an open-end credit agreement, other than an overdraft facility, it shall be assumed that:
   (i) the credit is provided for a period of 1 year starting from the date of the initial drawdown, and that the final payment made by the consumer clears the balance of capital, interest and other charges, if any;
   (ii) the capital is repaid by the consumer in equal monthly payments, commencing 1 month after the date of the initial drawdown. However, in cases where the capital must be repaid only in full, in a single payment, within each payment period, successive drawdowns and repayments of the entire capital by the consumer shall be assumed to occur over the period of 1 year. Interest and other charges shall be applied in accordance with those drawdowns and repayments of capital and as provided for in the credit agreement.

For the purposes of this point, an open-end credit agreement is a credit agreement without fixed duration and includes credits which must be repaid in full within or after a period but, once repaid, become available to be drawn down again.

(f)   In the case of credit agreements other than overdrafts and open-end credits as referred to in the assumptions set out in points (d) and (e):

     (i)   if the date or amount of a repayment of capital to be made by the consumer cannot be ascertained, it shall be assumed that the repayment is made at the earliest date provided for in the credit agreement and is for the lowest amount for which the credit agreement provides;

     (ii)   if the date of conclusion of the credit agreement is not known, the date of the initial drawdown shall be assumed to be the date which results in the shortest interval between that date and the date of the first payment to be made by the consumer.

(g)   Where the date or amount of a payment to be made by the consumer cannot be ascertained on the basis of the credit agreement or the assumptions set out in points (d), (e) or (f), it shall be assumed that the payment is made in accordance with the dates and conditions required by the creditor and, when these are unknown:

     (i)   interest charges are paid together with the repayments of capital;

     (ii)   a non-interest charge expressed as a single sum is paid at the date of the conclusion of the credit agreement;

     (iii)   non-interest charges expressed as several payments are paid at regular intervals, commencing with the date of the first repayment of capital, and if the amount of such payments is not known they shall be assumed to be equal amounts;

     (iv)   the final payment clears the balance of capital, interest and other charges, if any.

(h)   If the ceiling applicable to the credit has not yet been agreed, that ceiling is assumed to be EUR 1 500.

(i)   If different borrowing rates and charges are offered for a limited period or amount, the borrowing rate and the charges shall be deemed to be the highest rate for the whole duration of the credit agreement.

(j)   For consumer credit agreements for which a fixed borrowing rate is agreed in relation to the initial period, at the end of which a new borrowing rate is determined and subsequently periodically adjusted according to an agreed indicator, the calculation of the annual percentage rate shall be based on the assumption that, at the end of the fixed borrowing rate period, the borrowing rate is the same as at the time of calculating the annual percentage rate, based on the value of the agreed indicator at that time.]

NOTES

   Point II: substituted by Commission Directive 2011/90/EU, Art 1, Annex.

ANNEX II
STANDARD EUROPEAN CONSUMER CREDIT INFORMATION

[4.464]

1.   Identity and contact details of the creditor/credit intermediary

Creditor	[Identity]
Address	[Geographical address to be used by the consumer]
Telephone number [*]	
E-mail address [*]	
Fax number [*]	
Web address [*]	
If applicable	
Credit intermediary	[Identity]
Address	[Geographical address to be used by the consumer]
Telephone number [*]	
E-mail address [*]	
Fax number [*]	
Web address [*]	
[*] This information is optional for the creditor.	

Wherever 'if applicable' is indicated, the creditor must fill in the box if the information is relevant to the credit product or delete the respective information or the entire row if the information is not relevant for the type of credit considered.

Indications between square brackets provide explanations for the creditor and must be replaced with the corresponding information.

2. Description of the main features of the credit product

The type of credit	
The total amount of credit *This means the ceiling or the total sums made available under the credit agreement.*	
The conditions governing the drawdown *This means how and when you will obtain the money.*	
The duration of the credit agreement	
Instalments and, where appropriate, the order in which instalments will be allocated	You will have to pay the following: [The amount, number and frequency of payments to be made by the consumer] Interest and/or charges will be payable in the following manner:
The total amount you will have to pay *This means the amount of borrowed capital plus interest and possible costs related to your credit.*	[Sum of total amount of credit and total cost of credit]
If applicable The credit is granted in the form of a deferred payment for a good or service or is linked to the supply of specific goods or the provision of a service Name of good/service Cash price	
If applicable Sureties required This is a description of the security to be provided by you in relation to the credit agreement.	[Kind of sureties]
If applicable Repayments do not give rise to immediate amortisation of the capital.	

3. Costs of the credit

The borrowing rate or, if applicable, different borrowing rates which apply to the credit agreement	[% —fixed, or —variable (with the index or reference rate applicable to the initial borrowing rate), —periods]
Annual Percentage Rate of Charge (APR) *This is the total cost expressed as an annual percentage of the total amount of credit.* *The APR is there to help you compare different offers.*	[% A representative example mentioning all the assumptions used for calculating the rate to be set out here]
Is it compulsory, in order to obtain the credit or to obtain it on the terms and conditions marketed, to take out —an insurance policy securing the credit, or	Yes/no [if yes, specify the kind of insurance]
—another ancillary service contract? If the costs of these services are not known by the creditor they are not included in the APR.	Yes/no [if yes, specify the kind of ancillary service]
Related costs	
If applicable Maintaining one or more accounts is required for recording both payment transactions and drawdowns	

If applicable Amount of costs for using a specific means of payment (eg a credit card)	
If applicable Any other costs deriving from the credit agreement	
If applicable Conditions under which the abovementioned costs related to the credit agreement can be changed	
If applicable Obligation to pay notarial fees	
Costs in the case of late payments *Missing payments could have severe consequences for you (eg forced sale) and make obtaining credit more difficult.*	You will be charged [. . . (applicable interest rate and arrangements for its adjustment and, where applicable, default charges)] for late payments.

4.   Other important legal aspects

Right of withdrawal *You have the right to withdraw from the credit agreement within a period of 14 calendar days.*	Yes/no
Early repayment *You have the right to repay the credit early at any time in full or partially.*	
If applicable The creditor is entitled to compensation in the case of early repayment	[Determination of the compensation (calculation method) in accordance with the provisions implementing Article 16 of Directive 2008/48/EC]
Consultation of a database *The creditor must inform you immediately and without charge of the result of a consultation of a database, if a credit application is rejected on the basis of such a consultation. This does not apply if the provision of such information is prohibited by European Community law or is contrary to objectives of public policy or public security.*	
Right to a draft credit agreement *You have the right, upon request, to obtain a copy of the draft credit agreement free of charge. This provision does not apply if the creditor is at the time of the request unwilling to proceed to the conclusion of the credit agreement with you.*	
If applicable The period of time during which the creditor is bound by the pre-contractual information	This information is valid from . . . until . . .

If applicable
5.   Additional information in the case of distance marketing of financial services

(a) concerning the creditor	
If applicable Representative of the creditor in your Member State of residence Address Telephone number [*] E-mail address [*] Fax number [*] Web address [*]	[Identity] [Geographical address to be used by the consumer]
If applicable	

Registration	[The trade register in which the creditor is entered and his registration number or an equivalent means of identification in that register]
If applicable The supervisory authority	
(b) concerning the credit agreement	
If applicable Exercise of the right of withdrawal	[Practical instructions for exercising the right of withdrawal indicating, inter alia, the period for exercising the right, the address to which notification of exercise of the right of withdrawal should be sent and the consequences of non-exercise of that right]
If applicable The law taken by the creditor as a basis for the establishment of relations with you before the conclusion of the credit contract	
If applicable Clause stipulating the governing law applicable to the credit agreement and/or the competent court	[Relevant clause to be set out here]
If applicable Language regime	Information and contractual terms will be supplied in [specific language]. With your consent, we intend to communicate in [specific language/languages] during the duration of the credit agreement.
(c) concerning redress	
Existence of and access to out-of-court complaint and redress mechanism	[Whether or not there is an out-of-court complaint and redress mechanism for the consumer who is party to the distance contract and, if so, the methods of access to it]
[*] This information is optional for the creditor.	

ANNEX III
EUROPEAN CONSUMER CREDIT INFORMATION FOR (1) OVERDRAFTS (2) CONSUMER CREDIT OFFERED BY CERTAIN CREDIT ORGANISATIONS (ARTICLE 2(5) OF DIRECTIVE 2008/48/EC) (3) DEBT CONVERSION

[4.465]
1.   Identity and contact details of the creditor/credit intermediary

Creditor Address Telephone number [*] E-mail address [*] Fax number [*] Web address [*]	[Identity] [Geographical address to be used by the consumer]
If applicable Credit intermediary Address Telephone number [*] E-mail address [*] Fax number [*] Web address [*]	[Identity] [Geographical address to be used by the consumer]
[*] This information is optional for the creditor.	

Wherever 'if applicable' is indicated, the creditor must fill in the box if the information is relevant to the credit product or delete the respective information or the entire row if the information is not relevant for the type of credit considered.

Indications between square brackets provide explanations for the creditor and must be replaced with the corresponding information.

2. Description of the main features of the credit product

The type of credit	
The total amount of credit *This means the ceiling or the total sums made available under the credit agreement.*	
The duration of the credit agreement	
If applicable You may be requested to repay the amount of credit in full on demand at any time.	

3. Costs of the credit

The borrowing rate or, if applicable, different borrowing rates which apply to the credit agreement	[% —fixed or, —variable (with the index or reference rate applicable to the initial borrowing rate)]
If applicable The annual percentage rate of charge (APR) [*] *This is the total cost of credit expressed as an annual percentage of the total amount of credit. The APR is there to help you compare different offers.*	[% A representative example mentioning all the assumptions used for calculating the rate to be set out here]
If applicable Costs If applicable The conditions under which those costs may be changed	[The costs applicable from the time the credit agreement is concluded]
Costs in the case of late payments	You will be charged [. . . . . (applicable interest rate and arrangements for its adjustment and, where applicable, default charges)] for late payments.
[*] Not applicable to European Consumer Credit Information for overdrafts in those Member States which decide on the basis of Article 6(2) of Directive 2008/48/EC that the APR need not be provided for overdrafts.	

4. Other important legal aspects

Termination of the credit agreement	[The conditions and procedure for terminating the credit agreement]
Consultation of a database *The creditor must inform you immediately and without charge of the result of a consultation of a database if a credit application is rejected on the basis of such a consultation. This does not apply if the provision of such information is prohibited by European Community law or is contrary to objectives of public policy or public security.*	
If applicable The period of time during which the creditor is bound by the pre-contractual information	This information is valid from . . . until . . . .

If applicable

5.   Additional information to be given where the pre-contractual information is provided by certain credit organisations (Article 2(5) of Directive 2008/48/EC or relates to a consumer credit for debt conversion

Instalments and, where appropriate, the order in which instalments will be allocated	You will have to pay the following: [Representative example of an instalment table including the amount, number and frequency of payments to be made by the consumer]
The total amount you will have to pay	
Early repayment *You have the right to repay the credit early at any time in full or partially.* If applicable The creditor is entitled to compensation in the case of early repayment	[Determination of the compensation (calculation method) in accordance with the provisions implementing Article 16 of Directive 2008/48/EC]

If applicable
6.   Additional information to be given in the case of distance marketing of financial services

(a) concerning the creditor	
If applicable Representative of the creditor in your Member State of residence Address Telephone number [*] E-mail address [*] Fax number [*] Web address [*]	[Identity] [Geographical address to be used by the consumer]
If applicable Registration	[The trade register in which the creditor is entered and his registration number or an equivalent means of identification in that register]
If applicable The supervisory authority	
(b) concerning the credit agreement	
Right of withdrawal *You have the right to withdraw from the credit agreement within a period of 14 calendar days.* If applicable Exercise of the right of withdrawal	Yes/no [Practical instructions for exercising the right of withdrawal indicating, inter alia, the address to which notification of exercise of the right of withdrawal should be sent and the consequences of non-exercise of that right]
If applicable The law taken by the creditor as a basis for the establishment of relations with you before the conclusion of the credit contract	
If applicable Clause stipulating the law applicable to the credit agreement and/or the competent court	[Relevant clause to be set out here]
If applicable Language regime	Information and contractual terms will be supplied in [specific language]. With your consent, we intend to communicate in [specific language/languages] during the duration of the credit agreement.
(c) concerning redress	

Existence of and access to out-of-court complaint and redress mechanism	[Whether or not there is an out-of-court complaint and redress mechanism for the consumer who is party to the distance contract and, if so, the methods of access to it]
[*] This information is optional for the creditor.	

DIRECTIVE OF THE EUROPEAN PARLIAMENT AND OF THE COUNCIL

(2008/122/EC)

of 14 January 2009

on the protection of consumers in respect of certain aspects of timeshare, long-term holiday product, resale and exchange contracts

(Text with EEA relevance)

NOTE

Date of publication in OJ: OJ L33, 3.2.2009, p 10.

This Directive has been implemented in the UK by the Timeshare, Holiday Products, Resale and Exchange Contracts Regulations 2010, SI 2010/2960 at **[2.841]**.

THE EUROPEAN PARLIAMENT AND THE COUNCIL OF THE EUROPEAN UNION,

Having regard to the Treaty establishing the European Community, and in particular Article 95 thereof,

Having regard to the proposal from the Commission,

Having regard to the opinion of the European Economic and Social Committee,[1]

Acting in accordance with the procedure laid down in Article 251 of the Treaty,[2]

Whereas:

(1) Since the adoption of Directive 94/47/EC of the European Parliament and of the Council of 26 October 1994 on the protection of purchasers in respect of certain aspects of contracts relating to the purchase of the right to use immovable properties on a timeshare basis,[3] timeshare has evolved and new holiday products similar to it have appeared on the market. These new holiday products and certain transactions related to timeshare, such as resale contracts and exchange contracts, are not covered by Directive 94/47/EC. In addition, experience with the application of Directive 94/47/EC has shown that some subjects already covered need to be updated or clarified, in order to prevent the development of products aiming at circumventing this Directive.

(2) The existing regulatory gaps create appreciable distortions of competition and cause serious problems for consumers, thus hindering the smooth functioning of the internal market. Directive 94/47/EC should therefore be replaced by a new up-to-date directive. Since tourism plays an increasingly important role in the economies of the Member States, greater growth and productivity in the timeshare and long-term holiday product industries should be encouraged by adopting certain common rules.

(3) In order to enhance legal certainty and fully achieve the benefits of the internal market for consumers and businesses, the relevant laws of the Member States need to be approximated further. Therefore, certain aspects of the marketing, sale and resale of timeshares and long-term holiday products as well as the exchange of rights deriving from timeshare contracts should be fully harmonised. Member States should not be allowed to maintain or introduce in their national legislation provisions diverging from those laid down in this Directive. Where no such harmonised provisions exist, Member States should remain free to maintain or introduce national legislation in conformity with Community law. Thus, Member States should, for instance, be able to maintain or introduce provisions on the effects of exercising the right of withdrawal in legal relationships falling outside the scope of this Directive or provisions according to which no commitment may be entered into between a consumer and a trader of a timeshare or long-term holiday product, nor any payment made between those persons, as long as the consumer has not signed a credit agreement to finance the purchase of those services.

(4) This Directive should be without prejudice to the application by Member States, in accordance with Community law, of the provisions of this Directive to areas not within its scope. Member States could therefore maintain or introduce national legislation corresponding to the provisions of this Directive or certain of its provisions in relation to transactions that fall outside the scope of this Directive.

(5) The different contracts covered by this Directive should be clearly defined in such a way as to preclude circumvention of its provisions.

(6) For the purposes of this Directive, timeshare contracts should not be understood as covering multiple reservations of accommodation, including hotel rooms, in so far as multiple reservations do not imply rights and obligations beyond those arising from separate reservations. Nor should timeshare contracts be understood as covering ordinary lease contracts since the latter refer to one single continuous period of occupation and not to multiple periods.

(7) For the purposes of this Directive, long-term holiday product contracts should not be understood as covering ordinary loyalty schemes which provide discounts on future stays in the hotels of a hotel chain, since membership in the scheme is not obtained for consideration nor is the consideration paid by the consumer primarily for the purpose of obtaining discounts or other benefits in respect of accommodation.

(8) This Directive should not affect the provisions of Council Directive 90/314/EEC of 13 June 1990 on package travel, package holidays and package tours.[4]

(9) Directive 2005/29/EC of the European Parliament and of the Council of 11 May 2005 concerning unfair business-to-consumer commercial practices in the internal market (Unfair Commercial Practices Directive)[5] prohibits misleading, aggressive and other unfair commercial business-to-consumer practices. Given the nature of the products and the commercial practices related to timeshares, long-term holiday products, resale and exchange, it is appropriate to adopt more detailed and specific provisions regarding information requirements and sales events. The commercial purpose of invitations to sales events should be made clear to consumers. The provisions concerning pre-contractual information and the contract should be clarified and updated. In order to give consumers the possibility to acquaint themselves with the information before the conclusion of the contract, it should be provided by means which are easily accessible to them at that time.

(10) Consumers should have the right, which should not be refused by traders, to be provided with pre-contractual information and the contract in a language, of their choice, with which they are familiar. In addition, in order to facilitate the execution and the enforcement of the contract, Member States should be allowed to determine that further language versions of the contract should be provided to consumers.

(11) In order to provide consumers with the opportunity of fully understanding their rights and obligations under the contract, they should be allowed a period during which they may withdraw from the contract without having to justify the withdrawal and without bearing any cost. Currently the length of this period varies between Member States, and experience shows that the length prescribed in Directive 94/47/EC is not sufficiently long. The period should therefore be extended in order to achieve a high level of consumer protection and more clarity for consumers and traders. The length of the period, the modalities for and the effects of exercising the right of withdrawal should be harmonised.

(12) Consumers should have effective remedies in the event that traders do not comply with the provisions regarding pre-contractual information or the contract, in particular those laying down that the contract should include all the information required and that the consumer should receive a copy of the contract at the time of its conclusion. In addition to the remedies existing under national law, consumers should benefit from an extended withdrawal period where information has not been provided by traders. The exercise of the right of withdrawal should remain free of charge during that extended period regardless of what services consumers may have enjoyed. The expiration of the withdrawal period does not preclude consumers from seeking remedies in accordance with national law for breaches of the information requirements.

(13) Council Regulation (EEC, Euratom) No 1182/71 of 3 June 1971 determining the rules applicable to periods, dates and time limits[6] should apply to the calculation of the periods set out in this Directive.

(14) The prohibition on advance payments to traders or any third party before the end of the withdrawal period should be clarified in order to improve consumer protection. For resale contracts, the prohibition of advance payment should apply until the actual sale takes place or the resale contract is terminated, but Member States should remain free to regulate the possibility and modalities of final payments to intermediaries where resale contracts are terminated.

(15) For long-term holiday product contracts, the price to be paid in the context of a staggered payment schedule could take into consideration the possibility that subsequent amounts could be adjusted after the first year in order to ensure that the real value of those instalments is maintained, for instance to take account of inflation.

(16) In the event of a consumer withdrawing from a contract where the price is entirely or partly covered by credit granted to the consumer by the trader or by a third party on the basis of an arrangement between that third party and the trader, the credit agreement should be terminated at no cost to the consumer. The same should apply to contracts for other related services provided by the trader or by a third party on the basis of an arrangement between that third party and the trader.

(17) Consumers should not be deprived of the protection granted by this Directive where the law applicable to the contract is that of a Member State. The law applicable to a contract should be determined in accordance with the Community rules on private international law, in particular Regulation (EC) No 593/2008 of the European Parliament and of the Council of 17 June 2008 on

the law applicable to contractual obligations (Rome I).[7] Under that Regulation, the law of a third country may be applicable, in particular where consumers are targeted by traders whilst on holiday in a country other than their country of residence. Given that such commercial practices are common in the area covered by this Directive and that the contracts involve considerable amounts of money, an additional safeguard should be provided in certain specific situations, in particular where the courts of any Member State have jurisdiction over the contract, to ensure that the consumer is not deprived of the protection granted by this Directive. This concept reflects the particular needs of consumer protection arising from the typical complexity, long-term nature and financial relevance of the contracts falling within the scope of this Directive.

(18) It should be determined in accordance with Council Regulation (EC) No 44/2001 of 22 December 2000 on jurisdiction and the recognition and enforcement of judgments in civil and commercial matters[8] which courts have jurisdiction in proceedings which have as their object matters covered by this Directive.

(19) In order to ensure that the protection afforded to consumers under this Directive is fully effective, in particular as regards compliance by traders with the information requirements both at the pre-contractual stage and in the contract, it is necessary that the Member States lay down effective, proportionate and dissuasive penalties for infringements of this Directive.

(20) It is necessary to ensure that persons or organisations having, under national law, a legitimate interest in the matter have legal remedies for initiating proceedings against infringements of this Directive.

(21) It is necessary to develop suitable and effective redress procedures in the Member States for settling disputes between consumers and traders. To this end, Member States should encourage the establishment of public or private bodies for settling disputes out of court.

(22) Member States should ensure that consumers are effectively informed of the national provisions transposing this Directive and encourage traders and code owners to inform consumers about their codes of conduct in this field. With the aim of pursuing a high level of consumer protection, consumer organisations could be informed of, and involved in, the drafting of codes of conduct.

(23) Since the objectives of this Directive cannot be sufficiently achieved by the Member States and can therefore be better achieved at Community level, the Community may adopt measures in accordance with the principle of subsidiarity as set out in Article 5 of the Treaty. In accordance with the principle of proportionality, as set out in that Article, this Directive does not go beyond what is necessary in order to eliminate the internal market barriers and achieve a high common level of consumer protection.

(24) This Directive respects the fundamental rights and observes the principles recognised in particular by the European Convention on Human Rights and Fundamental Freedoms and the Charter of Fundamental Rights of the European Union.

(25) In accordance with point 34 of the Interinstitutional agreement on better law-making,[9] Member States are encouraged to draw up, for themselves and in the interests of the Community, their own tables, which will, as far as possible, illustrate the correlation between this Directive and the transposition measures, and to make them public,

NOTES

[1]   OJ C44, 16.2.2008, p 27.

[2]   Opinion of the European Parliament of 22 October 2008 (not yet published in the Official Journal) and Council Decision of 18 December 2008.

[3]   OJ L280, 29.10.1994, p 83.

[4]   OJ L158, 23.6.1990, p 59.

[5]   OJ L149, 11.6.2005, p 22.

[6]   OJ L124, 8.6.1971, p 1.

[7]   OJ L177, 4.7.2008, p 6.

[8]   OJ L12, 16.1.2001, p 1.

[9]   OJ C321, 31.12.2003, p 1.

HAVE ADOPTED THIS DIRECTIVE:

[4.466]
Article 1
Purpose and scope

1. The purpose of this Directive is to contribute to the proper functioning of the internal market and to achieve a high level of consumer protection, by approximating the laws, regulations and administrative provisions of the Member States in respect of certain aspects of the marketing, sale and resale of timeshares and long-term holiday products as well as exchange contracts.

2. This Directive applies to trader-to-consumer transactions.

This Directive is without prejudice to national legislation which:

(a)   provides for general contract law remedies;

(b)   relates to the registration of immovable or movable property and conveyance of immovable property;

(c)   relates to conditions of establishment or authorisation regimes or licensing requirements; and

(d)   relates to the determination of the legal nature of the rights which are the subject of the contracts covered by this Directive.

[4.467]
Article 2
Definitions

1.   For the purposes of this Directive, the following definitions shall apply:

(a)   "timeshare contract" means a contract of a duration of more than one year under which a consumer, for consideration, acquires the right to use one or more overnight accommodation for more than one period of occupation;

(b)   "long-term holiday product contract" means a contract of a duration of more than one year under which a consumer, for consideration, acquires primarily the right to obtain discounts or other benefits in respect of accommodation, in isolation or together with travel or other services;

(c)   "resale contract" means a contract under which a trader, for consideration, assists a consumer to sell or buy a timeshare or a long-term holiday product;

(d)   "exchange contract" means a contract under which a consumer, for consideration, joins an exchange system which allows that consumer access to overnight accommodation or other services in exchange for granting to other persons temporary access to the benefits of the rights deriving from that consumer's timeshare contract;

(e)   "trader" means a natural or legal person who is acting for purposes relating to that person's trade, business, craft or profession and anyone acting in the name of or on behalf of a trader;

(f)   "consumer" means a natural person who is acting for purposes which are outside that person's trade, business, craft or profession;

(g)   "ancillary contract" means a contract under which the consumer acquires services which are related to a timeshare contract or long-term holiday product contract and which are provided by the trader or a third party on the basis of an arrangement between that third party and the trader;

(h)   "durable medium" means any instrument which enables the consumer or the trader to store information addressed personally to him in a way which is accessible for future reference for a period of time adequate for the purposes of the information and which allows the unchanged reproduction of the information stored;

(i)   "code of conduct" means an agreement or set of rules not imposed by law, regulation or administrative provision of a Member State which defines the behaviour of traders who undertake to be bound by the code in relation to one or more particular commercial practices or business sectors;

(j)   "code owner" means any entity, including a trader or group of traders, which is responsible for the formulation and revision of a code of conduct and/or for monitoring compliance with the code by those who have undertaken to be bound by it.

2.   In calculating the duration of a timeshare contract or a long-term holiday product contract, as defined in points (a) and (b) of paragraph 1 respectively, any provision in the contract allowing for tacit renewal or prolongation shall be taken into account.

[4.468]
Article 3
Advertising

1.   Member States shall ensure that any advertising specifies the possibility of obtaining the information referred to in Article 4(1) and indicates where it can be obtained.

2.   Where a timeshare, long-term holiday product, resale or exchange contract is to be offered to a consumer in person at a promotion or sales event, the trader shall clearly indicate in the invitation the commercial purpose and the nature of the event.

3.   The information referred to in Article 4(1) shall be available to the consumer at any time during the event.

4.   A timeshare or a long-term holiday product shall not be marketed or sold as an investment.

[4.469]
Article 4
Pre-contractual information

1.   In good time before the consumer is bound by any contract or offer, the trader shall provide the consumer, in a clear and comprehensible manner, with accurate and sufficient information, as follows:

(a)   in the case of a timeshare contract: by means of the standard information form as set out in Annex I and information as listed in Part 3 of that form;

(b)   in the case of a long-term holiday product contract: by means of the standard information form as set out in Annex II and information as listed in Part 3 of that form;

(c)   in the case of a resale contract: by means of the standard information form as set out in Annex III and information as listed in Part 3 of that form;

(d)   in the case of an exchange contract: by means of the standard information form as set out in Annex IV and information as listed in Part 3 of that form.

2.   The information referred to in paragraph 1 shall be provided, free of charge, by the trader on paper or on another durable medium which is easily accessible to the consumer.

3.   Member States shall ensure that the information referred to in paragraph 1 is drawn up in the language or one of the languages of the Member State in which the consumer is resident or a national, at the choice of the consumer, provided it is an official language of the Community.

[4.470]
Article 5
The timeshare, long-term holiday product, resale or exchange contract

1.   Member States shall ensure that the contract is in writing, on paper or on another durable medium, and drawn up in the language or one of the languages of the Member State in which the consumer is resident or a national, at the choice of the consumer, provided it is an official language of the Community.

However, the Member State in which the consumer is resident may require that in addition:

(a)   in every instance, the contract be provided to the consumer in the language or one of the languages of that Member State, provided it is an official language of the Community;

(b)   in the case of a timeshare contract concerning one specific immovable property, the trader provide the consumer with a certified translation of the contract in the language or one of the languages of the Member State in which the property is situated, provided it is an official language of the Community.

The Member State on whose territory the trader carries out sale activities may require that, in every instance, the contract be provided to the consumer in the language or one of the languages of that Member State, provided it is an official language of the Community.

2.   The information referred to in Article 4(1) shall form an integral part of the contract and shall not be altered unless the parties expressly agree otherwise or the changes result from unusual and unforeseeable circumstances beyond the trader's control, the consequences of which could not have been avoided even if all due care had been exercised.

These changes shall be communicated to the consumer on paper or on another durable medium easily accessible to him, before the contract is concluded.

The contract shall expressly mention any such changes.

3.   In addition to the information referred to in Article 4(1), the contract shall include:

(a)   the identity, place of residence and signature of each of the parties; and

(b)   the date and place of the conclusion of the contract.

4.   Before the conclusion of the contract, the trader shall explicitly draw the consumer's attention to the existence of the right of withdrawal, the length of the withdrawal period referred to in Article 6, and the ban on advance payments during the withdrawal period referred to in Article 9.

The corresponding contractual clauses shall be signed separately by the consumer.

The contract shall include a separate standard withdrawal form, as set out in Annex V, intended to facilitate the exercise of the right of withdrawal in accordance with Article 6.

5.   The consumer shall receive a copy or copies of the contract at the time of its conclusion.

[4.471]
Article 6
Right of withdrawal

1.   In addition to the remedies available to the consumer under national law in the event of breach of the provisions of this Directive, Member States shall ensure that the consumer is given a period of 14 calendar days to withdraw from the timeshare, long-term holiday product, resale or exchange contract, without giving any reason.

2.   The withdrawal period shall be calculated:

(a)   from the day of the conclusion of the contract or of any binding preliminary contract; or

(b)   from the day when the consumer receives the contract or any binding preliminary contract if it is later than the date referred to in point (a).

3.   The withdrawal period shall expire:

(a)   after one year and 14 calendar days from the day referred to in paragraph 2 of this Article, where a separate standard withdrawal form as required by Article 5(4) has not been filled in by the trader and provided to the consumer in writing, on paper or on another durable medium;

(b)   after three months and 14 calendar days from the day referred to in paragraph 2 of this Article, where the information referred to in Article 4(1), including the applicable standard information form set out in Annexes I to IV, has not been provided to the consumer in writing, on paper or on another durable medium.

In addition, Member States shall provide for appropriate penalties in accordance with Article 15, in particular in the event that, on expiry of the withdrawal period, the trader has failed to comply with the information requirements set out in this Directive.

4.   Where a separate standard withdrawal form as required by Article 5(4) has been filled in by the trader and provided to the consumer in writing, on paper or on another durable medium, within one year from the day referred to in paragraph 2 of this Article, the withdrawal period shall start from the day the consumer receives that form. Similarly, where the information referred to in Article 4(1), including the applicable standard information form set out in Annexes I to IV, has been provided to the consumer in writing, on paper or on another durable medium, within three months from the day referred to in paragraph 2 of this Article, the withdrawal period shall start from the day the consumer receives such information.

5.   In the event that the exchange contract is offered to the consumer together with and at the same time as the timeshare contract, only a single withdrawal period in accordance with paragraph 1 shall apply to both contracts. The withdrawal period for both contracts shall be calculated according to the provisions of paragraph 2 as they apply to the timeshare contract.

[4.472]
Article 7
Modalities for exercising the right of withdrawal
Where the consumer intends to exercise the right of withdrawal the consumer shall, before the expiry of the withdrawal period, notify the trader on paper or on another durable medium of the decision to withdraw. The consumer may use the standard withdrawal form set out in Annex V and provided by the trader in accordance with Article 5(4). The deadline is met if the notification is sent before the withdrawal period has expired.

[4.473]
Article 8
Effects of exercising the right of withdrawal
1.   The exercise of the right of withdrawal by the consumer terminates the obligation of the parties to perform the contract.
2.   Where the consumer exercises the right of withdrawal, the consumer shall neither bear any cost nor be liable for any value corresponding to the service which may have been performed before withdrawal.

[4.474]
Article 9
Advance payment
1.   Member States shall ensure that in relation to timeshare, long-term holiday product and exchange contracts any advance payment, provision of guarantees, reservation of money on accounts, explicit acknowledgement of debt or any other consideration to the trader or to any third party by the consumer before the end of the withdrawal period according to Article 6, is prohibited.
2.   Member States shall ensure that in relation to resale contracts any advance payment, provision of guarantees, reservation of money on accounts, explicit acknowledgement of debt or any other consideration to the trader or to any third party by the consumer before the actual sale takes place or the resale contract is otherwise terminated, is prohibited.

[4.475]
Article 10
Specific provisions relating to long-term holiday product contracts
1.   For long-term holiday product contracts, payment shall be made according to a staggered payment schedule. Any payment of the price specified in the contract otherwise than in accordance with the staggered payment schedule shall be prohibited. The payments, including any membership fee, shall be divided into yearly instalments, each of which shall be of equal value. The trader shall send a written request for payment, on paper or on another durable medium, at least fourteen calendar days in advance of each due date.
2.   From the second instalment payment onwards, the consumer may terminate the contract without incurring any penalty by giving notice to the trader within fourteen calendar days of receiving the request for payment of each instalment. This right shall not affect rights to terminate the contract under existing national legislation.

[4.476]
Article 11
Termination of ancillary contracts
1.   Member States shall ensure that, where the consumer exercises the right to withdraw from the timeshare or long-term holiday product contract, any exchange contract ancillary to it or any other ancillary contract is automatically terminated, at no cost to the consumer.
2.   Without prejudice to Article 15 of Directive 2008/48/EC of the European Parliament and of the Council of 23 April 2008 on credit agreements for consumers,[1] where the price is fully or partly covered by a credit granted to the consumer by the trader, or by a third party on the basis of an

arrangement between the third party and the trader, the credit agreement shall be terminated, at no cost to the consumer, where the consumer exercises the right to withdraw from the timeshare, long-term holiday product, resale or exchange contract.

3. The Member States shall lay down detailed rules on the termination of such contracts.

NOTES

1   OJ L133, 22.5.2008, p 66.

[4.477]
Article 12
Imperative nature of the Directive and application in international cases

1. Member States shall ensure that, where the law applicable to the contract is the law of a Member State, consumers may not waive the rights conferred on them by this Directive.

2. Where the applicable law is that of a third country, consumers shall not be deprived of the protection granted by this Directive, as implemented in the Member State of the forum if:
—   any of the immovable properties concerned is situated within the territory of a Member State, or,
—   in the case of a contract not directly related to immovable property, the trader pursues commercial or professional activities in a Member State or, by any means, directs such activities to a Member State and the contract falls within the scope of such activities.

[4.478]
Article 13
Judicial and administrative redress

1. Member States shall ensure that, in the interests of consumers, adequate and effective means exist to ensure compliance by traders with this Directive.

2. The means referred to in paragraph 1 shall include provisions whereby one or more of the following bodies, as determined by national law, shall be entitled to take action in accordance with national law before the courts or competent administrative bodies to ensure that the national provisions for implementing this Directive are applied:
   (a)   public bodies and authorities or their representatives;
   (b)   consumer organisations with a legitimate interest in protecting consumers;
   (c)   professional organisations with a legitimate interest in taking such action.

[4.479]
Article 14
Consumer information and out-of-court redress

1. Member States shall take appropriate measures to inform consumers of the national law transposing this Directive and shall encourage, where appropriate, traders and code owners to inform consumers of their codes of conduct.

The Commission shall encourage the drawing up at Community level, particularly by professional bodies, organisations and associations, of codes of conduct aimed at facilitating the implementation of this Directive, in conformity with Community law. It shall also encourage traders and their branch organisations to inform consumers of any such codes, including, where appropriate, by means of a specific marking.

2. Member States shall encourage the setting up or development of adequate and effective out-of-court complaints and redress procedures for the settlement of consumer disputes under this Directive and shall, where appropriate, encourage traders and their branch organisations to inform consumers of the availability of such procedures.

[4.480]
Article 15
Penalties

1. Member States shall provide for appropriate penalties in the event of a trader's failure to comply with the national provisions adopted pursuant to this Directive.

2. Those penalties shall be effective, proportionate and dissuasive.

[4.481]
Article 16
Transposition

1. Member States shall adopt and publish, by 23 February 2011, the laws, regulations and administrative provisions necessary to comply with this Directive. They shall forthwith communicate to the Commission the text of those provisions.

They shall apply those provisions from 23 February 2011.

When Member States adopt those provisions, they shall contain a reference to this Directive or be accompanied by such a reference on the occasion of their official publication. Member States shall determine how such reference is to be made.

2. Member States shall communicate to the Commission the text of the main provisions of national law which they adopt in the field covered by this Directive.

[4.482]
Article 17
Review

The Commission shall review this Directive and report to the European Parliament and the Council no later than 23 February 2014.

If necessary, it shall make further proposals to adapt it to developments in the area.

The Commission may request information from the Member States and the national regulatory authorities.

[4.483]
Article 18
Repeal

Directive 94/47/EC shall be repealed.

References to the repealed Directive shall be construed as references to this Directive and shall be read in accordance with the correlation table in Annex VI.

[4.484]
Article 19
Entry into force

This Directive shall enter into force on the 20th day following its publication in the *Official Journal of the European Union*.

[4.485]
Article 20
Addressees

This Directive is addressed to the Member States.

ANNEX I
STANDARD INFORMATION FORM FOR TIMESHARE CONTRACTS

[4.486]
Part 1:

Identity, place of residence and legal status of the trader(s) which will be party to the contract:
Short description of the product (eg description of the immovable property):
Exact nature and content of the right(s):
Exact period within which the right which is the subject of the contract may be exercised and, if necessary, its duration:
Date on which the consumer may start to exercise the contractual right:
If the contract concerns a specific property under construction, date when the accommodation and services/facilities will be completed/available:
Price to be paid by the consumer for acquiring the right(s):
Outline of additional obligatory costs imposed under the contract; type of costs and indication of amounts (eg annual fees, other recurrent fees, special levies, local taxes):
A summary of key services available to the consumer (eg electricity, water, maintenance, refuse collection) and an indication of the amount to be paid by the consumer for such services:
A summary of facilities available to the consumer (eg swimming pool or sauna):
Are these facilities included in the costs indicated above?
If not, specify what is included and what has to be paid for:
Is it possible to join an exchange scheme?

If yes, specify the name of the exchange scheme:

Indication of costs for membership/exchange:

Has the trader signed a code/codes of conduct and, if yes, where can it/they be found?

Part 2:

General information:
— The consumer has the right to withdraw from this contract without giving any reason within 14 calendar days from the conclusion of the contract or any binding preliminary contract or receipt of those contracts if that takes place later.
— During this withdrawal period, any advance payment by the consumer is prohibited. The prohibition concerns any consideration, including payment, provision of guarantees, reservation of money on accounts, explicit acknowledgement of debt etc. It includes not only payment to the trader, but also to third parties.
— The consumer shall not bear any costs or obligations other than those specified in the contract.
— In accordance with international private law, the contract may be governed by a law other than the law of the Member State in which the consumer is resident or is habitually domiciled and possible disputes may be referred to courts other than those of the Member State in which the consumer is resident or is habitually domiciled.

Signature of the consumer:

Part 3:

Additional information to which the consumer is entitled and where it can be obtained specifically (for instance, under which chapter of a general brochure) if not provided below:

1. INFORMATION ABOUT THE RIGHTS ACQUIRED
— conditions governing the exercise of the right which is the subject of the contract within the territory of the Member States(s) in which the property or properties concerned are situated and information on whether those conditions have been fulfilled or, if they have not, what conditions remain to be fulfilled,
— where the contract provides rights to occupy accommodation to be selected from a pool of accommodation, information on restrictions on the consumer's ability to use any accommodation in the pool at any time.

2. INFORMATION ON THE PROPERTIES
— where the contract concerns a specific immovable property, an accurate and detailed description of that property and its location; where the contract concerns a number of properties (multi-resorts), an appropriate description of the properties and their location; where the contract concerns accommodation other than immovable property, an appropriate description of the accommodation and the facilities,
— the services (eg electricity, water, maintenance, refuse collection) to which the consumer has or will have access to and under what conditions,
— where applicable, the common facilities, such as swimming pool, sauna, etc, to which the consumer has or may have access and under what conditions.

3. ADDITIONAL REQUIREMENTS FOR ACCOMMODATION UNDER CONSTRUCTION (where applicable)
— the state of completion of the accommodation and of the services rendering the accommodation fully operational (gas, electricity, water and telephone connections) and any facilities to which the consumer will have access,
— the deadline for completion of the accommodation and of the services rendering it fully operational (gas, electricity, water and telephone connections) and a reasonable estimate of the deadline for the completion of any facilities to which the consumer will have access,
— the number of the building permit and the name(s) and full address(es) of the competent authority or authorities,

Part 4 Other Materials

— a guarantee regarding completion of the accommodation or a guarantee regarding reimbursement of any payment made if the accommodation is not completed and, where appropriate, the conditions governing the operation of such guarantees.

4. INFORMATION ON THE COSTS
— an accurate and appropriate description of all costs associated with the timeshare contract; how these costs will be allocated to the consumer and how and when such costs may be increased; the method for the calculation of the amount of charges relating to occupation of the property, the mandatory statutory charges (for example, taxes and fees) and the administrative overheads (for example, management, maintenance and repairs),
— where applicable, information on whether there are any charges, mortgages, encumbrances or any other liens recorded against title to the accommodation.

5. INFORMATION ON TERMINATION OF THE CONTRACT
— where appropriate, information on the arrangements for the termination of ancillary contracts and the consequences of such termination,
— conditions for terminating the contract, the consequences of termination, and information on any liability of the consumer for any costs which might result from such termination.

6. ADDITIONAL INFORMATION
— information on how maintenance and repairs of the property and its administration and management are arranged, including whether and how consumers may influence and participate in the decisions regarding these issues,
— information on whether or not it is possible to join a system for the resale of the contractual rights, information about the relevant system and an indication of costs related to resale through this system,
— indication of the language(s) available for communication with the trader in relation to the contract, for instance in relation to management decisions, increase of costs and the handling of queries and complaints,
— where applicable, the possibility for out-of-court dispute resolution.

Acknowledgement of receipt of information:

Signature of the consumer:

ANNEX II
STANDARD INFORMATION FORM FOR LONG-TERM HOLIDAY PRODUCT CONTRACTS

[4.487]
Part 1:

Identity, place of residence and legal status of the trader(s) which will be party to the contract:

Short description of the product:

Exact nature and content of the right(s):

Exact period within which the right which is the subject of the contract may be exercised and, if necessary, its duration:

Date on which the consumer may start to exercise the contractual right:

Price to be paid by the consumer for acquiring the right(s), including any recurring costs the consumer can expect to incur resulting from the right to obtain access to the accommodation, travel and any related products or services as specified:

The staggered payment schedule setting out equal amounts of instalments of this price for each year of the length of the contract and the dates on which they are due to be paid:

After year 1, subsequent amounts may be adjusted to ensure that the real value of those instalments is maintained, for instance to take account of inflation.

Outline of additional obligatory costs imposed under the contract; type of costs and indication of amounts (eg annual membership fees):

A summary of key services available to the consumer (eg discounted hotel stays and flights):

Are they included in the costs indicated above?

If not, specify what is included and what has to be paid for (eg three-night stay included in annual membership fee, all other accommodation must be paid for separately):

Has the trader signed a code/codes of conduct and, if yes, where can it/they be found?

Part 2:

General information:
— The consumer has the right to withdraw from this contract without giving any reason within 14 calendar days from the conclusion of the contract or any binding preliminary contract or receipt of those contracts if that takes place later.
— During this withdrawal period, any advance payment by the consumer is prohibited. The prohibition concerns any consideration, including payment, provision of guarantees, reservation of money on accounts, explicit acknowledgement of debt etc. It includes not only payment to the trader, but also to third parties.
— The consumer has the right to terminate the contract without incurring any penalty by giving notice to the trader within 14 calendar days of receiving the request for payment for each annual instalment.
— The consumer shall not bear any costs or obligations other than those specified in the contract.
— In accordance with international private law, the contract may be governed by a law other than the law of the Member State in which the consumer is resident or is habitually domiciled and possible disputes may be referred to courts other than those of the Member State in which the consumer is resident or is habitually domiciled.

Signature of the consumer:

Part 3:

Additional information to which the consumer is entitled and where it can be obtained specifically (for instance, under which chapter of a general brochure) if not provided below:

1. INFORMATION ABOUT THE RIGHTS ACQUIRED
— an appropriate and correct description of discounts available for future bookings, illustrated by a set of examples of recent offers,
— information on the restrictions on the consumer's ability to use the rights, such as limited availability or offers provided on a first-come-first-served basis, time limits on particular promotions and special discounts.

2. INFORMATION ON THE TERMINATION OF THE CONTRACT
— where appropriate, information on the arrangements for the termination of ancillary contracts and the consequences of such termination,
— conditions for terminating the contract, the consequences of termination, and information on any liability of the consumer for any costs which might result from such termination.

3. ADDITIONAL INFORMATION
— indication of the language(s) available for communication with the trader in relation to the contract, for instance in relation to the handling of queries and complaints,
— where applicable, the possibility for out-of-court dispute resolution.

Acknowledgement of receipt of information:

Signature of the consumer:

ANNEX III
STANDARD INFORMATION FORM FOR RESALE CONTRACTS

[4.488]

Part 1:

Identity, place of residence and legal status of the trader(s) which will be party to the contract:
Short description of the services (eg marketing):
Duration of the contract:
Price to be paid by the consumer for acquiring the services:
Outline of additional obligatory costs imposed under the contract; type of costs and indication of amounts (eg local taxes, notary fees, cost of advertising):
Has the trader signed a code/codes of conduct and, if yes, where can it/they be found?

Part 2:

General information:
   — The consumer has the right to withdraw from this contract without giving any reason within 14 calendar days from the conclusion of the contract or any binding preliminary contract or receipt of those contracts if that takes place later.
   — Any advance payment by the consumer is prohibited until the actual sale has taken place or the resale contract otherwise is terminated. The prohibition concerns any consideration, including payment, provision of guarantees, reservation of money on accounts, explicit acknowledgement of debt etc. It includes not only payment to the trader, but also to third parties.
   — The consumer shall not bear any costs or obligations other than those specified in the contract.
   — In accordance with international private law, the contract may be governed by a law other than the law of the Member State in which the consumer is resident or is habitually domiciled and possible disputes may be referred to courts other than those of the Member State in which the consumer is resident or is habitually domiciled.
Signature of the consumer:

Part 3:

Additional information to which the consumer is entitled and where it can be obtained specifically (for instance, under which chapter of a general brochure) if not provided below:
   — conditions for terminating the contract, the consequences of termination, and information on any liability of the consumer for any costs which might result from such termination,
   — indication of the language(s) available for communication with the trader in relation to the contract, for instance in relation to the handling of queries and complaints,
   — where applicable, the possibility for out-of-court dispute resolution.

Acknowledgement of receipt of information:

Signature of the consumer:

ANNEX IV
STANDARD INFORMATION FORM FOR EXCHANGE CONTRACTS

[4.489]

Part 1:

Identity, place of residence and legal status of the trader(s) which will be party to the contract:
Short description of the product:
Exact nature and content of the right(s):
Exact period within which the right which is the subject of the contract may be exercised and, if necessary, its duration:
Date on which the consumer may start to exercise the contractual right:
Price to be paid by the consumer for the exchange membership fees:
Outline of additional obligatory costs imposed under the contract; type of costs and indication of amounts (eg renewal fees, other recurrent fees, special levies, local taxes):
A summary of key services available to the consumer:
Are they included in the costs indicated above?
If not, specify what is included and what has to be paid for (type of costs and indication of amounts; eg an estimate of the price to be paid for individual exchange transactions, including any additional charges):
Has the trader signed a code/codes of conduct and, if yes, where can it/they be found?

Part 2:

General information:
— The consumer has the right to withdraw from this contract without giving any reason within 14 calendar days from the conclusion of the contract or any binding preliminary contract or receipt of those contracts if that takes place later. In cases where the exchange contract is offered together with and at the same time as the timeshare contract, only a single withdrawal period shall apply to both contracts.
— During this withdrawal period, any advance payment by the consumer is prohibited. The prohibition concerns any consideration, including payment, provision of guarantees, reservation of money on accounts, explicit acknowledgement of debt etc. It includes not only payment to the trader, but also to third parties.
— The consumer shall not bear any costs or obligations other than those specified in the contract,
— In accordance with international private law, the contract may be governed by a law other than the law of the Member State in which the consumer is resident or is habitually domiciled and possible disputes may be referred to courts other than those of the Member State in which the consumer is resident or is habitually domiciled.

Signature of the consumer:

Part 3:

Additional information to which the consumer is entitled and where it can be obtained specifically (for instance, under which chapter of a general brochure) if not provided below:

1. INFORMATION ABOUT THE RIGHTS ACQUIRED
— explanation of how the exchange system works; the possibilities and modalities for exchange; an indication of the value allotted to the consumer's timeshare in the exchange system and a set of examples of concrete exchange possibilities,
— an indication of the number of resorts available and the number of members in the exchange system, including any limitations on the availability of particular accommodation selected by the consumer, for example, as the result of peak periods of demand, the potential need to book a long time in advance, and indications of any restrictions on the choice resulting from the timeshare rights deposited into the exchange system by the consumer.

2. INFORMATION ON THE PROPERTIES
— a brief and appropriate description of the properties and their location; where the contract concerns accommodation other than immovable property, an appropriate description of the accommodation and the facilities; description of where the consumer can obtain further information.

3. INFORMATION ON THE COSTS
— information on the obligation on the trader to provide details before an exchange is arranged, in respect of each proposed exchange, of any additional charges for which the consumer is liable in respect of the exchange.

4. INFORMATION ON THE TERMINATION OF THE CONTRACT
— where appropriate, information on the arrangements for the termination of ancillary contracts and the consequences of such termination,
— conditions for terminating the contract, the consequences of termination, and information on any liability of the consumer for any costs which might result from such termination.

5. ADDITIONAL INFORMATION
— indication of the language(s) available for communication with the trader in relation to the contract, for instance in relation to the handling of queries and complaints,
— where applicable, the possibility for out-of-court dispute resolution.

Acknowledgement of receipt of information:

Signature of the consumer:

ANNEX V
SEPARATE STANDARD WITHDRAWAL FORM TO FACILITATE THE RIGHT
OF WITHDRAWAL

[4.490]

Right of withdrawal
The consumer has the right to withdraw from this contract within 14 calendar days without giving any reason.
The right of withdrawal starts from . . . . (to be filled in by the trader before providing the form to the consumer).
Where the consumer has not received this form, the withdrawal period starts when the consumer has received this form, but expires in any case after one year and 14 calendar days.
Where the consumer has not received all the required information, the withdrawal period starts when the consumer has received that information, but expires in any case after three months and 14 calendar days.
To exercise the right of withdrawal, the consumer shall notify the trader using the name and address indicated below by using a durable medium (eg written letter sent by post, e-mail). The consumer may use this form, but it is not obligatory.
Where the consumer exercises the right of withdrawal, the consumer shall not be liable for any costs.
In addition to the right of withdrawal, national contract law rules may provide for consumer rights, eg to terminate the contract in case of omission of information.
Ban on advance payment
During the withdrawal period any advance payment by the consumer is prohibited. The prohibition concerns any consideration, including payment, provision of guarantees, reservation of money on accounts, explicit acknowledgement of debt, etc.
It includes not only payment to the trader, but also to third parties.
Notice of withdrawal
— To (Name and address of the trader) (*):

— I/We (**) hereby give notice that I/We (**) withdraw from the contract,

— Date of conclusion of contract (*):

— Name(s) of consumer(s) (***):

— Address(es) of consumer(s) (***):

— Signature(s) of consumer(s) (only if this form is notified on paper) (***):

— Date (***):

(*) To be filled in by the trader before providing the form to the consumer.

(**) Delete as appropriate.

(***) To be filled in by the consumer(s) where this form is used to withdraw from the contract.

Acknowledgement of receipt of information:

Signature of the consumer:

ANNEX VI
CORRELATION TABLE BETWEEN PROVISIONS OF THIS DIRECTIVE AND DIRECTIVE 94/47/EC
[4.491]

Directive 94/47/EC	*This Directive*
Article 1, first paragraph	Article 1(1) and Article 1(2), first subparagraph
Article 1, second paragraph	—
Article 1, third paragraph	Article 1(2), second subparagraph
Article 2, first indent	Article 2(1)(a)
—	Article 2(1)(b) (new)
—	Article 2(1)(c) (new)
—	Article 2(1)(d) (new)
Article 2, second indent	—
Article 2, third indent	Article 2(1)(e)
Article 2, fourth indent	Article 2(1)(f)
—	Article 2(1)(g) (new)
—	Article 2(1)(h) (new)
—	Article 2(1)(i) (new)
—	Article 2(1)(j) (new)
—	Article 2(2) (new)
Article 3(1)	Article 4(1)
Article 3(2)	Article 5(2)
Article 3(3)	Article 3(1)
—	Article 3(2) (new)
—	Article 3(3) (new)
—	Article 3(4) (new)
Article 4, first indent	Article 5(1), first subparagraph, and Article 5(2), first subparagraph
Article 4, second indent	Article 4(3) and Article 5(1)
—	Article 4(2) (new)
—	Article 5(4) (new)
—	Article 5(5) (new)
Article 5(1), introductory sentence	Article 6(1)
Article 5(1), first indent	Article 6(1) and Article 6(2)
Article 5(1), second indent	Article 6(3) and Article 6(4)
Article 5(1), third indent	Article 6(3)
—	Article 6(5) (new)
Article 5(2)	Article 7
—	Article 8(1) (new)

Directive 94/47/EC	*This Directive*
Article 5(3)	Article 8(2)
Article 5(4)	Article 8(2)
Article 6	Article 9(1)
—	Article 9(2) (new)
—	Article 10(1) (new)
—	Article 10(2) (new)
—	Article 11(1) (new)
Article 7, first paragraph	Article 11(2)
Article 7, second paragraph	Article 11(3)
Article 8	Article 12(1)
Article 9	Article 12(2)
Article 10	Articles 13 and 15
Article 11	—
—	Article 14(1) (new)
—	Article 14(2) (new)
Article 12	Article 16
—	Article 17 (new)
—	Article 18 (new)
—	Article 19 (new)
Article 13	Article 20
Annex	Annex I
Annex, point (a)	Article 5(3)(a), and Annex I, Part 1, first box
Annex, point (b)	Annex I, Part 1, third box, and Annex I, Part 3, point 1, first indent
Annex, point (c)	Annex I, Part 1, second box, and Annex I, Part 3, point 2, first indent
Annex, point (d)(1)	Annex I, Part 3, point 3, first indent
Annex, point (d)(2)	Annex I, Part 1, fourth box, and Annex I, Part 3, point 3, second indent
Annex, point (d)(3)	Annex I, Part 3, point 3, third indent
Annex, point (d)(4)	Annex I, Part 3, point 3, first indent
Annex, point (d)(5)	Annex I, Part 3, point 3, fourth indent
Annex, point (e)	Annex I, Part 1, sixth box, and Annex I, Part 3, point 2, second indent
Annex, point (f)	Annex I, Part 1, sixth box, and Annex I, Part 3, point 2, third indent
Annex, point (g)	Annex I, Part 3, point 6, first indent
Annex, point (h)	Annex I, Part 1, fourth box
Annex, point (i)	Annex I, Part 1, fifth and sixth boxes, and Annex I, Part 3, point 4, first indent
Annex, point (j)	Annex I, Part 2, third indent
Annex, point (k)	Annex I, Part 2, seventh box, and Annex I, Part 3, point 6, second indent
Annex, point (l)	Annex I, Part 2, first and third indents, Annex I, Part 3, point 5, first indent, and Annex V (new)
Annex, point (m)	Article 5(3)(b)
—	Annex I, Part 1, eighth box (new)
—	Annex I, Part 2, second indent (new)
—	Annex I, Part 2, fourth indent (new)
—	Annex I, Part 3, point 1, second indent (new)

Directive 94/47/EC	*This Directive*
—	Annex I, Part 3, point 4, second indent (new)
—	Annex I, Part 3, point 5, second indent (new)
—	Annex I, Part 3, point 6, third indent (new)
—	Annex I, Part 3, point 6, fourth indent (new)
—	Annexes II to V (new)

DIRECTIVE OF THE EUROPEAN PARLIAMENT AND OF THE COUNCIL

(2009/22/EC)

of 23 April 2009

on injunctions for the protection of consumers' interests

(Text with EEA relevance)

NOTE

Date of publication in OJ: OJ L110, 1.5.2009, p 30.
As at 1 October 2015 this Directive had not been implemented in the UK.

THE EUROPEAN PARLIAMENT AND THE COUNCIL OF THE EUROPEAN UNION,
Having regard to the Treaty establishing the European Community, and in particular Article 95 thereof,
Having regard to the proposal from the Commission,
Having regard to the opinion of the European Economic and Social Committee,[1]
Acting in accordance with the procedure laid down in Article 251 of the Treaty,[2]
Whereas:

(1) Directive 98/27/EC of the European Parliament and of the Council of 19 May 1998 on injunctions for the protection of consumers' interests[3] has been substantially amended several times.[4] In the interests of clarity and rationality the said Directive should be codified.

(2) Certain Directives, listed in Annex I to this Directive, lay down rules with regard to the protection of consumers' interests.

(3) Current mechanisms available for ensuring compliance with those Directives, both at national and at Community level, do not always allow infringements harmful to the collective interests of consumers to be terminated in good time. Collective interests means interests which do not include the cumulation of interests of individuals who have been harmed by an infringement. This is without prejudice to individual actions brought by individuals who have been harmed by an infringement.

(4) As far as the purpose of bringing about the cessation of practices that are unlawful under the national provisions applicable is concerned, the effectiveness of national measures transposing the Directives in question, including protective measures that go beyond the level required by those Directives, provided they are compatible with the Treaty and allowed by those Directives, may be thwarted where those practices produce effects in a Member State other than that in which they originate.

(5) Those difficulties can disrupt the smooth functioning of the internal market, their consequence being that it is sufficient to move the source of an unlawful practice to another country in order to place it out of reach of all forms of enforcement. This constitutes a distortion of competition.

(6) Those difficulties are likely to diminish consumer confidence in the internal market and may limit the scope for action by organisations representing the collective interests of consumers or independent public bodies responsible for protecting the collective interests of consumers, adversely affected by practices that infringe Community law.

(7) Those practices often extend beyond the frontiers between the Member States. There is an urgent need for some degree of approximation of national provisions designed to enjoin the cessation of the unlawful practices irrespective of the Member State in which the unlawful practice has produced its effects. With regard to jurisdiction, this is without prejudice to the rules of private international law and the Conventions in force between Member States, while respecting the general obligations of the Member States deriving from the Treaty, in particular those related to the smooth functioning of the internal market.

(8)   The objective of the action envisaged can only be attained by the Community. It is therefore incumbent on the Community to act.

(9)   The third paragraph of Article 5 of the Treaty makes it incumbent on the Community not to go beyond what is necessary to achieve the objectives of the Treaty. In accordance with that Article, the specific features of national legal systems must be taken into account to every extent possible by leaving Member States free to choose between different options having equivalent effect. The courts or administrative authorities competent to rule on the proceedings referred to in this Directive should have the right to examine the effects of previous decisions.

(10)   One option should consist in requiring one or more independent public bodies, specifically responsible for the protection of the collective interests of consumers, to exercise the rights of action set out in this Directive. Another option should provide for the exercise of those rights by organisations whose purpose is to protect the collective interests of consumers, in accordance with criteria laid down by national law.

(11)   Member States should be able to choose between or combine these two options in designating at national level the bodies and/or organisations qualified for the purposes of this Directive.

(12)   For the purposes of intra-Community infringements the principle of mutual recognition should apply to these bodies and/or organisations. The Member States should, at the request of their national entities, communicate to the Commission the name and purpose of their national entities which are qualified to bring an action in their own country according to the provisions of this Directive.

(13)   It is the business of the Commission to ensure the publication of a list of these qualified entities in the *Official Journal of the European Union*. Until a statement to the contrary is published, a qualified entity is assumed to have legal capacity if its name is included in that list.

(14)   Member States should be able to require that a prior consultation be undertaken by the party that intends to bring an action for an injunction, in order to give the defendant an opportunity to bring the contested infringement to an end. Member States should be able to require that this prior consultation take place jointly with an independent public body designated by those Member States.

(15)   Where the Member States have established that there should be prior consultation, a deadline of two weeks after the request for consultation is received should be set after which, should the cessation of the infringement not be achieved, the applicant shall be entitled to bring an action, without any further delay, before the competent court or administrative authority.

(16)   It is appropriate that the Commission report on the functioning of this Directive and in particular on its scope and on the operation of prior consultation.

(17)   The application of this Directive should not prejudice the application of Community competition rules.

(18)   This Directive should be without prejudice to the obligations of the Member States concerning the time limits for transposition and application in national law of the Directives set out in Annex II, Part B,

NOTES

¹   OJ C161, 13.7.2007, p 39.

²   Opinion of the European Parliament of 19 June 2007 (OJ C146 E, 12.6.2008, p 73) and Council Decision of 23 March 2009.

³   OJ L166, 11.6.1998, p 51.

⁴   See Annex II, Part A.

HAVE ADOPTED THIS DIRECTIVE:

[4.492]
Article 1
Scope
1.   The purpose of this Directive is to approximate the laws, regulations and administrative provisions of the Member States relating to actions for an injunction referred to in Article 2 aimed at the protection of the collective interests of consumers included in the *Directives listed in Annex I*, with a view to ensuring the smooth functioning of the internal market.
2.   For the purposes of this Directive, an infringement means any act contrary to the *Directives listed in Annex I* as transposed into the internal legal order of the Member States which harms the collective interests referred to in paragraph 1.

NOTES
   For the words in italics there are substituted the words "Union acts listed in Annex I" by European Parliament and Council Regulation 524/2013/EU, art 20(1), as from 9 January 2016.

[4.493]
Article 2
Actions for an injunction
1. Member States shall designate the courts or administrative authorities competent to rule on proceedings commenced by qualified entities within the meaning of Article 3 seeking:

  (a) an order with all due expediency, where appropriate by way of summary procedure, requiring the cessation or prohibition of any infringement;

  (b) where appropriate, measures such as the publication of the decision, in full or in part, in such form as deemed adequate and/or the publication of a corrective statement with a view to eliminating the continuing effects of the infringement;

  (c) in so far as the legal system of the Member State concerned so permits, an order against the losing defendant for payments into the public purse or to any beneficiary designated in or under national legislation, in the event of failure to comply with the decision within a time limit specified by the courts or administrative authorities, of a fixed amount for each day's delay or any other amount provided for in national legislation, with a view to ensuring compliance with the decisions.

2. This Directive shall be without prejudice to the rules of private international law with respect to the applicable law, that is, normally, either the law of the Member State where the infringement originated or the law of the Member State where the infringement has its effects.

[4.494]
Article 3
Entities qualified to bring an action
For the purposes of this Directive, a 'qualified entity' means any body or organisation which, being properly constituted according to the law of a Member State, has a legitimate interest in ensuring that the provisions referred to in Article 1 are complied with, in particular:

  (a) one or more independent public bodies, specifically responsible for protecting the interests referred to in Article 1, in Member States in which such bodies exist; and/or

  (b) organisations whose purpose is to protect the interests referred to in Article 1, in accordance with the criteria laid down by the national law.

[4.495]
Article 4
Intra-Community infringements
1. Each Member State shall take the measures necessary to ensure that, in the event of an infringement originating in that Member State, any qualified entity from another Member State where the interests protected by that qualified entity are affected by the infringement, may apply to the court or administrative authority referred to in Article 2, on presentation of the list provided for in paragraph 3 of this Article. The courts or administrative authorities shall accept this list as proof of the legal capacity of the qualified entity without prejudice to their right to examine whether the purpose of the qualified entity justifies its taking action in a specific case.

2. For the purposes of intra-Community infringements, and without prejudice to the rights granted to other entities under national legislation, the Member States shall, at the request of their qualified entities, communicate to the Commission that these entities are qualified to bring an action under Article 2. The Member States shall inform the Commission of the name and purpose of these qualified entities.

3. The Commission shall draw up a list of the qualified entities referred to in paragraph 2, with the specification of their purpose. This list shall be published in the *Official Journal of the European Union*; changes to this list shall be published without delay and the updated list shall be published every six months.

[4.496]
Article 5
Prior consultation
1. Member States may introduce or maintain in force provisions whereby the party that intends to seek an injunction can only start this procedure after it has tried to achieve the cessation of the infringement in consultation either with the defendant or with both the defendant and a qualified entity within the meaning of Article 3(a) of the Member State in which the injunction is sought. It shall be for the Member State to decide whether the party seeking the injunction must consult the qualified entity. If the cessation of the infringement is not achieved within two weeks after the request for consultation is received, the party concerned may bring an action for an injunction without any further delay.

2. The rules governing prior consultation adopted by Member States shall be notified to the Commission and shall be published in the *Official Journal of the European Union*.

[4.497]
Article 6
Reports
1. Every three years and for the first time no later than 2 July 2003 the Commission shall submit to the European Parliament and to the Council a report on the application of this Directive.

2. In its first report the Commission shall examine in particular:

(a) the scope of this Directive in relation to the protection of the collective interests of persons exercising a commercial, industrial, craft or professional activity;

(b) the scope of this Directive as determined by the *Directives listed in Annex I*;

(c) whether the prior consultation provided for in Article 5 has contributed to the effective protection of consumers.

Where appropriate, this report shall be accompanied by proposals with a view to amending this Directive.

NOTES

Para 2: for the words in italics there are substituted the words "Union acts listed in Annex I" by European Parliament and Council Regulation 524/2013/EU, art 20(1), as from 9 January 2016.

[4.498]
Article 7
Provisions for wider action

This Directive shall not prevent Member States from adopting or maintaining in force provisions designed to grant qualified entities and any other person concerned more extensive rights to bring action at national level.

[4.499]
Article 8
Implementation

Member States shall communicate to the Commission the provisions of national law which they adopt in the field covered by this Directive.

[4.500]
Article 9
Repeal

Directive 98/27/EC, as amended by the Directives set out in Annex II, Part A, is repealed, without prejudice to the obligations of the Member States concerning the time limits for transposition into national law and application of the Directives set out in Annex II, Part B.

References to the repealed Directive shall be construed as references to this Directive and shall be read in accordance with the correlation table in Annex III.

[4.501]
Article 10
Entry into force

This Directive shall enter into force on 29 December 2009.

[4.502]
Article 11
Addressees

This Directive is addressed to the Member States.

ANNEX I
LIST OF DIRECTIVES REFERRED TO IN ARTICLE 1[1]

[4.503]

1. Council Directive 85/577/EEC of 20 December 1985 to protect the consumer in respect of contracts negotiated away from business premises (OJ L372, 31.12.1985, p 31).

2. Council Directive 87/102/EEC of 22 December 1986 for the approximation of the laws, regulations and administrative provisions of the Member States concerning consumer credit (OJ L42, 12.2.1987, p 48).[2]

3. Council Directive 89/552/EEC of 3 October 1989 on the coordination of certain provisions laid down by law, regulation or administrative action in Member States concerning the pursuit of television broadcasting activities: Articles 10 to 21 (OJ L298, 17.10.1989, p 23).

4. Council Directive 90/314/EEC of 13 June 1990 on package travel, package holidays and package tours (OJ L158, 23.6.1990, p 59).

5. Council Directive 93/13/EEC of 5 April 1993 on unfair terms in consumer contracts (OJ L95, 21.4.1993, p 29).

6. Directive 97/7/EC of the European Parliament and of the Council of 20 May 1997 on the protection of consumers in respect of distance contracts (OJ L144, 4.6.1997, p 19).

7. Directive 1999/44/EC of the European Parliament and of the Council of 25 May 1999 on certain aspects of the sale of consumer goods and associated guarantees (OJ L171, 7.7.1999, p 12).

8.   Directive 2000/31/EC of the European Parliament and of the Council of 8 June 2000 on certain legal aspects on information society services, in particular electronic commerce, in the internal market (Directive on electronic commerce) (OJ L178, 17.7.2000, p 1).

9.   Directive 2001/83/EC of the European Parliament and of the Council of 6 November 2001 on the Community code relating to medicinal products for human use: Articles 86 to 100 (OJ L311, 28.11.2001, p 67).

10.   Directive 2002/65/EC of the European Parliament and of the Council of 23 September 2002 concerning the distance marketing of consumer financial services (OJ L271, 9.10.2002, p 16).

11.   Directive 2005/29/EC of the European Parliament and of the Council of 11 May 2005 concerning unfair business-to-consumer commercial practices in the internal market (OJ L149, 11.6.2005, p 22).

12.   Directive 2006/123/EC of the European Parliament and of the Council of 12 December 2006 on services in the internal market (OJ L376, 27.12.2006, p 36).

13.   Directive 2008/122/EC of the European Parliament and of the Council of 14 January 2009 on the protection of consumers in respect of certain aspects of timeshare, long-term holiday product, resale and exchange contracts (OJ L33, 3.2.2009, p 10).

[14.   Directive 2013/11/EU of the European Parliament and of the Council of 21 May 2013 on alternative dispute resolution for consumer disputes (OJ L 165, 18.6.2013, p. 63): Article 13.]

[15.   Regulation (EU) No 524/2013 of the European Parliament and of the Council of 21 May 2013 on online dispute resolution for consumer disputes (Regulation on consumer ODR) (OJ L 165, 18.6.2013, p. 1): Article 14.]

NOTES

   Para 14: added by European Parliament and Council Directive 2013/11/EU, art 23.
   For the words in italics in the heading there are substituted the words "List of Union Acts", and para 15 added, by European Parliament and Council Regulation 524/2013/EU, art 20(2), (3), as from 9 January 2016.

[1]   The Directives referred to in points 5, 6, 9 and 11 contain specific provisions concerning injunctions.

[2]   The said Directive was repealed and replaced, with effect from 12 May 2010, by Directive 2008/48/EC of the European Parliament and of the Council of 23 April 2008 on credit agreements for consumers (OJ L133, 22.5.2008, p 66).

ANNEX II

PART A
REPEALED DIRECTIVE AND ITS AMENDMENTS

[4.504]
(referred to in Article 9)

Directive 98/27/EC of the European Parliament and of the Council (OJ L166, 11.6.1998, p 51).	
Directive 1999/44/EC of the European Parliament and of the Council (OJ L171, 7.7.1999, p 12).	Article 10 only
Directive 2000/31/EC of the European Parliament and of the Council (OJ L178, 17.7.2000, p 1).	Article 18(2) only
Directive 2002/65/EC of the European Parliament and of the Council (OJ L271, 9.10.2002, p 16).	Article 19 only
Directive 2005/29/EC of the European Parliament and of the Council (OJ L149, 11.6.2005, p 22).	Article 16(1) only
Directive 2006/123/EC of the European Parliament and of the Council (OJ L376, 27.12.2006, p 36).	Article 42 only

PART B
LIST OF TIME LIMITS FOR TRANSPOSITION INTO NATIONAL LAW AND APPLICATION

[4.505]
(referred to in Article 9)

Directive	Time limit for transposition	Date of application
98/27/EC	1 January 2001	—
1999/44/EC	1 January 2002	—
2000/31/EC	16 January 2002	—
2002/65/EC	9 October 2004	—
2005/29/EC	12 June 2007	12 December 2007
2006/123/EC	28 December 2009	—

ANNEX III
CORRELATION TABLE
[4.506]

Directive 98/27/EC	This Directive
Articles 1 to 5	Articles 1 to 5
Article 6(1)	Article 6(1)
Article 6(2), first subparagraph, first indent	Article 6(2), first subparagraph, point (a)
Article 6(2), first subparagraph, second indent	Article 6(2), first subparagraph, point (b)
Article 6(2), first subparagraph, third indent	Article 6(2), first subparagraph, point (c)
Article 6(2), second subparagraph	Article 6(2), second subparagraph
Article 7	Article 7
Article 8(1)	—
Article 8(2)	Article 8
—	Article 9
Article 9	Article 10
Article 10	Article 11
Annex	Annex I
—	Annex II
—	Annex III

DIRECTIVE OF THE EUROPEAN PARLIAMENT AND OF THE COUNCIL

(2011/7/EU)

of 16 February 2011

on combating late payment in commercial transactions

(recast)

(Text with EEA relevance)

NOTES
Date of publication in OJ: OJ L48 23.2.2011, p 1.
This Directive has been implemented in the UK by the Late Payment of Commercial Debts Regulations 2013, SI 2013/395.

THE EUROPEAN PARLIAMENT AND THE COUNCIL OF THE EUROPEAN UNION,
Having regard to the Treaty on the Functioning of the European Union, and in particular Article 114 thereof,
Having regard to the proposal from the European Commission,
Having regard to the opinion of the European Economic and Social Committee,[1]
Acting in accordance with the ordinary legislative procedure,[2]
Whereas:

(1) A number of substantive changes are to be made to Directive 2000/35/EC of the European

Parliament and of the Council of 29 June 2000 on combating late payment in commercial transactions.[3] It is desirable, for reasons of clarity and rationalisation, that the provisions in question be recast.

(2) Most goods and services are supplied within the internal market by economic operators to other economic operators and to public authorities on a deferred payment basis whereby the supplier gives its client time to pay the invoice, as agreed between parties, as set out in the supplier's invoice or as laid down by law.

(3) Many payments in commercial transactions between economic operators or between economic operators and public authorities are made later than agreed in the contract or laid down in the general commercial conditions. Although the goods are delivered or the services performed, many corresponding invoices are paid well after the deadline. Such late payment negatively affects liquidity and complicates the financial management of undertakings. It also affects their competitiveness and profitability when the creditor needs to obtain external financing because of late payment. The risk of such negative effects strongly increases in periods of economic downturn when access to financing is more difficult.

(4) Judicial claims related to late payment are already facilitated by Council Regulation (EC) No 44/2001 of 22 December 2000 on jurisdiction and the recognition and enforcement of judgments in civil and commercial matters,[4] Regulation (EC) No 805/2004 of the European Parliament and of the Council of 21 April 2004 creating a European Enforcement Order for uncontested claims,[5] Regulation (EC) No 1896/2006 of the European Parliament and of the Council of 12 December 2006 creating a European order for payment procedure[6] and Regulation (EC) No 861/2007 of the European Parliament and of the Council of 11 July 2007 establishing a European Small Claims Procedure.[7] However, in order to discourage late payment in commercial transactions, it is necessary to lay down complementary provisions.

(5) Undertakings should be able to trade throughout the internal market under conditions which ensure that transborder operations do not entail greater risks than domestic sales. Distortions of competition would ensue if substantially different rules applied to domestic and transborder operations.

(6) In its Communication of 25 June 2008 entitled ' "Think Small First" — A "Small Business Act" for Europe', the Commission emphasised that small and medium-sized enterprises' (SMEs) access to finance should be facilitated and that a legal and business environment supportive of timely payments in commercial transactions should be developed. It should be noted that public authorities have a special responsibility in this regard. The criteria for the definition of SMEs are set out in Commission Recommendation 2003/361/EC of 6 May 2003 concerning the definition of micro, small and medium-sized enterprises.[8]

(7) One of the priority actions of the Commission Communication of 26 November 2008 entitled 'European Economic Recovery Plan' is the reduction of administrative burdens and the promotion of entrepreneurship by, inter alia, ensuring that, as a matter of principle, invoices, including to SMEs, for supplies and services are paid within 1 month to ease liquidity constraints.

(8) The scope of this Directive should be limited to payments made as remuneration for commercial transactions. This Directive should not regulate transactions with consumers, interest in connection with other payments, for instance payments under the laws on cheques and bills of exchange, or payments made as compensation for damages including payments from insurance companies. Furthermore, Member States should be able to exclude debts that are subject to insolvency proceedings, including proceedings aimed at debt restructuring.

(9) This Directive should regulate all commercial transactions irrespective of whether they are carried out between private or public undertakings or between undertakings and public authorities, given that public authorities handle a considerable volume of payments to undertakings. It should therefore also regulate all commercial transactions between main contractors and their suppliers and subcontractors.

(10) The fact that the liberal professions are covered by this Directive should not oblige Member States to treat them as undertakings or merchants for purposes outside the scope of this Directive.

(11) The delivery of goods and the provision of services for remuneration to which this Directive applies should also include the design and execution of public works and building and civil engineering works.

(12) Late payment constitutes a breach of contract which has been made financially attractive to debtors in most Member States by low or no interest rates charged on late payments and/or slow procedures for redress. A decisive shift to a culture of prompt payment, including one in which the exclusion of the right to charge interest should always be considered to be a grossly unfair contractual term or practice, is necessary to reverse this trend and to discourage late payment. Such a shift should also include the introduction of specific provisions on payment periods and on the compensation of creditors for the costs incurred, and, inter alia, that the exclusion of the right to compensation for recovery costs should be presumed to be grossly unfair.

(13) Accordingly, provision should be made for business-to-business contractual payment

periods to be limited, as a general rule, to 60 calendar days. However, there may be circumstances in which undertakings require more extensive payment periods, for example when undertakings wish to grant trade credit to their customers. It should therefore remain possible for the parties to expressly agree on payment periods longer than 60 calendar days, provided, however, that such extension is not grossly unfair to the creditor.

(14) In the interest of consistency of Union legislation, the definition of 'contracting authorities' in Directive 2004/17/EC of the European Parliament and of the Council of 31 March 2004 coordinating the procurement procedures of entities operating in the water, energy, transport and postal services sectors[9] and in Directive 2004/18/EC of the European Parliament and of the Council of 31 March 2004 on the coordination of procedures for the award of public works contracts, public supply contracts and public services contracts[10] should apply for the purposes of this Directive.

(15) Statutory interest due for late payment should be calculated on a daily basis as simple interest, in accordance with Regulation (EEC, Euratom) No 1182/71 of the Council of 3 June 1971 determining the rules applicable to periods, dates and time limits.[11]

(16) This Directive should not oblige a creditor to claim interest for late payment. In the event of late payment, this Directive should allow a creditor to resort to charging interest for late payment without giving any prior notice of non-performance or other similar notice reminding the debtor of his obligation to pay.

(17) A debtor's payment should be regarded as late, for the purposes of entitlement to interest for late payment, where the creditor does not have the sum owed at his disposal on the due date provided that he has fulfilled his legal and contractual obligations.

(18) Invoices trigger requests for payment and are important documents in the chain of transactions for the supply of goods and services, inter alia, for determining payment deadlines. For the purposes of this Directive, Member States should promote systems that give legal certainty as regards the exact date of receipt of invoices by the debtors, including in the field of e-invoicing where the receipt of invoices could generate electronic evidence and which is partly governed by the provisions on invoicing contained in Council Directive 2006/112/EC of 28 November 2006 on the common system of value added tax.[12]

(19) Fair compensation of creditors for the recovery costs incurred due to late payment is necessary to discourage late payment. Recovery costs should also include the recovery of administrative costs and compensation for internal costs incurred due to late payment for which this Directive should determine a fixed minimum sum which may be cumulated with interest for late payment. Compensation in the form of a fixed sum should aim at limiting the administrative and internal costs linked to the recovery. Compensation for the recovery costs should be determined without prejudice to national provisions according to which a national court may award compensation to the creditor for any additional damage regarding the debtor's late payment.

(20) In addition to an entitlement to payment of a fixed sum to cover internal recovery costs, creditors should also be entitled to reimbursement of the other recovery costs they incur as a result of late payment by a debtor. Such costs should include, in particular, those incurred by creditors in instructing a lawyer or employing a debt collection agency.

(21) This Directive should be without prejudice to the right of Member States to provide for fixed sums for compensation of recovery costs which are higher and therefore more favourable to the creditor, or to increase those sums, inter alia, in order to keep pace with inflation.

(22) This Directive should not prevent payments by instalments or staggered payments. However, each instalment or payment should be paid on the agreed terms and should be subject to the rules for late payment set out in this Directive.

(23) As a general rule, public authorities benefit from more secure, predictable and continuous revenue streams than undertakings. In addition, many public authorities can obtain financing at more attractive conditions than undertakings. At the same time, public authorities depend less than undertakings on building stable commercial relationships for the achievement of their aims. Long payment periods and late payment by public authorities for goods and services lead to unjustified costs for undertakings. It is therefore appropriate to introduce specific rules as regards commercial transactions for the supply of goods or services by undertakings to public authorities, which should provide in particular for payment periods normally not exceeding 30 calendar days, unless otherwise expressly agreed in the contract and provided it is objectively justified in the light of the particular nature or features of the contract, and in any event not exceeding 60 calendar days.

(24) However, account should be taken of the specific situation of public authorities carrying out economic activities of an industrial or commercial nature by offering goods or services on the market as a public undertaking. For that purpose, Member States should be allowed, under certain conditions, to extend the statutory payment period up to a maximum of 60 calendar days.

(25) A particular cause for concern in connection with late payment is the situation of health services in a large number of Member States. Healthcare systems, as a fundamental part of Europe's social infrastructure, are often obliged to reconcile individual needs with the available finances, as the population of Europe ages, as expectations rise, and as medicine advances. All systems have to deal with the challenge of prioritising healthcare in a way that balances the needs

of individual patients with the financial resources available. Member States should therefore be able to grant public entities providing healthcare a certain amount of flexibility in meeting their commitments. For that purpose, Member States should be allowed, under certain conditions, to extend the statutory payment period up to a maximum of 60 calendar days. Member States should, nonetheless, make every effort to ensure that payments in the healthcare sector are made within the statutory payment periods.

(26) In order not to jeopardise the achievement of the objective of this Directive, Member States should ensure that in commercial transactions the maximum duration of a procedure of acceptance or verification does not exceed, as a general rule, 30 calendar days. Nevertheless, it should be possible for a verification procedure to exceed 30 calendar days, for example in the case of particularly complex contracts, when expressly agreed in the contract and in any tender documents and if it is not grossly unfair to the creditor.

(27) The Union institutions are in a situation comparable to that of the public authorities of Member States with regard to their financing and commercial relationships. Council Regulation (EC, Euratom) No 1605/2002 of 25 June 2002 on the Financial Regulation applicable to the general budget of the European Communities[13] specifies that the validation, authorisation and payment of expenditure by Union institutions must be completed within the time limits laid down in its implementing rules. Those implementing rules are currently set out in Commission Regulation (EC, Euratom) No 2342/2002 of 23 December 2002 laying down detailed rules for the implementation of Council Regulation (EC, Euratom) No 1605/2002 on the Financial Regulation applicable to the general budget of the European Communities,[14] and specify the circumstances in which creditors which are paid late are entitled to receive default interest. In the context of the ongoing review of those Regulations, it should be ensured that the maximum time limits for payment by the Union institutions are aligned with statutory periods applicable to public authorities in accordance with this Directive.

(28) This Directive should prohibit abuse of freedom of contract to the disadvantage of the creditor. As a result, where a term in a contract or a practice relating to the date or period for payment, the rate of interest for late payment or the compensation for recovery costs is not justified on the grounds of the terms granted to the debtor, or it mainly serves the purpose of procuring the debtor additional liquidity at the expense of the creditor, it may be regarded as constituting such an abuse. For that purpose, and in accordance with the academic 'Draft Common Frame of Reference', any contractual term or practice which grossly deviates from good commercial practice and is contrary to good faith and fair dealing should be regarded as unfair to the creditor. In particular, the outright exclusion of the right to charge interest should always be considered as grossly unfair, whereas the exclusion of the right to compensation for recovery costs should be presumed to be grossly unfair. This Directive should not affect national provisions relating to the way contracts are concluded or regulating the validity of contractual terms which are unfair to the debtor.

(29) In the context of enhanced efforts to prevent the abuse of freedom of contract to the detriment of creditors, organisations officially recognised as representing undertakings and organisations with a legitimate interest in representing undertakings should be able to take action before national courts or administrative bodies in order to prevent the continued use of contract terms or practices which are grossly unfair to the creditor.

(30) In order to contribute to the achievement of the objective of this Directive, Member States should foster the spread of good practices, including by encouraging the publication of a list of prompt payers.

(31) It is desirable to ensure that creditors are in a position to exercise a retention of title clause on a non-discriminatory basis throughout the Union, if the retention of title clause is valid under the applicable national provisions designated by private international law.

(32) This Directive only defines the term 'enforceable title' but should not regulate the various procedures for forced execution of such a title or the conditions under which forced execution of such a title can be stopped or suspended.

(33) The consequences of late payment can be dissuasive only if they are accompanied by procedures for redress which are rapid and effective for the creditor. In accordance with the principle of non-discrimination set out in Article 18 of the Treaty on the Functioning of the European Union, those procedures should be available to all creditors who are established in the Union.

(34) In order to facilitate compliance with the provisions of this Directive, Member States should encourage recourse to mediation or other means of alternative dispute resolution. Directive 2008/52/EC of the European Parliament and of the Council of 21 May 2008 on certain aspects of mediation in civil and commercial matters[15] already sets a framework for systems of mediation at Union level, especially for cross-border disputes, without preventing its application to internal mediation systems. Member States should also encourage interested parties to draw up voluntary codes of conduct aimed, in particular, at contributing to the implementation of this Directive.

(35) It is necessary to ensure that the recovery procedures for unchallenged claims related to late payment in commercial transactions be completed within a short period of time, including through an expedited procedure and irrespective of the amount of the debt.

(36)   Since the objective of this Directive, namely combating late payment in the internal market, cannot be sufficiently achieved by the Member States and can, therefore, by reason of its scale and effect, be better achieved at the Union level, the Union may adopt measures, in accordance with the principle of subsidiarity as set out in Article 5 of the Treaty on European Union. In accordance with the principle of proportionality, as set out in that Article, this Directive does not go beyond what is necessary in order to achieve that objective.

(37)   The obligation to transpose this Directive into national law should be confined to those provisions which represent a substantive change as compared with Directive 2000/35/EC. The obligation to transpose the provisions which are unchanged arises under that Directive.

(38)   This Directive should be without prejudice to the obligations of the Member States relating to the time limits for transposition into national law and application of Directive 2000/35/EC.

(39)   In accordance with point 34 of the Interinstitutional Agreement on better law-making,[16] Member States are encouraged to draw up, for themselves and in the interest of the Union, their own tables which will, as far as possible, illustrate the correlation between this Directive and their transposition measures, and to make those tables public,

NOTES

[1]   OJ C255, 22.9.2010, p 42.

[2]   Position of the European Parliament of 20 October 2010 (not yet published in the Official Journal) and decision of the Council of 24 January 2011.

[3]   OJ L200, 8.8.2000, p 35.

[4]   OJ L12, 16.1.2001, p 1.

[5]   OJ L143, 30.4.2004, p 15.

[6]   OJ L399, 30.12.2006, p 1.

[7]   OJ L199, 31.7.2007, p 1.

[8]   OJ L124, 20.5.2003, p 36.

[9]   OJ L134, 30.4.2004, p 1.

[10]   OJ L134, 30.4.2004, p 114.

[11]   OJ L124, 8.6.1971, p 1.

[12]   OJ L347, 11.12.2006, p 1.

[13]   OJ L248, 16.9.2002, p 1.

[14]   OJ L357, 31.12.2002, p 1.

[15]   OJ L136, 24.5.2008, p 3.

[16]   OJ C321, 31.12.2003, p 1.

HAVE ADOPTED THIS DIRECTIVE

[4.507]
Article 1
Subject matter and scope
1.   The aim of this Directive is to combat late payment in commercial transactions, in order to ensure the proper functioning of the internal market, thereby fostering the competitiveness of undertakings and in particular of SMEs.
2.   This Directive shall apply to all payments made as remuneration for commercial transactions.
3.   Member States may exclude debts that are subject to insolvency proceedings instituted against the debtor, including proceedings aimed at debt restructuring.

[4.508]
Article 2
Definitions
For the purposes of this Directive, the following definitions shall apply:
   (1)   'commercial transactions' means transactions between undertakings or between undertakings and public authorities which lead to the delivery of goods or the provision of services for remuneration;
   (2)   'public authority' means any contracting authority, as defined in point (a) of Article 2(1) of Directive 2004/17/EC and in Article 1(9) of Directive 2004/18/EC, regardless of the subject or value of the contract;
   (3)   'undertaking' means any organisation, other than a public authority, acting in the course of its independent economic or professional activity, even where that activity is carried out by a single person;
   (4)   'late payment' means payment not made within the contractual or statutory period of payment and where the conditions laid down in Article 3(1) or Article 4(1) are satisfied;
   (5)   'interest for late payment' means statutory interest for late payment or interest at a rate agreed upon between undertakings, subject to Article 7;

(6)   'statutory interest for late payment' means simple interest for late payment at a rate which is equal to the sum of the reference rate and at least eight percentage points;

(7)   'reference rate' means either of the following:

    (a)   for a Member State whose currency is the euro, either:

        (i)   the interest rate applied by the European Central Bank to its most recent main refinancing operations; or

        (ii)   the marginal interest rate resulting from variable-rate tender procedures for the most recent main refinancing operations of the European Central Bank;

    (b)   for a Member State whose currency is not the euro, the equivalent rate set by its national central bank;

(8)   'amount due' means the principal sum which should have been paid within the contractual or statutory period of payment, including the applicable taxes, duties, levies or charges specified in the invoice or the equivalent request for payment;

(9)   'retention of title' means the contractual agreement according to which the seller retains title to the goods in question until the price has been paid in full;

(10)   'enforceable title' means any decision, judgment or order for payment issued by a court or other competent authority, including those that are provisionally enforceable, whether for immediate payment or payment by instalments, which permits the creditor to have his claim against the debtor collected by means of forced execution.

[4.509]
Article 3
Transactions between undertakings

1.   Member States shall ensure that, in commercial transactions between undertakings, the creditor is entitled to interest for late payment without the necessity of a reminder, where the following conditions are satisfied:

    (a)   the creditor has fulfilled its contractual and legal obligations; and

    (b)   the creditor has not received the amount due on time, unless the debtor is not responsible for the delay.

2.   Member States shall ensure that the applicable reference rate:

    (a)   for the first semester of the year concerned shall be the rate in force on 1 January of that year;

    (b)   for the second semester of the year concerned shall be the rate in force on 1 July of that year.

3.   Where the conditions set out in paragraph 1 are satisfied, Member States shall ensure the following:

    (a)   that the creditor is entitled to interest for late payment from the day following the date or the end of the period for payment fixed in the contract;

    (b)   where the date or period for payment is not fixed in the contract, that the creditor is entitled to interest for late payment upon the expiry of any of the following time limits:

        (i)   30 calendar days following the date of receipt by the debtor of the invoice or an equivalent request for payment;

        (ii)   where the date of the receipt of the invoice or the equivalent request for payment is uncertain, 30 calendar days after the date of receipt of the goods or services;

        (iii)   where the debtor receives the invoice or the equivalent request for payment earlier than the goods or the services, 30 calendar days after the date of the receipt of the goods or services;

        (iv)   where a procedure of acceptance or verification, by which the conformity of the goods or services with the contract is to be ascertained, is provided for by statute or in the contract and if the debtor receives the invoice or the equivalent request for payment earlier or on the date on which such acceptance or verification takes place, 30 calendar days after that date.

4.   Where a procedure of acceptance or verification, by which the conformity of the goods or services with the contract is to be ascertained, is provided for, Member States shall ensure that the maximum duration of that procedure does not exceed 30 calendar days from the date of receipt of the goods or services, unless otherwise expressly agreed in the contract and provided it is not grossly unfair to the creditor within the meaning of Article 7.

5.   Member States shall ensure that the period for payment fixed in the contract does not exceed 60 calendar days, unless otherwise expressly agreed in the contract and provided it is not grossly unfair to the creditor within the meaning of Article 7.

[4.510]
Article 4
Transactions between undertakings and public authorities

1.   Member States shall ensure that, in commercial transactions where the debtor is a public authority, the creditor is entitled upon expiry of the period defined in paragraphs 3, 4 or 6 to statutory interest for late payment, without the necessity of a reminder, where the following conditions are satisfied:

    (a)   the creditor has fulfilled its contractual and legal obligations; and

(b)   the creditor has not received the amount due on time, unless the debtor is not responsible for the delay.

2.   Member States shall ensure that the applicable reference rate:

(a)   for the first semester of the year concerned shall be the rate in force on 1 January of that year;

(b)   for the second semester of the year concerned shall be the rate in force on 1 July of that year.

3.   Member States shall ensure that in commercial transactions where the debtor is a public authority:

(a)   the period for payment does not exceed any of the following time limits:

    (i)   30 calendar days following the date of receipt by the debtor of the invoice or an equivalent request for payment;

    (ii)   where the date of receipt of the invoice or the equivalent request for payment is uncertain, 30 calendar days after the date of the receipt of the goods or services;

    (iii)   where the debtor receives the invoice or the equivalent request for payment earlier than the goods or the services, 30 calendar days after the date of the receipt of the goods or services;

    (iv)   where a procedure of acceptance or verification, by which the conformity of the goods or services with the contract is to be ascertained, is provided for by statute or in the contract and if the debtor receives the invoice or the equivalent request for payment earlier or on the date on which such acceptance or verification takes place, 30 calendar days after that date;

(b)   the date of receipt of the invoice is not subject to a contractual agreement between debtor and creditor.

4.   Member States may extend the time limits referred to in point (a) of paragraph 3 up to a maximum of 60 calendar days for:

(a)   any public authority which carries out economic activities of an industrial or commercial nature by offering goods or services on the market and which is subject, as a public undertaking, to the transparency requirements laid down in Commission Directive 2006/111/EC of 16 November 2006 on the transparency of financial relations between Member States and public undertakings as well as on financial transparency within certain undertakings;[1]

(b)   public entities providing healthcare which are duly recognised for that purpose.

If a Member State decides to extend the time limits in accordance with this paragraph, it shall send a report on such extension to the Commission by 16 March 2018.

On that basis, the Commission shall submit a report to the European Parliament and the Council indicating which Member States have extended the time limits in accordance with this paragraph and taking into account the impact on the functioning of the internal market, in particular on SMEs. That report shall be accompanied by any appropriate proposals.

5.   Member States shall ensure that the maximum duration of a procedure of acceptance or verification referred to in point (iv) of point (a) of paragraph 3 does not exceed 30 calendar days from the date of receipt of the goods or services, unless otherwise expressly agreed in the contract and any tender documents and provided it is not grossly unfair to the creditor within the meaning of Article 7.

6.   Member States shall ensure that the period for payment fixed in the contract does not exceed the time limits provided for in paragraph 3, unless otherwise expressly agreed in the contract and provided it is objectively justified in the light of the particular nature or features of the contract, and that it in any event does not exceed 60 calendar days.

NOTES

[1]   OJ L318, 17.11.2006, p 17.

[4.511]
Article 5
Payment schedules
This Directive shall be without prejudice to the ability of parties to agree, subject to the relevant provisions of applicable national law, on payment schedules providing for instalments. In such cases, where any of the instalments is not paid by the agreed date, interest and compensation provided for in this Directive shall be calculated solely on the basis of overdue amounts.

[4.512]
Article 6
Compensation for recovery costs
1.   Member States shall ensure that, where interest for late payment becomes payable in commercial transactions in accordance with Article 3 or 4, the creditor is entitled to obtain from the debtor, as a minimum, a fixed sum of EUR 40.

2.   Member States shall ensure that the fixed sum referred to in paragraph 1 is payable without the necessity of a reminder and as compensation for the creditor's own recovery costs.

3.   The creditor shall, in addition to the fixed sum referred to in paragraph 1, be entitled to obtain reasonable compensation from the debtor for any recovery costs exceeding that fixed sum and incurred due to the debtor's late payment. This could include expenses incurred, inter alia, in instructing a lawyer or employing a debt collection agency.

[4.513]
Article 7
Unfair contractual terms and practices
1.   Member States shall provide that a contractual term or a practice relating to the date or period for payment, the rate of interest for late payment or the compensation for recovery costs is either unenforceable or gives rise to a claim for damages if it is grossly unfair to the creditor.
In determining whether a contractual term or a practice is grossly unfair to the creditor, within the meaning of the first subparagraph, all circumstances of the case shall be considered, including:

(a)   any gross deviation from good commercial practice, contrary to good faith and fair dealing;
(b)   the nature of the product or the service; and
(c)   whether the debtor has any objective reason to deviate from the statutory rate of interest for late payment, from the payment period as referred to in Article 3(5), point (a) of Article 4(3), Article 4(4) and Article 4(6) or from the fixed sum as referred to in Article 6(1).

2.   For the purpose of paragraph 1, a contractual term or a practice which excludes interest for late payment shall be considered as grossly unfair.
3.   For the purpose of paragraph 1, a contractual term or a practice which excludes compensation for recovery costs as referred to in Article 6 shall be presumed to be grossly unfair.
4.   Member States shall ensure that, in the interests of creditors and competitors, adequate and effective means exist to prevent the continued use of contractual terms and practices which are grossly unfair within the meaning of paragraph 1.
5.   The means referred to in paragraph 4 shall include provisions whereby organisations officially recognised as representing undertakings, or organisations with a legitimate interest in representing undertakings may take action according to the applicable national law before the courts or before competent administrative bodies on the grounds that contractual terms or practices are grossly unfair within the meaning of paragraph 1, so that they can apply appropriate and effective means to prevent their continued use.

[4.514]
Article 8
Transparency and awareness raising
1.   Member States shall ensure transparency regarding the rights and obligations stemming from this Directive, including by making publicly available the applicable rate of statutory interest for late payment.
2.   The Commission shall make publicly available on the Internet details of the current statutory rates of interest which apply in all the Member States in the event of late payment in commercial transactions.
3.   Member States shall, where appropriate, use professional publications, promotion campaigns or any other functional means to increase awareness of the remedies for late payment among undertakings.
4.   Member States may encourage the establishment of prompt payment codes which set out clearly defined payment time limits and a proper process for dealing with any payments that are in dispute, or any other initiatives that tackle the crucial issue of late payment and contribute to developing a culture of prompt payment which supports the objective of this Directive.

[4.515]
Article 9
Retention of title
1.   Member States shall provide in conformity with the applicable national provisions designated by private international law that the seller retains title to goods until they are fully paid for if a retention of title clause has been expressly agreed between the buyer and the seller before the delivery of the goods.
2.   Member States may adopt or retain provisions dealing with down payments already made by the debtor.

[4.516]
Article 10
Recovery procedures for unchallenged claims
1.   Member States shall ensure that an enforceable title can be obtained, including through an expedited procedure and irrespective of the amount of the debt, normally within 90 calendar days of the lodging of the creditor's action or application at the court or other competent authority, provided that the debt or aspects of the procedure are not disputed. Member States shall carry out this duty in accordance with their respective national laws, regulations and administrative provisions.

2.   National laws, regulations and administrative provisions shall apply the same conditions for all creditors who are established in the Union.

3.   When calculating the period referred to in paragraph 1, the following shall not be taken into account:

    (a)   periods for service of documents;

    (b)   any delays caused by the creditor, such as periods devoted to correcting applications.

4.   This Article shall be without prejudice to the provisions of Regulation (EC) No 1896/2006.

[4.517]
Article 11
Report
By 16 March 2016, the Commission shall submit a report to the European Parliament and the Council on the implementation of this Directive. The report shall be accompanied by any appropriate proposals.

[4.518]
Article 12
Transposition
1.   Member States shall bring into force the laws, regulations and administrative provisions necessary to comply with Articles 1 to 8 and 10 by 16 March 2013. They shall forthwith communicate to the Commission the text of those provisions.

When Member States adopt those measures, they shall contain a reference to this Directive or shall be accompanied by such reference on the occasion of their official publication. They shall also include a statement that references in existing laws, regulations and administrative provisions to the repealed Directive shall be construed as references to this Directive. The methods of making such reference and the formulation of such statement shall be laid down by Member States.

2.   Member States shall communicate to the Commission the text of the main provisions of national law which they adopt in the field covered by this Directive.

3.   Member States may maintain or bring into force provisions which are more favourable to the creditor than the provisions necessary to comply with this Directive.

4.   In transposing the Directive, Member States shall decide whether to exclude contracts concluded before 16 March 2013.

[4.519]
Article 13
Repeal
Directive 2000/35/EC is repealed with effect from 16 March 2013, without prejudice to the obligations of the Member States relating to the time limit for its transposition into national law and its application. However, it shall remain applicable to contracts concluded before that date to which this Directive does not apply pursuant to Article 12(4).

References to the repealed Directive shall be construed as references to this Directive and be read in accordance with the correlation table set out in the Annex.

[4.520]
Article 14
Entry into force
This Directive shall enter into force on the 20th day following its publication in the *Official Journal of the European Union*.

[4.521]
Article 15
Addressees
This Directive is addressed to the Member States.

ANNEX
CORRELATION TABLE

[4.522]

Directive 2000/35/EC	*This Directive*
—	Article 1(1)
Article 1	Article 1(2)
Article 2(1), first subparagraph	Article 2(1)
Article 2(1), second subparagraph	Article 2(2)
Article 2(1), third subparagraph	Article 2(3)
Article 2(2)	Article 2(4)
—	Article 2(5)
—	Article 2(6)

Directive 2000/35/EC	This Directive
—	Article 2(7), introductory part
—	Article 2(8)
Article 2(3)	Article 2(9)
Article 2(4)	Article 2(7)(a)
Article 2(5)	Article 2(10)
Article 3(l)(a)	Article 3(3)(a)
Article 3(l)(b), introductory part	Article 3(3)(b), introductory part
Article 3(l)(b)(i)	Article 3(3)(b)(i)
Article 3(l)(b)(ii)	Article 3(3)(b)(ii)
Article 3(l)(b)(iii)	Article 3(3)(b)(iii)
Article 3(l)(b)(iv)	Article 3(3)(b)(iv)
—	Article 3(4)
—	Article 3(5)
Article 3(1)(c)	Article 3(1)
Article 3(1)(d), first and third sentences	—
Article 3(1)(d), second sentence	Article 2(7)(b)
—	Article 3(2)
—	Article 4
—	Article 5
—	Article 6(1)
—	Article 6(2)
—	Article 6(3)
Article 3(1)(e)	—
Article 3(2)	—
Article 3(3)	Article 7(1)
—	Article 7(2)
—	Article 7(3)
Article 3(4)	Article 7(4)
Article 3(5)	Article 7(5)
—	Article 8
Article 4	Article 9
Article 5(1), (2) and (3)	Article 10(1), (2) and (3)
Article 5(4)	—
—	Article 10(4)
—	Article 11
Article 6(1)	—
—	Article 12(1)
Article 6(2)	Article 12(3)
Article 6(3)	Article 1(3)
Article 6(4)	Article 12(2)
Article 6(5)	—
—	Article 12(4)
—	Article 13
Article 7	Article 14
Article 8	Article 15
—	Annex

DIRECTIVE OF THE EUROPEAN PARLIAMENT AND OF THE COUNCIL

(2011/83/EU)

of 25 October 2011

on consumer rights, amending Council Directive 93/13/EEC and Directive 1999/44/EC of the European Parliament and of the Council and repealing Council Directive 85/577/EEC and Directive 97/7/EC of the European Parliament and of the Council

(Text with EEA relevance)

NOTES

Date of publication in OJ: OJ L304, 22.11.2011, p 64.

This Directive has been implemented in the UK by the Consumer Rights (Payment Surcharges) Regulations 2012, SI 2012/3110 and by the Consumer Contracts (Information, Cancellation and Additional Charges) Regulations 2013, SI 2013/3134 at [2.1059].

THE EUROPEAN PARLIAMENT AND THE COUNCIL OF THE EUROPEAN UNION,

Having regard to the Treaty on the Functioning of the European Union, and in particular Article 114 thereof,

Having regard to the proposal from the European Commission,

Having regard to the opinion of the European Economic and Social Committee,[1]

Having regard to the opinion of the Committee of Regions,[2]

Acting in accordance with the ordinary legislative procedure,[3]

Whereas:

(1)   Council Directive 85/577/EEC of 20 December 1985 to protect the consumer in respect of contracts negotiated away from business premises[4] and Directive 97/7/EC of the European Parliament and of the Council of 20 May 1997 on the protection of consumers in respect of distance contracts[5] lay down a number of contractual rights for consumers.

(2)   Those Directives have been reviewed in the light of experience with a view to simplifying and updating the applicable rules, removing inconsistencies and closing unwanted gaps in the rules. That review has shown that it is appropriate to replace those two Directives by a single Directive. This Directive should therefore lay down standard rules for the common aspects of distance and off-premises contracts, moving away from the minimum harmonisation approach in the former Directives whilst allowing Member States to maintain or adopt national rules in relation to certain aspects.

(3)   Article 169(1) and point (a) of Article 169(2) of the Treaty on the Functioning of the European Union (TFEU) provide that the Union is to contribute to the attainment of a high level of consumer protection through the measures adopted pursuant to Article 114 thereof.

(4)   In accordance with Article 26(2) TFEU, the internal market is to comprise an area without internal frontiers in which the free movement of goods and services and freedom of establishment are ensured. The harmonisation of certain aspects of consumer distance and off-premises contracts is necessary for the promotion of a real consumer internal market striking the right balance between a high level of consumer protection and the competitiveness of enterprises, while ensuring respect for the principle of subsidiarity.

(5)   The cross-border potential of distance selling, which should be one of the main tangible results of the internal market, is not fully exploited. Compared with the significant growth of domestic distance sales over the last few years, the growth in cross-border distance sales has been limited. This discrepancy is particularly significant for Internet sales for which the potential for further growth is high. The cross-border potential of contracts negotiated away from business premises (direct selling) is constrained by a number of factors including the different national consumer protection rules imposed upon the industry. Compared with the growth of domestic direct selling over the last few years, in particular in the services sector, for instance utilities, the number of consumers using this channel for cross-border purchases has remained flat. Responding to increased business opportunities in many Member States, small and medium-sized enterprises (including individual traders) or agents of direct selling companies should be more inclined to seek business opportunities in other Member States, in particular in border regions. Therefore the full harmonisation of consumer information and the right of withdrawal in distance and off-premises contracts will contribute to a high level of consumer protection and a better functioning of the business-to-consumer internal market.

(6)   Certain disparities create significant internal market barriers affecting traders and consumers. Those disparities increase compliance costs to traders wishing to engage in the cross-border sale of goods or provision of services. Disproportionate fragmentation also undermines consumer confidence in the internal market.

(7)   Full harmonisation of some key regulatory aspects should considerably increase legal

certainty for both consumers and traders. Both consumers and traders should be able to rely on a single regulatory framework based on clearly defined legal concepts regulating certain aspects of business-to-consumer contracts across the Union. The effect of such harmonisation should be to eliminate the barriers stemming from the fragmentation of the rules and to complete the internal market in this area. Those barriers can only be eliminated by establishing uniform rules at Union level. Furthermore consumers should enjoy a high common level of protection across the Union.

(8) The regulatory aspects to be harmonised should only concern contracts concluded between traders and consumers. Therefore, this Directive should not affect national law in the area of contracts relating to employment, contracts relating to succession rights, contracts relating to family law and contracts relating to the incorporation and organisation of companies or partnership agreements.

(9) This Directive establishes rules on information to be provided for distance contracts, off-premises contracts and contracts other than distance and off-premises contracts. This Directive also regulates the right of withdrawal for distance and off-premises contracts and harmonises certain provisions dealing with the performance and some other aspects of business-to-consumer contracts.

(10) This Directive should be without prejudice to Regulation (EC) No 593/2008 of the European Parliament and of the Council of 17 June 2008 on the law applicable to contractual obligations (Rome I).[6]

(11) This Directive should be without prejudice to Union provisions relating to specific sectors, such as medicinal products for human use, medical devices, privacy and electronic communications, patients' rights in cross-border healthcare, food labelling and the internal market for electricity and natural gas.

(12) The information requirements provided for in this Directive should complete the information requirements of Directive 2006/123/EC of the European Parliament and of the Council of 12 December 2006 on services in the internal market[7] and Directive 2000/31/EC of the European Parliament and of the Council of 8 June 2000 on certain legal aspects of information society services, in particular electronic commerce, in the Internal Market ('Directive on electronic commerce').[8] Member States should retain the possibility to impose additional information requirements applicable to service providers established in their territory.

(13) Member States should remain competent, in accordance with Union law, to apply the provisions of this Directive to areas not falling within its scope. Member States may therefore maintain or introduce national legislation corresponding to the provisions of this Directive, or certain of its provisions, in relation to contracts that fall outside the scope of this Directive. For instance, Member States may decide to extend the application of the rules of this Directive to legal persons or to natural persons who are not consumers within the meaning of this Directive, such as non-governmental organisations, start-ups or small and medium-sized enterprises. Similarly, Member States may apply the provisions of this Directive to contracts that are not distance contracts within the meaning of this Directive, for example because they are not concluded under an organised distance sales or service-provision scheme. Moreover, Member States may also maintain or introduce national provisions on issues not specifically addressed in this Directive, such as additional rules concerning sales contracts, including in relation to the delivery of goods, or requirements for the provision of information during the existence of a contract.

(14) This Directive should not affect national law in the area of contract law for contract law aspects that are not regulated by this Directive. Therefore, this Directive should be without prejudice to national law regulating for instance the conclusion or the validity of a contract (for instance in the case of lack of consent). Similarly, this Directive should not affect national law in relation to the general contractual legal remedies, the rules on public economic order, for instance rules on excessive or extortionate prices, and the rules on unethical legal transactions.

(15) This Directive should not harmonise language requirements applicable to consumer contracts. Therefore, Member States may maintain or introduce in their national law language requirements regarding contractual information and contractual terms.

(16) This Directive should not affect national laws on legal representation such as the rules relating to the person who is acting in the name of the trader or on his behalf (such as an agent or a trustee). Member States should remain competent in this area. This Directive should apply to all traders, whether public or private.

(17) The definition of consumer should cover natural persons who are acting outside their trade, business, craft or profession. However, in the case of dual purpose contracts, where the contract is concluded for purposes partly within and partly outside the person's trade and the trade purpose is so limited as not to be predominant in the overall context of the contract, that person should also be considered as a consumer.

(18) This Directive does not affect the freedom of Member States to define, in conformity with Union law, what they consider to be services of general economic interest, how those services should be organised and financed, in compliance with State aid rules, and which specific obligations they should be subject to.

(19) Digital content means data which are produced and supplied in digital form, such as

computer programs, applications, games, music, videos or texts, irrespective of whether they are accessed through downloading or streaming, from a tangible medium or through any other means. Contracts for the supply of digital content should fall within the scope of this Directive. If digital content is supplied on a tangible medium, such as a CD or a DVD, it should be considered as goods within the meaning of this Directive. Similarly to contracts for the supply of water, gas or electricity, where they are not put up for sale in a limited volume or set quantity, or of district heating, contracts for digital content which is not supplied on a tangible medium should be classified, for the purpose of this Directive, neither as sales contracts nor as service contracts. For such contracts, the consumer should have a right of withdrawal unless he has consented to the beginning of the performance of the contract during the withdrawal period and has acknowledged that he will consequently lose the right to withdraw from the contract. In addition to the general information requirements, the trader should inform the consumer about the functionality and the relevant interoperability of digital content. The notion of functionality should refer to the ways in which digital content can be used, for instance for the tracking of consumer behaviour; it should also refer to the absence or presence of any technical restrictions such as protection via Digital Rights Management or region coding. The notion of relevant interoperability is meant to describe the information regarding the standard hardware and software environment with which the digital content is compatible, for instance the operating system, the necessary version and certain hardware features. The Commission should examine the need for further harmonisation of provisions in respect of digital content and submit, if necessary, a legislative proposal for addressing this matter.

(20) The definition of distance contract should cover all cases where a contract is concluded between the trader and the consumer under an organised distance sales or service-provision scheme, with the exclusive use of one or more means of distance communication (such as mail order, Internet, telephone or fax) up to and including the time at which the contract is concluded. That definition should also cover situations where the consumer visits the business premises merely for the purpose of gathering information about the goods or services and subsequently negotiates and concludes the contract at a distance. By contrast, a contract which is negotiated at the business premises of the trader and finally concluded by means of distance communication should not be considered a distance contract. Neither should a contract initiated by means of distance communication, but finally concluded at the business premises of the trader be considered a distance contract. Similarly, the concept of distance contract should not include reservations made by a consumer through a means of distance communications to request the provision of a service from a professional, such as in the case of a consumer phoning to request an appointment with a hairdresser. The notion of an organised distance sales or service-provision scheme should include those schemes offered by a third party other than the trader but used by the trader, such as an online platform. It should not, however, cover cases where websites merely offer information on the trader, his goods and/or services and his contact details.

(21) An off-premises contract should be defined as a contract concluded with the simultaneous physical presence of the trader and the consumer, in a place which is not the business premises of the trader, for example at the consumer's home or workplace. In an off-premises context, the consumer may be under potential psychological pressure or may be confronted with an element of surprise, irrespective of whether or not the consumer has solicited the trader's visit. The definition of an off-premises contract should also include situations where the consumer is personally and individually addressed in an off-premises context but the contract is concluded immediately afterwards on the business premises of the trader or through a means of distance communication. The definition of an off-premises contract should not cover situations in which the trader first comes to the consumer's home strictly with a view to taking measurements or giving an estimate without any commitment of the consumer and where the contract is then concluded only at a later point in time on the business premises of the trader or via means of distance communication on the basis of the trader's estimate. In those cases, the contract is not to be considered as having been concluded immediately after the trader has addressed the consumer if the consumer has had time to reflect upon the estimate of the trader before concluding the contract. Purchases made during an excursion organised by the trader during which the products acquired are promoted and offered for sale should be considered as off-premises contracts.

(22) Business premises should include premises in whatever form (such as shops, stalls or lorries) which serve as a permanent or usual place of business for the trader. Market stalls and fair stands should be treated as business premises if they fulfil this condition. Retail premises where the trader carries out his activity on a seasonal basis, for instance during the tourist season at a ski or beach resort, should be considered as business premises as the trader carries out his activity in those premises on a usual basis. Spaces accessible to the public, such as streets, shopping malls, beaches, sports facilities and public transport, which the trader uses on an exceptional basis for his business activities as well as private homes or workplaces should not be regarded as business premises. The business premises of a person acting in the name or on behalf of the trader as defined in this Directive should be considered as business premises within the meaning of this Directive.

(23) Durable media should enable the consumer to store the information for as long as it is necessary for him to protect his interests stemming from his relationship with the trader. Such media

should include in particular paper, USB sticks, CD-ROMs, DVDs, memory cards or the hard disks of computers as well as e-mails.

(24) A public auction implies that traders and consumers attend or are given the possibility to attend the auction in person. The goods or services are offered by the trader to the consumer through a bidding procedure authorised by law in some Member States, to offer goods or services at public sale. The successful bidder is bound to purchase the goods or services. The use of online platforms for auction purposes which are at the disposal of consumers and traders should not be considered as a public auction within the meaning of this Directive.

(25) Contracts related to district heating should be covered by this Directive, similarly to the contracts for the supply of water, gas or electricity. District heating refers to the supply of heat, inter alia, in the form of steam or hot water, from a central source of production through a transmission and distribution system to multiple buildings, for the purpose of heating.

(26) Contracts related to the transfer of immovable property or of rights in immovable property or to the creation or acquisition of such immovable property or rights, contracts for the construction of new buildings or the substantial conversion of existing buildings as well as contracts for the rental of accommodation for residential purposes are already subject to a number of specific requirements in national legislation. Those contracts include for instance sales of immovable property still to be developed and hire-purchase. The provisions of this Directive are not appropriate to those contracts, which should be therefore excluded from its scope. A substantial conversion is a conversion comparable to the construction of a new building, for example where only the façade of an old building is retained. Service contracts in particular those related to the construction of annexes to buildings (for example a garage or a veranda) and those related to repair and renovation of buildings other than substantial conversion, should be included in the scope of this Directive, as well as contracts related to the services of a real estate agent and those related to the rental of accommodation for non-residential purposes.

(27) Transport services cover passenger transport and transport of goods. Passenger transport should be excluded from the scope of this Directive as it is already subject to other Union legislation or, in the case of public transport and taxis, to regulation at national level. However, the provisions of this Directive protecting consumers against excessive fees for the use of means of payment or against hidden costs should apply also to passenger transport contracts. In relation to transport of goods and car rental which are services, consumers should benefit from the protection afforded by this Directive, with the exception of the right of withdrawal.

(28) In order to avoid administrative burden being placed on traders, Member States may decide not to apply this Directive where goods or services of a minor value are sold off-premises. The monetary threshold should be established at a sufficiently low level as to exclude only purchases of small significance. Member States should be allowed to define this value in their national legislation provided that it does not exceed EUR 50. Where two or more contracts with related subjects are concluded at the same time by the consumer, the total cost thereof should be taken into account for the purpose of applying this threshold.

(29) Social services have fundamentally distinct features that are reflected in sector-specific legislation, partially at Union level and partially at national level. Social services include, on the one hand, services for particularly disadvantaged or low income persons as well as services for persons and families in need of assistance in carrying out routine, everyday tasks and, on the other hand, services for all people who have a special need for assistance, support, protection or encouragement in a specific life phase. Social services cover, inter alia, services for children and youth, assistance services for families, single parents and older persons, and services for migrants. Social services cover both short-term and long-term care services, for instance services provided by home care services or provided in assisted living facilities and residential homes or housing ('nursing homes'). Social services include not only those provided by the State at a national, regional or local level by providers mandated by the State or by charities recognised by the State but also those provided by private operators. The provisions of this Directive are not appropriate to social services which should be therefore excluded from its scope.

(30) Healthcare requires special regulations because of its technical complexity, its importance as a service of general interest as well as its extensive public funding. Healthcare is defined in Directive 2011/24/EU of the European Parliament and of the Council of 9 March 2011 on the application of patients' rights in cross-border healthcare[9] as 'health services provided by health professionals to patients to assess, maintain or restore their state of health, including the prescription, dispensation and provision of medicinal products and medical devices'. Health professional is defined in that Directive as a doctor of medicine, a nurse responsible for general care, a dental practitioner, a midwife or a pharmacist within the meaning of Directive 2005/36/EC of the European Parliament and of the Council of 7 September 2005 on the recognition of professional qualifications[10] or another professional exercising activities in the healthcare sector which are restricted to a regulated profession as defined in point (a) of Article 3(1) of Directive 2005/36/EC, or a person considered to be a health professional according to the legislation of the Member State of treatment. The provisions of this Directive are not appropriate to healthcare which should be therefore excluded from its scope.

(31)   Gambling should be excluded from the scope of this Directive. Gambling activities are those which involve wagering at stake with pecuniary value in games of chance, including lotteries, gambling in casinos and betting transactions. Member States should be able to adopt other, including more stringent, consumer protection measures in relation to such activities.

(32)   The existing Union legislation, inter alia, relating to consumer financial services, package travel and timeshare contains numerous rules on consumer protection. For this reason, this Directive should not apply to contracts in those areas. With regard to financial services, Member States should be encouraged to draw inspiration from existing Union legislation in that area when legislating in areas not regulated at Union level, in such a way that a level playing field for all consumers and all contracts relating to financial services is ensured.

(33)   The trader should be obliged to inform the consumer in advance of any arrangement resulting in the consumer paying a deposit to the trader, including an arrangement whereby an amount is blocked on the consumer's credit or debit card.

(34)   The trader should give the consumer clear and comprehensible information before the consumer is bound by a distance or off-premises contract, a contract other than a distance or an off-premises contract, or any corresponding offer. In providing that information, the trader should take into account the specific needs of consumers who are particularly vulnerable because of their mental, physical or psychological infirmity, age or credulity in a way which the trader could reasonably be expected to foresee. However, taking into account such specific needs should not lead to different levels of consumer protection.

(35)   The information to be provided by the trader to the consumer should be mandatory and should not be altered. Nevertheless, the contracting parties should be able to expressly agree to change the content of the contract subsequently concluded, for instance the arrangements for delivery.

(36)   In the case of distance contracts, the information requirements should be adapted to take into account the technical constraints of certain media, such as the restrictions on the number of characters on certain mobile telephone screens or the time constraint on television sales spots. In such cases the trader should comply with a minimum set of information requirements and refer the consumer to another source of information, for instance by providing a toll free telephone number or a hypertext link to a webpage of the trader where the relevant information is directly available and easily accessible. As to the requirement to inform the consumer of the cost of returning goods which by their nature cannot normally be returned by post, it will be considered to have been met, for example, if the trader specifies one carrier (for instance the one he assigned for the delivery of the good) and one price concerning the cost of returning the goods. Where the cost of returning the goods cannot reasonably be calculated in advance by the trader, for example because the trader does not offer to arrange for the return of the goods himself, the trader should provide a statement that such a cost will be payable, and that this cost may be high, along with a reasonable estimation of the maximum cost, which could be based on the cost of delivery to the consumer.

(37)   Since in the case of distance sales, the consumer is not able to see the goods before concluding the contract, he should have a right of withdrawal. For the same reason, the consumer should be allowed to test and inspect the goods he has bought to the extent necessary to establish the nature, characteristics and the functioning of the goods. Concerning off-premises contracts, the consumer should have the right of withdrawal because of the potential surprise element and/or psychological pressure. Withdrawal from the contract should terminate the obligation of the contracting parties to perform the contract.

(38)   Trading websites should indicate clearly and legibly at the latest at the beginning of the ordering process whether any delivery restrictions apply and which means of payment are accepted.

(39)   It is important to ensure for distance contracts concluded through websites that the consumer is able to fully read and understand the main elements of the contract before placing his order. To that end, provision should be made in this Directive for those elements to be displayed in the close vicinity of the confirmation requested for placing the order. It is also important to ensure that, in such situations, the consumer is able to determine the moment at which he assumes the obligation to pay the trader. Therefore, the consumer's attention should specifically be drawn, through an unambiguous formulation, to the fact that placing the order entails the obligation to pay the trader.

(40)   The current varying lengths of the withdrawal periods both between the Member States and for distance and off-premises contracts cause legal uncertainty and compliance costs. The same withdrawal period should apply to all distance and off-premises contracts. In the case of service contracts, the withdrawal period should expire after 14 days from the conclusion of the contract. In the case of sales contracts, the withdrawal period should expire after 14 days from the day on which the consumer or a third party other than the carrier and indicated by the consumer, acquires physical possession of the goods. In addition the consumer should be able to exercise the right to withdraw before acquiring physical possession of the goods. Where multiple goods are ordered by the consumer in one order but are delivered separately, the withdrawal period should expire after 14 days from the day on which the consumer acquires physical possession of the last good. Where goods are delivered in multiple lots or pieces, the withdrawal period should expire after 14 days from the day

on which the consumer acquires the physical possession of the last lot or piece.

(41) In order to ensure legal certainty, it is appropriate that Council Regulation (EEC, Euratom) No 1182/71 of 3 June 1971 determining the rules applicable to periods, dates and time limits[11] should apply to the calculation of the periods contained in this Directive. Therefore, all periods contained in this Directive should be understood to be expressed in calendar days. Where a period expressed in days is to be calculated from the moment at which an event occurs or an action takes place, the day during which that event occurs or that action takes place should not be considered as falling within the period in question.

(42) The provisions relating to the right of withdrawal should be without prejudice to the Member States' laws and regulations governing the termination or unenforceability of a contract or the possibility for the consumer to fulfil his contractual obligations before the time determined in the contract.

(43) If the trader has not adequately informed the consumer prior to the conclusion of a distance or off-premises contract, the withdrawal period should be extended. However, in order to ensure legal certainty as regards the length of the withdrawal period, a 12-month limitation period should be introduced.

(44) Differences in the ways in which the right of withdrawal is exercised in the Member States have caused costs for traders selling cross-border. The introduction of a harmonised model withdrawal form that the consumer may use should simplify the withdrawal process and bring legal certainty. For these reasons, Member States should refrain from adding any presentational requirements to the Union-wide model form relating for example to the font size. However, the consumer should remain free to withdraw in his own words, provided that his statement setting out his decision to withdraw from the contract to the trader is unequivocal. A letter, a telephone call or returning the goods with a clear statement could meet this requirement, but the burden of proof of having withdrawn within the time limits fixed in the Directive should be on the consumer. For this reason, it is in the interest of the consumer to make use of a durable medium when communicating his withdrawal to the trader.

(45) As experience shows that many consumers and traders prefer to communicate via the trader's website, there should be a possibility for the trader to give the consumer the option of filling in a web-based withdrawal form. In this case the trader should provide an acknowledgement of receipt for instance by e-mail without delay.

(46) In the event that the consumer withdraws from the contract, the trader should reimburse all payments received from the consumer, including those covering the expenses borne by the trader to deliver goods to the consumer. The reimbursement should not be made by voucher unless the consumer has used vouchers for the initial transaction or has expressly accepted them. If the consumer expressly chooses a certain type of delivery (for instance 24-hour express delivery), although the trader had offered a common and generally acceptable type of delivery which would have incurred lower delivery costs, the consumer should bear the difference in costs between these two types of delivery.

(47) Some consumers exercise their right of withdrawal after having used the goods to an extent more than necessary to establish the nature, characteristics and the functioning of the goods. In this case the consumer should not lose the right to withdraw but should be liable for any diminished value of the goods. In order to establish the nature, characteristics and functioning of the goods, the consumer should only handle and inspect them in the same manner as he would be allowed to do in a shop. For example, the consumer should only try on a garment and should not be allowed to wear it. Consequently, the consumer should handle and inspect the goods with due care during the withdrawal period. The obligations of the consumer in the event of withdrawal should not discourage the consumer from exercising his right of withdrawal.

(48) The consumer should be required to send back the goods not later than 14 days after having informed the trader about his decision to withdraw from the contract. In situations where the trader or the consumer does not fulfil the obligations relating to the exercise of the right of withdrawal, penalties provided for by national legislation in accordance with this Directive should apply as well as contract law provisions.

(49) Certain exceptions from the right of withdrawal should exist, both for distance and off-premises contracts. A right of withdrawal could be inappropriate for example given the nature of particular goods or services. That is the case for example with wine supplied a long time after the conclusion of a contract of a speculative nature where the value is dependent on fluctuations in the market ('vin en primeur'). The right of withdrawal should neither apply to goods made to the consumer's specifications or which are clearly personalised such as tailor-made curtains, nor to the supply of fuel, for example, which is a good, by nature inseparably mixed with other items after delivery. The granting of a right of withdrawal to the consumer could also be inappropriate in the case of certain services where the conclusion of the contract implies the setting aside of capacity which, if a right of withdrawal were exercised, the trader may find difficult to fill. This would for example be the case where reservations are made at hotels or concerning holiday cottages or cultural or sporting events.

(50)   On the one hand, the consumer should benefit from his right of withdrawal even in case he has asked for the provision of services before the end of the withdrawal period. On the other hand, if the consumer exercises his right of withdrawal, the trader should be assured to be adequately paid for the service he has provided. The calculation of the proportionate amount should be based on the price agreed in the contract unless the consumer demonstrates that that total price is itself disproportionate, in which case the amount to be paid shall be calculated on the basis of the market value of the service provided. The market value should be defined by comparing the price of an equivalent service performed by other traders at the time of the conclusion of the contract. Therefore the consumer should request the performance of services before the end of the withdrawal period by making this request expressly and, in the case of off-premises contracts, on a durable medium. Similarly, the trader should inform the consumer on a durable medium of any obligation to pay the proportionate costs for the services already provided. For contracts having as their object both goods and services, the rules provided for in this Directive on the return of goods should apply to the goods aspects and the compensation regime for services should apply to the services aspects.

(51)   The main difficulties encountered by consumers and one of the main sources of disputes with traders concern delivery of goods, including goods getting lost or damaged during transport and late or partial delivery. Therefore it is appropriate to clarify and harmonise the national rules as to when delivery should occur. The place and modalities of delivery and the rules concerning the determination of the conditions for the transfer of the ownership of the goods and the moment at which such transfer takes place, should remain subject to national law and therefore should not be affected by this Directive. The rules on delivery laid down in this Directive should include the possibility for the consumer to allow a third party to acquire on his behalf the physical possession or control of the goods. The consumer should be considered to have control of the goods where he or a third party indicated by the consumer has access to the goods to use them as an owner, or the ability to resell the goods (for example, when he has received the keys or possession of the ownership documents).

(52)   In the context of sales contracts, the delivery of goods can take place in various ways, either immediately or at a later date. If the parties have not agreed on a specific delivery date, the trader should deliver the goods as soon as possible, but in any event not later than 30 days from the day of the conclusion of the contract. The rules regarding late delivery should also take into account goods to be manufactured or acquired specially for the consumer which cannot be reused by the trader without considerable loss. Therefore, a rule which grants an additional reasonable period of time to the trader in certain circumstances should be provided for in this Directive. When the trader has failed to deliver the goods within the period of time agreed with the consumer, before the consumer can terminate the contract, the consumer should call upon the trader to make the delivery within a reasonable additional period of time and be entitled to terminate the contract if the trader fails to deliver the goods even within that additional period of time. However, this rule should not apply when the trader has refused to deliver the goods in an unequivocal statement. Neither should it apply in certain circumstances where the delivery period is essential such as, for example, in the case of a wedding dress which should be delivered before the wedding. Nor should it apply in circumstances where the consumer informs the trader that delivery on a specified date is essential. For this purpose, the consumer may use the trader's contact details given in accordance with this Directive. In these specific cases, if the trader fails to deliver the goods on time, the consumer should be entitled to terminate the contract immediately after the expiry of the delivery period initially agreed. This Directive should be without prejudice to national provisions on the way the consumer should notify the trader of his will to terminate the contract.

(53)   In addition to the consumer's right to terminate the contract where the trader has failed to fulfil his obligations to deliver the goods in accordance with this Directive, the consumer may, in accordance with the applicable national law, have recourse to other remedies, such as granting the trader an additional period of time for delivery, enforcing the performance of the contract, withholding payment, and seeking damages.

(54)   In accordance with Article 52(3) of Directive 2007/64/EC of the European Parliament and of the Council of 13 November 2007 on payment services in the internal market,[12] Member States should be able to prohibit or limit traders' right to request charges from consumers taking into account the need to encourage competition and promote the use of efficient payment instruments. In any event, traders should be prohibited from charging consumers fees that exceed the cost borne by the trader for the use of a certain means of payment.

(55)   Where the goods are dispatched by the trader to the consumer, disputes may arise, in the event of loss or damage, as to the moment at which the transfer of risk takes place. Therefore this Directive should provide that the consumer be protected against any risk of loss of or damage to the goods occurring before he has acquired the physical possession of the goods. The consumer should be protected during a transport arranged or carried out by the trader, even where the consumer has chosen a particular delivery method from a range of options offered by the trader. However, that provision should not apply to contracts where it is up to the consumer to take delivery of the goods himself or to ask a carrier to take delivery. Regarding the moment of the transfer of the risk, a consumer should be considered to have acquired the physical possession of the goods when he has received them.

(56) Persons or organisations regarded under national law as having a legitimate interest in protecting consumer contractual rights should be afforded the right to initiate proceedings, either before a court or before an administrative authority which is competent to decide upon complaints or to initiate appropriate legal proceedings.

(57) It is necessary that Member States lay down penalties for infringements of this Directive and ensure that they are enforced. The penalties should be effective, proportionate and dissuasive.

(58) The consumer should not be deprived of the protection granted by this Directive. Where the law applicable to the contract is that of a third country, Regulation (EC) No 593/2008 should apply, in order to determine whether the consumer retains the protection granted by this Directive.

(59) The Commission, following consultation with the Member States and stakeholders, should look into the most appropriate way to ensure that all consumers are made aware of their rights at the point of sale.

(60) Since inertia selling, which consists of unsolicited supply of goods or provision of services to consumers, is prohibited by Directive 2005/29/EC of the European Parliament and of the Council of 11 May 2005 concerning unfair business-to-consumer commercial practices in the internal market ('Unfair Commercial Practices Directive')[13] but no contractual remedy is provided therein, it is necessary to introduce in this Directive the contractual remedy of exempting the consumer from the obligation to provide any consideration for such unsolicited supply or provision.

(61) Directive 2002/58/EC of the European Parliament and of the Council of 12 July 2002 concerning the processing of personal data and the protection of privacy in the electronic communications sector (Directive on privacy and electronic communications)[14] already regulates unsolicited communications and provides for a high level of consumer protection. The corresponding provisions on the same issue contained in Directive 97/7/EC are therefore not needed.

(62) It is appropriate for the Commission to review this Directive if some barriers to the internal market are identified. In its review, the Commission should pay particular attention to the possibilities granted to Member States to maintain or introduce specific national provisions including in certain areas of Council Directive 93/13/EEC of 5 April 1993 on unfair terms in consumer contracts[15] and Directive 1999/44/EC of the European Parliament and of the Council of 25 May 1999 on certain aspects of the sale of consumer goods and associated guarantees.[16] That review could lead to a Commission proposal to amend this Directive; that proposal may include amendments to other consumer protection legislation reflecting the Commission's Consumer Policy Strategy commitment to review the Union acquis in order to achieve a high, common level of consumer protection.

(63) Directives 93/13/EEC and 1999/44/EC should be amended to require Member States to inform the Commission about the adoption of specific national provisions in certain areas.

(64) Directives 85/577/EEC and 97/7/EC should be repealed.

(65) Since the objective of this Directive, namely, through the achievement of a high level of consumer protection, to contribute to the proper functioning of the internal market, cannot be sufficiently achieved by the Member States and can therefore be better achieved at Union level, the Union may adopt measures, in accordance with the principle of subsidiarity as set out in Article 5 of the Treaty on European Union. In accordance with the principle of proportionality, as set out in that Article, this Directive does not go beyond what is necessary in order to achieve that objective.

(66) This Directive respects the fundamental rights and observes the principles recognised in particular by the Charter of Fundamental Rights of the European Union.

(67) In accordance with point 34 of the Interinstitutional agreement on better law-making,[17] Member States are encouraged to draw up, for themselves and in the interests of the Union, their own tables, which will, as far as possible, illustrate the correlation between this Directive and the transposition measures, and to make them public,

NOTES

1   OJ C317, 23.12.2009, p 54.

2   OJ C200, 25.8.2009, p. 76.

3   Position of the European Parliament of 23 June 2011 (not yet published in the Official Journal) and decision of the Council of 10 October 2011.

4   OJ L372, 31.12.1985, p 31.

5   OJ L144, 4.6.97, p 19..

6   OJ L177, 4.7.2008, p 6.

7   OJ L 376, 27.12.2006, p 36.

8   OJ L178, 17.7.2000, p 1.

9   OJ L88, 4.4.2011, p 45.

10   OJ L255, 30.9.2005, p 22.

11   OJ L124, 8.6.1971, p 1.

12   OJ L319, 5.12.2007, p 1.

13   OJ L149, 11.6.2005, p 22.

14   OJ L201, 31.7.2002, p 37.

15   OJ L95, 21.4.93, p29..

16   OJ L171, 7.7.99, p 12.

17   OJ C321, 31.12.2003, p 1.

HAVE ADOPTED THIS DIRECTIVE:

CHAPTER I
SUBJECT MATTER, DEFINITIONS AND SCOPE

[4.523]
Article 1
Subject matter

The purpose of this Directive is, through the achievement of a high level of consumer protection, to contribute to the proper functioning of the internal market by approximating certain aspects of the laws, regulations and administrative provisions of the Member States concerning contracts concluded between consumers and traders.

[4.524]
Article 2
Definitions

For the purpose of this Directive, the following definitions shall apply:

(1)   'consumer' means any natural person who, in contracts covered by this Directive, is acting for purposes which are outside his trade, business, craft or profession;

(2)   'trader' means any natural person or any legal person, irrespective of whether privately or publicly owned, who is acting, including through any other person acting in his name or on his behalf, for purposes relating to his trade, business, craft or profession in relation to contracts covered by this Directive;

(3)   'goods' means any tangible movable items, with the exception of items sold by way of execution or otherwise by authority of law; water, gas and electricity shall be considered as goods within the meaning of this Directive where they are put up for sale in a limited volume or a set quantity;

(4)   'goods made to the consumer's specifications' means non-prefabricated goods made on the basis of an individual choice of or decision by the consumer;

(5)   'sales contract' means any contract under which the trader transfers or undertakes to transfer the ownership of goods to the consumer and the consumer pays or undertakes to pay the price thereof, including any contract having as its object both goods and services;

(6)   'service contract' means any contract other than a sales contract under which the trader supplies or undertakes to supply a service to the consumer and the consumer pays or undertakes to pay the price thereof;

(7)   'distance contract' means any contract concluded between the trader and the consumer under an organised distance sales or service-provision scheme without the simultaneous physical presence of the trader and the consumer, with the exclusive use of one or more means of distance communication up to and including the time at which the contract is concluded;

(8)   'off-premises contract' means any contract between the trader and the consumer:

    (a)   concluded in the simultaneous physical presence of the trader and the consumer, in a place which is not the business premises of the trader;

    (b)   for which an offer was made by the consumer in the same circumstances as referred to in point (a);

    (c)   concluded on the business premises of the trader or through any means of distance communication immediately after the consumer was personally and individually addressed in a place which is not the business premises of the trader in the simultaneous physical presence of the trader and the consumer; or

    (d)   concluded during an excursion organised by the trader with the aim or effect of promoting and selling goods or services to the consumer;

(9)   'business premises' means:

    (a)   any immovable retail premises where the trader carries out his activity on a permanent basis; or

    (b)   any movable retail premises where the trader carries out his activity on a usual basis;

(10) 'durable medium' means any instrument which enables the consumer or the trader to store information addressed personally to him in a way accessible for future reference for a period of time adequate for the purposes of the information and which allows the unchanged reproduction of the information stored;

(11) 'digital content' means data which are produced and supplied in digital form;

(12) 'financial service' means any service of a banking, credit, insurance, personal pension, investment or payment nature;

(13) 'public auction' means a method of sale where goods or services are offered by the trader to consumers, who attend or are given the possibility to attend the auction in person, through a transparent, competitive bidding procedure run by an auctioneer and where the successful bidder is bound to purchase the goods or services;

(14) 'commercial guarantee' means any undertaking by the trader or a producer (the guarantor) to the consumer, in addition to his legal obligation relating to the guarantee of conformity, to reimburse the price paid or to replace, repair or service goods in any way if they do not meet the specifications or any other requirements not related to conformity set out in the guarantee statement or in the relevant advertising available at the time of, or before the conclusion of the contract;

(15) 'ancillary contract' means a contract by which the consumer acquires goods or services related to a distance contract or an off-premises contract and where those goods are supplied or those services are provided by the trader or by a third party on the basis of an arrangement between that third party and the trader.

[4.525]
Article 3
Definitions
(1) This Directive shall apply, under the conditions and to the extent set out in its provisions, to any contract concluded between a trader and a consumer. It shall also apply to contracts for the supply of water, gas, electricity or district heating, including by public providers, to the extent that these commodities are provided on a contractual basis.

(2) If any provision of this Directive conflicts with a provision of another Union act governing specific sectors, the provision of that other Union act shall prevail and shall apply to those specific sectors.

(3) This Directive shall not apply to contracts:
    (a) for social services, including social housing, childcare and support of families and persons permanently or temporarily in need, including long-term care;
    (b) for healthcare as defined in point (a) of Article 3 of Directive 2011/24/EU, whether or not they are provided via healthcare facilities;
    (c) for gambling, which involves wagering a stake with pecuniary value in games of chance, including lotteries, casino games and betting transactions;
    (d) for financial services;
    (e) for the creation, acquisition or transfer of immovable property or of rights in immovable property;
    (f) for the construction of new buildings, the substantial conversion of existing buildings and for rental of accommodation for residential purposes;
    (g) which fall within the scope of Council Directive 90/314/EEC of 13 June 1990 on package travel, package holidays and package tours;[1]
    (h) which fall within the scope of Directive 2008/122/EC of the European Parliament and of the Council of 14 January 2009 on the protection of consumers in respect of certain aspects of timeshare, long-term holiday product, resale and exchange contracts;[2]
    (i) which, in accordance with the laws of Member States, are established by a public office-holder who has a statutory obligation to be independent and impartial and who must ensure, by providing comprehensive legal information, that the consumer only concludes the contract on the basis of careful legal consideration and with knowledge of its legal scope;
    (j) for the supply of foodstuffs, beverages or other goods intended for current consumption in the household, and which are physically supplied by a trader on frequent and regular rounds to the consumer's home, residence or workplace;
    (k) for passenger transport services, with the exception of Article 8(2) and Articles 19 and 22;
    (l) concluded by means of automatic vending machines or automated commercial premises;
    (m) concluded with telecommunications operators through public payphones for their use or concluded for the use of one single connection by telephone, Internet or fax established by a consumer.

(4) Member States may decide not to apply this Directive or not to maintain or introduce corresponding national provisions to off-premises contracts for which the payment to be made by the consumer does not exceed EUR 50. Member States may define a lower value in their national legislation.

(5) This Directive shall not affect national general contract law such as the rules on the validity, formation or effect of a contract, in so far as general contract law aspects are not regulated in this Directive.

(6) This Directive shall not prevent traders from offering consumers contractual arrangements which go beyond the protection provided for in this Directive.

NOTES
[1]   OJ L158, 23.6.1990, p 59.
[2]   OJ L33, 3.2.2009, p 10.

[4.526]
Article 4
Level of harmonisation
Member States shall not maintain or introduce, in their national law, provisions diverging from those laid down in this Directive, including more or less stringent provisions to ensure a different level of consumer protection, unless otherwise provided for in this Directive.

CHAPTER II
CONSUMER INFORMATION FOR CONTRACTS OTHER THAN DISTANCE OR OFF-PREMISES CONTRACTS

[4.527]
Article 5
Information requirements for contracts other than distance or off-premises contracts
1.   Before the consumer is bound by a contract other than a distance or an off-premises contract, or any corresponding offer, the trader shall provide the consumer with the following information in a clear and comprehensible manner, if that information is not already apparent from the context:
-   (a)   the main characteristics of the goods or services, to the extent appropriate to the medium and to the goods or services;
-   (b)   the identity of the trader, such as his trading name, the geographical address at which he is established and his telephone number;
-   (c)   the total price of the goods or services inclusive of taxes, or where the nature of the goods or services is such that the price cannot reasonably be calculated in advance, the manner in which the price is to be calculated, as well as, where applicable, all additional freight, delivery or postal charges or, where those charges cannot reasonably be calculated in advance, the fact that such additional charges may be payable;
-   (d)   where applicable, the arrangements for payment, delivery, performance, the time by which the trader undertakes to deliver the goods or to perform the service, and the trader's complaint handling policy;
-   (e)   in addition to a reminder of the existence of a legal guarantee of conformity for goods, the existence and the conditions of after-sales services and commercial guarantees, where applicable;
-   (f)   the duration of the contract, where applicable, or, if the contract is of indeterminate duration or is to be extended automatically, the conditions for terminating the contract;
-   (g)   where applicable, the functionality, including applicable technical protection measures, of digital content;
-   (h)   where applicable, any relevant interoperability of digital content with hardware and software that the trader is aware of or can reasonably be expected to have been aware of.
2.   Paragraph 1 shall also apply to contracts for the supply of water, gas or electricity, where they are not put up for sale in a limited volume or set quantity, of district heating or of digital content which is not supplied on a tangible medium.
3.   Member States shall not be required to apply paragraph 1 to contracts which involve day-to-day transactions and which are performed immediately at the time of their conclusion.
4.   Member States may adopt or maintain additional pre-contractual information requirements for contracts to which this Article applies.

CHAPTER III
CONSUMER INFORMATION AND RIGHT OF WITHDRAWAL FOR DISTANCE OR OFF-PREMISES CONTRACTS

[4.528]
Article 6
Information requirements for distance and off-premises contracts
1.   Before the consumer is bound by a distance or off-premises contract, or any corresponding offer, the trader shall provide the consumer with the following information in a clear and comprehensible manner:
-   (a)   the main characteristics of the goods or services, to the extent appropriate to the medium and to the goods or services;
-   (b)   the identity of the trader, such as his trading name;
-   (c)   the geographical address at which the trader is established and the trader's telephone number, fax number and e-mail address, where available, to enable the consumer to contact the trader quickly and communicate with him efficiently and, where applicable, the geographical address and identity of the trader on whose behalf he is acting;
-   (d)   if different from the address provided in accordance with point (c), the geographical address of the place of business of the trader, and, where applicable, that of the trader on whose behalf he is acting, where the consumer can address any complaints;
-   (e)   the total price of the goods or services inclusive of taxes, or where the nature of the goods or services is such that the price cannot reasonably be calculated in advance, the manner in which the price is to be calculated, as well as, where applicable, all additional freight,

delivery or postal charges and any other costs or, where those charges cannot reasonably be calculated in advance, the fact that such additional charges may be payable. In the case of a contract of indeterminate duration or a contract containing a subscription, the total price shall include the total costs per billing period. Where such contracts are charged at a fixed rate, the total price shall also mean the total monthly costs. Where the total costs cannot be reasonably calculated in advance, the manner in which the price is to be calculated shall be provided;

(f)   the cost of using the means of distance communication for the conclusion of the contract where that cost is calculated other than at the basic rate;

(g)   the arrangements for payment, delivery, performance, the time by which the trader undertakes to deliver the goods or to perform the services and, where applicable, the trader's complaint handling policy;

(h)   where a right of withdrawal exists, the conditions, time limit and procedures for exercising that right in accordance with Article 11(1), as well as the model withdrawal form set out in Annex I(B);

(i)   where applicable, that the consumer will have to bear the cost of returning the goods in case of withdrawal and, for distance contracts, if the goods, by their nature, cannot normally be returned by post, the cost of returning the goods;

(j)   that, if the consumer exercises the right of withdrawal after having made a request in accordance with Article 7(3) or Article 8(8), the consumer shall be liable to pay the trader reasonable costs in accordance with Article 14(3);

(k)   where a right of withdrawal is not provided for in accordance with Article 16, the information that the consumer will not benefit from a right of withdrawal or, where applicable, the circumstances under which the consumer loses his right of withdrawal;

(l)   a reminder of the existence of a legal guarantee of conformity for goods;

(m)   where applicable, the existence and the conditions of after sale customer assistance, after-sales services and commercial guarantees;

(n)   the existence of relevant codes of conduct, as defined in point (f) of Article 2 of Directive 2005/29/EC, and how copies of them can be obtained, where applicable;

(o)   the duration of the contract, where applicable, or, if the contract is of indeterminate duration or is to be extended automatically, the conditions for terminating the contract;

(p)   where applicable, the minimum duration of the consumer's obligations under the contract;

(q)   where applicable, the existence and the conditions of deposits or other financial guarantees to be paid or provided by the consumer at the request of the trader;

(r)   where applicable, the functionality, including applicable technical protection measures, of digital content;

(s)   where applicable, any relevant interoperability of digital content with hardware and software that the trader is aware of or can reasonably be expected to have been aware of;

(t)   where applicable, the possibility of having recourse to an out-of-court complaint and redress mechanism, to which the trader is subject, and the methods for having access to it.

2.   Paragraph 1 shall also apply to contracts for the supply of water, gas or electricity, where they are not put up for sale in a limited volume or set quantity, of district heating or of digital content which is not supplied on a tangible medium.

3.   In the case of a public auction, the information referred to in points (b), (c) and (d) of paragraph 1 may be replaced by the equivalent details for the auctioneer.

4.   The information referred to in points (h), (i) and (j) of paragraph 1 may be provided by means of the model instructions on withdrawal set out in Annex I(A). The trader shall have fulfilled the information requirements laid down in points (h), (i) and (j) of paragraph 1 if he has supplied these instructions to the consumer, correctly filled in.

5.   The information referred to in paragraph 1 shall form an integral part of the distance or off-premises contract and shall not be altered unless the contracting parties expressly agree otherwise.

6.   If the trader has not complied with the information requirements on additional charges or other costs as referred to in point (e) of paragraph 1, or on the costs of returning the goods as referred to in point (i) of paragraph 1, the consumer shall not bear those charges or costs.

7.   Member States may maintain or introduce in their national law language requirements regarding the contractual information, so as to ensure that such information is easily understood by the consumer.

8.   The information requirements laid down in this Directive are in addition to information requirements contained in Directive 2006/123/EC and Directive 2000/31/EC and do not prevent Member States from imposing additional information requirements in accordance with those Directives.

Without prejudice to the first subparagraph, if a provision of Directive 2006/123/EC or Directive 2000/31/EC on the content and the manner in which the information is to be provided conflicts with a provision of this Directive, the provision of this Directive shall prevail.

9.   As regards compliance with the information requirements laid down in this Chapter, the burden of proof shall be on the trader.

Part 4   Other Materials

[4.529]
Article 7
Formal requirements for off-premises contracts
1.   With respect to off-premises contracts, the trader shall give the information provided for in Article 6(1) to the consumer on paper or, if the consumer agrees, on another durable medium. That information shall be legible and in plain, intelligible language.
2.   The trader shall provide the consumer with a copy of the signed contract or the confirmation of the contract on paper or, if the consumer agrees, on another durable medium, including, where applicable, the confirmation of the consumer's prior express consent and acknowledgement in accordance with point (m) of Article 16.
3.   Where a consumer wants the performance of services or the supply of water, gas or electricity, where they are not put up for sale in a limited volume or set quantity, or of district heating to begin during the withdrawal period provided for in Article 9(2), the trader shall require that the consumer makes such an express request on a durable medium.
4.   With respect to off-premises contracts where the consumer has explicitly requested the services of the trader for the purpose of carrying out repairs or maintenance for which the trader and the consumer immediately perform their contractual obligations and where the payment to be made by the consumer does not exceed EUR 200:
   (a)   the trader shall provide the consumer with the information referred to in points (b) and (c) of Article 6(1) and information about the price or the manner in which the price is to be calculated together with an estimate of the total price, on paper or, if the consumer agrees, on another durable medium. The trader shall provide the information referred to in points (a), (h) and (k) of Article 6(1), but may choose not to provide it on paper or another durable medium if the consumer expressly agrees;
   (b)   the confirmation of the contract provided in accordance with paragraph 2 of this Article shall contain the information provided for in Article 6(1).
Member States may decide not to apply this paragraph.
5.   Member States shall not impose any further formal pre-contractual information requirements for the fulfilment of the information obligations laid down in this Directive.

[4.530]
Article 8
Formal requirements for distance contracts
1.   With respect to distance contracts, the trader shall give the information provided for in Article 6(1) or make that information available to the consumer in a way appropriate to the means of distance communication used in plain and intelligible language. In so far as that information is provided on a durable medium, it shall be legible.
2.   If a distance contract to be concluded by electronic means places the consumer under an obligation to pay, the trader shall make the consumer aware in a clear and prominent manner, and directly before the consumer places his order, of the information provided for in points (a), (e), (o) and (p) of Article 6(1).
The trader shall ensure that the consumer, when placing his order, explicitly acknowledges that the order implies an obligation to pay. If placing an order entails activating a button or a similar function, the button or similar function shall be labelled in an easily legible manner only with the words "order with obligation to pay" or a corresponding unambiguous formulation indicating that placing the order entails an obligation to pay the trader. If the trader has not complied with this subparagraph, the consumer shall not be bound by the contract or order.
3.   Trading websites shall indicate clearly and legibly at the latest at the beginning of the ordering process whether any delivery restrictions apply and which means of payment are accepted.
4.   If the contract is concluded through a means of distance communication which allows limited space or time to display the information, the trader shall provide, on that particular means prior to the conclusion of such a contract, at least the pre-contractual information regarding the main characteristics of the goods or services, the identity of the trader, the total price, the right of withdrawal, the duration of the contract and, if the contract is of indeterminate duration, the conditions for terminating the contract, as referred to in points (a), (b), (e), (h) and (o) of Article 6(1). The other information referred to in Article 6(1) shall be provided by the trader to the consumer in an appropriate way in accordance with paragraph 1 of this Article.
5.   Without prejudice to paragraph 4, if the trader makes a telephone call to the consumer with a view to concluding a distance contract, he shall, at the beginning of the conversation with the consumer, disclose his identity and, where applicable, the identity of the person on whose behalf he makes that call, and the commercial purpose of the call.
6.   Where a distance contract is to be concluded by telephone, Member States may provide that the trader has to confirm the offer to the consumer who is bound only once he has signed the offer or has sent his written consent. Member States may also provide that such confirmations have to be made on a durable medium.
7.   The trader shall provide the consumer with the confirmation of the contract concluded, on a durable medium within a reasonable time after the conclusion of the distance contract, and at the latest at the time of the delivery of the goods or before the performance of the service begins. That confirmation shall include:

(a)   all the information referred to in Article 6(1) unless the trader has already provided that information to the consumer on a durable medium prior to the conclusion of the distance contract; and

(b)   where applicable, the confirmation of the consumer's prior express consent and acknowledgment in accordance with point (m) of Article 16.

8.   Where a consumer wants the performance of services, or the supply of water, gas or electricity, where they are not put up for sale in a limited volume or set quantity, or of district heating, to begin during the withdrawal period provided for in Article 9(2), the trader shall require that the consumer make an express request.

9.   This Article shall be without prejudice to the provisions on the conclusion of e-contracts and the placing of e-orders set out in Articles 9 and 11 of Directive 2000/31/EC.

10.   Member States shall not impose any further formal pre-contractual information requirements for the fulfilment of the information obligations laid down in this Directive.

[4.531]
Article 9
Right of withdrawal

1.   Save where the exceptions provided for in Article 16 apply, the consumer shall have a period of 14 days to withdraw from a distance or off-premises contract, without giving any reason, and without incurring any costs other than those provided for in Article 13(2) and Article 14.

2.   Without prejudice to Article 10, the withdrawal period referred to in paragraph 1 of this Article shall expire after 14 days from:

(a)   in the case of service contracts, the day of the conclusion of the contract;

(b)   in the case of sales contracts, the day on which the consumer or a third party other than the carrier and indicated by the consumer acquires physical possession of the goods or:

     (i)   in the case of multiple goods ordered by the consumer in one order and delivered separately, the day on which the consumer or a third party other than the carrier and indicated by the consumer acquires physical possession of the last good;

     (ii)   in the case of delivery of a good consisting of multiple lots or pieces, the day on which the consumer or a third party other than the carrier and indicated by the consumer acquires physical possession of the last lot or piece;

     (iii)   in the case of contracts for regular delivery of goods during defined period of time, the day on which the consumer or a third party other than the carrier and indicated by the consumer acquires physical possession of the first good;

(c)   in the case of contracts for the supply of water, gas or electricity, where they are not put up for sale in a limited volume or set quantity, of district heating or of digital content which is not supplied on a tangible medium, the day of the conclusion of the contract.

3.   The Member States shall not prohibit the contracting parties from performing their contractual obligations during the withdrawal period. Nevertheless, in the case of off-premises contracts, Member States may maintain existing national legislation prohibiting the trader from collecting the payment from the consumer during the given period after the conclusion of the contract.

[4.532]
Article 10
Omission of information on the right of withdrawal

1.   If the trader has not provided the consumer with the information on the right of withdrawal as required by point (h) of Article 6(1), the withdrawal period shall expire 12 months from the end of the initial withdrawal period, as determined in accordance with Article 9(2).

2.   If the trader has provided the consumer with the information provided for in paragraph 1 of this Article within 12 months from the day referred to in Article 9(2), the withdrawal period shall expire 14 days after the day upon which the consumer receives that information.

[4.533]
Article 11
Exercise of the right of withdrawal

1.   Before the expiry of the withdrawal period, the consumer shall inform the trader of his decision to withdraw from the contract. For this purpose, the consumer may either:

(a)   use the model withdrawal form as set out in Annex I(B); or

(b)   make any other unequivocal statement setting out his decision to withdraw from the contract.

Member States shall not provide for any formal requirements applicable to the model withdrawal form other than those set out in Annex I(B).

2.   The consumer shall have exercised his right of withdrawal within the withdrawal period referred to in Article 9(2) and Article 10 if the communication concerning the exercise of the right of withdrawal is sent by the consumer before that period has expired.

3.   The trader may, in addition to the possibilities referred to in paragraph 1, give the option to the consumer to electronically fill in and submit either the model withdrawal form set out in Annex I(B) or any other unequivocal statement on the trader's website. In those cases the trader shall communicate to the consumer an acknowledgement of receipt of such a withdrawal on a durable medium without delay.

4.   The burden of proof of exercising the right of withdrawal in accordance with this Article shall be on the consumer.

[4.534]
Article 12
Effects of withdrawal
The exercise of the right of withdrawal shall terminate the obligations of the parties:
   (a)   to perform the distance or off-premises contract; or
   (b)   to conclude the distance or off-premises contract, in cases where an offer was made by the consumer.

[4.535]
Article 13
Obligations of the trader in the event of withdrawal
1.   The trader shall reimburse all payments received from the consumer, including, if applicable, the costs of delivery without undue delay and in any event not later than 14 days from the day on which he is informed of the consumer's decision to withdraw from the contract in accordance with Article 11.
The trader shall carry out the reimbursement referred to in the first subparagraph using the same means of payment as the consumer used for the initial transaction, unless the consumer has expressly agreed otherwise and provided that the consumer does not incur any fees as a result of such reimbursement.
2.   Notwithstanding paragraph 1, the trader shall not be required to reimburse the supplementary costs, if the consumer has expressly opted for a type of delivery other than the least expensive type of standard delivery offered by the trader.
3.   Unless the trader has offered to collect the goods himself, with regard to sales contracts, the trader may withhold the reimbursement until he has received the goods back, or until the consumer has supplied evidence of having sent back the goods, whichever is the earliest.

[4.536]
Article 14
Obligations of the consumer in the event of withdrawal
1.   Unless the trader has offered to collect the goods himself, the consumer shall send back the goods or hand them over to the trader or to a person authorised by the trader to receive the goods, without undue delay and in any event not later than 14 days from the day on which he has communicated his decision to withdraw from the contract to the trader in accordance with Article 11. The deadline shall be met if the consumer sends back the goods before the period of 14 days has expired.
The consumer shall only bear the direct cost of returning the goods unless the trader has agreed to bear them or the trader failed to inform the consumer that the consumer has to bear them.
In the case of off-premises contracts where the goods have been delivered to the consumer's home at the time of the conclusion of the contract, the trader shall at his own expense collect the goods if, by their nature, those goods cannot normally be returned by post.
2.   The consumer shall only be liable for any diminished value of the goods resulting from the handling of the goods other than what is necessary to establish the nature, characteristics and functioning of the goods. The consumer shall in any event not be liable for diminished value of the goods where the trader has failed to provide notice of the right of withdrawal in accordance with point (h) of Article 6(1).
3.   Where a consumer exercises the right of withdrawal after having made a request in accordance with Article 7(3) or Article 8(8), the consumer shall pay to the trader an amount which is in proportion to what has been provided until the time the consumer has informed the trader of the exercise of the right of withdrawal, in comparison with the full coverage of the contract. The proportionate amount to be paid by the consumer to the trader shall be calculated on the basis of the total price agreed in the contract. If the total price is excessive, the proportionate amount shall be calculated on the basis of the market value of what has been provided.
4.   The consumer shall bear no cost for:
   (a)   the performance of services or the supply of water, gas or electricity, where they are not put up for sale in a limited volume or set quantity, or of district heating, in full or in part, during the withdrawal period, where:
      (i)   the trader has failed to provide information in accordance with points (h) or (j) of Article 6(1); or
      (ii)   the consumer has not expressly requested performance to begin during the withdrawal period in accordance with Article 7(3) and Article 8(8); or

   (b)   the supply, in full or in part, of digital content which is not supplied on a tangible medium where:

      (i)   the consumer has not given his prior express consent to the beginning of the performance before the end of the 14-day period referred to in Article 9;

      (ii)   the consumer has not acknowledged that he loses his right of withdrawal when giving his consent; or

      (iii)   the trader has failed to provide confirmation in accordance with Article 7(2) or Article 8(7).

5.   Except as provided for in Article 13(2) and in this Article, the consumer shall not incur any liability as a consequence of the exercise of the right of withdrawal.

[4.537]
Article 15
Effects of the exercise of the right of withdrawal on ancillary contracts

1.   Without prejudice to Article 15 of Directive 2008/48/EC of the European Parliament and of the Council of 23 April 2008 on credit agreements for consumers,[1] if the consumer exercises his right of withdrawal from a distance or an off-premises contract in accordance with Articles 9 to 14 of this Directive, any ancillary contracts shall be automatically terminated, without any costs for the consumer, except as provided for in Article 13(2) and in Article 14 of this Directive.

2.   The Member States shall lay down detailed rules on the termination of such contracts.

NOTES
[1]   OJ L133, 22.5.2008, p 66.

[4.538]
Article 16
Exceptions from the right of withdrawal

Member States shall not provide for the right of withdrawal set out in Articles 9 to 15 in respect of distance and off-premises contracts as regards the following:

   (a)   service contracts after the service has been fully performed if the performance has begun with the consumer's prior express consent, and with the acknowledgement that he will lose his right of withdrawal once the contract has been fully performed by the trader;

   (b)   the supply of goods or services for which the price is dependent on fluctuations in the financial market which cannot be controlled by the trader and which may occur within the withdrawal period;

   (c)   the supply of goods made to the consumer's specifications or clearly personalised;

   (d)   the supply of goods which are liable to deteriorate or expire rapidly;

   (e)   the supply of sealed goods which are not suitable for return due to health protection or hygiene reasons and were unsealed after delivery;

   (f)   the supply of goods which are, after delivery, according to their nature, inseparably mixed with other items;

   (g)   the supply of alcoholic beverages, the price of which has been agreed upon at the time of the conclusion of the sales contract, the delivery of which can only take place after 30 days and the actual value of which is dependent on fluctuations in the market which cannot be controlled by the trader;

   (h)   contracts where the consumer has specifically requested a visit from the trader for the purpose of carrying out urgent repairs or maintenance. If, on the occasion of such visit, the trader provides services in addition to those specifically requested by the consumer or goods other than replacement parts necessarily used in carrying out the maintenance or in making the repairs, the right of withdrawal shall apply to those additional services or goods;

   (i)   the supply of sealed audio or sealed video recordings or sealed computer software which were unsealed after delivery;

   (j)   the supply of a newspaper, periodical or magazine with the exception of subscription contracts for the supply of such publications;

   (k)   contracts concluded at a public auction;

   (l)   the provision of accommodation other than for residential purpose, transport of goods, car rental services, catering or services related to leisure activities if the contract provides for a specific date or period of performance;

   (m)   the supply of digital content which is not supplied on a tangible medium if the performance has begun with the consumer's prior express consent and his acknowledgment that he thereby loses his right of withdrawal.

CHAPTER IV
OTHER CONSUMER RIGHTS

[4.539]
Article 17
Scope

1.   Articles 18 and 20 shall apply to sales contracts. Those Articles shall not apply to contracts for the supply of water, gas or electricity, where they are not put up for sale in a limited volume or set quantity, of district heating or the supply of digital content which is not supplied on a tangible medium.

2.   Articles 19, 21 and 22 shall apply to sales and service contracts and to contracts for the supply of water, gas, electricity, district heating or digital content.

[4.540]
Article 18
Delivery

1.   Unless the parties have agreed otherwise on the time of delivery, the trader shall deliver the goods by transferring the physical possession or control of the goods to the consumer without undue delay, but not later than 30 days from the conclusion of the contract.

2.   Where the trader has failed to fulfil his obligation to deliver the goods at the time agreed upon with the consumer or within the time limit set out in paragraph 1, the consumer shall call upon him to make the delivery within an additional period of time appropriate to the circumstances. If the trader fails to deliver the goods within that additional period of time, the consumer shall be entitled to terminate the contract.

The first subparagraph shall not be applicable to sales contracts where the trader has refused to deliver the goods or where delivery within the agreed delivery period is essential taking into account all the circumstances attending the conclusion of the contract or where the consumer informs the trader, prior to the conclusion of the contract, that delivery by or on a specified date is essential. In those cases, if the trader fails to deliver the goods at the time agreed upon with the consumer or within the time limit set out in paragraph 1, the consumer shall be entitled to terminate the contract immediately.

3.   Upon termination of the contract, the trader shall, without undue delay, reimburse all sums paid under the contract.

4.   In addition to the termination of the contract in accordance with paragraph 2, the consumer may have recourse to other remedies provided for by national law.

[4.541]
Article 19
Fees for the use of means of payment

Member States shall prohibit traders from charging consumers, in respect of the use of a given means of payment, fees that exceed the cost borne by the trader for the use of such means.

[4.542]
Article 20
Passing of risk

In contracts where the trader dispatches the goods to the consumer, the risk of loss of or damage to the goods shall pass to the consumer when he or a third party indicated by the consumer and other than the carrier has acquired the physical possession of the goods. However, the risk shall pass to the consumer upon delivery to the carrier if the carrier was commissioned by the consumer to carry the goods and that choice was not offered by the trader, without prejudice to the rights of the consumer against the carrier.

[4.543]
Article 21
Communication by telephone

Member States shall ensure that where the trader operates a telephone line for the purpose of contacting him by telephone in relation to the contract concluded, the consumer, when contacting the trader is not bound to pay more than the basic rate.

The first subparagraph shall be without prejudice to the right of telecommunication services providers to charge for such calls.

[4.544]
Article 22
Additional payments

Before the consumer is bound by the contract or offer, the trader shall seek the express consent of the consumer to any extra payment in addition to the remuneration agreed upon for the trader's main contractual obligation. If the trader has not obtained the consumer's express consent but has inferred it by using default options which the consumer is required to reject in order to avoid the additional payment, the consumer shall be entitled to reimbursement of this payment.

CHAPTER V
GENERAL PROVISIONS

[4.545]
Article 23
Enforcement

1. Member States shall ensure that adequate and effective means exist to ensure compliance with this Directive.

2. The means referred to in paragraph 1 shall include provisions whereby one or more of the following bodies, as determined by national law, may take action under national law before the courts or before the competent administrative bodies to ensure that the national provisions transposing this Directive are applied:

   (a)   public bodies or their representatives;

   (b)   consumer organisations having a legitimate interest in protecting consumers;

   (c)   professional organisations having a legitimate interest in acting.

[4.546]
Article 24
Penalties

1. Member States shall lay down the rules on penalties applicable to infringements of the national provisions adopted pursuant to this Directive and shall take all measures necessary to ensure that they are implemented. The penalties provided for must be effective, proportionate and dissuasive.

2. Member States shall notify those provisions to the Commission by 13 December 2013 and shall notify it without delay of any subsequent amendment affecting them.

[4.547]
Article 25
Imperative nature of the Directive

If the law applicable to the contract is the law of a Member State, consumers may not waive the rights conferred on them by the national measures transposing this Directive.

Any contractual terms which directly or indirectly waive or restrict the rights resulting from this Directive shall not be binding on the consumer.

[4.548]
Article 26
Information

Member States shall take appropriate measures to inform consumers and traders of the national provisions transposing this Directive and shall, where appropriate, encourage traders and code owners as defined in point (g) of Article 2 of Directive 2005/29/EC, to inform consumers of their codes of conduct.

[4.549]
Article 27
Inertia selling

The consumer shall be exempted from the obligation to provide any consideration in cases of unsolicited supply of goods, water, gas, electricity, district heating or digital content or unsolicited provision of services, prohibited by Article 5(5) and point 29 of Annex I to Directive 2005/29/EC. In such cases, the absence of a response from the consumer following such an unsolicited supply or provision shall not constitute consent.

[4.550]
Article 28
Transposition

1. Member States shall adopt and publish, by 13 December 2013, the laws, regulations and administrative provisions necessary to comply with this Directive. They shall forthwith communicate to the Commission the text of these measures in the form of documents. The Commission shall make use of these documents for the purposes of the report referred to in Article 30.

They shall apply those measures from 13 June 2014.

When Member States adopt those measures, they shall contain a reference to this Directive or be accompanied by such a reference on the occasion of their official publication. Member States shall determine how such reference is to be made.

2. The provisions of this Directive shall apply to contracts concluded after 13 June 2014.

[4.551]
Article 29
Reporting requirements

1. Where a Member State makes use of any of the regulatory choices referred to in Article 3(4), Article 6(7), Article 6(8), Article 7(4), Article 8(6) and Article 9(3), it shall inform the Commission thereof by 13 December 2013, as well as of any subsequent changes.

2. The Commission shall ensure that the information referred to in paragraph 1 is easily accessible to consumers and traders, inter alia, on a dedicated website.

3. The Commission shall forward the information referred to in paragraph 1 to the other Member States and the European Parliament. The Commission shall consult stakeholders on that information.

[4.552]
Article 30
Reporting by the Commission and review
By 13 December 2016, the Commission shall submit a report on the application of this Directive to the European Parliament and the Council. That report shall include in particular an evaluation of the provisions of this Directive regarding digital content including the right of withdrawal. The report shall be accompanied, where necessary, by legislative proposals to adapt this Directive to developments in the field of consumer rights.

CHAPTER VI
FINAL PROVISIONS

[4.553]
Article 31
Repeals
Directive 85/577/EEC and Directive 97/7/EC, as amended by Directive 2002/65/EC of the European Parliament and of the Council of 23 September 2002 concerning the distance marketing of consumer financial services[1] and by Directives 2005/29/EC and 2007/64/EC, are repealed as of 13 June 2014.

References to the repealed Directives shall be construed as references to this Directive and shall be read in accordance with the correlation table set out in Annex II.

NOTES
[1]   OJ L271, 9.10.2006, p 16.

Articles 32, 33   *(Art 32 inserts Directive 93/13/EEC, Art 8a at* **[4.230]***; Art 33 inserts Directive 1999/44/EC, Art 8a at* **[4.259]***.)*

[4.554]
Article 34
Entry into force
This Directive shall enter into force on the 20th day following its publication in the *Official Journal of the European Union.*

[4.555]
Article 35
Addresses
This Directive is addressed to the Member States.

ANNEX I
INFORMATION CONCERNING THE EXERCISE OF THE RIGHT OF WITHDRAWAL
[4.556]

A.   MODEL INSTRUCTIONS ON WITHDRAWAL

RIGHT OF WITHDRAWAL

You have the right to withdraw from this contract within 14 days without giving any reason.

The withdrawal period will expire after 14 days from the day [1].

To exercise the right of withdrawal, you must inform us [2] of your decision to withdraw from this contract by an unequivocal statement (e.g. a letter sent by post, fax or e-mail). You may use the attached model withdrawal form, but it is not obligatory. [3]

To meet the withdrawal deadline, it is sufficient for you to send your communication concerning your exercise of the right of withdrawal before the withdrawal period has expired.

EFFECTS OF WITHDRAWAL

If you withdraw from this contract, we shall reimburse to you all payments received from you, including the costs of delivery (with the exception of the supplementary costs resulting from your choice of a type of delivery other than the least expensive type of standard delivery offered by us), without undue delay and in any event not later than 14 days from the day on which we are informed about your decision to withdraw from this contract. We will carry out such reimbursement using the same means of payment as you used for the initial transaction, unless you have expressly agreed otherwise; in any event, you will not incur any fees as a result of such reimbursement. [4]

[5]

[6]

Instructions for completion:

[1.]   Insert one of the following texts between inverted commas:

    (a)   in the case of a service contract or a contract for the supply of water, gas or electricity, where they are not put up for sale in a limited volume or set quantity, of district heating or of digital content which is not supplied on a tangible medium: 'of the conclusion of the contract.';

    (b)   in the case of a sales contract: 'on which you acquire, or a third party other than the carrier and indicated by you acquires, physical possession of the goods.';

    (c)   in the case of a contract relating to multiple goods ordered by the consumer in one order and delivered separately: 'on which you acquire, or a third party other than the carrier and indicated by you acquires, physical possession of the last good.';

    (d)   in the case of a contract relating to delivery of a good consisting of multiple lots or pieces: 'on which you acquire, or a third party other than the carrier and indicated by you acquires, physical possession of the last lot or piece.';

    (e)   in the case of a contract for regular delivery of goods during a defined period of time: 'on which you acquire, or a third party other than the carrier and indicated by you acquires, physical possession of the first good.'.

[2.]   Insert your name, geographical address and, where available, your telephone number, fax number and e-mail address.

[3.]   If you give the option to the consumer to electronically fill in and submit information about his withdrawal from the contract on your website, insert the following: 'You can also electronically fill in and submit the model withdrawal form or any other unequivocal statement on our website [insert Internet address]. If you use this option, we will communicate to you an acknowledgement of receipt of such a withdrawal on a durable medium (e.g. by e-mail) without delay.'.

[4.]   In the case of sales contracts in which you have not offered to collect the goods in the event of withdrawal insert the following: 'We may withhold reimbursement until we have received the goods back or you have supplied evidence of having sent back the goods, whichever is the earliest.'.

[5.]   If the consumer has received goods in connection with the contract:

    (a)   insert:
        —   'We will collect the goods.'; or,
        —   'You shall send back the goods or hand them over to us or . . . [insert the name and geographical address, where applicable, of the person authorised by you to receive the goods], without undue delay and in any event not later than 14 days from the day on which you communicate your withdrawal from this contract to us. The deadline is met if you send back the goods before the period of 14 days has expired.'

    (b)   insert:
        —   'We will bear the cost of returning the goods.',
        —   'You will have to bear the direct cost of returning the goods.',
        —   If, in a distance contract, you do not offer to bear the cost of returning the goods and the goods, by their nature, cannot normally be returned by post: 'You will have to bear the direct cost of returning the goods, . . . EUR [insert the amount].'; or if the cost of returning the goods cannot reasonably be calculated in advance: 'You will have to bear the direct cost of returning the goods. The cost is estimated at a maximum of approximately . . . EUR [insert the amount].'; or
        —   If, in an off-premises contract, the goods, by their nature, cannot normally be returned by post and have been delivered to the consumer's home at the time of the conclusion of the contract: 'We will collect the goods at our own expense.'; and,

    (c)   insert: 'You are only liable for any diminished value of the goods resulting from the handling other than what is necessary to establish the nature, characteristics and functioning of the goods.'

[6.]   In the case of a contract for the provision of services or the supply of water, gas or electricity, where they are not put up for sale in a limited volume or set quantity, or of district heating, insert the following: 'If you requested to begin the performance of services or the supply of water/gas/electricity/district heating [delete where inapplicable] during the withdrawal period, you shall pay us an amount which is in proportion to what has been provided until you have communicated us your withdrawal from this contract, in comparison with the full coverage of the contract.'.

B.   MODEL WITHDRAWAL FORM

(COMPLETE AND RETURN THIS FORM ONLY IF YOU WISH TO WITHDRAW FROM THE CONTRACT)

— To [here the trader's name, geographical address and, where available, his fax number and e-mail address are to be inserted by the trader]:

— I/We (*) hereby give notice that I/We (*) withdraw from my/our (*) contract of sale of the following goods (*)/for the provision of the following service (*),

— Ordered on (*)/received on (*),

— Name of consumer(s),

— Address of consumer(s),

— Signature of consumer(s) (only if this form is notified on paper),

— Date

(*) Delete as appropriate.

ANNEX II
CORRELATION TABLE

[4.557]

Directive 85/577/EEC	Directive 97/7/EC	This Directive
Article 1		Article 3 read in conjunction with Article 2, points 8 and 9, and Article 16, point (h)
	Article 1	Article 1 read in conjunction with Article 2, point 7
Article 2		Article 2, points 1 and 2
	Article 2, point 1	Article 2, point 7
	Article 2, point 2	Article 2, point 1
	Article 2, point 3	Article 2, point 2
	Article 2, point 4, first sentence	Article 2, point 7
	Article 2, point 4, second sentence	—
	Article 2, point 5	—
Article 3(1)		Article 3(4)
Article 3(2), point (a)		Article 3(3), points (e) and (f)
Article 3(2), point (b)		Article 3(3), point (j)
Article 3(2), point (c)		—
Article 3(2), point (d)		Article 3(3), point (d)
Article 3(2), point (e)		Article 3(3), point (d)
Article 3(3)		—
	Article 3(1), first indent	Article 3(3), point (d)
	Article 3(1), second indent	Article 3(3), point (l)
	Article 3(1), third indent	Article 3(3), point (m)
	Article 3(1), fourth indent	Article 3(3), points (e) and (f)
	Article 3(1), fifth indent	Article 6(3) and Article 16, point (k) read in conjunction with Article 2, point 13
	Article 3(2), first indent	Article 3(3), point (j)
	Article 3(2), second indent	Article 3(3), point (f) (for rental of accommodation for residential purposes), point (g) (for package travel), point (h) (for timeshare), point (k) (for passenger transport with some exceptions) and Article 16, point (l) (exemption from the right of withdrawal)

Directive 85/577/EEC	Directive 97/7/EC	This Directive
Article 4, first sentence		Article 6(1), points (b), (c) and (h), and Article 7(1) and (2)
Article 4, second sentence		Article 6(1), point a and Article 7(1)
Article 4, third sentence		Article 6(1)
Article 4, fourth sentence		Article 10
	Article 4(1), point (a)	Article 6(1), points (b) and (c)
	Article 4(1), point (b)	Article 6(1), point (a)
	Article 4(1), point (c)	Article 6(1), point (e)
	Article 4(1), point (d)	Article 6(1), point (e)
	Article 4(1), point (e)	Article 6(1), point (g)
	Article 4(1), point (f)	Article 6(1), point (h)
	Article 4(1), point (g)	Article 6(1), point (f)
	Article 4(1), point (h)	—
	Article 4(1), point (i)	Article 6(1), points (o) and (p)
	Article 4(2)	Article 6(1) read in conjunction with Article 8(1), (2) and (4)
	Article 4(3)	Article 8(5)
	Article 5(1)	Article 8(7)
	Article 5(2)	Article 3(3), point m
	Article 6(1)	Article 9(1) and (2), Article 10, Article 13(2), Article 14
	Article 6(2)	Article 13 and Article 14(1), second and third subparagraphs
	Article 6(3), first indent	Article 16, point (a)
	Article 6(3), second indent	Article 16, point (b)
	Article 6(3), third indent	Article 16, points (c) and (d)
	Article 6(3), fourth indent	Article 16, point (i)
	Article 6(3), fifth indent	Article 16, point (j)
	Article 6(3), sixth indent	Article 3(3), point (c)
	Article 6(4)	Article 15
	Article 7(1)	Article 18(1) (for sales contracts)
	Article 7(2)	Article 18(2), (3) and (4)
	Article 7(3)	—
	Article 8	—
	Article 9	Article 27
	Article 10	— (but see Article 13 of Directive 2002/58/EC)
	Article 11(1)	Article 23(1)
	Article 11(2)	
	Article 11(3), point (a)	Article 6(9) for the burden of proof concerning pre-contractual information; for the rest: –
	Article 11(3), point (b)	Article 24(1)
	Article 11(4)	—
	Article 12(1)	Article 25
	Article 12(2)	—

Directive 85/577/EEC	Directive 97/7/EC	This Directive
	Article 13	Article 3(2)
	Article 14	Article 4
	Article 15(1)	Article 28(1)
	Article 15(2)	Article 28(1)
	Article 15(3)	Article 28(1)
	Article 15(4)	Article 30
	Article 16	Article 26
	Article 17	—
	Article 18	Article 34
	Article 19	Article 35
Article 5(1)		Articles 9 and 11
Article 5(2)		Article 12
Article 6		Article 25
Article 7		Articles 13, 14 and 15
Article 8		Article 4

Annex to Regulation (EC) No 2006/2004 of the European Parliament and of the Council of 27 October 2004 on cooperation between national authorities responsible for the enforcement of consumer protection laws (the Regulation on consumer protection cooperation)[1]	To be construed as a reference to
Paragraphs 2 and 11	This Directive

[1]   OJ L 364, 9.12.2004, p 1.

COMPETITION COMMISSION: PAYMENT PROTECTION INSURANCE MARKET INVESTIGATION ORDER 2011

CONTENTS

[4.558]

Notice of making of an Order under section 161 of the Enterprise Act issued under section 165 of and Schedule 10 to the Enterprise Act 2002

(1)   On 5 February 2007, the Office of Fair Trading (OFT), in exercise of its duty under section 131 of the Enterprise Act 2002 (the Act), referred to the Competition Commission (CC) the supply of all payment protection insurance (PPI), except store card PPI, to non-business customers in the UK. The OFT made the reference to the CC following receipt of a super-complaint about PPI on 13 September 2005 from Citizens Advice.

(2)   The CC investigated the matters referred to it in accordance with section 131 of the Act and concluded, in accordance with section 134(1), that there were features of the market, either alone or in combination, which prevented, restricted or distorted competition within the relevant market, and in accordance with section 134(2) that an adverse effect on competition existed.

(3)   The CC regarded the following as features of the market which adversely affected competition:

      (a)   Distributors and intermediaries fail actively to seek to win customers by using the price or quality of their PPI policies as a competitive variable.

      (b)   Consumers who want to compare PPI policies (including PPI combined with credit), stand-alone PPI or short-term IP policies are hindered in doing so. Product complexity (the variations in pricing structures—in particular in relation to single-premium policies—and in terms and conditions, the way information on PPI is presented to customers); the perception that taking PPI would increase their chances of being given credit; the bundling of PPI with credit; and the limited scale of stand-alone provision, act as barriers to search for all types of PPI policies. The bundling of retail PPI with credit accounts and with merchandise cover (also known as purchase protection insurance) acts as a barrier to search for retail PPI. In addition, the time taken to obtain accurate price information is a barrier in relation to the provision of PLPPI, MPPI and SMPPI. These barriers to search impede the ability of consumers to make comparisons, and therefore effective choices, between PPI policies. They also, therefore, act as barriers to expansion for other PPI providers, in particular providers of stand-alone PPI.

(c)   Consumers who want to switch PPI policies to alternative PPI providers or to alternative insurance products are hindered in doing so. Terms which make switching expensive (in the case of single-premium policies) act as barriers to switching for PLPPI and SMPPI policies. Terms which risk leaving consumers uninsured (for a short period of time or in case they suffer a recurrence of a condition) act as barriers to switching for all types of PPI policies. In addition, the lack of access to consumers' balance information acts as a barrier for switching for CCPPI and retail PPI, and the bundling of retail PPI with merchandise cover acts as a barrier to switching for retail PPI. These barriers to switching limit consumer choice. They also, therefore, act as barriers to expansion for other PPI providers, in particular providers of stand-alone PPI.

(d)   The sale of PPI at the point of sale further restricts the extent to which other PPI providers can compete effectively.

(4)   The CC found that there was a detrimental effect on customers resulting from the adverse effect on competition and considered, in accordance with section 134(4), whether action should be taken by it, or whether it should recommend the taking of action by others, for the purpose of remedying, mitigating or preventing the adverse effect on competition concerned or the detrimental effect on customers so far as it had resulted from, or may be expected to result from, the adverse effect on competition.

(5)   The CC consulted on a range of possible actions and in its report published on 29 January 2009, the CC decided to impose a package of remedies, which included a prohibition on selling PPI at the point of sale of credit—a point-of-sale prohibition (POSP)—which would be effective and proportionate in remedying the various features of the market identified as having an adverse effect on competition.

(6)   Barclays Bank plc challenged the lawfulness of the CC's decision to impose the package of remedies in the Competition Appeal Tribunal (the Tribunal). The Tribunal partly upheld Barclays' challenge as is set out in its judgment of 16 October 2009. As a result the CC's decision to include the POSP as part of the package of remedies was quashed by the Tribunal and remitted to the CC for reconsideration. The CC's findings as to an adverse effect on competition in the PPI market, as set out in paragraph 3 above, were not disturbed.

(7)   The CC reconsidered its decision to impose the POSP as part of its package of remedies. In its report dated 14 October 2010 the CC decided that in order to achieve as comprehensive a solution to the adverse effect on competition as was reasonable and practicable it was necessary for the POSP to form part of the package of remedies for PLPPI, MPPI, CCPPI and SMPPI.

(8)   Accordingly, the CC decided that the package of remedies for PLPPI, MPPI, CCPPI and SMPPI would contain the following key elements:

(a)   *POSP*—PPI cannot be sold by the credit arranger (or any business covered by the prohibition) at the same time as the credit product, nor within seven days of the conclusion of the credit sale period, or the provision of a personal PPI quote, if one were not provided during the credit sale period. As a limited exception to this POSP, the distributor or intermediary arranging the credit (or any business covered by the prohibition) may sell PPI to the consumer the day after the conclusion of the credit sale provided that the consumer has initiated the transaction over the Internet or telephone and the consumer has confirmed that they have seen the personal PPI quote.

(b)   *Provision of a personal quote*—all credit arrangers must provide a personal PPI quote to the consumer in a durable medium, if the credit arranger provides information about PPI to the consumer during the credit sale. If the credit arranger does not provide a personal PPI quote during the credit sale period, but subsequently contacts the consumer to offer PPI, a personal PPI quote must be provided at that time. Stand-alone providers are required to provide a personal PPI quote to the consumer in a durable medium if the consumer asks the provider about the cost and/or features of a stand-alone policy, including short-term IP, sold by that provider.

(c)   *Information provision in marketing materials*—all PPI providers must disclose prominently the following information in any PPI marketing materials that include pricing claims or cost information, any indication of the benefits of the PPI product or its main characteristics: the monthly cost of PPI per £100 of monthly benefit[1] (CCPPI providers must also show the cost of PPI per £100 of outstanding balance); that PPI is optional (stand-alone providers do not have to include this statement) and available from other providers (without specifying those other providers); and that information on PPI, alternative providers and other forms of protection can be found on the Consumer Financial Education Body's (CFEB) moneymadeclear website.

(d)   *Provision of information to third parties*—all PPI providers must provide comparative data to the CFEB, as specified by, and in the format requested by, the CFEB. In addition to the information that the OFT may request from time to time for the purposes of monitoring and reviewing the operation of the remedy package, all PPI providers that meet a specified threshold must provide the following information to the OFT on an annual basis: annual gross written premium (GWP), split by product type; distributor penetration rates, split by product type; and aggregate claims ratios for each provider, split by product type. In addition, all PPI providers must provide to any person on request aggregate claims ratios, split by product type, for the previous year. These can be provided in the form of a range to be specified by the CC.

(e)   *Recommendation to use information for price comparison tables*—the CC will recommend to the CFEB that it uses the information provided to it pursuant to this remedy package to populate its PPI price comparison tables with data on all PPI and short-term IP products.

(f)   *A prohibition on the selling of single-premium PPI policies*—PPI cannot be charged on a single-premium basis. Subject to the prohibition on charging PPI on a single-premium basis, premiums can be charged monthly or annually. Where an annual premium is paid by a consumer, then a rebate must be paid to consumers on a pro-rata basis if the consumer terminates the policy during the year. No separate charges can be levied on a customer for administration or for the set-up or early termination of a PPI policy.

(g)   *Annual reviews*—PPI providers must provide an annual review for PPI customers. Provision of this annual review will be the responsibility of the company that sold the PPI policy to the consumer, other than for sales made by intermediaries where provision of this annual review will be the responsibility of the company with whom the consumer has an ongoing relationship.

(h)   *Compliance reporting requirements to support the above elements.*

(9)   For retail PPI, the CC decided, as is set out in its report dated 14 October 2010, that the POSP should not form part of the remedy package. The key elements which form the remedy package for retail PPI are:

(a)   *Unbundling PPI from merchandise cover*—an obligation to offer PPI separately from merchandise cover if both are offered as a bundled product.

(b)   *Information provision in marketing materials*—an obligation to provide information above the cost of PPI and 'key messages' in marketing materials.

(c)   *Provision of information to third parties*—an obligation to provide information to the CFEB for publication and to provide information about claims ratios to any party on request.

(d)   *Recommendation to the CFEB*—a recommendation to the CFEB that it uses the information provided to it under the above obligation to populate its PPI price comparison tables.

(e)   *Personal PPI quote*—an obligation to provide a personal PPI quote to customers before the end of the cooling-off period.

(f)   *Annual review*—an obligation to provide customers who have spent more than £50 on retail PPI premiums in the preceding 12 months with a written annual review of PPI costs including a reminder of the customer's right to cancel.

(g)   *Annual reminder*—an obligation to remind all active customers who have spent less than £50 in the preceding 12 months of their cancellation rights and of key messages with their next retail credit account statement.

(h)   *Single-premium prohibition*—a prohibition on selling single-premium PPI policies and on charges which have a similar economic effect.

(10)   The CC indicated in its reports of 29 January 2009 and 14 October 2010 that it intended to implement the remedy package by making an Order.

(11)   On 25 November 2010 in accordance with paragraph 2 of Schedule 10 to the Act the CC gave notice of its intention to make an Order, and invited representations on the draft Order.

(12)   In light of the representations received following the November 2010 consultation, the CC revised the Order and on 14 February 2011, in accordance with paragraph 2 of Schedule 10 to the Act, invited representations on the revised draft Order.

(13)   In light of the representations the CC received following the 14 February 2011 consultation some modifications were made to the Order. The CC does not consider those modifications to be material in any respect and has decided, in accordance with paragraph 5 to Schedule 10 of the Act that the Order, as modified, does not require further consultation.

(14)   The CC now gives notice of the making of the attached Order. The Order is made in accordance with section 138 and in exercise of the powers conferred by section 161 of and Schedule 8 to the Act. The Order is made for the purpose of remedying, mitigating or preventing the adverse effect on competition which the CC identified within the market for the supply of PPI, except store card PPI, to non-business customers in the UK and for the purpose of remedying, mitigating or preventing detrimental effects on consumers so far as they have resulted from or may be expected to result from the adverse effect of competition.

(15)   The Order will come into force on 6 April 2011.

(signed) PETER DAVIS

Group Chairman

24 March 2011

NOTES

[1] If the benefit pays out for less than 12 months, notice of this fact must also be clearly disclosed to consumers alongside the cost of the policy.

BACKGROUND

[4.559]

(1) On 5 February 2007, the Office of Fair Trading (OFT) in exercise of its powers under sections 131 and 133 of the Enterprise Act 2002 (the Act) referred the supply of all payment protection insurance services (except store card payment protection insurance services) to non-business customers in the UK ('the supply of PPI') to the Competition Commission (CC) for investigation.

(2) The CC investigated the matters referred to it pursuant to section 131 of the Act and concluded, in accordance with section 134(1) of the Act, that there are features of the market either alone or in combination which prevent, restrict or distort competition in connection with the relevant market and, in accordance with section 134(2) of the Act, that an adverse effect on competition existed.

(3) The CC found that there is a detrimental effect on Consumers resulting from the adverse effect on competition and considered, in accordance with section 134(4) of the Act, whether *(a)* action should be taken by it for the purpose of remedying, mitigating or preventing the adverse effect on competition concerned or the detrimental effect on Consumers so far as it has resulted, or may be expected to result, from the adverse effect on competition, and whether *(b)* it should recommend the taking of action by others for the purpose of remedying, mitigating or preventing the adverse effect on competition concerned or any detrimental effect on Consumers so far as it has resulted from, or may be expected to result from, the adverse effect on competition.

(4) In accordance with section 165 of the Act and paragraph 2(1)(a) of Schedule 10, the CC on 25 November 2010 and again on 14 February 2011 published a Notice of its intention to make this Order to remedy the adverse effects on competition that it had identified, indicating the nature of its provisions and stating that any interested person who wished to make representations should do so in writing by 5.00 pm on 6 January 2011 and 5.00 pm on 22 February 2011 respectively.

(5) The CC received a number of responses and having considered the representations it received in both consultations is now issuing this Order.

THE ORDER

[4.561]

The CC makes this Order in performance of its duty under section 138 and in exercise of the powers it has in section 86(1) to (5) and section 87 (each applicable by virtue of section 164), section 161(1), (3) and (4) and paragraphs 1, 2, 10, 11 15, 17, 18, 19, 21 and 22 of Schedule 8 to the Enterprise Act 2002, for the purpose of remedying, mitigating or preventing the adverse effect on competition and any detrimental effects on customers so far as they have resulted, or may be expected to result, from the adverse effect on competition specified in the reports of the CC entitled *Payment Protection Insurance market investigation* (29 January 2009) *and Payment Protection Insurance market investigation: remittal of the point-of-sale prohibition remedy by the Competition Appeal Tribunal* (14 October 2010).[1]

NOTES

[1] www.competition-commission.org.uk/rep_pub/reports/2009/fulltext/542.pdf and
www.competition-commission.org.uk/inquiries/ ref2010/ppi_remittal/pdf/report.pdf.

PART 1
GENERAL

1. TITLE, COMMENCEMENT, APPLICATION AND SCOPE

[4.562]

1.1 The title of this Order is the 'Payment Protection Insurance Market Investigation Order 2011' and it commences on 6 April 2011 (the 'Commencement Date') except:

(a) Articles 3, 5 and 6 which commence on 1 October 2011; and
(b) Articles 4, 7, 8, 9, 10 and 11 which commence on 6 April 2012.

1.2 This Order applies to any PPI Provider or Administrator who whether from an establishment in the United Kingdom or otherwise either provides PPI to a Consumer or administers a PPI policy on behalf of a PPI Provider in the United Kingdom and applies to an Insurer whether operating from an establishment in the United Kingdom or otherwise in so far as specific obligations arise under this Order.

2. INTERPRETATION

[4.563]
2.1 In this Order:

Additional Statement	means the statement set out in Schedule 2.
Administrator	means a person who administers a PPI policy on behalf of a PPI Provider by conducting certain functions including but not limited to sending renewal notices, collecting premiums, processing of claims or customer amendments and in performing these functions has no direct contractual relationship with the Policyholder.
Annual Premium	means a payment which may be paid by regular instalments of the Premium for a PPI policy which is renewable on an annual basis made once a year which is not a Single Premium.
Annual Reminder	means a written statement made in accordance with Article 4 and using the words in Schedule 3d(ii).
Annual Review	means a document required by Article 4 and completed in accordance with the instructions and in the format set out in Schedule 3 that summarizes information relating to a PPI policy for the preceding 12 calendar months.
APR	means the annual percentage rate of charge calculated in accordance with the Consumer Credit (Disclosure of Information) Regulations 2010 or the Consumer Credit (Agreements) Regulations 1983, as applicable or in the case of mortgage Credit, the Mortgages and Home Finance: Conduct of Business Sourcebook MCOB 10.
Associate	means a PPI Provider who has a Commercial Referral Relationship with a Credit Arranger for the sale of PPI and either:
	(a) is mentioned by the Credit Arranger to the Consumer as a PPI Provider after commencement of the Credit Sale; or
	(b) to whom the Credit Arranger has given or allowed access to information concerning a specific sale of Credit for the purposes of selling PPI.
Business Year	means a period of more than 6 months for which the PPI Provider publishes or prepares accounts.
CC	means the Competition Commission.
CCPPI	means PPI taken out to enable a Policyholder to protect the ability to make payments due on a Credit Card.
CFEB	means Consumer Financial Education Body.
Claims Ratio	means the ratio of Incurred Claims to Earned Premiums during a Business Year.
Combined APR	means the combined cost of Credit with PPI expressed as an annual percentage rate and calculated by applying the formula used to calculate the APR and assuming that PPI is a compulsory ancillary service.
Commencement Date	means 6 April 2011.
Commercial Referral Relationship	means an arrangement where one party receives payment or other benefit from another party (other than the Consumer) as a result of a Consumer purchasing PPI and includes an arrangement between members of a Corporate Group which results in a beneficial effect for one member as a result of the action of another member.
Compliance Officer	means a natural person employed by a PPI Provider whose duties include those set out in Article 15.2.
Compliance Report	means a report required by Article 12.
Consumer	means a natural person who, in transactions covered by this Order, is acting for purposes which are outside any trade, business or profession carried on by that person.
Corporate Group	means a group of companies which are required by the Companies Act 2006 to file group accounts.

Credit	means any kind of loan, or any other kind of accommodation or facility in the nature of credit granted to a Consumer and for the purposes of this Order includes a Mortgage, Credit Card and Retail Credit Account but does not include a Store Card or a facility offered by a Store Card or a facility which enables a Consumer to overdraw on a current account.
Credit Arranger	means a Distributor or Intermediary arranging the sale of Credit to a Consumer.
Credit Card	means a Credit agreement which is a credit-token agreement within the meaning of the Consumer Credit Act 1974, other than a Store Card.
Credit Provider	means a person who provides Credit.
Credit Sale	means the period determined in accordance with Article 8.2.
Distributor	means a Credit Provider who also provides PPI for the Credit provided by that person.
Durable Medium	means paper or any instrument or medium which enables the recipient to store information addressed personally to the recipient in a way accessible for future reference for a period of time adequate for the purposes of the information and which allows the unchanged reproduction of the information stored.
Electronic Communication	has the same meaning as in the Electronic Communications Act 2000.
Earned Premiums	means the value of actual Premiums earned in a Business Year exclusive of any taxes or duties levied with no deductions for expenses relating to acquisition or administration of the policy and with no adjustment for any risks being reinsured and are that proportion of written premiums attributable to the risks borne by the Insurer during that Business Year and including where relevant those written in previous Business Years.
GWP	means the annual gross written Premium from PPI exclusive of Insurance Premium Tax and for the purposes of Part 5, annual gross written Premium from PPI sold direct to Consumers.
ICOBS	means Insurance: Conduct of Business Sourcebook.
Incurred Claims	means the value of total claims incurred during a Business Year, exclusive of external and internal claims management costs and with no adjustment for any risks being reinsured and includes paid claims and the difference between outstanding claims (both reported and incurred but not reported) brought forward from previous Business Years and outstanding claims carried forward at the end of the Business Year with all amounts being stated before any adjustment for discounting.
Independent Market Research Agency	means an organization which has as its primary business carrying out research with Consumers, is certified to ISO 20252/2006 or equivalent and is a separate legal entity from and not in the same Corporate Group as any PPI Provider and in which a PPI Provider does not have a beneficial and/or controlling interest.
Insurer	means a person who effects or carries out a contract of insurance, agreeing to take responsibility on its own account for or as principal for paying the sum insured to the Policyholder pursuant to a PPI policy.
Intermediary	means a person other than a Distributor through whom a Consumer is able to select or purchase or arrange to purchase PPI, whether or not in conjunction with Credit and for the purposes of this Order does not include a Price Comparison Website.
Intermediary Network	means an organization consisting of more than one Intermediary.
IPT	means Insurance Premium Tax on general insurance premiums introduced on 1 October 1994.
Marketing Communication	means an oral or written communication containing a Marketing Statement and may be either:

(a) made directly to a particular Consumer or included in addressed mail to a particular Consumer; or

(b) made to Consumers in general indirectly by using intervening media such as newspaper and broadcast advertisements.

Marketing Statement	means a promotional message, invitation or inducement to purchase PPI consisting of or including any of the items of information listed in Schedule 1.
Merchandise Cover	means insurance against loss as a result of accidental damage or theft of goods purchased on a Retail Credit Account.
Monthly Benefit	means the benefit that is payable to a Policyholder on a monthly basis in the event of an accident, sickness or unemployment claim on a PPI policy.
Monthly Cost	means the cost of the Premium per month.
Monthly Premium	means payment of the Premium for a PPI policy which does not have an annual renewal date by regular monthly payments or regular four-weekly payments where failure to make the payments may result in the lapsing of the PPI policy.
Mortgage	means Credit where the obligation to repay is secured by a first mortgage on a residential property.
MPPI	means PPI taken out to enable a Policyholder to protect the ability to make payments due on a first Mortgage.
OFT	means the Office of Fair Trading.
Penetration Rates	means the number of Consumers who take out a PPI Product Type in a Business Year with the Credit Arranger, including those who subsequently cancel but excluding those who purchased Stand-Alone PPI, expressed as a percentage of the total number of Consumers who take out Credit with the Credit Arranger in that Business Year.
Personal Loan	means unsecured Credit which is not a Credit Card, Store Card, or Retail Credit Account.
Personal PPI Quote	means a document required by Article 7 and completed in accordance with the instructions in and in the format set out in Schedule 4.
PLPPI	means PPI taken out to enable a Policyholder to protect the ability to make payments due for a Personal Loan.
Policyholder	means a Consumer who is the holder of a PPI policy.
PPI	means a contract of insurance taken out to enable a Policyholder to protect the ability to make payments due to third parties in respect of Credit, in the event the Policyholder experiences involuntary unemployment or incapacity as a result of accident or sickness and which:
	(*a*) provides benefits determined by the payments due to third parties which may not always be paid directly to the Policyholder;
	(*b*) may be combined with other forms of insurance cover; and
	(*c*) for the purposes of this Order includes Short-Term IP but does not include PPI for a Store Card or a facility offered by a Store Card or a facility which enables a Consumer to overdraw on a current account or a facility which enables the payment of an annual premium for insurance which is not PPI.
PPI Comparison Tables	means the tables produced by the CFEB containing price and non-price information about PPI policies.
PPI Product Type	means an individual type of PPI policy being PLPPI, SMPPI, CCPPI, Retail PPI and MPPI.
PPI Provider	means either a Distributor, an Intermediary, a Stand-Alone Provider or a Short-Term IP Provider and includes an Insurer when providing PPI direct to a Consumer.
Premium	means all payments receivable under a contract of insurance by the Insurer, including IPT.
Prescribed Statement	means the statement set out in Schedule 1a or 1b as applicable.
Price Comparison Website	means an Internet site which, as its primary business, gathers and presents to Consumers price and/or non-price information about financial products from many different providers but does not sell its own financial products or those of another member of the Corporate Group of which it is part to the Consumer.

Prohibition Period	means the period determined in accordance with Article 8.3.
Retail Credit Account	means a Credit agreement, other than a Store Card or Credit Card, between a retailer or a member of the retailer's Corporate Group and a Consumer which enables the Consumer to purchase the retailer's goods or services before payment and permits the Consumer to discharge less than the whole of any outstanding balance on or before the expiry of a specified period and also known as a home shopping account and described as such in Schedules 3d(i) and 3d(ii) and 4d.
Retail PPI	means PPI taken out to enable a Policyholder to protect the ability to make payments due on a Retail Credit Account.
Retail PPI Provider	means a person who in the course of a trade, business or profession provides Retail PPI to a Consumer.
Short-Term IP	means a contract of insurance which provides a pre-agreed amount paid directly to the Policyholder or the Policyholder's nominee in the event the Policyholder experiences involuntary unemployment or incapacity as a result of accident or sickness and which:

(a) has a maximum time limited benefit duration;

(b) may include or combine other forms of insurance cover or include other benefits;

(c) is written for a term which is less than 5 years and not predetermined by the term of any Credit; and

(d) can be terminated by the Insurer.

Short-Term IP Provider	means a person who in the course of a trade, business or profession provides Short-Term IP direct to a Consumer.
Single Premium	means a payment of the total Premium payable for the PPI policy covering a period of more than 12 consecutive months made as one amount at or after the start of a PPI policy.
SMPPI	means PPI taken out to enable a Policyholder to protect the ability to make payments due for Credit where the obligation to repay is secured by a second or lower-ranking Mortgage.
Stand-Alone PPI	means either:

(a) any PPI Product Type or Short-Term IP which is provided by a PPI Provider which is not the Credit Provider or the Credit Arranger or an Associate; or

(b) any PPI Product Type or Short-Term IP provided in the circumstances set out in Article 8.5.

Stand-Alone Provider	means a person who in the course of a trade, business or profession provides Stand-Alone PPI to a Consumer and who either:

(a) sources the PPI Product Type or Short-Term IP from an Insurer; or

(b) is an Insurer.

Store Card	has the same meaning as in the Store Cards Market Investigation Order 2006.
Working Day	means any day except for Saturday, Sunday, Christmas Day, Good Friday or a bank holiday under the Banking and Financial Dealings Act 1971.

2.2   In this Order any reference to:

(a)   '**annual**' means any 12 consecutive months and any reference to '**annual basis**' or '**annually**' is construed on a cognate basis;

(b)   '**day**' means calendar day;

(c)   '**month**' means calendar month;

(d)   '**oral**' means a communication made orally either in person or by telephone or by using intervening media such as broadcast media;

(e)   a '**person**' includes any individual, firm, partnership, body corporate or association;

(f)   '**provide**' includes to sell or an offer or promise to provide, sell or otherwise supply and for the purposes of Articles 1, 4, 6 and Part 5, has provided, sold or otherwise supplied;

(g)   '**written**' means a communication in writing and made by any means including an Electronic Communication;

(h)   any reference to a government department or organization or person or place or thing includes a reference to its successor in title; and

(i)   a requirement to give the name of a government department or organization or person or place or thing, will apply to give the name of the successor in title to the government department or organization or person or place or thing.

2.3 The Interpretation Act 1978 applies to this Order except where words and expressions are expressly defined.

PART 2
INFORMATION REQUIREMENTS

3. OBLIGATION TO PROVIDE INFORMATION ABOUT PPI

[4.564]
3.1 When a PPI Provider makes a Marketing Statement except about Retail PPI in a Marketing Communication the PPI Provider must, subject to Article 3.6, ensure that the following information is included prominently within the same Marketing Communication as the Marketing Statement:
(a)   the cost of PPI to the Consumer, expressed in the format of the Monthly Cost for every £100 of Monthly Benefit; and
(b)   for PLPPI, CCPPI, SMPPI and MPPI, the Prescribed Statement in Schedule 1a; or
(c)   for Stand-Alone PPI or Short-Term IP, the Prescribed Statement in Schedule 1b.

3.2 When a PPI Provider makes a Marketing Statement about Retail PPI in a Marketing Communication, the PPI Provider must, subject to Articles 3.5 and 3.6, ensure that the information in Article 3.2(a) or Article 3.2(b) as appropriate is included prominently within the same Marketing Communication as the Marketing Statement:
(a)   when the Marketing Communication is made in writing:
     (i)   the prescribed statement in Schedule 1a; and
     (ii)   display the cost of Retail PPI to the Consumer expressed in the format of the Monthly Cost for every £100 of Monthly Benefit and the Monthly Cost for every £100 of the balance owed by the Consumer on the account; or
(b)   when the Marketing Communication is made orally, the prescribed statement in Schedule 1a.

3.3 When a PPI Provider makes a Marketing Statement about CCPPI in a Marketing Communication the PPI Provider must, in addition to the obligations arising under Article 3.1, ensure that the cost of CCPPI to the Consumer is expressed in the format of the Monthly Cost for every £100 of the balance owed by the Consumer on the account and is displayed prominently within the same Marketing Communication as the Marketing Statement.

3.4 When a PPI Provider makes a Marketing Statement in a Marketing Communication about a PPI policy under which the Monthly Benefit to the Consumer is only payable for a duration of less than 12 months, the PPI Provider in addition to the obligations arising under Articles 3.1, 3.2 or 3.3, must ensure that the Additional Statement in Schedule 2 is included prominently within the same Marketing Communication as the Marketing Statement.

3.5 Article 3.4 does not apply to Retail PPI where:
(a)   the Marketing Statement is made in an oral Marketing Communication; and
(b)   the Retail PPI policy pays the total balance owed by the Consumer on the Retail Credit Account within 12 months.

3.6 When an Intermediary makes a Marketing Statement in a Marketing Communication about a PPI policy which is provided by an Insurer or a PPI Provider other than the Intermediary, the person producing the Marketing Communication has the responsibility for complying with the obligations in Articles 3.1, 3.2, 3.3 and 3.4.

3.7 When an Intermediary makes a Marketing Statement in a Marketing Communication about a PPI policy which is specifically or exclusively designed for that Intermediary or Intermediary Network, the Intermediary or the Intermediary Network which provides the PPI policy must ensure that the Marketing Communication containing the Marketing Statement relating to that PPI policy complies with the obligations in Articles 3.1, 3.2, 3.3 and 3.4.

3.8 For the purposes of this article, '**prominently**' means when assessing the Marketing Communication as a whole, in a manner that ensures as far as is reasonably possible that it is likely that a Consumer's attention will be drawn to it and no less prominently than the Marketing Statement itself.

4. OBLIGATION TO PROVIDE AN ANNUAL REVIEW OR ANNUAL REMINDER

[4.565]
4.1 For any PPI policy which starts on or after 6 April 2012 except a Retail PPI policy, a PPI Provider or Administrator must, subject to Article 4.7, send an Annual Review to a Policyholder in accordance with paragraphs (a) to (b) below:
(a)   where a PPI policy has an annual renewal date or the Premium is paid by an Annual Premium the first and each subsequent Annual Review must be sent not less than 2 weeks and not more than 4 weeks before the date by which the PPI policy must be renewed or the date by which the Annual Premium must be paid as the case may be; and

Part 4 Other Materials

(b)   where a PPI policy is paid by Monthly Premium:
   (i)   the first Annual Review must be sent at any time during the first 13 months following the commencement of the PPI policy; and
   (ii)   each subsequent Annual Review must be sent on a date which is either within 2 weeks before or within 2 weeks after the anniversary of the date on which the first Annual Review was sent.

4.2   For a Retail PPI policy which starts on or after 6 April 2012 if the total amount of Premium paid on the first 12-month anniversary of the start of the Retail PPI policy is £50 or more, a PPI Provider or Administrator must, subject to Article 4.8, send the first Annual Review to a Policyholder at any time during the 13th month following the start of the Policy and if on any subsequent 12-month anniversary of the start of the Retail PPI policy the total amount of Premium paid in the preceding 12 months is either:
(a)   £50 or more, send an Annual Review at any time in the month following the 12-month anniversary of the start of the Retail PPI policy; or
(b)   less than £50, send an Annual Reminder with the next Retail Credit Account statement.

4.3   For a Retail PPI policy which starts on or after 6 April 2012 if the total amount of Premium paid on the first 12-month anniversary of the start of the Retail PPI policy is less than £50 a PPI Provider or Administrator must, subject to Article 4.8, send the first Annual Reminder with the next Retail Credit Account statement and if on any subsequent 12-month anniversary of the start of the Retail PPI policy the total amount of Premium paid in the preceding 12 months is either:
(a)   less than £50, send an Annual Reminder with the next Retail Credit Account statement; or
(b)   £50 or more, send an Annual Review in accordance with Article 4.2*(a)*.

4.4   For any SMPPI policy which is not paid by a Single Premium or any CCPPI policy or any MPPI policy any of which are in force on 6 April 2012, a PPI Provider or Administrator must, subject to Article 4.7, send an Annual Review to a Policyholder in accordance with paragraphs *(a)* to *(b)* below:
(a)   the first Annual Review must be sent at any time during the 12 months following 6 April 2012; and
(b)   each subsequent Annual Review must be sent within 2 weeks before or after the anniversary of the date on which the first Annual Review was sent.

4.5   For a Retail PPI policy which is in force on 6 April 2012 a Retail PPI Provider or Administrator must, subject to Article 4.8, send an Annual Review to a Policyholder in accordance with either paragraphs *(a)* or *(b)*:
(a)   where the start date of the Retail PPI policy is known by the Retail PPI Provider, in accordance with paragraphs (i) to (iii) below:
   (i)   if on the first 12-month anniversary of the start date of the Retail PPI policy after 6 April 2012, the total amount of Premium paid is £50 or more, send the first Annual Review at any time during the following month and if on any subsequent 12-month anniversary of the start date of the Retail PPI policy the total amount of Premium paid in the preceding 12 months is either:
   (ii)   £50 or more, send an Annual Review at any time in the following month; or
   (iii)   less than £50, send an Annual Reminder with the next Retail Credit Account statement; or
(b)   where the start date of the Retail PPI policy is not known by the Retail PPI Provider, in accordance with paragraphs (i) to (iii) below:
   (i)   if on 6 July 2012 ('the reference date'), the total amount of Premium paid in the preceding 12 months is £50 or more, send the first Annual Review at any time during the following month and if on any subsequent 12-month anniversary of the reference date the total amount of Premium paid in the preceding 12 months is either:
   (ii)   £50 or more, send an Annual Review at any time in the following month; or
   (iii)   less than £50, send an Annual Reminder with the next Retail Credit Account statement.

4.6   For a Retail PPI policy which is in force at 6 April 2012 a PPI Provider or Administrator must, subject to Article 4.8, send an Annual Reminder to a Policyholder in accordance with either paragraphs *(a)* or *(b)*:
(a)   where the start date of the Retail PPI policy is known by the Retail PPI Provider, in accordance with paragraphs (i) to (iii) below:
   (i)   if on the first 12-month anniversary of the commencement date of the Retail PPI policy after 6 April 2012 the total amount of Premium paid is less than £50, send the first Annual Reminder with the next Retail Credit Account statement and if on any subsequent 12-month anniversary of the start date of the Retail PPI policy the total amount of Premium paid in the preceding 12 months is either:
   (ii)   less than £50, send an Annual Reminder with the next Retail Credit Account statement; or
   (iii)   £50 or more, send an Annual Review at any time in the following month; or
(b)   where the start date of the Retail PPI policy is not known by the Retail PPI Provider, in accordance with paragraphs (i) to (iii) below:

> (i)   if on 6 July 2012 ('the reference date') the total amount of Premium paid in the preceding 12 months is less than £50, send the first Annual Reminder with the next Retail Credit Account statement and if on any subsequent 12-month anniversary of the reference date the total amount of Premium paid in the preceding 12 months is either:
>> (ii)   less than £50, send an Annual Reminder with the next Retail Credit Account statement; or
>> (iii)   £50 or more, send an Annual Review at any time in the following month.

4.7   The obligations in Article 4.1 and Article 4.4 do not apply, if in the 12 months preceding the date when the Annual Review would have been sent either:
(a)   the PPI Policyholder has:
> (i)   not paid nor been required to pay any PPI Premium;
> (ii)   cancelled the PPI policy; or
> (iii)   permitted the PPI policy to lapse; or

(b)   the PPI Provider has:
> (i)   cancelled the PPI policy in accordance with contractual rights;
> (ii)   received notice of the death of the Policyholder; or
> (iii)   received notice that the Policyholder has left the current address and no notice of the Policyholder's new address has been received by the PPI Provider.

4.8   The obligations in Article 4.2, Article 4.3, Article 4.5 and Article 4.6 do not apply if in the 12 months preceding the calculation date either:
(a)   the Retail PPI Policyholder has:
> (i)   not paid nor been required to pay any Retail PPI Premium;
> (ii)   cancelled the Retail PPI policy; or
> (iii)   permitted the Retail PPI policy to lapse; or

(b)   the Retail PPI Provider has:
> (i)   cancelled the PPI policy in accordance with contractual rights;
> (ii)   received notice of the death of the Policyholder; or
> (iii)   received notice that the Policyholder has left the current address and no notice of the Policyholder's new address has been received by the PPI Provider.

4.9   Articles 4.1 to 4.8 do not apply to an Intermediary when the Intermediary no longer maintains direct contact with the Policyholder following the provision of a PPI policy but apply to whichever of the Insurer, PPI Provider or Administrator is in direct contact with the Policyholder.

4.10   Whenever a PPI Provider or Administrator is required to send an Annual Review or Annual Reminder, the PPI Provider or Administrator must:
(a)   use the format of Annual Review as set out below:
> (i)   for PLPPI use the form set out in Schedule 3a;
> (ii)   for SMPPI or MPPI use the form set out in Schedule 3b(i) or Schedule 3(b)(ii) where an MPPI or SMPPI policy is provided to joint Policyholders;
> (iii)   for CCPPI use the form set out in Schedule 3c;
> (iv)   for Retail PPI use the form set out in Schedule 3d(i); and
> (v)   for Stand-Alone PPI or Short-Term IP and for any PPI Product Type or Short-Term IP sold by an Intermediary use the form set out in Schedule 3e, except for CCPPI that constitutes Stand-Alone PPI where the form set out in Schedule 3c must be used;

(b)   include a policy summary for policies dated after 14 January 2005 with any Annual Review;
(c)   follow the instructions in Schedule 3 when completing the Annual Review; and
(d)   for an Annual Reminder for Retail PPI include the words in Schedule 3d(ii) prominently on the Retail Credit Account statement.

4.11   Whenever an Annual Review is sent to the Policyholder the PPI Provider or Administrator must not:
(a)   include with the Annual Review any information on or about or relating to the Credit to which the PPI policy relates; or
(b)   send the Annual Review as an Electronic Communication except where the Policyholder has made an explicit request that the Annual Review be sent as an Electronic Communication.

4.12   Where a PPI policy is provided to joint Policyholders, a PPI Provider or Administrator need not send a separate Annual Review to each of the Policyholders unless either of the Policyholders specifically request this.

4.13   Whenever a PPI Provider or Administrator requires and requests information from another PPI Provider or an Insurer in order to produce an Annual Review, the information requested must be provided to the PPI Provider within 7 days of the request being made.

4.14   For the purposes of this article:
(a)   **'calculation date'** means the date when it is determined whether an Annual Review or Annual Reminder must be sent for a Retail PPI policy;
(b)   **'direct contact'** means written or oral communication concerning the carrying out of a PPI policy that takes place between the Administrator, Insurer or PPI Provider as the case may be and the Policyholder;

(c)   '**explicit request**' means a written communication by the Policyholder instructing that the Annual Review be provided electronically which may not be a term or condition of an agreement, but may be made by the Policyholder indicating agreement to receive all communications from the PPI Provider or Administrator as Electronic Communications;

(d)   '**policy summary**' means a document containing a summary of the PPI policy in the format and containing the information in ICOBS 6 Annex 2; and

(e)   '**prominently**' means when assessing the Retail Credit Account statement as a whole, in a manner that ensures as far as is reasonably possible that it is likely that a Consumer's attention will be drawn to it.

5. OBLIGATION TO PROVIDE INFORMATION TO THE CFEB

[4.566]
5.1   A PPI Provider must provide to the CFEB such data, in such format, as the CFEB may need from time to time in connection with the preparation of and publication by the CFEB of the PPI Comparison Tables.

6. OBLIGATION TO DISCLOSE CLAIMS RATIOS

[4.567]
6.1   A PPI Provider must produce a Claims Ratio within 3 months after the end of a Business Year for each PPI Product Type, Stand-Alone PPI and Short-Term IP provided in that Business Year.

6.2   A PPI Provider which is required to submit a Compliance Report must disclose the Claims Ratio produced in accordance with Article 6.1 to the OFT in the Compliance Report.

6.3   A PPI Provider may disclose the Claims Ratio produced in accordance with Article 6.1 on its website in the format of a range of 10 percentile increments commencing with 0-10% and continuing up to 80% and then in one aggregate banding.

6.4   A PPI Provider must disclose the Claims Ratio produced in accordance with Article 6.1 to any person requesting it (an '**enquirer**') in accordance with Article 6.5 and in the format of a range of 10 percentile increments commencing with 0-10% and continuing up to 80% and then in one aggregate banding.

6.5   A PPI Provider must respond to an oral request from an enquirer as follows:
(a)   by disclosing the Claims Ratio produced in accordance with Article 6.1 orally to the enquirer within 24 hours or by close of business the next Working Day whichever is the later after receiving the request;
(b)   by disclosing the Claims Ratio produced in accordance with Article 6.1 in writing to the enquirer within 7 days after receiving the request; or
(c)   by directing the enquirer either orally or in writing within the timescale stipulated in *(a)* or *(b)* above to the Claims Ratio produced in accordance with Article 6.1 published on the PPI Provider's website if it has done so.

6.6   A PPI Provider must respond to a written request either:
(a)   by disclosing the Claims Ratio produced in accordance with Article 6.1 in writing to the enquirer within 7 days of receiving the request; or
(b)   by directing the enquirer within 7 days of receiving the request orally or in writing to the Claims Ratio produced in accordance with Article 6.1 published on the PPI Provider's website if it has done so.

6.7   Whenever a PPI Provider requires and requests information from another PPI Provider or Insurer in order to produce a Claims Ratio in accordance with Article 6.1, the information requested must be provided to the PPI Provider within 7 days of receiving the request.

7. OBLIGATION TO PROVIDE A PERSONAL PPI QUOTE

[4.568]
7.1   A PPI Provider which makes a written or oral Marketing Statement direct to a Consumer either during a Credit Sale or when otherwise promising, offering or arranging to provide Short-Term IP or any other PPI Product Type except for Retail PPI or Stand-Alone PPI, must, subject to Article 7.3, on the same occasion as making the Marketing Statement or as soon as practicable afterwards give the Consumer a Personal PPI Quote in accordance with Article 7.4.

7.2   A PPI Provider which makes a Marketing Statement orally or in writing direct to a Consumer either during a Credit Sale or when otherwise providing Retail PPI or Stand-Alone PPI must, subject to Article 7.3:
(a)   give the Consumer a Personal PPI Quote in a Durable Medium on the same occasion or no later than 14 days after providing the PPI policy; and
(b)   use the Personal PPI Quote format set out in:
   (i)   Schedule 4c(i) for CCPPI provided in the circumstances set out in Article 8.5;
   (ii)   Schedule 4d for Retail PPI; or
   (iii)   Schedule 4e(i) for Stand-Alone PPI other than CCPPI provided in the circumstances set out in Article 8.5; and

(c)   in each case follow the instructions in Schedule 4.

7.3   The obligations in Articles 7.1 or 7.2 do not apply where after making the Marketing Statement:

(a)   the PPI Provider discovers:

     (i)   that the Consumer is ineligible for or does not intend to take out the Credit to which the PPI policy would relate;

     (ii)   that the Consumer is ineligible for the PPI of the kind to which the Marketing Statement relates or the PPI is not suitable for the Consumer; or

     (iii)   that the Consumer does not intend to purchase PPI and does not want to receive a Personal PPI Quote; or

(b)   the PPI Provider is unable to produce a Personal PPI Quote where despite making reasonable endeavours to obtain information from the Consumer in order to provide a Personal PPI Quote, the Consumer does not provide the information; and

(c)   in each case the PPI Provider is able to provide the OFT should the OFT request it with a record of and reasons for the exemption relied upon.

7.4   Where the obligations in Article 7.1 apply, a PPI Provider must give a separate Personal PPI Quote in a Durable Medium to the Consumer for each PPI Product Type or Short-Term IP offered to the Consumer and in each case must follow the instructions in Schedule 4 when completing the Personal PPI Quote and:

(a)   for PLPPI give the Personal PPI Quote in the format set out in Schedule 4a;

(b)   for SMPPI or MPPI give the Personal PPI Quote in the format set out in Schedule 4b(i) or Schedule 4b(ii) where an MPPI or SMPPI policy is provided to joint Policyholders;

(c)   for CCPPI excluding CCPPI sold in the circumstances set out in Article 8.5 give the Personal PPI Quote in the format set out in Schedule 4c(ii);

(d)   for Short-Term IP give the Personal PPI Quote in the format set out in Schedule 4e(ii); and

(e)   for any PPI Product Type or Short-Term IP sold by an Intermediary give the Personal PPI Quote in the format set out in Schedule 4e(ii).

7.5   A PPI Provider may '**give**' the Consumer a Personal PPI Quote by any of the following means:

(a)   direct to the Consumer in person;

(b)   by using Electronic Communication; or

(c)   by post.

7.6   In all cases the PPI Provider must allow the Consumer to buy the PPI at the price stated in the Personal PPI Quote for at least 14 days commencing on the day the Personal PPI Quote is received by the Consumer provided the Consumer remains eligible for the PPI for which the Personal PPI Quote was given.

7.7   The PPI Provider must give the Consumer a new Personal PPI Quote where the previous Personal PPI Quote becomes inaccurate due to:

(a)   material changes to the eligibility of the Consumer for the PPI, which the Consumer notifies to the PPI Provider or the PPI Provider otherwise discovers; or

(b)   material changes to the costs or the benefits of the PPI.

7.8   In any circumstance other than the Consumer receiving the Personal PPI Quote in person or by recorded receipt, the date of receipt after the PPI Provider gives the Personal PPI Quote to the Consumer is deemed to be:

(a)   in the case of posting, the second postal delivery day following the day on which the Personal PPI Quote was posted; or

(b)   in the case of Electronic Communication, the same day.

7.9   For the purposes of this article:

(a)   '**material change**' means a change which could reasonably be expected to influence the Consumer's decision to purchase; and

(b)   '**postal delivery day**' means any day except a Sunday or a Bank Holiday as determined pursuant to the Banking and Financial Dealings Act 1971 in the location of the Consumer.

PART 3
THE PROHIBITIONS

8. PROHIBITION ON SALE OF PPI AT THE CREDIT SALE

[4.569]

8.1   Subject to Articles 8.4 and 8.6 from the start of a Credit Sale determined in accordance with Article 8.2 until the end of the Prohibition Period determined in accordance with Article 8.3 a Credit Arranger or an Associate may provide a Personal PPI Quote to a Consumer but must not provide PPI to a Consumer.

8.2   A Credit Sale starts when a Consumer makes an application for Credit and ends when the Consumer receives confirmation in a Durable Medium that the Credit Provider is bound unconditionally to provide the Credit which is the subject of the application, and in deciding whether:

(a) an application for Credit has been made, no account is taken of:
    (i) an application, request or notification by the Consumer to utilize Credit or vary the amount of Credit which has been approved or agreed under an existing Credit agreement and which does not give rise to a new Credit agreement; or
    (ii) replacement of a Credit Card;
(b) the Credit Provider is bound unconditionally to provide Credit, no account is taken of the conditions in Article 8.2*(b)*(i) to (iii) and a condition is not treated as falling outside the scope of Article 8.2*(b)*(i) to (iii) merely because a matter or a thing needs to be demonstrated or done to the reasonable satisfaction of the Credit Provider or Credit Arranger:
    (i) conditions relating to the value of, title to or any rights or obligations attaching to any property to be offered by way of security for the Credit;
    (ii) conditions which are within the power of the Consumer to fulfil (including conditions relating to actions to be taken by the Consumer to activate a Credit Card or commencing to use a Retail Credit Account); or
    (iii) conditions which are within the power of a third party (other than the Credit Provider or Credit Arranger) to fulfil.

8.3 A Prohibition Period starts at the end of a Credit Sale determined in accordance with Article 8.2 and ends at the later of either:
(a) the start of the 7th consecutive day following the day when the Credit Sale ends; or
(b) the start of the 7th consecutive day following the day the Consumer receives a Personal PPI Quote from the Credit Arranger or Associate.

8.4 Article 8.1 and Article 8.6 do not apply to providing:
(a) Retail PPI which may be provided at any time after the start of a Credit Sale;
(b) Stand-Alone PPI or any PPI Product Type or Short-Term IP deemed to be Stand-Alone in accordance with Article 8.5;
(c) any PPI Product Type or Short-Term IP where all the conditions in Article 8.7 are met.

8.5 Except in the case of Retail PPI, when any PPI Product Type or Short-Term IP is provided to the Consumer by a Credit Arranger or Associate in the circumstances set out in Article 8.5*(a)* and *(b)*, it is deemed to be Stand-Alone PPI and the prohibition in Article 8.1 does not apply:
(a) where the PPI Product Type or Short-Term IP is provided:
    (i) not less than 1 month after the end of a Credit Sale to the Policyholder by the Credit Arranger or Associate; or
    (ii) within 1 month of a Credit Sale where the Credit Arranger or Associate after making reasonable efforts including making inquiries of the Customer and of the Credit Arranger's or Associate's internal records of Credit sales cannot determine if a Credit Sale has been made within the preceding month; and
(b) in each case the Policyholder has received a Personal PPI Quote in accordance with Article 7.2 on the same occasion as, or no later than 14 days after, the PPI Product Type or Short-Term IP is provided.

8.6 A Credit Arranger or Associate who meets all the conditions in Article 8.7 may provide any PPI Product Type or Short-Term IP the day after the later of either the end of the Credit Sale or the receipt by the Consumer of a Personal PPI Quote in accordance with Article 7.4.

8.1 The conditions are:
(a) the Consumer initiates the provision of PPI by contacting the Credit Arranger or Associate by using only either of the two following means:
    (i) in writing using the Internet; or
    (ii) orally by telephone;
(b) the Credit Arranger or Associate does not encourage, suggest or in any other way induce the Consumer to initiate the provision of PPI during the Prohibition Period;
(c) the Consumer confirms to the Credit Arranger or Associate that the Consumer has received the Personal PPI Quote; and
(d) the Credit Arranger or Associate is able to provide the OFT, should the OFT request it, with a record that all of these conditions were met prior to the provision of PPI.

8.8 A Consumer does not 'initiate the provision of PPI' for the purposes of Article 8.7*(a)* where the Consumer's decision to purchase PPI is demonstrably:
(a) confirmation of a pre-agreed sale; or
(b) an affirmative response to a question from the Credit Arranger or Associate.

8.9 The provision of PPI initiated by a Consumer in accordance with Article 8.7*(a)* may be concluded through any sales channel including in-branch.

8.10 If before or after the start of this Order a Consumer enters into an insurance arrangement which has the same effect as PPI but which has the sole, dominant or substantial purpose to avoid the operation of this Order or can reasonably be expected to have that purpose, that insurance arrangement will be regarded as PPI and this Order will apply.

9. PROHIBITION ON SALE OF PPI BEFORE THE START OF THE CREDIT SALE

[4.570]
9.1 Whenever a Credit Arranger has discussed orally or in writing a type of Credit with

a Consumer and has reasonable grounds to believe that the Consumer will make an application for that type of Credit from the Credit Arranger within 7 days of the discussion, the Credit Arranger or an Associate of the Credit Arranger may provide a Personal PPI Quote but must not provide PPI that could provide cover for the type of Credit discussed with the Consumer before the application for the Credit is made.

9.2 Article 9.1 does not apply:
(a) to providing Retail PPI for a Retail Credit Account; or
(b) where the Credit Arranger after making reasonable inquiries of the Consumer and its own internal records does not have reasonable grounds to believe that the Consumer will make an application for the type of Credit discussed.

9.3 For the purposes of Article 9.1, a Credit Arranger or Associate will have 'reasonable grounds to believe' that the Consumer will make an application for the type of Credit discussed if the Credit Arranger has discussed any of the following with the Consumer:
(a) the amount of Credit that may be provided; and
(b) either:
  (i) the terms of repayment of that Credit; or
  (ii) the interest rate or charges payable on that Credit.

10. PROHIBITION OF PAYMENT BY SINGLE PREMIUM AND REQUIREMENT TO PAY A REBATE

[4.571]
10.1 A PPI Provider must not enter into an agreement with a Consumer to provide PPI which requires payment by a Single Premium.

10.2 A PPI policy must not require payment of the Premium other than by Monthly or Annual Premium but payment may be made by any arrangement provided that the arrangement does not result in a payment which constitutes a Single Premium or can reasonably be construed to do so.

10.3 A PPI policy must not require the Policyholder to pay any additional charges for set up, administration or early termination of a PPI policy for any reason.

10.4 Where a PPI policy paid by Annual Premium is terminated by the Policyholder, the PPI Provider must pay a rebate to the Policyholder in direct proportion to the remaining period of cover.

PART 4
REQUIREMENT AS TO SEPARATE SUPPLY

11. DUTY TO OFFER RETAIL PPI SEPARATELY WHEN SOLD IN A PACKAGE OF INSURANCE

[4.572]
11.1 Whenever a PPI Provider offers a package of insurance which contains Retail PPI and Merchandise Cover, the PPI Provider must also:
(a) offer Retail PPI as a separate insurance; and
(b) promote the separate Retail PPI with equal prominence in all written Marketing Communications as the package of insurance.

11.2 A Retail PPI Provider must offer to provide Retail PPI through all sales channels through which it also provides the package of insurance which contains Retail PPI and Merchandise Cover.

PART 5
COMPLIANCE

12. OBLIGATION TO SUBMIT COMPLIANCE REPORTS

[4.573]
12.1 A Compliance Report must be submitted to the OFT in accordance with Article 12.2 by any PPI Provider which in 2007 achieved on a Corporate Group basis either:
(a) a total GWP of £30 million or more; or
(b) a GWP of £10 million or more in relation to any PPI Product Type, Stand-Alone PPI orShort-Term IP.

12.2 A PPI Provider which satisfies the conditions in Article 12.1 must submit a Compliance Report to the OFT subject to Article 12.11:
(a) on the following dates: 6 April 2012, 1 October 2012, 6 April 2013, 1 October 2013 ('**Six-Monthly Compliance Report**'); and
(b) then annually from 6 April 2014 ('**Annual Compliance Report**') provided either of the amounts in Article 12.1*(a)* or *(b)* continue to be achieved in the preceding year.

12.3 Any other PPI Provider that on 6 April 2013 satisfies the conditions in Article 12.4*(a)* or *(b)* must submit a Compliance Report ('**Annual Compliance Report**') to the OFT and annually thereafter on 6 April, subject to Article 12.11, provided the conditions in Article 12.4*(a)* or *(b)* continue to be satisfied.

12.4   The conditions are that in the year preceding 6 April a PPI Provider achieves either:
(a)   a total GWP of £30 million or more; or
(b)   a GWP of £10 million or more in relation to any PPI Product Type, Stand-Alone PPI or Short-Term IP.

12.5   On 6 April 2012 and annually thereafter on 6 April for each year in which both the conditions in *(a)* and *(b)* are satisfied a Compliance Report must be submitted to the OFT, subject to Article 12.11, by a PPI Provider which:
(a)   does not meet the conditions in Articles 12.1*(a)* or *(b)* or 12.4*(a)* or *(b)*; and
(b)   achieves on a Corporate Group basis a total GWP of £10 million or more in the preceding year.

12.6   The Compliance Report submitted by a PPI Provider that meets the conditions in Article 12.5 must set out the annual breakdown of GWP by PPI Product Type, Stand-Alone PPI and Short-Term IP in a format to be determined and advised by the OFT.

12.7   Where PPI Providers are members of the same Corporate Group:
(a)   only one Compliance Report for the Corporate Group must be submitted; and
(b)   the Compliance Report must identify the information in Schedule 5b separately for each PPI Provider.

12.8   A Compliance Report must be prepared at the PPI Provider's election either:
(a)   by an Independent Party; or
(b)   by the PPI Provider.

12.9   A PPI Provider must ensure that:
(a)   where the Compliance Report is prepared by the PPI Provider it includes a certificate signed by an Independent Party verifying that the Compliance Report is true and correct;
(b)   the Compliance Report includes a signed certificate stating that:
    (i)   the Compliance Report has been prepared in accordance with the requirements of this Order; and
    (ii)   for the period to which the Compliance Report relates, the PPI Provider has complied in all material aspects with the requirements of this Order and is reasonably expected to continue to do so; and
(c)   the certificate is signed as follows:
    (i)   for an incorporated PPI Provider, by a director and non-executive director or where there are no non-executive directors, two directors of the PPI Provider;
    (ii)   for an unincorporated PPI Provider, by two principals who are both Approved Persons; or
    (iii)   for a sole trader PPI Provider, by an Approved Person.

12.10   Subject to any additional or different requirements that the OFT may impose pursuant to Schedule 6:
(a)   the Six-Monthly Compliance Report must report on the matters listed in Schedule 5a; and
(b)   the Annual Compliance Report must report on the matters listed in Schedule 5b.

12.11   The obligation to provide a Compliance Report will be satisfied if it is submitted within 1 week of the due date in each case.

12.12   In this article:
(a)   '**Approved Person**' means a person in relation to whom the FSA has given approval under section 59 of the Financial Services and Markets Act 2000 for the performance of activities regulated by section 22;
(b)   '**Independent Party**' means a person expert in the preparation of compliance reports and which is a separate legal entity from and not in the same Corporate Group as any PPI Provider and in which a PPI Provider does not have a beneficial and/or controlling interest; and
(c)   '**preceding year**' means the year which precedes the year for which the Compliance Report is to be submitted.

13. OBLIGATION TO CONDUCT A MYSTERY SHOPPING EXERCISE

[4.574]
13.1   Starting with the year from 6 April 2012 and annually afterwards in addition to any requirements arising under Article 12, a PPI Provider which achieves a total GWP of £60 million or more in a preceding year must commission and conduct an independent mystery shopping exercise in accordance with the requirements in Schedule 5c.

13.2   The independent mystery shopping exercise must not be conducted unless the OFT has agreed to the design.

13.3   A PPI Provider must include a report of the results of the mystery shopping exercise in the Compliance Report prepared in accordance with Article 12.

13.4   In this article '**preceding year**' means the year which precedes the year for which the report of the results of the independent mystery shopping exercise is to be submitted.

14. OBLIGATION TO REPORT ON CLARITY OF MARKETING COMMUNICATION

[4.575]
14.1   A PPI Provider required by Article 12 to submit a Compliance Report must include a report confirming that the Marketing Communications used in the previous year were prepared using easily understandable words and in a clear and comprehensible form.

14.2   A Marketing Communication is 'prepared using easily understandable words and in a clear and comprehensible form' only if it has been either:
(a)   certified as such by an independent organization specializing in plain English; or
(b)   tested with Consumers by an Independent Market Research Agency and found to be using easily understandable words and in a clear and comprehensible form.

15. OBLIGATION TO APPOINT A COMPLIANCE OFFICER

[4.576]
15.1   A PPI Provider within 21 days after 6 April 2011 must:
(a)   appoint a Compliance Officer who is a natural person; and
(b)   notify the name of the Compliance Officer to the OFT.

15.2   In addition to any others, the duties of the Compliance Officer must include:
(a)   monitoring compliance by the PPI Provider with this Order;
(b)   responsibility for compilation and submission of the Compliance Report to the OFT;
(c)   facilitation of the provision of information to the OFT; and
(d)   acting as a point of contact for the OFT with the PPI Provider.

PART 6
THE CC

16. DIRECTIONS BY THE CC AS TO COMPLIANCE

[4.577]
16.1   The CC may give directions falling within Article 16.2 to:
(a)   a person specified in the directions; or
(b)   a holder for the time being of an office so specified in any body of persons corporate or unincorporate.

16.2   Directions fall within this paragraph if they are directions:
(a)   to take such actions as may be specified or described in the directions for the purpose of carrying out, or ensuring compliance with, this Order; or
(b)   to do, or refrain from doing, anything so specified or described which the person might be required by this Order to do or refrain from doing.

16.3   In Article 16.2 above, 'actions' includes steps to introduce and maintain arrangements to ensure that any director, employee or agent of a PPI Provider carries out, or secures compliance with, this Order.

16.4   The CC may vary or revoke any directions so given.

SCHEDULE 1
INFORMATION GIVING RISE TO A MARKETING STATEMENT

[4.578]
Price Information

'Price Information' includes, but is not limited to, the expression of the price or cost of PPI as an exact, indicative or illustrative amount.

Significant benefits of PPI

'Significant benefits of PPI' includes, but is not limited to, claims of 'peace of mind', details of PPI cover and any other claim or assertion which is intended to influence or induce the Consumer to buy PPI.

Significant exclusions or limitations

A significant exclusion or limitation is one that may have an adverse effect on the benefit payable under the PPI policy or affect the Consumer's decision to buy PPI.

Duration

Length of time of the PPI policy or time that benefits are paid under the policy.

SCHEDULE 1A
PRESCRIBED STATEMENT FOR PLPPI, SMPPI, MPPI, CCPPI OR RETAIL PPI FOR INCLUSION IN A MARKETING COMMUNICATION

[4.579]
The Prescribed Statement is:

This Payment Protection Insurance is optional. There are other providers of Payment Protection Insurance and other products designed to protect you against loss of income. For impartial information about insurance, please visit the website at www.moneymadeclear.org.uk.

SCHEDULE 1B
PRESCRIBED STATEMENT FOR STAND-ALONE PPI AND SHORT-TERM IP FOR INCLUSION IN A MARKETING COMMUNICATION

[4.580]
The Prescribed Statement is:

There are other providers of Payment Protection Insurance [Short-Term Income Protection] and other products designed to protect you against loss of income. For impartial information about insurance, please visit the website at www.moneymadeclear.org.uk.

SCHEDULE 2
ADDITIONAL STATEMENT

[4.581]
The Additional Statement is:

'The monthly benefit payable under this policy is for a duration of less than 12 months.'

SCHEDULE 3
ANNUAL REVIEW

INSTRUCTIONS FOR THE ANNUAL REVIEW

[4.582]

(1)   The format of the Annual Review that follows must be used as the basis of the Annual Review provided pursuant to Article 4 and in particular:

    (a)   no text should be omitted or amended but amendments to update the name of a government department or organization or person or place or thing (including a website), may be made;

    (b)   presentation should be clear and easily legible and prominence must be given to text shown in bold;

    (c)   where square brackets or italics indicate that specific information is to be provided (for example, company logo, details of PPI cover, required notice for termination or telephone number), then the PPI Provider's specific information should be used to complete these sections. If a particular section is not applicable to the PPI Provider (for example, if no additional types of PPI cover are provided), then this section can be deleted or completed as 'none' or 'not applicable', as appropriate. If information is unknown to the PPI Provider at the time of issuing the Annual Review (for example, if the PPI Provider does not keep information about its customers' age or employment status) then those sections can be completed as 'not known';

    (d)   colour and shading of the text can be adjusted so long as the other instructions of this schedule are not affected;

    (e)   additional markings such as a bar code may be included provided these markings are solely for the purpose of facilitating processing for the benefit of Consumers and do not detract from the presentation of the required text; and

    (f)   modifications to the placement of the Policyholder's name and address may be made in order to comply with existing systems designed for Consumer communications.

(2)   The Annual Review must always specify Life, Accident & Sickness and Unemployment cover and, where offered, include additional types of cover. If the PPI does not include one or more of Life, Accident & Sickness and Unemployment cover this must be specified as not provided. Details of any additional types of cover must follow the specification of Life, Accident & Sickness and Unemployment cover. If no additional types of cover are offered then the section headed 'other' can be deleted or completed as 'none' or 'not applicable', as appropriate. For each type of cover, state what benefit is paid in the event of a claim.

(3)   Where statements for Credit are provided on a 4-week basis (instead of monthly) instead of the average monthly balance, the average balance of the statement must be used as the basis for the calculations for 'Average Monthly Cost of Payment Protection Insurance in the past year' and 'Average Monthly Cost of Payment Protection Insurance for every £100 of outstanding balance covered'. The description on the form must not be changed, though a note may be included on the form to indicate the basis on which calculations have been made.

(4)   Where instalments are not required by a Credit Provider, the section headed 'instalments' can be deleted.

(5)   Where the Annual Review is for a Short-Term Income Protection Insurance policy, the words 'Payment Protection Insurance' may be replaced with 'Short-term Income Protection'.

(6)   Where a policy summary is sufficiently succinct to be printed on the reverse of the Annual Review, this can be done and the text 'are in the attached policy summary' should be replaced with 'is on the reverse of this page'.

(7)   The title of the form cannot be changed but the name of the product may be given in the line immediately following the title in place of the words 'this insurance'.

(8)   Age should be given as a whole number as at the Policyholder's last birthday. Date of birth may be substituted for Age.

(9)   Annual cost is the calculation of those payments received over the course of the previous year. The average Monthly Cost is the calculation of the mean Monthly Cost over the period the Annual Review refers to. Average outstanding balance is the mean of the outstanding balances shown on the monthly Credit Card or Retail Credit statements over the period the Annual Review refers to.

(10)   The estimated total cost of PPI for the remainder of the credit agreement does not need to be included for policies that are annually renewable and this section can be deleted for such policies.

(11)   'Start date' may be the date of first movement on the account or date of agreement as may be applicable.

(12)   Where no notice is required before cancellation the words 'You can cancel your Payment Protection Policy at any time' may be used.

SCHEDULE 3A

[4.584]

[Name]
[Address Line 1]
[Address Line 2]
[Address Line 3]
[Address Line 4]
[Postcode]

Reference   [x]
Date   [x]

Logo

Annual Review of Optional Payment Protection Insurance on your Personal Loan
This form gives you information about how much this insurance has cost in the past year

Things you should know about your Optional Payment Protection Insurance

You can cancel your policy at any time and it will not affect your credit.

Cheaper or more appropriate cover may be available from other providers. You can compare product features and costs using the Consumer Financial Education Body's comparison tables at www.moneymadeclear.org.uk/tables/bespoke/PPI.

There are other products which can protect you against loss of your income. For impartial information about insurance, please visit the website at: www.moneymadeclear.org.uk/products/insurance/insurance.html.

Further details of cover, including any significant exclusions and limitations, are in the attached policy summary. You should check this form to make sure that all the recorded details are correct, otherwise your insurance cover may be affected.

Payment Protection Insurance cover
Type of cover included

Life	[Repays outstanding balance on loan]
Accident & Sickness	[Up to 12 months of monthly instalments in any claim]
Unemployment	[Up to 12 months of monthly instalments in any claim]
[Other]	[Not included]

We have recorded your current employment status as	[Employed 16+ hours a week]
We have recorded your current age [or Date of birth] as	[Age] or [Date of birth]

Cost of Payment Protection Insurance cover

Annual cost of Payment Protection Insurance in the past year	£[xxx]
Estimated total cost of Payment Protection Insurance for the remainder of the credit agreement	£[xxx]
Average monthly cost of Payment Protection Insurance in the past year	£[xxx]

We have calculated the cost of our Payment Protection Insurance as a **monthly cost for every £100 of monthly benefit below**. This number explains how much this insurance costs you each month for every £100 in benefit that you would receive each month if you made a successful claim for accident, sickness or unemployment. For example, if the number is £5 this means that for every £5 that you pay as a monthly premium, you will get £100 for each [full] month that the claim lasts [less the waiting period on the policy]. This number can be used to make comparisons with the cost of insurance from other providers. You should also compare the cover offered and the way in which benefits are paid out.

Monthly cost of Payment Protection Insurance for every £100 of monthly benefit	£[xxx]

The credit protected by this cover

Original start date	[Date]	Total amount payable	£[xxx]
The term of the credit agreement	[xx] months	Instalments	£[xxx]/month
The total amount of credit	£[xxx]	Amount of monthly repayment covered [if different from instalment]	£[xxx]/month
Total charge for credit	£[xxx]		

Cancellation rights
You can cancel your Payment Protection Insurance at any time [by providing [X] days' notice to your insurer]. To cancel, call [xxx xxxx xxxx] or write to [Customer Services at [X]]. There is no charge for cancellation.
For general enquiries, please call: [xxx xxxx xxxx].

SCHEDULE 3B(I)

[4.585]

[Name]
[Address Line 1]
[Address Line 2]
[Address Line 3]
[Address Line 4]
[Postcode]

Reference   [x]
Date   [x]

Logo

Annual Review of Optional Payment Protection Insurance on your Mortgage

This form gives you information about how much this insurance has cost in the past year

---

Things you should know about your Optional Payment Protection Insurance

You can cancel your policy at any time and it will not affect your credit.

Cheaper or more appropriate cover may be available from other providers. You can compare product features and costs using the Consumer Financial Education Body's comparison tables at **www.moneymadeclear.org.uk/tables/bespoke/PPI**.

There are other products which can protect you against loss of your income. For impartial information about insurance, please visit the website at: **www.moneymadeclear.org.uk/products/insurance/insurance.html**.

Further details of cover, including any significant exclusions and limitations, are in the attached policy summary. You should check this form to make sure that all the recorded details are correct, otherwise your insurance cover may be affected.

Payment Protection Insurance cover

Type of cover included

Life	[Not included]
Accident & Sickness	[Up to 12 months of monthly instalments per claim]
Unemployment	[Up to 12 months of monthly instalments per claim]
[Other]	[Not included]

We have recorded your current employment status as   [Employed 16+ hours a week]

We have recorded your current age [or Date of birth] as   [Age] or [Date of birth]

Cost of Payment Protection Insurance cover

Annual cost of Payment Protection Insurance in the past year	£[xxx]
Estimated total cost of Payment Protection Insurance for the remainder of the loan agreement	£[xxx]
Average monthly cost of Payment Protection Insurance in the past year	£[xxx]

We have calculated the cost of our Payment Protection Insurance as a **monthly cost for every £100 of monthly benefit below**. This number explains how much this insurance costs you each month for every £100 in benefit that you would receive each month if you made a successful claim for accident, sickness or unemployment. For example, if the number is £5 this means that for every £5 that you pay as a monthly premium, you will get £100 for each [full] month that the claim lasts [less the waiting period on the policy]. This number can be used to make comparisons with the cost of insurance from other providers. You should also compare the cover offered and the way in which benefits are paid out.

Monthly cost of Payment Protection Insurance for every £100 of monthly benefit	£[xxx]

The mortgage protected by this cover

Original start date	[Date]	The total remaining amount you must pay back including the amount borrowed as at [date]	£[xxx]
Remaining term of the loan agreement	[xx] years	Payments	£[xxx]/month
Total outstanding loan as at [date]	£[xxx]	Amount of monthly payment covered [if different from monthly payment]	£[xxx]/month
[Estimated] Total remaining charge for loan as at [date]	£[xxx]		

Cancellation rights
You can cancel your Payment Protection Insurance at any time [by providing [X] days' notice to your insurer]. To cancel, call [xxx xxxx xxxx] or write to [Customer Services at [X]]. There is no charge for cancellation.
For general enquiries, please call: [xxx xxxx xxxx].

SCHEDULE 3B(II)

[4.586]

[Name]
[Address Line 1]
[Address Line 2]
[Address Line 3]
[Address Line 4]   Reference   [x]
[Postcode]   Date   [x]

Logo

Annual Review of Optional Payment Protection Insurance on your Joint Mortgage
This form gives you information about how much this insurance has cost in the past year

Things you should know about your Optional Payment Protection Insurance
You can cancel your policy at any time and it will not affect your credit.

Cheaper or more appropriate cover may be available from other providers. You can compare product features and costs using the Consumer Financial Education Body's comparison tables at **www.moneymadeclear.org.uk/tables/bespoke/PPI.**

There are other products which can protect you against loss of your income. For impartial information about insurance, please visit the website at: **www.moneymadeclear.org.uk/products/insurance/insurance.html.**

Further details of cover, including any significant exclusions and limitations, are in the attached policy summary. You should check this form to make sure that all the recorded details are correct, otherwise your insurance cover may be affected.

Payment Protection Insurance cover

Type of cover included	Beneficiary 1	Beneficiary 2
Life	[Not included]	[Not included]
Accident & Sickness	[Up to 12 months of monthly instalments per claim]	[Up to 12 months of monthly instalments per claim]
Unemployment	[Up to 12 months of monthly instalments per claim]	[Up to 12 months of monthly instalments per claim]
[Other]	[Not included]	[Not included]
We have recorded your current employment status as	[Employed 16+ hours a week]	[Employed 16+ hours a week]
We have recorded your current age [or Date of birth] as	[Age] or [Date of birth]	[Age] or [Date of birth]

Cost of Payment Protection Insurance cover

Annual cost of Payment Protection Insurance in the past year	£[xxx]	£[xxx]
Estimated total cost of Payment Protection Insurance for the remainder of the loan agreement	£[xxx]	£[xxx]
Average monthly cost of Payment Protection Insurance	£[xxx]	£[xxx]

We have calculated the cost of our Payment Protection Insurance as a **monthly cost for every £100 of monthly benefit below.** This number explains how much this insurance costs you each month for every £100 in benefit that you would receive each month if you made a successful claim for accident, sickness or unemployment. For example, if the number is £5 this means that for every £5 that you pay as a monthly premium, you will get £100 for each [full] month that the claim lasts [less the waiting period on the policy]. This number can be used to make comparisons with the cost of insurance from other providers. You should also compare the cover offered and the way in which benefits are paid out.

Monthly cost of Payment Protection Insurance for every £100 of monthly benefit	£[xxx]	£[xxx]

The mortgage protected by this cover

Original start date	[Date]	The total remaining amount you must pay back including the amount borrowed as at [date]	£[xxx]
Remaining term of the loan agreement	[xx] years	Payments	£[xxx]/month
Total outstanding loan as at [date]	£[xxx]	Amount of monthly payment covered [if different from monthly payment]	£[xxx]/month
[Estimated] Total remaining charge for loan as at [date]	£[xxx]		

Cancellation rights
You can cancel your Payment Protection Insurance at any time [by providing [X] days' notice to your insurer]. To cancel, call [xxx xxxx xxxx] or write to [Customer Services at [X]]. There is no charge for cancellation.
For general enquiries, please call: [xxx xxxx xxxx].

SCHEDULE 3C

[4.587]

[Name]
[Address Line 1]
[Address Line 2]
[Address Line 3]
[Address Line 4]   Reference   [x]
[Postcode]   Date   [x]

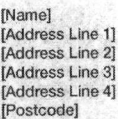
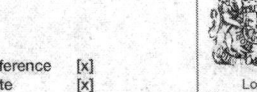

Logo

Annual Review of Optional Payment Protection Insurance on your Credit Card

This form gives you information about how much this insurance has cost in the past year

Things you should know about your Optional Payment Protection Insurance

You can cancel your policy at any time and it will not affect your credit.

Cheaper or more appropriate cover may be available from other providers. You can compare product features and costs using the Consumer Financial Education Body's comparison tables at **www.moneymadeclear.org.uk/tables/bespoke/PPI**.

There are other products which can protect you against loss of your income. For impartial information about insurance, please visit the website at: **www.moneymadeclear.org.uk/products/insurance/insurance.html**.

Further details of cover, including any significant exclusions and limitations, are in the attached policy summary. You should check this form to make sure that all the recorded details are correct, otherwise your insurance cover may be affected.

Payment Protection Insurance cover
Type of cover included

Life	[Repays outstanding balance up to a maximum of £10,000]
Accident & Sickness	[Repays 10% of your outstanding balance for up to 12 months in any claim]
Unemployment	[Repays 10% of your outstanding balance for up to 12 months in any claim]
[Other]	[Not included]
We have recorded your current employment status as	[Employed 16+ hours a week]
We have recorded your current age [or Date of birth] as	[Age] or [Date of birth]

Cost of Payment Protection Insurance cover

Annual cost of Payment Protection Insurance in the past year	£[xxx]
Average monthly cost of Payment Protection Insurance in the past year	£[xxx]
Monthly cost of Payment Protection Insurance for every £100 outstanding balance covered	£[xxx]

We have calculated the cost of our Payment Protection Insurance as a **monthly cost for every £100 of monthly benefit below**. This number explains how much this insurance costs you each month for every £100 in benefit that you would receive each month if you made a successful claim for accident, sickness or unemployment. For example, if the number is £5 this means that for every £5 that you pay as a monthly premium, you will get £100 for each [full] month that the claim lasts [less the waiting period on the policy]. This number can be used to make comparisons with the cost of insurance from other providers. You should also compare the cover offered and the way in which benefits are paid out.

Monthly cost of Payment Protection Insurance for every £100 of monthly benefit	£[xxx]

The credit protected by this cover

Credit limit, as at the date of this annual review	£[xxx]
Average outstanding balance in past year	£[xxx]

Cancellation rights

You can cancel your Payment Protection Insurance at any time [by providing [X] days' notice to your insurer]. To cancel, call [xxx xxxx xxxx] or write to [Customer Services at [X]]. There is no charge for cancellation.
For general enquiries, please call: [xxx xxxx xxxx].

SCHEDULE 3D(I)

[4.588]

[Name]
[Address Line 1]
[Address Line 2]
[Address Line 3]
[Address Line 4]
[Postcode]

Reference [x]
Date [x]

Logo

Annual Review of Optional Payment Protection Insurance on your Home Shopping Account

This form gives you information about how much this insurance has cost in the past year

Things you should know about your Optional Payment Protection Insurance

You can cancel your policy at any time and it will not affect your credit.

Cheaper or more appropriate cover may be available from other providers. You can compare product features and costs using the Consumer Financial Education Body's comparison tables at **www.moneymadeclear.org.uk/tables/bespoke/PPI**.

There are other products which can protect you against loss of your income. For impartial information about insurance, please visit the website at: **www.moneymadeclear.org.uk/products/insurance/insurance.html**.

Further details of cover, including any exclusions and limitations, are in the attached policy summary. You should check this form to make sure that all the recorded details are correct, otherwise your insurance cover may be affected.

Payment Protection Insurance cover

Type of cover included

Life	[Repays outstanding balance up to a maximum of £10,000]
Accident & Sickness	[Repays 10% of your outstanding balance for up to 6 months in any claim]
Unemployment	[Repays 10% of your outstanding balance for up to 6 months in any claim]
[Other]	[Not included]

We have recorded your current employment status as [Employed 16+ hours a week]

We have recorded your current age or [Date of birth] as [Age] or [Date of birth]

Cost of Payment Protection Insurance cover

Annual cost of Payment Protection Insurance in past year	£[xxx]
Average monthly cost of Payment Protection Insurance in past year	£[xxx]
Average monthly cost of Payment Protection Insurance for every £100 outstanding balance covered	£[xxx]

We have calculated the cost of our Payment Protection Insurance as a **monthly cost for every £100 of monthly benefit below**. This number explains how much this insurance costs you each month for every £100 in benefit that you would receive each month if you made a successful claim for accident, sickness or unemployment. For example, if the number is £5 this means that for every £5 that you pay as a monthly premium, you will get £100 for each [full] month that the claim lasts [less the waiting period on the policy]. This number can be used to make comparisons with the cost of insurance from other providers. You should also compare the cover offered and the way in which benefits are paid out.

Monthly cost of Payment Protection Insurance for every £100 of monthly benefit £[xxx]

The credit protected by this cover

Credit limit, as at the date of this annual review	£[xxx]
Average outstanding balance in past year	£[xxx]

Cancellation rights
You can cancel your Payment Protection Insurance at any time [by providing [X] days' notice to your insurer]. To cancel, call [xxx xxxx xxxx] or write to [Customer Services at [X]]. There is no charge for cancellation.
For general enquiries, please call: [xxx xxxx xxxx].

SCHEDULE 3D(II)
ANNUAL REMINDER FOR RETAIL PPI

[4.589]

Payment Protection Insurance is optional. Cheaper or more appropriate cover may be available from other providers. You can compare product features and costs using the Consumer Financial Education Body's comparison tables at www.moneymadeclear.org.uk/tables/bespoke/PPI. You can cancel your Payment Protection Insurance at any time [by providing X days' notice]. To cancel, call [xxx xxx xxx] or write to Customer Services at [X]. There is no charge for cancellation.

SCHEDULE 3E

[4.590]

<table>
<tr><td>

[Name]
[Address Line 1]
[Address Line 2]
[Address Line 3]
[Address Line 4]
[Postcode]

</td><td>

Reference   [x]
Date   [x]

</td><td>

Logo

</td></tr>
</table>

Annual Review of your Optional Payment Protection Insurance [Stand Alone]
This form gives you information about how much this insurance has cost in the past year

Things you should know about your Optional Payment Protection Insurance
You can cancel your policy at any time.

Cheaper or more appropriate cover may be available from other providers. You can compare product features and costs using the Consumer Financial Education Body's comparison tables at **www.moneymadeclear.org.uk/tables/bespoke/PPI.**

There are other products which can protect you against loss of your income. For impartial information about insurance, please visit the website at: **www.moneymadeclear.org.uk/products/insurance/insurance.html.**

Further details of cover, including any exclusions and limitations, are in the attached policy summary. You should check this form to make sure that all the recorded details are correct, otherwise your insurance cover may be affected.

Payment Protection Insurance cover
Type of cover included

Life	[Repays up to a maximum of £10,000]
Accident & Sickness	[Up to 12 months' benefit]
Unemployment	[Up to 12 months' benefit]
[Other]	[Not included]

We have recorded your current employment status as	[Employed 16+ hours a week]
We have recorded your current age [or Date of birth] as	[Age] or [Date of birth]

Cost of Payment Protection Insurance cover

Annual cost of Payment Protection Insurance in past year	£[xxx]
Average monthly cost of Payment Protection Insurance in the past year	£[xxx]

We have calculated the cost of our Payment Protection Insurance as a **monthly cost for every £100 of monthly benefit below.** This number explains how much this insurance costs you each month for every £100 in benefit that you would receive each month if you made a successful claim for accident, sickness or unemployment. For example, if the number is £5 this means that for every £5 that you pay as a monthly premium, you will get £100 for each [full] month that the claim lasts [less the excess period on the policy]. This number can be used to make comparisons with the cost of insurance from other providers. You should also compare the cover offered and the way in which benefits are paid out.

Monthly cost of Payment Protection Insurance for every £100 of monthly benefit	£[xxx]

Monthly income [or monthly repayment] protected by this cover [or monthly benefit]

Amount of monthly income [or repayment] protected	£[xxx]
or	
[Your monthly benefit is]	£[xxx]

Cancellation rights
You can cancel your Payment Protection Insurance at any time [by providing [X] days' notice to your insurer]. To cancel, call [xxx xxxx xxxx] or write to [Customer Services at [X]]. There is no charge for cancellation.
For general enquiries, please call: [xxx xxxx xxxx].

SCHEDULE 4
PERSONAL PPI QUOTE

INSTRUCTIONS FOR QUOTES

[4.591]

(1)   The form of the quotes that follow must be used for the format of the quote provided by any PPI Provider and in particular:

      (a)   no text should be omitted or amended but amendments to update the name of a government department or organization or person or place or thing (including a website), may be made;

      (b)   presentation must be clear and legible and prominence must be given to text shown in bold;

      (c)   where square brackets or italics indicate that certain specific information is to be provided (for example, company logo, reference, dates, how long the quote is valid for, PPI details, website address or telephone number), then the PPI Provider should use its own PPI Provider-specific information to complete these sections where this is relevant. If a particular section is not applicable to the PPI Provider (for example, if PPI is not sold via the Internet or if no additional types of cover are offered) then this section can be deleted or completed as 'none' or 'not applicable', as appropriate. If information is unknown to the PPI Provider at the time of issuing the quote (for example, if the details of the Credit have not yet been finalized) then those sections can be completed as 'not known'; and

      (d)   colour and shading of the text can be adjusted so long as the other instructions of this schedule are not affected.

(2)   The quote must always specify Life, Accident & Sickness and Unemployment cover and, where offered, include additional types of cover. If the PPI does not include one or more of Life, Accident & Sickness and Unemployment cover this must be specified as not provided. Details of any additional types of cover must follow the specification of Life, Accident & Sickness and Unemployment cover. If no additional types of cover are offered then the section headed 'other' can be deleted or completed as 'none' or 'not applicable', as appropriate. For each type of cover, state what benefit is paid in the event of a claim.

(3)   If the total cost of PPI is the same as the annual cost of PPI, it need not be included separately.

(4)   If the Monthly Cost for every £100 Monthly Benefit varies with the payment terms on which goods are purchased using a Retail Credit Account and this is not known at the time of issuing the Personal PPI Quote, Retail PPI Providers may use an illustrative value in Schedule 4d. (This may be based on the most frequently used payment terms on which goods are purchased using the Retail Credit Account in question.)

(5)   Where instalments are not required by a Credit Provider, the section headed 'instalments' can be deleted.

(6)   Where the Personal PPI Quote is for a Short-Term IP Policy, the words 'Payment Protection Insurance' may be replaced with 'Short-term Income Protection'.

(7)   Where a policy summary is sufficiently succinct to be printed on the reverse of the Personal PPI Quote, this can be done and the text 'are in the attached policy summary' should be replaced with 'are on the reverse of this page'.

(8)   The title of the form cannot be changed but the name of the product may be given in the line immediately following the title in place of the words 'this insurance'.

(9)   Annual cost is the estimated or actual annual cost of the PPI being quoted. Monthly cost is the estimated or actual Monthly Cost of the PPI being quoted.

(10)   The estimated total cost of PPI for the remainder of the credit agreement does not need to be included for policies that are annually renewable and this section can be deleted for such policies.

(11)   Where PPI is offered to more than one Consumer including a joint or group discount, the Personal PPI Quote for each Consumer will include that portion of any such discount as is appropriate.

(12)   The Personal PPI Quote issued for Retail PPI may display both the price of PPI as a separate insurance and the price of PPI together with Merchandise Cover.

SCHEDULE 4A

[4.593]

[Name]
[Address Line 1]
[Address Line 2]
[Address Line 3]
[Address Line 4]
[Postcode]   Reference   [x]
                                                    Date   [x]

Logo

Quote for Optional Payment Protection Insurance on your Personal Loan
This form gives you information about how much this insurance will cost

Things you should know about Optional Payment Protection Insurance

Taking out this insurance is optional and does not increase your chances of obtaining credit.

Cheaper or more appropriate cover may be available from other providers. You can compare product features and costs using the Consumer Financial Education Body's comparison tables at **www.moneymadeclear.org.uk/tables/bespoke/PPI.**

There are other products which can protect you against loss of your income. For impartial information about insurance, please visit the website at: **www.moneymadeclear.org.uk/products/insurance/insurance.html.**

Further details of cover, including any significant exclusions and limitations, are in the attached policy summary. This quote is valid [for [X] days] provided that you remain eligible for this product. Before we are allowed to sell you Payment Protection Insurance we will need to tell you about its key features, significant benefits, exclusions and limitations and tell you about any parts of the policy you may not be eligible to make a claim under given your personal circumstances.

Payment Protection Insurance quote
Type of cover included

Life	[Repays outstanding balance on loan]
Accident & Sickness	[Up to 12 months of monthly instalments in any claim]
Unemployment	[Up to 12 months of monthly instalments in any claim]
[Other]	[Not included]

Cost of Payment Protection Insurance cover

Annual cost of Payment Protection Insurance	£[xxx]
Estimated total cost of Payment Protection Insurance for the duration of the credit agreement	£[xxx]
Monthly cost of Payment Protection Insurance	£[xxx]

We have calculated a **combined APR** to illustrate the cost of taking the credit and Payment Protection Insurance together. Comparing this measure with the APR of the credit alone gives an indication of the additional cost of Payment Protection Insurance over a period.

| Combined APR (credit and Payment Protection Insurance) | [xx]% |

We have calculated the cost of our Payment Protection Insurance as a **monthly cost for every £100 of monthly benefit below**. This number explains how much this insurance costs you each month for every £100 in benefit that you would receive each month if you made a successful claim for accident, sickness or unemployment. For example, if the number is £5 this means that for every £5 that you pay as a monthly premium, you will get £100 for each [full] month that the claim lasts [less the waiting period on the policy]. This number can be used to make comparisons with the cost of insurance from other providers. You should also compare the cover offered and the way in which benefits are paid out.

| Monthly cost of Payment Protection Insurance for every £100 of monthly benefit | £[xxx] |

The credit on which this quote is based

Start date (if known)	[date]	Total amount payable	£[xxx]
The term of the credit agreement	[xx] months	Annual Percentage Rate of Charge (APR)	[xx]%
The total amount of credit	£[xxx]	Instalments	£[xxx]/month
Total charge for credit	£[xxx]	Amount of monthly repayment covered [if different from instalment]	£[xxx]/month

As the provider of this credit we are not allowed to complete the sale of Payment Protection Insurance at the same time as you take out the credit. This is to give you time to compare this policy against alternatives. If you decide that you would like to take out this Payment Protection Insurance policy from us, please [ring [xxx xxxx xxxx] or visit [www.xxx.com] on or after [the next day after the later of the end of the credit sale or the date of quote]].

© Competition Commission   Published by LexisNexis.

SCHEDULE 4B(I)

[4.594]

[Name]
[Address Line 1]
[Address Line 2]
[Address Line 3]
[Address Line 4]
[Postcode]

Reference　　[x]
Date　　　　[x]

Logo

Quote for Optional Payment Protection Insurance on your Mortgage
This form gives you information about how much this insurance will cost

Things you should know about Optional Payment Protection Insurance

Taking out this insurance is optional and does not increase your chances of obtaining credit.

Cheaper or more appropriate cover may be available from other providers. You can compare product features and costs using the Consumer Financial Education Body's comparison tables at **www.moneymadeclear.org.uk/tables/bespoke/PPI**.

There are other products which can protect you against loss of your income. For impartial information about insurance, please visit the website at: **www.moneymadeclear.org.uk/products/insurance/insurance.html**.

Further details of cover, including any significant exclusions and limitations, are in the attached policy summary. This quote is valid [for [X] days] provided that you remain eligible for this product. Before we are allowed to sell you Payment Protection Insurance we will need to tell you about its key features, significant benefits, exclusions and limitations and tell you about any parts of the policy you may not be eligible to make a claim under given your personal circumstances.

Payment Protection Insurance quote

Type of cover included

Life	[Not included]
Accident & Sickness	[Up to 12 months of monthly instalments in any claim]
Unemployment	[Up to 12 months of monthly instalments in any claim]
[Other]	[Not included]

Cost of Payment Protection Insurance cover

Annual cost of Payment Protection Insurance	£[xxx]
Total cost of Payment Protection Insurance for the duration of the loan agreement	£[xxx]
Monthly cost of Payment Protection Insurance	£[xxx]

We have calculated a **combined APR** to illustrate the cost of taking the mortgage and Payment Protection Insurance together. Comparing this measure with the APR of the mortgage alone gives an indication of the additional cost of Payment Protection Insurance over a period.

Combined APR (mortgage and Payment Protection Insurance)	[xx]%

We have calculated the cost of our Payment Protection Insurance as a **monthly cost for every £100 of monthly benefit below**. This number explains how much this insurance costs you each month for every £100 in benefit that you would receive each month if you made a successful claim for accident, sickness or unemployment. For example, if the number is £5 this means that for every £5 that you pay as a monthly premium, you will get £100 for each [full] month that the claim lasts [less the waiting period on the policy]. This number can be used to make comparisons with the cost of insurance from other providers. You should also compare the cover offered and the way in which benefits are paid out.

Monthly cost of Payment Protection Insurance for every £100 of monthly benefit	£[xxx]

The mortgage on which this quote is based

Start date (if known)	[date]	The total amount you must pay back including the amount borrowed	£[xxx]
The term of the loan agreement	[xx] years	Annual Percentage Rate of Charge (APR)	[xx]%
Total loan	£[xxx]	Payments	£[xxx]/month
Total charge for loan	£[xxx]	Amount of monthly payment covered [if different from monthly payment]	£[xxx]/month

As the provider of this mortgage we are not allowed to complete the sale of Payment Protection Insurance at the same time as you take out the mortgage. This is to give you time to compare this policy against alternatives. If you decide that you would like to take out this Payment Protection Insurance policy from us, please [ring [xxx xxxx xxxx] or visit [www.xxx.com] on or after [the next day after the later of the end of the credit sale or the date of quote]].

SCHEDULE 4B(II)

[4.595]

[Name]
[Address Line 1]
[Address Line 2]
[Address Line 3]
[Address Line 4]
[Postcode]

Reference   [x]
Date   [x]

Logo

Quote for Optional Payment Protection Insurance on your Joint Mortgage
This form gives you information about how much this insurance will cost

Things you should know about Optional Payment Protection Insurance

Taking out this insurance is optional and does not increase your chances of obtaining credit.

Cheaper or more appropriate cover may be available from other providers. You can compare product features and costs using the Consumer Financial Education Body's comparison tables at **www.moneymadeclear.org.uk/tables/bespoke/PPI**.

There are other products which can protect you against loss of your income. For impartial information about insurance, please visit the website at: **www.moneymadeclear.org.uk/products/insurance/insurance.html**.

Further details of cover, including any significant exclusions and limitations, are in the attached policy summary. This quote is valid [for [X] days] provided that you remain eligible for this product. Before we are allowed to sell you Payment Protection Insurance we will need to tell you about its key features, significant benefits, exclusions and limitations and tell you about any parts of the policy you may not be eligible to make a claim under given your personal circumstances.

Payment Protection Insurance quote

Type of cover included	Beneficiary 1	Beneficiary 2
Life	[Not included]	[Not included]
Accident & Sickness	[Up to 12 months of monthly instalments in any claim]	[Up to 12 months of monthly instalments in any claim]
Unemployment	[Up to 12 months of monthly instalments in any claim]	[Up to 12 months of monthly instalments in any claim]
[Other]	[Not included]	[Not included]

Cost of Payment Protection Insurance cover

	Beneficiary 1	Beneficiary 2
Annual cost of Payment Protection Insurance	£[xxx]	£[xxx]
Total cost of Payment Protection Insurance for the duration of the credit agreement	£[xxx]	£[xxx]
Monthly cost of Payment Protection Insurance	£[xxx]	£[xxx]

We have calculated a **combined APR** to illustrate the cost of taking the mortgage and Payment Protection Insurance together. Comparing this measure with the APR of the mortgage alone gives an indication of the additional cost of Payment Protection Insurance over a period.

Combined APR (mortgage and Payment Protection Insurance)	[xx]%	[xx]%

We have calculated the cost of our Payment Protection Insurance as a **monthly cost for every £100 of monthly benefit below**. This number explains how much this insurance costs you each month for every £100 in benefit that you would receive each month if you made a successful claim for accident, sickness or unemployment. For example, if the number is £5 this means that for every £5 that you pay as a monthly premium, you will get £100 for each [full] month that the claim lasts [less the waiting period on the policy]. This number can be used to make comparisons with the cost of insurance from other providers. You should also compare the cover offered and the way in which benefits are paid out.

Monthly cost of Payment Protection Insurance for every £100 of monthly benefit	£[xxx]	£[xxx]

The mortgage on which this quote is based

Start date (if known)	[date]	The total amount you must pay back including the amount borrowed	£[xxx]
The term of the loan agreement	[xx] years	Annual Percentage Rate of Charge (APR)	[xx]%
Total loan	£[xxx]	Payments	£[xxx]/month
Total charge for loan	£[xxx]	Amount of monthly payment covered [if different from monthly payment]	£[xxx]/month

As the provider of this mortgage we are not allowed to complete the sale of Payment Protection Insurance at the same time as you take out the mortgage. This is to give you time to compare this policy against alternatives. If you decide that you would like to take out this Payment Protection Insurance policy from us, please [ring [xxx xxxx xxxx] or visit [www.xxx.com] on or after [the next day after the later of the end of the credit sale or the date of quote]].

SCHEDULE 4C(I)

[4.596]

[Name]
[Address Line 1]
[Address Line 2]
[Address Line 3]
[Address Line 4]
[Postcode]

Reference   [X]
Date   [X]

Logo

Quote for Optional Payment Protection Insurance on your Credit Card [Stand-Alone]

This form gives you information about how much this insurance will cost

Things you should know about Optional Payment Protection Insurance

Cheaper or more appropriate cover may be available from other providers. You can compare product features and costs using the Consumer Financial Education Body's comparison tables at **www.moneymadeclear.org.uk/tables/bespoke/PPI.**

There are other products which can protect you against loss of your income. For impartial information about insurance, please visit the website at: **www.moneymadeclear.org.uk/products/insurance/insurance.html.**

Further details of cover, including any significant exclusions and limitations, are in the attached policy summary. This quote is valid [for [X] days] provided that you remain eligible for this product.

Payment Protection Insurance quote

Type of cover included

Life	[Repays outstanding balance up to a maximum of £10,000]
Accident & Sickness	[Repays 10% of your outstanding balance for up to 12 months in any claim]
Unemployment	[Repays 10% of your outstanding balance for up to 12 months in any claim]
[Other]	[Not included]

Cost of Payment Protection Insurance cover

Illustrative annual cost of Payment Protection Insurance (based on a typical outstanding balance of £1,000 each month for one year)	£[xxx]
Illustrative monthly cost of Payment Protection Insurance (based on a typical outstanding balance of £1,000 for each month)	£[xxx]
Monthly cost of Payment Protection Insurance for every £100 outstanding balance covered	£[xxx]

We have calculated a **combined APR** to illustrate the cost of taking the credit and Payment Protection Insurance together. Comparing this measure with the APR of the credit alone gives an indication of the additional cost of Payment Protection Insurance over a period.

Combined APR (credit and Payment Protection Insurance)	[xx]%

We have calculated the cost of our Payment Protection Insurance as a **monthly cost for every £100 of monthly benefit below.** This number explains how much this insurance costs you each month for every £100 in benefit that you would receive each month if you made a successful claim for accident, sickness or unemployment. For example, if the number is £5 this means that for every £5 that you pay as a monthly premium, you will get £100 for each [full] month that the claim lasts [less the waiting period on the policy]. This number can be used to make comparisons with the cost of insurance from other providers. You should also compare the cover offered and the way in which benefits are paid out.

Monthly cost of Payment Protection Insurance for every £100 of monthly benefit	£[xxx]

The credit on which this quote is based

Credit limit (if known)	£[xxx]
Annual Percentage Rate of Charge (APR)	[xx]%

Cancellation rights
You can cancel your Payment Protection Insurance at any time [by providing [X] days' notice to your insurer]. To cancel, call [xxx xxxx xxxx] or write to [Customer Services at [X]]. There is no charge for cancellation.

For general enquiries, please call: [xxx xxxx xxxx].

SCHEDULE 4C(II)

[4.597]

[Name]
[Address Line 1]
[Address Line 2]
[Address Line 3]
[Address Line 4]
[Postcode]

Reference   [x]
Date   [x]

Logo

Quote for Optional Payment Protection Insurance on your Credit Card
This form gives you information about how much this insurance will cost

Things you should know about Optional Payment Protection Insurance
Taking out this insurance is optional and does not increase your chances of obtaining credit.

Cheaper or more appropriate cover may be available from other providers. You can compare product features and costs using the Consumer Financial Education Body's comparison tables at **www.moneymadeclear.org.uk/tables/bespoke/PPI**.

There are other products which can protect you against loss of your income. For impartial information about insurance, please visit the website at: **www.moneymadeclear.org.uk/products/insurance/insurance.html**.

Further details of cover, including any significant exclusions and limitations, are in the attached policy summary. This quote is valid [for [X] days] provided that you remain eligible for this product. Before we are allowed to sell you Payment Protection Insurance we will need to tell you about its key features, significant benefits, exclusions and limitations and tell you about any parts of the policy you may not be eligible to make a claim under given your personal circumstances.

Payment Protection Insurance quote
Type of cover included

Life	[Repays outstanding balance up to a maximum of £10,000]
Accident & Sickness	[Repays 10% of your outstanding balance for up to 12 months in any claim]
Unemployment	[Repays 10% of your outstanding balance for up to 12 months in any claim]
[Other]	[Not included]

Cost of Payment Protection Insurance cover

Illustrative annual cost of Payment Protection Insurance (based on a typical outstanding balance of £1,000 each month for one year)	£[xxx]
Illustrative monthly cost of Payment Protection Insurance (based on a typical outstanding balance of £1,000 for each month)	£[xxx]
Monthly cost of Payment Protection Insurance for every £100 outstanding balance covered	£[xxx]

We have calculated a **combined APR** to illustrate the cost of taking the credit and Payment Protection Insurance together. Comparing this measure with the APR of the credit alone gives an indication of the additional cost of Payment Protection Insurance over a period.

Combined APR (credit and Payment Protection Insurance)	[xx]%

We have calculated the cost of our Payment Protection Insurance as a **monthly cost for every £100 of monthly benefit below**. This number explains how much this insurance costs you each month for every £100 in benefit that you would receive each month if you made a successful claim for accident, sickness or unemployment. For example, if the number is £5 this means that for every £5 that you pay as a monthly premium, you will get £100 for each [full] month that the claim lasts [less the waiting period on the policy]. This number can be used to make comparisons with the cost of insurance from other providers. You should also compare the cover offered and the way in which benefits are paid out.

Monthly cost of Payment Protection Insurance for every £100 of monthly benefit	£[xxx]

The credit on which this quote is based

Credit limit (if known)	£[xxx]
Annual Percentage Rate of Charge (APR)	[xx]%

As the provider of this credit we are not allowed to complete the sale of Payment Protection Insurance at the same time as you take out the credit. This is to give you time to compare this policy against alternatives. If you decide that you would like to take out this Payment Protection Insurance policy from us, please [ring [xxx xxxx xxxx] or visit [www.xxx.com] on or after [the next day after the later of the end of the credit sale or the date of quote]].

SCHEDULE 4D

[4.598]

[Name]
[Address Line 1]
[Address Line 2]
[Address Line 3]
[Address Line 4]
[Postcode]

Reference   [X]
Date   [X]

Logo

Quote for Optional Payment Protection Insurance on your Home Shopping Account

This form gives you information about how much this insurance will cost

Things you should know about Optional Payment Protection Insurance

Taking out this insurance is optional and does not increase your chances of obtaining credit.

Cheaper or more appropriate cover may be available from other providers. You can compare product features and costs using the Consumer Financial Education Body's comparison tables at **www.moneymadeclear.org.uk/tables/bespoke/PPI**.

There are other products which can protect you against loss of your income. For impartial information about insurance, please visit the website at: **www.moneymadeclear.org.uk/products/insurance/insurance.html**.

Further details of cover, including any significant exclusions and limitations, are in the attached policy summary. This quote is valid [for [X] days] provided that you remain eligible for this product.

Payment Protection Insurance quote

Type of cover included

Life	[Repays outstanding balance up to a maximum of £10,000]
Accident & Sickness	[Repays 10% of your outstanding balance for up to 6 months in any claim]
Unemployment	[Repays 10% of your outstanding balance for up to 6 months in any claim]
[Other]	[Not included]

Cost of Payment Protection Insurance cover

Illustrative annual cost of Payment Protection Insurance (based on a typical outstanding balance of £300 each month for one year)	£[xxx]
Illustrative monthly cost of Payment Protection Insurance (based on a typical outstanding balance of £300 for each month)	£[xxx]
Monthly cost of Payment Protection Insurance for every £100 outstanding balance covered	£[xxx]

We have calculated a **combined APR** to illustrate the cost of taking the credit and Payment Protection Insurance together. Comparing this measure with the APR of the credit alone gives an indication of the additional cost of Payment Protection Insurance over a period.

Combined APR (credit and Payment Protection Insurance)	[xx]%

We have calculated the cost of our Payment Protection Insurance as a **monthly cost for every £100 of monthly benefit below**. This number explains how much this insurance costs you each month for every £100 in benefit that you would receive each month if you made a successful claim for accident, sickness or unemployment. For example, if the number is £5 this means that for every £5 that you pay as a monthly premium, you will get £100 for each [full] month that the claim lasts [less the waiting period on the policy]. This number can be used to make comparisons with the cost of insurance from other providers. You should also compare the cover offered and the way in which benefits are paid out.

Monthly cost of Payment Protection Insurance for every £100 of monthly benefit	£[xxx]

The credit on which this quote is based

Credit limit	£[xxx]
Annual Percentage Rate of Charge (APR)	[xx]%

Cancellation rights
You can cancel your Payment Protection Insurance at any time [by providing [X] days' notice to your insurer]. To cancel, call [xxx xxxx xxxx] or write to [Customer Services at [X]]. There is no charge for cancellation.

For general enquiries, please call: [xxx xxxx xxxx].

SCHEDULE 4E(I)

[4.599]

[Name]
[Address Line 1]
[Address Line 2]
[Address Line 3]
[Address Line 4]
[Postcode]

Reference   [x]
Date   [x]

Logo

....

Quote for your Optional Payment Protection Insurance [Stand-Alone]
This form gives you information about how much this insurance will cost

> ### Things you should know about Optional Payment Protection Insurance
>
> Cheaper or more appropriate cover may be available from other providers. You can compare product features and costs using the Consumer Financial Education Body's comparison tables at **www.moneymadeclear.org.uk/tables/bespoke/PPI**.
>
> There are other products which can protect you against loss of your income. For impartial information about insurance, please visit the website at: **www.moneymadeclear.org.uk/products/insurance/insurance.html**.

Further details of cover, including any significant exclusions and limitations, are in the attached policy summary. This quote is valid [for [X] days] provided that you remain eligible for this product.

....

Payment Protection Insurance quote
Type of cover included

Life	[Repays a maximum of £10,000]
Accident & Sickness	[Up to 12 months' benefit]
Unemployment	[Up to 12 months' benefit]
[Other]	[Not included]

Cost of Payment Protection Insurance cover

Annual cost of Payment Protection Insurance	£[xxx]
Monthly cost of Payment Protection Insurance	£[xxx]

We have calculated the cost of our Payment Protection Insurance as a **monthly cost for every £100 of monthly benefit below**. This number explains how much this insurance costs you each month for every £100 in benefit that you would receive each month if you made a successful claim for accident, sickness or unemployment. For example, if the number is £5 this means that for every £5 that you pay as a monthly premium, you will get £100 for each [full] month that the claim lasts [less the waiting period on the policy]. This number can be used to make comparisons with the cost of insurance from other providers. You should also compare the cover offered and the way in which benefits are paid out.

Monthly cost of Payment Protection Insurance for every £100 of monthly benefit	£[xxx]

....

Monthly income [or monthly repayment] protected by this cover [or monthly benefit]

Amount of monthly income [or repayment] protected	£[xxx]
or	
[Your monthly benefit is]	£[xxx]

SCHEDULE 4E(II)

[4.600]

[Name] [Address Line 1] [Address Line 2] [Address Line 3] [Address Line 4] [Postcode]	Reference [x] Date [x]

Logo

Quote for your Optional Payment Protection Insurance
This form gives you information about how much this insurance will cost

> **Things you should know about Optional Payment Protection Insurance**
>
> Taking out this insurance is optional and does not increase your chances of obtaining credit.
>
> Cheaper or more appropriate cover may be available from other providers. You can compare product features and costs using the Consumer Financial Education Body's comparison tables at **www.moneymadeclear.org.uk/tables/bespoke/PPI**.
>
> There are other products which can protect you against loss of your income. For impartial information about insurance, please visit the website at: **www.moneymadeclear.org.uk/products/insurance/insurance.html**.

Further details of cover, including any significant exclusions and limitations, are in the attached policy summary. This quote is valid [for [X] days] provided that you remain eligible for this product. Before we are allowed to sell you Payment Protection Insurance we will need to tell you about its key features, significant benefits, exclusions and limitations and tell you about any parts of the policy you may not be eligible to make a claim under given your personal circumstances.

Payment Protection Insurance quote
Type of cover included

Life	[Repays a maximum of £10,000]
Accident & Sickness	[Up to 12 months' benefit]
Unemployment	[Up to 12 months' benefit]
[Other]	[Not included]

Cost of Payment Protection Insurance cover

Annual cost of Payment Protection Insurance	£[xxx]
Monthly cost of Payment Protection Insurance	£[xxx]

We have calculated the cost of our Payment Protection Insurance as a **monthly cost for every £100 of monthly benefit below**. This number explains how much this insurance costs you each month for every £100 in benefit that you would receive each month if you made a successful claim for accident, sickness or unemployment. For example, if the number is £5 this means that for every £5 that you pay as a monthly premium, you will get £100 for each [full] month that the claim lasts [less the waiting period on the policy]. This number can be used to make comparisons with the cost of insurance from other providers. You should also compare the cover offered and the way in which benefits are paid out.

Monthly cost of Payment Protection Insurance for every £100 of monthly benefit	£[xxx]

Monthly income [or monthly repayment] protected by this cover [or monthly benefit]

Amount of monthly income [or repayment] protected or	£[xxx]
[Your monthly benefit is]	£[xxx]

As we have recently arranged credit for you, we are not allowed to complete the sale of Payment Protection Insurance at the same time as you take out the credit. This is to give you time to compare this policy against alternatives. If you decide that you would like to take out this Payment Protection Insurance policy from us, please [ring [xxx xxxx xxxx] or visit [www.xxx.com] on or after [the next day after the later of the end of the credit sale or the date of quote]].

SCHEDULE 5A
CONTENTS OF SIX-MONTHLY COMPLIANCE REPORT

[4.601]

(1)   The Compliance Report must, subject to any additional or different requirements that the OFT may impose pursuant to Schedule 6, include for the 6-month reporting period:
    (a)   GWP by PPI Product Type and for Stand-Alone PPI or Short-Term IP;
    (b)   Penetration Rates, by PPI Product Type;
    (c)   Claims Ratio, by PPI Product Type and for Stand-Alone PPI or Short-Term IP;

(d)   the percentage of the PPI Provider's PPI Policyholders for whom they are not the Credit Provider;

(e)   the percentage of the PPI Provider's Credit customers who received a Personal PPI Quote from the PPI Provider and subsequently purchased PPI from the PPI Provider;

(f)   the percentage of the PPI Provider's Credit customers who received a Personal PPI Quote and follow-up from the PPI Provider at or after the end of the Prohibition Period and did not subsequently take PPI from the PPI Provider;

(g)   steps taken to ensure compliance, including:
- details of training of staff regarding compliance; and
- details of internal compliance monitoring systems;

(h)   representative samples of Marketing Communications including sales scripts; and

(i)   details of any incidences of non-compliance and steps taken to rectify this.

SCHEDULE 5B
CONTENTS OF ANNUAL COMPLIANCE REPORT

[4.603]

(1)   The Compliance Report must, subject to any additional or different requirements that the OFT may impose pursuant to Schedule 6, include for the annual reporting period:

(a)   annual GWP by PPI Product Type and for Stand-Alone PPI or Short-Term IP;

(b)   Penetration Rates, by PPI Product Type;

(c)   Claims Ratio, by PPI Product Type and for Stand-Alone PPI or Short-Term IP;

(d)   the percentage of the PPI Provider's PPI Policyholders for whom they are not the Credit Provider;

(e)   the percentage of the PPI Provider's Credit customers who received a Personal PPI Quote from the PPI Provider and subsequently purchased PPI from the PPI Provider;

(f)   the percentage of the PPI Provider's Credit customers who receive a Personal PPI Quote and follow-up from the PPI Provider at or after the end of the Prohibition Period and did not subsequently take PPI from the PPI Provider;

(g)   steps taken to ensure compliance including:
- details of training of staff regarding compliance; and
- details of internal compliance monitoring systems;

(h)   representative samples of Marketing Communications including sales scripts;

(i)   for a PPI Provider meeting the requirements in Schedule 5a, a report on the clarity of Marketing Communication in accordance with Article 14;

(j)   details of any incidences of non-compliance and steps taken to rectify this; and

(k)   for a PPI Provider meeting the requirement, a report of the annual mystery shopping exercise as required by Article 13.

SCHEDULE 5C
SPECIFICATIONS OF MYSTERY SHOPPING EXERCISE

[4.605]

(1)   The mystery shopping exercise must be undertaken by an Independent Market Research Agency.

(2)   The Independent Market Research Agency must apply for PPI from the Credit Arranger for each PPI Product Type or Short-Term IP offered by the Credit Arranger in each of the following ways (where PPI is offered in any of these ways):

(a)   at least 20 separate applications by telephone;

(b)   at least 20 separate applications by personal branch visits; and

(c)   at least 20 separate applications through the Credit Arranger's website.

(3)   The mystery shopping exercise must provide information on the following issues, in so far as these are relevant to the PPI Product Type or Short-Term IP:

(a)   whether the Consumer was prompted to buy PPI at the same time as arranging the Credit;

(b)   whether it is made clear to the Consumer that:

(i)   the Consumer could return to purchase PPI from the next day after the conclusion of the Credit Sale or, if later, the provision of a Personal PPI Quote; and

(ii)   the Personal PPI Quote continues to be valid for at least 14 days after it was provided;

(c)   whether the oral disclosures required by Article 3.2 were made prominently;

(d)   whether the Personal PPI Quote was received in the form relevant for the PPI Product Type and consistent with the requirements of Article 7 and Schedule 4; and

(e)   where the Consumer obtains Retail PPI, if Retail PPI is offered separately to Merchandise Cover.

(4)   Any information on any issues identified by the Independent Market Research Agency may be investigated and commented on by the Credit Arranger alongside the report which is provided to the OFT. Any one mystery shop which is verified by the OFT as non-compliant will constitute evidence of non-compliance with the Order.

SCHEDULE 6
SUPPLY OF INFORMATION TO THE OFT

[4.607]

(1)   Any person to whom this Order applies is required to provide to the OFT any information and documents required for the purposes of enabling the OFT to monitor the carrying out of this Order or any provisions of this Order and/or to review the effectiveness of the operation of this Order, or any provision of this Order.

(2)   Any person to whom this Order applies may be required by the OFT to keep and produce those records specified in writing by the OFT that relate to the operation of any provisions of this Order.

(3)   Any person to whom this Order applies and whom the OFT believes to have information which may be relevant to the monitoring or the review of the operation of any provisions of this Order may be required by the OFT to attend and provide such information in person.

(4)   Subject always to Part 9 of the Act, the OFT may publish any information or documents that it has received in connection with the monitoring or the review of this Order or any provisions of this Order for the purpose of assisting the OFT in the discharge of its functions under or in connection with this Order.

DIRECTIVE OF THE EUROPEAN PARLIAMENT AND OF THE COUNCIL

(2013/11/EU)

of 21 May 2013

on alternative dispute resolution for consumer disputes and amending Regulation (EC) No 2006/2004 and Directive 2009/22/EC

(Directive on consumer ADR)

[4.609]

THE EUROPEAN PARLIAMENT AND THE COUNCIL OF THE EUROPEAN UNION,

Having regard to the Treaty on the Functioning of the European Union, and in particular Article 114 thereof,

Having regard to the proposal from the European Commission,

After transmission of the draft legislative act to the national Parliaments,

Having regard to the opinion of the European Economic and Social Committee,[1]

Acting in accordance with the ordinary legislative procedure,[2]

Whereas:

(1)   Article 169(1) and point (a) of Article 169(2) of the Treaty on the Functioning of the European Union (TFEU) provide that the Union is to contribute to the attainment of a high level of consumer protection through measures adopted pursuant to Article 114 TFEU. Article 38 of the Charter of Fundamental Rights of the European Union provides that Union policies are to ensure a high level of consumer protection.

(2)   In accordance with Article 26(2) TFEU, the internal market is to comprise an area without internal frontiers in which the free movement of goods and services is ensured. The internal market should provide consumers with added value in the form of better quality, greater variety, reasonable prices and high safety standards for goods and services, which should promote a high level of consumer protection.

(3)   Fragmentation of the internal market is detrimental to competitiveness, growth and job creation within the Union. Eliminating direct and indirect obstacles to the proper functioning of the internal market and improving citizens' trust is essential for the completion of the internal market.

(4)   Ensuring access to simple, efficient, fast and low-cost ways of resolving domestic and cross-border disputes which arise from sales or service contracts should benefit consumers and therefore boost their confidence in the market. That access should apply to online as well as to offline transactions, and is particularly important when consumers shop across borders.

(5)   Alternative dispute resolution (ADR) offers a simple, fast and low-cost out-of-court solution to disputes between consumers and traders. However, ADR is not yet sufficiently and consistently developed across the Union. It is regrettable that, despite Commission Recommendations 98/257/EC of 30 March 1998 on the principles applicable to the bodies responsible for out-of-court settlement

of consumer disputes[3] and 2001/310/EC of 4 April 2001 on the principles for out-of-court bodies involved in the consensual resolution of consumer disputes,[4] ADR has not been correctly established and is not running satisfactorily in all geographical areas or business sectors in the Union. Consumers and traders are still not aware of the existing out-of-court redress mechanisms, with only a small percentage of citizens knowing how to file a complaint with an ADR entity. Where ADR procedures are available, their quality levels vary considerably in the Member States and cross-border disputes are often not handled effectively by ADR entities.

(6)   The disparities in ADR coverage, quality and awareness in Member States constitute a barrier to the internal market and are among the reasons why many consumers abstain from shopping across borders and why they lack confidence that potential disputes with traders can be resolved in an easy, fast and inexpensive way. For the same reasons, traders might abstain from selling to consumers in other Member States where there is no sufficient access to high-quality ADR procedures. Furthermore, traders established in a Member State where high-quality ADR procedures are not sufficiently available are put at a competitive disadvantage with regard to traders that have access to such procedures and can thus resolve consumer disputes faster and more cheaply.

(7)   In order for consumers to exploit fully the potential of the internal market, ADR should be available for all types of domestic and cross-border disputes covered by this Directive, ADR procedures should comply with consistent quality requirements that apply throughout the Union, and consumers and traders should be aware of the existence of such procedures. Due to increased cross-border trade and movement of persons, it is also important that ADR entities handle cross-border disputes effectively.

(8)   As advocated by the European Parliament in its resolutions of 25 October 2011 on alternative dispute resolution in civil, commercial and family matters and of 20 May 2010 on delivering a single market to consumers and citizens, any holistic approach to the single market which delivers results for its citizens should as a priority develop simple, affordable, expedient and accessible system of redress.

(9)   In its Communication of 13 April 2011 entitled 'Single Market Act — Twelve levers to boost growth and strengthen confidence — "Working together to create new growth" ', the Commission identified legislation on ADR which includes an electronic commerce (e-commerce) dimension, as one of the twelve levers to boost growth, strengthen confidence and make progress towards completing the Single Market.

(10)   In its conclusions of 24–25 March and 23 October 2011, the European Council invited the European Parliament and the Council to adopt, by the end of 2012, a first set of priority measures to bring a new impetus to the Single Market. Moreover, in its Conclusions of 30 May 2011 on the Priorities for relaunching the Single Market, the Council of the European Union highlighted the importance of e-commerce and agreed that consumer ADR schemes can offer low-cost, simple and quick redress for both consumers and traders. The successful implementation of those schemes requires sustained political commitment and support from all actors, without compromising the affordability, transparency, flexibility, speed and quality of decision-making by the ADR entities falling within the scope of this Directive.

(11)   Given the increasing importance of online commerce and in particular cross-border trade as a pillar of Union economic activity, a properly functioning ADR infrastructure for consumer disputes and a properly integrated online dispute resolution (ODR) framework for consumer disputes arising from online transactions are necessary in order to achieve the Single Market Act's aim of boosting citizens' confidence in the internal market.

(12)   This Directive and Regulation (EU) No 524/2013 of the European Parliament and of the Council of 21 May 2013 on online dispute resolution for consumer disputes[5] are two interlinked and complementary legislative instruments. Regulation (EU) No 524/2013 provides for the establishment of an ODR platform which offers consumers and traders a single point of entry for the out-of-court resolution of online disputes, through ADR entities which are linked to the platform and offer ADR through quality ADR procedures. The availability of quality ADR entities across the Union is thus a precondition for the proper functioning of the ODR platform.

(13)   This Directive should not apply to non-economic services of general interest. Non-economic services are services which are not performed for economic consideration. As a result, non-economic services of general interest performed by the State or on behalf of the State, without remuneration, should not be covered by this Directive irrespective of the legal form through which those services are provided.

(14)   This Directive should not apply to health care services as defined in point (a) of Article 3 of Directive 2011/24/EU of the European Parliament and of the Council of 9 March 2011 on the application of patients' rights in cross-border healthcare.[6]

(15)   The development within the Union of properly functioning ADR is necessary to strengthen consumers' confidence in the internal market, including in the area of online commerce, and to fulfil the potential for and opportunities of cross-border and online trade. Such development should build on existing ADR procedures in the Member States and respect their legal traditions. Both existing and newly established properly functioning dispute resolution entities that comply with the quality

requirements set out in this Directive should be considered as 'ADR entities' within the meaning of this Directive. The dissemination of ADR can also prove to be important in those Member States in which there is a substantial backlog of cases pending before the courts, preventing Union citizens from exercising their right to a fair trial within a reasonable time.

(16) This Directive should apply to disputes between consumers and traders concerning contractual obligations stemming from sales or services contracts, both online and offline, in all economic sectors, other than the exempted sectors. This should include disputes arising from the sale or provision of digital content for remuneration. This Directive should apply to complaints submitted by consumers against traders. It should not apply to complaints submitted by traders against consumers or to disputes between traders. However, it should not prevent Member States from adopting or maintaining in force provisions on procedures for the out-of-court resolution of such disputes.

(17) Member States should be permitted to maintain or introduce national provisions with regard to procedures not covered by this Directive, such as internal complaint handling procedures operated by the trader. Such internal complaint handling procedures can constitute an effective means for resolving consumer disputes at an early stage.

(18) The definition of 'consumer' should cover natural persons who are acting outside their trade, business, craft or profession. However, if the contract is concluded for purposes partly within and partly outside the person's trade (dual purpose contracts) and the trade purpose is so limited as not to be predominant in the overall context of the supply, that person should also be considered as a consumer.

(19) Some existing Union legal acts already contain provisions concerning ADR. In order to ensure legal certainty, it should be provided that, in the event of conflict, this Directive is to prevail, except where it explicitly provides otherwise. In particular, this Directive should be without prejudice to Directive 2008/52/EC of the European Parliament and of the Council of 21 May 2008 on certain aspects of mediation in civil and commercial matters,[7] which already sets out a framework for systems of mediation at Union level for cross-border disputes, without preventing the application of that Directive to internal mediation systems. This Directive is intended to apply horizontally to all types of ADR procedures, including to ADR procedures covered by Directive 2008/52/EC.

(20) ADR entities are highly diverse across the Union but also within the Member States. This Directive should cover any entity that is established on a durable basis, offers the resolution of a dispute between a consumer and a trader through an ADR procedure and is listed in accordance with this Directive. This Directive may also cover, if Member States so decide, dispute resolution entities which impose solutions which are binding on the parties. However, an out-of-court procedure which is created on an ad hoc basis for a single dispute between a consumer and a trader should not be considered as an ADR procedure.

(21) Also ADR procedures are highly diverse across the Union and within Member States. They can take the form of procedures where the ADR entity brings the parties together with the aim of facilitating an amicable solution, or procedures where the ADR entity proposes a solution or procedures where the ADR entity imposes a solution. They can also take the form of a combination of two or more such procedures. This Directive should be without prejudice to the form which ADR procedures take in the Member States.

(22) Procedures before dispute resolution entities where the natural persons in charge of dispute resolution are employed or receive any form of remuneration exclusively from the trader are likely to be exposed to a conflict of interest. Therefore, those procedures should, in principle, be excluded from the scope of this Directive, unless a Member State decides that such procedures can be recognised as ADR procedures under this Directive and provided that those entities are in complete conformity with the specific requirements on independence and impartiality laid down in this Directive. ADR entities offering dispute resolution through such procedures should be subject to regular evaluation of their compliance with the quality requirements set out in this Directive, including the specific additional requirements ensuring their independence.

(23) This Directive should not apply to procedures before consumer-complaint handling systems operated by the trader, nor to direct negotiations between the parties. Furthermore, it should not apply to attempts made by a judge to settle a dispute in the course of a judicial proceeding concerning that dispute.

(24) Member States should ensure that disputes covered by this Directive can be submitted to an ADR entity which complies with the requirements set out in this Directive and is listed in accordance with it. Member States should have the possibility of fulfilling this obligation by building on existing properly functioning ADR entities and adjusting their scope of application, if needed, or by providing for the creation of new ADR entities. This Directive should not preclude the functioning of existing dispute resolution entities operating within the framework of national consumer protection authorities of Member States where State officials are in charge of dispute resolution. State officials should be regarded as representatives of both consumers' and traders' interests. This Directive should not oblige Member States to create a specific ADR entity in each retail sector. When necessary, in order to ensure full sectoral and geographical coverage by and access to ADR, Member States should have the possibility to provide for the creation of a residual

ADR entity that deals with disputes for the resolution of which no specific ADR entity is competent. Residual ADR entities are intended to be a safeguard for consumers and traders by ensuring that there are no gaps in access to an ADR entity.

(25) This Directive should not prevent Member States from maintaining or introducing legislation on procedures for out-of-court resolution of consumer contractual disputes which is in compliance with the requirements set out in this Directive. Furthermore, in order to ensure that ADR entities can operate effectively, those entities should have the possibility of maintaining or introducing, in accordance with the laws of the Member State in which they are established, procedural rules that allow them to refuse to deal with disputes in specific circumstances, for example where a dispute is too complex and would therefore be better resolved in court. However, procedural rules allowing ADR entities to refuse to deal with a dispute should not impair significantly consumers' access to ADR procedures, including in the case of cross- border disputes. Thus, when providing for a monetary threshold, Member States should always take into account that the real value of a dispute may vary among Member States and, consequently, setting a disproportionately high threshold in one Member State could impair access to ADR procedures for consumers from other Member States. Member States should not be required to ensure that the consumer can submit his complaint to another ADR entity, where an ADR entity to which the complaint was first submitted has refused to deal with it because of its procedural rules. In such cases Member States should be deemed to have fulfilled their obligation to ensure full coverage of ADR entities.

(26) This Directive should allow traders established in a Member State to be covered by an ADR entity which is established in another Member State. In order to improve the coverage of and consumer access to ADR across the Union, Member States should have the possibility of deciding to rely on ADR entities established in another Member State or regional, transnational or pan-European ADR entities, where traders from different Member States are covered by the same ADR entity. Recourse to ADR entities established in another Member State or to transnational or pan-European ADR entities should, however, be without prejudice to Member States' responsibility to ensure full coverage by and access to ADR entities.

(27) This Directive should be without prejudice to Member States maintaining or introducing ADR procedures dealing jointly with identical or similar disputes between a trader and several consumers. Comprehensive impact assessments should be carried out on collective out-of-court settlements before such settlements are proposed at Union level. The existence of an effective system for collective claims and easy recourse to ADR should be complementary and they should not be mutually exclusive procedures.

(28) The processing of information relating to disputes covered by this Directive should comply with the rules on the protection of personal data laid down in the laws, regulations and administrative provisions of the Member States adopted pursuant to Directive 95/46/EC of the European Parliament and of the Council of 24 October 1995 on the protection of individuals with regard to the processing of personal data and on the free movement of such data.[8]

(29) Confidentiality and privacy should be respected at all times during the ADR procedure. Member States should be encouraged to protect the confidentiality of ADR procedures in any subsequent civil or commercial judicial proceedings or arbitration.

(30) Member States should nevertheless ensure that ADR entities make publicly available any systematic or significant problems that occur frequently and lead to disputes between consumers and traders. The information communicated in this regard could be accompanied by recommendations as to how such problems can be avoided or resolved in future, in order to raise traders' standards and to facilitate the exchange of information and best practices.

(31) Member States should ensure that ADR entities resolve disputes in a manner that is fair, practical and proportionate to both the consumer and the trader, on the basis of an objective assessment of the circumstances in which the complaint is made and with due regard to the rights of the parties.

(32) The independence and integrity of ADR entities is crucial in order to gain Union citizens' trust that ADR mechanisms will offer them a fair and independent outcome. The natural person or collegial body in charge of ADR should be independent of all those who might have an interest in the outcome and should have no conflict of interest which could impede him or it from reaching a decision in a fair, impartial and independent manner.

(33) The natural persons in charge of ADR should only be considered impartial if they cannot be subject to pressure that potentially influences their attitude towards the dispute. In order to ensure the independence of their actions, those persons should also be appointed for a sufficient duration, and should not be subject to any instructions from either party or their representative.

(34) In order to ensure the absence of any conflict of interest, natural persons in charge of ADR should disclose any circumstances that might affect their independence and impartiality or give rise to a conflict of interest with either party to the dispute they are asked to resolve. This could be any financial interest, direct or indirect, in the outcome of the ADR procedure or any personal or business relationship with one or more of the parties during the three years prior to assuming the post,

including any capacity other than for the purposes of ADR in which the person concerned has acted for one or more of the parties, for a professional organisation or a business association of which one of the parties is a member or for any other member thereof.

(35) There is a particular need to ensure the absence of such pressure where the natural persons in charge of ADR are employed or receive any form of remuneration from the trader. Therefore, specific requirements should be provided for in the event that Member States decide to allow dispute resolution procedures in such cases to qualify as ADR procedures under this Directive. Where natural persons in charge of ADR are employed or receive any form of remuneration exclusively from a professional organisation or a business association of which the trader is a member, they should have at their disposal a separate and dedicated budget sufficient to fulfil their tasks.

(36) It is essential for the success of ADR, in particular in order to ensure the necessary trust in ADR procedures, that the natural persons in charge of ADR possess the necessary expertise, including a general understanding of law. In particular, those persons should have sufficient general knowledge of legal matters in order to understand the legal implications of the dispute, without being obliged to be a qualified legal professional.

(37) The applicability of certain quality principles to ADR procedures strengthens both consumers' and traders' confidence in such procedures. Such quality principles were first developed at Union level in Recommendations 98/257/EC and 2001/310/EC. By making some of the principles established in those Commission Recommendations binding, this Directive establishes a set of quality requirements which apply to all ADR procedures carried out by an ADR entity which has been notified to the Commission.

(38) This Directive should establish quality requirements of ADR entities, which should ensure the same level of protection and rights for consumers in both domestic and cross-border disputes. This Directive should not prevent Member States from adopting or maintaining rules that go beyond what is provided for in this Directive.

(39) ADR entities should be accessible and transparent. In order to ensure the transparency of ADR entities and of ADR procedures it is necessary that the parties receive the clear and accessible information they need in order to take an informed decision before engaging in an ADR procedure. The provision of such information to traders should not be required where their participation in ADR procedures is mandatory under national law.

(40) A properly functioning ADR entity should conclude online and offline dispute resolution proceedings expeditiously within a timeframe of 90 calendar days starting on the date on which the ADR entity has received the complete complaint file including all relevant documentation pertaining to that complaint, and ending on the date on which the outcome of the ADR procedure is made available. The ADR entity which has received a complaint should notify the parties after receiving all the documents necessary to carry out the ADR procedure. In certain exceptional cases of a highly complex nature, including where one of the parties is unable, on justified grounds, to take part in the ADR procedure, ADR entities should be able to extend the timeframe for the purpose of undertaking an examination of the case in question. The parties should be informed of any such extension, and of the expected approximate length of time that will be needed for the conclusion of the dispute.

(41) ADR procedures should preferably be free of charge for the consumer. In the event that costs are applied, the ADR procedure should be accessible, attractive and inexpensive for consumers. To that end, costs should not exceed a nominal fee.

(42) ADR procedures should be fair so that the parties to a dispute are fully informed about their rights and the consequences of the choices they make in the context of an ADR procedure. ADR entities should inform consumers of their rights before they agree to or follow a proposed solution. Both parties should also be able to submit their information and evidence without being physically present.

(43) An agreement between a consumer and a trader to submit complaints to an ADR entity should not be binding on the consumer if it was concluded before the dispute has materialised and if it has the effect of depriving the consumer of his right to bring an action before the courts for the settlement of the dispute. Furthermore, in ADR procedures which aim at resolving the dispute by imposing a solution, the solution imposed should be binding on the parties only if they were informed of its binding nature in advance and specifically accepted this. Specific acceptance by the trader should not be required if national rules provide that such solutions are binding on traders.

(44) In ADR procedures which aim at resolving the dispute by imposing a solution on the consumer, in a situation where there is no conflict of laws, the solution imposed should not result in the consumer being deprived of the protection afforded to him by the provisions that cannot be derogated from by agreement by virtue of the law of the Member State where the consumer and the trader are habitually resident. In a situation involving a conflict of laws, where the law applicable to the sales or service contract is determined in accordance with Article 6(1) and (2) of Regulation (EC) No 593/2008 of the European Parliament and of the Council of 17 June 2008 on the law applicable to contractual obligations (Rome I),[9] the solution imposed by the ADR entity should not result in the consumer being deprived of the protection afforded to him by the provisions that cannot be derogated from by agreement by virtue of the law of the Member State in which the consumer is

habitually resident. In a situation involving a conflict of laws, where the law applicable to the sales or service contract is determined in accordance with Article 5(1) to (3) of the Rome Convention of 19 June 1980 on the law applicable to contractual obligations,[10] the solution imposed by the ADR entity should not result in the consumer being deprived of the protection afforded to the consumer by the mandatory rules of the law of the Member State in which the consumer is habitually resident.

(45)   The right to an effective remedy and the right to a fair trial are fundamental rights laid down in Article 47 of the Charter of Fundamental Rights of the European Union. Therefore, ADR procedures should not be designed to replace court procedures and should not deprive consumers or traders of their rights to seek redress before the courts. This Directive should not prevent parties from exercising their right of access to the judicial system. In cases where a dispute could not be resolved through a given ADR procedure whose outcome is not binding, the parties should subsequently not be prevented from initiating judicial proceedings in relation to that dispute. Member States should be free to choose the appropriate means to achieve this objective. They should have the possibility to provide, inter alia, that limitation or prescription periods do not expire during an ADR procedure.

(46)   In order to function efficiently, ADR entities should have sufficient human, material and financial resources at their disposal. Member States should decide on an appropriate form of funding for ADR entities on their territories, without restricting the funding of entities that are already operational. This Directive should be without prejudice to the question of whether ADR entities are publicly or privately funded or funded through a combination of public and private funding. However, ADR entities should be encouraged to specifically consider private forms of funding and to utilise public funds only at Member States' discretion. This Directive should not affect the possibility for businesses or for professional organisations or business associations to fund ADR entities.

(47)   When a dispute arises it is necessary that consumers are able to identify quickly which ADR entities are competent to deal with their complaint and to know whether or not the trader concerned will participate in proceedings submitted to an ADR entity. Traders who commit to use ADR entities to resolve disputes with consumers should inform consumers of the address and website of the ADR entity or entities by which they are covered. That information should be provided in a clear, comprehensible and easily accessible way on the trader's website, where one exists, and if applicable in the general terms and conditions of sales or service contracts between the trader and the consumer. Traders should have the possibility of including on their websites, and in the terms and conditions of the relevant contracts, any additional information on their internal complaint handling procedures or on any other ways of directly contacting them with a view to settling disputes with consumers without referring them to an ADR entity. Where a dispute cannot be settled directly, the trader should provide the consumer, on paper or another durable medium, with the information on relevant ADR entities and specify if he will make use of them.

(48)   The obligation on traders to inform consumers about the ADR entities by which those traders are covered should be without prejudice to provisions on consumer information on out-of-court redress procedures contained in other Union legal acts, which should apply in addition to the relevant information obligation provided for in this Directive.

(49)   This Directive should not require the participation of traders in ADR procedures to be mandatory or the outcome of such procedures to be binding on traders, when a consumer has lodged a complaint against them. However, in order to ensure that consumers have access to redress and that they are not obliged to forego their claims, traders should be encouraged as far as possible to participate in ADR procedures. Therefore, this Directive should be without prejudice to any national rules making the participation of traders in such procedures mandatory or subject to incentives or sanctions or making their outcome binding on traders, provided that such legislation does not prevent the parties from exercising their right of access to the judicial system as provided for in Article 47 of the Charter of Fundamental Rights of the European Union.

(50)   In order to avoid an unnecessary burden being placed on ADR entities, Member States should encourage consumers to contact the trader in an effort to solve the problem bilaterally before submitting a complaint to an ADR entity. In many cases, doing so would allow consumers to settle their disputes swiftly and at an early stage.

(51)   Member States should involve the representatives of professional organisations, business associations and consumer organisations when developing ADR, in particular in relation to the principles of impartiality and independence.

(52)   Member States should ensure that ADR entities cooperate on the resolution of cross-border disputes.

(53)   Networks of ADR entities, such as the financial dispute resolution network 'FIN-NET' in the area of financial services, should be strengthened within the Union. Member States should encourage ADR entities to become part of such networks.

(54)   Close cooperation between ADR entities and national authorities should strengthen the effective application of Union legal acts on consumer protection. The Commission and the Member States should facilitate cooperation between the ADR entities, in order to encourage the exchange of best practice and technical expertise and to discuss any problems arising from the

operation of ADR procedures. Such cooperation should be supported, inter alia, through the Union's forthcoming Consumer Programme.

(55) In order to ensure that ADR entities function properly and effectively, they should be closely monitored. For that purpose, each Member States should designate a competent authority or competent authorities which should perform that function. The Commission and competent authorities under this Directive should publish and update a list of ADR entities that comply with this Directive. Member States should ensure that ADR entities, the European Consumer Centre Network, and, where appropriate, the bodies designated in accordance with this Directive publish that list on their website by providing a link to the Commission's website, and whenever possible on a durable medium at their premises. Furthermore, Member States should also encourage relevant consumer organisations and business associations to publish the list. Member States should also ensure the appropriate dissemination of information on what consumers should do if they have a dispute with a trader. In addition, competent authorities should publish regular reports on the development and functioning of ADR entities in their Member States. ADR entities should notify to competent authorities specific information on which those reports should be based. Member States should encourage ADR entities to provide such information using Commission Recommendation 2010/304/EU of 12 May 2010 on the use of a harmonised methodology for classifying and reporting consumer complaints and enquiries.[11]

(56) It is necessary for Member States to lay down rules on penalties for infringements of the national provisions adopted to comply with this Directive and to ensure that those rules are implemented. The penalties should be effective, proportionate and dissuasive.

(57) Regulation (EC) No 2006/2004 of the European Parliament and of the Council of 27 October 2004 on cooperation between national authorities responsible for the enforcement of consumer protection laws (the Regulation on consumer protection cooperation)[12] should be amended to include a reference to this Directive in its Annex so as to reinforce cross-border cooperation on enforcement of this Directive.

(58) Directive 2009/22/EC of the European Parliament and of the Council of 23 April 2009 on injunctions for the protection of consumers' interests[13] (Injunctions Directive) should be amended to include a reference to this Directive in its Annex so as to ensure that the consumers' collective interests laid down in this Directive are protected.

(59) In accordance with the Joint Political Declaration of 28 September 2011 of Member States and the Commission on explanatory documents,[14] Member States have undertaken to accompany, in justified cases, the notification of their transposition measures with one or more documents explaining the relationship between the components of a directive and the corresponding parts of national transposition instruments. With regard to this Directive, the legislator considers the transmission of such documents to be justified.

(60) Since the objective of this Directive, namely to contribute, through the achievement of a high level of consumer protection and without restricting consumers' access to the courts, to the proper functioning of the internal market, cannot be sufficiently achieved by the Member States and can therefore be better achieved at Union level, the Union may adopt measures, in accordance with the principle of subsidiarity as set out in Article 5 of the Treaty on European Union. In accordance with the principle of proportionality, as set out in that Article, this Directive does not go beyond what is necessary in order to achieve that objective.

(61) This Directive respects fundamental rights and observes the principles recognised in particular by the Charter of Fundamental Rights of the European Union and specifically Articles 7, 8, 38 and 47 thereof.

(62) The European Data Protection Supervisor was consulted in accordance with Article 28(2) of Regulation (EC) No 45/2001 of the European Parliament and of the Council of 18 December 2000 on the protection of individuals with regard to the processing of personal data by the Community institutions and bodies and on the free movement of such data[15] and delivered an opinion on 12 January 2012,[16]

HAVE ADOPTED THIS DIRECTIVE:

NOTES

1   OJ C181, 21.6.2012, p 93.

2   Position of the European Parliament of 12 March 2013 (not yet published in the Official Journal) and decision of the Council of 22 April 2013.

3   OJ L115, 17.4.1998, p 31.

4   OJ L109, 19.4.2001, p 56.

5   See page 1 of this Official Journal.

6   OJ L88, 4.4.2011, p 45.

7   OJ L136, 24.5.2008, p 3.

8   OJ L281, 23.11.1995, p 31.

9   OJ L177, 4.7.2008, p 6.

[10]	OJ L266, 9.10.1980, p 1.
[11]	OJ L136, 2.6.2010, p 1.
[12]	OJ L364, 9.12.2004, p 1.
[13]	OJ L110, 1.5.2009, p 30.
[14]	OJ C369, 17.12.2011, p 14.
[15]	OJ L8, 12.1.2001, p 1.
[16]	OJ C136, 11.5.2012, p 1.

CHAPTER I
GENERAL PROVISIONS

[4.610]
Article 1
Subject matter

The purpose of this Directive is, through the achievement of a high level of consumer protection, to contribute to the proper functioning of the internal market by ensuring that consumers can, on a voluntary basis, submit complaints against traders to entities offering independent, impartial, transparent, effective, fast and fair alternative dispute resolution procedures. This Directive is without prejudice to national legislation making participation in such procedures mandatory, provided that such legislation does not prevent the parties from exercising their right of access to the judicial system.

[4.611]
Article 2
Scope

1.   This Directive shall apply to procedures for the out-of- court resolution of domestic and cross-border disputes concerning contractual obligations stemming from sales contracts or service contracts between a trader established in the Union and a consumer resident in the Union through the intervention of an ADR entity which proposes or imposes a solution or brings the parties together with the aim of facilitating an amicable solution.

2.   This Directive shall not apply to:
   (a)   procedures before dispute resolution entities where the natural persons in charge of dispute resolution are employed or remunerated exclusively by the individual trader, unless Member States decide to allow such procedures as ADR procedures under this Directive and the requirements set out in Chapter II, including the specific requirements of independence and transparency set out in Article 6(3), are met;
   (b)   procedures before consumer complaint-handling systems operated by the trader;
   (c)   non-economic services of general interest;
   (d)   disputes between traders;
   (e)   direct negotiation between the consumer and the trader;
   (f)   attempts made by a judge to settle a dispute in the course of a judicial proceeding concerning that dispute;
   (g)   procedures initiated by a trader against a consumer;
   (h)   health services provided by health professionals to patients to assess, maintain or restore their state of health, including the prescription, dispensation and provision of medicinal products and medical devices;
   (i)   public providers of further or higher education.

3.   This Directive establishes harmonised quality requirements for ADR entities and ADR procedures in order to ensure that, after its implementation, consumers have access to high-quality, transparent, effective and fair out-of-court redress mechanisms no matter where they reside in the Union. Member States may maintain or introduce rules that go beyond those laid down by this Directive, in order to ensure a higher level of consumer protection.

4.   This Directive acknowledges the competence of Member States to determine whether ADR entities established on their territories are to have the power to impose a solution.

[4.612]
Article 3
Relationship with other Union legal acts

1.   Save as otherwise set out in this Directive, if any provision of this Directive conflicts with a provision laid down in another Union legal act and relating to out-of-court redress procedures initiated by a consumer against a trader, the provision of this Directive shall prevail.

2.   This Directive shall be without prejudice to Directive 2008/52/EC.

3.   Article 13 of this Directive shall be without prejudice to provisions on consumer information on out-of-court redress procedures contained in other Union legal acts which shall apply in addition to that Article.

[4.613]
Article 4
Definitions

1. For the purposes of this Directive:
   (a) 'consumer' means any natural person who is acting for purposes which are outside his trade, business, craft or profession;
   (b) 'trader' means any natural persons, or any legal person irrespective of whether privately or publicly owned, who is acting, including through any person acting in his name or on his behalf, for purposes relating to his trade, business, craft or profession;
   (c) 'sales contract' means any contract under which the trader transfers or undertakes to transfer the ownership of goods to the consumer and the consumer pays or undertakes to pay the price thereof, including any contract having as its object both goods and services;
   (d) 'service contract' means any contract other than a sales contract under which the trader supplies or undertakes to supply a service to the consumer and the consumer pays or undertakes to pay the price thereof;
   (e) 'domestic dispute' means a contractual dispute arising from a sales or service contract where, at the time the consumer orders the goods or services, the consumer is resident in the same Member State as that in which the trader is established;
   (f) 'cross-border dispute' means a contractual dispute arising from a sales or service contract where, at the time the consumer orders the goods or services, the consumer is resident in a Member State other than the Member State in which the trader is established;
   (g) 'ADR procedure' means a procedure, as referred to in Article 2, which complies with the requirements set out in this Directive and is carried out by an ADR entity;
   (h) 'ADR entity' means any entity, however named or referred to, which is established on a durable basis and offers the resolution of a dispute through an ADR procedure and that is listed in accordance with Article 20(2);
   (i) 'competent authority' means any public authority designated by a Member State for the purposes of this Directive and established at national, regional or local level.

2. A trader is established:
   — if the trader is a natural person, where he has his place of business,
   — if the trader is a company or other legal person or association of natural or legal persons, where it has its statutory seat, central administration or place of business, including a branch, agency or any other establishment.

3. An ADR entity is established:
   — if it is operated by a natural person, at the place where it carries out ADR activities,
   — if the entity is operated by a legal person or association of natural or legal persons, at the place where that legal person or association of natural or legal persons carries out ADR activities or has its statutory seat,
   — if it is operated by an authority or other public body, at the place where that authority or other public body has its seat.

CHAPTER II
ACCESS TO AND REQUIREMENTS APPLICABLE TO ADR ENTITIES AND ADR PROCEDURES

[4.614]
Article 5
Access to ADR entities and ADR procedures

1. Member States shall facilitate access by consumers to ADR procedures and shall ensure that disputes covered by this Directive and which involve a trader established on their respective territories can be submitted to an ADR entity which complies with the requirements set out in this Directive.

2. Member States shall ensure that ADR entities:
   (a) maintain an up-to-date website which provides the parties with easy access to information concerning the ADR procedure, and which enables consumers to submit a complaint and the requisite supporting documents online;
   (b) provide the parties, at their request, with the information referred to in point (a) on a durable medium;
   (c) where applicable, enable the consumer to submit a complaint offline;
   (d) enable the exchange of information between the parties via electronic means or, if applicable, by post;
   (e) accept both domestic and cross-border disputes, including disputes covered by Regulation (EU) No 524/2013; and
   (f) when dealing with disputes covered by this Directive, take the necessary measures to ensure that the processing of personal data complies with the rules on the protection of personal data laid down in the national legislation implementing Directive 95/46/EC in the Member State in which the ADR entity is established.

3.   Member States may fulfil their obligation under paragraph 1 by ensuring the existence of a residual ADR entity which is competent to deal with disputes as referred to in that paragraph for the resolution of which no existing ADR entity is competent. Member States may also fulfil that obligation by relying on ADR entities established in another Member State or regional, transnational or pan-European dispute resolution entities, where traders from different Member States are covered by the same ADR entity, without prejudice to their responsibility to ensure full coverage and access to ADR entities.

4.   Member States may, at their discretion, permit ADR entities to maintain and introduce procedural rules that allow them to refuse to deal with a given dispute on the grounds that:

  (a)   the consumer did not attempt to contact the trader concerned in order to discuss his complaint and seek, as a first step, to resolve the matter directly with the trader;

  (b)   the dispute is frivolous or vexatious;

  (c)   the dispute is being or has previously been considered by another ADR entity or by a court;

  (d)   the value of the claim falls below or above a pre-specified monetary threshold;

  (e)   the consumer has not submitted the complaint to the ADR entity within a pre-specified time limit, which shall not be set at less than one year from the date upon which the consumer submitted the complaint to the trader;

  (f)   dealing with such a type of dispute would otherwise seriously impair the effective operation of the ADR entity.

Where, in accordance with its procedural rules, an ADR entity is unable to consider a dispute that has been submitted to it, that ADR entity shall provide both parties with a reasoned explanation of the grounds for not considering the dispute within three weeks of receiving the complaint file.

Such procedural rules shall not significantly impair consumers' access to ADR procedures, including in the case of cross-border disputes.

5.   Member States shall ensure that, when ADR entities are permitted to establish pre-specified monetary thresholds in order to limit access to ADR procedures, those thresholds are not set at a level at which they significantly impair the consumers' access to complaint handling by ADR entities.

6.   Where, in accordance with the procedural rules referred to in paragraph 4, an ADR entity is unable to consider a complaint that has been submitted to it, a Member State shall not be required to ensure that the consumer can submit his complaint to another ADR entity.

7.   Where an ADR entity dealing with disputes in a specific economic sector is competent to consider disputes relating to a trader operating in that sector but which is not a member of the organisation or association forming or funding the ADR entity, the Member State shall be deemed to have fulfilled its obligation under paragraph 1 also with respect to disputes concerning that trader.

[4.615]
Article 6
Expertise, independence and impartiality

1.   Member States shall ensure that the natural persons in charge of ADR possess the necessary expertise and are independent and impartial. This shall be guaranteed by ensuring that such persons:

  (a)   possess the necessary knowledge and skills in the field of alternative or judicial resolution of consumer disputes, as well as a general understanding of law;

  (b)   are appointed for a term of office of sufficient duration to ensure the independence of their actions, and are not liable to be relieved from their duties without just cause;

  (c)   are not subject to any instructions from either party or their representatives;

  (d)   are remunerated in a way that is not linked to the outcome of the procedure;

  (e)   without undue delay disclose to the ADR entity any circumstances that may, or may be seen to, affect their independence and impartiality or give rise to a conflict of interest with either party to the dispute they are asked to resolve. The obligation to disclose such circumstances shall be a continuing obligation throughout the ADR procedure. It shall not apply where the ADR entity comprises only one natural person.

2.   Member States shall ensure that ADR entities have in place procedures to ensure that in the case of circumstances referred to in point (e) of paragraph 1:

  (a)   the natural person concerned is replaced by another natural person that shall be entrusted with conducting the ADR procedure; or failing that

  (b)   the natural person concerned refrains from conducting the ADR procedure and, where possible, the ADR entity proposes to the parties to submit the dispute to another ADR entity which is competent to deal with the dispute; or failing that

  (c)   the circumstances are disclosed to the parties and the natural person concerned is allowed to continue to conduct the ADR procedure only if the parties have not objected after they have been informed of the circumstances and their right to object.

This paragraph shall be without prejudice to point (a) of Article 9(2).

Where the ADR entity comprises only one natural person, only points (b) and (c) of the first subparagraph of this paragraph shall apply.

3.   Where Member States decide to allow procedures referred to in point (a) of Article 2(2) as ADR procedures under this Directive, they shall ensure that, in addition to the general requirements set out in paragraphs 1 and 5, those procedures comply with the following specific requirements:

(a) the natural persons in charge of dispute resolution are nominated by, or form part of, a collegial body composed of an equal number of representatives of consumer organisations and of representatives of the trader and are appointed as result of a transparent procedure;

(b) the natural persons in charge of dispute resolution are granted a period of office of a minimum of three years to ensure the independence of their actions;

(c) the natural persons in charge of dispute resolution commit not to work for the trader or a professional organisation or business association of which the trader is a member for a period of three years after their position in the dispute resolution entity has ended;

(d) the dispute resolution entity does not have any hierarchical or functional link with the trader and is clearly separated from the trader's operational entities and has a sufficient budget at its disposal, which is separate from the trader's general budget, to fulfil its tasks.

4. Where the natural persons in charge of ADR are employed or remunerated exclusively by a professional organisation or a business association of which the trader is a member, Member States shall ensure that, in addition to the general requirements set out in paragraphs 1 and 5, they have a separate and dedicated budget at their disposal which is sufficient to fulfil their tasks.

This paragraph shall not apply where the natural persons concerned form part of a collegial body composed of an equal number of representatives of the professional organisation or business association by which they are employed or remunerated and of consumer organisations.

5. Member States shall ensure that ADR entities where the natural persons in charge of dispute resolution form part of a collegial body provide for an equal number of representatives of consumers' interests and of representatives of traders' interests in that body.

6. For the purposes of point (a) of paragraph 1, Member States shall encourage ADR entities to provide training for natural persons in charge of ADR. If such training is provided, competent authorities shall monitor the training schemes established by ADR entities, on the basis of information communicated to them in accordance with point (g) of Article 19(3).

[4.616]
Article 7
Transparency
1. Member States shall ensure that ADR entities make publicly available on their websites, on a durable medium upon request, and by any other means they consider appropriate, clear and easily understandable information on:

(a) their contact details, including postal address and e-mail address;

(b) the fact that ADR entities are listed in accordance with Article 20(2);

(c) the natural persons in charge of ADR, the method of their appointment and the length of their mandate;

(d) the expertise, impartiality and independence of the natural persons in charge of ADR, if they are employed or remunerated exclusively by the trader;

(e) their membership in networks of ADR entities facilitating cross-border dispute resolution, if applicable;

(f) the types of disputes they are competent to deal with, including any threshold if applicable;

(g) the procedural rules governing the resolution of a dispute and the grounds on which the ADR entity may refuse to deal with a given dispute in accordance with Article 5(4);

(h) the languages in which complaints can be submitted to the ADR entity and in which the ADR procedure is conducted;

(i) the types of rules the ADR entity may use as a basis for the dispute resolution (for example legal provisions, considerations of equity, codes of conduct);

(j) any preliminary requirements the parties may have to meet before an ADR procedure can be instituted, including the requirement that an attempt be made by the consumer to resolve the matter directly with the trader;

(k) whether or not the parties can withdraw from the procedure;

(l) the costs, if any, to be borne by the parties, including any rules on awarding costs at the end of the procedure;

(m) the average length of the ADR procedure;

(n) the legal effect of the outcome of the ADR procedure, including the penalties for non-compliance in the case of a decision having binding effect on the parties, if applicable;

(o) the enforceability of the ADR decision, if relevant.

2. Member States shall ensure that ADR entities make publicly available on their websites, on a durable medium upon request, and by any other means they consider appropriate, annual activity reports. Those reports shall include the following information relating to both domestic and cross-border disputes:

(a) the number of disputes received and the types of complaints to which they related;

(b) any systematic or significant problems that occur frequently and lead to disputes between consumers and traders; such information may be accompanied by recommendations as to how such problems can be avoided or resolved in future, in order to raise traders' standards and to facilitate the exchange of information and best practices;

(c) the rate of disputes the ADR entity has refused to deal with and the percentage share of the types of grounds for such refusal as referred to in Article 5(4);

(d)   in the case of procedures referred to in point (a) of Article 2(2), the percentage shares of solutions proposed or imposed in favour of the consumer and in favour of the trader, and of disputes resolved by an amicable solution;

(e)   the percentage share of ADR procedures which were discontinued and, if known, the reasons for their discontinuation;

(f)   the average time taken to resolve disputes;

(g)   the rate of compliance, if known, with the outcomes of the ADR procedures;

(h)   cooperation of ADR entities within networks of ADR entities which facilitate the resolution of cross-border disputes, if applicable.

[4.617]
Article 8
Effectiveness

Member States shall ensure that ADR procedures are effective and fulfil the following requirements:

(a)   the ADR procedure is available and easily accessible online and offline to both parties irrespective of where they are;

(b)   the parties have access to the procedure without being obliged to retain a lawyer or a legal advisor, but the procedure shall not deprive the parties of their right to independent advice or to be represented or assisted by a third party at any stage of the procedure;

(c)   the ADR procedure is free of charge or available at a nominal fee for consumers;

(d)   the ADR entity which has received a complaint notifies the parties to the dispute as soon as it has received all the documents containing the relevant information relating to the complaint;

(e)   the outcome of the ADR procedure is made available within a period of 90 calendar days from the date on which the ADR entity has received the complete complaint file. In the case of highly complex disputes, the ADR entity in charge may, at its own discretion, extend the 90 calendar days' time period. The parties shall be informed of any extension of that period and of the expected length of time that will be needed for the conclusion of the dispute.

[4.618]
Article 9
Fairness

1.   Member States shall ensure that in ADR procedures:

(a)   the parties have the possibility, within a reasonable period of time, of expressing their point of view, of being provided by the ADR entity with the arguments, evidence, documents and facts put forward by the other party, any statements made and opinions given by experts, and of being able to comment on them;

(b)   the parties are informed that they are not obliged to retain a lawyer or a legal advisor, but they may seek independent advice or be represented or assisted by a third party at any stage of the procedure;

(c)   the parties are notified of the outcome of the ADR procedure in writing or on a durable medium, and are given a statement of the grounds on which the outcome is based.

2.   In ADR procedures which aim at resolving the dispute by proposing a solution, Member States shall ensure that:

(a)   The parties have the possibility of withdrawing from the procedure at any stage if they are dissatisfied with the performance or the operation of the procedure. They shall be informed of that right before the procedure commences. Where national rules provide for mandatory participation by the trader in ADR procedures, this point shall apply only to the consumer.

(b)   The parties, before agreeing or following a proposed solution, are informed that:

(i)   they have the choice as to whether or not to agree to or follow the proposed solution;

(ii)   participation in the procedure does not preclude the possibility of seeking redress through court proceedings;

(iii)   the proposed solution may be different from an outcome determined by a court applying legal rules.

(c)   The parties, before agreeing to or following a proposed solution, are informed of the legal effect of agreeing to or following such a proposed solution.

(d)   The parties, before expressing their consent to a proposed solution or amicable agreement, are allowed a reasonable period of time to reflect.

3.   Where, in accordance with national law, ADR procedures provide that their outcome becomes binding on the trader once the consumer has accepted the proposed solution, Article 9(2) shall be read as applicable only to the consumer.

[4.619]
Article 10
Liberty
1. Member States shall ensure that an agreement between a consumer and a trader to submit complaints to an ADR entity is not binding on the consumer if it was concluded before the dispute has materialised and if it has the effect of depriving the consumer of his right to bring an action before the courts for the settlement of the dispute.

2. Member States shall ensure that in ADR procedures which aim at resolving the dispute by imposing a solution the solution imposed may be binding on the parties only if they were informed of its binding nature in advance and specifically accepted this. Specific acceptance by the trader is not required if national rules provide that solutions are binding on traders.

[4.620]
Article 11
Legality
1. Member States shall ensure that in ADR procedures which aim at resolving the dispute by imposing a solution on the consumer:

  (a) in a situation where there is no conflict of laws, the solution imposed shall not result in the consumer being deprived of the protection afforded to him by the provisions that cannot be derogated from by agreement by virtue of the law of the Member State where the consumer and the trader are habitually resident;

  (b) in a situation involving a conflict of laws, where the law applicable to the sales or service contract is determined in accordance with Article 6(1) and (2) of Regulation (EC) No 593/2008, the solution imposed by the ADR entity shall not result in the consumer being deprived of the protection afforded to him by the provisions that cannot be derogated from by agreement by virtue of the law of the Member State in which he is habitually resident;

  (c) in a situation involving a conflict of laws, where the law applicable to the sales or service contract is determined in accordance with Article 5(1) to (3) of the Rome Convention of 19 June 1980 on the law applicable to contractual obligations, the solution imposed by the ADR entity shall not result in the consumer being deprived of the protection afforded to him by the mandatory rules of the law of the Member State in which he is habitually resident.

2. For the purposes of this Article, 'habitual residence' shall be determined in accordance with Regulation (EC) No 593/2008.

[4.621]
Article 12
Effect of ADR procedures on limitation and prescription periods
1. Member States shall ensure that parties who, in an attempt to settle a dispute, have recourse to ADR procedures the outcome of which is not binding, are not subsequently prevented from initiating judicial proceedings in relation to that dispute as a result of the expiry of limitation or prescription periods during the ADR procedure.

2. Paragraph 1 shall be without prejudice to provisions on limitation or prescription contained in international agreements to which Member States are party.

CHAPTER III
INFORMATION AND COOPERATION

[4.622]
Article 13
Consumer information by traders
1. Member States shall ensure that traders established on their territories inform consumers about the ADR entity or ADR entities by which those traders are covered, when those traders commit to or are obliged to use those entities to resolve disputes with consumers. That information shall include the website address of the relevant ADR entity or ADR entities.

2. The information referred to in paragraph 1 shall be provided in a clear, comprehensible and easily accessible way on the traders' website, where one exists, and, if applicable, in the general terms and conditions of sales or service contracts between the trader and a consumer.

3. Member States shall ensure that, in cases where a dispute between a consumer and a trader established in their territory could not be settled further to a complaint submitted directly by the consumer to the trader, the trader provides the consumer with the information referred to in paragraph 1, specifying whether he will make use of the relevant ADR entities to settle the dispute. That information shall be provided on paper or on another durable medium.

[4.623]
Article 14
Assistance for consumers
1.   Member States shall ensure that, with regard to disputes arising from cross-border sales or service contracts, consumers can obtain assistance to access the ADR entity operating in another Member State which is competent to deal with their cross-border dispute.
2.   Member States shall confer responsibility for the task referred to in paragraph 1 on their centres of the European Consumer Centre Network, on consumer organisations or on any other body.

[4.624]
Article 15
General information
1.   Member States shall ensure that ADR entities, the centres of the European Consumer Centre Network and, where appropriate, the bodies designated in accordance with Article 14(2) make publicly available on their websites, by providing a link to the Commission's website, and whenever possible on a durable medium at their premises, the list of ADR entities referred to in Article 20(4).
2.   Member States shall encourage relevant consumer organisations and business associations to make publicly available on their websites, and by any other means they consider appropriate, the list of ADR entities referred to in Article 20(4).
3.   The Commission and Member States shall ensure appropriate dissemination of information on how consumers can access ADR procedures for resolving disputes covered by this Directive.
4.   The Commission and the Member States shall take accompanying measures to encourage consumer organisations and professional organisations, at Union and at national level, to raise awareness of ADR entities and their procedures and to promote ADR take-up by traders and consumers. Those bodies shall also be encouraged to provide consumers with information about competent ADR entities when they receive complaints from consumers.

[4.625]
Article 16
Cooperation and exchanges of experience between ADR entities
1.   Member States shall ensure that ADR entities cooperate in the resolution of cross-border disputes and conduct regular exchanges of best practices as regards the settlement of both cross-border and domestic disputes.
2.   The Commission shall support and facilitate the networking of national ADR entities and the exchange and dissemination of their best practices and experiences.
3.   Where a network of ADR entities facilitating the resolution of cross-border disputes exists in a sector-specific area within the Union, Member States shall encourage ADR entities that deal with disputes in that area to become a member of that network.
4.   The Commission shall publish a list containing the names and contact details of the networks referred to in paragraph 3. The Commission shall, when necessary, update this list.

[4.626]
Article 17
Cooperation between ADR entities and national authorities enforcing Union legal acts on consumer protection
1.   Member States shall ensure cooperation between ADR entities and national authorities entrusted with the enforcement of Union legal acts on consumer protection.
2.   This cooperation shall in particular include mutual exchange of information on practices in specific business sectors about which consumers have repeatedly lodged complaints. It shall also include the provision of technical assessment and information by such national authorities to ADR entities where such assessment or information is necessary for the handling of individual disputes and is already available.
3.   Member States shall ensure that cooperation and mutual information exchanges referred to in paragraphs 1 and 2 comply with the rules on the protection of personal data laid down in Directive 95/46/EC.
4.   This Article shall be without prejudice to provisions on professional and commercial secrecy which apply to the national authorities enforcing Union legal acts on consumer protection. ADR entities shall be subject to rules of professional secrecy or other equivalent duties of confidentiality laid down in the legislation of the Member States where they are established.

CHAPTER IV
THE ROLE OF COMPETENT AUTHORITIES AND THE COMMISSION

[4.627]
Article 18
Designation of competent authorities
1.   Each Member State shall designate a competent authority which shall carry out the functions set out in Articles 19 and 20. Each Member State may designate more than one competent authority. If a Member State does so, it shall determine which of the competent authorities designated is the

single point of contact for the Commission. Each Member State shall communicate the competent authority or, where appropriate, the competent authorities, including the single point of contact it has designated, to the Commission.

2.   The Commission shall establish a list of the competent authorities including, where appropriate, the single point of contact communicated to it in accordance with paragraph 1, and publish that list in the *Official Journal of the European Union*.

[4.628]
Article 19
Information to be notified to competent authorities by dispute resolution entities
1.   Member States shall ensure that dispute resolution entities established on their territories, which intend to qualify as ADR entities under this Directive and be listed in accordance with Article 20(2), notify to the competent authority the following:
   (a)   their name, contact details and website address;
   (b)   information on their structure and funding, including information on the natural persons in charge of dispute resolution, their remuneration, term of office and by whom they are employed;
   (c)   their procedural rules;
   (d)   their fees, if applicable;
   (e)   the average length of the dispute resolution procedures;
   (f)   the language or languages in which complaints can be submitted and the dispute resolution procedure conducted;
   (g)   a statement on the types of disputes covered by the dispute resolution procedure;
   (h)   the grounds on which the dispute resolution entity may refuse to deal with a given dispute in accordance with Article 5(4);
   (i)   a reasoned statement on whether the entity qualifies as an ADR entity falling within the scope of this Directive and complies with the quality requirements set out in Chapter II.
In the event of changes to the information referred to in points (a) to (h), ADR entities shall without undue delay notify those changes to the competent authority.
2.   Where Member States decide to allow procedures as referred to in point (a) of Article 2(2), they shall ensure that ADR entities applying such procedures notify to the competent authority, in addition to the information and statements referred to in paragraph 1, the information necessary to assess their compliance with the specific additional requirements of independence and transparency set out in Article 6(3).
3.   Member States shall ensure that ADR entities communicate to the competent authorities every two years information on:
   (a)   the number of disputes received and the types of complaints to which they related;
   (b)   the percentage share of ADR procedures which were discontinued before an outcome was reached;
   (c)   the average time taken to resolve the disputes received;
   (d)   the rate of compliance, if known, with the outcomes of the ADR procedures;
   (e)   any systematic or significant problems that occur frequently and lead to disputes between consumers and traders. The information communicated in this regard may be accompanied by recommendations as to how such problems can be avoided or resolved in future;
   (f)   where applicable, an assessment of the effectiveness of their cooperation within networks of ADR entities facilitating the resolution of cross-border disputes;
   (g)   where applicable, the training provided to natural persons in charge of ADR in accordance with Article 6(6);
   (h)   an assessment of the effectiveness of the ADR procedure offered by the entity and of possible ways of improving its performance.

[4.629]
Article 20
Role of the competent authorities and of the Commission
1.   Each competent authority shall assess, in particular on the basis of the information it has received in accordance with Article 19(1), whether the dispute resolution entities notified to it qualify as ADR entities falling within the scope of this Directive and comply with the quality requirements set out in Chapter II and in national provisions implementing it, including national provisions going beyond the requirements of this Directive, in conformity with Union law.
2.   Each competent authority shall, on the basis of the assessment referred to in paragraph 1, list all the ADR entities that have been notified to it and fulfil the conditions set out in paragraph 1.
That list shall include the following:
   (a)   the name, the contact details and the website addresses of the ADR entities referred to in the first subparagraph;
   (b)   their fees, if applicable;
   (c)   the language or languages in which complaints can be submitted and the ADR procedure conducted;
   (d)   the types of disputes covered by the ADR procedure;
   (e)   the sectors and categories of disputes covered by each ADR entity;

(f)   the need for the physical presence of the parties or of their representatives, if applicable, including a statement by the ADR entity on whether the ADR procedure is or can be conducted as an oral or a written procedure;

(g)   the binding or non-binding nature of the outcome of the procedure; and

(h)   the grounds on which the ADR entity may refuse to deal with a given dispute in accordance with Article 5(4).

Each competent authority shall notify the list referred to in the first subparagraph of this paragraph to the Commission. If any changes are notified to the competent authority in accordance with the second subparagraph of Article 19(1), that list shall be updated without undue delay and the relevant information notified to the Commission.

If a dispute resolution entity listed as ADR entity under this Directive no longer complies with the requirements referred to in paragraph 1, the competent authority concerned shall contact that dispute resolution entity, stating the requirements the dispute resolution entity fails to comply with and requesting it to ensure compliance immediately. If the dispute resolution entity after a period of three months still does not fulfil the requirements referred to in paragraph 1, the competent authority shall remove the dispute resolution entity from the list referred to in the first subparagraph of this paragraph. That list shall be updated without undue delay and the relevant information notified to the Commission.

3.   If a Member State has designated more than one competent authority, the list and its updates referred to in paragraph 2 shall be notified to the Commission by the single point of contact referred to in Article 18(1). That list and those updates shall relate to all ADR entities established in that Member State.

4.   The Commission shall establish a list of the ADR entities notified to it in accordance with paragraph 2 and update that list whenever changes are notified to the Commission. The Commission shall make publicly available that list and its updates on its website and on a durable medium. The Commission shall transmit that list and its updates to the competent authorities. Where a Member State has designated a single point of contact in accordance with Article 18(1), the Commission shall transmit that list and its updates to the single point of contact.

5.   Each competent authority shall make publicly available the consolidated list of ADR entities referred to in paragraph 4 on its website by providing a link to the relevant Commission website. In addition, each competent authority shall make publicly available that consolidated list on a durable medium.

6.   By 9 July 2018, and every four years thereafter, each competent authority shall publish and send to the Commission a report on the development and functioning of ADR entities. That report shall in particular:

(a)   identify best practices of ADR entities;

(b)   point out the shortcomings, supported by statistics, that hinder the functioning of ADR entities for both domestic and cross-border disputes, where appropriate;

(c)   make recommendations on how to improve the effective and efficient functioning of ADR entities, where appropriate.

7.   If a Member State has designated more than one competent authority in accordance with Article 18(1), the report referred to in paragraph 6 of this Article shall be published by the single point of contact referred to in Article 18(1). That report shall relate to all ADR entities established in that Member State.

CHAPTER V
FINAL PROVISIONS

[4.630]
Article 21
Penalties
Member States shall lay down the rules on penalties applicable to infringements of the national provisions adopted in particular pursuant to Article 13 and shall take all measures necessary to ensure that they are implemented. The penalties provided for shall be effective, proportionate and dissuasive.

[4.631]
Article 24
Communication
1.   By 9 July 2015, Member States shall communicate to the Commission:

(a)   where appropriate, the names and contact details of the bodies designated in accordance with Article 14(2); and

(b)   the competent authorities including, where appropriate, the single point of contact, designated in accordance with Article 18(1).

Member States shall inform the Commission of any subsequent changes to this information.

2.   By 9 January 2016, Member States shall communicate to the Commission the first list referred to in Article 20(2).

3.   The Commission shall transmit to the Member States the information referred to in point (a) of paragraph 1.

[4.632]
Article 25
Transposition
1.   Member States shall bring into force the laws, regulations and administrative provisions necessary to comply with this Directive by 9 July 2015. They shall forthwith communicate to the Commission the text of those provisions.

When Member States adopt those provisions, they shall contain a reference to this Directive or be accompanied by such a reference on the occasion of their official publication. Member States shall determine how such reference is to be made.

2.   Member States shall communicate to the Commission the text of the main provisions of national law which they adopt in the field covered by this Directive.

[4.633]
Article 26
Report
By 9 July 2019, and every four years thereafter, the Commission shall submit to the European Parliament, the Council and the European Economic and Social Committee a report on the application of this Directive. That report shall consider the development and the use of ADR entities and the impact of this Directive on consumers and traders, in particular on the awareness of consumers and the level of adoption by traders. That report shall be accompanied, where appropriate, by proposals for amendment of this Directive.

[4.634]
Article 27
Entry into force
This Directive shall enter into force on the twentieth day following that of its publication in the *Official Journal of the European Union*.

[4.635]
Article 28
Addressees
This Directive is addressed to the Member States.

APPENDIX

CCA 1974 (pre CCA 2006)

CONSUMER CREDIT ACT 1974 (PRE CCA 2006)

(1974 c 39)

ARRANGEMENT OF SECTIONS

PART IV
SEEKING BUSINESS

Advertising

Canvassing etc

Miscellaneous

PART V
ENTRY INTO CREDIT OR HIRE AGREEMENTS

Preliminary matters

Making the agreement

Cancellation of certain agreements within cooling-off period

Exclusion of certain agreements from Part V

PART VI
MATTERS ARISING DURING CURRENCY OF CREDIT OR HIRE AGREEMENTS

PART VII
DEFAULT AND TERMINATION

Default notices

Further restriction of remedies for default

Early payment by debtor

Termination of agreements

PART VIII
SECURITY

General

Pledges

Negotiable instruments

Land mortgages

PART IX
JUDICIAL CONTROL

Enforcement of certain regulated agreements and securities

Extension of time

PART X
ANCILLARY CREDIT BUSINESS

Definitions

PART XI
ENFORCEMENT OF ACT

PART XII
SUPPLEMENTAL

General

Regulations, orders, etc

Interpretation

Miscellaneous

SCHEDULES

An Act to establish for the protection of consumers a new system, administered by the Director General of Fair Trading, of licensing and other control of traders concerned with the provision of credit, or the supply of goods on hire or hire-purchase, and their transactions, in place of the present enactments regulating moneylenders, pawnbrokers and hire-purchase traders and their transactions, and for related matters

[31st July 1974]

NOTES

    The text of the Consumer Credit Act 1974 reproduced in this Appendix is as it had effect on 15 June 2006, prior to amendments made by the Consumer Credit Act 2006, and subsequent amendments. For the text of the 1974 Act as it has effect on 1 August 2015, with all amendments incorporated, see [1.520] et seq and the notes to individual provisions below.

    Substitution of references to the Director General of Fair Trading: the Enterprise Act 2002, s 2(1) (now repealed), provided that, as from 1 April 2003, the functions of the Director General of Fair Trading, his property, rights and liabilities were transferred to the Office of Fair Trading. Accordingly, (by virtue of s 2(2), (3) of the 2002 Act) the office of the Director was abolished, and amendments made to this Act by the 2002 Act to take account of this (see Sch 25, para 6). Consequently, throughout this Act, unless noted otherwise, the words "OFT", "OFT's", "it", "it" and "its" were substituted for the original words "Director", "Director's", "he", "him" and "his" respectively. For transitional provisions in connection with the transfer, see s 276(1) of, and Sch 24, para 6 to, the 2002 Act.

PART I
[OFFICE OF FAIR TRADING]

NOTES

    Part heading: words in square brackets substituted by the Enterprise Act 2002, s 278(1), Sch 25, para 6(1), (2), as from 1 April 2003.

[A.1]
1   General functions of [OFT]

(1)   It is the duty of the [Office of Fair Trading ("the OFT")]—
    (a)   to administer the licensing system set up by this Act,
    (b)   to exercise the adjudicating functions conferred on [it] by this Act in relation to the issue, renewal, variation, suspension and revocation of licences, and other matters,

(c)   generally to superintend the working and enforcement of this Act, and regulations made under it, and

(d)   where necessary or expedient, [itself] to take steps to enforce this Act, and regulations so made.

(2)   It is the duty of the [OFT], so far as appears to [it] to be practicable and having regard both to the national interest and the interests of persons carrying on businesses to which this Act applies and their customers, to keep under review and from time to time advise the Secretary of State about—

(a)   social and commercial developments in the United Kingdom and elsewhere relating to the provision of credit or bailment or (in Scotland) hiring of goods to individuals, and related activities; and

(b)   the working and enforcement of this Act and orders and regulations made under it.

NOTES

Sub-s (1): words in first pair of square brackets and words in square brackets in para (d) substituted by the Enterprise Act 2002, s 278(1), Sch 25, para 6(1), (2)(a)(i), (iii), as from 1 April 2003.

References to the OFT, etc: as to the abolition of the office of the Director General of Fair Trading and the substitution of the original references to the Director (and related expressions), see the note preceding s 1 at **[A.1]**.

[A.2]
2   Powers of Secretary of State

(1)   The Secretary of State may by order—

(a)   confer on the [OFT] additional functions concerning the provision of credit or bailment or (in Scotland) hiring of goods to individuals, and related activities, and

(b)   regulate the carrying out by the [OFT] of [its] functions under this Act.

(2)   The Secretary of State may give general directions indicating considerations to which the [OFT] should have particular regard in carrying out [its] functions under this Act, and may give specific directions on any matter connected with the carrying out by the [OFT] of those functions.

(3)   The Secretary of State, on giving any directions under subsection (2), shall arrange for them to be published in such manner as he thinks most suitable for drawing them to the attention of interested persons.

(4)   With the approval of the Secretary of State and the Treasury, the [OFT] may charge, for any service or facility provided by [it] under this Act, a fee of an amount specified by general notice (the "specified fee").

(5)   Provision may be made under subsection (4) for reduced fees, or no fees at all, to be paid for certain services or facilities by persons of a specified description, and references in this Act to the specified fee shall, in such cases, be construed accordingly.

(6)   An order under subsection (1)(a) shall be made by statutory instrument and shall be of no effect unless a draft of the order has been laid before and approved by each House of Parliament.

(7)   References in subsection (2) to the functions of the [OFT] under this Act do not include the making of a determination to which section 41 or 150 (appeals from [OFT] to the Secretary of State) applies.

NOTES

References to the OFT, etc: as to the abolition of the office of the Director General of Fair Trading and the substitution of the original references to the Director (and related expressions), see the note preceding s 1 at **[A.1]**.

Order: the Consumer Credit Licensing (Representations) Order 1976, SI 1976/191.

3   (*Repealed by the Tribunals and Inquiries Act 1992, s 18(2), Sch 4, Pt I, as from 1 October 1992.*)

[A.3]
4   Dissemination of information and advice

The [OFT] shall arrange for the dissemination, in such form and manner as [it] considers appropriate, of such information and advice as it may appear to [it] expedient to give to the public in the United Kingdom about the operation of this Act, the credit facilities available to them, and other matters within the scope of [its] functions under this Act.

NOTES

References to the OFT, etc: as to the abolition of the office of the Director General of Fair Trading and the substitution of the original references to the Director (and related expressions), see the note preceding s 1 at **[A.1]**.

5   (*Repealed by the Enterprise Act 2002, s 278(2), Sch 26, as from 20 June 2003.*)

[A.4]
6   Form etc of application

(1)   An application to the [OFT] under this Act is of no effect unless the requirements of this section are satisfied.

(2)   The application must be in writing, and in such form, and accompanied by such particulars, as the [OFT] may specify by general notice, and must be accompanied by the specified fee.

(3) After giving preliminary consideration to an application, the [OFT] may by notice require the applicant to furnish [it] with such further information relevant to the application as may be described in the notice, and may require any information furnished by the applicant (whether at the time of the application or subsequently) to be verified in such manner as the [OFT] may stipulate.
(4) The [OFT] may by notice require the applicant to publish details of his application at a time or times and in a manner specified in the notice.

NOTES
  References to the OFT, etc: as to the abolition of the office of the Director General of Fair Trading and the substitution of the original references to the Director (and related expressions), see the note preceding s 1 at **[A.1]**.

[A.5]
7 Penalty for false information
A person who, in connection with any application or request to the [OFT] under this Act, or in response to any invitation or requirement of the [OFT] under this Act, knowingly or recklessly gives information to the [OFT] which, in a material particular, is false or misleading, commits an offence.

NOTES
  References to the OFT, etc: as to the abolition of the office of the Director General of Fair Trading and the substitution of the original references to the Director (and related expressions), see the note preceding s 1 at **[A.1]**.

PART II
CREDIT AGREEMENTS, HIRE AGREEMENTS AND LINKED TRANSACTIONS

[A.6]
8 Consumer credit agreements
(1) A personal credit agreement is an agreement between an individual ("the debtor") and any other person ("the creditor") by which the creditor provides the debtor with credit of any amount.
(2) A consumer credit agreement is a personal credit agreement by which the creditor provides the debtor with credit not exceeding [£25,000].
(3) A consumer credit agreement is a regulated agreement within the meaning of this Act if it is not an agreement (an "exempt agreement") specified in or under section 16.

NOTES
  Sub-s (2): sum in square brackets substituted by the Consumer Credit (Increase of Monetary Limits) Order 1983, SI 1983/1878, Schedule, Pt II (as amended by SI 1998/996, art 2), as from 1 May 1998.

[A.7]
9 Meaning of credit
(1) In this Act "credit" includes a cash loan, and any other form of financial accommodation.
(2) Where credit is provided otherwise than in sterling, it shall be treated for the purposes of this Act as provided in sterling of an equivalent amount.
(3) Without prejudice to the generality of subsection (1), the person by whom goods are bailed or (in Scotland) hired to an individual under a hire-purchase agreement shall be taken to provide him with fixed-sum credit to finance the transaction of an amount equal to the total price of the goods less the aggregate of the deposit (if any) and the total charge for credit.
(4) For the purposes of this Act, an item entering into the total charge for credit shall not be treated as credit even though time is allowed for its payment.

[A.8]
10 Running-account credit and fixed-sum credit
(1) For the purposes of this Act—
  (a) running-account credit is a facility under a personal credit agreement whereby the debtor is enabled to receive from time to time (whether in his own person, or by another person) from the creditor or a third party cash, goods and services (or any of them) to an amount or value such that, taking into account payments made by or to the credit of the debtor, the credit limit (if any) is not at any time exceeded; and
  (b) fixed-sum credit is any other facility under a personal credit agreement whereby the debtor is enabled to receive credit (whether in one amount or by instalments).
(2) In relation to running-account credit, "credit limit" means, as respects any period, the maximum debit balance which, under the credit agreement, is allowed to stand on the account during that period, disregarding any term of the agreement allowing that maximum to be exceeded merely temporarily.
(3) For the purposes of section 8(2), running-account credit shall be taken not to exceed the amount specified in that subsection ("the specified amount") if—
  (a) the credit limit does not exceed the specified amount; or
  (b) whether or not there is a credit limit, and if there is, notwithstanding that it exceeds the specified amount,—

(i) the debtor is not enabled to draw at any one time an amount which, so far as (having regard to section 9(4)) it represents credit, exceeds the specified amount, or

(ii) the agreement provides that, if the debit balance rises above a given amount (not exceeding the specified amount), the rate of the total charge for credit increases or any other condition favouring the creditor or his associate comes into operation, or

(iii) at the time the agreement is made it is probable, having regard to the terms of the agreement and any other relevant considerations, that the debit balance will not at any time rise above the specified amount.

[A.9]

11   Restricted-use credit and unrestricted-use credit

(1) A restricted-use credit agreement is a regulated consumer credit agreement—

   (a) to finance a transaction between the debtor and the creditor, whether forming part of that agreement or not, or

   (b) to finance a transaction between the debtor and a person (the "supplier") other than the creditor, or

   (c) to refinance any existing indebtedness of the debtor's, whether to the creditor or another person,

and "restricted-use credit" shall be construed accordingly.

(2) An unrestricted-use credit agreement is a regulated consumer credit agreement not falling within subsection (1), and "unrestricted-use credit" shall be construed accordingly.

(3) An agreement does not fall within subsection (1) if the credit is in fact provided in such a way as to leave the debtor free to use it as he chooses, even though certain uses would contravene that or any other agreement.

(4) An agreement may fall within subsection (1)(b) although the identity of the supplier is unknown at the time the agreement is made.

[A.10]

12   Debtor-creditor-supplier agreements

A debtor-creditor-supplier agreement is a regulated consumer credit agreement being—

   (a) a restricted-use credit agreement which falls within section 11(1)(a), or

   (b) a restricted-use credit agreement which falls within section 11(1)(b) and is made by the creditor under pre-existing arrangements, or in contemplation of future arrangements, between himself and the supplier, or

   (c) an unrestricted-use credit agreement which is made by the creditor under pre-existing arrangements between himself and a person (the "supplier") other than the debtor in the knowledge that the credit is to be used to finance a transaction between the debtor and the supplier.

[A.11]

13   Debtor-creditor agreements

A debtor-creditor agreement is a regulated consumer credit agreement being—

   (a) a restricted-use credit agreement which falls within section 11(1)(b) but is not made by the creditor under pre-existing arrangements, or in contemplation of future arrangements, between himself and the supplier, or

   (b) a restricted-use credit agreement which falls within section 11(1)(c), or

   (c) an unrestricted-use credit agreement which is not made by the creditor under pre-existing arrangements between himself and a person (the "supplier") other than the debtor in the knowledge that the credit is to be used to finance a transaction between the debtor and the supplier.

[A.12]

14   Credit-token agreements

(1) A credit-token is a card, check, voucher, coupon, stamp, form, booklet or other document or thing given to an individual by a person carrying on a consumer credit business, who undertakes—

   (a) that on the production of it (whether or not some other action is also required) he will supply cash, goods and services (or any of them) on credit, or

   (b) that where, on the production of it to a third party (whether or not any other action is also required), the third party supplies cash, goods and services (or any of them), he will pay the third party for them (whether or not deducting any discount or commission), in return for payment to him by the individual.

(2) A credit-token agreement is a regulated agreement for the provision of credit in connection with the use of a credit-token.

(3) Without prejudice to the generality of section 9(1), the person who gives to an individual an undertaking falling within subsection (1)(b) shall be taken to provide him with credit drawn on whenever a third party supplies him with cash, goods or services.

(4) For the purposes of subsection (1), use of an object to operate a machine provided by the person giving the object or a third party shall be treated as the production of the object to him.

[A.13]
15 Consumer hire agreements
(1)   A consumer hire agreement is an agreement made by a person with an individual (the "hirer") for the bailment or (in Scotland) the hiring of goods to the hirer, being an agreement which—
   (a)   is not a hire-purchase agreement, and
   (b)   is capable of subsisting for more than three months, and
   (c)   does not require the hirer to make payments exceeding [£25,000].
(2)   A consumer hire agreement is a regulated agreement if it is not an exempt agreement.

NOTES
   Sub-s (1): sum in square brackets in para (c) substituted by the Consumer Credit (Increase of Monetary Limits) Order 1983, SI 1983/1878, Schedule, Pt II (as amended by SI 1998/996, art 2), as from 1 May 1998.

[A.14]
16 Exempt agreements
(1)   This Act does not regulate a consumer credit agreement where the creditor is a local authority . . . , or a body specified, or of a description specified, in an order made by the Secretary of State, being—
   [(a)   an insurer,]
   (b)   a friendly society,
   (c)   an organisation of employers or organisation of workers,
   (d)   a charity,
   (e)   a land improvement company, . . .
   (f)   a body corporate named or specifically referred to in any public general Act
   [(ff)   a body corporate named or specifically referred to in an order made under—
            section 156(4), *444(1)* or 447(2)(a) of the Housing Act 1985,
            [section 156(4) of that Act as it has effect by virtue of section 17 of the Housing Act 1996 (the right to acquire),]
            (*applies to Scotland only.*)
            Article 154(1)(a) or 156AA of the Housing (Northern Ireland) Order 1981 or Article 10(6A) of the Housing (Northern Ireland) Order 1983; or]
   [(g)   a building society][, or
   [(h)   a deposit-taker]].
(2)   Subsection (1) applies only where the agreement is—
   (a)   a debtor-creditor-supplier agreement financing—
            (i)   the purchase of land, or
            (ii)   the provision of dwellings on any land,
            and secured by a land mortgage on that land, or
   (b)   a debtor-creditor agreement secured by any land mortgage; or
   (c)   a debtor-creditor-supplier agreement financing a transaction which is a linked transaction in relation to—
            (i)   an agreement falling within paragraph (a), or
            (ii)   an agreement falling within paragraph (b) financing—
                     (aa)   the purchase of any land, or
                     (bb)   the provision of dwellings on any land,
            and secured by a land mortgage on the land referred to in paragraph (a) or, as the case may be, the land referred to in sub-paragraph (ii).
[(3)   Before he makes, varies or revokes an order under subsection (1), the Secretary of State must undertake the necessary consultation.
(3A)   The necessary consultation means consultation with the bodies mentioned in the following table in relation to the provision under which the order is to be made, varied or revoked:

TABLE

Provision of subsection (1)	Consultee
Paragraph (a) or (b)	The Financial Services Authority
Paragraph (d)	Charity Commissioners
Paragraph (e), (f) or (ff)	Any Minister of the Crown with responsibilities in relation to the body in question
Paragraph (g) or (h)	The Treasury and the Financial Services Authority]

(4)   An order under subsection (1) relating to a body may be limited so as to apply only to agreements by that body of a description specified in the order.
(5)   The Secretary of State may by order provide that this Act shall not regulate other consumer credit agreements where—
   (a)   the number of payments to be made by the debtor does not exceed the number specified for that purpose in the order, or

(b)   the rate of the total charge for credit does not exceed the rate so specified, or

(c)   an agreement has a connection with a country outside the United Kingdom.

(6)   The Secretary of State may by order provide that this Act shall not regulate consumer hire agreements of a description specified in the order where—

(a)   the owner is a body corporate authorised by or under any enactment to supply electricity, gas or water, and

(b)   the subject of the agreement is a meter or metering equipment,

[or where the owner is a [provider of a public electronic communications service who is specified in the order]].

[(6A)   This Act does not regulate a consumer credit agreement where the creditor is a housing authority and the agreement is secured by a land mortgage of a dwelling.

(6B)   In subsection (6A) "housing authority" means—

(a)   as regards England and Wales, [the Housing Corporation . . . and] an authority or body within section 80(1) of the Housing Act 1985 (the landlord condition for secure tenancies), other than a housing association or a housing trust which is a charity;

(b)   *(applies to Scotland only)*;

(c)   as regards Northern Ireland, the Northern Ireland Housing Executive.]

[(6C)   This Act does not regulate a consumer credit agreement if—

(a)   it is secured by a land mortgage; and

(b)   entering into that agreement as lender is a regulated activity for the purposes of the Financial Services and Markets Act 2000.

(6D)   But section 126, and any other provision so far as it relates to section 126, applies to an agreement which would (but for subsection (6C) be a regulated agreement.

(6E)   Subsection (6C) must be read with—

(a)   section 22 of the Financial Services and Markets Act 2000 (regulated activities: power to specify classes of activity and categories of investment);

(b)   any order for the time being in force under that section; and

(c)   Schedule 2 to that Act.]

(7)   Nothing in this section affects the application of sections 137 to 140 (extortionate credit bargains).

(8)   *(Applies to Scotland only.)*

(9)   In the application of this section to Northern Ireland [subsection (3A)] shall have effect as if any reference to a Minister of the Crown were a reference to a Northern Ireland department, . . . and any reference to the Charity Commissioners were a reference to the Department of Finance for Northern Ireland.

[(10)   In this section—

(a)   "deposit-taker" means—

(i)   a person who has permission under Part 4 of the Financial Services and Markets Act 2000 to accept deposits,

(ii)   an EEA firm of the kind mentioned in paragraph 5(b) of Schedule 3 to that Act which has permission under paragraph 15 of that Schedule (as a result of qualifying for authorisation under paragraph 12 of that Schedule) to accept deposits,

(iii)   any wholly owned subsidiary (within the meaning of the Companies Act 1985) of a person mentioned in sub-paragraph (i), or

(iv)   any undertaking which, in relation to a person mentioned in sub-paragraph (ii), is a subsidiary undertaking within the meaning of any rule of law in force in the EEA State in question for purposes connected with the implementation of the European Council Seventh Company Law Directive of 13 June 1983 on consolidated accounts (No 83/349/EEC), and which has no members other than that person;

(b)   "insurer" means—

(i)   a person who has permission under Part 4 of the Financial Services and Markets Act 2000 to effect or carry out contracts of insurance, or

(ii)   an EEA firm of the kind mentioned in paragraph 5(d) of Schedule 3 to that Act, which has permission under paragraph 15 of that Schedule (as a result of qualifying for authorisation under paragraph 12 of that Schedule) to effect or carry out contracts of insurance,

but does not include a friendly society or an organisation of workers or of employers.

(11)   Subsection (10) must be read with—

(a)   section 22 of the Financial Services and Markets Act 2000;

(b)   any relevant order under that section; and

(c)   Schedule 2 to that Act.]

NOTES

Sub-s (1): first words omitted repealed, and para (g) added, by the Building Societies Act 1986, s 120, Sch 18, Pt I, para 10(2), Sch 19, Pt I, as from 1 January 1987; para (a) substituted by the Financial Services and Markets Act 2000 (Consequential Amendments and Repeals) Order 2001, SI 2001/3649, art 165(1), (2)(a), as from 1 December 2001; para (ff) inserted by the Housing and Planning Act 1986, s 22(2), (4), as from 7 January 1987 with respect to agreements made after that date, number in italics repealed by the Housing Act 1996, s 227, Sch 19, Pt XIV, as from a day to be appointed, and words in square brackets inserted by the Housing Act 1996 (Consequential Amendments) (No 2) Order 1997, SI 1997/627, art 2,

Schedule, para 2, as from 1 April 1997; para (h) added by the Banking Act 1987, s 88 as from 1 October 1987, and substituted by SI 2001/3649, art 165(1), (2)(b), as from 1 December 2001.

Sub-ss (3), (3A): substituted for original sub-s (3), by SI 2001/3649, art 165(1), (3), as from 1 December 2001.

Sub-s (6): words in first (outer) pair of square brackets substituted by the Telecommunications Act 1984, s 109, Sch 4, para 60(1), as from 5 August 1984; words in second (inner) pair of square brackets substituted by the Communications Act 2003, s 406(1), Sch 17, para 47, as from 29 December 2003.

Sub-s (6A): inserted, together with sub-s (6B), by the Housing and Planning Act 1986, s 22(3), (4), as from 7 January 1987 with respect to agreements made after that date.

Sub-s (6B): inserted as noted to sub-s (6A); words in square brackets inserted by the Housing Act 1988, s 140(1), Sch 17, Pt I, para 20, as from 15 January 1989; words omitted repealed, subject to transitional provisions, by the Government of Wales Act 1998, ss 141, 152, Sch 18, Pt VI, as from 1 November 1998.

Sub-ss (6C)–(6E): inserted by the Financial Services and Markets Act 2000 (Regulated Activities) Order 2001, SI 2001/544, art 90(1), (2), as from 31 October 2004.

Sub-s (9): words in square brackets substituted, and words omitted repealed, by SI 2001/3649, art 165(1), (5), as from 1 December 2001.

Sub-ss (10), (11): added by SI 2001/3649, art 165(1), (6), as from 1 December 2001.

Order: the Consumer Credit (Exempt Agreements) Order 1989, SI 1989/869.

[A.15]
17 Small agreements
(1) A small agreement is—
   (a)   a regulated consumer credit agreement for credit not exceeding [£50], other than a hire-purchase or conditional sale agreement; or
   (b)   a regulated consumer hire agreement which does not require the hirer to make payments exceeding [£50],

being an agreement which is either unsecured or secured by a guarantee or indemnity only (whether or not the guarantee or indemnity is itself secured).
(2) Section 10(3)(a) applies for the purposes of subsection (1) as it applies for the purposes of section 8(2).
(3) Where—
   (a)   two or more small agreements are made at or about the same time between the same parties, and
   (b)   it appears probable that they would instead have been made as a single agreement but for the desire to avoid the operation of provisions of this Act which would have applied to that single agreement but, apart from this subsection, are not applicable to the small agreements,

this Act applies to the small agreements as if they were regulated agreements other than small agreements.
(4) If, apart from this subsection, subsection (3) does not apply to any agreements but would apply if, for any party or parties to any of the agreements, there were substituted an associate of that party, or associates of each of those parties, as the case may be, then subsection (3) shall apply to the agreements.

NOTES
Sub-s (1): sums in square brackets substituted by the Consumer Credit (Increase of Monetary Limits) Order 1983, SI 1983/1878, art 3, Schedule, Pt I, as from 1 May 1998.

[A.16]
18 Multiple agreements
(1) This section applies to an agreement (a "multiple agreement") if its terms are such as—
   (a)   to place a part of it within one category of agreement mentioned in this Act, and another part of it within a different category of agreements so mentioned, or within a category of agreement not so mentioned, or
   (b)   to place it, or a part of it, within two or more categories of agreement so mentioned.
(2) Where a part of an agreement falls within subsection (1), that part shall be treated for the purposes of this Act as a separate agreement.
(3) Where an agreement falls within subsection (1)(b), it shall be treated as an agreement in each of the categories in question, and this Act shall apply to it accordingly.
(4) Where under subsection (2) a part of a multiple agreement is to be treated as a separate agreement, the multiple agreement shall (with any necessary modifications) be construed accordingly; and any sum payable under the multiple agreement, if not apportioned by the parties, shall for the purposes of proceedings in any court relating to the multiple agreement be apportioned by the court as may be requisite.
(5) In the case of an agreement for running-account credit, a term of the agreement allowing the credit limit to be exceeded merely temporarily shall not be treated as a separate agreement or as providing fixed-sum credit in respect of the excess.
(6) This Act does not apply to a multiple agreement so far as the agreement relates to goods if under the agreement payments are to be made in respect of the goods in the form of rent (other than a rent-charge) issuing out of land.

[A.17]
19 Linked transactions

(1)   A transaction entered into by the debtor or hirer, or a relative of his, with any other person ("the other party"), except one for the provision of security, is a linked transaction in relation to an actual or prospective regulated agreement (the "principal agreement") of which it does not form part if—

(a)   the transaction is entered into in compliance with a term of the principal agreement; or

(b)   the principal agreement is a debtor-creditor-supplier agreement and the transaction is financed, or to be financed, by the principal agreement; or

(c)   the other party is a person mentioned in subsection (2), and a person so mentioned initiated the transaction by suggesting it to the debtor or hirer, or his relative, who enters into it—

(i)   to induce the creditor or owner to enter into the principal agreement, or

(ii)   for another purpose related to the principal agreement, or

(iii)   where the principal agreement is a restricted-use credit agreement, for a purpose related to a transaction financed, or to be financed, by the principal agreement.

(2)   The persons referred to in subsection (1)(c) are—

(a)   the creditor or owner, or his associate;

(b)   a person who, in the negotiation of the transaction, is represented by a credit-broker who is also a negotiator in antecedent negotiations for the principal agreement;

(c)   a person who, at the time the transaction is initiated, knows that the principal agreement has been made or contemplates that it might be made.

(3)   A linked transaction entered into before the making of the principal agreement has no effect until such time (if any) as that agreement is made.

(4)   Regulations may exclude linked transactions of the prescribed description from the operation of subsection (3).

NOTES

Regulations: the Consumer Credit (Linked Transactions) (Exemptions) Regulations 1983, SI 1983/1560.

[A.18]
20 Total charge for credit

(1)   The Secretary of State shall make regulations containing such provisions as appear to him appropriate for determining the true cost to the debtor of the credit provided or to be provided under an actual or prospective consumer credit agreement (the "total charge for credit"), and regulations so made shall prescribe—

(a)   what items are to be treated as entering into the total charge for credit, and how their amount is to be ascertained;

(b)   the method of calculating the rate of the total charge for credit.

(2)   Regulations under subsection (1) may provide for the whole or part of the amount payable by the debtor or his relative under any linked transaction to be included in the total charge for credit, whether or not the creditor is a party to the transaction or derives benefit from it.

NOTES

Regulations: the Consumer Credit (Total Charge for Credit) Regulations 1980, SI 1980/51.

PART III
LICENSING OF CREDIT AND HIRE BUSINESSES

Licensing principles

[A.19]
21 Businesses needing a licence

(1)   Subject to this section, a licence is required to carry on a consumer credit business or consumer hire business.

(2)   A local authority does not need a licence to carry on a business.

(3)   A body corporate empowered by a public general Act naming it to carry on a business does not need a licence to do so.

[A.20]
22 Standard and group licences

(1)   A licence may be—

(a)   a standard licence, that is a licence, issued by the [OFT] to a person named in the licence on an application made by him, which, during the prescribed period, covers such activities as are described in the licence, or

(b)   a group licence, that is a licence, issued by the [OFT] (whether on the application of any person or of [its] own motion), which, during such period as the [OFT] thinks fit or, if [it] thinks fit, indefinitely, covers such persons and activities as are described in the licence.

(2)   A licence is not assignable or, subject to section 37, transmissible on death or in any other way.

(3)   Except in the case of a partnership or an unincorporated body of persons, a standard licence shall not be issued to more than one person.

(4)   A standard licence issued to a partnership or an unincorporated body of persons shall be issued in the name of the partnership or body.

(5)   The [OFT] may issue a group licence only if it appears to [it] that the public interest is better served by doing so than by obliging the persons concerned to apply separately for standard licences.

(6)   The persons covered by a group licence may be described by general words, whether or not coupled with the exclusion of named persons, or in any other way the [OFT] thinks fit.

(7)   The fact that a person is covered by a group licence in respect of certain activities does not prevent a standard licence being issued to him in respect of those activities or any of them.

(8)   A group licence issued on the application of any person shall be issued to that person, and general notice shall be given of the issue of any group licence (whether on application or not).

[(9)   Subsection (10) applies if a standard licence is issued to an EEA consumer credit firm.

(10)   The activities described in the licence are not to include an activity for which the firm has, or could obtain, permission under paragraph 15 of Schedule 3 to the Financial Services and Markets Act 2000.]

NOTES

Sub-ss (9), (10): added by the Financial Services and Markets Act 2000 (Consequential Amendments and Repeals) Order 2001, SI 2001/3649, art 166, as from 1 December 2001.

References to the OFT, etc: as to the abolition of the office of the Director General of Fair Trading and the substitution of the original references to the Director (and related expressions), see the note preceding s 1 at **[A.1]**.

Regulations: the Consumer Credit (Termination of Licences) Regulations 1976, SI 1976/1002.

[A.21]
23   Authorisation of specific activities

(1)   Subject to this section, a licence to carry on a business covers all lawful activities done in the course of that business, whether by the licensee or other persons on his behalf.

(2)   A licence may limit the activities it covers, whether by authorising the licensee to enter into certain types of agreement only, or in any other way.

(3)   A licence covers the canvassing off trade premises of debtor-creditor-supplier agreements or regulated consumer hire agreements only if, and to the extent that, the licence specifically so provides; and such provision shall not be included in a group licence.

(4)   Regulations may be made specifying other activities which, if engaged in by or on behalf of the person carrying on a business, require to be covered by an express term in his licence.

[A.22]
24   Control of name of business

A standard licence authorises the licensee to carry on a business under the name or names specified in the licence, but not under any other name.

[A.23]
25   Licensee to be a fit person

(1)   A standard licence shall be granted on the application of any person if he satisfies the [OFT] that—
   (a)   he is a fit person to engage in activities covered by the licence, and
   (b)   the name or names under which he applies to be licensed is or are not misleading or otherwise undesirable.

[(1A)   The [OFT] shall refuse an application for the grant of standard licence made by a consumer credit EEA firm if all of the activities described in the licence are activities for which the firm has permission, or could obtain, under paragraph 15 of Schedule 3 to the Financial Services and Markets Act 2000.

(1B)   If an application for the grant of a standard licence—
   (a)   is made by a person with permission under Part 4 of the Financial Services and Markets Act 2000 to accept deposits, and
   (b)   relates to a listed activity,
the Financial Services Authority may, if it considers that the [OFT] ought to refuse the application, notify him of that fact.

(1C)   In subsection (1B) "listed activity" means an activity listed in Annex 1 to the banking consolidation directive (2000/12/EC) or in the Annex to the investment services directive (93/22/EEC) and references to deposits and to their acceptance must be read with—
   (a)   section 22 of the Financial Services and Markets Act 2000;
   (b)   any relevant order under that section; and
   (c)   Schedule 2 to that Act.]

(2)   In determining whether an applicant for a standard licence is a fit person to engage in any activities, the [OFT] shall have regard to any circumstances appearing to [it] to be relevant, and in particular any evidence tending to show that the applicant, or any of the applicant's employees, agents or associates (whether past or present) or, where the applicant is a body corporate, any person appearing to the [OFT] to be a controller of the body corporate or an associate of any such person, has—

(a) committed any offence involving fraud or other dishonesty, or violence,

(b) contravened any provision made by or under this Act, or by or under any other enactment regulating the provision of credit to individuals or other transactions with individuals,

[(bb) contravened any provision in force in an EEA State which corresponds to a provision of the kind mentioned in paragraph (b);]

(c) practised discrimination on grounds of sex, colour, race or ethnic or national origins in, or in connection with, the carrying on of any business, or

(d) engaged in business practices appearing to the [OFT] to be deceitful or oppressive, or otherwise unfair or improper (whether unlawful or not).

(3) In subsection (2), "associate", in addition to the persons specified in section 184, includes a business associate.

NOTES

Sub-s (1A)–(1C): inserted by the Financial Services and Markets Act 2000 (Consequential Amendments and Repeals) Order 2001, SI 2001/3649, art 167(1), (2), as from 1 December 2001.

Sub-s (2): para (bb) inserted by SI 2001/3649, art 167(1), (3), as from 1 December 2001.

References to the OFT, etc: as to the abolition of the office of the Director General of Fair Trading and the substitution of the original references to the Director (and related expressions), see the note preceding s 1 at **[A.1]**.

[A.24]

[26 Conduct of business

(1) Regulations may be made as to—

(a) the conduct by a licensee of his business; and

(b) the conduct by a consumer credit EEA firm of its business in the United Kingdom.

(2) The regulations may in particular specify—

(a) the books or other records to be kept by any person to whom the regulations apply;

(b) the information to be furnished by such a person to those persons with whom—

(i) that person does business, or

(ii) that person seeks to do business,

and the way in which that information is to be furnished.]

NOTES

Substituted by the Financial Services and Markets Act 2000 (Consequential Amendments and Repeals) Order 2001, SI 2001/3649, art 168, as from 1 December 2001.

Regulations: the Consumer Credit (Conduct of Business) (Credit References) Regulations 1977, SI 1977/330; the Consumer Credit (Conduct of Business) (Pawn Records) Regulations 1983, SI 1983/1565.

Issue of licences

[A.25]

27 Determination of applications

(1) Unless the [OFT] determines to issue a licence in accordance with an application [it] shall, before determining the application, by notice—

(a) inform the applicant, giving [its] reasons, that, as the case may be, [it] is minded to refuse the application, or to grant it in terms different from those applied for, describing them, and

(b) invite the applicant to submit to the [OFT] representations in support of his application in accordance with section 34.

(2) If the [OFT] grants the application in terms different from those applied for then, whether or not the applicant appeals, the [OFT] shall issue the licence in the terms approved by [it] unless the applicant by notice informs [it] that he does not desire a licence in those terms.

NOTES

References to the OFT, etc: as to the abolition of the office of the Director General of Fair Trading and the substitution of the original references to the Director (and related expressions), see the note preceding s 1 at **[A.1]**.

[A.26]

28 Exclusion from group licence

Where the [OFT] is minded to issue a group licence (whether on the application of any person or not), and in doing so to exclude any person from the group by name, [it] shall, before determining the matter,—

(a) give notice of that fact to the person proposed to be excluded, giving [its] reasons, and

(b) invite that person to submit to the [OFT] representations against his exclusion in accordance with section 34.

NOTES

References to the OFT, etc: as to the abolition of the office of the Director General of Fair Trading and the substitution of the original references to the Director (and related expressions), see the note preceding s 1 at **[A.1]**.

Renewal, variation, suspension and revocation of licences

[A.27]
29 Renewal

(1) If the licensee under a standard licence, or the original applicant for, or any licensee under, a group licence of limited duration, wishes the [OFT] to renew the licence, whether on the same terms (except as to expiry) or on varied terms, he must, during the period specified by the [OFT] by general notice or such longer period as the [OFT] may allow, make an application to the [OFT] for its renewal.

(2) The [OFT] may of [its] own motion renew any group licence.

(3) The preceding provisions of this Part apply to the renewal of a licence as they apply to the issue of a licence, except that section 28 does not apply to a person who was already excluded in the licence up for renewal.

(4) Until the determination of an application under subsection (1) and, where an appeal lies from the determination, until the end of the appeal period, the licence shall continue in force, notwithstanding that apart from this subsection it would expire earlier.

(5) On the refusal of an application under this section, the [OFT] may give directions authorising a licensee to carry into effect agreements made by him before the expiry of the licence.

(6) General notice shall be given of the renewal of a group licence.

NOTES

References to the OFT, etc: as to the abolition of the office of the Director General of Fair Trading and the substitution of the original references to the Director (and related expressions), see the note preceding s 1 at **[A.1]**.

[A.28]
30 Variation by request

(1) On an application made by the licensee, the [OFT] may if [it] thinks fit by notice to the licensee vary a standard licence in accordance with the application.

(2) In the case of a group licence issued on the application of any person, the [OFT], on an application made by that person, may if [it] thinks fit by notice to that person vary the terms of the licence in accordance with the application; but the [OFT] shall not vary a group licence under this subsection by excluding a named person, other than the person making the request, unless that named person consents in writing to his exclusion.

(3) In the case of a group licence from which (whether by name or description) a person is excluded, the [OFT], on an application made by that person, may if [it] thinks fit, by notice to that person, vary the terms of the licence so as to remove the exclusion.

(4) Unless the [OFT] determines to vary a licence in accordance with an application [it] shall, before determining the application, by notice—

    (a) inform the applicant, giving [its] reasons, that [it] is minded to refuse the application, and

    (b) invite the applicant to submit to the [OFT] representations in support of his application in accordance with section 34.

(5) General notice shall be given that a variation of a group licence has been made under this section.

NOTES

References to the OFT, etc: as to the abolition of the office of the Director General of Fair Trading and the substitution of the original references to the Director (and related expressions), see the note preceding s 1 at **[A.1]**.

[A.29]
31 Compulsory variation

(1) Where at a time during the currency of a licence the [OFT] is of the opinion that, if the licence had expired at that time, [it] would, on an application for its renewal or further renewal on the same terms (except as to expiry), have been minded to grant the application but on different terms, and that therefore the licence should be varied, [it] shall proceed as follows.

(2) In the case of a standard licence the [OFT] shall, by notice—

    (a) inform the licensee of the variations the [OFT] is minded to make in the terms of the licence, stating [its] reasons, and

    (b) invite him to submit to the [OFT] representations as to the proposed variations in accordance with section 34.

(3) In the case of a group licence the [OFT] shall—

    (a) give general notice of the variations [it] is minded to make in the terms of the licence, stating [its] reasons, and

    (b) in the notice invite any licensee to submit to [it] representations as to the proposed variations in accordance with section 34.

(4) In the case of a group licence issued on application the [OFT] shall also—

    (a) inform the original applicant of the variations the [OFT] is minded to make in the terms of the licence, stating [its] reasons, and

    (b) invite him to submit to the [OFT] representations as to the proposed variations in accordance with section 34.

(5) If the [OFT] is minded to vary a group licence by excluding any person (other than the original applicant) from the group by name the [OFT] shall, in addition, take the like steps under section 28 as are required in the case mentioned in that section.

(6) General notice shall be given that a variation of any group licence has been made under this section.

(7) A variation under this section shall not take effect before the end of the appeal period.

NOTES

References to the OFT, etc: as to the abolition of the office of the Director General of Fair Trading and the substitution of the original references to the Director (and related expressions), see the note preceding s 1 at **[A.1]**.

[A.30]

32 Suspension and revocation

(1) Where at a time during the currency of a licence the [OFT] is of the opinion that if the licence had expired at that time [it] would have been minded not to renew it, and that therefore it should be revoked or suspended, [it] shall proceed as follows.

(2) In the case of a standard licence the [OFT] shall, by notice—
  (a) inform the licensee that, as the case may be, the [OFT] is minded to revoke the licence, or suspend it until a specified date or indefinitely, stating [its] reasons, and
  (b) invite him to submit representations as to the proposed revocation or suspension in accordance with section 34.

(3) In the case of a group licence the [OFT] shall—
  (a) give general notice that, as the case may be, [it] is minded to revoke the licence, or suspend it until a specified date or indefinitely, stating [its] reasons, and
  (b) in the notice invite any licensee to submit to [it] representations as to the proposed revocation or suspension in accordance with section 34.

(4) In the case of a group licence issued on application the [OFT] shall also—
  (a) inform the original applicant that, as the case may be, the [OFT] is minded to revoke the licence, or suspend it until a specified date or indefinitely, stating [its] reasons, and
  (b) invite him to submit representations as to the proposed revocation or suspension in accordance with section 34.

(5) If [it] revokes or suspends the licence, the [OFT] may give directions authorising a licensee to carry into effect agreements made by him before the revocation or suspension.

(6) General notice shall be given of the revocation or suspension of a group licence.

(7) A revocation or suspension under this section shall not take effect before the end of the appeal period.

(8) Except for the purposes of section 29, a licensee under a suspended licence shall be treated, in respect of the period of suspension, as if the licence had not been issued; and where the suspension is not expressed to end on a specified date it may, if the [OFT] thinks fit, be ended by notice given by [it] to the licensee or, in the case of a group licence, by general notice.

NOTES

References to the OFT, etc: as to the abolition of the office of the Director General of Fair Trading and the substitution of the original references to the Director (and related expressions), see the note preceding s 1 at **[A.1]**.

[A.31]

33 Application to end suspension

(1) On an application made by a licensee the [OFT] may, if [it] thinks fit, by notice to the licensee end the suspension of a licence, whether the suspension was for a fixed or indefinite period.

(2) Unless the [OFT] determines to end the suspension in accordance with the application [it] shall, before determining the application, by notice—
  (a) inform the applicant, giving [its] reasons, that [it] is minded to refuse the application, and
  (b) invite the applicant to submit to the [OFT] representations in support of his application in accordance with section 34.

(3) General notice shall be given that a suspension of a group licence has been ended under this section.

(4) In the case of a group licence issued on application—
  (a) the references in subsection (1) to a licensee include the original applicant;
  (b) the [OFT] shall inform the original applicant that a suspension of a group licence has been ended under this section.

NOTES

References to the OFT, etc: as to the abolition of the office of the Director General of Fair Trading and the substitution of the original references to the Director (and related expressions), see the note preceding s 1 at **[A.1]**.

Miscellaneous

[A.32]

34   Representations to [OFT]

(1) Where this section applies to an invitation by the [OFT] to any person to submit representations, the [OFT] shall invite that person, within 21 days after the notice containing the invitation is given to him or published, or such longer period as the [OFT] may allow,—

    (a)   to submit his representations in writing to the [OFT], and

    (b)   to give notice to the [OFT], if he thinks fit, that he wishes to make representations orally, and where notice is given under paragraph (b) the [OFT] shall arrange for the oral representations to be heard.

(2) In reaching [its] determination the [OFT] shall take into account any representations submitted or made under this section.

(3) The [OFT] shall give notice of [its] determination to the persons who were required to be invited to submit representations about it or, where the invitation to submit representations was required to be given by general notice, shall give general notice of the determination.

NOTES

References to the OFT, etc: as to the abolition of the office of the Director General of Fair Trading and the substitution of the original references to the Director (and related expressions), see the note preceding s 1 at **[A.1]**.

[A.33]

35   The register

(1) The [OFT] shall establish and maintain a register, in which [it] shall cause to be kept particulars of—

    (a)   applications not yet determined for the issue, variation or renewal of licences, or for ending the suspension of a licence;

    (b)   licences which are in force, or have at any time been suspended or revoked, with details of any variation of the terms of a licence;

    (c)   decisions given by [it] under this Act, and any appeal from those decisions; and

    (d)   such other matters (if any) as [it] thinks fit.

[(1A) The [OFT] shall also cause to be kept in the register any copy of any notice or other document relating to a consumer credit EEA firm which is given to the [OFT] by the Financial Services Authority for inclusion in the register.]

(2) The [OFT] shall give general notice of the various matters required to be entered in the register, and of any change in them made under subsection (1)(d).

(3) Any person shall be entitled, on payment of the specified fee—

    (a)   to inspect the register during ordinary office hours and take copies of any entry, or

    (b)   to obtain from the [OFT] a copy, certified by the [OFT] to be correct, of any entry in the register.

(4) The [OFT] may, if [it] thinks fit, determine that the right conferred by subsection (3)(a) shall be exercisable in relation to a copy of the register instead of, or in addition to, the original.

(5) The [OFT] shall give general notice of the place or places where, and times when, the register or a copy of it may be inspected.

NOTES

Sub-s (1A): inserted by the Financial Services and Markets Act 2000 (Consequential Amendments and Repeals) Order 2001, SI 2001/3649, art 169, as from 1 December 2001.

References to the OFT, etc: as to the abolition of the office of the Director General of Fair Trading and the substitution of the original references to the Director (and related expressions), see the note preceding s 1 at **[A.1]**.

[A.34]

36   Duty to notify changes

(1) Within 21 working days after a change takes place in any particulars entered in the register in respect of a standard licence or the licensee under section 35(1)(d) (not being a change resulting from action taken by the [OFT]), the licensee shall give the [OFT] notice of the change; and the [OFT] shall cause any necessary amendment to be made in the register.

(2) Within 21 working days after—

    (a)   any change takes place in the officers of—

        (i)   a body corporate, or an unincorporated body of persons, which is the licensee under a standard licence, or

        (ii)   a body corporate which is a controller of a body corporate which is such a licensee, or

    (b)   a body corporate which is such a licensee becomes aware that a person has become or ceased to be a controller of the body corporate, or

    (c)   any change takes place in the members of a partnership which is such a licensee (including a change on the amalgamation of the partnership with another firm, or a change whereby the number of partners is reduced to one),

the licensee shall give the [OFT] notice of the change.

(3)   Within 14 working days after any change takes place in the officers of a body corporate which is a controller of another body corporate which is a licensee under a standard licence, the controller shall give the licensee notice of the change.

(4)   Within 14 working days after a person becomes or ceases to be a controller of a body corporate which is a licensee under a standard licence, that person shall give the licensee notice of the fact.

(5)   Where a change in a partnership has the result that the business ceases be carried on under the name, or any of the names, specified in a standard licence the licence shall cease to have effect.

(6)   Where the [OFT] is given notice under subsection (1) or (2) of any change, and subsection (5) does not apply, the [OFT] may by notice require the licensee to furnish [it] with such information, verified in such manner, as the [OFT] may stipulate.

NOTES

References to the OFT, etc: as to the abolition of the office of the Director General of Fair Trading and the substitution of the original references to the Director (and related expressions), see the note preceding s 1 at **[A.1]**.

[A.35]
37   Death, bankruptcy etc of licensee
(1)   A licence held by one individual terminates if he—
   (a)   dies, or
   (b)   is adjudged bankrupt, or
   (c)   becomes a patient within the meaning of Part VIII of the Mental Health Act 1959.
(2)   In relation to a licence held by one individual, or a partnership or other unincorporated body of persons, or a body corporate, regulations may specify other events relating to the licensee on the occurrence of which the licence is to terminate.
(3)   Regulations may—
   (a)   provide for the termination of a licence by subsection (1), or under subsection (2), to be deferred for a period not exceeding 12 months, and
   (b)   authorise the business of the licensee to be carried on under the licence by some other person during the period of deferment, subject to such conditions as may be prescribed.
(4)   This section does not apply to group licences.

NOTES

Regulations: the Consumer Credit (Termination of Licences) Regulations 1976, SI 1976/1002.

38   (*Application of s 37 to Northern Ireland and Scotland; outside the scope of this work.*)

[A.36]
39   Offences against Part III
(1)   A person who engages in any activities for which a licence is required when he is not a licensee under a licence covering those activities commits an offence.
(2)   A licensee under a standard licence who carries on business under a name not specified in the licence commits an offence.
(3)   A person who fails to give the [OFT] or a licensee notice under section 36 within the period required commits an offence.

NOTES

References to the OFT, etc: as to the abolition of the office of the Director General of Fair Trading and the substitution of the original references to the Director (and related expressions), see the note preceding s 1 at **[A.1]**.

[A.37]
40   Enforcement of agreements made by unlicensed trader
(1)   A regulated agreement, other than a non-commercial agreement, if made when the creditor or owner was unlicensed, is enforceable against the debtor or hirer only where the [OFT] has made an order under this section which applies to the agreement.
(2)   Where during any period an unlicensed person (the "trader") was carrying on a consumer credit business or consumer hire business, he or his successor in title may apply to the [OFT] for an order that regulated agreements made by the trader during that period are to be treated as if he had been licensed.
(3)   Unless the [OFT] determines to make an order under subsection (2) in accordance with the application, [it] shall, before determining the application, by notice—
   (a)   inform the applicant, giving his reasons, that, as the case may be, [it] is minded to refuse the application, or to grant it in terms different from those applied for, describing them, and
   (b)   invite the applicant to submit to the [OFT] representations in support of [its] application in accordance with section 34.
(4)   In determining whether or not to make an order under subsection (2) in respect of any period the [OFT] shall consider, in addition to any other relevant factors—
   (a)   how far, if at all, debtors or hirers under regulated agreements made by the trader during that period were prejudiced by the trader's conduct,

(b)   whether or not the [OFT] would have been likely to grant a licence covering that period on an application by the trader, and

(c)   the degree of culpability for the failure to obtain a licence.

(5) If the [OFT] thinks fit, [it] may in an order under subsection (2)—

(a)   limit the order to specified agreements, or agreements of a specified description or made at a specified time;

(b)   make the order conditional on the doing of specified acts by the applicant.

[(6) This section does not apply to a regulated agreement, other than a non-commercial agreement, made by a consumer credit EEA firm unless at the time it was made that firm was precluded from entering into it as a result of

(a)   a consumer credit prohibition imposed under section 203 of the Financial Services and Markets Act 2000; or

(b)   a restriction imposed on the firm under section 204 of that Act.]

NOTES

Sub-s (6): added by the Financial Services and Markets Act 2000 (Consequential Amendments and Repeals) Order 2001, SI 2001/3649, art 170, as from 1 December 2001.

References to the OFT, etc: as to the abolition of the office of the Director General of Fair Trading and the substitution of the original references to the Director (and related expressions), see the note preceding s 1 at **[A.1]**.

[A.38]
41 Appeals to Secretary of State under Part III

(1) If, in the case of a determination by the [OFT] such as is mentioned in column 1 of the table set out at the end of this section, a person mentioned in relation to that determination in column 2 of the table is aggrieved by the determination he may, within the prescribed period, and in the prescribed manner, appeal to the Secretary of State.

(2) Regulations may make provision as to the persons by whom (on behalf of the Secretary of State) appeals under this section are to be heard, the manner in which they are to be conducted, and any other matter connected with such appeals.

(3) On an appeal under this section, the Secretary of State may give such directions for disposing of the appeal as he thinks just, including a direction for the payment of costs by any party to the appeal.

(4) A direction under subsection (3) for payment of costs may be made a rule of the High Court on the application of the party in whose favour it is given.

(5) (*Applies to Scotland only.*)

TABLE

Determination	Appellant
Refusal to issue, renew or vary licence in accordance with terms of application.	The applicant.
Exclusion of person from group licence.	The person excluded.
Refusal to give directions in respect of a licensee under section 29(5) or 32(5)	The licensee.
Compulsory variation, or suspension or revocation, of standard licence.	The licensee.
Compulsory variation, or suspension or revocation, of group licence.	The original applicant or any licensee.
Refusal to end suspension of licence in accordance with terms of application.	The applicant.
Refusal to make order under section 40(2) in accordance with terms of application.	The applicant.
[Imposition of, or refusal to withdraw, consumer credit prohibition under section 203 of the Financial Services and Markets Act 2000.	The consumer credit EEA firm concerned.
Imposition of, or refusal to withdraw, a restriction under section 204 of the Financial Services and Markets Act 2000.	The consumer credit EEA firm concerned.]

NOTES

References to the OFT, etc: as to the abolition of the office of the Director General of Fair Trading and the substitution of the original references to the Director (and related expressions), see the note preceding s 1 at **[A.1]**.

Table: entries relating to the Financial Services and Markets Act 2000, ss 203, 204 added by the Financial Services and Markets Act 2000 (Consequential Amendments and Repeals) Order 2001, SI 2001/3649, art 171, as from 1 December 2001.

Regulations: the Consumer Credit Licensing (Appeals) Regulations 1998, SI 1998/1203.

42 (*Repealed by the Tribunals and Inquiries Act 1992, s 18(2), Sch 4, Pt I, as from 1 October 1992.*)

PART IV
SEEKING BUSINESS
Advertising

[A.39]
43 Advertisements to which Part IV applies

(1) This Part applies to any advertisement, published for the purposes of a business carried on by the advertiser, indicating that he is willing—

    (a)   to provide credit, or

    (b)   to enter into an agreement for the bailment or (in Scotland) the hiring of goods by him.

(2) An advertisement does not fall within subsection (1) if the advertiser does not carry on—

    (a)   a consumer credit business or consumer hire business, or

    (b)   a business in the course of which he provides credit to individuals secured on land, or

    (c)   a business which comprises or relates to unregulated agreements where—

        (i)   the [law applicable to] the agreement is the law of a country outside the United Kingdom, and

        (ii) if the [law applicable to] the agreement were the law of a part of the United Kingdom it would be a regulated agreement.

(3) An advertisement does not fall within subsection (1)(a) if it indicates—

    (a)   that the credit must exceed [£25,000], and that no security is required, or the security is to consist of property other than land, or

    (b)   that the credit is available only to a body corporate.

[(3A) An advertisement does not fall within subsection (1)(a) in so far as it is a communication of an invitation or inducement to engage in investment activity within the meaning of section 21 of the Financial Services and Markets Act 2000, other than an exempt generic communication.

(3B) An "exempt generic communication" is a communication to which subsection (1) of section 21 of the Financial Services and Markets Act 2000 does not apply, as a result of an order under subsection (5) of that section, because it does not identify a person as providing an investment or as carrying on an activity to which the communication relates.]

(4) An advertisement does not fall within subsection (1)(b) if it indicates that the advertiser is not willing to enter into a consumer hire agreement.

(5) The Secretary of State may by order provide that this Part shall not apply to other advertisements of a description specified in the order.

NOTES

Sub-s (2): words in square brackets substituted by the Contracts (Applicable Law) Act 1990, s 5, Sch 4, para 2, as from 1 April 1991.

Sub-s (3): sum in square brackets in para (a) substituted by the Consumer Credit (Increase of Monetary Limits) Order 1983, SI 1983/1878, Schedule, Pt II (as amended by SI 1998/996, art 2, as from 1 May 1998.

Sub-ss (3A), (3B): inserted by the Financial Services and Markets Act 2000 (Regulated Activities) Order 2001, SI 2001/544, art 90(1), (3), as from 31 October 2004.

Order: the Consumer Credit (Exempt Advertisements) Order 1985, SI 1985/621.

[A.40]
44 Form and content of advertisements

(1) The Secretary of State shall make regulations as to the form and content of advertisements to which this Part applies, and the regulations shall contain such provisions as appear to him appropriate with a view to ensuring that, having regard to its subject-matter and the amount of detail included in it, an advertisement conveys a fair and reasonably comprehensive indication of the nature of the credit or hire facilities offered by the advertiser and of their true cost to persons using them.

(2) Regulations under subsection (1) may in particular—

    (a)   require specified information to be included in the prescribed manner in advertisements, and other specified material to be excluded;

    (b)   contain requirements to ensure that specified information is clearly brought to the attention of persons to whom advertisements are directed, and that one part of an advertisement is not given insufficient or excessive prominence compared with another.

NOTES

Regulations: the Consumer Credit (Advertisements) Regulations 2004, SI 2004/1484.

[A.41]
45   Prohibition of advertisement where goods etc not sold for cash
If an advertisement to which this Part applies indicates that the advertiser is willing to provide credit under a restricted-use credit agreement relating to goods or services to be supplied by any person, but at the time when the advertisement is published that person is not holding himself out as prepared to sell the goods or provide the services (as the case may be) for cash, the advertiser commits an offence.

[A.42]
46   False or misleading advertisements
(1)   If an advertisement to which this Part applies conveys information which in a material respect is false or misleading the advertiser commits an offence.

(2)   Information stating or implying an intention on the advertiser's part which he has not got is false.

[A.43]
47   Advertising infringements
(1)   Where an advertiser commits an offence against regulations made under section 44 or against section 45 or 46, or would be taken to commit such an offence but for the defence provided by section 168, a like offence is committed by—
    (a)   the publisher of the advertisement, and
    (b)   any person who, in the course of a business carried on by him, devised the advertisement, or a part of it relevant to the first-mentioned offence, and
    (c)   where the advertiser did not procure the publication of the advertisement, the person who did procure it.
(2)   In proceedings for an offence under subsection (1)(a) it is a defence for the person charged to prove that—
    (a)   the advertisement was published in the course of a business carried on by him, and
    (b)   he received the advertisement in the course of that business, and did not know and had no reason to suspect that its publication would be an offence under this Part.

Canvassing etc

[A.44]
48   Definition of canvassing off trade premises (regulated agreements)
(1)   An individual (the "canvasser") canvasses a regulated agreement off trade premises if he solicits the entry (as debtor or hirer) of another individual (the "consumer") into the agreement by making oral representations to the consumer, or any other individual, during a visit by the canvasser to any place (not excluded by subsection (2)) where the consumer, or that other individual, as the case may be, is, being a visit—
    (a)   carried out for the purpose of making such oral representations to individuals who are at that place, but
    (b)   not carried out in response to a request made on a previous occasion.
(2)   A place is excluded from subsection (1) if it is a place where a business is carried on (whether on a permanent or temporary basis) by—
    (a)   the creditor or owner, or
    (b)   a supplier, or
    (c)   the canvasser, or the person whose employee or agent the canvasser is, or
    (d)   the consumer.

[A.45]
49   Prohibition of canvassing debtor-creditor agreements off trade premises
(1)   It is an offence to canvass debtor-creditor agreements off trade premises.
(2)   It is also an offence to solicit the entry of an individual (as debtor) into a debtor-creditor agreement during a visit carried out in response to a request made on a previous occasion, where—
    (a)   the request was not in writing signed by or on behalf of the person making it, and
    (b)   if no request for the visit had been made, the soliciting would have constituted the canvassing of a debtor-creditor agreement off trade premises.
(3)   Subsections (1) and (2) do not apply to any soliciting for an agreement enabling the debtor to overdraw on a current account of any description kept with the creditor, where—
    (a)   the [OFT] has determined that current accounts of that description kept with the creditor are excluded from subsections (1) and (2), and
    (b)   the debtor already keeps an account with the creditor (whether a current account or not).
(4)   A determination under subsection (3)(a)—
    (a)   may be made subject to such conditions as the [OFT] thinks fit, and
    (b)   shall be made only where the [OFT] is of opinion that it is not against the interests of debtors.
(5)   If soliciting is done in breach of a condition imposed under subsection (4)(a), the determination under subsection (3)(a) does not apply to it.

NOTES
References to the OFT, etc: as to the abolition of the office of the Director General of Fair Trading and the substitution of the original references to the Director (and related expressions), see the note preceding s 1 at **[A.1]**.

[A.46]
50   Circulars to minors
(1)   A person commits an offence who, with a view to financial gain, sends to a minor any document inviting him to—
- (a)   borrow money, or
- (b)   obtain goods on credit or hire, or
- (c)   obtain services on credit, or
- (d)   apply for information or advice on borrowing money or otherwise obtaining credit, or hiring goods.

(2)   In proceedings under subsection (1) in respect of the sending of a document to a minor, it is a defence for the person charged to prove that he did not know, and had no reasonable cause to suspect, that he was a minor.

(3)   Where a document is received by a minor at any school or educational establishment for minors, a person sending it to him at that establishment knowing or suspecting it to be such an establishment shall be taken to have reasonable cause to suspect that he is a minor.

[A.47]
51   Prohibition of unsolicited credit-tokens
(1)   It is an offence to give a person a credit-token if he has not asked for it.

(2)   To comply with subsection (1) a request must be contained in a document signed by the person making the request, unless the credit-token agreement is a small debtor-creditor-supplier agreement.

(3)   Subsection (1) does not apply to the giving of a credit-token to a person—
- (a)   for use under a credit-token agreement already made, or
- (b)   in renewal or replacement of a credit-token previously accepted by him under a credit-token agreement which continues in force, whether or not varied.

Miscellaneous

[A.48]
52   Quotations
(1)   Regulations may be made—
- (a)   as to the form and content of any document (a "quotation") by which a person who carries on a consumer credit business or consumer hire business, or a business in the course of which he provides credit to individuals secured on land, gives prospective customers information about the terms on which he is prepared to do business;
- (b)   requiring a person carrying on such a business to provide quotations to such persons and in such circumstances as are prescribed.

(2)   Regulations under subsection (1)(a) may in particular contain provisions relating to quotations such as are set out in relation to advertisements in section 44.

[(3)   In this section, "quotation" does not include—
- (a)   any document which is a communication of an invitation or inducement to engage in investment activity within the meaning of section 21 of the Financial Services and Markets Act 2000; or
- (b)   any document (other than one falling within paragraph (a)) provided by an authorised person (within the meaning of that Act) in connection with an agreement which would or might be an exempt agreement as a result of section 16(6C).]

NOTES
Sub-s (3): added by the Financial Services and Markets Act 2000 (Regulated Activities) Order 2001, SI 2001/544, art 90(1), (4), as from 31 October 2004.
Regulations: the Consumer Credit (Quotations) (Revocation) Regulations 1997, SI 1997/211.

[A.49]
53   Duty to display information
Regulations may require a person who carries on a consumer credit business or consumer hire business, or a business in the course of which he provides credit to individuals secured on land [(other than credit provided under an agreement which is an exempt agreement as a result of section 16(6C))], to display in the prescribed manner, at any premises where the business is carried on to which the public have access, prescribed information about the business.

NOTES
Words in square brackets inserted by the Financial Services and Markets Act 2000 (Regulated Activities) Order 2001, SI 2001/544, art 90(1), (5), as from 31 October 2004.

[A.50]
54   Conduct of business regulations
Without prejudice to the generality of section 26, regulations under that section may include provisions further regulating the seeking of business by [a person to whom the regulations apply] who carries on a consumer credit business or a consumer hire business.

NOTES

Words in square brackets substituted by the Financial Services and Markets Act 2000 (Consequential Amendments and Repeals) Order 2001, SI 2001/3649, art 172, as from 1 December 2001.

PART V
ENTRY INTO CREDIT OR HIRE AGREEMENTS
Preliminary matters

[A.51]
55   Disclosure of information
(1)   Regulations may require specified information to be disclosed in the prescribed manner to the debtor or hirer before a regulated agreement is made.

(2)   A regulated agreement is not properly executed unless regulations under subsection (1) were complied with before the making of the agreement.

NOTES

Regulations: the Consumer Credit (Disclosure of Information) Regulations 2004, SI 2004/1481.

[A.52]
56   Antecedent negotiations
(1)   In this Act "antecedent negotiations" means any negotiations with the debtor or hirer—
    (a)   conducted by the creditor or owner in relation to the making of any regulated agreement, or

    (b)   conducted by a credit-broker in relation to goods sold or proposed to be sold by the credit-broker to the creditor before forming the subject-matter of a debtor-creditor-supplier agreement within section 12(a), or

    (c)   conducted by the supplier in relation to a transaction financed or proposed to be financed by a debtor-creditor-supplier agreement within section 12(b) or (c),

and "negotiator" means the person by whom negotiations are so conducted with the debtor or hirer.

(2)   Negotiations with the debtor in a case falling within subsection (1)(b) or (c) shall be deemed to be conducted by the negotiator in the capacity of agent of the creditor as well as in his actual capacity.

(3)   An agreement is void if, and to the extent that, it purports in relation to an actual or prospective regulated agreement—
    (a)   to provide that a person acting as, or on behalf of, a negotiator is to be treated as the agent of the debtor or hirer, or

    (b)   to relieve a person from liability for acts or omissions of any person acting as, or on behalf of, a negotiator.

(4)   For the purposes of this Act, antecedent negotiations shall be taken to begin when the negotiator and the debtor or hirer first enter into communication (including communication by advertisement), and to include any representations made by the negotiator to the debtor or hirer and any other dealings between them.

[A.53]
57   Withdrawal from prospective agreement
(1)   The withdrawal of a party from a prospective regulated agreement shall operate to apply this Part to the agreement, any linked transaction and any other thing done in anticipation of the making of the agreement as it would apply if the agreement were made and then cancelled under section 69.

(2)   The giving to a party of a written or oral notice which, however expressed, indicates the intention of the other party to withdraw from a prospective regulated agreement operates as a withdrawal from it.

(3)   Each of the following shall be deemed to be the agent of the creditor or owner for the purpose of receiving a notice under subsection (2)—
    (a)   a credit-broker or supplier who is the negotiator in antecedent negotiations, and

    (b)   any person who, in the course of a business carried on by him, acts on behalf of the debtor or hirer in any negotiations for the agreement.

(4)   Where the agreement, if made, would not be a cancellable agreement, subsection (1) shall nevertheless apply as if the contrary were the case.

NOTES

Regulations: the Consumer Credit (Repayment of Credit on Cancellation) Regulations 1983, SI 1983/1559.

[A.54]
58 Opportunity for withdrawal from prospective land mortgage
(1)   Before sending to the debtor or hirer, for his signature, an unexecuted agreement in a case where the prospective regulated agreement is to be secured on land (the "mortgaged land"), the creditor or owner shall give the debtor or hirer a copy of the unexecuted agreement which contains a notice in the prescribed form indicating the right of the debtor or hirer to withdraw from the prospective agreement, and how and when the right is exercisable, together with a copy of any other document referred to in the unexecuted agreement.
(2)   Subsection (1) does not apply to—
  (a)   a restricted-use credit agreement to finance the purchase of the mortgaged land, or
  (b)   an agreement for a bridging loan in connection with the purchase of the mortgaged land or other land.

NOTES
  Regulations: the Consumer Credit (Cancellation Notices and Copies of Documents) Regulations 1983, SI 1983/1557.

[A.55]
59 Agreement to enter future agreement void
(1)   An agreement is void if, and to the extent that, it purports to bind a person to enter as debtor or hirer into a prospective regulated agreement.
(2)   Regulations may exclude from the operation of subsection (1) agreements such as are described in the regulations.

NOTES
  Regulations: the Consumer Credit (Agreements to Enter Prospective Agreements) (Exemptions) Regulations 1983, SI 1983/1552.

Making the agreement

[A.56]
60 Form and content of agreements
(1)   The Secretary of State shall make regulations as to the form and content of documents embodying regulated agreements, and the regulations shall contain such provisions as appear to him appropriate with a view to ensuring that the debtor or hirer is made aware of—
  (a)   the rights and duties conferred or imposed on him by the agreement,
  (b)   the amount and rate of the total charge for credit (in the case of a consumer credit agreement),
  (c)   the protection and remedies available to him under this Act, and
  (d)   any other matters which, in the opinion of the Secretary of State, it is desirable for him to know about in connection with the agreement.
(2)   Regulations under subsection (1) may in particular—
  (a)   require specified information to be included in the prescribed manner in documents, and other specified material to be excluded;
  (b)   contain requirements to ensure that specified information is clearly brought to the attention of the debtor or hirer, and that one part of a document is not given insufficient or excessive prominence compared with another.
(3)   If, on an application made to the [OFT] by a person carrying on a consumer credit business or a consumer hire business, it appears to the [OFT] impracticable for the applicant to comply with any requirement of regulations under subsection (1) in a particular case, [it] may, by notice to the applicant, direct that the requirement be waived or varied in relation to such agreements, and subject to such conditions (if any), as [it] may specify, and this Act and the regulations shall have effect accordingly.
(4)   The [OFT] shall give a notice under subsection (3) only if [it] is satisfied that to do so would not prejudice the interests of debtors or hirers.

NOTES
  References to the OFT, etc: as to the abolition of the office of the Director General of Fair Trading and the substitution of the original references to the Director (and related expressions), see the note preceding s 1 at **[A.1]**.
  Regulations: the Consumer Credit (Agreements) Regulations 1983, SI 1983/1553.

[A.57]
61 Signing of agreement
(1)   A regulated agreement is not properly executed unless—
  (a)   a document in the prescribed form itself containing all the prescribed terms and conforming to regulations under section 60(1) is signed in the prescribed manner both by the debtor or hirer and by or on behalf of the creditor or owner, and
  (b)   the document embodies all the terms of the agreement, other than implied terms, and
  (c)   the document is, when presented or sent to the debtor or hirer for signature, in such a state that all its terms are readily legible.
(2)   In addition, where the agreement is one to which section 58(1) applies, it is not properly executed unless—

    (a)   the requirements of section 58(1) were complied with, and

    (b)   the unexecuted agreement was sent, for his signature, to the debtor or hirer [by an appropriate method] not less than seven days after a copy of it was given to him under section 58(1), and

    (c)   during the consideration period, the creditor or owner refrained from approaching the debtor or hirer (whether in person, by telephone or letter, or in any other way) except in response to a specific request made by the debtor or hirer after the beginning of the consideration period, and

    (d)   no notice of withdrawal by the debtor or hirer was received by the creditor or owner before the sending of the unexecuted agreement.

(3)   In subsection (2)(c), "the consideration period" means the period beginning with the giving of the copy under section 58(1) and ending—

    (a)   at the expiry of seven days after the day on which the unexecuted agreement is sent, for his signature, to the debtor or hirer, or

    (b)   on its return by the debtor or hirer after signature by him,

whichever first occurs.

(4)   Where the debtor or hirer is a partnership or an unincorporated body of persons, subsection (1)(a) shall apply with the substitution for "by the debtor or hirer" of "by or on behalf of the debtor or hirer".

NOTES

Sub-s (2): in para (b) words in square brackets substituted by the Consumer Credit Act 1974 (Electronic Communications) Order 2004, SI 2004/3236, art 2(1), (2), as from 31 December 2004.

    Regulations: the Consumer Credit (Agreements) Regulations 1983, SI 1983/1553.

[A.58]
62 Duty to supply copy of unexecuted agreement

(1)   If the unexecuted agreement is presented personally to the debtor or hirer for his signature, but on the occasion when he signs it the document does not become an executed agreement, a copy of it, and of any other document referred to in it, must be there and then delivered to him.

(2)   If the unexecuted agreement is sent to the debtor or hirer for his signature, a copy of it, and of any other document referred to in it, must be sent to him at the same time.

(3)   A regulated agreement is not properly executed if the requirements of this section are not observed.

[A.59]
63 Duty to supply copy of executed agreement

(1)   If the unexecuted agreement is presented personally to the debtor or hirer for his signature, and on the occasion when he signs it the document becomes an executed agreement, a copy of the executed agreement, and of any other document referred to in it, must be there and then delivered to him.

(2)   A copy of the executed agreement, and of any other document referred to in it, must be given to the debtor or hirer within the seven days following the making of the agreement unless—

    (a)   subsection (1) applies, or

    (b)   the unexecuted agreement was sent to the debtor or hirer for his signature and, on the occasion of his signing it, the document became an executed agreement.

(3)   In the case of a cancellable agreement, a copy under subsection (2) must be sent [by an appropriate method].

(4)   In the case of a credit-token agreement, a copy under subsection (2) need not be given within the seven days following the making of the agreement if it is given before or at the time when the credit-token is given to the debtor.

(5)   A regulated agreement is not properly executed if the requirements of this section are not observed.

NOTES

Sub-s (3): words in square brackets substituted by the Consumer Credit Act 1974 (Electronic Communications) Order 2004, SI 2004/3236, art 2(1), (3), as from 31 December 2004.

[A.60]
64 Duty to give notice of cancellation rights

(1)   In the case of a cancellable agreement, a notice in the prescribed form indicating the right of the debtor or hirer to cancel the agreement, how and when that right is exercisable, and the name and address of a person to whom notice of cancellation may be given,—

    (a)   must be included in every copy given to the debtor or hirer under section 62 or 63, and

    (b)   except where section 63(2) applied, must also be sent [by an appropriate method] to the debtor or hirer within the seven days following the making of the agreement.

(2)   In the case of a credit-token agreement, a notice under subsection (1)(b) need not be sent [by an appropriate method] within the seven days following the making of the agreement if either—

    (a)   it is sent [by an appropriate method] to the debtor or hirer before the credit-token is given to him, or

(b)   it is sent [by an appropriate method] to him together with the credit-token.

(3)   Regulations may provide that except where section 63(2) applied a notice sent under subsection (1)(b) shall be accompanied by a further copy of the executed agreement, and of any other document referred to in it.

(4)   Regulations may provide that subsection (1)(b) is not to apply in the case of agreements such as are described in the regulations, being agreements made by a particular person, if—

(a)   on an application by that person to the [OFT], the [OFT] has determined that, having regard to—

(i)   the manner in which antecedent negotiations for agreements with the applicant of that description are conducted, and

(ii)   the information provided to debtors or hirers before such agreements are made,

the requirement imposed by subsection (1)(b) can be dispensed with without prejudicing the interests of debtors or hirers; and

(b)   any conditions imposed by the [OFT] in making the determination are complied with.

(5)   A cancellable agreement is not properly executed if the requirements of this section are not observed.

NOTES

Sub-ss (1), (2): words in square brackets substituted by the Consumer Credit Act 1974 (Electronic Communications) Order 2004, SI 2004/3236, art 2(1), (4), as from 31 December 2004.

References to the OFT, etc: as to the abolition of the office of the Director General of Fair Trading and the substitution of the original references to the Director (and related expressions), see the note preceding s 1 at **[A.1]**.

Regulations: the Consumer Credit (Cancellation Notices and Copies of Documents) Regulations 1983, SI 1983/1557; the Consumer Credit (Notice of Cancellation Rights) (Exemptions) Regulations 1983, SI 1983/1558.

[A.61]
65   Consequences of improper execution

(1)   An improperly-executed regulated agreement is enforceable against the debtor or hirer on an order of the court only.

(2)   A retaking of goods or land to which a regulated agreement relates is an enforcement of the agreement.

[A.62]
66   Acceptance of credit-tokens

(1)   The debtor shall not be liable under a credit-token agreement for use made of the credit-token by any person unless the debtor had previously accepted the credit-token, or the use constituted an acceptance of it by him.

(2)   The debtor accepts a credit-token when—

(a)   it is signed, or

(b)   a receipt for it is signed, or

(c)   it is first used,

either by the debtor himself or by a person who, pursuant to the agreement, is authorised by him to use it.

Cancellation of certain agreements within cooling-off period

[A.63]
67   Cancellable agreements

A regulated agreement may be cancelled by the debtor or hirer in accordance with this Part if the antecedent negotiations included oral representations made when in the presence of the debtor or hirer by an individual acting as, or on behalf of, the negotiator, unless—

(a)   the agreement is secured on land, or is a restricted-use credit agreement to finance the purchase of land or is an agreement for a bridging loan in connection with the purchase of land, or

(b)   the unexecuted agreement is signed by the debtor or hirer at premises at which any of the following is carrying on any business (whether on a permanent or temporary basis)—

(i)   the creditor or owner;

(ii)   any party to a linked transaction (other than the debtor or hirer or a relative of his);

(iii)   the negotiator in any antecedent negotiations.

[A.64]
68   Cooling-off period

The debtor or hirer may serve notice of cancellation of a cancellable agreement between his signing of the unexecuted agreement and—

(a)   the end of the fifth day following the day on which he received a copy under section 63(2) or a notice under section 64(1)(b), or

(b)   if (by virtue of regulations made under section 64(4)) section 64(1)(b) does not apply, the end of the fourteenth day following the day on which he signed the unexecuted agreement.

[A.65]
69   Notice of cancellation
(1)   If within the period specified in section 68 the debtor or hirer under a cancellable agreement serves on—

(a)   the creditor or owner, or

(b)   the person specified in the notice under section 64(1), or

(c)   a person who (whether by virtue of subsection (6) or otherwise) is the agent of the creditor or owner,

a notice (a "notice of cancellation") which, however expressed and whether or not conforming to the notice given under section 64(1), indicates the intention of the debtor or hirer to withdraw from the agreement, the notice shall operate—

(i)   to cancel the agreement, and any linked transaction, and

(ii)   to withdraw any offer by the debtor or hirer, or his relative, to enter into a linked transaction.

(2)   In the case of a debtor-creditor-supplier agreement for restricted-use credit financing—

(a)   the doing of work or supply of goods to meet an emergency, or

(b)   the supply of goods which, before service of the notice of cancellation, had by the act of the debtor or his relative become incorporated in any land or thing not comprised in the agreement or any linked transaction,

subsection (1) shall apply with the substitution of the following for paragraph (i)—

> "(i)   to cancel only such provisions of the agreement and any linked transaction as—
>
> (aa)   relate to the provision of credit, or
>
> (bb)   require the debtor to pay an item in the total charge for credit, or
>
> (cc)   subject the debtor to any obligation other than to pay for the doing of the said work, or the supply of the said goods".

(3)   Except so far as is otherwise provided, references in this Act to the cancellation of an agreement or transaction do not include a case within subsection (2).

(4)   Except as otherwise provided by or under this Act, an agreement or transaction cancelled under subsection (1) shall be treated as if it had never been entered into.

(5)   Regulations may exclude linked transactions of the prescribed description from subsection (1)(i) or (ii).

(6)   Each of the following shall be deemed to be the agent of the creditor or owner for the purpose of receiving a notice of cancellation—

(a)   a credit-broker or supplier who is the negotiator in antecedent negotiations, and

(b)   any person who, in the course of a business carried on by him, acts on behalf of the debtor or hirer in any negotiations for the agreement.

[(7)   Whether or not it is actually received by him, a notice of cancellation sent to a person shall be deemed to be served on him—.

(a)   in the case of a notice sent by post, at the time of posting, and

(b)   in the case of a notice transmitted in the form of an electronic communication in accordance with section 176A(1), at the time of the transmission.]

NOTES

Sub-s (7): substituted by the Consumer Credit Act 1974 (Electronic Communications) Order 2004, SI 2004/3236, art 2(1), (5), as from 31 December 2004.

Regulations: the Consumer Credit (Linked Transactions) (Exemptions) Regulations 1983, SI 1983/1560.

[A.66]
70   Cancellation: recovery of money paid by debtor or hirer
(1)   On the cancellation of a regulated agreement, and of any linked transaction,—

(a)   any sum paid by the debtor or hirer, or his relative, under or in contemplation of the agreement or transaction, including any item in the total charge for credit, shall become repayable, and

(b)   any sum, including any item in the total charge for credit, which but for the cancellation is, or would or might become, payable by the debtor or hirer, or his relative, under the agreement or transaction shall cease to be, or shall not become, so payable, and

(c)   in the case of a debtor-creditor-supplier agreement falling within section 12(b) any sum paid on the debtor's behalf by the creditor to the supplier shall become repayable to the creditor.

(2)   If, under the terms of a cancelled agreement or transaction, the debtor or hirer, or his relative, is in possession of any goods, he shall have a lien on them for any sum repayable to him under subsection (1) in respect of that agreement or transaction, or any other linked transaction.

(3)   A sum repayable under subsection (1) is repayable by the person to whom it was originally paid, but in the case of a debtor-creditor-supplier agreement falling within section 12(b) the creditor and the supplier shall be under a joint and several liability to repay sums paid by the debtor, or his relative, under the agreement or under a linked transaction falling within section 19(1)(b) and accordingly, in such a case, the creditor shall be entitled, in accordance with rules of court, to have the supplier made a party to any proceedings brought against the creditor to recover any such sums.

(4)   Subject to any agreement between them, the creditor shall be entitled to be indemnified by the supplier for loss suffered by the creditor in satisfying his liability under subsection (3), including costs reasonably incurred by him in defending proceedings instituted by the debtor.

(5)   Subsection (1) does not apply to any sum which, if not paid by a debtor, would be payable by virtue of section 71, and applies to a sum paid or payable by a debtor for the issue of a credit-token only where the credit-token has been returned to the creditor or surrendered to a supplier.

(6)   If the total charge for credit includes an item in respect of a fee or commission charged by a credit-broker, the amount repayable under subsection (1) in respect of that item shall be the excess over [£5] of the fee or commission.

(7)   If the total charge for credit includes any sum payable or paid by the debtor to a credit-broker otherwise than in respect of a fee or commission charged by him, that sum shall for the purposes of subsection (6) be treated as if it were such a fee or commission.

(8)   So far only as is necessary to give effect to section 69(2), this section applies to an agreement or transaction within that subsection as it applies to a cancelled agreement or transaction.

NOTES

Sub-s (6): sum in square brackets substituted by the Consumer Credit (Further Increase of Monetary Amounts) Order 1998, SI 1998/997, art 3, Schedule, as from 1 May 1998.

[A.67]
71   Cancellation: repayment of credit

(1)   Notwithstanding the cancellation of a regulated consumer credit agreement, other than a debtor-creditor-supplier agreement for restricted-use credit, the agreement shall continue in force so far as it relates to repayment of credit and payment of interest.

(2)   If, following the cancellation of a regulated consumer credit agreement, the debtor repays the whole or a portion of a credit—

   (a)   before the expiry of one month following service of the notice of cancellation, or
   (b)   in the case of a credit repayable by instalments, before the date on which the first instalment is due,

no interest shall be payable on the amount repaid.

(3)   If the whole of a credit repayable by instalments is not repaid on or before the date specified in subsection (2) (b), the debtor shall not be liable to repay any of the credit except on receipt of a request in writing in the prescribed form, signed by or on behalf of the creditor, stating the amounts of the remaining instalments (recalculated by the creditor as nearly as may be in accordance with the agreement and without extending the repayment period), but excluding any sum other than principal and interest.

(4)   Repayment of a credit, or payment of interest, under a cancelled agreement shall be treated as duly made if it is made to any person on whom, under section 69, a notice of cancellation could have been served, other than a person referred to in section 69(6)(b).

NOTES

Regulations: the Consumer Credit (Repayment of Credit on Cancellation) Regulations 1983, SI 1983/1559.

[A.68]
72   Cancellation: return of goods

(1)   This section applies where any agreement or transaction relating to goods, being—

   (a)   a restricted-use debtor-creditor-supplier agreement, a consumer hire agreement, or a linked transaction to which the debtor or hirer under any regulated agreement is a party, or
   (b)   a linked transaction to which a relative of the debtor or hirer under any regulated agreement is a party,

is cancelled after the debtor or hirer (in a case within paragraph (a)) or the relative (in a case within paragraph (b)) has acquired possession of the goods by virtue of the agreement or transaction.

(2)   In this section—

   (a)   "the possessor" means the person who has acquired possession of the goods as mentioned in subsection (1),
   (b)   "the other party" means the person from whom the possessor acquired possession, and
   (c)   "the pre-cancellation period" means the period beginning when the possessor acquired possession and ending with the cancellation.

(3)   The possessor shall be treated as having been under a duty throughout the pre-cancellation period—

   (a)   to retain possession of the goods, and
   (b)   to take reasonable care of them.

(4)   On the cancellation, the possessor shall be under a duty, subject to any lien, to restore the goods to the other party in accordance with this section, and meanwhile to retain possession of the goods and take reasonable care of them.

(5)   The possessor shall not be under any duty to deliver the goods except at his own premises and in pursuance of a request in writing signed by or on behalf of the other party and served on the possessor either before, or at the time when, the goods are collected from those premises.

(6)   If the possessor—

(a)   delivers the goods (whether at his own premises or elsewhere) to any person on whom, under section 69, a notice of cancellation could have been served (other than a person referred to in section 69(6)(b)), or

(b)   sends the goods at his own expense to such a person,

he shall be discharged from any duty to retain the goods or deliver them to any person.

(7)   Where the possessor delivers the goods as mentioned in subsection (6)(a) his obligation to take care of the goods shall cease; and if he sends the goods as mentioned in subsection (6)(b), he shall be under a duty to take reasonable care to see that they are received by the other party and not damaged in transit, but in other respects his duty to take care of the goods shall cease.

(8)   Where, at any time during the period of 21 days following the cancellation, the possessor receives such a request as is mentioned in subsection (5), and unreasonably refuses or unreasonably fails to comply with it, his duty to take reasonable care of the goods shall continue until he delivers or sends the goods as mentioned in subsection (6), but if within that period he does not receive such a request his duty to take reasonable care of the goods shall cease at the end of that period.

(9)   The preceding provisions of this section do not apply to—

(a)   perishable goods, or

(b)   goods which by their nature are consumed by use and which, before the cancellation, were so consumed, or

(c)   goods supplied to meet an emergency, or

(d)   goods which, before the cancellation, had become incorporated in any land or thing not comprised in the cancelled agreement or a linked transaction.

(10)   Where the address of the possessor is specified in the executed agreement, references in this section to his own premises are to that address and no other.

(11)   Breach of a duty imposed by this section is actionable as a breach of statutory duty.

[A.69]
73   Cancellation: goods given in part-exchange

(1)   This section applies on the cancellation of a regulated agreement where, in antecedent negotiations, the negotiator agreed to take goods in part-exchange (the "part-exchange goods") and those goods have been delivered to him.

(2)   Unless, before the end of the period of ten days beginning with the date of cancellation, the part-exchange goods are returned to the debtor or hirer in a condition substantially as good as when they were delivered to the negotiator, the debtor or hirer shall be entitled to recover from the negotiator a sum equal to the part-exchange allowance (as defined in subsection (7)(b)).

(3)   In the case of a debtor-creditor-supplier agreement within section 12(b), the negotiator and the creditor shall be under a joint and several liability to pay to the debtor a sum recoverable under subsection (2).

(4)   Subject to any agreement between them, the creditor shall be entitled to be indemnified by the negotiator for loss suffered by the creditor in satisfying his liability under subsection (3), including costs reasonably incurred by him in defending proceedings instituted by the debtor.

(5)   During the period of ten days beginning with the date of cancellation, the debtor or hirer, if he is in possession of goods to which the cancelled agreement relates, shall have a lien on them for—

(a)   delivery of the part-exchange goods, in a condition substantially as good as when they were delivered to the negotiator, or

(b)   a sum equal to the part-exchange allowance;

and if the lien continues to the end of that period it shall thereafter subsist only as a lien for a sum equal to the part-exchange allowance.

(6)   Where the debtor or hirer recovers from the negotiator or creditor, or both of them jointly, a sum equal to the part-exchange allowance, then, if the title of the debtor or hirer to the part-exchange goods has not vested in the negotiator, it shall so vest on the recovery of that sum.

(7)   For the purposes of this section—

(a)   the negotiator shall be treated as having agreed to take goods in part-exchange if, in pursuance of the antecedent negotiations, he either purchased or agreed to purchase those goods or accepted or agreed to accept them as part of the consideration for the cancelled agreement, and

(b)   the part-exchange allowance shall be the sum agreed as such in the antecedent negotiations or, if no such agreement was arrived at, such sum as it would have been reasonable to allow in respect of the part-exchange goods if no notice of cancellation had been served.

(8)   In an action brought against the creditor for a sum recoverable under subsection (2), he shall be entitled, in accordance with rules of court, to have the negotiator made a party to the proceedings.

Exclusion of certain agreements from Part V

[A.70]
74   Exclusion of certain agreements from Part V

(1)   This Part (except section 56) does not apply to—

(a)   a non-commercial agreement, or

(b)   a debtor-creditor agreement enabling the debtor to overdraw on a current account, or

(c)   a debtor-creditor agreement to finance the making of such payments arising on, or connected with, the death of a person as may be prescribed.

(2)   This Part (except sections 55 and 56) does not apply to a small debtor-creditor-supplier agreement for restricted-use credit.

[(2A)   In the case of an agreement to which the Consumer Protection (Cancellation of Contracts Concluded away from Business Premises) Regulations 1987 apply the reference in subsection (2) to a small agreement shall be construed as if in section 17(1)(a) and (b) "£35" were substituted for "£50".]

(3)   Subsection (1)(b) or (c) applies only where the [OFT] so determines, and such a determination—

(a)   may be made subject to such conditions as the [OFT] thinks fit, and

(b)   shall be made only if the [OFT] is of opinion that it is not against the interests of debtors.

[(3A)   Notwithstanding anything in subsection (3)(b) above, in relation to a debtor-creditor agreement under which the creditor is the Bank of England or a bank within the meaning of the Bankers' Books Evidence Act 1879, the [OFT] shall make a determination that subsection (1)(b) above applies unless [it] considers that it would be against the public interest to do so.]

(4)   If any term of an agreement falling within subsection [(1)(c)] or (2) is expressed in writing, regulations under section 60(1) shall apply to that term (subject to section 60(3)) as if the agreement was a regulated agreement not falling within subsection [(1)(c)] or (2).

NOTES

Sub-s (2A): inserted by the Consumer Protection (Cancellation of Contracts Concluded away from Business Premises) Regulations 1987, SI 1987/2117, reg 9, as from 1 July 1988.

Sub-s (3A): added by the Banking Act 1979, s 38(1), as from 1 October 1979.

Sub-s (4): words in square brackets substituted by the Banking Act 1979, s 38(1), as from 1 October 1979.

References to the OFT, etc: as to the abolition of the office of the Director General of Fair Trading and the substitution of the original references to the Director (and related expressions), see the note preceding s 1 at **[A.1]**.

Regulations: the Consumer Credit (Payments Arising on Death) Regulations 1983, SI 1983/1554.

PART VI
MATTERS ARISING DURING CURRENCY OF CREDIT OR HIRE AGREEMENTS

[A.71]
75   Liability of creditor for breaches by supplier

(1)   If the debtor under a debtor-creditor-supplier agreement falling within section 12(b) or (c) has, in relation to a transaction financed by the agreement, any claim against the supplier in respect of a misrepresentation or breach of contract, he shall have a like claim against the creditor, who, with the supplier, shall accordingly be jointly and severally liable to the debtor.

(2)   Subject to any agreement between them, the creditor shall be entitled to be indemnified by the supplier for loss suffered by the creditor in satisfying his liability under subsection (1), including costs reasonably incurred by him in defending proceedings instituted by the debtor.

(3)   Subsection (1) does not apply to a claim—

(a)   under a non-commercial agreement, or

(b)   so far as the claim relates to any single item to which the supplier has attached a cash price not exceeding [£100] or more than [£30,000].

(4)   This section applies notwithstanding that the debtor, in entering into the transaction, exceeded the credit limit or otherwise contravened any term of the agreement.

(5)   In an action brought against the creditor under subsection (1) he shall be entitled, in accordance with rules of court, to have the supplier made a party to the proceedings.

NOTES

Sub-s (3): sums in first and second pairs of square brackets in para (b) substituted by the Consumer Credit (Increase of Monetary Limits) Order 1983, SI 1983/1878, arts 3, 4, Schedule, Pts I, II, as from 1 May 1998.

[A.72]
76   Duty to give notice before taking certain action

(1)   The creditor or owner is not entitled to enforce a term of a regulated agreement by—

(a)   demanding earlier payment of any sum, or

(b)   recovering possession of any goods or land, or

(c)   treating any right conferred on the debtor or hirer by the agreement as terminated, restricted or deferred,

except by or after giving the debtor or hirer not less than seven days' notice of intention to do so.

(2)   Subsection (1) applies only where—

(a)   a period for the duration of the agreement is specified in the agreement, and

(b)   that period has not ended when the creditor or owner does an act mentioned in subsection (1),

but so applies notwithstanding that, under the agreement, any party is entitled to terminate it before the end of the period so specified.

(3)   A notice under subsection (1) is ineffective if not in the prescribed form.

(4) Subsection (1) does not prevent a creditor from treating the right to draw on any credit as restricted or deferred and taking such steps as may be necessary to make the restriction or deferment effective.

(5) Regulations may provide that subsection (1) is not to apply to agreements described by the regulations.

(6) Subsection (1) does not apply to a right of enforcement arising by reason of any breach by the debtor or hirer of the regulated agreement.

NOTES

Regulations: the Consumer Credit (Enforcement, Default and Termination Notices) Regulations 1983, SI 1983/1561.

[A.73]
77 Duty to give information to debtor under fixed-sum credit agreement

(1) The creditor under a regulated agreement for fixed-sum credit, within the prescribed period after receiving a request in writing to that effect from the debtor and payment of a fee of [£1], shall give the debtor a copy of the executed agreement (if any) and of any other document referred to in it, together with a statement signed by or on behalf of the creditor showing, according to the information to which it is practicable for him to refer,—

    (a) the total sum paid under the agreement by the debtor;

    (b) the total sum which has become payable under the agreement by the debtor but remains unpaid, and the various amounts comprised in that total sum, with the date when each became due; and

    (c) the total sum which is to become payable under the agreement by the debtor, and the various amounts comprised in that total sum, with the date, or mode of determining the date, when each becomes due.

(2) If the creditor possesses insufficient information to enable him to ascertain the amounts and dates mentioned in subsection (1)(c), he shall be taken to comply with that paragraph if his statement under subsection (1) gives the basis on which, under the regulated agreement, they would fall to be ascertained.

(3) Subsection (1) does not apply to—

    (a) an agreement under which no sum is, or will or may become, payable by the debtor, or

    (b) a request made less than one month after a previous request under that subsection relating to the same agreement was complied with.

(4) If the creditor under an agreement fails to comply with subsection (1)—

    (a) he is not entitled, while the default continues, to enforce the agreement; . . .

    (b) . . .

(5) This section does not apply to a non-commercial agreement.

NOTES

Sub-s (1): sum in square brackets substituted by the Consumer Credit (Further Increase in Monetary Amounts) Order 1998, SI 1998/997, art 3, Schedule, as from 1 May 1998.

Sub-s (4): words omitted repealed by the Consumer Protection from Unfair Trading Regulations 2008, SI 2008/1277, reg 30(1), (3), Sch 2, Pt 1, paras 17, 19, Sch 4, as from 26 May 2008.

Regulations: the Consumer Credit (Prescribed Periods for Giving Information) Regulations 1983, SI 1983/1569.

[A.74]
78 Duty to give information to debtor under running-account credit agreement

(1) The creditor under a regulated agreement for running-account credit, within the prescribed period after receiving a request in writing to that effect from the debtor and payment of a fee of [£1], shall give the debtor a copy of the executed agreement (if any) and of any other document referred to in it, together with a statement signed by or on behalf of the creditor showing, according to the information to which it is practicable for him to refer,—

    (a) the state of the account, and

    (b) the amount, if any, currently payable under the agreement by the debtor to the creditor, and

    (c) the amounts and due dates of any payments which, if the debtor does not draw further on the account, will later become payable under the agreement by the debtor to the creditor.

(2) If the creditor possesses insufficient information to enable him to ascertain the amounts and dates mentioned in subsection (1)(c), he shall be taken to comply with that paragraph if his statement under subsection (1) gives the basis on which, under the regulated agreement, they would fall to be ascertained.

(3) Subsection (1) does not apply to—

    (a) an agreement under which no sum is, or will or may become, payable by the debtor, or

    (b) a request made less than one month after a previous request under that subsection relating to the same agreement was complied with.

(4) Where running-account credit is provided under a regulated agreement, the creditor shall give the debtor statements in the prescribed form, and with the prescribed contents—

    (a) showing according to the information to which it is practicable for him to refer, the state of the account at regular intervals of not more than twelve months, and (b)　where the agreement provides, in relation to specified periods, for the making of payments by the debtor, or the charging against him of interest or any other sum, showing according to the information to which it is practicable for him to refer the state of the account at the end of each of those periods during which there is any movement in the account.

(5)　A statement under subsection (4) shall be given within the prescribed period after the end of the period to which the statement relates.

(6)　If the creditor under an agreement fails to comply with subsection (1)—

(a)　he is not entitled, while the default continues, to enforce the agreement; and

(b)　if the default continues for one month he commits an offence.

(7)　This section does not apply to a non-commercial agreement, and subsections (4) and (5) do not apply to a small agreement.

NOTES

Sub-s (1): sum in square brackets substituted by the Consumer Credit (Further Increase in Monetary Amounts) Order 1998, SI 1998/997, art 3, Schedule, as from 1 May 1998.

Regulations: the Consumer Credit (Prescribed Periods for Giving Information) Regulations 1983, SI 1983/1569; the Consumer Credit (Running-Account Credit) Information Regulations 1983, SI 1983/1570.

[A.75]
79　Duty to give hirer information

(1)　The owner under a regulated consumer hire agreement, within the prescribed period after receiving a request in writing to that effect from the hirer and payment of a fee of [£1], shall give to the hirer a copy of the executed agreement and of any other document referred to in it, together with a statement signed by or on behalf of the owner showing, according to the information to which it is practicable for him to refer, the total sum which has become payable under the agreement by the hirer but remains unpaid and the various amounts comprised in that total sum, with the date when each became due.

(2)　Subsection (1) does not apply to—

(a)　an agreement under which no sum is, or will or may become, payable by the hirer, or

(b)　a request made less than one month after a previous request under that subsection relating to the same agreement was complied with.

(3)　If the owner under an agreement fails to comply with subsection (1)—

(a)　he is not entitled, while the default continues, to enforce the agreement; and

(b)　if the default continues for one month he commits an offence.

(4)　This section does not apply to a non-commercial agreement.

NOTES

Sub-s (1): sum in square brackets substituted by the Consumer Credit (Further Increase in Monetary Amounts) Order 1998, SI 1998/997, art 3, Schedule, as from 1 May 1998.

Regulations: the Consumer Credit (Prescribed Periods for Giving Information) Regulations 1983, SI 1983/1569.

[A.76]
80　Debtor or hirer to give information about goods

(1)　Where a regulated agreement, other than a non-commercial agreement, requires the debtor or hirer to keep goods to which the agreement relates in his possession or control, he shall, within seven working days after he has received a request in writing to that effect from the creditor or owner, tell the creditor or owner where the goods are.

(2)　If the debtor or hirer fails to comply with subsection (1), and the default continues for 14 days, he commits an offence.

[A.77]
81　Appropriation of payments

(1)　Where a debtor or hirer is liable to make to the same person payments in respect of two or more regulated agreements, he shall be entitled, on making any payment in respect of the agreements which is not sufficient to discharge the total amount then due under all the agreements, to appropriate the sum so paid by him—

(a)　in or towards the satisfaction of the sum due under any one of the agreements, or

(b)　in or towards the satisfaction of the sums due under any two or more of the agreements in such proportions as he thinks fit.

(2)　If the debtor or hirer fails to make any such appropriation where one or more of the agreements is—

(a)　a hire-purchase agreement or conditional sale agreement, or

(b)　a consumer hire agreement, or

(c)　an agreement in relation to which any security is provided,

the payment shall be appropriated towards the satisfaction of the sums due under the several agreements respectively in the proportions which those sums bear to one another.

[A.78]
82   Variation of agreements
(1)   Where, under a power contained in a regulated agreement, the creditor or owner varies the agreement, the variation shall not take effect before notice of it is given to the debtor or hirer in the prescribed manner.

(2)   Where an agreement (a "modifying agreement") varies or supplements an earlier agreement, the modifying agreement shall for the purposes of this Act be treated as—

    (a)   revoking the earlier agreement, and

    (b)   containing provisions reproducing the combined effect of the two agreements,

and obligations outstanding in relation to the earlier agreement shall accordingly be treated as outstanding instead in relation to the modifying agreement.

[(2A)   Subsection (2) does not apply if the modifying agreement is an exempt agreement as a result of section 16(6C).]

(3)   If the earlier agreement is a regulated agreement but (apart from this subsection) the modifying agreement is not then, [unless the modifying agreement is—

    (a)   for running account credit; or

    (b)   an exempt agreement as a result of section 16(6C),

it shall be treated as a regulated agreement.]

(4)   If the earlier agreement is a regulated agreement for running-account credit, and by the modifying agreement the creditor allows the credit limit to be exceeded but intends the excess to be merely temporary, Part V (except section 56) shall not apply to the modifying agreement.

(5)   If—

    (a)   the earlier agreement is a cancellable agreement, and

    (b)   the modifying agreement is made within the period applicable under section 68 to the earlier agreement,

then, whether or not the modifying agreement would, apart from this subsection, be a cancellable agreement, it shall be treated as a cancellable agreement in respect of which a notice may be served under section 68 not later than the end of the period applicable under that section to the earlier agreement.

[(5A)   Subsection (5) does not apply where the modifying agreement is an exempt agreement as a result of section 16(6C).]

(6)   Except under subsection (5), a modifying agreement shall not be treated as a cancellable agreement.

(7)   This section does not apply to a non-commercial agreement.

NOTES
Sub-s (2A): inserted by the Financial Services and Markets Act 2000 (Consequential Amendments) Order 2005, SI 2005/2967, art 2(1), (2), as from 16 November 2005.
Sub-s (3): words in square brackets substituted by SI 2005/2967, art 2(1), (3), as from 16 November 2005.
Sub-s (5A): inserted by SI 2005/2967, art 2(1), (4), as from 16 November 2005.
Regulations: the Consumer Credit (Notice of Variation of Agreements) Regulations 1977, SI 1977/328.

[A.79]
83   Liability for misuse of credit facilities
(1)   The debtor under a regulated consumer credit agreement shall not be liable to the creditor for any loss arising from use of the credit facility by another person not acting, or to be treated as acting, as the debtor's agent.

(2)   This section does not apply to a non-commercial agreement, or to any loss in so far as it arises from misuse of an instrument to which section 4 of the Cheques Act 1957 applies.

[A.80]
84   Misuse of credit-tokens
(1)   Section 83 does not prevent the debtor under a credit-token agreement from being made liable to the extent of [£50] (or the credit limit if lower) for loss to the creditor arising from use of the credit-token by other persons during a period beginning when the credit-token ceases to be in the possession of any authorised person and ending when the credit-token is once more in the possession of an authorised person.

(2)   Section 83 does not prevent the debtor under a credit-token agreement from being made liable to any extent for loss to the creditor from use of the credit-token by a person who acquired possession of it with the debtor's consent.

(3)   Subsections (1) and (2) shall not apply to any use of the credit-token after the creditor has been given oral or written notice that it is lost or stolen, or is for any other reason liable to misuse.

[(3A)   Subsections (1) and (2) shall not apply to any use, in connection with a distance contract (other than an excepted contract), of a card which is a credit-token.

(3B)   In subsection (3A), "distance contract" and "excepted contract" have the meanings given in the Consumer Protection (Distance Selling) Regulations 2000.]

[(3C)   Subsections (1) and (2) shall not apply to any use, in connection with a distance contract within the meaning of the Financial Services (Distance Marketing) Regulations 2004, of a card which is a credit-token.]

(4)   Subsections (1) and (2) shall not apply unless there are contained in the credit-token agreement in the prescribed manner particulars of the name, address and telephone number of a person stated to be the person to whom notice is to be given under subsection (3).

(5)   Notice under subsection (3) takes effect when received, but where it is given orally, and the agreement so requires, it shall be treated as not taking effect if not confirmed in writing within seven days.

(6)   Any sum paid by the debtor for the issue of the credit-token, to the extent (if any) that it has not been previously offset by use made of the credit token, shall be treated as paid towards satisfaction of any liability under subsection (1) or (2).

(7)   The debtor, the creditor, and any person authorised by the debtor to use the credit-token, shall be authorised persons for the purposes of subsection (1).

(8)   Where two or more credit-tokens are given under one credit-token agreement, the preceding provisions of this section apply to each credit-token separately.

NOTES

Sub-s (1): sum in square brackets substituted by the Consumer Credit (Further Increase in Monetary Amounts) Order 1998, SI 1998/997, art 3, Schedule, as from 1 May 1998.

Sub-ss (3A), (3B): inserted by the Consumer Protection (Distance Selling) Regulations 2000, SI 2000/2334, reg 21(5), as from 31 October 2000.

Sub-s (3C): inserted by the Financial Services (Distance Marketing) Regulations 2004, SI 2004/2095, reg 14(4), as from 31 October 2004 (in relation to distance contracts made on or after that date).

Regulations: the Consumer Credit (Credit-Token Agreements) Regulations 1983, SI 1983/1555.

[A.81]
85   Duty on issue of new credit-tokens

(1)   Whenever, in connection with a credit-token agreement, a credit-token (other than the first) is given by the creditor to the debtor, the creditor shall give the debtor a copy of the executed agreement (if any) and of any other document referred to in it.

(2)   If the creditor fails to comply with this section—
(a)   he is not entitled, while the default continues, to enforce the agreement; and
(b)   if the default continues for one month he commits an offence.

(3)   This section does not apply to a small agreement.

[A.82]
86   Death of debtor or hirer

(1)   The creditor or owner under a regulated agreement is not entitled, by reason of the death of the debtor or hirer, to do an act specified in paragraphs (a) to (e) of section 87(1) if at the death the agreement is fully secured.

(2)   If at the death of the debtor or hirer a regulated agreement is only partly secured or is unsecured, the creditor or owner is entitled, by reason of the death of the debtor or hirer, to do an act specified in paragraphs (a) to (e) of section 87(1) on an order of the court only.

(3)   This section applies in relation to the termination of an agreement only where—
(a)   a period for its duration is specified in the agreement, and
(b)   that period has not ended when the creditor or owner purports to terminate the agreement,
but so applies notwithstanding that, under the agreement, any party is entitled to terminate it before the end of the period so specified.

(4)   This section does not prevent the creditor from treating the right to draw on any credit as restricted or deferred, and taking such steps as may be necessary to make the restriction or deferment effective.

(5)   This section does not affect the operation of any agreement providing for payment of sums—
(a)   due under the regulated agreement, or
(b)   becoming due under it on the death of the debtor or hirer,
out of the proceeds of a policy of assurance on his life.

(6)   For the purposes of this section an act is done by reason of the death of the debtor or hirer if it is done under a power conferred by the agreement which is—
(a)   exercisable on his death, or
(b)   exercisable at will and exercised at any time after his death.

PART VII
DEFAULT AND TERMINATION

Default notices

[A.83]
87   Need for default notice

(1)   Service of a notice on the debtor or hirer in accordance with section 88 (a "default notice") is necessary before the creditor or owner can become entitled, by reason of any breach by the debtor or hirer of a regulated agreement,—
(a)   to terminate the agreement, or
(b)   to demand earlier payment of any sum, or
(c)   to recover possession of any goods or land, or

(d)   to treat any right conferred on the debtor or hirer by the agreement as terminated, restricted or deferred, or

(e)   to enforce any security.

(2)   Subsection (1) does not prevent the creditor from treating the right to draw upon any credit as restricted or deferred, and taking such steps as may be necessary to make the restriction or deferment effective.

(3)   The doing of an act by which a floating charge becomes fixed is not enforcement of a security.

(4)   Regulations may provide that subsection (1) is not to apply to agreements described by the regulations.

NOTES

Regulations: the Consumer Credit (Enforcement, Default and Termination Notices) Regulations 1983, SI 1983/1561.

[A.84]
88   Contents and effect of default notice

(1)   The default notice must be in the prescribed form and specify—

(a)   the nature of the alleged breach;

(b)   if the breach is capable of remedy, what action is required to remedy it and the date before which that action is to be taken;

(c)   if the breach is not capable of remedy, the sum (if any) required to be paid as compensation for the breach, and the date before which it is to be paid.

(2)   A date specified under subsection (1) must not be less than seven days after the date of service of the default notice, and the creditor or owner shall not take action such as is mentioned in section 87(1) before the date so specified or (if no requirement is made under subsection (1)) before those seven days have elapsed.

(3)   The default notice must not treat as a breach failure to comply with a provision of the agreement which becomes operative only on breach of some other provision, but if the breach of that other provision is not duly remedied or compensation demanded under subsection (1) is not duly paid, or (where no requirement is made under subsection (1)) if the seven days mentioned in subsection (2) have elapsed, the creditor or owner may treat the failure as a breach and section 87(1) shall not apply to it.

(4)   The default notice must contain information in the prescribed terms about the consequences of failure to comply with it.

(5)   A default notice making a requirement under subsection (1) may include a provision for the taking of action such as is mentioned in section 87(1) at any time after the restriction imposed by subsection (2) will cease, together with a statement that the provision will be ineffective if the breach is duly remedied or the compensation duly paid.

NOTES

Regulations: the Consumer Credit (Enforcement, Default and Termination Notices) Regulations 1983, SI 1983/1561.

[A.85]
89   Compliance with default notice

If before the date specified for that purpose in the default notice the debtor or hirer takes the action specified under section 88(1)(b) or (c) the breach shall be treated as not having occurred.

Further restriction of remedies for default

[A.86]
90   Retaking of protected hire-purchase etc goods

(1)   At any time when—

(a)   the debtor is in breach of a regulated hire-purchase or a regulated conditional sale agreement relating to goods, and

(b)   the debtor has paid to the creditor one-third or more of the total price of the goods, and

(c)   the property in the goods remains in the creditor,

the creditor is not entitled to recover possession of the goods from the debtor except on an order of the court.

(2)   Where under a hire-purchase or conditional sale agreement the creditor is required to carry out any installation and the agreement specifies, as part of the total price, the amount to be paid in respect of the installation (the "installation charge") the reference in subsection (1)(b) to one third of the total price shall be construed as a reference to the aggregate of the installation charge and one third of the remainder of the total price.

(3)   In a case where—

(a)   subsection (1)(a) is satisfied, but not subsection (1)(b), and

(b)   subsection (1)(b) was satisfied on a previous occasion in relation to an earlier agreement, being a regulated hire-purchase or regulated conditional sale agreement, between the same parties, and relating to any of the goods comprised in the later agreement (whether or not other goods were also included),

subsection (1) shall apply to the later agreement with the omission of paragraph (b).

(4) If the later agreement is a modifying agreement, subsection (3) shall apply with the substitution, for the second reference to the later agreement, of a reference to the modifying agreement.

(5) Subsection (1) shall not apply, or shall cease to apply, to an agreement if the debtor has terminated, or terminates, the agreement.

(6) Where subsection (1) applies to an agreement at the death of the debtor, it shall continue to apply (in relation to the possessor of the goods) until the grant of probate or administration, or (in Scotland) confirmation (on which the personal representative would fall to be treated as the debtor).

(7) Goods falling within this section are in this Act referred to as "protected goods".

[A.87]
91 Consequences of breach of s 90
If goods are recovered by the creditor in contravention of section 90—
    (a)   the regulated agreement, if not previously terminated, shall terminate, and
    (b)   the debtor shall be released from all liability under the agreement, and shall be entitled to recover from the creditor all sums paid by the debtor under the agreement.

[A.88]
92 Recovery of possession of goods or land
(1) Except under an order of the court, the creditor or owner shall not be entitled to enter any premises to take possession of goods subject to a regulated hire-purchase agreement, regulated conditional sale agreement or regulated consumer hire agreement.

(2) At any time when the debtor is in breach of a regulated conditional sale agreement relating to land, the creditor is entitled to recover possession of the land from the debtor, or any person claiming under him, on an order of the court only.

(3) An entry in contravention of subsection (1) or (2) is actionable as a breach of statutory duty.

[A.89]
93 Interest not to be increased on default
The debtor under a regulated consumer credit agreement shall not be obliged to pay interest on sums which, in breach of the agreement, are unpaid by him at a rate—
    (a)   where the total charge for credit includes an item in respect of interest, exceeding the rate of that interest, or
    (b)   in any other case, exceeding what would be the rate of the total charge for credit if any items included in the total charge for credit by virtue of section 20(2) were disregarded.

93A *(Applies to Scotland only.)*

Early payment by debtor

[A.90]
94 Right to complete payments ahead of time
(1) The debtor under a regulated consumer credit agreement is entitled at any time, by notice to the creditor and the payment to the creditor of all amounts payable by the debtor to him under the agreement (less any rebate allowable under section 95), to discharge the debtor's indebtedness under the agreement.

(2) A notice under subsection (1) may embody the exercise by the debtor of any option to purchase goods conferred on him by the agreement, and deal with any other matter arising on, or in relation to, the termination of the agreement.

[A.91]
95 Rebate on early settlement
(1) Regulations may provide for the allowance of a rebate of charges for credit to the debtor under a regulated consumer credit agreement where, under section 94, on refinancing, on breach of the agreement, or for any other reason, his indebtedness is discharged or becomes payable before the time fixed by the agreement, or any sum becomes payable by him before the time so fixed.

(2) Regulations under subsection (1) may provide for calculation of the rebate by reference to any sums paid or payable by the debtor or his relative under or in connection with the agreement (whether to the creditor or some other person), including sums under linked transactions and other items in the total charge for credit.

NOTES
  Regulations: the Consumer Credit (Early Settlement) Regulations 2004, SI 2004/1483.

[A.92]
96 Effect on linked transactions
(1) Where for any reason the indebtedness of the debtor under a regulated consumer credit agreement is discharged before the time fixed by the agreement, he, and any relative of his, shall at the same time be discharged from any liability under a linked transaction, other than a debt which has already become payable.

(2) Subsection (1) does not apply to a linked transaction which is itself an agreement providing the debtor or his relative with credit.

(3) Regulations may exclude linked transactions of the prescribed description from the operation of subsection (1).

NOTES

Regulations: the Consumer Credit (Enforcement, Default and Termination Notices) Regulations 1983, SI 1983/1561.

[A.93]

97 Duty to give information

(1) The creditor under a regulated consumer credit agreement, within the prescribed period after he has received a request in writing to that effect from the debtor, shall give the debtor a statement in the prescribed form indicating, according to the information to which it is practicable for him to refer, the amount of the payment required to discharge the debtor's indebtedness under the agreement, together with the prescribed particulars showing how the amount is arrived at.

(2) Subsection (1) does not apply to a request made less than one month after a previous request under that subsection relating to the same agreement was complied with.

(3) If the creditor fails to comply with subsection (1)—

    (a) he is not entitled, while the default continues, to enforce the agreement; and

    (b) if the default continues for one month he commits an offence.

NOTES

Regulations: the Consumer Credit (Settlement Information) Regulations 1983, SI 1983/1564; the Consumer Credit (Early Settlement) Regulations 2004, SI 2004/1483.

Termination of agreements

[A.94]

98 Duty to give notice of termination (non-default cases)

(1) The creditor or owner is not entitled to terminate a regulated agreement except by or after giving the debtor or hirer not less than seven days' notice of the termination.

(2) Subsection (1) applies only where—

    (a) a period for the duration of the agreement is specified in the agreement, and

    (b) that period has not ended when the creditor or owner does an act mentioned in subsection (1),

but so applies notwithstanding that, under the agreement, any party is entitled to terminate it before the end of the period so specified.

(3) A notice under subsection (1) is ineffective if not in the prescribed form.

(4) Subsection (1) does not prevent a creditor from treating the right to draw on any credit as restricted or deferred and taking such steps as may be necessary to make the restriction or deferment effective.

(5) Regulations may provide that subsection (1) is not to apply to agreements described by the regulations.

(6) Subsection (1) does not apply to the termination of a regulated agreement by reason of any breach by the debtor or hirer of the agreement.

NOTES

Regulations: the Consumer Credit (Enforcement, Default and Termination Notices) Regulations 1983, SI 1983/1561.

[A.95]

99 Right to terminate hire-purchase etc agreements

(1) At any time before the final payment by the debtor under a regulated hire-purchase or regulated conditional sale agreement falls due, the debtor shall be entitled to terminate the agreement by giving notice to any person entitled or authorised to receive the sums payable under the agreement.

(2) Termination of an agreement under subsection (1) does not affect any liability under the agreement which has accrued before the termination.

(3) Subsection (1) does not apply to a conditional sale agreement relating to land after the title to the land has passed to the debtor.

(4) In the case of a conditional sale agreement relating to goods, where the property in the goods, having become vested in the debtor, is transferred to a person who does not become the debtor under the agreement, the debtor shall not thereafter be entitled to terminate the agreement under subsection (1).

(5) Subject to subsection (4), where a debtor under a conditional sale agreement relating to goods, terminates the agreement under this section after the property in the goods has become vested in him, the property in the goods shall thereupon vest in the person (the "previous owner") in whom it was vested immediately before it became vested in the debtor:

Provided that if the previous owner has died, or any other event has occurred whereby that property, if vested in him immediately before that event, would thereupon have vested in some other person, the property shall be treated as having devolved as if it had been vested in the previous owner immediately before his death or immediately before that event, as the case may be.

[A.96]
100 Liability of debtor on termination of hire-purchase etc agreement
(1)   Where a regulated hire-purchase or regulated conditional sale agreement is terminated under section 99 the debtor shall be liable, unless the agreement provides for a smaller payment, or does not provide for any payment, to pay to the creditor the amount (if any) by which one-half of the total price exceeds the aggregate of the sums paid and the sums due in respect of the total price immediately before the termination.
(2)   Where under a hire-purchase or conditional sale agreement the creditor is required to carry out any installation and the agreement specifies, as part of the total price, the amount to be paid in respect of the installation (the "installation charge") the reference in subsection (1) to one-half of the total price shall be construed as a reference to the aggregate of the installation charge and one-half of the remainder of the total price.
(3)   If in any action the court is satisfied that a sum less than the amount specified in subsection (1) would be equal to the loss sustained by the creditor in consequence of the termination of the agreement by the debtor, the court may make an order for the payment of that sum in lieu of the amount specified in subsection (1).
(4)   If the debtor has contravened an obligation to take reasonable care of the goods or land, the amount arrived at under subsection (1) shall be increased by the sum required to recompense the creditor for that contravention, and subsection (2) shall have effect accordingly.
(5)   Where the debtor, on the termination of the agreement, wrongfully retains possession of goods to which the agreement relates, then, in any action brought by the creditor to recover possession of the goods from the debtor, the court, unless it is satisfied that having regard to the circumstances it would not be just to do so, shall order the goods to be delivered to the creditor without giving the debtor an option to pay the value of the goods.

[A.97]
101 Right to terminate hire agreement
(1)   The hirer under a regulated consumer hire agreement is entitled to terminate the agreement by giving notice to any person entitled or authorised to receive the sums payable under the agreement.
(2)   Termination of an agreement under subsection (1) does not affect any liability under the agreement which has accrued before the termination.
(3)   A notice under subsection (1) shall not expire earlier than eighteen months after the making of the agreement, but apart from that the minimum period of notice to be given under subsection (1), unless the agreement provides for a shorter period, is as follows.
(4)   If the agreement provides for the making of payments by the hirer to the owner at equal intervals, the minimum period of notice is the length of one interval or three months, whichever is less.
(5)   If the agreement provides for the making of such payments at differing intervals, the minimum period of notice is the length of the shortest interval or three months, whichever is less.
(6)   In any other case, the minimum period of notice is three months.
(7)   This section does not apply to—
  (a)   any agreement which provides for the making by the hirer of payments which in total (and without breach of the agreement) exceed [£1,500] in any year, or
  (b)   any agreement where—
    (i)   goods are bailed or (in Scotland) hired to the hirer for the purposes of a business carried on by him, or the hirer holds himself out as requiring the goods for those purposes, and
    (ii)   the goods are selected by the hirer, and acquired by the owner for the purposes of the agreement at the request of the hirer from any person other than the owner's associate, or
  (c)   any agreement where the hirer requires, or holds himself out as requiring, the goods for the purpose of bailing or hiring them to other persons in the course of a business carried on by him.
(8)   If, on an application made to the [OFT] by a person carrying on a consumer hire business, it appears to the [OFT] that it would be in the interest of hirers to do so, [it] may by notice to the applicant direct that this section shall not apply to consumer hire agreements made by the applicant, and subject to such conditions (if any) as the [OFT] may specify, this Act shall have effect accordingly.
(9)   In the case of a modifying agreement subsection (3) shall apply with the substitution, for "the making of the agreement" of "the making of the original agreement".

NOTES
  References to the OFT, etc: as to the abolition of the office of the Director General of Fair Trading and the substitution of the original references to the Director (and related expressions), see the note preceding s 1 at **[A.1]**.
  Sub-s (7): sum in square brackets substituted by the Consumer Credit (Further Increase in Monetary Amounts) Order 1998, SI 1998/997, art 3, Schedule, as from 1 May 1998.

Appendix

[A.98]

102 Agency for receiving notice of rescission

(1) Where the debtor or hirer under a regulated agreement claims to have a right to rescind the agreement, each of the following shall be deemed to be the agent of the creditor or owner for the purpose of receiving any notice rescinding the agreement which is served by the debtor or hirer—

   (a) a credit-broker or supplier who was the negotiator in antecedent negotiations, and

   (b) any person who, in the course of a business carried on by him, acted on behalf of the debtor or hirer in any negotiations for the agreement.

(2) In subsection (1) "rescind" does not include—

   (a) service of a notice of cancellation, or

   (b) termination of an agreement under section 99 or 101, or by the exercise of a right or power in that behalf expressly conferred by the agreement.

[A.99]

103 Termination statements

(1) If an individual (the "customer") serves on any person (the "trader") a notice—

   (a) stating that—

      (i) the customer was the debtor or hirer under a regulated agreement described in the notice, and the trader was the creditor or owner under the agreement, and

      (ii) the customer has discharged his indebtedness to the trader under the agreement, and

      (iii) the agreement has ceased to have any operation; and

   (b) requiring the trader to give the customer a notice, signed by or on behalf of the trader, confirming that those statements are correct,

the trader shall, within the prescribed period after receiving the notice, either comply with it or serve on the customer a counter-notice stating that, as the case may be, he disputes the correctness of the notice or asserts that the customer is not indebted to him under the agreement.

(2) Where the trader disputes the correctness of the notice he shall give particulars of the way in which he alleges it to be wrong.

(3) Subsection (1) does not apply in relation to any agreement if the trader has previously complied with that subsection on the service of a notice under it with respect to that agreement.

(4) Subsection (1) does not apply to a non-commercial agreement.

(5) If the trader fails to comply with subsection (1), and the default continues for one month, he commits an offence.

NOTES

Regulations: the Consumer Credit (Prescribed Periods for Giving Information) Regulations 1983, SI 1983/1569.

104 (*Applies to Scotland only.*)

PART VIII
SECURITY

General

[A.100]

105 Form and content of securities

(1) Any security provided in relation to a regulated agreement shall be expressed in writing.

(2) Regulations may prescribe the form and content of documents ("security instruments") to be made in compliance with subsection (1).

(3) Regulations under subsection (2) may in particular—

   (a) require specified information to be included in the prescribed manner in documents, and other specified material to be excluded;

   (b) contain requirements to ensure that specified information is clearly brought to the attention of the surety, and that one part of a document is not given insufficient or excessive prominence compared with another.

(4) A security instrument is not properly executed unless—

   (a) a document in the prescribed form, itself containing all the prescribed terms and conforming to regulations under subsection (2), is signed in the prescribed manner by or on behalf of the surety, and

   (b) the document embodies all the terms of the security, other than implied terms, and

   (c) the document, when presented or sent for the purpose of being signed by or on behalf of the surety, is in such a state that its terms are readily legible, and

   (d) when the document is presented or sent for the purpose of being signed by or on behalf of the surety there is also presented or sent a copy of the document.

(5) A security instrument is not properly executed unless—

   (a) where the security is provided after, or at the time when, the regulated agreement is made, a copy of the executed agreement, together with a copy of any other document referred to in it, is given to the surety at the time the security is provided, or

(b)   where the security is provided before the regulated agreement is made, a copy of the executed agreement, together with a copy of any other document referred to in it, is given to the surety within seven days after the regulated agreement is made.

(6) Subsection (1) does not apply to a security provided by the debtor or hirer.

(7) If—

  (a)   in contravention of subsection (1) a security is not expressed in writing, or

  (b)   a security instrument is improperly executed,

the security (so far as provided in relation to a regulated agreement) is enforceable against the surety on an order of the court only.

(8) If an application for an order under subsection (7) is dismissed (except on technical grounds only) section 106 (ineffective securities) shall apply to the security.

(9) Regulations under section 60(1) shall include provision requiring documents embodying regulated agreements also to embody any security provided in relation to a regulated agreement by the debtor or hirer.

NOTES

Regulations: the Consumer Credit (Agreements) Regulations 1983, SI 1983/1553; the Consumer Credit (Guarantees and Indemnities) Regulations 1983, SI 1983/1556.

[A.101]
106 Ineffective securities

Where, under any provision of this Act, this section is applied to any security provided in relation to a regulated agreement, then, subject to section 177 (saving for registered charges),—

  (a)   the security, so far as it is so provided, shall be treated as never having effect;

  (b)   any property lodged with the creditor or owner solely for the purposes of the security as so provided shall be returned by him forthwith;

  (c)   the creditor or owner shall take any necessary action to remove or cancel an entry in any register, so far as the entry relates to the security as so provided; and

  (d)   any amount received by the creditor or owner on realisation of the security shall, so far as it is referable to the agreement, be repaid to the surety.

[A.102]
107 Duty to give information to surety under fixed-sum credit agreement

(1) The creditor under a regulated agreement for fixed-sum credit in relation to which security is provided, within the prescribed period after receiving a request in writing to that effect from the surety and payment of a fee of [£1], shall give to the surety (if a different person from the debtor)—

  (a)   a copy of the executed agreement (if any) and of any other document referred to in it;

  (b)   a copy of the security instrument (if any); and

  (c)   a statement signed by or on behalf of the creditor showing, according to the information to which it is practicable for him to refer,—

      (i)   the total sum paid under the agreement by the debtor,

      (ii)   the total sum which has become payable under the agreement by the debtor but remains unpaid, and the various amounts comprised in that total sum, with the date when each became due, and

      (iii)   the total sum which is to become payable under the agreement by the debtor, and the various amounts comprised in that total sum, with the date, or mode of determining the date, when each becomes due.

(2) If the creditor possesses insufficient information to enable him to ascertain the amount and dates mentioned in subsection (1)(c) (iii), he shall be taken to comply with that sub-paragraph if his statement under subsection (1)(c) gives the basis on which, under the regulated agreement, they would fall to be ascertained.

(3) Subsection (1) does not apply to—

  (a)   an agreement under which no sum is, or will or may become, payable by the debtor, or

  (b)   a request made less than one month after a previous request under that subsection relating to the same agreement was complied with.

(4) If the creditor under an agreement fails to comply with subsection (1)—

  (a)   he is not entitled, while the default continues, to enforce the security, so far as provided in relation to the agreement; and

  (b)   if the default continues for one month he commits an offence.

(5) This section does not apply to a non-commercial agreement.

NOTES

Sub-s (1): sum in square brackets substituted by the Consumer Credit (Further Increase in Monetary Amounts) Order 1998, SI 1998/997, art 3, Schedule, as from 1 May 1998.

Regulations: the Consumer Credit (Prescribed Periods for Giving Information) Regulations 1983, SI 1983/1569.

[A.103]
108 Duty to give information to surety under running-account credit agreement

(1) The creditor under a regulated agreement for running-account credit in relation to which security is provided, within the prescribed period after receiving a request in writing to that effect from the surety and payment of a fee of [£1], shall give to the surety (if a different person from the debtor)—

(a) a copy of the executed agreement (if any) and of any other document referred to in it;

(b) a copy of the security instrument (if any); and

(c) a statement signed by or on behalf of the creditor showing, according to the information to which it is practicable for him to refer,—

    (i) the state of the account, and

    (ii) the amount, if any, currently payable under the agreement by the debtor to the creditor, and

    (iii) the amounts and due dates of any payments which, if the debtor does not draw further on the account, will later become payable under the agreement by the debtor to the creditor.

(2) If the creditor possesses insufficient information to enable him to ascertain the amounts and dates mentioned in subsection (1)(c)(iii), he shall be taken to comply with that sub-paragraph if his statement under subsection (1)(c) gives basis on which, under the regulated agreement, they would fall to be ascertained.

(3) Subsection (1) does not apply to—

(a) an agreement under which no sum is, or will or may become, payable by the debtor, or

(b) a request made less than one month after a previous request under that subsection relating to the same agreement was complied with.

(4) If the creditor under an agreement fails to comply with subsection (1)—

(a) he is not entitled, while the default continues, to enforce the security, so far as provided in relation to the agreement; and

(b) if the default continues for one month he commits an offence.

(5) This section does not apply to a non-commercial agreement.

NOTES

    Sub-s (1): sum in square brackets substituted by the Consumer Credit (Further Increase in Monetary Amounts) Order 1998, SI 1998/997, art 3, Schedule, as from 1 May 1998.

    Regulations: the Consumer Credit (Prescribed Periods for Giving Information) Regulations 1983, SI 1983/1569.

[A.104]
109 Duty to give information to surety under consumer hire agreement

(1) The owner under a regulated consumer hire agreement in relation to which security is provided, within the prescribed period after receiving a request in writing to that effect from the surety and payment of a fee of [£1], shall give to the surety (if a different person from the hirer)—

(a) a copy of the executed agreement and of any other document referred to in it;

(b) a copy of the security instrument (if any); and

(c) a statement signed by or on behalf of the owner showing, according to the information to which it is practicable for him to refer, the total sum which has become payable under the agreement by the hirer but remains unpaid and the various amounts comprised in that total sum, with the date when each became due.

(2) Subsection (1) does not apply to—

(a) an agreement under which no sum is, or will or may become, payable by the hirer, or

(b) a request made less than one month after a previous request under that subsection relating to the same agreement was complied with.

(3) If the owner under an agreement fails to comply with subsection (1)—

(a) he is not entitled, while the default continues, to enforce the security, so far as provided in relation to the agreement; and

(b) if the default continues for one month he commits an offence.

(4) This section does not apply to a non-commercial agreement.

NOTES

    Sub-s (1): sum in square brackets substituted by the Consumer Credit (Further Increase in Monetary Amounts) Order 1998, SI 1998/997, art 3, Schedule, as from 1 May 1998.

    Regulations: the Consumer Credit (Prescribed Periods for Giving Information) Regulations 1983, SI 1983/1569.

[A.105]
110 Duty to give information to debtor or hirer

(1) The creditor or owner under a regulated agreement, within the prescribed period after receiving a request in writing to that effect from the debtor or hirer and payment of a fee of [£1], shall give the debtor or hirer a copy of any security instrument executed in relation to the agreement after the making of the agreement.

(2) Subsection (1) does not apply to—

(a) a non-commercial agreement, or

(b)   an agreement under which no sum is, or will or may become, payable by the debtor or hirer, or

(c)   a request made less than one month after a previous request under subsection (1) relating to the same agreement was complied with.

(3)   If the creditor or owner under an agreement fails to comply with subsection (1)—

(a)   he is not entitled, while the default continues, to enforce the security (so far as provided in relation to the agreement); . . .

(b)   . . .

NOTES

Sub-s (1): sum in square brackets substituted by the Consumer Credit (Further Increase in Monetary Amounts) Order 1998, SI 1998/997, art 3, Schedule, as from 1 May 1998.

Sub-s (3): words omitted repealed by the Consumer Protection from Unfair Trading Regulations 2008, SI 2008/1277, reg 30(1), (3), Sch 2, Pt 1, paras 17, 28, Sch 4, as from 26 May 2008.

Regulations: the Consumer Credit (Prescribed Periods for Giving Information) Regulations 1983, SI 1983/1569.

[A.106]
111   Duty to give surety copy of default etc notice

(1)   When a default notice or a notice under section 76(1) or 98(1) is served on a debtor or hirer, a copy of the notice shall be served by the creditor or owner on any surety (if a different person from the debtor or hirer).

(2)   If the creditor or owner fails to comply with subsection (1) in the case of any surety, the security is enforceable against the surety (in respect of the breach or other matter to which the notice relates) on an order of the court only.

[A.107]
112   Realisation of securities

Subject to section 121, regulations may provide for any matters relating to the sale or other realisation, by the creditor or owner, of property over which any right has been provided by way of security in relation to an actual or prospective regulated agreement, other than a non-commercial agreement.

[A.108]
113   Act not to be evaded by use of security

(1)   Where a security is provided in relation to an actual or prospective regulated agreement, the security shall not be enforced so as to benefit the creditor or owner, directly or indirectly, to an extent greater (whether as respects the amount of any payment or the time or manner of its being made) than would be the case if the security were not provided and any obligations of the debtor or hirer, or his relative, under or in relation to the agreement were carried out to the extent (if any) to which they would be enforced under this Act.

(2)   In accordance with subsection (1), where a regulated agreement is enforceable on an order of the court or the [OFT] only, any security provided in relation to the agreement is enforceable (so far as provided in relation to the agreement) where such an order has been made in relation to the agreement, but not otherwise.

(3)   Where—

(a)   a regulated agreement is cancelled under section 69(1) or becomes subject to section 69(2), or

(b)   a regulated agreement is terminated under section 91, or

(c)   in relation to any agreement an application for an order under section 40(2), 65(1), 124(1) or 149(2) is dismissed (except on technical grounds only), or

(d)   a declaration is made by the court under section 142(1) (refusal of enforcement order) as respects any regulated agreement,

section 106 shall apply to any security provided in relation to the agreement.

(4)   Where subsection (3)(d) applies and the declaration relates to a part only of the regulated agreement, section 106 shall apply to the security only so far as it concerns that part.

(5)   In the case of a cancelled agreement, the duty imposed on the debtor or hirer by section 71 or 72 shall not be enforceable before the creditor or owner has discharged any duty imposed on him by section 106 (as applied by subsection (3)(a)).

(6)   If the security is provided in relation to a prospective agreement or transaction, the security shall be enforceable in relation to the agreement or transaction only after the time (if any) when the agreement is made; and until that time the person providing the security shall be entitled, by notice to the creditor or owner, to require that section 106 shall thereupon apply to the security.

(7)   Where an indemnity [or guarantee] is given in a case where the debtor or hirer is a minor, or [an indemnity is given in a case where he] is otherwise not of full capacity, the reference in subsection (1) to the extent to which his obligations would be enforced shall be read in relation to the indemnity [or guarantee] as a reference to the extent to which [those obligations] would be enforced if he were of full capacity.

(8)   Subsections (1) to (3) also apply where a security is provided in relation to an actual or prospective linked transaction, and in that case—

(a)   references to the agreement shall be read as references to the linked transaction, and

(b)   references to the creditor or owner shall be read as references to any person (other than the debtor or hirer, or his relative) who is a party, or prospective party, to the linked transaction.

NOTES

Sub-s (7): words in square brackets inserted or substituted by the Minors' Contracts Act 1987, s 4(1), as from 9 June 1987.

References to the OFT, etc: as to the abolition of the office of the Director General of Fair Trading and the substitution of the original references to the Director (and related expressions), see the note preceding s 1 at **[A.1]**.

Pledges

[A.109]

114   Pawn-receipts

(1)   At the time he receives the article, a person who takes any article in pawn under a regulated agreement shall give to the person from whom he receives it a receipt in the prescribed form (a "pawn-receipt").

(2)   A person who takes any article in pawn from an individual whom he knows to be, or who appears to be and is, a minor commits an offence.

(3)   This section and sections 115 to 122 do not apply to—

   (a)   a pledge of documents of title [or of bearer bonds], or

   (b)   a non-commercial agreement.

NOTES

Sub-s (3): words in square brackets inserted by the Banking Act 1979, s 38(2), as from 1 October 1979.

Regulations: the Consumer Credit (Agreements) Regulations 1983, SI 1983/1553; the Consumer Credit (Pawn Receipts) Regulations 1983, SI 1983/1566.

[A.110]

115   Penalty for failure to supply copies of pledge agreement, etc

If the creditor under a regulated agreement to take any article in pawn fails to observe the requirements of sections 62 to 64 or 114(1) in relation to the agreement he commits an offence.

[A.111]

116   Redemption period

(1)   A pawn is redeemable at any time within six months after it was taken.

(2)   Subject to subsection (1), the period within which a pawn is redeemable shall be the same as the period fixed by the parties for the duration of the credit secured by the pledge, or such longer period as they may agree.

(3)   If the pawn is not redeemed by the end of the period laid down by subsections (1) and (2) (the "redemption period"), it nevertheless remains redeemable until it is realised by the pawnee under section 121, except where under section 120(1)(a) the property in it passes to the pawnee.

(4)   No special charge shall be made for redemption of a pawn after the end of the redemption period, and charges in respect of the safe keeping of the pawn shall not be at a higher rate after the end of the redemption period than before.

[A.112]

117   Redemption procedure

(1)   On surrender of the pawn-receipt, and payment of the amount owing, at any time when the pawn is redeemable, the pawnee shall deliver the pawn to the bearer of the pawn-receipt.

(2)   Subsection (1) does not apply if the pawnee knows or has reasonable cause to suspect that the bearer of the pawn-receipt is neither the owner of the pawn nor authorised by the owner to redeem it.

(3)   The pawnee is not liable to any person in tort or delict for delivering the pawn where subsection (1) applies, or refusing to deliver it where the person demanding delivery does not comply with subsection (1) or, by reason of subsection (2), subsection (1) does not apply.

[A.113]

118   Loss etc of pawn-receipt

(1)   A person (the "claimant") who is not in possession of the pawn-receipt but claims to be the owner of the pawn, or to be otherwise entitled or authorised to redeem it, may do so at any time when it is redeemable by tendering to the pawnee in place of the pawn-receipt—

   (a)   a statutory declaration made by the claimant in the prescribed form, and with the prescribed contents, or

   (b)   where the pawn is security for fixed-sum credit not exceeding [£75] or running-account credit on which the credit limit does not exceed [£75], and the pawnee agrees, a statement in writing in the prescribed form, and with the prescribed contents, signed by the claimant.

(2)   On compliance by the claimant with subsection (1), section 117 shall apply as if the declaration or statement were the pawn-receipt, and the pawn-receipt itself shall become inoperative for the purposes of section 117.

NOTES

Sub-s (1): sums in square brackets substituted by the Consumer Credit (Further Increase in Monetary Amounts) Order 1998, SI 1998/997, art 3, Schedule, as from 1 May 1998.

Regulations: the Consumer Credit (Loss of Pawn Receipts) Regulations 1983, SI 1983/1567.

[A.114]
119 Unreasonable refusal to deliver pawn

(1) If a person who has taken a pawn under a regulated agreement refuses without reasonable cause to allow the pawn to be redeemed, he commits an offence.

(2) On the conviction in England or Wales of a pawnee under subsection (1) where the offence does not amount to theft, [section 148 of the Powers of Criminal Courts (Sentencing) Act 2000 (restitution orders)] shall apply as if the pawnee had been convicted of stealing the pawn.

(3) On the conviction in Northern Ireland of a pawnee under subsection (1) where the offence does not amount to theft, section 27 (orders for restitution) of the Theft Act (Northern Ireland) 1969, and any provision of the Theft Act (Northern Ireland) 1969 relating to that section, shall apply as if the pawnee had been convicted of stealing the pawn.

NOTES

Sub-s (2): words in square brackets substituted by the Powers of Criminal Courts (Sentencing) Act 2000, s 165(1), Sch 9, para 45, as from 25 August 2000.

[A.115]
120 Consequence of failure to redeem

(1) If at the end of the redemption period the pawn has not been redeemed—
   (a) notwithstanding anything in section 113, the property in the pawn passes to the pawnee where the redemption period is six months and the pawn is security for fixed-sum credit not exceeding [£75] or running-account credit on which the credit limit does not exceed [£75]; or
   (b) in any other case the pawn becomes realisable by the pawnee.

(2) Where the debtor or hirer is entitled to apply to the court for a time order under section 129, subsection (1) shall apply with the substitution, for "at the end of the redemption period" of "after the expiry of five days following the end of the redemption period".

NOTES

Sub-s (1): sums in square brackets substituted by the Consumer Credit (Further Increase in Monetary Amounts) Order 1998, SI 1998/997, art 3, Schedule, as from 1 May 1998.

[A.116]
121 Realisation of pawn

(1) When a pawn has become realisable by him, the pawnee may sell it, after giving to the pawnor (except in such cases as may be prescribed) not less than the prescribed period of notice of the intention to sell, indicating in the notice the asking price and such other particulars as may be prescribed.

(2) Within the prescribed period after the sale takes place, the pawnee shall give the pawnor the prescribed information in writing as to the sale, its proceeds and expenses.

(3) Where the net proceeds of sale are not less than the sum which, if the pawn had been redeemed on the date of the sale, would have been payable for its redemption, the debt secured by the pawn is discharged and any surplus shall be paid by the pawnee to the pawnor.

(4) Where subsection (3) does not apply, the debt shall be treated as from the date of sale as equal to the amount by which the net proceeds of sale fall short of the sum which would have been payable for the redemption of the pawn on that date.

(5) In this section the "net proceeds of sale" is the amount realised (the "gross amount") less the expenses (if any) of the sale.

(6) If the pawnor alleges that the gross amount is less than the true market value of the pawn on the date of sale, it is for the pawnee to prove that he and any agents employed by him in the sale used reasonable care to ensure that the true market value was obtained, and if he fails to do so subsections (3) and (4) shall have effect as if the reference in subsection (5) to the gross amount were a reference to the true market value.

(7) If the pawnor alleges that the expenses of the sale were unreasonably high, it is for the pawnee to prove that they were reasonable, and if he fails to do so subsections (3) and (4) shall have effect as if the reference in subsection (5) to expenses were a reference to reasonable expenses.

NOTES

Regulations: the Consumer Credit (Realisation of Pawn) Regulations 1983, SI 1983/1568.

122 (*Applies to Scotland only.*)

Negotiable instruments

[A.117]
123 Restrictions on taking and negotiating instruments

(1) A creditor or owner shall not take a negotiable instrument, other than a bank note or cheque, in discharge of any sum payable—

   (a) by the debtor or hirer under a regulated agreement, or

   (b) by any person as surety in relation to the agreement.

(2) The creditor or owner shall not negotiate a cheque taken by him in discharge of a sum payable as mentioned in subsection (1), except to a banker (within the meaning of the Bills of Exchange Act 1882).

(3) The creditor or owner shall not take a negotiable instrument as security for the discharge of any sum payable as mentioned in subsection (1).

(4) A person takes a negotiable instrument as security for the discharge of a sum if the sum is intended to be paid in some other way, and the negotiable instrument is to be presented for payment only if the sum is not paid in that way.

(5) This section does not apply where the regulated agreement is a non-commercial agreement.

(6) The Secretary of State may by order provide that this section shall not apply where the regulated agreement has a connection with a country outside the United Kingdom.

NOTES

Order: the Consumer Credit (Negotiable Instruments) (Exemption) Order 1984, SI 1984/435.

[A.118]
124 Consequences of breach of s 123

(1) After any contravention of section 123 has occurred in relation to a sum payable as mentioned in section 123(1)(a), the agreement under which the sum is payable is enforceable against the debtor or hirer on an order of the court only.

(2) After any contravention of section 123 has occurred in relation to a sum payable by any surety, the security is enforceable on an order of the court only.

(3) Where an application for an order under subsection (2) is dismissed (except on technical grounds only) section 106 shall apply to the security.

[A.119]
125 Holders in due course

(1) A person who takes a negotiable instrument in contravention of section 123(1) or (3) is not a holder in due course, and is not entitled to enforce the instrument.

(2) Where a person negotiates a cheque in contravention of section 123(2), his doing so constitutes a defect in his title within the meaning of the Bills of Exchange Act 1882.

(3) If a person mentioned in section 123(1)(a) or (b) ("the protected person") becomes liable to a holder in due course of an instrument taken from the protected person in contravention of section 123(1) or (3), or taken from the protected person and negotiated in contravention of section 123(2), the creditor or owner shall indemnify the protected person in respect of that liability.

(4) Nothing in this Act affects the rights of the holder in due course of any negotiable instrument.

Land mortgages

[A.120]
126 Enforcement of land mortgages

A land mortgage securing a regulated agreement is enforceable (so far as provided in relation to the agreement) on an order of the court only.

PART IX
JUDICIAL CONTROL

Enforcement of certain regulated agreements and securities

[A.121]
127 Enforcement orders in cases of infringement

(1) In the case of an application for an enforcement order under—

   (a) section 65(1) (improperly executed agreements), or

   (b) section 105(7)(a) or (b) (improperly executed security instruments), or

   (c) section 111(2) (failure to serve copy of notice on surety), or

   (d) section 124(1) or (2) (taking of negotiable instrument in contravention of section 123),

the court shall dismiss the application if, but (subject to subsections (3) and (4)) only if, it considers it just to do so having regard to—

   (i) prejudice caused to any person by the contravention in question, and the degree of culpability for it; and

   (ii) the powers conferred on the court by subsection (2) and sections 135 and 136.

(2) If it appears to the court just to do so, it may in an enforcement order reduce or discharge any sum payable by the debtor or hirer, or any surety, so as to compensate him for prejudice suffered as a result of the contravention in question.

(3)   The court shall not make an enforcement order under section 65(1) if section 61(1)(a) (signing of agreements) was not complied with unless a document (whether or not in the prescribed form and complying with regulations under section 60(1)) itself containing all the prescribed terms of the agreement was signed by the debtor or hirer (whether or not in the prescribed manner).

(4)   The court shall not make an enforcement order under section 65(1) in the case of a cancellable agreement if—

(a)   a provision of section 62 or 63 was not complied with, and the creditor or owner did not give a copy of the executed agreement, and of any other document referred to in it, to the debtor or hirer before the commencement of the proceedings in which the order is sought, or

(b)   section 64(1) was not complied with.

(5)   Where an enforcement order is made in a case to which subsection (3) applies, the order may direct that the regulated agreement is to have effect as if it did not include a term omitted from the document signed by the debtor or hirer.

NOTES

Regulations: the Consumer Credit (Agreements) Regulations 1983, SI 1983/1553.

[A.122]
128   Enforcement orders on death of debtor or hirer
The court shall make an order under section 86(2) if, but only if, the creditor or owner proves that he has been unable to satisfy himself that the present and future obligations of the debtor or hirer under the agreement are likely to be discharged.

Extension of time

[A.123]
129   Time orders
(1)   [Subject to subsection (3) below,] if it appears to the court just to do so—

(a)   on an application for an enforcement order; or

(b)   on an application made by a debtor or hirer under this paragraph after service on him of—

(i)   a default notice, or

(ii)   a notice under section 76(1) or 98(1); or

(c)   in an action brought by a creditor or owner to enforce a regulated agreement or any security, or recover possession of any goods or land to which a regulated agreement relates,

the court may make an order under this section (a "time order").

(2)   A time order shall provide for one or both of the following, as the court considers just—

(a)   the payment by the debtor or hirer or any surety of any sum owed under a regulated agreement or a security by such instalments, payable at such times, as the court, having regard to the means of the debtor or hirer and any surety, considers reasonable;

(b)   the remedying by the debtor or hirer of any breach of a regulated agreement (other than the non-payment of money) within such period as the court may specify.

[(3)   *(Applies to Scotland only.)*]

NOTES

Sub-s (1): words in square brackets inserted by Debtors (Scotland) Act 1987, s 108(1), Sch 6, para 17, in relation to Scotland only.

[A.124]
130   Supplemental provisions about time orders
(1)   Where in accordance with rules of court an offer to pay any sum by instalments is made by the debtor or hirer and accepted by the creditor or owner, the court may in accordance with rules of court make a time order under section 129(2)(a) giving effect to the offer without hearing evidence of means.

(2)   In the case of a hire-purchase or conditional sale agreement only, a time order under section 129(2)(a) may deal with sums which, although not payable by the debtor at the time the order is made, would if the agreement continued in force become payable under it subsequently.

(3)   A time order under section 129(2)(a) shall not be made where the regulated agreement is secured by a pledge if, by virtue of regulations made under section 76(5), 87(4) or 98(5), service of a notice is not necessary for enforcement of the pledge.

(4)   Where, following the making of a time order in relation to a regulated hire-purchase or conditional sale agreement or a regulated consumer hire agreement, the debtor or hirer is in possession of the goods, he shall be treated (except in the case of a debtor to whom the creditor's title has passed) as a bailee or (in Scotland) a custodier of the goods under the terms of the agreement, notwithstanding that the agreement has been terminated.

(5)   Without prejudice to anything done by the creditor or owner before the commencement of the period specified in a time order made under section 129(2)(b) ("the relevant period"),—

(a)   he shall not while the relevant period subsists take in relation to the agreement any action such as is mentioned in section 87(1);

(b)   where—

(i)   a provision of the agreement ("the secondary provision") becomes operative only on breach of another provision of the agreement ("the primary provision"), and

(ii)   the time order provides for the remedying of such a breach of the primary provision within the relevant period,

he shall not treat the secondary provision as operative before the end of that period;

(c)   if while the relevant period subsists the breach to which the order relates is remedied it shall be treated as not having occurred.

(6)   On the application of any person affected by a time order, the court may vary or revoke the order.

Protection of property pending proceedings

[A.125]
131   Protection orders
The court, on the application of the creditor or owner under a regulated agreement, may make such orders as it thinks just for protecting any property of the creditor or owner, or property subject to any security, from damage or depreciation pending the determination of any proceedings under this Act, including orders restricting or prohibiting use of the property or giving directions as to its custody.

Hire and hire-purchase etc agreements

[A.126]
132   Financial relief for hirer
(1)   Where the owner under a regulated consumer hire agreement recovers possession of goods to which the agreement relates otherwise than by action, the hirer may apply to the court for an order that—

(a)   the whole or part of any sum paid by the hirer to the owner in respect of the goods shall be repaid, and

(b)   the obligation to pay the whole or part of any sum owed by the hirer to the owner in respect of the goods shall cease,

and if it appears to the court just to do so, having regard to the extent of the enjoyment of the goods by the hirer, the court shall grant the application in full or in part.

(2)   Where in proceedings relating to a regulated consumer hire agreement the court makes an order for the delivery to the owner of goods to which the agreement relates the court may include in the order the like provision as may be made in an order under subsection (1).

[A.127]
133   Hire-purchase etc agreements: special powers of court
(1)   If, in relation to a regulated hire-purchase or conditional sale agreement, it appears to the court just to do so—

(a)   on an application for an enforcement order or time order; or

(b)   in an action brought by the creditor to recover possession of goods to which the agreement relates,

the court may—

(i)   make an order (a "return order") for the return to the creditor of goods to which the agreement relates,

(ii)   make an order (a "transfer order") for the transfer to the debtor of the creditor's title to certain goods to which the agreement relates ("the transferred goods"), and the return to the creditor of the remainder of the goods.

(2)   In determining for the purposes of this section how much of the total price has been paid ("the paid-up sum"), the court may—

(a)   treat any sum paid by the debtor, or owed by the creditor, in relation to the goods as part of the paid-up sum;

(b)   deduct any sum owed by the debtor in relation to the goods (otherwise than as part of the total price) from the paid-up sum,

and make corresponding reductions in amounts so owed.

(3)   Where a transfer order is made, the transferred goods shall be such of the goods to which the agreement relates as the court thinks just; but a transfer order shall be made only where the paid-up sum exceeds the part of the total price referable to the transferred goods by an amount equal to at least one-third of the unpaid balance of the total price.

(4)   Notwithstanding the making of a return order or transfer order, the debtor may at any time before the goods enter the possession of the creditor, on payment of the balance of the total price and the fulfilment of any other necessary conditions, claim the goods ordered to be returned to the creditor.

(5)   When, in pursuance of a time order or under this section, the total price of goods under a regulated hire-purchase agreement or regulated conditional sale agreement is paid and any other necessary conditions are fulfilled, the creditor's title to the goods vests in the debtor.

(6)   If, in contravention of a return order or transfer order, any goods to which the order relates are not returned to the creditor, the court, on the application of the creditor, may—

(a)   revoke so much of the order as relates to those goods, and

(b) order the debtor to pay the creditor the unpaid portion of so much of the total price as is referable to those goods.

(7) For the purposes of this section, the part of the total price referable to any goods is the part assigned to those goods by the agreement or (if no such assignment is made) the part determined by the court to be reasonable.

[A.128]
134 Evidence of adverse detention in hire-purchase etc cases

(1) Where goods are comprised in a regulated hire-purchase agreement, regulated conditional sale agreement or regulated consumer hire agreement, and the creditor or owner—

(a) brings an action or makes an application to enforce a right to recover possession of the goods from the debtor or hirer, and

(b) proves that a demand for the delivery of the goods was included in the default notice under section 88(5), or that, after the right to recover possession of the goods accrued but before the action was begun or the application was made, he made a request in writing to the debtor or hirer to surrender the goods,

then, for the purposes of the claim of the creditor or owner to recover possession of the goods, the possession of them by the debtor or hirer shall be deemed to be adverse to the creditor or owner.

(2) In subsection (1) "the debtor or hirer" includes a person in possession of the goods at any time between the debtor's or hirer's death and the grant of probate or administration, or (in Scotland) confirmation.

(3) Nothing in this section affects a claim for damages for conversion or (in Scotland) for delict.

Supplemental provisions as to orders

[A.129]
135 Power to impose conditions, or suspend operation of order

(1) If it considers it just to do so, the court may in an order made by it in relation to a regulated agreement include provisions—

(a) making the operation of any term of the order conditional on the doing of specified acts by any party to the proceedings;

(b) suspending the operation of any term of the order either—
   (i) until such time as the court subsequently directs, or
   (ii) until the occurrence of a specified act or omission.

(2) The court shall not suspend the operation of a term requiring the delivery up of goods by any person unless satisfied that the goods are in his possession or control.

(3) In the case of a consumer hire agreement, the court shall not so use its powers under subsection (1)(b) as to extend the period for which, under the terms of the agreement, the hirer is entitled to possession of the goods to which the agreement relates.

(4) On the application of any person affected by a provision included under subsection (1), the court may vary the provision.

[A.130]
136 Power to vary agreements and securities

The court may in an order made by it under this Act include such provision as it considers just for amending any agreement or security in consequence of a term of the order.

Extortionate credit bargains

[A.131]
137 Extortionate credit bargains

(1) If the court finds a credit bargain extortionate it may reopen the credit agreement so as to do justice between the parties.

(2) In this section and sections 138 to 140—

(a) "credit agreement" means any agreement [(other than an agreement which is an exempt agreement as a result of section 16(6C))] between an individual (the "debtor") and any other person (the "creditor") by which the creditor provides the debtor with credit of any amount, and

(b) "credit bargain"—
   (i) where no transaction other than the credit agreement is to be taken into account in computing the total charge for credit, means the credit agreement, or
   (ii) where one or more other transactions are to be so taken into account, means the credit agreement and those other transactions, taken together.

NOTES

Sub-s (2): words in square brackets in para (a) inserted by the Financial Services and Markets Act 2000 (Regulated Activities) Order 2001, SI 2001/544, art 90(1), (6), as from 31 October 2004.

[A.132]
138 When bargains are extortionate

(1) A credit bargain is extortionate if it—

    (a)   requires the debtor or a relative of his to make payments (whether unconditionally, or on certain contingencies) which are grossly exorbitant, or

    (b)   otherwise grossly contravenes ordinary principles of fair dealing.

(2)   In determining whether a credit bargain is extortionate, regard shall be had to such evidence as is adduced concerning—

    (a)   interest rates prevailing at the time it was made,

    (b)   the factors mentioned in subsections (3) to (5), and

    (c)   any other relevant considerations.

(3)   Factors applicable under subsection (2) in relation to the debtor include—

    (a)   his age, experience, business capacity and state of health; and

    (b)   the degree to which, at the time of making the credit bargain, he was under financial pressure, and the nature of that pressure.

(4)   Factors applicable under subsection (2) in relation to the creditor include—

    (a)   the degree of risk accepted by him, having regard to the value of any security provided;

    (b)   his relationship to the debtor; and

    (c)   whether or not a colourable cash price was quoted for any goods or services included in the credit bargain.

(5)   Factors applicable under subsection (2) in relation to a linked transaction include the question how far the transaction was reasonably required for the protection of debtor or creditor, or was in the interest of the debtor.

[A.133]
139   Reopening of extortionate agreements

(1)   A credit agreement may, if the court thinks just, be reopened on the ground that the credit bargain is extortionate—

    (a)   on an application for the purpose made by the debtor or any surety to the High Court, county court or sheriff court; or

    (b)   at the instance of the debtor or a surety in any proceedings to which the debtor and creditor are parties, being proceedings to enforce the agreement, any security relating to it, or any linked transaction; or

    (c)   at the instance of the debtor or a surety in other proceedings in any court where the amount paid or payable under the credit agreement is relevant.

(2)   In reopening the agreement, the court may, for the purpose of relieving the debtor or a surety from payment of any sum in excess of that fairly due and reasonable, by order—

    (a)   direct accounts to be taken, or (in Scotland) an accounting to be made, between any persons,

    (b)   set aside the whole or part of any obligation imposed on the debtor or surety by the credit bargain or any related agreement,

    (c)   require the creditor to repay the whole or part of any sum paid under the credit bargain or any related agreement by the debtor or a surety, whether paid to the creditor or any other person,

    (d)   direct the return to the surety of any property provided for the purposes of the security, or

    (e)   alter the terms of the credit agreement or any security instrument.

(3)   An order may be made under subsection (2) notwithstanding that its effect is to place a burden on the creditor in respect of an advantage unfairly enjoyed by another person who is a party to a linked transaction.

(4)   An order under subsection (2) shall not alter the effect of any judgment.

(5)   In England and Wales, an application under subsection (1)(a) shall be brought only in the county court in the case of—

    (a)   a regulated agreement, or

    (b)   an agreement (not being a regulated agreement) under which the creditor provides the debtor with fixed-sum credit . . . or running-account credit . . .

[(5A)   . . .]

(6)   (*Applies to Scotland only.*)

(7)   In Northern Ireland an application under subsection (1)(a) may be brought in the county court in the case of—

    (a)   a regulated agreement, or

    (b)   an agreement (not being a regulated agreement) under which the creditor provides the debtor with fixed-sum credit not exceeding [£105,000] or running-account credit on which the credit limit does not exceed [£105,000].

NOTES

   Sub-s (5): words omitted repealed by the High Court and County Courts Jurisdiction Order 1991, SI 1991/724, art 2(1), (8), Schedule, Pt I, as from 1 July 1991.

   Sub-s (5A): inserted by the Administration of Justice Act 1982, s 37, Sch 3, Pt II, para 4; repealed by SI 1991/724, art 2(1), (8), Schedule, Pt I, as from 1 July 1991.

   Sub-s (7): sums in square brackets substituted by virtue of the County Courts (Financial Limits) Order (Northern Ireland) 1993, SR 1993/282, art 2, Schedule, as from 1 September 1993.

[A.134]
140 Interpretation of sections 137 to 139
Where the credit agreement is not a regulated agreement, expressions used in sections 137 to 139 which, apart from this section, apply only to regulated agreements, shall be construed as nearly as may be as if the credit agreement were a regulated agreement.

Miscellaneous

[A.135]
141 Jurisdiction and parties
(1)   In England and Wales, the county court shall have jurisdiction to hear and determine—
   (a)   any action by the creditor or owner to enforce a regulated agreement or any security relating to it;
   (b)   any action to enforce any linked transaction against the debtor or hirer or his relative;
and such an action shall not be brought in any other court.
(2)   Where an action or application is brought in the High Court which, by virtue of this Act, ought to have been brought in the county court it shall not be treated as improperly brought, but shall be transferred to the county court.
(3)–(3B)   (*Apply to Scotland only.*)
(4)   In Northern Ireland the county court shall have jurisdiction to hear and determine any action or application falling within subsection (1).
(5)   Except as may be provided by rules of court, all the parties to a regulated agreement, and any surety, shall be made parties to any proceedings relating to the agreement.

[A.136]
142 Power to declare rights of parties
(1)   Where under any provision of this Act a thing can be done by a creditor or owner on an enforcement order only, and either—
   (a)   the court dismisses (except on technical grounds only) an application for an enforcement order, or
   (b)   where no such application has been made or such an application has been dismissed on technical grounds only, an interested party applies to the court for a declaration under this subsection,
the court may if it thinks just make a declaration that the creditor or owner is not entitled to do that thing, and thereafter no application for an enforcement order in respect of it shall be entertained.
(2)   Where—
   (a)   a regulated agreement or linked transaction is cancelled under section 69(1), or becomes subject to section 69(2), or
   (b)   a regulated agreement is terminated under section 91, and an interested party applies to the court for a declaration under this subsection, the court may make a declaration to that effect.

143, 144   (*Apply to Northern Ireland only.*)

PART X
ANCILLARY CREDIT BUSINESS

Definitions

[A.137]
145 Types of ancillary credit business
(1)   An ancillary credit business is any business so far as it comprises or relates to—
   (a)   credit brokerage,
   (b)   debt-adjusting,
   (c)   debt-counselling,
   (d)   debt-collecting, or
   (e)   the operation of a credit reference agency.
(2)   Subject to section 146(5) [and (5A)], credit brokerage is the effecting of introductions—
   (a)   of individuals desiring to obtain credit—
      (i)   to persons carrying on businesses to which this sub-paragraph applies, or
      (ii)   in the case of an individual desiring to obtain credit to finance the acquisition or provision of a dwelling occupied or to be occupied by himself or his relative, to any person carrying on a business in the course of which he provides credit secured on land, or
   (b)   of individuals desiring to obtain goods on hire to persons carrying on businesses to which this paragraph applies, or
   (c)   of individuals desiring to obtain credit, or to obtain goods on hire, to other credit-brokers.
(3)   Subsection (2)(a)(i) applies to—
   (a)   a consumer credit business;
   (b)   a business which comprises or relates to consumer credit agreements being, otherwise than by virtue of section 16(5)(a), exempt agreements;
   (c)   a business which comprises or relates to unregulated agreements where—

      (i)   the [law applicable to] the agreement is the law of a country outside the United Kingdom, and

      (ii) if the [law applicable to] the agreement were the law of a part of the United Kingdom it would be a regulated consumer credit agreement.

(4)   Subsection (2)(b) applies to—

   (a)   a consumer hire business;

   (b)   a business which comprises or relates to unregulated agreements where—

      (i)   the [law applicable to] the agreement is the law of a country outside the United Kingdom, and

      (ii) if the [law applicable to] the agreement were the law of a part of the United Kingdom it would be a regulated consumer hire agreement.

(5)   Subject to [section 146(5B) and (6)], debt-adjusting is, in relation to debts due under consumer credit agreements or consumer hire agreements,—

   (a)   negotiating with the creditor or owner, on behalf of the debtor or hirer, terms for the discharge of a debt, or

   (b)   taking over, in return for payments by the debtor or hirer, his obligation to discharge a debt, or

   (c)   any similar activity concerned with the liquidation of a debt.

(6)   Subject to [section 146(5C) and (6)], debt-counselling is the giving of advice to debtors or hirers about the liquidation of debts due under consumer credit agreements or consumer hire agreements.

(7)   Subject to section 146(6), debt-collecting is the taking of steps to procure payment of debts due under consumer credit agreements or consumer hire agreements.

(8)   A credit reference agency is a person carrying on a business comprising the furnishing of persons with information relevant to the financial standing of individuals, being information collected by the agency for that purpose.

NOTES

Sub-s (2): words in square brackets inserted by the Financial Services and Markets Act 2000 (Regulated Activities) (Amendment) (No 1) Order 2003, SI 2003/1475, art 21(1)(a), as from 31 October 2004.

Sub-s (3): words in square brackets substituted by the Contracts (Applicable Law) Act 1990, s 5, Sch 4, para 2, as from 1 April 1991.

Sub-s (4): words in square brackets in para (b) substituted by the Contracts (Applicable Law) Act 1990, s 5, Sch 4, para 2, as from 1 April 1991.

Sub-ss (5), (6): words in square brackets substituted by SI 2003/1475, art 21(1)(b), (c), as from 31 October 2004.

[A.138]
146   Exceptions from section 145

(1)   A barrister or advocate acting in that capacity is not to be treated as doing so in the course of any ancillary credit business.

(2)   A solicitor engaging in contentious business (as defined in [section 87(1) of the Solicitors Act 1974]) is not to be treated as doing so in the course of any ancillary credit business.

(3)   (*Applies to Scotland only.*)

(4)   A solicitor in Northern Ireland engaging in [contentious business (as defined in Article 3(2) of the Solicitors (Northern Ireland) Order 1976], is not to be treated as doing so in the course of any ancillary credit business.

(5)   For the purposes of section 145(2), introductions effected by an individual by canvassing off trade premises either debtor-creditor-supplier agreements falling within section 12(a) or regulated consumer hire agreements shall be disregarded if—

   (a)   the introductions are not effected by him in the capacity of an employee, and

   (b)   he does not by any other method effect introductions falling within section 145(2).

[(5A)   It is not credit brokerage for a person to effect the introduction of an individual desiring to obtain credit if the introduction is made—

   (a)   to an authorised person, within the meaning of the 2000 Act, who has permission under that Act to enter as lender into relevant agreements; or

   (b)   to a qualifying broker, with a view to that individual obtaining credit under a relevant agreement.

(5B)   It is not debt-adjusting for a person to carry on an activity mentioned in paragraph (a), (b) or (c) of section 145(5) if—

   (a)   the debt in question is due under a relevant agreement; and

   (b)   that activity is a regulated activity for the purposes of the 2000 Act.

(5C)   It is not debt-counselling for a person to give advice to debtors about the liquidation of debts if—

   (a)   the debt in question is due under a relevant agreement; and

   (b)   giving that advice is a regulated activity for the purposes of the 2000 Act.

(5D)   In this section—

   "the 2000 Act" means the Financial Services and Markets Act 2000;

   "relevant agreement" means [an] agreement which is secured by a land mortgage, where entering into that agreement as lender is a regulated activity for the purposes of the 2000 Act;

"qualifying broker" means a person who may effect introductions of the kind mentioned in subsection (5A) without contravening the general prohibition, within the meaning of section 19 of the 2000 Act,

and references to "regulated activities" and the definition of "qualifying broker" must be read with—

(a)   section 22 of the 2000 Act (regulated activities: power to specify classes of activity and categories of investment);

(b)   any order for the time being in force under that section; and

(c)   Schedule 2 to that Act.]

(6)   It is not debt-adjusting, debt-counselling or debt-collecting for a person to do anything in relation to a debt arising under an agreement if—

(a)   he is the creditor or owner under the agreement, otherwise than by virtue of an assignment, or

(b)   he is the creditor or owner under the agreement by virtue of an assignment made in connection with the transfer to the assignee of any business other than a debt-collecting business, or

(c)   he is the supplier in relation to the agreement, or

(d)   he is a credit-broker who has acquired the business of the person who was the supplier in relation to the agreement, or

(e)   he is a person prevented by subsection (5) from being treated as a credit-broker, and the agreement was made in consequence of an introduction (whether made by him or another person) which, under subsection (5), is to be disregarded.

NOTES

Sub-ss (2), (4): words in square brackets substituted by the Arbitration Act 1996, s 107(1), Sch 3, para 28, as from 31 January 1997.

Sub-ss (5A)–(5C): inserted, together with sub-s (5D), by the Financial Services and Markets Act 2000 (Regulated Activities) (Amendment) (No 1) Order 2003, SI 2003/1475, art 21(2), as from 31 October 2004.

Sub-s (5D): inserted as noted above; in definition "relevant agreement" word in square brackets substituted by the Financial Services and Markets Act 2000 (Consequential Amendments) Order 2005, SI 2005/2967, art 3, as from 16 November 2005.

Solicitors: references to solicitors are modified so as to include references to recognised bodies within the meaning of the Administration of Justice Act 1985, s 9, by the Solicitors' Incorporated Practices Order 1991, SI 1991/2684, arts 3–5, Sch 1.

Licensing

[A.139]
147   Application of Part III
(1)   The provisions of Part III (except section 40) apply to an ancillary credit business as they apply to a consumer credit business.

(2)   Without prejudice to the generality of section 26, regulations under that section (as applied by subsection (1)) may include provisions regulating the collection and dissemination of information by credit reference agencies.

NOTES

Regulations: the Consumer Credit (Termination of Licences) Regulations 1976, SI 1976/1002; the Consumer Credit (Conduct of Business) (Credit References) Regulations 1977, SI 1977/330; the Consumer Credit Licensing (Appeals) Regulations 1998, SI 1998/1203.

[A.140]
148   Agreement for services of unlicensed trader
(1)   An agreement for the services of a person carrying on an ancillary credit business (the "trader"), if made when the trader was unlicensed, is enforceable against the other party (the "customer") only where the [OFT] has made an order under subsection (2) which applies to the agreement.

(2)   The trader or his successor in title may apply to the [OFT] for an order that agreements within subsection (1) are to be treated as if made when the trader was licensed.

(3)   Unless the [OFT] determines to make an order under subsection (2) in accordance with the application, [it] shall, before determining the application, by notice—

(a)   inform the trader, giving [its] reasons, that, as the case may be, [it] is minded to refuse the application, or to grant it in terms different from those applied for, describing them, and

(b)   invite the trader to submit to the [OFT] representations in support of his application in accordance with section 34.

(4)   In determining whether or not to make an order under subsection (2) in respect of any period the [OFT] shall consider, in addition to any other relevant factors,—

(a)   how far, if at all, customers under agreements made by the trader during that period were prejudiced by the trader's conduct,

(b)   whether or not the [OFT] would have been likely to grant a licence covering that period on an application by the trader, and

(c)   the degree of culpability for the failure to obtain a licence.

(5)   If the [OFT] thinks fit, [it] may in an order under subsection (2)—

(a)   limit the order to specified agreements, or agreements of a specified description or made at a specified time;

(b)   make the order conditional on the doing of specified acts by the trader.

[(6)   This section does not apply to an agreement made by a consumer credit EEA firm unless at the time it was made that firm was precluded from entering into it as a result of—

(a)   a consumer credit prohibition imposed under section 203 of the Financial Services and Markets Act 2000; or

(b)   a restriction imposed on the firm under section 204 of that Act.]

NOTES

Sub-s (6): added by the Financial Services and Markets Act 2000 (Consequential Amendments and Repeals) Order 2001, SI 2001/3649, art 173, as from 1 December 2001.

References to the OFT, etc: as to the abolition of the office of the Director General of Fair Trading and the substitution of the original references to the Director (and related expressions), see the note preceding s 1 at **[A.1]**.

[A.141]
149   Regulated agreements made on introductions by unlicensed credit-broker

(1)   A regulated agreement made by a debtor or hirer who, for the purpose of making that agreement, was introduced to the creditor or owner by an unlicensed credit-broker is enforceable against the debtor or hirer only where—

(a)   on the application of the credit-broker, the [OFT] has made an order under section 148(2) in respect of a period including the time when the introduction was made, and the order does not (whether in general terms or specifically) exclude the application of this paragraph to the regulated agreement, or

(b)   the [OFT] has made an order under subsection (2) which applies to the agreement.

(2)   Where during any period individuals were introduced to a person carrying on a consumer credit business or consumer hire business by an unlicensed credit-broker for the purpose of making regulated agreements with the person carrying on that business, that person or his successor in title may apply to the [OFT] for an order that regulated agreements so made are to be treated as if the credit-broker had been licensed at the time of the introduction.

(3)   Unless the [OFT] determines to make an order under subsection (2) in accordance with the application, [it] shall, before determining the application, by notice—

(a)   inform the applicant, giving [its] reasons, that, as the case may be, [it] is minded to refuse the application, or to grant it in terms different from those applied for, describing them, and

(b)   invite the applicant to submit to the [OFT] representations in support of his application in accordance with section 34.

(4)   In determining whether or not to make an order under subsection (2) the [OFT] shall consider, in addition to any other relevant factors—

(a)   how far, if at all, debtors or hirers under regulated agreements to which the application relates were prejudiced by the credit-broker's conduct, and

(b)   the degree of culpability of the applicant in facilitating the carrying on by the credit-broker of his business when unlicensed.

(5)   If the [OFT] thinks fit, [it] may in an order under subsection (2)—

(a)   limit the order to specified agreements, or agreements of a specified description or made at a specified time;

(b)   make the order conditional on the doing of specified acts by the applicant.

[(6)   For the purposes of this section, "unlicensed credit-broker" does not include a consumer credit EEA firm unless at the time the introduction was made that firm was precluded from making it as a result of—

(a)   a consumer credit prohibition imposed under section 203 of the Financial Services and Markets Act 2000; or

(b)   a restriction imposed on the firm under section 204 of that Act.]

NOTES

Sub-s (6): added by the Financial Services and Markets Act 2000 (Consequential Amendments and Repeals) Order 2001, SI 2001/3649, art 174, as from 1 December 2001.

References to the OFT, etc: as to the abolition of the office of the Director General of Fair Trading and the substitution of the original references to the Director (and related expressions), see the note preceding s 1 at **[A.1]**.

[A.142]
150   Appeals to Secretary of State against licensing decisions

Section 41 (as applied by section 147(1)) shall have effect as if the following entry were included in the table set out at the end—

Determination	Appellant
Refusal to make order under section 148(2) or 149(2) in accordance with terms of application	The applicant

Seeking business

[A.143]
151 Advertisements
(1) Sections 44 to 47 apply to an advertisement published for the purposes of a business of credit brokerage carried on by any person, whether it advertises the services of that person or the services of persons to whom he effects introductions, as they apply to an advertisement to which Part IV applies.
(2) Sections 44, 46 and 47 apply to an advertisement, published for the purposes of a business carried on by the advertiser, indicating that he is willing to advise on debts, or engage in transactions concerned with the liquidation of debts, as they apply to an advertisement to which Part IV applies.
[(2A) An advertisement does not fall within subsection (1) or (2) in so far as it is a communication of an invitation or inducement to engage in investment activity within the meaning of section 21 of the Financial Services and Markets Act 2000, other than an exempt generic communication (as defined in section 43(3B)).]
(3) The Secretary of State may by order provide that an advertisement published for the purposes of a business of credit brokerage, debt-adjusting or debt-counselling shall not fall within subsection (1) or (2) if it is of a description specified in the order.
(4) An advertisement does not fall within subsection (2) if it indicates that the advertiser is not willing to act in relation to consumer credit agreements and consumer hire agreements.
(5) In subsections (1) and (3) "credit brokerage" includes the effecting of introductions of individuals desiring to obtain credit to any person carrying on a business in the course of which he provides credit secured on land.

NOTES
Sub-s (2A): inserted by the Financial Services and Markets Act 2000 (Regulated Activities) Order 2001, SI 2001/544, art 90(1), (7), as from 31 October 2004.
Regulations: the Consumer Credit (Advertisements) Regulations 2004, SI 2004/1484.

[A.144]
152 Application of sections 52 to 54 to credit brokerage etc
(1) Sections 52 to 54 apply to a business of credit brokerage, debt-adjusting or debt-counselling as they apply to a consumer credit business.
(2) In their application to a business of credit brokerage, sections 52 and 53 shall apply to the giving of quotations and information about the business of any person to whom the credit-broker effects introductions as well as to the giving of quotations and information about his own business.

[A.145]
153 Definition of canvassing off trade premises (agreements for ancillary credit services)
(1) An individual (the "canvasser") canvasses off trade premises the services of a person carrying on an ancillary credit business if he solicits the entry of another individual (the "consumer") into an agreement for the provision to the consumer of those services by making oral representations to the consumer, or any other individual, during a visit by the canvasser to any place (not excluded by subsection (2)) where the consumer, or that other individual, as the case may be, is, being a visit—
   (a) carried out for the purpose of making such oral representations to individuals who are at that place, but
   (b) not carried out in response to a request made on a previous occasion.
(2) A place is excluded from subsection (1) if it is a place where (whether on a permanent or temporary basis)—
   (a) the ancillary credit business is carried on, or
   (b) any business is carried on by the canvasser or the person whose employee or agent the canvasser is, or by the consumer.

[A.146]
154 Prohibition of canvassing certain ancillary credit services off trade premises
It is an offence to canvass off trade premises the services of a person carrying on a business of credit brokerage, debt-adjusting or debt-counselling.

[A.147]
155 Right to recover brokerage fees
(1) [Subject to subsection (2A),] the excess over [£5] of a fee or commission for his services charged by a credit-broker to an individual to whom this subsection applies shall cease to be payable or, as the case may be, shall be recoverable by the individual if the introduction does not result in his entering into a relevant agreement within the six months following the introduction (disregarding any agreement which is cancelled under section 69(1) or becomes subject to section 69(2)).
(2) Subsection (1) applies to an individual who sought an introduction for a purpose which would have been fulfilled by his entry into—
   (a) a regulated agreement, or

(b)   in the case of an individual such as is referred to in section 145(2)(a)(ii), an agreement for credit secured on land, or

(c)   an agreement such as is referred to in section 145(3)(b) or (c) or (4)(b).

[(2A)   But subsection (1) does not apply where—

(a)   the fee or commission relates to the effecting of an introduction of a kind mentioned in section 146(5A); and

(b)   the person charging that fee or commission is an authorised person or an appointed representative, within the meaning of the Financial Services and Markets Act 2000.]

(3)   An agreement is a relevant agreement for the purposes of subsection (1) in relation to an individual if it is an agreement such as is referred to in subsection (2) in relation to that individual.

(4)   In the case of an individual desiring to obtain credit under a consumer credit agreement, any sum payable or paid by him to a credit-broker otherwise than as a fee or commission for the credit-broker's services shall for the purposes of subsection (1) be treated as such a fee or commission if it enters, or would enter, into the total charge for credit.

NOTES

Sub-s (1): words in first pair of square brackets inserted by the Financial Services and Markets Act 2000 (Regulated Activities) (Amendment) (No 1) Order 2003, SI 2003/1475, art 22(1), (2), as from 31 October 2004; sum in square brackets substituted by the Consumer Credit (Further Increase in Monetary Amounts) Order 1998, SI 1998/997, art 3, Schedule, as from 1 May 1998.

Sub-s (2A): inserted by SI 2003/1475, art 22(1), (3), as from 31 October 2004.

Entry into agreements

[A.148]

156   Entry into agreements

Regulations may make provision, in relation to agreements entered into in the course of a business of credit brokerage, debt-adjusting or debt-counselling, corresponding, with such modifications as the Secretary of State thinks fit, to the provision which is or may be made by or under sections 55, 60, 61, 62, 63, 65, 127, 179 or 180 in relation to agreements to which those sections apply.

Credit reference agencies

[A.149]

157   Duty to disclose name etc of agency

(1)   A creditor, owner or negotiator, within the prescribed period after receiving a request in writing to that effect from the debtor or hirer, shall give him notice of the name and address of any credit reference agency from which the creditor, owner or negotiator has, during the antecedent negotiations, applied for information about his financial standing.

(2)   Subsection (1) does not apply to a request received more than 28 days after the termination of the antecedent negotiations, whether on the making of the regulated agreement or otherwise.

(3)   If the creditor, owner or negotiator fails to comply with subsection (1) he commits an offence.

NOTES

Regulations: the Consumer Credit (Credit Reference Agency) Regulations 2000, SI 2000/290.

[A.150]

158   Duty of agency to disclose filed information

(1)   A credit reference agency, within the prescribed period after receiving,

(a)   a request in writing to that effect from any individual [partnership or other unincorporated body of persons not consisting entirely of bodies corporate] (the "consumer") and

(b)   such particulars as the agency may reasonably require to enable them to identify the file, and

(c)   a fee of [£2],

shall give the consumer a copy of the file relating to [it] kept by the agency.

(2)   When giving a copy of the file under subsection (1), the agency shall also give the consumer a statement in the prescribed form of [the consumer's] rights under section 159.

(3)   If the agency does not keep a file relating to the consumer it shall give [the consumer] notice of that fact, but need not return any money paid.

(4)   If the agency contravenes any provision of this section it commits an offence.

(5)   In this Act "file", in relation to an individual, means all the information about him kept by a credit reference agency, regardless of how the information is stored and "copy of the file", as respects information not in plain English, means a transcript reduced into plain English.

NOTES

Sub-s (1): words in first and third pairs of square brackets substituted by the Data Protection Act 1998, s 62(1)(a), as from 1 March 2000, subject to savings in Sch 14, para 20 to that Act; sum in square brackets in para (c) substituted by the Consumer Credit (Further Increase of Monetary Amounts) Order 1998, SI 1998/997, Schedule, para 3, as from 1 May 1998.

Sub-s (2), (3): words in square brackets substituted by the Data Protection Act 1998, s 62(1)(b), (c), as from 1 March 2000, subject to savings in Sch 14, para 20 to that Act.

Regulations: the Consumer Credit (Credit Reference Agency) Regulations 2000, SI 2000/290.

[A.151]
159 Correction of wrong information
[(1) Any individual (the "objector") given—
   (a) information under section 7 of the Data Protection Act 1998 by a credit reference agency, or
   (b) information under section 158,
who considers that an entry in his file is incorrect, and that if it is not corrected he is likely to be prejudiced, may give notice to the agency requiring it either to remove the entry from the file or amend it.]
(2) Within 28 days after receiving a notice under subsection (1), the agency shall by notice inform the [objector] that it has—
   (a) removed the entry from the file, or
   (b) amended the entry, or
   (c) taken no action,
and if the notice states that the agency has amended the entry it shall include a copy of the file so far as it comprises the amended entry.
(3) Within 28 days after receiving a notice under subsection (2) or, where no such notice was given, within 28 days after the expiry of the period mentioned in subsection (2), the [objector] may, unless he has been informed by the agency that it has removed the entry from his file, serve a further notice on the agency requiring it to add to the file an accompanying notice of correction (not exceeding 200 words) drawn up by the [objector] and include a copy of it when furnishing information included in or based on that entry.
(4) Within 28 days after receiving a notice under subsection (3), the agency, unless it intends to apply to the [the relevant authority] under subsection (5), shall by notice inform the [objector] that it has received the notice under subsection (3) and intends to comply with it.
(5) If—
   (a) the [objector] has not received a notice under subsection (4) within the time required, or
   (b) it appears to the agency that it would be improper for it to publish a notice of correction because it is incorrect, or unjustly defames any person, or is frivolous or scandalous, or is for any other reason unsuitable,
the [objector] or, as the case may be, the agency may, in the prescribed manner and on payment of the specified fee, apply to the [the relevant authority], who may make such order on the application as he thinks fit.
(6) If a person to whom an order under this section is directed fails to comply with it within the period specified in the order he commits an offence.
[(7) The [Information Commissioner] may vary or revoke any order made by him under this section.
(8) In this section "the relevant authority" means—
   (a) where the objector is a partnership or other unincorporated body of persons, the [OFT], and
   (b) in any other case, the [Information Commissioner].]

NOTES
   Sub-s (1): substituted by the Data Protection Act 1998, s 62(1), (2), as from 1 March 2000; for savings see Sch 14, para 20 to that Act and the Data Protection Act 1998 (Commencement) Order 2000, SI 2000/183, art 2(2).
   Sub-ss (2)–(5): words in square brackets substituted by the Data Protection Act 1998, s 62(3), as from 1 March 2000; for savings see Sch 14, para 20 thereto and SI 2000/183, art 2(2).
   Sub-s (7): added, together with sub-s (8), by the Data Protection Act 1998, s 62(4), as from 1 March 2000 (for savings see Sch 14, para 20 thereto and SI 2000/183, art 2(2)); words in square brackets substituted by the Freedom of Information Act 2000, s 18(4), Sch 2, Pt I, para 7, as from 30 January 2001.
   Sub-s (8): added as noted to sub-s (7) above; words final pair of in square brackets substituted by the Freedom of Information Act 2000, s 18(4), Sch 2, Pt I, para 7, as from 30 January 2001.
   References to the OFT, etc: as to the abolition of the office of the Director General of Fair Trading and the substitution of the original references to the Director (and related expressions), see the note preceding s 1 at **[A.1]**.
   Regulations: the Consumer Credit (Credit Reference Agency) Regulations 2000, SI 2000/290.

[A.152]
160 Alternative procedure for business consumers
(1) The [OFT], on an application made by a credit reference agency, may direct that this section shall apply to the agency if [it] is satisfied—
   (a) that compliance with section 158 in the case of consumers who carry on a business would adversely affect the service provided to its customers by the agency, and
   (b) that, having regard to the methods employed by the agency and to any other relevant factors, it is probable that consumers carrying on a business would not be prejudiced by the making of the direction.
(2) Where an agency to which this section applies receives a request, particulars and a fee under section 158(1) from a consumer who carries on a business, and section 158(3) does not apply, the agency, instead of complying with section 158, may elect to deal with the matter under the following subsections.

(3)   Instead of giving the consumer a copy of the file, the agency shall within the prescribed period give notice to the consumer that it is proceeding under this section, and by notice give the consumer such information included in or based on entries in the file as the [OFT] may direct, together with a statement in the prescribed form of the consumer's rights under subsections (4) and (5).

(4)   If within 28 days after receiving the information given [to the consumer] under subsection (3), or such longer period as the [OFT] may allow, the consumer—

(a)   gives notice to the [OFT] that [the consumer] is dissatisfied with the information, and

(b)   satisfies the [OFT] that [the consumer] has taken such steps in relation to the agency as may be reasonable with a view to removing the cause of [the consumer's] dissatisfaction, and

(c)   pays the [OFT] the specified fee,

the [OFT] may direct the agency to give the [OFT] a copy of the file, and the [OFT] may disclose to the consumer such of the information on the file as the [OFT] thinks fit.

(5)   Section 159 applies with any necessary modifications to information given to the consumer under this section as it applies to information given under section 158.

(6)   If an agency making an election under subsection (2) fails to comply with subsection (3) or (4) it commits an offence.

[(7)   In this section "consumer" has the same meaning as in section 158.]

NOTES

Sub-s (4): words in first, fourth, sixth and seventh pairs of square brackets substituted by the Data Protection Act 1998, s 62(5)(a), as from 1 March 2000; for savings see Sch 14, para 20 to that Act and the Data Protection Act 1998 (Commencement) Order 2000, SI 2000/183, art 2(2).

Sub-s (7): added by the Data Protection Act 1998, s 62(5)(b), as from 1 March 2000; for savings see Sch 14, para 20 thereto and SI 2000/183, art 2(2).

References to the OFT, etc: as to the abolition of the office of the Director General of Fair Trading and the substitution of the original references to the Director (and related expressions), see the note preceding s 1 at **[A.1]**.

Regulations: the Consumer Credit (Credit Reference Agency) Regulations 2000, SI 2000/290.

PART XI
ENFORCEMENT OF ACT

[A.153]
161   Enforcement authorities

(1)   The following authorities ("enforcement authorities") have a duty to enforce this Act and regulations made under it—

(a)   the [OFT],

(b)   in Great Britain, the local weights and measures authority,

(c)   in Northern Ireland, the Department of Commerce for Northern Ireland.

(2)   . . .

(3)   Every local weights and measures authority shall, whenever the [OFT] requires, report to [it] in such form and with such particulars as [it] requires on the exercise of their functions under this Act.

(4)–(6)   . . .

NOTES

Sub-s (2): repealed by the Enterprise Act 2002, s 278, Sch 25, para 6(1), (32)(b), Sch 26, as from 1 April 2003.

Sub-ss (4)–(6): repealed by the Local Government, Planning and Land Act 1980, ss 1(4), 194, Sch 4, para 10, Sch 34, Pt IV, as from 13 November 1980.

References to the OFT, etc: as to the abolition of the office of the Director General of Fair Trading and the substitution of the original references to the Director (and related expressions), see the note preceding s 1 at **[A.1]**.

[A.154]
162   Powers of entry and inspection

(1)   A duly authorised officer of an enforcement authority, at all reasonable hours and on production, if required, of his credentials, may—

(a)   in order to ascertain whether a breach of any provision of or under this Act has been committed, inspect any goods and enter any premises (other than premises used only as a dwelling);

(b)   if he has reasonable cause to suspect that a breach of any provision of or under this Act has been committed, in order to ascertain whether it has been committed, require any person—

(i)   carrying on, or employed in connection with, a business to produce any books or documents relating to it; or

(ii)   having control of any information relating to a business recorded otherwise than in a legible form to provide a document containing a legible reproduction of the whole or any part of the information,

and take copies of, or of any entry in, the books or documents;

(c)   if he has reasonable cause to believe that a breach of any provision of or under this Act has been committed, seize and detain any goods in order to ascertain (by testing or otherwise) whether such a breach has been committed;

(d)   seize and detain any goods, books or documents which he has reason to believe may be required as evidence in proceedings for an offence under this Act;

(e)   for the purpose of exercising his powers under this subsection to seize goods, books or documents, but only if and to the extent that it is reasonably necessary for securing that the provisions of this Act and of any regulations made under it are duly observed, require any person having authority to do so to break open any container and, if that person does not comply, break it open himself.

(2)   An officer seizing goods, books or documents in exercise of his powers under this section shall not do so without informing the person he seizes them from.

(3)   If a justice of the peace, on sworn information in writing, or, in Scotland, a sheriff or a magistrate or justice of the peace, on evidence on oath,—

(a)   is satisfied that there is reasonable ground to believe either—

(i)   that any goods, books or documents which a duly authorised officer has power to inspect under this section are on any premises and their inspection is likely to disclose evidence of a breach of any provision of or under this Act; or

(ii)   that a breach of any provision of or under this Act has been, is being or is about to be committed on any premises; and

(b)   is also satisfied either—

(i)   that admission to the premises has been or is likely to be refused and that notice of intention to apply for a warrant under this subsection has been given to the occupier; or

(ii)   that an application for admission, or the giving of such a notice, would defeat the object of the entry or that the premises are unoccupied or that the occupier is temporarily absent and it might defeat the object of the entry to wait for his return,

the justice or, as the case may be, the sheriff or magistrate may by warrant under his hand, which shall continue in force for a period of one month, authorise an officer of an enforcement authority to enter the premises (by force if need be).

(4)   An officer entering premises by virtue of this section may take such other persons and equipment with him as he thinks necessary; and on leaving premises entered by virtue of a warrant under subsection (3) shall, if they are unoccupied or the occupier is temporarily absent, leave them as effectively secured against trespassers as he found them.

(5)   Regulations may provide that, in cases described by the regulations, an officer of a local weights and measures authority is not to be taken to be duly authorised for the purposes of this section unless he is authorised by the [OFT].

(6)   A person who is not a duly authorised officer of an enforcement authority, but purports to act as such under this section, commits an offence.

(7)   Nothing in this section compels a barrister, advocate or solicitor to produce a document containing a privileged communication made by or to him in that capacity or authorises the seizing of any such document in his possession.

NOTES

References to the OFT, etc: as to the abolition of the office of the Director General of Fair Trading and the substitution of the original references to the Director (and related expressions), see the note preceding s 1 at **[A.1]**.

Seize and detain goods, etc: the powers of seizure conferred by sub-s (1)(c), (d) are powers to which the Criminal Justice and Police Act 2001, s 50 apply (additional powers of seizure from premises); see s 50 of, and Sch 1, Pt 1, para 19 to, that Act.

Regulations: the Consumer Credit (Entry and Inspection) Regulations 1977, SI 1977/331.

[A.155]

163   Compensation for loss

(1)   Where, in exercising his powers under section 162, an officer of an enforcement authority seizes and detains goods and their owner suffers loss by reason of—

(a)   that seizure, or

(b)   the loss, damage or deterioration of the goods during detention,

then, unless the owner is convicted of an offence under this Act committed in relation to the goods, the authority shall compensate him for the loss so suffered.

(2)   Any dispute as to the right to or amount of any compensation under subsection (1) shall be determined by arbitration.

[A.156]

164   Power to make test purchases etc

(1)   An enforcement authority may—

(a)   make, or authorise any of their officers to make on their behalf, such purchases of goods; and

(b)   authorise any of their officers to procure the provision of such services or facilities or to enter into such agreements or other transactions,

as may appear to them expedient for determining whether any provisions made by or under this Act are being complied with.

(2)   Any act done by an officer authorised to do it under subsection (1) shall be treated for the purposes of this Act as done by him as an individual on his own behalf.

(3) Any goods seized by an officer under this Act may be tested, and in the event of such a test he shall inform the person mentioned in section 162(2) of the test results.

(4) Where any test leads to proceedings under this Act, the enforcement authority shall—
  (a) if the goods were purchased, inform the person they were purchased from of the test results, and
  (b) allow any person against whom the proceedings are taken to have the goods tested on his behalf if it is reasonably practicable to do so.

[A.157]
165   Obstruction of authorised officers
(1) Any person who—
  (a) wilfully obstructs an officer of an enforcement authority acting in pursuance of this Act; or
  (b) wilfully fails to comply with any requirement properly made to him by such an officer under section 162; or
  (c) without reasonable cause fails to give such an officer (so acting) other assistance or information he may reasonably require in performing his functions under this Act,
commits an offence.

(2) If any person, in giving such information as is mentioned in subsection (1)(c), makes any statement which he knows to be false, he commits an offence.

(3) Nothing in this section requires a person to answer any question or give any information if to do so might incriminate that person or (where that person is [married or a civil partner) the spouse or civil partner] of that person.

NOTES
Sub-s (3): words in square brackets substituted by the Civil Partnership Act 2004, s 261(1), Sch 27, para 50, as from 5 December 2005.

[A.158]
166   Notification of convictions and judgments to [OFT]
Where a person is convicted of an offence or has a judgment given against him by or before any court in the United Kingdom and it appears to the court—
  (a) having regard to the functions of the [OFT] under this Act, that the conviction or judgment should be brought to the [OFT's] attention, and
  (b) that it may not be brought to [its] attention unless arrangements for that purpose are made by the court,
the court may make such arrangements notwithstanding that the proceedings have been finally disposed of.

NOTES
References to the OFT, etc: as to the abolition of the office of the Director General of Fair Trading and the substitution of the original references to the Director (and related expressions), see the note preceding s 1 at **[A.1]**.

[A.159]
167   Penalties
(1) An offence under a provision of this Act specified in column 1 of Schedule 1 is triable in the mode or modes indicated in column 3, and on conviction is punishable as indicated in column 4 (where a period of time indicates the maximum term of imprisonment, and a monetary amount indicates the maximum fine, for the offence in question).

(2) A person who contravenes any regulations made under section 44, 52, 53, or 112, or made under section 26 by virtue of section 54, commits an offence.

[A.160]
168   Defences
(1) In any proceedings for an offence under this Act it is a defence for the person charged to prove—
  (a) that his act or omission was due to a mistake, or to reliance on information supplied to him, or to an act or omission by another person, or to an accident or some other cause beyond his control, and
  (b) that he took all reasonable precautions and exercised all due diligence to avoid such an act or omission by himself or any person under his control.

(2) If in any case the defence provided by subsection (1) involves the allegation that the act or omission was due to an act or omission by another person or to reliance on information supplied by another person, the person charged shall not, without leave of the court, be entitled to rely on that defence unless, within a period ending seven clear days before the hearing, he has served on the prosecutor a notice giving such information identifying or assisting in the identification of that other person as was then in his possession.

[A.161]
169 Offences by bodies corporate
Where at any time a body corporate commits an offence under this Act with the consent or connivance of, or because of neglect by, any individual, the individual commits the like offence if at that time—
- (a) he is a director, manager, secretary or similar officer of the body corporate, or
- (b) he is purporting to act as such an officer, or
- (c) the body corporate is managed by its members, of whom he is one.

[A.162]
170 No further sanctions for breach of Act
(1) A breach of any requirement made (otherwise than by any court) by or under this Act shall incur no civil or criminal sanction as being such a breach, except to the extent (if any) expressly provided by or under this Act.
(2) In exercising [its] functions under this Act the [OFT] may take account of any matter appearing to [it] to constitute a breach of a requirement made by or under this Act, whether or not any sanction for that breach is provided by or under this Act and, if it is so provided, whether or not proceedings have been brought in respect of the breach.
(3) Subsection (1) does not prevent the grant of an injunction, or the making of an order of certiorari, mandamus or prohibition or as respects Scotland the grant of an interdict or of an order under section 91 of the Court of Session Act 1868 (order for specific performance of statutory duty).

___

NOTES
References to the OFT, etc: as to the abolition of the office of the Director General of Fair Trading and the substitution of the original references to the Director (and related expressions), see the note preceding s 1 at **[A.1]**.
Court of Session Act 1868, s 91: repealed by the Court of Session Act 1988.

___

[A.163]
171 Onus of proof in various proceedings
(1) If an agreement contains a term signifying that in the opinion of the parties section 10(3)(b)(iii) does not apply to the agreement, it shall be taken not to apply unless the contrary is proved.
(2) It shall be assumed in any proceedings, unless the contrary is proved, that when a person initiated a transaction as mentioned in section 19(1)(c) he knew the principal agreement had been made, or contemplated that it might be made.
(3) Regulations under section 44 or 52 may make provision as to the onus of proof in any proceedings to enforce the regulations.
(4) In proceedings brought by the creditor under a credit-token agreement—
- (a) it is for the creditor to prove that the credit-token was lawfully supplied to the debtor, and was accepted by him, and
- (b) if the debtor alleges that any use made of the credit-token was not authorised by him, it is for the creditor to prove either—
  - (i) that the use was so authorised, or
  - (ii) that the use occurred before the creditor had been given notice under section 84(3).

(5) In proceedings under section 50(1) in respect of a document received by a minor at any school or other educational establishment for minors, it is for the person sending it to him at that establishment to prove that he did not know or suspect it to be such an establishment.
(6) In proceedings under section 119(1) it is for the pawnee to prove that he had reasonable cause to refuse to allow the pawn to be redeemed.
(7) If, in proceedings referred to in section 139(1), the debtor or any surety alleges that the credit bargain is extortionate it is for the creditor to prove the contrary.

[A.164]
172 Statements by creditor or owner to be binding
(1) A statement by a creditor or owner is binding on him if given under—
    section 77(1),
    section 78(1),
    section 79(1),
    section 97(1),
    section 107(1)(c),
    section 108(1)(c), or
    section 109(1)(c).
(2) Where a trader—
- (a) gives a customer a notice in compliance with section 103(1)(b), or
- (b) gives a customer a notice under section 103(1) asserting that the customer is not indebted to him under an agreement,

the notice is binding on the trader.
(3) Where in proceedings before any court—
- (a) it is sought to rely on a statement or notice given as mentioned in subsection (1) or (2), and

(b)   the statement or notice is shown to be incorrect,

the court may direct such relief (if any) to be given to the creditor or owner from the operation of subsection (1) or (2) as appears to the court to be just.

[A.165]
173   Contracting-out forbidden

(1)   A term contained in a regulated agreement or linked transaction, or in any other agreement relating to an actual or prospective regulated agreement or linked transaction, is void if, and to the extent that, it is inconsistent with a provision for the protection of the debtor or hirer or his relative or any surety contained in this Act or in any regulation made under this Act.

(2)   Where a provision specifies the duty or liability of the debtor or hirer or his relative or any surety in certain circumstances, a term is inconsistent with that provision if it purports to impose, directly or indirectly, an additional duty or liability on him in those circumstances.

(3)   Notwithstanding subsection (1), a provision of this Act under which a thing may be done in relation to any person on an order of the court or the [OFT] only shall not be taken to prevent its being done at any time with that person's consent given at that time, but the refusal of such consent shall not give rise to any liability.

NOTES

References to the OFT, etc: as to the abolition of the office of the Director General of Fair Trading and the substitution of the original references to the Director (and related expressions), see the note preceding s 1 at **[A.1]**.

PART XII
SUPPLEMENTAL

General

174   (*Repealed by the Enterprise Act 2002, ss 247(d), 278(2), Sch 26, as from 20 June 2003.*)

[A.166]
175   Duty of persons deemed to be agents

Where under this Act a person is deemed to receive a notice or payment as agent of the creditor or owner under a regulated agreement, he shall be deemed to be under a contractual duty to the creditor or owner to transmit the notice, or remit the payment, to him forthwith.

[A.167]
176   Service of documents

(1)   A document to be served under this Act by one person ("the server") on another person ("the subject") is to be treated as properly served on the subject if dealt with as mentioned in the following subsections.

(2)   The document may be delivered or sent [by an appropriate method] to the subject, or addressed to him by name and left at his proper address.

(3)   For the purposes of this Act, a document sent by post to, or left at, the address last known to the server as the address of a person shall be treated as sent by post to, or left at, his proper address.

(4)   Where the document is to be served on the subject as being the person having any interest in land, and it is not practicable after reasonable inquiry to ascertain the subject's name or address, the document may be served by—

     (a)   addressing it to the subject by the description of the person having that interest in the land (naming it), and

     (b)   delivering the document to some responsible person on the land or affixing it, or a copy of it, in a conspicuous position on the land.

(5)   Where a document to be served on the subject as being a debtor, hirer or surety, or as having any other capacity relevant for the purposes of this Act, is served at any time on another person who—

     (a)   is the person last known to the server as having that capacity, but

     (b)   before that time had ceased to have it,

the document shall be treated as having been served at that time on the subject.

(6)   Anything done to a document in relation to a person who (whether to the knowledge of the server or not) has died shall be treated for the purposes of subsection (5) as service of the document on that person if it would have been so treated had he not died.

[(7)   The following enactments shall not be construed as authorising service on the Public Trustee (in England and Wales) or the Probate Judge (in Northern Ireland) of any document which is to be served under this Act—

     section 9 of the Administration of Estates Act 1925;

     section 3 of the Administration of Estates Act (Northern Ireland) 1955.]

(8)   References in the preceding subsections to the serving of a document on a person include the giving of the document to that person.

NOTES

Sub-s (2): words in square brackets substituted by the Consumer Credit Act 1974 (Electronic Communications) Order 2004, SI 2004/3236, art 2(1), (6), as from 31 December 2004.

Sub-s (7): substituted by the Law of Property (Miscellaneous Provisions) Act 1994, s 21(1), Sch 1, para 6, as from 1 July 1995.

[A.168]
[176A Electronic transmission of documents
(1)   A document is transmitted in accordance with this subsection if—
   (a)   the person to whom it is transmitted agrees that it may be delivered to him by being transmitted to a particular electronic address in a particular electronic form,
   (b)   it is transmitted to that address in that form, and
   (c)   the form in which the document is transmitted is such that any information in the document which is addressed to the person to whom the document is transmitted is capable of being stored for future reference for an appropriate period in a way which allows the information to be reproduced without change.
(2)   A document transmitted in accordance with subsection (1) shall, unless the contrary is proved, be treated for the purposes of this Act, except section 69, as having been delivered on the working day immediately following the day on which it is transmitted.
(3)   In this section, "electronic address" includes any number or address used for the purposes of receiving electronic communications.]

NOTES
Inserted by the Consumer Credit Act 1974 (Electronic Communications) Order 2004, SI 2004/3236, art 2(1), (7), as from 31 December 2004.

[A.169]
177   Saving for registered charges
(1)   Nothing in this Act affects the rights of a proprietor of a registered charge (within the meaning of the [Land Registration Act 2002]), who—
   (a)   became the proprietor under a transfer for valuable consideration without notice of any defect in the title arising (apart from this section) by virtue of this Act, or
   (b)   derives title from such a proprietor.
(2)   Nothing in this Act affects the operation of section 104 of the Law of Property Act 1925 (protection of purchaser where mortgagee exercises power of sale).
(3)   Subsection (1) does not apply to a proprietor carrying on a business of debt-collecting.
(4)   Where, by virtue of subsection (1), a land mortgage is enforced which apart from this section would be treated as never having effect, the original creditor or owner shall be liable to indemnify the debtor or hirer against any loss thereby suffered by him.
(5)   (*Applies to Scotland only.*)
(6)   In the application of this section to Northern Ireland—
   (a)   any reference to the proprietor of a registered charge (within the meaning of the [Land Registration Act 2002]) shall be construed as a reference to the registered owner of a charge under the Local Registration of Title (Ireland) Act 1891 or Part IV of the Land Registration Act (Northern Ireland) 1970, and
   (b)   for the reference to section 104 of the Law of Property Act 1925 there shall be substituted a reference to section 21 of the Conveyancing and Law of Property Act 1881 and section 5 of the Conveyancing Act 1911.

NOTES
Sub-ss (1), (6): words in square brackets substituted by the Land Registration Act 2002, s 133, Sch 11, para 11, as from 13 October 2003.
Conveyancing and Law of Property Act 1881, s 21: repealed by the Law of Property Act 1925, s 207, Sch 7.
Conveyancing Act 1911: repealed by the Settled Land Act 1925, the Trustee Act 1925 and the Law of Property Act 1925.

[A.170]
178   Local Acts
The Secretary of State or the Department of Commerce for Northern Ireland may by order make such amendments or repeals of any provision of any local Act as appears to the Secretary of State or, as the case may be, the Department, necessary or expedient in consequence of the replacement by this Act of the enactments relating to pawnbrokers and moneylenders.

NOTES
Order: the Consumer Credit (Local Acts) Order 1984, SI 1984/1107.

Regulations, orders, etc

[A.171]
179   Power to prescribe form etc of secondary documents
(1)   Regulations may be made as to the form and content of credit-cards, trading-checks, receipts, vouchers and other documents or things issued by creditors, owners or suppliers under or in connection with regulated agreements or by other persons in connection with linked transactions, and may in particular—

(a)   require specified information to be included in the prescribed manner in documents, and other specified material to be excluded;

(b)   contain requirements to ensure that specified information is clearly brought to the attention of the debtor or hirer, or his relative, and that one part of a document is not given insufficient or excessive prominence compared with another.

(2)   If a person issues any document or thing in contravention of regulations under subsection (1) then, as from the time of the contravention but without prejudice to anything done before it, this Act shall apply as if the regulated agreement had been improperly executed by reason of a contravention of regulations under section 60(1).

[A.172]

180   Power to prescribe form etc of copies

(1)   Regulations may be made as to the form and content of documents to be issued as copies of any executed agreement, security instrument or other document referred to in this Act, and may in particular—

     (a)   require specified information to be included in the prescribed manner in any copy, and contain requirements to ensure that such information is clearly brought to the attention of a reader of the copy;

     (b)   authorise the omission from a copy of certain material contained in the original, or the inclusion of such material in condensed form.

(2)   A duty imposed by any provision of this Act (except section 35) to supply a copy of any document—

     (a)   is not satisfied unless the copy supplied is in the prescribed form and conforms to the prescribed requirements;

     (b)   is not infringed by the omission of any material, or its inclusion in condensed form, if that is authorised by regulations;

and references in this Act to copies shall be construed accordingly.

(3)   Regulations may provide that a duty imposed by this Act to supply a copy of a document referred to in an unexecuted agreement or an executed agreement shall not apply to documents of a kind specified in the regulations.

NOTES

    Regulations: the Consumer Credit (Cancellation Notices and Copies of Documents) Regulations 1983, SI 1983/1557.

[A.173]

181   Power to alter monetary limits etc

(1)   The Secretary of State may by order made by statutory instrument amend, or further amend, any of the following provisions of this Act so as to reduce or increase a sum mentioned in that provision, namely, sections 8(2), 15(1)(c), 17(1), 43(3)(a), 70(6), 75(3)(b), 77(1), 78(1), 79(1), 84(1), 101(7)(a), 107(1), 108(1), 109(1), 110(1), 118(1)(b), 120(1)(a), 139(5) and (7), 155(1) and 158(1).

(2)   An order under subsection (1) amending section 8(2), 15(1)(c), 17(1), 43(3)(a), 75(3)(b) or 139(5) and (7) shall be of no effect unless a draft of the order has been laid before and approved by each House of Parliament.

NOTES

    Orders: the Consumer Credit (Increase of Monetary Limits) Order 1983, SI 1983/1878; the Consumer Credit (Further Increase of Monetary Amounts) Order 1998, SI 1998/997.

[A.174]

182   Regulations and orders

(1)   Any power of the Secretary of State to make regulations or orders under this Act, except the power conferred by sections 2(1)(a), 181 and 192, shall be exercisable by statutory instrument subject to annulment in pursuance of a resolution of either House of Parliament.

(2)   Where a power to make regulations or orders is exercisable by the Secretary of State by virtue of this Act, regulations or orders made in the exercise of that power may—

     (a)   make different provision in relation to different cases or classes of case, and

     (b)   exclude certain cases or classes of case, and

     (c)   contain such transitional provisions as the Secretary of State thinks fit.

(3)   Regulations may provide that specified expressions, when used as described by the regulations, are to be given the prescribed meaning, notwithstanding that another meaning is intended by the person using them.

(4)   Any power conferred on the Secretary of State by this Act to make orders includes power to vary or revoke an order so made.

[A.175]

183   Determinations etc by [OFT]

The [OFT] may vary or revoke any determination or direction made or given by [it] under this Act (other than Part III, or Part III as applied by section 147).

NOTES

References to the OFT, etc: as to the abolition of the office of the Director General of Fair Trading and the substitution of the original references to the Director (and related expressions), see the note preceding s 1 at **[A.1]**.

Interpretation

[A.176]
184 Associates
[(1) A person is an associate of an individual if that person is—
  (a) the individual's husband or wife or civil partner,
  (b) a relative of—
    (i)   the individual, or
    (ii) the individual's husband or wife or civil partner, or
  (c) the husband or wife or civil partner of a relative of—
    (i)   the individual, or
    (ii) the individual's husband or wife or civil partner.]
(2) A person is an associate of any person with whom he is in partnership, and of the husband or wife [or civil partner] or a relative of any individual with whom he is in partnership.
(3) A body corporate is an associate of another body corporate—
  (a) if the same person is a controller of both, or a person is a controller of one and persons who are his associates, or he and persons who are his associates, are the controllers of the other; or
  (b) if a group of two or more persons is a controller of each company, and the groups either consist of the same persons or could be regarded as consisting of the same persons by treating (in one or more cases) a member of either group as replaced by a person of whom he is an associate.
(4) A body corporate is an associate of another person if that person is a controller of it or if that person and persons who are his associates together are controllers of it.
(5) In this section "relative" means brother, sister, uncle, aunt, nephew, niece, lineal ancestor or lineal descendant, . . . references to a husband or wife include a former husband or wife and a reputed husband [or wife, and references to a civil partner include a former civil partner] [and a reputed civil partner]; and for the purposes of this subsection a relationship shall be established as if any illegitimate child, step-child or adopted child of a person [were the legitimate child of the relationship in question].

NOTES

Sub-s (1): substituted by the Civil Partnership Act 2004, s 261(1), Sch 27, para 51(1), (2), as from 5 December 2005.

Sub-s (2): words in square brackets inserted by the Civil Partnership Act 2004, s 261(1), Sch 27, para 51(1), (3), as from 5 December 2005.

Sub-s (5): word omitted repealed and words in first and third pairs of square brackets substituted by the Civil Partnership Act 2004, s 261(1), (4), Sch 27, para 51(1), (4), Sch 30; words in second pair of square brackets inserted by the Civil Partnership Act 2004 (Overseas Relationships and Consequential, etc Amendments) Order 2005, SI 2005/3129, art 4(4), Sch 4, para 2, as from 5 December 2005.

[A.177]
185 Agreement with more than one debtor or hirer
(1) Where an actual or prospective regulated agreement has two or more debtors or hirers (not being a partnership or an unincorporated body of persons)—
  (a) anything required by or under this Act to be done to or in relation to the debtor or hirer shall be done to or in relation to each of them; and
  (b) anything done under this Act by or on behalf of one of them shall have effect as if done by or on behalf of all of them.
(2) Notwithstanding subsection (1)(a), where running-account credit is provided to two or more debtors jointly, any of them may by a notice signed by him (a "dispensing notice") authorise the creditor not to comply in his case with section 78(4) (giving of periodical statement of account); and the dispensing notice shall have effect accordingly until revoked by a further notice given by the debtor to the creditor:
  Provided that:
  (a) a dispensing notice shall not take effect if previous dispensing notices are operative in the case of the other debtor, or each of the other debtors, as the case may be;
  (b) any dispensing notices operative in relation to an agreement shall cease to have effect if any of the debtors dies.
(3) Subsection (1)(b) does not apply for the purposes of section 61(1)(a) or 127(3).
(4) Where a regulated agreement has two or more debtors or hirers (not being a partnership or an unincorporated body of persons), section 86 applies to the death of any of them.
(5) An agreement for the provision of credit, or the bailment or (in Scotland) the hiring of goods, to two or more persons jointly where—
  (a) one or more of those persons is an individual, and
  (b) one or more of them is a body corporate,

is a consumer credit agreement or consumer hire agreement if it would have been one had they all been individuals; and the body corporate or bodies corporate shall accordingly be included among the debtors or hirers under the agreement.

(6)   Where subsection (5) applies, references in this Act to the signing of any document by the debtor or hirer shall be construed in relation to a body corporate as referring to a signing on behalf of the body corporate.

[A.178]
186   Agreement with more than one creditor or owner

Where an actual or prospective regulated agreement has two or more creditors or owners, anything required by or under this Act to be done to, or in relation to, or by, the creditor or owner shall be effective if done to, or in relation to, or by, any one of them.

[A.179]
187   Arrangements between creditor and supplier

(1)   A consumer credit agreement shall be treated as entered into under pre-existing arrangements between a creditor and a supplier if it is entered into in accordance with, or in furtherance of, arrangements previously made between persons mentioned in subsection (4)(a), (b) or (c).

(2)   A consumer credit agreement shall be treated as entered into in contemplation of future arrangements between a creditor and a supplier if it is entered into in the expectation that arrangements will subsequently be made between persons mentioned in subsection (4)(a), (b) or (c) for the supply of cash, goods and services (or any of them) to be financed by the consumer credit agreement.

(3)   Arrangements shall be disregarded for the purposes of subsection (1) or (2) if—
    (a)   they are arrangements for the making, in specified circumstances, of payments to the supplier by the creditor, and
    (b)   the creditor holds himself out as willing to make, in such circumstances, payments of the kind to suppliers generally.

[(3A)   Arrangements shall also be disregarded for the purposes of subsections (1) and (2) if they are arrangements for the electronic transfer of funds from a current account at a bank within the meaning of the Bankers' Books Evidence Act 1879.]

(4)   The persons referred to in subsections (1) and (2) are—
    (a)   the creditor and the supplier;
    (b)   one of them and an associate of the other's;
    (c)   an associate of one and an associate of the other's.

(5)   Where the creditor is an associate of the supplier's, the consumer credit agreement shall be treated, unless the contrary is proved, as entered into under pre-existing arrangements between the creditor and the supplier.

NOTES

Sub-s (3A): inserted by the Banking Act 1987, s 89, as from 1 October 1987.

[A.180]
188   Examples of use of new terminology

(1)   Schedule 2 shall have effect for illustrating the use of terminology employed in this Act.

(2)   The examples given in Schedule 2 are not exhaustive.

(3)   In the case of conflict between Schedule 2 and any other provision of this Act, that other provision shall prevail.

(4)   The Secretary of State may by order amend Schedule 2 by adding further examples or in any other way.

[A.181]
189   Definitions

(1)   In this Act, unless the context otherwise requires—
    "advertisement" includes every form of advertising, whether in a publication, by television or radio, by display of notices, signs, labels, showcards or goods, by distribution of samples, circulars, catalogues, price lists or other material, by exhibition of pictures, models or films, or in any other way, and references to the publishing of advertisements shall be construed accordingly;
    "advertiser" in relation to an advertisement, means any person indicated by the advertisement as willing to enter into transactions to which the advertisement relates;
    "ancillary credit business" has the meaning given by section 145(1);
    "antecedent negotiations" has the meaning given by section 56;
    "appeal period" means the period beginning on the first day on which an appeal to the Secretary of State may be brought and ending on the last day on which it may be brought or, if it is brought, ending on its final determination, or abandonment;
    ["appropriate method" means—
       (a)   post, or
       (b)   transmission in the form of an electronic communication in accordance with section 176A(1);]

"assignment", in relation to Scotland, means assignation;

"associate" shall be construed in accordance with section 184;

[. . .]

"bill of sale" has the meaning given by section 4 of the Bills of Sale Act 1878 or, for Northern Ireland, by section 4 of the Bills of Sale (Ireland) Act 1879;

["building society" means a building society within the meaning of the Building Societies Act 1986;]

"business" includes profession or trade, and references to a business apply subject to subsection (2);

"cancellable agreement" means a regulated agreement which, by virtue of section 67, may be cancelled by the debtor or hirer;

"canvass" shall be construed in accordance with sections 48 and 153;

"cash" includes money in any form;

"charity" means as respects England and Wales a charity registered under [the Charities Act 1993] or an exempt charity (within the meaning of that Act), [as respects] Northern Ireland an institution or other organisation established for charitable purposes only ("organisation" including any persons administering a trust and "charitable" being construed in the same way as if it were contained in the Income Tax Acts) [and as respects Scotland a body entered in the Scottish Charity Register];

"conditional sale agreement" means an agreement for the sale of goods or land under which the purchase price or part of it is payable by instalments, and the property in the goods or land is to remain in the seller (notwithstanding that the buyer is to be in possession of the goods or land) until such conditions as to the payment of instalments or otherwise as may be specified in the agreement are fulfilled;

"consumer credit agreement" has the meaning given by section 8, and includes a consumer credit agreement which is cancelled under section 69(1), or becomes subject to section 69(2), so far as the agreement remains in force;

"consumer credit business" means any business so far as it comprises or relates to the provision of credit under regulated consumer credit agreements;

"consumer hire agreement" has the meaning given by section 15;

"consumer hire business" means any business so far as it comprises or relates to the bailment or (in Scotland) the hiring of goods under regulated consumer hire agreements;

"controller", in relation to a body corporate, means a person—

    (a)   in accordance with whose directions or instructions the directors of the body corporate or of another body corporate which is its controller (or any of them) are accustomed to act, or

    (b)   who, either alone or with any associate or associates, is entitled to exercise or control the exercise of, one third or more of the voting power at any general meeting of the body corporate or of another body corporate which is its controller;

"copy" shall be construed in accordance with section 180;

"costs", in relation to Scotland, means expenses;

"court" means in relation to England and Wales the county court, in relation to Scotland the sheriff court and in relation to Northern Ireland the High Court or the county court;

"credit" shall be construed in accordance with section 9;

"credit-broker" means a person carrying on a business of credit brokerage;

"credit brokerage" has the meaning given by section 145(2);

"credit limit" has the meaning given by section 10(2);

"creditor" means the person providing credit under a consumer credit agreement or the person to whom his rights and duties under the agreement have passed by assignment or operation of law, and in relation to a prospective consumer credit agreement, includes the prospective creditor;

"credit reference agency" has the meaning given by section 145(8);

"credit-sale agreement" means an agreement for the sale of goods, under which the purchase price or part of it is payable by instalments, but which is not a conditional sale agreement;

"credit-token" has the meaning given by section 14(1);

"credit-token agreement" means a regulated agreement for the provision of credit in connection with the use of a credit-token;

"debt-adjusting" has the meaning given by section 145(5);

"debt-collecting" has the meaning given by section 145(7);

"debt-counselling" has the meaning given by section 145(6);

"debtor" means the individual receiving credit under a consumer credit agreement or the person to whom his rights and duties under the agreement have passed by assignment or operation of law, and in relation to a prospective consumer credit agreement includes the prospective debtor;

"debtor-creditor agreement" has the meaning given by section 13;

"debtor-creditor-supplier agreement" has the meaning given by section 12;

"default notice" has the meaning given by section 87(1);

"deposit" means [(except in section 16(10) and 25(1B))] any sum payable by a debtor or hirer by way of deposit or down-payment, or credited or to be credited to him on account of any deposit or down-payment, whether the sum is to be or has been paid to the creditor or owner or any other person, or is to be or has been discharged by a payment of money or a transfer or delivery of goods or by any other means;

. . .

"electric line" has the meaning given by [the Electricity Act 1989] or, for Northern Ireland, [the Electricity (Northern Ireland) Order 1992];

["electronic communication" means an electronic communication within the meaning of the Electronic Communications Act 2000 (c 7);]

"embodies" and related words shall be construed in accordance with subsection (4);

"enforcement authority" has the meaning given by section 161(1);

"enforcement order" means an order under section 65(1), 105(7)(a) or (b), 111(2) or 124(1) or (2);

"executed agreement" means a document, signed by or on behalf of the parties, embodying the terms of a regulated agreement, or such of them as have been reduced to writing;

"exempt agreement" means an agreement specified in or under section 16;

"finance" means to finance wholly or partly and "financed" and "refinanced" shall be construed accordingly;

"file" and "copy of the file" have the meanings given by section 158(5);

"fixed-sum credit" has the meaning given by section 10(1)(b);

"friendly society" means a society registered [or treated as registered under the Friendly Societies Act 1974 or the Friendly Societies Act 1992] . . . ;

"future arrangements" shall be construed in accordance with section 187;

"general notice" means a notice published by the [OFT] at a time and in a manner appearing to [it] suitable for securing that the notice is seen within a reasonable time by persons likely to be affected by it;

"give", means, deliver or send [by an appropriate method] to;

"goods" has the meaning given by [section 61(1) of the Sale of Goods Act 1979];

"group licence" has the meaning given by section 22(1)(b);

"High Court" means Her Majesty's High Court of Justice, or the Court of Session in Scotland or the High Court of Justice in Northern Ireland;

"hire-purchase agreement" means an agreement, other than a conditional sale agreement, under which—

    (a)   goods are bailed or (in Scotland) hired in return for periodical payments by the person to whom they are bailed or hired, and

    (b)   the property in the goods will pass to that person if the terms of the agreement are complied with and one or more of the following occurs—

        (i)   the exercise of an option to purchase by that person,

        (ii)   the doing of any other specified act by any party to the agreement,

        (iii)   the happening of any other specified event;

"hirer" means the individual to whom goods are bailed or (in Scotland) hired under a consumer hire agreement, or the person to whom his rights and duties under the agreement have passed by assignment or operation of law, and in relation to a prospective consumer hire agreement includes the prospective hirer;

"individual" includes a partnership or other unincorporated body of persons not consisting entirely of bodies corporate;

"installation" means—

    (a)   the installing of any electric line or any gas or water pipe,

    (b)   the fixing of goods to the premises where they are to be used, and the alteration of premises to enable goods to be used on them,

    (c)   where it is reasonably necessary that goods should be constructed or erected on the premises where they are to be used, any work carried out for the purpose of constructing or erecting them on those premises;

. . .

"judgment" includes an order or decree made by any court;

"land", includes an interest in land, and in relation to Scotland includes heritable subjects of whatever description;

"land improvement company" means an improvement company as defined by section 7 of the Improvement of Land Act 1899;

"land mortgage" includes any security charged on land;

"licence" means a licence under Part III (including that Part as applied to ancillary credit businesses by section 147);

"licensed", in relation to any act, means authorised by a licence to do the act or cause or permit another person to do it;

"licensee", in the case of a group licence, includes any person covered by the licence;

"linked transaction" has the meaning given by section 19(1);

"local authority", in relation to England . . . , means . . . a county council, a London borough council, a district council, the Common Council of the City of London, or the Council of Isles of Scilly, [in relation to Wales means a county council or a county borough council,] and in relation to Scotland, means a [council constituted under section 2 of the Local Government etc (Scotland) Act 1994], and, in relation to Northern Ireland, means a district council;

. . .

"modifying agreement" has the meaning given by section 82(2);

"mortgage", in relation to Scotland, includes any heritable security;

"multiple agreement" has the meaning given by section 18(1);

"negotiator" has the meaning given by section 56(1);

"non-commercial agreement" means a consumer credit agreement or a consumer hire agreement not made by the creditor or owner in the course of a business carried on by him;

"notice" means notice in writing;

"notice of cancellation" has the meaning given by section 69(1);

["OFT" means the Office of Fair Trading;]

"owner" means a person who bails or (in Scotland) hires out goods under a consumer hire agreement or the person to whom his rights and duties under the agreement have passed by assignment or operation of law, and in relation to a prospective consumer hire agreement, includes the prospective bailor or persons from whom the goods are to be hired;

"pawn" means any article subject to a pledge;

"pawn-receipt" has the meaning given by section 114;

"pawnee" and "pawnor" include any person to whom the rights and duties of the original pawnee or the original pawnor, as the case may be, have passed by assignment or operation of law;

"payment" includes tender;

"personal credit agreement" has the meaning given by section 8(1);

"pledge" means the pawnee's rights over an article taken in pawn;

"prescribed" means prescribed by regulations made by the Secretary of State;

"pre-existing arrangements" shall be construed in accordance with section 187;

"principal agreement" has the meaning given by section 19(1);

"protected goods" has the meaning given by section 90(7);

"quotation" has the meaning given by section 52(1)(a);

"redemption period" has the meaning given by section 116(3);

"register" means the register kept by the [OFT] under section 35;

"regulated agreement" means a consumer credit agreement, or consumer hire agreement, other than an exempt agreement, and "regulated" and "unregulated" shall be construed accordingly;

"regulations" means regulations made by the Secretary of State;

"relative", except in section 184, means a person who is an associate by virtue of section 184(1);

"representation" includes any condition or warranty, and any other statement or undertaking, whether oral or in writing;

"restricted-use credit agreement" and "restricted-use credit" have the meanings given by section 11(1);

"rules of court", in relation to Northern Ireland means, in relation to the High Court, rules made under section 7 of the Northern Ireland Act 1962, and, in relation to any other court, rules made by the authority having for the time being power to make rules regulating the practice and procedure in that court;

"running-account credit" shall be construed in accordance with section 10;

"security", in relation to an actual or prospective consumer credit agreement or consumer hire agreement, or any linked transaction, means a mortgage, charge, pledge, bond, debenture, indemnity, guarantee, bill, note or other right provided by the debtor or hirer, or at his request (express or implied), to secure the carrying out of the obligations of the debtor or hirer under the agreement;

"security instrument" has the meaning given by section 105(2);

"serve on" means deliver or send [by an appropriate method] to;

"signed" shall be construed in accordance with subsection (3);

"small agreement" has the meaning given by section 17(1), and "small" in relation to an agreement within any category shall be construed accordingly;

"specified fee" shall be construed in accordance with section 2(4) and (5);

"standard licence" has the meaning given by section 22(1)(a);

"supplier" has the meaning given by section 11(1)(b) or 12(c) or 13(c) or, in relation to an agreement falling within section 11(1)(a), means the creditor, and includes a person to whom the rights and duties of a supplier (as so defined) have passed by assignment or operation of law, or (in relation to a prospective agreement) the prospective supplier;

"surety" means the person by whom any security is provided, or the person to whom his rights and duties in relation to the security have passed by assignment or operation of law;

"technical grounds" shall be construed in accordance with subsection (5);

"time order" has the meaning given by section 129(1);

"total charge for credit" means a sum calculated in accordance with regulations under section 20(1);

"total price" means the total sum payable by the debtor under a hire-purchase agreement or a conditional sale agreement, including any sum payable on the exercise of an option to purchase, but excluding any sum payable as a penalty or as compensation or damages for a breach of the agreement;

. . .

"unexecuted agreement" means a document embodying the terms of a prospective regulated agreement, or such of them as it is intended to reduce to writing;

"unlicensed" means without a licence but applies only in relation to acts for which a licence is required;

"unrestricted-use credit agreement" and "unrestricted-use credit" have the meanings given by section 11(2);

"working day" means any day other than—

    (a)   Saturday or Sunday,

    (b)   Christmas Day or Good Friday,

    (c)   a bank holiday within the meaning given by section 1 of the Banking and Financial Dealings Act 1971.

(2)   A person is not to be treated as carrying on a particular type of business merely because occasionally he enters into transactions belonging to a business of that type.

(3)   Any provision of this Act requiring a document to be signed is complied with by a body corporate if the document is sealed by that body.

This subsection does not apply to Scotland.

(4)   A document embodies a provision if the provision is set out either in the document itself or in another document referred to in it.

(5)   An application dismissed by the court or the [OFT] shall, if the court or the [OFT] (as the case may be) so certifies, be taken to be dismissed on technical grounds only.

(6)   Except in so far as the context otherwise requires, any reference in this Act to an enactment shall be construed as a reference to that enactment as amended by or under any other enactment, including this Act.

(7)   In this Act, except where otherwise indicated—

    (a)   a reference to a numbered Part, section or Schedule is a reference to the Part or section of, or the Schedule to, this Act so numbered, and

    (b)   a reference in a section to a numbered subsection is a reference to the subsection of that section so numbered, and

    (c)   a reference in a section, subsection or Schedule to a numbered paragraph is a reference to the paragraph of that section, subsection or Schedule so numbered.

NOTES

Sub-s (1) is amended as follows:

definitions "appropriate method", "electronic communication" inserted and in definitions "give" and "serve on", words in square brackets substituted by the Consumer Credit Act 1974 (Electronic Communications) Order 2004, SI 2004/3236, art 2(1), (8), (9), as from 31 December 2004;

definition "authorised institution" inserted by the Banking Act 1987, s 88, as from 1 October 1987, and repealed by the Financial Services and Markets Act 2000 (Consequential Amendments and Repeals) Order 2001, SI 2001/3649, art 176(a), as from 1 December 2001;

definition "building society" substituted by the Building Societies Act 1986, s 120, Sch 18, Pt I, para 10(4), as from 1 January 1987;

in definition "charity" words in first pair of square brackets substituted by the Charities Act 1993, s 98(1), Sch 6, para 30, as from 1 March 1996, words in second pair of square brackets substituted and words in third pair of square brackets added by the Charities and Trustee Investment (Scotland) Act 2005 (Consequential Provisions and Modifications) Order 2006, SI 2006/242, art 5, Schedule, Pt 1, para 1, as from 1 April 2006;

in definition "deposit" words in square brackets inserted by SI 2001/3649, art 176(b), as from 1 December 2001;

definition "Director" (omitted) repealed by the Enterprise Act 2002, s 278, Sch 25, para 6(1), (38)(a)(i), Sch 26, as from 1 April 2003;

in definition "electric line" words in first pair of square brackets substituted by the Electricity Act 1989, s 112(1), Sch 16, para 17(1), (3), as from 31 March 1990, words in second pair of square brackets substituted by the Electricity (Northern Ireland) Order 1992, SI 1992/231, art 95(1), Sch 12, para 15;

in definition "friendly society" words in square brackets substituted by SI 2001/3649, art 176(c), as from 1 December 2001, words omitted repealed by the Friendly Societies Act 1992, s 120, Sch 22, Pt I, as from 1 January 1994;

in definition "goods" words in square brackets substituted by the Sale of Goods Act 1979, s 63, Sch 2, para 18, as from 1 January 1980;

definition "insurance company" (omitted) repealed by SI 2001/3649, art 176(a), as from 1 December 2001;

in definition "local authority" words omitted in the first place repealed, and words in first pair of square brackets inserted, by the Local Government (Wales) Act 1994, s 66(6), (8), Sch 16, para 45, Sch 18, as from 1 April 1996, words omitted in the second place repealed by the Local Government Act 1985, s 102, Sch 17, as from 16 July 1985, and words in second pair of square brackets substituted by the Local Government etc (Scotland) Act 1994, s 180(1), Sch 13, para 94, as from 1 April 1996;

definition "minor" (omitted) repealed by the Age of Legal Capacity (Scotland) Act 1991, s 10, Sch 2; and

definition "OFT" inserted by the Enterprise Act 2002, s 278(1), Sch 25, para 6(1), (38)(a)(iii), as from 1 April 2003;

References to the OFT, etc: as to the abolition of the office of the Director General of Fair Trading and the substitution of the original references to the Director (and related expressions), see the note preceding s 1 at **[A.1]**.

[A.182]
[189A Meaning of "consumer credit EEA firm"
In this Act "consumer credit EEA firm" means an EEA firm falling within sub-paragraph (a), (b) or
(c) of paragraph 5 of Schedule 3 to the Financial Services and Markets Act 2000 carrying on, or
seeking to carry on, consumer credit business, consumer hire business or ancillary credit business
for which a licence would be required under this Act but for paragraph 15(3) of Schedule 3 to the
Financial Services and Markets Act 2000.]

NOTES
Inserted by the Financial Services and Markets Act 2000 (Consequential Amendments and Repeals) Order 2001,
SI 2001/3649, art 177, as from 1 December 2001.

Miscellaneous

[A.183]
190 Financial provisions
(1) There shall be defrayed out of money provided by Parliament—
  (a) all expenses incurred by the Secretary of State in consequence of the provisions of this Act;
  (b) any expenses incurred in consequence of those provisions by any other Minister of the
      Crown or Government department;
  (c) any increase attributable to this Act in the sums payable out of money so provided under
      the Superannuation Act 1972 or the Fair Trading Act 1973.
(2) Any fees received by the [OFT] under this Act shall be paid into the Consolidated Fund.

NOTES
References to the OFT, etc: as to the abolition of the office of the Director General of Fair Trading and the substitution of the
original references to the Director (and related expressions), see the note preceding s 1 at **[A.1]**.

191 (*Applies to Northern Ireland only.*)

[A.184]
192 Transitional and commencement provisions, amendments and repeals
(1) The provisions of Schedule 3 shall have effect for the purposes of this Act.
(2) The appointment of a day for the purposes of any provision of Schedule 3 shall be effected by
an order of the Secretary of State made by statutory instrument; and any such order shall include a
provision amending Schedule 3 so as to insert an express reference to the day appointed.
(3) Subject to subsection (4)—
  (a) the enactments specified in Schedule 4 shall have effect subject to the amendments
      specified in that Schedule (being minor amendments or amendments consequential on the
      preceding provisions of this Act), and
  (b) the enactments specified in Schedule 5 are hereby repealed to the extent shown in column
      3 of that Schedule.
(4) The Secretary of State shall by order made by statutory instrument provide for the coming into
operation of the amendments contained in Schedule 4 and the repeals contained in Schedule 5, and
those amendments and repeals shall have effect only as provided by an order so made.

NOTES
Orders: the Consumer Credit Act 1974 (Commencement No 1) Order 1975, SI 1975/2123; the Consumer Credit Act 1974
(Commencement No 2) Order 1977, SI 1977/325; the Consumer Credit Act 1974 (Commencement No 3) Order 1977,
SI 1977/802; the Consumer Credit Act 1974 (Commencement No 4) Order 1977, SI 1977/2163; the Consumer Credit Act 1974
(Commencement No 5) Order 1979, SI 1979/1685; the Consumer Credit Act 1974 (Commencement No 6) Order 1980,
SI 1980/50; the Consumer Credit Act 1974 (Commencement No 7) Order 1981, SI 1981/280; the Consumer Credit Act 1974
(Commencement No 8) Order 1983, SI 1983/1551; the Consumer Credit Act 1974 (Commencement No 9) Order 1984,
SI 1984/436; the Consumer Credit Act 1974 (Commencement No 10) Order 1989, SI 1989/1128

[A.185]
193 Short title and extent
(1) This Act may be cited as the Consumer Credit Act 1974.
(2) This Act extends to Northern Ireland.

SCHEDULES

SCHEDULE 1
PROSECUTION AND PUNISHMENT OF OFFENCES

Section 167

[A.186]

1 Section	2 Offence	3 Mode of prosecution	4 Imprisonment or fine
7	Knowingly or recklessly giving false information to [OFT].	(a) Summarily. (b) On indictment.	[The prescribed sum]. 2 years or a fine or both.
39(1)	Engaging in activities requiring a licence when not a licensee.	(a) Summarily. (b) On indictment.	[The prescribed sum]. 2 years or a fine or both.
39(2)	Carrying on business under a name not specified in licence.	(a) Summarily. (b) On indictment.	[The prescribed sum]. 2 years or a fine or both.
39(3)	Failure to notify changes in registered particulars.	(a) Summarily. (b) On indictment.	[The prescribed sum]. 2 years or a fine or both.
45	Advertising credit where goods etc not available for cash.	(a) Summarily. (b) On indictment.	[The prescribed sum]. 2 years or a fine or both.
46(1)	False or misleading advertisements.	(a) Summarily. (b) On indictment.	[The prescribed sum]. 2 years or a fine or both.
47(1)	Advertising infringements.	(a) Summarily. (b) On indictment.	[The prescribed sum]. 2 years or a fine or both.
49(1)	Canvassing debtor-creditor agreements off trade premises.	(a) Summarily. (b) On indictment.	[The prescribed sum]. 1 year or a fine or both.
49(2)	Soliciting debtor-creditor agreements during visits made in response to previous oral requests.	(a) Summarily. (b) On indictment.	[The prescribed sum]. 1 year or a fine or both.
50(1)	Sending circulars to minors.	(a) Summarily. (b) On indictment.	[The prescribed sum]. 1 year or a fine or both.
51(1)	Supplying unsolicited credit-tokens.	(a) Summarily. (b) On indictment.	[The prescribed sum]. 2 years or a fine or both.
77(4)	Failure of creditor under fixed-sum credit agreement to supply copies of documents etc.	Summarily.	[Level 4 on the standard scale].
78(6)	Failure of creditor under running-account credit agreement to supply copies of documents etc.	Summarily.	[Level 4 on the standard scale].
79(3)	Failure of owner under consumer hire agreement to supply copies of documents etc.	Summarily.	[Level 4 on the standard scale].
80(2)	Failure to tell creditor or owner whereabouts of goods.	Summarily.	[Level 3 on the standard scale].
85(2)	Failure of creditor to supply copy of credit-token agreement.	Summarily.	[Level 4 on the standard scale.].

1 Section	2 Offence	3 Mode of prosecution	4 Imprisonment or fine
97(3)	Failure to supply debtor with statement of amount required to discharge agreement.	Summarily.	[Level 3 on the standard scale].
103(5)	Failure to deliver notice relating to discharge of agreements.	Summarily.	[Level 3 on the standard scale].
107(4)	Failure of creditor to give information to surety under fixed-sum credit agreement.	Summarily.	[Level 4 on the standard scale].
108(4)	Failure of creditor to give information to surety under running-account credit agreement.	Summarily.	[Level 4 on the standard scale].
109(3)	Failure of owner to give information to surety under consumer hire agreement.	Summarily.	[Level 4 on the standard scale].
110(3)	Failure of creditor or owner to supply a copy of any security instrument to debtor or hirer.	Summarily.	[Level 4 on the standard scale].
114(2)	Taking pledges from minors.	(a) Summarily. (b) On indictment.	[The prescribed sum]. 1 year or a fine or both.
115	Failure to supply copies of a pledge agreement or pawn-receipt.	Summarily.	[Level 4 on the standard scale.]
119(1)	Unreasonable refusal to allow pawn to be redeemed.	Summarily.	[Level 4 on the standard scale.]
154	Canvassing ancillary credit services off trade premises.	(a) Summarily. (b) On indictment.	[The prescribed sum]. 1 year or a fine or both.
157(3)	Refusal to give name etc of credit reference agency.	Summarily.	[Level 4 on the standard scale.]
158(4)	Failure of credit reference agency to disclose filed information.	Summarily.	[Level 4 on the standard scale.]
159(6)	Failure of credit reference agency to correct information.	Summarily.	[Level 4 on the standard scale.]
160(6)	Failure of credit reference agency to comply with section 160(3) or (4).	Summarily.	[Level 4 on the standard scale.]
162(6)	Impersonation of enforcement authority officers.	(a) Summarily. (b) On indictment.	[The prescribed sum]. 2 years or a fine or both.
165(1)	Obstruction of enforcement authority officers.	Summarily.	[Level 4 on the standard scale.]
165(2)	Giving false information to enforcement authority officers.	(a) Summarily. (b) On indictment.	[The prescribed sum]. 2 years or a fine or both.
167(2)	Contravention of regulations under section 44, 52, 53, 54 or 112.	(a) Summarily. (b) On indictment.	[The prescribed sum]. 2 years or a fine or both.

1 Section	2 Offence	3 Mode of prosecution	4 Imprisonment or fine
174(5)	Wrongful disclosure of information.	(a) Summarily. (b) On indictment.	[The prescribed sum]. 2 years or a fine or both.

NOTES

References to the prescribed sum substituted by virtue of the Magistrates' Courts Act 1980, s 32(2).

References to a level on the standard scale substituted by virtue of the Criminal Justice Act 1982, ss 38, 46.

References to the OFT, etc: as to the abolition of the office of the Director General of Fair Trading and the substitution of the original references to the Director (and related expressions), see the note preceding s 1 at **[A.1]**.

SCHEDULE 2
EXAMPLES OF USE OF NEW TERMINOLOGY

Section 188(1)

PART I
LIST OF TERMS

[A.187]

Term	*Defined in section*	*Illustrated by example(s)*
Advertisement	189(1)	2
Advertiser	189(1)	2
Antecedent negotiations	56	1, 2, 3, 4
Cancellable agreement	67	4
Consumer credit agreement	8	5, 6, 7, 15, 19, 21
Consumer hire agreement	15	20, 24
Credit	9	16, 19, 21
Credit-broker	189(1)	2
Credit limit	10(2)	6, 7, 19, 22, 23
Creditor	189(1)	1, 2, 3, 4
Credit-sale agreement	189(1)	5
Credit-token	14	3, 14, 16
Credit-token agreement	14	3, 14, 16, 22
Debtor-creditor agreement	13	8, 16, 17, 18
Debtor-creditor-supplier agreement	12	8, 16
Fixed-sum credit	10	9, 10, 17, 23
Hire-purchase agreement	189(1)	10
Individual	189(1)	19, 24
Linked transaction	19	11
Modifying agreement	82(2)	24
Multiple agreement	18	16, 18
Negotiator	56(1)	1, 2, 3, 4
Personal credit agreement	8(1)	19
Pre-existing arrangements	187	8, 21
Restricted-use credit	11	10, 12, 13, 14, 16
Running-account credit	10	15, 16, 18, 23
Small agreement	17	16, 17, 22
Supplier	189(1)	3, 14
Total charge for credit	20	5, 10
Total price	189(1)	10
Unrestricted-use credit	11	8, 12, 16, 17, 18

PART II
EXAMPLES

Example 1

[A.188]

Facts. Correspondence passes between an employee of a moneylending company (writing on behalf of the company) and an individual about the terms on which the company would grant him a loan under a regulated agreement.

Analysis. The correspondence constitutes antecedent negotiations falling within section 56(1)(a), the moneylending company being both creditor and negotiator.

Example 2

Facts. Representations are made about goods in a poster displayed by a shopkeeper near the goods, the goods being selected by a customer who has read the poster and then sold by the shopkeeper to a finance company introduced by him (with whom he has a business relationship). The goods are disposed of by the finance company to the customer under a regulated hire-purchase agreement.

Analysis. The representations in the poster constitute antecedent negotiations falling within section 56(1)(b), the shopkeeper being the credit-broker and negotiator and the finance company being the creditor. The poster is an advertisement and the shopkeeper is the advertiser.

Example 3

Facts. Discussions take place between a shopkeeper and a customer about goods the customer wishes to buy using a credit-card issued by the D Bank under a regulated agreement.

Analysis. The discussions constitute antecedent negotiations falling within section 56(1)(c), the shopkeeper being the supplier and negotiator and the D Bank the creditor. The credit-card is a credit-token as defined in section 14(1), and the regulated agreement under which it was issued is a credit-token agreement as defined in section 14(2).

Example 4

Facts. Discussions take place and correspondence passes between a secondhand car dealer and a customer about a car, which is then sold by the dealer to the customer under a regulated conditional sale agreement. Subsequently, on a revocation of that agreement by consent, the car is resold by the dealer to a finance company introduced by him (with whom he has a business relationship), who in turn dispose of it to the same customer under a regulated hire-purchase agreement.

Analysis. The discussions and correspondence constitute antecedent negotiations in relation both to the conditional sale agreement and the hire-purchase agreement. They fall under section 56(1)(a) in relation to the conditional sale agreement, the dealer being the creditor and the negotiator. In relation to the hire-purchase agreement they fall within section 56(1)(b), the dealer continuing to be treated as the negotiator but the finance company now being the creditor. Both agreements are cancellable if the discussions took place when the individual conducting the negotiations (whether the "negotiator" or his employee or agent) was in the presence of the debtor, unless the unexecuted agreement was signed by the debtor at trade premises (as defined in section 67(b)). If the discussions all took place by telephone however, or the unexecuted agreement was signed by the debtor on trade premises (as so defined) the agreements are not cancellable.

Example 5

Facts. E agrees to sell to F (an individual) an item of furniture in return for 24 monthly instalments of £10 payable in arrears. The property in the goods passes to F immediately.

Analysis. This is a credit-sale agreement (see definition of "credit-sale agreement" in section 189(1)). The credit provided amounts to £240 less the amount which, according to regulations made under section 20(1), constitutes the total charge for credit. (This amount is required to be deducted by section 9(4)). Accordingly the agreement falls within section 8(2) and is a consumer credit agreement.

Example 6

Facts. The G Bank grants H (an individual) an unlimited overdraft, with an increased rate of interest on so much of any debit balance as exceeds £2,000.

Analysis. Although the overdraft purports to be unlimited, the stipulation for increased interest above £2,000 brings the agreement within section 10(3)(b)(ii) and it is a consumer credit agreement.

Example 7

Facts. J is an individual who owns a small shop which usually carries a stock worth about £1,000. K makes a stocking agreement under which he undertakes to provide on short-term credit the stock needed from time to time by J without any specified limit.

Analysis. Although the agreement appears to provide unlimited credit, it is probable, having regard to the stock usually carried by J, that his indebtedness to K will not at any time rise above £5,000. Accordingly the agreement falls within section 10(3)(b)(iii) and is a consumer credit agreement.

Example 8

Facts. U, a moneylender, lends £500 to V (an individual) knowing he intends to use it to buy office equipment from W. W introduced V to U, it being his practice to introduce customers needing finance to him. Sometimes U gives W a commission for this and sometimes not. U pays the £500 direct to V.

Analysis. Although this appears to fall under section 11(1)(b), it is excluded by section 11(3) and is therefore (by section 11(2)) an unrestricted-use credit agreement. Whether it is a debtor-creditor agreement (by section 13(c)) or a debtor-creditor-supplier agreement (by section 12(c)) depends on whether the previous dealings between U and W amount to "pre-existing arrangements", that is whether the agreement can be taken to have been entered into "in accordance with, or in furtherance of" arrangements previously made between U and W, as laid down in section 187(1).

Example 9

Facts. A agrees to lend B (an individual) £4,500 in nine monthly instalments of £500.

Analysis. This is a cash loan and is a form of credit (see section 9 and definition of "cash" in section 189(1)). Accordingly it falls within section 10(1)(b) and is fixed-sum credit amounting to £4,500.

Example 10

Facts. C (in England) agrees to bail goods to D (an individual) in return for periodical payments. The agreement provides for the property in the goods to pass to D on payment of a total of £7,500 and the exercise by D of an option to purchase. The sum of £7,500 includes a down-payment of £1,000. It also includes an amount which, according to regulations made under section 20(1), constitutes a total charge for credit of £1,500.

Analysis. This is a hire-purchase agreement with a deposit of £1,000 and a total price of £7,500 (see definitions of "hire-purchase agreement", "deposit" and "total price" in section 189(1)). By section 9(3), it is taken to provide credit amounting to £7,500 – (£1,500 + £1,000), which equals £5,000. Under section 8(2), the agreement is therefore a consumer credit agreement, and under sections 9(3) and 11(1) it is a restricted-use credit agreement for fixed-sum credit. A similar result would follow if the agreement by C had been a hiring agreement in Scotland.

Example 11

Facts. X (an individual) borrows £500 from Y (Finance). As a condition of the granting of the loan X is required—

    (a)   to execute a second mortgage on his house in favour of Y (Finance), and

    (b)   to take out a policy of insurance on his life with Y (Insurances).

In accordance with the loan agreement, the policy is charged to Y (Finance) as collateral security for the loan. The two companies are associates within the meaning of section 184(3).

Analysis. The second mortgage is a transaction for the provision of security and accordingly does not fall within section 19(1), but the taking out of the insurance policy is a linked transaction falling within section 19(1)(a). The charging of the policy is a separate transaction (made between different parties) for the provision of security and again is excluded from section 19(1). The only linked transaction is therefore the taking out of the insurance policy. If X had not been required by the loan agreement to take out the policy, but it had been done at the suggestion of Y (Finance) to induce them to enter into the loan agreement, it would have been a linked transaction under section 19(1)(c)(i) by virtue of section 19(2)(a).

Example 12

Facts. The N Bank agrees to lend O (an individual) £2,000 to buy a car from P. To make sure the loan is used as intended, the N Bank stipulates that the money must be paid by it direct to P.

Analysis. The agreement is a consumer credit agreement by virtue of section 8(2). Since it falls within section 11(1)(b), it is a restricted-use credit agreement, P being the supplier. If the N Bank had not stipulated for direct payment to the supplier, section 11(3) would have operated and made the agreement into one for unrestricted-use credit.

Example 13

Facts. Q, a debt-adjuster, agrees to pay off debts owed by R (an individual) to various moneylenders. For this purpose the agreement provides for the making of a loan by Q to R in return for R's agreeing to repay the loan by instalments with interest. The loan money is not paid over to R but retained by Q and used to pay off the moneylenders.

Analysis. This is an agreement to refinance existing indebtedness of the debtor's, and if the loan by Q does not exceed £5,000 is a restricted-use credit agreement falling within section 11(1)(c).

Example 14

Facts. On payment of £1, S issues to T (an individual) a trading check under which T can spend up to £20 at any shop which has agreed, or in future agrees, to accept S's trading checks.

Analysis. The trading check is a credit-token falling within section 14(1)(b). The credit-token agreement is a restricted-use credit agreement within section 11(1)(b), any shop in which the credit-token is used being the "supplier". The fact that further shops may be added after the issue of the credit-token is irrelevant in view of section 11(4).

Example 15

Facts. A retailer, L, agrees with M (an individual) to open an account in M's name and, in return for M's promise to pay a specified minimum sum into the account each month and to pay a monthly charge for credit, agrees to allow to be debited to the account, in respect of purchases made by M from L, such sums as will not increase the debit balance at any time beyond the credit limit, defined in the agreement as a given multiple of the specified minimum sum.

Analysis. This arrangement provides credit falling within the definition of running-account credit in section 10(1)(a). Provided the credit limit is not over £5,000, the agreement falls within section 8(2) and is a consumer credit agreement for running-account credit.

Example 16

Facts. Under an unsecured agreement, A (Credit), an associate of the A Bank, issues to B (an individual) a credit-card for use in obtaining cash on credit from A (Credit), to be paid by branches of the A Bank (acting as agent of A (Credit)), or goods or cash from suppliers or banks who have agreed to honour credit-cards issued by A (Credit). The credit limit is £30.

Analysis. This is a credit-token agreement falling within section 14(1)(a) and (b). It is a regulated consumer credit agreement for running-account credit. Since the credit limit does not exceed £30, the agreement is a small agreement. So far as the agreement relates to goods it is a debtor-creditor-supplier agreement within section 12(b), since it provides restricted-use credit under section 11(1)(b). So far as it relates to cash it is a debtor-creditor agreement within section 13(c) and the credit it provides is unrestricted-use credit. This is therefore a multiple agreement. In that the whole agreement falls within several of the categories of agreement mentioned in this Act, it is, by section 18(3), to be treated as an agreement in each of those categories. So far as it is a debtor-creditor-supplier agreement providing restricted-use credit it is, by section 18(2), to be treated as a separate agreement; and similarly so far as it is a debtor-creditor agreement providing unrestricted-used credit. (See also Example 22.)

Example 17

Facts. The manager of the C Bank agrees orally with D (an individual) to open a current account in D's name. Nothing is said about overdraft facilities. After maintaining the account in credit for some weeks, D draws a cheque in favour of E for an amount exceeding D's credit balance by £20. E presents the cheque and the Bank pay it.

Analysis. In drawing the cheque D, by implication, requests the Bank to grant him an overdraft of £20 on its usual terms as to interest and other charges. In deciding to honour the cheque, the Bank by implication accepts the offer. This constitutes a regulated small consumer credit agreement for unrestricted-use, fixed-sum credit. It is a debtor-creditor agreement, and falls within section 74(1)(b) if covered by a determination under section 74(3). (Compare Example 18.)

Example 18

Facts. F (an individual) has had a current account with the G Bank for many years. Although usually in credit, the account has been allowed by the Bank to become overdrawn from time to time. The maximum such overdraft has been is about £1,000. No explicit agreement has ever been made about overdraft facilities. Now, with a credit balance of £500, F draws a cheque for £1,300.

Analysis. It might well be held that the agreement with F (express or implied) under which the Bank operate his account includes an implied term giving him the right to overdraft facilities up to say £1,000. If so, the agreement is a regulated consumer credit agreement for unrestricted-use, running-account credit. It is a debtor-creditor agreement, and falls within section 74(1)(b) if covered by a direction under section 74(3). It is also a multiple agreement, part of which (i.e. the part not dealing with the overdraft), as referred to in section 18(1)(a), falls within a category of agreement not mentioned in this Act. (Compare Example 17.)

Example 19

Facts. H (a finance house) agrees with J (a partnership of individuals) to open an unsecured loan account in J's name on which the debit balance is not to exceed £7,000 (having regard to payments into the account made from time to time by J). Interest is to be payable in advance on this sum, with provision for yearly adjustments. H is entitled to debit the account with interest, a "setting-up" charge, and other charges. Before J has an opportunity to draw on the account it is initially debited with £2,250 for advance interest and other charges.

Analysis. This is a personal running-account credit agreement (see sections 8(1) and 10(1)(a), and definition of "individual" in section 189(1)). By section 10(2) the credit limit is £7,000. By section 9(4) however the initial debit of £2,250, and any other charges later debited to the account by H, are not to be treated as credit even though time is allowed for their payment. Effect is given to this by section 10(3). Although the credit limit of £7,000 exceeds the amount (£5,000) specified in section 8(2) as the maximum for a consumer credit agreement, so that the agreement is not within section 10(3)(a), it is caught by section 10(3)(b)(i). At the beginning J can effectively draw (as credit) no more than £4,750, so the agreement is a consumer credit agreement.

Example 20

Facts. K (in England) agrees with L (an individual) to bail goods to L for a period of three years certain at £2,000 a year, payable quarterly. The agreement contains no provision for the passing of the property in the goods to L.

Analysis. This is not a hire-purchase agreement (see paragraph (b) of the definition of that term in section 189(1)) and is capable of subsisting for more than three months. Paragraphs (a) and (b) of section 15(1) are therefore satisfied, but paragraph (c) is not. The payments by L must exceed £5,000 if he conforms to the agreement. It is true that under section 101 L has a right to terminate the agreement on giving K three months' notice expiring not earlier than eighteen months after the making of the agreement, but that section applies only where the agreement is a regulated consumer hire agreement apart from the section (see subsection (1)). So the agreement is not a consumer hire agreement, though it would be if the hire charge were say £1,500 a year, or there were a "break" clause in it operable by either party before the hire charges exceeded £5,000. A similar result would follow if the agreement by K had been a hiring agreement in Scotland.

Example 21

Facts. The P Bank decides to issue cheque cards to its customers under a scheme whereby the Bank undertakes to honour cheques of up to £30 in every case where the payee has taken the cheque in reliance on the cheque card, whether the customer has funds in his account or not. The P Bank writes to the major retailers advising them of this scheme and also publicises it by advertising. The Bank issues a cheque card to Q (an individual), who uses it to pay by cheque for goods costing £20 bought by Q from R, a major retailer. At the time, Q has £500 in his account at the P Bank.

Analysis. The agreement under which the cheque card is issued to Q is a consumer credit agreement even though at all relevant times Q has more than £30 in his account. This is because Q is free to draw out his whole balance and then use the cheque card, in which case the Bank has bound itself to honour the cheque. In other words the cheque card agreement provides Q with credit, whether he avails himself of it or not. Since the amount of the credit is not subject to any express limit, the cheque card can be used any number of times. It may be presumed however that section 10(3)(b)(iii) will apply. The agreement is an unrestricted-use debtor-creditor agreement (by section 13(c)). Although the P Bank wrote to R informing R of the P Bank's willingness to honour any cheque taken by R in reliance on a cheque card, this does not constitute pre-existing arrangements as mentioned in section 13(c) because section 187(3) operates to prevent it. The agreement is not a credit-token agreement within section 14(1)(b) because payment by the P Bank to R, would be a payment of the cheque and not a payment for the goods.

Example 22

Facts. The facts are as in Example 16. On one occasion B uses the credit-card in a way which increases his debit balance with A (Credit) to £40. A (Credit) writes to B agreeing to allow the excess on that occasion only, but stating that it must be paid off within one month.

Analysis. In exceeding his credit limit B, by implication, requests A (Credit) to allow him a temporary excess (compare Example 17). A (Credit) is thus faced by B's action with the choice of treating it as a breach of contract or granting his implied request. He does the latter. If he had done the former, B would be treated as taking credit to which he was not entitled (section 14(3)) and, subject to the terms of his contract with A (Credit), would be liable to damages for breach of contract. As it is, the agreement to allow the excess varies the original credit-token agreement by adding a new term. Under section 10(2), the new term is to be disregarded in arriving at the credit limit, so that the credit-token agreement at no time ceases to be a small agreement. By section 82(2) the later agreement is deemed to revoke the original agreement and contain provisions reproducing the combined effect of the two agreements. By section 82(4), this later agreement is exempted from Part V (except section 56).

Example 23

Facts. Under an oral agreement made on 10th January, X (an individual) has an overdraft on his current account at the Y Bank with a credit limit of £100. On 15th February, when his overdraft standards at £90, X draws a cheque for £25. It is the first time that X has exceeded his credit limit, and on 16th February the bank honours the cheque.

Analysis. The agreement of 10th January is a consumer credit agreement for running-account credit. The agreement of 15th–16th February varies the earlier agreement by adding a term allowing the credit limit to be exceeded merely temporarily. By section 82(2) the later agreement is deemed to revoke the earlier agreement and reproduce the combined effect of the two agreements. By section 82(4), Part V of this Act (except section 56) does not apply to the later agreement. By section 18(5), a term allowing a merely temporary excess over the credit limit is not to be treated as a separate agreement, or as providing fixed-sum credit. The whole of the £115 owed to the Bank by X on 16th February is therefore running-account credit.

Example 24

Facts. On 1st March 1975 Z (in England) enters into an agreement with A (an unincorporated body of persons) to bail to A equipment consisting of two components (component P and component Q). The agreement is not a hire-purchase agreement and is for a fixed term of 3 years, so paragraphs (a) and (b) of section 15(1) are both satisfied. The rental is payable monthly at a rate of £2,400 a year, but the agreement provides that this is to be reduced to £1,200 a year for the remainder of the agreement if at any time during its currency A returns component Q to the owner Z. On 5th May 1976 A is incorporated as A Ltd., taking over A's assets and liabilities. On 1st March

1977, A Ltd. returns component Q. On 1st January 1978, Z and A Ltd. agree to extend the earlier agreement by one year, increasing the rental for the final year by £250 to £1,450.

Analysis. When entered into on 1st March 1975, the agreement is a consumer hire agreement. A falls within the definition of "individual" in section 189(1) and if A returns component Q before 1st May 1976 the total rental will not exceed £5,000 (see section 15(1)(c)). When this date is passed without component Q having been returned it is obvious that the total rental must now exceed £5,000. Does this mean that the agreement then ceases to be a consumer hire agreement? The answer is no, because there has been no change in the terms of the agreement, and without such a change the agreement cannot move from one category to the other. Similarly, the fact that A's rights and duties under the agreement pass to a body corporate on 5th May 1976 does not cause the agreement to cease to be a consumer hire agreement (see the definition of "hirer" in section 189(1)).

The effect of the modifying agreement of 1st January 1978 is governed by section 82(2), which requires it to be treated as containing provisions reproducing the combined effect of the two actual agreements, that is to say as providing that—

(a) obligations outstanding on 1st January 1978 are to be treated as outstanding under the modifying agreement;

(b) the modifying agreement applies at the old rate of hire for the months of January and February 1978, and

(c) for the year beginning 1st March 1978 A Ltd. will be the bailee of component P at a rental of £1,450.

The total rental under the modifying agreement is £1,850. Accordingly the modifying agreement is a regulated agreement. Even if the total rental under the modifying agreement exceeded £5,000 it would still be regulated because of the provisions of section 82(3).

SCHEDULES 3 AND 4

(Sch 3 (Transitional and Commencement Provisions), Sch 4 (Minor and Consequential Amendments) outside the scope of this work.)

Index